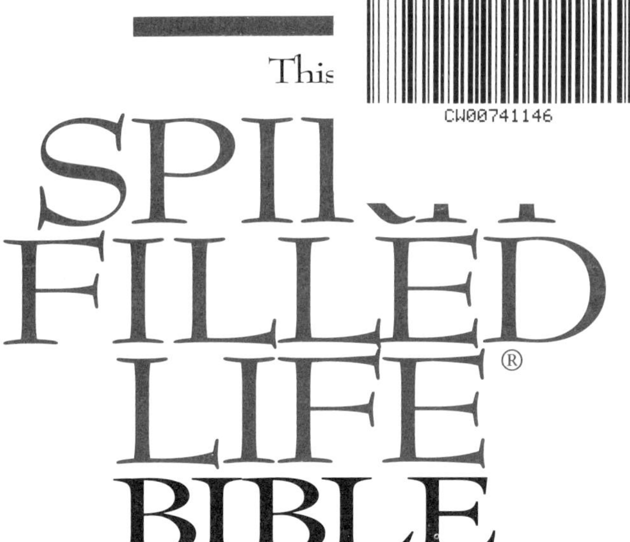

Is presented to

____
(name)

On the occasion of

____
(event)

By

____
(name)

On

____
(date)

SPIRIT FILLED LIFE® BIBLE

NKJV

A Personal Study Bible Unveiling All God's Fullness In All God's Word

General Editor
Jack W. Hayford, Litt.D.

Old Testament Editor
Sam Middlebrook, D.Min.

New Testament Editor
Jerry Horner, Th.D.

Assistant Editor
Gary Matsdorf, M.A.

THOMAS NELSON PUBLISHERS
Nashville

Printed in the United States of America

12 13 14 15—01 00

Table of Contents

The *Spirit-Filled Life*® *Bible*
Introduction

The waves of successive seasons of revival blessing throughout church history have left recurring high-water marks. These signs of the Holy Spirit's surgings across the Earth and throughout time have, as a rule, been the result of God's signal use of anointed men, whose leadership not only was the spearhead making a holy penetration in their world, but whose name became the designation of that revival era. Accordingly we note the strata of church history by the mention of names, such as Augustine, Aquinas, Luther, Calvin, Knox, Huss, Wesley, Finney, and Moody.

But with the opening of the twentieth century, from out of the wellsprings of the holiness tradition, a revival broke forth, which is distinctive in two ways. First, the wave of renewal it gave rise to in the church internationally has not receded; rather, it has continued to roll forward and to engulf leaders and laity in every historic tradition and contemporary circle of Christianity. Second, this revival has not been characterized by the leadership of any primary personality to set its agenda or establish its style. One historian has called the Pentecostal-Charismatic revival of this century "a movement without a man," thereby noting the phenomenon that its broadening tide of influence seems linked to this fact. No one can proscribe the movement's boundaries, none can inscribe his name upon it, and who can describe it in any other way than by Peter's words at Pentecost: "This is what was spoken by the prophet Joel: ' . . . in the last days . . . I will pour out of My Spirit on all flesh' " (Acts 2:16, 17)?

As the waves of this renewal have spread, the common denominator of those it engulfs is not a doctrinal position as much as it is a mutual sharing in a new dynamic. This "new" is neither novel nor unprecedented, but simply a rekindling and release of the simplicity and power inherent in the New Testament church—the life and ministry of Jesus continuing in His body today after the manner of the Book of Acts. Because of this, it has characteristically been difficult to prepare a single study Bible to serve this broad community. Their convictions about the Person of Jesus Christ, His virgin birth, sinless life, atoning death, literal resurrection, and majestic ascension are essentially in agreement. Their view of the authority of the Word of God and its divine inspiration is basically the same. And their experience of the contemporary operations of the Holy Spirit—whose fullness, fruit, gifts, and works of power are welcomed and realized today as at the church's inception—is held in general accord. However, by reason of the breadth of their denominational backgrounds, a wide diversity characterizes this band. They will be found at all points of the spectrum on such issues as: 1) Calvinism contrasted with Arminianism; 2) Dispensational contrasted with Covenant theology; 3) Premillennial, Postmillennial, and Amillennial differences; and even 4) the meaning of "speaking with tongues" with reference to the believer's initial infilling with the Holy Spirit.

The striking fact, given this widely diverse group, is that their movement together reflects not a lack of conviction about those points wherein they view Scripture and experience differently, but a response to the Holy Spirit's compulsion to give place to another overarching conviction. They choose to let brotherly love prevail in the church, to seek peace and pursue it, and to acknowledge that the prayer of our Lord Jesus "that they may be one" will never be answered around the text of a theology but at the Table of His Testimony. As we remember His Cross—His body to which we have been called, and His blood that has redeemed, washed, and justified us from our sins—we find oneness under His lordship. It is here we stand together, "till we all come to the unity of the faith and of the knowledge of the Son of God, to a perfect man, to the measure of the stature of the fullness of Christ . . . speaking the truth in love" (Eph. 4:13–15).

From this broad context and at this point in God's dealings throughout Christ's church globally, we have come to study and to serve, hoping that this Bible may contribute to the ongoing stream of the Holy Spirit's workings today and tomorrow.

The team of scholars, pastor-teachers, writers and editors express gratitude to God and to the executive leadership and editors of Thomas Nelson Publishers for the privilege of involvement in this historic project. The *Spirit-Filled Life® Bible* is the first of its kind, in which a broadly representative team from more than twenty denominations and independent fellowships has been banded together to produce a study Bible integrating the Pentecostal-Charismatic viewpoint. In noting this, the General Editor and his associates wish to acknowledge the earlier efforts of several Pentecostal teachers and scholars who have provided study Bible resources prior to the landmark event the *Spirit-Filled Life® Bible* occasions. While its uniqueness in scope and persons involved distinguishes this present work, it is with gratitude and humility that we salute that worthy group who preceded us in such efforts at leading the people of God into His Word at greater depth.

As General Editor, I offer my most respectful thanks to my Christian brothers and sisters who have accomplished the written and editorial work herein. Special personal acknowledgment is also appropriate to my son, Jack Hayford III, for his arduous labors in this project, as well as to Janet Kemp, Susanne Mahdi, Renee McCarter, and John Silver.

May God be pleased to multiply the fruit of the labor of all who have given themselves to present you, the reader-student, with the *Spirit-Filled Life® Bible.* We commit this work to Him with the psalmist's prayer: "And let the beauty of the LORD our God be upon us, and establish the work of our hands for us; yes, establish the work of our hands" (Ps. 90:17).

Jack W. Hayford
General Editor

Contributors

General Editor
Jack W. Hayford, B.A., B.Th., D.D., Litt.D.

Old Testament Editor
Sam Middlebrook, B.Th., B.A., M.Div., Th.D.

New Testament Editor
Jerry Horner, B.A., M.Div., Th.D.

Assistant Editor
Gary Matsdorf, B.A., M.A.

Kingdom Dynamics, Word Wealth, Truth-In-Action

Charles Blake, B.A., M.Div., D.Th.
Senior Pastor/Bishop
West Angeles Church of God in Christ
The Worth of the Human Personality

Jamie Buckingham, A.B., B.D., M.R.E., D.H.L.
Senior Pastor, Tabernacle Church
Melbourne, FL
The Traits of Spiritual Leadership

Larry Christenson, B.A., B.Th.
Chairman, International Lutheran Renewal Center
St. Paul, MN
God's Order for Family Life

Glen Cole, B.A., D.D.
Senior Pastor, Capital Christian Center
Sacramento, CA
Assigned to World Evangelism

Dennis Corrigan, B.A., B.Div., M.Div.
Senior Pastor, The Carpenter's Company
San Dimas, CA
Truth-In-Action Charts

Dick Eastman, B.A., D.D.
President, Every Home For Christ
Advancing in Spiritual Warfare

Charles Green, B.A., D.Th., Litt.D., D.H.L.
Senior Pastor, Word of Faith Fellowship
New Orleans, LA
The Pathway of Praise

Jack W. Hayford, B.A., B.Th., D.D., Litt.D.
Senior Pastor, The Church On The Way
Van Nuys, CA
The Kingdom of God
The Word of God
Prophecy and the Scriptures

Jack Hayford III, B.S., M.S.
Research Chemist, Kimberly-Clark
Neenah, WI
Messianic Promises and Christ's Coming

Marilyn Hickey, B.A., D.D.
Chairman of Board,
Oral Roberts University/
International Bible Teacher,
Marilyn Hickey Ministries
Denver, CO
The Ministry of Angels

Roy Hicks, Sr., G.Th., D.D.
Speaker/International Bible Teacher/Author
Faith's Confession of God's Word

Larry Lea, B.A., M.Div., D.D.
Senior Pastor
Larry Lea Ministries
Rockwall, TX
Prayer and Spiritual Attainment

Freda Lindsay, B.A., D.D., D.H.L.
Founder and Chairman of the Board
Christ For The Nations
Dallas, TX
The Work and Ministry of Women

Dick Mills, B.A., D.D.
Evangelist and Adjunct Professor
San Jacinto, CA
Word Wealth (assisted by David Mills)

Frederick K. C. Price, D.D.
Senior Pastor, Crenshaw Christian Center
Los Angeles, CA
God's Plan for Prosperity

Oral Roberts, D.H.L.
Founder and President/Evangelist
Oral Roberts University
Tulsa, OK
Principles of Seed Faith

M. G. "Pat" Robertson, B.A., M.Div., J.D., D.D.
President and Chief Executive Officer
The Christian Broadcasting Network, Inc.
Spiritual Answers to Hard Questions

James Robison, D.D.
President/Evangelist
James Robison Evangelistic Association
Fort Worth, TX
The Holy Spirit and Restoration

Demos Shakarian, D.H.L.
Founder and President
Full Gospel Business Men's Fellowship International
Brotherly Love

Charles V. Simpson, B.A.
General Overseer/Bible Teacher
Covenant Church
Mobile, AL
The Blood of the Covenant

Nathaniel M. Van Cleave, B.A., Th.D., D.D.
Special Conference Speaker/Faculty/Facultad de Teología
Spanish Bible College
Montebello, CA
The Ministry of Divine Healing

Paul Walker, B.A., M.Div., M.Ed., Ph.D.
Senior Pastor, Mount Paran Church of God
Atlanta, GA
Holy Spirit Gifts and Power

Book Introductions, Outlines, and Notes

Arden Conrad Autry, B.A., M.A., Ph.D.
Associate Professor
Oral Roberts University
Tulsa, OK
2 Corinthians

James Lee Beall, B.A., M.Th., Th.D.
Senior Pastor, Bethesda Christian Church
Sterling Heights, MI
1 and 2 Timothy, Titus

R. Russell Bixler, B.A., M.A., M.Div.
President, Cornerstone TeleVision, Inc.
Pittsburgh, PA
Genesis

Charles E. Blair, Th.B., D.D., Litt.D.
Senior Pastor, Calvary Temple
Denver, CO
Job

Paul G. Chappell, B.A., M.Div., Th.M., M.Phil., Ph.D.
Dean of the School of Theology
Oral Roberts University
Tulsa, OK
Deuteronomy

Jerry Cook, B.A., B.D.
Staff Pastor, Eastside Foursquare Church
Bothell, WA
1 and 2 Samuel, Joel

A. Joy Dawson
International Bible Teacher/Author
Youth With A Mission
Tujunga, CA
Esther

Guy P. Duffield, S.T.D., D.D.
Professor/Faculty
LIFE Bible College
Los Angeles, CA
Hebrews

Willard S. Elijahson, B.A., M.A., B.D., S.T.M., Th.D.
Author
Front Royal, VA
Micah

Howard M. Ervin, A.B., Th.B., B.D., M.A., Th.D.
Professor of Old Testament
Graduate School of Theology and Mission
Oral Roberts University
Tulsa, OK
Ezekiel (coauthored with Roy E. Hayden)

John Garlock, B.A., M.A.
Traveling Speaker and Teacher
Christ For The Nations Institute
Dallas, TX
Proverbs

Trevor L. Grizzle, B.A., M.Div., Ph.D.
Professor of New Testament
Oral Roberts University
Tulsa, OK
Colossians

Wayne A. Grudem, B.A., M.Div., Ph.D.
Professor of Biblical and Systematic Theology
Trinity Evangelical Divinity School
Deerfield, IL
Romans

Roy Edmund Hayden, A.A., B.A., B.Th., B.D., Th.M., M.A., Ph.D.
Professor of Old Testament
Oral Roberts University
Tulsa, OK
Jeremiah, Amos; Ezekiel (coauthored with Howard M. Ervin)

Jack W. Hayford, B.A., B.Th., D.D., Litt.D.
Senior Pastor, The Church On The Way
Van Nuys, CA
Ruth, Ephesians

Cheryl Lynn Hetherington, S.T.D., M.A., M.Phil., Ph.D.
Professor of Old Testament
Oral Roberts University
Tulsa, OK
Judges

Charles L. Holman, B.A., B.D., Th.M., Ph.D.
Associate Professor of Biblical Interpretation
Regent University
Virginia Beach, VA
1 and 2 Peter, Jude

Jerry Horner, B.A., M.Div., Th.D.
Dean of the College of Theology and Ministry
Regent University
Virginia Beach, VA
Galatians, Philippians, 3 John

Richard Duane Israel, B.A., M.Div., M.A., Ph.D.
Assistant Professor
Bethany Bible College
Scotts Valley, CA
Numbers

K. R. "Dick" Iverson, D.Th.
Senior Pastor, Bible Temple
Portland, OR
Psalms

Gary Kinnaman, B.A., M.A.
Senior Pastor, Word of Grace Church
Mesa, AZ
Acts

John Louwerse, B.S., B.C.A., M.A. Ling., M.A. Miss., M.Div., Ph.D.
Professor of Anthropology and World Mission, LIFE Bible College/Adjunct Professor of Linguistics and Bible Translation (Fuller Theological Seminary/Biola University)
Malachi

David Charles Mainse, S.T.M.
President and Television Host
Crossroads Christian Communications, Inc.
Peterboro, Ontario, Canada
Nehemiah

Gary Matsdorf, B.A., M.A.
Senior Pastor, Medford Foursquare Church
Medford, OR
Ezra

Ronald Mehl, B.Th., D.D.
Senior Pastor, Beaverton Foursquare Church
Beaverton, OR
Joshua

Sam Middlebrook, B.Th., B.A., M.Div., D.Min.
Dean and Executive Director
The King's Institute, The Church On The Way
Van Nuys, CA
Hosea, Habakkuk, Haggai

Earl Wesley Morey, B.A., M.Div., Ph.D.
International Teaching Ministry/Author
Clifton, VA
Revelation

Coleman Cox Phillips, B.Th., B.A., M.Ed., D.D.
Senior Pastor, Cathedral of the Valley
Escondido, CA
Daniel, additional notes for Revelation

Mary LaVonne Phillips, B.R.E., B.S., M.A.
Author/Retreat Speaker, Cathedral of the Valley
Escondido, CA
Zephaniah

Donald Pickerill, B.Th., B.A., M.A.
Professor
LIFE Bible College
San Dimas, CA
Song of Solomon, 1 Corinthians

Timothy Mark Powell, B.S., M.Div., Ph.D.
Senior Pastor, Christian Life Assembly
Fresno, CA
Obadiah, Nahum

Larry D. Powers, A.A., B.A., M.A.
Professor
LIFE Bible College
Los Angeles, CA
1 and 2 Kings, 1 and 2 Chronicles

Peter E. Prosser, B.A., B.Th., M.A., Ph.D.
Assistant Professor of Church History
Regent University
Virginia Beach, VA
1 and 2 John

Jon Mark Ruthven, B.A., M.A., B.D., Ph.D.
Assistant Professor of Theology
Regent University
Virginia Beach, VA
James

Siegfried Schatzmann, B.A., M.Div., Ph.D.
Director of Studies, Elim Bible College
Nantwich, England
John

David Warren Shibley, B.A., M.Div.
Founder and President
Global Advance
Rockwall, TX
Zechariah

Bob G. Slosser, B.A., L.H.D.
President Emeritus
Regent University
Virginia Beach, VA
Philemon

Charles W. Snow, Jr., B.S., M.A., Ed.D.
Dean of Doctoral Studies
School of Theology and Missions
Oral Roberts University
Tulsa, OK
Jonah

Russell P. Spittler, B.A., M.A., B.D., Ph.D.
Professor of New Testament
Fuller Theological Seminary
Pasadena, CA
1 and 2 Thessalonians

J. Lyle Story, B.A., M.Div., Ph.D.
Associate Professor of Biblical Studies
Regent University
Virginia Beach, VA
Matthew, Mark, Luke

James Caroll Tollett, B.A., M.Div., D.Min.
Senior Pastor, Freedom Church/
Assistant Professor of Evangelism,
Oral Roberts University
Tulsa, OK
Exodus

Nathaniel M. Van Cleave, B.A., Th.D., D.D.
Special Conference Speaker/Faculty/Facultad de Teología
Spanish Bible College
Montebello, CA
Isaiah

Paul B. Watney, B.A., M.A., D.Miss., Ph.D.
Professor/School of Theology and Missions
Oral Roberts University
Tulsa, OK
Lamentations

William C. Williams, B.A., M.A., Ph.D.
Bible Translator/Editor/
Professor of Old Testament,
Southern California College
Ecclesiastes

Brad H. Young, B.A., M.A., Ph.D.
Professor of New Testament Studies
Oral Roberts University
Leviticus

Kingdom Dynamics

Included throughout the *Spirit-Filled Life® Bible* is a treasury of insight developed by some of today's most respected Christian leaders. Kingdom Dynamics focuses 22 challenging and crucial Bible topics, providing enlightening discussions of these topics at more than 350 passages in the Scripture. The central goal of the subjects presented is to relate "power points" of the Holy Spirit-filled life that touch 1) Foundational Precepts, 2) Life-Releasing Promises, 3) Relational Priorities, and 4) practical Power Principles.

Wherever one of these timeless topics is mentioned in Scripture, it is highlighted (keyed with a dove symbol and gray-screened to set it apart from the Bible text). Each entry follows this format: chapter(s) and verse(s) being referenced, title of the particular article under its larger topic (abbreviated form in capital letters), and commentary.

ourselves (as though *our authority*
did not extend to you), [a]for it was to
you that we came with the gospel of
Christ;
15 not boasting of things beyond measure, *that is,* [a]in other men's labors,
but having hope, *that* as your faith is
increased, we shall be greatly *enlarged by you in our sphere,
16 to preach the gospel in the *regions*
beyond you, *and* not to boast in another man's sphere of accomplishment.

KINGDOM DYNAMICS

10:15, 16 The Continuing Call "Beyond," WORLD EVANGELISM. Paul's words of "having hope ... to preach the gospel in the regions beyond you" reveal he was never content to keep the message within the Christian community. As John Wesley said, "The world is my parish." This text models the church's mandate to reach "beyond you." Christ's orders are clear: "Make disciples of all the nations" (Matt. 28:19); "preach the gospel to every creature" (Mark 16:15); "[preach] repentance and remission of sins" (Luke 24:47); and go "as the Father has sent Me" (John 20:21) "to the end of the earth" (Acts 1:8). When the full command is obeyed, the full promise will be fulfilled.

(Rom. 10:13–15/Gal. 6:7, 8) G.C.

4 17 But [a]*"he who glories, let him glory*
in the LORD."

15 [a]Rom. 15:20 *See WW at Acts 5:13.
17 [a]Jer. 9:24
18 [a]Prov. 27:2 [b]Rom. 2:29

CHAPTER 11

1 [a]2 Cor. 11:4, 16, 19 *See WW at 2 Thess. 1:4.
2 [a]Gal. 4:17 [b]Hos. 2:19 [c]Col. 1:28 [d]Lev. 21:13 *See WW at 1 Cor. 14:1. • See WW at 1 John 3:3.
3 [a]Gen. 3:4, 13 [b]Eph. 6:24 [1]NU adds *and purity* *See WW at 1 Cor. 3:19.
4 [a]Gal. 1:6–8 *See WW at John 14:16. • See WW at Acts 4:12.
5 [a]2 Cor. 12:11 *See WW at Luke 22:35.

11:2 jea
#2205:
"zeal."
asm, in
ment. T
zeal (7:
(Acts 5:

3 But
serpent
ness, so
from the
4 For i
other J
preache
spirit wh
a [a]differ
accepted
it!

Paul and

5 For I
*inferior
6 Even
speech,
But [c]we
fested ar
7 Did I
self that
cause I
you [a]fre
8 I rob
wages *fr*
9 And

Following a Kingdom Dynamics chain is easy to do. The last line of each entry includes references separated by a slash (/). The reference before the slash takes you to the passage where the preceding Kingdom Dynamic is found (an asterisk in this position indicates that the Kingdom Dynamic you are currently reading is the first in the chain). The reference after the slash takes you to the next passage under that particular theme (an asterisk following the last reference indicates that you have completed the chain and takes you back to the beginning of it).

Most of the Kingdom Dynamics themes have been addressed by a leader noted for his or her study or emphasis in that area. The initials at the end of an entry indicate its author. NOTE: We realize that some of the themes treated are subject to differences in interpretation and application. The *Spirit-Filled Life®* *Bible* has included these

Foundational Precepts

Undergirding all of life are essential points of understanding absolutely necessary to our spiritual freedom, growth, and effectiveness.

The Word of God provides footings for faith. Jack W. Hayford (J.W.H.)

The Blood of the Covenant provides salvation for the soul. Charles Simpson (C.S.)

The Kingdom of God focuses life's intended purposes. Jack W. Hayford (J.W.H.)

Prayer and Spiritual Development sustains fellowship with God. Larry Lea (L.L.)

Assigned to World Evangelism keeps our vision beyond ourselves. Glen Cole (G.C.)

Prophecy and the Scriptures keeps vibrancy in our response to the Word and the Spirit. Jack W. Hayford (J.W.H.)

Spiritual Answers to Hard Questions focuses on questions related to God's nature and our salvation, Spirit-filled living, and laws of the kingdom of God. M. G. "Pat" Robertson (P.R.)

Life-Releasing Promises

God has given rich realms of promise to assist in the expansion of our potential in our personal, daily life and faithful service for Christ. While He has called us to forgiveness and eternal life, He has also opened the door to ever-increasing dimensions of fulfillment.

The Holy Spirit and Restoration—God wills to recover every loss and realize every purpose He has for us. James Robison (J.R.)

God's Plan for Prosperity—God wills to insure our sufficiency for every good work. Frederick K. C. Price (F.P.)

The Ministry of Angels—God assures our protection, defense, and advance in warfare. Marilyn Hickey (M.H.)

Principles of Seed Faith—God calls us to generosity in living and giving. Oral Roberts (O.R.)

Messianic Promises and Christ's Coming—God reminds us His covenants are true and faithful and our hope for ultimate joy and victory are secured.

Jack Hayford III (J.H.)

Spiritual Answers to Hard Questions addresses questions on the end times. M. G. "Pat" Robertson (P.R.)

nonetheless, not as a conclusive endorsement of any but as a representation of truth as applied by some, that we all may study together even at points of difference. Often to do so is to discover that one presumed to be a doctrinal opponent is seen on closer examination to be more in line with one's own thinking than was first supposed. Thus, the diversity of the themes and approaches offered here may contribute to better understanding as well as expanded enrichment to us all.

Relational Priorities

Just as Jesus summarized the Ten Commandments in two phrases, "Love God . . . love your neighbor," so we as His disciples are required to prioritize human relationships as well as our relationship with God. Maturity is impossible without learning and applying these principles:

God's Order for Family Life cultivates the roots of relationship in our homes.
Larry Christenson (L.C.)

The Worth of the Human Personality stimulates the mindset governing our relationship with individuals and all mankind. Charles Blake (C.B.)

Brotherly Love pulsates the breath of the Spirit into the words of Jesus' Greatest Commandments.
Demos Shakarian (D.S.)

The Work and Ministry of Women liberates women on God's holy terms rather than politicized human terms.
Freda Lindsay (F.L.)

The Traits of Spiritual Leadership initiates the multiplying of effective relationships through maturing leaders who relate maturely and beget maturing disciples.
Jamie Buckingham (J.B.)

Spiritual Answers to Hard Questions examines questions on morality and ethics.
M. G. "Pat" Robertson (P.R.)

Power Principles

Godly living is not only intended to be devoted and disciplined but also dynamic. The command of Jesus to "receive the Holy Spirit" is His call to enter the realm of Kingdom Dynamics in which the Spirit of God not only indwells us fruitfully but overflows us powerfully.

Holy Spirit Gifts and Power—Through these we are enabled with supernatural abilities for edifying the church and evangelizing the world.
Paul Walker (P.W.)

The Pathway of Praise—Praise explodes strongholds and paves the path to victory. Charles Green (C.G.)

The Ministry of Divine Healing—God still works through human instruments to extend this gentle grace.
Nathaniel Van Cleave (N.V.)

Faith's Confession of God's Word—The appropriating of God's promises is essential if we are to apply them to our circumstances.
Roy Hicks, Sr. (R.H.)

Advancing in Spiritual Warfare—The victory of His Cross is extended only as faithful intercessors "wrestle" against dark powers and win through the power of Jesus' name and blood.
Dick Eastman (D.E.)

Spiritual Answers to Hard Questions answers questions on the demonic.
M. G. "Pat" Robertson (P.R.)

THE WORD OF GOD (THE WORD OF GOD)

Jack W. Hayford

God's Word has been unscrolled in both the Scriptures and in His incarnate Son—Jesus Christ. Jesus, in describing the importance of the eternal Scriptures said, "Man shall not live by bread alone, but by every word that proceeds from the mouth of God" (Matt. 4:4). He also commended the steadfast inquiry into the Word of God: "Search the Scriptures . . . they . . . testify of Me" (John 5:39). There is no such thing as health or growth in Christian living apart from a clear priority on the place of the Bible in the life of the individual or the group. The Scriptures are the conclusive standard for our faith, morals, and practical living and are the nourishment for our rising to strength in faith, holiness in living, and effectiveness in service. The Holy Spirit who comes to fill us is the same Person who has given us the Book to guide and sustain us. The writer of this study has demonstrated the balance the Bible brings to living in his life, in his teaching ministry, and in his leadership.

THE SOURCE AND NATURE OF GOD'S WORD

1. **The Divine Inspiration of the Bible** (2 Tim. 3:16)
The Bible is "God-breathed" and the words planned by God's creative design.
2. **The Complete Trustworthiness of the Bible** (Ps. 19:7)
The Word of God is "perfect" in its accuracy and "sure" in its dependability.
3. **The Content of God's Word Is Completed** (Prov. 30:5, 6)
The Bible is complete, completely trustworthy, and sufficient to completely answer anything we need to know about eternal salvation or practical wisdom concerning relationships, morality, character, and conduct.
4. **Jesus and the Holy Scriptures** (Luke 16:17)
Jesus confirms that every word of Scripture is given by God, every truth is to be held inviolable, that the Scriptures are indissoluble and credible.
5. **The Way God's Word Is to Be Ministered** (2 Cor. 3:5–8)
The Word of God is to be ministered literally and life-givingly in the Spirit of Truth and the Spirit of Life.

THE ESSENTIAL PLACE AND POWER OF GOD'S WORD

6. **The Regenerating Power of God's Word** (1 Pet. 1:23)
The Word of God regenerates new spiritual life where man has, by nature, died spiritually.
7. **The Authority of God's Word over Our Lives** (Ps. 119:89–91)
As "spiritual" people we are to refuse the "natural" inclinations of fallen man, giving place instead to hearing and yielding to the authority of God's own Word.
8. **God's Word and Our Soul's Nourishment** (Deut. 8:3)
Spiritual survival is not possible for long without feeding upon the Word of God.
9. **God's Word and Practical, Fruitful Living** (Ps. 119:105)
The regular application of the Word of God is the pathway to success and prosperity in living.
10. **True Spiritual Growth Requires God's Word** (1 Cor. 3:1–5)
True spiritual growth requires the Word of God, which makes spiritual maturity genuine.
11. **Loving God's Word As Jesus' Follower** (John 14:21)
To follow Jesus and to know God a continuing requirement of steadfast commitment to hearing, heeding, and studying the Bible is necessary.
12. **God's Word: Purifier unto Holy Living** (James 1:23–25)
The Bible shows us Christ's likeness so that we can be ordered and shaped into that image.
13. **God's Word, Evangelism, and Expansion** (Is. 55:10, 11)
The spreading of God's Word and the fulfillment of our personal potential come by the Word of God.
14. **God's Word: Read It! Study It! Memorize It!** (2 Tim. 2:15)
God's Word is the only conclusive source of wisdom, knowledge, and understanding concerning ultimate realities waiting to liberate and enrich those who will pursue its wealth.

THE BLOOD OF THE COVENANT (THE BLOOD)

Charles Simpson

From the Garden of Eden to the garden in heaven's paradise, the blood of sacrifice is the constant Testimony of God's grace. As fallen man was clothed with skins of animals sacrificed by God Himself for such provision (Gen. 3:21), so the blood of the Lamb was shed to clothe in the righteousness of God every member of mankind who will receive His gift. This is the song of those who make this covenant with God "by sacrifice." Thus God will gather to Himself "those who have made a covenant with Me by sacrifice" (Ps. 50:5), and forever they shall sing the song of the redeemed: "To Him who loved us and washed us from our sins in His own blood . . . " (Rev. 1:5). This writer has studied God's pathways of covenant and has taught those principles as a pastor, teacher, and leader for over thirty years, demonstrating that the covenant-life is a steadfastly committed one.

1. **God the Covenant-Maker** (Gen. 1:3–5)
From the beginning God is revealed as the covenant-maker.
2. **"Covenant" First Appears with Noah** (Gen. 8:20)
Noah sacrifices to God, and we see the term "covenant" appear as God covenants never to destroy creation by flood again.
3. **Isaac, the Result of Covenant** (Gen. 22:13)
God's covenant gave Abraham a son, and covenant love provided a substitutionary sacrifice.
4. **Circumcision's Significance** (Gen. 17:10)
Circumcision speaks of cutting away of fleshly dependence and placing hope for future prosperity in God.
5. **The First Blood Sacrifice Covenant** (Gen. 15:10)
God originates the covenant bond; sacrifice is offered in a prescribed manner, and God takes sovereign administration of the oath.
6. **No Blood, No Atonement** (Lev. 17:11)
Life is in the blood. Apart from shedding of blood (giving of life), there was no atonement.
7. **Developing the Importance of Blood Sacrifice** (Ex. 12:13)
Sacrifice was a means of deliverance, sin offering, and consecrative act.
8. **The Blood, Essential for Right Standing Before God** (Gen. 4:1–10)
Right standing before a covenant-making God is shown to be a matter of life and death, not merely a matter of one's good efforts.
9. **The Issue of Blood Is Right Relationship** (Is. 1:11)
God's holiness required blood for cleansing, but right relationship is the ultimate goal of His covenant.
10. **Christ's Sacrifice, Permanent Relief** (Heb. 9:12)
Christ's blood was applied to a heavenly altar, where once and for all redemption was provided.
11. **The Blood, the Covering** (Gen. 3:21)
Blood is the only God-ordained covering for sin.
12. **God Sovereignly Inaugurates the New Covenant** (Matt. 26:28)
A new and eternal bond was established by the blood of Jesus.
13. **Right Relationship with God Through Blood** (Rom. 3:25)
The blood of Christ is forever the only means of right relationship with the holy God.
14. **Gentiles Embraced by Christ's Sacrifice** (Eph. 2:13)
Gentiles are now grafted into the patriarchs and covenants of promise and are included as heirs of all of God's promises.
15. **Bought Back By the Blood** (1 Pet. 1:18, 19)
The blood of Christ is the price for our purchase, or redemption.
16. **Partaking in the Blood** (John 6:53, 54)
Partaking in the covenant blood of Christ means being joined to God and receiving the benefits of His life.
17. **Christ's Blood Satisfies Holiness, Thereby Making Peace** (Col. 1:20)
Jesus Christ gave divine life in blood to satisfy mankind's sin debts and restore covenant peace.
18. **The Blood, Reconciliation, and Victorious Living** (Rom. 5:9)
The blood of Christ deals with the issue of man's separation from God, and faith in His blood infuses divine life for triumph over sin.
19. **The Weapon of the Blood** (Rev. 12:11)
The blood of Christ provides every believer with the necessary provision to defeat Satan.

20. **The Significance of Communion's Covenant** (1 Cor. 10:16)
Blessings and responsibilities of the covenant are extended laterally among those who partake of Christ together.

THE KINGDOM OF GOD

Jack W. Hayford

The whole of Jesus' own preaching, teaching, and ministry centered in these words: "The kingdom of God is at hand" (Mark 1:15). He came as the Savior-Lamb to rescue and redeem mankind to know his original estate in the divine order. The dynamic of Christian life and ministry is found in understanding the kingdom of God, which is not in "eating and drinking" (that is, ritual performance), but in "righteousness and peace and joy in the Holy Spirit" (Rom. 14:17). In a thoroughgoing development constituting 39 brief articles under eight headings, the 1) Foundations, 2) Terminology, 3) Message, 4) Character, 5) Ministry, 6) Conflict, 7) Worship, and 8) Prophecy of (and) the Kingdom are elaborated. Here is a wealth of material to establish a full-orbed perspective on the kingdom of God, the essence of the church's message and life. The writer of this study unfolds the balance that calls us to kingdom life and power in the present, while still anticipating the kingdom's final fullness and consummation in the future.

FOUNDATIONS OF THE KINGDOM

1. **God's Sovereignty** (Gen. 1:1)
God's realm is transcendent; His reign is exercised by His will, word, and works; and His regency (authority to rule) is His preexistence and holiness.

2. **Man's Delegated "Dominion"** (Gen. 1:26–28; 2:16, 17)
God has delegated His rule, and it extends as far as man's faithfulness to obey God's law.

3. **Before the Fall** (Gen. 1:31)
The perfect will of God is not manifest in the presence of death, disease, discord, or disaster.

4. **Impact of the Fall** (Gen. 3:16–24)
Man's dominion is forfeited to Satan; the curse spreads through all the Earth, but God moves redemptively to recover man's lost estate.

5. **After the Flood** (Gen. 8:20—9:17)
A renewed order is established: animals now fear man. A cleansed realm for seeking first God's kingdom is established, and new hope dawns.

6. **Prototype "Kingdom" Person** (Gen. 12:1–3)
Abraham demonstrates two key points: faith relationship with God and God's plan to restore man's "reign in life."

7. **Patriarchal Examples** (Gen. 26:1–5; 28:1–22)
The patriarchs reveal the duality of redemption: restored relationship with God and rulership in life under God.

8. **Human Responsibility** (1 Chr. 29:10–16)
Man is held accountable for Earth. The redeemed may partner with God and thereby decisively assist in the reestablishment of God's rule.

TERMINOLOGY OF THE KINGDOM

9. **Defining the Hope** (Matt. 3:1, 2)
"The kingdom" refers to God's sovereign rule and the entry of the Messiah, which means an end to the rule of death and deadening human systems.

10. **Synonymous Expressions** (Matt. 19:23, 24)
"The kingdom of God" and "the kingdom of heaven" are synonymous to "the kingdom," and labored effort to make significant distinctions between them is unnecessary.

11. **John's Writings** (John 18:36)
John uses the term "eternal life" to show his readers that the kingdom is spiritual, not that the kingdom passed with Jesus' ministry or the birth of the church.

12. **Paul's Writings** (Col. 1:27, 28)
Paul uses the expression "in Christ," which is how a believer enters the kingdom and shares in all the benefits of this new rule.

THE MESSAGE OF THE KINGDOM

13. **The Gospel of the Kingdom** (Mark 1:14, 15)
The synoptic Gospels and Acts show that Jesus preached "the gospel of the kingdom" and transmitted it to His

disciples who experienced confirming signs.

14. Repentance (Matt. 3:1, 2; 4:17)
The first call to the kingdom is repentance for birth, growth, and fruit.

15. New Birth (John 3:1–5)
A new order of life comes upon the believer, which births relationship with God and new perspective.

16. Present and Future Kingdom (Matt. 13:1–52)
The present kingdom is now, where God is recovering man's lost relationship with and rulership under God. The future kingdom is Christ's coming reign.

17. People of the Kingdom (Col. 1:13)
People who have received Jesus have been transferred into another kingdom where they operate as citizens, ambassadors, and militia of this kingdom.

18. The Kingdom Within You (Luke 17:20, 21)
The kingdom of God is a spiritual reality that is in one's life, over one's affairs, and expressed through one's life, love, and service.

CHARACTER AND THE KINGDOM

19. Basic Traits (Matt. 5:1—7:27)
In the Sermon on the Mount, Jesus outlines nine primary characteristics of people who receive the rule of God's kingdom.

20. Childlikeness (Matt. 18:1–4)
Christ's call to childlikeness establishes a spirit by which authority of the believer is to be exercised as an agent of God's kingdom power.

21. Forgiveness (Matt. 18:18–35)
Not forgiving can restrict what God would do in others, and can reap penalties for the unforgiving one as well as take toll on bodies, minds, and emotions.

22. Integrity and Morality (1 Cor. 6:9, 10)
Holiness of heart and life keep channels of communication open with God and insure the Holy Spirit's free access to fulfilling the Father's will.

MINISTRY OF THE KINGDOM

23. The Holy Spirit (Mark 1:15)
Having been born again does not qualify us for ministry; we need spiritual enduement for ministry.

24. Authority for Ministry (Luke 9:1, 2)
We may expect power over darkness; we are Christ's authorized representatives and God will provide us with peace and power.

25. Prayer and Intercession (Luke 11:2–4)
Prayer is our role of functioning as "kingdom administrators" to see ministry birthed and triumphed.

26. Casting Out Demons (Luke 11:20)
Power over demons is a signal of true ministry, but rejoicing is to be over salvation.

27. Receiving Kingdom Power (Acts 1:3–8)
The Holy Spirit is the One who brings power to man and must be received; it is not an automatic experience.

CONFLICT AND THE KINGDOM

28. Earth's Evil "Ruler" (Luke 4:1–12)
The present world systems are grounded by the destructive rule of Satan.

29. Taking It by Force (Matt. 11:12)
The kingdom of God enters by a kind of force, opposing human status quo by the entry of the Holy Spirit's power working in people.

30. Grounds of Authority (Col. 2:13–15)
The Cross is man's only hope for relationship with God and reinstatement to his place of "reigning in life."

31. Pressing In (Luke 16:16)
The kingdom of God is advanced through preaching, impassioned prayer, confrontation with the demonic, expectation for the miraculous, and a flaming heart.

32. Suffering, Tribulation (Acts 14:21, 22)
The power and the kingdom do not make one immune to life's struggles, but they do bring the promise of victory.

WORSHIP AND THE KINGDOM

33. A Kingdom of Priests (Ex. 19:5–7)
Through worship "kingdom priests" will discover means for their future victories.

34. "Establishing" God's Throne (Ps. 22:3)
God's is the power; ours is the privilege to praisefully invite His "enthroned" presence.

35. Inviting God's Rule (Ps. 93:2)
God's mighty Spirit is invited into any difficult situation by praying, "Your kingdom come. Your will be done—here," and then filling your life's setting with praise.

36. Worship and Praise (Rev. 1:5, 6)
The authority we are called to move in as "priests to God" is only fully accomplished in the spirit of praiseful worship.

37. Priority of Worship (1 Pet. 2:9)
The priority and growth in worship births powerful evangelism and spiritual victories.

PROPHECY AND THE KINGDOM

38. **Old Testament: Possessing the Kingdom** (Daniel 7:21, 22)
Saints possess the kingdom by steadfast battle, a mixture of victory and defeat with consummate triumph anticipated at Christ's coming.

39. **New Testament: Agelong Warfare** (Rev. 12:10, 11)
This age is an agelong battle where the believer is supplied with resources for kingdom victories.

PRAYER AND SPIRITUAL DEVELOPMENT (PRAYER)

Larry Lea

The night before His crucifixion, Jesus underscored the privileged pathway of prayer now being opened to His own through His Cross: "Until now you have asked nothing in My name. Ask, and you will receive, that your joy may be full" (John 16:24). By His own emphasis, Jesus placed prayer at the heart of Christian living. When the pulse is steady and the body exercised in this practice, every other facet of life flows with health as the individual is fed by God's Word. Yet, prayer is a puzzle to some who think it too mystical and a problem for others who find the habit hard to establish. But the writer of this study has been uniquely gifted to help people to practical, applicable-to-life patterns of prayer, as well as unveiling prayer secrets that help for habits by igniting understanding which prompts believers into dynamic prayer-patterns, rather than merely issuing rules. The result is prayer that builds blessing and fruitfulness in your life.

1. **Prayer Principles from God's Conversation with Abraham** (Gen. 18:17–33)
God saves by many or few: The absence of good brings the end of God's longsuffering. Our intercession is to be in line with God's character.

2. **The Heart of the Intercessor** (Ex. 32:11–14, 30–34)
Moses demonstrates unselfish, life-surrendering intercession that prevails beyond otherwise destructive effects of human weakness and sinning.

3. **Joshua and His Warriors Stand in the Gap** (Josh. 10:12–14)
Joshua and his warriors stood in the gap, contending for God's eternal purposes, teaching the triumph such faith may realize in spiritual warfare.

4. **God Intervenes with Power** (Is. 36:1—37:38)
Hezekiah and Isaiah demonstrate the power of prayer to face troublesome times and break evil powers.

5. **Intercessors (Gap People) Link God's Mercy with Human Need** (Ezek. 22:30)
God is looking for intercessors to stand "in the gap," bar intruders, and usher in God's mercy.

6. **Spiritual Leaders: Pray As Well As Teach** (Eph. 3:14–21)
Knowing the strength of Christianity is inward character, Paul prayed that Christ would imprint His nature upon the people's minds, wills, and emotions.

7. **Prayer and Fasting Birth Signs and Wonders** (Acts 13:1—14:28)
Ministries stand between God's abundance and human need. Supporting them by prayer and fasting will birth signs and wonders as God confirms His word.

8. **Prayer, the Proving Grounds of Our Faith** (Acts 4:1–37)
Prayer, not debate or argument, is the proving grounds of our faith.

9. **God's Holy Fire Falls** (2 Chr. 6:12–42; 7:1)
The moment we lay our choicest gifts upon the altar, God's holy fire falls; and whenever we make room for God, He always comes and fills.

10. **Unceasing Prayer Is a Key to Deliverance** (Acts 12:1–17)
Great deliverance comes through prayer, sometimes so surprisingly we may find it difficult to believe it ourselves!

11. **The Lord's Prayer** (Matt. 6:9–13)
The Lord's Prayer outlines seven major topics, each representing a basic human need.

12. **Prayer Is Agreeing with God's Will** (1 John 5:14, 15)
Immature faith tries to manipulate God; mature faith seeks to move under the banner of God's will.

13. **A Prayerful Quest for God Is the Pathway to Satisfaction** (John 4:34)
Earnestly seeking God will lead to our finding spiritual strength and satisfaction.

14. **David Asks for Joy and God's Presence** (Ps. 1–19)
David cried out, not only for pardon, but for purity; not only for acquittal, but for acceptance; not only for comfort, but for complete cleansing.

ASSIGNED TO WORLD EVANGELISM (WORLD EVANGELISM)

Glen Cole

From the earliest expression of God's intent to redeem fallen man, He has appointed a "Seed" that would accomplish the task (Gen. 3:15). That "Seed of the woman" fulfilled in Jesus Christ, was destined to become the "Seed of Abraham" through whom all the nations of the Earth are intended to be blessed (Gal. 3:29; Gen. 12:3). When the Lord says to Israel, just delivered from Egypt, "All the earth *is* Mine," He links it to a mission: "You shall be to Me a kingdom of priests" (Ex. 19:5, 6). There is no question as to their call being from bondage and into mission. So it is, from the beginning of the Bible story of redemption, the redeemed are assigned to world evangelization. The writer of this study leads one of today's mega-churches in living this truth: 1) receiving God's grace and then 2) sending God's truth; in 1) being filled with the Spirit and then 2) going to the uttermost part of the Earth.

1. **God's Promise to His Messiah** (Ps. 2:8)
God invites His Son to "ask" for the nations, and so we ask in His name and receive the inheritance of nations.
2. **Committed Action to Our Generation** (Prov. 24:11, 12)
We are responsible to our generation and accountable to God to spread the gospel.
3. **Spread the Good Tidings—Fearlessly** (Is. 40:8–11)
Answering our call to spread "good tidings," we are wise to be fearlessly obedient, believing God to confirm His Word.
4. **His Field—A Promise of Harvest** (Matt. 13:37, 38)
"The field is the world." Christ's own imagery points to the process of world evangelism: Go and sow.
5. **The Gospel and "The End"** (Matt. 24:14)
God cares for all people; Jesus died for every person, and the Word of God is for every nation—before "the end."
6. **Commissioned Under the King's Call** (Matt. 28:18–20)
Jesus leads His followers to think, live, and pray that His kingdom come to our entire planet.
7. **Commissioned in Christ's Servant Spirit** (Mark 16:15–18)
God seeks those who will serve without seeking recognition, selflessly and obediently seeking to exalt Christ, making Him known.
8. **Commissioned to Go with Christ's Compassion** (Luke 24:45–48)
Our fulfillment of the Great Commission requires a worldwide scope in ministering compassion and human concern.
9. **Commissioned with a Mandate and a Message** (John 20:21–23)
We are not only sent with the substance of the message—salvation; we are sent to bring the spirit of its truth—forgiveness.
10. **Christ's Final Charter and Promise** (Acts 1:8)
Let us first receive the Holy Spirit's anointing—power to act—then we shall find the lost and boldly declare Jesus as the Son of God.
11. **The Sole Avenue of Salvation** (Acts 4:12)
There is no authority, personality, system, or philosophy that can effect the rescue of the human soul other than personal trust in Christ.
12. **Christ—The Absolute Need of Every Man** (Rom. 3:23)
A clear look into the Word of God will help us capture and retain the conviction that all mankind desperately needs the gospel of Christ.
13. **The Absolute Need for a Messenger** (Rom. 10:13–15)
Someone must be sent to preach so that people will hear and believe.
14. **The Continuing Call "Beyond"** (2 Cor. 10:15, 16)
God calls His people to go "beyond" the

Christian community and reach people on new frontiers.

15. **The Seedtime of Our Lifetime** (Gal. 6:7, 8)
A God-possessed life guarantees partnership with God in worldwide fruitfulness.

16. **Destined for Victory** (Rev. 5:8–10)
The ultimate triumph of the Great Commission at work, as an innumerable people gather at God's eternal throne.

PROPHECY AND THE SCRIPTURES (PROPHECY)

Jack W. Hayford

What should be the believer's stance toward the potential of every Spirit-filled Christian to prophesy (Acts 2:17, 18; 1 Cor. 14:31)? What is the relative authority of the Bible in the giving of "words" of prophecy and in the judging or evaluation of their truth or merit? Here are keys to unlock the potential of this ministry without being detoured to dead-end streets of folly or error. The writer of this study has led and pastored for decades, modeling and teaching a way of balance, 1) employing the gift of prophecy as the Holy Spirit appoints and 2) keeping the eternal Word of Scripture central and sovereign in that exercise.

1. **The Holy Scriptures and the Spirit of Prophecy** (Rev. 19:10)
The Bible is prophetic: a book that reveals God's will through His Word and His Works, as well as a Book that reveals God's plans and predictions.

2. **Prophecy Not Christ-Centered Is Disqualified** (1 John 4:1–6)
Jesus Christ is to be presented and honored in a way that is consistent with the whole of Scriptures.

3. **The Spirit of Revelation** (Eph. 1:17–19)
Paul desires for a type of revelation that will enable people to know Christ and come to understand God's purposes and power in their lives.

4. **The Propriety and Desirability of Prophecy** (1 Cor. 14:1)
In fulfillment of Joel's prophecy and Moses' expressed hope, prophecy is to be welcomed for edification, exhortation, and comfort.

5. **Prophecy and the Sufficiency of God's Word** (2 Pet. 1:16–19)
No prophecy or experience holds a greater authority than the Word of God.

6. **The Issue of Personal Prophecy** (Acts 21:11)
Personal prophecy will usually be confirmative and the character of the giver weighed. The word is not to be viewed as "controlling" and may only be "in part," not bearing the whole story.

7. **The Office of the Prophet** (Acts 11:27–30)
The office of a prophet is for edification of the body: to enlarge and refresh the body, whether locally or beyond.

8. **The Purposes of Predictive Prophecies** (Deut. 28:1)
The purposes of predictive prophecies are to teach, to warn, and to instruct toward obedience and fruitful living.

9. **The Prophecies of Last Things** (1 John 2:18)
God is sovereign over all history, which shall reveal Him as all-wise and all-just as everyone stands before Him.

10. **Interpretive Approaches to the Book of Revelation** (Rev. 4:1)
The Book of Revelation tolerates a wide spectrum of approaches, which have the common denominator of the ultimate triumph of Jesus Christ.

11. **The "Day of the Lord" in Prophecy** (Obad. 15)
The "Day of the Lord" refers to the time when God intervenes to bring salvation to His people and punishment to the rebellious.

12. **Prophecy and the Future of Israel** (Ps. 122:6)
Differences of position concerning the future of Israel center on the question: Does Israel, as the ancient people of God, still hold a preferred place in His economy, or have they lost that place through unbelief?

13. **The Church and Present-Day Israel** (Rom. 11:19–24)
It is wise for believers to avoid the presumption of passivity toward Israel, since the evidence of all history is that God has not forgotten this people.

SPIRITUAL ANSWERS TO HARD QUESTIONS (SPIRITUAL ANSWERS)

Pat Robertson

Popular Christian talk show host and president of the Christian Broadcasting Network answers thirty-eight crucial and interesting questions, selected because of the frequency of their occurrence and the teaching value the answers provide. The questions touch all four of the Kingdom Dynamics "power points": 1) Foundational Precepts, 2) Life-Releasing Promises, 3) Relational Priorities, and 4) Power Principles. *This article begins on page 1996.*

THE HOLY SPIRIT AND RESTORATION (RESTORATION)

James Robison

Divine hope is the hallmark of the Holy Spirit's working. Inherent in the prophesied promise of Pentecost is the everlasting word, "I will restore the years that the swarming locust has eaten" (Joel 2:25–27). The whole of the passage promises a wholeness of recovery—a primary trait of the era of the Holy Spirit. In a fashion that characterizes the hope-filled qualities of his global ministry of evangelism, the writer of this study calls attention to the trail of promise that relentlessly proceeds through the whole of Scripture, offering hope when reason argues against it and promising restoration when it is obvious only God could bring such promise about. *This article begins on page 2012.*

1. **New Testament Prophecy** (Acts 3:19–21)
   This text unfolds the NT prophecy of restoration.
2. **Biblical Definition** (Job 40:10–12)
   This text gives the biblical definition of restoration.
3. **Restoration "In the Beginning"** (Gen. 3:21)
   This text shows the restoration "in the beginning."
4. **Man's Plunge into Degradation** (Gen. 6:5)
   This text reveals man's plunge into degradation.
5. **Restoration Foreshadowed** (Gen. 41:42–43)
   This text offers a foreshadowing of restoration.
6. **Man's Futile Efforts at Self-Restoration** (Jer. 8:8, 9)
   This text demonstrates man's futile efforts at self-restoration.
7. **Restoration and the Corruption of Leadership** (Ezek. 34:1–10)
   This text displays the corruption of leadership.
8. **Restoration and the Futility of Religious Ritual** (Amos 5:21–23)
   This text reminds of the futility of religious ritual.
9. **Restoration and the Shaking of Man's Works** (Heb. 12:26, 27)
   This text warns of God's shaking the works of man's hands.
10. **Repentance in Restoration** (Is. 58:1–14)
    This text emphasizes the place of repentance in restoration.
11. **Restoration of David's Tabernacle** (Acts 15:16–18)
    This text prophesies of the restoration of the tabernacle of David.
12. **Restoration of the God-Image** (Is. 4:2, 3)
    This text prophesies the restoration of the God-image.
13. **Restoration of Intimacy with God** (Rev. 19:7–9)
    This text promises intimacy with God.
14. **The Holy Spirit: The Agent of Restoration** (Joel 2:28, 29)
    This text designates the agent of restoration: the Holy Spirit.
15. **The Meaning of Restoration to an Individual** (John 10:10)
    This text describes what restoration means to the individual.
16. **The Meaning of Restoration to the Church** (John 13:34, 35)
    This text describes what restoration means to the church.

GOD'S PLAN FOR PROSPERITY (GOD'S PROSPERITY)

Fred Price

A trail of models mark the price of following the pathway of faith: the price is unselfishness, service, sacrifice, and giving. From Abraham to the apostles the highway of holy power is seen. But another fact becomes inescapably clear: God's bounty of blessing attends these sacrificial, self-giving servants of His. He covenants to 1) bless, 2) prosper, and 3) abound. The law is irretrievably set in Divine Order: faithfulness in giving and service results in a return and reward of abundance, and such prosperity continues to recycle as faith and giving continue. The writer of this study has held forth this principle at the price of being frequently misunderstood to suggest "cheap" prosperity. But examining his teaching of this truth one finds a biblical evidence for expecting to prosper; however, the pathway is one of discipleship, and it is not cheap.

1. **God's Prosperity Plan Includes Tithing** (Mal. 3:8–10)
   Not tithing is robbing God and robbing ourselves of His blessings.
2. **The Law of Divine Reciprocity** (Luke 6:38)
   You give to God and God gives to you; prosperity begins with investment.

3. **Prosperity Is a Result** (3 John 2)
Prosperity is not an end of itself but a result of a quality of life, commitment and dedication to God.
4. **Happy, Holy, Healthy, and at Peace** (Ps. 35:27)
God is pleased when His servants prosper, which means to be safe, happy, healthy, and at peace.
5. **Using Things, Not Loving Them** (Mark 10:17–27)
God is not opposed to His people having things but to things controlling His people.
6. **Riches Are a Responsibility** (1 Tim. 6:17)
It is a great responsibility to have wealth.
7. **Riches Are Not to Be Trusted** (Phil. 4:12, 13)
Our trust is to remain in God and our lives geared to His Word.
8. **Prospered to Bless** (Deut. 8:18)
Abundance is God's intent so that the believer can bless others.
9. **Abundant Life** (John 10:10)
God's plan was for man to be enriched; Jesus declares His intention to recover this.
10. **Responsible Commitment in God's Prosperity Plan** (Ps. 1:1–3)
No promise of God is without responsible action to be taken on our part.
11. **Sharpening Our Priorities** (Luke 12:15)
We should seek first the kingdom of God; then the things we need will be added to us.
12. **Do Whatever He Says; Then You Will Prosper** (Phil. 4:19)
God is not stingy, but we are to do all the Scripture tells us so as to prosper.
13. **God's Heart to Prosper His People** (Gen. 12:1–3)
Each believer is to receive the blessings of Abraham, which include spiritual, emotional, physical, and material blessings.

THE MINISTRY OF ANGELS (ANGELS)

Marilyn Hickey

The unseen realm is constantly described in the Bible as immediately present in our midst, not as a distant reality but as a present one. Angels are not occasionally present in the Bible; they are constantly manifest! The word "angel" occurs over 250 times in the pages of God's eternal revelation of the Scriptures, not only describing things they have done but unfolding things they are assigned to do in our day, as well as in the past. The writer of this study is a world-renowned Bible teacher who brings the force of these invisible servants and warriors to bear upon our present day: "Are they not all ministering spirits sent forth to minister for those who will inherit salvation?" (Heb. 1:14). The answer from the Bible is "Yes," and that means their ministry applies to us—today.

1. **Fivefold Ministry of Angels** (Ps. 103:20, 21)
Angels exist to serve God in at least these five ways.
2. **Variety in the Appearance of Angels** (Judg. 13:6)
Angels appear in different forms, depending upon their order of creation.
3. **Organized Structure in the Angelic Realm** (Col. 1:16)
Angels are a structured society with different levels of authority, according to God's creative order.
4. **Angels' Influence over Nations** (Dan. 10:13)
Some angels have influence over nations and national issues.
5. **Angels as Messengers** (Acts 8:26)
Angels are still active in building God's kingdom on Earth through messages.
6. **Guardian Angels Watch Over Us** (Ps. 91:11, 12)
Each believer has his own guardian angel.
7. **The Angel of the Lord Receives Worship** (Ex. 3:2, 4)
The Lord God is referred to as the "Angel of the LORD" and therefore receives worship.
8. **Jesus and Angels** (Rev. 1:1)
Jesus is closely associated with angels at birth, the forty-day fast, His agony on the night of His betrayal, the Resurrection, the Ascension, and His Second Coming.

9. **Fallen Angels** (Rev. 12:7, 9)
Fallen angels have their minds and understandings covered with horrible deception, making them instruments of Satan's rebellion.
10. **Ministering Spirits** (Heb. 1:14)
Angels are ministering spirits that advance the ministry of Jesus and His church.
11. **Seraphim** (Is. 6:2)
Seraphim are constantly seen glorifying God, supervising heaven's worship, and hovering above the throne of God.
12. **The Cherubim** (Gen. 3:24)
Cherubim guard the throne of God and are closely related to presence and withdrawal of the glory of God.
13. **Archangels** (Jude 9)
Archangel means "to be first (in political rank or power)" and is the highest rank of heavenly hosts.
14. **Lucifer** (Is. 14:12–14)
Satan was once an angel. He fell into pride and spoke five "I will" statements against God, who made five responses.
15. **Believers Accompanied by Angels** (Luke 16:22)
Angels accompany believers into God's presence at death and gather them to Christ at His return.

PRINCIPLES OF SEED FAITH (SEED FAITH)

Oral Roberts

Jesus is called "The Seed" (Gen. 3:15), the Word of God is designated as "Seed" (Luke 8:11; 1 Pet. 1:23), the growth of the believer is likened to a plant (John 15), and the evangelism of the world to a harvest (Matt. 13:30). This only begins the imagery of "seed faith" in the Bible, a theme that is biblically developed in this study by one of this century's best-known healing evangelists. It is altogether desirable to capture a firm grasp of this truth, the essence of which is that the little we have to bring to God is not a limit to faith's possibilities. When we bring Him the smallest of our strength, faith resource, and ability, when it is placed in Him—sown like a seed—there is a guaranteed fruitfulness and harvest forthcoming. It is within the laws of God's creation—both the natural and the spiritual realm—and worthy to be applied in practical living.

1. **God Established the Principle of the Seed and the Law of Seedtime and Harvest** (Gen. 8:22)
To overcome your problems, become fruitful and reach your potential; follow God's law of seedtime and you will harvest.
2. **Give God Your Best—Then Expect His Best** (2 Sam. 24:24)
Give to God first, generously, and of your best; then you will experience harvest.
3. **God Is a Good God. He Desires Only His Best for You!** (Ex. 15:26)
God's goodness is abundantly promised to those who listen and do what He says.
4. **You Must Give God an Opportunity** (1 Kin. 17:8–16)
Your giving causes something to happen according to God's eternal purposes.
5. **God Has Unlimited Resources, and the Good News Is That He Makes Them Available to You** (2 Chr. 25:9)
There are no shortages in God's supply; when you give, you put yourself into a position for increase.
6. **God Has a Way for Getting Your Need Met, Your Problem Solved. That Way Is Rooted In Your Faith's Becoming a Seed** (Matt. 17:19, 20)
When we release our faith to God in action, it takes on the nature of a miracle in the making.
7. **God Desires Biblical Abundance for You** (John 10:10)
Believe God wants you to have abundance, and line up your highest desire with His.
8. **God Expects You to Receive a Harvest from Your Giving. He Wants Us to Expect a Miracle Return!** (Luke 6:38)
Our giving is not a debt we owe but a seed we sow, and giving and receiving go together.
9. **God Has a Due Season for All of the Seeds You Plant—Good Seeds As Well As Bad Seeds** (Gal. 6:7–9)
Whether good or bad, the seeds we sow will bring a harvest—some quickly, others later.
10. **Your Giving Proves God, Opens the Windows of Heaven to You, and Causes the Devourer to Be Rebuked** (Mal. 3:10, 11)
God invites people to verify His trustworthiness by their giving.

11. **Your Faith in God Is the Key to Your Receiving** (Mark 11:22–24)
Expectancy opens your life to God to receive everything good from Him.
12. **All of Our Giving Is to Be as to God Our Source** (Matt. 25:34–40)
As we give to others, we look to God, offering it as a service of love to Him.
13. **Be Wise As to Where You Plant Your Seeds of Faith. God Multiplies Seed Sown in Good Soil** (Mark 4:1–20)
We are responsible to plant our giving in places where there is fruit to God.
14. **God Multiplies Your Seed to More Than Meet Your Greatest Need** (Luke 5:1–11)
Not only does God multiply what you give Him, but you will find God in the midst of your multiplication.
15. **Give What You Have in Your Hand to Give** (2 Cor. 9:8–10)
God makes all bounty, self-satisfaction, and contentedness abound toward us so we can share with others.
16. **You Can Always Give a Seed of Prayer . . . A Seed of Forgiveness . . . A Seed of Love and Joy** (James 5:15, 16)
There is always something to give: prayer, love, forgiveness—so keep planting.
17. **God Gave to Us First. He Is Our Role Model for Giving and Receiving** (John 3:16)
God gave sacrificially of His best and gave expecting to receive. So should we.

MESSIANIC PROMISES AND CHRIST'S COMING (MESSIAH'S COMING)

Jack Hayford III

Two prophetic stars shine brightest in God's Word: the "Morningstar" and the "Daystar." The first heralds the coming of the new day (Rev. 22:16—Greek, *astar*) fulfilled in our Lord Jesus Christ who has already fulfilled the promised coming Messiah, heralding a yet future day when He shall come again. He who fulfilled the Old Testament prophecies has been announced as the other "Morningstar" (2 Pet. 1:19—Greek, *phosphoros*), the rising sun that not only heralds the coming day but rules it! In the New Testament, Jesus promises, "I will come again," and with that promise He holds in form a cluster of attendant promises to be fulfilled when He does. The writer of this study is a chemical scientist who has verified the trustworthiness of the prophetic truths of the Bible through systematic study. He offers this development of both the above truths.

1. **The Gospel's First Proclamation** (Gen. 3:15)
All the richness, mercy, sorrow, and glory of God's redeeming work is immediately proclaimed with the judgment on the Fall.
2. **Jesus, the Prophet of the Greater Covenant** (Deut. 18:18, 19)
Jesus is the Mediator of the New Covenant and the Prophet who fulfilled the requirements of the Old Covenant.
3. **Messiah's Becoming a Man** (Is. 9:6)
This verse contains reference to one of the greatest incomprehensible truths, the Incarnation.
4. **Christ Birthed by a Young, Virgin Woman** (Is. 7:14)
Christ is shown to come through a virgin, young woman.
5. **Messiah Born at Bethlehem** (Mic. 5:2, 4, 5)
Scribes knew where Christ would be born, yet did not go; we must be willing to follow God's leading and word to see promises fulfilled.
6. **The Lord of Lords or a Rabbi on a Colt?** (Zech. 9:9)
Men were looking for a great king, while the Lord of Lords rode by on the way to history's greatest triumph.
7. **Detailed Account of Judas's Betrayal** (Ps. 41:9; Zech. 11:12, 13)
David, 1,000 years before Christ, and Zechariah, 500 years before Christ, gave detailed prophecies of Judas's betrayal of Christ.
8. **Details of Messiah's Death** (Ps. 22:1–31)
The ridicule by the people, the pierced hands and feet, lots cast for His clothes, and the separation from the Father are mentioned here.
9. **Purposes of the Crucifixion, Atonement, and Abundant Life** (Is. 53:1–12)
Christ suffered for our sins, but also for our healing and peace today.

10. **"Declared to Be the Son of God with Power"** (Ps. 16:10)
The sufficiency of Christ's atonement is declared with power by the Resurrection.
11. **Messiah's Peace, Place, and Promise for His People** (John 14:1–3)
The Peace in God's trustworthiness, the place He is preparing, and the promise of His return.
12. **Confirmed: Jesus Will Return** (Acts 1:10, 11)
Angels confirm that Jesus is to return; the promise is to motivate us to be faithful to the assignment He has given each of us to do.
13. **The Threefold Announcement of the Lord's Coming** (1 Thess. 4:15–18)
A shout, the voice of an archangel, and the trumpet of God detail the announcement of the Lord's return.
14. **Only the Father Knows When Christ Will Return** (Matt. 25:13)
We are to be about the Father's business on Earth, in hope of Christ's return; and we are to be done with superstitious and speculative date-setting.
15. **"Surely I Am Coming Quickly"** (Rev. 22:20)
There is much in God's Word we are to attend to, but we should not let the hope of His return be overshadowed.

GOD'S ORDER FOR FAMILY LIFE (FAMILY ORDER)

Larry Christenson

No theme is more likely to touch God's heart than that which is capturing the renewed attention of every sensitive Spirit-filled person today: The Priority of the Family. As redeemed souls walk in renewed relationship with God through Christ, it is consistent with the whole of Scripture that they prioritize their learning of the biblical pathway to fulfilling and divinely ordered family living. The Bible unfolds its story with a dual display of health in family relationships. Most obviously, the first pair (Adam and Eve) are at peace, in union, and experiencing the perfect intention of God's creative design as the "two shall be made one" married relationship. But another family is clearly present, as God—the heavenly Father of all Earth and heaven's family (Eph. 3:14, 15)—is seen in His foundational role as Giver, Nourisher, Protector of mankind's destiny. The writer of this study is renowned as author of "The Christian Family," and as a pastor whose skills and teaching help toward the recovering of the pristine pattern of divine design for relationships—in the home and with the loving Father God of all.

1. **God Created Man (Male/Female) in His Own Image** (Gen. 1:26–28)
God created man as male and female, not a solitary individual, but two people.
2. **The Identity of Family Is in God** (Eph. 3:14, 15)
The name of "family" belongs to God, and He extends it to a man and woman.
3. **Jesus and the Father Model Relationship for Marriage** (1 Cor. 11:3)
When the Bible shows how the Father and Jesus relate, it is showing husbands and wives how to relate.
4. **Christ and the Church Model Husband/Wife Relationships** (Eph. 5:22–33)
The husband's model is the divine Bridegroom; the wife's model is the church.
5. **Attitudes Toward God Determine Attitudes Toward Mates** (1 Pet. 3:1–7)
Spouses are to continue their role regardless of the other's shortcomings.
6. **Husbands and Wives Called to Operate in God's Order** (Col. 3:18, 19, 23, 24)
The roles in marriage are not self-chosen, nor are they culturally assigned. God has ordered them.
7. **Forgiveness Can Save and Transform a Marriage** (Hos. 2:16, 17, 19, 20)
Marriage is a state in which imperfect people often hurt one another; forgiveness can allow God's redemptive power to transform that marriage.
8. **Three Sides of Sex: Unity, Symbol of Love, Reserved for Marriage** (1 Cor. 7:3, 4)
Sex is a powerful symbol of the love between Christ and the church, the pure sharing of delight, but is destructive outside of marriage.
9. **The Husband, Protector and Provider** (Is. 54:5)
God is the Protector and Provider; the husband who looks to God will find the inspiration and power to be that for his family.
10. **God Backs Up the Covenant of Marriage** (Mal. 2:13, 14, 16)
God's power and authority stand against every enemy that would threaten marriage.

11. **Divorce Is a Case of a Heart Hardened Toward God** (Matt. 19:1–9)
Behind every divorce is hardness of heart toward God and then one's mate, which gives place for the Devil to exaggerate the other mate's failures and to indulge your self-pity.
12. **Divine Appointment Places People in Families** (Ps. 68:5, 6)
Placement into human families is no accident: it is God's appointment.
13. **God's Nurturing Heart in Parents Flows to Children** (Hos. 11:1, 3, 4)
God allows His own nurturing heart to flow through parents to their children.
14. **Loving and Caring for Children Honors God** (Ps. 127:3–5)
To care for children is a principal way of honoring God and building His kingdom.
15. **Parents Responsible to Raise Children** (Eph. 6:4)
God holds parents responsible for raising children, providing a right attitude and foundation.
16. **Corrective Discipline for the Rebellious** (Prov. 13:24)
A teachable child needs guidance; a rebellious one needs disciplined correction.
17. **Receiving One Another Is the Way to Oneness** (Rom. 15:5–7)
The power of receiving one another can transform two imperfect people into one life.

THE WORTH OF THE HUMAN PERSONALITY (HUMAN WORTH)

Charles E. Blake

Fallen though he be, man is still deemed by the Almighty to be of inestimable worth. Though incapable of saving himself, man—as creature—represents God's highest and best, made in His image and intended for His glory. In the light of Christ's will to spend His own life for man's redemption, an eternal insight into the worth of man from God's viewpoint is gained (1 Pet. 1:18, 19). Thus, in our understanding, essential to personal growth and relational development with both God and man is a biblical perspective on the fundamental value of the individual, both in God's sight and in your own. Having created man in His image, God has invested unmeasurable worth in each being. His quest for the redemption of sinful, fallen man is evidence not only of God's love but of His wisdom in working to retrieve that which is of infinite value to Him. The writer of this study has influenced Christians on every continent toward a biblical balance in humility before our Creator-Redeemer, joined to a holy learning of mutual esteem for one another as members of Christ's body. May we learn how personal worth may be learned and recovered on God's terms.

1. **Man's Intrinsic Value** (Gen. 1:26–28)
The nature in which man was created and his position in creation show his intrinsic worth, calling forth accountability and responsibility.
2. **Man's Dominion over Creation** (Ps. 8:4–8)
Our ability to fulfill our responsibility over the Earth is dependent on our willingness to submit and serve the living God.
3. **Man's Critical Role in the Affairs of the Earth** (Gen. 3:17)
The world literally stands or falls on man's actions—each believer has strategic significance to maximize the impact of good.
4. **The Sacredness of Life** (Gen. 9:5, 6)
Human life is God's unique, spiritual, immortal creation, and should be deeply respected.
5. **The Unity of the Human Race** (Acts 17:26)
All mankind proceeds from one blood, both figuratively and literally.
6. **All Believers Are Members of the Body of Christ** (1 Cor. 12:12)
All Christian brothers and sisters are needed, and all contribute to the well-being of the body.
7. **Love—The Testing of Discipleship** (John 13:34, 35)
Love is not a feeling or preference but a decision and a way of behaving.
8. **Christ Mandates Social Concern** (Matt. 25:37–40)
Concern for the hungry, homeless, diseased, and imprisoned cannot be divorced from our Christian walk.
9. **One Should Not Think Too Highly of Himself** (Rom. 12:3–5)
Man has a high position, but no one should think he is more worthy or more important than anyone else.

10. **Respect of Persons** (James 2:1–9)
The Bible teaches that we are to respect all persons equally, without partiality.
11. **Help from a Despised Source** (Luke 10:33)
The tragedy of prejudice is that it may separate one from a potential source of help.
12. **The Cross-Cultural Nature of God's Word and Work** (Matt. 27:32)
Black hands were extended to help the Savior bear His cross; and an Ethiopian was the first Gentile mentioned in Acts to be converted, and he later founded a church.
13. **Man's Greatest Need Is for Salvation** (1 Pet. 1:18, 19)
The price of Christ's death reveals the value of the human personality and the importance of salvation.
14. **Abundant Life** (John 10:10)
The Savior, Jesus, came to restore the quality and potential of human life.

BROTHERLY LOVE (BROTHERLY LOVE)

Demos Shakarian

Perhaps no wiser warning of the danger to experiencing the power of God is that registered in Paul's epistle to the Corinthians. Here is a people he at once commends and then strongly corrects. As much as he welcomes their experience in the gifts of the Spirit, he commands that they learn the grace of the Spirit—love. Foundational to every other value and goal in Christian life is the call to grow in love. 1 Cor. 13 charts the way, noting the absence of value in any accomplishment, gifts, or sacrifice unless love is the fountainhead and the flavor of it all. The writer of this study founded a worldwide network of fellowships whose theme was, "His banner over us is love" (Song 2:4), and through growing in that love, knit together multitudes of Christian communions. Such brotherly love is to be nurtured and becomes a proven source of joyful service.

1. **Responsibility for One Another** (Gen. 4:9)
We are held accountable for our treatment of our brothers and sisters (blood and spiritual).
2. **Love Embraces Those Who Have Wronged Us** (Gen. 45:4)
God expects us to demonstrate a forgiving and expressive love to those who have wronged us.
3. **Unselfish Christian Love Toward Strangers** (Lev. 19:34)
Remember how rejection feels and never manifest it. Treat others as family.
4. **To Get Closer to God, Love Others** (Ps. 15:3)
To "abide" in God's presence, speak kindly, and never gossip or discredit your neighbor.
5. **Abundantly Forgiven, Abundantly Forgive** (Ps. 86:5)
God wants us to abundantly give mercy just as we have abundantly received it.
6. **Love Those Who Have Animosity Toward You** (Matt. 5:44)
Jesus clearly calls forth love from us toward those who show animosity toward us.
7. **God's Love Loves the Unlovable** (Luke 6:31–35)
Through the transformation of God's love we are empowered to sincerely love the unlovable.
8. **Love Is Servant-Spirited** (John 12:26)
Love forsakes social status and accepts a place beneath those we serve.
9. **The Priority and Pathway of Brotherly Love** (John 15:12, 13)
The love of God enables us to give up comforts, to bear with others' treatment and pain.
10. **Brotherly Love Flows from the Divine Nature** (2 Pet. 1:7, 8)
The divine nature dissolves personal fighting and releases affection and benevolence.

THE WORK AND MINISTRY OF WOMEN (WOMEN)

Freda Lindsay

An inescapably blessed fact fills the Scriptures: God has ordained that every believer realize the significance of their mission and ministry as His servants. Gender is no restriction intended to limit significance or breadth of dimension in living for or serving Christ: "I will pour out My Spirit upon your sons and daughters . . . upon your menservants and your maidservants" (Acts 2:17, 18). Sensitive to the need for grace and balance in pursuing this theme, the writer of this study unfolds the uniqueness and dynamic of many of the Bible's key women. She herself is a case study in the mighty ways in which the Holy Spirit anoints women: she leads one of the world's largest ministry-training centers and missionary sending works.

1. **The First Woman: A Redemptive Instrument—Eve** (Gen. 4:25)
The woman, first scarred by sin, is selected to be the one first promised to become an instrument of God's redemptive working.
2. **The Submission That Bears Fruit—Sarah** (Gen. 16:1)
Submission means responding to authority in a biblical manner that is the pathway of rising beyond personal limitations.
3. **The Blessing of an Unselfish Woman—Rebekah** (Gen. 24:15–67)
Rebekah is a lesson in the way God provides surprising rewards for servant-spirited souls.
4. **A Godly Quest for Equal Rights—Daughters of Zelophehad** (Num. 27:1–11)
The daughters of Zelophehad reveal the pathway to overcoming inequality while sustaining a godly spirit.
5. **The Spirit-filled, Multitalented Woman—Deborah** (Judg. 4:4, 5)
Deborah demonstrates the possibilities of any woman today who would allow the Spirit of God to fill and form her life and allow her full capacities to shape the world around her.
6. **Tenacity That Takes the Throne—Ruth** (Ruth 1:1—4:22)
Ruth's primary virtue is tenacity to purpose: she was a woman who was steadfast.
7. **The Woman and Today's Prophetic Possibilities—Huldah** (2 Kin. 22:3–20)
Huldah's example of respectful, trust-begetting, forthright living, teaches the grounds for wise and effective spiritual ministry.
8. **Rising to Meet Your Destiny—Esther** (Esth. 4:1)
Esther met her destiny through trust in God, prayer, fasting, and a willingness to lay down her life for others, while keeping wisdom and patience when the pressure was on.
9. **Faithful Mother: Obedient Disciple—Mary** (Luke 1:26–56)
Mary is a model of responsive obedience, modeling her own words to the servants at Cana, "Whatever He [Jesus] says to you, do it."
10. **An Effective Older Woman and Widow—Anna** (Luke 2:36–38)
Anna exemplified the qualities of anointing and steadfastness while her prophetic anointing was untainted by the spirit of the age.
11. **Freed to Become Fruitful—Mary Magdalene** (Luke 8:2)
Mary Magdalene's life testifies that no dimension of satanic bondage can prohibit any woman from being released to fruitful service for Jesus Christ.
12. **Balancing Devotion and Duty—Martha and Mary** (Luke 10:38–42)
Martha and Mary remind us of the proper place of balancing personal devotion with practical duties.
13. **A "Radiant" Woman "Minister"—Phoebe** (Rom. 16:1)
Phoebe was a "Radiant Minister" of the gospel.
14. **Women and New Testament Ministry—Philip's Daughters** (Acts 21:9)
Philip's daughters make clear that women did bring God's Word and "words" by the power of the Holy Spirit in the early church.
15. **A Word of Wisdom to Wives** (1 Pet. 3:1)
Wives at home and women in ministry will win victories and rise in importance through a gracious, loving, servant-spirit.

TRAITS OF SPIRITUAL LEADERSHIP (LEADER TRAITS)

Jamie Buckingham

The apostolic directive laid the groundwork for the role of the leader: 1) equip the saints or assist them to fruitful life and service (Eph. 4:11, 12); and 2) transmit the truth to each successive "generation" of converts, that is, discipling those whom you touch, that they may in turn disciple those they touch (2 Tim. 2:2). But that same directive is only effective in its multiplying the life of the gospel through others as it is obeyed by leaders who live the truth in the purity and power of the gospel first! The writer of this study is a pastor, author, and editor who contends for godliness in leadership, that godly offspring may be multiplied. Thus, each new echelon of believers and leaders in the body of Christ will retain the likeness of the Founder—Jesus, whose life and character are not only preached but present in those who lead in His name.

1. **Call of God** (Is. 6:8, 9)
While all are called, leaders are divinely called or appointed to lead.
2. **Hearing God** (Matt. 16:13–20)
The ability to lead is not in human reason but receptivity to hear God's promptings.
3. **Faith** (Gen. 12:1–20; 17:1–27; 22:1–19)
Abraham's ability was tested in three areas of faith: faith to risk, trust, and surrender.
4. **The High Standard for Leadership** (James 3:1)
Leaders are under a higher standard to exemplify Jesus in their behavior, words, and deeds.
5. **Character Qualifications** (1 Tim. 3:1–13)
Leaders are to be mature and demonstrate sustained ethical character; failure in these outlined areas should cause a leader to accept removal until reverification is accomplished.
6. **Total Commitment** (Acts 26:19)
Paul demonstrates total commitment to the spirit of his call, discipleship, and adaptability.
7. **Humility** (Judg. 6:1—8:35)
Gideon demonstrates seven key traits of godly leadership, which were characterized by humility and willingness.
8. **A Teachable Spirit** (Acts 13:22)
David was humble and teachable; he listened to his critics and the prophets.
9. **Vulnerability** (Matt. 26:47–54)
Vulnerability means being totally open, hiding nothing, and refusing to defend oneself.
10. **Secure** (John 13:1–17)
Jesus shows the psychological security essential to be a servant-leader.
11. **Leading God's Way** (Judg. 8:22, 23; 9:1–57)
Leading is not through natural charisma but through doing things God's way.
12. **Resisting Popular Opinion** (Num. 13:1—14:45)
The godly leader is to call people to increase their faith in God, not appeal to the mood of the times.
13. **Fasting and Prayer** (Acts 13:1–3)
Disciplined fasting and prayer are mandatory in the lives of leaders.
14. **Dreams and Visions** (Acts 16:6–10)
The Word of God and having a transformed mind and affections on things above are needed for God's leading through dreams and visions.
15. **Miracles, Signs, and Wonders** (Acts 2:22)
Miracles, signs, and wonders are not occasional random events but evidences of God's anointing and therefore to be sought and welcomed.
16. **Unity and Harmony** (Acts 1:14)
The agreement of NT leaders was both spiritual and practical and deeply unifying.
17. **Taking Charge** (Ex. 27:1—28:43)
Taking charge is expressed in various manners, which the wise leader uses.
18. **Authority** (Ex. 28:1, 2)
The dual type of spiritual authority as represented by Moses and Aaron are necessary and complementary.
19. **Inspiration** (Judg. 4:1—5:31)
The inspirational leader provides a model of integrity and courage while setting a high standard for performance.
20. **Boldness** (Luke 3:1–20)
John the Baptist's ministry was marked by boldness and daring to preach what was unpopular.
21. **The Administrative Leader** (1 Cor. 12:28)
The NT recognizes three types of administrative leaders: the deacon, the steward leader, and the steersman/overseer.

HOLY SPIRIT GIFTS AND POWER (SPIRITUAL GIFTS)

Paul Walker

The miraculous works of the Holy Spirit have been in operation since creation when God commanded, "Let there be light." His creative presence is the avenue of God's creative power. Now, as the new creation of God's redemptive workings are the contemporary counterpart of His creative works, the same Holy Spirit is present as the avenue of redemptive gifts and power. His first works came in conjunction with God's Word (as He confirms its truth and promise) and with the declaration of the gospel of Jesus, the Light of the World. The writer of this study has pastored one of the historic Pentecostal churches in America for nearly thirty years, and brings his teaching gift to this examination of how God today flows His gifts and power through human vessels open to His workings. *This article begins on page 2018.*

1. **Speaking with Tongues Prophesied** (Is. 28:11, 12)
Isaiah prophesied the spiritual experience of speaking in known and unknown languages.
2. **The Person of the Holy Spirit** (John 14:16, 17)
The Holy Spirit has all the characteristics of a person.
3. **Holy Spirit Baptism: Case Histories** (Acts 2:4)
The Books of Acts contains case history accounts of being filled with the Holy Spirit.
4. **Tongues as a Sign** (Acts 10:46)
Tongues function as a sign of the indwelling presence of the Holy Spirit.
5. **Receiving the Holy Spirit Baptism** (Acts 19:2)
This passage brings up the question of receiving the Holy Spirit after believing in Christ.
6. **Names/Symbols of the Holy Spirit** (Rom. 8:2, 9, 15)
The Holy Spirit is given several names and symbols in the Scriptures.
7. **The Father's Gifts to You** (Rom. 12:6–8)
Gifts that are available to minister to the needs of the body and extend the witness.
8. **The Holy Spirit's Gifts to You** (1 Cor. 12:8–10, 28)
Gifts that are available to minister to the needs of the body and extend the witness.
9. **The Gifts Christ Gives** (Eph. 4:11)
Gifts that are available to minister to the needs of the body and extend the witness.
10. **Love: The Qualifying Factor** (1 Cor. 13:1)
The basis of all gifts is love; leaders are to see if those exercising gifts do so by love.
11. **Limits to Exercising Tongues** (1 Cor. 14:27)
Tongues in limited sequence, two or three at the most.
12. **A Call to Character** (Gal. 5:22, 23)
Being filled with the Spirit calls us as much to character as it does to charismatic activity.
13. **Benefits of Prayer in the Spirit** (Jude 20)
The practice of "tongues" in private devotions is for personal edification.
14. **The Pentecostal/Charismatic Context** (1 Cor. 14:1–40)
Love is the foundation of gifts; integrity is the key to their sacred preservation.

THE PATHWAY OF PRAISE (PRAISE PATHWAY)

Charles Green

Man was created to live and breathe in an atmosphere of praise-filled worship to His Creator. The avenue of sustained inflow of divine power was to be kept by the sustained outflow of joyous and humble praise to his Maker. The severance of the bond of blessing-through-obedience that sin brought silenced man's praise-filled fellowship with God and introduced self-centeredness, self-pitying, and complaint (see Gen. 3:9–12). But now has come salvation and life in Christ, and now upon receiving Jesus Christ as Savior, daily living calls us to prayer and the Word for fellowship and wisdom in living. But our daily approach to God in that communion is to be paved with praise: "Enter into His gates with thanksgiving, *and* into His courts with praise" (Ps. 100:4). Such a walk of praise-filled openness to Him will cultivate deep devotion, faithful obedience, and constant joy. The writer has established a record of leadership that models the manner in which praise brings steadfastness in godly living while teaching a praise-walk that is neither fanatical, glib, nor reduced to mere ritual, but one of life-delivering power available to each believer.

1. **"Judah" Means "Praise"** (Gen. 29:35)
Jacob gives Judah the highest blessing and will have royal and legal authority besides bringing forth the Messiah.
2. **Praise Cures "Dry Times"** (Num. 21:16, 17)
In times of pressure, anxiety, or depression gather with God's praising people.
3. **Power in Unity of Praise** (2 Chr. 5:13)
There is power in praise, thanksgiving, and music; and anything that takes attention away from God to the praiser/worshiper should be reconsidered.
4. **Powerful Praise Births Victory** (2 Chr. 20:15–22)
Faced with mortal enemies, the Levites responded to the Word of the Lord with "loud and high" voices of praise; total victory followed.
5. **Praise Stops the Advancement of Wickedness** (Ps. 7:14–17)
Self-induced, sincere, powerful, and audible praise will bring the presence of Jesus, driving out the desire to identify with sinful acts, thoughts, or deeds.
6. **Praise Spotlights God** (Ps. 18:3)
Praise toward Him who is worthy spotlights God and so we radiate with joy.
7. **Praise, the Pathway to God's Presence** (Ps. 22:3, 4)
Praise, however simple, brings the abiding presence of God and thereby our edification.
8. **Sing Praises with Understanding** (Ps. 47:7)
When we sing praises with understanding (intelligence, wisdom), we are testifying to God's love for us and our love for God, and others will be touched.
9. **Praise, the Road to Success** (Ps. 50:22, 23)
The focus of praise is toward God, but we are the ultimate beneficiaries as we receive power to order our conduct, revelation, and understanding.
10. **Praise Releases Blessings and Satisfaction** (Ps. 63:1–5)
The type of expressed praise that releases blessings is full of passion and desire for God.
11. **Creative Praise Stays Lively** (Ps. 71:14)
God wants us to be creative in our praise and not to fall prey to careless praise.
12. **Teach Your Children Praise** (Ps. 145:4)
We are to constantly praise God and raise (by words, deeds, and example) the next praisers.
13. **A Mighty Appeal to Praise** (Ps. 150:1–6)
We are called to praise God for His mighty acts and greatness throughout all His creation.
14. **The Glorious Garment of Praise** (Is. 61:3)
The garment of praise repels and replaces a heavy spirit and brings hope, warmth, and covering.
15. **Perfected Praise Produces Power** (Matt. 21:16)
Young people captivated by who Jesus was, responded with loud and powerful praise.
16. **Praise Springs Open Prison Doors** (Acts 16:25, 26)
Praise directed toward God opened prison doors, converted a man, saved a household, and overthrew satanic captivity.
17. **Encouraging One Another in Praise** (Eph. 5:18, 19)
Worship is magnified as we join with one another, mutually encouraging one another; therefore, we should assemble often and praise much.
18. **Praise Releases the Spirit of Prophecy** (Heb. 2:11, 12)
As people praise, Jesus joins the song Himself and releases a spirit of prophecy.
19. **The Sacrifice of Praise** (Heb. 13:10–15)
Praise is confrontive, requiring us to kill our pride, fear, or sloth.
20. **Worshipful Walk with God** (1 Pet. 2:9)
As a chosen generation, a priesthood, a nation, and "special" to God, we proclaim His praise and propagate His blessing throughout the Earth.

THE MINISTRY OF DIVINE HEALING (DIVINE HEALING)

Nathaniel M. Van Cleave

The dynamic ministry of Jesus not only revealed God's heart of love for mankind's need of a Redeemer, but unveiled God's compassionate heart of mercy for mankind's need of a Healer. The will of God was perfectly disclosed in His Son: ours is to seek how to most fully convey that full and perfect revelation. Just as the Fall of man introduced sickness as a part of the curse, the Cross of Christ has opened a door to healing as a part of salvation's provision. Healing encompasses God's power to restore broken hearts, broken homes, broken lives, and broken bodies. Suffering assumes a multiplicity of forms, but Christ's blood not only covers our sin with redemptive love; His stripes release a resource of healing at every dimension of our need. The writer of this study is a missionary, pastor, teacher, and theologian, who has seen and helped multitudes to faith without presumption.

1. **The Old Testament Healing Covenant** (Ex. 15:26)
   Gods promises to keep His people free of diseases if they obey Him.
2. **Healing Repentance and Humility** (Num. 12:1–6)
   The healing of Miriam points to the importance of repentance and humility in healing.
3. **The Focus of Divine Healing** (Num. 21:5–9)
   Our healing, both spiritual and physical, comes from looking to and identifying with Christ crucified, "by [whose] stripes we are healed."
4. **Lessons in Sharing Healing Hope** (2 Kin. 5:1–15)
   In some cases healing may involve obedience and persistence.
5. **Healing by Miracle or Medicine?** (2 Kin. 20:1–11)
   God is the Author of all healing benefits; medical remedies are an act of obedience.
6. **Job's Affliction and Total Recovery** (Job 42:10–13)
   Repentance and forgiving others have a place in receiving healing.
7. **A Promise of Divinely Protected Health** (Ps. 91:9, 10)
   Protection from sickness and plagues is conditioned upon intimate fellowship with God.
8. **Saving and Healing Benefit** (Ps. 103:3)
   The Lord not only forgives iniquity but physically heals as well.
9. **Deliverance from Our "Destructions"** (Ps. 107:20)
   Some sickness is a punishment of transgression; repentance can bring healing.
10. **Healing Prophesied Through Christ's Atonement** (Is. 53:4, 5)
    Bodily healing is included in the atoning work of Christ.
11. **The Extent of Jesus' Healing Ministry and Commission** (Matt. 4:23–25)
    Jesus healed extensively and made it part of the Christian mission of deliverance.
12. **The Biblical Grounds for Divine Healing** (Matt. 8:16, 17)
    Jesus has borne all our sicknesses, as well as our sins.
13. **The Lord's Willingness to Heal** (Mark 1:40–45)
    Saints are to be certain of the Lord's willingness to heal.
14. **The Place of Persistent Faith** (Mark 5:24–34)
    The Bible records many who were certain and persistent and thereby were healed.
15. **Cultivating a Climate of Faith for Healing** (Mark 9:22, 23)
    Continuance in prayer and praise builds faith that brings deliverance.
16. **Which Is Easier, Pardon or Healing?** (Luke 5:16–26)
    The linking of healing with forgiveness evidences Jesus' concern for human need at every point.
17. **The Healing of Spirit, Soul, and Body** (Luke 8:36)
    God has a concern to restore every part of man—his personality, his health, his relationship with God—and to save him from ultimate death.
18. **The Disciples Instructed to Heal** (Luke 10:8, 9)
    The authority to heal has been given to Jesus' disciples as they are willing to exercise the privileges of being messengers and participants in the kingdom of God.
19. **Healing as They Went** (Luke 17:12–19)
    The nature of some healing is "progressive" so that a doctor's confirmation is not faithlessness.
20. **Divine Healing Never Outdated** (John 8:58)
    Christ ties all facets of His Person and ministry to His own unchanging timelessness.
21. **Healing in Jesus' Incomparable Name** (Acts 3:16)
    Jesus' character and office is the authoritative grounds for extending healing grace.

22. **Paul's Healing Ministry in Malta** (Acts 28:8, 9)
God heals by many means: the prayer of faith, natural recuperative powers, medical aid, and miracles.
23. **The Gift of Healing** (1 Cor. 12:9, 28)
The Holy Spirit energizes the gift of healing, and it should be established in the church.
24. **The New Testament Divine Healing Covenant** (James 5:13–18)
Sick persons whom the elders of the church anoint with oil and pray for will be healed.

FAITH'S CONFESSION OF GOD'S WORD (FAITH'S CONFESSION)

Roy Hicks, Sr.

Jesus Himself established the importance of understanding how faith operates, when He said, "According to your faith let it be to you" (Matt. 9:29). Faith that believes is called to become faith that appropriates. The present day has seen a rise of understanding on this subject, but mixed with a confusing and distracting flurry of ideas that have often brought misunderstanding and criticism. Is there a biblically balanced approach to "confessing God's Word in faith"? The writer of this study has moved within the circles of both movements—classical Pentecostal and Charismatic "word of faith" fellowships, and invites examination of a study that may bring hope for such balance.

1. **The Words We Speak** (Gen. 17:5)
God spoke a new name to Abram and thus was arranging that Abram would remember God's promise each time he heard his new name, "Abraham."
2. **Faith When Facing Delays** (Num. 13:30; 14:6–9)
Caleb knew they could enter the land God gave them; and thus, forty years later, he did possess God's provision.
3. **Silencing Unbelief** (Josh. 6:10)
We cannot help what we see and hear, but our refusal to speak doubt and fear will keep our heart inclined to what God can do.
4. **The Meaning of "Faith's Confession"** (2 Chr. 6:24–31)
Surrender and peaceful submission to God is a pathway to your prayer's being received by God.
5. **"Acceptable" Speech Before God** (Ps. 19:14)
We are to speak the words that confirm what we believe about God, His love, and His power.
6. **Wise Words Bring Health** (Prov. 16:23, 24)
God's wisdom teaches our hearts and then flows out of our words and conduct.
7. **Keeping Your Confession Without Hypocrisy** (Matt. 15:7–9)
Living faith requires that the mouth and heart be together to avoid hypocrisy.
8. **Jesus on "Faith's Confession"** (Mark 11:22–24)
Faith's confession first seeks God's intention and is spoken as a release of God's creative word of promise.
9. **Jesus' Name: Faith's Complete Authority** (Acts 3:6)
When we pray in faith, let us confess His deity and lordship as we speak His name.
10. **Calling for "Great Grace"** (Acts 4:33)
Grace may also refer to operations of "the power of God" to move mountains.
11. **Continuing in Faith As We Have Begun** (Rom. 10:9, 10)
We accept God's provisions (contracts) for our needs by signing them with our words.
12. **Faith At the Lord's Table** (1 Cor. 11:23–26)
Faith confesses and appropriates today the benefits that Christ has provided through His Cross (forgiveness, wholeness, strength, health).
13. **Faith Exalting Jesus' Lordship** (Phil. 2:9–11)
Our praiseful confession of Jesus releases His power over all evil we face.
14. **Understanding *Rhema* and *Logos*** (Heb. 4:11–13)
"Logos" has to do with the whole Bible being always true, and "Rhema" has to do with the particular verse or truth that the Holy Spirit makes lively to us in our maturity or service.
15. **Faith's Confession Is Steadfast** (Heb. 11:13–16)
Our worship and walk in His lordship remains a daily celebration.
16. **Declaring the Ultimate Victory in Christ** (Rev. 12:11)
The heart of faith's confession is in the Word of God and the blood of the Lamb.

ADVANCING IN SPIRITUAL WARFARE (FAITH'S WARFARE)

Dick Eastman

Few truths have become so pronouncedly vibrant to the renewed church's life in this century as the place and power of prayer warfare. This call in no wise reduces the conviction that the Cross of Jesus Christ has accomplished all victory over the Devil (Col. 3:14, 15). To the contrary, this order of warfare depends on what He has finished! Just as the mission to evangelize the world is founded in the complete provision of salvation, the mission to precede our evangelistic endeavor with prayer power that paves the way to the overthrow of contemporary works of darkness is founded in the blood of the Lamb (Rev. 12:9–12). The writer of this study has taught hundreds of thousands of Christians in over 100 different denominations in scores of nations to pray with increased effectiveness.

1. **Spiritual Warfare** (Eph. 6:10–18)
There is a battle and we are armed to offensively approach the confrontation.
2. **The Invisible Realm and Victorious Warfare** (2 Kin. 6:8–17)
Seeing into the invisible (discerning the spiritual issues and God's perspective) is a key to victorious praying.
3. **Divine Revelation and Spiritual Warfare** (Jer. 33:3)
Prayer brings revelational insight that is necessary for victorious spiritual warfare.
4. **Intimacy and Spiritual Breakthrough** (Prov. 3:5, 6)
Intimacy with God in prayer births blessings and victories.
5. **Faithfulness in Prayer and Spiritual Warfare** (Acts 6:1–4)
The early church learned quickly that their prayer had to be continuous because spiritual warfare is continuous.
6. **Intercession in Spiritual Warfare** (Ezek. 22:30)
The intercessor stands before God on the behalf of others and averts judgment.
7. **Patterns in Prayer and Spiritual Breakthrough** (Ps. 5:1–3)
Consistency and order in daily prayers are needed for spiritual breakthrough.
8. **Faith's Victory Through Prayer** (Acts 4:31–34)
Prayer births supernatural boldness, unity, fruitfulness, and fullness.
9. **Physical Acts in Warfare Prayer** (2 Kin. 19:8–19)
Physical acts parallel the establishment of spiritual authority in the invisible realm.
10. **Effectivity in Spiritual Warfare** (James 5:13–18)
A righteous man's praying is energized by the Holy Spirit, and things happen.
11. **Seeking God and Spiritual Warfare** (Jer. 29:11–14)
Earnestness, intensity, and diligence are part of God's emphasis for prayer.
12. **Fasting to Spiritual Breakthrough** (Ezra 8:21–23)
Fasting is referred to as a sacrificial form of prayer that produces results.
13. **Angelic Activity in Spiritual Warfare** (Rev. 12:7–11)
God may use angels to administer the victory for saints engaged in prayer warfare.
14. **Taking Authority and Victorious Warfare** (Mark 11:20–24)
It is necessary to take authority in the spiritual realm to impact the natural realm.
15. **Trumpets and Spiritual Warfare** (Num. 10:1–10)
Trumpets have a unique place of sounding spiritual authority.
16. **Tears and Brokenness in Victorious Warfare** (Ps. 126:5, 6)
Tears of sorrow, joy, compassion, travail, and repentance have a place in warfare.

Word Wealth

Understanding important key words helps you better understand God's Word. That is why detailed, easy-to-understand definitions are included for more than 550 important terms.

Each Word Wealth listing is located within the Bible text, near the verse where the featured word appears. English spellings of original Greek and Hebrew words are given, along with helpful insight into the derivation, as well as the *Strong's Concordance* numerical listing for each word. *Strong's* numbers in regular type refer to the numbers from the Hebrew dictionary in the back of *Strong's. Strong's* numbers in italicized (slanted) type refer to numbers from the Greek dictionary in the back of *Strong's.* In the center column, you will also find cross-referencing to the locations of related Word Wealth entries. Word Wealth illuminates key passages and expands your overall understanding of Scripture.

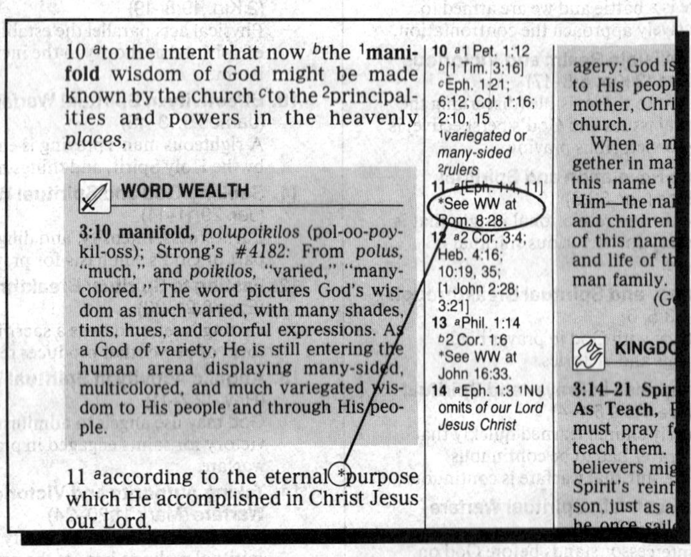

10 [a]to the intent that now [b]the [1]**manifold** wisdom of God might be made known by the church [c]to the [2]principalities and powers in the heavenly *places,*

WORD WEALTH

3:10 manifold, *polupoikilos* (pol-oo-poy-kil-oss); Strong's *#4182:* From *polus,* "much," and *poikilos,* "varied," "many-colored." The word pictures God's wisdom as much varied, with many shades, tints, hues, and colorful expressions. As a God of variety, He is still entering the human arena displaying many-sided, multicolored, and much variegated wisdom to His people and through His people.

11 [a]according to the eternal *purpose which He accomplished in Christ Jesus our Lord,

10 [a]1 Pet. 1:12 [b][1 Tim. 3:16] [c]Eph. 1:21; 6:12; Col. 1:16; 2:10, 15 [1]*variegated or many-sided* [2]*rulers*
11 [a][Eph. 1:4, 11] *See WW at Rom. 8:28.
12 [a]2 Cor. 3:4; Heb. 4:16; 10:19, 35; [1 John 2:28; 3:21]
13 [a]Phil. 1:14 [b]2 Cor. 1:6 *See WW at John 16:33.
14 [a]Eph. 1:3 [1]NU omits *of our Lord Jesus Christ*

Following is an index providing this information about each entry: 1) English word treated; 2) Greek or Hebrew transliteration; and 3) the Scripture reference where the Word Wealth definition is located.

Word Wealth Index

anger (observable, fierce), *'aph* . . . Judg. 10:7
anger (from repeated irritation), *cha'as* . . . 1 Kin. 16:2
anointed, *mashach* . . . Is. 61:1
another, *allos* . . . John 14:16
apostles, *apostolos* . . . 1 Cor. 12:28
appears, *phaneroo* . . . Col. 3:4
appointed time, *mo'ed* . . . Num. 9:2
ashamed, *bush* . . . Ezek. 16:63
ask, *aiteo* . . . Matt. 7:7
assembly, *qahal* . . . Lev. 16:17
atonement (make), *chaphar* . . . Num. 15:25
authority, *dunastes* . . . Acts 8:27
Baal, *ba'al* . . . Hos. 2:8
babbler, *spermologos* . . . Acts 17:18
backslidings, *meshubah* . . . Jer. 5:6
baptism, *baptisma* . . . Matt. 21:25
beauty, *yophi* . . . Ezek. 28:12
been done, *ergazomai* . . . John 3:21
believe, *aman* . . . 2 Chr. 20:20
believe, *pisteuo* . . . Rom. 10:9
blasphemous, *blaspemos* . . . Acts 6:11
blemish (without), *tamim* . . . Lev. 23:12
bless, *barach* . . . Ps. 145:2
bless, *eulogeo* . . . Luke 6:28
blessed, *'ashar* . . . Prov. 31:28
blessed, *makarios* . . . Matt. 5:3
blindness, *porosis* . . . Rom. 11:25
blood, *dam* . . . Lev. 17:11
blood, *haima* . . . 1 John 1:7
boldness, *parrhesia* . . . Acts 4:31
breath, *neshamah* . . . Ps. 150:6
brethren, *'ach* . . . Ps. 133:1
brotherly love, *philadelphia* . . . Heb. 13:1
built, *banah* . . . Zech. 1:16
call (cry out, shout, proclaim), *qara'* . . . Jer. 33:3
called (invite, summons), *kaleo* . . . Gal. 1:6
care, *merimna* . . . 1 Pet. 5:7
caught up, *harpadzo* . . . 1 Thess. 4:17
charge, *parangelia* . . . Acts 16:24
cheerful, *hilaros* . . . 2 Cor. 9:7
cheerfulness, *hilarotes* . . . Rom. 12:8
cherubim, *keruvim* . . . Ex. 25:18
chose, *bachar* . . . 1 Kin. 11:34
chosen, *eklektos* . . . 1 Pet. 2:9
Christ, *Christos* . . . 2 Tim. 4:22
church, *ecclesia* . . . Acts 8:1
clap, *taqa'* . . . Ps. 47:1
cleansed, *taher* . . . Lev. 14:31
clears, *naqah* . . . Num. 14:18
comfort (console, deep empathy), *nacham* . . . Ps. 23:4
comfort (strengthening presence), *paraklesis* . . . Acts 9:31
coming, *parousia* . . . 1 Cor. 15:23
commandments, *mitsvah* . . . Ps. 119:35
commit, *galal* . . . Prov. 16:3
committed fornication, *porneuo* . . . Rev. 17:2
companion, *chaber* . . . Ps. 119:63
company, *tsaba'* . . . Ps. 68:11
compassion (moved with), *splanchnizomai* . . . Matt. 14:14
compels, *angareuo* . . . Matt. 5:41
compels, *sunecho* . . . 2 Cor. 5:14
complete, *katartisis* . . . 2 Cor. 13:9
comprehend, *katalambano* . . . John 1:5
confidence, *peitho* . . . 2 Thess. 3:4
confirming, *bebaioo* . . . Mark 16:20
conformed, *suschematizo* . . . Rom. 12:2
congregation, *'edah* . . . Josh. 22:17
conquerors (more than), *hupernikao* . . . Rom. 8:37
continually, *tamid* . . . Ex. 28:30
correct, *yasar* . . . Jer. 10:24
counsel, *'etsah* . . . Zech. 6:13
courtesy, *epieikeia* . . . Acts 24:4
covenant (pledge, treaty, agreement), *berit* . . . Gen. 17:7
covenant (will, testament, pact), *diatheke* . . . Mark 14:24
covetous, *pleonektes* . . . 1 Cor. 6:10
craftiness, *panourgia* . . . 1 Cor. 3:19
created, *bara'* . . . Gen. 1:1
creation, *ktisis* . . . Col. 1:15
creature, *ktisma* . . . Rev. 5:13
crush, *suntribo* . . . Rom. 16:20
cures, *iasis* . . . Luke 13:32
darkness, *skotos* . . . Luke 11:35
darkness, *scotia* . . . John 12:46
day, *yom* . . . Zeph. 1:7
delights, *chafets* . . . Ps. 112:1
delivered, *paradidomi* . . . Luke 23:25
desire, *zeloo* . . . 1 Cor. 14:1
desired, *epithumeo* . . . Matt. 13:17
despised, *ma'as* . . . Amos 2:4
destroy, *apollumi* . . . Luke 9:56
direct, *yashar* . . . Prov. 3:6
disaster, *hubris* . . . Acts 27:10
disciples, *mathetes* . . . Matt. 10:1
dominion, *moshel* . . . Zech. 9:10
done no wrong (I have), *adikeo* . . . Acts 25:10
doubting, *diakrino* . . . Acts 11:12
downcast, *tapeinos* . . . 2 Cor. 7:6
dreams, *chalom* . . . Joel 2:28
dwell (temporarily reside), *gur* . . . Jer. 42:17
dwellings, *mishchan* . . . Is. 32:18
eager, *spoudazo* . . . Gal. 2:10
easy, *chresto* . . . Matt. 11:30
effectively, *energeo* . . . 1 Thess. 2:13
eldership, *presbuterion* . . . 1 Tim. 4:14
endurance, *hupomone* . . . Heb. 10:36
endure (stand firm under pressure), *anechomai* . . . 2 Thess. 1:4
endures (hold out under stress), *hupomeno* . . . Matt. 24:13
enraged, *orgizo* . . . Rev. 12:17
ephod, *'ephod* . . . Ex. 35:27
equipping, *katartismos* . . . Eph. 4:12
error, *plane* . . . Jude 11

esteemed, *megaluno* . . . . . Acts 5:13
ever, *'ad* . . . . . Mic. 4:5
everlasting, *aionios* . . . . . Rev. 14:6
evil, *ra'* . . . . . Ps. 5:4
exalted (elevate, lift up, extol), *rum* . . . . . Ps. 18:46
exalted (highly; to highest position), *huperupsoo* . . . . . Phil. 2:9
example, *hupogrammos* . . . . . 1 Pet. 2:21
excellence, *huperbole* . . . . . 2 Cor. 4:7
faith, *pistis* . . . . . Mark 11:22
faithful, *'emunah* . . . . . Prov. 28:20
families, *mishpachah* . . . . . Gen. 12:3
fast, *tsom* . . . . . Jon. 3:5
father, *'ab* . . . . . Ps. 68:5
favor, *ratson* . . . . . Deut. 33:23
fear (reverence, awe), *morah* . . . . . Is. 8:13
fear (startled, sudden fear), *pachad* . . . . . Hos. 3:5
fear (panic, alarm), *phobeo* . . . . . Matt. 10:26
fear (of terror, flight), *phobos* . . . 1 John 4:18
feared, *yare'* . . . . . Ex. 1:17
feed, *ra'ah* . . . . . Is. 40:11
fellowship, *koinonia* . . . . . Acts 2:42
fervent, *zeo* . . . . . Acts 18:25
fill (fill up, fulfill), *male'* . . . . . Jer. 23:24
fill (satisfied with abundance), *chortazo* . . . . . Matt. 15:33
flesh (body), *basar* . . . . . Job 19:26
flesh (literal—body, spiritual—lower nature), *sarx* . . . . . Matt. 26:41
forgives, *salach* . . . . . Ps. 103:3
follow, *akoloutheo* . . . . . John 13:36
foreigners, *paroikos* . . . . . Eph. 2:19
forever, *olam* . . . . . Ps. 136:1
forgiving, *charizomai* . . . . . Col. 3:13
formed, *morphoo* . . . . . Gal. 4:19
fornications, *porneia* . . . . . Matt. 15:19
framed, *katartizo* . . . . . Heb. 11:3
free (loosen, unshackle), *patach* . . . Jer. 40:4
free (setting at liberty), *eleutheroo* . . . . . Rom. 8:2
free (freedom to come and go), *eleutheros* . . . . . Rev. 6:15
friend (companion, neighbor), *re'a* . . . . . Prov. 17:17
friend (affectionate friend), *philos* . . . . . John 11:11
fullness, *pleroma* . . . . . Eph. 3:19
futile, *mataioo* . . . . . Rom. 1:21
gap, *perets* . . . . . Ezek. 22:30
generation, *dor* . . . . . Esth. 9:28
Gentiles, *goyim* . . . . . Ps. 106:47
gentle, *epieikes* . . . . . 1 Tim. 3:3
gentleness, *praotes* . . . . . 1 Tim. 6:11
gift, *charisma* . . . . . 1 Cor. 1:7
give, *didomi* . . . . . Acts 20:35
give rest, *nu'ach* . . . . . Ex. 33:14
glory (renown and visible splendor), *chabod* . . . . . Is. 60:1
glory (majestic, perfection), *doxa* . . . . . John 2:11
God (Eternal Creator), *'elohim* . . . . . 2 Kin. 19:15
good (right, pleasant, happy), *tob* . . . . . Ezek. 34:14
good (physical and moral sense), *kalos* . . . . . Matt. 13:48
good (that which produces benefits), *agathos* . . . . . Phil. 1:6
goodness (being and doing good), *agathosune* . . . . . Rom. 15:14
gospel, *euangelion* . . . . . Mark 1:1
grace (act merciful, compassionate toward), *chen* . . . . . Zech. 12:10
grace (unmerited favor, undeserved blessing), *charis* . . . . . 2 Cor. 12:9
gracious (be), *chanan* . . . . . Mal. 1:9
grain offering, *minchah* . . . . . Num. 29:6
grave, *she'ol* . . . . . Hos. 13:14
great, *rab* . . . . . Ps. 31:19
groaning, *embrimaomai* . . . . . John 11:38
guarantee, *arrabon* . . . . . 2 Cor. 1:22
guilty, *'asham* . . . . . Lev. 4:13
hand, *yad* . . . . . Josh. 4:24
hardened, *poroo* . . . . . Mark 8:17
head, *rosh* . . . . . Gen. 3:15
healed, *therapeuo* . . . . . Matt. 12:22
healing, *marpe'* . . . . . Mal. 4:2
heals (who heals you), *rapha'* . . . . . Ex. 15:26
health, *hugiaino* . . . . . 3 John 2
heart, *leb* . . . . . Ps. 37:4
hearts, *kardia* . . . . . Rev. 2:23
heaven (expanse above Earth), *shamayim* . . . . . 1 Kin. 8:23
heaven (regions above Earth, God's abode), *ouranos* . . . . . Rev. 21:1
heirs, *sunkleronomos* . . . . . Heb. 11:9
Helper (alongside for strength, guidance), *parakletos* . . . . . John 15:26
helper (comes running to cry for help), *boethos* . . . . . Heb. 13:6
heresies, *haireseis* . . . . . 2 Pet. 2:1
high places, *bamah* . . . . . Ezek. 6:3
holiness, *hagiosune* . . . . . 1 Thess. 3:13
holy (set aside for holy purposes), *qadosh* . . . . . Lev. 19:2
holy (purity), *hagios* . . . . . Acts 7:33
honor, *hadar* . . . . . Ps. 8:5
hope (yearning for), *tiqvah* . . . . . Hos. 2:15
hope (confident expectation with sure basis), *elpis* . . . . . 1 Thess. 1:3
horn, *qeren* . . . . . Ezek. 29:21
house, *bayit* . . . . . 2 Sam. 7:11
humble, *shaphel* . . . . . Jer. 13:18
humbles, *tapeinoo* . . . . . Matt. 18:4
humility, *tapeinophrosune* . . . . . Acts 20:19
hypocrisy, *hupokrisis* . . . . . Gal. 2:13
hypocrites, *hupokrites* . . . . . Matt. 6:2
idle talk, *mataiologia* . . . . . 1 Tim. 1:6

idle talkers, *mataiologos* . . . . Titus 1:10
immediately, *eutheos* . . . . John 6:21
impart, *metadidomi* . . . . Rom. 1:11
in vain, *tohu* . . . . Is. 45:18
inheritance, *cheleq* . . . . Zech. 2:12
iniquities (crooked direction, warped deeds), *'avon* . . . . Ps. 130:3
instruction, *musar* . . . . Prov. 4:13
insulted, *hubrizo* . . . . Luke 18:32
intercession (make; reaching God with urgent request), *paga'* . . . . Jer. 27:18
intercession (make; plead on behalf of another), *enthunchano* . . . . Heb. 7:25
jealousy, *zelos* . . . . 2 Cor. 11:2
Jesus, *Iesous* . . . . Phil. 4:23
joined, *proskollao* . . . . Mark 10:7
joy (laud, cheering in triumph), *rinnah* . . . . Ps. 30:5
joy (rejoice, glad, sugg. of dancing, leaping), *gil* . . . . Hab. 3:18
joyful, *sameach* . . . . 2 Chr. 7:10
judge (rule, legislate, govern), *din* . . . . Deut. 32:36
judge (decide a matter and verdict), *shaphat* . . . . Judg. 2:18
judge (make opinion, pass decision), *krino* . . . . John 18:31
judgment, *krisis* . . . . Matt. 5:22
judgment, *krima* . . . . Rev. 20:4
judgment seat, *bema* . . . . Matt. 27:19
judgments, *mishpat* . . . . Num. 36:13
just, *dikaios* . . . . Matt. 1:19
justified, *dikaioo* . . . . Matt. 12:37
keep a feast, *chagag* . . . . Ex. 23:14
kept, *phroureo* . . . . 1 Pet. 1:5
kindness, *philanthropia* . . . . Acts 28:2
kindness, *chrestotes* . . . . Gal. 5:22
know (perceive, be acquainted with), *yada'* . . . . Ex. 3:7
know (recognition of truth by personal experience), *ginosko* . . . . John 8:32
knowledge, *da'at* . . . . Mal. 2:7
lack, *hustereo* . . . . Luke 22:35
lamb, *arnion* . . . . Rev. 6:1
land, *'eretz* . . . . Ex. 32:13
laugh, *sachaq* . . . . Eccl. 3:4
law, *torah* . . . . Is. 42:21
layers, *ma'alah* . . . . Amos 9:6
left, *aphiemi* . . . . Mark 1:20
lewdness, *aselgeia* . . . . 1 Pet. 4:3
liberty (release, set free), *deror* . . . . Lev. 25:10
liberty (negation of domination), *eleutheria* . . . . 1 Cor. 10:29
life, *zoe* . . . . 1 John 5:20
lift up, *hupsoo* . . . . James 4:10
listen, *shama'* . . . . 1 Kin. 20:8
little faith, *oligopistos* . . . . Matt. 8:26
looked, *apoblepo* . . . . Heb. 11:26
looking, *aphorao* . . . . Heb. 12:2
Lord (master), *'adon* . . . . Mic. 4:13
Lord (owner, controller), *kurios* . . . . John 6:68
Lord (absolute dominion, supreme authority), *despotes* . . . . Jude 4
love (affection for friend, idea, pleasure, etc.), *'ahab* . . . . Ps. 97:10
love (fond of, affection), *phileo* . . . . John 21:15
love (undefeatable benevolence, unconquerable goodwill), *agape* . . . . Rom. 5:5
loved, *agapao* . . . . John 3:16
lowly, *praus* . . . . Matt. 21:5
lusts, *epithumia* . . . . 2 Tim. 2:22
made, *karat* . . . . Ex. 34:27
majesty (royalty, glorious, spendor), *hod* . . . . 1 Chr. 29:11
majesty (magnificence), *megaleiotes* . . . . Luke 9:43
man (mankind, humanness), *'adam* . . . . Gen. 1:26
man (maleness, man, with sense of dignity), *'ish* . . . . Is. 32:2
man (champion, mighty), *geber* . . . Jer. 31:22
manifest, *emphanidzo* . . . . John 14:21
manifold, *polupoikilos* . . . . Eph. 3:10
mediator, *mesites* . . . . Gal. 3:19
meditates, *hagah* . . . . Ps. 1:2
memorial, *zikron* . . . . Ex. 39:7
mention (make), *zachar* . . . . Is. 62:6
merciful, *eleemon* . . . . Matt. 5:7
mercy (unfailing love, kindness, tenderness), *chesed* . . . . Mic. 6:8
mercy (outward expression of pity), *eleos* . . . . 2 Tim. 1:16
mercy (have; to show compassion, pity, love), *racham* . . . . Hos. 2:23
mercy (have; active desire to remove distress), *eleeo* . . . . Rom. 9:15
mercy seat, *hilasterion* . . . . Heb. 9:5
Messiah, *mashiach* . . . . Dan. 9:25
might, *chayil* . . . . Zech. 4:6
mighty, *dunateo* . . . . 2 Cor. 13:3
mind (right; sane, controlled), *sophroneo* . . . . Mark 5:15
mind (insight, perception), *dianoia* . . . . Mark 12:30
mind (sound; disciplined thought patterns), *sophronismos* . . . . . . 2 Tim. 1:7
minister, *sharat* . . . . 1 Chr. 15:2
ministered, *leitourgeo* . . . . Acts 13:2
ministers, *leitourgos* . . . . Heb. 1:7
moment, *atomos* . . . . 1 Cor. 15:52
mortal, *'enosh* . . . . Job 4:17
Most High, *'elyon* . . . . Gen. 14:18
mourn (over death, sin, tragedy), *'abal* . . . . Joel 1:9
mourn (over loss of something valuable), *pentheo* . . . . Rev. 18:11
mystery, *musterion* . . . . Mark 4:11

name (marking of fame, memorial, character), *shem* . . . . . Deut. 18:5
name (identity of intrinsic values), *onoma* . . . . . John 12:13
needy, *'ebyon* . . . . . Ps. 70:5
new, *kainos* . . . . . 2 Cor. 5:17
obedience, *hupakoe* . . . . . 2 Cor. 10:5
obeyed, *hupakouo* . . . . . Rom. 6:17
offended, *skandalizo* . . . . . Matt. 11:6
offense, *skandalon* . . . . . Matt. 16:23
offered, *prosphero* . . . . . Heb. 9:28
offering, *prosphora* . . . . . Acts 21:26
one, *'echad* . . . . . Deut. 6:4
other, *heteros* . . . . . Acts 4:12
partaker, be, *metecho* . . . . . 1 Cor. 9:10
partakers, *metochos* . . . . . Heb. 3:14
partiality (exhibiting bias), *prosopoleptes* . . . . . Acts 10:34
partiality (favoritism), *prosopolepsia* . . . . . Col. 3:25
partiality (show; making distinctions among people), *prosopolepteo* . . James 2:9
passed, *abar* . . . . . Josh. 3:4
patience, *makrothumia* . . . . . Heb. 6:12
peace (rest, harmony, wholeness man seeks), *shalom* . . . . . Nah. 1:15
peace (calmness, perfect well-being), *eirene* . . . . . Luke 1:79
people, *'am* . . . . . Ruth 1:16
perceived, *epiginosko* . . . . . Luke 5:22
perfect (finish, fulfilled), *gamar* . . . Ps. 138:8
perfect (finished, complete, consummate soundness), *teleios* . . . . . James 3:2
perfected, *teleioo* . . . . . 1 John 2:5
perilous, *chalepos* . . . . . 2 Tim. 3:1
perish, *'abad* . . . . . Judg. 5:31
poor, *'ani* . . . . . Ps. 40:17
poor (became), *ptocheuo* . . . . . 2 Cor. 8:9
possess, *yarash* . . . . . Deut. 8:1
possession, *'achuzzah* . . . . . Josh. 22:9
possible, *dunatos* . . . . . Matt. 19:26
poverty, *ptocheia* . . . . . Rev. 2:9
power (capacity, ability), *koach* . . . . . Deut. 8:18
power (authority, right to act), *exousia* . . . . . Mark 3:15
power (might, great force), *dunamis* . . . . . Acts 4:33
power (effective power shown in reigning), *kratos* . . . . . 1 Tim. 6:16
powerful, *energes* . . . . . Heb. 4:12
praise (boast about with words and singing), *halal* . . . . . 1 Chr. 23:30
praise (to glory in and calm, sooth), *shabach* . . . . . Ps. 63:3
praise (celebration, lauding, exaltation), *tehillah* . . . . . Ps. 100:4
praise (recognition of God's glory), *epainos* . . . . . Eph. 1:6
pray (asking for or inquiring about), *sha'al* . . . . . Ps. 122:6
pray (request toward God), *proseuchomai* . . . . . Matt. 6:6
prayed, *palal* . . . . . Job 42:10
prayer, *tephillah* . . . . . 2 Chr. 6:20
preach, *nataph* . . . . . Ezek. 21:2
preached, *kerusso* . . . . . Acts 9:20
precepts, *piqud* . . . . . Ps. 119:15
prepared, *hetoimazo* . . . . . Rev. 21:2
preserved, *shamar* . . . . . Job 10:12
pride, *huperephania* . . . . . Mark 7:22
priest, *kohen* . . . . . Lev. 5:6
promise (with assurance of accomplishment), *epangelia* . . . Acts 13:32
promise (a pledge made), *epangelma* . . . . . 2 Pet. 3:13
promised, *epangello* . . . . . Acts 7:5
prophecies, *propheteia* . . . . . 1 Thess. 5:20
prophet, *nabi'* . . . . . 1 Sam. 3:20
prophet, *prophetes* . . . . . Matt. 2:5
propitiation, *hilasmos* . . . . . 1 John 4:10
prosper, *chashar* . . . . . Eccl. 11:6
proverb, *mashal* . . . . . Prov. 1:6
provision, *pronoia* . . . . . Rom. 13:14
psalm, *mizmor* . . . . . Ps. 3: title
pure (ethical purity, cleanliness), *katharos* . . . . . Matt. 5:8
pure (free from falsehood and hidden motives), *eilikrines* . . . . . 2 Pet. 3:1
pure (morally faultless, undefiled), *hagnos* . . . . . 1 John 3:3
purpose, *prothesis* . . . . . Rom. 8:28
put out, *methistemi* . . . . . Luke 16:4
quickly, *tachu* . . . . . Rev. 22:20
ransom, *lutron* . . . . . Matt. 20:28
reader, *anaginosko* . . . . . Mark 13:14
ready, *shaqad* . . . . . Jer. 1:12
receive, *apecho* . . . . . Philem. 15
recognized, *phaneros* . . . . . 1 Cor. 11:19
reconciled, *katallasso* . . . . . 1 Cor. 7:11
redeemed (liberate, free, release), *padah* . . . . . Neh. 1:10
redeemed (repurchase, buy back), *ga'al* . . . . . Is. 52:9
redemption, *apolutrosis* . . . . . Rom. 3:24
refine, *tsaraph* . . . . . Zech. 13:9
refuge, *machseh* . . . . . Prov. 14:26
reigned, *malach* . . . . . 2 Sam. 8:15
rejoices, *sus* . . . . . Is. 64:5
remain, *yashab* . . . . . Lam. 5:19
remission, *aphesis* . . . . . Heb. 9:22
render, *apodidomi* . . . . . Matt. 22:21
renewing, *anakainosis* . . . . . Titus 3:5
repent, *metanoeo* . . . . . Matt. 3:2
report (good), *euphemos* . . . . . Phil. 4:8
reproach, *oneidizo* . . . . . James 1:5
rest (place of stillness, peace, comfort), *menuchah* . . . . . Is. 28:12

rest (cessation from toil, refreshing), *anapauo* . . . . Rev. 14:13
rested, *shabat* . . . . Ex. 16:30
restorer, *shub* . . . . Ruth 4:15
resurrection, *anastasis* . . . . Acts 23:6
reveals, *galah* . . . . Amos 3:7
reverent, *semnos* . . . . 1 Tim. 3:11
reward, *misthos* . . . . Rev. 22:12
righteous, *tsaddiq* . . . . Lam. 1:18
righteousness, *dikaiosune* . . . . 2 Tim. 4:8
roar, *sha'ag* . . . . Joel 3:16
***room* enough,** *day* . . . . Mal. 3:10
sacrifice, *zabach* . . . . Deut. 16:2
safety, *betach* . . . . Deut. 33:12
salvation (soundness, prosperity, rescuing), *soteria* . . . . Luke 19:9
salvation (releasing, deliverance, liberation), *soterion* . . . . Acts 28:28
sanctified, *hagiadzo* . . . . John 10:36
Satan, *Satan* . . . . Job 1:6
satisfied, *sabe'a* . . . . Amos 4:8
save, *yasha'* . . . . Jer. 17:14
saved, *sozo* . . . . Luke 7:50
savior, *soter* . . . . John 4:42
saw, *theoreo* . . . . John 20:14
Scriptures, *graphe* . . . . John 5:39
seek, *baqash* . . . . Hos. 5:15
seer, *ro'eh* . . . . 1 Sam. 9:9
selfish ambition, *eritheia* . . . . Phil. 1:16
sensual, *psuchikos* . . . . James 3:15
sent, *apostello* . . . . John 20:21
seraphim, *seraphim* . . . . Is. 6:2
servants, *doulos* . . . . Rev. 19:5
serve, *'abad* . . . . Ps. 100:2
service, *leitourgia* . . . . Luke 1:23
settled down, *shachan* . . . . Num. 10:12
shall live, *chayah* . . . . Hab. 2:4
shepherd, *poimen* . . . . John 10:2
Shiloh, *shiloh* . . . . Gen. 49:10
shout (great), *teru'ah* . . . . Ezra 3:11
sign, *'ot* . . . . Ps. 86:17
signs, *semeion* . . . . Rev. 16:14
sin, *hamartia* . . . . John 1:29
sin offering, *chatta't* . . . . Lev. 9:2
sincere, *anupokritos* . . . . 1 Pet. 1:22
sincerity, *eilikrineia* . . . . 1 Cor. 5:8
sing, *shir* . . . . Judg. 5:3
sing praises, *zamar* . . . . Ps. 149:3
sinner, *hamartolos* . . . . James 5:20
sinners, *opheiletes* . . . . Luke 13:4
slightly, *qalal* . . . . Jer. 8:11
soberly, *sophronos* . . . . Titus 2:12
***son* (only;** only child, single), *yachid* . . . . Gen. 22:2
son (builder of future generations), *ben* . . . . Gen. 29:32
sorceries, *pharmakeia* . . . . Rev. 9:21
sorrow, *'aven* . . . . Prov. 22:8
soul, *nephesh* . . . . Prov. 10:3
souls, *psuche* . . . . Luke 21:19
sow, *zara'* . . . . Hos. 10:12
special, *segullah* . . . . Deut. 26:18
Spirit (breath of "life"), *ruach* . . . . 2 Sam. 23:2
Spirit (capacity to respond to God), *pneuma* . . . . Rom. 7:6
spiritually, *pneumatikos* . . . . Rev. 11:8
statutes, *choq* . . . . Neh. 9:13
stewards, *oikonomos* . . . . 1 Pet. 4:10
stirred up, *'ur* . . . . Hag. 1:14
strangers, *paroikia* . . . . Acts 13:17
strength, *'oz* . . . . Jer. 16:19
strengthened, *dunamoo* . . . . Col. 1:11
strong (be), *chazaq* . . . . Josh. 1:9
subject, *hupotasso* . . . . 1 Cor. 14:32
suffer, *pascho* . . . . Acts 17:3
supplies, *epichoregeo* . . . . Gal. 3:5
sustain, *chul* . . . . Ps. 55:22
swore, *shaba'* . . . . Gen. 26:3
take, *airo* . . . . John 16:22
taste (choose and delight in good), *ta'am* . . . . Ps. 34:8
taste (experiences), *geuomai* . . . . John 8:52
teach, *yarah* . . . . Ps. 32:8
teaches, *lamad* . . . . Is. 48:17
temple, *heychal* . . . . Hag. 2:15
tempted, *nasah* . . . . Ps. 78:41
tested, *peirazo* . . . . Rev. 2:10
testimony (account of what one has seen, heard or known), *marturia* . . . . John 19:35
testimony (proclamation of personal experience), *marturion* . . . . Rev. 15:5
thank, *yadah* . . . . 1 Chr. 16:7
thanks (given), *eucharisteo* . . . . John 6:11
thanksgiving, *todah* . . . . Ps. 95:2
thoughts, *dialogismos* . . . . Luke 2:35
time (quality of time, *that is,* appointed), *kairos* . . . . Col. 4:5
times (small space of time or season), *et* . . . . Is. 33:6
times (quantity of time, *that is,* lapse, span), *chronos* . . . . Acts 1:7
transgression, *parabaino* . . . . Acts 1:25
transgressions, *pesha* . . . . Ezek. 18:31
tread, *darach* . . . . Deut. 11:25
tribe, *matteh* . . . . Ex. 38:22
tribulation, *thlipsis* . . . . John 16:33
trimmed, *kosmeo* . . . . Matt. 25:7
trouble, *'amal* . . . . Job 5:7
troubled, *tarasso* . . . . Luke 24:38
true, *alethes* . . . . Rom. 3:4
trumpet, *shophar* . . . . Hos. 8:1
trust, *chasah* . . . . Zeph. 3:12
truth (dependability, reliability), *'emet* . . . . Ps. 25:5
truth (reality, accuracy, integrity), *aletheia* . . . . John 4:24
unclean, *tame'* . . . . Lev. 10:10
understand, *bin* . . . . Neh. 8:8

understanding (intelligent thinking process), *sachal* . . . . Jer. 3:15
understanding (faculty of clear apprehension), *sunesis* . . . . Luke 2:47
unrighteousness, *adikia* . . . . John 7:18
useless, *mataios* . . . . Acts 14:15
virgins, *betulah* . . . . Ps. 45:14
virtue, *arete* . . . . 2 Pet. 1:5
vision, *chazon* . . . . 2 Chr. 32:32
void, *kenoo* . . . . 1 Cor. 9:15
wait (hopefully), *qavah* . . . . Lam. 3:25
wait (tarry, expect), *yachal* . . . . Mic. 7:7
watchman, *tsaphah* . . . . Hos. 9:8
waters, *mayim* . . . . Is. 43:2
went up, *'alah* . . . . Ex. 19:20
wicked, *rasha'* . . . . Prov. 10:16
will, *thelema* . . . . Matt. 12:50
willing, *thelo* . . . . Matt. 8:2
wiped out, *exaleipho* . . . . Col. 2:14
wisdom (principals of right living made action), *chochmah* . . . . Is. 11:2
wisdom (right application of truth), *sophia* . . . . Acts 6:10
withdrawn, *ekneuo* . . . . John 5:13
withstand, *anthistemi* . . . . Eph. 6:11
witness, *martus* . . . . Rev. 1:5
witnessing, *martureo* . . . . Acts 26:22
wonders, *teras* . . . . Acts 15:12
wondrous sign, *mophet* . . . . Zech. 3:8
wondrous thing (did a), *pala'* . . . Judg. 13:19
word (communication, utterance), *rhema* . . . . Matt. 4:4
word (speech, dictum), *'imrah* . . . . 2 Sam. 22:31
word (transmission of thought, revelation), *logos* . . . . Acts 19:20
words, *davar* . . . . Deut. 1:1
working together, *sunergeo* . . . . . James 2:22
working, *energeia* . . . . Col. 1:29
workmanship, *poiema* . . . . Eph. 2:10
works, *ergon* . . . . John 9:4
works (wonderful), *megaleios* . . . . . Acts 2:11
world (Earth, globe, land), *tebel* . . . Jer. 51:15
world (Earth and world system), *kosmos* . . . . John 18:36
worry, *merimnao* . . . . Matt. 6:25
worship (stoop as act of submission), *shachah* . . . . Ps. 99:5
worship (prostrate, bow down), *proskuneo* . . . . Rev. 4:10
wrath, *thumos* . . . . Luke 4:28
wrote, *chatab* . . . . Deut. 31:9
YAH, *Yah* . . . . Is. 12:2
zealous (full of emotion, passionate), *qanah* . . . . Zech. 8:2
zealous (deep commitment, eager, devotion), *zelotes* . . . . Acts 22:3

Truth-In-Action

Truth-In-Action is an intensely practical feature showing you ways to apply the Bible's great truths. Appearing in chart form, this study help summarizes the foundations and teachings of each book, then invites you—and shows you how—to act upon the summons the Holy Spirit is issuing in the Word.

Climaxing the books (or major divisions of the books), key "Action" truths are listed in numerical order, with each "Truth" listed, noting those verses that invite the believer's response. Within the text, each key verse is referenced by a symbol (**1**), directing you to note similarly highlighted verses and to discover passages of parallel emphasis. Together these passages are summarized with action words that offer specific steps you can take to let God guide your life—at work, at home—at all times.

Walk in Love

1 5 Therefore[a] be imitators of God as dear [b]children.
2 And [a]walk in love,
has loved us and *given
an *offering and a sa
[c]for a sweet-smelling a
4 3 But *fornication and
ness or [b]covetousness,
be named among you,
saints;
4 [a]neither filthiness, n
ing, nor coarse jesting,
fitting, but rather [d]givin

See WW at Col. 3:13.

CHAPTER 5

14 T

TRUTH-IN-ACTION through EPHESIANS

Letting the LIFE of the Holy Spirit Bring Faith's Works

Truth Ephesians Teaches	Text	Ac
1 **Guidelines for Growing in Godliness** Simply put, godliness is living the way God wants us to. Few books speak as clearly and succinctly to this subject as does Eph. Here godliness is exhorted in terms of be-	4:1 5:1, 2	**Unders** most ef preach. sistent, truth o **Model** Him ra

Old Testament Truth-In-Action Charts

New Testament Truth-In-Action Charts

Charts

In-Text Maps

Preface

Purpose

In the preface to the 1611 edition, the translators of the Authorized Version, known popularly as the King James Bible, state that it was not their purpose "to make a new translation ... but to make a good one better." Indebted to the earlier work of William Tyndale and others, they saw their best contribution to consist in revising and enhancing the excellence of the English versions which had sprung from the Reformation of the sixteenth century. In harmony with the purpose of the King James scholars, the translators and editors of the present work have not pursued a goal of innovation. They have perceived the Holy Bible, New King James Version, as a continuation of the labors of the earlier translators, thus unlocking for today's readers the spiritual treasures found especially in the Authorized Version of the Holy Scriptures.

A Living Legacy

For nearly four hundred years, and throughout several revisions of its English form, the King James Bible has been deeply revered among the English-speaking peoples of the world. The precision of translation for which it is historically renowned, and its majesty of style, have enabled that monumental version of the Word of God to become the mainspring of the religion, language, and legal foundations of our civilization.

Although the Elizabethan period and our own era share in zeal for technical advance, the former period was more aggressively devoted to classical learning. Along with this awakened concern for the classics came a flourishing companion interest in the Scriptures, an interest that was enlivened by the conviction that the manuscripts were providentially handed down and were a trustworthy record of the inspired Word of God. The King James translators were committed to producing an English Bible that would be a precise translation, and by no means a paraphrase or a broadly approximate rendering. On the one hand, the scholars were almost as familiar with the original languages of the Bible as with their native English. On the other hand, their reverence for the divine Author and His Word assured a translation of the Scriptures in which only a principle of utmost accuracy could be accepted.

In 1786 Catholic scholar Alexander Geddes said of the King James Bible, "If accuracy and strictest attention to the letter of the text be supposed to constitute an excellent version, this is of all versions the most excellent." George Bernard Shaw became a literary legend in our century because of his severe and often humorous criticisms of our most cherished values. Surprisingly, however, Shaw pays the following tribute to the scholars commissioned by King James: "The translation was extraordinarily well done because to the translators what they were translating was not merely a curious collection of ancient books written by different authors in different stages of culture, but the Word of God divinely revealed through His chosen and expressly inspired scribes. In this conviction they carried out their work with boundless reverence and care and achieved a beautifully artistic result." History agrees with these estimates. Therefore, while seeking to unveil the excellent *form* of the traditional English Bible, special care has also been taken in the present edition to preserve the work of *precision* which is the legacy of the 1611 translators.

Complete Equivalence in Translation

Where new translation has been necessary in the New King James Version, the most complete representation of the original has been rendered by considering the history of usage and etymology of words in their contexts. This principle of complete equivalence seeks to preserve *all* of the information in the text, while presenting it in good literary form. Dynamic equivalence, a recent procedure in Bible translation, commonly results in paraphrasing where a more literal rendering is needed to reflect a specific and vital sense. For example, complete equivalence truly renders the original text in expressions such as "lifted her voice and wept" (Gen. 21:16); "I gave you cleanness of teeth" (Amos 4:6); "Jesus met them, saying, 'Rejoice!' " (Matt. 28:9); and " 'Woman, what does your concern have to do with Me?' " (John 2:4). Complete equivalence translates fully, in order to provide an English text that is both accurate and readable.

In keeping with the principle of complete equivalence, it is the policy to translate interjections which are commonly omitted in modern language renderings of the Bible. As an example, the interjection *behold,* in the older King James editions, continues to have a place in English usage, especially in dramatically calling attention to a spectacular scene, or an event of profound importance such as the Immanuel prophecy of Isaiah 7:14. Consequently, *behold* is retained for these occasions in the present edition. However, the Hebrew and Greek originals for this word can be translated variously, depending on the circumstances in the passage. Therefore, in addition to *behold,* words such as *indeed, look, see,* and *surely* are also rendered to convey the appropriate sense suggested by the context in each case.

In faithfulness to God and to our readers, it was deemed appropriate that all participating scholars sign a statement affirming their belief in the verbal and plenary inspiration of Scripture, and in the inerrancy of the original autographs.

Devotional Quality

The King James scholars readily appreciated the intrinsic beauty of divine revelation. They accordingly disciplined their talents to render well-chosen English words of their time, as well as a graceful, often musical arrangement of language, which has stirred the hearts of Bible readers through the years. The translators, the committees, and the editors of the present edition, while sensitive to the late-twentieth-century English idiom, and while adhering faithfully to the Hebrew, Aramaic, and Greek texts, have sought to maintain those lyrical and devotional qualities that are so highly regarded in the Authorized Version. This devotional quality is especially apparent in the poetic and prophetic books, although even the relatively plain style of the Gospels and Epistles cannot strictly be likened, as sometimes suggested, to modern newspaper style. The Koine Greek of the New Testament is influenced by the Hebrew background of the writers, for whom even the gospel narratives were not merely flat utterance, but often song in various degrees of rhythm.

The Style

Students of the Bible applaud the timeless devotional character of our historic Bible. Yet it is also universally understood that our language, like all living languages, has undergone profound change since 1611. Subsequent revisions of the King James Bible have sought to keep abreast of changes in English speech. The present work is a further step toward this objective. Where obsolescence and other reading difficulties exist, present-day vocabulary, punctuation, and grammar have been carefully integrated. Words representing ancient objects, such as *chariot* and *phylactery,* have no modern substitutes and are therefore retained.

A special feature of the New King James Version is its conformity to the thought flow of the 1611 Bible. The reader discovers that the sequence and selection of words, phrases, and clauses of the new edition, while much clearer, are so close to the traditional that there is remarkable ease in listening to the reading of either edition while following with the other.

In the discipline of translating biblical and other ancient languages, a standard method of transliteration, that is, the English spelling of untranslated words, such as names of persons and places, has never been commonly adopted. In keeping with the design of the present work, the King James spelling of untranslated words is retained, although made uniform throughout. For example, instead of the spellings *Isaiah* and *Elijah* in the Old Testament, and *Esaias* and *Elias* in the New Testament, *Isaiah* and *Elijah* now appear in both Testaments.

King James doctrinal and theological terms, for example, *propitiation, justification,* and *sanctification,* are generally familiar to English-speaking peoples. Such terms have been retained except where the original language indicates need for a more precise translation.

Readers of the Authorized Version will immediately be struck by the absence of several pronouns: *thee, thou,* and *ye* are replaced by the simple *you,* while *your* and *yours* are substituted for *thy* and *thine* as applicable. *Thee, thou, thy* and *thine* were once forms of address to express a special relationship to human as well as divine persons. These pronouns are no longer part of our language. However, reverence for God in the present work is preserved by capitalizing pronouns, including *You, Your,* and *Yours,* which refer to Him. Additionally, capitalization of these pronouns benefits the reader by clearly distinguishing divine and human persons referred to in a passage. Without such capitalization the distinction is often obscure, because the antecedent of a pronoun is not always clear in the English translation.

In addition to the pronoun usages of the seventeenth century, the *-eth* and *-est* verb endings, so familiar in the earlier King James editions, are now obsolete. Unless a speaker is schooled in these verb endings, there is common difficulty in selecting the correct form to be used with a given subject of the verb in vocal prayer. That is, should we use *love, loveth,* or *lovest? do, doeth, doest,* or *dost? have, hath,* or *hast?* Because these forms are obsolete, contemporary English usage has been substituted for the previous verb endings.

In older editions of the King James Version, the frequency of the connective *and* far exceeded the limits of present English usage. Also, biblical linguists agree that the Hebrew and Greek original words for this conjunction may commonly be translated otherwise, depending on the immediate context. Therefore, instead of *and,* alternatives such as *also, but, however, now, so, then,* and *thus* are accordingly rendered in the present edition, when the original language permits.

The real character of the Authorized Version does not reside in its archaic pronouns or verbs or other grammatical forms of the seventeenth century, but rather in the care taken by its scholars to impart the letter and spirit of the original text in a majestic and reverent style.

The Format

The format of the New King James Version is designed to enhance the vividness and devotional quality of the Holy Scriptures:

- Subject headings assist the reader to identify topics and transitions in the biblical content.
- Words or phrases in *italics* indicate expressions in the original language which require clarification by additional English words, as also done throughout the history of the King James Bible.
- Verse numbers in **bold** type indicate the beginning of a paragraph.
- *Oblique type* in the New Testament indicates a quotation from the Old Testament.
- Poetry is structured as contemporary verse to reflect the poetic form and beauty of the passage in the original language.
- The covenant name of God was usually translated from the Hebrew as "LORD" or "GOD" (using capital letters as shown) in the King James Old Testament. This tradition is maintained. In the present edition the name is so capitalized whenever the covenant name is quoted in the New Testament from a passage in the Old Testament.

The Old Testament Text

The Hebrew Bible has come down to us through the scrupulous care of ancient scribes who copied the original text in successive generations. By the sixth century A.D. the scribes were succeeded by a group known as the Masoretes, who continued to preserve the sacred Scriptures for another five hundred years in a form known as the Masoretic Text. Babylonia, Palestine, and Tiberias were the main centers of Masoretic activity; but by the tenth century A.D. the Masoretes of Tiberias, led by the family of ben Asher, gained the ascendancy. Through subsequent editions, the ben Asher text became in the twelfth century the only recognized form of the Hebrew Scriptures.

Daniel Bomberg printed the first Rabbinic Bible in 1516–17; that work was followed in 1524–25 by a second edition prepared by Jacob ben Chayyim and also published by Bomberg. The text of ben Chayyim was adopted in most subsequent Hebrew Bibles, including those used by the King James translators. The ben Chayyim text was also used for the first two editions of Rudolph Kittel's *Biblia Hebraica* of 1906 and 1912. In 1937 Paul Kahle published a third edition of *Biblia Hebraica.* This edition was based on the oldest dated manuscript of the ben Asher text, the Leningrad Manuscript B19a (A.D. 1008), which Kahle regarded as superior to that used by ben Chayyim.

For the New King James Version the text used was the 1967/1977 Stuttgart edition of the *Biblia Hebraica,* with frequent comparisons being made with the Bomberg edition of 1524–25. The Septuagint (Greek) Version of the Old Testament and the Latin Vulgate also were consulted. In addition to referring to a variety of ancient versions of the Hebrew Scriptures, the New King James Version draws on the resources of relevant manuscripts from the Dead Sea caves. In the few places where the Hebrew was so obscure that the 1611 King James was compelled to follow one of the versions, but where information is now available to resolve the problems, the New King James Version follows the Hebrew text. Significant variations are recorded in the center reference column.

The New Testament Text

There is more manuscript support for the New Testament than for any other body of ancient literature. Over five thousand Greek, eight thousand Latin, and many more manuscripts in other languages attest the integrity of the New Testament. There is only one basic New Testament used by Protestants, Roman Catholics, and Orthodox, by conservatives and liberals. Minor variations in hand copying have appeared through the centuries, before mechanical printing began about A.D. 1450.

Some variations exist in the spelling of Greek words, in word order, and in similar details. These ordinarily do not show up in translation and do not affect the sense of the text in any way.

Other manuscript differences such as omission or inclusion of a word or a clause, and two paragraphs in the Gospels, should not overshadow the overwhelming degree of *agreement* which exists among the ancient records. Bible readers may be assured that the most important differences in English New Testaments of today are due, not to manuscript divergence, but to the way in which translators view the task of translation: How literally should the text be rendered? How does the translator view the matter of biblical inspiration? Does the translator adopt a paraphrase when a literal rendering would be quite clear and more to the point? The New King James Version follows the historic precedent of the Authorized Version in maintaining a literal approach to translation, except where the idiom of the original language cannot be translated directly into our tongue.

The King James New Testament was based on the traditional text of the Greek-speaking churches, first published in 1516, and later called the Textus Receptus or Received Text. Although based on the relatively few available manuscripts, these were representative of many more which existed at the time but only became known later. In the late nineteenth century, B. Westcott and F. Hort taught that this text had been officially edited by the fourth-century church, but a total lack of historical evidence for this event has forced a revision of the theory. It is now widely held that the Byzantine Text that largely supports the Textus Receptus has as much right as the Alexandrian or any other tradition to be weighed in determining the text of the New Testament. Those readings in the Textus Receptus which have weak support are indicated in the center reference column as being opposed by both Critical and Majority Texts (see "Center-Column Notes").

Since the 1880s most contemporary translations of the New Testament have relied upon a relatively few manuscripts discovered chiefly in the late nineteenth and early twentieth centuries. Such translations depend primarily on two manuscripts, Codex Vaticanus and Codex Sinaiticus, because of their greater age. The Greek text obtained by using these sources and the related papyri (our most ancient manuscripts) is known as the Alexandrian Text. However, some scholars have grounds for doubting the faithfulness of Vaticanus and Sinaiticus, since they often disagree with one another, and Sinaiticus exhibits excessive omission.

A third viewpoint of New Testament scholarship holds that the best text is based on the consensus of the majority of existing Greek manuscripts. This text is called the Majority Text. Most of these manuscripts are in substantial agreement. Even though many are late, and none is earlier than the fifth century, usually their readings are verified by papyri, ancient versions, quotations from the early church fathers, or a combination of these. The Majority Text is similar to the Textus Receptus, but it corrects those readings which have little or no support in the Greek manuscript tradition.

Today, scholars agree that the science of New Testament textual criticism is in a state of flux. Very few scholars still favor the Textus Receptus as such, and then often for its historical prestige as the text of Luther, Calvin, Tyndale, and the King James Version. For about a century most have followed a Critical Text (so called because it is edited according to specific principles of textual criticism) which depends heavily upon the Alexandrian type of text. More recently many have abandoned this Critical Text (which is quite similar to the one edited by Westcott and Hort) for one that is more eclectic. Finally, a small but growing number of scholars prefer the Majority Text, which is close to the traditional text except in the Revelation.

In light of these facts, and also because the New King James Version is the fifth revision of a historic document translated from specific Greek texts, the editors decided to retain the traditional text in the body of the New Testament and to indicate major Critical and Majority Text variant readings in the center reference column. Although these variations are duly indicated in the center-column notes of the present edition, it is most important to emphasize that fully eighty-five percent of the New Testament text is the same in the Textus Receptus, the Alexandrian Text, and the Majority Text.

Center-Column Notes

Significant explanatory notes, alternate translations, and cross-references, as well as New Testament citations of Old Testament passages, are supplied in the center reference column. Cross-references enclosed in square brackets identify passages similar in concept to the referenced passage in the text.

Important textual variants in the Old Testament are identified in a standard form.

The textual notes in the present edition of the New Testament make no evaluation of readings, but do clearly indicate the manuscript sources of readings. They objectively present the facts without such tendentious remarks as "the best manuscripts omit" or "the most reliable manuscripts read." Such notes are value judgments that differ according to varying viewpoints on the text. By giving a clearly defined set of variants the New King James Version benefits readers of all textual persuasions.

Where significant variations occur in the New Testament Greek manuscripts, textual notes are classified as follows:

1. NU-Text
These variations from the traditional text generally represent the Alexandrian or Egyptian type of text described previously in "The New Testament Text." They are found in the Critical Text published in the twenty-sixth edition of the Nestle-Aland Greek New Testament (N) and in the United Bible Societies' third edition (U), hence the acronym, "NU-Text."

2. M-Text
This symbol indicates points of variation in the Majority Text from the traditional text, as also previously discussed in "The New Testament Text." It should be noted that M stands for whatever reading is printed in the published *Greek New Testament According to the Majority Text,* whether supported by overwhelming, strong, or only a divided majority textual tradition.

The textual notes reflect the scholarship of the past 150 years and will assist the reader to observe the variations between the different manuscript traditions of the New Testament. Such information is generally not available in English translations of the New Testament.

Special Abbreviations

Arab. Arabic

Aram. Aramaic

Bg. the 1524–25 edition of the Hebrew Old Testament published by Daniel Bomberg (see Preface, "The Old Testament Text")

cf. compare

ch., chs. chapter, chapters

DSS Dead Sea Scrolls

e.g. for example

et al. and others

etc. and so forth

fem. feminine

f., ff. following verse, following verses

Gr. Greek

Heb. Hebrew

i.e. that is

Kt. Kethib (literally, in Aramaic, "written")—the written words of the Hebrew Old Testament preserved by the Masoretes (see "Qr.")

Lat. Latin

lit. literally

LXX Septuagint—an ancient translation of the Old Testament into Greek

M Majority Text (see Preface, "The New Testament Text")

ms., mss. manuscript, manuscripts

masc. masculine

MT Masoretic Text—the traditional Hebrew Old Testament (see Preface, "The Old Testament Text")

NU the most prominent modern Critical Text of the Greek New Testament, published in the twenty-sixth edition of the *N*estle-Aland Greek New Testament and in the third edition of the *U*nited Bible Societies' Greek New Testament (see Preface, "The New Testament Text")

pl. plural

Qr. Qere (literally, in Aramaic, "read")—certain words read aloud, differing from the written words, in the Masoretic tradition of the Hebrew Old Testament (see "Kt.")

Sam. Samaritan Pentateuch—a variant Hebrew edition of the books of Moses, used by the Samaritan community

sing. singular

Syr. Syriac

Tg. Targum—an Aramaic paraphrase of the Old Testament

TR Textus Receptus or Received Text (see Preface, "The New Testament Text")

v., vv. verse, verses

vss. versions—ancient translations of the Bible

Vg. Vulgate—an ancient translation of the Bible into Latin, translated and edited by Jerome

Books of the Old and New Testaments and Their Abbreviations

The Old Testament

The New Testament

THE
OLD TESTAMENT

The First Book of Moses Called GENESIS

Author: Traditionally Moses
Date: About 1440 B.C.
Theme: Beginnings
Key Words: Create, Covenant, Genealogy

Author Jewish tradition lists Moses as the author of Genesis and of the next four books. Together these books are called the Pentateuch. Jesus said, "If you believed Moses, you would believe Me; for he wrote about Me" (John 5:46). The Pentateuch itself depicts Moses as having written extensively. See Exodus 17:14; 24:4; Deuteronomy 31:24. Acts 7:22 tells us that "Moses was learned in all the wisdom of the Egyptians." In the notes accompanying the text we observe a number of loanwords from Egyptian that are found in Genesis, a fact which suggests that the original author had his roots in Egypt, as did Moses.

Date The traditional date of the Exodus from Egypt is the mid-fifteenth century B.C. First Kings 6:1 states that Solomon began building the temple "in the four hundred and eightieth year after the children of Israel had come out of the land of Egypt." Solomon is thought to have begun construction about 960 B.C., dating the Exodus about 1440 B.C. So Moses wrote Genesis after 1440 B.C., during the forty years in the wilderness.

Content Genesis opens with the formation of the solar system, the preparation of the land for habitation, and the creation of life on the Earth. All of the eight acts of creation are accomplished in six days.

The subsequent ten chapters explain the origins of many mysterious qualities of life: human sexuality, marriage, sin, sickness, pain in childbearing, death, the wrath of God, man's enmity toward man, and the dispersion of races and languages throughout the Earth.

Genesis, beginning in chapter 12, recounts the call of Abraham and the inauguration of God's covenant with him, a glorious, eternal covenant renewed with Isaac and Jacob. Genesis is remarkable for its exquisite narrative, highlighted by the inspiring account of Joseph and the divine preservation and multiplication of the people of God in Egypt. It is a lesson in divine election, as Paul recounts in Romans 9.

Genesis in many ways anticipates the New Testament: the very personal God, the Trinity, the institution of marriage, the seriousness of sin, divine judgment, and righteousness by faith. The Tree of Life, lost in Genesis, is restored in Revelation 22.

Genesis concludes with the blessing of Jacob upon Judah, from whose tribe was to come the Messiah: "The scepter shall not depart from Judah, nor a lawgiver from between his feet, until Shiloh comes; and to Him *shall be* the obedience of the people" (49:10). Many centuries and many struggles will follow before this prophecy finds its fulfillment in Jesus Christ.

Personal Application Genesis immediately brings into question many secular world views, so serious Genesis students must become accustomed to thinking differently. We must perceive the world and its history as the ancient biblical authors reveal it. For example, the narratives of chapters 1—3 are not to be understood allegorically but as actual history. The Word of God must always stand above the word of man; we are not to judge His Word, but rather, it judges us. Therefore, ancient Hebrews should not be thought of as primitive simply because they relate reality differently. Rationalized Greek thinking about world realities may be our heritage, but it is not always true.

Genesis teaches many other lessons as well: Abraham is our example of faith (15:6; Gal. 3:7); Joseph's life is an exquisite sermon for all who suffer unfairly and is a challenge to faithfulness in this age of undisciplined permissiveness.

Finally, we understand human nature properly only as we grasp the truth of "original sin." When Adam sinned, all of us not only sinned but inherited a resident sin nature (8:21; Rom. 5:19; 7:18). Only a Savior can deal effectively with this inherited natural corruption.

Christ Revealed The preexistent Christ, the living Word, was very much involved in the creation. "All things were made through Him, and without Him nothing was made that was made" (John 1:3). Jesus' ministry is anticipated in Genesis 3:15, suggesting that the "Seed" of the woman who will bruise the Serpent's (Satan's) head is Jesus Christ, the "Seed" of Abraham mentioned by Paul in Galatians 3:16. Melchizedek is the mysterious king-priest of chapter 14. Since Jesus Christ is both King and High Priest, the letter to the Hebrews makes this appropriate identification (Heb. 6:20).

The greatest revelation of Christ in Genesis is found in God's establishment of His covenant with Abraham in chapters 15 and 17. God made glorious promises to Abraham, and Jesus is the major fulfillment of those promises, a truth explained in detail by Paul in Galatians. Much of the Bible is built upon the Abrahamic covenant and its flowering in Jesus Christ.

The dramatic story of Abraham's willingness to sacrifice Isaac at God's command bears a startling similarity to the crucial event of the New Testament. "Take . . . your only *son* Isaac, whom you love . . . and offer him there as a burnt offering" (22:2), reminds us of God's willingness to sacrifice *His* only Son for the sins of the world.

Finally, Jacob's blessing upon Judah anticipates the coming of "Shiloh," to be identified as the Messiah. "And to Him *shall be* the obedience of the people" (49:10).

The Holy Spirit at Work "The Spirit of God was hovering over the face of the waters" (1:2). Thus we find the Spirit involved in creation. The Holy Spirit also worked in Joseph, a fact obvious to Pharaoh: "Can we find *such a one* as this, a man in whom *is* the Spirit of God?" (41:38).

Although the Holy Spirit is otherwise not mentioned in Genesis, we see His work in drawing the animals from the four corners of the Earth into Noah's ark. We also perceive His working throughout the lives of the patriarchs as He protected them and their families and as He blessed them materially. All sorts of difficulties and impossible situations beset the chosen family, frustrating, if possible, the fulfillment of God's promises to Abraham; but the Spirit of God supernaturally resolved every challenge.

Outline of Genesis

The History of Creation

1 IN the [a]beginning [b]God* **created** the *heavens and the *earth.

CHAPTER 1

1 [a]Ps. 102:25; Is. 40:21; [John 1:1–3; Heb. 1:10] [b]Gen. 2:4; [Ps. 8:3; 89:11; 90:2]; Is. 44:24; Acts 17:24; Rom. 1:20; [Heb. 1:2; 11:3]; Rev. 4:11
*See WW at 2 Kin. 19:15. • See WW at 1 Kin. 8:23. • See WW at Ex. 32:13.

WORD WEALTH

1:1 created, *bara'* (bah-*rah*); Strong's #1254: To form or fashion, to produce, to create. Originally this verb carried the idea of "carving" or "cutting out," and that concept is still expressed by the intensive verbal form in Josh. 17:18, referring to "cutting" down trees to "clear out" the land. This suggests that creating is similar to sculpturing. Thus *bara'* is a fitting word to describe both creating by bringing into existence and creating by fashioning existing matter into something new, as God did in "creating" man (Gen. 1:27) out of dust from the ground. God is always the subject of the verb *bara'* in its standard form; creating is therefore a divine capacity.

KINGDOM DYNAMICS

1:1 God's Sovereignty, FOUNDATIONS OF THE KINGDOM. The necessary beginning point in studying the theme of "the kingdom of God" is the Bible's opening verse. Here we meet the Sover-
(*cont. on next page*)

1:1—2:25 See section 1 of Truth-In-Action at the end of Gen.

1:1 In the beginning God created is the traditional translation of what is a somewhat complex and debated Hebrew sentence structure. Other translation possibilities have appeared in the last century, but they presuppose the existence of chaotic matter or even a pre-Adamic race before the creation described in ch. 1 began. Nothing in the remainder of Gen., nor in the Bible as a whole, requires or necessarily recommends this view, even though such opinions are biblically tolerable. Still, the most direct and fully acceptable translation is the traditional one adopted here.

(cont. from preceding page)
eign of all the Universe, whose realm, reign, and regency are described at the outset. 1) His realm (or scope of His rule) is transcendent; that is, not only does it include the entire physical universe, but it exceeds it. He existed before all creation, He expands beyond it, and by virtue of having begotten it, He encompasses all that it is. 2) His reign (or the power by which He rules) is exercised by His will, His word, and His works. By His own will He creatively decides and designs; by His own word He speaks creation into being; and by His own works, His Spirit displays His unlimited power. 3) His regency (or authority to rule) is in His preexistence and holiness. He is there before creation "in the beginning." Thus, as its Creator, He deserves to be its Potentate. His benevolent intent in creating things "good" reveals His holy nature (that is, complete and perfect), and thus His moral right to be creation's King. All kingdom power and authority flow from Him.

(*/Gen. 1:26–28; 2:16, 17) J.W.H.

2 The earth was [a]without form, and
*void; and darkness [1]*was* on the face of
the deep. [b]And the Spirit of God was
hovering over the face of the waters.
3 [a]Then God said, [b]"Let there be
[c]light"; and there was light.
4 And God saw the light, that *it was*
good; and God divided the light from
the darkness.
5 God called the light Day, and the
[a]darkness He called Night. [1]So the evening and the morning were the first
day.

KINGDOM DYNAMICS

1:3–5 God the Covenant-Maker, THE BLOOD. From the beginning, God is revealed as the covenant-maker. Jeremiah referred to God's activity in creation as acts of covenant (Jer. 33:20), speaking of God's "covenant with the day" and "covenant with the night." Thereby, the unchangeable character of God's nature is emphasized as His relationship with all of His creation is portrayed as an immutable bond under His sovereign administration.

(*/Gen. 8:20) C.S.

6 Then God said, [a]"Let there be a
[1]firmament in the midst of the waters,
and let it divide the waters from the
waters."
7 Thus God made the firmament,
[a]and divided the waters which *were*
under the firmament from the waters
which *were* [b]above the firmament; and
it was so.
8 And God called the firmament
Heaven. So the evening and the morning were the second day.
9 Then God said, [a]"Let the waters under the heavens be gathered together
into one place, and [b]let the dry *land*
appear"; and it was so.
10 And God called the dry *land* Earth,
and the gathering together of the waters He called Seas. And God saw that
it was good.
11 Then God said, "Let the earth
[a]bring forth grass, the herb *that* yields
seed, *and* the [b]fruit tree *that* yields
fruit according to its kind, whose seed

2 [a]Jer. 4:23 [b][Gen. 6:3]; Job 26:13; Ps. 33:6; 104:30; Is. 40:13, 14 [1]Words in italic type have been added for clarity. They are not found in the original Hebrew or Aramaic. *See WW at Is. 45:18.
3 [a]Ps. 33:6, 9 [b]2 Cor. 4:6 [c][Heb. 11:3]
5 [a]Job 37:18; Ps. 19:2; 33:6; 74:16; 104:20; 136:5; Jer. 10:12 [1]Lit. *And evening was, and morning was, a day, one.*
6 [a]Job 37:18; Jer. 10:12; 2 Pet. 3:5 [1]*expanse*
7 [a]Job 38:8–11; Prov. 8:27–29 [b]Ps. 148:4
9 [a]Job 26:10; Ps. 104:6–9; Prov. 8:29; Jer. 5:22; 2 Pet. 3:5 [b]Ps. 24:1, 2; 33:7; 95:5
11 [a]Ps. 65:9–13; 104:14; Heb. 6:7 [b]2 Sam. 16:1; Luke 6:44

1:2 We are given here the consequence of God's first creative act—**the earth was without form** (lacking the order it would have when God's commands were complete) and **darkness *was* on the face of the deep** (a further description of the lack of complete order and beauty that would emerge within six days). Both statements reveal that creation reflected God's normal process of bringing order out of chaos. The deep is the primeval ocean that underlies the Earth (see 7:11). **Hovering** connotes "sweeping" or "moving" rather than staying stationary. The Holy Spirit is the "executive arm" of the Trinity, so He was quite active as God spoke each word. An alternate view, which recommends the possibility of the initial Gen. 1:1 creation becoming disordered (possibly by reason of Lucifer's fall), is not biblically objectionable, but neither is it verifiable.

1:3 God's first divine command begins the process of transforming the chaos. **God said** will occur 10 times in ch. 1 as the means of bringing about life and order. The exact working relationship among the members of the Trinity in this process is not clearly defined in the Bible (see Col. 1:16). **Light** is the presence of illumination in general. The luminary bodies are created on the fourth day (vv. 14–19).

1:4 ***Was* good** is the divine approval formula that will occur seven times to emphasize creation's quality and aptness for its purpose. It stands in contrast to the condition described following the Fall (ch. 3).

1:5 The evening and the morning: The Hebrews began each new **day** at sunset. This time designation, along with the numbering of the days and the Sabbath rest on day seven, shows that the author views creation as happening in the course of six consecutive 24-hour periods, followed by a seventh of divine rest.

1:6, 7 Let it divide the waters from the waters: The water-covered Earth was apparently surrounded by vapor. God used **the firmament,** the space between the surface and the clouds, to separate the two "waters," creating a massive vapor canopy high above the Earth (Hebrew *mabbul*). These **waters which *were* above** provided a protective greenhouse effect over the world of that period.

1:8 Heaven: See definition of firmament in note on v. 6.

1:9, 10 The third day marked the appearance of **Earth** by defining the boundaries (**be gathered together into one place**) of the **Seas.**

1:11, 12 God commanded **the earth,** with its productive power, to **bring forth** the plant kingdom. **According to its kind:** God's laws of genetics were impressed upon the plant kingdom.

is in itself, on the earth"; and it was so.
12 And the earth brought forth grass,
the herb *that* yields seed according to
its kind, and the tree *that* yields fruit,
whose seed *is* in itself according to its
kind. And God saw that *it was* good.
13 So the evening and the morning
were the third day.
14 Then God said, "Let there be
[a]lights in the firmament of the heavens
to divide the day from the night; and
let them be for signs and [b]seasons,*
and for days and years;
15 "and let them be for lights in the
firmament of the heavens to give light
on the earth"; and it was so.
16 Then God made two great [1]lights:
the [a]greater light to rule the day, and
the [b]lesser light to rule the night. *He
made* [c]the stars also.
17 God set them in the firmament of
the [a]heavens to give light on the earth,
18 and to [a]rule over the day and over
the night, and to divide the light from
the darkness. And God saw that *it was*
good.
19 So the evening and the morning
were the fourth day.
20 Then God said, "Let the waters
abound with an abundance of living
[1]creatures, and let birds fly above the
earth across the face of the [2]firmament
of the heavens."
21 So [a]God created great sea creatures
and every living thing that moves, with
which the waters abounded, according
to their kind, and every winged bird
according to its kind. And God saw
that *it was* good.
22 And God blessed them, saying,
[a]"Be fruitful and multiply, and *fill the
waters in the seas, and let birds multiply on the earth."
23 So the evening and the morning
were the fifth day.
24 Then God said, "Let the earth bring
forth the living creature according to
its kind: cattle and creeping thing and
beast of the earth, *each* according to
its kind"; and it was so.
25 And God made the beast of the
earth according to its kind, cattle according to its kind, and everything that
creeps on the earth according to its
kind. And God saw that *it was* good.
26 Then God said, [a]"Let Us make **man**
in Our image, according to Our likeness; [b]let them have dominion over the
fish of the sea, over the birds of the
air, and over the cattle, over [1]all the
earth and over every creeping thing
that creeps on the earth."

14 [a]Deut. 4:19; Ps. 74:16; 136:5–9 [b]Ps. 104:19 *See WW at Num. 9:2.
16 [a]Ps. 136:8 [b]Deut. 17:3; Ps. 8:3 [c]Deut. 4:19; Job 38:7; Is. 40:26 [1]*luminaries*
17 [a]Gen. 15:5; Jer. 33:20, 25
18 [a]Jer. 31:35
20 [1]*souls* [2]*expanse*
21 [a]Ps. 104:25–28
22 [a]Gen. 8:17 *See WW at Jer. 23:24.
26 [a]Gen. 9:6; Ps. 100:3; Eccl. 7:29; [Eph. 4:24]; James 3:9 [b]Gen. 9:2; Ps. 8:6–8 [1]Syr. *all the wild animals of*
27 [a]Gen. 5:2; 1 Cor. 11:7 [b]Matt. 19:4; [Mark 10:6–8] *See WW at Gen. 1:1.
28 [a]Gen. 9:1, 7; Lev. 26:9 [b]1 Cor. 9:27 [1]*moves about on*

WORD WEALTH

1:26 man, *'adam* (ah-*dahm*); Strong's #120: Man, mankind, Adam the first man, or humanity at large. *'Adam* is translated as "Adam" (the proper name) about 20 times in the OT, and as "man" more than 500 times. When referring to the whole human race, the Bible often uses the phrase *b'nay 'adam,* the "children of Adam." As with English "man," *'adam* in its general sense has nothing to do with maleness and everything to do with humanness. For example, in one case *'adam* refers exclusively to women! (Num. 31:35). *'Adam* is probably related to the verb *'adom,* to be red, referring to the ruddiness of man's complexion. *'Adamah,* "soil" or "ground," may also be derived from this verb. Thus Gen. 2:7 says, "The LORD God formed *'adam* of the dust of the *'adamah.*" Paul sees Adam as earth man or earthy man in 1 Cor. 15:47. *'Adam* is one of the four major Hebrew words for "man" used in the Bible. See also *'enosh, 'ish,* and *geber.*

27 So God *created man [a]in His *own*
image; in the image of God He created
him; [b]male and female He created
them.
28 Then God blessed them, and God
said to them, [a]"Be fruitful and multiply; fill the earth and [b]subdue it; have
dominion over the fish of the sea, over
the birds of the air, and over every living thing that [1]moves on the earth."

KINGDOM DYNAMICS

1:26–28 God Created Man (Male/Female) in His Own Image, FAMILY ORDER. These verses introduce a phrase that is the cornerstone of the biblical understanding of man: image of God. The image of God is presented first and fore-

(*cont. on next page*)

1:21 Great sea creatures are the more magnificent ocean creatures, such as whales and dolphins. **According to their kind:** Again, the laws of genetics that preclude any evolution into another kind; a sparrow can never produce a vulture.
1:24 Cattle is generic for all domestic animals; **creeping thing** represents mice, reptiles, insects, and so on; **beast of the earth** represents wild animals. Together with those in v. 21 they represent the totality of the animal kingdom.
1:26 Let Us: God was speaking, not only to what the NT reveals to be the rest of the Trinity, but to the entire host of heaven, the angels, as well. **Our image** likely refers to such qualities as reason, personality, and intellect, and to the capacity to relate, to hear, to see, and to speak. All of these are characteristics of God, which He chose to reproduce in mankind. **Dominion over . . . the earth:** God created **man** to be His kingdom agent, to rule and subdue the rest of creation, including the aggressive satanic forces, which would soon infringe upon it.

(*cont. from preceding page*)
most in relation to a unique social or community concept of God. "Then God [singular] said, 'Let Us [plural] make man in Our [plural] image.'" Many scholars interpret this use of both the singular and the plural as an allusion to the Trinity: one God, yet a community of Persons.

God then proceeds to create man in His own image. At this all-important beginning point, Scripture highlights a particular aspect of man's nature, namely, that which corresponds to the social or community aspect of God's nature: God creates man as male and female—not a solitary individual, but two people. Yet, as we read on, we discover that the two are, nevertheless, "one" (see 2:24).

The "community" that reflects God's image is a special community: the community of a man and a woman. When God chose to create man in His own image, He created a marriage, a family. The community of the family is a reflection of the community in the Godhead. Its identity, life, and power come from God.
(*/Eph. 3:14, 15) L.C.

KINGDOM DYNAMICS

1:26–28; 2:16, 17 Man's Delegated "Dominion," FOUNDATIONS OF THE KINGDOM. In creating man, the Sovereign of the universe makes a choice to delegate to man "dominion . . . on the earth" (v. 28). Man's power and authority for exercising this rule originate in God's intent to make man in His own image and likeness. Man's ability to sustain his role as delegated ruler of Earth will rest in his continued obedience to God's rule as King of all. His power to reign in life will extend only as far as his faithfulness to obey God's law. See also 1 Chr. 29:10–16. (Gen. 1:1/Gen. 1:31) J.W.H.

KINGDOM DYNAMICS

1:26–28 Man's Intrinsic Value, HUMAN WORTH. Man is distinct from the rest of creation. The Divine Triune Counsel determined that man was to have God's image and likeness. Man is a spiritual being who is not only body, but also soul and spirit. He is a moral being whose intelligence, perception, and self-determination far exceed that of any other earthly being.

These properties or traits possessed by mankind and his prominence in the order of creation imply the intrinsic worth, not only of the family of mankind, but also of each human individual.

Capacity and ability constitute accountability and responsibility. We should never be pleased to dwell on a level of existence lower than that on which God has made it possible for us to dwell. We should strive to be the best we can be and to reach the highest levels we can reach. To do less is to be unfaithful stewards of the life entrusted to us. See Ps. 8:4, 5; 139:13, 14.
(*/Ps. 8:4–8) C.B.

29 And God said, "See, I have given
you every herb *that* yields seed which
is on the face of all the earth, and every
tree whose fruit yields seed; [a]to you it
shall be for food.
30 "Also, to [a]every beast of the earth,
to every [b]bird of the air, and to everything that creeps on the earth, in which
there is [1]life, *I have given* every green
herb for food"; and it was so.
31 Then [a]God saw everything that He
had made, and indeed *it was* very
good. So the evening and the morning
were the sixth day.

KINGDOM DYNAMICS

1:31 Before the Fall, FOUNDATIONS OF THE KINGDOM. The original order of man's environment on Earth must be distinguished from what it became following the impact of man's fall, the curse, and the eventual deluge (Is. 45:18; Rom. 8:20; 2 Pet. 3:4–7). The agricultural, zoological, geological, and meteorological disharmony to which creation became subject must not be attributed to God. The perfect will of God, as founding King of creation, is not manifest in the presence of death, disease, discord, and disaster any more than it is manifest in human sin. Our present world does not reflect the kingdom order He originally intended for man's enjoyment on Earth, nor does it reflect God's kingdom as it shall ultimately be experienced on this planet. Understanding this, we should be cautious not to attribute to "God's will" or to "acts of God" those characteristics of our world that resulted from the ruin of God's original order by reason of man's fall.
(Gen. 1:26–28; 2:16, 17/Gen. 3:16–24) J.W.H.

2 Thus the heavens and the earth,
and [a]all the *host of them, were finished.
2 [a]And on the seventh day God ended

29 [a]Gen. 9:3; Ps. 104:14, 15
30 [a]Ps. 145:15 [b]Job 38:41 [1]*a living soul*
31 [a][Ps. 104:24; 1 Tim. 4:4]

CHAPTER 2

1 [a]Ps. 33:6 *See WW at Ps. 68:11.
2 [a]Ex. 20:9–11; 31:17; Heb. 4:4, 10

2:1 The work of creation week is **finished: earth** is habitable, life has been created, man is in charge, and food has been provided for all. God's involvement is not ended, however; the Sustainer's power continues to work to this day.

2:2, 3 He rested means God abstained from further creating, having **ended His work. The seventh day:** Designed for the good of man, the Sabbath was ordained by God to be a day for rest and special covenant celebration. It is **sanctified** in the sense that those who observe its true

His work which He had done, and He
*rested on the seventh day from all His
work which He had done.
3 Then God [a]blessed the seventh day
and sanctified it, because in it He
rested from all His work which God
had created and made.
4 [a]This *is* the [1]history of the heavens
and the *earth when they were created,
in the day that the LORD God made the
earth and the heavens,
5 before any [a]plant of the field was
in the earth and before any herb of the
field had grown. For the LORD God had
not [b]caused it to rain on the earth, and
there was no man [c]to till the ground;
6 but a mist went up from the earth
and watered the whole face of the
ground.
7 And the LORD God formed man *of*
the [a]dust of the ground, and [b]breathed
into his [c]nostrils the *breath of life; and
[d]man became a living being.

Life in God's Garden

8 The LORD God planted [a]a garden
[b]eastward in [c]Eden, and there He put
the man whom He had formed.
9 And out of the ground the LORD God
made [a]every tree grow that is pleasant
to the sight and good for food. [b]The
tree of life *was* also in the midst of the
garden, and the tree of the knowledge
of good and [c]evil.*
10 Now a river went out of Eden to water the garden, and from there it parted
and became four riverheads.
11 The name of the first *is* Pishon; it
is the one which skirts [a]the whole land
of Havilah, where *there is* gold.
12 And the gold of that land *is* good.
[a]Bdellium and the onyx stone *are*
there.
13 The name of the second river *is* Gihon; it *is* the one which goes around
the whole land of Cush.
14 The name of the third river *is*
[a]Hiddekel;[1] it *is* the one which goes toward the east of [2]Assyria. The fourth
river *is* the Euphrates.
15 Then the LORD God took [1]the man
and put him in the garden of Eden to
[2]tend and keep it.
16 And the LORD God commanded the
man, saying, "Of every tree of the garden you may freely eat;
17 "but of the tree of the knowledge
of good and evil [a]you shall not eat, for
in the day that you eat of it [b]you[1] shall
surely [c]die."
18 And the LORD God said, "*It is* not
good that man should be alone;
[a]I will make him a helper comparable
to him."
19 [a]Out of the ground the LORD God
formed every beast of the field and
every bird of the air, and [b]brought
them to [1]Adam to see what he would
call them. And whatever Adam called
each living creature, that *was* its name.
20 So Adam gave names to all cattle,
to the birds of the air, and to every
beast of the field. But for Adam there
was not found a helper comparable to
him.

2 *See WW at Ex. 16:30.
3 [a][Is. 58:13]
4 [a]Gen. 1:1; Ps. 90:1, 2 [1]Heb. *toledoth,* lit. *generations* *See WW at Ex. 32:13.
5 [a]Gen. 1:11, 12 [b]Gen. 7:4; Job 5:10; 38:26–28 [c]Gen. 3:23
7 [a]Gen. 3:19, 23; Ps. 103:14 [b]Job 33:4 [c]Gen. 7:22 [d]1 Cor. 15:45 *See WW at Ps. 150:6.
8 [a]Is. 51:3 [b]Gen. 3:23, 24 [c]Gen. 4:16
9 [a]Ezek. 31:8 [b][Gen. 3:22; Rev. 2:7; 22:2, 14] [c][Deut. 1:39] *See WW at Ps. 5:4.
11 [a]Gen. 25:18
12 [a]Num. 11:7
14 [a]Dan. 10:4 [1]Or *Tigris* [2]Heb. *Ashshur*
15 [1]Or *Adam* [2]*cultivate*
17 [a]Gen. 3:1, 3, 11, 17 [b]Gen. 3:3, 19; [Rom. 6:23] [c]Rom. 5:12; 1 Cor. 15:21, 22 [1]Lit. *dying you shall die*
18 [a]1 Cor. 11:8, 9; 1 Tim. 2:13
19 [a]Gen. 1:20, 24 [b]Ps. 8:6 [1]Or *the man*

---

intent enjoy divine blessings. Thus God built the seven-day week into the order of the universe.

2:4 History is literally "generations," meaning "offspring," a word appearing 11 times in Gen., usually introducing a new narrative or genealogy. This chapter depicts creation from a different perspective, more localized and man-centered.

2:5, 6 Skipping over a host of details from ch. 1 these verses correspond to 1:2. **A mist:** Probably "a spring" or "fresh-water ocean"; underground water was apparently surging up through the as yet undistinguished **ground** (continents).

2:7 Formed: Six Hebrew words found in these early chapters to describe the creation process are quite similar, so modern translators use varied English words to let the reader know a different Hebrew word is being rendered. All six words are normally used of God's creative activity: *bara'* (1:1), "create"; *'asah* (1:7), "make"; *nathan* (1:17), "set"; *yatsar* (2:7), "form"; *banah* (2:22), "make" or "build"; and *qanah* (4:1; 14:19), "create," "possess," or "acquire." A most intimate moment occurred when the Creator **breathed into his nostrils the breath of life.** "In Him was life" (John 1:4), and He gave mankind the precious life that only God has to give.

2:8 A garden describes a real place, not an allegorical image. It was apparently a reserve, or enclosed, parklike area. **Eastward in Eden** indicates that the area of Eden lay east of present-day Israel, somewhere in Mesopotamia or Arabia.

2:9 In this lush natural reserve were found the two trees that are key to everything that follows in all of human history. They were the physical means God used to transact spiritual realities. **The tree of life** is the tree associated with experiencing the life of God, including immortality. **The tree of the knowledge of good and evil** represents human autonomy, that is, self-rule and an assumed independence from God in all areas of life.

2:10–14 Two of the four rivers are identified today: the **Hiddekel** (the Tigris) and **the Euphrates. Bdellium** is a yellowish aromatic resin.

2:17 The tragedy of human autonomy is seen in God's warning, **you shall surely die.** In that man's self-rule is all-inclusive, so the death is inclusive of man's spiritual, moral, social, relational, and ultimately, his physical being.

2:18 A helper indicates that Adam's strength for all he was called to be and do was inadequate in itself. **Comparable to him** denotes complementarity. The needed help is for daily work, procreation, and mutual support through companionship.

2:19 That *was* its name restates what God had already instructed man in ch. 1: "Have dominion over" the Earth and its creatures. The one in authority is entitled to name the members of the community for which he is responsible.

21 And the LORD God caused a [a]deep sleep to fall on Adam, and he slept; and He took one of his ribs, and closed up the flesh in its place.
22 Then the rib which the LORD God had taken from man He [1]made into a woman, [a]and He [b]brought her to the man.
23 And Adam said:

> "This *is* now [a]bone of my bones
> And flesh of my flesh;
> She shall be called [1]Woman,
> Because she was [b]taken out of
> [2]Man."*

24 [a]Therefore a man shall leave his father and mother and [b]be[1] joined to his wife, and they shall become *one flesh.
25 [a]And they were both naked, the man and his wife, and were not [b]ashamed.*

The Temptation and Fall of Man

2 **3** Now [a]the serpent was [b]more cunning than any beast of the field which the LORD God had made. And he said to the woman, "Has God indeed said, 'You shall not eat of every tree of the garden'?"
2 And the woman said to the serpent, "We may eat the [a]fruit of the trees of the garden;
3 "but of the fruit of the tree which *is* in the midst of the garden, God has said, 'You shall not eat it, nor shall you [a]touch it, lest you die.' "
4 [a]Then the serpent said to the woman, "You will not surely die.
5 "For God knows that in the *day you eat of it your eyes will be opened, and you will be like God, knowing good and evil."
6 So when the woman [a]saw that the 2
tree *was* good for food, that it *was* [1]pleasant to the eyes, and a tree desirable to make *one* *wise, she took of its fruit [b]and ate. She also gave to her husband with her, and he ate.
7 Then the eyes of both of them were opened, [a]and they knew that they *were* naked; and they sewed fig leaves together and made themselves [1]coverings.
8 And they heard [a]the [1]sound of the LORD God walking in the garden in the [2]cool of the day, and Adam and his wife [b]hid themselves from the presence of the LORD God among the trees of the garden.
9 Then the LORD God called to Adam and said to him, "Where *are* you?"
10 So he said, "I heard Your voice in the garden, [a]and I was afraid because I was naked; and I hid myself."
11 And He said, "Who told you that you *were* naked? Have you eaten from the tree of which I commanded you that you should not eat?"
12 Then the man said, [a]"The woman whom You gave *to be* with me, she gave me of the tree, and I ate."
13 And the LORD God said to the woman, "What *is* this you have done?"

21 [a]1 Sam. 26:12
22 [a]1 Tim. 2:13 [b]Heb. 13:4 [1]Lit. *built*
23 [a]Gen. 29:14 [b]1 Cor. 11:8, 9 [1]Heb. *Ishshah* [2]Heb. *Ish* *See WW at Is. 32:2.
24 [a]Matt. 19:5 [b]Mark 10:6–8 [1]Lit. *cling* *See WW at Deut. 6:4.
25 [a]Gen. 3:7, 10 [b]Is. 47:3 *See WW at Ezek. 16:63.

CHAPTER 3

1 [a]1 Chr. 21:1 [b]2 Cor. 11:3
2 [a]Gen. 2:16, 17
3 [a]Ex. 19:12, 13
4 [a][2 Cor. 11:3]
5 *See WW at Zeph. 1:7.
6 [a]1 John 2:16 [b]1 Tim. 2:14 [1]Lit. *a desirable thing* *See WW at Jer. 3:15.
7 [a]Gen. 2:25 [1]*girding coverings*
8 [a]Job 38:1 [b]Job 31:33 [1]Or *voice* [2]Or *wind, breeze*
10 [a]Gen. 2:25
12 [a][Prov. 28:13]

2:21 One of his ribs: As in other creative miracles of Scripture, God begins with "a seed," such as the jar of meal from which Elijah ate for two and a half years and the fish and loaves of bread with which Jesus fed the 5,000. The rib was likely chosen as representative of an intimate part of Adam's makeup.
2:24 Leave connotes a priority change on the part of the husband. **Be joined** has the idea of both passion and permanence. **One flesh** carries a number of implications, including sexual union, child conception, spiritual and emotional intimacy, and showing each other the same respect shown other close kin, such as one's parents and siblings. This is enhanced in the NT where it is clear that Christian mates are also each other's brother and sister.
3:1–24 This chapter, the Fall of man, introduces two dominant themes of OT theology: 1) God is personal and redemptive, and 2) man is sinful. The reader will not fully understand the Bible without grasping these two great truths.
3:1–5 See section 2 of Truth-In-Action at the end of Gen.
3:1 The serpent is identified in Rev. 12:9 as Satan himself, here in corporeal form. It is not clear why he chose to indwell this particular **beast . . . which the LORD God had made.** Later OT history lists the snake among the unclean animals (Lev. 11). He is **cunning,** crafty, and shrewd. **Has God indeed said:** "All this is not enough," suggested the tempter. "You could have more!" The question was shrewdly overstated: **Every tree?**
3:2, 3 The woman's response shows initial innocence, but **the serpent** caused her to begin pondering the matter.
3:4 This bold lie could be translated, "Die? You will not die!" In other words, "God has falsely threatened you with death."
3:5 You will be like God: The tempting thirst for power can be unquenchable, even when people have all of their needs met. **Knowing** carries the sense of "experiencing"; thus the challenge grew yet greater: "God is withholding a good thing from you (self-rule) in order to keep you dependent on Him."
3:6 See section 2 of Truth-In-Action at the end of Gen.
3:6 The desire to become **wise** seemed quite reasonable to **the woman.** Unfortunately, her definition of wise was human self-rule, not God-dependency as taught in Prov. 1:7.
3:7 They *were* naked: Adam and Eve's newly gained awareness brought them not the promised knowledge of good and evil, but embarrassment over their nakedness.
3:8 Sinners have always **hid themselves from the presence of the LORD God,** as they will continue to do: "Hide us from the face of Him who sits on the throne!" (Rev. 6:16).
3:9 The LORD God was not asking out of ignorance, but rather as a parent would demand knowingly of a disobedient child: "What have you been doing now?"
3:12, 13 Another human frailty appears for the first time: **the man** blamed his wife *and* God. **The woman,** too, tried to shift the blame.

The woman said, [a]"The serpent deceived me, and I ate."
14 So the LORD God said to the serpent:

"Because you have done this,
You *are* cursed more than all cattle,
And more than every beast of the field;
On your belly you shall go,
And [a]you shall eat dust
All the days of your life.
15 And I will put enmity
Between you and the woman,
And between [a]your seed and [b]her Seed;
[c]He shall bruise your **head,**
And you shall bruise His heel."

WORD WEALTH

3:15 head, *rosh* (*rohsh*); Strong's #7218: Head, the head (of the human body), the head of a line; what is principal or supreme; first, top, prince, the highest part, summit, beginning, foremost, leader, and chief. Just as the "head" of a company refers to its chief person, *rosh* is used to show headship. In 3:15, the promise is that the Seed of woman would someday crush the Serpent's head, that woman in particular would play a part in undoing the effects of the Fall. In its most specific sense the Lord Jesus has trampled Satan at the Cross. In its wider sense, the human race will eventually completely triumph over the Evil One (Rom. 16:20).

KINGDOM DYNAMICS

3:15 The Gospel's First Proclamation, MESSIAH'S COMING. This verse contains the first proclamation of the gospel. All of the richness, the mercy, the sorrow, and the glory of God's redeeming work with man is here in miniature. God promises to bring a Redeemer from the Seed of the woman; He will be completely human yet divinely begotten. "That serpent of old, called the Devil," would war with the Seed (see Rev. 12) and would smite Him. But even as the Serpent struck at His heel, His foot would descend crushing the Serpent's head. In Christ's life and death this scripture was fulfilled. Divinely begotten, yet fully human, by His death and resurrection He has defeated and made a public spectacle of the powers of hell (Col. 2:15). This first messianic promise is one of the most succinct statements of the gospel to be found anywhere.

(*/Deut. 18:18, 19) J.H.

16 To the woman He said:

"I will greatly multiply your sorrow and your conception;
[a]In pain you shall bring forth children;
[b]Your desire *shall be* [1]for your husband,
And he shall [c]rule over you."

17 Then to Adam He said, [a]"Because you have heeded the voice of your wife, and have eaten from the tree [b]of which I commanded you, saying, 'You shall not eat of it':

[c]"Cursed *is* the ground for your sake;
[d]In toil you shall eat *of* it
All the days of your life.

13 [a]Gen. 3:4; 2 Cor. 11:3; 1 Tim. 2:14
14 [a]Deut. 28:15–20; Is. 65:25; Mic. 7:17
15 [a]John 8:44; Acts 13:10; 1 John 3:8 [b]Is. 7:14; Luke 1:31, 34, 35; Gal. 4:4 [c]Rom. 16:20; [Rev. 12:7, 17]
16 [a]Is. 13:8; John 16:21 [b]Gen. 4:7 [c]1 Cor. 11:3; Eph. 5:22; 1 Tim. 2:12, 15 [1]Lit. *toward*
17 [a]1 Sam. 15:23 [b]Gen. 2:17 [c]Gen. 5:29; Rom. 8:20–22; Heb. 6:8 [d]Job 5:7; 14:1; Eccl. 2:23

3:14, 15 You *are* cursed carries the idea of coming under God's judgment. Although the exact meaning of the serpent's being cursed **more than** the rest of the animal kingdom is unclear, Paul later reinforces the idea that all creation was affected by the Fall (Rom. 8:20–22). **On your belly you shall go** does not insist that the serpent previously had legs; it is equally likely to be poetic language supporting the fact that the animal kingdom will not be able to reverse its post-Fall condition on its own. **You shall eat dust** is also figurative for extreme humiliation.

NT allusions to v. 15 (Rom. 16:20; Heb. 2:14; Rev. 12) seem to indicate that the curse to the serpent has a broader application. Interpreted messianically, **enmity** represents the conflict between Satan (**your seed**) and God's people, especially Jesus Christ (**her Seed**). **He shall bruise your head . . . you shall bruise His heel** depicts the long struggle between good and evil, with God ultimately winning through Jesus Christ, the last Adam. V. 15 is often referred to as the first messianic prophecy in the OT, the *Protoevangelium*.

3:16 The woman is not *directly* cursed, although it is obvious she comes under God's general curse. Rather, there will be a major marring of her appointed roles as wife and mother. Maternity will be with great suffering, a particularly disappointing consequence to OT women who saw large families as a sign of blessing. **Your desire *shall be* for your husband** is difficult in the Hebrew. Most likely the expression carries the idea that, remembering their joint-rule in the Garden, she would desire to dominate her husband. **He shall rule over you** asserts the divine assignment of the husband's servant-leader role. There is no evidence that this was ever intended as a diminishing of the woman's person or giftedness, but rather as a redemptive role assigned the husband toward the wife as a means toward reinstating the original partnership. Note: the passage does not assert male dominance over females. It does assign husbandly responsibility for leadership in the marriage relationship. See Eph. 5:22–33.

3:17–19 Adam is also spared a *direct* cursing. His major mistake was in heeding **the voice of** his **wife** rather than the voice of God. As the one having the greatest responsibility, his sentence is the longest and most comprehensive. **In toil you shall eat of it** notes a marring of man's fundamental role as laborer/provider; work shall be with difficulties and futilities (**thorns and thistles . . . in the sweat of your face**). This lifelong struggle will then end in death.

KINGDOM DYNAMICS

3:17 Man's Critical Role in the Affairs of the Earth, HUMAN WORTH. From the perspective of man's strategic role we must assume him to be more valuable than anything on Earth. No other form of earthly life plays such a cosmic role as mankind. The world literally stands or falls based on the actions of men. Only man has the power to deplete the Earth's resources and to pollute its atmosphere. The sin of one man, Adam, corrupted the world. The continued sinfulness of mankind caused the Flood (6:12, 13). In contrast, the obedience of one Man, Jesus Christ, brought justification and righteousness to many (Rom. 5:18, 19). If redeemed men were to walk in that justification and righteousness, could they not cause the world to bloom and blossom? God wants to reveal His truth and beauty to the world only through redeemed mankind. Each believer has strategic significance in his own sphere. He or she must strive to maximize the impact of the good and encourage others to do the same. (Ps. 8:4–8/Gen. 9:5, 6) C.B.

18 Both thorns and thistles it shall
[1]bring forth for you,
And [a]you shall eat the herb of the
field.
19 [a]In the sweat of your face you shall
eat bread
Till you return to the ground,
For out of it you were taken;
[b]For dust you *are,*
And [c]to dust you shall return."

20 And Adam called his wife's name
[a]Eve,[1] because she was the mother of
all living.
21 Also for Adam and his wife the
LORD God made tunics of skin, and
clothed them.

KINGDOM DYNAMICS

3:21 The Blood, the Covering, THE BLOOD. The covenant love of God required that innocent animals be sacrificed to provide garments of skin as a covering for Adam and Eve. This early foreshadowing of substitutionary atonement points toward the necessity of judgment upon the innocent to provide a covering for the guilty. Adam and Eve made a vain attempt to cover themselves with their own efforts by sewing together fig leaves. However, God's order provided covering by means of a sacrifice. Under the New Covenant, we are required to be clothed with Christ rather than with our good works (Gal. 3:27).
(Heb. 9:12/Matt. 26:28) C.S.

18 [a]Ps. 104:14 [1]*cause to grow*
19 [a]2 Thess. 3:10 [b]Gen. 2:7; 5:5 [c]Job 21:26; Eccl. 3:20
20 [a]2 Cor. 11:3; 1 Tim. 2:13 [1]Lit. *Life* or *Living*

KINGDOM DYNAMICS

3:21 Restoration "In the Beginning," RESTORATION. Chs. 1—3 unveil God's ways of restoration "in the beginning." The entire concept of "The Holy Spirit and Restoration" is developed in the study article, which begins on page 2012.
(Job 42:10–12/Gen. 6:5) J.R.

22 Then the LORD God said, "Behold,
the man has become like one of Us,
to know good and evil. And now, lest
he put out his *hand and take also of
the tree of life, and eat, and live *forever"—
23 therefore the LORD God sent him out
of the garden of Eden [a]to till the
ground from which he was taken.
24 So [a]He drove out the man; and He
placed [b]cherubim [c]at the east of the
garden of Eden, and a flaming sword
which turned every way, to guard the
way to the tree of [d]life.

22 *See WW at Josh. 4:24. • See WW at Ps. 136:1.
23 [a]Gen. 4:2; 9:20
24 [a]Ezek. 31:3, 11 [b]Ex. 25:18–22; Ps. 104:4; Ezek. 10:1–20; Heb. 1:7 [c]Gen. 2:8 [d]Gen. 2:9; [Rev. 22:2]

KINGDOM DYNAMICS

3:16–24 Impact of the Fall, FOUNDATIONS OF THE KINGDOM. Through disobedience to the terms of his rule, man "falls," thus experiencing the loss of his "dominion" (vv. 22, 23). Everything of his delegated realm (Earth) comes under a curse as his relationship with God, the fountainhead of his power to rule, is severed (vv. 17, 18). Thus, man loses the "life" power essential to ruling in God's kingdom (vv. 19, 22). Beyond the tragedy of man's loss, two other facts unfold. First, through his disobedience to God and submission to the Serpent's suggestions, man's rule has been forfeited to the Serpent. Rev. 12:9 verifies that the spirit employing the snake's form was Satan himself. The domain originally delegated to man now falls to Satan, who becomes administrator of this now-cursed realm. The Serpent's "seed" and "head" indicate a continual line (seed) of evil offspring extending Satan's rule (head) (v. 15). However, a second fact offers hope. Amid the tragedy of this sequence of events, God begins to move redemptively, and a plan for recovering man's lost estate is promised (v. 15) and

3:22–24 The curse is reinforced by the expulsion of Adam and Eve from **the garden**, the place of their unique communion with **the LORD God. Cherubim,** wielding a zigzagging **sword,** sure to hit and bring death, prevented their return. The lesson is clear: there will be no communion with God without His initiative.

set in motion with the first sacrifice (v. 21).

(Gen. 1:31/Gen. 8:20—9:17) J.W.H.

KINGDOM DYNAMICS

3:24 The Cherubim, ANGELS. Cherubim are the created beings assigned to guard the throne of God (Ps. 99:1) as well as the ark of the covenant and the mercy seat (Ex. 25:18–22; 37:7–9). Cherubim (plural for cherub) guarded the Tree of Life to keep man from eating of it and, therefore, living forever in his sins. Thus, contrary to popular belief, more than one angel guarded the entrance to Eden. The fullest description of cherubim is in Ezek. 10, where they are closely related to the glory of God and have a part in its presence and its withdrawal, moving at the Almighty's direction.

(Is. 6:2/Jude 9) M.H.

Cain Murders Abel

4 Now Adam knew Eve his wife, and
she conceived and bore [1]Cain, and
said, "I have acquired a *man from the
LORD."
2 Then she bore again, this time his
brother [1]Abel. Now [a]Abel was a keeper
of sheep, but Cain was a tiller of the
ground.
3 And [1]in the process of time it came
to pass that Cain brought an offering
of the fruit [a]of the ground to the LORD.
4 Abel also brought of [a]the firstborn
of his flock and of [b]their fat. And the
LORD [c]respected Abel and his *offering,
5 but He did not respect Cain and his
offering. And Cain was very angry,
and his countenance fell.
6 So the LORD said to Cain, "Why are
you angry? And why has your countenance fallen?
7 "If you do well, will you not be accepted? And if you do not do well, *sin
lies at the door. And its desire *is*
[1]for you, but you should rule over it."
8 Now Cain [1]talked with Abel his
[2]brother; and it came to pass, when
they were in the field, that Cain rose
up against Abel his brother and
[a]killed him.
9 Then the LORD said to Cain, "Where
is Abel your brother?" He said, [a]"I
do not *know. *Am* I [b]my brother's
keeper?"

CHAPTER 4

1 [1]Lit. *Acquire* *See WW at Is. 32:2.
2 [a]Luke 11:50, 51 [1]Lit. *Breath* or *Nothing*
3 [a]Num. 18:12 [1]Lit. *at the end of days*
4 [a]Num. 18:17 [b]Lev. 3:16 [c]Heb. 11:4 *See WW at Num. 29:6.
7 [1]Lit. *toward* *See WW at Lev. 9:2.
8 [a]Matt. 23:35; Luke 11:51; [1 John 3:12–15]; Jude 11 [1]Lit. *said to* [2]Sam., LXX, Syr., Vg. add *"Let us go out to the field."*
9 [a]John 8:44 [b]1 Cor. 8:11–13 *See WW at Ex. 3:7.
10 [a]Num. 35:33; Deut. 21:1–9; Heb. 12:24; Rev. 6:9, 10 *See WW at Lev. 17:11.

KINGDOM DYNAMICS

4:9 Responsibility for One Another, BROTHERLY LOVE. The theme of brotherhood emerges early in Scripture; and from the very beginning, it is clear that God places a high priority on how brothers treat each other. In this passage the question of responsibility for one another first emerges. Cain asks, *"Am I my brother's keeper?"* The word used for "keeper" (Hebrew *shamar*) means "to guard, to protect, to attend, or to regard." Are we responsible? "Absolutely," is God's answer. Not only are we our brother's keeper, we are held accountable for our treatment of and our ways of relating to our brothers (blood and spiritual).

For Cain's sins against his brother, God curses him throughout the Earth, takes away his ability to farm, and sentences him to a life as a fugitive and a vagabond (v. 12). This clearly indicates that unbrotherliness destines one to fruitlessness and frustration of purpose.

(*/Gen. 45:4) D.S.

10 And He said, "What have you done?
The voice of your brother's *blood
[a]cries out to Me from the ground.

KINGDOM DYNAMICS

4:1–10 The Blood, Essential for Right Standing Before God, THE BLOOD. The issue of blood sacrifice as being essential for right standing with God is conveyed through the offerings of Cain and Abel. Pursuant upon the founding lesson God gave in dealing with Adam and Eve's sin (3:21), Cain's vegetable offering, the fruit of his own efforts, was an offering of self-righteous refusal to live under God's revealed covenant. As Adam's attempt to use fig leaves for a covering was rejected, so was Cain's offering; but Abel's offering of a blood sacrifice was pleasing to God. God's sacrifice of animals in the Garden had established the blood sacrifice as necessary for approaching Him. Right standing before a covenant-making God was shown to be a matter of life and death, not merely a matter of one's good efforts.

(Ex. 12:13/Is. 1:11) C.S.

4:1 Adam knew Eve expresses the close sexual experience of marriage.

4:5 God most likely **did not respect Cain** because he was offering poor quality worship—"an offering of the fruit" (v. 3) as opposed to Abel's "firstborn of his flock" (v. 4).

4:7 Sin lies at the door: Crouches or hides at the door. The language virtually personifies sin as a demon crouching like a crazed animal at Cain's doorstep.

4:8 Cain had no thought of repentance, only revenge.

4:10 What have you done? As in the previous chapter, God knew, yet He asked a demanding question. "The life . . . *is* in the blood" (Lev. 17:11); the One who gives that life can hear its cry. See Job 16:18; Is. 26:21; Ezek. 24:7, 8; Matt. 23:35; Rev. 6:10.

11 "So now [a]you *are* cursed from the
earth, which has opened its mouth to
receive your brother's blood from your
hand.
12 "When you till the ground, it shall
no longer yield its strength to you. A
fugitive and a vagabond you shall be
on the earth."
13 And Cain said to the LORD, "My
[1]punishment *is* greater than I can bear!
14 "Surely You have driven me out
this day from the face of the ground;
[a]I shall be [b]hidden from Your face; I
shall be a fugitive and a vagabond on
the earth, and it will happen *that*
[c]anyone who finds me will kill me."
15 And the LORD said to him, [1]"Therefore, whoever kills Cain, vengeance
shall be taken on him [a]sevenfold." And
the LORD set a [b]mark on Cain, lest anyone finding him should kill him.

The Family of Cain

16 Then Cain [a]went out from the
[b]presence of the LORD and dwelt in the
land of [1]Nod on the east of Eden.
17 And Cain knew his wife, and she
conceived and bore Enoch. And he
built a city, [a]and called the name of
the city after the name of his son—
Enoch.
18 To Enoch was born Irad; and Irad
begot Mehujael, and Mehujael begot
Methushael, and Methushael begot Lamech.
19 Then Lamech took for himself
[a]two wives: the name of one *was* Adah,
and the name of the second *was* Zillah.
20 And Adah bore Jabal. He was the
father of those who dwell in tents and
have livestock.
21 His brother's name *was* Jubal. He
was the father of all those who play
the harp and [1]flute.
22 And as for Zillah, she also bore
Tubal-Cain, an instructor of every
craftsman in bronze and iron. And the
sister of Tubal-Cain *was* Naamah.
23 Then Lamech said to his wives:

"Adah and Zillah, hear my voice;
Wives of Lamech, *listen to my
speech!
For I have [1]killed a man for
wounding me,
Even a young man [2]for hurting
me.
24 [a]If Cain shall be avenged
sevenfold,
Then Lamech seventy-
sevenfold."

11 [a]Gen. 3:14; Deut. 11:28; 28:15–20; Gal. 3:10
13 [1]*iniquity*
14 [a]Ps. 51:11 [b]Deut. 31:18; Is. 1:15 [c]Gen. 9:6; Num. 35:19, 21, 27
15 [a]Gen. 4:24; Ps. 79:12 [b]Gen. 9:6; Ezek. 9:4, 6 [1]So with MT, Tg.; LXX, Syr., Vg. *Not so;*
16 [a]2 Kin. 13:23; 24:20; Jer. 23:39; 52:3 [b]Jon. 1:3 [1]Lit. *Wandering*
17 [a]Ps. 49:11
19 [a]Gen. 2:24; 16:3; 1 Tim. 3:2
21 [1]*pipe*
23 [1]*slain a man for my wound* [2]*for my hurt* *See WW at 1 Kin. 20:8.
24 [a]Gen. 4:15
25 [a]Gen. 5:3 [1]Lit. *Appointed* *See WW at Deut. 18:5.
26 [a]Gen. 5:6 [b]Gen. 12:8; 26:25; 1 Kin. 18:24; Ps. 116:17; Joel 2:32; Zeph. 3:9; 1 Cor. 1:2 [1]Gr. *Enos,* Luke 3:38

A New Son

25 And Adam knew his wife again,
and she bore a son and [a]named* him
[1]Seth, "For God has appointed another
seed for me instead of Abel, whom
Cain killed."

KINGDOM DYNAMICS

4:25 The First Woman: A Redemptive Instrument (Eve), WOMEN. The Bible reveals that God created male and female, and that all mankind are descendants of that first pair. While Eve was deceived by the Serpent, and the first to violate the divine regulations governing their life (2:16, 17; 3:6), the Word of God holds Adam as the disobedient one, who knowingly broke trust with God (Rom. 5:12, 17; 1 Tim. 2:14). This fact does not intimate that the woman was less intelligent or more vulnerable to deception than the man, but that under the circumstances in which the Fall of man occurred, deception of the woman preceded active disobedience of the man.

It is a remarkable token of divine grace that God, in His mercy and in His giving of the first promise of a Deliverer/Messiah (Gen. 3:15), chose to bring this about by Seed of the woman. In short, the one first scarred by sin is selected to be the one first promised to become an instrument of God's redemptive working.

The birth of Seth, the "seed" given to replace the murdered Abel, was the first in the "bloodline" that will trace to the birth of the Lord Jesus Christ. Eve's distinct place in the failure of the first couple becomes the soil in which God's mercy plants the first seed of promise. The message is obvious: God is able to "make all grace abound" toward any of us. However deep the failure, Eve's testimony declares God's grace goes deeper yet. (*/Gen. 16:1) F.L./J.W.H.

26 And as for Seth, [a]to him also a son
was born; and he named him [1]Enosh.
Then *men* began [b]to call on the name
of the LORD.

4:11–15 The **mark on Cain** is unidentifiable, since his descendants perished in the Flood. The mark was not a stigma, but rather a protection for Cain and shows God's incredible love for even impenitent sinners.

4:16, 17 A city: Even villages are called cities in the Bible.

4:20–22 Lamech's three sons were pioneers, each in his own specialty. **Tubal-Cain** developed ironworking, a skill that both Scripture and archaeology demonstrate to have been lost for centuries after the Flood (until about 1500 B.C.).

4:23, 24 This irreverent poem shows sin is progressing quickly. Lamech's depravity surpassed even Cain's—boasting for killing **a young man for** merely **hurting** him.

4:26 Amid the depravity were those seeking to know **the LORD**. Gen. goes on to develop God's revelation of Himself to such human seekers.

The Family of Adam

5 This is the book of the [a]genealogy
of Adam. In the day that God created *man, He made him in [b]the likeness of God.
2 He *created them [a]male and female,
and [b]blessed them and called them
Mankind in the day they were created.
3 And Adam lived one hundred and
thirty years, and begot *a son* [a]in his
own likeness, after his image, and
[b]named him Seth.
4 After he begot Seth, [a]the days of
Adam were eight hundred years;
[b]and he had sons and daughters.
5 So all the days that Adam lived
were nine hundred and thirty years;
[a]and he died.
6 Seth lived one hundred and five
years, and begot [a]Enosh.
7 After he begot Enosh, Seth lived
eight hundred and seven years, and
had sons and daughters.
8 So all the days of Seth were nine
hundred and twelve years; and he died.
9 Enosh lived ninety years, and begot
[1]Cainan.
10 After he begot Cainan, Enosh lived
eight hundred and fifteen years, and
had sons and daughters.
11 So all the days of Enosh were nine
hundred and five years; and he died.
12 Cainan lived seventy years, and begot Mahalalel.
13 After he begot Mahalalel, Cainan
lived eight hundred and forty years,
and had sons and daughters.
14 So all the days of Cainan were nine
hundred and ten years; and he died.
15 Mahalalel lived sixty-five years,
and begot Jared.
16 After he begot Jared, Mahalalel
lived eight hundred and thirty years,
and had sons and daughters.
17 So all the days of Mahalalel were
eight hundred and ninety-five years;
and he died.
18 Jared lived one hundred and sixty-
two years, and begot [a]Enoch.
19 After he begot Enoch, Jared lived
eight hundred years, and had sons and
daughters.
20 So all the days of Jared were nine
hundred and sixty-two years; and he
died.
21 Enoch lived sixty-five years, and begot Methuselah.

CHAPTER 5

1 [a]Gen. 2:4; 6:9; 1 Chr. 1:1; Matt. 1:1 [b]Gen. 1:26; 9:6; [Eph. 4:24; Col. 3:10] *See WW at Gen. 1:26.
2 [a]Gen. 1:27; Deut. 4:32; Matt. 19:4; Mark 10:6 [b]Gen. 1:28; 9:1 *See WW at Gen. 1:1.
3 [a]1 Cor. 15:48, 49 [b]Gen. 4:25
4 [a]1 Chr. 1:1–4; Luke 3:36–38 [b]Gen. 1:28; 4:25
5 [a]Gen. 2:17; 3:19; 6:17; [Heb. 9:27]
6 [a]Gen. 4:26
9 [1]Heb. *Qenan*
18 [a]Jude 14, 15

5:1 In the day that means "when."
5:4–32 The purpose of these genealogies is twofold: to record that real people lived before the Flood, and to record their physical death fulfillment of the curse. They link Creation with the Flood through 10 patriarchs.
5:5 930 years shows Adam lived during much of the antediluvian period.

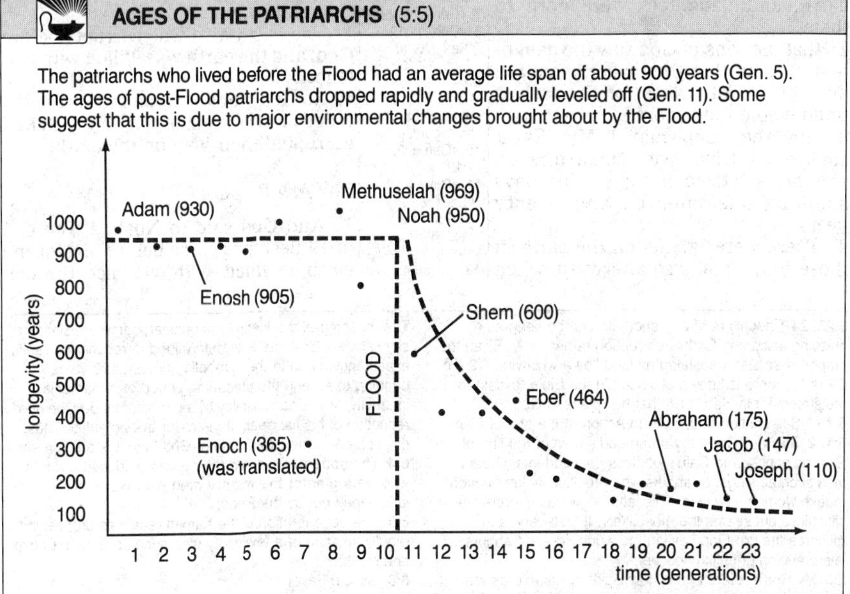

22 After he begot Methuselah, Enoch
[a]walked with God three hundred
years, and had sons and daughters.
23 So all the days of Enoch were three
hundred and sixty-five years.
24 And [a]Enoch walked with God; and
he *was* not, for God [b]took him.
25 Methuselah lived one hundred and
eighty-seven years, and begot Lamech.
26 After he begot Lamech, Methuselah
lived seven hundred and eighty-two
years, and had sons and daughters.
27 So all the days of Methuselah were
nine hundred and sixty-nine years; and
he died.
28 Lamech lived one hundred and
eighty-two years, and had a son.
29 And he called his name [a]Noah,[1]
saying, "This *one* will comfort us concerning our work and the toil of our
hands, because of the ground [b]which
the LORD has cursed."
30 After he begot Noah, Lamech lived
five hundred and ninety-five years, and
had sons and daughters.
31 So all the days of Lamech were
seven hundred and seventy-seven
years; and he died.
32 And Noah was five hundred years
old, and Noah begot [a]Shem, Ham,
[b]and Japheth.

The Wickedness and Judgment of Man

3 **6** Now it came to pass, [a]when men
began to multiply on the face of the
earth, and daughters were born to
them,
2 that the sons of God saw the daughters of men, that they *were* beautiful;
and they [a]took wives for themselves
of all whom they chose.
3 And the LORD said, [a]"My *Spirit
shall not [b]strive[1] with *man forever,
[c]for he *is* indeed flesh; yet his days
shall be one hundred and twenty
years."
4 There were [1]giants on the earth in
those [a]days, and also afterward, when
the sons of God came in to the daughters of men and they bore *children* to
them. Those *were* the mighty men who
were of old, men of renown.
5 Then [1]the LORD saw that the wickedness of man *was* *great in the earth,
and *that* every [a]intent[2] of the thoughts
of his heart *was* only evil [3]continually.

KINGDOM DYNAMICS

6:5 Man's Plunge into Degradation, RESTORATION. Chs. 4—12 reveal man's plunge into degradation and his absolute need for redemption and restoration. The entire concept of "The Holy Spirit and Restoration" is developed in the study article that begins on page 2012.
(Gen. 3:21/Gen. 41:42, 43) J.R.

6 And [a]the LORD was sorry that He
had made man on the earth, and
[b]He was grieved in His [c]heart.
7 So the LORD said, "I will [a]destroy
man whom I have created from the
face of the earth, both man and beast,
creeping thing and birds of the air, for
I am sorry that I have made them."
8 But Noah [a]found *grace in the eyes
of the LORD.

Noah Pleases God

9 This is the genealogy of Noah.
[a]Noah was a just man, [1]perfect in his
generations. Noah [b]walked with God.
10 And Noah begot three sons: [a]Shem,
Ham, and Japheth.
11 The earth also was corrupt [a]before
God, and the earth was [b]filled with violence.
12 So God [a]looked upon the earth, and
indeed it was corrupt; for [b]all flesh had
corrupted their way on the earth.

The Ark Prepared

13 And God said to Noah, [a]"The end
of all flesh has come before Me, for the
earth is filled with violence through

22 [a]Gen. 6:9; 17:1; 24:40; 48:15
24 [a]2 Kin. 2:11 [b]Heb. 11:5
29 [a]Luke 3:36 [b]Gen. 3:17–19; 4:11 [1]Lit. *Rest*
32 [a]Gen. 6:10; 7:13 [b]Gen. 10:21

CHAPTER 6

1 [a]Gen. 1:28
2 [a]Deut. 7:3, 4
3 [a][Gal. 5:16, 17] [b]2 Thess. 2:7 [c]Ps. 78:39 [1]LXX, Syr., Tg., Vg. *abide* *See WW at 2 Sam. 23:2. • See WW at Gen. 1:26.
4 [a]Num. 13:32, 33 [1]Heb. *nephilim, fallen* or *mighty ones*
5 [a]Gen. 8:21 [1]So with MT, Tg.; Vg. *God;* LXX LORD *God* [2]*thought* [3]*all the day* *See WW at Ps. 31:19.
6 [a]1 Sam. 15:11, 29 [b]Is. 63:10 [c]Mark 3:5
7 [a]Gen. 7:4, 23
8 [a]Gen. 19:19 *See WW at Zech. 12:10.
9 [a]2 Pet. 2:5 [b]Gen. 5:22, 24 [1]*blameless* or *having integrity*
10 [a]Gen. 5:32; 7:13
11 [a]Rom. 2:13 [b]Ezek. 8:17
12 [a]Ps. 14:2; 53:2, 3 [b]Ps. 14:1–3
13 [a]1 Pet. 4:7

5:23, 24 Enoch's relatively short life can be seen as a blessing, escaping Earth's corruption rather early. Elijah the prophet was also translated by God "by a whirlwind" (2 Kin. 2:11). No more is known of Enoch in the Bible, except for the statement in Heb. 11:5 that he "pleased God."

6:1–7 See section 3 of Truth-In-Action at the end of Gen.

6:1, 2 Sons of God may mean godly men of the line of Seth as opposed to Cain's godless descendants, superior men such as kings, or angels who rebelliously left heaven to take women as wives. This latter view has interpretive difficulties but seems the most likely. It also serves to reinforce the pre-Flood evil in the world, for God abhors interbreeding of unlike species.

6:3 My Spirit refers to the Holy Spirit in His role as the life-sustaining breath given to man at creation (2:7). **Strive:** The meaning of the Hebrew is unclear; some translations say "abide." God has now determined to reduce man's life expectancy, seen in the symbolic number, **120** years, bringing to an end the preceding period of remarkable longevity. Man's corruptibility by sin recommended the divine reduction of his life span of years for evil potential. Thus, this is more a merciful action of God than it is a judgment.

6:4 The **sons of God** and their wives produced children who were **giants; the mighty men who were of old** were later wiped out by the Flood.

6:5 The degeneration of the human race was proceeding rapidly, in spite of a few godly men such as Enosh, Enoch, and Noah.

6:8 Grace: Favor.

6:11 Violence: More accurately, "lawlessness."

them; [b]and behold, [c]I will destroy them
with the earth.
14 "Make yourself an ark of gopher-
wood; make [1]rooms in the ark, and
*cover it inside and outside with pitch.
15 "And this is how you shall make it:
The length of the ark *shall be* three
hundred [1]cubits, its width fifty cubits,
and its height thirty cubits.
16 "You shall make a window for the
ark, and you shall finish it to a cubit
from above; and set the door of the ark
in its side. You shall make it *with*
lower, second, and third *decks*.
17 [a]"And behold, I Myself am bringing
[b]floodwaters on the earth, to destroy
from under heaven all flesh in which
is the breath of life; everything that *is*
on the earth shall [c]die.
18 "But I will establish My [a]covenant
with you; and [b]you shall go into the
ark—you, your sons, your wife, and
your sons' wives with you.
19 "And of every living thing of all
flesh you shall bring [a]two of every *sort*
into the ark, to keep *them* alive with
you; they shall be male and female.
20 "Of the birds after their kind, of
animals after their kind, and of every
creeping thing of the earth after its
kind, two of every *kind* [a]will come to
you to keep *them* alive.
21 "And you shall take for yourself of
all food that is eaten, and you shall
gather *it* to yourself; and it shall be
food for you and for them."
22 [a]Thus Noah did; [b]according to all
that [c]God commanded him, so he did.

The Great Flood

7 Then the [a]LORD said to Noah,
[b]"Come into the ark, you and all
your household, because I have seen
that [c]you *are* *righteous before Me in
this generation.
2 "You shall take with you seven
each of every [a]clean animal, a male
and his female; [b]two each of animals
that *are* unclean, a male and his female;
3 "also seven each of birds of the air,
male and female, to keep [1]the species
alive on the face of all the *earth.
4 "For after [a]seven more days I will
cause it to rain on the earth [b]forty days
and forty nights, and I will [1]destroy
from the face of the earth all living
things that I have made."
5 [a]And Noah did according to all that
the LORD commanded him.
6 Noah *was* [a]six hundred years old
when the *floodwaters were on the
earth.
7 [a]So Noah, with his sons, his wife,
and his sons' wives, went into the ark
because of the waters of the flood.
8 Of clean animals, of animals that
are unclean, of birds, and of everything
that creeps on the earth,
9 two by two they went into the ark
to Noah, male and female, as God had
commanded Noah.
10 And it came to pass after seven days
that the waters of the flood were on
the earth.
11 In the six hundredth year of Noah's
life, in the second month, the seventeenth day of the month, on [a]that day
all [b]the fountains of the great deep
were broken up, and the [c]windows of
heaven were opened.
12 [a]And the rain was on the earth forty
days and forty nights.
13 On the very same day Noah and
Noah's sons, Shem, Ham, and Japheth,
and Noah's wife and the three wives of
his sons with them, entered the ark—
14 [a]they and every beast after its kind,
all cattle after their kind, every creeping thing that creeps on the earth after
its kind, and every bird after its kind,
every bird of every [b]sort.
15 And they [a]went into the ark to
Noah, two by two, of all flesh in which
is the breath of life.
16 So those that entered, male and

13 [b]Gen. 6:17 [c]2 Pet. 2:4–10
14 [1]Lit. *compartments* or *nests* *See WW at Num. 15:25.
15 [1]A cubit is about 18 inches.
17 [a]2 Pet. 2:5 [b]2 Pet. 3:6 [c]Luke 16:22
18 [a]Gen. 8:20—9:17; 17:7 [b]Gen. 7:1, 7, 13
19 [a]Gen. 7:2, 8, 9, 14–16
20 [a]Gen. 7:9, 15
22 [a]Gen. 7:5; 12:4, 5 [b]Gen. 7:5, 9, 16 [c][1 John 5:3]

CHAPTER 7

1 [a]Matt. 11:28 [b]Matt. 24:38 [c]Gen. 6:9 *See WW at Lam. 1:18.
2 [a]Lev. 11 [b]Lev. 10:10
3 [1]Lit. *seed* *See WW at Ex. 32:13.
4 [a]Gen. 7:10 [b]Gen. 7:12, 17 [1]Lit. *blot out*
5 [a]Gen. 6:22
6 [a]Gen. 5:4, 32 *See WW at Is. 43:2.
7 [a]Matt. 24:38
11 [a]Matt. 24:39 [b]Gen. 8:2 [c]Ps. 78:23
12 [a]Gen. 7:4, 17
14 [a]Gen. 6:19 [b]Gen. 1:21
15 [a]Gen. 6:19, 20; 7:9

6:15, 16 The dimensions of the **ark** were roughly 450 feet long, 75 feet wide, and 45 feet high, with a capacity exceeding that of 500 railroad stock cars. The ark's bargelike shape made it difficult to capsize.

6:17 Every ancient culture has its memory of the worldwide Flood.

6:18 My covenant is the first mention of a biblical covenant. God's protection through the impending Flood is His first installment of the covenant promise.

6:19–21 The gathering of **every living thing** and **all food,** as well as everyone's survival inside **the ark,** were obvious miracles under God's sovereign control (vv. 17, 18).

6:22 Noah's obedience is a patriarchal model of God's working in tandem with man for the establishing of His kingdom purposes on Earth.

7:2, 3 The additional **clean** animals and **birds** were for later sacrifices (8:20) and for preliminary surveying of the Earth (8:7–12).

7:4 Forty days and forty nights may be taken literally or as a conventional expression for "a long time" (see Ex. 24:18). Subsequent numbering seems to indicate the former.

7:11 The Flood began as **the fountains of the great deep were broken up.** Worldwide undersea earthquakes and volcanic eruptions occurred almost simultaneously, throwing massive ocean waves surging back and forth across the Earth. This may also refer to the cataclysm that created the continents separating and spreading these giant land masses from the original, single land mass (1:9, 10).

7:12 The rain in Hebrew signifies "heavy or abnormal rainfall." In v. 17 it is called "the flood." It accompanied the massive water surges from the Earth.

female of all flesh, went in [a]as God had
commanded him; and the LORD shut
him in.
17 [a]Now the flood was on the earth
forty days. The waters increased and
lifted up the ark, and it rose high above
the earth.
18 The waters prevailed and greatly increased on the earth, [a]and the ark
moved about on the surface of the waters.
19 And the waters prevailed exceedingly on the earth, and all the high hills
under the whole heaven were covered.
20 The waters prevailed fifteen cubits
upward, and the mountains were covered.
21 [a]And all flesh died that moved on
[1]the earth: birds and cattle and beasts
and every creeping thing that creeps
on the earth, and every man.
22 All in [a]whose nostrils *was* the
*breath [1]of the spirit of life, all that *was*
on the dry *land,* died.
23 So He destroyed all living things
which were on the face of the ground:
both man and cattle, creeping thing
and bird of the air. They were destroyed from the earth. Only [a]Noah
and those who *were* with him in the
ark remained *alive.*
24 [a]And the waters prevailed on the
earth one hundred and fifty days.

Noah's Deliverance

8 Then God [a]remembered Noah, and
every living thing, and all the animals that *were* with him in the ark.
[b]And God made a wind to pass over
the earth, and the waters subsided.
2 [a]The fountains of the deep and
the windows of heaven were also
[b]stopped, and [c]the rain from heaven
was restrained.
3 And the waters receded continually
from the earth. At the end [a]of the
hundred and fifty days the waters decreased.
4 Then the ark rested in the seventh
month, the seventeenth day of the
month, on the mountains of Ararat.
5 And the waters decreased continually until the tenth month. In the tenth
month, on the first *day* of the month,
the tops of the mountains were seen.
6 So it came to pass, at the end of
forty days, that Noah opened [a]the window of the ark which he had made.
7 Then he sent out a raven, which
kept going to and fro until the waters
had dried up from the earth.
8 He also sent out from himself a
dove, to see if the waters had receded
from the face of the ground.
9 But the dove found no resting place
for the sole of her foot, and she returned into the ark to him, for the waters *were* on the face of the whole
earth. So he put out his hand and took
her, and drew her into the ark to himself.
10 And he waited yet another seven
days, and again he sent the dove out
from the ark.
11 Then the dove came to him in the
evening, and behold, a freshly plucked
olive leaf *was* in her mouth; and Noah
knew that the waters had receded from
the earth.
12 So he *waited yet another seven
days and sent out the dove, which did
not return again to him anymore.
13 And it came to pass in the six hundred and first year, in the first *month,*
the first *day* of the month, that the waters were dried up from the earth; and
Noah removed the covering of the ark
and looked, and indeed the surface of
the ground was dry.
14 And in the second month, on the
twenty-seventh day of the month, the
earth was dried.
15 Then God spoke to Noah, saying,
16 "Go out of the ark, [a]you and your
wife, and your sons and your sons'
wives with you.
17 "Bring out with you every living
thing of all flesh that *is* with you: birds

16 [a]Gen. 7:2, 3 **17** [a]Gen. 7:4, 12; 8:6 **18** [a]Ps. 104:26 **21** [a]Gen. 6:7, 13, 17; 7:4 [1]*the land* **22** [a]Gen. 2:7 [1]LXX, Vg. omit *of the spirit* *See WW at Ps. 150:6. **23** [a]Matt. 24:38, 39; Luke 17:26, 27; Heb. 11:7; 1 Pet. 3:20; 2 Pet. 2:5 **24** [a]Gen. 8:3, 4

CHAPTER 8

1 [a]Gen. 19:29; Ex. 2:24; 1 Sam. 1:19; Ps. 105:42; 106:4 [b]Ex. 14:21; 15:10; Job 12:15; Ps. 29:10; Is. 44:27; Nah. 1:4 **2** [a]Gen. 7:11 [b]Deut. 11:17 [c]Gen. 7:4, 12; Job 38:37 **3** [a]Gen. 7:24

6 [a]Gen. 6:16 **12** *See WW at Mic. 7:7. **16** [a]Gen. 7:13

7:19, 20 Even **the high hills** were being swept by the enormous waves. **Fifteen cubits upward** indicates the water covered the highest **mountains** by at least 22 feet (7 meters). This would have allowed the ark to float freely in that it probably had a 15-cubit draft (6:15).

7:23 The face of the ground: Marine life apparently survived in spite of the upheaval as there is no indication of their subsequent re-creation.

7:24 150 days includes the 40 days of deluge. The ark floated on calmer water 110 days.

8:1 Then God remembered expresses concisely the faithfulness of God.

8:3–5 During the 110-day period, the winds (v. 1) caused **the waters** to begin receding. Exactly five months after the Flood began (v. 4), the water level had fallen below 15 cubits of the highest mountains and **the ark rested . . . on the mountains of Ararat.** This indicates it landed on an unidentified peak of a mountain chain in the Ararat region—modern eastern Turkey, southern Russia, and northwestern Iran. It took over two more months of gradual receding for a sufficient portion of **the tops of the mountains** to be **seen** (v. 5).

8:6–12 These verses give additional details of Noah's actions during the time the waters were subsiding. The birds were God's means of informing Noah of the conditions outside the ark.

8:11 An **olive leaf** can sprout quickly and is a symbol of fertility.

8:14, 15 Noah spent more than a year in the ark.

and cattle and every creeping thing
that creeps on the earth, so that they
may abound on the earth, and [a]be fruitful and multiply on the earth."
18 So Noah went out, and his sons and
his wife and his sons' wives with him.
19 Every animal, every creeping thing,
every bird, *and* whatever creeps on the
earth, according to their families, went
out of the ark.

God's Covenant with Creation

20 Then Noah built an [a]altar* to the
LORD, and took of [b]every clean animal
and of every clean bird, and offered
[c]burnt offerings on the altar.

KINGDOM DYNAMICS

8:20 "Covenant" First Appears with Noah, THE BLOOD. Prior to Noah, covenant is presented in the Bible only by inference. The use of the term "covenant" appears first in God's dealings with Noah (6:18; 9:9) and is tied to and established by his sacrificial offering after the Flood. In gratitude for his deliverance, Noah built an altar and offered blood sacrifices. There is no direct command specifically instructing Noah to offer a blood sacrifice, clearly suggesting the precedent had been established, reaching back through Abel to the lessons of the Garden, where a blood sacrifice was required for the clothing of Adam and Eve. Noah's sacrifice was pleasing to God, and in response, God covenanted not to destroy creation again by flood. This is the first instance in biblical history where the term "covenant" is applied to the relationship between God and an individual, as well as his descendants; and it is established in blood.
(Gen. 1:3–5/Gen. 22:13) C.S.

21 And the LORD smelled [a]a soothing
aroma. Then the LORD said in His
heart, "I will never again [b]curse the
ground for man's sake, although the
[c]imagination[1] of man's heart *is* evil
from his youth; [d]nor will I again destroy every living thing as I have done.

22 "While the earth [a]remains,
Seedtime and harvest,
Cold and heat,
Winter and summer,
And [b]day and night
Shall not cease."

KINGDOM DYNAMICS

8:22 God Established the Principle of the Seed and the Law of Seedtime and Harvest, SEED FAITH. Noah's first acts after the Flood were to build an altar and sacrifice to the Lord. God was pleased and made promises to the human family through the faith of Noah. He also instituted the Law of Seedtime and Harvest: "While the earth remains, seedtime and harvest . . . shall not cease" (v. 22).

When God created the first living thing, He gave it the ability to grow and multiply. How? Through the *Seed.* Your life began by the seed principle. Every act of your life since your birth has operated by the seed principle—springing from good seeds or bad seeds you have sown—whether or not you were consciously aware of your seed-planting. The principle continues today. To overcome life's problems, reach your potential in life, see your life become fruitful, multiplied, replenished (that is, in health, finance, spiritual renewal, family, or your entire being), determine to follow God's law of seedtime and harvest. Sow the seed of His promise in the soil of your need.
(*/2 Sam. 24:24) O.R.

9 So God blessed Noah and his sons,
and said to them: [a]"Be fruitful and
multiply, and fill the earth.
2 [a]"And the *fear of you and the
dread of you shall be on every beast
of the earth, on every bird of the air,
on all that move *on* the earth, and on
all the fish of the sea. They are given
into your hand.
3 [a]"Every moving thing that lives
shall be food for you. I have given you
[b]all things, even as the [c]green herbs.
4 [a]"But you shall not eat flesh with
its life, *that is,* its blood.
5 "Surely for your lifeblood I will demand *a reckoning;* [a]from the hand
of every beast I will require it, and
[b]from the hand of man. From the hand
of every [c]man's brother I will require
the life of man.

6 "Whoever [a]sheds *man's blood,
By man his blood shall be shed;

17 [a]Gen. 1:22, 28; 9:1, 7
20 [a]Gen. 12:7; Ex. 29:18, 25 [b]Gen. 7:2; Lev. 11 [c]Gen. 22:2; Ex. 10:25 *See WW at 2 Kin. 12:9.
21 [a]Ex. 29:18, 25; Lev. 1:9; Ezek. 20:41; 2 Cor. 2:15; Eph. 5:2 [b]Gen. 3:17; 6:7, 13, 17; Is. 54:9 [c]Gen. 6:5; 11:6; Job 14:4; Ps. 51:5; Jer. 17:9; Rom. 1:21; 3:23; Eph. 2:1–3 [d]Gen. 9:11, 15 [1]*intent* or *thought*
22 [a]Is. 54:9 [b]Ps. 74:16; Jer. 33:20, 25

CHAPTER 9

1 [a]Gen. 1:28, 29; 8:17; 9:7, 19; 10:32
2 [a]Gen. 1:26, 28; Ps. 8:6 *See WW at Is. 8:13.
3 [a]Deut. 12:15; 14:3, 9, 11; Acts 10:12, 13 [b]Rom. 14:14, 20; 1 Cor. 10:23, 26; Col. 2:16; [1 Tim. 4:3, 4] [c]Gen. 1:29
4 [a]Lev. 7:26; 17:10–16; 19:26; Deut. 12:16, 23; 15:23; 1 Sam. 14:33, 34; Acts 15:20, 29
5 [a]Ex. 21:28 [b]Gen. 4:9, 10; Ps. 9:12 [c]Acts 17:26
6 [a]Ex. 21:12–14; Lev. 24:17; Num. 35:33; Matt. 26:52 *See WW at Gen. 1:26.

8:19 Families means the animals left in groups of similar types. There is no indication of reproduction during the year.
8:21 I will never again curse the ground can be translated, "I will not curse the ground any further," meaning God will not add to the curse of 3:17. This seems the best understanding. God's mercy here is in spite of the fact He knows the Flood will not change man's heart; he will still be **evil from his youth**.
9:1–3 Man's original dominion over **the earth** was reaffirmed.
9:4 The earliest command not to drink **blood** (see also Lev. 3:17).
9:6 Of all creation, man's life is most sacred to God. Willful violation of another's life calls for retribution by fellowmen—God's agents.

[b]For in the image of God
He made man.

KINGDOM DYNAMICS

9:5, 6 The Sacredness of Life, HUMAN WORTH. Life was breathed into man by God. Man was made in the "image" of God, and after God's "likeness" (1:26; 9:6). Man was God's unique, spiritual, immortal, intelligent creation. Thus, God commands, "You shall not murder" (Ex. 20:13). To take human life is to assault the image of God in man. Human life should be respected and reverenced. Life, even prenatal life, is always a miracle; and no one should feel he has the right to shed the blood of an innocent human being. The word "require" (Gen. 9:5) indicates that God was doing more than simply stating a rule. He was saying that He will actually "pursue" (Hebrew *darash*) or "seek" a man's life in payment for the innocent life he has taken. Let no disrespect for human life invade any mind. Let us proclaim the value and the sacredness of life.

(Gen. 3:17/Acts 17:26) C.B.

7 And as for you, [a]be fruitful and
multiply;
Bring forth abundantly in the
earth
And multiply in it."

8 Then God spoke to Noah and to his
sons with him, saying:
9 "And as for Me, [a]behold, I establish
[b]My covenant with you and with your
[1]descendants after you,
10 [a]"and with every living creature
that *is* with you: the birds, the cattle,
and every beast of the earth with you,
of all that go out of the ark, every beast
of the earth.
11 "Thus [a]I establish My covenant
with you: Never again shall all flesh
be cut off by the waters of the flood;
never again shall there be a flood to
destroy the earth."
12 And God said: [a]"This *is* the sign of
the covenant which I make between
Me and you, and every living creature
that *is* with you, for perpetual generations:
13 "I set [a]My rainbow in the cloud, and
it shall be for the sign of the covenant
between Me and the earth.
14 "It shall be, when I bring a cloud
over the earth, that the rainbow shall
be seen in the cloud;
15 "and [a]I will *remember My covenant which *is* between Me and you
and every living creature of all flesh;
the waters shall never again become
a flood to destroy all flesh.
16 "The rainbow shall be in the cloud,
and I will look on it to remember [a]the
everlasting covenant between God and
every living creature of all flesh that
is on the earth."
17 And God said to Noah, "This *is* the
*sign of the covenant which I have es-
tablished between Me and all flesh that
is on the earth."

6 [b]Gen. 1:26, 27 **7** [a]Gen. 9:1, 19 **9** [a]Gen. 6:18 [b]Is. 54:9 [1]Lit. *seed* **10** [a]Ps. 145:9 **11** [a]Gen. 8:21; Is. 54:9 **12** [a]Gen. 9:13, 17; 17:11 **13** [a]Ezek. 1:28; Rev. 4:3 **15** [a]Lev. 26:42, 45; Deut. 7:9; Ezek. 16:60 *See WW at Is. 62:6. **16** [a]Gen. 17:13, 19; 2 Sam. 23:5; Is. 55:3; Jer. 32:40; Heb. 13:20 **17** *See WW at Ps. 86:17. **18** [a]Gen. 9:25–27; 10:6 **19** [a]Gen. 5:32

KINGDOM DYNAMICS

8:20—9:17 After the Flood, FOUNDATIONS OF THE KINGDOM. Following the deluge, a renewed order is established. Noah's faith, which occasioned his deliverance, is now manifest in an expression of worship to God as he disembarks from the ark (8:20–22). God declares His covenant with Noah (9:8–17) after restating His purpose to make man to be fruitful and multiply, as at the beginning. However, other factors are not as at the beginning; notably the relationship of God with man, as well as of man with creation. The Flood has not reversed the loss of man's original dominion. He is still fallen, though thankfully a recipient of God's mercy. Further, the animals will fear mankind from this time on (9:2), which was not characteristic of their relationship prior to this. In the ultimate restoration of God's kingdom on Earth, the original fearless order will be regained (Is. 11:6–9). Notwithstanding these deficiencies, a cleansed realm for seeking God's kingdom first is newly available to man, and again God asserts man's responsibility for administrating Earth with an accountability to Him (9:1–7). The Flood has not neutralized the influence of the Serpent, nor has it changed mankind's capacity for rebellion against God's rule. Nevertheless, new hope dawns with promise for the eventual recovery of what was lost of his first estate.

(Gen. 3:16–24/Gen. 12:1–3) J.W.H.

Noah and His Sons

18 Now the sons of Noah who went out
of the ark were Shem, Ham, and Japheth. [a]And Ham *was* the father of Canaan.
19 [a]These three *were* the sons of Noah,

9:8–10 I establish My covenant with you: The first of the five OT covenants between God and man, it was an unconditional promise to all of life that God would never again destroy the Earth by water.

9:12–17 Biblical covenants normally include these elements: the covenant sacrifice, with the shedding of blood (8:20), the covenant meal (also 8:20), the final establishment of the covenant (9:9), and **the sign of the covenant** (9:13), here the **rainbow**, apparently a new phenomenon of nature.

[b]and from these the whole earth was populated.
20 And Noah began *to be* [a]a farmer, and he planted a vineyard.
21 Then he drank of the wine [a]and was drunk, and became uncovered in his tent.
22 And Ham, the father of Canaan, saw the nakedness of his father, and told his two *brothers outside.
23 [a]But Shem and Japheth took a garment, laid *it* on both their shoulders, and went backward and covered the nakedness of their father. Their faces *were* [1]turned away, and they did not see their father's nakedness.
24 So Noah awoke from his wine, and knew what his younger son had done to him.
25 Then he said:

> [a]"Cursed *be* Canaan;
> A [b]servant of servants
> He shall be to his brethren."

26 And he said:

> [a]"Blessed *be* the LORD,
> The God of Shem,
> And may Canaan be his servant.
> 27 May God [a]enlarge Japheth,
> [b]And may he dwell in the tents of Shem;
> And may Canaan be his servant."

28 And Noah lived after the flood three hundred and fifty years.
29 So all the days of Noah were nine hundred and fifty years; and he died.

Nations Descended from Noah

10 Now this *is* the genealogy of the sons of Noah: Shem, Ham, and Japheth. [a]And sons were born to them after the flood.
2 [a]The sons of Japheth *were* Gomer, Magog, Madai, Javan, Tubal, Meshech, and Tiras.

19 [b]Gen. 9:1, 7; 10:32; 1 Chr. 1:4
20 [a]Gen. 3:19, 23; 4:2; Prov. 12:11; Jer. 31:24
21 [a]Prov. 20:1; Eph. 5:18
22 *See WW at Ps. 133:1.
23 [a]Ex. 20:12; Gal. 6:1 [1]Lit. *backwards*
25 [a]Deut. 27:16; Josh. 9:23, 27 [b]Josh. 9:23; 1 Kin. 9:20, 21
26 [a]Gen. 14:20; 24:27; Ps. 144:15; Heb. 11:16
27 [a]Gen. 10:2–5; 39:3; Is. 66:19 [b]Luke 3:36; John 1:14; Eph. 2:13, 14; 3:6

CHAPTER 10

1 [a]Gen. 9:1, 7, 19
2 [a]1 Chr. 1:5–7

9:22 Ham's actions were somehow a form of dishonoring **his father**.
9:25–27 Noah's curse of Ham's descendants is the first recorded human curse (see note on 3:14, 15). It is not clear exactly what is meant, but the Canaanites did become slaves of **Shem** (father of the Hebrews) during Israel's monarchy. **God enlarge Japheth** is also difficult; it may represent God's incorporation of Gentiles, which awaited the New Covenant.
10:1–32 The table of nations is written from the viewpoint of an author living some centuries after the **flood,** but still too early to include later nationalities, such as the Ishmaelites, the Moabites, the Ammonites, the Edomites, and the Chaldeans.
10:2, 3 The sons of **Japheth** (**Gomer, Magog, Tubal,** and **Meshech**) and his grandson **Togarmah** loom large in Ezekiel's prophecy of the final battle of the ages (Ezek. 38; 39).

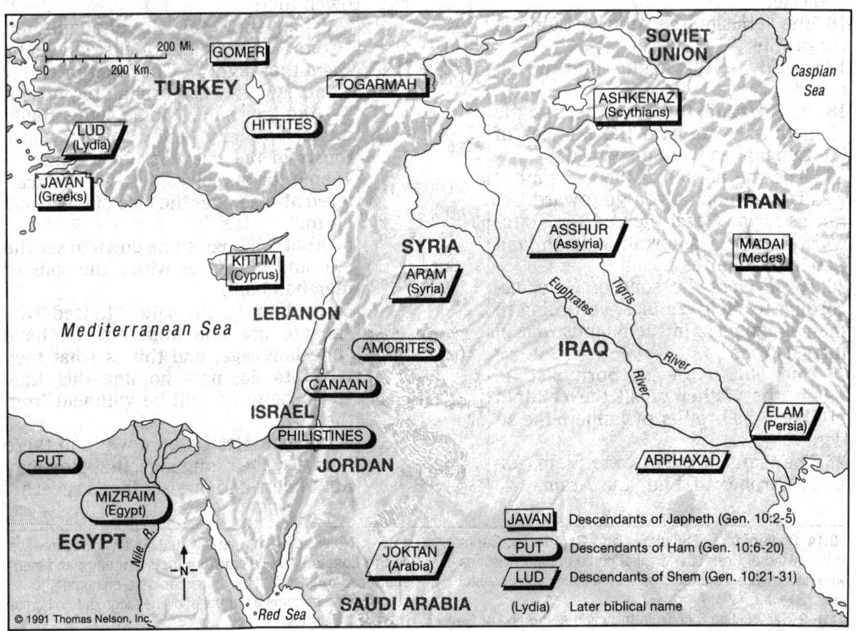

The Nations of Genesis 10

3 The sons of Gomer *were* Ashkenaz,
[1]Riphath, and Togarmah.
4 The sons of Javan *were* Elishah,
Tarshish, Kittim, and [1]Dodanim.
5 From these [a]the coastland *peoples*
of the *Gentiles were separated into
their lands, everyone according to his
language, according to their families,
into their nations.
6 [a]The sons of Ham *were* Cush,
Mizraim, [1]Put, and Canaan.
7 The sons of Cush *were* Seba, Havilah, Sabtah, Raamah, and Sabtechah;
and the sons of Raamah *were* Sheba
and Dedan.
8 Cush begot [a]Nimrod; he began to
be a mighty one on the earth.
9 He was a mighty [a]hunter [b]before
the LORD; therefore it is said, "Like
Nimrod the mighty hunter before the
LORD."
10 [a]And the beginning of his kingdom
was [b]Babel, Erech, Accad, and Calneh,
in the land of Shinar.
11 From that land he went [a]to Assyria
and built Nineveh, Rehoboth Ir, Calah,
12 and Resen between Nineveh and
Calah (that *is* the principal city).
13 Mizraim begot Ludim, Anamim, Le-
habim, Naphtuhim,
14 Pathrusim, and Casluhim [a](from
whom came the Philistines and Caphtorim).
15 Canaan begot Sidon his firstborn,
and [a]Heth;
16 [a]the Jebusite, the Amorite, and the
Girgashite;
17 the Hivite, the Arkite, and the Si-
nite;
18 the Arvadite, the Zemarite, and the
Hamathite. Afterward the families of
the Canaanites were dispersed.
19 [a]And the border of the Canaanites
was from Sidon as you go toward Gerar, as far as Gaza; then as you go toward Sodom, Gomorrah, Admah, and
Zeboiim, as far as Lasha.
20 These *were* the sons of Ham, according to their families, according to
their languages, in their lands *and* in
their nations.
21 And *children* were born also to
Shem, the *father of all the children
of Eber, [1]the brother of Japheth the elder.
22 The [a]sons of Shem *were* Elam, Asshur, [b]Arphaxad, Lud, and Aram.
23 The sons of Aram *were* Uz, Hul,
Gether, and [1]Mash.
24 [1]Arphaxad begot [a]Salah, and Salah
begot Eber.
25 [a]To Eber were born two sons: the
name of one *was* [1]Peleg, for in his
days the earth was divided; and his
brother's name *was* Joktan.
26 Joktan begot Almodad, Sheleph,
Hazarmaveth, Jerah,
27 Hadoram, Uzal, Diklah,
28 [1]Obal, Abimael, Sheba,
29 Ophir, Havilah, and Jobab. All
these *were* the sons of Joktan.
30 And their dwelling place was from
Mesha as you go toward Sephar, the
mountain of the east.
31 These *were* the sons of Shem, according to their families, according to
their languages, in their lands, according to their nations.
32 [a]These *were* the families of the sons
of Noah, according to their generations, in their nations; [b]and from these
the nations were divided on the earth
after the flood.

The Tower of Babel

11 Now the whole earth had one 3
language and one [1]speech.
2 And it came to pass, as they journeyed from the east, that they found a
plain in the land [a]of Shinar, and they
dwelt there.
3 Then they said to one another,
"Come, let us make bricks and [1]bake
them thoroughly." They had brick for
stone, and they had asphalt for mortar.
4 And they said, "Come, let us *build
ourselves a city, and a tower [a]whose
top *is* in the heavens; let us make a
[b]name for ourselves, lest we [c]be scattered abroad over the face of the whole
earth."
5 [a]But the LORD came down to see the
city and the tower which the sons of
men had built.
6 And the LORD said, "Indeed [a]the
*people *are* one and they all have
[b]one language, and this is what they
begin to do; now nothing that they
[c]propose to do will be withheld from
them.
7 "Come, [a]let Us go down and there
[b]confuse their language, that they may
not understand one another's speech."

3 [1]*Diphath,* 1 Chr. 1:6
4 [1]Sam. *Rodanim* and 1 Chr. 1:7
5 [a]Ps. 72:10 *See WW at Ps. 106:47.
6 [a]1 Chr. 1:8–16 [1]Or *Phut*
8 [a]Mic. 5:6
9 [a]Jer. 16:16 [b]Gen. 21:20
10 [a]Mic. 5:6 [b]Gen. 11:9
11 [a]Mic. 5:6
14 [a]1 Chr. 1:12
15 [a]Gen. 23:3
16 [a]Gen. 14:7; 15:19–21
19 [a]Num. 34:2–12
21 [1]Or *the older brother of Japheth* *See WW at Ps. 68:5.
22 [a]1 Chr. 1:17–28 [b]Luke 3:36
23 [1]LXX *Meshech* and 1 Chr. 1:17
24 [a]Gen. 11:12 [1]So with MT, Vg., Tg.; LXX *Arphaxad begot Cainan, and Cainan begot Salah* (cf. Luke 3:35, 36)
25 [a]1 Chr. 1:19 [1]Lit. *Division*
28 [1]*Ebal,* 1 Chr. 1:22
32 [a]Gen. 10:1 [b]Gen. 9:19; 11:8

CHAPTER 11

1 [1]Lit. *lip*
2 [a]Gen. 10:10; 14:1
3 [1]Lit. *burn*
4 [a]Deut. 1:28; 9:1 [b]Gen. 6:4 [c]Deut. 4:27 *See WW at Zech. 1:16.
5 [a]Gen. 18:21
6 [a]Gen. 9:19 [b]Gen. 11:1 [c]Ps. 2:1 *See WW at Ruth 1:16.
7 [a]Gen. 1:26 [b]Ex. 4:11

10:14 Casluhim . . . Philistines and Caphtorim: Caphtor is the island of Crete, the original home of the Philistines who later invaded and conquered the Palestinian coastal area. See Jer. 47:4; Amos 9:7.

11:1–9 See section 3 of Truth-In-Action at the end of Gen.

11:2 The land of Shinar is unknown.

11:5–8 Noah's descendants reverted quickly to pagan ways, so **the LORD** decided to **confuse their language** and then **scattered them.** What they intended as a monument to human effort became a symbol of divine judgment on human pride and self-rule.

8 So [a]the LORD scattered them abroad
from there [b]over the face of all the
earth, and they ceased building the
city.
9 Therefore its name is called [1]Babel,
[a]because there the LORD confused the
language of all the earth; and from
there the LORD scattered them abroad
over the face of all the earth.

Shem's Descendants

10 [a]This *is* the genealogy of Shem:
Shem *was* one hundred years old, and
begot Arphaxad two years after the
flood.
11 After he begot Arphaxad, Shem
lived five hundred years, and begot
sons and daughters.
12 Arphaxad lived thirty-five years,
[a]and begot Salah.
13 After he begot Salah, Arphaxad
lived four hundred and three years,
and begot sons and daughters.
14 Salah lived thirty years, and begot
Eber.
15 After he begot Eber, Salah lived
four hundred and three years, and begot sons and daughters.
16 [a]Eber lived thirty-four years, and
begot [b]Peleg.
17 After he begot Peleg, Eber lived
four hundred and thirty years, and begot sons and daughters.
18 Peleg lived thirty years, and begot
Reu.
19 After he begot Reu, Peleg lived two
hundred and nine years, and begot
sons and daughters.
20 Reu lived thirty-two years, and begot [a]Serug.
21 After he begot Serug, Reu lived two
hundred and seven years, and begot
sons and daughters.
22 Serug lived thirty years, and begot
Nahor.
23 After he begot Nahor, Serug lived
two hundred years, and begot sons and
daughters.
24 Nahor lived twenty-nine years, and
begot [a]Terah.
25 After he begot Terah, Nahor lived
one hundred and nineteen years, and
begot sons and daughters.
26 Now Terah lived seventy years, and
[a]begot [1]Abram, Nahor, and Haran.

Terah's Descendants

27 This *is* the genealogy of Terah:
Terah begot [a]Abram, Nahor, and
Haran. Haran begot Lot.
28 And Haran died before his father
Terah in his native land, in Ur of the
Chaldeans.
29 Then Abram and Nahor took wives:
the name of Abram's wife *was* [a]Sarai,[1]
and the name of Nahor's wife, [b]Milcah,

8 [a]Gen. 11:4; Deut. 32:8; Ps. 92:9; [Luke 1:51] [b]Gen. 10:25, 32
9 [a]1 Cor. 14:23 [1]Lit. *Confusion*, Babylon
10 [a]Gen. 10:22–25; 1 Chr. 1:17
12 [a]Luke 3:35
16 [a]1 Chr. 1:19 [b]Luke 3:35
20 [a]Luke 3:35
24 [a]Gen. 11:31; Josh. 24:2; Luke 3:34
26 [a]Josh. 24:2; 1 Chr. 1:26 [1]*Abraham*, Gen. 17:5
27 [a]Gen. 11:31; 17:5
29 [a]Gen. 17:15; 20:12 [b]Gen. 22:20, 23; 24:15 [1]*Sarah*, Gen. 17:15

11:9 Babel is derived from the Hebrew *balal*, which means "mixed up" or "confused." The Babylonians later interpreted "Babel" to mean "the gate of the god." Most scholars link this city with Babylon, which eventually became synonymous with the final evil city that persecutes God's people (Rev. 17; 18). We find here the answers to why there are so many languages on **the earth** and why the human race spread so rapidly across the Earth after the Flood. From the birth of **Arphaxad** to Abraham's migration is nine generations, 365 years.
11:10–32 The genealogies here serve as a transitional link from the primeval period of man to the patriarchal period whereby God begins His ultimate redemptive process.
11:14 Eber is probably Shem's descendant from whom the Hebrews came.
11:10–26 Longevity was dropping sharply, from Noah's 950 years to Abraham's 175 years, in just 10 generations. This reduction was symbolically portrayed in 6:3 (120 years). Ps. 90:10 will later reduce the span of a person's life to a symbolic 70 years.
11:27 Abram was born five generations after Babel.
11:28 Ur is found three times in Gen. It was likely in modern southern Iraq. Josh. 24:2 states that **Terah** served "other gods" while dwelling beyond the Euphrates River, in Haran.

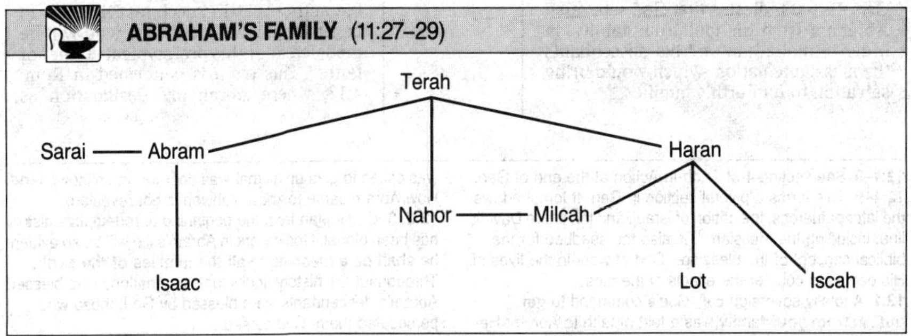

the daughter of Haran the father of
Milcah and the father of Iscah.
30 But [a]Sarai was barren; she had no
child.
31 And Terah [a]took his son Abram and
his grandson Lot, the son of Haran,
and his daughter-in-law Sarai, his son
Abram's wife, and they went out with
them from [b]Ur of the Chaldeans to go
to [c]the land of Canaan; and they came
to Haran and dwelt there.
32 So the days of Terah were two hundred and five years, and Terah died in
Haran.

Promises to Abram

4 **12** Now the [a]LORD had said to Abram:

"Get [b]out of your country,
From your family
And from your father's *house,
To a land that I will show
you.
2 [a]I will make you a great nation;
[b]I will *bless you
And make your name great;
[c]And you shall be a blessing.
3 [a]I will bless those who bless
you,
And I will curse him who *curses
you;
And in [b]you all the **families** of the
earth shall be [c]blessed."

30 [a]Gen. 16:1, 2; Luke 1:36
31 [a]Gen. 12:1 [b]Gen. 15:7; Neh. 9:7; Acts 7:4 [c]Gen. 10:19

CHAPTER 12

1 [a]Gen. 15:7; Acts 7:2, 3; [Heb. 11:8] [b]Gen. 13:9 *See WW at 2 Sam. 7:11.
2 [a][Gen. 17:4–6]; 18:18; 46:3; Deut. 26:5; 1 Kin. 3:8 [b]Gen. 22:17; 24:35 [c]Gen. 28:4; Zech. 8:13; Gal. 3:14 *See WW at Ps. 145:2.
3 [a]Gen. 24:35; 27:29; Ex. 23:22; Num. 24:9 [b]Gen. 18:18; 22:18; 26:4; 28:14; Ps. 72:17; Matt. 1:1; Luke 3:34; Acts 3:25; [Gal. 3:8] [c]Is. 41:27 *See WW at Jer. 8:11.

WORD WEALTH

12:3 families, *mishpachah* (meesh-pah-*chah*); Strong's #4940: A family of people, a type, class, or kind of people or things; a species of animals, a group of related individuals (a tribe), or a group of related things (a category). The main concept of *mishpachah* is that people, animals, or things that share a kinship or similarity of kind form a family, clan, or species. Thus its scope can be as narrow as an immediate family, or as broad as a whole nation (10:31, 32; Amos 3:2). Gen. 12:1–3 indicates that God separated Abraham from his idolatrous family, in order to make him and his descendants the messianic nation, which would bring salvation to *all* Earth's families.

KINGDOM DYNAMICS

12:1–3 God's Heart to Prosper His People, GOD'S PROSPERITY. In this passage God promises to make Abraham great; and God did bless Abraham in many ways, including material blessing. See 13:1, 2, where we see how Abraham was made very rich. See also 24:35, where Abraham's servant reports that "the LORD has blessed my master greatly," and then enumerates the material blessings that God had given to Abraham. The dynamic of this historic fact becomes pertinent to every believer today.

In Gal. 3:13, 14, God promises to give all believers the blessings of Abraham, telling us that Jesus became a curse for us so that we might receive "the blessings of Abraham." This begins, of course, with our being born again, or becoming new creatures in Christ Jesus. But "the blessings of Abraham" involve other things as well. The Lord wants us to prosper—spiritually, emotionally and physically, and materially. The blessings are ours by His promise, and we need make no apology for the fact that prosperity is included.

(Phil. 4:19/Mal. 3:8–10*) F.P.

KINGDOM DYNAMICS

12:1–3 Prototype "Kingdom" Person, FOUNDATIONS OF THE KINGDOM. Abraham is shown in both OT and NT as the prototype of all who experience God's processes of seeking to reinstate man through redemption, first and foremost, in his relationship to God by faith, without works (Rom. 4:1–25). But too seldom is the second facet of redemption noted. Abraham is also shown as a case of God's program to recover man's "reign in life" (Rom. 5:17). Abraham is designated as the "father" of all who walk his pathway of faith (Rom. 4:12). As such, he is God's revealed example of His plan to eventually reestablish His kingdom's rule in all the Earth through people of His covenant. Through Abraham, whom He wills to become "a great nation" (restoring rule) and to whom He chooses to give a "great name" (restoring authority), God declares His plans to beget innumerable children who will be modeled after this prototypical "father of faith." This truth is confirmed in Rom. 4:13, where Abraham's designation as

12:1–9 See section 4 of Truth-In-Action at the end of Gen.
12:1–9 This forms a pivotal section in Gen. It foreshadows the later patriarchs, the nation of Israel, and the entire Davidic line, including the Messiah. It is also the seedbed for the biblical concept of the blessing—God at work in the lives of His people to counter the effects of the curse.
12:1 A totally sovereign call, God's command to **get out . . . from your family** was a test of faith to Abram. He was called to give up all that was dear for an unknown **land.** How Abram came to know Yahweh is not revealed.
12:2, 3 God's plan from the beginning of redemptive history has been global. God's work in Abram's life will be so evident he **shall be a blessing** to **all the families of the earth.** Throughout OT history, individuals and nations who blessed Abram's descendants were blessed by God; those who persecuted them, God cursed.

"heir of the world" parallels Jesus' promise that His followers, who humble themselves in faith, shall also be recipients of "the kingdom" and shall "inherit the earth" (Matt. 5:3–5).
(Gen. 8:20—9:17/Gen. 26:1–5; 28:1–22)
J.W.H.

4 So Abram departed as the LORD had
spoken to him, and Lot went with him.
And Abram *was* seventy-five years old
when he departed from Haran.
5 Then Abram took Sarai his wife and
Lot his brother's son, and all their possessions that they had gathered, and
[a]the [1]people whom they had acquired
[b]in Haran, and they [c]departed to go
to the land of Canaan. So they came
to the land of Canaan.
6 Abram [a]passed* through the land
to the place of Shechem, [b]as far as
[1]the terebinth tree of Moreh. [c]And the
Canaanites *were* then in the land.
7 [a]Then the LORD appeared to Abram
and said, [b]"To your [1]descendants I will
give this land." And there he built an
[c]altar to the LORD, who had appeared
to him.
8 And he moved from there to the
mountain east of Bethel, and he

5 [a]Gen. 14:14 [b]Gen. 11:31 [c]Gen. 13:18 [1]Lit. *souls*
6 [a]Heb. 11:9 [b]Deut. 11:30 [c]Gen. 10:18, 19 [1]Heb. *Alon Moreh* *See WW at Josh. 3:4.
7 [a]Gen. 17:1; 18:1 [b]Gen. 13:15; 15:18; 17:8 [c]Gen. 13:4, 18; 22:9 [1]Lit. *seed*
8 [a]Gen. 4:26; 13:4; 21:33
9 [a]Gen. 13:1, 3; 20:1; 24:62 [1]Heb. *Negev*
10 [a]Gen. 26:1 [b]Ps. 105:13 [c]Gen. 43:1 *See WW at Jer. 42:17.
11 [a]Gen. 12:14; 26:7; 29:17
12 [a]Gen. 20:11; 26:7
13 [a]Gen. 20:1–18; 26:6–11 [b]Gen. 20:12 [1]Lit. *my soul* *See WW at Prov. 10:3. • See WW at Hab. 2:4.

pitched his tent *with* Bethel on the west
and Ai on the east; there he built an
altar to the LORD and [a]called on the
name of the LORD.
9 So Abram journeyed, [a]going on still
toward the [1]South.

Abram in Egypt

10 Now there was [a]a famine in the
land, and Abram [b]went down to Egypt
to *dwell there, for the famine *was*
[c]severe in the land.
11 And it came to pass, when he was
close to entering Egypt, that he said
to Sarai his wife, "Indeed I know
that you *are* [a]a woman of beautiful
countenance.
12 "Therefore it will happen, when the
Egyptians see you, that they will say,
'This *is* his wife'; and they [a]will kill me,
but they will let you live.
13 [a]"Please say you *are* my [b]sister,
that it may be well with me for your
sake, and that [1]I* may *live because
of you."
14 So it was, when Abram came into
Egypt, that the Egyptians saw the
woman, that she *was* very beautiful.
15 The princes of Pharaoh also saw

12:5 People whom they had acquired in Haran: Slaves and others who had attached themselves to Abram for protection and provision.

12:6, 7 From Haran to Shechem was a 400-mile journey.

12:11–13 My sister: Sarai was indeed his half sister, as we learn from 20:12. But she was his "sister" in another manner also: Abram had just come from Haran, with its custom of "adopting" one's wife as sister in order to confer special privileges, including inheritance, upon her. Nonetheless, it was deceptive, unnecessary, and faithless.

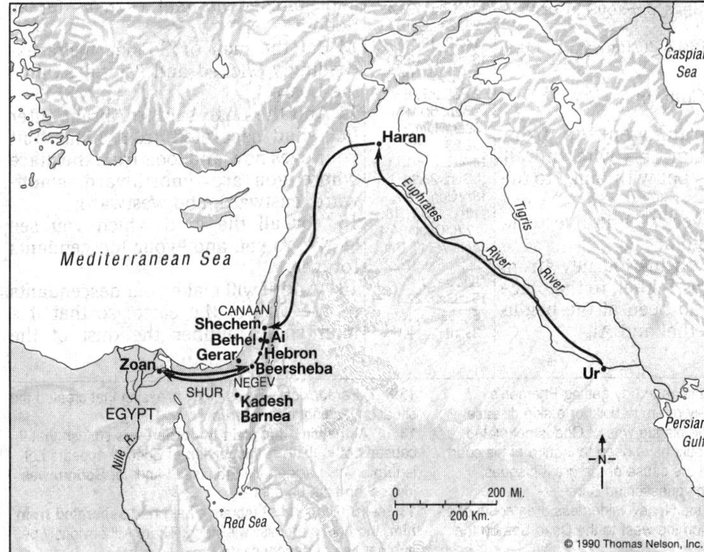

Abraham's Journey of Faith. Abraham's 1,500-mile journey was fueled by faith. "And he went out, not knowing where he was going. By faith he dwelt in the land of promise as *in* a foreign country, . . . for he waited for the city which has foundations, whose builder and maker is God" (Heb. 11:8–10).

her and commended her to Pharaoh.
And the woman was taken to Pharaoh's house.
16 He [a]treated Abram well for her
sake. He [b]had sheep, oxen, male donkeys, male and female servants, female donkeys, and camels.
17 But the LORD [a]plagued Pharaoh and
his house with great plagues because of Sarai, Abram's wife.
18 And Pharaoh called Abram and
said, [a]"What *is* this you have done to me? Why did you not tell me that she *was* your wife?
19 "Why did you say, 'She *is* my sis-
ter'? I might have taken her as my wife. Now therefore, here is your wife; take *her* and go your way."
20 [a]So Pharaoh commanded *his* men
concerning him; and they sent him away, with his wife and all that he had.

KINGDOM DYNAMICS

12:1–20; 17:1–27; 22:1–19 Faith, LEADER TRAITS. Abraham's ability to lead was tested in three areas of faith: 1) Faith to risk (12:1–5): A wealthy man, Abraham risked all to follow God. The godly leader is willing to risk everything on God's faithfulness, and venture into the unknown. 2) Faith to trust (17:1–27): Abraham and Sarah were long past the age of child-bearing. The godly leader does not rely on facts alone, but goes beyond facts to faith. 3) Faith to surrender (22:1–19). Abraham knew the sacrifice of his son would destroy any hope of fulfilling God's promise that he would father many nations. The godly leader is willing to sacrifice all things precious in order to please God.

(Matt. 16:13–20/James 3:1) J.B.

Abram Inherits Canaan

13 Then Abram went up from Egypt, he and his wife and all that he had, and [a]Lot with him, [b]to the [1]South.
2 [a]Abram *was* very rich in livestock,
in silver, and in gold.
3 And he went on his journey [a]from
the South as far as Bethel, to the place where his tent had been at the beginning, between Bethel and Ai,
4 to the [a]place of the altar which he
had made there at first. And there Abram [b]called on the name of the LORD.
5 Lot also, who went with Abram,
had flocks and herds and tents.
6 Now [a]the land was not able to
[1]support them, that they might dwell together, for their possessions were so great that they could not dwell together.
7 And there was [a]strife between the
herdsmen of Abram's livestock and the herdsmen of Lot's livestock. [b]The Canaanites and the Perizzites then dwelt in the land.
8 So Abram said to Lot, [a]"Please let
there be no strife between you and me, and between my herdsmen and your herdsmen; for we *are* brethren.
9 [a]"*Is* not the whole land before you?
Please [b]separate from me. [c]If *you take* the left, then I will go to the right; or, if *you go* to the right, then I will go to the left."
10 And Lot lifted his eyes and saw all
[a]the plain of Jordan, that it *was* well watered everywhere (before the LORD [b]destroyed Sodom and Gomorrah) [c]like the garden of the LORD, like the land of Egypt as you go toward [d]Zoar.
11 Then Lot *chose for himself all the
plain of Jordan, and Lot journeyed east. And they separated from each other.
12 Abram dwelt in the land of Canaan,
and Lot [a]dwelt in the cities of the plain and [b]pitched *his* tent even as far as Sodom.
13 But the men of Sodom [a]*were* ex-
ceedingly wicked and [b]sinful against the LORD.
14 And the LORD said to Abram, after
Lot [a]had separated from him: "Lift your eyes now and look from the place where you are—[b]northward, southward, eastward, and westward;
15 "for all the land which you see
[a]I give to you and [b]your [1]descendants forever.
16 "And [a]I will make your descendants
as the dust of the earth; so that if a man could number the dust of the

16 [a]Gen. 20:14 [b]Gen. 13:2
17 [a]Gen. 20:18; 1 Chr. 16:21; [Ps. 105:14]
18 [a]Gen. 20:9, 10; 26:10
20 [a][Prov. 21:1]

CHAPTER 13

1 [a]Gen. 12:4; 14:12, 16 [b]Gen. 12:9 [1]Heb. *Negev*
2 [a]Gen. 24:35; 26:14; Ps. 112:3; Prov. 10:22
3 [a]Gen. 12:8, 9
4 [a]Gen. 12:7, 8; 21:33 [b]Ps. 116:17
6 [a]Gen. 36:7 [1]Lit. *bear*
7 [a]Gen. 26:20 [b]Gen. 12:6; 15:20, 21
8 [a]1 Cor. 6:7; [Phil. 2:14, 15]
9 [a]Gen. 20:15; 34:10 [b]Gen. 13:11, 14 [c][Rom. 12:18]
10 [a]Gen. 19:17–29; Deut. 34:3 [b]Gen. 19:24 [c]Gen. 2:8, 10; Is. 51:3 [d]Gen. 14:2, 8; 19:22; Deut. 34:3
11 *See WW at 1 Kin. 11:34.
12 [a]Gen. 19:24, 25, 29 [b]Gen. 14:12; 19:1
13 [a]Gen. 18:20, 21; Ezek. 16:49; 2 Pet. 2:7, 8 [b]Gen. 6:11; 39:9; Num. 32:23
14 [a]Gen. 13:11 [b]Gen. 28:14
15 [a]Gen. 12:7; 13:17; 15:7, 18; 17:8; Deut. 34:4; Acts 7:5 [b]2 Chr. 20:7; Ps. 37:22 [1]Lit. *seed*
16 [a]Gen. 22:17; Ex. 32:13; Num. 23:10

12:17, 18 The LORD intervened by getting Pharaoh's attention. **Plagued** likely refers to boils or a skin disease. How **Pharaoh** knew the plague was of God is not stated. The normal method would have been to inquire of his court magician-priests about the cause of the great plagues, confirming their word by questioning Sarai.

13:1 The South was the Negev wilderness area south of a line drawn from Gaza on the west to the Dead Sea on the east.

13:5–7 Paradoxically it was God's blessing that created the situation leading to their **strife.**

13:10 At that time **the plain of Jordan** was so lush that it caused Lot to think of **the garden** of Eden. It appears Lot is turning his back on the Promised Land, for **Sodom** was just beyond the borders.

13:14–18 Though **Lot** (Abram's heir) **had separated from him,** the Lord's promise will stand. There will obviously be another line of **descendants.**

earth, *then* your descendants also
could be numbered.
17 "Arise, walk in the land through its
length and its width, for I give it to
you."
18 [a]Then Abram moved *his* tent, and
went and [b]dwelt by [1]the terebinth trees
of Mamre, [c]which *are* in Hebron, and
built an [d]altar there to the LORD.

Lot's Captivity and Rescue

14 And it came to pass in the days
of Amraphel king [a]of Shinar,
Arioch king of Ellasar, Chedorlaomer
king of [b]Elam, and Tidal king of
[1]nations,
2 *that* they made war with Bera king
of Sodom, Birsha king of Gomorrah,
Shinab king of [a]Admah, Shemeber
king of Zeboiim, and the king of Bela
(that is, [b]Zoar).
3 All these joined together in the Valley of Siddim [a](that is, the Salt Sea).
4 Twelve years [a]they *served Chedorlaomer, and in the thirteenth year they
rebelled.
5 In the fourteenth year Chedorlaomer and the kings that *were* with
him came and attacked [a]the Rephaim
in Ashteroth Karnaim, [b]the Zuzim in
Ham, [c]the Emim in Shaveh Kiriathaim,
6 [a]and the Horites in their mountain
of Seir, as far as El Paran, which *is*
by the wilderness.
7 Then they turned back and came to
En Mishpat (that *is*, Kadesh), and attacked all the country of the Amalekites, and also the Amorites who dwelt
[a]in Hazezon Tamar.
8 And the king of Sodom, the king of
Gomorrah, the king of Admah, the
king of Zeboiim, and the king of Bela
(that *is*, Zoar) went out and joined together in battle in the Valley of Siddim
9 against Chedorlaomer king of
Elam, Tidal king of [1]nations, Amraphel
king of Shinar, and Arioch king of Ellasar—four kings against five.
10 Now the Valley of Siddim *was full*
of [a]asphalt pits; and the kings of
Sodom and Gomorrah fled; *some* fell
there, and the remainder fled [b]to the
mountains.
11 Then they took [a]all the goods of
Sodom and Gomorrah, and all their
provisions, and went their way.
12 They also took Lot, Abram's
[a]brother's son [b]who dwelt in Sodom,
and his goods, and departed.
13 Then one who had escaped came
and told Abram the [a]Hebrew, for
[b]he dwelt by [1]the terebinth trees of
Mamre the Amorite, brother of Eshcol
and brother of Aner; [c]and they *were*
allies with Abram.
14 Now [a]when Abram heard that
[b]his brother was taken captive, he
armed his three hundred and eighteen
trained *servants* who were [c]born in his
own house, and went in pursuit
[d]as far as Dan.
15 He divided his forces against them
by night, and he and his servants
[a]attacked them and pursued them as
far as Hobah, which *is* [1]north of Damascus.
16 So he [a]brought back all the goods,
and also brought back his brother Lot
and his goods, as well as the women
and the people.
17 And the king of Sodom [a]went out
to meet him at the Valley of Shaveh
(that *is*, the [b]King's Valley), [c]after his
return from [1]the defeat of Chedorlaomer and the kings who *were* with him.

Abram and Melchizedek

18 Then [a]Melchizedek king of Salem **5**
brought out [b]bread and wine; he *was*
[c]the *priest of [d]God **Most High.**

18 [a]Gen. 26:17 [b]Gen. 14:13 [c]Gen. 23:2; 35:27 [d]Gen. 8:20; 22:8, 9 [1]Heb. *Alon Mamre*

CHAPTER 14

1 [a]Gen. 10:10; 11:2 [b]Is. 11:11; 21:2 [1]Heb. *goyim*
2 [a]Deut. 29:23 [b]Gen. 13:10; 19:22
3 [a]Num. 34:12
4 [a]Gen. 9:26 *See WW at Ps. 100:2.
5 [a]Gen. 15:20 [b]Deut. 2:20 [c]Deut. 2:10
6 [a]Deut. 2:12, 22
7 [a]2 Chr. 20:2
9 [1]Heb. *goyim*
10 [a]Gen. 11:3 [b]Gen. 19:17, 30
11 [a]Gen. 14:16, 21
12 [a]Gen. 11:27; 12:5 [b]Gen. 13:12
13 [a]Gen. 39:14; 40:15 [b]Gen. 13:18 [c]Gen. 14:24; 21:27, 32 [1]Heb. *Alon Mamre*
14 [a]Gen. 19:29 [b]Gen. 13:8; 14:12 [c]Gen. 12:5; 15:3; 17:27 [d]Deut. 34:1
15 [a]Is. 41:2, 3 [1]Lit. *on the left hand of*
16 [a]Gen. 31:18
17 [a]1 Sam. 18:6 [b]2 Sam. 18:18 [c]Heb. 7:1 [1]Lit. *striking*
18 [a]Heb. 7:1–10 [b]Gen. 18:5 [c]Ps. 110:4 [d]Acts 16:17 *See WW at Lev. 5:6.

14:1–16 This narrative roots **Abram** firmly in the international scene. The four kings came quite a distance, likely from modern Iran, Iraq, and Turkey. On a raid to quell a rebellion in the Dead Sea area against their eastern alliance (v. 2), they take **Lot** (v. 12).

14:5, 6 Chedorlaomer and the kings traveled southward in Transjordan, first conquering three tribes. **The Rephaim** and **the Emim** were the very tall people who were destroyed finally by the Israelites under Moses; their king had a bed more than 12 feet long (Deut. 3:11). Then the kings marched south to conquer the **Horites** (who would later be dispossessed by the descendants of Esau).

14:10 The five allied armies were defeated by the invaders from the east; some of the survivors fell into the **asphalt pits.** To this day, occasional chunks of asphalt (or bitumen) float to the surface at the southern end of the Dead Sea.

14:13 Abram the Hebrew: "Hebrew" appears to be the name by which other people identified the chosen family; it was not a title they would have called themselves, except to identify themselves to foreigners. See 39:14, 17; 40:15; 41:12; 43:32.

14:14, 15 His brother: "Kinsman," "relative." That his servants were already **trained** for war is indicative of the political conditions of the time, and of the need for strong patriarchal leaders like **Abram.** Abram was not only wealthy, he was also a mighty military man.

14:15 North of Damascus indicates Abram drove them somewhere outside the Promised Land.

14:18–24 See section 5 of Truth-In-Action at the end of Gen.

14:18–20 Abram's seemingly routine encounter with the regional **king of Salem** is revealed centuries later as being an encounter with an antetype of Jesus Christ in His role as Priest (Ps. 110:4; Heb. 7:1–10). **Melchizedek** means "My King Is Righteous or Legitimate," and he greets **Abram** with a royal banquet (**bread and wine**). Uniquely occupying the

WORD WEALTH

14:18 Most High, *'elyon* (el-*yohn*); Strong's #5945: Most High, uppermost; pertaining to the heights, in the highest; highness; supreme, lofty, elevated, high in rank, exalted. *'Elyon* is derived from the verb *'alah* meaning "to ascend." It appears as an adjective more than 20 times, describing exalted rulers and even the highest rooms in the wall of the temple (Ezek. 41:7). It becomes a divine title when paired with one of the names of God, such as *'El 'Elyon* or *'Elohim 'Elyon,* "God Most High." Compare the angels' declaration at the birth of Jesus: "Glory to God in the **highest**, and on earth peace, goodwill toward men!" (Luke 2:14).

19 And he blessed him and said:

[a]"Blessed be Abram of God Most
High,
[b]Possessor of heaven and earth;
20 And [a]blessed be God Most High,
Who has delivered your enemies
into your hand."

And he [b]gave him [1]a tithe of all.
21 Now the king of Sodom said to
Abram, "Give me the [1]persons, and
take the goods for yourself."
22 But Abram [a]said to the king of
Sodom, "I [b]have raised my hand to the
LORD, God Most High, [c]the Possessor
of heaven and earth,
23 "that [a]I *will take* nothing, from a
thread to a sandal strap, and that I will
not take anything that *is* yours, lest you
should say, 'I have made Abram rich'—
24 "except only what the young men
have eaten, and the *portion of the men
who went with me: Aner, Eshcol, and
Mamre; let them take their portion."

God's Covenant with Abram

15 After these things the *word of
the LORD came to Abram [a]in
a vision, saying, [b]"Do not be afraid,

19 [a]Ruth 3:10 [b]Gen. 14:22
20 [a]Gen. 24:27 [b]Heb. 7:4 [1]*one-tenth*
21 [1]Lit. *souls*
22 [a]Gen. 14:2, 8, 10 [b]Dan. 12:7 [c]Gen. 14:19
23 [a]2 Kin. 5:16
24 *See WW at Zech. 2:12.

CHAPTER 15

1 [a]Dan. 10:1 [b]Gen. 21:17; 26:24 [c]Deut. 33:29 [d]Prov. 11:18 [1]Or *your reward shall be very great* *See WW at Deut. 1:1.
2 [a]Gen. 17:18 [b]Acts 7:5 [1]*am childless*
3 [a]Gen. 14:14 [1]*a servant*
4 [a]2 Sam. 7:12
5 [a]Ps. 147:4 [b]Jer. 33:22 [c]Ex. 32:13 [d]Gen. 17:19 *See WW at Num. 13:30.
6 [a]Rom. 4:3, 9, 22 [b]Ps. 32:2; 106:31 *See WW at 2 Chr. 20:20.
7 [a]Gen. 12:1 [b]Gen. 11:28, 31 [c]Ps. 105:42, 44
8 [a]Luke 1:18

Abram. I *am* your [c]shield, [1]your exceedingly [d]great reward."
2 [a]But Abram said, "Lord GOD, what
will You give me, [b]seeing I [1]go childless, and the heir of my house *is* Eliezer
of Damascus?"
3 Then Abram said, "Look, You have
given me no offspring; indeed [a]one[1]
born in my house is my heir!"
4 And behold, the word of the LORD
came to him, saying, "This one shall
not be your heir, but one who [a]will
come from your own body shall be
your heir."
5 Then He brought him outside and
said, "Look now toward heaven, and
[a]count the [b]stars if you are *able to
number them." And He said to him,
[c]"So shall your [d]descendants be."
6 And he [a]believed* in the LORD, 4
and He [b]**accounted** it to him for righteousness.

WORD WEALTH

15:6 accounted, *chashab* (kah-*shahv*); Strong's #2803: To think, reckon, put together, calculate, imagine, impute, make account; to lay one's thoughts together, to form a judgment; to devise, to plan, to produce something in the mind, to invent. This verb is normally the equivalent of the English word "to think," but also contains a strong suggestion of "counting." *Chashab* is the consideration of a great number of elements, which results in a conclusion based on a wide overview. In this verse, God added up everything that Abraham's belief meant to Him, and computing it all together, determined that it was equal to righteousness.

7 Then He said to him, "I *am* the
LORD, who [a]brought you out of [b]Ur of
the Chaldeans, [c]to give you this land
to inherit it."
8 And he said, "Lord GOD, [a]how shall
I know that I will inherit it?"
9 So He said to him, "Bring Me a
three-year-old heifer, a three-year-old

offices of king and **priest,** he worships **God Most High** (somewhat of a rarity in the area at that time). Prior to any legal requirement, Abram responds to his office, generosity, and blessing by giving him **a tithe** of all the spoils gathered in the recent war.
14:21–24 In spite of the rudeness of Salem's neighboring **king of Sodom, Abram** gives him the remaining 90 percent of the booty. The same generosity is not required of the booty taken by Abram's allies, **Aner, Eshcol, and Mamre.**
15:1–21 This is one of the most important chapters in the OT because it depicts the establishment of the Abrahamic covenant, a covenant ultimately fulfilled in Jesus Christ.
15:2, 3 Childless is the word often used to describe God's closing a womb in judgment. *How does this reckon with the promise?* is Abram's complaint. The culture permitted a senior slave to become **heir** of a childless man.
15:6 See section 4 of Truth-In-Action at the end of Gen.
15:6 Abram's silence was his way of giving credence to God's word (**believed**). This resulted in a legal reckoning (**accounted it to him for righteousness**). This statement is quoted twice by Paul (Rom. 4:3; Gal. 3:6) and once by James (2:23). It is the basis for the NT teaching that God's way has always been responsive trust in His word, which then produces right living.
15:9, 10 God is setting the stage for a "covenant-cutting" ceremony, almost exactly as was done in contemporary cultures of the Near East. Biblical as well as major secular covenants were established in blood.

female goat, a three-year-old ram, a
turtledove, and a young pigeon."
10 Then he brought all these to Him
and [a]cut them in two, down the middle,
and placed each piece opposite the
other; but he did not cut [b]the birds in
two.

KINGDOM DYNAMICS

15:10 The First Blood Sacrifice Covenant, THE BLOOD. The direct requirement of a blood sacrifice as the means of establishing covenant first appears in this episode (vv. 1–21) and God's instruction to Abraham. The animals to be offered were selected, cut in halves, and arranged in proper order opposite one another. The covenant parties then passed between the halves indicating that they were irrevocably bound together in blood. The cutting in halves of the sacrifice spoke of the end of existing lives for the sake of establishing a new bond or covenant. The sacred nature of this bond was attested to by the shedding of lifeblood. In this instance, only God passed between the pieces, indicating that it was His covenant and He would assume responsibility for its administration. Present in this account of covenant-making are three essential ingredients: 1) a bond that originates from God's initiative, 2) the offering of a blood sacrifice as a requirement of covenant, and 3) God's sovereign administration of the outcome of His oath.

(Gen. 17:10/Lev. 17:11) C.S.

11 And when the vultures came down
on the carcasses, Abram drove them
away.
12 Now when the sun was going down,
[a]a deep sleep fell upon Abram; and behold, horror *and* great darkness fell
upon him.
13 Then He said to Abram: "Know cer-

10 [a]Gen. 15:17; Jer. 34:18 [b]Lev. 1:17
12 [a]Gen. 2:21; 28:11; Job 33:15
13 [a]Ex. 1:11; Acts 7:6 [b]Ex. 12:40
14 [a]Ex. 6:6 [b]Ex. 12:36 *See WW at Deut. 32:36.
15 [a]Job 5:26 [b]Gen. 25:8; 47:30 [c]Gen. 25:8 [1]Die and join your ancestors *See WW at Nah. 1:15.
16 [a]Gen. 15:13; Ex. 12:41 [b]Gen. 48:22; Lev. 18:24–28; 1 Kin. 21:26 [c]1 Kin. 11:12; Matt. 23:32
17 [a]Jer. 34:18, 19
18 [a]Gen. 24:7 [b]Gen. 12:7; 17:8; Ex. 23:31; Num. 34:3; Deut. 11:24; Josh. 1:4; 21:43; Acts 7:5

CHAPTER 16

1 [a]Gen. 11:30; 15:2, 3 [b]Gen. 12:16; 21:9 [c]Gal. 4:24

tainly [a]that your descendants will be
strangers in a land *that is* not theirs,
and will serve them, and [b]they will afflict them four hundred years.
14 "And also the nation whom they
serve [a]I will *judge; afterward [b]they
shall come out with great possessions.
15 "Now as for you, [a]you shall [1]go
[b]to your fathers in *peace; [c]you shall
be buried at a good old age.
16 "But [a]in the fourth generation they
shall return here, for the iniquity
[b]of the Amorites [c]*is* not yet complete."
17 And it came to pass, when the sun
went down and it was dark, that behold, there appeared a smoking oven
and a burning torch that [a]passed between those pieces.
18 On the same day the LORD [a]made
a covenant with Abram, saying:
[b]"To your descendants I have given
this land, from the river of Egypt to
the great river, the River Euphrates—
19 "the Kenites, the Kenezzites, the
Kadmonites,
20 "the Hittites, the Perizzites, the
Rephaim,
21 "the Amorites, the Canaanites, the
Girgashites, and the Jebusites."

Hagar and Ishmael

16 Now Sarai, Abram's wife, 4
[a]had borne him no *children.*
And she had [b]an Egyptian maidservant
whose name was [c]Hagar.

KINGDOM DYNAMICS

16:1 The Submission That Bears Fruit (Sarah), WOMEN. Sarah was originally called "Sarai," which means "Princess." When God changed Sarai's name to "Sarah," He named her "The Princess"

(*cont. on next page*)

15:12–16 While Abram was in **a deep sleep,** God informed him of the future. **Four hundred years . . . the fourth generation:** These statements appear contradictory, but they are apparently to be understood in different contexts. "Four hundred years" is an approximation. Gal. 3:17 counts the 430 years much the same, from the establishment of this covenant with Abram. Such a dating appears more reasonable, placing these events about 1870 B.C. (assuming the dating of the Mosaic covenant at Sinai to be 1440 B.C.). The four generations of v. 16 were Levi, Kohath, Amram, and Moses.

15:16 The Amorites represent all the inhabitants of Canaan. God's judgment must await its perfect timing.

15:17 During a most dramatic scene God humbled Himself to accept the role of the inferior party to this covenant. In the ancient Hittite suzerainty covenant, a puppet ruler, the inferior party, would walk **between** the bleeding **pieces** of split animals, taking an oath of loyalty to his superior: "May the gods do so to me (and more also) as I have done to these animals if I do not fulfill the terms of this covenant!" See Jer. 34:8–22. Here **the LORD** voluntarily made Himself lower than Abram for the establishment of the covenant. This dramatic act prefigures the precious gift of His own Son, who condescended to die on a degrading cross for all humanity. **A smoking oven and a burning torch:** A figure of speech, a hendiadys, where one noun modifies the other, so that not two but a single blazing fire, the Shekinah Himself, **passed between those pieces.** The LORD was the promising Party; God's oath was unilateral, unconditional, with *no requirements* demanded of Abram as his part in this mighty covenant. Abram simply believed. The Abrahamic covenant is the OT model for the New Covenant in Jesus Christ.

15:18 Made a covenant: The Hebrew says "cut" a covenant, because the animals were split.

16:1–4 See section 4 of Truth-In-Action at the end of Gen.

16:1–3 Ten years earlier **Abram** had believed God for a son. **Sarai,** at the age of 75, had exhausted her faith, and now Abram weakened also. With 15 more years to wait, they devised their own scheme, which the NT identifies as "according to the flesh" (Gal. 4:23).

(cont. from preceding page)
or "Queen," linking her in corulership with her husband Abraham (formerly Abram), the "Father of Many Nations," and including her in His covenant promise (17:15, 16).

Sarah, the beautiful (12:14) wife of Abraham, was barren (16:1), a condition considered a curse in the ancient world. She is a positive lesson 1) in faith that rises above personal limitations (Heb. 11:11); and 2) in a submitted spirit that responds biblically to her husband, without becoming depersonalized (1 Pet. 3:5, 6).

Sarah is also an illustration of the dangers of taking God's promises into our own hands. Her suggestion that Abraham take her handmaid as wife, in view of Sarah's barrenness, resulted in the birth of Ishmael—a child who occasioned jealousy and conflict between the two women, eventually between their two sons, and to this day, among their offspring.
(Gen. 4:25/Gen. 24:15–67) F.L.

2 [a]So Sarai said to Abram, "See now,
the LORD [b]has restrained me from
bearing *children*. Please, [c]go in to my
maid; perhaps I shall [1]obtain children
by her." And Abram [d]heeded the voice
of Sarai.
3 Then Sarai, Abram's wife, took Hagar her maid, the Egyptian, and gave
her to her husband Abram to be his
wife, after Abram [a]had dwelt ten years
in the land of Canaan.
4 So he went in to Hagar, and she
conceived. And when she saw that she
had conceived, her mistress became
[a]despised in her [1]eyes.
5 Then Sarai said to Abram, [1]"My
wrong *be* upon you! I gave my maid
into your embrace; and when she saw
that she had conceived, I became despised in her eyes. [a]The LORD judge between you and me."
6 [a]So Abram said to Sarai, "Indeed
your maid *is* in your hand; do to her
as you please." And when Sarai dealt
harshly with her, [b]she fled from her
presence.
7 Now the [a]Angel* of the LORD found
her by a spring of water in the wilderness, [b]by the spring on the way to
[c]Shur.

2 [a]Gen. 30:3 [b]Gen. 20:18 [c]Gen. 30:3, 9 [d]Gen. 3:17 [1]Lit. *be built up from*
3 [a]Gen. 12:4, 5
4 [a]1 Sam. 1:6, 7; [Prov. 30:21, 23] [1]*sight*
5 [a]Gen. 31:53; Ex. 5:21 [1]*The wrong done to me be*
6 [a]1 Pet. 3:7 [b]Gen. 16:9; Ex. 2:15
7 [a]Gen. 21:17, 18; 22:11, 15; 31:11 [b]Gen. 20:1; 25:18 [c]Ex. 15:22 *See WW at 2 Chr. 32:21.
9 [a][Titus 2:9]
10 [a]Gen. 17:20
11 [a]Luke 1:13, 31 [1]Lit. *God Hears*
12 [a]Gen. 21:20; Job 24:5; 39:5–8 [b]Gen. 25:18
13 [a]Gen. 31:42 [1]Heb. *El Roi* [2]Seen the back of
14 [a]Gen. 24:62 [b]Gen. 14:7; Num. 13:26 [1]Lit. *Well of the One Who Lives and Sees Me*
15 [a]Gal. 4:22

CHAPTER 17
1 [a]Gen. 12:7; 18:1 [b]Gen. 28:3; 35:11; Ex. 6:3; Job 42:2 [c]2 Kin. 20:3 [d]Gen. 6:9; Deut. 18:13 [1]Heb. *El Shaddai* *See WW at Ps. 91:1.
2 [a]Gen. 15:18; Ex. 6:4; [Gal. 3:19] [b]Gen. 12:2; 13:16; 15:5; 18:18

8 And He said, "Hagar, Sarai's maid,
where have you come from, and where
are you going?" She said, "I am fleeing
from the presence of my mistress Sarai."
9 The Angel of the LORD said to her,
"Return to your mistress, and [a]submit
yourself under her hand."
10 Then the Angel of the LORD said to
her, [a]"I will multiply your descendants
exceedingly, so that they shall not be
counted for multitude."
11 And the Angel of the LORD said to
her:

"Behold, you *are* with child,
[a]And you shall bear a son.
You shall call his name [1]Ishmael,
Because the LORD has heard your
affliction.
12 [a]He shall be a wild man;
His hand *shall be* against every
man,
And every man's hand against
him.
[b]And he shall dwell in the
presence of all his brethren."

13 Then she called the name of the
LORD who spoke to her, You-Are-[1]the-
God-Who-Sees; for she said, "Have I
also here [2]seen Him [a]who sees me?"
14 Therefore the well was called
[a]Beer Lahai Roi;[1] observe, *it is* [b]be-
tween Kadesh and Bered.
15 So [a]Hagar bore Abram a son; and
Abram named his son, whom Hagar
bore, Ishmael.
16 Abram *was* eighty-six years old
when Hagar bore Ishmael to Abram.

The Sign of the Covenant

17 When Abram was ninety-nine
years old, the LORD [a]appeared
to Abram and said to him, [b]"I *am*
[1]Almighty* God; [c]walk before Me and
be [d]blameless.
2 "And I will make My [a]covenant between Me and you, and [b]will multiply
you exceedingly."
3 Then Abram fell on his face, and
God talked with him, saying:
4 "As for Me, behold, My covenant

16:7 Hagar was fleeing to her home in Egypt; **the Angel** found her about halfway there.

16:12 The Ishmaelites were to roam freely across the desert, often in conflict with others. Modern-day Arabs claim descent from Ishmael; **his brethren** are the Israelites.

16:13 The-God-Who-Sees: In a vision the Hebrews did not distinguish an "Angel of God" (v. 7) from God Himself. Theophanies (manifestations of God) were sometimes accomplished through intermediary angels. See Acts 7:30–32, 38, 53; Heb. 2:2.

16:15 Abram honored **Hagar** by giving **Ishmael** the name that the maid claimed an angel had chosen.

17:1, 2 Thirteen more years passed before God affirmed the **covenant** with **Abram. Almighty God** is translated from the Hebrew *El Shaddai* whose root emphasizes God's might over against the frailty of man. In Gen. it is used particularly in situations where people are hard-pressed and need assurance (28:3; 35:11; 49:25).

is with you, and you shall be [a]a father
of [1]many nations.
5 "No longer shall [a]your *name be
called [1]Abram, but your name shall be
[2]Abraham; [b]for I have made you a father of [3]many nations.

KINGDOM DYNAMICS

17:5 The Words We Speak, FAITH'S CONFESSION. One of the explicit teachings of the Bible is the importance of the words we speak. In this text God changes Abram's name to Abraham and promises Abraham that he will become the father of many nations. "Abram" means "High Father" or "Patriarch." "Abraham" means "Father of a Multitude." Thus, God was arranging that every time Abraham heard or spoke his own name, he would be reminded of God's promise. Adam Clarke's Commentary states it well: "God [associates] the patriarch more nearly to Himself, by thus imparting to him a portion of His own name," noting God added this to Abraham "for the sake of dignity." The principle: Let God's words, which designated His will and promise for your life, become as fixed in your mind and as governing of your speech as God's changing Abraham's name was in shaping his concept of himself. Do not "name" yourself anything less than God does.

(*/Num. 13:30; 14:6–9) R.H.

6 "I will make you exceedingly fruitful; and I will make [a]nations of you,
and [b]kings shall come from you.
7 "And I will [a]establish My **covenant**
between Me and you and your descendants after you in their *generations, for an everlasting covenant,
[b]to be God to you and [c]your descendants after you.

WORD WEALTH

17:7 covenant, *berit* (beh-*reet*); Strong's #1285: A covenant, compact, pledge, treaty, agreement. This is one of the most theologically important words in the Bible, appearing more than 250 times in the OT. A *berit* may be made between individuals, between a king and his people, or by God with His people. Here God's irrevocable pledge is that He will be God to Abraham and his descendants *forever.* The greatest provision of the Abrahamic covenant, this is the foundation stone of Israel's eternal relationship to God, a truth affirmed by David (2 Sam. 7:24), by the Lord Himself (Jer. 33:24–26), and by Paul (Rom. 9:4; 11:2, 29). All other Bible promises are based on this one.

4 [a][Rom. 4:11, 12, 16] [1]Lit. *multitude of nations*
5 [a]Neh. 9:7 [b]Rom. 4:17 [1]Lit. *Exalted Father* [2]Lit. *Father of a Multitude* [3]*a multitude of* *See WW at Deut. 18:5.
6 [a]Gen. 17:16; 35:11 [b]Matt. 1:6
7 [a][Gal. 3:17] [b]Gen. 26:24; 28:13; Lev. 11:45; 26:12, 45; Heb. 11:16 [c]Rom. 9:8; Gal. 3:16 *See WW at Esth. 9:28.
8 [a]Gen. 12:7; 13:15, 17; Acts 7:5 [b]Gen. 23:4; 28:4 [c]Ex. 6:7; 29:45; Lev. 26:12; Deut. 29:13; Rev. 21:7 [1]Lit. *of your sojournings* *See WW at Josh. 22:9.
9 [a]Ex. 19:5 *See WW at Job 10:12.
10 [a]John 7:22; Acts 7:8
11 [a]Ex. 12:13, 48; [Rom. 4:11]

8 "Also [a]I give to you and your descendants after you the land [b]in[1] which
you are a stranger, all the land of Canaan, as an everlasting *possession;
and [c]I will be their God."
9 And God said to Abraham: "As for
you, [a]you shall *keep My covenant,
you and your descendants after you
throughout their generations.
10 "This *is* My covenant which you
shall keep, between Me and you and
your descendants after you: [a]Every
male child among you shall be circumcised;

KINGDOM DYNAMICS

17:10 Circumcision's Significance, THE BLOOD. The act of circumcision was required as a sign of the covenant previously established with Abraham. This was not a new covenant but an external sign that Abraham and his descendants were to execute to show that they were God's covenant people. The fact that this was performed upon the male reproductive organ had at least a twofold significance: 1) the cutting away of the foreskin spoke of the cutting away of fleshly dependence, and 2) their hope for the future posterity and prosperity was not to rest upon their own ability. Circumcision was a statement that confidence was being placed in the promise of God and His faithfulness rather than in their own flesh.

(Gen. 22:13/Gen. 15:10) C.S.

11 "and you shall be circumcised in the
flesh of your foreskins, and it shall be
[a]a sign of the covenant between Me
and you.
12 "He who is eight days old among

17:5 Name changes correspond to either character change or a major call from God. Abram's name is changed from "Exalted Father" to "Father of a Multitude." In spite of his new name, **Abraham** still did not have the promised son through Sarai (Sarah, v. 15), who was almost 90 years of age.

17:8 An everlasting possession: The land was given to the chosen people by this unending promise. **God** established a covenant that is unconditional, valid whether Abraham's **descendants** are faithful or not. The land belongs to God, and He gives it to whom He chooses.

17:11 A sign of the covenant was not mentioned during its establishment in ch. 15. Circumcision was not uncommon in the ancient Near East, but God chose it as a sign to identify the people of the Abrahamic covenant for it literally touches the male at his point of propagating life. Later, pride made circumcision into an idolatrous symbol, which the Hebrews assumed would demand God's continued favor. Just as Christian baptism without faith is meaningless for justification, so it is with mere physical circumcision. See Rom. 2:25–29.

17:12 Circumcision is administered early because it marks entrance into the covenant.

you [a]shall be circumcised, every male child in your generations, he who is born in your house or bought with money from any foreigner who is not your descendant.

13 "He who is born in your house and he who is bought with your money must be circumcised, and My covenant shall be in your flesh for an everlasting covenant.

14 "And the uncircumcised male child, who is not circumcised in the flesh of his foreskin, that person [a]shall be cut off from his people; he has broken My covenant."

15 Then God said to Abraham, "As for Sarai your wife, you shall not call her name Sarai, but [1]Sarah *shall be* her name.

16 "And I will bless her [a]and also give you a son by her; then I will bless her, and she shall be *a mother* [b]*of* nations; [c]kings of peoples shall be from her."

17 Then Abraham fell on his face [a]and laughed, and said in his heart, "Shall *a child* be born to a man who is one hundred years old? And shall Sarah, who is ninety years old, bear *a child?*"

18 And Abraham [a]said to God, "Oh, that Ishmael might live before You!"

19 Then God said: "No, [a]Sarah your wife shall bear you a son, and you shall call his name Isaac; I will establish My [b]covenant with him for an everlasting covenant, *and* with his descendants after him.

20 "And as for Ishmael, I have heard you. Behold, I have blessed him, and will make him fruitful, and [a]will multiply him exceedingly. He shall beget [b]twelve princes, [c]and I will make him a great nation.

21 "But My [a]covenant I will establish with Isaac, [b]whom Sarah shall bear to you at this [c]set time next year."

22 Then He finished talking with him, and God went up from Abraham.

23 So Abraham took Ishmael his son, all who were born in his house and all who were bought with his money, every male among the men of Abraham's house, and circumcised the flesh of their foreskins that very same day, as God had said to him.

24 Abraham *was* ninety-nine years old when he was circumcised in the flesh of his foreskin.

25 And Ishmael his son *was* thirteen years old when he was circumcised in the flesh of his foreskin.

26 That very same day Abraham was circumcised, and his son Ishmael;

27 and [a]all the men of his house, born in the house or bought with money from a foreigner, were circumcised with him.

12 [a]Lev. 12:3
14 [a]Ex. 4:24–26
15 [1]Lit. *Princess*
16 [a]Gen. 18:10 [b]Gen. 35:11; Gal. 4:31; 1 Pet. 3:6 [c]Gen. 17:6; 36:31; 1 Sam. 8:22
17 [a]Gen. 17:3; 18:12; 21:6
18 [a]Gen. 18:23
19 [a]Gen. 18:10; 21:2; [Gal. 4:28] [b]Gen. 22:16; Matt. 1:2; Luke 3:34
20 [a]Gen. 16:10 [b]Gen. 25:12–16 [c]Gen. 21:13, 18
21 [a]Gen. 26:2–5 [b]Gen. 21:2 [c]Gen. 18:14
27 [a]Gen. 18:19

CHAPTER 18

1 [a]Gen. 13:18; 14:13 [1]Heb. *Alon Mamre*
2 [a]Gen. 18:16, 22; 32:24; Josh. 5:13; Judg. 13:6–11; Heb. 13:2 [b]Gen. 19:1; 1 Pet. 4:9
4 [a]Gen. 19:2; 24:32; 43:24
5 [a]Judg. 6:18, 19; 13:15, 16 [b]Judg. 19:5; Ps. 104:15 [c]Gen. 19:8; 33:10
8 [a]Gen. 19:3

The Son of Promise

18 Then the LORD appeared to him by [1]the [a]terebinth trees of Mamre, as he was sitting in the tent door in the heat of the day.

2 [a]So he lifted his eyes and looked, and behold, three men were standing by him; [b]and when he saw *them,* he ran from the tent door to meet them, and bowed himself to the ground,

3 and said, "My Lord, if I have now found favor in Your sight, do not pass on by Your servant.

4 "Please let [a]a little water be brought, and wash your feet, and rest yourselves under the tree.

5 "And [a]I will bring a morsel of bread, that [b]you may refresh your hearts. After that you may pass by, [c]inasmuch as you have come to your servant." They said, "Do as you have said."

6 So Abraham hurried into the tent to Sarah and said, "Quickly, make ready three measures of fine meal; knead *it* and make cakes."

7 And Abraham ran to the herd, took a tender and good calf, gave *it* to a young man, and he hastened to prepare it.

8 So [a]he took butter and milk and the calf which he had prepared, and set *it* before them; and he stood by them under the tree as they ate.

9 Then they said to him, "Where *is*

17:15 Since both names mean "Princess," Sarai's name change to **Sarah** served to bring her into the covenant in her own right.

17:17 Abraham . . . laughed because all of this was incredible. His laughter is somewhat ironic in that "Isaac" means "May God Smile upon Him."

17:20 Twelve princes refers to the tribal chieftains of the Ishmaelites (25:16).

17:24–27 For **Abraham** this sealed his transaction (15:6); for the others it was their initiation. Some see this as the birth of God's OT people, the OT counterpart to Pentecost.

18:1–8 This is typical Bedouin hospitality, both ancient and modern. Nothing is too good for a guest. It is still Bedouin custom in some areas for the host to stand while the visitors eat. The **three men** were two angels (19:1) and **the LORD** (vv. 13, 17), apparently as a theophany (see note on 16:13). Abraham did not appear to recognize who they were for a while (see Heb. 13:2).

18:9–15 Abraham earlier had laughed (17:17), and now **Sarah** laughs also. God's harsher reaction with her (see 17:19) indicates that Sarah was in persistent unbelief, not mere astonishment.

Sarah your wife?" So he said, "Here,
[a]in the tent."
10 And He said, "I will certainly return
to you [a]according to the time of life,
and behold, [b]Sarah your wife shall
have a son." (Sarah was listening in
the tent door which *was* behind him.)
11 Now [a]Abraham and Sarah were
old, well advanced in age; *and* [1]Sarah
[b]had passed the age of childbearing.
12 Therefore Sarah [a]laughed within
herself, saying, [b]"After I have grown
old, shall I have pleasure, my [c]lord being old also?"
13 And the LORD said to Abraham,
"Why did Sarah laugh, saying, 'Shall
I surely bear *a child,* since I am old?'
14 [a]"Is anything too hard for the LORD?
[b]At the appointed time I will return to
you, according to the time of life, and
Sarah shall have a son."
15 But Sarah denied *it,* saying, "I did
not laugh," for she was afraid. And He
said, "No, but you did laugh!"

Abraham Intercedes for Sodom

16 Then the men rose from there and
looked toward Sodom, and Abraham
went with them [a]to send them on the
way.
17 And the LORD said, [a]"Shall I hide
from Abraham what I am doing,
18 "since Abraham shall surely become a great and mighty nation, and
all the nations of the earth shall be
[a]blessed in him?
19 "For I have known him, in order
[a]that he may command his children
and his household after him, that they
keep the way of the LORD, to do righteousness and justice, that the LORD
may bring to Abraham what He has
spoken to him."
20 And the LORD said, "Because
[a]the outcry against Sodom and Gomorrah is great, and because their [b]sin is
very grave,
21 [a]"I will go down now and see
whether they have done altogether according to the outcry against it that has
come to Me; and if not, [b]I will know."
22 Then the men turned away from
there [a]and went toward Sodom, but
Abraham still stood before the LORD.
23 And Abraham [a]came near and said,
[b]"Would You also [c]destroy the [d]righ-
teous with the *wicked?
24 "Suppose there were fifty righteous
within the city; would You also destroy
the place and not spare *it* for the fifty
righteous that were in it?
25 "Far be it from You to do such a
thing as this, to slay the righteous with
the wicked, so [a]that the righteous
should be as the wicked; far be it from
You! [b]Shall not the *Judge of all the
earth do right?"
26 So the LORD said, [a]"If I find in
Sodom fifty righteous within the city,
then I will spare all the place for their
sakes."
27 Then Abraham answered and said,
"Indeed now, I who *am* [a]*but* dust and
ashes have taken it upon myself to
speak to the Lord:
28 "Suppose there were five less than
the fifty righteous; would You destroy
all of the city for *lack of* five?" So He
said, "If I find there forty-five, I will
not destroy *it.*"
29 And he spoke to Him yet again and
said, "Suppose there should be forty
found there?" So He said, "I will not
do *it* for the sake of forty."
30 Then he said, "Let not the Lord be
angry, and I will speak: Suppose thirty
should be found there?" So He said,
"I will not do *it* if I find thirty there."
31 And he said, "Indeed now, I have
taken it upon myself to speak to the
Lord: Suppose twenty should be found
there?" So He said, "I will not destroy
it for the sake of twenty."
32 Then he said, [a]"Let not the Lord be
angry, and I will speak but once more:
Suppose ten should be found there?"
[b]And He said, "I will not destroy *it* for
the sake of ten."
33 So the LORD went His way as soon
as He had finished speaking with
Abraham; and Abraham returned to
his place.

9 [a]Gen. 24:67
10 [a]2 Kin. 4:16 [b]Gen. 17:19, 21; 21:2; Rom. 9:9
11 [a]Gen. 17:17; Luke 1:18; Rom. 4:19; Heb. 11:11, 12, 19 [b]Gen. 31:35 [1]Lit. *the manner of women had ceased to be with Sarah*
12 [a]Gen. 17:17 [b]Luke 1:18 [c]1 Pet. 3:6
14 [a]Num. 11:23; Jer. 32:17; Zech. 8:6; Matt. 3:9; 19:26; Luke 1:37; Rom. 4:21 [b]Gen. 17:21; 18:10; 2 Kin. 4:16
16 [a]Acts 15:3; Rom. 15:24
17 [a]Gen. 18:22, 26, 33; Ps. 25:14; Amos 3:7; [John 15:15]
18 [a][Gen. 12:3; 22:18]; Matt. 1:1; Luke 3:34; [Acts 3:25, 26; Gal. 3:8]
19 [a][Deut. 4:9, 10; 6:6, 7]
20 [a]Gen. 4:10; 19:13; Ezek. 16:49, 50 [b]Gen. 13:13
21 [a]Gen. 11:5; Ex. 3:8; Ps. 14:2 [b]Deut. 8:2; 13:3; Josh. 22:22; Luke 16:15; 2 Cor. 11:11
22 [a]Gen. 18:16; 19:1
23 [a][Heb. 10:22] [b]Ex. 23:7; Num. 16:22; 2 Sam. 24:17; Ps. 11:4–7 [c]Job 9:22 [d]Gen. 20:4 *See WW at Prov. 10:16.
25 [a]Job 8:20; Is. 3:10, 11 [b]Deut. 1:16, 17; 32:4; Job 8:3, 20; 34:17; Ps. 58:11; 94:2; Is. 3:10, 11; Rom. 3:5, 6 *See WW at Judg. 2:18.
26 [a]Jer. 5:1; Ezek. 22:30
27 [a][Gen. 3:19]; Job 4:19; 30:19; 42:6; [1 Cor. 15:47, 48]
32 [a]Judg. 6:39 [b]James 5:16

KINGDOM DYNAMICS

18:17–33 Prayer Principles from God's Conversation with Abraham, PRAYER. At least three important principles emerge from God's conversation with Abraham in ch. 18. 1) We learn that wicked Sodom could have been spared for the sake of only 10 righteous people. From this we learn that it is not the presence of evil that brings God's mercy and long-suffering to an end; rather, it is the (*cont. on next page*)

18:16–33 The LORD honored **Abraham** by telling of His plan to destroy the evil cities, although Abraham was concerned only with the safety of his nephew Lot. Having initiated the process, Abraham demonstrates the principle of partnership with God by tenaciously questioning. He is feeling his way forward in faith.

18:21 The outcry against it confirms that God's judgment is perfect and accurately weighed.

(cont. from preceding page)
absence of good! 2) Although God sometimes inspires us to pray by showing us things to come (v. 17), our intercession must be in line with God's character and covenant with men. Like Abraham, we may appeal to God to preserve His name, honor, and perfect justice before the world (v. 25). 3) Although we often measure influence by numbers, man's arithmetic cannot be used to estimate the impact of the righteous. God saves by many or by few.
(*/Ex. 32:11–14, 30–34) L.L.

Sodom's Depravity

3 **19** Now [a]the two angels came to
Sodom in the evening, and
[b]Lot was sitting in the gate of Sodom.
When Lot saw *them*, he rose to meet
them, and he bowed himself with his
face toward the ground.
2 And he said, "Here now, my lords,
please [a]turn in to your servant's house
and spend the night, and [b]wash your
feet; then you may rise early and go on
your way." And they said, [c]"No, but we
will spend the night in the open square."
3 But he insisted strongly; so they
turned in to him and entered his house.
[a]Then he made them a feast, and baked
[b]unleavened bread, and they ate.
4 Now before they lay down, the men
of the city, the men of Sodom, both old
and young, all the people from every
quarter, surrounded the house.
5 [a]And they called to Lot and said to
him, "Where are the men who came
to you tonight? [b]Bring them out to us
that we [c]may know them *carnally*."
6 So [a]Lot went out to them through
the doorway, shut the door behind him,
7 and said, "Please, my brethren, do
not do so wickedly!
8 [a]"See now, I have two daughters
who have not known a man; please,
let me bring them out to you, and you
may do to them as you wish; only do
nothing to these men, [b]since this is the
reason they have come under the
shadow of my roof."
9 And they said, "Stand back!" Then
they said, "This one [a]came in to
[1]stay *here*, [b]and he keeps acting as a
judge; now we will deal worse with you
than with them." So they pressed hard
against the man Lot, and came near
to break down the door.
10 But the men reached out their hands
and pulled Lot into the house with
them, and shut the door.
11 And they [a]struck the men who *were*
at the doorway of the house with blindness, both small and great, so that they
became weary *trying* to find the door.

Sodom and Gomorrah Destroyed

12 Then the men said to Lot, "Have
you anyone else here? Son-in-law,
your sons, your daughters, and whomever you have in the city—[a]take *them*
out of this place!
13 "For we will destroy this place, because the [a]outcry against them has
grown great before the face of the
LORD, and [b]the LORD has sent us to destroy it."
14 So Lot went out and spoke to his
sons-in-law, [a]who had married his
daughters, and said, [b]"Get up, get out
of this place; for the LORD will destroy
this city!" [c]But to his sons-in-law he
seemed to be joking.
15 When the morning dawned, the angels urged Lot to hurry, saying, [a]"Arise,
take your wife and your two daughters who are here, lest you be consumed in the punishment of the city."
16 And while he lingered, the men
[a]took hold of his hand, his wife's hand,
and the hands of his two daughters, the
[b]LORD being merciful to him, [c]and they
brought him out and set him outside
the city.
17 So it came to pass, when they had
brought them outside, that [1]he said,
[a]"Escape for your life! [b]Do not look
behind you nor stay anywhere in the
plain. Escape [c]to the mountains, lest
you be [2]destroyed."
18 Then Lot said to them, "Please,
[a]no, my lords!
19 "Indeed now, your servant has

CHAPTER 19
1 [a]Gen. 18:2, 16, 22 [b]Gen. 18:1–5
2 [a]Gen. 24:31; [Heb. 13:2] [b]Gen. 18:4; 24:32 [c]Luke 24:28
3 [a]Gen. 18:6–8; Ex. 23:15; Num. 9:11; 28:17 [b]Ex. 12:8
5 [a]Is. 3:9 [b]Judg. 19:22 [c]Gen. 4:1; Rom. 1:24, 27; Jude 7
6 [a]Judg. 19:23
8 [a]Judg. 19:24 [b]Gen. 18:5
9 [a]2 Pet. 2:7, 8 [b]Ex. 2:14 [1]As a resident alien
11 [a]Gen. 20:17, 18
12 [a]Gen. 7:1; 2 Pet. 2:7, 9
13 [a]Gen. 18:20 [b]Lev. 26:30–33; Deut. 4:26; 28:45; 1 Chr. 21:15
14 [a]Matt. 1:18 [b]Num. 16:21, 24, 26, 45; Rev. 18:4 [c]Ex. 9:21; Jer. 43:1, 2; Luke 17:28; 24:11
15 [a]Ps. 37:2; Rev. 18:4
16 [a]Deut. 5:15; 6:21; 7:8; 2 Pet. 2:7 [b]Ex. 34:7; Ps. 32:10; 33:18, 19; Luke 18:13 [c]Ps. 34:22
17 [a]1 Kin. 19:3; Jer. 48:6 [b]Gen. 19:26; Matt. 24:16–18; Luke 9:62; Phil. 3:13, 14 [c]Gen. 14:10 [1]LXX, Syr., Vg. *they* [2]Lit. *swept away*
18 [a]Acts 10:14

19:1–28 See section 3 of Truth-In-Action at the end of Gen.
19:1–3 See note on 18:1–8. **Unleavened bread** indicates that the meal was prepared hastily.
19:4, 5 The men of the city wanted to abuse Lot's visitors in a sadistic, homosexual manner. Homosexuality is the only reason given here for Sodom's judgment; Jude 7 confirms it, although Ezek. 16:49, 50 adds further grounds. The culture demanded that travelers not be victimized. This was later codified in the Mosaic Law (Deut. 10:18, 19), and homosexuality was to be punished by death (Lev. 20:13). See also the note on Judg. 19:22.
19:8 I have two daughters: The virtue of hospitality flared into a vice of incredible behavior. Lot's next step, if necessary, would have been to risk his own life in order to protect his guests.
19:11 Blindness: This is not the ordinary Hebrew word for blindness; it probably means a brilliant flash of light, leading to temporary blindness, as occurred to Saul of Tarsus on the road to Damascus.
19:16 He lingered: Like most of the human race, Lot was tied to his possessions.
19:19 Lest some evil . . . I die: Lot wanted more security than **the mountains** afforded him. In many respects he

found favor in your sight, and you have increased your *mercy which you have shown me by saving my life; but I cannot escape to the mountains, lest some evil overtake me and I die.
20 "See now, this city *is* near *enough* to flee to, and it *is* a little one; please let me escape there (*is* it not a little one?) and my soul shall live."
21 And he said to him, "See, [a]I have favored you concerning this thing also, in that I will not overthrow this city for which you have spoken.
22 "Hurry, escape there. For [a]I cannot do anything until you arrive there." Therefore [b]the name of the city was called [1]Zoar.
23 The sun had risen upon the earth when Lot entered Zoar.
24 Then the LORD rained [a]brimstone and [b]fire on Sodom and Gomorrah, from the LORD out of the heavens.
25 So He [1]overthrew those cities, all the plain, all the inhabitants of the cities, and [a]what grew on the ground.
26 But his wife looked back behind him, and she became [a]a pillar of salt.
27 And Abraham went early in the morning to the place where [a]he had stood before the LORD.
28 Then he looked toward Sodom and Gomorrah, and toward all the land of the plain; and he saw, and behold, [a]the smoke of the land which went up like the smoke of a furnace.
29 And it came to pass, when God destroyed the cities of the plain, that God [a]remembered Abraham, and sent Lot out of the midst of the overthrow, when He overthrew the cities in which Lot had dwelt.

The Descendants of Lot

30 Then Lot went up out of Zoar and [a]dwelt in the mountains, and his two daughters were with him; for he was afraid to dwell in Zoar. And he and his two daughters dwelt in a cave.
31 Now the firstborn said to the younger, "Our father *is* old, and *there is* no man on the earth [a]to come in to us as is the custom of all the earth.
32 "Come, let us make our father drink wine, and we will lie with him, that we [a]may preserve the [1]lineage of our father."
33 So they made their father drink wine that night. And the firstborn went in and lay with her father, and he did not know when she lay down or when she arose.
34 It happened on the next day that the firstborn said to the younger, "Indeed I lay with my father last night; let us make him drink wine tonight also, and you go in *and* lie with him, that we may preserve the [1]lineage of our father."
35 Then they made their father drink wine that night also. And the younger arose and lay with him, and he did not know when she lay down or when she arose.
36 Thus both the daughters of Lot were with child by their father.
37 The firstborn bore a son and called his name Moab; [a]he *is* the father of the Moabites to this day.
38 And the younger, she also bore a son and called his name Ben-Ammi; [a]he *is* the father of the people of Ammon to this day.

Abraham and Abimelech

20 And Abraham journeyed from [a]there to the South, and dwelt between [b]Kadesh and Shur, and [c]stayed in Gerar.
2 Now Abraham said of Sarah his wife, [a]"She *is* my sister." And Abimelech king of Gerar sent and [b]took Sarah.
3 But [a]God came to Abimelech [b]in a *dream by night, and said to him, [c]"Indeed you *are* a dead man because of the woman whom you have taken, for she *is* [1]a man's wife."

19 *See WW at Mic. 6:8.
21 [a]Job 42:8, 9; Ps. 145:19
22 [a]Ex. 32:10; Deut. 9:14 [b]Gen. 13:10; 14:2 [1]Lit. *Little* or *Insignificant*
24 [a]Deut. 29:23; Ps. 11:6; Is. 13:19; Jer. 20:16; 23:14; 49:18; 50:40; Ezek. 16:49, 50; Hos. 11:8; Amos 4:11; Zeph. 2:9; Matt. 10:15; Mark 6:11; Luke 17:29; Rom. 9:29; 2 Pet. 2:6; Jude 7; Rev. 11:8 [b]Lev. 10:2
25 [a]Ps. 107:34 [1]*devastated*
26 [a]Gen. 19:17; Luke 17:32
27 [a]Gen. 18:22
28 [a]Rev. 9:2; 18:9
29 [a]Gen. 8:1; 18:23; Deut. 7:8; 9:5, 27
30 [a]Gen. 19:17, 19
31 [a]Gen. 16:2, 4; 38:8, 9; Deut. 25:5
32 [a][Mark 12:19] [1]Lit. *seed*
34 [1]Lit. *seed*
37 [a]Num. 25:1; Deut. 2:9
38 [a]Num. 21:24; Deut. 2:19

CHAPTER 20

1 [a]Gen. 18:1 [b]Gen. 12:9; 16:7, 14 [c]Gen. 26:1, 6
2 [a]Gen. 12:11–13; 26:7 [b]Gen. 12:15
3 [a]Ps. 105:14 [b]Job 33:15 [c]Gen. 20:7 [1]Lit. *married to a husband* *See WW at Joel 2:28.

models the grip of "this present evil age" (Gal. 1:4). The futility of seeking safety in temporal things is seen in Lot's rapid departure (v. 30).
19:24 Brimstone and fire likely refer to sulfurous fire. Many postulate that God sent a severe earthquake, accompanied by lightning, that ignited bitumen and petroleum. See also v. 28.
19:26 A pillar of salt was likely chosen since salt was a major trade of the area. Judgment engulfed her because her affections were with Sodom, not with Yahweh.
19:29 God remembered Abraham: Lot was saved, not because he was chosen (although he was declared "righteous," 2 Pet. 2:7), but for the sake of his uncle Abraham.
19:31 No man on the earth: All the land the girls could see was devastated. In their fear they chose incest rather than prayer or investigation of facts.
19:37, 38 Moab derives from a Hebrew root meaning "through our father." The Moabites were later responsible for the most carnal seduction in Israel's history (Num. 25). **Ben-Ammi** means "Son of My Kin." The Ammonites were responsible for human sacrifice to Molech (Lev. 18:21).
20:1 Gerar was on a caravan route, north of **Shur** on the way to Gaza.
20:2–18 On the eve of Isaac's conception, Abraham's faithless scheming stands in contrast to God's sovereignty (v. 6). See note on 12:11–13.

4 But Abimelech had not come near
her; and he said, "Lord, [a]will You slay
a righteous nation also?
5 "Did he not say to me, 'She *is* my
sister'? And she, even she herself said,
'He *is* my brother.' [a]In the [1]integrity
of my heart and innocence of my hands
I have done this."
6 And God said to him in a dream,
"Yes, I know that you did this in the
integrity of your heart. For [a]I also withheld you from sinning [b]against Me;
therefore I did not let you touch her.
7 "Now therefore, restore the man's
wife; [a]for he *is* a prophet, and he will
pray for you and you shall live. But if
you do not restore *her,* [b]know that you
shall surely die, you [c]and all who *are*
yours."
8 So Abimelech rose early in the
morning, called all his servants, and
told all these things in their hearing;
and the men were very much afraid.
9 And Abimelech called Abraham
and said to him, "What have you done
to us? How have I [1]offended you,
[a]that you have brought on me and on
my kingdom a great sin? You have
done deeds to me [b]that ought not to
be done."
10 Then Abimelech said to Abraham,
"What did you have in view, that you
have done this thing?"
11 And Abraham said, "Because I
thought, surely [a]the fear of God *is* not
in this place; and [b]they will kill me on
account of my wife.
12 "But indeed [a]*she is* truly my sister.
She *is* the daughter of my father, but
not the daughter of my mother; and
she became my wife.
13 "And it came to pass, when [a]God
caused me to wander from my father's
house, that I said to her, 'This *is* your
kindness that you should do for me:
in every place, wherever we go,
[b]say of me, "He *is* my brother." ' "
14 Then Abimelech [a]took sheep, oxen,
and male and female servants, and
gave *them* to Abraham; and he restored Sarah his wife to him.
15 And Abimelech said, "See, [a]my
land *is* before you; dwell where it
pleases you."
16 Then to Sarah he said, "Behold, I
have given your brother a thousand
pieces of silver; [a]indeed this [1]vindi-
cates you [b]before all who *are* with you
and before everybody." Thus she was
[2]rebuked.
17 So Abraham [a]prayed to God; and
God [b]healed Abimelech, his wife, and
his female servants. Then they bore
children;
18 for the LORD [a]had closed up all the
wombs of the house of Abimelech because of Sarah, Abraham's wife.

Isaac Is Born

21 And the LORD [a]visited Sarah as
He had said, and the LORD did
for Sarah [b]as He had spoken.
2 For Sarah [a]conceived and bore
Abraham a son in his old age, [b]at the
set time of which God had spoken to
him.
3 And Abraham called the name of
his son who was born to him—whom
Sarah bore to him—[a]Isaac.[1]
4 Then Abraham [a]circumcised his
son Isaac when he was eight days old,
[b]as God had commanded him.
5 Now [a]Abraham was one hundred
years old when his son Isaac was born
to him.
6 And Sarah said, [a]"God has [1]made
me laugh, *and* all who hear [b]will laugh
with me."
7 She also said, "Who would have
said to Abraham that Sarah would
nurse children? [a]For I have borne *him*
a son in his old age."

Hagar and Ishmael Depart

8 So the child grew and was weaned.
And Abraham made a great feast
on the same day that Isaac was
weaned.
9 And Sarah saw the son of Hagar

4 [a]Gen. 18:23–25
5 [a]2 Kin. 20:3 [1]*innocence*
6 [a]1 Sam. 25:26, 34 [b]Gen. 39:9
7 [a]1 Sam. 7:5 [b]Gen. 2:17 [c]Num. 16:32, 33
9 [a]Gen. 26:10; 39:9 [b]Gen. 34:7 [1]*sinned against*
11 [a]Prov. 16:6 [b]Gen. 12:12; 26:7
12 [a]Gen. 11:29
13 [a]Gen. 12:1–9, 11 [b]Gen. 12:13; 20:5
14 [a]Gen. 12:16
15 [a]Gen. 13:9; 34:10; 47:6
16 [a]Gen. 26:11 [b]Mal. 2:9 [1]Lit. *is a covering of the eyes for you to all* [2]Or *justified*
17 [a]Job 42:9 [b]Gen. 21:2
18 [a]Gen. 12:17

CHAPTER 21

1 [a]1 Sam. 2:21 [b][Gal. 4:23, 28]
2 [a]Heb. 11:11, 12 [b]Gen. 17:21; 18:10, 14
3 [a]Gen. 17:19, 21 [1]Lit. *Laughter*
4 [a]Acts 7:8 [b]Gen. 17:10, 12
5 [a]Gen. 17:1, 17
6 [a]Is. 54:1 [b]Luke 1:58 [1]Lit. *made laughter for me*
7 [a]Gen. 18:11, 12

20:7 He *is* a prophet in the sense of one who has a special gift from God for intercession and for wisdom.

20:12 Abraham revealed what the genealogy of Terah (11:27–32) did not tell, that Sarah was actually his half **sister,** a common marriage in tightly knit societies, such as those of the patriarchal age.

20:14–18 Abimelech was both terrified and angry. He gave large gifts in order to gain favor with **God** and with **Abraham.** V. 16 is difficult (see marginal note), but the meaning is nevertheless clear: "Here is compensation for any injury to your personal honor."

20:17, 18 Infertility in either home or field would have been frightening to **Abimelech.** It was vitally important that he as ruler set the example for his people by having many children, and animals bearing fruitfully.

21:3 Isaac: "Laughter," so named because "God has made me laugh" (v. 6). This was happy laughter, but **Abraham**'s earlier laughter (17:17) as well as **Sarah**'s (18:12) were unbelieving responses to the miracle of Isaac's birth, which to them still lay in the realm of impossibility.

21:4 See note on 17:12.

21:9 Ishmael was doing something to Isaac that deeply offended **Sarah.** The Hebrew word translated **scoffing** can mean "playing," "laughing," or "reproaching" (see this use in 39:14). Paul later used the word "persecuted" in describing Ishmael's treatment of Isaac (Gal. 4:29).

[a]the Egyptian, whom she had borne to
Abraham, [b]scoffing.[1]
10 Therefore she said to Abraham,
[a]"Cast out this bondwoman and her
son; for the son of this bondwoman
shall not be heir with my son, *namely*
with Isaac."
11 And the matter was very [1]dis-
pleasing in Abraham's sight [a]because
of his son.
12 But God said to Abraham, "Do not
let it be displeasing in your sight because of the lad or because of your
bondwoman. Whatever Sarah has said
to you, listen to her voice; for [a]in Isaac
your seed shall be called.
13 "Yet I will also make [a]a nation of
the son of the bondwoman, because he
is your [1]seed."
14 So Abraham rose early in the morning, and took bread and [1]a skin of water; and putting *it* on her shoulder, he
gave *it* and the boy to Hagar, and
[a]sent her away. Then she departed and
wandered in the Wilderness of Beersheba.
15 And the water in the skin was used
up, and she placed the boy under one
of the shrubs.
16 Then she went and sat down across
from *him* at a distance of about a bow-
shot; for she said to herself, "Let me
not see the death of the boy." So she
sat opposite *him*, and lifted her voice
and wept.
17 And [a]God heard the voice of the lad.
Then the [b]angel of God called to Hagar
out of heaven, and said to her, "What
ails you, Hagar? Fear not, for God
has heard the voice of the lad where
he *is*.
18 "Arise, lift up the lad and hold him
with your hand, for [a]I will make him
a great nation."
19 Then [a]God opened her eyes, and
she saw a well of water. And she went
and filled the skin with water, and gave
the lad a drink.
20 So God [a]was with the lad; and he
grew and dwelt in the wilderness,
[b]and became an archer.
21 He dwelt in the Wilderness of
Paran; and his mother [a]took a wife for
him from the land of Egypt.

9 [a]Gen. 16:1, 4, 15 [b][Gal. 4:29] [1]Lit. *laughing*
10 [a]Gal. 3:18; 4:30
11 [a]Gen. 17:18 [1]*distressing*
12 [a][Rom. 9:7, 8]
13 [a]Gen. 16:10; 17:20; 21:18; 25:12–18 [1]*descendant*
14 [a]John 8:35 [1]A water bottle made of skins
17 [a]Ex. 3:7 [b]Gen. 22:11
18 [a]Gen. 16:10; 21:13; 25:12–16
19 [a]Num. 22:31
20 [a]Gen. 28:15; 39:2, 3, 21 [b]Gen. 16:12
21 [a]Gen. 24:4
22 [a]Gen. 20:2, 14; 26:26 [b]Gen. 26:28
23 [a]Josh. 2:12 [1]*take an oath* *See WW at Gen. 26:3.
25 [a]Gen. 26:15, 18, 20–22
27 [a]Gen. 26:31; 31:44 [1]*treaty*
29 [a]Gen. 33:8
30 [a]Gen. 31:48, 52
31 [a]Gen. 21:14; 26:33 [1]Lit. *Well of the Oath* or *Well of the Seven* *See WW at Jer. 33:3.
33 [a]Gen. 4:26; 12:8; 13:4; 26:25 [b]Deut. 32:40; 33:27

CHAPTER 22
1 [a]Heb. 11:17

A Covenant with Abimelech

22 And it came to pass at that time that
[a]Abimelech and Phichol, the commander of his army, spoke to Abraham, saying, [b]"God *is* with you in all
that you do.
23 "Now therefore, [a]swear[1]* to me by
God that you will not deal falsely with
me, with my offspring, or with my posterity; but that according to the kindness that I have done to you, you will
do to me and to the land in which you
have dwelt."
24 And Abraham said, "I will swear."
25 Then Abraham rebuked Abimelech
because of a well of water which
Abimelech's servants [a]had seized.
26 And Abimelech said, "I do not
know who has done this thing; you did
not tell me, nor had I heard *of it* until
today."
27 So Abraham took sheep and oxen
and gave them to Abimelech, and the
two of them [a]made a [1]covenant.
28 And Abraham set seven ewe lambs
of the flock by themselves.
29 Then Abimelech asked Abraham,
[a]"What *is the meaning of* these seven
ewe lambs which you have set by
themselves?"
30 And he said, "You will take *these*
seven ewe lambs from my hand, that
[a]they may be my witness that I have
dug this well."
31 Therefore he [a]called* that place
[1]Beersheba, because the two of them
swore an oath there.
32 Thus they made a covenant at Beersheba. So Abimelech rose with Phichol, the commander of his army, and
they returned to the land of the Philistines.
33 Then *Abraham* planted a tamarisk
tree in Beersheba, and [a]there called on
the name of the LORD, [b]the Everlasting
God.
34 And Abraham stayed in the land of
the Philistines many days.

Abraham's Faith Confirmed

22 Now it came to pass after these 4
things that [a]God tested Abra-

21:10 The NT sees in this historical incident a type of the two covenants—law and grace (Gal. 4:28–31).
21:12, 13 God was telling **Abraham** that He would provide for Ishmael on his behalf. See note on 16:12.
21:16, 17 God has heard is another wordplay on the name of Ishmael, "God Hears."
21:21 The Wilderness of Paran is a desert plateau south of Canaan.
21:22–34 In contrast to his earlier interchange with **Abimelech** (ch. 20), **Abraham** learns here the value of frankness. The scene here at Beersheba is about 25 miles from the former one at Gerar.
21:33 Beersheba: The most important town of the Negev, both ancient and modern, was a religious center and home base to ***Abraham*** and Isaac who worshiped there; Amos refers centuries later to Beersheba's status as a shrine (5:5; 8:14).
22:1–14 See section 4 of Truth-In-Action at the end of Gen.

ham, and said to him, "Abraham!" And he said, "Here I am."

2 Then He said, "Take now your son, [a]your **only *son*** Isaac, whom you [b]love, and go [c]to the land of Moriah, and offer him there as a [d]burnt offering on one of the mountains of which I shall tell you."

WORD WEALTH

22:2 only *son*, *yachid* (yah-*cheed*); Strong's #3173: An only one, an only child, a precious life. *Yachid* comes from the verb *yachad*, "to be one." *Yachid* describes Abraham's unique miracle child, Isaac. Zechariah describes what the Messiah will one day become to Israel's repentant, weeping citizens: a previous, only son (Zech. 12:10). Here the place where God told Abraham to sacrifice his son Isaac is the same place where God sacrificed *His* own Son: the hills of Moriah in Jerusalem. Equally noteworthy is that the phrase "His only begotten Son" in John 3:16 in the Hebrew NT is: "His Son, His *Yachid*."

3 So Abraham rose early in the morning and saddled his donkey, and took two of his young men with him, and Isaac his son; and he split the wood for the burnt offering, and arose and went to the place of which God had told him.

4 Then on the third day Abraham lifted his eyes and saw the place afar off.

5 And Abraham said to his young men, "Stay here with the donkey; the [1]lad and I will go yonder and *worship, and we will [a]come back to you."

6 So Abraham took the wood of the burnt offering and [a]laid *it* on Isaac his son; and he took the fire in his hand, and a knife, and the two of them went together.

7 But Isaac spoke to Abraham his father and said, "My father!" And he said, "Here I am, my son." Then he said, "Look, the fire and the wood, but where *is* the [1]lamb for a burnt offering?"

8 And Abraham said, "My son, God will provide for Himself the [a]lamb for a [b]burnt offering." So the two of them went together.

2 [a]Gen. 22:12, 16; John 3:16; Heb. 11:17; 1 John 4:9 [b]John 5:20 [c]2 Chr. 3:1 [d]Gen. 8:20; 31:54
5 [a][Heb. 11:19] [1]Or *young man* *See WW at Ps. 99:5.
6 [a]John 19:17
7 [1]Or *goat*
8 [a]John 1:29, 36 [b]Ex. 12:3–6

9 [a][Heb. 11:17–19; James 2:21]
11 [a]Gen. 16:7–11; 21:17, 18; 31:11
12 [a]1 Sam. 15:22 [b]Gen. 26:5; James 2:21, 22 [c]Gen. 22:2, 16; John 3:16
14 [1]Heb. *YHWH Yireh*
15 *See WW at 2 Chr. 32:21.

9 Then they came to the place of which God had told him. And Abraham built an altar there and placed the wood in order; and he bound Isaac his son and [a]laid him on the altar, upon the wood.

10 And Abraham stretched out his hand and took the knife to slay his son.

11 But the [a]Angel of the LORD called to him from heaven and said, "Abraham, Abraham!" So he said, "Here I am."

12 And He said, [a]"Do not lay your hand on the lad, or do anything to him; for [b]now I know that you fear God, since you have not [c]withheld your son, your only *son*, from Me."

13 Then Abraham lifted his eyes and looked, and there behind *him was* a ram caught in a thicket by its horns. So Abraham went and took the ram, and offered it up for a burnt offering instead of his son.

KINGDOM DYNAMICS

22:13 Isaac, the Result of Covenant, THE BLOOD. Isaac was born to Abraham and Sarah as a result of covenant promise (17:1). God's requirement of Abraham to sacrifice Isaac was the supreme test that would demonstrate both Abraham's reverence for God and his confidence in God's faithfulness to keep His covenant promise. He prepared to offer up Isaac with the assurance that God would raise him from death itself (Heb. 11:19). God made a timely intervention and provided a ram to be sacrificed instead of Isaac. This is a dramatic foreshadowing of God's offering His only begotten Son to die in our place (John 3:16). God's covenant love gave Abraham a son, and covenant love provided a substitutionary sacrifice to save that son. Centuries later covenant love would cause God to give His own Son as a blood sacrifice for the sons of men.

(Gen. 8:20/Gen. 17:10) C.S.

14 And Abraham called the name of 1
the place, [1]The-LORD-Will-Provide; as it is said *to* this day, "In the Mount of the LORD it shall be provided."

15 Then the *Angel of the LORD called to Abraham a second time out of heaven,

22:2 The land of Moriah may be what later came to be Mt. Zion, location of the temple in Jerusalem. **A burnt offering** (see note on Lev. 1:3) belonged entirely to God. It is not clear why God chose a potential human sacrifice as Abraham's test. He clearly forbids such practice (Deut. 18:10). The main point is obviously the test of faith.

22:3 Abraham told no one about his orders, certainly not Isaac. The drama builds with each verse.

22:6 The fire in his hand refers to some burning material, perhaps a firestone or flint.

22:11–14 A vision from God must often first die, and then the Lord resurrects the vision from its ashes. **The-LORD-Will-Provide** (Hebrew *YHWH Yireh*) carries the idea of God's making provision when He sees the need.

22:14 See section 1 of Truth-In-Action at the end of Gen.

16 and said: [a]"By Myself I have sworn,
says the LORD, because you have done
this thing, and have not withheld your
son, your *only *son*—
17 "blessing I will [a]bless you, and multiplying I will multiply your descendants [b]as the stars of the heaven
[c]and as the sand which *is* on the seashore; and [d]your descendants shall
*possess the gate of their enemies.
18 [a]"In your seed all the nations of the
earth shall be blessed, [b]because you
have obeyed My voice."
19 So Abraham returned to his young
men, and they rose and went together
to [a]Beersheba; and Abraham dwelt at
Beersheba.

The Family of Nahor

20 Now it came to pass after these
things that it was told Abraham, saying, "Indeed [a]Milcah also has borne
children to your brother Nahor:

16 [a]Ps. 105:9 *See WW at Gen. 22:2. **17** [a]Gen. 17:16; 26:3, 24 [b]Gen. 15:5; 26:4 [c]Gen. 13:16; 32:12 [d]Gen. 24:60 *See WW at Deut. 8:1. **18** [a]Gen. 12:3; 18:18; 26:4 [b]Gen. 18:19; 22:3, 10; 26:5 **19** [a]Gen. 21:31 **20** [a]Gen. 11:29; 24:15 **21** [a]Job 1:1 [b]Job 32:2 **23** [a]Gen. 24:15 [1]*Rebecca,* Rom. 9:10

CHAPTER 23

2 [a]Josh. 14:15; 15:13; 21:11 [b]Gen. 13:18; 23:19 **3** [a]Gen. 10:15; 15:20 **4** [a][Gen. 17:8]

21 [a]"Huz his firstborn, Buz his brother,
Kemuel the father [b]of Aram,
22 "Chesed, Hazo, Pildash, Jidlaph,
and Bethuel."
23 And [a]Bethuel begot [1]Rebekah.
These eight Milcah bore to Nahor,
Abraham's brother.
24 His concubine, whose name was
Reumah, also bore Tebah, Gaham,
Thahash, and Maachah.

Sarah's Death and Burial

23 Sarah lived one hundred and
twenty-seven years; *these were*
the years of the life of Sarah.
2 So Sarah died in [a]Kirjath Arba (that
is, [b]Hebron) in the land of Canaan, and
Abraham came to mourn for Sarah and
to weep for her.
3 Then Abraham stood up from before his dead, and spoke to the sons
of [a]Heth, saying,
4 [a]"I *am* a foreigner and a visitor

22:16 By Myself I have sworn: "Because He could swear by no one greater, He swore by Himself" (Heb. 6:13). God also used this incident to settle the issue for all time: He does not approve of human sacrifice.
22:20–24 This section serves to give a list of Aramean tribes and to give background for Isaac's return to Abraham's family for a wife (ch. 24).
23:2 Kirjath Arba: The "city of Arba" was the earlier name for **Hebron,** named for a former great chieftain Arba who had settled there (see Josh. 14:15).
23:3 The sons of Heth (see 10:15) apparently are the Hittites, who years before had moved south from Asia Minor, dispossessing the earlier occupants, the sons of Arba.
23:4–20 A fascinating story of Near Eastern bargaining. **Abraham** was quite aware that the Hittites did not intend to give him a free burial ground, nor would he have dared to accept their pretended offer. The issue at stake—will Abraham gain a permanent holding in **Canaan,** or will he remain a landless dependent?

THE ABRAHAMIC COVENANT (22:15–18)

Genesis 12:1–3	God initiated His covenant with Abram when he was living in Ur of the Chaldeans, promising a land, descendants, and blessing.
Genesis 12:4, 5	Abram went with his family to Haran, lived there for a time, and left at the age of 75.
Genesis 13:14–17	After Lot separated from Abram, God again promised the land to him and his descendants.
Genesis 15:1–21	This covenant was ratified when God passed between the sacrificial animals Abram laid before God.
Genesis 17:1–27	When Abram was 99 God renewed His covenant, changing Abram's name to Abraham ("Father of a Multitude"). Sign of the covenant: circumcision.
Genesis 22:15–18	Confirmation of the covenant because of Abraham's obedience.

The Abrahamic covenant was foundational to other covenants:
- The promise of land in the Palestinian Covenant (Deut. 30:1–10)
- The promise of kingly descendants in the Davidic Covenant (2 Sam. 7:12–16)
- The promise of blessing in the "Old" and "New" Covenants (Ex. 19:3–6; Jer. 31:31–40)

among you. [b]Give me *property for a
burial place among you, that I may
bury my dead out of my sight."
5 And the sons of Heth answered
Abraham, saying to him,
6 "Hear us, my lord: You *are* [a]a
[1]mighty prince among us; bury your
dead in the choicest of our burial
places. None of us will withhold from
you his burial place, that you may bury
your dead."
7 Then Abraham stood up and bowed
himself to the people of the land, the
sons of Heth.
8 And he spoke with them, saying, "If
it is your wish that I bury my dead out
of my sight, hear me, and [1]meet with
Ephron the son of Zohar for me,
9 "that he may give me the cave of
[a]Machpelah which he has, which *is* at
the end of his field. Let him give it to
me at the full price, as property for a
burial place among you."
10 Now Ephron dwelt among the sons
of Heth; and Ephron the Hittite answered Abraham in the presence of the
sons of Heth, all who [a]entered at the
gate of his city, saying,
11 [a]"No, my lord, hear me: I give you
the field and the cave that *is* in it; I
give it to you in the presence of the
sons of my people. I give it to you. Bury
your dead!"
12 Then Abraham bowed himself
down before the people of the land;
13 and he spoke to Ephron in the hearing of the people of the land, saying,
"If you *will give it,* please hear me. I
will give you money for the field; take
it from me and I will bury my dead
there."
14 And Ephron answered Abraham,
saying to him,
15 "My lord, listen to me; the land *is*
worth four hundred [a]shekels of silver.
What *is* that between you and me? So
bury your dead."
16 And Abraham listened to Ephron;
and Abraham [a]weighed out the silver
for Ephron which he had named in the
hearing of the sons of Heth, four hundred shekels of silver, currency of the
merchants.
17 So [a]the field of Ephron which *was*
in Machpelah, which *was* before
Mamre, the field and the cave which

4 [b]Acts 7:5, 16 *See WW at Josh. 22:9.
6 [a]Gen. 13:2; 14:14; 24:35 [1]Lit. *prince of God*
8 [1]*entreat*
9 [a]Gen. 25:9
10 [a]Gen. 23:18; 34:20, 24; Ruth 4:1, 4, 11
11 [a]2 Sam. 24:21–24
15 [a]Ex. 30:13; Ezek. 45:12
16 [a]2 Sam. 14:26; Jer. 32:9, 10; Zech. 11:12
17 [a]Gen. 25:9; 49:29–32; 50:13; Acts 7:16
20 [a]Jer. 32:10, 11

CHAPTER 24

1 [a]Gen. 18:11; 21:5 [b]Gen. 12:2; 13:2; 24:35; Ps. 112:3; Prov. 10:22; [Gal. 3:9]
2 [a]Gen. 15:2 [b]Gen. 24:10; 39:4–6 [c]Gen. 47:29; 1 Chr. 29:24
3 [a]Gen. 14:19, 22 [b]Gen. 26:35; 28:2; Ex. 34:16; Deut. 7:3; 2 Cor. 6:14–17 [1]*take an oath*
4 [a]Gen. 28:2 [b]Gen. 12:1; Heb. 11:15
7 [a]Gen. 12:1; 24:3 [b]Gen. 12:7; 13:15; 15:18; 17:8; Ex. 32:13; Deut. 1:8; 34:4; Acts 7:5 [c]Gen. 16:7; 21:17; 22:11; Ex. 23:20, 23; 33:2; Heb. 1:4, 14 [1]Lit. *seed*
8 [a]Josh. 2:17–20 *See WW at Num. 14:18.
9 *See WW at Mic. 4:13.
10 [a]Gen. 24:2, 22

was in it, and all the trees that *were*
in the field, which *were* within all the
surrounding borders, were deeded
18 to Abraham as a possession in the
presence of the sons of Heth, before
all who went in at the gate of his city.
19 And after this, Abraham buried
Sarah his wife in the cave of the field
of Machpelah, before Mamre (that *is,*
Hebron) in the land of Canaan.
20 So the field and the cave that *is* in
it [a]were deeded to Abraham by the
sons of Heth as property for a burial
place.

A Bride for Isaac

24 Now Abraham [a]was old, well
advanced in age; and the LORD
[b]had blessed Abraham in all things.
2 So Abraham said [a]to the oldest servant of his house, who [b]ruled over all
that he had, "Please, [c]put your hand
under my thigh,
3 "and I will make you [a]swear[1] by the
LORD, the God of heaven and the God
of the earth, that [b]you will not take a
wife for my son from the daughters of
the Canaanites, among whom I dwell;
4 [a]"but you shall go [b]to my country
and to my family, and take a wife for
my son Isaac."
5 And the servant said to him, "Perhaps the woman will not be willing to
follow me to this land. Must I take your
son back to the land from which you
came?"
6 But Abraham said to him, "Beware
that you do not take my son back there.
7 "The LORD God of heaven, who
[a]took me from my father's house and
from the land of my family, and who
spoke to me and swore to me, saying,
[b]'To your [1]descendants I give this
land,' [c]He will send His angel before
you, and you shall take a wife for my
son from there.
8 "And if the woman is not willing
to follow you, then [a]you will be *released from this oath; only do not take
my son back there."
9 So the servant put his hand under
the thigh of Abraham his *master, and
swore to him concerning this matter.
10 Then the servant took ten of his
master's camels and departed, [a]for all

23:14, 15 Bargaining from a position of strength, **Ephron** carefully slipped his exorbitant price (**400 shekels of silver**) into the delicate negotiations.
23:19 Sarah's bones **in . . . Canaan** testified to possessing the promise. See Joseph's request in 50:25.
24:2, 3 Put your hand under my thigh: These words were part of an important oath used by a man who thinks he is dying, although **Abraham** still had many years ahead. The thigh represented privacy and was associated with procreation. Perhaps **the oldest servant** was the Eliezer of 15:2.
24:4 To my country: To Haran (Syria) Abraham's home country. The idea is to maintain the purity of the bloodline.
24:10 Many archaeologists have claimed that **camels** were

his master's goods *were in* his hand.
And he arose and went to Mesopotamia, to [b]the city of Nahor.
11 And he made his camels kneel
down outside the city by a well of water at evening time, the time [a]when
women go out to draw *water.*
12 Then he [a]said, "O LORD God of my
master Abraham, please [b]give me success this day, and show kindness to my
master Abraham.
13 "Behold, *here* [a]I stand by the well
of water, and [b]the daughters of the
men of the city are coming out to draw
water.
14 "Now let it be that the young
woman to whom I say, 'Please let down
your pitcher that I may drink,' and she
says, 'Drink, and I will also give your
camels a drink'—*let* her *be the one*
You have appointed for Your servant
Isaac. And [a]by this I will know that
You have shown kindness to my master."
15 And it happened, [a]before he had
finished speaking, that behold, [b]Re-
bekah,[1] who was born to Bethuel, son
of [c]Milcah, the wife of Nahor, Abraham's brother, came out with her
pitcher on her shoulder.

KINGDOM DYNAMICS

24:15–67 The Blessing of an Unselfish Woman (Rebekah), WOMEN. Rebekah, the Syrian, was the granddaughter of Nahor, Abraham's brother (22:23). Rebekah's name refers to "tying or binding up," implying that her beauty was so great, it could literally "captivate" or "fascinate" men. She is introduced as a diligently industrious and beautifully sensitive girl. Her willingness to serve Eleazar and her readiness to draw water for all 10 of the thirsty camels dramatize this. A lesson in the way God provides surprising rewards for servant-spirited souls is seen in what happened to Rebekah. Little did she know those camels were carrying untold gifts for her and her family. Her will to wait for her family's blessing before accepting the invitation to leave for a marriage to Isaac, who was a wealthy prince of the ancient world, is a model for today. How many marriages today would be different 1) if the Holy Spirit were the guide, 2) if prayer and worship were the order of the day, and 3) if the couple had the blessing of the family?

(Gen. 16:1/Num. 27:1–11) F.L.

16 Now the young woman [a]*was* very
beautiful to behold, a *virgin; no man
had known her. And she went down
to the well, filled her pitcher, and came
up.
17 And the servant ran to meet her and
said, "Please let me drink a little water
from your pitcher."
18 [a]So she said, "Drink, my lord."
Then she quickly let her pitcher
down to her hand, and gave him a
drink.
19 And when she had finished giving
him a drink, she said, "I will draw *water* for your camels also, until they
have finished drinking."
20 Then she quickly emptied her
pitcher into the trough, ran back to the
well to draw *water,* and drew for all
his camels.
21 And the man, wondering at her, remained silent so as to know whether
[a]the LORD had made his journey prosperous or not.
22 So it was, when the camels had finished drinking, that the man took a
golden [a]nose ring weighing half a
shekel, and two bracelets for her wrists
weighing ten *shekels* of gold,
23 and said, "Whose daughter *are*
you? Tell me, please, is there room *in*
your father's house for us [1]to lodge?"
24 So she said to him, [a]"I *am* the
daughter of Bethuel, Milcah's son,
whom she bore to Nahor."
25 Moreover she said to him, "We
have both straw and feed enough, and
room to lodge."
26 Then the man [a]bowed down his
head and worshiped the LORD.
27 And he said, [a]"Blessed *be* the LORD
God of my master Abraham, who has
not forsaken [b]His mercy and His *truth
toward my master. As for me, being

10 [b]Gen. 11:31, 32; 22:20; 27:43; 29:5
11 [a]Ex. 2:16; 1 Sam. 9:11
12 [a]Gen. 24:27, 42, 48; 26:24; 32:9; Ex. 3:6, 15 [b]Gen. 27:20; Neh. 1:11; Ps. 37:5
13 [a]Gen. 24:43 [b]Ex. 2:16
14 [a]Judg. 6:17, 37; 1 Sam. 14:10; 16:7; 20:7; 2 Kin. 20:9; Prov. 16:33; Acts 1:26
15 [a]Is. 65:24 [b]Gen. 24:45; 25:20 [c]Gen. 22:20, 23 [1]*Rebecca,* Rom. 9:10
16 [a]Gen. 12:11; 26:7; 29:17 *See WW at Ps. 45:14.
18 [a]Gen. 24:14, 46; [1 Pet. 3:8, 9]
21 [a]Gen. 24:12–14, 27, 52
22 [a]Gen. 24:47; Ex. 32:2, 3; Is. 3:19–21
23 [1]*to spend the night*
24 [a]Gen. 22:23; 24:15
26 [a]Gen. 24:48, 52; Ex. 4:31
27 [a]Gen. 24:12, 42, 48; Ex. 18:10; Ruth 4:14; 1 Sam. 25:32, 39; 2 Sam. 18:28; Luke 1:68 [b]Gen. 32:10; Ps. 98:3 *See WW at Ps. 25:5.

not being domesticated at this time and for several centuries to come, in spite of a continuing record of camels through the early books of the OT. However, camel bones have been dug from houses near Haran, and a record of expenditure for camel feed has been found in southern Turkey, both excavations dating from the patriarchal age. **Mesopotamia** is a Greek word meaning "the Land between the Waters," translated from the Hebrew, "Aram of the Two Rivers," the area of the Tigris and the Euphrates (modern Iraq). **The city of Nahor** was close to Haran.

24:12–14 Normally such a prayer is inadvisable but occasionally God will honor it, as He did in this case. The servant knew full well that **Abraham**'s God was a God of miracles; he had been observing His blessings through the years.

24:22 Golden nose ring: As much a part of a woman's jewelry as earrings today.

24:27 As for me, being on the way is a literal translation. It may be interpreted as the ecstatic servant's remark: "The Lord led me—*me*—straight to the house!" His initial response was a few moments of joyous worship.

on the way, the LORD [c]led me to the
house of my master's brethren."
28 So the young woman ran and told
her mother's household these things.
29 Now Rebekah had a brother whose
name *was* [a]Laban, and Laban ran out
to the man by the well.
30 So it came to pass, when he saw the
nose ring, and the bracelets on his sister's wrists, and when he heard the
words of his sister Rebekah, saying,
"Thus the man spoke to me," that he
went to the man. And there he stood
by the camels at the well.
31 And he said, "Come in, [a]O blessed
of the LORD! Why do you stand outside? For I have prepared the house,
and a place for the camels."
32 Then the man came to the house.
And he unloaded the camels, and
[a]provided straw and feed for the camels, and water to [b]wash his feet and
the feet of the men who *were* with him.
33 *Food* was set before him to eat, but
he said, [a]"I will not eat until I have told
about my errand." And he said, "Speak
on."
34 So he said, "I *am* Abraham's servant.
35 "The LORD [a]has blessed my master
greatly, and he has become great; and
He has given him flocks and herds, silver and gold, male and female servants, and camels and donkeys.
36 "And Sarah my master's wife
[a]bore a son to my master when she was
old; and [b]to him he has given all that
he has.
37 "Now my master [a]made me swear,
saying, 'You shall not take a wife for
my son from the daughters of the Canaanites, in whose land I dwell;
38 [a]'but you shall go to my father's
house and to my family, and take a
wife for my son.'
39 [a]"And I said to my master, 'Perhaps
the woman will not follow me.'
40 [a]"But he said to me, 'The LORD,
[b]before whom I walk, will send His angel with you and [1]prosper your way;
and you shall take a wife for my son
from my family and from my father's
house.
41 [a]'You will be clear from this oath
when you arrive among my family; for
if they will not give *her* to you, then
you will be released from my oath.'
42 "And this day I came to the well and

27 [c]Gen. 24:21, 48
29 [a]Gen. 29:5, 13
31 [a]Gen. 26:29; Judg. 17:2; Ruth 3:10; Ps. 115:15
32 [a]Gen. 43:24; Judg. 19:21 [b]Gen. 19:2; John 13:5, 13–15
33 [a]Job 23:12; John 4:34; Eph. 6:5–7
35 [a]Gen. 13:2; 24:1
36 [a]Gen. 21:1–7 [b]Gen. 21:10; 25:5
37 [a]Gen. 24:2–4
38 [a]Gen. 24:4
39 [a]Gen. 24:5
40 [a]Gen. 24:7 [b]Gen. 5:22, 24; 17:1; 1 Kin. 8:23 [1]*make your way successful*
41 [a]Gen. 24:8
42 [a]Gen. 24:12
43 [a]Gen. 24:13
45 [a]Gen. 24:15 [b]1 Sam. 1:13
48 [a]Gen. 24:26, 52 [b]Gen. 22:23; 24:27; Ps. 32:8; 48:14; Is. 48:17
49 [a]Gen. 47:29; Josh. 2:14
50 [a]Ps. 118:23; Matt. 21:42; Mark 12:11 [b]Gen. 31:24, 29
51 [a]Gen. 20:15
52 [a]Gen. 24:26, 48
53 [a]Gen. 24:10, 22; Ex. 3:22; 11:2; 12:35 [b]2 Chr. 21:3; Ezra 1:6

said, [a]'O LORD God of my master Abraham, if You will now prosper the way
in which I go,
43 [a]'behold, I stand by the well of water; and it shall come to pass that when
the virgin comes out to draw *water,*
and I say to her, "Please give me a little
water from your pitcher to drink,"
44 'and she says to me, "Drink, and I
will draw for your camels also,"—*let*
her *be* the woman whom the LORD has
appointed for my master's son.'
45 [a]"But before I had finished [b]speak-
ing in my heart, there was Rebekah,
coming out with her pitcher on her
shoulder; and she went down to the
well and drew *water.* And I said to her,
'Please let me drink.'
46 "And she made haste and let her
pitcher down from her *shoulder,* and
said, 'Drink, and I will give your camels a drink also.' So I drank, and she
gave the camels a drink also.
47 "Then I asked her, and said, 'Whose
daughter *are* you?' And she said, 'The
daughter of Bethuel, Nahor's son,
whom Milcah bore to him.' So I put
the nose ring on her nose and the
bracelets on her wrists.
48 [a]"And I bowed my head and worshiped the LORD, and blessed the LORD
God of my master Abraham, who had
led me in the way of truth to [b]take the
daughter of my master's brother for his
son.
49 "Now if you will [a]deal kindly and
truly with my master, tell me. And if
not, tell me, that I may turn to the right
hand or to the left."
50 Then Laban and Bethuel answered
and said, [a]"The thing comes from the
LORD; we cannot [b]speak to you either
bad or good.
51 [a]"Here *is* Rebekah before you; take
her and go, and let her be your master's
son's wife, as the LORD has spoken."
52 And it came to pass, when Abraham's servant heard their words, that
[a]he worshiped the LORD, *bowing himself* to the earth.
53 Then the servant brought out
[a]jewelry of silver, jewelry of gold, and
clothing, and gave *them* to Rebekah.
He also gave [b]precious things to her
brother and to her mother.
54 And he and the men who *were* with
him ate and drank and stayed all night.
Then they arose in the morning, and he

24:48 Brother is not as specific as our English "brother"; it could mean "nephew" or simply "relative" (see 14:14). Rebekah was actually **the daughter** of Abraham's nephew, Bethuel.

24:53 These were the wedding gifts, the dowry.

24:54 Abraham's servant was impatient to share the testimony of his miracle at home.

said, [a]"Send me away to my master."
55 But her brother and her mother
said, "Let the young woman stay with
us *a few* days, at least ten; after that
she may go."
56 And he said to them, "Do not
[1]hinder me, since the LORD has prospered my way; send me away so that
I may go to my master."
57 So they said, "We will call the
young woman and ask her personally."
58 Then they called Rebekah and said
to her, "Will you go with this man?"
And she said, "I will go."
59 So they sent away Rebekah their
sister [a]and her nurse, and Abraham's
servant and his men.
60 And they blessed Rebekah and said
to her:

"Our sister, *may* you *become*
[a]*The mother of* thousands of ten
thousands;
[b]And may your descendants
possess
The gates of those who hate
them."

61 Then Rebekah and her maids arose,
and they rode on the camels and followed the man. So the servant took Rebekah and departed.
62 Now Isaac came from the way of
[a]Beer Lahai Roi, for he dwelt in the
South.
63 And Isaac went out [a]to meditate in
the field in the evening; and he lifted
his eyes and looked, and there, the
camels *were* coming.
64 Then Rebekah lifted her eyes, and
when she saw Isaac [a]she dismounted
from her camel;
65 for she had said to the servant,
"Who *is* this man walking in the field
to meet us?" The servant said, "It *is*
my master." So she took a veil and covered herself.
66 And the servant told Isaac all the
things that he had done.
67 Then Isaac brought her into his
mother Sarah's tent; and he [a]took Rebekah and she became his wife, and
he loved her. So Isaac [b]was comforted
after his mother's *death.*

54 [a]Gen. 24:56, 59; 30:25
56 [1]*delay*
59 [a]Gen. 35:8
60 [a]Gen. 17:16 [b]Gen. 22:17; 28:14
62 [a]Gen. 16:14; 25:11
63 [a]Josh. 1:8; Ps. 1:2; 77:12; 119:15, 27, 48; 143:5; 145:5
64 [a]Josh. 15:18
67 [a]Gen. 25:20; 29:20; Prov. 18:22 [b]Gen. 23:1, 2; 38:12

CHAPTER 25

1 [a]1 Chr. 1:32, 33
2 [a]1 Chr. 1:32, 33
5 [a]Gen. 24:35, 36
6 [a]Gen. 21:14 [b]Judg. 6:3
8 [a]Gen. 15:15; 47:8, 9 [b]Gen. 25:17; 35:29; 49:29, 33
9 [a]Gen. 35:29; 50:13 [b]Gen. 23:9, 17; 49:30
10 [a]Gen. 23:3–16 [b]Gen. 49:31
11 [a]Gen. 16:14
12 [a]Gen. 11:10, 27; 16:15
13 [a]1 Chr. 1:29–31

Abraham and Keturah

25 Abraham again took a wife, and
her name *was* [a]Keturah.
2 And [a]she bore him Zimran, Jokshan, Medan, Midian, Ishbak, and
Shuah.
3 Jokshan begot Sheba and Dedan.
And the sons of Dedan were Asshurim,
Letushim, and Leummim.
4 And the sons of Midian *were*
Ephah, Epher, Hanoch, Abidah, and
Eldaah. All these *were* the children of
Keturah.
5 And [a]Abraham gave all that he had
to Isaac.
6 But Abraham gave gifts to the sons
of the concubines which Abraham had;
and while he was still living he [a]sent
them eastward, away from Isaac his
son, to [b]the country of the east.

Abraham's Death and Burial

7 This *is* the sum of the years of Abraham's life which he lived: one hundred
and seventy-five years.
8 Then Abraham breathed his last
and [a]died in a good old age, an old man
and full *of years,* and [b]was gathered
to his people.
9 And [a]his sons Isaac and Ishmael
buried him in the cave of [b]Machpelah,
which *is* before Mamre, in the field of
Ephron the son of Zohar the Hittite,
10 [a]the field which Abraham purchased from the sons of Heth. [b]There
Abraham was buried, and Sarah his
wife.
11 And it came to pass, after the death
of Abraham, that God blessed his son
Isaac. And Isaac dwelt at [a]Beer Lahai
Roi.

The Families of Ishmael and Isaac

12 Now this *is* the [a]genealogy of Ishmael, Abraham's son, whom Hagar the
Egyptian, Sarah's maidservant, bore to
Abraham.
13 And [a]these *were* the names of the
sons of Ishmael, by their names, according to their generations: The first-

24:62 Beer Lahai Roi was a well in the southern part of the country, perhaps about 12 miles northwest of Kadesh. See 16:13, 14.
24:63 Isaac was not colorful like his father Abraham, nor his son Jacob. He was quiet, thoughtful, 40 years old, and still unmarried. His life was primarily an interlude between two high points.
25:1 In v. 6 **Keturah** is identified, not as Abraham's **wife,** but as his concubine (see 1 Chr. 1:32). She shared the same status as Hagar. In light of this fact and Abraham's vitality in fathering these many sons, some scholars feel the events chronologically belong earlier in Gen., before Sarah died.
25:2 Some of these names are found today in ancient South-Arabian inscriptions. **Midian** appears often in the early books of the OT.
25:6 Abraham sent these sons **away from Isaac** to **the east,** into Arabia, in order to establish Isaac's unique status (v. 5).
25:9, 10 See note on 23:4–20.
25:12–18 See note on 16:12.

born of Ishmael, Nebajoth; then Kedar,
Adbeel, Mibsam,
14 Mishma, Dumah, Massa,
15 [1]Hadar, Tema, Jetur, Naphish, and
Kedemah.
16 These *were* the sons of Ishmael and
these *were* their names, by their towns
and their [1]settlements, [a]twelve princes
according to their nations.
17 These *were* the years of the life of
Ishmael: one hundred and thirty-seven
years; and [a]he breathed his last and
died, and was gathered to his people.
18 [a](They dwelt from Havilah as far as
Shur, which *is* east of Egypt as you go
toward Assyria.) He [1]died [b]in the presence of all his brethren.
19 This *is* the [a]genealogy of Isaac,
Abraham's son. [b]Abraham begot
Isaac.
20 Isaac was forty years old when he
took Rebekah as wife, [a]the daughter
of Bethuel the Syrian of Padan Aram,
[b]the sister of Laban the Syrian.
21 Now Isaac pleaded with the LORD
for his wife, because she *was* barren;
[a]and the LORD granted his plea,
[b]and Rebekah his wife conceived.
22 But the children struggled together
within her; and she said, "If *all is* well,
why *am I like* this?" [a]So she went to
inquire of the LORD.
23 And the LORD said to her:

[a]"Two nations *are* in your womb,
Two peoples shall be separated
from your body;
One people shall be stronger than
[b]the other,
[c]And the older shall serve the
younger."

24 So when her days were fulfilled *for
her* to give birth, indeed *there were*
twins in her womb.
25 And the first came out red. *He was*
[a]like a hairy garment all over; so they
called his name [1]Esau.
26 Afterward his brother came out,
and [a]his hand took hold of Esau's heel;
so [b]his name was called [1]Jacob. Isaac
was sixty years old when she bore
them.
27 So the boys grew. And Esau was
[a]a skillful hunter, a man of the field;
but Jacob was [b]a [1]mild man, [c]dwelling
in tents.
28 And Isaac loved Esau because he
[a]ate *of his* game, [b]but Rebekah loved
Jacob.

Esau Sells His Birthright

29 Now Jacob cooked a stew; and Esau
came in from the field, and he *was*
weary.
30 And Esau said to Jacob, "Please
feed me with that same red *stew,* for I
am weary." Therefore his name was
called [1]Edom.
31 But Jacob said, "Sell me your birthright as of this day."
32 And Esau said, "Look, I *am* about
to die; so [a]what *is* this birthright to
me?"
33 Then Jacob said, [1]"Swear to me as
of this day." So he swore to him, and
[a]sold his birthright to Jacob.
34 And Jacob gave Esau bread and
stew of lentils; then [a]he ate and drank,
arose, and went his way. Thus Esau
[b]despised *his* birthright.

Isaac and Abimelech

26 There was a famine in the land,
besides [a]the first famine that
was in the days of Abraham. And Isaac
went to [b]Abimelech king of the Philistines, in Gerar.
2 Then the LORD appeared to him and
said: [a]"Do not go down to Egypt; live
in [b]the land of which I shall tell you.
3 [a]"Dwell in this land, and [b]I will be
with you and [c]bless you; for to you and
your descendants [d]I give all these
lands, and I will perform [e]the oath
which I **swore** to Abraham your father.

15 [1]MT *Hadad*
16 [a]Gen. 17:20 [1]*camps*
17 [a]Gen. 25:8; 49:33
18 [a]1 Sam. 15:7 [b]Gen. 16:12 [1]*fell*
19 [a]Gen. 36:1, 9 [b]Matt. 1:2
20 [a]Gen. 22:23; 24:15, 29, 67 [b]Gen. 24:29
21 [a]1 Chr. 5:20 [b]Rom. 9:10–13
22 [a]1 Sam. 1:15; 9:9; 10:22
23 [a]Gen. 17:4–6, 16; 24:60 [b]2 Sam. 8:14 [c]Rom. 9:12
25 [a]Gen. 27:11, 16, 23 [1]Lit. *Hairy*
26 [a]Hos. 12:3 [b]Gen. 27:36 [1]*Supplanter* or *Deceitful,* lit. *One Who Takes the Heel*
27 [a]Gen. 27:3, 5 [b]Job 1:1, 8 [c]Heb. 11:9 [1]Lit. *complete*
28 [a]Gen. 27:4, 19, 25, 31 [b]Gen. 27:6–10
30 [1]Lit. *Red*
32 [a]Mark 8:36, 37
33 [a]Heb. 12:16 [1]*Take an oath*
34 [a]Eccl. 8:15 [b]Heb. 12:16, 17

CHAPTER 26

1 [a]Gen. 12:10 [b]Gen. 20:1, 2
2 [a]Gen. 12:7; 17:1; 18:1; 35:9 [b]Gen. 12:1
3 [a]Heb. 11:9 [b]Gen. 28:13, 15 [c]Gen. 12:2 [d]Gen. 12:7; 13:15; 15:18 [e]Gen. 22:16

WORD WEALTH

26:3 swore, *shaba'* (shah-*vah*); Strong's #7650: To swear, to give one's word, to

25:18 From Havilah as far as Shur: The location of Havilah is unknown, but is probably an oasis in Arabia, on the eastern side of the Red Sea. Shur is in the Sinai wilderness. The general area is the northern section of the Arabian peninsula.
25:22, 23 Rebekah must have been having a difficult pregnancy. Even in her **womb** the babies were struggling to be firstborn; literally, they "were crushing one another." **To inquire of the LORD:** We are not told how Rebekah asked God. The focus is on the Lord's response.
25:27 A mild man: The Hebrew word has the sense of "stable," or "solid." See marginal note.
25:29–34 According to Hurrian custom (the area around Haran), a man could sell **his birthright** to his brother. The birthright meant headship of the family and a double share of the inheritance (Deut. 21:17). Jacob is obviously ruthless, but the focal point is Esau's lust for the present and tangible at any cost (v. 34). The NT calls him a "profane person" (Heb. 12:16).
25:30 Edom later became a fierce enemy to Israel.
26:1 Isaac had an experience in **Gerar** much like his father **Abraham** had had earlier (12:10).
26:3–5 God repeated the Abrahamic covenant to Isaac.

bind oneself with an oath. The origin of this verb is evidently the noun *sheba'*, which means "seven." To swear (*shaba'*) meant either to "completely bind oneself" to fulfilling an oath, or to "seven oneself," that is, to repeat some detail of the oath seven times. Perhaps this is why Abraham gave *seven* lambs to Abimelech when entering into an agreement with him (21:28–31). The seven lambs were a witness that Abraham had dug a certain well, and he and Abimelech *swore* to each other to accept the fact that the well was Abraham's. The place was named Beersheba, normally translated "Well of the Oath" but sometimes "Well of the Seven." In 26:3, God by an irrevocable oath assures Isaac that he will have numberless descendants; they will inherit the Promised Land; and Isaac's seed will bless the whole world.

4 "And [a]I will make your descendants
multiply as the stars of heaven; I will
give to your descendants all these
lands; [b]and in your seed all the nations
of the earth shall be blessed;
5 [a]"because Abraham obeyed My
voice and kept My charge, My *commandments,
My statutes, and My
laws."

KINGDOM DYNAMICS

26:1–5; 28:1–22 Patriarchal Examples, FOUNDATIONS OF THE KINGDOM. The promise of God to Abraham that he would be "heir of the world" (Rom. 4:13) is repeated to his offspring, Isaac and Jacob, in succession. God's words and dealings in the lives of the patriarchs reveal that His unfolding program of redemption is dual: 1) restoring relationship to God to establish fellowship with Him, and 2) restoring rulership in life under God to reestablish human ability to "rule" in life's practical details of family and business. Thus, under His covenant, God promised these patriarchs both progeny—a family line, and property—an economic base. This illustrates God's progressive processing of His redemptive promise. He not only provides for restored fellowship with Himself (relationship), but covenants for human fulfillment and personal fruitfulness in life. This plan is geared not only to bless His people, but to make them a blessing to others.

Joseph's life elaborates this principle. God redeems him from the pit by His merciful providence, then raises him to rulership in Egypt, for the saving of nations (Gen. 37—50).

The "kingdom" concept of God's delegating His rule on Earth to be administrated through those who walk with Him is birthed at creation. Although damaged at man's fall, it is progressively being reinstated as a redemptive goal and is demonstrated in those who accept His covenant.

(Gen. 12:1–3/1 Chr. 29:10–16) J.W.H.

4 [a]Gen. 15:5; 22:17; Ex. 32:13 [b]Gen. 12:3; 22:18; Gal. 3:8
5 [a]Gen. 22:16, 18
*See WW at Ps. 119:35.

6 So Isaac dwelt in Gerar.
7 And the men of the place asked
about his wife. And [a]he said, "She *is*
my sister"; for [b]he was afraid to say,
"*She is* my wife," *because he thought,*
"lest the men of the place kill me for
Rebekah, because she *is* [c]beautiful to
behold."
8 Now it came to pass, when he had
been there a long time, that Abimelech
king of the Philistines looked through
a window, and saw, and there was
Isaac, [1]showing endearment to Rebekah
his wife.
9 Then Abimelech called Isaac and
said, "Quite obviously she *is* your wife;
so how could you say, 'She *is* my sister'?"
Isaac said to him, "Because I
said, 'Lest I die on account of her.' "
10 And Abimelech said, "What *is* this
you have done to us? One of the people
might soon have lain with your wife,
and [a]you would have brought guilt on
us."
11 So Abimelech charged all *his* people,
saying, "He who [a]touches this man
or his wife shall surely be put to
death."
12 Then Isaac sowed in that land, and
reaped in the same year [a]a hundredfold;
and the LORD [b]blessed him.
13 The man [a]began to prosper, and
continued prospering until he became
very prosperous;
14 for he had possessions of flocks and
possessions of herds and a great number
of servants. So the Philistines
[a]envied* him.
15 Now the Philistines had stopped up
all the wells [a]which his father's servants
had dug in the days of Abraham
his father, and they had filled them
with earth.

7 [a]Gen. 12:13; 20:2, 12, 13 [b]Prov. 29:25 [c]Gen. 12:11; 24:16; 29:17
8 [1]*caressing*
10 [a]Gen. 20:9
11 [a]Ps. 105:15
12 [a]Matt. 13:8, 23; Mark 4:8 [b]Gen. 24:1; 25:8, 11; 26:3; Job 42:12; Prov. 10:22
13 [a]Gen. 24:35; [Prov. 10:22]
14 [a]Gen. 37:11; Eccl. 4:4
*See WW at Zech. 8:2.
15 [a]Gen. 21:25, 30

26:7, 8 Isaac mixed fear and faith, an incompatible combination. See note on 12:11–13 for this same weakness in his father. **A long time** serves to show the error of his fear.

26:12 Isaac sowed . . . and reaped: This proves God's faithfulness (v. 3) in response to Isaac's obedience not to go to Egypt (v. 2).

26:15–22 Isaac's riches were not a cushion from reality. Instead, his prosperity angered his enemies and brought rejection from his allies (v. 16). Isaac responded by working diligently to preserve his inheritance.

16 And Abimelech said to Isaac, "Go
away from us, for [a]you are much
mightier than we."
17 Then Isaac departed from there and
[1]pitched his tent in the Valley of Gerar,
and dwelt there.
18 And Isaac dug again the wells of
water which they had dug in the days
of Abraham his father, for the Philistines had stopped them up after the
death of Abraham. [a]He called them by
the names which his father had called
them.
19 Also Isaac's servants dug in the valley, and found a well of running water
there.
20 But the herdsmen of Gerar [a]quar-
reled with Isaac's herdsmen, saying,
"The water *is* ours." So he called the
name of the well [1]Esek, because they
quarreled with him.
21 Then they dug another well, and
they quarreled over that *one* also. So
he called its name [1]Sitnah.
22 And he moved from there and dug
another well, and they did not quarrel
over it. So he called its name [1]Reho-
both, because he said, "For now the
LORD has made room for us, and we
shall [a]be fruitful in the land."
23 Then he went up from there to Beersheba.
24 And the LORD [a]appeared to him the
same night and said, [b]"I *am* the God
of your father Abraham; [c]do not fear,
for [d]I *am* with you. I will bless you and
multiply your descendants for My servant Abraham's sake."
25 So he [a]built an altar there and
[b]called on the name of the LORD, and
he pitched his tent there; and there
Isaac's servants dug a well.
26 Then Abimelech came to him from
Gerar with Ahuzzath, one of his
friends, [a]and Phichol the commander
of his army.
27 And Isaac said to them, "Why have
you come to me, [a]since you hate me
and have [b]sent me away from you?"
28 But they said, "We have certainly
seen that the LORD [a]is with you. So we
said, 'Let there now be an oath between us, between you and us; and let
us make a [1]covenant with you,
29 'that you will do us no harm, since
we have not touched you, and since we
have done nothing to you but good and
have sent you away in peace. [a]You *are*
now the blessed of the LORD.' "
30 [a]So he made them a feast, and they
ate and drank.
31 Then they arose early in the morning and [a]swore an oath with one another; and Isaac sent them away, and
they departed from him in peace.
32 It came to pass the same day that
Isaac's servants came and told him
about the well which they had dug,
and said to him, "We have found
water."
33 So he called it [1]Shebah. [a]Therefore
the name of the city *is* [2]Beersheba to
this day.
34 [a]When Esau was forty years old, he
took as wives Judith the daughter of
Beeri the Hittite, and Basemath the
daughter of Elon the Hittite.
35 And [a]they were a grief of mind to
Isaac and Rebekah.

Isaac Blesses Jacob

27 Now it came to pass, when Isaac
was [a]old and [b]his eyes were so
dim that he could not see, that he called
Esau his older son and said to him,
"My son." And he answered him,
"Here I am."
2 Then he said, "Behold now, I am
old. I [a]do not know the day of my
death.
3 [a]"Now therefore, please take your
weapons, your quiver and your bow,
and go out to the field and hunt game
for me.
4 "And make me [1]savory food, such
as I love, and bring *it* to me that I may
eat, that my soul [a]may bless you before
I die."
5 Now Rebekah was listening when
Isaac spoke to Esau his son. And Esau
went to the field to hunt game and to
bring *it*.

16 [a]Ex. 1:9 **17** [1]*camped* **18** [a]Gen. 21:31 **20** [a]Gen. 21:25 [1]Lit. *Quarrel* **21** [1]Lit. *Enmity* **22** [a]Gen. 17:6; 28:3; 41:52; Ex. 1:7 [1]Lit. *Spaciousness* **24** [a]Gen. 26:2 [b]Gen. 17:7, 8; 24:12; Ex. 3:6; Acts 7:32 [c]Gen. 15:1 [d]Gen. 26:3, 4 **25** [a]Gen. 12:7, 8; 13:4, 18; 22:9; 33:20 [b]Gen. 21:33; Ps. 116:17 **26** [a]Gen. 21:22 **27** [a]Judg. 11:7 [b]Gen. 26:16 **28** [a]Gen. 21:22, 23 [1]*treaty*

29 [a]Gen. 24:31; Ps. 115:15 **30** [a]Gen. 19:3 **31** [a]Gen. 21:31 **33** [a]Gen. 21:31; 28:10 [1]Lit. *Oath* or *Seven* [2]Lit. *Well of the Oath* or *Well of the Seven* **34** [a]Gen. 28:8; 36:2 **35** [a]Gen. 27:46; 28:1, 8

CHAPTER 27

1 [a]Gen. 35:28 [b]Gen. 48:10; 1 Sam. 3:2 **2** [a][Prov. 27:1; James 4:14] **3** [a]Gen. 25:27, 28 **4** [a]Gen. 27:19, 25, 27, 31; 48:9, 15, 16; 49:28; Deut. 33:1; Heb. 11:20 [1]*tasty*

26:23 Beersheba: See note on 21:33.

26:24–33 We see here Isaac's reward for hard work and tenacity. The **covenant** is a revival of one Abraham made earlier (21:22–24). **Abimelech** was an official name for a number of rulers, even as "Pharaoh" was in Egypt.

26:28 When a party to **a covenant** died, the covenant was automatically abrogated and had to be renewed.

26:30 A feast was one way of ratifying a covenant.

26:34, 35 Esau's marriage to foreign **wives** was another step away from the family's favor.

27:1–4 Isaac is apparently unaware that **Esau** has sold his birthright. He likely requests the meal to strengthen his waning vitality.

27:4 Savory food was some type of delicious meat Isaac liked. To **bless** meant to transfer from father to eldest son the family's material property, aspirations, and spiritual promises. Modeled after God's interaction with His people (see note on 12:1–9), the patriarchal concept of the blessing later becomes foundational in the transmission of emotional and spiritual vitality from generation to generation. As such, God formalized its major principles in the famous Aaronic blessing. See notes on Num. 6:24–26.

6 So Rebekah spoke to Jacob her son,
saying, "Indeed I heard your father
speak to Esau your brother, saying,
7 'Bring me game and make [1]savory
food for me, that I may eat it and bless
you in the presence of the LORD before
my death.'
8 "Now therefore, my son, [a]obey my
voice according to what I command
you.
9 "Go now to the flock and bring me
from there two choice kids of the goats,
and I will make [a]savory food from
them for your father, such as he loves.
10 "Then you shall take *it* to your father, that he may eat *it,* and that he
[a]may bless you before his death."
11 And Jacob said to Rebekah his
mother, "Look, [a]Esau my brother *is* a
hairy man, and I *am* a smooth-*skinned*
man.
12 "Perhaps my father will [a]feel me,
and I shall seem to be a deceiver to
him; and I shall bring [b]a curse on myself and not a blessing."
13 But his mother said to him, [a]"*Let*
your curse *be* on me, my son; only obey
my voice, and go, get *them* for me."
14 And he went and got *them* and
brought *them* to his mother, and his
mother [a]made [1]savory food, such as
his father loved.
15 Then Rebekah took [a]the choice
clothes of her elder son Esau, which
were with her in the house, and put
them on Jacob her younger son.
16 And she put the skins of the kids
of the goats on his hands and on the
smooth part of his neck.
17 Then she gave the savory food and
the bread, which she had prepared,
into the hand of her son Jacob.
18 So he went to his father and said,
"My father." And he said, "Here I am.
Who *are* you, my son?"
19 Jacob said to his father, "I *am* Esau
your firstborn; I have done just as you
told me; please arise, sit and eat of my
game, [a]that your soul may bless me."
20 But Isaac said to his son, "How *is*
it that you have found *it* so quickly,
my son?" And he said, "Because the
LORD your God brought *it* to me."

7 [1]*tasty*
8 [a]Gen. 27:13, 43
9 [a]Gen. 27:4
10 [a]Gen. 27:4; 48:16
11 [a]Gen. 25:25
12 [a]Gen. 27:21, 22 [b]Gen. 9:25; Deut. 27:18
13 [a]Gen. 43:9; 1 Sam. 25:24; 2 Sam. 14:9; Matt. 27:25
14 [a]Prov. 23:3; Luke 21:34 [1]*tasty*
15 [a]Gen. 27:27
19 [a]Gen. 27:4

21 [a]Gen. 27:12
23 [a]Gen. 27:16
25 [a]Gen. 27:4, 10, 19, 31
27 [a]Gen. 29:13 [b]Song 4:11; Hos. 14:6
28 [a]Heb. 11:20 [b]Gen. 27:39; Deut. 33:13, 28; 2 Sam. 1:21; Ps. 133:3; Prov. 3:20; Mic. 5:7; Zech. 8:12 [c]Gen. 45:18; Num. 18:12 [d]Deut. 7:13; 33:28
29 [a]Gen. 9:25; 25:23; Is. 45:14; 49:7; 60:12, 14 [b]Gen. 37:7, 10; 49:8 [c]Gen. 12:2, 3; Zeph. 2:8, 9
31 [a]Gen. 27:4 [1]*tasty*

21 Then Isaac said to Jacob, "Please
come near, that I [a]may feel you, my
son, whether you *are* really my son
Esau or not."
22 So Jacob went near to Isaac his father, and he felt him and said, "The
voice *is* Jacob's voice, but the hands
are the hands of Esau."
23 And he did not recognize him, because [a]his hands were hairy like his
brother Esau's hands; so he blessed
him.
24 Then he said, "*Are* you really my
son Esau?" He said, "I *am.*"
25 He said, "Bring *it* near to me, and
I will eat of my son's game, so [a]that
my soul may bless you." So he brought
it near to him, and he ate; and he
brought him wine, and he drank.
26 Then his father Isaac said to him,
"Come near now and kiss me, my son."
27 And he came near and [a]kissed him;
and he smelled the smell of his clothing, and blessed him and said:

"Surely, [b]the smell of my son
Is like the smell of a field
Which the LORD has blessed.
28 Therefore may [a]God give you
Of [b]the dew of heaven,
Of [c]the fatness of the earth,
And [d]plenty of grain and wine.
29 [a]Let peoples serve you,
And nations bow down to you.
Be master over your brethren,
And [b]let your mother's sons bow
down to you.
[c]Cursed *be* everyone who curses
you,
And blessed *be* those who bless
you!"

Esau's Lost Hope

30 Now it happened, as soon as Isaac
had finished blessing Jacob, and Jacob
had scarcely gone out from the presence of Isaac his father, that Esau his
brother came in from his hunting.
31 He also had made [1]savory food, and
brought it to his father, and said to his
father, "Let my father arise and
[a]eat of his son's game, that your soul
may bless me."

27:6 Rebekah wanted to ensure that her favorite son received Isaac's blessing. Strangely, in the course of this brazen deception, God's will was accomplished: Jacob was in the chosen lineage. See Mal. 1:2, 3; Rom. 9:6–13.
27:15 The availability of **the choice clothes** indicates that **Esau** and his wives lived under the same roof with Isaac and **Rebekah.** Reference to **the house** indicates that Isaac and his clan have abandoned the risks of living in tents in the open spaces for the safety of the walled town of Beersheba.
27:16–27 The tension built dramatically for **Jacob.** He uses God to further his selfish ambitions (v. 20) and exploits Isaac's blindness. See Deut. 27:18.
27:26 Isaac is still suspicious. This close proximity will enable Isaac to use his sense of smell (v. 27).
27:27–29 The blessing contains three important elements: material prosperity (v. 28), political supremacy (v. 29), and a cursing of all enemies (v. 29).
27:28 Fatness: Riches.

32 And his father Isaac said to him, "Who *are* you?" So he said, "I *am* your son, your firstborn, Esau."

33 Then Isaac trembled exceedingly, and said, "Who? Where *is* the one who hunted game and brought *it* to me? I ate all *of it* before you came, and I have blessed him—[a]*and* indeed he shall be blessed."

34 When Esau heard the words of his father, [a]he cried with an exceedingly great and bitter cry, and said to his father, "Bless me—me also, O my father!"

35 But he said, "Your brother came with deceit and has taken away your blessing."

36 And *Esau* said, [a]"Is he not rightly named [1]Jacob? For he has supplanted me these two times. He took away my birthright, and now look, he has taken away my blessing!" And he said, "Have you not reserved a blessing for me?"

37 Then Isaac answered and said to Esau, [a]"Indeed I have made him your master, and all his brethren I have given to him as servants; with [b]grain and wine I have [1]sustained him. What shall I do now for you, my son?"

38 And Esau said to his father, "Have you only one blessing, my father? Bless me—me also, O my father!" And Esau lifted up his voice [a]and wept.

39 Then Isaac his father answered and said to him:

"Behold, [a]your dwelling shall be of
the [1]fatness of the earth,
And of the dew of heaven from
above.

40 By your sword you shall live,
And [a]you shall serve your
brother;
And [b]it shall come to pass, when
you become restless,
That you shall break his yoke
from your neck."

Jacob Escapes from Esau

41 So Esau [a]hated Jacob because of the blessing with which his father blessed him, and Esau said in his heart, [b]"The days of mourning for my father [1]are at hand; [c]then I will kill my brother Jacob."

42 And the words of Esau her older son were told to Rebekah. So she sent and called Jacob her younger son, and said to him, "Surely your brother Esau [a]comforts himself concerning you *by intending* to kill you.

43 "Now therefore, my son, obey my voice: arise, flee to my brother Laban [a]in Haran.

44 "And stay with him a [a]few days, until your brother's fury turns away,

45 "until your brother's *anger turns away from you, and he forgets what you have done to him; then I will send and bring you from there. Why should I be bereaved also of you both in one day?"

46 And Rebekah said to Isaac, [a]"I am weary of my life because of the daughters of Heth; [b]if Jacob takes a wife of the daughters of Heth, like these *who are* the daughters of the land, what good will my life be to me?"

28

Then Isaac called Jacob and [a]blessed him, and [1]charged him, and said to him: [b]"You shall not take a wife from the daughters of Canaan.

2 [a]"Arise, go to [b]Padan Aram, to the house of [c]Bethuel your mother's father; and take yourself a wife from there of the daughters of [d]Laban your mother's brother.

3 "May [a]God Almighty bless you,
And make you [b]fruitful and
multiply you,
That you may be an assembly of
peoples;

4 And give you [a]the blessing of
Abraham,

33 [a]Gen. 25:23; 28:3, 4; Num. 23:20; Rom. 11:29
34 [a][Heb. 12:17]
36 [a]Gen. 25:26, 32–34 [1]*Supplanter* or *Deceitful*, lit. *One Who Takes the Heel*
37 [a]2 Sam. 8:14 [b]Gen. 27:28, 29 [1]*provided support for*
38 [a]Heb. 12:17
39 [a]Gen. 27:28; Heb. 11:20 [1]*fertility*
40 [a]Gen. 25:23; 27:29; 2 Sam. 8:14; [Obad. 18–20] [b]2 Kin. 8:20–22
41 [a]Gen. 26:27; 32:3–11; 37:4, 5, 8 [b]Gen. 50:2–4, 10 [c]Obad. 10 [1]*are soon here*
42 [a]Ps. 64:5
43 [a]Gen. 11:31; 25:20; 28:2, 5
44 [a]Gen. 31:41
45 *See WW at Judg. 10:7.
46 [a]Gen. 26:34, 35; 28:8 [b]Gen. 24:3

CHAPTER 28

1 [a]Gen. 27:33 [b]Gen. 24:3 [1]*commanded*
2 [a]Hos. 12:12 [b]Gen. 25:20 [c]Gen. 22:23 [d]Gen. 24:29; 27:43; 29:5
3 [a]Gen. 17:16; 35:11; 48:3 [b]Gen. 26:4, 24
4 [a]Gen. 12:2, 3; 22:17; Gal. 3:8

27:33 Though **Isaac** is very angry, he knows he has been fighting God's providence; **indeed he** [Jacob] **shall be blessed.**

27:34, 35 Isaac and **Esau** both recognized immediately what Jacob had done. The words of **blessing** had already been given; they could not be retracted or given again to another. The ancients knew far better than we moderns about the power of the spoken word. A blessing, a curse, a creative word, a destructive word, can all have great effects when spoken in faith. Heb. 12:16, 17 lays the responsibility on Esau's weakness (see note on 25:29–34), and Rom. 9:6–13 attributes it to God's providence.

27:37 Your master: For much of their history the descendants of **Esau** were subject to the descendants of Jacob. Finally, about 100 B.C., the Edomites were conquered by the Jews and forcibly merged into Judaism. See note on Obad. 10, 11.

27:39, 40 Isaac gave Esau as much of a blessing as he could without contradicting his previous blessing to Jacob. His descendants were to be cruel, untamed, savage people. **You shall break . . . yoke** likely refers to brief victories such as when the Edomites were a thorn to Solomon (1 Kin. 11:14–25).

27:41–46 Esau's hatred is not valid in light of his own responsibility in the matter. Rebekah's quick grasp and ingenuity sends Jacob away with blessing (28:1, 2), but at the cost of never seeing him again.

28:1 Isaac added to the blessing Jacob had received by guile. He was apparently persuaded by Rebekah.

28:2 Padan Aram: The "field" or "plain" of Aram, the homeland of the Arameans, whose language Aramaic was destined to become the dominant language of the Near East.

28:3 God Almighty: See note on 17:1, 2.

28:4 See note on 12:2, 3.

To you and your descendants
with you,
That you may inherit the land
[b]In[1] which you are a stranger,
Which God gave to Abraham."

5 So Isaac sent Jacob away, and he went to Padan Aram, to Laban the son of Bethuel the Syrian, the brother of Rebekah, the mother of Jacob and Esau.

Esau Marries Mahalath

6 Esau saw that Isaac had blessed Jacob and sent him away to Padan Aram to take himself a wife from there, *and that* as he blessed him he gave him a charge, saying, "You shall not take a wife from the daughters of Canaan,"
7 and that Jacob had obeyed his father and his mother and had gone to Padan Aram.
8 Also Esau saw [a]that the daughters of Canaan did not please his father Isaac.
9 So Esau went to Ishmael and [a]took [b]Mahalath the daughter of Ishmael, Abraham's son, [c]the sister of Nebajoth, to be his wife in addition to the wives he had.

Jacob's Vow at Bethel

10 Now Jacob [a]went out from Beersheba and went toward [b]Haran.
11 So he came to a certain place and stayed there all night, because the sun had set. And he took one of the stones of that place and put it at his head, and he lay down in that place to sleep.
12 Then he [a]dreamed, and behold, a ladder *was* set up on the earth, and its top reached to heaven; and there [b]the angels of God were ascending and descending on it.
13 [a]And behold, the LORD stood above it and said: [b]"I *am* the LORD God of Abraham your father and the God of Isaac; [c]the land on which you lie I will give to you and your descendants.
14 "Also your [a]descendants shall be as the dust of the earth; you shall spread abroad [b]to the west and the east, to the north and the south; and in you and [c]in your seed all the families of the earth shall be blessed.
15 "Behold, [a]I *am* with you and will [b]keep[1] you wherever you go, and will [c]bring you back to this land; for [d]I will not leave you [e]until I have done what I have spoken to you."
16 Then Jacob awoke from his sleep and said, "Surely the LORD is in [a]this place, and I did not know *it.*"
17 And he was afraid and said, "How awesome *is* this place! This *is* none other than the house of God, and this *is* the gate of heaven!"
18 Then Jacob rose early in the morn- 5
ing, and took the stone that he had put at his head, [a]set it up as a pillar, [b]and poured oil on top of it.
19 And he called the name of [a]that place [1]Bethel; but the name of that city had been Luz previously.
20 [a]Then Jacob made a vow, saying, "If [b]God will be with me, and keep me in this way that I am going, and give me [c]bread to eat and clothing to put on,
21 "so that [a]I come back to my father's house in peace, [b]then the LORD shall be my God.
22 "And this stone which I have set as a pillar [a]shall be God's house, [b]and of all that You give me I will surely give a [1]tenth to You."

Jacob Meets Rachel

29 So Jacob went on his journey [a]and came to the land of the people of the East.
2 And he looked, and saw a [a]well in the field; and behold, there *were* three flocks of sheep lying by it; for out of that well they watered the flocks. A large stone *was* on the well's mouth.
3 Now all the flocks would be gathered there; and they would roll the stone from the well's mouth, water the

4 [b]Gen. 17:8; 23:4; 36:7 [1]Lit. *Of your sojournings*
8 [a]Gen. 24:3; 26:34, 35; 27:46
9 [a]Gen. 26:34, 35 [b]Gen. 36:2, 3 [c]Gen. 25:13
10 [a]Hos. 12:12 [b]Gen. 12:4, 5; 27:43; 29:4
12 [a]Gen. 31:10; 41:1 [b]John 1:51
13 [a]Gen. 35:1; 48:3 [b]Gen. 26:24 [c]Gen. 13:15, 17; 26:3; 35:12
14 [a]Gen. 13:16; 22:17 [b]Gen. 13:14, 15 [c]Gen. 12:3; 18:18; 22:18; 26:4
15 [a]Gen. 26:3, 24; 31:3 [b]Gen. 48:16 [c]Gen. 35:6; 48:21 [d]Deut. 7:9; 31:6, 8 [e]Num. 23:19 [1]*protect*
16 [a]Ex. 3:5
18 [a]Gen. 31:13, 45 [b]Lev. 8:10–12
19 [a]Judg. 1:23, 26 [1]Lit. *House of God*
20 [a]Judg. 11:30 [b]Gen. 28:15 [c]1 Tim. 6:8
21 [a]Judg. 11:31 [b]Deut. 26:17
22 [a]Gen. 35:7, 14 [b]Gen. 14:20 [1]*tithe*

CHAPTER 29

1 [a]Num. 23:7
2 [a]Gen. 24:10, 11

28:5 Syrian is the Greek translation of "Aramean."

28:9 Esau's endeavor is futile for God is not working through **Ishmael.**

28:10–22 Jacob's dream emphasizes God's initiating grace as He assures him He is the Lord of the past and future. **Jacob** was the third generation to receive the promises of the Abrahamic covenant, not because he was righteous, but because of God's call and faithfulness to **Abraham.** Since Jacob had probably never heard God's voice before, **the LORD** identified Himself by His prior relationship with Abraham and **Isaac.**

28:18–22 See section 5 of Truth-In-Action at the end of Gen.

28:16–18 Jacob associated **God** with the **place** where he had the dream. He memorialized it with **the stone . . . at his head** and consecrated it with **oil.**

28:20, 21 Jacob was endeavoring to grasp the promise and to adopt **the LORD** as his **God,** by formalizing a relationship such as his father had enjoyed. His words are neither cynical nor are they a bribe.

28:22 A tenth to You: The tithe, although found in the later Mosaic Law, originated with the earlier patriarchs, Abraham (see note on 14:18–20) and Jacob. Therefore, the tithe is part of the Abrahamic covenant of grace, not merely of the Mosaic covenant of works.

sheep, and put the stone back in its
place on the well's mouth.
4 And Jacob said to them, "My brethren, where *are* you from?" And they
said, "We *are* from [a]Haran."
5 Then he said to them, "Do you
know [a]Laban the son of Nahor?" And
they said, "We know him."
6 So he said to them, [a]"Is he well?"
And they said, "*He is* well. And look,
his daughter Rachel [b]is coming with
the sheep."
7 Then he said, "Look, *it is* still
[1]high day; *it is* not time for the cattle
to be gathered together. Water the
sheep, and go and *feed *them.*"
8 But they said, "We cannot until all
the flocks are gathered together, and
they have *rolled the stone from the
well's mouth; then we water the
sheep."
9 Now while he was still speaking
with them, [a]Rachel came with her father's sheep, for she was a shep-
herdess.
10 And it came to pass, when Jacob
saw Rachel the daughter of Laban
his mother's brother, and the sheep
of Laban his mother's brother, that
Jacob went near and [a]rolled the
stone from the well's mouth, and watered the flock of Laban his mother's
brother.
11 Then Jacob [a]kissed Rachel, and
lifted up his voice and wept.
12 And Jacob told Rachel that he *was*
[a]her father's relative and that he *was*
Rebekah's son. [b]So she ran and told
her father.
13 Then it came to pass, when Laban
heard the report about Jacob his sister's son, that [a]he ran to meet him, and
embraced him and kissed him, and
brought him to his house. So he told
Laban all these things.
14 And Laban said to him, [a]"Surely
you *are* my bone and my flesh." And
he stayed with him for a month.

4 [a]Gen. 11:31; 28:10
5 [a]Gen. 24:24, 29; 28:2
6 [a]Gen. 43:27 [b]Gen. 24:11; Ex. 2:16, 17
7 [1]*early in the day* *See WW at Is. 40:11.
8 *See WW at Prov. 16:3.
9 [a]Ex. 2:16
10 [a]Ex. 2:17
11 [a]Gen. 33:4; 45:14, 15
12 [a]Gen. 13:8; 14:14, 16; 28:5 [b]Gen. 24:28
13 [a]Gen. 24:29–31; Luke 15:20
14 [a]Gen. 2:23; 37:27; Judg. 9:2; 2 Sam. 5:1; 19:12, 13
15 [a]Gen. 30:28; 31:41
17 [a]Gen. 12:11, 14; 26:7 [1]Or *weak*
18 [a]Gen. 31:41; 2 Sam. 3:14; Hos. 12:12
20 [a]Gen. 30:26; Hos. 12:12
21 [a]Judg. 15:1
22 [a]Judg. 14:10; John 2:1, 2
24 [a]Gen. 30:9, 10
25 [a]Gen. 27:35; 31:7; 1 Sam. 28:12
26 [1]Lit. *place*
27 [a]Gen. 31:41; Judg. 14:2

Jacob Marries Leah and Rachel

15 Then Laban said to Jacob, "Because
you *are* my relative, should you therefore serve me for nothing? Tell me,
[a]what *should* your wages *be?*"
16 Now Laban had two daughters: the
name of the elder *was* Leah, and the
name of the younger *was* Rachel.
17 Leah's eyes *were* [1]delicate, but Rachel was [a]beautiful of form and appearance.
18 Now Jacob loved Rachel; so he said,
[a]"I will serve you seven years for Rachel your younger daughter."
19 And Laban said, "*It is* better that
I give her to you than that I should
give her to another man. Stay with
me."
20 So Jacob [a]served seven years for
Rachel, and they seemed *only* a few
days to him because of the love he had
for her.
21 Then Jacob said to Laban, "Give *me*
my wife, for my days are fulfilled, that
I may [a]go in to her."
22 And Laban gathered together all
the men of the place and [a]made a feast.
23 Now it came to pass in the evening,
that he took Leah his daughter and
brought her to Jacob; and he went in
to her.
24 And Laban gave his maid [a]Zilpah
to his daughter Leah *as* a maid.
25 So it came to pass in the morning,
that behold, it *was* Leah. And he said
to Laban, "What is this you have done
to me? Was it not for Rachel that I
served you? Why then have you
[a]deceived me?"
26 And Laban said, "It must not be
done so in our [1]country, to give the
younger before the firstborn.
27 [a]"Fulfill her week, and we will give
you this one also for the service which
you will serve with me still another
seven years."
28 Then Jacob did so and fulfilled her

29:4 Haran: See note on 24:4.
29:9 Rachel means "Ewe."
29:11 Jacob's kiss reflected a patriarchal greeting between men and women (see v. 13). His tears were likely those of joy at finding his family.
29:13 Laban is often seen as Jacob's "match." He is obviously God's means of discipline for 20 years (31:41). Through Laban, Jacob tastes his own cunning, yet he displays more character than Esau and wins through tenacity.
29:17 Delicate ("weak," marginal reading) refers either to Leah's vision or to the fact that her eyes were not very attractive, that they lacked luster.
29:18 Such a custom is still common among the Bedouin when the young suitor has no money.
29:22–25 An ancient lamp provided little light, and the bride was always veiled, as Jacob's mother Rebekah had been (24:65). Further, **Leah** must have been eagerly cooperating in the deception. Our sins have a way of catching up to us: **Jacob** had pretended to be Esau and disguised himself thus. The whole idea of Jacob's deceiving Isaac had been his mother's, and Jacob discovered to his grief that **Laban** was just as scheming and dishonest as his younger sister, Rebekah.
29:24 A maid was provided as part of the marriage contract.
29:28 Her week was apparently the seven days of the marriage feast (see Judg. 14:17); after the feast **Jacob** received **Rachel** as his second **wife.** The difficulty of this dual marriage may have been behind the later prohibition of such marriage (Lev. 18:18).

week. So he gave him his daughter Rachel as wife also.
29 And Laban gave his maid [a]Bilhah
to his daughter Rachel as a maid.
30 Then *Jacob* also went in to Rachel,
and he also [a]loved Rachel more than
Leah. And he served with Laban
[b]still another seven years.

The Children of Jacob

31 When the LORD [a]saw that Leah *was*
[1]unloved, He [b]opened her womb; but
Rachel *was* barren.
32 So Leah conceived and bore a **son,**
and she called his name [1]Reuben; for
she said, "The LORD has surely [a]looked
on my affliction. Now therefore, my
husband will love me."

WORD WEALTH

29:32 son, *ben* (*behn*); Strong's #1121: A son, a child. The plural is not restricted to the meaning "sons," but often means "children" or "descendants" of both genders. An example is the phrase *b'nay yisrael* (literally, "sons of Israel"), generally translated "children of Israel." The root from which *ben* comes is possibly *banah,* meaning "to build up," or "to fortify." The idea is that a son is a builder of future generations.

33 Then she conceived again and bore
a son, and said, "Because the LORD has
heard that I *am* [1]unloved, He has therefore given me this *son* also." And she
called his name [2]Simeon.
34 She conceived again and bore a son,
and said, "Now this time my husband
will become attached to me, because I
have borne him three sons." Therefore
his name was called [1]Levi.
35 And she conceived again and bore
a son, and said, "Now I will *praise the
LORD." Therefore she *called his name
[a]Judah.[1] Then she stopped bearing.

KINGDOM DYNAMICS

29:35 "Judah" Means "Praise," PRAISE PATHWAY. "Judah" means "Praise," and out of this man comes a great tribe of Israel. This is one of the most significant praise verses in the Bible. Observe the following passages: 1) Jacob (49:8–12) speaks important words over Judah, giving him the highest blessing. His brothers will praise him. He will triumph over all his enemies. V. 10 says Judah will have royal authority (scepter) and legal authority (lawgiver) and will bring forth the Messiah. 2) Out of Judah, through David, comes the Christ, who in every action and detail is a praise to the Father (Luke 3:23–33). 3) The tribe of Judah (Praise) led Israel through the wilderness (Num. 2:3, 9). 4) They led in the conquest of Canaan (Judg. 1:1–19). 5) Judah is the first tribe to praise David, making him king (2 Sam. 2:1–11).

(*/Num. 21:16, 17) C.G.

29 [a]Gen. 30:3–5
30 [a]Gen. 29:17–20; Deut. 21:15–17 [b]Gen. 30:26; 31:41; Hos. 12:12
31 [a]Ps. 127:3 [b]Gen. 30:1 [1]Lit. *hated*
32 [a]Gen. 16:11; 31:42; Ex. 3:7; 4:31; Deut. 26:7; Ps. 25:18 [1]Lit. *See, a Son*
33 [1]Lit. *hated* [2]Lit. *Heard*
34 [1]Lit. *Attached*
35 [a]Gen. 49:8; Matt. 1:2 [1]Lit. *Praise* *See WW at 1 Chr. 16:7. • See WW at Jer. 33:3.

CHAPTER 30

1 [a]Gen. 16:1, 2; 29:31 [b]Gen. 37:11 [c]1 Sam. 1:5, 6; [Job 5:2]
2 [a]Gen. 16:2; 1 Sam. 1:5
3 [a]Gen. 16:2 [b]Gen. 50:23; Job 3:12 [c]Gen. 16:2, 3 [1]Lit. *be built up by her*
4 [a]Gen. 16:3, 4
6 [a]Gen. 18:25; Ps. 35:24; 43:1; Lam. 3:59 [1]Lit. *Judge* *See WW at Deut. 32:36.
8 [1]Lit. *wrestlings of God* [2]Lit. *My Wrestling*
9 [a]Gen. 30:4
11 [1]So with Qr., Syr., Tg.; Kt., LXX, Vg. *in fortune* [2]Lit. *Troop* or *Fortune*
13 [a]Prov. 31:28; Luke 1:48 [1]Lit. *Happy* *See WW at Prov. 31:28.

30

Now when Rachel saw that
[a]she bore Jacob no children, Rachel [b]envied her sister, and said to Jacob, "Give me children, [c]or else I die!"
2 And Jacob's anger was aroused
against Rachel, and he said, [a]"*Am* I in
the place of God, who has withheld
from you the fruit of the womb?"
3 So she said, "Here is [a]my maid Bilhah; go in to her, [b]and she will bear *a*
child on my knees, [c]that I also may
[1]have children by her."
4 Then she gave him Bilhah her maid
[a]as wife, and Jacob went in to her.
5 And Bilhah conceived and bore Jacob a son.
6 Then Rachel said, "God has
[a]judged* my case; and He has also
heard my voice and given me a son."
Therefore she called his name [1]Dan.
7 And Rachel's maid Bilhah conceived again and bore Jacob a second
son.
8 Then Rachel said, "With [1]great
wrestlings I have wrestled with my sister, *and* indeed I have prevailed." So
she called his name [2]Naphtali.
9 When Leah saw that she had
stopped bearing, she took Zilpah her
maid and [a]gave her to Jacob as wife.
10 And Leah's maid Zilpah bore Jacob
a son.
11 Then Leah said, [1]"A troop comes!"
So she called his name [2]Gad.
12 And Leah's maid Zilpah bore Jacob
a second son.
13 Then Leah said, "I am happy, for
the daughters [a]will call me *blessed."
So she called his name [1]Asher.
14 Now Reuben went in the days of

29:31–35 God's love for **Leah** is displayed in her becoming mother to the priestly and kingly tribes, **Levi** and **Judah.**

30:1, 2 A barren wife has reason for great shame in many cultures (see v. 23). **Rachel** implies that it is Jacob's fault; he reminds her it is God's providence (in response to Jacob's poor attitude, 29:31).

30:3 To set a child on one's **knees** was to claim it as one's own.

30:8 The **wrestlings** are obviously a carryover of the rivalry Jacob experienced with Esau. His family relationships continue to reap bitter harvest.

30:14 Mandrakes, like avocados, are considered in some

wheat harvest and found mandrakes in
the field, and brought them to his
mother Leah. Then Rachel said to
Leah, [a]"Please give me *some* of your
son's mandrakes."
15 But she said to her, [a]"*Is it* a small
matter that you have taken away my
husband? Would you take away my
son's mandrakes also?" And Rachel
said, "Therefore he will lie with you
tonight for your son's mandrakes."
16 When Jacob came out of the field
in the evening, Leah went out to meet
him and said, "You must come in to
me, for I have surely hired you with
my son's mandrakes." And he lay with
her that night.
17 And God listened to Leah, and she
conceived and bore Jacob a fifth son.
18 Leah said, "God has given me my
wages, because I have given my maid
to my husband." So she called his
name [1]Issachar.
19 Then Leah conceived again and
bore Jacob a sixth son.
20 And Leah said, "God has endowed
me *with* a good endowment; now my
husband will dwell with me, because I
have borne him six sons." So she
called his name [1]Zebulun.
21 Afterward she bore a [a]daughter,
and called her name [1]Dinah.
22 Then God [a]remembered Rachel,
and God listened to her and [b]opened
her womb.
23 And she conceived and bore a son,
and said, "God has taken away [a]my
reproach."
24 So she called his name [1]Joseph, and
said, [a]"The LORD shall add to me another son."

Jacob's Agreement with Laban

25 And it came to pass, when Rachel
had borne Joseph, that Jacob said to
Laban, [a]"Send me away, that I may go
to [b]my own place and to my country.
26 "Give *me* my wives and my children
[a]for whom I have served you, and let
me go; for you know my service which
I have done for you."
27 And Laban said to him, "Please
stay, if I have found favor in your eyes,
for [a]I have learned by experience that
the LORD has blessed me for your
sake."
28 Then he said, [a]"Name me your
wages, and I will give *it*."
29 So *Jacob* said to him, [a]"You know
how I have served you and how your
livestock has been with me.
30 "For what you had before I *came*
was little, and it has increased to a
great amount; the LORD has blessed
you [1]since my coming. And now, when
shall I also [a]provide for my own
house?"
31 So he said, "What shall I give you?"
And Jacob said, "You shall not give
me anything. If you will do this thing
for me, I will again feed and keep your
flocks:
32 "Let me pass through all your flock
today, removing from there all the
speckled and spotted sheep, and all
the brown ones among the lambs,
and the spotted and speckled among
the goats; and [a]*these* shall be my
wages.
33 "So my [a]righteousness will answer
for me in time to come, when the subject of my wages comes before you: every one that *is* not speckled and spotted
among the goats, and brown among
the lambs, will be considered stolen,
if *it is* with me."
34 And Laban said, "Oh, that it were
according to your word!"
35 So he removed that day the male
goats that were [a]speckled and spotted,
all the female goats that were speckled
and spotted, every one that had *some*
white in it, and all the brown ones
among the lambs, and gave *them* into
the hand of his sons.
36 Then he put three days' journey between himself and Jacob, and Jacob
fed the rest of Laban's flocks.
37 Now [a]Jacob took for himself rods
of green poplar and of the almond and
chestnut trees, peeled white strips in
them, and exposed the white which
was in the rods.
38 And the rods which he had peeled,
he set before the flocks in the gutters,
in the watering troughs where the
flocks came to drink, so that they

14 [a]Gen. 25:30 **15** [a][Num. 16:9, 13] **18** [1]Lit. *Wages* **20** [1]Lit. *Dwelling* **21** [a]Gen. 34:1 [1]Lit. *Judgment* **22** [a]Gen. 19:29; 1 Sam. 1:19, 20 [b]Gen. 29:31 **23** [a]1 Sam. 1:6; Is. 4:1; Luke 1:25 **24** [a]Gen. 35:16–18 [1]Lit. *He Will Add* **25** [a]Gen. 24:54, 56 [b]Gen. 18:33 **26** [a]Gen. 29:18–20, 27, 30; Hos. 12:12

27 [a]Gen. 26:24; 39:3; Is. 61:9 **28** [a]Gen. 29:15; 31:7, 41 **29** [a]Gen. 31:6, 38–40; Matt. 24:45; Titus 2:10 **30** [a][1 Tim. 5:8] [1]Lit. *at my foot* **32** [a]Gen. 31:8 **33** [a]Ps. 37:6 **35** [a]Gen. 31:9–12 **37** [a]Gen. 31:9–12

countries to be an aphrodisiac and to induce fertility. They are a fragrant plant with a small yellowish fruit. Rachel's request is obviously faithless and does not work; only God could help Rachel (v. 22).

30:22 Remembered connotes compassion.

30:27 Laban **learned by experience** or by divination (44:5) that he was **blessed** because of Jacob. He likely looked for omens.

30:32, 33 Jacob offered to take the least desirable of the animals, but those so easily identified that there could be no accusation of stealing.

30:35, 36 Laban continued to cheat **Jacob.** He tipped the scales in his favor.

30:37–42 Jacob was not practicing superstition; he was exercising faith which he somehow associated with **the rods.** God, having designed the laws of genetics, intervened and honored Jacob's faith (31:9).

should conceive when they came to
drink.
39 So the flocks conceived before the
rods, and the flocks brought forth
streaked, speckled, and spotted.
40 Then Jacob separated the lambs,
and made the flocks face toward the
streaked and all the brown in the flock
of Laban; but he put his own flocks by
themselves and did not put them with
Laban's flock.
41 And it came to pass, whenever the
stronger livestock conceived, that Jacob placed the rods before the eyes of
the livestock in the gutters, that they
might conceive among the rods.
42 But when the flocks were feeble, he
did not put *them* in; so the feebler were
Laban's and the stronger Jacob's.
43 Thus the man [a]became exceedingly
prosperous, and [b]had large flocks, female and male servants, and camels
and donkeys.

Jacob Flees from Laban

31 Now *Jacob* heard the words of
Laban's sons, saying, "Jacob
has taken away all that was our father's, and from what was our father's
he has acquired all this [a]wealth."
2 And Jacob saw the [a]countenance of
Laban, and indeed it *was* not [b]*favorable* toward him as before.
3 Then the LORD said to Jacob,
[a]"Return to the land of your fathers
and to your family, and I will [b]be with
you."
4 So Jacob sent and called Rachel and
Leah to the field, to his flock,
5 and said to them, [a]"I see your father's [1]countenance, that it *is* not *favorable* toward me as before; but the
God of my father [b]has been with me.
6 "And [a]you know that with all my
*might I have served your father.
7 "Yet your father has deceived me
and [a]changed my wages [b]ten times,
but God [c]did not allow him to hurt
me.
8 "If he said thus: [a]'The speckled
shall be your wages,' then all the flocks
bore speckled. And if he said thus: 'The
streaked shall be your wages,' then all
the flocks bore streaked.
9 "So God has [a]taken away the livestock of your father and given *them*
to me.
10 "And it happened, at the time when
the flocks conceived, that I lifted my
eyes and saw in a dream, and behold,
the rams which leaped upon the flocks
were streaked, speckled, and gray-
spotted.
11 "Then [a]the Angel of God spoke to
me in a dream, saying, 'Jacob.' And I
said, 'Here I am.'
12 "And He said, 'Lift your eyes now
and see, all the rams which leap on the
flocks *are* streaked, speckled, and
gray-spotted; for [a]I have seen all that
Laban is doing to you.
13 'I *am* the God of Bethel, [a]where you
anointed the pillar *and* where you
made a vow to Me. Now [b]arise, get out
of this land, and return to the land of
your family.' "
14 Then Rachel and Leah answered
and said to him, [a]"Is there still any portion or inheritance for us in our father's
house?
15 "Are we not considered strangers
by him? For [a]he has sold us, and also
completely consumed our money.
16 "For all these riches which God has
taken from our father are *really* ours
and our children's; now then, whatever
God has said to you, do it."
17 Then Jacob rose and set his sons
and his wives on camels.
18 And he carried away all his livestock and all his possessions which he
had gained, his acquired livestock
which he had gained in Padan Aram,
to go to his father Isaac in the land of
[a]Canaan.
19 Now Laban had gone to shear his
sheep, and Rachel had stolen the
[a]household[1] idols that were her father's.
20 And Jacob stole away, unknown to
Laban the Syrian, in that he did not
tell him that he intended to flee.
21 So he fled with all that he had. He
arose and crossed the river, and
[a]headed[1] toward the mountains of
Gilead.

Laban Pursues Jacob

22 And Laban was told on the third
day that Jacob had fled.

43 [a]Gen. 12:16; 30:30 [b]Gen. 13:2; 24:35; 26:13, 14

CHAPTER 31

1 [a]Ps. 49:16
2 [a]Gen. 4:5 [b]Deut. 28:54
3 [a]Gen. 28:15, 20, 21; 32:9 [b]Gen. 46:4
5 [a]Gen. 31:2, 3 [b]Gen. 21:22; 28:13, 15; 31:29, 42, 53; Is. 41:10; Heb. 13:5 [1]Lit. *face*
6 [a]Gen. 30:29; 31:38–41 *See WW at Deut. 8:18.
7 [a]Gen. 29:25; 31:41 [b]Num. 14:22; Neh. 4:12; Job 19:3; Zech. 8:23 [c]Gen. 15:1; 20:6; 31:29; Job 1:10; Ps. 37:28; 105:14
8 [a]Gen. 30:32
9 [a]Gen. 31:1, 16
11 [a]Gen. 16:7–11; 22:11, 15; 31:13; 48:16
12 [a]Gen. 31:42; Ex. 3:7; Ps. 139:3; Eccl. 5:8
13 [a]Gen. 28:16–22; 35:1, 6, 15 [b]Gen. 31:3; 32:9
14 [a]Gen. 2:24
15 [a]Gen. 29:15, 20, 23, 27; Neh. 5:8
18 [a]Gen. 17:8; 33:18; 35:27
19 [a]Gen. 31:30, 34; 35:2; Judg. 17:5; 1 Sam. 19:13; Hos. 3:4 [1]Heb. *teraphim*
21 [a]Gen. 46:28; 2 Kin. 12:17; Luke 9:51, 53 [1]Lit. *set his face toward*

30:43 God's blessings are always able to exceed man's defrauding.
31:7 Ten was a round number equal to "time after time."
31:13 Jacob's vow is honored by God.
31:19 Household idols: Laban spoke of them as his "gods" (v. 30). These *teraphim*, small figurines of the family gods, held great meaning for the heirs. According to the ancient law around Haran, the sons, particularly the eldest, had the privilege of inheriting the family "gods," as well as all the property that went with them. **Rachel** stole them either to ridicule her father's religion (vv. 14–16), to lay claim to the inheritance, or to remain attached to her native religion.
31:21 The river is the Euphrates. **Gilead** was east of the Jordan and south of the Sea of Galilee.

23 Then he took [a]his brethren with him and pursued him for seven days' journey, and he overtook him in the mountains of Gilead.

24 But God [a]had come to Laban the Syrian in a dream by night, and said to him, "Be careful that you [b]speak to Jacob neither good nor bad."

25 So Laban overtook Jacob. Now Jacob had pitched his tent in the mountains, and Laban with his brethren pitched in the mountains of Gilead.

26 And Laban said to Jacob: "What have you done, that you have stolen away unknown to me, and [a]carried away my daughters like captives *taken* with the sword?

27 "Why did you flee away secretly, and steal away from me, and not tell me; for I might have sent you away with joy and songs, with timbrel and harp?

28 "And you did not allow me [a]to kiss my sons and my daughters. Now [b]you have done foolishly in *so* doing.

29 "It is in my power to do you harm, but the [a]God of your father spoke to me [b]last night, saying, 'Be careful that you speak to Jacob neither good nor bad.'

30 "And now you have surely gone because you greatly long for your father's house, *but* why did you [a]steal my gods?"

31 Then Jacob answered and said to Laban, "Because I was [a]afraid, for I said, 'Perhaps you would take your daughters from me by force.'

32 "With whomever you find your gods, [a]do not let him live. In the presence of our brethren, identify what I have of yours and take *it* with you." For Jacob did not know that Rachel had stolen them.

33 And Laban went into Jacob's tent, into Leah's tent, and into the two maids' tents, but he did not find *them*. Then he went out of Leah's tent and entered Rachel's tent.

34 Now Rachel had taken the [1]household idols, put them in the camel's saddle, and sat on them. And Laban [2]searched all about the tent but did not find *them*.

35 And she said to her father, "Let it not displease my lord that I cannot [a]rise before you, for the manner of women *is* with me." And he searched but did not find the [1]household idols.

36 Then Jacob was angry and rebuked Laban, and Jacob answered and said to Laban: "What *is* my [1]trespass? What *is* my sin, that you have so hotly pursued me?

37 "Although you have searched all my things, what part of your household things have you found? Set *it* here before my brethren and your brethren, that they may judge between us both!

38 "These twenty years I *have been* with you; your ewes and your female goats have not miscarried their young, and I have not eaten the rams of your flock.

39 [a]"That which was torn *by beasts* I did not bring to you; I bore the loss of it. [b]You required it from my hand, *whether* stolen by day or stolen by night.

40 "*There* I was! In the day the drought consumed me, and the frost by night, and my sleep departed from my eyes.

41 "Thus I have been in your house twenty years; I [a]served you fourteen years for your two daughters, and six years for your flock, and [b]you have changed my wages ten times.

42 [a]"Unless the God of my father, the God of Abraham and [b]the Fear of Isaac, had been with me, surely now you would have sent me away empty-handed. [c]God has seen my affliction and the labor of my hands, and [d]rebuked *you* last night."

Laban's Covenant with Jacob

43 And Laban answered and said to Jacob, "*These* daughters *are* my daughters, and *these* children *are* my children, and *this* flock *is* my flock; all that you see *is* mine. But what can I do this day to these my daughters or

23 [a]Gen. 13:8
24 [a]Gen. 20:3; 31:29; 46:2–4; Job 33:15; Matt. 1:20 [b]Gen. 24:50; 31:7, 29
26 [a]1 Sam. 30:2
28 [a]Gen. 31:55; Ruth 1:9, 14; 1 Kin. 19:20; Acts 20:37 [b]1 Sam. 13:13
29 [a]Gen. 28:13; 31:5, 24, 42, 53 [b]Gen. 31:24
30 [a]Gen. 31:19; Josh. 24:2; Judg. 17:5; 18:24
31 [a]Gen. 26:7; 32:7, 11
32 [a]Gen. 44:9
34 [1]Heb. *teraphim* [2]Lit. *felt*
35 [a]Ex. 20:12; Lev. 19:32 [1]Heb. *teraphim*
36 [1]*transgression*
39 [a]Ex. 22:10 [b]Ex. 22:10–13
41 [a]Gen. 29:20, 27–30 [b]Gen. 31:7
42 [a]Gen. 31:5, 29, 53; Ps. 124:1, 2 [b]Gen. 31:53; Is. 8:13 [c]Gen. 29:32; Ex. 3:7 [d]Gen. 31:24, 29; 1 Chr. 12:17

31:24 Neither good nor bad is an idiomatic expression meaning not to speak any threats.

31:25 Jacob and his retinue must have been terrified, for **Laban**'s sons and servants were obviously fully armed and eager for a fight. The sons especially wanted to regain their father's idols.

31:35 The manner of women: Rachel claimed to be menstruating (see Lev. 15) in order to remain seated. Jacob was obviously unaware of Rachel's theft; otherwise, he would not have made so dangerous an oath in v. 32.

31:39 Hurrian law required that the owner, not the shepherd, bear these accidental losses. Laban obeyed the law only when it suited him.

31:41 Ten times: See note on 31:7.

31:42 The Fear of Isaac is seen by most translators as an early name of Yahweh. It means He is the God who inspired awe in Isaac. See Is. 8:13.

31:43–55 The **covenant** makes Jacob's departure much more peaceful. It also shows that Jacob should have trusted God to intervene rather than fleeing in fear (v. 31). Open communication is better than scheming.

to their children whom they have
borne?
44 "Now therefore, come, [a]let us make
a [1]covenant,* [b]you and I, and let it be
a witness between you and me."
45 So Jacob [a]took a stone and set it
up *as* a pillar.
46 Then Jacob said to his brethren,
"Gather stones." And they took stones
and made a heap, and they ate there
on the heap.
47 Laban called it [1]Jegar Sahadutha,
but Jacob called it [2]Galeed.
48 And Laban said, [a]"This heap *is* a
witness between you and me this day."
Therefore its name was called Galeed,
49 also [a]Mizpah,[1] because he said,
"May the LORD *watch between you
and me when we are absent one from
another.
50 "If you afflict my daughters, or if
you take *other* wives besides my
daughters, *although* no man *is* with
us—see, God *is* witness between you
and me!"
51 Then Laban said to Jacob, "Here is
this heap and here is *this* pillar, which
I have placed between you and me.
52 "This heap *is* a witness, and *this* pillar *is* a witness, that I will not pass beyond this heap to you, and you will not
pass beyond this heap and this pillar
to me, for harm.
53 "The God of Abraham, the God of
Nahor, and the God of their father
[a]judge between us." And Jacob [b]swore
by [c]the [1]Fear of his father Isaac.
54 Then Jacob offered a *sacrifice on
the mountain, and called his brethren
to eat bread. And they ate bread and
stayed all night on the mountain.
55 And early in the morning Laban
arose, and [a]kissed his sons and daughters and [b]blessed them. Then Laban
departed and [c]returned to his place.

Esau Comes to Meet Jacob

32 So Jacob went on his way, and
[a]the angels of God met him.
2 When Jacob saw them, he said,
"This *is* God's [a]camp." And he called
the name of that place [1]Mahanaim.
3 Then Jacob sent messengers before

44 [a]Gen. 21:27, 32; 26:28 [b]Josh. 24:27 [1]*treaty* *See WW at Gen. 17:7.
45 [a]Gen. 28:18; 35:14; Josh. 24:26, 27
47 [1]Lit., in Aram., *Heap of Witness* [2]Lit., in Heb., *Heap of Witness*
48 [a]Josh. 24:27
49 [a]Judg. 10:17; 11:29; 1 Sam. 7:5, 6 [1]Lit. *Watch* *See WW at Hos. 9:8.
53 [a]Gen. 16:5 [b]Gen. 21:23 [c]Gen. 31:42 [1]A reference to God
54 *See WW at Deut. 16:2.
55 [a]Gen. 29:11, 13; 31:28, 43 [b]Gen. 28:1 [c]Gen. 18:33; 30:25; Num. 24:25

CHAPTER 32

1 [a]Num. 22:31; 2 Kin. 6:16, 17; [Ps. 34:7; 91:1; Heb. 1:14]
2 [a]Josh. 5:14; Ps. 103:21; 148:2; Luke 2:13 [1]Lit. *Double Camp*
3 [a]Gen. 14:6; 33:14, 16 [b]Gen. 25:30; 36:6–9; Deut. 2:5; Josh. 24:4 [1]Lit. *field*
4 [a]Prov. 15:1
5 [a]Gen. 30:43 [b]Gen. 33:8, 15
6 [a]Gen. 33:1
7 [a]Gen. 32:11; 35:3
8 [1]Lit. *strikes*
9 [a][Ps. 50:15] [b]Gen. 28:13; 31:42 [c]Gen. 31:3, 13
10 [a]Gen. 24:27 [b]Job 8:7
11 [a]Ps. 59:1, 2 [b]Hos. 10:14 [1]Lit. *strike*
12 [a]Gen. 28:13–15 [b]Gen. 22:17
13 [a]Gen. 43:11 [1]*he had received*

him to Esau his brother [a]in the land
of Seir, [b]the [1]country of Edom.
4 And he commanded them, saying,
[a]"Speak thus to my lord Esau, 'Thus
your servant Jacob says: "I have dwelt
with Laban and stayed there until now.
5 [a]"I have oxen, donkeys, flocks, and
male and female servants; and I have
sent to tell my lord, that [b]I may find
favor in your sight." ' "
6 Then the messengers returned to
Jacob, saying, "We came to your
brother Esau, and [a]he also is coming
to meet you, and four hundred men *are*
with him."
7 So Jacob was greatly afraid and
[a]distressed; and he divided the people
that *were* with him, and the flocks and
herds and camels, into two companies.
8 And he said, "If Esau comes to the
one company and [1]attacks it, then the
other company which is left will escape."
9 [a]Then Jacob said, [b]"O God of my
father Abraham and God of my father
Isaac, the LORD [c]who said to me, 'Return to your country and to your family, and I will deal well with you':
10 "I am not worthy of the least of all
the [a]mercies and of all the truth which
You have shown Your servant; for I
crossed over this Jordan with [b]my
staff, and now I have become two companies.
11 [a]"Deliver me, I pray, from the hand
of my brother, from the hand of Esau;
for I fear him, lest he come and
[1]attack me *and* [b]the mother with the
children.
12 "For [a]You said, 'I will surely treat
you well, and make your descendants
as the [b]sand of the sea, which cannot
be numbered for multitude.' "
13 So he lodged there that same night,
and took what [1]came to his hand as
[a]a present for Esau his brother:
14 two hundred female goats and
twenty male goats, two hundred ewes
and twenty rams,
15 thirty milk camels with their colts,
forty cows and ten bulls, twenty female
donkeys and ten foals.
16 Then he delivered *them* to the hand
of his servants, every drove by itself,

31:45 A stone . . . a pillar: See note on 28:16–18.
31:46 A meal together was one way to establish a covenant.
31:52 The **heap . . . pillar** served as a type of boundary marker as well as a memorial.
32:1, 2 Jacob still had his greatest challenge ahead, knowing that he must face the brother he had cheated 20 years earlier, so the **angels of God** were reassuring.
32:6 Esau was bringing a sizable force; although the reason is not given, it apparently was not to attack as **Jacob** feared.
32:13 Jacob quickly selected from his wealth what he thought would be an appropriate **present for Esau,** trying to gain Esau's favor. He again lacks faith in God's promise, a prime example of the far-reaching implications of his treachery some 20 years earlier.
32:16 Pass over the Jabbok River (see v. 22), which flows into the Jordan River from the east, about 15 miles north of the Dead Sea.

and said to his servants, "Pass over before me, and put some distance between successive droves."
17 And he commanded the first one,
saying, "When Esau my brother meets
you and asks you, saying, 'To whom
do you belong, and where are you
going? Whose *are* these in front of
you?'
18 "then you shall say, 'They *are* your
servant Jacob's. It *is* a present sent to
my lord Esau; and behold, he also *is*
behind us.' "
19 So he commanded the second, the
third, and all who followed the droves,
saying, "In this manner you shall
speak to Esau when you find him;
20 "and also say, 'Behold, your servant
Jacob *is* behind us.' " For he said, "I
will [a]appease* him with the present
that goes before me, and afterward I
will see his face; perhaps he will accept
me."
21 So the present went on over before
him, but he himself lodged that night
in the camp.

Wrestling with God

22 And he arose that night and took
his two wives, his two female servants,
and his eleven sons, [a]and crossed over
the ford of Jabbok.
23 He took them, sent them [1]over the
brook, and sent over what he had.
24 Then Jacob was left alone; and
[a]a Man wrestled with him until the
[1]breaking of day.
25 Now when He saw that He did not
prevail against him, He [1]touched the
socket of his hip; and [a]the socket of
Jacob's hip was out of joint as He wrestled with him.
26 And [a]He said, "Let Me go, for the
day breaks." But he said, [b]"I will not
let You go unless You bless me!"
27 So He said to him, "What *is* your
name?" He said, "Jacob."
28 And He said, [a]"Your name shall no
longer be called Jacob, but [1]Israel; for
you have [b]struggled with God and
[c]with men, and have prevailed."
29 Then Jacob asked, saying, "Tell *me*
Your name, I pray." And He said,
[a]"Why *is* it *that* you ask about My
name?" And He [b]blessed him there.
30 So Jacob called the name of the
place [1]Peniel: "For [a]I have seen God
face to face, and my life is preserved."
31 Just as he crossed over [1]Penuel the
sun rose on him, and he limped on his
hip.
32 Therefore to this day the children
of Israel do not eat the muscle that
shrank, which *is* on the hip socket, because He [1]touched the socket of Jacob's hip in the muscle that shrank.

20 [a][Prov. 21:14] *See WW at Num. 15:25.
22 [a]Num. 21:24; Deut. 3:16; Josh. 12:2
23 [1]*across*
24 [a]Josh. 5:13–15; Hos. 12:2–4 [1]*dawn*
25 [a]Matt. 26:41; 2 Cor. 12:7 [1]*struck*
26 [a]Luke 24:28 [b]Hos. 12:4
28 [a]Gen. 35:10; 1 Kin. 18:31; 2 Kin. 17:34 [b]Hos. 12:3, 4 [c]Gen. 25:31; 27:33 [1]Lit. *Prince with God*
29 [a]Judg. 13:17, 18 [b]Gen. 35:9
30 [a]Gen. 16:13; Ex. 24:10, 11; 33:20; Num. 12:8; Deut. 5:24; Judg. 6:22; Is. 6:5; [Matt. 5:8; 1 Cor. 13:12] [1]Lit. *Face of God*
31 [1]Lit. *Face of God;* same as *Peniel,* v. 30
32 [1]*struck*

32:24–32 This is one of the Bible's mysterious narratives. The **Man** is identified by Hosea as an angel (Hos. 12:4). The importance of the narrative is Jacob's willingness to contend with God at his time of desperate need. He knows God has willed to bless him (v. 12) and he will settle for nothing less than his full inheritance (v. 26). His contending tenacity causes him to again prevail (v. 29; see note on 29:13).

32:27 The man obviously knew Jacob's **name.** He was made to say it because of its meaning—"Supplanter" or "Deceiver." He must acknowledge his weakness before he is transformed.

32:28 **Israel** can mean "Prince with God" (marginal reading), "He Strives with God," or "May God Persevere." In spite of his character weaknesses, God commends him for his prevailing attitude; he is a fighter. As such, Hosea sees him as a model to be emulated whenever one is facing difficulty or a need for character transformation (Hos. 12:2–6).

32:31 **He limped:** This symbolizes that character transformation costs God's people in terms of ego death. Although the emphasis is Jacob's contending (v. 28), his personal transformation is an important secondary element.

32:32 This custom is never again mentioned in Scripture, but it does appear in later rabbinic writings (after A.D. 150).

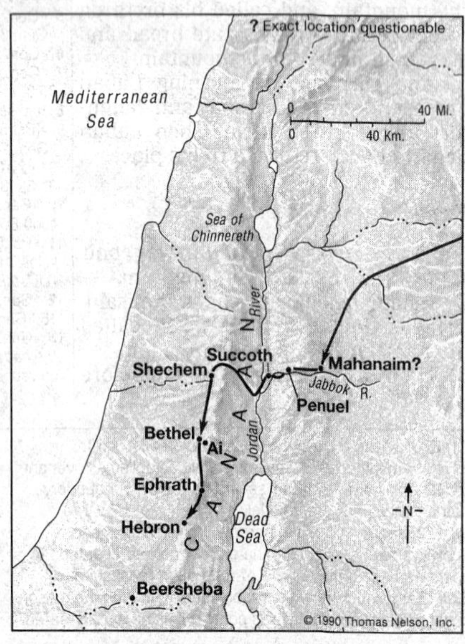

Jacob Returns to Canaan. After 20 years in northern Mesopotamia, Jacob returned to Canaan. On the way he encountered God face to face at Penuel (Gen. 32:30, 31).

Jacob and Esau Meet

33 Now Jacob lifted his eyes and
looked, and there, [a]Esau was
coming, and with him were four hundred men. So he divided the children
among Leah, Rachel, and the two
maidservants.
2 And he put the maidservants and
their children in front, Leah and her
children behind, and Rachel and Joseph last.
3 Then he crossed over before them
and [a]bowed himself to the ground
seven times, until he came near to his
brother.
4 [a]But Esau ran to meet him, and embraced him, [b]and fell on his neck and
kissed him, and they wept.
5 And he lifted his eyes and saw the
women and children, and said, "Who
are these with you?" So he said, "The
children [a]whom God has *graciously
given your servant."
6 Then the maidservants came near,
they and their children, and bowed
down.
7 And Leah also came near with her
children, and they bowed down. Afterward Joseph and Rachel came near,
and they bowed down.
8 Then Esau said, "What *do* you
mean by [a]all this company which I
met?" And he said, "*These are* [b]to find
favor in the sight of my lord."
9 But Esau said, "I have enough, my
brother; keep what you have for yourself."
10 And Jacob said, "No, please, if
I have now found favor in your
sight, then receive my present from my
hand, inasmuch as I [a]have seen your
face as though I had seen the face
of God, and you were pleased with
me.
11 "Please, take [a]my blessing that is
brought to you, because God has dealt
[b]graciously with me, and because I
have [1]enough." [c]So he urged him, and
he took *it*.
12 Then Esau said, "Let us take our
journey; let us go, and I will go before
you."
13 But Jacob said to him, "My lord
knows that the children *are* weak, and
the flocks and herds which are nursing
are with me. And if the men should
drive them hard one day, all the flock
will die.
14 "Please let my lord go on ahead before his servant. I will lead on slowly
at a pace which the livestock that go
before me, and the children, [1]are able
to endure, until I come to my lord
[a]in Seir."
15 And Esau said, "Now let me leave
with you *some* of the people who *are*
with me." But he said, "What need is
there? [a]Let me find favor in the sight
of my lord."
16 So Esau returned that day on his
way to Seir.
17 And Jacob journeyed to [a]Succoth,
built himself a house, and made
[1]booths for his livestock. Therefore the
name of the place is called [2]Succoth.

Jacob Comes to Canaan

18 Then Jacob came [1]safely to [a]the city
of [b]Shechem, which *is* in the land of
Canaan, when he came from Padan
Aram; and he pitched his tent before
the city.
19 And [a]he bought the parcel of
[1]land, where he had pitched his tent,
from the children of Hamor, Shechem's father, for one hundred pieces
of money.
20 Then he erected an altar there and
called it [a]El[1] Elohe Israel.

The Dinah Incident

34 Now [a]Dinah the daughter of
Leah, whom she had borne to
Jacob, went out to see the daughters
of the land.
2 And when Shechem the son of Hamor the Hivite, prince of the country,
saw her, he [a]took her and lay with her,
and violated her.

CHAPTER 33

1 [a]Gen. 32:6 **3** [a]Gen. 18:2; 42:6 **4** [a]Gen. 32:28 [b]Gen. 45:14, 15 **5** [a]Gen. 48:9; [Ps. 127:3]; Is. 8:18 *See WW at Mal. 1:9. **8** [a]Gen. 32:13–16 [b]Gen. 32:5 **10** [a]Gen. 43:3; 2 Sam. 3:13; 14:24, 28, 32 **11** [a]Judg. 1:15; 1 Sam. 25:27; 30:26 [b]Gen. 30:43; Ex. 33:19 [c]2 Kin. 5:23 [1]Lit. *all*

14 [a]Gen. 32:3; 36:8 [1]*can stand* **15** [a]Gen. 34:11; 47:25; Ruth 2:13 **17** [a]Josh. 13:27; Judg. 8:5; Ps. 60:6 [1]*shelters* [2]Lit. *Booths* **18** [a]John 3:23 [b]Gen. 12:6; 35:4; Josh. 24:1; Judg. 9:1; Ps. 60:6 [1]Or *to Shalem, a city of* **19** [a]Josh. 24:32; John 4:5 [1]Lit. *the field* **20** [a]Gen. 35:7 [1]Lit. *God, the God of Israel*

CHAPTER 34

1 [a]Gen. 30:21 **2** [a]Gen. 20:2

33:3 Seven times: This typical Eastern response represents complete submission.

33:4 Esau's response is such an incredible example of grace that some see it as the example behind the actions of the prodigal's father (Luke 15:20).

33:10 Jacob was so relieved of his anxiety that he described his feelings as those of having **seen the face of God** without being struck dead.

33:11 He took *it* shows Esau's goodwill; it also seals the reconciliation.

33:17 Instead of following Esau south to Seir (Edom), as promised, **Jacob** doubled back over the Jabbok River (where he had temporarily left the bulk of his flocks) and remained there for an extended period. It appears he is still somewhat devious.

33:18, 19 Jacob wished to maintain a discreet distance from Esau, so he moved westward across the Jordan River and settled in **Canaan. Shechem** was between Mt. Ebal and Mt. Gerizim in the central highlands.

34:2 The Hivite: We know nothing about the Hivites outside the Bible. They may be the same as the Horites. **Violated her** means "forcibly raped her," although Dinah may have consented (v. 26).

3 His soul [1]was strongly attracted to Dinah the daughter of Jacob, and he loved the young woman and spoke [2]kindly to the young woman.

4 So Shechem [a]spoke to his father Hamor, saying, "Get me this young woman as a wife."

5 And Jacob heard that he had defiled Dinah his daughter. Now his sons were with his livestock in the field; so Jacob [a]held[1] his peace until they came.

6 Then Hamor the father of Shechem went out to Jacob to speak with him.

7 And the sons of Jacob came in from the field when they heard *it;* and the men were grieved and very angry, because he [a]had done a disgraceful thing in Israel by lying with Jacob's daughter, [b]a thing which ought not to be done.

8 But Hamor spoke with them, saying, "The soul of my son Shechem longs for your daughter. Please give her to him as a wife.

9 "And make marriages with us; give your daughters to us, and take our daughters to yourselves.

10 "So you shall dwell with us, and the land shall be before you. Dwell and trade in it, and acquire possessions for yourselves in it."

11 Then Shechem said to her father and her brothers, "Let me find favor in your eyes, and whatever you say to me I will give.

12 "Ask me ever so much [a]dowry[1] and gift, and I will give according to what you say to me; but give me the young woman as a wife."

13 But the sons of Jacob answered Shechem and Hamor his father, and spoke [a]deceitfully, because he had defiled Dinah their sister.

14 And they said to them, "We cannot do this thing, to give our sister to one who is [a]uncircumcised, for [b]that *would be* a reproach to us.

15 "But on this *condition* we will consent to you: If you will become as we *are,* if every male of you is circumcised,

16 "then we will give our daughters to you, and we will take your daughters to us; and we will dwell with you, and we will become one people.

17 "But if you will not heed us and be circumcised, then we will take our daughter and be gone."

18 And their words pleased Hamor and Shechem, Hamor's son.

19 So the young man did not delay to do the thing, because he *delighted in Jacob's daughter. He *was* [a]more honorable than all the household of his father.

20 And Hamor and Shechem his son came to the [a]gate of their city, and spoke with the men of their city, saying:

21 "These men *are* at peace with us. Therefore let them dwell in the land and trade in it. For indeed the land *is* large enough for them. Let us take their daughters to us as wives, and let us give them our daughters.

22 "Only on this *condition* will the men consent to dwell with us, to be one people: if every male among us is circumcised as they *are* circumcised.

23 "*Will* not their livestock, their property, and every animal of theirs *be* ours? Only let us consent to them, and they will dwell with us."

24 And all who went out of the gate of his city heeded Hamor and Shechem his son; every male was circumcised, all who [a]went out of the gate of his city.

25 Now it came to pass on the third day, when they were in pain, that two of the sons of Jacob, [a]Simeon and Levi, Dinah's brothers, each took his sword and came *boldly upon the city and killed all the males.

26 And they [a]killed Hamor and Shechem his son with the edge of the sword, and took Dinah from Shechem's house, and went out.

27 The sons of Jacob came upon the slain, and plundered the city, because their sister had been defiled.

28 They took their sheep, their oxen, and their donkeys, what *was* in the city and what *was* in the field,

29 and all their wealth. All their little ones and their wives they took captive; and they plundered even all that *was* in the houses.

30 Then Jacob said to Simeon and

3 [1]Lit. *clung to* [2]*tenderly*
4 [a]Judg. 14:2
5 [a]2 Sam. 13:22 [1]*kept silent*
7 [a]Deut. 22:20–30; Josh. 7:15; Judg. 20:6 [b]Deut. 23:17; 2 Sam. 13:12
12 [a]Ex. 22:16, 17; Deut. 22:29 [1]*bride-price*
13 [a]Gen. 31:7; Ex. 8:29
14 [a]Ex. 12:48 [b]Josh. 5:2–9
19 [a]1 Chr. 4:9 *See WW at Ps. 112:1.
20 [a]Gen. 19:1; 23:10; Ruth 4:1, 11; 2 Sam. 15:2
24 [a]Gen. 23:10, 18
25 [a]Gen. 29:33, 34; 42:24; 49:5–7 *See WW at Deut. 33:12.
26 [a]Gen. 49:5, 6

34:7 A disgraceful thing in Israel is a very strong Hebrew expression for a sin that has injured the entire family or community, found a number of times later in the OT. See Josh. 7:15.

34:13 Jacob's sons carried on his deceitful nature. Nonetheless, God used their plan as a form of judgment against the sinful Hivites (v. 7).

34:14 The Hivites were perhaps somehow related to the Philistines, the only other Middle Easterners who did not practice circumcision.

34:21–24 The Hivites regarded circumcision as a minor price for an alliance that would potentially increase their wealth and power.

34:27–29 Simeon, Levi, and their armed men left nothing alive in Shechem, and with their brothers stole everything of value, even **their little ones and their wives.** See note on 48:22.

34:30, 31 This cruel act ultimately cost **Simeon and Levi**

Levi, [a]"You have [b]troubled me [c]by making me obnoxious among the inhabitants of the land, among the Canaanites and the Perizzites; [d]and since I *am* few in number, they will gather themselves together against me and kill me. I shall be destroyed, my household and I."

31 But they said, "Should he treat our sister like a harlot?"

Jacob's Return to Bethel

35 Then God said to Jacob, "Arise, go up to [a]Bethel and dwell there; and make an altar there to God, [b]who appeared to you [c]when you fled from the face of Esau your brother."

2 And Jacob said to his [a]household and to all who *were* with him, "Put away [b]the foreign gods that *are* among you, [c]purify yourselves, and change your garments.

3 "Then let us arise and go up to Bethel; and I will make an altar there to God, [a]who answered me in the day of my distress [b]and has been with me in the way which I have gone."

4 So they gave Jacob all the foreign [1]gods which *were* in their hands, and the [a]earrings which *were* in their ears; and Jacob hid them under [b]the terebinth tree which *was* by Shechem.

5 And they journeyed, and [a]the terror of God was upon the cities that *were* all around them, and they did not pursue the sons of Jacob.

6 So Jacob came to [a]Luz (that *is*, Bethel), which *is* in the land of Canaan, he and all the people who *were* with him.

7 And he [a]built an altar there and called the place [1]El Bethel, because [b]there God appeared to him when he fled from the face of his brother.

8 Now [a]Deborah, Rebekah's nurse, died, and she was buried below Bethel under the terebinth tree. So the name of it was called [1]Allon Bachuth.

9 Then [a]God appeared to Jacob again, when he came from Padan Aram, and [b]blessed him.

10 And God said to him, "Your name *is* Jacob; [a]your name shall not be called Jacob anymore, [b]but Israel shall be your name." So He called his name Israel.

11 Also God said to him: [a]"I *am* God Almighty. [b]Be fruitful and multiply; [c]a nation and a company of nations shall proceed from you, and kings shall come from your body.

12 "The [a]land which I gave Abraham and Isaac I give to you; and to your descendants after you I give this land."

13 Then God [a]went[1] up from him in the place where He talked with him.

14 So Jacob [a]set up a pillar in the place where He talked with him, a pillar of stone; and he poured a drink offering on it, and he poured oil on it.

15 And Jacob called the name of the place where God spoke with him, [a]Bethel.

Death of Rachel

16 Then they journeyed from Bethel. And when there was but a little distance to go to Ephrath, Rachel labored *in childbirth,* and she had hard labor.

17 Now it came to pass, when she was in hard labor, that the midwife said to her, "Do not fear; [a]you will have this son also."

18 And so it was, as her soul was departing (for she died), that she called his name [1]Ben-Oni; but his father called him [2]Benjamin.

19 So [a]Rachel died and was buried on the way to [b]Ephrath (that *is*, Bethlehem).

20 And Jacob set a pillar on her grave, which *is* the pillar of Rachel's grave [a]to this day.

30 [a]Gen. 49:6 [b]Josh. 7:25 [c]Ex. 5:21 [d]Deut. 4:27

CHAPTER 35

1 [a]Gen. 28:19; 31:13 [b]Gen. 28:13 [c]Gen. 27:43
2 [a]Josh. 24:15 [b]Josh. 24:2, 14, 23 [c]Ex. 19:10, 14
3 [a]Gen. 32:7, 24 [b]Gen. 28:15, 20; 31:3, 42
4 [a]Hos. 2:13 [b]Josh. 24:26 [1]*idols*
5 [a]Ex. 15:16; 23:27
6 [a]Gen. 28:19, 22; 48:3
7 [a]Eccl. 5:4 [b]Gen. 28:13 [1]Lit. *God of the House of God*
8 [a]Gen. 24:59 [1]Lit. *Terebinth of Weeping*
9 [a]Josh. 5:13 [b]Gen. 32:29
10 [a]Gen. 17:5 [b]Gen. 32:28
11 [a]Ex. 6:3 [b]Gen. 9:1, 7 [c]Gen. 17:5, 6, 16; 28:3; 48:4
12 [a]Gen. 12:7; 13:15; 26:3, 4; 28:13; 48:4
13 [a]Gen. 17:22; 18:33 [1]*departed*
14 [a]Gen. 28:18, 19; 31:45
15 [a]Gen. 28:19
17 [a]Gen. 30:24
18 [1]Lit. *Son of My Sorrow* [2]Lit. *Son of the Right Hand*
19 [a]Gen. 48:7 [b]Mic. 5:2
20 [a]1 Sam. 10:2

their father's blessing (see 49:5–7). **Jacob** was terrified of the expected vengeance by the neighboring communities, but his two sons were impenitent.

35:2–4 Jacob knew the truth that would ultimately be codified in the second Commandment, that God deeply hates images or pictures of Himself or of any other god. The prophets later spoke out harshly against the use of images in Israel. **Change your garments:** This act was intended to signify a repentant change of heart, as should Christian baptism, yet **the foreign gods** were hidden beneath a carefully identified **terebinth tree.** Thus paganism remained deeply rooted in their hearts.

35:4 The foreign gods: See note on 31:19. **The earrings** were apparently charms.

35:5 The terror of God may have been a natural disaster, a plague, or simply a great fear of **the sons of Jacob.** The expression normally indicated some kind of catastrophe attributed to the Lord. God continued to protect His chosen ones.

35:6, 7 Bethel: Again, **Jacob** worshiped his **God** at the spot where he had met Him many years before. See 28:11–22.

35:9–15 God reaffirmed the Abrahamic covenant for **Jacob,** and affirmed his new name, **Israel,** as well. See note on 32:28. From this point on the narrative interchanges "Jacob" and "Israel."

35:11 God Almighty: See note on 17:1, 2.

35:14 See note on 28:16–18.

35:20 To this day indicates that this clause was written centuries later. **Rachel's grave** is recorded as still having been there in Saul's time (see 1 Sam. 10:2), and the traditional place between Jerusalem and Bethlehem is the present site of a Crusader church.

21 Then Israel journeyed and pitched
his tent beyond [a]the tower of Eder.
22 And it happened, when Israel dwelt
in that land, that Reuben went and
[a]lay with Bilhah his father's concubine; and Israel heard *about it.*

Jacob's Twelve Sons

Now the sons of Jacob were twelve:
23 the sons of Leah *were* [a]Reuben, Jacob's firstborn, and Simeon, Levi, Judah, Issachar, and Zebulun;
24 the sons of Rachel *were* Joseph and
Benjamin;
25 the sons of Bilhah, Rachel's maidservant, *were* Dan and Naphtali;
26 and the sons of Zilpah, Leah's maidservant, *were* Gad and Asher. These
were the sons of Jacob who were born
to him in Padan Aram.

Death of Isaac

27 Then Jacob came to his father Isaac
at [a]Mamre, or [b]Kirjath Arba[1] (that *is,*
Hebron), where Abraham and Isaac
had dwelt.
28 Now the days of Isaac were one
hundred and eighty years.
29 So Isaac breathed his last and died,
and [a]was [1]gathered to his people, *being*
old and full of days. And [b]his sons
Esau and Jacob buried him.

The Family of Esau

36 Now this *is* the genealogy of
Esau, [a]who is Edom.
2 [a]Esau took his wives from the
daughters of Canaan: Adah the daughter of Elon the [b]Hittite; [c]Aholibamah[1]
the daughter of Anah, the daughter of
Zibeon the Hivite;
3 and [a]Basemath, Ishmael's daughter, sister of Nebajoth.
4 Now [a]Adah bore Eliphaz to Esau,
and Basemath bore Reuel.
5 And [1]Aholibamah bore Jeush, Jaalam, and Korah. These *were* the sons
of Esau who were born to him in the
land of Canaan.
6 Then Esau took his wives, his sons,
his daughters, and all the persons of
his household, his cattle and all his animals, and all his goods which he had
gained in the land of Canaan, and went
to a country away from the presence
of his brother Jacob.
7 [a]For their possessions were too
great for them to dwell together, and
[b]the land where they were strangers
could not support them because of
their livestock.
8 So Esau dwelt in [a]Mount Seir.
[b]Esau *is* Edom.
9 And this *is* the genealogy of Esau
the father of the Edomites in Mount
Seir.
10 These *were* the names of Esau's
sons: [a]Eliphaz the son of Adah the wife
of Esau, and Reuel the son of Basemath
the wife of Esau.
11 And the sons of Eliphaz were Teman, Omar, [1]Zepho, Gatam, and
Kenaz.
12 Now Timna was the concubine of
Eliphaz, Esau's son, and she bore
[a]Amalek to Eliphaz. These *were* the
sons of Adah, Esau's wife.
13 These *were* the sons of Reuel: Nahath, Zerah, Shammah, and Mizzah.
These were the sons of Basemath,
Esau's wife.
14 These were the sons of [1]Aholiba-
mah, Esau's wife, the daughter of
Anah, the daughter of Zibeon. And she
bore to Esau: Jeush, Jaalam, and
Korah.

The Chiefs of Edom

15 These *were* the chiefs of the sons
of Esau. The sons of Eliphaz, the firstborn *son* of Esau, were Chief Teman, Chief Omar, Chief Zepho, Chief
Kenaz,
16 [1]Chief Korah, Chief Gatam, *and*
Chief Amalek. These *were* the chiefs
of Eliphaz in the land of Edom. They
were the sons of Adah.
17 These *were* the sons of Reuel,
Esau's son: Chief Nahath, Chief Zerah,
Chief Shammah, and Chief Mizzah.
These *were* the chiefs of Reuel in the
land of Edom. These *were* the sons of
Basemath, Esau's wife.
18 And these *were* the sons of [1]Aholi-
bamah, Esau's wife: Chief Jeush, Chief

21 [a]Mic. 4:8
22 [a]Gen. 49:4; 1 Chr. 5:1
23 [a]Gen. 29:31–35; 30:18–20; 46:8; Ex. 1:1–4
27 [a]Gen. 13:18; 18:1; 23:19 [b]Josh. 14:15 [1]Lit. *Town* or *City of Arba*
29 [a]Gen. 15:15; 25:8; 49:33 [b]Gen. 25:9; 49:31 [1]Joined his ancestors

CHAPTER 36

1 [a]Gen. 25:30
2 [a]Gen. 26:34; 28:9 [b]2 Kin. 7:6 [c]Gen. 36:25 [1]Or *Oholibamah*
3 [a]Gen. 28:9
4 [a]1 Chr. 1:35
5 [1]Or *Oholibamah*
7 [a]Gen. 13:6, 11 [b]Gen. 17:8; 28:4; Heb. 11:9
8 [a]Gen. 32:3; Deut. 2:5; Josh. 24:4 [b]Gen. 36:1, 19
10 [a]1 Chr. 1:35
11 [1]*Zephi,* 1 Chr. 1:36
12 [a]Ex. 17:8–16; Num. 24:20; Deut. 25:17–19; 1 Sam. 15:2, 3
14 [1]Or *Oholibamah*
16 [1]Sam. omits *Chief Korah*
18 [1]Or *Oholibamah*

35:21 Eder's location is unknown.
35:22 Reuben's indiscretion later cost him his birthright (see 49:3, 4).
35:27 Jacob finally arrived at his **father**'s home, not merely for a visit, but with his full entourage. **Isaac** has apparently lived in ill health and totally blind for many years.
36:1–43 An interlude paves the way for the final section of Gen. It also serves as a further reminder of the brotherhood of **Esau** and Jacob and their respective nations. Some of these names figure elsewhere in Scripture, among which are several that appear in the Book of Job. The descendants of **Amalek** became bitter enemies of Israel for generations, until they were finally destroyed by Saul and David.
36:2 See note on 26:34, 35.
36:7, 8 Esau and his clan replaced the Horites (v. 20), the original inhabitants of **Seir.** Vv. 20–30 list the Horite kings.

Jaalam, and Chief Korah. These *were* the chiefs *who descended* from Aholibamah, Esau's wife, the daughter of Anah.
19 These *were* the sons of Esau, who is Edom, and these *were* their chiefs.

The Sons of Seir

20 [a]These *were* the sons of Seir [b]the Horite who inhabited the land: Lotan, Shobal, Zibeon, Anah,
21 Dishon, Ezer, and Dishan. These *were* the chiefs of the Horites, the sons of Seir, in the land of Edom.
22 And the sons of Lotan were Hori and [1]Hemam. Lotan's sister *was* Timna.
23 These *were* the sons of Shobal: [1]Alvan, Manahath, Ebal, [2]Shepho, and Onam.
24 These *were* the sons of Zibeon: both Ajah and Anah. This *was the* Anah who found the [1]water in the wilderness as he pastured [a]the donkeys of his father Zibeon.
25 These *were* the children of Anah: Dishon and [1]Aholibamah the daughter of Anah.
26 These *were* the sons of [1]Dishon: [2]Hemdan, Eshban, Ithran, and Cheran.
27 These *were* the sons of Ezer: Bilhan, Zaavan, and [1]Akan.
28 These *were* the sons of Dishan: [a]Uz and Aran.
29 These *were* the chiefs of the Horites: Chief Lotan, Chief Shobal, Chief Zibeon, Chief Anah,
30 Chief Dishon, Chief Ezer, and Chief Dishan. These *were* the chiefs of the Horites, according to their chiefs in the land of Seir.

The Kings of Edom

31 [a]Now these *were* the kings who *reigned in the land of Edom before any king reigned over the children of Israel:
32 Bela the son of Beor reigned in Edom, and the name of his city *was* Dinhabah.
33 And when Bela died, Jobab the son of Zerah of Bozrah reigned in his place.
34 When Jobab died, Husham of the land of the Temanites reigned in his place.
35 And when Husham died, Hadad the son of Bedad, who attacked Midian in the field of Moab, reigned in his place. And the name of his city *was* Avith.
36 When Hadad died, Samlah of Masrekah reigned in his place.
37 And when Samlah died, Saul of [a]Rehoboth-*by*-the-River reigned in his place.
38 When Saul died, Baal-Hanan the son of Achbor reigned in his place.
39 And when Baal-Hanan the son of Achbor died, [1]Hadar reigned in his place; and the name of his city *was* [2]Pau. His wife's name *was* Mehetabel, the daughter of Matred, the daughter of Mezahab.

The Chiefs of Esau

40 And these *were* the names of the chiefs of Esau, according to their families and their places, by their names: Chief Timnah, Chief [1]Alvah, Chief Jetheth,
41 Chief [1]Aholibamah, Chief Elah, Chief Pinon,
42 Chief Kenaz, Chief Teman, Chief Mibzar,
43 Chief Magdiel, and Chief Iram. These *were* the chiefs of Edom, according to their dwelling places in the land of their possession. Esau *was* the father of [1]the Edomites.

Joseph Dreams of Greatness

37 Now Jacob dwelt in the land [a]where his father was a [1]stranger, in the land of Canaan.
2 This *is* the history of Jacob. Joseph, *being* seventeen years old, was feeding the flock with his brothers. And the lad *was* with the sons of Bilhah and the sons of Zilpah, his father's wives; and Joseph brought [a]a bad report of them to his father.
3 Now Israel loved Joseph more than all his children, because he *was* [a]the son of his old age. Also he [b]made him a tunic of *many* colors.
4 But when his brothers saw that their father loved him more than all his brothers, they [a]hated him and could not speak peaceably to him.

20 [a]1 Chr. 1:38–42 [b]Gen. 14:6; Deut. 2:12, 22
22 [1]*Homam,* 1 Chr. 1:39
23 [1]*Alian,* 1 Chr. 1:40 [2]*Shephi,* 1 Chr. 1:40
24 [a]Lev. 19:19 [1]So with MT, Vg. (*hot springs*); LXX *Jamin;* Tg. *mighty men;* Talmud *mules*
25 [1]Or *Oholibamah*
26 [1]Heb. *Dishan* [2]*Hamran,* 1 Chr. 1:41
27 [1]*Jaakan,* 1 Chr. 1:42
28 [a]Job 1:1
31 [a]Gen. 17:6, 16; 35:11; 1 Chr. 1:43
*See WW at 2 Sam. 8:15.
37 [a]Gen. 10:11
39 [1]Sam., Syr. *Hadad* and 1 Chr. 1:50 [2]*Pai,* 1 Chr. 1:50
40 [1]*Aliah,* 1 Chr. 1:51
41 [1]Or *Oholibamah*
43 [1]Heb. *Edom*

CHAPTER 37

1 [a]Gen. 17:8; 23:4; 28:4; 36:7; Heb. 11:9 [1]*sojourner,* temporary resident
2 [a]Gen. 35:25, 26; 1 Sam. 2:22–24
3 [a]Gen. 44:20 [b]Gen. 37:23, 32; Judg. 5:30; 1 Sam. 2:19
4 [a]Gen. 27:41; 49:23; 1 Sam. 17:28; John 15:18–20

36:43 See Introduction to Obadiah: Background.
37:2 The account of **Jacob**'s people in Egypt had been revealed to Abraham (15:13–16). Hence, this is part of God's sovereignty, operating through **Joseph's brothers.**
37:3 Israel loved Joseph more: Being the firstborn of Jacob's favorite wife, Rachel, Joseph not surprisingly became his favorite son. We do not know the correct description of this **tunic of many colors.** The translation here follows the Septuagint's "many colors," but it may be "a long robe with sleeves." An inscription from another Semitic language, Akkadian, suggests "an ornamented tunic," as might be worn by royalty.

6 5 Now Joseph had a dream, and he told *it* to his brothers; and they hated him even more.

6 So he said to them, "Please hear this dream which I have dreamed:

7 [a]"There we were, binding sheaves in the field. Then behold, my sheaf arose and also stood upright; and indeed your sheaves stood all around and bowed down to my sheaf."

8 And his brothers said to him, "Shall you indeed reign over us? Or shall you indeed have dominion over us?" So they hated him even more for his dreams and for his words.

9 Then he dreamed still another dream and told it to his brothers, and said, "Look, I have dreamed another dream. And this time, [a]the sun, the moon, and the eleven stars bowed down to me."

10 So he told *it* to his father and his brothers; and his father rebuked him and said to him, "What *is* this dream that you have dreamed? Shall your mother and I and [a]your brothers indeed come to bow down to the earth before you?"

11 And [a]his brothers envied him, but his father [b]kept the matter *in mind.*

Joseph Sold by His Brothers

12 Then his brothers went to feed their father's flock in [a]Shechem.

13 And Israel said to Joseph, "Are not your brothers feeding *the flock* in Shechem? Come, I will send you to them." So he said to him, "Here I am."

14 Then he said to him, "Please go and see if it is well with your brothers and well with the flocks, and bring back word to me." So he sent him out of the Valley of [a]Hebron, and he went to Shechem.

15 Now a certain man found him, and there he was, wandering in the field. And the man asked him, saying, "What are you seeking?"

16 So he said, "I am *seeking my brothers. [a]Please tell me where they are feeding *their flocks.*"

17 And the man said, "They have departed from here, for I heard them say, 'Let us go to Dothan.' " So Joseph went after his brothers and found them in [a]Dothan.

18 Now when they saw him afar off, even before he came near them, [a]they conspired against him to kill him.

19 Then they said to one another, "Look, this [1]dreamer is coming!

20 [a]"Come therefore, let us now kill him and cast him into some pit; and we shall say, 'Some wild beast has devoured him.' We shall see what will become of his dreams!"

21 But [a]Reuben heard *it,* and he delivered him out of their hands, and said, "Let us not kill him."

7 [a]Gen. 42:6, 9; 43:26; 44:14
9 [a]Gen. 46:29; 47:25
10 [a]Gen. 27:29
11 [a]Matt. 27:17, 18; Acts 7:9 [b]Dan. 7:28; Luke 2:19, 51
12 [a]Gen. 33:18–20
14 [a]Gen. 13:18; 23:2, 19; 35:27; Josh. 14:14, 15; Judg. 1:10
16 [a]Song 1:7 *See WW at Hos. 5:15.
17 [a]2 Kin. 6:13
18 [a]1 Sam. 19:1; Ps. 31:13; 37:12, 32; Matt. 21:38; 26:3, 4; 27:1; Mark 14:1; John 11:53; Acts 23:12
19 [1]Lit. *master of dreams*
20 [a]Gen. 37:22; Prov. 1:11
21 [a]Gen. 42:22

37:5–10 See section 6 of Truth-In-Action at the end of Gen.
37:5 A dream confirms God's providence. He is acting through **Joseph.**
37:11 The two attitudes here are typical reactions to news from God.
37:17 Dothan was 15 miles (24 km) north of Shechem.

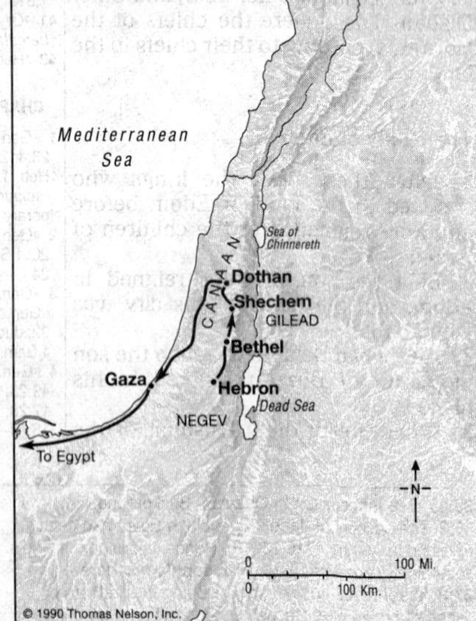

Joseph Becomes a Slave in Egypt. Joseph followed his shepherd brothers from Hebron to Dothan, where they sold him to merchants traveling to Egypt.

22 And Reuben said to them, "Shed no
blood, *but* cast him into this pit which
is in the wilderness, and do not lay a
hand on him"—that he might deliver
him out of their hands, and bring him
back to his father.
23 So it came to pass, when Joseph
had come to his brothers, that they
[a]stripped Joseph *of* his tunic, the tunic
of *many* colors that *was* on him.
24 Then they took him and cast him
into a pit. And the pit *was* empty; *there*
was no water in it.
25 [a]And they sat down to eat a meal.
Then they lifted their eyes and looked,
and there was a company of [b]Ishmael-
ites, coming from Gilead with their
camels, bearing spices, [c]balm, and
myrrh, on their way to carry *them*
down to Egypt.
26 So Judah said to his brothers,
"What profit *is there* if we kill our
brother and [a]conceal his blood?
27 "Come and let us sell him to the Ishmaelites, and [a]let not our hand be upon
him, for he *is* [b]our brother *and* [c]our
flesh." And his brothers listened.
28 Then [a]Midianite traders passed by;
so *the brothers* pulled Joseph up and
lifted him out of the pit, [b]and sold him
to the Ishmaelites for [c]twenty *shekels*
of silver. And they took Joseph to
Egypt.
29 Then Reuben returned to the pit,
and indeed Joseph *was* not in the pit;
and he [a]tore his clothes.
30 And he returned to his brothers and
said, "The lad [a]*is* no *more;* and I, where
shall I go?"
31 So they took [a]Joseph's tunic, killed
a kid of the goats, and dipped the tunic
in the blood.
32 Then they sent the tunic of *many*
colors, and they brought *it* to their father and said, "We have found this. Do
you know whether it *is* your son's tunic
or not?"
33 And he recognized it and said, "*It*
is my son's tunic. A [a]wild beast has
devoured him. Without doubt Joseph
is torn to pieces."
34 Then Jacob [a]tore his clothes, put
sackcloth on his waist, and [b]mourned
for his son many days.
35 And all his sons and all his daughters [a]arose to *comfort him; but he refused to be comforted, and he said,
"For [b]I shall go down into the *grave
to my son in mourning." Thus his father wept for him.
36 Now [a]the [1]Midianites had sold him
in Egypt to Potiphar, an officer of Pharaoh *and* captain of the guard.

Judah and Tamar

38 It came to pass at that time that
Judah departed from his
brothers, and [a]visited a certain Adullamite whose name *was* Hirah.
2 And Judah [a]saw there a daughter
of a certain Canaanite whose name
was [b]Shua, and he married her and
went in to her.
3 So she conceived and bore a son,
and he called his name [a]Er.
4 She conceived again and bore a son,
and she called his name [a]Onan.
5 And she conceived yet again and
bore a son, and called his name
[a]Shelah. He was at Chezib when she
bore him.
6 Then Judah [a]took a wife for Er his
firstborn, and her name *was* [b]Tamar.
7 But [a]Er, Judah's firstborn, was
wicked in the sight of the LORD,
[b]and the LORD killed him.
8 And Judah said to Onan, "Go in to
[a]your brother's wife and marry her,
and raise up an heir to your brother."
9 But Onan knew that the heir would
not be [a]his; and it came to pass, when
he went in to his brother's wife, that
he emitted on the ground, lest he
should give an heir to his brother.
10 And the thing which he did [1]dis-

23 [a]Matt. 27:28
25 [a]Prov. 30:20 [b]Gen. 16:11, 12; 37:28, 36; 39:1 [c]Jer. 8:22
26 [a]Gen. 37:20
27 [a]1 Sam. 18:17 [b]Gen. 42:21 [c]Gen. 29:14
28 [a]Gen. 37:25; Judg. 6:1–3; 8:22, 24 [b]Gen. 45:4, 5; Ps. 105:17; Acts 7:9 [c]Matt. 27:9
29 [a]Gen. 37:34; 44:13; Job 1:20
30 [a]Gen. 42:13, 36
31 [a]Gen. 37:3, 23
33 [a]Gen. 37:20
34 [a]Gen. 37:29; 2 Sam. 3:31 [b]Gen. 50:10
35 [a]2 Sam. 12:17 [b]Gen. 25:8; 35:29; 42:38; 44:29, 31 *See WW at Ps. 23:4. • See WW at Hos. 13:14.
36 [a]Gen. 39:1 [1]MT *Medanites*

CHAPTER 38

1 [a]2 Kin. 4:8
2 [a]Gen. 34:2 [b]1 Chr. 2:3
3 [a]Gen. 46:12; Num. 26:19
4 [a]Gen. 46:12; Num. 26:19
5 [a]Num. 26:20
6 [a]Gen. 21:21 [b]Ruth 4:12
7 [a]Gen. 46:12; Num. 26:19 [b]1 Chr. 2:3
8 [a]Deut. 25:5, 6; Matt. 22:24
9 [a]Deut. 25:6
10 [1]Lit. *was evil in the eyes of*

37:25 Spices, balm, and myrrh were Palestinian products popular in **Egypt** for embalming, cosmetics, and medicines.
37:28–32 Midianite traders: Midian and Medan were sons of Abraham by Keturah (25:1), and were later perceived by Israel to be members of the same tribe as their half brother Ishmael. See Judg. 8:22–24. Their action was a type of kidnapping, which Ex. 21:16 and Deut. 24:7 specify as punishable by death.
37:28 Twenty *shekels* of silver was fair price for a male slave under 20 (Lev. 27:5).
37:34 Sackcloth: A rough clothing of mourning, made of goat's or camel's hair.
38:1–30 The account of Joseph is interrupted to preserve this account of **Judah.** It is important because **Perez** (v. 29) was a direct ancestor of David (Ruth 4:18–22) and because Judah occupied an important role in Hebrew history. The account revolves around the "levirate marriage," a marriage provision intended to insure that a man who died childless could have his lineage continue through his brother (Deut. 25:5–10).
38:1 Adullam was located in the hills about 9 miles (14½ km) northwest of Hebron. A cave near there was David's headquarters while hunted by Saul (1 Sam. 22:1).
38:7 The LORD killed him: Israel attributed both good and evil, life and death, to God (see Is. 45:7). This premature death was a judgment for **Er**'s undefined wickedness.
38:9 The heir . . . be his: The first born to the levirate marriage was considered the child of the dead brother. **When** can mean "whenever," indicating **Onan** would never accept his responsibility to father a child.
38:10 Onan was judged for his continued, planned rebellion against the purpose of the marriage.

pleased the LORD; therefore He killed
[a]him also.
11 Then Judah said to Tamar his
daughter-in-law, [a]"Remain* a widow
in your father's house till my son Shelah is grown." For he said, "Lest he
also die like his brothers." And Tamar
went and dwelt [b]in her father's house.
12 Now in the process of time the
daughter of Shua, Judah's wife, died;
and Judah [a]was comforted, and went
up to his sheepshearers at Timnah, he
and his *friend Hirah the Adullamite.
13 And it was told Tamar, saying,
"Look, your father-in-law is going up
[a]to Timnah to shear his sheep."
14 So she took off her widow's garments, covered *herself* with a veil and
wrapped herself, and [a]sat in an open
place which *was* on the way to Timnah; for she saw [b]that Shelah was
grown, and she was not given to him
as a wife.
15 When Judah saw her, he thought
she *was* a harlot, because she had covered her face.
16 Then he turned to her by the way,
and said, "Please let me come in to
you"; for he did not know that she *was*
his daughter-in-law. So she said,
"What will you give me, that you may
come in to me?"
17 And he said, [a]"I will send a young
goat from the flock." So she said,
[b]"Will you give *me* a pledge till you
send *it?*"
18 Then he said, "What pledge shall I
give you?" So she said, [a]"Your signet
and cord, and your staff that *is* in your
hand." Then he gave *them* to her, and
went in to her, and she conceived by
him.
19 So she arose and went away, and
[a]laid aside her veil and put on the garments of her widowhood.
20 And Judah sent the young goat by
the hand of his friend the Adullamite,
to receive *his* pledge from the woman's
hand, but he did not find her.
21 Then he asked the men of that
place, saying, "Where is the harlot who
was [1]openly by the roadside?" And
they said, "There was no harlot in this
place."

10 [a]Gen. 46:12; Num. 26:19
11 [a]Ruth 1:12, 13 [b]Lev. 22:13 *See WW at Lam. 5:19.
12 [a]2 Sam. 13:39 *See WW at Prov. 17:17.
13 [a]Josh. 15:10, 57; Judg. 14:1
14 [a]Prov. 7:12 [b]Gen. 38:11, 26
17 [a]Judg. 15:1; Ezek. 16:33 [b]Gen. 38:20
18 [a]Gen. 38:25; 41:42
19 [a]Gen. 38:14
21 [1]*in full view*
24 [a]Judg. 19:2 [b]Lev. 20:14; 21:9; Deut. 22:21 [1]*pregnant*
25 [a]Gen. 37:32; 38:18
26 [a]Gen. 37:33 [b]1 Sam. 24:17 [c]Gen. 38:14 [d]Job 34:31, 32
29 [a]Gen. 46:12; Num. 26:20; Ruth 4:12; 1 Chr. 2:4; Matt. 1:3 [1]Lit. *Breach* or *Breakthrough* *See WW at Ezek. 22:30.
30 [a]Gen. 46:12; 1 Chr. 2:4; Matt. 1:3

CHAPTER 39

1 [a]Gen. 12:10; 43:15 [b]Gen. 37:36; Ps. 105:17 [c]Gen. 37:28; 45:4
2 [a]Gen. 26:24, 28; 28:15; 35:3; 39:3, 21, 23; 1 Sam. 16:18; 18:14, 28; Acts 7:9

22 So he returned to Judah and said,
"I cannot find her. Also, the men of the
place said there was no harlot in this
place."
23 Then Judah said, "Let her take
them for herself, lest we be shamed;
for I sent this young goat and you have
not found her."
24 And it came to pass, about three
months after, that Judah was told, saying, "Tamar your daughter-in-law has
[a]played the harlot; furthermore she *is*
[1]with child by harlotry." So Judah said,
"Bring her out [b]and let her be burned!"
25 When she *was* brought out, she sent
to her father-in-law, saying, "By the
man to whom these belong, I *am* with
child." And she said, [a]"Please determine whose these *are*—the signet and
cord, and staff."
26 So Judah [a]acknowledged *them* and
said, [b]"She has been more righteous
than I, because [c]I did not give her to
Shelah my son." And he [d]never knew
her again.
27 Now it came to pass, at the time for
giving birth, that behold, twins *were*
in her womb.
28 And so it was, when she was giving
birth, that *the one* put out *his* hand;
and the midwife took a scarlet *thread*
and bound it on his hand, saying, "This
one came out first."
29 Then it happened, as he drew back
his hand, that his brother came out
unexpectedly; and she said, "How did
you break through? *This* *breach *be*
upon you!" Therefore his name was
called [a]Perez.[1]
30 Afterward his brother came out
who had the scarlet *thread* on his
hand. And his name was called [a]Zerah.

Joseph a Slave in Egypt

39 Now Joseph had been taken
[a]down to Egypt. And [b]Potiphar,
an officer of Pharaoh, captain of the
guard, an Egyptian, [c]bought him from
the Ishmaelites who had taken him
down there.
2 [a]The LORD was with Joseph, and he
was a successful man; and he was in
the house of his master the Egyptian.

38:15 Harlot here indicates a cult-prostitute. This shows the depravity of both **Judah** and the world into which he married; it was not only an act of fornication, but of idolatry.
38:23 Shamed: Judah is ironically concerned about his reputation.
38:24 Let her be burned: Judah was using a legal expression. Again, the Mosaic Law later incorporated this earlier provision: death to an adulteress by fire (Lev. 21:9) or, more commonly, by stoning (Deut. 22:24).
38:25 The **signet** was a personal identification seal hanging from a **cord** about its owner's neck. The **staff** probably had a distinctive carving at the top. Tamar had a sense for the dramatic: she knew that anyone in the household could quickly identify their owner.
38:27–30 The **birth** events are obviously miraculous. This is another incident of God's providence whereby the younger receives preferred status.

3 And his master saw that the LORD
was with him and that the LORD
[a]made all he did [1]to prosper in his
hand.
6 4 So Joseph [a]found favor in his sight,
and *served him. Then he made him
[b]overseer of his house, and all *that* he
had he put [1]under his authority.
5 So it was, from the time *that* he had
made him overseer of his house and
all that he had, that [a]the LORD blessed
the Egyptian's house for Joseph's sake;
and the blessing of the LORD was on
all that he had in the house and in the
field.
6 Thus he left all that he had in Joseph's [1]hand, and he did not know
what he had except for the [2]bread
which he ate. Now Joseph [a]was handsome in form and appearance.
7 And it came to pass after these
things that his master's wife [1]cast longing eyes on Joseph, and she said,
[a]"Lie with me."
8 But he refused and said to his master's wife, "Look, my master does not
know what *is* with me in the house,
and he has committed all that he has
to my hand.
6 9 "*There is* no one greater in this
house than I, nor has he kept back anything from me but you, because you
are his wife. [a]How then can I do this
great wickedness, and [b]sin against
God?"
10 So it was, as she spoke to Joseph
day by day, that he [a]did not heed her,
to lie with her *or* to be with her.
11 But it happened about this time,
when Joseph went into the house to
do his work, and none of the men of
the house *was* inside,
12 that she [a]caught him by his garment, saying, "Lie with me." But he left
his garment in her hand, and fled and
ran outside.
13 And so it was, when she saw that
he had left his garment in her hand and
fled outside,
14 that she called to the men of her
house and spoke to them, saying, "See,
he has brought in to us a [a]Hebrew to
[1]mock us. He came in to me to lie with
me, and I cried out with a loud voice.
15 "And it happened, when he heard
that I lifted my voice and cried out, that
he left his garment with me, and fled
and went outside."
16 So she kept his garment with her
until his master came home.
17 Then she [a]spoke to him with words
like these, saying, "The Hebrew servant whom you brought to us came in
to me to mock me;
18 "so it happened, as I lifted my voice
and cried out, that he left his garment
with me and fled outside."
19 So it was, when his master heard
the words which his wife spoke to him,
saying, "Your servant did to me after
this manner," that his [a]anger was
aroused.
20 Then Joseph's master took him and
[a]put him into the [b]prison, a place
where the king's prisoners *were* confined. And he was there in the prison.
21 But the LORD was with Joseph and 6
showed him mercy, and He [a]gave[1] him
favor in the sight of the keeper of the
prison.
22 And the keeper of the prison
[a]committed to Joseph's hand all the
prisoners who *were* in the prison;
whatever they did there, it was his doing.
23 The keeper of the prison did not
look into anything *that was* under
[1]*Joseph's* authority, because [a]the LORD
was with him; and whatever he did, the
LORD made *it* prosper.

The Prisoners' Dreams

40 It came to pass after these
things *that* the [a]butler and the
baker of the king of Egypt offended
their lord, the king of Egypt.
2 And Pharaoh was [a]angry with his
two officers, the chief butler and the
chief baker.
3 [a]So he put them in custody in the
house of the captain of the guard, in
the prison, the place where Joseph *was*
confined.

3 [a]Ps. 1:3 [1]*to be a success*
4 [a]Gen. 18:3; 19:19; 39:21 [b]Gen. 24:2, 10; 39:8, 22; 41:40 [1]Lit. *in his hand* *See WW at 1 Chr. 15:2.
5 [a]Gen. 18:26; 30:27; 2 Sam. 6:11
6 [a]Gen. 29:17; 1 Sam. 16:12 [1]Care [2]Food
7 [a]2 Sam. 13:11 [1]Lit. *lifted up her eyes toward*
9 [a]Lev. 20:10; Prov. 6:29, 32 [b]Gen. 20:6; 42:18; 2 Sam. 12:13; Ps. 51:4
10 [a]Prov. 1:10
12 [a]Prov. 7:13
14 [a]Gen. 14:13; 41:12 [1]*laugh at*
17 [a]Ex. 23:1; Ps. 120:3; Prov. 26:28
19 [a]Prov. 6:34, 35
20 [a]Ps. 105:18; [1 Pet. 2:19] [b]Gen. 40:3, 15; 41:14
21 [a]Gen. 39:2; Ex. 3:21; Ps. 105:19; [Prov. 16:7]; Dan. 1:9; Acts 7:9, 10 [1]Caused him to be viewed with favor by
22 [a]Gen. 39:4; 40:3, 4
23 [a]Gen. 39:2, 3 [1]Lit. *his hand*

CHAPTER 40

1 [a]Gen. 40:11, 13; Neh. 1:11
2 [a]Prov. 16:14
3 [a]Gen. 39:1, 20, 23; 41:10

39:3 Potiphar was wise enough to note that every project he assigned to Joseph did indeed **prosper in his hand.** People in these ancient cultures actively sought such divinely empowered men.
39:4 See section 6 of Truth-In-Action at the end of Gen.
39:6 The bread which he ate: Joseph was excluded from oversight of the food possibly because of Egyptian prejudice against eating with Asiatics (43:32).
39:7–20 Joseph's honor was repaid with injustice. Yet **God** sees, remembers, and prospers Joseph. It is an obviously God-ordained test (Ps. 105:19).
39:9 See section 6 of Truth-In-Action at the end of Gen.
39:20 Joseph should have been executed. The imprisonment again shows God's providence and hints that Potiphar may not have fully believed his wife.
39:21 See section 6 of Truth-In-Action at the end of Gen.
39:23 In spite of **the LORD**'s prosperity, "they hurt his feet with fetters, he was laid in irons" (Ps. 105:18).
40:1 The butler was the cupbearer, the man who first tasted everything Pharaoh ate and drank; he did so in **the king**'s presence, to learn if it was poisoned. Such a one must be trustworthy, and thereby became quasi-counsellor to royalty,

4 And the captain of the guard charged Joseph with them, and he served them; so they were in custody for a while.

5 Then the butler and the baker of the king of Egypt, who *were* confined in the prison, [a]had a dream, both of them, each man's dream in one night *and* each man's dream with its *own* interpretation.

6 And Joseph came in to them in the morning and looked at them, and saw that they *were* [1]sad.

7 So he asked Pharaoh's officers who *were* with him in the custody of his lord's house, saying, [a]"Why do you look *so* sad today?"

8 And they said to him, [a]"We each have had a dream, and *there is* no interpreter of it." So Joseph said to them, [b]"Do not interpretations belong to God? Tell *them* to me, please."

9 Then the chief butler told his dream to Joseph, and said to him, "Behold, in my dream a vine *was* before me,

10 "and in the vine *were* three branches; it *was* as though it budded, its blossoms shot forth, and its clusters brought forth ripe grapes.

11 "Then Pharaoh's cup *was* in my hand; and I took the grapes and pressed them into Pharaoh's cup, and placed the cup in Pharaoh's hand."

12 And Joseph said to him, [a]"This *is* the interpretation of it: The three branches [b]*are* three days.

13 "Now within three days Pharaoh will [a]lift up your *head and restore you to your [1]place, and you will put Pharaoh's cup in his hand according to the former manner, when you were his butler.

14 "But [a]remember me when it is well with you, and [b]please show kindness to me; make mention of me to Pharaoh, and get me out of this house.

15 "For indeed I was [a]stolen away from the land of the Hebrews; [b]and also I have done nothing here that they should put me into the dungeon."

16 When the chief baker saw that the interpretation was good, he said to Joseph, "I also *was* in my dream, and there *were* three [1]white baskets on my head.

17 "In the uppermost basket *were* all kinds of baked goods for Pharaoh, and the birds ate them out of the basket on my head."

18 So Joseph answered and said, [a]"This *is* the interpretation of it: The three baskets *are* three days.

19 [a]"Within three days Pharaoh will lift [1]off your head from you and [b]hang you on a tree; and the birds will eat your flesh from you."

20 Now it came to pass on the third day, *which was* Pharaoh's [a]birthday, that he [b]made a feast for all his servants; and he [c]lifted up the head of the chief butler and of the chief baker among his servants.

21 Then he [a]restored the chief butler to his butlership again, and [b]he placed the cup in Pharaoh's hand.

22 But he [a]hanged the chief baker, as Joseph had interpreted to them.

23 Yet the chief butler did not remember Joseph, but [a]forgot him.

Pharaoh's Dreams

41 Then it came to pass, at the end of two full years, that [a]Pharaoh had a dream; and behold, he stood by the river.

2 Suddenly there came up out of the river seven cows, fine looking and fat; and they fed in the meadow.

3 Then behold, seven other cows came up after them out of the river, ugly and gaunt, and stood by the *other* cows on the bank of the river.

4 And the ugly and gaunt cows ate up the seven fine looking and fat cows. So Pharaoh awoke.

5 He slept and dreamed a second time; and suddenly seven heads of grain came up on one stalk, plump and good.

6 Then behold, seven thin heads, blighted by the [a]east wind, sprang up after them.

7 And the seven thin heads devoured the seven plump and full heads. So Pharaoh awoke, and indeed, *it was* a dream.

8 Now it came to pass in the morning [a]that his spirit was troubled, and he

5 [a]Gen. 37:5; 41:1
6 [1]*dejected*
7 [a]Neh. 2:2
8 [a]Gen. 41:15 [b][Gen. 41:16; Dan. 2:11, 20–22, 27, 28, 47]
12 [a]Gen. 40:18; 41:12, 25; Judg. 7:14; Dan. 2:36; 4:18, 19 [b]Gen. 40:18; 42:17
13 [a]2 Kin. 25:27; Ps. 3:3; Jer. 52:31 [1]*position* *See WW at Gen. 3:15.
14 [a]1 Sam. 25:31; Luke 23:42 [b]Gen. 24:49; 47:29; Josh. 2:12; 1 Sam. 20:14, 15; 2 Sam. 9:1; 1 Kin. 2:7
15 [a]Gen. 37:26–28 [b]Gen. 39:20
16 [1]Or *baskets of white bread*
18 [a]Gen. 40:12
19 [a]Gen. 40:13 [b]Deut. 21:22 [1]Lit. *up*
20 [a]Matt. 14:6–10 [b]Mark 6:21 [c]Gen. 40:13, 19; 2 Kin. 25:27; Jer. 52:31; Matt. 25:19
21 [a]Gen. 40:13 [b]Neh. 2:1
22 [a]Gen. 40:19; Deut. 21:23; Esth. 7:10
23 [a]Job 19:14; Ps. 31:12; Eccl. 9:15, 16; Is. 49:15; Amos 6:6

CHAPTER 41

1 [a]Gen. 40:5; Judg. 7:13
6 [a]Ex. 10:13; Ezek. 17:10
8 [a]Dan. 2:1, 3; 4:5, 19

as was Nehemiah, cupbearer to King Artaxerxes more than 1,000 years later. **The baker** also must be trustworthy.

40:6–8 In addition to being a man of integrity, Joseph was sensitive to others. **God** was also obviously at the forefront of his thinking.

40:15 Joseph's view of his being sold was that he was unjustly **stolen away.**

40:23 But forgot him stands in stark contrast to God who remembers Joseph (41:37–45).

41:1, 2 The river: The Nile River. The **cows** coming **up out of the river** would have been natural, for they liked to stand in the Nile as protection from the heat and flies.

41:6 The east wind: A scorching wind off the desert.

41:8 Dreams were assumed to be messages from God (see Job 7:14). The ancient Egyptians left many hieroglyphic writings with detailed instructions on how to **interpret** dreams; thus **the magicians** and **wise men** were expected to understand what God was telling Pharaoh. The magicians

sent and called for all [b]the magicians
of Egypt and all its [c]wise men. And
Pharaoh told them his dreams, but
there was no one who could interpret
them for Pharaoh.
9 Then the [a]chief butler spoke to Pharaoh, saying: "I remember my faults
this day.
10 "When Pharaoh was [a]angry with
his servants, [b]and put me in custody
in the house of the captain of the guard,
both me and the chief baker,
11 [a]"we each had a dream in one night,
he and I. Each of us dreamed according
to the interpretation of his *own* dream.
12 "Now there *was* a young [a]Hebrew
man with us there, a [b]servant of the
captain of the guard. And we told him,
and he [c]interpreted our dreams for us;
to each man he interpreted according
to his *own* dream.
13 "And it came to pass, just [a]as he
interpreted for us, so it happened. He
restored me to my office, and he
hanged him."
6 14 [a]Then Pharaoh sent and called Joseph, and they [b]brought him quickly
[c]out of the dungeon; and he shaved,
[d]changed his clothing, and came to
Pharaoh.
15 And Pharaoh said to Joseph, "I
have had a dream, and *there is* no one
who can interpret it. [a]But I have heard
it said of you *that* you can understand
a dream, to interpret it."
16 So Joseph answered Pharaoh, saying, [a]"*It is* not in me; [b]God will give
Pharaoh an answer of peace."
17 Then Pharaoh said to Joseph: "Behold, [a]in my dream I stood on the bank
of the river.
18 "Suddenly seven cows came up out
of the river, fine looking and fat; and
they fed in the meadow.
19 "Then behold, seven other cows
came up after them, poor and very ugly
and gaunt, such ugliness as I have
never seen in all the land of Egypt.
20 "And the gaunt and ugly cows ate
up the first seven, the fat cows.
21 "When they had eaten them up, no
one would have known that they had
eaten them, for they *were* just as ugly
as at the beginning. So I awoke.
22 "Also I saw in my dream, and suddenly seven [1]heads came up on one
stalk, full and good.
23 "Then behold, seven heads, withered, thin, *and* blighted by the east
wind, sprang up after them.
24 "And the thin heads devoured the
seven good heads. So [a]I told *this* to the
magicians, but *there was* no one who
could explain *it* to me."
25 Then Joseph said to Pharaoh, "The
dreams of Pharaoh *are* one; [a]God
has shown Pharaoh what He *is* about
to do:
26 "The seven good cows *are* seven
years, and the seven good [1]heads *are*
seven years; the dreams *are* one.
27 "And the seven thin and ugly cows
which came up after them *are* seven
years, and the seven empty heads
blighted by the east wind are [a]seven
years of famine.
28 [a]"This *is* the thing which I have spoken to Pharaoh. God has shown Pharaoh what He *is* about to do.
29 "Indeed [a]seven years of great
plenty will come throughout all the
land of Egypt;
30 "but after them seven years of famine will [a]arise, and all the plenty will
be forgotten in the land of Egypt; and
the famine [b]will deplete the land.
31 "So the plenty will not be known
in the land because of the famine following, for it *will be* very severe.
32 "And the dream was repeated to
Pharaoh twice because the [a]thing *is* established by God, and God will shortly
bring it to pass.
33 "Now therefore, let Pharaoh select
a discerning and wise man, and set him
over the land of Egypt.
34 "Let Pharaoh do *this*, and let him
appoint [1]officers over the land, [a]to collect one-fifth *of the produce* of the land
of Egypt in the seven plentiful years.
35 "And [a]let them gather all the food
of those good years that are coming,
and store up grain under the [1]authority
of Pharaoh, and let them keep food in
the cities.
36 "Then that food shall be as a
[1]reserve for the land for the seven
years of famine which shall be in the
land of Egypt, that the land [a]may not
[2]perish during the famine."

8 [b]Ex. 7:11, 22; Is. 29:14; Dan. 1:20; 2:2; 4:7 [c]Matt. 2:1
9 [a]Gen. 40:1, 14, 23
10 [a]Gen. 40:2, 3 [b]Gen. 39:20
11 [a]Gen. 40:5; Judg. 7:15
12 [a]Gen. 39:14; 43:32 [b]Gen. 37:36 [c]Gen. 40:12
13 [a]Gen. 40:21, 22
14 [a]Ps. 105:20 [b]Dan. 2:25 [c][1 Sam. 2:8] [d]2 Kin. 25:27–29
15 [a]Gen. 41:8, 12; Dan. 5:16
16 [a]Dan. 2:30; Acts 3:12; [2 Cor. 3:5] [b]Gen. 40:8; 41:25, 28, 32; Deut. 29:29; Dan. 2:22, 28, 47
17 [a]Gen. 41:1
22 [1]Heads of grain
24 [a]Gen. 41:8; Ex. 7:11; Is. 8:19; Dan. 4:7
25 [a]Gen. 41:28, 32; Dan. 2:28, 29, 45; Rev. 4:1
26 [1]Heads of grain
27 [a]2 Kin. 8:1
28 [a][Gen. 41:25, 32; Dan. 2:28]
29 [a]Gen. 41:47
30 [a]Gen. 41:54, 56 [b]Gen. 47:13; Ps. 105:16
32 [a]Gen. 41:25, 28; Num. 23:19; Is. 46:10, 11
34 [a][Prov. 6:6–8] [1]*overseers*
35 [a]Gen. 41:48 [1]Lit. *hand*
36 [a]Gen. 47:15, 19 [1]Lit. *supply* [2]*be cut off*

were expected to be experts in handling the ritual books of magic.
41:9 My faults refers to his ingratitude toward Joseph.
41:14–57 See section 6 of Truth-In-Action at the end of Gen.
41:14 Egyptian custom, as contrasted with Semitic, demanded that **Joseph** be cleanshaven. This also symbolized his transformation from a slave to a governor.
41:16 An answer of peace: A response that would be directed toward Pharaoh's *shalom,* "welfare."
41:31 There is no indication that **the famine** was a direct judgment; rather, it was part of God's subjecting creation to futility (Rom. 8:20).
41:32 The two dreams were connected in one message from **God;** the "doubling" indicated its certainty as well as its imminence.

Joseph's Rise to Power

37 So [a]the advice was good in the eyes
of Pharaoh and in the eyes of all his
servants.
38 And Pharaoh said to his servants,
"Can we find *such a one* as this, a man
[a]in whom *is* the Spirit of God?"
39 Then Pharaoh said to Joseph, "Inasmuch as God has shown you all this,
there is no one as discerning and wise
as you.
40 [a]"You shall be [1]over my house, and
all my people shall be ruled according
to your word; only in regard to the
throne will I be greater than you."
41 And Pharaoh said to Joseph, "See,
I have [a]set you over all the land of
Egypt."
42 Then Pharaoh [a]took his signet ring
off his hand and put it on Joseph's
hand; and he [b]clothed him in garments
of fine linen [c]and put a gold chain
around his neck.
43 And he had him ride in the second
[a]chariot which he had; [b]and they cried
out before him, "Bow the knee!" So he
set him [c]over all the land of Egypt.

KINGDOM DYNAMICS

41:42, 43 Restoration Foreshadowed, RESTORATION. The story of Joseph's life (chs. 34—46) is a grand foreshadowing of God's restoration process, especially of those whose loss is the result of their being victimized by others. The entire concept of "The Holy Spirit and Restoration" is developed in the study article, which begins on page 2012.

(Gen. 6:5/Jer. 8:8, 9) J.R.

44 Pharaoh also said to Joseph, "I *am*
Pharaoh, and without your consent no
man may lift his hand or foot in all the
land of Egypt."
45 And Pharaoh called Joseph's name
[1]Zaphnath-Paaneah. And he gave him
as a wife [a]Asenath, the daughter of
Poti-Pherah priest of On. So Joseph
went out over *all* the land of Egypt.
46 Joseph was thirty years old when
he [a]stood before Pharaoh king of
Egypt. And Joseph went out from the
presence of Pharaoh, and went
throughout all the land of Egypt.
47 Now in the seven plentiful years the
ground brought forth [1]abundantly.
48 So he gathered up all the food of
the seven years which were in the land
of Egypt, and laid up the food in
the cities; he laid up in every city the
food of the fields which surrounded
them.
49 Joseph gathered very much grain,
[a]as the sand of the sea, until he stopped
counting, for *it was* immeasurable.
50 [a]And to Joseph were born two sons
before the years of famine came, whom
Asenath, the daughter of Poti-Pherah
priest of On, bore to him.
51 Joseph called the name of the firstborn [1]Manasseh: "For God has made
me forget all my *toil and all my
[a]father's house."
52 And the name of the second he
called [1]Ephraim: "For God has caused
me to be [a]fruitful in the land of my affliction."
53 Then the seven years of plenty
which were in the land of Egypt ended,
54 [a]and the seven years of famine began to come, [b]as Joseph had said. The
famine was in all lands, but in all the
land of Egypt there was bread.
55 So when all the land of Egypt was
famished, the people cried to Pharaoh
for bread. Then Pharaoh said to all the
Egyptians, "Go to Joseph; [a]whatever
he says to you, do."
56 The famine was over all the face of
the earth, and Joseph opened [1]all the
storehouses and [a]sold to the Egyptians.
And the famine became severe in the
land of Egypt.

37 [a]Ps. 105:19; Acts 7:10
38 [a]Num. 27:18; [Job 32:8; Prov. 2:6]; Dan. 4:8, 9, 18; 5:11, 14; 6:3
40 [a]Ps. 105:21; Acts 7:10 [1]In charge of
41 [a]Gen. 42:6; Ps. 105:21; Dan. 6:3; Acts 7:10
42 [a]Esth. 3:10 [b]Esth. 8:2, 15 [c]Dan. 5:7, 16, 29
43 [a]Gen. 46:29 [b]Esth. 6:9 [c]Gen. 42:6
45 [a]Gen. 46:20 [1]Probably Egyptian for *God Speaks and He Lives*
46 [a]1 Sam. 16:21; 1 Kin. 12:6, 8; Dan. 1:19
47 [1]Lit. *by handfuls*
49 [a]Gen. 22:17; Judg. 7:12; 1 Sam. 13:5
50 [a]Gen. 46:20; 48:5
51 [a]Ps. 45:10 [1]Lit. *Making Forgetful* *See WW at Job 5:7.
52 [a]Gen. 17:6; 28:3; 49:22 [1]Lit. *Fruitfulness*
54 [a]Ps. 105:16; Acts 7:11 [b]Gen. 41:30
55 [a]John 2:5
56 [a]Gen. 42:6 [1]Lit. *all that was in them*

41:37 If **Pharaoh** had been impressed only by Joseph's ability to interpret dreams, he would have hired him as a magician; but Pharaoh was even more taken with Joseph's wisdom.

41:38 In whom *is* the Spirit of God: Coming from the lips of **Pharaoh,** he is either speaking by the providence of God without understanding (see John 11:49–52) or the phrase should be translated, "the spirit of a god." Scholars are divided.

41:42 His signet ring: Joseph was given the highest office dealing with *financial matters;* Egyptian inscriptions depict just such a trusted officer as "Sealbearer to the King." Some inscriptions describe Asiatic slaves as high Egyptian officials, one of which may represent Joseph. Joseph literally went from rags to riches in a day.

41:45 On was a famous religious center dedicated to the worship of the sun-god. **Joseph's** promotion unfortunately included a pagan marriage. There is no indication, however, that he abandoned faith in Yahweh.

41:50–52 The names of **Joseph**'s two sons are later memorialized in a blessing which Yahweh established to be used from antiquity throughout the church age. See note on 48:20.

41:53–55 Joseph's interpretations were accurate in every detail.

41:56 Over all the face of the earth: Some widespread natural catastrophe must have occurred, since **Egypt** receives almost all its water from seasonal rains deep in east Africa via the Nile River. Not only was the Near East rainless at this time, but the Nile, which always floods annually, apparently did not overflow its banks for several seasons, perhaps even the full seven years. Without the flooding, very little will grow in Egypt.

57 [a]So all countries came to Joseph in Egypt to [b]buy *grain,* because the famine was severe in all lands.

Joseph's Brothers Go to Egypt

42 When [a]Jacob saw that there was grain in Egypt, Jacob said to his sons, "Why do you look at one another?"
2 And he said, "Indeed I have heard that there is grain in Egypt; go down to that place and buy for us there, that we may [a]live and not die."
3 So Joseph's ten brothers went down to buy grain in Egypt.
4 But Jacob did not send Joseph's brother Benjamin with his brothers, for he said, [a]"Lest some calamity befall him."
5 And the sons of Israel went to buy *grain* among those who journeyed, for the famine was [a]in the land of Canaan.
6 Now Joseph *was* governor [a]over the land; and it was he who sold to all the people of the land. And Joseph's brothers came and [b]bowed down before him with *their* faces to the earth.
7 Joseph saw his brothers and recognized them, but he acted as [a]a stranger to them and spoke [1]roughly to them. Then he said to them, "Where do you come from?" And they said, "From the land of Canaan to buy food."
8 So Joseph recognized his brothers, but they did not recognize him.
9 Then Joseph [a]remembered the dreams which he had dreamed about them, and said to them, "You *are* spies! You have come to see the [1]nakedness of the land!"
10 And they said to him, "No, my lord, but your servants have come to buy food.
11 "We *are* all *one man's sons; we *are* honest *men;* your servants are not spies."
12 But he said to them, "No, but you have come to see the nakedness of the land."
13 And they said, "Your servants *are* twelve brothers, the sons of one man in the land of Canaan; and in fact, the youngest *is* with our father today, and one [a]*is* no more."
14 But Joseph said to them, "It *is* as I spoke to you, saying, 'You *are* spies!'
15 "In this *manner* you shall be tested: [a]By the life of Pharaoh, you shall not leave this place unless your youngest brother comes here.
16 "Send one of you, and let him bring your brother; and you shall be [1]kept in prison, that your words may be tested to see whether *there is* any truth in you; or else, by the life of Pharaoh, surely you *are* spies!"
17 So he [1]put them all together in prison [a]three days.
18 Then Joseph said to them the third day, "Do this and live, [a]*for* I fear God:
19 "If you *are* honest *men,* let one of your brothers be confined to your prison house; but you, go and carry grain for the famine of your houses.
20 "And [a]bring your youngest brother to me; so your words will be verified, and you shall not die." And they did so.
21 Then they said to one another, [a]"We *are* truly guilty concerning our brother, for we saw the anguish of his soul when he pleaded with us, and we would not hear; [b]therefore this distress has come upon us."
22 And Reuben answered them, saying, [a]"Did I not speak to you, saying, 'Do not sin against the boy'; and you would not listen? Therefore behold, his blood is now [b]required of us."
23 But they did not know that Joseph understood *them,* for he spoke to them through an interpreter.
24 And he turned himself away from them and [a]wept. Then he returned to them again, and talked with them. And he took [b]Simeon from them and bound him before their eyes.

57 [a]Ezek. 29:12 [b]Gen. 27:28, 37; 42:3

CHAPTER 42

1 [a]Acts 7:12
2 [a]Gen. 43:8; Ps. 33:18, 19; Is. 38:1
4 [a]Gen. 42:38
5 [a]Gen. 12:10; 26:1; 41:57; Acts 7:11
6 [a]Gen. 41:41, 55 [b]Gen. 37:7–10; 41:43; Is. 60:14
7 [a]Gen. 45:1, 2 [1]*harshly*
9 [a]Gen. 37:5–9 [1]Exposed parts
11 *See WW at Deut. 6:4.
13 [a]Gen. 37:30; 42:32; 44:20; Lam. 5:7
15 [a]1 Sam. 1:26; 17:55
16 [1]Lit. *bound*
17 [a]Gen. 40:4, 7, 12 [1]Lit. *gathered*
18 [a]Gen. 22:12; 39:9; Ex. 1:17; Lev. 25:43; Neh. 5:15; Prov. 1:7; 9:10
20 [a]Gen. 42:34; 43:5; 44:23
21 [a]Gen. 37:26–28; 44:16; 45:3; Job 36:8, 9; Hos. 5:15 [b]Prov. 21:13; Matt. 7:2
22 [a]Gen. 37:21, 22, 29 [b]Gen. 9:5, 6; 1 Kin. 2:32; 2 Chr. 24:22; Ps. 9:12; Luke 11:50, 51
24 [a]Gen. 43:30; 45:14, 15 [b]Gen. 34:25, 30; 43:14, 23

42:1–24 The reconciliation of **Joseph** and **his brothers** begins with **Jacob**'s need for **grain.** This was also the providential beginning of moving the Israelites into **Egypt** (15:13, 14).
42:6 Joseph's first dream had now come to pass (see 37:5–8).
42:7, 8 We are not told why Joseph's **brothers did not recognize him** or his accent. Perhaps it was the 20-year time lapse.
42:9 Although **Joseph** was somewhat harsh in his dealings, as any Egyptian would have been to Canaanites, there is no hint of vengeance or vindictiveness in the narrative. On the contrary, Joseph was affectionate (v. 24) and merciful (vv. 16–19). To see **the nakedness of the land** means to pry into Egypt's private affairs.
42:11 All one man's sons: A group of 10 **spies** would hardly be of one family.
42:15 By the life of Pharaoh: Since Pharaoh was thought to be a god, Joseph was using an Egyptian expression, much as "As the LORD lives" was later used in Israel.
42:18 Joseph had proven his authority; he is now expressing his concern and his submission to **God.**
42:22 His blood: Surprisingly, Jacob's sons associated this current predicament with their sin of more than 20 years earlier.
42:24 Joseph was obviously not vengeful and gives vent to long concealed emotions. However, God still has lessons for his brothers, so his identity remains concealed.

The Brothers Return to Canaan

25 Then Joseph [a]gave a command to
fill their sacks with grain, to [b]restore
every man's money to his sack, and to
give them provisions for the journey.
[c]Thus he did for them.
26 So they loaded their donkeys with
the grain and departed from there.
27 But as [a]one *of them* opened his sack
to give his donkey feed at the encampment, he saw his money; and there it
was, in the mouth of his sack.
28 So he said to his brothers, "My
money has been *restored, and there
it is, in my sack!" Then their hearts
[1]failed *them* and they were afraid, saying to one another, "What *is* this *that*
God has done to us?"
29 Then they went to Jacob their father
in the land of Canaan and told him all
that had happened to them, saying:
30 "The man *who is* lord of the land
[a]spoke [1]roughly to us, and took us for
spies of the country.
31 "But we said to him, 'We *are* honest
men; we are not spies.
32 'We *are* twelve brothers, sons of our
father; one *is* no *more,* and the youngest *is* with our father this day in the
land of Canaan.'
33 "Then the man, the lord of the country, said to us, [a]'By this I will know
that you *are* honest *men:* Leave one of
your brothers *here* with me, take *food
for* the famine of your households, and
be gone.
34 'And bring your [a]youngest brother
to me; so I shall know that you *are* not
spies, but *that* you *are* honest *men.* I
will grant your brother to you, and you
may [b]trade in the land.' "
35 Then it happened as they emptied
their sacks, that surprisingly [a]each
man's bundle of money *was* in his
sack; and when they and their father
saw the bundles of money, they were
afraid.
36 And Jacob their father said to them,
"You have [a]bereaved me: Joseph is no
more, Simeon is no *more,* and you
want to take [b]Benjamin. All these
things are against me."
37 Then Reuben spoke to his father,
saying, "Kill my two sons if I do not
bring him *back* to you; put him in my
hands, and I will bring him back to
you."
38 But he said, "My son shall not go
down with you, for [a]his brother is
dead, and he is left alone. [b]If any calamity should befall him along the way
in which you go, then you would
[c]bring down my gray hair with sorrow
to the *grave."

Joseph's Brothers Return with Benjamin

43 Now the famine *was* [a]severe in
the land.
2 And it came to pass, when they had
eaten up the grain which they had
brought from Egypt, that their father
said to them, "Go [a]back, buy us a little
food."
3 But Judah spoke to him, saying,
"The man solemnly warned us, saying,
'You shall not see my face unless your
[a]brother *is* with you.'
4 "If you send our brother with us,
we will go down and buy you food.
5 "But if you will not send *him,* we
will not go down; for the man said to
us, 'You shall not see my face unless
your brother *is* with you.' "
6 And Israel said, "Why did you deal
so [1]wrongfully with me *as* to tell the
man whether you had still *another*
brother?"
7 But they said, "The man asked us
pointedly about ourselves and our family, saying, '*Is* your father still alive?
Have you *another* brother?' And we
told him according to these words.
Could we possibly have known that he
would say, 'Bring your brother
down'?"
8 Then Judah said to Israel his father,
"Send the lad with me, and we will
arise and go, that we may [a]live and not
die, both we and you *and* also our little
ones.
9 "I myself will be surety for him;
from my hand you shall require him.
[a]If I do not bring him *back* to you and
set him before you, then let me bear
the blame forever.
10 "For if we had not lingered, surely

25 [a]Gen. 44:1 [b]Gen. 43:12 [c][Matt. 5:44; Rom. 12:17, 20, 21; 1 Pet. 3:9] **27** [a]Gen. 43:21, 22 **28** [1]*sank* *See WW at Ruth 4:15. **30** [a]Gen. 42:7 [1]*harshly* **33** [a]Gen. 42:15, 19, 20 **34** [a]Gen. 42:20; 43:3, 5 [b]Gen. 34:10 **35** [a]Gen. 43:12, 15, 21 **36** [a]Gen. 43:14 [b]Gen. 35:18; [Rom. 8:28, 31]
38 [a]Gen. 37:22; 42:13; 44:20, 28 [b]Gen. 42:4; 44:29 [c]Gen. 37:35; 44:31 *See WW at Hos. 13:14.

CHAPTER 43

1 [a]Gen. 41:54, 57; 42:5; 45:6, 11 **2** [a]Gen. 42:2; 44:25 **3** [a]Gen. 42:20; 43:5; 44:23 **6** [1]Lit. *wickedly* **8** [a]Gen. 42:2; 47:19 **9** [a]Gen. 42:37; 44:32; Philem. 18, 19

42:25–28 Joseph continues to instruct **his brothers** through the use of a type of shock therapy. Their sense of guilt prompts them to declare **God** must be punishing them; they could be accused of grand theft and made slaves (43:18).

42:38 Jacob would rather allow Simeon to languish in prison than risk sending Benjamin, his only other son by Rachel, to Egypt. **The grave** is Sheol, a place of darkness and gloom where man was cut off from God.

43:2, 3 Go back: Jacob was still closing his eyes to reality. Joseph (and Simeon) must have been wondering why the brothers were delayed, for Joseph had been counting on Simeon's value as a hostage. **Solemnly:** "Fiercely" or "repeatedly."

43:6 Israel: See note on 35:9–15.

by now we would have returned this
second time."
11 And their father Israel said to them,
"If *it must be* so, then do this: Take
some of the best fruits of the land in
your vessels and [a]carry down a present
for the man—a little [b]balm and a little
honey, spices and myrrh, pistachio
nuts and almonds.
12 "Take double money in your hand,
and take back in your hand the money
[a]that was returned in the mouth of
your sacks; perhaps it was an oversight.
13 "Take your brother also, and arise,
go back to the man.
14 "And may God [a]Almighty [b]give you
mercy before the man, that he may release your other brother and Benjamin.
[c]If I am bereaved, I am bereaved!"
15 So the men took that present and
Benjamin, and they took double money
in their hand, and arose and went
[a]down to Egypt; and they stood before
Joseph.
16 When Joseph saw Benjamin with
them, he said to the [a]steward of his
house, "Take *these* men to my home,
and slaughter [1]an animal and make
ready; for *these* men will dine with me
at noon."
17 Then the man did as Joseph ordered, and the man brought the men
into Joseph's house.
18 Now the men were [a]afraid because
they were brought into Joseph's house;
and they said, "*It is* because of the
money, which was returned in our
sacks the first time, that we are
brought in, so that he may [1]make a
case against us and seize us, to take
us as slaves with our donkeys."
19 When they drew near to the steward of Joseph's house, they talked with
him at the door of the house,
20 and said, "O sir, [a]we indeed came
down the first time to buy food;
21 "but [a]it happened, when we came
to the encampment, that we opened
our sacks, and there, *each* man's
money *was* in the mouth of his sack,
our money in full weight; so we have
brought it back in our hand.
22 "And we have brought down other
money in our hands to buy food. We
do not know who put our money in our
sacks."
23 But he said, "Peace *be* with you, do
not be afraid. Your God and the God
of your father has given you treasure
in your sacks; I had your money."
Then he brought [a]Simeon out to them.
24 So the man brought the men into
Joseph's house and [a]gave *them* water,
and they washed their feet; and he
gave their donkeys feed.
25 Then they made the present ready
for Joseph's coming at noon, for they
heard that they would eat bread there.
26 And when Joseph came home, they
brought him the present which *was* in
their hand into the house, and [a]bowed
down before him to the earth.
27 Then he asked them about *their*
well-being, and said, "*Is* your father
well, the old man [a]of whom you spoke?
Is he still alive?"
28 And they answered, "Your servant
our father *is* in good health; he *is* still
alive." [a]And they bowed their heads
down and prostrated themselves.
29 Then he lifted his eyes and saw his
brother Benjamin, [a]his mother's son,
and said, "*Is* this your younger brother
[b]of whom you spoke to me?" And he
said, "God be *gracious to you, my
son."
30 Now [a]his heart yearned for his
brother; so Joseph made haste and
sought *somewhere* to weep. And he
went into *his* chamber and [b]wept there.
31 Then he washed his face and came
out; and he restrained himself, and
said, "Serve the [a]bread."
32 So they set him a place by himself,
and them by themselves, and the Egyptians who ate with him by themselves;
because the Egyptians could not eat
food with the [a]Hebrews, for that *is*
[b]an abomination to the Egyptians.

11 [a]Gen. 32:20; 33:10; 43:25, 26; [Prov. 18:16] [b]Gen. 37:25; Jer. 8:22; Ezek. 27:17
12 [a]Gen. 42:25, 35; 43:21, 22
14 [a]Gen. 17:1; 28:3; 35:11; 48:3 [b]Gen. 39:21; Ps. 106:46 [c]Gen. 42:36; Esth. 4:16
15 [a]Gen. 39:1; 46:3, 6
16 [a]Gen. 24:2; 39:4; 44:1 [1]Lit. *a slaughter*
18 [a]Gen. 42:28 [1]Lit. *roll himself upon us*
20 [a]Gen. 42:3, 10
21 [a]Gen. 42:27, 35
23 [a]Gen. 42:24
24 [a]Gen. 18:4; 19:2; 24:32
26 [a]Gen. 37:7, 10; 42:6; 44:14
27 [a]Gen. 29:6; 42:11, 13; 43:7; 45:3; 2 Kin. 4:26
28 [a]Gen. 37:7, 10
29 [a]Gen. 35:17, 18 [b]Gen. 42:13 *See WW at Mal. 1:9.
30 [a]1 Kin. 3:26 [b]Gen. 42:24; 45:2, 14, 15; 46:29
31 [a]Gen. 43:25
32 [a]Gen. 41:12; Ex. 1:15 [b]Gen. 46:34; Ex. 8:26

43:11 If *it must be* so: Israel reluctantly accepted the inevitable, for all this was God's will. **Balm:** From Gilead (see Jer. 8:22). Wild **honey, spices and myrrh** were highly prized in Egypt for cosmetics, perfume, incense, and embalming the dead. **Pistachio nuts** were a rare delicacy, and **almonds** grew wild in Canaan. All the gifts proved they had returned to Canaan.

43:14 God Almighty: See note on 17:1, 2.

43:21 In full weight: Payment was normally made by weight, as coinage was still in the future.

43:28 Your servant expresses Near Eastern humility when in the presence of a threatening superior. Joseph was accomplishing his purpose of instructing his brothers.

43:32–34 Ancient inscriptions demonstrate this hostile attitude of **Egyptians** toward Asiatics. Egyptians were a dark-skinned Hamitic people; the **Hebrews** were Semites. It is possible that an invading tribe, the Asiatic "Hyksos," were the Semitic rulers of Egypt at this time, but v. 32 indicates the sharp difference between these Egyptian rulers and the Semitic Hebrews, confirming the fact that Pharaoh and his administration were of a native Egyptian dynasty. The brothers stared **in astonishment** as they were all seated in order of their ages. How could Joseph know this?

Since Joseph's skin color would betray him as an Asiatic, Jacob's sons might have recognized him. So he was maintaining a discreet distance from them (see 45:4).

33 And they sat before him, the firstborn according to his [a]birthright and
the youngest according to his youth;
and the men looked in astonishment
at one another.
34 Then he took servings to them from
before him, but Benjamin's serving
was [a]five times as much as any of
theirs. So they drank and were merry
with him.

Joseph's Cup

44 And he commanded [1]the [a]stew-
ard of his house, saying, [b]"Fill
the men's sacks with food, as much as
they can carry, and put each man's
money in the mouth of his sack.
2 "Also put my cup, the silver cup, in
the mouth of the sack of the youngest,
and his grain money." So he did according to the word that Joseph had
spoken.
3 As soon as the morning dawned, the
men were sent away, they and their
donkeys.
4 When they had gone out of the city,
and were not *yet* far off, Joseph said
to his steward, "Get up, follow the
men; and when you overtake them, say
to them, 'Why have you [a]repaid evil
for good?
5 '*Is* not this *the one* from which my
lord drinks, and with which he indeed
practices divination? You have done
evil in so doing.' "
6 So he overtook them, and he spoke
to them these same words.
7 And they said to him, "Why does
my lord say these words? Far be it from
us that your servants should do such
a thing.
8 "Look, we brought back to you
from the land of Canaan [a]the money
which we found in the mouth of our
sacks. How then could we steal silver
or gold from your lord's house?
9 "With whomever of your servants
it is found, [a]let him die, and we also
will be my lord's slaves."
10 And he said, "Now also *let* it *be* according to your words; he with whom
it is found shall be my slave, and you
shall be blameless."
11 Then each man speedily let down
his sack to the ground, and each
opened his sack.

33 [a]Gen. 27:36; 42:7; Deut. 21:16, 17
34 [a]Gen. 35:24; 45:22

CHAPTER 44

1 [a]Gen. 43:16 [b]Gen. 42:25 [1]Lit. *the one over*
4 [a]1 Sam. 25:21
8 [a]Gen. 43:21
9 [a]Gen. 31:32
12 [1]*finished with*
13 [a]Gen. 37:29, 34; Num. 14:6; 2 Sam. 1:11
14 [a]Gen. 37:7, 10
16 [a][Num. 32:23] [b]Gen. 44:9
17 [a]Prov. 17:15
18 [a]Gen. 18:30, 32; Ex. 32:22
20 [a]Gen. 37:3; 43:8; 44:30 [b]Gen. 42:38 [c]Gen. 46:19 [d]Gen. 42:4
21 [a]Gen. 42:15, 20
23 [a]Gen. 43:3, 5

12 So he searched. He began with the
oldest and [1]left off with the youngest;
and the cup was found in Benjamin's
sack.
13 Then they [a]tore their clothes, and
each man loaded his donkey and returned to the city.
14 So Judah and his brothers came to
Joseph's house, and he *was* still there;
and they [a]fell before him on the
ground.
15 And Joseph said to them, "What
deed *is* this you have done? Did you
not know that such a man as I can certainly practice divination?"
16 Then Judah said, "What shall we
say to my lord? What shall we speak?
Or how shall we clear ourselves? God
has [a]found out the iniquity of your servants; here [b]we are, my lord's slaves,
both we and *he* also with whom the
cup was found."
17 But he said, [a]"Far be it from me that
I should do so; the man in whose hand
the cup was found, he shall be my
slave. And as for you, go up in peace
to your father."

Judah Intercedes for Benjamin

18 Then Judah came near to him and
said: "O my lord, please let your servant speak a word in my lord's hearing, and [a]do not let your anger burn
against your servant; for you *are* even
like Pharaoh.
19 "My lord asked his servants, saying, 'Have you a father or a brother?'
20 "And we said to my lord, 'We have
a father, an old man, and [a]a child of
his old age, *who is* young; his brother
is [b]dead, and he [c]alone is left of his
mother's children, and his [d]father
loves him.'
21 "Then you said to your servants,
[a]'Bring him down to me, that I may set
my eyes on him.'
22 "And we said to my lord, 'The lad
cannot leave his father, for *if* he should
leave his father, *his father* would die.'
23 "But you said to your servants,
[a]'Unless your youngest brother comes
down with you, you shall see my face
no more.'
24 "So it was, when we went up to
your servant my father, that we told
him the words of my lord.

44:1–12 Joseph continued his plan of instructing and chastening his brothers according to his dream (37:5–8).
44:5 With which . . . practices divination: Either Joseph practiced something later prohibited in Israel (Deut. 18:10), or the Hebrew should be translated, "he would certainly have divined about this matter."
44:13 Tore their clothes: An ancient Semitic demonstration of grief, anger, or repentance.
44:15 See note on v. 5.

25 "And [a]our father said, 'Go back *and*
buy us a little food.'
26 "But we said, 'We cannot go down;
if our youngest brother is with us, then
we will go down; for we may not see
the man's face unless our youngest
brother *is* with us.'
27 "Then your servant my father said
to us, 'You know that [a]my wife bore
me two sons;
28 'and the one went out from me, and
I said, [a]"Surely he is torn to pieces";
and I have not seen him since.
29 'But if you [a]take this one also from
me, and calamity befalls him, you shall
bring down my gray hair with sorrow
to the grave.'
30 "Now therefore, when I come to
your servant my father, and the lad *is*
not with us, since [a]his life is bound up
in the lad's life,
31 "it will happen, when he sees that
the lad *is* not *with us,* that he will die.
So your servants will bring down the
gray hair of your servant our father
with sorrow to the grave.
32 "For your servant became surety for
the lad to my father, saying, [a]'If I do
not bring him *back* to you, then I shall
bear the blame before my father forever.'
33 "Now therefore, please [a]let your
servant remain instead of the lad as a
slave to my lord, and let the lad go up
with his brothers.
34 "For how shall I go up to my father
if the lad *is* not with me, lest perhaps
I see the evil that would [1]come upon
my father?"

Joseph Revealed to His Brothers

45 Then Joseph could not restrain
himself before all those who
stood by him, and he cried out, "Make
everyone go out from me!" So no one
stood with him [a]while Joseph made
himself known to his brothers.
2 And he [a]wept aloud, and the Egyptians and the house of Pharaoh heard *it.*
3 Then Joseph said to his brothers,
[a]"I *am* Joseph; does my father still
live?" But his brothers could not answer him, for they were dismayed in
his presence.
4 And Joseph said to his brothers,
"Please come near to me." So they
came near. Then he said: "I *am* Joseph
your brother, [a]whom you sold into
Egypt.

25 [a]Gen. 43:2
27 [a]Gen. 30:22–24; 35:16–18; 46:19
28 [a]Gen. 37:31–35
29 [a]Gen. 42:36, 38; 44:31
30 [a][1 Sam. 18:1; 25:29]
32 [a]Gen. 43:9
33 [a]Ex. 32:32
34 [1]Lit. *find*

CHAPTER 45

1 [a]Acts 7:13
2 [a]Gen. 43:30; 46:29
3 [a]Gen. 43:27; Acts 7:13
4 [a]Gen. 37:28; 39:1; Ps. 105:17
5 [a]Gen. 45:7, 8; 50:20; Ps. 105:16, 17
6 [a]Gen. 43:1; 47:4, 13
7 [a]Gen. 45:5; 50:20 [1]*remnant*
8 [a][Rom. 8:28] [b]Judg. 17:10; Is. 22:21 [c]Gen. 41:43; 42:6

KINGDOM DYNAMICS

45:4 Love Embraces Those Who Have Wronged Us, BROTHERLY LOVE. The story of Joseph is an early account of the forgiving nature God expects us to display in our treatment of those who have wronged us. It is a founding example of Christ-like love. Though Joseph's brothers sold him into slavery and deceived his father into thinking him dead, when he confronts his brothers during their time of need, his forgiveness and love burst forth from his heart. With uncanny faith in the overriding providence of God, he even professes his belief that God has used his brothers' betrayal of him as a means to deliver his family during the time of famine (v. 7). Joseph's forgiveness of his brothers' sin is so complete that he kisses all of them and weeps with joy at being united with them once again. Brotherly forgiveness is expressive, self-giving, and offered in a way that assists its being received.

(Gen. 4:9/Lev. 19:34) D.S.

5 "But now, do not therefore be
grieved or angry with yourselves because you sold me here; [a]for God sent
me before you to preserve life.
6 "For these two years the [a]famine
has been in the land, and *there are* still
five years in which *there will be* neither
plowing nor harvesting.
7 "And God [a]sent me before you to 6
preserve a [1]posterity for you in the
earth, and to save your lives by a great
deliverance.
8 "So now *it was* not you *who* sent
me here, but [a]God; and He has made
me [b]a father to Pharaoh, and lord of
all his house, and a [c]ruler throughout
all the land of Egypt.
9 "Hurry and go up to my father, and
say to him, 'Thus says your son Joseph:

44:27–29 See notes on 42:38 and 43:11.
45:1 Joseph's position was awkward. As an Asiatic himself, he was part of a scorned lower class, yet he was also governor of all Egypt. Joseph desired the welfare of **his brothers,** but he did not trust them; he was still working through his hurt and through his role as God's agent. He wished to bring them to Egypt where there was food, but they were shepherds; and the Egyptians, being cattlemen, despised shepherds (see 46:34). In the uncontrollable emotion of Judah's plea, Joseph broke and ordered **everyone . . . out,** that is, all of his Egyptian servants.
45:3 Still live means "Is he truly still in good health?" The **brothers . . . were dismayed:** speechless, astonished, dumbfounded.
45:4 He had to identify himself again; they were too shocked to grasp the fact that it really was **Joseph.**
45:5 The entire 20-year period is brought into focus.
45:7 See section 6 of Truth-In-Action at the end of Gen.
45:8 Note Joseph's developed perspective over that expressed in 40:15. **A father to Pharaoh** was a common designation of a high-ranking advisor.

"God has made me lord of all Egypt;
come down to me, do not [1]tarry.
10 [a]"You shall dwell in the land of Goshen, and you shall be near to me, you
and your children, your children's children, your flocks and your herds, and
all that you have.
11 "There I will [a]provide* for you, lest
you and your household, and all that
you have, come to poverty; for *there
are* still five years of famine." '
12 "And behold, your eyes and the
eyes of my brother Benjamin see that
it is [a]my mouth that speaks to you.
13 "So you shall tell my father of all
my glory in Egypt, and of all that you
have seen; and you shall hurry and
[a]bring my father down here."
14 Then he fell on his brother Benjamin's neck and wept, and Benjamin
wept on his neck.
15 Moreover he [a]kissed all his brothers
and wept over them, and after that his
brothers talked with him.
16 Now the report of it was heard in
Pharaoh's house, saying, "Joseph's
brothers have come." So it pleased
Pharaoh and his servants well.
17 And Pharaoh said to Joseph, "Say
to your brothers, 'Do this: Load your
animals and depart; go to the land of
Canaan.
18 'Bring your father and your households and come to me; I will give you
the best of the land of Egypt, and you
will eat [a]the [1]fat of the land.
19 'Now you are commanded—do this:
Take carts out of the land of Egypt for
your little ones and your wives; bring
your father and come.
20 'Also do not be concerned about
your goods, for the best of all the land
of Egypt *is* yours.' "
21 Then the sons of Israel did so; and
Joseph gave them [a]carts,[1] according to
the command of Pharaoh, and he gave
them provisions for the journey.
22 He gave to all of them, to each man,
[a]changes of garments; but to Benjamin
he gave three hundred *pieces* of silver
and [b]five changes of garments.
23 And he sent to his father these
things: ten donkeys loaded with the
good things of Egypt, and ten female
donkeys loaded with grain, bread, and
food for his father for the journey.
24 So he sent his brothers away, and
they departed; and he said to them,
"See that you do not become troubled
along the way."
25 Then they went up out of Egypt, and
came to the land of Canaan to Jacob
their father.
26 And they told him, saying, "Joseph
is still alive, and he *is* governor over
all the land of Egypt." [a]And Jacob's
heart stood still, because he did not believe them.
27 But when they told him all the
words which Joseph had said to them,
and when he saw the carts which Joseph had sent to carry him, the spirit
[a]of Jacob their father revived.
28 Then Israel said, "*It is* enough. Joseph my son *is* still alive. I will go and
see him before I die."

Jacob's Journey to Egypt

46 So Israel took his journey with
all that he had, and came to
[a]Beersheba, and offered sacrifices
[b]to the God of his father Isaac.
2 Then God spoke to Israel [a]in the visions of the night, and said, "Jacob, Jacob!" And he said, "Here I am."
3 So He said, "I *am* God, [a]the God
of your father; do not fear to go down
to Egypt, for I will [b]make of you a great
nation there.
4 [a]"I will go down with you to Egypt,
and I will also surely [b]bring you up
again; and [c]Joseph [1]will put his hand
on your eyes."
5 Then [a]Jacob arose from Beersheba;
and the sons of Israel carried their father Jacob, their little ones, and their
wives, in the [1]carts [b]which Pharaoh
had sent to carry him.
6 So they took their livestock and
their goods, which they had acquired
in the land of Canaan, and went to
Egypt, [a]Jacob and all his descendants
with him.
7 His sons and his sons' sons, his
daughters and his sons' daughters, and
all his descendants he brought with
him to Egypt.
8 Now [a]these *were* the names of the
children of Israel, Jacob and his sons,

9 [1]*delay*
10 [a]Gen. 46:28, 34; 47:1, 6; Ex. 9:26
11 [a]Gen. 47:12 *See WW at Ps. 55:22.
12 [a]Gen. 42:23
13 [a]Gen. 46:6–28; Acts 7:14
15 [a]Gen. 48:10
18 [a]Gen. 27:28; 47:6; Deut. 32:9–14 [1]The choicest produce
21 [a]Gen. 45:19; 46:5 [1]*wagons*
22 [a]2 Kin. 5:5 [b]Gen. 43:34
26 [a]Job 29:24; Ps. 126:1; Luke 24:11, 41
27 [a]Judg. 15:19; Is. 40:29

CHAPTER 46

1 [a]Gen. 21:31, 33; 26:32, 33; 28:10 [b]Gen. 26:24, 25; 28:13; 31:42; 32:9
2 [a]Gen. 15:1; 22:11; 31:11; Num. 12:6; Job 33:14, 15
3 [a]Gen. 17:1; 28:13 [b]Gen. 12:2; Ex. 1:9; 12:37; Deut. 26:5
4 [a]Gen. 28:15; 31:3; 48:21; Ex. 3:12 [b]Gen. 15:16; 50:12, 24, 25; Ex. 3:8 [c]Gen. 50:1 [1]Will close your eyes when you die
5 [a]Gen. 47:9; Acts 7:15 [b]Gen. 45:19–21 [1]*wagons*
6 [a]Deut. 26:5; Josh. 24:4; Ps. 105:23; Is. 52:4; Acts 7:15
8 [a]Ex. 1:1–4

45:16–20 Pharaoh's graciousness was unprecedented. No doubt it was due to God's providence, a providence that also included severe testing for Israel so as to manifest God's ultimate sovereignty over Egypt (15:13, 14).
45:24 Do not become troubled: "Do not quarrel among yourselves."
45:26 Jacob's heart stood still: He almost died of shock.
46:1 Beersheba: A trip to worship at an ancient shrine seemed appropriate for the occasion. See note on 21:33.
46:2–4 God has now spoken of this covenant seven times to Abraham, twice to Isaac, and three times to **Jacob. His hand on your eyes: Joseph** "will close your eyelids when you die."
46:8–25 The list here serves primarily to mark those involved in a significant turning point of Israel's history.

who went to Egypt: [b]Reuben *was* Jacob's firstborn.
9 The [a]sons of Reuben *were* Hanoch,
Pallu, Hezron, and Carmi.
10 [a]The sons of Simeon *were* [1]Jemuel,
Jamin, Ohad, [2]Jachin, [3]Zohar, and
Shaul, the son of a Canaanite woman.
11 The sons of [a]Levi *were* Gershon,
Kohath, and Merari.
12 The sons of [a]Judah *were* [b]Er, Onan,
Shelah, Perez, and Zerah (but Er and
Onan died in the land of Canaan).
[c]The sons of Perez were Hezron and
Hamul.
13 The sons of Issachar *were* Tola,
[1]Puvah, [2]Job, and Shimron.
14 The [a]sons of Zebulun *were* Sered,
Elon, and Jahleel.
15 These *were* the [a]sons of Leah,
whom she bore to Jacob in Padan
Aram, with his daughter Dinah. All the
persons, his sons and his daughters,
were thirty-three.
16 The sons of Gad *were* [1]Ziphion,
Haggi, Shuni, [2]Ezbon, Eri, [3]Arodi, and
Areli.
17 [a]The sons of Asher *were* Jimnah,
Ishuah, Isui, Beriah, and Serah, their
sister. And the sons of Beriah *were* Heber and Malchiel.
18 [a]These *were* the sons of Zilpah,
[b]whom Laban gave to Leah his daughter; and these she bore to Jacob: sixteen persons.
19 The [a]sons of Rachel, [b]Jacob's wife,
were Joseph and Benjamin.
20 [a]And to Joseph in the land of Egypt
were born Manasseh and Ephraim,
whom Asenath, the daughter of Poti-
Pherah priest of On, bore to him.
21 [a]The sons of Benjamin *were* Belah,
Becher, Ashbel, Gera, Naaman, [b]Ehi,
Rosh, [c]Muppim, [1]Huppim, and Ard.
22 These *were* the sons of Rachel, who
were born to Jacob: fourteen persons
in all.
23 The son of Dan *was* [1]Hushim.
24 [a]The sons of Naphtali *were* [1]Jah-
zeel, Guni, Jezer, and [2]Shillem.
25 [a]These *were* the sons of Bilhah,
[b]whom Laban gave to Rachel his
daughter, and she bore these to Jacob:
seven persons in all.
26 [a]All the persons who went with Jacob to Egypt, who came from his body,

8 [b]Num. 26:4, 5
9 [a]Ex. 6:14
10 [a]Ex. 6:15 [1]*Nemuel,* 1 Chr. 4:24 [2]*Jarib,* 1 Chr. 4:24 [3]*Zerah,* 1 Chr. 4:24
11 [a]1 Chr. 6:1, 16
12 [a]1 Chr. 2:3; 4:21 [b]Gen. 38:3, 7, 10 [c]Gen. 38:29
13 [1]*Puah,* Num. 26:23; 1 Chr. 7:1 [2]*Jashub,* Num. 26:24; 1 Chr. 7:1
14 [a]Num. 26:26
15 [a]Gen. 35:23; 49:31
16 [1]Sam., LXX *Zephon* and Num. 26:15 [2]*Ozni,* Num. 26:16 [3]*Arod,* Num. 26:17
17 [a]1 Chr. 7:30
18 [a]Gen. 30:10; 37:2 [b]Gen. 29:24
19 [a]Gen. 35:24 [b]Gen. 44:27
20 [a]Gen. 41:45, 50–52; 48:1
21 [a]1 Chr. 7:6; 8:1 [b]Num. 26:38 [c]Num. 26:39 [1]*Hupham,* Num. 26:39
23 [1]*Shuham,* Num. 26:42
24 [a]Num. 26:48 [1]*Jahziel,* 1 Chr. 7:13 [2]*Shallum,* 1 Chr. 7:13
25 [a]Gen. 30:5, 7 [b]Gen. 29:29
26 [a]Ex. 1:5 [b]Gen. 35:11
27 [a]Deut. 10:22
28 [a]Gen. 31:21 [b]Gen. 47:1
29 [a]Gen. 41:43 [b]Gen. 45:14, 15
30 [a]Luke 2:29, 30
31 [a]Gen. 47:1
32 [a]Gen. 47:3
33 [a]Gen. 47:2, 3
34 [a]Gen. 47:3 [b]Gen. 30:35; 34:5; 37:17 [c]Gen. 43:32 [1]*loathsome*

CHAPTER 47

1 [a]Gen. 46:31 [b]Gen. 45:10; 46:28; 50:8 **2** [a]Acts 7:13 **3** [a]Gen. 46:33

[b]besides Jacob's sons' wives, *were*
sixty-six persons in all.
27 And the sons of Joseph who were
born to him in Egypt *were* two persons.
[a]All the persons of the house of Jacob
who went to Egypt were seventy.

Jacob Settles in Goshen

28 Then he sent Judah before him to
Joseph, [a]to point out before him *the
way* to Goshen. And they came [b]to the
land of Goshen.
29 So Joseph made ready his [a]chariot
and went up to Goshen to meet his father Israel; and he presented himself
to him, and [b]fell on his neck and wept
on his neck a good while.
30 And Israel said to Joseph, [a]"Now
let me die, since I have seen your face,
because you *are* still alive."
31 Then Joseph said to his brothers
and to his father's household, [a]"I will
go up and tell Pharaoh, and say to him,
'My brothers and those of my father's
house, who *were* in the land of Canaan,
have come to me.
32 'And the men *are* [a]shepherds, for
their occupation has been to feed livestock; and they have brought their
flocks, their herds, and all that they
have.'
33 "So it shall be, when Pharaoh calls
you and says, [a]'What is your occupation?'
34 "that you shall say, 'Your servants'
[a]occupation has been with livestock
[b]from our youth even till now, both we
and also our fathers,' that you may
dwell in the land of Goshen; for every
shepherd *is* [c]an[1] abomination to the
Egyptians."

47 Then Joseph [a]went and told
Pharaoh, and said, "My father
and my brothers, their flocks and their
herds and all that they possess, have
come from the land of Canaan; and indeed they *are* in [b]the land of Goshen."
2 And he took five men from among
his brothers and [a]presented them to
Pharaoh.
3 Then Pharaoh said to his brothers,
[a]"What *is* your occupation?" And they

46:27 Jacob entered **Egypt** with a family of **seventy;** his descendants departed under Moses approximately 600,000 strong (Ex. 12:37). The additional four (see v. 26) include Ephraim, Manasseh, **Joseph,** and Jacob.

46:28 Goshen was a grazing area in the eastern Nile River delta. According to the monuments, Asiatics did sometimes settle in Egyptian pasturelands. Their presence in Egypt could, and soon would, cause serious friction (Ex. 1:8–11).

46:34 An abomination: Because of the traditional hostility between the cattleman and the **shepherd,** Joseph instructed his brothers to identify themselves **with livestock** (cattle).

47:3 Joseph's **brothers** appear to have violated their instructions not to mention that they are **shepherds.** Probably they were using the word in a generic sense, meaning people who care for any domesticated animals. **Pharaoh** seems to have understood it this way (v. 6).

said to Pharaoh, [b]"Your servants *are* shepherds, both we *and* also our fathers."

4 And they said to Pharaoh, [a]"We have come to dwell in the land, because your servants have no pasture for their flocks, [b]for the famine *is* severe in the land of Canaan. Now therefore, please let your servants [c]dwell in the land of Goshen."

5 Then Pharaoh spoke to Joseph, saying, "Your father and your brothers have come to you.

6 [a]"The land of Egypt *is* before you. Have your father and brothers dwell in the best of the land; let them dwell [b]in the land of Goshen. And if you know *any* competent men among them, then make them chief herdsmen over my livestock."

7 Then Joseph brought in his father Jacob and set him before Pharaoh; and Jacob [a]blessed Pharaoh.

8 Pharaoh said to Jacob, "How old *are* you?"

9 And Jacob said to Pharaoh, [a]"The days of the years of my [1]pilgrimage *are* [b]one hundred and thirty years; [c]few and evil have been the days of the years of my life, and [d]they have not attained to the days of the years of the life of my fathers in the days of their pilgrimage."

10 So Jacob [a]blessed Pharaoh, and went out from before Pharaoh.

11 And Joseph situated his father and his brothers, and gave them a possession in the land of Egypt, in the best of the land, in the land of [a]Rameses, [b]as Pharaoh had commanded.

12 Then Joseph provided [a]his father, his brothers, and all his father's household with bread, according to the number in *their* families.

Joseph Deals with the Famine

13 Now *there was* no bread in all the land; for the famine *was* very severe, [a]so that the land of Egypt and the land of Canaan languished because of the famine.

14 [a]And Joseph gathered up all the money that was found in the land of Egypt and in the land of Canaan, for the grain which they bought; and Joseph brought the money into Pharaoh's house.

15 So when the money failed in the land of Egypt and in the land of Canaan, all the Egyptians came to Joseph and said, "Give us bread, for [a]why should we die in your presence? For the money has failed."

16 Then Joseph said, "Give your livestock, and I will give you *bread* for your livestock, if the money is gone."

17 So they brought their livestock to Joseph, and Joseph gave them bread *in exchange* for the horses, the flocks, the cattle of the herds, and for the donkeys. Thus he [1]fed them with bread *in exchange* for all their livestock that year.

18 When that year had ended, they came to him the next year and said to him, "We will not hide from my lord that our money is gone; my lord also has our herds of livestock. There is nothing left in the sight of my lord but our bodies and our lands.

19 "Why should we die before your eyes, both we and our land? Buy us and our land for bread, and we and our land will be servants of Pharaoh; give *us* seed, that we may [a]live and not die, that the land may not be desolate."

20 Then Joseph [a]bought all the land of Egypt for Pharaoh; for every man of the Egyptians sold his field, because the famine was severe upon them. So the land became Pharaoh's.

21 And as for the people, he [1]moved them into the cities, from *one* end of the borders of Egypt to the *other* end.

22 [a]Only the land of the [b]priests he did not buy; for the priests had rations *allotted to them* by Pharaoh, and they ate their rations which Pharaoh gave them; therefore they did not sell their lands.

23 Then Joseph said to the people, "Indeed I have bought you and your land this day for Pharaoh. Look, *here is* seed

3 [b]Gen. 46:32, 34; Ex. 2:17, 19
4 [a]Gen. 15:13; Deut. 26:5; Ps. 105:23 [b]Gen. 43:1; Acts 7:11 [c]Gen. 46:34
6 [a]Gen. 20:15; 45:10, 18; 47:11 [b]Gen. 47:4
7 [a]Gen. 47:10; 48:15, 20; 2 Sam. 14:22; 1 Kin. 8:66; Heb. 7:7
9 [a]Ps. 39:12; [Heb. 11:9, 13] [b]Gen. 47:28 [c][Job 14:1] [d]Gen. 5:5; 11:10, 11; 25:7, 8; 35:28 [1]Lit. *sojourning*
10 [a]Gen. 47:7
11 [a]Ex. 1:11; 12:37 [b]Gen. 47:6, 27
12 [a]Gen. 45:11; 50:21
13 [a]Gen. 41:30; Acts 7:11
14 [a]Gen. 41:56; 42:6
15 [a]Gen. 47:19
17 [1]*supplied*
19 [a]Gen. 43:8
20 [a]Jer. 32:43
21 [1]So with MT, Tg.; Sam., LXX, Vg. *made the people virtual slaves*
22 [a]Lev. 25:34; Ezra 7:24 [b]Gen. 41:45

47:9 Pilgrimage: Literally, "camps" or "sojournings," places where one stays only temporarily. **Few and evil:** A typical statement in ancient Semitic wisdom literature.

47:11 The land of Rameses: The Egyptian name for the area called "Goshen" by the Hebrews.

47:18 *The Egyptians finally sold Pharaoh their homes and their* **lands,** even selling themselves as the king's slaves. Starvation was the only alternative. Voluntary slavery was often a means of keeping the poor alive. Joseph's behavior was not heartless; even the enslaved peasants would have considered him a wise man. We must understand the culture: after all, Pharaoh was considered to be a god. As the result of Joseph's efforts, Egypt now had a strong central government, probably marking the end of some anarchic conditions.

47:21–26 Joseph **moved them into the cities** where they could be fed, then distributed **seed** for planting as the drought was ending. He did not disturb **the priests;** they are a powerful political force in any primitive land. Years later Moses himself became a member of the Egyptian royal family and noted that these decrees by Joseph were **law over the land of Egypt to this day.**

for you, and you shall *sow the land.
24 "And it shall come to pass in the
harvest that you shall give one-fifth to
Pharaoh. Four-fifths shall be your own,
as seed for the field and for your food,
for those of your households and as
food for your little ones."
25 So they said, "You have saved
[a]our lives; let us find favor in the sight
of my lord, and we will be Pharaoh's
servants."
26 And Joseph made it a law over the
land of Egypt to this day, *that* Pharaoh
should have one-fifth, [a]except for the
land of the priests only, *which* did not
become Pharaoh's.

Joseph's Vow to Jacob

27 So Israel [a]dwelt in the land of
Egypt, in the country of Goshen; and
they had possessions there and [b]grew
and multiplied exceedingly.
28 And Jacob lived in the land of Egypt
seventeen years. So the length of Jacob's life was one hundred and forty-
seven years.
29 When the time [a]drew near that Israel must die, he called his son Joseph
and said to him, "Now if I have found
favor in your sight, please [b]put your
hand under my thigh, and [c]deal kindly
and truly with me. [d]Please do not bury
me in Egypt,
30 "but [a]let me lie with my fathers; you
shall carry me out of Egypt and
[b]bury me in their burial place." And
he said, "I will do as you have said."
31 Then he said, "Swear to me." And
he swore to him. So [a]Israel bowed himself on the head of the bed.

Jacob Blesses Joseph's Sons

48 Now it came to pass after these
things that Joseph was told, "Indeed your father *is* sick"; and he took
with him his two sons, [a]Manasseh and
Ephraim.
2 And Jacob was told, "Look, your
son Joseph is coming to you"; and Israel [1]strengthened* himself and sat up
on the bed.
3 Then Jacob said to Joseph: "God
[a]Almighty* appeared to me at [b]Luz in
the land of Canaan and blessed me,
4 "and said to me, 'Behold, I will
[a]make you fruitful and multiply you,
and I will make of you a multitude of
people, and [b]give this land to your descendants after you [c]*as* an everlasting
possession.'
5 "And now your [a]two sons, Ephraim
and Manasseh, who were born to you
in the land of Egypt before I came to
you in Egypt, *are* mine; as Reuben and
Simeon, they shall be mine.
6 "Your [1]offspring [2]whom you beget
after them shall be yours; they will be
called by the name of their brothers
in their inheritance.
7 "But as for me, when I came from
Padan, [a]Rachel died beside me in the
land of Canaan on the way, when *there
was* but a little distance to go to Ephrath; and I buried her there on the way
to Ephrath (that is, Bethlehem)."
8 Then Israel saw Joseph's sons, and
said, "Who *are* these?"
9 And Joseph said to his father,
"They *are* my sons, whom God has
given me in this *place*." And he said,
"Please bring them to me, and [a]I will
bless them."
10 Now [a]the eyes of Israel were dim
with age, *so that* he could not see.
Then Joseph brought them near him,
and he [b]kissed them and embraced
them.
11 And Israel said to Joseph, [a]"I had
not thought to see your face; but in
fact, God has also shown me your offspring!"
12 So Joseph brought them from beside his knees, and he bowed down
with his face to the earth.
13 And Joseph took them both,
Ephraim with his right hand toward Israel's left hand, and Manasseh with his
left hand toward Israel's right hand,
and brought *them* near him.
14 Then Israel stretched out his right

23 *See WW at Hos. 10:12
25 [a]Gen. 33:15
26 [a]Gen. 47:22
27 [a]Gen. 47:11 [b]Gen. 17:6; 26:4; 35:11; 46:3; Ex. 1:7; Deut. 26:5; Acts 7:17
29 [a]Deut. 31:14; 1 Kin. 2:1 [b]Gen. 24:2–4 [c]Gen. 24:49; Josh. 2:14 [d]Gen. 50:25
30 [a]2 Sam. 19:37 [b]Gen. 49:29; 50:5–13; Heb. 11:21
31 [a]Gen. 48:2; 1 Kin. 1:47; Heb. 11:21

CHAPTER 48

1 [a]Gen. 41:51, 56; 46:20; 50:23; Josh. 14:4
2 [1]Collected his strength *See WW at Josh. 1:9.
3 [a]Gen. 43:14; 49:25 [b]Gen. 28:13, 19; 35:6, 9 *See WW at Ps. 91:1.
4 [a]Gen. 46:3 [b]Gen. 35:12; Ex. 6:8 [c]Gen. 17:8
5 [a]Gen. 41:50; 46:20; 48:8; Josh. 13:7; 14:4
6 [1]*children* [2]Who are born to you
7 [a]Gen. 35:9, 16, 19, 20
9 [a]Gen. 27:4; 47:15
10 [a]Gen. 27:1; 1 Sam. 3:2 [b]Gen. 27:27; 45:15; 50:1
11 [a]Gen. 45:26

47:29 Under my thigh: Exactly as Jacob's grandfather Abraham had done earlier. See note on 24:2, 3.
47:30 Their burial place: See note on 23:19.
47:31 Bowed himself on the head of the bed: Heb. 11:21 reflects the Septuagint variation: "*leaning* on the top of his staff."
48:5, 6 Jacob claimed the perpetuation of his own name, not through his son Joseph, but through his two grandsons, then stated that the grandsons in turn would father entire tribes in their own names. Thus, by Jacob's dying decree the house of Joseph was to be split into two tribes.
48:8 Israel was likely aware of (**saw**) the presence of **Joseph's sons** and yet was not fully able to recognize them because of his poor eyesight (v. 10).
48:9 Bless them: To affirm God's will for them over that of the curse. See note on 12:1–9.
48:10 He kissed . . . embraced them: An integral part of blessing is physical affirmation.
48:13 Joseph was positioning them according to the traditional pattern of blessing.
48:14 His right hand was the hand with the greater anointing and blessing, used to bless the firstborn. Jacob was crossing his hands to bless the second born. This again

hand and [a]laid *it* on Ephraim's head, who *was* the younger, and his left hand on Manasseh's head, [b]guiding his hands knowingly, for Manasseh *was* the [c]firstborn.
15 And [a]he blessed Joseph, and said:

"God, [b]before whom my fathers
Abraham and Isaac walked,
The God who has fed me all my
life long to this day,
16 The Angel [a]who has redeemed
me from all evil,
Bless the lads;
Let [b]my name be named upon
them,
And the name of my fathers
Abraham and Isaac;
And let them [c]grow into a
multitude in the midst of the
earth."

17 Now when Joseph saw that his father [a]laid his right hand on the head of Ephraim, it displeased him; so he took hold of his father's hand to remove it from Ephraim's head to Manasseh's head.
18 And Joseph said to his father, "Not so, my father, for this *one is* the firstborn; put your right hand on his head."
19 But his father refused and said, [a]"I know, my son, I know. He also shall become a people, and he also shall be great; but truly [b]his younger brother shall be greater than he, and his descendants shall become a multitude of nations."
20 So he blessed them that day, saying, [a]"By you Israel will bless, saying, 'May God make you as Ephraim and as Manasseh!' " And thus he set Ephraim before Manasseh.
21 Then Israel said to Joseph, "Behold, I am dying, but [a]God will be with you and bring you back to the land of your fathers.
22 "Moreover [a]I have given to you one [1]portion above your brothers, which I took from the hand [b]of the Amorite with my sword and my bow."

Jacob's Last Words to His Sons

49 And Jacob called his sons and said, "Gather together, that I may [a]tell you what shall befall you [b]in the last days:

2 "Gather together and hear, you
sons of Jacob,
And listen to Israel your father.

3 "Reuben, you are [a]my firstborn,
My might and the beginning of
my strength,
The excellency of dignity and the
excellency of power.
4 Unstable as water, you shall not
excel,
Because you [a]went up to your
father's bed;
Then you defiled *it*—
He went up to my couch.

5 "Simeon and Levi *are* brothers;
Instruments of [1]cruelty *are in*
their dwelling place.
6 [a]Let not my soul enter their
council;
Let not my honor be united
[b]to their *assembly;

14 [a]Matt. 19:15; Mark 10:16 [b]Gen. 48:19 [c]Gen. 41:51, 52; Josh. 17:1 **15** [a]Gen. 47:7, 10; 49:24; [Heb. 11:21] [b]Gen. 17:1; 24:40; 2 Kin. 20:3 **16** [a]Gen. 22:11, 15–18; 28:13–15; 31:11; [Ps. 34:22; 121:7] [b]Amos 9:12; Acts 15:17 [c]Num. 26:34, 37 **17** [a]Gen. 48:14 **19** [a]Gen. 48:14 [b]Num. 1:33, 35; Deut. 33:17 **20** [a]Ruth 4:11, 12 **21** [a]Gen. 28:15; 46:4; 50:24 **22** [a]Gen. 14:7; Josh. 24:32; John 4:5 [b]Gen. 34:28 [1]Lit. *shoulder*

CHAPTER 49

1 [a]Deut. 33:1, 6–25; [Amos 3:7] [b]Num. 24:14; [Deut. 4:30]; Is. 2:2; 39:6; Jer. 23:20; Heb. 1:2 **3** [a]Gen. 29:32 **4** [a]Gen. 35:22; Deut. 27:20; 1 Chr. 5:1 **5** [1]*violence* **6** [a]Ps. 64:2; Prov. 1:15, 16 [b]Ps. 26:9; Eph. 5:11 *See WW at Lev. 16:17.

affirmed God's sovereignty and grace. Blessing is based on God's grace, not one's merit. See Rom. 9:6–13.
48:16 The lads were likely teenagers.
48:17 The sovereign breaking of tradition is what **displeased Joseph.**
48:20 Saying establishes this very important verse as a blessing that God intends to be literally perpetuated, much as the Aaronic blessing (Num. 6:23) and the Lord's Prayer (Luke 11:2). The importance of the blessing lies in the meanings of the names **Ephraim** and **Manasseh.** See marginal notes on 41:51, 52. By so blessing, one is asking God to cause one's negative past to be forgotten and his future to be fruitful.
48:22 The meaning of this verse is obscure. **One portion,** literally, one "shoulder" (Hebrew *shekem*), is perhaps referring back to 34:25, *the conquest of Shechem,* which *was part of* Manasseh's territory.
49:1–28 This is not only a prophecy, but also a blessing (see v. 28); it is even a curse for certain **sons. Jacob** spoke authoritatively, in faith; therefore his words were creative, and would have significant effect upon future generations. Jacob reserved his best blessings for **Judah** and **Joseph;** their descendants did indeed become the most dominant tribes in Israel, Judah in the south and Ephraim and Manasseh in the north. Typical of an ancient Semite's dying blessing, there is a collective quality to some of his statements, as if Jacob were sometimes speaking, not merely of individual sons, but of their descendants as well.
49:3, 4 Reuben should have received the preeminent blessing because he was the **firstborn.** But he **defiled** his **father's bed** when he "lay with Bilhah his father's concubine" (35:22). He therefore forfeited the place of prominence and became a pastoral people east of the Jordan (Num. 32:1–33).
49:5–7 Jacob actually feared his next two sons, **brothers,** "Two of a kind!" An illustration of their **cruelty** (or violence) and **anger** was the slaughter at Shechem (34:25–31). **Simeon** was overlooked in Moses' later blessing (Deut. 33); they were apparently absorbed into Judah (Josh. 15:20–63; 19:1–9). Because the Levites were the first to return to God after the golden calf incident, they did rise to prominence as the tribe to offer special priestly service (Num. 3:12, 13, 41). Their OT history was one of vacillating devotion.

[c]For in their anger they slew a
man,
And in their self-will they
[1]hamstrung an ox.
7 Cursed *be* their anger, for *it is*
fierce;
And their wrath, for it is
cruel!
[a]I will divide them in Jacob
And scatter them in Israel.

8 "Judah,[a] you *are he* whom your
brothers shall praise;
[b]Your hand *shall be* on the neck
of your enemies;
[c]Your father's children shall bow
down before you.
9 Judah *is* [a]a lion's whelp;
From the prey, my son, you have
gone up.
[b]He [1]bows down, he lies down as
a lion;
And as a lion, who shall rouse
him?
10 [a]The [1]scepter shall not depart from
Judah,
Nor [b]a lawgiver from between his
feet,
[c]Until **Shiloh** comes;
[d]And to Him *shall be* the obedience
of the people.

WORD WEALTH

49:10 Shiloh, *shiloh* (shee-*loh*); Strong's #7886: Shiloh was a city where the tabernacle was set up (Josh. 18:1). Here in Gen. it appears to be a proper name or title, which believers generally accept as a messianic designation of Jesus. The derivation is uncertain. One idea is that *shiloh* means "the peaceful one." Another view is that *shiloh* is a noun with a pronominal suffix that should be understood to mean "his son"; thus, lawgivers and princes would not depart from Judah until his son comes. Another possibility is to divide *shiloh* into the two words *shay* and *loh,* which would mean "the one to whom tribute is brought." The most likely meaning of *shiloh* is the one accepted by most of the ancient Jewish authorities who understood *shiloh* to be a word compounded from *shel* and *loh,* meaning "to whom it belongs." *Shelloh* may be expressed by the English phrases: "to whom dominion belongs," "whose is the kingdom," "he whose right it is to reign." See especially Ezek. 21:27.

6 [c]Gen. 34:26 [1]*lamed*
7 [a]Num. 18:24; Josh. 19:1, 9; 21:1–42; 1 Chr. 4:24–27
8 [a]Deut. 33:7; Rev. 5:5 [b]Ps. 18:40 [c]Gen. 27:29; 1 Chr. 5:2
9 [a]Deut. 33:22; Ezek. 19:5–7; Mic. 5:8; [Rev. 5:5] [b]Num. 23:24; 24:9 [1]*couches*
10 [a]Num. 24:17; Jer. 30:21; Matt. 1:3; 2:6; Luke 3:33; Rev. 5:5 [b]Ps. 60:7 [c]Is. 11:1; [Matt. 21:9] [d]Deut. 18:15; Ps. 2:6–9; 72:8–11; Is. 42:1, 4; 49:6; 60:1–5; [Luke 2:30–32] [1]A symbol of kingship
13 [a]Deut. 33:18, 19; Josh. 19:10, 11 [b]Gen. 10:19; Josh. 11:8
14 [a]1 Chr. 12:32
15 [a]1 Sam. 10:9 *See WW at Is. 28:12. • See WW at Ps. 100:2.
16 [a]Gen. 30:6; Deut. 33:22; Judg. 18:26, 27
17 [a]Judg. 18:27
18 [a]Ex. 15:2; Ps. 25:5; 40:1–3; 119:166, 174; Is. 25:9; Mic. 7:7 *See WW at Lam. 3:25.
19 [a]Gen. 30:11; Deut. 33:20; 1 Chr. 5:18 [1]Lit. *Troop* [2]Lit. *raid*

11 Binding his donkey to the vine,
And his donkey's colt to the
choice vine,
He washed his garments in
wine,
And his clothes in the blood of
grapes.
12 His eyes *are* darker than wine,
And his teeth whiter than milk.

13 "Zebulun[a] shall dwell by the haven
of the sea;
He *shall become* a haven for
ships,
And his border shall [b]adjoin
Sidon.

14 "Issachar[a] is a strong donkey,
Lying down between two
burdens;
15 He saw that *rest *was* good,
And that the land *was* pleasant;
He bowed [a]his shoulder to bear
a burden,
And became a band of *slaves.

16 "Dan[a] shall judge his people
As one of the tribes of Israel.
17 [a]Dan shall be a serpent by the way,
A viper by the path,
That bites the horse's heels
So that its rider shall fall
backward.
18 [a]I have *waited for your salvation,
O LORD!

19 "Gad,[a1] a troop shall [2]tramp upon
him,
But he shall [2]triumph at last.

49:8–12 Judah was next in order of birth, so Jacob granted him the blessing of the firstborn. He would be a ruler over Israel and the nations. Jacob's prediction was fulfilled in the fact that **Shiloh** (likely the Messiah) was to come from Judah.
49:11, 12 Using highly symbolic language, Jacob prophesies the messianic age to be one of paradise on Earth. There will be abundance of food, vitality, and health, overall bounty. People will have their fill of **wine** and **milk.**
49:13 Zebulun was to enjoy a mediocre maritime position; his descendants were instrumental in defeating Sisera (Judg. 4:6–10).
49:14, 15 Issachar was to be basically docile, accepting a happy, quiet life in Canaan. See Deut. 33:18. They were politically insightful, switching allegiance from Saul to David (1 Chr. 12:32).
49:16–18 Dan was a small tribe, but a little **serpent by the way** can destroy a mighty cavalryman. Dan unfortunately did not live up to its blessing of being a mighty warrior (Judg. 1:34) and seems to have had little interaction with the other tribes in later years (Judg. 5:17). Samson was a Danite.
49:19 Troop . . . tramp . . . triumph are all wordplays in Hebrew on the name **Gad.** His tribe later settled east of the Jordan, suffering much from Ammonite, Moabite, and Amalekite attacks.

20 "Bread from [a]Asher *shall be* rich,
And he shall yield royal dainties.

21 "Naphtali[a] *is* a deer let loose;
He uses beautiful words.

22 "Joseph *is* a fruitful bough,
A fruitful bough by a well;
His branches run over the
wall.
23 The archers have [a]bitterly
grieved him,
Shot *at him* and hated him.
24 But his [a]bow remained in
strength,
And the arms of his hands were
[1]made strong
By the hands of [b]the Mighty *God*
of Jacob
[c](From there [d]*is* the Shepherd,
[e]the Stone of Israel),
25 [a]By the God of your father who
will help you,
[b]And by the Almighty [c]who will
bless you
With blessings of heaven
above,
Blessings of the deep that lies
beneath,
Blessings of the breasts and of the
womb.
26 The blessings of your father
Have excelled the blessings of my
ancestors,
[a]Up to the utmost bound of the
everlasting hills.
[b]They shall be on the head of
Joseph,
And on the crown of the head of
him who was separate from his
brothers.

27 "Benjamin is a [a]ravenous wolf;
In the morning he shall devour
the prey,
[b]And at night he shall divide the
spoil."

20 [a]Deut. 33:24
21 [a]Deut. 33:23
23 [a]Gen. 37:4, 24
24 [a]Job 29:20 [b]Ps. 132:2, 5 [c]Gen. 45:11; 47:12 [d][Ps. 23:1; 80:1] [e]Is. 28:16 [1]Or *supple*
25 [a]Gen. 28:13; 32:9; 35:3; 43:23; 50:17 [b]Gen. 17:1; 35:11 [c]Deut. 33:13
26 [a]Deut. 33:15 [b]Deut. 33:16
27 [a]Judg. 20:21, 25 [b]Zech. 14:1

28 All these *are* the twelve tribes of Israel, and this *is* what their father spoke
to them. And he blessed them; he
blessed each one according to his own
blessing.

Jacob's Death and Burial

29 Then he charged them and said to
them: "I [a]am to be gathered to my people; [b]bury me with my fathers [c]in the
cave that *is* in the field of Ephron the
Hittite,
30 "in the cave that *is* in the field of
Machpelah, which *is* before Mamre in
the land of Canaan, [a]which Abraham
bought with the field of Ephron the Hittite as a possession for a burial place.
31 [a]"There they buried Abraham and
Sarah his wife, [b]there they buried
Isaac and Rebekah his wife, and there
I buried Leah.
32 "The field and the cave that *is* there
were purchased from the sons of
Heth."
33 And when Jacob had finished commanding his sons, he drew his feet up
into the bed and breathed his last, and
was gathered to his people.

50 Then Joseph [a]fell on his father's
face, and [b]wept over him, and
kissed him.
2 And Joseph commanded his servants the physicians to [a]embalm his
father. So the physicians embalmed
Israel.
3 Forty days were required for him,
for such are the days required for those
who are embalmed; and the Egyptians
[a]mourned[1] for him seventy days.
4 Now when the days of his mourning
were past, Joseph spoke to [a]the house-

29 [a]Gen. 15:15; 25:8; 35:29 [b]Gen. 47:30 [c]Gen. 23:16–20; 50:13
30 [a]Gen. 23:3–20
31 [a]Gen. 23:19, 20; 25:9 [b]Gen. 35:29; 50:13

CHAPTER 50

1 [a]Gen. 46:4, 29 [b]2 Kin. 13:14
2 [a]Gen. 50:26
3 [a]Deut. 34:8 [1]Lit. *wept*
4 [a]Esth. 4:2

49:20 The tribe of **Asher** inherited a choice area on the coast north of Mt. Carmel. It was near Phoenician merchant cities and became **rich,** yet they did not expel the Phoenicians (Judg. 1:31, 32).
49:21 Naphtali was also prosperous, located in a fertile northern mountain area (Josh. 20:7). They never drove out the Canaanites but received tribute.
49:22–26 Joseph received the longest blessing. He is pictured as **fruitful** (v. 22), hated (v. 23), strong (v. 24), and a leader among his brothers (v. 26). His descendants were leaders among the northern tribes (1 Kin. 12:25–33) but were also idolatrous and participated in treasonous alliances (2 Chr. 25:5–8; Hos. 4:17). Some settled east of the Jordan; Gideon was a Josephite.
49:24 These titles for Yahweh are rare in the OT.
49:25, 26 The **blessings** are strikingly similar to Moses' benediction upon **Joseph** in Deut. 33:13–16. **The Almighty:** See note on 17:1, 2.
49:27 Benjamin's blessing is actually positive; they shall be a spirited tribe whom Moses called "the beloved of the LORD" (Deut. 33:12). They showed some unrest under David (2 Sam. 20:1), but joined the southern kingdom when Israel divided (1 Kin. 12:21). King Saul and the apostle Paul were Benjamites.
49:29–32 See note on 23:4–20.
49:33 He drew . . . the bed means he took to his deathbed. Was **gathered to his people** stresses the unity of the patriarchal family, even in death.
50:2, 3 The embalmers were a secret profession in ancient Egypt; they knew their trade well, as we witness by the mummies still preserved after several thousand years. The process was lengthy and costly, requiring as many as **forty days. Seventy days** of mourning was the Egyptian custom, especially for people of stature.
50:4 Joseph was likely considered unfit to approach **Pharaoh** because of his contact with the dead. He had to request **the household of Pharaoh** to intercede for him so he could keep his promise to Jacob. See 47:29–31.

hold of Pharaoh, saying, "If now I have
found favor in your eyes, please speak
in the hearing of Pharaoh, saying,
5 [a]'My father made me *swear, saying, "Behold, I am dying; in my grave
[b]which I dug for myself in the land of
Canaan, there you shall bury me."
Now therefore, please let me go up and
bury my father, and I will come
back.' "
6 And Pharaoh said, "Go up and
bury your father, as he made you
swear."
7 So Joseph went up to bury his father; and with him went up all the servants of Pharaoh, the elders of his
house, and all the elders of the land
of Egypt,
8 as well as all the house of Joseph,
his brothers, and his father's house.
Only their little ones, their flocks, and
their herds they left in the land of Goshen.
9 And there went up with him both
chariots and horsemen, and it was a
very great gathering.
10 Then they came to the threshing
floor of Atad, which *is* beyond the Jordan, and they [a]mourned there with a
great and very solemn lamentation.
[b]He observed seven days of mourning
for his father.
11 And when the inhabitants of the
land, the Canaanites, saw the mourning at the threshing floor of Atad, they
said, "This *is* a deep mourning of the
Egyptians." Therefore its name was
called [1]Abel Mizraim, which *is* beyond
the Jordan.
12 So his sons did for him just as he
had commanded them.
13 For [a]his sons carried him to the land
of Canaan, and buried him in the cave
of the field of Machpelah, before
Mamre, which Abraham [b]bought with
the field from Ephron the Hittite as
property for a burial place.
14 And after he had buried his father,
Joseph returned to Egypt, he and his
brothers and all who went up with him
to bury his father.

Joseph Reassures His Brothers

15 When Joseph's brothers saw that
their father was dead, [a]they said, "Perhaps Joseph will hate us, and may
[1]actually repay us for all the evil which
we did to him."
16 So they sent *messengers* to Joseph,
saying, "Before your father died he
commanded, saying,
17 'Thus you shall say to Joseph: "I
beg you, please forgive the trespass of
your brothers and their sin; [a]for they
did evil to you." ' Now, please, forgive
the trespass of the servants of [b]the God
of your father." And Joseph wept when
they spoke to him.
18 Then his brothers also went and
[a]fell down before his face, and they said,
"Behold, we *are* your servants."
19 Joseph said to them, [a]"Do not be
afraid, [b]for *am* I in the place of
God?
20 [a]"But as for you, you meant evil 6
against me; *but* [b]God meant it for
good, in order to bring it about as *it is*
this day, to save many people alive.
21 "Now therefore, do not be afraid;
[a]I will provide for you and your little
ones." And he comforted them and
spoke [1]kindly to them.

Death of Joseph

22 So Joseph dwelt in Egypt, he and
his father's household. And Joseph
lived one hundred and ten years.
23 Joseph saw Ephraim's children
[a]to the third *generation.* [b]The children
of Machir, the son of Manasseh,
[c]were also brought up on Joseph's
knees.
24 And Joseph said to his brethren,

5 [a]Gen. 47:29–31 [b]2 Chr. 16:14; Is. 22:16 *See WW at Gen. 26:3. **10** [a]Acts 8:2 [b]1 Sam. 31:13; Job 2:13 **11** [1]Lit. *Mourning of Egypt* **13** [a]Gen. 49:29–31; Acts 7:16 [b]Gen. 23:16–20

15 [a][Job 15:21] [1]*fully* **17** [a][Prov. 28:13] [b]Gen. 49:25 **18** [a]Gen. 37:7–10; 41:43; 44:14 **19** [a]Gen. 45:5 [b]Gen. 30:2; 2 Kin. 5:7 **20** [a]Gen. 45:5, 7; Ps. 56:5 [b][Acts 3:13–15] **21** [a][Matt. 5:44] [1]Lit. *to their hearts* **23** [a]Gen. 48:1; Job 42:16 [b]Num. 26:29; 32:39 [c]Gen. 30:3

50:5 Dug means prepared, made ready, or bought. See 47:30.
50:7–9 The impressive funeral procession demonstrated **Egypt**'s love for **Joseph.** The next time Israel leaves, it will not be with Egyptian honor.
50:10 A threshing floor was a flat surface near a village, ideal for a stopping place. **Beyond the Jordan:** Why the **lamentation** was held across the river is unknown. There was also no need to travel so far out of the way, unless a wide detour was mandatory because the Philistines presented a hostile force.
50:13 See note on 23:4–20.
50:15–18 Joseph's brothers were once again terrified of him. **They sent *messengers*:** Those who fear retribution first send influential friends to intercede, perhaps even sending gifts, before they themselves appear. The message in Jacob's name seems fictitious, but we cannot be sure.
50:19–21 Joseph's response reflects maturity and insight. To be able to perceive the hand of **God** in a prolonged period of unfair suffering requires innumerable choices to deny bitterness and to pray. God's will was hence accomplished as the result of man's reprehensible behavior. See notes on 40:15 and 45:8 for the development of Joseph's attitude.
50:20 See section 6 of Truth-In-Action at the end of Gen.
50:23 Knees: See note on 30:3.
50:24 God will surely visit you: The attitude of the Egyptian court was obviously becoming more negative toward Joseph and his rapidly growing family. Already Joseph realized that a miraculous visitation would be necessary in order to leave Egypt for the Promised Land.

"I am dying; but [a]God will surely visit you, and bring you out of this land to the land [b]of which He swore to Abraham, to Isaac, and to Jacob."
25 Then [a]Joseph took an oath from the children of Israel, saying, *"God will surely [1]visit you, and [b]you shall carry up my [c]bones from here."
26 So Joseph died, *being* one hundred and ten years old; and they embalmed him, and he was put in a coffin in Egypt.

24 [a]Gen. 15:14; 46:4; 48:21; Ex. 3:16, 17; Josh. 3:17; Heb. 11:22 [b]Gen. 26:3; 35:12; 46:4; Ex. 6:8
25 [a]Gen. 47:29, 30; Ex. 13:19; Josh. 24:32; Acts 7:15, 16; Heb. 11:22 [b]Gen. 17:8; 28:13; 35:12; Deut. 1:8; 30:1–8 [c]Ex. 13:19 [1]*give attention to* *See WW at 2 Kin. 19:15.

50:25, 26 Moses brought **Joseph**'s body out of **Egypt** (Ex. 13:19), yet Joshua did not bury him with the patriarchs at Hebron. Rather, Joseph was buried in the field Jacob had bought at Shechem (33:19; Josh. 24:32).

Gen. concludes on a somber note, yet with a restrained hope that looks down the years toward God's deliverance.

TRUTH-IN-ACTION through GENESIS

Letting the LIFE of the Holy Spirit Bring Faith's Works Alive in You!

Truth Genesis Teaches	Text	**Action** Genesis Invites
1 Keys to Understanding God God is Creator, and only He has self-existence. We are created beings. God created all living things to reproduce *after their own kinds.*	1:1—2:25	**Understand** that as a creature, you are ultimately accountable to the Creator. **Understand** you can reproduce only what you are. Therefore, **pursue** Christlikeness.
	22:14	**Understand** that God's nature is to provide for His creation. He reveals Himself as "The LORD Who Provides."
2 Guidelines to Avoiding Sin Man fell by choice. The tempter is the father of lies (John 8:44), deceiving and seducing us to sin. The Lie questions God's Word, giving our opinion absolute authority. Our opinions are easy prey to Satan's deception.	3:1–5	**Do not challenge** God's Word. **Ask** instead, *What does God's Word mean to me? How can I apply it to my life?*
	3:6	**Suspect** urgings that come from carnal appetites, visual enticements that invite acquisition, and things that tug at personal ambition (see 1 John 2:16).
3 Steps in Hating Sin God hates sin perfectly, and thus it must be judged and punished. Civilizations have been judged for sin and collapsed as a result. Gen. teaches that faithfulness to God means hatred for sin.	6:1–7	**Avoid** ungodliness (life that is unconscious of God). God destroyed the Earth with a Flood because of it.
	11:1–9	**Turn away** from all appeals to personal power and recognition. God confused human speech because of them.
	19:1–28	**Flee** from all immorality and impurity. Because of them, God destroyed Sodom and Gomorrah.

Truth Genesis Teaches	Text	**Action** Genesis Invites
4 Key Lessons in Faith Abraham is the father of faith and the faithful. Through his life, faith is exemplified. From this "friend of God" (James 2:23), we learn that faith is not perfect character or integrity. Rather, it is simply taking God at His word. By doing so, Abraham became the model of faith for the believer. His life demonstrates how we benefit from believing what God says despite evidence to the contrary.	12:1–9	**Do not fear** when God's direction takes a turn you do not understand. He knows what He is doing.
	15:6	**Believe** God's promises to you. He knows how to bring them to pass although you may not.
	16:1–4	**Avoid** striving to fulfill God's promises by yourself. Doing so always backfires and produces undesired results.
	22:1–14	**Trust** that God will provide as He promises. His nature is to provide. **Remember:** God's provisions are strategically located along the pathway of faithful obedience.
5 Keys to Generous Living The lives of the patriarchs richly illustrate that encounters with God unavoidably result in men and women who are generous with God and with others. Later codified in the Law, tithing (giving a tenth) began as an act of faithful devotion to God to acknowledge that He alone is our resource.	14:18–24	**Tithe** as a basic expression of trust in and allegiance to God. Thus did Abraham lift up his hand (that is, show allegiance) "to the LORD, God Most High, the Possessor of heaven and earth."
	28:18–22	**Understand** that to the patriarchs, to tithe was an expression of loyalty to and faith in God; also it is an expression of covenant relationship with God.
6 Steps to Realize Fulfilled Vision Joseph was faithful to a vision. His life proves that vision restrains people from sin (Prov. 29:18). Because he believed what God had shown him, he remained steadfastly faithful and loyal in all his relationships, especially with God. Individuals who are faithful to God's vision will enjoy favor with Him and with others and will succeed in their endeavors. In the end they will realize their vision, experiencing vindication in spite of any adversity they may have faced.	37:5–10	**Hold fast** to the vision God gives you early in life. **Do not divert from** it. God can bring it to pass.
	39:4, 21	**Expect** God's favor in the sight of others. He grants favor and success to the faithful.
	39:9	**Remain faithful** to God in all you do. **Do not compromise,** especially when your vision is slow in coming.
	41:14–57	**Believe** that God is sufficient. He has given you the gifts you need to realize His purpose through you.
	45:7; 50:20	**Trust** in God's sovereign providence. He causes all things to work for your good as you remain faithful to His calling and purpose for you.

The Second Book of Moses Called EXODUS

Author: Traditionally Moses
Date: About 1400 B.C.
Theme: Deliverance
Key Words: Deliver, Sacrifice, Sign, Tabernacle, Sanctuary

Author Moses, whose name means "Drawn Out," is the central figure of Exodus. He is the Hebrew prophet who led the Israelites out of Egypt. Exodus is traditionally attributed to him. Four passages in Exodus lend strong support to Moses' authorship of at least most of it (17:14; 24:4, 7; 34:27). Through various events and face-to-face encounters with God, Moses received the revelation of those things God wanted to be known. Then, through the process of Holy Spirit inspiration, Moses communicated this revealed information to the Hebrew people both orally and in written form.

Date Conservative tradition dates Moses' death sometime around 1400 B.C., so the Book of Exodus was likely compiled during the forty years preceding, while in the wilderness.

Background Exodus is the continuation of the Genesis account, dealing with the development of a small family group of seventy people into a large nation of millions. For 430 years the Hebrews lived in Egypt, most of the time in bondage. Exodus records Moses' development, Israel's deliverance from their bondage, their trip from Egypt to Mount Sinai to receive God's law, and His instructions on the building of the tabernacle. It ends with the construction of the tabernacle as a dwelling place for God.

Content The Book of Exodus can be divided into three major sections: the miraculous deliverance of Israel (1:1—13:16), the miraculous journey to Sinai (13:17—18:27), and the miraculous revelations at Sinai (19:1—40:38).

Section one (1:1—13:16) opens with the Hebrews being oppressed in Egypt (1:10–14). Like any group under restraint, the Hebrews complained. Their complaint was made known not only to their captors, but to their God (2:23–25). God heard their plea and put in motion a plan to deliver them. He accomplished this deliverance through selecting a prophet named Moses (3:1–10).

Deliverance did not occur instantaneously; it was a process. A considerable amount of time and ten plagues were used to gain the release of the Hebrews from Pharaoh's grip. The plagues accomplished two important things: first, they demonstrated the superiority of the Hebrew God over Egyptian gods and, second, they brought freedom to the Hebrews.

The second division recounts the miraculous journey to Sinai (13:17—18:27). Four major events occur in this section. First, the Hebrews witness God's miraculous delivering power (13:17—15:21). Second, they experience firsthand God's ability to provide for His children (15:22—17:7). Third, they receive protection from their enemy, the Amalekites (17:8–16). Fourth, ruling elders are established to keep peace among the people (18:1–27). These four major events teach one major concept: God had His hand on the lives of His special people. Since they witnessed His presence and knew the way God worked in their behalf, they could adjust their lives to His way in order to continue receiving His blessings.

The final section deals with the miraculous revelations at Sinai (19:1—40:38). God's deliverance of the people is for the specific purpose of developing a covenant people. This section has three major components. First is the giving of the Ten Commandments and those instructions that explain in great detail how these commandments are to be expressed in the lives of God's covenant people (19:1—23:19). The results of living outside this covenant structure are demonstrated by the incident involving the golden calf (32:1–35). Second are instructions concerning the building of a tabernacle and its furniture (25:1—31:18). Third is the actual construction of the tabernacle, its furnishings, and the dwelling of God's presence in the completed structure (35:4—40:33).

Personal Application The first concept to be gleaned from the Book of Exodus is that God blesses those who remain in a covenant relationship with Him. He is their God and they become His holy people.

Second, God explains in great detail what is acceptable to Him.

Third, God delivers those who find themselves in bondage. The deliverance may not come instantaneously, but it will come to those who wait and make preparation for His deliverance. That deliverance is based upon obedience to God's expressed will and upon moving when He says to move. The children of Israel had to wait until after the Passover meal and the angel of death had passed over; after that, God gave the command to go. Thus, we also must wait, but be ready to move when God commands.

Christ Revealed Moses is a type of Christ, for he delivers from bondage. Aaron serves as a type for Jesus as the High Priest (28:1) making intercession at the altar of incense (30:1). The Passover indicates that Jesus is the Lamb of God who was slain for our redemption (12:1–22).

The "I AM" passages in John's Gospel find their primary source in Exodus. John states that Jesus is the Bread of Life; Moses speaks of the bread of God in two ways, the manna (16:35) and the showbread (25:30). John tells us that Jesus is the Light of the World; in the tabernacle the lampstand serves as a never-failing light (25:31–40).

The Holy Spirit at Work Oil in the Book of Exodus symbolically represents the Holy Spirit (27:20). For example, the anointing oil is a type of the Holy Spirit, which is used to prepare worshipers and priests for godly service (30:31).

The fruit of the Holy Spirit is listed in Galatians 5:22, 23. A parallel list can also be found in Exodus 34:6, 7, which lists the attributes of God as being merciful, gracious, longsuffering, good, truthful, and forgiving.

The most direct references to the Holy Spirit can be found in 31:3–11 and 35:30—36:1, when individuals are empowered by the Holy Spirit to become great artisans. Through the enabling work of the Holy Spirit, these individuals' natural abilities were enhanced and expanded to perform needed tasks with excellence and precision.

Outline of Exodus

I. The miraculous deliverance of Israel 1:1—13:16
- A. Oppression of the Israelites in Egypt 1:1–22
- B. The birth and early life of Moses 2:1—4:31
- C. The deliverance process 5:1—11:10
- D. The Exodus event 12:1—13:16

II. The miraculous journey to Sinai 13:17—18:27
- A. Deliverance at the Red Sea 13:17—15:21
- B. Provisions provided 15:22—17:7
- C. Protection from Amalekites 17:8–16
- D. Establishment of ruling elders 18:1–27

III. The miraculous revelations at Sinai 19:1—40:38
- A. Arrival at Sinai and God's appearing 19:1–25
- B. The Ten Commandments 20:1–21
- C. The Book of the Covenant 20:22—23:19
- D. God's Angel of protection 23:20–33
- E. Israel accepts the covenant 24:1–18
- F. Directions concerning the tabernacle 25:1—31:18
- G. The golden calf 32:1–35
- H. Repentance and renewal of covenant 33:1—35:3
- I. Building the tabernacle 35:4—40:33
- J. The glory of the Lord filling the tabernacle 40:34–38

Israel's Suffering in Egypt

CHAPTER 1

NOW [a]these *are* the names of the
children of Israel who came to
Egypt; each man and his household
came with Jacob:
2 Reuben, Simeon, Levi, and Judah;
3 Issachar, Zebulun, and Benjamin;
4 Dan, Naphtali, Gad, and Asher.
5 All those [1]who were descendants of
Jacob were [a]seventy[2] persons (for Joseph was in Egypt *already*).
6 And [a]Joseph died, all his *brothers,
and all that generation.
7 [a]But the children of Israel were
fruitful and increased abundantly, multiplied and [1]grew exceedingly mighty;
and the land was filled with them.
8 Now there arose a new king over
Egypt, [a]who did not know Joseph.
9 And he said to his people, "Look,
the people of the children of Israel *are*
more and [a]mightier than we;
10 [a]"come, let us [b]deal shrewdly with
them, lest they multiply, and it happen,
in the event of war, that they also join
our enemies and fight against us, and
so go up out of the land."
11 Therefore they set taskmasters
over them [a]to afflict them with their
[b]burdens. And they built for Pharaoh [c]supply cities, Pithom [d]and
Raamses.
12 But the more they afflicted them,
the more they multiplied and grew.
And they were in dread of the children
of Israel.
13 So the Egyptians made the children
of Israel [a]serve with [1]rigor.
14 And they [a]made their lives bitter
with hard bondage—[b]in mortar, in
brick, and in all manner of service in
the field. All their service in which they
made them serve *was* with rigor.
15 Then the king of Egypt spoke to the
[a]Hebrew midwives, of whom the name

1 [a]Gen. 46:8–27
5 [a]Gen. 46:26, 27 [1]Lit. *who came from the loins of* [2]DSS, LXX *seventy-five;* cf. Acts 7:14
6 [a]Gen. 50:26 *See WW at Ps. 133:1.
7 [a]Acts 7:17 [1]*became very numerous*
8 [a]Acts 7:18, 19
9 [a]Gen. 26:16
10 [a]Ps. 83:3, 4 [b]Acts 7:19
11 [a]Ex. 3:7; 5:6 [b]Ex. 1:14; 2:11; 5:4–9; 6:6 [c]1 Kin. 9:19 [d]Gen. 47:11
13 [a]Gen. 15:13 [1]*harshness*
14 [a]Num. 20:15 [b]Ps. 81:6
15 [a]Ex. 2:6

1:1 Egypt, situated in the northeast corner of Africa, is the site of the Exodus. The Book of Exodus is a continuation of the Gen. account, dealing with the 430-year development of a family group of 70 into a large nation. See Deut. 26:5.
1:7 The Egyptians did not associate with alien peoples, but considered themselves superior. However, because of Joseph, Israel was a tolerated and, at times, favored people (Gen. 43:32) until **the land** [Goshen] **was filled with them.**
1:8 A new king is never identified apart from his royal title, "Pharaoh." If the Exodus was about 1446 B.C. this would refer to Thutmosis III. Those who date it much later identify him as Sethos I.
1:11 Raamses was the royal city of the Egyptian kings located in the northeastern section of the Nile Delta. **Pithom,** a supply city, was in the same general area. **Taskmasters** were individuals responsible for controlling and managing a group of people in their performance of a specific task.
1:14 Mortar was a wet mud or clay mixture used to make bricks. These bricks were composed of the mud or clay along with other substances, like straw or sand, which tempered the strength of the bricks.
1:15–17 The **midwives** were to be the executioners of Pharaoh's murderous plan. However, because they **feared God** more than Pharaoh, they took care to see that the Hebrew women kept their children. They triumph as God's instruments to preserve His plan for Israel.

of one *was* Shiphrah and the name of
the other Puah;
16 and he said, "When you do the
duties of a midwife for the Hebrew
women, and see *them* on the birthstools, if it *is* a [a]son, then you shall kill
him; but if it *is* a daughter, then she
shall live."
17 But the midwives [a]**feared** God, and
did not do [b]as the king of Egypt commanded them, but saved the male children alive.

WORD WEALTH

1:17 feared, *yare'* (yah-*ray*); Strong's #3372: To fear, be afraid of someone or something; to stand in awe of something or someone possessing great power; to revere someone. The verb *yare'* and its derivatives occur more than 400 times. While there is some variation in the meaning of this word, its basic meaning is primarily "to be afraid." See 3:6; 14:13; 1 Sam. 18:12; 2 Sam. 6:9. The fear of God is not a terror that He is against us or will strike without cause or warning. Rather, the fear of the Lord produces wise, healthy actions, as in the present reference: the midwives were more afraid of angering God by destroying innocent babies than they were afraid of disobeying Pharaoh.

18 So the king of Egypt called for the
midwives and said to them, "Why have
you done this thing, and saved the
male children alive?"
19 And [a]the midwives said to Pharaoh,
"Because the Hebrew women *are* not
like the Egyptian women; for they
[1]*are* lively and give birth before the
midwives come to them."
20 [a]Therefore God dealt well with the
midwives, and the people multiplied
and [1]grew very mighty.
21 And so it was, because the midwives feared God, [a]that He [1]provided
households for them.
22 So Pharaoh commanded all his people, saying, [a]"Every son who is [1]born
you shall cast into the river, and every
daughter you shall save alive."

Moses Is Born

2 And [a]a man of the house of Levi
went and took *as wife* a daughter
of Levi.
2 So the woman conceived and bore
a son. And [a]when she saw that he *was*
a beautiful *child,* she hid him three
months.
3 But when she could no longer hide
him, she took an ark of [a]bulrushes for
him, daubed it with [b]asphalt and
[c]pitch, put the child in it, and laid *it*
in the reeds [d]by the river's bank.
4 [a]And his sister stood afar off, to
know what would be done to him.
5 Then the [a]daughter of Pharaoh
came down to bathe at the river. And
her maidens walked along the riverside; and when she saw the ark among
the reeds, she sent her maid to get it.
6 And when she opened *it,* she saw
the child, and behold, the baby wept.
So she had compassion on him, and
said, "This is one of the Hebrews' children."
7 Then his sister said to Pharaoh's
daughter, "Shall I go and call a nurse
for you from the Hebrew women, that
she may nurse the child for you?"
8 And Pharaoh's daughter said to her,
"Go." So the maiden went and called
the child's mother.
9 Then Pharaoh's daughter said to
her, "Take this child away and nurse
him for me, and I will give *you* your
wages." So the woman took the child
and nursed him.
10 And the child grew, and she
brought him to Pharaoh's daughter,
and he became [a]her son. So she *called
his name [1]Moses, saying, "Because I
drew him out of the water."

Moses Flees to Midian

11 Now it came to pass in those days,
[a]when Moses was grown, that he went

16 [a]Matt. 2:16; Acts 7:19
17 [a]Ex. 1:21; Prov. 16:6 [b]Dan. 3:16, 18; Acts 4:18–20; 5:29
19 [a]Josh. 2:4; 2 Sam. 17:19, 20 [1]*have vigor of life,* bear quickly, easily
20 [a]Gen. 15:1; Ruth 2:12; [Prov. 11:18]; Eccl. 8:12; [Is. 3:10]; Heb. 6:10 [1]*became very numerous*
21 [a]1 Sam. 2:35; 2 Sam. 7:11, 13, 27, 29; 1 Kin. 2:24; 11:38; [Ps. 127:1] [1]*gave them families*
22 [a]Acts 7:19 [1]Sam., LXX, Tg. add *to the Hebrews*

CHAPTER 2

1 [a]Ex. 6:16–20; Num. 26:59; 1 Chr. 23:14
2 [a]Acts 7:20; Heb. 11:23
3 [a]Is. 18:2 [b]Gen. 14:10 [c]Gen. 6:14; Is. 34:9 [d]Is. 19:6
4 [a]Ex. 15:20; Num. 26:59
5 [a]Ex. 7:15; Acts 7:21
10 [a]Acts 7:21 [1]Heb. *Mosheh,* lit. *Drawn Out* *See WW at Jer. 33:3.
11 [a]Acts 7:23, 24; Heb. 11:24–26

1:16 Birthstools were special stone chairs used by women when they gave birth. They may have been an Egyptian invention.
2:1 Moses' priestly ancestry later becomes crucial to his leadership role.
2:2 Beautiful means healthy.
2:3 Bulrushes are marsh plants, long hollow-stemmed grass similar to papyrus. **An ark** is an allusion to the ark that delivered Noah.
2:5 Pharaoh's **daughter** was probably the daughter of one of Pharaoh's concubines. Her identity is unknown.
2:7 A **nurse** was a hired woman who breast-fed an infant or helped to raise a child. She usually became a respected member of the household she served. Children were not weaned until they were three to five years of age, which allowed ample time for religious training about the God of the Hebrews. This training probably caused Moses to seek out his people (v. 11).
2:10 Adoption was not a practice among the Hebrews, but was a common practice among the Egyptians. The name **Moses** is related to a Hebrew root, meaning to "draw out."
2:11 He went out to his brethren is interpreted in Heb. 11:24 as he "refused to be called the son of Pharaoh's daughter." Although he was trained in Egypt, Moses never forgot his nurse or his heritage.

out to his brethren and looked at their
burdens. And he saw an Egyptian
beating a Hebrew, one of his brethren.
12 So he looked this way and that way,
and when he saw no one, he [a]killed
the Egyptian and hid him in the sand.
13 And [a]when he went out the second
day, behold, two Hebrew men [b]were
fighting, and he said to the one who
did the wrong, "Why are you striking
your companion?"
14 Then he said, [a]"Who made you a
prince and a *judge over us? Do you
intend to kill me as you killed the
Egyptian?" So Moses [b]feared and said,
"Surely this thing is known!"
15 When Pharaoh heard of this matter,
he sought to kill Moses. But [a]Moses
fled from [1]the face of Pharaoh and
dwelt in the land of [b]Midian; and he
sat down by [c]a well.
16 [a]Now the priest of Midian had
seven daughters. [b]And they came and
drew water, and they filled the
[c]troughs to water their father's flock.
17 Then the [a]shepherds came and
[b]drove them away; but Moses stood up
and helped them, and [c]watered their
flock.
18 When they came to [a]Reuel[1] their father, [b]he said, "How *is it that* you have
come so soon today?"
19 And they said, "An Egyptian delivered us from the hand of the shepherds, and he also drew enough water
for us and watered the flock."
20 So he said to his daughters, "And
where *is* he? Why *is* it *that* you have
left the man? Call him, that he may
[a]eat bread."
21 Then Moses was content to live with
the man, and he gave [a]Zipporah his
daughter to Moses.
22 And she bore *him* a son. He called
his name [a]Gershom,[1] for he said, "I
have been [b]a [2]stranger in a foreign
land."

12 [a]Acts 7:24, 25 **13** [a]Acts 7:26–28 [b]Prov. 25:8 **14** [a]Acts 7:27, 28 [b]Judg. 6:27 *See WW at Judg. 2:18. **15** [a]Acts 7:29 [b]Ex. 3:1 [c]Gen. 24:11; 29:2 [1]*the presence of Pharaoh* **16** [a]Ex. 3:1; 4:18; 18:12 [b]Gen. 24:11, 13, 19; 29:6–10 [c]Gen. 30:38 **17** [a]Gen. 47:3 [b]Gen. 26:19–21 [c]Gen. 29:3, 10 **18** [a]Num. 10:29 [b]Ex. 3:1; 4:18 [1]*Jethro,* Ex. 3:1 **20** [a]Gen. 31:54; 43:25 **21** [a]Ex. 4:25; 18:2 **22** [a]Ex. 4:20; 18:3, 4 [b]Acts 7:29 [1]Lit. *Stranger There* [2]*sojourner,* temporary resident

23 [a]Acts 7:34 [b]Deut. 26:7 [c]James 5:4 **24** [a]Ex. 6:5 [b]Gen. 15:13; 22:16–18; 26:2–5; 28:13–15 [c]Gen. 12:1–3; 15:14; 17:1–14 *See WW at 2 Kin. 19:15. **25** [a]Ex. 4:31 [b]Ex. 3:7

CHAPTER 3

1 [a]Ex. 4:18 [b]Ex. 2:16 [c]Ex. 17:6 [d]Ex. 18:5 *See WW at Lev. 5:6. **2** [a]Deut. 33:16

23 Now it happened [a]in the process of
time that the king of Egypt died. Then
the children of Israel [b]groaned because
of the bondage, and they cried out; and
[c]their cry came up to God because of
the bondage.
24 So *God [a]heard their groaning, and
God [b]remembered His [c]covenant with
Abraham, with Isaac, and with Jacob.
25 And God [a]looked upon the children
of Israel, and God [b]acknowledged
them.

Moses at the Burning Bush

3 Now Moses was tending the flock
of [a]Jethro his father-in-law, [b]the
*priest of Midian. And he led the flock
to the back of the desert, and came to
[c]Horeb, [d]the mountain of God.
2 And [a]the Angel of the LORD appeared to him in a flame of fire from
the midst of a bush. So he looked, and
behold, the bush was burning with fire,
but the bush *was* not consumed.

KINGDOM DYNAMICS

3:2, 4 The Angel of the Lord Receives Worship, ANGELS. One unusual "angel"—the Angel of the Lord—is different from all others in that this Angel received worship. How could this be? No angel can receive worship, which belongs to God alone. The angel Lucifer was expelled from heaven for trying to receive such worship. The mystery is solved in this text where the Angel of the Lord is revealed to be the Lord God (see Acts 7:30–32). But how could Moses and other OT persons have seen God face-to-face and lived since Scripture clearly states the contrary (Ex. 33:20)? The answer: because they saw the Son of God in a preincarnate form, known in the OT as the Angel of the Lord—the "Messenger [Angel] of the covenant" (Mal. 3:1).

(Ps. 91:11, 12/Rev. 1:1) M.H.

2:15 The Midianites were descendants of Abraham through his second wife, Keturah, and were therefore a kindred people to Moses. They lived in western Arabia and the eastern part of the Sinai peninsula. Wells were often situated outside the towns or villages. In addition to supplying water, they functioned as local landmarks and places of meeting.

2:16–22 Water, the source of life and wealth, was vital to survival in a hostile environment.

2:21 *Moses takes a wife from among this distant kindred people.*

2:22 Moses summarizes his life since leaving Egypt in the naming of his son. **Gershom** is from a Hebrew root meaning "driven or thrust out."

2:23–25 The death of the king serves as a turning point in the lives of the Hebrews. Some perhaps thought things would get better when Pharaoh died; however, things got worse. The severity of the situation once again causes the Hebrews to turn their minds toward God.

3:1 The location of Mt. **Horeb** is uncertain. Tradition identifies it with Gebel Musa ("Mountain of Moses"), a 7,500-foot mountain in the center of a granite range in the south of the Sinai peninsula.

3:2 Angels are supernatural creatures that exist in the heavenlies serving as messengers from God and as protectors for His chosen people. **The Angel of the LORD** was a visible manifestation of God, possibly the preincarnate Christ. The **flame of fire** was the glory of God's presence, the Shekinah, which transformed everything and everyone it touched.

3 3 Then Moses said, "I will now turn
aside and see this [a]great sight, why the
bush does not burn."
4 So when the LORD saw that he
turned aside to look, God called [a]to
him from the midst of the bush and
said, "Moses, Moses!" And he said,
"Here I am."
5 Then He said, "Do not draw near
this place. [a]Take your sandals off your
feet, for the place where you stand *is*
holy ground."
6 Moreover He said, [a]"I *am* the God
of your father—the God of Abraham,
the God of Isaac, and the God of Jacob." And Moses hid his face, for [b]he
was afraid to look upon God.
7 And the LORD said: [a]"I have surely
seen the oppression of My *people who
are in Egypt, and have heard their cry
[b]because of their taskmasters, [c]for I
know their [1]sorrows.

WORD WEALTH

3:7 know, *yada'* (yah-*dah*); Strong's #3045: To know, to perceive, to distinguish, to recognize, to acknowledge, to be acquainted with; in a few instances to "know intimately," that is, sexually; also to acknowledge, recognize, esteem, and endorse. When Scripture speaks of God's making known His name, it refers to His revealing (through deeds or events) what His name truly means. Thus, in 6:3, "I appeared to Abraham, to Isaac, and to Jacob as *'El Shaddai,* but *by* My name *Yahweh* I was not known to them," God did not mean that the Patriarchs had never heard the name *Yahweh,* but rather that He did not reveal the full meaning of His name *Yahweh* until the time of Moses and the Exodus.

8 "So [a]I have come down to [b]deliver
them out of the hand of the Egyptians,
and to bring them up from that land
[c]to a good and large land, to a land
[d]flowing with milk and honey, to the
place of [e]the Canaanites and the
Hittites and the Amorites and the
Perizzites and the Hivites and the Jebusites.
9 "Now therefore, behold, [a]the cry of
the children of Israel has come to Me,
and I have also seen the [b]oppression
with which the Egyptians oppress
them.
10 [a]"Come now, therefore, and I will
send you to Pharaoh that you may
bring My people, the children of Israel,
out of Egypt."
11 But Moses said to God, [a]"Who *am*
I that I should go to Pharaoh, and that
I should bring the children of Israel out
of Egypt?"
12 So He said, [a]"I will certainly be with
you. And this *shall be* a [b]sign to you
that I have sent you: When you have
brought the people out of Egypt, you
shall serve God on this mountain."
13 Then Moses said to God, "Indeed,
when I come to the children of Israel
and say to them, 'The God of your fathers has sent me to you,' and they say
to me, 'What *is* His name?' what shall
I say to them?"
14 And God said to Moses, "I AM 1
WHO I AM." And He said, "Thus you
shall say to the children of Israel,
[a]'I AM has sent me to you.'"
15 Moreover God said to Moses, "Thus
you shall say to the children of Israel:
'The LORD God of your fathers, the God
of Abraham, the God of Isaac, and the
God of Jacob, has sent me to you. This
is [a]My name *forever, and this *is* My
memorial to all generations.'
16 "Go and [a]gather the elders of Israel
together, and say to them, 'The LORD
God of your fathers, the God of Abraham, of Isaac, and of Jacob, appeared
to me, saying, [b]"I have surely visited
you and *seen* what is done to you in
Egypt;

3 [a]Acts 7:31 **4** [a]Deut. 33:16 **5** [a]Josh. 5:15 **6** [a][Matt. 22:32] [b]1 Kin. 19:13 **7** [a]Ex. 2:23–25 [b]Ex. 1:11 [c]Ex. 2:25 [1]*pain* *See WW at Ruth 1:16. **8** [a]Gen. 15:13–16; 46:4; 50:24, 25 [b]Ex. 6:6–8; 12:51 [c]Deut. 1:25; 8:7–9 [d]Jer. 11:5 [e]Gen. 15:19–21

9 [a]Ex. 2:23 [b]Ex. 1:11, 13, 14 **10** [a][Mic. 6:4] **11** [a]Ex. 4:10; 6:12 **12** [a]Gen. 31:3 [b]Ex. 4:8; 19:3 **14** [a][John 8:24, 28, 58] **15** [a]Ps. 30:4; 97:12; 102:12; 135:13 *See WW at Ps. 136:1. **16** [a]Ex. 4:29 [b]Ex. 2:25; 4:31

3:3 See section 3 of Truth-In-Action at the end of Ex.
3:3 God comes to Moses through the commonplace, which becomes special and holy when touched by God. Spontaneous combustion was not unusual in the desert, but a nonconsuming flame was an extraordinary and commanding event.
3:5 Take your sandals off: In the East, removing one's shoes (sandals) is a form of respect. **Holy ground:** The ground becomes holy because of God's visitation.
3:7–10 God acknowledges that He has **seen** and **heard** the problems of the Hebrews and intends to become personally involved. **A land flowing with milk and honey** poetically describes its lushness and fertility. The named peoples serve as geographic boundaries (v. 17). **Pharaoh** is again unidentified. He may be Thutmosis III or Ramses II. See note on 1:8.
3:11, 12 When Moses asks, **Who *am* I,** God responds that He will accompany Moses and His plans will be accomplished. Israel will **serve God** in freedom. At this encounter Moses is commissioned for service, a major turning point in Moses' life.
3:14, 15 See section 1 of Truth-In-Action at the end of Ex.
3:14 God identifies Himself as **I AM WHO I AM.** Revealing His divine name declares His character and attributes, reinforcing that the issue is not who Moses is, but who is *with* him. This name is related to the Hebrew verb meaning "to be," and so implies the absolute existence of God. The Hebrew here is also the source of the English, "Yahweh," "Jehovah," or "LORD" (v. 15). See note on 34:6, 7.
3:16 Elders of Israel refers to those of advanced age who, by great experience and authority, were the leaders of the Hebrew people.

17 "and I have said [a]I will bring you up out of the affliction of Egypt to the land of the Canaanites and the Hittites and the Amorites and the Perizzites and the Hivites and the Jebusites, to a land flowing with milk and honey." '

18 "Then [a]they will heed your voice; and [b]you shall come, you and the elders of Israel, to the king of Egypt; and you shall say to him, 'The LORD God of the Hebrews has [c]met with us; and now, please, let us go three days' journey into the wilderness, that we may sacrifice to the LORD our God.'

19 "But I am sure that the king of Egypt [a]will not let you go, no, not even by a mighty hand.

20 "So I will [a]stretch out My hand and strike Egypt with [b]all My wonders which I will do in its midst; and [c]after that he will let you go.

21 "And [a]I will give this people favor in the sight of the Egyptians; and it shall be, when you go, that you shall not go empty-handed.

22 [a]"But every woman shall ask of her neighbor, namely, of her who dwells near her house, [b]articles of silver, articles of gold, and clothing; and you shall put *them* on your sons and on your daughters. So [c]you shall plunder the Egyptians."

Miraculous Signs for Pharaoh

4 Then Moses answered and said, "But suppose they will not believe me or listen to my voice; suppose they say, 'The LORD has not appeared to you.' "

2 So the LORD said to him, "What *is* that in your hand?" He said, "A rod."

3 And He said, "Cast it on the ground." So he cast it on the ground, and it became a serpent; and Moses fled from it.

4 Then the LORD said to Moses, "Reach out your hand and take *it* by the tail" (and he reached out his hand and caught it, and it became a rod in his hand),

5 "that they may [a]believe that the [b]LORD God of their fathers, the God of Abraham, the God of Isaac, and the God of Jacob, has appeared to you."

6 Furthermore the LORD said to him, "Now put your hand in your bosom." And he put his hand in his bosom, and when he took it out, behold, his hand *was* leprous, [a]like snow.

7 And He said, "Put your hand in your bosom again." So he put his hand in his bosom again, and drew it out of his bosom, and behold, [a]it was restored like his *other* flesh.

8 "Then it will be, if they do not believe you, nor heed the message of the [a]first sign, that they may believe the message of the latter sign.

9 "And it shall be, if they do not believe even these two signs, or listen to your voice, that you shall take water from [1]the river and pour *it* on the dry *land.* [a]The water which you take from the river will become *blood on the dry *land.*"

10 Then Moses said to the LORD, "O my Lord, I *am* not eloquent, neither before nor since You have spoken to Your servant; but [a]I *am* slow of speech and [1]slow of tongue."

11 So the LORD said to him, [a]"Who has made man's mouth? Or who makes the mute, the deaf, the seeing, or the blind? *Have* not I, the LORD?

12 "Now therefore, go, and I will be [a]with your mouth and *teach you what you shall say."

17 [a]Gen. 15:13–21; 46:4; 50:24, 25
18 [a]Ex. 4:31 [b]Ex. 5:1, 3 [c]Num. 23:3, 4, 15, 16
19 [a]Ex. 5:2
20 [a]Ex. 6:6; 9:15 [b]Deut. 6:22 [c]Ex. 11:1; 12:31–37
21 [a]Ex. 11:3; 12:36
22 [a]Ex. 11:2 [b]Ex. 33:6 [c]Job 27:17

CHAPTER 4

5 [a]Ex. 4:31; 19:9 [b]Ex. 3:6, 15
6 [a]Num. 12:10
7 [a]Deut. 32:39
8 [a]Ex. 7:6–13
9 [a]Ex. 7:19, 20 [1]The Nile *See WW at Lev. 17:11.
10 [a]Ex. 3:11; 4:1; 6:12 [1]*heavy* or *dull of tongue;* cannot talk very well
11 [a]Ps. 94:9; 146:8
12 [a]Is. 50:4 *See WW at Ps. 32:8.

3:17 Canaanites were an ancient people who lived in the land of Canaan. The Canaanite religious ceremonies centered in fertility cults and in their many different gods. **Hittites** also lived in Canaan. They, too, were polytheistic and served as many as a thousand gods. The **Amorites** were among the larger groups in Canaan. The term was often used synonymously for any group of people found in Canaan. The term **Perizzites** may refer to those living in unwalled villages. **Hivites** were a small group of tent villagers in Canaan who often acted as servants. **Jebusites** was the name of those people who originally lived in the city of Jebus, later called Jerusalem.

3:18 Sacrifice *was, and is, the means by which sinful man* can approach a sinless, holy God. It denotes worship as the goal of the Exodus. **Three days' journey** would not take them to Horeb, but beyond the borders of their Egyptian delta region.

3:20 Wonders point to or represent things larger or more important than themselves. They are usually linked to the acts of God. In Ex., most uses of the word point to those miracles produced by God to deliver the Israelites out of Egyptian bondage.

4:1–9 The signs given to Moses were for his sake, to prove that God was with him. Often signs or miracles are given to prove God is on the scene on behalf of His people.

4:2 God takes the ordinary, such as a shepherd's **rod,** and uses it as an extraordinary rod of God. This rod was used to perform various miracles by God's power.

4:10 O my Lord is Moses' recognition that God has a right to command him. **Not eloquent . . . slow of speech and slow of tongue** is Moses' claim to being inadequate at persuasive, confrontational speech. **Neither before nor since** indicates his perspective that his problem is long-standing and that his encounter with Yahweh has not changed matters.

4:12 The promise made here is similar to Matt. 10:19, 20. When we do not know how to respond, God will give us boldness and the proper words.

13 But he said, "O my Lord, [a]please
send by the hand of whomever *else*
You may send."
14 So [a]the *anger of the LORD was kindled against Moses, and He said: "Is
not Aaron the Levite your [b]brother? I
know that he can speak well. And look,
[c]he is also coming out to meet you.
When he sees you, he will be glad in
his heart.
15 "Now [a]you shall speak to him and
[b]put the words in his mouth. And I will
be with your mouth and with his
mouth, and [c]I will teach you what you
shall do.
16 "So he shall be your spokesman to
the people. And he himself shall be as
a mouth for you, and [a]you shall be to
him as God.
17 "And you shall take this rod in your
hand, with which you shall do the
signs."

Moses Goes to Egypt

18 So Moses went and returned to
[a]Jethro his father-in-law, and said to
him, "Please let me go and return
to my brethren who *are* in Egypt, and
see whether they are still alive." And
Jethro said to Moses, [b]"Go in *peace."
19 Now the LORD said to Moses in
[a]Midian, "Go, return to [b]Egypt; for
[c]all the men who sought your life are
dead."
20 Then Moses [a]took his wife and his
sons and set them on a donkey, and
he returned to the land of Egypt. And
Moses took [b]the rod of God in his
*hand.
21 And the LORD said to Moses, "When
you go back to Egypt, see that you do
all those [a]wonders before Pharaoh
which I have put in your hand. But
[b]I will harden his heart, so that he will
not let the people go.

13 [a]Jon. 1:3
14 [a]Num. 11:1, 33 [b]Num. 26:59 [c]Ex. 4:27 *See WW at Judg. 10:7.
15 [a]Ex. 4:12, 30; 7:1, 2 [b]Num. 23:5, 12 [c]Deut. 5:31
16 [a]Ex. 7:1, 2
18 [a]Ex. 2:21; 3:1; 4:18 [b]Judg. 18:6 *See WW at Nah. 1:15.
19 [a]Ex. 3:1; 18:1 [b]Gen. 46:3, 6 [c]Ex. 2:15, 23
20 [a]Ex. 18:2–5 [b]Num. 20:8, 9, 11 *See WW at Josh. 4:24.
21 [a]Ex. 3:20; 11:9, 10 [b]John 12:40
22 [a]Ex. 5:1 [b]Hos. 11:1 [c]Jer. 31:9
23 [a]Ex. 11:5; 12:29
24 [a]Gen. 42:27 [b]Num. 22:22 [c]Gen. 17:14
25 [a]Ex. 2:21; 18:2 [b]Josh. 5:2, 3 [1]Lit. *made it touch* [2]Lit. *his*
26 [1]*bridegroom*
27 [a]Ex. 4:14 [b]Ex. 3:1; 18:5; 24:13
28 [a]Ex. 4:15, 16 [b]Ex. 4:8, 9 *See WW at Deut. 1:1.
29 [a]Ex. 3:16; 12:21
30 [a]Ex. 4:15, 16
31 [a]Ex. 3:18; 4:8, 9; 19:9 [b]Gen. 50:24 [c]Ex. 2:25; 3:7 [d]Gen. 24:26

22 "Then you shall [a]say to Pharaoh,
'Thus says the LORD: [b]"Israel *is* My
son, [c]My firstborn.
23 "So I say to you, let My son go that
he may serve Me. But if you refuse to
let him go, indeed [a]I will kill your son,
your firstborn." ' "
24 And it came to pass on the way, at
the [a]encampment, that the LORD
[b]met him and sought to [c]kill him.
25 Then [a]Zipporah took [b]a sharp stone
and cut off the foreskin of her son and
[1]cast *it* at [2]*Moses'* feet, and said,
"Surely you *are* a husband of blood to
me!"
26 So He let him go. Then she said,
"*You are* a [1]husband of blood!"—because of the circumcision.
27 And the LORD said to Aaron, "Go
into the wilderness [a]to meet Moses."
So he went and met him on [b]the mountain of God, and kissed him.
28 So Moses [a]told Aaron all the *words
of the LORD who had sent him, and all
the [b]signs which He had commanded
him.
29 Then Moses and Aaron [a]went and
gathered together all the elders of the
children of Israel.
30 [a]And Aaron spoke all the words
which the LORD had spoken to Moses.
Then he did the signs in the sight of
the people.
31 So the people [a]believed; and when
they heard that the LORD had [b]visited
the children of Israel and that He
[c]had looked on their affliction, then
[d]they bowed their heads and worshiped.

First Encounter with Pharaoh

5 Afterward Moses and Aaron went
in and told Pharaoh, "Thus says
the LORD God of Israel: 'Let My people

4:13–17 Although Moses asks God to send someone else, he is not released from his responsibility. God, however, changes the chain of communication. God will speak to Moses and Moses will speak to Aaron. Aaron will then speak to the people. Moses is the agent of God, and Aaron is the mouthpiece of Moses.

4:18 Moses, through marriage, becomes a son to Jethro. As an obedient son, he needs to ask permission to leave the geographic area where Jethro lives.

4:19 Upon learning of Pharaoh's death, Moses feels free to return to Egypt. This event in the life of Moses parallels the situation in the early life of Jesus; upon Herod's death, Jesus was able to return to Israel from Egypt (Matt. 2:19–21).

4:22 All of humanity is God's creation, but Israel has a special place and task in God's plan. To be the **firstborn** is to be regarded as God's special property, not only favored, but having unique responsibilities.

4:24–26 This is a difficult passage filled with obscurities. Apparently, Moses neglected to circumcise his son. **Circumcision** was an action that served as a sign of God's covenant relationship with His people as designated by God Himself (Gen. 17:10–14). Failure to perform this rite may have been caused by his wife's abhorrence of the practice, or by adhering to the Midianite rite, which called for males to be circumcised at puberty. However, as head of the house, Moses should have performed this rite when his son was eight days old. As he is now about to become Israel's deliverer, God is displeased and vicariously uses **Zipporah** to do what Moses should have done.

4:26 The meaning of **a husband of blood** probably refers to Zipporah's indignant feelings about the circumcision just performed.

4:30, 31 The **signs** validate the call of Moses and cause the people to **believe.** Bowing heads was a sign of respect.

5:1 Moses was able to go before the Pharaoh because he

go, that they may [1]hold* [a]a feast to Me
in the wilderness.' "
2 And Pharaoh said, [a]"Who *is* the
LORD, that I should obey His voice to
let Israel go? I do not know the LORD,
[b]nor will I let Israel go."
3 So they said, [a]"The God of the Hebrews has [b]met with us. Please, let us
go three days' journey into the desert
and sacrifice to the LORD our God, lest
He fall upon us with [c]pestilence or with
the sword."
4 Then the king of Egypt said to them,
"Moses and Aaron, why do you take
the people from their work? Get *back*
to your [a]labor."
5 And Pharaoh said, "Look, the people of the land *are* [a]many now, and you
make them *rest from their labor!"
6 So the same day Pharaoh commanded the [a]taskmasters of the people
and their officers, saying,
7 "You shall no longer give the people straw to make [a]brick as before. Let
them go and gather straw for themselves.
8 "And you shall lay on them the
quota of bricks which they made before. You shall not reduce it. For they
are idle; therefore they cry out, saying,
'Let us go *and* sacrifice to our God.'
9 "Let more work be laid on the men,
that they may labor in it, and let them
not regard false words."
10 And the taskmasters of the people
and their officers went out and spoke
to the people, saying, "Thus says Pharaoh: 'I will not give you straw.
11 'Go, get yourselves straw where you
can find it; yet none of your work will
be reduced.' "
12 So the people were scattered
abroad throughout all the land of
Egypt to gather stubble instead of
straw.
13 And the taskmasters forced *them* to
hurry, saying, "Fulfill your work, *your*
daily quota, as when there was straw."
14 Also the [a]officers of the children of
Israel, whom Pharaoh's taskmasters
had set over them, were [b]beaten *and*
were asked, "Why have you not fulfilled your task in making brick both
yesterday and today, as before?"
15 Then the officers of the children of
Israel came and cried out to Pharaoh,
saying, "Why are you dealing thus
with your servants?
16 "There is no straw given to your
servants, and they say to us, 'Make
brick!' And indeed your servants *are*
beaten, but the fault *is* in your *own* people."
17 But he said, "You *are* idle! Idle!
Therefore you say, 'Let us go *and* sacrifice to the LORD.'
18 "Therefore go now *and* work; for
no straw shall be given you, yet you
shall deliver the quota of bricks."
19 And the officers of the children of
Israel saw *that* they *were* in trouble
after it was said, "You shall not reduce
any bricks from your daily quota."
20 Then, as they came out from Pharaoh, they met Moses and Aaron who
stood there to meet them.
21 [a]And they said to them, "Let the
LORD look on you and judge, because
you have made [1]us abhorrent in the
sight of Pharaoh and in the sight of his
servants, to put a sword in their hand
to kill us."

Israel's Deliverance Assured

22 So Moses returned to the LORD and
said, "Lord, why have You brought
trouble on this people? Why *is* it You
have sent me?
23 "For since I came to Pharaoh to
speak in Your name, he has done evil
to this people; neither have You delivered Your people at all."

6 Then the LORD said to Moses,
"Now you shall see what I will do
to Pharaoh. For [a]with a strong hand
he will let them go, and with a strong
hand [b]he will drive them out of his
land."

CHAPTER 5

1 [a]Ex. 3:18; 7:16; 10:9 [1]*keep a pilgrim-feast* *See WW at Ex. 23:14.
2 [a]2 Kin. 18:35; 2 Chr. 32:14; Job 21:15 [b]Ex. 3:19; 7:14
3 [a]Ex. 3:18; 7:16 [b]Ex. 4:24; Num. 23:3 [c]Ex. 9:15
4 [a]Ex. 1:11; 2:11; 6:6
5 [a]Ex. 1:7, 9 *See WW at Ex. 16:30.
6 [a]Ex. 1:11; 3:7; 5:10, 13, 14
7 [a]Ex. 1:14
14 [a]Ex. 5:6 [b]Is. 10:24
21 [a]Ex. 6:9; 14:11; 15:24; 16:2 [1]Lit. *our scent to stink before*

CHAPTER 6

1 [a]Ex. 3:19 [b]Ex. 12:31, 33, 39

---

had been adopted by the previous Pharaoh's daughter. Thus, even though a new king was in the land, respect had to be paid to the former Pharaoh's offspring. Another possibility found in historical records states that one Pharaoh, Ramses II, made himself available to anyone who wanted to see him. Feasts were community activities when the community would stop its normal activities to offer *thanksgiving to certain deities* on specific occasions. It was usually a joyous time of eating and of worship. **Hold a feast** is the third term used to identify the purpose of their deliverance. See 3:12, 18.

5:2 Who *is* the LORD, that I should obey His voice: Pharaoh was considered to be divine. Thus, he had a difficult time believing that a God of an enslaved people, even if He did exist, could present a threat to him as long as that God and His people stayed captives.

5:3 Pharaoh's claim over the Hebrew slaves lasted only as long as they were on Egyptian soil. Once they had left the region, they would have been free men and would not have had to return.

5:10 Archaeological excavations have shown a difference in the bricks used in the buildings in northeast Egypt. As the buildings went up, less and less **straw** was used.

5:14 The **officers** were Hebrew foremen. Apparently, their privileged status lasted only as long as they were of service to Pharaoh. Perhaps for this reason they tried to discredit Moses and Aaron (v. 21).

2 And God spoke to Moses and said
to him: "I *am* [1]the LORD.
3 [a]"I appeared to Abraham, to Isaac,
and to Jacob, as [b]God Almighty, but
by My name [c]LORD[1] I was not known
to them.
4 [a]"I have also [1]established My covenant with them, [b]to give them the
land of Canaan, the land of their
[2]pilgrimage, [c]in which they were
[3]strangers.
5 "And [a]I have also heard the groaning of the children of Israel whom the
Egyptians keep in bondage, and I have
remembered My covenant.
6 "Therefore say to the children of Israel: [a]'I *am* the LORD; [b]I will bring you
out from under the burdens of the
Egyptians, I will [c]rescue you from their
bondage, and I will redeem you with
[1]an outstretched arm and with great
judgments.
7 'I will [a]take you as My people, and
[b]I will be your God. Then you shall
know that I *am* the LORD your God who
brings you out [c]from under the burdens of the Egyptians.
8 'And I will bring you into the land
which I [a]swore[1]* to give to Abraham,
Isaac, and Jacob; and I will give it to
you *as* a heritage: I *am* the LORD.' "
9 So Moses spoke thus to the children
of Israel; [a]but they did not heed Moses,
because of [b]anguish[1] of spirit and cruel
bondage.
10 And the LORD spoke to Moses, saying,
11 "Go in, tell Pharaoh king of Egypt
to let the children of Israel go out of
his land."
12 And Moses spoke before the LORD,
saying, "The children of Israel have
not heeded me. How then shall Pharaoh heed me, for [a]I *am* [1]of uncircumcised lips?"
13 Then the LORD spoke to Moses and
Aaron, and gave them a [a]command[1]
for the children of Israel and for Pharaoh king of Egypt, to bring the children of Israel out of the land of Egypt.

The Family of Moses and Aaron

14 These *are* the heads of their fathers'
houses: [a]The sons of Reuben, the firstborn of Israel, *were* Hanoch, Pallu,
Hezron, and Carmi. These are the
*families of Reuben.
15 [a]And the sons of Simeon *were*
[1]Jemuel, Jamin, Ohad, Jachin, Zohar,
and Shaul the son of a Canaanite
woman. These *are* the families of
Simeon.
16 These *are* the names of [a]the sons
of Levi according to their generations:
Gershon, Kohath, and Merari. And the
years of the life of Levi *were* one hundred and thirty-seven.
17 [a]The sons of Gershon *were* Libni
and Shimi according to their families.
18 And [a]the sons of Kohath *were* Amram, Izhar, Hebron, and Uzziel. And
the years of the life of Kohath *were* one
hundred and thirty-three.
19 [a]The sons of Merari *were* Mahli and
Mushi. These *are* the families of Levi
according to their generations.
20 Now [a]Amram took for himself
[b]Jochebed, his father's sister, as wife;
and she bore him [c]Aaron and Moses.
And the years of the life of Amram
were one hundred and thirty-seven.
21 [a]The sons of Izhar *were* Korah,
Nepheg, and Zichri.
22 And [a]the sons of Uzziel *were*
Mishael, Elzaphan, and Zithri.
23 Aaron took to himself Elisheba,
daughter of [a]Amminadab, sister of
Nahshon, as wife; and she bore him
[b]Nadab, Abihu, [c]Eleazar, and Ithamar.
24 And [a]the sons of Korah *were* Assir,
Elkanah, and Abiasaph. These are the
families of the Korahites.
25 Eleazar, Aaron's son, took for himself one of the daughters of Putiel as
wife; and [a]she bore him Phinehas.
These *are* the heads of the fathers'
houses of the Levites according to their
families.
26 These *are the same* Aaron and Moses to whom the LORD said, "Bring out
the children of Israel from the land of
Egypt according to their [a]armies."[1]
27 These *are* the ones who spoke to
Pharaoh king of Egypt, [a]to bring out
the children of Israel from Egypt.
These *are the same* Moses and
Aaron.

2 [1]Heb. *YHWH*
3 [a]Gen. 17:1; 35:9; 48:3 [b]Gen. 28:3; 35:11 [c]Ps. 68:4; 83:18 [1]Heb. *YHWH*, traditionally *Jehovah*
4 [a]Gen. 12:7; 15:18; 17:4, 7, 8; 26:3; 28:4, 13 [b]Lev. 25:23 [c]Gen. 28:4 [1]*made* or *ratified* [2]*sojournings* [3]*sojourners*, temporary residents
5 [a]Ex. 2:24
6 [a]Deut. 6:12 [b]Deut. 26:8 [c]Deut. 7:8 [1]Mighty power
7 [a]2 Sam. 7:24 [b]Ex. 29:45, 46 [c]Ex. 5:4, 5
8 [a]Gen. 15:18; 26:3 [1]*promised*, lit. *lifted up My hand* *See WW at Gen. 26:3.
9 [a]Ex. 5:21 [b]Ex. 2:23 [1]Lit. *shortness*
12 [a]Jer. 1:6 [1]One who does not speak well
13 [a]Deut. 31:14 [1]*charge*
14 [a]Gen. 46:9 *See WW at Gen. 12:3.
15 [a]Gen. 46:10 [1]*Nemuel*, Num. 26:12
16 [a]Gen. 46:11
17 [a]1 Chr. 6:17
18 [a]1 Chr. 6:2, 18
19 [a]1 Chr. 6:19; 23:21
20 [a]Ex. 2:1, 2 [b]Num. 26:59 [c]Num. 26:59
21 [a]1 Chr. 6:37, 38
22 [a]Lev. 10:4
23 [a]Ruth 4:19, 20 [b]Lev. 10:1 [c]Ex. 28:1
24 [a]Num. 26:11
25 [a]Num. 25:7, 11
26 [a]Ex. 7:4; 12:17, 51 [1]*hosts*
27 [a]Ps. 77:20

6:3 God Almighty translates the Hebrew *El-Shaddai*, that is, "The God Who Is Enough," "The All-Powerful," and "The One Who Is Self-Sufficient," signifying God as a source of all blessing and military prowess.

6:4 A covenant was an agreement of two parties. Usually one party was superior to the other. It contained certain permanent pledges made to each other, which were ratified by a ritual or ceremony, such as circumcision (Gen. 17:10, 11), passing through cut bodies of slain animals (Jer. 34:18), or sharing a special meal (Gen. 31:54).

6:14–25 This genealogy places **Moses** and **Aaron** as descendants of **Levi** and members of that tribe of the Hebrew people. This later becomes important when God calls this tribe into the priesthood.

6:26 Armies referred to their family clans.

Aaron Is Moses' Spokesman

28 And it came to pass, on the day the
LORD spoke to Moses in the land of
Egypt,
29 that the LORD spoke to Moses, saying, "I *am* the LORD. [a]Speak to Pharaoh
king of Egypt all that I say to you."
30 But Moses said before the LORD,
"Behold, [a]I *am* [1]of uncircumcised lips,
and how shall Pharaoh heed me?"
2 7 So the LORD said to Moses: "See, I
have made you [a]*as* God to Pharaoh, and Aaron your brother shall be
[b]your *prophet.
2 "You [a]shall speak all that I command you. And Aaron your brother
shall tell Pharaoh to send the children
of Israel out of his land.
3 "And [a]I will harden Pharaoh's
heart, and [b]multiply My [c]signs and My
wonders in the land of Egypt.
4 "But [a]Pharaoh will not heed you,
so [b]that I may lay My hand on Egypt
and bring My [1]armies *and* My people,
the children of Israel, out of the land
of Egypt [c]by great judgments.
5 "And the Egyptians [a]shall know
that I *am* the LORD, when I [b]stretch out
My hand on Egypt and [c]bring out the
children of Israel from among them."
6 Then Moses and Aaron [a]did *so;* just
as the LORD commanded them, so they
did.
7 And Moses *was* [a]eighty years old
and [b]Aaron eighty-three years old
when they spoke to Pharaoh.

Aaron's Miraculous Rod

8 Then the LORD spoke to Moses and
Aaron, saying,
9 "When Pharaoh speaks to you, saying, [a]'Show a *miracle for yourselves,'
then you shall say to Aaron, [b]'Take
your rod and cast *it* before Pharaoh,
and let it become a serpent.' "
10 So Moses and Aaron went in to Pharaoh, and they did so, just [a]as the LORD
commanded. And Aaron cast down his
rod before Pharaoh and before his servants, and it [b]became a serpent.
11 But Pharaoh also [a]called the wise
men and [b]the [1]sorcerers; so the magi-

29 [a]Ex. 6:11; 7:2
30 [a]Ex. 4:10; 6:12 [1]One who does not speak well

CHAPTER 7

1 [a]Ex. 4:16 [b]Ex. 4:15, 16 *See WW at 1 Sam. 3:20.
2 [a]Ex. 4:15
3 [a]Ex. 4:21; 9:12 [b]Ex. 11:9 [c]Deut. 4:34
4 [a]Ex. 3:19, 20; 10:1; 11:9 [b]Ex. 9:14 [c]Ex. 6:6; 12:12 [1]*hosts*
5 [a]Ps. 9:16 [b]Ex. 9:15 [c]Ex. 3:20; 6:6; 12:51
6 [a]Ex. 7:2
7 [a]Deut. 29:5; 31:2; 34:7 [b]Num. 33:39
9 [a]Is. 7:11 [b]Ex. 4:2, 3, 17 *See WW at Zech. 3:8.
10 [a]Ex. 7:9 [b]Ex. 4:3
11 [a]Gen. 41:8 [b]2 Tim. 3:8 [1]*soothsayers*

6:30 See note on 4:10.
7:1—11:10 See section 2 of Truth-In-Action at the end of Ex.
7:1, 2 A prophet was the middleman between God and His people. He acted as the mouthpiece of God to the people and represented the people to God.
7:3 I will harden Pharaoh's heart reinforces God's sovereignty. Pharaoh is already arrogantly unbelieving (5:2). God will intensify this to prove His presence to Egypt and Israel. See Rom. 9:14–18.
7:11 Egypt, like the rest of the Middle-Eastern cultures, was a land where magic flourished. The belief was that one, through the use of magic, could influence or control the gods. **Wise men** were those who knew the occultic arts; **sorcerers** muttered magic formulas and incantations; **magicians** were the bearers of magic books. Their temporary success shows Satan's power to imitate certain miracles. See 2 Thess. 2:9, 10.

THE TEN PLAGUES ON EGYPT (7:3, 5)

The Plague	The Effect
1. Blood (7:20)	Pharaoh hardened (7:22)
2. Frogs (8:6)	Pharaoh begs relief, promises freedom (8:8), but is hardened (8:15)
3. Lice (8:17)	Pharaoh hardened (8:19)
4. Flies (8:24)	Pharaoh bargains (8:28), but is hardened (8:32)
5. Livestock diseased (9:6)	Pharaoh hardened (9:7)
6. Boils (9:10)	Pharaoh hardened (9:12)
7. Hail (9:23)	Pharaoh begs relief (9:27), promises freedom (9:28), but is hardened (9:35)
8. Locusts (10:13)	Pharaoh bargains (10:11), begs relief (10:17), but is hardened (10:20)
9. Darkness (10:22)	Pharaoh bargains (10:24), but is hardened (10:27)
10. Death of firstborn (12:29)	Pharaoh and Egyptians beg Israel to leave Egypt (12:31–33)

God multiplied His signs and wonders in the land of Egypt that the Egyptians might know that He is the Lord.

cians of Egypt, they also [c]did in like manner with their [2]enchantments.

12 For every man threw down his rod, and they became serpents. But Aaron's rod swallowed up their rods.

13 And Pharaoh's heart grew hard, and he did not heed them, as the LORD had said.

The First Plague: Waters Become Blood

14 So the LORD said to Moses: [a]"Pharaoh's heart *is* hard; he refuses to let the people go.

15 "Go to Pharaoh in the morning, when he goes out to the [a]water, and you shall stand by the river's bank to meet him; and [b]the rod which was turned to a serpent you shall take in your hand.

16 "And you shall say to him, [a]'The LORD God of the Hebrews has sent me to you, saying, "Let My people go, [b]that they may [1]serve Me in the wilderness"; but indeed, until now you would not hear!

17 'Thus says the LORD: "By this [a]you shall know that I *am* the LORD. Behold, I will strike the waters which *are* in the river with the rod that *is* in my hand, and [b]they shall be turned [c]to blood.

18 "And the fish that *are* in the river shall die, the river shall stink, and the Egyptians will [a]loathe[1] to drink the water of the river." ' "

19 Then the LORD spoke to Moses, "Say to Aaron, 'Take your rod and [a]stretch out your hand over the waters of Egypt, over their streams, over their rivers, over their ponds, and over all their pools of water, that they may become blood. And there shall be blood throughout all the land of Egypt, both in *buckets of* wood and *pitchers of* stone.' "

20 And Moses and Aaron did so, just as the LORD commanded. So he [a]lifted up the rod and struck the waters that *were* in the river, in the sight of Pharaoh and in the sight of his servants. And all the [b]waters that *were* in the river were turned to blood.

11 [c]Ex. 7:22; 8:7, 18 [2]*secret arts*
14 [a]Ex. 8:15; 10:1, 20, 27
15 [a]Ex. 2:5; 8:20 [b]Ex. 4:2, 3; 7:10
16 [a]Ex. 3:13, 18; 4:22 [b]Ex. 3:12, 18; 4:23; 5:1, 3; 8:1 [1]*worship*
17 [a]Ex. 5:2; 7:5; 10:2 [b]Ex. 4:9; 7:20 [c]Rev. 11:6; 16:4, 6
18 [a]Ex. 7:24 [1]*be weary of drinking*
19 [a]Ex. 8:5, 6, 16; 9:22; 10:12, 21; 14:21, 26
20 [a]Ex. 17:5 [b]Ps. 78:44; 105:29, 30

21 The fish that *were* in the river died, the river stank, and the Egyptians [a]could not drink the water of the river. So there was blood throughout all the land of Egypt.

22 [a]Then the magicians of Egypt did [b]so with their [1]enchantments; and Pharaoh's heart grew hard, and he did not heed them, [c]as the LORD had said.

23 And Pharaoh turned and went into his house. Neither was his heart moved by this.

24 So all the Egyptians dug all around the river for water to drink, because they could not drink the water of the river.

25 And seven days passed after the LORD had struck the river.

The Second Plague: Frogs

8

And the LORD spoke to Moses, "Go to Pharaoh and say to him, 'Thus says the LORD: "Let My people go, [a]that they may serve Me.

2 "But if you [a]refuse to let *them* go, behold, I will smite all your territory with [b]frogs.

3 "So the river shall bring forth frogs abundantly, which shall go up and come into your house, into your [a]bedroom, on your bed, into the houses of your servants, on your people, into your ovens, and into your kneading bowls.

4 "And the frogs shall come up on you, on your people, and on all your servants." ' "

5 Then the LORD spoke to Moses, "Say to Aaron, [a]'Stretch out your hand with your rod over the streams, over the rivers, and over the ponds, and cause frogs to come up on the land of Egypt.' "

6 So Aaron stretched out his hand over the waters of Egypt, and [a]the frogs came up and covered the land of Egypt.

7 [a]And the magicians did so with their [1]enchantments, and brought up frogs on the land of Egypt.

8 Then Pharaoh called for Moses and Aaron, and said, [a]"Entreat[1] the LORD

21 [a]Ex. 7:18
22 [a]Ex. 7:11 [b]Ex. 8:7 [c]Ex. 3:19; 7:3 [1]*secret arts*

CHAPTER 8

1 [a]Ex. 3:12, 18; 4:23; 5:1, 3
2 [a]Ex. 7:14; 9:2 [b]Rev. 16:13
3 [a]Ps. 105:30
5 [a]Ex. 7:19
6 [a]Ps. 78:45; 105:30
7 [a]Ex. 7:11, 22 [1]*secret arts*
8 [a]Ex. 8:28; 9:28; 10:17 [1]*Pray to, Make supplication to*

7:13 The elders of Israel did not ask for signs, but when they saw them, they believed (4:30, 31). Pharaoh asked for a sign (v. 9), but when he saw one, he did not believe.

7:17—8:19 In addition to being called "wonders" (see note on 3:20), God's dealings with Egypt are commonly called "plagues" because of the main Hebrew verbs that describe His actions, **I will strike** (7:17) and **I will smite** (8:2). This reinforces God's judgment behind them. Many of the plagues are aimed at Egypt's nature gods as much as at the Egyptians themselves. With each plague, God demonstrates that the various Egyptian gods are powerless and judged by Him.

7:20 Some interpret this to mean the Nile was polluted by fine red earth God released through flooding. The text more likely indicates that the Nile actually turned to **blood.**

8:1–15 **Frogs** were associated with the goddess Heqt, who helped women in childbirth. This almost comical plague shows Yahweh is in charge of the land of Egypt.

that He may take away the frogs from
me and from my people; and I will let
the people [b]go, that they may sacrifice
to the LORD."
9 And Moses said to Pharaoh, "Accept the honor of saying when I shall
intercede for you, for your servants,
and for your people, to destroy the
frogs from you and your houses, *that*
they may remain in the river only."
10 So he said, "Tomorrow." And he
said, "*Let it be* according to your word,
that you may know that [a]*there is* no
one like the LORD our God.
11 "And the frogs shall depart from
you, from your houses, from your servants, and from your people. They
shall remain in the river only."
12 Then Moses and Aaron went out
from Pharaoh. And Moses [a]cried out
to the LORD concerning the frogs which
He had brought against Pharaoh.
13 So the LORD did according to the
word of Moses. And the frogs died out
of the houses, out of the courtyards,
and out of the fields.
14 They gathered them together in
heaps, and the land stank.
15 But when Pharaoh saw that there
was [a]relief, [b]he hardened his heart and
did not heed them, as the LORD had
said.

The Third Plague: Lice

16 So the LORD said to Moses, "Say to
Aaron, 'Stretch out your rod, and strike
the dust of the land, so that it may become [1]lice throughout all the land of
Egypt.'"
17 And they did so. For Aaron
stretched out his hand with his rod and
struck the dust of the earth, and
[a]it became lice on man and beast. All
the dust of the land became lice
throughout all the land of Egypt.
18 Now [a]the magicians so worked with
their [1]enchantments to bring forth lice,
but they [b]could not. So there were lice
on man and beast.
19 Then the magicians said to Pharaoh, "This *is* [a]the[1] finger of God." But
Pharaoh's [b]heart grew hard, and he did
not heed them, just as the LORD had
said.

The Fourth Plague: Flies

20 And the LORD said to Moses,
[a]"Rise early in the morning and stand
before Pharaoh as he comes out to the
water. Then say to him, 'Thus says the
LORD: [b]"Let My people go, that they
may serve Me.
21 "Or else, if you will not let My people go, behold, I will send swarms *of*
flies on you and your servants, on your
people and into your houses. The
houses of the Egyptians shall be full
of swarms *of flies,* and also the ground
on which they *stand.*
22 "And in that day [a]I will set apart
the land of [b]Goshen, in which My people dwell, that no swarms *of flies* shall
be there, in order that you may [c]know
that I *am* the LORD in the midst of the
[d]land.
23 "I will [1]make a difference between
My people and your people. Tomorrow
this [a]sign shall be."'"
24 And the LORD did so. [a]Thick
swarms *of flies* came into the house of
Pharaoh, *into* his servants' houses, and
into all the land of Egypt. The land was
corrupted because of the swarms *of*
flies.
25 Then Pharaoh called for Moses and
Aaron, and said, "Go, sacrifice to your
God in the land."
26 And Moses said, "It is not right to
do so, for we would be sacrificing
[a]the abomination of the Egyptians to
the LORD our God. If we sacrifice the
abomination of the Egyptians before
their eyes, then will they not [1]stone
us?
27 "We will go [a]three days' journey
into the wilderness and sacrifice to the
LORD our God as [b]He will command
us."
28 So Pharaoh said, "I will let you go,
that you may sacrifice to the LORD your

8 [b]Ex. 10:8, 24
10 [a]Ex. 9:14; 15:11; Deut. 4:35, 39; 33:26; 2 Sam. 7:22; 1 Chr. 17:20; Ps. 86:8; Is. 46:9; [Jer. 10:6, 7]
12 [a]Ex. 8:30; 9:33; 10:18; 32:11; [James 5:16–18]
15 [a]Eccl. 8:11 [b]Ex. 7:14, 22; 9:34; 1 Sam. 6:6
16 [1]*gnats*
17 [a]Ps. 105:31
18 [a]Ex. 7:11, 12; 8:7 [b]Dan. 5:8; 2 Tim. 3:8, 9 [1]*secret arts*
19 [a]Ex. 7:5; 10:7; 1 Sam. 6:3, 9; Ps. 8:3; Luke 11:20 [b]Ex. 8:15 [1]An act of God
20 [a]Ex. 7:15; 9:13 [b]Ex. 3:18; 4:23; 5:1, 3; 8:1
22 [a]Ex. 9:4, 6, 26; 10:23; 11:6, 7; 12:13 [b]Gen. 50:8 [c]Ex. 7:5, 17; 10:2; 14:4 [d]Ex. 9:29
23 [a]Ex. 4:8 [1]Lit. *set a ransom,* Ex. 9:4; 11:7
24 [a]Ps. 78:45; 105:31
26 [a]Gen. 43:32; 46:34; [Deut. 7:25, 26; 12:31] [1]Put us to death by stoning
27 [a]Ex. 3:18; 5:3 [b]Ex. 3:12

8:16–19 This could have been ticks, **lice,** gnats, or mosquitoes, all of which existed in the dry, hot climate of Egypt.

8:19 Finger of God speaks figuratively of the power of God. The magicians recognize the superiority of God's power and tell Pharaoh that the Hebrew God is behind all of these events. They are, in effect, surrendering. How can one fight the God who created and controls nature? This is Egypt's first move toward acknowledging that Yahweh is powerfully present at the very point their gods should be.

8:20—9:12 The next three plagues bring loss and physical suffering. In the first three plagues, all suffer; in the next three, the inhabitants of Goshen—the Hebrews—are spared.

8:22, 23 Goshen was a district of about 900 square miles with two major cities: Raamses and Pithom. The Hebrews lived in this region under the protection of God. This action sends out two messages: one to Pharaoh that God is in control and another to the Hebrews that God cares for them.

8:24 The great number of flies upsets the daily processes of life. Doing any work outside is impossible.

8:25–32 Pharaoh tries to persuade Moses to compromise.

8:26 The **abomination** to the Egyptians would have been sacrificing a cow, since in their minds a cow was sacred.

God in the wilderness; only you shall not go very far away. [a]Intercede for me."

29 Then Moses said, "Indeed I am going out from you, and I will entreat the LORD, that the swarms *of flies* may depart tomorrow from Pharaoh, from his servants, and from his people. But let Pharaoh not [a]deal deceitfully anymore in not letting the people go to sacrifice to the LORD."

30 So Moses went out from Pharaoh and [a]entreated the LORD.

31 And the LORD did according to the word of Moses; He removed the swarms *of flies* from Pharaoh, from his servants, and from his people. Not one remained.

32 But Pharaoh [a]hardened his heart at this time also; neither would he let the people go.

The Fifth Plague: Livestock Diseased

9 Then the LORD said to Moses, [a]"Go in to Pharaoh and tell him, 'Thus says the LORD God of the Hebrews: "Let My people go, that they may [b]serve Me.

2 "For if you [a]refuse to let *them* go, and still hold them,

3 "behold, the [a]hand of the LORD will be on your cattle in the field, on the horses, on the donkeys, on the camels, on the oxen, and on the sheep—a very severe pestilence.

4 "And [a]the LORD will make a difference between the livestock of Israel and the livestock of Egypt. So nothing shall die of all *that* belongs to the children of Israel." ' "

5 Then the LORD appointed a set time, saying, "Tomorrow the LORD will do this thing in the land."

6 So the LORD did this thing on the next day, and [a]all the livestock of Egypt died; but of the livestock of the children of Israel, not one died.

7 Then Pharaoh sent, and indeed, not even one of the livestock of the Israelites was dead. But the [a]heart of Pharaoh became hard, and he did not let the people go.

28 [a]Ex. 8:8, 15, 29, 32; 9:28; 1 Kin. 13:6
29 [a]Ex. 8:8, 15
30 [a]Ex. 8:12
32 [a]Ex. 4:21; 8:8, 15; Ps. 52:2

CHAPTER 9

1 [a]Ex. 4:23; 8:1 [b]Ex. 7:16
2 [a]Ex. 8:2
3 [a]Ex. 7:4; 1 Sam. 5:6; Ps. 39:10; Acts 13:11
4 [a]Ex. 8:22
6 [a]Ex. 9:19, 20, 25; Ps. 78:48, 50
7 [a]Ex. 7:14; 8:32
8 *See WW at 1 Kin. 8:23.
9 [a]Deut. 28:27; Rev. 16:2
10 [a]Deut. 28:27
11 [a][Ex. 8:18, 19; 2 Tim. 3:9] [b]Deut. 28:27; Job 2:7; Rev. 16:1, 2
12 [a]Ex. 7:13 [b]Ex. 4:21
13 [a]Ex. 8:20 [b]Ex. 9:1
14 [a]Ex. 8:10; Deut. 3:24; 2 Sam. 7:22; 1 Chr. 17:20; Ps. 86:8; Is. 45:5–8; 46:9; Jer. 10:6, 7
15 [a]Ex. 3:20; 7:5 [b]Ex. 5:3
16 [a]Ex. 14:17; Prov. 16:4; [Rom. 9:17, 18; 1 Pet. 2:8, 9] [b]Ex. 7:4, 5; 10:1; 11:9; 14:17 [c]1 Kin. 8:43 *See WW at Deut. 8:18.

The Sixth Plague: Boils

8 So the LORD said to Moses and Aaron, "Take for yourselves handfuls of ashes from a furnace, and let Moses scatter it toward the *heavens in the sight of Pharaoh.

9 "And it will become fine dust in all the land of Egypt, and it will cause [a]boils that break out in sores on man and beast throughout all the land of Egypt."

10 Then they took ashes from the furnace and stood before Pharaoh, and Moses scattered *them* toward heaven. And *they* caused [a]boils that break out in sores on man and beast.

11 And the [a]magicians could not stand before Moses because of the [b]boils, for the boils were on the magicians and on all the Egyptians.

12 But the LORD hardened the heart of Pharaoh; and he [a]did not heed them, just [b]as the LORD had spoken to Moses.

The Seventh Plague: Hail

13 Then the LORD said to Moses, [a]"Rise early in the morning and stand before Pharaoh, and say to him, 'Thus says the LORD God of the Hebrews: "Let My people go, that they may [b]serve Me,

14 "for at this time I will send all My plagues to your very heart, and on your servants and on your people, [a]that you may know that *there is* none like Me in all the earth.

15 "Now if I had [a]stretched out My hand and struck you and your people with [b]pestilence, then you would have been cut off from the earth.

16 "But indeed for [a]this *purpose* I have raised you up, that I may [b]show My *power *in* you, and that My [c]name may be declared in all the earth.

17 "As yet you exalt yourself against My people in that you will not let them go.

18 "Behold, tomorrow about this time I will cause very heavy hail to rain down, such as has not been in Egypt since its founding until now.

19 "Therefore send now *and* gather

9:3 The fifth plague that destroyed livestock could have been an attack on Hathor, the mother-goddess of Egypt, who was often portrayed in the form of a cow.

9:8 The scattered **handfuls of ashes** somehow symbolize the disease.

9:9 The **boils** were probably tumors, blisters, or running sores. See Deut. 28:27.

9:16 The intent of the plagues is clearly stated to Egypt.

9:18 The hailstorm itself was a miracle, for in a virtually rainless land, **hail** was rarely seen. Thus, with this miracle, God intensified the natural and made the hailstorm destructive. The hail could have been an attack on two Egyptian gods: Isis, the goddess of life, and Seth, the protector of crops.

9:19 An all-powerful, merciful God can bring judgment and mercy at the same time. Pharaoh is told how to save men and animals by heeding God's instructions.

your livestock and all that you have in the field, for the hail shall come down on every man and every animal which is found in the field and is not brought home; and they shall die." ' "

20 He who [a]feared the word of the LORD among the [b]servants of Pharaoh made his servants and his livestock flee to the houses.

21 But he who did not regard the word of the LORD left his servants and his livestock in the field.

22 Then the LORD said to Moses, "Stretch out your hand toward heaven, that there may be [a]hail in all the land of Egypt—on man, on beast, and on every herb of the field, throughout the land of Egypt."

23 And Moses stretched out his rod toward heaven; and [a]the LORD sent thunder and hail, and fire darted to the ground. And the LORD rained hail on the land of Egypt.

24 So there was hail, and fire mingled with the hail, so very heavy that there was none like it in all the land of Egypt since it became a nation.

25 And the [a]hail struck throughout the whole land of Egypt, all that *was* in the field, both man and beast; and the hail struck every herb of the field and broke every tree of the field.

26 [a]Only in the land of Goshen, where the children of Israel *were,* there was no hail.

27 And Pharaoh sent and [a]called for Moses and Aaron, and said to them, [b]"I have sinned this time. [c]The LORD *is* *righteous, and my people and I *are* wicked.

28 [a]"Entreat[1] the LORD, that there may be no *more* [2]mighty thundering and hail, for *it is* enough. I will let you [b]go, and you shall stay no longer."

29 So Moses said to him, "As soon as I have gone out of the city, I will [a]spread out my hands to the LORD; the thunder will cease, and there will be no more hail, that you may know that the [b]earth *is* the LORD's.

30 "But as for you and your servants, [a]I know that you will not yet fear the LORD God."

31 Now the flax and the barley were struck, [a]for the barley *was* in the head and the flax *was* in bud.

32 But the wheat and the spelt were not struck, for they *are* [1]late crops.

33 So Moses went out of the city from Pharaoh and [a]spread out his hands to the LORD; then the thunder and the hail ceased, and the rain was not poured on the earth.

34 And when Pharaoh saw that the rain, the hail, and the thunder had ceased, he sinned yet more; and he hardened his heart, he and his servants.

35 So [a]the heart of Pharaoh was hard; neither would he let the children of Israel go, as the LORD had spoken by Moses.

The Eighth Plague: Locusts

10 Now the LORD said to Moses, "Go in to Pharaoh; [a]for I have hardened his heart and the hearts of his servants, [b]that I may show these signs of Mine before him,

2 "and that [a]you may tell in the hearing of your son and your son's son the mighty things I have done in Egypt, and My signs which I have done among them, that you may [b]know that I *am* the LORD."

3 So Moses and Aaron came in to Pharaoh and said to him, "Thus says the LORD God of the Hebrews: 'How long will you refuse to [a]humble yourself before Me? Let My people go, that they may [b]serve Me.

4 'Or else, if you refuse to let My people go, behold, tomorrow I will bring [a]locusts into your territory.

5 'And they shall cover the face of the earth, so that no one will be able to see the earth; and [a]they shall eat the residue of what is left, which remains to you from the hail, and they shall eat every tree which grows up for you out of the field.

6 'They shall [a]fill your houses, the houses of all your servants, and the houses of all the Egyptians—which neither your fathers nor your fathers' fathers have seen, since the day that they were on the earth to this day.' " And he turned and went out from Pharaoh.

7 Then Pharaoh's [a]servants said to him, "How long shall this man be [b]a snare to us? Let the men go, that they may serve the LORD their God. Do

20 [a][Prov. 13:13] [b]Ex. 8:19; 10:7
22 [a]Rev. 16:21
23 [a]Josh. 10:11
25 [a]Ps. 78:47, 48; 105:32, 33
26 [a]Ex. 8:22, 23; 9:4, 6; 10:23; 11:7; 12:13
27 [a]Ex. 8:8 [b]Ex. 9:34; 10:16, 17 [c]2 Chr. 12:6 *See WW at Lam. 1:18.
28 [a]Ex. 8:8, 28; 10:17 [b]Ex. 8:25; 10:8, 24 [1]*Pray to, Make supplication to* [2]Lit. *voices of God* or *sounds of God*
29 [a]Is. 1:15 [b]Ps. 24:1
30 [a][Is. 26:10]
31 [a]Ruth 1:22; 2:23
32 [1]Lit. *darkened*
33 [a]Ex. 8:12; 9:29
35 [a]Ex. 4:21

CHAPTER 10

1 [a]John 12:40 [b]Ex. 7:4; 9:16
2 [a]Joel 1:3 [b]Ex. 7:5, 17; 8:22
3 [a][1 Kin. 21:29] [b]Ex. 4:23; 8:1; 9:1
4 [a]Rev. 9:3
5 [a]Ex. 9:32
6 [a]Ex. 8:3, 21
7 [a]Ex. 7:5; 8:19; 9:20; 12:33 [b]Ex. 23:33

9:20, 21 One can make one of two responses to any offer made by God: acceptance or rejection. Both carry different consequences.

9:27–35 Pharaoh acknowledges his and his people's sin and asks Moses for God's mercy. However, even though he and his people know their sinful state, he refuses repentance (v. 34).

10:2 Oral tradition and recitation are important parts of a Hebrew child's education and religious training that preserve the belief and experience of the people.

you not yet know that Egypt is destroyed?"

8 So Moses and Aaron were brought again to Pharaoh, and he said to them, "Go, serve the LORD your God. Who *are* the ones that are going?"

9 And Moses said, "We will go with our young and our old; with our sons and our daughters, with our flocks and our herds we will go, for [a]we must hold a feast to the LORD."

10 Then he said to them, "The LORD had better be with you when I let you and your little ones go! Beware, for evil is ahead of you.

11 "Not so! Go now, you *who are* men, and serve the LORD, for that is what you desired." And they were driven [a]out from Pharaoh's presence.

12 Then the LORD said to Moses, [a]"Stretch out your hand over the land of Egypt for the locusts, that they may come upon the land of Egypt, and [b]eat every herb of the land—all that the hail has left."

13 So Moses stretched out his rod over the land of Egypt, and the LORD brought an east wind on the land all that day and all *that* night. When it was morning, the east wind brought the locusts.

14 And [a]the locusts went up over all the land of Egypt and rested on all the territory of Egypt. *They were* very severe; [b]previously there had been no such locusts as they, nor shall there be such after them.

15 For they [a]covered the face of the whole earth, so that the land was darkened; and they [b]ate every herb of the land and all the fruit of the trees which the hail had left. So there remained nothing green on the trees or on the plants of the field throughout all the land of Egypt.

16 Then Pharaoh called [a]for Moses and Aaron in haste, and said, [b]"I have sinned against the LORD your God and against you.

17 "Now therefore, please forgive my sin only this once, and [a]entreat[1] the LORD your God, that He may take away from me this death only."

18 So he [a]went out from Pharaoh and entreated the LORD.

19 And the LORD turned a very strong west wind, which took the locusts away and blew them [a]into the Red Sea. There remained not one locust in all the territory of Egypt.

20 But the LORD [a]hardened Pharaoh's heart, and he did not let the children of Israel go.

The Ninth Plague: Darkness

21 Then the LORD said to Moses, [a]"Stretch out your hand toward heaven, that there may be darkness over the land of Egypt, [1]darkness *which* may even be felt."

22 So Moses stretched out his hand toward heaven, and there was [a]thick darkness in all the land of Egypt [b]three days.

23 They did not see one another; nor did anyone rise from his place for three days. [a]But all the children of Israel had light in their dwellings.

24 Then Pharaoh called to Moses and [a]said, "Go, serve the LORD; only let your flocks and your herds be kept back. Let your [b]little ones also go with you."

25 But Moses said, "You must also give [1]us sacrifices and burnt offerings, that we may sacrifice to the LORD our God.

26 "Our [a]livestock also shall go with us; not a hoof shall be left behind. For we must take some of them to serve the LORD our God, and even we do not know with what we must serve the LORD until we arrive there."

27 But the LORD [a]hardened Pharaoh's heart, and he would not let them go.

28 Then Pharaoh said to him, [a]"Get away from me! Take heed to yourself and see my face no more! For in the day you see my face you shall die!"

29 So Moses said, "You have spoken well. [a]I will never see your face again."

Death of the Firstborn Announced

11 And the LORD said to Moses, "I will bring one more plague on Pharaoh and on Egypt. [a]Afterward he

9 [a]Ex. 5:1; 7:16
11 [a]Ex. 10:28
12 [a]Ex. 7:19 [b]Ex. 10:5, 15
14 [a]Deut. 28:38; Ps. 78:46; 105:34 [b]Joel 1:4, 7; 2:1–11; Rev. 9:3
15 [a]Ex. 10:5 [b]Ps. 105:35
16 [a]Ex. 8:8 [b]Ex. 9:27
17 [a]Ex. 8:8, 28; 9:28; 1 Kin. 13:6 [1]*make supplication to*
18 [a]Ex. 8:30
19 [a]Joel 2:20
20 [a]Ex. 4:21; 10:1; 11:10
21 [a]Ex. 9:22 [1]Lit. *that one may feel the darkness*
22 [a]Ps. 105:28; Rev. 16:10 [b]Ex. 3:18
23 [a]Ex. 8:22, 23
24 [a]Ex. 8:8, 25; 10:8 [b]Ex. 10:10
25 [1]Lit. *into our hands*
26 [a]Ex. 10:9
27 [a]Ex. 4:21; 10:1, 20; 14:4, 8
28 [a]Ex. 10:11
29 [a]Ex. 11:8; Heb. 11:27

CHAPTER 11

1 [a]Ex. 12:31, 33, 39

10:11 Pharaoh proposes a further compromise with Moses: he will allow only the **men** to go and sacrifice to God, which is counter to both Hebrew and Egyptian understandings of worship. In both cultures the entire populace worships together. Without giving time for response, Moses and Aaron are banished from **Pharaoh's presence.** This action on Pharaoh's part is merely a psychological ploy.

10:13–15 Locusts come and eat what is left of the crops that were destroyed by the hailstorm, thus endangering life. In this manner God continued the attack on Isis and Seth.

10:21 The darkening of the sun had a twofold effect. First, God demonstrated His power over the sun, the most potent religious symbol of Egypt. Second, it was a direct frontal attack on Pharaoh himself, since he was considered to be the incarnation of Amon-Ra, the sun god.

will let you go from here. [b]When he
lets *you* go, he will surely drive you
out of here altogether.
2 "Speak now in the hearing of the
people, and let every man ask from his
neighbor and every woman from her
neighbor, [a]articles of silver and articles
of gold."
3 [a]And the LORD gave the people favor in the sight of the Egyptians. Moreover the man [b]Moses *was* very great
in the land of Egypt, in the sight of Pharaoh's servants and in the sight of the
people.
4 Then Moses said, "Thus says the
LORD: [a]'About midnight I will go out
into the midst of Egypt;
5 'and [a]all the firstborn in the land
of Egypt shall die, from the firstborn
of Pharaoh who sits on his throne, even
to the firstborn of the female servant
who *is* behind the handmill, and all the
firstborn of the animals.
6 [a]'Then there shall be a great cry
throughout all the land of Egypt,
[b]such as was not like it *before,* nor
shall be like it again.
7 [a]'But against none of the children
of Israel [b]shall a dog [1]move its tongue,
against man or beast, that you may
know that the LORD does make a difference between the Egyptians and Israel.'
8 "And [a]all these your servants shall
come down to me and bow down to
me, saying, 'Get out, and all the people
who follow you!' After that I will go
out." [b]Then he went out from Pharaoh
in great anger.
9 But the LORD said to Moses, [a]"Pharaoh will not heed you, so that [b]My
wonders may be multiplied in the land
of Egypt."
10 So Moses and Aaron did all these
wonders before Pharaoh; [a]and the
LORD hardened Pharaoh's heart, and
he did not let the children of Israel go
out of his land.

1 [c]Ex. 6:1; 12:39
2 [a]Ex. 3:22; 12:35, 36
3 [a]Ex. 3:21; 12:36 [b]Deut. 34:10–12
4 [a]Ex. 12:12, 23, 29
5 [a]Ex. 4:23; 12:12, 29
6 [a]Ex. 12:30 [b]Ex. 10:14
7 [a]Ex. 8:22 [b]Josh. 10:21 [1]*sharpen*
8 [a]Ex. 12:31–33 [b]Heb. 11:27
9 [a]Ex. 3:19; 7:4; 10:1 [b]Ex. 7:3; 9:16
10 [a]Rom. 2:5

CHAPTER 12

2 [a]Deut. 16:1
3 [a]Josh. 4:19 *See WW at Josh. 22:17.
5 [a][1 Pet. 1:19] [1]*perfect* or *sound* [2]*a year old* *See WW at Lev. 23:12.
6 [a]Lev. 23:5 *See WW at Lev. 16:17.
8 [a]Num. 9:12 [b]Deut. 16:7 [c]1 Cor. 5:8
9 [a]Deut. 16:7
10 [a]Ex. 16:19; 23:18; 34:25
11 [a]Ex. 12:13, 21, 27, 43 [1]Made ready to travel
12 [a]Ex. 11:4, 5 *See WW at Josh. 3:4.

The Passover Instituted

12 Now the LORD spoke to Moses
and Aaron in the land of Egypt,
saying,
2 [a]"This month *shall be* your beginning of months; it *shall be* the first
month of the year to you.
3 "Speak to all the *congregation of
Israel, saying: 'On the [a]tenth of this
month every man shall take for himself
a lamb, according to the house of *his*
father, a lamb for a household.
4 'And if the household is too small
for the lamb, let him and his neighbor
next to his house take *it* according to
the number of the persons; according
to each man's need you shall make
your count for the lamb.
5 'Your lamb shall be [a]without[1]*
blemish, a male [2]of the first year. You
may take *it* from the sheep or from the
goats.
6 'Now you shall keep it until the
[a]fourteenth day of the same month.
Then the whole *assembly of the congregation of Israel shall kill it at twilight.
7 'And they shall take *some* of the **2**
blood and put *it* on the two doorposts
and on the lintel of the houses where
they eat it.
8 'Then they shall eat the flesh on that
[a]night; [b]roasted in fire, with [c]unleav-
ened bread *and* with bitter *herbs* they
shall eat it.
9 'Do not eat it raw, nor boiled at all
with water, but [a]roasted in fire—its
head with its legs and its entrails.
10 [a]'You shall let none of it remain until morning, and what remains of it until morning you shall burn with fire.
11 'And thus you shall eat it: [1]*with* a
belt on your waist, your sandals on
your feet, and your staff in your hand.
So you shall eat it in haste. [a]It *is* the
LORD's Passover.
12 'For I [a]will *pass through the land

11:2 The Hebrews are told to ask from the Egyptians prized possessions and objects of value. This further humbled Pharaoh and his gods who were supposed to be caring for the Egyptians.

11:5 The final visitation showed God was not only the controlling force in nature, but was also the controlling force in life and death. Yahweh Himself brings the plague. This attack demonstrated that the God of the Hebrews was greater than Osiris, the Egyptian giver of life.

12:1–11 **Passover** *was originally a feast for* those about to be delivered by their direct obedience to the covenant God; it served as the final dynamic proof of God's presence and protective care. Its continued celebration by **all the congregation of Israel** would serve as a memorial for those who had been delivered and their offspring.

It is celebrated in the month of Nisan (also called Abib, March–April), and marks the new year because its beginning was the beginning of Israel's new life as a people. It is characterized by selecting a **lamb,** which is sacrificed four days later and eaten as part of a major commemorative meal. A feast of hope and life, the Passover represents deliverance and new beginnings; in many of its elements, it is a type of Christ our Redeemer, the Lamb of God.

12:7 See section 2 of Truth-In-Action at the end of Ex.

12:8 The **bitter *herbs*** have traditionally been regarded as representing the bitterness of Egyptian bondage. "Bitter *herbs*" could have been dandelions or horseradish.

12:11 The Passover meal was to be eaten **in haste,** with all the participants ready to move when God commanded them to leave.

12:12 Passover was a judgment **against all the gods of Egypt.** It was the final statement of God's power.

of Egypt on that night, and will strike
all the firstborn in the land of Egypt,
both man and beast; and [b]against all
the gods of Egypt I will execute judgment: [c]I *am* the LORD.
13 'Now the blood shall be a sign for
you on the houses where you *are*. And
when I see the blood, I will pass over
you; and the plague shall not be on you
to destroy *you* when I strike the land
of Egypt.

KINGDOM DYNAMICS

12:13 Developing the Importance of Blood Sacrifice, THE BLOOD. Ex. gives a more developed understanding of the importance of blood sacrifices. Sacrifice is seen as the means of deliverance for the individual, the family, and the nation. The blood of sacrificial animals was used regularly as an offering for sins as well as to consecrate the instruments of worship (20:24). It is first called "the blood of the covenant" in 24:5–8. It is in the Mosaic covenant and the Levitical priesthood that we see the most detailed administration of the blood of sacrifices. This developed significance of the role of the blood points toward the blood of Christ and its application for our redemption, justification, and sanctification (Heb. 9:14).

(Lev. 17:11/Gen. 4:1–10) C.S.

14 'So this day shall be to you [a]a *memorial; and you shall *keep it as a
[b]feast to the LORD throughout your
generations. You shall keep it as a
feast [c]by an everlasting ordinance.
3 15 [a]'Seven days you shall eat unleavened bread. On the first day you shall
remove leaven from your houses. For
whoever eats leavened bread from the
first day until the seventh day, [b]that
[1]person* shall be [2]cut off from Israel.
16 'On the first day *there shall be*
[a]a holy convocation, and on the seventh day there shall be a holy convocation for you. No manner of work shall
be done on them; but *that* which everyone must eat—that only may be prepared by you.
17 'So you shall observe *the Feast of*
Unleavened Bread, for [a]on this same
day I will have brought your [1]armies
[b]out of the land of Egypt. Therefore
you shall observe this day throughout

12 [b]Num. 33:4 [c]Ex. 6:2
14 [a]Ex. 13:9 [b]Lev. 23:4, 5; 2 Kin. 23:21 [c]Ex. 12:17, 24; 13:10 *See WW at Ex. 39:7. • See WW at Ex. 23:14.
15 [a]Ex. 13:6, 7; 23:15; 34:18; Lev. 23:6; Num. 28:17; Deut. 16:3, 8 [b]Gen. 17:14; Ex. 12:19; Num. 9:13 [1]*soul* [2]Put to death *See WW at Prov. 10:3.
16 [a]Lev. 23:2, 7, 8; Num. 28:18, 25
17 [a]Ex. 12:14; 13:3, 10 [b]Num. 33:1 [1]*hosts*
18 [a]Ex. 12:2; Lev. 23:5–8; Num. 28:16–25
19 [a]Ex. 12:15; 23:15; 34:18
21 [a][Heb. 11:28] [b]Ex. 3:16 [c]Ex. 12:3; Num. 9:4; Josh. 5:10; 2 Kin. 23:21; Ezra 6:20; Mark 14:12–16
22 [a]Heb. 11:28 [b]Ex. 12:7
23 [a]Ex. 11:4; 12:12, 13 [b]Ex. 24:8 [c]Ezek. 9:6; Rev. 7:3; 9:4 [d]1 Cor. 10:10; Heb. 11:28 [1]Crosspiece at top of door
24 [a]Ex. 12:14, 17; 13:5, 10
25 [a]Ex. 3:8, 17
26 [a]Ex. 10:2; 13:8, 14, 15; Deut. 32:7; Josh. 4:6; Ps. 78:6
27 [a]Ex. 12:11 [b]Ex. 4:31
28 [a][Heb. 11:28]

your generations as an everlasting ordinance.
18 [a]'In the first *month*, on the fourteenth day of the month at evening,
you shall eat unleavened bread, until
the twenty-first day of the month at
evening.
19 'For [a]seven days no leaven shall be 3
found in your houses, since whoever
eats what is leavened, that same person shall be cut off from the congregation of Israel, whether *he is* a stranger
or a native of the land.
20 'You shall eat nothing leavened; in
all your dwellings you shall eat unleavened bread.' "
21 Then [a]Moses called for all the
[b]elders of Israel and said to them,
[c]"Pick out and take lambs for yourselves according to your families, and
kill the Passover *lamb*.
22 [a]"And you shall take a bunch of
hyssop, dip *it* in the blood that *is* in
the basin, and [b]strike the lintel and the
two doorposts with the blood that *is*
in the basin. And none of you shall go
out of the door of his house until morning.
23 [a]"For the LORD will pass through to
strike the Egyptians; and when He sees
the [b]blood on the [1]lintel and on the two
doorposts, the LORD will pass over the
door and [c]not allow [d]the destroyer
to come into your houses to strike
you.
24 "And you shall [a]observe this thing
as an ordinance for you and your sons
forever.
25 "It will come to pass when you
come to the land which the LORD will
give you, [a]just as He promised, that
you shall keep this service.
26 [a]"And it shall be, when your children say to you, 'What do you mean
by this service?'
27 "that you shall say, [a]'It *is* the Passover sacrifice of the LORD, who passed
over the houses of the children of Israel
in Egypt when He struck the Egyptians
and delivered our households.' " So the
people [b]bowed their heads and worshiped.
28 Then the children of Israel went
away and [a]did *so;* just as the LORD had
commanded Moses and Aaron, so they
did.

12:15 See section 3 of Truth-In-Action at the end of Ex.
12:16 Convocation was a sacred assembly or calling together of people for rest and worship.
12:19, 20 See section 3 of Truth-In-Action at the end of Ex.
12:19 House can be applied to a tent or small hut.
12:21–28 A liturgical elaboration of vv. 1–13.
12:22 Hyssop is a member of the mint family, a shrublike plant. The **blood** used was symbolic of the blood of Christ, which brings salvation.
12:26–28 Children are to be a part of the Passover. They are to partake of it and be instructed in its meaning.

The Tenth Plague: Death of the Firstborn

29 [a]And it came to pass at midnight that [b]the LORD struck all the firstborn in the land of Egypt, from the firstborn of Pharaoh who sat on his throne to the firstborn of the captive who *was* [1]in the dungeon, and all the firstborn of [c]livestock.

30 So Pharaoh rose in the night, he, all his servants, and all the Egyptians; and there was a great cry in Egypt, for *there was* not a house where *there was* not one dead.

The Exodus

31 Then he [a]called for Moses and Aaron by night, and said, "Rise, go out from among my people, [b]both you and the children of Israel. And go, serve the LORD as you have [c]said.

32 [a]"Also take your flocks and your herds, as you have said, and be gone; and bless me also."

33 [a]And the Egyptians [b]urged the people, that they might send them out of the land in haste. For they said, "We *shall* all *be* dead."

34 So the people took their dough before it was leavened, having their kneading bowls bound up in their clothes on their shoulders.

35 Now the children of Israel had done according to the word of Moses, and they had asked from the Egyptians [a]articles of silver, articles of gold, and clothing.

36 [a]And the LORD had given the people favor in the sight of the Egyptians, so that they granted them *what they requested.* Thus [b]they plundered the Egyptians.

37 Then [a]the children of Israel journeyed from [b]Rameses to Succoth, about [c]six hundred thousand men on foot, besides children.

38 A [a]mixed multitude went up with them also, and flocks and herds—a great deal of [b]livestock.

39 And they baked unleavened cakes of the dough which they had brought out of Egypt; for it was not leavened, because [a]they were driven out of Egypt and could not wait, nor had they prepared provisions for themselves.

40 Now the [1]sojourn of the children of Israel who lived in [2]Egypt *was* [a]four hundred and thirty years.

41 And it came to pass at the end of the four hundred and thirty years—on that very same day—it came to pass that [a]all the armies of the LORD went out from the land of Egypt.

42 It *is* [a]a [1]night of solemn observance to the LORD for bringing them out of the land of Egypt. This *is* that night of the LORD, a solemn observance for all the children of Israel throughout their generations.

Passover Regulations

43 And the LORD said to Moses and Aaron, "This *is* [a]the ordinance of the Passover: No foreigner shall eat it.

44 "But every man's servant who is bought for money, when you have [a]circumcised him, then he may eat it.

45 [a]"A sojourner and a hired servant shall not eat it.

46 "In one house it shall be eaten; you shall not carry any of the flesh outside the house, [a]nor shall you break one of its bones.

47 [a]"All the congregation of Israel shall keep it.

48 "And [a]when a stranger [1]dwells with you *and wants* to keep the Passover to the LORD, let all his males be circumcised, and then let him come near and keep it; and he shall be as a native of the land. For no uncircumcised person shall eat it.

49 [a]"One law shall be for the native-born and for the stranger who dwells among you."

50 Thus all the children of Israel did; as the LORD commanded Moses and Aaron, so they did.

51 [a]And it came to pass, on that very same day, that the LORD brought the children of Israel out of the land of Egypt [b]according to their armies.

29 [a]Ex. 11:4, 5 [b]Num. 8:17; 33:4; Ps. 135:8; 136:10 [c]Ex. 9:6 [1]*in prison*
31 [a]Ex. 10:28, 29 [b]Ex. 8:25; 11:1 [c]Ex. 10:9
32 [a]Ex. 10:9, 26
33 [a]Ex. 10:7 [b]Ex. 11:8; Ps. 105:38
35 [a]Ex. 3:21, 22; 11:2, 3; Ps. 105:37
36 [a]Ex. 3:21 [b]Gen. 15:14
37 [a]Num. 33:3, 5 [b]Gen. 47:11; Ex. 1:11; Num. 33:3, 4 [c]Gen. 12:2; Ex. 38:26; Num. 1:46; 2:32; 11:21; 26:51
38 [a]Num. 11:4 [b]Ex. 17:3; Num. 20:19; 32:1; Deut. 3:19
39 [a]Ex. 6:1; 11:1; 12:31–33
40 [a]Gen. 15:13, 16; Acts 7:6; Gal. 3:17 [1]Length of the stay [2]Sam., LXX *Egypt and Canaan*
41 [a]Ex. 3:8, 10; 6:6; 7:4
42 [a]Ex. 13:10; 34:18; Deut. 16:1, 6 [1]*night of vigil*
43 [a]Ex. 12:11; Num. 9:14
44 [a]Gen. 17:12, 13; Lev. 22:11
45 [a]Lev. 22:10
46 [a]Num. 9:12; Ps. 34:20; [John 19:33, 36]
47 [a]Ex. 12:6; Num. 9:13, 14
48 [a]Num. 9:14 [1]As a resident alien
49 [a]Lev. 24:22; Num. 15:15, 16; [Gal. 3:28]
51 [a]Ex. 12:41; 20:2 [b]Ex. 6:26

12:29–32 Pharaoh was directly touched by the final plague. He requested that the Hebrews leave and also asked for a blessing. At this point he knew the God of the Hebrews was God and that he and the gods of Egypt were defeated.
12:35–37 See note on 11:2.
12:37 From Rameses to Succoth would have been eastward, the most direct route. The **six hundred thousand men,** plus women and children, could easily have made the number of the people who participated in the Exodus as many as from 1.5 to 2 million.
12:38 Mixed multitude: These were probably Egyptian slaves who followed Israel's example of offering the sacrificial lamb. They saw the God of Israel at work, and they believed and received God's blessing for obedience. This relationship would continue until the giving of the Law, when they would be excluded; yet, if males opted for circumcision all foreign origin would be obliterated and they could fully participate.
12:40 Four hundred and thirty years had passed from the migration of Jacob's family to the time of the Exodus. The traditional conservative date is 1446 B.C.

The Firstborn Consecrated

13 Then the LORD spoke to Moses, saying,

2 [a]"Consecrate[1] to Me all the firstborn, whatever opens the womb among the children of Israel, *both* of man and beast; it is Mine."

The Feast of Unleavened Bread

[3] 3 And Moses said to the people: [a]"Remember this day in which you went out of Egypt, out of the house of [1]bondage; for [b]by strength of hand the LORD brought you out of this *place.* [c]No leavened bread shall be eaten.

4 [a]"On this day you are going out, in the month Abib.

5 "And it shall be, when the LORD [a]brings you into the [b]land of the Canaanites and the Hittites and the Amorites and the Hivites and the Jebusites, which He [c]swore to your fathers to give you, a land flowing with milk and honey, [d]that you shall keep this service in this month.

[3] 6 [a]"Seven days you shall eat unleavened bread, and on the seventh day *there shall be* a feast to the LORD.

7 "Unleavened bread shall be eaten seven days. And [a]no leavened bread shall be seen among you, nor shall leaven be seen among you in all your quarters.

8 "And you shall [a]tell your son in that day, saying, '*This is done* because of what the LORD did for me when I came up from Egypt.'

9 "It shall be as [a]a *sign to you on your hand and as a memorial between your eyes, that the LORD's law may be in your mouth; for with a strong hand the LORD has brought you out of Egypt.

10 [a]"You shall therefore keep this [1]ordinance in its season from year to year.

The Law of the Firstborn

11 "And it shall be, when the LORD [a]brings you into the land of the [b]Canaanites, as He swore to you and your fathers, and gives it to you,

12 [a]"that you shall [1]set apart to the LORD all that open the womb, that is, every firstborn that comes from an animal which you have; the males *shall be* the LORD's.

13 "But [a]every firstborn of a donkey you shall *redeem with a lamb; and if you will not redeem *it,* then you shall break its neck. And all the firstborn of man among your sons [b]you shall redeem.

14 [a]"So it shall be, when your son asks you in time to come, saying, 'What *is* this?' that you shall say to him, [b]'By strength of hand the LORD brought us out of Egypt, out of the house of bondage.

15 'And it came to pass, when Pharaoh was stubborn about letting us go, that [a]the LORD killed all the firstborn in the land of Egypt, both the firstborn of man and the firstborn of beast. Therefore I sacrifice to the LORD all males that open the womb, but all the firstborn of my sons I redeem.'

16 "It shall be as [a]a sign on your hand and as frontlets between your eyes, for by strength of hand the LORD brought us out of Egypt."

The Wilderness Way

17 Then it came to pass, when Pharaoh had let the people go, that God did not lead them *by* way of the land of the Philistines, although that *was* near; for God said, "Lest perhaps the people [a]change their minds when they see war, and [b]return to Egypt."

18 So God [a]led the people around *by* way of the wilderness of the Red Sea. And the children of Israel went up in orderly ranks out of the land of Egypt.

19 And Moses took the [a]bones of [b]Joseph with him, for he had placed the children of Israel under solemn oath, saying, [c]"God will surely [1]visit you, and you shall carry up my bones from here with you."

CHAPTER 13

2 [a]Luke 2:23 [1]*Set apart*
3 [a]Deut. 16:3 [b]Ex. 3:20; 6:1 [c]Ex. 12:8, 19 [1]Lit. *slaves*
4 [a]Ex. 12:2; 23:15; 34:18
5 [a]Ex. 3:8, 17 [b]Gen. 17:8 [c]Ex. 6:8 [d]Ex. 12:25, 26
6 [a]Ex. 12:15–20
7 [a]Ex. 12:19
8 [a]Ex. 10:2; 12:26; 13:14
9 [a]Deut. 6:8; 11:18 *See WW at Ps. 86:17.
10 [a]Ex. 12:14, 24 [1]*regulation*
11 [a]Ex. 13:5 [b]Num. 21:3
12 [a]Lev. 27:26 [1]Lit. *cause to pass over*
13 [a]Ex. 34:20 [b]Num. 3:46, 47; 18:15, 16 *See WW at Neh. 1:10.
14 [a]Deut. 6:20 [b]Ex. 13:3, 9
15 [a]Ex. 12:29
16 [a]Ex. 13:9
17 [a]Ex. 14:11 [b]Deut. 17:16
18 [a]Num. 33:6
19 [a]Gen. 50:24, 25 [b]Ex. 1:6; Deut. 33:13–17 [c]Ex. 4:31 [1]*give attention to*

13:2 The **firstborn** sons belonged to God in a special way because He spared them in Egypt. They were to be as the firstfruit offering to God. See vv. 11–16.
13:3–10 A liturgical elaboration and reminder of the Feast of Unleavened Bread.
13:3 See section 3 of Truth-In-Action at the end of Ex.
13:6, 7 See section 3 of Truth-In-Action at the end of Ex.
13:9, 16 The later Jewish practice of wearing phylacteries while praying is based on these verses. Phylacteries are two small leather boxes attached by leather straps, one to the left hand and one to the forehead of an Israelite. They contain passages of the Law.
13:17 By way of ... Philistines likely refers to the road to Philistia. Although this was the most direct route to Canaan, it was heavily guarded by Egypt.
13:18 The Red Sea or "Sea of Reeds" is a narrow body of water that stretches about 1,300 miles from Suez to the Gulf of Aden. It has depths up to 9,500 feet. This would have been a southeasterly turn. **Orderly ranks** meant they were organized and in fighting formation. God's people were not disorganized and panic-stricken, fleeing for their lives.
13:19 The **bones of Joseph** were carried out of Egypt, fulfilling Gen. 50:25, 26.

20 So [a]they took their journey from
[b]Succoth and camped in Etham at the
edge of the wilderness.
21 And [a]the LORD went before them by
day in a pillar of cloud to lead the way,
and by night in a pillar of fire to give
them light, so as to go by day and
night.
22 He did not take away the pillar of
cloud by day or the pillar of fire by
night *from* before the people.

The Red Sea Crossing

14 Now the LORD spoke to Moses,
saying:
2 "Speak to the children of Israel,
[a]that they turn and camp before [b]Pi
Hahiroth, between [c]Migdol and the
sea, opposite Baal Zephon; you shall
camp before it by the sea.
3 "For Pharaoh will say of the children of Israel, [a]'They *are* bewildered
by the land; the wilderness has closed
them in.'
4 "Then [a]I will harden Pharaoh's
heart, so that he will pursue them; and
I [b]will gain honor over Pharaoh and
over all his army, [c]that the Egyptians
may know that I *am* the LORD." And
they did so.
5 Now it was told the king of Egypt
that the people had fled, and [a]the heart
of Pharaoh and his servants was
turned against the people; and they
said, "Why have we done this, that we
have let Israel go from serving us?"
6 So he [1]made ready his chariot and
took his people with him.
7 Also, he took [a]six hundred choice
chariots, and all the chariots of Egypt
with captains over every one of them.
8 And the LORD [a]hardened the heart
of Pharaoh king of Egypt, and he pursued the children of Israel; and [b]the
children of Israel went out with boldness.
9 So the [a]Egyptians pursued them, all
the horses *and* chariots of Pharaoh, his
horsemen and his army, and overtook
them camping by the sea beside Pi Hahiroth, before Baal Zephon.

20 [a]Num. 33:6–8 [b]Ex. 12:37
21 [a]Ex. 14:19, 24; 33:9, 10; Num. 9:15; 14:14; Deut. 1:33; Neh. 9:12; Ps. 78:14; 99:7; 105:39; [Is. 4:5]; 1 Cor. 10:1

CHAPTER 14

2 [a]Ex. 13:18 [b]Num. 33:7 [c]Jer. 44:1
3 [a]Ps. 71:11
4 [a]Ex. 4:21; 7:3; 14:17 [b]Ex. 9:16; 14:17, 18, 23; Rom. 9:17, 22, 23 [c]Ex. 7:5; 14:25
5 [a]Ps. 105:25
6 [1]*harnessed*
7 [a]Ex. 15:4
8 [a]Ex. 14:4 [b]Ex. 6:1; 13:9; Num. 33:3; Acts 13:17
9 [a]Ex. 15:9; Josh. 24:6

13:20 The Israelites are being led in an east-southeasterly direction by the most direct route free of armed resistance.
13:21 The **pillar of cloud** and the **pillar of fire** were manifestations of God's guiding presence.
14:1, 2 This divinely led turn, either due south or back toward Egypt, was to depict confusion (v. 3) so as to trick and defeat Pharaoh (v. 4).
14:7 Chariots were either two- or four-wheeled horse-drawn vehicles, used to carry a driver and one or more warriors. Equipped with bows, arrows, spears, and javelins, they were excessively heavy and became easily bogged down and immovable in muddy ground, trapping horses and men.

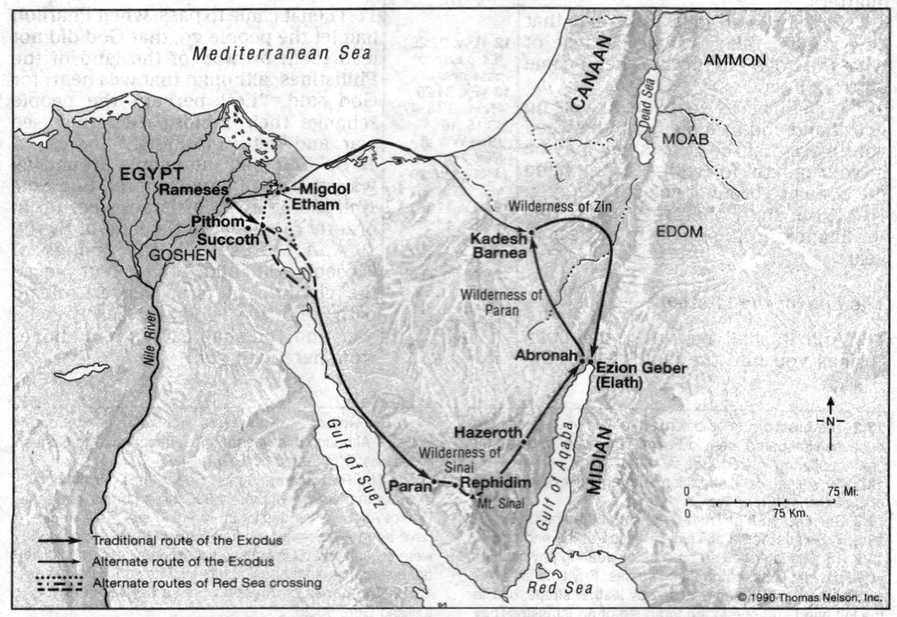

The Exodus from Egypt. Note that this map shows the site from which the waters of the Red Sea have receded.

10 And when Pharaoh drew near, the
children of Israel lifted their eyes, and
behold, the Egyptians marched after
them. So they were very afraid, and
the children of Israel [a]cried out to the
LORD.
11 [a]Then they said to Moses, "Because
there were no graves in Egypt, have
you taken us away to die in the wilderness? Why have you so dealt with us,
to bring us up out of Egypt?
12 [a]"*Is* this not the word that we told
you in Egypt, saying, 'Let us alone that
we may serve the Egyptians'? For *it
would have been* better for us to serve
the Egyptians than that we should die
in the wilderness."
3 13 And Moses said to the people,
[a]"Do not be afraid. [b]Stand still, and see
the [c]salvation[1] of the LORD, which He
will accomplish for you today. For the
Egyptians whom you see today, you
shall [d]see again no more forever.
14 [a]"The LORD will fight for you, and
you shall [b]hold[1] your peace."
15 And the LORD said to Moses, "Why
do you cry to Me? Tell the children of
Israel to go forward.
16 "But [a]lift up your rod, and stretch
out your hand over the sea and divide
it. And the children of Israel shall go
on dry *ground* through the midst of the
sea.
17 "And I indeed will [a]harden the
hearts of the Egyptians, and they shall
follow them. So I will [b]gain honor over
Pharaoh and over all his army, his
chariots, and his horsemen.
18 "Then the Egyptians shall know
that I *am* the LORD, when I have gained
honor for Myself over Pharaoh, his
chariots, and his horsemen."
19 And the Angel of God, [a]who went
before the camp of Israel, moved and
went behind them; and the pillar of
cloud went from before them and stood
behind them.
20 So it came between the camp of the
Egyptians and the camp of Israel. Thus
it was a cloud and darkness *to the one,*
and it gave light by night *to the other,*
so that the one did not come near the
other all that night.
21 Then Moses stretched out his hand

10 [a]Neh. 9:9
11 [a]Ps. 106:7, 8
12 [a]Ex. 5:21; 6:9
13 [a]2 Chr. 20:15, 17 [b]Ps. 46:10, 11 [c]Ex. 14:30; 15:2 [d]Deut. 28:68 [1]*deliverance*
14 [a]Deut. 1:30; 3:22 [b][Is. 30:15] [1]Lit. *be quiet*
16 [a]Num. 20:8, 9, 11
17 [a]Ex. 14:8 [b]Ex. 14:4
19 [a][Is. 63:9]
21 [a]Ps. 66:6; 106:9; 136:13, 14 [b]Is. 63:12, 13 *See WW at Is. 43:2.
22 [a]Ex. 15:19 [b]Ex. 14:29; 15:8
24 [a]Judg. 7:19 [b]Ex. 13:21 [1]*confused*
25 [a]Ex. 7:5; 14:4, 14, 18 [1]Sam., LXX, Syr. *bound*
27 [a]Josh. 4:18 [b]Ex. 15:1, 7 [1]Lit. *shook off*
28 [a]Ps. 78:53; 106:11
29 [a]Ps. 66:6; 78:52, 53
30 [a]Ps. 106:8, 10 [b]Ps. 58:10; 59:10 [1]*delivered*
31 [a]John 2:11; 11:45 [1]Lit. *hand with which the LORD worked* *See WW at 2 Chr. 20:20.

over the sea; and the LORD caused the
sea to go *back* by a strong east wind
all that night, and [a]made the sea into
dry *land,* and the *waters were [b]di-
vided.
22 So [a]the children of Israel went into
the midst of the sea on the dry *ground,*
and the waters *were* [b]a wall to them
on their right hand and on their left.
23 And the Egyptians pursued and
went after them into the midst of the
sea, all Pharaoh's horses, his chariots,
and his horsemen.
24 Now it came to pass, in the morning
[a]watch, that [b]the LORD looked down
upon the army of the Egyptians
through the pillar of fire and cloud, and
He [1]troubled the army of the Egyptians.
25 And He [1]took off their chariot
wheels, so that they drove them with
difficulty; and the Egyptians said, "Let
us flee from the face of Israel, for the
LORD [a]fights for them against the Egyptians."
26 Then the LORD said to Moses,
"Stretch out your hand over the sea,
that the waters may come back upon
the Egyptians, on their chariots, and
on their horsemen."
27 And Moses stretched out his hand
over the sea; and when the morning
appeared, the sea [a]returned to its full
depth, while the Egyptians were fleeing into it. So the LORD [b]overthrew[1] the
Egyptians in the midst of the sea.
28 Then [a]the waters returned and covered the chariots, the horsemen, *and*
all the army of Pharaoh that came into
the sea after them. Not so much as one
of them remained.
29 But [a]the children of Israel had
walked on dry *land* in the midst of the
sea, and the waters *were* a wall to them
on their right hand and on their left.
30 So the LORD [a]saved[1] Israel that day
out of the hand of the Egyptians, and
Israel [b]saw the Egyptians dead on the
seashore.
31 Thus Israel saw the great [1]work
which the LORD had done in Egypt; so
the people feared the LORD, and
[a]believed* the LORD and His servant
Moses.

14:10–18 Water was in front of them, and Pharaoh and his army behind them. They were trapped and had one of three options: surrender, fight, or trust God. The actual crossing probably took place somewhere between Qantir and just north of Suez, near the papyrus marshes.
14:13, 14 See section 3 of Truth-In-Action at the end of Ex.
14:19 Angel of God: The Angel, the cloud, and the fire were visible means of direction, protection, and assurance.
14:21 The Egyptians had to learn that God was no desert god, but was the controller of all human destiny and the God of all the elements.
14:24 "Watch" meant one of two things: 1) posting a guard, or 2) a unit of time that divided the night, such as the evening watch, midnight watch, cockcrow watch, and **morning watch.**
14:31 The proper response to the power of God is fear (awe), trust, and obedience, a lesson the Israelites would have to learn over and over again.

The Song of Moses

15 Then [a]Moses and the children of Israel sang this song to the LORD, and spoke, saying:

"I will [b]sing to the LORD,
For He has triumphed gloriously!
The horse and its rider
He has thrown into the sea!
2 The LORD *is* my strength and
[a]song,
And He has become my salvation;
He *is* my God, and [b]I will praise
Him;
My [c]father's God, and I [d]will exalt
Him.
3 The LORD *is* a man of [a]war;
The LORD *is* His [b]name.
4 [a]Pharaoh's chariots and his army
He has cast into the sea;
[b]His chosen captains also are
drowned in the Red Sea.
5 The depths have covered them;
[a]They sank to the bottom like a
stone.

6 "Your [a]right hand, O LORD, has
become glorious in power;
Your right hand, O LORD, has
dashed the enemy in pieces.
7 And in the greatness of Your
[a]excellence
You have overthrown those who
rose against You;
You sent forth [b]Your wrath;
It [c]consumed them [d]like stubble.
8 And [a]with the blast of Your
nostrils
The waters were gathered
together;
[b]The floods stood upright like a
heap;
The depths [1]congealed in the
heart of the sea.
9 [a]The enemy said, 'I will pursue,
I will overtake,
I will [b]divide the spoil;
My desire shall be satisfied on
them.
I will draw my sword,
My hand shall destroy them.'
10 You blew with Your wind,
The sea covered them;
They sank like lead in the mighty
waters.

CHAPTER 15

1 [a]Ps. 106:12 [b]Is. 12:1–6
2 [a]Is. 12:2 [b]Gen. 28:21, 22 [c]Ex. 3:6, 15, 16 [d]Is. 25:1
3 [a]Rev. 19:11 [b]Ps. 24:8; 83:18
4 [a]Ex. 14:28 [b]Ex. 14:7
5 [a]Neh. 9:11
6 [a]Ps. 17:7; 118:15
7 [a]Deut. 33:26 [b]Ps. 78:49, 50 [c]Ps. 59:13 [d]Is. 5:24
8 [a]Ex. 14:21, 22, 29 [b]Ps. 78:13 [1]*became firm*
9 [a]Judg. 5:30 [b]Is. 53:12
11 [a]1 Kin. 8:23 [b]Is. 6:3 [c]1 Chr. 16:25 [d]Ps. 77:11, 14 [1]*mighty ones*
13 [a][Ps. 77:20] [b]Ps. 78:54 *See WW at Mic. 6:8. • See WW at Is. 52:9.
14 [a]Josh. 2:9 [b]Ps. 48:6 [1]*Anguish*
15 [a]Gen. 36:15, 40 [b]Deut. 2:4 [c]Num. 22:3, 4 [d]Josh. 5:1 [e]Josh. 2:9–11, 24
16 [a]Josh. 2:9 [b]1 Sam. 25:37 [c]Jer. 31:11
17 [a]Ps. 44:2; 80:8, 15 [b]Ps. 2:6; 78:54, 68 [c]Ps. 68:16; 76:2; 132:13, 14
18 [a]Is. 57:15
19 [a]Ex. 14:23 [b]Ex. 14:28

11 "Who[a] *is* like You, O LORD, among
the [1]gods?
Who *is* like You, [b]glorious in
holiness,
Fearful in [c]praises, [d]doing
wonders?
12 You stretched out Your right
hand;
The earth swallowed them.
13 You in Your *mercy have
[a]led forth
The people whom You have
*redeemed;
You have guided *them* in Your
strength
To [b]Your holy habitation.

14 "The [a]people will hear *and* be
afraid;
[b]Sorrow[1] will take hold of the
inhabitants of Philistia.
15 [a]Then [b]the chiefs of Edom will be
dismayed;
[c]The mighty men of Moab,
Trembling will take hold of
them;
[d]All the inhabitants of Canaan will
[e]melt away.
16 [a]Fear and dread will fall on
them;
By the greatness of Your arm
They will be [b]*as* still as a stone,
Till Your people pass over, O
LORD,
Till the people pass over
[c]Whom You have purchased.
17 You will bring them in and
[a]plant them
In the [b]mountain of Your
inheritance,
In the place, O LORD, *which* You
have made
For Your own dwelling,
The [c]sanctuary, O LORD, *which*
Your hands have established.

18 "The[a] LORD shall reign forever and
ever."

19 For the [a]horses of Pharaoh went
with his chariots and his horsemen into
the sea, and [b]the LORD brought back
the waters of the sea upon them. But
the children of Israel went on dry *land*
in the midst of the sea.

15:1–18 *The Song of Moses is directed* completely to the praise of God for His saving presence, rescue, protection, and establishment of His people.
15:1 Rider refers to chariot driver.
15:3 Man of war was a warrior. It was the acknowledgment that God fought the battle.
15:5 That the Egyptians **sank . . . like a stone** probably reflected the fact that they were heavily armored (v. 10).
15:7 Wrath literally means "burning." God's action overtook them in the same fashion that a fire overtakes stubble.
15:10 Lead probably refers to their armament (v. 5).
15:17 A sanctuary is a holy place set apart for worshiping God and performing religious ceremonies.

The Song of Miriam

20 Then Miriam [a]the prophetess,
[b]the sister of Aaron, [c]took the timbrel
in her hand; and all the women went
out after her [d]with timbrels and with
dances.
21 And Miriam [a]answered them:

[b]"Sing* to the LORD,
For He has triumphed gloriously!
The horse and its rider
He has thrown into the sea!"

Bitter Waters Made Sweet

22 So Moses brought Israel from the
Red Sea; then they went out into the
Wilderness of [a]Shur. And they went
three days in the wilderness and found
no [b]water.
23 Now when they came to [a]Marah,
they could not drink the waters of Marah, for they *were* bitter. Therefore the
name of it was called [1]Marah.
24 And the people [a]complained
against Moses, saying, "What shall we
drink?"
1 25 So he cried out to the LORD, and the
LORD showed him a tree. [a]When he
cast *it* into the waters, the waters were
made sweet. There He [b]made a statute
and an [1]ordinance for them, and there
[c]He tested them,
26 and said, [a]"If you diligently heed
the voice of the LORD your God and do
what is right in His sight, give ear to
His *commandments and keep all His
statutes, I will put none of the [b]diseases
on you which I have brought on the
Egyptians. For I *am* the LORD [c]who
heals you."

WORD WEALTH

15:26 heals, *rapha'* (rah-*phah*); Strong's #7495: To cure, heal, repair, mend, restore health. Its participial form *rophe'*, "one who heals," is the Hebrew word for doctor. The main idea of the verb *rapha'* is physical healing. Some have tried to explain away the biblical teaching of divine healing, but all can see that this verse speaks of physical diseases and their divine cure. The first mention of *rapha'* in the Bible (Gen. 20:17) refers unquestionably to the cure of a physical condition, as do references to healing from leprosy and boils (Lev. 13:18; 14:3).

20 [a]Judg. 4:4 [b]Ex. 2:4; Num. 26:59; 1 Chr. 6:3; Mic. 6:4 [c]1 Sam. 18:6; 1 Chr. 15:16; Ps. 68:25; 81:2; 149:3; Jer. 31:4 [d]Judg. 11:34; 21:21; 2 Sam. 6:16; Ps. 30:11; 150:4
21 [a]1 Sam. 18:7 [b]Ex. 15:1 *See WW at Judg. 5:3.
22 [a]Gen. 16:7; 20:1; 25:18; Num. 33:8 [b]Ex. 17:1; Num. 20:2
23 [a]Num. 33:8; Ruth 1:20 [1]Lit. *Bitter*
24 [a]Ex. 14:11; 16:2; Ps. 106:13
25 [a]2 Kin. 2:21 [b]Josh. 24:25 [c]Ex. 16:4; Deut. 8:2, 16; Judg. 2:22; 3:1, 4; Ps. 66:10 [1]*regulation*
26 [a]Ex. 19:5, 6; Deut. 7:12, 15 [b]Deut. 28:27, 58, 60 [c]Ex. 23:25; Deut. 32:39; Ps. 41:3, 4; 103:3; 147:3 *See WW at Ps. 119:35.

Scripture affirms, "I am Yahweh your Physician."

KINGDOM DYNAMICS

15:26 God Is a Good God. He Desires Only His Best for You!, SEED FAITH. In promising His continuing, healing presence as our Covenant Healer, God places two great conditions before His people.

First, God asks us to heed Him. He wants us to listen for His voice, to have a hearing ear so we will hear Him. God has always spoken to His people and He will speak to you today, but you must cultivate an attitude of listening for His voice. He speaks in many ways: through His Word, through His anointed servants, and through direct revelation in your inner man (Eph. 1:17, 18). He is seeking a people who will listen for His voice and not try to run and hide from Him (see Gen. 3:8).

Second, God asks us to "do what is right in His sight." He is seeking people who will not only hear His words, but will take them to heart and act on them—people who will obey His word and not be hearers only (see James 1:22–25).

God's goodness is abundantly promised. It awaits those who "[sow] to the Spirit" (Gal. 6:7–9), hearing His voice and doing what He tells us to do.

(2 Sam. 24:24/1 Kin. 17:8–16) O.R.

KINGDOM DYNAMICS

15:26 The Old Testament Healing Covenant, DIVINE HEALING. This verse is widely referred to as the OT Divine Healing Covenant. It is called a "covenant," because in it God promises He will keep His people free from diseases, and conditions the promise upon their diligent obedience.

The words used here for "diseases" (Hebrew *makhaleh*) and "heals" (Hebrew *rapha*) are regularly used for physical sickness and bodily healing. This is not only a spiritual concept, but also an intensely physical one. The covenant is made absolutely certain by the fact that God joins His mighty name to the promise, calling Himself *Yahweh-Rapha*, meaning "the LORD who heals." *Yahweh-Rapha* is one of the compound names by which God revealed His attributes to Israel. Here His very name declares it is His nature to be the Healer to those who obey His word—to recover to health and to sustain in health.

(*cont. on next page*)

15:20 A timbrel was a tambourinelike percussion instrument used primarily by women.
15:23 Marah means "Bitter." Wells and pools in this region of the world were often brackish.
15:25, 26 See section 1 of Truth-In-Action at the end of Ex.
15:26 The LORD who heals you in Hebrew is *Yahweh-Ropheka.* This is one of the blessings enjoyed when one is in obedient, covenant relationship with God.

(cont. from preceding page)
While sin and disobedience are not always the direct causes of sickness, man's fall into sin is the original and underlying cause of all disease. Those who seek healing will benefit by looking to Christ Jesus our sin-bearer, along with pursuing renewed consecration. (See James 5:14–16; 1 Cor. 11:29–32.)
(*/Num. 12:1–16) N.V.

27 [a]Then they came to Elim, where
there *were* twelve wells of water and
seventy palm trees; so they camped
there by the waters.

Bread from Heaven

16 And they [a]journeyed from Elim,
and all the congregation of the
children of Israel came to the Wilderness of Sin, which is between Elim and
[b]Sinai, on the fifteenth day of the second month after they departed from
the land of Egypt.
2 Then the whole congregation of the
children of Israel [a]complained against
Moses and Aaron in the wilderness.
3 And the children of Israel said to
them, [a]"Oh, that we had died by the
hand of the LORD in the land of Egypt,
[b]when we sat by the pots of *meat *and*
when we ate bread to the full! For you
have brought us out into this wilderness to kill this whole assembly with
hunger."
3 4 Then the LORD said to Moses, "Behold, I will rain [a]bread from heaven
for you. And the people shall go out
and gather [1]a certain quota every day,
that I may [b]test* them, whether they
will [c]walk in My law or not.
5 "And it shall be on the sixth day
that they shall prepare what they bring
in, and [a]it shall be twice as much as
they gather daily."
6 Then Moses and Aaron said to all
the children of Israel, [a]"At evening you
shall know that the LORD has brought
you out of the land of Egypt.
7 "And in the morning you shall see
[a]the glory of the LORD; for He [b]hears

27 [a]Num. 33:9

CHAPTER 16

1 [a]Num. 33:10, 11 [b]Ex. 12:6, 51; 19:1
2 [a]1 Cor. 10:10
3 [a]Lam. 4:9 [b]Num. 11:4, 5 *See WW at Job 19:26.
4 [a][John 6:31–35] [b]Deut. 8:2, 16 [c]Judg. 2:22 [1]Lit. *the portion of a day in its day* *See WW at Ps. 78:41.
5 [a]Lev. 25:21
6 [a]Ex. 6:7
7 [a]John 11:4, 40 [b]Num. 14:27; 17:5 [c]Num. 16:11
8 [a]1 Sam. 8:7
9 [a]Num. 16:16
10 [a]Num. 16:19 *See WW at Is. 60:1.
12 [a]Ex. 16:8 [b]Ex. 16:6 [c]Ex. 16:7 *See WW at Amos 4:8.
13 [a]Num. 11:31 [b]Num. 11:9
14 [a]Num. 11:7, 8 [b]Ps. 147:16
15 [a]1 Cor. 10:3
16 [a]Ex. 12:4 [b]Ex. 16:32, 36

your complaints against the LORD. But
[c]what *are* we, that you complain
against us?"
8 Also Moses said, "*This shall be seen* 5
when the LORD gives you meat to eat
in the evening, and in the morning
bread to the full; for the LORD hears
your complaints which you make
against Him. And what *are* we? Your
complaints *are* not against us but
[a]against the LORD."
9 Then Moses spoke to Aaron, "Say
to all the congregation of the children
of Israel, [a]'Come near before the LORD,
for He has heard your complaints.' "
10 Now it came to pass, as Aaron
spoke to the whole congregation of the
children of Israel, that they looked toward the wilderness, and behold, the
*glory of the LORD [a]appeared in the
cloud.
11 And the LORD spoke to Moses, saying,
12 [a]"I have heard the complaints of the
children of Israel. Speak to them, saying, [b]'At twilight you shall eat meat,
and [c]in the morning you shall be *filled
with bread. And you shall know that I
am the LORD your God.' "
13 So it was that [a]quails came up at
evening and covered the camp, and in
the morning [b]the dew lay all around
the camp.
14 And when the layer of dew lifted,
there, on the surface of the wilderness,
was [a]a small round [b]substance, *as* fine
as frost on the ground.
15 So when the children of Israel saw
it, they said to one another, "What is
it?" For they did not know what it *was.*
And Moses said to them, [a]"This *is* the
bread which the LORD has given you
to eat.
16 "This is the thing which the LORD
has commanded: 'Let every man
gather it [a]according to each one's need,
one [b]omer for each person, *according
to the* number of persons; let every
man take for *those* who *are* in his
tent.' "
17 Then the children of Israel did so
and gathered, some more, some less.

16:1 This is a month and a half after leaving Egypt.
16:3 Although slaves while in Egypt, they had been well cared for. Now that they are in the **wilderness,** they forget God's goodness and their suffering and begin to complain *about the lack of foodstuffs.*
16:4 See section 3 of Truth-In-Action at the end of Ex.
16:4 God tests the people to see if they will do what they are told. One way He does this is by placing a restriction on the amount of heaven-sent food that they may gather.
16:8 See section 5 of Truth-In-Action at the end of Ex.
16:13–18 The food supply comes morning by morning in God's time, according to God's plan. The supply cannot be stored up for future use, except for the Sabbath. It is to be used only as God has specified (v. 20), a miraculous demonstration of His provision to meet the needs of His people. Each family has all that is needed. They are allowed to have an omer of the **bread** (v. 15) per day—a bowl holding about 4 pints (v. 16). This substance is Israel's staple food for 40 years (v. 35). The petition in the Lord's Prayer, "Give us day by day our daily bread" (Luke 11:3), in all likelihood, looks back to the bread provided by God for the Israelites as their daily sustenance.

18 So when they measured *it* by omers, [a]he who gathered much had nothing left over, and he who gathered little had no lack. Every man had gathered according to each one's need.

19 And Moses said, "Let no one [a]leave any of it till morning."

20 Notwithstanding they did not [1]heed Moses. But some of them left part of it until morning, and it bred worms and stank. And Moses was angry with them.

21 So they gathered it every morning, every man according to his need. And when the sun became hot, it melted.

22 And so it was, on the sixth day, *that* they gathered twice as much bread, two omers for each one. And all the rulers of the congregation came and told Moses.

23 Then he said to them, "This *is what* the LORD has said: 'Tomorrow *is* [a]a Sabbath rest, a holy Sabbath to the LORD. Bake what you will bake *today,* and boil what you will boil; and lay up for yourselves all that remains, to be kept until morning.' "

24 So they laid it up till morning, as Moses commanded; and it did not [a]stink, nor were there any worms in it.

25 Then Moses said, "Eat that today, for today *is* a Sabbath to the LORD; today you will not find it in the field.

26 [a]"Six days you shall gather it, but on the seventh day, the Sabbath, there will be none."

27 Now it happened *that some* of the people went out on the seventh day to gather, but they found none.

28 And the LORD said to Moses, "How long [a]do you refuse to keep My commandments and My laws?

29 "See! For the LORD has given you the Sabbath; therefore He gives you on the sixth day bread for two days. Let every man remain in his place; let no man go out of his place on the seventh day."

30 So the people **rested** on the seventh day.

18 [a]2 Cor. 8:15
19 [a]Ex. 12:10; 16:23; 23:18
20 [1]*listen to*
23 [a]Gen. 2:3; Ex. 20:8–11; 23:12; 31:15; 35:2; Lev. 23:3; Neh. 9:13, 14
24 [a]Ex. 16:20
26 [a]Ex. 20:9, 10
28 [a]2 Kin. 17:14; Ps. 78:10; 106:13

WORD WEALTH

16:30 rested, *shabat* (shah-*vat*); Strong's #7673: To stop, to rest, to cease, to end. This verb is of great importance in the OT, mainly because of the noun that is formed from it: shab-*bat,* or as we say, "Sabbath." The *shabbat* is the day when all work ceases, and Israel rests and meditates on the glories of God's creation (heaven and Earth), just as God rested on that first Sabbath (Gen. 2:1–3).

31 And the house of Israel called its name [1]Manna. And [a]it *was* like white coriander seed, and the taste of it *was* like wafers *made* with honey.

32 Then Moses said, "This *is* the thing which the LORD has commanded: 'Fill an omer with it, to be kept for your generations, that they may see the bread with which I fed you in the wilderness, when I brought you out of the land of Egypt.' "

33 And Moses said to Aaron, [a]"Take a pot and put an omer of manna in it, and lay it up before the LORD, to be kept for your generations."

34 As the LORD commanded Moses, so Aaron laid it up [a]before the Testimony, to be kept.

35 And the children of Israel [a]ate manna [b]forty years, [c]until they came to an inhabited land; they ate manna until they came to the border of the land of Canaan.

36 Now an omer *is* one-tenth of an ephah.

Water from the Rock

17 Then [a]all the congregation of the children of Israel set out on their journey from the Wilderness of [b]Sin, according to the commandment of the LORD, and camped in Rephidim; but *there was* no water for the people to [c]drink.

2 [a]Therefore the people contended with Moses, and said, "Give us water, that we may drink." So Moses said to

31 [a]Num. 11:7–9; Deut. 8:3, 16 [1]Lit. *What?* Ex. 16:15
33 [a]Heb. 9:4; Rev. 2:17
34 [a]Ex. 25:16, 21; 27:21; 40:20; Num. 17:10
35 [a]Deut. 8:3, 16 [b]Num. 33:38; John 6:31, 49 [c]Josh. 5:12; Neh. 9:20, 21

CHAPTER 17

1 [a]Ex. 16:1 [b]Num. 33:11–15 [c]Ex. 15:22; Num. 20:2
2 [a]Ex. 14:11; Num. 20:2, 3, 13

16:22, 23 Moses explains the sanctity and observance of the **Sabbath** and all that it entails. God gave a double portion of the food to provide for the Sabbath observance. Thus the people did not need to toil and gather it on the Sabbath.

16:31 Manna, the Hebrew name given by the Israelites, meant "what is it?" (see v. 15). **Coriander** is an herb that grows to be 2 to 3 feet tall. The plant produces seeds, which are used for flavoring food to this day.

16:32 A sample of **the bread** was commanded to be kept to show future generations the provision of God in the wilderness. This sample was more than a keepsake; it was a sign of the covenant.

16:35 Manna nurtured the people and gave life for 40 **years.** As such, it was a type of Christ. A direct correlation can be seen every time the Eucharist is observed and the one officiating repeats Christ's words, "Take, eat; this is My body which is broken for you" (1 Cor. 11:24).

17:1 These places, like most mentioned on the journey, are unknown today.

them, "Why do you contend with me?
Why do you [b]tempt the LORD?"
3 And the people thirsted there for
water, and the people [a]complained
against Moses, and said, "Why *is* it you
have brought us up out of Egypt, to kill
us and our children and our [b]livestock
with thirst?"
4 So Moses [a]cried out to the LORD,
saying, "What shall I do with this people? They are almost ready to [b]stone[1]
me!"
5 And the LORD said to Moses,
[a]"Go on before the people, and take
with you some of the elders of Israel.
Also take in your hand your rod with
which [b]you struck the river, and go.
6 [a]"Behold, I will stand before you
there on the rock in Horeb; and you
shall strike the rock, and water will
come out of it, that the people may
drink." And Moses did so in the sight
of the elders of Israel.
7 So he called the name of the place
[a]Massah[1] and [2]Meribah, because of the
contention of the children of Israel, and
because they [3]tempted the LORD, saying, "Is the LORD among us or not?"

Victory over the Amalekites

8 [a]Now Amalek came and fought
with Israel in Rephidim.
9 And Moses said to Joshua, "Choose
us some men and go out, fight with
Amalek. Tomorrow I will stand on the
top of the hill with [a]the rod of God in
my hand."
10 So Joshua did as Moses said to him,
and fought with Amalek. And Moses,
Aaron, and Hur went up to the top of
the hill.
11 And so it was, when Moses [a]held
up his hand, that Israel prevailed; and
when he let down his hand, Amalek
prevailed.
12 But Moses' hands *became* [1]heavy;
so they took a stone and put *it* under
him, and he sat on it. And Aaron and
Hur supported his hands, one on one
side, and the other on the other side;

2 [b][Deut. 6:16]
3 [a]Ex. 16:2, 3 [b]Ex. 12:38
4 [a]Ex. 14:15 [b]John 8:59; 10:31 [1]Put me to death by stoning
5 [a]Ezek. 2:6 [b]Num. 20:8
6 [a]Num. 20:10, 11
7 [a]Num. 20:13, 24; 27:14 [1]Lit. *Tempted* [2]Lit. *Contention* [3]*tested*
8 [a]Gen. 36:12
9 [a]Ex. 4:20
11 [a][James 5:16]
12 [1]Weary of being held up
14 [a]Ex. 24:4; 34:27 [b]1 Sam. 15:3
15 [1]Heb. *YHWH Nissi* *See WW at 2 Kin. 12:9.
16 [a]Gen. 22:14–16 [1]Lit. *a hand is upon the throne of the LORD*

CHAPTER 18

1 [a]Ex. 2:16, 18; 3:1 [b][Ps. 106:2, 8]
2 [a]Ex. 2:21; 4:20–26
3 [a]Acts 7:29 [b]Ex. 2:22 [1]Lit. *Stranger There* [2]*sojourner*, temporary resident
4 [a]Gen. 49:25 [1]Lit. *My God Is Help*
5 [a]Ex. 3:1, 12; 4:27; 24:13
7 [a]Gen. 18:2 [b]Ex. 4:27

and his hands were steady until the going down of the sun.
13 So Joshua defeated Amalek and his
people with the edge of the sword.
14 Then the LORD said to Moses,
[a]"Write this *for* a memorial in the book
and recount *it* in the hearing of Joshua,
that [b]I will utterly blot out the remembrance of Amalek from under heaven."
15 And Moses built an *altar and 1
called its name, [1]The-LORD-Is-My-
Banner;
16 for he said, "Because [1]the LORD has
[a]sworn: the LORD *will have* war with
Amalek from generation to generation."

Jethro's Advice

18 And [a]Jethro, the priest of Midian, Moses' father-in-law,
heard of all that [b]God had done for
Moses and for Israel His people—that
the LORD had brought Israel out of
Egypt.
2 Then Jethro, Moses' father-in-law,
took [a]Zipporah, Moses' wife, after he
had sent her back,
3 with her [a]two sons, of whom the
name of one *was* [1]Gershom (for he
said, [b]"I have been a [2]stranger in a foreign land")
4 and the name of the other *was*
[1]Eliezer (for *he said*, "The God of my
father *was* my [a]help, and delivered me
from the sword of Pharaoh");
5 and Jethro, Moses' father-in-law,
came with his sons and his wife to Moses in the wilderness, where he was encamped at [a]the mountain of God.
6 Now he had said to Moses, "I, your
father-in-law Jethro, am coming to you
with your wife and her two sons with
her."
7 So Moses [a]went out to meet his
father-in-law, bowed down, and [b]kissed
him. And they asked each other about
their well-being, and they went into the
tent.
8 And Moses told his father-in-law all
that the LORD had done to Pharaoh and

17:3 The people complained continually. Their suffering in Egypt had been of a different nature. Now they complain about the lack of **water.** Their despair is evident in the fact that they are ready to stone Moses. They had stopped trusting God and were looking to Moses the man as their source and provider.

17:8 The Amalekites were a wandering tribe located in the arid area between Canaan and Egypt.

17:9 Joshua appears for the first time as the leader of a volunteer army.

17:10 Hur is mentioned here and in 24:14 as an assistant to Moses.

17:15 See section 1 of Truth-In-Action at the end of Ex.

17:15 The-LORD-Is-My-Banner (Hebrew *YAHWEH NISSI*): A banner is the polelike standard beneath which armies or communities rallied. When lifted up, it called the people together for battle, for meeting, or for instruction. This phrase also could have been a battle cry. Erecting an **altar** was Moses' recognition of the presence of God. At this altar, he was honoring God as the giver of victory over the Amalekites.

18:2–7 Moses probably had sent his wife and sons back to Jethro for protection at some time during the Egyptian plagues.

18:8 Moses bears testimony to the fact that all that was

to the Egyptians for Israel's sake, all
the hardship that had come upon them
on the way, and *how* the LORD had
[a]delivered them.
9 Then Jethro rejoiced for all the
[a]good which the LORD had done for Israel, whom He had delivered out of the
hand of the Egyptians.
10 And Jethro said, [a]"Blessed *be* the
LORD, who has delivered you out of the
hand of the Egyptians and out of
the hand of Pharaoh, *and* who has delivered the people from under the hand
of the Egyptians.
11 "Now I know that the LORD *is*
[a]greater than all the gods; [b]for in the
very thing in which they [1]behaved
[c]proudly, *He was* above them."
12 Then Jethro, Moses' father-in-law,
[1]took a burnt [a]offering and *other* sacrifices *to offer* to God. And Aaron came
with all the elders of Israel [b]to eat
bread with Moses' father-in-law before
God.
13 And so it was, on the next day, that
Moses [a]sat to judge the people; and the
people stood before Moses from morning until evening.
14 So when Moses' father-in-law saw
all that he did for the people, he said,
"What *is* this thing that you are doing
for the people? Why do you alone
[1]sit, and all the people stand before you
from morning until evening?"
15 And Moses said to his father-in-law,
"Because [a]the people come to me to
inquire of God.
16 "When they have [a]a [1]difficulty, they
come to me, and I judge between one
and another; and I make known the
statutes of God and His laws."
17 So Moses' father-in-law said to him,
"The thing that you do *is* not good.
18 "Both you and these people who *are*
with you will surely wear yourselves
out. For this thing *is* too much for you;
[a]you are not able to perform it by yourself.
19 "Listen now to my voice; I will give
you [1]counsel, and God will be with
you: Stand [a]before God for the people,
so that you may [b]bring the difficulties
to God.
20 "And you shall [a]teach them the statutes and the laws, and show them the
way in which they must walk and
[b]the work they must do.
21 "Moreover you shall select from all
the people [a]able men, such as [b]fear
God, [c]men of truth, [d]hating covetousness; and place *such* over them *to be*
rulers of thousands, rulers of hundreds, rulers of fifties, and rulers of
tens.
22 "And let them judge the people at
all times. [a]Then it will be *that* every
great matter they shall bring to you,
but every small matter they themselves
shall judge. So it will be easier for you,
for [b]they will bear *the burden* with
you.
23 "If you do this thing, and God so
commands you, then you will be able
to endure, and all this people will also
go to their [a]place in peace."
24 So Moses heeded the voice of his
father-in-law and did all that he had
said.
25 And [a]Moses chose able men out of
all Israel, and made them heads over
the people: rulers of thousands, rulers
of hundreds, rulers of fifties, and rulers
of tens.
26 So they judged the people at all
times; the [a]hard[1] cases they brought
to Moses, but they judged every small
case themselves.
27 Then Moses let his father-in-law depart, and [a]he went his way to his own
land.

Israel at Mount Sinai

19 In the third month after the children of Israel had gone out of
the land of Egypt, on the same day,
[a]they came *to* the Wilderness of Sinai.
2 For they had departed from [a]Rephi-
dim, had come *to* the Wilderness of Sinai, and camped in the wilderness. So
Israel camped there before [b]the mountain.

8 [a]Ex. 15:6, 16; Ps. 81:7
9 [a][Is. 63:7–14]
10 [a]Gen. 14:20; 2 Sam. 18:28; 1 Kin. 8:56; Ps. 68:19, 20
11 [a]Ex. 12:12; 15:11; 2 Chr. 2:5; Ps. 95:3; 97:9; 135:5 [b]Ex. 1:10, 16, 22; 5:2, 7 [c]Luke 1:51 [1]*acted presumptuously*
12 [a]Ex. 24:5 [b]Gen. 31:54; Deut. 12:7 [1]So with MT, LXX; Syr., Tg., Vg. *offered*
13 [a]Deut. 33:4, 5; Matt. 23:2
14 [1]*Sit as judge*
15 [a]Lev. 24:12; Num. 9:6, 8; 27:5; Deut. 17:8–13
16 [a]Ex. 24:14; Deut. 19:17 [1]*dispute*
18 [a]Num. 11:14, 17; Deut. 1:12
19 [a]Ex. 4:16; 20:19 [b]Num. 9:8; 27:5 [1]*advice*
20 [a]Deut. 5:1 [b]Deut. 1:18
21 [a]Ex. 18:24, 25; Deut. 1:13, 15; 2 Chr. 19:5–10; Ps. 15:1–5; Acts 6:3 [b]Gen. 42:18; 2 Sam. 23:3 [c]Ezek. 18:8 [d]Deut. 16:19
22 [a]Lev. 24:11; Deut. 1:17 [b]Num. 11:17
23 [a]Ex. 16:29
25 [a]Ex. 18:21; Deut. 1:15
26 [a]Job 29:16 [1]*difficult matters*
27 [a]Num. 10:29, 30

CHAPTER 19

1 [a]Num. 33:15
2 [a]Ex. 17:1 [b]Ex. 3:1, 12; 18:5

---

done by God took place **for Israel's sake.** Prior to Moses' account, Jethro had only heard of his son-in-law's exploits through scattered reports (18:1).

18:9–11 Jethro blesses God for His acts of deliverance and confessed he now knew that the almighty God of Moses was the true God.

18:12 Burnt offering: See note on Lev. 1:3. **Elders of Israel,** representatives of all the people, shows tribal organization.

18:15 In looking to Moses for wisdom from God, the people now accept his counsel as the Lord's counsel.

18:16–19 Three detrimental effects resulted from Moses' acting as judge over everything, everyone, and all situations commonplace, religious, and legal: he was overworked, the people did not receive justice quickly, and the elders were deprived of the opportunity to use their talents.

18:20 As God's representative, Moses is to teach and enlighten the people in four areas: the **statutes** of God, His **laws** and regulations pertaining to the statutes, the way the Israelites are to live in light of the statutes and laws, and what work they are to do.

18:21 Rulers are to be God-fearing, trustworthy, and honest, those who govern or dispense justice, judgment, and protection.

3 And [a]Moses went up to God, and
the LORD [b]called to him from the mountain, saying, "Thus you shall say to the
house of Jacob, and tell the children
of Israel:
4 [a]'You have seen what I did to the
Egyptians, and *how* [b]I [1]bore you on eagles' wings and brought you to Myself.
2 5 'Now [a]therefore, if you will indeed
obey My voice and [b]keep My *covenant, then [c]you shall be a *special
treasure to Me above all people; for all
the earth *is* [d]Mine.
6 'And you shall be to Me a [a]kingdom
of priests and a [b]holy nation.' These
are the words which you shall speak
to the children of Israel."
7 So Moses came and called for the
[a]elders of the people, and [1]laid before
them all these words which the LORD
commanded him.

KINGDOM DYNAMICS

19:5–7 A Kingdom of Priests, WORSHIP AND THE KINGDOM. In these verses the Lord indicates His objective for His delivered people. His purpose for their destiny requires their understanding His essential priority for them: worship—His redemptive goal and kingdom reinstatement. As they learn to worship as a nation of priests, they will discover His foundational means for their possessing their future victories (as ones whose domain, or "kingdom," He has promised). Their restored rule, from sharing to "kingdom" possession, extends from their walk before God in worship. Israel's deliverance from Egypt is not only a triumphant testimony; it is God's timeless type, showing His plans and methods for the church's deliverance and intended conquest (1 Cor. 10:11).

(Acts 14:21, 22/Ps. 22:3) J.W.H.

4 8 Then [a]all the people answered together and said, "All that the LORD has
spoken we will do." So Moses *brought
back the words of the people to the
LORD.

3 [a]Acts 7:38 [b]Ex. 3:4
4 [a]Deut. 29:2 [b]Is. 63:9 [1]*sustained*
5 [a]Ex. 15:26; 23:22 [b]Deut. 5:2 [c]Ps. 135:4 [d]Ex. 9:29 *See WW at Gen. 17:7. • See WW at Deut. 26:18.
6 [a][1 Pet. 2:5, 9] [b]Deut. 7:6; 14:21; 26:19
7 [a]Ex. 4:29, 30 [1]*set*
8 [a]Deut. 5:27; 26:17 *See WW at Ruth 4:15.
9 [a]Ex. 19:16; 20:21; 24:15 [b]Deut. 4:12, 36
10 [a]Lev. 11:44, 45
12 [a]Heb. 12:20
15 [a][1 Cor. 7:5]
16 [a]Heb. 12:18, 19 [b]Heb. 12:21 *See WW at Hos. 8:1.
17 [a]Deut. 4:10
18 [a]Deut. 4:11 [b]Ex. 3:2; 24:17 [c]Gen. 15:17; 19:28 [d]Ps. 68:8 [1]LXX *all the people*

9 And the LORD said to Moses, "Behold, I come to you [a]in the thick cloud,
[b]that the people may hear when I
speak with you, and believe you forever." So Moses told the words of the
people to the LORD.
10 Then the LORD said to Moses, "Go
to the people and [a]consecrate them today and tomorrow, and let them wash
their clothes.
11 "And let them be ready for the third
day. For on the third day the LORD will
come down upon Mount Sinai in the
sight of all the people.
12 "You shall set bounds for the people
all around, saying, 'Take heed to yourselves *that* you do *not* go up to the
mountain or touch its base. [a]Whoever
touches the mountain shall surely be
put to death.
13 'Not a hand shall touch him, but he
shall surely be stoned or shot *with an
arrow;* whether man or beast, he shall
not live.' When the trumpet sounds
long, they shall come near the mountain."
14 So Moses went down from the
mountain to the people and sanctified
the people, and they washed their
clothes.
15 And he said to the people, "Be
ready for the third day; [a]do not come
near *your* wives."
16 Then it came to pass on the third
day, in the morning, that there were
[a]thunderings and lightnings, and a
thick cloud on the mountain; and the
sound of the *trumpet was very loud,
so that all the people who *were* in the
camp [b]trembled.
17 And [a]Moses brought the people out
of the camp to meet with God, and they
stood at the foot of the mountain.
18 Now [a]Mount Sinai *was* completely
in smoke, because the LORD descended
upon [b]it in fire. [c]Its smoke ascended
like the smoke of a furnace, and
[1]the [d]whole mountain quaked greatly.
19 And when the blast of the trumpet

19:5, 6 God placed His requirements and stipulations on those who were chosen to be His people. This type of covenant was common during this period of history between an overlord and his subjects. The overlord blessed and protected the people in exchange for loyalty and obedience.
19:5 See section 2 of Truth-In-Action at the end of Ex.
19:5 You shall be a special treasure to Me: This was what their relationship would be to Him if they accepted the covenant.
19:6 Kingdom of priests: God had complete sway in all things, since all the Earth was His (v. 5), and His obedient loyal people would have dominion in the Earth. **Holy nation** describes a people set apart from the world, dedicated to the Lord God and His service, indwelt by His presence.
19:8 See section 4 of Truth-In-Action at the end of Ex.
19:10 To prepare for God's presence, the people were instructed to purify themselves by washing their clothes. In addition to this physical consecration was an implied spiritual preparation (v. 14). They were told to separate themselves from those things in which they normally participated.
19:15 Do not come near your wives instructed the men not to have sexual relations with their wives. Sexual relations involved their whole being, and would distract from the sanctification process (1 Cor. 7:5).
19:16–25 Here all Israel has the experience Moses had known at **Mount Sinai.** The intent is clear: God is coming to His people to give instruction. Though personal, their relationship with God will have definite boundaries.

sounded long and became louder and
louder, [a]Moses spoke, and [b]God answered him by voice.
20 Then the LORD came down upon
Mount Sinai, on the top of the mountain. And the LORD called Moses to the
top of the mountain, and Moses **went
up.**

WORD WEALTH

19:20 went up, *'alah* (ah-*lah*); Strong's #5927: To ascend, to go up, to rise. This verb appears more than 800 times in the OT. In addition to the obvious meaning of "go up," *'alah* can mean "bring up" or "offer up," when referring to sacrifices. Furthermore, the whole burnt offering is called *'olah* because the smoke from the offering ascended to heaven. In Ps. 24:3, *'alah* refers to ascending God's holy hill by the righteous. *'Alah* is also the root of the word *'aliyah,* "ascension" or "going up," which especially refers to going up to Zion, or to returning to Israel from the lands of dispersion. Finally, *'alah* is the root of *'elyon* (highest), which is part of the divine title *'El 'Elyon* (the Most High God).

21 And the LORD said to Moses, "Go
down and warn the people, lest they
break through [a]to gaze at the LORD,
and many of them perish.
22 "Also let the [a]priests who come
near the LORD [b]consecrate themselves,
lest the LORD [c]break out against
them."
23 But Moses said to the LORD, "The
people cannot come up to Mount Sinai;
for You warned us, saying, [a]'Set
bounds around the mountain and consecrate it.' "
24 Then the LORD said to him, "Away!
Get down and then come up, you and
Aaron with you. But do not let the
priests and the people break through
to come up to the LORD, lest He break
out against them."
25 So Moses went down to the people
and spoke to them.

The Ten Commandments

20 And God spoke [a]all these 4
words, saying:
2 [a]"I *am* the LORD your God, who
brought you out of the land of
Egypt, [b]out of the house of
[1]bondage.
3 [a]"You shall have no other gods before Me.
4 [a]"You shall not make for yourself
a carved image—any likeness
of anything that *is* in heaven
above, or that *is* in the earth
beneath, or that *is* in the water
under the earth;
5 [a]you shall not bow down to
them nor [1]serve them. [b]For I,
the LORD your God, *am* a jealous God, [c]visiting[2] the iniquity
of the fathers upon the children to the third and fourth
generations of those who hate
Me,
6 but [a]showing mercy to thousands, to those who love Me
and *keep My command-
ments.
7 [a]"You shall not take the *name of
the LORD your God in vain, for
the LORD [b]will not hold *him*
guiltless who takes His name
in vain.
8 [a]"Remember the Sabbath *day, to
keep it holy.
9 [a]Six days you shall labor and
do all your work,
10 but the [a]seventh day *is* the
Sabbath of the LORD your God.
In it you shall do no work: you,

19 [a]Heb. 12:21 [b]Neh. 9:13; Ps. 81:7
21 [a]1 Sam. 6:19
22 [a]Ex. 19:24; 24:5 [b]Lev. 10:3; 21:6–8 [c]2 Sam. 6:7, 8
23 [a]Ex. 19:12

CHAPTER 20

1 [a]Deut. 5:22
2 [a]Hos. 13:4 [b]Ex. 13:3; Deut. 7:8 [1]*slaves*
3 [a]Deut. 6:14; 2 Kin. 17:35; Jer. 25:6; 35:15
4 [a]Lev. 19:4; 26:1; Deut. 4:15–19; 27:15
5 [a]Is. 44:15, 19 [b]Ex. 34:14; Deut. 4:24; Josh. 24:19; Nah. 1:2 [c]Num. 14:18, 33; Deut. 5:9, 10; 1 Kin. 21:29; Ps. 79:8; Jer. 32:18 [1]*worship* [2]*punishing*
6 [a]Deut. 7:9; Rom. 11:28 *See WW at Job 10:12.
7 [a]Lev. 19:12; Deut. 6:13; 10:20; [Matt. 5:33–37] [b]Mic. 6:11 *See WW at Deut. 18:5.
8 [a]Ex. 23:12; 31:13–16; Lev. 26:2; Deut. 5:12 *See WW at Zeph. 1:7.
9 [a]Ex. 34:21; 35:2, 3; Lev. 23:3; Deut. 5:13; Luke 13:14
10 [a]Gen. 2:2, 3

19:23, 24 The boundaries were due to God's holiness; this separation can be bridged only by Jesus Christ who enables redeemed men to enter "the Presence *behind* the veil" (Heb. 6:19).

20:1–17 See section 4 of Truth-In-Action at the end of Ex.

20:1 These 10 **words** (the Ten Commandments) are absolute law, principles that are all-encompassing and allow for no exception. Jesus confirms their timeless application (Matt. 5:21–37).

20:2 God proclaims triumph for His people, not over them. **I am the LORD your God** identified the speaker with the one who performed the miracles of the Exodus event.

20:3 God's character demands loyalty. The believer demonstrates loyalty by worshiping the only one, true God.

20:4 Israel was surrounded by peoples who worshiped images also called gods. Since no human effort could represent God adequately, God forbade creating any image of Him, either literally or conceptually. The Israelites, in this regard, became unique among their neighbors.

20:5 Third and fourth *generations:* It was possible for four generations to live around the aged head of the family. Because of the close ties of a patriarchal family, the influence of the patriarch, good or evil, affected all generations under his control.

20:7 The name of the LORD should not be misused, for His name and His character are inseparable. The name of God has been misused in magic, in substantiating truth through the use of oaths and in profane utterances. The Third Commandment deals not only with the use of God's name, but with controlling one's tongue as well.

20:8 The Sabbath is to be a holy day, set aside to God. The Hebrew word means to "desist." One who is in a covenantal position with God is to stop the everyday activities of life and honor God with rest every seventh day. God had set the pattern in creation: six days He worked; on the seventh day He rested.

nor your son, nor your daughter, nor your male servant, nor
your female servant, nor your
cattle, [b]nor your stranger who
is within your gates.
11 For [a]*in* six days the LORD made
the heavens and the earth, the
sea, and all that *is* in them, and
rested the seventh day. Therefore the LORD blessed the Sabbath day and hallowed it.
12 [a]"Honor your father and your
mother, that your days may be
[b]long upon the land which the
LORD your God is giving you.
13 [a]"You shall not murder.
14 [a]"You shall not commit [b]adultery.
15 [a]"You shall not steal.
16 [a]"You shall not bear false witness
against your neighbor.
17 [a]"You shall not covet your neighbor's house; [b]you shall not
covet your neighbor's wife,
nor his male servant, nor his
female servant, nor his ox, nor
his donkey, nor anything that
is your neighbor's."

The People Afraid of God's Presence

18 Now [a]all the people [b]witnessed the
thunderings, the lightning flashes, the
sound of the trumpet, and the mountain [c]smoking; and when the people
saw *it*, they trembled and stood afar
off.
19 Then they said to Moses, [a]"You
speak with us, and we will hear; but
[b]let not God speak with us, lest we
die."
4 20 And Moses said to the people,
[a]"Do not fear; [b]for God has come to
*test you, and [c]that His fear may be
before you, so that you may not sin."
21 So the people stood afar off, but Moses drew near [a]the thick darkness
where God *was*.

The Law of the Altar

22 Then the LORD said to Moses, "Thus
you shall say to the children of Israel:
'You have seen that I have talked with
you [a]from heaven.
23 'You shall not make *anything to be*
[a]with Me—gods of silver or gods of
gold you shall not make for yourselves.
24 'An altar of [a]earth you shall make
for Me, and you shall sacrifice on it
your burnt offerings and your peace offerings, [b]your sheep and your oxen. In
every [c]place where I [1]record My name
I will come to you, and I will [d]bless
you.
25 'And [a]if you make Me an altar of
stone, you shall not build it of hewn
stone; for if you [b]use your tool on it,
you have profaned it.
26 'Nor shall you go up by *steps to
My altar, that your [a]nakedness may
not be exposed on it.'

The Law Concerning Servants

21 "Now these *are* the [1]judgments
which you shall [a]set before
them:
2 [a]"If you buy a Hebrew servant, he
shall serve six years; and in the seventh he shall go out free and pay nothing.
3 "If he comes in by himself, he shall
go out by himself; if he *comes in* married, then his wife shall go out with
him.
4 "If his master has given him a wife,
and she has borne him sons or daughters, the wife and her children shall be
her master's, and he shall go out by
himself.

10 [b]Neh. 13:16–19
11 [a]Ex. 31:17
12 [a]Lev. 19:3 [b]Deut. 5:16, 33; 6:2; 11:8, 9
13 [a]Rom. 13:9
14 [a]Matt. 5:27 [b]Deut. 5:18
15 [a]Lev. 19:11, 13
16 [a]Deut. 5:20
17 [a][Eph. 5:3, 5] [b][Matt. 5:28]
18 [a]Heb. 12:18, 19 [b]Rev. 1:10, 12 [c]Ex. 19:16, 18
19 [a]Heb. 12:19 [b]Deut. 5:5, 23–27
20 [a][Is. 41:10, 13] [b][Deut. 13:3] [c]Is. 8:13 *See WW at Ps. 78:41.
21 [a]Ex. 19:16
22 [a]Deut. 4:36; 5:24, 26
23 [a]Ex. 32:1, 2, 4
24 [a]Ex. 20:25; 27:1–8 [b]Ex. 24:5 [c]2 Chr. 6:6 [d]Gen. 12:2 [1]*cause My name to be remembered*
25 [a]Deut. 27:5 [b]Josh. 8:30, 31
26 [a]Ex. 28:42, 43 *See WW at Amos 9:6.

CHAPTER 21

1 [a]Deut. 4:14; 6:1 [1]*ordinances*
2 [a]Jer. 34:14

20:12 Since the family is the key component to society, proper relationships must be maintained. **Honor** means to prize highly, to show respect, to glorify and exalt.
20:13 Murder is an intentional, wanton taking of someone's life. This Commandment is not speaking of accidental killing, wartime killing, or capital punishment, the latter two being essential, God-ordained sanctions of government in administrating a fallen world. This Commandment is aimed at the sanctity of human life in the eyes of God.
20:14 Adultery covers any form of unfaithfulness. While aimed at maintaining the sexual sanctity and holiness of marriage, it also deals with the concept of a proper relationship with God and others. This purity also includes our thoughts (Matt. 5:27, 28).
20:15 The positive side to this Commandment is making sure that all you possess is gained through proper means.
20:16 The Ninth Commandment calls one to be trustworthy and truthful.
20:17 Covet means desire or lust. It is not the wanting of something that is wrong, but wanting it at the expense of others or from a motive of jealousy or envy.
20:20 See section 4 of Truth-In-Action at the end of Ex.
20:22—23:19 This section, often called the Book of the Covenant, explains in great detail how the Ten Commandments are to be lived and expressed in the lives of God's covenant people.
20:24 Sacrifice provided the center around which all worship revolved. **Burnt offerings:** See note on Lev. 1:3. Portions of the **peace offerings** were eaten by the priest, which demonstrated God's acceptance of such offerings, and the other parts were eaten by those who offered them.
20:25, 26 These prohibitions are so Israel's altars will not be like the Canaanites'.
21:1 Judgments referred to the decisions of the law.
21:2 One became a **servant** by being sold by his impoverished parents, by being sold for theft, or by selling himself.

2 5 [a]"But if the servant plainly says, 'I
love my master, my wife, and my children; I will not go out free,'
6 "then his master shall bring him to
the [a]judges. He shall also bring him to
the door, or to the doorpost, and his
master shall pierce his ear with an awl;
and he shall serve him forever.
7 "And if a man [a]sells his daughter
to be a female slave, she shall not go
out as the male slaves do.
8 "If she [1]does not please her master,
who has betrothed her to himself, then
he shall let her be redeemed. He shall
have no right to sell her to a foreign
people, since he has dealt deceitfully
with her.
9 "And if he has betrothed her to his
son, he shall deal with her according
to the custom of daughters.
10 "If he takes another *wife,* he shall
not diminish her food, her clothing,
[a]and her marriage rights.
11 "And if he does not do these three
for her, then she shall go out free, without *paying* money.

The Law Concerning Violence

12 [a]"He who strikes a man so that he
dies shall surely be put to death.
13 "However, [a]if he did not lie in wait,
but God [b]delivered *him* into his hand,
then [c]I will appoint for you a place
where he may flee.
14 "But if a man acts with [a]premedita-
tion against his neighbor, to kill him
by treachery, [b]you shall take him from
My altar, that he may die.
15 "And he who strikes his father or
his mother shall surely be put to
death.
16 [a]"He who kidnaps a man and
[b]sells him, or if he is [c]found in his
hand, shall surely be put to death.
17 "And [a]he who curses his father or
his mother shall surely be put to death.
18 "If men contend with each other,
and one strikes the other with a stone
or with *his* fist, and he does not die
but is confined to *his* bed,
19 "if he rises again and walks about
outside [a]with his staff, then he who
struck *him* shall be [1]acquitted. He shall
only pay *for* the loss of his time, and
shall provide *for him* to be thoroughly
healed.
20 "And if a man beats his male or female servant with a rod, so that he dies
under his hand, he shall surely be punished.
21 "Notwithstanding, if he remains
alive a day or two, he shall not be punished; for he *is* his [a]property.
22 "If men [1]fight, and hurt a woman
with child, so that [2]she gives birth
prematurely, yet no harm follows, he
shall surely be punished accordingly as
the woman's *husband imposes on
him; and he shall [a]pay as the judges
determine.
23 "But if *any* harm follows, then you
shall give life for life,
24 [a]"eye for eye, tooth for tooth, hand
for hand, foot for foot,
25 "burn for burn, wound for wound,
stripe for stripe.
26 "If a man strikes the eye of his male
or female servant, and destroys it, he
shall let him go free for the sake of his
eye.
27 "And if he knocks out the tooth of
his male or female servant, he shall
let him go free for the sake of his
tooth.

Animal Control Laws

28 "If an ox gores a man or a woman
to death, then [a]the ox shall surely be
stoned, and its flesh shall not be eaten;
but the owner of the ox *shall be*
[1]acquitted.
29 "But if the ox [1]tended to thrust with
its horn in times past, and it has been
made known to his owner, and he has
not kept it confined, so that it has killed
a man or a woman, the ox shall be
stoned and its owner also shall be put
to death.
30 "If there is imposed on him a sum
of money, then he shall pay [a]to redeem
his life, whatever is imposed on him.
31 "Whether it has gored a son or
gored a daughter, according to this
judgment it shall be done to him.

5 [a]Deut. 15:16, 17
6 [a]Ex. 12:12; 22:8, 9
7 [a]Neh. 5:5
8 [1]Lit. *is evil in the eyes of*
10 [a][1 Cor. 7:3, 5]
12 [a]Gen. 9:6; Lev. 24:17; Num. 35:30; [Matt. 26:52]
13 [a]Deut. 19:4, 5 [b]1 Sam. 24:4, 10, 18 [c]Num. 35:11; Deut. 19:3; Josh. 20:2
14 [a]Deut. 19:11, 12; [Heb. 10:26] [b]1 Kin. 2:28–34
16 [a]Deut. 24:7 [b]Gen. 37:28 [c]Ex. 22:4
17 [a]Lev. 20:9; Prov. 20:20; Matt. 15:4; Mark 7:10
19 [a]2 Sam. 3:29 [1]*exempt from punishment*
21 [a]Lev. 25:44–46
22 [a]Ex. 18:21, 22; 21:30; Deut. 22:18 [1]*struggle* [2]Lit. *her children come out* *See WW at Hos. 2:8.
24 [a]Lev. 24:20; Deut. 19:21; [Matt. 5:38–44; 1 Pet. 2:19–21]
28 [a]Gen. 9:5 [1]*exempt from punishment*
29 [1]*was inclined*
30 [a]Ex. 21:22; Num. 35:31

21:5 See section 2 of Truth-In-Action at the end of Ex.
21:7–11 God's concern for people is seen in His loving provision for even slave-brides, a provision not known among the heathen.
21:12–14 Those who accidentally killed someone had a place of sanctuary, safety, or protection. Those guilty of murder had no place of safety, not even at the altar of God.
21:18–27 Insofar as possible, restitution was to be made for an injury done to another. An individual who is personally responsible for his actions, and therefore must care for those whom he injures, is much more careful in his dealings with others.
21:19 Walks about outside referred to the ability to get around, even if it was with a stick. If the person injured could walk around, he had recovered.
21:23–27 See note on Lev. 24:20.
21:26, 27 Freedom was the payment for personal injury to a servant.
21:28, 29 Killing an animal that kills a human speaks highly of God's view of the sanctity of human life.

32 "If the ox gores a male or female servant, he shall give to their master [a]thirty shekels of silver, and the [b]ox shall be stoned.

33 "And if a man *opens a pit, or if a man digs a pit and does not cover it, and an ox or a donkey falls in it,

34 "the owner of the pit shall make *it* good; he shall give money to their owner, but the dead *animal* shall be his.

35 "If one man's ox hurts another's, so that it dies, then they shall sell the live ox and divide the money from it; and the dead *ox* they shall also divide.

36 "Or if it was known that the ox tended to thrust in time past, and its owner has not kept it confined, he shall surely pay ox for ox, and the dead animal shall be his own.

Responsibility for Property

22 "If a man steals an ox or a sheep, and slaughters it or sells it, he shall [a]restore five oxen for an ox and four sheep for a sheep.

2 "If the thief is found [a]breaking in, and he is struck so that he dies, *there shall be* [b]no guilt for his bloodshed.

3 "If the sun has risen on him, *there shall be* guilt for his bloodshed. He should make full restitution; if he has nothing, then he shall be [a]sold[1] for his theft.

4 "If the theft is certainly [a]found alive in his hand, whether it is an ox or donkey or sheep, he shall [b]restore double.

5 "If a man causes a field or vineyard to be grazed, and lets loose his animal, and it feeds in another man's field, he shall make restitution from the best of his own field and the best of his own vineyard.

6 "If fire breaks out and catches in thorns, so that stacked grain, standing grain, or the field is consumed, he who kindled the fire shall surely make restitution.

7 "If a man [a]delivers to his neighbor money or articles to keep, and it is stolen out of the man's house, [b]if the thief is found, he shall pay double.

8 "If the thief is not found, then the *master of the house shall be brought to the [a]judges *to see* whether he has put his hand into his neighbor's goods.

9 "For any kind of trespass, *whether it concerns* an ox, a donkey, a sheep, or clothing, *or* for any kind of lost thing which *another* claims to be his, the [a]cause of both parties shall come before the judges; *and* whomever the judges condemn shall pay double to his neighbor.

10 "If a man delivers to his neighbor a donkey, an ox, a sheep, or any animal to keep, and it dies, is hurt, or driven away, no one seeing *it,*

11 "*then* an [a]oath of the LORD shall be between them both, that he has not put his hand into his neighbor's goods; and the owner of it shall accept *that,* and he shall not make *it* good.

12 "But [a]if, in fact, it is stolen from him, he shall make restitution to the owner of it.

13 "If it is [a]torn to pieces *by a beast, then* he shall bring it as evidence, *and* he shall not make good what was torn.

14 "And if a man borrows *anything* from his neighbor, and it becomes injured or dies, the owner of it not *being* with it, he shall surely make *it* good.

15 "If its owner *was* with it, he shall not make *it* good; if it *was* hired, it came for its hire.

Moral and Ceremonial Principles

16 [a]"If a man entices a virgin who is not betrothed, and lies with her, he shall surely pay the bride-price for her *to be* his wife.

17 "If her father utterly refuses to give her to him, he shall pay money according to the [a]bride-price of virgins.

18 [a]"You shall not permit a sorceress 5
to *live.

19 [a]"Whoever lies with an animal shall surely be put to death.

20 [a]"He who sacrifices to *any* god, ex-

---

32 [a]Zech. 11:12, 13; Matt. 26:15; 27:3, 9 [b]Ex. 21:28
33 *See WW at Jer. 40:4.

CHAPTER 22

1 [a]2 Sam. 12:6; Prov. 6:31; Luke 19:8
2 [a]Job 24:16; Matt. 6:19; 24:43; 1 Pet. 4:15 [b]Num. 35:27
3 [a]Ex. 21:2; Matt. 18:25 [1]Sold as a slave
4 [a]Ex. 21:16 [b]Prov. 6:31
7 [a]Lev. 6:1–7 [b]Ex. 22:4
8 [a]Ex. 21:6, 22; 22:28; Deut. 17:8, 9; 19:17 *See WW at Hos. 2:8.
9 [a]Deut. 25:1; 2 Chr. 19:10
11 [a]Heb. 6:16
12 [a]Gen. 31:39
13 [a]Gen. 31:39
16 [a]Deut. 22:28, 29
17 [a]Gen. 34:12; 1 Sam. 18:25
18 [a]Lev. 19:31; 20:6, 27; Deut. 18:10, 11; 1 Sam. 28:3–10; Jer. 27:9, 10 *See WW at Hab. 2:4.
19 [a]Lev. 18:23; 20:15, 16; Deut. 27:21
20 [a]Ex. 32:8; 34:15; Lev. 17:7; Num. 25:2; Deut. 17:2, 3, 5; 1 Kin. 18:40; 2 Kin. 10:25

21:32 Thirty shekels of silver was the price of a good slave.

21:33, 34 The **pit** referred to here was likely a well. Short walls of protection were required to be erected around the opening to prevent a person or animal from falling into it.

22:1 The thief had to make restitution.

22:2–4 If a **thief** broke into a home at night and was killed, the person who killed him was free of wrath. If a thief came into a home in the daylight and was killed, the one doing the slaying was treated as a murderer (21:12). The rationale behind this is based upon the ability of the witness to identify the thief and take him before the judges for restitution.

22:13 The carcass proved that a wild beast did attack the animal and that the one charged with the animal's safety did attempt to protect it.

22:16, 17 Sex was viewed as a gift of God. Godly sex allowed one to imitate God as a creator by giving life to another human being in God's image. Thus, all improper sexual activity was looked upon as an affront to God and a lowering of human dignity.

22:18 See section 5 of Truth-In-Action at the end of Ex.

22:18 Sorcery was trying to force a deity or spirits to do the bidding of the sorcerer.

cept to the LORD only, he shall be utterly destroyed.
21 [a]"You shall neither mistreat a
[1]stranger nor oppress him, for you
were strangers in the land of Egypt.
22 [a]"You shall not afflict any widow
or fatherless child.
23 "If you afflict them in any way, *and*
they [a]cry at all to Me, I will surely
[b]hear their cry;
24 "and My [a]wrath will become hot,
and I will kill you with the sword;
[b]your wives shall be widows, and your
children fatherless.
25 [a]"If you lend money to *any of* My
people *who are* *poor among you, you
shall not be like a moneylender to him;
you shall not charge him [b]interest.
26 [a]"If you ever take your neighbor's
garment as a pledge, you shall return
it to him before the sun goes down.
27 "For that *is* his only covering, it *is*
his garment for his skin. What will he
sleep in? And it will be that when he
cries to Me, I will hear, for I *am*
[a]gracious.
5 28 [a]"You shall not *revile God, nor
curse a [b]ruler of your people.
29 "You shall not delay *to offer*
[a]the first of your ripe produce and your
juices. [b]The firstborn of your sons you
shall give to Me.
30 [a]"Likewise you shall do with your
oxen *and* your sheep. It shall be with
its mother [b]seven days; on the eighth
day you shall give it to Me.
31 "And you shall be [a]holy men to Me:
[b]you shall not eat meat torn *by beasts*
in the field; you shall throw it to the
dogs.

Justice for All

23 "You [a]shall not circulate a false
report. Do not put your hand
with the wicked to be an [b]unrighteous
witness.
4 2 [a]"You shall not follow a crowd to
do evil; [b]nor shall you testify in a dispute so as to turn aside after many to
pervert *justice.*
3 "You shall not show partiality to a
[a]poor man in his dispute.
4 [a]"If you *meet your enemy's ox or
his donkey going astray, you shall
surely bring it back to him again.

21 [a]Deut. 10:19 [1]*sojourner*
22 [a][James 1:27]
23 [a][Luke 18:7] [b]Ps. 18:6
24 [a]Ps. 69:24 [b]Ps. 109:9
25 [a]Lev. 25:35–37 [b]Ps. 15:5 *See WW at Ps. 40:17.
26 [a]Deut. 24:6, 10–13
27 [a]Ex. 34:6, 7
28 [a]Eccl. 10:20 [b]Acts 23:5 *See WW at Jer. 8:11.
29 [a]Ex. 23:16, 19 [b]Ex. 13:2, 12, 15
30 [a]Deut. 15:19 [b]Lev. 22:27
31 [a]Lev. 11:44; 19:2 [b]Ezek. 4:14

CHAPTER 23

1 [a]Ps. 101:5 [b]Deut. 19:16–21
2 [a]Gen. 7:1 [b]Lev. 19:15
3 [a]Deut. 1:17; 16:19
4 [a][Rom. 12:20] *See WW at Jer. 27:18.
5 [a]Deut. 22:4
6 [a]Eccl. 5:8 *See WW at Num. 36:13. • See WW at Ps. 70:5.
7 [a]Eph. 4:25 [b]Matt. 27:4 [c]Rom. 1:18
8 [a]Prov. 15:27; 17:8, 23
9 [a]Ex. 22:21 [1]*sojourner* *See WW at Ex. 3:7.
10 [a]Lev. 25:1–7 *See WW at Hos. 10:12.
11 [1]*olive yards*
12 [a]Luke 13:14 *See WW at Ex. 16:30. • See WW at Ex. 33:14.
13 [a]1 Tim. 4:16 [b]Josh. 23:7
14 [a]Ex. 23:17; 34:22–24

5 [a]"If you see the donkey of one who
hates you lying under its burden, and
you would refrain from helping it, you
shall surely help him with it.
6 [a]"You shall not pervert the *judgment of your *poor in his dispute.
7 [a]"Keep yourself far from a false
matter; [b]do not kill the innocent and
righteous. For [c]I will not justify the
wicked.
8 "And [a]you shall take no bribe, for
a bribe blinds the discerning and perverts the words of the righteous.
9 "Also [a]you shall not oppress a
[1]stranger, for you *know the heart of
a stranger, because you were strangers
in the land of Egypt.

The Law of Sabbaths

10 [a]"Six years you shall *sow your
land and gather in its produce,
11 "but the seventh *year* you shall let
it rest and lie fallow, that the poor of
your people may eat; and what they
leave, the beasts of the field may eat.
In like manner you shall do with your
vineyard *and* your [1]olive grove.
12 [a]"Six days you shall do your work,
and on the seventh day you shall *rest,
that your ox and your donkey may
*rest, and the son of your female ser-
vant and the stranger may be refreshed.
13 "And in all that I have said to you,
[a]be circumspect and [b]make no mention of the name of other gods, nor let
it be heard from your mouth.

Three Annual Feasts

14 [a]"Three times you shall **keep a feast**
to Me in the year:

WORD WEALTH

23:14 keep a feast, *chagag* (cha-*gahg*); Strong's #2287: To celebrate, keep a feast, be festive, dance, assemble for rejoicing and celebration. This verb occurs 15 times. It is translated as "dancing" in 1 Sam. 30:16, and "kept a pilgrim feast" in Ps. 42:4. An important derivative is *chag,* "feast," especially referring to the seven feasts God gave to Israel. The name "Haggai" comes from *chagag* and (*cont. on next page*)

22:22 To **afflict** meant to treat with contempt.
22:25–27 The duty of the rich was to **lend** to the poor, but usually without interest. Surety could be asked for, but not if it would cause the borrower to suffer.
22:28 See section 5 of Truth-In-Action at the end of Ex.
22:28 The same honor paid to God was also to be paid to His representatives.
23:2, 3 See section 4 of Truth-In-Action at the end of Ex.
23:4 An enemy was one with whom one was having a dispute before the Law.
23:10, 11 See note on Lev. 25:1–55.
23:14–17 Feasting was a time of resting from common tasks and dwelling on God's mercy and grace.

(cont. from preceding page) means "Festive One" or "Celebrating One." The OT abounds in feasts and celebrations, ordained by God and resulting in human happiness.

4 15 [a]"You shall keep the Feast of Unleavened Bread (you shall eat unleavened bread seven days, as I commanded you, at the time appointed in the month of Abib, for in it you came out of Egypt; [b]none shall appear before Me empty);
3 16 [a]"and the Feast of Harvest, the firstfruits of your labors which you have sown in the field; and [b]the Feast of Ingathering at the end of the year, when you have gathered in *the fruit of* your labors from the field.
17 [a]"Three times in the year all your males shall appear before the Lord [1]GOD.
18 [a]"You shall not offer the blood of My sacrifice with leavened [b]bread; nor shall the fat of My [1]sacrifice remain until morning.
19 [a]"The first of the firstfruits of your land you shall bring into the house of the LORD your God. [b]You shall not boil a young goat in its mother's milk.

The Angel and the Promises

20 [a]"Behold, I send an *Angel before you to keep you in the way and to bring you into the place which I have prepared.
21 "Beware of Him and obey His voice; [a]do not provoke Him, for He will [b]not pardon your *transgressions; for [c]My name *is* in Him.
22 "But if you indeed obey His voice and do all that I speak, then [a]I will be an enemy to your enemies and an adversary to your adversaries.
23 [a]"For My Angel will go before you and [b]bring you in to the Amorites and the Hittites and the Perizzites and the Canaanites and the Hivites and the Jebusites; and I will [1]cut them off.

15 [a]Ex. 12:14–20 [b]Ex. 22:29; 34:20
16 [a]Ex. 34:22 [b]Deut. 16:13
17 [a]Deut. 16:16 [1]Heb. *YHWH,* usually translated LORD
18 [a]Ex. 34:25 [b]Deut. 16:4 [1]*feast*
19 [a]Deut. 26:2, 10 [b]Deut. 14:21
20 [a]Ex. 3:2; 13:15; 14:19 *See WW at 2 Chr. 32:21.
21 [a]Ps. 78:40, 56 [b]Deut. 18:19 [c]Is. 9:6 *See WW at Ezek. 18:31.
22 [a]Deut. 30:7
23 [a]Ex. 23:20 [b]Josh. 24:8, 11 [1]*annihilate them*
24 [a]Ex. 20:5; 23:13, 33 [b]Deut. 12:30, 31 [c]Num. 33:52
25 [a]Deut. 6:13 [b]Deut. 28:5 [c]Ex. 15:26
26 [a]Deut. 7:14; 28:4 [b]1 Chr. 23:1
27 [a]Ex. 15:16 [b]Deut. 7:23
28 [a]Josh. 24:12
29 [a]Deut. 7:22
31 [a]Gen. 15:18 [b]Josh. 21:44 [1]*boundaries* [2]Heb. *Nahar,* the Euphrates
32 [a]Ex. 34:12, 15 [1]*treaty*
33 [a]Ps. 106:36

CHAPTER 24

1 [a]Lev. 10:1, 2 [b]Num. 11:16

24 "You shall not [a]bow down to their gods, nor serve them, [b]nor do according to their works; [c]but you shall utterly overthrow them and completely break down their *sacred* pillars.
25 "So you shall [a]serve the LORD your God, and [b]He will bless your bread and your water. And [c]I will take sickness away from the midst of you.
26 [a]"No one shall suffer miscarriage or be barren in your land; I will [b]fulfill the number of your days.
27 "I will send [a]My fear before you, I will [b]cause confusion among all the people to whom you come, and will make all your enemies turn *their* backs to you.
28 "And [a]I will send hornets before you, which shall drive out the Hivite, the Canaanite, and the Hittite from before you.
29 [a]"I will not drive them out from before you in one year, lest the land become desolate and the beasts of the field become too numerous for you.
30 "Little by little I will drive them out from before you, until you have increased, and you inherit the land.
31 "And [a]I will set your [1]bounds from the Red Sea to the sea, Philistia, and from the desert to the [2]River. For I will [b]deliver the inhabitants of the land into your hand, and you shall drive them out before you.
32 [a]"You shall make no [1]covenant with them, nor with their gods.
33 "They shall not dwell in your land, lest they make you sin against Me. For *if* you serve their gods, [a]it will surely be a snare to you."

Israel Affirms the Covenant

24 Now He said to Moses, "Come up to the LORD, you and Aaron, [a]Nadab and Abihu, [b]and seventy of the elders of Israel, and worship from afar.
2 "And Moses alone shall come near the LORD, but they shall not come near; nor shall the people go up with him."
3 So Moses came and told the people 4

23:15 See section 4 of Truth-In-Action at the end of Ex.
23:15 See notes on 12:1–11, 14–20.
23:16 See section 3 of Truth-In-Action at the end of Ex.
23:16 The Feast of Harvest is also called the Feast of Weeks (Num. 28:26–31) or the Day of Pentecost (Acts 2:1). It was observed in the third month (May–June), 50 days after the Feast of Unleavened Bread and commemorated the early harvest. **The Feast of Ingathering,** also known as the Feast of Tabernacles (Booths), was an autumn feast (September–October) to celebrate the completed harvest. Following Israel's wilderness experience, it was a commemoration of their wandering as well and included living in small temporary booths in honor of Israel's life in temporary shelters in the wilderness.
23:19 The first of the firstfruits meant the best and the first of the products of Israel's labors. **Boil a young . . . mother's milk:** See note on Deut. 14:21.
23:25 See note on 15:26.
23:31–33 The Israelites were told to avoid all influences that would cause them to leave the worship of the true God and holy living.
23:31 These ideal boundaries of Israel were only briefly realized under David and Solomon.
24:3 See section 4 of Truth-In-Action at the end of Ex.

all the words of the LORD and all the
[1]judgments. And all the people answered with one voice and said,
[a]"All the words which the LORD has
said we will do."
4 And Moses [a]wrote* all the words of
the LORD. And he rose early in the
morning, and built an altar at the foot
of the mountain, and twelve [b]pillars according to the twelve tribes of Israel.
5 Then he sent young men of the children of Israel, who offered [a]burnt offerings and sacrificed peace offerings
of oxen to the LORD.
6 And Moses [a]took half the blood and
put *it* in basins, and half the blood he
sprinkled on the altar.
4 7 Then he [a]took the Book of the Covenant and read in the hearing of the
people. And they said, "All that the
LORD has said we will do, and be obedient."
8 And Moses took the blood, sprinkled *it* on the people, and said, "This
is [a]the blood of the covenant which the
LORD has made with you according to
all these words."

On the Mountain with God

9 Then Moses went up, also Aaron,
Nadab, and Abihu, and seventy of the
elders of Israel,
10 and they [a]saw the God of Israel.
And *there was* under His feet as it were
a paved work of [b]sapphire stone, and
it was like the [c]very[1] heavens in *its*
clarity.
11 But on the nobles of the children of
Israel He [a]did not [1]lay His hand. So
[b]they saw God, and they [c]ate and
drank.
12 Then the LORD said to Moses,
[a]"Come up to Me on the mountain and
be there; and I will give you [b]tablets
of stone, and the *law and commandments which I have written, that you
may teach them."
13 So Moses arose with [a]his assistant

3 [a]Ex. 19:8; 24:7 [1]*ordinances*
4 [a]Deut. 31:9 [b]Gen. 28:18 *See WW at Deut. 31:9.
5 [a]Ex. 18:12; 20:24
6 [a]Heb. 9:18
7 [a]Heb. 9:19
8 [a][Luke 22:20]
10 [a][John 1:18; 6:46] [b]Ezek. 1:26 [c]Matt. 17:2 [1]Lit. *substance of heaven*
11 [a]Ex. 19:21 [b]Gen. 32:30 [c]1 Cor. 10:18 [1]*stretch out His*
12 [a]Ex. 24:2, 15 [b]Ex. 31:18; 32:15 *See WW at Is. 42:21.
13 [a]Ex. 32:17
14 [a]Ex. 17:10, 12
15 [a]Ex. 19:9
16 [a]Ex. 16:10; 33:18
17 [a]Deut. 4:26, 36; 9:3
18 [a]Ex. 34:28

CHAPTER 25

2 [a]Ex. 35:4–9, 21 [1]*heave offering*
5 [1]Or *dolphin*
6 [a]Ex. 27:20 [b]Ex. 30:23
7 [a]Ex. 28:4, 6–14 *See WW at Ex. 35:27.
8 [a]Heb. 9:1, 2 [b][2 Cor. 6:16] [1]*sacred place* *See WW at Num. 10:12.
9 *See WW at Is. 32:18.

Joshua, and Moses went up to the
mountain of God.
14 And he said to the elders, "Wait
here for us until we come back to you.
Indeed, Aaron and [a]Hur *are* with you.
If any man has a difficulty, let him go
to them."
15 Then Moses went up into the mountain, and [a]a cloud covered the mountain.
16 Now [a]the glory of the LORD rested
on Mount Sinai, and the cloud covered
it six days. And on the seventh day He
called to Moses out of the midst of the
cloud.
17 The sight of the glory of the LORD
was like [a]a consuming fire on the top
of the mountain in the eyes of the children of Israel.
18 So Moses went into the midst of the
cloud and went up into the mountain.
And [a]Moses was on the mountain forty
days and forty nights.

Offerings for the Sanctuary

25 Then the LORD spoke to Moses,
saying:
2 "Speak to the children of Israel, that
they bring Me an [1]offering. [a]From everyone who gives it willingly with his
heart you shall take My offering.
3 "And this *is* the offering which you
shall take from them: gold, silver, and
bronze;
4 "blue, purple, and scarlet *thread,*
fine linen, and goats' *hair;*
5 "ram skins dyed red, [1]badger skins,
and acacia wood;
6 [a]"oil for the light, and [b]spices for
the anointing oil and for the sweet incense;
7 "onyx stones, and stones to be set
in the [a]ephod* and in the breastplate.
8 "And let them make Me a [a]sanc- 3
tuary,[1] that [b]I may *dwell among
them.
9 "According to all that I show you,
that is, the pattern of the *tabernacle

24:4–6 The sealing of the covenant was completed. Moses acted as mediator between God and the people. The dividing of the **blood** pointed to a twofold aspect of the covenant: blood splashed on the altar demonstrated God's gracious forgiveness in accepting the offering; blood sprinkled on the people bound them to God.

24:4 The **twelve pillars** or "standing-stones" represented the **twelve tribes of Israel** with whom God was making the covenant.

24:7 See section 4 of Truth-In-Action at the end of Ex.

24:9–11 The chief leaders were allowed to see only God's footstool, a worship experience allowing them to have intimate contact, even as Moses had. This would solidify their leadership.

24:11 He did . . . hand means they survived the ordained, intimate experience (see 19:21). Their worship was sealed by a covenant meal.

24:12 Traditionally the **tablets of stone** are thought to have contained the Ten Commandments, but this is not clearly stated. If so, this is chronologically before ch. 20.

25:2 The offering was to be a freewill offering of worship from the heart, not a tax that was imposed.

25:8 See section 3 of Truth-In-Action at the end of Ex.

25:9 The **tabernacle** was a tent or dwelling place that was sacred, dedicated to God for His presence. This is why God gave to the Israelites **the pattern** or precise plans for its construction and furnishings.

and the pattern of all its furnishings, just so you shall make *it*.

The Ark of the Testimony

10 [a]"And they shall make an ark of acacia wood; two and a half cubits *shall be* its length, a cubit and a half its width, and a cubit and a half its height.
11 "And you shall overlay it with pure gold, inside and out you shall overlay it, and shall make on it a molding of [a]gold all around.
12 "You shall cast four rings of gold for it, and put *them* in its four corners; two rings *shall be* on one side, and two rings on the other side.
13 "And you shall make poles *of* acacia wood, and overlay them with gold.
14 "You shall put the poles into the rings on the sides of the ark, that the ark may be carried by them.
15 [a]"The poles shall be in the rings of the ark; they shall not be taken from it.
16 "And you shall put into the ark [a]the Testimony which I will give you.
17 [a]"You shall make a mercy seat of pure gold; two and a half cubits *shall be* its length and a cubit and a half its width.
18 "And you shall make two **cherubim** of gold; of hammered work you shall make them at the two ends of the mercy seat.

WORD WEALTH

25:18 cherubim, *keruvim* (keh-roo-*veem*), plural of *keruv;* Strong's #3742: A heavenly being represented by carved gold figures on the ark of the covenant. *Keruv* may be related to an Akkadian verb, meaning "to bless, praise, adore." *Keruvim* are mentioned 90 times in the OT, in Gen., Ex., Num., 1 and 2 Sam., 1 and 2 Kin., 1 and 2 Chr., Ps., Is., and especially Ezek. (more than 30 times). *Keruvim* were observed from Adam's time to Ezekiel's time. See the description in Ezek. 10. The idea persists that *keruv* means "covering angel" (Ezek. 28:14). A *keruv* does cover, as Ex. 25:20 states. (Compare the two angels facing each other, who covered and guarded the Lord of Glory, as His body lay quietly in death, John 20:12.)

19 "Make one cherub at one end, and the other cherub at the other end; you shall make the cherubim at the two ends of it *of one piece* with the mercy seat.
20 "And [a]the cherubim shall stretch out *their* wings above, covering the mercy seat with their wings, and they shall face one another; the faces of the cherubim *shall be* toward the mercy seat.
21 [a]"You shall put the mercy seat on top of the ark, and [b]in the ark you shall put the Testimony that I will give you.
22 "And [a]there I will meet with you, and I will speak with you from above the mercy seat, from [b]between the two cherubim which *are* on the ark of the Testimony, about everything which I will give you in commandment to the children of Israel.

The Table for the Showbread

23 [a]"You shall also make a table of acacia wood; two cubits *shall be* its length, a cubit its width, and a cubit and a half its height.
24 "And you shall overlay it with pure gold, and make a molding of gold all around.
25 "You shall make for it a frame of a handbreadth all around, and you shall make a gold molding for the frame all around.
26 "And you shall make for it four rings of gold, and put the rings on the four corners that *are* at its four legs.
27 "The rings shall be close to the frame, as holders for the poles to bear the table.
28 "And you shall make the poles of acacia wood, and overlay them with gold, that the table may be carried with them.
29 "You shall make [a]its dishes, its pans, its pitchers, and its bowls for pouring. You shall make them of pure gold.

10 [a]Ex. 37:1–9; Deut. 10:3; Heb. 9:4
11 [a]Ex. 37:2; Heb. 9:4
15 [a]Num. 4:6; 1 Kin. 8:8
16 [a]Ex. 16:34; 31:18; Deut. 10:2; 31:26; 1 Kin. 8:9; Heb. 9:4
17 [a]Ex. 37:6; Heb. 9:5
20 [a]1 Kin. 8:7; 1 Chr. 28:18; Heb. 9:5
21 [a]Ex. 26:34; 40:20 [b]Ex. 25:16
22 [a]Ex. 29:42, 43; 30:6, 36; Lev. 16:2; Num. 17:4 [b]Num. 7:89; 1 Sam. 4:4; 2 Sam. 6:2; 2 Kin. 19:15; Ps. 80:1; Is. 37:16
23 [a]Ex. 37:10–16; 1 Kin. 7:48; 2 Chr. 4:8; Heb. 9:2
29 [a]Ex. 37:16; Num. 4:7

25:10 The **ark** was a chest about 3¾ feet long and 2¼ feet wide and high. It was the symbol of God's presence, the place where He would meet and speak with Moses (v. 22).
25:17 The **mercy seat** or atonement cover was 3¾ feet long and 2¼ feet wide. It was the symbol of God's throne protected by cherubim. On the Day of Atonement, the high priest sprinkled blood on and in front of the mercy seat (Lev. 16:14, 15). Tradition holds that this sprinkling was in the shape of a cross. Here atonement was made by God for His people.
25:18 **Cherubim** were angelic beings associated with guarding and bearing God's throne. They were associated with the worship of God Almighty.
25:23 The **table** of showbread served as a symbol of God as the provider of food. This table was about 3 feet long, 1½ feet wide, and 2¼ feet high.

30 "And you shall set the [a]showbread
on the table before Me always.

The Gold Lampstand

31 [a]"You shall also make a lampstand
of pure gold; the lampstand shall be
of hammered work. Its shaft, its
branches, its bowls, its *ornamental*
knobs, and flowers shall be *of one*
piece.
32 "And six branches shall come out
of its sides: three branches of the lampstand out of one side, and three
branches of the lampstand out of the
other side.
33 [a]"Three bowls *shall be* made like
almond *blossoms* on one branch, *with*
an *ornamental* knob and a flower, and
three bowls made like almond *blos-*
soms on the other branch, *with* an *or-*
namental knob and a flower—and so
for the six branches that come out of
the lampstand.
34 [a]"On the lampstand itself four
bowls *shall be* made like almond *blos-*
soms, each with its *ornamental* knob
and flower.
35 "And *there shall be* a knob under
the *first* two branches of the same, a
knob under the *second* two branches
of the same, and a knob under the *third*
two branches of the same, according
to the six branches that extend from
the lampstand.
36 "Their knobs and their branches
shall be of one piece; all of it *shall be*
one hammered piece of pure gold.
37 "You shall make seven lamps for
it, and [a]they shall arrange its lamps so
that they [b]give light in front of it.
38 "And its wick-trimmers and their
trays *shall be* of pure gold.
39 "It shall be made of a talent of pure
gold, with all these utensils.
40 "And [a]see to it that you make *them*
according to the pattern which was
shown you on the mountain.

The Tabernacle

26 "Moreover [a]you shall make the
tabernacle *with* ten curtains of
fine woven linen, and blue, purple, and
scarlet *thread;* with artistic designs of
cherubim you shall weave them.
2 "The length of each curtain *shall be*
twenty-eight cubits, and the width of
each curtain four cubits. And every one
of the curtains shall have [1]the same
measurements.
3 "Five curtains shall be coupled to
one another, and *the other* five curtains *shall be* coupled to one another.
4 "And you shall make loops of blue
yarn on the edge of the curtain on the
selvedge of *one* set, and likewise you
shall do on the outer edge of *the other*
curtain of the second set.
5 "Fifty loops you shall make in the
one curtain, and fifty loops you shall
make on the edge of the curtain that
is on the end of the second set, that
the loops may be clasped to one another.
6 "And you shall make fifty clasps of
gold, and couple the curtains together
with the clasps, so that it may be one
tabernacle.
7 [a]"You shall also make curtains of
goats' *hair,* to be a tent over the tabernacle. You shall make eleven curtains.
8 "The length of each curtain *shall be*
thirty cubits, and the width of each curtain four cubits; and the eleven curtains shall all have the same measurements.
9 "And you shall couple five curtains
by themselves and six curtains by
themselves, and you shall double over
the sixth curtain at the forefront of the
tent.
10 "You shall make fifty loops on the
edge of the curtain that is outermost
in *one* set, and fifty loops on the edge
of the curtain of the second set.
11 "And you shall make fifty bronze
clasps, put the clasps into the loops,
and couple the tent together, that it
may be one.
12 "The remnant that remains of the
curtains of the tent, the half curtain
that remains, shall hang over the back
of the tabernacle.
13 "And a cubit on one side and a cubit
on the other side, of what remains of
the length of the curtains of the tent,
shall hang over the sides of the tabernacle, on this side and on that side, to
cover it.
14 [a]"You shall also make a covering
of ram skins dyed red for the tent, and

30 [a]Ex. 39:36; 40:23; Lev. 24:5–9
31 [a]Ex. 37:17–24; 1 Kin. 7:49; Zech. 4:2; Heb. 9:2; Rev. 1:12
33 [a]Ex. 37:19
34 [a]Ex. 37:20–22
37 [a]Ex. 27:21; 30:8; Lev. 24:3, 4; 2 Chr. 13:11 [b]Num. 8:2
40 [a]Ex. 25:9; 26:30; Num. 8:4; 1 Chr. 28:11, 19; Acts 7:44; [Heb. 8:5]

CHAPTER 26

1 [a]Ex. 36:8–19
2 [1]Lit. *one measure*
7 [a]Ex. 36:14
14 [a]Ex. 35:7, 23; 36:19

25:30 Showbread was a type of Christ, the Bread of Life.
25:31–40 The **lampstand** served as a symbol of God as the light that was the guide for the children of Israel during the Exodus. It was a type of Christ, who is our light. It was made of about 75 pounds of gold.
26:1, 2 The first set of **curtains** were about 42 feet long and 6 feet wide and made of expensive materials.
26:7 The **tent over the tabernacle** was a goats' hair curtain about 45 feet long and 6 feet wide used to protect the first expensive set of curtains.
26:14 These two sets protected the first two sets of curtains,

a covering of badger skins above that.
15 "And for the tabernacle you shall [a]make the boards of acacia wood, standing upright.
16 "Ten cubits *shall be* the length of a board, and a cubit and a half *shall be* the width of each board.
17 "Two [1]tenons *shall be* in each board for binding one to another. Thus you shall make for all the boards of the tabernacle.
18 "And you shall make the boards for the tabernacle, twenty boards for the south side.
19 "You shall make forty sockets of silver under the twenty boards: two sockets under each of the boards for its two tenons.
20 "And for the second side of the tabernacle, the north side, *there shall be* twenty boards
21 "and their forty sockets of silver: two sockets under each of the boards.
22 "For the far side of the tabernacle, westward, you shall make six boards.
23 "And you shall also make two boards for the two back corners of the tabernacle.
24 "They shall be [1]coupled together at the bottom and they shall be coupled together at the top by one ring. Thus it shall be for both of them. They shall be for the two corners.
25 "So there shall be eight boards with their sockets of silver—sixteen sockets—two sockets under each of the boards.
26 "And you shall make bars of acacia wood: five for the boards on one side of the tabernacle,
27 "five bars for the boards on the other side of the tabernacle, and five bars for the boards of the side of the tabernacle, for the far side westward.

15 [a]Ex. 36:20–34
17 [1]Projections for joining, lit. *hands*
24 [1]Lit. *doubled*

the outermost being of **badger skins** and the innermost being of **ram skins.**
26:15, 16 The **upright boards** (frames) for the tabernacle were to be 15 feet long and 2¼ feet wide.
26:26 The **bars** were 15 cross-members that held the upright supports in place.

THE PLAN OF THE TABERNACLE (26:1)

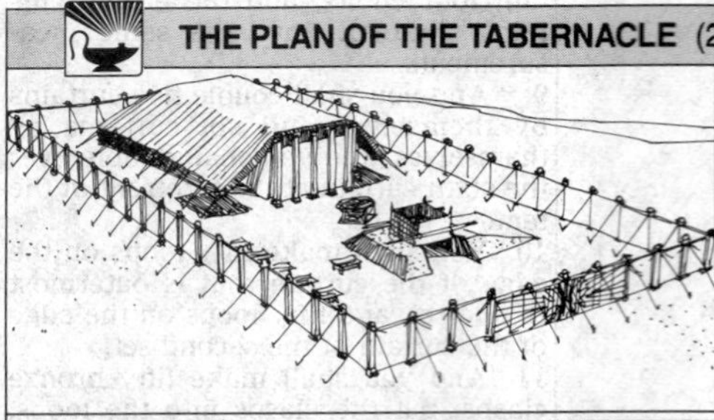

The tabernacle was to provide a place where God might dwell among His people. The term *tabernacle* sometimes refers to the tent, including the holy place and the Most Holy, which was covered with embroidered curtains. But in other places it refers to the entire complex, including the curtained court in which the tent stood.

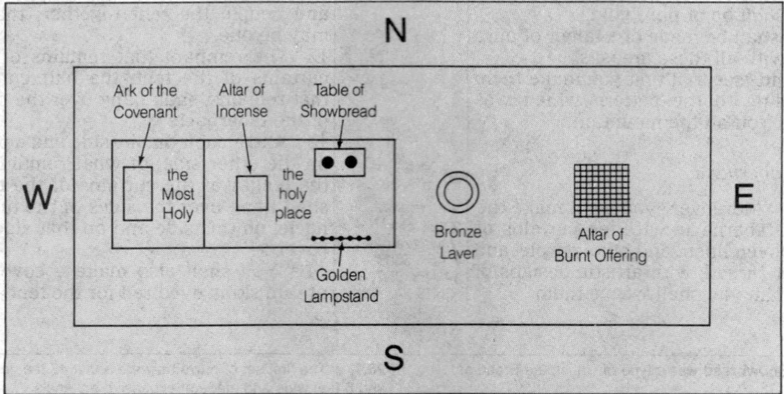

This illustration shows the relative positions of the tabernacle furniture used in Israelite worship. The tabernacle is enlarged for clarity. See also Chart: The Furniture of the Tabernacle (37:1).

28 "The [a]middle bar shall pass
through the midst of the boards from
end to end.
29 "You shall overlay the boards with
gold, make their rings of gold *as* holders for the bars, and overlay the bars
with gold.
30 "And you shall raise up the tabernacle [a]according to its pattern which you
were shown on the mountain.
31 [a]"You shall make a veil woven of
blue, purple, and scarlet *thread,* and
fine woven linen. It shall be woven
with an artistic design of cherubim.
32 "You shall hang it upon the four pillars of acacia *wood* overlaid with gold.
Their hooks *shall be* gold, upon four
sockets of silver.
33 "And you shall hang the veil from
the clasps. Then you shall bring
[a]the ark of the Testimony in there, behind the veil. The veil shall be a divider
for you between [b]the holy *place* and
the Most Holy.
34 [a]"You shall put the mercy seat upon
the ark of the Testimony in the Most
Holy.
35 [a]"You shall set the table outside the
veil, and [b]the lampstand across from
the table on the side of the tabernacle
toward the south; and you shall put the
table on the north side.
36 [a]"You shall make a screen for the
door of the tabernacle, *woven of* blue,
purple, and scarlet *thread,* and fine
woven linen, made by a weaver.
37 "And you shall make for the screen
[a]five pillars of acacia *wood,* and overlay them with gold; their hooks *shall
be* gold, and you shall cast five sockets
of bronze for them.

The Altar of Burnt Offering

27 "You shall make [a]an altar of
acacia wood, five cubits long
and five cubits wide—the altar shall be
square—and its height *shall be* three
cubits.

KINGDOM DYNAMICS

27:1—28:43 Taking Charge, LEADER TRAITS. God called Moses with a direct command to "take charge" (Hebrew *veatta*). 1) "You shall command" (Hebrew *veatta tezave,* 27:20). The overseer must step in and take charge any time he feels his delegated leader is moving in the wrong direction or confusion is beginning to find entrance. 2) "You shall bring close" (Hebrew *veatta hakrev,* 28:1). At times the leader leads by merely putting an arm around his subordinate's shoulder, to affirm, identify with, or encourage. 3) "You shall speak to all *who are* gifted artisans [the leaders]" (Hebrew *veatta tedeber,* 28:3). The literal statement is "speak to the wise in heart."

Occasionally, in order to avoid misunderstanding, an overseer needs to "take charge" by directly addressing the entire cadre of the workers rather than by speaking through delegated leadership. The wise leader knows when to let the reins of authority hang slack that his delegates may learn, but he should not relinquish full control until God tells him to do so.

(Acts 1:14/Ex. 28:1, 2) J.B.

28 [a]Ex. 36:33
30 [a]Ex. 25:9, 40; 27:8; 39:32; Num. 8:4; Acts 7:44; [Heb. 8:2, 5]
31 [a]Ex. 27:21; 36:35–38; Lev. 16:2; 2 Chr. 3:14; Matt. 27:51; Heb. 9:3; 10:20
33 [a]Ex. 25:10–16; 40:21 [b]Lev. 16:2; Heb. 9:2, 3
34 [a]Ex. 25:17–22; 40:20; Heb. 9:5
35 [a]Ex. 40:22; Heb. 9:2 [b]Ex. 40:24
36 [a]Ex. 36:37
37 [a]Ex. 36:38

CHAPTER 27

1 [a]Ex. 38:1; Ezek. 43:13
8 [a]Ex. 25:40; 26:30; Acts 7:44; [Heb. 8:5]
9 [a]Ex. 38:9–20

2 "You shall make its horns on its
four corners; its horns shall be of one
piece with it. And you shall overlay it
with bronze.
3 "Also you shall make its pans to receive its ashes, and its shovels and its
basins and its forks and its firepans;
you shall make all its utensils of
bronze.
4 "You shall make a grate for it, a network of bronze; and on the network
you shall make four bronze rings at its
four corners.
5 "You shall put it under the rim of
the altar beneath, that the network
may be midway up the altar.
6 "And you shall make poles for the
altar, poles of acacia wood, and overlay them with bronze.
7 "The poles shall be put in the rings,
and the poles shall be on the two sides
of the altar to bear it.
8 "You shall make it hollow with
boards; [a]as it was shown you on the
mountain, so shall they make *it.*

The Court of the Tabernacle

9 [a]"You shall also make the court of
the tabernacle. For the south side *there
shall be* hangings for the court *made*

26:31–34 The **veil** was an inner curtain made like the general first set (see vv. 1, 2) which further subdivided the 810-square-foot structure. It was hung 30 feet from the tabernacle's opening.
26:33 The Most Holy was the place behind the inner veil and is often called "the Holy of Holies."
27:1 The **altar** was 7½ feet long, 7½ feet wide, and 4½ feet tall. The altar was a type of the cross where Christ would offer Himself as a pure offering before God on behalf of sinners.
27:9–19 The court around the tabernacle was 150 feet long and 75 feet wide and marked the outer limits of the holy precincts. It was a large, open-air place of sacrifices.

of fine woven linen, one hundred cubits
long for one side.
10 "And its twenty pillars and their
twenty sockets *shall be* bronze. The
hooks of the pillars and their bands
shall be silver.
11 "Likewise along the length of the
north side *there shall be* hangings one
hundred *cubits* long, with its twenty
pillars and their twenty sockets of
bronze, and the hooks of the pillars
and their bands of silver.
12 "And along the width of the court
on the west side *shall be* hangings of
fifty cubits, with their ten pillars and
their ten sockets.
13 "The width of the court on the east
side *shall be* fifty cubits.
14 "The hangings on *one* side *of the
gate shall be* fifteen cubits, *with* their
three pillars and their three sockets.
15 "And on the other side *shall be*
hangings of fifteen *cubits, with* their
three pillars and their three sockets.
16 "For the gate of the court *there shall
be* a screen twenty cubits long, *woven
of* blue, purple, and scarlet *thread,* and
fine woven linen, made by a weaver.
It *shall have* four pillars and four sockets.
17 "All the pillars around the court
shall have bands of silver; their
[a]hooks *shall be* of silver and their sockets of bronze.
18 "The length of the court *shall be* one
hundred cubits, the width fifty
throughout, and the height five cubits,
made of fine woven linen, and its sockets of bronze.
19 "All the utensils of the tabernacle
for all its service, all its pegs, and all
the pegs of the court, *shall be* of
bronze.

The Care of the Lampstand

20 "And [a]you shall command the children of Israel that they bring you pure
oil of pressed olives for the light, to
cause the lamp to [1]burn continually.
21 "In the tabernacle of meeting,
[a]outside the veil which *is* before the
Testimony, [b]Aaron and his sons shall
tend it from evening until morning before the LORD. [c]*It shall be* a statute forever to their generations on behalf of
the children of Israel.

17 [a]Ex. 38:19
20 [a]Ex. 35:8, 28; Lev. 24:1–4 [1]Lit. *ascend*
21 [a]Ex. 26:31, 33 [b]Ex. 30:8; 1 Sam. 3:3; 2 Chr. 13:11 [c]Ex. 28:43; 29:9; Lev. 3:17; 16:34; Num. 18:23; 19:21; 1 Sam. 30:25

Garments for the Priesthood

28 "Now take [a]Aaron your
brother, and his sons with him,
from among the children of Israel, that
he may minister to Me as [b]priest,
Aaron *and* Aaron's sons: [c]Nadab,
Abihu, [d]Eleazar, and Ithamar.
2 "And [a]you shall make [1]holy garments for Aaron your brother, for
glory and for beauty.

KINGDOM DYNAMICS

28:1, 2 Authority, LEADER TRAITS. Moses' authority came from God with direct revelation (33:11), while Aaron's came from his office, through God's appointment. Moses had no special garments, but Aaron needed "holy garments," which endowed him with glory and beauty (28:2). Aaron's office and his attire were essential in designating his authority over the people, while Moses had none of these trappings. He was humble and self-effacing, yet at crucial moments of decision, he was powerful and authoritative. This dual type of spiritual authority causes misunderstanding and, at times, even conflict. However, there is no confusion in God's order if we will see that there are both types of leaders in the Bible, and both are necessary in a healthy, balanced church or organization. Every strong-willed, highly popular, visionary or prophetic type needs an Aaron—a priest-type who will minister more directly to the needs of the people. The level of apparent authority should not be held in competition, but seen as complementary.

(Ex. 27:1—28:43/Judg. 4:1—5:31) J.B.

3 "So [a]you shall speak to all *who are*
gifted artisans, [b]whom I have filled
with the spirit of *wisdom, that they
may make Aaron's garments, to consecrate him, that he may minister to Me
as priest.
4 "And these *are* the garments which
they shall make: [a]a breastplate, [b]an
[1]ephod,* [c]a robe, [d]a skillfully woven
tunic, a turban, and [e]a sash. So they
shall make holy garments for Aaron

CHAPTER 28

1 [a]Num. 3:10; 18:7 [b]Ps. 99:6; Heb. 5:4 [c]Ex. 24:1, 9; Lev. 10:1 [d]Ex. 6:23; Lev. 10:6, 16
2 [a]Ex. 29:5, 29; 31:10; 39:1–31; Lev. 8:7–9, 30 [1]*sacred*
3 [a]Ex. 31:6; 36:1 [b]Ex. 31:3; 35:30, 31; Is. 11:2; Eph. 1:17 *See WW at Is. 11:2.
4 [a]Ex. 28:15 [b]Ex. 28:6 [c]Ex. 28:31 [d]Ex. 28:39 [e]Lev. 8:7 [1]Ornamented vest *See WW at Ex. 35:27.

27:19 Of bronze shows that the farther one got from the Most Holy, the lesser the value of materials; this symbolized the need to be "special" to approach God fully.

27:20, 21 The **oil** to be burned in the lamp tended by Aaron and his sons was symbolic of the Holy Spirit. Beaten olive oil, which was the best, was used in the tabernacle. To obtain the oil, olives were gently pounded in a bowl and the oil was extracted from the pulp.

27:21 The **tabernacle of meeting** here is an alternate name for the tabernacle.

28:1–43 Aaron's garments were different from those of the others because he was the highest representative. All others were subordinate to him. As high priest, Aaron was Israel's chief representative before God; conversely, he was God's representative before the people.

28:1 Aaron was a type of Christ, who is our High Priest.

your brother and his sons, that he may
minister to Me as priest.

The Ephod

5 "They shall take the gold, blue, purple, and scarlet *thread,* and the fine
linen,
6 [a]"and they shall make the ephod of
gold, blue, purple, *and* scarlet *thread,*
and fine woven linen, artistically
worked.
7 "It shall have two shoulder straps
joined at its two edges, and *so* it shall
be joined together.
8 "And the [1]intricately woven band
of the ephod, which *is* on it, shall be
of the same workmanship, *made of*
gold, blue, purple, and scarlet *thread,*
and fine woven linen.
9 "Then you shall take two onyx
[a]stones and engrave on them the
names of the sons of Israel:
10 "six of their names on one stone
and six names on the other stone, in
order of their [a]birth.
11 "With the work of an [a]engraver in
stone, *like* the engravings of a signet,
you shall engrave the two stones with
the names of the sons of Israel. You
shall set them in settings of gold.
12 "And you shall put the two stones
on the shoulders of the ephod *as* *memorial stones for the sons of Israel. So
[a]Aaron shall bear their names before
the LORD on his two shoulders [b]as a
memorial.
13 "You shall also make settings of
gold,
14 "and you shall make two chains of
pure gold like braided cords, and fasten the braided chains to the settings.

The Breastplate

15 [a]"You shall make the breastplate of
judgment. Artistically woven according to the workmanship of the ephod
you shall make it: of gold, blue, purple,
and scarlet *thread,* and fine woven
linen, you shall make it.
16 "It shall be doubled into a square:
a span *shall be* its length, and a span
shall be its width.
17 [a]"And you shall put settings of
stones in it, four rows of stones: *The
first* row *shall be* a [1]sardius, a topaz,
and an emerald; *this shall be* the first
row;
18 "the second row *shall be* a turquoise, a sapphire, and a diamond;
19 "the third row, a [1]jacinth, an agate,
and an amethyst;
20 "and the fourth row, a [1]beryl, an
[2]onyx, and a jasper. They shall be set
in gold settings.
21 "And the stones shall have the
names of the sons of Israel, twelve according to their names, *like* the engravings of a signet, each one with its own
name; they shall be according to the
twelve tribes.
22 "You shall make chains for the
breastplate at the end, like braided
cords of pure gold.
23 "And you shall make two rings of
gold for the breastplate, and put the
two rings on the two ends of the breastplate.
24 "Then you shall put the two braided
chains of gold in the two rings which
are on the ends of the breastplate;
25 "and the *other* two ends of the
two braided *chains* you shall fasten
to the two settings, and put them on
the shoulder straps of the ephod in
the front.
26 "You shall make two rings of gold,
and put them on the two ends of the
breastplate, on the edge of it, which is
on the inner side of the ephod.
27 "And two *other* rings of gold you
shall make, and put them on the two
shoulder straps, underneath the ephod
toward its front, right at the seam
above the [1]intricately woven band of
the ephod.
28 "They shall bind the breastplate by
means of its rings to the rings of the
ephod, using a blue cord, so that it is
above the intricately woven band of
the ephod, and so that the breastplate does not come loose from the
ephod.
29 "So Aaron shall [a]bear the names of
the sons of Israel on the breastplate of
judgment over his heart, when he goes
into the holy *place,* as a memorial before the LORD continually.
30 "And [a]you shall put in the breastplate of judgment the [1]Urim and the
Thummim, and they shall be over Aaron's heart when he goes in before the
LORD. So Aaron shall bear the judg-

6 [a]Ex. 39:2–7; Lev. 8:7
8 [1]*ingenious work of*
9 [a]Ex. 35:27
10 [a]Gen. 29:31—30:24; 35:16–18
11 [a]Ex. 35:35
12 [a]Ex. 28:29, 30; 39:6, 7 [b]Lev. 24:7; Num. 31:54; Josh. 4:7; Zech. 6:14; 1 Cor. 11:24 *See WW at Ex. 39:7.
15 [a]Ex. 39:8–21
17 [a]Ex. 39:10 [1]Or *ruby*
19 [1]Or *amber*
20 [1]Or *yellow jasper* [2]Or *carnelian*
27 [1]*ingenious work of*
29 [a]Ex. 28:12
30 [a]Lev. 8:8; Num. 27:21; Deut. 33:8; 1 Sam. 28:6; Ezra 2:63; Neh. 7:65 [1]Lit. *Lights and the Perfections*

28:5–14 The ephod was an elaborate four-piece, vestlike garment by which Aaron symbolically bore Israel on his shoulders into God's presence (v. 12).

28:15–30 The **breastplate** was a single piece of fabric, folded over to form a nine-by-nine-inch square. Twelve stones again symbolized Aaron's bearing Israel before God, this time over his heart.

28:30 The Urim and the Thummim were put in the breastplate. These were some type of device used to understand messages from Yahweh.

ment of the children of Israel over his
heart before the LORD **continually.**

WORD WEALTH

28:30 continually, *tamid* (tah-*meed*); Strong's #8548: Constantly, always, evermore, perpetually. It is assumed that this adverb comes from a root, meaning "to stretch out to eternity," "to extend forever." *Tamid* occurs more than 100 times in the OT with the primary idea of something permanent and unceasing. In 29:42, *tamid* describes the burnt offering as "continual"; "permanent," "daily," or "regular" may also fit here. *Tamid* occurs in several well-loved verses: "My eyes *are* **ever** toward the LORD" (Ps. 25:15). "His praise *shall* **continually** *be* in my mouth" (Ps. 34:1). "The LORD will guide you **continually,** and satisfy your soul in drought" (Is. 58:11).

Other Priestly Garments

31 [a]"You shall make the robe of the
ephod all of blue.
32 "There shall be an opening for his
head in the middle of it; it shall have
a woven binding all around its opening, like the opening in a coat of mail,
so that it does not tear.
33 "And upon its hem you shall make
pomegranates of blue, purple, and
scarlet, all around its hem, and bells
of gold between them all around:
34 "a golden bell and a pomegranate,
a golden bell and a pomegranate, upon
the hem of the robe all around.
35 "And it shall be upon Aaron when
he ministers, and its sound will be
heard when he goes into the holy *place*
before the LORD and when he comes
out, that he may not die.
36 [a]"You shall also make a plate of
pure gold and engrave on it, *like* the
engraving of a signet:

HOLINESS TO THE LORD.

37 "And you shall put it on a blue cord,
that it may be on the turban; it shall
be on the front of the turban.
38 "So it shall be on Aaron's forehead,
that Aaron may [a]bear the iniquity of
the holy things which the children of
Israel hallow in all their [1]holy gifts;
and it shall always be on his forehead,
that they may be [b]accepted before the
LORD.
39 "You shall [a]skillfully weave the
tunic of fine linen *thread,* you shall
make the turban of fine linen, and you
shall make the sash of woven work.
40 [a]"For Aaron's sons you shall make
tunics, and you shall make sashes for
them. And you shall make [1]hats for
them, for glory and [b]beauty.
41 "So you shall put them on Aaron
your brother and on his sons with him.
You shall [a]anoint* them, [b]consecrate
them, and [1]sanctify them, that they
may minister to Me as priests.
42 "And you shall make [a]for them
linen trousers to cover their [1]naked-
ness; they shall [2]reach from the waist
to the thighs.
43 "They shall be on Aaron and on his
sons when they come into the tabernacle of meeting, or when they come near
[a]the altar to minister in the holy *place,*
that they [b]do not incur [1]iniquity and
die. [c]*It shall be* a statute forever to him
and his descendants after him.

Aaron and His Sons Consecrated

29 "And this is what you shall do
to them to hallow them for ministering to Me as priests: [a]Take one
young bull and two rams *without
blemish,
2 "and [a]unleavened bread, unleavened cakes mixed with oil, and unleavened wafers anointed with oil (you
shall make them of wheat flour).
3 "You shall put them in one basket
and bring them in the basket, with the
bull and the two rams.
4 "And Aaron and his sons you shall
bring to the door of the tabernacle of
meeting, [a]and you shall wash them
with water.
5 [a]"Then you shall take the garments,
put the tunic on Aaron, and the robe
of the ephod, the *ephod, and the
breastplate, and gird him with [b]the intricately woven band of the ephod.

31 [a]Ex. 39:22–26 **36** [a]Ex. 39:30, 31; Lev. 8:9; Zech. 14:20 **38** [a]Ex. 28:43; Lev. 10:17; 22:9, 16; Num. 18:1; [Is. 53:11]; Ezek. 4:4–6; [John 1:29; Heb. 9:28; 1 Pet. 2:24] [b]Lev. 1:4; 22:27; 23:11; Is. 56:7 [1]*sacred*
39 [a]Ex. 35:35; 39:27–29 **40** [a]Ex. 28:4; 39:27–29, 41; Ezek. 44:17, 18 [b]Ex. 28:2 [1]*headpieces* or *turbans* **41** [a]Ex. 29:7–9; 30:30; 40:15; Lev. 10:7 [b]Ex. 29:9; Lev. 8; Heb. 7:28 [1]*set them apart* *See WW at Is. 61:1. **42** [a]Ex. 39:28; Lev. 6:10; 16:4; Ezek. 44:18 [1]*bare flesh* [2]Lit. *be* **43** [a]Ex. 20:26 [b]Lev. 5:1, 17; 20:19, 20; 22:9; Num. 9:13; 18:22 [c]Ex. 27:21; Lev. 17:7 [1]*guilt*

CHAPTER 29

1 [a]Lev. 8; [Heb. 7:26–28] *See WW at Lev. 23:12. **2** [a]Lev. 2:4; 6:19–23 **4** [a]Ex. 40:12; Lev. 8:6; [Heb. 10:22] **5** [a]Ex. 28:2; Lev. 8:7 [b]Ex. 28:8 *See WW at Ex. 35:27.

28:31–35 The robe of the ephod was worn under the ephod and breastplate to remind Aaron of God's nearness.
28:33, 34 Pomegranates are a round, sweet fruit with a hard rind, *which suggested God's fruitful provision.*
28:36 HOLINESS TO THE LORD spoke of the devotion and life-style of the high priest and Israel by virtue of God's choosing.
28:40, 41 All priests needed special garments to establish their authority. Those of **Aaron's sons** were much less opulent.
28:42, 43 Both **Aaron** and **his sons** wore a plain linen undergarment so as to **cover their nakedness.** Exposed genitalia were common in Canaanite worship (see 20:26).
29:1 Hallow literally means "to make holy." A priest was consecrated, that is, made holy or set apart entirely for God's service, by a special ceremony.
29:4 The ritual cleansings dealt with the outward or external cleansing of a person. They foreshadowed NT baptism (Rom. 6:4).

6 [a]"You shall put the turban on his *head, and put the holy crown on the turban.
7 "And you shall take the anointing [a]oil, pour *it* on his head, and anoint him.
8 "Then [a]you shall bring his sons and put tunics on them.
9 "And you shall gird them with sashes, Aaron and his sons, and put the hats on them. [a]The priesthood shall be theirs for a perpetual statute. So you shall [b]consecrate Aaron and his sons.
10 "You shall also have the bull brought before the tabernacle of meeting, and [a]Aaron and his sons shall put their hands on the head of the bull.
11 "Then you shall kill the bull before the LORD, *by* the door of the tabernacle of meeting.
12 "You shall take *some* of the blood of the bull and put *it* on [a]the horns of the altar with your finger, and [b]pour all the blood beside the base of the altar.
13 "And [a]you shall take all the fat that covers the entrails, the fatty lobe *attached* to the liver, and the two kidneys and the fat that *is* on them, and burn *them* on the altar.
14 "But [a]the flesh of the bull, with its skin and its offal, you shall burn with fire outside the camp. It *is* a sin offering.
15 [a]"You shall also take one ram, and Aaron and his sons shall [b]put their hands on the head of the ram;
16 "and you shall kill the ram, and you shall take its blood and [a]sprinkle *it* all around on the altar.
17 "Then you shall cut the ram in pieces, wash its entrails and its legs, and put *them* with its pieces and with its head.
18 "And you shall burn the whole ram on the altar. It *is* a [a]burnt offering to the LORD; it *is* a sweet aroma, an offering made by fire to the LORD.
19 [a]"You shall also take the other ram, and Aaron and his sons shall put their hands on the head of the ram.
20 "Then you shall kill the ram, and take some of its blood and put *it* on the tip of the right ear of Aaron and on the tip of the right ear of his sons, on the thumb of their right hand and on the big toe of their right foot, and sprinkle the blood all around on the altar.
21 "And you shall take some of the blood that is on the altar, and some of [a]the anointing oil, and sprinkle *it* on Aaron and on his garments, on his sons and on the garments of his sons with him; and [b]he and his garments shall be hallowed, and his sons and his sons' garments with him.
22 "Also you shall take the fat of the ram, the fat tail, the fat that covers the entrails, the fatty lobe *attached to* the liver, the two kidneys and the fat on them, the right thigh (for it *is* a ram of consecration),
23 [a]"one loaf of bread, one cake *made with* oil, and one wafer from the basket of the unleavened bread that *is* before the LORD;
24 "and you shall put all these in the hands of Aaron and in the hands of his sons, and you shall [a]wave them *as* a wave offering before the LORD.
25 [a]"You shall receive them back from their hands and burn *them* on the altar as a burnt offering, as a sweet aroma before the LORD. It *is* an offering made by fire to the LORD.
26 "Then you shall take [a]the breast of the ram of Aaron's consecration and wave it *as* a wave offering before the LORD; and it shall be your portion.
27 "And from the ram of the consecration you shall consecrate [a]the breast of the wave offering which is waved, and the thigh of the heave offering which is raised, of *that* which *is* for Aaron and of *that* which is for his sons.
28 "It shall be from the children of Israel *for* Aaron and his sons [a]by a statute forever. For it is a heave offering; [b]it shall be a heave offering from the children of Israel from the sacrifices of their peace offerings, *that is,* their heave offering to the LORD.
29 "And the [a]holy garments of Aaron [b]shall be his sons' after him, [c]to be anointed in them and to be consecrated in them.
30 [a]"That son who becomes priest in

6 [a]Ex. 28:36, 37; Lev. 8:9 *See WW at Gen. 3:15. **7** [a]Ex. 25:6; 30:25–31; Lev. 8:12; 10:7; 21:10; Num. 35:25; Ps. 133:2 **8** [a]Ex. 28:39, 40; Lev. 8:13 **9** [a]Ex. 40:15; Num. 3:10; 18:7; 25:13; Deut. 18:5 [b]Ex. 28:41; Lev. 8 **10** [a]Lev. 1:4; 8:14 **12** [a]Lev. 8:15 [b]Ex. 27:2; 30:2; Lev. 4:7 **13** [a]Lev. 1:8; 3:3, 4 **14** [a]Lev. 4:11, 12, 21; Heb. 13:11 **15** [a]Lev. 8:18 [b]Lev. 1:4–9 **16** [a]Ex. 24:6; Lev. 1:5, 11 **18** [a]Ex. 20:24 **19** [a]Lev. 8:22 **21** [a]Ex. 30:25, 31; Lev. 8:30 [b]Ex. 28:41; 29:1; [Heb. 9:22] **23** [a]Lev. 8:26 **24** [a]Lev. 7:30; 10:14 **25** [a]Lev. 8:28 **26** [a]Lev. 7:31, 34; 8:29 **27** [a]Lev. 7:31, 34; Num. 18:11, 18; Deut. 18:3 **28** [a]Lev. 10:15 [b]Lev. 3:1; 7:34 **29** [a]Ex. 28:2 [b]Num. 20:26, 28 [c]Ex. 28:41; 30:30; Num. 18:8 **30** [a]Num. 20:28

29:10–14 The **sin offering,** also known as a guilt offering, was offered for unintentional and intentional sins for which there was no possible restitution. The guilt for the wrongdoing was symbolically transferred from the worshiper to the animal through the laying on of hands. The animal was then killed, and the sin was thus covered.

29:15–18 The **burnt offering** was a symbol of the new priest's dedication to God. See notes on Lev. 1:3 and 1:4.

29:19, 20 In the ordination ceremony of the priest, the blood of a ram was applied to the priest's **ear** to signify that he would hear only the Word of the Lord, to his **thumb** to signify he would rightly perform the duties of a priest, and to the **toe** to signify that he would walk in the path of righteousness.

29:24 Wave offering: See note on Lev. 3:1.

29:28 A heave offering: See note on Lev. 3:1.

29:29 Priestly succession by Aaron's descendants was instituted here.

his place shall put them on for [b]seven
days, when he enters the tabernacle of
meeting to minister in the [1]holy *place.*
31 "And you shall take the ram of the
consecration and [a]boil its flesh in the
*holy place.
32 "Then Aaron and his sons shall eat
the flesh of the ram, and the [a]bread
that *is* in the basket, *by* the door of the
tabernacle of meeting.
33 [a]"They shall eat those things with
which the atonement was made, to
consecrate *and* to sanctify them;
[b]but an outsider shall not eat *them,* because they *are* holy.
34 "And if any of the flesh of the consecration offerings, or of the bread, remains until the morning, then [a]you
shall burn the remainder with fire. It
shall not be eaten, because it *is* holy.
35 "Thus you shall do to Aaron and
his sons, according to all that I have
commanded you. [a]Seven days you
shall consecrate them.
36 "And you [a]shall offer a bull every
day *as* a sin offering for atonement.
[b]You shall cleanse the altar when you
*make atonement for it, and you shall
anoint it to sanctify it.
37 "Seven days you shall make atonement for the altar and sanctify it. And
the altar shall be most holy. [a]Whatever
touches the altar must be holy.

The Daily Offerings

38 "Now this *is* what you shall offer
on the altar: [a]two lambs of the first
year, [b]day by day continually.
39 "One lamb you shall offer [a]in the
morning, and the other lamb you shall
offer [1]at twilight.
40 "With the one lamb shall be one-
tenth *of an ephah* of flour mixed with
one-fourth of a hin of pressed oil, and
one-fourth of a hin of wine *as* a drink
offering.
41 "And the other lamb you shall
[a]offer [1]at twilight; and you shall offer
with it the grain offering and the drink
offering, as in the morning, for a sweet
aroma, an offering made by fire to the
LORD.
42 "*This shall be* [a]a continual burnt offering throughout your generations *at*
the door of the tabernacle of meeting
before the LORD, [b]where I will meet you
to speak with you.
43 "And there I will meet with the children of Israel, and *the tabernacle*
[a]shall be sanctified by My glory.
44 "So I will consecrate the tabernacle
of meeting and the altar. I will also
[a]consecrate both Aaron and his sons
to minister to Me as priests.
45 [a]"I will *dwell among the children
of Israel and will [b]be their God.
46 "And they shall know that [a]I *am* the
LORD their God, who [b]brought them up
out of the land of Egypt, that I may
dwell among them. I *am* the LORD their
God.

The Altar of Incense

30 "You shall make [a]an altar to
burn incense on; you shall make
it of acacia wood.
2 "A cubit *shall be* its length and a
cubit its width—it shall be square—and
two cubits *shall be* its height. Its horns
shall be of one piece with it.
3 "And you shall overlay its top, its
sides all around, and its horns with
pure gold; and you shall make for it a
[1]molding of gold all around.
4 "Two gold rings you shall make for
it, under the molding on both its sides.
You shall place *them* on its two sides,
and they will be holders for the poles
with which to bear it.
5 "You shall make the poles of acacia
wood, and overlay them with gold.
6 "And you shall put it before the
[a]veil that *is* before the ark of the Testimony, before the [b]mercy seat that *is*
over the Testimony, where I will meet
with you.
7 "Aaron shall burn on it [a]sweet incense every morning; when [b]he tends
the lamps, he shall burn incense on it.
8 "And when Aaron lights the lamps
[1]at twilight, he shall burn incense on
it, a perpetual incense before the LORD
throughout your generations.
9 "You shall not offer [a]strange incense on it, or a burnt offering, or a
grain offering; nor shall you pour a
drink offering on it.
10 "And [a]Aaron shall make atonement
upon its horns once a year with the
blood of the sin offering of atonement;

30 [b]Lev. 8:35 [1]*sanctuary*
31 [a]Lev. 8:31 *See WW at Lev. 19:2.
32 [a]Matt. 12:4
33 [a]Lev. 10:14, 15, 17 [b]Ex. 12:43; Lev. 22:10
34 [a]Ex. 12:10; 23:18; 34:25; Lev. 7:18; 8:32
35 [a]Lev. 8:33–35
36 [a]Heb. 10:11 [b]Ex. 30:26–29; 40:10, 11 *See WW at Num. 15:25.
37 [a]Num. 4:15; Hag. 2:11–13; Matt. 23:19
38 [a]Num. 28:3–31; 29:6–38; 1 Chr. 16:40; Ezra 3:3 [b]Dan. 12:11
39 [a]Ezek. 46:13–15 [1]Lit. *between the two evenings*
41 [a]1 Kin. 18:29, 36; 2 Kin. 16:15; Ezra 9:4, 5; Ps. 141:2 [1]Lit. *between the two evenings*
42 [a]Ex. 30:8 [b]Ex. 25:22; 33:7, 9; Num. 17:4
43 [a]Ex. 40:34; 1 Kin. 8:11; 2 Chr. 5:14; Ezek. 43:5; Hag. 2:7, 9
44 [a]Lev. 21:15
45 [a]Ex. 25:8; Lev. 26:12; Num. 5:3; Deut. 12:11; Zech. 2:10; [John 14:17, 23; Rev. 21:3] [b]Gen. 17:8; Lev. 11:45 *See WW at Num. 10:12.
46 [a]Ex. 16:12; 20:2; Deut. 4:35 [b]Lev. 11:45

CHAPTER 30

1 [a]Ex. 37:25–29
3 [1]*border*
6 [a]Ex. 26:31–35 [b]Ex. 25:21, 22
7 [a]Ex. 30:34; 1 Sam. 2:28; 1 Chr. 23:13; Luke 1:9 [b]Ex. 27:20, 21
8 [1]Lit. *between the two evenings*
9 [a]Lev. 10:1
10 [a]Lev. 16:3–34

29:38–46 The twice daily offerings here served to signify each day was to be opened and closed with gifts of worship to God.

30:1–10 The altar of **incense,** which symbolized daily prayer to God, was a type of Christ as our Intercessor.

30:9 **Strange incense** was any not made according to formula in vv. 34–38.

30:10 The Day of **Atonement** was instituted as the time of year when the high priest offered a sacrifice to atone for the sins of the nation. This sacrifice was man's recognition of the fact that he could not atone for his own sins. See note on Lev. 16:1–34.

once a year he shall make atonement
upon it throughout your generations.
It *is* most holy to the LORD."

The Ransom Money

11 Then the LORD spoke to Moses, saying:
12 [a]"When you take the census of the
children of Israel for their number,
then every man shall give [b]a[1] ransom
for himself to the LORD, when you number them, that there may be no [c]plague
among them when *you* number them.
13 [a]"This is what everyone among
those who are numbered shall give:
half a shekel according to the shekel
of the sanctuary [b](a shekel *is* twenty
gerahs). [c]The half-shekel *shall be* an
offering to the LORD.
14 "Everyone included among those
who are numbered, from twenty years
old and above, shall give an [1]offering
to the LORD.
15 "The [a]rich shall not give more and
the poor shall not give less than half
a shekel, when *you* give an offering to
the LORD, to make atonement for yourselves.
16 "And you shall take the atonement
money of the children of Israel, and
[a]shall [1]appoint it for the service of the
tabernacle of meeting, that it may be
[b]a memorial for the children of Israel
before the LORD, to make atonement
for yourselves."

The Bronze Laver

17 Then the LORD spoke to Moses, saying:
18 [a]"You shall also make a [1]laver of
bronze, with its base also of bronze,
for washing. You shall [b]put it between
the tabernacle of meeting and the altar.
And you shall put water in it,
19 "for Aaron and his sons [a]shall wash
their hands and their feet in water from
it.
20 "When they go into the tabernacle
of meeting, or when they come near
the altar to minister, to burn an offering made by fire to the LORD, they shall
wash with water, lest they die.
21 "So they shall wash their hands and
their feet, lest they die. And [a]it shall
be a [1]statute forever to them—to him
and his descendants throughout their
generations."

The Holy Anointing Oil

22 Moreover the LORD spoke to Moses,
saying:
23 "Also take for yourself [a]quality
spices—five hundred *shekels* of liquid
[b]myrrh, half as much sweet-smelling
cinnamon (two hundred and fifty *shekels*), two hundred and fifty *shekels* of
sweet-smelling [c]cane,
24 "five hundred *shekels* of [a]cassia, according to the shekel of the sanctuary,
and a [b]hin of olive oil.
25 "And you shall make from these a
holy anointing oil, an ointment compounded according to the art of the
perfumer. It shall be [a]a holy anointing
oil.
26 [a]"With it you shall anoint the tabernacle of meeting and the ark of the Testimony;
27 "the table and all its utensils, the
lampstand and its utensils, and the altar of incense;
28 "the altar of burnt offering with all
its utensils, and the laver and its base.
29 "You shall consecrate them, that
they may be most holy; [a]whatever
touches them must be holy.
30 [a]"And you shall *anoint Aaron and
his sons, and consecrate them, that
they may minister to Me as priests.
31 "And you shall speak to the children of Israel, saying: 'This shall be a
holy anointing oil to Me throughout
your generations.
32 'It shall not be poured on man's
flesh; nor shall you make *any other*
like it, according to its composition.
[a]It *is* holy, *and* it shall be holy to you.
33 [a]'Whoever [1]compounds *any* like it,
or whoever puts *any* of it on an outsider, [b]shall be [2]cut off from his people.' "

The Incense

34 And the LORD said to Moses:
[a]"Take sweet spices, stacte and onycha
and galbanum, and pure frankincense

12 [a]Ex. 38:25, 26; Num. 1:2; 26:2; 2 Sam. 24:2 [b]Num. 31:50; [Matt. 20:28; 1 Pet. 1:18, 19] [c]2 Sam. 24:15 [1]*the price of a life*
13 [a]Matt. 17:24 [b]Lev. 27:25; Num. 3:47; Ezek. 45:12 [c]Ex. 38:26
14 [1]*contribution*
15 [a]Job 34:19; Prov. 22:2; [Eph. 6:9]
16 [a]Ex. 38:25–31 [b]Num. 16:40 [1]*give*
18 [a]Ex. 38:8; 1 Kin. 7:38 [b]Ex. 40:30 [1]*basin*
19 [a]Ex. 40:31, 32; Ps. 26:6; Is. 52:11; John 13:8, 10; Heb. 10:22
21 [a]Ex. 28:43 [1]*requirement*
23 [a]Song 4:14; Ezek. 27:22 [b]Ps. 45:8; Prov. 7:17 [c]Song 4:14; Jer. 6:20
24 [a]Ps. 45:8 [b]Ex. 29:40
25 [a]Ex. 37:29; 40:9; Lev. 8:10; Num. 35:25; Ps. 89:20; 133:2
26 [a]Ex. 40:9; Lev. 8:10; Num. 7:1
29 [a]Ex. 29:37; Num. 4:15; Hag. 2:11–13
30 [a]Ex. 29:7; Lev. 8:12 *See WW at Is. 61:1.
32 [a]Ex. 30:25, 37
33 [a]Ex. 30:38 [b]Gen. 17:14; Ex. 12:15; Lev. 7:20, 21 [1]*mixes* [2]Put to death
34 [a]Ex. 25:6; 37:29

30:11–16 The tabernacle was partially supported with this atonement tax. All paid the same atonement fee to ransom their lives, for all are sinners. The tax was paid by weight, approximately $\frac{2}{10}$ of an ounce of various metals.
30:17–21 The **laver** was used by the priests to cleanse their hands and their feet. This was a type of Christ's cleansing us from the impurities of the world.
30:23 **Myrrh** is an extract from a myrrh tree. **Cane** is a reedlike grass smelling like ginger, that grows along streams.
30:24 **Cassia** is a flowering plant that smells like cinnamon.
30:31 **Anointing oil,** a type of the Holy Spirit, prepared one for service; it was also part of the service (ch. 29).
30:34–38 **Incense** was used widely in religious ceremonies in the East. The rare and expensive ingredients symbolize that Yahweh is entitled to the best available.
30:34 **Stacte** is a resin from the storax tree. **Onycha** is a

with *these* sweet spices; there shall be
equal amounts of each.
35 "You shall make of these an incense, a compound [a]according to the
art of the perfumer, salted, pure, *and*
holy.
36 "And you shall beat *some* of it very
fine, and put some of it before the Testimony in the tabernacle of meeting
[a]where I will meet with you. [b]It shall
be most holy to you.
37 "But *as for* the incense which you
shall make, [a]you shall not make any
for yourselves, according to its
[1]composition. It shall be to you holy
for the LORD.
38 [a]"Whoever makes *any* like it, to
smell it, he shall be cut off from his
people."

Artisans for Building the Tabernacle

31 Then the LORD spoke to Moses,
saying:
2 [a]"See, I have called by name Bezalel the [b]son of Uri, the son of Hur, of
the *tribe of Judah.
3 "And I have [a]filled him with the
Spirit of God, in wisdom, in understanding, in *knowledge, and in all
manner of workmanship,
4 "to design artistic works, to work
in gold, in silver, in bronze,
5 "in cutting jewels for setting, in
carving wood, and to work in all *manner of* workmanship.
6 "And I, indeed I, have appointed
with him [a]Aholiab the son of Ahisamach, of the tribe of Dan; and I have
put wisdom in the hearts of all the
[b]gifted artisans, that they may make
all that I have commanded you:
7 [a]"the tabernacle of meeting, [b]the
ark of the Testimony and [c]the mercy
seat that *is* on it, and all the furniture
of the tabernacle—
8 [a]"the table and its utensils, [b]the
pure *gold* lampstand with all its utensils, the altar of incense,
9 [a]"the altar of burnt offering with all

35 [a]Ex. 30:25
36 [a]Ex. 29:42 [b]Lev. 2:3
37 [a]Ex. 30:32 [1]Lit. *proportion*
38 [a]Ex. 30:33

CHAPTER 31

2 [a]Ex. 35:30—36:1 [b]1 Chr. 2:20 *See WW at Ex. 38:22.
3 [a]1 Kin. 7:14 *See WW at Mal. 2:7.
6 [a]Ex. 35:34 [b]Ex. 28:3; 35:10, 35; 36:1
7 [a]Ex. 36:8 [b]Ex. 37:1–5 [c]Ex. 37:6–9
8 [a]Ex. 37:10–16 [b]Ex. 37:17–24
9 [a]Ex. 38:1–7 [b]Ex. 38:8
10 [a]Ex. 39:1, 41 [1]Or *woven garments*
11 [a]Ex. 30:23–33 [b]Ex. 30:34–38
13 [a]Ezek. 20:12, 20 [b]Lev. 20:8 [1]*consecrates*
14 [a]Ex. 20:8 [b]Num. 15:32–36 [1]*defiles*
15 [a]Ex. 20:9–11 [b]Gen. 2:2
17 [a]Ex. 31:13 [b]Gen. 1:31; 2:2, 3 *See WW at Ex. 16:30.
18 [a][Ex. 24:12; 32:15, 16]

CHAPTER 32

1 [a]Ex. 24:18; Deut. 9:9–12

its utensils, and [b]the laver and its
base—
10 [a]"the [1]garments of ministry, the
holy garments for Aaron the priest and
the garments of his sons, to minister
as priests,
11 [a]"and the anointing oil and [b]sweet
incense for the holy *place*. According
to all that I have commanded you they
shall do."

The Sabbath Law

12 And the LORD spoke to Moses, say- 3
ing,
13 "Speak also to the children of Is- 1
rael, saying: [a]'Surely My Sabbaths you
shall keep, for it *is* a sign between Me
and you throughout your generations,
that *you* may know that I *am* the LORD
who [b]sanctifies[1] you.
14 [a]'You shall keep the Sabbath, therefore, for *it is* holy to you. Everyone
who [1]profanes it shall surely be put to
death; for [b]whoever does *any* work on
it, that person shall be cut off from
among his people.
15 'Work shall be done for [a]six days,
but the [b]seventh *is* the Sabbath of rest,
holy to the LORD. Whoever does *any*
work on the Sabbath day, he shall
surely be put to death.
16 'Therefore the children of Israel
shall keep the Sabbath, to observe the
Sabbath throughout their generations
as a perpetual covenant.
17 'It *is* [a]a sign between Me and the
children of Israel forever; for [b]*in* six
days the LORD made the heavens and
the earth, and on the seventh day He
*rested and was refreshed.' "
18 And when He had made an end of
speaking with him on Mount Sinai, He
gave Moses [a]two tablets of the Testimony, tablets of stone, written with the
finger of God.

The Gold Calf

32 Now when the people saw that 4
Moses [a]delayed coming down

---

dark brown gum resin. **Galbanum** originally comes out of the plant as a milky substance that changes into a gum. **Frankincense** is an aromatic gum resin.

31:3 This is one of the earliest references in Scripture to being filled with **the Spirit of God.** The idea here is that God's Spirit enhanced these men's native abilities with **wisdom** to fulfill His instructions; **understanding** to solve the project's *complex problems;* and **workmanship,** skill to accomplish the labor with accuracy.

31:12–17 See section 3 of Truth-In-Action at the end of Ex.

31:12–17 Even though the tabernacle needed to be constructed quickly, that need did not outweigh obedience to observe the **Sabbath.**

31:13 See section 1 of Truth-In-Action at the end of Ex.

31:13 The **Sabbath** was the covenant sign between God and Israel of their relationship and sanctification. He was the Sanctifier, the One who strengthened them for obedience.

32:1–6 Some believe that in the fashioning of the **molded calf** no attempt was made to abandon worshiping the one true God. Rather, the molded calf was to serve as a sign of His presence. The belief has been proposed that the choice of the calf was due to the people's familiarity with bull worship in Egypt. This is highly unlikely, however. The calf clearly represents the Hebrews' impatience and intent to worship Yahweh on their terms rather than on His. It was also an affront to Moses' leadership.

32:1 See section 4 of Truth-In-Action at the end of Ex.

from the mountain, the people [b]gath-
ered together to Aaron, and said to
him, [c]"Come, make us [1]gods that shall
[d]go before us; for *as for* this Moses,
the man who [e]brought us up out of the
land of Egypt, we do not know what
has become of him."
2 And Aaron said to them, "Break off
the [a]golden earrings which *are* in the
ears of your wives, your sons, and your
daughters, and bring *them* to me."
3 So all the people broke off the
golden earrings which *were* in their
ears, and brought *them* to Aaron.
4 [a]And he received *the gold* from
their hand, and he fashioned it with an
engraving tool, and made a molded
calf. Then they said, "This *is* your god,
O Israel, that [b]brought you out of the
land of Egypt!"
5 So when Aaron saw *it,* he built an
altar before it. And Aaron made a
[a]proclamation and said, "Tomorrow *is*
a feast to the LORD."
6 Then they rose early on the next
day, offered burnt offerings, and
brought peace offerings; and the people [a]sat down to eat and drink, and
rose up to play.
7 And the LORD said to Moses,
[a]"Go, get down! For your people whom
you brought out of the land of Egypt
[b]have corrupted *themselves.*
8 "They have turned aside quickly
out of the way which [a]I commanded
them. They have made themselves a
molded calf, and worshiped it and sacrificed to it, and said, [b]'This *is* your
god, O Israel, that brought you out of
the land of Egypt!' "
9 And the LORD said to Moses,
[a]"I have seen this people, and indeed
it *is* a [1]stiff-necked people!
10 "Now therefore, [a]let Me alone, that
[b]My wrath may burn hot against them
and I may [1]consume them. And [c]I
will make of you a great nation."
11 [a]Then Moses pleaded with [1]the
LORD his God, and said: "LORD, why
does Your wrath burn hot against Your
people whom You have brought out of
the land of Egypt with great power and
with a mighty hand?
12 [a]"Why should the Egyptians speak,
and say, 'He brought them out to harm
them, to kill them in the mountains,
and to consume them from the face of
the earth'? Turn from Your fierce
wrath, and [b]relent from this harm to
Your people.
13 "Remember Abraham, Isaac, and
Israel, Your servants, to whom You
[a]swore by Your own self, and said to
them, [b]'I will multiply your descendants as the stars of heaven; and all
this **land** that I have spoken of I give
to your descendants, and they shall inherit *it* forever.' "
14 So the LORD [a]relented from the
harm which He said He would do to
His people.

WORD WEALTH

32:13 land, *'eretz* (*eh*-retz); Strong's #776: Earth, land, ground. This noun occurs more than 2,500 times in the OT. Its broadest meaning refers to the whole Earth, and especially to the dry ground, as in Gen. 1:1, 10. Less specifically, it refers to any particular land; *'eretz mitzraim* is the land of Egypt, *'artzot* (the plural form) *goyim* are the lands of the Gentiles, and so forth. The most specific use concerns the "land of Israel," *'eretz Yisrael,* which is the Promised Land. God's promises concerning the land of Israel are emphasized throughout the OT.

KINGDOM DYNAMICS

32:11–14, 30–34 The Heart of the Intercessor, PRAYER. Moses' true character was revealed in the response he made in prayer when he learned of Israel's ingratitude and rejection. Focusing on God's honor, not his own, Moses begged God not to destroy Israel. After renewing Israel's commitment to God, Moses stood in the gap for Israel, offering his life for theirs (Ps. 106:23).

Afterward, Moses returned to the mountain another 40 days to receive again God's commandments (Ex. 34:1–28). But Israel could not blame God for the delay; their own sins had delayed God's purposes for them. Yet those purposes remained intact because Moses had stood between Israel's sin and God's wrath. Unselfish intercession prevails beyond the otherwise destructive effects of human weakness and sin.

(Gen. 18:17–33/Josh. 10:12–14) L.L.

15 And [a]Moses turned and went down
from the mountain, and the two tablets
of the Testimony *were* in his hand. The

1 [b]Ex. 17:1–3 [c]Acts 7:40 [d]Ex. 13:21 [e]Ex. 32:8 [1]Or *a god*
2 [a]Ex. 11:2; 35:22; Judg. 8:24–27
4 [a]Ex. 20:3, 4, 23; Deut. 9:16; Judg. 17:3, 4; 1 Kin. 12:28; Neh. 9:18; Ps. 106:19; Acts 7:41 [b]Ex. 29:45, 46
5 [a]Lev. 23:2, 4, 21, 37; 2 Kin. 10:20; 2 Chr. 30:5
6 [a]Ex. 32:17–19; Num. 25:2; 1 Cor. 10:7
7 [a]Deut. 9:8–21; Dan. 9:14 [b]Gen. 6:11, 12
8 [a]Ex. 20:3, 4, 23; Deut. 32:17 [b]1 Kin. 12:28
9 [a]Ex. 33:3, 5; 34:9; Deut. 9:6; 2 Chr. 30:8; Is. 48:4; [Acts 7:51] [1]*stubborn*
10 [a]Deut. 9:14, 19 [b]Ex. 22:24 [c]Num. 14:12 [1]*destroy*
11 [a]Deut. 9:18, 26–29 [1]Lit. *the face of the LORD*
12 [a]Num. 14:13–19; Deut. 9:28; Josh. 7:9 [b]Ex. 32:14
13 [a]Gen. 22:16–18; [Heb. 6:13] [b]Gen. 12:7; 13:15; 15:7, 18; 22:17; 26:4; 35:11, 12; Ex. 13:5, 11; 33:1
14 [a]2 Sam. 24:16
15 [a]Deut. 9:15

32:7–14 Moses accepted God's verdict on the wayward Hebrews, but pleaded that God would not deal with them in a way that would taint His honor or break His promises to them. Moses' request was granted by God.

32:14 Relented means "moved to pity." It shows the tension that exists between God's judgment and mercy. His decision was not totally reversed, merely tempered (v. 35).

tablets *were* written on both sides; on the one *side* and on the other they were written.

16 Now the [a]tablets *were* the work of God, and the writing *was* the writing of God engraved on the tablets.

17 And when Joshua heard the noise of the people as they shouted, he said to Moses, "*There is* a noise of war in the camp."

18 But he said:

"*It is* not the noise of the shout of
victory,
Nor the noise of the cry of defeat,
But the sound of singing I hear."

19 So it was, as soon as he came near the camp, that [a]he saw the calf *and* the dancing. So Moses' anger became hot, and he cast the tablets out of his hands and broke them at the foot of the mountain.

20 [a]Then he took the calf which they had made, burned *it* in the fire, and ground *it* to powder; and he scattered *it* on the water and made the children of Israel drink *it*.

21 And Moses said to Aaron, [a]"What did this people do to you that you have brought *so* great a sin upon them?"

22 So Aaron said, "Do not let the anger of my lord become hot. [a]You know the people, that they *are set* on evil.

23 "For they said to me, 'Make us gods that shall go before us; *as for* this Moses, the man who brought us out of the land of Egypt, we do not know what has become of him.'

24 "And I said to them, 'Whoever has any gold, let them break *it* off.' So they gave *it* to me, and I cast it into the fire, and this calf came out."

25 Now when Moses saw that the people *were* [a]unrestrained (for Aaron [b]had not restrained them, to *their* shame among their enemies),

2 26 then Moses stood in the entrance of the camp, and said, "Whoever *is* on the LORD's side—*come* to me!" And all the sons of Levi gathered themselves together to him.

27 And he said to them, "Thus says the LORD God of Israel: 'Let every man put his sword on his side, and go in and out from entrance to entrance throughout the camp, and [a]let every man kill his brother, every man his companion, and every man his neighbor.' "

28 So the sons of Levi did according to the word of Moses. And about three thousand men of the people fell that day.

29 [a]Then Moses said, [1]"Consecrate yourselves today to the LORD, that He may bestow on you a blessing this day, for every man has opposed his son and his brother."

30 Now it came to pass on the next day that Moses said to the people, [a]"You have committed a great sin. So now I will go up to the LORD; [b]perhaps I can [c]make atonement for your sin."

31 Then Moses [a]returned to the LORD and said, "Oh, these people have committed a great sin, and have [b]made for themselves a god of gold!

32 "Yet now, if You will forgive their sin—but if not, I pray, [a]blot me [b]out of Your book which You have written."

33 And the LORD said to Moses, [a]"Whoever has sinned against Me, I will [b]blot him out of My book.

34 "Now therefore, go, lead the people to *the place* of which I have [a]spoken to you. [b]Behold, My Angel shall go before you. Nevertheless, [c]in the day when I [d]visit for punishment, I will visit punishment upon them for their sin."

35 So the LORD plagued the people because of [a]what they did with the calf which Aaron made.

The Command to Leave Sinai

33 Then the LORD said to Moses, "Depart *and* go up from here, you [a]and the people whom you have brought out of the land of Egypt, to the land of which I swore to Abraham, Isaac, and Jacob, saying, [b]'To your descendants I will give it.'

2 [a]"And I will send *My* Angel before you, [b]and I will drive out the Canaanite

16 [a]Ex. 31:18
19 [a]Deut. 9:16, 17
20 [a]Num. 5:17, 24; Deut. 9:21
21 [a]Gen. 26:10
22 [a]Ex. 14:11; Deut. 9:24
25 [a]Ex. 33:4, 5 [b]2 Chr. 28:19
27 [a]Num. 25:5–13
29 [a]Ex. 28:41; 1 Sam. 15:18, 22; Prov. 21:3; Zech. 13:3 [1]Lit. *Fill your hand*
30 [a]1 Sam. 12:20, 23 [b]2 Sam. 16:12 [c]Num. 25:13
31 [a]Deut. 9:18 [b]Ex. 20:23
32 [a]Ps. 69:28; Is. 4:3; Mal. 3:16; Rom. 9:3 [b]Dan. 12:1; Phil. 4:3; Rev. 3:5; 21:27
33 [a]Lev. 23:30; [Ezek. 18:4; 33:2, 14, 15] [b]Ex. 17:14; Deut. 29:20; Ps. 9:5; Rev. 3:5; 21:27
34 [a]Ex. 3:17 [b]Ex. 23:20; Josh. 5:14 [c]Deut. 32:35; Rom. 2:5, 6 [d]Ps. 89:32
35 [a]Neh. 9:18

CHAPTER 33

1 [a]Ex. 32:1, 7, 13; Josh. 3:17 [b]Gen. 12:7
2 [a]Ex. 32:34; Josh. 5:14 [b]Ex. 23:27–31; Josh. 24:11

32:19 The shattered **tablets** symbolized their shattered relationship with Yahweh.
32:20 Drinking the gold dust was to serve as a sign to the people that the golden image was totally destroyed.
32:21–35 Those who *sin must be punished.* If God had not *punished idolatrous* Israel, He would not have been true to His nature and would have seemed to condone this sin.
32:25 Aaron's lack of leadership resulted in the people's being out of control and vulnerable to evil.
32:26–29 See section 2 of Truth-In-Action at the end of Ex.
32:26–28 Those who had remained loyal to Yahweh's way brought control back by killing 3,000 of those caught in the very act of calf worship. The group was led by loyal **sons of Levi**.
32:33–35 Yahweh's response, that only He can blot out their sin and that only at their request, shows the importance of individual, personal repentance. The undefined punishment was temporarily stayed (v. 34), coming sometime later in the form of a plague (v. 35).
33:1–6 Yahweh's intent was that Israel continue on, in spite of her sin.

and the Amorite and the Hittite and the Perizzite and the Hivite and the Jebusite.
3 "*Go up* [a]to a land flowing with milk and honey; for I will not go up in your midst, lest [b]I [1]consume you on the way, for you *are* a [c]stiff-necked[2] people."
4 And when the people heard this bad news, [a]they mourned, [b]and no one put on his ornaments.
5 For the LORD had said to Moses, "Say to the children of Israel, 'You *are* a stiff-necked people. I could come up into your midst in one moment and consume you. Now therefore, take off your [1]ornaments, that I may [a]know what to do to you.' "
6 So the children of Israel stripped themselves of their ornaments by Mount Horeb.

Moses Meets with the LORD

7 Moses took his tent and pitched it outside the camp, far from the camp, and [a]called it the tabernacle of meeting. And it came to pass *that* everyone who [b]sought the LORD went out to the tabernacle of meeting which *was* outside the camp.
8 So it was, whenever Moses went out to the tabernacle, *that* all the people rose, and each man stood [a]*at* his tent door and watched Moses until he had gone into the tabernacle.
9 And it came to pass, when Moses entered the tabernacle, that the pillar of cloud descended and stood *at* the door of the tabernacle, and *the LORD* [a]talked with Moses.
10 All the people saw the pillar of cloud standing *at* the tabernacle door, and all the people rose and [a]worshiped, each man *in* his tent door.
11 So [a]the LORD spoke to Moses face to face, as a man speaks to his *friend. And he would return to the camp, but [b]his *servant Joshua the son of Nun, a young man, did not depart from the tabernacle.

The Promise of God's Presence

12 Then Moses said to the LORD, "See, [a]You say to me, 'Bring up this people.' But You have not let me know whom You will send with me. Yet You have said, [b]'I know you by name, and you have also found *grace in My sight.'
13 "Now therefore, I pray, [a]if I have found grace in Your sight, [b]show me now Your way, that I may know You and that I may find grace in Your sight. And consider that this nation *is* [c]Your people."
14 And He said, [a]"My Presence will go 3
with you, and I will **give** you [b]**rest.**"

> **WORD WEALTH**
>
> **33:14 give rest,** *nu'ach* (noo-*ahch*); Strong's #5117: To rest, settle down; to be soothed or quieted; to be secure; to be still; to dwell peacefully. This verb occurs about 65 times, first in Gen. 8:4, which states that the ark rested on the mountains of Ararat. *Nu'ach* is the verb that describes the Spirit of God resting upon the Messiah (Is. 11:2), or upon the 70 elders of Israel (Num. 11:25). The name "Noah" ("Rest-Giver," or "Comforter") is derived from *nu'ach;* see Gen. 5:29. In the present reference, God's presence will give rest to His people, that is, His presence soothes, comforts, settles, consoles, and quiets us.

15 Then he said to Him, [a]"If Your Pres- 3
ence does not go *with us*, do not bring us up from here.
16 "For how then will it be known that Your people and I have found grace in Your sight, [a]except You go with us? So we [b]shall be separate, Your people and I, from all the people who *are* upon the face of the earth."
17 So the LORD said to Moses, [a]"I will also do this thing that you have spoken; for you have found grace in My sight, and I know you by name."
18 And he said, "Please, show me [a]Your glory."
19 Then He said, "I will make all My [a]goodness pass before you, and I will

3 [a]Ex. 3:8 [b]Num. 16:21, 45 [c]Ex. 32:9; 33:5 [1]*destroy* [2]*stubborn*
4 [a]Num. 14:1, 39 [b]Ezra 9:3; Esth. 4:1, 4; Ezek. 24:17, 23
5 [a][Ps. 139:23] [1]*jewelry*
7 [a]Ex. 29:42, 43 [b]Deut. 4:29
8 [a]Num. 16:27
9 [a]Ex. 25:22; 31:18; Ps. 99:7
10 [a]Ex. 4:31
11 [a]Num. 12:8; Deut. 34:10 [b]Ex. 24:13
*See WW at Prov. 17:17. • See WW at 1 Chr. 15:2.
12 [a]Ex. 3:10; 32:34 [b]Ex. 33:17; John 10:14, 15; 2 Tim. 2:19
*See WW at Zech. 12:10.
13 [a]Ex. 34:9 [b]Ps. 25:4; 27:11; 86:11; 119:33 [c]Ex. 3:7, 10; 5:1; 32:12, 14; Deut. 9:26, 29
14 [a]Ex. 3:12; Deut. 4:37; Is. 63:9 [b]Deut. 12:10; 25:19; Josh. 21:44; 22:4
15 [a]Ex. 33:3
16 [a]Num. 14:14 [b]Ex. 34:10; Deut. 4:7, 34
17 [a][James 5:16]
18 [a]Ex. 24:16, 17; [1 Tim. 6:16]
19 [a]Ex. 34:6, 7

33:5 God decided to withdraw Himself from their **midst,** news so dreadful the people could not wear any festive dress. **That . . . to do to you** shows there was an indefinite time in which they were unaware of God's final verdict.
33:7 The tabernacle of meeting here was the place of God's presence. It was a sort of portable, small-scale tabernacle for special times of communion with God, especially before the full tabernacle was complete. It had none of the tabernacle furnishings, however, and is different from that named in 27:21 (see note). Moses placed it a great distance from the camp because of the desecration by the molded calf.
33:12–17 This completes the scenario suspended in v. 6.
33:14 See section 3 of Truth-In-Action at the end of Ex.
33:15 See section 3 of Truth-In-Action at the end of Ex.
33:18 Moses desired to see God's **glory** (literally "weight") that is, the inner reality that makes God who He is.
33:19–23 God cannot grant Moses' full request. He does, however, reveal to Moses that He is partially understood through His actions in history and through various characteristics associated with His name (v. 19; see notes on 3:14 and 34:6, 7).

proclaim the name of the LORD before
you. [b]I will *be gracious to whom I will
be [c]gracious, and I will have compassion on whom I will have compassion."
20 But He said, "You cannot see My
face; for [a]no man shall see Me, and
live."
21 And the LORD said, "Here is a place
by Me, and you shall stand on the rock.
22 "So it shall be, while My glory
passes by, that I will put you [a]in the
cleft of the rock, and will [b]cover you
with My hand while I pass by.
23 "Then I will take away My hand,
and you shall see My back; but My face
shall [a]not be seen."

Moses Makes New Tablets

34 And the LORD said to Moses,
[a]"Cut two tablets of stone like
the first *ones*, and [b]I will write on *these*
tablets the words that were on the first
tablets which you broke.
2 "So be ready in the morning, and
come up in the morning to Mount Sinai, and present yourself to Me there
[a]on the top of the mountain.
3 "And no *man shall [a]come up with
you, and let no man be seen throughout
all the mountain; let neither flocks nor
herds *feed before that mountain."
4 So he cut two tablets of stone like
the first *ones*. Then Moses rose early
in the morning and *went up Mount
Sinai, as the LORD had commanded
him; and he took in his hand the two
tablets of stone.
5 Now the LORD descended in the
[a]cloud and stood with him there, and
[b]proclaimed the name of the LORD.
6 And the LORD passed before him
and proclaimed, "The LORD, the LORD
[a]God, merciful and gracious, longsuffering, and abounding in [b]goodness
and [c]truth,
7 [a]"keeping mercy for thousands,
[b]forgiving iniquity and transgression
and sin, [c]by no means *clearing *the
guilty*, visiting the iniquity of the fathers upon the children and the children's children to the third and the
fourth generation."
8 So Moses made haste and [a]bowed
his head toward the earth, and worshiped.

19 [b][Rom. 9:15, 16, 18] [c][Rom. 4:4, 16] *See WW at Mal. 1:9.
20 [a][Gen. 32:30]
22 [a]Is. 2:21 [b]Ps. 91:1, 4
23 [a][John 1:18]

CHAPTER 34

1 [a][Ex. 24:12; 31:18; 32:15, 16, 19] [b]Deut. 10:2, 4
2 [a]Ex. 19:11, 18, 20
3 [a]Ex. 19:12, 13; 24:9–11 *See WW at Is. 32:2. • See WW at Is. 40:11.
4 *See WW at Ex. 19:20.
5 [a]Ex. 19:9 [b]Ex. 33:19
6 [a]Neh. 9:17 [b]Rom. 2:4 [c]Ps. 108:4
7 [a]Ex. 20:6 [b]Ps. 103:3, 4 [c]Job 10:14 *See WW at Num. 14:18.
8 [a]Ex. 4:31

9 [a]Ex. 33:12–16 [b]Ex. 33:3 [c]Ps. 33:12; 94:14 [1]*stubborn* *See WW at Ps. 103:3.
10 [a]Deut. 5:2 [b]Ps. 77:14 [c]Ps. 145:6 [1]*wonderful acts* *See WW at Judg. 13:19.
11 [a]Deut. 6:25 [b]Ex. 23:20–33; 33:2
12 [a]Ex. 23:32, 33
13 [a]Deut. 12:3 [b]2 Kin. 18:4
14 [a][Ex. 20:3–5] [b][Is. 9:6; 57:15] [c][Deut. 4:24]
15 [a]Judg. 2:17 [b]Num. 25:1, 2 [c]1 Cor. 8:4, 7, 10
16 [a]Gen. 28:1 [b]Num. 25:1, 2
17 [a]Ex. 20:4, 23; 32:8
18 [a]Ex. 12:15, 16 [b]Ex. 12:2; 13:4 *See WW at Num. 9:2.

9 Then he said, "If now I have found
grace in Your sight, O Lord, [a]let my
Lord, I pray, go among us, even though
we *are* a [b]stiff-necked[1] people; and
*pardon our iniquity and our sin, and
take us as [c]Your inheritance."

The Covenant Renewed

10 And He said: "Behold, [a]I make a
covenant. Before all your people I will
[b]do [1]marvels* such as have not been
done in all the earth, nor in any nation;
and all the people among whom you
are shall see the work of the LORD. For
it *is* [c]an awesome thing that I will do
with you.
11 [a]"Observe what I command you
this day. Behold, [b]I am driving out
from before you the Amorite and the
Canaanite and the Hittite and the Perizzite and the Hivite and the Jebusite.
12 [a]"Take heed to yourself, lest you
make a covenant with the inhabitants
of the land where you are going, lest
it be a snare in your midst.
13 "But you shall [a]destroy their altars,
break their *sacred* pillars, and [b]cut
down their wooden images
14 "(for you shall worship [a]no other
god, for the LORD, whose [b]name *is* Jealous, *is* a [c]jealous God),
15 "lest you make a covenant with the
inhabitants of the land, and they
[a]play the harlot with their gods and
make sacrifice to their gods, and *one
of them* [b]invites you and you [c]eat of
his sacrifice,
16 "and you take of [a]his daughters for
your sons, and his daughters [b]play the
harlot with their gods and make your
sons play the harlot with their gods.
17 [a]"You shall make no molded gods
for yourselves.
18 "The Feast of [a]Unleavened Bread
you shall keep. Seven days you shall
eat unleavened bread, as I commanded
you, in the *appointed time of the
month of Abib; for in the [b]month of
Abib you came out from Egypt.
19 [a]"All [1]that open the womb *are*
Mine, and every male firstborn among
your livestock, *whether* ox or sheep.
20 "But [a]the firstborn of a donkey you

19 [a]Ex. 13:2; 22:29 [1]*the firstborn* 20 [a]Ex. 13:13

34:6, 7 In a more complete definition of His name, **the LORD** (see note on 3:14), God defines Himself in terms of eight characteristics displayed to Israel. These would have been readily apparent in the molded calf incident.

34:10–28 The covenant is renewed.

34:13 ***Sacred* pillars,** or Asherim, were wooden poles that symbolized various gods.

34:14 The first two Commandments are reinforced through the revelation of another covenant name.

34:18 See notes on 12:1–11 and 12:14–20.

34:19, 20 See note on 13:2.

shall redeem with a lamb. And if you
will not redeem *him,* then you shall
break his neck. All the firstborn of
your sons you shall redeem. And none
shall appear before Me [b]empty-
handed.
21 [a]"Six days you shall work, but on
the seventh day you shall *rest; in
plowing time and in harvest you shall
rest.
3 22 "And you shall observe the Feast of
Weeks, of the firstfruits of wheat harvest, and the Feast of Ingathering at
the year's end.
23 [a]"Three times in the year all your
men shall appear before the Lord, the
LORD God of Israel.
24 "For I will [a]cast out the nations before you and enlarge your borders; neither will any man covet your land
when you go up to appear before
the LORD your God three times in the
year.
25 "You shall not offer the blood of My
sacrifice with leaven, [a]nor shall the
sacrifice of the Feast of the Passover
be left until morning.
26 [a]"The first of the firstfruits of your
land you shall bring to the house of
the LORD your God. You shall not boil
a young goat in its mother's milk."
27 Then the LORD said to Moses,
"Write [a]these words, for according to
the tenor of these words I have **made**
a covenant with you and with Israel."

WORD WEALTH

34:27 made, *karat* (kah-*rat*); Strong's #3772: To cut, cut down, cut off, cut in pieces; to cut a covenant. This verb appears almost 300 times in the OT. Frequently the meaning is cutting something off, or cutting something down. The most important use of *karat* is in the often used phrase "cut a covenant," translated "make a covenant." *Karat* was the most fitting verb to use due to the "cutting up" of sacrificial animals when a covenant was inaugurated. See especially Gen. 15:7–21 for a good illustration of "cutting" a covenant. Circumcision, another instance of cutting, is the covenant that admits a Hebrew male into the congregation of the Lord. In the NT, the everlasting covenant was made when God's Lamb was pierced to death for His people. See Heb. 9:15; 10:10–22.

20 [b]Ex. 22:29; 23:15
21 [a]Ex. 20:9; 23:12; 31:15; 35:2
*See WW at Ex. 16:30.
23 [a]Ex. 23:14–17
24 [a][Ex. 33:2]
25 [a]Ex. 12:10
26 [a]Ex. 23:19
27 [a]Deut. 31:9

28 [a]So he was there with the LORD
forty days and forty nights; he neither
ate bread nor drank water. And [b]He
wrote on the tablets the words of
the covenant, the [1]Ten Commandments.

The Shining Face of Moses

29 Now it was so, when Moses came
down from Mount Sinai (and the
[a]two tablets of the Testimony *were* in
Moses' hand when he came down from
the mountain), that Moses did not
know that [b]the skin of his face shone
while he talked with Him.
30 So when Aaron and all the children
of Israel saw Moses, behold, the skin
of his face shone, and they were afraid
to come near him.
31 Then Moses called to them, and
Aaron and all the rulers of the congregation returned to him; and Moses
talked with them.
32 Afterward all the children of Israel
came near, [a]and he gave them as commandments all that the LORD had spoken with him on Mount Sinai.
33 And when Moses had finished
speaking with them, he put [a]a veil on
his face.
34 But [a]whenever Moses went in before the LORD to speak with Him, he
would take the veil off until he came
out; and he would come out and speak
to the children of Israel whatever he
had been commanded.
35 And whenever the children of Israel
saw the face of Moses, that the skin
of Moses' face shone, then Moses
would put the veil on his face again,
until he went in to speak with Him.

Sabbath Regulations

35 Then Moses gathered all the
congregation of the children of
Israel together, and said to them,
[a]"These *are* the words which the LORD
has commanded *you* to do:
2 "Work shall be done for [a]six days,

28 [a]Ex. 24:18
[b]Ex. 34:1, 4 [1]Lit. *Ten Words*
29 [a]Ex. 32:15
[b]2 Cor. 3:7
32 [a]Ex. 24:3
33 [a][2 Cor. 3:13, 14]
34 [a][2 Cor. 3:13–16]

CHAPTER 35

1 [a]Ex. 34:32
2 [a]Lev. 23:3

34:21 See note on 20:8.
34:22 See section 3 of Truth-In-Action at the end of Ex.
34:22 See note on 23:16.
34:29–35 The shining of Moses' **face** symbolized God's acceptance of his leadership in contrast to Israel's earlier rejection (see note on 32:1–6). We are not told why Moses veiled his face. Paul says it was so the Israelites might not see the end of its fading splendor (2 Cor. 3:13).

35:1—40:33 A repetition of what was covered in chs. 25—31, with the exception that instead of merely describing the tabernacle and its content, it is now being built. For approximately 300 years the tabernacle would be the focal point of Israel's religious life, until it was replaced by Solomon's temple. See note on 25:9.
35:1–3 See note on 20:8.

but the seventh day shall be a holy day
for you, a Sabbath of rest to the LORD.
Whoever does any work on it shall be
put to [b]death.
3 [a]"You shall kindle no fire throughout your dwellings on the Sabbath
day."

Offerings for the Tabernacle

4 And Moses spoke to all the congregation of the children of Israel, saying,
[a]"This *is* the thing which the LORD
commanded, saying:
5 'Take from among you an offering
to the LORD. [a]Whoever *is* of a willing
*heart, let him bring it as an offering
to the LORD: [b]gold, silver, and bronze;
6 [a]'blue, purple, and scarlet *thread,*
fine linen, and [b]goats' *hair;*
7 'ram skins dyed red, badger skins,
and acacia wood;
8 'oil for the light, [a]and spices for the
anointing oil and for the sweet incense;
9 'onyx stones, and stones to be set
in the ephod and in the breastplate.

Articles of the Tabernacle

10 [a]'All *who are* gifted artisans among
you shall come and make all that the
LORD has commanded:
11 [a]'the tabernacle, its tent, its covering, its clasps, its boards, its bars, its
pillars, and its sockets;
12 [a]'the ark and its poles, *with* the
mercy seat, and the veil of the covering;
13 'the [a]table and its poles, all its utensils, [b]and the showbread;
14 'also [a]the lampstand for the light,
its utensils, its lamps, and the oil for
the light;
15 [a]'the incense altar, its poles, [b]the
anointing oil, [c]the sweet incense, and
the screen for the door at the entrance
of the tabernacle;
16 [a]'the altar of burnt offering with its
bronze grating, its poles, all its utensils, *and* the laver and its base;
17 [a]'the hangings of the court, its pillars, their sockets, and the screen for
the gate of the court;
18 'the pegs of the tabernacle, the pegs
of the court, and their cords;
19 [a]'the [1]garments of ministry, for
ministering in the holy *place*—the holy
garments for Aaron the priest and the
garments of his sons, to minister as
priests.' "

2 [b]Num. 15:32–36
3 [a]Ex. 12:16; 16:23
4 [a]Ex. 25:1, 2
5 [a]Ex. 25:2; 1 Chr. 29:14; Mark 12:41–44; 2 Cor. 8:10–12; 9:7 [b]Ex. 38:24 *See WW at Ps. 37:4.
6 [a]Ex. 36:8 [b]Ex. 36:14
8 [a]Ex. 25:6; 30:23–25
10 [a]Ex. 31:2–6; 36:1, 2
11 [a]Ex. 26:1, 2; 36:14
12 [a]Ex. 25:10–22
13 [a]Ex. 25:23 [b]Ex. 25:30; Lev. 24:5, 6
14 [a]Ex. 25:31
15 [a]Ex. 30:1 [b]Ex. 30:25 [c]Ex. 30:34–38
16 [a]Ex. 27:1–8
17 [a]Ex. 27:9–18
19 [a]Ex. 31:10; 39:1, 41 [1]Or *woven garments*

The Tabernacle Offerings Presented

20 And all the congregation of the chil- 5
dren of Israel departed from the presence of Moses.
21 Then everyone came [a]whose
heart [1]was stirred, and everyone
whose spirit was willing, *and* they
[b]brought the LORD's offering for the
work of the tabernacle of meeting, for
all its service, and for the holy garments.
22 They came, both men and women,
as many as had a willing heart, *and*
brought [a]earrings and nose rings, rings
and necklaces, all [b]jewelry of gold, that
is, every man who *made* an offering
of gold to the LORD.
23 And [a]every man, with whom was
found blue, purple, and scarlet *thread,*
fine linen, and goats' *hair,* red skins
of rams, and [1]badger skins, brought
them.
24 Everyone who offered an offering
of silver or bronze brought the LORD's
offering. And everyone with whom
was found acacia wood for any work
of the service, brought *it.*
25 All the women *who were* [a]gifted
artisans spun yarn with their hands,
and brought what they had spun, of
blue, purple, *and* scarlet, and fine
linen.
26 And all the women whose hearts
[1]stirred with wisdom spun yarn of
goats' *hair.*
27 [a]The rulers brought onyx stones,
and the stones to be set in the **ephod**
and in the breastplate,

WORD WEALTH

35:27 ephod, *'ephod* (ay-*phode*); Strong's #646: Ephod, a vest or robe, a priestly garment probably extending from the shoulders to the waist; an extended piece called the "robe of the ephod" attached to the upper part, thus making a full-length garment. The ephod was ornately woven and decorated with attached pieces, such as the breastplate. The ephod consisted of intricate linen work, a woven waistband, and two gold chains, which securely fastened the two onyx stones on which were written the names of the tribes of Israel. The breastplate itself contained twelve precious stones, each stone representing one of the tribes. Thus the high priest carried the names and the concerns of Israel's twelve families over his heart (28:29).

21 [a]Ex. 25:2; 35:5, 22, 26, 29; 36:2 [b]Ex. 35:24 [1]Lit. *lifted him up*
22 [a]Ex. 32:2, 3 [b]Ex. 11:2
23 [a]1 Chr. 29:8 [1]Or *dolphin*
25 [a]Ex. 28:3; 31:6; 36:1
26 [1]Lit. *lifted them up*
27 [a]1 Chr. 29:6; Ezra 2:68

35:4–9 See note on 25:2.
35:10–29 Emphasis was placed on the willingness of the people to work and the presentation of the offerings (v. 22).
35:20–29 See section 5 of Truth-In-Action at the end of Ex.

28 and [a]spices and oil for the light, for
the anointing oil, and for the sweet incense.
29 The children of Israel brought a
[a]freewill offering to the LORD, all the
men and women whose hearts were
willing to bring *material* for all kinds
of work which the LORD, by the hand
of Moses, had commanded to be done.

The Artisans Called by God

4 **30** And Moses said to the children of
Israel, "See, [a]the LORD has called by
name Bezalel the son of Uri, the son
of Hur, of the tribe of Judah;
31 "and He has filled him with the
Spirit of God, in wisdom and understanding, in knowledge and all manner
of workmanship,
32 "to design artistic works, to work
in gold and silver and bronze,
33 "in cutting jewels for setting, in
carving wood, and to work in all manner of artistic workmanship.
34 "And He has put in his heart the
ability to teach, *in* him and [a]Aholiab
the son of Ahisamach, of the tribe of
Dan.
35 "He has [a]filled them with skill to
do all manner of work of the engraver
and the designer and the tapestry
maker, in blue, purple, and scarlet
thread, and fine linen, and of the
weaver—those who do every work and
those who design artistic works.
36 "And Bezalel and Aholiab, and
every [a]gifted artisan in whom
the LORD has put wisdom and understanding, to know how to do all manner of work for the service of the
[b]sanctuary,[1] shall do according to all
that the LORD has commanded."

The People Give More than Enough

2 Then Moses called Bezalel and
Aholiab, and every gifted artisan in
whose heart the LORD had put wisdom,
everyone [a]whose heart [1]was stirred, to
come and do the work.
3 And they received from Moses all
the [a]offering which the children of Israel [b]had brought for the work of the
service of making the sanctuary. So
they continued bringing to him freewill
offerings every morning.
4 Then all the craftsmen who were
doing all the work of the sanctuary
came, each from the work he was doing,
5 and they spoke to Moses, saying,
[a]"The people bring much more than
*enough for the service of the work
which the LORD commanded *us* to do."
6 So Moses gave a commandment,
and they caused it to be proclaimed
throughout the camp, saying, "Let neither man nor woman do any more
work for the offering of the sanctuary."
And the people were restrained from
bringing,
7 for the material they had was *sufficient for all the work to be done—
indeed too [a]much.

Building the Tabernacle

8 [a]Then all the gifted artisans among
them who worked on the tabernacle
made ten curtains woven of fine linen,
and of blue, purple, and scarlet *thread;*
with artistic designs of cherubim they
made them.
9 The length of each curtain *was*
twenty-eight cubits, and the width of
each curtain four cubits; the curtains
were all the same size.
10 And he coupled five curtains to one
another, and *the other* five curtains he
coupled to one another.
11 He made loops of blue *yarn* on the
edge of the curtain on the selvedge of
one set; likewise he did on the outer
edge of *the other* curtain of the second
set.
12 [a]Fifty loops he made on one curtain,
and fifty loops he made on the edge
of the curtain on the end of the second
set; the loops held one *curtain* to another.
13 And he made fifty clasps of gold,
and coupled the curtains to one another with the clasps, that it might be
one tabernacle.
14 [a]He made curtains of goats' *hair* for
the tent over the tabernacle; he made
eleven curtains.
15 The length of each curtain *was*
thirty cubits, and the width of each curtain four cubits; the eleven curtains
were the same size.
16 He coupled five curtains by themselves and six curtains by themselves.
17 And he made fifty loops on the edge
of the curtain that is outermost in one
set, and fifty loops he made on the edge
of the curtain of the second set.

28 [a]Ex. 30:23
29 [a]Ex. 35:5, 21; 36:3; 1 Chr. 29:9
30 [a]Ex. 31:1–6
34 [a]Ex. 31:6
35 [a]Ex. 31:3, 6; 35:31; 1 Kin. 7:14; 2 Chr. 2:14; Is. 28:26

CHAPTER 36

1 [a]Ex. 28:3; 31:6; 35:10, 35 [b]Ex. 25:8 [1]*holy place*
2 [a]Ex. 35:21, 26; 1 Chr. 29:5, 9, 17 [1]*lifted him up*
3 [a]Ex. 35:5 [b]Ex. 35:27
5 [a]2 Chr. 24:14; 31:6–10; [2 Cor. 8:2, 3] *See WW at Mal. 3:10.
7 [a]1 Kin. 8:64 *See WW at Mal. 3:10.
8 [a]Ex. 26:1–14
12 [a]Ex. 26:5
14 [a]Ex. 26:7

35:30—36:1 See note on 31:3.
35:30–35 See section 4 of Truth-In-Action at the end of Ex.
36:2–7 The tabernacle was completed free of debt because of the people's willingness.
36:8–19 See notes on 26:1, 2 and 26:7, 14.

18 He also made fifty bronze clasps to
couple the tent together, that it might
be one.
19 [a]Then he made a covering for the
tent of ram skins dyed red, and a covering of [1]badger skins above *that*.
20 For the tabernacle [a]he made boards
of acacia wood, standing upright.
21 The length of each board *was* ten
cubits, and the width of each board a
cubit and a half.
22 Each board had two [1]tenons [a]for
binding one to another. Thus he made
for all the boards of the tabernacle.
23 And he made boards for the tabernacle, twenty boards for the south side.
24 Forty sockets of silver he made to
go under the twenty boards: two sockets under each of the boards for its two
tenons.
25 And for the other side of the tabernacle, the north side, he made twenty
boards
26 and their forty sockets of silver: two
sockets under each of the boards.
27 For the west side of the tabernacle
he made six boards.
28 He also made two boards for the
two back corners of the tabernacle.
29 And they were coupled at the bottom and [1]coupled together at the top
by one ring. Thus he made both of
them for the two corners.
30 So there were eight boards and
their sockets—sixteen sockets of silver—two sockets under each of the
boards.
31 And he made [a]bars of acacia wood:
five for the boards on one side of the
tabernacle,
32 five bars for the boards on the other
side of the tabernacle, and five bars for
the boards of the tabernacle on the far
side westward.
33 And he made the middle bar to pass
through the boards from one end to the
other.
34 He overlaid the boards with gold,
made their rings of gold *to be* holders
for the bars, and overlaid the bars with
gold.
35 And he made [a]a veil of blue, purple,
and scarlet *thread*, and fine woven
linen; it was worked *with* an artistic
design of cherubim.
36 He made for it four pillars of acacia
wood, and overlaid them with gold,
with their hooks of gold; and he cast
four *sockets of* silver for them.
37 He also made a [a]screen for the tabernacle door, of blue, purple, and scarlet *thread*, and fine woven linen, made
by a [1]weaver,
38 and its five pillars with their hooks.
And he overlaid their capitals and their
rings with gold, but their five sockets
were bronze.

Making the Ark of the Testimony

37 Then [a]Bezalel made [b]the ark of
acacia wood; two and a half cubits *was* its length, a cubit and a half
its width, and a cubit and a half its
height.
2 He overlaid it with pure gold inside
and outside, and made a molding of
gold all around it.
3 And he cast for it four rings of gold
to be set in its four corners: two rings
on one side, and two rings on the other
side of it.
4 He made poles of acacia wood, and
overlaid them with gold.
5 And he put the poles into the rings
at the sides of the ark, to bear the ark.
6 He also made the [a]mercy seat of
pure gold; two and a half cubits *was*
its length and a cubit and a half its
width.
7 He made two cherubim of beaten
gold; he made them of one piece at the
two ends of the mercy seat:
8 one *cherub at one end on this side,
and the other cherub at the *other* end
on that side. He made the cherubim at
the two ends *of one piece* with the
mercy seat.
9 The cherubim spread out *their*
wings above, *and* covered the [a]mercy
seat with their wings. They faced one
another; the faces of the cherubim
were toward the mercy seat.

Making the Table for the Showbread

10 He made [a]the table of acacia wood;
two cubits *was* its length, a cubit its
width, and a cubit and a half its height.
11 And he overlaid it with pure gold,
and made a molding of gold all around
it.
12 Also he made a frame of a handbreadth all around it, and made a
molding of gold for the frame all
around it.
13 And he cast for it four rings of gold,
and put the rings on the four corners
that *were* at its four legs.

19 [a]Ex. 26:14 [1]Or *dolphin*
20 [a]Ex. 26:15–29
22 [a]Ex. 26:17 [1]Projections for joining, lit. *hands*
29 [1]Lit. *doubled*
31 [a]Ex. 26:26–29
35 [a]Ex. 26:31–37
37 [a]Ex. 26:36 [1]Lit. *variegator*, a weaver in colors

CHAPTER 37

1 [a]Ex. 35:30; 36:1 [b]Ex. 25:10–20
6 [a]Ex. 25:17
8 *See WW at Ex. 25:18.
9 [a]Ex. 25:20
10 [a]Ex. 25:23–29

36:20–38 See notes on 26:15, 16 and 26:26.
37:1–9 See notes on 25:10; 25:17; 25:18.
37:10–16 See notes on 25:23 and 25:30.

14 The rings were close to the frame,
as holders for the poles to bear the table.
15 And he made the poles of acacia
wood to bear the table, and overlaid
them with gold.
16 He made of pure gold the utensils
which were on the table: its [a]dishes,
its cups, its bowls, and its pitchers for
pouring.

16 [a]Ex. 25:29

17 [a]Ex. 25:31–39

Making the Gold Lampstand

17 He also made the [a]lampstand of
pure gold; of hammered work he made
the lampstand. Its shaft, its branches,
its bowls, its *ornamental* knobs, and
its flowers were of the same piece.
18 And six branches came out of its
sides: three branches of the lampstand
out of one side, and three branches

37:17–24 See note on 25:31–40.

THE FURNITURE OF THE TABERNACLE (37:1)

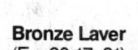

Ark of the Covenant
(Ex. 25:10–22)
The ark was most sacred of all the furniture in the tabernacle. Here the Hebrews kept a copy of the Ten Commandments, which summarized the whole covenant.

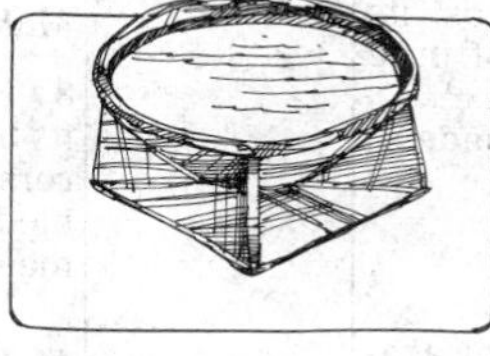

Bronze Laver
(Ex. 30:17–21)
It was to the laver of bronze that the priests would come for cleansing. They must be pure to enter the presence of God.

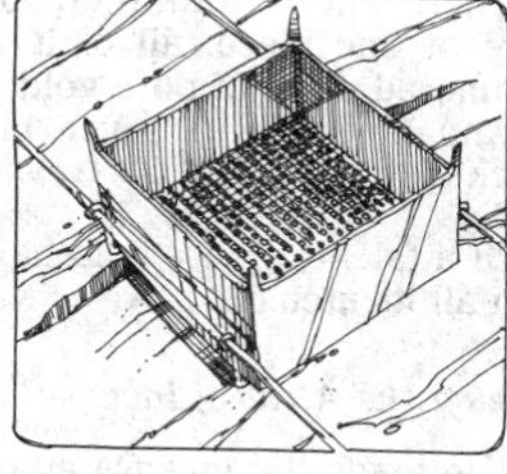

Altar of Burnt Offering
(Ex. 27:1–8)
Animal sacrifices were offered on this altar, located in the court in front of the tabernacle. The blood of the sacrifice was sprinkled on the four horns of the altar.

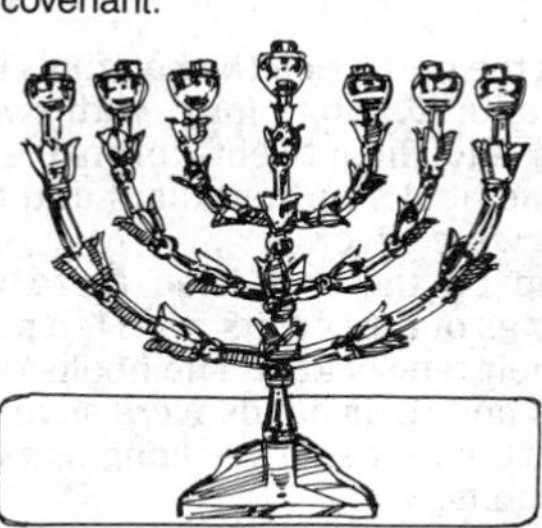

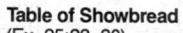

Gold Lampstand
(Ex. 25:31–40)
The gold lampstand stood in the holy place, opposite the table of showbread. It held seven lamps, flat bowls in which a wick lay with one end in the oil of the bowl and the lighted end hanging out.

Table of Showbread
(Ex. 25:23–30)
The table of showbread was a stand on which the offerings were placed. Always in God's presence on the table were the 12 loaves of bread representing the 12 tribes.

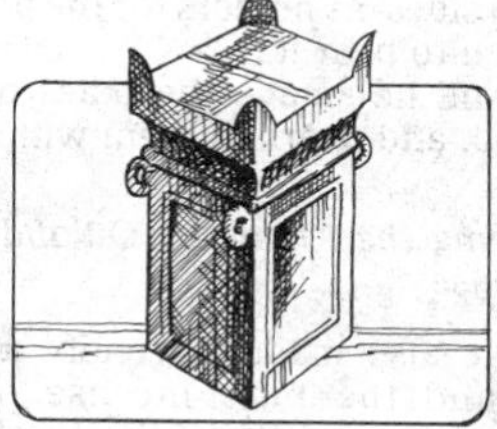

Altar of Incense
(Ex. 30:1–10)
The altar of incense inside the tabernacle was much smaller than the altar of burnt offering outside. The incense burned on the altar was a perfume of a sweet-smelling aroma.

See also Chart: The Plan of the Tabernacle (26:1).

of the lampstand out of the other side.

19 There were three bowls made like almond *blossoms* on one branch, with an *ornamental* knob and a flower, and three bowls made like almond *blossoms* on the other branch, with an *ornamental* knob and a flower—and so for the six branches coming out of the lampstand.

20 And on the lampstand itself *were* four bowls made like almond *blossoms, each with* its *ornamental* knob and flower.

21 *There was* a knob under the *first* two branches of the same, a knob under the *second* two branches of the same, and a knob under the *third* two branches of the same, according to the six branches extending from it.

22 Their knobs and their branches were of one piece; all of it *was* one hammered piece of pure gold.

23 And he made its seven lamps, its [a]wick-trimmers, and its trays of pure gold.

24 Of a talent of pure gold he made it, with all its utensils.

Making the Altar of Incense

25 [a]He made the incense altar of acacia wood. Its length *was* a cubit and its width a cubit—*it was* square—and two cubits *was* its height. Its horns were *of one piece* with it.

26 And he overlaid it with pure gold: its top, its sides all around, and its horns. He also made for it a molding of gold all around it.

27 He made two rings of gold for it under its molding, by its two corners on both sides, as holders for the poles with which to bear it.

28 And he [a]made the poles of acacia wood, and overlaid them with gold.

Making the Anointing Oil and the Incense

29 He also made [a]the holy anointing oil and the pure incense of sweet spices, according to the work of the perfumer.

Making the Altar of Burnt Offering

38 He made [a]the altar of burnt offering of acacia wood; five cubits *was* its length *and* five cubits its width—*it was* square—and its height *was* three cubits.

2 He made its horns on its four corners; the horns were *of one piece* with it. And he overlaid it with bronze.

3 He made all the utensils for the altar: the pans, the shovels, the basins, the forks, and the firepans; all its utensils he made of bronze.

4 And he made a grate of bronze network for the altar, under its rim, midway from the bottom.

5 He cast four rings for the four corners of the bronze grating, *as* holders for the poles.

6 And he made the poles of acacia wood, and overlaid them with bronze.

7 Then he put the poles into the rings on the sides of the altar, with which to bear it. He made the altar hollow with boards.

Making the Bronze Laver

8 He made [a]the laver of bronze and its base of bronze, from the bronze mirrors of the serving women who assembled at the door of the tabernacle of meeting.

Making the Court of the Tabernacle

9 Then he made [a]the court on the south side; the hangings of the court *were of* fine woven linen, one hundred cubits long.

10 There *were* twenty pillars for them, with twenty bronze sockets. The hooks of the pillars and their bands *were* silver.

11 On the north side *the hangings were* one hundred cubits *long*, with twenty pillars and their twenty bronze sockets. The hooks of the pillars and their bands *were* silver.

12 And on the west side *there were* hangings of fifty cubits, with ten pillars and their ten sockets. The hooks of the pillars and their bands *were* silver.

13 For the east side *the hangings were* fifty cubits.

14 The hangings of one side *of the gate were* fifteen cubits *long, with* their three pillars and their three sockets,

15 and the same for the other side of the court gate; on this side and that *were* hangings of fifteen cubits, *with* their three pillars and their three sockets.

23 [a]Num. 4:9
25 [a]Ex. 30:1–5
28 [a]Ex. 30:5
29 [a]Ex. 30:23–25

CHAPTER 38

1 [a]Ex. 27:1–8
8 [a]Ex. 30:18
9 [a]Ex. 27:9–19

37:25–28 See notes on 30:1–10.
37:29 Oil and . . . incense: See notes on 30:22–38.
38:1–7 See note on 27:1.
38:8 See note on 30:17–21.
38:9–20 See note on 27:9–19.

16 All the hangings of the court all around *were of* fine woven linen.
17 The sockets for the pillars *were* bronze, the hooks of the pillars and their bands *were* silver, and the overlay of their capitals *was* silver; and all the pillars of the court had bands of silver.
18 The screen for the gate of the court *was* woven of blue, purple, and scarlet *thread,* and of fine woven linen. The length *was* twenty cubits, and the height along its width *was* five cubits, corresponding to the hangings of the court.
19 And *there were* four pillars *with* their four sockets of bronze; their hooks *were* silver, and the overlay of their capitals and their bands *was* silver.
20 All the [a]pegs of the tabernacle, and of the court all around, *were* bronze.

Materials of the Tabernacle

21 [1]This is the inventory of the tabernacle, [a]the tabernacle of the Testimony, which was counted according to the commandment of Moses, for the service of the Levites, [b]by the hand of [c]Ithamar, son of Aaron the priest.
22 [a]Bezalel the son of Uri, the son of Hur, of the **tribe** of Judah, made all that the LORD had commanded Moses.

WORD WEALTH

38:22 tribe, *matteh* (mat-*teh*); Strong's #4294: Rod, staff, branch, tribe. Originally *matteh* meant "branch," as in a tree or on a vine. Since a patriarch's rod or staff comes from a branch, *matteh* naturally describes such a rod. Finally, *matteh* is used for a tribe of people, possibly because a tribe was united under a tribal staff, but more likely because it was seen as a "branch" of the family. This is certainly true of the tribes of Israel, which developed from the growing families of Jacob's twelve sons. In English, we also refer to a certain "branch" of one's family. This concept receives further reinforcement in Rom. 11:17–24, where Paul speaks of the "branches" as groups of people, showing that the family tree of God's household consists of branches from two sources: the native Jewish branches, and the branches God has chosen from among the Gentiles. Another word for "tribe" is *shevet,* which means "rod, staff, tribe." *Matteh* and *shevet* are used interchangeably in reference to the tribes of Israel.

20 [a]Ex. 27:19
21 [a]Num. 1:50, 53; 9:15; 10:11; 17:7, 8; 2 Chr. 24:6; Acts 7:44 [b]Num. 4:28, 33 [c]Ex. 28:1; Lev. 10:6, 16 [1]Lit. *These are the things appointed for*
22 [a]Ex. 31:2, 6; 1 Chr. 2:18–20
23 [a]Ex. 31:6; 36:1 [1]*skillful workman*
24 [a]Ex. 35:5, 22 [b]Ex. 30:13, 24; Lev. 5:15; 27:3, 25; Num. 3:47; 18:16
25 [a]Ex. 30:11–16; Num. 1:2
26 [a]Ex. 30:13, 15 [b]Ex. 12:37; Num. 1:46; 26:51 [1]Lit. *a head*
27 [a]Ex. 26:19, 21, 25, 32
28 [a]Ex. 27:17

CHAPTER 39

1 [a]Ex. 25:4; 35:23 [b]Ex. 31:10; 35:19 [c]Ex. 28:4 [1]Or *woven garments* [2]*sanctuary*

23 And with him *was* [a]Aholiab the son of Ahisamach, of the tribe of Dan, an engraver and [1]designer, a weaver of blue, purple, and scarlet *thread,* and of fine linen.
24 All the gold that was used in all the work of the holy *place,* that is, the gold of the [a]offering, was twenty-nine talents and seven hundred and thirty shekels, according to [b]the shekel of the sanctuary.
25 And the silver from those who were [a]numbered of the congregation *was* one hundred talents and one thousand seven hundred and seventy-five shekels, according to the shekel of the sanctuary:
26 [a]a bekah for [1]each man (*that is,* half a shekel, according to the shekel of the sanctuary), for everyone included in the numbering from twenty years old and above, for [b]six hundred and three thousand, five hundred and fifty *men.*
27 And from the hundred talents of silver were cast [a]the sockets of the sanctuary and the bases of the veil: one hundred sockets from the hundred talents, one talent for each socket.
28 Then from the one thousand seven hundred and seventy-five *shekels* he made hooks for the pillars, overlaid their capitals, and [a]made bands for them.
29 The offering of bronze *was* seventy talents and two thousand four hundred shekels.
30 And with it he made the sockets for the door of the tabernacle of meeting, the bronze altar, the bronze grating for it, and all the utensils for the altar,
31 the sockets for the court all around, the bases for the court gate, all the pegs for the tabernacle, and all the pegs for the court all around.

Making the Garments of the Priesthood

39 Of the [a]blue, purple, and scarlet *thread* they made [b]garments[1] of ministry, for ministering in the [2]holy *place,* and made the holy garments for Aaron, [c]as the LORD had commanded Moses.

38:21–31 This summary of the materials used in the tabernacle emphasizes its opulence and the people's freewill giving.
39:1 See note on 28:1–43.

Making the Ephod

2 [a]He made the [b]ephod of gold, blue,
purple, and scarlet *thread,* and of fine
woven linen.
3 And they beat the gold into thin
sheets and cut *it into* threads, to work
it in *with* the blue, purple, and scarlet
thread, and the fine linen, *into* artistic
designs.
4 They made shoulder straps for it to
couple *it* together; it was coupled together at its two edges.
5 And the intricately woven band of
his ephod that *was* on it *was* of the
same workmanship, *woven of* gold,
blue, purple, and scarlet *thread,* and
of fine woven linen, as the LORD had
commanded Moses.
6 [a]And they set onyx stones, enclosed
in [1]settings of gold; they were engraved, as signets are engraved, with
the names of the sons of Israel.
7 He put them on the shoulders of the
ephod *as* [a]**memorial** stones for the sons
of Israel, as the LORD had commanded
Moses.

> **WORD WEALTH**
>
> **39:7 memorial,** *zikron* (zeek-*roan*); Strong's #2146: A memorial, remembrance, record, memento; a written record; a momentous event, which is long to be remembered. Occurring 24 times, *zikron* is derived from the verb *zakar,* "to remember." The first occurrence of *zikron* in Scripture concerns the Passover; the day, the ceremony, and the meal constitute a memorial of God's mighty deeds (12:14). In the present reference, the stones representing the 12 tribes were placed on the ephod, which served to remind the high priest of each tribe by name. Compare Josh. 4:7. In Mal. 3:16, God made up a book of "remembrance," where those who think often of Him are listed, and will someday be like the jewels over Aaron's heart (v. 17).

Making the Breastplate

8 [a]And he made the breastplate, artistically woven like the workmanship
of the ephod, of gold, blue, purple,
and scarlet *thread,* and of fine woven
linen.
9 They made the breastplate square
by doubling it; a span *was* its length
and a span its width *when doubled.*
10 [a]And they set in it four rows of
stones: a row with a sardius, a topaz,
and an emerald was the first row;
11 the second row, a turquoise, a sapphire, and a diamond;
12 the third row, a jacinth, an agate,
and an amethyst;
13 the fourth row, a beryl, an onyx,
and a jasper. *They were* enclosed in
settings of gold in their mountings.
14 *There were* [a]twelve stones according to the names of the sons of Israel:
according to their names, *engraved like*
a signet, each one with its own name
according to the twelve tribes.
15 And they made chains for the
breastplate at the ends, like braided
cords of pure gold.
16 They also made two settings of gold
and two gold rings, and put the two
rings on the two ends of the breastplate.
17 And they put the two braided *chains*
of gold in the two rings on the ends
of the breastplate.
18 The two ends of the two braided
chains they fastened in the two settings, and put them on the shoulder
straps of the ephod in the front.
19 And they made two rings of gold
and put *them* on the two ends of the
breastplate, on the edge of it, which
was on the inward side of the ephod.
20 They made two *other* gold rings and
put them on the two shoulder straps,
underneath the ephod toward its front,
right at the seam above the intricately
woven band of the ephod.
21 And they bound the breastplate by
means of its rings to the rings of the
ephod with a blue cord, so that it would
be above the intricately woven band
of the ephod, and that the breastplate would not come loose from the
ephod, as the LORD had commanded
Moses.

Making the Other Priestly Garments

22 [a]He made the [b]robe of the ephod
of woven work, all of blue.
23 And *there was* an opening in the
middle of the robe, like the opening in
a coat of mail, *with* a woven binding
all around the opening, so that it would
not tear.
24 They made on the hem of the robe
pomegranates of blue, purple, and
scarlet, and of fine woven *linen.*
25 And they made [a]bells of pure gold,
and put the bells between the pome-

2 [a]Ex. 28:6–14 [b]Lev. 8:7
6 [a]Ex. 28:9–11 [1]*plaited work*
7 [a]Ex. 28:12, 29; Josh. 4:7
8 [a]Ex. 28:15–30
10 [a]Ex. 28:17
14 [a]Rev. 21:12
22 [a]Ex. 28:31–35 [b]Ex. 29:5; Lev. 8:7
25 [a]Ex. 28:33

39:2–7 See note on 28:5–14.
39:8–21 See note on 28:15–30.
39:22–26 See notes on 28:31–35 and 28:33, 34.

granates on the hem of the robe all
around between the pomegranates:
26 a bell and a pomegranate, a bell and
a pomegranate, all around the hem of
the robe to [1]minister in, as the LORD
had commanded Moses.
27 [a]They made tunics, artistically
woven of fine linen, for Aaron and his
sons,
28 [a]a turban of fine linen, exquisite
hats of fine linen, [b]short trousers of
fine woven linen,
29 [a]and a sash of fine woven linen with
blue, purple, and scarlet *thread*, made
by a weaver, as the LORD had commanded Moses.
30 [a]Then they made the plate of the
holy crown of pure gold, and wrote on
it an inscription *like* the engraving of
a signet:

[b]HOLINESS TO THE LORD.

31 And they tied to it a blue cord, to
fasten *it* above on the turban, as the
LORD had commanded Moses.

The Work Completed

32 Thus all the work of the tabernacle
of the tent of meeting was [a]finished.
And the children of Israel did [b]accord-
ing to all that the LORD had commanded Moses; so they did.
33 And they brought the tabernacle to
Moses, the tent and all its furnishings:
its clasps, its boards, its bars, its pillars,
and its sockets;
34 the covering of ram skins dyed red,
the covering of badger skins, and the
veil of the covering;
35 the ark of the Testimony with its
poles, and the mercy seat;
36 the table, all its utensils, and the
[a]showbread;
37 the pure *gold* lampstand with its
lamps (the lamps set in order), all its
utensils, and the oil for light;
38 the gold altar, the anointing oil, and
the sweet incense; the screen for the
tabernacle door;
39 the bronze altar, its grate of bronze,
its poles, and all its utensils; the laver
with its base;
40 the hangings of the court, its pillars
and its sockets, the screen for the court
gate, its cords, and its pegs; all the
utensils for the service of the tabernacle, for the tent of meeting;
41 and the [1]garments of ministry, to
[2]minister in the holy *place:* the holy
garments for Aaron the priest, and his
sons' garments, to minister as priests.
42 According to all that the LORD had
commanded Moses, so the children of
Israel [a]did all the work.
43 Then Moses looked over all the
work, and indeed they had done it; as
the LORD had commanded, just so they
had done it. And Moses [a]blessed them.

The Tabernacle Erected and Arranged

40 Then the LORD [a]spoke to Moses,
saying:
2 "On the first day of the [a]first month
you shall set up [b]the tabernacle of the
tent of meeting.
3 [a]"You shall put in it the ark of the
Testimony, and [1]partition off the ark
with the veil.
4 [a]"You shall bring in the table and
[b]arrange the things that are to be set
in order on it; [c]and you shall bring in
the lampstand and [1]light its lamps.
5 [a]"You shall also set the altar of gold
for the incense before the ark of the
Testimony, and put up the screen for
the door of the tabernacle.
6 "Then you shall set the [a]altar of the
burnt offering before the door of the
tabernacle of the tent of meeting.
7 "And [a]you shall set the laver between the tabernacle of meeting and
the altar, and put water in it.
8 "You shall set up the court all
around, and hang up the screen at the
court gate.
9 "And you shall take the anointing
oil, and [a]anoint the tabernacle and all
that *is* in it; and you shall hallow it and
all its utensils, and it shall be holy.
10 "You shall [a]anoint the altar of the
burnt offering and all its utensils, and
consecrate the altar. [b]The altar shall
be most holy.
11 "And you shall anoint the laver and
its base, and consecrate it.
12 [a]"Then you shall bring Aaron and
his sons to the door of the tabernacle
of meeting and wash them with water.
13 "You shall put the holy [a]garments
on Aaron, [b]and anoint him and consecrate him, that he may minister to
Me as priest.
14 "And you shall bring his sons and
clothe them with tunics.

26 [1]*serve*
27 [a]Ex. 28:39, 40
28 [a]Ex. 28:4, 39; Lev. 8:9; Ezek. 44:18 [b]Ex. 28:42; Lev. 6:10
29 [a]Ex. 28:39
30 [a]Ex. 28:36, 37 [b]Zech. 14:20
32 [a]Ex. 40:17 [b]Ex. 25:40; 39:42, 43
36 [a]Ex. 25:23–30
41 [1]Or *woven garments* [2]*serve*
42 [a]Ex. 35:10
43 [a]Lev. 9:22, 23; Num. 6:23–26; Josh. 22:6; 2 Sam. 6:18; 1 Kin. 8:14; 2 Chr. 30:27

CHAPTER 40

1 [a]Ex. 25:1—31:18
2 [a]Ex. 12:2; 13:4 [b]Ex. 26:1, 30; 40:17
3 [a]Ex. 26:33; 40:21; Lev. 16:2; Num. 4:5 [1]*screen*
4 [a]Ex. 26:35; 40:22 [b]Ex. 25:30; 40:23 [c]Ex. 40:24, 25 [1]*set up*
5 [a]Ex. 40:26
6 [a]Ex. 39:39
7 [a]Ex. 30:18; 40:30
9 [a]Ex. 30:26; Lev. 8:10
10 [a]Ex. 30:26–30 [b]Ex. 29:36, 37
12 [a]Ex. 29:4–9; Lev. 8:1–13
13 [a]Ex. 29:5; 39:1, 41 [b][Ex. 28:41]; Lev. 8:12

39:27–29 See notes on 28:40–43.
39:30, 31 See note on 28:36.
39:32–43 Moses finished the tabernacle God had commanded him to build.
40:1–33 The tabernacle is carefully assembled and inaugurated.

15 "You shall anoint them, as you
anointed their father, that they may
minister to Me as priests; for their
anointing shall surely be [a]an everlasting priesthood throughout their generations."
16 Thus Moses did; according to all
that the LORD had commanded him, so
he did.
17 And it came to pass in the first
month of the second year, on the first
day of the month, *that* the [a]tabernacle
was [1]raised up.
18 So Moses raised up the tabernacle,
fastened its sockets, set up its boards,
put in its bars, and raised up its pillars.
19 And he spread out the tent over the
tabernacle and put the covering of the
tent on top of it, as the LORD had commanded Moses.
20 He took [a]the Testimony and put *it*
into the ark, inserted the poles through
the rings of the ark, and put the mercy
seat on top of the ark.
21 And he brought the ark into the tabernacle, [a]hung up the veil of the covering, and partitioned off the ark of the
Testimony, as the LORD had commanded Moses.
22 [a]He put the table in the tabernacle
of meeting, on the north side of the tabernacle, outside the veil;
23 [a]and he set the bread in order upon
it before the LORD, as the LORD had
commanded Moses.
24 [a]He put the lampstand in the tabernacle of meeting, across from the table,
on the south side of the tabernacle;
25 and [a]he lit the lamps before the
LORD, as the LORD had commanded
Moses.
26 [a]He put the gold altar in the tabernacle of meeting in front of the veil;
27 [a]and he burned sweet incense on it,
as the LORD had commanded Moses.
28 [a]He hung up the screen *at* the door
of the tabernacle.
29 [a]And he put the altar of burnt offering *before* the door of the tabernacle
of the tent of meeting, and [b]offered
upon it the burnt offering and the grain
offering, as the LORD had commanded
Moses.
30 [a]He set the laver between the tabernacle of meeting and the altar, and put
water there for washing;
31 and Moses, Aaron, and his sons
would [a]wash their hands and their feet
with water from it.
32 Whenever they went into the tabernacle of meeting, and when they came
near the altar, they washed, [a]as the
LORD had commanded Moses.
33 [a]And he raised up the court all
around the tabernacle and the altar, and hung up the screen of the
court gate. So Moses [b]finished the
work.

The Cloud and the Glory

34 [a]Then the [b]cloud covered the tabernacle of meeting, and the [c]glory of the
LORD filled the tabernacle.
35 And Moses [a]was not able to enter
the tabernacle of meeting, because the
cloud rested above it, and the glory of
the LORD filled the tabernacle.
36 [a]Whenever the cloud was taken up
from above the tabernacle, the children
of Israel would [1]go onward in all their
journeys.
37 But [a]if the cloud was not taken up,
then they did not journey till the day
that it was taken up.
38 For [a]the cloud of the LORD *was*
above the tabernacle by day, and fire
was over it by night, in the sight of all
the house of Israel, throughout all their
journeys.

15 [a]Ex. 29:9; Num. 25:13
17 [a]Ex. 40:2; Num. 7:1
[1]*erected*
20 [a]Ex. 25:16; Deut. 10:5; 1 Kin. 8:9; 2 Chr. 5:10; Heb. 9:4
21 [a]Ex. 26:33
22 [a]Ex. 26:35
23 [a]Ex. 40:4; Lev. 24:5, 6
24 [a]Ex. 26:35
25 [a]Ex. 25:37; 30:7, 8; 40:4; Lev. 24:3, 4
26 [a]Ex. 30:1, 6; 40:5
27 [a]Ex. 30:7
28 [a]Ex. 26:36; 40:5
29 [a]Ex. 40:6 [b]Ex. 29:38–42
30 [a]Ex. 30:18; 40:7
31 [a]Ex. 30:19, 20; John 13:8
32 [a]Ex. 30:19
33 [a]Ex. 27:9–18; 40:8 [b][Heb. 3:2–5]
34 [a]Ex. 29:43; Lev. 16:2; Num. 9:15; 2 Chr. 5:13; Is. 6:4 [b]1 Kin. 8:10, 11 [c]Lev. 9:6, 23
35 [a][Lev. 16:2]; 1 Kin. 8:11; 2 Chr. 5:13, 14
36 [a]Ex. 13:21, 22; Num. 9:17; Neh. 9:19
[1]*journey*
37 [a]Num. 9:19–22
38 [a]Ex. 13:21; Num. 9:15; Ps. 78:14; Is. 4:5

40:29 The offering was prepared and presented to God as a meal, symbolically presenting the best fruits of human living to God to be consumed and used as He desired.

40:34–38 God's glory filled the tabernacle. Without His glory and presence, the work was not finished and the tabernacle was useless. The central message of Ex. is reiterated: God is personally present in their midst.

TRUTH-IN-ACTION through EXODUS

Letting the LIFE of the Holy Spirit Bring Faith's Works Alive in You!

Truth Exodus Teaches	Text	**Action** Exodus Invites
1 Four Keys to Understanding God Successful Christian living begins with knowing who God is. In Ex., God reveals part of His nature and character. Knowing God in truth will affect our behavior. Ex. gives four keys to make our lives more faithful and fruitful.	3:14, 15	**Understand** that God is! His Name is "I AM WHO I AM." **Rest** on this foundation. **Be grounded** and established in Him.
	15:25, 26	**Receive** God as "The Lord Who Heals You." To heal is His nature; His will is to make us whole.
	17:15	**Rely upon** God who is "The Lord Your Banner." As you surrender to Him—your Victory, Miracle, and Protection—your battle against the flesh will succeed.
	31:13	**Pursue** God who is "The Lord Who Makes You Holy." His life in us makes our holiness possible.
2 Steps to Holiness God calls us to be holy, "set apart to Him and His purposes." God intends His people to be distinguished in nature and in character from the world—different in the way we think, act, and live. This difference will be visible and bring God glory.	7:1—11:10	**Know** that God deals differently with us than with the world (see 8:23; 9:26; 10:23; 11:7).
	12:7	**Rely** on the blood of Jesus to protect you from all evil (see 1 Pet. 1:18, 19).
	19:5	**Obey** God's Word and you will become His "special treasure."
	21:5	**Be Jesus' bondslave.** He will open your ears to hear His voice clearly and understand His Word.
	32:26–29	**Be zealous** for God's holiness. He honors those who honor Him.
3 Guidelines to Godly Living Godly living is living with God in your life and His Life in you. He gives guidelines to help us build our lives on His precepts. God calls us to acts of faith that build godliness. Without faith, our acts become vain religion. Godliness embraces godly practice and shuns vain religious acts.	3:3	**Stay alert** to **seek** out God's working. It often comes in a way we do not expect.
	12:15, 19, 20; 13:3, 6, 7	**Participate** regularly in the Lord's Supper. We thus share in His deliverance and life.
	14:13, 14	**Be still** as God works. You will see His deliverance.
	16:4	**Be careful** to apply God's Word. He wants us to follow His instructions.
	23:16; 34:22	**Celebrate** God's blessings to you.
	25:8; 33:15	**Dwell in** and **esteem** God's Presence. It distinguishes us from everyone else.
	31:12–17; 33:14	**Rest** in God's Sabbath. His rest gives us rest from our own works (see Heb. 4:10, 11).

Truth Exodus Teaches	Text	**Action** Exodus Invites
4 Keys to Wise Living God calls His people to wisdom. Wisdom is knowing how to apply truth. Ex. gives principles that teach us how to live wisely and please God. It also teaches us certain wise practices. The Holy Spirit will train us to practice wisdom as a discipline that will lead to the fullness of life.	19:8; 24:3, 7	**Do not trust** yourself to obey God's Word. Depend upon His Holy Spirit.
	20:1–17	**Meditate** on the Ten Commandments regularly to learn God's moral nature and character.
	20:20	**Learn** reverence for the Lord; it will keep you from sinning.
	23:2, 3	**Suspect** majority opinion that proposes deviance. Evil is often popular but disobeys God.
	23:15	**Give** every time you gather with God's people for worship. It shows faith that He provides for you.
	32:1	**Do not become impatient** with God. It leads to sin.
	35:30–35	**Recognize** that any skill or ability you have is God's gift. **Be grateful** for His gifts, avoiding pride.
5 Keys to Understanding Authority God rules His people through delegated authority. All authority is from God (see Rom. 13). To distrust those He places over us is to distrust Him. God calls His people to a submissive attitude toward His leaders. He cautions us to be careful how we speak about them.	16:8; 22:28	**Do not grumble** against spiritual leadership. You thus grumble against the Lord and rebel.
	22:18	**Avoid** and **shun** the occult. To seek out spiritual direction from evil leads to death.
	35:20–29	**Listen** to those God sends to speak to and lead us. **Do not rebel** against their leadership. To disregard godly leaders is to disregard Him.

The Third Book of Moses Called
LEVITICUS

Author: Traditionally Moses
Date: About 1445 B.C.
Theme: The Sanctity of God and Holiness in Everyday Life
Key Words: Holiness, Offering, Sacrifice

Author The Book of Leviticus is the third book ascribed to Moses from the Hebrew Scriptures of the Old Testament. In 1:1, the text refers to the word of the Lord, which was spoken to Moses from the tabernacle of meeting; this forms the basis for this entire book of Scripture. The priests and Levites have preserved its contents.

Date Scholars have dated the Book of Leviticus from the time of Moses' activities (earlier dating in the fifteenth century B.C. and the later alternative dating in the twelfth century B.C.) to the time of Ezra during the return (sixth century B.C.). Acceptance of Mosaic authorship for Leviticus would date its writing to about 1445 B.C. The book describes the sacrificial system and worship that precedes the time of Ezra and recalls the institution of the sacrificial system. The book contains little historical information that would give an exact date.

Background The theology of the Book of Leviticus links the idea of holiness to everyday life. It goes beyond the issue of sacrifice though the sacrificial worship and the work of the priests is explained with great care. The concept of holiness affects not only the relationship that each individual has with God, but also the relationship of love and respect that each person must have for his neighbor. The code of holiness permeates the work because each individual must be pure even as God Himself is pure and because the purity of each individual is the foundation of the holiness of the entire covenant community. The teaching of Jesus Christ, "Therefore, whatever you want men to do to you, do also to them, for this is the Law and the Prophets" (Matt. 7:12), reflects the text of Leviticus 19:18, "Love your neighbor as yourself."

Content In Hebrew the Book of Leviticus was named *Vayikra*, which means "And He Called." The Hebrew title is taken from the first word of the book, which was a customary way of naming ancient works. The English title "Leviticus" is derived from the Greek version of the work and means "Matters Pertaining to the Levites." The title is somewhat misleading because the book deals with many more issues relating to purity, holiness, the whole priesthood, the sanctity of God, and holiness in everyday life. The word "holy" appears more than eighty times in the book.

Sometimes the Book of Leviticus has been viewed as a difficult work to grasp; however, according to early tradition, in Jewish education it was the first book to be taught to children. It deals with

God's character and will, especially in matters of holiness, which the Jewish sages considered to be of primary importance. They felt that before proceeding to other biblical texts, children should first be educated concerning the sanctity of God and the responsibility of each individual to live a holy life. Holiness (Hebrew *kedushah*) is a key word in Leviticus, describing the sanctity of the divine presence. Holiness is being set apart from the profane, and holy is the opposite of the common or secular.

Another major theme of the Book of Leviticus is the sacrificial system. The Burnt Sacrifice (Hebrew *olah*) refers to the only sacrifice that is entirely consumed upon the altar, and therefore it is sometimes called the whole offering. The Grain Offering (Hebrew *minchah*) is a tribute offering made in order to secure or maintain the divine favor, indicating that the fruits of a person's labor should be dedicated to God. The Peace Offering (Hebrew *shelamim*) is designed to provide expiation and permits the one who makes the offering to eat the meat of the sacrifice. It was often given on a joyous occasion. The Sin Offering (Hebrew *chatta't*) is employed to remove impurity from the sanctuary. The Trespass Offering (Hebrew *asham*), also referred to as the Guilt Offering or the Offering of Reparation, is prepared for violation of the sanctity of the property of God or of another person, usually by use of a false oath. The trespass had desecrated the sanctity of God and an offering is required.

In addition to the sacrifices, the liturgical calendar holds a significant place in the Book of Leviticus. The Sabbath year refers to the emancipation of Israelite slaves, and people in debt, as well as the redemption of the land (see also Ex. 21:2–6; 23:10, 11; Deut. 15:1–11, 12–18). The Jubilee Year refers to the fact that the land of Israel, as well as the people, belongs to God and not to any individual. The land, therefore, must have rest after each period of forty-nine years (Lev. 25:8–17), which teaches God's ownership. The entire Book of Leviticus is permeated with the sanctity of God, the holiness of His character, and the necessity of the congregation to approach Him in purity of heart and mind.

Personal Application The Book of Leviticus has a powerful contemporary and personal application for the life of the church today. The sanctity of God and His great desire for fellowship with His people are clearly seen in the descriptions of the sacrificial system. Holiness, being set apart for a saintly life in fellowship with God, is the primary issue for the people of ancient Israel as it is for the people of God today.

Christ Revealed Christ is not specifically mentioned in Leviticus. However, the sacrificial system and the high priest in the Book of Leviticus are types that picture the work of Christ. The Book of Hebrews describes Christ as the High Priest and uses the text of Leviticus as a basis for illustrating His work. Some have used extreme forms of allegorization of the Book of Leviticus in order to reveal Christ; however, this method of Bible interpretation should be used cautiously in order to insure that the book's original historical and cultural meaning are preserved. The Book of Leviticus focuses on the life and the worship of ancient Israel.

The Holy Spirit at Work Though the term "Holy Spirit" is never mentioned in the Book of Leviticus, God's presence is felt throughout the book. The holiness of God's character is constantly referred to in the designation of holiness to the people's actions and worship. He is not seen as in pagan cults of the period where idols were venerated, but He is in the midst of the people as they worship Him. They must be holy even as He is holy.

Outline of Leviticus

I. The description of the sacrificial system **1:1—7:38**
- A. The burnt offering 1:1–17
- B. The grain offering 2:1–16
- C. The peace offering 3:1–17
- D. The sin offering 4:1—5:13
- E. The trespass offering 5:14—6:7
- F. Other instructions 6:8—7:38

II. The service of the priests in the sanctuary **8:1—10:20**
- A. Ordination of Aaron and his sons 8:1–36
- B. The priests take office 9:1–24
- C. The sin of Nadab and Abihu 10:1–11
- D. The sin of Eleazar and Ithamar 10:12–20

III. The laws of impurities **11:1—16:34**
- A. Animal impurities 11:1–47
- B. Childbirth impurities 12:1–8
- C. Skin impurities 13:1—14:57
- D. Discharge impurities 15:1–33
- E. Moral impurities 16:1–34

IV. The holiness code **17:1—26:46**
- A. Killing for food 17:1–16
- B. On being holy 18:1—20:27
- C. Laws for priests and sacrifices 21:1—22:33
- D. Holy days and religious feasts 23:1–44
- E. Laws for holy elements of worship 24:1–9
- F. Punishment for blasphemy 24:10–23
- G. The Sabbath and Jubilee years 25:1–55
- H. Blessing for obedience and punishment for disobedience 26:1–46

V. Gifts to the sanctuary **27:1–34**

The Burnt Offering

NOW the LORD [a]called to Moses,
and spoke to him [b]from the tabernacle of meeting, saying,
2 "Speak to the children of Israel, and
say to them: [a]'When any one of you
brings an offering to the LORD, you
shall bring your offering of the
livestock—of the herd and of the
flock.
3 'If his offering *is* a burnt sacrifice
of the herd, let him offer a male
[a]without blemish; he shall offer it of
his own free will at the door of the tabernacle of meeting before the LORD.
4 [a]'Then he shall put his hand on the
head of the burnt offering, and it will
be [b]accepted on his behalf [c]to make
atonement for him.
5 'He shall kill the [a]bull before the
LORD; [b]and the priests, Aaron's sons,
shall bring the blood [c]and sprinkle the
blood all around on the *altar that *is*
by the door of the tabernacle of meeting.

CHAPTER 1

1 [a]Ex. 19:3; 25:22 [b]Ex. 40:34
2 [a]Lev. 22:18, 19
3 [a]Eph. 5:27
4 [a]Lev. 3:2, 8, 13; 4:15 [b][Rom. 12:1] [c]2 Chr. 29:23, 24
5 [a]Mic. 6:6 [b]2 Chr. 35:11 [c][Heb. 12:24] *See WW at 2 Kin. 12:9.

1:1 Now the LORD called to Moses and spoke to him: God called to Moses, and Moses spoke to the people as God's messenger. The code of holiness and the message that is spoken are ordained by God. **The tabernacle of meeting** is the place where God meets with His servants. See Ex. 25:22, "And there I will meet with you, and I will speak with you from above the mercy seat." It was within the tabernacle proper and housed the ark and other sacred furniture (Ex. 37).

1:2 Bring your offering: Lev. 1:1–7:38 deals with the offerings that were presented by the individual people of Israel to the LORD their God. Lev. 1:1–17 explains the burnt sacrifice; 2:1–16, the grain offering; 3:1–17, the peace offering; 4:1–35, the sin offering; 5:14–19, the trespass offering.

1:3 See section 2 of Truth-In-Action at the end of Lev.

1:3 The **burnt sacrifice** was the most common of the sacrifices, being offered twice daily according to the meticulous instructions of this chapter. It included bulls, sheep, goats, pigeons, and turtledoves. The entire animal (except the skin) was burned on the altar.

1:4 The purpose for the burnt sacrifice was **to make atonement** for the person bringing the sacrifice. It did not remove sin's presence but made possible fellowship with a holy God. It foreshadowed Jesus Christ, the true Burnt Sacrifice, who, as the sacrificial Lamb, once and for all "takes away the sin of the world!" (John 1:29).

6 'And he shall [a]skin the burnt offering and cut it into its pieces.

7 'The sons of Aaron the priest shall put [a]fire on the altar, and [b]lay the wood in order on the fire.

8 'Then the priests, Aaron's sons, shall lay the parts, the head, and the fat in order on the wood that *is* on the fire upon the altar;

9 'but he shall wash its entrails and its legs with water. And the priest shall burn all on the altar as a burnt sacrifice, an offering made by fire, a [a]sweet[1] aroma to the LORD.

10 'If his offering *is* of the flocks—of the sheep or of the goats—as a burnt sacrifice, he shall bring a male [a]without blemish.

11 [a]'He shall kill it on the north side of the altar before the LORD; and the priests, Aaron's sons, shall sprinkle its blood all around on the altar.

12 'And he shall cut it into its pieces, with its head and its fat; and the priest shall lay them in order on the wood that *is* on the fire upon the altar;

13 'but he shall wash the entrails and the legs with water. Then the priest shall bring *it* all and burn *it* on the altar; it *is* a burnt sacrifice, an [a]offering made by fire, a sweet aroma to the LORD.

14 'And if the burnt sacrifice of his offering to the LORD *is* of birds, then he shall bring his offering of [a]turtledoves or young pigeons.

15 'The priest shall bring it to the altar, [1]wring off its head, and burn *it* on the altar; its blood shall be drained out at the side of the altar.

16 'And he shall remove its crop with its feathers and cast it [a]beside the altar on the east side, into the place for ashes.

17 'Then he shall split it at its wings, *but* [a]shall not divide *it* completely; and the priest shall burn it on the altar, on the wood that *is* on the fire. [b]It *is* a burnt sacrifice, an offering made by fire, a [1]sweet aroma to the LORD.

The Grain Offering

[2] **2** 'When anyone offers [a]a grain offering to the LORD, his offering shall be *of* fine flour. And he shall pour oil on it, and put [b]frankincense on it.

2 'He shall bring it to Aaron's sons, the priests, one of whom shall take from it his handful of fine flour and oil with all the frankincense. And the priest shall burn [a]*it as* a memorial on the altar, an offering made by fire, a sweet aroma to the LORD.

3 [a]'The rest of the grain offering *shall be* Aaron's and his [b]sons'. [c]*It is* most holy of the offerings to the LORD made by fire.

4 'And if you bring as an offering a grain offering baked in the oven, *it shall be* unleavened cakes of fine flour mixed with oil, or unleavened wafers [a]anointed[1] with oil.

5 'But if your offering *is* a grain offering *baked* in a [1]pan, *it shall be of* fine flour, unleavened, mixed with oil.

6 'You shall break it in pieces and pour oil on it; it *is* a grain offering.

7 'If your offering *is* a grain offering *baked* in a [a]covered pan, it shall be made *of* fine flour with oil.

8 'You shall bring the grain offering that is made of these things to the LORD. And when it is presented to the priest, he shall bring it to the altar.

9 'Then the priest shall take from the grain offering [a]a memorial portion, and burn *it* on the altar. *It is* an [b]offering made by fire, a sweet aroma to the LORD.

10 'And [a]what is left of the grain offering *shall be* Aaron's and his sons'. *It is* most holy of the offerings to the LORD made by fire.

11 'No grain offering which you bring to the LORD shall be made with [a]leaven, for you shall burn no leaven nor any honey in any offering to the LORD made by fire.

12 [a]'As for the offering of the firstfruits, you shall offer them to the LORD, but they shall not be burned on the altar for a sweet aroma.

13 'And every offering of your grain offering [a]you shall season with salt; you shall not allow [b]the salt of the *covenant of your God to be lacking from your grain offering. [c]With all your offerings you shall offer salt.

14 'If you offer a grain offering of your

---

6 [a]Lev. 7:8
7 [a]Lev. 6:8–13; Mal. 1:10 [b]Gen. 22:9
9 [a]Gen. 8:21; [Ezek. 20:28, 41; 2 Cor. 2:15] [1]*soothing* or *pleasing aroma*
10 [a]Ex. 12:5; Lev. 1:3; Ezek. 43:22; [1 Pet. 1:19]
11 [a]Ex. 24:6; 40:22; Lev. 1:5; Ezek. 8:5
13 [a]Num. 15:4–7; 28:12–14
14 [a]Gen. 15:9; Lev. 5:7, 11; 12:8; Luke 2:24
15 [1]Lit. *nip* or *chop off*
16 [a]Lev. 6:10
17 [a]Gen. 15:10; Lev. 5:8 [b]Lev. 1:9, 13 [1]*soothing* or *pleasing aroma*

CHAPTER 2

1 [a]Lev. 6:14; 9:17; Num. 15:4 [b]Lev. 5:11
2 [a]Lev. 2:9; 5:12; 6:15; 24:7; Acts 10:4
3 [a]Lev. 7:9 [b]Lev. 6:6; 10:12, 13 [c]Ex. 29:37; Num. 18:9
4 [a]Ex. 29:2 [1]*spread*
5 [1]*flat plate* or *griddle*
7 [a]Lev. 7:9
9 [a]Lev. 2:2, 16; 5:12; 6:15 [b]Ex. 29:18
10 [a]Lev. 2:3; 6:16
11 [a]Ex. 23:18; 34:25; Lev. 6:16, 17; [Matt. 16:12; Mark 8:15; Luke 12:1; 1 Cor. 5:8; Gal. 5:9]
12 [a]Ex. 22:29; 34:22; Lev. 23:10, 11, 17, 18
13 [a][Mark 9:49, 50; Col. 4:6] [b]Num. 18:19; 2 Chr. 13:5 [c]Ezek. 43:24 *See WW at Gen. 17:7.

2:1 See section 2 of Truth-In-Action at the end of Lev.

2:1 When anyone offers a grain offering to the LORD: The idea of the different types of offerings teaches that everything in the created universe belongs to God. The individual must take a portion of what he has and set it apart as holy to the Lord in recognition of the divine blessing in God's creation.

2:2–16 Only a **handful** of the grain offering was burned. The remainder was **Aaron's and his sons'** to eat (v. 3). **Fine flour and oil** were its main ingredients (v. 2), and it could be cooked one of four ways (vv. 4, 5, 7, 14). Offered twice daily, it was a dedicatory tribute to God (v. 9) and also served as income to the Levitical priesthood. It foreshadowed the Christian's giving himself in daily sacrificial consecration to God through Jesus Christ (see Rom. 12:1, 2; Heb. 13:15, 16).

firstfruits to the LORD, [a]you shall offer
for the grain offering of your firstfruits
green heads of grain roasted on the
fire, grain beaten from [b]full heads.
15 'And [a]you shall put oil on it, and
lay frankincense on it. It *is* a grain offering.
16 'Then the priest shall burn [a]the memorial portion: *part* of its beaten grain
and *part* of its oil, with all the frankincense, as an offering made by fire to
the LORD.

The Peace Offering

1 **3** 'When his offering *is* a [a]sacrifice
of a peace offering, if he offers *it*
of the herd, whether male or female,
he shall offer it [b]without [1]blemish before the LORD.
2 'And [a]he shall lay his hand on the
head of his offering, and kill it *at* the
door of the tabernacle of meeting; and
Aaron's sons, the priests, shall [b]sprin-
kle the blood all around on the altar.
3 'Then he shall offer from the sacrifice of the peace offering an offering
made by fire to the LORD. [a]The fat that
covers the entrails and all the fat that
is on the entrails,
4 'the two kidneys and the fat that *is*
on them by the flanks, and the fatty
lobe *attached* to the liver above the
kidneys, he shall remove;
5 'and Aaron's sons [a]shall burn it on
the altar upon the [b]burnt sacrifice,
which *is* on the wood that *is* on the fire,
as an [c]offering made by fire, a [d]sweet
aroma to the LORD.
6 'If his offering as a sacrifice of a
peace offering to the LORD *is* of the
flock, *whether* male or female, [a]he
shall offer it *without blemish.
7 'If he offers a [a]lamb as his offering,
then he shall [b]offer it [c]before the LORD.
8 'And he shall lay his hand on the
head of his offering, and kill it before

14 [a]Lev. 23:10, 14 [b]2 Kin. 4:42
15 [a]Lev. 2:1
16 [a]Lev. 2:2

CHAPTER 3

1 [a]Lev. 7:11, 29 [b]Lev. 1:3; 22:20–24 [1]*imperfection* or *defect*
2 [a]Ex. 29:10, 11, 16, 20; Lev. 1:4, 5; 16:21 [b]Lev. 1:5
3 [a]Ex. 29:13, 22; Lev. 1:8; 3:16; 4:8, 9
5 [a]Ex. 29:13; Lev. 6:12; 7:28–34 [b]2 Chr. 35:14 [c]Num. 28:3–10 [d]Num. 15:8–10
6 [a]Lev. 3:1; 22:20–24 *See WW at Lev. 23:12.
7 [a]Num. 15:4, 5 [b]1 Kin. 8:62 [c]Lev. 17:8, 9
11 [a]Lev. 21:6, 8, 17, 21, 22; 22:25; Num. 28:2; [Ezek. 44:7; Mal. 1:7, 12]
12 [a]Num. 15:6–11 [b]Lev. 3:1, 7
16 [a]Lev. 7:23–25; 1 Sam. 2:15; 2 Chr. 7:7
17 [a]Lev. 6:18; 7:36; 17:7; 23:14 [b]Gen. 9:4; Lev. 7:23, 26; 17:10, 14; 1 Sam. 14:33 [1]*everlasting* or *never-ending*

CHAPTER 4

2 [a]Lev. 5:15–18; Num. 15:22–30; 1 Sam. 14:27; Acts 3:17 [1]*through error*

the tabernacle of meeting; and Aaron's
sons shall sprinkle its blood all around
on the altar.
9 'Then he shall offer from the sacrifice of the peace offering, as an offering made by fire to the LORD, its fat
and the whole fat tail which he shall
remove close to the backbone. And the
fat that covers the entrails and all the
fat that *is* on the entrails,
10 'the two kidneys and the fat that *is*
on them by the flanks, and the fatty
lobe *attached* to the liver above the
kidneys, he shall remove;
11 'and the priest shall burn *them* on
the altar *as* [a]food, an offering made by
fire to the LORD.
12 'And if his [a]offering *is* a goat, then
[b]he shall offer it before the LORD.
13 'He shall lay his hand on its head
and kill it before the tabernacle of
meeting; and the sons of Aaron shall
sprinkle its blood all around on the altar.
14 'Then he shall offer from it his offering, as an offering made by fire to the
LORD. The fat that covers the entrails
and all the fat that *is* on the entrails,
15 'the two kidneys and the fat that *is*
on them by the flanks, and the fatty
lobe *attached* to the liver above the
kidneys, he shall remove;
16 'and the priest shall burn them on
the altar *as* food, an offering made by
fire for a sweet aroma; [a]all the fat *is*
the LORD's.
17 '*This shall be* a [a]perpetual[1] statute
throughout your generations in all
your dwellings: you shall eat neither
fat nor [b]blood.' "

The Sin Offering

4 Now the LORD spoke to Moses, saying,
2 "Speak to the children of Israel, 4
saying: [a]'If a person sins [1]uninten-

3:1 See section 1 of Truth-In-Action at the end of Lev.
3:1 A peace offering was an optional sacrifice, which could be brought in conjunction with a confession or vow or simply as a freewill offering of gratitude (7:11–21). It consisted of a sacrificed animal, some of which was burned, some eaten by the priests, and some returned to the worshiper to eat. It was a festive offering, foreshadowing the NT Communion meal as well as any other festive Christian meal commemorating salvation (see Acts 2:46). **Without blemish before the LORD** signifies that what is offered to the Lord in the sacrificial practices of ancient Israel must be perfect, separated as holy. Gifts of sacrifice to the Lord were strictly regulated so that this holiness to the Lord would characterize the entire sacrificial system.
3:5 Aaron's sons: The priests came from the household and family lineage of Aaron and were ordained for the service of sacrifice.
3:17 A perpetual statute . . . neither fat nor blood: The holiness of the nation was reflected in the laws of the community established by God to make them separate and distinct. Some of the laws were designed to insure the health of the community, and others were intended to give identity to the people for all generations.
4:2 See section 4 of Truth-In-Action at the end of Lev.
4:2 Sins unintentionally against any of the commandments of the LORD: Failure to observe the commandments of the Lord results in a violation in the holiness code and in the covenant relationship with God. The subsequent sin offering may then be given for the anointed priest (v. 3), the congregation of Israel (v. 13), the ruler of the people (v. 22), or an individual of the common people (v. 27).

tionally against any of the *commandments of the LORD *in anything* which ought not to be done, and does any of them,

3 [a]'if the *anointed priest sins, bringing guilt on the people, then let him offer to the LORD for his sin which he has sinned [b]a young bull without blemish as a [c]sin offering.

4 'He shall bring the bull [a]to the door of the tabernacle of meeting before the LORD, lay his hand on the bull's head, and kill the bull before the LORD.

5 'Then the anointed priest [a]shall take some of the bull's blood and bring it to the tabernacle of meeting.

6 'The priest shall dip his finger in the blood and sprinkle some of the blood seven times before the LORD, in front of the [a]veil of the sanctuary.

7 'And the priest shall [a]put some of the blood on the horns of the altar of sweet incense before the LORD, which is in the tabernacle of meeting; and he shall pour [b]the remaining blood of the bull at the base of the altar of the burnt offering, which is at the door of the tabernacle of meeting.

8 'He shall take from it all the fat of the bull as the sin offering. The fat that covers the entrails and all the fat which *is* on the entrails,

9 'the two kidneys and the fat that *is* on them by the flanks, and the fatty lobe *attached* to the liver above the kidneys, he shall remove,

10 [a]'as it was taken from the bull of the sacrifice of the peace offering; and the priest shall burn them on the altar of the burnt offering.

11 [a]'But the bull's hide and all its *flesh, with its head and legs, its entrails and offal—

12 'the whole bull he shall carry outside the camp to a clean place, [a]where the ashes are poured out, and [b]burn it on wood with fire; where the ashes are poured out it shall be burned.

4 13 'Now [a]if the whole *congregation of Israel sins unintentionally, [b]and the thing is hidden from the eyes of the *assembly, and they have done *something against* any of the commandments of the LORD *in anything* which should not be done, and are **guilty;**

2 *See WW at Ps. 119:35.
3 [a]Ex. 40:15; Lev. 8:12 [b]Lev. 3:1; 9:2 [c]Lev. 9:7 *See WW at Dan. 9:25.
4 [a]Lev. 1:3, 4; 4:15; Num. 8:12
5 [a]Lev. 16:14; Num. 19:4
6 [a]Ex. 40:21, 26
7 [a]Lev. 4:18, 25, 30, 34; 8:15; 9:9; 16:18 [b]Ex. 40:5, 6; Lev. 5:9
10 [a]Lev. 3:3–5
11 [a]Ex. 29:14; Lev. 9:11; Num. 19:5 *See WW at Job 19:26.
12 [a]Lev. 4:21; 6:10, 11; 16:27 [b][Heb. 13:11, 12]
13 [a]Num. 15:24–26; Josh. 7:11 [b]Lev. 5:2–4, 17 *See WW at Josh. 22:17. • See WW at Lev. 16:17.
15 [a]Lev. 1:3, 4
16 [a]Lev. 4:5; [Heb. 9:12–14]
20 [a]Lev. 4:3 [b]Lev. 1:4; Num. 15:25 [1]Lit. *covering* *See WW at Num. 15:25.
22 [a]Lev. 4:2, 13, 27 [1]*leader*

WORD WEALTH

4:13 guilty, *'asham* (ah-*sham*); Strong's #816: To be guilty, to be conscious of guilt; to become an offender, to trespass. In most instances, *'asham* means "guilt offering," "trespass offering." *'Asham* is similar to *chata'ah,* which may mean "sin" or "sin offering," depending on context. *'Asham* can portray the condition of guiltiness, guilt itself, the shame of being guilty, the punishment that guilt brings, and the offering that removes guilt. By far the most significant reference is Is. 53:10, where *'asham* appears in the description of the Messiah's atoning death. Jesus' death was the ultimate trespass offering for the sins of the whole world. See 1 John 2:2.

14 'when the sin which they have committed becomes known, then the assembly shall offer a young bull for the sin, and bring it before the tabernacle of meeting.

15 'And the elders of the congregation [a]shall lay their hands on the head of the bull before the LORD. Then the bull shall be killed before the LORD.

16 [a]'The anointed priest shall bring some of the bull's blood to the tabernacle of meeting.

17 'Then the priest shall dip his finger in the blood and sprinkle *it* seven times before the LORD, in front of the veil.

18 'And he shall put *some* of the blood on the horns of the altar which *is* before the LORD, which *is* in the tabernacle of meeting; and he shall pour the remaining blood at the base of the altar of burnt offering, which is at the door of the tabernacle of meeting.

19 'He shall take all the fat from it and burn *it* on the altar.

20 'And he shall do [a]with the bull as he did with the bull as a sin offering; thus he shall do with it. [b]So the priest shall *make [1]atonement for them, and it shall be forgiven them.

21 'Then he shall carry the bull outside the camp, and burn it as he burned the first bull. It *is* a sin offering for the assembly.

22 'When a [1]ruler has sinned, and 4
[a]done *something* unintentionally *against* any of the commandments of the LORD his God *in anything* which should not be done, and is guilty,

---

4:3 The **sin offering** was characterized by the sprinkling of the animal's blood (v. 6). It included a wide variety of male and female animals and emphasized purification before God. Offered to end a person's period of uncleanness (see 12:6; 14:19), to terminate certain vows (Num. 6:13, 14), or to purify from inadvertent sins (Lev. 4:2) or sins of omission (Lev. 5:1–4), it foreshadowed purification from sin's pollution by the blood of Jesus Christ (Heb. 9:12–14; 1 John 1:9).

4:13 See section 4 of Truth-In-Action at the end of Lev.

4:22 See section 4 of Truth-In-Action at the end of Lev.

23 'or [a]if his sin which he has committed [1]comes to his knowledge, he shall
bring as his offering a kid of the goats,
a male without blemish.
24 'And [a]he shall lay his hand on the
head of the goat, and kill it at the place
where they kill the burnt offering before the LORD. It *is* a sin offering.
25 [a]'The priest shall take some of the
blood of the sin offering with his finger, put *it* on the horns of the altar of
burnt offering, and pour its blood at
the base of the altar of burnt offering.
26 'And he shall burn all its fat on the
altar, like [a]the fat of the sacrifice of
the peace offering. [b]So the priest shall
make [1]atonement for him concerning
his sin, and it shall be forgiven him.
4 **27** [a]'If [1]anyone of the [2]common people
sins unintentionally by doing *something against* any of the commandments of the LORD *in anything* which
ought not to be done, and is guilty,
28 'or [a]if his sin which he has committed comes to his knowledge, then he
shall bring as his offering a kid of the
goats, a female without blemish, for his
sin which he has committed.
29 [a]'And he shall lay his hand on the
head of the sin offering, and kill the
sin offering at the place of the burnt
offering.
30 'Then the priest shall take *some* of
its blood with his finger, put *it* on the
horns of the altar of burnt offering, and
pour all *the remaining* blood at the
base of the altar.
31 [a]'He shall remove all its fat, [b]as fat
is removed from the sacrifice of the
peace offering; and the priest shall
burn it on the altar for a [c]sweet aroma
to the LORD. [d]So the priest shall make
atonement for him, and it shall be forgiven him.
32 'If he brings a lamb as his sin offering, [a]he shall bring a female without
blemish.
33 'Then he shall [a]lay his hand on the
head of the sin offering, and kill it as
a sin offering at the place where they
kill the burnt offering.
34 'The priest shall take *some* of the
blood of the sin offering with his finger, put *it* on the horns of the altar of
burnt offering, and pour all *the remaining* blood at the base of the altar.
35 'He shall remove all its fat, as the
fat of the lamb is removed from the
sacrifice of the peace offering. Then
the priest shall burn it on the altar,
[a]according to the offerings made by
fire to the LORD. [b]So the priest shall
make atonement for his sin that he has
committed, and it shall be forgiven
him.

23 [a]Lev. 4:14; 5:4 [1]*is made known to him*
24 [a]Lev. 4:4; [Is. 53:6]
25 [a]Lev. 4:7, 18, 30, 34
26 [a]Lev. 3:3–5 [b]Lev. 4:20; Num. 15:28 [1]Lit. *covering*
27 [a]Lev. 4:2; Num. 15:27 [1]Lit. *any soul* [2]Lit. *people of the land*
28 [a]Lev. 4:23
29 [a]Lev. 1:4; 4:4, 24
31 [a]Lev. 3:14 [b]Lev. 3:3, 4 [c]Gen. 8:21; Ex. 29:18; Lev. 1:9, 13; 2:2, 9, 12 [d]Lev. 4:26
32 [a]Lev. 4:28
33 [a]Lev. 1:4; Num. 8:12
35 [a]Lev. 3:5 [b]Lev. 4:26, 31

CHAPTER 5

1 [a]Prov. 29:24; [Jer. 23:10] [b]Lev. 5:17; 7:18; 17:16; 19:8; 20:17; Num. 9:13 [1]*his iniquity*
2 [a]Lev. 11:24, 28, 31, 39; Num. 19:11–16; Deut. 14:8 [b]Lev. 5:17
3 [a]Lev. 5:12, 13, 15
4 [a]1 Sam. 25:22; Acts 23:12 [b][Matt. 5:33–37]; Mark 6:23; [James 5:12] [1]*vows* *See WW at Gen. 26:3.
5 [a]Lev. 16:21; 26:40; Num. 5:7; Ezra 10:11, 12; Ps. 32:5; Prov. 28:13

The Trespass Offering

5 'If a person sins in [a]hearing the ut- 5
terance of an oath, and *is* a witness,
whether he has seen or known *of the
matter*—if he does not tell *it*, he
[b]bears [1]guilt.
2 'Or [a]if a person touches any un- 5
clean thing, whether *it is* the carcass
of an unclean beast, or the carcass of
unclean livestock, or the carcass of unclean creeping things, and he is unaware of it, he also shall be unclean
and [b]guilty.
3 'Or if he touches [a]human uncleanness—whatever uncleanness with
which a man may be defiled, and he
is unaware of it—when he realizes *it*,
then he shall be guilty.
4 'Or if a person [1]swears,* speaking
thoughtlessly with *his* lips [a]to do evil
or [b]to do good, whatever *it is* that a
man may pronounce by an oath, and
he is unaware of it—when he realizes
it, then he shall be guilty in any of
these *matters*.
5 'And it shall be, when he is guilty 5
in any of these *matters*, that he shall
[a]confess that he has sinned in that
thing;
6 'and he shall bring his trespass offering to the LORD for his sin which
he has committed, a female from the
flock, a lamb or a kid of the goats as
a sin offering. So the **priest** shall make
atonement for him concerning his sin.

WORD WEALTH

5:6 priest, *kohen* (ko-*hayn*); Strong's #3548: A priest; especially a chief priest; a minister, a personal attendant, an officer; specifically the high priest descended from Aaron. The *kohen* was the Lord's "personal attendant," one whose entire life revolved around Yahweh's service, both through ministering in the tabernacle (or temple in later times) and in carrying the burden of the people of Israel (see Ex. 28:29). A *kohen* ministers to the Lord as priest (Ex. 28:1). Notice the six appearances of the words "minister," "serve," or "service" in the references to the high priest in Heb. 8:1—9:10.
(cont. on next page)

4:27 See section 4 of Truth-In-Action at the end of Lev.
5:1 See section 5 of Truth-In-Action at the end of Lev.
5:2–4 See section 5 of Truth-In-Action at the end of Lev.
5:5 See section 5 of Truth-In-Action at the end of Lev.

(*cont. from preceding page*)
To this day the Jewish surname "Cohen" identifies a family descended from Aaron the high priest.

7 [a]'If he is not able to bring a lamb,
then he shall bring to the LORD, for his
trespass which he has committed, two
[b]turtledoves or two young pigeons: one
as a sin offering and the other as a
burnt offering.
8 'And he shall bring them to the
priest, who shall offer *that* which *is* for
the sin offering first, and [a]wring off its
head from its neck, but shall not divide
it [1]completely.
9 'Then he shall sprinkle *some* of the
blood of the sin offering on the side
of the altar, and the [a]rest of the blood
shall be drained out at the base of the
altar. It *is* a sin offering.
10 'And he shall offer the second *as* a
burnt offering according to the [a]pre-
scribed manner. So [b]the priest shall
make atonement on his behalf for his
sin which he has committed, and it
shall be forgiven him.
11 'But if he is [a]not able to bring two
turtledoves or two young pigeons, then
he who sinned shall bring for his offering one-tenth of an ephah of fine flour
as a sin offering. [b]He shall put no oil
on it, nor shall he put frankincense on
it, for it *is* a sin offering.
12 'Then he shall bring it to the priest,
and the priest shall take his handful
of it [a]as a memorial portion, and burn
it on the altar [b]according to the offerings made by fire to the LORD. It *is* a
sin offering.
13 [a]'The priest shall make atonement
for him, [1]for his sin that he has committed in any of these matters; and it
shall be forgiven him. [b]*The rest* shall
be the priest's as a grain offering.' "

Offerings with Restitution

14 Then the LORD spoke to Moses, saying:
15 [a]"If a person commits a trespass,
and sins unintentionally in regard to
the holy things of the LORD, then

7 [a]Lev. 12:6, 8; 14:21 [b]Lev. 1:14
8 [a]Lev. 1:15–17 [1]Lit. *apart*
9 [a]Lev. 4:7, 18, 30, 34
10 [a]Lev. 1:14–17 [b]Lev. 4:20, 26; 5:13, 16
11 [a]Lev. 14:21–32 [b]Lev. 2:1, 2; 6:15; Num. 5:15
12 [a]Lev. 2:2 [b]Lev. 4:35
13 [a]Lev. 4:26 [b]Lev. 2:3; 6:17, 26 [1]*concerning his sin*
15 [a]Lev. 4:2; 22:14; Num. 5:5–8 [b]Ezra 10:19 [c]Ex. 30:13; Lev. 27:25
16 [a]Lev. 6:5; 22:14; 27:13, 15, 27, 31; Num. 5:7 [b]Lev. 4:26
17 [a]Lev. 4:2, 13, 22, 27 [b]Lev. 5:1, 2 [1]*punishment*
18 [a]Lev. 5:15
19 [a]Ezra 10:2

CHAPTER 6

2 [a]Num. 5:6 [b]Lev. 19:11; Acts 5:4; Col. 3:9 [c]Ex. 22:7, 10 [d]Prov. 24:28 [1]*deceiving his associate* [2]*an entrusted security*
3 [a]Ex. 23:4; Deut. 22:1–4 [b]Ex. 22:11; Lev. 19:12; Jer. 7:9; Zech. 5:4
4 [a]Lev. 24:18, 21 [1]*return* *See WW at Lev. 4:13.
5 [a]Lev. 5:16; Num. 5:7, 8; 2 Sam. 12:6
6 [a]Lev. 1:3; 5:15

[b]he shall bring to the LORD as his trespass offering a ram without blemish
from the flocks, with your valuation in
shekels of silver according to [c]the
shekel of the sanctuary, as a trespass
offering.
16 "And he shall make restitution for
the harm that he has done in regard
to the holy thing, [a]and shall add one-
fifth to it and give it to the priest.
[b]So the priest shall make atonement
for him with the ram of the trespass
offering, and it shall be forgiven him.
17 "If a person sins, and commits any
of these things which are forbidden to
be done by the commandments of the
LORD, [a]though he does not know *it*,
yet he is [b]guilty and shall bear his
[1]iniquity.
18 [a]"And he shall bring to the priest
a ram without blemish from the flock,
with your valuation, as a trespass offering. So the priest shall make atonement for him regarding his ignorance
in which he erred and did not know
it, and it shall be forgiven him.
19 "It is a trespass offering; [a]he has
certainly trespassed against the LORD."

6 And the LORD spoke to Moses, saying:
2 "If a person sins and [a]commits a
trespass against the LORD by [b]lying[1] to
his neighbor about [c]what was delivered to him for safekeeping, or about
[2]a pledge, or about a robbery, or if he
has [d]extorted from his neighbor,
3 "or if he [a]has found what was lost
and lies concerning it, and [b]swears
falsely—in any one of these things that
a man may do in which he sins:
4 "then it shall be, because he has
sinned and is *guilty, that he shall
[1]restore [a]what he has stolen, or the
thing which he has extorted, or what
was delivered to him for safekeeping,
or the lost thing which he found,
5 "or all that about which he has **5**
sworn falsely. He shall [a]restore its full
value, add one-fifth more to it, *and* give
it to whomever it belongs, on the day
of his trespass offering.
6 "And he shall bring his trespass offering to the LORD, [a]a ram without

5:7 Two turtledoves or two young pigeons: The rule for purification of sin as a result of ritual uncleanness or in swearing an oath should not be linked to the economic status of the individual. The law therefore makes provision for the poor. Mary the mother of Jesus gave the offering of two turtledoves or two young pigeons instead of the more expensive sacrifice (Luke 2:24; for the ritual after childbirth, see Lev. 12:8).

5:15 The **trespass offering** was a compensatory offering restricted to a ram or male lamb. It was offered primarily for trespasses against the Lord's sacred property or His holy name (by giving false oaths in court). In addition to the animal sacrifice, the offender "shall make restitution" (v. 16), and so bring satisfaction for the sin.

It foreshadowed Christ's sacrificial death that compensated God for our sin, a compensation we could never pay (see Is. 53). It also denoted the Christian's charge to walk in forgiveness and responsible action toward his neighbor (see Matt. 5:23, 24).

6:5 See section 5 of Truth-In-Action at the end of Lev.

blemish from the flock, with your [1]valuation, as a trespass offering, to the priest.

7 [a]"So the priest shall make atonement for him before the LORD, and he shall be forgiven for any one of these things that he may have done in which he trespasses."

The Law of the Burnt Offering

8 Then the LORD spoke to Moses, saying,

9 "Command Aaron and his sons, saying, 'This *is* the [a]law of the burnt offering: The burnt offering *shall be* on the hearth upon the altar all night until morning, and the fire of the altar shall be kept burning on it.

10 [a]'And the priest shall put on his linen garment, and his linen trousers he shall put on his body, and take up the ashes of the burnt offering which the fire has consumed on the altar, and he shall put them [b]beside the altar.

11 'Then [a]he shall take off his garments, put on other garments, and carry the ashes outside the camp [b]to a clean place.

12 'And the fire on the altar shall be kept burning on it; it shall not be put out. And the priest shall burn wood on it every morning, and lay the burnt offering in order on it; and he shall burn on it [a]the fat of the peace offerings.

13 'A fire shall always be burning on the [a]altar; it shall never go out.

The Law of the Grain Offering

14 'This *is* the law of the grain offering: The sons of Aaron shall offer it on the altar before the LORD.

15 'He shall take from it his handful of the fine flour of the *grain offering, with its oil, and all the frankincense which *is* on the grain offering, and shall burn *it* on the altar *for* a sweet aroma, as a memorial to the LORD.

16 'And the remainder of it Aaron and his sons shall eat; with unleavened bread it shall be eaten in a holy place; in the court of the tabernacle of meeting they shall eat it.

17 'It shall not be baked with leaven. I have given it *as* their [1]portion* of My offerings made by fire; it *is* most holy, like the sin offering and the [a]trespass offering.

18 [a]'All the males among the children of Aaron may eat it. [b]*It shall be* a *statute *forever in your generations concerning the offerings made by fire to the LORD. [c]Everyone who touches them must be holy.' "

19 And the LORD spoke to Moses, saying,

20 [a]"This *is* the offering of Aaron and his sons, which they shall offer to the LORD, *beginning* on the day when he is anointed: one-tenth of an [b]ephah of fine flour as a daily grain offering, half of it in the morning and half of it at night.

21 "It shall be made in a [a]pan with oil. *When it is* mixed, you shall bring it in. The baked pieces of the grain offering you shall offer *for* a [1]sweet aroma to the LORD.

22 "The priest from among his sons, [a]who is anointed in his place, shall offer it. *It is* a statute forever to the LORD. [b]It shall be [1]wholly burned.

23 "For every grain offering for the priest shall be wholly burned. It shall not be eaten."

The Law of the Sin Offering

24 Also the LORD spoke to Moses, saying,

25 "Speak to Aaron and to his sons, saying, 'This *is* the law of the sin offering: [a]In the place where the burnt offering is killed, the sin offering shall be killed before the LORD. It *is* most holy.

26 [a]'The priest who offers it for sin shall eat it. In a holy place it shall be eaten, in the court of the tabernacle of meeting.

27 [a]'Everyone who touches its flesh [1]must be holy. And when its blood is sprinkled on any garment, you shall wash that on which it was sprinkled, in a holy place.

28 'But the earthen vessel in which it is boiled [a]shall be broken. And if it is boiled in a bronze pot, it shall be both scoured and rinsed in water.

29 'All the males among the priests may eat it. It *is* most holy.

30 [a]'But no sin offering from which

6 [1]*appraisal*
7 [a]Lev. 4:26
9 [a]Ex. 29:38–42; Num. 28:3–10
10 [a]Ex. 28:39–43; Lev. 16:4; Ezek. 44:17, 18 [b]Lev. 1:16
11 [a]Ezek. 44:19 [b]Lev. 4:12
12 [a]Lev. 3:3, 5, 9, 14
13 [a]Lev. 1:7
15 *See WW at Num. 29:6.
17 [a]Lev. 7:7 [1]*share* *See WW at Zech. 2:12.
18 [a]Lev. 6:29; 7:6; Num. 18:10; 1 Cor. 9:13 [b]Lev. 3:17 [c]Ex. 29:37; Lev. 22:3–7; Num. 4:15; Hag. 2:11–13 *See WW at Neh. 9:13. • See WW at Ps. 136:1.
20 [a]Ex. 29:2 [b]Ex. 16:36
21 [a]Lev. 2:5; 7:9 [1]*pleasing*
22 [a]Lev. 4:3 [b]Ex. 29:25 [1]*completely*
25 [a]Lev. 1:1, 3, 5, 11
26 [a][Lev. 10:17, 18]; Num. 18:9, 10; [Ezek. 44:28, 29]
27 [a]Ex. 29:37; Num. 4:15; Hag. 2:11–13 [1]Lit. *shall*
28 [a]Lev. 11:33; 15:12
30 [a]Lev. 4:7, 11, 12, 18, 21; 10:18; 16:27; [Heb. 13:11, 12]

6:9—7:38 These specific instructions for the priests supplement what has previously been stated about the various offerings.

6:9 Command Aaron and his sons saying: The strong imperative, "Command," means that an immediate response is expected. Aaron and his sons are required to begin this practice and to continue it. **Law** (Hebrew *torah*) denotes instruction. The English "law" is based in part upon the Latin Vulgate version, which translated *torah* by the Latin *lex* meaning "law." It is best, however, to see *torah* as referring to a general body of instructions.

6:12, 13 See section 1 of Truth-In-Action at the end of Lev.

any of the blood is brought into the tabernacle of meeting, to make atonement
in [1]the holy [b]*place*, shall be [c]eaten. It
shall be [d]burned in the fire.

The Law of the Trespass Offering

7 'Likewise [a]this *is* the law of the
trespass offering (it *is* most holy):
2 'In the place where they kill the
burnt offering they shall kill the trespass offering. And its blood he shall
sprinkle all around on the altar.
3 'And he shall offer from it all its fat.
The fat tail and the fat that covers the
entrails,
4 'the two kidneys and the fat that *is*
on them by the flanks, and the fatty
lobe *attached* to the liver above the
kidneys, he shall remove;
5 'and the priest shall burn them on
the altar *as* an offering made by fire
to the LORD. It *is* a trespass offering.
4 6 [a]'Every male among the priests may
eat it. It shall be eaten in a holy place.
[b]It *is* most holy.
7 [a]'The trespass offering *is* like the
sin offering; *there is* one law for them
both: the priest who makes atonement
with it shall have *it*.
8 'And the priest who offers anyone's
burnt offering, that priest shall have
for himself the skin of the burnt offering which he has offered.
9 'Also [a]every grain offering that is
baked in the oven and all that is prepared in the covered pan, or [1]in a pan,
shall be the priest's who offers it.
10 'Every grain offering, *whether*
mixed with oil or dry, shall belong to
all the sons of Aaron, to one *as much*
as the other.

The Law of Peace Offerings

11 [a]'This *is* the law of the sacrifice of
peace offerings which he shall offer to
the LORD:
12 'If he offers it for a thanksgiving,
then he shall offer, with the sacrifice
of thanksgiving, unleavened cakes
mixed with oil, unleavened wafers
[a]anointed with oil, or cakes of blended
flour mixed with oil.
13 'Besides the cakes, *as* his offering
he shall offer [a]leavened bread with the
sacrifice of thanksgiving of his peace
offering.
14 'And from it he shall offer one cake
from each offering *as* a heave offering
to the LORD. [a]It shall belong to the
priest who sprinkles the blood of the
peace offering.
15 [a]'The flesh of the sacrifice of his
peace offering for thanksgiving shall
be eaten the same day it is offered. He
shall not leave any of it until morning.
16 'But [a]if the sacrifice of his offering
is a vow or a voluntary offering, it shall
be eaten the same day that he offers
his sacrifice; but on the next day the
remainder of it also may be eaten;
17 'the remainder of the flesh of the
sacrifice on the third day must be
burned with fire.
18 'And if *any* of the flesh of the sacrifice of his peace offering is eaten at
all on the third day, it shall not be accepted, nor shall it be [a]imputed to him;
it shall be an [b]abomination *to* him who
offers it, and the person who eats of it
shall bear [1]guilt.
19 'The flesh that touches any *unclean
thing shall not be eaten. It shall be
burned with fire. And as for the *clean*
flesh, all who are [1]clean may eat of it.
20 'But the person who eats the flesh
of the sacrifice of the peace offering
that *belongs* to the [a]LORD, [b]while he
is unclean, that person [c]shall be cut off
from his people.
21 'Moreover the person who touches
any unclean thing, *such as* [a]human uncleanness, *an* [b]unclean animal, or any
[c]abominable[1] unclean thing, and who
eats the flesh of the sacrifice of the
peace offering that *belongs* to the
LORD, that person [d]shall be cut off from
his people.' "

Fat and Blood May Not Be Eaten

22 And the LORD spoke to Moses, saying,
23 "Speak to the children of Israel,
saying: [a]'You shall not eat any fat, of
ox or sheep or goat.
24 'And the fat of an animal that dies
naturally, and the fat of what is torn
by wild beasts, may be used in any
other way; but you shall by no means
eat it.

30 [b]Ex. 26:33 [c]Lev. 6:16, 23, 26 [d]Lev. 16:27 [1]The Most Holy Place when capitalized

CHAPTER 7

1 [a]Lev. 5:14—6:7
6 [a]Lev. 6:16–18, 29; Num. 18:9 [b]Lev. 2:3
7 [a]Lev. 6:24–30; 14:13
9 [a]Lev. 2:3, 10; Num. 18:9; Ezek. 44:29 [1]*on a griddle*
11 [a]Lev. 3:1; 22:18, 21; Ezek. 45:15
12 [a]Lev. 2:4; Num. 6:15
13 [a]Lev. 2:12; 23:17, 18; Amos 4:5
14 [a]Num. 18:8, 11, 19
15 [a]Lev. 22:29, 30
16 [a]Lev. 19:5–8
18 [a]Num. 18:27 [b]Lev. 11:10, 11, 41; 19:7; [Prov. 15:8] [1]*his iniquity*
19 [1]*pure* *See WW at Lev. 10:10.
20 [a][Heb. 2:17] [b]Lev. 5:3; 15:3; 22:3–7; Num. 19:13; [1 Cor. 11:28] [c]Gen. 17:14; Ex. 31:14
21 [a]Lev. 5:2, 3, 5 [b]Lev. 11:24, 28 [c]Ezek. 4:14 [d]Lev. 7:20 [1]So with MT, LXX, Vg.; Sam., Syr., Tg. *swarming thing* (cf. 5:2)
23 [a]Lev. 3:17; 17:10–15; Deut. 14:21; Ezek. 4:14; 44:31

7:1 It *is* most holy is literally, "holy of holies" (Hebrew *kodesh kodeshim*), signifying the sacredness of the trespass offering in comparison to all things holy and set apart to the Lord.
7:6 See section 4 of Truth-In-Action at the end of Lev.
7:10 Belong to all the sons of Aaron: The priests were permitted to eat some of the offerings. They must eat them, however, within the holy place (v. 6), which emphasized the sacredness of an offering set apart to the Lord. The sons of Aaron served as priests because of their family heritage and had to maintain their own purity and ritual cleanness.

25 'For whoever eats the fat of the animal of which men offer an offering made by fire to the LORD, the person who eats *it* shall be cut off from his people.

26 [a]'Moreover you shall not eat any blood in any of your dwellings, *whether* of bird or beast.

27 'Whoever eats any blood, that person shall be cut off from his people.' "

The Portion of Aaron and His Sons

4 **28** Then the LORD spoke to Moses, saying,

29 "Speak to the children of Israel, saying: [a]'He who offers the sacrifice of his peace offering to the LORD shall bring his offering to the LORD from the sacrifice of his peace offering.

30 [a]'His own hands shall bring the offerings made by fire to the LORD. The fat with the breast he shall bring, that the [b]breast may be waved *as* a wave offering before the LORD.

31 [a]'And the priest shall burn the fat on the altar, but the [b]breast shall be Aaron's and his sons'.

32 [a]'Also the right thigh you shall give to the priest *as* a heave offering from the sacrifices of your peace offerings.

33 'He among the sons of Aaron, who offers the blood of the peace offering and the fat, shall have the right thigh for *his* part.

34 'For [a]the breast of the wave offering and the thigh of the heave offering I have taken from the children of Israel, from the sacrifices of their peace offerings, and I have given them to Aaron the priest and to his sons from the children of Israel by a statute forever.' "

35 This *is* the consecrated portion for Aaron and his sons, from the offerings made by fire to the LORD, on the day when *Moses* presented them to [1]minister to the LORD as priests.

36 The LORD commanded this to be given to them by the children of Israel, [a]on the day that He anointed them, *by* a statute forever throughout their generations.

37 This *is* the law [a]of the burnt offering, [b]the grain offering, [c]the sin offering, [d]the trespass offering, [e]the consecrations, and [f]the sacrifice of the peace offering,

38 which the LORD commanded Moses on Mount Sinai, on the day when He commanded the children of Israel [a]to offer their offerings to the LORD in the Wilderness of Sinai.

26 [a]Gen. 9:4; Lev. 3:17; 17:10–16; 19:26; Deut. 12:23; 1 Sam. 14:33; Ezek. 33:25; [John 6:53]; Acts 15:20, 29
29 [a]Lev. 3:1; 22:21; Ezek. 45:15
30 [a]Lev. 3:3, 4, 9, 14 [b]Ex. 29:24, 27; Lev. 8:27; 9:21; Num. 6:20
31 [a]Lev. 3:5, 11, 16 [b]Num. 18:11; Deut. 18:3
32 [a]Ex. 29:27; Lev. 7:34; 9:21; Num. 6:20
34 [a]Ex. 29:28; Lev. 10:14, 15; Num. 18:18, 19; Deut. 18:3
35 [1]*serve*
36 [a]Ex. 40:13–15; Lev. 8:12, 30
37 [a]Lev. 6:9 [b]Lev. 6:14 [c]Lev. 6:25 [d]Lev. 7:1 [e]Ex. 29:1; Lev. 6:20 [f]Lev. 7:11
38 [a]Lev. 1:1, 2; Deut. 4:5

CHAPTER 8

2 [a]Ex. 29:1–3 [b]Ex. 28:2, 4 [c]Ex. 30:24, 25 [d]Ex. 29:10 [e]Ex. 29:15, 19
6 [a]Ex. 30:20; Heb. 10:22
7 [a]Ex. 39:1–31 *See WW at Ex. 35:27.
8 [a]Ex. 28:30; Num. 27:21; Deut. 33:8; 1 Sam. 28:6; Ezra 2:63; Neh. 7:65 [1]Lit. *Lights and the Perfections,* Ex. 28:30
9 [a]Ex. 28:36, 37; 29:6
10 [a]Ex. 30:26–29; 40:10, 11; Lev. 8:2
11 [1]*set them apart* for the LORD
12 [a]Ex. 29:7; 30:30; Lev. 21:10, 12; Ps. 133:2

Aaron and His Sons Consecrated

8 And the LORD spoke to Moses, saying:

2 [a]"Take Aaron and his sons with him, and [b]the garments, [c]the anointing oil, a [d]bull as the sin offering, two [e]rams, and a basket of unleavened bread;

3 "and gather all the congregation together at the door of the tabernacle of meeting."

4 So Moses did as the LORD commanded him. And the congregation was gathered together at the door of the tabernacle of meeting.

5 And Moses said to the congregation, "This *is* what the LORD commanded to be done."

6 Then Moses brought Aaron and his sons and [a]washed them with water.

7 And he [a]put the tunic on him, girded him with the sash, clothed him with the robe, and put the *ephod on him; and he girded him with the intricately woven band of the ephod, and with it tied *the ephod* on him.

8 Then he put the breastplate on him, and he [a]put the [1]Urim and the Thummim in the breastplate.

9 [a]And he put the turban on his head. Also on the turban, on its front, he put the golden plate, the holy crown, as the LORD had commanded Moses.

10 [a]Also Moses took the anointing oil, and anointed the tabernacle and all that *was* in it, and consecrated them.

11 He sprinkled some of it on the altar seven times, anointed the altar and all its utensils, and the laver and its base, to [1]consecrate them.

12 And he [a]poured some of the anoint-

7:26 You shall not eat any blood refers to eating meat without draining the blood (see 1 Sam. 14:33). This prohibition is because of the atoning significance of blood.

7:28–36 See section 4 of Truth-In-Action at the end of Lev.

8:2 A bull as the sin offering refers to the first step in the priestly ordination. It is the offering of purification (see note on 4:3). This installation is also explained in Ex. 29; 35—39.

8:12 Anointing oil on Aaron's head: The anointing set Aaron apart for designated service in the priestly worship (see also Ex. 29:7) for fulfillment of his divinely appointed task. Both kings and priests were anointed to serve the congregation as God's designated leaders. Even the pagan king Cyrus is referred to as the Lord's anointed (messiah) because of the task he was designated to perform (Is. 45:1). The writers of the Dead Sea Scrolls referred to the messiahs ("anointed ones") of Aaron and David, which seems to demonstrate their view that God would send both a priestly

ing oil on Aaron's *head and anointed
him, to consecrate him.
13 [a]Then Moses brought Aaron's sons
and put tunics on them, girded them
with sashes, and put [1]hats on them, as
the LORD had commanded Moses.
14 [a]And he brought the bull for the sin
offering. Then Aaron and his sons
[b]laid their hands on the head of the
bull for the sin offering,
15 and Moses killed *it*. [a]Then he took
the blood, and put *some* on the horns
of the altar all around with his finger,
and purified the altar. And he poured
the blood at the base of the altar, and
consecrated it, to make [1]atonement for
it.
16 [a]Then he took all the fat that *was*
on the entrails, the fatty lobe *attached
to* the liver, and the two kidneys with
their fat, and Moses burned *them* on
the altar.
17 But the bull, its hide, its flesh, and
its offal, he burned with fire outside the
camp, as the LORD [a]had commanded
Moses.
18 [a]Then he brought the ram as the
burnt offering. And Aaron and his sons
laid their hands on the head of the
ram,
19 and Moses killed *it*. Then he sprinkled the blood all around on the
altar.
20 And he cut the ram into pieces; and
Moses [a]burned the head, the pieces,
and the fat.
21 Then he washed the entrails and the
legs in water. And Moses burned the
whole ram on the altar. It *was* a burnt
sacrifice for a [1]sweet aroma, an offering made by fire to the LORD, [a]as the
LORD had commanded Moses.
22 And [a]he brought the second ram,
the ram of consecration. Then Aaron
and his sons laid their hands on the
head of the ram,
23 and Moses killed *it*. Also he took
some of [a]its blood and put it on the
tip of Aaron's right ear, on the thumb
of his right hand, and on the big toe
of his right foot.
24 Then he brought Aaron's sons. And
Moses put *some* of the [a]blood on the
tips of their right ears, on the thumbs
of their right hands, and on the big
toes of their right feet. And Moses
sprinkled the blood all around on the
altar.
25 [a]Then he took the fat and the fat
tail, all the fat that *was* on the entrails,
the fatty lobe *attached to* the liver, the
two kidneys and their fat, and the right
thigh;
26 [a]and from the basket of unleavened
bread that was before the LORD he took
one unleavened cake, a cake of bread
anointed with oil, and one wafer, and
put *them* on the fat and on the right
thigh;
27 and he put all *these* [a]in Aaron's
hands and in his sons' hands, and
waved them *as* a wave offering before
the LORD.
28 [a]Then Moses took them from their
hands and burned *them* on the altar,
on the burnt offering. They *were* consecration offerings for a sweet aroma.
That *was* an offering made by fire to
the LORD.
29 And [a]Moses took the [b]breast and
waved it *as* a wave offering before the
LORD. It was Moses' [c]part of the ram
of consecration, as the LORD had commanded Moses.
30 Then [a]Moses took some of the
anointing oil and some of the blood
which *was* on the altar, and sprinkled
it on Aaron, on his garments, on his
sons, and on the garments of his sons
with him; and he consecrated Aaron,
his garments, his sons, and the garments of his sons with him.
31 And Moses said to Aaron and his
sons, [a]"Boil the flesh *at* the door of the
tabernacle of meeting, and eat it there
with the bread that *is* in the basket
of consecration offerings, as I commanded, saying, 'Aaron and his sons
shall eat it.'
32 [a]"What remains of the flesh and of
the bread you shall burn with fire.
33 "And you shall not go outside the
door of the tabernacle of meeting *for*
seven days, until the days of your consecration are ended. For [a]seven days
he shall consecrate you.
34 [a]"As he has done this day, *so* the
LORD has commanded to do, to make
atonement for you.
35 "Therefore you shall stay *at* the
door of the tabernacle of meeting day
and night for seven days, and [a]keep
the [1]charge of the LORD, so that you
may not die; for so I have been commanded."
36 So Aaron and his sons did all the
things that the LORD had commanded
by the hand of Moses.

12 *See WW at Gen. 3:15.
13 [a]Ex. 29:8, 9 [1]*headpieces*
14 [a]Ex. 29:10; Ps. 66:15; Ezek. 43:19 [b]Lev. 4:4
15 [a]Ex. 29:12, 36; Lev. 4:7; Ezek. 43:20, 26; [Heb. 9:22] [1]Lit. *covering*
16 [a]Ex. 29:13; Lev. 4:8
17 [a]Ex. 29:14; Lev. 4:11, 12
18 [a]Ex. 29:15
20 [a]Lev. 1:8
21 [a]Ex. 29:18 [1]*pleasing*
22 [a]Ex. 29:19, 31; Lev. 8:2
23 [a]Ex. 29:20, 21; Lev. 14:14
24 [a][Heb. 9:13, 14, 18–23]
25 [a]Ex. 29:22
26 [a]Ex. 29:23
27 [a]Ex. 29:24; Lev. 7:30, 34
28 [a]Ex. 29:25
29 [a]Ps. 99:6 [b]Ex. 29:27 [c]Ex. 29:26
30 [a]Ex. 29:21; 30:30; Num. 3:3
31 [a]Ex. 29:31, 32
32 [a]Ex. 29:34
33 [a]Ex. 29:30, 35; Lev. 10:7; Ezek. 43:25, 26
34 [a][Heb. 7:16]
35 [a]Num. 1:53; 3:7; 9:19; Deut. 11:1; 1 Kin. 2:3; Ezek. 48:11 [1]*office*

and a kingly Messiah during the last days. Jesus used the term "anointed" from Is. 61:1 when He spoke of His messianic task (Luke 4:18). From this comes the term "christ," which is technically not a proper name but the Greek form of the Hebrew word *mashiach* (messiah).

The Priestly Ministry Begins

9 It came to pass on the [a]eighth day
that Moses called Aaron and his
sons and the elders of Israel.
2 And he said to Aaron, "Take for
yourself a young [a]bull as a **sin offering**
and a ram as a burnt offering, without
blemish, and offer *them* before the
LORD.

> **WORD WEALTH**
>
> **9:2 sin offering,** *chatta't* (kah-*taht*); Strong's #2403: A sin, an offense, a misdeed, also used to describe the punishment for sin, or the offering for sin. The root verb *chata'* means "to sin, to be at fault, to harm, to offend." The noun appears more than 270 times in the OT, and 112 times is translated "sin offering."

3 "And to the children of Israel you
shall speak, saying, [a]'Take a kid of the
goats as a sin offering, and a calf and
a lamb, *both* of the first year, without
blemish, as a burnt offering,
4 'also a bull and a ram as peace offerings, to *sacrifice before the LORD,
and [a]a grain offering mixed with oil;
for [b]today the LORD will appear to
you.' "
5 So they brought what Moses commanded before the tabernacle of meeting. And all the congregation drew
near and stood [1]before the LORD.
6 Then Moses said, "This *is* the thing
which the LORD commanded you to do,
and the *glory of the LORD will appear
to you."
7 And Moses said to Aaron, "Go to
the altar, [a]offer your sin offering and
your burnt offering, and make atonement for yourself and for the people.
[b]Offer the offering of the people, and
make atonement for them, as the LORD
commanded."
8 Aaron therefore went to the altar
and killed the calf of the sin offering,
which *was* for himself.
9 Then the sons of Aaron brought the
blood to him. And he dipped his finger
in the blood, put *it* on the horns of the
altar, and poured the blood at the base
of the altar.
10 [a]But the fat, the kidneys, and the
fatty lobe from the liver of the sin offering he burned on the altar, as the LORD
had commanded Moses.
11 [a]The flesh and the hide he burned
with fire outside the camp.
12 And he killed the burnt offering;
and Aaron's sons presented to him the
blood, [a]which he sprinkled all around
on the altar.
13 [a]Then they presented the burnt offering to him, with its pieces and head,
and he burned *them* on the altar.
14 [a]And he washed the entrails and the
legs, and burned *them* with the burnt
offering on the altar.
15 [a]Then he brought the people's offering, and took the goat, which *was* the
sin offering for the people, and killed
it and offered it for sin, like the first
one.
16 And he brought the burnt offering
and offered it [a]according to the [1]pre-
scribed manner.
17 Then he brought the grain offering,
took a handful of it, and burned *it* on
the altar, [a]besides the burnt sacrifice
of the morning.
18 He also killed the bull and the ram
as [a]sacrifices of peace offerings, which
were for the people. And Aaron's sons
presented to him the blood, which he
sprinkled all around on the altar,
19 and the fat from the bull and the
ram—the fatty tail, what covers *the entrails* and the kidneys, and the fatty
lobe *attached to* the liver;
20 and they put the fat on the breasts.
[a]Then he burned the fat on the altar;
21 but the breasts and the right thigh
Aaron waved [a]*as* a wave offering before the LORD, as Moses had commanded.
22 Then Aaron lifted his hand toward
the people, [a]blessed them, and came
down from offering the sin offering,
the burnt offering, and peace offerings.
23 And Moses and Aaron went into the
tabernacle of meeting, and came out
and blessed the people. Then the glory
of the LORD appeared to all the people,
24 and [a]fire came out from before the
LORD and consumed the burnt offering

CHAPTER 9
1 [a]Ezek. 43:27
2 [a]Ex. 29:21; Lev. 4:1–12
3 [a]Lev. 4:23, 28; Ezra 6:17; 10:19
4 [a]Lev. 2:4 [b]Ex. 29:43; Lev. 9:6, 23
*See WW at Deut. 16:2.
5 [1]*in the presence of*
6 *See WW at Is. 60:1.
7 [a]Lev. 4:3; 1 Sam. 3:14; [Heb. 5:3–5; 7:27] [b]Lev. 4:16, 20; Heb. 5:1
10 [a]Ex. 23:18; Lev. 8:16
11 [a]Lev. 4:11, 12; 8:17
12 [a]Lev. 1:5; 8:19
13 [a]Lev. 8:20
14 [a]Lev. 8:21
15 [a][Is. 53:10; Heb. 2:17; 5:3]
16 [a]Lev. 1:1–13 [1]*ordinance*
17 [a]Ex. 29:38, 39
18 [a]Lev. 3:1–11
20 [a]Lev. 3:5, 16
21 [a]Ex. 29:24, 26, 27; Lev. 7:30–34
22 [a]Num. 6:22–26; Deut. 21:5; Luke 24:50
24 [a]Gen. 4:4; Judg. 6:21; 2 Chr. 7:1; Ps. 20:3

9:8 The sin offering: The entire process of the slaughter, the sprinkling of the blood and the offering of the fat, as described with precision in ch. 4, is here carried out in exact detail by the newly ordained Aaron.

9:22 Then Aaron lifted his hand toward the people, blessed them: The blessing of Aaron, recited while he stood by the altar, is recorded in Num. 6:22–27. He would turn to the people, raise his hands, and pronounce the blessing. The people would then respond. The Aaronic blessing is still recited today in the modern synagogue; in the time of Jesus, the people in the temple responded with the blessing, "Blessed be the Name of His Honor; His kingdom is forever and ever."

9:24 God's approval is seen in **fire that came out from before the LORD and consumed the burnt offering.** This miraculous display of God's presence was repeated at Elijah's confrontation with the prophets of Baal (1 Kin. 18:38).

and the fat on the altar. When all the people saw *it*, they [b]shouted and fell on their [c]faces.

The Profane Fire of Nadab and Abihu

10 Then [a]Nadab and Abihu, the sons of Aaron, [b]each took his censer and put fire in it, put incense on it, and offered [c]profane fire before the LORD, which He had not commanded them.
2 So [a]fire went out from the LORD and devoured them, and they died before the LORD.
3 And Moses said to Aaron, "This is what the LORD spoke, saying:

'By those [a]who come near Me
I must be regarded as holy;
And before all the people
I must be glorified.' "

So Aaron held his peace.
4 Then Moses called Mishael and Elzaphan, the sons of Uzziel the uncle of Aaron, and said to them, "Come near, [a]carry your *brethren from [1]before the sanctuary out of the camp."
5 So they went near and carried them by their tunics out of the camp, as Moses had said.
6 And Moses said to Aaron, and to Eleazar and Ithamar, his sons, "Do not [1]uncover your heads nor tear your clothes, lest you die, and [a]wrath come upon all the people. But let your brethren, the whole house of Israel, [2]bewail the burning which the LORD has kindled.
7 [a]"You shall not go out from the door of the tabernacle of meeting, lest you die, [b]for the anointing oil of the LORD *is* upon you." And they did according to the word of Moses.

Conduct Prescribed for Priests

8 Then the LORD spoke to Aaron, saying:
9 [a]"Do not drink wine or intoxicating drink, you, nor your sons with you, when you go into the tabernacle of meeting, lest you die. *It shall be* a statute forever throughout your generations,
10 "that you may [a]distinguish between holy and unholy, and between **unclean** and clean,

WORD WEALTH

10:10 unclean, *tame'* (tah-*may*); Strong's #2931: Defiled, contaminated, polluted, unclean. This adjective comes from a root verb, also spelled *tame'*, meaning "to defile" or to make unclean." The adjective *tame* occurs more than 80 times (usually translated "unclean"), 75 percent of these in Lev., Num., and Deut. The cause for uncleanness is contact with unclean things (7:21). In addition, God restricted Israel from eating a number of species of birds, mammals, fish, and insects, which were to be considered unclean. This emphasis on cleanness or uncleanness was a part of God's design to impress the Israelites with the difference between the two conditions. Not only were the priests to learn to distinguish between holy and unholy, between clean and unclean, but they were to teach that differentiation to all Israel (10:10, 11).

11 [a]"and that you may teach the children of Israel all the statutes which the LORD has spoken to them by the hand of Moses."
12 And Moses spoke to Aaron, and to Eleazar and Ithamar, his sons who were left: [a]"Take the grain offering that remains of the offerings made by fire to the LORD, and eat it without leaven beside the altar; [b]for it *is* most holy.
13 "You shall eat it in a [a]holy* place, because it *is* your [1]due and your sons' due, of the sacrifices made by fire to the LORD; for [b]so I have been commanded.
14 [a]"The breast of the wave offering

24 [b]Ezra 3:11 [c]1 Kin. 18:38, 39

CHAPTER 10

1 [a]Ex. 24:1, 9; Num. 3:2–4; 1 Chr. 24:2 [b]Lev. 16:12 [c]Ex. 30:9; 1 Sam. 2:17
2 [a]Gen. 19:24; Num. 11:1; 16:35; Rev. 20:9
3 [a]Ex. 19:22; Lev. 21:6; Is. 52:11; Ezek. 20:41
4 [a]Acts 5:6, 10 [1]*in front of* *See WW at Ps. 133:1.
6 [a]Num. 1:53; 16:22, 46; 18:5; Josh. 7:1; 22:18, 20; 2 Sam. 24:1 [1]An act of mourning [2]*weep bitterly*
7 [a]Lev. 8:33; 21:12 [b]Lev. 8:30
9 [a]Gen. 9:21; [Prov. 20:1; 31:5]; Is. 28:7; Ezek. 44:21; Hos. 4:11; Luke 1:15; [Eph. 5:18]; 1 Tim. 3:3; Titus 1:7
10 [a]Lev. 11:47; 20:25; Ezek. 22:26; 44:23
11 [a]Deut. 24:8; Neh. 8:2, 8; Jer. 18:18; Mal. 2:7
12 [a]Num. 18:9 [b]Lev. 21:22
13 [a]Num. 18:10 [b]Lev. 2:3; 6:16 [1]*portion* *See WW at Lev. 19:2.
14 [a]Ex. 29:24, 26, 27; Lev. 7:30–34; Num. 18:11

10:1 Nadab and Abihu also appear in Ex. 24:1, 9, where they are within a select group of representatives of the people who were close to Moses and able to view the Lord's glory. A conflict may have existed within the priesthood between a group led by Nadab and Abihu and a group of the priests mentioned here who remained faithful to the sacred worship, led by Mishael and Elzaphan (v. 4). The nature of their wrong, that is to offer **profane fire** (Hebrew *esh zarah,* literally "strange" or "foreign" fire), seems to make reference to idolatrous worship. Apparently they had taken fire for their censers from a place other than the altar fire, which was the only legitimate fire for the worship.

Ancient Jewish interpretation taught that they were intoxicated when they came before the **LORD,** which intensified the gravity of their actions (see v. 9). The holiness of the worship was in jeopardy when the priests offered fire other than that commanded by God. The same manifestation of fire which had earlier shown approval is now sent by God in judgment (v. 2).

10:6 Do not uncover . . . clothes are prohibitions against mourning their deaths. Instead they were to remain totally dedicated to God's task (v. 7).

10:9 Priests were commanded **not** to **drink wine or intoxicating drink** while ministering in the tabernacle. It impaired their ability to make wise decisions.

and the thigh of the heave offering you
shall eat in a clean place, you, your
sons, and your [b]daughters with you;
for *they are* your due and your sons'
[c]due, *which* are given from the sacrifices of peace offerings of the children
of Israel.
15 [a]"The thigh of the heave offering
and the breast of the wave offering
they shall bring with the offerings of
fat made by fire, to offer *as* a wave offering before the LORD. And it shall be
yours and your sons' with you, by a
statute forever, as the LORD has commanded."
16 Then Moses made careful inquiry
about [a]the goat of the sin offering, and
there it was—burned up. And he was
angry with Eleazar and Ithamar, the
sons of Aaron *who were* left, saying,
17 [a]"Why have you not eaten the sin
offering in a holy place, since it *is* most
holy, and *God* has given it to you to
bear [b]the guilt of the congregation, to
make atonement for them before the
LORD?
18 "See! [a]Its blood was not brought inside [1]the holy *place;* indeed you should
have eaten it in a holy *place,* [b]as I commanded."
19 And Aaron said to Moses, "Look,
[a]this day they have offered their sin
offering and their burnt offering before
the LORD, and such things have befallen me! *If* I had eaten the sin offering
today, [b]would it have been accepted in
the sight of the LORD?"
20 So when Moses heard *that,* he was
content.

Foods Permitted and Forbidden

11 Now the LORD spoke to Moses
and Aaron, saying to them,
2 "Speak to the children of Israel,
saying, [a]'These *are* the animals which
you may eat among all the animals that
are on the earth:
3 'Among the animals, whatever divides the hoof, having cloven hooves
and chewing the cud—that you may
eat.
4 'Nevertheless these you shall
[a]not eat among those that chew the cud
or those that have cloven hooves: the
camel, because it chews the cud but
does not have cloven hooves, is
[1]unclean to you;
5 'the [1]rock hyrax, because it chews
the cud but does not have cloven
hooves, *is* [2]unclean to you;
6 'the hare, because it chews the cud
but does not have cloven hooves, *is* unclean to you;
7 'and the swine, though it divides the
hoof, having cloven hooves, yet does
not chew the cud, [a]*is* unclean to you.
8 'Their flesh you shall not eat, and
their carcasses you shall not touch.
[a]They *are* unclean to you.
9 [a]'These you may eat of all that *are*
in the water: whatever in the water has
fins and scales, whether in the seas or
in the rivers—that you may eat.
10 'But all in the seas or in the rivers
that do not have fins and scales, all that
move in the water or any living thing
which *is* in the water, they *are* [1]an
[a]abomination to you.
11 'They shall be an abomination to
you; you shall not eat their flesh, but
you shall regard their carcasses as an
abomination.
12 'Whatever in the water does not
have fins or scales—that *shall be* an
abomination to you.
13 [a]'And these you shall regard as an
abomination among the birds; they
shall not be eaten, they *are* an abomination: the eagle, the vulture, the buzzard,
14 'the kite, and the falcon after its
kind;
15 'every raven after its kind,
16 'the ostrich, the short-eared owl, the
sea gull, and the hawk after its kind;
17 'the little owl, the fisher owl, and
the screech owl;
18 'the white owl, the jackdaw, and the
carrion vulture;
19 'the stork, the heron after its kind,
the hoopoe, and the bat.
20 'All flying insects that creep on *all*
fours *shall be* an abomination to you.
21 'Yet these you may eat of every flying insect that creeps on *all* fours:
those which have jointed legs above
their feet with which to leap on the
earth.
22 'These you may eat: [a]the locust after its kind, the destroying locust after
its kind, the cricket after its kind, and
the grasshopper after its kind.
23 'But all *other* flying insects which
have four feet *shall be* an abomination
to you.

14 [b]Lev. 22:13 [c]Num. 18:10
15 [a]Lev. 7:29, 30, 34
16 [a]Lev. 9:3, 15
17 [a]Lev. 6:24–30 [b]Ex. 28:38; Lev. 22:16; Num. 18:1
18 [a]Lev. 6:30 [b]Lev. 6:26, 30 [1]The Most Holy Place when capitalized
19 [a]Lev. 9:8, 12 [b][Is. 1:11–15]; Jer. 6:20; 14:12; Hos. 9:4; [Mal. 1:10, 13; 3:1–4]

CHAPTER 11

2 [a]Deut. 14:4; Ezek. 4:14; Dan. 1:8; [Matt. 15:11]; Acts 10:12, 14; [Rom. 14:14; Heb. 9:10; 13:9]
4 [a]Acts 10:14 [1]*impure*
5 [1]*rock badger* [2]*impure*
7 [a]Is. 65:4; 66:3, 17; Mark 5:1–17
8 [a]Is. 52:11; [Mark 7:2, 15, 18]; Acts 10:14, 15; 15:29
9 [a]Deut. 14:9
10 [a]Lev. 7:18, 21; Deut. 14:3 [1]*detestable*
13 [a]Deut. 14:12–19; Is. 66:17
22 [a]Matt. 3:4; Mark 1:6

11:1 The LORD spoke to Moses and Aaron: The Lord now speaks directly to both Moses and Aaron, following the ordination of Aaron into the priestly service (see also 13:1; 15:1).

11:2 Animals which you may eat: These restrictions of the community are paralleled in Deut. 14:3–21. The people are set apart in a holy relationship to the Lord, which requires a conscious awareness of the divine presence in daily living, including foods which are acceptable to be eaten (see vv. 43–47). See also the notes on Deut. 14:3–21.

Unclean Animals

24 'By these you shall become [1]unclean; whoever touches the carcass of any of them shall be unclean until evening;

25 'whoever carries part of the carcass of any of them [a]shall wash his clothes and be unclean until evening:

26 '*The carcass* of any animal which divides the foot, but is not cloven-hoofed or does not chew the cud, *is* unclean to you. Everyone who touches it shall be unclean.

27 'And whatever goes on its paws, among all kinds of animals that go on *all* fours, those *are* unclean to you. Whoever touches any such carcass shall be unclean until evening.

28 'Whoever carries *any such* carcass shall wash his clothes and be unclean until evening. It *is* unclean to you.

29 'These also *shall be* unclean to you among the creeping things that creep on the earth: the mole, [a]the mouse, and the large lizard after its kind;

30 'the gecko, the monitor lizard, the sand reptile, the sand lizard, and the chameleon.

31 'These *are* unclean to you among all that creep. Whoever [a]touches them when they are dead shall be unclean until evening.

32 'Anything on which *any* of them falls, when they are dead shall be [1]unclean, whether *it is* any item of wood or clothing or skin or sack, whatever item *it is,* in which *any* work is done, [a]it must be put in water. And it shall be unclean until evening; then it shall be clean.

33 'Any [a]earthen vessel into which *any* of them falls [b]you shall break; and whatever *is* in it shall be unclean:

34 'in such a vessel, any edible food upon which water falls becomes unclean, and any drink that may be drunk from it becomes unclean.

35 'And everything on which *a part* of *any such* carcass falls shall be unclean; *whether it is* an oven or cooking stove, it shall be broken down; *for* they *are* unclean, and shall be unclean to you.

36 'Nevertheless a spring or a cistern, *in which there is* plenty of water, shall be clean, but whatever touches any such carcass becomes unclean.

37 'And if a part of *any such* carcass falls on any planting seed which is to be sown, it *remains* clean.

38 'But if water is put on the seed, and if *a part* of *any such* carcass falls on it, it *becomes* [1]unclean to you.

39 'And if any animal which you may eat dies, he who touches its carcass shall be [a]unclean until evening.

40 [a]'He who eats of its carcass shall wash his clothes and be unclean until evening. He also who carries its carcass shall wash his clothes and be unclean until evening.

41 'And every creeping thing that creeps on the earth *shall be* [1]an abomination. It shall not be eaten.

42 'Whatever crawls on its belly, whatever goes on *all* fours, or whatever has many feet among all creeping things that creep on the earth—these you shall not eat, for they *are* an abomination.

43 [a]'You shall not make [1]yourselves [2]abominable with any creeping thing that creeps; nor shall you make yourselves unclean with them, lest you be defiled by them.

44 'For I *am* the LORD your [a]God. You shall therefore consecrate yourselves, and [b]you shall be holy; for I *am* holy. Neither shall you defile yourselves with any creeping thing that creeps on the earth.

45 [a]'For I *am* the LORD who brings you up out of the land of Egypt, to be your God. [b]You shall therefore be holy, for I *am* holy.

46 'This *is* the law [1]of the animals and the birds and every living creature that moves in the waters, and of every creature that creeps on the earth,

47 [a]'to distinguish between the unclean and the clean, and between the animal that may be eaten and the animal that may not be eaten.'" 3

The Ritual After Childbirth

12 Then the LORD spoke to Moses, saying,

24 [1]*impure*
25 [a]Lev. 14:8; 15:5; Num. 19:10, 21, 22; 31:24; Zech. 13:1; [Heb. 9:10; 10:22; Rev. 7:14]
29 [a]Is. 66:17
31 [a]Hag. 2:13
32 [a]Lev. 15:12 [1]*impure*
33 [a]Lev. 6:28 [b]Lev. 15:12; Ps. 2:9; Jer. 48:38; [2 Tim. 2:21]; Rev. 2:27
38 [1]*impure*
39 [a]Hag. 2:11–13
40 [a]Ex. 22:31; Lev. 17:15; 22:8; Deut. 14:21; Ezek. 4:14; 44:31
41 [1]*detestable*
43 [a]Lev. 20:25 [1]Lit. *your souls* [2]*impure*
44 [a]Ex. 6:7; Lev. 22:33; 25:38; 26:45 [b]Ex. 19:6; Lev. 19:2; 20:7, 26; [Amos 3:3]; Matt. 5:48; 1 Thess. 4:7; 1 Pet. 1:15, 16; [Rev. 22:11, 14]
45 [a]Ex. 6:7; 20:2; Lev. 22:33; 25:38; 26:45; Ps. 105:43–45; Hos. 11:1 [b]Lev. 11:44
46 [1]*concerning*
47 [a]Lev. 10:10; Ezek. 44:23; Mal. 3:18

11:44 You shall be holy; for I *am* holy: The people recognized the difference between the sacred and the profane. They imitated God by living lives according to the code of holiness.

11:45 The LORD who brings you up out of the land of Egypt, to be your God: The salvation of the people from Egypt is considered a present reality. He saved that generation in order that all generations of the people of Israel would recognize Him as their God and realize that they too were redeemed from the bondage of Egypt along with their mothers and fathers. As a result, the people were to respond to Him as the one God worthy of worship and service, who brings a new way of life, thus connecting the response of the children of Israel to live a holy life with divine acts of salvation (see Ex. 6:7, 8; 29:45, 46).

11:47 See section 3 of Truth-In-Action at the end of Lev.

2 "Speak to the children of Israel,
saying: 'If a [a]woman has conceived,
and borne a male child, then [b]she shall
be [1]unclean seven days; [c]as in the days
of her customary impurity she shall be
unclean.
3 'And on the [a]eighth day the flesh
of his foreskin shall be circumcised.
4 'She shall then continue in the
blood of *her* purification thirty-three
days. She shall not touch any [1]hal-
lowed thing, nor come into the
sanctuary until the days of her purification are fulfilled.
5 'But if she bears a female child, then
she shall be unclean two weeks, as in
her customary impurity, and she shall
continue in the blood of *her* purification sixty-six days.
6 [a]'When the days of her purification
are fulfilled, whether for a son or a
daughter, she shall bring to the priest
a [b]lamb [1]of the first year as a burnt
offering, and a young pigeon or a turtledove as a [c]sin offering, to the door
of the tabernacle of meeting.
7 'Then he shall offer it before the
LORD, and make [1]atonement for her.
And she shall be clean from the flow
of her blood. This *is* the law for her
who has borne a male or a female.
8 [a]'And if she is not able to bring a
lamb, then she may bring two turtledoves or two young pigeons—one as
a burnt offering and the other as a sin
offering. [b]So the priest shall make
atonement for her, and she will be
[1]clean.' "

The Law Concerning Leprosy

13 And the LORD spoke to Moses
and Aaron, saying:
2 "When a man has on the skin of
his body a swelling, [a]a scab, or a bright
spot, and it becomes on the skin of his
body *like* a [1]leprous sore, [b]then he
shall be brought to Aaron the priest or
to one of his sons the priests.
3 "The priest shall examine the sore
on the skin of the body; and if the hair
on the sore has turned white, and the
sore appears *to be* deeper than the skin
of his body, it *is* a leprous sore. Then
the priest shall examine him, and pronounce him [1]unclean.
4 "But if the bright spot *is* white on
the skin of his body, and does not appear *to be* deeper than the skin, and
its hair has not turned white, then the
priest shall isolate *the one who has* the
sore [a]seven days.
5 "And the priest shall examine him
on the seventh day; and indeed *if* the
sore appears to be as it was, *and* the
sore has not spread on the skin, then
the priest shall isolate him another
seven days.
6 "Then the priest shall examine him
again on the seventh day; and indeed
if the sore has faded, *and* the sore has
not spread on the skin, then the priest
shall pronounce him clean; it *is only* a
scab, and he [a]shall wash his clothes
and be clean.
7 "But if the scab should at all spread
over the skin, after he has been seen
by the priest for his cleansing, he shall
be seen by the priest again.
8 "And *if* the priest sees that the scab
has indeed spread on the skin, then the
priest shall pronounce him [1]unclean.
It *is* leprosy.
9 "When the leprous sore is on a person, then he shall be brought to the
priest.
10 [a]"And the priest shall examine *him;*
and indeed *if* the swelling on the skin
is white, and it has turned the hair
white, and *there is* a spot of raw flesh
in the swelling,
11 "it *is* an old leprosy on the skin of
his body. The priest shall pronounce
him [1]unclean, and shall not isolate him,
for he *is* unclean.

CHAPTER 12

2 [a]Lev. 15:19; [Job 14:4; Ps. 51:5] [b]Ex. 22:30; Lev. 8:33; 13:4; Luke 2:22 [c]Lev. 18:19 [1]*impure*
3 [a]Gen. 17:12; Luke 1:59; 2:21; John 7:22, 23; Gal. 5:3
4 [1]*consecrated*
6 [a]Luke 2:22 [b][John 1:29; 1 Pet. 1:18, 19] [c]Lev. 5:7 [1]Lit. *a son of his year*
7 [1]Lit. *covering*
8 [a]Lev. 5:7; Luke 2:22–24 [b]Lev. 4:26 [1]*pure*

CHAPTER 13

2 [a]Deut. 28:27; Is. 3:17 [b]Deut. 17:8, 9; 24:8; Mal. 2:7; Luke 17:14 [1]Heb. *saraath,* disfiguring skin diseases, including leprosy, and so in vv. 2–46 and 14:1–32
3 [1]*defiled*
4 [a]Lev. 14:8
6 [a]Lev. 11:25; 14:8; [John 13:8, 10]
8 [1]*defiled*
10 [a]Num. 12:10, 12; 2 Kin. 5:27; 2 Chr. 26:19, 20
11 [1]*defiled*

12:2 If a woman has conceived, and borne: The laws regarding ritual purification after childbirth emphasized the idea of separating the unclean from the holy. The people were to practice the holiness code in each aspect of natural life. Although it is not always clear to us today why God deemed certain activities as unclean, these customs were diligently observed and obviously had significance to the people of that time. Jesus Himself was brought to the temple for this ritual (Luke 2:22–24).

12:6 The **burnt offering** and **sin offering** served to purify the woman, secure any needed forgiveness, express her gratitude, and renew her dedication.

12:8 If she is not able to bring a lamb: The family of Jesus did not offer a lamb, but two small birds, the offering for those who did not possess the means for such expense (Luke 2:24). See text and note on 5:7.

13:2 On the skin of his body *like* a leprous sore: Vv. 2–28 deal with the diagnosis of 21 afflictions of the skin which are referred to in the inclusive term "leprosy." Leprosy (Hebrew *tsara'at*) denoted a variety of skin ailments, including psoriasis, favus, leukoderma, and the contagious Hansen's disease. Lev. associated holiness with wholeness; skin diseases therefore made one unclean because he was not pure and whole (vv. 12, 13, 20, 55).

13:4 The priest shall isolate *the one* who has the sore: The priest oversaw the treatment of the afflicted person in a way that both cared for the sick and also protected the community. The medical principles contained in Lev. view the ailment within parameters of personal and social hygiene that were unparalleled in other religions of the period.

12 "And if leprosy breaks out all over
the skin, and the leprosy covers all the
skin of *the one who has* the sore, from
his head to his foot, wherever the priest
looks,
13 "then the priest shall consider; and
indeed *if* the leprosy has covered all
his body, he shall pronounce *him* clean
who has the sore. It has all turned
[a]white. He *is* clean.
14 "But when raw flesh appears on
him, he shall be unclean.
15 "And the priest shall examine the
raw flesh and pronounce him to be unclean; *for* the raw flesh *is* unclean. It
is leprosy.
16 "Or if the raw flesh changes and
turns white again, he shall come to the
priest.
17 "And the priest shall examine him;
and indeed *if* the sore has turned white,
then the priest shall pronounce *him*
clean *who has* the sore. He *is* clean.
18 "If the body develops a [a]boil in the
skin, and it is healed,
19 "and in the place of the boil there
comes a white swelling or a bright
spot, reddish-white, then it shall be
shown to the priest;
20 "and *if*, when the priest sees it, it
indeed *appears* deeper than the skin,
and its hair has turned white, the priest
shall pronounce him unclean. It *is* a
leprous sore which has broken out of
the boil.
21 "But if the priest examines it, and
indeed *there are* no white hairs in it,
and it *is* not deeper than the skin, but
has faded, then the priest shall isolate
him seven days;
22 "and if it should at all spread over
the skin, then the priest shall pronounce him unclean. It *is* a [1]leprous
sore.
23 "But if the bright spot stays in one
place, *and* has not spread, it *is* the scar
of the boil; and the priest shall pronounce him clean.
24 "Or if the body receives a [a]burn on
its skin by fire, and the raw *flesh* of
the burn becomes a bright spot,
reddish-white or white,
25 "then the priest shall examine it;
and indeed *if* the hair of the bright spot
has turned white, and it appears
deeper than the skin, it *is* leprosy broken out in the burn. Therefore the
priest shall pronounce him unclean. It
is a leprous sore.
26 "But if the priest examines it, and
indeed *there are* no white hairs in the
bright spot, and it *is* not deeper than
the skin, but has faded, then the priest
shall isolate him seven days.

13 [a]Ex. 4:6
18 [a]Ex. 9:9; 15:26
22 [1]*infection*
24 [a]Is. 3:24

27 "And the priest shall examine him
on the seventh day. If it has at all
spread over the skin, then the priest
shall pronounce him unclean. It *is* a
leprous sore.
28 "But if the bright spot stays in one
place, *and* has not spread on the skin,
but has faded, it *is* a swelling from
the burn. The priest shall pronounce
him clean, for it *is* the scar from the
burn.
29 "If a man or woman has a sore on
the head or the beard,
30 "then the priest shall examine the
sore; and indeed if it appears deeper
than the skin, *and there is* in it thin
yellow hair, then the priest shall pronounce him unclean. It *is* a scaly leprosy of the head or beard.
31 "But if the priest examines the scaly
sore, and indeed it does not appear
deeper than the skin, and *there is* no
black hair in it, then the priest shall
isolate *the one who has* the scale seven
days.
32 "And on the seventh day the priest
shall examine the sore; and indeed *if*
the scale has not spread, and there is
no yellow hair in it, and the scale does
not appear deeper than the skin,
33 "he shall shave himself, but the
scale he shall not shave. And the priest
shall isolate *the one who has* the scale
another seven days.
34 "On the seventh day the priest shall
examine the scale; and indeed *if* the
scale has not spread over the skin, and
does not appear deeper than the skin,
then the priest shall pronounce him
clean. He shall wash his clothes and
be clean.
35 "But if the scale should at all spread
over the skin after his cleansing,
36 "then the priest shall examine him;
and indeed *if* the scale has spread over
the skin, the priest need not seek for
yellow hair. He *is* unclean.
37 "But if the scale appears to be at a
standstill, and there is black hair
grown up in it, the scale has healed.
He *is* clean, and the priest shall pronounce him clean.
38 "If a man or a woman has bright
spots on the skin of the body, *specifically* white bright spots,
39 "then the priest shall look; and indeed *if* the bright spots on the skin of
the body *are* dull white, it *is* a white
spot *that* grows on the skin. He *is*
clean.
40 "As for the man whose hair has
fallen from his head, he *is* bald, *but*
he *is* clean.
41 "He whose hair has fallen from his

forehead, he *is* bald on the forehead, *but* he *is* clean.

42 "And if there is on the bald head or bald [a]forehead a reddish-white sore, it *is* leprosy breaking out on his bald head or his bald forehead.

43 "Then the priest shall examine it; and indeed *if* the swelling of the sore *is* reddish-white on his bald head or on his bald forehead, as the appearance of leprosy on the skin of the body,

44 "he is a leprous man. He *is* unclean. The priest shall surely pronounce him [1]unclean; his sore *is* on his [a]head.

45 "Now the leper on whom the sore *is,* his clothes shall be torn and his head [a]bare; and he shall [b]cover his mustache, and cry, [c]'Unclean! Unclean!'

46 "He shall be unclean. All the days he has the sore he shall be unclean. He *is* unclean, and he shall [1]dwell alone; his dwelling *shall be* [a]outside the camp.

The Law Concerning Leprous Garments

47 "Also, if a garment has a [1]leprous plague in it, *whether it is* a woolen garment or a linen garment,

48 "whether *it is* in the warp or woof of linen or wool, whether in leather or in anything made of leather,

49 "and if the plague is greenish or reddish in the garment or in the leather, whether in the warp or in the woof, or in anything made of leather, it *is* a leprous [1]plague and shall be shown to the priest.

50 "The priest shall examine the plague and isolate *that which has* the plague seven days.

51 "And he shall examine the plague on the seventh day. If the plague has spread in the garment, either in the warp or in the woof, in the leather *or* in anything made of leather, the plague *is* [a]an active leprosy. It *is* unclean.

52 "He shall therefore burn that garment in which is the plague, whether warp or woof, in wool or in linen, or anything of leather, for it *is* an active leprosy; *the garment* shall be burned in the fire.

53 "But if the priest examines *it,* and indeed the plague has not spread in the garment, either in the warp or in the woof, or in anything made of leather,

54 "then the priest shall command that they wash *the thing* in which *is* the plague; and he shall isolate it another seven days.

55 "Then the priest shall examine the plague after it has been washed; and indeed *if* the plague has not changed its color, though the plague has not spread, it *is* unclean, and you shall burn it in the fire; it continues eating away, *whether* the damage *is* outside or inside.

56 "If the priest examines *it,* and indeed the plague has faded after washing it, then he shall tear it out of the garment, whether out of the warp or out of the woof, or out of the leather.

57 "But if it appears again in the garment, either in the warp or in the woof, or in anything made of leather, it *is* a spreading *plague;* you shall burn with fire that in which is the plague.

58 "And if you wash the garment, either warp or woof, or whatever is made of leather, if the plague has disappeared from it, then it shall be washed a second time, and shall be clean.

59 "This *is* the law of the leprous plague in a garment of wool or linen, either in the warp or woof, or in anything made of leather, to pronounce it clean or to pronounce it unclean."

The Ritual for Cleansing Healed Lepers

14 Then the LORD spoke to Moses, saying,

2 "This shall be the law of the [1]leper for the day of his cleansing: He [a]shall be brought to the priest.

3 "And the priest shall go out of the camp, and the priest shall examine *him;* and indeed, *if* the [1]leprosy is healed in the leper,

4 "then the priest shall command to take for him who is to be *cleansed two living *and* clean birds, [a]cedar wood, [b]scarlet, and [c]hyssop.

5 "And the priest shall command that one of the birds be killed in an earthen vessel over running water.

6 "As for the living bird, he shall take it, the cedar wood and the scarlet and the hyssop, and dip them and the living bird in the blood of the bird *that was* killed over the running water.

7 "And he shall [a]sprinkle it [b]seven times on him who is to be cleansed from the leprosy, and shall pronounce

42 [a]2 Chr. 26:19
44 [a]Is. 1:5 [1]*altogether defiled*
45 [a]Lev. 10:6; 21:10 [b]Ezek. 24:17, 22; Mic. 3:7 [c]Is. 6:5; 64:6; Lam. 4:15; Luke 5:8
46 [a]Num. 5:1–4; 12:14; 2 Kin. 7:3; 15:5; 2 Chr. 26:21; Ps. 38:11; Luke 17:12 [1]*live alone*
47 [1]A mold, fungus, or similar infestation, and so in vv. 47–59
49 [1]*mark*
51 [a]Lev. 14:44

CHAPTER 14

2 [a]Matt. 8:2, 4; Mark 1:40, 44; Luke 5:12, 14; 17:14 [1]See note at 13:2
3 [1]Heb. *saraath,* disfiguring skin diseases, including leprosy, and so in vv. 1–32
4 [a]Lev. 14:6, 49, 51, 52; Num. 19:6; Heb. 9:19 [b]Ex. 25:4 [c]Ex. 12:22; Ps. 51:7 *See WW at Lev. 14:31.
7 [a]Num. 19:18, 19; [Heb. 9:13, 21; 12:24] [b]2 Kin. 5:10, 14; Ps. 51:2

13:47 The Israelites saw a similarity between the wholeness of people's skin and the wholeness of **a garment,** many of which were made from animal skins, because both had the appearance of abnormality.

him clean, and shall let the living bird
loose in the open field.
8 "He who is to be cleansed [a]shall
wash his clothes, shave off all his hair,
and [b]wash himself in water, that he
may be clean. After that he shall come
into the camp, and [c]shall stay outside
his tent seven days.
9 "But on the [a]seventh day he shall
shave all the hair off his head and his
beard and his eyebrows—all his hair
he shall shave off. He shall wash his
clothes and wash his body in water,
and he shall be clean.
10 "And on the eighth day [a]he shall
take two male lambs without blemish,
one ewe lamb of the first year without
blemish, three-tenths *of an ephah* of
fine flour mixed with oil as [b]a grain
offering, and one log of oil.
11 "Then the priest who makes *him*
clean shall present the man who is to
be made clean, and those things, before the LORD, *at* the door of the tabernacle of meeting.
12 "And the priest shall take one male
lamb and [a]offer it as a trespass offering, and the log of oil, and [b]wave them
as a wave offering before the LORD.
13 "Then he shall kill the lamb [a]in the
place where he kills the sin offering
and the burnt offering, in a holy place;
for [b]as the sin offering *is* the priest's,
so *is* the trespass offering. [c]It *is* most
holy.
14 "The priest shall take *some* of the
blood of the trespass offering, and the
priest shall put *it* [a]on the tip of the right
ear of him who is to be cleansed, on
the thumb of his right hand, and on
the big toe of his right foot.
15 "And the priest shall take *some* of
the log of oil, and pour *it* into the palm
of his own left hand.
16 "Then the priest shall dip his right
finger in the oil that *is* in his left hand,
and shall [a]sprinkle some of the oil with
his finger seven times before the LORD.
17 "And of the rest of the oil in his
hand, the priest shall put *some* on the
tip of the right ear of him who is to
be cleansed, on the thumb of his right
hand, and on the big toe of his right
foot, on the blood of the trespass offering.
18 "The rest of the oil that *is* in the
priest's hand he shall put on the head

8 [a]Lev. 11:25; 13:6; Num. 8:7 [b]Lev. 11:25; [Eph. 5:26; Heb. 10:22; Rev. 1:5, 6] [c]Lev. 13:5; Num. 5:2, 3; 12:14, 15; 2 Chr. 26:21
9 [a]Num. 19:19
10 [a]Matt. 8:4; Mark 1:44; Luke 5:14 [b]Lev. 2:1; Num. 15:4
12 [a]Lev. 5:6, 18; 6:6; 14:19 [b]Ex. 29:22–24, 26
13 [a]Ex. 29:11; Lev. 1:5, 11; 4:4, 24 [b]Lev. 6:24–30; 7:7 [c]Lev. 2:3; 7:6; 21:22
14 [a]Ex. 29:20; Lev. 8:23, 24
16 [a]Lev. 4:6
18 [a]Lev. 4:26; 5:6; Num. 15:28; [Heb. 2:17] [1]Lit. *covering*
19 [a]Lev. 5:1, 6; 12:7; [2 Cor. 5:21]
20 [a]Lev. 14:8, 9
21 [a]Lev. 5:7, 11; 12:8; 27:8 [1]Approximately two dry quarts
22 [a]Lev. 12:8; 15:14, 15
23 [a]Lev. 14:10, 11
24 [a]Lev. 14:12
25 [a]Lev. 14:14, 17
30 [a]Lev. 14:22; 15:14, 15

of him who is to be cleansed. [a]So the
priest shall make [1]atonement for him
before the LORD.
19 "Then the priest shall offer [a]the sin
offering, and make atonement for him
who is to be cleansed from his uncleanness. Afterward he shall kill the burnt
offering.
20 "And the priest shall offer the burnt
offering and the grain offering on
the altar. So the priest shall make
atonement for him, and he shall be
[a]clean.
21 "But [a]if he *is* poor and cannot afford
it, then he shall take one male lamb
as a trespass offering to be waved, to
make atonement for him, [1]one-tenth *of
an ephah* of fine flour mixed with oil
as a grain offering, a log of oil,
22 [a]"and two turtledoves or two young
pigeons, such as he is able to afford:
one shall be a sin offering and the other
a burnt offering.
23 [a]"He shall bring them to the priest
on the eighth day for his cleansing, to
the door of the tabernacle of meeting,
before the LORD.
24 [a]"And the priest shall take the lamb
of the trespass offering and the log of
oil, and the priest shall wave them *as*
a wave offering before the LORD.
25 "Then he shall kill the lamb of the
trespass offering, [a]and the priest shall
take *some* of the blood of the trespass
offering and put *it* on the tip of the
right ear of him who is to be cleansed,
on the thumb of his right hand, and
on the big toe of his right foot.
26 "And the priest shall pour some of
the oil into the palm of his own left
hand.
27 "Then the priest shall sprinkle with
his right finger *some* of the oil that *is*
in his left hand seven times before the
LORD.
28 "And the priest shall put *some* of
the oil that *is* in his hand on the tip of
the right ear of him who is to be
cleansed, on the thumb of the right
hand, and on the big toe of his right
foot, on the place of the blood of the
trespass offering.
29 "The rest of the oil that *is* in the
priest's hand he shall put on the head
of him who is to be cleansed, to make
atonement for him before the LORD.
30 "And he shall offer one of [a]the

14:12 And the priest shall take one male lamb and offer it as a trespass offering: The Law of Moses made provision for the healing of a person afflicted with skin diseases. Vv. 1–32 describe the process of healing and the offering which is made to God for the recovery. When Jesus healed the leper (Luke 5:12–14), He commanded him to show himself to the priest and to make the offering which was commanded by Moses in the law. This indicates that the biblical regulations pertaining to skin diseases were being observed by the Jewish people during the time of Jesus.

turtledoves or young pigeons, such as he can afford—
31 "such as he is able to afford, the one *as* a sin offering and the other *as* a burnt offering, with the grain offering. So the priest shall make atonement for him who is to be **cleansed** before the LORD.

WORD WEALTH

14:31 cleansed, *taher* (tah-*hehr*); Strong's #2891: To make clean, to purify; to be pure, clean, uncontaminated. This verb and its related adjective *tahor* are used for cleansing physically, ceremonially, and morally, and thus can refer to pure gold (Ex. 25:11), pure offerings (Lev. 14:4), and a pure heart (Ps. 51:10).

32 "This *is* the law *for one* who had a leprous sore, who cannot afford [a]the usual cleansing."

The Law Concerning Leprous Houses

33 And the LORD spoke to Moses and Aaron, saying:
34 [a]"When you have come into the land of Canaan, which I give you as a *possession, and [b]I put the [1]leprous plague in a *house in the land of your possession,
35 "and he who owns the house comes and tells the priest, saying, 'It seems to me that *there is* [a]some plague in the house,'
36 "then the priest shall command that they empty the house, before the priest goes *into it* to examine the plague, that all that *is* in the house may not be made unclean; and afterward the priest shall go in to examine the house.
37 "And he shall examine the plague; and indeed *if* the plague *is* on the walls of the house with ingrained streaks, greenish or reddish, which appear to be [1]deep in the wall,
38 "then the priest shall go out of the house, to the door of the house, and [1]shut up the house seven days.
39 "And the priest shall come again on the seventh day and look; and indeed *if* the plague has spread on the walls of the house,
40 "then the priest shall command that they take away the stones in which *is* the plague, and they shall cast them into an unclean place outside the city.
41 "And he shall cause the house to be scraped inside, all around, and the dust that they scrape off they shall pour out in an unclean place outside the city.
42 "Then they shall take other stones and put *them* in the place of *those* stones, and he shall take other mortar and plaster the house.
43 "Now if the plague comes back and breaks out in the house, after he has taken away the stones, after he has scraped the house, and after it is plastered,
44 "then the priest shall come and look; and indeed *if* the plague has spread in the house, it *is* [a]an active leprosy in the house. It *is* unclean.
45 "And he shall break down the house, its stones, its timber, and all the plaster of the house, and he shall carry *them* outside the city to an unclean place.
46 "Moreover he who goes into the house at all while it is shut up shall be [1]unclean [a]until evening.
47 "And he who lies down in the house shall [a]wash his clothes, and he who eats in the house shall wash his clothes.
48 "But if the priest comes in and examines *it*, and indeed the plague has not spread in the house after the house was plastered, then the priest shall pronounce the house clean, because the plague is healed.
49 "And [a]he shall take, to cleanse the house, two birds, cedar wood, scarlet, and hyssop.
50 "Then he shall kill one of the birds in an earthen vessel over running water;
51 "and he shall take the cedar wood, the hyssop, the scarlet, and the living bird, and dip them in the blood of the slain bird and in the running water, and sprinkle the house seven times.
52 "And he shall [1]cleanse the house with the blood of the bird and the running water and the living bird, with the cedar wood, the hyssop, and the scarlet.
53 "Then he shall let the living bird loose outside the city in the open field, and [a]make atonement for the house, and it shall be clean.
54 "This *is* the law for any [a]leprous sore and scale,
55 "for the [a]leprosy of a garment [b]and of a house,
56 [a]"for a swelling and a scab and a bright spot,
57 "to [a]teach* when *it is* unclean and when *it is* clean. This *is* the law of leprosy."

32 [a]Lev. 14:10
34 [a]Gen. 12:7; 13:17; 17:8; Num. 32:22; Deut. 7:1; 32:49 [b][Prov. 3:33] [1]Decomposition by mildew, mold, dry rot, etc., and so in vv. 34–53 *See WW at Josh. 22:9. • See WW at 2 Sam. 7:11.
35 [a][Ps. 91:9, 10; Prov. 3:33; Zech. 5:4]
37 [1]Lit. *lower than the wall*
38 [1]*quarantine*
44 [a]Lev. 13:51; [Zech. 5:4]
46 [a]Lev. 11:24; 15:5 [1]*defiled*
47 [a]Lev. 14:8
49 [a]Lev. 14:4
52 [1]*ceremonially cleanse*
53 [a]Lev. 14:20
54 [a]Lev. 13:30; 26:21
55 [a]Lev. 13:47–52 [b]Lev. 14:34
56 [a]Lev. 13:2
57 [a]Lev. 11:47; 20:25; Deut. 24:8; Ezek. 44:23 *See WW at Ps. 32:8.

The Law Concerning Bodily Discharges

15 And the LORD spoke to Moses
and Aaron, saying,
2 "Speak to the children of Israel, and
say to them: [a]'When any man has a
discharge from his body, his discharge
is unclean.
3 'And this shall be his uncleanness
in regard to his discharge—whether his
body runs with his discharge, or his
body is stopped up by his discharge,
it *is* his uncleanness.
4 'Every bed is [1]unclean on which he
who has the discharge lies, and everything on which he sits shall be unclean.
5 'And whoever [a]touches his bed
shall [b]wash his clothes and [c]bathe in
water, and be unclean until evening.
6 'He who sits on anything on which
he who has the [a]discharge sat shall
wash his clothes and bathe in water,
and be unclean until evening.
7 'And he who touches the body of
him who has the discharge shall wash
his clothes and bathe in water, and be
unclean until evening.
8 'If he who has the discharge [a]spits
on him who is clean, then he shall
wash his clothes and bathe in water,
and be unclean until evening.
9 'Any saddle on which he who has
the discharge rides shall be unclean.
10 'Whoever touches anything that
was under him shall be unclean until
evening. He who carries *any of* those
things shall wash his clothes and bathe
in water, and be unclean until evening.
11 'And whomever the one who has
the discharge touches, and has not
rinsed his hands in water, he shall
wash his clothes and bathe in water,
and be unclean until evening.
12 'The [a]vessel of earth that he who
has the discharge touches shall be broken, and every vessel of wood shall be
rinsed in water.
13 'And when he who has a discharge
is cleansed of his discharge, then
[a]he shall count for himself seven days
for his cleansing, wash his clothes, and
bathe his body in running water; then
he shall be clean.
14 'On the eighth day he shall take for
himself [a]two turtledoves or two young
pigeons, and come before the LORD, to

CHAPTER 15

2 [a]Lev. 22:4; Num. 5:2; 2 Sam. 3:29
4 [1]*defiled*
5 [a]Lev. 5:2; 14:46 [b]Lev. 14:8, 47 [c]Lev. 11:25; 17:15
6 [a]Lev. 15:10; Deut. 23:10
8 [a]Num. 12:14
12 [a]Lev. 6:28; 11:32, 33
13 [a]Lev. 14:8; 15:28; Num. 19:11, 12
14 [a]Lev. 14:22, 23, 30, 31
15 [a]Lev. 14:30, 31 [b]Lev. 14:19, 31 [1]Lit. *covering*
16 [a]Lev. 22:4; Deut. 23:10, 11
18 [a][Ex. 19:15; 1 Sam. 21:4; 1 Cor. 6:18]
19 [a]Lev. 12:2 [1]Lit. *in her impurity*
24 [a]Lev. 18:19; 20:18 [1]*defiled*
25 [a]Matt. 9:20; Mark 5:25; Luke 8:43

the door of the tabernacle of meeting,
and give them to the priest.
15 'Then the priest shall offer them,
[a]the one *as* a sin offering and the other
as a burnt offering. [b]So the priest shall
make [1]atonement for him before the
LORD because of his discharge.
16 [a]'If any man has an emission of semen, then he shall wash all his body
in water, and be unclean until evening.
17 'And any garment and any leather
on which there is semen, it shall be
washed with water, and be unclean until evening.
18 'Also, when a woman lies with a
man, and *there is* an emission of semen, they shall bathe in water, and
[a]be unclean until evening.
19 [a]'If a woman has a discharge, *and*
the discharge from her body is blood,
she shall be [1]set apart seven days; and
whoever touches her shall be unclean
until evening.
20 'Everything that she lies on during
her impurity shall be unclean; also everything that she sits on shall be unclean.
21 'Whoever touches her bed shall
wash his clothes and bathe in water,
and be unclean until evening.
22 'And whoever touches anything
that she sat on shall wash his clothes
and bathe in water, and be unclean until evening.
23 'If *anything* is on *her* bed or on anything on which she sits, when he
touches it, he shall be unclean until
evening.
24 'And [a]if any man lies with her at
all, so that her impurity is on him, he
shall be [1]unclean seven days; and every bed on which he lies shall be unclean.
25 'If [a]a woman has a discharge of
blood for many days, other than at the
time of her *customary* impurity, or if
it runs beyond her *usual time of* impurity, all the days of her unclean discharge shall be as the days of her *customary* impurity. She *shall be* unclean.
26 'Every bed on which she lies all the
days of her discharge shall be to her
as the bed of her impurity; and whatever she sits on shall be unclean, as
the uncleanness of her impurity.
27 'Whoever touches those things shall

15:1–33 This chapter deals with uncleanness associated with discharges from male and female sexual organs, also showing how objects or persons associated with unclean people become unclean. By Jesus' time the religious community had used various Levitical laws to so isolate people that they felt estranged from God Himself. Jesus countered this, demonstrating God's desire to draw near to the unclean and make them whole (see Mark 1:40, 41; 5:24–34).

be unclean; he shall wash his clothes and bathe in water, and be unclean until evening.

28 'But [a]if she is cleansed of her discharge, then she shall count for herself seven days, and after that she shall be clean.

29 'And on the eighth day she shall take for herself two turtledoves or two young pigeons, and bring them to the priest, to the door of the tabernacle of meeting.

30 'Then the priest shall offer the one *as* a sin offering and the other *as* a [a]burnt offering, and the priest shall make atonement for her before the LORD for the discharge of her uncleanness.

3 31 'Thus you shall [a]separate the children of Israel from their uncleanness, lest they die in their uncleanness when they [b]defile My tabernacle that *is* among them.

32 [a]'This *is* the law for one who has a discharge, [b]and *for him* who emits semen and is unclean thereby,

33 [a]'and for her who is indisposed because of her *customary* impurity, and for one who has a discharge, either man [b]or woman, [c]and for him who lies with her who is unclean.' "

The Day of Atonement

16 Now the LORD spoke to Moses after [a]the death of the two sons of Aaron, when they offered *profane fire* before the LORD, and died;

2 and the LORD said to Moses: "Tell Aaron your brother [a]not to come at *just* any *time into the Holy *Place* inside the veil, before the mercy seat which *is* on the ark, lest he die; for [b]I will appear in the cloud above the mercy seat.

3 [1]"Thus Aaron shall [a]come into the Holy *Place:* [b]with *the blood of* a young bull as a sin offering, and *of* a ram as a burnt offering.

4 "He shall put the [a]holy linen tunic and the linen trousers on his body; he shall be girded with a linen sash, and with the linen turban he shall be attired. These *are* holy garments. Therefore [b]he shall wash his body in water, and put them on.

5 "And he shall take from [a]the congregation of the children of Israel two kids of the goats as a sin offering, and one ram as a burnt offering.

6 "Aaron shall offer the bull as a sin offering, which *is* for himself, and [a]make atonement for himself and for his house.

7 "He shall take the two goats and present them before the LORD *at* the door of the tabernacle of meeting.

8 "Then Aaron shall cast lots for the two goats: one lot for the LORD and the other lot for the scapegoat.

9 "And Aaron shall bring the goat on which the LORD's lot fell, and offer it *as* a sin offering.

10 "But the goat on which the lot fell to be the scapegoat shall be presented alive before the LORD, to make [a]atonement upon it, *and* to let it go as the scapegoat into the wilderness.

11 "And Aaron shall bring the bull of the sin offering, which is for [a]himself, and make atonement for himself and for his house, and shall kill the bull as the sin offering which *is* for himself.

12 "Then he shall take [a]a censer full of burning coals of fire from the altar before the LORD, with his hands full of [b]sweet incense beaten fine, and bring *it* inside the veil.

13 [a]"And he shall put the incense on the fire before the LORD, that the cloud of incense may cover the [b]mercy seat that *is* on the Testimony, lest he [c]die.

14 [a]"He shall take some of the blood of the bull and [b]sprinkle *it* with his finger on the mercy seat on the east *side;* and before the mercy seat he shall sprinkle some of the blood with his finger seven times.

15 [a]"Then he shall kill the goat of the sin offering, which *is* for the people, bring its blood [b]inside the veil, do with

28 [a]Lev. 15:13–15
30 [a]Lev. 5:7
31 [a]Deut. 24:8 [b]Num. 5:3; 19:13, 20
32 [a]Lev. 15:2 [b]Lev. 15:16
33 [a]Lev. 15:19 [b]Lev. 15:25 [c]Lev. 15:24

CHAPTER 16

1 [a]Lev. 10:1, 2
2 [a]Ex. 30:10 [b]Ex. 25:21, 22; 40:34 *See WW at Is. 33:6.
3 [a][Heb. 9:7, 12, 24, 25] [b]Lev. 4:3 [1]Lit. *With this*
4 [a]Ex. 28:39, 42, 43 [b]Ex. 30:20
5 [a]Lev. 4:14
6 [a][Heb. 5:3; 7:27, 28; 9:7]
10 [a][1 John 2:2]
11 [a][Heb. 7:27; 9:7]
12 [a]Lev. 10:1 [b]Ex. 30:34–38
13 [a]Ex. 30:7, 8 [b]Ex. 25:21 [c]Ex. 28:43
14 [a][Heb. 9:25; 10:4] [b]Lev. 4:6, 17
15 [a][Heb. 2:17] [b][Heb. 6:19; 7:27; 9:3, 7, 12]

15:31 See section 3 of Truth-In-Action at the end of Lev.

16:1–34 The primary purposes of this chapter are to instruct the priest in the proper way to atone for the people's purification, how to approach God (**lest he die,** v. 2), and how to cleanse the tabernacle to make possible God's continued presence. On the Day of Atonement, the high priest wore special, less elaborate clothing (v. 4; see also Ex. 28), emphasizing his role as God's servant stripped of all natural honor in God's presence. The atoning ceremony itself consisted of four main elements: the sin offering for the priest's purification (v. 6), the casting of lots to determine which goat to sacrifice as a sin offering for the people (vv. 7, 8), the sacrificing of the goat (v. 9) and the dispatching of a second goat into the wilderness (v. 10). Vv. 11–22 then describe these elements in detail.

16:1 See text and note on 10:1.

16:8 The **scapegoat** was perhaps the most striking feature of the ceremony, symbolizing sending the nation's sins away from them (vv. 21, 22). This was the one facet observed by all the nation. This entire ceremony prefigured Christ's crucifixion and many of its elements are discussed in Heb. (see especially Heb. 9). The joyous NT news, however, is that whereas the OT ceremony was inadequate and temporary (having to be repeated annually and then only

that blood as he did with the blood of
the bull, and sprinkle it on the mercy
seat and before the mercy seat.
16 "So he shall [a]make atonement for
the Holy *Place,* because of the uncleanness of the children of Israel, and because of their transgressions, for all
their sins; and so he shall do for the
tabernacle of meeting which *remains
among them in the midst of their uncleanness.
17 "There shall be [a]no man in the tabernacle of meeting when he goes in to
make atonement in the Holy *Place,* until he comes out, that he may make
atonement for himself, for his household, and for all the **assembly** of Israel.

> **WORD WEALTH**
>
> **16:17 assembly,** *qahal* (kah-*hal*); Strong's #6951: A congregation, assembly, company; a multitude that has been "called together." The verb *qahal* which means "to call together, to assemble, to gather together, to convoke." *Qahal* is used in reference to the whole congregation of Israel nearly 30 times in Ex. through Deut. While the people comprised an actual family or nation, they were also a spiritual congregation. The NT word *ekklesia* (a congregation "called together") parallels *qahal. Ekklesia* is translated as "church," but "assembly" or "congregation" is more accurate. Thus God's dealing with the *qahal* in the OT prefigures His dealings with His assemblies in the NT. Thus the earliest pattern of congregational life is the "church" in the wilderness.

18 "And he shall go out to the altar that
is before the LORD, and make atonement for [a]it, and shall take some of the
blood of the bull and some of the blood
of the goat, and put *it* on the horns of
the altar all around.
19 "Then he shall sprinkle some of the
blood on it with his finger seven times,
cleanse it, and [a]consecrate[1] it from the
[2]uncleanness of the children of Israel.
20 "And when he has made an end of
atoning for the Holy *Place,* the tabernacle of meeting, and the altar, he shall
bring the live goat.
21 "Aaron shall lay both his hands on
the head of the live goat, [a]confess over

16 [a]Ex. 29:36; 30:10; Ezek. 45:18; [Heb. 9:22–24] *See WW at Num. 10:12. **17** [a]Ex. 34:3; Luke 1:10 **18** [a]Ex. 29:36 **19** [a]Lev. 16:14; Ezek. 43:20 [1]*set it apart* [2]*impurity* **21** [a]Lev. 5:5; 26:40 [b][Is. 53:6] *See WW at Ps. 130:3.

22 [a]Lev. 8:14; [Is. 53:6, 11, 12; John 1:29; Heb. 9:28; 1 Pet. 2:24] [b]Lev. 14:7 [1]*shall carry* [2]*solitary land* **23** [a]Lev. 6:11; 16:4; Ezek. 42:14; 44:19 **24** [1]Lit. *covering* **25** [a]Lev. 1:8; 4:10 **26** [a]Lev. 15:5 **27** [a]Lev. 4:12, 21; 6:30; Heb. 13:11 **29** [a]Ex. 30:10; Lev. 23:27–32; Num. 29:7 [1]*humble yourselves* [2]As a resident alien **30** [a]Ps. 51:2; Jer. 33:8; [Eph. 5:26; Heb. 9:13, 14; 1 John 1:7, 9] [1]Lit. *covering* **31** [a]Lev. 23:27, 32; Ezra 8:21; Is. 58:3, 5; Dan. 10:12 **32** [a]Lev. 4:3, 5, 16; 21:10 [b]Ex. 29:29, 30; Num. 20:26, 28

it all the *iniquities of the children of
Israel, and all their transgressions,
concerning all their sins, [b]putting them
on the head of the goat, and shall send
it away into the wilderness by the hand
of a suitable man.
22 "The goat [1]shall [a]bear on itself all
their iniquities to an [2]uninhabited land;
and he shall [b]release the goat in the
wilderness.
23 "Then Aaron shall come into the
tabernacle of meeting, [a]shall take off
the linen garments which he put on
when he went into the Holy *Place,* and
shall leave them there.
24 "And he shall wash his body with
water in a holy place, put on his garments, come out and offer his burnt offering and the burnt offering of the
people, and make [1]atonement for himself and for the people.
25 [a]"The fat of the sin offering he shall
burn on the altar.
26 "And he who released the goat as
the scapegoat shall wash his clothes
[a]and bathe his body in water, and afterward he may come into the camp.
27 [a]"The bull *for* the sin offering and
the goat *for* the sin offering, whose
blood was brought in to make atonement in the Holy *Place,* shall be carried
outside the camp. And they shall burn
in the fire their skins, their flesh, and
their offal.
28 "Then he who burns them shall
wash his clothes and bathe his body
in water, and afterward he may come
into the camp.
29 "*This* shall be a statute forever for
you: [a]In the seventh month, on the
tenth *day* of the month, you shall
[1]afflict your souls, and do no work at
all, *whether* a native of your own country or a stranger who [2]dwells among
you.
30 "For on that day *the priest* shall
make [1]atonement for you, to [a]cleanse
you, *that* you may be clean from all
your sins before the LORD.
31 [a]"It *is* a sabbath of solemn rest for
you, and you shall afflict your souls.
It is a statute forever.
32 [a]"And the priest, who is anointed
and [b]consecrated to minister as priest
in his father's place, shall make atone-

partially dealing with the people's sin problem), Jesus Christ's crucifixion was once and for all, completely dealing with the sin and purification issues before God.

16:23–28 These verses deal with the necessary washings of purification before returning to the routine of daily life.

16:29 The seventh month was approximately October.

16:30 You may be clean from all your sins before the LORD: The Day of Atonement became the most sacred day on the calendar of Israel. The people recognized their sins, confessed them before the Lord in fasting, in repentance, and in self-examination. The Jewish sages taught that each person must first forgive his or her neighbor before requesting forgiveness from the Lord. See 19:18; 23:26–32.

ment, and put on the linen clothes, the
holy garments;
33 "then he shall make [1]atonement for
[2]the Holy Sanctuary, and he shall
make atonement for the tabernacle of
meeting and for the altar, and he shall
make atonement for the priests and for
all the people of the assembly.
34 [a]"This shall be an everlasting statute for you, to make atonement for the
children of Israel, for all their sins,
[b]once a year." And he did as the LORD
commanded Moses.

The Sanctity of Blood

17 And the LORD spoke to Moses,
saying,
2 "Speak to Aaron, to his sons, and
to all the children of Israel, and say to
them, 'This *is* the thing which the LORD
has commanded, saying:
3 "Whatever man of the house of Israel who [a]kills an ox or lamb or goat
in the camp, or who kills *it* outside the
camp,
4 "and does not bring it to the door
of the tabernacle of meeting to offer
an offering to the LORD before the tabernacle of the LORD, the guilt of bloodshed shall be [a]imputed to that man. He
has shed blood; and that man shall be
[1]cut off from among his people,
5 "to the end that the children of Israel may bring their sacrifices [a]which
they offer in the open field, that they
may bring them to the LORD at the door
of the tabernacle of meeting, to the
priest, and offer them *as* peace offerings to the LORD.
6 "And the priest [a]shall sprinkle the
blood on the altar of the LORD *at* the
door of the tabernacle of meeting, and
[b]burn the fat for a sweet aroma to the
LORD.
7 "They shall no more offer their sacrifices [a]to [1]demons, after whom they
[b]have played the harlot. This shall be
a statute forever for them throughout
their generations." '
8 "Also you shall say to them: 'Whatever man of the house of Israel, or of
the strangers who dwell among you,
[a]who offers a burnt offering or sacrifice,
9 'and does not [a]bring it to the door
of the tabernacle of meeting, to offer
it to the LORD, that man shall be
[1]cut off from among his people.
10 [a]'And whatever man of the house
of Israel, or of the strangers who dwell
among you, who eats any blood,
[b]I will set My face against that person
who eats blood, and will cut him off
from among his people.
11 'For the [a]life of the flesh *is* in the
blood, and I have given it to you upon
the altar [b]to make atonement for your
souls; for [c]it *is* the blood *that* makes
atonement for the soul.'

33 [1]Lit. *covering* [2]The Most Holy Place
34 [a]Lev. 23:31; Num. 29:7 [b]Ex. 30:10; [Heb. 9:7, 25, 28]

CHAPTER 17

3 [a]Deut. 12:5, 15, 21
4 [a]Rom. 5:13 [1]Put to death
5 [a]Gen. 21:33; 22:2; 31:54; Deut. 12:1–27; Ezek. 20:28
6 [a]Lev. 3:2 [b]Ex. 29:13, 18; Num. 18:17
7 [a]Ex. 22:20; 32:8; 34:15; Deut. 32:17; 2 Chr. 11:15; Ps. 106:37; 1 Cor. 10:20 [b]Ex. 34:15; Deut. 31:16; Ezek. 23:8 [1]Having the form of a goat or satyr
8 [a]Lev. 1:2, 3; 18:26
9 [a]Lev. 14:23 [1]Put to death
10 [a]Gen. 9:4; Lev. 3:17; 7:26, 27; Deut. 12:16, 23–25; 15:23; 1 Sam. 14:33 [b]Lev. 20:3, 5, 6
11 [a]Gen. 9:4; Lev. 17:14 [b][Matt. 26:28; Rom. 3:25; Eph. 1:7; Col. 1:14, 20; 1 Pet. 1:2; 1 John 1:7] [c][Heb. 9:22]

WORD WEALTH

17:11 blood, *dam* (*dahm*); Strong's #1818: Blood (human or animal). This highly significant word appears 360 times in the OT, starting with the introduction of sacrifice (Gen. 4:4), continuing through the Law of Moses with the offering of the blood of sacrifices (appearing in Lev. about 60 times), and culminating in the sacrifice of God's sinless Lamb. Thus atonement through shed blood is an inescapable scriptural teaching. This text teaches the value of blood: it is the "life" of man and animal; therefore, sacrifice is a life for a life. God has provided blood to cover sin. Finally, the blood actually makes atonement for the "soul," that is to say, a human life. Accordingly, v. 12 shows that blood, being for these vital purposes, is much too sacred to be misused, especially by drinking it.

KINGDOM DYNAMICS

17:11 No Blood, No Atonement, THE BLOOD. This is the clearest statement of the necessity of blood as it relates to sacrificial offerings: the life is in the blood. Life and blood were given upon the altar for the specific purpose of making atonement, or attaining reconciliation with God. Apart from the shedding of blood or giving a life, there was no atonement. This established ordinance is reaffirmed in the New Covenant in Heb.

(*cont. on next page*)

17:1–16 The regulations of this chapter deal with issues of sacrifice, hunting and eating meat. They are more for the laity than the priests.

17:7 They shall no more offer their sacrifices to demons: The gravest sin in ancient Israel was idolatry (see also Deut. 32:17). The laws pertaining to the sanctity of blood prohibit involvement in the pagan practices of foreign worship. The essence of the Jewish monotheistic faith was contained in the verse, "Hear, O Israel: The LORD our God, the LORD *is* one!" (Deut. 6:4). The early church had similar concerns when they dealt with the question of Gentiles from pagan backgrounds coming to faith in Jesus as Messiah and Lord (see Acts 15:20, 29; 21:25).

17:11 For the life of the flesh is in the blood: The blood represents the life-force of the living soul (Gen. 4:10; 9:4–6; Deut. 12:23). The eating of blood was strictly prohibited. In pagan worship, the drinking of blood was sometimes incorporated into ritual practice where the participant was believed to capture the life-force of a creature by eating its blood.

(cont. from preceding page)
9:22. The New Covenant in Christ's blood fulfilled the requirements of the Old Covenant for redemption. The blood of Christ is seen as surpassing the blood sacrifices of the Old Covenant and eternally satisfying the requirements of a holy God (Heb. 9:12).
(Gen. 15:10/Ex. 12:13) C.S.

12 "Therefore I said to the children of
Israel, 'No one among you shall eat
blood, nor shall any stranger who
dwells among you eat blood.'
13 "Whatever man of the children of
Israel, or of the strangers who dwell
among you, who [a]hunts and catches
any animal or bird that may be eaten,
he shall [b]pour out its blood and
[c]cover it with dust;
14 [a]"for *it is* the life of all flesh. Its
blood sustains its life. Therefore I said
to the children of Israel, 'You shall not
eat the blood of any flesh, for the life
of all flesh is its blood. Whoever eats
it shall be cut off.'
15 [a]"And every person who eats what
died *naturally* or what was torn *by
beasts, whether he is* a native of your
own country or a stranger, [b]he shall
both wash his clothes and [c]bathe in
water, and be unclean until evening.
Then he shall be clean.
16 "But if he does not wash *them* or
bathe his body, then [a]he shall bear his
[1]guilt."

Laws of Sexual Morality

3 **18** Then the LORD spoke to Moses,
saying,
2 "Speak to the children of Israel, and
say to them: [a]'I am the LORD your God.
3 [a]'According to [1]the doings of the
land of Egypt, where you dwelt, you
shall not do; and [b]according to the doings of the land of Canaan, where I am
bringing you, you shall not do; nor
shall you walk in their [2]ordinances.
4 [a]'You shall observe My judgments
and keep My ordinances, to walk in
them: I *am* the LORD your God.
5 'You shall therefore keep My statutes and My judgments, which if a man
does, he shall live by them: I *am* the
LORD.
6 'None of you shall approach anyone
who is near of kin to him, to uncover
his nakedness: I *am* the LORD.
7 'The nakedness of your father or the
nakedness of your mother you shall
not uncover. She *is* your mother; you
shall not uncover her nakedness.
8 'The nakedness of your [a]father's
wife you shall not uncover; it *is* your
father's nakedness.
9 [a]'The nakedness of your sister, the
daughter of your father, or the daughter of your mother, *whether* born at
home or elsewhere, their nakedness
you shall not uncover.
10 'The nakedness of your son's
daughter or your daughter's daughter,
their nakedness you shall not uncover;
for theirs *is* your own nakedness.
11 'The nakedness of your father's
wife's daughter, begotten by your father—she *is* your sister—you shall not
uncover her nakedness.
12 [a]'You shall not uncover the nakedness of your father's sister; she *is* near
of kin to your father.
13 'You shall not uncover the nakedness of your mother's sister, for she *is*
near of kin to your mother.
14 [a]'You shall not uncover the nakedness of your father's brother. You shall
not approach his wife; she *is* your aunt.
15 'You shall not uncover the nakedness of your daughter-in-law—she *is*
your son's wife—you shall not uncover
her nakedness.
16 'You shall not uncover the nakedness of your brother's wife; it *is* your
brother's nakedness.
17 'You shall not uncover the nakedness of a woman and her [a]daughter,
nor shall you take her son's daughter
or her daughter's daughter, to uncover
her nakedness. They *are* near of kin
to her. It *is* wickedness.
18 'Nor shall you take a woman
[a]as a rival to her sister, to uncover her
nakedness while the other is alive.
19 'Also you shall not approach a
woman to uncover her nakedness as
[a]long as she is in her [b]*customary* impurity.

13 [a]Lev. 7:26 [b]Deut. 12:16, 24 [c]Ezek. 24:7
14 [a]Gen. 9:4; Lev. 17:11; Deut. 12:23
15 [a]Ex. 22:31; Lev. 7:24; 22:8; Deut. 14:21; Ezek. 4:14; 44:31 [b]Lev. 11:25 [c]Lev. 15:5
16 [a]Lev. 5:1 [1]*iniquity*

CHAPTER 18

2 [a]Ex. 6:7; Lev. 11:44, 45; 19:3; Ezek. 20:5, 7, 19, 20
3 [a]Josh. 24:14; Ezek. 20:7, 8 [b]Ex. 23:24; Lev. 18:24–30; 20:23; Deut. 12:30, 31 [1]*what is done in* [2]*statutes*
4 [a]Ezek. 20:19
8 [a]Gen. 35:22
9 [a]Lev. 18:11; 20:17; Deut. 27:22
12 [a]Lev. 20:19
14 [a]Lev. 20:20
17 [a]Lev. 20:14
18 [a]1 Sam. 1:6, 8
19 [a]Ezek. 18:6 [b]Lev. 15:24; 20:18

18:1–30 See section 3 of Truth-In-Action at the end of Lev.
18:3 According to the doings of the land of Egypt, where you dwelt, you shall not do: The redemption of the people from the land of Egypt involved not only bringing them out (see v. 1), but also the removal of Egypt and its idolatrous and pagan practices from the hearts of the people. The people became a nation dedicated to God and His holiness. God's deliverance acquired for Him a people for His very own, presenting a challenge to each person of the community. They have now become responsible to God their Redeemer who saved them from slavery. The people must determine to live holy, Godlike lives according to the covenant relationship (see Ex. 20:2 as the preamble for the Ten Commandments). Of specific concern in this chapter are proper sexual relations.
18:6 To uncover his nakedness means to have sexual intercourse.

20 [a]'Moreover you shall not lie carnally with your [b]neighbor's wife, to defile yourself with her.
21 'And you shall not let any of your
descendants [a]pass through [b]*the fire* to
[c]Molech, nor shall you profane the
*name of your God: I *am* the LORD.
22 'You shall not lie with [a]a male as
with a woman. It *is* an abomination.
23 'Nor shall you mate with any
[a]animal, to defile yourself with it. Nor
shall any woman stand before an animal to mate with it. It *is* perversion.
24 [a]'Do not defile yourselves with any
of these things; [b]for by all these the
nations are defiled, which I am casting
out before you.
25 'For [a]the land is defiled; therefore
I [b]visit[1] the punishment of its iniquity
upon it, and the land [c]vomits out its
inhabitants.
26 [a]'You shall therefore [1]keep My statutes and My judgments, and shall not
commit *any* of these abominations, *either* any of your own nation or any
stranger who dwells among you
27 '(for all these abominations the men
of the land have done, who *were* before
you, and thus the land is defiled),
28 'lest [a]the land vomit you out also
when you defile it, as it vomited out
the nations that *were* before you.
29 'For whoever commits any of these
abominations, the persons who commit *them* shall be [1]cut off from among
their people.
30 'Therefore you shall keep My
[1]ordinance, so [a]that *you* do not commit
any of these abominable customs
which were committed before you, and
that you do not defile yourselves by
them: [b]I *am* the LORD your God.' "

Moral and Ceremonial Laws

19 And the LORD spoke to Moses,
saying,
2 "Speak to all the congregation of
the children of Israel, and say to them:
[a]'You shall be **holy,** for I the LORD your
God *am* holy.

WORD WEALTH

19:2 holy, *qadosh* (kah-*dosh*); Strong's #6918: Set apart, dedicated to sacred purposes; holy, sacred, clean, morally or ceremonially pure. The verb *qadash* means "to set apart something or someone for holy purposes." Holiness is separation from everything profane and defiling; and at the same time, it is dedication to everything holy and pure. People or even objects, such as anointing oil or vessels, may be considered holy to the Lord (Ex. 30:25; Jer. 2:3; Zech. 14:20, 21). Lev. stresses "holy" and "holiness" most thoroughly. Lev. 10:10 shows that God desired that the priests be able to distinguish "holy" and "unholy" and teach Israel to do likewise. God is entirely holy in His nature, motives, thoughts, words, and deeds so that He is called *Qadosh,* "the Holy One" or *Qedosh Yisrael,* "the Holy One of Israel." Thus 19:2 can say, "You shall be *qedoshim* [holy ones] for I . . . *am* holy."

3 [a]'Every one of you shall revere his
mother and his father, and [b]keep My
Sabbaths: I *am* the LORD your God.
4 [a]'Do not turn to idols, [b]nor make
for yourselves [1]molded gods: I *am* the
LORD your God.
5 'And [a]if you offer a sacrifice of a
peace offering to the LORD, you shall
offer it of your own free will.
6 'It shall be eaten the same day you
offer *it,* and on the next day. And if
any remains until the third day, it shall
be burned in the fire.
7 'And if it is eaten at all on the third
day, it *is* an abomination. It shall not
be accepted.
8 'Therefore *everyone* who eats it
shall bear his iniquity, because he has
profaned the hallowed *offering* of the
LORD; and that person shall be cut off
from his people.
9 [a]'When you reap the harvest of
your land, you shall not wholly reap
the corners of your field, nor shall you
gather the gleanings of your harvest.
10 'And you shall not glean your vineyard, nor shall you gather *every* grape
of your vineyard; you shall leave them
for the poor and the stranger: I *am* the
LORD your God.
11 [a]'You shall not steal, nor deal
falsely, [b]nor lie to one another.
12 'And you shall not [a]swear by My
name falsely, [b]nor shall you profane
the name of your God: I *am* the LORD.
13 [a]'You shall not cheat your neighbor,

20 [a][Prov. 6:25–33] [b]Ex. 20:14; Lev. 20:10; [Matt. 5:27, 28; 1 Cor. 6:9; Heb. 13:4]
21 [a]Lev. 20:2–5; Deut. 12:31 [b]2 Kin. 16:3 [c]1 Kin. 11:7, 33; Acts 7:43 *See WW at Deut. 18:5.
22 [a]Lev. 20:13; Rom. 1:27
23 [a]Ex. 22:19; Lev. 20:15, 16; Deut. 27:21
24 [a]Matt. 15:18–20; 1 Cor. 3:17 [b]Lev. 18:3; 20:23; Deut. 18:12
25 [a]Num. 35:33, 34; Ezek. 36:17 [b]Is. 26:21; Jer. 5:9 [c]Lev. 18:28; 20:22 [1]*bring judgment for*
26 [a]Lev. 18:5, 30 [1]*obey*
28 [a]Jer. 9:19
29 [1]Put to death
30 [a]Lev. 18:3; 22:9 [b]Lev. 18:2 [1]*charge*

CHAPTER 19

2 [a]Ex. 19:6; Lev. 11:44; 20:7, 26; [Eph. 1:4]; 1 Pet. 1:16
3 [a]Ex. 20:12; Deut. 5:16; Matt. 15:4; Eph. 6:2 [b]Ex. 16:23; 20:8; 31:13
4 [a]Ex. 20:4; Ps. 96:5; 115:4–7; 1 Cor. 10:14; [Col. 3:5] [b]Ex. 34:17 [1]*molten*
5 [a]Lev. 7:16
9 [a]Lev. 23:22; Deut. 24:19–22
11 [a]Ex. 20:15, 16 [b]Jer. 9:3–5; Eph. 4:25
12 [a]Ex. 20:7; Deut. 5:11; [Matt. 5:33–37; James 5:12] [b]Lev. 18:21
13 [a]Ex. 22:7–15, 21–27; Mark 10:19

18:22 Lie with a male: All homosexual relationships were strictly forbidden (see 20:13).
19:2 You shall be holy: The people must imitate God in holiness by practicing numerous duties that reflect Him. This chapter emphasizes numerous commandments given to the people regarding religious life, good neighborliness, respect for the old and the alien, and trading. For a clearer understanding of vv. 1–18, see Ex. 20:1–17 and Deut. 5:6–21, where the importance of the Israelite ethic in a life of holiness dedicated to God is elaborated as fulfilling the requirements of God's absolutes.

nor rob *him.* [b]The wages of him who is hired shall not remain with you all night until morning.

14 'You shall not curse the deaf, [a]nor put a stumbling block before the blind, but shall *fear your God: I *am* the LORD.

15 'You shall do no injustice in [a]judgment. You shall not [b]be partial to the poor, nor honor the person of the mighty. In righteousness you shall judge your neighbor.

16 'You shall not go about *as* a [a]talebearer among your people; nor shall you [b]take a stand against the life of your neighbor: I *am* the LORD.

5 **17** [a]'You shall not hate your brother in your heart. [b]You shall surely [1]rebuke your neighbor, and not bear sin because of him.

18 [a]'You shall not take vengeance, nor bear any grudge against the children of your people, [b]but you shall love your neighbor as yourself: I *am* the LORD.

2 **19** 'You shall keep My statutes. You shall not let your livestock breed with another kind. You shall not sow your field with mixed seed. Nor shall a garment of mixed linen and wool come upon you.

20 'Whoever lies carnally with a woman who *is* [a]betrothed to a man as a concubine, and who has not at all been redeemed nor given her freedom, for this there shall be [1]scourging; *but* they shall not be put to death, because she was not free.

21 'And he shall bring his trespass offering to the LORD, to the door of the tabernacle of meeting, a ram as a trespass offering.

22 'The priest shall make [1]atonement for him with the ram of the trespass offering before the LORD for his sin which he has committed. And the sin which he has committed shall be forgiven him.

2 **23** 'When you come into the land, and have planted all kinds of trees for food, then you shall count their fruit as [1]uncircumcised. Three years it shall be as uncircumcised to you. *It* shall not be eaten.

24 'But in the fourth year all its fruit shall be holy, a praise to the LORD.

25 'And in the fifth year you may eat its fruit, that it may yield to you its increase: I *am* the LORD your God.

26 'You shall not eat *anything* with the blood, nor shall you practice divination or soothsaying.

27 'You shall not shave around the sides of your head, nor shall you disfigure the edges of your beard.

28 'You shall not [a]make any cuttings in your flesh for the dead, nor tattoo any marks on you: I *am* the LORD.

29 [a]'Do not prostitute your daughter, to cause her to be a harlot, lest the land fall into harlotry, and the land become full of wickedness.

30 'You shall [1]keep My Sabbaths and [a]reverence My sanctuary: I *am* the LORD.

31 'Give no regard to mediums and familiar spirits; do not *seek after [a]them, to be defiled by them: I *am* the LORD your God.

32 [a]'You shall [1]rise before the gray headed and honor the presence of an old man, and [b]fear your God: I *am* the LORD. 4

33 'And [a]if a stranger dwells with you in your land, you shall not mistreat him.

34 [a]'The stranger who dwells among you shall be to you as [1]one born among you, and [b]you shall love him as yourself; for you were strangers in the land of Egypt: I *am* the LORD your God.

13 [b]Deut. 24:15; Mal. 3:5; James 5:4
14 [a]Deut. 27:18 *See WW at Ex. 1:17.
15 [a]Deut. 16:19 [b]Ex. 23:3, 6; Deut. 1:17; 10:17; Ps. 82:2
16 [a]Prov. 11:13; 18:8; 20:19 [b]Ex. 23:7; Deut. 27:25; 1 Kin. 21:7–19
17 [a][1 John 2:9, 11; 3:15] [b]Matt. 18:15; [Luke 17:3]; Eph. 5:11 [1]*reprove*
18 [a][Deut. 32:35; 1 Sam. 24:12; Rom. 12:19; Heb. 10:30] [b]Matt. 5:43; 19:19; Mark 12:31; Luke 10:27; [Rom. 13:9; Gal. 5:14]; James 2:8
20 [a]Deut. 22:23–27 [1]*punishment*
22 [1]Lit. *covering*
23 [1]*unclean*
28 [a]1 Kin. 18:28; Jer. 16:6
29 [a]Lev. 21:9; Deut. 22:21; 23:17, 18
30 [a]Lev. 26:2; Eccl. 5:1 [1]*observe*
31 [a]Lev. 20:6, 27; Deut. 18:11; 1 Sam. 28:3; Is. 8:19 *See WW at Hos. 5:15.
32 [a]Prov. 23:22; Lam. 5:12; 1 Tim. 5:1 [b]Lev. 19:14 [1]*rise to give honor*
33 [a]Ex. 22:21; Deut. 24:17, 18
34 [a]Ex. 12:48 [b]Deut. 10:19 [1]*native among you*

KINGDOM DYNAMICS

19:34 Unselfish Christian Love Toward Strangers, BROTHERLY LOVE. In the timeless words of this text, God's Word clearly establishes definite guidelines on how to interact with strangers. The spirit of these guidelines recurs throughout both the OT and NT. God indicates that He expects us to relate to strangers in deep, unselfish, servant-spirited, Christian love. He reminds His people that they, who once were foreigners in the land of Egypt, should above all others remember how it feels to be treated as outsiders. Lesson 1: Remember how rejection feels, and never manifest it. His further instructions on the treatment of

19:17 See section 5 of Truth-In-Action at the end of Lev.

19:18 ***You shall love your neighbor as yourself:*** The word "love" (Hebrew *ahav*) could be understood as esteem. Love of one's neighbor begins with self-esteem. Then one esteems his neighbor. This general rule summarizes and fulfills the other commandments. The Jewish sages Hillel and Akiva taught that within this law is contained all the other laws of the Scriptures. Paul quotes the verse in a similar fashion (Rom. 13:8; Gal. 5:14). When Jesus cites the Golden Rule, which emphasizes positive action to assist others in need, He explains that "this is the Law and the Prophets" (Matt. 7:12).

19:19 See section 2 of Truth-In-Action at the end of Lev.

19:23–25 See section 2 of Truth-In-Action at the end of Lev.

19:32 See section 4 of Truth-In-Action at the end of Lev.

strangers are opposite to normal, worldly standards. The Lord says that when strangers come into our homes, they are to be treated as "one born among you," that is, as blood relatives! Since the Jews placed great emphasis upon bloodlines and lineage, God's use of this terminology had an extremely high impact, underscoring the significance of strangers in God's eyes. Lesson 2: All humanity is one family. Treat others that way.

(Gen. 45:4/Ps. 15:3) D.S.

35 'You shall do no injustice in judgment, in measurement of length,
weight, or volume.
36 'You shall have [a]honest scales, honest weights, an honest ephah, and an
honest hin: I *am* the LORD your God,
who brought you out of the land of
Egypt.
37 [a]'Therefore you shall observe all
My statutes and all My judgments, and
perform them: I *am* the LORD.' "

Penalties for Breaking the Law

20 Then the LORD spoke to Moses,
saying,
2 [a]"Again, you shall say to the children of Israel: [b]'Whoever of the children of Israel, or of the strangers who
[1]dwell in Israel, who gives *any* of his
descendants to Molech, he shall surely
be put to death. The people of the land
shall [c]stone him with stones.
3 [a]'I will set My face against that
man, and will [1]cut him off from his
people, because he has given *some* of
his descendants to Molech, to defile
My sanctuary and profane My holy
name.
4 'And if the people of the land should
in any way [1]hide their eyes from the
man, when he gives *some* of his descendants to Molech, and they do not
kill him,
5 'then I will set My face against that
man and against his family; and I will
cut him off from his people, and all
who prostitute themselves with him to
commit harlotry with Molech.
6 'And [a]the person who turns to mediums and familiar spirits, to prostitute
himself with them, I will set My face
against that person and cut him off
from his people.
7 [a]'Consecrate[1] yourselves therefore,
and be holy, for I *am* the LORD your
God.
8 'And you shall keep [a]My statutes,
and perform them: [b]I *am* the LORD who
[1]sanctifies you.
9 'For [a]everyone who *curses his father or his mother shall surely be put
to death. He has cursed his father or
his mother. [b]His blood *shall be* upon
him.
10 [a]'The man who commits adultery
with *another* man's wife, *he* who commits adultery with his neighbor's wife,
the adulterer and the adulteress, shall
surely be put to death.
11 'The man who lies with his [a]father's
wife has uncovered his father's nakedness; both of them shall surely be put
to death. Their blood *shall be* upon
them.
12 'If a man lies with his [a]daughter-in-
law, both of them shall surely be put
to death. They have committed perversion. Their blood *shall be* upon them.
13 [a]'If a man lies with a male as he **3**
lies with a woman, both of them have
committed an abomination. They shall
surely be put to death. Their blood
shall be upon them.
14 'If a man marries a woman and her
[a]mother, it *is* wickedness. They shall
be burned with fire, both he and they,
that there may be no wickedness
among you.
15 'If a man mates with an [a]animal, he
shall surely be put to death, and you
shall kill the animal.
16 'If a woman approaches any animal
and mates with it, you shall kill the
woman and the animal. They shall
surely be put to death. Their blood *is*
upon them.
17 'If a man takes his [a]sister, his father's daughter or his mother's daughter, and sees her nakedness and she
sees his nakedness, it *is* a wicked thing.
And they shall be [1]cut off in the sight
of their people. He has uncovered his
sister's nakedness. He shall bear his
[2]guilt.
18 [a]'If a man lies with a woman during
her [1]sickness and uncovers her nakedness, he has [2]exposed her flow, and she
has uncovered the flow of her blood.
Both of them shall be [3]cut off from
their people.
19 'You shall not uncover the nakedness of your [a]mother's sister nor of

36 [a]Deut. 25:13–15; Prov. 20:10 **37** [a]Lev. 18:4, 5; Deut. 4:5, 6; 5:1; 6:25

CHAPTER 20

2 [a]Lev. 18:2 [b]Lev. 18:21; 2 Kin. 23:10; 2 Chr. 33:6; Jer. 7:31 [c]Deut. 17:2–5 [1]As resident aliens **3** [a]Lev. 17:10 [1]Put him to death **4** [1]*disregard* **6** [a]Lev. 19:31; 1 Sam. 28:7–25 **7** [a]Lev. 19:2; Heb. 12:14 [1]*Set yourselves apart for the* LORD

8 [a]Lev. 19:19, 37 [b]Ex. 31:13; Deut. 14:2; Ezek. 37:28 [1]*sets you apart* **9** [a]Ex. 21:17; Deut. 27:16; Prov. 20:20; Matt. 15:4 [b]2 Sam. 1:16 *See WW at Jer. 8:11. **10** [a]Ex. 20:14; Lev. 18:20; Deut. 5:18; 22:22; John 8:4, 5 **11** [a]Lev. 18:7, 8; Deut. 27:20 **12** [a]Lev. 18:15 **13** [a]Lev. 18:22; Deut. 23:17; Judg. 19:22 **14** [a]Lev. 18:17 **15** [a]Lev. 18:23; Deut. 27:21 **17** [a]Lev. 18:9; Deut. 27:22 [1]Put to death [2]*iniquity* **18** [a]Lev. 15:24; 18:19 [1]Or *customary impurity* [2]Lit. *made bare* [3]Put to death **19** [a]Lev. 18:13

20:2 The ancient Phoenician worship of **Molech,** which often involved child sacrifice, sexual deviations (especially homosexuality, bestiality, and incest), and the consultation of mediums, as well as any sort of foreign religious practice, would break the bond of holiness between God and His people (see also v. 26). This is why the severe command that such a violator **shall surely be put to death.**

20:13 See section 3 of Truth-In-Action at the end of Lev.

your [b]father's sister, for that would uncover his near of kin. They shall bear
their guilt.
20 'If a man lies with his [a]uncle's wife,
he has uncovered his uncle's nakedness. They shall bear their sin; they
shall die childless.
21 'If a man takes his [a]brother's wife,
it *is* an [1]unclean thing. He has uncovered his brother's nakedness. They
shall be childless.
22 'You shall therefore keep all My
[a]statutes and all My judgments, and
perform them, that the land where I am
bringing you to dwell [b]may not vomit
you out.
23 [a]'And you shall not walk in the statutes of the nation which I am casting
out before you; for they commit all
these things, and [b]therefore I abhor
them.
24 'But [a]I have said to you, "You shall
inherit their land, and I will give it to
you to *possess, a land flowing with
milk and honey." I *am* the LORD your
God, [b]who has separated you from the
peoples.
25 [a]'You shall therefore distinguish between clean animals and unclean, between unclean birds and clean, [b]and
you shall not make yourselves [1]abom-
inable by beast or by bird, or by any
kind of living thing that creeps on
the ground, which I have separated
from you as [2]unclean.
26 'And you shall be holy to Me,
[a]for I the LORD *am* holy, and have separated you from the peoples, that you
should be Mine.
27 [a]'A man or a woman who is a medium, or who has familiar spirits, shall
surely be put to death; they shall stone
them with stones. Their blood *shall be*
upon them.' "

Regulations for Conduct of Priests

21 And the LORD said to Moses,
"Speak to the priests, the sons
of Aaron, and say to them: [a]'None shall
defile himself for the dead among his
people,
2 'except for his relatives who are
nearest to him: his mother, his father, his son, his daughter, and his
brother;
3 'also his virgin sister who is near
to him, who has had no husband, for
her he may defile himself.
4 '*Otherwise* he shall not defile himself, *being* a [1]chief man among his people, to profane himself.
5 [a]'They shall not make any bald
place on their heads, nor shall they
shave the edges of their beards nor
make any cuttings in their flesh.
6 'They shall be [a]holy to their God
and not profane the name of their God,
for they offer the offerings of the LORD
made by fire, *and* the [b]bread of their
God; [c]therefore they shall be holy.
7 [a]'They shall not take a wife *who is*
a harlot or a defiled woman, nor shall
they take a woman [b]divorced from her
husband; for [1]*the priest* is holy to his
God.
8 'Therefore you shall [1]consecrate
him, for he offers the bread of your
God. He shall be holy to you, for
[a]I the LORD, who [b]sanctify you, *am*
holy.
9 'The daughter of any priest, if she
profanes herself by playing the harlot,
she profanes her father. She shall be
[a]burned with fire.
10 '*He who is* the high priest among
his brethren, on whose head the
anointing oil was [a]poured and who is
consecrated to wear the garments,
shall not [b]uncover[1] his head nor tear
his clothes;
11 'nor shall he go [a]near any dead
body, nor defile himself for his father
or his mother;
12 [a]'nor shall he go out of the sanctuary, nor profane the sanctuary of his
God; for the [b]consecration of the
anointing oil of his God *is* upon him: I
am the LORD.
13 'And he shall take a wife in her virginity.
14 'A widow or a divorced woman or
a defiled woman *or* a harlot—these he
shall not marry; but he shall take a virgin of his own people as wife.
15 'Nor shall he profane his posterity

19 [b]Lev. 18:12
20 [a]Lev. 18:14
21 [a]Lev. 18:16; Matt. 14:3, 4 [1]*indecent, impure*
22 [a]Lev. 18:26; 19:37 [b]Lev. 18:25, 28; 2 Chr. 36:14–16
23 [a]Lev. 18:3, 24 [b]Deut. 9:5
24 [a]Ex. 3:17; 6:8; 13:5; 33:1–3 [b]Ex. 19:5; 33:16; Lev. 20:26; Deut. 7:6; 14:2; 1 Kin. 8:53 *See WW at Deut. 8:1.
25 [a]Lev. 10:10; 11:1–47; Deut. 14:3–21 [b]Lev. 11:43 [1]*detestable or loathsome* [2]*defiled*
26 [a]Lev. 19:2; 1 Pet. 1:16
27 [a]Lev. 19:31; 1 Sam. 28:9

CHAPTER 21

1 [a]Lev. 19:28; Ezek. 44:25
4 [1]Lit. *master* or *husband*
5 [a]Lev. 19:27; Deut. 14:1; Ezek. 44:20
6 [a]Ex. 22:31 [b]Lev. 3:11 [c]Is. 52:11
7 [a]Ezek. 44:22 [b]Deut. 24:1, 2 [1]Lit. *he*
8 [a]Lev. 11:44, 45 [b]Lev. 8:12, 30 [1]*set him apart*
9 [a]Deut. 22:21
10 [a]Lev. 8:12 [b]Lev. 10:6, 7 [1]In mourning
11 [a]Num. 19:14
12 [a]Lev. 10:7 [b]Ex. 29:6, 7

20:22 Vomit you out: The land itself is viewed as holy and it will not tolerate these sins, all of which undermine the code of holiness (see 26:32–35). Observing the divine commandments and judgments preserves the covenant relationship between God and His people in the land He promised to give to them.

21:1 Speak to the priests, the sons of Aaron: Membership in the priesthood was limited to sons of Aaron. The purity and holiness of the priests was carefully preserved to distinguish them from the common Israelite. Because the priests presented offerings for the rest of the people, their holiness as mediators was more strict (see v. 6). **Shall defile himself for the dead** means to take part in a funeral service.

21:10 The anointing oil: On the installation and the consecration of the priests, see the description in 8:12, 13; Ex. 29:1–46. The holy garments and the anointing are specifically mentioned in Ex. 29:29. Ps. 133:2 contains rich imagery of the ordination process that sets the priests apart for the holy service of the Lord in the sanctuary.

among his people, for I the LORD sanctify him.' "
16 And the LORD spoke to Moses, saying,
17 "Speak to Aaron, saying: 'No man
of your descendants in *succeeding* generations, who has *any* defect, may approach to offer the bread of his God.
18 'For any man who has a [a]defect
shall not approach: a man blind or
lame, who has a marred *face* or any
limb [b]too long,
19 'a man who has a broken foot or
broken hand,
20 'or is a hunchback or a dwarf, or *a
man* who has a defect in his eye, or
eczema or scab, or is a eunuch.
21 'No man of the descendants of
Aaron the priest, who has a defect,
shall come near to offer the offerings
made by fire to the LORD. He has a defect; he shall not come near to offer
the bread of his God.
22 'He may eat the bread of his God,
both the most holy and the holy;
23 'only he shall not go near the
[a]veil or approach the altar, because he
has a defect, lest [b]he profane My sanctuaries; for I the LORD sanctify them.' "
24 And Moses told *it* to Aaron and his
sons, and to all the children of Israel.
22 Then the LORD spoke to Moses,
saying,
2 "Speak to Aaron and his sons, that
they [a]separate[1] themselves from the
holy things of the children of Israel,
and that they [b]do not profane My holy
name *by* what they [c]dedicate to Me: I
am the LORD.
3 "Say to them: 'Whoever of all your
descendants throughout your generations, who goes near the holy things
which the children of Israel dedicate
to the LORD, [a]while he has [1]unclean-
ness upon him, that person shall be
cut off from My presence: I *am* the
LORD.
4 'Whatever man of the descendants
of Aaron, who *is* a [a]leper or has
[b]a discharge, shall not eat the holy offerings [c]until he is clean. And [d]who-
ever touches anything made *unclean
by a corpse, or [e]a man who has had
an emission of semen,
5 'or [a]whoever touches any creeping
thing by which he would be made unclean, or [b]any person by whom he
would become unclean, whatever his
uncleanness may be—

18 [a]Lev. 22:19–25 [b]Lev. 22:23
23 [a]Lev. 16:2 [b]Lev. 21:12

CHAPTER 22

2 [a]Num. 6:3 [b]Lev. 18:21 [c]Ex. 28:38; Lev. 16:19; 25:10; Num. 18:32; Deut. 15:19 [1]*keep themselves apart from*
3 [a]Lev. 7:20, 21; Num. 19:13 [1]*defilement*
4 [a]Num. 5:2 [b]Lev. 15:2 [c]Lev. 14:2; 15:13 [d]Lev. 11:24–28, 39, 40; Num. 19:11 [e]Lev. 15:16, 17 *See WW at Lev. 10:10.
5 [a]Lev. 11:23–28 [b]Lev. 15:7, 19
6 [a]Lev. 15:5
7 [a]Lev. 21:22; Num. 18:11, 13
8 [a]Ex. 22:31; Lev. 7:24; 11:39, 40; 17:15; Ezek. 44:31
9 [a]Lev. 18:30 [b]Ex. 28:43; Lev. 22:16; Num. 18:22 [1]*charge*
10 [a]Ex. 29:33; Lev. 22:13; Num. 3:10 [1]*As a visitor*
11 [a]Ex. 12:44
15 [a]Num. 18:32
18 [a]Lev. 1:2, 3, 10 [1]*brings his offering*
19 [a]Lev. 1:3; Deut. 15:21 *See WW at Lev. 23:12.

6 'the person who has touched any
such thing shall be unclean until evening, and shall not eat the holy *offerings* unless he [a]washes his body with
water.
7 'And when the sun goes down he
shall be clean; and afterward he may
eat the holy *offerings*, because [a]it *is* his
food.
8 [a]'Whatever dies *naturally* or is torn
by beasts he shall not eat, to defile himself with it: I *am* the LORD.
9 'They shall therefore keep [a]My
[1]ordinance, [b]lest they bear sin for it
and die thereby, if they profane it: I
the LORD sanctify them.
10 [a]'No outsider shall eat the holy *offering;* one who [1]dwells with the priest,
or a hired servant, shall not eat the
holy thing.
11 'But if the priest [a]buys a person
with his money, he may eat it; and one
who is born in his house may eat his
food.
12 'If the priest's daughter is married
to an outsider, she may not eat of the
holy offerings.
13 'But if the priest's daughter is a
widow or divorced, and has no child,
and has returned to her father's house
as in her youth, she may eat her father's food; but no outsider shall eat
it.
14 'And if a man eats the holy *offering*
unintentionally, then he shall restore
a holy *offering* to the priest, and add
one-fifth to it.
15 'They shall not profane the [a]holy *offerings* of the children of Israel, which
they offer to the LORD,
16 'or allow them to bear the guilt
of trespass when they eat their holy
offerings; for I the LORD sanctify
them.' "

Offerings Accepted and Not Accepted

17 And the LORD spoke to Moses, saying,
18 "Speak to Aaron and his sons, and
to all the children of Israel, and say to
them: [a]'Whatever man of the house of
Israel, or of the strangers in Israel, who
[1]offers his sacrifice for any of his vows
or for any of his freewill offerings,
which they offer to the LORD as a burnt
offering—
19 [a]'*you shall offer* of your own free
will a male *without blemish from the

22:2 That they separate themselves: The priests were addressed directly and instructed with the warning that they were required to preserve their own sanctity. The story of Nadab and Abihu reminded the priests of the sanctity of their task and the care that was required to preserve their individual holiness before the Lord (10:1–7).

cattle, from the sheep, or from the
goats.
20 [a]'Whatever has a defect, you shall
not offer, for it shall not be acceptable
on your behalf.
21 'And [a]whoever offers a sacrifice of
a peace offering to the LORD, [b]to fulfill
his vow, or a freewill offering from the
cattle or the sheep, it must be perfect
to be accepted; there shall be no defect
in it.
22 [a]'Those *that are* blind or broken or
maimed, or have an [1]ulcer or eczema
or scabs, you shall not offer to the
LORD, nor make [b]an offering by fire of
them on the altar to the LORD.
23 'Either a bull or a lamb that has any
limb [a]too long or too short you may
offer *as* a freewill offering, but for a
vow it shall not be accepted.
24 'You shall not offer to the LORD
what is bruised or crushed, or torn or
cut; nor shall you make *any offering
of them* in your land.
25 'Nor [a]from a foreigner's hand shall
you offer any of these as [b]the bread
of your God, because their [c]corruption
is in them, *and* defects *are* in them.
They shall not be accepted on your behalf.' "
26 And the LORD spoke to Moses, saying:
27 [a]"When a bull or a sheep or a goat
is born, it shall be seven days with its
mother; and from the eighth day and
thereafter it shall be accepted as an offering made by fire to the LORD.
28 "*Whether it is* a cow or ewe, do not
kill both her [a]and her young on the
same day.
29 "And when you [a]offer a sacrifice of
*thanksgiving to the LORD, offer *it* of
your own free will.
30 "On the same day it shall be eaten;
you shall leave [a]none of it until morning: I *am* the LORD.
31 [a]"Therefore you shall keep My
commandments, and perform them: I
am the LORD.
32 [a]"You shall not profane My holy
name, but [b]I will be [1]hallowed among
the children of Israel. I *am* the LORD
who [c]sanctifies you,
33 [a]"who brought you out of the land
of Egypt, to be your God: I *am* the
LORD."

20 [a]Deut. 15:21; 17:1; Mal. 1:8, 14; [Eph. 5:27; Heb. 9:14; 1 Pet. 1:19]
21 [a]Lev. 3:1, 6 [b]Num. 15:3, 8; Ps. 61:8; 65:1; Eccl. 5:4, 5
22 [a]Lev. 22:20; Mal. 1:8 [b]Lev. 1:9, 13; 3:3, 5 [1]*running sore*
23 [a]Lev. 21:18
25 [a]Num. 15:15, 16 [b]Lev. 21:6, 17 [c]Mal. 1:14
27 [a]Ex. 22:30
28 [a]Deut. 22:6, 7
29 [a]Lev. 7:12; Ps. 107:22; 116:17; Amos 4:5 *See WW at Ps. 95:2.
30 [a]Lev. 7:15
31 [a]Lev. 19:37; Num. 15:40; Deut. 4:40
32 [a]Lev. 18:21 [b]Lev. 10:3; Matt. 6:9; Luke 11:2 [c]Lev. 20:8 [1]*treated as holy*
33 [a]Lev. 19:36, 37; Num. 15:40; Deut. 4:40

CHAPTER 23

2 [a]Ex. 12:16 *See WW at Num. 9:2.
3 [a]Ex. 20:9; 23:12; 31:15; Lev. 19:3; Deut. 5:13, 14; Luke 13:14
4 [a]Ex. 23:14–16; Lev. 23:2, 37
5 [a]Ex. 12:1–28; Num. 9:1–5; 28:16–25; Deut. 16:1–8; Josh. 5:10
7 [a]Ex. 12:16; Num. 28:18, 25 [1]*occupational*
10 [a]Ex. 23:19; 34:26 [b][Rom. 11:16]; James 1:18; Rev. 14:4
11 [a]Ex. 29:24

Feasts of the LORD

23 And the LORD spoke to Moses,
saying,
2 "Speak to the children of Israel, and
say to them: 'The *feasts of the LORD,
which you shall proclaim *to be* [a]holy
convocations, these *are* My feasts.

The Sabbath

3 [a]'Six days shall work be done, but
the seventh day *is* a Sabbath of solemn
rest, a holy convocation. You shall do
no work *on it;* it *is* the Sabbath of the
LORD in all your dwellings.

The Passover and Unleavened Bread

4 [a]'These *are* the feasts of the LORD,
holy convocations which you shall proclaim at their appointed times.
5 [a]'On the fourteenth *day* of the first
month at twilight *is* the LORD's Passover.
6 'And on the fifteenth day of the
same month *is* the Feast of Unleavened
Bread to the LORD; seven days you
must eat unleavened bread.
7 [a]'On the first day you shall have a
holy convocation; you shall do no
[1]customary work on it.
8 'But you shall offer an offering
made by fire to the LORD for seven
days. The seventh day *shall be* a holy
convocation; you shall do no customary work *on it.*' "

The Feast of Firstfruits

9 And the LORD spoke to Moses, saying,
10 "Speak to the children of Israel, and
say to them: [a]'When you come into the
land which I give to you, and reap its
harvest, then you shall bring a sheaf
of [b]the firstfruits of your harvest to the
priest.
11 'He shall [a]wave the sheaf before the
LORD, to be accepted on your behalf;
on the day after the Sabbath the priest
shall wave it.
12 'And you shall offer on that day,
when you wave the sheaf, a male lamb
of the first year, **without blemish,** as a
burnt offering to the LORD.

23:2 The feasts of the LORD: The various feasts belonged to the Lord and emphasized His divine participation with the community.

23:3 The **Sabbath,** or seventh-day's rest, as a time of worship, study, reflection, and refreshing set apart for the Lord, became the basis for the other holy convocations of the Lord. The place of worship, whether it was the tent of meeting in the wilderness, the sanctuary at Shechem, or the temple in Jerusalem, became the center of gathering and involved the service of the priests who led the people in their celebration of God's presence.

23:5 See text and notes on Ex. 12:1–11.

23:6 See text and note on Ex. 12:14.

WORD WEALTH

23:12 without blemish, *tamim* (tah-*meem*); Strong's #8549: Unblemished, perfect, complete, full, upright, sincere, spotless, whole, healthy, blameless. This word first appears in Gen. 6:9: Noah was "perfect" in his generations. In Gen. 17:1, God tells Abram to walk before Him and be "blameless." *Tamim* is also used to describe animals fit for sacrifice, without blemish. The root verb *tamam* means "to finish, use up, accomplish, be spent, be completed." The dominant thought in all 90 occurrences of *tamim* is of someone or something complete, unblemished, and upright.

13 'Its grain offering *shall be* two-
tenths *of an ephah* of fine flour mixed
with oil, an offering made by fire to
the LORD, for a [1]sweet aroma; and its
drink offering *shall be* of wine, one-
fourth of a hin.
14 'You shall eat neither bread nor
parched grain nor fresh grain until the
same day that you have brought an offering to your God; *it shall be* a statute
forever throughout your generations
in all your dwellings.

The Feast of Weeks

15 'And you shall count for yourselves
from the day after the Sabbath, from
the day that you brought the sheaf of
the wave offering: seven Sabbaths
shall be completed.
16 'Count [a]fifty days to the day after
the seventh Sabbath; then you shall offer [b]a new grain offering to the LORD.
17 'You shall bring from your dwellings two wave *loaves* of two-tenths *of
an ephah.* They shall be of fine flour;
they shall be baked with leaven. *They
are* [a]the firstfruits to the LORD.
18 'And you shall offer with the bread
seven lambs of the first year, without
blemish, one young bull, and two rams.
They shall be *as* a burnt offering to the
LORD, with their grain offering and
their drink offerings, an offering made
by fire for a sweet aroma to the LORD.
19 'Then you shall sacrifice [a]one kid
of the goats as a sin offering, and two
male lambs of the first year as a sacrifice of a [b]peace offering.
20 'The priest shall wave them with the
bread of the firstfruits *as* a wave offering before the LORD, with the two
lambs. [a]They shall be holy to the LORD
for the priest.
21 'And you shall proclaim on the
same day *that* it is a holy convocation
to you. You shall do no customary
work *on it. It shall be* a statute forever
in all your dwellings throughout your
generations.
22 [a]'When you reap the harvest of
your land, you shall not wholly reap
the corners of your field when you
reap, nor shall you gather any gleaning
from your harvest. You shall leave
them for the *poor and for the stranger:
I *am* the LORD your God.' "

The Feast of Trumpets

23 Then the LORD spoke to Moses, saying,
24 "Speak to the children of Israel,
saying: 'In the [a]seventh month, on the
first *day* of the month, you shall have
a sabbath-*rest,* [b]a *memorial of blowing of trumpets, a holy convocation.
25 'You shall do no customary work
on it; and you shall offer an offering
made by fire to the LORD.' "

The Day of Atonement

26 And the LORD spoke to Moses, saying:
27 [a]"Also the tenth *day* of this seventh
month *shall be* the Day of Atonement.
It shall be a holy convocation for you;
you shall afflict your souls, and offer
an offering made by fire to the LORD.
28 "And you shall do no work on that
same day, for it *is* the Day of Atonement, [a]to make atonement for you before the LORD your God.
29 "For any person who is not
[a]afflicted *in soul* on that same day
[b]shall be cut off from his people.
30 "And any person who does any
work on that same day, [a]that person I
will destroy from among his people.
31 "You shall do no manner of work;
it shall be a statute forever throughout
your generations in all your dwellings.
32 "It *shall be* to you a sabbath of *solemn* rest, and you shall [1]afflict your
souls; on the ninth *day* of the month
at evening, from evening to evening,
you shall [2]celebrate your sabbath."

13 [1]*pleasing*
16 [a]Acts 2:1 [b]Num. 28:26
17 [a]Ex. 23:16, 19; Num. 15:17–21
19 [a]Lev. 4:23, 28; Num. 28:30; [2 Cor. 5:21] [b]Lev. 3:1
20 [a]Lev. 14:13; Num. 18:12; Deut. 18:4
22 [a]Lev. 19:9, 10; Deut. 24:19–22; Ruth 2:2, 15 *See WW at Ps. 40:17.
24 [a]Num. 29:1 [b]Lev. 25:9 *See WW at Ex. 39:7.
27 [a]Lev. 16:1–34; 25:9; Num. 29:7
28 [a]Lev. 16:34
29 [a]Is. 22:12; Jer. 31:9; Ezek. 7:16 [b]Gen. 17:14; Lev. 13:46; Num. 5:2
30 [a]Lev. 20:3–6
32 [1]*humble yourselves* [2]*observe your sabbath*

23:15–21 See text and note on Ex. 23:16.
23:24, 25 See text and note on Num. 29:1–6.
23:24 The seventh month was September–October and marked the end of one agricultural year and the beginning of another. A very special month, there were four extra rest days (vv. 24, 25, 27, 28, 34–36).

The Feast of Tabernacles

33 Then the LORD spoke to Moses, saying,
34 "Speak to the children of Israel,
saying: [a]'The fifteenth day of this seventh month *shall be* the Feast of Tabernacles *for* seven days to the LORD.
35 'On the first day *there shall be* a
holy convocation. You shall do no customary work *on it.*
36 '*For* seven days you shall offer an
[a]offering made by fire to the LORD.
[b]On the eighth day you shall have a
holy convocation, and you shall offer
an offering made by fire to the LORD.
It *is* a [c]sacred[1] assembly, *and* you shall
do no customary work *on it.*
37 [a]'These *are* the feasts of the LORD
which you shall proclaim *to be* holy
convocations, to offer an offering made
by fire to the LORD, a burnt offering
and a grain offering, a sacrifice and
drink offerings, everything on its day—

34 [a]Num. 29:12
36 [a]Num. 29:12–34 [b]Num. 29:35–38 [c]Deut. 16:8 [1]*solemn*
37 [a]Lev. 23:2, 4
38 [a]Num. 29:39
39 [a]Ex. 23:16 *See WW at Ex. 23:14.
40 [a]Neh. 8:15 [b]Deut. 12:7; 16:14, 15 [1]*foliage*
41 [a]Num. 29:12 *See WW at Ex. 23:14.
42 [a][Is. 4:6] [1]*tabernacles; shelters made of boughs*

38 [a]'besides the Sabbaths of the LORD,
besides your gifts, besides all your
vows, and besides all your freewill offerings which you give to the LORD.
39 'Also on the fifteenth day of the seventh month, when you have [a]gathered
in the fruit of the land, you shall *keep
the feast of the LORD *for* seven days;
on the first day *there shall be* a
sabbath-*rest*, and on the eighth day a
sabbath-*rest*.
40 'And [a]you shall take for yourselves
on the first day the [1]fruit of beautiful
trees, branches of palm trees, the
boughs of leafy trees, and willows of
the brook; [b]and you shall rejoice before the LORD your God for seven days.
41 [a]'You shall *keep it as a feast to the
LORD for seven days in the year. *It shall
be* a statute forever in your generations. You shall celebrate it in the seventh month.
42 [a]'You shall dwell in [1]booths for

23:33–36 See text and note on Num. 29:12–39.

ISRAEL'S ANNUAL FEASTS (23:44)

Feast	Month of Sacred Year	Day	Corresponding Month
Passover	1 (Abib)	14	Mar.–Apr.
Ex. 12:1–14; Lev. 23:5; Num. 9:1–14; 28:16; Deut. 16:1–7			
***Unleavened Bread**	1 (Abib)	15–21	Mar.–Apr.
Ex. 12:15–20; 13:3–10; Lev. 23:6–8; Num. 28:17–25; Deut. 16:3, 4, 8			
Firstfruits	1 (Abib) and 3 (Sivan)	16 6	Mar.–Apr. May–June
Lev. 23:9–14; Num. 28:26			
***Weeks** (Harvest or Pentecost)	3 (Sivan)	6 (50 days after barley harvest)	May–June
Ex. 23:16; 34:22; Lev. 23:15–21; Num. 28:26–31; Deut. 16:9–12			
Trumpets *Rosh Hashanah*	7 (Tishri)	1	Sept.–Oct.
Lev. 23:23–25; Num. 29:1–6			
Day of Atonement *Yom Kippur*	7 (Tishri)	10	Sept.–Oct.
Lev. 16; 23:26–32; Num. 29:7–11			
***Tabernacles** (Booths or Ingathering)	7 (Tishri)	15–22	Sept.–Oct.
Ex. 23:16; 34:22; Lev. 23:33–36, 39–43; Num. 29:12–38; Deut. 16:13–15			

*The three major feasts for which all males of Israel were required to travel to the temple in Jerusalem (Ex. 23:14–19).

seven days. [b]All who are native Israelites shall dwell in booths,
43 [a]'that your generations may [b]know
that I made the children of Israel dwell
in booths when [c]I brought them out of
the land of Egypt: I *am* the LORD your
God.' "
44 So Moses [a]declared to the children
of Israel the feasts of the LORD.

Care of the Tabernacle Lamps

2 **24** Then the LORD spoke to Moses,
saying:
2 [a]"Command the children of Israel
that they bring to you pure oil of
pressed olives for the light, to make the
lamps burn *continually.
3 "Outside the veil of the Testimony,
in the tabernacle of meeting, Aaron
shall be in charge of it from evening
until morning before the LORD continually; *it shall be* a statute forever in your
generations.
4 "He shall [1]be in charge of the lamps
on [a]the pure *gold* lampstand before the
LORD continually.

The Bread of the Tabernacle

5 "And you shall take fine flour and
bake twelve [a]cakes with it. Two-tenths
of an ephah shall be in each cake.
6 "You shall set them in two rows, six
in a row, [a]on the pure *gold* table before
the LORD.
7 "And you shall put pure frankincense on *each* row, that it may be on
the bread for a [a]memorial, an offering
made by fire to the LORD.
8 [a]"Every Sabbath he shall set it in
order before the LORD continually, *being taken* from the children of Israel
by an everlasting covenant.
9 "And [a]it shall be for Aaron and his
sons, [b]and they shall eat it in a holy
place; for it *is* most holy to him from
the offerings of the LORD made by fire,
by a perpetual statute."

The Penalty for Blasphemy

10 Now the son of an Israelite woman,
whose father *was* an Egyptian, went
out among the children of Israel; and
this Israelite *woman's* son and a man
of Israel fought each other in the camp.
11 And the Israelite woman's son
[a]blasphemed the *name *of the* LORD
and [b]cursed;* and so they [c]brought
him to Moses. (His mother's name *was*
Shelomith the daughter of Dibri, of the
*tribe of Dan.)
12 Then they [a]put him [1]in custody,
[b]that [2]the mind of the LORD might be
shown to them.
13 And the LORD spoke to Moses, saying,
14 "Take outside the camp him who
has cursed; then let all who heard *him*
[a]lay their hands on his head, and let
all the congregation stone him.
15 "Then you shall speak to the children of Israel, saying: 'Whoever curses
his God [a]shall [1]bear his sin.
16 'And whoever [a]blasphemes the
name of the LORD shall surely be put
to death. All the congregation shall
certainly stone him, the stranger as
well as him who is born in the land.
When he blasphemes the name *of the
LORD*, he shall be put to death.
17 [a]'Whoever kills any man shall
surely be put to death.
18 [a]'Whoever kills an animal shall
make it good, animal for animal.
19 'If a man causes disfigurement of
his neighbor, as [a]he has done, so shall
it be done to him—
20 'fracture for [a]fracture, [b]eye for eye,
tooth for tooth; as he has caused disfigurement of a man, so shall it be done
to him.
21 'And whoever kills an animal shall
restore it; but whoever kills a man shall
be put to death.
22 'You shall have [a]the[1] same law for
the stranger and for one from your
own country; for I *am* the LORD your
God.' "
23 Then Moses spoke to the children
of Israel; and they took outside the
camp him who had cursed, and stoned
him with stones. So the children of Israel did as the LORD commanded Moses.

The Sabbath of the Seventh Year

25 And the LORD spoke to Moses
on Mount [a]Sinai, saying,

42 [b]Neh. 8:14–16
43 [a]Deut. 31:13 [b]Ex. 10:2 [c]Lev. 22:33
44 [a]Lev. 23:2

CHAPTER 24

2 [a]Ex. 27:20, 21 *See WW at Ex. 28:30.
4 [a]Ex. 25:31; 31:8; 37:17 [1]*arrange or set in order*
5 [a]Ex. 25:30; 39:36; 40:23
6 [a]1 Kin. 7:48
7 [a]Lev. 2:2, 9, 16
8 [a]1 Chr. 9:32
9 [a]Matt. 12:4 [b]Ex. 29:33
11 [a]Ex. 22:28 [b]Is. 8:21 [c]Ex. 18:22, 26 *See WW at Deut. 18:5. • See WW at Jer. 8:11. • See WW at Ex. 38:22.
12 [a]Num. 15:34 [b]Num. 27:5 [1]*under guard* [2]Lit. *it might be declared to them from the mouth of the LORD*
14 [a]Deut. 13:9; 17:7
15 [a]Lev. 20:17 [1]*be responsible for*
16 [a][Mark 3:28, 29]
17 [a]Ex. 21:12
18 [a]Lev. 24:21
19 [a]Ex. 21:24
20 [a]Ex. 21:23 [b][Matt. 5:38, 39]
22 [a]Ex. 12:49 [1]*one standard of judgment*

CHAPTER 25

1 [a]Lev. 26:46

24:1–4 See section 2 of Truth-In-Action at the end of Lev.
24:20 Eye for eye, tooth for tooth: The principle of *lex talionis* was used to prevent extreme brutality in exacting retribution. In the ancient Near East, it had been the practice to take the life of one who had caused injury in retaliation for damages incurred. The Mosaic covenant limited retaliation. By the time of Jesus, the Pharisees had interpreted the law to mean that a person was required to pay to the injured person compensation equivalent to the damages caused.
25:1–55 This chapter describes the seventh-year Sabbath and the Year of Jubilee. It deals with a sabbath for the land

2 "Speak to the children of Israel, and
say to them: 'When you come into the
land which I give you, then the land
shall [a]keep a sabbath to the LORD.
3 'Six years you shall sow your field,
and six years you shall prune your
vineyard, and gather its fruit;
4 'but in the [a]seventh year there shall
be a sabbath of solemn [b]rest for the
land, a sabbath to the LORD. You shall
neither sow your field nor prune your
vineyard.
5 [a]'What grows of its own accord of
your harvest you shall not reap, nor
gather the grapes of your untended
vine, *for* it is a year of rest for the land.
6 'And the sabbath *produce* of the
land shall be food for you: for you,
your male and female servants, your
hired man, and the stranger who
dwells with you,
7 'for your livestock and the beasts
that *are* in your land—all its produce
shall be for food.

The Year of Jubilee

8 'And you shall count seven sabbaths of years for yourself, seven times
seven years; and the time of the seven
sabbaths of years shall be to you forty-nine years.
9 'Then you shall cause the *trumpet
of the Jubilee to sound on the tenth *day*
of the seventh month; [a]on the Day of
Atonement you shall make the trumpet
to sound throughout all your land.
10 'And you shall consecrate the fiftieth year, and [a]proclaim **liberty**
throughout *all* the land to all its inhabitants. It shall be a Jubilee for you;
[b]and each of you shall return to his

2 [a]Lev. 26:34, 35
4 [a]Deut. 15:1; Neh. 10:31 [b][Heb. 4:9]
5 [a]2 Kin. 19:29
9 [a]Lev. 23:24, 27 *See WW at Hos. 8:1.
10 [a]Is. 61:2; 63:4; Jer. 34:8, 15, 17; [Luke 4:19] [b]Lev. 25:13, 28, 54; Num. 36:4

(vv. 2–22), the redemption of property (vv. 23–38), and the redemption of slaves (vv. 39–55). The primary purpose for these regulations is to prevent the total ruin of the land and of indebted people.

25:2 The land shall keep a sabbath to the LORD: The land of Israel is considered holy to the Lord and is, therefore, also to rest every seventh year. The three foundations of the OT covenant can be seen in the land, the people, and the religious practices. All three are to be preserved as holy to the Lord, and the priests are instructed to maintain the sanctity of the covenant community through the Levitical code.

25:10 The fiftieth year . . . shall be a Jubilee, which apparently followed the seventh cycle of Sabbath years (v. 8), hence making two successive special years every 50 years. Jesus' proclamation from Is. 61:2 that He came "to proclaim the acceptable year of the LORD" (Luke 4:19) is against the backdrop of Jubilee principles taught in this chapter.

ISRAEL'S OTHER SACRED TIMES (25:1)

Sabbath Ex. 20:8–11; 31:12–17; Lev. 23:3; Deut. 5:12–15	Every seventh day was a solemn rest from all work.
Sabbath Year Ex. 23:10, 11; Lev. 25:1–7	Every seventh year was designated a "year of release" to allow the land to lie fallow.
Year of Jubilee Lev. 25:8–55; 27:17–24; Ezek. 46:17	The 50th year, which followed seven Sabbath years, was to proclaim liberty to those who were servants because of debt, and to return lands to their former owners.
The New Moon Num. 28:11–15; Ps. 81:3	The first day of the Hebrew 29 or 30-day month was a day of rest, special sacrifices, and the blowing of trumpets.
Dedication (Lights or *Hanukkah*) John 10:22	An eight-day feast in the ninth month (Chislev) commemorating the cleansing of the temple from defilement by Syria, and its rededication.
Purim (Lots) Esth. 9:18–32	A feast on the 14th and 15th of the 12th month (Adar). The name comes from Babylonian *Pur*, meaning "Lot."

possession, and each of you shall return to his family.

WORD WEALTH

25:10 liberty, *deror* (deh-*ror*); Strong's #1865: Freedom, liberty, release, setting free. Lev. 25:10 is the verse inscribed on the Liberty Bell. *Deror* is also the Hebrew word for "swallow," a bird swift in flight. In this reference, the details about the Year of Jubilee are given (vv. 8–17 and 39–55), indicating that *deror* is a technical term for the release of slaves and property every 50 years. The Lord Jesus in His first sermon quoted Is. 61:1, which states that the Messiah's anointing and divine commission enables Him to "proclaim liberty to the captives" (Luke 4:17–19).

11 'That fiftieth year shall be a Jubilee
to you; in it [a]you shall neither sow nor
reap what grows of its own accord, nor
gather *the grapes* of your untended
vine.
12 'For it *is* the Jubilee; it shall be holy
to you; [a]you shall eat its produce from
the field.
13 [a]'In this Year of Jubilee, each of you
shall return to his possession.
14 'And if you sell anything to your
neighbor or buy from your neighbor's
hand, you shall not [a]oppress one another.
15 [a]'According to the number of years
after the Jubilee you shall buy from
your neighbor, and according to the
number of years of crops he shall sell
to you.
16 'According to the multitude of years
you shall increase its price, and according to the fewer number of years
you shall diminish its price; for he sells
to you *according* to the number *of the
years* of the crops.
17 'Therefore [a]you shall not [1]oppress
one another, [b]but you shall fear your
God; for I *am* the LORD your God.

Provisions for the Seventh Year

18 [a]'So you shall observe My statutes
and keep My judgments, and perform
them; [b]and you will dwell in the land
in *safety.
19 'Then the land will yield its fruit,
and [a]you will eat your fill, and dwell
there in safety.
20 'And if you say, [a]"What shall we
eat in the seventh year, since [b]we shall
not sow nor gather in our produce?"
21 'Then I will [a]command My blessing
on you in the [b]sixth year, and it will
bring forth produce enough for three
years.
22 [a]'And you shall sow in the eighth
year, and eat [b]old produce until the
ninth year; until its produce comes in,
you shall eat *of* the old *harvest*.

Redemption of Property

23 'The land shall not be sold permanently, for [a]the land *is* Mine; for you
are [b]strangers and sojourners with
Me.
24 'And in all the land of your possession you shall grant redemption of the
land.
25 [a]'If one of your brethren becomes
poor, and has sold *some* of his possession, and if [b]his redeeming relative
comes to redeem it, then he may redeem what his brother sold.
26 'Or if the man has no one to redeem
it, but he himself becomes able to redeem it,
27 'then [a]let him count the years since
its sale, and restore the remainder to
the man to whom he sold it, that he
may return to his possession.
28 'But if he is not able to have *it* restored to himself, then what was sold
shall remain in the hand of him who
bought it until the Year of Jubilee;
[a]and in the Jubilee it shall be released,
and he shall return to his possession.
29 'If a man sells a house in a walled
city, then he may redeem it within a
whole year after it is sold; *within* a full
year he may redeem it.
30 'But if it is not *redeemed within the
space of a full year, then the house in
the walled city shall belong permanently to him who bought it, throughout his generations. It shall not be released in the Jubilee.
31 'However the houses of villages
which have no wall around them shall
be counted as the fields of the country.
They may be redeemed, and they shall
be released in the Jubilee.
32 'Nevertheless [a]the cities of the Levites, *and* the houses in the cities of
their possession, the Levites may redeem at any time.
33 'And if a man purchases a house
from the Levites, then the house that
was sold in the city of his possession
shall be released in the Jubilee; for the
houses in the cities of the Levites *are*
their possession among the children of
Israel.
34 'But [a]the field of the common-land
of their cities may not be [b]sold, for it
is their perpetual possession.

11 [a]Lev. 25:5
12 [a]Lev. 25:6, 7
13 [a]Lev. 25:10; 27:24; Num. 36:4
14 [a]Lev. 19:13
15 [a]Lev. 27:18, 23
17 [a]Lev. 25:14; Prov. 14:31; 22:22; Jer. 7:5, 6; 1 Thess. 4:6 [b]Lev. 19:14, 32; 25:43 [1]*mistreat*
18 [a]Lev. 19:37 [b]Lev. 26:5; Deut. 12:10; Ps. 4:8; Jer. 23:6 *See WW at Deut. 33:12.
19 [a]Lev. 26:5; Ezek. 34:25
20 [a]Matt. 6:25, 31 [b]Lev. 25:4, 5
21 [a]Deut. 28:8 [b]Ex. 16:29
22 [a]2 Kin. 19:29 [b]Lev. 26:10; Josh. 5:11
23 [a]Ex. 19:5; 2 Chr. 7:20 [b]Gen. 23:4; Ex. 6:4; 1 Chr. 29:15; Ps. 39:12; Heb. 11:13; 1 Pet. 2:11
25 [a]Ruth 2:20; 4:4, 6 [b]Num. 5:8; Ruth 3:2, 9, 12; [Job 19:25]; Jer. 32:7, 8
27 [a]Lev. 25:50–52
28 [a]Lev. 25:10, 13
30 *See WW at Is. 52:9.
32 [a]Num. 35:1–8; Josh. 21:2
34 [a]Num. 35:2–5 [b]Acts 4:36, 37

Lending to the Poor

35 'If one of your brethren becomes
poor, and [1]falls into poverty among
you, then you shall [a]help him, like a
stranger or a sojourner, that he may
live with you.
36 [a]'Take no usury or interest from
him; but [b]fear your God, that your
brother may live with you.
37 'You shall not lend him your money
for usury, nor lend him your food at a
profit.
38 [a]'I *am* the LORD your God, who
brought you out of the land of Egypt,
to give you the land of Canaan *and* to
be your God.

The Law Concerning Slavery

39 'And if *one of* your brethren *who
dwells* by you becomes poor, and sells
himself to you, you shall not compel
him to serve as a slave.
40 'As a hired servant *and* a sojourner
he shall be with you, *and* shall serve
you until the Year of Jubilee.
41 'And *then* he shall depart from
you—he and his children [a]with him—
and shall return to his own family. He
shall return to the possession of his fathers.
42 'For they *are* [a]My servants, whom
I brought out of the land of Egypt; they
shall not be sold as slaves.
43 [a]'You shall not rule over him
[b]with [1]rigor, but you [c]shall fear your
God.
44 'And as for your male and female
slaves whom you may have—from the
nations that are around you, from
them you may buy male and female
slaves.
45 'Moreover you may buy [a]the children of the strangers who dwell among
you, and their families who are with
you, which they beget in your land;
and they shall become your property.
2 46 'And [a]you may take them as an inheritance for your children after you,
to inherit *them as* a possession; they
shall be your permanent slaves. But regarding your brethren, the children of
Israel, you shall not rule over one another with rigor.
47 'Now if a sojourner or stranger
close to you becomes rich, and *one of*
your brethren *who dwells* by him
becomes poor, and sells himself to
the stranger *or* sojourner close to you,
or to a member of the stranger's family,
48 'after he is sold he may be redeemed
again. One of his brothers may redeem
him;
49 'or his uncle or his uncle's son may
redeem him; or *anyone* who is near of
kin to him in his family may redeem
him; or if he is able he may redeem
himself.
50 'Thus he shall reckon with him who
bought him: The price of his release
shall be according to the number of
years, from the year that he was sold
to him until the Year of Jubilee; *it shall
be* [a]according to the time of a hired
servant for him.
51 'If *there are* still many years
remaining, according to them he shall
repay the price of his redemption
from the money with which he was
bought.
52 'And if there remain but a few years
until the Year of Jubilee, then he shall
reckon with him, *and* according to his
years he shall repay him the price of
his redemption.
53 'He shall be with him as a yearly
hired servant, and he shall not rule
with rigor over him in your sight.
54 'And if he is not redeemed in these
years, then he shall be released in the
Year of Jubilee—he and his children
with him.
55 'For the children of Israel *are* servants to Me; they *are* My servants
whom I brought out of the land of
Egypt: I *am* the LORD your God.

Promise of Blessing and Retribution

26 'You shall [a]not make idols for 4
yourselves;
neither a carved image nor a *sacred* pillar shall you rear up for
yourselves;
nor shall you set up an engraved
stone in your land, to bow down
to it;
for I *am* the LORD your God.
2 [a]You shall [1]keep My Sabbaths and
reverence My sanctuary:
I *am* the LORD.

35 [a]Deut. 15:7–11; 24:14, 15; Luke 6:35; 1 John 3:17 [1]Lit. *his hand fails*
36 [a]Ex. 22:25; Deut. 23:19, 20 [b]Neh. 5:9
38 [a]Lev. 11:45; 22:32, 33
41 [a]Ex. 21:3
42 [a]Lev. 25:55; [Rom. 6:22; 1 Cor. 7:22, 23]
43 [a]Eph. 6:9; Col. 4:1 [b]Ex. 1:13, 14; Lev. 25:46, 53; Ezek. 34:4 [c]Ex. 1:17; Deut. 25:18; Mal. 3:5 [1]*severity*
45 [a][Is. 56:3, 6, 7]
46 [a]Is. 14:2
50 [a]Job 7:1; Is. 16:14

CHAPTER 26

1 [a]Ex. 20:4, 5; Deut. 4:15–18; 5:8
2 [a]Lev. 19:30 [1]*observe*

25:35 If one of your brethren becomes poor: The instruction of the Lord insures care for the poor and the needy in the priestly code. As has been seen, one's relationship to the Lord is not restricted by a person's wealth or poverty, because provisions are made within the code for offerings which cost less for those who have limited means (12:8; 14:21). Gifts of support for the less fortunate became a central part of Jewish faith and practice (see Deut. 15:7–11 and compare the teachings of Jesus, Matt. 6:1–4).

25:46 See section 2 of Truth-In-Action at the end of Lev.

26:1–46 See section 4 of Truth-In-Action at the end of Lev.

3 [a]'If you walk in My statutes and
keep My commandments, and
perform them,
4 [a]then I will give you rain in its season, [b]the land shall yield its
produce, and the trees of the
field shall yield their fruit.
5 [a]Your threshing shall last till the
time of vintage, and the vintage
shall last till the time of sowing;
you shall eat your bread to the
full, and [b]dwell in your land
safely.
6 [a]I will give *peace in the land, and
[b]you shall lie down, and none
will make *you* afraid;
I will rid the land of [c]evil[1] beasts,
and [d]the sword will not go
through your land.
7 You will chase your enemies, and
they shall fall by the sword before you.
8 [a]Five of you shall chase a hundred,
and a hundred of you shall put
ten thousand to flight;
your enemies shall fall by the
sword before you.

9 'For I will [a]look on you favorably
and [b]make you fruitful, multiply you and confirm My [c]cov-
enant with you.
10 You shall eat the [a]old harvest,
and clear out the old because
of the new.
11 [a]I will set My [1]tabernacle among
you, and My soul shall not abhor you.
12 [a]I will walk among you and be
your God, and you shall be My
*people.
13 I *am* the LORD your God, who
brought you out of the land of
Egypt, that *you* should not be
their slaves;
I have broken the bands of your
[a]yoke and made you walk [1]up-
right.

14 'But if you do not obey Me, and
do not observe all these commandments,

3 [a]Deut. 28:1–14 **4** [a]Is. 30:23 [b]Ps. 67:6 **5** [a]Amos 9:13 [b]Lev. 25:18, 19 **6** [a]Is. 45:7 [b]Job 11:19 [c]2 Kin. 17:25 [d]Ezek. 14:17 [1]*wild beasts* *See WW at Nah. 1:15. **8** [a]Deut. 32:30 **9** [a]Ex. 2:25 [b]Gen. 17:6, 7 [c]Gen. 17:1–7 **10** [a]Lev. 25:22 **11** [a]Ex. 25:8; 29:45, 46 [1]*dwelling place* **12** [a][2 Cor. 6:16] *See WW at Ruth 1:16. **13** [a]Gen. 27:40 [1]*erect*

15 *See WW at Amos 2:4. **16** [a]Deut. 28:22 [b]1 Sam. 2:33 [c]Ezek. 24:23; 33:10 [d]Judg. 6:3–6 [1]*without profit* **17** [a]Ps. 34:16 [b]Deut. 28:25 [c]Ps. 106:41 [d]Prov. 28:1 [1]*oppose you* **18** [a]1 Sam. 2:5 **19** [a]Is. 25:11 [b]Deut. 28:23 **20** [a]Ps. 127:1 [b]Gen. 4:12 **22** [a]Deut. 32:24 [b]Judg. 5:6 **23** [a]Amos 4:6–12 **24** [a]Lev. 26:28, 41

15 and if you *despise My statutes,
or if your soul abhors My judgments, so that you do not
perform all My command-
ments, *but* break My covenant,
16 I also will do this to you:
I will even appoint terror over
you, [a]wasting disease and fever
which shall [b]consume the eyes
and [c]cause sorrow of heart.
And [d]you shall sow your seed
[1]in vain, for your enemies shall
eat it.
17 I will [1]set [a]My face against you,
and [b]you shall be defeated by
your enemies.
[c]Those who hate you shall reign
over you, and you shall [d]flee
when no one pursues you.

18 'And after all this, if you do not
obey Me, then I will punish you
[a]seven times more for your
sins.
19 I will [a]break the pride of your
power;
I [b]will make your heavens like
iron and your earth like bronze.
20 And your [a]strength shall be spent
in vain;
for your [b]land shall not yield its
produce, nor shall the trees of
the land yield their fruit.

21 'Then, if you walk contrary to Me,
and are not willing to obey Me,
I will bring on you seven times
more plagues, according to
your sins.
22 [a]I will also send wild beasts among
you, which shall rob you of
your children, destroy your
livestock, and make you few in
number;
and [b]your highways shall be
desolate.

23 'And if [a]by these things you are
not reformed by Me, but walk
contrary to Me,
24 [a]then I also will walk contrary to
you, and I will punish you yet
seven times for your sins.

26:9 Confirm My covenant with you: The covenant is accentuated in ch. 26, as the consequences of disobedience (vv. 14–39) are explained, as well as the promised blessings for obedience (vv. 1–13 and 40–46). God has redeemed the people from bondage and He alone is to be worshiped. He has revealed His will to them. The higher purpose of the covenant relationship emerges in that, through the obedience and the holiness of the community, the Lord will walk among the people who are set apart for fellowship with Him and He will be their God (v. 12).

26:14 But if you do not obey: Compare the texts of Deut. 27:11–13 and Josh. 8:30–35, where one finds a description of the blessings and curses of those who have entered into the covenant relationship. These texts quite probably refer to an early ceremony that enabled the people to learn and to recite the laws of the blessings and of the curses by reciting the promises of the covenant. The people's response to the divine initiative will determine their future relationship with God. He invites them to accept the terms of the covenant.

25 And [a]I will bring a sword against you that will execute the vengeance of the covenant;
when you are gathered together within your cities [b]I will send pestilence among you;
and you shall be delivered into the hand of the enemy.
26 [a]When I have cut off your supply of bread, ten women shall bake your bread in one oven, and they shall bring back your bread by weight, [b]and you shall eat and not be *satisfied.

27 'And after all this, if you do not obey Me, but walk contrary to Me,
28 then I also will walk contrary to you in fury;
and I, even I, will chastise you seven times for your sins.
29 [a]You[1] shall eat the flesh of your sons, and you shall eat the flesh of your daughters.
30 [a]I will destroy your *high places, cut down your incense altars, and cast your carcasses on the lifeless forms of your idols;
and My soul shall abhor you.
31 I will lay your [a]cities waste and [b]bring your sanctuaries to desolation, and I will not [c]smell the fragrance of your [1]sweet aromas.
32 [a]I will bring the land to desolation, and your enemies who dwell in it shall be astonished at it.
33 [a]I will scatter you among the nations and draw out a sword after you;
your land shall be desolate and your cities waste.
34 [a]Then the land shall enjoy its sabbaths as long as it lies desolate and you *are* in your enemies' land;
then the land shall *rest and enjoy its sabbaths.
35 As long as *it* lies desolate it shall rest—
for the time it did not rest on your [a]sabbaths when you dwelt in it.

36 'And as for those of you who are left, I will send [a]faintness[1] into their hearts in the lands of their enemies;
the sound of a shaken leaf shall cause them to flee;
they shall flee as though fleeing from a sword, and they shall fall when no one pursues.
37 [a]They shall stumble over one another, as it were before a sword, when no one pursues;
and [b]you shall have no *power* to stand before your enemies.
38 You shall [a]perish* among the nations, and the land of your enemies shall eat you up.
39 And those of you who are left [a]shall [1]waste away in their iniquity in your enemies' lands;
also in their [b]fathers' iniquities, which are with them, they shall waste away.

40 '*But* [a]if they confess their iniquity and the iniquity of their fathers, with their unfaithfulness in which they were unfaithful to Me, and that they also have walked contrary to Me, **5**
41 and *that* I also have walked contrary to them and have brought them into the land of their enemies;
if their [a]uncircumcised hearts are [b]humbled, and they [c]accept their guilt—
42 then I will [a]remember My covenant with Jacob, and My covenant with Isaac and My covenant with Abraham I will remember;
I will [b]remember the land.
43 [a]The land also shall be left empty by them, and will enjoy its sabbaths while it lies desolate without them;
they will accept their guilt, because they [b]despised My judgments and because their soul abhorred My statutes.
44 Yet for all that, when they are in the land of their enemies, [a]I will not cast them away, nor shall I abhor them, to utterly destroy them and break My covenant with them;
for I *am* the LORD their God.
45 But [a]for their sake I will remember the covenant of their ancestors, [b]whom I brought out of the land of Egypt [c]in the

25 [a]Ezek. 5:17 [b]Deut. 28:21 **26** [a]Ps. 105:16 [b]Mic. 6:14 *See WW at Amos 4:8. **29** [a]2 Kin. 6:28, 29 [1]In time of famine **30** [a]2 Chr. 34:3 *See WW at Ezek. 6:3. **31** [a]2 Kin. 25:4, 10 [b]Ps. 74:7 [c]Is. 1:11–15 [1]*pleasing* **32** [a]Jer. 9:11; 18:16 **33** [a]Deut. 4:27 **34** [a]2 Chr. 36:21 *See WW at Ex. 16:30. **35** [a]Lev. 25:2 **36** [a]Ezek. 21:7, 12, 15 [1]*fear*

37 [a]1 Sam. 14:15, 16 [b]Josh. 7:12, 13 **38** [a]Deut. 4:26 *See WW at Judg. 5:31. **39** [a]Ezek. 4:17; 33:10 [b]Ex. 34:7 [1]*rot away* **40** [a]Neh. 9:2 **41** [a]Acts 7:51 [b]2 Chr. 12:6, 7, 12 [c]Dan. 9:7 **42** [a]Ex. 2:24; 6:5 [b]Ps. 136:23 **43** [a]Lev. 26:34, 35 [b]Lev. 26:15 **44** [a]Deut. 4:31 **45** [a][Rom. 11:28] [b]Lev. 22:33; 25:38 [c]Ps. 98:2

26:40 See section 5 of Truth-In-Action at the end of Lev.
26:42 Then I will remember My covenant: The theme that God remembers His promise and never goes back on His word is emphasized in the covenant relationship. The community of the covenant is never without hope. God is always ready to receive His people in repentance even after they have failed and abandoned Him.

sight of the nations, that I might
be their God:
I *am* the LORD.' "

46 [a]These *are* the statutes and judgments and laws which the LORD made between Himself and the children of Israel [b]on Mount Sinai by the hand of Moses.

Redeeming Persons and Property Dedicated to God

4 27 Now the LORD spoke to Moses, saying,
2 "Speak to the children of Israel, and say to them: [a]'When a man [1]consecrates by a vow certain persons to the LORD, according to your [2]valuation,
3 'if your valuation is of a male from twenty years old up to sixty years old, then your valuation shall be fifty shekels of silver, [a]according to the shekel of the sanctuary.
4 'If it *is* a female, then your valuation shall be thirty shekels;
5 'and if from five years old up to twenty years old, then your valuation for a male shall be twenty shekels, and for a female ten shekels;
6 'and if from a month old up to five years old, then your valuation for a male shall be five shekels of silver, and for a female your valuation shall be three shekels of silver;
7 'and if from sixty years old and above, if *it is* a male, then your valuation shall be fifteen shekels, and for a female ten shekels.
8 'But if he is too poor to pay your valuation, then he shall present himself before the priest, and the priest shall set a value for [a]him; according to the ability of him who vowed, the priest shall value him.
9 'If *it is* an animal that men may bring as an offering to the LORD, all that *anyone* gives to the LORD shall be holy.
10 'He shall not substitute it or exchange it, good for bad or bad for good; and if he at all exchanges animal for animal, then both it and the one exchanged for it shall be [a]holy.
11 'If *it is* an unclean animal which they do not offer as a sacrifice to the LORD, then he shall present the animal before the priest;
12 'and the priest shall set a value for it, whether it is good or bad; as you, the priest, value it, so it shall be.
13 [a]'But if he *wants* at all *to* redeem it, then he must add one-fifth to your valuation.
14 'And when a man [1]dedicates his house *to be* holy to the LORD, then the priest shall set a value for it, whether it is good or bad; as the priest values it, so it shall stand.
15 'If he who dedicated it *wants to* [1]redeem his house, then he must add one-fifth of the money of your valuation to it, and it shall be his.
16 'If a man [1]dedicates to the LORD *part* of a field of his possession, then your valuation shall be according to the seed for it. A homer of barley seed *shall be valued* at fifty shekels of silver.
17 'If he dedicates his field from the Year of Jubilee, according to your valuation it shall stand.
18 'But if he dedicates his field after the Jubilee, then the priest shall [a]reckon to him the money due according to the years that remain till the Year of Jubilee, and it shall be deducted from your valuation.
19 'And if he who dedicates the field ever wishes to redeem it, then he must add one-fifth of the money of your valuation to it, and it shall belong to him.
20 'But if he does not want to redeem the field, or if he has sold the field to another man, it shall not be redeemed anymore;
21 'but the field, [a]when it is released in the Jubilee, shall be holy to the LORD, as a [b]devoted field; it shall be [c]the possession of the priest.
22 'And if a man dedicates to the LORD a field which he has bought, which is not the field of [a]his possession,
23 'then the priest shall reckon to him the worth of your valuation, up to the Year of Jubilee, and he shall give your valuation on that day *as* a holy *offering* to the LORD.
24 [a]'In the Year of Jubilee the field shall return to him from whom it was bought, to the one who *owned* the land as a possession.
25 'And all your valuations shall be ac-

46 [a]Lev. 27:34; Deut. 6:1; 12:1; [John 1:17] [b]Lev. 25:1

CHAPTER 27

2 [a]Lev. 7:16; Num. 6:2; Deut. 23:21–23; Judg. 11:30, 31, 39 [1]*Or makes a difficult or extraordinary vow* [2]*appraisal*
3 [a]Ex. 30:13; Lev. 27:25; Num. 3:47; 18:16
8 [a]Lev. 5:11; 14:21–24
10 [a]Lev. 27:33
13 [a]Lev. 6:5; 22:14; 27:15, 19
14 [1]*sets apart*
15 [1]*buy back*
16 [1]*sets apart*
18 [a]Lev. 25:15, 16, 28
21 [a]Lev. 25:10, 28, 31 [b]Lev. 27:28 [c]Num. 18:14; Ezek. 44:29
22 [a]Lev. 25:10, 25
24 [a]Lev. 25:10–13, 28

27:1–8 See section 4 of Truth-In-Action at the end of Lev.
27:2–33 When a man consecrates by a vow: The Levitical code deals with dedicatory gifts and offerings consecrated for the sanctuary. They are considered "most holy" (v. 28) to the Lord and must be rendered to the service of God. The purpose of these regulations is to prevent foolish or rash commitments and to warn against the temptation to forget or alter vows (Eccl. 5:4, 5). This includes commitments regarding persons (vv. 2–8), animals (vv. 9–13), houses (vv. 14, 15), lands (vv. 16–24), and even tithes (vv. 30–33).

cording to the shekel of the sanctuary:
[a]twenty gerahs to the shekel.
26 'But the [a]firstborn of the animals,
which should be the LORD's firstborn,
no man shall dedicate; whether *it is* an
ox or sheep, it *is* the LORD's.
27 'And if *it is* an unclean animal, then
he shall *redeem *it* according to your
valuation, and [a]shall add one-fifth to
it; or if it is not *redeemed, then it shall
be sold according to your valuation.
28 [a]'Nevertheless no [1]devoted *offering*
that a man may devote to the LORD of
all that he has, *both* man and beast,
or the field of his possession, shall be
sold or redeemed; every devoted *offer-*
ing is most holy to the LORD.
29 [a]'No person under the ban, who
may become doomed to destruction
among men, shall be redeemed, *but*
shall surely be put to death.
30 'And [a]all the tithe of the land,
whether of the seed of the land *or* of
the fruit of the tree, *is* the LORD's. It *is*
holy to the LORD.
31 [a]'If a man wants at all to redeem
any of his tithes, he shall add one-fifth
to it.
32 'And concerning the tithe of the
herd or the flock, of whatever [a]passes
under the rod, the tenth one shall be
holy to the LORD.
33 'He shall not inquire whether it is
good or bad, [a]nor shall he exchange
it; and if he exchanges it at all, then
both it and the one exchanged for it
shall be holy; it shall not be redeemed.' "
34 [a]These *are* the commandments
which the LORD commanded Moses
for the children of Israel on Mount
[b]Sinai.

25 [a]Ex. 30:13
26 [a]Ex. 13:2, 12; 22:30
27 [a]Lev. 27:11, 12
*See WW at Neh. 1:10. • See WW at Is. 52:9.
28 [a]Josh. 6:17–19 [1]Given exclusively and irrevocably
29 [a]Num. 21:2
30 [a]Gen. 28:22
31 [a]Lev. 27:13
32 [a]Jer. 33:13
33 [a]Lev. 27:10
34 [a]Lev. 26:46 [b][Heb. 12:18–29]

27:34 The LORD commanded Moses for the children of Israel on Mount Sinai: Lev. receives its authority from the revelation of the Lord to Moses on Mt. Sinai. Though many of the principles of life and the legal code of conduct contained in Lev. deal with diverse issues directly related to the Israelites sojourning in the wilderness, this book also has meaning for readers today.

TRUTH-IN-ACTION through LEVITICUS

Letting the LIFE of the Holy Spirit Bring Faith's Works Alive in You!

Truth Leviticus Teaches	Text	**Action** Leviticus Invites
1 Steps to Dynamic Devotion God wants our devotion for Him to guide the way we live. The Bible suggests many ways to build a life that expresses zealous devotion for God. A devoted life focuses on knowing and pleasing God.	3:1	**Know** that fellowship with God requires time, energy, and resources we would normally use otherwise.
	6:12, 13	**Be constant** in your zeal for the Lord and His kingdom. Half-hearted devotion is unworthy (see Rev. 3:16).
2 Keys to Effective Service Lev. is a book on service. It has much to say to the believer about how God wants all spiritual ministry to be conducted. Since every believer is called to be a ministering person (see Eph. 4:11–16), these guidelines are highly important.	1:3	**Serve** the Lord with the best of your efforts. **Make sure** that your ministry is without the defects of pride, selfish ambition, or a personal lack of holiness.
	2:1	**Soak** all ministry with continuous prayer (incense) and **be filled** with the Holy Spirit (oil) while engaged in any ministry activity.
	19:19	**Avoid** mixing Spirit-filled and fleshly activity in the conduct of your ministry. God abhors such a mixture.
	19:23–25	**Do not urge** the immature to enter ministry prematurely. Long-term fruitfulness may be limited.
	24:1–4	**Be ready** constantly to bear witness to your faith in Jesus as Lord and Savior.

Truth Leviticus Teaches	Text	**Action** Leviticus Invites
	25:46	Leaders, **minister** with meekness, gentleness, and humility. Harsh, overbearing leadership misrepresents God's character and nature.
3 Keys to Moral Purity Moral impurity is extremely destructive to spiritual life and personal relationships. Sexual unfaithfulness is often an analogy for idolatry and unfaithfulness in the OT. Impurity compromises the integrity of our minds, hearts, and bodies. God tells us to flee from it because of its evil power.	11:47; 15:31 18:1–30 20:13	**Avoid** all spiritual and moral uncleanness. It will corrupt and defile every aspect of your life. **Know** what God's Word says about sexual conduct. **Flee** from and **avoid** every form of sexual and moral uncleanness. **Know** God's attitude about homosexuality. It is a serious perversion. Though He offers grace to the homosexual offender, He rejects his conduct.
4 Guidelines for Godly Living Though often concerned with the types of Hebrew ceremonial and ritual laws, Lev. can prove helpful for any believer who is serious about learning to live a life that is godly in Christ Jesus. Lev. makes it clear that godliness is not optional for those who want to live in a way that pleases their Lord.	4:2, 13, 22, 27 7:6, 28–36 19:32 26:1–46 27:1–8	**Acknowledge** that you are inclined to sin by your very nature. **Honor** God's servants with adequate financial support. **Honor** your parents. **Shun** the kind of disregard for elderly parents that the world promotes. **Study** and **know** God's Word. **Practice** it faithfully. God blesses obedience, but considers unfaithfulness hostility to Him. **Know** that God puts special value on everyone He has redeemed.
5 Keys to Dealing with Sin Like cancer, sin can spread quickly and defile a whole church or nation. God commands that we deal with sin forthrightly and thoroughly. Only through confronting sin can we ever be saved from its power. God cannot look upon sin because of His holiness, so we should not overlook it or deal with it lightly.	5:1; 19:17 5:2–4 5:5; 26:40 6:5	**Do not conceal** wrongdoing you are aware of. **Confront** sin. **Know** that you are accountable even for sins you are not aware of. **Be sensitive** to the Holy Spirit's conviction of sin, and **repent** when convicted. **Confess** your sins quickly, frankly, and openly. Hiding them will only harden your heart. Whenever possible, **make restitution** for sins you have committed against others, as a part of genuine repentance.

The Fourth Book of Moses Called NUMBERS

Author: Traditionally, Moses
Date: About 1400 B.C.
Theme: Yahweh's Guiding Presence for the Journey from Sinai to Transjordan
Key Words: Census, Murmuring, Purity, Tabernacle of Meeting

Author Authorship is traditionally ascribed to Moses, the central personality of the book. Numbers 33:2 makes specific reference to Moses writing down points about the wilderness journey.

The English title *Numbers* is taken from its title (*arithmoi*) in the Greek translation of the Old Testament (the Septuagint), followed by the Latin Vulgate (*numeri*). In the Hebrew text the name of the book is *In the Wilderness,* taken from the opening line, "The LORD spoke to Moses in the Wilderness of Sinai."

Date Assuming Mosaic authorship, it was likely written about 1400 B.C., shortly before his death. Events in the book span about 40 years, beginning shortly after the Exodus in 1440 B.C.

Content The division of the opening books of the Old Testament into five books or scrolls, (called "The Pentateuch," meaning "Five Scrolls"), should not obscure the point that each of the five books is a continuation of the preceding. Moses, whose birth is recounted in Exodus 2 and whose death is narrated in Deuteronomy 34, is the figure who unites the story from Exodus through Deuteronomy.

The Book of Numbers continues the account of the Mosaic period, which begins in Exodus. It begins with Israel still at Sinai. The Israelites' entry into the Wilderness of Sinai is recorded in Exodus 19:1. Israel leaves Sinai at Numbers 10:11.

Numbers has two major divisions: 1) the section containing instructions while still at Sinai (1:1—10:10); 2) the wilderness journey, which covers the itinerary from Sinai to the plains of Moab across the Jordan from the Promised Land (10:11—36:13). The instructions at Sinai deal with the preparation for the journey, and the rest of the book tells of the journey itself.

The instructions at Sinai (1:1—10:10) cover a variety of topics, but those dealing with the preparation for the journey dominate. Chapters 1—4 deal with a series of instructions to number (take a census of) various groups followed by a report of the compliance with the command. Chapters 5 and 6 deal with ritual uncleanness, marital unfaithfulness, and Nazirites. In chapter 7 the leaders of the people bring offerings for the tabernacle. Chapter 8 deals with the consecration of the Levites. Chapter 9 deals with Passover and the cloud and fire; the preparation motif is reconsidered in 10:1–10, where the instructions are given for signal trumpets to be made.

The section of Numbers that deals with the journey (10:11—36:13) has two major parts. First, 10:11—25:18 describes the perishing of the generation that experienced Yahweh's deliverance from Egypt. The key points in this part are the accounts of the complaints, rebellions, and disobedience of the first generation, which led to their deaths.

The second subsection (26—36) narrates the preparation of the second generation for entry into the Promised Land. It begins with a new census (compare ch. 1), noting that the entire first generation, except Joshua, Caleb, and Moses, had died in the wilderness. This section ends with the apportionment of the land among the tribes after they have entered the Promised Land.

Personal Application One of the most familiar events in Numbers is the negative report of the ten spies, as opposed to the positive one of Joshua and Caleb (13:25–33). This resulted in severe chastisement (14:20–38). From this we learn the profound consequences that can sometimes develop from being faithless and negative. When God speaks a promise, we need to respond with optimism, not pessimism.

The repeated grumblings of the Israelites, even in light of God's continuous provision, show us the need to maintain an attitude of thankfulness to God, even when we have great needs (Phil. 4:6).

Numbers also shows us the side of God that He is slow to reveal—His anger (14:20–38). Though He is loving and merciful, He is also just. When mankind repeatedly rejects Him, He must issue judgment (Heb. 9:27); when His children repeatedly disobey, He must chastise, sometimes severely (Heb. 12:3–11).

Christ Revealed Jesus Christ is pictured in Numbers as the Provider. The apostle Paul writes concerning Christ that He was the spiritual Rock that followed the Israelites through the wilderness and gave them spiritual drink (1 Cor. 10:4). The rock that gave water occurs twice in the story of the wilderness (ch. 20; Ex. 17). Paul emphasizes the provision of Christ for the needs of His people whom He has delivered from bondage.

The messianic figure of Israel's King is prophesied by Balaam in 24:17: "I see Him, but not now; I behold Him, but not near; a Star shall come out of Jacob; a Scepter shall rise out of Israel." Jewish tradition interpreted this verse messianically, as attested by the Qumran texts. Jesus Christ is the Messiah, according to the uniform witness of the New Testament, and the true King about whom Balaam speaks.

The Holy Spirit at Work The Holy Spirit is spoken of directly in chapter 11. There the Spirit is depicted as performing two functions: anointing for leadership and inspiring prophecy. In verse 16 Moses is asking the Lord for help in his leadership duties. The response is that Yahweh will take the Spirit that is upon Moses (identified in v. 29 as the Lord's Spirit) and pass it to his leaders. Even a leader like Moses was unable to do everything and needed Spirit-gifted leadership in the performance of his task.

When the Spirit is given to the elders, He causes prophesying (v. 25). Only the appointed seventy elders prophesy. When Joshua complains that two of the elders in the camp are also prophesying,

Moses expresses the longing that all God's people would also receive His Spirit and prophesy. This hope of Moses is picked up in Joel 2:28–32 and is ultimately fulfilled on the Day of Pentecost (Acts 2:16–21) when the Spirit was poured out and made available to all.

Outline of Numbers

I. Instructions for the journey from Sinai **1:1—10:10**

- A. Account of census taking 1:1—4:49
  - 1. Military census 1:1—2:34
  - 2. Nonmilitary census: Levites 3:1—4:49
- B. Further instructions and accounts 5:1—10:10
  - 1. Five instructions 5:1—6:27
  - 2. Leaders' offerings 7:1–89
  - 3. Dedicating Levites 8:1–26
  - 4. Second Passover 9:1–14
  - 5. Guidance by cloud and fire 9:15–23
  - 6. The silver trumpets 10:1–10

II. Account of the journey from Sinai **10:11—36:13**

- A. Rebellion and punishment of first generation 10:11—25:18
  - 1. Account of first march from Sinai 10:11–36
  - 2. Complaining of the people 11:1–3
  - 3. Craving for meat 11:4–35
  - 4. Challenge to Moses 12:1–16
  - 5. Refusal to enter the Promised Land 13:1—14:45
  - 6. Instruction concerning offerings 15:1–41
  - 7. Challenges to Aaron's authority 16:1—18:32
  - 8. Laws of purification 19:1–22
  - 9. Death of Miriam and Aaron 20:1–29
  - 10. From Mount Hor to the plains of Moab 21:1–35
  - 11. Balak and Balaam 22:1—25:18
- B. Preparation of the new generation 26:1—36:13
  - 1. A new census 26:1–65
  - 2. Instructions concerning inheritance, offerings, and vows 27:1—30:16
  - 3. Vengeance on the Midianites 31:1–54
  - 4. The Transjordanian tribes 32:1–42
  - 5. Itinerary from Egypt to Moab 33:1–49
  - 6. Instructions for the occupation of Canaan 33:50—36:13

The First Census of Israel

NOW the LORD spoke to Moses
[a]in the Wilderness of Sinai,
[b]in the tabernacle of meeting, on the
[c]first *day* of the second month, in the
second year after they had come out
of the land of Egypt, saying:
2 [a]"Take a census of all the *congregation of the children of Israel, by their
families, by their fathers' houses, according to the number of names, every
male [b]individually,
3 "from [a]twenty years old and
above—all who *are able to* go to war
in Israel. You and Aaron shall number
them by their armies.
4 "And with you there shall be a man
from every *tribe, each one the head
of his father's house.
5 "These are the names of the men
who shall stand with you: from Reuben, Elizur the son of Shedeur;
6 "from Simeon, Shelumiel the son of
Zurishaddai;

CHAPTER 1
1 [a]Ex. 19:1 [b]Ex. 25:22 [c]Num. 9:1; 10:11
2 [a]Num. 26:2, 63, 64 [b]Ex. 30:12, 13; 38:26
*See WW at Josh. 22:17.
3 [a]Ex. 30:14; 38:26
4 *See WW at Ex. 38:22.

1:1–50 The census reported in ch. 1 deals with the *formation* of an army for the invasion of the *Promised Land.*

1:1 Ex. 19:1 *dates the arrival* at Sinai three months to the *day after* they left Egypt. The **tabernacle of meeting** was completed nine months later in the first month of the second year (Ex. 40:17), and now Num. begins a month later. Nineteen days later (10:11) Israel leaves Sinai. Num. shows the people of God on the move toward their inheritance.

1:2–16 The command is given to take a census and form an army of males 20 years of age and older. The compliance is narrated in detail in vv. 17–46.

1:5–15 The mention of specific names shows the importance of the individual within the framework of the total community.

7 "from Judah, Nahshon the son of Amminadab;

8 "from Issachar, Nethanel the son of Zuar;

9 "from Zebulun, Eliab the son of Helon;

10 "from the sons of Joseph: from Ephraim, Elishama the son of Ammihud; from Manasseh, Gamaliel the son of Pedahzur;

11 "from Benjamin, Abidan the son of Gideoni;

12 "from Dan, Ahiezer the son of Ammishaddai;

13 "from Asher, Pagiel the son of Ocran;

14 "from Gad, Eliasaph the son of [a]Deuel;[1]

15 "from Naphtali, Ahira the son of Enan."

16 [a]These *were* [b]chosen[1] from the congregation, leaders of their fathers' tribes, [c]heads of the divisions in Israel.

17 Then Moses and Aaron took these men who had been [1]mentioned [a]by name,

18 and they assembled all the congregation together on the first *day* of the second month; and they recited their [a]ancestry by families, by their fathers' houses, according to the number of names, from twenty years old and above, each one individually.

19 As the LORD commanded Moses, so he numbered them in the Wilderness of Sinai.

20 Now the [a]children of Reuben, Israel's oldest son, their genealogies by their families, by their fathers' house, according to the number of names, every male individually, from twenty years old and above, all who *were able to* go to war:

21 those who were numbered of the tribe of Reuben *were* forty-six thousand five hundred.

22 From the [a]children of Simeon, their genealogies by their families, by their fathers' house, of those who were numbered, according to the number of names, every male individually, from twenty years old and above, all who *were able to* go to war:

23 those who were numbered of the tribe of Simeon *were* fifty-nine thousand three hundred.

24 From the [a]children of Gad, their genealogies by their families, by their fathers' house, according to the number of names, from twenty years old and above, all who *were able to* go to war:

25 those who were numbered of the tribe of Gad *were* forty-five thousand six hundred and fifty.

26 From the [a]children of Judah, their genealogies by their families, by their fathers' house, according to the number of names, from twenty years old and above, all who *were able to* go to war:

27 those who were numbered of the tribe of Judah *were* [a]seventy-four thousand six hundred.

28 From the [a]children of Issachar, their genealogies by their families, by their fathers' house, according to the number of names, from twenty years old and above, all who *were able to* go to war:

29 those who were numbered of the tribe of Issachar *were* fifty-four thousand four hundred.

30 From the [a]children of Zebulun, their genealogies by their families, by their fathers' house, according to the number of names, from twenty years old and above, all who *were able to* go to war:

31 those who were numbered of the tribe of Zebulun *were* fifty-seven thousand four hundred.

32 From the sons of Joseph, the [a]children of Ephraim, their genealogies by their families, by their fathers' house, according to the number of names, from twenty years old and above, all who *were able to* go to war:

33 those who were numbered of the tribe of Ephraim *were* forty thousand five hundred.

34 From the [a]children of Manasseh, their genealogies by their families, by their fathers' house, according to the number of names, from twenty years old and above, all who *were able to* go to war:

35 those who were numbered of the tribe of Manasseh *were* thirty-two thousand two hundred.

36 From the [a]children of Benjamin, their genealogies by their families, by their fathers' house, according to the number of names, from twenty years old and above, all who *were able to* go to war:

37 those who were numbered of the

14 [a]Num. 7:42 [1]*Reuel,* Num. 2:14
16 [a]Ex. 18:21; Num. 7:2; 1 Chr. 27:16–22 [b]Num. 16:2 [c]Ex. 18:21, 25; Jer. 5:5; Mic. 3:1, 9; 5:2 [1]*called*
17 [a]Is. 43:1 [1]*designated*
18 [a]Ezra 2:59; Heb. 7:3
20 [a]Num. 2:10, 11; 26:5–11; 32:6, 15, 21, 29
22 [a]Num. 2:12, 13; 26:12–14
24 [a]Gen. 30:11; Num. 26:15–18; Josh. 4:12; Jer. 49:1
26 [a]Gen. 29:35; Num. 26:19–22; 2 Sam. 24:9; Ps. 78:68; Matt. 1:2
27 [a]2 Chr. 17:14
28 [a]Num. 2:5, 6
30 [a]Num. 2:7, 8; 26:26, 27
32 [a]Gen. 48:1–22; Num. 26:28–37; Deut. 33:13–17; Jer. 7:15; Obad. 19
34 [a]Num. 2:20, 21; 26:28–34
36 [a]Gen. 49:27; Num. 26:38–41; 2 Chr. 17:17; Rev. 7:8

1:18 This public proclamation let all Israel know the analysis and character of the community. The census was not to rely on human strength; rather, it was to answer clearly the question, "Who are the people of God?" especially those who will be able to fight in Canaan (v. 45).

1:24–43 The order here corresponds to the arrangement of the armies around the camp detailed in 2:10–17.

tribe of Benjamin *were* thirty-five thousand four hundred.
38 From the [a]children of Dan, their genealogies by their families, by their fathers' house, according to the number
of names, from twenty years old and
above, all who *were able to* go to war:
39 those who were numbered of the
tribe of Dan *were* sixty-two thousand
seven hundred.
40 From the [a]children of Asher, their
genealogies by their families, by their
fathers' house, according to the number of names, from twenty years old
and above, all who *were able to* go to
war:
41 those who were numbered of the
tribe of Asher *were* forty-one thousand
five hundred.
42 From the children of Naphtali, their
genealogies by their families, by their
fathers' house, according to the number of names, from twenty years old
and above, all who *were able to* go to
war:
43 those who were numbered of the
tribe of Naphtali *were* fifty-three thousand four hundred.
44 [a]These are the ones who were numbered, whom Moses and Aaron numbered, with the leaders of Israel, twelve
men, each one representing his father's
house.
45 So all who were numbered of the
children of Israel, by their fathers'
houses, from twenty years old and
above, all who *were able to* go to war
in Israel—
46 all who were numbered were
[a]six hundred and three thousand five
hundred and fifty.
47 But [a]the Levites were not numbered
among them by their fathers' tribe;
48 for the LORD had spoken to Moses,
saying:
3 49 [a]"Only the tribe of Levi you shall
not number, nor take a census of them
among the children of Israel;
50 [a]"but you shall appoint the Levites
over the tabernacle of the Testimony,
over all its furnishings, and over all
things that belong to it; they shall carry
the tabernacle and all its furnishings;
they shall attend to it [b]and camp
around the tabernacle.
51 [a]"And when the tabernacle is to go
forward, the Levites shall take it down;
and when the tabernacle is to be set
up, the Levites shall set it [b]up. [c]The
outsider who comes near shall be put
to death.
52 "The children of Israel shall pitch
their tents, [a]everyone by his own
camp, everyone by his own standard,
according to their armies;
53 [a]"but the Levites shall camp around
the tabernacle of the Testimony, that
there may be no [b]wrath on the congregation of the children of Israel; and the
Levites shall [c]keep[1] charge of the tabernacle of the Testimony."
54 Thus the children of Israel did; according to all that the LORD commanded Moses, so they did.

38 [a]Gen. 30:6; 46:23; Num. 2:25, 26; 26:42, 43
40 [a]Num. 2:27, 28; 26:44–47
44 [a]Num. 26:64
46 [a]Ex. 12:37; 38:26; Num. 2:32; 26:51, 63; Heb. 11:12; Rev. 7:4–8
47 [a]Num. 2:33; 3:14–22; 26:57–62; 1 Chr. 6:1–47; 21:6
49 [a]Num. 2:33; 26:62
50 [a]Ex. 38:21; Num. 3:7, 8; 4:15, 25–27, 33 [b]Num. 3:23, 29, 35, 38
51 [a]Num. 4:5–15; 10:17, 21 [b]Num. 10:21 [c]Num. 3:10, 38; 4:15, 19, 20; 18:22
52 [a]Num. 2:2, 34; 24:2
53 [a]Num. 1:50 [b]Lev. 10:6; Num. 8:19; 16:46; 18:5; 1 Sam. 6:19 [c]Num. 8:24; 18:2–4; 1 Chr. 23:32 [1]*have in their care*

The Tribes and Leaders by Armies

2 And the LORD spoke to Moses and 5
Aaron, saying:
2 [a]"Everyone of the children of Israel 3
shall camp by his own [1]standard, beside the emblems of his father's house;
they shall camp [b]some distance from
the tabernacle of meeting.
3 "On the [a]east side, toward the rising
of the sun, those of the standard of the
forces with Judah shall camp according to their armies; and [b]Nahshon the
son of Amminadab *shall be* the leader
of the children of Judah."
4 And his *army was numbered at
seventy-four thousand six hundred.
5 "Those who camp next to him *shall
be* the tribe of Issachar, and Nethanel
the son of Zuar *shall be* the leader of
the children of Issachar."
6 And his army was numbered at
fifty-four thousand four hundred.

CHAPTER 2

2 [a]Num. 1:52; 24:2 [b]Josh. 3:4 [1]*banner*
3 [a]Num. 10:5 [b]Num. 1:7; 7:12; 10:14; Ruth 4:20; 1 Chr. 2:10; Matt. 1:4; Luke 3:32, 33
4 *See WW at Ps. 68:11.

1:46 The accuracy of the large number here has caused great debate among scholars. There is no reason, however, to doubt it.

1:49–51 See section 3 of Truth-In-Action at the end of Num.

1:50 The exemption from military duty for the Levites is based on their service for the **tabernacle of the Testimony,** a synonym for the tabernacle or tabernacle of meeting. See notes on Ex. 25—27; *36:8—39:43.*

2:1–34 See section 5 of Truth-In-Action at the end of Num.

2:1–34 With the military census completed in ch. 1, instructions for the organization of the tribes and their armies are given. The camp is organized with three tribes on each side of the tabernacle, so that Yahweh's dwelling place is in the midst of the camp. Further, when they break camp and march, the six tribes on the east and south set out, followed by the Levites with the tabernacle traveling in the center (v. 17), followed by the six tribes on the west and north respectively. Whether encamped or on the march, the tabernacle is central. One tribe is given priority among the three that camp on each side of the tabernacle, Judah on the east (v. 9), Reuben on the south (v. 16), Ephraim on the west (v. 24), and Dan on the north (v. 31).

2:2 See section 3 of Truth-In-Action at the end of Num.

2:2 Emblems of his father's house likely refers to the sign which the nonmilitary forces camped around, with the **standard** referring specifically to the military cohort's camp. In v. 2 the nonmilitary members of the camp are dealt with, while the rest of the chapter deals with military formations.

7 "Then *comes* the tribe of Zebulun, and Eliab the son of Helon *shall
be* the leader of the children of Zebulun."
8 And his army was numbered at
fifty-seven thousand four hundred.
9 "All who were numbered according
to their armies of the forces with Judah, one hundred and eighty-six thousand four hundred—[a]these shall
[1]break camp first.
10 "On the [a]south side *shall be* the
standard of the forces with Reuben according to their armies, and the leader
of the children of Reuben *shall be* Elizur the son of Shedeur."
11 And his army was numbered at
forty-six thousand five hundred.
12 "Those who camp next to him *shall
be* the tribe of Simeon, and the leader
of the children of Simeon *shall be* Shelumiel the son of Zurishaddai."
13 And his army was numbered at
fifty-nine thousand three hundred.
14 "Then *comes* the tribe of Gad, and
the leader of the children of Gad *shall
be* Eliasaph the son of [1]Reuel."
15 And his army was numbered at
forty-five thousand six hundred and
fifty.
16 "All who were numbered according to their armies of the forces with
Reuben, one hundred and fifty-one
thousand four hundred and fifty
—[a]they shall [1]be the second to break
camp.
17 [a]"And the tabernacle of meeting 3
shall move out with the [1]camp of the
Levites [b]in the middle of the [2]camps;
as they camp, so they shall move out,
everyone in his place, by their [3]stan-
dards.
18 "On the west side *shall be* the standard of the forces with Ephraim

9 [a]Num. 10:14 [1]Lit. *set forth*
10 [a]Num. 10:6
14 [1]*Deuel,* Num. 1:14; 7:42
16 [a]Num. 10:18 [1]Lit. *set forth second*
17 [a]Num. 10:17, 21 [b]Num. 1:53 [1]*company* [2]*whole company* [3]*banners*

2:17 See section 3 of Truth-In-Action at the end of Num.
2:17 This verse is the key to the chapter, indicating the centrality of the **tabernacle of meeting** (see note on 1:50) as the critical issue.

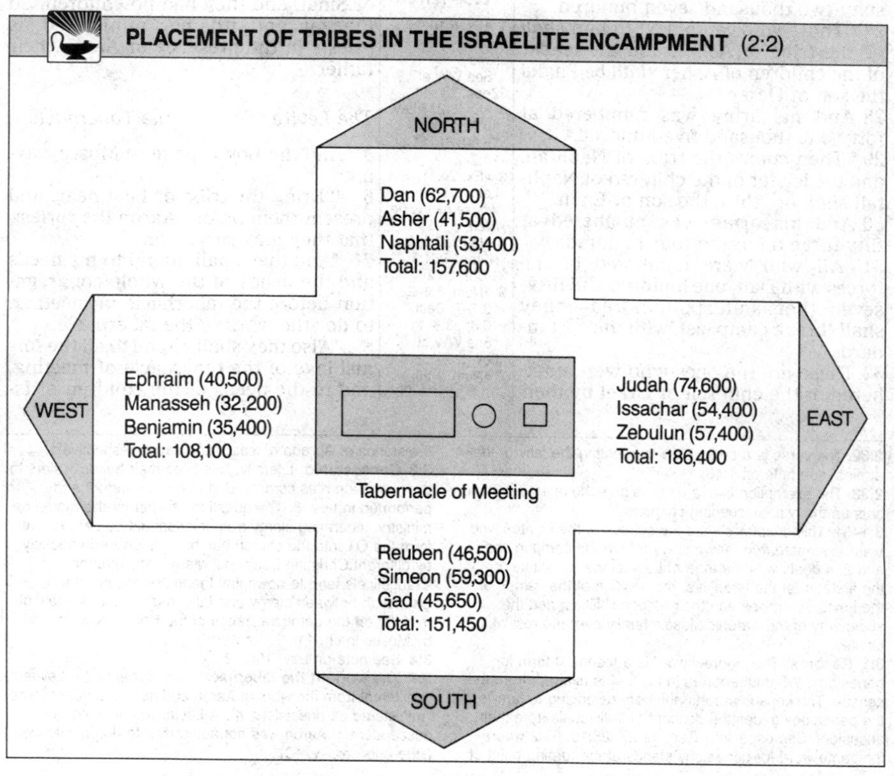

according to their armies, and the
leader of the children of Ephraim
shall be Elishama the son of Ammihud."
19 And his army was numbered at
forty thousand five hundred.
20 "Next to him *comes* the tribe of Manasseh, and the leader of the children
of Manasseh *shall be* Gamaliel the son
of Pedahzur."
21 And his army was numbered at
thirty-two thousand two hundred.
22 "Then *comes* the tribe of Benjamin,
and the leader of the children of Benjamin *shall be* Abidan the son of
Gideoni."
23 And his army was numbered at
thirty-five thousand four hundred.
24 "All who were numbered according
to their armies of the forces with
Ephraim, one hundred and eight thousand one hundred—[a]they shall [1]be the
third to break camp.
25 "The [1]standard of the forces with
Dan *shall be* on the north side according to their armies, and the leader of
the children of Dan *shall be* Ahiezer
the son of Ammishaddai."
26 And his army was numbered at
sixty-two thousand seven hundred.
27 "Those who camp next to him *shall
be* the tribe of Asher, and the leader
of the children of Asher *shall be* Pagiel
the son of Ocran."
28 And his army was numbered at
forty-one thousand five hundred.
29 "Then *comes* the tribe of Naphtali,
and the leader of the children of Naphtali *shall be* Ahira the son of Enan."
30 And his army was numbered at
fifty-three thousand four hundred.
31 "All who were numbered of the
forces with Dan, one hundred and fifty-
seven thousand six hundred—[a]they
shall [1]break camp last, with their [2]stan-
dards."
32 These *are* the ones who were numbered of the children of Israel by their
fathers' houses. [a]All who were numbered according to their armies of the
forces *were* six hundred and three
thousand five hundred and fifty.
33 But [a]the Levites were not numbered
among the children of Israel, just as
the LORD commanded Moses.
34 Thus the children of Israel [a]did according to all that the LORD commanded Moses; [b]so they camped by
their [1]standards and so they broke
camp, each one by his family, according to their fathers' houses.

The Sons of Aaron

3 Now these *are* the [a]records[1] of
Aaron and Moses *when the LORD
spoke with Moses on Mount Sinai.
2 And these *are* the names of the sons
of Aaron: Nadab, the [a]firstborn, and
[b]Abihu, Eleazar, and Ithamar.
3 These *are* the names of the sons of
Aaron, [a]the anointed priests, [1]whom
he consecrated to minister as priests.
4 [a]Nadab and Abihu had died before
the LORD when they offered profane
fire before the LORD in the Wilderness
of Sinai; and they had no children. So
Eleazar and Ithamar ministered as
priests in the presence of Aaron their
father.

The Levites Serve in the Tabernacle

5 And the LORD spoke to Moses, saying:
6 [a]"Bring the tribe of Levi near, and
present them before Aaron the *priest,
that they may serve him.
7 "And they shall attend to his needs
and the needs of the whole congregation before the tabernacle of meeting,
to do [a]the work of the tabernacle.
8 "Also they shall attend to all the furnishings of the tabernacle of meeting,
and to the needs of the children of Is-

24 [a]Num. 10:22 [1]Lit. *set forth third*
25 [1]*banner*
31 [a]Num. 10:25 [1]Lit. *set forth last* [2]*banners*
32 [a]Ex. 38:26; Num. 1:46; 11:21
33 [a]Num. 1:47; 26:57–62
34 [a]Num. 1:54 [b]Num. 24:2, 5, 6 [1]*banners*

CHAPTER 3

1 [a]Ex. 6:16–27 [1]Lit. *generations* *See WW at Zeph. 1:7.
2 [a]Ex. 6:23 [b]Lev. 10:1, 2; Num. 26:60, 61; 1 Chr. 24:2
3 [a]Ex. 28:41; Lev. 8 [1]Lit. *whose hands he filled*
4 [a]Lev. 10:1, 2; Num. 26:61; 1 Chr. 24:2
6 [a]Num. 8:6–22; 18:1–7; Deut. 10:8; 33:8–11 *See WW at Lev. 5:6.
7 [a]Num. 1:50; 8:11, 15, 24, 26

2:32 The verse is a conclusion, presenting the tally of the armies (see note on 1:46).
2:33 The exemption in this verse is an echo of 1:49–53 and sets up the two succeeding chapters.
3:1–51 This chapter covers the census of the Levites who were exempted from any military role in the camp in chs. 1 and 2. It deals with the tribe of Levi as the substitute for the firstborn of the Israelites, the position of the camps of the Levitical families and their responsibilities, and the superiority of the Aaronic/Mosaic family over the rest of the Levites.
3:1 Records: The Hebrew word is a technical term for *genealogy*. What is reported in vv. 1–4 is different from the census. The census reports numbers belonging to families; the genealogy traces the descent of individuals from their ancestors. See especially Gen. 11:27; 25:19; 37:2 where the same word for genealogy stands at the turning point of the stories of Abraham, Isaac, and Jacob respectively.
3:3 Consecrated: Literally, "He filled their hands" refers to the ordination rites commanded in Ex. 28 and 29 and performed in Lev. 8. The question of whether the model of ministry separating clergy from laity should be carried over from the OT into the church has been answered variously by different Christian traditions. Many contemporary evangelicals tend to downplay the importance of the distinction between clergy and laity, modeling their view of ministry on the democratization of the Spirit, as is desired by Moses in ch. 11.
3:4 See note on Lev. 10:1, 2.
3:7 The work of the tabernacle as the role of the Levites is different from the work of Aaron and his descendants who "ministered as priests" (v. 4). A Levite who was not a descendant of Aaron was not authorized to do priestly work ("the outsider," v. 10).

rael, to do the work of the tabernacle.
9 "And [a]you shall give the Levites to
Aaron and his sons; they *are* given entirely to [1]him from among the children
of Israel.
10 "So you shall appoint Aaron and his
sons, [a]and they shall attend to their
priesthood; [b]but the outsider who
comes near shall be put to death."
11 Then the LORD spoke to Moses, saying:
12 "Now behold, [a]I Myself have taken
the Levites from among the children
of Israel instead of every firstborn who
opens the womb among the children
of Israel. Therefore the Levites shall be
[b]Mine,
13 "because [a]all the firstborn *are*
Mine. [b]On the day that I struck all the
firstborn in the land of Egypt, I sanctified to Myself all the firstborn in Israel,
both *man and beast. They shall be
Mine: I *am* the LORD."

Census of the Levites Commanded

14 Then the LORD spoke to Moses in
the Wilderness of Sinai, saying:
15 "Number the children of Levi by
their fathers' houses, by their families;
you shall number [a]every male from a
month old and above."
16 So Moses numbered them according to the [1]word of the LORD, as he was
commanded.
17 [a]These were the sons of Levi by
their names: Gershon, Kohath, and
Merari.
18 And these *are* the names of the sons
of [a]Gershon by their families: [b]Libni
and Shimei.
19 And the sons of [a]Kohath by their
families: [b]Amram, Izehar, Hebron, and
Uzziel.
20 [a]And the sons of Merari by their
families: Mahli and Mushi. These *are*
the families of the Levites by their fathers' houses.
21 From Gershon *came* the family of
the Libnites and the family of the
Shimites; these *were* the families of the
Gershonites.
22 Those who were numbered, according to the number of all the males from
a month old and above—of those who
were numbered *there were* seven thousand five hundred.
23 [a]The families of the Gershonites
were to camp behind the tabernacle
westward.
24 And the leader of the father's house
of the Gershonites *was* Eliasaph the
son of Lael.
25 [a]The duties of the children of Gershon in the tabernacle of meeting *included* [b]the tabernacle, [c]the tent with
[d]its covering, [e]the screen for the door
of the tabernacle of meeting,
26 [a]the screen for the door of the court,
[b]the hangings of the court which *are*
around the tabernacle and the altar,
and [c]their cords, according to all the
work relating to them.
27 [a]From Kohath *came* the family of
the Amramites, the family of the Izharites, the family of the Hebronites, and
the family of the Uzzielites; these *were*
the families of the Kohathites.
28 According to the number of all the
males, from a month old and above,
there were eight thousand [1]six hundred [2]keeping charge of the sanctuary.
29 [a]The families of the children of Kohath were to camp on the south side
of the tabernacle.
30 And the leader of the fathers' house
of the families of the Kohathites *was*
Elizaphan the son of [a]Uzziel.
31 [a]Their duty *included* [b]the ark,
[c]the table, [d]the lampstand, [e]the altars,
the utensils of the sanctuary with
which they ministered, [f]the screen, and
all the work relating to them.
32 And Eleazar the son of Aaron the
priest *was to be* chief over the leaders
of the Levites, *with* oversight of those
who kept charge of the sanctuary.
33 From Merari *came* the family of the
Mahlites and the family of the Mu-
shites; these *were* the families of Merari.
34 And those who were numbered, according to the number of all the males
from a month old and above, *were* six
thousand two hundred.
35 The leader of the fathers' house of
the families of Merari *was* Zuriel the
son of Abihail. [a]These *were* to camp
on the north side of the tabernacle.
36 And [a]the appointed duty of the children of Merari *included* the boards of

9 [a]Num. 8:19; 18:6, 7 [1]Sam., LXX *Me*
10 [a]Ex. 29:9; Num. 18:7 [b]Num. 1:51; 3:38; 16:40
12 [a]Num. 3:41; 8:16; 18:6 [b]Ex. 13:2; Num. 3:45; 8:14
13 [a]Ex. 13:2; Lev. 27:26; Num. 8:16, 17; Neh. 10:36; Luke 2:23 [b]Ex. 13:12, 15; Num. 8:17 *See WW at Gen. 1:26.
15 [a]Num. 3:39; 26:62
16 [1]Lit. *mouth*
17 [a]Gen. 46:11; Ex. 6:16–22; Num. 26:57; 1 Chr. 6:1, 16; 23:6
18 [a]Num. 4:38–41 [b]Ex. 6:17
19 [a]Num. 4:34–37 [b]Ex. 6:18
20 [a]Ex. 6:19; Num. 4:42–45
23 [a]Num. 1:53
25 [a]Num. 4:24–26 [b]Ex. 25:9 [c]Ex. 26:1 [d]Ex. 26:7, 14 [e]Ex. 26:36
26 [a]Ex. 27:9, 12, 14, 15 [b]Ex. 27:16 [c]Ex. 35:18
27 [a]1 Chr. 26:23
28 [1]Some LXX mss. *three* [2]*taking care of*
29 [a]Ex. 6:18; Num. 1:53
30 [a]Lev. 10:4
31 [a]Num. 4:15 [b]Ex. 25:10 [c]Ex. 25:23 [d]Ex. 25:31 [e]Ex. 27:1; 30:1 [f]Ex. 26:31–33
35 [a]Num. 1:53; 2:25
36 [a]Num. 4:31, 32

3:12, 13 Firstborn: The firstborn are God's in recognition of man's dependence on Him for life. This special claim gave them high value in Israel's society. Because they were God's property, they had to be bought by their father. Here **the Levites** are the substitute for the human firstborn.

3:17–39 The pattern of the census report is the same for all three groups: 1) names of the families in the group; 2) number in the group; 3) place where they were to camp; 4) name of the leader; 5) the list of the duties of the group. Ch. 4 expands on the last element of the list and tells how the duties were to be executed.

the tabernacle, its bars, its pillars, its
sockets, its utensils, all the work relating to them,
37 and the pillars of the court all
around, with their sockets, their pegs,
and their cords.
38 [a]Moreover those who were to camp
before the tabernacle on the east, before the tabernacle of meeting, *were*
Moses, Aaron, and his sons, [b]keeping
charge of the sanctuary, [c]to meet the
needs of the children of Israel; but
[d]the outsider who came near was to
be put to death.
39 [a]All who were numbered of the Levites, whom Moses and Aaron numbered at the commandment of the
LORD, by their families, all the males
from a month old and above, *were*
twenty-two thousand.

Levites Dedicated Instead of the Firstborn

40 Then the LORD said to Moses:
[a]"Number[1] all the firstborn males of
the children of Israel from a month old
and above, and take the number of
their names.
41 [a]"And you shall take the Levites for
Me—I *am* the LORD—instead of all the
firstborn among the children of Israel,
and the livestock of the Levites instead
of all the firstborn among the livestock
of the children of Israel."
42 So Moses numbered all the firstborn among the children of Israel, as
the LORD commanded him.
43 And all the firstborn males, according to the number of names from a
month old and above, of those who
were numbered of them, were twenty-
two thousand two hundred and
seventy-three.
44 Then the LORD spoke to Moses, saying:
45 [a]"Take the Levites instead of all the
firstborn among the children of Israel,
and the livestock of the Levites instead
of their livestock. The Levites shall be
Mine: I *am* the LORD.
46 "And for [a]the redemption of the two
hundred and seventy-three of the first-

38 [a]Num. 1:53 [b]Num. 18:5 [c]Num. 3:7, 8 [d]Num. 3:10
39 [a]Num. 3:43; 4:48; 26:62
40 [a]Num. 3:15 [1]*Take a census of*
41 [a]Num. 3:12, 45
45 [a]Num. 3:12, 41
46 [a]Ex. 13:13, 15; Num. 18:15, 16 [b]Num. 3:39, 43
47 [a]Lev. 27:6; Num. 18:16 [b]Num. 1:2, 18, 20 [c]Ex. 30:13
50 [a]Num. 3:46, 47
51 [a]Num. 3:48

CHAPTER 4

2 [a]Num. 3:27–32
3 [a]Num. 4:23, 30, 35; 8:24; 1 Chr. 23:3, 24, 27; Ezra 3:8
4 [a]Num. 4:15 [b]Num. 4:19
5 [a]Ex. 26:31; Heb. 9:3 [b]Ex. 25:10, 16
6 [a]Ex. 39:1 [b]Ex. 25:13; 1 Kin. 8:7, 8
7 [a]Ex. 25:23, 29, 30 [b]Lev. 24:5–9 [1]*jars for the drink offering* [2]Lit. *continual bread*

born of the children of Israel, [b]who are
more than the number of the Levites,
47 "you shall take [a]five shekels for
each one [b]individually; you shall take
them in the currency of the shekel of
the sanctuary, [c]the shekel of twenty
gerahs.
48 "And you shall give the money,
with which the excess number of them
is redeemed, to Aaron and his sons."
49 So Moses took the redemption
money from those who were over and
above those who were redeemed by the
Levites.
50 From the firstborn of the children
of Israel he took the money, [a]one thousand three hundred and sixty-five
shekels, according to the shekel of the
sanctuary.
51 And Moses [a]gave their redemption
money to Aaron and his sons, according to the word of the LORD, as the
LORD commanded Moses.

Duties of the Sons of Kohath

4 Then the LORD spoke to Moses and
Aaron, saying:
2 "Take a census of the sons of
[a]Kohath from among the children of
Levi, by their families, by their fathers'
house,
3 [a]"from thirty years old and above,
even to fifty years old, all who enter
the service to do the work in the tabernacle of meeting.
4 [a]"This *is* the service of the sons of
Kohath in the tabernacle of meeting,
relating to [b]the most holy things:
5 "When the camp prepares to journey, Aaron and his sons shall come,
and they shall take down [a]the covering
veil and cover the [b]ark of the Testimony with it.
6 "Then they shall put on it a covering of badger skins, and spread over
that a cloth entirely of [a]blue; and they
shall insert [b]its poles.
7 "On the [a]table of showbread they
shall spread a blue cloth, and put on
it the dishes, the pans, the bowls, and
the [1]pitchers for pouring; and the
[b]showbread[2] shall be on it.

3:40–51 It was found that there were 273 more firstborn than Levites (v. 46). Therefore, these 273 had to be exchanged for money (v. 47) instead of Levites (*see note on vv. 12, 13*). *The money* helped finance the tabernacle.
4:1–49 This chapter details a census of the Levites, between the ages of 30 and 50, for the work of the tabernacle. The duties of the Kohathites focus on **the most holy things** (unspecified special holy objects within the tabernacle, v. 4). The Gershonites and the Merarites deal with the coverings and the structural pieces of the tabernacle.
4:4–20 Service of the sons of Kohath: The majority of instructions deal with the preparation by Aaron and his descendants of the implements for transport by the Kohathites. All of the items are covered and either have poles inserted into rings on the implement or are placed on a carrying beam by Aaron and his sons, so that the Kohathites have no need to touch the holy things.

8 "They shall spread over them a
scarlet cloth, and cover the same with
a covering of badger skins; and they
shall insert its poles.
9 "And they shall take a blue cloth
and cover the [a]lampstand of the light,
[b]with its lamps, its wick-trimmers, its
trays, and all its oil vessels, with which
they service it.
10 "Then they shall put it with all its
utensils in a covering of badger skins,
and put *it* on a carrying beam.
11 "Over [a]the golden altar they shall
spread a blue cloth, and cover it with
a covering of badger skins; and they
shall insert its poles.
12 "Then they shall take all the
[a]utensils of service with which they
minister in the sanctuary, put *them* in
a blue cloth, cover them with a covering of badger skins, and put *them* on
a carrying beam.
13 "Also they shall take away the
ashes from the altar, and spread a purple cloth over it.
14 "They shall put on it all its implements with which they minister there—
the firepans, the forks, the shovels, the
[1]basins, and all the utensils of the altar—and they shall spread on it a covering of badger skins, and insert its
poles.
15 "And when Aaron and his sons
have finished covering the sanctuary
and all the furnishings of the sanctuary, when the camp is set to go, then
[a]the sons of Kohath shall come to carry
them; [b]but they shall not touch any
holy thing, lest they die. [c]These *are* the
things in the tabernacle of meeting
which the sons of Kohath are to carry.
16 "The appointed duty of Eleazar the
son of Aaron the priest *is* [a]the oil for
the light, the [b]sweet incense, [c]the daily
grain offering, the [d]anointing oil, the
oversight of all the tabernacle, of all
that *is* in it, with the sanctuary and its
furnishings."
17 Then the LORD spoke to Moses and
Aaron, saying:
18 "Do not cut off the tribe of the families of the Kohathites from among the
Levites;
19 "but do this in regard to them, that
they may live and not die when they
approach [a]the most holy things: Aaron
and his sons shall go in and [1]appoint
each of them to his service and his
task.

9 [a]Ex. 25:31 [b]Ex. 25:37, 38
11 [a]Ex. 30:1–5
12 [a]Ex. 25:9; 1 Chr. 9:29
14 [1]*bowls*
15 [a]Num. 7:9; 10:21; Deut. 31:9; Josh. 4:10; 2 Sam. 6:13; 1 Chr. 15:2, 15 [b]2 Sam. 6:6, 7; 1 Chr. 13:9, 10 [c]Num. 3:31
16 [a]Ex. 25:6; Lev. 24:2 [b]Ex. 30:34 [c]Ex. 29:38 [d]Ex. 30:23–25
19 [a]Num. 4:4 [1]*assign*
20 [a]Ex. 19:21; 1 Sam. 6:19
22 [a]Num. 3:22
23 [a]Num. 4:3; 1 Chr. 23:3, 24, 27
24 [a]Num. 7:7
25 [a]Num. 3:25, 26 [b]Ex. 36:8 [c]Ex. 26:14
27 [1]*command* [2]*assign*
28 [a]Num. 4:33 [1]Lit. *hand*
29 [a]Num. 3:33–37
30 [a]Num. 4:3; 8:24–26
31 [a]Num. 3:36, 37 [b]Num. 7:8 [c]Ex. 26:15

20 [a]"But they shall not go in to watch
while the holy things are being covered, lest they die."

Duties of the Sons of Gershon

21 Then the LORD spoke to Moses, saying:
22 "Also take a census of the sons of
[a]Gershon, by their fathers' house, by
their families.
23 [a]"From thirty years old and above,
even to fifty years old, you shall number them, all who enter to perform the
service, to do the work in the tabernacle of meeting.
24 "This *is* the [a]service of the families
of the Gershonites, in serving and carrying:
25 [a]"They shall carry the [b]curtains of
the tabernacle and the tabernacle of
meeting *with* its covering, the covering
of [c]badger skins that *is* on it, the screen
for the door of the tabernacle of meeting,
26 "the screen for the door of the gate
of the court, the hangings of the court
which *are* around the tabernacle and
altar, and their cords, all the furnishings for their service and all that
is made for these things: so shall they
serve.
27 "Aaron and his sons shall [1]assign
all the service of the sons of the Gershonites, all their tasks and all their
service. And you shall [2]appoint to them
all their tasks as their duty.
28 "This *is* the service of the families
of the sons of Gershon in the tabernacle of meeting. And their duties *shall
be* [a]under the [1]authority of Ithamar the
son of Aaron the priest.

Duties of the Sons of Merari

29 "*As for* the sons of [a]Merari, you
shall number them by their families
and by their fathers' house.
30 [a]"From thirty years old and above,
even to fifty years old, you shall number them, everyone who enters the service to do the work of the tabernacle
of meeting.
31 "And [a]this *is* [b]what they must carry
as all their service for the tabernacle
of meeting: [c]the boards of the tabernacle, its bars, its pillars, its sockets,
32 "and the pillars around the court
with their sockets, pegs, and cords,
with all their furnishings and all their

4:21–28 The service of the families of the sons of Gershon: The external coverings are all handled by these under the authority of Ithamar, the son of Aaron.

4:29–33 Service of the families of the sons of Merari: Their duties relate to the structural pieces of the sanctuary and are also supervised by Ithamar, the son of Aaron.

service; and you shall [a]assign *to each*
man by name the items he must carry.
33 "This *is* the service of the families
of the sons of Merari, as all their service for the tabernacle of meeting, under the [1]authority of Ithamar the son
of Aaron the priest."

Census of the Levites

34 [a]And Moses, Aaron, and the leaders
of the congregation numbered the sons
of the Kohathites by their families and
by their fathers' house,
35 from thirty [a]years old and above,
even to fifty years old, everyone who
entered the service for work in the tabernacle of meeting;
36 and those who were numbered by
their families were two thousand seven
hundred and fifty.
37 These *were* the ones who were
numbered of the families of the Kohathites, all who might serve in the tabernacle of meeting, whom Moses and
Aaron numbered according to the commandment of the LORD by the hand of
Moses.
38 And those who were numbered of
the sons of Gershon, by their families
and by their fathers' house,
39 from thirty years old and above,
even to fifty years old, everyone who
entered the service for work in the tabernacle of meeting—
40 those who were numbered by their
families, by their fathers' house, were
two thousand six hundred and thirty.
41 [a]These *are* the ones who were numbered of the families of the sons of Gershon, of all who might serve in the tabernacle of meeting, whom Moses and
Aaron numbered according to the commandment of the LORD.
42 Those of the families of the sons of
Merari who were numbered, by their
families, by their fathers' [1]house,
43 from thirty years old and above,
even to fifty years old, everyone who
entered the service for work in the tabernacle of meeting—
44 those who were numbered by their
families were three thousand two hundred.
45 These *are* the ones who were numbered of the families of the sons of Merari, whom Moses and Aaron numbered [a]according to the word of the
LORD by the hand of Moses.
46 All who were [a]numbered of the Levites, whom Moses, Aaron, and the
leaders of Israel numbered, by their
families and by their fathers' houses,
47 [a]from thirty years old and above,
even to fifty years old, everyone who
came to do the work of service and the
work of bearing burdens in the tabernacle of meeting—
48 those who were numbered were
eight thousand five hundred and
eighty.
49 According to the commandment of
the LORD they were numbered by the
hand of Moses, [a]each according to his
service and according to his task; thus
were they numbered by him, [b]as the
LORD commanded Moses.

Ceremonially Unclean Persons Isolated

5 And the LORD spoke to Moses, saying:
2 "Command the children of Israel
that they put out of the camp every
[a]leper, everyone who has a [b]discharge,
and whoever becomes [c]defiled [1]by a
corpse.
3 "You shall put out both male and
female; you shall put them outside the
camp, that they may not defile their
camps [a]in the midst of which I dwell."
4 And the children of Israel did so,
and put them outside the camp; as the
LORD spoke to Moses, so the children
of Israel did.

Confession and Restitution

5 Then the LORD spoke to Moses, say- 4
ing,
6 "Speak to the children of Israel:

32 [a]Ex. 25:9; 38:21 **33** [1]Lit. *hand* **34** [a]Num. 4:2 **35** [a]Num. 4:47 **41** [a]Num. 4:22 **42** [1]*household*

45 [a]Num. 4:29 **46** [a]Num. 3:39; 26:57–62; 1 Chr. 23:3–23 **47** [a]Num. 4:3, 23, 30 **49** [a]Num. 4:15, 24, 31 [b]Num. 4:1, 21

CHAPTER 5

2 [a]Lev. 13:3, 8, 46; Num. 12:10, 14, 15 [b]Lev. 15:2 [c]Lev. 21:1; Num. 9:6, 10; 19:11, 13; 31:19 [1]*by contact with* **3** [a]Lev. 26:11, 12; Num. 35:34; [2 Cor. 6:16]

4:34–49 The results of the census are revealed. This helped to reiterate the importance of the Levitical ministry and establish who is truly a part of this line.

5:1—6:27 The previous chapters dealt with a temporary state of affairs, namely, the order of the march from Sinai to the Promised Land. Here, the instructions are not limited to the time of the journey, but apply to life *in the land.*

5:2 Leper: The quarantine for leprosy has been dealt with in detail in Lev. 13:1–46. Some sort of infection is the likely cause of the **discharge.** In Lev. 15 quarantine was not necessary. In the camp, because of the Holy Presence in their midst, perhaps the additional rigor was necessary. **Defiled by a corpse:** This is developed further in 19:11–19. It is to be assumed that the quarantines are in effect only until the uncleanness from leprosy, discharge, or defilement is removed.

5:5–8 See section 4 of Truth-In-Action at the end of Num.

5:6–8 In vv. 6, 7, **sin** refers to the theological aspect of the wrong (wrong against God), **trespass** refers to the social aspect of the wrong (wrong against another person), and **restitution** deals with the social dimension of sin, while **atonement** (v. 8) deals with the theological dimension of the sin.

5:6 Sin: An act committed **against the LORD,** which brings one into the state of being **guilty.**

[a]'When a man or woman commits any sin that men commit in unfaithfulness against the LORD, and that person is *guilty,

7 [a]'then he shall confess the sin which he has committed. He shall make restitution for his trespass [b]in full, plus one-fifth of it, and give *it* to the one he has wronged.

8 'But if the man has no [1]relative to whom restitution may be made for the wrong, the restitution for the wrong *must go* to the LORD for the priest, in addition to [a]the ram of the atonement with which *atonement is made for him.

9 'Every [a]offering[1] of all the holy things of the children of Israel, which they bring to the priest, shall be [b]his.

10 'And every man's [1]holy things shall be his; whatever any man gives the priest shall be [a]his.' "

Concerning Unfaithful Wives

11 And the LORD spoke to Moses, saying,

12 "Speak to the children of Israel, and say to them: 'If any man's wife goes astray and behaves unfaithfully toward him,

13 'and a man [a]lies with her carnally, and it is hidden from the eyes of her husband, and it is concealed that she has defiled herself, and *there was* no witness against her, nor was she [b]caught—

14 'if the spirit of jealousy comes upon him and he becomes [a]jealous of his wife, who has defiled herself; or if the spirit of jealousy comes upon him and he becomes jealous of his wife, although she has not defiled herself—

15 'then the man shall bring his wife to the priest. He shall [a]bring the offering required for her, one-tenth of an ephah of barley meal; he shall pour no oil on it and put no frankincense on it, because it *is* a grain offering of jealousy, an offering for remembering, for [b]bringing iniquity to *remembrance.

16 'And the priest shall bring her near, and set her before the LORD.

17 'The priest shall take holy water in an earthen vessel, and take some of the dust that is on the floor of the tabernacle and put *it* into the water.

18 'Then the priest shall stand the woman before the [a]LORD, uncover the woman's head, and put the offering for remembering in her hands, which *is* the grain offering of jealousy. And the priest shall have in his hand the bitter water that brings a curse.

19 'And the priest shall put her under oath, and say to the woman, "If no man has lain with you, and if you have not gone astray to uncleanness *while* under your husband's *authority*, *be free from this bitter water that brings a curse.

20 "But if you have gone astray *while* under your husband's *authority*, and if you have defiled yourself and some man other than your husband has lain with you"—

21 'then the priest shall [a]put the woman under the oath of the curse, and he shall say to the woman—[b]"the LORD make you a curse and an oath among your people, when the LORD makes your thigh [1]rot and your belly swell;

22 "and may this water that causes the curse [a]go into your stomach, and make *your* belly swell and *your* thigh rot."

[b]Then the woman shall say, "Amen, so be it."

23 'Then the priest shall write these curses in a book, and he shall scrape *them* off into the bitter water.

24 'And he shall make the woman drink the bitter water that brings a curse, and the water that brings the curse shall enter her *to become* bitter.

25 [a]'Then the priest shall take the grain offering of jealousy from the woman's hand, shall [b]wave the offering before the LORD, and bring it to the altar;

26 'and the priest shall take a handful of the offering, [a]as its memorial portion, burn *it* on the altar, and afterward make the woman drink the water.

27 'When he has made her drink the water, then it shall be, if she has defiled herself and behaved unfaithfully

6 [a]Lev. 5:14—6:7 *See WW at Lev. 4:13.
7 [a]Lev. 5:5; 26:40, 41; Josh. 7:19; Ps. 32:5; 1 John 1:9 [b]Lev. 6:4, 5
8 [a]Lev. 5:15; 6:6, 7; 7:7 [1]*redeemer*, Heb. *goel* *See WW at Num. 15:25.
9 [a]Ex. 29:28; Lev. 6:17, 18, 26; 7:6–14 [b]Lev. 7:32–34; 10:14, 15 [1]*heave offering*
10 [a]Lev. 10:13 [1]*consecrated*
13 [a]Lev. 18:20; 20:10 [b]John 8:4
14 [a]Prov. 6:34; Song 8:6
15 [a]Lev. 5:11 [b]1 Kin. 17:18; Ezek. 29:16; Heb. 10:3 *See WW at Ex. 39:7.
18 [a]Heb. 13:4
19 *See WW at Num. 14:18.
21 [a]Josh. 6:26; 1 Sam. 14:24; Neh. 10:29 [b]Jer. 29:22 [1]Lit. *fall away*
22 [a]Ps. 109:18 [b]Deut. 27:15–26
25 [a]Lev. 8:27 [b]Lev. 2:2, 9
26 [a]Lev. 2:2, 9

5:8 The ram of the atonement: See note on Lev. 5:15.

5:11–31 This instruction may seem to modern readers to be unfair to women. However, the intent of the instruction must be borne in mind, namely to regulate the jealousy of the husband. The ordeal provides a legal method for the guilt or innocence of the woman to be revealed.

5:12–14 These verses outline the conditions under which the ordeal should be carried out, assuming neither guilt nor innocence. **The spirit of jealousy** does not refer to any being or force outside of the husband, but to his own spirit dominated by jealous suspicion.

5:15–28 The ordeal is not assumed to operate on chance or fate, but the **oath** under which the woman is placed makes the ordeal effective. Its purpose was to bear witness to a desire for objective justice; it also removed suspicion or fear within relationships.

5:15 One-tenth of an ephah was 7½ pints (3 to 4 liters).

toward her husband, that the water that brings a [a]curse will enter her *and become* bitter, and her belly will swell, her thigh will rot, and the woman [b]will become a curse among her people.
28 'But if the woman has not defiled herself, and is clean, then she shall be free and may conceive children.
29 'This *is* the law of jealousy, when a wife, *while* under her husband's *authority*, [a]goes astray and defiles herself,
30 'or when the spirit of jealousy comes upon a man, and he becomes jealous of his wife; then he shall stand the woman before the LORD, and the priest shall execute all this law upon her.
31 'Then the man shall be free from [1]iniquity, but that woman [a]shall bear her [2]guilt.' "

The Law of the Nazirite

2 **6** Then the LORD spoke to Moses, saying,
2 "Speak to the children of Israel, and say to them: 'When either a man or woman [1]consecrates an offering to take the vow of a Nazirite, [a]to separate himself to the LORD,
3 [a]'he shall separate himself from wine and *similar* drink; he shall drink neither vinegar made from wine nor vinegar made from *similar* drink; neither shall he drink any grape juice, nor eat fresh grapes or raisins.
4 'All the days of his [1]separation he shall eat nothing that is produced by the grapevine, from seed to skin.
5 'All the days of the vow of his separation no [a]razor shall come upon his head; until the days are fulfilled for which he separated himself to the LORD, he shall be holy. *Then* he shall let the locks of the hair of his head grow.
6 'All the days that he separates himself to the LORD [a]he shall not go near a dead body.
7 [a]'He shall not [1]make himself unclean even for his father or his mother, for his brother or his sister, when they die, because his separation to God *is* on his head.
8 [a]'All the days of his separation he shall be holy to the LORD.
9 'And if anyone dies very suddenly beside him, and he defiles his consecrated head, then he shall [a]shave his head on the day of his cleansing; on the seventh day he shall shave it.
10 'Then [a]on the eighth day he shall bring two turtledoves or two young pigeons to the priest, to the door of the tabernacle of meeting;
11 'and the priest shall offer one as a *sin offering and *the* other as a burnt offering, and make atonement for him, because he sinned in regard to the corpse; and he shall sanctify his head that same day.
12 'He shall consecrate to the LORD the days of his separation, and bring a male lamb in its first year [a]as a trespass offering; but the former days shall be [1]lost, because his separation was defiled.
13 'Now this *is* the law of the Nazirite: [a]When the days of his separation are fulfilled, he shall be brought to the door of the tabernacle of meeting.
14 'And he shall present his offering to the LORD: one male lamb in its first year without blemish as a burnt offering, one ewe lamb in its first year without blemish [a]as a sin offering, one ram without blemish [b]as a peace offering,
15 'a basket of unleavened bread, [a]cakes of fine flour mixed with oil, unleavened wafers [b]anointed with oil, and their grain offering with their [c]drink offerings.
16 'Then the priest shall bring *them* before the LORD and offer his sin offering and his burnt offering;
17 'and he shall offer the ram as a sacrifice of a peace offering to the LORD, with the basket of unleavened bread; the priest shall also offer its grain offering and its drink offering.
18 [a]'Then the Nazirite shall shave his consecrated head *at* the door of the tabernacle of meeting, and shall take the hair from his consecrated head and

27 [a]Deut. 28:37; Is. 65:15; Jer. 24:9; 29:18, 22; 42:18 [b]Num. 5:21
29 [a]Num. 5:19
31 [a]Lev. 20:17, 19, 20 [1]*guilt* [2]*iniquity*

CHAPTER 6

2 [a]Lev. 27:2; Judg. 13:5; [Lam. 4:7; Amos 2:11, 12]; Acts 21:23; Rom. 1:1 [1]Or *makes a difficult vow*
3 [a]Lev. 10:9; Amos 2:12; Luke 1:15
4 [1]Separation as a Nazirite
5 [a]Judg. 13:5; 16:17; 1 Sam. 1:11
6 [a]Lev. 21:1–3, 11; Num. 19:11–22
7 [a]Lev. 21:1, 2, 11; Num. 9:6 [1]By touching a dead body
8 [a][2 Cor. 6:17, 18]
9 [a]Lev. 14:8, 9; Acts 18:18; 21:24
10 [a]Lev. 5:7; 14:22; 15:14, 29
11 *See WW at Lev. 9:2.
12 [a]Lev. 5:6 [1]*void*
13 [a]Acts 21:26
14 [a]Lev. 4:2, 27, 32 [b]Lev. 3:6
15 [a]Lev. 2:4 [b]Ex. 29:2 [c]Num. 15:5, 7, 10
18 [a]Num. 6:9; Acts 21:23, 24

6:1–21 The three aspects of **the vow of a Nazirite** are abstinence from the fruit of the vine (vv. 3, 4), abstinence from cutting one's hair (v. 5), and abstinence from defilement by contact with a dead body (vv. 6–12). These were apparently viewed as specific *acts of discipline* and *cleanness*.

6:1–8 See section 2 of Truth-In-Action at the end of Num.

6:2 Nazirite is a noun form of the verb **to separate.** The sense is clearly one who separates **himself to the LORD** for a specific time. This temporary Nazirite is probably distinct from the lifelong Nazirites of which Samson is the best example (see Judg. 13—16; Amos 2:11, 12).

6:14 Burnt offering, sin offering, and **peace offering** are a familiar trilogy from the beginning of Aaron's priestly ministry. See notes on Lev. 1:3, 4; 3:1; 4:3.

6:17 The **grain offering** and **drink offering** are not independent sacrifices but form part of the communion ritual of the **peace offering.** The need to observe these rituals (vv. 13–21) to absolve the vow reinforces its seriousness. See note on Lev. 3:1.

put *it* on the fire which is under the
sacrifice of the peace offering.
19 'And the priest shall take the
[a]boiled shoulder of the ram, one
[b]unleavened cake from the basket, and
one unleavened wafer, and [c]put *them*
upon the hands of the Nazirite after he
has shaved his consecrated *hair,*
20 'and the priest shall wave them as
a wave offering before the LORD;
[a]they *are* holy for the priest, together
with the breast of the wave offering
and the thigh of the heave offering. After that the Nazirite may drink wine.'
21 "This is the law of the Nazirite who
vows to the LORD the offering for his
separation, and besides that, whatever
else his hand is able to provide; according to the vow which he takes, so he
must do according to the law of his separation."

The Priestly Blessing

22 And the LORD spoke to Moses, saying:
23 "Speak to Aaron and his sons, saying, 'This is the way you shall *bless
the children of Israel. Say to them:

24 "The LORD [a]bless you and
[b]keep you;
25 The LORD [a]make His face shine
upon you,
And [b]be* gracious to you;
26 [a]The LORD [1]lift up His countenance
upon you,
And [b]give you *peace." '

27 [a]"So they shall [1]put My name on
the children of Israel, and [b]I will bless
them."

Offerings of the Leaders

7 Now it came to pass, when Moses
had finished [a]setting up the tabernacle, that he [b]anointed it and consecrated it and all its furnishings,
and the altar and all its utensils; so
he anointed them and consecrated
them.
2 Then [a]the leaders of Israel, the
heads of their fathers' houses, who
were the leaders of the tribes [1]and over
those who were numbered, made an offering.
3 And they brought their offering before the LORD, six covered carts and
twelve oxen, a cart for *every* two of the
leaders, and for each one an ox; and
they presented them before the tabernacle.
4 Then the LORD spoke to Moses, saying,
5 "Accept *these* from them, that they
may be used in doing the work of the
tabernacle of meeting; and you shall
give them to the Levites, *to* every man
according to his service."
6 So Moses took the carts and the
oxen, and gave them to the Levites.
7 Two carts and four oxen [a]he gave
to the sons of Gershon, according to
their service;
8 [a]and four carts and eight oxen he
gave to the sons of Merari, according
to their service, under the [1]authority
of Ithamar the son of Aaron the
priest.
9 But to the sons of Kohath he gave
none, because theirs *was* [a]the service
of the holy things, [b]*which* they carried
on their shoulders.
10 Now the leaders offered [a]the dedication *offering* for the altar when it was
anointed; so the leaders offered their
offering before the altar.
11 For the LORD said to Moses, "They
shall offer their offering, one leader
each day, for the dedication of the altar."
12 And the one who offered his

19 [a]1 Sam. 2:15 [b]Ex. 29:23, 24 [c]Lev. 7:30
20 [a]Ex. 29:27, 28
23 *See WW at Ps. 145:2.
24 [a]Deut. 28:3–6 [b]Ps. 121:7; John 7:11
25 [a]Ps. 31:16; 67:1; 80:3, 7, 19; 119:135; Dan. 9:17 [b]Gen. 43:29; Ex. 33:19; Mal. 1:9 *See WW at Mal. 1:9.
26 [a]Ps. 4:6; 89:15 [b]Lev. 26:6; Is. 26:3, 12; John 14:27; Phil. 4:7 [1]Look upon you with favor *See WW at Nah. 1:15.
27 [a]Deut. 28:10; 2 Sam. 7:23; 2 Chr. 7:14; Is. 43:7; Dan. 9:18, 19 [b]Ex. 20:24; Num. 23:20; Ps. 5:12; 67:7; 115:12, 13; Eph. 1:3 [1]*invoke*

CHAPTER 7

1 [a]Ex. 40:17–33 [b]Lev. 8:10, 11
2 [a]Num. 1:4 [1]Lit. *who stood over*
7 [a]Num. 4:24–28
8 [a]Num. 4:29–33 [1]Lit. *hand*
9 [a]Num. 4:15 [b]Num. 4:6–14
10 [a]Num. 7:1; Deut. 20:5; 1 Kin. 8:63; 2 Chr. 7:5, 9; Ezra 6:16; Neh. 12:27

6:20 Wave offering is a type of peace offering. See note on Lev. 3:1.
6:22–27 You is singular in Hebrew, hence addressed to an individual, though this may be understood in a collective sense to refer to all of Israel. There are three poetic lines, each with two verbs, Yahweh being the subject of both verbs. This is known as the Aaronic blessing and is used literally by many modern-day Christians.
6:24 To **bless** means an increase in prosperity because Yahweh will **keep** the worshiper from harm.
6:25 Make His face shine upon you implies taking pleasure in the worshiper, with the result that the Lord will be **gracious** or favorable to the worshiper.
6:26 To **lift up His countenance upon you,** similar to making His face shine in v. 25, results in **peace,** the provision of all things necessary for the well-being of the recipient.
7:1–89 The newly appointed leaders respond to their appointment with offerings for the newly dedicated tabernacle. The offering consisted of two parts, one for the **work of the tabernacle of meeting** (vv. 2–9), given at one time, and one for the **altar** (vv. 10–88), given in a twelve-day ceremony.
7:1 The chronology here alludes to the completing of the erection of the tabernacle (Ex. 40:17–33) and the consecration of the tabernacle and the altar (Lev. 8:10, 11).
7:2–9 The offering for the tabernacle provided the means for carrying the tabernacle on the journey, two carts for the hangings of the tabernacle and four carts for the boards and frames of the tabernacle. The Kohathites had to carry the most holy things on their shoulders by means of poles put through the rings attached to the holy things (4:4–15).
7:10–88 The leaders are those appointed by Moses in chs. 1 and 2, and they all bring identical gifts. The generosity of the offerings is stressed through the repetitions of vv. 12–83 and underlined by the sum totals given in vv. 84–88. Their generosity stands as an example for later generations.

offering on the first day *was* [a]Nahshon the son of Amminadab, from the tribe of Judah.

13 His offering *was* one silver platter, the weight of which *was* one hundred and thirty *shekels,* and one silver bowl of seventy shekels, according to [a]the shekel of the sanctuary, both of them full of fine flour mixed with oil as a [b]grain offering;

14 one gold pan of ten *shekels,* full of [a]incense;

15 [a]one young bull, one ram, and one male lamb [b]in its first year, as a burnt offering;

16 one kid of the goats as a [a]sin offering;

17 and for [a]the sacrifice of peace offerings: two oxen, five rams, five male goats, and five male lambs in their first year. This *was* the offering of Nahshon the son of Amminadab.

18 On the second day Nethanel the son of Zuar, leader of Issachar, presented *an offering.*

19 *For* his offering he offered one silver platter, the weight of which *was* one hundred and thirty *shekels,* and one silver bowl of seventy shekels, according to the shekel of the sanctuary, both of them full of fine flour mixed with oil as a grain offering;

20 one gold pan of ten *shekels,* full of incense;

21 one young bull, one ram, and one male lamb in its first year, as a burnt offering;

22 one kid of the goats as a sin offering;

23 and as the sacrifice of peace offerings: two oxen, five rams, five male goats, and five male lambs in their first year. This *was* the offering of Nethanel the son of Zuar.

24 On the third day Eliab the son of Helon, leader of the children of Zebulun, *presented an offering.*

25 His offering *was* one silver platter, the weight of which *was* one hundred and thirty *shekels,* and one silver bowl of seventy shekels, according to the shekel of the sanctuary, both of them full of fine flour mixed with oil as a grain offering;

26 one gold pan of ten *shekels,* full of incense;

27 one young bull, one ram, and one male lamb in its first year, as a burnt offering;

28 one kid of the goats as a sin offering;

29 and for the sacrifice of peace offerings: two oxen, five rams, five male goats, and five male lambs in their first year. This *was* the offering of Eliab the son of Helon.

30 On the fourth day [a]Elizur the son of Shedeur, leader of the children of Reuben, *presented an offering.*

31 His offering *was* one silver platter, the weight of which *was* one hundred and thirty *shekels,* and one silver bowl of seventy shekels, according to the shekel of the sanctuary, both of them full of fine flour mixed with oil as a grain offering;

32 one gold pan of ten *shekels,* full of incense;

33 one young bull, one ram, and one male lamb in its first year, as a burnt offering;

34 one kid of the goats as a sin offering;

35 and as the sacrifice of peace offerings: two oxen, five rams, five male goats, and five male lambs in their first year. This *was* the offering of Elizur the son of Shedeur.

36 On the fifth day [a]Shelumiel the son of Zurishaddai, leader of the children of Simeon, *presented an offering.*

37 His offering *was* one silver platter, the weight of which *was* one hundred and thirty *shekels,* and one silver bowl of seventy shekels, according to the shekel of the sanctuary, both of them full of fine flour mixed with oil as a grain offering;

38 one gold pan of ten *shekels,* full of incense;

39 one young bull, one ram, and one male lamb in its first year, as a burnt offering;

40 one kid of the goats as a sin offering;

41 and as the sacrifice of peace offerings: two oxen, five rams, five male goats, and five male lambs in their first year. This *was* the offering of Shelumiel the son of Zurishaddai.

42 On the sixth day [a]Eliasaph the son of [1]Deuel, leader of the children of Gad, *presented an offering.*

43 His offering *was* one silver platter, the weight of which *was* one hundred and thirty *shekels,* and one silver bowl of seventy shekels, according to the shekel of the sanctuary, both of them

12 [a]Num. 2:3
13 [a]Ex. 30:13 [b]Lev. 2:1
14 [a]Ex. 30:34, 35
15 [a]Lev. 1:2 [b]Ex. 12:5
16 [a]Lev. 4:23
17 [a]Lev. 3:1
30 [a]Num. 1:5; 2:10
36 [a]Num. 1:6; 2:12; 7:41
42 [a]Num. 1:14; 2:14; 10:20 [1]*Reuel,* Num. 2:14

7:13 The weight of the shekel varied. It is generally assumed it was equivalent at this time to about 12 to 15 grams. **Grain offering:** See note on 6:17.

7:15 Burnt offering: See note on 6:14.

7:16 Sin offering: See note on 6:14.

7:17 Peace offerings: See note on 6:14.

full of fine flour mixed with oil as a grain offering;
44 one gold pan of ten *shekels,* full of incense;
45 one young bull, one ram, and one male lamb in its first year, as [a]a burnt offering;
46 one kid of the goats as a sin offering;
47 and as the sacrifice of peace offerings: two oxen, five rams, five male goats, and five male lambs in their first year. This *was* the offering of Eliasaph the son of Deuel.
48 On the seventh day [a]Elishama the son of Ammihud, leader of the children of Ephraim, *presented an offering.*
49 His offering *was* one silver platter, the weight of which *was* one hundred and thirty *shekels,* and one silver bowl of seventy shekels, according to the shekel of the sanctuary, both of them full of fine flour mixed with oil as a grain offering;
50 one gold pan of ten *shekels,* full of incense;
51 one young bull, one ram, and one male lamb in its first year, as a burnt offering;
52 one kid of the goats as a sin offering;
53 and as the sacrifice of peace offerings: two oxen, five rams, five male goats, and five male lambs in their first year. This *was* the offering of Elishama the son of Ammihud.
54 On the eighth day [a]Gamaliel the son of Pedahzur, leader of the children of Manasseh, *presented an offering.*
55 His offering *was* one silver platter, the weight of which *was* one hundred and thirty *shekels,* and one silver bowl of seventy shekels, according to the shekel of the sanctuary, both of them full of fine flour mixed with oil as a grain offering;
56 one gold pan of ten *shekels,* full of incense;
57 one young bull, one ram, and one male lamb in its first year, as a burnt offering;
58 one kid of the goats as a sin offering;
59 and as the sacrifice of peace offerings: two oxen, five rams, five male goats, and five male lambs in their first year. This *was* the offering of Gamaliel the son of Pedahzur.
60 On the ninth day [a]Abidan the son of Gideoni, leader of the children of Benjamin, *presented an offering.*
61 His offering *was* one silver platter, the weight of which *was* one hundred and thirty *shekels,* and one silver bowl of seventy shekels, according to the shekel of the sanctuary, both of them full of fine flour mixed with oil as a grain offering;
62 one gold pan of ten *shekels,* full of incense;
63 one young bull, one ram, and one male lamb in its first year, as a burnt offering;
64 one kid of the goats as a sin offering;
65 and as the sacrifice of peace offerings: two oxen, five rams, five male goats, and five male lambs in their first year. This *was* the offering of Abidan the son of Gideoni.
66 On the tenth day [a]Ahiezer the son of Ammishaddai, leader of the children of Dan, *presented an offering.*
67 His offering *was* one silver platter, the weight of which *was* one hundred and thirty *shekels,* and one silver bowl of seventy shekels, according to the shekel of the sanctuary, both of them full of fine flour mixed with oil as a grain offering;
68 one gold pan of ten *shekels,* full of incense;
69 one young bull, one ram, and one male lamb in its first year, as a burnt offering;
70 one kid of the goats as a sin offering;
71 and as the sacrifice of peace offerings: two oxen, five rams, five male goats, and five male lambs in their first year. This *was* the offering of Ahiezer the son of Ammishaddai.
72 On the eleventh day [a]Pagiel the son of Ocran, leader of the children of Asher, *presented an offering.*
73 His offering *was* one silver platter, the weight of which *was* one hundred and thirty *shekels,* and one silver bowl of seventy shekels, according to the shekel of the sanctuary, both of them full of fine flour mixed with oil as a grain offering;
74 one gold pan of ten *shekels,* full of incense;
75 one young bull, one ram, and one male lamb in its first year, as a burnt offering;
76 one kid of the goats as a sin offering;
77 and as the sacrifice of peace offerings: two oxen, five rams, five male goats, and five male lambs in their first year. This *was* the offering of Pagiel the son of Ocran.
78 On the twelfth day [a]Ahira the son of Enan, leader of the children of Naphtali, *presented an offering.*
79 His offering *was* one silver platter,

45 [a]Ps. 40:6
48 [a]Num. 1:10; 2:18; 1 Chr. 7:26
54 [a]Num. 1:10; 2:20
60 [a]Num. 1:11; 2:22
66 [a]Num. 1:12; 2:25
72 [a]Num. 1:13; 2:27
78 [a]Num. 1:15; 2:29

the weight of which *was* one hundred and thirty *shekels,* and one silver bowl of seventy shekels, according to the shekel of the sanctuary, both of them full of fine flour mixed with oil as a grain offering;

80 one gold pan of ten *shekels,* full of incense;

81 one young bull, one ram, and one male lamb in its first year, as a burnt offering;

82 one kid of the goats as a sin offering;

83 and as the sacrifice of peace offerings: two oxen, five rams, five male goats, and five male lambs in their first year. This *was* the offering of Ahira the son of Enan.

84 This *was* [a]the dedication *offering* for the altar from the leaders of Israel, when it was anointed: twelve silver platters, twelve silver bowls, and twelve gold pans.

85 Each silver platter *weighed* one hundred and thirty *shekels* and each bowl seventy *shekels.* All the silver of the vessels *weighed* two thousand four hundred *shekels,* according to the shekel of the sanctuary.

86 The twelve gold pans full of incense *weighed* ten *shekels* apiece, according to the shekel of the sanctuary; all the gold of the pans *weighed* one hundred and twenty *shekels.*

87 All the oxen for the burnt offering *were* twelve young bulls, the rams twelve, the male lambs in their first year twelve, with their grain offering, and the kids of the goats as a sin offering twelve.

88 And all the oxen for the sacrifice of peace offerings were twenty-four bulls, the rams sixty, the male goats sixty, and the lambs in their first year sixty. This *was* the dedication *offering* for the altar after it was [a]anointed.

89 Now when Moses went into the tabernacle of meeting [a]to speak with Him, he heard [b]the voice of One speaking to him from above the mercy seat that *was* on the ark of the Testimony, from [c]between the two *cherubim; thus He spoke to him.

84 [a]Num. 7:10
88 [a]Num. 7:1, 10
89 [a][Ex. 33:9, 11]; Num. 12:8 [b]Ex. 25:21, 22 [c]Ps. 80:1; 99:1 *See WW at Ex. 25:18.

Arrangement of the Lamps

8 And the LORD spoke to Moses, saying:

2 "Speak to Aaron, and say to him, 'When you [a]arrange the lamps, the seven [b]lamps shall give light in front of the lampstand.' "

3 And Aaron did so; he arranged the lamps to face toward the front of the lampstand, as the LORD commanded Moses.

4 [a]Now this workmanship of the lampstand *was* hammered gold; from its shaft to its flowers it *was* [b]hammered work. [c]According to the pattern which the LORD had shown Moses, so he made the lampstand.

Cleansing and Dedication of the Levites

5 Then the LORD spoke to Moses, saying:

6 "Take the Levites from among the children of Israel and cleanse them *ceremonially.*

7 "Thus you shall do to them to cleanse them: Sprinkle [a]water of purification on them, and [b]let[1] them shave all their *body, and let them wash their clothes, and *so* make themselves clean.

8 "Then let them take a young bull with [a]its grain offering of fine flour mixed with oil, and you shall take another young bull as a sin offering.

9 [a]"And you shall bring the Levites before the tabernacle of meeting, [b]and you shall gather together the whole congregation of the children of Israel.

10 "So you shall bring the Levites before the LORD, and the children of Israel [a]shall lay their hands on the Levites;

11 "and Aaron shall [1]offer the Levites

CHAPTER 8

2 [a]Lev. 24:2–4 [b]Ex. 25:37; 40:25
4 [a]Ex. 25:31 [b]Ex. 25:18 [c]Ex. 25:40; Acts 7:44
7 [a]Num. 19:9, 13, 17, 20; Ps. 51:2, 7; [Heb. 9:13, 14] [b]Lev. 14:8, 9 [1]Heb. *let them cause a razor to pass over* *See WW at Job 19:26.
8 [a]Lev. 2:1; Num. 15:8–10
9 [a]Ex. 29:4; 40:12 [b]Lev. 8:3
10 [a]Lev. 1:4
11 [1]*present*

7:89 Describes the means by which Yahweh communicated with **Moses** in fulfillment of His promise in Ex. 25:21, 22. With this note, the tabernacle is fully operational.

8:1–4 A hierarchy is set up between Moses and Aaron when 7:89 and 8:1–4 are compared. Moses has access to the ark to hear God's voice; Aaron has access only to the anteroom where the table and lampstand *are,* except on the Day of Atonement.

8:5–22 This is the beginning of the Levitical service. Prior to this, only Moses, Aaron, and his sons did the work of the tabernacle; now they have assistance in the tasks of operating the worship system of ancient Israel.

8:6, 7 This is the preparatory cleansing and takes place prior to the ceremony. Purification and cleansing were requirements for these helpers of the priests. Compare the ordination of priests in Lev. 8. They were told to **shave all their body** as a symbol of being cut off from anything unclean.

8:10, 11 The laying on of hands signifies an identification of the ones making the offering with the sacrifice. **The Levites** function as Israel's sacrifice to Yahweh (see vv. 16–18 where they stand as Israel's sacrifice of the firstborn to Yahweh). The **wave offering** is the portion of the sacrifice that belongs to the officiating priest (see note on 6:20). Likewise, Yahweh has given the Levites to Aaron and his sons (see v. 19).

before the LORD, *like* a [a]wave offering
from the children of Israel, that they
may perform the work of the LORD.
12 [a]"Then the Levites shall lay their
hands on the heads of the young bulls,
and you shall offer one as a sin offering
and the other as a burnt offering to the
LORD, to make atonement for the Levites.
13 "And you shall stand the Levites before Aaron and his sons, and then offer
them *like* a wave offering to the LORD.
14 "Thus you shall [a]separate the Levites from among the children of Israel,
and the Levites shall be [b]Mine.
15 "After that the Levites shall go in
to service the tabernacle of meeting.
So you shall cleanse them and [a]offer
them, *like* a wave offering.
16 "For they *are* [a]wholly given to Me
from among the children of Israel; I
have taken them for Myself [b]instead
of all who open the womb, the firstborn
of all the children of Israel.
17 [a]"For all the firstborn among the
children of Israel *are* Mine, *both* man
and beast; on the day that I struck all
the firstborn in the land of Egypt I
[1]sanctified them to Myself.
18 "I have taken the Levites instead of
all the firstborn of the children of Israel.
19 "And [a]I have given the Levites as
a gift to Aaron and his sons from
among the children of Israel, to do the
work for the children of Israel in the
tabernacle of meeting, and to make
atonement for the children of Israel,
[b]that there be no plague among the
children of Israel when the children of
Israel come near the sanctuary."
20 Thus Moses and Aaron and all the
congregation of the children of Israel
did to the Levites; according to all that
the LORD commanded Moses concerning the Levites, so the children of Israel
did to them.
21 [a]And the Levites purified themselves and washed their clothes; then
Aaron presented them, *like* a wave offering before the LORD, and Aaron

11 [a]Num. 18:6
12 [a]Ex. 29:10
14 [a]Num. 16:9
[b]Num. 3:12, 45; 16:9
15 [a]Num. 8:11, 13
16 [a]Num. 3:9
[b]Ex. 13:2; Num. 3:12, 45
17 [a]Ex. 12:2, 12, 13, 15; Num. 3:13; Luke 2:23
[1]*set them apart*
19 [a]Num. 3:9
[b]Num. 1:53; 16:46; 18:5; 2 Chr. 26:16
21 [a]Num. 8:7
22 [a]Num. 8:15
[b]Num. 8:5
24 [a]Num. 4:3; 1 Chr. 23:3, 24, 27
26 [a]Num. 1:53
*See WW at Ps. 133:1.

CHAPTER 9

2 [a]Ex. 12:1–16; Lev. 23:5; Num. 28:16; Deut. 16:1, 2 [b]2 Chr. 30:1–15; Luke 22:7; [1 Cor. 5:7, 8]

made atonement for them to cleanse
them.
22 [a]After that the Levites went in to
do their work in the tabernacle of
meeting before Aaron and his sons;
[b]as the LORD commanded Moses concerning the Levites, so they did to
them.
23 Then the LORD spoke to Moses, saying,
24 "This *is* what *pertains* to the Levites: [a]From twenty-five years old and
above one may enter to perform service in the work of the tabernacle of
meeting;
25 "and at the age of fifty years they
must cease performing this work, and
shall work no more.
26 "They may minister with their
*brethren in the tabernacle of meeting,
[a]to attend to needs, but they *themselves* shall do no work. Thus you shall
do to the Levites regarding their duties."

The Second Passover

9 Now the LORD spoke to Moses in
the Wilderness of Sinai, in the first
month of the second year after they
had come out of the land of Egypt, saying:
2 "Let the children of Israel keep 3
[a]the Passover at its **appointed** [b]**time.**

WORD WEALTH

9:2 appointed time, *mo'ed* (mo-*ed*); Strong's #4150: A fixed time, appointment, appointed season, festival, feast, solemn assembly, appointed place. The root of *mo'ed* is the verb *ya'ad,* which means to "set" or "fix," as in setting a time, or fixing a date, or appointing a place for meeting. The first occurrence of *mo'ed* is Gen. 1:14, where the stars and heavenly bodies are created to serve for "seasons" (*mo'adim*) and as "signs." The books of Moses frequently refer to the tent of "meeting"; the best transla-
(*cont. on next page*)

8:16–18 See note on 3:12, 13.
8:19 To make atonement means that the Levites atone for the Israelites, standing as the firstborn dedicated to Yahweh. **That there be no plague** is the consequence of the Levites' surrounding the tabernacle to insulate the Israelites (see 1:53).
8:23–26 Here the age to begin service is 25, compared with age 30 in 4:3. The reason for the change to the lower age limit is not given. Since the older age limit was given before the initiation of the Levitical service, it may have proved insufficient for the actual need once the Levitical service began, hence the change. Or, there may have been a training period between ages 25 and 30.
9:1–14 This passage refines instructions concerning **the Passover** on the occasion of its first commemoration, anticipating the settlement in the land, so that the Book of Numbers is not simply a history of the past. The concern of the instructions is to make participation in Passover accessible to as many as possible, since it commemorated the salvation of the Israelites from their bondage and was the formative event of Israel's relationship to God. See notes on Ex. 12:1–11.
9:2, 3 See section 3 of Truth-In-Action at the end of Num.

(cont. from preceding page)
tion of *mo'ed* in those contexts might be "meeting place." *Mo'ed* is used for the seven "feasts" of the Lord (Lev. 23:2), actually Yahweh's seven sacred appointments, the times He meets with Israel. The entire plan of redemption is revealed in the progression of the seven mileposts, which unfold yearly in the Hebrew calendar. Furthermore, every major event in the life of Jesus occurred during one of Israel's seven feasts.

3 "On the fourteenth day of this
month, [1]at twilight, you shall [2]keep it
at its appointed time. According to all
its [3]rites and ceremonies you shall
keep it."
4 So Moses told the children of Israel
that they should keep the Passover.
5 And [a]they kept the Passover on the
fourteenth day of the first month, at
twilight, in the Wilderness of Sinai; according to all that the LORD commanded Moses, so the children of Israel did.
6 Now there were *certain* men who
were [a]defiled by a human corpse, so
that they could not keep the Passover
on that day; [b]and they came before
Moses and Aaron that day.
7 And those men said to him, "We *became* defiled by a human corpse. Why
are we kept from presenting the offering of the LORD at its appointed time
among the children of Israel?"
8 And Moses said to them, "Stand
still, that [a]I may *hear what the LORD
will command concerning you."
9 Then the LORD spoke to Moses, saying,
10 "Speak to the children of Israel,
saying: 'If anyone of you or your
[1]posterity is *unclean because of a
corpse, or *is* far away on a journey, he
may still keep the LORD's Passover.
11 'On [a]the fourteenth day of the second month, at twilight, they may keep
it. They shall [b]eat it with unleavened
bread and bitter herbs.
12 [a]'They shall leave none of it until
morning, [b]nor break one of its bones.
[c]According to all the [1]ordinances of the
Passover they shall keep it.
13 'But the man who *is* clean and is
not on a journey, and ceases to keep
the Passover, that same person [a]shall
be cut off from among his people, because he [b]did not bring the offering of
the LORD at its appointed time; that
man shall [c]bear his sin.
14 'And if a stranger [1]dwells among
you, and would keep the LORD's Passover, he must do so according to the
rite of the Passover and according to
its ceremony; [a]you shall have one
[2]ordinance, both for the stranger and
the native of the land.' "

The Cloud and the Fire

15 Now [a]on the day that the tabernacle
was raised up, the cloud [b]covered the
tabernacle, the tent of the Testimony;
[c]from evening until morning it was
above the tabernacle like the appearance of fire.
16 So it was always: the cloud covered
it *by day*, and the appearance of fire
by night.
17 Whenever the cloud [a]was [1]taken up
from above the tabernacle, after that
the children of Israel would journey;
and in the place where the cloud settled, there the children of Israel would
pitch their tents.
18 At the [1]command of the LORD the
children of Israel would journey, and
at the command of the LORD they
would camp; [a]as long as the cloud
stayed above the tabernacle they remained encamped.
19 Even when the cloud continued
long, many days above the tabernacle,
the children of Israel [a]kept the charge
of the LORD and did not journey.
20 So it was, when the cloud was
above the tabernacle a few days: according to the command of the LORD
they would remain encamped, and according to the command of the LORD
they would journey.
21 So it was, when the cloud remained
only from evening until morning: when
the cloud was taken up in the morning,
then they would journey; whether by
day or by night, whenever the cloud
was taken up, they would journey.
22 *Whether it was* two days, a month,
or a year that the cloud remained
above the tabernacle, the children of
Israel [a]would remain encamped and

3 [1]Lit. *between the evenings* [2]*observe* [3]*statutes*
5 [a]Josh. 5:10
6 [a]Num. 5:2; 19:11–22; John 18:28 [b]Ex. 18:15, 19, 26; Num. 27:2
8 [a]Ex. 18:22; Num. 27:5 *See WW at 1 Kin. 20:8.
10 [1]*descendants* *See WW at Lev. 10:10.
11 [a]2 Chr. 30:2, 15 [b]Ex. 12:8
12 [a]Ex. 12:10 [b]Ex. 12:46; [John 19:36] [c]Ex. 12:43 [1]*statutes*
13 [a]Gen. 17:14; Ex. 12:15, 47 [b]Num. 9:7 [c]Num. 5:31
14 [a]Ex. 12:49; Lev. 24:22; Num. 15:15, 16, 29 [1]As a resident alien [2]*statute*
15 [a]Ex. 40:33, 34; Neh. 9:12, 19; Ps. 78:14 [b]Is. 4:5 [c]Ex. 13:21, 22; 40:38
17 [a]Ex. 40:36–38; Num. 10:11, 12, 33, 34; Ps. 80:1 [1]*lifted up*
18 [a]1 Cor. 10:1 [1]Lit. *mouth*
19 [a]Num. 1:53; 3:8
22 [a]Ex. 40:36, 37

9:10, 11 The allowance to celebrate Passover *a month* later *emphasizes the obligation* to keep the feast regardless of extenuating circumstances.

9:15–23 This text concerning divine guidance in the wilderness anticipates the accounts of the wilderness wanderings found later in the book. Vv. 15–17 look back to Ex. 40:34–38, when the cloud descended on the tabernacle. Prior to that it had gone before the people (see Ex. 14:19, 20); now it would be in the midst of the people above the tabernacle. The **command of the LORD** came **by the hand of Moses** (v. 23), stressing that there is no conflict between the leading of the Lord's own presence in the cloud and the leading by Moses through the word of the Lord.

not journey; but when it was taken up, they would journey.

23 At the command of the LORD they remained encamped, and at the command of the LORD they journeyed; they [a]kept the charge of the LORD, at the command of the LORD by the hand of Moses.

Two Silver Trumpets

10 And the LORD spoke to Moses, saying:

2 "Make two silver trumpets for yourself; you shall make them of hammered work; you shall use them for [a]calling the congregation and for directing the movement of the camps.

3 "When [a]they *blow both of them, all the congregation shall gather before you at the door of the tabernacle of meeting.

4 "But if they blow *only* one, then the leaders, the [a]heads of the divisions of Israel, shall gather to you.

5 "When you sound the [a]advance, [b]the camps that lie on the east side shall then begin their journey.

6 "When you sound the advance the second time, then the camps that lie [a]on the south side shall begin their journey; they shall sound the call for them to begin their journeys.

7 "And when the assembly is to be gathered together, [a]you shall blow, but not [b]sound the advance.

8 [a]"The sons of Aaron, the priests, shall blow the trumpets; and these shall be to you as an [1]ordinance *forever throughout your generations.

9 [a]"When you go to war in your land against the enemy who [b]oppresses you, then you shall sound an alarm with the trumpets, and you will be [c]remembered before the LORD your God, and you will be saved from your enemies.

10 "Also [a]in the day of your gladness, in your appointed feasts, and at the beginning of your months, you shall blow the trumpets over your burnt offerings and over the sacrifices of your peace offerings; and they shall be [b]a *memorial for you before your God: I *am* the LORD your God."

23 [a]Num. 9:19

CHAPTER 10

2 [a]Is. 1:13
3 [a]Jer. 4:5; Joel 2:15 *See WW at Ps. 47:1.
4 [a]Ex. 18:21; Num. 1:16; 7:2
5 [a]Joel 2:1 [b]Num. 2:3
6 [a]Num. 2:10
7 [a]Num. 10:3 [b]Joel 2:1
8 [a]Num. 31:6; Josh. 6:4; 1 Chr. 15:24; 2 Chr. 13:12 [1]*statute* *See WW at Ps. 136:1.
9 [a]Num. 31:6; Josh. 6:5; 2 Chr. 13:14 [b]Judg. 2:18; 4:3; 6:9; 10:8, 12 [c]Gen. 8:1; Ps. 106:4
10 [a]Lev. 23:24; Num. 29:1; 1 Chr. 15:24; 2 Chr. 5:12; Ps. 81:3 [b]Lev. 23:24; Num. 10:9 *See WW at Ex. 39:7.

KINGDOM DYNAMICS

10:1–10 Trumpets and Spiritual Warfare, FAITH'S WARFARE. The employing of trumpets has a unique relationship to the exercise of spiritual authority in prayer. Here two silver trumpets were sanctified for use by spiritual leadership in Israel. One was appointed for the calling forth of the assembly and the other for the mobilization of the camps when they were about to journey (v. 2). Thus, the first trumpet's use was primarily to gather the people together, while the second trumpet meant it was time to "move forward," usually in the sense of moving forward into battle. Regarding employment of the second trumpet, note especially the words of v. 9: "you shall sound an alarm with the trumpets . . . and you will be saved from your enemies."

The sounding of trumpets in victorious spiritual warfare is especially significant in God's final plan for the ages (Rev. 8—12). All of the culminating events of Rev. 12 result from the sounding of the seventh trumpet. Further, the sounding of the seven trumpets does not occur until the prayers of God's saints are released with much incense (symbolic of worship) before the throne of God (see Rev. 8:1–6), quite possibly indicating that the prayers of God's people release the final trumpet blasts that herald the coming and establishing of Christ's eternal kingdom on Earth. Hearing the clear sound of the trumpet alerts us to the Holy Spirit's call to battle (see 1 Cor. 14:8).

(Mark 11:20–24/Ps. 126:5, 6) D.E.

Departure from Sinai

11 Now it came to pass on the twentieth *day* of the second month, in the

10:1–10 The final element in the preparation for the journey—the signal trumpets—enabled the camp to be directed from the center for assemblies (vv. 3, 4) and for moving in and out of camp formation (vv. 5–8). When the Israelites were settled in their land, the trumpets would have a military function (v. 9) and a worship function (v. 10).

10:5–8 Only **the east** and **south** sides of the camp are mentioned, due to their preceding the tabernacle in the march according to the order of ch. 2.

10:11—36:13 This is the major turning point in the book, and one of the primary turning points of the entire Pentateuch. Israel now departs from Sinai and moves toward the Promised Land. These chapters are characterized by disobedience, murmuring, and rebellion on the part of the people as the unity of Mt. Sinai gives way to the strife of the journey. The problems culminate in the death of the entire first generation.

10:11–36 The departure from Sinai is told three times in this section in different ways: 1) a summary statement (vv. 10–13); 2) a detailed order of the march (vv. 4–28); 3) a statement of the general pattern for breaking camp.

10:11–13 Twentieth *day* . . . second year: The date is from the time of the Exodus. Since they entered into Sinai in the third month (Ex. 19:1), they were camped at Sinai about a year. After these verses the chronology is abandoned until 20:1, where an incomplete chronological reference is given. Later (33:38), Aaron's death is dated in the fortieth year from the Exodus. Otherwise, we know nothing of the chronological sequence of the events of the wilderness wanderings.

second year, that the cloud [a]was taken up from above the tabernacle of the Testimony.

12 And the children of Israel set out from the [a]Wilderness of Sinai on [b]their journeys; then the cloud **settled down** in the [c]Wilderness of Paran.

WORD WEALTH

10:12 settled down, *shachan* (shah-*chahn*); Strong's #7931: To dwell, abide, remain, stay, tabernacle. This verb occurs more than 120 times. People dwell in tents (Ps. 120:5) or in a certain land (Jer. 7:7); God dwells in Mt. Zion (Is. 8:18); glory dwells in the Holy Land (Ps. 85:9). *Mishkan,* "tabernacle," God's "place of dwelling," is derived from *shakan.* This term also refers to the tabernacle of Moses and to other dwelling places as well. *Mishkan* occurs more than 50 times in Ex. alone. Another derivative of *shakan* is *shekinah,* the "abiding presence of Almighty God." Sometimes the *shekinah* appears in a visible way. Not found in Scripture, *shekinah* comes to us from Judaic writings.

13 So they started out for the first time [a]according to the command of the LORD by the hand of Moses.

14 The [1]standard of the camp of the children of Judah [a]set out first according to their armies; over their army was [b]Nahshon the son of Amminadab.

15 Over the *army of the tribe of the children of Issachar *was* Nethanel the son of Zuar.

16 And over the army of the tribe of the children of Zebulun *was* Eliab the son of Helon.

17 Then [a]the tabernacle was taken down; and the sons of Gershon and the sons of Merari set out, [b]carrying the tabernacle.

18 And [a]the standard of the camp of Reuben set out according to their armies; over their army *was* Elizur the son of Shedeur.

19 Over the army of the tribe of the children of Simeon *was* Shelumiel the son of Zurishaddai.

20 And over the army of the tribe of the children of Gad *was* Eliasaph the son of Deuel.

21 Then the Kohathites set out, carrying the [a]holy things. (The tabernacle would be [1]prepared for their arrival.)

22 And [a]the standard of the camp of the children of Ephraim set out according to their armies; over their army *was* Elishama the son of Ammihud.

23 Over the army of the tribe of the children of Manasseh *was* Gamaliel the son of Pedahzur.

24 And over the army of the tribe of the children of Benjamin *was* Abidan the son of Gideoni.

25 Then [a]the standard of the camp of the children of Dan (the rear guard of all the camps) set out according to their armies; over their army *was* Ahiezer the son of Ammishaddai.

26 Over the army of the tribe of the children of Asher *was* Pagiel the son of Ocran.

27 And over the army of the tribe of the children of Naphtali *was* Ahira the son of Enan.

28 [a]Thus *was* the order of march of the children of Israel, according to their armies, when they began their journey.

29 Now Moses said to [a]Hobab the son of [b]Reuel[1] the Midianite, Moses' father-in-law, "We are setting out for the place of which the LORD said, [c]'I will give it to you.' Come with us, and [d]we will treat you well; for [e]the LORD has promised good things to Israel."

30 And he said to him, "I will not go, but I will depart to my *own* land and to my relatives."

31 So *Moses* said, "Please do not leave, inasmuch as you know how we are to camp in the wilderness, and you can [1]be our [a]eyes.

32 "And it shall be, if you go with us—indeed it shall be—that [a]whatever good the LORD will do to us, the same we will do to you."

33 So they departed from [a]the mountain of the LORD on a journey of three days; and the ark of the *covenant of the LORD [b]went before them for the three days' journey, to search out a *resting place for them.

11 [a]Num. 9:17
12 [a]Ex. 19:1; Num. 1:1; 9:5 [b]Ex. 40:36 [c]Gen. 21:21; Num. 12:16; Deut. 1:1
13 [a]Num. 10:5, 6
14 [a]Num. 2:3–9 [b]Num. 1:7 [1]*banner*
15 *See WW at Ps. 68:11.
17 [a]Num. 1:51 [b]Num. 4:21–32; 7:7–9
18 [a]Num. 2:10–16
21 [a]Num. 4:4–20; 7:9 [1]Prepared by the Gershonites and the Merarites
22 [a]Num. 2:18–24
25 [a]Num. 2:25–31; Josh. 6:9
28 [a]Num. 2:34
29 [a]Judg. 4:11 [b]Ex. 2:18; 3:1; 18:12 [c]Gen. 12:7; Ex. 6:4–8 [d]Judg. 1:16 [e]Gen. 32:12; Ex. 3:8 [1]*Jethro,* Ex. 3:1; LXX *Raguel*
31 [a]Job 29:15 [1]Act as our guide
32 [a]Ex. 18:9; Lev. 19:34; Judg. 1:16
33 [a]Ex. 3:1; Deut. 1:6 [b]Deut. 1:33; Josh. 3:3–6; Ezek. 20:6 *See WW at Gen. 17:7. • See WW at Is. 28:12.

The cloud was taken up in v. 11 is supplemented by **the command of the LORD by the hand of Moses** in v. 13. Showing the conformity of the human leader with the divine leading is the concern here and in 9:15–23.

Wilderness of Paran: A general reference to the area north of the traditional location of Sinai. It includes all of the locales until their entrance into the Wilderness of Zin at 20:1.

10:14–28 Beginning in v. 17 and continuing through v. 27, the Hebrew construction behind **set out** indicates what would typically happen; hence we may translate "would set out."

10:29–32 Hobab: See note on Judg. 4:11. **Be our eyes:** Hobab apparently knew the terrain and could provide a valuable service for the Israelites.

10:33–36 The ark accompanied by the cloud constituted the vanguard of the congregation. Apparently Hobab and a contingent would scout for a suitable campsite. The congregation would then await the lifting of the cloud and depart for the next destination. The role of the ark in war is also suggested here.

34 And [a]the cloud of the LORD *was*
above them by day when they went out
from the camp.
35 So it was, whenever the ark set out,
that Moses said:

[a]"Rise up, O LORD!
Let Your enemies be scattered,
And let those who hate You flee
before You."

36 And when it rested, he said:

"Return, O LORD,
To the many thousands of Israel."

The People Complain

5 **11** Now [a]*when* the people complained, it displeased the LORD;
[b]for the LORD heard *it,* and His *anger
was aroused. So the [c]fire of the LORD
burned among them, and consumed
some in the outskirts of the camp.
2 Then the people [a]cried out to Moses, and when Moses [b]prayed to the
LORD, the fire was [1]quenched.
3 So he called the name of the place
[1]Taberah, because the fire of the LORD
had burned among them.
4 Now the [a]mixed multitude who
were among them [1]yielded to [b]intense
craving; so the children of Israel also
wept again and said: [c]"Who will give
us meat to eat?
5 [a]"We remember the fish which we
ate freely in Egypt, the cucumbers, the
melons, the leeks, the onions, and the
garlic;
6 "but now [a]our whole being *is* dried
up; *there is* nothing at all except this
manna *before* our eyes!"
7 Now [a]the manna *was* like coriander
seed, and its color like the color of
bdellium.
8 The people went about and gathered *it,* ground *it* on millstones or beat
it in the mortar, cooked *it* in pans, and
made cakes of it; and [a]its taste was like
the taste of pastry prepared with oil.
9 And [a]when the dew fell on the camp
in the night, the manna fell on it.
10 Then Moses heard the people weeping throughout their families, everyone
at the door of his tent; and [a]the anger
of the LORD was greatly aroused; Moses also was displeased.
11 [a]So Moses said to the LORD, "Why
have You afflicted Your servant? And
why have I not found favor in Your
sight, that You have laid the [1]burden
of all these people on me?
12 "Did I conceive all these people?
Did I beget them, that You should say
to me, [a]'Carry them in your bosom, as
a [b]guardian carries a nursing child,' to
the land which You [c]swore[1] to their
fathers?
13 [a]"Where am I to get meat to give
to all these people? For they weep all
over me, saying, 'Give us meat, that we
may eat.'
14 [a]"I am not able to bear all these peo- 6
ple alone, because the burden *is* too
heavy for me.
15 "If You treat me like this, please kill
me here and now—if I have found favor in Your sight—and [a]do not let me
see my wretchedness!"

The Seventy Elders

16 So the LORD said to Moses: "Gather
to Me [a]seventy men of the elders of
Israel, whom you know to be the elders
of the people and [b]officers over them;

34 [a]Ex. 13:21; Neh. 9:12, 19
35 [a]Ps. 68:1, 2; 132:8; Is. 17:12–14

CHAPTER 11

1 [a]Num. 14:2; 16:11; 17:5; Deut. 9:22 [b]Ps. 78:21 [c]Lev. 10:2; 2 Kin. 1:12 *See WW at Judg. 10:7.
2 [a]Num. 12:11, 13; 21:7 [b][James 5:16] [1]*extinguished*
3 [1]Lit. *Burning*
4 [a]Ex. 12:38 [b]1 Cor. 10:6 [c][Ps. 78:18] [1]Lit. *lusted intensely*
5 [a]Ex. 16:3
6 [a]Num. 21:5
7 [a]Ex. 16:14, 31
8 [a]Ex. 16:31
9 [a]Ex. 16:13, 14
10 [a]Ps. 78:21
11 [a]Ex. 5:22; Deut. 1:12 [1]*responsibility*
12 [a]Is. 40:11 [b]Is. 49:23; 1 Thess. 2:7 [c]Gen. 26:3 [1]*solemnly promised*
13 [a]Matt. 15:33; Mark 8:4
14 [a]Ex. 18:18; Deut. 1:12
15 [a]Rev. 3:17
16 [a]Ex. 18:25; 24:1, 9 [b]Deut. 16:18

11:1–35 This chapter contains two accounts of campsites that were remembered for the punishment of the Lord on the people: **Taberah** (vv. 1–3) and **Kibroth Hattaavah** (vv. 4–35).

11:1 See section 5 of Truth-In-Action at the end of Num.

11:1 The complaint is generic. A hint at the issue may be contained in the reference that the punishment begins on the fringes of the camp rather than the center. If we assume that the people assigned to camp on the edges were complaining that they were exposed to greater dangers, the locale of the punishment makes sense. **The fire of the LORD** refers to God's manifested presence. See note on Lev. 10:1.

11:4–35 Two issues are interwoven in this account: 1) the complaint of the people about the lack of meat and 2) Moses' frustration with his responsibilities. Vv. 4–10 report the people's complaint; vv. 11–23 report a conversation between Yahweh and Moses in which Yahweh answers Moses' question about his leadership responsibilities as well as the lack of meat; vv. 24–34 report the implementation of the answers to the two problems.

11:4 Mixed multitude refers either to non-Israelites who joined themselves to the camp at the Exodus (Ex. 12:38) or to Israelite riffraff, those governed by sensual appetite. The origin of the problem lies with them, but it soon spreads. **Meat:** According to Ex. 16:13 quails originally accompanied the manna. Apparently the quails did not continue. It is also not clear why the people did not kill of their flocks and herds (Ex. 12:32, 38).

11:6 Our whole being: The relationship between physical and nonphysical aspects of humans is very close in Hebrew thought. Physical want generates emotional consequences.

11:7 Manna: See notes on Ex. 16:13–18, 31.

11:14–25 See section 6 of Truth-In-Action at the end of Num.

11:15 The bitterness of Moses' complaint is reminiscent of similar complaints among OT figures: Elijah (1 Kin. 19:4), Job (Job 3:20, 21), and Jonah (Jon. 4:3). It is important to note that they did not consider their deaths to be their own prerogative. In all instances, God was gracious not to grant their petitions.

11:16, 17 The **elders** are selected from those who are already functioning as leaders. The Spirit brings new

bring them to the tabernacle of meeting, that they may stand there with
you.
17 "Then I will come down and talk
with you there. [a]I will take of the Spirit
that *is* upon you and will put *the same*
upon them; and they shall bear the burden of the people with you, that you
may not bear *it* yourself alone.
18 "Then you shall say to the people,
[1]'Consecrate yourselves for tomorrow,
and you shall eat meat; for you have
wept [a]in the hearing of the LORD, saying, "Who will give us meat to eat? For
it was well with us in Egypt." Therefore the LORD will give you meat, and
you shall eat.
19 'You shall eat, not one day, nor two
days, nor five days, nor ten days, nor
twenty days,
20 [a]'but *for* a whole month, until it
comes out of your nostrils and becomes loathsome to you, because you
have [b]despised the LORD who is among
you, and have wept before Him, saying, [c]"Why did we ever come up out
of Egypt?" ' "
21 And Moses said, [a]"The people
whom I *am* among *are* six hundred
thousand men on foot; yet You have
said, 'I will give them meat, that they
may eat *for* a whole month.'
22 [a]"Shall flocks and herds be slaughtered for them, to provide enough for
them? Or shall all the fish of the sea
be gathered together for them, to provide enough for them?"
23 And the LORD said to Moses,
[a]"Has[1] the LORD's arm been shortened?
Now you shall see whether [b]what* I
say will happen to you or not."
24 So Moses went out and told the people the words of the LORD, and he
[a]gathered the seventy men of the elders of the people and placed them
around the tabernacle.
25 Then the LORD came down in the
cloud, and spoke to him, and took of
the Spirit that *was* upon him, and
placed *the same* upon the seventy el-

17 [a]1 Sam. 10:6; 2 Kin. 2:15; [Joel 2:28]
18 [a]Ex. 16:7 [1]*Set yourselves apart*
20 [a]Ps. 78:29; 106:15 [b]1 Sam. 10:19 [c]Num. 21:5
21 [a]Gen. 12:2; Ex. 12:37; Num. 1:46; 2:32
22 [a]2 Kin. 7:2
23 [a]Is. 50:2; 59:1 [b]Num. 23:19 [1]Is the LORD's power limited? *See WW at Deut. 1:1.
24 [a]Num. 11:16
25 [a]2 Kin. 2:15 [b]1 Sam. 10:5, 6, 10; Joel 2:28; Acts 2:17, 18; 1 Cor. 14:1 [1]Tg., Vg. *and they did not cease*
26 [a]Jer. 36:5
28 [a][Mark 9:38–40; Luke 9:49]
29 [a]1 Cor. 14:5 [1]*jealous*
31 [a]Ex. 16:13; Ps. 78:26–28; 105:40
32 [a]Ex. 16:36; Ezek. 45:11
33 [a]Ps. 78:29–31; 106:15
34 [1]Lit. *Graves of Craving*

ders; and it happened, [a]when the Spirit
rested upon them, that [b]they prophesied, [1]although they never did *so* again.
26 But two men had remained in the
camp: the name of one *was* Eldad, and
the name of the other Medad. And the
Spirit rested upon them. Now they
were among those listed, but who
[a]had not gone out to the tabernacle;
yet they prophesied in the camp.
27 And a young man ran and told Moses, and said, "Eldad and Medad are
prophesying in the camp."
28 So Joshua the son of Nun, Moses'
assistant, *one* of his choice men, answered and said, "Moses my lord,
[a]forbid them!"
29 Then Moses said to him, "Are you
[1]zealous for my sake? [a]Oh, that all the
LORD's people were prophets *and* that
the LORD would put His Spirit upon
them!"
30 And Moses returned to the camp,
both he and the elders of Israel.

The LORD Sends Quail

31 Now a [a]wind went out from the
LORD, and it brought quail from the sea
and left *them* fluttering near the camp,
about a day's journey on this side and
about a day's journey on the other side,
all around the camp, and about two cubits above the surface of the ground.
32 And the people stayed up all that
day, all night, and all the next day, and
gathered the quail (he who gathered
least gathered ten [a]homers); and they
spread *them* out for themselves all
around the camp.
33 But while the [a]meat *was* still between their teeth, before it was
chewed, the wrath of the LORD was
aroused against the people, and the
LORD struck the people with a very
great plague.
34 So he called the name of that place
[1]Kibroth Hattaavah, because there
they buried the people who had yielded
to craving.

authority for the exercise of their leadership. The passing of the Spirit from Moses to the 70 elders is an ordination for an official function, not the bestowal of a charisma.

11:25 They prophesied: This is an unexpected consequence. It is unrelated to the leadership function of the 70 elders, for it *was a onetime phenomenon*. The prophesying may have been manifested either as a Spirit-induced ecstasy or as an utterance, as in the case of Saul's prophesying in 1 Sam. 10. On that occasion Saul was anointed king and the prophesying was a sign (1 Sam. 10:9, 10) which yielded no message or utterance. So here in ch. 11 the prophesying appears to be a sign of the ordination of the 70 elders.

11:29 Joshua apparently wants to control. Though Eldad and Medad were legitimate elders, they were not present at the tabernacle. The Spirit is not confined to particular persons, but is free to rest upon whom He wills. This met with the approval of Moses, who desired a democratization of the Spirit and envisioned a nation of prophets (see Joel 2:28–32).

11:32 Ten homers was approximately 2,000 liters.

11:34 Kibroth Hattaavah means "Graves of Craving." Hattaavah refers to the introduction of the account in v. 4.

35 [a]From Kibroth Hattaavah the people moved to Hazeroth, and camped at
Hazeroth.

Dissension of Aaron and Miriam

7 12 Then [a]Miriam and Aaron
[1]spoke [b]against Moses because
of the [2]Ethiopian woman whom he had
married; for [c]he had married an Ethiopian woman.
2 So they said, "Has the LORD indeed
spoken only through [a]Moses? [b]Has He
not spoken through us also?" And the
LORD [c]heard *it*.
3 (Now the man Moses *was* very
humble, more than all men who *were*
on the face of the earth.)
4 [a]Suddenly the LORD said to Moses,
Aaron, and Miriam, "Come out, you
three, to the tabernacle of meeting!" So
the three came out.
5 [a]Then the LORD came down in the
pillar of cloud and stood *in* the door
of the tabernacle, and called Aaron and
Miriam. And they both went forward.
6 Then He said,

"Hear now My words:
If there is a prophet among you,
I, the LORD, make Myself known
to him [a]in a vision;
I speak to him [b]in a *dream.
7 Not so with [a]My servant Moses;
[b]He *is* faithful in all [c]My house.
8 I speak with him [a]face to face,
Even [b]plainly,[1] and not in
[2]dark sayings;
And he sees [c]the form of the
LORD.
Why then [d]were you not afraid
To speak against My servant
Moses?"

35 [a]Num. 33:17

CHAPTER 12

1 [a]Num. 20:1 [b]Num. 11:1 [c]Ex. 2:21 [1]*criticized* [2]*Cushite*
2 [a]Num. 16:3 [b]Mic. 6:4 [c]Ezek. 35:12, 13
4 [a][Ps. 76:9]
5 [a]Ex. 19:9; 34:5
6 [a]Gen. 46:2 [b]Gen. 31:10 *See WW at Joel 2:28.
7 [a]Josh. 1:1 [b]Heb. 3:2, 5 [c]1 Tim. 1:12
8 [a]Deut. 34:10 [b][1 Cor. 13:12] [c]Ex. 33:19–23 [d]2 Pet. 2:10 [1]*appearing* [2]*riddles*
10 [a]Deut. 24:9 [b]2 Kin. 5:27; 15:5
11 [a]2 Sam. 19:19; 24:10 [1]*the penalty for this*
12 [a]Ps. 88:4
13 [a]Ps. 103:3
14 [a]Deut. 25:9 [b]Lev. 13:46 [1]*exiled*
15 [a]Deut. 24:9
16 [a]Num. 11:35; 33:17, 18

9 So the anger of the LORD was
aroused against them, and He departed.
10 And when the cloud departed from
above the tabernacle, [a]suddenly Miriam *became* [b]leprous, as *white as*
snow. Then Aaron turned toward
Miriam, and there she was, a leper.
11 So Aaron said to Moses, "Oh, my
lord! Please [a]do not lay [1]*this* sin on us,
in which we have done foolishly and
in which we have sinned.
12 "Please [a]do not let her be as one
dead, whose flesh is half consumed
when he comes out of his mother's
womb!"
13 So Moses cried out to the LORD, saying, "Please [a]heal her, O God, I pray!"
14 Then the LORD said to Moses, "If her
father had but [a]spit in her face, would
she not be shamed seven days? Let her
be [b]shut[1] out of the camp seven days,
and afterward she may be received
again."
15 [a]So Miriam was shut out of the
camp seven days, and the people did
not journey till Miriam was brought in
again.
16 And afterward the people moved
from [a]Hazeroth and camped in the
Wilderness of Paran.

KINGDOM DYNAMICS

12:1–16 Healing Repentance and Humility, DIVINE HEALING. This passage relates how Moses' sister, Miriam, was healed of leprosy. She received physical healing through the intercession of Moses. However, her healing was delayed seven days because of her sin in defying the God-given leadership of Moses.

(cont. on next page)

11:35 Hazeroth is somewhere north of Mt. Sinai (v. 10), but south of the Wilderness of Paran (12:16).

12:1–16 The theme of prophetic authority is continued from ch. 11 with the rebellion of **Miriam and Aaron.** The issue is the marriage of **Moses** to a non-Israelite, leading Miriam and Aaron to challenge the legitimacy of Moses as the mouthpiece of the Lord (vv. 1–3). The Lord asserts that the status of Moses is above even the prophets (vv. 4–8), and Miriam is stricken with leprosy and subsequently healed (vv. 9–15). Moses' special status above other prophetic figures is emphasized. The Mosaic Law, then, is above critique from the prophets. So also today the Scriptures have a primacy over the prophetic gifts of the Spirit.

12:1, 2 See section 7 of Truth-In-Action at the end of Num.

12:1 Ethiopian woman: If the Hebrew word for Cushite, translated here as Ethiopian, refers to the country south of Egypt, then it would be a second wife of Moses, not Zipporah the daughter of the Midianite Jethro mentioned in Ex. 2:16–21. Cush may be a short form of Cushan, however, a word used as a synonym for Midian in Hab. 3:7, and thus would then refer to Zipporah the Midianite, Moses' wife.

12:2 The intent of this verse is to legitimize Miriam and Aaron's right to criticize Moses as they did in v. l. (For Miriam as a prophetess, see Ex. 15:20; for Aaron as one through whom Yahweh speaks, see Ex. 4, where he speaks to Pharaoh for Moses.)

12:4–8 Yahweh's revelation to Moses is unique. It is direct (**plainly**) and immediate (**face to face**); the prophets' revelations are in mediated forms. The clear lesson is that even prophets cannot presume to claim that their message is equal to that of Moses.

12:9–15 The punishment of leprosy affects only Miriam, but it is important to note that Aaron is the one to confess the sin of both of them (v. 11).

12:14 Seven days: This is the length of elapsed time prescribed for the priest's first and second inspections of leprosy in Lev. 13. The implication is that she was healed in response to Moses' prayer and would be pronounced clean after seven days. For spitting in the face as a sign of contempt, see Deut. 25:9.

12:16 The Wilderness of Paran is immediately to the south of Judah's tribal claim, hence the stories of chs. 13 and 14 take place while preparing for an invasion of the Promised Land from the south.

(cont. from preceding page)

Is it possible that delays in receiving answers to our prayer may sometimes be the result of a sinful attitude? Is there instruction in the fact that the progress of the whole camp was delayed until Miriam was restored? Repentance and humility will not earn healing, but they may—as with Miriam—clear the way for God's grace to be revealed more fully (see 1 Cor. 12:20–27).

(Ex. 15:26/Num. 21:5–9) N.V.

Spies Sent into Canaan

13 And the LORD spoke to Moses,
saying,

KINGDOM DYNAMICS

13:1—14:45; Josh. 6:1–27; 10:1–43 Resisting Popular Opinion, LEADER TRAITS. Joshua was continually faced with choices, and most of his decisions went against popular opinion. Yet in each instance he called on the people to increase their faith in God's promises rather than look at the impossible circumstances. The leader does not condition his appeal to the sentiment or mood of the times. Spiritual advance requires faith, and unbelief will never see beyond the difficulties. Unbelief sees "walled cities and giants" rather than the presence and power of God. Unbelief looks at obstacles; faith looks at God. Joshua and Caleb were willing to do the unpopular thing and call the people to positive faith. They led the way into the future by confronting a negative report and helping a new generation rise to serve God in faith.

(Judg. 8:22, 23; 9:1–57/Acts 13:1–3) J.B.

2 [a]"Send men to spy out the land of
Canaan, which I am giving to the children of Israel; from each tribe of their
fathers you shall send a man, every one
a leader among them."
3 So Moses sent them [a]from the Wilderness of Paran according to the command of the LORD, all of them men who
were heads of the children of Israel.
4 Now these *were* their names: from
the tribe of Reuben, Shammua the son
of Zaccur;
5 from the tribe of Simeon, Shaphat
the son of Hori;
6 [a]from the tribe of Judah, [b]Caleb the
son of Jephunneh;
7 from the tribe of Issachar, Igal the
son of Joseph;
8 from the tribe of Ephraim, [1]Hoshea
the son of Nun;
9 from the tribe of Benjamin, Palti the
son of Raphu;
10 from the tribe of Zebulun, Gaddiel
the son of Sodi;
11 from the tribe of Joseph, *that is,*
from the tribe of Manasseh, Gaddi the
son of Susi;
12 from the tribe of Dan, Ammiel the
son of Gemalli;
13 from the tribe of Asher, Sethur the
son of Michael;
14 from the tribe of Naphtali, Nahbi
the son of Vophsi;
15 from the tribe of Gad, Geuel the son
of Machi.
16 These *are* the names of the men
whom Moses sent to [1]spy out the land.
And Moses called [a]Hoshea[2] the son of
Nun, Joshua.
17 Then Moses sent them to spy out
the land of Canaan, and said to them,
"Go up this *way* into the South, and
go up to [a]the mountains,
18 "and see what the land is like:
whether the people who dwell in it *are*
strong or weak, few or many;
19 "whether the land they dwell in *is*
good or bad; whether the cities they
inhabit *are* like camps or strongholds;
20 "whether the land *is* [1]rich or poor;
and whether there are forests there or
not. [a]Be* of good courage. And bring
some of the fruit of the land." Now the
time *was* the season of the first ripe
grapes.
21 So they went up and spied out the
land [a]from the Wilderness of Zin as
far as [b]Rehob, near the entrance of
[c]Hamath.
22 And they went up through the
South and came to [a]Hebron; Ahiman,
Sheshai, and Talmai, the descendants
of [b]Anak, *were* there. (Now Hebron
was built seven years before Zoan in
Egypt.)

CHAPTER 13

2 [a]Num. 32:8; Deut. 1:22; 9:23
3 [a]Num. 12:16; 32:8; Deut. 1:19; 9:23
6 [a]Num. 34:19 [b]Num. 14:6, 30; Josh. 14:6, 7; Judg. 1:12; 1 Chr. 4:15
8 [1]LXX, Vg. *Oshea*
16 [a]Ex. 17:9; Deut. 32:44 [1]*secretly search* [2]LXX, Vg. *Oshea*
17 [a]Judg. 1:9
20 [a]Deut. 31:6, 7, 23 [1]*fertile or barren* *See WW at Josh. 1:9.
21 [a]Num. 20:1; 27:14; 33:36; Josh. 15:1 [b]Josh. 19:28 [c]Num. 34:8; Josh. 13:5
22 [a]Josh. 15:13, 14; Judg. 1:10 [b]Josh. 11:21, 22

13:3 Wilderness of Paran: Kadesh Barnea is the campsite according to Deut. 1:19 (see also Num. 13:26). According to 20:1, Kadesh Barnea is located in the Wilderness of Zin. The apparent reason for locating Kadesh in both wildernesses is that the borders of wilderness areas are not distinct. Since Kadesh apparently lay on the fringe of both areas, it could be referred to as belonging to either. **Heads of the children of Israel** shows why the report of the 10 carried such weight. They were key leaders.

13:16 Hoshea . . . Joshua: The original name means "Salvation." Moses changes it to "Yahweh (the Lord) Is Salvation."

13:21 From Josh. 13:5 we can deduce that the **entrance of Hamath** was in the north of Israel toward Lebanon; apparently the spies traversed all of what later became Israel.

13:22 Hebron is mentioned here probably because it became Caleb's inheritance (see Josh. 14:6–15).

23 [a]Then they came to the [1]Valley of
Eshcol, and there cut down a branch
with one cluster of grapes; they carried
it between two of them on a pole. *They*
also *brought* some of the pomegranates and figs.
24 The place was called the Valley of
[1]Eshcol, because of the cluster which
the men of Israel cut down there.
25 And they returned from spying out
the land after forty days.
26 Now they departed and came back
to Moses and Aaron and all the congregation of the children of Israel in the
Wilderness of Paran, at [a]Kadesh; they
brought back word to them and to all
the congregation, and showed them
the fruit of the land.
27 Then they told him, and said: "We
went to the land where you sent us. It
truly [1]flows with [a]milk and honey,
[b]and this *is* its fruit.
28 "Nevertheless the [a]people who
dwell in the land *are* strong; the cities
are fortified *and* very large; moreover
we saw the descendants of [b]Anak
there.
29 [a]"The Amalekites dwell in the land
of the South; the Hittites, the Jebusites,
and the Amorites dwell in the mountains; and the Canaanites dwell by the
sea and along the banks of the Jordan."
30 Then [a]Caleb quieted the people before Moses, and said, "Let us go up at
once and take *possession, for we are
well **able** to overcome it."

WORD WEALTH

13:30 able, *yakol* (yah-*kole*); Strong's #3201: To be able, to have power; having the capacity to prevail or succeed. This verb is used 200 times in the OT. Generally it is translated by such English words as "can," "could," or "be able"; in a few references, "prevail" (1 Kin. 22:22; Esth. 6:13); sometimes, "to have power." In Esth. 8:6, it is translated as "endure"; the compassionate queen asks, "How can I endure to see the evil that will come to my people?" Here in Num. 13, Caleb uses the intensive repetition of *yakol:* "Let us go up ... for we are well able to overcome it."

KINGDOM DYNAMICS

13:30; 14:6–9 Faith When Facing Delays, FAITH'S CONFESSION. Caleb saw the same giants and walled city as the other spies, but the 10 spies brought back an "evil report" of unbelief. Caleb's words declared a conviction—a "confession"—before all Israel: "We are well able to overcome." He had surveyed the land, a reminder that faith is not blind. Faith does not deny the reality of difficulty; it declares the power of God in the face of the problem.

There is a message in the spirit of Caleb's response to the rejection of his faith-filled report. Some use their confession of faith to cultivate schism, but Caleb stood his ground in faith and still moved in partnership and support—for 40 years—beside many whose unbelief delayed his own experience. What patience as well as faith! His eventual actual possession of the land at a later date indicates that even though delays come, faith's confession will ultimately bring victory to the believer.

(Gen. 17:5/Josh. 6:10) R.H.

31 [a]But the men who had gone up with
him said, "We are not able to go up
against the people, for they *are* stronger than we."
32 And they [a]gave the children of Israel a bad report of the land which they
had spied out, saying, "The land
through which we have gone as spies
is a land that devours its inhabitants,
and [b]all the people whom we saw in
it *are* men of *great* stature.
33 "There we saw the [1]giants ([a]the descendants of Anak came from the
giants); and we were [b]like[2] grasshoppers in our own sight, and so we
were [c]in their sight."

Israel Refuses to Enter Canaan

14 So all the congregation lifted up
their voices and cried, and the
people [a]wept that night.

23 [a]Gen. 14:13; Num. 13:24; 32:9; Deut. 1:24, 25 [1]*Wadi*
24 [1]Lit. *Cluster*
26 [a]Num. 20:1, 16; 32:8; 33:36; Deut. 1:19; Josh. 14:6
27 [a]Ex. 3:8, 17; 13:5; 33:3 [b]Deut. 1:25 [1]Has an abundance of food
28 [a]Deut. 1:28; 9:1, 2 [b]Josh. 11:21, 22
29 [a]Ex. 17:8; Judg. 6:3
30 [a]Num. 14:6, 24
*See WW at Deut. 8:1.
31 [a]Num. 32:9; Deut. 1:28; 9:1–3; Josh. 14:8
32 [a]Num. 14:36, 37; Ps. 106:24 [b]Amos 2:9
33 [a]Deut. 1:28; 9:2; Josh. 11:21 [b]Is. 40:22 [c]1 Sam. 17:42 [1]Heb. *nephilim* [2]As mere insects

CHAPTER 14

1 [a]Num. 11:4; Deut. 1:45

13:26–33 The positive report (v. 30) is framed by negative reports (vv. 27–29, 31–33). Caleb alone is mentioned. Joshua does not speak until 14:6. Likewise, when Yahweh commends the two spies, Caleb is mentioned alone in 14:24 and then together with Joshua in 14:30.
13:28 Anak: See note on Josh. 11:21.
13:32 The **bad report** was a faithless one that defamed Yahweh's delivering abilities.
13:33 The Hebrew word for **giants** is the same used in Gen. 6:4 (see note). In that they were probably destroyed in the Flood, Anak's ancestral reference is not given.
14:1–45 This chapter narrates the people's two reactions to the spies' report narrated in ch. 13: return to Egypt (vv. 1–5) and kill the two spies who had faith (vv. 6–10). These were saved by divine intervention and the people sentenced to death instead (vv. 10–38). The people then attempt to invade the Promised Land against Yahweh's command (vv. 39–45).

2 [a]And all the children of Israel complained against Moses and Aaron, and the whole congregation said to them, "If only we had died in the land of Egypt! Or if only we had died in this wilderness!
3 "Why has the LORD brought us to this land to [1]fall by the sword, that our wives and [a]children should become victims? Would it not be better for us to return to Egypt?"
4 So they said to one another, [a]"Let us select a leader and [b]return to Egypt."
5 Then Moses and Aaron [1]fell on their faces before all the *assembly of the congregation of the children of Israel.
2 6 But Joshua the son of Nun and Caleb the son of Jephunneh, *who were* among those who had spied out the land, tore their clothes;
7 and they spoke to all the congregation of the children of Israel, saying: [a]"The land we *passed through to spy out *is* an exceedingly good land.
8 "If the LORD [a]delights in us, then He will bring us into this land and give it to us, [b]'a land which flows with milk and honey.'
9 "Only [a]do not rebel against the LORD, [b]nor fear the people of the land, for [c]they[1] *are* our bread; their protection has departed from them, [d]and the LORD *is* with us. Do not fear them."
10 [a]And all the congregation said to stone them with stones. Now [b]the glory of the LORD appeared in the tabernacle of meeting before all the children of Israel.

Moses Intercedes for the People

11 Then the LORD said to Moses: "How long will these people [a]reject[1] Me? And how long will they not [b]believe Me, with all the [2]signs which I have performed among them?
12 "I will strike them with the pestilence and disinherit them, and I will [a]make of you a nation greater and mightier than they."

2 [a]Ex. 16:2; 17:3
3 [a]Deut. 1:39 [1]*be killed in battle*
4 [a]Neh. 9:17 [b]Acts 7:39
5 [1]*prostrated themselves* *See WW at Lev. 16:17.
7 [a]Num. 13:27 *See WW at Josh. 3:4.
8 [a]Deut. 10:15 [b]Num. 13:27
9 [a]Deut. 1:26; 9:7, 23, 24 [b]Deut. 7:18 [c]Num. 24:8 [d]Deut. 20:1, 3, 4; 31:6–8 [1]They shall be as food for our consumption.
10 [a]Ex. 17:4 [b]Ex. 16:10
11 [a]Heb. 3:8 [b]Deut. 9:23 [1]*despise* [2]*miraculous signs*
12 [a]Ex. 32:10

13 [a]Ps. 106:23 [b]Ex. 32:12
14 [a]Deut. 2:25
16 [a]Deut. 9:28
18 [a]Ex. 34:6, 7 [b]Ex. 20:5
19 [a]Ex. 32:32; 34:9 [b]Ps. 51:1; 106:45 [c]Ps. 78:38 *See WW at Ps. 103:3.

13 And [a]Moses said to the LORD: [b]"Then the Egyptians will hear *it*, for by Your might You brought these people up from among them,
14 "and they will tell *it* to the inhabitants of this land. They have [a]heard that You, LORD, *are* among these people; that You, LORD, are seen face to face and Your cloud stands above them, and You go before them in a pillar of cloud by day and in a pillar of fire by night.
15 "Now *if* You kill these people as one man, then the nations which have heard of Your fame will speak, saying,
16 'Because the LORD was not [a]able to bring this people to the land which He swore to give them, therefore He killed them in the wilderness.'
17 "And now, I pray, let the power of my Lord be great, just as You have spoken, saying,
18 [a]'The LORD is longsuffering and abundant in mercy, forgiving iniquity and transgression; but He by no means **clears** *the guilty*, [b]visiting the iniquity of the fathers on the children to the third and fourth *generation*.'

WORD WEALTH

14:18 clears, *naqah* (nah-*kah*); Strong's #5352: To clear, acquit, cleanse, make clean; to make blameless; to free, exempt; also, to empty by pouring out the contents of something. This verb may have originally meant to "empty out a cup," then developed the meaning of "emptying any charges" against one, thus leaving him clean and clear. Most of the 40 references to *naqah* have the suggestion of clearing or declaring one innocent. The adjective *naqi* means "innocent, blameless, and guiltless." *Naqi* occurs 42 times and refers to innocent people, innocent blood, and to those who are exempt from an oath.

19 [a]"Pardon* the iniquity of this people, I pray, [b]according to the greatness of Your mercy, just [c]as You have for-

14:2 Life and death as slaves in Egypt were preferable to the death in the wilderness, according to the people's complaint (Ex. 14:11; 16:3; 17:3). Now death in the wilderness seems better than death in the Promised Land.
14:5 Fell on their faces: Either a sign of despair on the part of Moses and Aaron or of intercession.
14:6 Tore their clothes: A response of grief.
14:6–9 See section 2 of Truth-In-Action at the end of Num.
14:9 They *are* our bread: Probably a retort to the spies who had said the land eats its inhabitants in 13:32. **Their protection:** Literally, "their shadow," a pictorial reference to the inhabitants' idols, which would shade them from the destructive sun.
14:10 The congregation's decision to execute Joshua and Caleb is not carried out due to Yahweh's intervention. Instead, the other 10 spies are executed by Yahweh, and Joshua and Caleb live (vv. 36–38).
14:11–25 Moses again intercedes for the people (see Ex. 32:12–14). In v. 18, Moses cites Yahweh's own words from Ex. 34:6, 7. The issue of the Lord's mercy and the Lord's punishment of sin is raised. Both aspects of Yahweh's character are affirmed, in that Yahweh is merciful to Israel since He did not disinherit the nation, but the people who sinned must pay the consequences (vv. 22–24).

given this people, from Egypt even until now."
20 Then the LORD said: "I have pardoned, [a]according to your word;
21 "but truly, as I live, [a]all the *earth
shall be filled with the glory of the
LORD—
22 [a]"because all these men who have
seen My glory and the signs which I
did in Egypt and in the wilderness, and
*have put Me to the test now [b]these
ten times, and have not heeded My
voice,
23 "they certainly shall not [a]see the
land of which I [1]swore to their fathers,
nor shall any of those who rejected Me
see it.
2 24 "But My servant [a]Caleb, because he
has a different spirit in him and
[b]has followed Me fully, I will bring into
the land where he went, and his descendants shall inherit it.
25 "Now the Amalekites and the Canaanites dwell in the valley; tomorrow
turn and [a]move out into the wilderness
by the Way of the Red Sea."

Death Sentence on the Rebels

26 And the LORD spoke to Moses and
Aaron, saying,
27 [a]"How long *shall I bear with* this
evil congregation who complain
against Me? [b]I have heard the complaints which the children of Israel
make against Me.
28 "Say to them, [a]'As I live,' says the
LORD, 'just as you have spoken in My
hearing, so I will do to you:
29 'The carcasses of you who have
complained against Me shall fall in this
wilderness, [a]all of you who were numbered, according to your entire number, from twenty years old and above.
2 30 [a]'Except for Caleb the son of Jephunneh and Joshua the son of Nun,
you shall by no means enter the land

20 [a]Mic. 7:18–20
21 [a]Ps. 72:19 *See WW at Ex. 32:13.
22 [a]Deut. 1:35 [b]Gen. 31:7 *See WW at Ps. 78:41.
23 [a]Num. 26:65; 32:11 [1]*solemnly promised*
24 [a]Josh. 14:6, 8, 9 [b]Num. 32:12
25 [a]Deut. 1:40
27 [a]Ex. 16:28 [b]Ex. 16:12
28 [a]Heb. 3:16–19
29 [a]Num. 1:45, 46; 26:64
30 [a]Deut. 1:36–38 [1]*solemnly promised*
31 [a]Deut. 1:39 [b]Ps. 106:24 [1]*be acquainted with*
32 [a]Num. 26:64, 65; 32:13 [1]You shall die.
33 [a]Ps. 107:40 [b]Deut. 2:14 [c]Ezek. 23:35 [1]Vg. *wanderers*
34 [a]Num. 13:25 [b]Ezek. 4:6 [c][Heb. 4:1] [1]*iniquity* [2]*opposition* *See WW at Ps. 130:3.
35 [a]Num. 23:19 [b]1 Cor. 10:5
37 [a][1 Cor. 10:10]
38 [a]Josh. 14:6, 10
39 [a]Ex. 33:4
40 [a]Deut. 1:41–44

which I [1]swore I would make you dwell
in.
31 [a]'But your little ones, whom you
said would be victims, I will bring in,
and they shall [1]know the land which
[b]you have despised.
32 'But *as for* you, [a]your[1] carcasses
shall fall in this wilderness.
33 'And your sons shall [a]be [1]shepherds
in the wilderness [b]forty years, and
[c]bear the brunt of your infidelity, until
your carcasses are consumed in the
wilderness.
34 [a]'According to the number of the
days in which you spied out the land,
[b]forty days, for each day you shall bear
your [1]guilt* one year, *namely* forty
years, [c]and you shall know My [2]re-
jection.
35 [a]'I the LORD have spoken this. I will
surely do so to all [b]this evil congregation who are gathered together against
Me. In this wilderness they shall be
consumed, and there they shall die.'"
36 Now the men whom Moses sent to
spy out the land, who returned and
made all the congregation complain
against him by bringing a bad report
of the land,
37 those very men who brought the
evil report about the land, [a]died by the
plague before the LORD.
38 [a]But Joshua the son of Nun and Caleb the son of Jephunneh remained
alive, of the men who went to spy out
the land.

A Futile Invasion Attempt

39 Then Moses told these words to all
the children of Israel, [a]and the people
mourned greatly.
40 And they rose early in the morning
and went up to the top of the mountain,
saying, [a]"Here we are, and we will go
up to the place which the LORD has
promised, for we have sinned!"

14:20 According to your word shows the power of intercessory prayer based on a firm confidence in God's word.

14:22 These ten times: Ten is apparently not literal, but means "often" or "lots of times."

14:24 See section 2 of Truth-In-Action at the end of Num.

14:24 Different spirit in him: A reference to Caleb's spirit or attitude, not to the Holy Spirit.

14:25 The Way of the Red Sea: The east finger of the Red Sea is apparently their destination, namely toward the Gulf of Aqabah. Their direction of travel is reversed, from north to south.

14:26–38 The overlap of this material with that of vv. 11–25 is obvious. The difference is that vv. 11–25 are addressed to Moses; in these verses, however, Moses and Aaron receive a command to address the Israelites informing them of Yahweh's decision (vv. 26–35).

14:30 See section 2 of Truth-In-Action at the end of Num.

14:30 See note on 13:26–33.

14:33 Shepherds speaks of the nomadic life-style they would have to assume since they would not be able to raise crops or herds in the Promised Land as they had hoped.

14:36–38 The first of the faithless generation to perish are the 10 unbelieving spies who die by **the plague** before the Lord, a special punishment for rebellion during this wilderness time (Ex. 32:35; Num. 11:33).

14:39–45 When Moses complies with the command of the Lord in vv. 26–35, the people attempt the task in disobedience of the Lord's command and without His presence. They are defeated and driven back to **Hormah** (v. 45). The place is unknown today.

41 And Moses said, "Now why do you
[1]transgress the command of the LORD?
For this will not succeed.
42 [a]"Do not go up, lest you be defeated
by your enemies, for the LORD *is* not
among you.
43 "For the Amalekites and the Canaanites *are* there before you, and you
shall fall by the sword; [a]because you
have turned away from the LORD, the
LORD will not be with you."
44 [a]But they presumed to go up to the
mountaintop. Nevertheless, neither the
ark of the covenant of the LORD nor
Moses departed from the camp.
45 Then the Amalekites and the Canaanites who dwelt in that mountain
came down and attacked them, and
drove them back as far as [a]Hormah.

Laws of Grain and Drink Offerings

15 And the LORD spoke to Moses,
saying,
2 [a]"Speak to the children of Israel,
and say to them: 'When you have come
into the land you are to inhabit, which
I am giving to you,
3 'and you [a]make an offering by fire
to the LORD, a burnt offering or a sacrifice, [b]to fulfill a vow or as a freewill
offering or [c]in your appointed feasts,
to make a [d]sweet[1] aroma to the LORD,
from the herd or the flock,
4 'then [a]he who presents his offering
to the LORD shall bring [b]a grain offering of one-tenth *of an ephah* of fine
flour mixed [c]with one-fourth of a hin
of oil;
5 [a]'and one-fourth of a hin of wine
as a drink offering you shall prepare
with the burnt offering or the sacrifice,
for each [b]lamb.
6 [a]'Or for a ram you shall prepare as
a grain offering two-tenths *of an ephah*
of fine flour mixed with one-third of a
hin of oil;
7 'and as a drink offering you shall
offer one-third of a hin of wine as a
sweet aroma to the LORD.

41 [1]*overstep*
42 [a]Deut. 1:42; 31:17
43 [a]2 Chr. 15:2
44 [a]Deut. 1:43
45 [a]Num. 21:3

CHAPTER 15

2 [a]Lev. 23:10; Num. 15:18; Deut. 7:1
3 [a]Lev. 1:2, 3 [b]Lev. 7:16; 22:18, 21 [c]Lev. 23:2, 8, 12, 38; Num. 28:18, 19, 27; Deut. 16:10 [d]Gen. 8:21; Ex. 29:18; Lev. 1:9 [1]*pleasing*
4 [a]Lev. 2:1; 6:14 [b]Ex. 29:40; Lev. 23:13 [c]Lev. 14:10; Num. 28:5
5 [a]Num. 28:7, 14 [b]Lev. 1:10; 3:6; Num. 15:11; 28:4, 5
6 [a]Num. 28:12, 14
8 [a]Lev. 7:11
9 [a]Num. 28:12, 14
11 [a]Num. 28
14 [1]As a resident alien
15 [a]Ex. 12:49; Num. 9:14; 15:29 [1]*statute*
18 [a]Num. 15:2; Deut. 26:1
19 [a]Josh. 5:11, 12
20 [a]Ex. 34:26; Lev. 23:10, 14, 17; Deut. 26:2, 10; Prov. 3:9, 10 [b]Lev. 2:14; 23:10, 16

8 'And when you prepare a young
bull as a burnt offering, or as a sacrifice to fulfill a vow, or as a [a]peace offering to the LORD,
9 'then shall be offered [a]with the
young bull a grain offering of three-
tenths *of an ephah* of fine flour mixed
with half a hin of oil;
10 'and you shall bring as the drink offering half a hin of wine as an offering
made by fire, a sweet aroma to the
LORD.
11 [a]'Thus it shall be done for each
young bull, for each ram, or for each
lamb or young goat.
12 'According to the number that you
prepare, so you shall do with everyone
according to their number.
13 'All who are native-born shall do
these things in this manner, in
presenting an offering made by fire, a
sweet aroma to the LORD.
14 'And if a stranger [1]dwells with you,
or whoever *is* among you throughout
your generations, and would present
an offering made by fire, a sweet
aroma to the LORD, just as you do, so
shall he do.
15 [a]'One [1]ordinance *shall be* for you
of the assembly and for the stranger
who dwells *with you,* an ordinance forever throughout your generations; as
you are, so shall the stranger be before
the LORD.
16 'One law and one custom shall be
for you and for the stranger who dwells
with you.' "
17 Again the LORD spoke to Moses,
saying,
18 [a]"Speak to the children of Israel,
and say to them: 'When you come into
the land to which I bring you,
19 'then it will be, when you eat of
[a]the bread of the land, that you shall
offer up a heave offering to the LORD.
20 [a]'You shall offer up a cake of the
first of your ground meal *as* a heave
offering; as [b]a heave offering of the
threshing floor, so shall you offer it up.
21 'Of the first of your ground meal

15:1–41 The instructions and events narrated from here to 20:1 take place in unspecified settings. Following the death sentence of ch. 14, however, they inject a note of hope that Yahweh is still preparing His people for life in the Promised Land. The chapter includes: 1) instructions concerning offerings to accompany sacrifices (vv. 1–16); 2) instructions for a heave offering from the threshing floor (vv. 17–21); 3) instructions for intentional and unintentional sin (vv. 22–31); 4) the story of a Sabbath violation (vv. 32–36); 5) instructions for tassels for remembrance (vv. 37–41).

15:1–16 The kind of sacrifice under discussion here is an **offering by fire** (v. 3). This category includes the **burnt offering,** where the whole animal is burned (see note on Lev. 1:3, 4), and the **sacrifice** where only part of the animal is burned. The occasions for such a fire offering to Yahweh include fulfillment of a vow, a voluntary offering, or a festival offering. These must be accompanied by a **grain offering** (see note on Lev. 2:2–16) and **drink offering.**

15:4 ***An ephah*** was about 22 liters. **One-fourth of a hin** was about 3 pints (1.8 liters).

15:8 Peace offering: See note on Lev. 3:1.

15:17–21 This offering claims the first bread made from the grain of the threshing floor for the Lord.

15:21 A heave offering is a type of peace offering. See note on Lev. 3:1.

you shall give to the LORD a heave offering throughout your generations.

Laws Concerning Unintentional Sin

22 [a]'If you sin unintentionally, and do
not observe all these *commandments
which the LORD has spoken to Moses—
23 'all that the LORD has commanded
you by the hand of Moses, from the
day the LORD gave commandment and
onward throughout your generations—
24 'then it will be, [a]if it is unintentionally committed, [1]without the knowledge of the congregation, that the whole congregation shall offer one young bull as a burnt offering, as a sweet aroma to the LORD, [b]with its grain offering and its drink offering, according to the ordinance, and
[c]one kid of the goats as a sin offering.
25 [a]'So the priest shall **make atonement** for the whole congregation of the children of Israel, and it shall be forgiven them, for it was unintentional; they shall bring their offering, an offering made by fire to the LORD, and their sin offering before the LORD, for their unintended sin.

WORD WEALTH

15:25 make atonement, *chaphar* (kah-*far*); Strong's #3722: To cover, make atonement, make reconciliation; to pacify or appease; to clear, purge, or cleanse. This verb occurs 100 times. The primary meaning of *chaphar* may be "to cover." The verb is used in Gen. 6:14, where Noah was instructed to cover the ark with pitch. An important derivative is the word *kippur* (atonement), a familiar term due to its use in *Yom Kippur,* the Day of Atonement; see Lev. 23:27, 28. "Appease" and "make reconciliation" translate *chaphar* in Gen. 32:20 and Dan. 9:24, respectively.

26 'It shall be forgiven the whole congregation of the children of Israel and the stranger who dwells among them, because all the people *did it* unintentionally.
27 'And [a]if a person sins unintentionally, then he shall bring a female goat in its first year as a sin offering.
28 [a]'So the priest shall make atonement for the person who sins unintentionally, when he sins unintentionally before the LORD, to make atonement for him; and it shall be forgiven him.
29 [a]'You shall have one law for him who sins unintentionally, *for* him who is native-born among the children of Israel and for the stranger who dwells among them.

Law Concerning Presumptuous Sin

30 [a]'But the person who does *anything*
[1]presumptuously, *whether he is* native-born or a stranger, that one [2]brings reproach on the LORD, and he shall be
[3]cut off from among his people.
31 'Because he has [a]despised the word of the LORD, and has broken His commandment, that person shall be completely cut off; his [1]guilt *shall be* upon him.' "

Penalty for Violating the Sabbath

32 Now while the children of Israel were in the wilderness, [a]they found a man gathering sticks on the Sabbath day.
33 And those who found him gathering sticks brought him to Moses and Aaron, and to all the congregation.
34 They put him [a]under guard, because it had not been explained what should be done to him.
35 Then the LORD said to Moses,
[a]"The man must surely be put to death; all the congregation shall [b]stone him with stones outside the camp."
36 So, as the LORD commanded Moses, all the congregation brought him outside the camp and stoned him with stones, and he died.

Tassels on Garments

37 Again the LORD spoke to Moses, saying,
38 "Speak to the children of Israel: Tell
[a]them to make tassels on the corners

22 [a]Lev. 4:2 *See WW at Ps. 119:35. **24** [a]Lev. 4:13 [b]Num. 15:8–10 [c]Lev. 4:23 [1]Lit. *away from the eyes* **25** [a]Lev. 4:20; [Heb. 2:17] **27** [a]Lev. 4:27–31 **28** [a]Lev. 4:35 **29** [a]Num. 15:15 **30** [a]Num. 14:40–44; Deut. 1:43; 17:12; Ps. 19:13; Heb. 10:26 [1]*defiantly,* lit. *with a high hand* [2]*blasphemes* [3]Put to death **31** [a]2 Sam. 12:9; Prov. 13:13 [1]*iniquity* **32** [a]Ex. 31:14, 15; 35:2, 3 **34** [a]Lev. 24:12 **35** [a]Ex. 31:14, 15 [b]Lev. 24:14; Deut. 21:21; 1 Kin. 21:13; Acts 7:58 **38** [a]Deut. 22:12; Matt. 23:5

15:22–31 Now the regulations turn to sin offerings. Two instructions are given regarding unintentional sin, one for the whole congregation (vv. 22–26) and one for an individual (vv. 27–29). Vv. 30, 31 indicate the consequences of intentional sin. One who sins **presumptuously** (willfully violates the Law) is contrasted with the one who sins **unintentionally.**

15:24 Sin offering: See note on Lev. 4:3.

15:32–36 The severity of the law in vv. 30, 31 is soon enforced when a Sabbath violator is executed. The sin was not just an individual matter, but in principle threatened the entire community and hence had to be rooted out.

15:37–41 This visual reminder of the duty to obey the Law was given because of the serious consequences of failure to obey. The chapter thus concludes with the duty and responsibility of obedient faith.

15:38 Tassels were worn around the hem of the clothes to remind people to do God's will. They apparently had an upper garment folded into a quadrangular shape. Tassels were to be put on each of these **corners.**

of their garments throughout their generations, and to put a blue thread in
the tassels of the corners.
39 "And you shall have the tassel, that
you may look upon it and [a]remember
all the commandments of the LORD and
do them, and that you [b]*may* not
[c]follow the harlotry to which your own
heart and your own eyes are inclined,
40 "and that you may remember and
do all My commandments, and be
[a]holy for your God.
41 "I *am* the LORD your God, who
brought you out of the land of Egypt,
to be your God: I *am* the LORD your
God."

Rebellion Against Moses and Aaron

7 **16** Now [a]Korah the son of Izhar,
the son of Kohath, the son of
Levi, with [b]Dathan and Abiram the
sons of Eliab, and On the son of Peleth,
sons of Reuben, took *men;*
2 and they rose up before Moses with
some of the children of Israel, two hundred and fifty leaders of the congregation, [a]representatives of the congregation, men of renown.
3 [a]They gathered together against
Moses and Aaron, and said to them,
"*You* [1]*take* too much upon yourselves,
for [b]all the congregation *is* *holy, every
one of them, [c]and the LORD *is* among
them. Why then do you exalt yourselves above the assembly of the
LORD?"
4 So when Moses heard *it*, he [a]fell on
his face;
5 and he spoke to Korah and all his
company, saying, "Tomorrow morning
the LORD will show who *is* [a]His and
who is [b]holy,[1] and will cause *him* to
come near to Him. That one whom He
chooses He will cause to [c]come near
to Him.

39 [a]Ps. 103:18 [b]Deut. 29:19 [c]Ps. 73:27; 106:39; James 4:4
40 [a][Lev. 11:44, 45; Rom. 12:1; Col. 1:22; 1 Pet. 1:15, 16]

CHAPTER 16

1 [a]Ex. 6:21 [b]Num. 26:9; Deut. 11:6
2 [a]Num. 1:16; 26:9
3 [a]Num. 12:2; 14:2; Ps. 106:16 [b]Ex. 19:6 [c]Ex. 29:45 [1]*assume too much for* *See WW at Lev. 19:2.
4 [a]Num. 14:5; 20:6
5 [a][2 Tim. 2:19] [b]Lev. 21:6–8, 12 [c]Ezek. 40:46; 44:15, 16 [1]*set aside* for His use only
9 [a]1 Sam. 18:23; Is. 7:13 [b]Num. 3:41, 45; 8:13–16; Deut. 10:8
11 [a]Ex. 16:7, 8
13 [a]Ex. 16:3; Num. 11:4–6 [b]Ex. 2:14; Acts 7:27, 35
14 [a]Num. 14:1–4 [b]Ex. 3:8; Lev. 20:24
15 [a]Gen. 4:4, 5 [b]1 Sam. 12:3; Acts 20:33 [1]*graciously regard*

6 "Do this: Take censers, Korah and
all your company;
7 "put fire in them and put incense
in them before the LORD tomorrow, and
it shall be *that* the man whom the LORD
chooses *is* the holy one. *You take* too
much upon yourselves, you sons of
Levi!"
8 Then Moses said to Korah, "Hear
now, you sons of Levi:
9 "*Is it* [a]a small thing to you that the
God of Israel has [b]separated you from
the congregation of Israel, to bring
you near to Himself, to do the work
of the tabernacle of the LORD, and to
stand before the congregation to serve
them;
10 "and that He has brought you near
to Himself, you and all your brethren,
the sons of Levi, with you? And are
you seeking the priesthood also?
11 "Therefore you and all your company *are* gathered together against the
LORD. [a]And what *is* Aaron that you
complain against him?"
12 And Moses sent to call Dathan and
Abiram the sons of Eliab, but they said,
"We will not come up!
13 "*Is it* a small thing that you have
brought us up out of [a]a land flowing
with milk and honey, to kill us in the
wilderness, that you should [b]keep acting like a prince over us?
14 "Moreover [a]you have not brought
us into [b]a land flowing with milk and
honey, nor given us inheritance of
fields and vineyards. Will you put out
the eyes of these men? We will not
come up!"
15 Then Moses was very angry, and
said to the LORD, [a]"Do not [1]respect
their offering. [b]I have not taken one
donkey from them, nor have I hurt one
of them."
16 And Moses said to Korah, "Tomorrow, you and all your company be

---

16:1—18:32 These three chapters narrate the events that reaffirmed the divinely appointed structure of Moses as political leader and Aaron (and his descendants) as the worship leader superior to the Levites, who, in turn, are chosen from the Israelites to minister in the sanctuary.

16:1–50 See section 7 of Truth-In-Action at the end of Num.

16:1–50 Vv. 1–40 narrate a twofold rebellion against Mosaic and Aaronic authority, the end of which was the making of a memorial covering for the altar to assert the choice of Aaron and his descendants as priests. In vv. 41–50, the people complain about the punishment of the rebels, and a plague is unleashed against them until Aaron atones for them.

16:1–3 The people mentioned are working in collusion, but **Korah** is later described as Aaron's antagonist, and **Dathan and Abiram** are Moses' antagonists. It is a religious as well as a civil rebellion, grounded in a contest of the unique, exclusive roles Moses has introduced (v. 3).

16:4–11 Moses deals with Korah, who represented a faction of the Levites who wanted priestly prerogatives as well as their own duties (see chs. 3; 4). First he devises a test to prove Aaron's right to bear the incense in the tabernacle (vv. 4–7), and then he rebukes them for not appreciating the significance of the ministry to which the Lord called them (vv. 8–11).

16:12–15 Moses turns to deal with those who challenge his own position, but they refuse to appear before him, fearing reprisal. Their objection to Moses' leadership is that he backed away from the Promised Land and returned to the wilderness (v. 13) and had not been successful in entering it since then (v. 14). To apply a secular standard of success to a spiritual leader is to miss the point. The successful spiritual leader is one who follows divine guidance.

16:16–35 The confrontation occurs in two places: the tent of meeting (vv. 18–24, 35) and the individual tents of the leaders of the rebellion (vv. 25–34).

present [a]before the LORD—you and
they, as well as Aaron.
17 "Let each take his censer and put
incense in it, and each of you bring his
censer before the LORD, two hundred
and fifty censers; both you and Aaron,
each *with* his censer."
18 So every man took his censer, put
fire in it, laid incense on it, and stood
at the door of the tabernacle of meeting
with Moses and Aaron.
19 And Korah gathered all the congregation against them at the door of the
tabernacle of meeting. Then [a]the glory
of the LORD appeared to all the congregation.
20 And the LORD spoke to Moses and
Aaron, saying,
21 [a]"Separate yourselves from among
this congregation, that I may [b]consume
them in a moment."
22 Then they [a]fell[1] on their faces, and
said, "O God, [b]the God of the spirits
of all flesh, shall one man sin, and You
be angry with all the [c]congregation?"
23 So the LORD spoke to Moses, saying,
24 "Speak to the congregation, saying,
'Get away from the tents of Korah, Dathan, and Abiram.' "
25 Then Moses rose and went to Dathan and Abiram, and the elders of Israel followed him.
26 And he spoke to the congregation,
saying, [a]"Depart now from the tents
of these wicked men! Touch nothing
of theirs, lest you be consumed in all
their sins."
27 So they got away from around the
tents of Korah, Dathan, and Abiram;
and Dathan and Abiram came out and
stood at the door of their tents, with
their wives, their sons, and their little
[a]children.
28 And Moses said: [a]"By this you shall
know that the LORD has sent me to do
all these works, for *I have* not *done
them* [b]of my own will.
29 "If these men die naturally like all
men, or if they are [a]visited by the common fate of all men, *then* the LORD has
not sent me.
30 "But if the LORD creates [a]a new
thing, and the earth opens its mouth
and swallows them up with all that belongs to them, and they [b]go down alive
into the pit, then you will understand
that these men have rejected the
LORD."
31 [a]Now it came to pass, as he finished
speaking all these words, that the
ground split apart under them,
32 and the earth opened its mouth and
swallowed them up, with their households and [a]all the men with Korah,
with all *their* goods.
33 So they and all those with them
went down alive into the pit; the earth
closed over them, and they perished
from among the assembly.
34 Then all Israel who *were* around
them fled at their cry, for they said,
"Lest the earth swallow us up *also!*"
35 And [a]a fire came out from the LORD
and consumed the two hundred and
fifty men who were offering incense.
36 Then the LORD spoke to Moses, saying:
37 "Tell Eleazar, the son of Aaron the
priest, to pick up the censers out of the
blaze, for [a]they are holy, and scatter
the fire some distance away.
38 "The censers of [a]these men who
sinned [1]against their own souls, let
them be made into hammered plates
as a covering for the altar. Because
they presented them before the LORD,
therefore they are holy; [b]and they shall
be a sign to the children of Israel."
39 So Eleazar the priest took the
bronze censers, which those who were
burned up had presented, and they
were hammered out as a covering on
the altar,
40 *to be* a [1]memorial to the children
of Israel [a]that no outsider, who *is* not
a descendant of Aaron, should come
near to offer incense before the LORD,
that he might not become like Korah
and his companions, just as the LORD
had said to him through Moses.

Complaints of the People

41 On the next day [a]all the congregation of the children of Israel complained against Moses and Aaron, saying, "You have killed the people of the
LORD."

16 [a]1 Sam. 12:3, 7
19 [a]Ex. 16:7, 10; Lev. 9:6, 23; Num. 14:10
21 [a]Gen. 19:17; Jer. 51:6 [b]Ex. 32:10; 33:5
22 [a]Num. 14:5 [b]Num. 27:16; Job 12:10; Eccl. 12:7; Heb. 12:9 [c]Gen. 18:23–32; 20:4 [1]*prostrated themselves*
26 [a]Gen. 19:12, 14, 15, 17
27 [a]Ex. 20:5; Num. 26:11
28 [a]Ex. 3:12; John 5:36 [b]Num. 24:13; John 5:30
29 [a]Ex. 20:5; Job 35:15; Is. 10:3
30 [a]Job 31:3; Is. 28:21 [b][Ps. 55:15]
31 [a]Num. 26:10; Ps. 106:17
32 [a]Num. 26:11; 1 Chr. 6:22, 37
35 [a]Lev. 10:2; Num. 11:1–3; 26:10; Ps. 106:18
37 [a]Lev. 27:28
38 [a]Prov. 20:2; Hab. 2:10 [b]Num. 17:10; Ezek. 14:8 [1]Or *at the cost of their own lives*
40 [a]Num. 3:10; 2 Chr. 26:18 [1]*reminder*
41 [a]Num. 14:2; Ps. 106:25

16:22 The spirits of all flesh refers to the vital power that distinguishes the living from the dead. God, as the giver of life, is appealed to in order to preserve the congregation from death.
16:30 The pit is Sheol, the OT abode of the dead.
16:38 Even profane fire offered before the Lord here is holy, so the materials could not be used for profane purposes again. According to Ex. 27:2, the altar already had been overlaid with bronze. This text implies a double overlay of bronze, the second serving as a memorial sign.
16:41–50 Again we see **the plague** as punishment from Yahweh against a people slow to learn vital lessons. The **censer** as a means of atonement on Aaron's part is fitting since that was the source of the earlier dispute. The Lord honored the legitimate offering of Aaron in contrast to those He destroyed earlier, who had offered unauthorized incense (v. 35). Aaron's ministry is steadfastly confirmed.

42 Now it happened, when the congregation had gathered against Moses and
Aaron, that they turned toward the tabernacle of meeting; and suddenly [a]the
cloud covered it, and the glory of the
LORD appeared.
43 Then Moses and Aaron came before
the tabernacle of meeting.
44 And the LORD spoke to Moses, saying,
45 "Get away from among this congregation, that I may consume them in
a moment." And they fell on their
faces.
46 So Moses said to Aaron, "Take a
censer and put fire in it from the altar,
put incense *on it,* and take it quickly
to the congregation and make [1]atone-
ment for them; [a]for wrath has gone out
from the LORD. The plague has begun."
47 Then Aaron took *it* as Moses commanded, and ran into the midst of the
assembly; and already the plague had
begun among the people. So he put in
the incense and made atonement for
the people.
48 And he stood between the dead and
the living; so [a]the plague was stopped.
49 Now those who died in the plague
were fourteen thousand seven hundred, besides those who died in the Korah incident.
50 So Aaron returned to Moses at the
door of the tabernacle of meeting, for
the plague had stopped.

The Budding of Aaron's Rod

17 And the LORD spoke to Moses,
saying:
2 "Speak to the children of Israel, and
get from them a rod from each father's
house, all their leaders according to
their fathers' houses—twelve rods.
*Write each man's name on his rod.
3 "And you shall write Aaron's name
on the rod of Levi. For there shall be
one rod for the head of *each* father's
house.
4 "Then you shall place them in the
tabernacle of meeting before [a]the Testimony, [b]where I meet with you.
5 "And it shall be *that* the rod of the
man [a]whom I choose will blossom;
thus I will rid Myself of the complaints
of the children of Israel, [b]which they
make against you."
6 So Moses spoke to the children of
Israel, and each of their leaders gave
him a rod apiece, for each leader according to their fathers' houses, twelve
rods; and the rod of Aaron *was* among
their rods.
7 And Moses placed the rods before
the LORD in [a]the tabernacle of witness.
8 Now it came to pass on the next day
that Moses went into the tabernacle of
witness, and behold, the [a]rod of Aaron,
of the house of Levi, had sprouted and
put forth buds, had produced blossoms
and yielded ripe almonds.
9 Then Moses brought out all the rods
from before the LORD to all the children
of Israel; and they looked, and each
man took his rod.
10 And the LORD said to Moses, "Bring
[a]Aaron's rod back before the Testimony, to be kept [b]as a sign against the
rebels, [c]that you may put their complaints away from Me, lest they die."
11 Thus did Moses; just as the LORD
had commanded him, so he did.
12 So the children of Israel spoke to
Moses, saying, "Surely we die, we perish, we all perish!
13 [a]"Whoever even comes near the
tabernacle of the LORD must die. Shall
we all utterly die?"

Duties of Priests and Levites

18 Then the LORD said to Aaron:
[a]"You and your sons and your
father's house with you shall [b]bear the

42 [a]Ex. 40:34 **46** [a]Lev. 10:6; Num. 18:5 [1]Lit. *covering* **48** [a]Num. 25:8; Ps. 106:30

CHAPTER 17

2 *See WW at Deut. 31:9. **4** [a]Ex. 25:16 [b]Ex. 25:22; 29:42, 43; 30:36; Num. 17:7 **5** [a]Num. 16:5 [b]Num. 16:11 **7** [a]Ex. 38:21; Num. 1:50, 51; 9:15; 18:2; Acts 7:44 **8** [a][Ezek. 17:24]; Heb. 9:4 **10** [a]Heb. 9:4 [b]Num. 16:38; Deut. 9:7, 24 [c]Num. 17:5 **13** [a]Num. 1:51, 53; 18:4, 7

CHAPTER 18

1 [a]Num. 17:13 [b]Ex. 28:38; Lev. 10:17; 22:16

17:1–13 The authority of Aaron is established beyond dispute in vv. 1–11, as Moses' authority was in ch. 12. The deaths in ch. 16 discouraged the people, so that they despaired of being able to live with the Lord in their midst (vv. 12, 13).

17:2 All their leaders refers to those who filled the positions created in 1:5–15. **Aaron** stands as the leader of the Levites. The number of rods would total 13 when Aaron's rod was added.

17:4 The Testimony refers to the ark where Yahweh's presence dwelt in the Holy of Holies.

17:7 Tabernacle of witness: Usually this is called the tabernacle of meeting. The change emphasizes the presence of the ark of the testimony inside the tabernacle of meeting, since that is where the rods are to be placed. See note on 1:50.

17:8 The full cycle of the almond tree had transpired. Aaron's **rod** had gone beyond the requirements of the test, a strong affirmation of his authority.

17:10 The **sign against the rebels** is similar to the "memorial" in 16:40 and the "tassels" of 15:38–41.

17:13 The question was pressing for any person needing to offer a sacrifice.

18:1–32 The Lord addresses three speeches to Aaron and one to Moses. The first speech (vv. 1–7) answers the question of the people in 17:13, namely, how the lay people can avoid death when they are bringing sacrifices to the tabernacle. The other speeches deal with the support of the priests and the Levites, since they will receive no allotment of land.

18:1 The special status of the Aaronites and the Levites did not allow them to act inappropriately in their sacred tasks.

[1]iniquity *related to* the sanctuary, and you and your sons with you shall bear the iniquity *associated with* your priesthood.

2 "Also bring with you your brethren of the [a]tribe of Levi, the tribe of your father, that they may be [b]joined with you and serve you while you and your sons *are* with you before the tabernacle of [1]witness.

3 "They shall attend to your [1]needs and [a]all the needs of the tabernacle; [b]but they shall not come near the articles of the sanctuary and the altar, [c]lest they die—they and you also.

4 "They shall be joined with you and attend to the needs of the tabernacle of meeting, for all the work of the tabernacle; [a]but an outsider shall not come near you.

5 "And you shall attend to [a]the duties of the sanctuary and the duties of the altar, [b]that there *may* be no more wrath on the children of Israel.

6 "Behold, I Myself have [a]taken your brethren the Levites from among the children of Israel; [b]*they are* a gift to you, given by the LORD, to do the work of the tabernacle of meeting.

7 "Therefore [a]you and your sons with you shall attend to your priesthood for everything at the altar and [b]behind the veil; and you shall serve. I give your priesthood *to you* as a [c]gift for service, but the outsider who comes near shall be put to death."

Offerings for Support of the Priests

8 And the LORD spoke to Aaron: "Here, [a]I Myself have also given you [1]charge of My heave offerings, all the holy gifts of the children of Israel; I have given them [b]as a portion to you and your sons, as an ordinance forever.

9 "This shall be yours of the most holy things *reserved* from the fire: every offering of theirs, every [a]grain offering and every [b]sin offering and every [c]trespass offering which they render to Me, *shall be* most holy for you and your sons.

10 [a]"In a most holy *place* you shall eat it; every male shall eat it. It shall be holy to you.

11 "This also *is* yours: [a]the heave offering of their gift, with all the wave offerings of the children of Israel; I have given them to you, and your sons and daughters with you, as an ordinance forever. [b]Everyone who is [1]clean in your house may eat it.

12 [a]"All the [1]best of the oil, all the best of the new wine and the grain, [b]their firstfruits which they offer to the LORD, I have given them to you.

13 "Whatever first ripe fruit is in their land, [a]which they bring to the LORD, shall be yours. Everyone who is clean in your house may eat it.

14 [a]"Every [1]devoted thing in Israel shall be yours.

15 "Everything that first opens [a]the womb of all flesh, which they bring to the LORD, whether man or beast, shall be yours; nevertheless [b]the firstborn of man you shall surely *redeem, and the firstborn of unclean animals you shall redeem.

16 "And those redeemed of the devoted things you shall redeem when one month old, [a]according to your valuation, for five shekels of silver, according to the shekel of the sanctuary, which *is* [b]twenty gerahs.

17 [a]"But the firstborn of a cow, the firstborn of a sheep, or the firstborn of a goat you shall not redeem; they *are* holy. [b]You shall sprinkle their *blood on the altar, and burn their fat *as* an offering made by fire for a sweet aroma to the LORD.

18 "And their flesh shall be yours, just as the [a]wave[1] breast and the right thigh are yours.

19 "All the heave offerings of the holy

1 [1]*guilt*
2 [a]Gen. 29:34; Num. 1:47 [b]Num. 3:5–10 [1]*testimony*
3 [a]Num. 3:25, 31, 36 [b]Num. 16:40 [c]Num. 4:15 [1]*service*
4 [a]Num. 3:10
5 [a]Ex. 27:21; 30:7; Lev. 24:3 [b]Num. 8:19; 16:46
6 [a]Num. 3:12, 45 [b]Num. 3:9
7 [a]Num. 3:10; 18:5 [b]Heb. 9:3, 6 [c]Matt. 10:8; 1 Pet. 5:2, 3
8 [a]Lev. 6:16, 18; 7:28–34; Num. 5:9 [b]Ex. 29:29; 40:13, 15 [1]*custody*
9 [a]Lev. 2:2, 3; 10:12, 13 [b]Lev. 6:25, 26 [c]Lev. 7:7; Num. 5:8–10
10 [a]Lev. 6:16, 26
11 [a]Ex. 29:27, 28; Deut. 18:3–5 [b]Lev. 22:1–16 [1]*purified*
12 [a]Ex. 23:19; Neh. 10:35, 36 [b]Ex. 22:29; Lev. 23:20 [1]Lit. *fat*
13 [a]Ex. 22:29; 23:19; 34:26
14 [a]Lev. 27:1–33 [1]*consecrated*
15 [a]Ex. 13:2 [b]Ex. 13:12–15; Num. 3:46; Luke 2:22–24 *See WW at Neh. 1:10.
16 [a]Lev. 27:6 [b]Ex. 30:13
17 [a]Deut. 15:19 [b]Lev. 3:2, 5 *See WW at Lev. 17:11.
18 [a]Ex. 29:26–28; Lev. 7:31–36 [1]*breast of the wave offering*

18:2–6 This is a reaffirmation of what was stated in 3:5–13. On **tabernacle of witness** see note on 17:7.

18:7 The priestly status for Aaronites is **a gift for service.** The Hebrew text is difficult here, but it affirms: 1) the freedom of the Lord's choice of the Aaronites for priestly duties; 2) the purpose for which they were chosen. A priest is a servant, which is also the NT understanding of minister.

18:8–19 After a general statement in v. 8, the provisions for the priests are divided into two categories: 1) provisions for officiating priests (vv. 9, 10); 2) provisions for priests and families when not officiating (vv. 11–19).

18:9 The most holy things *reserved* from the fire refers to sacrifices where only part of the offering is burned. Only priests could partake of the **grain offering** (see note on Lev. 2:1), **sin offering** (see note on Lev. 4:3), and **trespass offering** (see note on Lev. 5:14).

18:11 The heave offering (see note on 15:21) was typically the right thigh of the sacrificial animal (see Lev. 7:32), which was lifted or heaved out of the sacrifice. The offerer of the sacrifice would contribute it to the priest. **The wave offerings** were the breasts of the sacrifices, which were ceremonially waved (see note on Lev. 3:1).

18:12–18 Firstfruits (vv. 12, 13) and firstborn (vv. 14–18), including the redemption price of firstborn humans in vv. 15, 16, belong to the priests (see notes on 3:12, 13, 40–51). This is distinct from the tithe, which would be given for the support of the Levites.

18:19 A covenant of salt probably refers to the salt eaten in the solemnizing of a contract. It attests the permanence of the agreement.

things, which the children of Israel offer to the LORD, I have given to you
and your sons and daughters with you
as an ordinance forever; [a]it *is* a covenant of salt forever before the LORD
with you and your descendants with
you."
5 20 Then the LORD said to Aaron: "You
shall have [a]no inheritance in their
land, nor shall you have any portion
among them; [b]I *am* your portion and
your inheritance among the children of
Israel.

Tithes for Support of the Levites

21 "Behold, [a]I have given the children
of Levi all the tithes in Israel as
[1]an inheritance in return for the work
which they perform, [b]the work of the
tabernacle of meeting.
22 [a]"Hereafter the children of Israel
shall not come near the tabernacle of
meeting, [b]lest they bear sin and die.
23 "But the Levites shall perform the
work of the tabernacle of meeting, and
they shall bear their iniquity; *it shall
be* a statute forever, throughout your
generations, that among the children
of Israel they shall have no inheritance.
24 "For the tithes of the children of Israel, which they offer up *as* a heave
offering to the LORD, I have given to
the Levites [1]as an inheritance; therefore I have said to them, 'Among the
children of Israel they shall have no
inheritance.' "

The Tithe of the Levites

25 Then the LORD spoke to Moses, saying,
26 "Speak thus to the Levites, and say
to them: 'When you take from the children of Israel the tithes which I have
given you from them as your inheritance, then you shall offer up a heave
offering of it to the LORD, [a]a tenth of
the tithe.
27 'And your heave offering shall be
reckoned to you as though *it were* the
grain of the [a]threshing floor and as the
fullness of the winepress.
28 'Thus you shall also offer a heave
offering to the LORD from all your
tithes which you receive from the children of Israel, and you shall give the
LORD's heave offering from it to Aaron
the priest.
29 'Of all your gifts you shall offer up
every heave offering due to the LORD,
from all the [1]best of them, the consecrated part of them.'
30 "Therefore you shall say to them:
'When you have lifted up the best of
it, then *the rest* shall be accounted to
the Levites as the produce of the
threshing floor and as the produce of
the winepress.
31 'You may eat it in any place, you
and your households, for it *is* [a]your
[1]reward for your work in the tabernacle of meeting.
32 'And you shall [a]bear no sin because
of it, when you have lifted up the best
of it. But you shall not [b]profane the
holy gifts of the children of Israel, lest
you die.' "

Laws of Purification

19 Now the LORD spoke to Moses 4
and Aaron, saying,
2 "This *is* the [1]ordinance of the law
which the LORD has commanded, saying: 'Speak to the children of Israel,
that they bring you a red heifer without
[2]blemish, in which there *is* no [a]defect
[b]*and* on which a yoke has never come.
3 'You shall give it to Eleazar the
priest, that he may take it [a]outside the
camp, and it shall be slaughtered before him;
4 'and Eleazar the priest shall take

19 [a]Lev. 2:13; 2 Chr. 13:5; [Mark 9:49, 50]
20 [a]Deut. 10:8, 9; 12:12; 14:27–29; 18:1, 2; Josh. 13:14, 33 [b]Ps. 16:5; Ezek. 44:28
21 [a]Lev. 27:30–33; Deut. 14:22–29; Neh. 10:37; 12:44; Mal. 3:8–10; [Heb. 7:4–10] [b]Num. 3:7, 8 [1]*a possession*
22 [a]Num. 1:51 [b]Lev. 22:9
24 [1]*for a possession*
26 [a]Neh. 10:38
27 [a]Num. 15:20; [2 Cor. 8:12]
29 [1]Lit. *fat*
31 [a][Matt. 10:10; Luke 10:7]; 1 Cor. 9:13; [1 Tim. 5:18] [1]*wages*
32 [a]Lev. 19:8; 22:16; Ezek. 22:26 [b]Lev. 22:2, 15

CHAPTER 19

2 [a]Lev. 22:20–25 [b]Deut. 21:3; 1 Sam. 6:7 [1]*statute* [2]*defect*
3 [a]Lev. 4:12, 21; Num. 19:9; Heb. 13:11

18:20 See section 5 of Truth-In-Action at the end of Num.
18:21 **Tithes** means 1/10, but what it is 1/10 of (net worth, yearly increase, etc.) is not specified. This would be a much larger amount of goods than the priests would receive from the offerings mentioned in vv. 8–19.
18:22, 23 See 17:12, 13; 18:1.
18:24 **Heave offering** again is the portion that is lifted out and contributed, in this case the tithe from all Israel. See note on v. 11.
18:25–32 This speech to Moses deals with the disposition of the tithes received by the Levites. They had to tithe from their receipts (vv. 26–29) and then could use the remainder freely for their livelihood (vv. 30–32). After **a tenth of the tithe** was taken, the offering lost its holy character and could then be put to mundane use like any of the other crops in Israel (v. 27). If they failed to give the tithe, they would profane **the holy gifts** and would **die** (v. 32).
19:1–22 See section 4 of Truth-In-Action at the end of Num.
19:1–22 The chapter is a body of instructions concerning water for purification of people who touch corpses, and it demonstrates that God is not on the side of death. It is appropriate in this section in light of the deaths of so many in ch. 16.
19:3 **Eleazar,** Aaron's successor, performs the rite that produces the ashes. This is probably to protect Aaron (or the high priest in succeeding generations) from defilement and the chance of incurring iniquity and dying in the performance of his duties. Eleazar does not slaughter it himself or participate in the burning in order to avoid touching the corpse, since he has to return to the tabernacle to sprinkle blood before it.

some of its blood with his finger, and
[a]sprinkle some of its blood seven times
directly in front of the tabernacle of
meeting.
5 'Then the heifer shall be burned in
his sight: [a]its hide, its flesh, its blood,
and its offal shall be burned.
6 'And the priest shall take [a]cedar
wood and [b]hyssop and scarlet, and
cast *them* into the midst of the fire
burning the heifer.
7 [a]'Then the priest shall wash his
clothes, he shall bathe in water, and
afterward he shall come into the camp;
the priest shall be unclean until evening.
8 'And the one who burns it shall
wash his clothes in water, bathe in water, and shall be unclean until evening.
9 'Then a man *who is* clean shall
gather up [a]the ashes of the heifer, and
store *them* outside the camp in a clean
place; and they shall be kept for the
congregation of the children of Israel
[b]for the water of [1]purification; it *is* for
purifying from sin.
10 'And the one who gathers the ashes
of the heifer shall wash his clothes, and
be unclean until evening. It shall be a
statute forever to the children of Israel
and to the stranger who dwells among
them.
11 [a]'He who touches the dead [1]body
of anyone shall be unclean seven days.
12 [a]'He shall purify himself with the
water on the third day and on the
seventh day; *then* he will be clean. But
if he does not purify himself on the
third day and on the seventh day, he
will not be clean.
13 'Whoever touches the body of anyone who has died, and [a]does not purify
himself, [b]defiles the *tabernacle of the
LORD. That person shall be cut off from
Israel. He shall be unclean, because
[c]the water of purification was not
sprinkled on him; [d]his uncleanness *is*
still on him.
14 'This *is* the law when a man dies
in a tent: All who come into the tent
and all who *are* in the tent shall be unclean seven days;

4 [a]Lev. 4:6; Heb. 9:13
5 [a]Ex. 29:14; Lev. 4:11, 12; 9:11
6 [a]Lev. 14:4, 6, 49 [b]Ex. 12:22; 1 Kin. 4:33
7 [a]Lev. 11:25; 15:5; 16:26, 28
9 [a][Heb. 9:13, 14] [b]Num. 19:13, 20, 21 [1]Lit. *impurity*
11 [a]Lev. 21:1, 11; Num. 5:2; 6:6; 9:6, 10; 31:19; Lam. 4:14; Hag. 2:13 [1]Lit. *soul of man*
12 [a]Num. 19:19; 31:19
13 [a]Lev. 22:3–7 [b]Lev. 15:31 [c]Num. 8:7; 19:9 [d]Lev. 7:20; 22:3 *See WW at Is. 32:18.
15 [a]Lev. 11:32; Num. 31:20 *See WW at Jer. 40:4.
16 [a]Num. 19:11; 31:19
17 [a]Num. 19:9 [1]Lit. *living*
18 [a]Ps. 51:7
19 [a]Lev. 14:9
20 [a]Num. 19:13
22 [a]Hag. 2:11–13 [b]Lev. 15:5

CHAPTER 20

1 [a]Num. 13:21; 33:36 [b]Num. 13:26 [c]Ex. 15:20; Num. 26:59
2 [a]Ex. 17:1 [b]Num. 16:19, 42

15 'and every [a]open* vessel, which has
no cover fastened on it, *is* unclean.
16 [a]'Whoever in the open field touches
one who is slain by a sword or who
has died, or a bone of a man, or a
grave, shall be unclean seven days.
17 'And for an unclean *person* they
shall take some of the [a]ashes of the
heifer burnt for purification from sin,
and [1]running water shall be put on
them in a vessel.
18 'A clean person shall take [a]hyssop
and dip *it* in the water, sprinkle *it* on
the tent, on all the vessels, on the persons who were there, or on the one
who touched a bone, the slain, the
dead, or a grave.
19 'The clean *person* shall sprinkle the
unclean on the third day and on the
seventh day; [a]and on the seventh day
he shall purify himself, wash his
clothes, and bathe in water; and at
evening he shall be clean.
20 'But the man who is unclean and
does not purify himself, that person
shall be cut off from among the assembly, because he has [a]defiled the sanctuary of the LORD. The water of purification has not been sprinkled on him; he
is unclean.
21 'It shall be a perpetual statute for
them. He who sprinkles the water of
purification shall wash his clothes;
and he who touches the water of purification shall be unclean until evening.
22 [a]'Whatever the unclean *person* touches shall be unclean; and [b]the person
who touches *it* shall be unclean until
evening.' "

Moses' Error at Kadesh

20 Then[a] the children of Israel, the
whole congregation, came into
the Wilderness of Zin in the first
month, and the people stayed in
[b]Kadesh; and [c]Miriam died there and
was buried there.
2 [a]Now there was no water for the
congregation; [b]so they gathered together against Moses and Aaron.

19:6 Cedar wood and hyssop and scarlet are used in the cleansing of a leper in Lev. 14. There they are instruments of the cleansing; here they are ingredients in the cleansing (see also v. 18). "Scarlet" refers to a material dyed red.

19:11–13 The unclean person himself or herself may do the purificatory rite. This contrasts with the special cases in vv. 14–19 where a clean person must perform the act on behalf of the unclean person.

20:1–29 The theme of the chapter is the deaths of the three leaders of the Israelites. Miriam's death (v. 1) and Aaron's death (vv. 22–29) are reported at the beginning and end; Moses' failure which led to his death outside the Promised Land is sandwiched between these two reports (vv. 2–21).

20:1 The Wilderness of Zin lies to the north of the Wilderness of Paran in the Sinai Peninsula. **In the first month** is an incomplete dating, probably the first month of the fortieth year (see 33:38). **Kadesh** is the same Kadesh of ch. 13, from which the spies were sent out 40 years earlier.

Miriam died there is a simple report. Presumably the reason was that she was part of the first generation that came under the death penalty.

3 And the people [a]contended with Moses and spoke, saying: "If only we had died [b]when our brethren died before the LORD!
4 [a]"Why have you brought up the assembly of the LORD into this wilderness, that we and our animals should die here?
5 "And why have you made us come up out of Egypt, to bring us to this evil place? It *is* not a place of grain or figs or vines or pomegranates; nor *is* there any water to drink."
6 So Moses and Aaron went from the presence of the assembly to the door of the tabernacle of meeting, and [a]they [1]fell on their faces. And [b]the glory of the LORD appeared to them.
6 7 Then the LORD spoke to Moses, saying,
8 [a]"Take the rod; you and your brother Aaron gather the congregation together. Speak to the rock before their eyes, and it will yield its water; thus [b]you shall bring water for them out of the rock, and give drink to the congregation and their animals."
9 So Moses took the rod [a]from before the LORD as He commanded him.
10 And Moses and Aaron gathered the assembly together before the rock; and he said to them, [a]"Hear now, you rebels! Must we bring water for you out of this rock?"
11 Then Moses lifted his hand and struck the rock twice with his rod; [a]and water came out abundantly, and the congregation and their animals drank.
12 Then the LORD spoke to Moses and Aaron, "Because [a]you did not believe Me, to [b]hallow Me in the eyes of the children of Israel, therefore you shall not bring this assembly into the land which I have given them."
13 [a]This *was* the water of [1]Meribah, because the children of Israel contended with the LORD, and He was hallowed among them.

3 [a]Ex. 17:2; Num. 14:2 [b]Num. 11:1, 33; 14:37; 16:31–35, 49
4 [a]Ex. 17:3
6 [a]Num. 14:5; 16:4, 22, 45 [b]Num. 14:10 [1]*prostrated themselves*
8 [a]Ex. 4:17, 20; 17:5, 6 [b]Neh. 9:15; Ps. 78:15, 16; 105:41; Is. 43:20; 48:21; [1 Cor. 10:4]
9 [a]Num. 17:10
10 [a]Ps. 106:33
11 [a]Ex. 17:6; Deut. 8:15; Ps. 78:16; Is. 48:21; [1 Cor. 10:4]
12 [a]Num. 20:28; 27:14; Deut. 1:37; 3:26, 27; 34:5 [b]Lev. 10:3; Ezek. 20:41; 36:23; 1 Pet. 3:15
13 [a]Deut. 33:8; Ps. 106:32 [1]Lit. *Contention*

Passage Through Edom Refused

14 [a]Now Moses sent messengers from Kadesh to the king of [b]Edom. [c]"Thus says your brother Israel: 'You know all the hardship that has befallen us,
15 [a]'how our fathers went down to Egypt, [b]and we dwelt in Egypt a long time, [c]and the Egyptians [1]afflicted us and our fathers.
16 [a]'When we cried out to the LORD, He heard our voice and [b]sent the Angel and brought us up out of Egypt; now here we are in Kadesh, a city on the edge of your border.
17 'Please [a]let us pass through your country. We will not pass through fields or vineyards, nor will we drink water from wells; we will go along the King's Highway; we will not turn aside to the right hand or to the left until we have passed through your territory.' "
18 Then [a]Edom said to him, "You shall not pass through my *land,* lest I come out against you with the sword."
19 So the children of Israel said to him, "We will go by the Highway, and if I or my livestock drink any of your water, [a]then I will pay for it; let me only pass through on foot, nothing *more.*"
20 Then he said, [a]"You shall not pass through." So Edom came out against them with many men and with a strong hand.
21 Thus Edom [a]refused to give Israel passage through his territory; so Israel [b]turned away from him.

14 [a]Judg. 11:16, 17 [b]Gen. 36:31–39 [c]Deut. 2:4; Obad. 10–12
15 [a]Gen. 46:6; Acts 7:15 [b]Ex. 12:40 [c]Ex. 1:11; Deut. 26:6; Acts 7:19 [1]*did evil to*
16 [a]Ex. 2:23; 3:7 [b]Ex. 3:2; 14:19
17 [a]Num. 21:22
18 [a]Num. 24:18; Ps. 137:7; Ezek. 25:12, 13; Obad. 10–15
19 [a]Deut. 2:6, 28
20 [a]Judg. 11:17
21 [a]Deut. 2:27, 30 [b]Deut. 2:8; Judg. 11:18

Death of Aaron

22 Now the children of Israel, the whole congregation, journeyed from

20:3 When our brethren died before the LORD is a reference to the Korah incident of ch. 16.

20:7–12 See section 6 of Truth-In-Action at the end of Num.

20:8 Take the rod: This would be the rod of Aaron that was now before the ark in the Holy of Holies. **Speak to the rock** shows a different means of performing the miracle. The rod was no magic instrument; rather it was the vehicle of the divine power. In this instance, though, the spoken word was to be the vehicle of the miracle.

20:11 Moses . . . struck the rock: Moses failed to be open to the new avenue through which God intended to move. He acted on the basis of his past experience. The method worked, but the Lord was displeased at Moses' disobedience. The measure of success in the Lord's eyes is not the outcome of the effort, but the obedience of His servant.

20:12 To hallow Me means to make the Lord holy in the eyes of the people.

20:13 He was hallowed: This appears to be in direct contradiction of the previous verse where Moses and Aaron are judged for not causing the Lord to be hallowed. The text tells us that the Lord was indeed hallowed among the Israelites as a result of the miracle. Moses and Aaron, however, did not themselves cause the children of Israel to hallow Him.

20:14 Your brother Israel: The Edomites were descendants of Esau, Jacob's brother, hence addressed here as relatives.

20:16 The Angel refers to the angel of the burning bush as well as the death angel in the last plague.

20:17–21 Two rounds of negotiation are tried, one a simple request, the other an offer to pay for their passage through Edom.

20:22 Mount Hor is unknown, but according to v. 23, it is not far from Kadesh Barnea on the border of Edom.

[a]Kadesh [b]and came to Mount Hor.
23 And the LORD spoke to Moses and
Aaron in Mount Hor by the border of
the land of Edom, saying:
24 "Aaron shall [1]be [a]gathered to his
people, for he shall not enter the land
which I have given to the children of
Israel, because you rebelled against
My word at the water of Meribah.
25 [a]"Take Aaron and Eleazar his son,
and bring them up to Mount Hor;
26 "and strip Aaron of his garments
and put them on Eleazar his son; for
Aaron shall be gathered *to his people*
and die there."
27 So Moses did just as the LORD commanded, and they *went up to Mount
Hor in the sight of all the congregation.
28 [a]Moses stripped Aaron of his garments and put them on Eleazar his son;
and [b]Aaron died there on the top of
the mountain. Then Moses and Eleazar
came down from the mountain.
29 Now when all the congregation saw
that Aaron was dead, all the house of
Israel mourned for Aaron [a]thirty days.

22 [a]Num. 33:37 [b]Num. 21:4
24 [a]Gen. 25:8; Deut. 32:50 [1]Die and join his ancestors
25 [a]Num. 33:38; Deut. 32:50
27 *See WW at Ex. 19:20.
28 [a]Ex. 29:29, 30; Deut. 10:6 [b]Num. 33:38
29 [a]Gen. 50:3, 10; Deut. 34:8

CHAPTER 21

1 [a]Num. 33:40; Josh. 12:14; Judg. 1:16
2 [a]Gen. 28:20; Judg. 11:30 [b]Deut. 2:34
3 [1]Lit. *Utter Destruction*

Canaanites Defeated at Hormah

21 The [a]king of Arad, the Canaanite, who dwelt in the South,
heard that Israel was coming on the
road to Atharim. Then he fought
against Israel and took *some* of them
prisoners.
2 [a]So Israel made a vow to the LORD,
and said, "If You will indeed deliver
this people into my hand, then [b]I will
utterly destroy their cities."
3 And the LORD listened to the voice
of Israel and delivered up the Canaanites, and they utterly destroyed them
and their cities. So the name of that
place was called [1]Hormah.

The Bronze Serpent

4 Then they journeyed from Mount
Hor by the Way of the Red Sea, to

20:24 You rebelled against My word: The failure to follow the Lord's instruction (see v. 11) is defined as rebellion here. Moses called the people "rebels" in v. 10; here the Lord says Moses and Aaron are guilty of rebellion.
20:29 Thirty days is an extraordinarily long period of mourning, showing the esteem in which Aaron was held. See Deut. 34:8, where Moses' death was mourned for the same period.
21:1–35 This chapter narrates the journey to the last stage before the conquest of the Promised Land, from Mt. Hor to the plains of Moab. Everything else in the book from ch. 22 to the end occurs on the plains of Moab (see Deut. 1:5).
21:1 Arad is actually in the Promised Land. The king thought that Israel was on the way to Canaan, though they were not planning to enter from the South (see 20:14–21, where their intent was to pass through Edom). The Canaanites launch something of a preemptive strike and Israel counterattacks (vv. 2, 3).
21:2 A vow is not unusual prior to military actions. **Utterly destroy** translates the Hebrew verb from which the noun Hormah (utter destruction) is derived. It is a consecration of the spoils of war to the Lord through total destruction.
21:4 To go around the land of Edom: The story of 20:14–21 is continued. Scholars are divided as to whether they

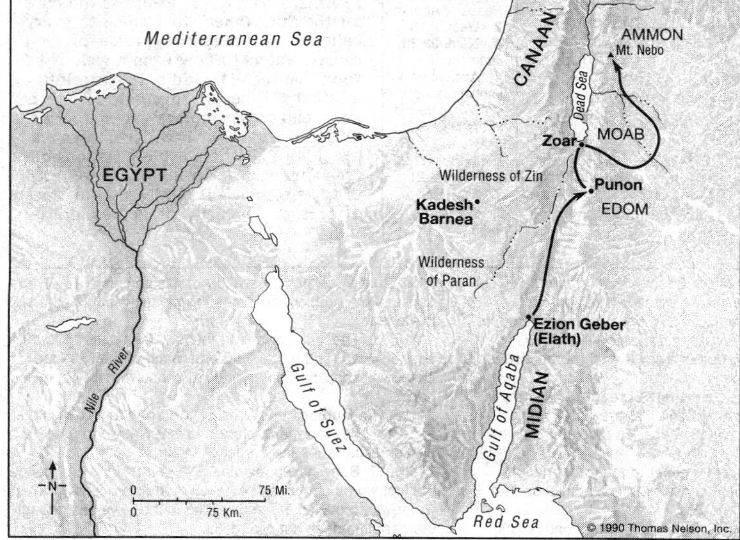

From the Wilderness to Canaan

[a]go around the land of Edom; and the
soul of the people became very [1]dis-
couraged on the way.
5 And the people [a]spoke against God
and against Moses: "Why have you
brought us up out of Egypt to die in
the wilderness? For *there is* no food
and no water, and our soul [1]loathes
this worthless bread."
6 So [a]the LORD sent [b]fiery* serpents
among the people, and they bit the people; and many of the people of Israel
died.
7 [a]Therefore the people came to Moses, and said, "We have [b]sinned, for
we have spoken against the LORD and
against you; [c]pray to the LORD that He
take away the serpents from us." So
Moses prayed for the people.
3 8 Then the LORD said to Moses,
[a]"Make a [b]fiery* *serpent,* and set it on
a pole; and it shall be that everyone
who is bitten, when he looks at it, shall
live."
9 So [a]Moses made a bronze serpent,
and put it on a pole; and so it was, if
a serpent had bitten anyone, when he
looked at the bronze serpent, he lived.

KINGDOM DYNAMICS

21:5–9 The Focus of Divine Healing, DIVINE HEALING. The plague of fiery serpents sent upon God's people was, in reality, a self-inflicted punishment, resulting from their frequent murmuring. God's judgment was in allowing what their own presumption invited, and many died from the bites of the serpents. But in answer to the repentance of His people, God prescribed the erecting of a bronze serpent to which any might look in faith and be healed. Jesus referred to this account in John 3:14, 15. He clearly implied that the bronze serpent typified His being raised upon the Cross. Our healing, both spiritual and physical, comes from looking to and identifying with Christ crucified, "by whose stripes you were healed" (1 Pet. 2:24).

(Num. 12:1–16/2 Kin. 5:1–15) N.V.

4 [a]Judg. 11:18 [1]*impatient*
5 [a]Num. 20:4, 5 [1]*detests*
6 [a]1 Cor. 10:9 [b]Deut. 8:15 *See WW at Is. 6:2.
7 [a]Num. 11:2; Ps. 78:34; Is. 26:16; Hos. 5:15 [b]Lev. 26:40 [c]Ex. 8:8; 1 Sam. 12:19; 1 Kin. 13:6; Acts 8:24
8 [a][John 3:14, 15] [b]Is. 14:29; 30:6 *See WW at Is. 6:2.
9 [a]2 Kin. 18:4; John 3:14, 15

From Mount Hor to Moab

10 Now the children of Israel moved
on and [a]camped in Oboth.
11 And they journeyed from Oboth
and camped at [1]Ije Abarim, in the wilderness which *is* east of Moab, toward
the sunrise.
12 [a]From there they moved and
camped in the Valley of Zered.
13 From there they moved and camped
on the other side of the Arnon, which
is in the wilderness that extends from
the border of the Amorites; for [a]the Arnon *is* the border of Moab, between
Moab and the Amorites.
14 Therefore it is said in the Book of
the Wars of the LORD:

[1]"Waheb in Suphah,
The brooks of the Arnon,
15 And the slope of the brooks
That reaches to the dwelling of
[a]Ar,
And lies on the border of Moab."

16 From there *they went* [a]to Beer,
which *is* the well where the LORD said
to Moses, "Gather the people together,
and I will give them water."
17 [a]Then Israel *sang this song:

"Spring up, O well!
All of you sing to it—

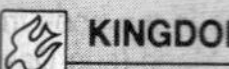

KINGDOM DYNAMICS

21:16, 17 Praise Cures "Dry Times," PRAISE PATHWAY. Praise is the cure for the "dry times" that come to every believer, for here the praise of God caused waters to flow from a well. Note four truths: 1) God's instruction—"Gather the people together." There is unity and power in corporate gathering. 2) God's promise—"I will give them water [life]." 3) The people's responsibility—They sang, "Spring up, O well! All of you sing to it." 4) Our lesson—In times of pressure, anxiety, or depression, do

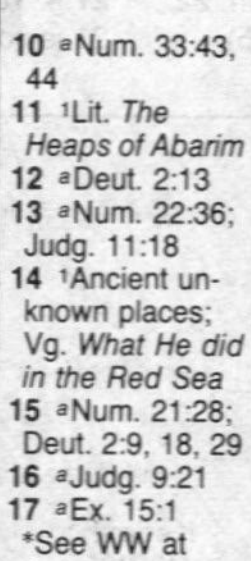

10 [a]Num. 33:43, 44
11 [1]Lit. *The Heaps of Abarim*
12 [a]Deut. 2:13
13 [a]Num. 22:36; Judg. 11:18
14 [1]Ancient unknown places; Vg. *What He did in the Red Sea*
15 [a]Num. 21:28; Deut. 2:9, 18, 29
16 [a]Judg. 9:21
17 [a]Ex. 15:1 *See WW at Judg. 5:3.

went around to the south of Edom or to the north, between Edom and Moab. The people's discouragement is understandable after a military victory, which appeared to open the door to the Promised Land (vv. 1–3), was abandoned and a long detour away from the Promised Land was required.

21:5 Against God . . . worthless bread displays the progressive sinful dissatisfaction that grew as a result of the rebellious decision in ch. 13. Rebellion is a lethal leaven in the human heart.

21:6 Fiery serpents refers either to the inflammation produced by the venomous bite or it could describe the creatures themselves.

21:8 See section 3 of Truth-In-Action at the end of Num.

21:9 Bronze serpent: As with Aaron's censer in 16:47, the cause of the problem becomes the means by which the sin is atoned.

21:10–20 The itinerary shows the Israelites passing to the east of Moab (and possibly Edom). Most of the sites are unknown. It depicts a determined march toward the Promised Land.

21:14 The Book of the Wars of the LORD functions like a footnote. The document referred to is unknown to us. The citation establishes the border of Moab.

21:16, 17 Beer in Hebrew means "Spring" or "Well," hence the first words of the song in v. 17. A festive occasion when water was provided is remembered in these verses, though the narrative does not give details.

not stay alone. Gather with God's people, especially a praising people. Regardless of your personal feelings, join in audible praise, and sing to your well—the living God. Let your song be one of thanksgiving for past blessings and a song of faith in God's promises for the present and the future!

(Gen. 29:35/2 Chr. 5:13) C.G.

18 The well the leaders sank,
Dug by the nation's nobles,
By the [a]lawgiver, with their
staves."

And from the wilderness *they went* to Mattanah,
19 from Mattanah to Nahaliel, from Nahaliel to Bamoth,
20 and from Bamoth, *in* the valley that *is* in the [1]country of Moab, to the top of Pisgah which looks [a]down on the [2]wasteland.

King Sihon Defeated

21 Then [a]Israel sent messengers to Sihon king of the Amorites, saying,
22 [a]"Let me pass through your land. We will not turn aside into fields or vineyards; we will not drink water from wells. We will go by the King's Highway until we have passed through your territory."
23 [a]But Sihon would not allow Israel to pass through his territory. So Sihon gathered all his people together and [1]went out against Israel in the wilderness, [b]and he came to Jahaz and fought against Israel.
24 Then [a]Israel defeated him with the edge of the sword, and took possession of his land from the Arnon to the Jabbok, as far as the people of Ammon; for the border of the people of Ammon *was* fortified.
25 So Israel took all these cities, and Israel [a]dwelt in all the cities of the Amorites, in Heshbon and in all its villages.
26 For Heshbon *was* the city of Sihon king of the Amorites, who had fought against the former king of Moab, and had taken all his land from his hand as far as the Arnon.
27 Therefore those who speak in [1]proverbs say:

"Come to Heshbon, let it be built;
Let the city of Sihon be repaired.

28 "For [a]fire went out from Heshbon,
A flame from the city of Sihon;
It consumed [b]Ar of Moab,
The lords of the [c]heights of the
Arnon.
29 Woe to you, [a]Moab!
You have perished, O people of
[b]Chemosh!
He has given his [c]sons as
fugitives,
And his [d]daughters into captivity,
To Sihon king of the Amorites.

30 "But we have shot at them;
Heshbon has perished [a]as far as
Dibon.
Then we laid waste as far as
Nophah,
Which *reaches* to [b]Medeba."

31 Thus Israel dwelt in the land of the Amorites.
32 Then Moses sent to [1]spy out [a]Jazer; and they took its villages and drove out the Amorites who *were* there.

King Og Defeated

33 [a]And they turned and went up by the way to [b]Bashan. So Og king of Bashan went out against them, he and all his people, to battle [c]at Edrei.
34 Then the LORD said to Moses, [a]"Do not fear him, for I have [1]delivered him into your hand, with all his people and his land; and [b]you shall do to him as you did to Sihon king of the Amorites, who dwelt at Heshbon."
35 [a]So they defeated him, his sons, and all his people, until there was no survivor left him; and they took possession of his land.

18 [a]Is. 33:22 **20** [a]Num. 23:28 [1]Lit. *field* [2]Heb. *Jeshimon* **21** [a]Num. 32:33; Deut. 2:26–37; Judg. 11:19 **22** [a]Num. 20:16, 17 **23** [a]Deut. 29:7 [b]Deut. 2:32; Judg. 11:20 [1]*attacked* **24** [a]Deut. 2:33; Josh. 12:1; Neh. 9:22; Ps. 135:10; 136:19; Amos 2:9 **25** [a]Amos 2:10

27 [1]*parables* **28** [a]Jer. 48:45, 46 [b]Deut. 2:9, 18; Is. 15:1 [c]Num. 22:41; 33:52 **29** [a]Jer. 48:46 [b]Judg. 11:24; 1 Kin. 11:33; 2 Kin. 23:13 [c]Is. 15:2, 5 [d]Is. 16:2 **30** [a]Num. 32:3, 34; Jer. 48:18, 22 [b]Is. 15:2 **32** [a]Num. 32:1, 3, 35; Jer. 48:32 [1]*secretly search* **33** [a]Deut. 29:7 [b]Deut. 3:1 [c]Josh. 13:12 **34** [a]Deut. 3:2 [b]Num. 21:24; Ps. 135:10; 136:20 [1]*given you victory over him* **35** [a]Deut. 3:3, 4; 29:7; Josh. 13:12

21:21–26 North of Moab lived a group of Amorites through whom Israel had to pass to gain access to the Jordan and hence to the Promised Land. The defeat of these Amorites is narrated here. The territory later went to the tribe of Reuben (32:33).

21:27–30 The proverb or parable is a song of victory detailing how the Amorites in Heshbon defeated the Moabites to the south (vv. 28, 29). Now Israel has defeated the Amorites, hence giving them rights of ownership (v. 30). The issue is that the border of Moab and Israel is the Arnon River (vv. 14, 15). Israel's claim to this land was disputed from time to time (see Judg. 11).

21:33–35 Og's kingdom lay north of the Amorite kingdom of Sihon, but still east of the Jordan. The territory went to the tribe of Gad and Manasseh (32:33).

Balak Sends for Balaam

22 Then [a]the children of Israel moved, and camped in the plains of Moab on the side of the Jordan *across from* Jericho.

2 Now [a]Balak the son of Zippor saw all that Israel had done to the Amorites.

3 And [a]Moab was exceedingly afraid of the people because they *were* many, and Moab was sick with dread because of the children of Israel.

4 So Moab said to [a]the elders of Midian, "Now this company will [1]lick up everything around us, as an ox licks up the grass of the field." And Balak the son of Zippor *was* king of the Moabites at that time.

5 Then [a]he sent messengers to Balaam the son of Beor at [b]Pethor, which *is* near [1]the River in the land of [2]the sons of his people, to call him, saying: "Look, a people has come from Egypt. See, they cover the face of the earth, and are settling next to me!

6 [a]"Therefore please come at once, [b]curse this people for me, for they *are* too mighty for me. Perhaps I shall be able to defeat them and drive them out of the land, for I know that he whom you bless *is* blessed, and he whom you curse is cursed."

7 So the elders of Moab and the elders of Midian departed with [a]the diviner's fee in their hand, and they came to Balaam and spoke to him the words of Balak.

8 And he said to them, [a]"Lodge here tonight, and I will bring back word to you, as the LORD speaks to me." So the princes of Moab stayed with Balaam.

9 [a]Then God came to Balaam and said, "Who *are* these men with you?"

10 So Balaam said to God, "Balak the son of Zippor, king of Moab, has sent to me, *saying,*

11 'Look, a people has come out of Egypt, and they cover the face of the earth. Come now, curse them for me; perhaps I shall be able to overpower them and drive them out.' "

12 And God said to Balaam, "You shall not go with them; you shall not curse the people, for [a]they *are* blessed."

13 So Balaam rose in the morning and said to the princes of Balak, "Go back to your land, for the LORD has refused to give me permission to go with you."

14 And the princes of Moab rose and went to Balak, and said, "Balaam refuses to come with us."

15 Then Balak again sent princes, more numerous and more [1]honorable than they.

16 And they came to Balaam and said to him, "Thus says Balak the son of Zippor: 'Please let nothing hinder you from coming to me;

17 'for I will certainly [a]honor you greatly, and I will do whatever you say to me. [b]Therefore please come, curse this people for me.' "

18 Then Balaam answered and said to the servants of Balak, [a]"Though Balak were to give me his house full of silver and gold, [b]I could not go beyond the word of the LORD my God, to do less or more.

19 "Now therefore, please, you also [a]stay here tonight, that I may know what more the LORD will say to me."

20 [a]And God came to Balaam at night and said to him, "If the men come to call you, rise *and* go with them; but

CHAPTER 22

1 [a]Num. 33:48, 49
2 [a]Josh. 24:9; Judg. 11:25; Mic. 6:5; Rev. 2:14
3 [a]Ex. 15:15
4 [a]Num. 25:15–18; 31:1–3; Josh. 13:21 [1]*consume*
5 [a]Num. 31:8, 16; Deut. 23:4; Josh. 13:22; 24:9; Neh. 13:1, 2; Mic. 6:5; 2 Pet. 2:15; Jude 11; Rev. 2:14 [b]Deut. 23:4 [1]The Euphrates [2]Or *the people of Amau*
6 [a]Num. 22:17; 23:7, 8 [b]Num. 22:12; 24:9
7 [a]1 Sam. 9:7, 8
8 [a]Num. 22:19
9 [a]Gen. 20:3
12 [a]Num. 23:20; [Rom. 11:28]
15 [1]*distinguished*
17 [a]Num. 24:11 [b]Num. 22:6
18 [a]Num. 22:38; 24:13 [b]1 Kin. 22:14; 2 Chr. 18:13
19 [a]Num. 22:8
20 [a]Num. 22:9

22:1—31:54 This story of the Israelites and the Moabites involves three scenes: 1) the Moabites recruit a prophet from Mesopotamia to curse Israel, though he can only bless them (chs. 22—24); 2) the Israelites fall prey to the worship of Baal of Peor, which involved sacred prostitution with Moabite women (ch. 25); 3) the attack on Midian in vengeance for their role in the Baal of Peor apostasy (ch. 31). Chs. 26—30 deal with another census and miscellaneous laws.

22:1–41 The subject of this passage is the recruitment of Balaam. Vv. 2–21 tell how Balaam was recruited; vv. 22–35 narrate a stern warning that Balaam receives on the way; and vv. 36–41 prepare for the oracles of Balaam that follow in chs. 23 and 24.

22:1 The plains of Moab was the traditional name of the area. It had been taken from Moab by Sihon the Amorite (see 21:26) who was defeated by Israel. Now Israelite territory and a staging area for the conquest of the Promised Land, it later became part of the Promised Land. The remaining events of the books of Num. and Deut. take place here.

22:4 The elders of Midian are from the territory south and east of Moab. They are shown here as coconspirators, hence their destruction in ch. 31 (see also 21:7).

22:5 Balaam was from Mesopotamia, near the Euphrates. This is a distance of about 400 miles, nearly a month's journey one way.

22:6 Balak, like all warriors in the ancient world, believes that the outcome of battles is determined by the gods; therefore, he believes the **curse** will enable him **to defeat** the Israelites.

22:8 The LORD in Hebrew is *Yahweh,* the name of the Israelite God. Balaam is seen as one who hears Yahweh, a prophet, even though not an Israelite (see v. 18).

22:9 God came to Balaam does not specify the means of revelation. Since it is at night, probably it is a vision or a dream.

22:13 In this first instance Yahweh forbids Balaam to go. Since Yahweh later lets Balaam go, this refusal is best seen as a means of stressing the intention of Yahweh for the Israelites (see v. 12).

22:20 Permission is given to go, but **Balaam** is held in tight rein as the first refusal (v. 12) has shown.

[b]only the word which I speak to you—
that you shall do."
21 So Balaam rose in the morning, saddled his donkey, and went with the
princes of Moab.

Balaam, the Donkey, and the Angel

22 Then God's anger was aroused because he went, [a]and the Angel of the
LORD took His stand in the way as an
adversary against him. And he was riding on his donkey, and his two servants
were with him.
23 Now [a]the donkey saw the Angel of
the LORD standing in the way with His
drawn sword in His hand, and the donkey turned aside out of the way and
went into the field. So Balaam struck
the donkey to turn her back onto the
road.
24 Then the Angel of the LORD stood
in a narrow path between the vineyards, *with* a wall on this side and a
wall on that side.
25 And when the donkey saw the Angel of the LORD, she pushed herself
against the wall and crushed Balaam's
foot against the wall; so he struck her
again.
26 Then the Angel of the LORD went
further, and stood in a narrow place
where there *was* no way to turn either
to the right hand or to the left.
27 And when the donkey saw the Angel of the LORD, she lay down under
Balaam; so Balaam's anger was
aroused, and he struck the donkey with
his staff.
28 Then the LORD [a]opened the mouth
of the donkey, and she said to Balaam,
"What have I done to you, that you
have struck me these three times?"
29 And Balaam said to the donkey,
"Because you have [1]abused me. I wish
there were a sword in my hand,
[a]for now I would kill you!"
30 [a]So the donkey said to Balaam,
"*Am* I not your donkey on which you
have ridden, ever since *I became*
yours, to this day? Was I ever [1]dis-

20 [b]Num. 22:35; 23:5, 12, 16, 26; 24:13
22 [a]Ex. 4:24
23 [a]Josh. 5:13; 2 Kin. 6:17; Dan. 10:7; Acts 22:9
28 [a]2 Pet. 2:16
29 [a][Prov. 12:10; Matt. 15:19] [1]*mocked*
30 [a]2 Pet. 2:16 [1]*accustomed*
31 [a]Gen. 21:19; 2 Kin. 6:17; Luke 24:16, 31
32 [a][2 Pet. 2:14, 15] [1]*as an adversary* [2]*contrary*
34 [a]1 Sam. 15:24, 30; 26:21; 2 Sam. 12:13 [1]Lit. *is evil in your eyes*
35 [a]Num. 22:20
36 [a]Gen. 14:17 [b]Num. 21:13
37 [a]Num. 22:17; 24:11
38 [a]Num. 23:26; 24:13; 1 Kin. 22:14; 2 Chr. 18:13
40 *See WW at Deut. 16:2.

posed to do this to you?" And he said,
"No."
31 Then the LORD [a]opened Balaam's
eyes, and he saw the Angel of the LORD
standing in the way with His drawn
sword in His hand; and he bowed his
head and fell flat on his face.
32 And the Angel of the LORD said to 1
him, "Why have you struck your donkey these three times? Behold, I have
come out [1]to stand against you, because *your* way is [a]perverse[2] before
Me.
33 "The donkey saw Me and turned
aside from Me these three times. If she
had not turned aside from Me, surely
I would also have killed you by now,
and let her live."
34 And Balaam said to the Angel of the
LORD, [a]"I have sinned, for I did not
know You stood in the way against me.
Now therefore, if it [1]displeases You, I
will turn back."
35 Then the Angel of the LORD said to
Balaam, "Go with the men, [a]but only
the word that I speak to you, that you
shall speak." So Balaam went with the
princes of Balak.
36 Now when Balak heard that Balaam
was coming, [a]he went out to meet him
at the city of Moab, [b]which *is* on the
border at the Arnon, the boundary of
the territory.
37 Then Balak said to Balaam, "Did I
not earnestly send to you, calling for
you? Why did you not come to me? Am
I not able [a]to honor you?"
38 And Balaam said to Balak, "Look,
I have come to you! Now, have I any
power at all to say anything? [a]The
word that God puts in my mouth, that
I must speak."
39 So Balaam went with Balak, and
they came to Kirjath Huzoth.
40 Then Balak *offered oxen and
sheep, and he sent *some* to Balaam and
to the princes who *were* with him.

Balaam's First Prophecy

41 So it was, the next day, that Balak
took Balaam and brought him up to the

22:22–35 The account concerning Balaam's donkey serves as a warning to Balaam. Balaam, as a prophet, should have been the one to see the Angel of the Lord; instead, his donkey does. Balaam's desire to kill his donkey with a sword (v. 29) is ironic since he is the one whose life is threatened by the sword of the Angel. Balaam's prophetic insight has been blinded by the prospect of reward.

22:22 God is apparently angry because of Balaam's readiness to go without questioning the implications for Israel. Balaam is later chastised for his reckless attitude (v. 32); there is also a hint he may not fully obey and that he may speak more than God says (v. 35).

22:32 See section 1 of Truth-In-Action at the end of Num.

22:32 Perverse connotes a recklessness or willingness to profit by gain.

22:39 Kirjath Huzoth's location is unknown.

22:40 Offered means to offer as a pagan sacrifice. Balaam and the princes who had recruited him apparently ate these animals.

22:41 The high places of Baal were sanctuaries where the Moabites worshiped. Some take this as a place name, Bamoth Baal (see Josh. 13:17).

[a]high places of Baal, that from there
he might observe [1]the extent of the
people.

23 Then Balaam said to Balak,
[a]"Build seven altars for me
here, and prepare for me here seven
bulls and seven rams."
2 And Balak did just as Balaam had
spoken, and Balak and Balaam [a]of-
fered a bull and a ram on *each* altar.
3 Then Balaam said to Balak, [a]"Stand
by your burnt offering, and I will go;
perhaps the LORD will come [b]to meet
me, and whatever He shows me I will
tell you." So he went to a desolate
height.
4 [a]And God met Balaam, and he said
to Him, "I have prepared the seven altars, and I have offered on *each* altar
a bull and a ram."
5 Then the LORD [a]put a word in Balaam's mouth, and said, "Return to Balak, and thus you shall speak."
6 So he returned to him, and there he
was, standing by his burnt offering, he
and all the princes of Moab.
7 And he [a]took up his [1]oracle and
said:

"Balak the king of Moab has
brought me from Aram,
From the mountains of the east.
[b]'Come, curse Jacob for me,
And come, [c]denounce Israel!'

8 "How[a] shall I curse whom God has
not cursed?
And how shall I denounce *whom*
the LORD has not denounced?
3 9 For from the top of the rocks I see
him,
And from the hills I behold him;
There! [a]A people dwelling alone,
[b]Not reckoning itself among the
nations.

10 "Who[a] can count the [1]dust of
Jacob,
Or number one-fourth of Israel?

41 [a]Num. 21:28; Deut. 12:2 [1]*the farthest extent*

CHAPTER 23

1 [a]Num. 23:29
2 [a]Num. 23:14, 30
3 [a]Num. 23:15 [b]Num. 23:4, 16
4 [a]Num. 23:16
5 [a]Num. 22:20, 35, 38; 23:16; Deut. 18:18; Jer. 1:9
7 [a]Deut. 23:4; Job 27:1; 29:1; Ps. 78:2 [b]Num. 22:6, 11, 17 [c]1 Sam. 17:10 [1]*prophetic discourse*
8 [a]Num. 22:12
9 [a]Deut. 32:8; 33:28; Josh. 11:23 [b]Ex. 33:16; Ezra 9:2; [Eph. 2:14]
10 [a]Gen. 13:16; 22:17; 28:14; 2 Chr. 1:9 [b]Ps.116:15 [1]Or *dust cloud*
11 [a]Num. 22:11
12 [a]Num. 22:38
14 [a]Num. 23:1, 2
15 [1]So with MT, Tg., Vg.; Syr. *call;* LXX *go and ask God*
16 [a]Num. 22:35; 23:5
18 [a]Judg. 3:20
19 [a]1 Sam. 15:29; Mal. 3:6; James 1:17 [b]Num. 11:23; 1 Kin. 8:56

Let me die [b]the death of the
righteous,
And let my end be like his!"

11 Then Balak said to Balaam, "What
have you done to me? [a]I took you to
curse my enemies, and look, you have
blessed *them* bountifully!"
12 So he answered and said, [a]"Must I
not take heed to speak what the LORD
has put in my mouth?"

Balaam's Second Prophecy

13 Then Balak said to him, "Please
come with me to another place from
which you may see them; you shall see
only the outer part of them, and shall
not see them all; curse them for me
from there."
14 So he brought him to the field of
Zophim, to the top of Pisgah, [a]and built
seven altars, and offered a bull and a
ram on *each* altar.
15 And he said to Balak, "Stand here
by your burnt offering while I [1]meet
the LORD over there."
16 Then the LORD met Balaam, and
[a]put a word in his mouth, and said, "Go
back to Balak, and thus you shall
speak."
17 So he came to him, and there he
was, standing by his burnt offering,
and the princes of Moab were with
him. And Balak said to him, "What has
the LORD spoken?"
18 Then he took up his oracle and said:

[a]"Rise up, Balak, and hear!
Listen to me, son of Zippor!

19 "God[a] *is* not a man, that He should 1
lie,
Nor a son of man, that He should
repent.
Has He [b]said, and will He not do?
Or has He spoken, and will He not
make it good?

23:1—24:25 Balaam gives four utterances: the first three are oriented toward the present and are oracles of blessing; the last one is for the distant future, specifically the Davidic kingdom.
23:1 Seven altars: This sacrifice is repeated in each new attempt (see vv. 14, 29). There already would have been altars at the sanctuary, but Balaam had new ones built since they probably were Baal altars.
23:3 Balaam leaves the pagan altars in order for the Lord to speak to him without accepting the pagan sacrifices.
23:7, 8 The power of a **curse** is subject to the Lord; Balaam's words alone would be of no effect. **Aram** is Syria, whose territory reached to the Euphrates and Pethor.
23:9, 10 Not reckoning itself among the nations shows the uniqueness of Israel's status as the people of God. The **dust of Jacob** is a word-picture showing the greatness of their number, like the phrase "sands of the sea."
23:9 See section 3 of Truth-In-Action at the end of Num.
23:13 Another place from which you may see them: It was necessary to see the object of a curse. **Balak** hoped that in seeing only a part of the Israelites Balaam would have more power to speak a curse.
23:14 Pisgah is also part of the mountain range that contains Mt. Nebo, from which Moses viewed the Promised Land before he died (Deut. 34).
23:19, 20 This is a rebuke of Balak who hoped that Balaam would curse the Israelites. The message from the Lord is that Balak is dealing with God, not a man, and God remains true to His first intention.
23:19 See section 1 of Truth-In-Action at the end of Num.

20 Behold, I have received *a*
command to bless;
[a]He has blessed, and I cannot
reverse it.

21 "He[a] has not observed *iniquity in
Jacob,
Nor has He seen [1]wickedness in
Israel.
The LORD his God *is* with him,
[b]And the *shout of a King *is* among
them.
22 [a]God brings them out of Egypt;
He has [b]strength like a wild ox.

[1] 23 "For *there is* no [1]sorcery against
Jacob,
Nor any [2]divination against
Israel.
It now must be said of Jacob
And of Israel, 'Oh, [a]what God has
done!'
24 Look, a people rises [a]like a
lioness,
And lifts itself up like a lion;
[b]It shall not lie down until it
devours the prey,
And drinks the blood of the
slain."

25 Then Balak said to Balaam, "Neither curse them at all, nor bless them
at all!"
26 So Balaam answered and said to
Balak, "Did I not tell you, saying,
[a]'All that the LORD speaks, that I must
do'?"

Balaam's Third Prophecy

27 Then Balak said to Balaam, "Please
come, I will take you to another place;
perhaps it will please God that you
may curse them for me from there."
28 So Balak took Balaam to the top of
Peor, that [a]overlooks [1]the wasteland.
29 Then Balaam said to Balak, "Build
for me here seven altars, and prepare
for me here seven bulls and seven
rams."

30 And Balak did as Balaam had said,
and offered a bull and a ram on *every*
altar.

24 Now when Balaam saw that it
pleased the LORD to bless Israel,
he did not go as at [a]other times, to seek
to use [1]sorcery, but he set his face toward the wilderness.
2 And Balaam raised his eyes, and
saw Israel [a]encamped according to
their tribes; and [b]the Spirit of God
came upon him.
3 [a]Then he took up his oracle and
said:

"The utterance of Balaam the son
of Beor,
The utterance of the *man whose
eyes are opened,
4 The utterance of him who hears
the words of God,
Who sees the vision of the
*Almighty,
Who [a]falls down, with eyes wide
open:

5 "How lovely are your tents, O
Jacob!
Your dwellings, O Israel!
6 Like valleys that stretch out,
Like gardens by the riverside,
[a]Like aloes [b]planted by the LORD,
Like cedars beside the waters.
7 He shall pour water from his
buckets,
And his seed *shall be* [a]in many
waters.

"His king shall be higher than
[b]Agag,
And his [c]kingdom shall be
exalted.

8 "God[a] brings him out of Egypt;
He has strength like a wild ox;
He shall [b]consume the nations,
his enemies;
He shall [c]break their bones
And [d]pierce *them* with his
arrows.

20 [a]Gen. 12:2; 22:17; Num. 22:12
21 [a]Ps. 32:2; [Rom. 4:7, 8] [b]Ps. 89:15–18 [1]*trouble* *See WW at Prov. 22:8. • See WW at Ezra 3:11.
22 [a]Num. 24:8 [b]Deut. 33:17; Job 39:10
23 [a]Ps. 31:19; 44:1 [1]*enchantment* [2]*fortune-telling*
24 [a]Gen. 49:9 [b]Gen. 49:27; Josh. 11:23
26 [a]Num. 22:38
28 [a]Num. 21:20 [1]Heb. *Jeshimon*

CHAPTER 24

1 [a]Num. 23:3, 15 [1]*enchantments*
2 [a]Num. 2:2, 34 [b]Num. 11:25; 1 Sam. 10:10; 19:20, 23; 2 Chr. 15:1
3 [a]Num. 23:7, 18 *See WW at Jer. 31:22.
4 [a]Ezek. 1:28 *See WW at Ps. 91:1.
6 [a]Ps. 1:3; Jer. 17:8 [b]Ps. 104:16
7 [a]Jer. 51:13; Rev. 17:1, 15 [b]1 Sam. 15:8, 9 [c]2 Sam. 5:12; 1 Chr. 14:2
8 [a]Num. 23:22 [b]Num. 14:9; 23:24 [c]Ps. 2:9; Jer. 50:17 [d]Ps. 45:5

23:21 The shout of a King *is* among them means that the Lord is Israel's king. As the previous line of poetry says, **The LORD his God *is* with him.**
23:23 See section 1 of Truth-In-Action at the end of Num.
23:23 Sorcery . . . divination: This assumes that Balaam's typical means of cursing through the use of occult media were powerless against Israel. In a confrontation with the occult, the Lord's protection renders occult powers harmless.
23:25, 26 Balak expects that if **Balaam** will not **curse** Israel, at least he will not **bless them.** Balaam replies that the prophetic responsibility prohibits him from remaining silent when a word is given. As Amos said, "The Lord GOD has spoken! Who can but prophesy?" (Amos 3:8).
23:28 The top of Peor is also a Baal shrine, which led to the apostasy of Israel in ch. 25.
24:1 He did not go . . . to seek to use sorcery: In light of 23:23, Balaam now knew that the sorcerer's means were futile.
24:2 The Spirit of God came upon him refers to an ecstatic state where the person of the prophet is overcome and displaced by the Spirit, as the language of vv. 3, 4 shows. See note on 11:25.
24:7 King in this context means the human king. **Agag** is the Amalekite king whom Saul conquers in 1 Sam. 15. See 24:20, the prophecy against Amalek in Balaam's last oracle.

9 'He[a] bows down, he lies down as
a lion;
And as a lion, who shall rouse
him?'
[b]"Blessed *is* he who blesses you,
And cursed *is* he who curses
you."

1 **10** Then Balak's anger was aroused
against Balaam, and he [a]struck his
hands together; and Balak said to Balaam, [b]"I called you to curse my enemies, and look, you have bountifully
blessed *them* these three times!
11 "Now therefore, flee to your place.
[a]I said I would greatly honor you, but
in fact, the LORD has kept you back
from honor."
12 So Balaam said to Balak, "Did I not
also speak to your messengers whom
you sent to me, saying,
13 'If Balak were to give me his house
full of silver and gold, I could not go
beyond the word of the LORD, to do
good or bad of my own will. What the
LORD says, that I must speak'?
14 "And now, indeed, I am going to my
people. Come, [a]I will advise you what
this people will do to your people in
the [b]latter days."

Balaam's Fourth Prophecy

15 So he took up his oracle and said:

"The utterance of Balaam the son
of Beor,
And the utterance of the man
whose eyes are opened;
16 The utterance of him who hears
the words of God,
And has the *knowledge of the
Most High,
Who sees the vision of the
Almighty,
Who falls down, with eyes wide
open:

17 "I[a] see Him, but not now;
I behold Him, but not near;
[b]A Star shall come out of Jacob;
[c]A Scepter shall rise out of Israel,
And [1]batter the brow of Moab,
And destroy all the sons of
[2]tumult.

18 "And [a]Edom shall be a possession;
Seir also, his enemies, shall be a
possession,
While Israel does [1]valiantly.
19 [a]Out of Jacob One [1]shall have
dominion,
And destroy the remains of the
city."

20 Then he looked on Amalek, and he
took up his oracle and said:

"Amalek *was* first among the
nations,
But *shall be* last *until he
perishes."

21 Then he looked on the Kenites, and
he took up his oracle and said:

"Firm is your dwelling place,
And your nest is set in the rock;
22 Nevertheless Kain shall be
burned.
How long until Asshur carries
you away captive?"

23 Then he took up his oracle and said:

"Alas! Who shall live when God
does this?
24 But ships *shall come* from the
coasts of [a]Cyprus,[1]
And they shall afflict Asshur and
afflict [b]Eber,
And so shall [2]*Amalek,* until he
perishes."

25 So Balaam rose and departed and
[a]returned to his place; Balak also went
his way.

9 [a]Gen. 49:9; Num. 23:24 [b]Gen. 12:3; 27:29 **10** [a]Ezek. 21:14, 17 [b]Num. 23:11; Neh. 13:2 **11** [a]Num. 22:17, 37 **14** [a][Mic. 6:5] [b]Gen. 49:1; Deut. 4:30; Dan. 2:28 **16** *See WW at Mal. 2:7.

17 [a]Rev. 1:7; Matt. 1:2; Luke 3:34 [b]Matt. 2:2 [c]Gen. 49:10 [1]*shatter the forehead* [2]Heb. *Sheth,* Jer. 48:45 **18** [a]2 Sam. 8:14 [1]*mightily* **19** [a]Gen. 49:10; Amos 9:11, 12 [1]*shall rule* **20** *See WW at Mic. 4:5. **24** [a]Gen. 10:4; Ezek. 27:6; Dan. 11:30 [b]Gen. 10:21, 25 [1]Heb. *Kittim* [2]Lit. *he* or *that one* **25** [a]Num. 22:5; 31:8

24:9 The blessing or cursing of Israel has a reciprocal power. Balak's attempt to curse would bring a curse on his people, hence Balaam's proclamation of future judgment on Moab and the other nations in the unsolicited oracle of vv. 17–24.
24:10 See section 1 of Truth-In-Action at the end of Num.
24:15, 16 Again, the ecstatic trance is the means of revelation.
24:17 The reference is to David's conquest of the Moabites (see 2 Sam. 8:2).
24:18, 19 The Edomites had refused Israel permission to pass through their land (20:1–18) and King David subdued them as well (2 Sam. 8:14).
24:20–24 These are three independent oracles with their own introductions, which are like postscripts to the previous oracles.
24:20 Saul defeated the Amalekites (1 Sam. 15:2), in punishment for their ambush of Israel mentioned in Deut. 25:17–19.
24:21, 22 Kenites were traditionally friendly to Israel, and some accompanied Israel to the Promised Land (Judg. 1:16). The Hebrew word for **nest** makes a pun on the names "Kenites" and **Kain. Asshur** is Assyria, which did not become a dominant power in the area until the late ninth or early eighth century B.C.
24:23, 24 These obscure words state one clear message: God is in control of the fate of nations (**God does this**).
24:25 Balaam . . . returned to his place: This would seem to put him out of reach of Israel's vengeance on Midian (see 31:8 where it is reported that he was killed; also, Balaam is

Israel's Harlotry in Moab

25 Now Israel remained in [a]Acacia Grove,[1] and the [b]people began to commit harlotry with the women of Moab.

2 [a]They invited the people to [b]the sacrifices of their gods, and the people ate and [c]bowed down to their gods.

3 So Israel was joined to Baal of Peor, and [a]the anger of the LORD was aroused against Israel.

4 Then the LORD said to Moses, [a]"Take all the leaders of the people and hang the offenders before the LORD, out in the sun, [b]that the fierce anger of the LORD may turn away from Israel."

5 So Moses said to [a]the *judges of Israel, [b]"Every one of you kill his men who were joined to Baal of Peor."

6 And indeed, one of the children of Israel came and presented to his brethren a Midianite woman in the sight of Moses and in the sight of all the congregation of the children of Israel, [a]who *were* weeping at the door of the tabernacle of meeting.

7 Now [a]when Phinehas [b]the son of Eleazar, the son of Aaron the priest, saw *it*, he rose from among the congregation and took a javelin in his hand;

8 and he went after the man of Israel into the tent and thrust both of them through, the man of Israel, and the woman through her body. So [a]the plague was [b]stopped among the children of Israel.

9 And [a]those who died in the plague were twenty-four thousand.

10 Then the LORD spoke to Moses, saying:

11 [a]"Phinehas the son of Eleazar, the son of Aaron the priest, has turned back My wrath from the children of Israel, because he was *zealous with My zeal among them, so that I did not consume the children of Israel in [b]My zeal.

12 "Therefore say, [a]'Behold, I give to him My [b]covenant of peace;

13 'and it shall be to him and [a]his descendants after him a covenant of [b]an everlasting priesthood, because he was [c]zealous* for his God, and [d]made [1]atonement for the children of Israel.' "

14 Now the name of the Israelite who was killed, who was killed with the Midianite woman, *was* Zimri the son of Salu, a leader of a father's house among the Simeonites.

15 And the name of the Midianite woman who was killed *was* Cozbi the daughter of [a]Zur; he *was* head of the people of a father's house in Midian.

16 Then the LORD spoke to Moses, say- 4
ing:

17 [a]"Harass the Midianites, and [1]attack them;

18 "for they harassed you with their [a]schemes[1] by which they seduced you in the matter of Peor and in the matter of Cozbi, the daughter of a leader of Midian, their sister, who was killed in the day of the plague because of Peor."

The Second Census of Israel

26 And it came to pass, after the [a]plague, that the LORD spoke to

CHAPTER 25

1 [a]Josh. 2:1 [b]Rev. 2:14 [1]Heb. *Shittim*
2 [a]Hos. 9:10 [b]Ex. 34:15 [c]Ex. 20:5
3 [a]Ps. 106:28, 29
4 [a]Deut. 4:3 [b]Num. 25:11
5 [a]Ex. 18:21 [b]Deut. 13:6, 9 *See WW at Judg. 2:18.
6 [a]Joel 2:17
7 [a]Ps. 106:30 [b]Ex. 6:25
8 [a]Ps. 106:30 [b]Num. 16:46–48
9 [a]Deut. 4:3
11 [a]Ps. 106:30 [b][Ex. 20:5] *See WW at Zech. 8:2.
12 [a][Mal. 2:4, 5; 3:1] [b]Is. 54:10
13 [a]1 Chr. 6:4–15 [b]Ex. 40:15 [c]Acts 22:3 [d][Heb. 2:17] [1]Lit. *covering* *See WW at Zech. 8:2.
15 [a]Num. 31:8
17 [a]Num. 31:1–3 [1]*be hostile toward*
18 [a]Rev. 2:14 [1]*tricks*

CHAPTER 26

1 [a]Num. 25:9

---

the subject of severe warnings in the NT: 2 Pet. 2:15; Jude 11; Rev. 2:14).

25:1–18 The Moabites and Midianites seduce the Israelites into apostasy. The occurrence of this story immediately after the blessing of Balaam is striking; it puts the Lord's resolve to bless Israel to the test. The story has three episodes: 1) the apostasy (vv. 1–3); 2) the punishment (vv. 4, 5); 3) repentance by the majority and defiance by some (vv. 6–13).

25:4 The leaders of the people were the ones to be hung out in the sun. That is the first stage of the punishment, apparently for the leaders of the apostasy.

25:5 The **judges** are responsible to execute the apostates, the people who followed the leaders who were punished (v. 4).

25:6 Presented . . . a Midianite woman: Exactly what this means is uncertain. It is apparently a matter of brazen defiance, an attempt to introduce an unbeliever into the most sacred aspect of Israel's faith, **the tabernacle.** It may also imply an effort to introduce the fertility cult of Baal religion with its ritual prostitution into Israelite worship. Note, also, it is a Midianite woman, not a Moabitess. This sets up the vengeance on the Midianites in ch. 31.

25:8 Into the tent: The word translated "tent" occurs only here in the Bible. It probably refers to an inner room in the tent of the Israelite where the couple were involved in the harlotry described in v. 1.

25:9 The plague, as elsewhere, is a means of divine punishment.

25:12 Phinehas, by this act of zeal, becomes the next in line for the high priesthood.

25:16–18 See section 4 of Truth-In-Action at the end of Num.

25:17 The **Midianites,** not the Moabites, are singled out for vengeance. Perhaps this is because the judgment on the Moabites was already given in Balaam's fourth oracle (24:17).

25:18 The seduction of Israel at Baal Peor is attributed to the Midianites here. The Moabites attempted the curse by Balaam, which was unsuccessful; the Midianites attempted a more sinister plan, apparently on the advice of Balaam, who was now living among the Midianites (see 31:8).

26:1–65 The new census was necessary because all of the first generation had perished (vv. 64, 65). This chapter begins the second major section after the departure from Sinai (see Introduction to Numbers: Outline) with the preparation of a new generation for the Promised Land. No more murmurings, complaints, or rebellions are recorded. The apportionment of the land and preparation for conquest along with various

Moses and Eleazar the son of Aaron
the priest, saying:
2 [a]"Take a census of all the congregation of the children of Israel [b]from
twenty years old and above, by their
fathers' houses, all who are able to go
to war in Israel."
3 So Moses and Eleazar the priest
spoke with them [a]in the plains of Moab
by the Jordan, *across from* Jericho,
saying:
4 "*Take a census of the people* from
twenty years old and above, just as the
LORD [a]commanded Moses and the children of Israel who came out of the land
of Egypt."
5 [a]Reuben *was* the firstborn of Israel.
The children of Reuben *were: of* Hanoch, the family of the Hanochites; *of*
Pallu, the family of the Palluites;
6 *of* Hezron, the family of the Hezronites; *of* Carmi, the family of the Car-
mites.
7 These *are* the families of the Reubenites: those who were numbered of
them were forty-three thousand seven
hundred and thirty.
8 And the son of Pallu *was* Eliab.
9 The sons of Eliab *were* Nemuel, Dathan, and Abiram. These *are* the Dathan and Abiram, [a]representatives of
the congregation, who contended
against Moses and Aaron in the company of Korah, when they contended
against the LORD;
10 [a]and the earth opened its mouth
and swallowed them up together with
Korah when that company died, when
the fire devoured two hundred and fifty
men; [b]and they became a sign.
11 Nevertheless [a]the children of Korah
did not die.
12 The sons of Simeon according to
their families *were: of* [1]Nemuel, the
family of the Nemuelites; *of* Jamin, the
family of the Jaminites; *of* [2]Jachin, the
family of the Jachinites;
13 *of* [1]Zerah, the family of the Zarhites; *of* Shaul, the family of the Sha-
ulites.
14 These *are* the families of the Sim-

2 [a]Ex. 30:12; 38:25, 26; Num. 1:2; 14:29 [b]Num. 1:3
3 [a]Num. 22:1; 31:12; 33:48; 35:1
4 [a]Num. 1:1
5 [a]Gen. 46:8; Ex. 6:14; 1 Chr. 5:1–3
9 [a]Num. 1:16; 16:1, 2
10 [a]Num. 16:32–35 [b]Num. 16:38–40; 1 Cor. 10:6; 2 Pet. 2:6
11 [a]Ex. 6:24; 1 Chr. 6:22, 23
12 [1]*Jemuel,* Gen. 46:10; Ex. 6:15 [2]*Jarib,* 1 Chr. 4:24
13 [1]*Zohar,* Gen. 46:10
15 [1]*Ziphion,* Gen. 46:16
16 [1]*Ezbon,* Gen. 46:16
17 [1]Sam., Syr. *Arodi* and Gen. 46:16
19 [a]Gen. 38:2; 46:12
20 [a]1 Chr. 2:3
23 [1]So with Sam., LXX, Syr., Vg.; Heb. *Puvah,* Gen. 46:13; 1 Chr. 7:1 [2]Sam., LXX, Syr., Vg. *Puaites*
24 [1]*Job,* Gen. 46:13
26 [a]Gen. 46:14

eonites: twenty-two thousand two hundred.
15 The sons of Gad according to their
families *were: of* [1]Zephon, the family
of the Zephonites; *of* Haggi, the family
of the Haggites; *of* Shuni, the family
of the Shunites;
16 *of* [1]Ozni, the family of the Oznites;
of Eri, the family of the Erites;
17 *of* [1]Arod, the family of the Arodites;
of Areli, the family of the Arelites.
18 These *are* the families of the sons
of Gad according to those who were
numbered of them: forty thousand five
hundred.
19 [a]The sons of Judah *were* Er and
Onan; and Er and Onan died in the
land of Canaan.
20 And [a]the sons of Judah according
to their families were: *of* Shelah, the
family of the Shelanites; *of* Perez, the
family of the Parzites; *of* Zerah, the
family of the Zarhites.
21 And the sons of Perez were: *of*
Hezron, the family of the Hezronites;
of Hamul, the family of the Hamu-
lites.
22 These *are* the families of Judah according to those who were numbered
of them: seventy-six thousand five
hundred.
23 The sons of Issachar according to
their families *were: of* Tola, the family
of the Tolaites; of [1]Puah, the family of
the [2]Punites;
24 of [1]Jashub, the family of the Ja-
shubites; of Shimron, the family of the
Shimronites.
25 These *are* the families of Issachar
according to those who were numbered of them: sixty-four thousand
three hundred.
26 [a]The sons of Zebulun according to
their families *were:* of Sered, the family of the Sardites; of Elon, the family
of the Elonites; of Jahleel, the family
of the Jahleelites.
27 These *are* the families of the Zebu-
lunites according to those who were
numbered of them: sixty thousand five
hundred.

---

new instructions make up the remainder of the Book of Numbers.

Vv. 1–51 give the results of the census. The names of the families are those of the first generation of the 12 tribal ancestors. Those families serve as the basis for the land division and inheritance rights.

Vv. 52–56 tell the purpose of the census, namely the division of the land among the tribes. This differs from the census of the first generation, which was to determine marching orders and battle ranks. Vv. 57–62 give the census of the Levites who would not be part of the land allotment.

26:2 All who are able to go to war envisions the conquest of the land.

26:8 Only three generations are listed from Reuben to Dathan and Abiram. Obviously the genealogy is abbreviated here since Israel was in Egypt for several hundred years. This should serve as a warning against assuming that biblical genealogies are complete enough to accurately date the exact history of humanity back to Adam.

26:11 Korah was a Levite mentioned here because of his association with Dathan and Abiram, who were Reubenites. Korah apparently was killed in front of the tent of meeting, hence his children were not swallowed up. See 16:27 where the children of Korah are not mentioned.

28 [a]The sons of Joseph according to their families, by Manasseh and Ephraim, *were:*

29 The sons of [a]Manasseh: of [b]Machir, the family of the Machirites; and Machir begot Gilead; of Gilead, the family of the Gileadites.

30 These *are* the sons of Gilead: *of* [1]Jeezer, the family of the Jeezerites; of Helek, the family of the Helekites;

31 *of* Asriel, the family of the Asrielites; *of* Shechem, the family of the Shechemites;

32 *of* Shemida, the family of the Shemidaites; *of* Hepher, the family of the Hepherites.

33 Now [a]Zelophehad the son of Hepher had no sons, but daughters; and the names of the daughters of Zelophehad *were* Mahlah, Noah, Hoglah, Milcah, and Tirzah.

34 These *are* the families of Manasseh; and those who were numbered of them *were* fifty-two thousand seven hundred.

35 These *are* the sons of Ephraim according to their families: of Shuthelah, the family of the Shuthalhites; of [1]Becher, the family of the Bachrites; of Tahan, the family of the Tahanites.

36 And these *are* the sons of Shuthelah: of Eran, the family of the Eranites.

37 These *are* the families of the sons of Ephraim according to those who were numbered of them: thirty-two thousand five hundred. These *are* the sons of Joseph according to their families.

38 [a]The sons of Benjamin according to their families were: of Bela, the family of the Belaites; of Ashbel, the family of the Ashbelites; of [b]Ahiram, the family of the Ahiramites;

39 of [a]Shupham,[1] the family of the Shuphamites; of [2]Hupham, the family of the Huphamites.

40 And the sons of Bela were [1]Ard and Naaman: [a]*of Ard,* the family of the Ardites; of Naaman, the family of the Naamites.

41 These *are* the sons of Benjamin according to their families; and those who were numbered of them *were* forty-five thousand six hundred.

42 These *are* the sons of Dan according to their families: of [1]Shuham, the family of the Shuhamites. These *are* the families of Dan according to their families.

43 All the families of the Shuhamites, according to those who were numbered of them, *were* sixty-four thousand four hundred.

44 [a]The sons of Asher according to their families *were:* of Jimna, the family of the Jimnites; of Jesui, the family of the Jesuites; of Beriah, the family of the Beriites.

45 Of the sons of Beriah: of Heber, the family of the Heberites; of Malchiel, the family of the Malchielites.

46 And the name of the daughter of Asher *was* Serah.

47 These *are* the families of the sons of Asher according to those who were numbered of them: fifty-three thousand four hundred.

48 [a]The sons of Naphtali according to their families *were:* of [1]Jahzeel, the family of the Jahzeelites; of Guni, the family of the Gunites;

49 of Jezer, the family of the Jezerites; of [a]Shillem, the family of the Shillemites.

50 These *are* the families of Naphtali according to their families; and those who were numbered of them *were* forty-five thousand four hundred.

51 [a]These *are* those who were numbered of the children of Israel: six hundred and one thousand seven hundred and thirty.

52 Then the LORD spoke to Moses, saying:

53 [a]"To these the land shall be [b]divided as an inheritance, according to the number of names.

54 [a]"To a large *tribe* you shall give a larger inheritance, and to a small *tribe* you shall give a smaller inheritance. Each shall be given its inheritance according to those who were numbered of them.

55 "But the land shall be [a]divided by lot; they shall inherit according to the names of the tribes of their fathers.

56 "According to the lot their inheri-

28 [a]Gen. 46:20; Deut. 33:16
29 [a]Josh. 17:1 [b]1 Chr. 7:14, 15
30 [1]*Abiezer,* Josh. 17:2
33 [a]Num. 27:1; 36:11
35 [1]*Bered,* 1 Chr. 7:20
38 [a]Gen. 46:21; 1 Chr. 7:6 [b]Gen. 46:21; 1 Chr. 8:1, 2
39 [a]1 Chr. 7:12 [1]MT *Shephupham; Shephuphan,* 1 Chr. 8:5 [2]*Huppim,* Gen. 46:21
40 [a]1 Chr. 8:3 [1]*Addar,* 1 Chr. 8:3
42 [1]*Hushim,* Gen. 46:23
44 [a]Gen. 46:17; 1 Chr. 7:30
48 [a]Gen. 46:24; 1 Chr. 7:13 [1]*Jahziel,* 1 Chr. 7:13
49 [a]1 Chr. 7:13
51 [a]Ex. 12:37; 38:26; Num. 1:46; 11:21
53 [a]Josh. 11:23; 14:1 [b]Num. 33:54
54 [a]Num. 33:54
55 [a]Num. 33:54; 34:13; Josh. 11:23; 14:2

26:28 The family tree of **Manasseh** is traced to the current generation (allowing for possible omissions) because of the problem of inheritance rights for those who have no sons.

26:33 The absence of a male descendant from a family of the Exodus generation caused problems for rights of inheritance, since women were provided for by their brothers or husbands. The fact that no brother existed meant the loss of an Israelite family from one tribe. The case is adjudicated in 27:1–12.

26:54–56 The proportion of the allotment depended on the preceding census. The division of the land was to be by lot, yet the assignment of the lots to the tribes was to be by size of the tribe. These two principles of allotment could cause a conflict if they differed. The text assumes that the Lord controls the lot and that the lot would correspond to the proportional size of the tribes. Thereafter there would be no ground for a tribe's expanding its borders as its size increased, because the borders were established by lot (a divinely authorized principle of division) as well as by size (a pragmatic principle of division).

tance shall be divided between the
larger and the smaller."
57 [a]And these *are* those who were
numbered of the Levites according to
their families: of Gershon, the family
of the Gershonites; of Kohath, the family of the Kohathites; of Merari, the
family of the Merarites.
58 These *are* the families of the Levites: the family of the Libnites, the
family of the Hebronites, the family of
the Mahlites, the family of the Mu-
shites, and the family of the Korathites.
And Kohath begot Amram.
59 The name of Amram's wife *was*
[a]Jochebed the daughter of Levi, who
was born to Levi in Egypt; and to Amram she bore Aaron and Moses and
their sister Miriam.
60 [a]To Aaron were born Nadab and
Abihu, Eleazar and Ithamar.
61 And [a]Nadab and Abihu died when
they offered profane fire before the
LORD.
62 [a]Now those who were numbered of
them were twenty-three thousand,
every male from a month old and
above; [b]for they were not numbered
among the other children of Israel, because there was [c]no inheritance given
to them among the children of Israel.
63 These *are* those who were numbered by Moses and Eleazar the priest,
who numbered the children of Israel
[a]in the plains of Moab by the Jordan,
across from Jericho.
64 [a]But among these there was not a
man of those who were numbered by
Moses and Aaron the priest when they
numbered the children of Israel in the
[b]Wilderness of Sinai.
65 For the LORD had said of them,
"They [a]shall surely die in the wilderness." So there was not left a man of
them, [b]except Caleb the son of Jephunneh and Joshua the son of Nun.

Inheritance Laws

27 Then came the daughters of
[a]Zelophehad the son of Hepher,
the son of Gilead, the son of Machir,
the son of Manasseh, from the families

57 [a]Gen. 46:11; Ex. 6:16–19; Num. 3:15; 1 Chr. 6:1, 16
59 [a]Ex. 2:1, 2; 6:20
60 [a]Num. 3:2
61 [a]Lev. 10:1, 2; Num. 3:3, 4; 1 Chr. 24:2
62 [a]Num. 3:39 [b]Num. 1:49 [c]Num. 18:20, 23, 24
63 [a]Num. 26:3
64 [a]Num. 14:29–35; Deut. 2:14–16; Heb. 3:17 [b]Num. 1:1–46
65 [a]Num. 14:26–35; [1 Cor. 10:5, 6] [b]Num. 14:30

CHAPTER 27

1 [a]Num. 26:33; 36:1, 11; Josh. 17:3
3 [a]Num. 14:35; 26:64, 65 [b]Num. 16:1, 2
4 [a]Deut. 25:6 [b]Josh. 17:4 [1]*withdrawn* [2]*inheritance*
5 [a]Ex. 18:13–26
7 [a]Num. 36:2; Josh. 17:4
11 [a]Num. 35:29

of Manasseh the son of Joseph; and
these *were* the names of his daughters:
Mahlah, Noah, Hoglah, Milcah, and
Tirzah.
2 And they stood before Moses, before Eleazar the priest, and before the
leaders and all the congregation, *by* the
doorway of the tabernacle of meeting,
saying:
3 "Our father [a]died in the wilderness;
but he was not in the company of those
who gathered together against the
LORD, [b]in company with Korah, but he
died in his own sin; and he had no sons.
4 "Why should the name of our father
be [a]removed[1] from among his family
because he had no son? [b]Give us a
[2]possession among our father's
brothers."
5 So Moses [a]brought their case before
the LORD.
6 And the LORD spoke to Moses, saying:
7 "The daughters of Zelophehad
speak *what is* right; [a]you shall surely
give them a possession of inheritance
among their father's brothers, and
cause the inheritance of their father to
pass to them.
8 "And you shall speak to the children of Israel, saying: 'If a man dies
and has no son, then you shall cause
his inheritance to pass to his daughter.
9 'If he has no daughter, then you
shall give his inheritance to his
brothers.
10 'If he has no brothers, then you
shall give his inheritance to his father's
brothers.
11 'And if his father has no brothers,
then you shall give his inheritance to
the relative closest to him in his family,
and he shall possess it.'" And it shall
be to the children of Israel [a]a statute
of judgment, just as the LORD commanded Moses.

KINGDOM DYNAMICS

27:1–11 A Godly Quest for Equal Rights (Daughters of Zelophehad), WOMEN. Zelophehad, of the tribe of Manasseh, had five daughters and no sons. Their

26:62 The males are listed from a month old, rather than 20 years, because the military service did not apply to the Levites, nor did the allotment of the land.

27:1–23 This chapter continues the preparation of the new generation for the inheritance of the land. The problem of a lack of male heirs is addressed in vv. 1–12, and a precedent for rights of inheritance is established. The preparation of Joshua to be the next leader of the new generation is the focus of vv. 12–23.

27:3 He died in his own sin: The intention is to underline that their father was no worse than others of the Exodus generation and did not deserve an unfair loss of identity among the clans of Israel.

27:9–11 The common principle in all these cases is that of the next closest relative's receiving one's inheritance. Daughters are the only females who are mentioned in the succession. The intent is to ensure that the land does not leave the domain of the clan.

names were: Mahlah, meaning "Sickness or Disease"; Noah, meaning "Rest or Comfort"; Hoglah, meaning "Partridge or Boxer"; Milcah, meaning "Queen or Counsel"; and Tirzah, meaning "Pleasantness." If we accept these women's names as pictures of their abilities, natures, or the adversities they had overcome, we see all the qualities necessary for the tenacity, tact, courage, wisdom, and grace they needed to request—and receive—an inheritance for themselves. Their presentation of their case to Moses and the leaders of Israel (v. 2), when the land was being divided to the tribes, is the Bible's first instance of an appeal for equal rights for women. The power of their example is in their wisdom of trusting God to see that they were not denied. All five daughters manifest a balance between a spirit of confrontation and a spirit of cooperation. The former is illustrated by their attack on injustice and the latter by their compliance with the elders' decision (36:2–12) that they should marry within their tribe. God defended them (v. 7) when they allowed Him to be their Deliverer/Provider. They reveal a contemporary pathway to overcoming inequality while sustaining a godly spirit.

(Gen. 24:15–67/Judg. 4:4, 5) F.L.

Joshua the Next Leader of Israel

12 Now the LORD said to Moses: [a]"Go up into this Mount Abarim, and see the land which I have given to the children of Israel.
13 "And when you have seen it, you also [a]shall [1]be gathered to your people, as Aaron your brother was gathered.
14 "For in the Wilderness of Zin, during the strife of the congregation, you [a]rebelled against My command to hallow Me at the waters before their eyes." (These *are* the [b]waters of Meribah, at Kadesh in the Wilderness of Zin.)

12 [a]Num. 33:47; Deut. 3:23–27; 32:48–52; 34:1–4
13 [a]Num. 20:12, 24, 28; 31:2; Deut. 10:6; 34:5, 6 [1]Die and join your ancestors
14 [a]Num. 20:12, 24; Deut. 1:37; 32:51; Ps. 106:32, 33 [b]Ex. 17:7
16 [a]Num. 16:22; Heb. 12:9
17 [a]Deut. 31:2; 1 Sam. 8:20; 18:13; 2 Chr. 1:10 [b]1 Kin. 22:17; Zech. 10:2; Matt. 9:36; Mark 6:34
18 [a]Gen. 41:38; Judg. 3:10; 1 Sam. 16:13, 18 [b]Deut. 34:9
19 [a]Deut. 3:28; 31:3, 7, 8, 23 [1]*commission*
20 [a]Num. 11:17 [b]Josh. 1:16–18 *See WW at 1 Chr. 29:11.
21 [a]Judg. 20:18, 23, 26; 1 Sam. 23:9; 30:7 [b]Ex. 28:30; 1 Sam. 28:6 [c]Josh. 9:14; 1 Sam. 22:10
23 [a]Deut. 3:28; 31:7, 8 [1]*commissioned*

CHAPTER 28

2 [a]Lev. 3:11; 21:6, 8; [Mal. 1:7, 12]

15 Then Moses spoke to the LORD, saying: 6
16 "Let the LORD, [a]the God of the spirits of all flesh, set a man over the congregation,
17 [a]"who may go out before them and go in before them, who may lead them out and bring them in, that the congregation of the LORD may not be [b]like sheep which have no shepherd."
18 And the LORD said to Moses: "Take Joshua the son of Nun with you, a man [a]in whom *is* the Spirit, and [b]lay your hand on him;
19 "set him before Eleazar the priest and before all the congregation, and [a]inaugurate[1] him in their sight.
20 "And [a]you shall give *some* of your *authority to him, that all the congregation of the children of Israel [b]may be obedient.
21 [a]"He shall stand before Eleazar the priest, who shall inquire before the LORD for him [b]by the judgment of the Urim. [c]At his word they shall go out, and at his word they shall come in, he and all the children of Israel with him—all the congregation."
22 So Moses did as the LORD commanded him. He took Joshua and set him before Eleazar the priest and before all the congregation.
23 And he laid his hands on him [a]and [1]inaugurated him, just as the LORD commanded by the hand of Moses.

Daily Offerings

28 Now the LORD spoke to Moses, saying,
2 "Command the children of Israel, and say to them, 'My offering, [a]My food for My offerings made by fire as a sweet aroma to Me, you shall be careful to offer to Me at their appointed time.'

27:12 Mount Abarim is the area in which Mt. Nebo is found (see 33:47). This then is an alternative way of describing Mt. Nebo, as in Deut. 34, where the command given here (vv. 12–14) is obeyed.
27:15–23 See section 6 of Truth-In-Action at the end of Num.
27:16 The God of the spirits of all flesh: See note on 16:22.
27:18 A man in whom *is* the Spirit refers back to ch. 11 where Joshua was present when the Spirit was imparted to the elders and they prophesied. It speaks of possessing discernment, wisdom, and insight.
27:19 Inaugurate means, literally, "command" or "give a charge" to Joshua.
27:20 *Some* of your authority: The phrase underlines the uniqueness of Moses as leader. Joshua, on the other hand, will share leadership with Eleazar as stated in v. 21. The distinction between religious and military leaders is made here for the first time.
28:1—30:42 Once again a section of instructions is included between the movements of the story. Chs. 28 and 29 contain regulations on the food offerings that are to be offered by the people as a whole rather than as individuals. Ch. 30 regulates the fulfillment of vows, particularly the vows of women and the rights of a father or husband to confirm or veto her vows.
28:1–15 This passage regulates offerings for the daily (vv. 1–8), weekly (vv. 9, 10), and monthly (vv. 11–15) offerings.
28:1–8 This is a **burnt offering** (see note on Lev. 1:3, 4), offered twice a day, by which the cycle of day and night, and therefore the whole of the 24-hour period, is dedicated to the worship of the Lord.

3 "And you shall say to them, [a]'This *is* the offering made by fire which you shall offer to the LORD: two male lambs in their first year *without blemish, day by day, as a regular burnt offering.

4 'The one lamb you shall offer in the morning, the other lamb you shall offer in the evening,

5 'and [a]one-tenth of an ephah of fine flour as a [b]grain offering mixed with one-fourth of a hin of pressed oil.

6 '*It is* [a]a regular burnt offering which was ordained at Mount Sinai for a sweet aroma, an offering made by fire to the LORD.

7 'And its drink offering *shall be* one-fourth of a hin for each lamb; [a]in a holy *place* you shall pour out the drink to the LORD as an offering.

8 'The other lamb you shall offer in the evening; as the morning grain offering and its drink offering, you shall offer *it* as an offering made by fire, a [1]sweet aroma to the LORD.

Sabbath Offerings

9 'And on the Sabbath day two lambs in their first year, without blemish, and two-tenths *of an ephah* of fine flour as a grain offering, mixed with oil, with its drink offering—

10 '*this is* [a]the burnt offering for every Sabbath, besides the regular burnt offering with its drink offering.

Monthly Offerings

11 [a]'At the beginnings of your months you shall present a burnt offering to the LORD: two young bulls, one ram, and seven lambs in their first year, without blemish;

12 [a]'three-tenths *of an ephah* of fine flour as a grain offering, mixed with oil, for each bull; two-tenths *of an ephah* of fine flour as a grain offering, mixed with oil, for the one ram;

13 'and one-tenth *of an ephah* of fine flour, mixed with oil, as a grain offering for each lamb, as a burnt offering of sweet aroma, an offering made by fire to the LORD.

14 'Their drink offering shall be half a hin of wine for a bull, one-third of a hin for a ram, and one-fourth of a hin for a lamb; this *is* the burnt offering for each month throughout the months of the year.

15 'Also [a]one kid of the goats as a sin offering to the LORD shall be offered, besides the regular burnt offering and its drink offering.

Offerings at Passover

16 [a]'On the fourteenth day of the first month *is* the Passover of the LORD.

17 [a]'And on the fifteenth day of this month *is* the feast; unleavened bread shall be eaten for seven days.

18 'On the [a]first day *you shall have* a holy [1]convocation. You shall do no [2]customary work.

19 'And you shall present an offering made by fire as a burnt offering to the LORD: two young bulls, one ram, and seven lambs in their first year. [a]Be sure they are without blemish.

20 'Their grain offering shall be of fine flour mixed with oil: three-tenths *of an ephah* you shall offer for a bull, and two-tenths for a ram;

21 'you shall offer one-tenth *of an ephah* for each of the seven lambs;

22 'also [a]one goat *as* a sin offering, to make [1]atonement for you.

23 'You shall offer these besides the burnt offering of the morning, which *is* for a regular burnt offering.

24 'In this manner you shall offer the food of the offering made by fire daily for seven days, as a sweet aroma to the LORD; it shall be offered besides the regular burnt offering and its drink offering.

25 'And [a]on the seventh day you shall have a holy convocation. You shall do no customary work.

Offerings at the Feast of Weeks

26 'Also [a]on the day of the firstfruits, when you bring a new grain offering to the LORD at your *Feast of* Weeks,

---

3 [a]Ex. 29:38–42 *See WW at Lev. 23:12. **5** [a]Ex. 16:36; Num. 15:4 [b]Lev. 2:1 **6** [a]Ex. 29:42; Amos 5:25 **7** [a]Ex. 29:42 **8** [1]*pleasing* **10** [a]Ezek. 46:4 **11** [a]Num. 10:10; 1 Sam. 20:5; 1 Chr. 23:31; 2 Chr. 2:4; Ezra 3:5; Neh. 10:33; Is. 1:13, 14; Ezek. 45:17; 46:6, 7; Hos. 2:11; Col. 2:16 **12** [a]Num. 15:4–12 **15** [a]Num. 15:24; 28:3, 22 **16** [a]Ex. 12:1–20; Lev. 23:5–8; Num. 9:2–5; Deut. 16:1–8; Ezek. 45:21 **17** [a]Lev. 23:6 **18** [a]Ex. 12:16; Lev. 23:7 [1]*assembly* or *gathering* [2]*occupational* **19** [a]Lev. 22:20; Num. 28:31; 29:8; Deut. 15:21 **22** [a]Num. 28:15 [1]Lit. *covering* **25** [a]Ex. 12:16; 13:6; Lev. 23:8 **26** [a]Ex. 23:16; 34:22; Lev. 23:10–21; Deut. 16:9–12; Acts 2:1

28:5 See note on 15:4.

28:9, 10 Besides the regular burnt offering: A doubling of the daily offering is meant here. The weekly cycle is acknowledged in worship.

28:11–15 The beginning of a month is an independent cycle of time, distinct from a week. It, too, has its appropriate expression in worship of the Lord. Thus each period of time (day, week, month) is committed to the Lord by an act of worship.

28:15 The sin offering included in v. 15 works like a monthly day of atonement. See note on Lev. 4:3.

28:16—29:40 This passage regulates the offerings for the great annual feasts. The order corresponds closely to Lev. 23.

28:16–25 The focus of the passage here is not so much on the Passover (v. 16), but on the Feast of Unleavened Bread (vv. 17–25). See notes on Ex. 12:1–11, 14–20.

28:26–31 The ***Feast of* Weeks,** here also called **the day of the firstfruits,** celebrated the end of the wheat harvest. See note on Ex. 23:16.

you shall have a holy convocation. You
shall do no customary work.
27 'You shall present a burnt offering
as a sweet aroma to the LORD: [a]two
young bulls, one ram, and seven lambs
in their first year,
28 'with their grain offering of fine
flour mixed with oil: three-tenths *of an
ephah* for each bull, two-tenths for the
one ram,
29 'and one-tenth for each of the seven
lambs;
30 '*also* one kid of the goats, to make
[1]atonement for you.
31 [a]'Be sure they are without [1]blemish.
You shall present *them* with their
drink offerings, besides the regular
burnt offering with its grain offering.

Offerings at the Feast of Trumpets

29 'And in the seventh month, on
the first *day* of the month, you
shall have a holy convocation. You
shall do no customary work. For you
[a]it is a day of blowing the trumpets.
2 'You shall offer a burnt offering as
a sweet aroma to the LORD: one young
bull, one ram, *and* seven lambs in their
first year, without blemish.
3 'Their grain offering *shall be* fine
flour mixed with oil: three-tenths *of an
ephah* for the bull, two-tenths for the
ram,
4 'and one-tenth for each of the seven
lambs;
5 'also one kid of the goats *as* a sin
offering, to make atonement for you;
6 'besides [a]the burnt offering with its
grain offering for the New Moon,
[b]the regular burnt offering with its
grain offering, and their drink offerings, [c]according to their ordinance, as
a sweet aroma, an offering made by
fire to the LORD.

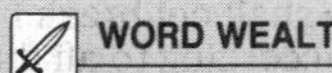
WORD WEALTH

29:6 grain offering, *minchah* (min-*khah*); Strong's #4503: An offering, gift, tribute, present, sacrifice, portion, or donation. Although the offerings of Cain and Abel are termed *minchah* in Gen. 4:4, 5, *minchah* is usually translated "grain offering" (Lev. 6:14). Elsewhere, it is translated "gifts," "presents," or "tribute," as in 1 Kin. 4:21. The *minchah* is primarily a religious offering, but may also be a personal gift that one gives to his ruler.

Offerings on the Day of Atonement

7 [a]'On the tenth *day* of this seventh
month you shall have a holy convocation. You shall [b]afflict your souls; you
shall not do any work.
8 'You shall present a burnt offering
to the LORD *as* a sweet aroma: one
young bull, one ram, *and* seven lambs
in their first year. [a]Be sure they are
without blemish.
9 'Their grain offering *shall be of* fine
flour mixed with oil: three-tenths *of an
ephah* for the bull, two-tenths for the
one ram,
10 'and one-tenth for each of the seven
lambs;
11 'also one kid of the goats *as* a sin
offering, besides [a]the sin offering for
atonement, the regular burnt offering
with its grain offering, and their drink
offerings.

Offerings at the Feast of Tabernacles

12 [a]'On the fifteenth day of the seventh
month you shall have a holy convocation. You shall do no customary work,
and you shall *keep a feast to the LORD
seven days.
13 [a]'You shall present a burnt offering,
an offering made by fire as a sweet
aroma to the LORD: thirteen young
bulls, two rams, *and* fourteen lambs in
their first year. They shall be without
blemish.
14 'Their grain offering *shall be of* fine
flour mixed with oil: three-tenths *of an
ephah* for each of the thirteen bulls,
two-tenths for each of the two rams,
15 'and one-tenth for each of the fourteen lambs;
16 'also one kid of the goats *as* a sin
offering, besides the regular burnt

27 [a]Lev. 23:18, 19
30 [1]Lit. *covering*
31 [a]Num. 28:3, 19 [1]*defect*

CHAPTER 29

1 [a]Ex. 23:16; 34:22; Lev. 23:23–25
6 [a]Num. 28:11–15 [b]Num. 28:3 [c]Num. 15:11, 12
7 [a]Lev. 16:29–34; 23:26–32 [b]Ps. 35:13; Is. 58:5
8 [a]Num. 28:19
11 [a]Lev. 16:3, 5
12 [a]Lev. 23:33–35; Deut. 16:13–15; Ezek. 45:25 *See WW at Ex. 23:14.
13 [a]Ezra 3:4

29:1–40 The common theme of this chapter is the festivals of the seventh month, which corresponds approximately to the month of September. This month begins the new year for the agricultural calendar.
29:1–6 The **day of blowing the trumpets** heralded the new agricultural year. The months of the year were numbered from the time of the Exodus, but the beginning of the year was celebrated, according to the agricultural cycle, in the seventh month.
29:6 **The New Moon** was the first day of their 28-day month. It was a day of rest, special sacrifices, and the blowing of trumpets.
29:7–11 See notes on Lev. 16.
29:12–39 The Feast of Tabernacles commemorated Israel's wandering in the wilderness and the end of the harvest. The observance began on the fifteenth day of Ethanim (September). There was a holy assembly on the first and eighth days and the Israelites lived in booths of palm trees to commemorate the wilderness wandering. It is also called the Feast of Booths.

offering, its grain offering, and its
drink offering.
17 'On the [a]second day *present* twelve
young bulls, two rams, fourteen lambs
in their first year without blemish,
18 'and their grain offering and their
drink offerings for the bulls, for the
rams, and for the lambs, by their number, [a]according to the ordinance;
19 'also one kid of the goats *as* a sin
offering, besides the regular burnt offering with its grain offering, and their
drink offerings.
20 'On the third day *present* eleven
bulls, two rams, fourteen lambs in their
first year without blemish,
21 'and their grain offering and their
drink offerings for the bulls, for the
rams, and for the lambs, by their number, [a]according to the ordinance;
22 'also one goat *as* a sin offering, besides the regular burnt offering, its
grain offering, and its drink offering.
23 'On the fourth day *present* ten bulls,
two rams, *and* fourteen lambs in their
first year, without blemish,
24 'and their grain offering and their
drink offerings for the bulls, for the
rams, and for the lambs, by their number, according to the ordinance;
25 'also one kid of the goats *as* a sin
offering, besides the regular burnt offering, its grain offering, and its drink
offering.
26 'On the fifth day *present* nine bulls,
two rams, *and* fourteen lambs in their
first year without blemish,
27 'and their grain offering and their
drink offerings for the bulls, for the
rams, and for the lambs, by their number, according to the ordinance;
28 'also one goat *as* a sin offering, besides the regular burnt offering, its
grain offering, and its drink offering.
29 'On the sixth day *present* eight
bulls, two rams, *and* fourteen lambs in
their first year without blemish,
30 'and their grain offering and their
drink offerings for the bulls, for the
rams, and for the lambs, by their number, according to the ordinance;
31 'also one goat *as* a sin offering, besides the regular burnt offering, its
grain offering, and its drink offering.
32 'On the seventh day *present* seven
bulls, two rams, *and* fourteen lambs in
their first year without blemish,
33 'and their grain offering and their
drink offerings for the bulls, for the
rams, and for the lambs, by their number, according to the ordinance;
34 'also one goat *as* a sin offering, besides the regular burnt offering, its
grain offering, and its drink offering.
35 'On the eighth day you shall have
a [a]sacred[1] assembly. You shall do no
customary work.
36 'You shall present a burnt offering,
an offering made by fire as a sweet
aroma to the LORD: one bull, one ram,
seven lambs in their first year *without
blemish,
37 'and their grain offering and their
drink offerings for the bull, for the ram,
and for the lambs, by their number, according to the ordinance;
38 'also one goat *as* a sin offering, besides the regular burnt offering, its
grain offering, and its drink offering.
39 'These you shall present to the LORD
at your [a]appointed feasts (besides your
[b]vowed offerings and your freewill offerings) as your burnt offerings and
your grain offerings, as your drink offerings and your peace offerings.' "
40 So Moses told the children of Israel
everything, just as the LORD commanded Moses.

The Law Concerning Vows

30 Then Moses spoke to [a]the heads
of the tribes concerning the children of Israel, saying, "This *is* the thing
which the LORD has commanded:
2 [a]"If a man makes a vow to the LORD,
or [b]swears* an oath to bind himself by
some agreement, he shall not break his
word; he shall [c]do according to all that
proceeds out of his mouth.
3 "Or if a woman makes a vow to the
LORD, and binds *herself* by some agree-

17 [a]Lev. 23:36
18 [a]Num. 15:12; 28:7, 14; 29:3, 4, 9, 10
21 [a]Num. 29:18
35 [a]Lev. 23:36 [1]*solemn*
36 *See WW at Lev. 23:12.
39 [a]Lev. 23:1–44; 1 Chr. 23:31; 2 Chr. 31:3; Ezra 3:5; Neh. 10:33; Is. 1:14 [b]Lev. 7:16; 22:18, 21, 23; 23:38

CHAPTER 30

1 [a]Num. 1:4, 16; 7:2
2 [a]Lev. 27:2; Deut. 23:21–23; Judg. 11:30, 31, 35; Eccl. 5:4 [b]Lev. 5:4; Matt. 14:9; Acts 23:14 [c]Job 22:27; Ps. 22:25; 50:14; 66:13, 14; Nah. 1:15 *See WW at Gen. 26:3.

30:1–16 The conditions under which a release from a **vow** may be granted are discussed here. There are no releases for a male, even a male dependent on his father's care. Likewise, an independent woman, who has never been married, is not addressed. These omissions underline the concern of the chapter, the relation between the institutions of family and the worship forms. A woman may be released from her vow in one of three ways: 1) by her father, providing she is still a dependent (vv. 3–5); 2) by her husband at the time of her marriage to him if she has made a vow prior to the marriage (vv. 6–8); or 3) by her husband if the vow is made while married (vv. 10–15). The father or husband affirms the vow by inaction, but he must actively negate such a vow and the negation must take place immediately upon hearing of it (v. 14). Widows and divorced women may not be released from vows they have made (v. 9).

The hierarchical family structure of the culture is evident here. It is important to note that the woman has an independent relationship to God. Her vow is conditioned by the parental or marital relationship, but it is not determined by it.

30:1 Heads of the tribes is used only here in the entire Pentateuch. The authoritarian structure of tribe and family is thus introduced at the outset of this section.

ment while in her father's house in her
youth,
4 "and her father hears her vow and
the agreement by which she has bound
herself, and her father [1]holds his
peace, then all her vows shall stand,
and every agreement with which she
has bound herself shall stand.
5 "But if her father overrules her on
the day that he hears, then none of her
vows nor her agreements by which she
has bound herself shall stand; and the
LORD will release her, because her father overruled her.
6 "If indeed she takes a husband,
while bound by her vows or by a rash
utterance from her lips by which she
bound herself,
7 "and her husband hears *it,* and
makes no response to her on the day
that he hears, then her vows shall
stand, and her agreements by which
she bound herself shall stand.
8 "But if her husband [a]overrules her
on the day that he hears *it,* he shall
make void her vow which she took and
what she uttered with her lips, by
which she bound herself, and the LORD
will release her.
9 "Also any vow of a widow or a divorced woman, by which she has
bound herself, shall stand against her.
10 "If she vowed in her husband's
house, or bound herself by an agreement with an oath,
11 "and her husband heard *it,* and
made no response to her *and* did not
overrule her, then all her vows shall
stand, and every agreement by which
she bound herself shall stand.
12 "But if her husband truly made
them void on the day he heard *them,*
then whatever proceeded from her lips
concerning her vows or concerning the
agreement binding her, it shall not
stand; her husband has made them
[1]void, and the LORD will release her.
13 "Every vow and every binding oath
to afflict her soul, her husband may
confirm it, or her husband may make
it void.
14 "Now if her husband makes no response whatever to her from day to
day, then he confirms all her vows or
all the agreements that bind her; he
confirms them, because he made no response to her on the day that he heard
them.
15 "But if he does make them void after he has heard *them,* then he shall
bear her guilt."
16 These *are* the *statutes which the
LORD commanded Moses, between a
man and his wife, and between a father
and his daughter in her youth in her
father's house.

Vengeance on the Midianites

31 And the LORD spoke to Moses,
saying:
2 [a]"Take vengeance on the Midianites for the children of Israel. Afterward you shall [b]be gathered to your
people."
3 So Moses spoke to the people, saying, "Arm some of yourselves for war,
and let them go against the Midianites
to take vengeance for the LORD on
[a]Midian.
4 "A thousand from each tribe of all
the tribes of Israel you shall send to
the war."
5 So there were recruited from the divisions of Israel one thousand from
each tribe, twelve thousand armed for
war.
6 Then Moses sent them to the war,
one thousand from *each* tribe; he sent
them to the war with Phinehas the son
of Eleazar the priest, with the holy articles and [a]the signal trumpets in his
hand.
7 And they warred against the

4 [1]*says nothing to interfere*
8 [a][Gen. 3:16]
12 [1]*annulled* or *invalidated*
16 *See WW at Neh. 9:13.

CHAPTER 31

2 [a]Num. 25:17 [b]Num. 27:12, 13
3 [a]Josh. 13:21
6 [a]Num. 10:9

30:5 The LORD will release her means the Lord will forgive her. The vow is not made null and void, but it is an unfulfilled promise that is forgiven (see vv. 8, 12 and the case in v. 15 where there is no forgiveness, but guilt is incurred by the husband).
30:13 To afflict her soul is an expression often associated with fasting (see Is. 58:3, 5). It refers to any act of self-denial.
30:15 He shall bear her guilt: See note on v. 5.
31:1–54 This chapter completes the account of Balaam, the Moabites, and the Midianites that began when Israel entered the plains of Moab in ch. 22. It is narrated in two parts: an account of the battle (vv. 1–11) and regulations concerning the division of the plunder (vv. 12–54). Vv. 12–24 are also concerned with two things: who among the Midianites should survive (vv. 12–18), and purification of the spoils of war (vv. 19–24). Vv. 25–47 include a command (vv. 25–30) and a compliance report (vv. 31–47) concerning the division of the booty among warriors, people, the high priest, and the Levites as the Lord's representatives. Vv. 48–54 narrate a freewill offering in thanks for the preservation of all the fighting men of Israel's army.
31:2 Vengeance on the Midianites: The Midianites are only collaborators in the Balaam story of chs. 22—25. The Moabites are the primary players; yet it was a Midianite woman who, together with an Israelite man, brought the plague of ch. 25 (note especially 25:16–18).
31:6 The holy war was led by a priest rather than a military leader, perhaps because it was a war of vengeance for the profanation of the tabernacle (ch. 25).
31:7 They killed all the males must be taken as hyperbole to emphasize the magnitude of the victory, or else the Midianites would have passed from history. This was not the case as their reappearance in the Book of Judges shows.

Midianites, just as the LORD commanded Moses, and [a]they killed all the
[b]males.
8 They killed the kings of Midian with
the rest of those who were killed—
[a]Evi, Rekem, [b]Zur, Hur, and Reba, the
five kings of Midian. [c]Balaam the son
of Beor they also killed with the sword.
9 And the children of Israel took the
women of Midian captive, with their little ones, and took as spoil all their cattle,
all their flocks, and all their goods.
10 They also burned with fire all the
cities where they dwelt, and all their
forts.
11 And [a]they took all the spoil and all
the booty—of man and beast.

Return from the War

12 Then they brought the captives, the
booty, and the spoil to Moses, to Eleazar the priest, and to the congregation
of the children of Israel, to the camp
in the plains of Moab by the Jordan,
across from Jericho.
13 And Moses, Eleazar the priest, and
all the leaders of the congregation,
went to meet them outside the camp.
14 But Moses was angry with the officers of the army, *with* the captains
over thousands and captains over hundreds, who had come from the battle.
15 And Moses said to them: "Have you
kept [a]all the women alive?
16 "Look, [a]these *women* caused the
children of Israel, through the [b]counsel
of Balaam, to trespass against the LORD
in the incident of Peor, and [c]there was
a plague among the congregation of
the LORD.
17 "Now therefore, [a]kill every male
among the little ones, and kill every
woman who has known a man intimately.
18 "But keep alive [a]for yourselves all
the young girls who have not known
a man intimately.
19 "And as for you, [a]remain outside
the camp seven days; whoever has
killed any person, and [b]whoever has
touched any slain, purify yourselves
and your captives on the third day and
on the seventh day.

7 [a]Deut. 20:13; Judg. 21:11; 1 Sam. 27:9; 1 Kin. 11:15, 16 [b]Gen. 34:25
8 [a]Josh. 13:21 [b]Num. 25:15 [c]Num. 31:16; Josh. 13:22
11 [a]Deut. 20:14
15 [a]Deut. 20:14
16 [a]Num. 25:2 [b]Num. 24:14; 2 Pet. 2:15; Rev. 2:14 [c]Num. 25:9
17 [a]Deut. 7:2; 20:16–18; Judg. 21:11
18 [a]Deut. 21:10–14
19 [a]Num. 5:2 [b]Num. 19:11–22
21 [1]*statute*
23 [a]Num. 19:9, 17
24 [a]Lev. 11:25 *See WW at Lev. 14:31.
26 [1]*captured*
27 [a]Josh. 22:8; 1 Sam. 30:24
28 [a]Num. 31:30, 47 [1]*tax*
29 [a]Deut. 18:1–5
30 [a]Num. 31:42–47 [b]Num. 3:7, 8, 25, 31, 36; 18:3, 4 [1]*perform the service*

20 "Purify every garment, everything
made of leather, everything woven of
goats' *hair,* and everything made of
wood."
21 Then Eleazar the priest said to the
men of war who had gone to the battle,
"This *is* the [1]ordinance of the law
which the LORD commanded Moses:
22 "Only the gold, the silver, the
bronze, the iron, the tin, and the lead,
23 "everything that can endure fire,
you shall put through the fire, and it
shall be clean; and it shall be purified
[a]with the water of purification. But all
that cannot endure fire you shall put
through water.
24 [a]"And you shall wash your clothes
on the seventh day and be *clean, and
afterward you may come into the
camp."

Division of the Plunder

25 Now the LORD spoke to Moses, saying:
26 "Count up the plunder that was
[1]taken—of man and beast—you and Eleazar the priest and the chief fathers
of the congregation;
27 "and [a]divide the plunder into two
parts, between those who took part in
the war, who went out to battle, and
all the congregation.
28 "And levy a [1]tribute for the LORD
on the men of war who went out to
battle: [a]one of every five hundred of
the persons, the cattle, the donkeys,
and the sheep;
29 "take *it* from their half, and [a]give
it to Eleazar the priest as a heave offering to the LORD.
30 "And from the children of Israel's
half you shall take [a]one of every fifty,
drawn from the persons, the cattle, the
donkeys, and the sheep, from all the
livestock, and give them to the Levites
[b]who [1]keep charge of the tabernacle
of the LORD."
31 So Moses and Eleazar the priest did
as the LORD commanded Moses.
32 The booty remaining from the plunder, which the men of war had taken,
was six hundred and seventy-five thousand sheep,

31:8 The text does not make clear how **Balaam** came to be among the Midianites, since he had gone home to *Mesopotamia (24:25).* It is also difficult to know why they should kill him, since he only blessed Israel. It appears that Balaam had returned to the Midianites and advised them in the matter of Baal Peor (see 31:16).

31:21 Eleazar instructs the people on the appropriate means of purifying different categories of booty, after Moses gives the primary command. This clearly depicts the priests' duty of instructing the people on how to carry out the law commanded by Moses.

31:25–47 This section governs the distribution of the spoils of war: 50 percent to the military and 50 percent to the nonmilitary, which are taxed for Yahweh (whose portion the high priest receives) and the Levites, respectively. The Midianite booty is the specific conquest, which becomes the basis for customary distribution after Israel's later battles.

33 seventy-two thousand cattle,
34 sixty-one thousand donkeys,
35 and thirty-two thousand persons in
all, of women who had not known a
man intimately.
36 And the half, the *portion for those
who had gone out to war, was in number three hundred and thirty-seven
thousand five hundred sheep;
37 and the LORD's [1]tribute of the sheep
was six hundred and seventy-five.
38 The cattle *were* thirty-six thousand,
of which the LORD's tribute *was*
seventy-two.
39 The donkeys *were* thirty thousand
five hundred, of which the LORD's tribute *was* sixty-one.
40 The persons *were* sixteen thousand,
of which the LORD's tribute *was* thirty-
two persons.
41 So Moses gave the tribute *which*
was the LORD's heave offering to Eleazar the priest, [a]as the LORD commanded Moses.
42 And from the children of Israel's
half, which Moses separated from the
men who fought—
43 now the half belonging to the congregation was three hundred and
thirty-seven thousand five hundred
sheep,
44 thirty-six thousand cattle,
45 thirty thousand five hundred donkeys,
46 and sixteen thousand persons—
47 and [a]from the children of Israel's
half Moses took one of every fifty,
drawn from man and beast, and gave
them to the Levites, who kept charge
of the tabernacle of the LORD, as the
LORD commanded Moses.
48 Then the officers who *were* over
thousands of the *army, the captains
of thousands and captains of hundreds,
came near to Moses;
49 and they said to Moses, "Your servants have taken a count of the men
of war who *are* under our command,
and not a man of us is missing.
50 "Therefore we have brought an offering for the LORD, what every man
found of ornaments of gold: armlets
and bracelets and signet rings and earrings and necklaces, [a]to make [1]atone-
ment for ourselves before the LORD."
51 So Moses and Eleazar the priest received the gold from them, all the fashioned ornaments.
52 And all the gold of the offering that
they offered to the LORD, from the captains of thousands and captains of hundreds, was sixteen thousand seven
hundred and fifty shekels.
53 [a](The men of war had taken spoil,
every man for himself.)
54 And Moses and Eleazar the priest
received the gold from the captains of
thousands and of hundreds, and
brought it into the tabernacle of meeting [a]as a memorial for the children of
Israel before the LORD.

36 *See WW at Zech. 2:12. **37** [1]*tax* **41** [a]Num. 5:9, 10; 18:8, 19 **47** [a]Num. 31:30 **48** *See WW at Ps. 68:11.

50 [a]Ex. 30:12–16 [1]Lit. *covering* **53** [a]Num. 31:32; Deut. 20:14 **54** [a]Ex. 30:16

CHAPTER 32

1 [a]Num. 21:32; Josh. 13:25; 2 Sam. 24:5 [b]Deut. 3:13 **3** [a]Num. 32:36 [b]Josh. 13:17, 26 [c]Num. 32:38 [d]Num. 32:38 **4** [a]Num. 21:24, 34, 35 **5** *See WW at Zech. 12:10. **7** [a]Num. 13:27—14:4

The Tribes Settling East of the Jordan

32 Now the children of Reuben and
the children of Gad had a very
great multitude of livestock; and when
they saw the land of [a]Jazer and the
land of [b]Gilead, that indeed the region
was a place for livestock,
2 the children of Gad and the children
of Reuben came and spoke to Moses,
to Eleazar the priest, and to the leaders
of the congregation, saying,
3 "Ataroth, Dibon, Jazer, [a]Nimrah,
[b]Heshbon, Elealeh, [c]Shebam, Nebo,
and [d]Beon,
4 "the country [a]which the LORD defeated before the congregation of Israel, *is* a land for livestock, and your
servants have livestock."
5 Therefore they said, "If we have
found *favor in your sight, let this land
be given to your servants as a possession. Do not take us over the Jordan."
6 And Moses said to the children of
Gad and to the children of Reuben:
"Shall your brethren go to war while
you sit here?
7 "Now why will you [a]discourage the
heart of the children of Israel from

31:48–54 A miraculous preservation of the soldiers' lives motivates a special offering to Yahweh. Its purpose is **to make atonement for** (v. 50) the soldiers whose lives have been spared. Atonement is used here in the sense of "payment for," as in the tax at Ex. 30:15, 16, rather than in the sense of "covering for sin." The offering is kept for the tabernacle itself (v. 54).

32:1–42 This chapter begins the occupation of the land, at least as it pertains to the east side of the Jordan River. Two and a half tribes choose to settle in the territory recently conquered, which was suitable for livestock (vv. 1–5). The concern of Moses is whether the real motive for their desire to stay on the other side of the Jordan is a fear of entering the Promised Land, which had been the downfall of the first generation (vv. 6–15). When that issue is resolved by a commitment on the part of the two and a half tribes to participate in the conquest of the Promised Land, their request to live east of the Jordan is granted (vv. 16–42).

32:7 To **discourage the heart** of the other tribes by not participating in the conquest of the land west of the Jordan would be tantamount to what the spies did in chs. 13 and 14, as v. 9 makes clear. Their actions would have implications for all Israel (v. 15).

going over into the land which the
LORD has given them?
8 "Thus your fathers did [a]when I sent
them away from Kadesh Barnea
[b]to see the land.
9 "For [a]when they went up to the Valley of Eshcol and saw the land, they
discouraged the heart of the children
of Israel, so that they did not go into
the land which the LORD had given
them.
10 [a]"So the LORD's anger was aroused
on that day, and He swore an oath, saying,
11 'Surely none of the men who came
up from Egypt, [a]from twenty years old
and above, shall see the land of which
I swore to Abraham, Isaac, and Jacob,
because [b]they have not wholly followed Me,
12 'except Caleb the son of Jephunneh,
the Kenizzite, and Joshua the son of
Nun, [a]for they have wholly followed
the LORD.'
13 "So the LORD's anger was aroused
against Israel, and He made them
[a]wander in the wilderness forty years,
until [b]all the generation that had done
evil in the sight of the LORD was
gone.
14 "And look! You have risen in your
fathers' place, a brood of sinful men,
to increase still more the [a]fierce anger
of the LORD against Israel.
15 "For if you [a]turn away from following Him, He will once again leave
them in the wilderness, and you will
destroy all these people."
16 Then they came near to him and
said: "We will build sheepfolds here
for our livestock, and cities for our little ones,
17 "but [a]we ourselves will be armed,
ready *to go* before the children of Israel until we have brought them to
their place; and our little ones will
dwell in the fortified cities because of
the inhabitants of the land.
18 [a]"We will not return to our homes
until every one of the children of Israel
has [1]received his inheritance.
19 "For we will not inherit with them
on the other side of the Jordan and beyond, [a]because our inheritance has
fallen to us on this eastern side of the
Jordan."
20 Then [a]Moses said to them: "If you
do this thing, if you arm yourselves before the LORD for the war,
21 "and all your armed men cross over
the Jordan before the LORD until He
has driven out His enemies from before
Him,
22 "and [a]the land is subdued before
the LORD, then afterward [b]you may return and be blameless before the LORD
and before Israel; and [c]this land shall
be your *possession before the LORD.
23 "But if you do not do so, then take
note, you have sinned against the
LORD; and be sure [a]your sin will find
you out.
24 [a]"Build cities for your little ones
and folds for your sheep, and do
[1]what has proceeded out of your
mouth."
25 And the children of Gad and the
children of Reuben spoke to Moses,
saying: "Your servants will do as my
lord commands.
26 [a]"Our little ones, our wives, our
flocks, and all our livestock will be
there in the cities of Gilead;
27 [a]"but your servants will cross over,
every man armed for war, before the
LORD to battle, just as my lord says."
28 So Moses gave command [a]concern-
ing them to Eleazar the priest, to
Joshua the son of Nun, and to the chief
fathers of the tribes of the children of
Israel.
29 And Moses said to them: "If the
children of Gad and the children of
Reuben cross over the Jordan with
you, every man armed for battle before
the LORD, and the land is subdued before you, then you shall give them the
land of Gilead as a possession.
30 "But if they do not cross over armed
with you, they shall have possessions
among you in the land of Canaan."
31 Then the children of Gad and the
children of Reuben answered, saying:
"As the LORD has said to your servants,
so we will do.
32 "We will cross over armed before
the LORD into the land of Canaan, but
the possession of our inheritance *shall
remain* with us on this side of the Jordan."
33 So [a]Moses gave to the children of
Gad, to the children of Reuben, and to
half the tribe of Manasseh the son of
Joseph, [b]the kingdom of Sihon king of

8 [a]Num. 13:3, 26 [b]Deut. 1:19–25
9 [a]Num. 13:24, 31; Deut. 1:24, 28
10 [a]Num. 14:11; Deut. 1:34–36
11 [a]Num. 14:28, 29; 26:63–65; Deut. 1:35 [b]Num. 14:24, 30
12 [a]Num. 14:6–9, 24, 30; Deut. 1:36; Josh. 14:8, 9
13 [a]Num. 14:33–35 [b]Num. 26:64, 65
14 [a]Num. 11:1; Deut. 1:34
15 [a]Deut. 30:17, 18; Josh. 22:16–18; 2 Chr. 7:19; 15:2
17 [a]Josh. 4:12, 13
18 [a]Josh. 22:1–4 [1]*possessed*
19 [a]Josh. 12:1; 13:8
20 [a]Deut. 3:18; Josh. 1:14
22 [a]Deut. 3:20; Josh. 11:23 [b]Josh. 22:4 [c]Deut. 3:12, 15, 16, 18; Josh. 1:15; 13:8, 32; 22:4, 9 *See WW at Josh. 22:9.
23 [a]Gen. 4:7; 44:16; Josh. 7:1–26; Is. 59:12; [Gal. 6:7]
24 [a]Num. 32:16 [1]*what you said you would do*
26 [a]Josh. 1:14
27 [a]Josh. 4:12
28 [a]Josh. 1:13
33 [a]Deut. 3:8–17; 29:8; Josh. 12:1–6; 13:8–31; 22:4 [b]Num. 21:24, 33, 35

32:8–13 See notes on ch. 13.

32:23 Be sure your sin will find you out is often misunderstood. It is not that their sin will be uncovered in a day of judgment and punished by Yahweh, but that an evil deed will come back on the head of the evildoer. What they sow, they will reap.

32:28–30 In light of Moses' impending death (see 31:2), **Eleazar** and **Joshua,** the leaders of the second generation, are informed of the settler's obligations.

the Amorites and the kingdom of Og
king of Bashan, the land with its cities
within the borders, the cities of the surrounding country.
34 And the children of Gad built
[a]Dibon and Ataroth and [b]Aroer,
35 Atroth and Shophan and [a]Jazer and
Jogbehah,
36 [a]Beth Nimrah and Beth Haran,
[b]fortified cities, and folds for sheep.
37 And the children of Reuben built
[a]Heshbon and Elealeh and Kirjathaim,
38 [a]Nebo and [b]Baal Meon [c](*their*
names being changed) and Shibmah;
and they gave *other* names to the cities
which they built.
39 And the children of [a]Machir the son
of Manasseh went to Gilead and took
it, and [1]dispossessed the Amorites who
were in it.
40 So Moses [a]gave Gilead to Machir
the son of Manasseh, and he dwelt in
it.
41 Also [a]Jair the son of Manasseh
went and took its small towns, and
called them [b]Havoth Jair.[1]
42 Then Nobah went and took Kenath
and its villages, and he called it Nobah,
after his own name.

Israel's Journey from Egypt Reviewed

33 These *are* the journeys of the
children of Israel, who went out
of the land of Egypt by their armies
under the [a]hand of Moses and Aaron.
2 Now Moses wrote down the starting
points of their journeys at the command of the LORD. And these *are* their
journeys according to their starting
points:
3 They [a]departed from Rameses in
[b]the first month, on the fifteenth day
of the first month; on the day after the
Passover the children of Israel went
out [c]with boldness in the sight of all
the Egyptians.
4 For the Egyptians were burying all
their firstborn, [a]whom the LORD had
killed among them. Also [b]on their gods
the LORD had executed judgments.
5 [a]Then the children of Israel moved
from Rameses and camped at Succoth.
6 They departed from [a]Succoth and
camped at Etham, which *is* on the edge
of the wilderness.
7 [a]They moved from Etham and
turned back to Pi Hahiroth, which *is*
east of Baal Zephon; and they camped
near Migdol.
8 They departed [1]from before Hahiroth and [a]passed through the midst of
the sea into the wilderness, went three
days' journey in the Wilderness of
Etham, and camped at Marah.
9 They moved from Marah and
[a]came to Elim. At Elim *were* twelve
springs of water and seventy palm
trees; so they camped there.
10 They moved from Elim and camped
by the Red Sea.
11 They moved from the Red Sea and
camped in the [a]Wilderness of Sin.
12 They journeyed from the Wilderness of Sin and camped at Dophkah.
13 They departed from Dophkah and
camped at Alush.
14 They moved from Alush and
camped at [a]Rephidim, where there was
no water for the people to drink.
15 They departed from Rephidim and
camped in the [a]Wilderness of Sinai.
16 They moved from the Wilderness of
Sinai and camped [a]at [1]Kibroth Hattaavah.
17 They departed from Kibroth Hattaavah and [a]camped at Hazeroth.
18 They departed from Hazeroth and
camped at [a]Rithmah.
19 They departed from Rithmah and
camped at Rimmon Perez.
20 They departed from Rimmon Perez
and camped at Libnah.
21 They moved from Libnah and
camped at Rissah.
22 They journeyed from Rissah and
camped at Kehelathah.
23 They went from Kehelathah and
camped at Mount Shepher.
24 They moved from Mount Shepher
and camped at Haradah.
25 They moved from Haradah and
camped at Makheloth.
26 They moved from Makheloth and
camped at Tahath.

34 [a]Num. 33:45, 46 [b]Deut. 2:36
35 [a]Num. 32:1, 3
36 [a]Num. 32:3 [b]Num. 32:24
37 [a]Num. 21:27
38 [a]Is. 46:1 [b]Ezek. 25:9 [c]Ex. 23:13; Josh. 23:7
39 [a]Gen. 50:23; Num. 27:1; 36:1 [1]*drove out*
40 [a]Deut. 3:12, 13, 15; Josh. 13:31
41 [a]Deut. 3:14; Josh. 13:30 [b]Judg. 10:4; 1 Kin. 4:13 [1]Lit. *Towns of Jair*

CHAPTER 33

1 [a]Ps. 77:20
3 [a]Ex. 12:37 [b]Ex. 12:2; 13:4 [c]Ex. 14:8
4 [a]Ex. 12:29 [b][Ex. 12:12; 18:11]; Is. 19:1
5 [a]Ex. 12:37
6 [a]Ex. 13:20
7 [a]Ex. 14:1, 2, 9
8 [a]Ex. 14:22; 15:22, 23 [1]Many Heb. mss., Sam., Syr., Tg., Vg. *from Pi Hahiroth;* cf. Num. 33:7
9 [a]Ex. 15:27
11 [a]Ex. 16:1
14 [a]Ex. 17:1; 19:2
15 [a]Ex. 16:1; 19:1, 2
16 [a]Num. 11:34 [1]Lit. *Graves of Craving*
17 [a]Num. 11:35
18 [a]Num. 12:16

32:38 *Their* names being changed refers to the two preceding names, which contained the names of pagan deities, thus necessitating a name change for the followers of Yahweh.

33:1–56 The chapter has two parts: a review of the itinerary from Egypt to the plains of Moab (vv. 1–49), and the Lord's speech to Moses instructing the Israelites to clear the land of the inhabitants for the preservation of the true worship of Yahweh.

33:1–49 The itinerary listed here is attributed to Moses (vv. 1, 2). The only events recorded are the Lord's judgments on the Egyptians (v. 4) and the death of Aaron (vv. 38, 39). A few locations are briefly described (vv. 9, 14). Otherwise it is pure itinerary. Many of the places cannot be identified, so that no mapping of the exact route of the Exodus has achieved a consensus among historians. Since some names are not mentioned in the recounting of the journey, the selection of material shows that the purpose of the narratives is not simply to recount the history of the journey, but to serve as examples (1 Cor. 10:6).

27 They departed from Tahath and
camped at Terah.
28 They moved from Terah and
camped at Mithkah.
29 They went from Mithkah and
camped at Hashmonah.
30 They departed from Hashmonah
and [a]camped at Moseroth.
31 They departed from Moseroth and
camped at Bene Jaakan.
32 They moved from [a]Bene Jaakan
and [b]camped at Hor Hagidgad.
33 They went from Hor Hagidgad and
camped at Jotbathah.
34 They moved from Jotbathah and
camped at Abronah.
35 They departed from Abronah
[a]and camped at Ezion Geber.
36 They moved from Ezion Geber and
camped in the [a]Wilderness of Zin,
which *is* Kadesh.
37 They moved from [a]Kadesh and
camped at Mount Hor, on the boundary of the land of Edom.
38 Then [a]Aaron the priest went up to
Mount Hor at the command of the
LORD, and died there in the fortieth
year after the children of Israel had
come out of the land of Egypt, on the
first *day* of the fifth month.
39 Aaron *was* one hundred and
twenty-three years old when he died
on Mount Hor.
40 Now [a]the king of Arad, the Canaanite, who dwelt in the South in the land
of Canaan, heard of the coming of the
children of Israel.
41 So they departed from Mount Hor
and camped at Zalmonah.
42 They departed from Zalmonah and
camped at Punon.
43 They departed from Punon and
[a]camped at Oboth.
44 [a]They departed from Oboth and
camped at Ije Abarim, at the border of
Moab.
45 They departed from [1]Ijim and
camped [a]at Dibon Gad.
46 They moved from Dibon Gad and
camped at [a]Almon Diblathaim.

30 [a]Deut. 10:6
32 [a]Deut. 10:6 [b]Deut. 10:7
35 [a]Deut. 2:8; 1 Kin. 9:26; 22:48
36 [a]Num. 20:1; 27:14
37 [a]Num. 20:22, 23; 21:4
38 [a]Num. 20:25, 28; Deut. 10:6; 32:50
40 [a]Num. 21:1
43 [a]Num. 21:10
44 [a]Num. 21:11
45 [a]Num. 32:34 [1]Same as *Ije Abarim*, v. 44
46 [a]Jer. 48:22; Ezek. 6:14
47 [a]Num. 21:20; Deut. 32:49
48 [a]Num. 22:1; 31:12; 35:1
49 [a]Num. 25:1; Josh. 2:1 [1]Heb. *Abel Shittim*
51 [a]Deut. 7:1, 2; 9:1; Josh. 3:17
52 [a]Ex. 23:24, 33; 34:13; Deut. 7:2, 5; 12:3; Judg. 2:2; Ps. 106:34–36 [1]Places for pagan worship *See WW at Ezek. 6:3.
53 [a]Deut. 11:31; Josh. 21:43
54 [a]Num. 26:53–56
55 [a]Josh. 23:13; Judg. 2:3

47 They moved from Almon Diblathaim [a]and camped in the mountains
of Abarim, before Nebo.
48 They departed from the mountains
of Abarim and [a]camped in the plains
of Moab by the Jordan, *across from*
Jericho.
49 They camped by the Jordan, from
Beth Jesimoth as far as the [a]Abel Acacia Grove[1] in the plains of Moab.

Instructions for the Conquest of Canaan

50 Now the LORD spoke to Moses in the
plains of Moab by the Jordan, *across*
from Jericho, saying,
51 "Speak to the children of Israel, and
say to them: [a]'When you have crossed
the Jordan into the land of Canaan,
52 [a]'then you shall drive out all the
inhabitants of the land from before
you, destroy all their engraved stones,
destroy all their molded images, and
demolish all their [1]high* places;
53 'you shall dispossess *the inhab-*
itants of the land and dwell in it, for I
have given you the land to [a]possess.
54 'And [a]you shall divide the land by
lot as an inheritance among your families; to the larger you shall give a larger
inheritance, and to the smaller you
shall give a smaller inheritance; there
everyone's *inheritance* shall be whatever falls to him by lot. You shall inherit according to the tribes of your fathers.
55 'But if you do not drive out the 4
inhabitants of the land from before
you, then it shall be that those whom
you let remain *shall be* [a]irritants in
your eyes and thorns in your sides, and
they shall harass you in the land where
you dwell.
56 'Moreover it shall be *that* I will do
to you as I thought to do to them.' "

The Appointed Boundaries of Canaan

34 Then the LORD spoke to Moses,
saying,

33:50–56 The Israelites must **drive out** (v. 52) or **dispossess** (v. 53) (the verbs are the same in the Hebrew text) the inhabitants of the land. Failure to do so will result in the Israelites' being driven from the land, as Yahweh intended to do to the Canaanites (v. 56). This concern illustrates the incompatibility of the old way of life with the new life of faith. V. 54 speaks of the land as an **inheritance** for the Israelites and lays the groundwork for many of the prophets' indictments against the wealthy Israelites who dispossess the poor from their inheritance (see Mic. 2:1–5).
33:55, 56 See section 4 of Truth-In-Action at the end of Num.
34:1—36:13 With the command to dispossess the inhabitants and to possess the land (33:50–56) serving as an introduction, the remaining chapters in Num. deal with the boundaries (34:1–15), division (34:16–29), allotment (ch. 35), and inheritance of the land (ch. 36).
34:1–15 The verses relate the Lord's instructions (vv. 1–12) and the speech of Moses complying with them (vv. 13–15). The borders discussed in the Lord's speech do not include the land east of the Jordan (see ch. 32), but are accounted for in the speech of Moses. It is an ideal description of the border, one that was never fully realized. In fact, the Philistines occupied the coastal areas throughout the period of the monarchy.

2 "Command the children of Israel,
and say to them: 'When you come into
[a]the land of Canaan, this *is* the land
that shall fall to you as an inheritance—the land of Canaan to its
boundaries.
3 [a]'Your southern border shall be
from the Wilderness of Zin along the
border of Edom; then your southern
border shall extend eastward to the
end of [b]the Salt Sea;
4 'your border shall turn from the
southern side of [a]the Ascent of Akrabbim, continue to Zin, and be on the
south of [b]Kadesh Barnea; then it shall
go on to [c]Hazar Addar, and continue
to Azmon;
5 'the border shall turn from Azmon
[a]to the Brook of Egypt, and it shall end
at the Sea.
6 'As for the [a]western border, you
shall have the Great Sea for a border;
this shall be your western border.
7 'And this shall be your northern
border: From the Great Sea you shall
mark out your *border* line to [a]Mount
Hor;
8 'from Mount Hor you shall mark out
your border [a]to the entrance of Hamath; then the direction of the border
shall be toward [b]Zedad;
9 'the border shall proceed to Ziph-
ron, and it shall end at [a]Hazar Enan.
This shall be your northern border.
10 'You shall mark out your eastern
border from Hazar Enan to Sheph-
ham;
11 'the border shall go down from
Shepham [a]to Riblah on the east side
of Ain; the border shall go down and
reach to the eastern [1]side of the Sea
[b]of Chinnereth;
12 'the border shall go down along the
Jordan, and it shall end at [a]the Salt
Sea. This shall be your land with its
surrounding boundaries.' "
13 Then Moses commanded the children of Israel, saying: [a]"This *is* the
land which you shall inherit by lot,
which the LORD has commanded to
give to the nine tribes and to the half-
tribe.
14 [a]"For the tribe of the children of
Reuben according to the house of their
fathers, and the tribe of the children
of Gad according to the house of their
fathers, have received *their inheritance;* and the half-tribe of Manasseh
has received its inheritance.
15 "The two tribes and the half-tribe
have received their inheritance on this
side of the Jordan, *across from* Jericho
eastward, toward the sunrise."

The Leaders Appointed to Divide the Land

16 And the LORD spoke to Moses, saying,
17 "These *are* the names of the men
who shall divide the land among you
as an inheritance: [a]Eleazar the priest
and Joshua the son of Nun.
18 "And you shall take one [a]leader of
every tribe to divide the land for the
inheritance.
19 "These *are* the names of the men:
from the tribe of Judah, Caleb the son
of Jephunneh;
20 "from the tribe of the children of
Simeon, Shemuel the son of Ammihud;
21 "from the tribe of Benjamin, Elidad
the son of Chislon;
22 "a leader from the tribe of the children of Dan, Bukki the son of Jogli;
23 "from the sons of Joseph: a leader
from the tribe of the children of Manasseh, Hanniel the son of Ephod,
24 "and a leader from the tribe of the
children of Ephraim, Kemuel the son
of Shiphtan;
25 "a leader from the tribe of the children of Zebulun, Elizaphan the son of
Parnach;
26 "a leader from the tribe of the children of Issachar, Paltiel the son of Az-
zan;
27 "a leader from the tribe of the children of Asher, Ahihud the son of She-
lomi;
28 "and a leader from the tribe of the
children of Naphtali, Pedahel the son
of Ammihud."
29 These *are* the ones the LORD commanded to [1]divide the inheritance
among the children of Israel in the land
of Canaan.

Cities for the Levites

35 And the LORD spoke to Moses
in [a]the plains of Moab by the
Jordan *across from* Jericho, saying:

CHAPTER 34

2 [a]Gen. 17:8; Deut. 1:7, 8; Ps. 78:54, 55; 105:11
3 [a]Josh. 15:1–3; Ezek. 47:13, 19 [b]Gen. 14:3; Josh. 15:2
4 [a]Josh. 15:3 [b]Num. 13:26; 32:8 [c]Josh. 15:3, 4
5 [a]Gen. 15:18; Josh. 15:4, 47; 1 Kin. 8:65; Is. 27:12
6 [a]Ex. 23:31; Josh. 15:12; Ezek. 47:20
7 [a]Num. 33:37
8 [a]Num. 13:21; Josh. 13:5; 2 Kin. 14:25 [b]Ezek. 47:15
9 [a]Ezek. 47:17
11 [a]2 Kin. 23:33; Jer. 39:5, 6 [b]Deut. 3:17; Josh. 11:2; 12:3; 13:27; 19:35; Matt. 14:34; Luke 5:1 [1]Lit. *shoulder*
12 [a]Num. 34:3
13 [a]Gen. 15:18; Num. 26:52–56; Deut. 11:24; Josh. 14:1–5
14 [a]Num. 32:33
17 [a]Josh. 14:1, 2; 19:51
18 [a]Num. 1:4, 16
29 [1]*apportion*

CHAPTER 35

1 [a]Num. 33:50

34:16–29 The task of dividing the land is delegated to a member from every tribe. Presumably the people mentioned in this chapter would subdivide the tribal territory by family after the division of Josh. 13—19. The order of the tribes is given by geographical arrangement from south to north.

35:1–34 The chapter deals with the portion of the Levites who are to receive 48 cities (vv. 6, 7), six of which are to be cities of refuge (vv. 6, 9–34). The Levitical cities and cities of refuge described in ch. 35 correspond to Josh. 20 and 21.

2 [a]"Command the children of Israel
that they give the Levites cities to dwell
in from the inheritance of their possession, and you shall *also* give the Levites [b]common-land around the cities.
3 "They shall have the cities to dwell
in; and their common-land shall be for
their cattle, for their herds, and for all
their animals.
4 "The common-land of the cities
which you will give the Levites *shall
extend* from the wall of the city outward a thousand cubits all around.
5 "And you shall measure outside the
city on the east side two thousand cubits, on the south side two thousand
cubits, on the west side two thousand
cubits, and on the north side two thousand cubits. The city *shall be* in the
middle. This shall belong to them as
common-land for the cities.
6 "Now among the cities which you
will give to the Levites *you shall appoint* [a]six cities of refuge, to which a
manslayer may flee. And to these you
shall add forty-two cities.
7 "So all the cities you will give to
the Levites *shall be* [a]forty-eight; these
you shall give with their common-
land.
8 "And the cities which you will give
shall be [a]from the possession of the
children of Israel; [b]from the larger
tribe you shall give many, from the
smaller you shall give few. Each shall
give some of its cities to the Levites,
in proportion to the inheritance that
each receives."

Cities of Refuge

9 Then the LORD spoke to Moses, saying,
10 "Speak to the children of Israel, and
say to them: [a]'When you cross the Jordan into the land of Canaan,
11 'then [a]you shall appoint cities to be
cities of refuge for you, that the manslayer who kills any person accidentally may flee there.
12 [a]'They shall be cities of refuge for
you from the avenger, that the manslayer may not die until he stands before the congregation in judgment.
13 'And of the cities which you give,
you shall have [a]six cities of refuge.
14 [a]'You shall appoint three cities on
this side of the Jordan, and three cities
you shall appoint in the land of Canaan, *which* will be cities of refuge.
15 'These six cities shall be for refuge
for the children of Israel, [a]for the stranger, and for the sojourner among them,
that anyone who kills a person accidentally may flee there.
16 [a]'But if he strikes him with an iron
implement, so that he dies, he *is* a murderer; the murderer shall surely be put
to death.
17 'And if he strikes him with a stone
in the hand, by which one could die,
and he does die, he *is* a murderer;
the murderer shall surely be put to
death.
18 'Or *if* he strikes him with a wooden
hand weapon, by which one could die,
and he does die, he *is* a murderer;
the murderer shall surely be put to
death.
19 [a]'The[1] avenger of blood himself
shall put the murderer to death; when
he meets him, he shall put him to
death.
20 [a]'If he pushes him out of hatred or,
[b]while lying in wait, hurls something
at him so that he dies,
21 'or in enmity he strikes him with his
hand so that he dies, the one who
struck *him* shall surely be put to death.
He *is* a murderer. The avenger of blood
shall put the murderer to death when
he meets him.
22 'However, if he pushes him suddenly [a]without enmity, or throws anything at him without lying in wait,
23 'or uses a stone, by which a man

2 [a]Josh. 14:3, 4; 21:2, 3; Ezek. 45:1; 48:10–20 [b]Lev. 25:32–34
6 [a]Deut. 4:41; Josh. 20:2, 7, 8; 21:3, 13
7 [a]Josh. 21:41
8 [a]Josh. 21:3 [b]Num. 26:54; 33:54
10 [a]Deut. 19:2; Josh. 20:1–9
11 [a]Ex. 21:13; Num. 35:22–25; Deut. 19:1–13
12 [a]Deut. 19:6; Josh. 20:3, 5, 6
13 [a]Num. 35:6
14 [a]Deut. 4:41; Josh. 20:8
15 [a]Num. 15:16
16 [a]Ex. 21:12, 14; Lev. 24:17; Deut. 19:11, 12
19 [a]Num. 35:21, 24, 27; Deut. 19:6, 12 [1]A family member who is to avenge the victim
20 [a]Gen. 4:8; 2 Sam. 3:27; 20:10; 1 Kin. 2:31, 32 [b]Ex. 21:14; Deut. 19:11, 12
22 [a]Ex. 21:13

35:2 Common-land derives from a word meaning "a place to herd cattle" and is appropriate for the use of the land in this context. More important, though, is the connotation that it is not to be owned by individuals but is for use by all Levites in the city.

35:4, 5 Apparently the **thousand cubits** of space in v. 4 was to remain open land, and the **two thousand cubits** in v. 5 could be used for planting.

35:6 The **cities of refuge** introduce the topic of vv. 9–34.

35:9–34 These verses do not specify the locations of the cities of refuge, but they regulate their function. Upon causing the death of another human being, the killer had to flee to a sanctuary city until he could stand trial. If he was found guilty of murder, he would be executed by the next of kin. If he was found guilty of manslaughter, he could find sanctuary within the city of refuge from then until the death of the reigning high priest. At that point he could return to his home. There is no distinction between civil and religious law. The whole land is the Lord's, and they are His people. See the notes on Josh. 20.

35:12 The **congregation** is the legal authority to try the case. See also v. 25.

35:16–24 The legal distinction between murder and manslaughter is formulated in a series of examples of what is murder (vv. 16–21) and what is manslaughter (vv. 22, 23).

35:19 The **avenger of blood** (vv. 19, 25, 27) is a legal role that fell to a near relative whose duty it was to execute the killer.

could die, throwing *it* at him without
seeing *him,* so that he dies, while he
was not his enemy or seeking his harm,
24 'then [a]the congregation shall judge
between the manslayer and the avenger of blood according to these judgments.
25 'So the congregation shall deliver
the manslayer from the hand of the
avenger of blood, and the congregation
shall return him to the city of refuge
where he had fled, and [a]he shall remain there until the death of the high
priest [b]who was *anointed with the
holy oil.
26 'But if the manslayer at any time
goes outside the limits of the city of
refuge where he fled,
27 'and the avenger of blood finds him
outside the limits of his city of refuge,
and the avenger of blood kills the manslayer, he shall not be guilty of [1]blood,
28 'because he should have remained
in his city of refuge until the death of
the high priest. But after the death of
the high priest the manslayer may return to the land of his possession.
29 'And these *things* shall be [a]a statute
of judgment to you throughout your
generations in all your dwellings.
30 'Whoever kills a person, the murderer shall be put to death on the
[a]testimony of witnesses; but *one witness is not *sufficient* testimony against
a person for the death *penalty*.
31 'Moreover you shall take no ransom
for the life of a murderer who *is* guilty
of death, but he shall surely be put to
death.
32 'And you shall take no ransom for
him who has fled to his city of refuge,
that he may return to dwell in the land
before the death of the priest.
33 'So you shall not pollute the land
where you *are;* for blood [a]defiles the
land, and no [1]atonement can be made
for the land, for the blood that is shed
on it, except [b]by the blood of him who
shed it.
34 'Therefore [a]do not defile the land
which you inhabit, in the midst of
which I dwell; for [b]I the LORD dwell
among the children of Israel.' "

24 [a]Num. 35:12; Josh. 20:6
25 [a]Josh. 20:6 [b]Ex. 29:7; Lev. 4:3; 21:10 *See WW at Is. 61:1.
27 [1]Murder
29 [a]Num. 27:11
30 [a]Deut. 17:6; 19:15; Matt. 18:16; John 7:51; 8:17, 18; 2 Cor. 13:1; Heb. 10:28 *See WW at Deut. 6:4.
33 [a]Deut. 21:7, 8; Ps. 106:38 [b]Gen. 9:6 [1]Lit. *covering*
34 [a]Lev. 18:24, 25; Deut. 21:23 [b]Ex. 29:45, 46

CHAPTER 36

1 [a]Num. 26:29 [b]Num. 27:1–11
2 [a]Num. 26:55; 33:54; Josh. 17:4 [b]Num. 27:1, 5–7
3 [a]Num. 27:4
4 [a]Lev. 25:10
5 [a]Num. 27:7
6 [a]Num. 36:11, 12 [1]Lit. *be wives to*
7 [a]1 Kin. 21:3
8 [a]1 Chr. 23:22

Marriage of Female Heirs

36 Now the chief fathers of the
families of the [a]children of
Gilead the son of Machir, the son of
Manasseh, of the families of the sons
of Joseph, came near and [b]spoke before Moses and before the leaders,
the chief fathers of the children of Israel.
2 And they said: [a]"The LORD commanded my lord *Moses* to give the land
as an inheritance by lot to the children
of Israel, and [b]my lord was commanded by the LORD to give the inheritance of our brother Zelophehad to his
daughters.
3 "Now if they are married to any of
the sons of the *other* tribes of the children of Israel, then their inheritance
will be [a]taken from the inheritance of
our fathers, and it will be added to the
inheritance of the tribe into which they
marry; so it will be taken from the lot
of our inheritance.
4 "And when [a]the Jubilee of the children of Israel comes, then their inheritance will be added to the inheritance
of the tribe into which they marry; so
their inheritance will be taken away
from the inheritance of the tribe of our
fathers."
5 Then Moses commanded the children of Israel according to the word
of the LORD, saying: [a]"What the tribe
of the sons of Joseph speaks is
right.
6 "This *is* what the LORD commands
concerning the daughters of Zelophehad, saying, 'Let them [1]marry whom
they think best, [a]but they may marry
only within the family of their father's
tribe.'
7 "So the inheritance of the children
of Israel shall not change hands from
tribe to tribe, for every one of the children of Israel shall [a]keep the inheritance of the tribe of his fathers.
8 "And [a]every daughter who possesses an inheritance in any tribe of
the children of Israel shall be the wife
of one of the family of her father's
tribe, so that the children of Israel each

35:25 It is implied that the trial is held in the town of the killer. If he is found guilty of manslaughter, he is then returned to the city of refuge to which he had fled.

The death of the high priest is not an arbitrary designation. Death must be atoned for by death (vv. 33, 34). The high priest's death is apparently substitutionary atonement for the life of the manslayer.

35:31, 32 Ransom money is inadequate payment for the death of a person. Neither murderer nor manslayer may buy off his sentence.

35:33, 34 Murder pollutes **the land** and must be atoned for (v. 33), or the land will be defiled (v. 34).

36:1–13 This chapter returns to possible loopholes in the situation of 27:1–11. It serves as an appendix to the entire book by preserving the integrity of each tribe as a unique entity.

36:6 This law applied only to daughters who inherited property under the provisions of 27:1–11.

may possess the inheritance of his fathers.
9 "Thus no inheritance shall change hands from *one* tribe to another, but every tribe of the children of Israel shall keep its own inheritance."
10 Just as the LORD commanded Moses, so did the daughters of Zelophehad;
11 [a]for Mahlah, Tirzah, Hoglah, Milcah, and Noah, the daughters of Zelophehad, were married to the sons of their father's brothers.
12 They were married into the families of the children of Manasseh the son of Joseph, and their inheritance remained in the tribe of their father's family.
13 These *are* the commandments and the **judgments** which the LORD commanded the children of Israel by the hand of Moses [a]in the plains of Moab by the Jordan, *across from* Jericho.

11 [a]Num. 26:33; 27:1
13 [a]Num. 26:3; 33:50

WORD WEALTH

36:13 judgments, *mishpat* (meesh-*paht*); Strong's #4941: Decision, determination, judgment; a personal cause or right; justice, rectification, correction, punishment. Occurring more than 400 times, *mishpat* is from the verb *shaphat,* "to decide, decree, judge, rule, determine." Judgment is that faculty (found always in God and sometimes in man) that produces decisions based on justice, rightness, truth, fairness, and equity. Judgment rectifies imbalance and sets things right again. If punishment is what is required to rectify things, then judgment brings punishment. Princes are expected to rule with justice or judgment (Is. 32:2). God Himself is called "a God of judgment" (Is. 30:18). In Is. 26:9, God's just decisions fill the Earth and instruct the peoples in righteousness.

TRUTH-IN-ACTION through Numbers

Letting the LIFE of the Holy Spirit Bring Faith's Works Alive in You!

Truth Numbers Teaches	Text	**Action** Numbers Invites
1 Keys to Knowing God and His Ways Num. reveals much about the character and ways of God. Moses' prayer in Ex. 33:13 should be dominant in the heart of every believer. Much can be learned about God and His ways as we observe His dealings with Israel.	22:32	**Know** that not all restraint or opposition is from the Devil. God will often oppose those whose ways are reckless before Him.
	23:19	**Understand** that God is immutable, never changing in nature, character, or in what He says (see Heb. 13:8).
	23:23; 24:10	**Know** that God is for you. He will even turn curses into blessings and use evil shaped against you for your good (see Rom. 8:28).
2 Steps to Dynamic Devotion The devotion God desires from His people is a theme that continues in Num. The Nazirite Law and the lives of Caleb and Joshua provide outstanding examples of the devotion God honors. They stand in bold contrast to Israel's general unfaithfulness.	6:1–8	**Commit yourself** to be wholly devoted to the Lord. God calls all His people to live lives fully separated unto Him.
	14:6–9, 24, 30	**Allow** the Lord to develop in you the spirit of Caleb and Joshua. **Follow** the Lord wholeheartedly.
3 Guidelines for Growing in Godliness Num. gives several important guidelines for building a life that increases its capacity for God. Becoming godly does not happen automatically through exposure to religious exercise. Rather, it is the result of	1:49–51	**Honor** the gifts of ministry the Lord has given to the church (see Eph. 4:10–13).
	2:2, 17	**Gather** frequently with God's people. **Make** the gathering of God's people a central part of your life in Christ.

Truth Numbers Teaches	Text	**Action** Numbers Invites
3 a conscious pursuit of God. From the way we regard the community of God to the way we embrace the truths of our redemption, every aspect of godly living is important.	9:2, 3 21:8 23:9	**Set apart** certain regular times to celebrate God's redemptive acts on your behalf. **Celebrate** with all of your heart. **Look to** Jesus' sacrifice (see John 3:14, 15). **Trust** His death as sufficient to cover all your sin. **Live** so that others will know that you do not consider yourself as one of the worldly.
4 **Steps to Dealing with Sin** Num. reiterates that it is important for God's people to know how to deal with sin. The seducing Midianites and the fiery serpents are among the analogies that show sin's vicious and virulent nature. God deals with sin ruthlessly and calls His people to deal with it similarly in their own personal lives. Sin must not be allowed to remain, but must be irradicated wherever possible.	5:5–8 19:1–22 25:16–18 33:55, 56	**Confess** your sins, and **make restitution.** Your restitution also belongs to God. **Confess** your sin quickly, and **avail yourself** often of God's provision for us to be purified from all our sin (see 1 John 1:7, 9). **Deal ruthlessly** with your own sin. **Search** it out in your own heart, and **repent** from it. **Give it no place** to stay or grow in you. **Deal thoroughly** with sin. Any sin you fail to deal with may well be your undoing.
5 **Keys to Contentment** Num. underlines that God's people are to be contented with God's provision. Discontent reveals a lack of faith in God. He knows what we need and will meet that need in His perfect time. Faith is willing to wait for that time and rest in His present provision.	2:1–34 11:1 18:20	**Accept** where God has placed you in His body. **Rest** in the fact that He has placed you just where He wants you to be (see 1 Cor. 12:18). **Do not complain** because of hardships. God designs them to train us for maturity. **Rejoice! Know** that the Lord is your inheritance because He has given you His Son and eternal life.
6 **Lessons for Leaders** Num. presents a number of crucial lessons for His leaders. Because leaders serve as examples, His Word has much to say about them specifically. All of God's people can learn from these passages and profit through their application.	11:14–25 20:7–12 27:15–23	**Share** the load of ministry with others God has put under your charge in order to increase, rather than limit, the ministry. **Honor** the Lord as holy among His people. **Never take credit** for something God has done through you. **Remember** that you are responsible to raise up successors to your leadership (see 2 Tim. 2:2).
7 **Keys to Relating Authority** Num. says much about relationship to those who bear God's delegated authority. Some of God's most severe judgments come for Israel's rebellion against Moses and Aaron. These incidents present clear lessons for believers today.	12:1, 2 16:1–50	**Do not talk** against God's appointed leadership. It will bring His judgment and chastisement. **Never align** in rebellion against God's appointed leadership. He hates and deals severely with this offense. Such rebellion often results in judgment on the rebellious community.

The Fifth Book of Moses Called
DEUTERONOMY

Author: Traditionally Moses
Date: Approximately 1400 B.C.
Theme: Obedience Brings Blessing, Disobedience Cursing
Key Words: Covenant, Obey, Remember, Blessed, Cursed

Author Deuteronomy identifies the book's content with Moses: "These *are* the words which Moses spoke to all Israel" (1:1). "Moses wrote this law and delivered it to the priests" (31:9) may well refer to his writing of the entire book as well. Moses' name appears nearly forty times in the volume, and the book clearly reflects Moses' personality. The first person pronoun used freely throughout its pages further supports Mosaic authorship.

Both Jewish and Samaritan tradition are unanimous in identifying Moses as the author. Christ expressly acknowledges Moses as the author of the book's content as do Peter and Stephen (Matt. 19:7, 8; Mark 10:3, 4; Acts 3:22; 7:37).

The last chapter, which contains the account of Moses' death, was probably written by his intimate friend Joshua.

Date Moses and the Israelites began the Exodus from Egypt about 1440 B.C. They arrived on the plains of Moab where Deuteronomy was likely written about 1400 B.C. on the occasion of the speaking of its content to the people "in the eleventh month, on the first *day* of the month," of the fortieth year of their wilderness wandering (1:3). This was just before Moses' death and Joshua's leading of the Israelites into Canaan. Deuteronomy therefore covers less than a two-month period, which includes the thirty days of mourning for Moses' death.

Background Moses was now 120 years old and the Promised Land lay ahead. He had led the Israelites out of captivity from Egypt and through the wilderness to receive God's Law at Mount Sinai. Because of Israel's disobedience in refusing to enter the land of Canaan, which God had promised them, they had wandered aimlessly in the desert for thirty-eight years. Now they were camped on the eastern border of Canaan, in the valley opposite Beth Peor in the uplands of Moab overlooking Jericho and the plain of Jordan. As the Israelites prepared to enter the Promised Land, they faced a turning point in their history—new foes, new temptations, and new leadership. Moses called the people together to remind them of the Lord's faithfulness and to challenge them to be faithful and obedient to their God as they possessed the Promised Land.

Content Deuteronomy is a series of farewell addresses by Moses to the Israelites as he prepares to die and as they make ready to enter the Promised Land. Although God had forbidden him to enter Canaan, Moses experiences a strong sense of anticipation for the people. What God had promised Abraham, Isaac, and Jacob centuries before is about to come true. Deuteronomy is the proclamation of a second chance for Israel. Israel's lack of faith and disloyalty had prevented the conquest of Canaan earlier. The majority of the people with Moses at the threshold of the Promised Land had not witnessed the scenes at Sinai; they had been born and reared in the wilderness. Thus Moses exhorts them thirty-five times to "go in and possess" the land. Thirty-four times he reminds them that this is the land that the Lord is giving them.

As this new generation of Israelites poised to enter the Promised Land, Moses vividly recalls with them God's faithfulness throughout their history and reminds them of their unique covenant relationship with the Lord. Moses realizes that the Israelites' greatest temptation in the new land will be to forsake God and to take up the worship of the Canaanite idols. Thus he is concerned for the perpetuation of the covenant relationship. To prepare the nation for life in the new land, Moses expounds the commandments and statutes God had given in His covenant. Obedience to God is equated with life, blessing, health, and prosperity. Disobedience is equated with death, cursing, disease, and poverty. The covenant showed God's children the way to live in fellowship with Him and with each other. So powerful is Deuteronomy's message that it is quoted over eighty times in the New Testament.

Personal Application Deuteronomy is characterized by a strong sense of urgency. Even to the contemporary reader the challenge is decisive: "I have set before you life and death, blessing and cursing; therefore choose life, that both you and your descendants may live" (30:19). The decision is ours.

Deuteronomy teaches that the relation of God to His people is far more than law. The indispensable conditions of our covenant relationship with God are obedience and loyalty. Our love, affection, and devotion to the Lord must be the true foundation of all our actions. Loyalty to God is the essence of true piety and holiness. Success, victory, prosperity, and happiness all depend upon our obedience to the Father. The book is a plea for our obedience to God based upon the motives of love and fear. "What does the LORD your God require of you, but to fear the LORD your God, to walk in all His ways and to love Him, to serve the LORD your God with all your heart and with all your soul, *and* to keep the commandments of the LORD and His statutes" (10:12, 13).

Christ Revealed Moses was the first to prophesy the coming of the Messiah, a Prophet like Moses himself (18:15). Notably, Moses is the only person with whom Jesus ever compared Himself. "For if you believed Moses, you would believe Me; for he wrote about Me. But if you do not believe his writings, how will you believe My words?" (John 5:46, 47). Jesus often quoted from Deuteronomy. When asked to name the most important commandment, He responded with Deuteronomy 6:5. When confronted by Satan at His temptation, He quoted exclusively from Deuteronomy (8:3; 6:16; 6:13; and 10:20).

How significant that Christ, who was perfectly obedient to the Father, even unto death, used this book on obedience to demonstrate His submission to the Father's will.

The Holy Spirit at Work The unifying theme throughout the Bible is the redemptive activity of God. Deuteronomy reminds the people that the Spirit of God had been with them from the time of their deliverance from Egypt to the present and that He would continue to guide and protect them if only they would be obedient to the stipulations of the covenant.

Second Peter 1:21 clearly describes Moses, "holy men of God spoke *as they were* moved by the Holy Spirit." As a spokesman for God, Moses demonstrated the presence of the Holy Spirit as he prophesied to the people. Several of his most significant prophecies included the coming of the Messiah (18:15), the dispersion of Israel (30:1), the repentance (30:2) and restoration (30:5) of Israel, Israel's future national restoration and conversion (30:5, 6), and Israel's national prosperity (30:9).

Outline of Deuteronomy

I. Moses' first message	**1:1—4:43**
A. Introduction	1:1–5
B. The past remembered	1:6—3:29
C. A call of obedience given	4:1–40
D. Cities of refuge appointed	4:41–43
II. Moses' second message	**4:44—26:19**
A. Exposition of the Ten Commandments	4:44—11:32
B. Exposition of the ceremonial laws	12:1—16:17
C. Exposition of the civil law	16:18—18:22
D. Exposition of the criminal laws	19:1—21:9
E. Exposition of the social laws	21:10—26:19
III. Moses' third message	**27:1—30:20**
A. Ratification ceremony	27:1–26
B. Covenant sanctions	28:1–68
C. The covenant oath	29:1—30:20
IV. Moses' final words and death	**31:1—34:12**
A. Perpetuation of the covenant	31:1–29
B. The song of witness	31:30—32:47
C. Moses' blessing on Israel	32:48—33:29
D. Moses' death and successor	34:1–12

The Previous Command to Enter Canaan

THESE *are* the **words** which Moses spoke to all Israel [a]on this side of the Jordan in the wilderness, in the [1]plain opposite [2]Suph, between Paran, Tophel, Laban, Hazeroth, and Dizahab.

WORD WEALTH

1:1 words, *davar* (*dah-vahr*); Strong's #1697: A word, a speech; a matter or thing; a commandment, a report, a message. This multifaceted noun may be translated by dozens of English words, but "word," "speech," and "matter" are most commonly used for *davar.* Frequently in the OT the phrase "the word [*davar*] of the LORD" occurs, particularly in Jer. and Ezek. The first verse of Deut. explains the contents of the book: "These *are* the words [speeches, matters, or messages] which Moses spoke to all Israel." The Hebrew title of Deut. is taken from this first sentence, and is *devarim,* or "words." Note the similarity between the

CHAPTER 1

1 [a]Deut. 4:44–46; Josh. 9:1, 10 [1]Heb. *arabah* [2]One LXX ms., Tg., Vg. *Red Sea*

1:1 Spoke to all Israel: Deut. is essentially for the laity, just as Lev. was a manual essentially for the priests and Levites. **The plain** is the Arabah, the valley running north and south of the Dead Sea. **Suph** is the Gulf of Aqabah.

Hebrew *davar* and the Greek *logos* (the Word, John 1:1). Jesus is the *davar* of the OT and the *logos* of the NT. He is the message of the entire Book.

2 *It is* eleven days' *journey* from Horeb by way of Mount Seir [a]to Kadesh
Barnea.
3 Now it came to pass [a]in the fortieth
year, in the eleventh month, on the first
day of the month, *that* Moses spoke
to the children of Israel according to
all that the LORD had given him as commandments to them,
4 [a]after he had killed Sihon king of
the Amorites, who dwelt in Heshbon,
and Og king of Bashan, who dwelt at
Ashtaroth [b]in[1] Edrei.
5 On this side of the Jordan in the
land of Moab, Moses began to explain
this law, saying,
6 "The LORD our God spoke to us
[a]in Horeb, saying: 'You have dwelt
long [b]enough at this mountain.
7 'Turn and take your journey, and
go to the mountains of the Amorites,
to all the neighboring *places* in the
[1]plain, in the mountains and in the lowland, in the South and on the seacoast,
to the land of the Canaanites and to
Lebanon, as far as the great river, the
River Euphrates.
8 'See, I have set the land before
you; go in and possess the land which
the LORD [1]swore to your fathers—to
[a]Abraham, Isaac, and Jacob—to give
to them and their descendants after
them.'

Tribal Leaders Appointed

9 "And [a]I spoke to you at that time,
saying: 'I [1]alone am not able to bear
you.
10 'The LORD your God has multiplied
you, [a]and here you *are* today, as the
stars of *heaven in multitude.
11 [a]'May the LORD God of your fathers
make you a thousand times more numerous than you are, and *bless you
[b]as He has promised you!
12 [a]'How can I alone bear your problems and your burdens and your complaints?
13 'Choose wise, understanding, and
knowledgeable men from among your
tribes, and I will make them [1]heads
over you.'
14 "And you answered me and said,
'The thing which you have told *us* to
do *is* good.'
15 "So I took [a]the heads of your tribes,
wise and knowledgeable men, and
[1]made them heads over you, leaders of
thousands, leaders of hundreds, leaders of fifties, leaders of tens, and officers for your tribes.
16 "Then I commanded your judges at
that time, saying, 'Hear *the cases* between your *brethren, and [a]judge righteously between a man and his
[b]brother or the stranger who is with
him.
17 [a]'You shall not show partiality in
*judgment; you shall hear the small as
well as the great; you shall not be
afraid in any man's presence, for
[b]the judgment *is* God's. The case that
is too hard for you, [c]bring to me, and
I will hear it.'
18 "And I commanded you at that time
all the things which you should do.

Israel's Refusal to Enter the Land

19 "So we departed from Horeb,
[a]and went through all that great and
terrible wilderness which you saw on
the way to the mountains of the Amorites, as the LORD our God had commanded us. Then [b]we came to Kadesh
Barnea.
20 "And I said to you, 'You have come
to the mountains of the Amorites,
which the LORD our God is giving us.
21 'Look, the LORD your God has set
the land before you; go up *and* possess
it, as the LORD God of your fathers has
spoken to you; [a]do not fear or be discouraged.'
22 "And every one of you came near
to me and said, 'Let us send men before
us, and let them search out the land
for us, and bring back word to us of
the way by which we should go up, and
of the cities into which we shall come.'

2 [a]Num. 13:26; 32:8; Deut. 9:23
3 [a]Num. 33:38
4 [a]Num. 21:23, 24, 33–35; Deut. 2:26–35; Josh. 13:10; Neh. 9:22 [b]Josh. 13:12 [1]LXX, Syr., Vg. *and;* cf. Josh. 12:4
6 [a]Ex. 3:1, 12 [b]Ex. 19:1, 2
7 [1]Heb. *arabah*
8 [a]Gen. 12:7; 15:5; 22:17; 26:3; 28:13; Ex. 33:1; Num. 14:23; 32:11 [1]*promised*
9 [a]Ex. 18:18, 24; Num. 11:14, 24 [1]*am not able to bear you by myself*
10 [a]Gen. 15:5; 22:17; Ex. 32:13; Deut. 7:7; 10:22; 26:5; 28:62 *See WW at 1 Kin. 8:23.
11 [a]2 Sam. 24:3 [b]Gen. 15:5 *See WW at Ps. 145:2.
12 [a]1 Kin. 3:8, 9
13 [1]*rulers*
15 [a]Ex. 18:25 [1]*appointed*
16 [a]Deut. 16:18; John 7:24 [b]Lev. 24:22 *See WW at Ps. 133:1.
17 [a]Lev. 19:15; Deut. 10:17; 16:19; 24:17; 1 Sam. 16:7; Prov. 24:23–26; Acts 10:34; James 2:1, 9 [b]2 Chr. 19:6 [c]Ex. 18:22, 26 *See WW at Num. 36:13.
19 [a]Num. 10:12; Deut. 2:7; 8:15; 32:10; Jer. 2:6 [b]Num. 13:26
21 [a]Josh. 1:6, 9

1:2 Eleven days: It had taken Israel 38 years to make this journey and an entire generation of Israelites had died. **Horeb** is used throughout Deut. (except in 33:2) to designate Sinai. The name occurs 12 times in the Pentateuch, 9 of these in Deut.
1:5 Began to explain indicates that Deut. is an exposition of the Law, not a word-for-word repetition of God's words.
1:6 The LORD our God is literally "Yahweh our God." "Yahweh" is the covenant name of Israel's God. "Our God" emphasizes the close covenant relationship between God and Israel.
1:22 In Num. 13:1, 2, God told Moses to send forth the spies. This verse states that the initiative came from the people. The Hebrew in Num. actually says "Send for yourself" which the Jewish rabbis interpret as "If you wish to send spies, do so." Thus God did not command this, but permitted it.

23 "The plan pleased me well; so
[a]I took twelve of your men, one man
from *each* tribe.
24 [a]"And they departed and went up
into the mountains, and came to the
Valley of Eshcol, and spied it out.
25 "They also took *some* of the fruit
of the land in their hands and brought
it down to us; and they brought back
word to us, saying, '*It is* a [a]good land
which the LORD our God is giving us.'
26 [a]"Nevertheless you would not go
up, but rebelled against the command
of the LORD your God;
27 "and you [a]complained in your tents,
and said, 'Because the LORD [b]hates us,
He has brought us out of the land of
Egypt to deliver us into the hand of the
Amorites, to destroy us.
28 'Where can we go up? Our brethren
have [1]discouraged our hearts, saying,
[a]"The people *are* greater and taller
than we; the cities *are* great and fortified up to heaven; moreover we have
seen the sons of the [b]Anakim there." '
29 "Then I said to you, 'Do not be terrified, [a]or afraid of them.
30 [a]'The LORD your God, who goes before you, He will fight for you, according to all He did for you in Egypt before
your eyes,
31 'and in the wilderness where you
saw how the LORD your God carried
you, as a [a]man carries his son, in all
the way that you went until you came
to this place.'
32 "Yet, for all that, [a]you did not believe the LORD your God,
33 [a]"who went in the way before you
[b]to search out a place for you to pitch
your tents, to show you the way you
should go, in the fire by night and in
the cloud by day.

The Penalty for Israel's Rebellion

34 "And the LORD heard the sound of
your words, and was angry, [a]and took
an oath, saying,
35 [a]'Surely not one of these men of this
evil generation shall see that good land
of which I [1]swore to give to your fathers,
36 [a]'except Caleb the son of Jephunneh; he shall see it, and to him and his
children I am giving the land on which
he *walked, because [b]he [1]wholly followed the LORD.'
37 [a]"The LORD was also angry with me
for your sakes, saying, 'Even you shall
not go in there.
38 [a]'Joshua the son of Nun, [b]who
stands before you, he shall go in there.
[c]Encourage him, for he shall cause Israel to inherit it.
39 [a]'Moreover your little ones and
your children, who [b]you say will be
victims, who today [c]have no knowledge of good and evil, they shall go in
there; to them I will give it, and they
shall possess it.
40 [a]'But *as for* you, turn and take your
journey into the wilderness by the Way
of the Red Sea.'
41 "Then you answered and said to
me, [a]'We have sinned against the
LORD; we will go up and fight, just as
the LORD our God commanded us.' And
when everyone of you had girded on
his weapons of war, you were ready
to go up into the mountain.
42 "And the LORD said to me, 'Tell 2
them, [a]"Do not go up nor fight, for I
am not among you; lest you be defeated before your enemies." '
43 "So I spoke to you; yet you would
not listen, but [a]rebelled against the
command of the LORD, and [b]pre-
sumptuously[1] went up into the mountain.
44 "And the Amorites who dwelt in
that mountain came out against you
and chased you [a]as bees do, and drove
you back from Seir to Hormah.
45 "Then you returned and wept before the LORD, but the LORD would not
listen to your voice nor give ear to you.
46 [a]"So you remained in Kadesh many
days, according to the days that you
spent *there*.

The Desert Years

2 "Then we turned and [a]journeyed
into the wilderness of the Way of
the Red Sea, [b]as the LORD spoke to me,

23 [a]Num. 13:2, 3
24 [a]Num. 13:21–25
25 [a]Num. 13:27
26 [a]Num. 14:1–4
27 [a]Ps. 106:25 [b]Deut. 9:28
28 [a]Deut. 9:1, 2 [b]Num. 13:28 [1]Lit. *melted*
29 [a]Num. 14:9
30 [a]Ex. 14:14
31 [a]Is. 46:3, 4; 63:9
32 [a]Jude 5
33 [a]Ex. 13:21 [b]Num. 10:33
34 [a]Deut. 2:14, 15
35 [a]Num. 14:22, 23 [1]*promised*
36 [a][Josh. 14:9] [b]Num. 32:11, 12 [1]*fully* *See WW at Deut. 11:25.
37 [a]Deut. 3:26; 4:21; 34:4
38 [a]Num. 14:30 [b]1 Sam. 16:22 [c]Deut. 31:7, 23
39 [a]Num. 14:31 [b]Num. 14:3 [c]Is. 7:15, 16
40 [a]Num. 14:25
41 [a]Num. 14:40
42 [a]Num. 14:41–43
43 [a]Num. 14:44 [b]Deut. 17:12, 13 [1]*willfully*
44 [a]Ps. 118:12
46 [a]Deut. 2:7, 14

CHAPTER 2

1 [a]Deut. 1:40 [b]Num. 14:25

1:28 Fortified up to heaven: This is hyperbole. Cities were built on mounds and seemed to be higher than they were. The walls of the Canaanite cities rose from 30 to 50 feet high and added to this perception.

1:36–39 A manifestation of God's covenant mercy is demonstrated in promising Caleb, Joshua, and the second generation entrance to Canaan. This act is the promise of a new beginning, a second chance, that is being fulfilled in the Deuteronomic covenant.

1:41–46 It is characteristic of human behavior not to appreciate the good until it is lost. In their attempt to correct their wrong, however, the Israelites continued their rebellion against God. In their vain attempt to circumvent God's judgment, they are disastrously defeated and driven to **Hormah,** which means "Destruction." It is the responsibility of God's people to act when God provides the opportunity.

1:42 See section 2 of Truth-In-Action at the end of Deut.

1:44 Num. 14:45 states that both the Amalekites and the Canaanites participated. The two terms are sometimes used interchangeably.

and we [1]skirted Mount Seir for many
days.
2 "And the LORD spoke to me, saying:
3 'You have skirted this mountain
[a]long enough; turn northward.
4 'And command the people, saying,
[a]"You *are about to* pass through the
territory of [b]your brethren, the descendants of Esau, who live in Seir; and
they will be afraid of you. Therefore
watch yourselves carefully.
5 "Do not meddle with them, for I will
not give you *any* of their land, no, not
so much as one footstep, [a]because I
have given Mount Seir to Esau *as* a
possession.
6 "You shall buy food from them with
money, that you may eat; and you shall
also buy water from them with money,
that you may drink.
7 "For the LORD your God has blessed
you in all the work of your *hand. He
knows your [1]trudging through this
great wilderness. [a]These forty years
the LORD your God *has been* with you;
you have lacked nothing." '
8 "And when we passed beyond our
brethren, the descendants of Esau who
dwell in Seir, away from the road of
the plain, away from [a]Elath and Ezion
Geber, we [b]turned and passed by way
of the Wilderness of Moab.
9 "Then the LORD said to me, 'Do not
harass Moab, nor contend with them
in battle, for I will not give you *any* of
their land *as* a possession, because I
have given [a]Ar to [b]the descendants of
Lot *as* a possession.' "
10 [a](The Emim had dwelt there in
times past, a people as great and numerous and tall as [b]the Anakim.
11 They were also *regarded as
[1]giants, like the Anakim, but the Moabites call them Emim.
12 [a]The Horites formerly dwelt in Seir,
but the descendants of Esau dispossessed them and destroyed them
from before them, and dwelt in their
[1]place, just as Israel did to the land of
their possession which the LORD gave
them.)
13 " 'Now rise and cross over [a]the
[1]Valley of the Zered.' So we crossed
over the Valley of the Zered.
1 14 "And the time we took to come
[a]from Kadesh Barnea until we crossed
over the Valley of the Zered *was* thirty-

1 [1]*circled around*
3 [a]Deut. 2:7, 14
4 [a]Num. 20:14–21 [b]Deut. 23:7
5 [a]Gen. 36:8
7 [a]Deut. 8:2–4 [1]Lit. *goings* *See WW at Josh. 4:24.
8 [a]Judg. 11:18 [b]Num. 21:4
9 [a]Deut. 2:18, 29 [b]Gen. 19:36–38
10 [a]Gen. 14:5 [b]Deut. 9:2
11 [1]Heb. *rephaim* *See WW at Gen. 15:6.
12 [a]Deut. 2:22 [1]*stead*
13 [a]Num. 21:12 [1]*Wadi* or *Brook*
14 [a]Num. 13:26 [b]Deut. 1:34, 35 [c]Num. 14:35 [1]*perished*
15 [1]*perished*
19 [a]Gen. 19:38
20 [a]Gen. 14:5 [1]Heb. *rephaim* *See WW at Gen. 15:6.
21 [a]Deut. 2:10
22 [a]Gen. 36:8 [b]Gen. 14:6; 36:20–30
23 [a]Josh. 13:3 [b]Gen. 10:14
24 [a]Judg. 11:18 [b]Deut. 1:4 [1]*to take possession*
25 [a]Ex. 23:27 [b]Ex. 15:14–16 [1]*everywhere under the heavens*
26 [a]Num. 21:21–32

eight years, [b]until all the generation of
the men of war [1]was consumed from
the midst of the camp, [c]just as the LORD
had sworn to them.
15 "For indeed the hand of the LORD
was against them, to destroy them
from the midst of the camp until they
[1]were consumed.
16 "So it was, when all the men of war
had finally perished from among the
people,
17 "that the LORD spoke to me, saying:
18 'This day you are to cross over at
Ar, the boundary of Moab.
19 'And *when* you come near the people of Ammon, do not harass them or
meddle with them, for I will not give
you *any* of the land of the people of
Ammon *as* a possession, because I
have given it to [a]the descendants of Lot
as a possession.' "
20 (That was also *regarded as a land
of [1]giants; giants formerly dwelt there.
But the Ammonites call them [a]Zam-
zummim,
21 [a]a people as great and numerous
and tall as the Anakim. But the LORD
destroyed them before them, and they
dispossessed them and dwelt in their
place,
22 just as He had done for the descendants of Esau, [a]who dwelt in Seir,
when He destroyed [b]the Horites from
before them. They dispossessed them
and dwelt in their place, even to this
day.
23 And [a]the Avim, who dwelt in villages as far as Gaza—[b]the Caphtorim,
who came from Caphtor, destroyed
them and dwelt in their place.)
24 " 'Rise, take your journey, and
[a]cross over the River Arnon. Look, I
have given into your hand [b]Sihon the
Amorite, king of Heshbon, and his
land. Begin [1]to possess *it,* and engage
him in battle.
25 [a]'This day I will begin to put the
dread and fear of you upon the nations
[1]under the whole heaven, who shall
hear the report of you, and shall
[b]tremble and be in anguish because of
you.'

King Sihon Defeated

26 "And I [a]sent messengers from the
Wilderness of Kedemoth to Sihon king

2:6, 7 The Lord blessed and prospered the Israelites even in their wilderness wanderings. They prospered sufficiently to be able to buy their food and water; they lacked nothing.
2:11, 20 The Anakim people were also known as Rephaim, the Hebrew for "giants."
2:14 See section 1 of Truth-In-Action at the end of Deut.
2:19 Ancient kinships existed between Israel and Ammon (Gen. 19:36–38).
2:23 **Caphtorim** refers to the Philistines; **Caphtor** is Crete.

of Heshbon, [b]with words of *peace,
saying,
27 [a]'Let me pass through your land; I
will keep strictly to the road, and I will
turn neither to the right nor to the left.
28 'You shall sell me food for money,
that I may eat, and give me water for
money, that I may drink; [a]only let me
pass through on foot,
29 [a]'just as the descendants of Esau
who dwell in Seir and the Moabites
who dwell in Ar did for me, until I cross
the Jordan to the land which the LORD
our God is giving us.'
30 [a]"But Sihon king of Heshbon would
not let us pass through, for [b]the LORD
your God [c]hardened his spirit and
made his heart obstinate, that He
might deliver him into your hand, as
it is this day.
31 "And the LORD said to me, 'See, I
have begun to [a]give Sihon and his land
over to you. Begin to possess *it*, that
you may inherit his land.'
32 [a]"Then Sihon and all his people
came out against us to fight at Jahaz.
33 "And [a]the LORD our God delivered
him [1]over to us; so [b]we defeated him,
his sons, and all his people.
34 "We took all his cities at that time,
and we [a]utterly destroyed the men,
women, and little ones of every city;
we left none remaining.
35 "We took only the livestock as plunder for ourselves, with the spoil of the
cities which we took.
36 [a]"From Aroer, which *is* on the bank
of the River Arnon, and *from* [b]the city
that *is* in the ravine, as far as Gilead,
there was not one city too strong for
us; [c]the LORD our God delivered all to
us.
37 "Only you did not go near the land
of the people of Ammon—anywhere
along the River [a]Jabbok, or to the cities
of the mountains, or [b]wherever the
LORD our God had forbidden us.

King Og Defeated

3 "Then we turned and went up the
road to Bashan; and [a]Og king of
Bashan came out against us, he and
all his people, to battle [b]at Edrei.
2 "And the LORD said to me, 'Do not
fear him, for I have delivered him and
all his people and his land into your
hand; you shall do to him as you did
to [a]Sihon king of the Amorites, who
dwelt at Heshbon.'
3 "So the LORD our God also delivered
into our hands Og king of Bashan, with
all his people, and we [1]attacked him
until he had no survivors remaining.
4 "And we took all his cities at that
time; there was not a city which we
did not take from them: sixty cities,
[a]all the region of Argob, the kingdom
of Og in Bashan.
5 "All these cities *were* fortified with
high walls, gates, and bars, besides a
great many rural towns.
6 "And we utterly destroyed them, as
we did to Sihon king [a]of Heshbon, utterly destroying the men, women, and
children of every city.
7 "But all the livestock and the spoil
of the cities we took as booty for ourselves.
8 "And at that time we took the
[a]land from the hand of the two kings
of the Amorites who *were* on this side
of the Jordan, from the River Arnon
to Mount [b]Hermon
9 "(the Sidonians call [a]Hermon Sirion, and the Amorites call it Senir),
10 [a]"all the cities of the plain, all Gilead, and [b]all Bashan, as far as Salcah
and Edrei, cities of the kingdom of Og
in Bashan.
11 [a]"For only Og king of Bashan remained of the remnant of [b]the [1]giants.
Indeed his bedstead *was* an iron bedstead. (*Is* it not in [c]Rabbah of the people of Ammon?) Nine cubits *is* its
length and four cubits its width, according to the standard cubit.

The Land East of the Jordan Divided

12 "And this [a]land, *which* we possessed at that time, [b]from Aroer, which
is by the River Arnon, and half the
mountains of Gilead and [c]its cities, I
gave to the Reubenites and the Gadites.
13 [a]"The rest of Gilead, and all Bashan, the kingdom of Og, I gave to
half the tribe of Manasseh. (All the region of Argob, with all Bashan, was
called the land of the [1]giants.
14 [a]"Jair the son of Manasseh took all
the region of Argob, [b]as far as the border of the Geshurites and the Maachathites, and [c]called Bashan after

26 [b]Deut. 20:10 *See WW at Nah. 1:15.
27 [a]Judg. 11:19
28 [a]Num. 20:19
29 [a]Deut. 23:3, 4
30 [a]Num. 21:23 [b]Josh. 11:20 [c]Ex. 4:21
31 [a]Deut. 1:3, 8
32 [a]Num. 21:23
33 [a]Deut. 7:2 [b]Num. 21:24 [1]Lit. *before us*
34 [a]Lev. 27:28
36 [a]Deut. 3:12; 4:48 [b]Josh. 13:9, 16 [c]Ps. 44:3
37 [a]Gen. 32:22 [b]Deut. 2:5, 9, 19

CHAPTER 3

1 [a]Num. 21:33–35 [b]Deut. 1:4
2 [a]Num. 21:34
3 [1]*struck*
4 [a]Deut. 3:13, 14
6 [a]Deut. 2:24, 34, 35
8 [a]Josh. 12:6; 13:8–12 [b]1 Chr. 5:23
9 [a]1 Chr. 5:23
10 [a]Deut. 4:49 [b]Josh. 12:5; 13:11
11 [a]Amos 2:9 [b]Deut. 2:11, 20 [c]Jer. 49:2 [1]Heb. *rephaim*
12 [a]Num. 32:33 [b]Deut. 2:36 [c]Num. 34:14
13 [a]Josh. 13:29–31; 17:1 [1]Heb. *rephaim*
14 [a]1 Chr. 2:22 [b]Josh. 13:13 [c]Num. 32:41

2:30 Note the parallels here with Pharaoh in Ex. 4:21.

2:34, 35 In accordance with 20:10–18, one aspect of a holy war was the total destruction of the enemy and all their possessions, including women and children. This law was called *herem.* The law of *herem* (7:1–5) required Israel to utterly destroy those cities in the heart of the conquest area to prevent the continuation of their false religions and to be God's instrument in executing judgment upon the Canaanites for their sinfulness.

3:1–3 A repetition of Num. 21:33–35.

his own name, [1]Havoth Jair, to this
day.)
15 "Also I gave [a]Gilead to Machir.
16 "And to the Reubenites [a]and the
Gadites I gave from Gilead as far as
the River Arnon, the middle of the river
as *the* border, as far as the River Jabbok, [b]the border of the people of Ammon;
17 "the plain also, with the Jordan as
the border, from Chinnereth [a]as far as
the east side of the Sea of the Arabah
[b](the Salt Sea), below the slopes of Pisgah.
18 "Then I commanded you at that
time, saying: 'The LORD your God has
given you this land to possess. [a]All you
men of valor shall cross over armed
before your brethren, the children of
Israel.
19 'But your wives, your little ones,
and your livestock (I know that you
have much livestock) shall stay in your
cities which I have given you,
20 'until the LORD *has given [a]rest to
your brethren as to you, and they also
possess the land which the LORD your
God is giving them beyond the Jordan.
Then each of you may [b]return to his
possession which I have given you.'
7 21 "And [a]I commanded Joshua at that
time, saying, 'Your eyes have seen all
that the LORD your God has done to
these two kings; so will the LORD do
to all the kingdoms through which you
pass.
22 'You must not fear them, for
[a]the LORD your God Himself fights for
you.'

Moses Forbidden to Enter the Land

23 "Then [a]I pleaded with the LORD at
that time, saying:
24 'O Lord GOD, You have begun to
show Your servant [a]Your greatness
and Your [1]mighty hand, for [b]what god
is there in heaven or on earth who can
do *anything* like Your works and Your
mighty *deeds?*
25 'I pray, let me cross over and see
[a]the good land beyond the Jordan,
those pleasant mountains, and Lebanon.'
26 "But the LORD [a]was angry with me
on your account, and would not listen
to me. So the LORD said to me: 'Enough
of that! Speak no more to Me of this
matter.
27 [a]'Go up to the top of Pisgah, and
lift your eyes toward the west, the
north, the south, and the east; behold
it with your eyes, for you shall not
cross over this Jordan.
28 'But [a]command[1] Joshua, and encourage him and strengthen him; for
he shall go over before this people, and
he shall cause them to inherit the land
which you will see.'
29 "So we stayed in [a]the valley opposite Beth Peor.

Moses Commands Obedience

4 "Now, O Israel, listen to [a]the *stat- 2
utes and the judgments which I
*teach you to observe, that you may
*live, and go in and [1]possess the land
which the LORD God of your fathers is
giving you.
2 [a]"You shall not add to the word
which I command you, nor take from
it, that you may keep the *commandments of the LORD your God which I
command you.
3 "Your eyes have seen what the
LORD did at [a]Baal Peor; for the LORD
your God has destroyed from among
you all the men who followed Baal of
Peor.
4 "But you who held fast to the LORD
your God *are* alive today, every one of
you.
5 "Surely I have taught you statutes
and judgments, just as the LORD my
God commanded me, that you should
act according *to them* in the land
which you go to possess.
6 "Therefore be careful to observe 2
them; for this *is* [a]your *wisdom and
your understanding in the sight of the
peoples who will hear all these statutes, and say, 'Surely this great nation
is a wise and understanding people.'
7 "For [a]what great nation *is there*
that has [b]God[1] *so* near to it, as the LORD
our God *is* to us, for whatever *reason*
we may call upon Him?
8 "And what great nation *is there* that
has *such* statutes and *righteous judgments as are in all this law which I set
before you this day?

14 [1]Lit. *Towns of Jair* **15** [a]Num. 32:39, 40 **16** [a]2 Sam. 24:5 [b]Num. 21:24 **17** [a]Num. 34:11, 12 [b]Gen. 14:3 **18** [a]Num. 32:20 **20** [a]Deut. 12:9, 10 [b]Josh. 22:4 *See WW at Ex. 33:14. **21** [a][Num. 27:22, 23] **22** [a]Ex. 14:14 **23** [a][2 Cor. 12:8, 9] **24** [a]Deut. 5:24; 11:2 [b]2 Sam. 7:22 [1]*strong* **25** [a]Deut. 4:22 **26** [a]Num. 20:12; 27:14 **27** [a]Num. 23:14; 27:12 **28** [a]Num. 27:18, 23 [1]*charge* **29** [a]Deut. 4:46; 34:6

CHAPTER 4

1 [a][Rom. 10:5] [1]*take possession of* *See WW at Neh. 9:13. • See WW at Is. 48:17. • See WW at Hab. 2:4. **2** [a]Prov. 30:6 *See WW at Ps. 119:35. **3** [a]Num. 25:1–9 **6** [a][2 Tim. 3:15] *See WW at Is. 11:2. **7** [a][2 Sam. 7:23] [b][Is. 55:6] [1]Or *a god* **8** *See WW at Lam. 1:18.

3:17 Chinnereth is a city on the Sea of Chinnereth, or the Sea of Galilee. The **Salt Sea** is the Dead Sea.
3:18–22 Joshua later quotes this passage to the Reubenites, Gadites, and half-tribe of Manasseh as a reminder of their responsibility to the tribes west of the Jordan. They ardently obeyed (Josh. 1:12–18).
3:21, 22 See section 7 of Truth-In-Action at the end of Deut.
4:1, 2 See section 2 of Truth-In-Action at the end of Deut.
4:1 Statutes and **judgments** as used in this verse are synonymous and describe all the law contained in chs. 5—26.
4:3 Baal means "Lord." Each geographical location had its own local god.
4:6–8 See section 2 of Truth-In-Action at the end of Deut.

9 "Only take heed to yourself, and diligently [a]keep *yourself, lest you [b]forget the things your eyes have seen, and lest they depart from your heart all the days of your life. And [c]teach them to your children and your grandchildren,

10 "*especially concerning* [a]the day you stood before the LORD your God in Horeb, when the LORD said to me, 'Gather the people to Me, and I will let them hear My words, that they may learn to fear Me all the days they live on the earth, and *that* they may teach their children.'

11 "Then you came near and stood at the foot of the mountain, and the mountain burned with fire to the midst of heaven, with darkness, cloud, and thick darkness.

12 [a]"And the LORD spoke to you out of the midst of the fire. You heard the sound of the words, but saw no [1]form; [b]*you* only *heard* a voice.

13 [a]"So He declared to you His covenant which He commanded you to perform, [b]the Ten Commandments; and [c]He *wrote them on two tablets of stone.

14 "And [a]the LORD commanded me at that time to teach you statutes and judgments, that you might [1]observe them in the land which you cross over to possess.

Beware of Idolatry

15 [a]"Take careful heed to yourselves, for you saw no [b]form when the LORD spoke to you at Horeb out of the midst of the fire,

16 "lest you [a]act corruptly and [b]make for yourselves a carved image in the [1]form of any figure: [c]the likeness of male or female,

17 "the likeness of any animal that *is* on the earth or the likeness of any winged bird that flies in the air,

18 "the likeness of anything that creeps on the ground or the likeness of any fish that *is* in the water beneath the earth.

19 "And *take heed,* lest you [a]lift your eyes to heaven, and *when* you see the sun, the moon, and the stars, [b]all the *host of heaven, you feel driven to [c]worship them and serve them, which the LORD your God has [1]given to all the peoples under the whole heaven as a heritage.

20 "But the LORD has taken you and [a]brought you out of the iron furnace, out of Egypt, to be [b]His people, an inheritance, as you are this day.

21 "Furthermore [a]the LORD was angry with me for your sakes, and swore that [b]I would not cross over the Jordan, and that I would not enter the good land which the LORD your God is giving you as an inheritance.

22 "But [a]I must die in this land, [b]I must not cross over the Jordan; but you shall cross over and [1]possess [c]that good land.

23 "Take heed to yourselves, lest you forget the covenant of the LORD your God which He *made with you, [a]and make for yourselves a carved image in the form of anything which the LORD your God has forbidden you.

24 "For [a]the LORD your God *is* a consuming fire, [b]a jealous God.

25 "When you beget children and grandchildren and have grown old in the land, and act corruptly and make a carved image in the form of anything, and [a]do evil in the sight of the LORD your God to provoke Him to anger,

26 [a]"I call heaven and earth to witness against you this day, that you will soon utterly perish from the land which you cross over the Jordan to possess; you will not [1]prolong *your* days in it, but will be utterly destroyed.

27 "And the LORD [a]will scatter you among the peoples, and you will be left few in number among the nations where the LORD will drive you.

28 "And [a]there you will serve gods, the work of men's hands, wood and stone, [b]which neither see nor hear nor eat nor smell.

29 [a]"But from there you will seek the LORD your God, and you will find *Him* if you seek Him with all your heart and with all your soul. 2

30 "When you are in [1]distress, and all these things come upon you in the [a]latter days, when you [b]turn to the LORD your God and obey His voice

9 [a]Prov. 4:23 [b]Deut. 29:2–8 [c]Gen. 18:19 *See WW at Prov. 10:3.
10 [a]Ex. 19:9, 16, 17
12 [a]Deut. 5:4, 22 [b]1 Kin. 19:11–18 [1]*similitude*
13 [a]Deut. 9:9, 11 [b]Ex. 34:28 [c]Ex. 24:12 *See WW at Deut. 31:9.
14 [a]Ex. 21:1 [1]*do or perform*
15 [a]Josh. 23:11 [b]Is. 40:18
16 [a]Deut. 9:12; 31:29 [b]Ex. 20:4, 5 [c]Rom. 1:23 [1]*similitude*
19 [a]Deut. 17:3 [b]2 Kin. 21:3 [c][Rom. 1:25] [1]*divided* *See WW at Ps. 68:11.
20 [a]Jer. 11:4 [b]Deut. 7:6; 27:9
21 [a]Num. 20:12 [b]Num. 27:13, 14
22 [a]2 Pet. 1:13–15 [b]Deut. 3:27 [c]Deut. 3:25 [1]*take possession of*
23 [a]Deut. 4:16 *See WW at Ex. 34:27.
24 [a]Deut. 9:3 [b]Ex. 20:5; 34:14
25 [a]2 Kin. 17:17
26 [a]Deut. 30:18, 19 [1]*live long on it*
27 [a]Deut. 28:62
28 [a]Jer. 16:13 [b]Ps. 115:4–7; 135:15–17
29 [a][2 Chr. 15:4]
30 [a]Hos. 3:5 [b]Joel 2:12 [1]*tribulation*

4:9–14 Moses recalls the experience of Israel at Mt. Sinai recorded in Ex. 19:16–19. His warning in v. 9 presupposes their difficulty being faithful to God in Canaan.

4:10 Fear refers to a holy reverence before God. Reverence is recognized as the proper response of men to God and expresses itself in worship and in obedience. The fear of the Lord is one of the major OT themes.

4:15–31 The revelation of God must not be corrupted with idolatry. This passage is a commentary on the second commandment and emphasizes that God is a Spirit.

4:23, 24 Jealous indicates an active zeal for righteousness that arose from God's holiness. Because of this, God could tolerate no form of idolatry.

4:29 See section 2 of Truth-In-Action at the end of Deut.

4:29 See Jer. 29:12–14.

31 "(for the LORD your God *is* a merciful God), He will not forsake you nor
[a]destroy you, nor forget the covenant
of your fathers which He swore to
them.
32 "For [a]ask now concerning the days
that are past, which were before you,
since the day that God *created *man
on the earth, and *ask* [b]from one end
of heaven to the other, whether *any*
great *thing* like this has happened, or
anything like it has been heard.
33 [a]"Did *any* people *ever* hear the
voice of God speaking out of the midst
of the fire, as you have heard, and
live?
34 "Or did God *ever* try to go *and* take
for Himself a nation from the midst of
another nation, [a]by trials, [b]by signs,
by wonders, by war, [c]by a mighty hand
and [d]an outstretched arm, [e]and by
great [1]terrors, according to all that the
LORD your God did for you in Egypt
before your eyes?
35 "To you it was shown, that you
might know that the LORD Himself *is*
God; [a]*there is* none other besides Him.
36 [a]"Out of heaven He let you hear His
voice, that He might instruct you; on
earth He showed you His great fire,
and you heard His words out of the
midst of the fire.
37 "And because [a]He loved your fathers, therefore He chose their [1]de-
scendants after them; and [b]He
brought you out of Egypt with His
Presence, with His mighty power,
38 [a]"driving out from before you nations greater and mightier than you, to
bring you in, to give you their land *as*
an inheritance, as *it is* this day.
39 "Therefore *know this day, and
consider *it* in your heart, that [a]the
LORD Himself *is* God in heaven above
and on the earth beneath; *there is* no
other.
40 [a]"You shall therefore keep His statutes and His commandments which I
command you today, that [1]it may go
well with you and with your children
after you, and that you may [2]prolong
your days in the land which the LORD
your God is giving you for all time."

Cities of Refuge East of the Jordan

41 Then Moses [a]set apart three cities
on this side of the Jordan, toward the
rising of the sun,
42 [a]that the manslayer might flee
there, who kills his neighbor unintentionally, without having hated him in
time past, and that by fleeing to one
of these cities he might live:
43 [a]Bezer in the wilderness on the plateau for the Reubenites, Ramoth in
Gilead for the Gadites, and Golan in
Bashan for the Manassites.

Introduction to God's Law

44 Now this *is* the law which Moses
set before the children of Israel.
45 These *are* the testimonies, the statutes, and the judgments which Moses
spoke to the children of Israel after
they came out of Egypt,
46 on this side of the Jordan, [a]in the
valley opposite Beth Peor, in the land
of Sihon king of the Amorites, who
dwelt at Heshbon, whom Moses and
the children of Israel [b]defeated[1] after
they came out of Egypt.
47 And they took possession of his
land and the land [a]of Og king of Bashan, two kings of the Amorites, who
were on this side of the Jordan, toward
the [1]rising of the sun,
48 [a]from Aroer, which *is* on the bank
of the River Arnon, even to Mount
[1]Sion (that is, [b]Hermon),
49 and all the plain on the east side of
the Jordan as far as the Sea of the Arabah, below the [a]slopes of Pisgah.

The Ten Commandments Reviewed

5 And Moses *called all Israel, and
said to them: "Hear, O Israel, the
statutes and judgments which I speak
in your hearing today, that you may
learn them and be careful to observe
them.
2 [a]"The LORD our God *made a covenant with us in Horeb.
3 "The LORD [a]did not make this covenant with our fathers, but with us,
those who *are* here today, all of us who
are alive.
4 [a]"The LORD talked with you face to
face on the mountain from the midst
of the fire.
5 [a]"I stood between the LORD and you
at that time, to declare to you the word
of the LORD; for [b]you were afraid because of the fire, and you did not go
up the mountain. *He* said:

31 [a]Lev. 26:44; Jer. 30:11
32 [a]Deut. 32:7; Job 8:8 [b]Deut. 28:64; Matt. 24:31 *See WW at Gen. 1:1. • See WW at Gen. 1:26.
33 [a]Ex. 20:22; 24:11; Deut. 5:24–26
34 [a]Deut. 7:19 [b]Ex. 7:3 [c]Ex. 13:3 [d]Ex. 6:6 [e]Deut. 26:8 [1]*calamities*
35 [a]Ex. 8:10; 9:14; [Deut. 4:39; 32:12, 39; 1 Sam. 2:2; Is. 43:10–12; 44:6–8; 45:5–7]; Mark 12:32
36 [a]Ex. 19:9, 19; 20:18, 22; Deut. 4:33; Neh. 9:13; Heb. 12:19, 25
37 [a]Deut. 7:7, 8; 10:15; 33:3 [b]Ex. 13:3, 9, 14 [1]Lit. *seed*
38 [a]Deut. 7:1
39 [a]Deut. 4:35; Josh. 2:11 *See WW at Ex. 3:7.
40 [a]Lev. 22:31; Deut. 5:16; 32:46, 47 [1]*you may prosper* [2]*live long*
41 [a]Num. 35:6; Deut. 19:2–13; Josh. 20:7–9
42 [a]Deut. 19:4
43 [a]Josh. 20:8
46 [a]Deut. 3:29 [b]Num. 21:24; Deut. 1:4 [1]*struck*
47 [a]Num. 21:33–35 [1]*east*
48 [a]Deut. 2:36; 3:12 [b]Deut. 3:9; Ps. 133:3 [1]Syr. *Sirion*
49 [a]Deut. 3:17

CHAPTER 5

1 *See WW at Jer. 33:3.
2 [a]Ex. 19:5; Deut. 4:23; Mal. 4:4 *See WW at Ex. 34:27.
3 [a]Jer. 31:32; Matt. 13:17; Heb. 8:9
4 [a]Ex. 19:9
5 [a]Ex. 20:21; Gal. 3:19 [b]Ex. 19:16

4:34 Great terrors are terrifying demonstrations of divine power. Note that of the three Greek words used in the NT for miracles, two are used here in the Septuagint, *semeion* for "sign" and *teras* for "wonder."

4:41–43 See note on 19:11–13.

6 [a]'I *am* the LORD your God who
brought you out of the land of
Egypt, out of the house of
[1]bondage.
7 [a]'You shall have no other gods
[1]before Me.
8 [a]'You shall not make for yourself
a carved image—any likeness
of anything that *is* in heaven
above, or that *is* in the earth
beneath, or that *is* in the water
under the earth;
9 you shall not [a]bow[1] down to
them nor serve them. For I, the
LORD your God, *am* a jealous
God, [2]visiting the iniquity of
the fathers upon the children
to the third and fourth *generations*
of those who hate
Me,
10 [a]but showing *mercy to thousands,
to those who love Me
and [1]keep My commandments.
11 [a]'You shall not take the name of
the LORD your God in vain, for
the LORD will not hold *him*
[1]guiltless who takes His name
in vain.
12 [a]'Observe the Sabbath day, to
[1]keep it holy, as the LORD your
God commanded you.
13 [a]Six days you shall labor and
do all your work,
14 but the seventh day *is* the
[a]Sabbath of the LORD your
God. *In it* you shall do no
work: you, nor your son, nor
your daughter, nor your male
servant, nor your female servant,
nor your ox, nor your
donkey, nor any of your cattle,
nor your stranger who *is*
within your gates, that your
male servant and your female
servant may rest as well as
you.
15 [a]And remember that you were
a slave in the land of Egypt,
and the LORD your God
brought you out from there
[b]by a mighty hand and by an
outstretched arm; therefore
the LORD your God commanded
you to keep the Sabbath
day.
16 [a]'Honor your father and your
mother, as the LORD your God
has commanded you, [b]that
your days may be long, and
that it may be well with
[c]you in the land which the
LORD your God is giving you.
17 [a]'You shall not murder.
18 [a]'You shall not commit adultery.
19 [a]'You shall not steal.
20 [a]'You shall not bear false witness
against your neighbor.
21 [a]'You shall not covet your neighbor's
wife; and you shall not
desire your neighbor's house,
his field, his male servant, his
female servant, his ox, his
donkey, or anything that *is*
your neighbor's.'
22 "These words the LORD spoke to all
your *assembly, in the mountain from
the midst of the fire, the cloud, and the
thick darkness, with a loud voice; and
He added no more. And [a]He wrote
them on two tablets of stone and gave
them to me.

The People Afraid of God's Presence

23 [a]"So it was, when you heard the
voice from the midst of the darkness,
while the mountain was burning with
fire, that you came near to me, all
the heads of your tribes and your elders.
24 "And you said: 'Surely the LORD our
God has shown us His glory and His
greatness, and [a]we have heard His
voice from the midst of the fire. We
have seen this day that God speaks
with man; yet he [b]*still* lives.
25 'Now therefore, why should we die?
For this great fire will consume us;
[a]if we hear the voice of the LORD our
God anymore, then we shall die.
26 [a]'For who *is there* of all *flesh who
has heard the voice of the living God
speaking from the midst of the fire, as
we *have*, and lived?
27 'You go near and hear all that the
LORD our God may say, and [a]tell us all
that the LORD our God says to you, and
we will hear and do *it*.'
28 "Then the LORD heard the voice of
your words when you spoke to me, and
the LORD said to me: 'I have heard the
voice of the words of this people which
they have spoken to you. [a]They are
right *in* all that they have spoken.

6 [a]Ex. 20:2–17; Lev. 26:1; Deut. 6:4; Ps. 81:10 [1]*slavery*
7 [a]Ex. 20:2, 3; 23:13; Hos. 13:4 [1]*besides*
8 [a]Ex. 20:4
9 [a]Ex. 34:7, 14–16; Num. 14:18; Deut. 7:10 [1]*worship them* [2]*punishing*
10 [a]Num. 14:18; Deut. 7:9; Jer. 32:18; Dan. 9:4 [1]*observe* *See WW at Mic. 6:8.
11 [a]Ex. 20:7; Lev. 19:12; Deut. 6:13; 10:20; Matt. 5:33 [1]*innocent*
12 [a]Ex. 20:8; Ezek. 20:12; Mark 2:27 [1]*sanctify it*
13 [a]Ex. 23:12; 35:2
14 [a][Gen. 2:2]; Ex. 16:29; [Heb. 4:4]
15 [a]Deut. 15:15 [b]Deut. 4:34, 37
16 [a]Ex. 20:12; Lev. 19:3; Matt. 15:4; Eph. 6:2, 3; Col. 3:20 [b]Deut. 6:2 [c]Deut. 4:40
17 [a]Ex. 20:13; Matt. 5:21
18 [a]Ex. 20:14; Mark 10:19; Luke 18:20; [Rom. 13:9]; James 2:11
19 [a]Ex. 20:15; Lev. 19:11; [Rom. 13:9]
20 [a]Ex. 20:16; 23:1; Matt. 19:18
21 [a]Ex. 20:17; [Rom. 7:7; 13:9]
22 [a]Ex. 24:12; 31:18; Deut. 4:13 *See WW at Lev. 16:17.
23 [a]Ex. 20:18, 19
24 [a]Ex. 19:19 [b]Deut. 4:33; Judg. 13:22
25 [a]Ex. 20:18, 19; Deut. 18:16
26 [a]Deut. 4:33 *See WW at Job 19:26.
27 [a]Ex. 20:19; Heb. 12:19
28 [a]Deut. 18:17

5:6–21 A recital of the Ten Commandments (originally given in Ex. 20:2–17) with Moses providing interpretation for the new situation in Canaan. This is an exposition or selective paraphrase of the Law by Moses and is not meant to be a word-for-word reproduction of the Law.

5:8, 9 These two verses should be taken together. This is not a prohibition against carving statues, but against making them for worship.

5:23–28 The leaders of Israel wanted Moses to act as an intermediary between themselves and God. In this role, Moses is a type of the "one Mediator between God and men, *the* Man Christ Jesus" (1 Tim. 2:5).

29 [a]'Oh, that they had such a heart in
them that they would fear Me and
[b]always keep all My commandments,
[c]that it might be well with them and
with their children forever!
30 'Go and say to them, "Return to
your tents."
31 'But as for you, stand here by Me,
[a]and I will speak to you all the commandments, the statutes, and the
judgments which you shall *teach
them, that they may observe *them* in
the land which I am giving them to possess.'
32 "Therefore you shall [1]be careful to
do as the LORD your God has commanded you; [a]you shall not turn aside
to the right hand or to the left.
33 "You shall walk in [a]all the ways
which the LORD your God has commanded you, that you may live [b]and
that it may be well with you, and *that*
you may prolong *your* days in the land
which you shall possess.

29 [a]Ps. 81:13 [b]Deut. 11:1 [c]Deut. 4:40
31 [a][Gal. 3:19] *See WW at Is. 48:17.
32 [a]Deut. 17:20; 28:14 [1]*observe*
33 [a]Deut. 10:12 [b]Deut. 4:40

CHAPTER 6

1 [a]Deut. 12:1
2 [a][Eccl. 12:13] [b]Deut. 4:40
3 [a]Deut. 7:13 [b]Gen. 22:17 [c]Ex. 3:8, 17 [1]Lit. *observe to do*
4 [a][1 Cor. 8:4, 6] [1]Or *The LORD is our God, the LORD alone,* i.e., the only one *See WW at 2 Kin. 19:15.

WORD WEALTH

6:4 one, *'echad* (eh-*chahd*): Strong's #259: One, a unit; united; unity. *'Echad* comes from the root *'achad,* "to bring together, to unify; to collect one's thoughts." *'Echad* serves to portray the same range of meaning as "one" does in English, from the very narrowest sense (one and one only, as in Eccl. 9:18, "one sinner destroys much good") to the broadest sense (one made up of many, as in Gen. 2:24, where a man and his wife "shall become one flesh"). Deut. 6:4–6 is the most important text in the OT. Jesus called it the greatest commandment of Scripture, and it remains the central confession of Judaism to the day. The foundational truth for world redemption is that there is one God who creates and redeems, and yet the NT shows that God is Father, Son, and Holy Spirit. Compare the unity of God to the unity of man made in His image: man is comprised of spirit, soul, and body (1 Thess. 5:23). Man is not three "beings" but "one being" with physical, emotional, and spiritual elements.

The Greatest Commandment

6 "Now this *is* [a]the commandment,
and these are the statutes and judgments which the LORD your God has
commanded to teach you, that you may
observe *them* in the land which you
are crossing over to possess,
2 [a]"that you may fear the LORD your
God, to keep all His statutes and His
commandments which I command
you, you and your son and your grandson, all the days of your life, [b]and that
your days may be prolonged.
3 "Therefore hear, O Israel, and
[1]be careful to observe *it,* that it
may be well with you, and that you
may [a]multiply greatly [b]as the LORD
God of your fathers has promised
you—[c]'a land flowing with milk and
honey.'
2 4 [a]"Hear, O Israel: [1]The LORD our
*God, the LORD *is* **one!**
5 [a]"You shall *love the LORD your
God with all your heart, [b]with all your
soul, and with all your strength.
6 "And [a]these words which I command you today shall be in your heart.
7 [a]"You shall teach them diligently to
your children, and shall talk of them
when you sit in your house, when you
walk by the way, when you lie down,
and when you rise up.
8 [a]"You shall bind them as a sign on
your hand, and they shall be as frontlets between your eyes.
9 [a]"You shall write them on the doorposts of your house and on your gates.

5 [a]Matt. 22:37 [b]2 Kin. 23:25 *See WW at Ps. 97:10.
6 [a]Deut. 11:18–20
7 [a]Deut. 4:9; 11:19
8 [a]Prov. 3:3; 6:21; 7:3
9 [a]Deut. 11:20
10 [1]*promised*

Caution Against Disobedience

10 "So it shall be, when the LORD your
God brings you into the land of which
He [1]swore to your fathers, to Abraham,

6:3 Flowing with milk and honey is an ancient idiom denoting the land's richness.

6:4–9 These verses have been known in Jewish tradition for centuries as "The Shema," which contains the fundamental truth of Israel's religion. They are recited as a daily prayer along with 11:13–21 and Num. 15:37–41.

6:4, 5 See section 2 of Truth-In-Action at the end of Deut.

6:4 This is the creed of Judaism. **The LORD** translates the Hebrew *Yahweh,* but later the Jews substituted the word *Adonai* ("my Lord") since they considered *Yahweh* too sacred to be pronounced. The word **God** is used here in its plural form in the Hebrew text. Thus, **our God, the LORD *is* one** likely emphasizes the Christian doctrine of the Trinity, three Persons of the same substance in the one Godhead; this understanding, however, would not have been apparent to the people of the OT.

6:5 Israel's obedience was to arise from a relationship based upon love. This verse is considered by Jesus to be the first and greatest commandment. The **heart** was considered the seat of the mind and will. When Jesus quotes this passage in Mark 12:30 and Luke 10:27, He adds "mind," probably to emphasize "understanding."

6:8, 9 At some point in time the Hebrews started putting this passage, along with 11:13–21, Ex. 13:1–10, and Ex. 13:11–16, into leather cubes on straps (phylacteries) and binding them on their left hands and on their foreheads during morning prayers. They also placed these scriptures in small metal or glass cases and fixed them to the right-hand doorposts of each home as literal fulfillments of the command to be a people of the commandments.

Isaac, and Jacob, to give you large and
beautiful cities [a]which you did not
build,
11 "houses full of all good things,
which you did not fill, hewn-out wells
which you did not dig, vineyards and
olive trees which you did not plant—
[a]when you have eaten and are full—
12 "*then* beware, lest you forget the
[a]LORD who brought you out of the land
of Egypt, from the house of bondage.
13 "You shall [a]fear the LORD your God
and serve Him, and [b]shall take oaths
in His name.
14 "You shall not go after other gods,
[a]the gods of the peoples who *are* all
around you
15 "(for [a]the LORD your God *is* a jealous God [b]among you), lest the *anger
of the LORD your God be aroused
against you and destroy you from the
face of the earth.
16 [a]"You shall not [1]tempt* the LORD
your God [b]as you [2]tempted *Him* in
Massah.
17 "You shall [a]diligently keep the
commandments of the LORD your God,
His testimonies, and His statutes which
He has commanded you.
18 "And you [a]shall do *what is* right
and good in the sight of the LORD, that
it may be well with you, and that you
may go in and possess the good land
of which the LORD swore to your fathers,
19 [a]"to cast out all your enemies from
before you, as the LORD has spoken.
20 [a]"When your son asks you in time
to come, saying, 'What *is the meaning
of* the testimonies, the statutes, and the
judgments which the LORD our God has
commanded you?'
21 "then you shall say to your son: 'We
were slaves of Pharaoh in Egypt, and
the LORD brought us out of Egypt
[a]with a mighty hand;
22 'and the LORD showed signs and
wonders before our eyes, great and severe, against Egypt, Pharaoh, and all
his household.
23 'Then He brought us out from there,
that He might bring us in, to give us
the land of which He [1]swore to our fathers.
24 'And the LORD commanded us to
[1]observe all these [2]statutes, [a]to fear the
LORD our God, [b]for our good always,
that [c]He might preserve us alive, as *it
is* [3]this day.
25 'Then [a]it will be righteousness for
us, if we are careful to observe all these
commandments before the LORD our
God, as He has commanded us.'

A Chosen People

7 "When the LORD your God brings
you into the land which you go to
[a]possess, and has cast out many
[b]nations before you, [c]the Hittites and
the Girgashites and the Amorites and
the Canaanites and the Perizzites and
the Hivites and the Jebusites, seven nations greater and mightier than you,
2 "and when the LORD your God delivers [a]them over to you, you shall conquer them *and* utterly destroy them.
[b]You shall make no covenant with
them nor show mercy to them.
3 [a]"Nor shall you make marriages
with them. You shall not give your
daughter to their son, nor take their
daughter for your son.
4 "For they will turn your sons away
from following Me, to serve other gods;
[a]so the anger of the LORD will be
aroused against you and destroy you
suddenly.
5 "But thus you shall deal with them:
you shall [a]destroy their altars, and
break down their *sacred* pillars, and
cut down their [1]wooden images, and
burn their carved images with fire.
6 "For you *are* a [1]holy* people to the
LORD your God; [a]the LORD your God
has chosen you to be a people for Himself, a *special treasure above all the
peoples on the face of the earth.
7 "The LORD did not set His [a]love on
you nor choose you because you were
more in number than any other people,
for you were [b]the least of all peoples;

10 [a]Josh. 24:13
11 [a]Deut. 8:10; 11:15; 14:29
12 [a]Deut. 8:11–18
13 [a]Matt. 4:10 [b]Deut. 5:11
14 [a]Deut. 13:7
15 [a]Ex. 20:5 [b]Ex. 33:3 *See WW at Judg. 10:7.
16 [a]Luke 4:12 [b][1 Cor. 10:9] [1]*test* [2]*tested* *See WW at Ps. 78:41.
17 [a]Deut. 11:22
18 [a]Ex. 15:26
19 [a]Num. 33:52, 53
20 [a]Ex. 13:8, 14
21 [a]Ex. 13:3
23 [1]*promised*
24 [a]Deut. 6:2 [b]Jer. 32:39 [c]Deut. 4:1 [1]*do* [2]*ordinances* [3]*today*
25 [a][Rom. 10:3, 5]

CHAPTER 7

1 [a]Deut. 6:10 [b]Gen. 15:19–21 [c]Ex. 33:2
2 [a]Num. 31:17 [b]Josh. 2:14
3 [a]1 Kin. 11:2
4 [a]Deut. 6:15
5 [a]Ex. 23:24; 34:13 [1]Heb. *Asherim*, Canaanite deities
6 [a]Ex. 19:5, 6 [1]*set-apart* *See WW at Lev. 19:2. • See WW at Deut. 26:18.
7 [a]Deut. 4:37 [b]Deut. 10:22

6:16 At **Massah** (Ex. 17:1–7) the Israelites sought to put God to the test by imposing demands upon Him to prove Himself in ways that they proposed. They demanded God provide them with drinking water as a sign that He was among them and thus as a condition for their continued loyalty. Jesus in His day refused to offer such signs to the scribes and Pharisees.

7:1 This list of nations is traditional and with minor changes appears frequently in the OT. Israel was forbidden from entering into any kind of association with them. Each of these seven states was relatively small, but taken together they were larger in population and more powerful than Israel.

7:2, 3 Utterly destroy is a verb derived from the Hebrew noun *herem* (see note on 2:34, 35). These prohibitions were to prevent Israel from endangering its covenant relationship with God.

7:5 The total destruction of these religious items would remove future temptation for Israel to adopt these foreign gods and enter into idolatry.

7:6 Holy refers to a separated **people.** Israel was a holy people because of their relationship to God. Their relationship was a result of divine choice, a choice whose essence remains a mystery.

8 "but [a]because the LORD loves you,
and because He would keep [b]the oath
which He swore to your fathers,
[c]the LORD has brought you out with a
mighty hand, and *redeemed you from
the house of [1]bondage, from the hand
of Pharaoh king of Egypt.
9 "Therefore know that the LORD
your God, He *is* God, [a]the faithful God
[b]who keeps covenant and mercy for a
thousand generations with those who
love Him and keep His commandments;
10 "and He repays those who hate Him
to their face, to destroy them. He will
not [1]be [a]slack with him who hates Him;
He will repay him to his face.
11 "Therefore you shall keep the commandment, the statutes, and the judgments which I command you today, to
observe them.

Blessings of Obedience

12 "Then it shall come to pass, because
you listen to these judgments, and keep
and do them, that the LORD your God
will keep with you the covenant and
the mercy which He swore to your fathers.
13 "And He will [a]love you and bless
you and [1]multiply you; [b]He will also
bless the fruit of your womb and the
fruit of your land, your grain and your
new wine and your oil, the increase of
your cattle and the offspring of your
flock, in the land of which He [2]swore
to your fathers to give you.
14 "You shall be blessed above all peoples; there shall not be a male or female [a]barren among you or among
your livestock.
15 "And the LORD will take away from
you all sickness, and will afflict you
with none of the [a]terrible diseases of
Egypt which you have known, but will
lay *them* on all those who hate you.
16 "Also you shall [1]destroy all the peoples whom the LORD your God delivers
over to you; your eye shall have no pity
on them; nor shall you serve their gods,
for that *will* [a]*be* a snare to you.
17 "If you should say in your heart,

8 [a]Deut. 10:15 [b]Luke 1:55, 72, 73 [c]Ex. 13:3, 14 [1]*slavery* *See WW at Neh. 1:10.
9 [a]1 Cor. 1:9; 2 Thess. 3:3; 2 Tim. 2:13 [b]Ex. 20:6; Deut. 5:10; Neh. 1:5; Dan. 9:4
10 [a][2 Pet. 3:9, 10] [1]*delay*
13 [a]Ps. 146:8; Prov. 15:9; John 14:21 [b]Deut. 28:4 [1]*cause you to increase* [2]*promised*
14 [a]Ex. 23:26
15 [a]Ex. 9:14; 15:26; Deut. 28:27, 60
16 [a]Ex. 23:33; Judg. 8:27; Ps. 106:36 [1]*consume*
18 [a]Ps. 105:5
19 [a]Deut. 4:34; 29:3
20 [a]Ex. 23:28; Josh. 24:12
22 [a]Ex. 23:29, 30 [1]*consume*
24 [a]Josh. 10:24, 42; 12:1–24 [b]Josh. 23:9 [1]*before*
25 [a]Prov. 23:6 [1]*desire*
26 [a]Deut. 13:17 [1]*devoted* or *banned*

CHAPTER 8

1 [a]Deut. 4:1; 6:24 [b]Deut. 30:16 [1]*observe to do* [2]*increase in number* [3]*promised*

'These nations are greater than I; how
can I dispossess them?'—
18 "you shall not be afraid of them, *but*
you shall [a]remember well what the
LORD your God did to Pharaoh and to
all Egypt:
19 [a]"the great trials which your eyes
saw, the signs and the wonders, the
mighty hand and the outstretched arm,
by which the LORD your God brought
you out. So shall the LORD your God
do to all the peoples of whom you are
afraid.
20 [a]"Moreover the LORD your God will
send the hornet among them until
those who are left, who hide themselves from you, are destroyed.
21 "You shall not be terrified of them;
for the LORD your God, the great and
awesome God, *is* among you.
22 "And the LORD your God will drive 1
out those nations before you [a]little by
little; you will be unable to [1]destroy
them at once, lest the beasts of the field
become *too* numerous for you.
23 "But the LORD your God will deliver
them over to you, and will inflict defeat
upon them until they are destroyed.
24 "And [a]He will deliver their kings
into your hand, and you will destroy
their name from under heaven; [b]no one
shall be able to stand [1]against you until
you have destroyed them.
25 "You shall burn the carved images
of their gods with fire; you shall not
[a]covet[1] the silver or gold *that is* on
them, nor take *it* for yourselves, lest
you be snared by it; for it *is* an abomination to the LORD your God.
26 "Nor shall you bring an abomination into your house, lest you be
doomed to destruction like it. You shall
utterly detest it and utterly abhor it,
[a]for it *is* an [1]accursed thing.

Remember the LORD Your God

8 "Every commandment which I
command you today [a]you must
[1]be careful to observe, that you may
live and [b]multiply,[2] and go in and
possess the land of which the LORD
[3]swore to your fathers.

7:12–16 Israel's health, prosperity, and success are based upon maintaining the covenant relationship with God.
7:16, 17 Success will be the result of God's involvement on their behalf. Their military action was to be without **pity,** for to spare any part of the enemy would be to open the door for future idolatry. This is a clear example of Israel's being used as God's instrument of judgment (**whom the LORD . . . over to you).** Though loving, God is also righteous and must judge those who reject Him and His covenant.
7:22 See section 1 of Truth-In-Action at the end of Deut.
7:22 The initial conquest of the land would be sudden, but the settlement and complete conquest would be a gradual process. This will allow the Israelites to grow in numbers and to take over the land in an orderly fashion without its reverting to a primitive state (**lest the beasts . . . for you**).
7:25, 26 Under the ban of *herem* (see note on 2:34, 35) the Israelites were to take no possessions from the idolatrous people they defeated lest they partake of the character and nature of those items. See notes on Josh. 7:1, 10–12.

WORD WEALTH

8:1 possess, *yarash* (yah-*rash*); Strong's #3423: To inherit, possess, seize, occupy. This verb occurs more than 250 times in the OT. Its great importance is seen in God's promises to Abraham, Isaac, and Jacob. Repeatedly in Gen., God pledges to give the land of Canaan to Abraham's descendants as an everlasting possession.

2 "And you shall remember that the
LORD your God [a]led you all the way
these forty years in the wilderness, to
humble you *and* [b]test you, [c]to know
what *was* in your heart, whether you
would keep His commandments or not.
3 "So He humbled you, [a]allowed you
to hunger, and [b]fed you with manna
which you did not know nor did your
fathers know, that He might make you
know that man shall [c]not live by bread
alone; but man lives by every *word* that
proceeds from the mouth of the LORD.

KINGDOM DYNAMICS

8:3 God's Word and Our Soul's Nourishment, THE WORD OF GOD. Jesus quoted this text in Matt. 4:4, when He faced Satan's snares in the wilderness. The obvious message of the passage is that there is no survival of the soul without God's Word—daily. That the parallel is used of Israel's receiving the daily supply of manna makes clear that a regular, daily portion of God's Word is to be sought and fed upon by the believer.

This is not a matter of legal duty, determining one's salvation, but a matter of personal responsibility, determining one's obedience to the pathway of discipleship. However, let no one suppose spiritual survival is possible for long without nourishment from the Word of God. 1 Pet. 2:2 declares that God's Word is as essential to the believer as milk is to a newborn child. But as we come to terms with His Word as key to our survival, let us also see that God has given its pleasantness as a joyful source of sweetness for our living (Ps. 19:10).

(Ps. 119:89–91/Ps. 119:105) J.W.H.

4 [a]"Your garments did not wear out
on you, nor did your foot swell these
forty years.
5 [a]"You should [1]know in your heart
that as a man *chastens his son, *so* the
LORD your God chastens you.
6 "Therefore you shall keep the commandments of the LORD your God,
[a]to walk in His ways and to fear
Him.
7 "For the LORD your God is bringing
you into a good land, [a]a land of brooks
of water, of fountains and springs, that
flow out of valleys and hills;
8 "a land of wheat and barley, of
vines and fig trees and pomegranates,
a land of olive oil and honey;
9 "a land in which you will eat bread
without scarcity, in which you will lack
nothing; a land whose stones *are* iron
and out of whose hills you can dig copper.
10 [a]"When you have eaten and are 4
full, then you shall bless the LORD your
God for the good land which He has
given you.
11 "Beware that you do not forget the
LORD your God by not keeping His
commandments, His judgments, and
His statutes which I command you today,
12 [a]"lest—*when* you have eaten and
are [1]full, and have built beautiful
houses and dwell *in them;*
13 "and *when* your herds and your
flocks multiply, and your silver and
your gold are [1]multiplied, and all that
you have is multiplied;
14 [a]"when your heart [1]is lifted up, and
you [b]forget the LORD your God who
brought you out of the land of Egypt,
from the house of bondage;
15 "who [a]led you through that great
and terrible wilderness, [b]*in which were*
*fiery serpents and scorpions and
thirsty land where there was no water;
[c]who brought water for you out of the
flinty rock;
16 "who fed you in the wilderness with
[a]manna, which your fathers did not
know, that He might humble you and
that He might test you, [b]to do you good
in the end—
17 "then you say in your heart, 'My
power and the might of my hand have
gained me this wealth.'
18 "And you shall remember the LORD
your God, [a]for *it is* He who gives you
power to get wealth, [b]that He may

2 [a]Deut. 1:3; 2:7; 29:5; Ps. 136:16; Amos 2:10 [b]Ex. 16:4 [c][John 2:25]
3 [a]Ex. 16:2, 3 [b]Ex. 16:12, 14, 35 [c]Matt. 4:4; Luke 4:4
4 [a]Deut. 29:5; Neh. 9:21
5 [a]2 Sam. 7:14; Ps. 89:30–33; Prov. 3:11, 12; Heb. 12:5–11; Rev. 3:19 [1]*consider* *See WW at Jer. 10:24.
6 [a][Deut. 5:33]
7 [a]Deut. 11:9–12; Jer. 2:7
10 [a]Deut. 6:11, 12
12 [a]Deut. 28:47; Prov. 30:9; Hos. 13:6 [1]*satisfied*
13 [1]*increased*
14 [a]1 Cor. 4:7 [b]Deut. 8:11; Ps. 106:21 [1]*becomes proud*
15 [a]Is. 63:12–14 [b]Num. 21:6 [c]Ex. 17:6; Num. 20:11 *See WW at Is. 6:2.
16 [a]Ex. 16:15 [b]Jer. 24:5, 6; [Heb. 12:11]
18 [a]Prov. 10:22; Hos. 2:8 [b]Deut. 7:8, 12

8:2 In this chapter Moses emphasizes that the people are to remember the faithfulness of God. The purpose for **the wilderness** experience was divine discipline; they must not forget what they were taught. **Heart** refers to the basic attitudes of the people toward God and His commandments. It took testing **to know** such inner attitudes.

8:3, 4 The experience of manna allowed Israel to realize that their basic source of life was God. Jesus in His temptation experience (Matt. 4:4; Luke 4:4) quotes from v. 3.

8:10–20 See section 4 of Truth-In-Action at the end of Deut.

[1]establish His covenant which He swore to your fathers, as *it is* this day.

WORD WEALTH

8:18 power, *koach* (*ko*-akh); Strong's #3581: Vigor, strength, force, capacity, power, wealth, means, or substance. Generally the word means "capacity" or "ability," whether physical, mental, or spiritual. Here Moses informs Israel that it is God who gives to them the "ability" (power, means, endurance, capacity) to obtain wealth, for material blessings are included in the promises to the patriarchs and their descendants. Moses strictly warns Israel in v. 17 not to falsely conclude that this capacity for success is an innate talent, but to humbly acknowledge that it is a God-given ability.

KINGDOM DYNAMICS

8:18 Prospered to Bless, GOD'S PROSPERITY. This text tells us that wealth should exist to establish and verify the covenant. It should not be squandered selfishly. Clearly God wants our needs to be met, and He wants us to have our heart's desires; but after our needs are met, what can be done with the surplus of His blessing? Can you live in more than one house at a time? God desires that we use our abundance to bless others.

God wants us to have wealth, but money is only a part of wealth. A person can have millions and still be poor: poor in health, poor in peacefulness, and poor in friendships. Wealth is more than money and possessions. We need the wisdom both 1) to receive God's covenant of prosperity—to receive wealth without its controlling us; and 2) to see its breadth and intent for our whole being—that with wealth and health, peace and friends—we serve others. God's covenanted prosperity is always a means to an end and never an end in itself.

(Phil. 4:12, 13/John 10:10) F.P.

19 "Then it shall be, if you by any means forget the LORD your God, and follow other gods, and serve them and worship them, [a]I testify against you this day that you shall surely perish.
20 "As the nations which the LORD destroys before you, [a]so you shall perish, because you would not be obedient to the voice of the LORD your God.

18 [1]*confirm*
19 [a]Deut. 4:26; 30:18
20 [a][Dan. 9:11, 12]

CHAPTER 9

2 [a]Num. 13:22, 28, 33; Josh. 11:21, 22
3 [a]Deut. 1:33; 31:3; Josh. 3:11; 5:14; John 10:4 [b]Deut. 4:24; Heb. 12:29 [c]Deut. 7:24 [d]Ex. 23:31
4 [a]Deut. 8:17; [Rom. 11:6, 20; 1 Cor. 4:4, 7] [b]Gen. 15:16; Lev. 18:3, 24–30; Deut. 12:31; 18:9–14
5 [a][Titus 3:5] [b]Gen. 50:24 [1]*perform*
6 [a]Ex. 34:9; Deut. 31:27 [1]*stubborn* or *rebellious*
7 [a]Num. 14:22 [b]Ex. 14:11
8 [a]Ex. 32:1–8; Ps. 106:19
9 [a]Ex. 24:12, 15; Deut. 5:2–22 [b]Ex. 24:18

Israel's Rebellions Reviewed

9 "Hear, O Israel: You *are* to cross over the Jordan today, and go in to dispossess nations greater and mightier than yourself, cities great and fortified up to heaven,
2 "a people great and tall, the [a]descendants of the Anakim, whom you know, and *of whom* you heard *it said,* 'Who can stand before the descendants of Anak?'
3 "Therefore understand today that the LORD your God *is* He who [a]goes over before you *as* a [b]consuming fire. [c]He will destroy them and bring them down before you; [d]so you shall drive them out and destroy them quickly, as the LORD has said to you.
4 [a]"Do not think in your heart, after the LORD your God has cast them out before you, saying, 'Because of my righteousness the LORD has brought me in to possess this land'; but *it is* [b]because of the wickedness of these nations *that* the LORD is driving them out from before you.
5 [a]"*It is* not because of your righteousness or the uprightness of your heart *that* you go in to possess their land, but because of the wickedness of these nations *that* the LORD your God drives them out from before you, and that He may [1]fulfill the [b]word which the LORD swore to your fathers, to Abraham, Isaac, and Jacob.
6 "Therefore understand that the LORD your God is not giving you this good land to possess because of your righteousness, for you *are* a [a]stiff-necked[1] people.
7 "Remember! Do not forget how you [a]provoked the LORD your God to wrath in the wilderness. [b]From the day that you departed from the land of Egypt until you came to this place, you have been rebellious against the LORD.
8 "Also [a]in Horeb you provoked the LORD to wrath, so that the LORD was angry *enough* with you to have destroyed you.
9 [a]"When I went up into the mountain to receive the tablets of stone, the tablets of the covenant which the LORD made with you, then I stayed on the mountain forty days and [b]forty nights. I neither ate bread nor drank water.

9:4–6 The people are reminded three times that their righteousness was not the cause for their receiving the Promised Land. It was the faithful fulfillment of God's promise to Abraham, Isaac, and Jacob.
9:6, 13 Stiff-necked can be translated as "stubborn." In vv. 7–14 Moses uses the Mt. Sinai experience to illustrate Israel's history of provocation and their unworthiness in and of themselves to receive the gift of the Promised Land. Any claim to a state of self-righteousness on the part of the Israelites was misleading.
9:7, 8 Wrath connotes judgment.
9:9, 25 Refers to the same period of prayer and fasting.

10 [a]"Then the LORD delivered to me
two tablets of stone written with the
finger of God, and on them *were* all
the words which the LORD had spoken
to you on the mountain from the midst
of the fire [b]in[1] the day of the assembly.
11 "And it came to pass, at the end of
forty days and forty nights, *that* the
LORD gave me the two tablets of stone,
the tablets of the covenant.
12 "Then the LORD said to me, [a]'Arise,
go down quickly from here, for your
people whom you brought out of Egypt
have acted corruptly; they have
[b]quickly turned aside from the way
which I commanded them; they have
made themselves a molded image.'
13 "Furthermore [a]the LORD spoke to
me, saying, 'I have seen this people,
and indeed [b]they are a [1]stiff-necked
people.
14 [a]'Let Me alone, that I may destroy
them and [b]blot out their name from under heaven; [c]and I will make of you a
nation mightier and greater than they.'
15 [a]"So I turned and came down from
the mountain, and [b]the mountain
burned with fire; and the two tablets
of the covenant *were* in my two hands.
16 "And [a]I looked, and behold, you
had sinned against the LORD your
God—had made for yourselves a
molded calf! You had turned aside
quickly from the way which the LORD
had commanded you.
17 "Then I took the two tablets and
threw them out of my two hands and
[a]broke them before your eyes.
18 "And I [a]fell[1] down before the LORD,
as at the first, forty days and forty
nights; I neither ate bread nor drank
water, because of all your sin which
you committed in doing wickedly in
the sight of the LORD, to provoke Him
to anger.
19 [a]"For I was afraid of the anger and
hot displeasure with which the LORD
was angry with you, to destroy you.
[b]But the LORD listened to me at that
time also.
20 "And the LORD was very angry with
Aaron *and* would have destroyed him;
so I prayed for Aaron also at the same
time.
21 "Then I took your sin, the calf
which you had made, and burned it

10 [a]Ex. 31:18; Deut. 4:13 [b]Ex. 19:17 [1]*when you were all gathered together*
12 [a]Ex. 32:7, 8 [b]Deut. 31:29
13 [a]Ex. 32:9 [b]Deut. 9:6 [1]*stubborn or rebellious*
14 [a]Ex. 32:10 [b]Deut. 29:20 [c]Num. 14:12
15 [a]Ex. 32:15–19 [b]Ex. 19:18
16 [a]Ex. 32:19
17 [a]Ex. 32:19
18 [a]Ex. 34:28; Ps. 106:23 [1]*prostrated myself*
19 [a]Ex. 32:10, 11; Heb. 12:21 [b]Ex. 32:14
21 [a]Ex. 32:20
22 [a]Num. 11:1, 3 [b]Ex. 17:7 [c]Num. 11:4, 34 [1]*caused the LORD to be angry*
23 [a]Num. 13:3 [b]Ps. 106:24, 25
24 [a]Deut. 9:7; 31:27
25 [a]Deut. 9:18 [1]*fell down*
26 [a]Deut. 32:9

CHAPTER 10

1 [a]Ex. 25:10 [1]*Cut out*
2 [a]Ex. 25:16, 21

with fire and crushed it *and* ground *it*
very small, until it was as fine as dust;
and I [a]threw its dust into the brook that
descended from the mountain.
22 "Also at [a]Taberah and [b]Massah and
[c]Kibroth Hattaavah you [1]provoked the
LORD to wrath.
23 "Likewise, [a]when the LORD sent you
from Kadesh Barnea, saying, 'Go up
and possess the land which I have
given you,' then you rebelled against
the commandment of the LORD your
God, and [b]you did not believe Him nor
obey His voice.
24 [a]"You have been rebellious against
the LORD from the day that I knew you.
25 [a]"Thus I [1]prostrated myself before
the LORD; forty days and forty nights
I kept prostrating myself, because the
LORD had said He would destroy you.
26 "Therefore I prayed to the LORD,
and said: 'O Lord GOD, do not destroy
Your people and [a]Your inheritance
whom You have redeemed through
Your greatness, whom You have
brought out of Egypt with a mighty
hand.
27 'Remember Your servants, Abraham, Isaac, and Jacob; do not look on
the stubbornness of this people, or on
their wickedness or their sin,
28 'lest the land from which You
brought us should say, "Because the
LORD was not able to bring them to the
land which He promised them, and because He hated them, He has brought
them out to kill them in the wilderness."
29 'Yet they *are* Your people and Your
inheritance, whom You brought out by
Your mighty power and by Your outstretched arm.'

The Second Pair of Tablets

10 "At that time the LORD said to
me, [1]'Hew for yourself two tablets of stone like the first, and come
up to Me on the mountain and make
yourself an [a]ark of wood.
2 'And I will write on the tablets the
words that were on the first tablets,
which you broke; and [a]you shall put
them in the ark.'
3 "So I made an ark of acacia wood,
hewed two tablets of stone like the

9:20 Moses' intercession for **Aaron** is not presented in Ex. If Israel's high priest, who was guilty of making the golden calf, had to be spared from God's judgment of death, consider how dependent upon God's mercy the common people were.

9:22 At Taberah the people complained of their difficulties and misfortunes (Num. 11:1–3); **Kibroth Hattaavah** ("Graves of Craving") was where God sent the quail, as well as a great plague of judgment "because there they buried the people who had yielded to craving" (Num. 11:31–35). On **Massah**, see note on 6:16.

first, and went up the mountain, having
the two tablets in my hand.
4 "And He wrote on the tablets according to the first writing, the Ten
[1]Commandments, [a]which the LORD had
spoken to you in the mountain from
the midst of the fire in the day of the
assembly; and the LORD gave them to
me.
5 "Then I turned and [a]came down
from the mountain, and [b]put the tablets
in the ark which I had made; [c]and
there they are, just as the LORD commanded me."
6 (Now the children of Israel journeyed from the wells of Bene Jaakan
to Moserah, where Aaron [a]died, and
where he was buried; and Eleazar
his son ministered as priest in his
[1]stead.
7 [a]From there they journeyed to Gudgodah, and from Gudgodah to Jotbathah, a land of [1]rivers of water.
8 At that time [a]the LORD [1]separated
the tribe of Levi [b]to bear the ark of
the covenant of the LORD, [c]to stand before the LORD to minister to Him and
[d]to bless in His name, to this day.
9 [a]Therefore Levi has no portion nor
inheritance with his brethren; the LORD
is his inheritance, just as the LORD your
God promised him.)
10 "As at the first time, [a]I stayed in
the mountain forty days and forty
nights; [b]the LORD also heard me at that
time, *and* the LORD chose not to destroy
you.
11 [a]"Then the LORD said to me, 'Arise,
begin *your* journey before the people,
that they may go in and possess the
land which I swore to their fathers to
give them.'

The Essence of the Law

12 "And now, Israel, [a]what does the
LORD your God require of you, but to
fear the LORD your God, to walk in all
His ways and to [b]love Him, to serve
the LORD your God with all your heart
and with all your soul,
13 "*and* to keep the commandments of
the LORD and His statutes which I command you today [a]for your [1]good?
14 "Indeed heaven and the highest
heavens belong to the [a]LORD your God,
also the earth with all that *is* in it.
15 "The LORD delighted only in your
fathers, to love them; and He chose
their [1]descendants after them, you
above all *peoples, as *it is* this day.
16 "Therefore circumcise the foreskin
of your [a]heart, and be [b]stiff-necked[1] no
longer.
17 "For the LORD your God *is* [a]God of
gods and [b]Lord of lords, the great God,
[c]mighty and awesome, who [d]shows no
partiality nor takes a bribe.
18 [a]"He administers justice for the
fatherless and the widow, and loves
the stranger, giving him food and
clothing.
19 "Therefore love the stranger, for
you were strangers in the land of
Egypt.
20 [a]"You shall fear the LORD your God;
you shall serve Him, and to Him you
shall hold fast, and take oaths in His
name.
21 "He *is* your *praise, and He *is* your
God, who has done for you these great
and awesome things which your eyes
have seen.
22 "Your fathers went down to Egypt
with seventy persons, and now the
LORD your God has made you as the
stars of heaven in multitude.

Love and Obedience Rewarded

11 "Therefore you shall love the
LORD your God, and keep His
charge, His statutes, His judgments,
and His commandments always.
2 "Know today that *I do* not *speak*

4 [a]Ex. 20:1; 34:28 [1]Lit. *Words*
5 [a]Ex. 34:29 [b]Ex. 40:20 [c]1 Kin. 8:9
6 [a]Num. 20:25–28; 33:38 [1]*place*
7 [a]Num. 33:32–34 [1]*brooks*
8 [a]Num. 3:6 [b]Num. 4:5, 15; 10:21 [c]Deut. 18:5 [d]Num. 6:23 [1]*set apart*
9 [a]Num. 18:20, 24; Deut. 18:1, 2; Ezek. 44:28
10 [a]Ex. 34:28; Deut. 9:18 [b]Ex. 32:14
11 [a]Ex. 33:1
12 [a]Mic. 6:8 [b]Deut. 6:5; Matt. 22:37; 1 Tim. 1:5
13 [a]Deut. 6:24 [1]*benefit* or *welfare*
14 [a][Neh. 9:6; Ps. 68:33; 115:16]
15 [1]Lit. *seed* *See WW at Ruth 1:16.
16 [a]Lev. 26:41; Deut. 30:6; Jer. 4:4; Rom. 2:28, 29 [b]Deut. 9:6, 13 [1]*rebellious*
17 [a]Deut. 4:35, 39; Is. 44:8; 46:9; Dan. 2:47; 1 Cor. 8:5, 6 [b]Rev. 19:16 [c]Deut. 7:21 [d]Acts 10:34
18 [a]Ex. 22:22–24; Ps. 68:5; 146:9
20 [a]Matt. 4:10
21 *See WW at Ps. 100:4.

10:6 Here it is stated that Aaron died at **Moserah.** According to Num. 20:28 and 33:38, he died at the top of Mt. Hor. This is not a contradiction in that Moserah was the name of the district in which Mt. Hor was located.

10:12, 13 What does the LORD your God require of you presents God's requirements by means of active verbs that represent interrelated attitudes: **to fear, to walk, to love, to serve,** and **to keep.** The verbs denote allegiance to God and are explained in 10:14—11:32.

10:16 An uncircumcised **heart** is one that is closed to God, lacking committed allegiance to His presence or word. If they will cut away that which hinders open allegiance to God, then the heart will become pliable to the direction of God. Without a circumcision of the heart, there can be no true reverence and love of God.

10:17 These remarkable titles for **God** are a basic affirmation of monotheism.

10:19 Although not formally stated in Deut., the mandate "You shall love your neighbor as yourself" is presented in principle.

10:20 To Him you shall hold fast indicates a very close and intimate relationship. The same verb is used for the relationship between a husband and wife.

10:21 The Lord Himself is to be the sole object of Israel's **praise.** The worship of God is a vital part of covenant requirements. Through worship man gives an inward response and an outward expression of his relationship to God.

11:1 Moses calls the people to the twin commands to **love** God and to **keep . . . His commandments.**

with your children, who have not
known and who have not seen the
[1]chastening of the LORD your God, His
greatness and His mighty hand and His
outstretched arm—
3 "His signs and His acts which He
did in the midst of Egypt, to Pharaoh
king of Egypt, and to all his land;
4 "what He did to the army of Egypt,
to their horses and their chariots:
[a]how He made the waters of the Red
Sea overflow them as they pursued
you, and *how* the LORD has destroyed
them to this day;
5 "what He did for you in the wilderness until you came to this place;
6 "and [a]what He did to Dathan and
Abiram the sons of Eliab, the son of
Reuben: how the earth opened its
mouth and swallowed them up, their
households, their tents, and all the substance that *was* [1]in their possession, in
the midst of all Israel—
7 "but your eyes have [a]seen every
great [1]act of the LORD which He did.
8 "Therefore you shall keep every
commandment which I command you
today, that you may [a]be* strong, and
go in and possess the land which you
cross over to possess,
9 "and [a]that you may prolong *your*
days in the land [b]which the LORD
[1]swore to give your fathers, to them
and their descendants, [c]'a land flowing
with milk and honey.'
10 "For the land which you go to possess *is* not like the land of Egypt from
which you have come, where you
sowed your seed and watered *it* by
foot, as a vegetable garden;
11 [a]"but the land which you cross over
to possess *is* a land of hills and valleys,
which drinks water from the rain of
heaven,
12 "a land for which the LORD your
God cares; [a]the eyes of the LORD your
God *are* always on it, from the beginning of the year to the very end of the
year.
13 'And it shall be that if you earnestly
[1]obey My commandments which I
command you today, to love the LORD
your God and serve Him with all your
heart and with all your soul,
14 'then [a]I[1] will give *you* the rain for
your land in its season, [b]the early rain
and the latter rain, that you may gather
in your grain, your new wine, and your
oil.
15 [a]'And I will send grass in your fields
for your livestock, that you may
[b]eat and be [1]filled.'
16 "Take heed to yourselves, [a]lest your
heart be deceived, and you turn aside
and [b]serve* other gods and worship
them,
17 "lest [a]the LORD's anger be aroused
against you, and He [b]shut up the heavens so that there be no rain, and the
land yield no produce, and [c]you perish
quickly from the good land which the
LORD is giving you.
18 "Therefore [a]you shall [1]lay up these 3
words of mine in your heart and in
your [b]soul, and [c]bind them as a sign
on your hand, and they shall be as
frontlets between your eyes.
19 [a]"You shall *teach them to your
children, speaking of them when you
sit in your house, when you walk by
the way, when you lie down, and when
you rise up.
20 [a]"And you shall write them on the
doorposts of your house and on your
gates,
21 "that [a]your days and the days of
your children may be multiplied in the
land of which the LORD swore to your
fathers to give them, like [b]the days of
the heavens above the earth.
22 "For if [a]you carefully keep all these
commandments which I command you
to do—to love the LORD your God, to
walk in all His ways, and [b]to hold fast
to Him—
23 "then the LORD will [a]drive out all
these nations from before you, and you
will [b]dispossess greater and mightier
nations than yourselves.
24 [a]"Every place on which the sole of
your foot treads shall be yours: [b]from
the wilderness and Lebanon, from the
river, the River Euphrates, even to
the [1]Western Sea, shall be your territory.
25 "No man shall be able to [a]stand
[1]against you; the LORD your God will
put the [b]dread of you and the fear of
you upon all the land where you **tread,**
just as He has said to you.

CHAPTER 11
2 [1]*discipline*
4 [a]Ex. 14:28; Ps. 106:11
6 [a]Num. 16:1–35; Ps. 106:16–18 [1]*at their feet*
7 [a]Deut. 10:21; 29:2 [1]*work*
8 [a]Deut. 31:6, 7, 23; Josh. 1:6, 7 *See WW at Josh. 1:9.
9 [a]Deut. 4:40; 5:16, 33; 6:2; Prov. 10:27 [b]Deut. 9:5 [c]Ex. 3:8 [1]*promised*
11 [a]Deut. 8:7
12 [a]1 Kin. 9:3
13 [1]Lit. *listen to*
14 [a]Lev. 26:4; Deut. 28:12 [b]Joel 2:23; James 5:7 [1]So with MT, Tg.; Sam., LXX, Vg. *He*
15 [a]Ps. 104:14 [b]Deut. 6:11; Joel 2:19 [1]*satisfied*
16 [a]Deut. 29:18; Job 31:27 [b]Deut. 8:19 *See WW at Ps. 100:2.
17 [a]Deut. 6:15; 9:19 [b]Deut. 28:24; 1 Kin. 8:35; 2 Chr. 6:26; 7:13 [c]Deut. 4:26; 2 Chr. 36:14–20
18 [a]Deut. 6:6–9 [b]Ps. 119:2, 34 [c]Deut. 6:8 [1]Lit. *put*
19 [a]Deut. 4:9, 10; 6:7; Prov. 22:6 *See WW at Is. 48:17.
20 [a]Deut. 6:9
21 [a]Deut. 4:40 [b]Ps. 72:5; 89:29; Prov. 3:2; 4:10; 9:11
22 [a]Deut. 11:1 [b]Deut. 10:20
23 [a]Deut. 4:38 [b]Deut. 9:1
24 [a]Josh. 1:3; 14:9 [b]Gen. 15:18; Ex. 23:31; Deut. 1:7, 8 [1]*Mediterranean*
25 [a]Deut. 7:24 [b]Ex. 23:27; Deut. 2:25; Josh. 2:9–11 [1]*before*

11:6 Moses used the rebellion of **Dathan** and **Abiram** (Num. 16) to stress Israel's failure and God's judgment. These men rebelled against the authority of God's chosen leader, Moses, and were destroyed by God. In their rebellion, Dathan and Abiram claimed Moses had brought them out of the land flowing with milk and honey (Egypt) and into desolation.

11:9–12 These verses contrast the Promised Land with Egypt.

11:14, 15 Moses abruptly switches in his presentation to the use of the words God had spoken to him, **I** [God] **will give *you* . . . I** [God] **will send.**

11:18–21 See section 3 of Truth-In-Action at the end of Deut.

WORD WEALTH

11:25 tread, *darach* (dah-*rahch*); Strong's #1869: To walk, go, tread, trample, march. This word, occurring more than 60 times in the OT, suggests a more forceful activity than mere walking. "Marching" or "treading" would best render *darach*. From this verb comes the noun *derech*, meaning "road," "path," or "way," whether an actual street or the path one habitually treads in life.

26 [a]"Behold, I set before you today a
blessing and a curse:
27 [a]"the blessing, if you obey the commandments of the LORD your God
which I command you today;
28 "and the [a]curse, if you do not obey
the commandments of the LORD your
God, but turn aside from the way
which I command you today, to go after other gods which you have not
known.
29 "Now it shall be, when the LORD
your God has brought you into the land
which you go to possess, that you shall
put the [a]blessing on Mount Gerizim
and the [b]curse on Mount Ebal.
30 "*Are* they not on the other side of
the Jordan, toward the setting sun, in
the land of the Canaanites who dwell
in the plain opposite Gilgal, [a]beside the
terebinth trees of Moreh?
31 "For you will cross over the Jordan
and go in to possess the land which
the LORD your God is giving you, and
you will possess it and dwell in it.
32 "And you shall be careful to observe all the statutes and judgments
which I set before you today.

A Prescribed Place of Worship

12 "These [a]*are* the statutes and
judgments which you shall be
careful to observe in the land which
the LORD God of your fathers is giving
you to possess, [b]all[1] the days that you
live on the earth.
2 [a]"You shall utterly destroy all the
places where the nations which you
shall dispossess served their gods,
[b]on the high mountains and on the hills
and under every green tree.
3 "And [a]you shall destroy their altars,
break their *sacred* pillars, and burn
their [1]wooden images with fire; you
shall cut down the carved images of
their gods and destroy their names
from that place.
4 "You shall not [a]worship the LORD 4
your God *with* such *things*.
5 "But you shall seek the [a]place
where the LORD your God chooses, out
of all your tribes, to put His name for
His [b]dwelling[1] place; and there you
shall go.
6 [a]"There you shall take your burnt
offerings, your sacrifices, your tithes,
the heave offerings of your hand, your
vowed offerings, your freewill offerings, and the [b]firstborn of your herds
and flocks.
7 "And [a]there you shall eat before the
LORD your God, and [b]you shall rejoice
in [1]all to which you have put your
hand, you and your households, in
which the LORD your God has blessed
you.
8 "You shall not at all do as we are 4
doing here today—[a]every man doing
whatever *is* right in his own eyes—
9 "for as yet you have not come to
the [a]rest[1]* and the inheritance which
the LORD your God is giving you.
10 "But *when* you cross over the Jordan and dwell in the land which the
LORD your God is giving you to inherit,
and He gives you [a]rest from all your
enemies round about, so that you dwell
in safety,
11 "then there will be the place where
the LORD your God chooses to make
His name abide. There you shall bring
all that I command you: your burnt offerings, your sacrifices, your tithes, the
heave offerings of your hand, and all
your choice offerings which you vow
to the LORD.
12 "And [a]you shall rejoice before the

26 [a]Deut. 30:1, 15, 19
27 [a]Deut. 28:1–14
28 [a]Deut. 28:15–68
29 [a]Deut. 27:12, 13; Josh. 8:33 [b]Deut. 27:13–26
30 [a]Gen. 12:6

CHAPTER 12
1 [a]Deut. 6:1 [b]Deut. 4:9, 10; 1 Kin. 8:40 [1]As long as
2 [a]Ex. 34:13 [b]2 Kin. 16:4; 17:10, 11
3 [a]Num. 33:52; Deut. 7:5; Judg. 2:2 [1]Heb. *Asherim*
4 [a]Deut. 12:31
5 [a]Ex. 20:24 [b]Ex. 15:13; 1 Sam. 2:29 [1]*home*
6 [a]Lev. 17:3, 4 [b]Deut. 14:23
7 [a]Deut. 14:26 [b]Deut. 12:12, 18 [1]*all that you undertake*
8 [a]Judg. 17:6; 21:25
9 [a]Deut. 3:20; 25:19; Ps. 95:11 [1]Or *place of rest* *See WW at Is. 28:12.
10 [a]Josh. 11:23
12 [a]Deut. 12:18; 26:11

11:26–32 These verses conclude the address Moses started in 5:1. The Israelites are placed in the position of decision as Moses sets before them a blessing or a curse that is conditioned upon their response to God and His Law. The opposing realities of blessing and cursing are so important that two mountains in Canaan were to serve as perpetual reminders of these dynamics.

11:30 The location described here is probably Shechem, which lies between Mt. Gerizim and Mt. Ebal (v. 29).

12:2–4 Places of idolatry were to be totally destroyed in order to divest them of any semblance of sanctity. This act of destruction was seen as a symbolic act of rejecting the foreign deities. Total destruction removed future temptations for the Israelites and removed any relationship of these gods with a particular geographical location.

12:4 See section 4 of Truth-In-Action at the end of Deut.

12:6 Burnt offerings: See note on Lev. 1:3, 4. The **sacrifices** consisted of **the heave offerings, vowed offerings,** and **freewill offerings,** all of which were different kinds of "peace offerings" (see note on Lev. 3:1). **The firstborn of your herds and flocks** refers to the firstborn during the bearing life of an animal. They were to be used in numerous sacrifices, including the vowed offerings.

12:8 See section 4 of Truth-In-Action at the end of Deut.

12:12 The **Levite** was cared for out of the sacrifices of the people.

LORD your God, you and your sons and
your daughters, your male and female
servants, and the [b]Levite who *is* within
your gates, since he has no portion nor
inheritance with you.
4 13 "Take heed to yourself that you do
not offer your burnt offerings in every
place that you see;
14 "but in the place which the LORD
chooses, in one of your tribes, there
you shall offer your burnt offerings,
and there you shall do all that I command you.
15 "However, [a]you may slaughter and
eat meat within all your gates, whatever your heart desires, according to
the blessing of the LORD your God
which He has given you; [b]the *unclean
and the clean may eat of it, [c]of the gazelle and the deer alike.
16 [a]"Only you shall not eat the blood;
you shall pour it on the earth like water.
17 "You may not eat within your gates
the tithe of your grain or your new
wine or your oil, of the firstborn of
your herd or your flock, of any of your
offerings which you vow, of your freewill offerings, or of the [1]heave offering
of your hand.
18 "But you must eat them before the
LORD your God in the place which the
LORD your God chooses, you and your
son and your daughter, your male servant and your female servant, and the
Levite who *is* within your gates; and
you shall rejoice before the LORD your
God in [1]all to which you put your
hands.
19 [1]"Take heed to yourself that you do
not forsake the Levite as long as you
live in your land.
20 "When the LORD your God [a]en-
larges your border as He has promised
you, and you say, 'Let me eat meat,'
because you long to eat meat, you may
eat as much meat as your heart desires.
21 "If the place where the LORD your
God chooses to put His name is too far
from [a]you, then you may slaughter
from your herd and from your flock
which the LORD has given you, just as
I have commanded you, and you may
eat within your gates as much as your
heart desires.

12 [b]Deut. 10:9; 14:29
15 [a]Deut. 12:21 [b]Deut. 12:22 [c]Deut. 14:5 *See WW at Lev. 10:10.
16 [a]Gen. 9:4; Lev. 7:26; 17:10–12; 1 Sam. 14:33; Acts 15:20, 29
17 [1]*contribution*
18 [1]*all your undertakings*
19 [1]*Be careful*
20 [a]Gen. 15:18; Ex. 34:24; Deut. 11:24; 19:8
21 [a]Deut. 14:24
23 [a]Gen. 9:4; Lev. 17:10–14; Deut. 12:16 *See WW at Lev. 17:11.
25 [a]Deut. 4:40; 6:18; Is. 3:10 [b]Ex. 15:26; 1 Kin. 11:38
26 [a]Num. 5:9, 10; 18:19
27 [a]Lev. 1:5, 9, 13, 17
28 [a]Deut. 12:25
29 [a]Ex. 23:23; Deut. 19:1; Josh. 23:4
31 [a]Lev. 18:3, 26, 30; 20:1, 2 [b]Deut. 18:10; Ps. 106:37; Jer. 32:35 [1]*detestable action*
32 [a]Deut. 4:2; 13:18; Josh. 1:7; Prov. 30:6; Rev. 22:18, 19

CHAPTER 13

1 [a]Num. 12:6; Jer. 23:28; Zech. 10:2

22 "Just as the gazelle and the deer are
eaten, so you may eat them; the unclean and the clean alike may eat them.
23 "Only be sure that you do not eat
the *blood, [a]for the blood *is* the life;
you may not eat the life with the meat.
24 "You shall not eat it; you shall pour
it on the earth like water.
25 "You shall not eat it, [a]that it may 3
go well with you and your children after you, [b]when you do *what is* right
in the sight of the LORD.
26 "Only the [a]holy things which you
have, and your vowed offerings, you
shall take and go to the place which
the LORD chooses.
27 "And [a]you shall offer your burnt offerings, the meat and the blood, on the
altar of the LORD your God; and the
blood of your sacrifices shall be poured
out on the altar of the LORD your God,
and you shall eat the meat.
28 "Observe and obey all these words 3
which I command you, [a]that it may go
well with you and your children after
you forever, when you do *what is* good
and right in the sight of the LORD your
God.

Beware of False Gods

29 "When [a]the LORD your God cuts off
from before you the nations which you
go to dispossess, and you displace
them and dwell in their land,
30 "take heed to yourself that you are
not ensnared to follow them, after they
are destroyed from before you, and
that you do not inquire after their gods,
saying, 'How did these nations serve
their gods? I also will do likewise.'
31 [a]"You shall not worship the LORD
your God in that way; for every
[1]abomination to the LORD which He
hates they have done to their gods; for
[b]they burn even their sons and daughters in the fire to their gods.
32 "Whatever I command you, be care- 3
ful to observe it; [a]you shall not add to
it nor take away from it.

Punishment of Apostates

13 "If there arises among you a 4
prophet or a [a]dreamer of

12:13 See section 4 of Truth-In-Action at the end of Deut.
12:16 Blood symbolized life, which God imparted to all living creatures; thus it was to be treated with respect by ritually pouring **it on the earth like water.**
12:23–25 The only prohibition placed upon the eating of meat was the mandate not to consume the animal's **blood.**
12:25 See section 3 of Truth-In-Action at the end of Deut.
12:28 See section 3 of Truth-In-Action at the end of Deut.
12:31 The practice of child sacrifice was a heinous **abomination** and was a capital crime to Israel (Lev. 18:21; 20:2–5).
12:32 See section 3 of Truth-In-Action at the end of Deut.
13:1–3 Prophecy and dreams are normal means for God to use in speaking to His people, but both gifts can be abused. True prophets have the power to perform signs and wonders, but others can also exercise such power (see Ex.

*dreams, [b]and he gives you a sign or a *wonder,
2 "and [a]the sign or the wonder comes to pass, of which he spoke to you, saying, 'Let us go after other gods'—which you have not known—'and let us serve them,'
3 "you shall not listen to the words of that prophet or that dreamer of dreams, for the LORD your God [a]is testing you to know whether you love the LORD your God with all your heart and with all your soul.
4 "You shall [a]walk[1] after the LORD your God and fear Him, and keep His commandments and obey His voice; you shall serve Him and [b]hold fast to Him.
5 "But [a]that prophet or that dreamer of dreams shall be put to death, because he has spoken in order to turn *you* away from the LORD your God, who brought you out of the land of Egypt and redeemed you from the house of bondage, to entice you from the way in which the LORD your God commanded you to walk. [b]So you shall [1]put away the evil from your midst.
6 [a]"If your brother, the son of your mother, your son or your daughter, [b]the wife [1]of your bosom, or your *friend [c]who is as your own soul, secretly entices you, saying, 'Let us go and serve other gods,' which you have not known, neither you nor your fathers,
7 "of the gods of the people which *are* all around you, near to you or far off from you, from *one* end of the earth to the *other* end of the earth,
8 "you shall [a]not [1]consent to him or listen to him, nor shall your eye pity him, nor shall you spare him or conceal him;
9 "but you shall surely kill him; your hand shall be first against him to put him to [a]death, and afterward the hand of all the people.
10 "And you shall stone him with stones until he dies, because he sought to entice you away from the LORD your God, who brought you out of the land of Egypt, from the house of bondage.
11 "So all Israel shall hear and [a]fear, and not again do such wickedness as this among you.
12 [a]"If you hear someone in one of your cities, which the LORD your God gives you to dwell in, saying,
13 [1]'Corrupt men have gone out from among you and enticed the inhabitants of their city, saying, "Let us go and serve other gods" '—which you have not known—
14 "then you shall inquire, search out, and *ask diligently. And *if it is* indeed *true *and* certain *that* such an [1]abomination was committed among you,
15 "you shall surely strike the inhabitants of that city with the edge of the sword, utterly destroying it, all that is in it and its livestock—with the edge of the sword.
16 "And you shall gather all its plunder into the middle of the street, and [1]completely [a]burn with fire the city and all its plunder, for the LORD your God. It shall be [b]a [2]heap forever; it shall not be built again.
17 [a]"So none of the accursed things shall remain in your hand, that the LORD may [b]turn from the fierceness of His anger and show you *mercy, have compassion on you and [1]multiply you, just as He swore to your fathers,
18 "because you have listened to the voice of the LORD your God, [a]to keep all His commandments which I command you today, to do *what is* right in the eyes of the LORD your God.

Improper Mourning

14 "You *are* [a]the children of the LORD your God; [b]you shall not cut yourselves nor [1]shave the front of your head for the dead.
2 [a]"For you *are* a holy people to the LORD your God, and the LORD has chosen you to be a people for Himself, a *special treasure above all the peoples who *are* on the face of the earth.

Clean and Unclean Meat

3 [a]"You shall not eat any [1]detestable thing.

1 [b]Matt. 24:24; Mark 13:22; 2 Thess. 2:9 *See WW at Joel 2:28. • See WW at Zech. 3:8.
2 [a]Deut. 18:22
3 [a]Ex. 20:20; Deut. 8:2, 16
4 [a]Deut. 10:12, 20; 2 Kin. 23:3 [b]Deut. 30:20 [1]*follow the LORD*
5 [a]Deut. 18:20; Jer. 14:15 [b]Deut. 17:5, 7; 1 Cor. 5:13 [1]*exterminate*
6 [a]Deut. 17:2 [b]Gen. 16:5 [c]1 Sam. 18:1, 3 [1]Whom you cherish *See WW at Prov. 17:17.
8 [a]Deut. 7:16; Prov. 1:10 [1]*yield*
9 [a]Lev. 24:14; Deut. 17:7
11 [a]Deut. 17:13
12 [a]Judg. 20:1–48
13 [1]Lit. *Sons of Belial*
14 [1]*detestable action* *See WW at Ps. 122:6. • See WW at Ps. 25:5.
16 [a]Josh. 6:24 [b]Josh. 8:28; Is. 17:1; 25:2; Jer 49:2 [1]Or *as a whole-offering* [2]Lit. *mound* or *ruin*
17 [a]Josh. 6:18 [b]Josh. 7:26 [1]*increase* *See WW at Hos. 2:23.
18 [a]Deut. 12:25, 28, 32

CHAPTER 14

1 [a][Rom. 8:16; Gal. 3:26] [b]Lev. 19:28; 21:1–5 [1]*make any baldness between your eyes*
2 [a]Lev. 20:26; Deut. 7:6; [Rom. 12:1] *See WW at Deut. 26:18.
3 [a]Ezek. 4:14 [1]*abominable*

7:10–12). One's gifts and powers are not the only test of being a true prophet; for, if any seek to move the people's loyalty away from God and **after other gods,** he is a false prophet.
13:1–5 See section 4 of Truth-In-Action at the end of Deut.
13:5, 9, 15 God so totally abhors the worship of false gods that He commands any city among the Israelites worshiping them to be utterly destroyed. He commands that false prophets (v. 5), family members (v. 9), or inhabitants of cities (v. 12) seeking to lead the Israelites into idolatry be destroyed.
14:1 These prohibitions are against mourning customs of the pagan cults for the dead.
14:3–21 The OT is not clear regarding the principle behind the selecting of **clean** and **unclean** or **detestable** animals. Some scholars think it was a matter of hygiene; others think the unclean animals were sacred to Canaanite religions. Jesus' teaching "purifying all foods" (Mark 7:19) and God's

4 [a]"These *are* the animals which you may eat: the ox, the sheep, the goat,

5 "the deer, the gazelle, the roe deer, the wild goat, the [1]mountain goat, the antelope, and the mountain sheep.

6 "And you may eat every animal with cloven hooves, having the hoof split into two parts, *and that* chews the cud, among the animals.

7 "Nevertheless, of those that chew the cud or have cloven hooves, you shall not eat, *such as* these: the camel, the hare, and the rock hyrax; for they chew the cud but do not have cloven hooves; they *are* unclean for you.

8 "Also the swine is unclean for you, because it has cloven hooves, yet *does* not *chew* the cud; you shall not eat their flesh [a]or touch their dead carcasses.

9 [a]"These you may eat of all that *are* in the waters: you may eat all that have fins and scales.

10 "And whatever does not have fins and scales you shall not eat; it *is* unclean for you.

11 "All clean birds you may eat.

12 [a]"But these you shall not eat: the eagle, the vulture, the buzzard,

13 "the red kite, the falcon, and the kite after their kinds;

14 "every raven after its kind;

15 "the ostrich, the short-eared owl, the sea gull, and the hawk after their kinds;

16 "the little owl, the screech owl, the white owl,

17 "the jackdaw, the carrion vulture, the fisher owl,

18 "the stork, the heron after its kind, and the hoopoe and the bat.

19 "Also [a]every [1]creeping thing that flies is unclean for you; [b]they shall not be eaten.

20 "You may eat all clean birds.

21 [a]"You shall not eat anything that dies *of itself;* you may give it to the alien who *is* within your gates, that he may eat it, or you may sell it to a foreigner; [b]for you *are* a holy people to the LORD your God. [c]You shall not boil a young goat in its mother's milk.

Tithing Principles

22 [a]"You shall truly tithe all the increase of your grain that the field produces year by year.

23 [a]"And you shall eat before the LORD your God, in the place where He chooses to make His name abide, the tithe of your grain and your new wine and your oil, of [b]the firstborn of your herds and your flocks, that you may learn to fear the LORD your God always.

24 "But if the journey is too long for you, so that you are not able to carry *the tithe, or* [a]if the place where the LORD your God chooses to put His name is too far from you, when the LORD your God has blessed you,

25 "then you shall exchange *it* for money, take the money in your hand, and go to the place which the LORD your God chooses.

26 "And you shall spend that money for whatever your heart desires: for oxen or sheep, for wine or similar drink, for whatever your heart desires; you shall eat there before the LORD your God, and you shall [a]rejoice, you and your household.

27 "You shall not [1]forsake the [a]Levite who *is* within your gates, for he has no part nor inheritance with you.

28 [a]"At the end of *every* third year you shall bring out the [b]tithe of your produce of that year and store *it* up within your gates.

29 "And the Levite, because he has no portion nor inheritance with you, and the stranger and the fatherless and the widow who *are* within your gates, may come and eat and be satisfied, that the LORD your God may bless you in all the work of your hand which you do.

4 [a]Lev. 11:2–45
5 [1]Or *addax*
8 [a]Lev. 11:26, 27
9 [a]Lev. 11:9
12 [a]Lev. 11:13
19 [a]Lev. 11:20 [b]Lev. 11:23 [1]*swarming*
21 [a]Lev. 17:15; 22:8; Ezek. 4:14; 44:31 [b]Deut. 14:2 [c]Ex. 23:19; 34:26
22 [a]Lev. 27:30; Deut. 12:6, 17; Neh. 10:37
23 [a]Deut. 12:5–7 [b]Deut. 15:19, 20
24 [a]Deut. 12:5, 21
26 [a]Deut. 12:7
27 [a]Deut. 12:12 [1]*neglect*
28 [a]Deut. 26:12; Amos 4:4 [b]Num. 18:21–24

command to Peter to "kill and eat" unclean animals (Acts 10:13) favor the latter view.

14:21 This seems to be a clear indicator that the dietary rules presented in this chapter were not solely for hygienic purposes, but existed because God's holy people, those set apart strictly to Him, were to be distinct in Canaan. For example, the law forbidding the boiling of **a young goat in its mother's milk** (also given in Ex. 23:19; 34:26) existed as a rejection of a Canaanite religious rite, possibly associated with a fertility cult.

14:22–27 The giving of the **tithe** ("a tenth") is an act of worship to honor God as the Provider of the harvest. Giving the tithe regularly teaches the people to recognize and remember that their prosperity is not their own doing. The emphasis of this tithe, in contrast to the more detailed principles in Num. 18:21–32 and Lev. 27:30–33, highlights the celebration of God's provision by eating a joyful family meal.

14:24–26 This special provision was to accommodate those living a great distance from the sanctuary who had such a large tithe that it was impractical to transport.

14:29 Throughout the Bible the interests of the poor and needy are connected with the interests of God. The reason for caring for the underprivileged was that God would bless the giver.

Debts Canceled Every Seven Years

15 "At the end of [a]*every* seven
years you shall grant a [1]release
of debts.
2 "And this *is* the form of the release:
Every creditor who has lent *anything*
to his neighbor shall [1]release *it;* he
shall not [2]require *it* of his neighbor or
his brother, because it is called the
LORD's release.
3 "Of a foreigner you may require *it;*
but you shall give up your claim to
what is owed by your brother,
4 "except when there may be no poor
among you; for the LORD will greatly
[a]bless you in the land which the LORD
your God is giving you to possess *as*
an inheritance—
5 "only if you carefully obey the voice
of the LORD your God, to observe with
care all these commandments which I
command you today.
6 "For the LORD your God will bless
you just as He promised you; [a]you
shall lend to many nations, but you
shall not borrow; you shall reign over
many nations, but they shall not reign
over you.

Generosity to the Poor

7 "If there is among you a poor man
of your brethren, within any of the
[1]gates in your land which the LORD
your God is giving you, [a]you shall not
harden your heart nor shut your hand
from your poor brother,
8 "but [a]you shall [1]open* your hand
wide to him and willingly lend him
*sufficient for his need, whatever he
needs.
9 "Beware lest there be a wicked
thought in your heart, saying, 'The seventh year, the year of release, is at
hand,' and your [a]eye be evil against
your poor brother and you give him
nothing, and [b]he cry out to the LORD
against you, and [c]it become sin among
you.
10 "You shall surely give to him, and
[a]your heart should not be grieved
when you give to him, because [b]for this
thing the LORD your God will bless you
in all your works and in all to which
you put your hand.
11 "For [a]the poor will never cease
from the land; therefore I command

CHAPTER 15

1 [a]Ex. 21:2; 23:10, 11; Lev. 25:4; Jer. 34:14 [1]*remission*
2 [1]*cancel the debt* [2]*exact it*
4 [a]Deut. 7:13
6 [a]Deut. 28:12, 44
7 [a]Ex. 23:6; Lev. 25:35–37; Deut. 24:12–14; [1 John 3:17] [1]*towns*
8 [a]Matt. 5:42; Gal. 2:10 [1]*freely open*
*See WW at Jer. 40:4. • See WW at Mal. 3:10.
9 [a]Deut. 28:54, 56 [b]Ex. 22:23; Deut. 24:15; Job 34:28; Ps. 12:5; James 5:4 [c][Matt. 25:41, 42]
10 [a]2 Cor. 9:5, 7 [b]Deut. 14:29; Ps. 41:1; Prov. 22:9
11 [a]Matt. 26:11; Mark 14:7; John 12:8 [1]*freely open*
*See WW at Ps. 40:17. • See WW at Ps. 70:5.
12 [a]Ex. 21:2–6; Jer. 34:14 [b]Lev. 25:39–46
13 [1]*set him free*
14 [a]Prov. 10:22
15 [a]Deut. 5:15
16 [a]Ex. 21:5, 6
18 [a]Is. 16:14
19 [a]Ex. 13:2, 12 [1]*set apart or consecrate*
20 [a]Lev. 7:15–18; Deut. 12:5; 14:23
21 [a]Lev. 22:19–25; Deut. 17:1

you, saying, 'You shall [1]open your
hand wide to your brother, to your
*poor and your *needy, in your land.'

The Law Concerning Bondservants

12 [a]"If your brother, a Hebrew man,
or a Hebrew woman, is [b]sold to you
and serves you six years, then in the
seventh year you shall let him go free
from you.
13 "And when you [1]send him away
free from you, you shall not let him go
away empty-handed;
14 "you shall supply him liberally from
your flock, from your threshing floor,
and from your winepress. *From what*
the LORD has [a]blessed you with, you
shall give to him.
15 [a]"You shall remember that you
were a slave in the land of Egypt, and
the LORD your God redeemed you;
therefore I command you this thing today.
16 "And [a]if it happens that he says to
you, 'I will not go away from you,' because he loves you and your house,
since he prospers with you,
17 "then you shall take an awl and
thrust *it* through his ear to the door,
and he shall be your servant forever.
Also to your female servant you shall
do likewise.
18 "It shall not seem hard to you when
you send him away free from you; for
he has been worth [a]a double hired servant in serving you six years. Then the
LORD your God will bless you in all that
you do.

The Law Concerning Firstborn Animals

19 [a]"All the firstborn males that come
from your herd and your flock you
shall [1]sanctify to the LORD your God;
you shall do no work with the firstborn
of your herd, nor shear the firstborn
of your flock.
20 [a]"You and your household shall eat
it before the LORD your God year by
year in the place which the LORD
chooses.
21 [a]"But if there is a defect in it, *if it
is* lame or blind *or has* any serious defect, you shall not sacrifice it to the
LORD your God.
22 "You may eat it within your gates;

15:4, 5, 11: Moses' statement **when there may be no poor among you** (v. 4) is conditional upon **carefully** obeying (v. 5; see also 14:29). Thus perfect and consistent obedience to God's commandments will make possible a society in which all poverty is eliminated by God's blessing. Realizing that Israel may not fulfill this requirement to its fullest, Moses goes on to say realistically, **the poor will never cease from the land** (v. 11).

[a]the unclean and the clean *person* alike *may eat it,* as *if it were* a gazelle or a deer.
23 "Only you shall not eat its blood; you shall pour it on the ground like water.

The Passover Reviewed

16 "Observe the [a]month of Abib, and keep the Passover to the LORD your God, for [b]in the month of Abib the LORD your God brought you out of Egypt by night.
2 "Therefore you shall **sacrifice** the Passover to the LORD your God, from the flock and [a]the herd, in the [b]place where the LORD chooses to put His name.
3 "You shall eat no leavened bread with it; [a]seven days you shall eat unleavened bread with it, *that is,* the bread of affliction (for you came out of the land of Egypt in haste), that you may [b]remember the day in which you

22 [a]Deut. 12:15, 16, 22

CHAPTER 16

1 [a]Ex. 12:2 [b]Ex. 13:4
2 [a]Num. 28:19 [b]Deut. 12:5, 26; 15:20
3 [a]Num. 29:12 [b]Ex. 13:3; Deut. 4:9

WORD WEALTH

16:2 sacrifice, *zabach* (zah-*vakh*); Strong's #2076: To slay, slaughter, or sacrifice. From this verb comes the noun *zebach,* "a sacrifice." Whereas sacrifice in English sometimes suggests merely an inconvenience or the giving of a costly gift, in Hebrew it involves the offering of a life. From *zabach* also comes the word for "altar," *mizbeach,* which is literally "place of sacrificing."

16:1 Abib, which was later called Nisan, occurred in the spring of the year around March or April. Ex. 12:18 states that the **Passover** celebration was to be held on the fourteenth day of Abib and that the Unleavened Bread celebration was to be observed the following seven days. Thus Passover and the Feast of Unleavened Bread were two parts of a single major festival. Detailed legislation for this festival is provided in Ex. 12, Lev. 23:5–8, and Num. 28:16–25. Passover was the celebration of the Israelites' deliverance from Egypt, thus a celebration of freedom and the commemoration of the establishment of the covenant community of God.
16:2 Passover here indicates the Passover animal, the *pesah* that was to be sacrificed. This is the same word used in v. 1 to designate the celebration. The Passover in Egypt had been celebrated within the family unit in their own homes. Now God was calling for the celebration to be enacted in one location, after Israel possessed the Promised Land, **in the place** where His sanctuary would be located. Thus God's covenant people were to come together in one place as one family under the leadership of one God.
16:3 Bread of affliction: The **unleavened bread** was symbolic of the hardships in Egypt and the oppression of the Pharaoh. The bread reminded them of the hasty departure from Egypt in which there was not even time to leaven the dough (Ex. 12:34).

THE JEWISH CALENDAR (16:1)

The Jews used two kinds of calendars:
Civil Calendar—official calendar of kings, childbirth, and contracts.
Sacred Calendar—from which festivals were computed.

Names of Months	Corresponds with	No. of Days	Month of Civil Year	Month of Sacred Year
Tishri	Sept.–Oct.	30	1st	7th
Heshvan	Oct.–Nov.	29 or 30	2nd	8th
Chislev	Nov.–Dec.	29 or 30	3rd	9th
Tebeth	Dec.–Jan.	29	4th	10th
Shebat	Jan.–Feb.	30	5th	11th
Adar	Feb.–Mar.	29 or 30	6th	12th
Nisan	Mar.–Apr.	30	7th	1st
Iyar	Apr.–May	29	8th	2nd
Sivan	May–June	30	9th	3rd
Tammuz	June–July	29	10th	4th
Ab	July–Aug.	30	11th	5th
***Elul**	Aug.–Sept.	29	12th	6th

*Hebrew months were alternately 30 and 29 days long. Their year, shorter than ours, had 354 days. Therefore, about every 3 years (7 times in 19 years) an extra 29-day month, Veadar, was added between Adar and Nisan.

came out of the land of Egypt all the
days of your life.
4 [a]"And no leaven shall be seen
among you in all your territory for
seven days, nor shall *any* of the meat
which you sacrifice the first day at twilight remain overnight until [b]morning.
5 "You may not sacrifice the Passover within any of your gates which
the LORD your God gives you;
6 "but at the place where the LORD
your God chooses to make His name
abide, there you shall sacrifice the
Passover [a]at twilight, at the going
down of the sun, at the *time you came
out of Egypt.
7 "And you shall roast and eat *it*
[a]in the place which the LORD your God
chooses, and in the morning you shall
turn and go to your tents.
8 "Six days you shall eat unleavened
bread, and [a]on the seventh day there
shall be a [1]sacred assembly to the LORD
your God. You shall do no work *on it.*

The Feast of Weeks Reviewed

9 "You shall count seven weeks for
yourself; begin to count the seven
weeks from *the time* you begin *to put*
the sickle to the grain.
10 "Then you shall keep the [a]Feast of
Weeks to the LORD your God with the
tribute of a freewill offering from your
hand, which you shall give [b]as the
LORD your God blesses you.
11 [a]"You shall rejoice before the LORD
your God, you and your son and your
daughter, your male servant and your
female servant, the Levite who *is*
within your gates, the stranger and the
fatherless and the widow who *are*
among you, at the place where the
LORD your God chooses to make His
name abide.
12 [a]"And you shall remember that you
were a slave in Egypt, and you shall
be careful to observe these statutes.

The Feast of Tabernacles Reviewed

13 [a]"You shall observe the Feast of
Tabernacles seven days, when you
have gathered from your threshing
floor and from your winepress.
14 "And [a]you shall rejoice in your
feast, you and your son and your
daughter, your male servant and your
female servant and the Levite, the
stranger and the fatherless and the
widow, who *are* within your [1]gates.
15 [a]"Seven days you shall *keep a sacred feast to the LORD your God in the
place which the LORD chooses, because
the LORD your God will bless you in
all your produce and in all the work
of your hands, so that you surely *rejoice.
16 [a]"Three times a year all your males
shall appear before the LORD your God
in the place which He chooses: at the
Feast of Unleavened Bread, at the
Feast of Weeks, and at the Feast of
Tabernacles; and [b]they shall not appear before the LORD empty-handed.
17 "Every man *shall give* as he is able,
[a]according to the blessing of the LORD
your God which He has given you.

Justice Must Be Administered

18 "You shall appoint [a]judges* and officers in all your [1]gates, which the
LORD your God gives you, according
to your tribes, and they shall judge the
people with just judgment.
19 [a]"You shall not pervert justice;
[b]you shall not [1]show partiality, [c]nor
take a bribe, for a bribe blinds the eyes
of the wise and [2]twists the words of
the righteous.
20 "You shall follow what is altogether
just, that you may [a]live and inherit the
land which the LORD your God is giving
you.
21 [a]"You shall not plant for yourself
any tree, as a [1]wooden image, near the
altar which you build for yourself to
the LORD your God.
22 [a]"You shall not set up a *sacred*
pillar, which the LORD your God
hates.

17 "You [a]shall not sacrifice to the
LORD your God a bull or sheep
which has any [1]blemish *or* defect, for

4 [a]Ex. 13:7 [b]Num. 9:12
6 [a]Ex. 12:7–10 *See WW at Num. 9:2.
7 [a]2 Kin. 23:23
8 [a]Ex. 12:16; 13:6; Lev. 23:8, 36 [1]Lit. *restraint*
10 [a]Ex. 34:22; Lev. 23:15, 16; Num. 28:26 [b]1 Cor. 16:2
11 [a]Deut. 16:14
12 [a]Deut. 15:15
13 [a]Ex. 23:16
14 [a]Neh. 8:9 [1]*towns*
15 [a]Lev. 23:39–41 *See WW at Ex. 23:14. • See WW at 2 Chr. 7:10.
16 [a]Ex. 23:14–17; 34:22–24 [b]Ex. 23:15
17 [a]Lev. 14:30, 31; Deut. 16:10
18 [a]Ex. 23:1–8; Deut. 1:16, 17; John 7:24 [1]*towns* *See WW at Judg. 2:18.
19 [a]Ex. 23:2, 6 [b]Deut. 1:17 [c]Ex. 23:8 [1]Lit. *regard faces* [2]*perverts*
20 [a]Ezek. 18:5–9
21 [a]Ex. 34:13 [1]Or *Asherah*
22 [a]Lev. 26:1

CHAPTER 17

1 [a]Deut. 15:21; Mal. 1:8, 13 [1]Lit. *evil thing*

16:4 The prohibition of leaven and the complete consumption of the meat symbolized the emphasis upon purity in this celebration.

16:10 The Feast of Weeks is the second major annual harvest festival to be celebrated by Israel. It is called the Feast of Harvest in Ex. 23:16, the Day of Firstfruits in Num. 28:26, and Pentecost (based upon the Greek translation of "fifty days") in Lev. 23:16. The details of this feast are provided in Ex. 23:16, 34:22, Lev. 23:15–21, and Num. 28:26–31. The celebration was in honor of God's gracious providence in the harvest.

16:13 Feast of Tabernacles: This harvest festival occurred in the autumn when all the produce had been gathered. In Ex. 23:16 and 34:22 it is called the Feast of Ingathering. Details about the observation of this feast are given in Lev. 23:33–43 and Num. 29:12–38. Every sabbatical year the Law was read to all Israel during this feast (31:9–13).

16:18; 17:8 Local courts were to be set up in all their **gates** (towns). These lower courts could appeal for a decision to a higher tribunal at the central sanctuary. The verdict of the higher tribunal was final (17:10, 11).

that *is* an [2]abomination to the LORD
your God.
2 [a]"If there is found among you,
within any of your [1]gates which the
LORD your God gives you, a man or a
woman who has been wicked in the
sight of the LORD your God, [b]in transgressing His covenant,
3 "who has gone and served other
gods and worshiped them, either [a]the
sun or moon or any of the host of
heaven, [b]which I have not commanded,
4 [a]"and it is told you, and you hear
of it, then you shall inquire diligently.
And if *it is* indeed true *and* certain that
such an [1]abomination has been committed in Israel,
5 "then you shall bring out to your
gates that man or woman who has
committed that wicked thing, and
[a]shall stone [b]to death that man or
woman with stones.
6 "Whoever is deserving of death
shall be put to death on the testimony
of two or three [a]witnesses; he shall not
be put to death on the testimony of one
witness.
7 "The hands of the witnesses shall
be the first against him to put him to
death, and afterward the hands of all
the people. So you shall put away the
evil from among [a]you.
8 [a]"If a matter arises which is too
hard for you to judge, between degrees
of guilt for bloodshed, between one
judgment or another, or between one
punishment or another, matters of controversy within your gates, then you
shall arise and go up to the [b]place
which the LORD your God chooses.
9 "And [a]you shall come to the
*priests, the Levites, and [b]to the judge
there in those days, and inquire *of
them;* [c]they shall pronounce upon you
the sentence of judgment.
10 "You shall do according to the sentence which they pronounce upon you
in that place which the LORD chooses.
And you shall be careful to do according to all that they order you.
11 "According to the sentence of the
law in which they instruct you, according to the judgment which they tell
you, you shall do; you shall not turn
aside *to* the right hand or *to* the left
from the sentence which they pronounce upon you.
12 "Now [a]the man who acts presumptuously and will not heed the priest
who stands to minister there before the
LORD your God, or the judge, that man
shall die. So you shall put away the
evil from Israel.
13 [a]"And all the people shall hear and
fear, and no longer act presumptuously.

Principles Governing Kings

14 "When you come to the land which
the LORD your God is giving you, and
possess it and dwell in it, and say,
[a]'I will set a king over me like all the
nations that *are* around me,'
15 "you shall surely set a king over
you [a]whom the LORD your God
chooses; *one* [b]from among your brethren you shall set as king over you; you
may not set a foreigner over you, who
is not your brother.
16 "But he shall not multiply [a]horses
for himself, nor cause the people
[b]to return to Egypt to multiply horses,
for [c]the LORD has said to you, [d]'You
shall not return that way again.'
17 "Neither shall he multiply wives for
himself, lest his heart turn away; nor
shall he greatly multiply silver and
[a]gold for himself.
18 "Also it shall be, when he sits on
the throne of his kingdom, that he shall
write for himself a copy of this law in
a book, from *the one* [a]before the
priests, the Levites.
19 "And [a]it shall be with him, and he
shall read it all the days of his life, that
he may learn to fear the LORD his God
and be careful to observe all the words
of this law and these statutes,
20 "that his heart may not [1]be lifted
above his brethren, that he [a]may not
turn aside from the commandment *to*
the right hand or *to* the left, and that
he may [2]prolong *his* days in his kingdom, he and his children in the midst
of Israel.

The Portion of the Priests and Levites

18 "The priests, the Levites—all
the tribe of Levi—shall have

1 [2]*detestable thing*
2 [a]Deut. 13:6 [b]Josh. 7:11 [1]*towns*
3 [a]Deut. 4:19 [b]Jer. 7:22
4 [a]Deut. 13:12, 14 [1]*detestable thing*
5 [a]Lev. 24:14–16; Josh. 7:25 [b]Deut. 13:6–18
6 [a]Num. 35:30; Deut. 19:15; Matt. 18:16; John 8:17; 2 Cor. 13:1; 1 Tim. 5:19; Heb. 10:28
7 [a]Deut. 13:5; 19:19; 1 Cor. 5:13
8 [a]Deut. 1:17; 2 Chr. 19:10 [b]Deut. 12:5; 16:2
9 [a]Jer. 18:18 [b]Deut. 19:17–19 [c]Ezek. 44:24 *See WW at Lev. 5:6.
12 [a]Num. 15:30; Deut. 1:43
13 [a]Deut. 13:11
14 [a]1 Sam. 8:5, 19, 20; 10:19
15 [a]1 Sam. 9:15, 16; 10:24; 16:12, 13; 1 Chr. 22:8–10; Hos. 8:4 [b]Jer. 30:21
16 [a]1 Kin. 4:26; 10:26–29; Ps. 20:7 [b]Is. 31:1; Ezek. 17:15 [c]Ex. 13:17, 18; Hos. 11:5 [d]Deut. 28:68
17 [a]1 Kin. 10:14
18 [a]Deut. 31:24–26
19 [a]Ps. 119:97, 98
20 [a]Deut. 5:32; 1 Kin. 15:5 [1]*become proud* [2]*continue long in his kingdom*

17:7 The witness was required to initiate the penalty by casting the first stones, thus subjecting himself to blood revenge should his testimony prove to be false (19:15–21).

17:14 This is the only passage in the Pentateuch that mentions the idea of a monarchy. Israel was a theocratic state with God as her only King. But here, Moses predicted that Israel would eventually ask for a king. Israel's kings would be distinguished from those of her neighbors by the guidelines of personal character set down in the Law. This anticipated the establishment of the Davidic throne and the reign of Christ.

17:16, 17 A sad commentary on Israel's subsequent monarchies is that many violated all three prohibitions.

18:1–8 This section gives detailed legislation about

[1]no part nor [a]inheritance with Israel;
they shall eat the offerings of the LORD
made by fire, and His portion.
2 "Therefore they shall have no inheritance among their brethren; the
LORD is their inheritance, as He said
to them.
3 "And this shall be the priest's
[a]due[1] from the people, from those who
offer a sacrifice, whether *it is* bull or
sheep: they shall give to the priest the
shoulder, the cheeks, and the stomach.
4 [a]"The firstfruits of your grain and
your new wine and your oil, and the
first of the fleece of your sheep, you
shall give him.
5 "For [a]the LORD your God has chosen him out of all your tribes [b]to stand
to minister in the **name** of the LORD,
him and his sons forever.

WORD WEALTH

18:5 name, *shem* (*shem*); Strong's #8034: Name, renown, fame, memorial, character. Possibly *shem* comes from a root that suggests "marking" or "branding." Thus a person was named because of something that marked him, whether physical features, or accomplishments he had made or was expected to make. *Shem* appears more than 800 times in the OT, its most important use being in the phrase "the name of the LORD," sometimes abbreviated to *ha-shem* ("the name," that is, *Yahweh*). See Lev. 24:11, where one man blasphemed "the name," meaning that he blasphemed the Lord. Thus, in Judaic tradition, *Yahweh* God is often simply called *hashem*.

6 "So if a Levite comes from any of
your [1]gates, from where he [a]dwells
among all Israel, and comes with all
the desire of his mind [b]to the place
which the LORD chooses,
7 "then he may serve in the name of
the LORD his God [a]as all his brethren
the Levites *do,* who stand there before
the LORD.
8 "They shall have equal [a]portions to
eat, besides what comes from the sale
of his inheritance.

Avoid Wicked Customs

9 "When you come into the land
which the LORD your God is giving you,
[a]you shall not learn to follow the
[1]abominations of those nations.
10 "There shall not be found among
you *anyone* who makes his son or his
daughter [a]pass[1] through the fire, [b]*or
one* who practices witchcraft, *or* a
soothsayer, or one who interprets
omens, or a sorcerer,
11 [a]"or one who conjures spells, or a
medium, or a spiritist, or [b]one who
calls up the dead.
12 "For all who do these things *are*
[1]an abomination to the LORD, and
[a]because of these abominations the
LORD your God drives them out from
before you.
13 "You shall be [1]blameless before the
LORD your God.
14 "For these nations which you will
dispossess listened to soothsayers and
diviners; but as for you, the LORD your
God has not [1]appointed such for you.

A New Prophet Like Moses

15 [a]"The LORD your God will raise up
for you a Prophet like me from your
midst, from your brethren. Him you
shall hear,
16 "according to all you desired of the
LORD your God in Horeb [a]in the day
of the assembly, saying, [b]'Let me not
hear again the voice of the LORD my
God, nor let me see this great fire anymore, lest I die.'
17 "And the LORD said to me: [a]'What
they have spoken is good.
18 [a]'I will raise up for them a Prophet
like you from among their brethren,
and [b]will put My words in His mouth,
[c]and He shall speak to them all that I
command Him.
19 [a]'And it shall be *that* whoever will
not hear My words, which He speaks
in My name, I will require *it* of him.

KINGDOM DYNAMICS

18:18, 19 Jesus, the Prophet of the Greater Covenant, MESSIAH'S COMING. To the religious Jews of Jesus' time, no one was greater than Moses. Through Moses God had given the Law; he was the person God used to transmit their whole religious system. But they were (*cont. on next page*)

CHAPTER 18

1 [a]Deut. 10:9; 1 Cor. 9:13 [1]*no portion*
3 [a]Lev. 7:32–34; Num. 18:11, 12; 1 Sam. 2:13–16, 29 [1]*right*
4 [a]Ex. 22:29
5 [a]Ex. 28:1 [b]Deut. 10:8
6 [a]Num. 35:2 [b]Deut. 12:5; 14:23 [1]*towns*
7 [a]Num. 1:50; 2 Chr. 31:2
8 [a]Lev. 27:30–33; Num. 18:21–24; 2 Chr. 31:4; Neh. 12:44
9 [a]Lev. 18:26, 27, 30; Deut. 12:29, 30; 20:16–18 [1]*detestable acts*
10 [a]Lev. 18:21; Deut. 12:31 [b]Ex. 22:18; Lev. 19:26, 31; 20:6, 27; Is. 8:19 [1]Be burned as an offering to an idol
11 [a]Lev. 20:27 [b]1 Sam. 28:7
12 [a]Lev. 18:24; Deut. 9:4 [1]*detestable*
13 [1]Lit. *perfect*
14 [1]*allowed you to do so*
15 [a]Matt. 21:11; Luke 1:76; 2:25–34; 7:16; 24:19; Acts 3:22
16 [a]Deut. 5:23–27 [b]Ex. 20:18, 19; Heb. 12:19
17 [a]Deut. 5:28
18 [a]Deut. 34:10; John 1:45; Acts 3:22 [b]Num. 23:5; Is. 49:2; 51:16; John 17:8 [c][John 4:25; 8:28]
19 [a]Acts 3:23; [Heb. 12:25]

---

providing for the Levites' food and material to make their clothing.
18:9–14 The prohibitions against accepting illegitimate religious personages or adopting illegitimate practices are because Israel is to be a unique (**blameless**) people.
18:15 Moses was followed by many genuine prophets, but his prophecy that a **Prophet** like himself would one day come forth found its fulfillment in Jesus Christ. Peter, in his sermon recorded in Acts 3:22, 23, quotes this prophecy as being fulfilled in Christ.
18:16 Horeb: See note on 5:23–28.

(cont. from preceding page)
also aware that God said He would send another Prophet like Moses. When the Pharisees inquired of John the Baptist whether he was "the Prophet" (John 1:21), they were referring to this passage of Scripture.

As Moses gave the Old Covenant so Jesus came to bring the New Covenant. John says, "For the law was given through Moses, *but* grace and truth came through Jesus Christ" (John 1:17). The writer of Heb. tells us that Christ became the Mediator of a better covenant (Heb. 8:6). Jesus, as the Prophet, came to fulfill the requirements of the Old Covenant so that a New Covenant could be established between God and man.

(Gen. 3:15/Is. 9:6) J.H.

20 'But [a]the prophet who presumes to
speak a word in My name, which I
have not commanded him to speak, or
[b]who speaks in the name of other gods,
that prophet shall die.'
4 21 "And if you say in your heart, 'How
shall we know the word which the
LORD has not spoken?'—
22 [a]"when a prophet speaks in the
name of the LORD, [b]if the thing does
not happen or come to pass, that *is* the
thing which the LORD has not spoken;
the prophet has spoken it [c]presumptuously; you shall not be afraid of him.

Three Cities of Refuge

19 "When the LORD your God
[a]has cut off the nations whose
land the LORD your God is giving you,
and you dispossess them and dwell in
their cities and in their houses,
2 [a]"you shall separate three cities for
yourself in the midst of your land
which the LORD your God is giving you
to possess.
3 "You shall prepare roads for yourself, and divide into three parts the territory of your land which the LORD your God is giving you to inherit, that any manslayer may flee there.
4 "And [a]this *is* the case of the manslayer who flees there, that he may live: Whoever kills his neighbor [1]unintentionally, not having hated him in time past—
5 "as when *a man* goes to the woods
with his neighbor to cut timber, and his hand swings a stroke with the ax to cut down the tree, and the head slips from the handle and strikes his neighbor so that he dies—he shall flee to one of these cities and live;
6 [a]"lest the avenger of blood, while
his anger is hot, pursue the manslayer and overtake him, because the way is long, and kill him, though he *was* not deserving of death, since he had not hated the victim in time past.
7 "Therefore I command you, saying,
'You shall separate three cities for yourself.'
8 "Now if the LORD your God [a]enlarges your territory, as He swore to [b]your fathers, and gives you the land which He promised to give to your fathers,
9 "and if you keep all these commandments and do them, which I command you today, to love the LORD your God and to walk always in His ways, [a]then you shall add three more cities for yourself besides these three,
10 [a]"lest innocent blood be shed in the
midst of your land which the LORD your God is giving you *as* an inheritance, and *thus* guilt of bloodshed be upon you.
11 "But [a]if anyone hates his neighbor,
lies in wait for him, rises against him and strikes him mortally, so that he dies, and he flees to one of these cities,
12 "then the elders of his city shall
send and bring him from there, and deliver him over to the hand of the avenger of blood, that he may die.
13 [a]"Your eye shall not pity him,
[b]but you shall [1]put away *the guilt of* innocent blood from Israel, that it may go well with you.

Property Boundaries

14 [a]"You shall not remove your neighbor's landmark, which the men of old have set, in your inheritance which you

20 [a]Deut. 13:5; Jer. 14:14, 15; Zech. 13:2–5 [b]Deut. 13:1–3; Jer. 2:8
22 [a]Jer. 28:9 [b]Deut. 13:2 [c]Deut. 18:20

CHAPTER 19

1 [a]Deut. 12:29
2 [a]Ex. 21:13; Num. 35:10–15; Deut. 4:41; Josh. 20:2
4 [a]Num. 35:9–34; Deut. 4:42 [1]*ignorantly*, lit. *without knowledge*
6 [a]Num. 35:12
8 [a]Deut. 12:20 [b]Gen. 15:18–21
9 [a]Josh. 20:7–9
10 [a]Num. 35:33; Deut. 21:1–9
11 [a]Num. 35:16, 24; Deut. 27:24; [1 John 3:15]
13 [a]Deut. 13:8 [b]Num. 35:33, 34; 1 Kin. 2:31 [1]*purge the blood of the innocent*
14 [a]Deut. 27:17; Job 24:2; Prov. 22:28; Hos. 5:10

18:21, 22 See section 4 of Truth-In-Action at the end of Deut.

19:2 In 4:41–43 Moses commanded that three cities of refuge be established on the east side of the Jordan. Here he instructed the Israelites to establish **three** such **cities** on the west side as they took possession of the land. These cities replaced the altar (see Ex. 21:12–14) as a refuge for the manslayer since the altar would be too far away for most of the people.

19:3, 4 The **manslayer** is he who kills without premeditation (**unintentionally**).

19:6 The avenger of blood refers to the closest male relative of the deceased. It was his responsibility to bring the **manslayer** before the courts of law in his hometown to be judged. The danger existed that the relative might kill the responsible party **while his anger is hot,** rather than bring him to the courts.

19:11–13 Premeditated murder required severe punishment because it violated the sanctity of life and defiled the land where God dwelt with His people.

will inherit in the land that the LORD your God is giving you to possess.

The Law Concerning Witnesses

15 [a]"One witness shall not rise against a man concerning any iniquity or any sin that he commits; by the mouth of two or three witnesses the matter shall be established.
16 "If a false witness [a]rises against any man to testify against him of wrongdoing,
17 "then both men in the controversy shall stand before the LORD, [a]before the priests and the judges who serve in those days.
18 "And the judges shall make careful inquiry, and indeed, *if* the witness *is* a false witness, who has testified falsely against his brother,
19 [a]"then you shall do to him as he thought to have done to his brother; so [b]you shall put away the evil from among you.
20 [a]"And those who remain shall hear and fear, and hereafter they shall not again commit such evil among you.
21 [a]"Your eye shall not pity: [b]life *shall be* for life, eye for eye, tooth for tooth, hand for hand, foot for foot.

Principles Governing Warfare

20 "When you go out to battle against your enemies, and see [a]horses and chariots *and* people more numerous than you, do not be [b]afraid of them; for the LORD your God *is* [c]with you, who brought you up from the land of Egypt.
2 "So it shall be, when you are on the verge of battle, that the priest shall approach and speak to the people.
3 "And he shall say to them, 'Hear, O Israel: Today you are on the verge of battle with your enemies. Do not let your heart faint, do not be afraid, and do not tremble or be terrified because of them;
4 'for the LORD your God *is* He who goes with you, [a]to fight for you against your enemies, to *save you.'
5 "Then the officers shall speak to the people, saying: 'What man *is there* who has built a new house and has not [a]dedicated it? Let him go and return to his house, lest he die in the battle and another man dedicate it.
6 'Also what man *is there* who has planted a vineyard and has not eaten of it? Let him go and return to his house, lest he die in the battle and another man eat of it.
7 [a]'And what man *is there* who is betrothed to a woman and has not married her? Let him go and return to his house, lest he die in the battle and another man marry her.'
8 "The officers shall speak further to the people, and say, [a]'What man *is there who is* fearful and fainthearted? Let him go and return to his house, [1]lest the heart of his brethren faint like his heart.'
9 "And so it shall be, when the officers have finished speaking to the people, that they shall make captains of the armies to lead the people.
10 "When you go near a city to fight against it, [a]then proclaim an offer of peace to it.
11 "And it shall be that if they accept your offer of peace, and open to you, then all the people *who are* found in it shall be placed under tribute to you, and serve you.
12 "Now if *the city* will not make peace with you, but makes war against you, then you shall besiege it.
13 "And when the LORD your God delivers it into your hands, [a]you shall strike every male in it with the edge of the sword.
14 "But the women, the little ones, [a]the livestock, and all that is in the city, all its spoil, you shall plunder for yourself; and [b]you shall eat the enemies' plunder which the LORD your God gives you.
15 "Thus you shall do to all the cities *which are* very far from you, which *are* not of the cities of these nations.
16 "But [a]of the cities of these peoples which the LORD your God gives you *as* an inheritance, you shall let nothing that breathes remain alive,
17 "but you shall utterly destroy them: the Hittite and the Amorite and the Canaanite and the Perizzite and the Hivite and the Jebusite, just as the LORD your God has commanded you,

15 [a]Num. 35:30; Deut. 17:6; Matt. 18:16; John 8:17; 2 Cor. 13:1; 1 Tim. 5:19; Heb. 10:28 **16** [a]Ex. 23:1; Ps. 27:12; 35:11 **17** [a]Deut. 17:8–11; 21:5 **19** [a]Prov. 19:5; Dan. 6:24 [b]Deut. 13:5; 17:7; 21:21; 22:21 **20** [a]Deut. 17:13; 21:21 **21** [a]Deut. 19:13 [b]Ex. 21:23, 24; Lev. 24:20; Matt. 5:38, 39

CHAPTER 20

1 [a]Ps. 20:7; Is. 31:1 [b]Deut. 7:18 [c]Num. 23:21; Deut. 5:6; 31:6, 8; 2 Chr. 13:12; 32:7, 8; Ps. 23:4; Is. 41:10 **4** [a]Deut. 1:30; 3:22; Josh. 23:10 *See WW at Jer. 17:14.
5 [a]Neh. 12:27 **7** [a]Deut. 24:5 **8** [a]Judg. 7:3 [1]So with MT, Tg.; Sam., LXX, Syr., Vg. *lest he make his brother's heart faint* **10** [a]2 Sam. 10:19 **13** [a]Num. 31:7 **14** [a]Josh. 8:2 [b]1 Sam. 14:30 **16** [a]Ex. 23:31–33; Num. 21:2, 3; Deut. 7:1–5; Josh. 11:14

19:21 See note on Lev. 24:20.
20:1–20 This chapter, along with 21:10–14, 23:9–14, and 25:17–19, provides significant instructions about conduct in holy wars. Israel is conquering the Promised Land; the presence of God on her side will give her the assurance of victory, but will be maintained only by obedience to His standards.
20:5–9 The subject is laws of exemption from military service. **People** refers to the army.
20:10–18 These verses are God's instructions for dealing with enemy cities.

18 "lest [a]they teach you to do according to all their [1]abominations which
they have done for their gods, and you
[b]sin against the LORD your God.
19 "When you besiege a city for a long
time, while making war against it to
take it, you shall not destroy its trees
by wielding an ax against them; if you
can eat of them, do not cut them down
to use in the siege, for the tree of the
field *is* man's *food.*
20 "Only the trees which you know *are*
not trees for food you may destroy and
cut down, to build siegeworks against
the city that makes war with you, until
it is subdued.

The Law Concerning Unsolved Murder

21 "If *anyone* is found slain, lying
in the field in the land which the
LORD your God is giving you to possess, *and* it is not known who killed
him,
2 "then your elders and your judges
shall go out and measure *the distance*
from the slain man to the surrounding
cities.
3 "And it shall be *that* the elders of
the city nearest to the slain man will
take a heifer which has not been
worked *and* which has not pulled with
a [a]yoke.
4 "The elders of that city shall bring
the heifer down to a valley with flowing water, which is neither plowed nor
sown, and they shall break the heifer's
neck there in the valley.
5 "Then the priests, the sons of Levi,
shall come near, for [a]the LORD your
God has chosen them to minister to
Him and to bless in the name of the
LORD; [b]by their word every controversy and every [1]assault shall be *settled.*
6 "And all the elders of that city nearest to the slain *man* [a]shall wash their
hands over the heifer whose neck was
broken in the valley.
7 "Then they shall answer and say,
'Our hands have not shed this blood,
nor have our eyes seen *it.*
8 'Provide atonement, O LORD, for
Your people Israel, whom You have redeemed, [a]and do not lay innocent
blood to the charge of Your people Israel.' And atonement shall be provided
on their behalf for the blood.
9 "So [a]you shall put away the *guilt
of* innocent blood from among you
when you do *what is* right in the sight
of the LORD.

Female Captives

10 "When you go out to war against
your enemies, and the LORD your God
delivers them into your hand, and you
take them captive,
11 "and you see among the captives a
beautiful woman, and desire her and
would take her for your [a]wife,
12 "then you shall bring her home to
your house, and she shall [a]shave her
head and trim her nails.
13 "She shall put off the clothes of her
captivity, remain in your house, and
[a]mourn her father and her mother a
full month; after that you may go in
to her and be her husband, and she
shall be your wife.
14 "And it shall be, if you have no delight in her, then you shall set her free,
but you certainly shall not sell her for
money; you shall not treat her brutally,
because you have [a]humbled her.

Firstborn Inheritance Rights

15 "If a man has two wives, one loved
[a]and the other unloved, and they have
borne him children, *both* the loved and
the unloved, and *if* the firstborn son is
of her who is unloved,
16 "then it shall be, [a]on the day he be-
queaths his possessions to his sons,
that he must not bestow firstborn status on the son of the loved wife in preference to the son of the unloved, the
true firstborn.
17 "But he shall acknowledge the son
of the unloved wife *as* the firstborn
[a]by giving him a double portion of all
that he has, for he [b]*is* the beginning
of his strength; [c]the right of the firstborn *is* his.

18 [a]Ex. 34:12–16; Deut. 7:4; 12:30; 18:9 [b]Ex. 23:33; 2 Kin. 21:3–15; Ps. 106:34–41 [1]*detestable things*

CHAPTER 21

3 [a]Num. 19:2
5 [a]Deut. 10:8; 1 Chr. 23:13 [b]Deut. 17:8, 9 [1]Lit. *stroke*
6 [a]Ps. 19:12; 26:6; Matt. 27:24
8 [a]Deut. 19:10, 13; Jon. 1:14
9 [a]Deut. 19:13
11 [a]Num. 31:18
12 [a]Lev. 14:8, 9; Num. 6:9
13 [a]Ps. 45:10
14 [a]Gen. 34:2; Deut. 22:29; Judg. 19:24
15 [a]Gen. 29:33
16 [a]1 Chr. 5:2; 26:10
17 [a]2 Kin. 2:9 [b]Gen. 49:3 [c]Gen. 25:31, 33

20:19, 20 Israel, unlike other armies which wasted lands, was to be discriminating, using good sense and discretion with reference to the land God created and in which He will dwell with His people.

21:1–9 Anonymous murder involved the entire community in blood guilt and the community as a whole had to seek **atonement.** The legal and religious procedures were carried out by **elders and judges,** members of a central legal tribunal, **elders of the city** who accepted responsibility, and **the priests.** The **heifer's neck** was broken as a sign of the punishment the crime deserved.

21:10–14 God allowed the Israelites to take women captive from distant cities (20:13–15), but they were to forsake paganism for Judaism before marrying (vv. 12, 13). The reason for God's allowing divorce if the husband subsequently did not **delight in her** is not given.

The Rebellious Son

4 18 "If a man has a stubborn and rebellious son who will not obey the voice of his father or the voice of his mother, and *who,* when they have chastened him, will not heed them,

19 "then his father and his mother shall take hold of him and bring him out to the elders of his city, to the gate of his city.

20 "And they shall say to the elders of his city, 'This son of ours is stubborn and rebellious; he will not obey our voice; he is a glutton and a drunkard.'

21 "Then all the men of his city shall stone him to death with stones; [a]so you shall put away the evil from among you, [b]and all Israel shall *hear and fear.

Miscellaneous Laws

22 "If a man has committed a sin [a]deserving of death, and he is put to death, and you hang him on a tree,

23 [a]"his body shall not remain overnight on the tree, but you shall surely bury him that day, so that [b]you do not defile the land which the LORD your God is giving you *as* an inheritance; for [c]he who is hanged *is* accursed of God.

22 "You [a]shall not see your brother's ox or his sheep going astray, and [1]hide yourself from them; you shall certainly bring them back to your brother.

2 "And if your brother *is* not near you, or if you do not know him, then you shall bring it to your own house, and it shall remain with you until your brother seeks it; then you shall restore it to him.

3 "You shall do the same with his donkey, and so shall you do with his garment; with any lost thing of your brother's, which he has lost and you have found, you shall do likewise; you [1]must not hide yourself.

4 [a]"You shall not see your brother's donkey or his ox fall down along the road, and hide yourself from them; you shall surely help him lift *them* up again.

5 "A woman shall not wear anything that pertains to a *man, nor shall a man put on a woman's garment, for all who do so *are* [1]an abomination to the LORD your God.

6 "If a bird's nest happens to be before you along the way, in any tree or on the ground, with young ones or eggs, with the mother sitting on the young or on the eggs, [a]you shall not take the mother with the young;

7 "you shall surely let the mother go, and take the young for yourself, [a]that it may be well with you and *that* you may prolong *your* days.

8 "When you build a new house, then you shall make a parapet for your roof, that you may not bring guilt of bloodshed on your household if anyone falls from it.

9 [a]"You shall not sow your vineyard with different kinds of seed, lest the yield of the seed which you have sown and the fruit of your vineyard be defiled.

10 [a]"You shall not plow with an ox and a donkey together.

11 [a]"You shall not wear a garment of different sorts, *such as* wool and linen mixed together.

12 "You shall make [a]tassels on the four corners of the clothing with which you cover *yourself.*

Laws of Sexual Morality

13 "If any man takes a wife, and goes in to her, and [a]detests her, 6

21 [a]Deut. 13:5; 19:19, 20; 22:21, 24 [b]Deut. 13:11 *See WW at 1 Kin. 20:8.
22 [a]Deut. 22:26; Matt. 26:66; Mark 14:64; Acts 23:29
23 [a]Josh. 8:29; 10:26, 27; John 19:31 [b]Lev. 18:25; Num. 35:34 [c]Gal. 3:13

CHAPTER 22

1 [a]Ex. 23:4 [1]*ignore them*
3 [1]*may not avoid responsibility*
4 [a]Ex. 23:5
5 [1]*detestable* *See WW at Jer. 31:22.
6 [a]Lev. 22:28
7 [a]Deut. 4:40
9 [a]Lev. 19:19
10 [a][2 Cor. 6:14–16]
11 [a]Lev. 19:19
12 [a]Num. 15:37–41; Matt. 23:5
13 [a]Deut. 21:15; 24:3

21:18–21 See section 4 of Truth-In-Action at the end of Deut.

21:18–21 These verses show the importance of the fifth *commandment* (Ex. 20:12).

21:22, 23 Hanging was not a method of execution among the Israelites. According to this sequence, the man was killed and then hung on a tree as a stern warning to the people that breaking God's laws was costly. **He who is hanged is accursed of God:** The apostle Paul used this injunction in Gal. 3:13 to draw an analogy to Christ. Just as the corpse of the criminal was under the curse of God, so Christ hanging on the Cross bore the judgment of God, the same shame as every condemned criminal. By taking upon Himself the curse of the Law, He redeemed us from that curse.

22:1–4 A man is not to **hide** or ignore the situation when he sees his neighbor's animals stray. He is, rather, to take action and retrieve the animal. This law addresses the natural human tendency not to get involved.

22:5 The basic principle presented here is that males and females are to honor the dignity of their own sex and not attempt to adopt the appearance or role of the other. This verse clearly forbids transvestism, which is a deviant form of sexual behavior.

22:6, 7 This law taught Israel basic food conservation.

22:8 The requirement for a **parapet** (a retaining wall or protective barrier) on the flat roofs of houses was a demonstration of concern for the value and protection of human life.

22:9–11 These miscellaneous laws teach the importance of maintaining disciplined order.

22:12 Tassels designates the twisted threads attached to one's garments. See note on Num. 15:38.

22:13–30 These miscellaneous laws pertain to the sanctity of virginity (vv. 13–21) and the penalties of illicit sexual

14 "and charges her with shameful conduct, and brings a bad name on her, and says, 'I took this woman, and when I came to her I found she *was* not a virgin,'

15 "then the father and mother of the young woman shall take and bring out *the evidence of* the young woman's virginity to the elders of the city at the gate.

16 "And the young woman's father shall say to the elders, 'I gave my daughter to this man as wife, and he detests her.

17 'Now he has charged her with shameful conduct, saying, "I found your daughter *was* not a virgin," and yet these *are the evidences of* my daughter's virginity.' And they shall spread the cloth before the elders of the city.

18 "Then the elders of that city shall take that man and punish him;

19 "and they shall fine him one hundred *shekels* of silver and give *them* to the father of the young woman, because he has brought a bad name on a virgin of Israel. And she shall be his wife; he cannot divorce her all his days.

20 "But if the thing is true, *and evidences of* virginity are not found for the young woman,

21 "then they shall bring out the young woman to the door of her father's house, and the men of her city shall stone her to death with [a]stones, because she has [b]done a disgraceful thing in Israel, to play the harlot in her father's house. [c]So you shall [1]put away the evil from among you.

6 **22** [a]"If a man is found lying with a woman married to a *husband, then both of them shall die—the man that lay with the woman, and the woman; so you shall put away the evil from Israel.

23 "If a young woman *who is* a virgin is [a]betrothed to a husband, and a man finds her in the city and lies with her,

24 "then you shall bring them both out to the gate of that city, and you shall stone them to death with stones, the young woman because she did not cry out in the city, and the man because he [a]humbled his neighbor's wife; [b]so you shall put away the evil from among you.

25 "But if a man finds a betrothed young woman in the countryside, and the man forces her and lies with her, then only the man who lay with her shall die.

26 "But you shall do nothing to the young woman; *there is* in the young woman no sin *deserving* of death, for just as when a man rises against his neighbor and kills him, even so *is* this matter.

27 "For he found her in the countryside, *and* the betrothed young woman cried out, but *there was* no one to save her.

28 [a]"If a man finds a young woman *who is* a virgin, who is not betrothed, and he seizes her and lies with her, and they are found out,

29 "then the man who lay with her shall give to the young woman's father [a]fifty *shekels* of silver, and she shall be his wife [b]because he has humbled her; he shall not be permitted to divorce her all his days.

30 [a]"A man shall not take his father's wife, nor [b]uncover his father's bed.

Those Excluded from the Congregation

23

"He who is emasculated by crushing or mutilation shall [a]not enter the assembly of the LORD.

2 "One of illegitimate birth shall not enter the assembly of the LORD; even to the tenth generation none of his *descendants* shall enter the assembly of the LORD.

3 [a]"An Ammonite or Moabite shall not enter the assembly of the LORD; even to the tenth generation none of his *descendants* shall enter the assembly of the LORD forever,

4 [a]"because they did not meet you with bread and water on the road when you came out of Egypt, and [b]because they hired against you Balaam the son of Beor from Pethor of [1]Mesopotamia, to curse you.

5 "Nevertheless the LORD your God would not listen to Balaam, but the LORD your God turned the curse into

21 [a]Deut. 21:21 [b]Gen. 34:7; Judg. 20:5–10; 2 Sam. 13:12, 13 [c]Deut. 13:5 [1]*purge the evil person*
22 [a]Lev. 20:10; Num. 5:22–27; Ezek. 16:38; [Matt. 5:27, 28]; John 8:5; [1 Cor. 6:9; Heb. 13:4] *See WW at Hos. 2:8.
23 [a]Lev. 19:20–22; Matt. 1:18, 19
24 [a]Deut. 21:14 [b]Deut. 22:21, 22; 1 Cor. 5:2, 13
28 [a]Ex. 22:16, 17
29 [a]Ex. 22:16, 17 [b]Deut. 22:24
30 [a]Lev. 18:8; 20:11; Deut. 27:20; 1 Cor. 5:1 [b]Ruth 3:9; Ezek. 16:8

CHAPTER 23

1 [a]Lev. 21:20; 22:24
3 [a]Neh. 13:1, 2
4 [a]Deut. 2:27–30 [b]Num. 22:5, 6; 23:7; Josh. 24:9; 2 Pet. 2:15; Jude 11 [1]Heb. *Aram Naharaim*

behavior (vv. 22–30). The latter section is an elaboration of the seventh commandment (Ex. 20:14).

22:13–21 See section 6 of Truth-In-Action at the end of Deut.

22:22 See section 6 of Truth-In-Action at the end of Deut.

22:30 Shall not . . . uncover his father's bed means no man shall encroach on his father's marital rights.

23:1-9 These verses deal with admission to **the assembly,** here referring to Israel as a worshiping community. The Greek equivalent is *ekklesia,* the word used in the NT to designate a local congregation of believers. God's exact reasons for the prohibitions are no longer totally clear.

a blessing for you, because the LORD
your God [a]loves you.
6 [a]"You shall not seek their peace nor
their prosperity all your days forever.
7 "You shall not abhor an Edomite,
[a]for he *is* your brother. You shall not
abhor an Egyptian, because [b]you were
an alien in his land.
8 "The children of the third generation born to them may enter the assembly of the LORD.

Cleanliness of the Camp Site

9 "When the army goes out against
your enemies, then keep yourself from
every wicked thing.
10 [a]"If there is any man among you
who becomes unclean by some occurrence in the night, then he shall go outside the camp; he shall not come inside
the camp.
11 "But it shall be, when evening
comes, that [a]he shall wash with water;
and when the sun sets, he may come
into the camp.
12 "Also you shall have a place outside
the camp, where you may go out;
13 "and you shall have an implement
among your equipment, and when you
sit down outside, you shall dig with it
and turn and cover your refuse.
14 "For the LORD your God [a]walks in
the midst of your camp, to deliver you
and give your enemies over to you;
therefore your camp shall be holy, that
He may see no unclean thing among
you, and turn away from you.

Miscellaneous Laws

15 [a]"You shall not give back to his
master the slave who has escaped from
his master to you.
16 "He may dwell with you in your
midst, in the place which he chooses
within one of your gates, where it
[1]seems best to him; [a]you shall not oppress him.
17 "There shall be no *ritual* [1]harlot
[a]of the daughters of Israel, or a [b]per-
verted[2] one of the sons of Israel.

5 [a]Deut. 4:37
6 [a]Ezra 9:12
7 [a]Gen. 25:24–26; Deut. 2:4, 8; Amos 1:11; Obad. 10, 12 [b]Ex. 22:21; 23:9; Lev. 19:34; Deut. 10:19
10 [a]Lev. 15:16
11 [a]Lev. 15:5
14 [a]Lev. 26:12; Deut. 7:21
15 [a]1 Sam. 30:15
16 [a]Ex. 22:21; Prov. 22:22 [1]*pleases him best*
17 [a]Lev. 19:29; Deut. 22:21 [b]Gen. 19:5; 2 Kin. 23:7 [1]Heb. *qedeshah,* fem. of *qadesh* (note 2) [2]Heb. *qadesh,* one practicing sodomy and prostitution in religious rituals
18 [1]*detestable*
19 [a]Ex. 22:25; Lev. 25:35–37; Neh. 5:2–7; Ps. 15:5
20 [a]Deut. 15:3 [b]Deut. 15:10
21 [a]Num. 30:1, 2; Job 22:27; Ps. 61:8; Eccl. 5:4, 5; Matt. 5:33
23 [a]Num. 30:2; Ps. 66:13, 14
25 [a]Matt. 12:1; Mark 2:23; Luke 6:1

CHAPTER 24

1 [a][Matt. 5:31; 19:7; Mark 10:4] [b][Jer. 3:8] [1]*indecency,* lit. *nakedness of a thing*

18 "You shall not bring the wages of
a harlot or the price of a dog to the
house of the LORD your God for any
vowed offering, for both of these *are*
[1]an abomination to the LORD your God.
19 [a]"You shall not charge interest to
your brother—interest on money *or*
food *or* anything that is lent out at interest.
20 [a]"To a foreigner you may charge interest, but to your brother you shall not
charge interest, [b]that the LORD your
God may bless you in all to which you
set your hand in the land which you
are entering to possess.
21 [a]"When you make a vow to the
LORD your God, you shall not delay to
pay it; for the LORD your God will
surely require it of you, and it would
be sin to you.
22 "But if you abstain from vowing, it
shall not be sin to you.
23 [a]"That which has gone from your
lips you shall keep and perform, for
you voluntarily vowed to the LORD
your God what you have promised
with your mouth.
24 "When you come into your neighbor's vineyard, you may eat your fill
of grapes at your pleasure, but you
shall not put *any* in your container.
25 "When you come into your neighbor's standing grain, [a]you may pluck
the heads with your hand, but you shall
not use a sickle on your neighbor's
standing grain.

Law Concerning Divorce

24 "When a [a]man takes a wife and
marries her, and it happens that
she finds no favor in his eyes because
he has found some [1]uncleanness in her,
and he writes her a [b]certificate of divorce, puts *it* in her hand, and sends
her out of his house,
2 "when she has departed from his
house, and goes and becomes another
man's *wife,*
3 "*if* the latter husband detests her
and writes her a certificate of divorce,
puts *it* in her hand, and sends her out

23:7 According to Hebrew tradition, the Edomites were descendants of Esau (Gen. 36:1–19).
23:9–14 During war, rules of hygiene were to be maintained as a symbol of purity, a prerequisite to God's presence.
23:17 Women and men of Israel were not to become prostitutes with the heathen cult fertility gods.
23:18 A female prostitute is identified as a **harlot** and a male prostitute as a **dog.** Legislation prohibited money obtained by sinful means to be given as a **vowed offering** to God.

24:1–4 This passage does not provide divine sanction for **divorce;** rather, it simply recognizes that divorce was practiced among the Israelites. The requirement of a **certificate of divorce** for the wife had the effect of nullifying all the husband's rights to the dowry she had brought into the marriage.

When Jesus discussed this passage with the Pharisees, He declared that Moses permitted divorce because of the hardness of human hearts, though God never intended for divorce to occur. See note on Matt. 5:31, 32.

of his house, or if the latter husband dies who took her as his wife,

4 [a]"*then* her former *husband who divorced her must not take her back to be his wife after she has been defiled; for that *is* [1]an abomination before the LORD, and you shall not bring sin on the land which the LORD your God is giving you *as* an inheritance.

Miscellaneous Laws

5 [a]"When a man has taken a new wife, he shall not go out to war or be charged with any business; he shall be free at home one year, and [b]bring happiness to his wife whom he has taken.

6 "No man shall take the lower or the upper millstone in pledge, for he takes [1]*one's* living in pledge.

7 "If a man is [a]found [1]kidnapping any of his brethren of the children of Israel, and mistreats him or sells him, then that kidnapper shall die; [b]and you shall put away the evil from among you.

8 "Take heed in [a]an outbreak of leprosy, that you carefully observe and do according to all that the priests, the Levites, shall teach you; just as I commanded them, *so* you shall be careful to do.

9 [a]"Remember what the LORD your God did [b]to Miriam on the way when you came out of Egypt!

10 "When you [a]lend your brother anything, you shall not go into his house to get his pledge.

11 "You shall stand outside, and the man to whom you lend shall bring the pledge out to you.

12 "And if the man *is* *poor, you shall not [1]keep his pledge overnight.

13 [a]"You shall in any case return the pledge to him again when the sun goes down, that he may sleep in his own garment and [b]bless you; and [c]it shall be righteousness to you before the LORD your God.

14 "You shall not [a]oppress a hired servant *who is* poor and needy, *whether* one of your brethren or one of the aliens who *is* in your land within your gates.

15 "Each day [a]you shall give *him* his wages, and not let the sun go down on it, for he *is* poor and has set his heart on it; [b]lest he cry out against you to the LORD, and it be sin to you.

16 [a]"Fathers shall not be put to death for *their* children, nor shall children be put to death for *their* fathers; a person shall be put to death for his own sin.

17 [a]"You shall not pervert justice due the stranger or the fatherless, [b]nor take a widow's garment as a pledge.

18 "But [a]you shall remember that you were a slave in Egypt, and the LORD your God redeemed you from there; therefore I command you to do this thing.

19 [a]"When you reap your harvest in your field, and forget a sheaf in the field, you shall not go back to get it; it shall be for the stranger, the fatherless, and the widow, that the LORD your God may [b]bless you in all the work of your hands.

20 "When you beat your olive trees, you shall not go over the boughs again; it shall be for the stranger, the fatherless, and the widow.

21 "When you gather the grapes of your vineyard, you shall not glean *it* afterward; it shall be for the stranger, the fatherless, and the widow.

22 "And you shall remember that you were a slave in the land of Egypt; therefore I command you to do this thing.

25

"If there is a [a]dispute between men, and they come to [1]court, that *the judges* may judge them, and they [b]justify the righteous and condemn the *wicked,

2 "then it shall be, if the wicked man [a]deserves to be beaten, that the judge will cause him to lie down [b]and be beaten in his presence, according to his guilt, with a certain number of blows.

3 [a]"Forty blows he may give him *and* no more, lest he should exceed this and beat him with many blows above these, and your brother [b]be humiliated in your sight.

4 [a][Jer. 3:1] [1]*a detestable thing* *See WW at Hos. 2:8. **5** [a]Deut. 20:7 [b]Prov. 5:18 **6** [1]*life* **7** [a]Ex. 21:16 [b]Deut. 19:19 [1]Lit. *stealing* **8** [a]Lev. 13:2; 14:2 **9** [a][1 Cor. 10:6] [b]Num. 12:10 **10** [a]Matt. 5:42 **12** [1]Lit. *sleep with his pledge* *See WW at Ps. 40:17. **13** [a]Ex. 22:26; Ezek. 18:7 [b]Job 29:11; 2 Tim. 1:18 [c]Deut. 6:25; Ps. 106:31; Dan. 4:27 **14** [a]Lev. 19:13; Deut. 15:7–18; [Prov. 14:31]; Amos 4:1; [Mal. 3:5; 1 Tim. 5:18]

15 [a]Lev. 19:13; Jer. 22:13 [b]Ex. 22:23; Deut. 15:9; Job 35:9; James 5:4 **16** [a]2 Kin. 14:6; 2 Chr. 25:4; Jer. 31:29, 30; Ezek. 18:20 **17** [a]Ex. 23:6 [b]Ex. 22:26 **18** [a]Deut. 24:22 **19** [a]Lev. 19:9, 10 [b]Deut. 15:10; Ps. 41:1; Prov. 19:17

CHAPTER 25

1 [a]Deut. 17:8–13; 19:17; Ezek. 44:24 [b]Prov. 17:15 [1]Lit. *the judgment* *See WW at Prov. 10:16. **2** [a]Prov. 19:29; Luke 12:48 [b]Matt. 10:17 **3** [a]2 Cor. 11:24 [b]Job 18:3

24:6 Every Israelite owned a small milling machine to *prepare flour for daily bread. To take this* as collateral on a loan was forbidden, since the **millstone** would be confiscated if the loan was not repaid and the person left without his means of livelihood.

24:7 Kidnapping here means seizing a fellow Israelite and mistreating or selling him into slavery.

24:10–13 This legislation protects the poor who were sometimes forced to request loans.

24:16 Sin here refers to crimes punishable by capital punishment. It is not to be confused with the spiritual consequences of sins addressed in 5:9.

24:19–22 This provision for feeding the underprivileged is beautifully exemplified in the Book of Ruth.

25:1–3 This same principle of God's leaders handling a legal **dispute** among fellow believers is addressed by Paul in 1 Cor. 6:1–8.

4 [a]"You shall not muzzle an ox while it [1]treads out *the grain.*

Marriage Duty of the Surviving Brother

5 [a]"If brothers dwell together, and one of them dies and has no son, the widow of the dead man shall not be *married* to a stranger outside *the family;* her husband's brother shall go in to her, take her as his wife, and perform the duty of a husband's brother to her.
6 "And it shall be *that* the firstborn son which she bears [a]will succeed to the name of his dead brother, that [b]his name may not be blotted out of Israel.
7 "But if the man does not want to take his brother's wife, then let his brother's wife go up to the [a]gate to the elders, and say, 'My husband's brother refuses to raise up a name to his brother in Israel; he will not perform the duty of my husband's brother.'
8 "Then the elders of his city shall call him and speak to him. But *if* he stands firm and says, [a]'I do not want to take her,'
9 "then his brother's wife shall come to him in the presence of the elders, [a]remove his sandal from his foot, spit in his face, and answer and say, 'So shall it be done to the man who will not [b]build up his brother's house.'
10 "And his name shall be called in Israel, 'The house of him who had his sandal removed.'

Miscellaneous Laws

11 "If *two* men fight together, and the wife of one draws near to rescue her husband from the hand of the one attacking him, and puts out her hand and seizes him by the genitals,
12 "then you shall cut off her hand; [a]your eye shall not pity *her.*
13 [a]"You shall not have in your bag differing weights, a heavy and a light.
14 "You shall not have in your house differing measures, a large and a small.
15 "You shall have a perfect and just weight, a perfect and just measure, [a]that your days may be lengthened in the land which the LORD your God is giving you.
16 "For [a]all who do such things, all who behave unrighteously, *are* [1]an abomination to the LORD your God.

Destroy the Amalekites

17 [a]"Remember what Amalek did to you on the way as you were coming out of Egypt,
18 "how he met you on the way and attacked your rear ranks, all the stragglers at your rear, when you *were* tired and weary; and he [a]did not fear God.
19 "Therefore it shall be, [a]when the LORD your God has given you rest from your enemies all around, in the land which the LORD your God is giving you to possess *as* an inheritance, *that* you will [b]blot out the remembrance of Amalek from under heaven. You shall not forget.

Offerings of Firstfruits and Tithes

26 "And it shall be, when you come into the land which the LORD your God is giving you *as* an inheritance, and you possess it and dwell in it,
2 [a]"that you shall take some of the first of all the produce of the ground, which you shall bring from your land that the LORD your God is giving you, and put *it* in a basket and [b]go to the place where the LORD your God chooses to make His name abide.
3 "And you shall go to the one who is priest in those days, and say to him, 'I declare today to the LORD [1]your God that I have come to the country which the LORD swore to our fathers to give us.'
4 "Then the priest shall take the basket out of your hand and set it down before the altar of the LORD your God.
5 "And you shall answer and say before the LORD your God: 'My father *was* [a]a [1]Syrian, [b]about to perish, and [c]he went down to Egypt and [2]dwelt

4 [a][Prov. 12:10; 1 Cor. 9:9; 1 Tim. 5:18] [1]*threshes*
5 [a]Matt. 22:24; Mark 12:19; Luke 20:28
6 [a]Gen. 38:9 [b]Ruth 4:5, 10
7 [a]Ruth 4:1, 2
8 [a]Ruth 4:6
9 [a]Ruth 4:7, 8 [b]Ruth 4:11
12 [a]Deut. 7:2; 19:13
13 [a]Lev. 19:35–37; Prov. 11:1; 20:23; Ezek. 45:10; Mic. 6:11
15 [a]Ex. 20:12
16 [a]Prov. 11:1; [1 Thess. 4:6] [1]*detestable*
17 [a]Ex. 17:8–16; 1 Sam. 15:1–3
18 [a][Ps. 36:1]; Rom. 3:18
19 [a]1 Sam. 15:3 [b]Ex. 17:14

CHAPTER 26

2 [a]Ex. 22:29; 23:16, 19; Num. 18:13; Deut. 16:10; Prov. 3:9 [b]Deut. 12:5
3 [1]LXX *my*
5 [a]Gen. 25:20; Hos. 12:12 [b]Gen. 43:1, 2; 45:7, 11 [c]Gen. 46:1, 6; Acts 7:15 [1]Or *Aramean* [2]As a resident alien

25:4 To muzzle an ox while it was threshing prevented it from eating while working on behalf of man. Paul quotes this verse in 1 Tim. 5:18 to illustrate the principle that "the laborer is worthy of his wages."
25:9 The removing of the sandal indicated that the brother had abandoned his responsibility and thus deserved the shame symbolized by the spitting.
25:13–16 Business activities are to be conducted in accordance with the highest ethical principles.
26:1–15 This section deals with one's attitude in giving an offering of **firstfruits** and **the tithe.** It teaches that both should be given with an attitude of joyful worship, as a testimony to God's personal provision and deliverance.
26:5 A Syrian is an unusual designation of Jacob, likely referring to his marriage to Leah and Rachel, both of whom were Syrians. **Few in number** refers to the 70 in Jacob's family when he entered Egypt (Gen. 46:8–27).

there, [d]few in number; and there he became a nation, [e]great, mighty, and populous.

6 'But the [a]Egyptians mistreated us, afflicted us, and laid hard bondage on us.

7 [a]'Then we cried out to the LORD God of our fathers, and the LORD heard our voice and looked on our affliction and our *labor and our oppression.

8 'So [a]the LORD brought us out of Egypt with a mighty hand and with an outstretched arm, [b]with great terror and with signs and wonders.

9 'He has brought us to this place and has given us this land, [a]"a land flowing with milk and honey";

10 'and now, behold, I have brought the firstfruits of the land which you, O LORD, have given me.' Then you shall set it before the LORD your God, and *worship before the LORD your God.

11 "So [a]you shall rejoice in every good *thing* which the LORD your God has given to you and your house, you and the Levite and the stranger who *is* among you.

12 "When you have finished laying aside all the [a]tithe of your increase in the third year—[b]the year of tithing—and have given *it* to the Levite, the stranger, the fatherless, and the widow, so that they may eat within your gates and be filled,

13 "then you shall say before the LORD your God: 'I have removed the [1]holy *tithe* from *my* house, and also have given them to the Levite, the stranger, the fatherless, and the widow, according to all Your commandments which You have commanded me; I have not transgressed Your commandments, [a]nor have I forgotten *them.*

14 [a]'I have not eaten any of it [1]when in *mourning, nor have I removed *any* of it [2]for an unclean *use,* nor given *any* of it for the dead. I have obeyed the voice of the LORD my God, and have done according to all that You have commanded me.

15 [a]'Look down from Your holy [1]habitation, from heaven, and bless Your people Israel and the land which You have given us, just as You swore to our fathers, [b]"a land flowing with milk and honey." '

5 [d]Gen. 46:27; Deut. 10:22 [e]Deut. 1:10
6 [a]Ex. 1:8–11, 14
7 [a]Ex. 2:23–25; 3:9; 4:31 *See WW at Job 5:7.
8 [a]Ex. 12:37, 51; 13:3, 14, 16; Deut. 5:15 [b]Deut. 4:34; 34:11, 12
9 [a]Ex. 3:8, 17
10 *See WW at Ps. 99:5.
11 [a]Deut. 12:7; 16:11; Eccl. 3:12, 13; 5:18–20
12 [a]Lev. 27:30; Num. 18:24 [b]Deut. 14:28, 29
13 [a]Ps. 119:141, 153, 176 [1]*hallowed things*
14 [a]Lev. 7:20; Jer. 16:7; Hos. 9:4 [1]Lit. *in my mourning* [2]Or *while I was unclean* *See WW at Prov. 22:8.
15 [a]Ps. 80:14; Is. 63:15; Zech. 2:13 [b]Ex. 3:8 [1]*home*
17 [a]Ex. 20:19 [b]Deut. 15:5
18 [a]Ex. 6:7; 19:5; Deut. 7:6; 14:2; 28:9; [Titus 2:14; 1 Pet. 2:9]
19 [a]Deut. 4:7, 8; 28:1 [b]Ex. 19:6; Deut. 7:6; 28:9; Is. 62:12; [1 Pet. 2:9] [1]*consecrated*

CHAPTER 27

2 [a]Josh. 4:1 [b]Josh. 8:32
3 [a]Ex. 3:8

A Special People of God

16 "This day the LORD your God commands you to observe these statutes and judgments; therefore you shall be careful to observe them with all your heart and with all your soul.

17 "Today you have [a]proclaimed the LORD to be your God, and that you will walk in His ways and keep His statutes, His commandments, and His judgments, and that you will [b]obey His voice.

18 "Also today [a]the LORD has proclaimed you to be His **special** people, just as He promised you, that *you* should keep all His commandments,

WORD WEALTH

26:18 special, *segullah* (seh-goo-*lah*); Strong's #5459: Possession, personal property, special treasure. This noun occurs eight times in the OT: in five of those references, it speaks of Israel as God's special treasure; in two references, it speaks of the prized possessions of kings, or "royal treasures"; the one remaining reference is Mal. 3:17, which speaks of the people God will regard as His "jewels." Man's treasure is material objects, but consistently in Scripture, God's treasure is human beings!

19 "and that He will set you [a]high above all nations which He has made, in praise, in name, and in honor, and that you may be [b]a [1]holy people to the LORD your God, just as He has spoken."

The Law Inscribed on Stones

27 Now Moses, with the elders of Israel, commanded the people, saying: "Keep all the commandments which I command you today.

2 "And it shall be, on the day [a]when you cross over the Jordan to the land which the LORD your God is giving you, that [b]you shall set up for yourselves large stones, and whitewash them with lime.

3 "You shall write on them all the words of this law, when you have crossed over, that you may enter the land which the LORD your God is giving you, [a]'a land flowing with milk and

26:12 A tithing ceremony was to begin the third year in Canaan. The offering of firstfruits (vv. 1–11) began the first year.

27:1–10 This joint address by **Moses, with the elders** is unusual since Moses normally addressed the people by himself. However, since Moses would not be crossing **over the Jordan,** the address seems designed to impress upon the elders their future responsibilities as leaders. The specific responsibility addressed is that of the renewal of the covenant **on Mount Ebal** in the Promised Land. Josh. 8:30–35 describes the renewal.

honey,' just as the LORD God of your fathers promised you.

4 "Therefore it shall be, when you have crossed over the Jordan, *that* [a]on Mount Ebal you shall set up these stones, which I command you today, and you shall whitewash them with lime.

5 "And there you shall build an altar to the LORD your God, an altar of stones; [a]you shall not use an iron *tool* on them.

6 "You shall build with [1]whole stones the altar of the LORD your God, and offer burnt offerings on it to the LORD your God.

7 "You shall offer peace offerings, and shall eat there, and [a]rejoice before the LORD your God.

8 "And you shall [a]write very plainly on the stones all the words of this law."

9 Then Moses and the priests, the Levites, spoke to all Israel, saying, "Take heed and listen, O Israel: [a]This day you have become the people of the LORD your God.

10 "Therefore you shall obey the voice of the LORD your God, and observe His commandments and His statutes which I command you today."

Curses Pronounced from Mount Ebal

11 And Moses commanded the people on the same day, saying,

12 "These shall stand [a]on Mount Gerizim to bless the people, when you have crossed over the Jordan: Simeon, Levi, Judah, Issachar, Joseph, and Benjamin;

13 "and [a]these shall stand on Mount Ebal to curse: Reuben, Gad, Asher, Zebulun, Dan, and Naphtali.

14 "And [a]the Levites shall speak with a loud voice and say to all the men of Israel:

15 [a]'Cursed *is* the one who makes a carved or molded image, [1]an abomination to the LORD, the work of the hands of the craftsman, and sets *it* up in secret.'

[b]"And all the people shall answer and say, 'Amen!'

16 [a]'Cursed *is* the one who treats his father or his mother with contempt.'

"And all the people shall say, 'Amen!'

17 [a]'Cursed *is* the one who moves his neighbor's landmark.'

"And all the people shall say, 'Amen!'

18 [a]'Cursed *is* the one who makes the blind to wander off the road.'

"And all the people shall say, 'Amen!'

19 [a]'Cursed *is* the one who perverts the justice due the stranger, the fatherless, and widow.'

"And all the people shall say, 'Amen!'

20 [a]'Cursed *is* the one who lies with his father's wife, because he has uncovered his father's bed.'

"And all the people shall say, 'Amen!'

21 [a]'Cursed *is* the one who lies with any kind of animal.'

"And all the people shall say, 'Amen!'

22 [a]'Cursed *is* the one who lies with his sister, the daughter of his father or the daughter of his mother.'

"And all the people shall say, 'Amen!'

23 [a]'Cursed *is* the one who lies with his mother-in-law.'

"And all the people shall say, 'Amen!'

24 [a]'Cursed *is* the one who attacks his neighbor secretly.'

"And all the people shall say, 'Amen!'

25 [a]'Cursed *is* the one who takes a bribe to slay an innocent person.'

"And all the people shall say, 'Amen!'

26 [a]'Cursed *is* the one who does not confirm *all* the words of this law by observing them.'

"And all the people shall say, 'Amen!'

Blessings on Obedience

28 "Now it shall come to pass, [a]if you diligently obey the voice of the LORD your God, to observe

4 [a]Deut. 11:29; Josh. 8:30, 31
5 [a]Ex. 20:25; Josh. 8:31
6 [1]*uncut*
7 [a]Deut. 26:11
8 [a]Josh. 8:32
9 [a]Deut. 26:18
12 [a]Deut. 11:29; Josh. 8:33; Judg. 9:7
13 [a]Deut. 11:29; Josh. 8:33
14 [a]Deut. 33:10; Josh. 8:33; Dan. 9:11
15 [a]Ex. 20:4, 23; 34:17; Lev. 19:4; 26:1; Deut. 4:16, 23; Is. 44:9; Hos. 13:2 [b]Num. 5:22; Jer. 11:5; 1 Cor. 14:16 [1]*a detestable thing*
16 [a]Ex. 20:12; Lev. 19:3; 20:9; Deut. 5:16; 21:18–21; Ezek. 22:7
17 [a]Deut. 19:14; Prov. 22:28
18 [a]Lev. 19:14
19 [a]Ex. 22:21, 22; 23:9; Lev. 19:33; Deut. 10:18; 24:17
20 [a]Lev. 18:8; 20:11; Deut. 22:30; 1 Cor. 5:1
21 [a]Ex. 22:19; Lev. 18:23; 20:15, 16
22 [a]Lev. 18:9
23 [a]Lev. 18:17; 20:14
24 [a]Ex. 20:13; 21:12; Lev. 24:17; Num. 35:30, 31
25 [a]Ex. 23:7; Ps. 15:5; Ezek. 22:12
26 [a]Ps. 119:21; Jer. 11:3; Gal. 3:10

CHAPTER 28

1 [a]Ex. 15:26; Lev. 26:3–13; Deut. 7:12–26; 11:13

27:4 Mount Ebal was a significant location for the renewal of the covenant. Located about 30 miles north of Jerusalem, it was where Abraham had built an altar and was associated with God's promise of the land since the days of the patriarchs.

27:9 This day you have become the people of the LORD. This ceremony would remind Israel of her special status with God.

27:11–26 This accompanying ceremony would serve to reinforce the two alternatives that would be available to Israel in her new land. See note on 11:26–32.

27:14 The Levites here are those with the specific duty of attending to the ark. They are not the whole tribe of Levi, who had already taken their place on Mt. Gerizim to represent the blessing (v. 12).

27:26 Paul quotes this verse in Gal. 3:10 as part of his argument that Christ has removed the curse of the Law and that we must not rely upon our own obedience or works for salvation, but upon the grace of God.

28:1–68 This chapter is another listing of blessings and

carefully all His commandments which
I command you today, that the LORD
your God [b]will set you high above all
nations of the earth.

KINGDOM DYNAMICS

28:1 The Purposes of Predictive Prophecies, PROPHECY. Promise and prophecy are abundant in the Bible. God gives many assurances of His readiness to bless, and often speaks of things He plans to do in the future. In both cases there are always conditions: God's call to align with His will so His word of promise can bless the obedient. Ch. 28 is a classic study of both God's promises and His prophecies. Compare vv. 1, 2 and vv. 58, 59 to note the blessings that are a promised potential to the obedient, and the judgments that are a predicted certainty for the disobedient.

This exemplifies the purpose of predictive prophecy in the Bible. It is to teach, to warn, and to instruct toward obedience and fruitful living. It is never given to arouse curiosity or promote guesswork. In Matt. 24 Jesus makes several prophecies about things to come, but tells His disciples that His purpose is only to elicit practical responses of obedient living (v. 42), not guessing at the possible schedule of forthcoming events (v. 36).

Elsewhere, our Lord indicates that predictive prophecies are also given to undergird our confidence in God's sovereignty and omniscience—that He is in control and that He does know the end from the beginning. Note His words in John 13:19, 14:20, and 16:4, where His triple emphasis on this purpose of His prediction occurs—"that when it does come to pass, you may believe that I am *He*" (that is, God's Son, the Messiah).

(Acts 11:27–30/1 John 2:18) J.W.H.

2 "And all these blessings shall come
upon you and [a]overtake you, because
you obey the voice of the LORD your
God:
3 [a]"Blessed *shall* you *be* in the city,
and blessed *shall* you *be* [b]in the country.
4 "Blessed *shall be* [a]the [1]fruit of your
body, the produce of your ground and
the increase of your herds, the increase
of your cattle and the offspring of your
flocks.
5 "Blessed *shall be* your basket and
your kneading bowl.
6 [a]"Blessed *shall* you *be* when you
come in, and blessed *shall* you *be* when
you go out.
7 "The LORD [a]will cause your enemies
who rise against you to be defeated before your face; they shall come out
against you one way and flee before
you seven ways.
8 "The LORD will [a]command the
blessing on you in your storehouses
and in all to which you [b]set your hand,
and He will bless you in the land which
the LORD your God is giving you.
9 [a]"The LORD will establish you as a
holy people to Himself, just as He has
sworn to you, if you keep the commandments of the LORD your God and
walk in His ways.
10 "Then all peoples of the earth shall
see that you are [a]called by the name
of the LORD, and they shall be [b]afraid
of you.
11 "And [a]the LORD will grant you
plenty of goods, in the fruit of your
body, in the increase of your livestock,
and in the produce of your ground, in
the land of which the LORD [1]swore to
your fathers to give you.
12 "The LORD will open to you His
good [1]treasure, the heavens, [a]to give
the rain to your land in its season, and
[b]to bless all the work of your hand.
[c]You shall lend to many nations, but
you shall not borrow.
13 "And the LORD will make [a]you the
*head and not the tail; you shall be
above only, and not be beneath, if you
[1]heed the commandments of the LORD
your God, which I command you
today, and are careful to observe
them.
14 [a]"So you shall not turn aside from
any of the words which I command you
this day, *to* the right or the left, to go
after other gods to serve them.

Curses on Disobedience

15 "But it shall come to pass, [a]if you
do not obey the voice of the LORD your
God, to observe carefully all His commandments and His statutes which I
command you today, that all these

1 [b]Deut. 26:19; 1 Chr. 14:2
2 [a]Deut. 28:15
3 [a]Ps. 128:1, 4 [b]Gen. 39:5
4 [a]Gen. 22:17 [1]*offspring*
6 [a]Ps. 121:8
7 [a]Lev. 26:7, 8
8 [a]Lev. 25:21 [b]Deut. 15:10
9 [a]Ex. 19:5, 6
10 [a]Num. 6:27; 2 Chr. 7:14; Is. 63:19; Dan. 9:18, 19 [b]Deut. 11:25
11 [a]Deut. 30:9 [1]*promised*
12 [a]Lev. 26:4; Deut. 11:14 [b]Deut. 14:29 [c]Deut. 15:6 [1]*storehouse*
13 [a][Is. 9:14, 15] [1]*listen to* *See WW at Gen. 3:15.
14 [a]Deut. 5:32; Josh. 1:7
15 [a]Lev. 26:14–39; Josh. 23:15; Dan. 9:10–14; Mal. 2:2

cursings, given by Moses himself during a covenant renewing ceremony on the plains of Moab (29:1). This ceremony foreshadowed the one they were to carry out later on Mt. Ebal (ch. 27).

28:9 Perhaps the most important blessing of the entire book is that **the LORD will establish you as a holy people to Himself . . . if you keep the commandments.**

28:15–68 The best comment on this lengthy series of curses is Paul's word in Rom. 1:18, "For the wrath of God is revealed from heaven against all ungodliness and unrighteousness of men." The inevitability of these curses would be real for believers today were it not removed by Jesus who "has redeemed us from the curse of the law, having become a curse for us" (Gal. 3:13).

curses will come upon you and overtake you:
16 "Cursed *shall* you *be* in the city, and
cursed *shall* you *be* in the country.
17 "Cursed *shall be* your basket and
your kneading bowl.
18 "Cursed *shall be* the [1]fruit of your
body and the produce of your land, the
increase of your cattle and the offspring of your flocks.
19 "Cursed *shall* you *be* when you
come in, and cursed *shall* you *be* when
you go out.
20 "The LORD will send on you [a]curs-
ing, [b]confusion, and [c]rebuke in all that
you set your hand to do, until you are
destroyed and until you perish quickly,
because of the wickedness of your doings in which you have forsaken Me.
21 "The LORD will make the [1]plague
cling to you until He has consumed you
from the land which you are going to
possess.
22 [a]"The LORD will strike you with
consumption, with fever, with inflammation, with severe burning fever,
with the sword, with [b]scorching,[1] and
with mildew; they shall pursue you until you perish.
23 "And [a]your heavens which *are* over
your head shall be bronze, and the
earth which is under you *shall be*
iron.
24 "The LORD will change the rain of
your land to powder and dust; from the
heaven it shall come down on you until
you are destroyed.
25 [a]"The LORD will cause you to be defeated before your enemies; you shall
go out one way against them and flee
seven ways before them; and you shall
become [1]troublesome to all the kingdoms of the earth.
26 [a]"Your carcasses shall be food for
all the birds of the air and the beasts
of the earth, and no one shall frighten
them away.
27 "The LORD will strike you with
[a]the boils of Egypt, with [b]tumors, with
the scab, and with the itch, from which
you cannot be healed.
28 "The LORD will strike you with madness and blindness and [a]confusion of
heart.
29 "And you shall [a]grope at noonday,
as a blind man gropes in darkness; you
shall not prosper in your ways; you
shall be only oppressed and plundered
continually, and no one shall save *you.*

18 [1]*offspring*
20 [a]Mal. 2:2 [b]Is. 65:14 [c]Ps. 80:16; Is. 30:17
21 [1]*pestilence*
22 [a]Lev. 26:16 [b]Amos 4:9 [1]*blight*
23 [a]Lev. 26:19
25 [a]Deut. 32:30 [1]*a terror*
26 [a]1 Sam. 17:44; Ps. 79:2
27 [a]Ex. 15:26 [b]1 Sam. 5:6
28 [a]Jer. 4:9
29 [a]Job 5:14

30 [a]2 Sam. 12:11; Job 31:10; Jer. 8:10 [b]Amos 5:11; Zeph. 1:13 [c]Deut. 20:6; Job 31:8; Jer. 12:13; Mic. 6:15
32 [a]2 Chr. 29:9 [b]Ps. 119:82 [c]Neh. 5:5 [1]*nothing you can do*
33 [a]Lev. 26:16; Jer. 5:15, 17
36 [a]2 Kin. 17:4, 6; 24:12, 14; 25:7, 11; 2 Chr. 36:1–21; Jer. 39:1–9 [b]Deut. 4:28; Jer. 16:13
37 [a]1 Kin. 9:7, 8; Jer. 24:9; 25:9 [b]Ps. 44:14 [1]*a thing of horror* *See WW at Prov. 1:6.
38 [a]Mic. 6:15; Hag. 1:6 [b]Ex. 10:4; Joel 1:4 [1]*devour*
39 [a]Zeph. 1:13
41 [a]Lam. 1:5
42 [1]*possess*

30 [a]"You shall betroth a wife, but another man shall lie with her; [b]you shall
build a house, but you shall not dwell
in it; [c]you shall plant a vineyard, but
shall not gather its grapes.
31 "Your ox *shall be* slaughtered before your eyes, but you shall not eat
of it; your donkey *shall be* violently
taken away from before you, and shall
not be restored to you; your sheep *shall
be* given to your enemies, and you shall
have no one to rescue *them.*
32 "Your sons and your daughters
shall be given to [a]another people, and
your eyes shall look and [b]fail *with
longing* for them all day long; and
there shall be [1]no strength in your
[c]hand.
33 "A nation whom you have not
known shall eat [a]the fruit of your land
and the produce of your labor, and you
shall be only oppressed and crushed
continually.
34 "So you shall be driven mad because of the sight which your eyes
see.
35 "The LORD will strike you in the
knees and on the legs with severe boils
which cannot be healed, and from the
sole of your foot to the top of your
head.
36 "The LORD will [a]bring you and the
king whom you set over you to a nation
which neither you nor your fathers
have known, and [b]there you shall
serve other gods—wood and stone.
37 "And you shall become [a]an[1] astonishment, a *proverb, [b]and a byword
among all nations where the LORD will
drive you.
38 [a]"You shall carry much seed out to
the field but gather little in, for [b]the
locust shall [1]consume it.
39 "You shall plant vineyards and tend
them, but you shall neither drink *of* the
[a]wine nor gather the *grapes;* for the
worms shall eat them.
40 "You shall have olive trees throughout all your territory, but you shall not
anoint *yourself* with the oil; for your
olives shall drop off.
41 "You shall beget sons and daughters; but they shall not be yours; for
[a]they shall go into captivity.
42 "Locusts shall [1]consume all your
trees and the produce of your land.
43 "The alien who *is* among you shall
rise higher and higher above you, and
you shall come down lower and lower.

28:32 ***Shall be* given to another people** refers to their children's being sold into slavery to a foreign nation. Unfortunately, this came to pass through Israel's disobedience. The northern kingdom of Israel fell to Assyria in 721 B.C., and Judah fell to Babylon in 587 B.C.

44 "He shall lend to you, but you shall
not lend to him; he shall be the head,
and you shall be the tail.
45 "Moreover all these curses shall
come upon you and pursue and overtake you, until you are destroyed, because you [1]did not obey the voice of
the LORD your God, to keep His commandments and His statutes which He
commanded you.
46 "And they shall be upon [a]you for a
sign and a *wonder, and on your descendants forever.
47 [a]"Because you did not serve the
LORD your God with joy and gladness
of heart, [b]for the abundance of everything,
48 "therefore you shall serve your enemies, whom the LORD will send against
you, in [a]hunger, in thirst, in nakedness,
and in need of everything; and He
[b]will put a yoke of iron on your neck
until He has destroyed you.
49 [a]"The LORD will bring a nation
against you from afar, from the end of
the earth, [b]*as swift* as the eagle flies,
a nation whose language you will not
understand,
50 "a nation of fierce countenance,
[a]which does not respect the elderly nor
show favor to the young.
51 "And they shall eat the increase of
your livestock and the produce of your
land, until you are destroyed; they
shall not leave you grain or new wine
or oil, *or* the increase of your cattle or
the offspring of your flocks, until they
have destroyed you.
52 "They shall [a]besiege you at all your
gates until your high and fortified
walls, in which you trust, come down
throughout all your land; and they
shall besiege you at all your gates
throughout all your land which the
LORD your God has given you.
53 [a]"You shall eat the [1]fruit of your
own body, the flesh of your sons and
your daughters whom the LORD your
God has given you, in the siege and
desperate straits in which your enemy
shall distress you.
54 "The [1]sensitive and very refined
man among you [a]will[2] be hostile
toward his brother, toward [b]the
wife of his bosom, and toward the
rest of his children whom he leaves behind,
55 "so that he will not give any of them
the flesh of his children whom he will
eat, because he has nothing left in the

45 [1]*did not listen to*
46 [a]Num. 26:10; Is. 8:18; Ezek. 14:8
*See WW at Zech. 3:8.
47 [a]Deut. 12:7; Neh. 9:35–37 [b]Deut. 32:15
48 [a]Lam. 4:4–6 [b]Jer. 28:13, 14
49 [a]Is. 5:26–30; 7:18–20; Jer. 5:15 [b]Jer. 48:40; 49:22; Lam. 4:19; Hos. 8:1
50 [a]2 Chr. 36:17
52 [a]2 Kin. 25:1, 2, 4
53 [a]Lev. 26:29; 2 Kin. 6:28, 29; Jer. 19:9; Lam. 2:20; 4:10 [1]*offspring*
54 [a]Deut. 15:9 [b]Deut. 13:6 [1]Lit. *tender* [2]Lit. *his eye shall be evil toward*
56 [1]*sensitive* [2]*refined* [3]Lit. *her eye shall be evil toward*
57 [a]Gen. 49:10 [1]*afterbirth*
58 [a]Ex. 6:3
59 [a]Dan. 9:12
60 [a]Deut. 7:15
62 [a]Deut. 4:27 [b]Deut. 10:22; Neh. 9:23
63 [a]Deut. 30:9; Jer. 32:41 [b]Prov. 1:26; [Is. 1:24] [c]Jer. 12:14; 45:4 [1]*torn*
*See WW at Is. 64:5.
64 [a]Lev. 26:33; Deut. 4:27, 28; Neh. 1:8; Jer. 16:13; Amos 9:9 [b]Deut. 28:36
65 [a]Lam. 1:3; Amos 9:4 [b]Lev. 26:36 [c]Lev. 26:16 [1]*anxious*

siege and desperate straits in which
your enemy shall distress you at all
your gates.
56 "The [1]tender and [2]delicate woman
among you, who would not venture to
set the sole of her foot on the ground
because of her delicateness and sensitivity, [3]will refuse to the husband of her
bosom, and to her son and her daughter,
57 "her [1]placenta which comes out
[a]from between her feet and her children whom she bears; for she will eat
them secretly for lack of everything in
the siege and desperate straits in which
your enemy shall distress you at all
your gates.
58 "If you do not carefully observe all
the words of this law that are written
in this book, that you may fear [a]this
glorious and awesome name, THE
LORD YOUR GOD,
59 "then the LORD will bring upon
you and your descendants [a]extraordi-
nary plagues—great and prolonged
plagues—and serious and prolonged
sicknesses.
60 "Moreover He will bring back on
you all [a]the diseases of Egypt, of which
you were afraid, and they shall cling
to you.
61 "Also every sickness and every
plague, which *is* not written in this
Book of the Law, will the LORD bring
upon you until you are destroyed.
62 "You [a]shall be left few in number,
whereas you were [b]as the stars of
heaven in multitude, because you
would not obey the voice of the LORD
your God.
63 "And it shall be, *that* just as the
LORD [a]rejoiced* over you to do you
good and multiply you, so the LORD
[b]will rejoice over you to destroy you
and bring you to nothing; and you shall
be [c]plucked[1] from off the land which
you go to possess.
64 "Then the LORD [a]will scatter you
among all peoples, from one end of the
earth to the other, and [b]there you shall
serve other gods, which neither you
nor your fathers have known—wood
and stone.
65 "And [a]among those nations you
shall find no rest, nor shall the sole of
your foot have a resting place; [b]but
there the LORD will give you a
[1]trembling heart, failing eyes, and
[c]anguish of soul.
66 "Your life shall hang in doubt be-

28:58 Moses forthrightly states the purpose of the Law, that Israel **may fear this glorious and awesome name, THE LORD YOUR GOD.**

fore you; you shall *fear day and night,
and have no assurance of life.
67 [a]"In the morning you shall say, 'Oh,
that it were evening!' And at evening
you shall say, 'Oh, that it were morning!' because of the fear which terrifies
your heart, and [b]because of the sight
which your eyes see.
68 "And the LORD [a]will take you back
to Egypt in ships, by the way of which
I said to you, [b]'You shall never see it
again.' And there you shall be offered
for sale to your enemies as male and female slaves, but no one will buy *you*."

The Covenant Renewed in Moab

29 These *are* the words of the *covenant which the LORD com-
manded Moses to make with the children of Israel in the land of Moab,
besides the [a]covenant which He made
with them in Horeb.
2 Now Moses called all Israel and
said to them: [a]"You have seen all that
the LORD did before your eyes in the
land of Egypt, to Pharaoh and to all
his servants and to all his land—
3 [a]"the great trials which your eyes
have seen, the signs, and those great
wonders.
4 "Yet [a]the LORD has not given you
a heart to [1]perceive and eyes to see and
ears to hear, to this *very* day.
5 [a]"And I have led you forty years in
the wilderness. [b]Your clothes have not
worn out on you, and your sandals
have not worn out on your feet.
6 [a]"You have not eaten bread, nor
have you drunk wine or *similar* drink,
that you may know that I *am* the LORD
your God.
7 "And when you came to this place,
[a]Sihon king of Heshbon and Og king
of Bashan came out against us to battle, and we conquered them.
8 "We took their land and [a]gave it as
an inheritance to the Reubenites, to the
Gadites, and to half the tribe of Manasseh.
9 "Therefore [a]keep the words of this
covenant, and do them, that you may
[b]prosper in all that you do.
10 "All of you stand today before the

66 *See WW at Hos. 3:5.
67 [a]Job 7:4 [b]Deut. 28:34
68 [a]Jer. 43:7; Hos. 8:13 [b]Deut. 17:16

CHAPTER 29

1 [a]Lev. 26:46; Deut. 5:2, 3 *See WW at Gen. 17:7.
2 [a]Ex. 19:4; Deut. 11:7
3 [a]Deut. 4:34; 7:19
4 [a][Is. 6:9, 10; Ezek. 12:2]; Matt. 13:14; [Acts 28:26, 27]; Rom. 11:8; [Eph. 4:18] [1]*understand* or *know*
5 [a]Deut. 1:3; 8:2 [b]Deut. 8:4
6 [a]Ex. 16:12; Deut. 8:3
7 [a]Num. 21:23, 24; Deut. 2:26—3:3
8 [a]Num. 32:33; Deut. 3:12, 13
9 [a]Deut. 4:6; 1 Kin. 2:3 [b]Josh. 1:7
11 [a]Josh. 9:21, 23, 27
12 [a]Neh. 10:29
13 [a]Deut. 28:9 [b]Ex. 6:7 [c]Gen. 17:7, 8
14 [a][Jer. 31:31; Heb. 8:7, 8]
15 [a]Acts 2:39
17 [1]*detestable things*
18 [a]Deut. 11:16 [b]Heb. 12:15 [c]Deut. 32:32; Acts 8:23
19 [a]Jer. 3:17; 7:24 [b]Is. 30:1 [1]*walk in the stubbornness* or *imagination*
20 [a]Ezek. 14:7 [b]Ps. 74:1 [c]Ps. 79:5; Ezek. 23:25 [d]Ex. 32:33; Deut. 9:14; 2 Kin. 14:27 *See WW at Ps. 103:3.
21 [a][Matt. 24:51]

LORD your God: your leaders and your
tribes and your elders and your officers, all the men of Israel,
11 "your little ones and your wives—
also the stranger who *is* in your camp,
from [a]the one who cuts your wood to
the one who draws your water—
12 "that you may enter into covenant
with the LORD your God, and [a]into His
oath, which the LORD your God makes
with you today,
13 "that He may [a]establish you today
as a people for Himself, and *that* He
may be God to you, [b]just as He has
spoken to you, and [c]just as He has
sworn to your fathers, to Abraham,
Isaac, and Jacob.
14 "I make this covenant and this oath,
[a]not with you alone,
15 "but with *him* who stands here with
us today before the LORD our God,
[a]as well as with *him* who *is* not here
with us today
16 (for you know that we dwelt in the
land of Egypt and that we came
through the nations which you passed
by,
17 and you saw their [1]abominations
and their idols which *were* among
them—wood and stone and silver and
gold);
18 "so that there may not be among 5
you man or woman or family or tribe,
[a]whose heart turns away today from
the LORD our God, to go *and* serve the
gods of these nations, [b]and that there
may not be among you a root bearing
[c]bitterness or wormwood;
19 "and so it may not happen, when
he hears the words of this curse, that
he blesses himself in his heart, saying,
'I shall have peace, even though I
[1]follow the [a]dictates of my heart'—[b]as
though the drunkard could be included
with the sober.
20 [a]"The LORD would not *spare him;
for then [b]the anger of the LORD and
[c]His jealousy would burn against that
man, and every curse that is written
in this book would settle on him, and
the LORD [d]would blot out his name
from under heaven.
21 "And the LORD [a]would separate him
from all the tribes of Israel for adver-

29:1–29 This chapter contains a summary of God's acts from the Exodus to Israel's current arrival on the plains of Moab. It is followed by another rehearsal of the meaning of Israel's covenant relationship with God (vv. 9–15) and further warnings of the consequences should there be in Canaan those **whose heart turns away today from the LORD** (vv. 16–29).

29:1 The covenant renewing ceremony at **Moab** reinforced the earlier ceremony **in Horeb** (5:2).

29:11 The one who cuts . . . draws your water refers to a class within the resident aliens (**stranger**) who were assigned menial tasks. See Josh. 9:21–27.

29:15 With *him* who *is* not here with us today refers to generations to be born. This reference is sobering since not only the future of the Israelites who were present, but that of their posterity, was contingent upon their obedience.

29:18 See section 5 of Truth-In-Action at the end of Deut.

sity, according to all the curses of the
covenant that are written in this Book
of the [b]Law,
22 "so that the coming generation of
your children who rise up after you,
and the foreigner who comes from a
far land, would say, when they [a]see the
plagues of that land and the sicknesses
which the LORD has laid on it:
23 'The whole land *is* brimstone,
[a]salt, and burning; it is not sown, nor
does it bear, nor does any grass grow
there, [b]like the overthrow of Sodom
and Gomorrah, Admah, and Zeboiim,
which the LORD overthrew in His anger
and His wrath.'
24 "All nations would say, [a]'Why has
the LORD done so to this land? What
does the heat of this great anger
mean?'
25 "Then *people* would say: 'Because
they have forsaken the covenant of the
LORD God of their fathers, which He
made with them when He brought
them out of the land of Egypt;
26 'for they went and served other
gods and worshiped them, gods that
they did not know and that He had not
given to them.
27 'Then the anger of the LORD was
aroused against this land, [a]to bring on it
every curse that is written in this book.
28 'And the LORD [a]uprooted them from
their land in anger, in wrath, and in
great indignation, and cast them into
another land, as *it is* this day.'
29 "The secret *things belong* to the
LORD our God, but those *things which
are* *revealed *belong* to us and to our
children forever, that *we* may do all the
words of this law.

The Blessing of Returning to God

30 "Now [a]it shall come to pass,
when [b]all these things come
upon you, the blessing and the [c]curse
which I have set before you, and
[d]you [1]call *them* to mind among all the
nations where the LORD your God
drives you,

21 [b]Deut. 30:10
22 [a]Jer. 19:8; 49:17; 50:13
23 [a]Jer. 17:6; Zeph. 2:9 [b]Gen. 19:24, 25; Is. 1:9; Jer. 20:16; Hos. 11:8
24 [a]1 Kin. 9:8; Jer. 22:8
27 [a]Dan. 9:11
28 [a]1 Kin. 14:15; 2 Chr. 7:20; Ps. 52:5; Prov. 2:22
29 *See WW at Amos 3:7.

CHAPTER 30

1 [a]Lev. 26:40 [b]Deut. 28:2 [c]Deut. 28:15–45 [d]Deut. 4:29, 30 [1]Lit. *cause them to return to your heart*
2 [a]Deut. 4:29, 30; Neh. 1:9; Is. 55:7; Lam. 3:40; Joel 2:12
3 [a]Ps. 106:45; Jer. 29:14; Lam. 3:22, 32 [b]Ps. 147:2; Jer. 32:37; Ezek. 34:13
4 [a]Deut. 28:64; Neh. 1:9; Is. 62:11
6 [a]Deut. 10:16; Jer. 32:39; Ezek. 11:19 *See WW at Ps. 97:10.
7 [a]Is. 54:15–17; Jer. 30:16, 20
8 [a]Zeph. 3:20
9 [a]Deut. 28:11 [b]Deut. 28:63; Jer. 32:41 [1]*offspring*
11 [a]Is. 45:19 [1]*not hidden from*

2 "and you [a]return to the LORD your
God and obey His voice, according to
all that I command you today, you and
your children, with all your heart and
with all your soul,
3 [a]"that the LORD your God will bring
you back from captivity, and have
compassion on you, and [b]gather you
again from all the nations where the
LORD your God has scattered you.
4 [a]"If *any* of you are driven out to the
farthest *parts* under heaven, from
there the LORD your God will gather
you, and from there He will bring
you.
5 "Then the LORD your God will bring
you to the land which your fathers possessed, and you shall possess it. He will
prosper you and multiply you more
than your fathers.
6 "And [a]the LORD your God will circumcise your heart and the heart of
your descendants, to *love the LORD
your God with all your heart and with
all your soul, that you may live.
7 "Also the LORD your God will put
all these [a]curses on your enemies and
on those who hate you, who persecuted
you.
8 "And you will [a]again obey the voice
of the LORD and do all His commandments which I command you today.
9 [a]"The LORD your God will make you
abound in all the work of your hand,
in the [1]fruit of your body, in the increase of your livestock, and in the produce of your land for good. For the
LORD will again [b]rejoice over you for
good as He rejoiced over your fathers,
10 "if you obey the voice of the LORD
your God, to keep His commandments
and His statutes which are written in
this Book of the Law, *and* if you turn
to the LORD your God with all your
heart and with all your soul.

The Choice of Life or Death

11 "For this commandment which I 7
command you today [a]*is* [1]not *too* mysterious for you, nor *is* it far off.

29:23 The details of the hypothetical scene that is described are related to the Hebrew terms commonly used to represent God's anger—fire (**brimstone**), scorching (**salt**), **and burning. Admah** and **Zeboiim** were located near the south end of the Dead Sea, close to **Sodom** and **Gomorrah.**

30:1–10 This passage is predictive, seeing beyond a future captivity brought on by disobedience to a period of repentance and restoration. The steps to restoration will include: remembering that they are in captivity as an inevitable consequence of disobeying the covenant (v. 1), repenting (v. 2), and wholeheartedly committing to **obey His voice** (v. 2). God would then bring them **back from captivity** (v. 3), **have compassion** on them (v. 3), **bring** them **to the land** (v. 5), and **circumcise** their **heart** (v. 6), a reference to the messianic covenant when God would deal with man's spiritual problem through an internal transformation.

30:11–14 See section 7 of Truth-In-Action at the end of Deut.

30:11–14 Returning to the ceremony in Moab, Moses reminds them that the **commandment** did not impose upon the people conditions they could not understand or fulfill. It was practical and realistic; thus, there was no excuse for disobedience.

12 [a]"It *is* not in heaven, that you
should say, 'Who will ascend into
heaven for us and bring it to us, that
we may hear it and do it?'
13 "Nor *is* it beyond the sea, that you
should say, 'Who will go over the sea
for us and bring it to us, that we may
hear it and do it?'
14 "But the word *is* very near you,
[a]in your mouth and in your heart, that
you may do it.
3 15 "See, [a]I have set before you today
life and good, death and evil,
16 "in that I command you today to
love the LORD your God, to walk in
His ways, and to keep His commandments, His statutes, and His judgments,
that you may live and multiply; and the
LORD your God will bless you in the
land which you go to possess.
17 "But if your heart turns away so
that you do not hear, and are drawn
away, and worship other gods and
serve them,
18 [a]"I announce to you today that you
shall surely perish; you shall not prolong *your* days in the land which you
cross over the Jordan to go in and possess.
19 [a]"I call heaven and earth as witnesses today against you, *that* [b]I have
set before you life and death, blessing
and cursing; therefore choose life, that
both you and your descendants may
live;
20 "that you may love the LORD your
God, that you may obey His voice, and
that you may cling to Him, for He *is*
your [a]life and the length of your days;
and that you may dwell in the land
which the LORD swore to your fathers,
to Abraham, Isaac, and Jacob, to give
them."

Joshua the New Leader of Israel

31 Then Moses went and spoke
these words to all Israel.
2 And he said to them: "I [a]*am* one
hundred and twenty years old today. I
can no longer [b]go out and come in.
Also the LORD has said to me, [c]'You
shall not cross over this Jordan.'
3 "The LORD your God [a]Himself
crosses over before you; He will destroy these nations from before you,
and you shall dispossess them.
[b]Joshua himself crosses over before
you, just [c]as the LORD has said.
4 [a]"And the LORD will do to them
[b]as He did to Sihon and Og, the kings
of the Amorites and their land, when
He destroyed them.
5 [a]"The LORD will give them over to 5
you, that you may do to them according to every commandment which I
have commanded you.
6 [a]"Be strong and of good courage,
[b]do not fear nor be afraid of them; for
the LORD your God, [c]He *is* the One who
goes with you. [d]He will not leave you
nor forsake you."
7 Then Moses called Joshua and said
to him in the sight of all Israel, [a]"Be
strong and of good courage, for you
must go with this people to the land
which the LORD has sworn to their fathers to give them, and you shall cause
them to inherit it.
8 "And the LORD, [a]He *is* the One who
goes before you. [b]He will be with you,
He will not leave you nor forsake you;
do not fear nor be dismayed."

The Law to Be Read Every Seven Years

9 So Moses **wrote** this law [a]and delivered it to the priests, the sons of Levi,
[b]who bore the ark of the covenant of
the LORD, and to all the elders of Israel.

12 [a]Prov. 30:4; Rom. 10:6–8
14 [a]Rom. 10:8
15 [a]Deut. 30:1, 19
18 [a]Deut. 4:26; 8:19
19 [a]Deut. 4:26 [b]Deut. 30:15
20 [a]Ps. 27:1; [John 11:25; 14:6; Col. 3:4]

CHAPTER 31

2 [a]Ex. 7:7; Deut. 34:7 [b]Num. 27:17; 1 Kin. 3:7 [c]Num. 20:12
3 [a]Deut. 9:3; Josh. 11:23 [b]Num. 27:18 [c]Num. 27:21
4 [a]Deut. 3:21 [b]Num. 21:24, 33
5 [a]Deut. 7:2; 20:10–20
6 [a]Josh. 10:25; 1 Chr. 22:13 [b]Deut. 1:29 [c]Deut. 20:4 [d]Josh. 1:5; Heb. 13:5
7 [a]Num. 27:19; Deut. 31:23; Josh. 1:6
8 [a]Ex. 13:21 [b]Deut. 31:6; Josh. 1:5; 1 Chr. 28:20; Heb. 13:5
9 [a]Deut. 17:18; 31:25, 26 [b]Num. 4:5, 6, 15; Deut. 10:8; 31:25, 26; Josh. 3:3

WORD WEALTH

31:9 wrote, *chatab* (kah-*tahv*); Strong's #3789: To write, inscribe, engrave, record; to document in written form. *Chatab* refers to inscribing words on some type of material (such as sheepskin), which serves to document and preserve the things written for future reference. Here Moses wrote this Torah and handed (*cont. on next page*)

30:15–20 See section 3 of Truth-In-Action at the end of Deut.
30:15–20 The chapter closes with a call to choose the way of life.
31:1—34:12 These chapters detail events connected with Moses' approaching death and funeral.
31:2 I can no longer go out and come in refers to Moses' inability to continue to discharge his duties. It is because of his advancing age and God's command that he **shall not cross over this Jordan.**
31:3–6 Soon the Israelites will cross the Jordan and begin the conquest of the Promised Land. Moses reminds the people that God will be with them in battle, just as He has been with them in the wilderness against **Sihon and Og** (2:26–37; 3:1–11), whose land they now occupy.
31:5–8 See section 5 of Truth-In-Action at the end of Deut.
31:7–13 Moses turns over the leadership of the Israelites to **Joshua,** who had already been designated (1:38; Num. 27:23). He also assigns to the Levitical **priests** and to **all the elders** (the ecclesiastical and civil heads of the nation) the responsibility of teaching the **law** and enforcing its observance.

(cont. from preceding page)
it to the Levitical priests for safekeeping. This began the scribal tradition, which has preserved the Scriptures for more than 3,000 years. Because of the nature of the Torah, and of all the Word of God, it was essential that the words be kept in written form, as opposed to some other means, such as tribal songs and stories. In John 5:46, 47, Jesus stated, "[Moses] wrote about Me. But if you do not believe his writings, how will you believe My words?" Jesus stymied Satan by appealing to the fixedness of the divine record: "It is written!"

10 And Moses commanded them, saying: "At the end of *every* seven years, at the appointed time in the [a]year of release, [b]at the Feast of Tabernacles,

11 "when all Israel comes to [a]appear before the LORD your God in the [b]place which He chooses, [c]you shall read this law before all Israel in their hearing.

12 [a]"Gather the people together, men and women and little ones, and the stranger who *is* within your gates, that they may hear and that they may learn to fear the LORD your God and carefully observe all the words of this law,

13 "and *that* their children, [a]who have not known it, [b]may hear and learn to fear the LORD your God as long as you live in the land which you cross the Jordan to possess."

Prediction of Israel's Rebellion

14 Then the LORD said to Moses, [a]"Behold, the days approach when you must die; call Joshua, and present yourselves in the tabernacle of meeting, that [b]I may [1]inaugurate him." So Moses and Joshua went and presented themselves in the tabernacle of meeting.

15 Now [a]the LORD appeared at the tabernacle in a pillar of cloud, and the pillar of cloud stood above the door of the tabernacle.

16 And the LORD said to Moses: "Behold, you will [1]rest with your fathers; and this people will [a]rise and [b]play the harlot with the gods of the foreigners of the land, where they go *to be* among them, and they will [c]forsake Me and [d]break My covenant which I have made with them.

17 "Then My anger shall be [a]aroused against them in that day, and [b]I will forsake them, and I will [c]hide My face from them, and they shall be [1]devoured. And many evils and troubles shall befall them, so that they will say in that day, [d]'Have not these evils come upon us because our God *is* [e]not among us?'

18 "And [a]I will surely hide My face in that day because of all the evil which they have done, in that they have turned to other gods.

19 "Now therefore, write down this song for yourselves, and teach it to the children of Israel; put it in their mouths, that this song may be [a]a witness for Me against the children of Israel.

20 "When I have brought them to the land flowing with milk and honey, of which I swore to their fathers, and they have eaten and filled themselves [a]and grown fat, [b]then they will turn to other gods and serve them; and they will provoke Me and break My covenant.

21 "Then it shall be, [a]when many evils and troubles have come upon them, that this song will testify against them as a witness; for it will not be forgotten in the mouths of their descendants, for [b]I know the inclination [c]of their behavior today, even before I have brought them to the land of which I swore *to give them*."

22 Therefore Moses wrote this song the same day, and taught it to the children of Israel.

23 [a]Then He inaugurated Joshua the son of Nun, and said, [b]"Be strong and of good courage; for you shall bring the children of Israel into the land of which I swore to them, and I will be with you."

24 So it was, when Moses had completed writing the words of this law in a book, when they were finished,

25 that Moses commanded the Levites, who bore the ark of the covenant of the LORD, saying:

26 "Take this Book of the Law, [a]and put it beside the ark of the covenant

10 [a]Deut. 15:1, 2 [b]Lev. 23:34; Deut. 16:13
11 [a]Deut. 16:16 [b]Deut. 12:5 [c]Josh. 8:34; 2 Kin. 23:2
12 [a]Deut. 4:10
13 [a]Deut. 11:2 [b]Ps. 78:6, 7
14 [a]Num. 27:13 [b]Num. 27:19; Deut. 3:28 [1]*commission*
15 [a]Ex. 33:9
16 [a]Deut. 29:22 [b]Ex. 34:15; Deut. 4:25–28; Judg. 2:11, 12, 17 [c]Deut. 32:15 [d]Judg. 2:20 [1]Die and join your ancestors
17 [a]Judg. 2:14; 6:13 [b]2 Chr. 15:2 [c]Deut. 32:20 [d]Judg. 6:13 [e]Num. 14:42 [1]*consumed*
18 [a]Deut. 31:17; [Is. 1:15, 16]
19 [a]Deut. 31:22, 26
20 [a]Deut. 32:15–17 [b]Deut. 31:16
21 [a]Deut. 31:17 [b]Hos. 5:3 [c]Amos 5:25, 26
23 [a]Num. 27:23; Deut. 31:14 [b]Deut. 31:7
26 [a]2 Kin. 22:8

31:14–23 The events in this private ceremony may be regarded as confirming Joshua in his commission by the immediate presence of **the LORD.** He had been commissioned or inaugurated earlier (Num. 27:22, 23).
31:16 The future apostasy of the Israelites is announced in the presence of Joshua so that he will be aware of the danger and strive in his day to avert it. This he faithfully does (Josh. 24:31); but in his own last address to Israel (Josh. 23:15, 16), he repeats the same prediction and warning.
31:20 It is instructive to note that the very prosperity that God would give the Israelites would contribute to a sense of ease and security in which the Source of that prosperity would be forgotten.

of the LORD your God, that it may be
there [b]as a witness against you;
27 [a]"for I know your rebellion and
your [b]stiff neck. *If* today, while I am
yet alive with you, you have been rebellious against the LORD, then how
much more after my death?
28 "Gather to me all the elders of your
tribes, and your officers, that I may
speak these words in their hearing
[a]and call heaven and earth to witness
against them.
5 29 "For I know that after my death you
will [a]become utterly corrupt, and turn
aside from the way which I have commanded you. And [b]evil will befall you
[c]in the latter days, because you will do
evil in the sight of the LORD, to provoke
Him to anger through the work of your
hands."

The Song of Moses

30 Then Moses spoke in the hearing
of all the assembly of Israel the words
of this song until they were ended:

32 "Give [a]ear, O heavens, and I will
speak;
And hear, O [b]earth, the words of
my mouth.
2 Let [a]my [1]teaching drop as the
rain,
My speech distill as the dew,
[b]As raindrops on the tender herb,
And as showers on the grass.
3 For I proclaim the [a]name of the
LORD:
[b]Ascribe greatness to our God.
4 *He is* [a]the Rock, [b]His work *is*
perfect;
For all His ways *are* justice,
[c]A God of truth and [d]without
injustice;
Righteous and upright *is* He.

5 "They[a] have corrupted
themselves;
They are not His children,
Because of their blemish:
A [b]perverse and crooked
generation.
6 Do you thus [a]deal[1] with the LORD,
O foolish and unwise people?
Is He not [b]your Father, *who*
[c]bought you?
Has He not [d]made you and
established you?

7 "Remember[a] the days of old,
Consider the years of many
generations.
[b]Ask your father, and he will show
you;
Your elders, and they will tell
you:
8 When the *Most High [a]divided
their inheritance to the nations,
When He [b]separated the sons of
Adam,
He set the boundaries of the
peoples
According to the number of the
[1]children of Israel.
9 For [a]the LORD's portion *is* His
people;
Jacob *is* the place of His
*inheritance.

10 "He found him [a]in a desert land
And in the *wasteland, a howling
wilderness;
He encircled him, He instructed
him,
He [b]kept him as the [1]apple of His
eye.
11 [a]As an eagle stirs up its nest, 1
Hovers over its young,
Spreading out its wings, taking
them up,
Carrying them on its wings,
12 *So* the LORD alone led him,
And *there was* no foreign god
with him.

13 "He[a] made him ride in the heights
of the earth,
That he might eat the produce of
the fields;
He made him draw honey from
the rock,
And oil from the flinty rock;
14 Curds from the cattle, and milk
of the flock,
[a]With fat of lambs;
And rams of the breed of Bashan,
and goats,

26 [b]Deut. 31:19
27 [a]Deut. 9:7, 24 [b]Ex. 32:9; Deut. 9:6, 13
28 [a]Deut. 30:19
29 [a]Deut. 32:5; Judg. 2:19; [Acts 20:29, 30] [b]Deut. 28:15 [c]Gen. 49:1; Deut. 4:30

CHAPTER 32

1 [a]Deut. 4:26; Ps. 50:4; Is. 1:2 [b]Jer. 6:19
2 [a]Is. 55:10, 11 [b]Ps. 72:6 [1]*doctrine*
3 [a]Deut. 28:58 [b]1 Chr. 29:11
4 [a]Deut. 32:15, 18, 30; Ps. 18:2 [b]2 Sam. 22:31 [c]Deut. 7:9; Is. 65:16; Jer. 10:10 [d]Job 34:10
5 [a]Deut. 4:25; 31:29 [b]Phil. 2:15
6 [a]Ps. 116:12 [b]Ex. 4:22; Deut. 1:31; Is. 63:16 [c]Ps. 74:2 [d]Deut. 32:15 [1]*repay the*
7 [a]Ps. 44:1 [b]Ex. 12:26; 13:14; Ps. 78:5–8
8 [a]Acts 17:26 [b]Gen. 11:8 [1]LXX, DSS *angels of God;* Symmachus, Lat. *sons of God* *See WW at Gen. 14:18.
9 [a]Ex. 19:5 *See WW at Zech. 2:12.
10 [a]Jer. 2:6; Hos. 13:5 [b]Ps. 17:8; Prov. 7:2; Zech. 2:8 [1]*pupil* *See WW at Is. 45:18.
11 [a]Is. 31:5
13 [a]Is. 58:14
14 [a]Ps. 81:16

31:28–30 The central commands in this chapter were that the covenant be read regularly, the song of witness be written and taught to Israel, and the covenant document be placed by the side of the ark. All of these embody one significant concern, that Israel would forget her covenant with God and break it.
31:29 See section 5 of Truth-In-Action at the end of Deut.
32:1–47 This poetic song was to be learned and repeated by the Israelites as an ongoing witness of their understanding of the covenant.
32:4 The Lord is described five times in this song as **the Rock,** the essence of stability and reliability (vv. 4, 15, 18, 30, 31). This descriptive title stresses the permanent, unchanging nature of the God of the covenant.
32:9 Israel is here called **Jacob,** a common poetic synonym for Israel.
32:11, 12 See section 1 of Truth-In-Action at the end of Deut.

With the choicest wheat;
And you drank wine, the
[b]blood of the grapes.

15 "But Jeshurun grew fat and
kicked;
[a]You grew fat, you grew thick,
You are obese!
Then he [b]forsook God *who*
[c]made him,
And scornfully esteemed the
[d]Rock of his salvation.
16 [a]They provoked Him to jealousy
with foreign *gods;*
With [1]abominations they
provoked Him to *anger.
17 [a]They sacrificed to demons, not to
God,
To gods they did not know,
To new *gods,* new arrivals
That your fathers did not fear.
18 [a]Of the Rock *who* begot you, you
are unmindful,
And have [b]forgotten the God who
fathered you.

19 "And[a] when the LORD saw *it,* He
spurned *them,*
Because of the provocation of His
sons and His daughters.
20 And He said: 'I will hide My face
from them,
I will see what their end *will be,*
For they *are* a perverse
generation,
[a]Children in whom *is* no faith.
21 [a]They have provoked Me to
*jealousy by *what* is not God;
They have moved Me to anger
[b]by their [1]foolish idols.
But [c]I will provoke them to
jealousy by *those who are* not
a nation;
I will move them to anger by a
foolish nation.
22 For [a]a fire is kindled in My anger,
And shall burn to the [1]lowest
[2]hell;
It shall consume the earth with
her increase,
And set on fire the foundations of
the mountains.

23 'I will [a]heap disasters on them;
[b]I will spend My arrows on them.
24 *They shall be* wasted with hunger,
Devoured by pestilence and bitter
destruction;

14 [b]Gen. 49:11
15 [a]Deut. 31:20 [b]Is. 1:4 [c]Is. 51:13 [d]Ps. 95:1
16 [a]Ps. 78:58; 1 Cor. 10:22 [1]*detestable acts* *See WW at 1 Kin. 16:2.
17 [a]Rev. 9:20
18 [a]Is. 17:10 [b]Jer. 2:32
19 [a]Judg. 2:14
20 [a]Matt. 17:17
21 [a]Ps. 78:58 [b]Ps. 31:6 [c]Rom. 10:19 [1]*foolishness,* lit. *vanities* *See WW at Zech. 8:2.
22 [a]Num. 16:33–35; Ps. 18:7, 8; Lam. 4:11 [1]*lowest part of* [2]Or *Sheol*
23 [a]Ex. 32:12; Deut. 29:21, 24 [b]Ps. 7:12, 13
24 [a]Lev. 26:22
26 [a]Ezek. 20:23
27 [a]Is. 10:12–15
28 *See WW at Zech. 6:13.
29 [a]Ps. 81:13; [Luke 19:42] [b]Deut. 31:29 *See WW at Jer. 3:15.
30 [a]Judg. 2:14; Ps. 44:12 *See WW at Deut. 6:4.
31 [a][1 Sam. 4:7, 8; Jer. 40:2, 3]
32 [a]Is. 1:8–10
33 [a]Ps. 58:4 [b]Rom. 3:13
34 [a][Jer. 2:22]
35 [a]Ps. 94:1; Rom. 12:19; Heb. 10:30 [b]2 Pet. 2:3

I will also send against them the
[a]teeth of beasts,
With the poison of serpents of the
dust.
25 The sword shall destroy outside;
There shall be terror within
For the young man and virgin,
The nursing child with the man
of gray hairs.
26 [a]I would have said, "I will dash
them in pieces,
I will make the memory of them
to cease from among men,"
27 Had I not feared the wrath of the
enemy,
Lest their adversaries should
misunderstand,
Lest they should say, [a]"Our hand
is high;
And it is not the LORD who has
done all this." '

28 "For they *are* a nation void of
*counsel,
Nor *is there any* understanding in
them.
29 [a]Oh, that they were wise, *that* they
*understood this,
That they would consider their
[b]latter end!
30 How could *one chase a
thousand,
And two put ten thousand to
flight,
Unless their Rock [a]had sold
them,
And the LORD had surrendered
them?
31 For their rock *is* not like our Rock,
[a]Even our enemies themselves
being judges.
32 For [a]their vine *is* of the vine of
Sodom
And of the fields of Gomorrah;
Their grapes *are* grapes of gall,
Their clusters *are* bitter.
33 Their wine *is* [a]the poison of
serpents,
And the cruel [b]venom of cobras.

34 '*Is* this not [a]laid up in store with
Me,
Sealed up among My treasures?
35 [a]Vengeance is Mine, and
recompense;
Their foot shall slip in *due* time;
[b]For the day of their calamity *is*
at hand,

32:15 Jeshurun is a poetic name for Israel. Israel's ingratitude to God is clearly noted as she **grew fat** on the bountiful provision of God and **kicked,** resisting His love and control. Israel abandoned her source of creation and scorned the basis of her salvation.

32:17 The idol worship of the pagan world is clearly more than superstition. Such worship submits the worshiper to demon power. See also Lev. 17:7; 2 Chr. 11:15; Ps. 106:37.

And the things to come hasten
upon them.'

36 "For[a] the LORD will **judge** His
people
[b]And have compassion on His
servants,
When He sees that *their* power is
gone,
And [c]*there is* no one *remaining,*
bond or free.

WORD WEALTH

32:36 judge, *din* (*deen*); Strong's #1777: Rule, govern, legislate, judge, strive, plead the cause of someone; contend with someone, contend for something. The noun derived from this word is translated as "plea," "judgment," or "cause." *Dayan* is another derivative and means "a judge." Finally, from *din* comes *medinah,* meaning "state," "province," or "government"; it is literally "place of judgment or justice."

37 He will say: [a]'Where *are* their
gods,
The rock in which they sought
refuge?
38 Who ate the fat of their sacrifices,
And drank the wine of their drink
offering?
Let them rise and help you,
And be your refuge.

39 'Now see that [a]I, *even* I, *am* He,
And [b]*there is* no God besides
Me;
[c]I kill and I make alive;
I wound and I *heal;
Nor *is there any* who can deliver
from My hand.
40 For I raise My hand to heaven,
And say, "*As* I live forever,
41 [a]If I [1]whet My glittering sword,
And My hand takes hold on
judgment,
I will render vengeance to My
enemies,
And repay those who hate Me.
42 I will make My arrows drunk with
blood,
And My sword shall devour flesh,
With the blood of the slain and
the captives,
From the heads of the leaders of
the enemy." '

43 "Rejoice,[a] O Gentiles, *with* His
[1]people;
For He will [b]avenge the blood of
His servants,
And render vengeance to His
adversaries;
He [c]will provide atonement for
His land *and* His people."

44 So Moses came with [1]Joshua the
son of Nun and spoke all the words of
this song in the hearing of the people.
45 Moses finished speaking all these
words to all Israel,
46 and he said to them: [a]"Set your
hearts on all the words which I testify
among you today, which you shall
command your [b]children to be careful
to observe—all the words of this law.
47 "For it *is* not a [1]futile thing for you,
because it *is* your [a]life, and by this
word you shall prolong *your* days in
the land which you cross over the Jordan to possess."

Moses to Die on Mount Nebo

48 Then the LORD spoke to Moses that
very same day, saying:
49 [a]"Go up this mountain of the
Abarim, Mount Nebo, which *is* in the
land of Moab, across from Jericho;
view the land of Canaan, which I give
to the children of Israel as a possession;
50 "and die on the mountain which
you ascend, and be [1]gathered to your
people, just as [a]Aaron your brother
died on Mount Hor and was gathered
to his people;
51 "because [a]you trespassed against
Me among the children of Israel at the
waters of [1]Meribah Kadesh, in the Wilderness of Zin, because you [b]did not
hallow Me in the midst of the children
of Israel.
52 [a]"Yet you shall see the land before
you, though you shall not go there, into
the land which I am giving to the children of Israel."

Moses' Final Blessing on Israel

33 Now this *is* [a]the blessing with
which Moses [b]the man of God
blessed the children of Israel before his
death.

36 [a]Ps. 135:14; Heb. 10:30 [b]Ps. 106:45; Jer. 31:20 [c]2 Kin. 14:26
37 [a]Judg. 10:14; Jer. 2:28
39 [a]Is. 41:4; 43:10 [b]Deut. 32:12; Is. 45:5 [c]1 Sam. 2:6; Ps. 68:20 *See WW at Ex. 15:26.
41 [a]Is. 1:24; 66:16; Jer. 50:28–32 [1]*sharpen*
43 [a]Rom. 15:10 [b]2 Kin. 9:7; Rev. 6:10; 19:2 [c]Ps. 65:3; 79:9; 85:1 [1]DSS fragment adds *And let all the gods (angels) worship Him;* cf. LXX and Heb. 1:6
44 [1]Heb. *Hoshea,* Num. 13:8, 16
46 [a]Ezek. 40:4; 44:5 [b]Deut. 11:19
47 [a]Deut. 8:3; 30:15–20 [1]*vain*
49 [a]Num. 27:12–14; Deut. 3:27
50 [a]Num. 20:25, 28; 33:38 [1]Join your ancestors
51 [a]Num. 20:11–13 [b]Lev. 10:3 [1]Lit. *Contention at Kadesh*
52 [a]Num. 27:12; Deut. 34:1–5

CHAPTER 33

1 [a]Gen. 49:28 [b]Ps. 90

32:49 Abarim means "the mountain of the borderlands" and constitutes a range of mountains of which Nebo is the highest peak.

33:1–29 Moses invokes blessings upon each of the tribes of Israel except Simeon, which was soon to be absorbed by Judah (Josh. 19:2–9). In contrast to the last chapter, this passage is striking in that a tone of positiveness and happiness prevails throughout. Totally absent are the warnings and reproofs. As the song of ch. 32 sets forth the calamities with which God's justice will fall upon Israel for her faithlessness, so the blessings of ch. 33 describe the glory and greatness that will crown Israel's faithfulness. Thus

2 And he said:

[a]"The LORD came from Sinai,
And dawned on them from [b]Seir;
He shone forth from [c]Mount Paran,
And He came with [d]ten thousands of saints;
From His right hand
Came a fiery law for them.
3 Yes, [a]He loves the people;
[b]All His saints *are* in Your hand;
They [c]sit down at Your feet;
Everyone [d]receives Your words.
4 [a]Moses [1]commanded a law for us,
[b]A heritage of the congregation of Jacob.
5 And He was [a]King in [b]Jeshurun,
When the leaders of the people were gathered,
All the tribes of Israel together.

6 "Let [a]Reuben live, and not die,
Nor let his men be few."

7 And this he said of [a]Judah:

"Hear, LORD, the voice of Judah,
And bring him to his people;
[b]Let his hands be sufficient for him,
And may You be [c]a help against his enemies."

8 And of [a]Levi he said:

[b]"*Let* Your [1]Thummim and Your Urim *be* with Your holy one,
[c]Whom You tested at Massah,
And with whom You contended at the waters of Meribah,
9 [a]Who says of his father and mother,
'I have not [b]seen them';
[c]Nor did he acknowledge his brothers,
Or know his own children;
For [d]they have observed Your *word
And kept Your covenant.
10 [a]They shall teach Jacob Your judgments,
And Israel Your law.
They shall put incense before You,
[b]And a whole burnt sacrifice on Your altar.
11 Bless his substance, LORD,
And [a]accept the work of his hands;
Strike the loins of those who rise against him,
And of those who hate him, that they rise not again."

12 Of Benjamin he said:

"The beloved of the LORD shall dwell in **safety** by Him,
Who shelters him all the day long;
And he shall dwell between His shoulders."

WORD WEALTH

33:12 safety, *betach* (*beh*-tahch); Strong's #983: Securely, in safety, confidently, in peace, trustingly; the state of confidence, security, and safety that belongs to those who trust and rely upon the Lord. *Betach* occurs more than 40 times in the OT and is most often translated "in safety," "securely," or "confidently"; occasionally, "boldly" (Gen. 34:25), or "in hope" (Ps. 16:9). From *betach* comes *bittachon,* which means "trust," "confidence," or "hope."

13 And of Joseph he said:

[a]"Blessed of the LORD *is* his land,
With the precious things of heaven, with the [b]dew,
And the deep lying beneath,
14 With the precious fruits of the sun,
With the precious produce of the months,
15 With the best things of [a]the ancient mountains,
With the precious things [b]of the everlasting hills,
16 With the precious things of the earth and its fullness,
And the favor of [a]Him who dwelt in the bush.
Let *the blessing* come [b]'on the head of Joseph,
And on the crown of the head of him *who was* separate from his brothers.'
17 His *glory *is like* a [a]firstborn bull,
And his horns *like* the [b]horns of the wild ox;
Together with them
[c]He shall push the peoples
To the ends of the earth;

2 [a]Ex. 19:18, 20; Ps. 68:8, 17; Hab. 3:3 [b]Deut. 2:1, 4 [c]Num. 10:12 [d]Dan. 7:10; Acts 7:53; Rev. 5:11
3 [a]Ps. 47:4; Hos. 11:1 [b]1 Sam. 2:9 [c][Luke 10:39] [d]Prov. 2:1
4 [a]Deut. 4:2; John 1:17; 7:19 [b]Ps. 119:111 [1]*charged us with*
5 [a]Ex. 15:18 [b]Deut. 32:15
6 [a]Gen. 49:3, 4
7 [a]Gen. 49:8–12 [b]Gen. 49:8 [c]Ps. 146:5
8 [a]Gen. 49:5 [b]Ex. 28:30; Lev. 8:8 [c]Num. 20:2–13; Deut. 6:2, 3, 16; Ps. 81:7 [1]Lit. *Perfections and Your Lights*
9 [a][Num. 25:5–8; Matt. 10:37; 19:29] [b][Gen. 29:32] [c]Ex. 32:26–28 [d]Mal. 2:5, 6 *See WW at 2 Sam. 22:31.
10 [a]Lev. 10:11; Deut. 31:9–13; Mal. 2:7 [b]Lev. 1:9; Ps. 51:19
11 [a]2 Sam. 24:23; Ezek. 20:40
13 [a]Gen. 49:22–26 [b]Gen. 27:28
15 [a]Gen. 49:26 [b]Hab. 3:6
16 [a]Ex. 3:2–4; Acts 7:30–35 [b]Gen. 49:26
17 [a]1 Chr. 5:1 [b]Num. 23:22 [c]1 Kin. 22:11; Ps. 44:5 *See WW at Ps. 8:5.

the song of ch. 32 and the blessings of ch. 33 are correspondent and supplemental. The foundation of these positive blessings is the strong confidence in Israel's unique, incomparable God, who **rides the heavens** to help Israel. He is an **eternal God** whose **everlasting arms** are never exhausted and who is their **refuge** and **safety.**

[d]They *are* the ten thousands of
Ephraim,
And they *are* the thousands of
Manasseh."

18 And of Zebulun he said:

[a]"Rejoice, Zebulun, in your going
out,
And Issachar in your tents!
19 They shall [a]call the peoples *to* the
mountain;
There [b]they shall offer sacrifices
of righteousness;
For they shall partake *of* the
abundance of the seas
And *of* treasures hidden in the
sand."

20 And of Gad he said:

"Blessed *is* he who [a]enlarges Gad;
He dwells as a lion,
And tears the arm and the crown
of his head.
21 [a]He provided the first *part* for
himself,
Because a lawgiver's portion was
reserved there.
[b]He came *with* the heads of the
people;
He administered the justice of the
LORD,
And His judgments with Israel."

22 And of Dan he said:

"Dan *is* a lion's whelp;
[a]He shall leap from Bashan."

23 And of Naphtali he said:

"O Naphtali, [a]satisfied with **favor,**
And full of the blessing of the
LORD,
[b]Possess the west and the south."

WORD WEALTH

33:23 favor, *ratson* (rah-*tzoan*); Strong's #7522: Pleasure, desire, delight, favor. The noun *ratson* comes from the verb *ratsa,* which means "to be pleased with" or "to be favorable toward something." *Ratson* refers especially to what is pleasing and desirable to God. The idea here is that Naphtali is to be satisfied with the pleasure, delight, and favor of God.

17 [d]Gen. 48:19
18 [a]Gen. 49:13–15
19 [a]Ex. 15:17; Ps. 2:6; Is. 2:3 [b]Ps. 4:5; 51:19
20 [a]1 Chr. 12:8
21 [a]Num. 32:16, 17 [b]Josh. 4:12
22 [a]Gen. 49:16, 17; Josh. 19:47
23 [a]Gen. 49:21 [b]Josh. 19:32
24 [a]Gen. 49:20 [b]Job 29:6
25 [a]Deut. 8:9
26 [a]Ex. 15:11; Deut. 4:35; Ps. 86:8; Jer. 10:6 [b]Deut. 32:15 [c]Deut. 10:14; Ps. 68:3, 33, 34; 104:3
27 [a][Ps. 90:1; 91:2, 9] [b]Deut. 9:3–5
28 [a]Deut. 33:12; Jer. 23:6; 33:16 [b]Deut. 8:7, 8 [c]Num. 23:9 [d]Gen. 27:28
29 [a]Ps. 144:15 [b]Deut. 4:32–34; 2 Sam. 7:23 [c]Gen. 15:1; Ps. 115:9 [d]Ps. 18:44; 66:3 [e]Num. 33:52 [1]Places for pagan worship

CHAPTER 34

1 [a]Num. 27:12; Deut. 32:49 *See WW at Ex. 19:20.
2 [1]Mediterranean
3 [a]2 Chr. 28:15
4 [a]Gen. 12:7 [b]Deut. 3:27
5 [a]Num. 20:12; Deut. 32:50; Josh. 1:1, 2

24 And of Asher he said:

[a]"Asher *is* most blessed of sons;
Let him be favored by his
brothers,
And let him [b]dip his foot in oil.
25 Your sandals *shall be* [a]iron and
bronze;
As your days, *so shall* your
strength *be.*

26 "*There is* [a]no one like the God of
[b]Jeshurun,
[c]*Who* rides the heavens to help
you,
And in His excellency on the
clouds.
27 The eternal God *is your* [a]refuge,
And underneath *are* the
everlasting arms;
[b]He will thrust out the enemy from
before you,
And will say, 'Destroy!'
28 Then [a]Israel shall dwell in safety,
[b]The fountain of Jacob [c]alone,
In a land of grain and new wine;
His [d]heavens shall also drop dew.
29 [a]Happy *are* you, O Israel!
[b]Who *is* like you, a people saved
by the LORD,
[c]The shield of your help
And the sword of your majesty!
Your enemies [d]shall submit to
you,
And [e]you shall tread down their
[1]high places."

Moses Dies on Mount Nebo

34 Then Moses *went up from the
plains of Moab [a]to Mount Nebo,
to the top of Pisgah, which is across
from Jericho. And the LORD showed
him all the land of Gilead as far as Dan,
2 all Naphtali and the land of
Ephraim and Manasseh, all the land of
Judah as far as the [1]Western Sea,
3 the South, and the plain of the Valley of Jericho, [a]the city of palm trees,
as far as Zoar.
4 Then the LORD said to him, [a]"This
is the land of which I swore to give
Abraham, Isaac, and Jacob, saying, 'I
will give it to your descendants.'
[b]I have caused you to see *it* with your
eyes, but you shall not cross over
there."
5 [a]So Moses the servant of the LORD

34:1–8 The land Moses was allowed to see from **Mount Nebo** was that which God had promised to the patriarchs. In Hebrew thought **to see *it* with your eyes** was a symbol of acquisition by which property became legally that of the viewer (Gen. 13:14, 15). Thus, Moses was accepting, from God, ownership of the Promised Land on behalf of all Israel.

34:1 The top of Pisgah likely refers to the summit of the ridge of mountains.

died there in the land of Moab, according to the word of the LORD.
6 And He buried him in a valley in
the land of Moab, opposite Beth Peor;
but [a]no one knows his grave to this
day.
7 [a]Moses *was* one hundred and
twenty years old when he died. [b]His
[1]eyes were not dim nor his natural
vigor [2]diminished.
8 And the children of Israel wept for
Moses in the plains of Moab [a]thirty
days. So the days of weeping *and*
mourning for Moses ended.
9 Now Joshua the son of Nun was full
of the [a]spirit of wisdom, for [b]Moses
had laid his hands on him; so the children of Israel heeded him, and did as
the LORD had commanded Moses.
10 But since then there [a]has not arisen
in Israel a prophet like Moses, [b]whom
the LORD knew face to face,
11 in all [a]the signs and wonders which
the LORD sent him to do in the land of
Egypt, before Pharaoh, before all his
servants, and in all his land,
12 and by all that mighty power and
all the great terror which Moses performed in the sight of all Israel.

6 [a]Jude 9
7 [a]Deut. 31:2 [b]Gen. 27:1; 48:10 [1]*eyesight was not weakened* [2]*reduced*
8 [a]Gen. 50:3, 10
9 [a]Is. 11:2 [b]Num. 27:18, 23
10 [a]Deut. 18:15, 18 [b]Ex. 33:11; Num. 12:8; Deut. 5:4
11 [a]Deut. 7:19

34:9–12 Moses' epitaph emphasizes God's unparalleled intimate knowledge of him.

TRUTH-IN-ACTION through Deuteronomy

Letting the LIFE of the Holy Spirit Bring Faith's Works Alive in You!

Truth Deuteronomy Teaches	Text	**Action** Deuteronomy Invites
1 Steps to Knowing God and His Ways Deut. focuses on how God brings His people to maturity. He will not allow us to skip any of the steps in the process and will make sure we complete it.	2:14	**Know** that God will always bring you back to face any area of growth you have tried to skip.
	7:22	**Do not despise** small advances. The process toward maturity is made up mostly of small steps, rather than major ones.
	32:11, 12	**Rest** in God's nurturing care. **Know** that He has committed Himself to care for you, guide you, and bring you to maturity.
2 Steps to Dynamic Devotion Deut. adds much to our understanding of being devoted to God with all of our heart and soul. It emphasizes the need for wholehearted commitment. God calls His people to pursue Him with all of their strength.	1:42	**Seek out** and **depend upon** God's presence. Without it, victory is unlikely, if not impossible.
	4:1, 2, 6–8	**Study** God's Word faithfully and carefully. **Apply** it to all you think and do. God will show His goodness and greatness.
	4:29; 6:4, 5	**Seek** God's face continually. **Do not neglect** prayer and Scripture meditation.
3 Steps to Holiness Holiness means being separated from and distinct from the world. Deut. gives much insight into the positive disciplines for building lives that are fully dedicated to God.	11:18–21	**Practice** Scripture memorization and meditation to fix God's Word in your consciousness and allow it to change your behavior.
	12:25, 28, 32	**Seek out** from the Scriptures the ways God wants you to live, and **practice them** so that your life will be pleasing to Him.
	30:15–20	**Understand** that when you choose any action, you choose its consequences as well. God cannot bless and prosper disobedience and unfaithfulness.

Truth Deuteronomy Teaches	Text	**Action** Deuteronomy Invites
4 Guidelines for Growing in Godliness Deut. gives much attention to the practices that will help you live with a continual God-consciousness, making more and more room for Him in your life. Godly people are careful to maintain proper attitudes and disciplines in their relationships. Deut. also explores how to maintain a proper regard for the authority God's Word has in life and conduct.	8:10–20	**Guard against** pride amid God's blessings. **Know** that prosperity often brings arrogance, causing us to forget that God is the source of all blessing.
	12:4, 8, 13	**Measure** your conduct and attitudes regularly according to God's Word.
	13:1–5; 18:21, 22	**Test** all ministry by God's Word. **Reject** any ministry that does not measure up to the Bible.
	21:18–21	**Give attention** to proper parental discipline. Rebellious children bring shame to their parents and dishonor the Lord.
5 Steps to Dealing with Sin It is important to deal with sins of heart and attitude before they fester, poisoning our lives and resulting in hateful actions.	29:18	**Guard against** bitterness in your own heart and among God's people. It most often causes people to turn away from God.
	31:5–8	**Turn away** from fear, faintheartedness, and discouragement. All unbelief is sin. **Trust** in God's presence. He promises to be with you always to keep you from fear.
	31:29	**Remain mindful** of your proneness to sin and turning away from God. **Acknowledge** and **rely** on God's strength and abundant provision.
6 Keys to Moral Purity Deut. reiterates that moral and sexual purity are essential to covenant loyalty to God. God's standards cannot be compromised and are usually in stark contrast to social standards of those among whom God's people dwell.	22:13–21	**Value** virginity; **do not be ashamed** of it. **Shun** today's casual attitude toward sexual relationships. **Realize** that God places a high premium on sexual purity.
	22:22	**Flee from** and **detest** adultery, and **honor** marital fidelity. **Understand** that God rejects adultery and will always judge it severely.
7 Guidelines to Gaining Victory Many scriptures point to our involvement in active spiritual combat, in which we must conduct ourselves as good soldiers. No wonder, then, that learning how to gain victory in this warfare is so important.	3:21, 22	**Remember,** the battle is the Lord's. **Trust** your battles to Him, and **rest** in His victory. He will fight for you.
	30:11–14	**Be confident** that God will supply the dynamic for all He demands. **Understand** that our life in Christ is a life of faith. **Depend** upon His constant provision.

The Book of JOSHUA

Author: Uncertain
Date: 1400–1375 B.C.
Theme: Possessing the Inheritance
Key Words: Obedience, Covenant, Courage

Author The author of the Book of Joshua cannot be determined from the Scripture. Use of the pronouns "we" and "us" in 5:1, 6 supports the theory that the author must have been an eyewitness to some of the events that occurred during this period. Joshua 24:26 suggests that the author of at least large sections was Joshua himself.

Other passages, however, could not have been written by Joshua. His death is recorded in the final chapter (24:29–32). Several other events are mentioned that did not occur until after his death: Caleb's conquest of Hebron (14:6–15); Othniel's victory (15:13–17); and the Danite migration (19:47). Parallel passages in Judges 1:10–16 and Judges 18 confirm that these events occurred after Joshua's death.

It is most probable that the book was composed in its final form by a later scribe or editor, but was founded on recorded documents written by Joshua.

Date The Book of Joshua covers some twenty-five years of Israel's history under the leadership of Joshua, Moses' assistant and successor.

The commonly accepted date of Joshua's death is about 1375 B.C. Therefore, the book covers Israel's history between 1400 B.C. and 1375 B.C. and was likely compiled shortly thereafter.

Background The book opens at the doorstep of Israel's entrance into Canaan. Politically, Canaan was divided into many city-states, each with its own autocratic government and all feuding with each other. Morally, the people were depraved; lawlessness and brutality were commonplace. Canaanite religion emphasized fertility and sex, serpent worship, and child sacrifice. The stage was set and the land ripe for conquest.

By contrast, the people of Israel had been without a homeland for four hundred years (Gen. 15:13). They had lived in bondage to Egyptian pharaohs, then had wandered aimlessly in the desert for over forty years. Yet they remained faithful, though imperfectly, to the one true God and clung to the promise He had made to their forefather, Abraham. Centuries before, God had promised to make Abraham and his descendants into a great nation and to give them Canaan as a homeland on the condition that they remain faithful and obedient to Him (Gen. 17). Now, they were at the threshold of experiencing the fulfillment of that promise.

Content The Book of Joshua is the sixth book of the Old Testament and the first in a group of books called the Former Prophets. Collectively, these books trace the development of God's kingdom in the Promised Land until the Babylonian captivity—a period of some nine hundred years. Joshua chronicles the period from Israel's entrance into Canaan through the conquest, division, and settlement of the Promised Land.

Personal Application The Book of Joshua teaches that the fulfillment of God's promises of blessing to Israel depend on their cooperation. The blessings of victory, inheritance, abundant provision, peace, and rest all came to the people of God as they obeyed Him. Faithful meditation on His Word and faithful obedience to His commands are the key to blessing and abundance (1:8). Near the end of his book, also, Joshua called the people to a life of obedience and faith (22:5).

Today, this abiding trust provides a clear foundation for our growth and blessing. As surely as blessing follows obedience, judgment follows disobedience. Achan's sin reveals the principle that no man lives to himself (ch. 7), but the sin of one affects the lives of many. God hates sin and is just as faithful to punish the disobedient as He is to bless the steadfast. These principles of blessing and cursing are object lessons for us on our pathway to maturity. Joshua's life and leadership demonstrated that spiritual maturity is not independence from God, but responsive dependence on God. To be victorious, we must surrender to Him; to lead others, we must follow Him.

The Book of Joshua provides other valuable lessons: attitudes essential for God-given victory; principles of leadership; the fatal result of pride; the relevance of memorials; God's faithfulness to His Word; examples of His miracle power.

Christ Revealed Christ is revealed in the Book of Joshua in three ways: by direct revelation, by types, and by illuminating aspects of His nature.

In 5:13–15, the triune God appeared to Joshua as the "Commander of the army of the LORD." By His appearance, Joshua was made aware that God Himself was in charge. It was Joshua's task, as ours, not so much to follow the Commander's plans as to know the Commander. We need to be on His side, not He on ours.

A type is a symbol, an object lesson. Types can be found in a person, in a religious ritual, even in a historical event. Joshua himself was a type of Christ. His name, which means "Yahweh Is Salvation," is a Hebrew equivalent to the Greek "Jesus." Joshua led the Israelites into the possession of their promised inheritance, just as Christ leads us into possession of eternal life.

The scarlet cord in Rahab's window (2:18, 21) illustrates Christ's redemptive work on the Cross. The blood-red cloth hanging in the window saved Rahab and her household from death. So, too, Christ shed His blood and hung on the Cross to save us from death.

One of the aspects of Christ's nature revealed in Joshua is that of fulfilled promise. At the end of his life, Joshua testified, "not one thing has failed of all the good things which the LORD your God spoke concerning you" (23:14). God, in His grace and faithfulness, had sustained and preserved His people by bringing them out of the wilderness and into the Land of Promise. He will do the same for us through Christ, who is The Promise.

The Holy Spirit at Work A consistent stream of the Holy Spirit's work flows through the Book of Joshua. His presence initially surfaces in 1:5, where God, knowing the overwhelming task of leading the nation Israel, provided Joshua with the promise of His ever-present Spirit.

The work of the Holy Spirit was the same then as it is now: He draws people into a saving relationship with God and accomplishes the purposes of the Father. His objective in Joshua, as in all the Old Testament, was the salvation of Israel; for it was through this nation that God chose to save the world (Is. 63:7–9).

Several characteristics of the way in which the Spirit works can be seen in Joshua. The Holy Spirit's work is *continual.* "I will not leave you nor forsake you" (1:5). The Holy Spirit is committed to accomplishing the task, no matter how long it takes. His continued presence is necessary for the success of God's plan in the lives of men. The Holy Spirit's work is *mutual.* "Only be strong and very courageous, that you may observe to do according to all the law which Moses My servant commanded you; do not turn from it to the right hand or to the left, that you may prosper wherever you go" (1:7). It has been said, "Without Him, we cannot; without us, He will not." Cooperation with the Holy Spirit is essential to victory. He empowers *us* to fulfill our calling and complete the task at hand. The Holy Spirit's work is *supernatural.* The fall of Jericho was wrought by the miraculous destruction of its walls (6:20). Victory was attained at Gibeon when the Spirit stayed the sun (10:12, 13). No true work of God, whether deliverance from bondage or possession of blessing, is accomplished without the Spirit's help.

Outline of Joshua

I. Preparing for the inheritance 1:1—5:15
- A. Through choosing the army's leader 1:1–18
  1. Joshua hears the call 1:1–9
  2. Joshua gives the command 1:10–15
  3. Joshua receives encouragement 1:16–18
- B. Through readying the army for battle 2:1—5:15
  1. By searching out the enemy's morale 2:1–24
  2. By positioning the people for battle 3:1—5:1
  3. By strengthening the troops for war 5:2–12
  4. By convincing a leader to serve 5:13–15

II. Possessing the inheritance 6:1—12:24
- A. The central territory 6:1—8:35
  1. Obedience brings conquest—Jericho 6:1–27
  2. Sin brings defeat—Achan 7:1–26
  3. Repentance brings victory—Ai 8:1–29
  4. The law brings blessing—Mount Ebal and Mount Gerizim 8:30–35
- B. The southern territory 9:1—10:43
  1. Deception brings bondage—Gibeonites 9:1–27
  2. Miracles bring deliverance—Amorites 10:1–43
- C. The northern territory 11:1–15
- D. Reviewing the conquered territories 11:16—12:24
  1. The territories 11:16–23
  2. The kings 12:1–24

III. Partaking of the inheritance 13:1—22:34
- A. Distributing the inheritance 13:1—21:45
  1. Portions yet unconquered 13:1–7
  2. Portions for Reuben, Gad, and Manasseh 13:8–33
  3. Dividing the portions west of the Jordan 14:1–5
  4. A portion for Caleb 14:6–15
  5. A portion for Judah 15:1–63
  6. A portion for Ephraim and Manasseh 16:1—17:18
  7. Portions for the remaining tribes 18:1—19:48
  8. A portion for Joshua 19:49–51
  9. Cities for refuge and the Levites 20:1—21:42
  10. Epilogue 21:43–45
- B. Discussing the future 22:1–34
  1. A blessing for the eastern tribes 22:1–9
  2. A clarification of the altar 22:10–34

IV. Joshua's final discourse and death 23:1—24:33
A. Joshua counsels the leaders 23:1–16
B. Joshua challenges the people 24:1–28
C. Joshua dies 24:29–33

God's Commission to Joshua

AFTER the death of Moses the servant of the LORD, it came to pass
that the LORD spoke to Joshua the *son
of Nun, Moses' [a]assistant, saying:
2 [a]"Moses My servant is dead. Now
therefore, arise, go over this Jordan,
you and all this people, to the land
which I am giving to them—the children of Israel.
3 [a]"Every place that the sole of your
foot will *tread upon I have given you,
as I said to Moses.
4 [a]"From the wilderness and this
Lebanon as far as the great river, the
River Euphrates, all the land of the Hittites, and to the Great Sea toward the
going down of the sun, shall be your
territory.
5 [a]"No man shall *be able to* stand before you all the days of your life;
[b]as I was with Moses, *so* [c]I will be with
you. [d]I will not leave you nor forsake
you.
5 6 [a]"Be strong and of good courage,
for to this people you shall [1]divide as
an inheritance the land which I swore
to their fathers to give them.
4 7 "Only be strong and very courageous, that you may observe to do according to all the law [a]which Moses
My servant commanded you; [b]do not
turn from it to the right hand or to the
left, that you may [1]prosper wherever
you go.
8 [a]"This Book of the Law shall not
depart from your mouth, but [b]you[1]
shall *meditate in it day and night, that
you may observe to do according to all
that is written in it. For then you will
make your way prosperous, and then
you will have good success.
9 [a]"Have I not commanded you? **Be 5**
strong and of good courage; [b]do not
be afraid, nor be dismayed, for the
LORD your God *is* with you wherever
you go."

WORD WEALTH

1:9 be strong, *chazaq* (kah-*zahk*); Strong's #2388: Be strong, courageous, valiant, manly, strengthened, established, firm, fortified, obstinate, mighty. Generally the words "strong" or "strengthened" define *chazaq*, but there is a wide range of meaning for this word, which occurs nearly 300 times in the OT; for example, "to encourage," as when David encouraged himself (literally, "made himself strong") in the Lord (1 Sam. 30:6). *Chazaq* is the root of several Hebrew names, including "Hezekiah," meaning "Strengthened by Yahweh."

The Order to Cross the Jordan

10 Then Joshua commanded the officers of the people, saying,
11 "Pass through the camp and command the people, saying, 'Prepare
provisions for yourselves, for [a]within
three days you will cross over this Jordan, to go in to possess the land which
the LORD your God is giving you to possess.'"
12 And to the Reubenites, the Gadites,
and half the tribe of Manasseh Joshua
spoke, saying,
13 "Remember [a]the word which Moses
the servant of the LORD commanded

CHAPTER 1
1 [a]Ex. 24:13; Num. 13:16; 14:6, 29, 30, 37, 38; Deut. 1:38; Acts 7:45 *See WW at Gen. 29:32.
2 [a]Num. 12:7; Deut. 34:5
3 [a]Deut. 11:24; Josh. 11:23 *See WW at Deut. 11:25.
4 [a]Gen. 15:18; Ex. 23:31; Num. 34:3–12
5 [a]Deut. 7:24 [b]Ex. 3:12 [c]Deut. 31:8, 23 [d]Deut. 31:6, 7; Heb. 13:5
6 [a]Deut. 31:7, 23 [1]*give as a possession*
7 [a]Num. 27:23; Deut. 31:7; Josh. 11:15 [b]Deut. 5:32 [1]*have success or act wisely*
8 [a]Deut. 17:18, 19; 31:24, 26; Josh. 8:34 [b]Deut. 29:9; Ps. 1:1–3 [1]*you shall be constantly in* *See WW at Ps. 1:2.
9 [a]Deut. 31:7 [b]Ps. 27:1
11 [a]Deut. 9:1; Josh. 3:17
13 [a]Num. 32:20–28

1:2–4 The land given to Abraham stretched from the Brook of Egypt (Wadi el-Arish) to the Euphrates River (Gen. 15:18). The **Great Sea** is the Mediterranean Sea. According to Ezek. 47:13–21, the Promised Land extended far beyond the boundaries ever possessed by Israel.

1:2 This Jordan: Most of the year this river was about 100 feet wide, tame, shallow, and easy to cross. In the spring, it swelled to roughly a mile wide and became a raging impasse.

1:5 I will not leave you nor forsake you is God's guarantee of success because of His presence and help. He will not allow Joshua to sink or fail.

1:6, 7 See section 5 of Truth-In-Action at the end of Josh.

1:6 Be strong and of good courage: This phrase occurs four times in this chapter (vv. 6, 7, 9, 18) and is God's encouragement to Joshua concerning his future tasks. Moses had previously received a command from God to encourage Joshua (Deut. 1:38; 3:28).

1:7, 8 See section 4 of Truth-In-Action at the end of Josh.

1:8 Meditate: The Hebrew word denotes an active recitation, a respeaking of God's words; thus they **shall not depart from your mouth.**

1:9 See section 5 of Truth-In-Action at the end of Josh.

1:11 Prepare: To this point, God's people had been provided for and had survived totally by His hand. Now God was developing in His people a mentality of personal responsibility, for the manna would soon cease.

1:12–18 The land would be conquered only by a united Israel. This interchange also links Joshua with Moses who gave the original command (Deut. 3:18–20).

you, saying, 'The LORD your God is giving you rest and is giving you this
land.'
14 "Your wives, your little ones, and
your livestock shall *remain in the land
which Moses gave you on this side of
the Jordan. But you shall [1]pass before
your brethren armed, all your mighty
men of valor, and help them,
15 "until the LORD has given your
brethren rest, as He *gave* you, and they
also have taken possession of the land
which the LORD your God is giving
them. [a]Then you shall return to the
land of your possession and enjoy it,
which Moses the LORD's servant gave
you on this side of the Jordan toward
the sunrise."
16 So they answered Joshua, saying,
"All that you command us we will do,
and wherever you send us we will go.
17 "Just as we heeded Moses in all
things, so we will heed you. Only the
LORD your God [a]be with you, as He was
with Moses.
18 "Whoever rebels against your command and does not heed your *words,
in all that you command him, shall be
put to death. Only be strong and of
good courage."

Rahab Hides the Spies

2 Now Joshua the son of Nun sent
out two men [a]from [1]Acacia Grove
to spy secretly, saying, "Go, view the
land, especially Jericho." So they went,
and [b]came to the house of a harlot
named [c]Rahab, and [2]lodged there.
2 And [a]it was told the king of Jericho,
saying, "Behold, men have come here
tonight from the children of Israel to
search out the country."

14 [1]*cross over ahead of* *See WW at Lam. 5:19. **15** [a]Josh. 22:1–4 **17** [a]1 Sam. 20:13; 1 Kin. 1:37 **18** *See WW at Deut. 1:1.

CHAPTER 2

1 [a]Num. 25:1; Josh. 3:1 [b]Heb. 11:31; James 2:25 [c]Matt. 1:5 [1]Heb. *Shittim* [2]Lit. *lay down* **2** [a]Josh. 2:22

4 [a]2 Sam. 17:19, 20 **6** [a]Ex. 1:17; 2 Sam. 17:19 **9** [a]Deut. 1:8 [b]Gen. 35:5; Ex. 23:27; Deut. 2:25; 11:25; Josh. 9:9, 10 [c]Ex. 15:15; Josh. 5:1 **10** [a]Ex. 14:21; Josh. 4:23 [b]Num. 21:21–35 [c]Deut. 20:17; Josh. 6:21 **11** [a]Ex. 15:14, 15 [b]Josh. 5:1; 7:5; Ps. 22:14; Is. 13:7 [c]Deut. 4:39 *See WW at 1 Kin. 8:23. **12** [a]1 Sam. 20:14, 15, 17

3 So the king of Jericho sent to Rahab, saying, "Bring out the men who
have come to you, who have entered
your house, for they have come to
search out all the country."
4 [a]Then the woman took the two men
and hid them. So she said, "Yes, the
men came to me, but I did not know
where they *were* from.
5 "And it happened as the gate was
being shut, when it was dark, that the
men went out. Where the men went I
do not know; pursue them quickly, for
you may overtake them."
6 (But [a]she had brought them up to
the roof and hidden them with the
stalks of flax, which she had laid in
order on the roof.)
7 Then the men pursued them by the
road to the Jordan, to the fords. And
as soon as those who pursued them
had gone out, they shut the gate.
8 Now before they lay down, she 1
came up to them on the roof,
9 and said to the men: [a]"I know that
the LORD has given you the land,
that [b]the terror of you has fallen on
us, and that all the inhabitants of
the land [c]are fainthearted because of
you.
10 "For we have heard how the LORD
[a]dried up the water of the Red Sea for
you when you came out of Egypt, and
[b]what you did to the two kings of the
Amorites who *were* on the other side
of the Jordan, Sihon and Og, whom
you [c]utterly destroyed.
11 "And as soon as we [a]heard *these
things*, [b]our hearts melted; neither did
there remain any more courage in anyone because of you, for [c]the LORD your
God, He *is* God in *heaven above and
on earth beneath.
12 "Now therefore, I beg you, [a]swear

1:18 Put to death: Strict discipline was imposed during times of hardship and war. Those who violated orders or were disloyal to Joshua were subject to severe punishment, even death.
2:1 Acacia Grove, also known as Shittim, was a site in Moab east of the Jordan River and opposite Jericho. **Secretly:** This classified mission reveals that Joshua intended to take Jericho by force and was unaware of the miracle before him. **The house of . . . Rahab** was a perfect place for the spies to stay because of the constant flow of traffic. Because it was a public house, it was common for people to come and go. God had sovereignly led them to the one person in all Jericho who believed in Him. See Heb. 11:31.
2:2 King of Jericho: The Amarna Tablets, fourteenth-century B.C. correspondence between Canaanite kings and Egyptian pharaohs, suggest that Canaan consisted of city-states, each with its own king, army, and government.
2:4–6 Lying is never justifiable; but in this case, because of Rahab's immature faith, it is understandable.
2:6 Flax was a native plant used for making cloth and candlewicks. When mature, it was soaked to separate the fibers, then dried on the rooftops. A typical **roof** in Canaan was flat and was used as a place for casual conversation and for sleeping during the heat of the summer.
2:7 Perhaps the king's messengers were so easily convinced that Rahab was telling the truth because of her respected position in this pagan society. Harlots (prostitutes) were often priestesses of the Canaanite religion, and their profession was considered honorable.
2:8–11 See section 1 of Truth-In-Action at the end of Josh.
2:8 The narrative is interrupted here to deal with Rahab's request and the details of the oath between her and the spies. It does not resume again until v. 22. This is typical of the Hebrew episodic style.
2:9–11 As soon as we heard: The Canaanites had heard of the Hebrew defeat of over 60 fortified cities east of the Jordan River.
2:12 Swear to me by the LORD: Swearing an oath was an appeal to God to witness the binding nature of a promise.

to me by the LORD, since I have shown you kindness, that you also will show kindness to [b]my father's house, and [c]give me [1]a true token,

13 "and [a]spare my father, my mother, my brothers, my sisters, and all that they have, and deliver our lives from death."

14 So the men answered her, "Our lives for yours, if none of you tell this business of ours. And it shall be, when the LORD has given us the land, that [a]we will deal kindly and truly with you."

15 Then she [a]let them down by a rope through the window, for her house *was* on the city wall; she dwelt on the wall.

16 And she said to them, "Get to the mountain, lest the pursuers *meet you. Hide there three days, until the pursuers have returned. Afterward you may go your way."

17 So the men said to her: "We *will be* [a]blameless[1] of this oath of yours which you have made us swear,

18 [a]"unless, *when* we come into the land, you bind this *line of scarlet cord in the window through which you let us down, [b]and unless you [1]bring your father, your mother, your brothers, and all your father's household to your own home.

19 "So it shall be *that* whoever goes outside the doors of your house into the street, his blood *shall be* on his own head, and we *will be* [1]guiltless. And whoever is with you in the house, [a]his [2]blood *shall be* on our head if a hand is laid on him.

20 "And if you tell this business of ours, then we will be [1]free from your oath which you made us swear."

21 Then she said, "According to your words, so *be* it." And she sent them away, and they departed. And she bound the scarlet cord in the window.

22 They departed and went to the mountain, and stayed there three days until the pursuers returned. The pursuers sought *them* all along the way, but did not find *them*.

23 So the two men returned, descended from the mountain, and crossed over; and they came to Joshua the son of Nun, and told him all that had befallen them.

24 And they said to Joshua, "Truly 1
[a]the LORD has delivered all the land into our hands, for indeed all the inhabitants of the country are fainthearted because of us."

Israel Crosses the Jordan

3 Then Joshua rose early in the morning; and they set out [a]from [1]Acacia Grove and came to the Jordan, he and all the children of Israel, and lodged there before they crossed over.

2 So it was, [a]after three days, that the officers went through the camp;

3 and they commanded the people, saying, [a]"When you see the ark of the covenant of the LORD your God, [b]and the priests, the Levites, [1]bearing it, then you shall set out from your place and go after it.

4 [a]"Yet there shall be a space between you and it, about two thousand cubits by measure. Do not come near it, that you may know the way by which you must go, for you have not **passed** *this* way before."

WORD WEALTH

3:4 passed, *'abar* (ah-*var*); Strong's #5674: To cross over, go over, go beyond, get over, go through, pass through, pass along, come over, pass beyond, transgress. *'Abar,* translated in the KJV by more than 60 English words and phrases, occurs more than 500 times. One of its meanings is "to pass from one side to the other side," pictured most easily by the crossing of a river, as in the present text. An important derivative is *'Ibri* ("Hebrew"), the ethnic description of Abraham and, by extension, of his descendants. See Gen. 14:13; Ex. 7:16; 1 Sam. 29:3. *'Ibri* has been regarded as a name for Eber's descendants. Eber was the great-grandson of Noah's son Shem, who was the father of all the Semitic peoples, and a direct ancestor of Abraham. See Gen. 11:10–26. Thus, "Hebrews"

(*cont. on next page*)

12 [b]1 Tim. 5:8 [c]Ex. 12:13; Josh. 2:18 [1]*a pledge of truth*
13 [a]Josh. 6:23–25
14 [a]Gen. 47:29; Judg. 1:24; [Matt. 5:7]
15 [a]Acts 9:25
16 *See WW at Jer. 27:18.
17 [a]Ex. 20:7 [1]*free from obligation to this oath*
18 [a]Josh. 2:12 [b]Josh. 6:23 [1]Lit. *gather* *See WW at Hos. 2:15.
19 [a]1 Kin. 2:32; Matt. 27:25 [1]*free from obligation* [2]*guilt of bloodshed*
20 [1]*free from obligation to*
24 [a]Ex. 23:31; Josh. 6:2; 21:44

CHAPTER 3

1 [a]Josh. 2:1 [1]Heb. *Shittim*
2 [a]Josh. 1:10, 11
3 [a]Num. 10:33 [b]Deut. 31:9, 25 [1]*carrying*
4 [a]Ex. 19:12

Although we do not know how Rahab came to possess faith, her request is further indication of a level of faith in the only true God.

2:15 Portions of Jericho's walls were 12 feet thick, allowing for individual dwellings to be built into them.

2:18 The **scarlet cord** would enable Israel's army to identify Rahab's house and spare all within (vv. 12, 13). The cord is symbolic of the redemptive work of Christ that saves us all. See Introduction to Joshua: Christ Revealed.

2:24 See section 1 of Truth-In-Action at the end of Josh.

3:3 The **ark** was made of acacia wood overlaid with gold and contained manna, Aaron's rod, and the Ten Commandments. It represented the presence of God and was Israel's most sacred possession.

3:4 Until now, they were led by a cloud during the day and a pillar of fire by night. Now, the ark would show them the way. The **space** of **about two thousand cubits** (about 1,000 yards) was to impress on the people the sacredness of the ark.

(*cont. from preceding page*)
would simply be one band or tribe of Semites. *'Ibri* may also refer to one who had "crossed over" the Euphrates River from the eastern lands as Abraham did.

5 And Joshua said to the people, [a]"Sanctify[1] yourselves, for tomorrow the LORD will do *wonders among you."

6 Then Joshua spoke to the *priests, saying, [a]"Take up the ark of the covenant and cross over before the people." So they took up the ark of the covenant and went before the people.

1 7 And the LORD said to Joshua, "This *day I will begin to [a]exalt[1] you in the sight of all Israel, that they may know that, [b]as I was with Moses, *so* I will be with you.

8 "You shall command [a]the priests who bear the ark of the covenant, saying, 'When you have come to the edge of the water of the Jordan, [b]you shall stand in the Jordan.' "

9 So Joshua said to the children of Israel, "Come here, and *hear the words of the LORD your God."

10 And Joshua said, "By this you shall *know that [a]the living God *is* among you, and *that* He will without fail [b]drive out from before you the [c]Canaanites and the Hittites and the Hivites and the Perizzites and the Girgashites and the Amorites and the Jebusites:

11 "Behold, the ark of the covenant of [a]the Lord of all the earth is crossing over before you into the Jordan.

12 "Now therefore, [a]take for yourselves twelve *men from the tribes of Israel, one man from every tribe.

13 "And it shall come to pass, [a]as soon as the soles of the feet of the priests who bear the ark of the LORD, [b]the Lord of all the earth, shall rest in the *waters of the Jordan, *that* the waters of the Jordan shall be cut off, the waters that come down from upstream, and they [c]shall stand as a heap."

14 So it was, when the people set out from their camp to cross over the Jordan, with the priests bearing the [a]ark of the covenant before the people,

15 and as those who bore the ark came to the Jordan, and [a]the feet of the priests who bore the ark dipped in the edge of the water (for the [b]Jordan overflows all its banks [c]during the whole time of harvest),

16 that the waters which came down from upstream stood *still, and* rose in a heap very far away [1]at Adam, the city that *is* beside [a]Zaretan. So the waters that went down [b]into the Sea of the Arabah, [c]the Salt Sea, failed, *and* were cut off; and the people crossed over opposite Jericho.

17 Then the priests who bore the ark of the covenant of the LORD stood firm on dry ground in the midst of the Jordan; [a]and all Israel crossed over on dry ground, until all the people had crossed completely over the Jordan.

The Memorial Stones

4 And it came to pass, when all the people had completely crossed [a]over the Jordan, that the LORD spoke to Joshua, saying:

2 [a]"Take for yourselves twelve men from the people, one man from every tribe,

3 "and command them, saying, 'Take for yourselves twelve stones from here, out of the midst of the Jordan, from the place where [a]the priests' feet stood firm. You shall carry them over with you and leave them in [b]the lodging place where you lodge tonight.' "

4 Then Joshua called the twelve men 4
whom he had appointed from the children of Israel, one man from every tribe;

5 and Joshua said to them: "Cross over before the ark of the LORD your God into the midst of the Jordan, and each one of you take up a stone on his shoulder, according to the number of the tribes of the children of Israel,

6 "that this may be [a]a *sign among you [b]when your children ask in time

---

5 [a]Josh. 7:13 [1]*Consecrate* *See WW at Judg. 13:19.
6 [a]Num. 4:15 *See WW at Lev. 5:6.
7 [a]Josh. 4:14 [b]Josh. 1:5, 9 [1]*make you great* *See WW at Zeph. 1:7.
8 [a]Josh. 3:3 [b]Josh. 3:17
9 *See WW at 1 Kin. 20:8.
10 [a]1 Thess. 1:9 [b]Ex. 33:2 [c]Acts 13:19 *See WW at Ex. 3:7.
11 [a]Zech. 4:14; 6:5
12 [a]Josh. 4:2, 4 *See WW at Is. 32:2.
13 [a]Josh. 3:15, 16 [b]Josh. 3:11 [c]Ps. 78:13; 114:3 *See WW at Is. 43:2.
14 [a]Acts 7:44, 45
15 [a]Josh. 3:13 [b]1 Chr. 12:15 [c]Josh. 4:18; 5:10, 12
16 [a]1 Kin. 4:12; 7:46 [b]Deut. 3:17 [c]Gen. 14:3 [1]Qr., many mss. and vss., *from Adam*
17 [a]Ex. 3:8; 6:1–8; 14:21, 22, 29; 33:1

CHAPTER 4

1 [a]Deut. 27:2
2 [a]Josh. 3:12
3 [a]Josh. 3:13 [b]Josh. 4:19, 20
6 [a]Deut. 27:2 [b]Deut. 6:20 *See WW at Ps. 86:17.

3:5 Sanctify yourselves: The people were asked to divorce themselves from anything that was unclean and to devote themselves wholly to the Lord.
3:7–13 *These verses represent a parenthetical break in the central narrative and give insight into the significance of the miracle that was about to occur.*
3:7 See section 1 of Truth-In-Action at the end of Josh.
3:7 Exalt: Through the ensuing miracle, the people came to trust that God's hand was upon their new leader Joshua.
3:14–17 The main thrust of the action is resumed, with the centrality of **the ark** again stressed. The detail concerning **the Jordan** overflowing **all its banks** enhances the miracle by focusing on the seemingly impossible situation.
3:16 Adam was about 19 miles upstream. **The Sea of the Arabah** (the Salt Sea or Dead Sea) was a continuation of the Jordan.
4:1–8 After crossing the Jordan, Joshua restated the command of 3:12. God ordered the building of two memorials: one where the priests stood in the river; the other, at the campsite.
4:4–7 See section 4 of Truth-In-Action at the end of Josh.

to come, saying, 'What do these stones *mean* to you?'

7 "Then you shall answer them that [a]the waters of the Jordan were cut off before the ark of the covenant of the LORD; when it crossed over the Jordan, the waters of the Jordan were cut off. And these stones shall be for [b]a *memorial to the children of Israel forever."

8 And the children of Israel did so, just as Joshua commanded, and took up twelve stones from the midst of the Jordan, as the LORD had spoken to Joshua, according to the number of the tribes of the children of Israel, and carried them over with them to the place where they lodged, and laid them down there.

9 Then Joshua set up twelve stones in the midst of the Jordan, in the place where the feet of the priests who bore the ark of the covenant stood; and they are there to this day.

10 So the priests who bore the ark stood in the midst of the Jordan until everything was finished that the LORD had commanded Joshua to speak to the people, according to all that Moses had commanded Joshua; and the people hurried and crossed over.

11 Then it came to pass, when all the people had completely crossed over, that the [a]ark of the LORD and the priests crossed over in the presence of the people.

12 And [a]the men of Reuben, the men of Gad, and half the tribe of Manasseh crossed over armed before the children of Israel, as Moses had spoken to them.

13 About forty thousand [1]prepared for war crossed over before the LORD for battle, to the plains of Jericho.

14 On that day the LORD [a]exalted[1] Joshua in the sight of all Israel; and they feared him, as they had feared Moses, all the days of his life.

15 Then the LORD spoke to Joshua, saying,

16 "Command the priests who bear [a]the ark of the Testimony to come up from the Jordan."

17 Joshua therefore commanded the priests, saying, "Come up from the Jordan."

18 And it came to pass, when the priests who bore the ark of the covenant of the LORD had come from the midst of the Jordan, *and* the soles of the priests' feet touched the dry land, that the waters of the Jordan returned to their place [a]and overflowed all its banks as before.

19 Now the people came up from the 1
Jordan on the tenth *day* of the first month, and they camped [a]in Gilgal on the east border of Jericho.

20 And [a]those twelve stones which they took out of the Jordan, Joshua set up in Gilgal.

21 Then he spoke to the children of Israel, saying: [a]"When your children ask their fathers in time to come, saying, 'What *are* these stones?'

22 "then you shall let your children know, saying, [a]'Israel crossed over this Jordan on [b]dry land';

23 "for the LORD your *God dried up the waters of the Jordan before you until you had crossed over, as the LORD your God did to the Red Sea, [a]which He dried up before us until we had crossed over,

24 [a]"that all the peoples of the earth may know the **hand** of the LORD, that it *is* [b]mighty, that you may [c]fear the LORD your God [1]forever."

7 [a]Josh. 3:13, 16 [b]Ex. 12:14; Num. 16:40 *See WW at Ex. 39:7.
11 [a]Josh. 3:11; 6:11
12 [a]Num. 32:17, 20, 27, 28; Josh. 1:14
13 [1]*equipped*
14 [a]Josh. 3:7; 1 Chr. 29:25 [1]*made Joshua great*
16 [a]Ex. 25:16, 22
18 [a]Josh. 3:15; 1 Chr. 12:15
19 [a]Josh. 5:9
20 [a]Deut. 11:30; Josh. 4:3; 5:9, 10
21 [a]Josh. 4:6
22 [a]Ex. 12:26, 27; 13:8–14; Deut. 26:5–9 [b]Josh. 3:17
23 [a]Ex. 14:21 *See WW at 2 Kin. 19:15.
24 [a]1 Kin. 8:42; 2 Kin. 19:19; Ps. 106:8 [b]Ex. 15:16; 1 Chr. 29:12; Ps. 89:13 [c]Ex. 14:31; Deut. 6:2; Ps. 76:7; Jer. 10:7 [1]Lit. *all days*

WORD WEALTH

4:24 hand, *yad* (*yahd*); Strong's #3027: The hand; means by which a work is accomplished; strength, power. This noun occurs more than 1,500 times in the OT and is found in a great number of figures of speech. For instance, to be "given into the hands" of someone denotes coming under his authority; being rescued "out of the hands" of someone is descriptive of deliverance and freedom. A "high hand" may describe either haughtiness or triumphant rejoicing. One interesting derivative of this noun is the verb *yadah,*

(cont. on next page)

4:9 To this day means the time when the Book of Joshua was written.

4:13 About one-third of the men went to war, leaving 70,580 men in the territories east of the Jordan for protection and defense (Num. 26:2, 7, 18, 34).

4:15–18 This passage expands upon the events of 4:11. The ark was taken out of the Jordan with as much ceremony as its entry to fix in the people's minds the sacred value of the ark and the significance of the miracle.

4:16 The Testimony, in Hebrew, is used only of God, and refers to the two tablets of stone contained in **the ark.** "Testimony" and "covenant" are used interchangeably.

4:19–24 See section 1 of Truth-In-Action at the end of Josh.

4:19 The tenth *day* of the first month (March–April) was traditionally the day when the paschal lamb was selected to be slain—four days before the annual observance of Passover (see 5:10). God chose this significant day to remind the people of their entry into the Promised Land and the completion of His promise.

4:20–24 Building monuments was a common practice in OT times. The monuments were visible reminders to coming generations of the power of God.

(cont. from preceding page)
generally translated "thank" or "praise"; its original meaning was probably "to praise by lifting up the hand."

The Second Generation Circumcised

5 So it was, when all the kings of the Amorites who *were* on the west side of the Jordan, and all the kings of the Canaanites [a]who *were* by the sea, [b]heard that the LORD had dried up the waters of the Jordan from before the children of Israel until [1]we had crossed over, that [2]their heart melted; [c]and there was no spirit in them any longer because of the children of Israel.

4 2 At that time the LORD said to Joshua, "Make [a]flint knives for yourself, and circumcise the sons of Israel again the second time."

3 So Joshua made flint knives for himself, and circumcised the sons of Israel at [1]the hill of the foreskins.

4 And this *is* the reason why Joshua circumcised them: [a]All the people who came out of Egypt *who were* males, all the men of war, had died in the wilderness on the way, after they had come out of Egypt.

5 For all the people who came out had been circumcised, but all the people born in the wilderness, on the way as they came out of Egypt, had not been circumcised.

6 For the children of Israel walked [a]forty years in the wilderness, till all the people *who were* men of war, who came out of Egypt, were [1]consumed, because they did not obey the voice of the LORD—to whom the LORD swore that [b]He would not show them the land which the LORD had sworn to their fathers that He would give us, [c]"a land flowing with milk and honey."

7 Then Joshua circumcised [a]their sons *whom* He raised up in their place; for they were uncircumcised, because they had not been circumcised on the way.

8 So it was, when they had finished circumcising all the people, that they stayed in their places in the camp [a]till they were healed.

9 Then the LORD said to Joshua, "This day I have *rolled away [a]the reproach of Egypt from you." Therefore the name of the place is called [b]Gilgal[1] to this day.

10 Now the children of Israel camped in Gilgal, and kept the Passover [a]on the fourteenth day of the month at twilight on the plains of Jericho.

11 And they ate of the produce of the land on the day after the Passover, unleavened bread and [1]parched grain, on the very same day.

12 Then [a]the manna ceased on the day after they had eaten the produce of the land; and the children of Israel no longer had manna, but they ate the food of the land of Canaan that year.

The Commander of the Army of the LORD

13 And it came to pass, when Joshua was by Jericho, that he lifted his eyes and looked, and behold, [a]a Man stood opposite him [b]with His sword drawn in His hand. And Joshua went to Him and said to Him, "*Are* You for us or for our adversaries?"

14 So He said, "No, but *as* Commander 7
of the *army of the LORD I have now come." And Joshua [a]fell on his face to the earth and [b]worshiped, and said to Him, "What does my Lord say to His servant?"

15 Then the Commander of the LORD's army said to Joshua, [a]"Take your san-

CHAPTER 5

1 [a]Num. 13:29 [b]Ex. 15:14, 15 [c]Josh. 2:10, 11; 9:9; 1 Kin. 10:5 [1]So with Kt.; Qr., some Heb. mss. and editions, LXX, Syr., Tg., Vg. *they* [2]*their courage failed*
2 [a]Ex. 4:25
3 [1]Heb. *Gibeath Haaraloth*
4 [a]Num. 14:29; 26:64, 65; Deut. 2:14–16
6 [a]Num. 14:33; Deut. 1:3; 29:5 [b]Num. 14:23, 29–35; 26:23–65; Heb. 3:11 [c]Ex. 3:8 [1]*destroyed*
7 [a]Num. 14:31; Deut. 1:39
8 [a]Gen. 34:25
9 [a]Gen. 34:14 [b]Josh. 4:19 [1]Lit. *Rolling* *See WW at Prov. 16:3.
10 [a]Ex. 12:6; Num. 9:5
11 [1]*roasted*
12 [a]Ex. 16:35
13 [a]Gen. 18:1, 2; 32:24, 30; Ex. 23:23; Num. 22:31; Zech. 1:8; Acts 1:10 [b]Num. 22:23; 1 Chr. 21:16
14 [a]Gen. 17:3; Num. 20:6 [b]Ex. 34:8 *See WW at Ps. 68:11.
15 [a]Ex. 3:5; Acts 7:33

5:1 We had crossed: Use of the pronoun "we" brings supporting evidence to the viewpoint that Joshua was the author of at least parts of this book. **Their heart melted:** God fulfilled His promise recorded in Ex. 23:27.

5:2–9 See section 4 of Truth-In-Action at the end of Josh.

5:2–8 Circumcise: Circumcision began as a sign of the covenant between God and Abraham (Gen. 17). Its practice, however, had been in suspension for 40 years, most likely as another sign of apathy and disobedience to the Law. The cutting away of the foreskin of the male sex organ was to mark them as a people in covenant with God. This outward sign was meaningless, however, unless coupled with an inward severing of fleshly deeds or "circumcision of the heart" (Deut. 30:6).

5:9 Although it is not clear why uncircumcision was associated with **the reproach of Egypt,** what is clear is that their circumcision cut all ties they had to Egyptian slavery. Their bondage was completely removed.

5:10 The people demonstrated their obedience and faith in God by celebrating the **Passover** (Ex. 12:1–28) to remind them that the inheritance of the Promised Land would be by simple faith in the blood of the Lamb.

5:12 Manna ceased: A manna miracle had been provided 6 days a week for 40 years. Upon entering the land, God's promise of provision would take on a new form. While God would still be their Provider, they would learn personal responsibility from working the land and eating from it.

5:13–15 This private encounter with heaven preceded Joshua's public role at Jericho. He discovered that there is a Commander, mightier than he, who stands ready to lead the nation in conquest. (See Introduction to Joshua: Christ Revealed.) **Take your sandal off your foot:** Like removing a hat this was a sign of humility and respect.

5:14, 15 See section 7 of Truth-In-Action at the end of Josh.

dal off your foot, for the place where
you stand *is* holy." And Joshua did so.

The Destruction of Jericho

6 Now [a]Jericho was securely shut up
because of the children of Israel;
none went out, and none came in.
2 And the LORD said to Joshua: "See!
[a]I have given Jericho into your hand,
its [b]king, *and* the mighty men of valor.
3 "You shall march around the city,
all *you* men of war; you shall go all
around the city once. This you shall do
six days.
4 "And seven priests shall bear seven
[a]trumpets of rams' horns before the
ark. But the seventh day you shall
march around the city [b]seven times,
and [c]the priests shall *blow the trumpets.
5 "It shall come to pass, when they
make a long *blast* with the ram's *horn,
and when you hear the sound of the
*trumpet, that all the people shall shout
with a *great shout; then the wall of
the city will fall down flat. And the people shall go up every man straight before him."
6 Then Joshua the son of Nun called
the priests and said to them, "Take up
the ark of the covenant, and let seven
priests bear seven trumpets of rams'
horns before the ark of the LORD."
7 And he said to the people, "Proceed,
and march around the city, and let him
who is armed advance before the ark
of the LORD."
8 So it was, when Joshua had spoken
to the people, that the seven priests
bearing the seven trumpets of rams'
horns before the LORD advanced and
blew the trumpets, and the ark of the
covenant of the LORD followed them.
9 The armed men went before the
priests who blew the trumpets, [a]and
the rear guard came after the ark,
while *the priests* continued blowing
the trumpets.
10 Now Joshua had commanded the
people, saying, "You shall not shout or
make any noise with your voice, nor
shall a word proceed out of your
mouth, until the day I say to you,
'Shout!' Then you shall shout."

CHAPTER 6
1 [a]Josh. 2:1
2 [a]Josh. 2:9, 24; 8:1 [b]Deut. 7:24
4 [a]Lev. 25:9; Judg. 7:16, 22 [b]1 Kin. 18:43; 2 Kin. 4:35; 5:10 [c]Num. 10:8 *See WW at Ps. 47:1.
5 *See WW at Ezek. 29:21. • See WW at Hos. 8:1. • See WW at Ezra 3:11.
9 [a]Num. 10:25

KINGDOM DYNAMICS

6:10 Silencing Unbelief, FAITH'S CONFESSION. Many texts in God's Word instruct us to "wait on God," to stand still, to be silent before Him (Moses, Ex. 14:13, 14; Jehoshaphat, 2 Chr. 20:15–17; David, Ps. 37:7, 8). In this text, Joshua commands the children of Israel to maintain total silence as they walk around the city of Jericho. The memory that Israel's 40-year punishment in the wilderness was a result of the people's murmuring in unbelief was doubtless in Joshua's mind. At that time, the spies had returned with a report motivated by what man sees without Holy Spirit-given vision. Their unbelief that they could take the land had sealed their fate in the wilderness.

Now, with the lessons of history in mind, Joshua's directive to keep silent is a precaution that teaches us. When facing great challenges, do not permit your lips to speak unbelieving words. Prohibit demoralizing speech from your lips. Words can bind up or set free, hence the order to silence! Later, they would see the salvation of the Lord following their shout of triumph (6:20).

We cannot help what we see and hear, but our refusal to speak doubt and fear will keep our hearts more inclined to what God can do, rather than to what we cannot (see Prov. 30:32).
(Num. 13:30; 14:6–9/2 Chr. 6:24–31) R.H.

11 So he had [a]the ark of the LORD circle the city, going around *it* once. Then
they came into the camp and [1]lodged
in the camp.
12 And Joshua rose early in the morning, [a]and the priests took up the ark
of the LORD.
13 Then seven priests bearing seven
trumpets of rams' horns before the ark
of the LORD went on continually and
blew with the trumpets. And the armed
men went before them. But the rear
guard came after the ark of the LORD,
while *the priests* continued blowing
the trumpets.
14 And the second day they marched
around the city once and returned to
the camp. So they did six days.
15 But it came to pass on the seventh
day that they rose early, about the
dawning of the day, and marched

11 [a]Josh. 4:11 [1]*spent the night*
12 [a]Deut. 31:25

6:1, 2 Jericho is one of the most ancient cities on Earth. It is first mentioned in the biblical record in Num. 22:1. The walls of this fortified city enclosed only about seven acres; thus, a large portion of its people lived in the surrounding countryside. They retreated inside the walls, not wishing to fight **Israel** because of their fear.

6:8–15 God's unconventional strategy included waiting, walking, and no talking. This peculiar march, day after day with no apparent result, was a test of their obedience and trust (Ps. 37:34). It also demonstrates the power of worship as seen in the leading of the ark and the continual trumpet blowing.

6:15 The number **seven** symbolized perfection and the mighty work of God. Its first mention in the biblical record is at creation (Gen. 2:2, 3).

around the city seven times in the same
manner. On that day only they
marched around the city seven times.
16 And the seventh time it happened,
when the priests blew the trumpets, that Joshua said to the people:
"Shout, for the LORD has given you
the city!
17 "Now the city shall be [a]doomed by
the LORD to destruction, it and all who
are in it. Only [b]Rahab the harlot shall
live, she and all who *are* with her in
the house, because [c]she hid the messengers that we sent.
3 18 "And you, [a]by all means abstain
from the accursed things, lest you become accursed when you take of the
accursed things, and make the camp
of Israel a curse, [b]and trouble it.
19 "But all the silver and gold, and vessels of bronze and iron, *are* [1]conse-
crated to the LORD; they [2]shall come
into the treasury of the LORD."
20 So the people shouted when *the
priests* blew the trumpets. And it happened when the people heard the
sound of the trumpet, and the people
shouted with a great shout, that
[a]the wall fell down flat. Then the people *went up into the city, every man
straight before him, and they took the
city.
21 And they [a]utterly destroyed all that
was in the city, both man and woman,
young and old, ox and sheep and donkey, with the edge of the sword.
22 But Joshua had said to the two men
who had spied out the country, "Go
into the harlot's house, and from there
bring out the woman and all that she
has, [a]as you swore to her."
23 And the young men who had been
spies went in and brought out Rahab,
[a]her father, her mother, her brothers,
and all that she had. So they brought
out all her relatives and left them outside the camp of Israel.
24 But they burned the city and all that
was in it with fire. Only the silver and
gold, and the vessels of bronze and

17 [a]Deut. 13:17; Josh. 7:1 [b]Josh. 2:1; Matt. 1:5 [c]Josh. 2:4, 6
18 [a]Deut. 7:26 [b]Josh. 7:1, 12, 25; 1 Kin. 18:17, 18; [Jon. 1:12]
19 [1]*set apart* [2]*shall go*
20 [a]Heb. 11:30 *See WW at Ex. 19:20.
21 [a]Deut. 7:2; 20:16, 17
22 [a]Josh. 2:12–19; Heb. 11:31
23 [a]Josh. 2:13
25 [a][Matt. 1:5]
26 [a]1 Kin. 16:34 [1]*warned*

CHAPTER 7

1 [a]Josh. 7:20, 21 [b]Josh. 6:17–19 [c]Josh. 22:20 [1]*acted unfaithfully* [2]*devoted* [3]*Zimri*, 1 Chr. 2:6
4 [a]Lev. 26:17; Deut. 28:25
5 [a]Lev. 26:36; Josh. 2:9, 11 [1]*the people's courage failed*

iron, they put into the treasury of the
house of the LORD.
25 And Joshua spared Rahab the harlot, her father's household, and all that
she had. So [a]she dwells in Israel to
this day, because she hid the messengers whom Joshua sent to spy out Jericho.
26 Then Joshua [1]charged *them* at that
time, saying, [a]"Cursed *be* the man before the LORD who rises up and builds
this city Jericho; he shall lay its foundation with his firstborn, and with his
youngest he shall set up its gates."
27 So the LORD was with Joshua, and
his fame spread throughout all the
country.

Defeat at Ai

7 But the children of Israel [1]com-
mitted a [a]trespass regarding the
[b]accursed[2] things, for [c]Achan the son
of Carmi, the son of [3]Zabdi, the son
of Zerah, of the tribe of Judah, took of
the accursed things; so the anger of
the LORD burned against the children
of Israel.
2 Now Joshua sent men from Jericho
to Ai, which *is* beside Beth Aven, on
the east side of Bethel, and spoke to
them, saying, "Go up and spy out the
country." So the men went up and
spied out Ai.
3 And they returned to Joshua and
said to him, "Do not let all the people
go up, but let about two or three thousand men go up and attack Ai. Do not
weary all the people there, for *the people of Ai are* few."
4 So about three thousand men went
up there from the people, [a]but they fled
before the men of Ai.
5 And the men of Ai struck down
about thirty-six men, for they chased
them *from* before the gate as far as
Shebarim, and struck them down on
the descent; therefore [a]the[1] hearts of
the people melted and became like water.

6:17–19 The firstfruits of the harvest were to be set apart for God (Lev. 23:10). So, too, the spoils of Jericho, being the firstfruits of conquest, must be totally devoted to God (**abstain from the accursed things**).
6:18, 19 See section 3 of Truth-In-Action at the end of Josh.
6:21 Utterly destroyed: The Canaanite civilization was so totally corrupt that coexisting with them would have been a serious threat to the survival and spiritual welfare of the Hebrew nation. Israel here is God's instrument of judgment against those who refuse to honor Him.
6:22–25 As promised (2:12–21), not only did God spare **Rahab** and her family when the walls collapsed, but also during the rampage (2:12–21). Rahab was the great-great-grandmother of David (Matt. 1:5).
6:26, 27 The curse was to invoke God's woe on someone. The fulfillment of this curse comes over 500 years later in the death of Abiram, son of Hiel of Bethel (1 Kin. 16:34).
7:1–26 The narrative of this chapter moves between two stories: one of Achan's sin, the other of the defeat at Ai.
7:1 Joshua had pronounced a divine ban on the spoils of Jericho (6:18). See note on Deut. 2:34, 35. Achan alone defied the ban, but his disobedience is seen as that of the whole nation because of the OT principle of corporate solidarity. No person sins alone.
7:2–5 Ai was a small, fortified city in the mountainous region northwest of Jericho.

6 Then Joshua [a]tore his clothes, and fell to the earth on his face before the ark of the LORD until evening, he and the elders of Israel; and they [b]put dust on their heads.

7 And Joshua said, "Alas, Lord [1]GOD, [a]why have You brought this people over the Jordan at all—to deliver us into the hand of the Amorites, to destroy us? Oh, that we had been content, and dwelt on the other side of the Jordan!

8 "O Lord, what shall I say when Israel turns its [1]back before its enemies?

9 "For the Canaanites and all the inhabitants of the land will hear *it,* and surround us, and [a]cut off our name from the earth. Then [b]what will You do for Your great name?"

The Sin of Achan

6 **10** So the LORD said to Joshua: "Get up! Why do you lie thus on your face?

11 "Israel has sinned, and they have also transgressed My covenant which I commanded them. [a]For they have even taken some of the [1]accursed things, and have both stolen and [b]deceived; and they have also put *it* among their own stuff.

12 [a]"Therefore the children of Israel could not stand before their enemies, *but* turned *their* backs before their enemies, because [b]they have become doomed to destruction. Neither will I be with you anymore, unless you destroy the accursed from among you.

13 "Get up, [a]sanctify[1] the people, and say, [b]'Sanctify yourselves for tomorrow, because thus says the LORD God of Israel: "*There is* an accursed thing in your midst, O Israel; you cannot stand before your enemies until you take away the accursed thing from among you."

14 'In the morning therefore you shall be brought according to your tribes. And it shall be *that* the tribe which [a]the LORD takes shall come according to families; and the family which the LORD takes shall come by households; and the household which the LORD takes shall come *man by man.

15 [a]'Then it shall be *that* he who is taken with the accursed thing shall be burned with fire, he and all that he has, because he has [b]transgressed[1] the covenant of the LORD, and because he [c]has done a disgraceful thing in Israel.' "

16 So Joshua rose early in the morning and brought Israel by their tribes, and the tribe of Judah was taken.

17 He brought the clan of Judah, and he took the family of the Zarhites; and he brought the family of the Zarhites man by man, and Zabdi was taken.

18 Then he brought his household man by man, and Achan the son of Carmi, the son of Zabdi, the son of Zerah, of the tribe of Judah, [a]was taken.

19 Now Joshua said to Achan, "My son, I beg you, [a]give glory to the LORD God of Israel, [b]and make confession to Him, and [c]tell me now what you have done; do not hide *it* from me."

20 And Achan answered Joshua and said, "Indeed [a]I have sinned against the LORD God of Israel, and this is what I have done:

21 "When I saw among the spoils a beautiful Babylonian garment, two hundred shekels of silver, and a wedge of gold weighing fifty shekels, I [1]coveted them and took them. And there they are, hidden in the earth in the midst of my tent, with the silver under it."

22 So Joshua sent messengers, and they ran to the tent; and there it was, hidden in his tent, with the silver under it.

23 And they took them from the midst of the tent, brought them to Joshua and to all the children of Israel, and laid them out before the LORD.

24 Then Joshua, and all Israel with him, took Achan the son of Zerah, the silver, the garment, the wedge of gold, his sons, his daughters, his oxen, his donkeys, his sheep, his tent, and [a]all that he had, and they brought them to [b]the Valley of Achor.

25 And Joshua said, [a]"Why have you

6 [a]Gen. 37:29, 34 [b]1 Sam. 4:12
7 [a]Ex. 17:3; Num. 21:5 [1]Heb. *YHWH, LORD*
8 [1]Lit. *neck*
9 [a]Deut. 32:26 [b]Ex. 32:12; Num. 14:13
11 [a]Josh. 6:17–19 [b]Acts 5:1, 2 [1]*devoted*
12 [a]Judg. 2:14 [b]Deut. 7:26; [Hag. 2:13, 14]
13 [a]Ex. 19:10 [b]Josh. 3:5 [1]*set apart*
14 [a][Prov. 16:33] *See WW at Jer. 31:22.
15 [a]1 Sam. 14:38, 39 [b]Josh. 7:11 [c]Gen. 34:7; Judg. 20:6 [1]*overstepped*
18 [a]1 Sam. 14:42
19 [a]1 Sam. 6:5; Jer. 13:16; John 9:24 [b]Num. 5:6, 7; 2 Chr. 30:22; Ezra 10:10, 11; Ps. 32:5; Prov. 28:13; Jer. 3:12, 13; Dan. 9:4 [c]1 Sam. 14:43
20 [a]Num. 22:34; 1 Sam. 15:24
21 [1]*desired*
24 [a]Num. 16:32, 33; Dan. 6:24 [b]Josh. 7:26; 15:7
25 [a]Josh. 6:18; 1 Chr. 2:7; [Gal. 5:12]

7:6 Tore his clothes: This was a customary, outward expression of deep sorrow and grief, as was sprinkling dirt on the head.

7:10–13 See section 6 of Truth-In-Action at the end of Josh.

7:10–12 The breach of their covenant (6:17–19) through Achan's trespass was the cause of their being **doomed to destruction.** The people were promised success and prosperity, but only if they acted in obedience (1:8, 9).

7:13–15 Sanctify the people: In order that the people might be consecrated to God, they were to separate themselves from the offender.

7:16 By their tribes: The Hebrew nation was a tribal society. The 12 tribes of Israel were descended from the 12 sons of Jacob and consisted of many clans and families.

7:24 Achor means "Trouble." It was likely named after this event as a reminder of Achan's trouble.

7:25 They burned them: Achan's family was destroyed because of a common knowledge of the sin as well as the principle of corporate guilt (Deut. 5:9).

troubled us? The LORD will trouble you
this day." [b]So all Israel stoned him
with stones; and they burned them
with fire after they had stoned them
with stones.
26 Then they [a]raised over him a great
heap of stones, still there to this day.
So [b]the LORD turned from the fierceness of His anger. Therefore the name
of that place has been called [c]the Valley of [1]Achor to this day.

The Fall of Ai

8 Now the LORD said to Joshua:
[a]"Do not be afraid, nor be dismayed; take all the people of war with
you, and arise, go up to Ai. See,
[b]I have given into your hand the king
of Ai, his people, his city, and his
land.
2 "And you shall do to Ai and its king
as you did to [a]Jericho and its king.
Only [b]its spoil and its cattle you shall
take as booty for yourselves. Lay an
ambush for the city behind it."
3 So Joshua arose, and all the people of war, to go up against Ai; and
Joshua *chose thirty thousand mighty
men of valor and sent them away by
night.
4 And he commanded them, saying:
"Behold, [a]you shall lie in ambush
against the city, behind the city. Do not
go very far from the city, but all of you
be ready.
5 "Then I and all the people who *are*
with me will approach the city; and it
will come about, when they come out
against us as at the first, that [a]we shall
flee before them.
6 "For they will come out after us till
we have drawn them from the city, for
they will say, '*They are* fleeing before
us as at the first.' Therefore we will flee
before them.
7 "Then you shall rise from the ambush and *seize the city, for the LORD
your God will deliver it into your
hand.
8 "And it will be, when you have
taken the city, *that* you shall set the
city on fire. According to the commandment of the LORD you shall do.
[a]See, I have commanded you."

25 [b]Deut. 17:5
26 [a]Josh. 8:29; 2 Sam. 18:17; Lam. 3:53 [b]Deut. 13:17 [c]Josh. 7:24; Is. 65:10; Hos. 2:15 [1]Lit. *Trouble*

CHAPTER 8

1 [a]Deut. 1:21; 7:18; 31:8; Josh. 1:9; 10:8 [b]Josh. 6:2
2 [a]Josh. 6:21 [b]Deut. 20:14; Josh. 8:27
3 *See WW at 1 Kin. 11:34.
4 [a]Judg. 20:29
5 [a]Josh. 7:5; Judg. 20:32
7 *See WW at Deut. 8:1.
8 [a]2 Sam. 13:28
11 [a]Josh. 8:5
12 [1]Ai
14 [a]Judg. 20:34; Eccl. 9:12 *See WW at Num. 9:2.
15 [a]Judg. 20:36
17 *See WW at Jer. 40:4.

9 Joshua therefore sent them out; and
they went to lie in ambush, and stayed
between Bethel and Ai, on the west
side of Ai; but Joshua lodged that night
among the people.
10 Then Joshua rose up early in the
morning and mustered the people, and
went up, he and the elders of Israel,
before the people to Ai.
11 [a]And all the people of war who
were with him went up and drew near;
and they came before the city and
camped on the north side of Ai. Now
a valley *lay* between them and Ai.
12 So he took about five thousand men
and set them in ambush between
Bethel and Ai, on the west side of [1]the
city.
13 And when they had set the people,
all the army that *was* on the north of
the city, and its rear guard on the west
of the city, Joshua went that night into
the midst of the valley.
14 Now it happened, when the king of
Ai saw *it*, that the men of the city hurried and rose early and went out
against Israel to battle, he and all his
people, at an *appointed place before
the plain. But he [a]did not know that
there was an ambush against him behind the city.
15 And Joshua and all Israel [a]made as
if they were beaten before them, and
fled by the way of the wilderness.
16 So all the people who *were* in Ai
were called together to pursue them.
And they pursued Joshua and were
drawn away from the city.
17 There was not a man left in Ai or
Bethel who did not go out after Israel.
So they left the city *open and pursued
Israel.
18 Then the LORD said to Joshua,
"Stretch out the spear that *is* in your
hand toward Ai, for I will give it into
your hand." And Joshua stretched out
the spear that *was* in his hand toward
the city.
19 So *those in* ambush arose quickly
out of their place; they ran as soon as
he had stretched out his hand, and they
entered the city and took it, and hurried to set the city on fire.
20 And when the men of Ai looked behind them, they saw, and behold, the

7:26 The **great heap of stones** served as a reminder that repentance brings restoration.
8:2 Israel was to learn that obedience brings reward. God told them they could **take** of the **spoil** at Ai, which they had been unable to do at **Jericho.**
8:10 The **elders of Israel** were the heads of clans and families representing the nation on special occasions.
8:12 These 5,000 **men** were a separate contingent from the 30,000 of v. 3 and were dispatched to **ambush** any reinforcements from **Bethel.**
8:13, 14 Joshua's nocturnal tactics were visible enough to stir the **king of Ai** who **rose early** to challenge **Israel.**
8:17 **Bethel** and **Ai** were less than 2 miles apart, but only Ai was conquered. Bethel was taken later (12:16).

smoke of the city ascended to heaven. So they had no power to flee this way or that way, and the people who had fled to the wilderness turned back on the pursuers.

21 Now when Joshua and all Israel saw that the ambush had taken the city and that the smoke of the city ascended, they turned back and struck down the men of Ai.

22 Then the others came out of the city against them; so they were *caught* in the midst of Israel, some on this side and some on that side. And they struck them down, so that they [a]let none of them remain or escape.

23 But the king of Ai they took alive, and brought him to Joshua.

24 And it came to pass when Israel had made an end of slaying all the inhabitants of Ai in the field, in the wilderness where they pursued them, and when they all had fallen by the edge of the sword until they were consumed, that all the Israelites returned to Ai and struck it with the edge of the sword.

25 So it was *that* all who fell that day, both men and women, *were* twelve thousand—all the people of Ai.

26 For Joshua did not draw back his hand, with which he stretched out the spear, until he had [a]utterly destroyed all the inhabitants of Ai.

27 [a]Only the livestock and the spoil of that city Israel took as booty for themselves, according to the word of the LORD which He had [b]commanded Joshua.

28 So Joshua burned Ai and made it [a]a heap forever, a desolation to this day.

29 [a]And the king of Ai he hanged on a tree until evening. [b]And as soon as the sun was down, Joshua commanded that they should take his corpse down from the tree, cast it at the entrance of the gate of the city, and [c]raise over it a great heap of stones *that remains* to this day.

22 [a]Deut. 7:2
26 [a]Josh. 6:21
27 [a]Num. 31:22, 26 [b]Josh. 8:2
28 [a]Deut. 13:16
29 [a]Josh. 10:26 [b]Deut. 21:22, 23; Josh. 10:27 [c]Josh. 7:26; 10:27
30 [a]Deut. 27:4–8 *See WW at 2 Kin. 12:9.
31 [a]Ex. 20:25; Deut. 27:5, 6 [b]Ex. 20:24
32 [a]Deut. 27:2, 3, 8
33 [a]Deut. 31:9, 25 [b]Deut. 31:12 [c]Deut. 11:29; 27:12 *See WW at Ps. 145:2.
34 [a]Deut. 31:11; Neh. 8:3 [b]Deut. 28:2, 15, 45; 29:20, 21; 30:19 [c]Josh. 1:8
35 [a]Ex. 12:38; Deut. 31:12 [b]Josh. 8:33

CHAPTER 9
1 [a]Num. 13:29; Josh. 3:10 [b]Num. 34:6 [c]Ex. 3:17; 23:23
2 [a]Josh. 10:5; Ps. 83:3, 5

Joshua Renews the Covenant

30 Now Joshua built an *altar to the LORD God of Israel [a]in Mount Ebal,

31 as Moses the servant of the LORD had commanded the children of Israel, as it is written in the Book of the Law of Moses: [a]"an altar of whole stones over which no man has wielded an iron *tool*." And [b]they offered on it burnt offerings to the LORD, and sacrificed peace offerings.

32 And there, in the presence of the children of Israel, [a]he wrote on the stones a copy of the law of Moses, which he had written.

33 Then all Israel, with their elders and officers and judges, stood on either side of the ark before the priests, the Levites, [a]who bore the ark of the covenant of the LORD, [b]the stranger as well as he who was born among them. Half of them *were* in front of Mount Gerizim and half of them in front of Mount Ebal, [c]as Moses the servant of the LORD had commanded before, that they should *bless the people of Israel.

34 And afterward [a]he read all the 4
words of the law, [b]the blessings and
the cursings, according to all that is
written in the [c]Book of the Law.

35 There was not a word of all that Moses had commanded which Joshua did not read before all the assembly of Israel, [a]with the women, the little ones, [b]and the strangers who were living among them.

The Treaty with the Gibeonites

9 And it came to pass when [a]all the kings who *were* on this side of the Jordan, in the hills and in the lowland and in all the coasts of [b]the Great Sea toward Lebanon—[c]the Hittite, the Amorite, the Canaanite, the Perizzite, the Hivite, and the Jebusite—heard *about it,*

2 that they [a]gathered together to fight

8:23 The fact that they took **the king of Ai . . . alive** was not a violation of God's command (v. 2); rather, it was to emphasize his death by hanging him on a tree (v. 29). Displaying a body by hanging it was an indication of God's curse (Deut. 21:22, 23).

8:30–35 Mount Ebal was about 20 miles north of Ai. In accordance with the Law of Moses, Joshua built an altar to honor God and renew the covenant (Deut. 27:1–10).

8:31, 32 The **burnt offerings** were all for God. Animals were killed, drained of their blood, then burned to ashes on the altar. They represented the total consecrating of self to God. (See Lev. 1:1–17.) The **peace offerings** were also animal sacrifices, but the meat was eaten by the priests and the people. They symbolized gratitude, commitment to God, and fellowship with Him (Lev. 7:11–18).

8:34, 35 See section 4 of Truth-In-Action at the end of Josh.

8:34 The blessings and the cursings were integral to the covenant relationship. The blessings would come if the covenant was obeyed; the cursings, if not. See Deut. 11:26–28.

9:1, 2 These two verses introduce the events of chs. 9—11. This chapter reveals two different reactions of the Canaanites to God and His people. One was to attempt to unify the otherwise divided cities and take **Israel** by force. The other was to use deception and diplomacy to unite with Israel.

with Joshua and Israel with one [1]ac-
cord.
3 But when the inhabitants of [a]Gib-
eon [b]heard what Joshua had done to
Jericho and Ai,
4 they worked craftily, and went and
[1]pretended to be ambassadors. And
they took old sacks on their donkeys,
old wineskins torn and [2]mended,
5 old and patched sandals on their
feet, and old garments on themselves;
and all the bread of their provision was
dry *and* moldy.
6 And they went to Joshua, [a]to the
camp at Gilgal, and said to him and
to the men of Israel, "We have come
from a far country; now therefore,
make a [1]covenant with us."
7 Then the men of Israel said to the
[a]Hivites, "Perhaps you dwell among
us; so [b]how can we make a covenant
with you?"
8 But they said to Joshua, [a]"We *are*
your servants." And Joshua said to
them, "Who *are* you, and where do you
come from?"
9 So they said to him: [a]"From a very
far country your servants have come,
because of the name of the LORD your
God; for we have [b]heard of His fame,
and all that He did in Egypt,
10 "and [a]all that He did to the two
kings of the Amorites who *were* beyond the Jordan—to Sihon king of
Heshbon, and Og king of Bashan, who
was at Ashtaroth.

2 [1]Lit. *mouth*
3 [a]Josh. 9:17, 22; 10:2; 21:17; 2 Sam. 21:1, 2 [b]Josh. 6:27
4 [1]*acted as envoys* [2]Lit. *tied up*
6 [a]Josh. 5:10 [1]*treaty*
7 [a]Josh. 9:1; 11:19 [b]Ex. 23:32; Deut. 7:2
8 [a]Deut. 20:11; 2 Kin. 10:5
9 [a]Deut. 20:15 [b]Ex. 15:14; Josh. 2:9, 10; 5:1
10 [a]Num. 21:24, 33
14 [a]Num. 27:21; Is. 30:1 [1]Lit. *did not inquire at the mouth of*
15 [a]2 Sam. 21:2
16 *See WW at Ex. 34:27.
17 [a]Josh. 18:25
18 [a]Ps. 15:4 [1]*strike* *See WW at Gen. 26:3.

11 "Therefore our elders and all the
inhabitants of our country spoke to us,
saying, 'Take provisions with you for
the journey, and go to meet them, and
say to them, "We *are* your servants;
now therefore, make a covenant with
us." '
12 "This bread of ours we took hot *for*
our provision from our houses on the
day we departed to come to you. But
now look, it is dry and moldy.
13 "And these wineskins which we
filled *were* new, and see, they are torn;
and these our garments and our sandals have become old because of the
very long journey."
14 Then the men of Israel took some 2
of their provisions; [a]but they [1]did not
ask counsel of the LORD.
15 So Joshua [a]made peace with them,
and made a covenant with them to let
them live; and the rulers of the congregation swore to them.
16 And it happened at the end of three
days, after they had *made a covenant
with them, that they heard that they
were their neighbors who dwelt near
them.
17 Then the children of Israel journeyed and came to their cities on the
third day. Now their cities *were*
[a]Gibeon, Chephirah, Beeroth, and Kirjath Jearim.
18 But the children of Israel did not
[1]attack them, [a]because the rulers of the
congregation had *sworn to them by

9:3 Gibeon was one of 4 Hivite cities, about 6 miles northwest of Jerusalem.
9:3–15 The desire of the Gibeonites to make peace suggests they knew the biblical stipulation in Deut. 7:2 and 20:10–16: The Canaanites must be utterly destroyed, but Israel was permitted to make treaties with distant peoples.
9:14 See section 2 of Truth-In-Action at the end of Josh.
9:14 For the second time Joshua acted without **counsel of the LORD.** The first time was at Ai (7:2–4).
9:15–18 Illustrated here is the integrity of one's word. Had Joshua broken his **covenant** with the Gibeonites—sworn to before God Himself—it would have been tantamount to breaking a promise to God and would eventually bring God's wrath upon them (Ezek. 17:12–19).
9:17 The distance between Gilgal and **Gibeon** was about 19 miles.

The Conquest of Canaan (Central and Southern Campaigns). From the military camp at Gilgal Joshua launched two campaigns, thus conquering central and southern Canaan.

the LORD God of Israel. And all the congregation complained against the rulers.
19 Then all the rulers said to all the
congregation, "We have sworn to them
by the LORD God of Israel; now therefore, we may not touch them.
20 "This we will do to them: We will
let them live, lest [a]wrath be upon us
because of the oath which we swore
to them."
21 And the rulers said to them, "Let
them live, but let them be [a]woodcutters
and water carriers for all the congregation, as the rulers had [b]promised
them."
22 Then Joshua called for them, and
he spoke to them, saying, "Why have
you deceived us, saying, [a]'We *are* very
far from you,' when [b]you dwell near
us?
23 "Now therefore, you *are* [a]cursed,
and none of you shall be freed from
being slaves—woodcutters and water
carriers for the house of my God."
24 So they answered Joshua and said,
"Because your servants were clearly
told that the LORD your God [a]com-
manded His servant Moses to give you
all the land, and to destroy all the
inhabitants of the land from before
you; therefore [b]we were very much
afraid for our lives because of you, and
have done this thing.
25 "And now, here we are, [a]in your
hands; do with us as it seems *good
and right to do to us."
26 So he did to them, and delivered
them out of the hand of the children
of Israel, so that they did not kill them.
27 And that day Joshua made them
[a]woodcutters and water carriers for
the congregation and for the altar of
the LORD, [b]in the place which He would
choose, even to this day.

The Sun Stands Still

10 Now it came to pass when
Adoni-Zedek king of Jerusalem
[a]heard how Joshua had taken [b]Ai and
had utterly destroyed it—[c]as he had
done to Jericho and its king, so he had

20 [a]2 Sam. 21:1, 2, 6; Ezek. 17:13, 15
21 [a]Deut. 29:11 [b]Josh. 9:15
22 [a]Josh. 9:6, 9 [b]Josh. 9:16
23 [a]Gen. 9:25
24 [a]Ex. 23:31–33; Deut. 7:1, 2 [b]Ex. 15:14
25 [a]Gen. 16:6 *See WW at Ezek. 34:14.
27 [a]Josh. 9:21, 23 [b]Deut. 12:5

CHAPTER 10

1 [a]Josh. 9:1 [b]Josh. 8:1 [c]Josh. 6:21 [d]Josh. 8:22, 26, 28 [e]Josh. 9:15

2 [a]Ex. 15:14–16; Deut. 11:25; 1 Chr. 14:17
4 [a]Josh. 9:15; 10:1
5 [a]Num. 13:29 [b]Josh. 9:2
6 [a]Josh. 5:10; 9:6
7 [a]Josh. 8:1
8 [a]Josh. 11:6; Judg. 4:14 [b]Josh. 1:5, 9 [c]Josh. 21:44
10 [a]Judg. 4:15; 1 Sam. 7:10, 12; Is. 28:21 [b]Josh. 16:3, 5 [c]Josh. 15:35
11 [a]Is. 30:30; Rev. 16:21

done to [d]Ai and its king—and [e]how the
inhabitants of Gibeon had made peace
with Israel and were among them,
2 that they [a]feared greatly, because
Gibeon *was* a great city, like one of the
royal cities, and because it *was* greater
than Ai, and all its men *were* mighty.
3 Therefore Adoni-Zedek king of Jerusalem sent to Hoham king of Hebron, Piram king of Jarmuth, Japhia
king of Lachish, and Debir king of
Eglon, saying,
4 "Come up to me and help me, that
we may attack Gibeon, for [a]it has made
peace with Joshua and with the children of Israel."
5 Therefore the five kings of the
[a]Amorites, the king of Jerusalem, the
king of Hebron, the king of Jarmuth,
the king of Lachish, *and* the king of
Eglon, [b]gathered together and went up,
they and all their armies, and camped
before Gibeon and made war against
it.
6 And the men of Gibeon sent to
Joshua at the camp [a]at Gilgal, saying,
"Do not forsake your servants; come
up to us quickly, save us and help us,
for all the kings of the Amorites who
dwell in the mountains have gathered
together against us."
7 So Joshua ascended from Gilgal, he
and [a]all the people of war with him,
and all the mighty men of valor.
8 And the LORD said to Joshua, [a]"Do
not fear them, for I have delivered
them into your hand; [b]not a man of
them shall [c]stand before you."
9 Joshua therefore came upon them
suddenly, having marched all night
from Gilgal.
10 So the LORD [a]routed them before Israel, killed them with a great slaughter
at Gibeon, chased them along the road
that goes [b]to Beth Horon, and struck
them down as far as [c]Azekah and Makkedah.
11 And it happened, as they fled before
Israel *and* were on the descent of Beth
Horon, [a]that the LORD cast down large
hailstones from heaven on them as far
as Azekah, and they died. *There were*
more who died from the hailstones

9:22–27 Although the Gibeonites were spared, they were denied their liberty. They were to be **slaves** to supply wood and water **for the altar.** Sacrifices and ritual washing required a great deal of both.

10:1, 2 With the defeat of **Jericho** and **Ai** and the surrender of **Gibeon** and its confederated cities (9:17), the Israelites were driving a wedge between north and south. Little by little, they were possessing the land (Ex. 23:30).

10:3–5 Gibeon had surrendered to **Joshua** rather than fight. Their desertion enraged the **king of Jerusalem,** so he formed a confederacy with four of the neighboring **kings** to attack Gibeon. This is Canaan's first serious attempt at resistance.

10:10, 11 The four verbs used in v. 10 assume Yahweh as the subject, the One who brings victory decisively and supernaturally. **Beth Horon** was a town 4 miles northwest of **Gibeon** on the road leading to **Azekah** and on to the coast. It was in mountainous country and consisted of two sites—one 800 feet higher than the other. **Descent** was the lower site.

than the children of Israel killed with
the sword.
12 Then Joshua spoke to the LORD in
the day when the LORD delivered up
the Amorites before the children of
Israel, and he said in the sight of
Israel:

[a]"Sun, stand still over Gibeon;
And Moon, in the Valley of
[b]Aijalon."
13 So the sun stood still,
And the moon stopped,
Till the people had revenge
Upon their enemies.

[a]*Is* this not written in the Book of
Jasher? So the sun stood still in the
midst of heaven, and did not hasten to
go *down* for about a whole day.
14 And there has been [a]no day like
that, before it or after it, that the LORD
heeded the voice of a man; for [b]the
LORD fought for Israel.

KINGDOM DYNAMICS

10:12–14 Joshua and His Warriors Stand in the Gap, PRAYER. Strengthened by God's assurance of victory, but knowing they must fight to possess that promise, Joshua's select warriors responded to Gibeon's plea for help. Their struggle illustrates a classic syndrome of spiritual life. No sooner had Joshua and Israel conquered Jericho and Ai than five Amorite kings attacked Gibeon to punish it and to block Israel's advance. (In a similar way, Satan forges weapons to war upon those who are moving in conquest for Christ.) The battle was long and fierce. Fearful that the sun would set before the enemy was annihilated, Joshua's prayer of faith touched God's omnipotence: the sun and moon—worshiped by the Amorites—stood still at Joshua's command, not only allowing Israel's success in battle, but demonstrating the ineffectiveness of the demon-gods embraced by their opponents. Joshua and his warriors stood in the gap, contending for God's eternal purposes and teaching the triumph such faith and tenacity may realize in our spiritual warfare!
(Ex. 32:11–14, 30–34/Is. 36:1—37:38) L.L.

12 [a]Is. 28:21; Hab. 3:11 [b]Judg. 12:12
13 [a]2 Sam. 1:18
14 [a]Is. 38:7, 8 [b]Ex. 14:14; Deut. 1:30; 20:4; Josh. 10:42; 23:3
15 [a]Josh. 10:43
18 *See WW at Prov. 16:3.
21 [a]Ex. 11:7 [1]*criticized*, lit. *sharpened his tongue*
24 [a]Ps. 107:40; Is. 26:5, 6; Mal. 4:3
25 [a]Deut. 31:6–8; Josh. 1:9 [b]Deut. 3:21; 7:19 [1]The captains
26 [1]The kings

15 [a]Then Joshua returned, and all
Israel with him, to the camp at Gilgal.

The Amorite Kings Executed

16 But these five kings had fled and
hidden themselves in a cave at Makkedah.
17 And it was told Joshua, saying,
"The five kings have been found hidden in the cave at Makkedah."
18 So Joshua said, *"Roll large stones
against the mouth of the cave, and set
men by it to guard them.
19 "And do not stay *there* yourselves,
but pursue your enemies, and attack
their rear *guard.* Do not allow them to
enter their cities, for the LORD your
God has delivered them into your
hand."
20 Then it happened, while Joshua and
the children of Israel made an end of
slaying them with a very great slaughter, till they had finished, that those
who escaped entered fortified cities.
21 And all the people returned to the
camp, to Joshua at Makkedah, in
peace. [a]No one [1]moved his tongue
against any of the children of Israel.
22 Then Joshua said, "Open the mouth
of the cave, and bring out those five
kings to me from the cave."
23 And they did so, and brought out
those five kings to him from the cave:
the king of Jerusalem, the king of Hebron, the king of Jarmuth, the king of
Lachish, *and* the king of Eglon.
24 So it was, when they brought out
those kings to Joshua, that Joshua
called for all the men of Israel, and said
to the captains of the men of war who
went with him, "Come near, put your
feet on the necks of these kings." And
they drew near and [a]put their feet on
their necks.
25 Then Joshua said to [1]them, [a]"Do
not be afraid, nor be dismayed; be
strong and of good courage, for
[b]thus the LORD will do to all your enemies against whom you fight."
26 And afterward Joshua struck
[1]them and killed them, and hanged

10:12, 13 This great miracle is clearly the result of God's sovereign power in response to Joshua's authority in prayer. He speaks directly to the **sun** and **moon.** They obeyed (obviously at God's command) and the delayed sunset enabled Israel to have **revenge upon their enemies.** If one eliminates the supernatural from this account, one is left to speculation and human reason. **The Book of Jasher** was an ancient, classical book of poetry about Israel's heroes and exploits. It is also mentioned in 2 Sam. 1:18.

10:16–27 These verses add detail to the general battle description of vv. 10 and 11 and represent Christ's victory over the powers of darkness. Israel now had control of the strategic central region.

10:24 Put their feet on their necks was an ancient custom for victorious kings who put their feet on the necks of the conquered enemy. This action exemplifies God's promise to "make your enemies your footstool" (Ps. 110:1).

them on five trees; and they [a]were
hanging on the trees until evening.
27 So it was at the time of the going
down of the sun *that* Joshua commanded, and they [a]took them down
from the trees, cast them into the cave
where they had been hidden, and laid
large stones against the cave's mouth,
which remain until this very day.

Conquest of the Southland

28 On that day Joshua took Makkedah, and struck it and its king with the
edge of the sword. He utterly [a]de-
stroyed [1]them—all the people who
were in it. He let none remain. He also
did to the king of Makkedah [b]as he had
done to the king of Jericho.
29 Then Joshua passed from Makkedah, and all Israel with him, to [a]Lib-
nah; and they fought against Libnah.
30 And the LORD also delivered it and
its king into the hand of Israel; he
struck it and all the people who *were*
in it with the edge of the sword. He
let none remain in it, but did to its king
as he had done to the king of Jericho.
31 Then Joshua passed from Libnah,
and all Israel with him, to Lachish; and
they encamped against it and fought
against it.
32 And the LORD delivered Lachish
into the hand of Israel, who took it on
the second day, and struck it and all
the people who *were* in it with the edge
of the sword, according to all that he
had done to Libnah.
33 Then Horam king of Gezer came up
to help Lachish; and Joshua struck him
and his people, until he left him none
remaining.
34 From Lachish Joshua passed to
Eglon, and all Israel with him; and they
encamped against it and fought against
it.
35 They took it on that day and struck
it with the edge of the sword; all the
people who *were* in it he utterly destroyed that day, according to all that
he had done to Lachish.
36 So Joshua went up from Eglon, and
all Israel with him, to [a]Hebron; and
they fought against it.
37 And they took it and struck it with
the edge of the sword—its king, all its
cities, and all the people who *were* in
it; he left none remaining, according
to all that he had done to Eglon, but
utterly destroyed it and all the people
who *were* in it.
38 Then Joshua returned, and all Israel
with him, to [a]Debir; and they fought
against it.
39 And he took it and its king and all
its cities; they struck them with the
edge of the sword and utterly destroyed all the people who *were* in it.
He left none remaining; as he had done
to Hebron, so he did to Debir and its
king, as he had done also to Libnah
and its king.
40 So Joshua conquered all the land:
the [a]mountain country and the [1]South
and the lowland and the wilderness
slopes, and [b]all their kings; he left
none remaining, but [c]utterly destroyed
all that breathed, as the LORD God of
Israel had commanded.
41 And Joshua conquered them from
[a]Kadesh Barnea as far as [b]Gaza, [c]and
all the country of Goshen, even as far
as Gibeon.
42 All these kings and their land
Joshua took at one time, [a]because the
LORD God of Israel fought for Israel.
43 Then Joshua returned, and all Israel
with him, to the camp at Gilgal.

The Northern Conquest

11 And it came to pass, when Jabin
king of Hazor heard *these
things,* that he [a]sent to Jobab king of
Madon, to the king [b]of Shimron, to the
king of Achshaph,
2 and to the kings who *were* from the
north, in the mountains, in the plain
south of [a]Chinneroth, in the lowland,
and in the heights [b]of Dor on the west,
3 to the Canaanites in the east and
in the west, the [a]Amorite, the Hittite,
the Perizzite, the Jebusite in the mountains, [b]and the Hivite below [c]Hermon
[d]in the land of Mizpah.
4 So they went out, they and all their
armies with them, *as* many people
[a]*as* the sand that *is* on the seashore in
multitude, with very many horses and
chariots.

26 [a]Josh. 8:29; 2 Sam. 21:9
27 [a]Deut. 21:22, 23; Josh. 8:29
28 [a]Deut. 7:2, 16 [b]Josh. 6:21 [1]So with MT and most authorities; many Heb. mss., some LXX mss., and some Tg. mss. *it*
29 [a]Josh. 15:42; 21:13; 2 Kin. 8:22; 19:8
36 [a]Num. 13:22; Josh. 14:13–15; 15:13; Judg. 1:10, 20; 2 Sam. 5:1, 3, 5, 13; 2 Chr. 11:10
38 [a]Josh. 15:15; Judg. 1:11; 1 Chr. 6:58
40 [a]Deut. 1:7 [b]Deut. 7:24 [c]Deut. 20:16, 17 [1]Heb. *Negev,* and so throughout the book
41 [a]Num. 13:26; Deut. 9:23 [b]Gen. 10:19; Josh. 11:22 [c]Josh. 11:16; 15:51
42 [a]Josh. 10:14

CHAPTER 11

1 [a]Josh. 10:3 [b]Josh. 19:15
2 [a]Num. 34:11 [b]Josh. 17:11; Judg. 1:27; 1 Kin. 4:11
3 [a]Josh. 9:1 [b]Deut. 7:1; Judg. 3:3, 5; 1 Kin. 9:20 [c]Josh. 11:17; 13:5, 11 [d]Gen. 31:49
4 [a]Gen. 22:17; 32:12; Judg. 7:12; 1 Sam. 13:5

10:28–43 Joshua's southern campaign was swift and victorious. Seven more cities were conquered, but the land was not occupied by Israel. The cities were eventually repopulated and later battles were necessary to subdue them again (Judg. 1).

11:1–23 Vv. 1–15 center on Joshua's northern campaign, and vv. 16–23 summarize his entire conquests.

11:1–5 Hearing of the victories of Joshua in the south, **Jabin, king of Hazor,** gathered together a coalition of northern kings to do battle against Joshua. Hazor was a large, important city some 10 miles northwest of the Sea of Galilee.

11:4 Horses and chariots: The combined enemy forces had use of a superior quality of weaponry.

5 And when all these kings had
[1]met together, they came and camped
together at the waters of Merom to
fight against Israel.
6 But the LORD said to Joshua,
[a]"Do not be afraid because of them,
for tomorrow about this time I will deliver all of them slain before Israel.
You shall [b]hamstring their horses and
burn their chariots with fire."
7 So Joshua and all the people of war
with him came against them suddenly
by the waters of Merom, and they attacked them.
8 And the LORD delivered them into
the hand of Israel, who defeated them
and chased them to [1]Greater [a]Sidon,
to the [2]Brook [b]Misrephoth, and to the
Valley of Mizpah eastward; they attacked them until they left none of
them remaining.
9 So Joshua did to them as the LORD
had told him: he hamstrung their
horses and burned their chariots with
fire.
10 Joshua turned back at that time and
took Hazor, and struck its king with
the sword; for Hazor was formerly the
head of all those kingdoms.
6 11 And they struck all the people who
were in it with the edge of the sword,
[a]utterly destroying *them*. There was
none left [b]breathing.* Then he burned
Hazor with fire.
12 So all the cities of those kings, and
all their kings, Joshua took and struck
with the edge of the sword. He utterly
destroyed them, [a]as Moses the servant
of the LORD had commanded.
13 But *as for* the cities that stood on
their [1]mounds, Israel burned none of
them, except Hazor only, *which* Joshua
burned.
14 And all the [a]spoil of these cities and
the livestock, the children of Israel
took as booty for themselves; but they
struck every man with the edge of the
sword until they had destroyed them,
and they left none breathing.
15 [a]As the LORD had commanded Moses his servant, so [b]Moses commanded
Joshua, and [c]so Joshua did. [1]He left
nothing undone of all that the LORD
had commanded Moses.

Summary of Joshua's Conquests

16 Thus Joshua took all this land:
[a]the mountain country, all the South,
[b]all the land of Goshen, the lowland,
and the Jordan [1]plain—the mountains
of Israel and its lowlands,
17 [a]from [1]Mount Halak and the ascent
to Seir, even as far as Baal Gad in the
Valley of Lebanon below Mount Hermon. He captured [b]all their kings, and
struck them down and killed them.
18 Joshua made war a long time with
all those kings.
19 There was not a city that made
peace with the children of Israel, except [a]the Hivites, the inhabitants of

5 [1]Lit. *assembled by appointment*
6 [a]Josh. 10:8 [b]2 Sam. 8:4
8 [a]Gen. 49:13 [b]Josh. 13:6 [1]Heb. *Sidon Rabbah* [2]Heb. *Misrephoth Maim*, lit. *Burnings of Water*
11 [a]Deut. 20:16 [b]Josh. 10:40 *See WW at Ps. 150:6.
12 [a]Num. 33:50–56; Deut. 7:2; 20:16
13 [1]Heb. *tel*, a heap of successive city ruins
14 [a]Deut. 20:14–18
15 [a]Ex. 34:10–17 [b]Deut. 31:7, 8 [c]Josh. 1:7 [1]Lit. *He turned aside from nothing*
16 [a]Josh. 12:8 [b]Josh. 10:40, 41 [1]Heb. *arabah*
17 [a]Josh. 12:7 [b]Deut. 7:24 [1]Lit. *The Smooth* or *Bald Mountain*
19 [a]Josh. 9:3–7

11:6 To **hamstring** is to permanently cripple horses by cutting the tendon on the back of the legs.

11:10 Joshua's victory at **Hazor** ranked as one of his most significant. It was a large, secure fortress, strategically located on the main trade route from Egypt to Mesopotamia.

11:11 See section 6 of Truth-In-Action at the end of Josh.

11:13 Mounds (Hebrew *tel*) were hills created by building one city on top of the ruins of another. The mound had a distinct defense advantage.

11:16, 17 The territory Joshua had conquered was bounded by **Mount Halak,** south of the Dead Sea, to **Mount Hermon** on the north; from the Mediterranean Sea to the Jordan Valley. God's promise to Abraham had been fulfilled (Gen. 15:18–20).

11:18 A long time: The northern campaign took five to seven years.

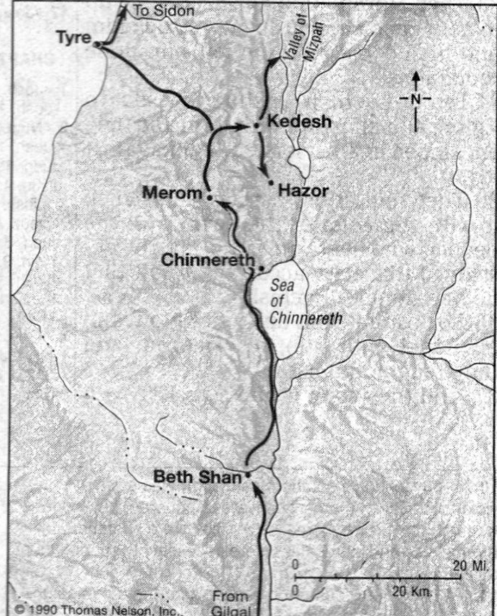

The Conquest of Canaan (Northern Campaign)

Gibeon. All *the others* they took in battle.
20 For [a]it was of the LORD [1]to harden
their hearts, that they should come
against Israel in battle, that He might
utterly destroy them, *and* that they
might receive no mercy, but that He
might destroy them, [b]as the LORD had
commanded Moses.
21 And at that time Joshua came and
cut off [a]the Anakim from the mountains: from Hebron, from Debir, from
Anab, from all the mountains of Judah,
and from all the mountains of Israel;
Joshua utterly destroyed them with
their cities.
22 None of the Anakim were left in the
land of the children of Israel; they remained only [a]in Gaza, in Gath, [b]and
in Ashdod.
23 So Joshua took the whole land,
[a]according to all that the LORD had said
to Moses; and Joshua gave it as an inheritance to Israel [b]according to their
divisions by their tribes. Then the land
[c]rested from war.

The Kings Conquered by Moses

12 These *are* the kings of the land
whom the children of Israel defeated, and whose land they possessed
on the other side of the Jordan toward
the rising of the sun, [a]from the River
Arnon [b]to Mount Hermon, and all the
eastern Jordan plain:
2 *One king was* [a]Sihon king of the
Amorites, who dwelt in Heshbon *and*
ruled half of Gilead, from Aroer, which
is on the bank of the River Arnon, from
the middle of that river, even as far as
the River Jabbok, *which is* the border
of the Ammonites,
3 and [a]the eastern Jordan plain from
the [1]Sea of Chinneroth as far as the
[2]Sea of the Arabah (the Salt Sea),
[b]the road to Beth Jeshimoth, and
[3]southward below [c]the[4] slopes of Pisgah.
4 *The other king was* [a]Og king of
Bashan and his territory, *who was* of
[b]the remnant of the giants, [c]who dwelt
at Ashtaroth and at Edrei,
5 and reigned over [a]Mount Hermon,
[b]over Salcah, over all Bashan, [c]as far
as the border of the Geshurites and the
Maachathites, and over half of Gilead
to the border of Sihon king of Heshbon.
6 [a]These Moses the servant of the
LORD and the children of Israel had
conquered; and [b]Moses the servant of
the LORD had given it *as* a possession
to the Reubenites, the Gadites, and half
the tribe of Manasseh.

The Kings Conquered by Joshua

7 And these *are* the kings of the country [a]which Joshua and the children of
Israel conquered on this side of the Jordan, on the west, from Baal Gad in the
Valley of Lebanon as far as [1]Mount Halak and the ascent to [b]Seir, which
Joshua [c]gave to the tribes of Israel *as*
a possession according to their divisions,
8 [a]in the mountain country, in the
lowlands, in the *Jordan* plain, in the
slopes, in the wilderness, and in the
South—[b]the Hittites, the Amorites,
the Canaanites, the Perizzites, the Hivites, and the Jebusites:
9 [a]the king of Jericho, one; [b]the king
of Ai, which *is* beside Bethel, one;
10 [a]the king of Jerusalem, one; the
king of Hebron, one;
11 the king of Jarmuth, one; the king
of Lachish, one;
12 the king of Eglon, one; [a]the king of
Gezer, one;
13 [a]the king of Debir, one; the king of
Geder, one;
14 the king of Hormah, one; the king
of Arad, one;
15 [a]the king of Libnah, one; the king
of Adullam, one;
16 [a]the king of Makkedah, one;
[b]the king of Bethel, one;
17 the king of Tappuah, one; [a]the king
of Hepher, one;

20 [a]Deut. 2:30 [b]Deut. 20:16, 17 [1]Lit. *to make strong*
21 [a]Num. 13:22, 33
22 [a]1 Sam. 17:4 [b]Josh. 15:46
23 [a]Num. 34:2–15 [b]Num. 26:53 [c]Deut. 12:9, 10; 25:19

CHAPTER 12

1 [a]Num. 21:24 [b]Deut. 3:8
2 [a]Deut. 2:24–27
3 [a]Deut. 3:17 [b]Josh. 13:20 [c]Deut. 3:17; 4:49 [1]Sea of Galilee [2]Lit. *Sea of the Plain,* the Dead Sea [3]Or *Teman* [4]Or *Ashdoth Pisgah*
4 [a]Num. 21:33 [b]Deut. 3:11 [c]Deut. 1:4
5 [a]Deut. 3:8 [b]Deut. 3:10 [c]Deut. 3:14
6 [a]Num. 21:24, 35 [b]Num. 32:29–33
7 [a]Josh. 11:17 [b]Gen. 14:6; 32:3 [c]Josh. 11:23 [1]Lit. *The Bald Mountain*
8 [a]Josh. 10:40; 11:16 [b]Ex. 3:8; 23:23
9 [a]Josh. 6:2 [b]Josh. 8:29
10 [a]Josh. 10:23
12 [a]Josh. 10:33
13 [a]Josh. 10:38, 39
15 [a]Josh. 10:29, 30
16 [a]Josh. 10:28 [b]Judg. 1:22
17 [a]1 Kin. 4:10

11:20 Harden their hearts: The Canaanites, like Pharaoh (Ex. 8:32), persisted in their unrepentant, pagan ways. This unavoidably led them to their destruction.

11:21 The **Anakim,** which means "the long-necked men," were the most dreaded inhabitants of Canaan. These giants were descendants of those who, 40 years earlier, had brought much terror to the hearts of Israel (Num. 13:27–33).

11:23 Joshua's military presence had been so profoundly established that none dared challenge him. When **Israel . . . rested from war** she was allowed to settle and enjoy her promised inheritance.

12:1–6 Sihon and **Og** were two kings defeated under the leadership of Moses. Their territories, located on the east side of the Jordan, extended from **Arnon** in Sihon's portion on the south to **Mount Hermon** in Og's portion on the north. The land of these two defeated kings was given to **the Reubenites, the Gadites, and half the tribe of Manasseh.**

12:4 Og king of Bashan: The defeat of this king is often mentioned in Scripture as an example of the mighty power of God (Ps. 135:10, 11).

12:7–24 Listed are the 31 kings, west of the Jordan, conquered by Joshua. The triumphs over these kings are the fulfillment of the Abrahamic covenant.

18 the king of Aphek, one; the king of
[1]Lasharon, one;
19 the king of Madon, one; [a]the king
of Hazor, one;
20 the king of [a]Shimron Meron, one;
the king of Achshaph, one;
21 the king of Taanach, one; the king
of Megiddo, one;
22 [a]the king of Kedesh, one; the king
of Jokneam in Carmel, one;
23 the king of Dor in the [a]heights of
Dor, one; the king of [b]the people of Gilgal, one;
24 the king of Tirzah, one—[a]all the
kings, thirty-one.

Remaining Land to Be Conquered

13 Now Joshua [a]was old, advanced
in years. And the LORD said to
him: "You are old, advanced in years,
and there remains very much land yet
to be possessed.
2 [a]"This is the land that yet remains:
[b]all the territory of the Philistines and
all [c]*that of* the Geshurites,
3 [a]"from Sihor, which *is* east of
Egypt, as far as the border of Ekron
northward (*which* is counted as Canaanite); the [b]five lords of the Philistines—the Gazites, the Ashdodites, the
Ashkelonites, the Gittites, and the Ekronites; also [c]the Avites;
4 "from the south, all the land of the
Canaanites, and Mearah that belongs
to the Sidonians [a]as far as Aphek, to
the border of [b]the Amorites;
5 "the land of [a]the [1]Gebalites, and all
Lebanon, toward the sunrise, [b]from
Baal Gad below Mount Hermon as far
as the entrance to Hamath;
6 "all the inhabitants of the mountains from Lebanon as far as [a]the
[1]Brook Misrephoth, *and* all the Sidonians—them [b]I will drive out from before
the children of Israel; only [c]divide[2] it
by lot to Israel as an inheritance, as I
have commanded you.
7 "Now therefore, divide this land as
an inheritance to the nine tribes and
half the tribe of Manasseh."

The Land Divided East of the Jordan

8 With the other half-tribe the Reubenites and the Gadites received their
inheritance, [a]which Moses had given
them, [b]beyond the Jordan eastward, as
Moses the servant of the LORD had
given them:
9 from Aroer which *is* on the bank of
the River Arnon, and the town that *is*
in the midst of the ravine, [a]and all the
plain of Medeba as far as Dibon;
10 [a]all the cities of Sihon king of the
Amorites, who reigned in Heshbon, as
far as the border of the children of Ammon;
11 [a]Gilead, and the border of the Geshurites and Maachathites, all Mount
Hermon, and all Bashan as far as Salcah;
12 all the kingdom of Og in Bashan,
who reigned in Ashtaroth and Edrei,
who remained of [a]the remnant of the
giants; [b]for Moses had [1]defeated and
[2]cast out these.
13 Nevertheless the children of Israel
[a]did not drive out the Geshurites or the
Maachathites, but the Geshurites and
the Maachathites dwell among the Israelites until this day.
14 [a]Only to the tribe of Levi he had
given [1]no inheritance; the sacrifices of
the LORD God of Israel made by fire
are their inheritance, [b]as He said to
them.

The Land of Reuben

15 [a]And Moses had given to the tribe
of the children of Reuben *an inheritance* according to their families.
16 Their territory was [a]from Aroer,
which *is* on the bank of the River Ar-

18 [1]Or *Sharon*
19 [a]Josh. 11:10
20 [a]Josh. 11:1; 19:15
22 [a]Josh. 19:37; 20:7; 21:32
23 [a]Josh. 11:2 [b]Is. 9:1
24 [a]Deut. 7:24

CHAPTER 13

1 [a]Josh. 14:10; 23:1, 2
2 [a]Judg. 3:1–3 [b]Joel 3:4 [c]2 Sam. 3:3
3 [a]Jer. 2:18 [b]Judg. 3:3 [c]Deut. 2:23
4 [a]Josh. 12:18; 19:30 [b]Judg. 1:34
5 [a]1 Kin. 5:18; Ezek. 27:9 [b]Josh. 12:7 [1]Or *Giblites*
6 [a]Josh. 11:8 [b]Josh. 23:13 [c]Josh. 14:1, 2 [1]Heb. *Misrephoth Maim,* lit. *Burnings of Water* [2]*apportion*
8 [a]Num. 32:33 [b]Josh. 12:1–6
9 [a]Num. 21:30
10 [a]Num. 21:24, 25
11 [a]Josh. 12:5
12 [a]Deut. 3:11 [b]Num. 21:24, 34, 35 [1]Lit. *struck* [2]*dispossessed*
13 [a]Josh. 13:11
14 [a]Josh. 14:3, 4 [b]Josh. 13:33 [1]*no land as a possession*
15 [a]Num. 34:14
16 [a]Josh. 12:2

13:1—21:45 In the ancient Hebrew society, real property was owned by the family, not the individual. The land was given by God. It was to remain in the family and could not pass from one tribe to another. Mosaic Law provided specific rules regarding the right of inheritance and the birthright. Legal wills and contracts were unnecessary to designate ownership, but family genealogies were carefully preserved. These chapters reflect that care.

13:1–7 These verses introduce the next division of the book: possessing the land. For over 40 years, Israel had been a homeless people, but now they were about to receive their inheritance. The author spares no detail in describing it.

13:1 To be possessed: God gave Joshua the task of allotting to the remaining nine and one-half tribes the land they were to occupy west of the Jordan.

13:2 The land that yet remains was territory that had so far been unconquered. It extended from north of Damascus to the Egyptian border. The tribes were to occupy the conquered land and extend their conquests into these outer regions.

13:8–12 This is a general description of the conquered territories east of Jordan. This land had already been divided among the tribes of Reuben and Gad, and half the tribe of Manasseh.

13:14, 33 According to Num. 18:20, the tribe of **Levi** received no allotment of land. Their inheritance was a share of the sacrifices offered to the Lord. They were to be supported by all the tribes (Deut. 18:1–8).

13:15–23 Reuben was given the southern portion to the border of Moab.

non, [b]and the city that *is* in the midst
of the ravine, [c]and all the plain by
Medeba;
17 [a]Heshbon and all its cities that *are*
in the plain: Dibon, Bamoth Baal, Beth
Baal Meon,
18 [a]Jahaza, Kedemoth, Mephaath,
19 [a]Kirjathaim, [b]Sibmah, Zereth Sha-
har on the mountain of the valley,
20 Beth Peor, [a]the slopes of Pisgah,
and Beth Jeshimoth—
21 [a]all the cities of the plain and all
the kingdom of Sihon king of the Amorites, who reigned in Heshbon, [b]whom
Moses had struck [c]with the princes of
Midian: Evi, Rekem, Zur, Hur, and
Reba, who *were* princes of Sihon
dwelling in the country.
22 The children of Israel also killed
with the sword [a]Balaam the son of
Beor, the [1]soothsayer, among those
who were killed by them.
23 And the border of the children of
Reuben was the bank of the Jordan.
This *was* the inheritance of the
children of Reuben according to
their families, the cities and their
villages.

The Land of Gad

24 [a]Moses also had given *an inheritance* to the tribe of Gad, to the
children of Gad according to their families.
25 [a]Their territory was Jazer, and all
the cities of Gilead, [b]and half the land
of the Ammonites as far as Aroer,
which *is* before [c]Rabbah,
26 and from Heshbon to Ramath Mizpah and Betonim, and from Mahanaim
to the border of Debir,
27 and in the valley [a]Beth Haram, Beth
Nimrah, [b]Succoth, and Zaphon, the
rest of the kingdom of Sihon king of
Heshbon, with the Jordan as *its* border, as far as the edge [c]of the [1]Sea of
Chinnereth, on the other side of the
Jordan eastward.
28 This *is* the inheritance of the children of Gad according to their families,
the cities and their villages.

16 [b]Num. 21:28 [c]Num. 21:30
17 [a]Num. 21:28, 30
18 [a]Num. 21:23
19 [a]Num. 32:37 [b]Num. 32:38
20 [a]Deut. 3:17
21 [a]Deut. 3:10 [b]Num. 21:24 [c]Num. 31:8
22 [a]Num. 22:5; 31:8 [1]*diviner*
24 [a]Num. 34:14
25 [a]Num. 32:1, 35 [b]Judg. 11:13, 15 [c]Deut. 3:11
27 [a]Num. 32:36 [b]Gen. 33:17 [c]Num. 34:11 [1]Sea of Galilee

29 [a]Num. 34:14
30 [a]Num. 32:41
31 [a]Josh. 9:10; 12:4; 13:12 [b]Num. 32:39, 40
32 [1]*apportioned*
33 [a]Josh. 13:14; 18:7 [b]Num. 18:20

CHAPTER 14

1 [a]Num. 34:16–29 *See WW at Ex. 38:22.
2 [a]Num. 26:55; 33:54; 34:13
3 [a]Josh. 13:8, 32, 33
4 [a]2 Chr. 30:1 [b]Num. 35:2–8
5 [a]Josh. 21:2

Half the Tribe of Manasseh (East)

29 [a]Moses also had given *an inheritance* to half the tribe of Manasseh; it
was for half the tribe of the children
of Manasseh according to their families:
30 Their territory was from Mahanaim, all Bashan, all the kingdom of
Og king of Bashan, and [a]all the towns
of Jair which are in Bashan, sixty
cities;
31 half of Gilead, and [a]Ashtaroth and
Edrei, cities of the kingdom of Og in
Bashan, *were* for the [b]children of Machir the son of Manasseh, for half of
the children of Machir according to
their families.
32 These *are the areas* which Moses
had [1]distributed as an inheritance
in the plains of Moab on the other
side of the Jordan, by Jericho eastward.
33 [a]But to the tribe of Levi Moses had
given no inheritance; the LORD God of
Israel *was* their inheritance, [b]as He
had said to them.

The Land Divided West of the Jordan

14 These *are the areas* which the
children of Israel inherited in
the land of Canaan, [a]which Eleazar the
priest, Joshua the son of Nun, and the
heads of the fathers of the *tribes of
the children of Israel distributed as an
inheritance to them.
2 Their inheritance *was* [a]by lot, as the
LORD had commanded by the hand of
Moses, for the nine tribes and the half-
tribe.
3 [a]For Moses had given the inheritance of the two tribes and the half-
tribe on the other side of the Jordan;
but to the Levites he had given no inheritance among them.
4 For [a]the children of Joseph were
two tribes: Manasseh and Ephraim.
And they gave no part to the Levites
in the land, except [b]cities to dwell *in*,
with their common-lands for their livestock and their property.
5 [a]As the LORD had commanded

13:24–28 Gad was given the land of Gilead in the central area.

13:29–33 Half the tribe of Manasseh was given the land of Bashan in the north.

14:1–5 This is an account of how the land west of the Jordan River was divided among the remaining 9½ tribes. The 12 tribes of Israel were descended from the 12 sons of Jacob. Levi did not receive a portion, leaving 11. But Joseph's descendants were divided into 2 tribes, Ephraim and Manasseh, again bringing the number of landed tribes to 12.

14:1 The dividing of the land was to be executed before God and presided over by Joshua, **Eleazar** (the spiritual leader in matters of this nature), and a representative from each tribe (Num. 34:16–18).

14:2 Casting lots was a respected means of determining God's will. It could have been by drawing straws or throwing small stones. However it was done, the people honored the outcome as God's decision.

Moses, so the children of Israel did; and they divided the land.

Caleb Inherits Hebron

6 Then the children of Judah came to Joshua in Gilgal. And Caleb the son of Jephunneh the [a]Kenizzite said to him: "You know [b]the word which the LORD said to Moses the man of God concerning [c]you and me in Kadesh Barnea.

7 "I *was* forty years old when Moses the servant of the LORD [a]sent me from Kadesh Barnea to spy out the land, and I brought back word to him as *it was* in my heart.

2 8 "Nevertheless [a]my brethren who went up with me made the [1]heart* of the people melt, but I wholly [b]followed the LORD my God.

9 "So Moses swore on that day, saying, [a]'Surely the land [b]where your foot has trodden shall be your inheritance and your children's forever, because you have wholly followed the LORD my God.'

10 "And now, behold, the LORD has kept me [a]alive, [b]as He said, these forty-five years, ever since the LORD spoke this word to Moses while Israel [1]wandered in the wilderness; and now, here I am this day, eighty-five years old.

11 [a]"As yet I *am as* strong this day as on the day that Moses sent me; just as my strength *was* then, so now *is* my strength for war, both [b]for going out and for coming in.

12 "Now therefore, give me this mountain of which the LORD spoke in that day; for you heard in that day how [a]the Anakim *were* there, and *that* the cities *were* great *and* fortified. [b]It may be that the LORD *will be* with me, and [c]I shall be able to drive them out as the LORD said."

13 And Joshua [a]blessed him, [b]and gave Hebron to Caleb the son of Jephunneh as an inheritance.

2 14 [a]Hebron therefore became the inheritance of Caleb the son of Jephunneh the Kenizzite to this day, because he [b]wholly followed the LORD God of Israel.

15 And [a]the name of Hebron formerly was Kirjath Arba (*Arba was* the greatest man among the Anakim). [b]Then the land had rest from war.

The Land of Judah

15 So *this* was the [1]lot of the tribe of the children of Judah according to their families: [a]The border of Edom at the [b]Wilderness of Zin southward *was* the extreme southern boundary.

2 And their [a]southern border began at the shore of the Salt Sea, from the bay that faces southward.

3 Then it went out to the southern side of [a]the Ascent of Akrabbim, passed along to Zin, ascended on the south side of Kadesh Barnea, passed along to Hezron, went up to Adar, and went around to Karkaa.

4 *From there* it passed [a]toward Azmon and went out to the Brook of Egypt; and the border ended at the sea. This shall be your southern border.

5 The east border *was* the Salt Sea as far as the mouth of the Jordan. And the [a]border on the northern quarter *began* at the bay of the sea at the mouth of the Jordan.

6 The border went up to [a]Beth Hoglah and passed north of Beth Arabah; and the border went up [b]to the stone of Bohan the son of Reuben.

7 Then the border went up toward [a]Debir from [b]the Valley of Achor, and it turned northward toward Gilgal, which *is* before the Ascent of Adummim, which *is* on the south side of the valley. The border continued toward the waters of En Shemesh and ended at [c]En Rogel.

8 And the border went up [a]by the Valley of the Son of Hinnom to the southern slope of the [b]Jebusite *city* (which *is* Jerusalem). The border went up to the top of the mountain that *lies* before the Valley of Hinnom westward, which *is* at the end of the Valley [c]of [1]Rephaim northward.

9 Then the border went around from the top of the hill to [a]the fountain of the water of Nephtoah, and extended to the cities of Mount Ephron. And the

6 [a]Num. 32:11, 12 [b]Num. 14:24, 30 [c]Num. 13:26
7 [a]Num. 13:6, 17; 14:6
8 [a]Num. 13:31, 32; Deut. 1:28 [b]Num. 14:24; Deut. 1:36 [1]*courage of the people fail* *See WW at Ps. 37:4.
9 [a]Num. 14:23, 24 [b]Num. 13:22; Deut. 1:36
10 [a]Num. 14:24, 30, 38 [b]Josh. 5:6; Neh. 9:21 [1]Lit. *walked*
11 [a]Deut. 34:7 [b]Deut. 31:2
12 [a]Num. 13:28, 33 [b]Rom. 8:31 [c]Josh. 15:14; Judg. 1:20
13 [a]Josh. 22:6 [b]Josh. 10:37; 15:13
14 [a]Josh. 21:12 [b]Josh. 14:8, 9
15 [a]Gen. 23:2; Josh. 15:13 [b]Josh. 11:23

CHAPTER 15

1 [a]Num. 34:3 [b]Num. 33:36 [1]*allotment*
2 [a]Num. 34:3, 4
3 [a]Num. 34:4
4 [a]Num. 34:5
5 [a]Josh. 18:15–19
6 [a]Josh. 18:19, 21 [b]Josh. 18:17
7 [a]Josh. 13:26 [b]Josh. 7:26 [c]2 Sam. 17:17; 1 Kin. 1:9
8 [a]Josh. 18:16; 2 Kin. 23:10; Jer. 19:2, 6 [b]Josh. 15:63; 18:28; Judg. 1:21; 19:10 [c]Josh. 18:16 [1]Lit. *Giants*
9 [a]Josh. 18:15

14:6–12 At the age of 85, **Caleb** asked for the city promised him by God 45 years earlier (Deut. 1:36).
14:8, 9 See section 2 of Truth-In-Action at the end of Josh.
14:13 Hebron was located 19 miles southwest of Jerusalem. For a period in their lives, Abraham, Isaac, and Jacob lived here (Gen. 35:27); no fewer than six OT saints were buried here; and it was here that Abraham established an altar following his separation from Lot.
14:14 See section 2 of Truth-In-Action at the end of Josh.
15:1–12 The portion of land allotted to the tribe of **Judah** extended from Bethel on the north to the Egyptian border on the south; from the Dead Sea on the east to the Mediterranean Sea on the west.

border went around [b]to Baalah (which
is [c]Kirjath Jearim).
10 Then the border [1]turned westward
from Baalah to Mount Seir, passed
along to the side of Mount Jearim on
the north (which *is* Chesalon), went
down to Beth Shemesh, and passed on
to [a]Timnah.
11 And the border went out to the side
of [a]Ekron northward. Then the border
went around to Shicron, passed along
to Mount Baalah, and extended to Jabneel; and the border ended at the sea.
12 The west border *was* [a]the coastline
of the Great Sea. This *is* the boundary
of the children of Judah all around according to their families.

Caleb Occupies Hebron and Debir

13 [a]Now to Caleb the son of Jephunneh he gave a share among the children of [b]Judah, according to the commandment of the LORD to Joshua,
namely, [c]Kirjath Arba, which *is* Hebron (*Arba was* the father of Anak).
14 Caleb drove out [a]the three sons of
Anak from there: [b]Sheshai, Ahiman,
and Talmai, the children of Anak.
15 Then [a]he went up from there to the
inhabitants of Debir (formerly the
name of Debir *was* Kirjath Sepher).
16 [a]And Caleb said, "He who [1]attacks
Kirjath Sepher and takes it, to him I
will give Achsah my daughter as wife."
17 So [a]Othniel the [b]son of Kenaz, the
brother of Caleb, took it; and he gave
him [c]Achsah his daughter as wife.
18 [a]Now it was so, when she came *to
him,* that she persuaded him to ask her
father for a field. So [b]she dismounted
from *her* donkey, and Caleb said to
her, "What do you wish?"
19 She answered, "Give me a [a]bless-
ing; since you have given me land in
the South, give me also springs of water." So he gave her the upper springs
and the lower springs.

The Cities of Judah

20 This *was* the inheritance of the tribe
of the children of Judah according to
their families:
21 The cities at the limits of the tribe
of the children of Judah, toward the
border of Edom in the South, were
Kabzeel, [a]Eder, Jagur,
22 Kinah, Dimonah, Adadah,
23 Kedesh, Hazor, Ithnan,
24 [a]Ziph, Telem, Bealoth,
25 Hazor, Hadattah, Kerioth, Hezron
(which *is* Hazor),
26 Amam, Shema, Moladah,
27 Hazar Gaddah, Heshmon, Beth
Pelet,
28 Hazar Shual, [a]Beersheba, Bizjoth-
jah,
29 Baalah, Ijim, Ezem,
30 Eltolad, Chesil, [a]Hormah,
31 [a]Ziklag, Madmannah, Sansannah,
32 Lebaoth, Shilhim, Ain, and [a]Rim-
mon: all the cities *are* twenty-nine, with
their villages.
33 In the lowland: [a]Eshtaol, Zorah,
Ashnah,
34 Zanoah, En Gannim, Tappuah,
Enam,
35 Jarmuth, [a]Adullam, Socoh, Azekah,
36 Sharaim, Adithaim, Gederah, and
Gederothaim: fourteen cities with their
villages;
37 Zenan, Hadashah, Migdal Gad,
38 Dilean, Mizpah, [a]Joktheel,
39 [a]Lachish, Bozkath, [b]Eglon,
40 Cabbon, [1]Lahmas, Kithlish,
41 Gederoth, Beth Dagon, Naamah,
and Makkedah: sixteen cities with
their villages;
42 [a]Libnah, Ether, Ashan,
43 Jiphtah, Ashnah, Nezib,
44 Keilah, Achzib, and Mareshah: nine
cities with their villages;
45 Ekron, with its towns and villages;
46 from Ekron to the sea, all that *lay*
near [a]Ashdod, with their villages;
47 Ashdod with its towns and villages,
Gaza with its towns and villages—as
far as [a]the Brook of Egypt and [b]the
Great Sea with *its* coastline.
48 And in the mountain country: Shamir, Jattir, Sochoh,
49 Dannah, Kirjath Sannah (which *is*
Debir),
50 Anab, Eshtemoh, Anim,
51 [a]Goshen, Holon, and Giloh: eleven
cities with their villages;
52 Arab, Dumah, Eshean,
53 Janum, Beth Tappuah, Aphekah,
54 Humtah, [a]Kirjath Arba (which *is*
Hebron), and Zior: nine cities with
their villages;

9 [b]1 Chr. 13:6 [c]Judg. 18:12
10 [a]Gen. 38:13; Judg. 14:1 [1]*turned around*
11 [a]Josh. 19:43
12 [a]Num. 34:6, 7; Josh. 15:47
13 [a]Josh. 14:13 [b]Num. 13:6 [c]Josh. 14:15
14 [a]Judg. 1:10, 20 [b]Num. 13:22
15 [a]Josh. 10:38; Judg. 1:11
16 [a]Judg. 1:12 [1]Lit. *strikes*
17 [a]Judg. 1:13; 3:9 [b]Num. 32:12; Josh. 14:6 [c]Judg. 1:12
18 [a]Judg. 1:14 [b]Gen. 24:64; 1 Sam. 25:23
19 [a]Gen. 33:11
21 [a]Gen. 35:21
24 [a]1 Sam. 23:14
28 [a]Gen. 21:31; Josh. 19:2
30 [a]Josh. 19:4
31 [a]Josh. 19:5; 1 Sam. 27:6; 30:1
32 [a]Judg. 20:45, 47
33 [a]Judg. 13:25; 16:31
35 [a]1 Sam. 22:1
38 [a]2 Kin. 14:7
39 [a]2 Kin. 14:19 [b]Josh. 10:3
40 [1]Or *Lahmam*
42 [a]Josh. 21:13
46 [a]Josh. 11:22
47 [a]Josh. 15:4 [b]Num. 34:6
51 [a]Josh. 10:41; 11:16
54 [a]Josh. 14:15

15:13–19 Hebron and **Debir** had been captured earlier by Joshua, but apparently were repopulated in the interim. **Caleb** advanced on the giants (the Anakim) with great courage and faith.

15:16, 17 As was the custom, Caleb promised his **daughter** in marriage to the man who took the city of Debir. Caleb's nephew, **Othniel,** accepted the challenge, took the city, and received **Achsah** as his **wife.**

15:20–62 The portion given to **Judah** contained 124 cities and towns divided into 4 major districts: the southland (vv. 21–32), the lowland hills to the west (vv. 33–47), the hill country (vv. 48–60), and the wilderness (vv. 61, 62).

55 [a]Maon, Carmel, Ziph, Juttah,
56 Jezreel, Jokdeam, Zanoah,
57 Kain, Gibeah, and Timnah: ten cities with their villages;
58 Halhul, Beth Zur, Gedor,
59 Maarath, Beth Anoth, and Eltekon:
six cities with their villages;
60 [a]Kirjath Baal (which *is* Kirjath
Jearim) and Rabbah: two cities with
their villages.
61 In the wilderness: Beth Arabah,
Middin, Secacah,
62 Nibshan, the City of Salt, and
[a]En Gedi: six cities with their villages.
5 63 As for the Jebusites, the inhabitants
of Jerusalem, [a]the children of Judah
could not drive them out; [b]but the
Jebusites dwell with the children of
Judah at Jerusalem to this day.

Ephraim and West Manasseh

16 The lot [1]fell to the children of
Joseph from the Jordan, by Jericho, to the waters of Jericho on the
east, to the [a]wilderness that goes up
from Jericho through the mountains to
[2]Bethel,
2 then went out [1]from [a]Bethel to Luz,
passed along to the border of the Ar-
chites at Ataroth,
3 and went down westward to the
boundary of the Japhletites, [a]as far as
the boundary of Lower Beth Horon to
[b]Gezer; and [1]it ended at the sea.
4 [a]So the children of Joseph, Manasseh and Ephraim, took their [1]inheri-
tance.

The Land of Ephraim

5 [a]The border of the children of
Ephraim, according to their families,
was *thus:* The border of their inheritance on the east side was [b]Ataroth
Addar [c]as far as Upper Beth Horon.
6 And the border went out toward the
sea on the north side of [a]Michmethath;
then the border went around eastward
to Taanath Shiloh, and passed by it on
the east of Janohah.
7 Then it went down from Janohah
to Ataroth and [1]Naarah, reached to
Jericho, and came out at the Jordan.
8 The border went out from [a]Tappuah
westward to the [b]Brook Kanah, and
[1]it ended at the sea. This *was* the inheritance of the tribe of the children of
Ephraim according to their families.
9 [a]The separate cities for the children
of Ephraim *were* among the inheritance of the children of Manasseh, all
the cities with their villages.
10 [a]And they did not drive out the Ca- 5
naanites who dwelt in Gezer; but the
Canaanites dwell among the Ephraimites to this day and have become forced
laborers.

The Other Half-Tribe of Manasseh (West)

17 There was also a lot for the tribe
of Manasseh, for he *was* the
[a]firstborn of Joseph: *namely* for
[b]Machir the firstborn of Manasseh, the
father of Gilead, because he was a man
of war; therefore he was given [c]Gilead
and Bashan.
2 And there was *a lot* for [a]the rest of
the children of Manasseh according to
their families: [b]for the children of
[1]Abiezer, the children of Helek, [c]the
children of Asriel, the children of Shechem, [d]the children of Hepher, and the
children of Shemida; these *were* the
male children of Manasseh the son of
Joseph according to their families.
3 But [a]Zelophehad the son of Hepher,
the son of Gilead, the son of Machir,

55 [a]1 Sam. 23:24, 25
60 [a]Josh. 18:14
62 [a]1 Sam. 23:29
63 [a]2 Sam. 5:6 [b]Judg. 1:21

CHAPTER 16

1 [a]Josh. 8:15; 18:12 [1]Lit. *went out* [2]LXX *Bethel Luz*
2 [a]Josh. 18:13 [1]LXX *to Bethel,*
3 [a]2 Chr. 8:5 [b]1 Kin. 9:15 [1]Lit. *the goings out of it were at the sea*
4 [a]Josh. 17:14 [1]*possession*
5 [a]Judg. 1:29 [b]Josh. 18:13 [c]2 Chr. 8:5
6 [a]Josh. 17:7
7 [1]*Naaran,* 1 Chr. 7:28
8 [a]Josh. 17:8 [b]Josh. 17:9 [1]Lit. *the goings out of it were at the sea*
9 [a]Josh. 17:9
10 [a]Judg. 1:29

CHAPTER 17

1 [a]Gen. 41:51; 46:20; 48:18 [b]Gen. 50:23 [c]Deut. 3:15
2 [a]Num. 26:29–33 [b]1 Chr. 7:18 [c]Num. 26:31 [d]Num. 26:32 [1]*Jeezer,* Num. 26:30
3 [a]Num. 26:33; 27:1; 36:2

15:63 See section 5 of Truth-In-Action at the end of Josh.
15:63 The children of Judah could not drive them out: Here is the first hint of the deficiency of Israel's conquests. This failure would affect the moral and social fiber of their lives for generations.
16:1–3 Chs. 16 and 17 describe the land given to the descendants of Joseph's two sons, Ephraim and Manasseh. See the note on 14:1–5. They drew one **lot,** but the land was divided between the two tribes. These introductory verses describe the southern boundary of Ephraim: roughly from the Jordan River east of Jericho, then westward to the Mediterranean Sea.
16:4 *Even though* **Manasseh** was Joseph's firstborn, Jacob had blessed **Ephraim** as his favorite (Gen. 48:19). Thus Ephraim received his birthright first.
16:5–8 Ephraim settled between Benjamin and Dan on the south and West Manasseh on the north.
16:9 Separate cities: They were also given cities within Manasseh's borders, possibly because Ephraim's area was proportionately too small for its population.
16:10 See section 5 of Truth-In-Action at the end of Josh.
16:10 Did not drive out: Although reduced to slave labor, these Canaanites would remain in Gezer nearly 400 years until subdued by Solomon. This mention is intended to show Ephraim's failure, even as Judah had failed to drive out the Jebusites (15:63). Deut. 7:1–5 had warned that such failure would eventually turn the Israelites from following God.
17:1 Machir was Manasseh's oldest son and the father of Gilead. Because he was a military hero, his family received a lush and mountainous territory east of the Sea of Galilee.
17:2 All the names mentioned were sons of Gilead (Num. 26:29–32). Their families received land west of the Jordan River.
17:3–6 Customarily, a man's inheritance was passed only to sons. But **Zelophehad,** the grandson of Gilead, had no sons—only five daughters. These daughters had come boldly before Moses to claim God's provision for them (Num. 27:1–11). In harmony with the Lord's instruction, Joshua gave

the son of Manasseh, had no sons, but
only daughters. And these *are* the
names of his daughters: Mahlah, Noah,
Hoglah, Milcah, and Tirzah.
4 And they came near before [a]Ele-
azar the priest, before Joshua the son
of Nun, and before the rulers, saying,
[b]"The LORD commanded Moses to give
us an [1]inheritance among our brothers." Therefore, according to the commandment of the LORD, he gave them
an inheritance among their father's
brothers.
5 Ten shares fell to [a]Manasseh, besides the land of Gilead and Bashan,
which *were* on the other side of the Jordan,
6 because the daughters of Manasseh
received an inheritance among his
sons; and the rest of Manasseh's sons
had the land of Gilead.
7 And the territory of Manasseh was
from Asher to [a]Michmethath, that *lies*
east of Shechem; and the border went
along south to the inhabitants of En
Tappuah.
8 Manasseh had the land of Tappuah,
but [a]Tappuah on the border of Manasseh *belonged* to the children of
Ephraim.
9 And the [1]border descended to the
[2]Brook Kanah, southward to the
brook. [a]These cities of Ephraim *are*
among the cities of Manasseh. The border of Manasseh *was* on the north side
of the brook; and it ended at the sea.
10 Southward *it was* Ephraim's, northward *it was* Manasseh's, and the sea
was its border. Manasseh's territory
was adjoining Asher on the north and
Issachar on the east.
11 And in Issachar and in Asher,
[a]Manasseh had [b]Beth Shean and its
towns, Ibleam and its towns, the inhabitants of Dor and its towns, the inhabitants of En Dor and its towns, the inhabitants of Taanach and its towns,
and the inhabitants of Megiddo and its
towns—three hilly regions.

4 [a]Josh. 14:1 [b]Num. 27:2–11 [1]*possession*
5 [a]Josh. 22:7
7 [a]Josh. 16:6
8 [a]Josh. 16:8
9 [a]Josh. 16:9 [1]*boundary* [2]*Wadi*
11 [a]1 Chr. 7:29 [b]Judg. 1:27; 1 Sam. 31:10; 1 Kin. 4:12
12 [a]Judg. 1:19, 27, 28
13 [a]Josh. 16:10
14 [a]Josh. 16:4 [b]Gen. 48:22 [c]Gen. 48:19; Num. 26:34, 37 [1]*allotment*
16 [a]Josh. 17:18; Judg. 1:19; 4:3 [b]Josh. 19:18; 1 Kin. 4:12
17 [1]*allotment* *See WW at Deut. 8:18.
18 [a]Deut. 20:1 [1]Lit. *goings out* *See WW at Gen. 1:1.

CHAPTER 18

1 [a]Josh. 19:51; 21:2; 22:9; Jer. 7:12 [b]Judg. 18:31; 1 Sam. 1:3, 24; 4:3, 4 *See WW at Gen. 49:10.

12 Yet [a]the children of Manasseh **5**
could not drive out *the inhabitants of*
those cities, but the Canaanites were
determined to dwell in that land.
13 And it happened, when the children
of Israel grew strong, that they put the
Canaanites to [a]forced labor, but did
not utterly drive them out.

More Land for Ephraim and Manasseh

14 [a]Then the children of Joseph spoke
to Joshua, saying, "Why have you
given us *only* [b]one [1]lot and one share
to inherit, since we *are* [c]a great people,
inasmuch as the LORD has blessed us
until now?"
15 So Joshua answered them, "If you
are a great people, *then* go up to the
forest *country* and clear a place for
yourself there in the land of the Perizzites and the giants, since the mountains of Ephraim are too confined for
you."
16 But the children of Joseph said,
"The mountain country is not enough
for us; and all the Canaanites who
dwell in the land of the valley have
[a]chariots of iron, *both those* who *are*
of Beth Shean and its towns and *those*
who *are* [b]of the Valley of Jezreel."
17 And Joshua spoke to the house of
Joseph—to Ephraim and Manasseh—
saying, "You *are* a great people and
have great *power; you shall not have
only one [1]lot,
18 "but the mountain country shall be **7**
yours. Although it *is* wooded, you shall
*cut it down, and its [1]farthest extent
shall be yours; for you shall drive out
the Canaanites, [a]though they have iron
chariots *and* are strong."

The Remainder of the Land Divided

18 Now the whole congregation of
the children of Israel assembled
together [a]at *Shiloh, and [b]set up the

them an allotment, along with their male relatives, west of the Jordan.

17:7–13 These verses describe the territory of Manasseh. It was centrally located between Ephraim on the south and Issachar and Asher on the north.

17:12, 13 Once again, the Israelites did not follow God's command to "utterly destroy" the Canaanites. See also 15:63 and 16:10. Instead, they compromised and used their captives as slave labor. Soon they began to comingle, and the seeds of dissension were planted.

17:12 See section 5 of Truth-In-Action at the end of Josh.

17:14, 15 Though they had been given the largest share of land, the tribes of Ephraim and Manasseh began to grumble because they wanted more. They felt they could neither clear the forests within their boundaries nor defeat the Canaanites with their advanced weaponry.

17:16 Is not enough: At the last census, Ephraim numbered 32,500; half of Manasseh was 26,300; a combined total of 58,800 (Num. 26:34, 37). The population of Dan, Zebulun, and Issachar was much greater, but their territories were considerably smaller. Apparently, Israel judged their portions in terms of the cities and its cleared area rather than the size of the land.

17:18 See section 7 of Truth-In-Action at the end of Josh.

18:1 Shiloh was a city in Ephraim about 35 miles north of Jerusalem. This new site was chosen for the erection of the tabernacle, probably because of its central location. The ark of the covenant remained there for over 100 years until it was captured in a battle with the Philistines (1 Sam. 4:1–11).

tabernacle of meeting there. And the land was subdued before them.

2 But there remained among the children of Israel seven tribes which had not yet received their inheritance.

3 Then Joshua said to the children of Israel: [a]"How long will you neglect to go and possess the land which the LORD God of your fathers has given you?

4 "Pick out from among you three men for *each* tribe, and I will send them; they shall rise and go through the land, survey it according to their inheritance, and come *back* to me.

5 "And they shall divide it into seven parts. [a]Judah shall remain in their territory on the south, and the [b]house of Joseph shall remain in their territory on the north.

6 "You shall therefore [1]survey the land in seven parts and bring *the survey* here to me, [a]that I may cast lots for you here before the LORD our God.

7 [a]"But the Levites have no part among you, for the priesthood of the LORD *is* their inheritance. [b]And Gad, Reuben, and half the tribe of Manasseh have received their inheritance beyond the Jordan on the east, which Moses the servant of the LORD gave them."

8 Then the men arose to go away; and Joshua charged those who went to [1]survey the land, saying, "Go, walk [a]through the land, survey it, and come back to me, that I may cast lots for you here before the LORD in Shiloh."

9 So the men went, passed through the land, and [1]wrote the survey in a book in seven parts by cities; and they came to Joshua at the camp in Shiloh.

10 Then Joshua cast [a]lots for them in Shiloh before the LORD, and there [b]Joshua divided the land to the children of Israel according to their [1]divisions.

The Land of Benjamin

11 [a]Now the lot of the tribe of the children of Benjamin came up according to their families, and the territory of their lot came out between the children of Judah and the children of Joseph.

12 [a]Their border on the north side began at the Jordan, and the border went up to the side of Jericho on the north, and went up through the mountains westward; it ended at the Wilderness of Beth Aven.

13 The border went over from there toward Luz, to the side of Luz [a](which *is* Bethel) southward; and the border descended to Ataroth Addar, near the hill that *lies* on the south side [b]of Lower Beth Horon.

14 Then the border extended around the west side to the south, from the hill that *lies* before Beth Horon southward; and [1]it ended at [a]Kirjath Baal (which *is* Kirjath Jearim), a city of the children of Judah. This *was* the west side.

15 The south side *began* at the end of Kirjath Jearim, and the border extended on the west and went out to [a]the spring of the waters of Nephtoah.

16 Then the border came down to the end of the mountain that *lies* before [a]the Valley of the Son of Hinnom, which *is* in the Valley of the [1]Rephaim on the north, descended to the Valley of Hinnom, to the side of the Jebusite *city* on the south, and descended to [b]En Rogel.

17 And it went around from the north, went out to En Shemesh, and extended toward Geliloth, which is before the Ascent of Adummim, and descended to [a]the stone of Bohan the son of Reuben.

18 Then it passed along toward the north side of [1]Arabah, and went down to Arabah.

19 And the border passed along to the north side of Beth Hoglah; then [1]the border ended at the north bay at the [a]Salt Sea, at the south end of the Jordan. This *was* the southern boundary.

20 The Jordan was its border on the east side. This *was* the inheritance of the children of Benjamin, according to its boundaries all around, according to their families.

21 Now the cities of the tribe of the children of Benjamin, according to their families, were Jericho, Beth Hoglah, Emek Keziz,

22 Beth Arabah, Zemaraim, Bethel,

23 Avim, Parah, Ophrah,

24 Chephar Haammoni, Ophni, and Gaba: twelve cities with their villages;

3 [a]Judg. 18:9
5 [a]Josh. 15:1 [b]Josh. 16:1—17:18
6 [a]Josh. 14:2; 18:10 [1]*describe in writing*
7 [a]Num. 18:7, 20; Josh. 13:33 [b]Josh. 13:8
8 [a]Gen. 13:17 [1]*describe in writing*
9 [1]*described it in writing*
10 [a]Acts 13:19 [b]Num. 34:16–29; Josh. 19:51 [1]*portions*
11 [a]Judg. 1:21
12 [a]Josh. 16:1
13 [a]Gen. 28:19; Josh. 16:2; Judg. 1:23 [b]Josh. 16:3
14 [a]Josh. 15:9 [1]Lit. *its goings out were*
15 [a]Josh. 15:9
16 [a]Josh. 15:8 [b]Josh. 15:7 [1]Lit. *Giants*
17 [a]Josh. 15:6
18 [1]*Beth Arabah*, Josh. 15:6; 18:22
19 [a]Josh. 15:2, 5 [1]Lit. *the goings out of the border were*

18:2, 3 Seven tribes had not received their allotments. Joshua's rebuke suggests the reason: their own complacency and laziness.

18:4–8 Joshua proposed that three men from each of the seven tribes survey the remaining land, write a description of it, and divide it into seven parts. Joshua would then draw lots to determine which part the Lord wanted each of the seven tribes to receive.

18:11–28 Benjamin's portion was north of Judah and south of Ephraim. Their portion contained 26 cities, including Jerusalem. Though the territory was small, the land was strategically located, both militarily and commercially.

25 [a]Gibeon, [b]Ramah, Beeroth,
26 Mizpah, Chephirah, Mozah,
27 Rekem, Irpeel, Taralah,
28 Zelah, Eleph, [a]Jebus (which *is* Jerusalem), Gibeath, *and* Kirjath: fourteen
cities with their villages. This was the
inheritance of the children of Benjamin
according to their families.

Simeon's Inheritance with Judah

19 The [a]second lot came out for
Simeon, for the tribe of the children of Simeon according to their families. [b]And their inheritance was within
the inheritance of the children of Judah.
2 [a]They had in their inheritance Beersheba (Sheba), Moladah,
3 Hazar Shual, Balah, Ezem,
4 Eltolad, Bethul, Hormah,
5 Ziklag, Beth Marcaboth, Hazar
Susah,
6 Beth Lebaoth, and Sharuhen: thirteen cities and their villages;
7 Ain, Rimmon, Ether, and Ashan:
four cities and their villages;
8 and all the villages that *were* all
around these cities as far as Baalath
Beer, [a]Ramah of the South. This *was*
the inheritance of the tribe of the children of Simeon according to their families.
9 The inheritance of the children of
Simeon *was included* in the share of
the children of Judah, for the share of
the children of Judah was [1]too much
for them. [a]Therefore the children of
Simeon had *their* inheritance within
the inheritance of [2]that people.

The Land of Zebulun

10 The third lot came out for the children of Zebulun according to their
families, and the border of their inheritance was as far as Sarid.
11 [a]Their border went toward the west
and to Maralah, went to Dabbasheth,
and extended along the brook that is
[b]east of Jokneam.
12 Then from Sarid it went eastward
toward the sunrise along the border of
Chisloth Tabor, and went out toward
[a]Daberath, bypassing Japhia.
13 And from there it passed along on
the east of [a]Gath Hepher, toward Eth
Kazin, and extended to Rimmon,
which borders on Neah.
14 Then the border went around it on
the north side of Hannathon, and [1]it
ended in the Valley of Jiphthah El.
15 Included were Kattath, Nahallal,
Shimron, Idalah, and Bethlehem:
twelve cities with their villages.
16 This *was* the inheritance of the children of Zebulun according to their
families, these cities with their villages.

The Land of Issachar

17 The fourth lot came out to Issachar,
for the children of Issachar according
to their families.
18 And their territory went to Jezreel,
and *included* Chesulloth, Shunem,
19 Haphraim, Shion, Anaharath,
20 Rabbith, Kishion, Abez,
21 Remeth, En Gannim, En Haddah,
and Beth Pazzez.
22 And the border *reached to Tabor,
Shahazimah, and [a]Beth Shemesh;
their border ended at the Jordan: sixteen cities with their villages.
23 This *was* the inheritance of the tribe
of the children of Issachar according
to their families, the cities and their villages.

The Land of Asher

24 [a]The fifth lot came out for the tribe
of the children of Asher according to
their families.
25 And their territory included Helkath, Hali, Beten, Achshaph,
26 Alammelech, Amad, and Mishal; it
reached to [a]Mount Carmel westward,
along *the Brook* Shihor Libnath.
27 It turned toward the sunrise to Beth
Dagon; and it *reached to Zebulun and
to the Valley of Jiphthah El, then
northward beyond Beth Emek and

25 [a]Josh. 11:19; 21:17; 1 Kin. 3:4, 5 [b]Jer. 31:15
28 [a]Josh. 15:8, 63

CHAPTER 19

1 [a]Judg. 1:3 [b]Josh. 19:9
2 [a]1 Chr. 4:28
8 [a]1 Sam. 30:27
9 [a]Josh. 19:1 [1]too large [2]Lit. *them*
11 [a]Gen. 49:13 [b]Josh. 12:22
12 [a]1 Chr. 6:72
13 [a]2 Kin. 14:25
14 [1]Lit. *the goings out of it were*
22 [a]Josh. 15:10; Judg. 1:33 *See WW at Jer. 27:18.
24 [a]Judg. 1:31, 32
26 [a]1 Sam. 15:12; 1 Kin. 18:20; Is. 33:9; 35:2; Jer. 46:18
27 *See WW at Jer. 27:18.

19:1–9 Simeon received 17 cities and surrounding villages within the territory of Judah. These cities were scattered rather than neighboring. Eventually, the tribe of Simeon was assimilated into Judah, thus fulfilling the prophecy of Gen. 49:5–7.

19:10–16 Zebulun inherited 12 cities with their villages. **Bethlehem** here is in Galilee; it is not Bethlehem of Judah in the south. The territory was fertile and mountainous. It lay between the Sea of Galilee and the Mediterranean.

19:17–23 The inheritance of **Issachar** included 16 cities and their villages southwest of the Sea of Galilee. It also included part of the Jezreel Valley, a rich agricultural area and site of many battles throughout history.

19:24–31 The territory of **Asher** stretched from north of Sidon to Mt. Carmel on the south; from the Mediterranean on the west to the western slopes of the Galilean hills on the east. The tribe of Asher prospered as a result of its renowned olive groves in this fertile, well-watered area. However, they never succeeded in driving out the Phoenicians from the seaport cities of Acco, Tyre, and Sidon (Judg. 1:31, 32).

Neiel, bypassing [a]Cabul *which was* on
the left,
28 including [1]Ebron, Rehob, Hammon,
and Kanah, [a]as far as Greater Sidon.
29 And the border turned to Ramah
and to the fortified city of Tyre; then
the border turned to Hosah, and ended
at the sea by the region of [a]Achzib.
30 Also Ummah, Aphek, and Rehob
were included: twenty-two cities with
their villages.
31 This *was* the inheritance of the tribe
of the children of Asher according to
their families, these cities with their
villages.

The Land of Naphtali

32 [a]The sixth lot came out to the children of Naphtali, for the children of
Naphtali according to their families.
33 And their border began at Heleph,
enclosing the territory from the terebinth tree in Zaanannim, Adami
Nekeb, and Jabneel, as far as Lakkum;
[1]it ended at the Jordan.
34 [a]From Heleph the border extended
westward to Aznoth Tabor, and went
out from there toward Hukkok; it ad-
joined Zebulun on the south side and
Asher on the west side, and ended at
Judah by the Jordan toward the sunrise.
35 And the fortified cities *are* Ziddim,
Zer, Hammath, Rakkath, Chinnereth,
36 Adamah, Ramah, Hazor,
37 [a]Kedesh, Edrei, En Hazor,
38 Iron, Migdal El, Horem, Beth Anath,
and Beth Shemesh: nineteen cities with
their villages.
39 This *was* the inheritance of the tribe
of the children of Naphtali according
to their families, the cities and their villages.

The Land of Dan

40 [a]The seventh lot came out for the
tribe of the children of Dan according
to their families.
41 And the territory of their inheritance was Zorah, [a]Eshtaol, Ir Shemesh,
42 [a]Shaalabbin, [b]Aijalon, Jethlah,
43 Elon, Timnah, [a]Ekron,
44 Eltekeh, Gibbethon, Baalath,
45 Jehud, Bene Berak, Gath Rimmon,
46 Me Jarkon, and Rakkon, with the
region [1]near [2]Joppa.
47 And the [a]border of the children of
Dan went beyond these, because the
children of Dan went up to fight
against Leshem and took it; and they
struck it with the edge of the sword,
took possession of it, and dwelt in it.
They called Leshem, [b]Dan, after the
name of Dan their father.
48 This *is* the inheritance of the tribe
of the children of Dan according to
their families, these cities with their
villages.

Joshua's Inheritance

49 When they had [1]made an end of dividing the land as an inheritance according to their borders, the children
of Israel gave an inheritance among
them to Joshua the son of Nun.
50 According to the word of the LORD
they gave him the city which he asked
for, [a]Timnath [b]Serah in the mountains
of Ephraim; and he built the city and
dwelt in it.
51 [a]These *were* the inheritances which
Eleazar the priest, Joshua the son of
Nun, and the heads of the fathers of
the tribes of the children of Israel divided as an inheritance by lot [b]in *Shiloh before the LORD, at the door of the
tabernacle of meeting. So they made
an end of dividing the country.

The Cities of Refuge

20 The LORD also spoke to Joshua,
saying,
2 "Speak to the children of Israel,
saying: [a]'Appoint[1] for yourselves cities
of refuge, of which I spoke to you
through Moses,
3 'that the slayer who kills a person

27 [a]1 Kin. 9:13
28 [a]Gen. 10:19; Josh. 11:8; Judg. 1:31; Acts 27:3 [1]So with MT, Tg., Vg.; a few Heb. mss. *Abdon* (cf. 21:30 and 1 Chr. 6:74)
29 [a]Judg. 1:31
32 [a]Josh. 19:32–39; Judg. 1:33
33 [1]Lit. *its goings out were*
34 [a]Deut. 33:23
37 [a]Josh. 20:7
40 [a]Josh. 19:40–48; Judg. 1:34–36
41 [a]Josh. 15:33
42 [a]Judg. 1:35; 1 Kin. 4:9 [b]Josh. 10:12; 21:24
43 [a]Josh. 15:11; Judg. 1:18
46 [1]*over against* [2]Heb. *Japho*
47 [a]Judg. 18 [b]Judg. 18:29
49 [1]*finished*
50 [a]Josh. 24:30 [b]1 Chr. 7:24
51 [a]Num. 34:17; Josh. 14:1 [b]Josh. 18:1, 10 *See WW at Gen. 49:10.

CHAPTER 20

2 [a]Ex. 21:13; Num. 35:6–34; Deut. 19:2, 9 [1]*Designate*

19:32–39 Naphtali was given the northernmost territory. It was a long, narrow strip of land between Asher and the Jordan River. The land was mountainous and fertile. They did not drive out the Canaanites but lived among them.

19:40–48 The territory allotted to **Dan** lay in the west-central region of Canaan, bordering the Mediterranean. The tribe was never able to fully maintain control over the land. Many of them later migrated to the northeast, conquered the city of Leshem (or Laish), settled there, and renamed it Dan. They soon fell into idolatry (Judg. 18:30).

19:49, 50 Not until all had received their portions did Joshua choose his inheritance and final resting place. **Timnath Serah** is traditionally connected with the location where Joshua commanded the sun to stand still (10:13).

20:2–6 It was the custom among all the ancient Near Eastern peoples to demand equal punishment for a crime; e.g., a life for a life. No consideration was given to the circumstances. But God's laws considered intent. **Cities of refuge** were established to provide sanctuary for one who had killed another unwillfully. Here, he was protected until he stood trial; and, if judged innocent, he was required to live there until the death of the high priest.

20:3 Avenger of blood: It was the duty of the nearest male relative to avenge the death by killing the killer.

accidentally *or* unintentionally may
flee there; and they shall be your refuge from the avenger of blood.
4 'And when he flees to one of those
cities, and stands at the entrance of the
gate of the city, and [1]declares his case
in the hearing of the elders of that city,
they shall take him into the city as one
of them, and give him a place, that he
may dwell among them.
5 [a]'Then if the avenger of blood pursues him, they shall not deliver the
slayer into his hand, because he struck
his neighbor unintentionally, but did
not hate him beforehand.
6 'And he shall dwell in that city
[a]until he stands before the congregation for *judgment, *and* until the death
of the one who is high priest in those
days. Then the slayer may return and
come to his own city and his own
house, to the city from which he fled.' "

4 [1]*states*
5 [a]Num. 35:12
6 [a]Num. 35:12, 24, 25
*See WW at Num. 36:13.

20:4 Entrance of the gate: This prominent area in the city became the local city hall. Here, cases were heard and reviewed by the city elders, men of age and experience who represented the people.
20:6 Death of the . . . high priest: This is a picture of what Christ has done for us. Only the death of the high priest could release the offender to return home, just as Christ's death on the cross releases us from our sin that we might go to our heavenly home.

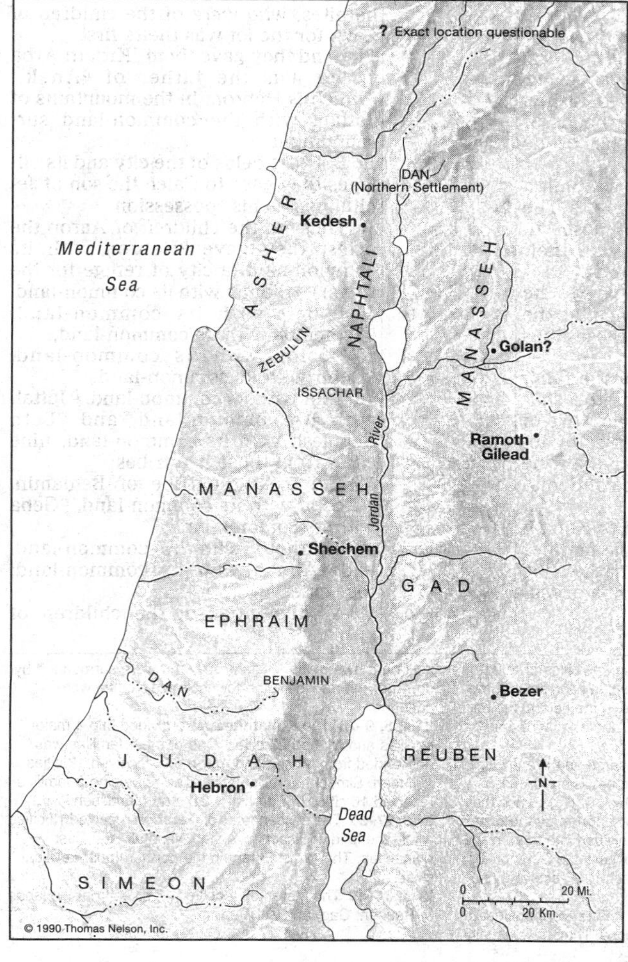

Division of Land Among the Twelve Tribes and Designation of the Cities of Refuge. From north to south and on both sides of the Jordan River, cities of refuge were strategically located to provide protection for those who had killed someone unintentionally.

7 So they appointed [a]Kedesh in Galilee, in the mountains of Naphtali,
[b]Shechem in the mountains of
Ephraim, and [c]Kirjath Arba (which *is*
Hebron) in [d]the mountains of Judah.
8 And on the other side of the Jordan,
by Jericho eastward, they assigned
[a]Bezer in the wilderness on the plain,
from the tribe of Reuben, [b]Ramoth in
Gilead, from the tribe of Gad, and
[c]Golan in Bashan, from the tribe of
Manasseh.
9 [a]These were the cities appointed for
all the children of Israel and for the
stranger who [1]dwelt among them, that
whoever killed a person accidentally
might flee there, and not die by the
hand of the avenger of blood [b]until he
stood before the congregation.

Cities of the Levites

21 Then the heads of the fathers'
houses of the [a]Levites came
near to [b]Eleazar the priest, to Joshua
the son of Nun, and to the heads of
the fathers' *houses* of the tribes of the
children of Israel.
2 And they spoke to them at [a]Shiloh
in the land of Canaan, saying, [b]"The
LORD commanded through Moses to
give us cities to dwell in, with their
common-lands for our livestock."
3 So the children of Israel gave to the
Levites from their inheritance, at the
commandment of the LORD, these cities
and their common-lands:
4 Now the lot came out for the families of the Kohathites. And [a]the children of Aaron the priest, *who were* of
the Levites, [b]had thirteen cities by lot
from the tribe of Judah, from the tribe
of Simeon, and from the tribe of Benjamin.
5 [a]The rest of the children of Kohath
had ten cities by lot from the families
of the tribe of Ephraim, from the tribe
of Dan, and from the half-tribe of Manasseh.

7 [a]Josh. 21:32; 1 Chr. 6:76 [b]Josh. 21:21; 2 Chr. 10:1 [c]Josh. 14:15; 21:11, 13 [d]Luke 1:39
8 [a]Deut. 4:43; Josh. 21:36; 1 Chr. 6:78 [b]Josh. 21:38; 1 Kin. 22:3 [c]Josh. 21:27
9 [a]Num. 35:15 [b]Josh. 20:6 [1]As a resident alien

CHAPTER 21

1 [a]Num. 35:1–8 [b]Num. 34:16–29; Josh. 14:1; 17:4
2 [a]Josh. 18:1 [b]Num. 35:2
4 [a]Josh. 21:8, 19 [b]Josh. 19:51
5 [a]Josh. 21:20
6 [a]Josh. 21:27
7 [a]Josh. 21:34
8 [a]Josh. 21:3 [b]Num. 35:2
9 [1]Lit. *called*
11 [a]Josh. 20:7; 1 Chr. 6:55 [b]Josh. 14:15; 15:13, 14 [c]Josh. 20:7; Luke 1:39 [1]Lit. *City of Arba*
12 [a]Josh. 14:14; 1 Chr. 6:56 *See WW at Josh. 22:9.
13 [a]1 Chr. 6:57 [b]Josh. 15:54; 20:2, 7 [c]Josh. 15:42; 2 Kin. 8:22
14 [a]Josh. 15:48 [b]Josh. 15:50
15 [a]1 Chr. 6:58 [b]Josh. 15:49
16 [a]1 Chr. 6:59 [b]Josh. 15:55 [c]Josh. 15:10
17 [a]Josh. 18:25 [b]Josh. 18:24
18 [a]1 Chr. 6:60

6 And [a]the children of Gershon had
thirteen cities by lot from the families
of the tribe of Issachar, from the tribe
of Asher, from the tribe of Naphtali,
and from the half-tribe of Manasseh in
Bashan.
7 [a]The children of Merari according
to their families had twelve cities from
the tribe of Reuben, from the tribe of
Gad, and from the tribe of Zebulun.
8 [a]And the children of Israel gave
these cities with their common-lands
by lot to the Levites, [b]as the LORD had
commanded by the hand of Moses.
9 So they gave from the tribe of the
children of Judah and from the tribe
of the children of Simeon these cities
which are [1]designated by name,
10 which were for the children of
Aaron, one of the families of the Kohathites, *who were* of the children of
Levi; for the lot was theirs first.
11 [a]And they gave them [1]Kirjath Arba
(*Arba was* the father of [b]Anak),
[c]which *is* Hebron, in the mountains of
Judah, with the common-land surrounding it.
12 But [a]the fields of the city and its villages they gave to Caleb the son of Jephunneh as his *possession.
13 Thus [a]to the children of Aaron the
priest they gave [b]Hebron with its
common-land (a city of refuge for the
slayer), [c]Libnah with its common-land,
14 [a]Jattir with its common-land,
[b]Eshtemoa with its common-land,
15 [a]Holon with its common-land,
[b]Debir with its common-land,
16 [a]Ain with its common-land, [b]Juttah
with its common-land, and [c]Beth
Shemesh with its common-land: nine
cities from those two tribes;
17 and from the tribe of Benjamin,
[a]Gibeon with its common-land, [b]Geba
with its common-land,
18 Anathoth with its common-land,
and [a]Almon with its common-land:
four cities.
19 All the cities of the children of

20:7, 8 Six Levitical cities were chosen as cities of refuge: three east of the Jordan and three west. In each set of three, one city was located in the north, one in the central region, and one in the south, so that it might not take more than half a day to reach a city of refuge.

21:1–45 The tribe of Levi was to disperse and live in cities throughout Israel. They were to make provision for the worship of God and teach the law (Deut. 33:10). Since they had no land of their own, they were supported by the tithe for God (Num. 18:24). The tribe was divided into three clans who descended from the three sons of Levi: the Gershonites, the Kohathites, and the Merarites. Each clan received its cities by sacred lot.

21:2 At this period in Israel's history, **cities** were enclosed places that had fortified walls for defense. They were usually built on a hill—again for defense—and were surrounded by **common-lands** where the townspeople's cattle were pastured.

21:4, 5, 9–26 The **Kohathites** were divided into 4 major families and allotted 23 cities. One of the 4 families was descended from Moses and Aaron and received 13 cities in Judah, Simeon, and Benjamin. The remaining 3 families received 10 cities in Ephraim, Dan, and Manasseh.

21:6, 27–33 The descendants of **Gershon** received 13 cities within the land of Issachar, Asher, Naphtali, and East Manasseh. This placed them in the northernmost Levitical cities.

21:7, 34–40 The Merarites received 12 cities from the lands of Reuben, Gad, and Zebulun.

Aaron, the priests, *were* thirteen cities
with their common-lands.
20 [a]And the families of the children of
Kohath, the Levites, the rest of the children of Kohath, even they had the
cities of their [1]lot from the tribe of
Ephraim.
21 For they gave them [a]Shechem with
its common-land in the mountains of
Ephraim (a city of refuge for the
slayer), [b]Gezer with its common-land,
22 Kibzaim with its common-land, and
Beth Horon with its common-land: four
cities;
23 and from the tribe of Dan, Eltekeh
with its common-land, Gibbethon with
its common-land,
24 [a]Aijalon with its common-land, *and*
Gath Rimmon with its common-land:
four cities;
25 and from the half-tribe of Manasseh, Tanach with its common-land and
Gath Rimmon with its common-land:
two cities.
26 All the ten cities with their
common-lands were for the rest of the
families of the children of Kohath.
27 [a]Also to the children of Gershon, of
the families of the Levites, from
the *other* half-tribe of Manasseh, *they
gave* [b]Golan in Bashan with its
common-land (a city of refuge for the
slayer), and Be Eshterah with its
common-land: two cities;
28 and from the tribe of Issachar, Kishion with its common-land, Daberath
with its common-land,
29 Jarmuth with its common-land, *and*
En Gannim with its common-land: four
cities;
30 and from the tribe of Asher, Mishal
with its common-land, Abdon with its
common-land,
31 Helkath with its common-land, and
Rehob with its common-land: four cities;
32 and from the tribe of Naphtali,
[a]Kedesh in Galilee with its common-
land (a city of refuge for the slayer),
Hammoth Dor with its common-land,
and Kartan with its common-land:
three cities.
33 All the cities of the Gershonites according to their families *were* thirteen
cities with their common-lands.
34 [a]And to the families of the children
of Merari, the rest of the Levites, from
the tribe of Zebulun, Jokneam with
its common-land, Kartah with its
common-land,
35 Dimnah with its common-land, *and*
Nahalal with its common-land: four
cities;
36 [1]and from the tribe of Reuben,
[a]Bezer with its common-land, Jahaz
with its common-land,
37 Kedemoth with its common-land,
and Mephaath with its common-land:
four cities;
38 and from the tribe of Gad, [a]Ramoth
in Gilead with its common-land (a city
of refuge for the slayer), Mahanaim
with its common-land,
39 Heshbon with its common-land, *and*
Jazer with its common-land: four cities
in all.
40 So all the cities for the children of
Merari according to their families, the
rest of the families of the Levites, were
by their lot twelve cities.
41 [a]All the cities of the Levites within
the possession of the children of Israel *were* forty-eight cities with their
common-lands.
42 Every one of these cities had its
common-land surrounding it; thus
were all these cities.

The Promise Fulfilled

43 So the LORD gave to Israel [a]all the
land of which He had sworn to give
to their fathers, and they [b]took possession of it and dwelt in it.
44 [a]The LORD gave them [b]rest all
around, according to all that He had
sworn to their fathers. And [c]not a man
of all their enemies stood against them;
the LORD delivered all their enemies
into their hand.
45 [a]Not a word failed of any good 1
thing which the LORD had spoken to
the house of Israel. All came to pass.

Eastern Tribes Return to Their Lands

22 Then Joshua called the Reubenites, the Gadites, and half
the tribe of Manasseh,
2 and said to them: "You have kept
[a]all that Moses the servant of the LORD
commanded you, [b]and have obeyed
my voice in all that I commanded you.
3 "You have not [1]left your brethren

20 [a]1 Chr. 6:66 [1]*allotment* **21** [a]Josh. 20:7 [b]Judg. 1:29 **24** [a]Josh. 10:12 **27** [a]Josh. 21:6; 1 Chr. 6:71 [b]Josh. 20:8 **32** [a]Josh. 20:7 **34** [a]Josh. 21:7; 1 Chr. 6:77–81

36 [a]Deut. 4:43; Josh. 20:8 [1]So with LXX, Vg. (cf. 1 Chr. 6:78, 79); MT, Bg., Tg. omit vv. 36, 37 **38** [a]Josh. 20:8 **41** [a]Num. 35:7 **43** [a]Gen. 12:7; 26:3, 4; 28:4, 13, 14 [b]Num. 33:53; Josh. 1:11 **44** [a]Deut. 7:23, 24; Josh. 11:23; 22:4 [b]Josh. 1:13, 15; 11:23 [c]Deut. 7:24 **45** [a][Num. 23:19]; Josh. 23:14; 1 Kin. 8:56

CHAPTER 22

2 [a]Num. 32:20–22; Deut. 3:18 [b]Josh. 1:12–18 **3** [1]*forsaken*

21:43–45 This passage summarizes the entire first part of the book and its basic message: God is faithful to the obedient. To the seed of Abraham, He had promised the land of Canaan (1:2, 3); He had promised victory (1:5); and He had promised rest (1:13). Everything the Lord had promised them had been fulfilled.

21:45 See section 1 of Truth-In-Action at the end of Josh.

22:1–9 Joshua began his conquest of the land by charging the 2½ eastern tribes to participate (1:12–15). He now ends his duties by dismissing them. Over 40,000 soldiers were given Joshua's blessing to return to their families who had waited for at least 7 (perhaps even 14) years.

these many days, up to this day, but
have kept the charge of the commandment of the LORD your God.
4 "And now the LORD your God has
given [a]rest to your brethren, as He
promised them; now therefore, return
and go to your tents *and* to the land
of your possession, [b]which Moses the
servant of the LORD gave you on the
other side of the Jordan.
2 5 "But [a]take[1] careful heed to do the
*commandment and the law which Mo-
ses the servant of the LORD commanded you, [b]to love the LORD your
God, to walk in all His ways, to keep
His commandments, to hold fast to
Him, and to serve Him with all your
heart and with all your *soul."
6 So Joshua [a]blessed them and sent
them away, and they went to their
tents.
7 Now to half the tribe of Manasseh
Moses had given a possession in Bashan, [a]but to the *other* half of it Joshua
gave *a possession* among their brethren on this side of the Jordan, westward. And indeed, when Joshua sent
them away to their tents, he blessed
them,
8 and spoke to them, saying, "Return
with much riches to your tents, with
very much livestock, with silver, with
gold, with bronze, with iron, and
with very much clothing. [a]Divide the
[1]spoil of your enemies with your brethren."
9 So the children of Reuben, the children of Gad, and half the tribe of Manasseh returned, and departed from
the children of Israel at Shiloh, which
is in the land of Canaan, to go to
[a]the country of Gilead, to the land of
their **possession,** which they had obtained according to the word of the
LORD by the hand of Moses.

WORD WEALTH

22:9 possession, *'achuzzah* (ah-*chooz*-zah); Strong's #272: Something obtained, seized, or held. *'Achuzzah* usually refers to the land of Israel (or any portion of it), which is to be held forever by Jacob's descendants. In Ps. 2:8, God promises His Messiah the remotest parts of the Earth (that is, the whole Earth) for His possession (*'achuzzah*). The related verb form is *'achaz*, meaning to seize, acquire, lay hold of, get, obtain, catch, take possession, grasp. This word is frequently translated "take hold of," as in Ex. 15:15 and Job 38:13.

4 [a]Josh. 21:44 [b]Num. 32:33
5 [a]Deut. 6:6, 17; 11:22; Jer. 12:16 [b]Deut. 10:12; 11:13, 22 [1]*be very careful to do*
*See WW at Ps. 119:35. • See WW at Prov. 10:3.
6 [a]Gen. 47:7; Ex. 39:43; Josh. 14:13; 2 Sam. 6:18; Luke 24:50
7 [a]Josh. 17:1–13
8 [a]Num. 31:27; 1 Sam. 30:24 [1]*plunder*
9 [a]Num. 32:1, 26, 29

An Altar by the Jordan

10 And when they came to the region
of the Jordan which *is* in the land of
Canaan, the children of Reuben, the
children of Gad, and half the tribe of
Manasseh built an altar there by the
Jordan—a great, impressive altar.
11 Now the children of Israel [a]heard
someone say, "Behold, the children of
Reuben, the children of Gad, and half
the tribe of Manasseh have built an altar on the [1]frontier of the land of Canaan, in the region of the Jordan—on
the children of Israel's side."
12 And when the children of Israel
heard *of it*, [a]the whole congregation of
the children of Israel gathered together
at Shiloh to go to war against them.
13 Then the children of Israel [a]sent
[b]Phinehas the son of Eleazar the priest
to the children of Reuben, to the children of Gad, and to half the tribe of
Manasseh, into the land of Gilead,
14 and with him ten rulers, one ruler
each from the chief house of every
tribe of Israel; and [a]each one *was* the
head of the house of his father among
the [1]divisions of Israel.
15 Then they came to the children of
Reuben, to the children of Gad, and to
half the tribe of Manasseh, to the land
of Gilead, and they spoke with them,
saying,
16 "Thus says the whole congregation
of the LORD: 'What [a]treachery[1] *is* this
that you have committed against the
God of Israel, to turn away this day
from following the LORD, in that you
have built for yourselves an altar,
[b]that you might rebel this day against
the LORD?
17 '*Is* the iniquity [a]of Peor not enough

11 [a]Deut. 13:12–18; Judg. 20:12, 13 [1]Lit. *front*
12 [a]Josh. 18:1; Judg. 20:1
13 [a]Deut. 13:14; Judg. 20:12 [b]Ex. 6:25; Num. 25:7, 11–13
14 [a]Num. 1:4 [1]Lit. *thousands*
16 [a]Deut. 12:5–14 [b]Lev. 17:8, 9 [1]*unfaithful act*
17 [a]Num. 25:1–9; Deut. 4:3

22:5 See section 2 of Truth-In-Action at the end of Josh.
22:9 Country of Gilead: This expression refers to all the land east of the Jordan.
22:10–20 On their way home, the eastern tribes built a huge altar somewhere near the Jordan River. The western tribes interpreted this action as an apostasy.
22:12 Mosaic Law prohibited sacrifices anywhere other than at the central tabernacle—then at Shiloh (Deut. 12—14). This law was meant to preserve purity of worship and keep the people unified. To have allowed sacrificial worship anywhere might have brought them dangerously close to pagan worship.
22:12–16 The western tribes responded immediately, again in obedience to the Law (Deut. 13:12–16). While the rest prepared for war, a delegation was sent to investigate.
22:17 Iniquity of Peor: An incident during the wilderness wanderings (Num. 25:1–9) when the Israelites were enticed to build an altar and worship the deity of Peor, a Canaanite

for us, from which we are not
*cleansed till this day, although there
was a plague in the **congregation** of the
LORD,

WORD WEALTH

22:17 congregation, *'edah* (ay-*dah*); Strong's #5712: Assembly, crowd, swarm, family, multitude, company. *'Edah* is from the verb *ya'ad,* "to appoint," thus implying a group assembled together by appointment, or acting together. The word occurs more than 140 times in the OT, most often in reference to the congregation of Israel.

18 'but that you must turn away this
day from following the LORD? And it
shall be, if you rebel today against the
LORD, that tomorrow [a]He will be angry with the whole congregation of
Israel.
19 [1]'Nevertheless, if the land of your
possession *is* *unclean, *then* cross over
to the land of the possession of the
LORD, [a]where the LORD's tabernacle
stands, and take possession among us;
but do not rebel against the LORD, nor
rebel against us, by building yourselves an altar besides the altar of the
LORD our God.
20 [a]'Did not Achan the son of Zerah
[1]commit a trespass in the [2]accursed
thing, and wrath fell on all the congregation of Israel? And that man did not
perish alone in his iniquity.' "
21 Then the children of Reuben, the
children of Gad, and half the tribe of
Manasseh answered and said to the
heads of the [1]divisions of Israel:
22 "The LORD [a]God of gods, the LORD
God of gods, He [b]knows, and let Israel
itself know—if *it is* in rebellion, or if
in treachery against the LORD, do not
*save us this day.
23 "If we have built ourselves an altar
to turn from following the LORD, or if
to offer on it burnt offerings or *grain
offerings, or if to offer peace offerings
on it, let the LORD Himself [a]require *an
account.*
24 "But in fact we have done it [1]for
fear, for a reason, saying, 'In time to

17 *See WW at Lev. 14:31.
18 [a]Num. 16:22
19 [a]Josh. 18:1 [1]*However* *See WW at Lev. 10:10.
20 [a]Josh. 7:1–26 [1]*act unfaithfully* [2]*devoted thing*
21 [1]Lit. *thousands*
22 [a]Deut. 4:35; 10:17; Is. 44:8; 45:5; 46:9; [1 Cor. 8:5, 6] [b][Job 10:7; 23:10; Jer. 12:3; 2 Cor. 11:11, 31] *See WW at Jer. 17:14.
23 [a]Deut. 18:19; 1 Sam. 20:16 *See WW at Num. 29:6.
24 [1]Lit. *from fear*
27 [a]Gen. 31:48; Josh. 22:34; 24:27 [b]Deut. 12:5, 14 [1]*testimony*
29 [a]Deut. 12:13, 14
30 [1]Lit. *thousands*
31 [a]Ex. 25:8; Lev. 26:11, 12; 2 Chr. 15:2; Zech. 8:23

come your descendants may speak to
our descendants, saying, "What have
you to do with the LORD God of Israel?
25 "For the LORD has made the Jordan
a border between you and us, *you* children of Reuben and children of Gad.
You have no part in the LORD." So your
descendants would make our descendants cease fearing the LORD.'
26 "Therefore we said, 'Let us now
prepare to build ourselves an altar, not
for burnt offering nor for sacrifice,
27 'but *that* it *may be* [a]a [1]witness between you and us and our generations
after us, that we may [b]perform the service of the LORD before Him with our
burnt offerings, with our sacrifices,
and with our peace offerings; that your
descendants may not say to our descendants in time to come, "You have
no part in the LORD." '
28 "Therefore we said that it will be,
when they say *this* to us or to our generations in time to come, that we may
say, 'Here is the replica of the altar of
the LORD which our fathers made,
though not for burnt offerings nor for
sacrifices; but it *is* a witness between
you and us.'
29 "Far be it from us that we should
rebel against the LORD, and turn from
following the LORD this day, [a]to build
an altar for burnt offerings, for grain
offerings, or for sacrifices, besides the
altar of the LORD our God which *is* before His tabernacle."
30 Now when Phinehas the priest and
the rulers of the congregation, the
heads of the [1]divisions of Israel who
were with him, heard the words that
the children of Reuben, the children of
Gad, and the children of Manasseh
spoke, it pleased them.
31 Then Phinehas the son of Eleazar
the priest said to the children of Reuben, the children of Gad, and the children of Manasseh, "This day we perceive that the LORD *is* [a]among us,
because you have not committed this
treachery against the LORD. Now you
have delivered the children of Israel
out of the hand of the LORD."
32 And Phinehas the son of Eleazar the
priest, and the rulers, returned from

god. As a result of God's wrath, 24,000 Israelites died in an epidemic. **Not cleansed:** The sin of idol worship was still prevalent among the people.

22:20 Did not perish alone: The western tribes knew that the sin of one man brings judgment on all and that unfaithfulness is infectious.

22:21–29 The eastern tribes vigorously denied the charge. The altar had been built as a witness that they worshiped the same God as the western tribes and not as a place to offer sacrifices.

22:24 The eastern tribes feared that, in generations to come, they would become separated from their brethren because of their location east of the Jordan. Remember, there were no bridges to span this 100-mile-long river. It posed a natural barrier to communication.

22:29 The three offerings mentioned are meant to represent all offerings made to the Lord.

the children of Reuben and the children of Gad, from the land of Gilead
to the land of Canaan, to the children
of Israel, and brought back word to
them.
33 So the thing pleased the children of
Israel, and the children of Israel
[a]blessed God; they spoke no more of
going against them in battle, to destroy
the land where the children of Reuben
and Gad dwelt.
34 The children of Reuben and the
children of [1]Gad called the altar, *Wit-*
ness, "For *it is* a witness between us
that the LORD *is* God."

Joshua's Farewell Address

23 Now it came to pass, a long time
after the LORD [a]had given rest
to Israel from all their enemies round
about, that Joshua [b]was old, advanced
in age.
2 And Joshua [a]called for all Israel, for
their elders, for their heads, for their
judges, and for their officers, and said
to them: "I am old, advanced in age.
3 "You have seen all that the [a]LORD
your God has done to all these nations
because of you, for the [b]LORD your God
is He who has fought for you.
4 "See, [a]I have divided to you by lot
these nations that remain, to be an inheritance for your tribes, from the Jordan, with all the nations that I have
cut off, as far as the Great Sea westward.
5 "And the LORD your God [a]will expel
them from before you and drive them
out of your sight. So you shall possess
their land, [b]as the LORD your God
promised you.
2 6 [a]"Therefore be very courageous to
keep and to do all that is written in
the Book of the Law of Moses, [b]lest
you turn aside from it to the right hand
or to the left,
3 7 "*and* lest you [a]go[1] among these nations, these who remain among you.
You shall not [b]make mention of the
name of their gods, nor cause *anyone*
to [c]swear *by them;* you shall not
[d]serve them nor bow down to them,
8 "but you shall [a]hold fast to the LORD
your God, as you have done to this day.
9 [a]"For the LORD has [1]driven out from
before you great and strong nations;
but *as for* you, no one has been able
to stand against you to this day.
10 [a]"One man of you shall chase a
thousand, for the LORD your God *is* He
who fights for you, [b]as He promised
you.
11 [a]"Therefore take careful heed to
yourselves, that you love the LORD your
God.
12 "Or else, if indeed you do [a]go back,
and cling to the remnant of these nations—these that remain among you—
and [b]make marriages with them, and
go in to them and they to you,
13 "know for certain that [a]the LORD
your God will no longer drive out these
nations from before you. [b]But they
shall be snares and traps to you, and
scourges on your sides and thorns in
your eyes, until you perish from this
good land which the LORD your God
has given you.
14 "Behold, this day [a]I[1] *am* going the 1
way of all the earth. And you know in
all your hearts and in all your souls
that [b]not one thing has failed of all the
good things which the LORD your God
spoke concerning you. All have come
to pass for you; not one word of them
has failed.
15 [a]"Therefore it shall come to pass,
that as all the good things have come
upon you which the LORD your God
promised you, so the LORD will bring
upon you [b]all harmful things, until He
has destroyed you from this good land
which the LORD your God has given
you.
16 [1]"When you have transgressed the
covenant of the LORD your God, which
He commanded you, and have gone
and served other gods, and bowed
down to them, then the [a]anger of the

33 [a]1 Chr. 29:20; Neh. 8:6; Dan. 2:19; Luke 2:28 **34** [1]LXX adds *and half the tribe of Manasseh*

CHAPTER 23

1 [a]Josh. 21:44; 22:4 [b]Josh. 13:1; 24:29 **2** [a]Deut. 31:28 **3** [a]Ps. 44:3 [b]Ex. 14:14; Deut. 1:30; Josh. 10:14, 42 **4** [a]Josh. 13:2, 6; 18:10 **5** [a]Ex. 23:30; 33:2 [b]Num. 33:53 **6** [a]Josh. 1:7 [b]Deut. 5:32 **7** [a]Ex. 23:33; Deut. 7:2, 3; [Prov. 4:14; Eph. 5:11] [b]Ex. 23:13; Ps. 16:4; Jer. 5:7; Hos. 2:17 [c]Deut. 6:13; 10:20 [d]Ex. 20:5 [1]*associate with*

8 [a]Deut. 10:20 **9** [a]Deut. 7:24; 11:23; Josh. 1:5 [1]*dispossessed* **10** [a]Lev. 26:8; Deut. 28:7; Is. 30:17 [b]Ex. 14:14 **11** [a]Josh. 22:5 **12** [a][2 Pet. 2:20, 21] [b]Deut. 7:3, 4; Ezra 9:2; Neh. 13:25 **13** [a]Judg. 2:3 [b]Ex. 23:33; 34:12; Deut. 7:16 **14** [a]1 Kin. 2:2 [b]Josh. 21:45; [Luke 21:33] [1]I am going to die. **15** [a]Deut. 28:63 [b]Lev. 26:14–39; Deut. 28:15–68 **16** [a]Deut. 4:24–28 [1]Or *if ever*

23:1–16 This is the first of two farewell messages by Joshua to the Israelites. The first was addressed to the leaders; the second, to all the people. In this chapter, his message was one of careful observance of God's Word. Three times he called them to obedience: (vv. 1–8; vv. 9–13; vv. 14–16). Each time he reminded them of what God had done, and each time he urged them *to be faithful.*

23:1, 2 Joshua was at the end of his life. Like a father, he wished to leave the benefit of his wisdom to those who would follow (Ps. 78:1–8). Israel was intended to be a blessing to the people around them (Gen. 12:3), but because these nations had resisted Israel as ambassadors of God's kingdom on Earth, they are here characterized as **enemies.**

23:5, 6 As had Moses, Joshua emphasized the need for obedience to keep and advance their inheritance.

23:6 See section 2 of Truth-In-Action at the end of Josh.

23:7 See section 3 of Truth-In-Action at the end of Josh.

23:11 Joshua's command to **love** God means a constant devotion to Him, developing a relationship with Him, being obedient, and guarding against corruption.

23:14 See section 1 of Truth-In-Action at the end of Josh.

23:14 I ***am going* . . . all the earth** reminded Israel of Joshua's impending death. These final two sermons were his last will and testament.

23:15, 16 God's grace has always been in tension with His strict justice and His need to be a righteous Judge.

LORD will burn against you, and you shall perish quickly from the good land which He has given you."

The Covenant at Shechem

24 Then Joshua gathered all the tribes of Israel to [a]Shechem and [b]called for the elders of Israel, for their heads, for their judges, and for their officers; and they [c]presented themselves before God.

2 And Joshua said to all the people, "Thus says the LORD God of Israel: [a]'Your fathers, *including* Terah, the father of Abraham and the father of Nahor, dwelt on the other side of [1]the River in old times; and [b]they served other gods.

3 [a]'Then I took your father Abraham from the other side of [1]the River, led him throughout all the land of Canaan, and multiplied his [2]descendants and [b]gave him Isaac.

4 'To Isaac I gave [a]Jacob and Esau. To [b]Esau I gave the mountains of Seir to possess, [c]but Jacob and his children went down to Egypt.

5 [a]'Also I sent Moses and Aaron, and [b]I plagued Egypt, according to what I did among them. Afterward I brought you out.

6 'Then I [a]brought your fathers out of Egypt, and you came to the sea; and the Egyptians pursued your fathers with chariots and horsemen to the Red Sea.

7 'So they cried out to the LORD; and He put [a]darkness between you and the Egyptians, brought the sea upon them, and covered them. And [b]your eyes saw what I did in Egypt. Then you dwelt in the wilderness [c]a long time.

8 'And I brought you into the land of the Amorites, who dwelt on the other side of the Jordan, [a]and they fought with you. But I gave them into your hand, that you might possess their land, and I destroyed them from before you.

CHAPTER 24
1 [a]Gen. 35:4 [b]Josh. 23:2 [c]1 Sam. 10:19
2 [a]Gen. 11:7–32 [b]Josh. 24:14 [1]The Euphrates
3 [a]Gen. 12:1; Acts 7:2, 3 [b]Gen. 21:1–8; [Ps. 127:3] [1]The Euphrates [2]Lit. *seed*
4 [a]Gen. 25:24–26 [b]Gen. 36:8; Deut. 2:5 [c]Gen. 46:1, 3, 6
5 [a]Ex. 3:10 [b]Ex. 7—10
6 [a]Ex. 12:37, 51; 14:2–31
7 [a]Ex. 14:20 [b]Deut. 4:34 [c]Josh. 5:6
8 [a]Num. 21:21–35
9 [a]Judg. 11:25 [b]Num. 22:2–14
10 [a]Deut. 23:5 [b]Num. 23:11, 20; 24:10
11 [a]Josh. 3:14, 17 [b]Josh. 6:1; 10:1
12 [a]Ex. 23:28; Deut. 7:20 [b]Ps. 44:3
13 [a]Deut. 6:10, 11
14 [a]Deut. 10:12, 13; 1 Sam. 12:24 [b]2 Cor. 1:12 [c]Josh. 24:2, 23; Ezek. 20:18 [d]Ezek. 20:7, 8 [1]The Euphrates
15 [a]Ruth 1:15; 1 Kin. 18:21 [b]Josh. 24:2; Ezek. 20:39 [c]Ex. 23:24, 32 [d]Gen. 18:19; Ps. 101:2; [1 Tim. 3:4, 5] [1]The Euphrates
17 *See WW at Job 10:12.

9 'Then [a]Balak the son of Zippor, king of Moab, arose to make war against Israel, and [b]sent and called Balaam the son of Beor to curse you.

10 [a]'But I would not listen to Balaam; [b]therefore he continued to bless you. So I delivered you out of his hand.

11 'Then [a]you went over the Jordan and came to Jericho. And [b]the men of Jericho fought against you—*also* the Amorites, the Perizzites, the Canaanites, the Hittites, the Girgashites, the Hivites, and the Jebusites. But I delivered them into your hand.

12 [a]'I sent the hornet before you which drove them out from before you, *also* the two kings of the Amorites, *but* [b]not with your sword or with your bow.

13 'I have given you a land for which you did not labor, and [a]cities which you did not build, and you dwell in them; you eat of the vineyards and olive groves which you did not plant.'

14 [a]"Now therefore, fear the LORD, serve Him in [b]sincerity and in truth, and [c]put away the gods which your fathers served on the other side of [1]the River and [d]in Egypt. Serve the LORD!

15 "And if it seems evil to you to serve the LORD, [a]choose for yourselves this day whom you will serve, whether [b]the gods which your fathers served that *were* on the other side of [1]the River, or [c]the gods of the Amorites, in whose land you dwell. [d]But as for me and my house, we will serve the LORD."

16 So the people answered and said: "Far be it from us that we should forsake the LORD to serve other gods;

17 "for the LORD our God *is* He who brought us and our fathers up out of the land of Egypt, from the house of bondage, who did those great signs in our sight, and *preserved us in all the way that we went and among

24:1 Shechem was located in the valley between Mt. Ebal and Mt. Gerizim. It provided a large, natural amphitheater for a gathering of all the tribes and may have been chosen because of its religious significance (see 8:30–35).

24:2 Thus says the LORD: Joshua spoke to them prophetically; that is, God was speaking to them through him.

24:9, 10 Balaam was a celebrated Mesopotamian who, although he did not have a pure relationship with God, was a recognized prophet of Yahweh. This episode (Num. 22—24) was so significant that Balaam is mentioned three times in the NT (2 Pet. 2:15; Jude 11; Rev. 2:14). **To curse** was to invoke God's woe on someone.

24:12 The hornet: This term is used here to describe fear or panic (Ex. 23:27, 28).

24:14, 15 Fear the LORD: Reverence and respect toward One who loves but is also just. The word **serve** is used seven times in these two verses and means to give allegiance exclusively to God. Joshua did not call the people to **choose for yourselves** because he believed there were two options from God's perspective. Doing so offered him the opportunity to affirm his own loyalty to God and to urge a similar response from the people.

24:16–18 The people's strong covenant response was undoubtedly sincere; however, for most it did not develop. Many soon did **forsake the LORD.**

all the people through whom we
passed.
18 "And the LORD drove out from before us all the people, including the
Amorites who dwelt in the land.
[a]We also will serve the LORD, for He
is our God."
19 But Joshua said to the people,
[a]"You cannot serve the LORD, for He
is a [b]holy God. He *is* [c]a jealous God;
[d]He will not forgive your *transgressions nor your sins.
20 [a]"If you forsake the LORD and serve
foreign gods, [b]then He will turn and
do you harm and consume you, after
He has done you good."
21 And the people said to Joshua, "No,
but we will serve the LORD!"
22 So Joshua said to the people, "You
are witnesses against yourselves that
[a]you have chosen the LORD for yourselves, to serve Him." And they said,
"*We are* witnesses!"
3 23 "Now therefore," *he said,* [a]"put
away the foreign gods which *are*
among you, and [b]incline your heart to
the LORD God of Israel."
24 And the people [a]said to Joshua,
"The LORD our God we will serve, and
His voice we will obey!"
25 So Joshua [a]made[1] a *covenant with
the people that day, and made for them
a *statute and an ordinance [b]in Shechem.
26 Then Joshua [a]wrote* these words
in the Book of the Law of God. And
he took [b]a large stone, and [c]set it up
there [d]under the oak that *was* by the
sanctuary of the LORD.

18 [a]Ps. 116:16
19 [a]Matt. 6:24 [b]1 Sam. 6:20 [c]Ex. 20:5 [d]Ex. 23:21 *See WW at Ezek. 18:31.
20 [a]Ezra 8:22 [b]Deut. 4:24–26
22 [a]Ps. 119:173
23 [a]Gen. 35:2 [b]1 Kin. 8:57, 58
24 [a]Deut. 5:24–27
25 [a]Ex. 15:25 [b]Josh. 24:1 [1]Lit. *cut a covenant* *See WW at Gen. 17:7. • See WW at Neh. 9:13.
26 [a]Deut. 31:24 [b]Judg. 9:6 [c]Gen. 28:18 [d]Gen. 35:4 *See WW at Deut. 31:9.
27 [a]Gen. 31:48 [b]Deut. 32:1
28 [a]Judg. 2:6, 7
29 [a]Judg. 2:8
30 [a]Josh. 19:50
31 [a]Judg. 2:7 [b]Deut. 11:2
32 [a]Gen. 50:25 [b]Gen. 33:19 [1]Heb. *qesitah,* an unknown ancient measure of weight
33 [a]Ex. 28:1 [b]Ex. 6:25

27 And Joshua said to all the people,
"Behold, this stone shall be [a]a witness
to us, for [b]it has heard all the words
of the LORD which He spoke to us. It
shall therefore be a witness to you, lest
you deny your God."
28 So [a]Joshua let the people depart,
each to his own inheritance.

Death of Joshua and Eleazar

29 [a]Now it came to pass after these
things that Joshua the son of Nun, the
servant of the LORD, died, *being* one
hundred and ten years old.
30 And they buried him within the border of his inheritance at [a]Timnath
Serah, which *is* in the mountains of
Ephraim, on the north side of Mount
Gaash.
31 [a]Israel served the LORD all the days
of Joshua, and all the days of the elders
who outlived Joshua, who had [b]known
all the works of the LORD which He had
done for Israel.
32 [a]The bones of Joseph, which the
children of Israel had brought up out
of Egypt, they buried at Shechem, in
the plot of ground [b]which Jacob had
bought from the sons of Hamor the father of Shechem for one hundred
[1]pieces of silver, and which had become an inheritance of the children of
Joseph.
33 And [a]Eleazar the son of Aaron died.
They buried him in a hill *belonging to*
[b]Phinehas his son, which was given to
him in the mountains of Ephraim.

24:19 You cannot serve the LORD is Joshua's way of sternly warning them of the seriousness of their covenant promise. **Forgive:** The Incarnation was predestined from eternity, and Christ's atonement was retroactive (Heb. 10:14). God's dealings with His people, however, are conditional. If Israel gave her allegiance to God and then rebelled against Him, they would be punished.

24:23 See section 3 of Truth-In-Action at the end of Josh.

24:25 Joshua represented the people in making a **covenant** with the Lord. Like the covenant at Mt. Sinai, it contained laws which the people were to obey (Ex. 24:3).

24:26–28 To preserve the evidence of the agreement, the proceedings were written down in an unidentified book of which **God** was witness. **A large stone** was **set up** near the holy place of the Lord in memory of the occasion.

24:32 The burial of **Joseph at Shechem** was in fulfillment of Joseph's request at the time of his death (Gen. 50:25).

24:33 The book concludes with the death and burial of three great men of Israel: Joshua, Joseph, and Eleazar. Israel had gained her inheritance, and God's covenant had been fulfilled.

TRUTH-IN-ACTION through Joshua

Letting the LIFE of the Holy Spirit Bring Faith's Works Alive in You!

Truth Joshua Teaches	Text	**Action** Joshua Invites
1 Keys to Knowing God and His Ways Joshua shows much about how God responds to godly lives. Prov. 16:7 says, "When a man's ways please the LORD, He makes even his enemies to be at peace with him." Joshua reveals many benefits of knowing the ways of God with men whose ways please Him.	2:8–11, 24; 3:7 4:19–24 21:45; 23:14	**Expect** God's favor when you follow His Word and the Spirit's direction and when your ways please Him. **Know** that you will encounter no obstacle God cannot work in and through you to overcome. **Rest** in the confidence that God will never fail to fulfill His promises to you when your ways please Him.
2 Steps to Dynamic Devotion Joshua continues to call God's people to devote themselves completely to the Lord. In a day when so many follow the Lord with only partial devotion, Joshua and Caleb "who wholly followed the LORD" provide challenging examples of the life the Lord honors.	9:14 14:8, 9, 14 22:5; 23:6	**Seek** the Lord prayerfully for every decision you make. **Know** that you cannot consistently make good decisions without His Word and Spirit. **Follow** God wholeheartedly and be devoted to Him. Doing so will yield a rich inheritance. **Be careful** faithfully to apply all of God's Word to all of your life. **Follow** Him with all of your heart and soul.
3 Steps to Holiness Joshua continually exhorts God's people to live holy lives. God's holy people will live unto Him and apart from the world. Joshua demonstrates that our failure to live in holiness can and will have dire consequences.	6:18, 19 23:7 24:23	**Do not covet** this world's goods. **Understand** that things we strive to get for ourselves will seriously weaken our walk with God. **Be careful** to not adopt this world's way of thinking and behavior. **Hold fast,** rather, to God's ways and serve Him wholeheartedly. **Reject** and **turn away** from this world and its ways. **Be assured** that you will thus be free to fully yield your heart to God.
4 Guidelines for Growing in Godliness Growing in godliness through knowing and applying God's Word is a recurring theme in Josh. Simply knowing God's Word is not enough. We must know God's Word well enough to apply it to life's situations. God promises that this kind of faithfulness to His Word will result in a successful and prosperous life.	1:7, 8 4:4–7 5:2–9 8:34, 35	**Practice regularly** Scripture memorization and meditation. Then **determine beforehand** to put it into practice. This promises sure success. **Establish memorials** in your spiritual journey. **Keep a record** of your experiences with God. **Share** these to instruct and encourage others. As God's people were circumcised for a sign, **be baptized. Rehearse** baptism's meaning and benefits (Col. 2:11–15). **Know** that this is a key to spiritual victory. **Incorporate** regular Scripture reading as a part of personal and corporate worship.

Truth Joshua Teaches	Text	**Action** Joshua Invites
5 Keys to Wise Living Good theology must always impact the way we live. Knowing God's Word but not knowing how to apply it is foolish and futile. Josh. helps us apply faithfully what we know about God's Word.	1:6, 7, 9 15:63; 16:10; 17:12	**Rely** on God's strength and wisdom, not your own. **Allow** God's abiding presence to give you courage: **Know** that Jesus' promise to be ever with you will keep you from terror and discouragement. **Do not rely** on your own strength and wisdom when dealing with sin. **Be assured** that without God you will have no success.
6 Steps to Dealing with Sin The failure to detect and deal with sin caused Israel's defeat at Ai. Past successes can cause us to be less careful about sin. None of us can afford to drop our guard, for even one person's sins can weaken the life of a whole church.	7:10–13 11:11	**Understand** that individual sin weakens the whole church. **Deal with sin** quickly and forthrightly. **Leave** no sin unconfessed or undealt with. **Be aware** that unconfessed sin will become a snare.
7 Guidelines to Gaining Victory Joshua is a type of Christ who always leads His people in victory and triumph. Our victories result from surrendering to Jesus' lordship and allowing Him to work through us to overcome our obstacles and adversities.	5:14, 15 17:18	**Submit yourself** continually to Jesus' lordship in your life. **Acknowledge** that He comes as the Captain of His army to lead us to victory (see Ex. 17:14, 15). **Be assured** that regardless of the strength of the enemy, God can and will enable you to prevail.

The Book of JUDGES

Author: Unknown
Date: About 1050–1000 B.C.
Theme: Apostasy, Oppression, Repentance, Deliverance
Key Words: Did Evil, Cried Out, Delivered, Judged, Spirit of the Lord

Author The author of Judges is unknown. The Talmud ascribes the Book of Judges to Samuel. He may have written portions of the book for it is recorded that he was a writer (1 Sam. 10:25). The inspired author carefully selected oral and written sources to provide a history of Israel with theological import.

Date The Book of Judges covers the period between Joshua's death and the rise of the monarchy. The actual date of composition is unknown. Internal evidence, however, indicates that it was written during the early part of the monarchy following Saul's coronation but prior to David's conquest of Jerusalem, about 1050 to 1000 B.C. This date is supported by two facts: 1) The words "In those days *there was* no king in Israel" (17:6) were penned from a period when Israel did have a king. 2) The declaration that "the Jebusites dwell with the children of Benjamin in Jerusalem to this day" (1:21) points to a time before David conquered the city (2 Sam. 5:6, 7).

Background The Book of Judges covers a chaotic period in Israel's history from about 1380 to 1050 B.C. Under the leadership of Joshua, Israel had generally conquered and occupied the land of Canaan, but large areas remained yet to be possessed by the individual tribes. Israel did evil in the sight of the Lord continually and "*there was* no king in Israel; everyone did *what was* right in his own eyes" (21:25). By deliberately serving foreign gods, the people of Israel broke their covenant with the Lord. As a result, the Lord delivered them into the hands of various oppressors. Each time the people cried out to the Lord, He faithfully raised up a judge to bring deliverance to His people. These judges whom the Lord chose and anointed with His Spirit were military and civil leaders. The Book of Judges not only looks back to the conquest of Canaan led by Joshua and records the conditions in Canaan during the period of the judges but it also anticipates the establishment of the monarchy in Israel.

Purpose The purpose of the Book of Judges is threefold: 1) historical, 2) theological, and 3) spiritual. Historically, the book describes the events that transpired during a specific period in Israel's history and provides a link between the conquest of Canaan and the monarchy. Theologically, the book underscores the principle established in the Law that obedience to the Law brings peace and life, and disobedience brings oppression and death. Moreover, the book points to the need for a centralized hereditary monarchy in Israel.

Israel's disobedience of the Lord's kingship throughout the time of the inspired leadership of the judges resulted in apostasy and anarchy, which consequently demonstrated the need for a permanent, centralized, hereditary monarchy through which the Lord would continue to exert His kingship over the nation of Israel. Spiritually, the book serves to show the faithfulness of the Lord to His covenant. Whenever His people repented and turned from their evil ways, the Lord always forgave them and raised up Spirit-empowered leaders to deliver them from their oppressors.

Content The Book of Judges is divided into three main sections: 1) a prologue (1:1—3:6); 2) a main body (3:7—16:31); and 3) an epilogue (17:1—21:25). The first part of the prologue (1:1—2:5) establishes the historical scene for the narratives that follow. It describes Israel's incomplete conquest of the Promised Land (1:1–36) and the Lord's rebuke for her unfaithfulness to His covenant (2:1–5). The second part of the prologue (2:6—3:6) provides an overview of the main body of the book. It portrays Israel's rebellious ways during the first centuries in the Promised Land and shows how the Lord dealt with her in that period, a time characterized by a recurring cycle of apostasy, oppression, repentance, and deliverance.

The main body of the book (3:7—16:31) illustrates this recurring pattern within Israel's early history. The Israelites did evil in the sight of the Lord (apostasy); the Lord delivered them into the hands of enemies (oppression); the people of Israel cried out to the Lord (repentance); and in response to their cry, the Lord raised up deliverers whom He empowered with His Spirit (deliverance). Six individuals—Othniel, Ehud, Deborah, Gideon, Jephthah, and Samson—whose role as deliverers is related in some detail are classified as the "major" judges. Six others who are only briefly mentioned—Shamgar, Tola, Jair, Ibzan, Elon, and Abdon—are referred to as the "minor" judges. The thirteenth individual, Abimelech, is supplemental to the story of Gideon.

Two stories are appended to the Book of Judges (17:1—21:25) in the form of an epilogue. The purpose of these appendices is not to establish an end to the period of the judges but to depict the religious and moral corruption that existed during this period. The first story illustrates the corruption in Israel's religion. Micah established in Ephraim a paganized form of worship of the Lord, which was adopted by the Danites when they abandoned their appointed inheritance and migrated into northern Israel. The second story in the epilogue illustrates Israel's moral corruption by relating the unfortunate experience of a Levite at Gibeah in Benjamin and the ensuing Benjamite War. Apparently, the purpose of this concluding section of the book is to illustrate the consequences of Israel's apostasy and anarchy when "*there was* no king in Israel."

Personal Application The Book of Judges illustrates the disastrous consequences of breaking fellowship with God through idolatrous worship. Sin separates from God. The Lord requires commitment from His people. When we commit sin, the Lord in His love chastises us until we come to full repentance. When we cry out to Him, the Lord faithfully responds to us. He forgives us, brings deliverance to us, and restores fellowship with us.

The Lord is our Judge—our Deliverer. He is able to do impossible things. Just as He appointed deliverers and empowered them with

His Spirit to do exploits, He is able to endue us with His Holy Spirit and to use us to bring deliverance to those who are bound in sin and despair. He responds to the cry of a penitent heart. The Lord is faithful and His love is constant.

Christ Revealed The Book of Judges graphically portrays the character of the Lord in His dealings with the children of Israel. In righteousness, the Lord punished them for their sin; but, in His love and mercy, He delivered them in response to their penitent cry. Though the judges are called the deliverers or saviors of the people, God ultimately is their Savior. "God *is* the Judge" (Ps. 75:7). He is "a just God and a Savior" (Is. 45:21).

Humankind's need of a divine deliverer or savior is emphasized in the Book of Judges. Throughout history, God's people have sinned. God as the Lord of history has always delivered His people from oppression when they repented and turned their hearts toward Him. In the fullness of time, God in His love sent forth His Son Jesus Christ as our Deliverer, our Savior, to redeem us from the bondage of sin and death. Our Lord is a righteous Judge (2 Tim. 4:8) who will one day "judge the world in righteousness" (Acts 17:31).

The Holy Spirit at Work The activity of the Spirit of the Lord in the Book of Judges is clearly portrayed in the charismatic leadership of the period. The following heroic deeds of Othniel, Gideon, Jephthah, and Samson are attributed to the Spirit of the Lord:

1. The Spirit of the Lord came upon Othniel (3:10) and enabled him to deliver the Israelites from the hand of Cushan-Rishathaim, king of Mesopotamia.

2. Through the personal presence of the Spirit of the Lord, Gideon (6:34) delivered God's people from the oppression of the Midianites. Literally, the Spirit of the Lord clothed Himself with Gideon. The Spirit empowered this divinely appointed leader and acted through him to accomplish the Lord's saving act on behalf of His people.

3. The Spirit of the Lord equipped Jephthah (11:29) with leadership skills in his military pursuit against the Ammonites. Jephthah's victory over the Ammonites was the Lord's act of deliverance on behalf of Israel.

4. The Spirit of the Lord empowered Samson to perform extraordinary deeds. He began to stir Samson (13:25). The Spirit of the Lord came mightily upon him on several occasions. He tore a lion apart with his bare hands (14:6). At one time he killed thirty Philistines (14:19) and at another time he freed himself from ropes that bound his hands and killed a thousand Philistines with the jawbone of a donkey (15:14, 15).

The same Holy Spirit who enabled these deliverers to do exploits and fulfill the Lord's plans and purposes is at work today. He desires to move upon His people so that they too can do impossible things. The Lord wants to bring deliverance to His people, and He is looking for consecrated men and women whom He can empower with His Holy Spirit.

Outline of Judges

I. Prologue: Conditions in Canaan after the death of Joshua 1:1—3:6
A. Continuing conquests by Israelite tribes 1:1–26
B. Incomplete conquests of the land 1:27–36
C. Covenant of the Lord broken 2:1–5

- D. Introduction to the period of the judges 2:6—3:6

II. History of oppressions and deliverances during the period of the judges 3:7—16:31

- A. Mesopotamian oppression and deliverance by Othniel 3:7–11
- B. Moabite oppression and deliverance by Ehud 3:12–30
- C. Philistine oppression and deliverance by Shamgar 3:31
- D. Canaanite oppression and deliverance by Deborah and Barak 4:1—5:31
- E. Midianite oppression and deliverance by Gideon 6:1—8:35
- F. Brief reign of Abimelech 9:1–57
- G. Tola's judgeship 10:1, 2
- H. Jair's judgeship 10:3–5
- I. Ammonite oppression and deliverance by Jephthah 10:6—12:7
- J. Ibzan's judgeship 12:8–10
- K. Elon's judgeship 12:11, 12
- L. Abdon's judgeship 12:13–15
- M. Philistine oppression and the exploits of Samson 13:1—16:31

III. Epilogue: Conditions illustrating the period of the judges 17:1—21:25

- A. Apostasy: The idolatry of Micah and the migration of the Danites 17:1—18:31
- B. Immorality: The atrocity at Gibeah and the Benjamite War 19:1—21:25

The Continuing Conquest of Canaan

NOW after the [a]death of Joshua it came to pass that the children of Israel [b]asked the LORD, saying, "Who shall be first to go up for us against the [c]Canaanites to fight against them?"

2 And the LORD said, [a]"Judah shall go up. Indeed I have delivered the land into his hand."

3 So Judah said to [a]Simeon his brother, "Come up with me to my allotted territory, that we may fight against the Canaanites; and [b]I will likewise go with you to your allotted territory." And Simeon went with him.

4 Then Judah went up, and the LORD delivered the Canaanites and the Perizzites into their hand; and they killed ten thousand men at [a]Bezek.

5 And they found Adoni-Bezek in Bezek, and fought against him; and they defeated the Canaanites and the Perizzites.

6 Then Adoni-Bezek fled, and they pursued him and caught him and cut off his thumbs and big toes.

7 And Adoni-Bezek said, "Seventy kings with their thumbs and big toes cut off used to gather *scraps* under my table; [a]as I have done, so God has repaid me." Then they brought him to Jerusalem, and there he died.

8 Now [a]the children of Judah fought against Jerusalem and took it; they struck it with the edge of the sword and set the city on fire.

9 [a]And afterward the children of Judah went down to fight against the Canaanites who dwelt in the mountains, in the [1]South, and in the lowland.

10 Then Judah [1]went against the Canaanites who dwelt in [a]Hebron. (Now the name of Hebron *was* formerly

CHAPTER 1

1 [a]Josh. 24:29 [b]Num. 27:21; Judg. 20:18 [c]Josh. 17:12, 13
2 [a]Gen. 49:8, 9; Rev. 5:5
3 [a]Josh. 19:1 [b]Judg. 1:17
4 [a]1 Sam. 11:8
7 [a]Lev. 24:19; 1 Sam. 15:33; [James 2:13]
8 [a]Josh. 15:63; Judg. 1:21
9 [a]Josh. 10:36; 11:21; 15:13 [1]Heb. *Negev*, and so throughout the book
10 [a]Josh. 15:13–19 [1]*attacked*

Prologue: The actual account of the heroic judges is preceded by an introduction in two parts (1:1—2:5; 2:6—3:6). The first section provides an account of Israel's failure to complete the conquest of the Promised Land as the Lord commanded them (1:1–36) and relates His displeasure concerning their unfaithfulness (2:1–5). The second section provides an overview of the main section of the book (3:7—16:31), giving an account of Israel's rebellion following Joshua's death and relating the way in which the Lord dealt with Israel during this time (2:6—3:6).

1:1 After the death of Joshua is a phrase that indicates the conclusion of the former period of *conquest and the beginning of a new period.* **Asked the LORD:** Probably involved the priestly use of the Urim and Thummim (see note on Ex. 28:30) or a verbal form of divine guidance.

1:2 Judah shall go up: The selection of the tribe of Judah corresponds with the divine preeminence of Judah in Jacob's patriarchal blessing (Gen. 49:8).

1:4 Bezek is Khirbet Bezqa near Gezer or northeast of Shechem.

1:6 Cut off his thumbs and big toes: Similar practices were common in the ancient Near East. These kings would no longer be able to lead in battle. Without thumbs they would have difficulty holding weapons, and without toes they would lose their footing in battle.

1:8 Jerusalem: Although the city was taken at this time, the Israelites did not occupy it until David captured it about 1000 B.C. (2 Sam. 5:6–9). According to Josh. 15:63, Judah failed to clear out the Jebusites though they initially **took** Jerusalem.

1:10 Kirjath Arba: The former name of Hebron (meaning "Confederacy"), which means "City of Four." It has been identified with Arba, the father of the Anakites (Josh. 15:13), who may have established it. According to Josh. 15:14, these three men were sons of Anak whom "Caleb drove out."

[b]Kirjath Arba.) And they killed Sheshai, Ahiman, and Talmai.
11 [a]From there they went against the
inhabitants of Debir. (The name of Debir *was* formerly Kirjath Sepher.)
12 [a]Then Caleb said, "Whoever attacks Kirjath Sepher and takes it, to
him I will give my daughter Achsah as
wife."
13 And Othniel the son of Kenaz,
[a]Caleb's younger brother, took it; so
he gave him his daughter Achsah as
wife.
14 [a]Now it happened, when she came
to him, that [1]she urged him to ask her
father for a field. And she dismounted
from *her* donkey, and Caleb said to
her, "What do you wish?"
15 So she said to him, [a]"Give me a
blessing; since you have given me land
in the South, give me also springs of
water." And Caleb gave her the upper
springs and the lower springs.
16 [a]Now the children of the Kenite,
Moses' father-in-law, *went up [b]from
the City of Palms with the children of
Judah into the Wilderness of Judah,
which *lies* in the South *near* [c]Arad;
[d]and they went and dwelt among the
people.
17 [a]And Judah went with his brother
Simeon, and they attacked the Canaanites who inhabited Zephath, and utterly destroyed it. So the name of the
city was called [b]Hormah.
18 Also Judah took [a]Gaza with its territory, Ashkelon with its territory, and
Ekron with its territory.
19 So the LORD was with Judah. And
they drove out the mountaineers, but
they could not drive out the inhabitants
of the lowland, because they had
[a]chariots of iron.
20 [a]And they gave Hebron to Caleb,
as Moses had said. Then he [1]expelled
from there the [b]three sons of Anak.
21 [a]But the children of Benjamin did
not drive out the Jebusites who inhabited Jerusalem; so the Jebusites dwell
with the children of Benjamin in Jerusalem to this day.

22 And the [1]house of Joseph also went
up against Bethel, [a]and the LORD *was*
with them.
23 So the [1]house of Joseph [a]sent men
to spy out Bethel. (The name of the city
was formerly [b]Luz.)
24 And when the spies saw a man coming out of the city, they said to him,
"Please show us the entrance to the
city, and [a]we will show you *mercy."
25 So he showed them the entrance to
the city, and they struck the city with
the edge of the sword; but they let the
man and all his family go.
26 And the man went to the land of
the Hittites, built a city, and called its
name Luz, which *is* its name to this
day.

Incomplete Conquest of the Land

27 [a]However, Manasseh did not drive
out *the inhabitants of* Beth Shean and
its villages, or [b]Taanach and its villages, or the inhabitants of [c]Dor and
its villages, or the inhabitants of Ibleam and its villages, or the inhabitants
of Megiddo and its villages; for the Canaanites were determined to dwell in
that land.
28 And it came to pass, when Israel
was strong, that they put the Canaanites [1]under tribute, but did not completely drive them out.
29 [a]Nor did Ephraim drive out the Canaanites who dwelt in Gezer; so the
Canaanites dwelt in Gezer among
them.
30 Nor did [a]Zebulun drive out the
inhabitants of Kitron or the inhabitants
of Nahalol; so the Canaanites dwelt
among them, and [1]were put under tribute.
31 [a]Nor did Asher drive out the inhabitants of Acco or the inhabitants of
Sidon, or of Ahlab, Achzib, Helbah,
Aphik, or Rehob.
32 So the Asherites [a]dwelt among the
Canaanites, the inhabitants of the land;
for they did not drive them out.
33 [a]Nor did Naphtali drive out the

10 [b]Josh. 14:15
11 [a]Josh. 15:15
12 [a]Josh. 15:16, 17
13 [a]Judg. 3:9
14 [a]Josh. 15:18, 19 [1]LXX, Vg. *he urged her*
15 [a]Gen. 33:11
16 [a]Num. 10:29–32; Judg. 4:11, 17; 1 Sam. 15:6; 1 Chr. 2:55 [b]Deut. 34:3; Judg. 3:13 [c]Josh. 12:14 [d]1 Sam. 15:6 *See WW at Ex. 19:20.
17 [a]Judg. 1:3 [b]Num. 21:3; Josh. 19:4
18 [a]Josh. 11:22
19 [a]Josh. 17:16, 18; Judg. 4:3, 13
20 [a]Num. 14:24; Josh. 14:9, 14 [b]Josh. 15:14; Judg. 1:10 [1]*drove out from there*
21 [a]Josh. 15:63; Judg. 1:8
22 [a]Judg. 1:19 [1]*family*
23 [a]Josh. 2:1; 7:2 [b]Gen. 28:19 [1]*family*
24 [a]Josh. 2:12, 14 *See WW at Mic. 6:8.
27 [a]Josh. 17:11–13 [b]Josh. 21:25 [c]Josh. 17:11
28 [1]*to forced labor*
29 [a]Josh. 16:10; 1 Kin. 9:16
30 [a]Josh. 19:10–16 [1]*became forced laborers*
31 [a]Josh. 19:24–31
32 [a]Ps. 106:34, 35
33 [a]Josh. 19:32–39

1:11–15 See Josh. 15:15–19.
1:13 Othniel: The first major judge (see 3:7–11). A victory in battle was one way of providing payment for a bride.
1:16 The **children of the Kenite** were associated with the Amalekites and the Midianites. Jethro, **Moses' father-in-law,** was a priest of Midian. The **City of Palms** probably refers to Jericho and its oasis.
1:17 Hormah, which means "Devotion" or "Destruction," was a new name given to **Zephath,** likely the valley region in southern Judah mentioned in 2 Chr. 14:10.
1:18 Gaza, Ashkelon, and **Ekron:** Three of the five main cities occupied by the Philistines, the others being Ashdod and Gath.
1:19 Judah took possession of the hill country, but **they could not drive out** the people from the plains because the enemies had iron chariots (wooden vehicles with iron fittings). The real reason, however, was Israel's disobedience to the Mosaic covenant (2:1–3, 20, 21).
1:21 In light of v. 8, **Benjamin** apparently fought on the eastern hill, which they bordered. Their success was no greater than Judah's (Josh. 15:63).
1:27–36 The conquest of Canaan was incomplete because the Israelites were disobedient and failed to carry out God's plan (Ex. 34:11–16).
1:28 Put the Canaanites under tribute: The tribe of Manasseh put the Canaanites to forced labor.

inhabitants of Beth Shemesh or the
inhabitants of Beth Anath; but they
dwelt among the Canaanites, the
inhabitants of the land. Nevertheless
the inhabitants of Beth Shemesh and
Beth Anath were put under tribute to
them.
34 And the Amorites forced the children of Dan into the mountains, for
they would not allow them to come
down to the valley;
35 and the Amorites were determined
to dwell in Mount Heres, [a]in Aijalon,
and in [1]Shaalbim; yet when the
strength of the house of Joseph became
greater, they [2]were put under tribute.
36 Now the boundary of the Amorites
was [a]from the Ascent of Akrabbim,
from Sela, and upward.

Israel's Disobedience

2 Then the Angel of the LORD came
up from Gilgal to Bochim, and said:
[a]"I led you up from Egypt and
[b]brought you to the land of which I
swore to your fathers; and [c]I said, 'I
will never break My covenant with
you.
3 2 'And [a]you shall make no [1]covenant
with the inhabitants of this land;
[b]you shall tear down their altars.'
[c]But you have not obeyed My voice.
Why have you done this?
3 "Therefore I also said, 'I will not
drive them out before you; but they
shall be [a]*thorns*[1] in your side, and
[b]their gods shall [2]be a [c]snare to you.' "
4 So it was, when the Angel of the
LORD spoke these *words to all the children of Israel, that the people lifted up
their voices and wept.
5 Then they called the name of that
place [1]Bochim; and they sacrificed
there to the LORD.
6 And when [a]Joshua had dismissed
the people, the children of Israel went

35 [a]Josh. 19:42 [1]*Shaalabbin,* Josh. 19:42 [2]*became forced laborers*
36 [a]Josh. 15:3

CHAPTER 2

1 [a]Ex. 20:2 [b]Deut. 1:8 [c]Gen. 17:7, 8
2 [a]Deut. 7:2 [b]Deut. 12:3 [c]Ps. 106:34 [1]*treaty*
3 [a]Josh. 23:13 [b]Judg. 3:6 [c]Ps. 106:36 [1]LXX, Tg., Vg. *enemies to you* [2]*entrap you*
4 *See WW at Deut. 1:1.
5 [1]Lit. *Weeping*
6 [a]Josh. 22:6; 24:28–31 *See WW at Deut. 8:1.
7 [a]Josh. 24:31
8 [a]Josh. 24:29
9 [a]Josh. 24:30 [b]Josh. 19:49, 50
10 [a]1 Sam. 2:12 [1]Died and joined their ancestors
11 [a]Judg. 3:7, 12; 4:1; 6:1
12 [a]Deut. 31:16 [b]Deut. 6:14 [c]Ex. 20:5 *See WW at 1 Kin. 16:2.
13 [a]Judg. 10:6 [1]A Canaanite god [2]Canaanite goddesses
14 [a]Deut. 31:17 [b]2 Kin. 17:20 [c]Is. 50:1 [d]Lev. 26:37
15 [a]Lev. 26:14–26

each to his own inheritance to *possess
the land.

Death of Joshua

7 [a]So the people served the LORD all
the days of Joshua, and all the days
of the elders who outlived Joshua, who
had seen all the great works of the
LORD which He had done for Israel.
8 Now [a]Joshua the son of Nun, the
servant of the LORD, died *when he was*
one hundred and ten years old.
9 [a]And they buried him within the
border of his inheritance at [b]Timnath
Heres, in the mountains of Ephraim,
on the north side of Mount Gaash.
10 When all that generation had 4
[1]been gathered to their fathers, another generation arose after them who
[a]did not know the LORD nor the work
which He had done for Israel.

Israel's Unfaithfulness

11 Then the children of Israel did
[a]evil in the sight of the LORD, and
served the Baals;
12 and they [a]forsook the LORD God of
their fathers, who had brought them
out of the land of Egypt; and they followed [b]other gods from *among* the
gods of the people who *were* all around
them, and they [c]bowed down to them;
and they provoked the LORD to *anger.
13 They forsook the LORD [a]and served
[1]Baal and the [2]Ashtoreths.
14 [a]And the anger of the LORD was hot
against Israel. So He [b]delivered them
into the hands of plunderers who de-
spoiled them; and [c]He sold them into
the hands of their enemies all around,
so that they [d]could no longer stand before their enemies.
15 Wherever they went out, the hand
of the LORD was against them for calamity, as the LORD had said, and as
the LORD had [a]sworn to them. And they
were greatly distressed.

1:34–36 Amorites: See note on 6:10.
2:1 Angel of the LORD: At times this messenger is described as the Lord Himself (6:11–18; Ex. 3:2–6), whereas at other times as one sent from God.
2:2, 3 See section 3 of Truth-In-Action at the end of Judg.
2:2 Make no covenant: By making such a covenant with the inhabitants of the land, Israel would break their covenant with the Lord (Ex. 23:32).
2:5 Bochim in Hebrew literally means "Weeping." The weeping of the people here *did not express true* repentance, *nor did their sacrifices* represent true faith, for they continued to be disobedient.
2:8 The servant of the LORD: Joshua is identified with other divine servants, such as Moses (Josh. 1:1) and the promised Messiah (Is. 53:11).
2:10–15 See section 4 of Truth-In-Action at the end of Judg.
2:10 Did not know connotes "Did not acknowledge or serve."
2:11 Did evil in the sight of the LORD: This refrain is part of a recurring sequence of events in the period of the judges: 1) apostasy of Israel (3:7); 2) punishment at the hands of foreign peoples (3:8); 3) repentance of Israel (3:9); 4) deliverance through a Spirit-empowered deliverer (3:9, 10).
2:13 Baal was a fertility and nature god of the Canaanites. The plural "Baals" in v. 11 suggests that there were several local representatives of the worship of Baal (Baal-Berith, 9:4). **Ashtoreths** were female deities, such as Ashtoreth (consort of Baal), who was the goddess of war and fertility and Asherah (consort of El, the chief Canaanite god).
2:14 Into the hands of their enemies: This expression means that God gave the enemies victory over Israel.

16 Nevertheless, [a]the LORD raised up
judges who delivered them out of the
hand of those who plundered them.
17 Yet they would not listen to their
judges, but they [a]played the harlot with
other gods, and bowed down to them.
They turned quickly from the way in
which their fathers walked, in obeying
the *commandments of the LORD; they
did not do so.
18 And when the LORD raised up
judges for them, [a]the LORD was with
the **judge** and delivered them out of the
hand of their enemies all the days of
the judge; [b]for the LORD was moved to
pity by their groaning because of those
who oppressed them and harassed
them.

WORD WEALTH

2:18 judge, *shaphat* (shah-*faht*); derived from Strong's #8199: One who judges, governs, passes down judgment, pronounces sentence, and decides matters. The root is *shaphat,* to "judge," "decide," and "pronounce sentence." In English, both "to judge" and "judgment" have negative associations, but not so in Hebrew. Judgment is the balance, ethics, and wisdom, which, if present in a ruler's mind, enables him to govern equitably and to keep the land free from injustice. Judgment, when used of God, is that divine faculty whereby He runs the universe righteously, handing down decisions that will maintain or bring about a right state of affairs. Abraham described God as the Judge of the whole Earth (Gen. 18:25). In the Book of Judges, God raised up human judges (*shophtim*) who governed Israel, executed justice, and handed down decisions.

19 And it came to pass, [a]when the
judge was dead, that they reverted and
behaved more corruptly than their fathers,
by following other gods, to
*serve them and bow down to them.
They did not cease from their own doings
nor from their stubborn way.

16 [a]Judg. 3:9, 10, 15; Ps. 106:43–45
17 [a]Ex. 34:15 *See WW at Ps. 119:35.
18 [a]Josh. 1:5 [b]Gen. 6:6
19 [a]Judg. 3:12 *See WW at Ps. 100:2.
20 [a][Josh. 23:16]
21 [a]Josh. 23:4, 5, 13
22 [a]Judg. 3:1, 4 [b]Deut. 8:2, 16; 13:3

CHAPTER 3

1 [a]Judg. 1:1; 2:21, 22 [1]*experienced*
2 *See WW at Is. 48:17.
3 [a]Josh. 13:3
4 [1]*find out*
5 [a]Ps. 106:35
6 [a]Ex. 34:15, 16; Deut. 7:3, 4; Josh. 23:12
7 [a]Judg. 2:11 [b]Deut. 32:18

20 Then the anger of the LORD was hot
against Israel; and He said, "Because
this nation has [a]transgressed My covenant
which I commanded their fathers,
and has not heeded My voice,
21 "I also will no longer drive out before
them any of the nations which
Joshua [a]left when he died,
22 "so [a]that through them I may 5
[b]test Israel, whether they will keep the
ways of the LORD, to walk in them as
their fathers kept *them,* or not."
23 Therefore the LORD left those nations,
without driving them out immediately;
nor did He deliver them into
the hand of Joshua.

The Nations Remaining in the Land

3 Now these *are* [a]the nations which
the LORD left, that He might test Israel
by them, *that is,* all who had not
[1]known any of the wars in Canaan
2 (*this was* only so that the generations 5
of the children of Israel might be
*taught to know war, at least those
who had not formerly known it),
3 *namely,* [a]five lords of the Philistines,
all the Canaanites, the Sidonians,
and the Hivites who dwelt in Mount
Lebanon, from Mount Baal Hermon to
the entrance of Hamath.
4 And they were *left, that He might*
test Israel by them, to [1]know whether
they would obey the commandments
of the LORD, which He had commanded
their fathers by the hand of Moses.
5 [a]Thus the children of Israel dwelt
among the Canaanites, the Hittites, the
Amorites, the Perizzites, the Hivites,
and the Jebusites.
6 And [a]they took their daughters to
be their wives, and gave their daughters
to their sons; and they served their
gods.

Othniel

7 So the children of Israel did [a]evil
in the sight of the LORD. They [b]forgot

2:16 Raised up judges: In response to Israel's supplication (v. 18), the Lord was faithful to raise up deliverers to save them from their oppression. The Lord must chastise the disobedience of His people. When they learn their lesson, He renews His blessing and restores His covenant relationship with them.

2:22 See section 5 of Truth-In-Action at the end of Judg.

2:22 The Lord tested Israel's loyalty through the invasions and temptations of the remaining nations.

3:1, 2 The Lord left the nations in Canaan, not only to test the children of Israel but also to teach them how to engage in battle. The Lord wanted them to learn how to be victorious in battle by depending on Him.

3:2–4 See section 5 of Truth-In-Action at the end of Judg.

3:3 Five lords of the Philistines: The Philistines were organized into a confederacy occupying the cities of Ashdod, Ashkelon, Ekron, Gath, and Gaza on the southern coast of Palestine. **Sidonians** were Phoenicians who dwelt in Sidon, a dominant city in the coastal plain in northern Palestine. **Hivites** are identified with the hill country of Lebanon in the northern region of Palestine. **Mount Baal Hermon** is probably Mt. Hermon.

3:5, 6 The disobedience and downfall of the children of Israel resulted from three factors: 1) they dwelt among the people of foreign nations; 2) they intermarried with them; and 3) they served their gods.

3:7—16:31 This main section illustrates the recurring pattern of Israel's apostasy, oppression, repentance, and deliverance.

3:7 Did evil in the sight of the LORD is a recurring

the LORD their God, and served the
Baals and [1]Asherahs.
8 Therefore the anger of the LORD
was hot against Israel, and He [a]sold
them into the hand of [b]Cushan-
Rishathaim king of Mesopotamia; and
the children of Israel served Cushan-
Rishathaim eight years.
9 When the children of Israel [a]cried
out to the LORD, the LORD [b]raised up a
deliverer for the children of Israel, who
delivered them: [c]Othniel the son of
Kenaz, Caleb's younger brother.
10 [a]The Spirit of the LORD came upon
him, and he judged Israel. He went out
to war, and the LORD delivered Cushan-
Rishathaim king of Mesopotamia into
his *hand; and his hand prevailed over
Cushan-Rishathaim.
11 So the land had rest for forty years.
Then Othniel the son of Kenaz died.

Ehud

12 [a]And the children of Israel again
did *evil in the sight of the LORD. So
the LORD strengthened [b]Eglon king of
Moab against Israel, because they had
done evil in the sight of the LORD.
13 Then he gathered to himself the
people of Ammon and [a]Amalek, went
and [1]defeated Israel, and took possession of [b]the City of Palms.
14 So the children of Israel [a]served
Eglon king of Moab eighteen years.
15 But when the children of Israel
[a]cried out to the LORD, the LORD raised
up a deliverer for them: Ehud the son
of Gera, the Benjamite, a [b]left-handed
man. By him the children of Israel sent
tribute to Eglon king of Moab.
16 Now Ehud made himself a dagger
(it was double-edged and a cubit in
length) and fastened it under his
clothes on his right thigh.
17 So he brought the tribute to Eglon
king of Moab. (Now Eglon *was* a very
fat man.)
18 And when he had finished presenting the tribute, he sent away the
people who had carried the tribute.
19 But he himself turned back [a]from
the [1]stone images that *were* at Gilgal,
and said, "I have a secret message for
you, O king." He said, "Keep silence!"
And all who attended him went out
from him.
20 So Ehud came to him (now he was
sitting upstairs in his cool private
chamber). Then Ehud said, "I have a
message from God for you." So he
arose from *his* seat.
21 Then Ehud reached with his left
hand, took the dagger from his right
thigh, and thrust it into his belly.
22 Even the [1]hilt went in after the
blade, and the fat closed over the
blade, for he did not draw the dagger
out of his belly; and his entrails came
out.
23 Then Ehud went out through the
porch and shut the doors of the upper
room behind him and locked them.
24 When he had gone out, [1]*Eglon's* servants came to look, and *to their* surprise, the doors of the upper room were
locked. So they said, "He is probably
[a]attending[2] to his needs in the cool
chamber."
25 So they waited till they were
[a]embarrassed,* and still he had not
opened the doors of the upper room.
Therefore they took the key and
opened *them*. And there was their master, fallen dead on the floor.
26 But Ehud had escaped while they
delayed, and passed beyond the
[1]stone images and escaped to Seirah.
27 And it happened, when he arrived,
that [a]he blew the trumpet in the
[b]mountains of Ephraim, and the children of Israel went down with him

7 [1]Name or symbol for Canaanite goddesses **8** [a]Deut. 32:30; Judg. 2:14 [b]Hab. 3:7 **9** [a]Judg. 3:15 [b]Judg. 2:16 [c]Judg. 1:13 **10** [a]Num. 27:18; 1 Sam. 11:6; 2 Chr. 15:1 *See WW at Josh. 4:24. **12** [a]Judg. 2:19 [b]1 Sam. 12:9 *See WW at Ps. 5:4. **13** [a]Judg. 5:14 [b]Deut. 34:3; Judg. 1:16; 2 Chr. 28:15 [1]*struck* **14** [a]Deut. 28:48 **15** [a]Ps. 78:34 [b]Judg. 20:16

19 [a]Josh. 4:20 [1]Tg. *quarries* **22** [1]*handle* **24** [a]1 Sam. 24:3 [1]Lit. *his* [2]Lit. *covering his feet* **25** [a]2 Kin. 2:17; 8:11 *See WW at Ezek. 16:63. **26** [1]Tg. *quarries* **27** [a]Judg. 6:34; 1 Sam. 13:3 [b]Josh. 17:15

expression, which introduces the cycles of the judges (v. 12; 4:1; 6:1; 10:6; 13:1).
3:8 Cushan-Rishathaim in Hebrew is literally "Cushan of Double Wickedness."
3:9 The children of Israel cried out is a recurring expression found in the cycles of the judges (v. 15; 4:3; 6:7; 10:10, 12).
3:10 The Spirit of the LORD: See Introduction to Judges: The Holy Spirit at Work. **Judged** is a military term meaning to mobilize Israel for God's holy wars.
3:11 Forty years likely includes Othniel's term.
3:12 Moab: The Moabites were descendants of Lot (Gen. 19:37). They lived along the eastern border of the Dead Sea.
3:13 Ammon: The Ammonites were also descendants of Lot (Gen. 19:38). They were the northeastern neighbors of the Moabites. **Amalek:** The Amalekites were descendants of Esau (Gen. 36:12). They inhabited the Sinai Peninsula and the Negev, the southern part of Palestine. **City of Palms:** See note on 1:16.
3:15 Benjamite: Ironically, Benjamin means "Son of the Right Hand." Several Benjamites were left-handed (20:15, 16). Ehud's left-handedness aided him in killing Eglon.
3:16 Ehud's dagger was more advantageous than a sword because it was smaller and could be concealed. The **cubit** was the standard unit of length, about 18 inches.
3:19 Gilgal was perhaps the place where idolatrous statues of stone were cut out of the quarry and made into idols.
3:20 Chamber: This upper room was built on the flat roof of a house and was favored because it provided a cool place in the hot summer.
3:24 Attending to his needs may refer either to resting with one's feet elevated or to using the restroom. The Hebrew phrase is obscure.
3:25 Embarrassed indicates they were at their wits' end, not knowing what to make of the situation.

from the mountains; and [1]he led them.
28 Then he said to them, "Follow *me,*
for [a]the LORD has delivered your enemies the Moabites into your hand." So
they went down after him, seized the
[b]fords of the Jordan leading to Moab,
and did not allow anyone to cross over.
29 And at that time they killed about
ten thousand men of Moab, all stout
men of valor; not a man escaped.
30 So Moab was subdued that day under the hand of Israel. And [a]the land
had rest for eighty years.

Shamgar

31 After him was [a]Shamgar the son of
Anath, who killed six hundred men of
the Philistines [b]with an ox goad;
[c]and he also delivered [d]Israel.

Deborah

4 When Ehud was dead, [a]the children of Israel again did [b]evil in the
sight of the LORD.

> **KINGDOM DYNAMICS**
>
> **4:1—5:31 Inspiration,** LEADER TRAITS. Godly leaders lead by inspiration. Deborah convinced her followers to extend themselves beyond their own vision. The inspirational leader provides a model of integrity and courage and sets a high standard of performance. He gives his followers autonomy and not only treats them as individuals, but encourages individualism. There is no better way to develop leadership than to give an individual a job involving responsibility and let him work it out. Deborah did this with young Barak. She appointed him as her field commander and assigned him the task of recruiting an army to defeat Sisera. She was not afraid to set the example of courage and heroism by using herself as bait for the ambush.
>
> (Ex. 28:1, 2/Luke 3:1–20) J.B.

2 So the LORD [a]sold them into the
hand of Jabin king of Canaan, who

27 [1]Lit. *he went before them*
28 [a]Judg. 7:9, 15; 1 Sam. 17:47 [b]Josh. 2:7; Judg. 12:5
30 [a]Judg. 3:11
31 [a]Judg. 5:6 [b]1 Sam. 17:47 [c]Judg. 2:16 [d]1 Sam. 4:1

CHAPTER 4

1 [a]Judg. 2:19 [b]Judg. 2:11
2 [a]Judg. 2:14 [b]Josh. 11:1, 10 [c]1 Sam. 12:9; Ps. 83:9 [d]Judg. 4:13, 16
3 [a]Deut. 20:1; Judg. 1:19 [b]Ps. 106:42
5 [a]Gen. 35:8 *See WW at Num. 36:13.
6 [a]Heb. 11:32 [b]Josh. 19:37; 21:32 [c]Judg. 8:18 [1]*march*
7 [a]Ex. 14:4

reigned in [b]Hazor. The commander of
his army *was* [c]Sisera, who dwelt in
[d]Harosheth Hagoyim.
3 And the children of Israel cried out
to the LORD; for Jabin had nine hundred [a]chariots of iron, and for twenty
years [b]he had harshly oppressed the
children of Israel.
4 Now Deborah, a prophetess, the
wife of Lapidoth, was judging Israel at
that time.
5 [a]And she would sit under the palm
tree of Deborah between Ramah and
Bethel in the mountains of Ephraim.
And the children of Israel came up to
her for *judgment.

> **KINGDOM DYNAMICS**
>
> **4:4, 5 The Spirit-Filled, Multitalented Woman (Deborah),** WOMEN. Deborah literally means "Bee," reminding us of this woman's wisdom, how she liberally shared with her friends, and how her influence and authority were used by God to "sting" Israel's enemies. Her creative talents and leadership abilities distinguish her. Deborah wrote songs and sang them (ch. 5), and she was a patriotic woman of God who judged (or led) Israel for 40 years. She might be called the first woman military commander and first female Supreme Court Justice! The keys to Deborah's effectiveness were her spiritual commitment and walk with God, seen in the fact she is called a prophetess. She demonstrates the possibilities for any woman today who will allow the Spirit of God to fill and form her life, developing her full capacities to shape the world around her.
>
> (Num. 27:1–11/Ruth 1:1—4:22) F.L.

6 Then she sent and called for [a]Barak
the son of Abinoam from [b]Kedesh in
Naphtali, and said to him, "Has not the
LORD God of Israel commanded, 'Go
and [1]deploy *troops* at Mount [c]Tabor;
take with you ten thousand men of the
sons of Naphtali and of the sons of
Zebulun;
7 'and against you [a]I will deploy

3:31 Shamgar is the first of six minor judges. **Son of Anath** is an expression that identifies Shamgar with the town of Beth Anath in Galilee. **Ox goad:** A long wooden pole with a sharpened metal tip, used by farmers for driving animals.
4:2 The northern tribes of Israel were now oppressed by the Canaanites under the leadership of **Jabin** who reigned in **Hazor,** an important Canaanite stronghold in northern Galilee. In the narrative, attention is focused on the role of **Sisera,** the Canaanite commander, who dwelt in **Harosheth Hagoyim,** a town in Galilee situated on the Kishon River.
4:4 Deborah, whose name means "Honeybee," was a prophetess and a judge in Israel. God raised her up and gave her leadership abilities. **Judging** here refers to functioning in a recognized office, including rendering decisions on people's inquiries (v. 5). She also played an undefined role in battle (v. 9).
4:6 Barak, whose name means "Lightning," was the commander of the Israelite army. **Mount Tabor:** Because of its height and strategic location in the northeastern part of the Valley of Jezreel, 10 miles from the beginning of the Kishon River, it was ideally suited for deploying troops.
4:7 The River Kishon flows through the Plain of Esdraelon and the Valley of Jezreel. Often it floods much of the valley in the rainy season. Sisera wisely chose this area along the river because he was able to move his chariots freely. However, the Lord sent a storm and a flood, which swept away the forces of Sisera and they were defeated (5:20, 21).

Sisera, the commander of Jabin's
army, with his chariots and his multitude at the [b]River Kishon; and I will
[1]deliver him into your hand'?"
8 And Barak said to her, "If you will
go with me, then I will go; but if you
will not go with me, I will not go!"
5 9 So she said, "I will surely go with
you; nevertheless there will be no glory
for you in the journey you are taking,
for the LORD will [a]sell Sisera into the
hand of a woman." Then Deborah
arose and went with Barak to Kedesh.
10 And Barak called [a]Zebulun and
Naphtali to Kedesh; he went up with
ten thousand men [b]under[1] his command, and Deborah went up with him.
11 Now Heber [a]the Kenite, of the children of [b]Hobab the father-in-law of
Moses, had separated himself from the
Kenites and pitched his tent near the
terebinth tree at Zaanaim, [c]which *is*
beside Kedesh.
12 And they reported to Sisera that
Barak the son of Abinoam had gone up
to Mount Tabor.
13 So Sisera gathered together all his
chariots, nine hundred chariots of iron,
and all the people who *were* with him,
from Harosheth Hagoyim to the River
Kishon.
14 Then Deborah said to Barak,
[1]"Up! For this *is* the day in which the
LORD has delivered Sisera into your
hand. [a]Has not the LORD gone out before you?" So Barak went down from
Mount Tabor with ten thousand men
following him.
15 And the LORD routed Sisera and all
his chariots and all *his* army with the
edge of the sword before Barak; and
Sisera alighted from *his* chariot and
fled away on foot.
16 But Barak pursued the chariots and
the army as far as Harosheth Hagoyim,
and all the army of Sisera fell by the
edge of the sword; not a man was
[a]left.
17 However, Sisera had fled away on
foot to the tent of [a]Jael, the wife of Heber the Kenite; for *there was* peace between Jabin king of Hazor and the
house of Heber the Kenite.
18 And Jael went out to meet Sisera,
and said to him, "Turn aside, my lord,
turn aside to me; do not fear." And
when he had turned aside with her into
the tent, she covered him with a
[1]blanket.
19 Then he said to her, "Please give
me a little water to drink, for I am
thirsty." So she opened [a]a jug of
milk, gave him a drink, and covered
him.
20 And he said to her, "Stand at the
door of the tent, and if any man comes
and inquires of you, and says, 'Is there
any man here?' you shall say, 'No.'"
21 Then Jael, Heber's wife, [a]took a tent
peg and took a hammer in her hand,
and went softly to him and drove the
peg into his temple, and it went down
into the ground; for he was fast asleep
and weary. So he died.
22 And then, as Barak pursued Sisera,
Jael came out to meet him, and said
to him, "Come, I will show you the man
whom you seek." And when he went
into her *tent,* there lay Sisera, dead
with the peg in his temple.
23 So on that day God subdued Jabin
king of Canaan in the presence of the
children of Israel.
24 And the hand of the children of Israel grew stronger and stronger
against Jabin king of Canaan, until
they had destroyed Jabin king of Canaan.

The Song of Deborah

5 Then Deborah and Barak the son
of Abinoam [a]sang on that day,
saying:

2 "When[1] leaders [a]lead in Israel,
[b]When the people [2]willingly offer
themselves,
Bless the LORD!

3 "Hear,[a] O kings! Give ear,
O princes!

7 [b]Judg. 5:21; 1 Kin. 18:40; Ps. 83:9, 10 [1]Lit. *draw*
9 [a]Judg. 2:14
10 [a]Judg. 5:18 [b]Ex. 11:8; 1 Kin. 20:10 [1]Lit. *at his feet*
11 [a]Judg. 1:16 [b]Num. 10:29 [c]Judg. 4:6
14 [a]Deut. 9:3; 31:3; 2 Sam. 5:24; Ps. 68:7; Is. 52:12 [1]*Arise!*
16 [a]Ex. 14:28; Ps. 83:9
17 [a]Judg. 5:6
18 [1]*rug*
19 [a]Judg. 5:24–27
21 [a]Judg. 5:24–27

CHAPTER 5

1 [a]Ex. 15:1; Judg. 4:4
2 [a]Ps. 18:47 [b]2 Chr. 17:16 [1]Or *When locks are loosed* [2]*volunteer*
3 [a]Deut. 32:1, 3

4:8, 9 Barak's hesitation to go to battle without Deborah showed a lack of trust in the Lord. Consequently, the honor of victory over Sisera, according to Deborah's prophetic word, would go to a woman. Nonetheless, Barak is mentioned as one of the heroes of faith (Heb. 11:32).
4:9 See section 5 of Truth-In-Action at the end of Judg.
4:11 **Heber the Kenite** migrated north *with his wife Jael* from the *Negev, the southern* region of Palestine and became an ally of King Jabin (v. 17). Jael, on the other hand, did not share her husband's allegiance. When she killed Sisera (vv. 21, 22), Jael demonstrated her faithfulness to the alliance of the Kenites with the Israelites, which had existed since the time of Moses. **Hobab** is more commonly known as Jethro (Ex. 3:1).
4:15 **Routed:** The Lord confused or troubled **Sisera** and his army by curtailing the mobility of their chariots during the flooding of the Kishon River. This same verb is used with reference to the Egyptian army and their chariots in the Red Sea (Ex. 14:24–26).
4:18, 19 Jael invited Sisera into her tent and concealed him with a blanket. She offered him **milk,** a sign of hospitality.
5:1–31 Songs were written to celebrate national victories (Ex. 15:1–8). This song of victory, known as the "Song of Deborah," is one of the oldest examples in biblical literature. This poem which ascribes to the Lord the victory over Sisera and the Canaanites may have been written by Deborah.

I, *even* [b]I, will **sing** to the LORD;
I will *sing praise to the LORD God
of Israel.

WORD WEALTH

5:3 sing, *shir* (*sheer*); Strong's #7891: To sing. *Shir* refers specifically to the kind of song that is sung with the human voice, as contrasted with an instrumental song. There is another common OT word for "sing," *zamar,* and from this word is derived *mizmor,* usually translated "psalm" or "song." *Mizmor* may be vocal as well as instrumental. *Shir* is found in the Hebrew title of The Song of Solomon: *Shir ha-Shirim,* literally, "The Song of Songs."

4 "LORD, [a]when You went out from
Seir,
When You marched from
[b]the field of Edom,
The earth trembled and the
heavens *poured,
The clouds also poured water;
5 [a]The mountains [1]gushed before
the LORD,
[b]This Sinai, before the LORD God
of Israel.

6 "In the days of [a]Shamgar, son of
Anath,
In the days of [b]Jael,
[c]The highways were deserted,
And the travelers walked along
the byways.
7 Village life ceased, it ceased in
Israel,
Until I, Deborah, arose,
Arose a mother in Israel.
8 They chose [a]new gods;
Then *there was* war in the gates;
Not a shield or spear was seen
among forty thousand in Israel.
9 My heart *is* with the rulers of
Israel
Who offered themselves willingly
with the people.
Bless the LORD!

10 "Speak, you who ride on white
[a]donkeys,
Who sit in judges' attire,
And who walk along the road.
11 Far from the noise of the archers,
among the watering places,
There they shall recount the
righteous acts of the LORD,
The righteous acts *for* His
villagers in Israel;
Then the people of the LORD shall
go down to the gates.

12 "Awake,[a] awake, Deborah!
Awake, awake, sing a song!
Arise, Barak, and lead your
captives away,
O son of Abinoam!

13 "Then the survivors came down,
the people against the nobles;
The LORD came down for me
against the mighty.
14 From Ephraim *were* those whose
roots were in [a]Amalek.
After you, Benjamin, with your
peoples,
From Machir rulers came down,
And from Zebulun those who
bear the recruiter's staff.
15 And [1]the princes of Issachar *were*
with Deborah;
As Issachar, so *was* Barak
Sent into the valley [2]under his
command;
Among the divisions of Reuben
There were great resolves of
heart.
16 Why did you sit among the
sheepfolds,
To hear the pipings for the
flocks?
The divisions of Reuben have
great searchings of heart.
17 [a]Gilead stayed beyond the Jordan,
And why did Dan remain
[1]on ships?
[b]Asher continued at the seashore,
And stayed by his inlets.
18 [a]Zebulun *is* a people *who*
jeopardized their lives to the
point of death,
Naphtali also, on the heights of
the battlefield.

3 [b]Ps. 27:6 *See WW at Ps. 149:3. **4** [a]Deut. 33:2; Ps. 68:7 [b]Ps. 68:8 *See WW at Ezek. 21:2. **5** [a]Ps. 97:5 [b]Ex. 19:18 [1]*flowed* **6** [a]Judg. 3:31 [b]Judg. 4:17 [c]Is. 33:8 **8** [a]Deut. 32:17 **10** [a]Judg. 10:4; 12:14

12 [a]Ps. 57:8 **14** [a]Judg. 3:13 **15** [1]So with LXX, Syr., Tg., Vg.; MT *And my princes in Issachar* [2]Lit. *at his feet* **17** [a]Josh. 22:9 [b]Josh. 19:29, 31 [1]Or *at ease* **18** [a]Judg. 4:6, 10

5:4, 5 The poem recalls the appearance of the Lord when He brought the children through the wilderness into Canaan (Deut. 33:2).
5:4 Seir originally referred to a mountain in Edom and later signified the territory of Edom south of the Dead Sea.
5:5 This Sinai: When the Lord appeared on Mt. Sinai, a thunderstorm and earthquake took place (Ex. 19:16–18).
5:7 Village life ceased: The villagers sought refuge in the fortified (walled) cities.
5:10, 11 These verses describe how the troops were mustered under Deborah's inspired leadership.
5:10 Who ride on white donkeys refers to the wealthy. **Who walk along the road** alludes to the lowly class.
5:11 Noise of the archers is an expression that may refer to the singers who encouraged the warriors by relating the former outstanding achievements of the Lord.
5:12 Awake, awake is a command to take action.
5:13–18 These verses review the responses of various tribes during the crisis with the Canaanites. The tribes of Ephraim, Benjamin, Zebulun, Issachar, and Naphtali were blessed because they mustered for battle. Reuben, Gilead (Gad), Dan, and Asher were reproved for their lack of participation.

19 "The kings came *and* fought,
Then the kings of Canaan fought
In [a]Taanach, by the waters of Megiddo;
They took no spoils of silver.
20 They fought from the *heavens;
The stars from their courses fought against Sisera.
21 [a]The torrent of Kishon swept them away,
That ancient torrent, the torrent of Kishon.
O my soul, *march on in strength!
22 Then the horses' hooves pounded,
The galloping, galloping of his steeds.
23 'Curse Meroz,' said the [1]angel of the LORD,
'Curse its inhabitants bitterly,
Because they did not come to the help of the LORD,
To the help of the LORD against the mighty.'

24 "Most blessed among women is Jael,
The wife of Heber the Kenite;
[a]Blessed is she among women in tents.
25 He asked for water, she gave milk;
She brought out cream in a lordly bowl.
26 She stretched her hand to the tent peg,
Her right hand to the workmen's hammer;
She pounded Sisera, she pierced his head,
She split and struck through his temple.
27 At her feet he sank, he fell, he lay still;
At her feet he sank, he fell;
Where he sank, there he fell [a]dead.

28 "The mother of Sisera looked through the window,
And cried out through the lattice,
'Why is his chariot *so* long in coming?
Why tarries the clatter of his chariots?'

19 [a]Judg. 1:27
20 *See WW at 1 Kin. 8:23.
21 [a]Judg. 4:7 *See WW at Deut. 11:25.
23 [1]Or *Angel*
24 [a][Luke 1:28]
27 [a]Judg. 4:18–21

29 [1]*princesses* [2]Lit. *repeats her words to herself*
30 *See WW at Jer. 31:22.
31 [a]Ps. 92:9 [b]2 Sam. 23:4 [c]Ps. 37:6; 89:36, 37 [d]Ps. 19:5

CHAPTER 6

1 [a]Judg. 2:11 [b]Num. 22:4; 31:1–3

29 Her wisest [1]ladies answered her,
Yes, she [2]answered herself,
30 'Are they not finding and dividing the spoil:
To every *man a girl *or* two;
For Sisera, plunder of dyed garments,
Plunder of garments embroidered and dyed,
Two pieces of dyed embroidery for the neck of the looter?'

31 "Thus let all Your enemies [a]**perish,** O LORD!
But *let* those who love Him *be*
[b]like the [c]sun
When it comes out in full [d]strength."

So the land had rest for forty years.

WORD WEALTH

5:31 perish, *'abad* (ah-*vahd*); Strong's #6: Destroy; be destroyed, perish, be ruined, be lost, fail. *'Abad* appears about 180 times in the OT. Its range of meaning stretches from the destruction of a kingdom (2 Kin. 24:2) to the destruction, punishment, and ruination of the satanic figure in Ezek. 28:16. *'Abad* is used to describe a "lost" sheep, or "perishing" sheep, Ps. 119:176. From *'abad* is derived "Abaddon." Generally regarded as destruction personified, Abaddon is a demonic prince in Rev. 9:11. In all six occurrences in the OT, this word is translated "destruction."

Midianites Oppress Israel

6 Then the children of Israel did [a]evil in the sight of the LORD. So the LORD delivered them into the hand of [b]Midian for seven years,

KINGDOM DYNAMICS

6:1—8:35 Humility, LEADER TRAITS. Gideon demonstrates seven traits of godly leadership: 1) unwillingness to lead unless God calls (6:36–40); 2) dependence on God at every turn (7:1–8); 3) willingness to turn faith into action (6:25–27; 7:15–22); 4) willingness to use the gifts God had given him to lead others. He told the 300 who stuck with him

5:20 The stars from their courses fought: *The expression* here does not mean *that the stars* caused the rain but that *the Lord* intervened in this battle by sending a torrential rain. On occasion in the Scriptures, "stars" may refer to angelic messengers (for example, Job 38:7).
5:23 The location of **Meroz** is unknown. It was likely a city near the scene of the action.

6:1—8:32 The deliverance from the oppression of the Midianites by Gideon is described in these chapters.
6:1 Midian: The Midianites were descendants of Midian, a son of Abraham and Keturah. They were a nomadic people who lived east of the Jordan River and the Dead Sea. Israel's seven-year oppression was God's punishment for their idolatry.

to watch him and follow his example (7:17); 5) he gave God glory before and after his victory (7:15; 8:3, 23); 6) he humbly gave others credit that belonged to him (8:1–3); 7) he refused to establish a dynasty after he had fulfilled God's charge (8:22, 23).
(Acts 26:19/Acts 13:22) J.B.

2 and the hand of Midian prevailed
against Israel. Because of the Midianites, the children of Israel made for
themselves the dens, [a]the caves, and
the strongholds which *are* in the mountains.
3 So it was, whenever Israel had
sown, Midianites would come up; also
Amalekites and the [a]people of the East
would come up against them.
4 Then they would encamp against
them and [a]destroy the produce of the
earth as far as Gaza, and leave no
sustenance for Israel, neither sheep
nor ox nor [b]donkey.
5 For they would come up with their
livestock and their tents, coming in as
numerous as locusts; both they and
their camels were [1]without number;
and they would enter the land to destroy it.
6 So Israel was greatly impoverished
because of the Midianites, and the children of Israel [a]cried out to the LORD.
7 And it came to pass, when the children of Israel cried out to the LORD because of the Midianites,

2 [a]1 Sam. 13:6; Heb. 11:38
3 [a]Judg. 7:12
4 [a]Lev. 26:16 [b]Deut. 28:31
5 [1]*innumerable*
6 [a]Ps. 50:15; Hos. 5:15
8 [a]Josh. 24:17 [1]*slavery*
9 [a]Ps. 44:2, 3
10 [a]2 Kin. 17:35, 37, 38; Jer. 10:2 [b]Judg. 2:1, 2
11 [a]Josh. 17:2; Judg. 6:15 [b]Judg. 7:1; Heb. 11:32 *See WW at 2 Chr. 32:21.
12 [a]Judg. 13:3; Luke 1:11, 28 [b]Josh. 1:5
13 [a][Is. 59:1] [b]Josh. 4:6, 21; Ps. 44:1 [c]Deut. 31:17; 2 Chr. 15:2; Ps. 44:9–16 [1]Heb. *adoni,* used of man

8 that the LORD sent a prophet to the
children of Israel, who said to them,
"Thus says the LORD God of Israel: 'I
brought you up from Egypt and
brought you out of the [a]house of
[1]bondage;
9 'and I delivered you out of the hand
of the Egyptians and out of the hand
of all who oppressed you, and [a]drove
them out before you and gave you their
land.
10 'Also I said to you, "I *am* the LORD
your God; [a]do not fear the gods of the
Amorites, in whose land you dwell."
But you have not obeyed My [b]voice.' "

Gideon

11 Now the *Angel of the LORD came
and sat under the terebinth tree which
was in Ophrah, which *belonged* to
Joash [a]the Abiezrite, while his son
[b]Gideon threshed wheat in the winepress, in order to hide *it* from the Midianites.
12 And the [a]Angel of the LORD appeared to him, and said to him, "The
LORD *is* [b]with you, you mighty man of
valor!"
13 Gideon said to Him, "O [1]my lord,
if the LORD is with us, why then has
all this happened to us? And [a]where
are all His miracles [b]which our fathers
told us about, saying, 'Did not the LORD
bring us up from Egypt?' But now the
LORD has [c]forsaken us and delivered

6:3 Amalekites: This ancient nomadic tribe, located in the Negev and in the Sinai Peninsula, descended from Esau's grandson Amalek (Gen. 36:12, 16). The Midianites formed a coalition with them and other eastern peoples.
6:5 As numerous as locusts: The invaders were so numerous and their devastation so extensive in the land that they were compared to swarms of locusts. **Camels:** This is the first reference in the OT to the use of camels in warfare.
6:8 The Lord sent an unnamed **prophet** to remind Israel of how He had delivered them from Egypt and given them their land, and to rebuke Israel for their disobedience to His covenant stipulations.
6:10 Amorites refers to the Canaanite nations in general.
6:11 Angel of the LORD: See note on 2:1. **Ophrah** was a city west of the Jordan. **Abiezrite:** A clan of the tribe of Manasseh (Josh. 17:2). **Threshed wheat in the winepress:** Normally, wheat was threshed in an open space. **Gideon** felt the wheat was more secure hidden in the enclosed winepress.
6:12 You mighty man of valor: The Angel pointed to Gideon's potential as a mighty deliverer through the Lord's enabling power, as well as to his noble status in the community in spite of Gideon's disclaimer (v. 15).
6:13 If the LORD is with us: While the Angel of the Lord assured Gideon of the Lord's presence with him, Gideon felt that the Lord had forsaken the Israelites in view of their present circumstances.

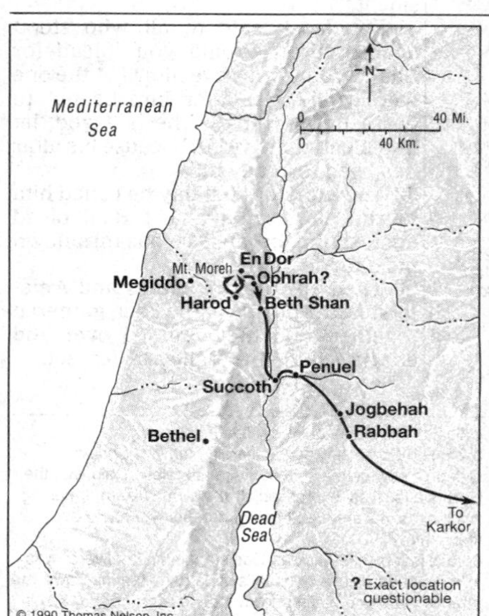

Gideon's Campaign

us into the hands of the Midianites."
1 14 Then the LORD turned to him and
said, [a]"Go in this might of yours, and
you shall *save Israel from the hand
of the Midianites. [b]Have I not sent
you?"
15 So he said to Him, "O [1]my Lord,
how can I save Israel? Indeed [a]my clan
is the weakest in Manasseh, and I *am*
the least in my father's house."
1 16 And the LORD said to him, [a]"Surely
I will be with you, and you shall
[1]defeat the Midianites as one man."
17 Then he said to Him, "If now I have
found *favor in Your sight, then
[a]show me a *sign that it is You who
talk with me.
18 [a]"Do not depart from here, I pray,
until I come to You and bring out my
offering and set *it* before You." And
He said, "I will wait until you come
back."
19 [a]So Gideon went in and prepared
a young goat, and unleavened bread
from an ephah of flour. The meat he
put in a basket, and he put the broth
in a pot; and he brought *them* out to
Him under the terebinth tree and presented *them*.
20 The Angel of God said to him,
"Take the meat and the unleavened
bread and [a]lay *them* on this rock, and
[b]pour out the broth." And he did so.
21 Then the Angel of the LORD put out
the end of the staff that *was* in His
hand, and touched the meat and the
unleavened bread; and [a]fire rose out
of the rock and consumed the meat and
the unleavened bread. And the Angel
of the LORD departed out of his sight.
22 Now Gideon [a]perceived that He
was the Angel of the LORD. So Gideon
said, "Alas, O Lord GOD! [b]For I have
seen the Angel of the LORD face to
face."
23 Then the LORD said to him, [a]"Peace
be with you; do not fear, you shall not
die."
24 So Gideon built an *altar there to
the LORD, and called it [1]The-LORD-*Is*-
Peace. To this day it *is* still [a]in Ophrah
of the Abiezrites.
25 Now it came to pass the same night
that the LORD said to him, "Take your
father's young bull, the second bull of
seven years old, and [a]tear down the
altar of [b]Baal that your father has, and
[c]cut down the [1]wooden image that *is*
beside it;
26 "and build an altar to the LORD your
God on top of this [1]rock in the proper
arrangement, and take the second bull
and offer a burnt sacrifice with the
wood of the image which you shall cut
down."
27 So Gideon took ten men from
among his servants and did as the
LORD had said to him. But because he
feared his father's household and the
men of the city too much to do *it* by
day, he did *it* by night.

Gideon Destroys the Altar of Baal

28 And when the men of the city arose
early in the morning, there was the altar of Baal, torn down; and the wooden
image that *was* beside it was cut down,
and the second bull was being offered
on the altar *which had been* built.
29 So they said to one another, "Who
has done this thing?" And when they
had inquired and asked, they said,
"Gideon the son of Joash has done this
thing."
30 Then the men of the city said to
Joash, "Bring out your son, that he
may die, because he has torn down the
altar of Baal, and because he has cut
down the wooden image that *was* beside it."
31 But Joash said to all who stood
against him, "Would you [1]plead for
Baal? Would you save him? Let the one
who would plead for him be put to
death by morning! If he *is* a god, let
him plead for himself, because his altar
has been torn down!"
32 Therefore on that day he called him
[a]Jerubbaal,[1] saying, "Let Baal plead
against him, because he has torn down
his altar."
33 Then all [a]the Midianites and Amalekites, the people of the East, gathered
together; and they crossed over and
encamped in [b]the Valley of Jezreel.

14 [a]1 Sam. 12:11 [b]Josh. 1:9 *See WW at Jer. 17:14.
15 [a]1 Sam. 9:21 [1]Heb. *Adonai*, used of God
16 [a]Ex. 3:12; Josh. 1:5 [1]Lit. *strike*
17 [a]Judg. 6:36, 37; 2 Kin. 20:8; Ps. 86:17; Is. 7:11; 38:7, 8 *See WW at Zech. 12:10. • See WW at Ps. 86:17.
18 [a]Gen. 18:3, 5
19 [a]Gen. 18:6–8
20 [a]Judg. 13:19 [b]1 Kin. 18:33, 34
21 [a]Lev. 9:24
22 [a]Gen. 32:30; Ex. 33:20; Judg. 13:21, 22 [b]Gen. 16:13
23 [a]Dan. 10:19
24 [a]Judg. 8:32 [1]Heb. *YHWH Shalom* *See WW at 2 Kin. 12:9.
25 [a]Judg. 2:2 [b]Judg. 3:7 [c]Ex. 34:13; Deut. 7:5 [1]Heb. *Asherah*, a Canaanite goddess
26 [1]*stronghold*
31 [1]*contend*
32 [a]Judg. 7:1; 1 Sam. 12:11; 2 Sam. 11:21 [1]Lit. *Let Baal Plead*
33 [a]Judg. 6:3 [b]Josh. 17:16; Hos. 1:5

6:14 See section 1 of Truth-In-Action at the end of Judg.
6:14 The LORD turned to him: The Angel of the Lord, now speaking to him as the Lord Himself, commissioned Gideon to deliver the people of Israel.
6:16 *See section* 1 of Truth-In-Action at the end of Judg.
6:19 The large amount of food (**an ephah** is over a bushel) presented in Gideon's offering reflects either his wealth or a special sacrifice in this destitute time.
6:21 Consumed the meat . . . bread: The consuming of the sacrifice fulfilled the sign Gideon had requested and indicated the acceptance of Gideon's offering.
6:24 The-LORD-*Is*-Peace is literally *Yahweh Shalom*. Gideon's new sense of security in his relationship with the Lord is effectively expressed by the term *shalom*, meaning wholeness, security, well-being, prosperity, peace, and friendship.
6:25 Gideon's first task as God's appointed deliverer was to remove the cause of Israel's idolatry by tearing down **the altar of Baal** and cutting down the **wooden image**, a cult object representing the Canaanite goddess Asherah.

34 But [a]the Spirit of the LORD came
upon Gideon; then he [b]blew the trumpet, and the Abiezrites gathered behind him.
35 And he sent messengers throughout
all Manasseh, who also gathered behind him. He also sent messengers to
[a]Asher, [b]Zebulun, and Naphtali; and
they came up to meet them.

The Sign of the Fleece

[2] 36 So Gideon said to God, "If You will
save Israel by my hand as You have
said—
37 [a]"look, I shall put a fleece of wool
on the threshing floor; if there is dew
on the fleece only, and *it is* dry on all
the ground, then I shall know that You
will save Israel by my hand, as You
have said."
38 And it was so. When he rose early
the next morning and squeezed the
fleece together, he wrung the dew out
of the fleece, a bowlful of water.
39 Then Gideon said to God, [a]"Do not
be angry with me, but let me speak just
once more: Let me test, I pray, just
once more with the fleece; let it now
be dry only on the fleece, but on all
the ground let there be dew."
40 And God did so that night. It was
dry on the fleece only, but there was
dew on all the ground.

Gideon's Valiant Three Hundred

[6] 7 Then [a]Jerubbaal (that *is,* Gideon)
and all the people who *were* with
him rose early and encamped beside
the well of Harod, so that the camp of
the Midianites was on the north side
of them by the hill of Moreh in the valley.
2 And the LORD said to Gideon, "The
people who *are* with you *are* too many
for Me to give the Midianites into their
hands, lest Israel [a]claim glory for itself
against Me, saying, 'My own hand has
saved me.'

34 [a]Judg. 3:10; 1 Chr. 12:18; 2 Chr. 24:20 [b]Num. 10:3; Judg. 3:27
35 [a]Judg. 5:17; 7:23 [b]Judg. 4:6, 10; 5:18
37 [a][Ex. 4:3–7]
39 [a]Gen. 18:32

CHAPTER 7

1 [a]Judg. 6:32
2 [a]Deut. 8:17; Is. 10:13

3 [a]Deut. 20:8
4 *See WW at Zech. 13:9.
7 [a]1 Sam. 14:6 [1]*home*
9 [a]Gen. 46:2, 3; Judg. 6:25
11 [a]Gen. 24:14; 1 Sam. 14:9, 10 [1]*you shall be encouraged*

3 "Now therefore, proclaim in the
hearing of the people, saying, [a]'Whoever *is* fearful and afraid, let him
turn and depart at once from Mount
Gilead.'" And twenty-two thousand of
the people returned, and ten thousand
remained.
4 But the LORD said to Gideon, "The
people *are* still *too* many; bring them
down to the water, and I will *test them
for you there. Then it will be, *that* of
whom I say to you, 'This one shall go
with you,' the same shall go with you;
and of whomever I say to you, 'This
one shall not go with you,' the same
shall not go."
5 So he brought the people down to
the water. And the LORD said to Gideon, "Everyone who laps from the water with his tongue, as a dog laps, you
shall set apart by himself; likewise everyone who gets down on his knees to
drink."
6 And the number of those who
lapped, *putting* their hand to their
mouth, was three hundred men; but all
the rest of the people got down on their
knees to drink water.
7 Then the LORD said to Gideon,
[a]"By the three hundred men who
lapped I will save you, and deliver the
Midianites into your hand. Let all the
other people go, every man to his
[1]place."
8 So the people took provisions and
their trumpets in their hands. And he
sent away all *the rest of* Israel, every
man to his tent, and retained those
three hundred men. Now the camp
of Midian was below him in the valley.
9 It happened on the same [a]night that
the LORD said to him, "Arise, go down
against the camp, for I have delivered
it into your hand.
10 "But if you are afraid to go down,
go down to the camp with Purah your
servant,
11 "and you shall [a]hear what they say;
and afterward [1]your hands shall be

6:34 The Spirit of the LORD came upon Gideon: In Hebrew this literally means "The Spirit of the Lord clothed Himself with Gideon." See Introduction to Judges: The Holy Spirit at Work.

6:36–40 See section 2 of Truth-In-Action at the end of Judg.

6:36–40 Gideon did not request the sign of **the fleece** to determine God's will but to gain deepened assurance. Through divine revelation, he already knew that he was appointed to deliver Israel. He wanted confirmation of the Lord's presence and power to enable him to accomplish the task.

6:39, 40 The fulfillment of Gideon's second request is more miraculous than the first. Normally, the wool fleece would have absorbed water more readily than the beaten earth of the threshing floor. To have **dry on the fleece only** with **dew on all the ground** would indeed be supernatural. The Lord was patient with Gideon and provided the assurance that he needed.

7:1–8 See section 6 of Truth-In-Action at the end of Judg.

7:1 Harod was a well or spring probably situated near Mt. Gilboa. **Moreh** was a prominent hill located at the entrance of the Valley of Jezreel.

7:5 How could the people who lapped like a dog acquire water without bending down and putting their faces in the water? V. 6 suggests they stayed on their feet, brought the water to their mouths with their hands, and lapped the water with their tongues. Whatever the exact explanation, the test was designed to reveal those who were more alert.

strengthened to go down against the
camp." Then he went down with Purah
his servant to the outpost of the armed
men who *were* in the camp.
12 Now the Midianites and Amalekites, [a]all the people of the East, were
lying in the valley [b]as numerous as locusts; and their camels *were* [1]without
number, as the sand by the seashore
in multitude.
13 And when Gideon had come, there
was a man telling a *dream to his companion. He said, "I have had a dream:
To my surprise, a loaf of barley bread
tumbled into the camp of Midian; it
came to a tent and struck it so that it
fell and overturned, and the tent collapsed."
14 Then his companion answered and
said, "This *is* nothing else but the
sword of Gideon the son of Joash, a
man of Israel! Into his hand [a]God has
delivered Midian and the whole camp."
15 And so it was, when Gideon heard
the telling of the dream and its interpretation, that he worshiped. He returned to the camp of Israel, and said,
"Arise, for the LORD has delivered the
camp of Midian into your hand."
16 Then he divided the three hundred
men *into* three companies, and he put
a trumpet into every man's hand, with
empty pitchers, and torches inside the
pitchers.
17 And he said to them, "Look at me
and do likewise; watch, and when I
come to the edge of the camp you shall
do as I do:
18 "When I *blow the trumpet, I and
all who *are* with me, then you also
blow the trumpets on every side of the
whole camp, and say, '*The sword of* the
LORD and of Gideon!' "
19 So Gideon and the hundred men
who *were* with him came to the outpost
of the camp at the beginning of the
middle watch, just as they had posted
the watch; and they blew the trumpets
and broke the pitchers that *were* in
their hands.
20 Then the three companies blew the
trumpets and broke the pitchers—they
held the torches in their left hands and
the trumpets in their right hands for
blowing—and they cried, "The sword
of the LORD and of Gideon!"
21 And [a]every man stood in his place
all around the camp; [b]and the whole
army ran and cried out and fled.
22 When the three hundred [a]blew the
trumpets, [b]the LORD set [c]every man's
sword against his companion throughout the whole camp; and the army fled
to [1]Beth Acacia, toward Zererah, as far
as the border of [d]Abel Meholah, by
Tabbath.
23 And the men of Israel gathered together from [a]Naphtali, Asher, and all
Manasseh, and pursued the Midianites.
24 Then Gideon sent messengers
throughout all the [a]mountains of
Ephraim, saying, "Come down against
the Midianites, and seize from them
the watering places as far as Beth
Barah and the Jordan." Then all the
men of Ephraim gathered together and
[b]seized the watering places as far as
[c]Beth Barah and the Jordan.
25 And they captured [a]two princes of
the Midianites, [b]Oreb and Zeeb. They
killed Oreb at the rock of Oreb, and
Zeeb they killed at the winepress of
Zeeb. They pursued Midian and
brought the heads of Oreb and Zeeb
to Gideon on the [c]other side of the Jordan.

Gideon Subdues the Midianites

8 Now [a]the men of Ephraim said to
him, "Why have you done this to
us by not calling us when you went
to fight with the Midianites?" And they
reprimanded him sharply.
2 So he said to them, "What have I
done now in comparison with you? *Is*

12 [a]Judg. 6:3, 33; 8:10 [b]Judg. 6:5 [1]*innumerable*
13 *See WW at Joel 2:28.
14 [a]Judg. 6:14, 16
18 *See WW at Ps. 47:1.
21 [a]Ex. 14:13, 14; 2 Chr. 20:17 [b]2 Kin. 7:7
22 [a]Josh. 6:4, 16, 20 [b]Ps. 83:9; Is. 9:4 [c]1 Sam. 14:20; 2 Chr. 20:23 [d]1 Kin. 4:12 [1]Heb. *Beth Shittah*
23 [a]Judg. 6:35
24 [a]Judg. 3:27 [b]Judg. 3:28 [c]John 1:28
25 [a]Judg. 8:3 [b]Ps. 83:11; Is. 10:26 [c]Judg. 8:4

CHAPTER 8

1 [a]Judg. 12:1; 2 Sam. 19:41

7:13 A loaf of barley bread: Barley was considered an inferior grain, which was used by the poor. This loaf symbolized Israel, who appeared inferior and smaller in number than the Midianite army. The barley represents agriculture. The Israelites who engaged in this form of livelihood had a settlement life-style. **Tent:** The tent represents the entire Midianite camp. The use of tents suggests that the Midianites had a nomadic life-style.
7:15 He worshiped means he bowed *on his knees* before *Yahweh, offering* vocal adoration and gratitude for God's encouragement.
7:19 The middle watch: There must have been three watches in the OT period. At the beginning of the middle watch, the new guards would have taken their posts and the army would have settled down to sleep.
7:22 Beth Acacia is also referred to as Beth Shittah. It was probably a town in the Jordan Valley. **Abel Meholah** was a town situated east of the Jordan River.
7:24 Beth Barah was a site in the Jordan Valley.
7:25 Oreb means "Raven," and **Zeeb** means "Wolf." The heads of these two Midianite princes were brought back to Gideon. It was a common practice in the ancient Near East to bring back body parts from dead victims to indicate the number of people killed.
8:1–3 Gideon was very diplomatic in his encounter with the Ephraimites and appeased their wrath with his gentle answer whereas Jephthah responded harshly to them and defeated them through a cruel scheme (12:1–6).
8:2 The gleaning of the grapes: Gideon was probably referring to Ephraim's mop-up work following the initial battle.

not the [1]gleaning *of the grapes* of
Ephraim better than [2]the vintage of
[a]Abiezer?
3 [a]"God has delivered into your
hands the princes of Midian, Oreb and
Zeeb. And what was I able to do in
comparison with you?" Then their
[b]anger toward him subsided when he
said that.
4 When Gideon came [a]to the Jordan,
he and [b]the three hundred men who
were with him *crossed over, exhausted but still in pursuit.
5 Then he said to the men of [a]Suc-
coth, "Please give loaves of bread to
the people who follow me, for they are
exhausted, and I am pursuing Zebah
and Zalmunna, kings of Midian."
6 And the leaders of Succoth said,
[a]"*Are*[1] the hands of Zebah and Zalmunna now in your hand, that [b]we
should give bread to your army?"
7 So Gideon said, "For this cause,
when the LORD has delivered Zebah
and Zalmunna into my hand, [a]then I
will tear your flesh with the thorns of
the wilderness and with briers!"
8 Then he went up from there [a]to Penuel and spoke to them in the same way.
And the men of Penuel answered him
as the men of Succoth had answered.
9 So he also spoke to the men of Penuel, saying, "When I [a]come back in
peace, [b]I will tear down this tower!"
10 Now Zebah and Zalmunna *were* at
Karkor, and their armies with them,
about fifteen thousand, all who were
left of [a]all the army of the people of
the East; for [b]one hundred and twenty
thousand men who drew the sword had
fallen.
11 Then Gideon went up by the road
of those who dwell in tents on the east
of [a]Nobah and Jogbehah; and he
[1]attacked the army while the camp felt
[b]secure.
12 When Zebah and Zalmunna fled, he
pursued them; and he [a]took the two
kings of Midian, Zebah and Zalmunna,
and routed the whole army.
13 Then Gideon the son of Joash returned from battle, from the Ascent of
Heres.
14 And he caught a young man of the
men of Succoth and interrogated him;
and he wrote down for him the leaders
of Succoth and its elders, seventy-
seven men.
15 Then he came to the men of Succoth
and said, "Here are Zebah and Zalmunna, about whom you [a]ridiculed
me, saying, '*Are* the hands of Zebah
and Zalmunna now in your hand, that
we should give bread to your weary
men?' "
16 [a]And he took the elders of the city,
and thorns of the wilderness and briers, and with them he [1]taught the men
of Succoth.
17 [a]Then he tore down the tower of
[b]Penuel and killed the men of the city.
18 And he said to Zebah and Zalmunna, "What kind of men *were they*
whom you killed at [a]Tabor?" So they
answered, "As you *are*, so *were* they;
each one resembled the son of a king."
19 Then he said, "They *were* my
brothers, the sons of my mother. As
the LORD lives, if you had let them live,
I would not kill you."
20 And he said to Jether his firstborn,
"Rise, kill them!" But the youth would
not draw his sword; for he was afraid,
because he *was* still a youth.
21 So Zebah and Zalmunna said, "Rise
yourself, and kill us; for as a man *is,*
so is his strength." So Gideon arose
and [a]killed Zebah and Zalmunna, and
took the crescent ornaments that *were*
on their camels' necks.

Gideon's Ephod

22 Then the men of Israel said to Gideon, [a]"Rule over us, both you and your
son, and your grandson also; for you
have [b]delivered us from the hand of
Midian."
23 But Gideon said to them, "I will not
rule over you, nor shall my son rule

2 [a]Judg. 6:11 [1]Few grapes left after the harvest [2]The whole harvest
3 [a]Judg. 7:24, 25 [b]Prov. 15:1
4 [a]Judg. 7:25 [b]Judg. 7:6 *See WW at Josh. 3:4.
5 [a]Gen. 33:17; Ps. 60:6
6 [a]1 Kin. 20:11; Judg. 8:15 [b]1 Sam. 25:11 [1]Lit. *Is the palm*
7 [a]Judg. 8:16
8 [a]Gen. 32:30, 31; 1 Kin. 12:25
9 [a]1 Kin. 22:27 [b]Judg. 8:17
10 [a]Judg. 7:12 [b]Judg. 6:5
11 [a]Num. 32:35, 42 [b]Judg. 18:27; [1 Thess. 5:3] [1]Lit. *struck*
12 [a]Ps. 83:11
15 [a]Judg. 8:6
16 [a]Judg. 8:7 [1]*disciplined*
17 [a]Judg. 8:9 [b]1 Kin. 12:25
18 [a]Judg. 4:6; Ps. 89:12
21 [a]Ps. 83:11
22 [a][Judg. 9:8] [b]Judg. 3:9; 9:17

Vintage of Abiezer: Gideon, an Abiezrite, was referring to his personal involvement in the victory over the Midianites. Ephraim outshone him.

8:5 Succoth was an ancient town located in the Transjordan north of the Jabbok River.

8:6 Perhaps the people of Succoth refused to help Gideon because they doubted his ability to defeat the two Midianite kings and they feared a reprisal by the Midianites.

8:7 I will tear your flesh: It is difficult to determine whether Gideon was speaking figuratively or indeed intended to draw threshing sledges over them or drag them over thorns and briers like a threshing sledge over grain.

8:8 Penuel was a town east of Succoth in the land of Gad. It was named by Jacob following his wrestling with the Angel (Gen. 32:30, 31).

8:9 I will tear down this tower may refer to part of Penuel's fortifications or to its temple.

8:11 Nobah and Jogbehah were cities in Gilead, east of the Jordan River.

8:19 My brothers, the sons of my mother: The term "brother" in a society where men had many wives usually signified half brothers.

8:23 The LORD shall rule over you: Gideon rejected the invitation given at one of the tribal assemblies to rule and establish a monarchy because he supported the theocratic kingship of the Lord. Gideon is listed as one of the heroes of faith (Heb. 11:32).

over you; [a]the LORD shall rule over
you."

KINGDOM DYNAMICS

8:22, 23; 9:1–57 Leading God's Way, LEADER TRAITS. Although Gideon wisely refused to serve as king of Israel (8:23), upon his death, his son Abimelech hired assassins to murder his brothers, in hope of seizing rule for himself. His youngest brother, Jotham, who escaped, climbed Mt. Gerizim and prophesied that a kingdom founded on sin would soon shatter; and within three years this happened. Gideon understood that God intended Israel to be a theocracy (God is King); but Abimelech, though possessing a natural charisma, did not have the mind of God, His appointment, or His anointing. Godly leaders do things God's way. Wickedness disqualifies from leading. The leader who seeks to benefit himself at the expense of others is on a path to self-destruction. Unlike his humble father, Abimelech was ambitious, believing the end justified the means. God judges leaders not on how much they accomplish, but on whether they do things His way.

(John 13:1–17/Num. 13:1—14:45) J.B.

24 Then Gideon said to them, "I would
like to [1]make a request of you, that
each of you would give me the earrings
from his plunder." For they had golden
earrings, [a]because they *were* Ishmaelites.
25 So they answered, "We will gladly
give *them*." And they spread out a garment, and each man threw into it the
earrings from his plunder.
26 Now the weight of the gold earrings
that he *requested was one thousand
seven hundred *shekels* of gold, besides
the crescent ornaments, pendants, and
purple robes which *were* on the kings
of Midian, and besides the chains that
were around their camels' necks.
27 Then Gideon [a]made it into an 6
*ephod and set it up in his city, [b]Ophrah.
And all Israel [c]played the harlot with
it there. It became [d]a snare to Gideon
and to his house.
28 Thus Midian was subdued before
the children of Israel, so that they lifted
their heads no more. [a]And the country
was quiet for forty years in the days
of Gideon.

Death of Gideon

29 Then [a]Jerubbaal the son of Joash
went and dwelt in his own house.
30 Gideon had [a]seventy sons who were
his own offspring, for he had many
wives.
31 [a]And his concubine who *was* in
Shechem also bore him a son, whose
name he called Abimelech.
32 Now Gideon the son of Joash died
[a]at a good old age, and was buried in
the tomb of Joash his father, [b]in Ophrah of the Abiezrites.
33 So it was, [a]as soon as Gideon was
dead, that the children of Israel again
[b]played the harlot with the Baals,
[c]and made Baal-Berith their god.
34 Thus the children of Israel [a]did not
remember the LORD their God, who had
delivered them from the hands of all
their enemies on every side;
35 [a]nor did they show kindness to the
house of Jerubbaal (Gideon) in accordance with the good he had done
for Israel.

Abimelech's Conspiracy

9 Then Abimelech the son of Jerubbaal went to Shechem, to [a]his
mother's brothers, and spoke with

23 [a]1 Sam. 8:7; 10:19; 12:12; Ps. 10:16
24 [a]Gen. 37:25, 28 [1]Lit. *request a request*
26 *See WW at Ps. 122:6.
27 [a]Judg. 17:5 [b]Judg. 6:11, 24 [c][Ps. 106:39] [d]Deut. 7:16 *See WW at Ex. 35:27.
28 [a]Judg. 5:31
29 [a]Judg. 6:32; 7:1
30 [a]Judg. 9:2, 5
31 [a]Judg. 9:1
32 [a]Gen. 25:8; Job 5:26 [b]Judg. 6:24; 8:27
33 [a]Judg. 2:19 [b]Judg. 2:17 [c]Judg. 9:4, 46
34 [a]Deut. 4:9; Judg. 3:7; Ps. 78:11, 42; 106:13, 21
35 [a]Judg. 9:16–18

CHAPTER 9

1 [a]Judg. 8:31, 35

8:24 Ishmaelites were descendants from Hagar (Gen. 16:15). The term here refers to the Midianites.
8:26 One thousand seven hundred *shekels* was approximately 73 pounds.
8:27 See section 6 of Truth-In-Action at the end of Judg.
8:27 Ephod: Gideon's ephod may have been a garment patterned after the short outer vest worn by the high priest. This golden ephod, however, was not worn as a garment; but it was erected in **Ophrah** and worshiped as an idol. Gideon, a man divinely appointed to deliver Israel from idolatry and oppression unfortunately became an instrument causing Israel to become an idolatrous *society once again.*
8:31 *Abimelech* *was a* son of Gideon by a concubine. A **concubine** was a female slave or mistress who became a man's wife. Often she remained in her father's house and her husband visited her occasionally. The name chosen by Gideon for his son means "My Father Is King." The first part of this name, "My Father," refers to the Lord, and the second part refers to the Lord's position as King in Israel.
8:33 Baal-Berith ("Lord of the Covenant") was worshiped also as El-Berith ("God of the Covenant") at a central shrine in Shechem.
9:1–3 Abimelech appealed to his kinsmen on his mother's side to speak on his behalf to the men of Shechem because he did not have any direct right to the throne. Shechem appears to have been ruled by an assembly which had the authority to designate kings (v. 3) as well as depose them (v. 23).
9:1 Shechem was an ancient city situated between Mt. Ebal and Mt. Gerizim in central Palestine. It had been an important city in Israel's religious history from the time of Abraham (Gen. 12:6, 7). After the conquest of Canaan, Joshua built an altar and conducted a covenant ceremony there. Offerings were given and the blessings and cursings of the Law were recited (Josh. 8:30–35).

them and with all the family of the
house of his mother's father, saying,
2 "Please speak in the hearing of all
the men of Shechem: 'Which is better
for you, that all [a]seventy of the sons
of Jerubbaal reign over you, or that
one reign over you?' Remember that I
am your own flesh and [b]bone."
3 And his mother's brothers spoke all
these words concerning him in the
hearing of all the men of Shechem; and
their heart was inclined to follow
Abimelech, for they said, "He is our
[a]brother."
4 So they gave him seventy *shekels*
of silver from the temple of [a]Baal-Berith,
with which Abimelech hired
[b]worthless and reckless men; and they
followed him.
5 Then he went to his father's house
[a]at Ophrah and [b]killed his brothers,
the seventy sons of Jerubbaal, on one
stone. But Jotham the youngest son of
Jerubbaal was left, because he hid himself.
6 And all the men of Shechem gathered
together, all of Beth Millo, and
they went and made Abimelech king
beside the terebinth tree at the pillar
that *was* in Shechem.

The Parable of the Trees

7 Now when they told Jotham, he
went and stood on top of [a]Mount Gerizim,
and lifted his voice and cried out.
And he said to them:

"Listen to me, you men of
Shechem,
That God may listen to you!

8 "The[a] trees once went forth to
anoint a king over them.
And they said to the olive tree,
[b]'Reign over us!'
9 But the olive tree said to them,
'Should I cease giving my oil,
[a]With which they honor God and
men,
And go to sway over trees?'

10 "Then the trees said to the fig tree,
'You come *and* reign over us!'
11 But the fig tree said to them,
'Should I cease my sweetness and
my good fruit,
And go to sway over trees?'

12 "Then the trees said to the vine,
'You come *and* reign over us!'
13 But the vine said to them,
'Should I cease my new wine,
[a]Which cheers *both* God and men,
And go to sway over trees?'

14 "Then all the trees said to the
bramble,
'You come *and* reign over us!'
15 And the bramble said to the trees,
'If in truth you anoint me as king
over you,
Then come *and* take *shelter in
my [a]shade;
But if not, [b]let fire come out of
the bramble
And devour the [c]cedars of
Lebanon!'

16 "Now therefore, if you have acted
in truth and sincerity in making
Abimelech king, and if you have dealt
well with Jerubbaal and his house, and
have done to him [a]as[1] he deserves—
17 "for my [a]father fought for you,
risked his life, and [b]delivered you out
of the hand of Midian;
18 [a]"but you have risen up against my
father's house this day, and killed his

2 [a]Judg. 8:30; 9:5, 18 [b]Gen. 29:14
3 [a]Gen. 29:15
4 [a]Judg. 8:33 [b]Judg. 11:3; 2 Chr. 13:7; Acts 17:5
5 [a]Judg. 6:24 [b]Judg. 8:30; 9:2, 18; 2 Kin. 11:1, 2
7 [a]Deut. 11:29; 27:12; Josh. 8:33; John 4:20
8 [a]2 Kin. 14:9 [b]Judg. 8:22, 23
9 [a][John 5:23]
13 [a]Ps. 104:15
15 [a]Is. 30:2; Dan. 4:12; Hos. 14:7 [b]Num. 21:28; Judg. 9:20; Ezek. 19:14 [c]2 Kin. 14:9; Is. 2:13; Ezek. 31:3 *See WW at Zeph. 3:12.
16 [a]Judg. 8:35 [1]Lit. *according to the doing of his hands*
17 [a]Judg. 7 [b]Judg. 8:22
18 [a]Judg. 8:30, 35; 9:2, 5, 6

9:2 Which is better for you implies that one ruler would be better than the corporate rule of Jerubbaal's (Gideon's) 70 sons.
9:4 Reckless men were mercenaries who could be hired for political and military enterprises.
9:5 On one stone: Abimelech killed his 70 half brothers in a public execution as though he were slaughtering animals for sacrifice. Whether he killed his brothers because he thought they would contend for leadership or because he was exercising personal vengeance is unclear.
9:6 Beth Millo: "Millo" is related to a Hebrew root word meaning "to fill." It may have been a fortified citadel, a large earthen platform upon which a wall or large structure was built, or even the temple of the deity Baal-Berith, which was located in or near Shechem (v. 20).
9:7 On top of Mount Gerizim: On the side of Mt. Gerizim is a projecting rock ledge that forms a triangular platform. This platform provided Jotham with a natural pulpit from which he related his fable (a short story in which plants or animals are personified and which teaches a useful truth).
9:8–15 Jotham used a popular ancient motif of trees vying for supremacy. The **olive tree,** the **fig tree,** and the **vine,** referred to in his fable, were valued highly in Palestine.
9:14 Bramble: A shrub with sharp thorns and runners. In the fable, the bramble represented Abimelech, who sought to exert power over others.
9:15 In my shade: The bramble's offer of shade (which it obviously could not give) symbolized the traditional role of the king who offered special protection to people who were traveling on behalf of the state (Is. 30:2; Dan. 4:12; Hos. 14:7). They were said to be "in his shadow." **Let fire come out of the bramble:** Farmers feared burning bramble bushes because the fire spread uncontrollably and caused much destruction. **Cedars of Lebanon:** These trees, which are highly valued in the Near East, probably represent the leaders of Shechem (v. 20).
9:16–20 Jotham used his fable to rebuke the Shechemites for accepting the unscrupulous Abimelech as their king.

seventy sons on one stone, and made
Abimelech, the son of his [b]female servant, king over the men of Shechem,
because he is your brother—
19 "if then you have acted in truth and
sincerity with Jerubbaal and with his
house this day, *then* [a]rejoice in Abimelech, and let him also rejoice in you.
20 "But if not, [a]let fire come from
Abimelech and devour the men of Shechem and Beth Millo; and let fire come
from the men of Shechem and from
Beth Millo and devour Abimelech!"
21 And Jotham ran away and fled; and
he went to [a]Beer and dwelt there, for
fear of Abimelech his brother.

Downfall of Abimelech

22 After Abimelech had reigned over
Israel three years,
23 [a]God sent a [b]spirit of ill will between Abimelech and the men of
Shechem; and the men of Shechem
[c]dealt treacherously with Abimelech,
24 [a]that the crime *done* to the seventy
sons of Jerubbaal might be settled and
their [b]blood be laid on Abimelech their
brother, who killed them, and on the
men of Shechem, who aided him in the
killing of his brothers.
25 And the men of Shechem set
[1]men in ambush against him on the
tops of the mountains, and they robbed
all who passed by them along that way;
and it was told Abimelech.
26 Now Gaal the son of Ebed came
with his brothers and went over to Shechem; and the men of Shechem put
their confidence in him.
27 So they went out into the fields, and
gathered *grapes* from their vineyards
and trod *them*, and [1]made merry. And
they went into [a]the house of their god,
and ate and drank, and cursed Abimelech.
28 Then Gaal the son of Ebed said,
[a]"Who *is* Abimelech, and who *is* Shechem, that we should serve him? *Is he*
not the son of Jerubbaal, and *is not*
Zebul his officer? Serve the men of

18 [b]Judg. 8:31
19 [a]Is. 8:6; [Phil. 3:3]
20 [a]Judg. 9:15, 45, 56, 57
21 [a]Num. 21:16
23 [a]1 Kin. 12:15; Is. 19:14 [b]1 Sam. 16:14; 18:9, 10; 1 Kin. 22:22; 2 Chr. 18:22 [c]Is. 33:1
24 [a]1 Kin. 2:32; Esth. 9:25; Matt. 23:35, 36 [b]Num. 35:33
25 [1]Lit. *liers-in-wait for*
27 [a]Judg. 9:4 [1]*rejoiced*
28 [a]1 Sam. 25:10; 1 Kin. 12:16 [b]Gen. 34:2, 6; Josh. 24:32
29 [a]2 Sam. 15:4 [1]Lit. *hand* [2]So with MT, Tg.; DSS *they;* LXX *I*
32 [1]Set up an ambush
33 [1]Lit. *as your hand can find*
34 [1]Set up an ambush
37 [1]Heb. *Meon-enim*
38 [a]Judg. 9:28, 29

[b]Hamor the father of Shechem; but
why should we serve him?
29 [a]"If only this people were under my
[1]authority! Then I would remove
Abimelech." So [2]he said to Abimelech,
"Increase your army and come out!"
30 When Zebul, the ruler of the city,
heard the words of Gaal the son of
Ebed, his anger was aroused.
31 And he sent messengers to Abimelech secretly, saying, "Take note! Gaal
the son of Ebed and his brothers have
come to Shechem; and here they are,
fortifying the city against you.
32 "Now therefore, get up by night,
you and the people who *are* with you,
and [1]lie in wait in the field.
33 "And it shall be, as soon as the sun
is up in the morning, *that* you shall
rise early and rush upon the city; and
when he and the people who are with
him come out against you, you may
then do to them [1]as you find opportunity."
34 So Abimelech and all the people
who *were* with him rose by night, and
[1]lay in wait against Shechem in four
companies.
35 When Gaal the son of Ebed went
out and stood in the entrance to the
city gate, Abimelech and the people
who *were* with him rose from lying in
wait.
36 And when Gaal saw the people, he
said to Zebul, "Look, people are coming down from the tops of the mountains!" But Zebul said to him, "You see
the shadows of the mountains as *if they
were* men."
37 So Gaal spoke again and said, "See,
people are coming down from the center of the land, and another company
is coming from the [1]Diviners' Terebinth Tree."
38 Then Zebul said to him, "Where indeed *is* your mouth now, with which
you [a]said, 'Who is Abimelech, that we
should serve him?' *Are* not these the
people whom you despised? Go out, if
you will, and fight with them now."
39 So Gaal went out, leading the men

9:21 Beer: The location of Beer (meaning "Well") is uncertain.
9:23 Spirit of ill will: Here the Hebrew word for "spirit" is used to describe a disposition. **Dealt treacherously:** The men of Shechem censured the leadership of Abimelech, which they had originally conferred *upon him*.
9:25 *Set men in ambush:* The men of Shechem began to plunder caravans on the strategic trade routes through Shechem.
9:26 Gaal and his kinsmen appear to have been Canaanites who moved to Shechem. He incited the Shechemites to revolt against King Abimelech, who was half Israelite, and to restore a Canaanite ruler (see v. 28).
9:27 The Shechemites held a pagan religious festival in the temple of their god at the time of the grape harvest.
9:28 The men of Hamor: Hamor, a native Canaanite, was their ancestor (Gen. 34:26). This would suggest that a large number of people in Shechem were Canaanites.
9:37 The center of the land, which, in the Hebrew, literally means "the navel of the land," is a geographical designation for the Shechem area and probably refers to Mt. Gerizim, located along the main north-south road in central Palestine. **Diviners' Terebinth Tree:** Likely a tree where magic and sorcery were performed.

of Shechem, and fought with Abimelech.
40 And Abimelech chased him, and he
fled from him; and many fell wounded,
to the *very* entrance of the gate.
41 Then Abimelech dwelt at Arumah,
and Zebul [1]drove out Gaal and his
brothers, so that they would not dwell
in Shechem.
42 And it came about on the next day
that the people went out into the field,
and they told Abimelech.
43 So he took his people, divided them
into three companies, and lay in wait
in the field. And he looked, and there
were the people, coming out of the city;
and he rose against them and [1]attacked
them.
44 Then Abimelech and the company
that *was* with him rushed forward and
stood at the entrance of the gate of the
city; and the *other* two companies
rushed upon all who *were* in the fields
and killed them.
45 So Abimelech fought against the
city all that day; [a]he took the city and
killed the people who *were* in it; and
he [b]demolished the city and *sowed it
with salt.
46 Now when all the men of the tower
of Shechem had heard *that*, they entered the [1]stronghold of the temple
[a]of the god Berith.
47 And it was told Abimelech that all
the men of the tower of Shechem were
gathered together.
48 Then Abimelech went up to Mount
[a]Zalmon, he and all the people who
were with him. And Abimelech took an
ax in his hand and cut down a bough
from the trees, and took it and laid *it*
on his shoulder; then he said to the
people who were with him, "What you
have seen me do, make haste *and* do
as I *have done*."
49 So each of the people likewise cut
down his own bough and followed
Abimelech, put *them* against the
[1]stronghold, and set the stronghold on
fire above them, so that all the people
of the tower of Shechem died, about a
thousand men and women.
50 Then Abimelech went to Thebez,
and he [1]encamped against Thebez and
took it.
51 But there was a strong tower in the
city, and all the men and women—all
the people of the city—fled there and
shut themselves in; then they went up
to the top of the tower.
52 So Abimelech came as far as the
tower and fought against it; and he
drew near the door of the tower to burn
it with fire.
53 But a certain woman [a]dropped an
upper millstone on Abimelech's head
and crushed his skull.
54 Then [a]he called quickly to the
young man, his armorbearer, and said
to him, "Draw your sword and kill me,
lest men say of me, 'A woman killed
him.' " So his young man thrust him
through, and he died.
55 And when the men of Israel saw
that Abimelech was dead, they departed, every man to his [1]place.
56 [a]Thus God repaid the wickedness
of Abimelech, which he had done to
his father by killing his seventy
brothers.
57 And all the evil of the men of Shechem God returned on their own
heads, and on them came [a]the curse
of Jotham the son of Jerubbaal.

Tola

10 After Abimelech there [a]arose to
save Israel Tola the son of Puah,
the son of Dodo, a man of Issachar;
and he dwelt in Shamir in the mountains of Ephraim.
2 He judged Israel twenty-three
years; and he died and was buried in
Shamir.

41 [1]*exiled*
43 [1]Lit. *struck*
45 [a]Judg. 9:20 [b]Deut. 29:23; 2 Kin. 3:25 *See WW at Hos. 10:12.
46 [a]Judg. 8:33 [1]*fortified room*
48 [a]Ps. 68:14
49 [1]*fortified room*
50 [1]*besieged*
53 [a]2 Sam. 11:21
54 [a]1 Sam. 31:4
55 [1]*home*
56 [a]Judg. 9:24; Job 31:3; Prov. 5:22
57 [a]Judg. 9:20

CHAPTER 10
1 [a]Judg. 2:16

9:45 Sowed it with salt: Scattering salt upon a destroyed city was an act of placing a curse of barrenness upon it. This twelfth-century B.C. destruction of Shechem has been confirmed by archaeologists. The city was eventually rebuilt by Jeroboam I and established as his capital (1 Kin. 12:25).
9:47 The tower of Shechem was probably the same as Beth Millo (v. 6).
9:48 Mount Zalmon may refer to Mt. Gerizim or Mt. Ebal.
9:50 Thebez was probably located northeast of Shechem. Apparently, this city had been under Abimelech's control but had joined in the revolt against him.
9:53 An upper millstone is the upper rotating part of a handmill used for grinding grain into flour.
9:54 A woman killed him: To die at the hand of a woman was a disgrace in the ancient Near East.
9:56 God repaid: God, as Israel's true King, was sovereignly in control of the events behind the destruction of Shechem and the death of Abimelech.
9:57 The curse: Jotham's words (v. 20) are here identified as God's judgment.
10:1–5 Tola and **Jair** were among the so-called "minor judges." They performed judicial functions in Israel and were responsible for maintaining and administering the law within the society. The "major judges," on the other hand, were predominantly military leaders, who delivered Israel from external enemies.
10:1 Arose to save Israel: Tola's acts of deliverance may have been confined to the internal strife and idolatrous conditions that resulted from Abimelech's reign. **Shamir** may be identified with Samaria, but it was more likely located in the hill country of Ephraim.

Jair

3 After him arose Jair, a Gileadite; and he judged Israel twenty-two years.
4 Now he had thirty sons who [a]rode on thirty donkeys; they also had thirty towns, [b]which are called [1]"Havoth Jair" to this day, which *are* in the land of Gilead.

4 [a]Judg. 5:10; 12:14 [b]Deut. 3:14 [1]Lit. *Towns of Jair,* Num. 32:41; Deut. 3:14

6 [a]Judg. 2:11; 3:7; 6:1; 13:1 [b]Judg. 2:13

5 And Jair died and was buried in Camon.

Israel Oppressed Again

6 Then [a]the children of Israel again did evil in the sight of the LORD, and [b]served the Baals and the Ashtoreths,

10:3 The judgeship of **Jair** anticipates the judgeship of Jephthah, the next major judge, who was also from Gilead.
10:4 Thirty donkeys: Jair appears to have been a man of wealth and position. **Havoth Jair,** "Towns or Villages of Jair," were located in the area of Gilead in the Transjordan.
10:5 Camon may be modern Qamm in Gilead.
10:6–16 These verses appear to be a theological introduction to the judgeships of both Jephthah (10:17—12:7) and Samson (13:1—16:31), which are established to bring deliverance from the Ammonites and the Philistines, respectively.
10:6 The Baals and the Ashtoreths were the Canaanites' gods, which were acknowledged as demon deities (Lev. 17:7; Deut. 32:17; 2 Chr. 11:15; Ps. 106:37). **The gods of**

The Judges of Israel

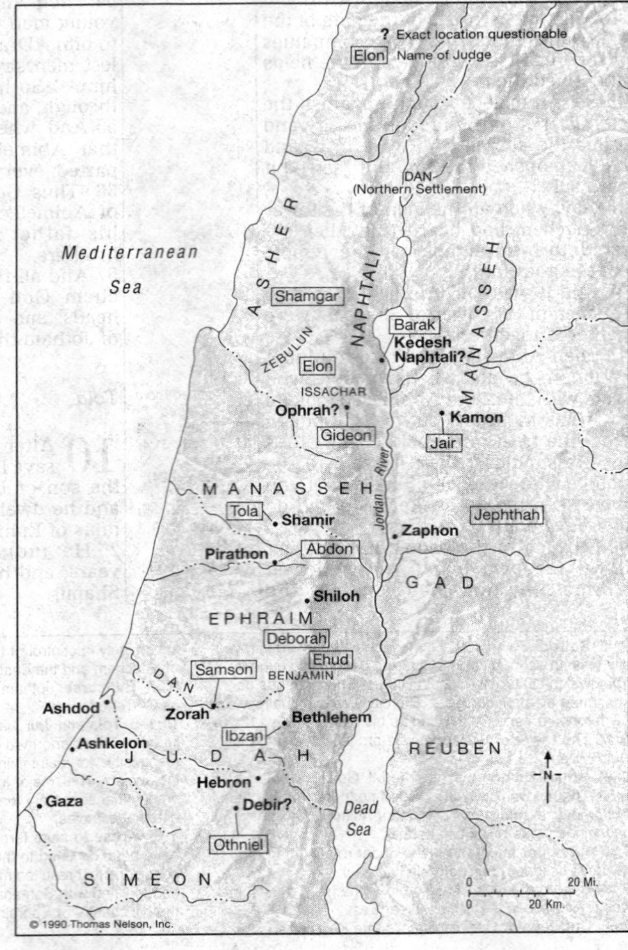

[c]the gods of Syria, the gods of [d]Sidon,
the gods of Moab, the gods of the people of Ammon, and the gods of the Philistines; and they forsook the LORD and
did not serve Him.
7 So the **anger** of the LORD was hot
against Israel; and He [a]sold them into
the hands of the [b]Philistines and into
the hands of the people of [c]Ammon.

> **WORD WEALTH**
>
> **10:7 anger,** *'aph* (*ahf*); Strong's #639: Anger; face, nostril, nose. This noun occurs approximately 250 times. Translated as "anger" in the great majority of occurrences, "wrath," "nose," and "nostril" may also translate *'aph.* (See Ps. 2:5; Song 7:4.) The connection between nose and anger exists through the verb *'anaph* "to be angry"), from which *'aph* is derived. The Hebrew figure of speech, which means "to grow angry," may be translated "his anger burned" or "his nose grew hot." See also Ps. 2:12; Prov. 22:24; Is. 42:25; 65:5. The idea is that anger is observable in the fierce breathing through the nose of an angry person.

8 From that year they [1]harassed and
oppressed the children of Israel for
eighteen years—all the children of Israel who *were* on the other side of the
Jordan in the [a]land of the Amorites,
in Gilead.
9 Moreover the people of Ammon
crossed over the Jordan to fight against
Judah also, against Benjamin, and
against the house of Ephraim, so that
Israel was severely distressed.
10 [a]And the children of Israel cried out
to the LORD, saying, "We have [b]sinned
against You, because we have both forsaken our God and served the Baals!"
11 So the LORD said to the children of
Israel, "*Did I* not *deliver you* [a]from the

6 [c]Judg. 2:12 [d]1 Kin. 11:33; Ps. 106:36
7 [a]Judg. 2:14; 4:2; 1 Sam. 12:9 [b]Judg. 13:1 [c]Judg. 3:13
8 [a]Num. 32:33 [1]Lit. *shattered*
10 [a]Judg. 6:6; 1 Sam. 12:10 [b]Deut. 1:41
11 [a]Ex. 14:30 [b]Num. 21:21, 24, 25 [c]Judg. 3:12, 13 [d]Judg. 3:31
12 [a]Judg. 1:31; 5:19 [b]Judg. 6:3; 7:12 [c]Ps. 106:42, 43 [1]LXX mss. *Midianites*
13 [a][Deut. 32:15; Judg. 2:12; Jer. 2:13]
14 [a]Deut. 32:37, 38
15 [a]1 Sam. 3:18; 2 Sam. 15:26
16 [a]2 Chr. 7:14; Jer. 18:7, 8 [b]Ps. 106:44, 45; Is. 63:9
17 [a]Gen. 31:49; Judg. 11:11, 29
18 [a]Judg. 11:8, 11

CHAPTER 11

1 [a]Heb. 11:32 [b]Judg. 6:12; 2 Kin. 5:1
2 [a]Gen. 21:10; Deut. 23:2

Egyptians and [b]from the Amorites and
[c]from the people of Ammon and
[d]from the Philistines?
12 "Also [a]the Sidonians [b]and Amalekites and [1]Maonites [c]oppressed you;
and you cried out to Me, and I delivered you from their hand.
13 [a]"Yet you have forsaken Me and 1
served other gods. Therefore I will deliver you no more.
14 "Go and [a]cry out to the gods which
you have chosen; let them deliver you
in your time of distress."
15 And the children of Israel said to
the LORD, "We have sinned! [a]Do to us
whatever seems best to You; only deliver us this day, we pray."
16 [a]So they put away the foreign gods
from among them and served the LORD.
And [b]His soul could no longer endure
the misery of Israel.
17 Then the people of Ammon gathered together and encamped in Gilead.
And the children of Israel assembled
together and encamped in [a]Mizpah.
18 And the people, the leaders of
Gilead, said to one another, "Who *is* the
man who will begin the fight against
the people of Ammon? He shall [a]be
head over all the inhabitants of Gilead."

Jephthah

11 Now [a]Jephthah the Gileadite
was [b]a mighty man of valor, but
he *was* the son of a harlot; and Gilead
begot Jephthah.
2 Gilead's wife bore sons; and when
his wife's sons grew up, they drove
Jephthah out, and said to him, "You
shall have [a]no inheritance in our father's house, for you *are* the son of another woman."
3 Then Jephthah fled from his

Syria: Hadad and Rimmon were among their gods (2 Kin. 5:18). **The gods of Sidon:** The Sidonians worshiped the same gods as the Canaanites. **The gods of Moab:** The chief deity of Moab was Chemosh. **The gods of the people of Ammon:** Milcom (or Molech) was the chief god of the Ammonites (1 Kin. 11:7). **The gods of the Philistines:** The chief deities of the Philistines were Dagon (16:23) and Baal-Zebub (2 Kin. 1:2, 3).
10:7 The author mentioned **the Philistines** either in retrospect with reference to Shamgar's judgeship or as a prelude to the Philistine oppression in the west during Samson's judgeship. **The people of Ammon:** The author may have mentioned the oppression of the Ammonites in the east at this point in anticipation of Jephthah's judgeship.
10:10 The children of Israel cried out: After 18 years of Ammonite oppression, the Israelites demonstrated true repentance. They acknowledged that they had forsaken God and had served the Baals.
10:12 Maonites: The Septuagint manuscripts read "Midianites." "Maon," however, may be connected with the Meunites, an Arab tribe from the same general area as the Midianites (2 Chr. 26:7).
10:13, 14 See section 1 of Truth-In-Action at the end of Judg.
10:16 And His soul . . . Israel portrays God's perspective in terms of human emotion. **Endure** carries the idea of both sympathy over Israel's suffering and impatience with it. The phrase could be translated, "The plight of Israel became intolerable to Him."
10:17 Mizpah was Jephthah's headquarters in Gilead.
11:1 Unlike Gideon, who was called directly by the Lord, Jephthah was called by the leaders of Gilead. The Lord did, however, witness their choice (vv. 10, 11) and empowered Jephthah with His Spirit (v. 29).
11:2 Another woman: A harlot (v. 1).
11:3 The land of Tob, which was east of the Jordan River, was probably north of Ammon and east of Manasseh.

brothers and dwelt in the land of
[a]Tob; and [b]worthless men banded together with Jephthah and went out
raiding with him.
4 It came to pass after a time that the
[a]people of Ammon made war against
Israel.
5 And so it was, when the people of
Ammon made war against Israel, that
the elders of Gilead went to get
Jephthah from the land of Tob.
6 Then they said to Jephthah, "Come
and be our commander, that we may
fight against the people of Ammon."
7 So Jephthah said to the elders of
Gilead, [a]"Did you not hate me, and expel
me from my father's house? Why have
you come to me now when you are in
[1]distress?"
8 [a]And the elders of Gilead said to
Jephthah, "That is why we have
[b]turned[1] again to you now, that you
may go with us and fight against the
people of Ammon, and be [c]our head
over all the inhabitants of Gilead."
9 So Jephthah said to the elders of
Gilead, "If you take me back home to
fight against the people of Ammon,
and the LORD delivers them to me, shall
I be your head?"
10 And the elders of Gilead said to
Jephthah, [a]"The LORD will be a witness
between us, if we do not do according
to your words."
11 Then Jephthah went with the elders
of Gilead, and the people made him
[a]head and commander over them; and
Jephthah spoke all his words [b]before
the LORD in Mizpah.
12 Now Jephthah sent messengers to
the king of the people of Ammon, saying, [a]"What do you have against me,
that you have come to fight against me
in my land?"
13 And the king of the people of Ammon answered the messengers of
Jephthah, [a]"Because Israel took away
my land when they came up out of
Egypt, from [b]the Arnon as far as
[c]the Jabbok, and to the Jordan. Now
therefore, restore those *lands* peaceably."

3 [a]2 Sam. 10:6, 8 [b]1 Sam. 22:2
4 [a]Judg. 10:9, 17
7 [a]Gen. 26:27 [1]*trouble*
8 [a]Judg. 10:18 [b][Luke 17:4] [c]Judg. 10:18 [1]*returned*
10 [a]Gen. 31:49, 50; Jer. 29:23; 42:5
11 [a]Judg. 11:8 [b]Judg. 10:17; 20:1; 1 Sam. 10:17
12 [a]2 Sam. 16:10
13 [a]Num. 21:24–26 [b]Josh. 13:9 [c]Gen. 32:22
15 [a]Deut. 2:9, 19
16 [a]Num. 13:26; 20:1
17 [a]Num. 20:14 [b]Num. 20:14–21 [c]Josh. 24:9 [d]Num. 20:1-
18 [a]Deut. 2:9, 18, 19 [b]Num. 21:4
19 [a]Num. 21:21; Deut. 2:26–36 [b]Num. 21:22; Deut. 2:27
20 [a]Num. 21:23; Deut. 2:27
21 [a]Josh. 24:8 [b]Num. 21:24, 25 [1]Lit. *struck*
22 [a]Deut. 2:36, 37
23 [1]*driven out*
24 [a]Num. 21:29; 1 Kin. 11:7; Jer. 48:7 [b][Deut. 9:4, 5; Josh. 3:10]

14 So Jephthah again sent messengers
to the king of the people of Ammon,
15 and said to him, "Thus says
Jephthah: [a]'Israel did not take away the
land of Moab, nor the land of the people of Ammon;
16 'for when Israel came up from
Egypt, they walked through the wilderness as far as the Red Sea and [a]came
to Kadesh.
17 'Then [a]Israel sent messengers to the
king of Edom, saying, "Please let me
pass through your land." [b]But the king
of Edom would not heed. And in like
manner they sent to the [c]king of Moab,
but he would not *consent*. So Israel
[d]remained in Kadesh.
18 'And they [a]went along through the
wilderness and [b]bypassed the land of
Edom and the land of Moab, came to
the east side of the land of Moab, and
encamped on the other side of the Arnon. But they did not enter the border
of Moab, for the Arnon *was* the border
of Moab.
19 'Then [a]Israel sent messengers to Sihon king of the Amorites, king of
Heshbon; and Israel said to him,
"Please [b]let us pass through your land
into our place."
20 [a]'But Sihon did not trust Israel to
pass through his territory. So Sihon
gathered all his people together, encamped in Jahaz, and fought against
Israel.
21 'And the LORD God of Israel [a]deliv-
ered Sihon and all his people into the
hand of Israel, and they [b]defeated[1]
them. Thus Israel gained possession of
all the land of the Amorites, who inhabited that country.
22 'They took possession of [a]all the
territory of the Amorites, from the Arnon to the Jabbok and from the wilderness to the Jordan.
23 'And now the LORD God of Israel
has [1]dispossessed the Amorites from
before His people Israel; should you
then possess it?
24 'Will you not possess whatever
[a]Chemosh your god gives you to possess? So whatever [b]the LORD our God

11:8 Be our head: "Head" refers to the highest place of leadership within a tribe. Initially, the Gileadites invited Jephthah to be their military leader (v. 6); they promised to make him their civil leader following the deliverance (vv. 8–11).

11:12, 13 Jephthah diplomatically sought *to settle the conflict with the Ammonites* without warfare.

11:13 My land: When Israel first entered Canaan, this region between the Arnon River and the Jabbok River was ruled by Sihon, king of the Amorites, who had taken the territory from the Moabites (Num. 21:29). The Israelites fought against Sihon. The Lord gave them the victory and they took over all the land of the Amorites from the Arnon to the Jabbok (vv. 21, 22). The Ammonites were now laying claim to all of the former Moabite territory.

11:14–23 Jephthah argued that the Lord gave Israel victory over the Amorites and enabled them to possess the Amorite territory between the Arnon and Jabbok rivers. Israel, therefore, acquired the disputed territory from the Amorites and not from the Moabites or the Ammonites (v. 15).

11:20 Jahaz: This city in the desert of Moab belonged first to the Amorite king, then to Israel, and finally to Moab.

11:24 Chemosh was the national god of the Moabites and Ammonites. Jephthah argued that the Ammonites should be

takes possession of before us, we will
possess.
25 'And now, *are* you any better than
[a]Balak the son of Zippor, king of
Moab? Did he ever strive against Israel? Did he ever fight against them?
26 'While Israel dwelt in [a]Heshbon and
its villages, in [b]Aroer and its villages,
and in all the cities along the banks
of the Arnon, for three hundred years,
why did you not recover *them* within
that time?
27 'Therefore I have not sinned against
you, but you wronged me by fighting
against me. May the LORD, [a]the Judge,
[b]render judgment this day between the
children of Israel and the people of
Ammon.' "
28 However, the king of the people of
Ammon did not heed the words which
Jephthah sent him.

Jephthah's Vow and Victory

29 Then [a]the Spirit of the LORD came
upon Jephthah, and he passed through
Gilead and Manasseh, and passed
through Mizpah of Gilead; and from
Mizpah of Gilead he advanced *toward*
the people of Ammon.
30 And Jephthah [a]made a vow to the
LORD, and said, "If You will indeed deliver the people of Ammon into my
hands,
31 "then it will be that whatever comes
out of the doors of my house to meet
me, when I return in peace from the
people of Ammon, [a]shall surely be the
LORD's, [b]and I will offer it up as a burnt
offering."
32 So Jephthah advanced toward the
people of Ammon to fight against
them, and the LORD delivered them into
his hands.
33 And he [1]defeated them from Aroer
as far as [a]Minnith—twenty cities—and
to [2]Abel Keramim, with a very great
slaughter. Thus the people of Ammon
were subdued before the children of Israel.

Jephthah's Daughter

34 When Jephthah came to his house
at [a]Mizpah, there was [b]his daughter,
coming out to meet him with timbrels
and dancing; and she *was his* *only
child. Besides her he had neither son
nor daughter.
35 And it came to pass, when he saw
her, that he [a]tore his clothes, and said,
"Alas, my daughter! You have brought
me very low! You are among those
who trouble me! For I [b]have [1]given my
word to the LORD, and [c]I cannot
[2]go back on it."
36 So she said to him, "My father, *if*
you have given your word to the LORD,
[a]do to me according to what has gone
out of your mouth, because [b]the LORD
has avenged you of your enemies, the
people of Ammon."
37 Then she said to her father, "Let
this thing be done for me: let me alone
for two months, that I may go and wander on the mountains and [1]bewail my
virginity, my [2]friends and I."
38 So he said, "Go." And he sent her
away *for* two months; and she went
with her friends, and bewailed her virginity on the mountains.
39 And it was so at the end of two

25 [a]Num. 22:2; Josh. 24:9; Mic. 6:5
26 [a]Num. 21:25, 26 [b]Deut. 2:36
27 [a]Gen. 18:25 [b]Gen. 16:5; 31:53; [1 Sam. 24:12, 15]
29 [a]Judg. 3:10
30 [a]Gen. 28:20; Num. 30:2; 1 Sam. 1:11
31 [a]Lev. 27:2, 3, 28; 1 Sam. 1:11 [b]Ps. 66:13
33 [a]Ezek. 27:17 [1]Lit. *struck* [2]Lit. *Plain of Vineyards*
34 [a]Judg. 10:17; 11:11 [b]Ex. 15:20; 1 Sam. 18:6; Ps. 68:25; Jer. 31:4 *See WW at Gen. 22:2.
35 [a]Gen. 37:29, 34 [b]Eccl. 5:2, 4, 5 [c]Num. 30:2 [1]Lit. *opened my mouth* [2]Lit. *take it back*
36 [a]Num. 30:2 [b]2 Sam. 18:19, 31
37 [1]*lament* [2]*companions*

satisfied with the land their god Chemosh had given them and not lay claim to the land that the Lord had given Israel. In the ancient Near East, success in warfare was a sign of divine favor and territories were seen as having been given to people by their particular deity.

11:25 Balak, king of Moab, to whom part of this disputed territory had belonged, agreed to Israel's claim on this area (see Num. 22—24). Jephthah pointed out that Israel had dwelt there for 300 years and that no one up until this time had contested their right to the land.

11:27 The final authority in this dispute is the **LORD, the Judge.** The singular noun "Judge," occurs only once in the Book of Judges.

11:29 The Spirit of the LORD: See Introduction to Judges: The Holy Spirit at Work.

11:30 Making **a vow** was common practice in Israel (Gen. 28:20), and keeping a vow was extremely important (Deut. 23:21–23; Eccl. 5:4, 5). In his zeal, Jephthah made a rash vow to the Lord.

11:31 Whatever comes out: Jephthah's home may have been planned to accommodate both families and livestock. A two-floor home from this period has been excavated. Archaeologists have suggested that one ground-floor room served as an entrance vestibule and another as a stairwell, while the other ground-floor rooms were probably used for storage and animals. If Jephthah's home had been constructed in this manner, it would have been possible for an animal, rather than his daughter, to come out first.

11:33 Aroer was a town of Gilead situated near the Ammonite capital of Rabbah-Ammon (modern Amman), which was strategically located east of the Jordan River alongside the King's Highway. **Minnith** and **Abel Keramim** were probably located near Rabbah-Ammon.

11:34 Dancing was a common custom by which women celebrated the triumphant return of an army after a successful battle (Ex. 15:20; 1 Sam. 18:6, 7).

11:35 Tore his clothes: Jephthah showed his overwhelming grief in a typical ancient Near Eastern manner.

11:37 The exact nature of the custom addressed here is not known. Apparently the girls retreated to a remote village where, under the care of seasoned matrons, they mourned the fact that Jephthah's daughter would be forever childless, a major reproach at the time.

11:39 He carried out his vow: The nature of Jephthah's vow is uncertain. Two feasible interpretations are that 1) his daughter remained a virgin and dedicated herself in service at Israel's central sanctuary; or 2) Jephthah offered her up as a burnt offering. Since there is no clear evidence

months that she returned to her father,
and he [a]carried out his vow with her
which he had vowed. She [1]knew no
man. And it became a custom in Israel
40 *that* the daughters of Israel went
four days each year to [1]lament the
daughter of Jephthah the Gileadite.

Jephthah's Conflict with Ephraim

12 Then [a]the men of Ephraim
[1]gathered together, crossed
over toward Zaphon, and said to
Jephthah, "Why did you cross over to
fight against the people of Ammon,
and did not call us to go with you? We
will burn your house down on you with
fire!"
2 And Jephthah said to them, "My
people and I were in a great struggle
with the people of Ammon; and when
I called you, you did not deliver me out
of their hands.
3 "So when I saw that you would not
deliver *me*, I [a]took my life in my hands
and crossed over against the people of
Ammon; and the LORD delivered them
into my hand. Why then have you
come up to me this day to fight against
me?"
4 Now Jephthah gathered together all
the men of Gilead and fought against
Ephraim. And the men of Gilead defeated Ephraim, because they said,
"You Gileadites [a]*are* fugitives of
Ephraim among the Ephraimites *and*
among the Manassites."
5 The Gileadites seized the [a]fords of
the Jordan before the Ephraimites *arrived*. And when *any* Ephraimite who
escaped said, "Let me cross over," the
men of Gilead would say to him, "*Are*
you an Ephraimite?" If he said, "No,"

39 [a]Judg. 11:31 [1]Remained a virgin
40 [1]*commemorate*

CHAPTER 12

1 [a]Judg. 8:1 [1]*were summoned*
3 [a]1 Sam. 19:5; 28:21; Job 13:14
4 [a]1 Sam. 25:10
5 [a]Josh. 22:11
6 [a]Ps. 69:2, 15 [1]Lit. *a flowing stream;* used as a test of dialect [2]Lit. *speak so*
14 [a]Judg. 5:10; 10:4
15 [a]Judg. 3:13, 27; 5:14

CHAPTER 13

1 [a]Judg. 2:11

6 then they would say to him, "Then
say, [a]'Shibboleth'!"[1] And he would
say, "Sibboleth," for he could not
[2]pronounce *it* right. Then they would
take him and kill him at the fords of
the Jordan. There fell at that time
forty-two thousand Ephraimites.
7 And Jephthah judged Israel six
years. Then Jephthah the Gileadite
died and was buried in among the cities of Gilead.

Ibzan, Elon, and Abdon

8 After him, Ibzan of Bethlehem
judged Israel.
9 He had thirty sons. And he gave
away thirty daughters in marriage, and
brought in thirty daughters from elsewhere for his sons. He judged Israel
seven years.
10 Then Ibzan died and was buried at
Bethlehem.
11 After him, Elon the Zebulunite
judged Israel. He judged Israel ten
years.
12 And Elon the Zebulunite died and
was buried at Aijalon in the country
of Zebulun.
13 After him, Abdon the son of Hillel
the Pirathonite judged Israel.
14 He had forty sons and thirty grandsons, who [a]rode on seventy young donkeys. He judged Israel eight years.
15 Then Abdon the son of Hillel the
Pirathonite died and was buried in Pirathon in the land of Ephraim, [a]in the
mountains of the Amalekites.

The Birth of Samson

13 Again the children of Israel
[a]did evil in the sight of the LORD,

---

concerning the former interpretation, the latter one, based upon Jephthah's statement in v. 31, seems a more natural interpretation even though human sacrifice was forbidden in the Mosaic Law (Deut. 12:31; 18:10). The episode reflects tragic deterioration of understanding God's ways, a condition resulting from the recurrent backslidings during this era.

12:1–7 Jephthah entered into a conflict with the Ephraimites, which resulted in the deaths of 42,000 people. The war may have been started because Ephraim was angry that Jephthah had not invited them to fight against the Ammonites (v. 1) or because Ephraim had insulted the Gileadites (v. 4).

12:1 Zaphon was probably situated east of the Jordan River in the territory of the tribe of Gad.

12:2, 3 Jephthah tried at first to use diplomacy with the Ephraimites. *Although there is* no record of an invitation to join with him in the battle, Jephthah stated that he had called them (v. 2). When they did not respond, he proceeded to fight with the Ammonites (v. 3).

12:4 You Gileads *are* fugitives: The meaning of this taunt is unclear. This insult, however, appears to have provoked the ensuing war between the Gileadites and the Ephraimites.

12:6 Shibboleth is a term meaning either "Ear of Grain" or "Flowing Stream." The Gildeadites used the pronunciation of this word to recognize the fleeing Ephraimites at the fords of the Jordan. The Ephraimites, having a different dialect, pronounced this word with a soft "s" sound, rather than a stronger "sh" sound.

12:8–13 Three minor judges followed Jephthah.

12:8 Ibzan of Bethlehem may have been from either Bethlehem in Judah or Bethlehem in Zebulun (Josh. 19:15). His large family indicates that he was a man of wealth and high status in the clan. His seeking wives for his sons outside the clan suggests that he was a man of influence and high esteem in surrounding regions (v. 9).

12:13 Abdon was a native of Pirathon in Ephraim (situated 7 miles southwest of Shechem). His large family and 70 donkeys (v. 14) suggest that he was a man of wealth and prominence.

13:1—16:31 The Lord raised up Samson to deliver Israel from a 40-year period of Philistine oppression. Israel had entered into another phase of idolatrous worship as

and the LORD delivered them [b]into the
hand of the Philistines for forty years.
2 Now there was a certain man from
[a]Zorah, of the family of the Danites,
whose name *was* Manoah; and his wife
was barren and had no children.
3 And the [a]Angel of the LORD appeared to the woman and said to her,
"Indeed now, you are barren and have
borne no children, but you shall conceive and bear a son.
4 "Now therefore, please be careful
[a]not to drink wine or *similar* drink, and
not to eat anything unclean.
5 "For behold, you shall conceive and
bear a son. And no [a]razor shall come
upon his head, for the child shall be
[b]a Nazirite to God from the womb; and
he shall [c]begin to deliver Israel out of
the hand of the Philistines."
6 So the woman came and told her
husband, saying, [a]"A Man of God
came to me, and His [b]countenance[1]
was like the countenance of the Angel
of God, very awesome; but I [c]did not
ask Him where He *was* from, and He
did not tell me His name.

KINGDOM DYNAMICS

13:6 Variety in the Appearance of Angels, ANGELS. What do angels look like? The appearance of angels is correctly rendered "very awesome." Angels appear in different forms depending upon their order of creation. For example, God's messenger angel, Gabriel, has the appearance of a man (Dan. 9:21). From Ezek. 28:13, 14 we learn that cherubim (plural for "cherub") are exotic and beautiful—covered with precious stones. Ezek. 1:23 tells us that cherubim have four wings, while seraphim (plural for "seraph") have six wings—two that cover the face, two that cover the feet, and two with which to fly (Is. 6:2).

(Ps. 103:20, 21/Col. 1:16) M.H.

7 "And He said to me, 'Behold, you
shall conceive and bear a son. Now

1 [b]Judg. 10:7; 1 Sam. 12:9 **2** [a]Josh. 19:41; Judg. 16:31 **3** [a]Judg. 6:12 **4** [a]Num. 6:2, 3, 20; Judg. 13:4; Luke 1:15 **5** [a]Num. 6:5; 1 Sam. 1:11 [b]Num. 6:2 [c]1 Sam. 7:13; 2 Sam. 8:1; 1 Chr. 18:1 **6** [a]Gen. 32:24–30 [b]Matt. 28:3; Luke 9:29; Acts 6:15 [c]Judg. 13:17, 18 [1]*appearance*

14 [a]Num. 6:3, 4; Judg. 13:4 **15** [a]Gen. 18:5; Judg. 6:18

drink no wine or *similar* drink, nor eat
anything unclean, for the child shall be
a Nazirite to God from the womb to
the day of his death.' "
8 Then Manoah prayed to the LORD,
and said, "O my Lord, please let the
Man of God whom You sent come to
us again and teach us what we shall
do for the child who will be born."
9 And God listened to the voice of
Manoah, and the Angel of God came
to the woman again as she was sitting
in the field; but Manoah her husband
was not with her.
10 Then the woman ran in haste and
told her husband, and said to him,
"Look, the Man who came to me the
other day has just now appeared to
me!"
11 So Manoah arose and followed his
wife. When he came to the Man, he
said to Him, "Are You the Man who
spoke to this woman?" And He said,
"I *am*."
12 Manoah said, "Now let Your words
come *to pass!* What will be the boy's
rule of life, and his work?"
13 So the Angel of the LORD said to Manoah, "Of all that I said to the woman
let her be careful.
14 "She may not eat anything that
comes from the vine, [a]nor may she
drink wine or *similar* drink, nor eat
anything unclean. All that I commanded her let her observe."
15 Then Manoah said to the Angel of
the LORD, "Please [a]let us detain You,
and we will prepare a young goat for
You."
16 And the Angel of the LORD said to
Manoah, "Though you detain Me, I will
not eat your food. But if you offer a
burnt offering, you must offer it to the
LORD." (For Manoah did not know He
was the Angel of the LORD.)
17 Then Manoah said to the Angel of
the LORD, "What *is* Your name, that
when Your words come *to pass* we
may honor You?"

described in 10:6, 7. The Lord used the Philistines to chasten Israel. Unlike the other accounts of Israel's apostasy, there is no record of Israel's repentance prior to God's raising up Samson as a deliverer unless Israel's crying out to God, recorded in 10:10–16, applies to the present Philistine oppression.

13:1 The **Philistines** arrived in Canaan during the invasion of the Sea Peoples around 1200 B.C. The Israelites accepted their domination (14:4; 15:11) until the time of Samuel (1 Sam. 7:10–14).

13:2 Zorah was a city, situated in the lowland of Judah, which was assigned to the tribe of Dan (Josh. 19:41). It marked the point of departure for the Danites when they migrated north (18:2, 8, 11). **Was barren:** Barrenness for women in Israel was a disgrace.

13:5 A **Nazirite** ("Devoted" or "Consecrated") was a person who took a vow of consecration to the Lord. The vow included 1) abstaining from wine or other intoxicating drinks; 2) refraining from cutting the hair; and 3) refusing to go near a dead body for a specified period of time or for a lifetime, as in the case of Samson. Samson began **to deliver** but, ultimately, the Lord completed it. The deliverance continued during Samuel's time (1 Sam. 7:10–14) and was completed in David's time (2 Sam. 5:17–25; 8:1).

13:6 Man of God: This expression, which was used of prophets (1 Sam. 9:6–10), refers in this instance to the Angel of the Lord (vv. 3, 21). See note on 2:1.

18 And the Angel of the LORD said to
him, [a]"Why do you ask My name, seeing it *is* wonderful?"
19 So Manoah took the young goat
with the grain offering, [a]and offered
it upon the rock to the LORD. And He
did a wondrous thing while Manoah
and his wife looked on—

> **WORD WEALTH**
>
> **13:19 did a wondrous thing,** *pala'* (pah-*lah*); Strong's #6381: To perform a miracle, marvel, wonder, or supernatural deed, that is, something beyond the human ability to grasp, do, or achieve. The verb *pala'* is part of a family of words that include the noun *pele'* (wonder, marvelous work) and the adjective *pil'iy* (wonderful). Is. 9:6 states that one of the Messiah's titles is "Wonderful." The psalmist prays that God will reveal to him "wondrous things" from the law of the Lord (Ps. 119:18), matters beyond normal human perception requiring supernatural insight to see them. For other examples of *pala'*, see Ex. 34:10; Ps. 107:8; Is. 29:14.

20 it happened as the flame went up
toward heaven from the altar—the Angel of the LORD ascended in the flame
of the altar! When Manoah and his
wife saw *this,* they [a]fell on their faces
to the ground.
21 When the Angel of the LORD appeared no more to Manoah and his
wife, [a]then Manoah knew that He *was*
the Angel of the LORD.
22 And Manoah said to his wife,
[a]"We shall surely die, because we have
seen God!"
23 But his wife said to him, "If the
LORD had desired to kill us, He would
not have accepted a burnt offering and
a grain offering from our hands, nor
would He have shown us all these
things, nor would He have told us *such*
things as these at this time."
24 So the woman bore a son and called
his name [a]Samson; and [b]the child
grew, and the LORD blessed him.
25 [a]And the Spirit of the LORD began
to move upon him at [1]Mahaneh Dan
[b]between Zorah and [c]Eshtaol.

Samson's Philistine Wife

14 Now Samson went down
[a]to Timnah, and [b]saw a woman
in Timnah of the daughters of the Philistines.
2 So he went up and told his father
and mother, saying, "I have seen a
woman in Timnah of the daughters of
the Philistines; now therefore, [a]get her
for me as a wife."
3 Then his father and mother said to
him, "*Is there* no woman among the
daughters of [a]your brethren, or among
all my people, that you must go and
get a wife from the [b]uncircumcised
Philistines?" And Samson said to his
father, "Get her for me, for [1]she
pleases me well."
4 But his father and mother did not
know that it was [a]of the LORD—that He
was seeking an occasion to move
against the Philistines. For at that time
[b]the Philistines had dominion over Israel.
5 So Samson went down to Timnah
with his father and mother, and came
to the vineyards of Timnah.
Now *to his* surprise, a young lion
came *roaring against him.
6 And [a]the Spirit of the LORD came
mightily upon him, and he tore the lion
apart as one would have torn apart a

18 [a]Gen. 32:29 **19** [a]Judg. 6:19–21 **20** [a]Lev. 9:24; 1 Chr. 21:16; Ezek. 1:28; Matt. 17:6 **21** [a]Judg. 6:22 **22** [a]Gen. 32:30; Ex. 33:20; Deut. 5:26; Judg. 6:22, 23
24 [a]Heb. 11:32 [b]1 Sam. 3:19; Luke 1:80 **25** [a]Judg. 3:10; 1 Sam. 11:6; Matt. 4:1 [b]Josh. 15:33; Judg. 18:11 [c]Judg. 16:31 [1]Lit. *Camp of Dan,* Judg. 18:12

CHAPTER 14

1 [a]Gen. 38:13; Josh. 15:10, 57 [b]Gen. 34:2 **2** [a]Gen. 21:21 **3** [a]Gen. 24:3, 4 [b]Gen. 34:14; Ex. 34:16; Deut. 7:3 [1]Lit. *she is right in my eyes* **4** [a]Josh. 11:20; 1 Kin. 12:15; 2 Kin. 6:33; 2 Chr. 10:15 [b]Deut. 28:48; Judg. 13:1 **5** *See WW at Joel 3:16. **6** [a]Judg. 3:10

13:18 It *is* wonderful is an expression meaning "beyond understanding." This Hebrew term, which is translated "Wonderful" in Is. 9:6, refers to the coming Messiah.
13:24 Samson's name is related to the Hebrew word for "sun."
13:25 The Spirit of the LORD began to move: The Lord began to empower Samson to deliver Israel (see Introduction to Judges: The Holy Spirit at Work). Samson was not a judge or deliverer who led the Israelites against the Philistines. He was a loner whose heroic exploits curtailed Philistine invasions and consequently helped the cause of his people. **Mahaneh Dan** is literally "Camp of Dan."
14:1–20 Samson's heroic demonstrations of physical prowess with the Philistines began at the time of his marriage to a Philistine woman. Samson appears to have violated his Nazirite vow on two accounts: 1) he scooped honey out of a lion's carcass, and 2) he conducted a feast where they drank wine.
14:1 Timnah: This city, generally identified with modern Tell el-Batashi, was probably located on the northern border of Judah near Beth Shemesh in the Sorek Valley.
14:2 Get her for me: Negotiations for marriage were customarily carried on by the parents. Samson's parents appear to be initially involved in this marriage contract (vv. 1–5). Then Samson took over the wedding plans (v. 10).
14:3 The uncircumcised Philistines: Samson's parents used this expression to deride the Philistines, apparently the only people around Israel who were not circumcised. According to the Mosaic Law, an Israelite was not to marry a Canaanite (Ex. 34:16; Deut. 7:3). Samson's parents, therefore, voiced their disapproval. **For she pleases me well** literally means "for she is right in my eyes." It is similar to the Hebrew expression in 17:6 and 21:25 that is translated "Everyone did *what was* right in his own eyes."
14:4 That it was of the LORD: God did not approve of Samson's decision to break the law, but He used the circumstances for His purposes and for His glory.
14:6 The Spirit of the LORD: See Introduction to Judges: The Holy Spirit at Work. **A young goat:** Tearing a goat in half by pulling apart its hind legs is still practiced in Arab countries.

young goat, though *he had* nothing in
his hand. But he did not tell his father
or his mother what he had done.
7 Then he went down and talked with
the woman; and she pleased Samson
well.
8 After some time, when he returned
to get her, he turned aside to see the
carcass of the lion. And behold, a
swarm of bees and honey *were* in the
carcass of the lion.
9 He took some of it in his hands and
went along, eating. When he came to
his father and mother, he gave *some*
to them, and they also ate. But he did
not tell them that he had taken the
honey out of the [a]carcass of the lion.
10 So his father went down to the
woman. And Samson gave a feast
there, for young men used to do so.
11 And it happened, when they saw
him, that they brought thirty companions to be with him.
12 Then Samson said to them, "Let me
[a]pose a riddle to you. If you can correctly solve and explain it to me
[b]within the seven days of the feast,
then I will give you thirty linen garments and thirty [c]changes of clothing.
13 "But if you cannot explain *it* to me,
then you shall give me thirty linen garments and thirty changes of clothing."
And they said to him, [a]"Pose your riddle, that we may hear it."
14 So he said to them:

"Out of the eater came something
to eat,
And out of the strong came
something sweet."

Now for three days they could not explain the riddle.
15 But it came to pass on the [1]seventh
day that they said to Samson's wife,
[a]"Entice your husband, that he may
explain the riddle to us, [b]or else we will
burn you and your father's house with
fire. Have you invited us in order to
take what is ours? *Is that* not *so*?"
16 Then Samson's wife wept on him,
and said, [a]"You only hate me! You do
not love me! You have posed a riddle
to the sons of my people, but you have
not explained *it* to me." And he said
to her, "Look, I have not explained *it*
to my father or my mother; so should
I explain *it* to you?"
17 Now she had wept on him the seven 3
days while their feast lasted. And it
happened on the seventh day that he
told her, because she pressed him so
much. Then she explained the riddle
to the sons of her people.
18 So the men of the city said to him
on the seventh day before the sun went
down:

"What *is* sweeter than honey?
And what *is* stronger than a
lion?"

And he said to them:

"If you had not plowed with my
heifer,
You would not have solved my
riddle!"

19 Then [a]the Spirit of the LORD came
upon him mightily, and he went down
to Ashkelon and killed thirty of their
men, took their apparel, and gave the
changes *of clothing* to those who had
explained the riddle. So his anger was
aroused, and he went back up to his
father's house.
20 And Samson's wife [a]was *given* to
his companion, who had been [b]his best
man.

Samson Defeats the Philistines

15 After a while, in the time of
wheat harvest, it happened that

9 [a]Lev. 11:27
12 [a]1 Kin. 10:1; Ezek. 17:2 [b]Gen. 29:27 [c]Gen. 45:22; 2 Kin. 5:22
13 [a]Ezek. 17:2
15 [a]Judg. 16:5 [b]Judg. 15:6 [1]So with MT, Tg., Vg.; LXX, Syr. *fourth*
16 [a]Judg. 16:15
19 [a]Judg. 3:10; 13:25
20 [a]Judg. 15:2 [b]John 3:29

14:8, 9 Samson violated his Nazirite vow by touching the carcass of the lion and thus became ceremonially unclean (Num. 6:6).

14:10 Feast: A seven-day marriage feast was common in the ancient Near East. Wine was usually served at such a feast, and Samson may have violated his Nazirite vow once again. Samson apparently gave the feast without involving his parents. These festivities normally would have taken place in the bridegroom's home, and Samson would have had Israelite companions and an Israelite best man. Samson's marriage would be called a *sadiqa* marriage in Arab society today, where arrangements are made directly with the bride's family. The wife continues to live at home with her father, and her husband visits her periodically.

14:11 They saw him: The antecedent for "they" is obscure. It probably refers to the Philistine family.

14:12 Linen garments were large rectangular sheets of linen which could be used as a garment or as a cover. **Thirty changes of clothing** were festal garments, which guests would wear at a wedding.

14:15 Seventh: Some ancient manuscripts read "fourth."

14:17 See section 3 of Truth-In-Action at the end of Judg.

14:19 The Spirit of the LORD: In spite of Samson's foolishness, the Lord empowered him with His Spirit for the purpose of humbling the Philistines and disrupting their domination of the Israelites (see Introduction to Judges: The Holy Spirit at Work). **Ashkelon,** one of the 5 principal cities of the Philistines, was located on the Mediterranean seacoast 12 miles north of Gaza.

15:1 The time of the wheat harvest took place in May. **Young goat:** The young goat Samson brought was probably the same type of gift that a husband brings when he visits his wife in a modern Arab *sadiqa* marriage (see note on 14:10).

Samson visited his wife with a [a]young
goat. And he said, "Let me go in to my
wife, into *her* room." But her father
would not permit him to go in.
2 Her father said, "I really thought
that you thoroughly [a]hated her; therefore I gave her to your companion. *Is*
not her younger sister better than she?
Please, take her instead."
3 And Samson said to them, "This
time I shall be *blameless regarding
the Philistines if I harm them!"
4 Then Samson went and caught
three hundred foxes; and he took
torches, turned *the foxes* tail to tail,
and put a torch between each pair of
tails.
5 When he had set the torches on fire,
he let *the foxes* go into the standing
grain of the Philistines, and burned up
both the shocks and the standing grain,
as well as the vineyards *and* olive
groves.
6 Then the Philistines said, "Who has
done this?" And they answered, "Samson, the son-in-law of the Timnite, because he has taken his wife and given
her to his companion." [a]So the Philistines came up and burned her and her
father with fire.
7 Samson said to them, "Since you
would do a thing like this, I will surely
take revenge on you, and after that I
will cease."
8 So he attacked them hip and thigh
with a great slaughter; then he went
down and dwelt in the cleft of the rock
of [a]Etam.
9 Now the Philistines went up, encamped in Judah, and deployed themselves [a]against Lehi.
10 And the men of Judah said, "Why
have you come up against us?" So they
answered, "We have come up to
[1]arrest Samson, to do to him as he has
done to us."
11 Then three thousand men of Judah
went down to the cleft of the rock of
Etam, and said to Samson, "Do you not
know that the Philistines [a]rule over us?
What *is* this you have done to us?" And
he said to them, "As they did to me,
so I have done to them."
12 But they said to him, "We have
come down to arrest you, that we may
deliver you into the hand of the Philistines." Then Samson said to them,
"Swear to me that you will not kill me
yourselves."
13 So they spoke to him, saying, "No,
but we will tie you securely and deliver
you into their hand; but we will surely
not kill you." And they bound him with
two [a]new ropes and brought him up
from the rock.
14 When he came to Lehi, the Philistines came shouting against him. Then
[a]the Spirit of the LORD came mightily
upon him; and the ropes that *were* on
his arms became like flax that is
burned with fire, and his bonds [1]broke
loose from his hands.
15 He found a fresh jawbone of a donkey, reached out his hand and took it,
and [a]killed a thousand men with it.
16 Then Samson said:

"With the jawbone of a donkey,
Heaps upon heaps,
With the jawbone of a donkey
I have slain a thousand men!"

17 And so it was, when he had finished
speaking, that he threw the jawbone
from his hand, and called that place
[1]Ramath Lehi.
18 Then he became very thirsty; so he
cried out to the LORD and said, [a]"You
have given this great deliverance by
the hand of Your servant; and now
shall I die of thirst and fall into the
hand of the uncircumcised?"
19 So God split the hollow place that
is in [1]Lehi, and water came out, and
he drank; and [a]his spirit returned, and
he revived. Therefore he called its
name [2]En Hakkore, which is in Lehi
to this day.
20 And [a]he judged Israel [b]twenty
years [c]in the days of the Philistines.

CHAPTER 15
1 [a]Gen. 38:17
2 [a]Judg. 14:20
3 *See WW at Num. 14:18.
6 [a]Judg. 14:15
8 [a]2 Chr. 11:6
9 [a]Judg. 15:19
10 [1]Lit. *bind*
11 [a]Lev. 26:25; Deut. 28:43; Judg. 13:1; 14:4; Ps. 106:40–42
13 [a]Judg. 16:11, 12
14 [a]Judg. 3:10; 14:6 [1]Lit. *were melted*
15 [a]Lev. 26:8; Josh. 23:10; Judg. 3:31
17 [1]Lit. *Jawbone Height*
18 [a]Ps. 3:7
19 [a]Gen. 45:27; Is. 40:29 [1]Lit. *Jawbone*, Judg. 15:14 [2]Lit. *Spring of the Caller*
20 [a]Judg. 10:2; 12:7–14 [b]Judg. 16:31 [c]Judg. 13:1

15:2 Hated her: The word "hate" was a technical term used in the context of divorce (Deut. 24:3). When Samson returned to his father's house, his father-in-law assumed that he had divorced his daughter (14:19, 20).

15:4 Foxes: This term in Hebrew can also mean "jackals." Jackals were more prevalent in Palestine. They ran in packs and could be caught more easily than foxes.

15:8 Hip and thigh: The meaning of this expression is not certain. It may have been a military expression or a wrestler's term used as a metaphor for a vicious attack. **Rock of Etam:** "Etam" means "Place of Birds of Prey." The location of this place is unknown.

15:9 Lehi: This place, meaning "Jawbone," was probably located in the region of Beth Shemesh.

15:14 The Spirit of the LORD gave Samson supernatural strength so that he could be saved from the hand of the Philistines. See Introduction to Judges: The Holy Spirit at Work.

15:15 A fresh jawbone would be strong, not dry and brittle. Samson violates his Nazirite vow again by touching part of a dead animal.

15:19 En Hakkore means "Spring of the Caller." It was a spring at Lehi.

15:20 Judged Israel: Samson's judgeship consisted of single-handed victories over the Philistines, which disrupted their domination over Israel. He did not liberate Israel from the Philistine oppression.

Samson and Delilah

16 Now Samson went to [a]Gaza and
saw a harlot there, and went in
to her.
2 *When* the Gazites *were told,* "Samson has come here!" they [a]surrounded
the place and lay in wait for him all
night at the gate of the city. They were
quiet all night, saying, "In the morning,
when it is daylight, we will kill him."
3 And Samson lay *low* till midnight;
then he arose at midnight, took hold
of the doors of the gate of the city and
the two gateposts, pulled them up, bar
and all, put *them* on his shoulders, and
carried them to the top of the hill that
faces Hebron.
3 4 Afterward it happened that he loved
a woman in the Valley of Sorek, whose
name *was* Delilah.
5 And the [a]lords of the Philistines
came up to her and said to her, [b]"Entice him, and find out where his great
strength *lies,* and by what *means* we
may overpower him, that we may bind
him to afflict him; and every one of us
will give you eleven hundred *pieces* of
silver."
6 So Delilah said to Samson, "Please
tell me where your great strength *lies,*
and with what you may be bound to
afflict you."
7 And Samson said to her, "If they
bind me with seven fresh bowstrings,
not yet dried, then I shall become
weak, and be like any *other* man."
8 So the lords of the Philistines
brought up to her seven fresh bowstrings, not yet dried, and she bound
him with them.
9 Now *men were* lying in wait, staying with her in the room. And she said
to him, "The Philistines *are* upon you,
Samson!" But he broke the bowstrings
as a strand of yarn breaks when it
touches fire. So the secret of his
strength was not known.
10 Then Delilah said to Samson,
"Look, you have mocked me and told
me lies. Now, please tell me what you
may be bound with."
11 So he said to her, "If they bind me
securely with [a]new ropes [1]that have
never been used, then I shall become
weak, and be like any *other* man."
12 Therefore Delilah took new ropes
and bound him with them, and said to
him, "The Philistines *are* upon you,
Samson!" And *men were* lying in wait,
staying in the room. But he broke them
off his arms like a thread.
13 Delilah said to Samson, "Until now
you have mocked me and told me lies.
Tell me what you may be bound with."
And he said to her, "If you weave the
seven locks of my head into the web
of the loom"—
14 So she wove *it* tightly with the batten of the loom, and said to him, "The
Philistines *are* upon you, Samson!" But
he awoke from his sleep, and pulled
out the batten and the web from the
loom.
15 Then she said to him, [a]"How can
you say, 'I love you,' when your heart
is not with me? You have mocked me
these three times, and have not told me
where your great strength *lies.*"
16 And it came to pass, when she pes-
tered him daily with her words and
pressed him, *so* that his soul was
[1]vexed to death,
17 that he [a]told her all his heart, and
said to her, [b]"No razor has ever come
upon my head, for I *have been* a Nazirite to God from my mother's womb.
If I am shaven, then my strength will
leave me, and I shall become weak, and
be like any *other* man."
18 When Delilah saw that he had told
her all his heart, she sent and called
for the lords of the Philistines, saying,
"Come up once more, for he has told
me all his heart." So the lords of the
Philistines came up to her and brought
the money in their hand.
19 [a]Then she lulled him to sleep on her
knees, and called for a man and had
him shave off the seven locks of his

CHAPTER 16
1 [a]Josh. 15:47
2 [a]1 Sam. 23:26; Ps. 118:10–12
5 [a]Josh. 13:3 [b]Judg. 14:15
11 [a]Judg. 15:13 [1]Lit. *with which work has never been done*
15 [a]Judg. 14:16
16 [1]Lit. *impatient to the point of*
17 [a][Mic. 7:5] [b]Num. 6:5; Judg. 13:5
19 [a]Prov. 7:26, 27

16:1 Gaza was one of the five principal cities of the Philistines located on the Mediterranean coast of southwest Palestine. **Harlot:** Samson's physical strength enabled him to do exploits, but his moral weakness led to his eventual destruction.
16:3 The hill that faces Hebron refers to an unknown hill in the direction of Hebron.
16:4–22 See section 3 of Truth-In-Action at the end of Judg.
16:4 The Valley of Sorek begins about 13 miles west-southwest of Jerusalem, continuing in a northwesterly direction toward the Mediterranean.
16:5 The lords of the Philistines: See note on 3:3. **Eleven hundred *pieces* of silver** was an exorbitant amount of money, especially when compared with the amount of money that Micah received for his priestly duties (17:10).
16:7 Seven fresh bowstrings: Bowstrings were made from the viscera of animals.
16:13 Into the web of the loom: Delilah wove Samson's hair into the fabric on the loom. Samson, lying in a prostrate position, was now fastened to the frame of the loom.
16:17 I *have been* a Nazirite: Samson finally revealed the source of his strength. His strength came from the supernatural empowerment of the Spirit of the Lord. This divine enabling was associated with his consecration to God as a Nazirite, which was symbolized by his unshaven hair.

head. Then [1]she began to torment him,
and his strength left him.
20 And she said, "The Philistines *are*
upon you, Samson!" So he awoke from
his sleep, and said, "I will go out as
before, at other times, and shake myself free!" But he did not know that the
LORD [a]had departed from him.
21 Then the Philistines took him and
[1]put out his [a]eyes, and brought him
down to Gaza. They bound him with
bronze fetters, and he became a
grinder in the prison.
22 However, the hair of his head began
to grow again after it had been shaven.

Samson Dies with the Philistines

23 Now the lords of the Philistines
gathered together to offer a great sacrifice to [a]Dagon their god, and to rejoice.
And they said:

"Our god has delivered into our
hands
Samson our enemy!"

24 When the people saw him, they
[a]praised* their god; for they said:

"Our god has delivered into our
hands our enemy,
The destroyer of our land,
And the one who multiplied our
dead."

25 So it happened, when their hearts
were [a]merry, that they said, "Call for
Samson, that he may perform for us."
So they called for Samson from the
prison, and he performed for them.
And they stationed him between the
pillars.
26 Then Samson said to the lad who
held him by the hand, "Let me feel the

19 [1]So with MT, Tg., Vg.; LXX *he began to be weak,*
20 [a]Num. 14:9, 42, 43; [Josh. 7:12]; 1 Sam. 16:14; 18:12; 28:15, 16; 2 Chr. 15:2
21 [a]2 Kin. 25:7 [1]Lit. *bored out*
23 [a]1 Sam. 5:2
24 [a]Dan. 5:4 *See WW at 1 Chr. 23:30.
25 [a]Judg. 9:27

27 [a]Deut. 22:8
28 [a]Jer. 15:15
31 [a]Judg. 13:25 [b]Judg. 15:20

CHAPTER 17

1 [a]Judg. 18:2
2 [a]Lev. 5:1 [b]Gen. 14:19

pillars which support the temple, so
that I can lean on them."
27 Now the temple was full of men and
women. All the lords of the Philistines
were there—about three thousand men
and women on the [a]roof watching
while Samson performed.
28 Then Samson called to the LORD, 3
saying, "O Lord GOD, [a]remember me,
I pray! Strengthen me, I pray, just this
once, O God, that I may with one *blow*
take vengeance on the Philistines for
my two eyes!"
29 And Samson took hold of the two
middle pillars which supported the
temple, and he braced himself against
them, one on his right and the other
on his left.
30 Then Samson said, "Let me die with
the Philistines!" And he pushed with
all his might, and the temple fell on the
lords and all the people who *were* in
it. So the dead that he killed at his
death were more than he had killed in
his life.
31 And his brothers and all his father's
household came down and took him,
and brought *him* up and [a]buried him
between Zorah and Eshtaol in the
tomb of his father Manoah. He had
judged Israel [b]twenty years.

Micah's Idolatry

17 Now there was a man from the
mountains of Ephraim, whose
name *was* [a]Micah.
2 And he said to his mother, "The
eleven hundred *shekels* of silver that
were taken from you, and on which
you [a]put a curse, even saying it in
my ears—here *is* the silver with me;
I took it." And his mother said,
[b]"*May you be* blessed by the LORD,
my son!"

16:20 The LORD had departed from him: Samson was discharged from his role as a judge for this ultimate violation of his vow.
16:22 This verse shows the mercy of God; He will restore Samson in spite of his sin.
16:23 Dagon, a grain and fertility god, was the chief god of the Philistines and was worshiped at the famous temples located in Gaza and Ashdod.
16:25 That he may perform, that is, be made a laughingstock.
16:26 Let me feel the pillars: Archaeologists have excavated a Philistine temple, similar to the one described in this narrative. It has a long inner chamber, its roof originally supported by two wooden pillars.
16:28 See section 3 of Truth-In-Action at the end of Judg.
16:31 Judged Israel: See note on 15:20. The Spirit of the Lord gave Samson supernatural strength and ability to enable him to perform many heroic deeds on behalf of Israel. He is listed without comment as one of the heroes of faith in Heb. 11:32.

Epilogue: Two stories are appended to the Book of Judges in the form of an epilogue (17:1—21:25). The first episode of the epilogue (17:1—18:31) depicts the corruption in Israelite worship. It tells the story of Micah's establishment of a paganized place of worship and the Danite adoption of this form of worship when they migrated north. The second episode of the epilogue (19:1—21:25) illustrates Israel's moral corruption. It relates the unfortunate story of the degenerate act of the men of Gibeah toward a Levite's concubine and the ensuing civil war against the tribe of Benjamin, which had supported the men who committed this atrocity.
17:1 Micah means "Who Is Like Yahweh?" It is ironic that a man with this name should establish an apostate place of worship and an illegitimate priesthood.
17:2 Blessed by the LORD: The mother counteracted the curse with the pronouncement of blessing upon her son.

2 3 So when he had returned the eleven
hundred *shekels* of silver to his mother,
his mother said, "I had wholly dedicated the silver from my hand to the
LORD for my son, to [a]make a carved
image and a molded image; now therefore, I will return it to you."
4 Thus he returned the silver to his
mother. Then his mother [a]took two
hundred *shekels* of silver and gave
them to the silversmith, and he made
it into a carved image and a molded
image; and they were in the house of
Micah.
5 The man Micah had a [a]shrine, and
made an [b]ephod and [c]household[1]
idols; and he consecrated one of his
sons, who became his *priest.

3 [a]Ex. 20:4, 23; 34:17; Lev. 19:4
4 [a]Is. 46:6
5 [a]Judg. 18:24 [b]Judg. 8:27; 18:14 [c]Gen. 31:19, 30; Hos. 3:4 [1]Heb. *teraphim*
*See WW at Lev. 5:6.
6 [a]Judg. 18:1; 19:1 [b]Deut. 12:8; Judg. 21:25
7 [a]Josh. 19:15; Judg. 19:1; Ruth 1:1, 2; Mic. 5:2; Matt. 2:1, 5, 6 [b]Deut. 18:6

6 [a]In those days *there was* no king 4
in Israel; [b]everyone did *what was* right
in his own eyes.
7 Now there was a young man from
[a]Bethlehem in Judah, of the family of
Judah; he *was* a Levite, and [b]was staying there.
8 The man departed from the city of
Bethlehem in Judah to stay wherever
he could find *a place*. Then he came
to the mountains of Ephraim, to the
house of Micah, as he journeyed.
9 And Micah said to him, "Where do
you come from?" So he said to him,
"I *am* a Levite from Bethlehem in Judah, and I am on my way to find *a*
place to stay."
10 Micah said to him, "Dwell with me,

17:3 See section 2 of Truth-In-Action at the end of Judg.
17:3 I had wholly dedicated the silver: The mother's consecration of the money to the Lord for making images was in disobedience to the Law (Ex. 20:4–6). The mother and her son's paganized view of the God of Israel was probably a result of the idolatrous influence of the Canaanites. **A carved image and a molded image:** The carved image was probably formed from stone or wood and overlaid with silver, and the molded image was made of melted silver poured into a mold.

17:5 An ephod was either an elaborate vest worn by a priest or an object of worship (see note on 8:27). **Household idols,** also referred to as teraphim, were used in divination.
17:6 See section 4 of Truth-In-Action at the end of Judg.
17:6 The author, likely writing from his perspective in the early monarchy, was explaining Micah's sacrilegious actions as a characteristic condition of this period when ***there was* no king.**
17:10 Father was a term of respect or an honorary title. **Ten *shekels* of silver:** The Levite appears to have been

THE PERIOD OF THE JUDGES (16:31)

Events and Judges	Years
Israel serves Cushan-Rishathaim (3:7, 8)	8
Peace following Othniel's deliverance (3:7–11)	40
Israel serves Moab (3:12)	18
Peace follows Ehud's deliverance (3:12–30)	80
Shamgar delivers Israel from Philistines (3:31)	1
Israel serves Canaan (4:1–3)	20
Peace following deliverance by Deborah and Barak (4:1—5:31)	40
Israel serves Midian (6:1–6)	7
Peace following Gideon's deliverance (6:1—8:35)	40
Abimelech, king of Israel (9:1–57)	3
Tola's career (10:1, 2)	23
Jair's career (10:3–5)	22
Israel serves Ammon and Philistia (10:6–10)	18
Jephthah's career (10:6—12:7)	6
Ibzan's career (12:8–10)	7
Elon's career (12:11, 12)	10
Abdon's career (12:13–15)	8
Israel serves Philistia (13:1)	40
Samson's career (12:1—16:31)	20

[a]and be a [b]father and a priest to me,
and I will give you ten *shekels* of silver
per year, a suit of clothes, and your
sustenance." So the Levite went in.
11 Then the Levite was content to
dwell with the man; and the young
man became like one of his sons to
him.
12 So Micah [a]consecrated[1] the Levite,
and the young man [b]became his priest,
and lived in the house of Micah.
13 Then Micah said, "Now I know that
the LORD will be good to me, since I
have a Levite as [a]priest!"

The Danites Adopt Micah's Idolatry

4 **18** In [a]those days *there was* no
king in Israel. And in those days
[b]the tribe of the Danites was seeking
an inheritance for itself to dwell in; for
until that day *their* inheritance among
the tribes of Israel had not fallen to
them.
2 So the children of Dan sent five men
of their family from their territory, men
of valor from [a]Zorah and Eshtaol,
[b]to spy out the land and search it. They
said to them, "Go, search the land." So
they went to the mountains of
Ephraim, to the [c]house of Micah, and
lodged there.
3 While they *were* at the house of Micah, they recognized the voice of the
young Levite. They turned aside and
said to him, "Who brought you here?
What are you doing in this *place*? What
do you have here?"
4 He said to them, "Thus and so Micah did for me. He has [a]hired me, and
I have become his priest."
5 So they said to him, "Please [a]in-
quire [b]of God, that we may know

10 [a]Judg. 18:19 [b]Gen. 45:8; Job 29:16
12 [a]Judg. 17:5 [b]Judg. 18:30 [1]Lit. *filled the hand of*
13 [a]Judg. 18:4

CHAPTER 18

1 [a]Judg. 17:6; 19:1; 21:25 [b]Josh. 19:40–48
2 [a]Judg. 13:25 [b]Num. 13:17; Josh. 2:1 [c]Judg. 17:1
4 [a]Judg. 17:10, 12
5 [a]1 Kin. 22:5; [Is. 30:1]; Hos. 4:12 [b]Judg. 1:1; 17:5; 18:14
6 [a]1 Kin. 22:6 [1]Lit. *The LORD is before the way in which you go*
7 [a]Josh. 19:47 [b]Judg. 18:27–29 [c]Judg. 10:12 [1]So with MT, Tg., Vg.; LXX *with Syria*
8 [a]Judg. 18:2
9 [a]Num. 13:30; Josh. 2:23, 24 [b]1 Kin. 22:3
10 [a]Judg. 18:7, 27 [b]Deut. 8:9
12 [a]Josh. 15:60 [b]Judg. 13:25 [1]Lit. *Camp of Dan*
13 [a]Judg. 18:2
14 [a]1 Sam. 14:28

whether the journey on which we go
will be prosperous."
6 And the priest said to them, [a]"Go
in peace. [1]The presence of the LORD *be*
with you on your way."
7 So the five men departed and went
to [a]Laish. They saw the people who
were there, [b]how they dwelt safely, in
the manner of the Sidonians, quiet and
secure. *There were* no rulers in the
land who might put *them* to shame for
anything. They *were* far from the
[c]Sidonians, and they had no ties
[1]with anyone.
8 Then *the spies* came back to their
brethren at [a]Zorah and Eshtaol, and
their brethren said to them, "What *is*
your *report*?"
9 So they said, [a]"Arise, let us go up
against them. For we have seen the
land, and indeed it *is* very good. *Would*
you [b]*do* nothing? Do not hesitate to go,
and enter to possess the land.
10 "When you go, you will come to a
[a]secure people and a large land. For
God has given it into your hands,
[b]a place where *there is* no lack of anything that *is* on the earth."
11 And six hundred men of the family
of the Danites went from there, from
Zorah and Eshtaol, armed with weapons of war.
12 Then they went up and encamped
in [a]Kirjath Jearim in Judah. (Therefore
they call that place [b]Mahaneh Dan[1] to
this day. There *it is*, west of Kirjath
Jearim.)
13 And they passed from there to the
mountains of Ephraim, and came to
[a]the house of Micah.
14 [a]Then the five men who had gone
to spy out the country of Laish answered and said to their brethren, "Do

---

motivated to serve as Micah's priest more by material concerns than by his devotion to the Lord. The money, clothing, and food Micah offered him apparently provided the incentive for him to become involved in an apostate form of worship. He eventually accepted an even more attractive offer (18:19, 20).

17:13 Micah had deceived himself into thinking that he would now have the Lord's blessing because he had a Levite priest. In reality he was disobeying God's Law.

18:1 See section 4 of Truth-In-Action at the end of Judg.

18:1 Seeking an inheritance: The Danites were unable to lay claim on their entire territory, located between Judah and Ephraim (Josh. 19:41–46), because of the opposition of the Amorites (1:34, 35) and later of the Philistines.

18:3 *Recognized the voice:* The Danites may have recognized his accent.

18:5 Please inquire of God: They were seeking an oracle from God that would assure them of success, though the Lord had already revealed His will to the Danites with regard to their inheritance. Perhaps their disobedience and lack of faith in the Lord prevented them from capturing their whole territory from the Amorites and Philistines. The Danites did not follow God's revealed plan for them when they captured Laish as an inheritance. In disobedience, they established an idolatrous center of worship at Dan (formerly Laish), which became prominent during the reign of Jeroboam I (vv. 30, 31; 1 Kin. 12:28–30).

18:6 Go in peace: The Levite proclaimed the message they wanted to hear and even authenticated it by using the Lord's name.

18:7 Laish was a Canaanite city in northern Palestine referred to as Leshem in Josh. 19:47. It was isolated from the Sidonians and did not have any close military alliances with anyone. **Sidonians:** The inhabitants of Laish had customs similar to those of the Sidonians, who were a Phoenician people interested more in agriculture and commerce than in war.

18:12 Kirjath Jearim was a city of Judah, which was about eight miles north of Jerusalem and six miles east of the Zorah-Eshtaol area. **Mahaneh Dan** was the place where the Spirit of the Lord first began to move on Samson's life (see note on 13:25).

you know that [b]there are in these
houses an ephod, household idols, a
carved image, and a molded image?
Now therefore, consider what you
should do."
15 So they turned aside there, and
came to the house of the young Levite
man—to the house of Micah—and
greeted him.
16 The [a]six hundred men armed with
their weapons of war, who *were* of the
children of Dan, stood by the entrance
of the gate.
17 Then [a]the five men who had gone
to spy out the land went up. Entering
there, they took [b]the carved image, the
ephod, the household idols, and the
molded image. The priest stood at
the entrance of the gate with the six
hundred men *who were* armed with
weapons of war.
18 When these went into Micah's
house and took the carved image, the
ephod, the household idols, and the
molded image, the priest said to them,
"What are you doing?"
19 And they said to him, "Be quiet,
[a]put your hand over your mouth, and
come with us; [b]be a father and a priest
to us. *Is it* better for you to be a priest
to the household of one man, or that
you be a priest to a tribe and a family
in Israel?"
20 So the priest's heart was glad; and
he took the *ephod, the household
idols, and the carved image, and took
his place among the people.
21 Then they turned and departed, and
put the little ones, the livestock, and
the goods in front of them.
22 When they were a good way from
the house of Micah, the men who *were*
in the houses near Micah's house gathered together and overtook the children of Dan.
23 And they called out to the children
of Dan. So they turned around and said
to Micah, [a]"What ails you, that you
have gathered such a company?"
24 So he said, "You have [a]taken away
my [1]gods which I made, and the priest,

14 [b]Judg. 17:5
16 [a]Judg. 18:11
17 [a]Judg. 18:2, 14 [b]Judg. 17:4, 5
19 [a]Job 21:5; 29:9; 40:4; Mic. 7:16 [b]Judg. 17:10
20 *See WW at Ex. 35:27.
23 [a]2 Kin. 6:28
24 [a]Gen. 31:30; Judg. 17:5 [1]*idols*
25 [1]Lit. *bitter of soul*
27 [a]Josh. 19:47
28 [a]Judg. 18:7 [b]Num. 13:21; 2 Sam. 10:6
29 [a]Josh. 19:47 [b]Judg. 20:1; 1 Kin. 12:29, 30; 15:20
30 [a]2 Kin. 15:29 [1]LXX, Vg. *Moses*
31 [a]Deut. 12:1–32; Josh. 18:1, 8; Judg. 19:18; 21:12 *See WW at Gen. 49:10.

CHAPTER 19

1 [a]Judg. 17:6; 18:1; 21:25 [b]Judg. 17:7; Ruth 1:1

and you have gone away. Now what
more do I have? How can you say to
me, 'What ails you?' "
25 And the children of Dan said to him,
"Do not let your voice be heard among
us, lest [1]angry men fall upon you, and
you lose your life, with the lives of your
household!"
26 Then the children of Dan went their
way. And when Micah saw that they
were too strong for him, he turned and
went back to his house.

Danites Settle in Laish

27 So they took *the things* Micah had
made, and the priest who had belonged
to him, and went to Laish, to a people
quiet and secure; [a]and they struck
them with the edge of the sword and
burned the city with fire.
28 *There was* no deliverer, because it
was [a]far from Sidon, and they had no
ties with anyone. It was in the valley
that belongs [b]to Beth Rehob. So they
rebuilt the city and dwelt there.
29 And [a]they called the name of the
city [b]Dan, after the name of Dan their
father, who was born to Israel. However, the name of the city formerly *was*
Laish.
30 Then the children of Dan set up for
themselves the carved image; and Jonathan the son of Gershom, the son of
[1]Manasseh, and his sons were priests
to the tribe of Dan [a]until the day of
the captivity of the land.
31 So they set up for themselves Micah's carved image which he made,
[a]all the time that the house of God was
in *Shiloh.

The Levite's Concubine

19 And it came to pass in those 4
days, [a]when *there was* no king
in Israel, that there was a certain Levite staying in the remote mountains of
Ephraim. He took for himself a concubine from [b]Bethlehem in Judah.
2 But his concubine played the harlot

18:21 In front of them: The Danites sent their families and possessions ahead to protect them against attack.
18:24 You have taken away my gods: Micah's gods were defenseless.
18:28 Beth Rehob was a town north of the Sea of Galilee near Dan. It was also called Rehob (Num. 13:21).
18:30 Set up for themselves the carved image: The Danites established a center of idolatrous worship. **Jonathan the son of Gershom** became the priest for this tribal center of worship. **The captivity of the land** refers either to the Assyrian captivity of Israel in 722 B.C. (2 Kin. 17:6) or to the campaign of Tiglath-Pileser III in 734–732 B.C. (2 Kin. 15:29).
18:31 All the time that the house of God was in Shiloh: These words suggest that the false worship at the Danite shrine was in opposition to the true worship of the Lord at Shiloh. Shiloh, a city north of Bethel, was Israel's religious center during the early settlement period in the twelfth century B.C.
19:1 See section 4 of Truth-In-Action at the end of Judg.
19:1 When *there was* no king in Israel: The narrative accounts in chs. 19—21 illustrate the anarchy that prevailed in Israel before the institution of the centralized monarchy. **Levite:** This unnamed Levite is not the same Levite who served Micah. **Concubine:** See note on 8:31.

against him, and went away from him
to her father's house at Bethlehem in
Judah, and was there four whole
months.
3 Then her husband arose and went
after her, to [a]speak [1]kindly to her *and*
bring her back, having his servant and
a couple of donkeys with him. So she
brought him into her father's house;
and when the father of the young
woman saw him, he was glad to meet
him.
4 Now his father-in-law, the young
woman's father, detained him; and he
stayed with him three days. So they ate
and drank and lodged there.
5 Then it came to pass on the fourth
day that they arose early in the morning, and he stood to depart; but the
young woman's father said to his son-
in-law, [a]"Refresh your heart with a
morsel of bread, and afterward go your
way."
6 So they sat down, and the two of
them ate and drank together. Then the
young woman's father said to the man,
"Please be content to stay all night, and
let your heart be merry."
7 And when the man stood to depart,
his father-in-law urged him; so he
lodged there again.
8 Then he arose early in the morning
on the fifth day to depart, but the
young woman's father said, "Please refresh your heart." So they delayed until afternoon; and both of them ate.
9 And when the man stood to depart—he and his concubine and his
servant—his father-in-law, the young
woman's father, said to him, "Look,
the day is now drawing toward evening; please spend the night. See, the
day is coming to an end; lodge here,
that your heart may be merry. Tomorrow go your way early, so that you may
get [1]home."
10 However, the man was not willing
to spend that night; so he rose and departed, and came to opposite [a]Jebus
(that *is,* Jerusalem). With him were the
two saddled donkeys; his concubine
was also with him.
11 They *were* near Jebus, and the day
was far spent; and the servant said to
his master, "Come, please, and let us
turn aside into this city [a]of the Jebusites and lodge in it."
12 But his master said to him, "We will
not turn aside here into a city of foreigners, who *are* not of the children of
Israel; we will go on [a]to Gibeah."
13 So he said to his servant, "Come,
let us draw near to one of these places,
and spend the night in Gibeah or in
[a]Ramah."
14 And they passed by and went their
way; and the sun went down on them
near Gibeah, which belongs to Benjamin.
15 They turned aside there to go in to
lodge in Gibeah. And when he went
in, he sat down in the open square of
the city, for no one would [a]take them
into *his* house to spend the night.
16 Just then an old man came in from
[a]his work in the field at evening, who
also *was* from the mountains of
Ephraim; he was staying in Gibeah,
whereas the men of the place *were*
Benjamites.
17 And when he raised his eyes, he
saw the traveler in the open square of
the city; and the old man said, "Where
are you going, and where do you come
from?"
18 So he said to him, "We *are* passing
from Bethlehem in Judah toward the
remote mountains of Ephraim; I *am*
from there. I went to Bethlehem in Judah; *now* I am going to [a]the house of
the LORD. But there *is* no one who will
take me into his house,
19 "although we have both straw and
fodder for our donkeys, and bread and
wine for myself, for your female servant, and for the young man *who is*
with your servant; *there is* no lack of
anything."
20 And the old man said, [a]"Peace *be*
with you! However, *let* all your needs
be my responsibility; [b]only do not
spend the night in the open square."
21 [a]So he brought him into his house,
and gave fodder to the donkeys.
[b]And they washed their feet, and ate
and drank.

3 [a]Gen. 34:3; 50:21 [1]Lit. *to her heart*
5 [a]Gen. 18:5; Judg. 19:8; Ps. 104:15
9 [1]Lit. *to your tent*
10 [a]Josh. 18:28; 1 Chr. 11:4, 5
11 [a]Josh. 15:8, 63; Judg. 1:21; 2 Sam. 5:6
12 [a]Josh. 18:28
13 [a]Josh. 18:25
15 [a]Matt. 25:43
16 [a]Ps. 104:23
18 [a]Josh. 18:1; Judg. 18:31; 20:18; 1 Sam. 1:3, 7
20 [a]Gen. 43:23; Judg. 6:23; 1 Sam. 25:6 [b]Gen. 19:2
21 [a]Gen. 24:32; 43:24 [b]Gen. 18:4; John 13:5

19:7–9 The father-in-law's extended hospitality is apparently mentioned as a type of pressure point to which the Levite succumbs. His poor decision is then assumed as a factor in the ensuing disaster (vv. 22–30).

19:10 Jebus was a name for Jerusalem used only here in vv. 10, 11 and in 1 Chr. 11:4, 5.

19:12 A city of foreigners: Since the Jebusites were in control of this city, the Levite may have felt that his life was endangered. **Gibeah** (modern Tell el-Ful) was located 3 miles north of Jerusalem. Archaeological excavations have revealed that Gibeah was destroyed by fire (20:37–40) and later rebuilt. It was Saul's home (1 Sam. 10:26) and later became the capital of his kingdom (1 Sam. 15:34).

19:15 For no one would take them into *his* house: The Benjamites were not willing to extend hospitality to the Levite and his concubine. The only man who was willing to take them into his home was a sojourner in Gibeah (vv. 16–21).

19:21 Washed their feet: Washing a guest's feet was a common custom of courtesy in the ancient Near East and a sign of hospitality.

Gibeah's Crime

22 As they were [a]enjoying themselves,
suddenly [b]certain men of the city,
[c]perverted[1] men, surrounded the house
and beat on the door. They spoke to
the master of the house, the old man,
saying, [d]"Bring out the man who came
to your house, that we may *know him
carnally!"
23 But [a]the man, the master of the
house, went out to them and said to
them, "No, my brethren! I beg you, do
not act *so* wickedly! Seeing this man
has come into my house, [b]do not commit this outrage.
24 [a]"Look, *here is* my virgin daughter
and [1]*the man's* concubine; let me bring
them out now. [b]Humble them, and do
with them as you please; but to this
man do not do such a vile thing!"
25 But the men would not heed him.
So the man took his concubine and
brought *her* out to them. And they
[a]knew her and abused her all night until morning; and when the day began
to break, they let her go.
26 Then the woman came as the day
was dawning, and fell down at the door
of the man's house where her master
was, till it was light.
27 When her master arose in the morning, and opened the doors of the house
and went out to go his way, there was
his concubine, fallen *at* the door of the
house with her hands on the threshold.
28 And he said to her, "Get up and let
us be going." But [a]there was no answer. So the man lifted her onto the
donkey; and the man got up and went
to his place.
29 When he entered his house he took
a knife, laid hold of his concubine, and
[a]divided her into twelve pieces, [1]limb
by limb, and sent her throughout all
the territory of Israel.
30 And so it was that all who saw it
said, "No such deed has been done or
seen from the day that the children of
Israel came up from the land of Egypt
until this day. Consider it, [a]confer, and
speak up!"

Israel's War with the Benjamites

20 So [a]all the children of Israel
came out, from [b]Dan to
[c]Beersheba, as well as from the land
of Gilead, and the *congregation gathered together as one man before the
LORD [d]at Mizpah.
2 And the leaders of all the people,
all the tribes of Israel, presented themselves in the *assembly of the people
of God, four hundred thousand foot
soldiers [a]who drew the sword.
3 (Now the children of Benjamin
heard that the children of Israel had
gone up to Mizpah.) Then the children
of Israel said, "Tell *us,* how did this
wicked deed happen?"
4 So the Levite, the husband of the
woman who was murdered, answered
and said, "My concubine and [a]I went
into Gibeah, which belongs to Benjamin, to spend the night.
5 [a]"And the men of Gibeah rose
against me, and surrounded the house
at night because of me. They intended
to kill me, [b]but instead they ravished
my concubine so that she died.
6 "So [a]I took hold of my concubine,
cut her in pieces, and sent her throughout all the territory of the inheritance
of Israel, because they [b]committed
lewdness and outrage in Israel.
7 "Look! All of you *are* children of
Israel; [a]give your advice and *counsel
here and now!"
8 So all the people arose as one man,
saying, "None *of us* will go to his tent,
nor will any turn back to his house;
9 "but now this *is* the thing which we
will do to Gibeah: *We will go up*
[a]against it by lot.
10 "We will take ten men out of *every*

22 [a]Judg. 16:25; 19:6, 9 [b]Gen. 19:4, 5; Judg. 20:5; Hos. 9:9; 10:9 [c]Deut. 13:13; 1 Sam. 2:12; 1 Kin. 21:10; [2 Cor. 6:15] [d]Gen. 19:5; [Rom. 1:26, 27] [1]Lit. *sons of Belial* *See WW at Ex. 3:7.
23 [a]Gen. 19:6, 7 [b]Gen. 34:7; Deut. 22:21; Judg. 20:6, 10; 2 Sam. 13:12
24 [a]Gen. 19:8 [b]Gen. 34:2; Deut. 21:14 [1]Lit. *his*
25 [a]Gen. 4:1
28 [a]Judg. 20:5
29 [a]Judg. 20:6; 1 Sam. 11:7 [1]Lit. *with her bones*
30 [a]Judg. 20:7; Prov. 13:10

CHAPTER 20

1 [a]Josh. 22:12; Judg. 20:11; 21:5 [b]Judg. 18:29; 1 Sam. 3:20; 2 Sam. 3:10; 24:2 [c]Josh. 19:2 [d]Judg. 10:17; 1 Sam. 7:5 *See WW at Josh. 22:17.
2 [a]Judg. 8:10 *See WW at Lev. 16:17.
4 [a]Judg. 19:15
5 [a]Judg. 19:22 [b]Judg. 19:25, 26
6 [a]Judg. 19:29 [b]Josh. 7:15
7 [a]Judg. 19:30 *See WW at Zech. 6:13.
9 [a]Judg. 1:3

19:22 Perverted men: This expression, which literally means "sons of Belial," refers to morally corrupt men who did not conform to either human or divine laws. **Bring out the man:** The sadistic intentions (20:5) of these wicked men who sought to satisfy their homosexual desires reveal the decadence of this period. The men of Sodom made a similar request (Gen. 19:5). **That we may know him *carnally:*** The Hebrew word for "know" here denotes sexual relations.
19:24 My virgin daughter and *the man's* concubine: The atrocity of this story lies not only in the degenerate intentions of the men of Gibeah but also in the willingness of the old man and the Levite to subject the defenseless women to brutal abuse. **Humble them** is a euphemistic expression. The old man was actually commanding the men to ravish the women.
19:29 Divided her into twelve pieces: The Levite literally cut his concubine into twelve pieces, one piece for each tribe. Doing so, he sought to mobilize the tribes of Israel to assemble for a judicial hearing. The purpose of the hearing was to determine the disciplinary action they should take against the perverted men of Gibeah and the Benjamites who supported them.
20:1 All the Israelites **gathered together** except the Benjamites (v. 3) and the people from Jabesh Gilead (21:8, 9). **Dan to Beersheba** was a conventional expression referring to the northern (Dan) and southern (Beersheba) boundaries of Israel. **From the land of Gilead** refers to the territory inhabited by the Transjordanian tribes. **Mizpah** was a town in Judah, north of Jerusalem. It was not the Mizpah of Gilead (10:17; 11:29).
20:9 By lot: Casting lots was a common way of determining God's will.

hundred throughout all the tribes of Israel, a hundred out of *every* thousand, and a thousand out of *every* ten thousand, to make provisions for the people, that when they come to Gibeah in Benjamin, they may repay all the vileness that they have done in Israel."

11 So all the men of Israel were gathered against the city, *united together as one man.

12 [a]Then the tribes of Israel sent men through all the tribe of Benjamin, saying, "What *is* this wickedness that has occurred among you?

13 "Now therefore, deliver up the men, [a]the [1]perverted men who *are* in Gibeah, that we may put them to death and [b]remove the evil from Israel!" But the children of Benjamin would not listen to the voice of their brethren, the children of Israel.

14 Instead, the children of Benjamin gathered together from their cities to Gibeah, to go to battle against the children of Israel.

15 And from their cities at that time [a]the children of Benjamin numbered twenty-six thousand men who drew the sword, besides the inhabitants of Gibeah, who numbered seven hundred select men.

16 Among all this people *were* seven hundred select men *who were* [a]left-handed; every one could sling a stone at a hair's *breadth* and not miss.

17 Now besides Benjamin, the men of Israel numbered four hundred thousand men who drew the sword; all of these *were* men of war.

18 Then the children of Israel arose and [a]went up to [1]the house of God to [b]inquire of God. They said, "Which of us shall go up first to battle against the children of Benjamin?" The LORD said, [c]"Judah first!"

19 So the children of Israel rose in the morning and encamped against Gibeah.

20 And the men of Israel went out to battle against Benjamin, and the men of Israel put themselves in battle array to fight against them at Gibeah.

21 Then [a]the children of Benjamin came out of Gibeah, and on that day cut down to the ground twenty-two thousand men of the Israelites.

22 And the people, that is, the men of Israel, encouraged themselves and again formed the battle line at the place where they had put themselves in array on the first day.

23 [a]Then the children of Israel went up and wept before the LORD until evening, and asked counsel of the LORD, saying, "Shall I again draw near for battle against the children of my brother Benjamin?" And the LORD said, "Go up against him."

24 So the children of Israel approached the children of Benjamin on the second day.

25 And [a]Benjamin went out against them from Gibeah on the second day, and cut down to the ground eighteen thousand more of the children of Israel; all these drew the sword.

26 Then all the children of Israel, that is, all the people, [a]went up and came to [1]the house of God and wept. They sat there before the LORD and fasted that day until evening; and they offered burnt offerings and peace offerings before the LORD.

27 So the children of Israel inquired of the LORD ([a]the ark of the covenant of God *was* there in those days,

28 [a]and Phinehas the son of Eleazar, the son of Aaron, [b]stood before it in those days), saying, "Shall I yet again go out to battle against the children of my brother Benjamin, or shall I cease?" And the LORD said, "Go up, for tomorrow I will deliver them into your hand."

29 Then Israel [a]set men in ambush all around Gibeah.

30 And the children of Israel went up against the children of Benjamin on the third day, and put themselves in battle

11 *See WW at Ps. 119:63.
12 [a]Deut. 13:14; Josh. 22:13, 16
13 [a]Deut. 13:13; Judg. 19:22 [b]Deut. 17:12; 1 Cor. 5:13 [1]Lit. *sons of Belial*
15 [a]Num. 1:36, 37; 2:23; 26:41
16 [a]Judg. 3:15; 1 Chr. 12:2
18 [a]Judg. 20:23, 26 [b]Num. 27:21 [c]Judg. 1:1, 2 [1]Or *Bethel*
21 [a][Gen. 49:27]
23 [a]Judg. 20:26, 27
25 [a]Judg. 20:21
26 [a]Judg. 20:18, 23; 21:2 [1]Or *Bethel*
27 [a]Josh. 18:1; 1 Sam. 1:3; 3:3; 4:3, 4
28 [a]Num. 25:7, 13; Josh. 24:33 [b]Deut. 10:8; 18:5
29 [a]Josh. 8:4

20:11 United together as one man: Israel was finally gathering together as a unified body (see also v. 8). Unfortunately, it took an atrocious event to bring them together.

20:13 Deliver up the men: This request of the tribes of Israel was not unreasonable because they had to punish the men of Gibeah in order to purge the evil from their midst. The matter might have been settled if the Benjamites had complied with their request. Their refusal provoked a war, which almost annihilated their tribe.

20:16 Being **left-handed** made them exceptional swordsmen.

20:18 House of God: This expression probably refers to Bethel, the place of that name, where the ark of the covenant and the high priest Phinehas were located at this time (vv. 27, 28). **To inquire of God:** They probably inquired of the Lord through the high priest's Urim and Thummim (see Lev. 8:8; Num. 27:21). **Judah first:** See note on 1:2.

20:26 Burnt offerings: See note on Lev. 1:3, 4. **Peace offerings:** See note on Lev. 3:1.

20:28 Phinehas was the priest at the time of Joshua (Josh. 22:13). The fact that he was still serving as priest suggests that this incident is not chronologically recorded. It took place during the early period of the judges, soon after Joshua's death.

array against Gibeah as at the other
times.
31 So the children of Benjamin went
out against the people, *and* were drawn
away from the city. They began to
strike down *and* kill some of the people, as at the other times, in the highways [a](one of which goes up to Bethel
and the other to Gibeah) and in the
field, about thirty men of Israel.
32 And the children of Benjamin said,
"They *are* defeated before us, as at
first." But the children of Israel said,
"Let us flee and draw them away from
the city to the highways."
33 So all the men of Israel rose from
their place and put themselves in battle
array at Baal Tamar. Then Israel's men
in ambush burst forth from their position in the plain of Geba.
34 And ten thousand select men from
all Israel came against Gibeah, and the
battle was fierce. [a]But [1]*the Benjamites*
did not know that disaster *was* upon
them.
35 The LORD [1]defeated Benjamin before Israel. And the children of Israel
destroyed that day twenty-five thousand one hundred Benjamites; all these
drew the sword.
36 So the children of Benjamin saw
that they were defeated. [a]The men of
Israel had given ground to the Benjamites, because they relied on the men in
ambush whom they had set against
Gibeah.
37 [a]And the men in ambush quickly
rushed upon Gibeah; the men in ambush spread out and struck the whole
city with the edge of the sword.
38 Now the appointed signal between
the men of Israel and the men in ambush was that they would make a great
cloud of [a]smoke rise up from the city,
39 whereupon the men of Israel would
turn in battle. Now Benjamin had begun [1]to strike *and* kill about thirty of
the men of Israel. For they said,
"Surely they are defeated before us, as
in the first battle."
40 But when the cloud began to rise
from the city in a column of smoke,
the Benjamites [a]looked behind them,
and there was the whole city going up
in smoke to heaven.

31 [a]Judg. 21:19
34 [a]Josh. 8:14; Job 21:13; Is. 47:11 [1]Lit. *they*
35 [1]Lit. *struck*
36 [a]Josh. 8:15
37 [a]Josh. 8:19
38 [a]Josh. 8:20
39 [1]Lit. *to strike the slain ones*
40 [a]Josh. 8:20

41 And when the men of Israel turned
back, the men of Benjamin panicked,
for they saw that disaster had come
upon them.
42 Therefore they [1]turned *their backs*
before the men of Israel in the direction
of the wilderness; but the battle overtook them, and whoever *came* out of
the cities they destroyed in their midst.
43 They surrounded the Benjamites,
chased them, *and* easily trampled them
down as far as the front of Gibeah toward the east.
44 And eighteen thousand men of Benjamin fell; all these *were* men of valor.
45 Then [1]they turned and fled toward
the wilderness to the rock of [a]Rimmon;
and they cut down five thousand of
them on the highways. Then they pursued them relentlessly up to Gidom,
and killed two thousand of them.
46 So all who fell of Benjamin that day
were twenty-five thousand men who
drew the sword; all these *were* [1]men
of valor.
47 [a]But six hundred men turned and
fled toward the wilderness to the rock
of Rimmon, and they stayed at the rock
of Rimmon for four months.
48 And the men of Israel turned back
against the children of Benjamin, and
struck them down with the edge of the
sword—from *every* city, men and
beasts, all who were found. They also
set fire to all the cities they came to.

Wives Provided for the Benjamites

21 Now [a]the men of Israel had
*sworn an oath at Mizpah, say-
ing, "None of us shall give his daughter
to Benjamin as a wife."
2 Then the people came [a]to [1]the
house of God, and remained there before God till evening. They lifted up
their voices and wept bitterly,
3 and said, "O LORD God of Israel,
why has this come to pass in Israel,
that today there should be one tribe
missing in Israel?"
4 So it was, on the next morning, that
the people rose early and [a]built an altar there, and offered burnt offerings
and peace offerings.
5 The children of Israel said, "Who

42 [1]*fled*
45 [a]Josh. 15:32; 1 Chr. 6:77; Zech. 14:10 [1]LXX *the rest*
46 [1]*valiant warriors*
47 [a]Judg. 21:13

CHAPTER 21

1 [a]Judg. 20:1 *See WW at Gen. 26:3.
2 [a]Judg. 20:18, 26 [1]Or *Bethel*
4 [a]Deut. 12:5; 2 Sam. 24:25

20:33 Baal Tamar was an unknown site near Gibeah.
20:45 The rock of Rimmon was a refuge near Gibeah.
20:46 This is an approximate number; the more precise one is given in v. 35.
21:1–25 The Israelites removed the bloodguiltiness from their midst by punishing the men of Gibeah through the deaths of the Benjamites (20:13, 35). They grieved for Benjamin when they realized that the tribe of Benjamin was almost extinct. Only 600 males survived. The 11 tribes, therefore, cunningly devised two schemes by which they could acquire wives for these survivors without violating their vow not to give them their daughters. The Benjamites acquired 400 young virgins from Jabesh Gilead (vv. 7–14) and 200 daughters of Shiloh (vv. 16–23).
21:2 House of God: See note on 20:18.
21:4 Offerings: See note on Lev. 1:3.

is there among all the tribes of Israel who did not come up with the assembly to the LORD?" [a]For they had made a great oath concerning anyone who had not come up to the LORD at Mizpah, saying, "He shall surely be put to death."

6 And the children of Israel grieved for Benjamin their brother, and said, "One tribe is cut off from Israel today.

7 "What shall we do for wives for those who remain, seeing we have sworn by the LORD that we will not give them our daughters as wives?"

8 And they said, "What one *is there* from the tribes of Israel who did not come up to Mizpah to the LORD?" And, in fact, no one had come to the camp from [a]Jabesh Gilead to the assembly.

9 For when the people were counted, indeed, not one of the inhabitants of Jabesh Gilead *was* there.

10 So the congregation sent out there twelve thousand of their most valiant men, and commanded them, saying, [a]"Go and strike the inhabitants of Jabesh Gilead with the edge of the sword, including the women and children.

11 "And this *is* the thing that you shall do: [a]You shall utterly destroy every male, and every woman who has known a man intimately."

12 So they found among the inhabitants of Jabesh Gilead four hundred young virgins who had not known a man intimately; and they brought them to the camp at [a]Shiloh, which is in the land of Canaan.

13 Then the whole congregation sent *word* to the children of Benjamin [a]who *were* at the rock of Rimmon, and announced peace to them.

14 So Benjamin came back at that time, and they gave them the women whom they had saved alive of the women of Jabesh Gilead; and yet they had not found enough for them.

15 And the people [a]grieved for Benjamin, because the LORD had made a *void in the tribes of Israel.

16 Then the elders of the *congregation said, "What shall we do for wives for those who remain, since the women of Benjamin have been destroyed?"

17 And they said, "*There must be* an inheritance for the survivors of Benjamin, that a tribe may not be destroyed from Israel.

18 "However, we cannot give them wives from our daughters, [a]for the children of Israel have sworn an oath, saying, 'Cursed *be* the one who gives a wife to Benjamin.' "

19 Then they said, "In fact, *there is* a yearly [a]feast of the LORD in [b]Shiloh, which *is* north of Bethel, on the east side of the [c]highway that goes up from Bethel to Shechem, and south of Lebonah."

20 Therefore they instructed the children of Benjamin, saying, "Go, lie in wait in the vineyards,

21 "and watch; and just when the daughters of Shiloh come out [a]to perform their dances, then come out from the vineyards, and every man catch a wife for himself from the daughters of Shiloh; then go to the land of Benjamin.

22 "Then it shall be, when their fathers or their brothers come to us to complain, that we will say to them, 'Be kind to them for our sakes, because we did not take a wife for any of them in the war; for *it is* not *as though* you have given the *women* to them at this time, making yourselves *guilty of your oath.' "

23 And the children of Benjamin did so; they took enough wives for their number from those who danced, whom they caught. Then they went and returned to their inheritance, and they [a]rebuilt the cities and dwelt in them.

24 So the children of Israel departed from there at that time, every man to his tribe and *family; they went out from there, every man to his inheritance.

25 [a]In those days *there was* no king 4
in Israel; [b]everyone did *what was* right in his own eyes.

5 [a]Judg. 20:1–3 **8** [a]1 Sam. 11:1; 31:11 **10** [a]Num. 31:17; Judg. 5:23; 1 Sam. 11:7 **11** [a]Num. 31:17; Deut. 20:13, 14 **12** [a]Josh. 18:1; Judg. 18:31 **13** [a]Judg. 20:47 **15** [a]Judg. 21:6 *See WW at Ezek. 22:30. **16** *See WW at Josh. 22:17.

18 [a]Judg. 11:35; 21:1 **19** [a]Lev. 23:2 [b]Deut. 12:5; Josh. 18:1; Judg. 18:31; 1 Sam. 1:3 [c]Judg. 20:31 **21** [a]Ex. 15:20; Judg. 11:34; 1 Sam. 18:6 **22** *See WW at Lev. 4:13. **23** [a]Judg. 20:48 **24** *See WW at Gen. 12:3. **25** [a]Judg. 17:6; 18:1; 19:1 [b]Deut. 12:8; Judg. 17:6

21:8 Jabesh Gilead was located in the Transjordan about 9 miles southeast of Beth Shan.

21:13 Announced peace to them: This offer of peace represents a covenantal restoration between the rebellious Benjamites and the other tribes.

21:19 Feast of the LORD in Shiloh: This was a local harvest festival in Shiloh, which was north of Bethel. **Lebonah** was a site about 3 miles north of Shiloh.

21:21 Catch a wife: The people of Israel realized that although they had vowed not to give their daughters to the Benjamites, the Benjamites could seize wives for themselves and not cause the vow to be violated.

21:25 See section 4 of Truth-In-Action at the end of Judg.

21:25 The Book of Judges concludes with a restatement of the apostate condition of Israel when they had no king (17:6; 18:1; 19:1).

TRUTH-IN-ACTION through JUDGES

Letting the LIFE of the Holy Spirit Bring Faith's Works Alive in You!

Truth Judges Teaches	Text	**Action** Judges Invites
1 Guidelines for Growing in Godliness Judg. emphasizes the necessity of trusting God's presence and divine resources rather than our own. Even those talents and abilities we have from birth are corrupted by sin and must be energized by the Holy Spirit to bear fruit for God.	6:14, 16 10:13, 14	**Believe** that God strengthens those He calls and commissions. **Trust** in the promise of His abiding presence **Heed God's warning: Do not** continue to **rely** upon your fleshly wisdom and ability lest God limit you to those resources rather than releasing His wisdom and power through you.
2 Keys to Wise Living Wisdom is knowing how to apply what you know to be true. Therefore, wisdom demands that you ascertain the Lord's direction and leadings for your life. Also, Judg. warns against assuming that all leadings are true. Self-righteousness and religious sentiment can be a source of serious deception.	6:36–40 17:3	**Test** and **confirm** any sense of divine leading. **Refuse** to move impulsively. **Be certain** of God's direction; it results in greater confidence. **Know that** God rejects any idolatry, regardless how religious or sincere one's sentiment may be. **Be wary** of religious deception.
3 Steps to Dealing with Sin Sin presents a constant struggle with which we must deal or risk downfall. When we resist sin, we often feel the battle is over only to be tempted by the same sin again and again. Sin never goes away, and so we must constantly be on guard against it. However, even when we are overcome with sin, we have hope. God always gives another chance to turn from sin and back to Him.	2:2, 3 14:17 16:4–22 16:28	**Understand** that sins not dealt with radically and ruthlessly ultimately weaken and may cause downfall. **Persist** for victory in your struggle against sin. **Guard** against the seductions of the world and the flesh. **Understand** that compromise will eventually weaken and wear you out, giving the Evil One an occasion to overpower you. **Repent quickly** when overcome by sin. **Be confident** that God is faithful to honor all truly heartfelt repentance.
4 Lessons for Leaders Good leadership is a key to the triumph of God's purposes. Judg. underlines the need for godly leaders who speak with prophetic, anointed voices. When there is a lack of such leadership among God's people, the people lead unrestrained lives guided by their own opinions rather than God's Word and godly wisdom.	2:10–15 17:6; 18:1; 19:1; 21:25	**Know** that a lack of godly leadership will cause God's people to become worldly and incur God's judgment. **Strive** to become godly in your leadership. **Pursue** a prophetic dimension in your ministry.
5 Key Lessons in Faith Faith sees beyond trials and obstacles, knowing that God is sovereign over such and uses them to shape us and strengthen us for future battles. Faith also relies on an ever-present God to bring the necessary answer and supply the present need.	2:22; 3:2–4 4:9	**Accept** adversity and **welcome** opposition. **Believe** that God will use them to train you in obedience and strengthen you in spiritual warfare. **Avoid** relying upon men due to a lack of confidence in God's presence. Faith in God honors Him and results in your receiving what He intends for you.

Truth Judges Teaches	Text	**Action** Judges Invites
6 Steps in Developing Humility Judg. stresses that humility is acknowledging that any good or righteous acts we accomplish result from God's working through us. We often think of humility as a weak self-abasement when, in fact, it is a bold confidence in a faithful God.	7:1–8 8:27	**Understand** that God's spiritual victory does not depend upon natural strength or ability. **Rely totally** upon God's enablement and strength. **Refuse** to build any monuments to your successes or victories. **Know** that they will likely become an occasion of stumbling for yourself and others.

The Book of RUTH

Author: Unknown. Jewish Tradition Ascribes It to Samuel.
Date: Between 1050 B.C. and 500 B.C.
Theme: God's Sovereign Intervention Brings Universal Redemption
Key Words: Sovereignty, The Almighty, Redeemer

Author and Date Scholars differ regarding the date of the book's writing, but its historical setting is obvious. Ruth occurs during the period of the judges, as a part of those events that occur between the death of Joshua and the rise of Samuel's influence (probably between 1150 and 1100 B.C.).

Rabbinic tradition holds that Samuel wrote the book in the latter half of the eleventh century B.C. While more recent criticism suggests a much later postexilic date (about 500 B.C.), there is sufficient evidence in the language of the book, as well as its references to unique customs dating to the twelfth century B.C., to recommend acceptance of the earlier date. It is also reasonable to suppose that Samuel, who witnessed the decline of Saul's rule and was directed by God to anoint David as God's heir-apparent to the throne, could have penned this himself. The lovely story would already have attracted oral retelling among the people of Israel, and the concluding genealogy would have secured a link with the patriarchs—thus giving a ready answer to all in Israel who would desire their king's family background.

Purpose Almost every commentator observes the Book of Ruth as a study in the sovereignty of God, emphasizing the sustaining mercy of God, which brings a fruitful end to a story that begins with famine, death, and loss. Unfortunately, such observations are often made on the basis of the recurrent laments of Naomi as she proposes "the hand of the LORD" as having been against her (1:13, 20, 21). Twice, in her lamentations, Naomi uses the name "the Almighty" with reference to God, emphasizing His irresistible might and sovereign power against her. However, it is not necessary to presume that Naomi's viewpoint is meant to be understood as a spiritual revelation intended as doctrine. Rather, her words are perhaps best understood as the historical record of what she said in her bewilderment.

This adjustment in viewing her words seems pivotal to a sound understanding. It does not seem consistent with the revelation of the whole of the Scripture and its disclosure of the nature of God to presume that the disastrous things in this book were either intended or initiated by God. The famine (1:1) was the natural by-product of sin, a judgment imposed by the people upon themselves through their disobedience. The Lord had previously warned that the land itself would turn against them if they were unfaithful to Him (Deut. 28:15, 16, 23, 24, 38–40). Further, Elimelech's choice to move his family to the country of Moab (1:2) is not evidenced as being God's direction but simply his own decision. Why suggest that the events that follow (his and his sons' deaths) are something of God's direct providence? There is more reason to propose that these unfortunate happenings, while not outside God's omniscience, are not direct divine judgments, but rather the natural result of exposure to circumstances outside the canopy of divine promise. God's protective canopy is to those who remain obedient to Him in the land of His appointment.

Naomi, therefore, represents more of a folklore theology. Though obviously a sincere and believing woman, she nonetheless reveals vulnerability to the practice common throughout history—the blaming or assigning to God's will those things that steal away, kill and destroy His people and over which unaided mankind has no power. But the revelation of the *whole* of Scripture shows that such besetting events are not directly brought by God on people. Instead, these are either 1) the fruit of the general curse resulting from man's fall; 2) the product of the flesh when having given place to its own will, however innocent or malicious the intent; or 3) the direct and assailing efforts of our adversary, the Devil (John 10:10).

That Ruth is a book demonstrating the sovereignty of God is not minimized by these observations; rather, what is underscored is the objective of God's sovereign grace and power. His almightiness is not revealed as man's opponent but rather as man's deliverer. He overthrows the restrictive or damning difficulties or devices into which we fall as the result of our sin, the flesh, or the Devil.

Content Johann Wolfgang von Goethe, the German writer-poet, described Ruth as "the loveliest complete work on a small scale." This poignant, fascinating, emotionally gripping, and historically significant narrative might be called the Crown Jewel of the Old Testament. Herein is not only a literary masterpiece, but a record of the genealogy of David, the crowned king of Israel appointed by God to sire the line leading to the Messiah's royal and endless rule.

Christ Revealed Boaz presents one of the most dramatic figures found anywhere in the Old Testament to foreshadow the redeeming work of Jesus Christ. The role of the "kinsman-redeemer," so beautifully fulfilled in Boaz's actions bringing about Ruth's personal restoration, speaks eloquently in this regard. His actions accomplish her enfranchisement in the blessings of Israel and bring her into the family line of the Messiah (Eph. 2:19). Here is a magnificent silhouette of the Master, foreshadowing His redemptive grace centuries in advance. As our "Kinsman," He becomes flesh—comes as a man (John 1:14; Phil. 2:5–8). By His willingness to identify with the human family (as Boaz assumed the duties of his human family), Christ has worked a thorough-going redemption of our plight. Further, Ruth's inability to do anything to alter her estate typifies absolute human helplessness (Rom. 5:6); and Boaz's willingness to pay the complete price (4:9) foreshadows Christ's full payment for our salvation (1 Cor. 6:20; Gal. 3:13; 1 Pet. 1:18, 19).

The Holy Spirit at Work There is no direct reference to the Holy Spirit in this book. There is, however, an interesting analogy in Naomi's concern for and guidance of Ruth through the process of her establishing her relationship with Boaz. Although Naomi's perception of God's dealings in her own life was limited, she nonetheless typifies the Holy Spirit's work in our interests. Naomi is seen as a gracious and tender woman who navigates great difficulties with an abiding fidelity. Notably, at the juncture of Ruth's first encounter with Boaz, Naomi's guidance may be seen as a representative way in which the Holy Spirit prompts and directs 1) to bring people to Christ (John 16:8; Rom. 2:4) and 2) to lead them to the accomplished purpose of God for human blessing (John 16:13–15; Gal. 5:5, 16–18, 22–25).

Personal Application The messages of Ruth transcend the immediately obvious purpose of providing the Davidic genealogy. Ruth presents several grand themes, each of which merit exploration and elaboration. 1) The Book of Ruth introduces the *universal* scope of redemption's purposes. The inclusion of the Moabitess, Ruth, as a Gentile participant in Israel's kingly line, pictures God's love as it reaches out to all the nations of the world. He not only incorporates Gentiles in His salvation, but employs non-Jewish people as instruments in His redemptive program. Ruth's message dissolves tendencies toward exclusivism, whether potential in Israel at that time or realized in any group's traditions in our time. 2) The Book of Ruth ennobles the beauty of *commitment and friendship* and underscores the values of family commitment. Both values are obviously important and desirably reinforced in our time. Ruth's prioritizing her daughter-servant role to the aging Naomi, Naomi's preoccupation with Ruth's best interest, and Boaz's self-effacing will to see the endowment of a foreign maid with what will bring her a promising future, are all worthy of examination in this regard.

3) Ruth is a book of glorious *redemptive imagery*. The principle God proposed through the tradition of the levirate marriage (Deut. 25:5–10) dramatically reveals His will that human loss always be recoverable and that we work with Him in extending such possibilities to those in need. While technically speaking no levirate marriage occurs in the Book of Ruth, it is this principle from which Boaz's actions spring and by which the spirit of God's redemptive ways is illustrated.

Outline for Ruth

I. A Hebrew family in Moab **1:1–22**
- A. Naomi's heartbreak 1:1–5
- B. Ruth's devotion and vow 1:6–18
- C. Return to Bethlehem 1:19–22

II. A humble gleaner **2:1–23**
- A. Ruth in the field of Boaz 2:1–3
- B. Boaz's provision and protection 2:4–17
- C. God's favor recognized by Naomi 2:18–23

III. A planned marriage **3:1–18**
- A. Naomi's instruction 3:1–5
- B. Ruth's obedience 3:6–13
- C. Reward of obedience 3:14–18

IV. A kinsman-redeemer **4:1–22**
- A. Boaz, God's chosen redeemer 4:1–12
- B. The marriage of Boaz to Ruth 4:13
- C. God's blessing upon Naomi 4:14–17
- D. The genealogy of David 4:18–22

Elimelech's Family Goes to Moab

NOW it came to pass, in the days
when [a]the *judges [1]ruled, that
there was [b]a famine in the land. And
a certain man of [c]Bethlehem, Judah,
went to [2]dwell* in the country of
[d]Moab, he and his wife and his two
sons.

 **KINGDOM DYNAMICS**

1:1—4:22 Tenacity That Takes the Throne (Ruth), WOMEN. "Ruth" literally means "Friendship" or "Female Friend." Nowhere else in the Bible do we find a lovelier picture of a true and loyal friend. Ruth's primary virtue is tenacity to purpose: she was a woman who was steadfast. See her constant in her commitment to her mother-in-law (1:16, 17) and tireless as she gleans in the fields (2:7, 17). The result of this constancy is her marriage to Boaz and the birth of Obed, who became the father of Jesse, whose son was David the king (4:17). Moreover, since Jesus was born of the seed of David, we see how Ruth, the alien Moabitess, became part of the lineage of the Messiah (Luke 3:31, 32).

(Judg. 4:4, 5/2 Kin. 22:3–20) F.L.

2 The name of the man *was* Elimelech, the name of his wife *was* Naomi,
and the names of his two sons *were*
Mahlon and Chilion—[a]Ephrathites of
Bethlehem, Judah. And they went
[b]to the country of Moab and remained
there.
3 Then Elimelech, Naomi's husband,
died; and she was left, and her two
sons.
4 Now they took wives of the women
of Moab: the name of the one *was*
Orpah, and the name of the other
Ruth. And they [1]dwelt there about ten
years.
5 Then both Mahlon and Chilion also
died; so the woman survived her two
sons and her husband.

Naomi Returns with Ruth

6 Then she arose with her daughters-
in-law that she might return from the
country of Moab, for she had heard in
the country of Moab that the LORD had
[a]visited[1] His people by [b]giving them
bread.
7 Therefore she went out from the
place where she was, and her two
daughters-in-law with her; and they
went on the way to return to the land
of Judah.
8 And Naomi said to her two daughters-in-law, [a]"Go, return each to her

CHAPTER 1

1 [a]Judg. 2:16–18 [b]Gen. 12:10; 26:1; 2 Kin. 8:1 [c]Judg. 17:8; Mic. 5:2 [d]Gen. 19:37 [1]Lit. *judged* [2]As a resident alien *See WW at Judg. 2:18. • See WW at Jer. 42:17.
2 [a]Gen. 35:19; 1 Sam. 1:1; 1 Kin. 11:26 [b]Judg. 3:30
4 [1]*lived*
6 [a]Ex. 3:16; 4:31; Jer. 29:10; Zeph. 2:7; Luke 1:68 [b]Ps. 132:15; Matt. 6:11 [1]*attended to*
8 [a]Josh. 24:15

1:1 When the judges ruled: Accepting an early date for the Exodus, this is the period from 1350 B.C. to 1100 B.C., a time of spiritual confusion, compromise, and apostasy. Against this backdrop, the story of Ruth presents a study of people who remained constant in their faith. **Country of Moab:** Though Moab was not far east of Bethlehem, it had not been touched by the drought. The Hebrew behind **dwell** indicates a temporary stay. See marginal note.
1:2 Elimelech means "My God Is King"; **Naomi,** "Pleasant, Delightful, Lovely"; **Mahlon,** "Weak, Sickly"; **Chilion,** "Failing, Pining." **The country,** literally "fields," suggests the family may have been migrant workers.
1:4 Took wives: Though Deut. 23:3 directs that a child born of Moabite background was not to be admitted to the congregation of Israel until the tenth generation, marriage was not prohibited. Deut. 7:1–3 only prohibited intermarriage with the seven Canaanite nations. **Orpah** means "Fawn"; **Ruth,** "Friend."
1:5 On the deaths of Elimelech and his sons, see Introduction to Ruth: Purpose.
1:8 The LORD translates "Yahweh." Naomi uses this name for God, rather than "Elohim," which would be impersonal or "Chemosh," the god of the Moabites. This choice of terms is a significant indicator of the piety that characterized Naomi's life and thought. **Kindly** translates the Hebrew *hesed,* which carries the idea of love and loyalty—a covenant of constancy. Naomi knows Yahweh's character and prays her daughter-in-law will experience His goodness, noting that the God of Israel is not only kind, but dependable.

From Outsider to Royal Ancestress. Ruth's loyalty to Naomi and to God moved her to leave her homeland Moab for Judah. Though a foreigner, she became an ancestress of David and Christ.

mother's house. [b]The LORD deal kindly
with you, as you have dealt [c]with the
dead and with me.
9 "The LORD grant that you may find
[a]rest, each in the house of her husband." So she kissed them, and they
lifted up their voices and wept.
1 10 And they said to her, "Surely we
will return with you to your people."
11 But Naomi said, "Turn back, my
daughters; why will you go with me?
Are there still sons in my womb,
[a]that they may be your husbands?
12 "Turn back, my daughters, go—for
I am too old to have a husband. If I
should say I have *hope, *if* I should
have a husband tonight and should
also bear sons,
13 "would you wait for them till they
were grown? Would you restrain yourselves from having husbands? No, my
daughters; for it grieves me very much
for your sakes that [a]the hand of the
LORD has gone out against me!"
14 Then they lifted up their voices and
wept again; and Orpah kissed her
mother-in-law, but Ruth [a]clung to
her.
15 And she said, "Look, your sister-in-
law has gone back to [a]her people and
to her gods; [b]return after your sister-
in-law."
1 16 But Ruth said:

[a]"Entreat[1] me not to leave you,
Or to turn back from following
after you;
For wherever you go, I will go;
And wherever you lodge, I will
lodge;
[b]Your **people** *shall be* my people,
And your God, my God.

8 [b]2 Tim. 1:16–18 [c]Ruth 2:20
9 [a]Ruth 3:1
11 [a]Gen. 38:11; Deut. 25:5
12 *See WW at Hos. 2:15.
13 [a]Judg. 2:15; Job 19:21; Ps. 32:4; 38:2
14 [a][Prov. 17:17]
15 [a]Judg. 11:24 [b]Josh. 1:15
16 [a]2 Kin. 2:2, 4, 6 [b]Ruth 2:11, 12 [1]*Urge me not*
17 [a]1 Sam. 3:17; 2 Sam. 19:13; 2 Kin. 6:31
18 [a]Acts 21:14 [1]Lit. *made herself strong to go*
19 [a]Matt. 21:10 [b]Is. 23:7; Lam. 2:15
20 [1]Lit. *Pleasant* [2]Lit. *Bitter* *See WW at Ps. 91:1.
21 [a]Job 1:21 [1]Heb. *Shaddai*
22 [a]Ruth 2:23; 2 Sam. 21:9

WORD WEALTH

1:16 people, *'am* (*ahm*); Strong's #5971: The people. This word, occurring nearly 2,000 times in the OT, refers to a body of human beings unified as a nation. Frequently, Israel is called by God *'ami,* literally "My people," as in Ex. 9:13, or *ha-'am,* "the people," as in Ex. 1:20. *'Am,* people viewed from within the group, contrasts with *goi,* a nation viewed from outside the group.

17 Where you die, I will die,
And there will I be buried.
[a]The LORD do so to me, and more
also,
If *anything but* death parts you
and me."

18 [a]When she saw that she [1]was determined to go with her, she stopped
speaking to her.
19 Now the two of them went until
they came to Bethlehem. And it happened, when they had come to Bethlehem, that [a]all the city was excited because of them; and the women said,
[b]"*Is* this Naomi?"
20 But she said to them, "Do not call
me [1]Naomi; call me [2]Mara, for the *Almighty has dealt very bitterly with me.
21 "I went out full, [a]and the LORD has
brought me home again empty. Why
do you call me Naomi, since the LORD
has testified against me, and [1]the Almighty has afflicted me?"
22 So Naomi returned, and Ruth the
Moabitess her daughter-in-law with
her, who returned from the country of
Moab. Now they came to Bethlehem
[a]at the beginning of barley harvest.

1:9 Find is literally "Go find." Naomi both releases and urges her daughters-in-law to pursue their futures without obligation to past family ties. **Rest** means not only an absence of strife, war, or struggle, but contains the idea of God's blessing bringing personal security to the individual. **In the house of her husband:** Naomi's directive that they return can only be interpreted as considerate on her part. Inasmuch as they were foreigners, she knew neither girl was likely to remarry in Israel.
1:10 See section 1 of Truth-In-Action at the end of Ruth.
1:10 Surely carries the idea of "No!" In short, "We are coming with you!"
1:12, 13 Naomi is referring to the custom of the levirate marriage. See Deut. 25:5–10; Matt. 22:24.
1:13 The hand of the LORD . . . against me: Naomi's perspective is understandable, given the limited revelation of God's true nature at the time (1 Sam. 3:1). However, her reaction should not be construed as a commentary either on the nature of God or on the actual cause of her condition. See Introduction to Ruth: Purpose.
1:14 Ruth's commendable commitment is not intended to reflect negatively on Orpah's submissive response to Naomi's repeated demands.
1:16, 17 Ruth is insistent, **Entreat me not to leave you.** Her oft-quoted poem of commitment is not mere emotion. She clearly is reaching beyond friendship to faith. **The LORD do so** indicates Ruth understands the nature of Yahweh. She invokes His name with an oath. Her commitment is rooted in an understanding of the living God, of whom she has learned from Naomi.
1:16 See section 1 of Truth-In-Action at the end of Ruth.
1:18 Was determined connotes being steadfastly minded.
1:19 The nature of their reception suggests that Naomi was of an old or aristocratic family in the region.
1:20 Naomi contrasts the lovely meaning of her name (see note on v. 2) with the bitterness of her plight.
1:21, 22 Testified against . . . afflicted me: Naomi reflects human nature in general as she blames God, rather than personal choices and sin nature, for the destructive and painful things she is experiencing. Naomi's behavior is characteristic of a person outside the covenant; thus she inappropriately indicates her circumstance to be the result of God's punitive action. See Introduction to Ruth: Purpose. **The Almighty:** See note on Gen. 17:1.

Ruth Meets Boaz

2 There was a [a]relative of Naomi's
husband, a man of great wealth, of
the *family of [b]Elimelech. His name
was [c]Boaz.
[1] 2 So Ruth the Moabitess said to Naomi, "Please let me go to the [a]field, and
glean heads of grain after *him* in whose
sight I may find favor." And she said
to her, "Go, my daughter."
3 Then she left, and went and gleaned
in the field after the reapers. And she
happened to come to the part of the
field *belonging* to Boaz, who *was* of the
family of Elimelech.
4 Now behold, Boaz came from
[a]Bethlehem, and said to the reapers,
[b]"The LORD *be* with you!" And they
answered him, "The LORD *bless
you!"
5 Then Boaz said to his servant who
was in charge of the reapers, "Whose
young woman *is* this?"
6 So the servant who was in charge
of the reapers answered and said, "It
is the young Moabite woman [a]who
came back with Naomi from the country of Moab.
7 "And she said, 'Please let me glean
and gather after the reapers among the
sheaves.' So she came and has continued from morning until now, though
she rested a little in the house."
[2] 8 Then Boaz said to Ruth, "You will
listen, my daughter, will you not? Do
not go to glean in another field, nor
go from here, but stay close by my
young women.
9 "*Let* your eyes *be* on the field which
they reap, and go after them. Have I
not commanded the young men not to
touch you? And when you are thirsty,
go to the vessels and drink from what
the young men have drawn."
10 So she [a]fell on her face, bowed
down to the ground, and said to him,
"Why have I found [b]favor* in your
eyes, that you should take notice of me,
since I *am* a foreigner?"
11 And Boaz answered and said to her,
"It has been fully reported to me,
[a]all that you have done for your
mother-in-law since the death of your
husband, and *how* you have left
your father and your mother and the
land of your birth, and have come to
a people whom you did not know before.
12 [a]"The LORD repay your work, and
a full reward be given you by the LORD
God of Israel, [b]under whose wings you
have come for *refuge."
13 Then she said, [a]"Let me find favor
in your sight, my lord; for you have
comforted me, and have spoken
[1]kindly to your maidservant, [b]though
I am not like *one of your maidservants."
14 Now Boaz said to her at mealtime,
"Come here, and eat of the bread, and
dip your piece of bread in the vinegar."
So she sat beside the reapers, and he
passed parched *grain* to her; and she

CHAPTER 2

1 [a]Ruth 3:2, 12 [b]Ruth 1:2 [c]Ruth 4:21 *See WW at Gen. 12:3.
2 [a]Lev. 19:9, 10; 23:22; Deut. 24:19
4 [a]Ruth 1:1 [b]Ps. 129:7, 8; Luke 1:28; 2 Thess. 3:16 *See WW at Ps. 145:2.
6 [a]Ruth 1:22
10 [a]1 Sam. 25:23 [b]1 Sam. 1:18 *See WW at Zech. 12:10.
11 [a]Ruth 1:14–18
12 [a]1 Sam. 24:19; Ps. 58:11 [b]Ruth 1:16; Ps. 17:8; 36:7; 57:1; 61:4; 63:7; 91:4 *See WW at Zeph. 3:12.
13 [a]Gen. 33:15; 1 Sam. 1:18 [b]1 Sam. 25:41 [1]Lit. *to the heart of* *See WW at Deut. 6:4.

2:1 Boaz means "Swiftness." Naomi was related to Boaz through her husband, **Elimelech,** a fact essential for his later exercise of the "kinsman-redeemer" role. **Of great wealth** in Hebrew encompasses more than economic prosperity. It reflects the possessor's power and social standing in the community. It also indicates that Boaz was probably a warrior earlier in life.

2:2 See section 1 of Truth-In-Action at the end of Ruth.

2:2 Glean: The law required that farmers leave the corners of their plots to be harvested by the poor. See Lev. 19:9; 23:22; Deut. 24:19.

2:3 Happened: Here is the providence of divine sovereignty working in Ruth's behalf; what was apparent happenstance was, in fact, the appointed blessing of God's purpose being advanced in her life. **Part of the field:** The picture is not of a cluster of farms surrounding Bethlehem, but of a common field wherein each man tilled the territory bequeathed to him. Boundaries were marked by stones, and such landmarks were viewed as sacred. See Deut 19:14; Prov. 22:28; Hos. 5:10.

2:4 The LORD *be* with you: This exchange between **Boaz** and his **reapers** suggests that even in this time of apostasy (the years of the judges) there were yet people whose daily language gloried in the God of Israel.

2:5, 6 Boaz had heard of Ruth (2:11) but had never seen her. **The young Moabite,** a reference to Ruth's national background, occurs throughout the narrative (1:22; 2:2, 21; 4:5, 10). Clearly, the author wants to emphasize that God integrated this Gentile girl into the circle of His own people and eventually into the royal line.

2:7 The house probably refers to a shelter in the field for the workers' relief from weariness and heat.

2:8 See section 2 of Truth-In-Action at the end of Ruth.

2:8 You will listen: Boaz appeals to Ruth's understanding, as well as to her physical hearing of the words. He clearly wants her to sense his sincere concern for her well-being. **My daughter** indicates the difference in their ages, a fact to which Boaz will later refer (3:10).

2:9 Boaz offers a courtesy (**commanded the young men**), promising Ruth's immunity to insensitive or rude actions or remarks. This was a particularly welcomed grace given the characteristic provincialism of mankind, which so commonly begets mistreatment and unkindness toward foreigners.

2:10–14 Ruth and Boaz's conversation characterizes the writer's style. Over half of the 85 verses in this book are dialogue; the story is essentially related through conversations.

2:11, 12 Boaz's spiritual priorities are indicated in his respect for Ruth's motivation in coming to Israel, both her supportive kindness to Naomi and her trust in **the LORD God of Israel.**

2:13 Spoken kindly indicates Ruth's gratefulness for her discovery of kindness in the face of difficulty.

2:14 Boaz acknowledges Ruth **at mealtime** by inviting her to sit with his **reapers,** a privilege the average gleaner would not have enjoyed.

ate and [a]was satisfied, and kept some
back.
15 And when she rose up to [1]glean,
Boaz commanded his young men, saying, "Let her glean even among the
sheaves, and do not [2]reproach her.
16 "Also let *grain* from the bundles fall
purposely for her; leave *it* that she may
glean, and do not rebuke her."
17 So she gleaned in the field until evening, and beat out what she had
gleaned, and it was about an ephah of
[a]barley.
18 Then she took *it* up and went into
the city, and her mother-in-law saw
what she had gleaned. So she brought
out and gave to her [a]what she had kept
back after she had been satisfied.
19 And her mother-in-law said to her,
"Where have you gleaned *today? And
where did you work? Blessed be the
one who [a]took notice of you." So she
told her mother-in-law with whom she
had worked, and said, "The man's
name with whom I worked today *is*
Boaz."
20 Then Naomi said to her daughter-
in-law, [a]"Blessed *be* he of the LORD,
who [b]has not forsaken His kindness to
the living and the dead!" And Naomi
said to her, "This man *is* a relation of
ours, [c]one of [1]our close relatives."
21 Ruth the Moabitess said, "He also
said to me, 'You shall stay close by my
young men until they have finished all
my harvest.'"
22 And Naomi said to Ruth her
daughter-in-law, "*It is* *good, my
daughter, that you go out with his
young women, and that people do not
[1]meet* you in any other field."

14 [a]Ruth 2:18
15 [1]Gather after the reapers [2]*rebuke*
17 [a]Ruth 1:22
18 [a]Ruth 2:14
19 [a]Ruth 2:10; [Ps. 41:1] *See WW at Zeph. 1:7.
20 [a]Ruth 3:10; 2 Sam. 2:5 [b]Prov. 17:17 [c]Ruth 3:9; 4:4, 6 [1]*our redeemers*, Heb. *goalenu*
22 [1]*encounter* *See WW at Ezek. 34:14. • See WW at Jer. 27:18.

CHAPTER 3

1 [a]1 Cor. 7:36; 1 Tim. 5:8 [b]Ruth 1:9 [1]Lit. *rest* *See WW at Hos. 5:15.
2 [a]Ruth 2:3, 8
3 [a]2 Sam. 14:2
7 [a]Judg. 19:6, 9, 22; 2 Sam. 13:28; Esth. 1:10

23 So she stayed close by the young
women of Boaz, to glean until the end
of barley harvest and wheat harvest;
and she dwelt with her mother-in-law.

Ruth's Redemption Assured

3 Then Naomi her mother-in-law
said to her, "My daughter, [a]shall I
not *seek [b]security[1] for you, that it may
be well with you?
2 "Now Boaz, [a]whose young women
you were with, *is he* not our relative?
In fact, he is winnowing barley tonight
at the threshing floor.
3 "Therefore wash yourself and
[a]anoint yourself, put on your *best* garment and go down to the threshing
floor; *but* do not make yourself known
to the man until he has finished eating
and drinking.
4 "Then it shall be, when he lies
down, that you shall notice the place
where he lies; and you shall go in, uncover his feet, and lie down; and he
will tell you what you should do."
5 And she said to her, "All that you 3
say to me I will do."
6 So she went down to the threshing
floor and did according to all that her
mother-in-law instructed her.
7 And after Boaz had eaten and
drunk, and [a]his heart was cheerful, he
went to lie down at the end of the heap
of grain; and she came softly, uncovered his feet, and lay down.
8 Now it happened at midnight that
the man was startled, and turned himself; and there, a woman was lying at
his feet.
9 And he said, "Who *are* you?" So she

2:15–17 Boaz's directive to his **young men** allows Ruth to garner far more than she could have otherwise. An **ephah** was about 4 gallons, the fruit of Boaz's generosity and Ruth's diligence to her task.
2:20 Naomi instinctively praises **the LORD,** recognizing that He is responsible for opening a door that may lead to their redemption: **This man . . . close relatives. Kindness:** See note on 1:8.
2:22, 23 Naomi's counsel as an older, wiser woman, who is also familiar with the customs of her people, is sensitively responded to by **Ruth.**
3:1 Inherent in **security** (Hebrew *manoah*) is rest and protection in one's own home.
3:2 Relative is the word central to the narrative and message of this book. Our language has no equivalent as the concept is related to the cultural obligation of a family member whose kinfolk have suffered loss. It involved the capacity of one relative who may be qualified to "redeem" another relative from slave status or recoup property once owned but now lost by reason of indebtedness. The expression "kinsman-redeemer" is often used for "relative," seeking in English to convey the combination of a human relationship with a divinely appointed role of recoverer. See Lev. 25:25, 47–55.

Winnowing refers to the practice of extracting grain from its surrounding husk. After the outer husk was broken, having been tread upon by animals walking over the **threshing floor** where the grain was poured, the mix was scooped up on flat, traylike baskets. Then, it was cast into the air at a location where a constant breeze would catch the lightweight husk (chaff) and blow it away, leaving the grain to fall back upon the tray. It was then poured into the containers for storing.
3:3–5 Naomi's direction and Ruth's ensuing action may appear to be seductive and inconsistent with the spiritual nobility of the book. To the contrary, however, Boaz's words, "You *are* a virtuous woman" (v. 11), make clear that he believed her to be highly moral.
3:5, 6 Ruth was completely submissive and obedient to Naomi's directive. That same spirit is needed by all who desire to realize the fullest benefits of Christ's redemptive workings toward them.
3:5 See section 3 of Truth-In-Action at the end of Ruth.
3:7, 8 Uncovered his feet: The obvious purpose was that the chill of the night would naturally awaken him in time and occasion his discovering her at his feet. **Was startled** may be translated "shivered with cold."
3:9 Under your wing is literally "spread the corner of your

answered, "I *am* Ruth, your maidservant. [a]Take[1] your maidservant under your wing, for you are [b]a [2]close relative."

10 Then he said, [a]"Blessed *are* you of the LORD, my daughter! For you have shown more kindness at the end than [b]at the beginning, in that you did not go after young men, whether poor or rich.

11 "And now, my daughter, do not fear. I will do for you all that you request, for all the people of my town know that you *are* [a]a virtuous woman.

12 "Now it is true that I *am* a [a]close relative; however, [b]there is a relative closer than I.

13 "Stay this night, and in the morning it shall be *that* if he will [a]perform the duty of a close relative for you—good; let him do it. But if he does not want to perform the duty for you, then I will perform the duty for you, [b]*as* the LORD lives! Lie down until morning."

14 So she lay at his feet until morning, and she arose before one could recognize another. Then he said, [a]"Do not let it be known that the woman came to the threshing floor."

15 Also he said, "Bring the [1]shawl that *is* on you and hold it." And when she held it, he measured six *ephahs* of barley, and laid *it* on her. Then [2]she went into the city.

16 When she came to her mother-in-law, she said, [1]"*Is* that you, my daughter?" Then she told her all that the man had done for her.

17 And she said, "These six *ephahs* of barley he gave me; for he said to me, 'Do not go empty-handed to your mother-in-law.' "

9 [a]Ezek. 16:8 [b]Ruth 2:20; 3:12 [1]Or *Spread the corner of your garment over your maidservant* [2]*redeemer*, Heb. *goel*
10 [a]Ruth 2:20 [b]Ruth 1:8
11 [a]Prov. 12:4; 31:10–31
12 [a]Ruth 3:9 [b]Ruth 4:1
13 [a]Deut. 25:5–10 [b]Jer. 4:2; 12:16
14 [a][1 Cor. 10:32]
15 [1]*cloak* [2]Many Heb. mss., Syr., Vg. *she*; MT, LXX, Tg. *he*
16 [1]Or *How are you,*
18 [a][Ps. 37:3, 5]

CHAPTER 4

1 [a]Ruth 3:12 [1]Heb. *peloni almoni*, lit. *so and so*
2 [a]1 Kin. 21:8
3 [a]Lev. 25:25
4 [a]Jer. 32:7, 8 [b]Gen. 23:18 [c]Lev. 25:25 [1]Lit. *uncover your ear* [2]So with many Heb. mss., LXX, Syr., Tg., Vg.; MT *he*
5 [a]Matt. 22:24 [1]Lit. *raise up*
6 [a]Ruth 3:12, 13
7 [a]Deut. 25:7–10

18 Then she said, [a]"Sit still, my daughter, until you know how the matter will turn out; for the man will not rest until he has concluded the matter this day."

Boaz Redeems Ruth

4 Now Boaz went up to the gate and sat down there; and behold, [a]the close relative of whom Boaz had spoken came by. So Boaz said, "Come aside, [1]friend, sit down here." So he came aside and sat down.

2 And he took ten men of [a]the elders of the city, and said, "Sit down here." So they sat down.

3 Then he said to the close relative, "Naomi, who has come back from the country of Moab, sold the piece of land [a]which *belonged* to our brother Elimelech.

4 "And I thought to [1]inform you, saying, [a]'Buy *it* back [b]in the presence of the inhabitants and the elders of my people. If you will redeem *it*, redeem *it;* but if [2]you will not redeem *it, then* tell me, that I may know; [c]for *there is* no one but you to redeem *it*, and I *am* next after you.' " And he said, "I will redeem *it*."

5 Then Boaz said, "On the day you buy the field from the hand of Naomi, you must also buy *it* from Ruth the Moabitess, the wife of the dead, [a]to [1]perpetuate the name of the dead through his inheritance."

6 [a]And the close relative said, "I cannot redeem *it* for myself, lest I ruin my own inheritance. You redeem my right of redemption for yourself, for I cannot redeem *it*."

7 [a]Now this *was the custom* in former

garment over." This is the most tender point of the account, and the most liable to misconstruction. The culture of the ancient Middle Eastern world involved the practice of the casting of a garment over one being claimed for marriage (see Ezek. 16:8), a tradition to which **Ruth** clearly refers. It does not imply anything so inappropriate as a midnight tryst.

3:10 Boaz's words seem to suggest that **young men** were attracted to Ruth. They also suggest that due to his age he may have been shy in approaching her, which necessitated Ruth's approaching him.

3:13 As the LORD lives is an oath of commitment assuring her acceptance.

3:14 Do not let it be known: This precaution was to avoid the possibility of anyone's misunderstanding Ruth's actions that night, just as they could be misunderstood today.

3:15 The large measure (possibly 80 to 90 lbs., not unbearable for field-workers) was not only an expression of Boaz's will to provide abundantly for her future (v. 17) but it also provided an apparent reason for Ruth's presence. People would conclude she came to secure a supply of grain to carry home prior to the heat of the day.

4:1 Numerous OT texts show **the gate** of the city as a place where legal matters and issues of civil counsel took place. See 2 Sam. 15:2; 1 Kin. 22:10; Amos 5:10.

4:2 A community's **elders** were endowed with the authority to confirm legal transactions and to exercise the role of contemporary judges in civil affairs.

4:6 Ruin my own inheritance: Since the property would belong to any son born of Ruth, **the relative** refers to issues of commitment already within his own family. These would be confused by any obligations potentially altering procedures already in place. It is also possible that he simply could not afford the financial impact of securing the field and taking a bride at the same time. Also conceivable is the possibility that his response reflects racial prejudice, Ruth being a Moabitess.

4:7–10 The author explains the cultural custom, which, by the time of the book's likely inscription, was no longer practiced. However, the use of a shoe or foot is not uncommon to demonstrate possession or authority. See Gen. 13:14–17; Deut. 11:24; Josh. 1:3; Ps. 60:8. The surrender of the **sandal** symbolized the surrendering of all rights to what went with it, in this case both the property and Ruth's hand in marriage.

times in Israel concerning redeeming
and exchanging, to confirm anything:
one man took off his sandal and gave
it to the other, and this *was* a confirmation in Israel.
8 Therefore the close relative said to
Boaz, "Buy *it* for yourself." So he took
off his sandal.
9 And Boaz said to the elders and all
the people, "You *are* witnesses this
day that I have bought all that was
Elimelech's, and all that *was* Chilion's and Mahlon's, from the hand of
Naomi.
10 "Moreover, Ruth the Moabitess, the
widow of Mahlon, I have acquired as
my wife, to perpetuate the name of the
dead through his inheritance, [a]that the
name of the dead may not be cut off
from among his brethren and from
[1]his position at the gate. You *are* witnesses this day."
11 And all the people who *were* at the
gate, and the elders, said, "*We are* witnesses. [a]The LORD make the woman
who is coming to your house like Rachel and Leah, the two who [b]built* the
house of Israel; and may you prosper
in [c]Ephrathah and be famous in
[d]Bethlehem.
12 "May your house be like the house
of [a]Perez, [b]whom Tamar bore to Judah, because of [c]the offspring which
the LORD will give you from this young
woman."

Descendants of Boaz and Ruth

13 So Boaz [a]took Ruth and she became
his wife; and when he went in to her,
[b]the LORD gave her conception, and
she bore a son.
14 Then [a]the women said to Naomi,
"Blessed *be* the LORD, who has not left
you this day without a [1]close relative;
and may his name be famous in Israel!
15 "And may he be to you a **restorer**
of life and a [1]nourisher* of your old
age; for your daughter-in-law, who
loves you, who is [a]better to you than
seven sons, has borne him."

WORD WEALTH

4:15 restorer, *shub* (*shoov*); Strong's #7725: To turn back; turn, return, restore, bring back, retrieve, reverse. *Shub* appears more than 1,000 times in the OT. In the KJV, *shub* was translated in more than 60 different ways. Its usual sense is "return" (Ex. 4:19), that is, to go back to a point of departure. In a spiritual sense, it can mean to "turn away" from God (Num. 14:43), or to "repent," to turn away from one's sin and toward God (Hos. 3:5).

16 Then Naomi took the child and laid
him on her bosom, and became a nurse
to him.
17 [a]Also the neighbor women gave
him a name, saying, "There is a *son
born to Naomi." And they called his
name Obed. He *is* the father of Jesse,
the father of David.
18 [a]Now this *is* the genealogy of Perez:
[b]Perez begot Hezron;
19 Hezron begot Ram, and Ram begot
Amminadab;
20 Amminadab begot [a]Nahshon, and
Nahshon begot [b]Salmon;[1]
21 Salmon begot Boaz, and Boaz begot
Obed;
22 Obed begot Jesse, and Jesse begot
[a]David.

10 [a]Deut. 25:6 [1]Probably his civic office
11 [a]Ps. 127:3; 128:3 [b]Gen. 29:25–30; Deut. 25:9 [c]Gen. 35:16–18 [d]1 Sam. 16:4–13; Mic. 5:2; Matt. 2:1–8 *See WW at Zech. 1:16.
12 [a]1 Chr. 2:4; Matt. 1:3 [b]Gen. 38:6–29 [c]1 Sam. 2:20
13 [a]Ruth 3:11 [b]Gen. 29:31; 33:5; Matt. 1:5
14 [a]Luke 1:58; [Rom. 12:15] [1]*redeemer*, Heb. *goel*
15 [a]1 Sam. 1:8 [1]*sustainer* *See WW at Ps. 55:22.
17 [a]Luke 1:58 *See WW at Gen. 29:32.
18 [a]1 Chr. 2:4, 5; Matt. 1:1–7 [b]Num. 26:20, 21
20 [a]Num. 1:7 [b]Matt. 1:4 [1]Heb. *Salmah*
22 [a]1 Chr. 2:15; Matt. 1:6

4:11, 12 The witnesses to the transaction also offer their blessing. In effect they congratulate Boaz on his marriage proposal.
4:12 The reference to **Tamar** (Gen. 38:6–29) reminds us of yet another disadvantaged woman whose circumstance God's providence not only recovered, but who also became part of the Messiah's bloodline. See Matt. 1:3.
4:13 The LORD gave may be more than a pious reference to God as life-giver; it may hint that **Ruth** seemed to be barren during the time of her marriage to Mahlon (1:4, 5). **Went in to her** is the common OT term for sexual relations.
4:14–17 The author describes what was probably the day of the child's presentation (Lev. 12) and the song of blessing by the older women of the community who had known **Naomi** before her loss and widowhood. They now revel with her in the complete reversal of her state.
4:17 Obed means "Servant."
4:18–22 Since this genealogy covers a span in excess of 600 years, it is likely that some names are omitted, not an unusual practice in biblical tradition. See Matt. 1:1–17. That the book concludes with the genealogy rather than with a dramatic flair should not puzzle us. It lends strong support to the proposition that the primary purpose of the Book of Ruth is to provide a historical base for the family background of **David,** from whose line the Messiah-Redeemer would come.

TRUTH-IN-ACTION through RUTH

Letting the LIFE of the Holy Spirit Bring Faith's Works Alive in You!

Truth Ruth Teaches	Text	**Action** Ruth Invites
1 Keys to Godly Relationships Ruth is replete with principles of righteous and godly relationships. Ruth is a supreme example of someone who prioritizes personal relationships. She exemplifies loyalty, servanthood, diligence, and moral righteousness. Much grief can be avoided when we learn to relate to one another in love and understand what this really implies about our relationships.	1:10	**Do not** make commitments too hastily. **Wait** until you understand the full implications of any commitment you make to another.
	1:16	**Practice** loyalty, and **understand** that a loyal person prioritizes his relationships over personal advantage or comfort. **Do not back out** of a commitment you make to a friend, even if it means personal sacrifice.
	2:2	**Learn** servanthood. **Know** that God calls us to serve those we love. **Believe** that God will honor those with a servant's heart.
2 Guidelines for Growing in Godliness Hospitality means showing kindness and generosity to strangers. Most will treat friends well, but godly persons treat strangers as they would treat friends.	2:8	**Practice** hospitality to strangers. **Do not withhold** blessings from those unfamiliar to you. **Know** that God rewards and honors such unselfishness.
3 Keys to Relating to Authority Proper relationship to authority is characteristic of godly people. Faithful, loving obedience is a key characteristic of such a right response to authority.	3:5	**Obey** legitimate authority. **Believe** that God will bless such obedience in ways you cannot expect.

The First Book of SAMUEL

Author: Uncertain
Date: Between 931 and 722 B.C.
Theme: God Is Working in History
Key People: Samuel, Saul, David

Author The author of 1 Samuel is not named in this book, but it is likely that Samuel either wrote or supplied the information for 1:1—25:1, which covers his life and ministry until his death. The authorship of the rest of 1 Samuel cannot certainly be determined, but some suppose that Abiathar the priest wrote it.

Date Because of the references to the city of Ziklag, which "has belonged to the kings of Judah to this day" (27:6) and other references to Judah and Israel, we know that it was written after the division of the nation in 931 B.C. Also, since there is no mention of the fall of Samaria in 722 B.C., it should be dated before this event. The Book of 1 Samuel covers a period of about 140 years, beginning with the birth of Samuel at about 1150 B.C., and ending with the death of Saul at about 1010 B.C.

Content Israel had been governed by judges whom God raised up at crucial times in the nation's history; however, the nation had degenerated both morally and politically. It had been under the merciless onslaught of the Philistines. The temple at Shiloh had been desecrated and the priesthood is corrupt and immoral. Into this religious and political confusion steps Samuel, the miraculous son of Hannah. In a remarkable way the renewal and joy that his birth brought to his mother prefigures the same for the nation.

Samuel's own sons do not share his godly character. The people do not have confidence in his sons' abilities; as Samuel grows old, they press him to give them a king. Reluctantly, he does so. Saul, a handsome and charismatic man, is chosen to become Israel's first king. His ego is as large as his stature. He impatiently steps into the office of priest, rather than wait for Samuel. After rejecting God's commands, he is rejected by God. After this rejection Saul becomes a tragic figure, consumed with jealousy and fear, gradually losing his sanity. His final years are spent relentlessly chasing David through the wilderness backcountry of his kingdom in an effort to kill him. David, however, has found an ally in Saul's son, Jonathan, who warns David of his father's plots to kill him. Ultimately, when both Saul and Jonathan are killed in battle, the stage is set for David to become the second king of Israel.

Personal Application It is clear in 1 Samuel that God is at work in history. Even the most sinful and rebellious occurrences can be used by Him to continue His divine plan. The corruption of Eli's sons and his unwillingness to deal with them becomes the schooling environment for the child Samuel. The rejection of God and the demand for a king by Israel becomes the basis for the establishment of an earthly royal line that will bring forth the entrance of God into human history in the person of the Messiah. Finally, Saul, who had such a wonderful beginning, ends his life in tragedy and suicide. Yet, because of Saul's insanity, David is brought from the sheepfold into the courts of the king. Saul's senseless jealousy and enraged pursuit of David provide the backdrop against which the greatest king of Israel, the "man after God's own heart," comes to the throne.

But it is not only in the broad sweeps of history that God's hand is obvious. The following lessons are also evident in 1 Samuel. God steps into the pain and misery of Hannah to give her, not only a son, but three sons and two daughters (2:21). Though men look on the outward appearance, God looks on the heart (16:7). Obedience is better than sacrifice (15:22, 23), indicating that God is concerned about men's hearts as well as their actions. God does not spare even those in high position when they have sinned, but He is still a God of patience and forgiveness.

Christ Revealed The similarities between Jesus and the boy Samuel are striking. Both were children of promise. Both were dedicated to God before birth. Both were the bridges of transition from one stage of the nation's history to another. Samuel combined the offices of prophet and priest; Christ is Prophet, Priest, and King.

The tragic end of Saul illustrates the ultimate result of earthly kingdoms. The only hope is a kingdom of God on Earth, whose ruler is God Himself. In David, the earthly lineage of God's King begins. In Christ, God comes as King and will come again as King of Kings.

David, the simple shepherd boy, prefigures Christ the Good Shepherd. Jesus becomes the ultimate Shepherd-King.

The Holy Spirit at Work First Samuel contains remarkable instances of the coming of the Holy Spirit upon the prophets, as well as upon Saul and his servants. In 10:6 the Holy Spirit comes upon Saul, who prophesies and is "turned into another man," that is, equipped by the Spirit to fulfill God's calling.

After David is anointed by Samuel, "the Spirit of the LORD came upon David from that day forward" (16:13).

The phenomenon of the Spirit inspiring worship occurs in chapter 10 and 19:20. This was not the emotionalized raving of the pagans, but true, Spirit-inspired worship and praise to God, not unlike what happened on the Day of Pentecost (Acts 2).

Even in the several uses of the ephod and the Urim and Thummim we look forward to the time when the "Spirit of truth" will guide us into "all truth," tell us of "things to come," and "take of what is Mine [Jesus'] and declare *it* to you" (John 16:13, 14).

Outline of 1 Samuel

I. Renewal under Samuel 1:1—7:17
- A. Birth and childhood of Samuel 1:1—2:36
  1. Birth and dedication of Samuel 1:1—2:11
  2. Growth of Samuel and the corruption of Eli's sons 2:12–36
- B. Beginning of Samuel's prophetic ministry 3:1—4:1
  1. His call from God 3:1–9
  2. His word for Eli 3:10–18
  3. His ministry to all Israel 3:19—4:1

The Family of Elkanah

NOW there was a certain man of Ramathaim Zophim, of the [a]mountains of Ephraim, and his name *was* [b]Elkanah the son of Jeroham, the son of [1]Elihu, the son of [2]Tohu, the son of Zuph, [c]an Ephraimite.
2 And he had [a]two wives: the name of one *was* Hannah, and the name of the other Peninnah. Peninnah had children, but Hannah had no children.
3 This man went up from his city [a]yearly [b]to worship and sacrifice to the LORD of hosts in [c]Shiloh.* Also the two sons of Eli, Hophni and Phinehas, the priests of the LORD, *were* there.
4 And whenever the time came for Elkanah to make an [a]offering, he would give portions to Peninnah his wife and to all her sons and daughters.
5 But to Hannah he would give a double portion, for he loved Hannah, [a]although the LORD had closed her womb.
6 And her rival also [a]provoked her severely, to make her miserable, because the LORD had closed her womb.
7 So it was, year by year, when she went up to the *house of the LORD, that she provoked her; therefore she wept and did not eat. 8

Hannah's Vow

8 Then Elkanah her husband said to her, "Hannah, why do you weep? Why do you not eat? And why is your heart grieved? *Am* I not [a]better to you than ten sons?"
9 So Hannah arose after they had finished eating and drinking in Shiloh. Now Eli the priest was sitting on the seat by the doorpost of [a]the [1]tabernacle* of the LORD.

CHAPTER 1
1 [a]Josh. 17:17, 18; 24:33 [b]1 Chr. 6:27, 33–38 [c]Ruth 1:2 [1]*Eliel,* 1 Chr. 6:34 [2]*Toah,* 1 Chr. 6:34
2 [a]Deut. 21:15–17
3 [a]Luke 2:41 [b]Deut. 12:5–7; 16:16 [c]Josh. 18:1 *See WW at Gen. 49:10.
4 [a]Deut. 12:17, 18
5 [a]Gen. 16:1; 30:1, 2
6 [a]Job 24:21
7 *See WW at 2 Sam. 7:11.
8 [a]Ruth 4:15
9 [a]1 Sam. 3:3 [1]*palace* or *temple,* Heb. *heykal* *See WW at Hag. 2:15.

1:1 Ramathaim Zophim, usually referred to as Ramah, is 15 miles north of Jerusalem in the hill country. It was *Samuel's birthplace, residence, and burial site.* **Elkanah . . . an Ephraimite:** Levites were usually referred to by the tribal area in which they lived. Actual lineage goes back to Levi; thus Samuel came from the priestly line of the Levites. See 1 Chr. 6:33–38.
1:2 It was customary, though not sanctioned by God, for a man to take a second wife when his first wife was barren.
1:3 LORD of hosts (Hebrew *Yahweh Sabaoth,* "God of the universe and ruler of the armies of heaven") is a name for God first used here in the OT. It expresses the infinite resources and power with which God acts for His people. **Shiloh** is located about 15 miles north of Ramah. The sanctuary located there was more substantial than the tabernacle, having doors and a doorpost (1:9; 3:15) and was a place of pilgrimage.
1:4, 5 Though the Hebrew text here is difficult, the sense apparently is that Elkanah gave **to Hannah . . . a double portion,** treating her as if she had a son who would have received a portion.
1:6, 7 Her rival, Peninnah, **provoked** Hannah, not so much to make her angry as to cause inner turmoil and pain. **The LORD had closed her womb:** A woman in OT times who could bear no children was viewed as cursed by God. For Hannah this time of infertility would end when God gave her a child.
1:7 See section 8 of Truth-In-Action at the end of 1 Sam.
1:9 Tabernacle, "palace," is used of the tabernacle at Shiloh and of Solomon's temple in Jerusalem (1 Kin. 6) and denotes a dwelling place, not a place of visitation.

8 10 [a]And she *was* in bitterness of soul,
and prayed to the LORD and [1]wept in
anguish.
11 Then she [a]made a vow and said, "O
LORD of hosts, if You will indeed
[b]look on the affliction of Your maidservant and [c]remember me, and not
forget Your maidservant, but will give
Your maidservant a male child, then I
will give him to the LORD all the days
of his life, and [d]no razor shall come
upon his *head."
12 And it happened, as she continued
praying before the LORD, that Eli
watched her mouth.
13 Now Hannah spoke in her heart;
only her lips moved, but her voice was
not heard. Therefore Eli thought she
was drunk.
14 So Eli said to her, "How long will
you be drunk? Put your wine away
from you!"
15 But Hannah answered and said,
"No, my lord, I *am* a woman of sorrowful spirit. I have drunk neither wine nor
intoxicating drink, but have [a]poured
out my soul before the LORD.
16 "Do not consider your maidservant
a [a]wicked[1] woman, for out of the abundance of my complaint and grief I have
spoken until now."
17 Then Eli answered and said, [a]"Go
in *peace, and [b]the God of Israel grant
your petition which you have asked of
Him."
18 And she said, [a]"Let your maidservant find *favor in your sight." So the
woman [b]went her way and ate, and her
face was no longer *sad*.

Samuel Is Born and Dedicated

19 Then they rose early in the morning
and worshiped before the LORD, and returned and came to their house at Ramah. And Elkanah [a]knew Hannah his
wife, and the LORD [b]remembered her.
20 So it came to pass in the process
of time that Hannah conceived and
bore a *son, and called his name
[1]Samuel, *saying*, "Because I have
asked for him from the LORD."
21 Now the man Elkanah and all his
house [a]went up to offer to the LORD
the yearly sacrifice and his vow.
22 But Hannah did not go up, for she 1
said to her husband, "*Not* until the
child is weaned; then I will [a]take him,
that he may appear before the LORD
and [b]remain there [c]forever."
23 So [a]Elkanah her husband said to
her, "Do what seems best to you; wait
until you have weaned him. Only let
the LORD [1]establish [2]His word." Then
the woman stayed and nursed her son
until she had weaned him.
24 Now when she had weaned him,
she [a]took him up with her, with
[1]three bulls, one ephah of flour, and a
skin of wine, and brought him to
[b]the house of the LORD in Shiloh. And
the child *was* young.
25 Then they slaughtered a bull, and
[a]brought the child to Eli.
26 And she said, "O my lord! [a]As your
soul lives, my lord, I *am* the woman
who stood by you here, praying to the
LORD.
27 [a]"For this child I prayed, and the
LORD has granted me my petition
which I asked of Him.
28 "Therefore I also have lent him to 1
the LORD; as long as he lives he shall
be [1]lent to the LORD." So they [a]wor-
shiped the LORD there.

Hannah's Prayer

2 And Hannah [a]prayed and said:

[b]"My heart rejoices in the LORD;
[c]My [1]horn is *exalted in the LORD.

10 [a]Job 7:11 [1]Lit. *wept greatly* **11** [a]Num. 30:6–11 [b]Ps. 25:18 [c]Gen. 8:1 [d]Num. 6:5 *See WW at Gen. 3:15. **15** [a]Ps. 42:4; 62:8 **16** [a]Deut. 13:13 [1]Lit. *daughter of Belial* **17** [a]Mark 5:34 [b]Ps. 20:3–5 *See WW at Nah. 1:15. **18** [a]Ruth 2:13 [b]Rom. 15:13 *See WW at Zech. 12:10. **19** [a]Gen. 4:1 [b]Gen. 21:1; 30:22
20 [1]Lit. *Heard by God* *See WW at Gen. 29:32. **21** [a]1 Sam. 1:3 **22** [a]Luke 2:22 [b]1 Sam. 1:11, 28 [c]Ex. 21:6 **23** [a]Num. 30:7, 10, 11 [1]*confirm* [2]So with MT, Tg., Vg.; DSS, LXX, Syr. *your* **24** [a]Num. 15:9, 10 [b]Josh. 18:1 [1]DSS, LXX, Syr. *a three-year-old bull* **25** [a]Luke 2:22 **26** [a]2 Kin. 2:2, 4, 6; 4:30 **27** [a][Matt. 7:7] **28** [a]Gen. 24:26, 52 [1]*granted*

CHAPTER 2

1 [a]Phil. 4:6 [b]Luke 1:46–55 [c]Ps. 75:10; 89:17, 24; 92:10; 112:9 [1]Strength *See WW at Ps. 18:46.

1:10–16 See section 8 of Truth-In-Action at the end of 1 Sam.
1:11 No razor shall come upon his head is part of the Nazirite vow described in Num. 6:1–8. It was normally a vow to separate someone to God for a specified period of time during which the hair would remain uncut.
1:13 That Eli **thought she was drunk** (meaning he misread the pious movement of her lips) likely reveals the sorry state into which worship had degenerated under Eli and his wicked sons.
1:16 Wicked, literally "daughter of Belial" is the same description given in the next chapter about Eli's own sons (2:12). It carries the idea of being good-for-nothing.
1:19 The LORD remembered does not imply that He has forgotten, but rather that He is now going to bring His answer to Hannah's prayer and unfold His purposes.
1:21 Presumably, this is one year after Hannah's vow to God regarding her son.
1:22 See section 1 of Truth-In-Action at the end of 1 Sam.
1:22 Until the child is weaned could be until he was 2 or 3 years old.
1:24 Three bulls are brought for the three sacrificial offerings involved: the burnt offering, the purification offering which was to follow childbirth, and the peace offering. (See Lev. 12.) An **ephah** is about one-half bushel.
1:28 See section 1 of Truth-In-Action at the end of 1 Sam.
1:28 Lent does not mean to give temporarily, but to give unconditionally in dedication **to the LORD.**
2:1–10 This beautiful song of praise provides a model for Mary's song of thanksgiving in Luke 1:46–55.
2:1 Her whole personality is involved in praising the Lord: **heart,** the very center of being; **horn,** strength. **I smile** is literally, "My mouth is opened wide." In Ps. 35:21, 25, the figure is used for defeating enemies by swallowing them.

[2]I smile at my enemies,
Because I [d]rejoice in Your
salvation.

2 "No[a] one is holy like the LORD,
For *there is* [b]none besides You,
Nor *is there* any [c]rock like our
God.

3 "Talk no more so very proudly;
[a]Let no arrogance come from your
mouth,
For the LORD *is* the God of
[b]knowledge;
And by Him actions are weighed.

4 "The[a] bows of the mighty men *are*
broken,
And those who stumbled are
girded with *strength.
5 *Those who were* full have hired
themselves out for bread,
And the hungry have ceased *to
hunger*.
Even [a]the barren has borne
seven,
And [b]she who has many children
has become feeble.

6 "The[a] LORD kills and makes alive;
He brings down to the *grave and
brings up.
7 The LORD [a]makes poor and
makes rich;
[b]He brings low and lifts up.
8 [a]He raises the poor from the dust
And lifts the beggar from the ash
heap,
[b]To set *them* among princes
And make them inherit the throne
of glory.

[c]"For the pillars of the earth *are* the
LORD's,
And He has set the *world upon
them.
9 [a]He will guard the feet of His
saints,
But the [b]wicked shall be silent in
darkness.

"For by strength no man shall
prevail.

10 The adversaries of the LORD shall
be [a]broken in pieces;
[b]From heaven He will thunder
against them.
[c]The LORD will *judge the ends of
the earth.

[d]"He will give [e]strength to His king,
And [f]exalt the [1]horn of His
anointed."

11 Then Elkanah went to his house at
Ramah. But the child [1]ministered to the
LORD before Eli the priest.

The Wicked Sons of Eli

12 Now the sons of Eli *were* [a]corrupt;[1]
[b]they did not know the LORD.
13 And the priests' custom with the
people *was that* when any man offered
a sacrifice, the priest's servant would
come with a three-pronged *fleshhook
in his hand while the meat was boiling.
14 Then he would thrust *it* into the
pan, or kettle, or caldron, or pot; and
the priest would take for himself all
that the fleshhook brought up. So they
did in [a]Shiloh to all the Israelites who
came there.
15 Also, before they [a]burned the fat,
the priest's servant would come and
say to the man who sacrificed, "Give
meat for roasting to the priest, for he
will not take boiled meat from you, but
raw."
16 And *if* the man said to him, "They
should really burn the fat first; *then*
you may take *as much* as your heart
desires," he would then answer him,
"*No*, but you must give *it* now; and if
not, I will take *it* by force."
17 Therefore the sin of the young men
was very great [a]before the LORD, for
men [b]abhorred[1] the offering of the
LORD.

Samuel's Childhood Ministry

18 [a]But Samuel ministered before the
LORD, *even as* a child, [b]wearing a linen
ephod.
19 Moreover his mother used to make

1 [d]Ps. 9:14; 13:5; 35:9 [2]Lit. *My mouth is enlarged*
2 [a]Ex. 15:11 [b]Deut. 4:35 [c]Deut. 32:4, 30, 31
3 [a]Ps. 94:4 [b]1 Sam. 16:7
4 [a]Ps. 37:15; 46:9 *See WW at Zech. 4:6.
5 [a]Ps. 113:9 [b]Is. 54:1
6 [a]Deut. 32:39 *See WW at Hos. 13:14.
7 [a]Deut. 8:17, 18 [b]Ps. 75:7
8 [a]Luke 1:52 [b]Job 36:7 [c]Job 38:4–6 *See WW at Jer. 51:15.
9 [a][1 Pet. 1:5] [b][Rom. 3:19]
10 [a]Ps. 2:9 [b]Ps. 18:13, 14 [c]Ps. 96:13; 98:9 [d][Matt. 28:18] [e]Ps. 21:1, 7 [f]Ps. 89:24 [1]Strength *See WW at Deut. 32:36.
11 [1]*served*
12 [a]Deut. 13:13 [b]Judg. 2:10 [1]Lit. *sons of Belial*
13 *See WW at Job 19:26.
14 [a]1 Sam. 1:3
15 [a]Lev. 3:3–5, 16
17 [a]Gen. 6:11 [b][Mal. 2:7–9] [1]*despised*
18 [a]1 Sam. 2:11; 3:1 [b]Ex. 28:4

2:5 This is a reference to Hannah and her adversary, Peninnah. The Lord can take circumstances and turn them completely around, as He did for Hannah.
2:6–8 Hannah can rejoice because she is in the hands of a sovereign God who finally determines the status of one's life.
2:10 Here is the first mention of the Messiah (Hebrew for "Anointed One") in conjunction with the idea of a **king.**
2:11 Samuel learns the function of a priest under Eli, whom he serves personally.
2:12 They did not know the LORD means that they did not fear or obey Him.
2:13–16 Demanding the meat before it was offered as sacrifice was robbing God.
2:18 Linen ephod is not the elaborate ephod mentioned in connection with specific guidance from the Lord (v. 28; 14:3), but a simple apron or loincloth worn by those priests attending to the sacred duties.

him a little robe, and bring *it* to him year by year when she [a]came up with her husband to offer the yearly sacrifice.
20 And Eli [a]would bless Elkanah and his wife, and say, "The LORD give you descendants from this woman for the [1]loan that was [b]given to the LORD." Then they would go to their own home.
21 And the LORD [a]visited[1] Hannah, so that she conceived and bore three sons and two daughters. Meanwhile the child Samuel [b]grew before the LORD.

Prophecy Against Eli's Household

22 Now Eli was very old; and he heard everything his sons did to all Israel, [1]and how they lay with [a]the women who assembled at the door of the tabernacle of meeting.
23 So he said to them, "Why do you do such things? For I hear of your evil dealings from all the people.
24 "No, my sons! For *it is* not a good report that I hear. You make the LORD's people transgress.
25 "If one *man sins against another, [a]God[1] will judge him. But if a man [b]sins against the LORD, who will intercede for him?" Nevertheless they did not heed the voice of their father, [c]because the LORD desired to kill them.
26 And the child Samuel [a]grew in stature, and [b]in favor both with the LORD and men.
27 Then a [a]man of God came to Eli and said to him, "Thus says the LORD: [b]'Did I not clearly reveal Myself to the house of your father when they were in Egypt in Pharaoh's house?
28 'Did I not [a]choose him out of all the tribes of Israel *to be* My priest, to offer upon My altar, to burn incense, and to wear an *ephod before Me? And [b]did I not give to the house of your father all the offerings of the children of Israel made by fire?
29 'Why do you [a]kick at My sacrifice and My offering which I have commanded *in My* [b]dwelling place, and honor your sons more than [c]Me, to make yourselves fat with the best of all the offerings of Israel My people?'
30 "Therefore the LORD God of Israel says: [a]'I said indeed *that* your house and the house of your father would walk before Me forever.' But now the LORD says: [b]'Far be it from Me; for those who honor Me I will honor, and [c]those who despise Me shall be lightly esteemed.
31 'Behold, [a]the days are coming that I will cut off your [1]arm and the arm of your father's house, so that there will not be an old man in your house.
32 'And you will see an enemy *in My* dwelling place, *despite* all the good which God does for Israel. And there shall not be [a]an old man in your house forever.
33 'But any of your men *whom* I do not cut off from My altar shall consume your eyes and grieve your heart. And all the descendants of your house shall die in the flower of their age.
34 'Now this *shall be* [a]a *sign to you that will come upon your two sons, on Hophni and Phinehas: [b]in one day they shall die, both of them.
35 'Then [a]I will raise up for Myself a faithful priest *who* shall do according to what *is* in My heart and in My mind. [b]I will build him a sure house, and he shall walk before [c]My *anointed forever.
36 [a]'And it shall come to pass that everyone who is left in your house will come *and* bow down to him for a piece of silver and a morsel of bread, and say, "Please, [1]put me in one of the priestly positions, that I may eat a piece of bread." ' "

Samuel's First Prophecy

3 Now [a]the boy Samuel ministered to the LORD before Eli. And [b]the

19 [a]1 Sam. 1:3, 21
20 [a]Gen. 14:19 [b]1 Sam. 1:11, 27, 28 [1]*gift*
21 [a]Gen. 21:1 [b]1 Sam. 2:26; 3:19–21 [1]*attended to*
22 [a]Ex. 38:8 [1]So with MT, Tg., Vg.; DSS, LXX omit rest of verse
25 [a]Deut. 1:17; 25:1, 2 [b]Num. 15:30 [c]Josh. 11:20 [1]Tg. *the Judge* *See WW at Is. 32:2.
26 [a]1 Sam. 2:21 [b]Prov. 3:4
27 [a]1 Kin. 13:1 [b]Ex. 4:14–16; 12:1
28 [a]Ex. 28:1, 4 [b]Num. 5:9 *See WW at Ex. 35:27.
29 [a]Deut. 32:15 [b]Deut. 12:5 [c]Matt. 10:37
30 [a]Ex. 29:9 [b]Jer. 18:9, 10 [c]Mal. 2:9–12
31 [a]1 Kin. 2:27, 35 [1]*strength*
32 [a]Zech. 8:4
34 [a]1 Kin. 13:3 [b]1 Sam. 4:11, 17 *See WW at Ps. 86:17.
35 [a]1 Kin. 2:35 [b]1 Kin. 11:38 [c]Ps. 18:50 *See WW at Dan. 9:25.
36 [a]1 Kin. 2:27 [1]*assign*

CHAPTER 3

1 [a]1 Sam. 2:11, 18 [b]Ps. 74:9

2:21 God repeatedly **visited** Hannah with a miracle in that, without Him, she was still barren.

2:22 According to 4:15, Eli was 98 years old when the ark was captured by the Philistines. **Women who assembled** were those who served in many of the menial tasks at the entrance to the tabernacle.

2:25 The LORD desired to kill them, or "the LORD was resolved to kill them," because they have gone beyond the limit of God's tolerance. This is a severe example of God's justice being mediated in personal history, a preview to His ultimate and just judgment at the end of this age.

2:26 Note the contrast between the wickedness of Eli's sons and the righteousness of the priest God was raising up. **Grew in stature, and in favor both with the LORD and men** is the same statement made of the boy Jesus (Luke 2:52).

2:27 There is no clue as to who the **man of God** may have been. **House of your father** refers to Aaron and the priests from his household.

2:29 Kick at My sacrifice is to treat with contempt. Eli, as high priest and father, is responsible for the sins of his sons.

2:35 The priesthood passed completely from Eli's line when Solomon removed Abiathar, a descendant of Eli, and replaced him with Zadok (1 Kin. 2:27, 35). The prophecy is ultimately messianic, however, pointing to Jesus Christ who is the ultimate **faithful priest,** and **My anointed forever,** combining the offices of priest and king. See Ps. 110; Heb. 5:6; Rev. 19:16.

3:1 This is the fourth statement that contrasts Samuel with the wicked sons of Eli (see 2:11, 21, 26). The **word . . .**

word of the LORD was rare in those
days; *there was* no widespread revelation.
2 And it came to pass at that time,
while Eli *was* lying down in his
place, and when his eyes had begun
to grow [a]so dim that he could not
see,
3 and before [a]the lamp of God went
out in the [1]tabernacle of the LORD
where the ark of God *was*, and while
Samuel was lying down,
4 that the LORD called Samuel. And
he answered, "Here I am!"
5 So he ran to Eli and said, "Here I
am, for you called me." And he said,
"I did not call; lie down again." And
he went and lay down.
6 Then the LORD called yet again,
"Samuel!" So Samuel arose and went
to Eli, and said, "Here I am, for you
called me." He answered, "I did not
call, my son; lie down again."
7 (Now Samuel [a]did not yet know the
LORD, nor was the word of the LORD
yet revealed to him.)
8 And the LORD called Samuel again
the third time. So he arose and went
to Eli, and said, "Here I am, for you
did call me." Then Eli perceived that
the LORD had called the boy.
9 Therefore Eli said to Samuel, "Go,
lie down; and it shall be, if He calls
you, that you must say, [a]'Speak, LORD,
for Your servant hears.'" So Samuel
went and lay down in his place.
3 10 Now the LORD came and stood and
called as at other times, "Samuel! Samuel!" And Samuel answered, "Speak,
for Your servant hears."
11 Then the LORD said to Samuel: "Behold, I will do something in Israel
[a]at which both ears of everyone who
hears it will tingle.
12 "In that day I will perform against
Eli [a]all that I have spoken concerning
his house, from beginning to end.
7 13 [a]"For I have told him that I will
[b]judge his house forever for the iniquity which he knows, because [c]his
sons made themselves vile, and he
[d]did not [1]restrain them.
14 "And therefore I have sworn to the
house of Eli that the iniquity of Eli's
house [a]shall not be atoned for by sacrifice or offering forever."
15 So Samuel lay down until [1]morning,
and opened the doors of the house of
the LORD. And Samuel was afraid to
tell Eli the vision.
16 Then Eli called Samuel and said,
"Samuel, my son!" He answered,
"Here I am."
17 And he said, "What *is* the word that
the LORD spoke to you? Please do not
hide *it* from me. [a]God do so to you,
and more also, if you hide anything
from me of all the things that He said
to you."
18 Then Samuel told him everything,
and hid nothing from him. And he said,
[a]"It *is* the LORD. Let Him do what
seems good to Him."
19 So Samuel [a]grew, and [b]the LORD
was with him [c]and let none of his
words [1]fall to the ground.
20 And all Israel [a]from Dan to Beersheba knew that Samuel *had been*
[1]established as a **prophet** of the LORD.

2 [a]Gen. 27:1; 48:10; 1 Sam. 4:15
3 [a]Ex. 27:20, 21 [1]*palace or temple*
7 [a]1 Sam. 2:12; Acts 19:2; 1 Cor. 13:11
9 [a]1 Kin. 2:17
11 [a]2 Kin. 21:12; Jer. 19:3
12 [a]1 Sam. 2:27–36; Ezek. 12:25; Luke 21:33
13 [a]1 Sam. 2:29–31 [b]1 Sam. 2:22; Ezek. 7:3; 18:30 [c]1 Sam. 2:12, 17, 22 [d]1 Sam. 2:23, 25 [1]Lit. *rebuke*
14 [a]Num. 15:30, 31; Is. 22:14; Heb. 10:4, 26–31
15 [1]So with MT, Tg., Vg.; LXX adds *and he arose in the morning*
17 [a]Ruth 1:17
18 [a]Gen. 24:50; Ex. 34:5–7; Lev. 10:3; Is. 39:8; Acts 5:39
19 [a]1 Sam. 2:21 [b]Gen. 21:22; 28:15; 39:2, 21, 23 [c]1 Sam. 9:6 [1]*fail*
20 [a]Judg. 20:1 [1]*confirmed*

WORD WEALTH

3:20 prophet, *nabi'* (nah-*vee*); Strong's #5030: Prophet; one who proclaims or tells a message he has received; a spokesman, herald, announcer. A prophet is someone who announces a message at the direction of another (usually the Lord God). *Nabi'* occurs more than 300 times in the OT. Six times the word is in the feminine form, *nebiyah*, and is translated "prophetess"; these six references are to Miriam, Deborah, Huldah (twice), Noadiah, and Isaiah's wife (doubtless a prophetess in her own capacity). In all other references, *nabi'* is masculine, "prophet." The word can refer to false prophets and to prophets of false gods, but nearly always refers to Yahweh's commissioned spokesmen.

was rare because sin blocked the revelation of God at the spiritual center of the nation.
3:3 The lamp of God refers to the golden candlestick, whose seven lamps were trimmed each evening and burned until the oil was exhausted in the morning. **Before the lamp . . . went out** indicates the time to be very early in the morning hours.
3:7 Samuel did not yet know the LORD in a personal or direct way.
3:10 See section 3 of Truth-In-Action at the end of 1 Sam.
3:10 It is important for Samuel to know, at his inauguration into the prophetic office, that the Lord has spoken and that the Lord knows him by name. **Your servant hears:** Samuel has learned servanthood and submission well. As he has been immediately available to Eli, he is now immediately available to the Lord. He is beginning to know the Lord (v. 7).
3:11 Ears . . . tingle is a figure of speech used to indicate the horror that is to occur to Eli and his sons.
3:13, 14 The sacrifices and offerings designed for forgiveness cannot atone for their sin because they have been corrupted and disdained by Eli and his sons.
3:13 See section 7 of Truth-In-Action at the end of 1 Sam.
3:19 His **words** do not **fall to the ground** because God fulfills the words that Samuel speaks in prophecy.
3:20 Samuel serves as priest, prophet, and judge. He is the last judge of Israel and provides the transition from rule by judges to rule by kings.

21 Then the LORD appeared again in
Shiloh. For the LORD *revealed Himself
to Samuel in Shiloh by [a]the word of
the LORD.
4 And the word of Samuel came to
all [1]Israel.

The Ark of God Captured

Now Israel went out to battle
against the Philistines, and encamped
beside [a]Ebenezer; and the Philistines
encamped in Aphek.
2 Then the [a]Philistines put themselves in battle array against Israel.
And when they joined battle, Israel
was [1]defeated by the Philistines, who
killed about four thousand men of the
army in the field.
3 And when the people had come into
the camp, the elders of Israel said,
"Why has the LORD defeated us today
before the Philistines? [a]Let us bring the
ark of the covenant of the LORD from
*Shiloh to us, that when it comes
among us it may save us from the hand
of our enemies."
4 So the people sent to Shiloh, that
they might bring from there the ark of
the covenant of the LORD of hosts,
[a]who dwells *between* [b]the cherubim.
And the [c]two sons of Eli, Hophni and
Phinehas, *were* there with the ark of
the covenant of *God.
5 And when the ark of the covenant
of the LORD came into the camp, all Israel *shouted so loudly that the earth
shook.
6 Now when the Philistines heard the
noise of the shout, they said, "What
does the sound of this great shout in
the camp of the Hebrews *mean?*" Then
they understood that the ark of the
LORD had come into the camp.
7 So the Philistines were afraid, for
they said, "God has come into the
camp!" And they said, [a]"Woe to us!
For such a thing has never happened
before.
8 "Woe to us! Who will deliver us
from the hand of these mighty gods?
These *are* the gods who struck the
Egyptians with all the plagues in the
wilderness.
9 [a]"Be* strong and conduct yourselves like men, you Philistines, that
you do not become servants of the Hebrews, [b]as they have been to you.
[1]Conduct yourselves like men, and
fight!"
10 So the Philistines fought, and
[a]Israel was [1]defeated, and every man
fled to his tent. There was a very great
slaughter, and there fell of Israel thirty
thousand foot soldiers.
11 Also [a]the ark of God was captured;
and [b]the two sons of Eli, Hophni and
Phinehas, died.

Death of Eli

12 Then a man of Benjamin ran from
the battle line the same day, and
[a]came to Shiloh with his clothes torn
and [b]dirt on his head.
13 Now when he came, there was Eli,
sitting on [a]a seat [1]by the wayside
*watching, for his heart [2]trembled for
the ark of God. And when the man
came into the city and told *it,* all the
city cried out.
14 When Eli heard the noise of the outcry, he said, "What *does* the sound of
this tumult *mean?*" And the man came
quickly and told Eli.
15 Eli was ninety-eight years old, and
[a]his eyes were so [1]dim that he could
not see.
16 Then the man said to Eli, "I *am* he
who came from the battle. And I fled
today from the battle line." And he
said, [a]"What happened, my son?"
17 So the messenger answered and
said, "Israel has fled before the Philistines, and there has been a great
slaughter among the people. Also your
two sons, Hophni and Phinehas, are
dead; and the ark of God has been captured."
18 Then it happened, when he made

21 [a]1 Sam.3:1, 4 *See WW at Amos 3:7.

CHAPTER 4

1 [a]1 Sam. 7:12 [1]So with MT, Tg.; LXX, Vg. add *And it came to pass in those days that the Philistines gathered themselves together to fight;* LXX adds further *against Israel*
2 [a]1 Sam. 12:9 [1]Lit. *struck*
3 [a]Josh. 6:6–21 *See WW at Gen. 49:10.
4 [a]1 Sam. 6:2 [b]Num. 7:89 [c]1 Sam. 2:12 *See WW at 2 Kin. 19:15.
5 *See WW at Ezra 3:11.
7 [a]Ex. 15:14
9 [a]1 Cor. 16:13 [b]Judg. 13:1 [1]Lit. *Be men* *See WW at Josh. 1:9.
10 [a]Deut. 28:15, 25 [1]Lit. *struck down*
11 [a]Ps. 78:60, 61 [b]1 Sam. 2:34
12 [a]2 Sam. 1:2 [b]Josh. 7:6
13 [a]1 Sam. 1:9; 4:18 [1]So with MT, Vg.; LXX *beside the gate watching the road* [2]*trembled with anxiety* *See WW at Hos. 9:8.
15 [a]1 Sam. 3:2 [1]*fixed*
16 [a]2 Sam. 1:4

3:21—4:1 We have moved from the word of God being "rare" (3:1) to a restoration of the Lord's word and His presence.
4:1 The Philistines, a non-Semitic people who migrated from Crete first in Abraham's time (2000 B.C.) and again in 1200 B.C., lived in five cities located in the southwestern part of Canaan: Gaza, Ashkelon, Ekron, Gath, and Ashdod. **Aphek** was in the foothills about 20 miles west of Shiloh.
4:3 Why has the LORD defeated us?: They blame the Lord for a defeat brought on by their own sin and ignorance.
4:4 The ark of the covenant was a chest, which contained the tablets of the Law of God, the basis of Israel's covenant relationship with God. The elders want the ark as a reminder of God's presence among them and to inspire courage in battle. **The cherubim** were two figures molded from pure gold, situated on each end of the ark.
4:8 These mighty gods: Though incorrect in their understanding of Yahweh, the Philistines' remark shows a greater respect and fear of the God of Israel than Israel has.
4:18 Excavations from this time have uncovered large stone benches without backs, which were often beside the city gates.

mention of the ark of God, that Eli fell
off the seat backward by the side of
the gate; and his neck was broken and
he died, for the man was old and
heavy. And he had judged Israel forty
years.

Ichabod

19 Now his daughter-in-law, Phinehas'
wife, was with child, *due* to be delivered; and when she heard the news
that the ark of God was captured, and
that her father-in-law and her husband
were dead, she bowed herself and gave
birth, for her labor pains came upon
her.
20 And about the time of her death
[a]the women who stood by her said to
her, "Do not fear, for you have borne
a son." But she did not answer, nor did
she [1]regard *it.*
21 Then she named the child [a]Icha-
bod,[1] saying, [b]"The *glory has departed from Israel!" because the ark
of God had been captured and because
of her father-in-law and her husband.
22 And she said, "The glory has departed from Israel, for the ark of God
has been captured."

The Philistines and the Ark

5 Then the Philistines took the ark
of God and brought it [a]from Ebenezer to Ashdod.
2 When the Philistines took the ark
of God, they brought it into the house
of [a]Dagon[1] and set it by Dagon.
3 And when the people of Ashdod
arose early in the morning, there was
Dagon, [a]fallen on its face to the earth
before the ark of the LORD. So they
took Dagon and [b]set it in its place
again.
4 And when they arose early the next
morning, there was Dagon, fallen on
its face to the ground before the ark
of the LORD. [a]The head of Dagon and
both the palms of its hands *were* broken off on the threshold; only [1]Dagon's
torso was left of it.
5 Therefore neither the priests of Dagon nor any who come into Dagon's
house [a]tread on the threshold of Dagon
in Ashdod to this day.
6 But the [a]hand of the LORD was
heavy on the people of Ashdod, and
He [b]ravaged them and struck them
with [c]tumors,[1] *both* Ashdod and its
[d]territory.
7 And when the men of Ashdod saw
how *it was,* they said, "The ark of the
[a]God of Israel must not remain with
us, for His hand is harsh toward us and
Dagon our god."
8 Therefore they sent and gathered to
themselves all the [a]lords of the Philistines, and said, "What shall we do with
the ark of the God of Israel?" And they
answered, "Let the ark of the God of
Israel be carried away to [b]Gath." So
they carried the ark of the God of Israel
away.
9 So it was, after they had carried it
away, that [a]the hand of the LORD was
against the city with a very great destruction; and He struck the men of the
city, both small and great, [1]and tumors
broke out on them.
10 Therefore they sent the ark of God
to Ekron. So it was, as the ark of God
came to Ekron, that the Ekronites cried
out, saying, "They have brought the
ark of the God of Israel to us, to kill
us and our people!"
11 So they sent and gathered together
all the lords of the Philistines, and said,
"Send away the ark of the God of Israel, and let it go back to its own place,
so that it does not kill us and our people." For there was a deadly destruction throughout all the city; the hand
of God was very heavy there.
12 And the men who did not die were
stricken with the tumors, and the
[a]cry of the city went up to heaven.

The Ark Returned to Israel

6 Now the ark of the LORD was in
the country of the Philistines seven
months.
2 And the Philistines [a]called for the

20 [a]Gen. 35:16–19 [1]*pay any attention to*
21 [a]1 Sam. 14:3 [b]Ps. 26:8; 78:61; [Jer. 2:11] [1]Lit. *Inglorious* *See WW at Is. 60:1.

CHAPTER 5

1 [a]1 Sam. 4:1; 7:12
2 [a]Judg. 16:23–30; 1 Chr. 10:8–10 [1]A Philistine idol
3 [a]Is. 19:1; 46:1, 2 [b]Is. 46:7
4 [a]Jer. 50:2; Ezek. 6:4, 6; Mic. 1:7 [1]So with LXX, Syr., Tg., Vg.; MT *Dagon*
5 [a]Zeph. 1:9
6 [a]Ex. 9:3; Deut. 2:15; 1 Sam. 5:7; 7:13; Ps. 32:4; 145:20; 147:6 [b]1 Sam. 6:5 [c]Deut. 28:27; Ps. 78:66 [d]Josh. 15:46, 47 [1]Probably bubonic plague. LXX, Vg. add *And in the midst of their land rats sprang up, and there was a great death panic in the city.*
7 [a]1 Sam. 6:5
8 [a]1 Sam. 6:4 [b]Josh. 11:22
9 [a]Deut. 2:15; 1 Sam. 5:11; 7:13; 12:15 [1]Vg. *and they had tumors in their secret parts*
12 [a]1 Sam. 9:16; Jer. 14:2

CHAPTER 6

2 [a]Gen. 41:8; Ex. 7:11; Is. 2:6; 47:13; Dan. 2:2; 5:7

4:22 Shiloh was never again the center of the nation's worship.
5:1 **Ashdod** is about 50 miles southwest of Shiloh.
5:2 **Dagon** was the primary god of the Philistine people, with the torso, arms, and head of a man and the lower body of a fish. He was worshiped as the father of Baal. See notes on 7:4; 12:10.
5:3 **Fallen on its face:** He fell prostrate on the ground as though worshiping before the ark.
5:4 **Broken off** is actually "cut off," indicating the idol had not simply fallen and broken but had been dismembered.
5:5 So profound was this catastrophe in the eyes of these Philistines that they would not even step on the **threshold** where the limbs and head of their god had lain in utter defeat.
5:6 God **struck them with tumors** may indicate swollen lymph glands, symptoms accompanying some form of the bubonic plague carried by rats.
5:8 **The lords of the Philistines** were the leaders of their city-states. **Gath** is 12 miles east of Ashdod.
5:12 **Cry of the city:** No prayer is addressed to the deposed Dagon, but heaven (Yahweh) is implored for help.

priests and the diviners, saying, "What
shall we do with the ark of the LORD?
Tell us how we should send it to its
place."
3 So they said, "If you send away the
ark of the God of Israel, do not send
it [a]empty; but by all means return *it*
to Him *with* [b]a trespass offering. Then
you will be healed, and it will be
known to you why His hand is not removed from you."
4 Then they said, "What *is* the trespass offering which we shall return to
Him?" They answered, [a]"Five golden
tumors and five golden rats, *according*
to the number of the lords of the Philistines. For the same plague *was* on all
of [1]you and on your lords.
5 "Therefore you shall make images
of your tumors and images of your rats
that [a]ravage the land, and you shall
[b]give glory to the God of Israel; perhaps He will [c]lighten[1] His hand from
you, from [d]your gods, and from your
land.
6 "Why then do you harden your
hearts [a]as the Egyptians and Pharaoh
hardened their hearts? When He did
mighty things among them, [b]did they
not let the people go, that they might
depart?
7 "Now therefore, make [a]a new cart,
take two milk cows [b]which have never
been yoked, and hitch the cows to the
cart; and take their calves home, away
from them.
8 "Then take the ark of the LORD and
set it on the cart; and put [a]the articles
of gold which you are returning to
Him *as* a trespass offering in a chest
by its side. Then send it away, and let
it go.
9 "And watch: if it goes up the road
to its own territory, to [a]Beth Shemesh,
then He has done [1]us this great evil.
But if not, then [b]we shall know that *it*
is not His hand *that* struck us—it happened to us by chance."
10 Then the men did so; they took two
milk cows and hitched them to the cart,
and shut up their calves at home.
11 And they set the ark of the LORD
on the cart, and the chest with the gold
rats and the images of their tumors.
12 Then the cows headed *straight for
the road to Beth Shemesh, *and* went
along the [a]highway, lowing as they
went, and did not turn aside to the right
hand or the left. And the lords of the
Philistines went after them to the border of Beth Shemesh.
13 Now *the people of* Beth Shemesh
were reaping their [a]wheat harvest in
the valley; and they lifted their eyes
and saw the ark, and rejoiced to see
it.
14 Then the cart came into the field of
Joshua of Beth Shemesh, and stood
there; a large stone *was* there. So they
split the wood of the cart and offered
the cows as a burnt offering to the
LORD.
15 The Levites took down the ark of
the LORD and the chest that *was* with
it, in which *were* the articles of gold,
and put *them* on the large stone. Then
the men of Beth Shemesh offered burnt
offerings and made *sacrifices the
same day to the LORD.
16 So when [a]the five lords of the Philistines had seen *it*, they returned to Ekron the same day.
17 [a]These *are* the golden tumors which
the Philistines returned *as* a trespass
offering to the LORD: one for Ashdod,
one for Gaza, one for Ashkelon, one
for [b]Gath, one for Ekron;
18 and the golden rats, *according to*
the number of all the cities of the Philistines *belonging* to the five lords, *both*
fortified cities and country villages,
even as far as the large *stone of* Abel
on which they set the ark of the LORD,
which stone remains to this day in the
field of Joshua of Beth Shemesh.
19 Then [a]He struck the men of Beth
Shemesh, because they had looked
into the ark of the LORD. [1]He [b]struck
fifty thousand and seventy men of the
people, and the people lamented because the LORD had struck the people
with a great slaughter.

3 [a]Ex. 23:15; Deut. 16:16 [b]Lev. 5:15, 16
4 [a]1 Sam. 5:6, 9, 12; 6:17 [1]Lit. *them*
5 [a]1 Sam. 5:6 [b]Josh. 7:19; 1 Chr. 16:28, 29; Is. 42:12; Jer. 13:16; Mal. 2:2; Rev. 14:7 [c]1 Sam. 5:6, 11; Ps. 39:10 [d]1 Sam. 5:3, 4, 7 [1]ease
6 [a]Ex. 7:13; 8:15; 9:34; 14:17 [b]Ex. 12:31
7 [a]2 Sam. 6:3 [b]Num. 19:2; Deut. 21:3, 4
8 [a]1 Sam. 6:4, 5
9 [a]Josh. 15:10; 21:16 [b]1 Sam. 6:3 [1]*this calamity to us*
12 [a]Num. 20:19 *See WW at Prov. 3:6.
13 [a]1 Sam. 12:17
15 *See WW at Deut. 16:2.
16 [a]Josh. 13:3; Judg. 3:3
17 [a]1 Sam. 6:4 [b]1 Sam. 5:8
19 [a]Ex. 19:21; Num. 4:5, 15, 16, 20 [b]2 Sam. 6:7 [1]Or *He struck seventy men of the people and fifty oxen of a man*

6:3 Trespass offering indicates they felt the need for an offering to expiate the crime of stealing the ark.
6:4 It was common among the pagan nations to make a representation of the part of the body that had been healed, or of the danger from which one had been delivered, and offer it to the gods as a gesture of thanksgiving.
6:5 Give glory to the God of Israel is to acknowledge His superiority over their gods.
6:6 Though this event happened many years later, the Exodus of the Israelites and the plagues of the **Egyptians** were well known outside the Hebrew community.
6:9 Beth Shemesh was about 14 miles west of Jerusalem.
6:12 The **border of Beth Shemesh** was about 12 miles from the Philistine city of Ekron. That these cows go 12 miles, taking the most direct route, not turning to the **right hand or the left,** is a miracle great enough to convince the Philistines that their troubles are from the hand of the God of Israel.
6:19 Though they are joyful at the return of the ark (v. 13), they still look at it as magical rather than as the holy presence of God. This verse contains an obscure Hebrew construction but the most likely understanding is that **seventy men,** then **fifty thousand,** were stricken, perhaps 70 in Beth Shemesh followed by thousands in the surrounding territory.

The Ark at Kirjath Jearim

20 And the men of Beth Shemesh said,
[a]"Who is *able to stand before this
holy LORD God? And to whom shall it
go up from us?"
21 So they sent messengers to the
inhabitants of [a]Kirjath Jearim, saying,
"The Philistines have brought back the
ark of the LORD; come down *and* take
it up with you."

7 Then the men of [a]Kirjath Jearim
came and took the ark of the LORD,
and brought it into the house of
[b]Abinadab on the hill, and [c]con-
secrated Eleazar his son to keep the
ark of the LORD.

Samuel Judges Israel

2 So it was that the ark remained in
Kirjath Jearim a long time; it was there
twenty years. And all the house of Israel lamented after the LORD.
3 Then Samuel spoke to all the house
of Israel, saying, "If you [a]return to
the LORD with all your hearts, *then*
[b]put away the foreign gods and the
[c]Ashtoreths[1] from among you, and
[d]prepare your hearts for the LORD,
and [e]serve Him only; and He will deliver you from the hand of the Philistines."
4 So the children of Israel put away
the [a]Baals and the [1]Ashtoreths, and
served the LORD only.
5 And Samuel said, [a]"Gather all Israel to Mizpah, and [b]I will *pray to the
LORD for you."
6 So they gathered together at Mizpah, [a]drew water, and poured *it* out before the LORD. And they [b]fasted that
day, and said there, [c]"We have sinned
against the LORD." And Samuel judged
the children of Israel at Mizpah.
7 Now when the Philistines heard
that the children of Israel had gathered
together at Mizpah, the lords of the
Philistines went up against Israel. And
when the children of Israel heard *of it*,
they were afraid of the Philistines.
8 So the children of Israel said to
Samuel, [a]"Do not cease to cry out to
the LORD our God for us, that He may
save us from the hand of the Philistines."
9 And Samuel took a [a]suckling lamb
and offered *it as* a whole burnt offering
to the LORD. Then [b]Samuel cried out
to the LORD for Israel, and the LORD
answered him.
10 Now as Samuel was offering up the
burnt offering, the Philistines drew
near to battle against Israel. [a]But the
LORD thundered with a loud thunder
upon the Philistines that day, and so
confused them that they were overcome before Israel.
11 And the men of Israel went out of
Mizpah and pursued the Philistines,
and [1]drove them back as far as below
Beth Car.

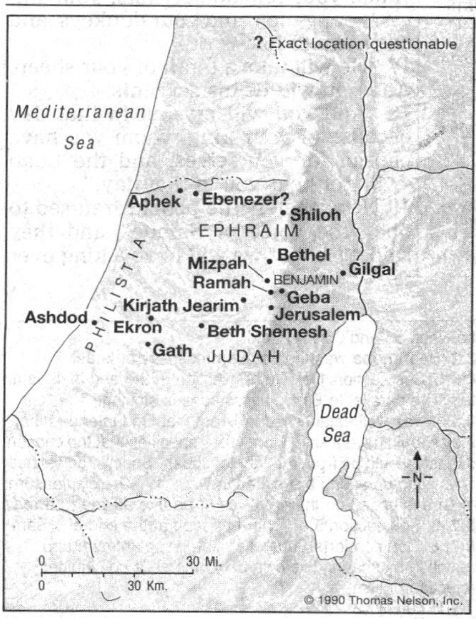

20 [a]Mal. 3:2 *See WW at Num. 13:30.
21 [a]1 Chr. 13:5, 6

CHAPTER 7

1 [a]1 Sam. 6:21 [b]2 Sam. 6:3, 4 [c]Lev. 21:8
3 [a]Deut. 30:2–10 [b]Gen. 35:2 [c]Judg. 2:13 [d]Job 11:13 [e]Luke 4:8 [1]Images of Canaanite goddesses
4 [a]Judg. 2:11; 10:16 [1]Images of Canaanite goddesses
5 [a]Judg. 10:17; 20:1 [b]1 Sam. 12:17–19 *See WW at Job 42:10.
6 [a]2 Sam. 14:14 [b]Neh. 9:1, 2 [c]1 Sam. 12:10
8 [a]Is. 37:4
9 [a]Lev. 22:27 [b]1 Sam. 12:18
10 [a]2 Sam. 22:14, 15
11 [1]*struck them down*

7:1 Kirjath Jearim is identified with modern Abu Ghosh, a village 9 miles west of Jerusalem.
7:2 Lamented indicates that a desire for God is growing in the heart of Israel.
7:3 Samuel waits 20 years before beginning his public ministry. Though undoubtedly continuing his regular duties as priest, he patiently waits for the exact moment God intends to call Israel to repentance.
7:4 Baals and Ashtoreths were Canaanite nature gods. Baal was a fertility god, and Ashtoreth was the goddess of love and war. See note on 5:2.
7:5 Mizpah was on the main north-south road through the hills 5 miles north of Jerusalem. The name **Mizpah** means "Watch."
7:6 Drew water . . . poured *it* out: A symbol of distress and brokenness. **Samuel judged:** Samuel calls the people to repentance, confession, and contrition before the Lord.
7:11 The location of **Beth Car** is unknown.

The Ministry of Samuel. As judge, Samuel visited yearly the cities of Bethel, Gilgal, and Mizpah.

12 Then Samuel [a]took a stone and set
it up between Mizpah and Shen, and
called its name [1]Ebenezer, saying,
"Thus far the LORD has helped us."
13 [a]So the Philistines were subdued,
and they [b]did not come anymore into
the territory of Israel. And the hand of
the LORD was against the Philistines all
the days of Samuel.
14 Then the cities which the Philistines
had taken from Israel were restored to
Israel, from Ekron to Gath; and Israel
recovered its territory from the hands
of the Philistines. Also there was peace
between Israel and the Amorites.
15 And Samuel [a]judged Israel all the
days of his life.
16 He went from year to year on a circuit to Bethel, Gilgal, and Mizpah, and
judged Israel in all those places.
17 But [a]he always returned to Ramah,
for his home *was* there. There he
judged Israel, and there he [b]built an
altar to the LORD.

Israel Demands a King

8 Now it came to pass when Samuel
was [a]old that he [b]made his [c]sons
*judges over Israel.
2 The name of his firstborn was Joel,
and the name of his second, Abijah;
they were judges in Beersheba.
1 3 But his sons [a]did not walk in his
ways; they turned aside [b]after dishonest gain, [c]took bribes, and perverted
justice.
4 Then all the elders of Israel gathered together and came to Samuel at
Ramah,
5 and said to him, "Look, you are old,
and your sons do not walk in your
ways. Now [a]make us a king to judge
us like all the nations."
6 But the thing [a]displeased Samuel
when they said, "Give us a king to
judge us." So Samuel [b]prayed to the
LORD.
5 7 And the LORD said to Samuel,
"Heed the voice of the people in all that

12 [a]Gen. 28:18; 35:14; Josh. 4:9; 24:26 [1]Lit. *Stone of Help*
13 [a]Judg. 13:1 [b]1 Sam. 13:5
15 [a]1 Sam. 12:11
17 [a]1 Sam. 8:4 [b]Judg. 21:4

CHAPTER 8

1 [a]1 Sam. 12:2 [b]Deut. 16:18, 19; 2 Chr. 19:5 [c]Judg. 10:4 *See WW at Judg. 2:18.
3 [a]Jer. 22:15–17 [b]Ex. 18:21 [c]Ex. 23:6–8; Deut. 16:19; 1 Sam. 12:3
5 [a]Deut. 17:14, 15; Hos. 13:10, 11; Acts 13:21
6 [a]1 Sam. 12:17 [b]1 Sam. 7:9
7 [a]Ex. 16:8 [b]1 Sam. 10:19
9 [a]1 Sam. 8:11–18
11 [a]Deut. 17:14–20 [b]1 Sam. 14:52 [c]2 Sam. 15:1
12 [a]1 Sam. 22:7
14 [a]1 Kin. 21:7; [Ezek. 46:18]
16 [1]LXX *cattle*
18 [a]Prov. 1:25–28; Is. 1:15; Mic. 3:4
19 [a]Is. 66:4; Jer. 44:16

they say to you; for [a]they have not rejected you, but [b]they have rejected Me,
that I should not reign over them.
8 "According to all the works which
they have done since the day that I
brought them up out of Egypt, even to
this day—with which they have forsaken Me and served other gods—so
they are doing to you also.
9 "Now therefore, heed their voice.
However, you shall solemnly forewarn
them, and [a]show them the behavior of
the king who will reign over them."
10 So Samuel told all the words of the
LORD to the people who asked him for
a king.
11 And he said, [a]"This will be the behavior of the king who will reign over
you: He will take your [b]sons and appoint *them* for his own [c]chariots and
to be his horsemen, and *some* will run
before his chariots.
12 "He will [a]appoint captains over his
thousands and captains over his fifties,
will set some to plow his ground and
reap his harvest, and *some* to make his
weapons of war and equipment for his
chariots.
13 "He will take your daughters *to be*
perfumers, cooks, and bakers.
14 "And [a]he will take the best of your
fields, your vineyards, and your olive
groves, and give *them* to his servants.
15 "He will take a tenth of your grain
and your vintage, and give it to his officers and servants.
16 "And he will take your male servants, your female servants, your finest [1]young men, and your donkeys, and
put *them* to his work.
17 "He will take a tenth of your sheep.
And you will be his servants.
18 "And you will cry out in that day
because of your king whom you have
chosen for yourselves, and the LORD
[a]will not hear you in that day."
19 Nevertheless the people [a]refused to
obey the voice of Samuel; and they
said, "No, but we will have a king over
us,

7:12 Ebenezer means "Stone of Help" and is the same battle site at which the Philistines had defeated Israel and captured the ark (4:1).
7:14 From Ekron to Gath indicates that all of Israel's land was restored right up to the borders of Philistia, which were marked by these two cities. The **Amorites** were the most powerful of the Canaanite tribes.
7:16 These may have been the sites of sanctuaries of worship in which Samuel ministered and directed the affairs of the nation.
7:17 After Shiloh and the death of Eli, Samuel returns to **Ramah,** the place of his birth and family, to live and minister.
8:1 The events of this chapter occur about 20 years after the victory at Ebenezer. Samuel at this time is probably between 55 and 65 years old.
8:2 Beersheba was the southernmost city of Israel.
8:3ff. See section 1 of Truth-In-Action at the end of 1 Sam.
8:3 The parallel to Eli's godless sons is striking.
8:5 It was well established in Israel that God intended that they should have a king. Gen. 49:10 specifies that the chosen dynasty would be from the tribe of Judah. Specific guidelines for setting up a king are stated in Deut. 17. The displeasure of God is based on their motives to be **like all the nations.**
8:7, 8 See section 5 of Truth-In-Action at the end of 1 Sam.
8:7, 8 God comforts Samuel in his disappointment and rejection by sharing His own pain in Israel's continuing rejection of Him.

20 "that we also may be [a]like all the nations, and that our king may judge us and go out before us and fight our battles."

21 And Samuel heard all the words of the people, and he repeated them in the hearing of the LORD.

4 22 So the LORD said to Samuel, [a]"Heed their voice, and make them a king." And Samuel said to the men of Israel, "Every man go to his city."

Saul Chosen to Be King

9 There was a man of Benjamin whose name *was* [a]Kish the son of Abiel, the son of Zeror, the son of Bechorath, the son of Aphiah, a Benjamite, a mighty man of [1]power.

2 And he had a choice and handsome son whose name *was* Saul. *There was* not a more handsome person than he among the children of Israel. [a]From his shoulders upward *he was* taller than any of the people.

3 Now the donkeys of Kish, Saul's father, were lost. And Kish said to his son Saul, "Please take one of the servants with you, and arise, go and *look for the donkeys."

4 So he passed through the mountains of Ephraim and through the land of [a]Shalisha, but they did not find *them.* Then they passed through the land of Shaalim, and *they were* not *there.* Then he passed through the land of the Benjamites, but they did not find *them.*

5 When they had come to the land of [a]Zuph, Saul said to his servant who *was* with him, "Come, let [b]us return, lest my father cease *caring* about the donkeys and become worried about us."

6 And he said to him, "Look now, *there is* in this city [a]a man of God, and *he is* an honorable man; [b]all that he says surely comes to pass. So let us go there; perhaps he can show us the way that we should go."

7 Then Saul said to his servant, "But look, *if* we go, [a]what shall we bring the man? For the bread in our vessels is all gone, and *there is* no present to bring to the man of God. What do we have?"

8 And the servant answered Saul again and said, "Look, I have here at hand one-fourth of a shekel of silver. I will give *that* to the man of God, to tell us our way."

9 (Formerly in Israel, when a man [a]went [1]to inquire of God, he spoke thus: "Come, let us go to the **seer**"; for *he who is* now *called* a prophet was formerly called [b]a seer.)

WORD WEALTH

9:9 seer, *ro'eh* (roh-*ay*); Strong's #7200, 7203: A visionary, a seer; one who sees visions; a prophet. *Ro'eh* comes from the verb *ra'ah,* which means "to see," but also has a wide range of meanings related to seeing (such as "perceive," "appear," "discern," "look," "stare," and many other nuances). It was only natural for Hebrew speakers to describe a prophet as a "seer," since prophets frequently received messages from God through visions. However, the word *nabi'* (spokesman) is the preferred Hebrew word for prophet.

10 Then Saul said to his servant, [1]"Well said; come, let us go." So they went to the city where the man of God *was.*

11 As they went up the hill to the city, [a]they met some young women going out to draw water, and said to them, "Is the seer here?"

12 And they answered them and said, "Yes, there he is, just ahead of you. Hurry now; for today he came to this city, because [a]there is a sacrifice of the people today [b]on the *high place.

13 "As soon as you come into the city, you will surely find him before he goes up to the high place to eat. For the people will not eat until he comes, because he must bless the sacrifice; afterward those who are invited will eat. Now therefore, go up, for about this time you will find him."

20 [a]1 Sam. 8:5
22 [a]1 Sam. 8:7; Hos. 13:11

CHAPTER 9

1 [a]1 Sam. 14:51; 1 Chr. 8:33; 9:36–39 [1]*wealth*
2 [a]1 Sam. 10:23
3 *See WW at Hos. 5:15.
4 [a]2 Kin. 4:42
5 [a]1 Sam. 1:1 [b]1 Sam. 10:2
6 [a]Deut. 33:1; 1 Kin. 13:1; 2 Kin. 5:8 [b]1 Sam. 3:19
7 [a]Judg. 6:18; 13:17; 1 Kin. 14:3; 2 Kin. 4:42; 8:8
9 [a]Gen. 25:22 [b]2 Sam. 24:11; 2 Kin. 17:13; 1 Chr. 26:28; 29:29; 2 Chr. 16:7, 10; Is. 30:10; Amos 7:12 [1]Lit. *to seek God*
10 [1]Lit. *Your word is good*
11 [a]Gen. 24:11, 15; 29:8, 9; Ex. 2:16
12 [a]Gen. 31:54; 1 Sam. 16:2 [b]1 Sam. 7:17; 10:5; 1 Kin. 3:2 *See WW at Ezek. 6:3.

8:22 See section 4 of Truth-In-Action at the end of 1 Sam.

8:22 Make them a king: There is a distinct difference between God's allowing Saul to be made king and His own choice of David. He says of David, "I have provided Myself a king" (16:1). In Saul He gives the people *their* king.

9:2 Saul at this time is a young, married man with a son, Jonathan.

9:4 The mountains of Ephraim were north of Gibeah, Saul's home. The exact locations of **Shalisha** and **Shaalim** are not clear.

9:5 Zuph is Ramah, where Samuel lived. See note on 1:1.

9:7 This verse gives insight into how the prophets were supported.

9:8 One-fourth of a shekel is about 1⁄10 ounce of silver.

9:9 Though previously having different meanings, **prophet** and **seer** came to be used interchangeably.

9:11 Towns were built on the tops of the hills, but the water would be in the valley or below the city. The job of carrying water fell to the **young women.**

9:12 To the pagans, the **high place** was their locale of worship to their idols. To the Israelites, it was a place of prayer and sacrifice.

14 So they went up to the city. As they
were coming into the city, there was
Samuel, coming out toward them on
his way up to the high place.
15 [a]Now the LORD had told Samuel in
his ear the day before Saul came, saying,
16 "Tomorrow about this time [a]I will
send you a man from the land of Benjamin, [b]and you shall *anoint him
[1]commander over My people Israel,
that he may save My people from the
hand of the Philistines; for I have
[c]looked upon My people, because their
cry has come to Me."
17 So when Samuel saw Saul, the LORD
said to him, [a]"There he is, the man of
whom I spoke to you. This one shall
reign over My people."
18 Then Saul drew near to Samuel in
the gate, and said, "Please tell me,
where *is* the seer's house?"
19 Samuel answered Saul and said, "I
am the seer. Go up before me to the
high place, for you shall eat with me
today; and tomorrow I will let you go
and will tell you all that *is* in your
heart.
20 "But as for [a]your donkeys that were
lost three days ago, do not be anxious
about them, for they have been found.
And [1]on whom [b]*is* all the desire of Israel? *Is it* not on you and on all your
father's house?"
21 And Saul answered and said,
[a]"*Am* I not a Benjamite, of the
[b]smallest of the tribes of Israel, and [c]my
family the least of all the families of
the [1]tribe of Benjamin? Why then do
you speak like this to me?"
22 Now Samuel took Saul and his servant and brought them into the hall,
and had them sit in the place of honor
among those who were invited; there
were about thirty persons.
23 And Samuel said to the cook,
"Bring the portion which I gave you,
of which I said to you, 'Set it apart.'"

15 [a]1 Sam. 15:1
16 [a]Deut. 17:15 [b]1 Sam. 10:1 [c]Ex. 2:23–25; 3:7, 9 [1]*prince or ruler* *See WW at Is. 61:1.
17 [a]1 Sam. 16:12
20 [a]1 Sam. 9:3 [b]1 Sam. 8:5, 19; 12:13 [1]*for whom*
21 [a]1 Sam. 15:17 [b]Judg. 20:46–48 [c]Judg. 6:15 [1]Lit. *tribes*
24 [a]Lev. 7:32, 33
25 [a]Deut. 22:8 [1]So with MT, Tg.; LXX omits *He spoke with Saul on top of the house;* LXX, Vg. afterward add *And he prepared a bed for Saul on top of the house, and he slept.*
27 [1]*now*

CHAPTER 10

1 [a]2 Kin. 9:3, 6 [b]Ps. 2:12 [c]Acts 13:21 [d]Deut. 32:9 [1]So with MT, Tg., Vg.; LXX *people Israel; and you shall rule the people of the Lord;* LXX, Vg. add *And you shall deliver His people from the hands of their enemies all around them. And this shall be a sign to you, that God has anointed you to be a prince.*
2 [a]Gen. 35:16–20; 48:7 [b]Josh. 18:28 [c]1 Sam. 9:3–5
3 [a]Gen. 28:22; 35:1, 3, 7

24 So the cook took up [a]the thigh with
its upper part and set *it* before Saul.
And *Samuel* said, "Here it is, what
was kept back. *It* was set apart for
you. Eat; for until this time it has been
kept for you, since I said I invited the
people." So Saul ate with Samuel that
day.
25 When they had come down from
the high place into the city, [1]*Samuel*
spoke with Saul on [a]the top of the
house.
26 They arose early; and it was about
the dawning of the day that Samuel
called to Saul on the top of the house,
saying, "Get up, that I may send you
on your way." And Saul arose, and
both of them went outside, he and
Samuel.

Saul Anointed King

27 As they were going down to the outskirts of the city, Samuel said to Saul,
"Tell the servant to go on ahead of us."
And he went on. "But you stand here
[1]awhile, that I may announce to you
the word of God."
10 Then [a]Samuel took a flask of oil
and poured *it* on his head,
[b]and kissed him and said: "*Is it* not
because [c]the LORD has anointed you
commander over [d]His [1]inheritance?
2 "When you have departed from me
today, you will find two men by [a]Ra-
chel's tomb in the territory of Benjamin [b]at Zelzah; and they will say to
you, 'The donkeys which you went to
look for have been found. And now
your father has ceased caring about
the donkeys and is worrying about
[c]you, saying, "What shall I do
about my son?"'
3 "Then you shall go on forward from
there and come to the terebinth tree
of Tabor. There three men going up
[a]to God at Bethel will meet you, one
carrying three young goats, another

9:15 In his ear is the equivalent to revealing something directly and intimately.
9:16 Commander is used of leaders in various government, military, and religious fields.
9:17 Reign means to "keep within bounds," the idea being to keep the nation within the limits of God's direction and purposes.
9:20 The desire of Israel for a king (8:5) rests on Saul.
9:21 Benjamin was the youngest of Jacob's 12 sons, and his tribe had also been severely reduced in number at a battle with all the other tribes of Israel because of the terrible sin committed in the Benjamite city of Gibeah (Judg. 19; 20).
9:22–24 Samuel, in anticipation of Saul's coming, had arranged this sacrificial banquet and invited 30 of the leading citizens of the city to join him. **The thigh with its upper part** is the portion of the sacrifice given to the priests. See Ex. 29:27; Lev. 7:32.
9:25 On the top of the house: The flat roofs were often used for relaxation in the evening.
10:1 Oil throughout Scripture typically symbolizes the Holy Spirit. This is the first recorded instance of any anointing with oil, other than for anointing the priests and the sanctuary. The monarchy was therefore given similar importance as the priesthood. **His inheritance** is the nation of Israel.
10:2 Rachel's tomb: Rachel was Jacob's wife who died in giving birth to her son Benjamin, after whom the tribe of Benjamin is named (Gen. 35). Her tomb is between Jerusalem and Bethlehem.
10:3 Terebinth tree: A large oaklike tree, which served as a landmark on the road to Bethel.

carrying three loaves of bread, and another carrying a skin of wine.

4 "And they will [1]greet you and give you two *loaves* of bread, which you shall receive from their hands.

5 "After that you shall come to the hill of God [a]where the Philistine garrison *is*. And it will happen, when you have come there to the city, that you will meet a group of prophets coming down [b]from the high place with a stringed instrument, a tambourine, a flute, and a harp before them; [c]and they will be prophesying.

6 "Then [a]the Spirit of the LORD will come upon you, and [b]you will prophesy with them and be turned into another man.

7 "And let it be, when these [a]signs come to you, *that* you do as the occasion demands; for [b]God *is* with you.

8 "You shall go down before me [a]to Gilgal; and surely I will come down to you to offer burnt offerings *and* make sacrifices of peace offerings. [b]Seven days you shall wait, till I come to you and show you what you should do."

9 So it was, when he had turned his back to go from Samuel, that God [1]gave him another heart; and all those signs came to pass that day.

10 [a]When they came there to the hill, there was [b]a group of prophets to meet him; then the Spirit of God came upon him, and he prophesied among them.

11 And it happened, when all who knew him formerly saw that he indeed prophesied among the prophets, that the people said to one another, "What *is* this *that* has come upon the son of Kish? [a]*Is* Saul also among the prophets?"

12 Then a man from there answered and said, "But [a]who *is* their father?" Therefore it became a *proverb: "*Is* Saul also among the prophets?"

13 And when he had finished prophesying, he went to the high place.

14 Then Saul's [a]uncle said to him and his servant, "Where did you go?" So he said, "To look for the donkeys. When we saw that *they were* nowhere *to be found,* we went to Samuel."

15 And Saul's uncle said, "Tell me, please, what Samuel said to you."

16 So Saul said to his uncle, "He told us plainly that the donkeys had been [a]found." But about the matter of the kingdom, he did not tell him what Samuel had said.

Saul Proclaimed King

17 Then Samuel called the people together [a]to the LORD [b]at Mizpah,

18 and said to the children of Israel, [a]"Thus says the LORD God of Israel: 'I brought up Israel out of Egypt, and delivered you from the hand of the Egyptians *and* from the hand of all kingdoms and from those who oppressed you.'

19 [a]"But you have today rejected your God, who Himself saved you from all your adversities and your tribulations; and you have said to Him, 'No, set a king over us!' Now therefore, present yourselves before the LORD by your tribes and by your [1]clans." **2**

20 And when Samuel had [a]caused all the tribes of Israel to come near, the tribe of Benjamin was chosen.

21 When he had caused the tribe of Benjamin to come near by their families, the family of Matri was chosen. And Saul the son of Kish was chosen. But when they sought him, he could not be found.

22 Therefore they [a]inquired of the LORD further, "Has the man come here

4 [1]*ask you about your welfare*
5 [a]1 Sam. 13:2, 3 [b]1 Sam. 19:12, 20; 2 Kin. 2:3, 5, 15 [c]Ex. 15:20, 21; 2 Kin. 3:15; 1 Chr. 25:1–6; 1 Cor. 14:1
6 [a]Num. 11:25, 29; Judg. 14:6; 1 Sam. 16:13 [b]1 Sam. 10:10; 19:23, 24
7 [a]Ex. 4:8; Luke 2:12 [b]Josh. 1:5; Judg. 6:12; 1 Sam. 3:19; [Heb. 13:5]
8 [a]1 Sam. 11:14, 15; 13:8 [b]1 Sam. 13:8–10
9 [1]*changed his heart*
10 [a]1 Sam. 10:5 [b]1 Sam. 19:20
11 [a]1 Sam. 19:24; Amos 7:14, 15; Matt. 13:54–57; John 7:15; Acts 4:13
12 [a]John 5:30, 36
*See WW at Prov. 1:6.
14 [a]1 Sam. 14:50
16 [a]1 Sam. 9:20
17 [a]Judg. 20:1 [b]1 Sam. 7:5, 6
18 [a]Judg. 6:8, 9; 1 Sam. 8:8; 12:6, 8
19 [a]1 Sam. 8:7, 19; 12:12 [1]*Lit. thousands*
20 [a]Acts 1:24, 26
22 [a]1 Sam. 23:2, 4, 10, 11

10:4 The greeting and the receiving of these sacrificial loaves was to be understood by Saul as homage being paid to God's anointed.

10:5 Gibeah, meaning **hill of God,** was Saul's home. Samuel was the first prophet around whom a colony of young men gathered for the purpose of learning to dedicate themselves to the service of God. Such a **group of prophets** formed in Ramah, Samuel's hometown. Music was a significant part of their expressions of praise and was often written under the spirit of prophecy, which came upon them from the Lord.

10:6 Saul will be **turned into another man,** that is, transformed and empowered by the Spirit of God.

10:7 The ability has been given by God, but Saul must choose to act upon it.

10:9 Both the transformation and empowering of the Holy Spirit (v. 6), as well as the regeneration of the heart, are essential if Saul is to lead Israel in the direction God intends.

10:12 Who *is* their father?: Does one become a prophet through lineage or through the power of God's Spirit? Saul's father, Kish, was not a prophet; therefore, the prophetic gift was given by God. This **proverb** came to be applied to anyone who appeared in any sphere of life that was radically different than his usual one.

10:19 See section 2 of Truth-In-Action at the end of 1 Sam.

10:19 Their rejection of God is shown in their desire to be like the other nations (see 8:19, 20). See note on 8:5.

10:20 The tribe, clan, family, and son were determined probably by casting lots. What Samuel had done in privately anointing Saul (v. 1) is now publicly confirmed so that both the people and Saul would have assurance of God's choice.

10:22 Saul was **hidden** because of an authentic modesty and shyness on his part.

yet?" And the LORD answered, "There
he is, hidden among the equipment."
23 So they ran and brought him from
there; and when he stood among the
people, [a]he was taller than any of the
people from his shoulders upward.
24 And Samuel said to all the people,
"Do you see him [a]whom the LORD has
chosen, that *there is* no one like him
among all the people?" So all the people shouted and said, [b]"Long[1] live the
king!"
25 Then Samuel explained to the people [a]the behavior of royalty, and wrote
it in a book and laid *it* up before the
LORD. And Samuel sent all the people
away, every man to his house.
26 And Saul also went home [a]to Gibeah; and valiant *men* went with him,
whose hearts God had touched.
27 [a]But some [b]rebels said, "How can
this man save us?" So they despised
him, [c]and brought him no presents. But
he [1]held his peace.

Saul Saves Jabesh Gilead

11 Then [a]Nahash the Ammonite
came up and [1]encamped against
[b]Jabesh Gilead; and all the men of Jabesh said to Nahash, [c]"Make a covenant with us, and we will serve you."
2 And Nahash the Ammonite answered them, "On this *condition* I will
make *a covenant* with you, that I may
put out all your right eyes, and bring
[a]reproach on all Israel."
3 Then the elders of Jabesh said to
him, "Hold off for seven days, that we
may send messengers to all the territory of Israel. And then, if *there is* no
one to [1]save us, we will come out to
you."
4 So the messengers came [a]to Gibeah
of Saul and told the news in the hearing of the people. And [b]all the people
lifted up their voices and wept.
5 Now there was Saul, coming behind
the herd from the field; and Saul said,
"What *troubles* the people, that they

23 [a]1 Sam. 9:2
24 [a]2 Sam. 21:6 [b]1 Kin. 1:25, 39 [1]Lit. *May the king live*
25 [a]1 Sam. 8:11–18
26 [a]Judg. 20:14
27 [a]1 Sam. 11:12 [b]Deut. 13:13 [c]1 Kin. 4:21; 10:25 [1]*kept silent*

CHAPTER 11

1 [a]1 Sam. 12:12 [b]Judg. 21:8 [c]Gen. 26:28 [1]*besieged*
2 [a]Gen. 34:14
3 [1]*deliver*
4 [a]1 Sam. 10:26; 15:34 [b]Judg. 2:4; 20:23, 26; 21:2
6 [a]Judg. 3:10; 6:34; 11:29; 13:25; 14:6
7 [a]Judg. 19:29 [b]Judg. 21:5, 8, 10 [1]Lit. *as one man*
8 [a]Judg. 1:5 [b]2 Sam. 24:9
11 [a]1 Sam. 31:11 [b]Judg. 7:16, 20
12 [a]1 Sam. 10:27 [b]Luke 19:27
13 [a]2 Sam. 19:22 [b]Ex. 14:13, 30
14 [a]1 Sam. 7:16; 10:8
15 [a]1 Sam. 10:17

weep?" And they told him the words
of the men of Jabesh.
6 [a]Then the Spirit of God came upon
Saul when he heard this news, and his
anger was greatly aroused.
7 So he took a yoke of oxen and
[a]cut them in pieces, and sent *them*
throughout all the territory of Israel by
the hands of messengers, saying,
[b]"Whoever does not go out with Saul
and Samuel to battle, so it shall be
done to his oxen." And the fear of the
LORD fell on the people, and they came
out [1]with one consent.
8 When he numbered them in [a]Bezek,
the children [b]of Israel were three hundred thousand, and the men of Judah
thirty thousand.
9 And they said to the messengers
who came, "Thus you shall say to the
men of Jabesh Gilead: 'Tomorrow, by
the time the sun is hot, you shall have
help.'" Then the messengers came and
reported *it* to the men of Jabesh, and
they were glad.
10 Therefore the men of Jabesh said,
"Tomorrow we will come out to you,
and you may do with us whatever
seems good to you."
11 So it was, on the next day, that
[a]Saul put the people [b]in three companies; and they came into the midst of
the camp in the morning watch, and
killed Ammonites until the heat of the
day. And it happened that those who
survived were scattered, so that no two
of them were left together.
12 Then the people said to Samuel,
[a]"Who *is* he who said, 'Shall Saul reign
over us?' [b]Bring the men, that we may
put them to death."
13 But Saul said, [a]"Not a man shall be
put to death this day, for today [b]the
LORD has accomplished salvation in Israel."
14 Then Samuel said to the people,
"Come, let us go [a]to Gilgal and renew
the kingdom there."
15 So all the people went to Gilgal, and
there they made Saul king [a]before the

10:24 No one like him refers to his attractive physical appearance.
10:25 The behavior of royalty is a prophetic description of how the monarchy, here established, is to conduct itself in relationship to the law and covenant of God.
10:27 That these **rebels . . . brought him no presents** was a serious breach of ethics bordering on outright rebellion.
11:1 The Ammonites inhabited the area east of the Jordan River. They were descended from Lot and were long-standing and bitter enemies of their distant relatives, Israel.
11:5 Though Saul had been acclaimed king (ch. 10), he had not taken any steps to form his government.
11:7 At this point **Saul** still sees **Samuel** as an integral part of the government of Israel. It is likely that this joining of the offices of prophet and king had been prescribed in the documents Samuel had read and placed in the sanctuary (10:25). Had this relationship continued, Saul's future would have turned out differently. "The Spirit of God" came on Saul (v. 6) and **the fear of the LORD** came on the people so that the newly formed monarchy was enjoying the power and presence of God.
11:11 The Israelites attacked from three directions between the hours of 3:00 and 6:00 A.M.
11:14, 15 To **renew the kingdom** means to unify the kingdom. **They made Saul king:** They renewed their original proclamation (10:24) in light of the first military victory under his rulership.

LORD in Gilgal. [b]There they made sacrifices of peace offerings before the
LORD, and there Saul and all the men
of Israel rejoiced greatly.

Samuel's Address at Saul's Coronation

12 Now Samuel said to all Israel:
"Indeed I have [1]heeded [a]your
voice in all that you said to me, and
[b]have made a king over you.
2 "And now here is the king, [a]walk-
ing before you; [b]and I am old and grayheaded, and look, my sons *are* with
you. I have walked before you from my
childhood to this day.
3 "Here I am. Witness against me
before the LORD and before [a]His
anointed: [b]Whose ox have I taken, or
whose donkey have I taken, or whom
have I cheated? Whom have I oppressed, or from whose hand have I received *any* [c]bribe with which to
[d]blind my eyes? I will restore *it* to
you."
4 And they said, [a]"You have not
cheated us or oppressed us, nor have
you taken anything from any man's
hand."
5 Then he said to them, "The LORD
is witness against you, and His
anointed *is* witness this day, [a]that you
have not found anything [b]in my hand."
And they answered, "*He is* witness."
6 Then Samuel said to the people,
[a]"*It is* the LORD who raised up Moses
and Aaron, and who brought your fathers up from the land of Egypt.
7 "Now therefore, stand still, that I
may [a]reason with you before the LORD
concerning all the [b]righteous acts of
the LORD which He did to you and your
fathers:
8 [a]"When Jacob had gone into
[1]Egypt, and your fathers [b]cried out to
the LORD, then the LORD [c]sent Moses
and Aaron, who brought your fathers
out of Egypt and made them dwell in
this place.
9 "And when they [a]forgot the LORD
their God, He sold them into the hand
of [b]Sisera, commander of the army of
Hazor, into the hand of the [c]Philistines,
and into the hand of the king of
[d]Moab; and they fought against them.
10 "Then they cried out to the LORD,
and said, [a]'We have sinned, because
we have forsaken the LORD [b]and
served the Baals and [1]Ashtoreths; but
now deliver us from the hand of our
enemies, and we will serve You.'
11 "And the LORD sent [1]Jerubbaal,
[2]Bedan, [a]Jephthah, and [b]Samuel,[3] and
delivered you out of the hand of your
enemies on every side; and you dwelt
in *safety.
12 "And when you saw that [a]Nahash
king of the Ammonites came against
you, [b]you said to me, 'No, but a king
shall reign over us,' when [c]the LORD
your God *was* your king.
13 "Now therefore, [a]here is the king
[b]whom you have chosen *and* whom
you have *desired. And take note,
[c]the LORD has set a king over you.
14 "If you [a]fear the LORD and serve
Him and obey His voice, and do not
rebel against the commandment of the
LORD, then both you and the king who
reigns over you will continue following
the LORD your God.
15 "However, if you do [a]not obey the
voice of the LORD, but [b]rebel against
the commandment of the LORD, then
the hand of the LORD will be against
you, as *it was* against your fathers.
16 "Now therefore, [a]stand and see this
great thing which the LORD will do before your eyes:
17 "*Is* today not the [a]wheat harvest?
[b]I will call to the LORD, and He will
send thunder and [c]rain, that you may
perceive and see that [d]your wickedness *is* great, which you have done in
the sight of the LORD, in asking a king
for yourselves."
18 So Samuel called to the LORD, and
the LORD sent thunder and rain that
day; and [a]all the people greatly feared
the LORD and Samuel.
19 And all the people said to Samuel,
[a]"Pray for your servants to the LORD
your God, that we may not die; for we
have added to all our sins the evil of
asking a king for ourselves."
20 Then Samuel said to the people,
"Do not fear. You have done all this

15 [b]1 Sam. 10:8

CHAPTER 12

1 [a]1 Sam. 8:5, 7, 9, 20, 22 [b]1 Sam. 10:24; 11:14, 15 [1]*listened to*
2 [a]Num. 27:17 [b]1 Sam. 8:1, 5
3 [a]1 Sam. 10:1; 24:6 [b]Num. 16:15 [c]Ex. 23:8 [d]Deut. 16:19
4 [a]Lev. 19:13
5 [a]Acts 23:9; 24:20 [b]Ex. 22:4
6 [a]Mic. 6:4
7 [a]Is. 1:18 [b]Judg. 5:11
8 [a]Gen. 46:5, 6 [b]Ex. 2:23–25 [c]Ex. 3:10; 4:14–16 [1]So with MT, Tg., Vg.; LXX adds *and the Egyptians afflicted them*
9 [a]Judg. 3:7 [b]Judg. 4:2 [c]Judg. 3:31; 10:7; 13:1 [d]Judg. 3:12–30
10 [a]Judg. 10:10 [b]Judg. 2:13; 3:7 [1]Images of Canaanite goddesses
11 [a]Judg. 11:1 [b]1 Sam. 7:13 [1]Gideon, cf. Judg. 6:25–32; Syr. *Deborah;* Tg. *Gideon* [2]LXX, Syr. *Barak;* Tg. *Simson* [3]Syr. *Simson* *See WW at Deut. 33:12.
12 [a]1 Sam. 11:1, 2 [b]1 Sam. 8:5, 19, 20 [c]Judg. 8:23
13 [a]1 Sam. 10:24 [b]1 Sam. 8:5; 12:17, 19 [c]Hos. 13:11 *See WW at Ps. 122:6.
14 [a]Josh. 24:14
15 [a]Deut. 28:15 [b]Is. 1:20
16 [a]Ex. 14:13, 31
17 [a]Gen. 30:14 [b][James 5:16–18] [c]Ezra 10:9 [d]1 Sam. 8:7
18 [a]Ex. 14:31
19 [a]Ex. 9:28

12:1 This chapter marks the end of the era of the judges, represented in Samuel. Political power now resides in the king. Even the office of prophet is subservient to the king.
12:2–6 Since Samuel's administration was completely upright, their rejection of him was also a rejection of Yahweh who had provided **Moses and Aaron** and all the other national rulers.
12:10 Baals and Ashtoreths were Canaanite nature gods. Baal was often identified with Dagon (see note on 5:2).
12:11 Jerubbaal was another name for Gideon (see Judg. 6:32).
12:12, 13 Samuel draws the contrast between their rejection of **God** as **your king** and **the king whom you have chosen.**
12:14, 15 An obedient heart, not the form of government, brings the blessing of God.
12:17 Wheat harvest was early summer, and thunder and rain were unheard of at this season.

wickedness; [a]yet do not turn aside
from following the LORD, but serve the
LORD with all your heart.
21 "And [a]do not turn aside; [b]for *then*
you would go after *empty things
which cannot profit or deliver, for they
are nothing.
22 "For [a]the LORD will not forsake
[b]His people, [c]for His great name's
sake, because [d]it has pleased the LORD
to make you His people.
6 23 "Moreover, as for me, far be it from
me that I should sin against the LORD
[a]in ceasing to pray for you; but [b]I will
teach you the [c]good and the right way.
24 [a]"Only fear the LORD, and serve
Him in *truth with all your heart; for
[b]consider what [c]great things He has
done for you.
25 "But if you still do wickedly,
[a]you shall be swept away, [b]both you
and your king."

Saul's Unlawful Sacrifice

13 Saul [1]reigned one year; and
when he had reigned two years
over Israel,
2 Saul *chose for himself three thousand *men* of Israel. Two thousand were
with Saul in [a]Michmash and in the
mountains of Bethel, and a thousand
were with [b]Jonathan in [c]Gibeah of
Benjamin. The rest of the people he
sent away, every man to his tent.
3 And Jonathan attacked [a]the garrison of the Philistines that *was* in
[b]Geba, and the Philistines heard *of it.*
Then Saul blew the trumpet throughout all the land, saying, "Let the Hebrews hear!"
4 Now all Israel heard it said *that*
Saul had attacked a garrison of the
Philistines, and *that* Israel had also become [1]an abomination to the Philistines. And the people were called together to Saul at Gilgal.

20 [a]Deut. 11:16
21 [a]2 Chr. 25:15 [b]Is. 41:29 *See WW at Is. 45:18.
22 [a]Deut. 31:6 [b]Is. 43:21 [c]Jer. 14:21 [d]Deut. 7:6–11
23 [a]Rom. 1:9 [b]Ps. 34:11 [c]1 Kin. 8:36
24 [a]Eccl. 12:13 [b]Is. 5:12 [c]Deut. 10:21 *See WW at Ps. 25:5.
25 [a]Josh. 24:20 [b]Deut. 28:36

CHAPTER 13

1 [1]Heb. is difficult; cf. 2 Sam. 5:4; 2 Kin. 14:2; see also 2 Sam. 2:10; Acts 13:21
2 [a]1 Sam. 14:5, 31 [b]1 Sam. 14:1 [c]1 Sam. 10:26 *See WW at 1 Kin. 11:34.
3 [a]1 Sam. 10:5 [b]2 Sam. 5:25
4 [1]*odious*
5 [a]Judg. 7:12 [b]Josh. 7:2 [1]So with MT, LXX, Tg., Vg.; Syr. and some mss. of LXX *three thousand*
6 [a]Judg. 6:2
7 [a]Num. 32:1–42
8 [a]1 Sam. 10:8
10 [1]Lit. *bless him*
13 [a]2 Chr. 16:9 [b]1 Sam. 15:11, 22, 28 *See WW at Ps. 119:35.

5 Then the Philistines gathered together to fight with Israel, [1]thirty thousand chariots and six thousand horsemen, and people [a]as the sand which
is on the seashore in multitude. And
they came up and encamped in Michmash, to the east of [b]Beth Aven.
6 When the men of Israel saw that
they were in danger (for the people
were distressed), then the people
[a]hid in caves, in thickets, in rocks, in
holes, and in pits.
7 And *some of* the Hebrews crossed
over the Jordan to the [a]land of Gad and
Gilead. As for Saul, he *was* still in Gilgal, and all the people followed him
trembling.
8 [a]Then he waited seven days, according to the time set by Samuel. But
Samuel did not come to Gilgal; and the
people were scattered from him.
9 So Saul said, "Bring a burnt offering and peace offerings here to me."
And he offered the burnt offering.
10 Now it happened, as soon as he had
finished presenting the burnt offering,
that Samuel came; and Saul went out
to meet him, that he might [1]greet
him.
11 And Samuel said, "What have you
done?" Saul said, "When I saw that the
people were scattered from me, and
that you did not come within the days
appointed, and *that* the Philistines
gathered together at Michmash,
12 "then I said, 'The Philistines will
now come down on me at Gilgal, and
I have not made supplication to the
LORD.' Therefore I felt compelled, and
offered a burnt offering."
13 And Samuel said to Saul, [a]"You 6
have done foolishly. [b]You have not
kept the *commandment of the LORD
your God, which He commanded you.
For now the LORD would have established your kingdom over Israel forever.

12:22–24 Samuel understood that God can bring redemption to areas where men have brought potential disaster by their own wrong motives.
12:23 See section 6 of Truth-In-Action at the end of 1 Sam.
13:1 This is a difficult passage because a number has dropped out of the Hebrew text.
13:2 Regardless of what the first number may have been, this event took place on the second anniversary of his reign. Saul forms a standing army at **Michmash,** 9 miles north of Jerusalem and 5 miles northeast of Gibeah, in extremely rugged terrain. It is 1,980 feet in elevation. **Bethel** is 5 miles northwest of Michmash at an elevation of 2,890 feet.
13:3 **Geba** is a town halfway between Michmash and Gibeah. Blowing **the trumpet** was an announcement of Jonathan's victory and a call to arms. Jonathan's attack was a signal for a war of independence from the Philistines.
13:5 The Hebrew number may be 3,000 as some ancient manuscripts indicate, rather than **30,000 chariots.** An army of 30,000 chariots would be the largest number ever recorded in the ancient world, and a minor power like Philistia would not have had that kind of strength.
13:8 The frightened soldiers are already beginning to abandon Saul, and he obviously feels his leadership was at stake.
13:9–12 The first rule of having authority over others is to be under authority oneself.
13:13, 14 See section 6 of Truth-In-Action at the end of 1 Sam.
13:13 The fool in Scripture is one devoid of moral and spiritual character. **Commandment of the LORD:** More than offering sacrifices or usurping the power of the priest is at stake here. God, not the king, was to be sovereign in Israel.

14 [a]"But now your kingdom shall not
continue. [b]The LORD has sought for
Himself a man [c]after His own heart,
and the LORD has commanded him *to
be* commander over His people, because you have [d]not kept what the
LORD commanded you."
15 Then Samuel arose and went up
from Gilgal to Gibeah of [1]Benjamin.
And Saul numbered the people present
with him, [a]about six hundred men.

No Weapons for the Army

16 Saul, Jonathan his son, and the people present with them remained in
[1]Gibeah of Benjamin. But the Philistines encamped in Michmash.
17 Then raiders came out of the camp
of the Philistines in three companies.
One company turned onto the road to
[a]Ophrah, to the land of Shual,
18 another company turned to the road
to [a]Beth Horon, and another company
turned *to* the road of the border that
overlooks the Valley of [b]Zeboim toward the wilderness.
19 Now [a]there was no blacksmith to
be found throughout all the land of Israel, for the Philistines said, "Lest the
Hebrews make swords or spears."
20 But all the Israelites would go down
to the Philistines to sharpen each
man's plowshare, his mattock, his ax,
and his sickle;
21 and the charge for a sharpening
was a [1]pim for the plowshares, the
mattocks, the forks, and the axes, and
to set the points of the goads.
22 So it came about, on the day of battle, that [a]there was neither sword nor
spear found in the hand of any of the
people who *were* with Saul and Jonathan. But they were found with Saul
and Jonathan his son.
23 [a]And the garrison of the Philistines
went out to the pass of Michmash.

14 [a]1 Sam. 15:28; 31:6 [b]1 Sam. 16:1 [c]Ps. 89:20; Acts 7:46; 13:22 [d]1 Sam. 15:11, 19
15 [a]1 Sam. 13:2, 6, 7; 14:2 [1]So with MT, Tg.; LXX, Vg. add *And the rest of the people went up after Saul to meet the people who fought against them, going from Gilgal to Gibeah in the hill of Benjamin.*
16 [1]Heb. *Geba*
17 [a]Josh. 18:23
18 [a]Josh. 16:3; 18:13, 14 [b]Gen. 14:2; Neh. 11:34
19 [a]Judg. 5:8; 2 Kin. 24:14; Jer. 24:1; 29:2
21 [1]About two-thirds shekel weight
22 [a]Judg. 5:8
23 [a]1 Sam. 14:1, 4

CHAPTER 14

1 [1]*carried*
2 [a]1 Sam. 13:15, 16
3 [a]1 Sam. 22:9, 11, 20 [b]1 Sam. 4:21 [c]1 Sam. 2:28
4 [a]1 Sam. 13:23
6 [a]1 Sam. 17:26, 36; Jer. 9:25, 26 [b]Judg. 7:4, 7; 1 Sam. 17:46, 47; 2 Chr. 14:11; [Ps. 115:3; 135:6; Zech. 4:6; Matt. 19:26; Rom. 8:31]

Jonathan Defeats the Philistines

14 Now it happened one day that
Jonathan the son of Saul said
to the young man who [1]bore his armor,
"Come, let us go over to the Philistines'
garrison that *is* on the other side." But
he did not tell his father.
2 And Saul was sitting in the outskirts
of [a]Gibeah under a pomegranate tree
which *is* in Migron. The people who
were with him *were* about six hundred
men.
3 [a]Ahijah the son of Ahitub, [b]Icha-
bod's brother, the son of Phinehas, the
son of Eli, the LORD's priest in Shiloh,
was [c]wearing an ephod. But the people
did not know that Jonathan had gone.
4 Between the passes, by which Jonathan sought to go over [a]to the Philistines' garrison, *there was* a sharp rock
on one side and a sharp rock on the
other side. And the name of one *was*
Bozez, and the name of the other Seneh.
5 The front of one faced northward
opposite Michmash, and the other
southward opposite Gibeah.
6 Then Jonathan said to the young 4
man who bore his armor, "Come, let
us go over to the garrison of these
[a]uncircumcised; it may be that the
LORD will work for us. For nothing restrains the LORD [b]from saving by many
or by few."
7 So his armorbearer said to him, "Do 5
all that is in your heart. Go then; here
I am with you, according to your
heart."
8 Then Jonathan said, "Very well, let
us cross over to *these* men, and we will
show ourselves to them.
9 "If they say thus to us, 'Wait until
we come to you,' then we will stand
still in our place and not go up to them.
10 "But if they say thus, 'Come up to
us,' then we will go up. For the LORD

13:14 Samuel rejects the idea of a successor to Saul's throne. The rejection of Saul himself comes later (see 15:10, 11).
13:16–18 Ophrah: One raiding party goes to the northeast. (Ophrah is about 5 miles east of Bethel.) The second party goes toward the west, the third toward the southeast. The strategy is to lure Saul and Jonathan and their soldiers out of their positions and force them to fight.
13:19–22 The Philistines owed their military superiority in part to their skills in metallurgy. This came from their contact with the Hittite nations and the nations around the Aegean Sea, the area from which they had migrated about 1200 B.C. Money was measured in weight rather than coins. **A pim** weighed about 1/4 ounce.
14:1 Other side: There was an extremely deep and rugged ravine separating the two encampments.
14:3 Saul now turns to **Ahijah,** Eli's great-grandson, even though Eli's line has been rejected by God.
14:4 The outcroppings were so rugged they were given names: **Bozez,** which means "Shining" or "Slippery," and **Seneh,** meaning "Thorny." It was the most improbable route one could choose, thus the surprise of the Philistines when Jonathan is discovered.
14:6 See section 4 of Truth-In-Action at the end of 1 Sam.
14:6 Uncircumcised was a term of derision often used by Israelites to designate Gentiles, or enemies. However, it is also a reminder of the covenant of God with His people. Jonathan and his armorbearer are covenant people of Yahweh; therefore, numerical odds do not apply, for the Lord is on their side.
14:7 See section 5 of Truth-In-Action at the end of 1 Sam.
14:7 The **armorbearer** was more than just an aide or servant; he was a loyal partner in battle.

has delivered them into our hand, and
[a]this *will be* a sign to us."
11 So both of them showed themselves
to the garrison of the Philistines. And
the Philistines said, "Look, the Hebrews are coming out of the holes
where they have [a]hidden."
12 Then the men of the garrison called
to Jonathan and his armorbearer, and
said, "Come up to us, and we will
[1]show you something." Jonathan said
to his armorbearer, "Come up after me,
for the LORD has delivered them into
the hand of Israel."
13 And Jonathan climbed up on his
hands and knees with his armorbearer
after him; and they [a]fell before Jonathan. And as he came after him, his
armorbearer killed them.
14 That first slaughter which Jonathan
and his armorbearer made was about
twenty men within about [1]half an acre
of land.
15 And [a]there was [1]trembling in the
camp, in the field, and among all the
people. The garrison and [b]the raiders
also trembled; and the earth quaked,
so that it was [c]a very great trembling.
16 Now the watchmen of Saul in
Gibeah of Benjamin looked, and *there*
was the multitude, melting away; and
they [a]went here and there.
17 Then Saul said to the people who
were with him, "Now call the roll and
see who has gone from us." And when
they had called the roll, surprisingly,
Jonathan and his armorbearer *were*
not *there*.
18 And Saul said to Ahijah, "Bring the
[1]ark of God here" (for at that time the
[1]ark of God was with the children of
Israel).
19 Now it happened, while Saul
[a]talked to the priest, that the noise
which *was* in the camp of the Philistines continued to increase; so Saul
said to the priest, "Withdraw your
hand."
20 Then Saul and all the people who
were with him assembled, and they
went to the battle; and indeed [a]every
man's sword was against his neighbor,
and there was very great confusion.

10 [a]Gen. 24:14; Judg. 6:36–40
11 [a]1 Sam. 13:6; 14:22
12 [1]*teach*
13 [a]Lev. 26:8; Josh. 23:10
14 [1]Lit. *half the area plowed by a yoke* of oxen in a day
15 [a]Deut. 28:7; 2 Kin. 7:6, 7; Job 18:11 [b]1 Sam. 13:17 [c]Gen. 35:5 [1]*terror*
16 [a]1 Sam. 14:20
18 [1]So with MT, Tg., Vg.; LXX *ephod*
19 [a]Num. 27:21
20 [a]Judg. 7:22; 2 Chr. 20:23
22 [a]1 Sam. 13:6
23 [a]Ex. 14:30; 2 Chr. 32:22; Hos. 1:7 [b]1 Sam. 13:5
24 [a]Josh. 6:26 *See WW at Ps. 34:8.
25 [a]Deut. 9:28; Matt. 3:5 [b]Ex. 3:8; Num. 13:27; Matt. 3:4
27 [1]Lit. *eyes* *See WW at Ex. 38:22.

21 Moreover the Hebrews *who* were
with the Philistines before that time,
who went up with them into the camp
from the surrounding *country*, they
also joined the Israelites who *were*
with Saul and Jonathan.
22 Likewise all the men of Israel who
[a]had hidden in the mountains of
Ephraim, *when* they heard that the Philistines fled, they also followed hard after them in the battle.
23 [a]So the LORD saved Israel that day,
and the battle shifted [b]to Beth Aven.

Saul's Rash Oath

24 And the men of Israel were distressed that day, for Saul had [a]placed
the people under oath, saying, "Cursed
is the man who eats *any* food until evening, before I have taken vengeance on
my enemies." So none of the people
*tasted food.
25 [a]Now all *the people* of the land
came to a forest; and there was [b]honey
on the ground.
26 And when the people had come into
the woods, there was the honey, dripping; but no one put his hand to
his mouth, for the people feared the
oath.
27 But Jonathan had not heard his father charge the people with the oath;
therefore he stretched out the end of
the *rod that *was* in his hand and
dipped it in a honeycomb, and put
his hand to his mouth; and his
[1]countenance brightened.
28 Then one of the people said, "Your
father strictly charged the people with
an oath, saying, 'Cursed *is* the man
who eats food this day.' " And the people were faint.
29 But Jonathan said, "My father has
troubled the land. Look now, how my
countenance has brightened because I
tasted a little of this honey.
30 "How much better if the people had
eaten freely today of the spoil of their
enemies which they found! For now
would there not have been a much
greater slaughter among the Philistines?"

14:12 Show you something is an invitation to fight. "We'll teach you a thing or two" is the spirit of this statement.
14:13 They climb up the face of the rock on their **hands and knees,** evidently a feat the Philistines thought could not be accomplished.
14:14 Half an acre could have been as little as 15–20 yards.
14:19 Withdraw your hand: Stop trying to get guidance for me; I do not have time.
14:20 The **confusion** is in the camp of the terrified Philistines as they begin fighting one another.
14:21 The Hebrews here are not Saul's men; this was a designation for groups of renegades and mercenaries that hired themselves out. As true hirelings, when the battle turns, they join the winning side and fight for Israel.
14:24 To be **distressed** is to be pressed or fatigued. Saul's foolish vow, which he imposes on his exhausted troops, further weakens them.
14:27 Jonathan's **countenance brightened,** meaning his eyes shone, because he had been refreshed and rejuvenated.

31 Now they had [1]driven back the Philistines that day from Michmash to Aijalon. So the people were very faint.

32 And the people rushed on the [1]spoil, and took sheep, oxen, and calves, and slaughtered *them* on the ground; and the people ate *them* [a]with the blood.

33 Then they told Saul, saying, "Look, the people are sinning against the LORD by eating with the blood!" So he said, "You have dealt treacherously; *roll a large stone to me this day."

34 Then Saul said, "Disperse yourselves among the people, and say to them, 'Bring me here every man's ox and every man's sheep, slaughter *them* here, and eat; and do not sin against the LORD by eating with the blood.' " So every one of the people brought his ox with him that night, and slaughtered *it* there.

35 Then Saul [a]built an altar to the LORD. This was the first altar that he built to the LORD.

36 Now Saul said, "Let us go down after the Philistines by night, and plunder them until the morning light; and let us not leave a man of them." And they said, "Do whatever seems good to you." Then the priest said, "Let us draw near to God here."

37 So Saul [a]asked counsel of God, "Shall I go down after the Philistines? Will You deliver them into the hand of Israel?" But [b]He did not answer him that day.

38 And Saul said, [a]"Come over here, all you chiefs of the people, and know and see what this sin was today.

39 "For [a]*as* the LORD lives, who saves Israel, though it be in Jonathan my son, he shall surely die." But not a man among all the people answered him.

40 Then he said to all Israel, "You be on one side, and my son Jonathan and I will be on the other side." And the people said to Saul, "Do what seems good to you."

41 Therefore Saul said to the LORD God of Israel, [a]"Give[1] a perfect *lot*." [b]So Saul and Jonathan were taken, but the people escaped.

42 And Saul said, "Cast *lots* between my son Jonathan and me." So Jonathan was taken.

43 Then Saul said to Jonathan, [a]"Tell me what you have done." And Jonathan told him, and said, [b]"I only *tasted a little honey with the end of the rod that *was* in my hand. So now I must die!"

44 Saul answered, [a]"God do so and more also; [b]for you shall surely die, Jonathan."

45 But the people said to Saul, "Shall Jonathan die, who has accomplished this great deliverance in Israel? Certainly not! [a]*As* the LORD lives, not one hair of his head shall fall to the ground, for he has worked [b]with God this day." So the people rescued Jonathan, and he did not die.

46 Then Saul returned from pursuing the Philistines, and the Philistines went to their own place.

Saul's Continuing Wars

47 So Saul established his sovereignty over Israel, and fought against all his enemies on every side, against Moab, against the people of [a]Ammon, against Edom, against the kings of [b]Zobah, and against the Philistines. Wherever he turned, he [1]harassed *them*.

48 And he gathered an army and [a]attacked[1] the Amalekites, and delivered Israel from the hands of those who plundered them.

49 [a]The sons of Saul were Jonathan, [1]Jishui, and Malchishua. And the names of his two daughters *were these:* the name of the firstborn Merab, and the name of the younger [b]Michal.

50 The name of Saul's wife *was* Ahinoam the daughter of Ahimaaz. And the name of the commander of his army *was* Abner the son of Ner, Saul's [a]uncle.

51 [a]Kish *was* the father of Saul, and Ner the father of Abner *was* the son of Abiel.

52 Now there was fierce war with the Philistines all the days of Saul. And when Saul saw any strong man or any valiant man, [a]he took him for himself.

31 [1]Lit. *struck*
32 [a]Gen. 9:4; Lev. 3:17; 17:10–14; 19:26; Deut. 12:16, 23, 24; Acts 15:20 [1]*plunder*
33 *See WW at Prov. 16:3.
35 [a]1 Sam. 7:12, 17; 2 Sam. 24:25
37 [a]Judg. 20:18 [b]1 Sam. 28:6
38 [a]Josh. 7:14; 1 Sam. 10:19
39 [a]1 Sam. 14:24, 44; 2 Sam. 12:5
41 [a]Prov. 16:33; Acts 1:24–26 [b]Josh. 7:16; 1 Sam. 10:20, 21 [1]So with MT, Tg.; LXX, Vg. *Why do You not answer Your servant today? If the injustice is with me or Jonathan my son, O LORD God of Israel, give proof; and if You say it is with Your people Israel, give holiness.*
43 [a]Josh. 7:19 [b]1 Sam. 14:27 *See WW at Ps. 34:8.
44 [a]Ruth 1:17; 1 Sam. 25:22 [b]1 Sam. 14:39
45 [a]2 Sam. 14:11; 1 Kin. 1:52; Luke 21:18; Acts 27:34 [b][2 Cor. 6:1; Phil. 2:12, 13]
47 [a]1 Sam. 11:1–13 [b]2 Sam. 10:6 [1]LXX, Vg. *prospered*
48 [a]Ex. 17:16; 1 Sam. 15:3–7 [1]Lit. *struck*
49 [a]1 Sam. 31:2; 1 Chr. 8:33 [b]1 Sam. 18:17–20, 27; 19:12 [1]*Abinadab,* 1 Chr. 8:33; 9:39
50 [a]1 Sam. 10:14
51 [a]1 Sam. 9:1, 21
52 [a]1 Sam. 8:11

14:31 From **Michmash to Aijalon** was about 3 miles.

14:32 Since it is now evening, the oath is no longer in effect.

14:33 **Eating with the blood** means eating the slaughtered animals without properly pouring out the blood on the altar of sacrifice as required in Lev. 19:26. This is why Saul builds the altar and oversees the sacrifice (vv. 33–35).

14:38 Saul rightly concludes that no answer has come from God because of sin in the camp.

14:45 **He has worked with God this day:** Though the discernment has pointed out Jonathan as the transgressor, God has proven to be with him rather than in the oath of Saul.

14:47 **Established his sovereignty** means that Saul has now secured himself as king. The list of nations is a summary statement of Saul's successes. **Moab, Ammon, Edom,** and **Zobah** were the nations east of the Jordan, beginning with Edom in the southeast and extending to Zobah, a district in northern Syria, east of present-day Lebanon.

Saul Spares King Agag

15 Samuel also said to Saul,
[a]"The LORD sent me to anoint
you king over His people, over Israel.
Now therefore, heed the voice of the
words of the LORD.
2 "Thus says the LORD of hosts: 'I will
punish Amalek *for* what he did to Israel, [a]how he ambushed him on the
way when he came up from Egypt.
3 'Now go and [a]attack[1] Amalek, and
[b]utterly destroy all that they have, and
do not spare them. But kill both man
and woman, infant and nursing child,
ox and sheep, camel and donkey.' "
4 So Saul gathered the people together and numbered them in Telaim,
two hundred thousand foot soldiers
and ten thousand men of Judah.
5 And Saul came to a city of Amalek,
and lay in wait in the valley.
6 Then Saul said to [a]the Kenites,
[b]"Go, depart, get down from among
the Amalekites, lest I destroy you with
them. For [c]you showed kindness to all
the children of Israel when they came
up out of Egypt." So the Kenites departed from among the Amalekites.
7 [a]And Saul attacked the Amalekites,
from [b]Havilah all the way to [c]Shur,
which is east of Egypt.
3 8 [a]He also took Agag king of the
Amalekites alive, and [b]utterly destroyed all the people with the edge of
the sword.
9 But Saul and the people [a]spared
Agag and the best of the sheep, the
oxen, the fatlings, the lambs, and all
that was good, and were unwilling to
utterly destroy them. But everything
despised and worthless, that they utterly destroyed.

Saul Rejected as King

10 Now the word of the LORD came to
Samuel, saying,
11 [a]"I greatly regret that I have set up
Saul *as* king, for he has [b]turned back
from following Me, [c]and has not performed My commandments." And it
[d]grieved Samuel, and he cried out to
the LORD all night.
12 So when Samuel rose early in the
morning to meet Saul, it was told Samuel, saying, "Saul went to [a]Carmel, and
indeed, he set up a monument for himself; and he has gone on around,
passed by, and gone down to Gilgal."
13 Then Samuel went to Saul, and Saul
said to him, [a]"Blessed *are* you of the
LORD! I have performed the commandment of the LORD."
14 But Samuel said, "What then *is* this
bleating of the sheep in my ears, and
the lowing of the oxen which I hear?"
15 And Saul said, "They have brought
them from the Amalekites; [a]for the
people spared the best of the sheep and
the oxen, to sacrifice to the LORD your
God; and the rest we have utterly destroyed."
16 Then Samuel said to Saul, "Be
quiet! And I will tell you what the LORD
said to me last night." And he said to
him, "Speak on."
17 So Samuel said, [a]"When you *were*
little in your own eyes, *were* you not
head of the tribes of Israel? And did
not the LORD anoint you king over Israel?
18 "Now the LORD sent you on a
mission, and said, 'Go, and utterly destroy the sinners, the Amalekites, and
fight against them until they are
[1]consumed.'
19 "Why then did you not obey the
voice of the LORD? Why did you swoop
down on the [1]spoil, and do evil in the
sight of the LORD?"
20 And Saul said to Samuel, [a]"But I
have obeyed the voice of the LORD, and
gone on the mission on which the LORD
sent me, and brought back Agag king
of Amalek; I have utterly destroyed the
Amalekites.
21 [a]"But the people took of the plun-

CHAPTER 15

1 [a]1 Sam. 9:16; 10:1
2 [a]Ex. 17:8, 14; Num. 24:20; Deut. 25:17–19
3 [a]Deut. 25:19 [b]Lev. 27:28, 29; Num. 24:20; Deut. 20:16–18; Josh. 6:17–21 [1]Lit. *strike*
6 [a]Num. 24:21; Judg. 1:16; 4:11–22; 1 Chr. 2:55 [b]Gen. 18:25; 19:12, 14; Rev. 18:4 [c]Ex. 18:10, 19; Num. 10:29, 32
7 [a]1 Sam. 14:48 [b]Gen. 2:11; 25:17, 18 [c]Gen. 16:7; Ex. 15:22; 1 Sam. 27:8
8 [a]1 Sam. 15:32, 33 [b]1 Sam. 27:8, 9
9 [a]1 Sam. 15:3, 15, 19
11 [a]Gen. 6:6, 7; 1 Sam. 15:35; 2 Sam. 24:16 [b]Josh. 22:16; 1 Kin. 9:6 [c]1 Sam. 13:13; 15:3, 9 [d]1 Sam. 15:35; 16:1
12 [a]Josh. 15:55; 1 Sam. 25:2
13 [a]Gen. 14:19; Judg. 17:2; Ruth 3:10; 2 Sam. 2:5
15 [a][Gen. 3:12, 13; Ex. 32:22, 23]; 1 Sam. 15:9, 21; [Prov. 28:13]
17 [a]1 Sam. 9:21; 10:22
18 [1]*exterminated*
19 [1]*plunder*
20 [a]1 Sam. 15:13; [Prov. 28:13]
21 [a]1 Sam. 15:15

15:2 I will punish Amalek: The Amalekites were descended from Esau, the father of the Edomites.
15:4 Telaim is on the southern border of Judah in the area of the Negev.
15:6 The Kenites, since the time of Moses, were friends of Israel, who had settled in the Negev of Judah. The name means "Smith" and they are thought to have been skilled in metal work. Jethro, Moses' father-in-law, was a Kenite (*Judg. 1:16*).
15:8–35 See section 3 of Truth-In-Action at the end of 1 Sam.
15:8, 9 In this holy war, all the spoil was considered a sacrifice to God (referred to as being put under "the ban") so that when Saul took the best for himself it was a direct rebellion against God.
15:11 I greatly regret does not mean that God was surprised and therefore sorry He had permitted Saul to be king, but refers to His deep emotions and concern for both Saul and Israel.
15:12 Carmel is in the Judean mountains, about 8 miles southeast of Hebron, not to be confused with Mt. Carmel. **Monument for himself:** While pretending to be sacrificing to God, Saul is sacrificing to his own ego. Samuel had delivered Saul's coronation message here at **Gilgal** (ch. 12). Now he was to announce the rejection of Saul by God.
15:14–21 These verses reveal a tragic character weakness in Saul. He first claims to have obeyed (v. 13), then blames the people (v. 15), and again seeks to justify himself and blame the people, the true mark of a worthless and hopeless leader (vv. 20, 21).

der, sheep and oxen, the best of the
things which should have been utterly
destroyed, to sacrifice to the LORD your
God in Gilgal."
3 22 So Samuel said:

[a]"Has the LORD *as great* delight in
burnt offerings and sacrifices,
As in obeying the voice of the
LORD?
Behold, [b]to obey is better than
sacrifice,
And to heed than the fat of rams.
23 For rebellion *is as* the sin of
[1]witchcraft,
And stubbornness *is as* *iniquity
and idolatry.
Because you have rejected the
word of the LORD,
[a]He also has rejected you from
being king."

24 [a]Then Saul said to Samuel, "I have
sinned, for I have transgressed the
commandment of the LORD and your
words, because I [b]feared* the people
and obeyed their voice.
25 "Now therefore, please pardon my
sin, and return with me, that I may
worship the LORD."
26 But Samuel said to Saul, "I will not
return with you, [a]for you have rejected
the word of the LORD, and the LORD has
rejected you from being king over Israel."
27 And as Samuel turned around to go
away, [a]*Saul* seized the edge of his robe,
and it tore.
28 So Samuel said to him, [a]"The LORD
has torn the kingdom of Israel from
you today, and has given it to a neighbor of yours, *who is* better than you.
29 "And also the Strength of Israel
[a]will not lie nor relent. For He *is* not a
man, that He should relent."
30 Then he said, "I have sinned; *yet*

22 [a]Ps. 50:8, 9; 51:16, 17; [Prov. 21:3; Is. 1:11–17; Jer. 7:22, 23; Mic. 6:6–8; Heb. 10:4–10] [b][Eccl. 5:1; Hos. 6:6; Matt. 5:24; 9:13; 12:7; Mark 12:33]
23 [a]1 Sam. 13:14;16:1 [1]*divination*
*See WW at Prov. 22:8.
24 [a]Num. 22:34; Josh. 7:20; 1 Sam. 26:21; 2 Sam. 12:13; Ps. 51:4 [b][Ex. 23:2; Prov. 29:25; Is. 51:12, 13]
*See WW at Ex. 1:17.
26 [a]1 Sam. 2:30
27 [a]1 Kin. 11:30, 31
28 [a]1 Sam. 28:17, 18; 1 Kin. 11:31
29 [a]Num. 23:19; Ezek. 24:14; 2 Tim. 2:13; Titus 1:2
30 [a][John 5:44; 12:43]
33 [a][Gen. 9:6]; Num. 14:45; Judg. 1:7; [Matt. 7:2]
34 [a]1 Sam. 7:17 [b]1 Sam. 11:4
35 [a]1 Sam. 19:24

CHAPTER 16

1 [a]1 Sam. 15:23, 35 [b]1 Sam. 9:16; 10:1; 2 Kin. 9:1 [c]Ruth 4:18–22 [d]Ps. 78:70, 71; Acts 13:22 [1]Lit. *seen*
*See WW at Joel 1:9.
2 [a]1 Sam. 9:12

[a]honor me now, please, before the elders of my people and before Israel, and
return with me, that I may worship the
LORD your God."
31 So Samuel turned back after Saul,
and Saul worshiped the LORD.
32 Then Samuel said, "Bring Agag
king of the Amalekites here to me." So
Agag came to him cautiously. And
Agag said, "Surely the bitterness of
death is past."
33 But Samuel said, [a]"As your sword
has made women childless, so shall
your mother be childless among
women." And Samuel hacked Agag in
pieces before the LORD in Gilgal.
34 Then Samuel went to [a]Ramah, and
Saul went up to his house at [b]Gibeah
of Saul.
35 And [a]Samuel went no more to see
Saul until the day of his death. Nevertheless Samuel mourned for Saul, and
the LORD regretted that He had made
Saul king over Israel.

David Anointed King

16 Now the LORD said to Samuel,
[a]"How long will you *mourn for
Saul, seeing I have rejected him from
reigning over Israel? [b]Fill your horn
with oil, and go; I am sending you to
[c]Jesse the Bethlehemite. For [d]I have
[1]provided Myself a king among his
sons."
2 And Samuel said, "How can I go?
If Saul hears *it*, he will kill me." But
the LORD said, "Take a heifer with you,
and say, [a]'I have come to sacrifice to
the LORD.'
3 "Then invite Jesse to the sacrifice,
and I will show you what you shall do;
you shall anoint for Me the one I name
to you."
4 So Samuel did what the LORD said,
and went to Bethlehem. And the elders

15:22, 23 See section 3 of Truth-In-Action at the end of 1 Sam.
15:22 Religious activity in itself has no value.
15:23 Saul's motives are shown to be **rebellion** and **stubbornness,** or standing in opposition to God's commands.
15:28 A neighbor of yours does not refer to a particular person, but simply means someone with whom you associate.
15:29 To **relent** is to repent or change one's mind.
15:30 Honor me now: Saul is concerned with his image and having Samuel with him would make it appear as though everything is all right.
15:32 The bitterness of death: Not having been immediately executed, Agag supposes he will be spared.
15:33 Made women childless indicates the cruelty of Agag and the Amalekites.
15:34 Ramah and **Gibeah** were only 10 miles apart, but Samuel was never to confront Saul again.
15:35 Though Saul reigned nearly 15 more years, he was deposed by the Lord at this moment.
16:1 Jesse the Bethlehemite was the grandson of Ruth and Boaz and so was in the line of the covenant with Abraham (Ruth 4:18–21). Bethlehem is about 10 miles from Ramah in the territory of Judah, thus bringing the monarchy into line with the prophecy in Gen. 49:10, "the scepter shall not depart from Judah." **I have provided Myself:** Saul had been the people's choice; God would now give the people His choice, "a man after His own heart" (13:14). Saul was anointed commander or prince (9:16), while David was to be anointed **king.**
16:2 Take a heifer: The Lord is not authorizing a lie on the part of Samuel, but Samuel is indeed to offer sacrifice to the Lord and takes the animal for that purpose. The full purpose of Samuel's journey is not disclosed to Saul.
16:4 The elders . . . trembled, indicating that Samuel has

of the town [a]trembled at his coming, and said, [b]"Do you come peaceably?"

5 And he said, "Peaceably; I have come to sacrifice to the LORD. [a]Sanctify[1] yourselves, and come with me to the sacrifice." Then he consecrated Jesse and his sons, and invited them to the sacrifice.

6 So it was, when they came, that he looked at [a]Eliab and [b]said, "Surely the LORD's anointed *is* before Him!"

4 7 But the LORD said to Samuel, [a]"Do not look at his appearance or at his physical stature, because I have [1]refused him. [b]For[2] *the LORD does* not *see* as man sees; for man [c]looks at the outward appearance, but the LORD looks at the [d]heart."

8 So Jesse called Abinadab, and made him pass before Samuel. And he said, "Neither has the LORD chosen this one."

9 Then Jesse made Shammah pass by. And he said, "Neither has the LORD chosen this one."

10 Thus Jesse made seven of his sons pass before Samuel. And Samuel said to Jesse, "The LORD has not chosen these."

11 And Samuel said to Jesse, "Are all the young men here?" Then he said, "There remains yet the youngest, and there he is, keeping the [a]sheep." And Samuel said to Jesse, "Send and bring him. For we will not [1]sit down till he comes here."

12 So he sent and brought him in. Now he *was* [a]ruddy, [b]with [1]bright eyes, and good-looking. [c]And the LORD said, "Arise, *anoint him; for this *is* the one!"

13 Then Samuel took the horn of oil and anointed him in the midst of his brothers; and [a]the Spirit of the LORD came upon David from that day forward. So Samuel arose and went to Ramah.

A Distressing Spirit Troubles Saul

14 [a]But the Spirit of the LORD departed from Saul, and [b]a distressing spirit from the LORD troubled him.

15 And Saul's servants said to him, "Surely, a distressing spirit from God is troubling you.

16 "Let our master now command your servants, *who are* before you, to seek out a man *who is* a skillful player on the harp. And it shall be that he will [a]play it with his hand when the [1]distressing spirit from God is upon you, and you shall be well."

17 So Saul said to his servants, [1]"Provide me now a man who can play well, and bring *him* to me."

18 Then one of the servants answered and said, "Look, I have seen a son of Jesse the Bethlehemite, *who is* skillful in playing, a mighty man of valor, a man of war, prudent in speech, and a handsome person; and [a]the LORD *is* with him."

19 Therefore Saul sent messengers to Jesse, and said, "Send me your son David, who *is* with the sheep."

20 And Jesse [a]took a donkey *loaded with* bread, a skin of wine, and a young goat, and sent *them* by his son David to Saul.

21 So David came to Saul and [a]stood before him. And he loved him greatly, and he became his armorbearer.

22 Then Saul sent to Jesse, saying, "Please let David stand before me, for he has found favor in my sight."

23 And so it was, whenever the spirit from God was upon Saul, that David would take a harp and play *it* with his hand. Then Saul would become re-

4 [a]1 Sam. 21:1 [b]1 Kin. 2:13; 2 Kin. 9:22
5 [a]Gen. 35:2; Ex. 19:10 [1]*Consecrate*
6 [a]1 Sam. 17:13, 28 [b]1 Kin. 12:26
7 [a]Ps. 147:10 [b]Is. 55:8, 9 [c]2 Cor. 10:7 [d]1 Kin. 8:39 [1]*rejected* [2]LXX *For God does not see as man sees;* Tg. *It is not by the appearance of a man;* Vg. *Nor do I judge according to the looks of a man*
11 [a]2 Sam. 7:8; Ps. 78:70–72 [1]So with LXX, Vg.; MT *turn around;* Tg., Syr. *turn away*
12 [a]1 Sam. 17:42 [b]Gen. 39:6; Ex. 2:2; Acts 7:20 [c]1 Sam. 9:17 [1]Lit. *beautiful* *See WW at Is. 61:1.
13 [a]Num. 27:18; 1 Sam. 10:6, 9, 10
14 [a]Judg. 16:20; 1 Sam. 11:6; 18:12; 28:15 [b]Judg. 9:23; 1 Sam. 16:15, 16; 18:10; 19:9; 1 Kin. 22:19–22
16 [a]1 Sam. 18:10; 19:9; 2 Kin. 3:15 [1]Lit. *evil*
17 [1]Lit. *Look now for a man for me*
18 [a]1 Sam. 3:19; 18:12, 14
20 [a]1 Sam. 10:4, 27; Prov. 18:16
21 [a]Gen. 41:46; Prov. 22:29

---

retained significant power as a judge as well as a priest during the time of Saul's rejection and decline.

16:7 See section 4 of Truth-In-Action at the end of 1 Sam.

16:12 Ruddy may refer to his fair skin as well as his reddish hair.

16:13 As in the case of Saul, **the Spirit of the LORD** accompanies the anointing by Samuel. From that moment God begins to equip David and direct the details of his life, though it will be some years before he ascends the throne. David is about 15 years old at this time. This is the first of three anointings that David will experience. He is anointed *king over Judah* (2 Sam. 2) and over all Israel seven years later (2 Sam. 5).

16:14 The **distressing spirit from the LORD** illustrates that in the absence of the Spirit of God, men are vulnerable to evil spirits. God is sovereign in all realms, physical and spiritual. However, unless we submit to Him and His rule, we are no longer protected from evil and its destructive effects. It is in this sense that God is said to have sent the spirit. Saul is not just suffering from a depressed mental state with periods of extreme anxiety; he is being driven by an evil spirit.

16:16 David's music, because "the LORD *is* with him" (v. 18), has power to drive out the evil spirit. **Harp,** or lyre, is the earliest instrument mentioned in Scripture (Gen. 4:21). Already mentioned in connection with the prophets (10:5), it played an important part in the life of Israel. See 2 Kin. 3:15 and 1 Chr. 25:1.

16:18 Man of war does not mean he has already fought in a war, but that David has proven his courage, probably by his dealing with the lion and the bear (17:34–36).

16:21 Saul **loved him greatly** because of David's natural attractiveness and because of the supernatural grace of the Holy Spirit in his life.

16:23 Spirit from God: See note on v. 14.

freshed and well, and the distressing spirit would depart from him.

David and Goliath

17 Now the Philistines gathered their armies together to battle, and were gathered at [a]Sochoh, which *belongs* to Judah; they encamped between Sochoh and Azekah, in Ephes Dammim.

2 And Saul and the men of Israel were gathered together, and they encamped in the Valley of Elah, and drew up in battle array against the Philistines.

3 The Philistines stood on a mountain on one side, and Israel stood on a mountain on the other side, with a valley between them.

4 And a champion went out from the camp of the Philistines, named [a]Goliath, from [b]Gath, whose height *was* six cubits and a span.

5 *He had* a bronze helmet on his head, and he *was* [1]armed with a coat of mail, and the weight of the coat *was* five thousand shekels of bronze.

6 And *he had* bronze armor on his legs and a bronze javelin between his shoulders.

7 Now the staff of his spear *was* like a weaver's beam, and his iron spearhead *weighed* six hundred shekels; and a shield-bearer went before him.

8 Then he stood and cried out to the armies of Israel, and said to them, "Why have you come out to line up for battle? *Am* I not a Philistine, and you the [a]servants of Saul? Choose a man for yourselves, and let him come down to me.

9 "If he is *able to fight with me and kill me, then we will be your servants. But if I prevail against him and kill him, then you shall be our servants and [a]serve us."

10 And the Philistine said, "I [a]defy the armies of Israel this day; give me a man, that we may fight together."

11 When Saul and all Israel heard these words of the Philistine, they were dismayed and greatly afraid.

12 Now David *was* [a]the son of that [b]Ephrathite of Bethlehem Judah, whose name *was* Jesse, and who had [c]eight sons. And the man was old, advanced *in years*, in the days of Saul.

13 The three oldest sons of Jesse had gone to follow Saul to the battle. The [a]names of his three sons who went to the battle *were* Eliab the firstborn, next to him Abinadab, and the third Shammah.

14 David *was* the youngest. And the three oldest followed Saul.

15 But David occasionally went and returned from Saul [a]to feed his father's sheep at Bethlehem.

16 And the Philistine drew near and presented himself forty days, morning and evening.

17 Then Jesse said to his son David, "Take now for your brothers an ephah of this dried *grain* and these ten loaves, and run to your brothers at the camp.

18 "And carry these ten cheeses to the captain of *their* thousand, and [a]see how your brothers fare, and bring back news of them."

19 Now Saul and they and all the men of Israel *were* in the Valley of Elah, fighting with the Philistines.

20 So David rose early in the morning, left the sheep with a keeper, and took *the things* and went as Jesse had commanded him. And he came to the camp as the army was going out to the fight and shouting for the battle.

21 For Israel and the Philistines had drawn up in battle array, army against army.

22 And David left his supplies in the hand of the supply keeper, ran to the army, and came and greeted his brothers.

23 Then as he talked with them, there was the champion, the Philistine of Gath, Goliath by name, coming up from the armies of the Philistines; and he spoke [a]according to the same words. So David heard *them*.

24 And all the men of Israel, when they saw the man, fled from him and were dreadfully afraid.

25 So the men of Israel said, "Have you seen this man who has come up? Surely he has come up to defy Israel;

CHAPTER 17

1 [a]Josh. 15:35; 2 Chr. 28:18
4 [a]2 Sam. 21:19 [b]Josh. 11:21, 22
5 [1]*clothed with scaled body armor*
8 [a]1 Sam. 8:17
9 [a]1 Sam. 11:1 *See WW at Num. 13:30.
10 [a]1 Sam. 17:26, 36, 45; 2 Sam. 21:21
12 [a]Ruth 4:22; 1 Sam. 16:1, 18; 17:58 [b]Gen. 35:19 [c]1 Sam. 16:10, 11; 1 Chr. 2:13–15
13 [a]1 Sam. 16:6, 8, 9; 1 Chr. 2:13
15 [a]1 Sam. 16:11, 19; 2 Sam. 7:8
18 [a]Gen. 37:13, 14
23 [a]1 Sam. 17:8–10

17:1 These events occur a considerable time after David has finished his duties as court musician and returned home, evidently because of the improved condition of Saul. **Sochoh** was about 14 miles west of Bethlehem in the foothills of the Judean mountains.

17:4 Champion is literally a "middle man," one who could decide the outcome of a particular battle by one single-handed fight with a similar champion from the opposing side. **Gath** was a major city of the Philistines not far to the west. **Six cubits and a span:** About 9 feet 9 inches.

17:5 Five thousand shekels of bronze: 126 pounds.

17:7 Six hundred shekels: Between 15 and 16 pounds.

17:15 David goes back and forth from supplying music for Saul's periods of insanity to his shepherding for his father, explaining why he is not present with Saul at this time.

17:17 Ephah: About ½ bushel.

17:21 Battle array: The two armies take up their battle formations on opposite sides of the ravine.

and it shall be *that* the man who kills
him the king will enrich with great
riches, [a]will give him his daughter, and
give his father's house exemption *from*
taxes in Israel."
26 Then David spoke to the men who
stood by him, saying, "What shall be
done for the man who kills this Philistine and takes away [a]the reproach
from Israel? For who *is* this [b]uncircum-
cised Philistine, that he should [c]defy
the armies of [d]the living God?"
27 And the people answered him in
this manner, saying, [a]"So shall it be
done for the man who kills him."
28 Now Eliab his oldest brother heard
when he spoke to the men; and Eliab's
[a]anger was aroused against David, and
he said, "Why did you come down
here? And with whom have you left
those few sheep in the wilderness? I
know your pride and the insolence of
your heart, for you have come down
to see the battle."
29 And David said, "What have I done
now? [a]*Is*[1] *there* not a cause?"
30 Then he turned from him toward
another and [a]said the same thing; and
these people answered him as the first
ones *did.*
31 Now when the words which David
spoke were heard, they reported *them*
to Saul; and he sent for him.
32 Then David said to Saul, [a]"Let no
man's heart fail because of him;
[b]your servant will go and fight with
this Philistine."
33 And Saul said to David, [a]"You are
not able to go against this Philistine
to fight with him; for you *are* a youth,
and he a man of war from his youth."
4 34 But David said to Saul, "Your servant used to keep his father's sheep,
and when a [a]lion or a bear came and
took a lamb out of the flock,
35 "I went out after it and struck it,
and delivered *the lamb* from its mouth;
and when it arose against me, I caught
it by its beard, and struck and killed it.
36 "Your servant has killed both lion
and bear; and this uncircumcised Philistine will be like one of them, seeing
he has defied the armies of the living
God."

25 [a]Josh. 15:16
26 [a]1 Sam. 11:2 [b]1 Sam. 14:6; 17:36; Jer. 9:25, 26 [c]1 Sam. 17:10 [d]Deut. 5:26; 2 Kin. 19:4; Jer. 10:10
27 [a]1 Sam. 17:25
28 [a]Gen. 37:4, 8–36; [Prov. 18:19; Matt. 10:36]
29 [a]1 Sam. 17:17 [1]Lit. *Is it not a word? or matter?*
30 [a]1 Sam. 17:26, 27
32 [a]Deut. 20:1–4 [b]1 Sam. 16:18
33 [a]Num. 13:31; Deut. 9:2
34 [a]Judg. 14:5
37 [a][2 Cor. 1:10; 2 Tim. 4:17, 18] [b]1 Sam. 20:13; 1 Chr. 22:11, 16
38 [1]Lit. *clothes*
42 [a][Ps. 123:4; Prov. 16:18; 1 Cor. 1:27, 28] [b]1 Sam. 16:12 [1]*belittled*
43 [a]1 Sam. 24:14; 2 Sam. 3:8; 9:8; 16:9; 2 Kin. 8:13
44 [a]1 Sam. 17:46; 1 Kin. 20:10, 11
45 [a]2 Sam. 22:33, 35; 2 Chr. 32:8; Ps. 124:8; [2 Cor. 10:4]; Heb. 11:33, 34 [b]1 Sam. 17:10
46 [a]Deut. 28:26 [b]Josh. 4:24; 1 Kin. 8:43; 18:36; 2 Kin. 19:19; Is. 52:10
47 [a]1 Sam. 14:6; 2 Chr. 14:11; 20:15; Ps. 44:6; Hos. 1:7; Zech. 4:6
*See WW at Lev. 16:17.

37 Moreover David said, [a]"The LORD,
who delivered me from the paw of the
lion and from the paw of the bear, He
will deliver me from the hand of this
Philistine." And Saul said to David,
[b]"Go, and the LORD be with you!"
38 So Saul clothed David with his
[1]armor, and he put a bronze helmet on
his head; he also clothed him with a
coat of mail.
39 David fastened his sword to his armor and tried to walk, for he had not
tested *them.* And David said to Saul,
"I cannot walk with these, for I have
not tested *them.*" So David took them
off.
40 Then he took his staff in his hand;
and he chose for himself five smooth
stones from the brook, and put them
in a shepherd's bag, in a pouch which
he had, and his sling was in his hand.
And he drew near to the Philistine.
41 So the Philistine came, and began
drawing near to David, and the man
who bore the shield *went* before
him.
42 And when the Philistine looked
about and saw David, he [a]disdained[1]
him; for he was *only* a youth, [b]ruddy
and good-looking.
43 So the Philistine [a]said to David,
"*Am* I a dog, that you come to me with
sticks?" And the Philistine cursed David by his gods.
44 And the Philistine [a]said to David,
"Come to me, and I will give your flesh
to the birds of the air and the beasts
of the field!"
45 Then David said to the Philistine, 3
"You come to me with a sword, with
a spear, and with a javelin. [a]But I come
to you in the name of the LORD of hosts,
the God of the armies of Israel, whom
you have [b]defied.
46 "This day the LORD will deliver you
into my hand, and I will strike you and
take your head from you. And this day
I will give [a]the carcasses of the camp
of the Philistines to the birds of the air
and the wild beasts of the earth,
[b]that all the earth may know that there
is a God in Israel.
47 "Then all this *assembly shall know
that the LORD [a]does not save with

17:28 Eliab reacts angrily to David's words about the giant (v. 26) because he saw them *as an insult to the army of* Israel.

17:34–37 See section 4 of Truth-In-Action at the end of 1 Sam.

17:38 Armor refers to the clothes that were worn under the actual armor.

17:39 Tested *them:* He has not learned to use them.

17:40 Sling: The sling was used with great accuracy as a weapon of war. The Benjamites were so accurate that they were able to split a hair with it (Judg. 20:16). It consisted of a small leather pouch with long leather cords attached at opposite ends. A stone in the pouch was whirled around the head and one end released, sending the stone with great velocity toward its target.

17:45–50 See section 3 of Truth-In-Action at the end of 1 Sam.

sword and spear; for [b]the battle *is* the
LORD's, and He will give you into our
hands."
48 So it was, when the Philistine arose
and came and drew near to meet David, that David hurried and [a]ran toward the army to meet the Philistine.
49 Then David put his hand in his bag
and took out a stone; and he slung *it*
and struck the Philistine in his forehead, so that the stone sank into his
forehead, and he fell on his face to the
earth.
50 So David prevailed over the Philistine with a [a]sling and a stone, and
struck the Philistine and killed him.
But *there was* no sword in the hand
of David.
51 Therefore David ran and stood over
the Philistine, took his [a]sword and
drew it out of its sheath and killed him,
and cut off his head with it. And when
the Philistines saw that their champion
was dead, [b]they fled.
52 Now the men of Israel and Judah
arose and shouted, and pursued the
Philistines as far as the entrance of
[1]the valley and to the gates of Ekron.
And the wounded of the Philistines fell
along the road to [a]Shaaraim, even as
far as Gath and Ekron.
53 Then the children of Israel returned
from chasing the Philistines, and they
plundered their tents.
54 And David took the head of the Philistine and brought it to Jerusalem, but
he put his armor in his tent.
55 When Saul saw David going out
against the Philistine, he said to
[a]Abner, the commander of the army,
"Abner, [b]whose son *is* this youth?"
And Abner said, "As your soul lives,
O king, I do not know."
56 So the king said, "Inquire whose
son this young man *is*."
57 Then, as David returned from the
slaughter of the Philistine, Abner took
him and brought him before Saul
[a]with the head of the Philistine in his
hand.
58 And Saul said to him, "Whose son
are you, young man?" So David answered, [a]"*I am* the son of your servant
Jesse the Bethlehemite."

47 [b]2 Chr. 20:15
48 [a]Ps. 27:3
50 [a]Judg. 3:31; 15:15; 20:16
51 [a]1 Sam. 21:9; 2 Sam. 23:21 [b]Heb. 11:34
52 [a]Josh. 15:36 [1]So with MT, Syr., Tg., Vg.; LXX *Gath*
55 [a]1 Sam. 14:50 [b]1 Sam. 16:21, 22
57 [a]1 Sam. 17:54
58 [a]1 Sam. 17:12

CHAPTER 18

1 [a]Gen. 44:30 [b]Deut. 13:6; 1 Sam. 20:17; 2 Sam. 1:26 [1]*life of Jonathan was bound up with the life of*
2 [a]1 Sam. 17:15
3 [a]1 Sam. 20:8–17
5 [1]*Or prospered* *See WW at Jer. 3:15.
6 [a]Ex. 15:20, 21; Judg. 11:34; Ps. 68:25; 149:3 [1]*Philistines*
7 [a]Ex. 15:21 [b]1 Sam. 21:11; 29:5
8 [a]Eccl. 4:4 [b]1 Sam. 15:28
9 [1]Viewed with suspicion
10 [a]1 Sam. 16:14 [b]1 Sam. 19:24; 1 Kin. 18:29; Acts 16:16 [c]1 Sam. 16:23 [d]1 Sam. 19:9, 10
11 [a]1 Sam. 19:10; 20:33
12 [a]1 Sam. 18:15, 29

Saul Resents David

18 Now when he had finished
speaking to Saul, [a]the [1]soul of
Jonathan was knit to the soul of David,
[b]and Jonathan loved him as his own
soul.
2 Saul took him that day, [a]and would
not let him go home to his father's
house anymore.
3 Then Jonathan and David made a
[a]covenant, because he loved him as his
own soul.
4 And Jonathan took off the robe that
was on him and gave it to David, with
his armor, even to his sword and his
bow and his belt.
5 So David went out wherever Saul
sent him, *and* [1]behaved* wisely. And
Saul set him over the men of war, and
he was accepted in the sight of all the
people and also in the sight of Saul's
servants.
6 Now it had happened as they were
coming *home*, when David was returning from the slaughter of the [1]Phi-
listine, that [a]the women had come out
of all the cities of Israel, singing and
dancing, to meet King Saul, with tambourines, with joy, and with musical
instruments.
7 So the women [a]sang as they
danced, and said:

[b]"Saul has slain his thousands,
And David his ten thousands."

8 Then Saul was very angry, and the
saying [a]displeased him; and he said,
"They have ascribed to David ten thousands, and to me they have ascribed
only thousands. Now *what* more can
he have but [b]the kingdom?"
9 So Saul [1]eyed David from that day
forward.
10 And it happened on the next day
that [a]the distressing spirit from God
came upon Saul, [b]and he prophesied
inside the house. So David [c]played *music* with his hand, as at other times;
[d]but *there was* a spear in Saul's hand.
11 And Saul [a]cast the spear, for he
said, "I will pin David to the wall!" But
David escaped his presence twice.
12 Now Saul was [a]afraid of David,

17:52 Gath was the hometown of Goliath. **Ekron** was about 5 miles north of Gath.
17:55 Saul is not discovering David for the first time, but since his intention is to bring David into his military leadership and make him a permanent member of his elite bodyguard, a thorough background check is in order.
18:1–4 In giving David his royal **robe, his armor, his sword and his bow and his belt,** Jonathan was giving his authority of succession to his father's throne to David.
18:2 This does not mean that David never again went home, but that he no longer resided at home, since his residence was the palace of Saul.
18:10 Prophesied is perhaps better understood as "raved" under the influence of the distressing spirit.

because [b]the LORD was with him, but had [c]departed from Saul.

13 Therefore Saul removed him from [1]his presence, and made him his captain over a thousand; and [a]he went out and came in before the people.

14 And David behaved wisely in all his ways, and [a]the LORD *was* with him.

15 Therefore, when Saul saw that he behaved very wisely, he was afraid of him.

16 But [a]all Israel and Judah loved David, because he went out and came in before them.

David Marries Michal

17 Then Saul said to David, "Here is my older daughter Merab; [a]I will give her to you as a wife. Only be valiant for me, and fight [b]the LORD's battles." For Saul thought, [c]"Let my hand not be against him, but let the hand of the Philistines be against him."

18 So David said to Saul, [a]"Who *am* I, and what *is* my life *or* my father's family in Israel, that I should be son-in-law to the king?"

19 But it happened at the time when Merab, Saul's daughter, should have been given to David, that she was given to [a]Adriel the [b]Meholathite as a wife.

20 [a]Now Michal, Saul's daughter, loved David. And they told Saul, and the thing pleased him.

21 So Saul said, "I will give her to him, that she may [1]be a snare to him, and that [a]the hand of the Philistines may be against him." Therefore Saul said to David a second time, [b]"You shall be my son-in-law today."

22 And Saul commanded his servants, "Communicate with David secretly, and say, 'Look, the king *has delight in you, and all his servants love you. Now therefore, become the king's son-in-law.'"

23 So Saul's servants spoke those words in the hearing of David. And David said, "Does it seem to you *a* light *thing* to be a king's son-in-law, seeing I *am* a poor and lightly esteemed man?"

24 And the servants of Saul told him, saying, [1]"In this manner David spoke."

25 Then Saul said, "Thus you shall say to David: 'The king does not desire any [a]dowry but one hundred foreskins of the Philistines, to take [b]vengeance on the king's enemies.'" But Saul [c]thought to make David fall by the hand of the Philistines.

26 So when his servants told David these words, it pleased David well to become the king's son-in-law. Now [a]the days had not expired;

27 therefore David arose and went, he and [a]his men, and killed two hundred men of the Philistines. And [b]David brought their foreskins, and they gave them in full count to the king, that he might become the king's son-in-law. Then Saul gave him Michal his daughter as a wife.

28 Thus Saul saw and knew that the LORD *was* with David, and *that* Michal, Saul's daughter, loved him;

29 and Saul was still more afraid of David. So Saul became David's enemy [1]continually.

30 Then the princes of the Philistines [a]went out *to war*. And so it was, whenever they went out, *that* David [b]behaved more wisely than all the servants of Saul, so that his name became highly esteemed.

Saul Persecutes David

19

Now Saul spoke to Jonathan his son and to all his servants, that they should kill [a]David; but Jonathan, Saul's son, [b]delighted greatly in David.

2 So Jonathan told David, saying, "My father Saul seeks to kill you. Therefore please be on your guard until morning, and stay in a secret *place* and hide.

3 "And I will go out and stand beside my father in the field where you *are*, and I will speak with my father about you. Then what I observe, I will tell [a]you."

4 Thus Jonathan [a]spoke well of David to Saul his father, and said to him, "Let not the king [b]sin against his servant, against David, because he has not sinned against you, and because his works *have been* very good toward you.

5 "For he took his [a]life in his hands

---

12 [b]1 Sam. 16:13, 18 [c]1 Sam. 16:14; 28:15
13 [a]Num. 27:17; 1 Sam. 18:16; 29:6; 2 Sam. 5:2 [1]Lit. *himself*
14 [a]Gen. 39:2, 3, 23; Josh. 6:27; 1 Sam. 16:18
16 [a]Num. 27:16, 17; 1 Sam. 18:5; 2 Sam. 5:2; 1 Kin. 3:7
17 [a]1 Sam. 14:49; 17:25 [b]Num. 32:20, 27, 29; 1 Sam. 25:28 [c]1 Sam. 18:21, 25; 2 Sam. 12:9
18 [a]1 Sam. 9:21; 18:23; 2 Sam. 7:18
19 [a]2 Sam. 21:8 [b]Judg. 7:22; 2 Sam. 21:8; 1 Kin. 19:16
20 [a]1 Sam. 18:28
21 [a]1 Sam. 18:17 [b]1 Sam. 18:26 [1]*be bait for*
22 *See WW at Ps. 112:1.
24 [1]Lit. *According to these words*
25 [a]Gen. 34:12; Ex. 22:17 [b]1 Sam. 14:24 [c]1 Sam. 18:17
26 [a]1 Sam. 18:21
27 [a]1 Sam. 18:13 [b]2 Sam. 3:14
29 [1]*all the days*
30 [a]2 Sam. 11:1 [b]1 Sam. 18:5

CHAPTER 19

1 [a]1 Sam. 8:8, 9 [b]1 Sam. 18:1
3 [a]1 Sam. 20:8–13
4 [a]1 Sam. 20:32; [Prov. 31:8, 9] [b]Gen. 42:22; [Prov. 17:13]; Jer. 18:20
5 [a]Judg. 9:17; 12:3

18:17 Saul's strategy is to place David in the major battles with the Philistines in order that he may be killed in battle.

18:19 Nothing more is known of **Adriel the Meholathite,** nor of Saul's reasons for giving his daughter in marriage to him. Meholah was located on the west bank of the Jordan about 23 miles south of the Sea of Galilee.

18:21 A snare to him: Saul presumes that David will put his own life in jeopardy in order to win Michal as his wife.

18:23 Poor and lightly esteemed means that his family has no high social standing, and he has no money for the dowry.

18:30 The **Philistines** inhabited what is the modern-day Gaza Strip. They were constantly trying to expand their borders and bring the Israelites under slavery and taxation.

and [b]killed the Philistine, and [c]the LORD brought about a great deliverance for all Israel. You saw *it* and rejoiced. [d]Why then will you [e]sin against innocent blood, to kill David without a cause?"
6 So Saul heeded the voice of Jonathan, and Saul swore, "*As* the LORD lives, he shall not be killed."
7 Then Jonathan called David, and Jonathan told him all these things. So Jonathan brought David to Saul, and he was in his presence [a]as in times past.
8 And there was war again; and David went out and fought with the Philistines, [a]and struck them with a mighty blow, and they fled from him.
9 Now [a]the distressing spirit from the LORD came upon Saul as he sat in his house with his spear in his hand. And David was playing *music* with *his* hand.
10 Then Saul sought to pin David to the wall with the spear, but he slipped away from Saul's presence; and he drove the spear into the wall. So David fled and escaped that night.
11 [a]Saul also sent messengers to David's house to watch him and to kill him in the morning. And Michal, David's wife, told him, saying, "If you do not save your life tonight, tomorrow you will be killed."
12 So Michal [a]let David down through a window. And he went and fled and escaped.
13 And Michal took [1]an image and laid *it* in the bed, put a cover of goats' *hair* for his head, and covered *it* with clothes.
14 So when Saul sent messengers to take David, she said, "He *is* sick."
15 Then Saul sent the messengers *back* to see David, saying, "Bring him up to me in the bed, that I may kill him."
16 And when the messengers had come in, there was the image in the bed, with a cover of goats' *hair* for his head.
17 Then Saul said to Michal, "Why have you deceived me like this, and sent my enemy away, so that he has escaped?" And Michal answered Saul, "He said to me, 'Let me go! [a]Why should I kill you?' "
18 So David fled and escaped, and went to [a]Samuel at [b]Ramah, and told him all that Saul had done to him. And he and Samuel went and stayed in Naioth.
19 Now it was told Saul, saying, "Take note, David *is* at Naioth in Ramah!"
20 Then [a]Saul sent messengers to take David. [b]And when they saw the group of prophets prophesying, and Samuel standing *as* leader over them, the Spirit of God came upon the messengers of Saul, and they also [c]prophesied.
21 And when Saul was told, he sent other messengers, and they prophesied likewise. Then Saul sent messengers again the third time, and they prophesied also.
22 Then he also went to Ramah, and came to the great well that *is* at Sechu. So he asked, and said, "Where *are* Samuel and David?" And *someone* said, "Indeed *they are* at Naioth in Ramah."
23 So he went there to Naioth in Ramah. Then [a]the Spirit of God was upon him also, and he went on and prophesied until he came to Naioth in Ramah.
24 [a]And he also stripped off his clothes and prophesied before Samuel in like manner, and lay down [b]naked all that day and all that night. Therefore they say, [c]"*Is* Saul also among the prophets?"

Jonathan's Loyalty to David

20 Then David fled from Naioth in Ramah, and went and said to Jonathan, "What have I done? What *is* my iniquity, and what *is* my sin before your father, that he seeks my life?"
2 So Jonathan said to him, "By no means! You shall not die! Indeed, my father will do nothing either great or small without first telling me. And why should my father hide this thing from me? It *is* not *so!*"
3 Then David took an oath again, and said, "Your father certainly knows that I have found favor in your eyes, and he has said, 'Do not let Jonathan know

5 [b]1 Sam. 17:49, 50 [c]1 Sam. 11:13; 1 Chr. 11:14 [d]1 Sam. 20:32 [e][Deut. 19:10–13]
7 [a]1 Sam. 16:21; 18:2, 10, 13
8 [a]1 Sam. 18:27; 23:5
9 [a]1 Sam. 16:14; 18:10, 11
11 [a]Judg. 16:2; Ps. 59:title
12 [a]Josh. 2:15; Acts 9:25; 2 Cor. 11:33
13 [1]*household idols,* Heb. *teraphim*
17 [a]2 Sam. 2:22
18 [a]1 Sam. 16:13 [b]1 Sam. 7:17
20 [a]1 Sam. 19:11, 14; John 7:32 [b]1 Sam. 10:5, 6, 10; [1 Cor. 14:3, 24, 25] [c]Num. 11:25; Joel 2:28
23 [a]1 Sam. 10:10
24 [a]Is. 20:2 [b]Mic. 1:8 [c]1 Sam. 10:10–12

19:9 Spirit from the LORD: See note on 16:14.
19:11 Ps. 59 describes the danger at this time.
19:13 An image was a teraphim, or a pagan idol. This one was evidently near life-size.
19:18 Ramah was about an hour's walk away. **Naioth** means "Tents" or "Camps" and is sometimes used for shepherds' huts or tents. Presumably, David and Samuel went together to such a place for rest and safety.
19:20–24 Samuel was leader over a group of prophets at Ramah. At times, when they were in worship, the Holy Spirit came upon these prophets and elevated their worship beyond their own enthusiasm. ***Is Saul also among the prophets?:*** This phrase had been used in 10:11 in a positive light, indicating that the Spirit of God was upon him and anointing him to be king. Here, it is to be understood sarcastically and tragically: Saul is not among the prophets.

this, lest he be grieved.' But [a]truly, *as*
the LORD lives and *as* your soul lives,
there is but a step between me and
death."
4 So Jonathan said to David, "Whatever you yourself desire, I will do *it*
for you."
5 And David said to Jonathan, "Indeed tomorrow *is* the [a]New Moon, and
I should not fail to sit with the king to
eat. But let me go, that I may [b]hide in
the field until the third *day* at evening.
6 "If your father misses me at all, then
say, 'David earnestly asked *permission*
of me that he might run over [a]to Bethlehem, his city, for *there is* a yearly
sacrifice there for all the family.'
7 [a]"If he says thus: '*It is* well,' your
servant will be safe. But if he is very
angry, be sure that [b]evil is determined
by him.
8 "Therefore you shall [a]deal kindly
with your servant, for [b]you have
brought your servant into a covenant
of the LORD with you. Nevertheless,
[c]if there is iniquity in me, kill me yourself, for why should you bring me to
your father?"
9 But Jonathan said, "Far be it from
you! For if I knew certainly that evil
was determined by my father to come
upon you, then would I not tell you?"
10 Then David said to Jonathan, "Who
will tell me, or what *if* your father answers you roughly?"
11 And Jonathan said to David,
"Come, let us go out into the field." So
both of them went out into the field.
12 Then Jonathan said to David: "The
LORD God of Israel *is witness!* When I
have [1]sounded out my father sometime
tomorrow, *or* the third *day,* and indeed
there is good toward David, and I do
not send to you and tell you,
13 "may [a]the LORD do so and much
more to Jonathan. But if it pleases my
father *to do* you evil, then I will report
it to you and send you away, that you
may go in safety. And [b]the LORD be
with you as He has [c]been with my father.
14 "And you shall not only show me
the kindness of the LORD while I still
live, that I may not die;
15 "but [a]you shall not [1]cut off your
kindness from my [2]house forever, no,
not when the LORD has cut off every
one of the enemies of David from the
face of the earth."
16 So Jonathan made *a covenant* with
the [1]house of David, *saying,* [a]"Let the
LORD require *it* at the hand of David's
enemies."
17 Now Jonathan again caused David
to vow, because he loved him; [a]for
he loved him as he loved his own
soul.
18 Then Jonathan said to David,
[a]"Tomorrow *is* the New Moon; and you
will be missed, because your seat will
be empty.
19 "And *when* you have stayed three
days, go down quickly and come to
[a]the place where you hid on the day
of the deed; and *remain by the stone
Ezel.
20 "Then I will shoot three arrows to
the side, as though I shot at a target;
21 "and there I will send a lad, *saying,*
'Go, find the arrows.' If I expressly say
to the lad, 'Look, the arrows *are* on this
side of you; get them and come'—then,
[a]as the LORD lives, *there is* safety for
you and no harm.
22 "But if I say thus to the young man,
'Look, the arrows *are* beyond you'—go
your way, for the LORD has sent you
away.
23 "And as for [a]the matter which you
and I have spoken of, indeed the LORD
be between you and me forever."
24 Then David hid in the field. And
when the New Moon had come, the
king sat down to eat the feast.
25 Now the king sat on his seat, as at
other times, on a seat by the wall. And
[1]Jonathan arose, and Abner sat by
Saul's side, but David's place was
empty.
26 Nevertheless Saul did not say anything that day, for he thought, "Something has happened to him; he *is* unclean, surely he *is* [a]unclean."
27 And it happened the next day, the
second *day* of the month, that David's
place was empty. And Saul said to Jonathan his son, "Why has the son of
Jesse not come to eat, either yesterday
or today?"
28 So Jonathan [a]answered Saul, "David earnestly asked *permission* of me
to go to Bethlehem.

CHAPTER 20

3 [a]1 Sam. 27:1; 2 Kin. 2:6
5 [a]Num. 10:10; 28:11–15 [b]1 Sam. 19:2, 3
6 [a]1 Sam. 16:4; 17:12; John 7:42
7 [a]Deut. 1:23; 2 Sam. 17:4 [b]1 Sam. 25:17; Esth. 7:7
8 [a]Josh. 2:14 [b]1 Sam. 18:3; 20:16; 23:18 [c]2 Sam. 14:32
12 [1]*searched out*
13 [a]Ruth 1:17; 1 Sam. 3:17 [b]Josh. 1:5; 1 Sam. 17:37; 18:12; 1 Chr. 22:11, 16 [c]1 Sam. 10:7
15 [a]1 Sam. 24:21; 2 Sam. 9:1, 3, 7; 21:7 [1]*stop being kind* [2]*family*
16 [a]Deut. 23:21; 1 Sam. 25:22; 31:2; 2 Sam. 4:7; 21:8 [1]*family*
17 [a]1 Sam. 18:1
18 [a]1 Sam. 20:5, 24
19 [a]1 Sam. 19:2 *See WW at Lam. 5:19.
21 [a]Jer. 4:2
23 [a]1 Sam. 20:14, 15
25 [1]So with MT, Syr., Tg., Vg.; LXX *he sat across from Jonathan*
26 [a]Lev. 7:20, 21; 15:5
28 [a]1 Sam. 20:6

20:5 The New Moon was a time of rest on the first day of each month. Saul had made it a three-day festival in his court.
20:12 The LORD God of Israel *is witness*: Jonathan takes an oath of loyalty to David, rather than to Saul, his own father and the king.
20:15 David kept this promise to Jonathan when he found Mephibosheth, Jonathan's crippled son, and brought him to live in the palace (see 2 Sam. 9).
20:19 Day of the deed refers to the conversation Saul and Jonathan had about David (19:2, 3).
20:26 He *is* unclean, that is, ceremonially unclean according to the Levitical law.

29 "And he said, 'Please let me go, for
our family has a sacrifice in the city,
and my brother has commanded me *to
be there*. And now, if I have found favor in your eyes, please let me get
away and see my brothers.' Therefore
he has not come to the king's table."
30 Then Saul's *anger was aroused
against Jonathan, and he said to him,
"You son of a perverse, rebellious
woman! Do I not know that you have
chosen the son of Jesse to your own
shame and to the shame of your
mother's nakedness?
31 "For as long as the son of Jesse lives
on the earth, you shall not be established, nor your kingdom. Now therefore, send and bring him to me, for he
[1]shall surely die."
32 And Jonathan answered Saul his father, and said to him, [a]"Why should
he be killed? What has he done?"
33 Then Saul [a]cast a spear at him to
[1]kill him, [b]by which Jonathan knew
that it was determined by his father to
kill David.
34 So Jonathan arose from the table
in fierce anger, and ate no food the second day of the month, for he was
grieved for David, because his father
had treated him shamefully.
35 And so it was, in the morning, that
Jonathan went out into the field at the
time appointed with David, and a little
lad *was* with him.
36 Then he said to his lad, "Now run,
find the arrows which I shoot." As the
lad ran, he shot an arrow beyond him.
37 When the lad had come to the place
where the arrow was which Jonathan
had shot, Jonathan cried out after the
lad and said, "*Is* not the arrow beyond
you?"
38 And Jonathan cried out after the
lad, "Make haste, hurry, do not delay!"
So Jonathan's lad gathered up the arrows and came back to his *master.
39 But the lad did not know anything.
Only Jonathan and David knew of the
matter.
40 Then Jonathan gave his [1]weapons
to his lad, and said to him, "Go, carry
them to the city."

30 *See WW at Judg. 10:7.
31 [1]Lit. *is a son of death*
32 [a]Gen. 31:36; 1 Sam. 19:5; [Prov. 31:9]; Matt. 27:23; Luke 23:22
33 [a]1 Sam. 18:11; 19:10 [b]1 Sam. 20:7 [1]*strike him down*
38 *See WW at Mic. 4:13.
40 [1]*equipment*
42 [a]1 Sam. 1:17

CHAPTER 21

1 [a]1 Sam. 14:3; Mark 2:26 [b]1 Sam. 16:4
4 [a]Ex. 25:30; Lev. 24:5–9; Matt. 12:4 [b]Ex. 19:15 [1]*ordinary* [2]*consecrated*
5 [a]Ex. 19:14, 15; 1 Thess. 4:4 [b]Lev. 8:26 [1]The young men are ceremonially undefiled
6 [a]Matt. 12:3, 4; Mark 2:25, 26; Luke 6:3, 4 [b]Lev. 24:8, 9

41 As soon as the lad had gone, David
arose from *a place* toward the south,
fell on his face to the ground, and
bowed down three times. And they
kissed one another; and they wept together, but David more so.
42 Then Jonathan said to David,
[a]"Go in peace, since we have both
sworn in the name of the LORD, saying,
'May the LORD be between you and me,
and between your descendants and my
descendants, forever.' " So he arose
and departed, and Jonathan went into
the city.

David and the Holy Bread

21 Now David came to Nob, to
Ahimelech the priest. And
[a]Ahimelech was [b]afraid when he
met David, and said to him, "Why
are you alone, and no one is with
you?"
2 So David said to Ahimelech the
priest, "The king has ordered me on
some business, and said to me, 'Do not
let anyone know anything about the
business on which I send you, or what
I have commanded you.' And I have
directed *my* young men to such and
such a place.
3 "Now therefore, what have you on
hand? Give *me* five *loaves of* bread in
my hand, or whatever can be found."
4 And the priest answered David and
said, "*There is* no [1]common bread on
hand; but there is [a]holy[2] bread, [b]if the
young men have at least kept themselves from women."
5 Then David answered the priest,
and said to him, "Truly, women *have
been* kept from us about three days
since I came out. And [1]the [a]vessels of
the young men are holy, and *the bread
is* in effect common, even though it was
consecrated [b]in the vessel this day."
6 So the priest [a]gave him holy *bread;*
for there was no bread there but the
showbread [b]which had been taken
from before the LORD, in order to put
hot bread *in its place* on the day when
it was taken away.
7 Now a certain man of the servants

20:29 My brother has commanded me: It was prerogative of the oldest brother to set these family occasions and command all the family members to attend.
20:31 Saul knows, as does Jonathan, that the kingdom has already been given to David.
21:1 David is now 20 years old. His exile lasts 10 years until he is crowned king over Judah in Hebron at age 30. **Nob** is halfway between Jerusalem and Gibeah. Though the ark was still at Kirjath Jearim (7:1), the tabernacle was standing at Nob and was the site of national worship. **Ahimelech,** referred to in 14:3 as Ahijah, is the great-grandson of Eli.
21:6 When the **showbread** was replaced it could be eaten but usually only by the priests. The showbread was 12 loaves made of pure wheat flour which was set in the sanctuary before Yahweh, fresh each Sabbath day. Jesus referred to this event in teaching that He was Lord of the Sabbath and that human need must be considered before ritual (Matt. 12:3, 4).

of Saul *was* there that day, detained
before the LORD. And his name *was*
[a]Doeg, an Edomite, the chief of the
herdsmen who *belonged* to Saul.
8 And David said to Ahimelech, "Is
there not here on hand a spear or a
sword? For I have brought neither my
sword nor my weapons with me, because the king's business required
haste."
9 So the priest said, "The sword of
Goliath the Philistine, whom you killed
in [a]the Valley of Elah, [b]there it is,
wrapped in a cloth behind the ephod.
If you will take that, take *it*. For *there*
is no other except that one here." And
David said, "*There is* none like it; give
it to me."

David Flees to Gath

10 Then David arose and fled that day
from before Saul, and went to Achish
the king of Gath.
11 And [a]the servants of Achish said to
him, "*Is* this not David the king of the
land? Did they not sing of him to one
another in dances, saying:

[b]'Saul has slain his thousands,
And David his ten thousands'?"

12 Now David [a]took these words
[1]to heart, and was very much afraid
of Achish the king of Gath.
13 So [a]he changed his behavior before
them, pretended [1]madness in their
hands, [2]scratched on the doors of the
gate, and let his saliva fall down on
his beard.
14 Then Achish said to his servants,
"Look, you see the man is insane. Why
have you brought him to me?
15 "Have I need of madmen, that you
have brought this *fellow* to play the
madman in my presence? Shall this *fel-*
low come into my house?"

David's Four Hundred Men

22 David therefore departed from
there and [a]escaped [b]to the cave
of Adullam. So when his brothers and
all his father's house heard *it*, they
went down there to him.
2 [a]And everyone *who was* in distress, 6
everyone who *was* in debt, and everyone *who was* [1]discontented gathered
to him. So he became captain over
them. And there were about [b]four hundred men with him.
3 Then David went from there to Mizpah of [a]Moab; and he said to the king
of Moab, "Please let my father and
mother come here with you, till I know
what God will do for me."
4 So he brought them before the king
of Moab, and they dwelt with him all
the time that David was in the stronghold.
5 Now the prophet [a]Gad said to David, "Do not stay in the stronghold; depart, and go to the land of Judah." So
David departed and went into the forest of Hereth.

Saul Murders the Priests

6 When Saul heard that David and
the men who *were* with him had been
discovered—now Saul was staying in
[a]Gibeah under a tamarisk tree in Ramah, with his spear in his hand, and
all his servants standing about him—
7 then Saul said to his servants who
stood about him, "Hear now, you Benjamites! Will the son of Jesse [a]give every one of you fields and vineyards,
and make you all captains of thousands and captains of hundreds?

7 [a]1 Sam. 14:47; 22:9; Ps. 52:title
9 [a]1 Sam. 17:2, 50 [b]1 Sam. 31:10
11 [a]Ps. 56:title [b]1 Sam. 18:6–8; 29:5
12 [a]Luke 2:19 [1]Lit. *in his heart*
13 [a]Ps. 34:title [1]*insanity* [2]*scribbled*

CHAPTER 22

1 [a]Ps. 57:title; 142:title [b]Josh. 12:15; 15:35; 2 Sam. 23:13
2 [a]Judg. 11:3 [b]1 Sam. 25:13 [1]Lit. *bitter of soul*
3 [a]2 Sam. 8:2
5 [a]2 Sam. 24:11; 1 Chr. 21:9; 29:29; 2 Chr. 29:25
6 [a]1 Sam. 15:34
7 [a]1 Sam. 8:14

21:9 It is not known how **the sword of Goliath** got to Nob. It had evidently been dedicated to the Lord after the great defeat by David.
21:10–12 David, concerned that Saul is still seeking his life, flees to the land of his enemies, the Philistines. Perhaps he thought that he would not be recognized, or could convince Achish the king of Gath of the genuineness of his break with Saul. Upon being recognized and even called **the king of the land,** he formulates a plan to extricate himself from this difficult situation.
21:10 Gath was the hometown of Goliath, 30 miles to the southwest of Jerusalem in Philistine territory.
21:14, 15 The ancient world regarded the insane as being an evil sign. They were exempt from harm, lest the gods become angry.
22:1 Adullam was about 20 miles southwest of Jerusalem and 10 miles south of the Philistine city of Gath. **All his father's house** move from Bethlehem and come to David for protection from Saul.
22:2 See section 6 of Truth-In-Action at the end of 1 Sam.
22:2 This is the beginning of the group of select and courageous fighting men that David gathers around himself. They are listed by name and by their amazing exploits in 2 Sam. 23:8–39 and 1 Chr. 11 and 12.
22:3, 4 Ruth, David's great-grandmother, was a Moabitess. Thus, perhaps his family stayed in safety with their relatives.
22:5 The prophet Gad probably came to David from Samuel's school of the prophets. It is possible that he also identified with David's cause and remained with David to assist him. See 1 Chr. 21:9; also 2 Sam. 24:11; 1 Chr. 29:29; 2 Chr. 29:25. **The forest of Hereth** was in the mountain area of Judah, east of Adullam.
22:6 The **tamarisk** tree is a soft-wooded desert tree seldom found in the mountains. This one was evidently well known because of its location in this hill country.
22:7 You Benjamites: That all Saul's retinue were from his own tribe of Benjamin, rather than a broader representation of the nation, may indicate the shrinking power of his rule.

8 "All of you have conspired against
me, and *there is* no one who reveals
to me that [a]my son has made a covenant with the son of Jesse; and *there
is* not one of you who is sorry for me
or reveals to me that my son has stirred
up my servant against me, to lie in
wait, as *it is* this day."
9 Then answered [a]Doeg the Edomite,
who was set over the servants of Saul,
and said, "I saw the son of Jesse going
to Nob, to [b]Ahimelech the son of
[c]Ahitub.
10 [a]"And he inquired of the LORD for
him, [b]gave him provisions, and gave
him the sword of Goliath the Philistine."
11 So the king sent to call Ahimelech
the priest, the son of Ahitub, and all
his father's house, the priests who *were*
in Nob. And they all came to the king.
12 And Saul said, "Hear now, son of

8 [a]1 Sam. 18:3; 20:16, 30
9 [a]1 Sam. 21:7; 22:22; Ps. 52:title [b]1 Sam. 21:1 [c]1 Sam. 14:3
10 [a]Num. 27:21; 1 Sam. 10:22 [b]1 Sam. 21:6, 9

22:8 Here is a tragic illustration of how twisted our view becomes when we give in to jealousy and rage. Saul invents his own reality, uses this myth to condemn his own servants, and orders the slaughter of the priests of God and their families.

22:9 Doeg the Edomite: The Edomites were descendants of Esau and long-standing enemies of Israel. See Introduction to Obadiah: Background.

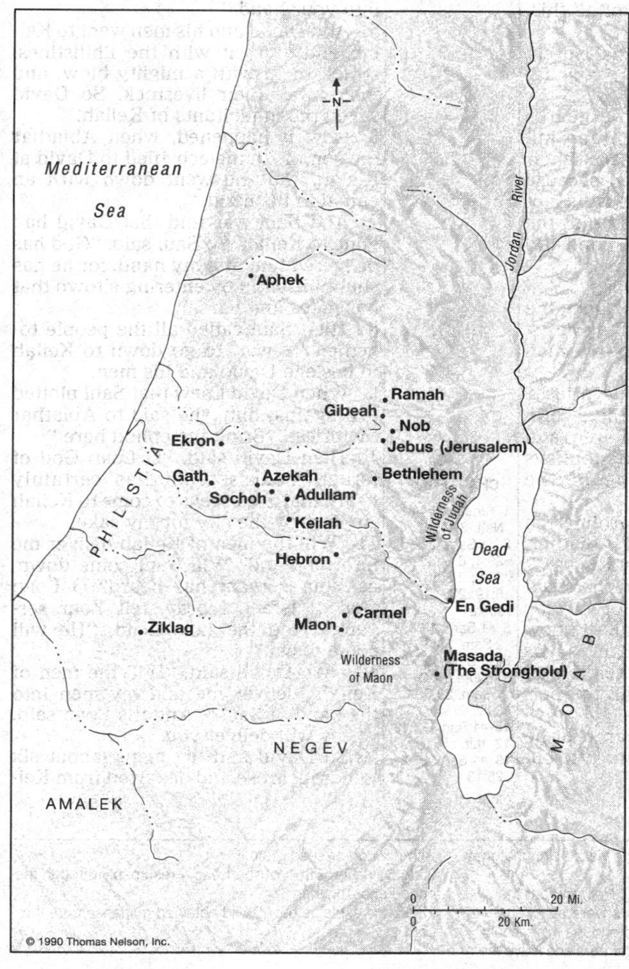

Before David Became King. Near Sochoh David defeated the giant Goliath (1 Sam. 17). Once Saul's wrath was kindled against the shepherd soldier, David fled Saul's presence and journeyed to Adullam. Taking his family to the safety of Moab, he established camp at the stronghold (1 Sam 22:4), now known as Masada. From there his activity took him north to Aphek and south to Amalek.

Ahitub!" He answered, "Here I am, my lord."

13 Then Saul said to him, "Why have you conspired against me, you and the son of Jesse, in that you have given him bread and a sword, and have inquired of God for him, that he should rise against me, to lie in wait, as it is this day?"

14 So Ahimelech answered the king and said, "And who among all your servants *is as* [a]faithful as David, who is the king's son-in-law, who goes at your bidding, and is honorable in your house?

15 "Did I then begin to inquire of God for him? Far be it from me! Let not the king impute anything to his servant, *or* to any in the house of my father. For your servant knew nothing of all this, little or much."

16 And the king said, "You shall surely die, Ahimelech, you and all [a]your father's house!"

17 Then the king said to the guards who stood about him, "Turn and kill the priests of the LORD, because their hand also *is* with David, and because they knew when he fled and did not tell it to me." But the servants of the king [a]would not lift their hands to strike the priests of the LORD.

18 And the king said to Doeg, "You turn and kill the priests!" So Doeg the Edomite turned and [1]struck the priests, and [a]killed on that day eighty-five men who wore a linen ephod.

19 [a]Also Nob, the city of the priests, he struck with the edge of the sword, both men and women, children and nursing infants, oxen and donkeys and sheep—with the edge of the sword.

20 [a]Now one of the sons of Ahimelech the son of Ahitub, named Abiathar, [b]escaped and fled after David.

21 And Abiathar told David that Saul had killed the LORD's priests.

22 So David said to Abiathar, "I knew that day, when Doeg the Edomite *was* there, that he would surely tell Saul. I have caused *the death* of all the persons of your father's [1]house.

23 "Stay with me; do not fear. [a]For he who seeks my life seeks your life, but with me you *shall be* safe."

14 [a]1 Sam. 19:4, 5; 20:32; 24:11
16 [a]Deut. 24:16
17 [a]Ex. 1:17
18 [a]1 Sam. 2:31 [1]*attacked*
19 [a]Josh. 21:1–45; 1 Sam. 22:9, 11
20 [a]1 Sam. 23:6, 9; 30:7; 1 Kin. 2:26, 27 [b]1 Sam. 2:33
22 [1]*family*
23 [a]1 Kin. 2:26

CHAPTER 23

1 [a]Josh. 15:44; Neh. 3:17, 18
2 [a]1 Sam. 22:10; 23:4, 6, 9; 28:6; 30:8; 2 Sam. 5:19, 23 [1]Lit. *strike*
5 [a]1 Sam. 19:8; 2 Sam. 5:20
6 [a]1 Sam. 22:20
9 [a]Num. 27:21; 1 Sam. 23:6; 30:7
10 [a]1 Sam. 22:19
12 [1]Lit. *shut up*
13 [a]1 Sam. 22:2; 25:13

David Saves the City of Keilah

23 Then they told David, saying, "Look, the Philistines are fighting against [a]Keilah, and they are robbing the threshing floors."

2 Therefore David [a]inquired of the LORD, saying, "Shall I go and [1]attack these Philistines?" And the LORD said to David, "Go and attack the Philistines, and save Keilah."

3 But David's men said to him, "Look, we are afraid here in Judah. How much more then if we go to Keilah against the armies of the Philistines?"

4 Then David inquired of the LORD once again. And the LORD answered him and said, "Arise, go down to Keilah. For I will deliver the Philistines into your hand."

5 And David and his men went to Keilah and [a]fought with the Philistines, struck them with a mighty blow, and took away their livestock. So David saved the inhabitants of Keilah.

6 Now it happened, when Abiathar the son of Ahimelech [a]fled to David at Keilah, *that* he went down *with* an ephod in his hand.

7 And Saul was told that David had gone to Keilah. So Saul said, "God has delivered him into my hand, for he has shut himself in by entering a town that has gates and bars."

8 Then Saul called all the people together for war, to go down to Keilah to besiege David and his men.

9 When David knew that Saul plotted evil against him, [a]he said to Abiathar the priest, "Bring the ephod here."

10 Then David said, "O LORD God of Israel, Your servant has certainly heard that Saul seeks to come to Keilah [a]to destroy the city for my sake.

11 "Will the men of Keilah deliver me into his hand? Will Saul come down, as Your servant has heard? O LORD God of Israel, I pray, tell Your servant." And the LORD said, "He will come down."

12 Then David said, "Will the men of Keilah [1]deliver me and my men into the hand of Saul?" And the LORD said, "They will deliver *you*."

13 So David and his men, [a]about six hundred, arose and departed from Kei-

22:18 Wearing **a linen ephod** was the visible sign that they spoke for Yahweh.

23:1 **Keilah** was 8 miles northwest of Hebron near the Philistine border. The **threshing floors** were attacked because they were not well defended and the grain could be stolen. This would demoralize the farmers and leave them with no food or seed grain.

23:2 **David inquired of the LORD,** presumably through the ephod and Abiathar.

23:6 This explains how David obtained guidance from the Lord.

lah and went wherever they could go.
Then it was told Saul that David had
escaped from Keilah; so he halted the
expedition.

David in Wilderness Strongholds

14 And David stayed in strongholds in
the wilderness, and remained in
[a]the mountains in the Wilderness of
[b]Ziph. Saul [c]sought him every day, but
God did not deliver him into his hand.
15 So David saw that Saul had come
out to seek his life. And David *was* in
the Wilderness of Ziph [1]in a forest.
16 Then Jonathan, Saul's son, arose
and went to David in the woods and
[1]strengthened his hand in God.
17 And he said to him, [a]"Do not fear,
for the hand of Saul my father shall
not find you. You shall be king over
Israel, and I shall be next to you.
[b]Even my father Saul knows that."
18 So the two of them [a]made a covenant
before the LORD. And David
stayed in the woods, and Jonathan
went to his own house.
19 Then the Ziphites [a]came up to Saul
at Gibeah, saying, "Is David not hiding
with us in strongholds in the woods,
in the hill of Hachilah, which *is* on the
south of Jeshimon?
20 "Now therefore, O king, come down
according to all the desire of your soul
to come down; and [a]our part *shall be*
to deliver him into the king's hand."
21 And Saul said, "Blessed *are* you of
the LORD, for you have compassion on
me.
22 "Please go and find out for sure,
and see the place where his hideout is,
and who has seen him there. For I am
told he is very crafty.
23 "See therefore, and take knowledge
of all the lurking places where he
hides; and come back to me with certainty,
and I will go with you. And it
shall be, if he is in the land, that I will
search for him throughout all the
[1]clans of Judah."
24 So they arose and went to Ziph before
Saul. But David and his men *were*
in the Wilderness [a]of Maon, in the
plain on the south of Jeshimon.
25 When Saul and his men went to
seek *him*, they told David. Therefore
he went down [1]to the rock, and stayed
in the Wilderness of Maon. And when
Saul heard *that*, he pursued David in
the Wilderness of Maon.
26 Then Saul went on one side of the
mountain, and David and his men on
the other side of the mountain. [a]So David
made haste to get away from Saul,
for Saul and his men [b]were encircling
David and his men to take them.
27 [a]But a messenger came to Saul, saying,
"Hurry and come, for the Philistines
have invaded the land!"
28 Therefore Saul returned from pursuing
David, and went against the Philistines;
so they called that place [1]the
Rock of Escape.
29 Then David went up from there and
dwelt in strongholds at [a]En Gedi.

David Spares Saul

24 Now it happened, [a]when Saul
had returned from following the
Philistines, that it was told him, saying,
"Take note! David *is* in the Wilderness
of En Gedi."
2 Then Saul took three thousand chosen
men from all Israel, and [a]went to
seek David and his men on the Rocks
of the Wild Goats.
3 So he came to the sheepfolds by the
road, where there *was* a cave; and
[a]Saul went in to [b]attend to his needs.
([c]David and his men were staying in
the recesses of the cave.)
4 [a]Then the men of David said to him,
"This is the day of which the LORD said
to you, 'Behold, I will deliver your enemy
into your hand, that you may do
to him as it seems good to you.'" And
David arose and secretly cut off a corner
of Saul's robe.
5 Now it happened afterward that
[a]David's heart troubled him because
he had cut Saul's *robe*.

14 [a]Ps. 11:1 [b]Josh. 15:55; 2 Chr. 11:8 [c]Ps. 32:7; 54:3, 4
15 [1]Or *in Horesh*
16 [1]*encouraged him*
17 [a][Ps. 27:1–3; Heb. 13:6] [b]1 Sam. 20:31; 24:20
18 [a]1 Sam. 18:3; 20:12–17, 42; 2 Sam. 9:1; 21:7
19 [a]1 Sam. 26:1; Ps. 54:title
20 [a]Ps. 54:3
23 [1]Lit. *thousands*
24 [a]Josh. 15:55; 1 Sam. 25:2
25 [1]Or *from the rock*
26 [a]Ps. 31:22 [b]Ps. 17:9
27 [a]2 Kin. 19:9
28 [1]Heb. *Sela Hammahlekoth*
29 [a]Josh. 15:62; 2 Chr. 20:2

CHAPTER 24

1 [a]1 Sam. 23:19, 28, 29
2 [a]1 Sam. 26:2; Ps. 38:12
3 [a]1 Sam. 24:10 [b]Judg. 3:24 [c]Ps. 57:title; 142:title
4 [a]1 Sam. 26:8–11
5 [a]2 Sam. 24:10

23:14 Strongholds were the mountain heights of the wilderness of Judah. **The Wilderness of Ziph** was part of the Judean desert near the town of Ziph, about 4 miles southeast of Hebron.
23:16 Jonathan's deep devotion to David leads him again to risk his life in seeking out David to strengthen **his hand in God.**
23:17 Next to you: That is, second in the kingdom. Only his death in battle against the Philistines at Mt. Gilboa (31:1) kept this from coming to reality.
23:19 Ps. 54 was composed by David during this difficult time, affirming his faith in God.
23:24 Maon is about 4 miles south of Ziph in the area known as the Arabah.
23:29 The strongholds (Masada, Hebrew *metzadot*) **at En Gedi** were in the area of the Dead Sea. This was the place where Jewish guerrillas took refuge during the revolts of A.D. 66 and 70. Masada is just to the south. The entire area is filled with caves which served as hiding places for David and his men.
24:2 There were then, as today, many **wild** mountain **goats** in this region.
24:4 Cut off a corner of Saul's robe: His outer garment which he had likely laid down.

5 6 And he said to his men, [a]"The LORD
forbid that I should do this thing to my
master, the LORD's anointed, to stretch
out my hand against him, seeing he *is*
the anointed of the LORD."
7 So David [a]restrained his servants
with *these* words, and did not allow
them to rise against Saul. And Saul got
up from the cave and went on *his* way.
8 David also arose afterward, went
out of the cave, and called out to Saul,
saying, "My lord the king!" And when
Saul looked behind him, David stooped
with his face to the earth, and bowed
down.
9 And David said to Saul: [a]"Why do
you listen to the words of men who say,
'Indeed David seeks your harm'?
10 "Look, this day your eyes have seen
that the LORD delivered you today into
my hand in the cave, and *someone*
urged *me* to kill you. But *my eye* spared
you, and I said, 'I will not stretch out
my hand against my lord, for he *is* the
LORD's anointed.'
11 "Moreover, my father, see! Yes, see
the corner of your robe in my hand!
For in that I cut off the corner of your
robe, and did not kill you, know and
see that *there is* [a]neither evil nor rebellion in my hand, and I have not sinned
against you. Yet you [b]hunt my life to
take it.
12 [a]"Let the LORD judge between you
and me, and let the LORD avenge me
on you. But my hand shall not be
against you.
13 "As the *proverb of the ancients
says, [a]'Wickedness proceeds from the
*wicked.' But my hand shall not be
against you.
14 "After whom has the king of Israel
come out? Whom do you pursue?
[a]A dead dog? [b]A flea?
15 [a]"Therefore let the LORD be judge,
and judge between you and me, and
[b]see and [c]plead my case, and deliver
me out of your hand."
16 So it was, when David had finished
speaking these words to Saul, that Saul
said, [a]"*Is* this your voice, my son Da-

6 [a]1 Sam. 26:11
7 [a]Ps. 7:4; [Matt. 5:44; Rom. 12:17, 19]
9 [a]Ps. 141:6; [Prov. 16:28; 17:9]
11 [a]Judg. 11:27; Ps. 7:3; 35:7 [b]1 Sam. 26:20
12 [a]Gen. 16:5; Judg. 11:27; 1 Sam. 26:10–23; Job 5:8
13 [a][Matt. 7:16–20] *See WW at Prov. 1:6. • See WW at Prov. 10:16.
14 [a]1 Sam. 17:43; 2 Sam. 9:8 [b]1 Sam. 26:20
15 [a]1 Sam. 24:12 [b]2 Chr. 24:22 [c]Ps. 35:1; 43:1; 119:154; Mic. 7:9
16 [a]1 Sam. 26:17
17 [a]1 Sam. 26:21 [b]Gen. 38:26 [c][Matt. 5:44] *See WW at Ezek. 34:14.
18 [a]1 Sam. 26:23
20 [a]1 Sam. 23:17
21 [a]Gen. 21:23; 1 Sam. 20:14–17 [b]2 Sam. 21:6–8
22 [a]1 Sam. 23:29

CHAPTER 25

1 [a]1 Sam. 28:3 [b]Num. 20:29; Deut. 34:8 [c]Gen. 21:21; Num. 10:12; 13:3 [1]So with MT, Syr., Tg., Vg.; LXX *Maon*
2 [a]1 Sam. 23:24 [b]Josh. 15:55
3 [a]Josh. 15:13; 1 Sam. 30:14

vid?" And Saul lifted up his voice and
wept.
17 [a]Then he said to David: "You *are*
[b]more righteous than I; for [c]you have
rewarded me with *good, whereas I
have rewarded you with evil.
18 "And you have shown this day how
you have dealt well with me; for when
[a]the LORD delivered me into your hand,
you did not kill me.
19 "For if a man finds his enemy, will
he let him get away safely? Therefore
may the LORD reward you with good
for what you have done to me this day.
20 "And now [a]I know indeed that you
shall surely be king, and that the kingdom of Israel shall be established in
your hand.
21 [a]"Therefore swear now to me by the
LORD [b]that you will not cut off my descendants after me, and that you will
not destroy my name from my father's
house."
22 So David swore to Saul. And Saul
went home, but David and his men
went up to [a]the stronghold.

Death of Samuel

25 Then [a]Samuel died; and the Israelites gathered together and
[b]lamented for him, and buried him at
his home in Ramah. And David arose
and went down [c]to the Wilderness of
[1]Paran.

David and the Wife of Nabal

2 Now *there was* a man [a]in Maon
whose business *was* in [b]Carmel, and
the man *was* very rich. He had three
thousand sheep and a thousand goats.
And he was shearing his sheep in Carmel.
3 The name of the man *was* Nabal,
and the name of his wife Abigail. And
she was a woman of good understanding and beautiful appearance; but the
man *was* harsh and evil in *his* doings.
He *was of the house of* [a]Caleb.
4 When David heard in the wilder-

24:6–22 See section 5 of Truth-In-Action at the end of 1 Sam.

24:6 The LORD's anointed does not imply that Saul still enjoyed the Lord's anointing. Rather, it shows that David had an unfailing reverence for the anointed (king) of the Lord.

24:14 A dead dog? A flea?: Saul was pursuing David with his choice 3,000 warriors, an army five times the size of David's men.

24:20 I know indeed that you shall surely be king: The real source of Saul's insane jealousy is that he knows he has been rejected by God.

25:1 Samuel died, and with him an entire era. He was the last of the judges and saw Israel through the transition to the monarchy. David also lost a dear friend and faithful ally. **The Wilderness of Paran** is the northern part of the Sinai desert which extends into the mountains of Judah.

25:2 Carmel here is not the famed Mt. Carmel, but the present-day Kurmul, in the mountains of Judah about a mile northwest of Maon.

25:3 Nabal means "Fool," perhaps a nickname given him because of his obvious lack of judgment.

25:4–9 David and his men had associated with these shepherds when they were in the desert. He had provided them protection and other services in return for food.

ness that Nabal was [a]shearing his sheep,

5 David sent ten young men; and David said to the young men, "Go up to Carmel, go to Nabal, and greet him in my name.

6 "And thus you shall say to him who lives *in prosperity:* [a]'Peace *be* to you, peace to your house, and peace to all that you have!

7 'Now I have heard that you have shearers. Your shepherds were with us, and we did not hurt them, [a]nor was there anything missing from them all the while they were in Carmel.

8 'Ask your young men, and they will tell you. Therefore [1]let *my* young men find favor in your eyes, for we come on [a]a feast day. Please give whatever comes to your hand to your servants and to your son David.' "

9 So when David's young men came, they spoke to Nabal according to all these words in the name of David, and waited.

10 Then Nabal answered David's servants, and said, [a]"Who *is* David, and who *is* the son of Jesse? There are many servants nowadays who break away each one from his master.

11 [a]"Shall I then take my bread and my water and my [1]meat that I have killed for my shearers, and give *it* to men when I do not know where they *are* from?"

12 So David's young men turned on their heels and went back; and they came and told him all these words.

13 Then David said to his men, "Every man gird on his sword." So every man girded on his sword, and David also girded on his sword. And about four hundred men went with David, and two hundred [a]stayed with the supplies.

14 Now one of the young men told Abigail, Nabal's wife, saying, "Look, David sent messengers from the wilderness to greet our master; and he [1]reviled them.

15 "But the men *were* very good to us, and [a]we were not hurt, nor did we miss anything as long as we accompanied them, when we were in the fields.

16 "They were [a]a wall to us both by night and day, all the time we were with them keeping the sheep.

17 "Now therefore, know and consider what you will do, for [a]harm is determined against our master and against all his household. For he *is such* a [b]scoundrel[1] that *one* cannot speak to him."

18 Then Abigail made haste and [a]took two hundred *loaves* of bread, two skins of wine, five sheep already dressed, five seahs of roasted *grain,* one hundred clusters of raisins, and two hundred cakes of figs, and loaded *them* on donkeys.

19 And she said to her servants, [a]"Go on before me; see, I am coming after you." But she did not tell her husband Nabal.

20 So it was, *as* she rode on the donkey, that she went down under cover of the hill; and there were David and his men, coming down toward her, and she met them.

21 Now David had said, "Surely in vain I have protected all that this *fellow* has in the wilderness, so that nothing was missed of all that *belongs* to him. And he has [a]repaid me evil for good.

22 [a]"May God do so, and more also, to the enemies of David, if I [b]leave [c]one male of all who *belong* to him by morning light."

23 Now when Abigail saw David, she [a]dismounted quickly from the donkey, fell on her face before David, and bowed down to the ground.

24 So she fell at his feet and said: "On me, my lord, *on* me *let* this iniquity *be!* And please let your maidservant [1]speak in your ears, and hear the words of your maidservant.

25 "Please, let not my lord [1]regard this scoundrel Nabal. For as his name *is,* so *is* he: [2]Nabal *is* his name, and folly *is* with him! But I, your maidservant, did not see the young men of my lord whom you sent.

26 "Now therefore, my lord, [a]*as* the LORD lives and *as* your soul lives, since the LORD has [b]held you back from coming to bloodshed and from [c]avenging[1] yourself with your own hand, now then, [d]let your enemies and those who seek harm for my lord be as Nabal.

27 "And now [a]this present which your maidservant has brought to my lord, let it be given to the young men who follow my lord.

28 "Please forgive the trespass of your

4 [a]Gen. 38:13; 2 Sam. 13:23
6 [a]Judg. 19:20; 1 Chr. 12:18; Ps. 122:7; Luke 10:5
7 [a]1 Sam. 25:15, 21
8 [a]Neh. 8:10–12; Esth. 8:17; 9:19, 22 [1]*be gracious to the young men*
10 [a]Judg. 9:28
11 [a]Judg. 8:6, 15 [1]Lit. *slaughter*
13 [a]1 Sam. 30:24
14 [1]*scolded* or *scorned at*
15 [a]1 Sam. 25:7, 21
16 [a]Ex. 14:22; Job 1:10
17 [a]1 Sam. 20:7 [b]Deut. 13:13; Judg. 19:22 [1]Lit. *son of Belial*
18 [a]Gen. 32:13; [Prov. 18:16; 21:14]
19 [a]Gen. 32:16, 20
21 [a]1 Sam. 24:17; Ps. 109:5; [Prov. 17:13]
22 [a]Ruth 1:17; 1 Sam. 3:17; 20:13, 16 [b]1 Sam. 25:34 [c]1 Kin. 14:10; 21:21; 2 Kin. 9:8
23 [a]Josh. 15:18; Judg. 1:14
24 [1]*speak to you*
25 [1]*pay attention to* [2]Lit. *Fool*
26 [a]2 Kin. 2:2 [b]Gen. 20:6; 1 Sam. 25:33 [c][Rom. 12:19] [d]2 Sam. 18:32 [1]Lit. *saving yourself*
27 [a]Gen. 33:11; 1 Sam. 30:26; 2 Kin. 5:15

25:10 Nabal slanders David as though he were a slave running away from his master.

25:14 Young men: One of Nabal's servants.

25:18 It is likely that these provisions were taken from the food already prepared for the feast.

25:21–31 This is one of several instances in Scripture where strong and extremely capable women are used by God in crucial situations. Abigail certainly shows herself worthy to be a queen, standing in stark contrast with Nabal "the fool."

maidservant. For [a]the LORD will certainly make for my lord an enduring
house, because my lord [b]fights the battles of the LORD, [c]and evil is not found
in you throughout your days.
29 "Yet a man has risen to pursue you
and seek your life, but the life of my
lord shall be [a]bound in the bundle of
the living with the LORD your God; and
the lives of your enemies He shall
[b]sling out, *as from* the pocket of a sling.
30 "And it shall come to pass, when
the LORD has done for my lord according to all the good that He has spoken
concerning you, and has appointed you
[a]ruler over Israel,
31 "that this will be no grief to you,
nor offense of heart to my lord, either
that you have shed blood without
cause, or that my lord has avenged
himself. But when the LORD has dealt
well with my lord, then remember your
maidservant."
32 Then David said to Abigail:
[a]"Blessed *is* the LORD God of Israel,
who sent you this day to meet me!
33 "And blessed *is* your advice and
blessed *are* you, because you have
[a]kept me this day from coming to
bloodshed and from avenging myself
with my own hand.
34 "For indeed, *as* the LORD God of Israel lives, who has [a]kept me back from
hurting you, unless you had hurried
and come to meet me, surely [b]by morning light no males would have been left
to Nabal!"
35 So David received from her hand
what she had brought him, and said
to her, [a]"Go up in peace to your house.
See, I have heeded your voice and
[b]respected your person."
36 Now Abigail went to Nabal, and
there he was, [a]holding a feast in his
house, like the feast of a king. And Nabal's heart *was* merry within him, for
he *was* very drunk; therefore she told
him nothing, little or much, until morning light.
37 So it was, in the morning, when the
wine had gone from Nabal, and his
wife had told him these things, that his
heart died within him, and he became
like a stone.
38 Then it happened, *after* about ten
days, that the LORD [a]struck Nabal, and
he died.
39 So when David heard that Nabal
was dead, he said, [a]"Blessed *be* the
LORD, who has [b]pleaded the cause of
my reproach from the hand of Nabal,
and has [c]kept His servant from evil!
For the LORD has [d]returned the wickedness of Nabal on his own head." And
David sent and proposed to Abigail, to
take her as his wife.
40 When the servants of David had
come to Abigail at Carmel, they spoke
to her saying, "David sent us to you,
to ask you to become his wife."
41 Then she arose, bowed her face to
the earth, and said, "Here is your maidservant, a servant to [a]wash the feet of
the servants of my lord."
42 So Abigail rose in haste and rode
on a donkey, [1]attended by five of her
maidens; and she followed the messengers of David, and became his wife.
43 David also took Ahinoam [a]of Jezreel, [b]and so both of them were his
wives.
44 But Saul had given [a]Michal his
daughter, David's wife, to [1]Palti the
son of Laish, who *was* from [b]Gallim.

David Spares Saul a Second Time

26 Now the Ziphites came to Saul
at Gibeah, saying, [a]"Is David
not hiding in the hill of Hachilah, opposite Jeshimon?"
2 Then Saul arose and went down to
the Wilderness of Ziph, having [a]three
thousand chosen men of Israel with
him, to seek David in the Wilderness
of Ziph.
3 And Saul encamped in the hill of
Hachilah, which *is* opposite Jeshimon,
by the road. But David stayed in the
wilderness, and he saw that Saul came
after him into the wilderness.
4 David therefore sent out spies, and
understood that Saul had indeed come.
5 So David arose and came to the
place where Saul had encamped. And
David saw the place where Saul lay,
and [a]Abner the son of Ner, the commander of his army. Now Saul lay
within the camp, with the people encamped all around him.
6 Then David answered, and said to
Ahimelech the Hittite and to Abishai
[a]the son of Zeruiah, brother of [b]Joab,
saying, "Who will [c]go down with me
to Saul in the camp?" And [d]Abishai
said, "I will go down with you."
7 So David and Abishai came to the
people by night; and there Saul lay

28 [a]2 Sam. 7:11–16, 27; 1 Kin. 9:5; 1 Chr. 17:10, 25 [b]1 Sam. 18:17 [c]1 Sam. 24:11; Ps. 7:3
29 [a][Ps. 66:9; Col. 3:3] [b]Jer. 10:18
30 [a]1 Sam. 13:14; 15:28
32 [a]Gen. 24:27; Ex. 18:10; 1 Kin. 1:48; Ps. 41:13; 72:18; 106:48; Luke 1:68
33 [a]1 Sam. 25:26
34 [a]1 Sam. 25:26 [b]1 Sam. 25:22
35 [a]1 Sam. 20:42; 2 Sam. 15:9; 2 Kin. 5:19; Luke 7:50; 8:48 [b]Gen. 19:21
36 [a]2 Sam. 13:28; Prov. 20:1; Is. 5:11; Dan. 5:1; [Hos. 4:11]
38 [a]1 Sam. 26:10; 2 Sam. 6:7; Ps. 104:29
39 [a]1 Sam. 25:32 [b]1 Sam. 24:15; Prov. 22:23 [c]1 Sam. 25:26, 34 [d]1 Kin. 2:44
41 [a][Prov. 15:33]; Luke 7:38, 44
42 [1]Lit. *with five of her maidens at her feet*
43 [a]Josh. 15:56 [b]1 Sam. 27:3; 30:5
44 [a]1 Sam. 18:20; 2 Sam. 3:14 [b]Is. 10:30 [1]*Paltiel*, 2 Sam. 3:15

CHAPTER 26

1 [a]1 Sam. 23:19; Ps. 54:title
2 [a]1 Sam. 13:2; 24:2
5 [a]1 Sam. 14:50, 51; 17:55
6 [a]1 Chr. 2:16 [b]2 Sam. 2:13 [c]Judg. 7:10, 11 [d]2 Sam. 2:18, 24

25:37 His heart died within him: He suffered either a stroke or heart attack and died 10 days later.
25:40 Proposals were often accomplished in the East through **servants.**
26:6 Abishai is the son of Zeruiah, David's sister. He became one of David's great generals. See 2 Sam. 23:18.

sleeping within the camp, with his
spear stuck in the ground by his head.
And Abner and the people lay all
around him.
8 Then Abishai said to David, [a]"God
has delivered your enemy into your
hand this day. Now therefore, please,
let me strike him [1]at once with the
spear, right to the earth; and I will not
have to strike him a second time!"
5 9 But David said to Abishai, "Do not
destroy him; [a]for who can stretch out
his hand against the LORD's anointed,
and *be guiltless?"
10 David said furthermore, "*As* the
LORD lives, [a]the LORD shall strike him,
or [b]his day shall come to die, or he
shall [c]go out to battle and perish.
11 [a]"The LORD forbid that I should
stretch out my hand against the LORD's
anointed. But please, take now the
spear and the jug of water that *are* by
his head, and let us go."
12 So David took the spear and the jug
of water *by* Saul's head, and they got
away; and no man saw or knew *it* or
awoke. For they *were* all asleep, because [a]a deep sleep from the LORD had
fallen on them.
13 Now David went over to the other
side, and stood on the top of a hill afar
off, a great distance *being* between
them.
14 And David called out to the people
and to Abner the son of Ner, saying,
"Do you not answer, Abner?" Then
Abner answered and said, "Who *are*
you, calling out to the king?"
15 So David said to Abner, "*Are* you
not a man? And who *is* like you in Israel? Why then have you not guarded
your lord the king? For one of the people came in to destroy your lord the
king.
16 "This thing that you have done *is*
not good. *As* the LORD lives, you deserve to die, because you have not
guarded your master, the LORD's
anointed. And now see where the
king's spear *is*, and the jug of water
that *was* by his head."

17 Then Saul knew David's voice, and
said, [a]"*Is* that your voice, my son David?" David said, "*It is* my voice, my
lord, O king."
18 And he said, [a]"Why does my lord
thus pursue his servant? For what have
I done, or what evil *is* in my hand?
19 "Now therefore, please, let my lord
the king hear the words of his servant:
If the LORD has [a]stirred you up against
me, let Him accept an offering. But if
it is the children of men, *may* they *be*
cursed before the LORD, [b]for they have
driven me out this day from sharing
in the [c]inheritance of the LORD, saying,
'Go, serve other gods.'
20 "So now, do not let my blood fall
to the earth before the face of the LORD.
For the king of Israel has come out to
seek [a]a flea, as when one hunts a partridge in the mountains."
21 Then Saul said, [a]"I have sinned. Return, my son David. For I will harm
you no more, because my life was precious in your eyes this day. Indeed I
have played the fool and erred exceedingly."
22 And David answered and said,
"Here is the king's spear. Let one of
the young men come over and get it.
23 [a]"May the LORD [b]repay every man
for his righteousness and his *faithfulness; for the LORD delivered you into
my hand today, but I would not stretch
out my hand against the LORD's
anointed.
24 "And indeed, as your life was valued much this day in my eyes, so let
my life be valued much in the eyes of
the LORD, and let Him deliver me out
of all tribulation."
25 Then Saul said to David, "*May* you
be blessed, my son David! You shall
both do great things and also still
[a]prevail." So David went on his way,
and Saul returned to his place.

David Allied with the Philistines

27 And David said in his heart,
"Now I shall perish someday by

8 [a]1 Sam. 24:4 [1]Or *one time*
9 [a]1 Sam. 24:6, 7; 2 Sam. 1:14, 16 *See WW at Num. 14:18.
10 [a][Deut. 32:35]; 1 Sam. 25:26, 38; [Luke 18:7; Rom. 12:19; Heb. 10:30] [b]Gen. 47:29; Deut. 31:14; [Job 7:1; 14:5]; Ps. 37:13 [c]1 Sam. 31:6
11 [a]1 Sam. 24:6–12; [Rom. 12:17, 19]
12 [a]Gen. 2:21; 15:12; Is. 29:10
17 [a]1 Sam. 24:16
18 [a]1 Sam. 24:9, 11–14
19 [a]2 Sam. 16:11; 24:1 [b]Deut. 4:27, 28 [c]2 Sam. 14:16; 20:19
20 [a]1 Sam. 24:14
21 [a]Ex. 9:27; 1 Sam. 15:24, 30; 24:17; 2 Sam. 12:13
23 [a]1 Sam. 24:19; Ps. 7:8; 18:20; 62:12 [b]2 Sam. 22:21 *See WW at Prov. 28:20.
25 [a]Gen. 32:28; 1 Sam. 24:20

26:9–25 See section 5 of Truth-In-Action at the end of 1 Sam.
26:12 The Lord assists David and attests to his innocence, as well as to his anointing, by giving them **sleep from the LORD.**
26:19 Accept an offering: The idea is that if God is behind Saul's wrath against David, Saul should offer a sacrifice to appease God's wrath. **Go, serve other gods:** Not that David would turn to other gods, but that through Saul's action he had been cut off from the place of the worship of the Lord and was forced to live in a foreign place.
26:21–25 Here is another of Saul's good intentions, which he never carried out.
26:24 David does not believe Saul's conciliatory words. It is in **the eyes of the LORD** that he wants to be valued.
26:25 Saul returned to his place does not mean that he returned home but that he continued his pursuit of David (ch. 27). However, David and Saul never saw each other again.
27:1 It has been two years since David pretended insanity in front of Achish the king of Gath to save his life (21:10). He returns as an outlaw and enemy of Saul and is accepted as politically beneficial to Achish (v. 12).

the hand of Saul. *There is* nothing better for me than that I should speedily
escape to the land of the Philistines;
and Saul will [1]despair of me, to seek
me anymore in any part of Israel. So I
shall escape out of his hand."
2 Then David arose [a]and went over
with the six hundred men who *were*
with him [b]to Achish the son of Maoch,
king of Gath.
3 So David dwelt with Achish at
Gath, he and his men, each man with
his household, *and* David [a]with his two
wives, Ahinoam the Jezreelitess, and
Abigail the Carmelitess, Nabal's
widow.
4 And it was told Saul that David had
fled to Gath; so he sought him no more.
5 Then David said to Achish, "If I
have now found favor in your eyes, let
them give me a place in some town in
the country, that I may dwell there. For
why should your servant dwell in the
royal city with you?"
6 So Achish gave him Ziklag that day.
Therefore [a]Ziklag has belonged to the
kings of Judah to this day.
7 Now [1]the time that David [a]dwelt in
the country of the Philistines was one
full year and four months.
8 And David and his men went up
and raided [a]the Geshurites, [b]the
[1]Girzites, and the [c]Amalekites. For
those nations were the inhabitants of
the land from [2]of old, [d]as you go to
Shur, even as far as the land of Egypt.
9 Whenever David [1]attacked the
land, he left neither man nor woman
alive, but took away the sheep, the
oxen, the donkeys, the camels, and the
apparel, and returned and came to
Achish.
10 Then Achish would say, "Where
have you made a raid today?" And David would say, "Against the southern
area of Judah, or against the southern
area of [a]the Jerahmeelites, or against
the southern *area* of [b]the Kenites."
11 David would save neither man nor
woman alive, to bring *news* to Gath,
saying, "Lest they should inform on us,
saying, 'Thus David did.' " And thus
was his behavior all the time he dwelt
in the country of the Philistines.
12 So Achish believed David, saying,
"He has made his people Israel utterly
abhor him; therefore he will be my servant forever."

28
Now [a]it happened in those days
that the Philistines gathered
their armies together for war, to fight
with Israel. And Achish said to David,
"You assuredly know that you will go
out with me to battle, you and your
men."
2 So David said to Achish, "Surely
you know what your servant can do."
And Achish said to David, "Therefore
I will make you one of my chief guardians forever."

Saul Consults a Medium

3 Now [a]Samuel had died, and all Israel had lamented for him and buried
him in [b]Ramah, in his own city. And
Saul had put [c]the mediums and the
spiritists out of the land.
4 Then the Philistines gathered together, and came and encamped at
[a]Shunem. So Saul gathered all Israel
together, and they encamped at
[b]Gilboa.
5 When Saul saw the army of the Philistines, he was [a]afraid, and his heart
trembled greatly.
6 And when Saul inquired of the
LORD, [a]the LORD did not answer him,
either by [b]dreams or [c]by Urim or by
the prophets.
7 Then Saul said to his servants,
"Find me a woman who is a medium,
[a]that I may go to her and inquire of
her." And his servants said to him, "In
fact, *there is* a woman who is a medium
at En Dor."
8 So Saul disguised himself and put
on other clothes, and he went, and two
men with him; and they came to the
woman by night. And [a]he said, "Please

CHAPTER 27

1 [1]*despair of searching for*
2 [a]1 Sam. 25:13 [b]1 Sam. 21:10; 1 Kin. 2:39
3 [a]1 Sam. 25:42, 43
6 [a]Josh. 15:31; 19:5; 1 Chr. 12:1; Neh. 11:28
7 [a]1 Sam. 29:3 [1]Lit. *the number of days*
8 [a]Josh. 13:2, 13 [b]Josh. 16:10; Judg. 1:29 [c]Ex. 17:8, 16; 1 Sam. 15:7, 8 [d]Gen. 25:18; Ex. 15:22 [1]Or *Gezrites* [2]*ancient times*
9 [1]Lit. *struck*
10 [a]1 Chr. 2:9, 25 [b]Judg. 1:16

CHAPTER 28

1 [a]1 Sam. 29:1, 2
3 [a]1 Sam. 25:1 [b]1 Sam. 1:19 [c]Ex. 22:18; Lev. 19:31; 20:27; Deut. 18:10, 11; 1 Sam. 15:23; 28:9
4 [a]Josh. 19:18; 1 Sam. 28:4; 1 Kin. 1:3; 2 Kin. 4:8 [b]1 Sam. 31:1
5 [a]Job 18:11; [Is. 57:20]
6 [a]1 Sam. 14:37; Prov. 1:28; Lam. 2:9 [b]Num. 12:6; Joel 2:28 [c]Ex. 28:30; Num. 27:21; Deut. 33:8
7 [a]1 Chr. 10:13
8 [a]Deut. 18:10, 11; 1 Chr. 10:13; Is. 8:19

27:6 David asks for and is given **Ziklag,** not just as his residence but as his possession. He was like a feudal lord over this area on the southern frontier of Philistia between Gaza and Beersheba.

27:8 These raids were in the modern area of the Gaza Strip. The desert of **Shur** is east of the present Suez Canal.

27:10 Judah, Jerahmeelites, Kenites were all in one way or other related to David. Judah was his own tribe. He was ensuring their support when he became king, while at the same time convincing Achish of his loyalty.

28:2 David's answer to Achish is ambiguous, not promising him anything, but leading Achish to think he has.

28:3 The entire scene is now seen from Israel's and Saul's perspective. **The mediums and the spiritists** are those who deal with spirits of the dead or ancestral spirits and those who contact the spirits. Resort to these is consistently prohibited by the law of God.

28:4 Gilboa refers to the hills running southeast on the south side of the Jezreel Valley. **Shunem** is nearly 60 miles north of the Philistine city of Ekron. This illustrates how far the Philistines had advanced into Israel's territory, threatening to divide the country in half.

28:6 When Saul killed the priests from Nob (ch. 22), he did away with any means by which he could receive guidance from God.

28:7 En Dor was about 6 miles north of Saul's position at Gilboa.

conduct a séance for me, and bring up
for me the one I shall name to you."
9 Then the woman said to him,
"Look, you know what Saul has done,
how he has [a]cut off the mediums and
the spiritists from the land. Why then
do you lay a snare for my life, to cause
me to die?"
10 And Saul swore to her by the LORD,
saying, "*As* the LORD lives, no punishment shall come upon you for this
thing."
11 Then the woman said, "Whom shall
I bring up for you?" And he said,
"Bring up Samuel for me."
12 When the woman saw Samuel, she
cried out with a loud voice. And the
woman spoke to Saul, saying, "Why
have you deceived me? For you *are*
Saul!"
13 And the king said to her, "Do not
be afraid. What did you see?" And the
woman said to Saul, "I saw [a]a[1] spirit
ascending out of the earth."
14 So he said to her, "What *is* his
form?" And she said, "An old man is
coming up, and he *is* covered with
[a]a mantle." And Saul perceived that it
was Samuel, and he stooped with *his*
face to the ground and bowed down.
15 Now Samuel said to Saul, "Why
have you [a]disturbed me by bringing
me up?" And Saul answered, "I am
deeply distressed; for the Philistines
make war against me, and [b]God has
departed from me and [c]does not answer me anymore, neither by prophets
nor by dreams. Therefore I have called
you, that you may reveal to me what I
should do."
16 Then Samuel said: "So why do you
ask me, seeing the LORD has departed
from you and has become your enemy?
17 "And the LORD has done for
[1]Himself [a]as He spoke by me. For the
LORD has torn the kingdom out of your
hand and given it to your neighbor, David.
18 [a]"Because you did not obey the
voice of the LORD nor execute His fierce
wrath upon [b]Amalek, therefore the
LORD has done this thing to you this
day.
19 "Moreover the LORD will also de-

9 [a]1 Sam. 28:3
13 [a]Ex. 22:28; Ps. 138:1 [1]Heb. *elohim*
14 [a]1 Sam. 15:27; 2 Kin. 2:8, 13
15 [a]Is. 14:9 [b]1 Sam. 16:14; 18:12 [c]1 Sam. 28:6
17 [a]1 Sam. 15:28 [1]Or *him*, i.e., David
18 [a]1 Sam. 13:9–13; 15:1–26; 1 Kin. 20:42; 1 Chr. 10:13; Jer. 48:10 [b]1 Sam. 15:3–9
19 [a]1 Sam. 31:1–6; Job 3:17–19
21 [a]Judg. 12:3; 1 Sam. 19:5; Job 13:14

CHAPTER 29

1 [a]1 Sam. 28:1 [b]Josh. 12:18; 19:30; 1 Sam. 4:1; 1 Kin. 20:30
2 [a]1 Sam. 6:4; 7:7 [b]1 Sam. 28:1, 2 [1]*passed on in the rear*
3 [a]1 Sam. 27:7 [b]1 Sam. 27:1–6; 1 Chr. 12:19, 20; Dan. 6:5

liver Israel with you into the hand of
the Philistines. And tomorrow you and
your sons *will be* with [a]me. The LORD
will also deliver the army of Israel into
the hand of the Philistines."
20 Immediately Saul fell full length on
the ground, and was dreadfully afraid
because of the words of Samuel. And
there was no strength in him, for he
had eaten no food all day or all night.
21 And the woman came to Saul and
saw that he was severely troubled, and
said to him, "Look, your maidservant
has obeyed your voice, and I have
[a]put my life in my hands and heeded
the words which you spoke to me.
22 "Now therefore, please, heed also
the voice of your maidservant, and let
me set a piece of bread before you; and
eat, that you may have strength when
you go on *your* way."
23 But he refused and said, "I will not
eat." So his servants, together with the
woman, urged him; and he heeded
their voice. Then he arose from the
ground and sat on the bed.
24 Now the woman had a fatted calf
in the house, and she hastened to kill
it. And she took flour and kneaded *it,*
and baked unleavened bread from it.
25 So she brought *it* before Saul and
his servants, and they ate. Then they
rose and went away that night.

The Philistines Reject David

29 Then [a]the Philistines gathered
together all their armies [b]at
Aphek, and the Israelites encamped by
a fountain which *is* in Jezreel.
2 And the [a]lords of the Philistines
[1]passed in review by hundreds and by
thousands, but [b]David and his men
passed in review at the rear with
Achish.
3 Then the princes of the Philistines
said, "What *are* these Hebrews *doing*
here?" And Achish said to the princes
of the Philistines, "*Is* this not David,
the servant of Saul king of Israel, who
has been with me [a]these days, or these
years? And to this day I have [b]found
no fault in him since he defected to
me."

28:10 The degree to which we can deceive ourselves and rationalize our sin is incredible. Saul swears to an outlaw necromancer **by the LORD!**

28:11–19 Before they can do anything Samuel appears, not a dead ghost conjured up, but a prophet of God again delivering God's message to the king. It is clear that the medium has not called him up, but that the Lord has again stepped into the life of Saul to speak to him. The woman was terrified and **cried out,** literally "screamed in terror," shocked at Samuel's appearance. Far from giving credence to any kind of spiritualist activity or contacting the dead, this passage shows that God is supreme. The medium is left terrified and Saul is paralyzed in fear, as both of them are rejected by the living God.

29:1 Aphek is the place where the Philistines had defeated Israel and captured the ark nearly 90 years before (4:1).

29:2 The lords of the Philistines were the leaders of the five main Philistine cities.

4 But the princes of the Philistines
were angry with him; so the princes
of the Philistines said to him, [a]"Make
this fellow return, that he may go back
to the place which you have appointed
for him, and do not let him go down
with us to [b]battle, lest [c]in the battle
he become our adversary. For with
what could he reconcile himself to his
master, if not with the heads of these
[d]men?
5 "*Is* this not David, [a]of whom they
sang to one another in dances, saying:

[b]'Saul has slain his thousands,
And David his ten thousands'?"

6 Then Achish called David and said
to him, "Surely, *as* the LORD lives, you
have been upright, and [a]your going out
and your coming in with me in the
army *is* good in my sight. For to this
day [b]I have not found evil in you since
the day of your coming to me. Nevertheless the lords do not favor you.
7 "Therefore return now, and go in
peace, that you may not displease the
lords of the Philistines."
8 So David said to Achish, "But what
have I done? And to this day what have
you found in your servant as long as I
have been with you, that I may not go
and fight against the enemies of my
lord the king?"
9 Then Achish answered and said to
David, "I know that you *are* as good
in my sight [a]as an angel of God; nevertheless [b]the princes of the Philistines
have said, 'He shall not go up with us
to the battle.'
10 "Now therefore, rise early in the
morning with your master's servants
[a]who have come with [1]you. And as
soon as you are up early in the morning and have light, depart."
11 So David and his men rose early to
depart in the morning, to return to the
land of the Philistines. [a]And the Philistines went up to Jezreel.

David's Conflict with the Amalekites

30 Now it happened, when David
and his men came to [a]Ziklag, on
the third day, that the [b]Amalekites had
invaded the South and Ziklag, attacked
Ziklag and burned it with fire,
2 and had taken captive the [a]women
and those who *were* there, from small
to great; they did not kill anyone, but
carried *them* away and went their way.
3 So David and his men came to the
city, and there it was, burned with fire;
and their wives, their sons, and their
daughters had been taken captive.
4 Then David and the people who
were with him lifted up their voices
and wept, until they had no more
power to weep.
5 And David's two [a]wives, Ahinoam
the Jezreelitess, and Abigail the widow
of Nabal the Carmelite, had been taken
captive.
6 Now David was greatly distressed,
for [a]the people spoke of stoning him,
because the soul of all the people was
[1]grieved, every man for his sons and
his daughters. [b]But David *strengthened himself in the LORD his God.
7 [a]Then David said to Abiathar the
priest, Ahimelech's son, "Please bring
the ephod here to me." And [b]Abiathar
brought the ephod to David.
8 [a]So David inquired of the LORD,
saying, "Shall I pursue this troop?
Shall I overtake them?" And He answered him, "Pursue, for you shall
surely overtake *them* and without fail
recover *all*."
9 So David went, he and the six hundred men who *were* with him, and
came to the Brook Besor, where those
stayed who were left behind.
10 But David pursued, he and four
hundred men; [a]for two hundred stayed
behind, who were so weary that they
could not cross the Brook Besor.
11 Then they found an Egyptian in the
field, and brought him to David; and
they gave him bread and he ate, and
they let him drink water.
12 And they gave him a piece of
[a]a cake of figs and two clusters of raisins. So [b]when he had eaten, his
strength came back to him; for he had
eaten no bread nor drunk water for
three days and three nights.

4 [a]1 Sam. 27:6 [b]1 Sam. 14:21 [c]1 Sam. 29:9 [d]1 Chr. 12:19, 20
5 [a]1 Sam. 21:11 [b]1 Sam. 18:7
6 [a]2 Sam. 3:25; 2 Kin. 19:27 [b]1 Sam. 29:3
9 [a]2 Sam. 14:17, 20; 19:27 [b]1 Sam. 29:4
10 [a]1 Chr. 12:19, 22 [1]So with MT, Tg., Vg.; LXX adds *and go to the place which I have selected for you there; and set no bothersome word in your heart, for you are good before me. And rise on your way*
11 [a]2 Sam. 4:4

CHAPTER 30

1 [a]1 Sam. 27:6 [b]1 Sam. 15:7; 27:8
2 [a]1 Sam. 27:2, 3
5 [a]1 Sam. 25:42, 43
6 [a]Ex. 17:4; John 8:59 [b]1 Sam. 23:16; Is. 25:4; Hab. 3:17–19 [1]Lit. *bitter* *See WW at Josh. 1:9.
7 [a]1 Sam. 23:2–9 [b]1 Sam. 23:6
8 [a]1 Sam. 23:2, 4; Ps. 50:15; 91:15
10 [a]1 Sam. 30:9, 21
12 [a]1 Sam. 25:18; 1 Kin. 20:7 [b]Judg. 15:19; 1 Sam. 14:27

29:4 Reconcile himself to his master: The fear is that, in the heat of battle, David will defect and take the heads of the Philistines, thereby gaining the favor of "his master," Saul.
30:1 *This was likely a retaliatory attack because of David's raids against them (27:8).*
30:6 Though grieving to the point of exhaustion, David uses the occasion to strengthen **himself in the LORD his God,** while the people, and very likely his soldiers, turn the energy of their grief to threats of assassination.
30:7, 8 Ps. 25 could have been composed at this time. It reflects David's trust in God at times of great danger and crisis.
30:7 Abiathar had escaped to David from Saul's massacre of the priests at Nob (22). He was the only living priest, and his was the only ephod.
30:9, 10 Brook Besor: 12–15 miles southwest of Ziklag, this is in addition to the 50 miles they had traveled from Aphek. Because their city had been burned, they had to leave with little or no rest or supplies. The exhaustion of the 200 was understandable.

13 Then David said to him, "To whom
do you *belong*, and where *are* you
from?" And he said, "I *am* a young
man from Egypt, servant of an Amalekite; and my master left me behind,
because three days ago I fell sick.
14 "We made an invasion of the southern *area* of [a]the Cherethites, in the *ter-*
ritory which *belongs* to Judah, and of
the southern *area* [b]of Caleb; and we
burned Ziklag with fire."
15 And David said to him, "Can you
take me down to this troop?" So he
said, "Swear to me by God that you
will neither kill me nor deliver me into
the hands of my [a]master, and I will
take you down to this troop."
16 And when he had brought him
down, there they were, spread out over
all the land, [a]eating and drinking and
*dancing, because of all the great spoil
which they had taken from the land of
the Philistines and from the land of Judah.
17 Then David attacked them from
twilight until the evening of the next
day. Not a man of them escaped, except four hundred young men who
rode on camels and fled.
18 So David recovered all that the
Amalekites had carried away, and David rescued his two wives.
19 And nothing of theirs was lacking,
either small or great, sons or daughters, spoil or anything which they had
taken from them; [a]David recovered all.
20 Then David took all the flocks and
herds they had driven before those
other livestock, and said, "This *is* David's spoil."
21 Now David came to the [a]two hundred men who had been so weary that
they could not follow David, whom
they also had made to stay at the Brook
Besor. So they went out to meet David
and to meet the people who *were* with
him. And when David came near the
people, he [1]greeted them.
22 Then all the wicked and [a]worthless[1]
men of those who went with David answered and said, "Because they did not
go with us, we will not give them *any*
of the spoil that we have recovered, except for every man's wife and children,
that they may lead *them* away and depart."

14 [a]2 Sam. 8:18; 1 Kin. 1:38, 44; Ezek. 25:16; Zeph. 2:5 [b]Josh. 14:13; 15:13
15 [a]Deut. 23:15
16 [a]1 Thess. 5:3 *See WW at Ex. 23:14.
19 [a]1 Sam. 30:8
21 [a]1 Sam. 30:10 [1]*asked them concerning their welfare*
22 [a]Deut. 13:13; Judg. 19:22 [1]Lit. *men of Belial*
24 [a]Num. 31:27; Josh. 22:8
25 *See WW at Neh. 9:13.
26 [1]*booty*
27 [a]Josh. 19:8 [b]Josh. 15:48; 21:14
28 [a]Josh. 13:16 [b]1 Chr. 27:27 [c]Josh. 15:50
29 [a]1 Sam. 27:10 [b]Judg. 1:16; 1 Sam. 15:6; 27:10
30 [a]Num. 14:45; 21:3; Josh. 12:14; 15:30; 19:4; Judg. 1:17 [1]Or *Borashan*
31 [a]Num. 13:22; Josh. 14:13–15; 21:11–13; 2 Sam. 2:1 [b]1 Sam. 23:22

CHAPTER 31

1 [a]1 Chr. 10:1–12 [b]1 Sam. 28:4
2 [a]1 Sam. 14:49; 1 Chr. 8:33
3 [a]2 Sam. 1:6 [1]Lit. *found him*
4 [a]Judg. 9:54; 1 Chr. 10:4 [b]Judg. 14:3; 1 Sam. 14:6; 17:26, 36 [c]2 Sam. 1:14 [d]2 Sam. 1:6, 10 [1]*torture*

23 But David said, "My brethren, you 6
shall not do so with what the LORD has
given us, who has preserved us and delivered into our hand the troop that
came against us.
24 "For who will heed you in this matter? But [a]as his part *is* who goes down
to the battle, so *shall* his part *be* who
stays by the supplies; they shall share
alike."
25 So it was, from that day forward;
he made it a *statute and an ordinance
for Israel to this day.
26 Now when David came to Ziklag,
he sent *some* of the [1]spoil to the elders
of Judah, to his friends, saying, "Here
is a present for you from the spoil of
the enemies of the LORD"—
27 to *those* who *were* in Bethel, *those*
who *were* in [a]Ramoth of the South,
those who *were* in [b]Jattir,
28 *those* who *were* in [a]Aroer, *those*
who *were* in [b]Siphmoth, *those* who
were in [c]Eshtemoa,
29 *those* who *were* in Rachal, *those*
who *were* in the cities of [a]the Jerahmeelites, *those* who *were* in the cities
of the [b]Kenites,
30 *those* who *were* in [a]Hormah, *those*
who *were* in [1]Chorashan, *those* who
were in Athach,
31 *those* who *were* in [a]Hebron, and to
all the places where David himself and
his men were accustomed to [b]rove.

The Tragic End of Saul and His Sons

31 Now [a]the Philistines fought
against Israel; and the men of
Israel fled from before the Philistines,
and fell slain on Mount [b]Gilboa.
2 Then the Philistines followed hard
after Saul and his sons. And the Philistines killed [a]Jonathan, Abinadab, and
Malchishua, Saul's sons.
3 [a]The battle became fierce against
Saul. The archers [1]hit him, and he was
severely wounded by the archers.
4 [a]Then Saul said to his armorbearer,
"Draw your sword, and thrust me
through with it, lest [b]these uncircumcised men come and thrust me through
and [1]abuse me." But his armorbearer
would not, [c]for he was greatly afraid.
Therefore Saul took a sword and
[d]fell on it.

30:17 The number of men who escaped is equal to the entire army of David.
30:23–31 See section 6 of Truth-In-Action at the end of 1 Sam.
30:26–31 The presents David sends to these cities in southern Judah are a gesture of gratitude toward those who have sustained him and his men during their exile, as well as some repayment of what they have given him. A further motive is likely political. These people were the first to crown David king in Hebron after the death of Saul.
31:1 David's victory is contrasted with Saul's defeat.
31:4 **He was greatly afraid** because the duty of the armorbearer was to keep the king alive.

5 And when his armorbearer saw that
Saul was dead, he also fell on his
sword, and died with him.
6 So Saul, his three sons, his armorbearer, and all his men died together
that same day.
7 And when the men of Israel who
were on the other side of the valley,
and *those* who *were* on the other side
of the Jordan, saw that the men of Israel had fled and that Saul and his sons
were dead, they forsook the cities and
fled; and the Philistines came and
dwelt in them.
8 So it happened the next day, when
the Philistines came to strip the slain,
that they found Saul and his three sons
fallen on Mount Gilboa.
9 And they cut off his head and
stripped off his armor, and sent *word*
throughout the land of the Philistines,
to [a]proclaim *it in* the temple of their
idols and among the people.
10 [a]Then they put his armor in the temple of the [b]Ashtoreths, and [c]they fastened his body to the wall of [d]Beth[1]
Shan.
11 [a]Now when the inhabitants of Jabesh Gilead heard what the Philistines
had done to Saul,
12 [a]all the valiant men arose and traveled all night, and took the body of
Saul and the bodies of his sons from
the wall of Beth Shan; and they came
to Jabesh and [b]burned them there.
13 Then they took their bones and
[a]buried *them* under the tamarisk tree
at Jabesh, [b]and fasted seven days.

9 [a]Judg. 16:23, 24; 2 Sam. 1:20
10 [a]1 Sam. 21:9 [b]Judg. 2:13; 1 Sam. 7:3 [c]2 Sam. 21:12 [d]Judg. 1:27 [1]*Beth Shean,* Josh. 17:11
11 [a]1 Sam. 11:1–13
12 [a]1 Sam. 11:1–11; 2 Sam. 2:4–7 [b]2 Chr. 16:14; Jer. 34:5; Amos 6:10
13 [a]2 Sam. 2:4, 5; 21:12–14 [b]Gen. 50:10

31:7 Men of Israel: The battle could be seen from across the valley. When these inhabitants of the surrounding cities see Israel is defeated, they evacuate the cities, leaving them to the Philistines.
31:9 The temple of their idols: The Philistines see this as a victory for their gods. They hang Saul's armor in their temple in much the same way as David had dedicated the sword of Goliath to the tabernacle at Nob.
31:11–13 Saul had saved the people of Jabesh Gilead from Nahash the Ammonite in his first military action as king (ch. 11). Here they risk their lives to express their gratitude and loyalty to Saul. The distance from **Beth Shan** to **Jabesh Gilead** is about 10 or 12 miles.
31:13 David later exhumed the bones of Saul and Jonathan and took them to the family tomb at Zela in Saul's homeland of Benjamin (2 Sam. 21:12–14). Saul was crowned at about 20 years of age. He reigned 40 years. Therefore he was about 60 years old at the time of his death.

TRUTH-IN-ACTION through 1 SAMUEL

Letting the LIFE of the Holy Spirit Bring Faith's Works Alive in You!

Truth 1 Samuel Teaches	Text	**Action** 1 Samuel Invites
1 Guidelines for Growing in Godliness As parents, we have much to do with our children's destiny. Give them over to God's purposes and continue to train them to become fruitful in godly living.	8:3ff.	**Raise** godly children. **Understand** that a failure to do so can result in greater ungodliness.
	1:22, 28	**Dedicate** your children to the Lord. **Remember** that they are an inheritance and gift from the Lord.
2 Steps to Holiness Holiness is saying "No!" to the world and its expectations and "Yes!" to God.	10:19	**Rely upon** God's wisdom, strength, and ingenuity rather than that of people.
3 Key Lessons in Faith Belief results in obedience; what we practice provides evidence of our faith. Faith is not merely a propositional affirmation. It determines action, produces obedience, and through overcoming, becomes fruitful.	3:10	**Be ready to obey** the words the Lord speaks to you. **Know** that God only continues to speak to those who do what He says.
	15:8–35	**Understand** that incomplete obedience is the same as disobedience. **Obey the Lord completely** and do not turn away from Him.
	15:22, 23	**Do not substitute** religion for obedience to God's Word. **Know** that disobedience and rebellion are as witchcraft in God's sight. **Understand** that to hear God's Word and not to practice it (obey) is to reject it.

Truth 1 Samuel Teaches	Text	**Action** 1 Samuel Invites
	17:45–50	**Do not fear** opposition even when it seems stronger or better supported. **Be assured** that God can use your minimal resources, when accompanied by great faith, to overcome whatever obstacles you face.
4 Keys to Wise Living Wisdom is in large measure understanding the principles by which God governs the moral universe. To gain wisdom means to learn to think God's thoughts after Him, esteeming the things He esteems and despising the things He despises. Learning wisdom is gaining the perspective that results from adopting God's values and rejecting the values this world espouses.	8:22	**Be aware** that if you persist in ungodly or unwise prayer, God may give you what you ask as a form of discipline, which would have been unnecessary otherwise.
	14:6	**Do not overvalue** size. **Remember,** the Lord accomplishes great things through small numbers.
	16:7	**Know** that God looks on the heart, not the outward appearance. **Do not judge** based upon what you see.
	17:34–37	**Do not despise** small opportunities. **Understand** that they prepare us for bigger battles.
5 Keys to Relating to Authority Learning to relate properly to God-ordained authority is an important part of spiritual maturity. Because our nature is sinful—in rebellion against God—we do not automatically know how to relate properly to authority. It is something we must be trained in and something for which we will experience much discipline from the Lord.	8:7, 8	**Receive** God-appointed authority, but **do not honor them above** God or His Word. **Know** that to do so is idolatry.
	14:7	**Practice loyalty** to God-appointed leaders in order to enhance their effectiveness on your behalf.
	24:6–22 26:9–25	**Do not speak against** or take up a cause against God-ordained leaders even if they seem to be wrong. **Leave** them to God's judgment and **intercede** for them. Each one of us must answer to God for our actions.
6 Lessons for Leaders Spiritual leadership differs radically from this world's ideas about how to lead. God's leaders must realize that they represent Him in their role, since He has given them their authority. In order to honor God, His servants must be faithful both to Him and to His people.	12:23	Leaders, **pray** for those whom you lead. Not to do so is to sin against God.
	13:13, 14	Leaders, **do not act presumptuously.** Obedience will establish your authority.
	22:2	Leaders, **do not despise** anyone the Lord brings to you. God is able to raise up even the lowliest through godly leadership.
	30:23–31	Leaders, **honor all ministry equally.** Those who support others are equally important to God.
7 Steps to Dealing with Sin Sin must be dealt with or it will become our downfall.	3:13	**Understand** that God holds us accountable for sins we know about but do not confront as we are able.
8 How to Tame the Tongue Taming the tongue involves knowing that things you should not say to men may often be said to God.	1:7, 10–16	**Voice** any complaints **only** to the Lord. **Remember** that vindication comes only from the Lord.

The Second Book of SAMUEL

Author: Possibly Abiathar the Priest
Date: Between 931 and 722 B.C.
Theme: King David, Forerunner of the Messiah
Key Persons: David, Nathan, Absalom, Joab, Bathsheba

Author The two books that now make up 1 and 2 Samuel were originally one book called "The Book of Samuel." The actual author is unknown. Samuel undoubtedly had written a great deal about this time in Israel's history. However, other materials had been collected from which the actual writer could draw. Three of these are mentioned in 1 Chronicles 29:29, namely: "the book of Samuel the seer," "the book of Nathan the prophet," and "the book of Gad the seer." Both Gad and Abiathar had access to the court events of David's reign and one or both may have given us these two books.

Date The book has to be dated after the division of the kingdoms following Solomon's reign, 931 B.C., because of the comment in 1 Samuel 27:6, "Ziklag has belonged to the kings of Judah to this day." Though a distinction was often drawn between Israel and Judah, and though David reigned in Judah for seven and one-half years before unifying the kingdom, there were no kings in Judah before this date.

There is no mention or reference to the fall of Samaria in 722 B.C., which makes a date after that event unlikely.

Content Second Samuel deals with the ascendance of David to the throne of Israel and the forty years of his reign. He is the focal point of the book.

The book begins with the death of Saul and Jonathan at the battlefield on Mount Gilboa. David is then anointed king over Judah, his own tribe. There is a power play by the house of Saul in the persons of Ishbosheth, Saul's son, and Abner, Saul's commander in chief of the armies. Though the rebellion is quelled, this summary statement describes the seven and one-half years before the nation is unified under David: "Now there was a long war between the house of Saul and the house of David. But David grew stronger and stronger, and the house of Saul grew weaker and weaker" (3:1).

David unifies both the political and religious life of the nation by bringing the ark of the covenant from the house of Abinadab, where it had rested since its return from the Philistines (6:1—7:1).

The theme of the coming King, the Messiah, is introduced as God establishes an everlasting covenant with David and his kingdom, "Your throne shall be established forever" (7:16).

David successfully defeats the enemies of Israel, and a time of stability and prosperity begins to emerge. Sadly however, his vulnerability and weakness lead him into his sin with Bathsheba and his murder of Uriah, her husband.

Though David repents after being confronted by the prophet Nathan, the consequences of his actions are spelled out: "The sword shall never depart from your house" (12:10).

David's son Absalom, after a long estrangement from his father, instigates a rebellion against the king, and David flees from Jerusalem. The rebellion ends when Absalom, hanging by his hair from a tree, is killed by Joab.

There is a quarrel between Israel and Judah concerning bringing the king back to Jerusalem. The rebel Sheba rouses Israel to desert David and go back to their homes. Although David makes a series of unfortunate and unwise decisions, the rebellion is quelled and David once again is established in Jerusalem.

The book ends with two beautiful poems, a list of David's mighty men, and David's sin in numbering the fighting men of Israel. David repents, buys the threshing floor of Araunah, and presents offerings to the Lord on the altar he builds there.

Personal Application This book unfolds God's working in history. Although human beings were sinful and must sometimes be punished by Him, God still worked through them to accomplish His redemptive purpose, fully realized in Jesus Christ, the Messiah and King of Kings. (See Rev. 22:16.)

Likewise, God has left the church in the world as the body of Christ to witness for Him and to carry out His purposes on the Earth today.

Christ Revealed David and his reign look to the coming of the Messiah. Chapter 7 especially anticipates the future King. God intercepts David's plans to build a house for the ark and explains that while David cannot build Him a house, God is building David a house, that is, a lineage that will last forever.

In his victory over all Israel's enemies, his humility and commitment to the Lord, his zeal for the house of God, his combining of the offices of prophet, priest, and king—David is a forerunner of the Root of Jesse, Jesus Christ.

The Holy Spirit at Work Jesus explained the work of the Spirit in John 16:8: "And when He has come, He will convict the world of sin, and of righteousness, and of judgment." We clearly see the working of the Holy Spirit in these ways in 2 Samuel. He functioned most often through the priest. He is seen working as counselor in the many times David would "inquire of the LORD" through the priest and the ephod.

The convincing or convicting work of the Spirit is seen clearly with Nathan the prophet confronting David about his sin with Bathsheba and Uriah. David's sin is laid bare, righteousness is accomplished, and the judgment is spelled out. This, in microcosm, illustrates the broad working of the Holy Spirit in the world, through the Spirit-empowered church.

Outline of 2 Samuel

I. The triumphs of David 1:1—10:19
- 1. The political triumphs of David 1:1—5:25
  - A. Reign of David in Hebron 1:1—4:12
  - B. Reign of David in Jerusalem 5:1–25
- 2. The spiritual triumphs of David 6:1—7:29
  - A. Moving the ark 6:1–23
  - B. God's covenant with David 7:1–29
- 3. The military triumphs of David 8:1—10:19
  - A. Triumphs over his enemies 8:1–12
  - B. David's righteous rule 8:13—9:13
  - C. Triumphs over Ammon and Syria 10:1–19

II. The transgressions of David 11:1–27
- 1. The sin of adultery 11:1–5
- 2. The sin of murder 11:6–27
  - A. Uriah's loyalty to David 11:6–13
  - B. David's command to murder Uriah 11:14–25
  - C. David and Bathsheba's marriage 11:26, 27

III. The troubles of David 12:1—24:25
- 1. Troubles in David's house 12:1—13:36
  - A. Prophecy by Nathan 12:1–14
  - B. Death of David's son 12:15–25
  - C. Joab's loyalty to David 12:26–31
  - D. Incest in David's house 13:1–20
  - E. Absalom's murder of Amnon 13:21–36
- 2. Troubles in David's kingdom 13:37—24:25
  - A. Rebellion of Absalom 13:37—17:29
  - B. Joab's murder of Absalom 18:1–33
  - C. David restored as king 19:1—20:26
  - D. Commentary of the reign of David 21:1—24:25

The Report of Saul's Death

NOW it came to pass after the
[a]death of Saul, when David had
returned from [b]the slaughter of the
Amalekites, and David had stayed two
days in Ziklag,
2 on the third day, behold, it happened that [a]a man came from Saul's
camp [b]with his clothes [1]torn and dust
on his head. So it was, when he came
to David, that he [c]fell to the ground
and prostrated himself.
3 And David said to him, "Where
have you come from?" So he said to
him, "I have escaped from the camp
of Israel."
4 Then David said to him, [a]"How did
the matter go? Please tell me." And he
answered, "The people have fled from
the battle, many of the people are
fallen and dead, and Saul and [b]Jona-
than his son are dead also."
5 So David said to the young man
who told him, "How do you know that
Saul and Jonathan his son are dead?"
6 Then the young man who told him
said, "As I happened by chance *to be*
on [a]Mount Gilboa, there was [b]Saul,
leaning on his spear; and indeed the
chariots and horsemen followed hard
after him.
7 "Now when he looked behind him,
he saw me and called to me. And I answered, 'Here I am.'
8 "And he said to me, 'Who *are* you?'
So I answered him, 'I *am* an Amalekite.'
9 "He said to me again, 'Please stand
over me and kill me, for [1]anguish has
come upon me, but my life still *remains*
in me.'
10 "So I stood over him and [a]killed
him, because I was sure that he could
not *live after he had fallen. And I took
the crown that *was* on his head and
the bracelet that *was* on his arm, and
have brought them here to my lord."
11 Therefore David took hold of his 4
own clothes and [a]tore them, and *so did*
all the men who *were* with him.
12 And they [a]mourned and wept and

CHAPTER 1

1 [a]1 Sam. 31:6 [b]1 Sam. 30:1, 17, 26
2 [a]2 Sam. 4:10 [b]1 Sam. 4:12 [c]1 Sam. 25:23 [1]To show grief
4 [a]1 Sam. 4:16; 31:3 [b]1 Sam. 31:2
6 [a]1 Sam. 31:1 [b]1 Sam. 31:2–4
9 [1]*agony*
10 [a]Judg. 9:54; 2 Kin. 11:12 *See WW at Hab. 2:4.
11 [a]2 Sam. 3:31; 13:31
12 [a]2 Sam. 3:31

1:2 Clothes torn and dust are signs of deep grief, an obvious ploy by the Amalekite to gain David's favor.

1:6–10 Saul's death as suicide is recorded in 1 Sam. 31. This Amalekite likely fabricated the story to make himself look good in David's eyes in order to get some reward (see 4:10).

1:11, 12 See section 4 of Truth-In-Action at the end of 2 Sam.

[b]fasted until evening for Saul and for
Jonathan his son, for the [c]people of the
LORD and for the house of Israel, because they had fallen by the sword.
13 Then David said to the young man
who told him, "Where *are* you from?"
And he answered, "I *am* the son of an
alien, an Amalekite."
4 14 So David said to him, "How [a]was
it you were not [b]afraid to [c]put forth
your hand to destroy the LORD's
anointed?"
15 Then [a]David called one of the
young men and said, "Go near, *and* execute him!" And he struck him so that
he died.
16 So David said to him, [a]"Your *blood
is on your own head, for [b]your own
mouth has testified against you,
saying, 'I have killed the LORD's
anointed.'"

The Song of the Bow

17 Then David lamented with this
lamentation over Saul and over Jonathan his son,
18 [a]and he told *them* to teach the children of Judah *the Song of* the Bow;
indeed *it is* written [b]in the Book
[1]of Jasher:

19 "The beauty of Israel is slain on
your high places!
[a]How the mighty have fallen!
20 [a]Tell *it* not in Gath,
Proclaim *it* not in the streets of
[b]Ashkelon—
Lest [c]the daughters of the
Philistines rejoice,
Lest the daughters of [d]the
uncircumcised triumph.

21 "O [a]mountains of Gilboa,
[b]*Let there be* no dew nor rain upon
you,
Nor fields of offerings.
For the shield of the mighty is
[1]cast away there!
The shield of Saul, not [c]anointed
with oil.
22 From the blood of the slain,
From the fat of the mighty,
[a]The bow of Jonathan did not turn
back,
And the sword of Saul did not
return empty.

23 "Saul and Jonathan *were* beloved
and pleasant in their lives,
And in their [a]death they were not
divided;
They were swifter than eagles,
They were [b]stronger than lions.

24 "O daughters of Israel, weep over
Saul,
Who clothed you in scarlet, with
luxury;
Who put ornaments of gold on
your apparel.

25 "How the mighty have fallen in the
midst of the battle!
Jonathan *was* slain in your high
places.
26 I am distressed for you, my
brother Jonathan;
You have been very pleasant to
me;
[a]Your love to me was wonderful,
Surpassing the love of women.

27 "How[a] the mighty have fallen,
And the weapons of war
perished!"

David Anointed King of Judah

2 It happened after this that David
[a]inquired of the LORD, saying,
"Shall I go up to any of the cities of
Judah?" And the LORD said to him, "Go
up." David said, "Where shall I go up?"
And He said, "To [b]Hebron."
2 So David went up there, and his
[a]two wives also, Ahinoam the

12 [b]1 Sam. 31:13 [c]2 Sam. 6:21
14 [a]Num. 12:8 [b]1 Sam. 31:4 [c]1 Sam. 24:6; 26:9
15 [a]2 Sam. 4:10, 12
16 [a]1 Sam. 26:9; 2 Sam. 3:28; 1 Kin. 2:32–37 [b]2 Sam. 1:10; Luke 19:22 *See WW at Lev. 17:11.
18 [a]1 Sam. 31:3 [b]Josh. 10:13 [1]Lit. *of the Upright*
19 [a]2 Sam. 1:27
20 [a]1 Sam. 27:2; 31:8–13; Mic. 1:10 [b]1 Sam. 6:17; Jer. 25:20 [c]Ex. 15:20; Judg. 11:34; 1 Sam. 18:6 [d]1 Sam. 31:4
21 [a]1 Sam. 31:1 [b]Ezek. 31:15 [c]1 Sam. 10:1 [1]Lit. *defiled*
22 [a]Deut. 32:42; 1 Sam. 18:4
23 [a]1 Sam. 31:2–4 [b]Judg. 14:18
26 [a]1 Sam. 18:1–4; 19:2; 20:17
27 [a]2 Sam. 1:19, 25

CHAPTER 2

1 [a]Judg. 1:1; 1 Sam. 23:2, 4, 9; 30:7, 8 [b]1 Sam. 30:31; 2 Sam. 2:11; 5:1–3; 1 Kin. 2:11
2 [a]1 Sam. 25:42, 43; 30:5

1:14–16 See section 4 of Truth-In-Action at the end of 2 Sam.
1:14 David always considered Saul as **God's anointed,** even though Saul was rejected by God, hated David, and sought to kill him. David's reverence was for God who had anointed Saul.
1:16 Your blood *is* on your own head: The lying Amalekite is responsible for his own death. This young man had presumed to do what David himself had twice refused to do, that is, to kill Saul, God's anointed.
1:18 *The Song of* the Bow was an appropriate title, for not only were the bow and arrow symbols of military might, but also the fighting men of Saul's tribe, Benjamin, were highly regarded for their ability with the bow and arrow. **The Book of Jasher,** or "The Book of the Upright," was a national songbook of Israel. It is referred to in Josh. 10:12–14 where Joshua's command, "Sun, stand still over Gibeon" is said to be recorded.
1:19 The words **How the mighty have fallen** are repeated in vv. 25 and 27 and mark the beginning of the three sections of the song. "The mighty" are Saul and Jonathan.
1:20 Gath and **Ashkelon** are two of the cities of the Philistines.
1:21 Gilboa: A ridge of high hills running diagonally from the northwest to southeast, forming the southern boundary of the Valley of Jezreel (Armageddon), with an elevation of 1,695 feet. The **fields of offerings** produced fruit for the firstfruit offerings. **The shield** was **not anointed with oil,** or cleaned with oil, but still had the blood of battle on it.

Jezreelitess, and Abigail the widow of
Nabal the Carmelite.
3 And David brought up [a]the men
who *were* with him, every man with
his household. So they dwelt in the cities of Hebron.
4 [a]Then the men of Judah came, and
there they [b]anointed David king over
the house of Judah. And they told David, saying, [c]"The men of Jabesh Gilead *were the ones* who buried Saul."
5 So David sent messengers to the
men of Jabesh Gilead, and said to
them, [a]"You *are* blessed of the LORD,
for you have shown this kindness to
your lord, to Saul, and have buried
him.
6 "And now may [a]the LORD show
kindness and truth to you. I also will
repay you this kindness, because you
have done this thing.
7 "Now therefore, let your hands be
strengthened, and be valiant; for your
master Saul is dead, and also the house
of Judah has anointed me king over
them."

Ishbosheth Made King of Israel

8 But [a]Abner the son of Ner, commander of Saul's army, took [1]Ishbo-
sheth the son of Saul and brought
him over to [b]Mahanaim;
9 and he made him king over [a]Gilead,
over the [b]Ashurites, over [c]Jezreel, over
Ephraim, over Benjamin, and over all
Israel.
10 Ishbosheth, Saul's son, *was* forty
years old when he began to reign over
Israel, and he reigned two years. Only
the house of Judah followed David.
11 And [a]the [1]time that David was king
in Hebron over the house of Judah was
seven years and six months.

Israel and Judah at War

12 Now Abner the son of Ner, and the
servants of Ishbosheth the son of Saul,
went out from Mahanaim to [a]Gibeon.
13 And [a]Joab the son of Zeruiah, and
the servants of David, went out and
met them by [b]the pool of Gibeon. So
they sat down, one on one side of the
pool and the other on the other side
of the pool.
14 Then Abner said to Joab, "Let the
young men now arise and compete before us." And Joab said, "Let them
arise."
15 So they arose and went over by
number, twelve from Benjamin, *followers* of Ishbosheth the son of Saul,
and twelve from the servants of David.
16 And each one grasped his opponent
by the head and *thrust* his sword in
his opponent's side; so they fell down
together. Therefore that place was
called [1]the Field of Sharp Swords,
which *is* in Gibeon.
17 So there was a very fierce battle
that day, and Abner and the men of
Israel were beaten before the servants
of David.
18 Now the [a]three sons of Zeruiah
were there: Joab and Abishai and Asahel. And Asahel *was* [b]*as* fleet of foot
[c]as a wild gazelle.
19 So Asahel pursued Abner, and in
going he did not turn to the right hand
or to the left from following Abner.
20 Then Abner looked behind him and
said, "*Are* you Asahel?" He answered,
"I *am*."
21 And Abner said to him, "Turn aside
to your right hand or to your left, and
lay hold on one of the young men and
take his armor for yourself." But Asahel would not turn aside from following him.
22 So Abner said again to Asahel,
"Turn aside from following me. Why
should I strike you to the ground? How
then could I face your brother Joab?"
23 However, he refused to turn aside.
Therefore Abner struck him [a]in the
stomach with the blunt end of the
spear, so that the spear came out of
his back; and he fell down there and
died on the spot. So it was *that* as
many as came to the place where Asa-

3 [a]1 Sam. 27:2, 3; 30:1; 1 Chr. 12:1
4 [a]1 Sam. 30:26; 2 Sam. 2:11; 5:5; 19:14, 41–43 [b]1 Sam. 16:13; 2 Sam. 5:3 [c]1 Sam. 31:11–13
5 [a]Ruth 2:20; 3:10
6 [a]Ex. 34:6; 2 Tim. 1:16, 18
8 [a]1 Sam. 14:50; 2 Sam. 3:6 [b]Gen. 32:2; Josh. 21:38; 2 Sam. 17:24 [1]*Esh-Baal*, 1 Chr. 8:33; 9:39
9 [a]Josh. 22:9 [b]Judg. 1:32 [c]1 Sam. 29:1
11 [a]2 Sam. 5:5; 1 Kin. 2:11 [1]Lit. *number of days*
12 [a]Josh. 10:2–12; 18:25
13 [a]1 Sam. 26:6; 2 Sam. 8:16; 1 Chr. 2:16; 11:6 [b]Jer. 41:12
16 [1]Heb. *Helkath Hazzurim*
18 [a]1 Chr. 2:16 [b]1 Chr. 12:8; Hab. 3:19 [c]Ps. 18:33
23 [a]2 Sam. 3:27; 4:6; 20:10

2:4 Jabesh Gilead: This is the city that Saul saved from the Ammonites in his first military action after being anointed king (1 Sam. 11:1–13). Because of this, they are kind to him.

2:8 Ishbosheth means "Man of Shame." His name originally was Esh-Baal, meaning "Fire of Baal," or "Destroyer of Baal."

2:10, 11 The discrepancy between the time that Ishbosheth ruled (2 years) and the time David was in Hebron before ruling over all Israel (7½ years) is best explained by David's refusal to seize the throne. He was content to wait until the people came to him, confirming God's anointing and timing.

2:12 The servants of Ishbosheth were the soldiers who had been defeated at Gilboa with Saul.

2:13 Zeruiah was David's sister (1 Chr. 2:16). **The pool of Gibeon** was one of the several large reservoirs in that area (also referred to in Jer. 41:12).

2:14 Abner wants the battle to be settled by 12 young warriors from each side. The assumption is that whoever wins this single match wins the war, an attractive plan to Abner because of the depletion of his army in the defeat at Mt. Gilboa.

2:17 After the young men savagely kill each other, the armies are engaged.

2:18 Abishai, a great warrior, is listed among David's mighty men in 23:18.

2:21 Abner does not want to kill **Asahel** because of his respect for Asahel's brother, Joab.

hel fell down and died, stood [b]still.
24 Joab and Abishai also pursued Abner. And the sun was going down when
they came to the hill of Ammah, which
is before Giah by the road to the Wilderness of Gibeon.
25 Now the children of Benjamin gathered together behind Abner and became [1]a unit, and took their stand on
top of a hill.
26 Then Abner called to Joab and said,
"Shall the sword devour forever? Do
you not know that it will be bitter in
the latter end? How long will it be then
until you tell the people to return from
pursuing their brethren?"
27 And Joab said, "*As* God lives,
[1]unless [a]you had spoken, surely then
by morning all the people would have
given up pursuing their brethren."
28 So Joab blew a *trumpet; and all the
people stood still and did not pursue
Israel anymore, nor did they fight anymore.
29 Then Abner and his men went on
all that night through the plain,
*crossed over the Jordan, and went
through all Bithron; and they came to
Mahanaim.
30 So Joab returned from pursuing Abner. And when he had gathered all the
people together, there were missing of
David's servants nineteen men and
Asahel.
31 But the servants of David had
struck down, of Benjamin and Abner's
men, three hundred and sixty men who
died.
32 Then they took up Asahel and buried him in his father's tomb, which *was*
in [a]Bethlehem. And Joab and his men
went all night, and they came to Hebron at daybreak.
3 Now there was a long [a]war between the house of Saul and the
house of David. But David grew stronger and stronger, and the house of Saul
grew weaker and weaker.

Sons of David

2 Sons were born [a]to David in Hebron: His firstborn was Amnon [b]by
Ahinoam the Jezreelitess;
3 his second, [1]Chileab, by Abigail the
widow of Nabal the Carmelite; the
third, [a]Absalom the son of Maacah, the
daughter of Talmai, king [b]of Geshur;
4 the fourth, [a]Adonijah the son of
Haggith; the fifth, Shephatiah the son
of Abital;
5 and the sixth, Ithream, by David's
wife Eglah. These were born to David
in Hebron.

Abner Joins Forces with David

6 Now it was so, while there was war
between the house of Saul and the
house of David, that Abner *was
strengthening *his hold* on the house of
Saul.
7 And Saul had a concubine, whose
name *was* [a]Rizpah, the daughter of
Aiah. So *Ishbosheth* said to Abner,
"Why have you [b]gone in to my father's
concubine?"
8 Then Abner became very angry at
the words of Ishbosheth, and said,
"*Am* I [a]a dog's head that belongs to
Judah? Today I show loyalty to the
house of Saul your father, to his
brothers, and to his friends, and have
not delivered you into the hand of David; and you charge me today with a
fault concerning this woman?
9 [a]"May God do so to Abner, and
more also, if I do not do for David
[b]as the LORD has sworn to him—
10 "to transfer the kingdom from the
[1]house of Saul, and set up the throne
of David over Israel and over Judah,
[a]from Dan to Beersheba."
11 And he could not answer Abner another word, because he feared him.
12 Then Abner sent messengers on his
behalf to David, saying, "Whose *is* the
land?" saying *also,* "Make your covenant with me, and indeed my hand
shall be with you to bring all Israel to
you."
13 And *David* said, "Good, I will make
a covenant with you. But one thing I
require of you: [a]you shall not see my
face unless you first bring [b]Michal,
Saul's daughter, when you come to see
my face."
14 So David sent messengers to

23 [b]2 Sam. 20:12
25 [1]*one band*
27 [a]2 Sam. 2:14 [1]*if you had not spoken*
28 *See WW at Hos. 8:1.
29 *See WW at Josh. 3:4.
32 [a]1 Sam. 20:6

CHAPTER 3

1 [a]1 Kin. 14:30; [Ps. 46:9]
2 [a]1 Chr. 3:1–4 [b]1 Sam. 25:42, 43
3 [a]2 Sam. 15:1–10 [b]Josh. 13:13; 1 Sam. 27:8; 2 Sam. 13:37; 14:32; 15:8 [1]*Daniel,* 1 Chr. 3:1
4 [a]1 Kin. 1:5
6 *See WW at Josh. 1:9.
7 [a]2 Sam. 21:8–11 [b]2 Sam. 16:21
8 [a]Deut. 23:18; 1 Sam. 24:14; 2 Sam. 9:8; 16:9
9 [a]Ruth 1:17; 1 Kin. 19:2 [b]1 Sam. 15:28; 16:1, 12; 28:17; 1 Chr. 12:23
10 [a]Judg. 20:1; 1 Sam. 3:20; 2 Sam. 17:11; 1 Kin. 4:25 [1]*family*
13 [a]Gen. 43:3 [b]1 Sam. 18:20; 19:11; 25:44; 2 Sam. 6:16

2:25 The children of Benjamin were the fellow tribesmen of Saul and Jonathan who had joined forces with Abner.
3:1 This does not mean that there was continued fighting, but that the hostility between **the house of David** and **the house of Saul** continued for a long time.
3:7, 8 Concubines were passed down from a king to his successor as part of the inherited property. Therefore, by taking Rizpah, Abner stakes his claim to the throne, which is treason in Ishbosheth's eyes. **Dog's head** represents something most contemptible.
3:10 From Dan to Beersheba was a common idiom to indicate the entire nation from the extreme north (Dan) to the extreme south (Beersheba).
3:13 Michal had been promised to David by Saul (1 Sam. 18:27; 19:11, 12), but Saul had broken his word and given her to Paltiel (1 Sam. 25:44). This renewal of his marriage to the king's daughter is a political statement that he bears no ill will toward the house of Saul.

[a]Ishbosheth, Saul's son, saying, "Give *me* my wife Michal, whom I betrothed to myself [b]for a hundred foreskins of the Philistines."
15 And Ishbosheth sent and took her from *her* husband, from [1]Paltiel the son of Laish.
16 Then her husband went along with her to [a]Bahurim, [1]weeping behind her. So Abner said to him, "Go, return!" And he returned.
17 Now Abner had communicated with the elders of Israel, saying, "In time past you were seeking for David *to be* king over you.
18 "Now then, do *it!* [a]For the LORD has spoken of David, saying, 'By the hand of My servant David, [1]I will save My people Israel from the hand of the Philistines and the hand of all their enemies.'"
19 And Abner also spoke in the hearing of [a]Benjamin. Then Abner also went to speak in the hearing of David in Hebron all that seemed good to Israel and the whole house of Benjamin.
20 So Abner and twenty men with him came to David at Hebron. And David made a feast for Abner and the men who *were* with him.
21 Then Abner said to David, "I will arise and go, and [a]gather all Israel to my lord the king, that they may make a covenant with you, and that you may [b]reign over all that your heart desires." So David sent Abner away, and he went in peace.

Joab Murders Abner

22 At that moment the servants of David and Joab came from a raid and brought much [1]spoil with them. But Abner *was* not with David in Hebron, for he had sent him away, and he had gone in peace.
23 When Joab and all the troops that *were* with him had come, they told Joab, saying, "Abner the son of Ner came to the king, and he sent him away, and he has gone in peace."
24 Then Joab came to the king and said, "What have you done? Look, Abner came to you; why *is* it *that* you sent him away, and he has already gone?
25 "Surely you realize that Abner the son of Ner came to deceive you, to know [a]your going out and your coming in, and to know all that you are doing."
26 And when Joab had gone from David's presence, he sent messengers after Abner, who brought him back from the well of Sirah. But David did not know *it.*
27 Now when Abner had returned to Hebron, Joab [a]took him aside in the gate to speak with him privately, and there [1]stabbed him [b]in the stomach, so that he died for the blood of [c]Asahel his brother.
28 Afterward, when David heard *it,* he said, "My kingdom and I *are* [1]guiltless before the LORD forever of the blood of Abner the son of Ner.
29 [a]"Let it rest on the head of Joab and on all his father's house; and let there never fail to be in the [1]house of Joab one [b]who has a discharge or is a leper, who leans on a staff or falls by the sword, or who lacks bread."
30 So Joab and Abishai his brother killed Abner, because he had killed their brother [a]Asahel at Gibeon in the battle.

David's Mourning for Abner

31 Then David said to Joab and to all the people who were with him, [a]"Tear your clothes, [b]gird yourselves with sackcloth, and mourn for Abner." And King David followed the coffin.
32 So they buried Abner in Hebron; and the king lifted up his voice and wept at the grave of Abner, and all the people wept.
33 And the king sang *a lament* over Abner and said:

"Should Abner die as a [a]fool dies?
34 Your hands were not bound
Nor your feet put into fetters;
As a man falls before wicked
men, *so* you fell."

Then all the people wept over him again.
35 And when all the people came [a]to persuade David to eat food while it was still day, David took an oath, saying, [b]"God do so to me, and more

14 [a]2 Sam. 2:10 [b]1 Sam. 18:25–27
15 [1]*Palti,* 1 Sam. 25:44
16 [a]2 Sam. 16:5; 19:16 [1]Lit. *going and weeping*
18 [a]2 Sam. 3:9 [1]So with many Heb. mss., LXX, Syr., Tg.; MT *he*
19 [a]1 Sam. 10:20, 21; 1 Chr. 12:29
21 [a]2 Sam. 3:10, 12 [b]1 Kin. 11:37
22 [1]*booty*
25 [a]Deut. 28:6; 1 Sam. 29:6; Is. 37:28
27 [a]2 Sam. 20:9, 10; 1 Kin. 2:5 [b]2 Sam. 4:6 [c]2 Sam. 2:23 [1]Lit. *struck*
28 [1]*innocent*
29 [a]Deut. 21:6–9; 1 Kin. 2:32, 33 [b]Lev. 15:2 [1]*family*
30 [a]2 Sam. 2:23
31 [a]Josh. 7:6; 2 Sam. 1:2, 11 [b]Gen. 37:34
33 [a]2 Sam. 13:12, 13
35 [a]2 Sam. 12:17; Jer. 16:7, 8 [b]Ruth 1:17

3:16 Bahurim was a city on the border of Judah, near Jerusalem. Paltiel follows Michal to the very border of David's kingdom.
3:19 The tribe of **Benjamin** is Saul's own tribe and the one least likely to accept David.
3:27 Abner feels safe in returning to **Hebron** not only because of David's disposition toward him, but because Hebron was a city of refuge in which no vengeance could be taken. See Num. 35:22–25 and Josh. 21:13.
3:31 Joab the assassin is made to mourn publicly while the man he has killed is buried with royal honors; a humiliation for this proud warrior and the beginning of a breach between him and David.
3:35–37 David's refusal to eat and his ongoing mourning

also, if I *taste bread or anything else
[c]till the sun goes down!"
36 Now all the people took note *of it*,
and it pleased them, since whatever the
king did pleased all the people.
37 For all the people and all Israel understood that day that it had not been
the king's *intent* to kill Abner the son
of Ner.
38 Then the king said to his servants,
"Do you not know that a prince and a
great man has fallen this day in Israel?
39 "And I *am* weak today, though
anointed king; and these men, the sons
of Zeruiah, [a]*are* too harsh for me.
[b]The LORD shall repay the evildoer according to his wickedness."

Ishbosheth Is Murdered

4 When Saul's [1]son heard that Abner
had died in Hebron, [a]he[2] lost heart,
and all Israel was [b]troubled.
2 Now Saul's son *had* two men *who*
were captains of troops. The name of
one *was* Baanah and the name of the
other Rechab, the sons of Rimmon the
Beerothite, of the children of Benjamin. (For [a]Beeroth also was [1]*part* of
Benjamin,
3 because the Beerothites fled to
[a]Gittaim and have been sojourners
there until this day.)
4 [a]Jonathan, Saul's son, had a son
who was lame in *his* feet. He was five
years old when the news about Saul
and Jonathan came [b]from Jezreel; and
his nurse took him up and fled. And it
happened, as she made haste to flee,
that he fell and became lame. His name
was [c]Mephibosheth.[1]
5 Then the sons of Rimmon the
Beerothite, Rechab and Baanah, set out
and came at about the heat of the day
to the [a]house of Ishbosheth, who was
lying on his bed at noon.
6 And they came there, all the way
into the house, *as though* to get wheat,
and they [1]stabbed him [a]in the stomach.
Then Rechab and Baanah his brother
escaped.
7 For when they came into the house,
he was lying on his bed in his bedroom;
then they struck him and killed him,
beheaded him and took his head, and
were all night escaping through the
plain.
8 And they brought the head of Ishbosheth to David at Hebron, and said to
the king, "Here is the head of Ishbosheth, the son of Saul your enemy,
[a]who sought your life; and the LORD
has avenged my lord the king this day
of Saul and his descendants."
9 But David answered Rechab and
Baanah his brother, the sons of Rimmon the Beerothite, and said to them,
"*As* the LORD lives, [a]who has redeemed
my life from all adversity,
10 "when [a]someone told me, saying,
'Look, Saul is dead,' thinking to have
brought good news, I arrested him and
had him executed in Ziklag—the one
who *thought* I would give him a reward for *his* news.
11 "How much more, when wicked
men have killed a *righteous person in
his own house on his bed? Therefore,
shall I not now [a]require his [1]blood at
your hand and [2]remove you from the
earth?"
12 So David [a]commanded his young
men, and they executed them, cut off
their hands and feet, and hanged *them*
by the pool in Hebron. But they took
the head of Ishbosheth and buried *it*
in the [b]tomb of Abner in Hebron.

David Reigns over All Israel

5 Then all the tribes of Israel [a]came
to David at Hebron and spoke, saying, "Indeed [b]we *are* your bone and
your flesh.
2 "Also, in time past, when Saul was
king over us, [a]you were the one who
led Israel out and brought them in; and
the LORD said to you, [b]'You shall shepherd My people Israel, and be ruler
over Israel.' "
3 [a]Therefore all the elders of Israel
came to the king at Hebron, [b]and King
David made a covenant with them at
Hebron [c]before the LORD. And they
anointed David king over Israel.
4 David *was* [a]thirty years old when
he began to reign, *and* [b]he reigned
forty years.
5 In Hebron he reigned over Judah
[a]seven years and six months, and in

35 [c]Judg. 20:26; 2 Sam. 1:12 *See WW at Ps. 34:8.
39 [a]2 Sam. 19:5–7 [b]1 Kin. 2:5, 6, 32–34; 2 Tim. 4:14

CHAPTER 4

1 [a]Ezra 4:4; Is. 13:7 [b]Matt. 2:3 [1]Ishbosheth [2]Lit. *his hands dropped*
2 [a]Josh. 18:25 [1]*considered part of*
3 [a]Neh. 11:33
4 [a]2 Sam. 9:3 [b]1 Sam. 29:1, 11 [c]2 Sam. 9:6 [1]*Merib-Baal*, 1 Chr. 8:34; 9:40
5 [a]2 Sam. 2:8, 9
6 [a]2 Sam. 2:23; 20:10 [1]Lit. *struck*
8 [a]1 Sam. 19:2, 10, 11; 23:15; 25:29
9 [a]Gen. 48:16; 1 Kin. 1:29; Ps. 31:7
10 [a]2 Sam. 1:2–16
11 [a][Gen. 9:5, 6; Ps. 9:12] [1]Or *bloodshed* [2]Lit. *consume you* *See WW at Lam. 1:18.
12 [a]2 Sam. 1:15 [b]2 Sam. 3:32

CHAPTER 5

1 [a]1 Chr. 11:1–3 [b]Gen. 29:14; Judg. 9:2; 2 Sam. 19:12, 13
2 [a]1 Sam. 18:5, 13, 16 [b]1 Sam. 16:1
3 [a]2 Sam. 3:17; 1 Chr. 11:3 [b]2 Sam. 2:4; 3:21; 2 Kin. 11:17 [c]Judg. 11:11; 1 Sam. 23:18
4 [a]Gen. 41:46; Num. 4:3; Luke 3:23 [b]1 Kin. 2:11; 1 Chr. 26:31; 29:27
5 [a]2 Sam. 2:11; 1 Chr. 3:4; 29:27

for Abner are important as public statements of his innocence in Abner's death—a crucial necessity if he is to gain the trust of the northern tribes.

4:1 Saul's son is Ishbosheth.

4:9–11 David views their act as a violent murder against a defenseless man, therefore warranting execution.

4:12 These radical measures send the message to the northern tribes that David holds no hatred for Saul, his tribe, or his descendants.

5:1 Hebron was a city with rich history for Israel, being the burial place of all the patriarchs and their wives, with the exception of Rachel (Gen. 23:2; 25:9; 35:27–29; 49:29–33).

5:4 Jesus also began His public ministry at the age of 30.

Jerusalem he reigned thirty-three years over all Israel and Judah.

The Conquest of Jerusalem

6 [a]And the king and his men went to Jerusalem against [b]the Jebusites, the inhabitants of the land, who spoke to David, saying, "You shall not come in here; but the blind and the lame will repel you," thinking, "David cannot come in here."
7 Nevertheless David took the stronghold of Zion [a](that *is,* the City of David).
8 Now David said on that day, "Whoever climbs up by way of the water shaft and defeats the Jebusites (the lame and the blind, *who are* hated by David's soul), [a]*he shall be chief and captain.*" Therefore they say, "The blind and the lame shall not come into the house."
9 Then David dwelt in the stronghold, and called it [a]the City of David. And David built all around from [1]the Millo and inward.

6 [a]Judg. 1:21 [b]Josh. 15:63
7 [a]1 Kin. 2:10; 8:1; 9:24
8 [a]1 Chr. 11:6–9
9 [a]2 Sam. 5:7 [1]Lit. *The Landfill*
10 [a]1 Sam. 17:45 [b]1 Sam. 18:12, 28
11 [a]1 Kin. 5:1–18 [b]1 Chr. 14:1
12 [a]Num. 24:7 [b]Is. 45:4
13 [a][Deut. 17:17]
14 [a]1 Chr. 3:5–8 [b]2 Sam. 12:24 [1]*Shimea,* 1 Chr. 3:5
15 [1]*Elishama,* 1 Chr. 3:6
17 [a]1 Chr. 11:16 *See WW at Is. 61:1.

10 So David went on and became great, and [a]the LORD God of hosts *was* with [b]him.
11 Then [a]Hiram [b]king of Tyre sent messengers to David, and cedar trees, and carpenters and masons. And they built David a house.
12 So David knew that the LORD had established him as king over Israel, and that He had [a]exalted His kingdom [b]for the sake of His people Israel.
13 And [a]David took more concubines and wives from Jerusalem, after he had come from Hebron. Also more sons and daughters were born to David.
14 Now [a]these *are* the names of those who were born to him in Jerusalem: [1]Shammua, Shobab, Nathan, [b]Solomon,
15 Ibhar, [1]Elishua, Nepheg, Japhia,
16 Elishama, Eliada, and Eliphelet.

The Philistines Defeated

17 [a]Now when the Philistines heard that they had *anointed David king over Israel, all the Philistines went up

5:6 Jerusalem had been in the control of the **Jebusites** since the times of Joshua (Josh. 15:63). Being on the border between the northern tribes and Judah, it symbolized unity.
5:9 The Millo was a large landfill, which made the city level. Joab was in charge of rebuilding the city itself (1 Chr. 11:8).
5:11, 12 This gift by Hiram signifies that David is now regarded as a national king, not just as the head of tribal Judah.
5:17 When the anointing is finished and the time for kingdom business is at hand, the enemy invariably shows up. **Went down:** Most assume this battle took place before the taking of Jerusalem. Consistently Scripture speaks of "going up" to Jerusalem because of its location on the hills and because of its spiritual significance. Had David been residing in Jerusalem there certainly would have been no reason to leave. **The stronghold,** therefore, may have been the familiar mountain stronghold in the desert of Judah where David defended himself from Saul (23:14; 1 Chr. 12:8).

Jerusalem: David's City. David took the fortress called Jebus and renamed it the "City of David." This established his kingship militarily and politically. He then established his religious leadership by moving the ark of the covenant to the City of David. Solomon later expanded northward to Mt. Moriah and built the temple and the royal palace.

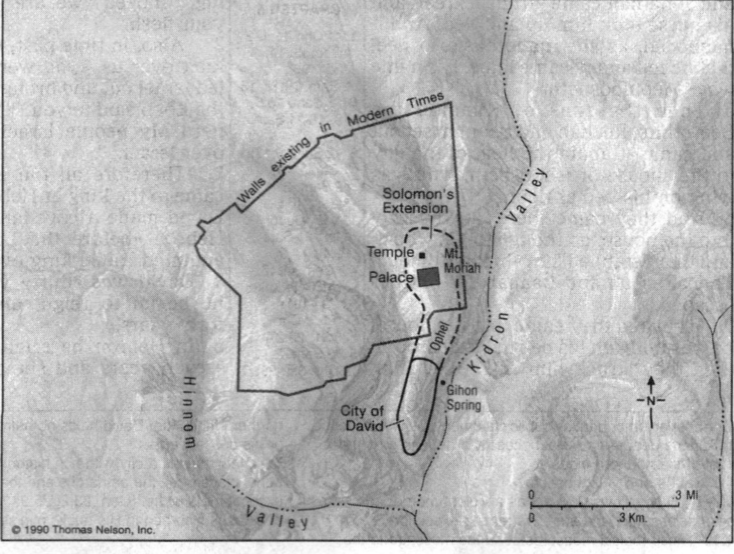

to search for David. And David heard
of it [b]and went down to the stronghold.
18 The Philistines also went and deployed themselves in [a]the Valley of
Rephaim.
19 So David [a]inquired of the LORD,
saying, "Shall I go up against the Philistines? Will You deliver them into my
hand?" And the LORD said to David,
"Go up, for I will doubtless deliver the
Philistines into your hand."
20 So David went to [a]Baal Perazim,
and David defeated them there; and he
said, "The LORD has broken through
my enemies before me, like a *breakthrough of water." Therefore he called
the name of that place [1]Baal Perazim.
21 And they left their [1]images there,
and David and his men [a]carried them
away.
22 [a]Then the Philistines went up once
again and deployed themselves in the
Valley of Rephaim.
23 Therefore [a]David inquired of the
LORD, and He said, "You shall not go
up; circle around behind them, and
come upon them in front of the mulberry trees.
24 "And it shall be, when you [a]hear
the sound of marching in the tops of
the mulberry trees, then you shall advance quickly. For then [b]the LORD will
go out before you to strike the camp
of the Philistines."
25 And David did so, as the LORD commanded him; and he drove back the
Philistines from [a]Geba[1] as far as
[b]Gezer.

The Ark Brought to Jerusalem

6 Again David gathered all *the*
choice *men* of Israel, thirty thousand.
2 And [a]David arose and went with all
the people who *were* with him from
[1]Baale Judah to bring up from there
the ark of God, whose name is called
[2]by the Name, the LORD of Hosts,
[b]who dwells *between* the *cherubim.
3 So they set the ark of God on a new
cart, and brought it out of the house
of Abinadab, which *was* on [a]the hill;
and Uzzah and Ahio, the sons of
Abinadab, drove the new [1]cart.
4 And they brought it out of [a]the
house of Abinadab, which *was* on the
hill, accompanying the ark of God; and
Ahio went before the ark.
5 Then David and all the house of Israel [a]played *music* before the LORD on
all kinds of *instruments of* fir wood,
on harps, on stringed instruments, on
tambourines, on sistrums, and on cymbals.
6 And when they came to [a]Nachon's
threshing floor, Uzzah put out *his*
[b]*hand* to the ark of God and [1]took hold
of it, for the oxen stumbled.
7 Then the anger of the LORD was 5
aroused against Uzzah, and God struck
him there for *his* [1]error; and he died
there by the ark of God.
8 And David became angry because
of the LORD's outbreak against Uzzah;
and he called the name of the place
[1]Perez Uzzah to this day.
9 [a]David was afraid of the LORD that
day; and he said, "How can the ark of
the LORD come to me?"
10 So David would not move the ark
of the LORD with him into the [a]City of
David; but David took it aside into the
house of Obed-Edom the [b]Gittite.
11 [a]The ark of the LORD remained in
the house of Obed-Edom the Gittite
three months. And the LORD [b]blessed
Obed-Edom and all his household.
12 Now it was told King David, saying,
"The LORD has blessed the house of
Obed-Edom and all that *belongs* to
him, because of the ark of God."

17 [b]2 Sam. 23:14
18 [a]1 Chr. 11:15
19 [a]1 Sam. 23:2
20 [a]Is. 28:21 [1]Lit. *Master of Breakthroughs* *See WW at Ezek. 22:30.
21 [a]Deut. 7:5, 25 [1]*idols*
22 [a]1 Chr. 14:13
23 [a]2 Sam. 5:19
24 [a]1 Chr. 14:15 [b]Judg. 4:14
25 [a]1 Chr. 14:16 [b]Josh. 16:10 [1]So with MT, Tg., Vg.; LXX *Gibeon*

CHAPTER 6

2 [a]1 Chr. 13:5, 6 [b]Ps. 80:1 [1]*Baalah, Kirjath Jearim,* Josh. 15:9; 1 Chr. 13:6 [2]LXX, Tg., Vg. omit *by the Name;* many Heb. mss., Syr. *there* *See WW at Ex. 25:18.
3 [a]1 Sam. 26:1 [1]LXX adds *with the ark*
4 [a]1 Sam. 7:1
5 [a]1 Sam. 18:6, 7
6 [a]1 Chr. 13:9 [b]Num. 4:15, 19, 20 [1]*held it*
7 [1]Or *irreverence*
8 [1]Lit. *Outburst Against Uzzah*
9 [a]Ps. 119:120
10 [a]2 Sam. 5:7 [b]1 Chr. 13:13; 26:4–8
11 [a]1 Chr. 13:14 [b]Gen. 30:27; 39:5

5:18 The Valley of Rephaim was about 3 or 4 miles south and west of Jerusalem.
5:20 Baal Perazim means "The LORD [in this case Yahweh] Who Breaks Out," or "The LORD Breaks Through."
5:21 The Philistines take **their images** into battle to ensure victory, since the ark has been taken by Israel.
5:23 Not go up: Not attack frontally, but rather from the rear this time. **Mulberry trees** are also called balsam trees.
5:24 The sound of marching is not merely wind blowing, but the sound of the angelic armies of God going ahead of them into battle.
5:25 From Geba to **Gezer** was about 15 miles.
6:1 The details of bringing the ark to Jerusalem are recorded in 1 Chr. 13, 15, and 16. About 70 years have passed since the ark was taken into the house of Abinadab after its capture by the Philistines (1 Sam. 4).
6:2 Baale Judah is the Canaanite name for the city of Kirjath Jearim. **By the Name:** The ark represented the very presence of God. "Name" here therefore represents everything God reveals Himself to be. The ark was the center of the nation's worship and the most sacred of its possessions.
6:3 Ex. 25 prescribed how to move this sacred ark.
6:6, 7 Error is literally "irreverence." Not even the priests were allowed to touch the ark or look into it because of its sacredness. Because the ark was not being handled according to God's directions, when the difficulties arose there was no acceptable way of dealing with them. Had the ark been carried on the shoulders of the priests, as the Law directed, this would not have happened.
6:7 See section 5 of Truth-In-Action at the end of 2 Sam.
6:10 Obed-Edom was from the Levitical city of Gath Rimmon. It is appropriate that the ark be with him, because his order of Levites were doorkeepers whose duties included watching over the ark in the sacred tent. His house is particularly blessed by its presence.

[a]So David went and brought up the ark
of God from the house of Obed-Edom
to the City of David with gladness.
13 And so it was, when [a]those bearing
the ark of the LORD had gone six paces,
that he sacrificed [b]oxen and fatted
sheep.
2 14 Then David [a]danced[1] before the
LORD with all *his* might; and David *was*
wearing [b]a linen *ephod.
15 [a]So David and all the house of Israel brought up the ark of the LORD
with *shouting and with the sound of
the trumpet.
2 **16** Now as the ark of the LORD came
into the City of David, [a]Michal, Saul's
daughter, looked through a window
and saw King David leaping and whirling before the LORD; and she despised
him in her heart.
17 So [a]they brought the ark of the
LORD, and set it in [b]its place in the
midst of the tabernacle that David had
erected for it. Then David [c]offered
burnt offerings and peace offerings before the LORD.
18 And when David had finished offering burnt offerings and peace offerings, [a]he blessed the people in the
name of the LORD of hosts.
19 [a]Then he distributed among all the
people, among the whole multitude of
Israel, both the women and the men,
to everyone a loaf of bread, a piece *of
meat,* and a cake of raisins. So all the
people departed, everyone to his
house.
20 [a]Then David returned to bless his
household. And Michal the daughter of
Saul came out to meet David, and said,
"How glorious was the king of Israel
today, [b]uncovering himself today in
the eyes of the maids of his servants,
as one of the [c]base fellows [1]shame-
lessly uncovers himself!"
21 So David said to Michal, "*It was* before the LORD, [a]who *chose me instead
of your father and all his house, to appoint me ruler over the [b]people of the
LORD, over Israel. Therefore I will play
music before the LORD.
22 "And I will be even more undigni-
fied than this, and will be humble in
my own sight. But as for the maidservants of whom you have spoken,
by them I will be held in honor."
23 Therefore Michal the daughter of 2
Saul had no children [a]to the day of her
death.

God's Covenant with David

7 Now it came to pass [a]when the
king was dwelling in his house,
and the LORD had given him rest from
all his enemies all around,
2 that the king said to Nathan the
*prophet, "See now, I dwell in [a]a house
of cedar, [b]but the ark of God dwells
inside tent [c]curtains."
3 Then Nathan said to the king, "Go,
do all that *is* in your [a]heart, for the
LORD *is* with you."
4 But it happened that night that the
word of the LORD came to Nathan, saying,
5 "Go and tell My servant David,
'Thus says the LORD: [a]"Would you
*build a house for Me to dwell in?
6 "For I have not dwelt in a house
[a]since the time that I brought the children of Israel up from Egypt, even to
this day, but have moved about in
[b]a tent and in a tabernacle.
7 "Wherever I have [a]moved about
with all the children of Israel, have I
ever spoken a word to anyone from the
tribes of Israel, whom I commanded
[b]to shepherd My people Israel, saying,
'Why have you not built Me a house
of cedar?' " '
8 "Now therefore, thus shall you say
to My servant David, 'Thus says the
LORD of hosts: [a]"I took you from the
sheepfold, from following the sheep, to
be ruler over My people, over Israel.
9 "And [a]I have been with you wherever you have gone, [b]and have [1]cut off
all your enemies from before you, and
have made you a great name, like the
name of the great men who *are* on the
earth.

12 [a]1 Chr. 15:25—16:3
13 [a]Num. 4:15; Josh. 3:3; 1 Sam. 6:15; 2 Sam. 15:24; 1 Chr. 15:2, 15 [b]1 Kin. 8:5
14 [a]Ps. 30:11; 149:3 [b]1 Sam. 2:18, 28 [1]*whirled about* *See WW at Ex. 35:27.
15 [a]1 Chr. 15:28 *See WW at Ezra 3:11.
16 [a]2 Sam. 3:14
17 [a]1 Chr. 16:1 [b]1 Chr. 15:1; 2 Chr. 1:4 [c]1 Kin. 8:5, 62, 63
18 [a]1 Kin. 8:14, 15, 55
19 [a]1 Chr. 16:3
20 [a]Ps. 30:title [b]2 Sam. 6:14, 16 [c]Judg. 9:4 [1]*openly*
21 [a]1 Sam. 13:14; 15:28 [b]2 Kin. 11:17 *See WW at 1 Kin. 11:34.
23 [a]1 Sam. 15:35; Is. 22:14

CHAPTER 7

1 [a]1 Chr. 17:1–27
2 [a]2 Sam. 5:11 [b]Acts 7:46 [c]Ex. 26:1 *See WW at 1 Sam. 3:20.
3 [a]1 Kin. 8:17, 18; 1 Chr. 22:7
5 [a]1 Kin. 5:3, 4; 8:19; 1 Chr. 22:8 *See WW at Zech. 1:16.
6 [a]Josh. 18:1; 1 Kin. 8:16 [b]Ex. 40:18, 34
7 [a]Lev. 26:11, 12 [b]2 Sam. 5:2; [Acts 20:28]
8 [a]1 Sam. 16:11, 12; Ps. 78:70, 71
9 [a]1 Sam. 18:14; 2 Sam. 5:10 [b]1 Sam. 31:6 [1]*destroyed*

6:13 Those bearing the ark: David finds the proper way to transport the ark, that is, on the shoulders of the priests. The presence of God is borne by people, not things.
6:14 See section 2 of Truth-In-Action at the end of 2 Sam.
6:14 David danced: Such rejoicing (literally, "spinning around") accompanied *all major* victories. In every other instance only women are mentioned as dancing, not men and certainly not the king. This accounts for some of Michal's embarrassment (v. 16), although her motive is obviously contempt.
6:16 See section 2 of Truth-In-Action at the end of 2 Sam.
6:16 Michal is here described as **Saul's daughter** rather than David's wife. She acts in the pride of her father, not the humility and joy of her husband.
6:20 Uncovering himself means divesting himself of his kingly robes and wearing only the shortened, priestly ephod. **Base fellows** refers to common men.
6:23 See section 2 of Truth-In-Action at the end of 2 Sam.
7:1 His house was the palace built by Hiram, king of Tyre (5:11).
7:7 God reminds David of His original intent in calling him **to shepherd My people Israel,** not to build Him a house.

10 "Moreover I will appoint a place for
My people Israel, and will [a]plant them,
that they may dwell in a place of their
own and move no more; [b]nor shall the
sons of wickedness oppress them anymore, as previously,
11 [a]"since the time that I commanded
judges *to be* over My people Israel, and
have caused you to rest from all your
enemies. Also the LORD [1]tells you
[b]that He will make you a [2]**house.**

WORD WEALTH

7:11 house, *bayit* (*by*-yeet); Strong's #1004: House, household, family, clan; temple, building, home. *Bayit* occurs about 2,000 times in the OT. *Bayit* may refer to a dwelling (Ruth 2:7) or a family (Gen. 7:1), and is also the word for the temple, the house of God at Jerusalem (2 Chr. 7:16).

12 [a]"When your days are fulfilled and
you [b]rest with your fathers, [c]I will set
up your seed after you, who will come
from your body, and I will establish his
kingdom.
13 [a]"He shall build a house for My
name, and I will [b]establish the throne
of his kingdom forever.
14 [a]"I will be his Father, and he shall
be [b]My son. If he commits iniquity, I
will chasten him with the rod of men
and with the [1]blows of the sons of men.
15 "But My *mercy shall not depart
from him, [a]as I took *it* from Saul,
whom I removed from before you.
16 "And [a]your house and your kingdom shall be established forever before
[1]you. Your throne shall be established
forever." ' "
17 According to all these words and
according to all this vision, so Nathan
spoke to David.

10 [a]Ps. 44:2; 80:8 [b]Ps. 89:22, 23
11 [a]Judg. 2:14–16 [b]2 Sam. 7:27 [1]*declares to you* [2]Royal dynasty
12 [a]1 Kin. 2:1 [b]Deut. 31:16 [c]Ps. 132:11
13 [a]1 Kin. 5:5; 8:19 [b][Is. 9:7; 49:8]
14 [a][Heb. 1:5] [b][Ps. 2:7; 89:26, 27, 30] [1]*strokes*
15 [a]1 Sam. 15:23, 28; 16:14 *See WW at Mic. 6:8.
16 [a]2 Sam. 7:13 [1]LXX *Me*

18 [a]Ex. 3:11
19 [a][Is. 55:8, 9]
20 [a]John 21:17
21 *See WW at Ps. 37:4.
22 [a]Deut. 10:17 [b]Ex. 15:11 [c]Ex. 10:2 [1]Tg., Syr. *O LORD God*
23 [a]Ps. 147:20 [b]Deut. 9:26; 33:29
24 [a][Deut. 26:18] [b]Ps. 48:14

David's Thanksgiving to God

18 Then King David went in and sat
before the LORD; and he said: [a]"Who
am I, O Lord GOD? And what is my
house, that You have brought me this
far?
19 "And yet this was a small thing in
Your sight, O Lord GOD; and You have
also spoken of Your servant's house
for a great while to come. [a]*Is* this the
manner of man, O Lord GOD?
20 "Now what more can David say to
You? For You, Lord GOD, [a]know Your
servant.
21 "For Your word's sake, and according to Your own *heart, You have done
all these great things, to make Your
servant know *them.*
22 "Therefore [a]You are great, [1]O Lord
GOD. For [b]*there is* none like You, nor
is there any God besides You, according to all that we have heard with our
[c]ears.
23 "And who *is* like Your people, like
Israel, [a]the one nation on the earth
whom God went to redeem for Himself
as a people, to make for Himself a
name—and to do for Yourself great
and awesome deeds for Your land—
before [b]Your people whom You redeemed for Yourself from Egypt, the
nations, and their gods?
24 "For [a]You have made Your people
Israel Your very own people forever;
[b]and You, LORD, have become their
God.
25 "Now, O LORD God, the word which
You have spoken concerning Your servant and concerning his house, establish *it* forever and do as You have
said.
26 "So let Your name be magnified forever, saying, 'The LORD of hosts *is* the
God over Israel.' And let the house of

7:12–16 The son of David (Solomon) and the Son of David (the Messiah) merge here. It is the Messiah's throne that will be established forever. See Ps. 45 and Heb. 1:8. In Israel it was generally held that the Messiah was to come from the tribe of Judah and the throne of David. See also Ps. 2:6, 7; 89:3, 4.

7:12 Seed can refer either to one child or a number of children. It can also be used for future generations in a line of succession. Here it is used for both Solomon and the Messiah.

7:14, 15 Because of Solomon's sin of idolatry at the end of his life, the kingdom was torn away from his son Jeroboam. However, one portion was reserved for David's sake, and the line of the Messiah continued (1 Kin. 11), thus fulfilling this promise.

7:14 I will be his Father: God as Father occurs over 200 times in the NT and is the exclusive way that Jesus refers to God.

7:16 Both **your house** and **your kingdom** are **established forever.** This cannot mean the physical house only, but reaches forward to Christ's statement, "Destroy this temple, and in three days I will raise it up" (John 2:19), speaking of His body. Read in connection with this chapter: Ps. 8; 72; 78; 89; 110; 132.

7:17 Vision: The OT always distinguished between a vision and a dream. A vision is received while awake.

7:18 Sat actually means "remained." David spends a lengthy time **before the LORD,** that is, in the tent where the ark stood.

7:19 The manner of man: That is, the law of man. The way God has treated David is the way God intends men to treat one another.

7:21 The two great motivations of God's blessings are faithfulness to His **word** and the loving generosity of His **heart.**

7:24 Not only is the kingdom of David to be forever, but Israel is **Your very own people forever.**

7:26, 27 LORD of hosts emphasizes the power of God. Hosts

Your servant David be established before You.
27 "For You, O LORD of hosts, God of
Israel, have *revealed *this* to Your servant, saying, 'I will build you a house.'
Therefore Your servant has found it in
his heart to *pray this *prayer to You.
28 "And now, O Lord GOD, You are
God, and [a]Your words are true, and
You have promised this goodness to
Your servant.
29 "Now therefore, let it please You to
bless the house of Your servant, that
it may continue before You forever; for
You, O Lord GOD, have spoken *it,* and
with Your blessing let the house of
Your servant be blessed [a]forever."

David's Further Conquests

8 After this it came to pass that David [1]attacked the Philistines and
subdued them. And David took
[2]Metheg Ammah from the hand of the
Philistines.
2 Then [a]he defeated Moab. Forcing
them down to the ground, he measured
them off with a line. With two lines he
measured off those to be put to death,
and with one full line those to be kept
alive. So the Moabites became David's
[b]servants, *and* [c]brought *tribute.
3 David also defeated Hadadezer the
son of Rehob, king of [a]Zobah, as he
went to recover [b]his territory at the
River Euphrates.
4 David took from him one thousand
chariots, [1]seven hundred horsemen,
and twenty thousand foot soldiers.
Also David [a]hamstrung all the chariot
horses, except that he spared *enough*
of them for one hundred chariots.
5 [a]When the Syrians of Damascus
came to help Hadadezer king of Zobah,
David killed twenty-two thousand of
the Syrians.
6 Then David put garrisons in Syria
of Damascus; and the Syrians became
David's servants, *and* brought tribute.

27 *See WW at Amos 3:7. • See WW at Job 42:10. • See WW at 2 Chr. 6:20.
28 [a]John 17:17
29 [a]2 Sam. 22:51

CHAPTER 8

1 [1]Lit. *struck* [2]Lit. *The Bridle of the Mother City*
2 [a]Num. 24:17 [b]2 Sam. 12:31 [c]1 Kin. 4:21 *See WW at Num. 29:6.
3 [a]1 Sam. 14:47 [b]2 Sam. 10:15–19
4 [a]Josh. 11:6, 9 [1]*seven thousand,* 1 Chr. 18:4
5 [a]1 Kin. 11:23–25
6 [a]2 Sam. 7:9; 8:14
7 [a]1 Kin. 10:16
8 [a]Ezek. 47:16 [1]*Tibhath,* 1 Chr. 18:8 [2]*Chun,* 1 Chr. 18:8
9 [a]1 Kin. 8:65 [1]*Tou,* 1 Chr. 18:9
10 [1]*Hadoram,* 1 Chr. 18:10 [2]Lit. *ask him of his welfare*
11 [a]1 Kin. 7:51
12 [a]2 Sam. 5:17–25 [1]LXX, Syr., Heb. mss. *Edom*
13 [a]2 Sam. 7:9 [b]2 Kin. 14:7 [c]1 Chr. 18:12 [1]LXX, Syr., Heb. mss. *Edomites* and 1 Chr. 18:12
14 [a]Gen. 27:29, 37–40
15 *See WW at Num. 36:13.

So [a]the LORD preserved David wherever he went.
7 And David took [a]the shields of gold
that had belonged to the servants of
Hadadezer, and brought them to Jerusalem.
8 Also from [1]Betah and from [a]Bero-
thai,[2] cities of Hadadezer, King David
took a large amount of bronze.
9 When [1]Toi king of [a]Hamath heard
that David had defeated all the army
of Hadadezer,
10 then Toi sent [1]Joram his son to King
David, to [2]greet him and bless him, because he had fought against Hadadezer
and defeated him (for Hadadezer had
been at war with Toi); and *Joram*
brought with him articles of silver, articles of gold, and articles of bronze.
11 King David also [a]dedicated these to
the LORD, along with the silver and
gold that he had dedicated from all the
nations which he had subdued—
12 from [1]Syria, from Moab, from the
people of Ammon, from the [a]Philis-
tines, from Amalek, and from the spoil
of Hadadezer the son of Rehob, king
of Zobah.
13 And David made *himself* a [a]name
when he returned from killing [b]eigh-
teen thousand [1]Syrians in [c]the Valley
of Salt.
14 He also put garrisons in Edom;
throughout all Edom he put garrisons,
and [a]all the Edomites became David's
servants. And the LORD preserved David wherever he went.

David's Administration

15 So David **reigned** over all Israel;
and David administered *judgment
and justice to all his people.

WORD WEALTH

8:15 reigned, *malach* (mah-*lach*); Strong's #4427: To reign, to be king, to

are the angelic armies of heaven. This powerful God will vanquish all enemies and fulfill the promises to David and his seed.

8:1 The Philistines had been Israel's enemy for more than 125 years, since the entry of Israel into Palestine under Joshua. **Metheg Ammah** means "The Bridle of the Mother City." The bridle of the Philistines is placed in David's hand, and they are now under his power.

8:2 David puts to death two out of three prisoners.

8:3–8 David defeats the Arameans, a loose federation of city-states who had come to power about the time of Saul in Israel.

8:3 Zobah is an area just north of Damascus in present-day Syria. **As he went** refers to **Hadadezer. David** attacks while the king is gone to secure his territories at the **River Euphrates.**

8:4 Hamstrung means that he cut the tendon behind the leg of the horses, making them useless as war or chariot horses. They were then only useful as work and farm horses. Concerning the number here different from 1 Chr. 18:4, see note on 1 Chr. 22:3.

8:6 David keeps occupational troops in **garrisons** throughout this entire area.

8:11 Dedicated these to the LORD means that David places them in the sanctuary treasury to be used in the building of the temple. From this gold and brass Solomon made the bronze Sea and the temple vessels (1 Chr. 18:8).

8:13 The Valley of Salt was an area south of the Dead Sea.

be established as king. *Melech,* "king," is what the sovereign is; *malach* is what he does. Two familiar Bible names derived from this root are "Abimelech" ("My Father Is King") and "Melchizedek" ("Righteous King.") A companion noun is *malkut,* "kingdom." The phrases "kingdom of God" and "kingdom of heaven" were used extensively by the Lord Jesus throughout the Gospels. Is. 9:7 states that the Messiah's kingdom is eternal. David reigned over all Israel (2 Sam. 8:15); the Messiah shall reign forever over Israel and all nations (Luke 1:33).

16 [a]Joab the son of Zeruiah *was* over
the army; [b]Jehoshaphat the son of Ahilud *was* recorder;
17 [a]Zadok the son of Ahitub and
Ahimelech the son of Abiathar *were*
the *priests; [1]Seraiah *was* the [2]scribe;
18 [a]Benaiah the son of Jehoiada *was*
over both the [b]Cherethites and the
Pelethites; and David's sons were [1]chief
ministers.

David's Kindness to Mephibosheth

9 Now David said, "Is there still anyone who is left of the house of Saul,
that I may [a]show him [1]kindness for
Jonathan's sake?"
2 And *there was* a servant of the
house of Saul whose name *was* [a]Ziba.
So when they had called him to David,
the king said to him, "*Are* you Ziba?"
He said, "At your service!"
3 Then the king said, "*Is* there not still
someone of the house of Saul, to whom
I may show [a]the kindness of God?"
And Ziba said to the king, "There is
still a son of Jonathan *who is* [b]lame
in *his* feet."
4 So the king said to him, "Where *is*
he?" And Ziba said to the king, "Indeed he *is* in the house of [a]Machir the
son of Ammiel, in Lo Debar."
5 Then King David sent and brought
him out of the house of Machir the son
of Ammiel, from Lo Debar.
6 Now when [a]Mephibosheth[1] the son
of Jonathan, the son of Saul, had come
to David, he fell on his face and prostrated himself. Then David said, "Mephibosheth?" And he answered, "Here
is your servant!"
7 So David said to him, "Do not fear,
for I will surely show you kindness for
Jonathan your father's sake, and will
restore to you all the land of Saul your
grandfather; and you shall eat bread
at my table *continually."
8 Then he bowed himself, and said,
"What *is* your servant, that you should
look upon such [a]a dead dog as I?"
9 And the king called to Ziba, Saul's
servant, and said to him, [a]"I have given
to your master's son all that belonged
to Saul and to all his house.
10 "You therefore, and your sons and
your servants, shall work the land for
him, and you shall bring in *the harvest,*
that your master's son may have food
to eat. But Mephibosheth your master's
son [a]shall eat bread at my table always." Now Ziba had [b]fifteen sons and
twenty servants.
11 Then Ziba said to the king, "According to all that my lord the king has
commanded his servant, so will your
servant do." "As for Mephibosheth,"
said the king, "he shall eat at [1]my table
like one of the king's sons."
12 Mephibosheth had a young son
[a]whose name *was* Micha. And all who
dwelt in the house of Ziba *were* servants of Mephibosheth.

16 [a]2 Sam. 19:13; 20:23; 1 Chr. 11:6 [b]1 Kin. 4:3
17 [a]1 Chr. 6:4–8; 24:3 [1]*Shavsha,* 1 Chr. 18:16 [2]*secretary* *See WW at Lev. 5:6.
18 [a]1 Kin. 1:8; 1 Chr. 18:17 [b]1 Sam. 30:14; 1 Kin. 1:38 [1]Lit. *priests*

CHAPTER 9

1 [a]1 Sam. 18:3; 20:14–16; 2 Sam. 21:7; [Prov. 27:10] [1]*covenant faithfulness*
2 [a]2 Sam. 16:1–4; 19:17, 29
3 [a]1 Sam. 20:14 [b]2 Sam. 4:4
4 [a]2 Sam. 17:27–29
6 [a]2 Sam. 16:4; 19:24–30 [1]Or *Merib-Baal*
7 *See WW at Ex. 28:30.
8 [a]2 Sam. 16:9
9 [a]2 Sam. 16:4; 19:29
10 [a]2 Sam. 9:7, 11, 13; 19:28 [b]2 Sam. 19:17
11 [1]LXX *David's table*
12 [a]1 Chr. 8:34

8:17 Zadok was from the family of Aaron through Eleazar and served at the tabernacle in Gibeon. His is the continuing line of priests through the rest of the OT.
8:18 Benaiah: See 2 Sam. 23:20. **The Cherethites and the Pelethites** were the king's bodyguard, an elite corps of fighting men, executioners, and couriers. The **chief ministers** were personal advisors.
9:1 See section 1 of Truth-In-Action at the end of 2 Sam.
9:1 For Jonathan's sake: This goes back to the covenant of friendship and kindness that David and Jonathan had made to one another in 1 Sam. 20:13–17.
9:2 Ziba probably farmed the lands of Saul in Gibeah with his 15 sons and 20 servants.
9:3 David sees himself as acting in behalf of God. In his graciousness to Mephibosheth he illustrates the **kindness of God.** When Mephibosheth was 5 years old, he and his nurse were fleeing for their lives after the death of Saul and Jonathan at the battle at Jezreel. Mephibosheth had fallen and become **lame in *his* feet.**
9:4 Machir is mentioned in 17:27. He was a wealthy man who took the young orphan into his house after Jonathan's death. His residence was **Lo Debar,** in the wilderness east of the Jordan River in Ammon, and near present-day Amman in Jordan.
9:7 The land that David restores is likely that which Ziba was farming near Gibeah. **Eat bread at my table:** Mephibosheth is put on the royal pension for the rest of his life, lives as one of the king's sons, and even eats at the king's table.
9:8 Dead dog represented a person of no value. Mephibosheth likely had never heard of David's friendship with Jonathan in that he was only 5 years old when his father died.
9:10 David gives to Mephibosheth as his inheritance the land Ziba was farming and which Ziba, his servants, and sons would now **work for him.**
9:11 Mephibosheth would be **like one of the king's sons.** In all of this David was a type of our Lord who redeems, restores, and returns us to our Father's table in peace.

13 So Mephibosheth dwelt in Jerusalem, [a]for he ate continually at the
king's table. And he [b]was lame in both
his feet.

The Ammonites and Syrians Defeated

10 It happened after this that the
[a]king of the people of Ammon
died, and Hanun his son reigned in his
place.
2 Then David said, "I will show
[a]kindness to Hanun the son of [b]Na-
hash, as his father showed kindness to
me." So David sent by the hand of his
servants to comfort him concerning his
father. And David's servants came into
the land of the people of Ammon.
3 And the princes of the people of
Ammon said to Hanun their lord, "Do
you think that David really honors
your father because he has sent comforters to you? Has David not *rather*
sent his servants to you to search the
city, to spy it out, and to overthrow it?"
4 Therefore Hanun took David's servants, shaved off half of their beards,
cut off their garments in the middle,
[a]at their buttocks, and sent them away.
5 When they told David, he sent to
meet them, because the men were
greatly [1]ashamed. And the king said,
"Wait at Jericho until your beards have
grown, and *then* return."
6 When the people of Ammon saw
that they [a]had made themselves repulsive to David, the people of Ammon
sent and hired [b]the Syrians of [c]Beth
Rehob and the Syrians of Zoba, twenty
thousand foot soldiers; and from the
king of [d]Maacah one thousand men,
and from [e]Ish-Tob twelve thousand
men.
7 Now when David heard of *it*, he
sent Joab and all the army of [a]the
mighty men.
8 Then the people of Ammon came
out and put themselves in battle array
at the entrance of the gate. And
[a]the Syrians of Zoba, Beth Rehob, Ish-
Tob, and Maacah *were* by themselves
in the field.
9 When Joab saw that the battle line
was against him before and behind, he
chose some of Israel's best and put
them in battle array against the Syrians.
10 And the rest of the people he put
under the command of [a]Abishai his
brother, that he might set *them* in battle array against the people of Ammon.
11 Then he said, "If the Syrians are too
strong for me, then you shall help me;
but if the people of Ammon are too
strong for you, then I will come and
help you.
12 [a]"Be of good courage, and let us
[b]be strong for our people and for the
cities of our God. And may [c]the LORD
do *what is* good in His sight."
13 So Joab and the people who *were*
with him drew near for the battle
against the Syrians, and they fled before him.
14 When the people of Ammon saw
that the Syrians were fleeing, they also
fled before Abishai, and entered the
city. So Joab returned from the people
of Ammon and went to [a]Jerusalem.
15 When the Syrians saw that they had
been defeated by Israel, they gathered
together.
16 Then [1]Hadadezer sent and brought
out the Syrians who *were* beyond
[2]the River, and they came to Helam.
And [3]Shobach the commander of
Hadadezer's army *went* before them.
17 When it was told David, he gathered all Israel, crossed over the Jordan,
and came to Helam. And the Syrians
set themselves in battle array against
David and fought with him.
18 Then the Syrians fled before Israel;
and David killed seven hundred charioteers and forty thousand [a]horsemen
of the Syrians, and struck Shobach the
commander of their army, who died
there.

13 [a]2 Sam. 9:7, 10, 11; 1 Kin. 2:7; 2 Kin. 25:29 [b]2 Sam. 9:3

CHAPTER 10

1 [a]2 Sam. 11:1; 1 Chr. 19:1
2 [a]2 Sam. 9:1; 1 Kin. 2:7 [b]1 Sam. 11:1
4 [a]Is. 20:4; 47:2
5 [1]*humiliated*
6 [a]Gen. 34:30; Ex. 5:21 [b]2 Sam. 8:3, 5 [c]Judg. 18:28 [d]Deut. 3:14; Josh. 13:11, 13 [e]Judg. 11:3, 5
7 [a]2 Sam. 23:8
8 [a]2 Sam. 10:6
10 [a]1 Sam. 26:6; 2 Sam. 3:30
12 [a]Deut. 31:6; Josh. 1:6, 7, 9; Neh. 4:14 [b]1 Sam. 4:9; 1 Cor. 16:13 [c]1 Sam. 3:18
14 [a]2 Sam. 11:1
16 [1]Heb. *Hadarezer* [2]The Euphrates [3]*Shophach,* 1 Chr. 19:16
18 [a]1 Chr. 19:18

10:1—22:51 The events of chs. 10—22 took place between the twentieth and thirtieth years of David's 40-year reign.
10:1 Ammon: The modern nation of Jordan. The Ammonites were descendants of Lot. Though related, great hostility had grown between them and Israel.
10:2 Nahash was the same king Saul had defeated at Jabesh Gilead (1 Sam. 11:1). What **kindness** he showed to David is not clear. Probably he had given him some assistance during David's flight from Saul. **Hanun:** Mephibosheth accepted David's offer of kindness and was blessed. Hanun rejects it and is destroyed. **David's servants** were ambassadors sent by David as his personal emissaries.
10:3 The **princes of the people** were the chiefs of the Ammonites. Likely, they were still outraged at David's harsh treatment of their allies, the Moabites (8:2).
10:4 Shaved off half of their beards: To the Hebrews and other nations, the beard was considered a man's greatest ornament or sign of honor. To shave it was the greatest possible insult. **Cut off their garments in the middle:** These were the long robelike garments, which covered the body to the ankles. The Hebrew wore no pants under them, so Hanun cut them at the most immodest and embarrassing length.
10:6 Beth Rehob was the capital of the Aramean kingdom. **Zoba:** See note on 8:3. Though defeated by David, this is a further rebellious alliance with Hanun.
10:7 Mighty men were the elite of David's fighting forces. For their names and exploits, see ch. 23.
10:16 Beyond the River: Hadadezer had occupational forces in Mesopotamia east of the Euphrates River.

19 And when all the kings *who were* servants to [1]Hadadezer saw that they were defeated by Israel, they made peace with Israel and [a]served them. So the Syrians were afraid to help the people of Ammon anymore.

David, Bathsheba, and Uriah

1 **11** It happened in the spring of the year, at the [a]time when kings go out *to battle,* that [b]David sent Joab and his servants with him, and all Israel; and they destroyed the people of Ammon and besieged [c]Rabbah. But David remained at Jerusalem.

6 2 Then it happened one evening that David arose from his bed [a]and walked on the roof of the king's house. And from the roof he [b]saw a woman bathing, and the woman *was* very beautiful to behold.

3 3 So David sent and inquired about the woman. And *someone* said, "*Is* this not [1]Bathsheba, the daughter of [2]Eliam, the wife [a]of Uriah the [b]Hittite?"

4 Then David sent messengers, and took her; and she came to him, and [a]he lay with her, for she was [b]cleansed from her impurity; and she returned to her house.

5 And the woman conceived; so she sent and told David, and said, "I *am* with child."

6 Then David sent to Joab, *saying,* "Send me Uriah the Hittite." And Joab sent Uriah to David.

7 When Uriah had come to him, David asked how Joab was doing, and how the people were doing, and how the war prospered.

8 And David said to Uriah, "Go down to your house and [a]wash your feet." So Uriah departed from the king's house, and a gift *of food* from the king followed him.

9 But Uriah slept at the [a]door of the king's house with all the servants of his lord, and did not go down to his house.

10 So when they told David, saying, "Uriah did not go down to his house," David said to Uriah, "Did you not come from a journey? Why did you not go down to your house?"

11 And Uriah said to David, [a]"The ark and Israel and Judah are dwelling in tents, and [b]my lord Joab and the servants of my lord are encamped in the open fields. Shall I then go to my house to eat and drink, and to lie with my wife? *As* you live, and *as* your soul lives, I will not do this thing."

12 Then David said to Uriah, "Wait here today also, and tomorrow I will let you depart." So Uriah remained in Jerusalem that day and the next.

13 Now when David called him, he ate and drank before him; and he made him [a]drunk. And at evening he went out to lie on his bed [b]with the servants of his lord, but he did not go down to his house.

14 In the morning it happened that David [a]wrote a letter to Joab and sent *it* by the hand of Uriah.

15 And he wrote in the letter, saying, "Set Uriah in the forefront of the [1]hottest battle, and retreat from him, that he may [a]be struck down and die."

16 So it was, while Joab besieged the city, that he assigned Uriah to a place where he knew there *were* valiant men.

17 Then the men of the city came out and fought with Joab. And *some* of the people of the servants of David fell; and Uriah the Hittite died also.

19 [a]2 Sam. 8:6 [1]Heb. *Hadarezer*

CHAPTER 11

1 [a]1 Kin. 20:22–26 [b]1 Chr. 20:1 [c]2 Sam. 12:26; Jer. 49:2, 3; Amos 1:14
2 [a]Deut. 22:8; 1 Sam. 9:25; Matt. 24:17; Acts 10:9 [b]Gen. 34:2; [Ex. 20:17]; Job 31:1; [Matt. 5:28]
3 [a]2 Sam. 23:39 [b]1 Sam. 26:6 [1]*Bathshua,* 1 Chr. 3:5 [2]*Ammiel,* 1 Chr. 3:5
4 [a][Lev. 20:10; Deut. 22:22]; Ps. 51:title; [James 1:14, 15] [b]Lev. 15:19, 28
8 [a]Gen. 18:4; 19:2
9 [a]1 Kin. 14:27, 28
11 [a]2 Sam. 7:2, 6 [b]2 Sam. 20:6–22
13 [a]Gen. 19:33, 35 [b]2 Sam. 11:9
14 [a]1 Kin. 21:8, 9
15 [a]2 Sam. 12:9 [1]*fiercest*

11:1–26 The watershed of David's reign. Here his kingdom begins a decline, as domestic tragedy plagues him and his final sin of numbering the nation brings his reign to an end.

11:1 See section 1 of Truth-In-Action at the end of 2 Sam.

11:1 Likely Joab returned to Jerusalem (10:14) because it was the rainy time of year. After the final rains, the battle and the siege of the Ammonites at Rabbah is renewed. There is no reason given for David's decision to stay in Jerusalem, though his place was with the armies. Had he been where he belonged, this tragedy with Bathsheba and Uriah would not have happened.

11:2–4 See section 6 of Truth-In-Action at the end of 2 Sam.

11:2 This event illustrates the sequence described in James 1:13–15: Desire, enticement, sin, death.

11:3–17 See section 3 of Truth-In-Action at the end of 2 Sam.

11:3 The powerful Hittite Empire ended about 1200 B.C. **Uriah the Hittite** was from one of the small groups of ethnic Hittites still remaining in Syria and Israel. He is also listed as one of David's 37 mighty men (23:39), which makes David's infamy even more appalling.

11:4 Cleansed from her impurity: According to Lev. 15:18, this involved ceremonial bathing and a period of "uncleanness" until evening.

11:6 Here begins the series of ploys, lies, and intrigue, especially shocking because of the great integrity shown by David in his dealings with Saul. This illustrates how quickly the entertaining of sin can pollute the heart of even the most noble of God's people.

11:8 The Hebrew custom was to wash their feet, take refreshment, and rest after returning from a long journey.

11:9 Door of the king's house: Another building adjoining the palace where the court servants lived.

11:11 The contrast is clearly drawn between David, who should be in the field with his troops, and Uriah, so committed to David and God that he will not even sleep one evening in the comfort of his own home with his wife.

11:14 David's callous heart is even further exposed by his sending the death sentence in the hands of Uriah himself.

18 Then Joab sent and told David all the things concerning the war,

19 and charged the messenger, saying, "When you have finished telling the matters of the war to the king,

20 "if it happens that the king's wrath rises, and he says to you: 'Why did you approach so near to the city when you fought? Did you not know that they would shoot from the wall?

21 'Who struck [a]Abimelech the son of [1]Jerubbesheth? Was it not a woman who cast a piece of a millstone on him from the wall, so that he died in Thebez? Why did you go near the wall?'—then you shall say, 'Your servant Uriah the Hittite is dead also.' "

22 So the messenger went, and came and told David all that Joab had sent by him.

23 And the messenger said to David, "Surely the men prevailed against us and came out to us in the field; then we drove them back as far as the entrance of the gate.

24 "The archers shot from the wall at your servants; and *some* of the king's servants are dead, and your servant Uriah the Hittite is dead also."

25 Then David said to the messenger, "Thus you shall say to Joab: 'Do not let this thing [1]displease you, for the sword devours one as well as another. Strengthen your attack against the city, and overthrow it.' So encourage him."

26 When the wife of Uriah heard that Uriah her *husband was dead, she mourned for her husband.

27 And when her mourning was over, David sent and brought her to his house, and she [a]became his wife and bore him a son. But the thing that David had done [b]displeased[1] the LORD.

Nathan's Parable and David's Confession

12 Then the LORD sent Nathan to David. And [a]he came to him, and [b]said to him: "There were two men in one city, one rich and the other poor.

2 "The rich *man* had exceedingly many flocks and herds.

3 "But the poor *man* had nothing, except one little ewe lamb which he had bought and nourished; and it grew up together with him and with his children. It ate of his own food and drank from his own cup and lay in his bosom; and it was like a daughter to him.

4 "And a traveler came to the rich man, who refused to take from his own flock and from his own herd to prepare one for the wayfaring man who had come to him; but he took the poor man's lamb and prepared it for the man who had come to him."

5 So David's anger was greatly 3
aroused against the man, and he said to Nathan, "*As* the LORD lives, the man who has done this [1]shall surely die!

6 "And he shall restore [a]fourfold for the lamb, because he did this thing and because he had no pity."

7 Then Nathan said to David, "You *are* the man! Thus says the LORD God of Israel: 'I [a]anointed you king over Israel, and I delivered you from the hand of Saul.

8 'I gave you your master's house and your master's wives into your keeping, and gave you the house of Israel and Judah. And if *that had been* too little, I also would have given you much more!

9 [a]'Why have you [b]despised the commandment of the LORD, to do evil in His sight? [c]You have killed Uriah the Hittite with the sword; you have taken his wife *to be* your wife, and have killed him with the sword of the people of Ammon.

10 'Now therefore, [a]the sword shall never depart from your house, because you have despised Me, and have taken the wife of Uriah the Hittite to be your wife.'

11 "Thus says the LORD: 'Behold, I will raise up adversity against you from your own house; and I will [a]take your wives before your eyes and give *them* to your neighbor, and he shall lie with your wives in the sight of this sun.

12 'For you did *it* secretly, [a]but I will do this thing before all Israel, before the sun.' "

13 [a]So David said to Nathan, [b]"I have

21 [a]Judg. 9:50–54 [1]Gideon; *Jerubbaal,* Judg. 6:32ff.
25 [1]Lit. *be evil in your sight*
26 *See WW at Hos. 2:8.
27 [a]2 Sam. 12:9 [b]1 Chr. 21:7; [Heb. 13:4] [1]Lit. *was evil in the eyes of*

CHAPTER 12
1 [a]Ps. 51:title [b]1 Kin. 20:35–41
5 [1]*deserves to die,* lit. *is a son of death*
6 [a][Ex. 22:1]; Luke 19:8
7 [a]1 Sam. 16:13; 2 Sam. 5:3
9 [a]1 Sam. 15:19 [b]Num. 15:31 [c]2 Sam. 11:14–17, 27
10 [a]2 Sam. 13:28; 18:14; 1 Kin. 2:25; [Amos 7:9]
11 [a]Deut. 28:30; 2 Sam. 16:21, 22
12 [a]2 Sam. 16:22
13 [a]1 Sam. 15:24 [b]2 Sam. 24:10; Job 7:20; Ps. 51; Luke 18:13

11:27 The usual period of mourning was seven days. She was brought as quickly as possible to the palace **and bore him a son.** David's plan had worked, but God was **displeased.** This is the first time it is recorded that David displeased the Lord.

12:1 Nathan's confrontation with David occurs about one year after the incident with Bathsheba and the murder of Uriah. Ps. 51 was written by David during this time.

12:3 The keeping of a **lamb** as a house pet was a common thing in Israel. To forcibly steal such a pet was considered a heinous and unthinkable crime.

12:5–14 See section 3 of Truth-In-Action at the end of 2 Sam.

12:6 To **restore fourfold** was according to the demands of the Law (Ex. 22:1). That David could be such a moralist against the rich man in the parable, while at the same time hiding his own sin, illustrates the deceitfulness of sin.

12:13 Death was required by the Law for both murder and

sinned against the LORD." And Nathan
said to David, "The LORD also has
[c]put away your sin; you shall not
die.
5 14 "However, because by this deed
you have given great occasion to the
enemies of the LORD [a]to blaspheme, the
child also *who is* born to you shall
surely die."
15 Then Nathan departed to his house.

The Death of David's Son

And the [a]LORD struck the child that
Uriah's wife bore to David, and it became ill.
16 David therefore pleaded with God
for the child, and David fasted and
went in and [a]lay all night on the
ground.
17 So the elders of his house arose *and*
went to him, to raise him up from the
ground. But he would not, nor did he
eat food with them.
18 Then on the seventh day it came to
pass that the child died. And the servants of David were afraid to tell him
that the child was dead. For they said,
"Indeed, while the child was alive, we
spoke to him, and he would not heed
our voice. How can we tell him that
the child is dead? He may do some
harm!"
19 When David saw that his servants
were whispering, David perceived that
the child was dead. Therefore David
said to his servants, "Is the child
dead?" And they said, "He is dead."
20 So David arose from the ground,
washed and [a]anointed himself, and
changed his clothes; and he went into
the house of the LORD and [b]worshiped.
Then he went to his own house; and
when he requested, they set food before him, and he ate.
21 Then his servants said to him,
"What *is* this that you have done? You
fasted and wept for the child *while he*
was alive, but when the child died, you
arose and ate food."
22 And he said, "While the child was
alive, I fasted and wept; [a]for I said,
'Who can tell *whether* [1]the LORD will
*be gracious to me, that the child may
live?'
23 "But now he is dead; why should I
fast? Can I bring him back again? I
shall go [a]to him, but [b]he shall not return to me."

Solomon Is Born

24 Then David *comforted Bathsheba
his wife, and went in to her and lay
with her. So [a]she bore a *son, and
[b]he[1] called his name Solomon. Now
the LORD loved him,
25 and He sent *word* by the hand of
Nathan the prophet: So [1]he called his
name [2]Jedidiah, because of the LORD.

Rabbah Is Captured

26 Now [a]Joab fought against [b]Rabbah
of the people of Ammon, and took the
royal city.
27 And Joab sent messengers to David,
and said, "I have fought against Rabbah, and I have taken the city's water
supply.
28 "Now therefore, gather the rest of
the people together and encamp
against the city and take it, lest I take
the city and it be called after my
name."
29 So David gathered all the people together and went to Rabbah, fought
against it, and took it.
30 [a]Then he took their king's crown
from his head. Its weight *was* a talent
of gold, with precious stones. And it
was *set* on David's head. Also he
brought out the [1]spoil of the city in
great abundance.
31 And he brought out the people who
were in it, and put *them to work* with

13 [c]2 Sam. 24:10; Job 7:21; [Ps. 32:1–5; Prov. 28:13; Mic. 7:18]; Zech. 3:4
14 [a]Is. 52:5; [Ezek. 36:20, 23]; Rom. 2:24
15 [a]1 Sam. 25:38
16 [a]2 Sam. 13:31
20 [a]Ruth 3:3; Matt. 6:17 [b]Job 1:20
22 [a]Is. 38:1–5; Joel 2:14; Jon. 3:9 [1]Heb. mss., Syr. *God* *See WW at Mal. 1:9.
23 [a]Gen. 37:35 [b]Job 7:8–10
24 [a]Matt. 1:6 [b]1 Chr. 22:9 [1]So with Kt., LXX, Vg.; Qr., a few Heb. mss., Syr., Tg. *she* *See WW at Ps. 23:4. • See WW at Gen. 29:32.
25 [1]Qr., some Heb. mss., Syr., Tg. *she* [2]Lit. *Beloved of the LORD*
26 [a]1 Chr. 20:1 [b]Deut. 3:11; 2 Sam. 11:1
30 [a]1 Chr. 20:2 [1]*plunder*

---

adultery, even for a king (Ex. 21:12; Lev. 20:10). However, because of David's deep repentance without making excuse and, more significantly, the promise of 5:12, God's grace is given, though his family will experience the tragic effects of his sin.

12:14 See section 5 of Truth-In-Action at the end of 2 Sam.

12:14 To blaspheme is to ridicule and devalue belief in God. It is sad indeed that one as zealous for God as David would by his own sin give occasion for God to be ridiculed.

12:16 David **went in** to his own house or chambers, not the sanctuary.

12:17 The elders of his house were the oldest, most trusted, and influential of his personal aides.

12:18 Do some harm: That is, harm himself in the throes of his grief.

12:20 When he **washed and anointed himself** David took away all the signs of grief. He goes to the **house of the LORD,** or the holy tent, which was on Mt. Zion.

12:23 Here is a wonderful promise for all who have lost young children to death: **I shall go to him.**

12:24 Solomon means "Peace."

12:25 Through Nathan God sends the name **Jedidiah,** which means "Loved By the Lord," as a testimony to the continuing grace of God.

12:26 Rabbah was the capital of Ammon, near the present city of Amman in Jordan. David now goes to battle as he should. Had he done so earlier, the terrible sin and its consequences might have been averted. The treachery and lust in David's heart had been dealt with, and his prayer, "Create in me a clean heart, O God, and renew a steadfast spirit within me," was answered (Ps. 51).

12:30 A talent of gold was about 75 pounds.

saws and iron picks and iron axes, and
made them cross over to the brick
works. So he did to all the cities of the
people of Ammon. Then David and all
the people returned to Jerusalem.

Amnon and Tamar

13 After this [a]Absalom the son of
David had a lovely sister, whose
name *was* [b]Tamar; and [c]Amnon the
son of David loved her.
2 Amnon was so distressed over his
sister Tamar that he became sick; for
she *was* a *virgin. And it was improper
for Amnon to do anything to her.
3 But Amnon had a *friend whose
name *was* Jonadab [a]the son of Shimeah, David's brother. Now Jonadab *was*
a very crafty man.
4 And he said to him, "Why *are* you,
the king's son, becoming thinner day
after day? Will you not tell me?" Amnon said to him, "I love Tamar, my
brother Absalom's sister."
5 So Jonadab said to him, "Lie down
on your bed and pretend to be ill. And
when your father comes to see you, say
to him, 'Please let my sister Tamar
come and give me food, and prepare
the food in my sight, that I may see *it*
and eat it from her hand.' "
6 Then Amnon lay down and pretended to be ill; and when the king
came to see him, Amnon said to the
king, "Please let Tamar my sister come
and [a]make a couple of cakes for me
in my sight, that I may eat from her
hand."
7 And David sent home to Tamar, saying, "Now go to your brother Amnon's
house, and prepare food for him."
8 So Tamar went to her brother Amnon's house; and he was lying down.
Then she took flour and kneaded *it*,
made cakes in his sight, and baked the
cakes.
9 And she took the pan and placed
them out before him, but he refused
to eat. Then Amnon said, [a]"Have everyone go out from me." And they all
went out from him.
10 Then Amnon said to Tamar, "Bring
the food into the bedroom, that I may
eat from your hand." And Tamar took
the cakes which she had made, and
brought *them* to Amnon her brother
in the bedroom.
11 Now when she had brought *them*
to him to eat, [a]he took hold of her and
said to her, "Come, lie with me, my sister."
12 But she answered him, "No, my
brother, do not [1]force me, for [a]no such
thing should be done in Israel. Do not
do this [b]disgraceful thing!
13 "And I, where could I take my
shame? And as for you, you would be
like one of the fools in Israel. Now
therefore, please speak to the king;
[a]for he will not withhold me from you."
14 However, he would not heed her
voice; and being stronger than she, he
[a]forced her and lay with her.
15 Then Amnon hated her [1]exceed-
ingly, so that the hatred with which
he hated her *was* greater than the
love with which he had loved her.
And Amnon said to her, "Arise, be
gone!"
16 So she said to him, "No, indeed!
This evil of sending me away *is* worse
than the other that you did to me." But
he would not listen to her.
17 Then he called his servant who attended him, and said, "Here! Put this
woman out, away from me, and bolt
the door behind her."
18 Now she had on [a]a robe of many
colors, for the king's virgin daughters
wore such apparel. And his servant put
her out and bolted the door behind her.
19 Then Tamar put [a]ashes on her head,
and tore her robe of many colors that
was on her, and [b]laid her hand on her
head and went away crying bitterly.
20 And Absalom her brother said to
her, "Has Amnon your brother been
with you? But now hold your peace,
my sister. He *is* your brother; do not
take this thing to heart." So Tamar remained desolate in her brother Absalom's house.
21 But when King David heard of all
these things, he was very angry.
22 And Absalom spoke to his brother

CHAPTER 13
1 [a]2 Sam. 3:2, 3; 1 Chr. 3:2 [b]1 Chr. 3:9 [c]2 Sam. 3:2
2 *See WW at Ps. 45:14.
3 [a]1 Sam. 16:9 *See WW at Prov. 17:17.
6 [a]Gen. 18:6
9 [a]Gen. 45:1
11 [a]Gen. 39:12; [Deut. 27:22]; Ezek. 22:11
12 [a][Lev. 18:9–11; 20:17] [b]Gen. 34:7; Judg. 19:23; 20:6 [1]Lit. *humble me*
13 [a]Gen. 20:12
14 [a]Lev. 18:9; [Deut. 22:25; 27:22]; 2 Sam. 12:11
15 [1]*with a very great hatred*
18 [a]Gen. 37:3; Judg. 5:30; Ps. 45:13, 14
19 [a]Josh. 7:6; 2 Sam. 1:2; Job 2:12; 42:6 [b]Jer. 2:37

13:1 This occurs two years later. David is 53 years of age, Amnon is 22, Absalom 20, Tamar 15, and Solomon 2. Amnon, the eldest, was considered by all to be the crown prince.
13:3 Jonadab was not only Amnon's friend, but his cousin.
13:15, 16 Sending me away: Not only had he stolen her virginity, a terrible curse in Israel, but he also rejected her as his wife, contrary to the Law (Deut. 22:29).
13:17, 18 Amnon's action leaves the impression that Tamar had tried to seduce him. Though she wears the coat unique to the king's daughters, the servant treats her as a commoner.
13:21 David is **very angry,** but he does not carry out the commands of the Law against Amnon as he should have. Incest was punishable by death (Lev. 20:17). The Septuagint Greek version adds, "He did not trouble the spirit of Amnon his son, because he loved him, for he was his firstborn," indicating the likely reason for his lack of action.
13:22 Neither good nor bad: Absalom does not speak to Amnon at all.

Amnon [a]neither good nor bad. For Absalom [b]hated Amnon, because he had
forced his sister Tamar.

Absalom Murders Amnon

23 And it came to pass, after two full
years, that Absalom [a]had sheepshearers in Baal Hazor, which *is* near
Ephraim; so Absalom invited all the
king's sons.
24 Then Absalom came to the king and
said, "Kindly note, your servant has
sheepshearers; please, let the king
and his servants go with your servant."
25 But the king said to Absalom, "No,
my son, let us not all go now, lest we
be a burden to you." Then he urged
him, but he would not go; and he
blessed him.
26 Then Absalom said, "If not, please
let my brother Amnon go with us."
And the king said to him, "Why should
he go with you?"
27 But Absalom urged him; so he let
Amnon and all the king's sons go with
him.
28 Now Absalom had commanded his
servants, saying, "Watch now, when
Amnon's [a]heart is merry with wine,
and when I say to you, 'Strike Amnon!'
then kill him. Do not be afraid. Have I
not commanded you? Be courageous
and [1]valiant."
29 So the servants of Absalom [a]did to
Amnon as Absalom had commanded.
Then all the king's sons arose, and
each one got on [b]his mule and fled.
30 And it came to pass, while they
were on the way, that news came to
David, saying, "Absalom has killed all
the king's sons, and not one of them
is left!"
31 So the king arose and [a]tore his garments and [b]lay on the ground, and all
his servants stood by with their clothes
torn.
32 Then [a]Jonadab the son of Shimeah,
David's brother, answered and said,
"Let not my lord suppose they have
killed all the young men, the king's
sons, for only Amnon is dead. For by
the command of Absalom this has been
determined from the day that he forced
his sister Tamar.
33 "Now therefore, [a]let not my lord the
king take the thing to his heart, to
think that all the king's sons are dead.
For only Amnon is dead."

Absalom Flees to Geshur

34 [a]Then Absalom fled. And the young
man *who was keeping watch lifted his
eyes and looked, and there, many people were coming from the road on the
hillside behind [1]him.
35 And Jonadab said to the king,
"Look, the king's sons are coming; as
your servant said, so it is."
36 So it was, as soon as he had finished
speaking, that the king's sons indeed
came, and they lifted up their voice and
wept. Also the king and all his servants
wept very bitterly.
37 But Absalom fled and went to
[a]Talmai the son of Ammihud, king of
Geshur. And *David* mourned for his
son every day.
38 So Absalom fled and went to
[a]Geshur, and was there three years.
39 And [1]King David [2]longed to go to
Absalom. For he had been [a]comforted
concerning Amnon, because he was
dead.

Absalom Returns to Jerusalem

14 So Joab the son of Zeruiah perceived that the king's heart *was*
concerned [a]about Absalom.
2 And Joab sent to [a]Tekoa and
brought from there a wise woman, and
said to her, "Please pretend to be a
mourner, [b]and put on mourning apparel; do not anoint yourself with oil,
but act like a woman who has been
mourning a long time for the dead.
3 "Go to the king and speak to him
in this manner." So Joab [a]put the
words in her mouth.
4 And when the woman of Tekoa
[1]spoke to the king, she [a]fell on her face
to the ground and prostrated herself,
and said, [b]"Help, O king!"
5 Then the king said to her, "What
troubles you?" And she answered,
[a]"Indeed I *am* a widow, my husband
is dead.
6 "Now your maidservant had two
sons; and the two fought with each
other in the field, and *there was* no one
to part them, but the one struck the
other and killed him.

22 [a]Gen. 24:50; 31:24 [b][Lev. 19:17, 18; 1 John 2:9, 11; 3:10, 12, 15]
23 [a]Gen. 38:12, 13; 1 Sam. 25:4
28 [a]Judg. 19:6, 9, 22; Ruth 3:7; 1 Sam. 25:36; Esth. 1:10 [1]Lit. *sons of valor*
29 [a]2 Sam. 12:10 [b]2 Sam. 18:9; 1 Kin. 1:33, 38
31 [a]2 Sam. 1:11 [b]2 Sam. 12:16
32 [a]2 Sam. 13:3–5
33 [a]2 Sam. 19:19
34 [a]2 Sam. 13:37, 38 [1]LXX adds *And the watchman went and told the king, and said, "I see men from the way of Horonaim, from the regions of the mountains."* *See WW at Hos. 9:8.
37 [a]2 Sam. 3:3; 1 Chr. 3:2
38 [a]2 Sam. 14:23, 32; 15:8
39 [a]Gen. 38:12; 2 Sam. 12:19, 23 [1]So with MT, Syr., Vg.; LXX *the spirit of the king;* Tg. *the soul of King David* [2]So with MT, Tg.; LXX, Vg. *ceased to pursue after*

CHAPTER 14

1 [a]2 Sam. 13:39
2 [a]2 Sam. 23:26; 2 Chr. 11:6; Amos 1:1 [b]Ruth 3:3
3 [a]Ex. 4:15; 2 Sam. 14:19
4 [a]1 Sam. 20:41; 25:23; 2 Sam. 1:2 [b]2 Kin. 6:26, 28 [1]Many Heb. mss., LXX, Syr., Vg. *came*
5 [a][Zech. 7:10]

13:23 Sheepshearers held a festival to celebrate the time of sheepshearing. **Baal Hazor** was about 6 miles south of Shiloh, where Absalom evidently had property and flocks.
13:32 Jonadab is the same man who had given Amnon the plan to seduce Tamar.
13:37 Talmai was Absalom's maternal grandfather.
14:2 Tekoa was about 7 miles south of Bethlehem. It later became the home of the prophet Amos.

7 "And now the whole family has risen up against your maidservant, and they said, 'Deliver him who struck his brother, that we may execute him [a]for the life of his brother whom he killed; and we will destroy the heir also.' So they would extinguish my ember that is left, and leave to my husband *neither* name nor remnant on the earth."

8 Then the king said to the woman, "Go to your house, and I will give orders concerning you."

9 And the woman of Tekoa said to the king, "My lord, O king, *let* [a]the [1]iniquity *be* on me and on my father's house, [b]and the king and his throne *be* guiltless."

10 So the king said, "Whoever says *anything* to you, bring him to me, and he shall not touch you anymore."

11 Then she said, "Please let the king remember the LORD your God, and do not permit [a]the avenger of blood to destroy anymore, lest they destroy my son." And he said, [b]"*As* the LORD lives, not one hair of your son shall fall to the ground."

12 Therefore the woman said, "Please, let your maidservant speak *another* word to my lord the king." And he said, "Say on."

13 So the woman said: "Why then have you schemed such a thing against [a]the people of God? For the king speaks this thing as one who is guilty, *in that* the king does not bring [b]his banished one home again.

[1] 14 "For we [a]will surely die and *become* like water spilled on the ground, which cannot be gathered up again. Yet God does not [b]take away a life; but He [c]devises means, so that His banished ones are not [1]expelled from Him.

15 "Now therefore, I have come to speak of this thing to my lord the king because the people have made me afraid. And your maidservant said, 'I will now speak to the king; it may be that the king will perform the request of his maidservant.

16 'For the king will hear and deliver his maidservant from the hand of the man *who would* destroy me and my son together from the [a]inheritance of God.'

17 "Your maidservant said, 'The word of my lord the king will now be comforting; for [a]as the angel of God, so *is* my lord the king in [b]discerning good and evil. And may the LORD your God be with you.' "

18 Then the king answered and said to the woman, "Please do not hide from me anything that I ask you." And the woman said, "Please, let my lord the king speak."

19 So the king said, "*Is* the hand of Joab with you in all this?" And the woman answered and said, "*As* *you live, my lord the king, no one can turn to the right hand or to the left from anything that my lord the king has spoken. For your servant Joab commanded me, and [a]he put all these words in the mouth of your maidservant.

20 "To bring about this change of affairs your servant Joab has done this thing; but my lord *is* wise, [a]according to the *wisdom of the angel of God, to know everything that *is* in the earth."

21 And the king said to Joab, "All right, I have granted this thing. Go therefore, bring back the young man Absalom."

22 Then Joab fell to the ground on his face and bowed himself, and [1]thanked the king. And Joab said, "Today your servant knows that I have found *favor in your sight, my lord, O king, in that the king has fulfilled the request of his servant."

23 So Joab arose [a]and went to Geshur, and brought Absalom to Jerusalem.

24 And the king said, "Let him return to his own house, but [a]do not let him see my face." So Absalom returned to his own house, but did not see the king's face.

David Forgives Absalom

25 Now in all Israel there was no one who was *praised as much as Absalom for his good looks. [a]From the sole of his foot to the crown of his head there was no blemish in him.

26 And when he cut the hair of his head—at the end of every year he cut *it* because it was heavy on him—when he cut it, he weighed the hair of his head at two hundred shekels according to the king's standard.

7 [a]Num. 35:19; Deut. 19:12, 13
9 [a]Gen. 27:13; 43:9; 1 Sam. 25:24; Matt. 27:25 [b]2 Sam. 3:28, 29; 1 Kin. 2:33 [1]*guilt*
11 [a]Num. 35:19, 21; [Deut. 19:4–10] [b]1 Sam. 14:45; 1 Kin. 1:52; Matt. 10:30; Acts 27:34
13 [a]Judg. 20:2 [b]2 Sam. 13:37, 38
14 [a]Job 30:23; 34:15; [Heb. 9:27] [b]Job 34:19; Matt. 22:16; Acts 10:34; Rom. 2:11 [c]Num. 35:15 [1]*cast out*
16 [a]Deut. 32:9; 1 Sam. 26:19; 2 Sam. 20:19
17 [a]1 Sam. 29:9; 2 Sam. 19:27 [b]1 Kin. 3:9
19 [a]2 Sam. 14:3 *See WW at Prov. 10:3.
20 [a]2 Sam. 14:17; 19:27 *See WW at Is. 11:2.
22 [1]Lit. *blessed* *See WW at Zech. 12:10.
23 [a]2 Sam. 13:37, 38
24 [a]Gen. 43:3; 2 Sam. 3:13
25 [a]Deut. 28:35; Job 2:7; Is. 1:6 *See WW at 1 Chr. 23:30.

14:7 Extinguish my ember: Cut off her only source of income, her husband. At issue is the law covering blood vengeance at the hands of relatives (see Num. 35:9–21).
14:14 See section 1 of Truth-In-Action at the end of 2 Sam.
14:25, 26 A heavy growth of hair was considered to be a sign of great manliness and power. **The king's standard:** Israel had a "sacred" standard and a "royal" standard of weights. The royal was about one-half of the sacred. Two hundred shekels would be about 3 pounds according to the royal standard.

27 [a]To Absalom were born three sons,
and one daughter whose name *was* Tamar. She was a woman of beautiful appearance.
28 And Absalom dwelt two full years
in Jerusalem, [a]but did not see the
king's face.
29 Therefore Absalom sent for Joab, to
send him to the king, but he would
not come to him. And when he sent
again the second time, he would not
come.
30 So he said to his servants, "See,
Joab's field is near mine, and he has
barley there; go and set it on fire." And
Absalom's servants set the field on fire.
31 Then Joab arose and came to Absalom's house, and said to him, "Why
have your servants set my field on
fire?"
32 And Absalom answered Joab,
"Look, I sent to you, saying, 'Come
here, so that I may send you to the
king, to say, "Why have I come from
Geshur? *It would be* better for me *to
be* there still." ' Now therefore, let me
see the king's face; but [a]if there is iniquity in me, let him execute me."
33 So Joab went to the king and told
him. And when he had called for Absalom, he came to the king and bowed
himself on his face to the ground before the king. Then the king [a]kissed
Absalom.

Absalom's Treason

4 **15** After this [a]it happened that Absalom [b]provided himself with
chariots and horses, and fifty men to
run before him.
2 Now Absalom would rise early and
stand beside the way to the gate. *So* it
was, whenever anyone who had a
[a]lawsuit[1] came to the king for a decision, that Absalom would call to him
and say, "What city *are* you from?"
And he would say, "Your servant *is*
from such and such a tribe of Israel."
3 Then Absalom would say to him,
"Look, your [1]case *is* good and right;
but *there is* no [2]deputy of the king to
hear you."
4 Moreover Absalom would say,
[a]"Oh, that I were made judge in the
land, and everyone who has any suit

27 [a]2 Sam. 13:1; 18:18
28 [a]2 Sam. 14:24
32 [a]1 Sam. 20:8; [Prov. 28:13]
33 [a]Gen. 33:4; 45:15; Luke 15:20

CHAPTER 15

1 [a]2 Sam. 12:11 [b]1 Kin. 1:5
2 [a]Deut. 19:17 [1]Lit. *contro-versy*
3 [1]Lit. *words* [2]Lit. *listener*
4 [a]Judg. 9:29
5 [a]2 Sam. 14:33; 20:9
6 [a][Rom. 16:18]
7 [a][Deut. 23:21] [b]2 Sam. 3:2, 3 [1]LXX mss., Syr., Josephus *four*
8 [a]1 Sam. 16:2 [b]Gen. 28:20, 21 [c]2 Sam. 13:38
10 [a]1 Kin. 1:34; 2 Kin. 9:13
11 [a]1 Sam. 16:3, 5 [b]Gen. 20:5
12 [a]2 Sam. 16:15; 1 Chr. 27:33; Ps. 41:9; 55:12–14 [b]Josh. 15:51 [c]Ps. 3:1
13 [a]Judg. 9:3; 2 Sam. 15:6 [1]Lit. *after*
14 [a]2 Sam. 12:11; Ps. 3:title
16 [a]Ps. 3:title

or cause would come to me; then I
would give him justice."
5 And *so* it was, whenever anyone
came near to bow down to him, that
he would put out his hand and take him
and [a]kiss him.
6 In this manner Absalom acted toward all Israel who came to the king
for judgment. [a]So Absalom stole the
hearts of the men of Israel.
7 Now it came to pass [a]after [1]forty
years that Absalom said to the king,
"Please, let me go to [b]Hebron and pay
the vow which I made to the LORD.
8 [a]"For your servant [b]took a vow
[c]while I dwelt at Geshur in Syria, saying, 'If the LORD indeed brings me back
to Jerusalem, then I will serve the
LORD.' "
9 And the king said to him, "Go in
peace." So he arose and went to Hebron.
10 Then Absalom sent spies throughout all the tribes of Israel, saying, "As
soon as you hear the sound of the trumpet, then you shall say, 'Absalom
[a]reigns in Hebron!' "
11 And with Absalom went two hundred men [a]invited from Jerusalem, and
they [b]went along innocently and did
not know anything.
12 Then Absalom sent for Ahithophel
the Gilonite, [a]David's counselor, from
his city—from [b]Giloh—while he offered sacrifices. And the conspiracy
grew strong, for the people with Absalom [c]continually increased in number.

David Escapes from Jerusalem

13 Now a messenger came to David,
saying, [a]"The hearts of the men of Israel are [1]with Absalom."
14 So David said to all his servants
who *were* with him at Jerusalem,
"Arise, and let us [a]flee, or we shall not
escape from Absalom. Make haste to
depart, lest he overtake us suddenly
and bring disaster upon us, and strike
the city with the edge of the sword."
15 And the king's servants said to the
king, "We *are* your servants, *ready to
do* whatever my lord the king commands."
16 Then [a]the king went out with all his

14:27 Tamar: The name of the daughter is given rather than the son's, showing his great love for his sister, Tamar.
15:1ff. See section 4 of Truth-In-Action at the end of 2 Sam.
15:1–30 The rebellion and death of Absalom are among the greatest pains and sorrows of David's life. Ps. 3 was written during his flight to the desert. Absalom was 24 years of age, David about 56.
15:1–9 The twofold deceit of Absalom is clear. He **stole the hearts** of Israel by professed devotion to them. He deceived David by professed devotion to God.
15:7 Forty years: The Greek and the Syriac versions of the OT have 4 years, rather than 40, though the 40 years may refer to the time of the anointing of David at Bethlehem.
15:12 Ahithophel may have been Bathsheba's grandfather (11:3; 23:34).

household after him. But the king left
[b]ten women, concubines, to keep the
house.
17 And the king went out with all the
people after him, and stopped at the
outskirts.
18 Then all his servants passed [1]before
him; [a]and all the Cherethites, all the
Pelethites, and all the Gittites, [b]six
hundred men who had followed him
from Gath, passed before the king.
19 Then the king said to [a]Ittai the Gittite, "Why are you also going with us?
Return and remain with the king. For
you *are* a foreigner and also an exile
from your own place.
20 "In fact, you came *only* yesterday.
Should I make you wander up and
down with us today, since I go [a]I know
not where? Return, and take your
brethren back. Mercy and truth *be* with
you."
21 But Ittai answered the king and
said, [a]"*As* the LORD lives, and *as* my
lord the king lives, surely in whatever
place my lord the king shall be,
whether in death or life, even there
also your servant will be."
22 So David said to Ittai, "Go, and
cross over." Then Ittai the Gittite and
all his men and all the little ones who
were with him crossed over.
23 And all the country wept with a
loud voice, and all the people crossed
over. The king himself also crossed
over the Brook Kidron, and all the people crossed over toward the way of the
[a]wilderness.
24 There was [a]Zadok also, and all the
Levites with him, bearing the [b]ark
of the covenant of God. And they
set down the ark of God, and [c]Abi-
athar went up until all the people
had finished crossing over from the
city.
25 Then the king said to Zadok, "Carry
the ark of God back into the city. If I
find favor in the eyes of the LORD, He
[a]will bring me back and show me *both*
it and [b]His dwelling place.
26 "But if He says thus: 'I have no
[a]delight in you,' here I am, [b]let Him
do to me as seems good to Him."
27 The king also said to Zadok the
priest, "*Are* you *not* a [a]seer?[1]* Return
to the city in peace, and [b]your two sons
with you, Ahimaaz your son, and Jonathan the son of Abiathar.
28 "See, [a]I will wait in the plains of
the wilderness until word comes from
you to inform me."
29 Therefore Zadok and Abiathar carried the ark of God back to Jerusalem.
And they remained there.
30 So David went up by the Ascent of
the *Mount of* Olives, and wept as he
went up; and he [a]had his head covered
and went [b]barefoot. And all the people
who *were* with him [c]covered their
heads and went up, [d]weeping as they
went up.
31 Then *someone* told David, saying,
[a]"Ahithophel *is* among the conspirators with Absalom." And David said,
"O LORD, I pray, [b]turn the *counsel of
Ahithophel into foolishness!"
32 Now it happened when David had
come to the top *of the mountain,* where
he worshiped God—there was Hushai
the [a]Archite coming to meet him
[b]with his robe torn and dust on his
head.
33 David said to him, "If you go on
with me, then you will become [a]a burden to me.
34 "But if you return to the city, and 7
say to Absalom, [a]'I will be your servant, O king; *as* I *was* your father's servant previously, so I *will* now also *be*
your servant,' then you may defeat the
counsel of Ahithophel for me.
35 "And *do* you not *have* Zadok and
Abiathar the priests with you there?
Therefore it will be *that* whatever you
hear from the king's house, you shall
tell to [a]Zadok and Abiathar the priests.
36 "Indeed *they have* there [a]with them
their two sons, Ahimaaz, Zadok's *son,*
and Jonathan, Abiathar's *son;* and by
them you shall send me everything you
hear."
37 So Hushai, [a]David's friend, went
into the city. [b]And Absalom came into
Jerusalem.

Mephibosheth's Servant

16 When[a] David was a little past
the top *of the mountain,* there
was [b]Ziba the servant of Mephibosheth, who met him with a couple of
saddled donkeys, and on them two
hundred *loaves* of bread, one hundred
clusters of raisins, one hundred summer fruits, and a skin of wine.
2 And the king said to Ziba, "What
do you mean to do with these?" So
Ziba said, "The donkeys *are* for the

16 [b]2 Sam. 12:11; 16:21, 22
18 [a]2 Sam. 8:18 [b]1 Sam. 23:13; 25:13; 30:1, 9 [1]Lit. *by his hand*
19 [a]2 Sam. 18:2
20 [a]1 Sam. 23:13
21 [a]Ruth 1:16, 17; [Prov. 17:17]
23 [a]2 Sam. 15:28; 16:2
24 [a]2 Sam. 8:17 [b]Num. 4:15; 1 Sam. 4:4 [c]1 Sam. 22:20
25 [a][Ps. 43:3] [b]Ex. 15:13; Jer. 25:30
26 [a]Num. 14:8; 2 Sam. 22:20; 1 Kin. 10:9; 2 Chr. 9:8; Is. 62:4 [b]1 Sam. 3:18
27 [a]1 Sam. 9:6–9 [b]2 Sam. 17:17–20 [1]*prophet* *See WW at 1 Sam. 9:9.
28 [a]Josh. 5:10; 2 Sam. 17:16
30 [a]2 Sam. 19:4; Esth. 6:12; Ezek. 24:17, 23 [b]Is. 20:2–4 [c]Jer. 14:3, 4 [d][Ps. 126:6]
31 [a]Ps. 3:1, 2; 55:12 [b]2 Sam. 16:23; 17:14, 23 *See WW at Zech. 6:13.
32 [a]Josh. 16:2 [b]2 Sam. 1:2
33 [a]2 Sam. 19:35
34 [a]2 Sam. 16:19
35 [a]2 Sam. 17:15, 16
36 [a]2 Sam. 15:27
37 [a]2 Sam. 16:16; 1 Chr. 27:33 [b]2 Sam. 16:15

CHAPTER 16

1 [a]2 Sam. 15:30, 32 [b]2 Sam. 9:2; 19:17, 29

15:18 These are David's "mighty men," the warriors of the king's bodyguard.

15:19 Ittai of Gath was David's Philistine mercenary officer, later used by David to lead his attack against Absalom (18:2).

15:34 See section 7 of Truth-In-Action at the end of 2 Sam.

king's household to ride on, the bread
and summer fruit for the young men
to eat, and the wine for [a]those who are
faint in the wilderness to drink."
3 Then the king said, "And where *is*
your [a]master's son?" [b]And Ziba said
to the king, "Indeed he is staying in
Jerusalem, for he said, 'Today the
house of Israel will restore the kingdom of my father to me.' "
4 So the king said to Ziba, "Here, all
that *belongs* to Mephibosheth *is*
yours." And Ziba said, "I humbly bow
before you, *that* I may find favor in
your sight, my lord, O king!"

Shimei Curses David

5 Now when King David came to
[a]Bahurim, there was a man from the
family of the house of Saul, whose
name *was* [b]Shimei the son of Gera,
coming from there. He came out, cursing continuously as he came.
6 And he threw stones at David and
at all the servants of King David. And
all the people and all the mighty men
were on his right hand and on his left.
7 Also Shimei said thus when he
cursed: "Come out! Come out! You
[1]bloodthirsty man, [a]you [2]rogue!
8 "The LORD has [a]brought upon you
all [b]the blood of the house of Saul, in
whose place you have reigned; and the
LORD has delivered the kingdom into
the hand of Absalom your son. So now
you *are caught* in your own evil, because you are a [1]bloodthirsty man!"
9 Then Abishai the son of Zeruiah
said to the king, "Why should this
[a]dead dog [b]curse my lord the king?
Please, let me go over and take off his
head!"
10 But the king said, [a]"What have I to
do with you, you sons of Zeruiah? So
let him curse, because [b]the LORD has
said to him, 'Curse David.' [c]Who then
shall say, 'Why have you done so?' "
11 And David said to Abishai and all
his servants, "See how [a]my son who
[b]came from my own body seeks my
life. How much more now *may this*
Benjamite? Let him alone, and let him
curse; for so the LORD has ordered him.
12 "It may be that the LORD will look

2 [a]2 Sam. 15:23; 17:29
3 [a]2 Sam. 9:9, 10 [b]2 Sam. 19:27
5 [a]2 Sam. 3:16 [b]2 Sam. 19:21; 1 Kin. 2:8, 9, 44–46
7 [a]Deut. 13:13 [1]Lit. *man of bloodshed* [2]*worthless man*
8 [a]Judg. 9:24, 56, 57; 1 Kin. 2:32, 33 [b]2 Sam. 1:16; 3:28, 29; 4:11, 12 [1]Lit. *man of bloodshed*
9 [a]1 Sam. 24:14; 2 Sam. 9:8 [b]Ex. 22:28
10 [a]2 Sam. 3:39; 19:22; [1 Pet. 2:23] [b]2 Kin. 18:25; [Lam. 3:38] [c][Rom. 9:20]
11 [a]2 Sam. 12:11 [b]Gen. 15:4
12 [a]Deut. 23:5; Neh. 13:2; Prov. 20:22 [b]Deut. 23:5; [Rom. 8:28; Heb. 12:10, 11] [1]So with Kt., LXX, Syr., Vg.; Qr. *my eyes;* Tg. *tears of my eyes*
13 [1]Lit. *dusted him with dust* *See WW at Jer. 8:11.
15 [a]2 Sam. 15:12, 37
16 [a]2 Sam. 15:37 [b]2 Sam. 15:34
17 [a]2 Sam. 19:25; [Prov. 17:17] *See WW at Prov. 17:17.
19 [a]2 Sam. 15:34
20 [a]2 Sam. 15:12
21 [a]2 Sam. 15:16; 20:3 [b]Gen. 34:30; 1 Sam. 13:4 [c]2 Sam. 2:7; Zech. 8:13
22 [a]2 Sam. 12:11, 12
23 [a]2 Sam. 15:12

on [1]my affliction, and that the LORD
will [a]repay me with [b]good for his cursing this day."
13 And as David and his men went
along the road, Shimei went along the
hillside opposite him and *cursed as he
went, threw stones at him and [1]kicked
up dust.
14 Now the king and all the people
who *were* with him became weary; so
they refreshed themselves there.

The Advice of Ahithophel

15 Meanwhile [a]Absalom and all the
people, the men of Israel, came to Jerusalem; and Ahithophel *was* with him.
16 And so it was, when Hushai the Archite, [a]David's friend, came to Absalom, that [b]Hushai said to Absalom,
"*Long* live the king! *Long* live the
king!"
17 So Absalom said to Hushai, "*Is* this
your loyalty to your *friend? [a]Why did
you not go with your friend?"
18 And Hushai said to Absalom, "No,
but whom the LORD and this people and
all the men of Israel choose, his I will
be, and with him I will remain.
19 "Furthermore, [a]whom should I
serve? *Should I* not *serve* in the presence of his son? As I have served in
your father's presence, so will I be in
your presence."
20 Then Absalom said to [a]Ahithophel,
"Give advice as to what we should do."
21 And Ahithophel said to Absalom,
"Go in to your father's [a]concubines,
whom he has left to keep the house;
and all Israel will hear that you
[b]are abhorred by your father. Then
[c]the hands of all who are with you will
be strong."
22 So they pitched a tent for Absalom
on the top of the house, and Absalom
went in to his father's concubines
[a]in the sight of all Israel.
23 Now the advice of Ahithophel,
which he gave in those days, *was* as
if one had inquired at the oracle of
God. So *was* all the advice of Ahithophel [a]both with David and with
Absalom.

17 Moreover Ahithophel said to
Absalom, "Now let me choose

16:3, 4 Your master's son is Mephibosheth. Ziba deceives David, so that David takes away the royal pension from Mephibosheth and returns his land to Ziba. See 19:24.

16:5 Shimei: A distant relative of Saul from **Bahurim,** a city east of the Mount of Olives. This was also the city to which Michal's husband pursued her when she was restored to David by Abner (3:16).

16:17 Your friend: That is, David.

16:21, 22 When Absalom took his father's **concubines,** he fulfilled the prophecy of Nathan (12:11, 12). Taking the concubines was also viewed as his taking succession to the throne.

16:23 Oracle of God: Indication of how highly respected Ahithophel's advice was, both to David and Absalom. His defection was at the highest level of David's administration.

twelve thousand men, and I will arise
and pursue David tonight.
2 "I will come upon him while he *is*
[a]weary and weak, and make him
[1]afraid. And all the people who *are*
with him will flee, and I will [b]strike
only the king.
3 "Then I will bring back all the people to you. When all return except the
man whom you seek, all the people will
be at peace."
4 And the saying pleased Absalom
and all the [a]elders of Israel.

The Advice of Hushai

5 Then Absalom said, "Now call Hushai the Archite also, and let us hear
what he [a]says too."
6 And when Hushai came to Absalom, Absalom spoke to him, saying,
"Ahithophel has spoken in this manner. Shall we do as he says? If not,
speak up."
7 So Hushai said to Absalom: "The
*advice that Ahithophel has given *is*
not good at this time.
8 "For," said Hushai, "you know your
father and his men, that they *are*
mighty men, and they *are* enraged in
their minds, like [a]a bear robbed of her
cubs in the field; and your father *is* a
man of war, and will not camp with
the people.
9 "Surely by now he is hidden in
some pit, or in some *other* place. And
it will be, when some of them are overthrown at the first, that whoever hears
it will say, 'There is a slaughter among
the people who follow Absalom.'
10 "And even he *who is* valiant, whose
heart *is* like the heart of a lion, will
[a]melt completely. For all Israel knows
that your father *is* a mighty man, and
those who *are* with him *are* valiant
men.
11 "Therefore I advise that all Israel
be fully gathered to you, [a]from Dan to
Beersheba, [b]like the sand that *is* by the
sea for multitude, and that you go to
battle in person.
12 "So we will come upon him in some
place where he may be found, and we
will fall on him as the dew falls on the
ground. And of him and all the men
who *are* with him there shall not be
left so much as one.
13 "Moreover, if he has withdrawn
into a city, then all Israel shall bring
ropes to that city; and we will [a]pull it
into the river, until there is not one
small stone found there."
14 So Absalom and all the men of Is- 7
rael said, "The advice of Hushai the
Archite *is* better than the advice of
Ahithophel." For [a]the LORD had
purposed to defeat the good advice of
Ahithophel, to the intent that the LORD
might bring disaster on Absalom.

Hushai Warns David to Escape

15 [a]Then Hushai said to Zadok and
Abiathar the priests, "Thus and so
Ahithophel advised Absalom and the
elders of Israel, and thus and so I
have advised.
16 "Now therefore, send quickly and
tell David, saying, 'Do not spend this
night [a]in the plains of the wilderness,
but speedily cross over, lest the king
and all the people who *are* with him
be swallowed up.' "
17 [a]Now Jonathan and Ahimaaz
[b]stayed at [c]En Rogel, for they dared
not be seen coming into the city; so a
female servant would come and tell
them, and they would go and tell King
David.
18 Nevertheless a lad saw them, and
told Absalom. But both of them went
away quickly and came to a man's
house [a]in Bahurim, who had a well in
his court; and they went down into it.
19 [a]Then the woman took and spread
a covering over the well's mouth, and
spread ground grain on it; and the
thing was not known.
20 And when Absalom's servants
came to the woman at the house, they
said, "Where *are* Ahimaaz and Jonathan?" So [a]the woman said to them,
"They have gone over the water
brook." And when they had searched
and could not find *them,* they returned
to Jerusalem.
21 Now it came to pass, after they had
departed, that they came up out of the
well and went and told King David,
and said to David, [a]"Arise and cross
over the water quickly. For thus has
Ahithophel advised against you."
22 So David and all the people who
were with him arose and crossed over
the Jordan. By morning light not one
of them was left who had not gone over
the Jordan.
23 Now when Ahithophel saw that his
advice was not followed, he saddled a
donkey, and arose and went home to

CHAPTER 17
2 [a]Deut. 25:18; 2 Sam. 16:14 [b]Zech. 13:7 [1]*tremble with fear*
4 [a]2 Sam. 5:3; 19:11
5 [a]2 Sam. 15:32–34
7 *See WW at Zech. 6:13.
8 [a]Hos. 13:8
10 [a]Josh. 2:11
11 [a]Judg. 20:1; 2 Sam. 3:10 [b]Gen. 22:17; Josh. 11:4; 1 Kin. 20:10
13 [a]Mic. 1:6
14 [a]2 Sam. 15:31, 34
15 [a]2 Sam. 15:35, 36
16 [a]2 Sam. 15:28
17 [a]2 Sam. 15:27, 36; 1 Kin. 1:42, 43 [b]Josh. 2:4–6 [c]Josh. 15:7; 18:16
18 [a]2 Sam. 3:16; 16:5
19 [a]Josh. 2:4–6
20 [a]Ex. 1:19; [Lev. 19:11]; Josh. 2:3–5
21 [a]2 Sam. 17:15, 16

17:14 See section 7 of Truth-In-Action at the end of 2 Sam.
17:17 Jonathan and Ahimaaz, the sons of the priests Zadok and Abiathar, were loyal to David. **En Rogel** was a well at the southeast corner of Jerusalem.

[a]his house, to his city. Then he [1]put
his [b]household in order, and [c]changed
himself, and died; and he was buried
in his father's tomb.
24 Then David went to [a]Mahanaim.
And Absalom crossed over the Jordan,
he and all the men of Israel with him.
25 And Absalom made [a]Amasa captain of the army instead of Joab. This
Amasa *was* the son of a man whose
name *was* [1]Jithra, an [2]Israelite, who
had gone in to [b]Abigail the daughter
of Nahash, sister of Zeruiah, Joab's
mother.
26 So Israel and Absalom encamped in
the land of Gilead.
27 Now it happened, when David had
come to Mahanaim, that [a]Shobi the
son of Nahash from Rabbah of the people of Ammon, [b]Machir the son of Ammiel from Lo Debar, and [c]Barzillai the
Gileadite from Rogelim,
28 brought beds and basins, earthen
vessels and wheat, barley and flour,
parched *grain* and beans, lentils and
parched *seeds,*
29 honey and curds, sheep and cheese
of the herd, for David and the people
who *were* with him to eat. For they
said, "The people are hungry and
weary and thirsty [a]in the wilderness."

Absalom's Defeat and Death

18 And David [1]numbered the people who *were* with him, and
[a]set captains of thousands and captains of hundreds over them.
2 Then David sent out one third of the
people under the hand of Joab, [a]one
third under the hand of Abishai the son
of Zeruiah, Joab's brother, and one
third under the hand of [b]Ittai the Gittite. And the king said to the people,
"I also will surely go out with you myself."
3 [a]But the people answered, "You
shall not go out! For if we flee away,
they will not care about us; nor if half
of us die, will they care about us. But
you are worth ten thousand of us now.
For you are now more help to us in
the city."
4 Then the king said to them, "Whatever seems best to you I will do." So
the king stood beside the gate, and all
the people went out by hundreds and
by thousands.
5 Now the king had commanded
Joab, Abishai, and Ittai, saying, "*Deal*
gently for my sake with the young man
Absalom." [a]And all the people heard
when the king gave all the captains orders concerning Absalom.
6 So the people went out into the field
of battle against Israel. And the battle
was in the [a]woods of Ephraim.
7 The people of Israel were overthrown there before the servants of David, and a great slaughter of twenty
thousand took place there that day.
8 For the battle there was scattered
over the face of the whole countryside,
and the woods devoured more people
that day than the sword devoured.
9 Then Absalom met the servants of
David. Absalom rode on a mule. The
mule went under the thick boughs of
a great terebinth tree, and [a]his head
caught in the terebinth; so he was left
hanging between heaven and earth.
And the mule which *was* under him
went on.
10 Now a certain man saw *it* and told
Joab, and said, "I just saw Absalom
hanging in a terebinth tree!"
11 So Joab said to the man who told
him, "You just saw *him!* And why did
you not strike him there to the ground?
I would have given you ten *shekels* of
silver and a belt."
12 But the man said to Joab, "Though
I were to receive a thousand *shekels*
of silver in my hand, I would not raise
my hand against the king's son.
[a]For in our hearing the king commanded you and Abishai and Ittai, saying, [1]'Beware lest anyone *touch* the
young man Absalom!'
13 "Otherwise I would have dealt
falsely against my own life. For there
is nothing hidden from the king, and
you yourself would have set yourself
against *me.*"
14 Then Joab said, "I cannot linger
with you." And he took three spears
in his hand and thrust them through
Absalom's heart, while he was *still*
alive in the midst of the terebinth tree.
15 And ten young men who bore

23 [a]2 Sam. 15:12 [b]2 Kin. 20:1 [c]Matt. 27:5 [1]Lit. *gave charge concerning his house*
24 [a]Gen. 32:2; Josh. 13:26; 2 Sam. 2:8; 19:32
25 [a]2 Sam. 19:13; 20:9–12; 1 Kin. 2:5, 32 [b]1 Chr. 2:16 [1]*Jether,* 1 Chr. 2:17 [2]So with MT, some LXX mss., Tg.; some LXX mss. *Ishmaelite* (cf. 1 Chr. 2:17); Vg. *of Jezrael*
27 [a]1 Sam. 11:1; 2 Sam. 10:1; 12:29 [b]2 Sam. 9:4 [c]2 Sam. 19:31, 32; 1 Kin. 2:7
29 [a]2 Sam. 16:2, 14

CHAPTER 18

1 [a]Ex. 18:25; Num. 31:14; 1 Sam. 22:7 [1]Lit. *attended to*
2 [a]Judg. 7:16; 1 Sam. 11:11 [b]2 Sam. 15:19–22
3 [a]2 Sam. 21:17
5 [a]2 Sam. 18:12
6 [a]Josh. 17:15, 18; 2 Sam. 17:26
9 [a]2 Sam. 14:26
12 [a]2 Sam. 18:5 [1]Vss. *'Protect the young man Absalom for me!'*

17:24 Mahanaim was a fortified city and the capital under Ishbosheth. The city was friendly to David because of David's favorable treatment to Saul's descendants, especially of Mephibosheth.
17:25 Since Joab has remained faithful to David, **Amasa** is put in charge of the army. Amasa's father, **Jithra,** had **gone in to Abigail,** that is, he had seduced her.
17:27 These men are chieftains and tributaries of David, indicating the significant support for David by wealthy and influential leaders in this area.
18:1 He **numbered** or organized them for battle.
18:6 The woods of Ephraim was a deserted and rugged area in the vicinity of Mahanaim. The severe terrain claimed more casualties than the battle (v. 8).
18:9 Terebinth tree: A large oak tree.

Joab's armor surrounded Absalom,
and struck and killed him.
16 So Joab blew the trumpet, and the
people returned from pursuing Israel.
For Joab held back the people.
17 And they took Absalom and cast
him into a large pit in the woods, and
[a]laid a very large heap of stones over
him. Then all Israel [b]fled, everyone to
his tent.
18 Now Absalom in his lifetime had
taken and set up a [1]pillar for himself,
which *is* in [a]the King's Valley. For he
said, [b]"I have no son to keep my name
in remembrance." He called the pillar
after his own name. And to this day it
is called Absalom's Monument.

David Hears of Absalom's Death

19 Then [a]Ahimaaz the son of Zadok
said, "Let me run now and take the
news to the king, how the LORD has
[1]avenged him of his enemies."
20 And Joab said to him, "You shall
not take the news this day, for you
shall take the news another day. But
today you shall take no news, because
the king's son is dead."
21 Then Joab said to the Cushite, "Go,
tell the king what you have seen." So
the Cushite bowed himself to Joab and
ran.
22 And Ahimaaz the son of Zadok said
again to Joab, "But [1]whatever happens, please let me also run after the
Cushite." So Joab said, "Why will you
run, my son, since you have no news
ready?"
23 "But whatever happens," *he said,*
"let me run." So he said to him, "Run."
Then Ahimaaz ran by way of the plain,
and outran the Cushite.
24 Now David was sitting between the
[a]two gates. And the watchman went
up to the roof over the gate, to the wall,
lifted his eyes and looked, and there
was a man, running alone.
25 Then the watchman cried out and
told the king. And the king said, "If
he *is* alone, *there is* news in his
mouth." And he came rapidly and
drew near.
26 Then the watchman saw *another*
man running, and the watchman called
to the gatekeeper and said, "There is
another man, running alone!" And the
king said, "He also brings news."
27 So the watchman said, [1]"I think the
running of the first is like the running
of Ahimaaz the son of Zadok." And the
king said, "He *is* a good man, and
comes with [a]good news."
28 So Ahimaaz called out and said to
the king, [1]"All is well!" Then he bowed
down with his face to the earth before
the king, and said, [a]"Blessed *be* the
LORD your God, who has delivered up
the men who raised their hand against
my lord the king!"
29 The king said, "Is the young man
Absalom safe?" Ahimaaz answered,
"When Joab sent the king's servant
and *me* your servant, I saw a great tumult, but I did not know what *it was*
about."
30 And the king said, "Turn aside *and*
stand here." So he turned aside and
stood still.
31 Just then the Cushite came, and the
Cushite said, "There is good news, my
lord the king! For the LORD has
avenged you this day of all those who
rose against you."
32 And the king said to the Cushite,
"Is the young man Absalom safe?" So
the Cushite answered, "May the enemies of my lord the king, and all who
rise against you to do harm, be like
that young man!"

David's Mourning for Absalom

33 Then the king was deeply moved,
and went up to the chamber over the
gate, and wept. And as he went, he said
thus: [a]"O my son Absalom—my son,
my son Absalom—if only I had died
in your place! O Absalom my son,
[b]my son!"

19

And Joab was told, "Behold, the
king is weeping and [a]mourning
for Absalom."
2 So the victory that day was *turned*
into [a]mourning for all the people. For

17 [a]Deut. 21:20, 21; Josh. 7:26; 8:29 [b]2 Sam. 19:8; 20:1, 22
18 [a]Gen. 14:17 [b]2 Sam. 14:27 [1]*monument*
19 [a]2 Sam. 15:36; 17:17 [1]*vindicated*
22 [1]Lit. *be what may*
24 [a]Judg. 5:11; 2 Sam. 13:34; 2 Kin. 9:17
27 [a]1 Kin. 1:42 [1]Lit. *I see the running*
28 [a]2 Sam. 16:12 [1]*Peace be to you*
33 [a]2 Sam. 12:10 [b]2 Sam. 19:4

CHAPTER 19

1 [a]Jer. 14:2
2 [a]Esth. 4:3

18:16 Held back the people: He spared the people. Because Absalom was dead, the rebellion was over.
18:17, 18 The **heap of stones** here is not an honored memorial, but a pile of stones like those placed on the body of Achan (Josh. 7:26). This stands in contrast to that erected by Absalom to himself in the **King's Valley,** or the Kidron Valley, immediately east of Jerusalem.
18:20, 21 Ahimaaz probably was not allowed to go because Joab did not know what David's response might be. He therefore chose an unnamed **Cushite,** a man from Ethiopia, probably a slave in Joab's service and known to David.
18:22 No news ready: It is possible that he had not actually seen the incident with Absalom, as indicated by his general description to David (v. 29).
18:23 By way of the plain: The Jordan plain.
18:33 David's sons, Amnon and Absalom, died violent deaths as a consequence of David's sins. Part of his grief had to be the awareness that his sin ultimately had killed his sons (12:10).

the people heard it said that day, "The
king is grieved for his son."
3 And the people [1]stole back [a]into the
city that day, as people who are
ashamed steal away when they flee in
battle.
4 But the king [a]covered his face, and
the king cried out with a loud voice,
[b]"O my son Absalom! O Absalom, my
son, my son!"
5 Then [a]Joab came into the house to
the king, and said, "Today you have
disgraced all your servants who today
have saved your life, the lives of your
sons and daughters, the lives of your
wives and the lives of your concubines,
6 "in that you love your enemies and
hate your friends. For you have declared today that you [1]regard neither
princes nor servants; for today I perceive that if Absalom had lived and all
of us had died today, then it would
have pleased you well.
7 "Now therefore, arise, go out and
speak [1]comfort to your servants. For I
swear by the LORD, if you do not go
out, not one will stay with you this
night. And that will be worse for you
than all the evil that has befallen you
from your youth until now."
8 Then the king arose and sat in the
[a]gate. And they told all the people, saying, "There is the king, sitting in the
gate." So all the people came before
the king. For everyone of Israel had
[b]fled to his tent.

David Returns to Jerusalem

9 Now all the people were in a dispute
throughout all the tribes of Israel, saying, "The king saved us from the hand
of our [a]enemies, he delivered us from
the hand of the [b]Philistines, and now
he has [c]fled from the land because of
Absalom.
10 "But Absalom, whom we anointed
over us, has died in battle. Now therefore, why do you say nothing about
bringing back the king?"
11 So King David sent to [a]Zadok and
Abiathar the priests, saying, "Speak to
the elders of Judah, saying, 'Why are
you the last to bring the king back to
his house, since the words of all Israel
have come to the king, to his *very*
house?
12 'You *are* my brethren, you *are*
[a]my bone and my flesh. Why then are
you the last to bring back the king?'
13 [a]"And say to Amasa, '*Are* you not
my bone and my flesh? [b]God do so to
me, and more also, if you are not commander of the army before me
[1]continually in place of Joab.'"
14 So he swayed the hearts of all the
men of Judah, [a]just as *the heart of* one
man, so that they sent *this word* to the
king: "Return, you and all your servants!"
15 Then the king returned and came
to the Jordan. And Judah came to
[a]Gilgal, to go to meet the king, to escort
the king [b]across the Jordan.
16 And [a]Shimei the son of Gera, a Benjamite, who *was* from Bahurim, hurried and came down with the men of
Judah to meet King David.
17 *There were* a thousand men of
[a]Benjamin with him, and [b]Ziba the servant of the house of Saul, and his fifteen sons and his twenty servants with
him; and they went over the Jordan before the king.
18 Then a ferryboat went across to
carry over the king's household, and
to do what he thought good.

David's Mercy to Shimei

Now Shimei the son of Gera fell
down before the king when he had
crossed the Jordan.
19 Then he said to the king, [a]"Do not
let my lord [1]impute iniquity to me, or
remember what [b]wrong your servant
did on the day that my lord the king
left Jerusalem, that the king should
[c]take *it* to heart.
20 "For I, your servant, know that I
have sinned. Therefore here I am, the
first to come today of all [a]the house
of Joseph to go down to meet my lord
the king."
21 But Abishai the son of Zeruiah answered and said, "Shall not Shimei be

3 [a]2 Sam. 17:24, 27; 19:32 [1]*went by stealth*
4 [a]2 Sam. 15:30 [b]2 Sam. 18:33
5 [a]2 Sam. 18:14
6 [1]*have no respect for*
7 [1]Lit. *to the heart of*
8 [a]2 Sam. 15:2; 18:24 [b]2 Sam. 18:17
9 [a]2 Sam. 8:1–14 [b]2 Sam. 3:18 [c]2 Sam. 15:14
11 [a]2 Sam. 15:24
12 [a]2 Sam. 5:1; 1 Chr. 11:1
13 [a]2 Sam. 17:25; 1 Chr. 2:17 [b]Ruth 1:17 [1]*permanently*
14 [a]Judg. 20:1
15 [a]Josh. 5:9; 1 Sam. 11:14, 15 [b]2 Sam. 17:22
16 [a]2 Sam. 16:5; 1 Kin. 2:8
17 [a]2 Sam. 3:19; 1 Kin. 12:21 [b]2 Sam. 9:2, 10; 16:1, 2
19 [a]1 Sam. 22:15 [b]2 Sam. 16:5, 6 [c]2 Sam. 13:33 [1]*charge me with iniquity*
20 [a]Judg. 1:22; 1 Kin. 11:28

19:3 Instead of a victorious return to reward, they creep back into the city as those who have been shamed in defeat.
19:8 All the people came before the king in an official review of the victorious troops. **Israel had fled to his tent** refers to those who had followed Absalom. They had gone home.
19:9, 10 These questions are addressed to the elders of the tribe of Judah, David's own tribe. Is there some reason why David is not being acknowledged by his own people? Judah's disposition is key, because the rebellion first began in that tribe with Absalom and those who followed him.
19:13 Amasa: Absalom's head general in the rebellion against David. See note on 17:25. This proved to be a disastrous as well as unnecessary decision. David is here pardoning Amasa for his crime and rewarding him as well.
19:14 All the men of Judah: He heals the breach that the rebellion had caused.
19:20 All the house of Joseph is used for all the tribes that opposed Judah.

put to death for this, [a]because he
[b]cursed the LORD's *anointed?"
22 And David said, [a]"What have I to
do with you, you sons of Zeruiah, that
you should be *adversaries to me today? [b]Shall any man be put to death
today in Israel? For do I not know that
today I *am* king over Israel?"
23 Therefore [a]the king said to Shimei,
"You shall not die." And the king
swore to him.

David and Mephibosheth Meet

24 Now [a]Mephibosheth the son of Saul
came down to meet the king. And he
had not cared for his feet, nor trimmed
his mustache, nor washed his clothes,
from the day the king departed until
the day he returned in peace.
25 So it was, when he had come to Jerusalem to meet the king, that the king
said to him, [a]"Why did you not go with
me, Mephibosheth?"
26 And he answered, "My lord, O king,
my servant deceived me. For your servant said, 'I will saddle a donkey for
myself, that I may ride on it and go to
the king,' because your servant *is* lame.
27 "And [a]he has slandered your servant to my lord the king, [b]but my lord
the king *is* like the angel of God. Therefore do *what is* good in your eyes.
28 "For all my father's house were but
dead men before my lord the king.
[a]Yet you set your servant among those
who eat at your own table. Therefore
what right have I still to [1]cry out anymore to the king?"
29 So the king said to him, "Why do
you speak anymore of your matters? I
have said, 'You and Ziba divide the
land.'"
30 Then Mephibosheth said to the
king, "Rather, let him take it all, inasmuch as my lord the king has come
back in peace to his own house."

David's Kindness to Barzillai

31 And [a]Barzillai the Gileadite came
down from Rogelim and went across
the Jordan with the king, to escort him
across the Jordan.
32 Now Barzillai was a very aged man,
eighty years old. And [a]he had *provided the king with supplies while he
stayed at Mahanaim, for he *was* a very
rich man.
33 And the king said to Barzillai,
"Come across with me, and I will provide for you while you are with me in
Jerusalem."
34 But Barzillai said to the king, "How
long have I to live, that I should go up
with the king to Jerusalem?
35 "I *am* today [a]eighty years old. Can
I discern between the good and *bad?
Can your servant *taste what I eat or
what I drink? Can I hear any longer
the voice of singing men and singing
women? Why then should your servant
be a further burden to my lord the
king?
36 "Your servant will go a little way
across the Jordan with the king. And
why should the king repay me *with*
such a reward?
37 "Please let your servant turn back
again, that I may die in my own city,
near the grave of my father and
mother. But here is your servant
[a]Chimham; let him cross over with my
lord the king, and do for him what
seems good to you."
38 And the king answered, "Chimham
shall cross over with me, and I will do
for him what seems good to you. Now
whatever you request of me, I will do
for you."
39 Then all the people went over the
Jordan. And when the king had
crossed over, the king [a]kissed Barzillai
and blessed him, and he returned to
his own place.

The Quarrel About the King

40 Now the king went on to Gilgal, and
[1]Chimham went on with him. And all
the people of Judah escorted the king,
and also half the people of Israel.
41 Just then all the men of Israel came
to the king, and said to the king, "Why
have our brethren, the men of Judah,
stolen you away and [a]brought the king,
his household, and all David's men
with him across the Jordan?"
42 So all the men of Judah answered
the men of Israel, "Because the king
is [a]a close relative of ours. Why then
are you angry over this matter? Have

21 [a][Ex. 22:28] [b][1 Sam. 26:9] *See WW at Dan. 9:25.
22 [a]2 Sam. 3:39; 16:10 [b]1 Sam. 11:13 *See WW at Job 1:6.
23 [a]1 Kin. 2:8, 9, 37, 46
24 [a]2 Sam. 9:6; 21:7
25 [a]2 Sam. 16:17
27 [a]2 Sam. 16:3, 4 [b]2 Sam. 14:17, 20
28 [a]2 Sam. 9:7–13 [1]*complain*
31 [a]2 Sam. 17:27–29; 1 Kin. 2:7
32 [a]2 Sam. 17:27–29 *See WW at Ps. 55:22.
35 [a]Ps. 90:10 *See WW at Ps. 5:4. • See WW at Ps. 34:8.
37 [a]2 Sam. 19:40; Jer. 41:17
39 [a]Gen. 31:55; Ruth 1:14; 2 Sam. 14:33
40 [1]MT *Chimhan*
41 [a]2 Sam. 19:15
42 [a]2 Sam. 19:12

19:24 Son of Saul: The grandson of Saul. It is not unusual in Scripture to refer to descendants as sons. **Had not cared for his feet:** Not washed. These were all signs of his deep mourning for David's absence from Jerusalem.

19:29 David had not originally divided the land, but rather had given Mephibosheth all the land, and had given Ziba to work it for Mephibosheth. David, in another act of weakness, does not reverse his word to Ziba, but hastily divides the land in half.

19:30 Mephibosheth's reply confirms his loyalty and honesty toward David.

19:31 Barzillai was a wealthy man from Gilead. See 17:27.

19:41 All the men of Israel: Representatives from the other tribes who had gone home after the defeat of Absalom.

we ever eaten at the king's *expense*?
Or has he given us any gift?"
43 And the men of Israel answered the
men of Judah, and said, "We have
[a]ten shares in the king; therefore we
also have more *right* to David than
you. Why then do you despise us—
were we not the first to advise bringing
back our king?" Yet [b]the words of the
men of Judah were [1]fiercer than the
words of the men of Israel.

The Rebellion of Sheba

20 And there happened to be there
a [1]rebel, whose name *was*
Sheba the son of Bichri, a Benjamite.
And he blew a trumpet, and said:

[a]"We have no share in David,
Nor do we have inheritance in the
son of Jesse;
[b]Every man to his tents, O Israel!"

2 So every man of Israel deserted David, *and* followed Sheba the son of
Bichri. But the [a]men of Judah, from the
Jordan as far as Jerusalem, remained
loyal to their king.
3 Now David came to his house at Jerusalem. And the king took the ten
women, [a]his concubines whom he had
left to keep the house, and put them
in seclusion and supported them, but
did not go in to them. So they were
shut up to the day of their death, living
in widowhood.
4 And the king said to Amasa,
[a]"Assemble the men of Judah for me
within three days, and be present here
yourself."
5 So Amasa went to assemble *the*
men of Judah. But he delayed longer
than the set time which David had appointed him.
6 And David said to [a]Abishai, "Now
Sheba the son of Bichri will do us more
harm than Absalom. Take [b]your lord's
servants and pursue him, lest he find
for himself fortified cities, and escape
us."
7 So Joab's men, with the [a]Chereth-
ites, the Pelethites, and [b]all the mighty
men, went out after him. And they
went out of Jerusalem to pursue Sheba
the son of Bichri.
8 When they *were* at the large stone
which *is* in Gibeon, Amasa came before them. Now Joab was dressed in
battle armor; on it was a belt *with* a
sword fastened in its sheath at his hips;
and as he was going forward, it fell out.
9 Then Joab said to Amasa, "*Are* you
in health, my brother?" [a]And Joab
took Amasa by the beard with his right
hand to kiss him.
10 But Amasa did not notice the sword
that *was* in Joab's hand. And [a]he
struck him with it [b]in the stomach, and
his entrails poured out on the ground;
and he did not *strike* him again. Thus
he died. Then Joab and Abishai his
brother pursued Sheba the son of
Bichri.
11 Meanwhile one of Joab's men stood
near Amasa, and said, "Whoever favors Joab and whoever *is* for David—
follow Joab!"
12 But Amasa wallowed in *his* blood
in the middle of the highway. And
when the man saw that all the people
stood still, he moved Amasa from the
highway to the field and threw a garment over him, when he saw that everyone who came upon him halted.
13 When he was removed from the
highway, all the people went on after
Joab to pursue Sheba the son of Bichri.
14 And he went through all the tribes
of Israel to [a]Abel and Beth Maachah
and all the Berites. So they were gathered together and also went after
[1]*Sheba*.
15 Then they came and besieged him
in Abel of Beth Maachah; and they
[a]cast up a siege mound against the city,
and it stood by the rampart. And all
the people who *were* with Joab bat-
tered the wall to throw it down.
16 Then a wise woman cried out from
the city, "Hear, hear! Please say to
Joab, 'Come nearby, that I may speak
with you.' "
17 When he had come near to her, the
woman said, "*Are* you Joab?" He answered, "I *am*." Then she said to him,
"Hear the words of your maidservant."
And he answered, "I am listening."

43 [a]1 Kin. 11:30, 31 [b]Judg. 8:1; 12:1 [1]*harsher*

CHAPTER 20

1 [a]2 Sam. 19:43; 1 Kin. 12:16 [b]1 Sam. 13:2; 2 Sam. 18:17; 2 Chr. 10:16 [1]Lit. *man of Belial*
2 [a]2 Sam. 19:14
3 [a]2 Sam. 15:16; 16:21, 22
4 [a]2 Sam. 17:25; 19:13
6 [a]2 Sam. 21:17 [b]2 Sam. 11:11; 1 Kin. 1:33
7 [a]2 Sam. 8:18; 1 Kin. 1:38, 44 [b]2 Sam. 15:18
9 [a]Matt. 26:49; Luke 22:47
10 [a]2 Sam. 3:27; 1 Kin. 2:5 [b]2 Sam. 2:23
14 [a]1 Kin. 15:20; 2 Kin. 15:29; 2 Chr. 16:4 [1]Lit. *him*
15 [a]2 Kin. 19:32; Ezek. 4:2

19:43 This shows the deep rift that was already apparent between Israel and Judah, which would ultimately produce two separate kingdoms after the death of Solomon.
20:3 These ten **concubines** were those Absalom had appropriated in his rebellion; therefore David remains aloof from them sexually, though they are kept on royal provision. This was not only an act of kindness, but a reassertion of his kingly powers.
20:5 This normally would have been Joab's assignment, but the newly appointed Amasa is sent. It is likely that the soldiers were obstinate, thus causing him to miss the three-day deadline.
20:7 Cherethites and Pelethites: See note on 8:18.
20:8 Gibeon is about 5 miles north of Jerusalem.
20:9 Taking another by the beard and kissing him is still a common practice among the Arabs.
20:14 Abel and Beth Maachah are two cities north of the Sea of Galilee, lying close together 4 miles west of Dan.

18 So she spoke, saying, "They used
to talk in former times, saying, 'They
shall surely seek *guidance* at Abel,'
and so they would end *disputes.*
19 "I *am among the* peaceable *and*
faithful in Israel. You seek to destroy
a city and a mother in Israel. Why
would you swallow up [a]the inheritance
of the LORD?"
20 And Joab answered and said, "Far
be it, far be it from me, that I should
swallow up or destroy!
21 "That *is* not so. But a man from the
mountains of Ephraim, Sheba the son
of Bichri by name, has raised his hand
against the king, against David. Deliver him only, and I will depart from
the city." So the woman said to Joab,
"Watch, his head will be thrown to you
over the wall."
22 Then the woman [a]in her wisdom
went to all the people. And they cut
off the head of Sheba the son of Bichri,
and threw *it* out to Joab. Then he blew
a trumpet, and they withdrew from the
city, every man to his tent. So Joab returned to the king at Jerusalem.

David's Government Officers

23 And [a]Joab *was* over all the army
of Israel; Benaiah the son of Jehoiada
was over the Cherethites and the Pelethites;
24 Adoram *was* [a]in charge of revenue;
[b]Jehoshaphat the son of Ahilud *was* recorder;
25 Sheva *was* scribe; [a]Zadok and Abiathar *were* the priests;
26 [a]and Ira the Jairite was [1]a chief
minister under David.

David Avenges the Gibeonites

21

Now there was a famine in the
days of David for three years,
year after year; and David [a]inquired
of the LORD. And the LORD answered,
"*It is* because of Saul and *his* [1]blood-
thirsty house, because he killed the
Gibeonites."
2 So the king called the Gibeonites
and spoke to them. Now the Gibeonites
were not of the children of Israel, but
[a]of the remnant of the Amorites; the
children of Israel had sworn protection
to them, but Saul had sought to kill
them [b]in his *zeal for the children of
Israel and Judah.
3 Therefore David said to the Gibeonites, "What shall I do for you? And with
what shall I *make atonement, that you
may bless [a]the inheritance of the
LORD?"
4 And the Gibeonites said to him,
"We will have no silver or gold from
Saul or from his house, nor shall you
kill any man in Israel for us." So he
said, "Whatever you say, I will do for
you."
5 Then they answered the king, "As
for the man who consumed us and plotted against us, *that* we should be destroyed from remaining in any of the
territories of Israel,
6 "let seven men of his descendants
be delivered [a]to us, and we will hang
them before the LORD [b]in Gibeah of
Saul, [c]*whom* the LORD chose." And the
king said, "I will give *them.*"
7 But the king spared [a]Mephibosheth
the son of Jonathan, the son of Saul,
because of [b]the LORD's oath that *was*
between them, between David and
Jonathan the son of Saul.
8 So the king took Armoni and Mephibosheth, the two sons of [a]Rizpah
the daughter of Aiah, whom she bore
to Saul, and the five sons of [1]Michal
the daughter of Saul, whom she
[2]brought up for Adriel the son of Barzillai the Meholathite;
9 and he delivered them into the

19 [a]1 Sam. 26:19; 2 Sam. 14:16; 21:3
22 [a]2 Sam. 20:16; [Eccl. 9:13–16]
23 [a]2 Sam. 8:16–18; 1 Kin. 4:3–6
24 [a]1 Kin. 4:6 [b]2 Sam. 8:16; 1 Kin. 4:3
25 [a]2 Sam. 8:17; 1 Kin. 4:4
26 [a]2 Sam. 8:18 [1]Or *David's priest*

CHAPTER 21

1 [a]Num. 27:21; 2 Sam. 5:19 [1]Lit. *house of bloodshed*
2 [a]Josh. 9:3, 15–20 [b][Ex. 34:11–16] *See WW at Zech. 8:2.
3 [a]1 Sam. 26:19; 2 Sam. 20:19 *See WW at Num. 15:25.
6 [a]Num. 25:4 [b]1 Sam. 10:26 [c]1 Sam. 10:24; [Hos. 13:11]
7 [a]2 Sam. 4:4; 9:10 [b]1 Sam. 18:3; 20:12–17; 23:18; 2 Sam. 9:1–7
8 [a]2 Sam. 3:7 [1]*Merab,* 1 Sam. 18:19; 25:44; 2 Sam. 3:14; 6:23 [2]Lit. *bore to Adriel*

20:18 Abel was well known in the region as a place where matters could be brought for wise counsel, and the wise woman is one of the people who gave such counsel.
20:19 A mother in Israel is a city of influence and respect.
20:22 This **woman in her wisdom,** whose name we do not know, withstands David's foremost general and convinces him of his error, determines a solution, convinces her neighbors as to the proper course to take, accomplishes what Joab has not been able to do, and saves her entire city from death. **Every man to his tent:** The soldiers disband and go back to their homes.
20:23–26 A reorganization for the final years of David's reign. Compare a similar list in 8:15–18. **Benaiah** was one of the "mighty men" who replaced Joab as commander in chief under Solomon (1 Kin. 2:35), and under orders from Solomon he would later execute Joab for the murders of Abner and Amasa (1 Kin. 2:31–34).
20:24 Adoram *was* in charge of revenue, the conscripted labor gangs used for the various building and work projects of the king.
21:3 Gibeonites: After the victories at Jericho and Ai at the very beginning of Joshua's conquest of Canaan, two Gibeonites tricked Joshua into making a covenant with them, ensuring they would never be harmed by Israel. In exchange for this protection they would perform menial work for Israel (Josh. 9). They are also called Hivites in Josh. 9:7.
21:8 Rizpah: A concubine of Saul. **Michal:** Other manuscripts have Merab, also a daughter of Saul who was given to Adriel as his wife (1 Sam. 18:19). This is more likely since Michal bore no children because of her anger at David upon the return of the ark of the covenant (6:23). The phrase **brought up for Adriel** is literally "bore to."
21:9 Beginning of barley harvest: The month of April.

hands of the Gibeonites, and they
hanged them on the hill [a]before the
LORD. So they fell, *all* seven together,
and were put to death in the days of
harvest, in the first *days,* in the beginning of barley harvest.
10 Now [a]Rizpah the daughter of Aiah
took sackcloth and spread it for herself
on the rock, [b]from the beginning of
harvest until the late rains poured on
them from heaven. And she did not allow the birds of the air to rest on them
by day nor the beasts of the field by
night.
11 And David was told what Rizpah
the daughter of Aiah, the concubine of
Saul, had done.
12 Then David went and took the
bones of Saul, and the bones of Jonathan his son, from the men of [a]Jabesh
Gilead who had stolen them from the
street of [1]Beth Shan, where the [b]Philis-
tines had hung them up, after the Philistines had struck down Saul in Gilboa.
13 So he brought up the bones of Saul
and the bones of Jonathan his son from
there; and they gathered the bones of
those who had been hanged.
14 They buried the bones of Saul and
Jonathan his son in the country of Benjamin in [a]Zelah, in the tomb of Kish
his father. So they performed all that
the king commanded. And after that
[b]God heeded the prayer for the land.

Philistine Giants Destroyed

5 15 When the Philistines were at war
again with Israel, David and his servants with him went down and fought
against the Philistines; and David grew
faint.
16 Then Ishbi-Benob, who *was* one of
the sons of [1]the [a]giant, the weight of
whose bronze spear *was* three hundred
shekels, who was bearing a new *sword,*
thought he could kill David.
17 But [a]Abishai the son of Zeruiah
came to his aid, and struck the Philistine and killed him. Then the men of
David swore to him, saying, [b]"You
shall go out no more with us to battle,
lest you quench the [c]lamp of Israel."
18 [a]Now it happened afterward that
there was again a battle with the Philistines at Gob. Then [b]Sibbechai the
Hushathite killed [1]Saph, who *was* one
of the sons of [2]the giant.
19 Again there was war at Gob with
the Philistines, where [a]Elhanan the son
of [1]Jaare-Oregim the Bethlehemite
killed [b]*the brother of* Goliath the Gittite, the shaft of whose spear *was* like
a weaver's beam.
20 Yet again [a]there was war at Gath,
where there was a man of *great* stature, who had six fingers on each hand
and six toes on each foot, twenty-four
in number; and he also was born to
[1]the giant.
21 So when he [a]defied Israel, Jonathan
the son of [1]Shimea, David's brother,
killed him.
22 [a]These four were born to [1]the giant
in Gath, and fell by the hand of David
and by the hand of his servants.

Praise for God's Deliverance

22 Then David [a]spoke to the LORD 2
the words of this song, on the
day when the LORD had [b]delivered him
from the hand of all his enemies, and
from the hand of Saul.
2 And he [a]said:

[b]"The LORD *is* my rock and my
[c]fortress and my deliverer;
3 The God of my strength,
[a]in whom I will *trust;
My [b]shield and the [c]horn[1] of my
salvation,
My [d]stronghold and my [e]refuge;
My Savior, You save me from
violence.
4 I will call upon the LORD, *who is*
worthy to be praised;
So shall I be saved from my
enemies.

5 "When the waves of death
surrounded me,

9 [a]2 Sam. 6:17 **10** [a]2 Sam. 3:7; 21:8 [b]Deut. 21:23 **12** [a]1 Sam. 31:11–13 [b]1 Sam. 31:8 [1]*Beth Shean,* Josh. 17:11 **14** [a]Josh. 18:28 [b]Josh. 7:26; 2 Sam. 24:25 **16** [a]Num. 13:22, 28; Josh. 15:14; 2 Sam. 21:18–22 [1]Or *Rapha* **17** [a]2 Sam. 20:6–10 [b]2 Sam. 18:3 [c]2 Sam. 22:29; 1 Kin. 11:36 **18** [a]1 Chr. 20:4–8 [b]1 Chr. 11:29; 27:11 [1]*Sippai,* 1 Chr. 20:4 [2]Or *Rapha* **19** [a]2 Sam. 23:24 [b]1 Sam. 17:4; 1 Chr. 20:5 [1]*Jair,* 1 Chr. 20:5 **20** [a]1 Chr. 20:6 [1]Or *Rapha* **21** [a]1 Sam. 17:10 [1]*Shammah,* 1 Sam. 16:9 and elsewhere **22** [a]1 Chr. 20:8 [1]Or *Rapha*

CHAPTER 22

1 [a]Ex. 15:1; Deut. 31:30; Judg. 5:1 [b]Ps. 18:title; 34:19 **2** [a]Ps. 18 [b]Deut. 32:4; 1 Sam. 2:2 [c]Ps. 91:2 **3** [a]Ps. 7:1; Heb. 2:13 [b]Gen. 15:1; Deut. 33:29; Ps. 84:11 [c]Luke 1:69 [d]Prov. 18:10 [e]Ps. 9:9; 46:1, 7, 11; Jer. 16:19 [1]Strength *See WW at Zeph. 3:12.

21:10 Spread it for herself: She spread the coarse blanket, likely for a bed, where she kept watch over the hanging corpses. To have the bodies ravaged by birds or wild animals was considered to be the worst possible insult and desecration of the dead. The coming of the rains signaled that the curse was lifted and Saul's sin was atoned for.

21:12–14 This remarkable act of kindness by Rizpah reminds David of the kindness of the men of Jabesh Gilead who had buried **Saul** and **Jonathan.** He performs one final gracious act toward the house of Saul.

21:15–22 See section 5 of Truth-In-Action at the end of 2 Sam.

21:15 David grew faint or physically weak.

21:16 Three hundred shekels was about 7½ pounds.

Sons of the giant: This was a race of giants from which the original Goliath had come.

21:17 Quench the lamp of Israel: David was the one through whom God's light and covenants were to be given. To lose him in battle would snuff out that light.

22:1–23:7 See section 2 of Truth-In-Action at the end of 2 Sam.

22:1–51 Here is David's reflective look at the power and working of God throughout his life and administration. This song is also found in Ps. 18.

The floods of ungodliness
[1]made me afraid.
6 The [a]sorrows of Sheol
surrounded me;
The snares of death confronted
me.
7 In my distress [a]I *called upon the
LORD,
And cried out to my God;
He [b]heard my voice from His
*temple,
And my cry *entered* His ears.

8 "Then [a]the earth shook and
trembled;
[b]The foundations of [1]heaven
quaked and were shaken,
Because He was angry.
9 Smoke went up from His nostrils,
And devouring [a]fire from His
mouth;
Coals were kindled by it.
10 He [a]bowed the heavens also, and
came down
With [b]darkness under His feet.
11 He rode upon a cherub, and flew;
And He [1]was seen [a]upon the
wings of the wind.
12 He made [a]darkness canopies
around Him,
Dark waters *and* thick clouds of
the skies.
13 From the brightness before Him
Coals of fire were kindled.

14 "The LORD [a]thundered from
heaven,
And the Most High uttered His
voice.
15 He sent out [a]arrows and scattered
them;
Lightning bolts, and He
vanquished them.
16 Then the channels of the sea
[a]were seen,
The foundations of the world
were uncovered,
At the [b]rebuke of the LORD,
At the blast of the breath of His
nostrils.

17 "He[a] sent from above, He took me,
He drew me out of many waters.
18 He delivered me from my strong
enemy,
From those who hated me;
For they were too strong for me.
19 They confronted me in the day of
my calamity,
But the LORD was my [a]support.
20 [a]He also brought me out into a
broad place;
He delivered me because He
[b]delighted in me.

21 "The[a] LORD rewarded me
according to my righteousness;
According to the [b]cleanness of
my hands
He has recompensed me.
22 For I have [a]kept the ways of the
LORD,
And have not wickedly departed
from my God.
23 For all His [a]judgments *were*
before me;
And *as for* His statutes, I did not
depart from them.
24 I was also [a]blameless before Him,
And I kept myself from my
iniquity.
25 Therefore [a]the LORD has
[1]recompensed me according to
my righteousness,
According to [2]my cleanness in
His eyes.

26 "With [a]the merciful You will show
Yourself merciful;
With a blameless man You will
show Yourself blameless;
27 With the pure You will show
Yourself pure;
And [a]with the devious You will
show Yourself shrewd.
28 You will save the [a]humble[1]
people;
But Your eyes *are* on [b]the
haughty, *that* You may bring
them down.

29 "For You *are* my [a]lamp, O LORD;
The LORD shall enlighten my
darkness.
30 For by You I can run against a
troop;
By my God I can leap over a
[a]wall.
31 *As for* God, [a]His way *is* perfect;
[b]The **word** of the LORD *is* proven;
He *is* a shield to all who trust in
Him.

5 [1]Or *overwhelmed*
6 [a]Ps. 116:3
7 [a]Ps. 116:4; 120:1 [b]Ex. 3:7 *See WW at Jer. 33:3. • See WW at Hag. 2:15.
8 [a]Judg. 5:4 [b]Job 26:11 [1]So with MT, LXX, Tg.; Syr., Vg. *hills* (cf. Ps. 18:7)
9 [a]Heb. 12:29
10 [a]Is. 64:1 [b]Ex. 20:21
11 [a]Ps. 104:3 [1]So with MT, LXX; many Heb. mss., Syr., Vg. *flew* (cf. Ps. 18:10); Tg. *spoke with power*
12 [a]Job 36:29
14 [a]Job 37:2–5
15 [a]Deut. 32:23
16 [a]Nah. 1:4 [b]Ex. 15:8
17 [a]Ps. 144:7
19 [a]Is. 10:20
20 [a]Ps. 31:8; 118:5 [b]2 Sam. 15:26
21 [a]1 Sam. 26:23 [b]Ps. 24:4
22 [a]Ps. 119:3
23 [a][Deut. 6:6–9; 7:12]
24 [a][Eph. 1:4]
25 [a]2 Sam. 22:21 [1]*rewarded* [2]LXX, Syr., Vg. *the cleanness of my hands in His sight* (cf. Ps. 18:24); Tg. *my cleanness before His word*
26 [a][Matt. 5:7]
27 [a][Lev. 26:23, 24]
28 [a]Ps. 72:12 [b]Job 40:11 [1]*afflicted*
29 [a]Ps. 119:105; 132:17
30 [a]2 Sam. 5:6–8
31 [a][Matt. 5:48] [b]Ps. 12:6

22:8 Though obviously a poetic characterization, David affirms that the prayer of God's anointed has monumental effect both on earth and in heaven.

22:21–25 That God saw David in this way is evidenced in 1 Kin. 14:8. That history so judged David is evidenced in 1 Kin. 15:4, 5. This does not gloss over David's sin (1 Kin. 15:5), but should be seen in two ways. First, David, even in his sin, had a heart for God and the ways of God. When accused, he quickly repented and did not complain when the obvious effects of his sin plagued his reign and family. Second, it is testimony to the fact that God utterly forgives and continues to accomplish His will, even in the face of human weakness (v. 51).

WORD WEALTH

22:31 word, *'imrah* (eem-*rah*); Strong's #565: Speech; word or words; commandment; dictum; answer; saying. This noun occurs 35 times and is derived from the verb *'amar,* "to speak" or "to say." *'Amar* occurs approximately 5,000 times in the OT, with many statements introduced by the words "and he said," or "he answered." See Ps. 12:6; 18:30. In Ps. 119, *'imrah* occurs 21 times, including v. 11. "Your word I have hidden in my heart, that I might not sin against You." Compare vv. 67, 154, 162; Ps. 138:2; Prov. 30:5.

32 "For [a]who *is* God, except the LORD?
And who *is* a rock, except our God?
33 [1]God *is* my [a]strength *and* power,
And He [b]makes [2]my way [c]perfect.
34 He makes [1]my feet [a]like the *feet* of deer,
And [b]sets me on my high places.
35 He teaches my hands [1]to make war,
So that my arms can bend a bow of bronze.

36 "You have also given me the shield of Your salvation;
Your gentleness has made me great.
37 You [a]enlarged my path under me;
So my feet did not slip.
38 "I have pursued my enemies and destroyed them;
Neither did I turn back again till they were destroyed.
39 And I have destroyed them and wounded them,
So that they could not rise;
They have fallen [a]under my feet.
40 For You have [a]armed me with *strength for the battle;
You have [1]subdued under me [b]those who rose against me.
41 You have also [1]given me the [a]necks of my enemies,
So that I destroyed those who hated me.
42 They looked, but *there was* none to save;
Even [a]to the LORD, but He did not answer them.
43 Then I beat them as fine [a]as the dust of the earth;
I trod them [b]like dirt in the streets,
And I [1]spread them out.

44 "You[a] have also delivered me from the [1]strivings of my people;
You have kept me as the [b]head of the nations.
[c]A people I have not known shall serve me.
45 The foreigners submit to me;
As soon as they hear, they obey me.
46 The foreigners fade away,
And [1]come frightened [a]from their hideouts.

47 "The LORD lives!
Blessed *be* my Rock!
Let God be *exalted,
The [a]Rock of my salvation!
48 *It is* God who avenges me,
And [a]subdues the peoples under me;
49 He delivers me from my enemies.
You also lift me up above those who rise against me;
You have delivered me from the [a]violent man.
50 Therefore I will *give thanks to You, O LORD, among [a]the Gentiles,
And sing praises to Your [b]name.

51 "*He*[a] *is* the tower of salvation to His king,
And shows mercy to His [b]anointed,
To David and [c]his descendants forevermore."

David's Last Words

23 Now these *are* the last words of David.

Thus says David the son of Jesse;
Thus says [a]the *man raised up on high,
[b]The anointed of the God of Jacob,
And the sweet psalmist of Israel:

2 "The[a] **Spirit** of the LORD spoke by me,
And His word *was* on my tongue.

32 [a]Is. 45:5, 6 **33** [a]Ps. 27:1 [b][Heb. 13:21] [c]Ps. 101:2, 6 [1]DSS, LXX, Syr., Vg. *It is God who arms me with strength* (cf. Ps. 18:32); Tg. *It is God who sustains me with strength* [2]So with Qr., LXX, Syr., Tg., Vg. (cf. Ps. 18:32); Kt. *His* **34** [a]2 Sam. 2:18 [b]Is. 33:16 [1]So with Qr., LXX, Syr., Tg., Vg. (cf. Ps. 18:33); Kt. *His* **35** [1]Lit. *for the war* **37** [a]Prov. 4:12 **39** [a]Mal. 4:3 **40** [a][Ps. 18:32] [b][Ps. 44:5] [1]Lit. *caused to bow down* *See WW at Zech. 4:6. **41** [a]Gen. 49:8 [1]*given me victory over* **42** [a]1 Sam. 28:6 **43** [a]Ps. 18:42 [b]Is. 10:6 [1]*scattered*

44 [a]2 Sam. 3:1 [b]Deut. 28:13 [c][Is. 55:5] [1]*contentions* **46** [a][Mic. 7:17] [1]So with LXX, Tg., Vg. (cf. Ps. 18:45); MT *gird themselves* **47** [a]Ps. 89:26 *See WW at Ps. 18:46. **48** [a]Ps. 144:2 **49** [a]Ps. 140:1, 4, 11 **50** [a]2 Sam. 8:1–14 [b]Rom. 15:9 *See WW at 1 Chr. 16:7. **51** [a]Ps. 144:10 [b]Ps. 89:20 [c]2 Sam. 7:12–16

CHAPTER 23

1 [a]2 Sam. 7:8, 9 [b]1 Sam. 16:12, 13 *See WW at Jer. 31:22. **2** [a][2 Pet. 1:21]

23:1–7 While ch. 22 looks over the past, ch. 23 begins with a look into the future.

23:2–4 The Spirit of the LORD spoke by me: David takes the voice of a prophet, presenting a King who rules in justice, **in the fear of God,** and **like the light of the morning.** It would take no prophetic gift simply to describe these general qualities in a ruler. It did take prophetic giftedness to reach through the centuries and see a future King ruling "like the

WORD WEALTH

23:2 Spirit, *ruach* (*roo*-ach); Strong's #7307: Spirit, wind, breath. This word occurs nearly 400 times. Job 37:21 and Ps. 148:8 speak about "winds" related to storms. In Gen. 6:17, "the *ruach* of life" is translated "the breath of life." Generally *ruach* is translated "spirit," whether concerning the human spirit, a distressing spirit (1 Sam. 16:23), or the Spirit of God. The Holy Spirit is especially presented in Is.: God puts His Spirit upon the Messiah (42:1); He will pour out His Spirit upon Israel's descendants (44:3); Yahweh and His Spirit both send the Anointed One (48:16, a reference to the triune God); the Spirit of God commissions and empowers the Messiah (61:1–3); see also 59:19, 21.

3 The God of Israel said,
[a]The Rock of Israel spoke to me:
'He who rules over men *must be* just,
Ruling [b]in the fear of God.
4 And [a]*he shall be* like the light of the morning *when* the sun rises,
A morning without clouds,
Like the tender grass *springing* out of the earth,
By clear shining after rain.'

5 "Although my house *is* not so with God,
[a]Yet He has made with me an everlasting covenant,
Ordered in all *things* and secure.
For *this is* all my salvation and all *my* desire;
Will He not make *it* increase?
6 But *the sons* of rebellion *shall* all *be* as thorns thrust away,
Because they cannot be taken with hands.
7 But the man *who* touches them
Must be [1]armed with iron and the shaft of a spear,
And they shall be utterly burned with fire in *their* place."

David's Mighty Men

8 These *are* the names of the mighty men whom David had: [1]Josheb-Basshebeth the Tachmonite, chief among [2]the captains. He was called Adino the Eznite, because he had killed eight hundred men at one time.

3 [a][Deut. 32:4] [b]Ex. 18:21; [Is. 11:1–5]
4 [a]Ps. 89:36; Is. 60:1
5 [a]2 Sam. 7:12; Ps. 89:29; Is. 55:3
7 [1]Lit. *filled*
8 [1]Lit. *One Who Sits in the Seat* (1 Chr. 11:11) [2]So with MT, Tg.; LXX, Vg. *the three*

9 [a]1 Chr. 11:12; 27:4 [1]*Dodai,* 1 Chr. 27:4
10 [a]Judg. 8:4 [b]1 Sam. 30:24, 25
11 [a]1 Chr. 11:27 [b]1 Chr. 11:13, 14
13 [a]1 Chr. 11:15 [b]1 Sam. 22:1 [c]2 Sam. 5:18
14 [a]1 Sam. 22:4, 5
17 [a][Lev. 17:10]
18 [a]2 Sam. 21:17; 1 Chr. 11:20 [1]So with MT, LXX, Vg.; some Heb. mss., Syr. *thirty;* Tg. *the mighty men*

9 And after him *was* [a]Eleazar the son
of [1]Dodo, the Ahohite, *one* of the three
mighty men with David when they defied the Philistines *who* were gathered
there for battle, and the men of Israel
had retreated.
10 He arose and attacked the Philistines until his hand was [a]weary, and
his hand stuck to the sword. The LORD
brought about a great victory that day;
and the people returned after him only
to [b]plunder.
11 And after him *was* [a]Shammah the
son of Agee the Hararite. [b]The Philistines had gathered together into a
troop where there was a piece of
ground full of lentils. So the people fled
from the Philistines.
12 But he stationed himself in the middle of the field, defended it, and killed
the Philistines. So the LORD brought
about a great victory.
13 Then [a]three of the thirty chief men
went down at harvest time and came
to David at [b]the cave of Adullam. And
the troop of Philistines encamped in
[c]the Valley of Rephaim.
14 David *was* then in [a]the stronghold,
and the garrison of the Philistines *was*
then *in* Bethlehem.
15 And David said with longing, "Oh,
that someone would give me a drink
of the water from the well of Bethlehem, which *is* by the gate!"
16 So the three mighty men broke
through the camp of the Philistines,
drew water from the well of Bethlehem
that *was* by the gate, and took it and
brought *it* to David. Nevertheless he
would not drink it, but poured it out
to the LORD.
17 And he said, "Far be it from me, O
LORD, that I should do this! Is *this not*
[a]the blood of the men who went in
jeopardy of their lives?" Therefore he
would not drink it. These things were
done by the three mighty men.
18 Now [a]Abishai the brother of Joab,
the son of Zeruiah, was chief of
[1]*another* three. He lifted his spear
against three hundred *men,* killed
them, and won a name among *these*
three.
19 Was he not the most honored of
three? Therefore he became their captain. However, he did not attain to the
first three.
20 Benaiah *was* the son of Jehoiada,
the son of a valiant man from

light of the morning." In Rev. 22:16 Christ looks back to David and declares, "I am the Root and the Offspring of David, the Bright and Morning Star."

23:8–39 A list of the elite warriors of David's personal bodyguard and special royal forces. See also 1 Chr. 11:10–47.

[a]Kabzeel, [1]who had done many deeds. [b]He had killed two lion-like heroes of Moab. He also had gone down and killed a lion in the midst of a pit on a snowy day.
21 And he killed an Egyptian, [1]a spectacular man. The Egyptian *had* a spear in his hand; so he went down to him with a staff, wrested the spear out of the Egyptian's hand, and killed him with his own spear.
22 These *things* Benaiah the son of Jehoiada did, and won a name among three mighty men.
23 He was more honored than the thirty, but he did not attain to the *first* three. And David appointed him [a]over his guard.
24 [a]Asahel the brother of Joab *was* one of the thirty; Elhanan the son of Dodo of Bethlehem,
25 [a]Shammah the Harodite, Elika the Harodite,
26 Helez the Paltite, Ira the son of Ikkesh the Tekoite,
27 Abiezer the Anathothite, Mebunnai the Hushathite,
28 Zalmon the Ahohite, Maharai the Netophathite,
29 Heleb the son of Baanah (the Netophathite), Ittai the son of Ribai from Gibeah of the children of Benjamin,
30 Benaiah a Pirathonite, Hiddai from the brooks of [a]Gaash,
31 Abi-Albon the Arbathite, Azmaveth the Barhumite,
32 Eliahba the Shaalbonite (of the sons of Jashen), Jonathan,
33 [a]Shammah the [1]Hararite, Ahiam the son of Sharar the Hararite,
34 Eliphelet the son of Ahasbai, the son of the Maachathite, Eliam the son of [a]Ahithophel the Gilonite,
35 [1]Hezrai the Carmelite, Paarai the Arbite,
36 Igal the son of Nathan of [a]Zobah, Bani the Gadite,
37 Zelek the Ammonite, Naharai the Beerothite (armorbearer of Joab the son of Zeruiah),
38 [a]Ira the Ithrite, Gareb the Ithrite,
39 *and* [a]Uriah the Hittite: thirty-seven in all.

20 [a]Josh. 15:21 [b]Ex. 15:15 [1]Lit. *great of acts*
21 [1]Lit. *a man of appearance*
23 [a]2 Sam. 8:18; 20:23
24 [a]2 Sam. 2:18; 1 Chr. 27:7
25 [a]1 Chr. 11:27
30 [a]Judg. 2:9
33 [a]2 Sam. 23:11 [1]Or *Ararite*
34 [a]2 Sam. 15:12
35 [1]*Hezro,* 1 Chr. 11:37
36 [a]2 Sam. 8:3
38 [a]1 Chr. 2:53
39 [a]2 Sam. 11:3, 6

CHAPTER 24

1 [a]2 Sam. 21:1, 2 [b]Num. 26:2; 1 Chr. 27:23, 24 [1]*take a census of*
2 [a]Judg. 20:1; 2 Sam. 3:10 [b][Jer. 17:5]
3 [a]Deut. 1:11
4 [1]*overruled*
5 [a]Deut. 2:36; Josh. 13:9, 16 [b]Num. 32:1, 3
6 [a]Josh. 19:47; Judg. 18:29 [b]Josh. 19:28; Judg. 18:28
7 [a]Josh. 19:29 [b]Josh. 11:3; Judg. 3:3
9 [a]1 Chr. 21:5
10 [a]1 Sam. 24:5 [b]2 Sam. 23:1 [c]2 Sam. 12:13

David's Census of Israel and Judah

24 Again [a]the anger of the LORD was aroused against Israel, and He moved David against them to say, [b]"Go, [1]number Israel and Judah." 5
2 So the king said to Joab the commander of the army who *was* with him, "Now go throughout all the tribes of Israel, [a]from Dan to Beersheba, and count the people, that [b]I may know the number of the people."
3 And Joab said to the king, "Now may the LORD your God [a]add to the people a hundred times more than there are, and may the eyes of my lord the king see *it*. But why does my lord the king desire this thing?"
4 Nevertheless the king's word [1]prevailed against Joab and against the captains of the army. Therefore Joab and the captains of the army went out from the presence of the king to count the people of Israel.
5 And they crossed over the Jordan and camped in [a]Aroer, on the right side of the town which *is* in the midst of the ravine of Gad, and toward [b]Jazer.
6 Then they came to Gilead and to the land of Tahtim Hodshi; they came to [a]Dan Jaan and around to [b]Sidon;
7 and they came to the stronghold of [a]Tyre and to all the cities of the [b]Hivites and the Canaanites. Then they went out to South Judah *as far as* Beersheba.
8 So when they had gone through all the land, they came to Jerusalem at the end of nine months and twenty days.
9 Then Joab gave the sum of the number of the people to the king. [a]And there were in Israel eight hundred thousand valiant men who drew the sword, and the men of Judah were five hundred thousand men.

The Judgment on David's Sin

10 And [a]David's heart condemned him after he had numbered the people. So [b]David said to the LORD, [c]"I have sinned greatly in what I have done; but now, I pray, O LORD, take away the

24:1–17 See section 5 of Truth-In-Action at the end of 2 Sam.
24:1 This event is placed by the writer of 1 Chr. 21 at the end of David's reign, during his final talks with Solomon and preparations for transferring the kingdom to him. See note on 1 Chr. 21:1 for a further explanation of this event.
24:3 Joab sees accurately the true nature of this command and its sin. The issue for David and for Israel had never been how many fighting men there were. Their strength was not in numbers, but in the Lord who went into battle with them. This command stands in contrast with his courageous and confident speech to Goliath, "The battle *is* the LORD's" (1 Sam. 17:47).
24:9 This number is smaller than the total in 1 Chr. 21. Since there is very little information as to how the census was actually conducted, the reason cannot be clearly given.
24:10 I have done very foolishly: David realized that considering Israel's strength on the basis of numbers of fighting men, as other nations did, was to violate Israel's relationship with Yahweh who was her true strength. David's

iniquity of Your servant, for I have
[d]done very foolishly."
11 Now when David arose in the morning, the word of the LORD came to the
prophet [a]Gad, David's [b]seer, saying,
12 "Go and tell David, 'Thus says the
LORD: "I offer you three *things;* choose
one of them for yourself, that I may
do *it* to you." ' "
13 So Gad came to David and told him;
and he said to him, "Shall [a]seven[1]
years of famine come to you in your
land? Or shall you flee three months
before your enemies, while they pursue
you? Or shall there be three days'
plague in your land? Now consider and
see what answer I should take back to
Him who sent me."
14 And David said to Gad, "I am in
great distress. Please let us fall into the

10 [d]1 Sam. 13:13; [2 Chr. 16:9]
11 [a]1 Sam. 22:5 [b]1 Sam. 9:9; 1 Chr. 29:29
13 [a]Ezek. 14:21 [1]So with MT, Syr., Tg., Vg.; LXX *three* (cf. 1 Chr. 21:12)

heart was always sensitive toward the Lord. He was easily convicted and quickly repented, qualities which earned him the accolades of 1 Kin. 14:8.

24:11 Seer: Spiritual advisor and prophet.

24:13 Seven: More likely understood to be three years as mentioned in 1 Chr. 21:12. These three plagues indicate that the Lord was not only displeased with David, but was angry with the nation. See in this regard v. 1. The exact reason for His anger is not given.

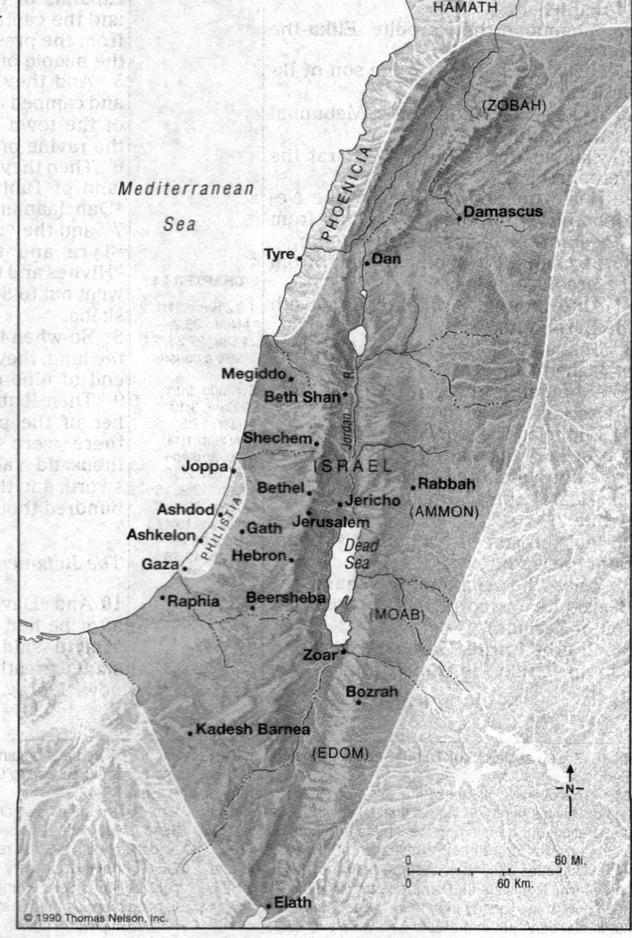

The Davidic Kingdom. David's military exploits successfully incorporated into the Israelite kingdom the powers of Edom, Moab, Ammon, and Zobah.

hand of the LORD, [a]for His mercies *are*
great; but [b]do not let me fall into the
hand of man."
15 So [a]the LORD sent a plague upon Israel from the morning till the appointed time. From Dan to Beersheba
seventy thousand men of the people
died.
16 [a]And when the [1]angel* stretched
out His hand over Jerusalem to destroy
it, [b]the LORD relented from the destruction, and said to the [1]angel who was
destroying the people, "It is enough;
now restrain your hand." And the
[1]angel of the LORD was by the threshing floor of [2]Araunah the Jebusite.
17 Then David spoke to the LORD when
he saw the angel who was striking the
people, and said, "Surely [a]I have
sinned, and I have done wickedly; but
these sheep, what have they done? Let
Your hand, I pray, be against me and
against my father's house."

The Altar on the Threshing Floor

18 And Gad came that day to David
and said to him, [a]"Go up, erect an altar
to the LORD on the threshing floor of
Araunah the Jebusite."
19 So David, according to the word of
Gad, went up as the LORD commanded.
20 Now Araunah looked, and saw the
king and his servants coming toward
him. So Araunah went out and bowed
before the king with his face to the
ground.
21 Then Araunah said, "Why has my
lord the king come to his servant?"
[a]And David said, "To buy the threshing floor from you, to build an altar to
the LORD, that [b]the plague may be
withdrawn from the people."
22 Now Araunah said to David, "Let
my lord the king take and offer up
whatever *seems* good to him. [a]Look,
here are oxen for burnt sacrifice, and
threshing implements and the yokes of
the oxen for wood.
23 "All these, O king, Araunah has
given to the king." And Araunah said

14 [a][Ps. 51:1; 103:8, 13, 14; 119:156; 130:4, 7] [b][Is. 47:6; Zech. 1:15]
15 [a]1 Chr. 21:14
16 [a]Ex. 12:23; 2 Kin. 19:35; Acts 12:23 [b]Gen. 6:6; 1 Sam. 15:11 [1]Or *Angel* [2]*Ornan*, 1 Chr. 21:15 *See WW at 2 Chr. 32:21.
17 [a]2 Sam. 7:8; 1 Chr. 21:17; Ps. 74:1
18 [a]1 Chr. 21:18
21 [a]Gen. 23:8–16 [b]Num. 16:48, 50
22 [a]1 Sam. 6:14; 1 Kin. 19:21
23 [a][Ezek. 20:40, 41]
24 [a]1 Chr. 21:24, 25
25 [a]2 Sam. 21:14 [b]2 Sam. 24:21

to the king, "May the LORD your God
[a]accept you."
24 Then the king said to Araunah, "No, 8
but I will surely buy *it* from you for a
price; nor will I offer burnt offerings
to the LORD my God with that which
costs me nothing." So [a]David bought
the threshing floor and the oxen for
fifty shekels of silver.

KINGDOM DYNAMICS

24:24 Give God Your Best—Then Expect His Best, SEED FAITH. David had sinned; and, as a result, a plague came on the people. To atone for this sin, the Lord told King David to build an altar on the threshing floor of Araunah and offer a burnt offering so that the plague might be stayed. Araunah tried to give David the land, the oxen, and other items to sacrifice. But David insisted on paying Araunah, saying that he could not present to God an offering that cost him nothing.

The very heart of Seed Faith is that unless you experience some sacrifice, you have not truly given. Unless your giving costs you something—something that represents a portion of your very life—then it is not a living gift and will not yield a good harvest. Our giving to the Lord must bear these three qualities.

First, it should be our best. When we give God our best, we are in a position to expect His best back into our lives.

Second, we should give to God first. The very first thought in our minds after we have received something should be how we can give a portion of our harvest to the work of the Lord.

Third, our giving should be generous, freely from our heart and without expecting anything back from the one to whom we give. As Jesus said to His disciples, "Freely you have received, freely give" (Matt. 10:8).

(Gen. 8:22/Ex. 15:26) O.R.

25 And David built there an altar to the
LORD, and offered burnt offerings and
peace offerings. [a]So the LORD heeded
the prayers for the land, and [b]the
plague was withdrawn from Israel.

24:17 Angel who was striking: Literally, the "destroying angel." This was further substantiation of the supernatural nature of the plague. This angel became visible. **Let Your hand, I pray, be against me:** The true penitent is always willing to take responsibility for the effects of his sin. Contrast Saul, who always had a ready alibi.

24:18 The threshing floor of Araunah was on Mt. Moriah, where Abraham offered Isaac (Gen. 22:2), and the location of Solomon's temple (2 Chr. 3:1).

24:24 See section 8 of Truth-In-Action at the end of 2 Sam.

24:24 Fifty shekels of silver: This seems to conflict with 1 Chr. 21:25, which says 600 shekels of gold. The figure in 2 Sam. specifically says that David bought the **threshing floor and the oxen** for 50 shekels of silver. The figure in 1 Chr. is for the entire site.

24:25 David . . . offered burnt offerings and peace offerings: In ch. 23 David functions as a prophet, here as a priest. David combines the three offices of prophet, priest, and king. These were again combined in David's relative, Christ the Messiah, and again combined in the Spirit-filled church, in whose members the Spirit of prophecy resides (Acts 2:14–21) and who are "kings and priests to our God" (Rev. 1:6; 5:10).

TRUTH-IN-ACTION through 2 SAMUEL

Letting the LIFE of the Holy Spirit Bring Faith's Works Alive in You!

Truth 2 Samuel Teaches	Text	**Action** 2 Samuel Invites
1 Guidelines for Growing in Godliness Godliness is living by God's Spirit, in the fear of God, under the eye of God, according to the will of God, with an uninterrupted consciousness of God's indwelling presence. Living this way will keep us from much trouble and tragedy.	14:14 9:1 11:1	**Continually practice forgiveness,** as this imitates the ways of God. **Be careful** to honor past vows and promises you have made. **Be assured** the Lord has heard them. **Be certain** that you are always where God wants you to be or you put yourself in jeopardy.
2 Steps to Dynamic Devotion God highly values His people's devotion in worship. David's humility in worship and Uzzah's presumption, along with Michal's criticism regarding worship, have much to teach us. Worship and praise must be our very highest priority.	22:1—23:7 6:14 6:16, 23	**Learn to praise God** for all victories and spiritual gains. **Understand** that this increases your chances for further victories. **Worship** the Lord with your whole being as an appropriate response to His presence. **Be careful** not to criticize forms of worship unfamiliar to you. To do so may cause future unfruitfulness.
3 Steps to Dealing with Sin The story of David and Bathsheba provides a negative, albeit poignant, object lesson on the importance of avoiding, repenting of, and forsaking sin. Its witness is consistent with the whole counsel of God: Confess and forsake sin quickly or it will prove to be your undoing.	11:3–17 12:5–14	**Confess** known sins. **Do not hide** them. Doing so usually leads to greater sin. **Understand** that continued refusal to deal with sin can lead to serious, even fatal consequences. **Learn** to see sin as God does. **Seek to develop** within yourself a godly hatred for sin.
4 Keys to Relating to Authority Since all authority comes from God (Rom. 13), how we relate to God-ordained and God-appointed authority can reveal much to us about how we, in fact, are relating to God. Whether we submit or rebel will test our true character.	1:11, 12 1:14–16 15:1ff.	**Honor** leadership. **Know** that the fall of any Christian leader is a defeat and shame for the whole church. **Understand** that taking up a cause against any leader is a serious offense. **Know** that God has His ways of dealing with His leaders. **Be diligent in loyalty. Refuse** to cultivate a following from those of another's ministry. **Understand** that doing so promotes disunity and division.
5 Lessons for Leaders Spiritual leadership is a sacred trust. How Christian leaders conduct themselves impacts far more than their own lives. This is why they will be more severely judged (see James 3:1). Also, godly leadership should grow and become stronger through its transmission to subsequent generations.	21:15–22 24:1–17 12:14 6:7	Leaders, **know** that you must eventually delegate a large measure of your authority to those you have raised up into ministry. Leaders, **be careful** not to overvalue the importance of numbers. Leaders, **understand** that sins you persist in can cause God's enemies to show utter contempt to the Lord and His people. Leaders, **regard** ministry as holy. **Do not act** presumptuously in carrying out assigned responsibilities.

Truth 2 Samuel Teaches	Text	**Action** 2 Samuel Invites
6 Keys to Moral Purity One pattern of attack on our moral purity comes through the improper glance that lodges in the mind.	11:2–4	**Guard** your eyes! **Be warned** that a lustful gaze will often lead to lustful thoughts and can result in immoral action.
7 Steps in Developing Humility Humility is a premium spiritual virtue. The humble man is not necessarily self-effacing; rather, he refuses to take credit for accomplishments, knowing that any good in his life has resulted from God's working through him.	15:34 17:14	**Pray** that the Lord will confuse and frustrate the advice of wicked and ungodly counsel. **Trust** that He will thwart them. **Know** that counsel against God's people originates from hell and is part of the Enemy's strategies against you.
8 Keys to Generous Living Sacrificial giving flows out of a godly and generous heart.	24:24	**Follow** David's example. **Learn** to give sacrificially.

The First Book of the KINGS

Author: Unknown, Attributed to Jeremiah
Date: Probably Between 560 B.C. and 538 B.C.
Theme: Lessons from the Dividing of the United Kingdom
Key Words: King, House, Prophet

Author Since 1 and 2 Kings were originally one book (see "Content" below), then this work had to be compiled some time after the capture of Judah by the Babylonians in 586 B.C. (see 2 Kin. 25). The book gives the impression that it is the product of one author and that this author was an eyewitness to the fall of Jerusalem. Though the authorship cannot be known with certainty, several suggestions have been made. Some have nominated Ezra as the compiler, while others point to Isaiah as the editor. Compare 2 Kings 18:19, 20 with Isaiah 36—39. A number of scholars say that the writer of 1 and 2 Kings was an unknown prophet or a Jewish captive in Babylon at about 550 B.C. Because Josephus (a prominent Jewish historian of the first century A.D.) ascribes Kings to "the prophets," many have abandoned the search for a specific author. However, the most probable position is that the prophet Jeremiah was author of 1 and 2 Kings. The early Jewish tradition of the Talmud states that Jeremiah wrote Kings. This famous prophet preached in Jerusalem before and after its fall, and 2 Kings 24 and 25 appear in Jeremiah 39—42; 52. Jeremiah could have written all but the contents of the last appendix (2 Kin. 25:27–30), which were probably added by one of his disciples.

Date Though the precise date for the composition of 1 and 2 Kings is uncertain, it is believed to have come into its final compilation sometime in the late sixth century B.C. The last event recorded in 2 Kings is the release of King Jehoiachin of Judah from imprisonment in Babylon. Since Jehoiachin was imprisoned in 597 B.C. (see 2 Kin. 24:8–17) and released thirty-seven years later (see 2 Kin. 25:27), then Kings must have been written after 560 B.C. to include this information. It is almost certain that the writer of Kings would have mentioned something as significant as the fall of Babylon to Persia in 538 B.C. had he known of these events. Since there is no mention of this prominent event in Kings, it is then concluded that 1 and 2 Kings probably was written before 538 B.C. Therefore the date of 1 and 2 Kings is fixed between 560 and 538 B.C., though the events recorded in 1 Kings occurred some three hundred years earlier.

Background The events covered in 1 Kings span a period of about one hundred and twenty years. First Kings records the turbulent experiences of God's people from the death of David around 971 B.C., to the reign of Jehoshaphat (the fourth king in the southern kingdom of Judah) and the reign of Ahaziah (the ninth king in the northern kingdom of Israel) around 853 B.C. This was a difficult period in the history of God's people, a time of great change and upheaval. There was struggle from within and pressure from without. The result was a dark moment in which the stable kingdom under a strong leader split in two.

Occasion and Purpose Contemplating the horror of the exile of God's people, the author compiles 1 and 2 Kings to answer the looming question of why both the northern kingdom of Israel and the southern kingdom of Judah had been taken captive. He writes with a prophetic message, showing that this punishment by captivity to foreign pagan nations was the inevitable consequence of the persistent violation of God's covenant with them. Kings was written to move the exiles to reflect on their history and return to the Lord. Perhaps this prophetic perspective is one reason why it was included in the "earlier prophets" in the Hebrew Bible.

Content First and 2 Kings were originally one unbroken book, which formed a sequel to 1 and 2 Samuel. The composers of the Greek Old Testament (the Septuagint, or LXX) divided the work into "3 and 4 Kingdoms" (1 and 2 Samuel were "1 and 2 Kingdoms"). The title "Kings" is derived from Jerome's Latin translation (the Vulgate) and is appropriate because of the emphasis of these books on the kings who reigned during this period.

The books of 1 and 2 Kings take up recording the historical events of God's people where the books of 1 and 2 Samuel leave off. However, Kings is more than just a compilation of the politically important or socially significant happenings in Israel and Judah. In fact, it is not as detailed a history as might be expected (four hundred years in only forty-seven chapters). Instead, 1 and 2 Kings is a selective history, one with a theological purpose. Therefore, the author selects and emphasizes the people and events that are morally and religiously significant. First and 2 Kings present God as the Lord of history. From history, these books establish God's providential working in and through the lives of His people for His redemptive purpose. They demonstrate the necessity of obedience to God's covenant and the painful consequence of disobedience. Therefore, the books of 1 and 2 Kings are not to be viewed as mere history, but as theology and lessons from history.

The united work of 1 and 2 Kings naturally divides into three main sections. The "Unified Kingdom" under Solomon in 1 Kings 1—11; the "Divided Kingdom" in 1 Kings 12—2 Kings 17; and finally, 2 Kings 18—25 focuses on the surviving "Kingdom of Judah."

The first half of 1 Kings records the glory of Solomon's reign, his wealth, wisdom, and the monumental accomplishment of the building of the temple. However, his disobedience in marrying foreign wives led him into idolatry; and the stage was set for the division of the kingdom. The king with a divided heart would leave behind a divided kingdom. On his death, those in the northern part of the empire rebelled and established their own nation, known as Israel. In the south, those who remained faithful to the house of David and Solomon formed the nation known as Judah.

In the second half of 1 Kings, which describes the divided kingdom, the narrative is difficult to follow. The author switches back and forth between the northern kingdom of Israel and the southern kingdom of Judah, tracing their histories simultaneously. There were nineteen regents in Israel, all of them bad. In Judah, there were twenty rulers, only eight of them good. First Kings records the first nine rulers in Israel and the first four kings in Judah. Some of these thirteen regents are only mentioned in a few verses, while whole chapters are devoted to others. Major attention is directed to those who either serve as a model of uprightness, or to those who illustrate why these nations eventually collapsed. When 1 Kings closes, Jehoshaphat is the king in Judah, and Ahaziah is on the throne in Israel.

Personal Application The message of 1 and 2 Kings is as relevant today as when it was written. God still controls human affairs. The nation, leader, or person who responds to and obeys the Lord will enjoy the benefits of a relationship with Him. Those who refuse and rebel will experience God's discipline. Though people are sinful, God is the author of redemption, and He graciously forgives those who will repent and return to Him.

Christ Revealed The failure of the prophets, priests, and kings of God's people points to the necessity of the advent of Christ. Christ Himself would be the ideal combination of these three offices. As a Prophet, Christ's word far surpasses that of the great prophet Elijah (Matt. 17:1–5). Many of the miracles of Jesus were reminiscent of the wonders God did through Elijah and Elisha in Kings. In addition, Christ is a Priest superior to any of those recorded in Kings (Heb. 7:22–27). First Kings vividly illustrates the need for Christ as our reigning King. When asked if He was King of the Jews, Jesus affirmed that He was (Matt. 27:11). However, Christ is a King "greater than Solomon" (Matt. 12:42). The name "Solomon" means "Peace"; Christ is the "Prince of Peace," and there will be no end to His peace (Is. 9:6). Solomon was noted for his wisdom, but Christ is the "wisdom of God" (1 Cor. 1:25, 29). Solomon's reign was temporary, but Christ will reign on the throne of David forever (1 Chr. 17:14; Is. 9:6), for He is "KING OF KINGS AND LORD OF LORDS" (Rev. 19:16). For a further study of allusions to Christ during the time of 1 Kings, read Introduction to 1 Chronicles: Christ Revealed and Introduction to 2 Chronicles: Christ Revealed.

The Holy Spirit at Work First Kings 18:12 is the only direct reference to the Holy Spirit in 1 Kings, where He is called the "Spirit of the LORD." The words of Obadiah there indicate that the Holy Spirit sometimes transported Elijah from one location to another (see also 2 Kin. 2:16). This is not unlike Acts 8:39, 40, where Philip is described as having a similar experience.

There is an allusion in 18:46 ("the hand of the LORD") to the Holy Spirit's work of enabling Elijah to do the miraculous. The formula "hand of the LORD" referred to the inspiration of the prophets by the Spirit of God (see 2 Kin. 3:15 and Ezek. 1:3; compare with 1 Sam. 10:6, 10 and 19:20, 23). Here "the hand of the LORD" refers to the Spirit of God who endowed Elijah with supernatural strength to do an amazing feat (for similar examples, see Judg. 14:6, 19; and 15:14).

In addition to these passages, 1 Kings 22:24 (see 1 Chr. 18:23) may be another reference to the Holy Spirit. This verse refers to a "spirit from the LORD" (see note on 22:24) and may indicate that the prophets understood that their ability to prophesy came by the Spirit of God (see 1 Sam. 10:6, 10; 19:20, 23). If this interpretation is taken, then it would correlate with 1 Corinthians 12:7–11, which confirms that the ability to prophesy is indeed a manifestation of the Holy Spirit.

For more on the Holy Spirit in the kingdom period, read Introduction to 2 Kings: The Holy Spirit at Work and Introduction to 2 Chronicles: The Holy Spirit at Work.

Outline of 1 Kings

- **I. The kingdom united 1:1—11:43**
  - A. The establishment of Solomon as king 1:1—2:46
  - B. The elevation of Solomon as king 3:1—8:66
  - C. The error of Solomon as king 9:1—11:43
- **II. The kingdom divided 12:1—22:53**
  - A. The revolt and reign of Jeroboam in Israel 12:1—14:20
  - B. The reign of Rehoboam in Judah 14:21–31
  - C. The reign of Abijam in Judah 15:1–8
  - D. The reign of Asa in Judah 15:9–24
  - E. The reign of Nadab in Israel 15:25–32
  - F. The reign of Baasha in Israel 15:33—16:7
  - G. The reign of Elah in Israel 16:8–14
  - H. The reign of Zimri in Israel 16:15–20
  - I. The reign of Omri in Israel 16:21–28
  - J. The reign of Ahab in Israel 16:29—22:40
  - K. The reign of Jehoshaphat in Judah 22:41–50
  - L. The reign of Ahaziah in Israel 22:51–53

Adonijah Presumes to Be King

NOW King David was [a]old,
[1]advanced in years; and they put
covers on him, but he could not get
warm.
2 Therefore his servants said to him,
"Let a young woman, a virgin, be
sought for our lord the king, and let
her [1]stand before the king, and let her
care for him; and let her lie in your
bosom, that our lord the king may be
warm."
3 So they sought for a lovely young
woman throughout all the territory of
Israel, and found [a]Abishag the [b]Shu-
nammite, and brought her to the king.
4 The young woman *was* very lovely;
and she cared for the king, and served
him; but the king did not know her.
5 Then [a]Adonijah the [1]son of Haggith 3
exalted himself, saying, "I will [2]be
king"; and [b]he prepared for himself
chariots and horsemen, and fifty men
to run before him.
6 (And his father had not [1]rebuked
him at any time by saying, "Why have
you done so?" He *was* also very good-
looking. [a]*His mother* had borne him after Absalom.)
7 Then he conferred with [a]Joab the
son of Zeruiah and with [b]Abiathar the
priest, and [c]they followed and helped
Adonijah.
8 But [a]Zadok the priest, [b]Benaiah the
son of Jehoiada, [c]Nathan the prophet,

CHAPTER 1

1 [a]1 Chr. 23:1 [1]Seventy years
2 [1]Or *serve*
3 [a]1 Kin. 2:17 [b]Josh. 19:18; 1 Sam. 28:4
5 [a]2 Sam. 3:4 [b]2 Sam. 15:1 [1]The fourth son [2]Lit. *reign*
6 [a]2 Sam. 3:3, 4; 1 Chr. 3:2 [1]Lit. *pained*
7 [a]1 Chr. 11:6 [b]2 Sam. 20:25 [c]1 Kin. 2:22, 28
8 [a]1 Kin. 2:35 [b]1 Kin. 2:25; 2 Sam. 8:18 [c]2 Sam. 12:1

1:4 Did not know her: David did not have sexual relations with her.

1:5 See section 3 of Truth-In-Action at the end of 1 Kin.

1:5 Adonijah . . . exalted himself: Even though Adonijah (the fourth son of David) was probably the oldest surviving son (compare 2 Sam. 3:2–4 with 2 Sam. 13:28; 18:15), there was no fixed pattern of succession. David had the right to appoint his own successor, and the kingdom had clearly been promised to Solomon (1 Chr. 22:9, 10; 28:4–7). In spite of this, Adonijah selfishly exalted himself in an attempt to bypass the Lord's will and David's choice. Therefore, Adonijah's statement **"I will be king"** does not mean that he would be king, just that he wanted the throne. However, as Adonijah discovered, it is futile to attempt to overrule God's providence. See note on 2:15.

1:7 In his rebellion, Adonijah is assisted by **Joab** (the general, and nephew of David) and **Abiathar the priest.** Abiathar was a descendant of Aaron through Ithamar (1 Chr. 24:3) and of the line of Eli (1 Sam. 2:31, 33). He was not loyal to David, and would be removed by Solomon (2:26, 27).

1:8 In contrast to Joab and Abiathar (v. 7), **Zadok the priest,**

[d]Shimei, Rei, and [e]the mighty men
who *belonged* to David were not with
Adonijah.
9 And Adonijah sacrificed sheep and
oxen and fattened cattle by the stone
of [1]Zoheleth, which *is* by [a]En Rogel;[2]
he also invited all his brothers, the
king's sons, and all the men of Judah,
the king's servants.
10 But he did not invite Nathan the
prophet, Benaiah, the mighty men, or
[a]Solomon his brother.
11 So Nathan spoke to Bathsheba the
mother of Solomon, saying, "Have you
not heard that Adonijah the son of
[a]Haggith has become king, and David
our lord does not know *it?*
12 "Come, please, let me now give you
*advice, that you may save your own
life and the life of your son Solomon.
13 "Go immediately to King David and
say to him, 'Did you not, my lord, O
king, swear to your maidservant, saying, [a]"Assuredly your son Solomon
shall reign after me, and he shall sit
on my throne"? Why then has Adonijah become king?'
14 "Then, while you are still talking
there with the king, I also will come
in after you and confirm your words."
15 So Bathsheba went into the chamber to the king. (Now the king was very
old, and Abishag the Shunammite was
serving the king.)
16 And Bathsheba bowed and did
homage to the king. Then the king said,
"What is your wish?"
17 Then she said to him, "My lord,
[a]you swore by the LORD your God to
your maidservant, *saying,* 'Assuredly
Solomon your son shall reign after me,
and he shall sit on my throne.'
18 "So now, look! Adonijah has become king; and now, my lord the king,
you do not know about *it.*
19 [a]"He has sacrificed oxen and fattened cattle and sheep in abundance,
and has invited all the sons of the king,
Abiathar the priest, and Joab the commander of the army; but Solomon your
servant he has not invited.
20 "And as for you, my lord, O king,
the eyes of all Israel *are* on you, that
you should tell them who will sit on
the throne of my lord the king after
him.
21 "Otherwise it will happen, when my
lord the king [a]rests with his fathers,
that I and my son Solomon will be
counted as offenders."
22 And just then, while she was still
talking with the king, Nathan the
prophet also came in.
23 So they told the king, saying, "Here
is Nathan the prophet." And when he
came in before the king, he bowed
down before the king with his face to
the ground.
24 And Nathan said, "My lord, O king,
have you said, 'Adonijah shall reign after me, and he shall sit on my throne'?
25 [a]"For he has gone down today, and
has sacrificed oxen and fattened cattle
and sheep in abundance, and has invited all the king's sons, and the commanders of the army, and Abiathar the
priest; and look! They are eating and
drinking before him; and they say,
[b]'*Long*[1] live King Adonijah!'
26 "But he has not invited me—me
your servant—nor Zadok the priest,
nor Benaiah the son of Jehoiada, nor
your servant Solomon.
27 "Has this thing been done by my
lord the king, and you have not told
your servant who should sit on the
throne of my lord the king after him?"

David Proclaims Solomon King

28 Then King David answered and
said, "Call Bathsheba to me." So she
came into the king's presence and
stood before the king.
29 And the king took an oath and said, 1
[a]"*As* the LORD lives, who has redeemed 3
my *life from every distress,
30 [a]"just as I swore to you by the LORD
God of Israel, saying, 'Assuredly Solomon your son shall be king after me,
and he shall sit on my throne in my
place,' so I certainly will do this day."

8 [d]1 Kin. 4:18 [e]2 Sam. 23:8
9 [a]Josh. 15:7; 18:16; 2 Sam. 17:17 [1]Lit. *Serpent* [2]A spring south of Jerusalem in the Kidron Valley
10 [a]2 Sam. 12:24
11 [a]2 Sam. 3:4
12 *See WW at Zech. 6:13.
13 [a]1 Kin. 1:30; 1 Chr. 22:9–13
17 [a]1 Kin. 1:13, 30
19 [a]1 Kin. 1:7–9, 25
21 [a]Deut. 31:16; 2 Sam. 7:12; 1 Kin. 2:10
25 [a]1 Kin. 1:9, 19 [b]1 Sam. 10:24 [1]Lit. *Let King Adonijah live*
29 [a]2 Sam. 4:9; 12:5 *See WW at Prov. 10:3.
30 [a]1 Kin. 1:13, 17

Benaiah (a military leader), and **Nathan the prophet** remain loyal to David and will anoint Solomon as king (v. 45). Zadok was a descendant of Aaron through Eleazar (1 Chr. 6:4–8, 50–52; 24:1–3), and would replace Abiathar (2:35). After Benaiah executed Adonijah (2:25) and Joab (2:26–34), he became Solomon's general (2:35).

1:9 In hope that he may usurp the throne, Adonijah seeks to gain support by holding a victory celebration at **En Rogel,** a spring south of Jerusalem in the Kidron Valley.

1:11–14 Since Adonijah had not officially been anointed or proclaimed king, Nathan's words **Adonijah . . . has become king** (vv. 11, 13) imply that Adonijah is gaining support and may take the throne (v. 25; 2:15) if something is not done to stop him.

1:29 See sections 1 and 3 of Truth-In-Action at the end of 1 Kin.

1:29 David's words are very representative of his language in the Psalms. God had allowed something redemptive to come out of David's failure with Bathsheba. God is a redeemer in every generation.

1:29–36 David adheres to his promise and enlists **Zadok the priest, Nathan the prophet,** and **Benaiah,** the captain of the guard, to anoint Solomon.

31 Then Bathsheba bowed with *her*
face to the earth, and paid homage to
the king, and said, [a]"Let my lord King
David live forever!"
32 And King David said, "Call to me
Zadok the priest, Nathan the prophet,
and Benaiah the son of Jehoiada." So
they came before the king.
33 The king also said to them, [a]"Take
with you the servants of your lord, and
have Solomon my son ride on my own
[b]mule, and take him down to [c]Gihon.[1]
34 "There let Zadok the priest and Nathan the prophet [a]anoint him king over
Israel; and [b]blow* the horn, and say,
[1]'*Long* live King Solomon!'
35 "Then you shall come up after him,
and he shall come and sit on my
throne, and he shall be king in my
place. For I have appointed him to be
ruler over Israel and Judah."
36 Benaiah the son of Jehoiada answered the king and said, [a]"Amen!
May the LORD God of my lord the king
say so *too*.
37 [a]"As the LORD has been with my
lord the king, even so may He be with
Solomon, and [b]make his throne
greater than the throne of my lord King
David."
38 So Zadok the priest, Nathan the
prophet, [a]Benaiah the son of Jehoiada,
the [b]Cherethites, and the Pelethites
went down and had Solomon ride on
King David's mule, and took him to Gihon.
39 Then Zadok the priest took a *horn
of [a]oil from the tabernacle and
[b]anointed Solomon. And they blew the
horn, [c]and all the people said, [1]"*Long*
live King Solomon!"
40 And all the people went up after
him; and the people played the flutes
and rejoiced with great joy, so that the
earth *seemed to* split with their sound.
41 Now Adonijah and all the guests
who *were* with him heard *it* as they
finished eating. And when Joab heard
the sound of the horn, he said, "Why
is the city in such a noisy uproar?"
42 While he was still speaking, there
came [a]Jonathan, the son of Abiathar
the priest. And Adonijah said to him,
"Come in, for [b]you *are* a prominent
man, and bring good news."
43 Then Jonathan answered and said
to Adonijah, "No! Our lord King David
has made Solomon king.
44 "The king has sent with him Zadok
the priest, Nathan the prophet, Benaiah the son of Jehoiada, the Cherethites, and the Pelethites; and they have
made him ride on the king's mule.
45 "So Zadok the priest and Nathan
the prophet have anointed him king at
Gihon; and they have gone up from
there rejoicing, so that the city is in an
uproar. This *is* the noise that you have
heard.
46 "Also Solomon [a]sits on the throne
of the kingdom.
47 "And moreover the king's servants
have gone to bless our lord King David,
saying, [a]'May God make the name of
Solomon better than your name, and
may He make his throne greater than
your throne.' [b]Then the king bowed
himself on the bed.
48 "Also the king said thus, 'Blessed
be the LORD God of Israel, who has
[a]given *one* to sit on my throne this day,
while my eyes see [b]*it!*' "
49 So all the guests who were with Adonijah were afraid, and arose, and each
one went his way.
50 Now Adonijah was afraid of Solomon; so he arose, and went and
[a]took hold of the horns of the altar.
51 And it was told Solomon, saying,
"Indeed Adonijah is afraid of King Solomon; for look, he has taken hold of
the horns of the altar, saying, 'Let King
Solomon swear to me today that he
will not put his servant to death with
the sword.' "
52 Then Solomon said, "If he proves
himself a worthy man, [a]not one hair
of him shall fall to the earth; but if
wickedness is found in him, he shall
die."
53 So King Solomon sent them to bring
him down from the altar. And he came
and fell down before King Solomon;
and Solomon said to him, "Go to your
house."

David's Instructions to Solomon

2 Now [a]the days of David drew near
that he should die, and he [1]charged
Solomon his son, saying:
2 [a]"I go the way of all the earth;

31 [a]Neh. 2:3; Dan. 2:4; 3:9
33 [a]2 Sam. 20:6 [b]Esth. 6:8 [c]2 Chr. 32:30; 33:14 [1]A spring east of Jerusalem in the Kidron Valley
34 [a]1 Sam. 10:1; 16:3, 12; 2 Sam. 2:4; 5:3; 1 Kin. 19:16; 2 Kin. 9:3; 11:12; 1 Chr. 29:22 [b]2 Sam. 15:10; 2 Kin. 9:13; 11:14 [1]Lit. *Let King Solomon live* *See WW at Ps. 47:1.
36 [a]Jer. 28:6
37 [a]Josh. 1:5, 17; 1 Sam. 20:13 [b]1 Kin. 1:47
38 [a]2 Sam. 8:18; 23:20–23 [b]2 Sam. 20:7; 1 Chr. 18:17
39 [a]Ex. 30:23, 25, 32; Ps. 89:20 [b]1 Chr. 29:22 [c]1 Sam. 10:24 [1]Lit. *Let King Solomon live* *See WW at Ezek. 29:21.
42 [a]2 Sam. 17:17, 20 [b]2 Sam. 18:27
46 [a]1 Kin. 2:12; 1 Chr. 29:23
47 [a]1 Kin. 1:37 [b]Gen. 47:31
48 [a]1 Kin. 3:6; [Ps. 132:11, 12] [b]2 Sam. 7:12
50 [a]Ex. 27:2; 30:10; 1 Kin. 2:28
52 [a]1 Sam. 14:45; 2 Sam. 14:11; Acts 27:34

CHAPTER 2

1 [a]Gen. 47:29; Deut. 31:14 [1]*commanded*
2 [a]Josh. 23:14

1:38 Cherethites . . . Pelethites: These are personal bodyguards that David chose from foreign mercenary troops (2 Sam. 8:18; 15:18; 20:7, 23; 23:22, 23; 1 Chr. 18:17), and Benaiah was their leader.

1:46 Solomon served as coregent with David for a period of time.

1:47 Bowed himself on the bed: He praised God while in bed.

1:50 Took hold of the horns of the altar: This ancient custom symbolized the seeking of sanctuary from execution.

2:2 Go the way of all the earth: David knew that he was going to die soon.

[b]be strong, therefore, and prove yourself a man.
[1] 3 "And keep the charge of the LORD
your God: to walk in His ways, to keep
His statutes, His *commandments, His
judgments, and His testimonies, as it
is written in the Law of Moses, that you
may [a]prosper in all that you do and
wherever you turn;
4 "that the LORD may [a]fulfill His word
which He spoke concerning me, saying, [b]'If your sons take heed to their
way, to [c]walk before Me in truth with
all their heart and with all their soul,'
He said, [d]'you shall not lack a man on
the throne of Israel.'
5 "Moreover you know also what
Joab the son of Zeruiah [a]did to me, *and*
what he did to the two commanders
of the armies of Israel, to [b]Abner the
son of Ner and [c]Amasa the son of Jether, whom he killed. And he shed the
blood of war in peacetime, and put the
blood of war on his belt that *was*
around his waist, and on his sandals
that *were* on his feet.
6 "Therefore do [a]according to your
wisdom, and do not let his gray hair
go down to the grave in peace.
7 "But show kindness to the sons of
[a]Barzillai the Gileadite, and let them
be among those who [b]eat at your table,
for so [c]they came to me when I fled
from Absalom your brother.
8 "And see, *you have* with you
[a]Shimei the son of Gera, a Benjamite
from Bahurim, who *cursed me with a
malicious curse in the day when I went
to Mahanaim. But [b]he came down to
meet me at the Jordan, and [c]I swore
to him by the LORD, saying, 'I will not
put you to death with the sword.'
9 "Now therefore, [a]do not hold him
*guiltless, for you *are* a wise man and
know what you ought to do to him; but
[b]bring his gray hair down to the grave
with blood."

Death of David

10 So [a]David [1]rested with his fathers,
and was buried in [b]the City of David.

2 [b]Deut. 31:7, 23; 1 Chr. 22:13
3 [a][Deut. 29:9; Josh. 1:7]; 1 Chr. 22:12, 13 *See WW at Ps. 119:35.
4 [a]2 Sam. 7:25 [b][Ps. 132:12] [c]2 Kin. 20:3 [d]2 Sam. 7:12, 13; 1 Kin. 8:25
5 [a]2 Sam. 3:39; 18:5, 12, 14 [b]2 Sam. 3:27; 1 Kin. 2:32 [c]2 Sam. 20:10
6 [a]1 Kin. 2:9; Prov. 20:26
7 [a]2 Sam. 19:31–39 [b]2 Sam. 9:7, 10; 19:28 [c]2 Sam. 17:17–29
8 [a]2 Sam. 16:5–13 [b]2 Sam. 19:18 [c]2 Sam. 19:23 *See WW at Jer. 8:11.
9 [a]Ex. 20:7; Job 9:28 [b]Gen. 42:38; 44:31 *See WW at Num. 14:18.
10 [a]1 Kin. 1:21; Acts 2:29; 13:36 [b]2 Sam. 5:7; 1 Kin. 3:1 [1]Died and joined his ancestors
11 [a]2 Sam. 5:4, 5; 1 Chr. 3:4; 29:26, 27 *See WW at 2 Sam. 8:15.
12 [a]1 Kin. 1:46; 1 Chr. 29:23 [b]1 Kin. 2:46; 2 Chr. 1:1
13 [a]1 Sam. 16:4, 5
15 [a]1 Kin. 1:11, 18 [b]1 Chr. 22:9, 10; 28:5–7; [Dan. 2:21]
16 [1]Lit. *turn away the face*
17 [a]1 Kin. 1:3, 4
19 [a][Ex. 20:12] [b]Ps. 45:9
20 [1]Lit. *turn away the face*
22 [a]1 Kin. 1:6; 2:15; 1 Chr. 3:2, 5

11 The period that David [a]reigned*
over Israel *was* forty years; seven
years he reigned in Hebron, and in Jerusalem he reigned thirty-three years.
12 [a]Then Solomon sat on the throne
of his father David; and his kingdom
was [b]firmly established.

Solomon Executes Adonijah

13 Now Adonijah the son of Haggith
came to Bathsheba the mother of Solomon. So she said, [a]"Do you come
peaceably?" And he said, "Peaceably."
14 Moreover he said, "I have something *to say* to you." And she said,
"Say it."
15 Then he said, "You know that the
kingdom was [a]mine, and all Israel had
set their expectations on me, that I
should reign. However, the kingdom
has been turned over, and has become
my brother's; for [b]it was his from the
LORD.
16 "Now I ask one petition of you; do
not [1]deny me." And she said to him,
"Say it."
17 Then he said, "Please speak to King
Solomon, for he will not refuse you,
that he may give me [a]Abishag the Shunammite as wife."
18 So Bathsheba said, "Very well, I
will speak for you to the king."
19 Bathsheba therefore went to King
Solomon, to speak to him for Adonijah.
And the king rose up to meet her and
[a]bowed down to her, and sat down on
his throne and had a throne set for the
king's mother; [b]so she sat at his right
hand.
20 Then she said, "I desire one small
petition of you; do not [1]refuse me."
And the king said to her, "Ask it, my
mother, for I will not refuse you."
21 So she said, "Let Abishag the Shunammite be given to Adonijah your
brother as wife."
22 And King Solomon answered and
said to his mother, "Now why do you
ask Abishag the Shunammite for Adonijah? Ask for him the kingdom also—
for he *is* my [a]older brother—for him,

2:3, 4 Success in the economy of God is always contingent on obedience to His Word.

2:3 See section 1 of Truth-In-Action at the end of 1 Kin.

2:13–25 **Adonijah**'s request to marry **Abishag** appears on the surface to be innocent, since she was a virgin (1:4; Deut. 22:30). However, Abishag was a member of David's harem, which was considered his royal property and was to be passed on to his successor (2 Sam. 3:7; 12:8; 16:21). Adonijah had not given up the hope that he would be king, and this was a clever maneuver to take the throne. **Solomon** wisely realized the implications (v. 22), and he promptly had Adonijah put to death.

2:15 Adonijah's words **the kingdom was mine** do not mean that he had become king, for he had never been officially crowned. He had gained the allegiance of Joab and Abiathar (1:7), and might have possessed the throne if he had gone unchecked (1:11). "The kingdom was mine" means Adonijah felt the kingdom was within his reach. Yet it was never really within reach, because God had chosen Solomon (1 Chr. 22:9, 10). Adonijah acknowledges this when he confesses that **the kingdom has become my brother's; for it was his from the LORD.** No man can overrule what God has determined to do.

and for [b]Abiathar the priest, and for Joab the son of Zeruiah."
23 Then King Solomon swore by the LORD, saying, [a]"May God do so to me, and more also, if Adonijah has not spoken this word against his own life!
24 "Now therefore, *as* the LORD lives, who has confirmed me and set me on the throne of David my father, and who has established a [1]house for me, as He [a]promised, Adonijah shall be put to death today!"
25 So King Solomon sent by the hand of [a]Benaiah the son of Jehoiada; and he struck him down, and he died.

Abiathar Exiled, Joab Executed

26 And to Abiathar the priest the king said, "Go to [a]Anathoth, to your own fields, for [1]you *are* deserving of death; but I will not put you to death at this time, [b]because you carried the ark of the Lord GOD before my father David, and because you were afflicted every time my father was afflicted."
27 So Solomon removed Abiathar from being priest to the LORD, that he might [a]fulfill the word of the LORD which He spoke concerning the house of Eli at *Shiloh.
28 Then news came to Joab, for Joab [a]had defected to Adonijah, though he had not defected to Absalom. So Joab fled to the tabernacle of the LORD, and [b]took hold of the horns of the altar.
29 And King Solomon was told, "Joab has fled to the tabernacle of the LORD; there *he is,* by the altar." Then Solomon sent Benaiah the son of Jehoiada, saying, "Go, [a]strike him down."
30 So Benaiah went to the tabernacle of the LORD, and said to him, "Thus says the king, [a]'Come out!' " And he said, "No, but I will die here." And Benaiah brought back word to the king, saying, "Thus said Joab, and thus he answered me."
31 Then the king said to him, [a]"Do as he has said, and strike him down and bury him, [b]that you may take away from me and from the house of my father the innocent blood which Joab shed.
32 "So the LORD [a]will return his [1]blood on his head, because he struck down two men more righteous [b]and better than he, and killed them with the sword—[c]Abner the son of Ner, the commander of the army of Israel, and [d]Amasa the son of Jether, the commander of the army of Judah—though my father David did not know *it.*
33 "Their blood shall therefore return upon the head of Joab and [a]upon the head of his descendants forever. [b]But upon David and his descendants, upon his house and his throne, there shall be peace forever from the LORD."
34 So Benaiah the son of Jehoiada went up and struck and killed him; and he was buried in his own house in the wilderness.
35 The king put Benaiah the son of Jehoiada in his place over the army, and the king put [a]Zadok the priest in the place of [b]Abiathar.

Shimei Executed

36 Then the king sent and called for [a]Shimei, and said to him, "Build yourself a house in Jerusalem and dwell there, and do not go out from there anywhere.
37 "For it shall be, on the day you go out and cross [a]the Brook Kidron, know for certain you shall surely die; [b]your [1]blood shall be on your own head."
38 And Shimei said to the king, "The saying *is* good. As my lord the king has said, so your servant will do." So Shimei dwelt in Jerusalem many days.
39 Now it happened at the end of three years, that two slaves of Shimei ran away to [a]Achish the son of Maachah, king of Gath. And they told Shimei, saying, "Look, your slaves *are* in Gath!"
40 So Shimei arose, saddled his donkey, and went to Achish at Gath to seek his slaves. And Shimei went and brought his slaves from Gath.
41 And Solomon was told that Shimei had gone from Jerusalem to Gath and had come back.
42 Then the king sent and called for Shimei, and said to him, "Did I not

22 [b]1 Kin. 1:7
23 [a]Ruth 1:17
24 [a]2 Sam. 7:11, 13; 1 Chr. 22:10 [1]Royal dynasty
25 [a]2 Sam. 8:18; 1 Kin. 4:4
26 [a]Josh. 21:18; Jer. 1:1 [b]1 Sam. 22:23; 23:6; 2 Sam. 15:14, 29 [1]Lit. *you are a man of death*
27 [a]1 Sam. 2:31–35 *See WW at Gen. 49:10.
28 [a]1 Kin. 1:7 [b]1 Kin. 1:50
29 [a]1 Kin. 2:5, 6
30 [a][Ex. 21:14]
31 [a][Ex. 21:14] [b][Num. 35:33; Deut. 19:13; 21:8, 9]
32 [a][Gen. 9:6]; Judg. 9:24, 57 [b]2 Chr. 21:13, 14 [c]2 Sam. 3:27 [d]2 Sam. 20:9, 10 [1]Or *bloodshed*
33 [a]2 Sam. 3:29 [b][Prov. 25:5]
35 [a]1 Sam. 2:35; 1 Kin. 4:4; 1 Chr. 6:53; 24:3; 29:22 [b]1 Kin. 2:27
36 [a]2 Sam. 16:5–13; 1 Kin. 2:8
37 [a]2 Sam. 15:23; 2 Kin. 23:6; John 18:1 [b]Lev. 20:9; Josh. 2:19; 2 Sam. 1:16; Ezek. 18:13 [1]Or *bloodshed*
39 [a]1 Sam. 27:2

2:27 Solomon's action was a fulfillment of God's prophetic word that the priestly line of **Eli,** of which **Abiathar** was a member, would terminate (1 Sam. 2:30–36).
2:28 See note on 1:50.
2:35 **Benaiah** and **Zadok** are here officially installed in the offices they unofficially occupied during the coregency. The descendants of Zadok were henceforth regarded as the priestly line.
2:36 **Shimei** was a descendant of King Saul (v. 8; 2 Sam. 16:5) and was resentful because David had taken the throne from Saul's family. He had insulted David during the revolt of Absalom (2 Sam. 16:5–13). When David regained control, Shimei recanted to save his life, since what he had done amounted to treason (2 Sam. 19:18–23). David allowed him to live even though Shimei's repentance was apparently insincere (v. 9). Therefore, in light of David's instruction (v. 9), Solomon confined Shimei to the city of Jerusalem. Shimei was executed when he violated this command.

THE KINGS AND PROPHETS OF ISRAEL AND JUDAH

The United Kingdom

Saul 1050–1010 B.C.
David 1010–970 B.C.
Solomon 970–930 B.C.

The Divided Kingdom

Judah Kings		Judah Prophets	B.C.	Israel Kings		Israel Prophets
			950			
Rehoboam	930–913			Jeroboam I	930–909	
			925			
Abijah	913–910					
Asa	910–869			Nadab	909–908	
				Baasha	908–886	
			900	Elah	886–885	
				Zimri	885	
				Tibni	885–880	
				Omri	885–874	
Jehoshaphat	872–848		875			
				Ahab	874–853	
				Ahaziah	853–852	
				Joram	852–841	
Jehoram	848–841		850	Jehu	841–814	
Ahaziah	841					
Athaliah	841–835	Joel				
Joash	835–796					
			825			
				Jehoahaz	814–798	
Amaziah	796–767		800	Jehoash	798–782	
Azariah	792–740			Jeroboam II	793–753	
			775			
						Amos
						Jonah
Jotham	750–735	Hosea	750	Zechariah	753	
		Isaiah		Shallum	752	
Ahaz	735–715	Micah		Menahem	752–742	
				Pekahiah	742–740	
			725	Pekah	752–732	
Hezekiah	715–686			Hoshea	732–722	

Judah: Kings		Judah: Prophets	B.C.	Israel: Kings	Israel: Prophets
Manasseh	697–642		700		
			675		
			650		
Amon	642–640	Nahum			
Josiah	640–609	Zephaniah			
			625		
Jehoahaz	609	Habakkuk			
Jehoiakim	609–598	Jeremiah	600		
Jehoiachin	598–597	Daniel			
Zedekiah	597–586	Ezekiel			
		Obadiah			
			575		
			550		
		Haggai	525		
		Zechariah			
			500		
			475		
		Malachi	450		
			425		
			400		

make you swear by the LORD, and warn
you, saying, 'Know for certain that on
the day you go out and travel anywhere, you shall surely die'? And you
said to me, 'The word I have heard *is*
good.'
43 "Why then have you not kept the
oath of the LORD and the commandment that I gave you?"
44 The king said moreover to Shimei,
"You know, as your heart acknowledges, [a]all the wickedness that you did
to my father David; therefore the LORD
will [b]return your wickedness on your
own head.
45 "But King Solomon *shall be*
blessed, and [a]the throne of David shall
be established before the LORD forever."
46 So the king commanded Benaiah
the son of Jehoiada; and he went out
and struck him down, and he died.
Thus the [a]kingdom was established in
the hand of Solomon.

Solomon Requests Wisdom

3 Now [a]Solomon made [1]a treaty with
Pharaoh king of Egypt, and married Pharaoh's daughter; then he
brought her [b]to the City of David until
he had finished building his [c]own
house, and [d]the house of the LORD, and
[e]the wall all around Jerusalem.
2 [a]Meanwhile the people sacrificed at
the high places, because there was no
house built for the name of the LORD
until those days.
2 3 And Solomon [a]loved the LORD,
[b]walking in the statutes of his father
David, except that he sacrificed and
burned incense at the high places.
4 Now [a]the king went to Gibeon to
sacrifice there, [b]for that *was* the great
high place: Solomon offered a thousand burnt offerings on that altar.
5 [a]At Gibeon the LORD appeared to
Solomon [b]in a *dream by night; and
God said, "Ask! What shall I give
you?"
6 [a]And Solomon said: "You have
shown great mercy to Your servant
David my father, because he [b]walked
before You in truth, in righteousness,
and in uprightness of heart with You;
You have continued this great kindness for him, and You [c]have given him
a son to sit on his throne, as *it is* this
day.
7 "Now, O LORD my God, You have 4
made Your servant king instead of my
father David, but I *am* a [a]little child; I
do not know *how* [b]to go out or come
in.
8 "And Your servant *is* in the midst
of Your people whom You [a]have chosen, a great people, [b]too numerous to
be numbered or counted.
9 [a]"Therefore give to Your servant an
[1]understanding heart [b]to judge Your
people, that I may [c]discern between
good and evil. For who is able to judge
this great people of Yours?"
10 The speech pleased the LORD, that
Solomon had asked this thing.
11 Then God said to him: "Because
you have asked this thing, and have
[a]not asked long life for yourself, nor
have asked riches for yourself, nor
have asked the life of your enemies,
but have asked for yourself understanding to discern justice,
12 [a]"behold, I have done according to
your words; [b]see, I have given you a
wise and understanding heart, so that
there has not been anyone like you before you, nor shall any like you arise
after you.
13 "And I have also [a]given you what
you have not asked: both [b]riches and
honor, so that there shall not be anyone like you among the kings all your
days.
14 "So [a]if you walk in My ways, to
keep My *statutes and My commandments, [b]as your father David walked,
then I will [c]lengthen[1] your days."

44 [a]2 Sam. 16:5–13 [b]1 Sam. 25:39
45 [a][Prov. 25:5]
46 [a]2 Chr. 1:1

CHAPTER 3

1 [a]1 Kin. 7:8; 9:24 [b]2 Sam. 5:7 [c]1 Kin. 7:1 [d]1 Kin. 6 [e]1 Kin. 9:15, 19 [1]*an alliance*
2 [a][Deut. 12:2–5, 13, 14]
3 [a][Rom. 8:28] [b][1 Kin. 3:6, 14]
4 [a]2 Chr. 1:3 [b]1 Chr. 16:39; 21:29
5 [a]1 Kin. 9:2; 11:9 [b]Num. 12:6 *See WW at Joel 2:28.
6 [a]2 Chr. 1:8 [b]1 Kin. 2:4; 9:4 [c]1 Kin. 1:48
7 [a]Jer. 1:6, 7 [b]Num. 27:17
8 [a][Deut. 7:6] [b]Gen. 13:6; 15:5; 22:17
9 [a]2 Chr. 1:10 [b]Ps. 72:1, 2 [c][Heb. 5:14] [1]Lit. *hearing*
11 [a][James 4:3]
12 [a][1 John 5:14, 15] [b]Eccl. 1:16
13 [a][Matt. 6:33] [b]1 Kin. 4:21, 24; 10:23
14 [a][1 Kin. 6:12] [b]1 Kin. 15:5 [c]Ps. 91:16 [1]*prolong* *See WW at Neh. 9:13.

3:1 In accord with ancient Eastern practices, Solomon sealed many of his political alliances with marriages.
3:2–4 During the time of the Book of Judges, Israel adopted the pagan custom of offering sacrifices at **high places** (elevated hilltops). The pagans believed the closer they were to heaven, the greater the chance their prayer and sacrifices would reach their gods. Since many of these high places were old Baal sites, this practice was expressly forbidden *to the Israelites* (Lev. 17:3, 4). But in certain exceptions the Lord gave His approval for His people to worship Him at a high place (1 Sam. 9:12–14). The high places in v. 2 and **the great high place** in v. 4 appear to fall under this unusual exception, **because there was no house built for the name of the LORD until those days** (v. 2). Since the tabernacle of Moses and the great bronze altar were at the great high place at **Gibeon** (1 Chr. 16:39; 21:29; 2 Chr. 1:3–6), Solomon's sacrifice there is not to be seen as idolatrous. However, in the later years of Solomon (after the temple was built), he built high places for his pagan wives (11:7, 8). This is what v. 3 refers to when it says **Solomon** walked **in the statutes of his father David, except that he sacrificed . . . at the high places.** After these exceptions in the early period of Israel's history, the high places were off limits to God's people. The high places were not done away with until the reign of Josiah (2 Kin. 23:8).
3:3 See section 2 of Truth-In-Action at the end of 1 Kin.
3:7–14 See section 4 of Truth-In-Action at the end of 1 Kin.
3:7 Little child; I do not know *how* to go out or come in: Solomon was not young in years, but this was a humble admission of his inexperience.

15 Then Solomon [a]awoke; and indeed it had been a dream. And he came to Jerusalem and stood before the ark of the covenant of the LORD, offered up burnt offerings, offered peace offerings, and [b]made a feast for all his servants.

Solomon's Wise Judgment

4 **16** Now two women *who were* harlots came to the king, and [a]stood before him.

17 And one woman said, "O my lord, this woman and I dwell in the same house; and I gave birth while she *was* in the house.

18 "Then it happened, the third day after I had given birth, that this woman also gave birth. And we *were* together; [1]no one *was* with us in the house, except the two of us in the house.

19 "And this woman's son died in the night, because she lay on him.

20 "So she arose in the middle of the night and took my son from my side, while your maidservant slept, and laid him in her bosom, and laid her dead child in my bosom.

21 "And when I rose in the morning to nurse my son, there he was, dead. But when I had examined him in the morning, indeed, he was not my son whom I had borne."

22 Then the other woman said, "No! But the living one *is* my son, and the dead one *is* your son." And the first woman said, "No! But the dead one *is* your son, and the living one *is* my son." Thus they spoke before the king.

23 And the king said, "The one says, 'This *is* my son, who lives, and your son *is* the dead one'; and the other says, 'No! But your son *is* the dead one, and my son *is* the living one.' "

24 Then the king said, "Bring me a sword." So they brought a sword before the king.

25 And the king said, "Divide the living child in two, and give half to one, and half to the other."

26 Then the woman whose son *was* living spoke to the king, for [a]she yearned with compassion for her son; and she said, "O my lord, give her the living child, and by no means kill him!" But the other said, "Let him be neither mine nor yours, *but* divide *him*."

27 So the king answered and said, "Give the first woman the living child, and by no means kill him; she *is* his mother."

28 And all Israel heard of the judgment which the king had rendered; and they feared the king, for they saw that the [a]wisdom of God *was* in him to administer justice.

Solomon's Administration

4 So King Solomon was king over all Israel.

2 And these *were* his officials: Azariah the son of Zadok, the priest;

3 Elihoreph and Ahijah, the sons of Shisha, [1]scribes; [a]Jehoshaphat the son of Ahilud, the recorder;

4 [a]Benaiah the son of Jehoiada, over the army; Zadok and [b]Abiathar, the priests;

5 Azariah the son of Nathan, over [a]the officers; Zabud the son of Nathan, [b]a priest *and* [c]the king's friend;

6 Ahishar, over the household; and [a]Adoniram the son of Abda, over the labor force.

7 And Solomon had twelve governors over all Israel, who provided food for the king and his household; each one made provision for one month of the year.

8 These *are* their names: [1]Ben-Hur, in the mountains of Ephraim;

9 [1]Ben-Deker, in Makaz, Shaalbim, Beth Shemesh, and Elon Beth Hanan;

10 [1]Ben-Hesed, in Arubboth; to him *belonged* Sochoh and all the land of Hepher;

11 [1]Ben-Abinadab, *in* all the regions of Dor; he had Taphath the daughter of Solomon as wife;

12 Baana the son of Ahilud, *in* Taanach, Megiddo, and all Beth Shean, which *is* beside Zaretan below Jezreel, from Beth Shean to Abel Meholah, as far as the other side of Jokneam;

13 [1]Ben-Geber, in Ramoth Gilead; to him *belonged* [a]the towns of Jair the son of Manasseh, in Gilead; to him *also belonged* [b]the region of Argob in

15 [a]Gen. 41:7 [b]Gen. 40:20; 1 Kin. 8:65; Esth. 1:3; Dan. 5:1; Mark 6:21
16 [a]Num. 27:2
18 [1]Lit. *no stranger*
26 [a]Gen. 43:30; Is. 49:15; Jer. 31:20; Hos. 11:8
28 [a]1 Kin. 3:9, 11, 12; 2 Chr. 1:12; Dan. 1:17; [Col. 2:2, 3]

CHAPTER 4

3 [a]2 Sam. 8:16; 20:24 [1]*secretaries*
4 [a]1 Kin. 2:35 [b]1 Kin. 2:27
5 [a]1 Kin. 4:7 [b]2 Sam. 8:18; 20:26 [c]2 Sam. 15:37; 16:16; 1 Chr. 27:33
6 [a]1 Kin. 5:14
8 [1]Lit. *Son of Hur*
9 [1]Lit. *Son of Deker*
10 [1]Lit. *Son of Hesed*
11 [1]Lit. *Son of Abinadab*
13 [a]Num. 32:41; 1 Chr. 2:22 [b]Deut. 3:4 [1]Lit. *Son of Geber*

3:15 Though the tabernacle of Moses and the bronze altar were in Gibeon, the **ark of the covenant** remained in **Jerusalem** at the tabernacle of David (2 Sam. 6:17).
3:16–28 See section 4 of Truth-In-Action at the end of 1 Kin.
3:16–28 This colorful account is a vivid demonstration of the gift of wisdom God had granted to Solomon, fulfilling vv. 9–12.
4:2–6 These verses list the **officials** of Solomon, the chief officers of his administration.
4:2 The word **son** often means "descendant." **Azariah** was actually the grandson of Zadok (1 Chr. 6:8, 9).
4:7–19 Here is a list of the 12 **governors** who made provisions for the royal household, one for each month of the year.

Bashan—sixty large cities with walls
and bronze gate-bars;
14 Ahinadab the son of Iddo, *in* Mahanaim;
15 [a]Ahimaaz, in Naphtali; he also took
Basemath the daughter of Solomon as
wife;
16 Baanah the son of [a]Hushai, in
Asher and Aloth;
17 Jehoshaphat the son of Paruah, in
Issachar;
18 [a]Shimei the son of Elah, in Benjamin;
19 Geber the son of Uri, in the land of
Gilead, *in* [a]the country of Sihon king
of the Amorites, and of Og king of Bashan. *He was* the only governor who
was in the land.

Prosperity and Wisdom of Solomon's Reign

20 Judah and Israel *were* as numerous
[a]as the sand by the sea in multitude,
[b]eating and drinking and rejoicing.
21 So [a]Solomon reigned over all kingdoms from [b]the[1] River *to* the land of
the Philistines, as far as the border of
Egypt. [c]*They* brought *tribute and
served Solomon all the days of his life.
22 [a]Now Solomon's [1]provision for one
day was thirty [2]kors of fine flour, sixty
kors of meal,
23 ten fatted oxen, twenty oxen from
the pastures, and one hundred sheep,
besides deer, gazelles, roebucks, and
fatted fowl.
24 For he had dominion over all *the
region* on this side of [1]the River from
Tiphsah even to Gaza, namely over
[a]all the kings on this side of the River;
and [b]he had peace on every side all
around him.
25 And Judah and Israel [a]dwelt[1]
*safely, [b]each man under his vine and
his fig tree, [c]from Dan as far as Beersheba, all the days of Solomon.
26 [a]Solomon had [1]forty thousand
stalls of [b]horses for his chariots, and
twelve thousand horsemen.
27 And [a]these governors, each man in
his month, provided food for King Solomon and for all who came to King
Solomon's table. There was no lack in
their supply.
28 They also brought barley and straw
to the proper place, for the horses and
steeds, each man according to his
charge.
29 And [a]God gave Solomon wisdom
and exceedingly great understanding,
and largeness of heart like the sand on
the seashore.
30 Thus Solomon's wisdom excelled
the wisdom of all the men [a]of the East
and all [b]the wisdom of Egypt.
31 For he was [a]wiser than all men—
[b]than Ethan the Ezrahite, [c]and Heman,
Chalcol, and Darda, the sons of Mahol;
and his fame was in all the surrounding
nations.
32 [a]He spoke three thousand proverbs,
and his [b]songs were one thousand and
five.
33 Also he spoke of trees, from the cedar tree of Lebanon even to the hyssop
that springs out of the wall; he spoke
also of animals, of birds, of creeping
things, and of fish.
34 And men of all nations, from all the
kings of the earth who had heard of
his wisdom, [a]came to hear the wisdom
of Solomon.

Solomon Prepares to Build the Temple

5 Now [a]Hiram king of Tyre sent his
servants to Solomon, because he
heard that they had anointed him king
in place of his father, [b]for Hiram had
always loved David.
2 Then [a]Solomon sent to Hiram, saying:

3 [a]You know how my father David
could not build a house for the
name of the LORD his God
[b]because of the wars which were
fought against him on every side,
until the LORD put [1]*his foes* under
the soles of his feet.
4 But now the LORD my God *has
given me [a]rest[1] on every side;
there is neither adversary nor
[2]evil occurrence.
5 [a]And behold, [1]I propose to build
a house for the name of the LORD
my God, [b]as the LORD spoke to
my father David, saying, "Your
son, whom I will set on your
throne in your place, he shall
build the house for My name."

15 [a]2 Sam. 15:27
16 [a]1 Chr. 27:33
18 [a]1 Kin. 1:8
19 [a]Deut. 3:8–10
20 [a]Gen. 22:17; 32:12 [b]Mic. 4:4
21 [a]Ps. 72:8 [b]Gen. 15:18 [c]Ps. 68:29 [1]The Euphrates *See WW at Num. 29:6.
22 [a]Neh. 5:18 [1]Lit. *bread* [2]Each about 5 bushels
24 [a]Ps. 72:11 [b]1 Chr. 22:9 [1]The Euphrates
25 [a][Jer. 23:6] [b][Mic. 4:4] [c]Judg. 20:1 [1]*lived in safety* *See WW at Deut. 33:12.
26 [a]1 Kin. 10:26 [b][Deut. 17:16] [1]So with MT, most other authorities; some LXX mss. *four thousand;* cf. 2 Chr. 9:25
27 [a]1 Kin. 4:7
29 [a]1 Kin. 3:12
30 [a]Gen. 25:6 [b]Is. 19:11, 12
31 [a]1 Kin. 3:12 [b]1 Chr. 15:19 [c]1 Chr. 2:6
32 [a]Eccl. 12:9 [b]Song 1:1
34 [a]1 Kin. 10:1

CHAPTER 5

1 [a]2 Chr. 2:3 [b]2 Sam. 5:11
2 [a]2 Chr. 2:3
3 [a]1 Chr. 28:2, 3 [b]1 Chr. 22:8; 28:3 [1]Lit. *them*
4 [a]1 Kin. 4:24 [1]*peace* [2]*misfortune* *See WW at Ex. 33:14.
5 [a]2 Chr. 2:4 [b]2 Sam. 7:12, 13 [1]Lit. *I am saying*

4:26 Forty thousand: *This is probably a copyist's error,* since 2 Chr. 9:25 says there were only "four thousand stalls." The copyist apparently misread the Hebrew word for "four" as "forty." Four thousand is probably the correct figure, since there were only "one thousand four hundred" chariots (10:26; 2 Chr. 1:14).

4:31 Ethan and **Heman** were musicians, and it is apparent from the titles of Ps. 88 and 89 that each of them wrote a psalm.

5:1, 12 Here another illustration of the **wisdom of Solomon** is set forth. Solomon capitalized on the friendly relationship that his father David had with Hiram of Tyre by obtaining the help of Hiram in building the temple.

6 Now therefore, command that
they cut down [a]cedars for me
from Lebanon; and my servants
will be with your servants, and I
will pay you wages for your
servants according to whatever
you say. For you know *there is*
none among us who has skill to
cut timber like the Sidonians.

7 So it was, when Hiram heard the
words of Solomon, that he rejoiced
greatly and said,

Blessed *be* the LORD this day, for
He has given David a wise son
over this great people!

8 Then Hiram sent to Solomon, saying:

I have considered *the message*
which you sent me, *and* I will do
all you desire concerning the
cedar and cypress logs.
9 My servants shall bring *them*
down [a]from Lebanon to the sea;
I will float them in rafts by sea
to the place you indicate to me,
and will have them broken apart
there; then you can take *them*
away. And you shall fulfill my
desire [b]by giving food for my
household.

10 Then Hiram gave Solomon cedar
and cypress logs *according to* all his
desire.
11 [a]And Solomon gave Hiram twenty
thousand [1]kors of wheat *as* food for
his household, and [2]twenty kors of
pressed oil. Thus Solomon gave to
Hiram year by year.
12 So the LORD gave Solomon wisdom,
[a]as He had promised him; and there
was peace between Hiram and Solomon, and the two of them made a
treaty together.
13 Then King Solomon raised up a labor force out of all Israel; and the labor
force was thirty thousand men.
14 And he sent them to Lebanon, ten
thousand a month in shifts: they were
one month in Lebanon *and* two months
at home; [a]Adoniram *was* in charge of
the labor force.
15 [a]Solomon had seventy thousand
who carried burdens, and eighty thousand who quarried *stone* in the mountains,
16 besides three thousand [1]three hundred from the [a]chiefs of Solomon's
deputies, who supervised the people
who labored in the work.
17 And the king commanded them to
quarry large stones, costly stones, *and*
[a]hewn stones, to lay the foundation of
the [1]temple.
18 So Solomon's builders, Hiram's
builders, and the Gebalites quarried
them; and they prepared timber and
stones to build the [1]temple.

Solomon Builds the Temple

6 And [a]it came to pass in the four
hundred and [1]eightieth year after
the children of Israel had come out of
the land of Egypt, in the fourth year
of Solomon's reign over Israel, in the
month of [2]Ziv, which *is* the second
month, [b]that he began to build the
house of the LORD.
2 Now [a]the house which King Solomon built for the LORD, its length *was*
sixty cubits, its width twenty, and its
height thirty cubits.
3 The vestibule in front of the [1]sanc-
tuary* of the house *was* [2]twenty cubits long across the width of the
house, *and* the width of [3]*the vestibule
extended* [4]ten cubits from the front of
the house.
4 And he made for the house [a]win-
dows with beveled frames.
5 Against the wall of the [1]temple he
built [a]chambers all around, *against* the
walls of the temple, all around the
sanctuary [b]and the [2]inner sanctuary.
Thus he made side chambers all
around it.
6 The lowest chamber *was* five cubits
wide, the middle *was* six cubits wide,
and the third *was* seven cubits wide;
for he made narrow ledges around the
outside of the temple, so that *the*

6 [a]2 Chr. 2:8, 10
9 [a]Ezra 3:7 [b]Ezek. 27:17; Acts 12:20
11 [a]2 Chr. 2:10 [1]Each about 5 bushels [2]So with MT, Tg., Vg.; LXX, Syr. *twenty thousand kors*
12 [a]1 Kin. 3:12
14 [a]1 Kin. 12:18
15 [a]1 Kin. 9:20–22; 2 Chr. 2:17, 18
16 [a]1 Kin. 9:23 [1]So with MT, Tg., Vg.; LXX *six hundred*
17 [a]1 Kin. 6:7; 1 Chr. 22:2 [1]Lit. *house*
18 [1]Lit. *house*

CHAPTER 6

1 [a]2 Chr. 3:1, 2 [b]Acts 7:47 [1]So with MT, Tg., Vg.; LXX *fortieth* [2]Or *Ayyar,* April or May
2 [a]Ezek. 41:1
3 [1]Heb. *heykal;* here the main room of the temple; elsewhere called the holy place, Ex. 26:33; Ezek. 41:1 [2]About 30 feet [3]Lit. *it* [4]About 15 feet *See WW at Hag. 2:15.
4 [a]Ezek. 40:16; 41:16
5 [a]Ezek. 41:6 [b]1 Kin. 6:16, 19–21, 31 [1]Lit. *house* [2]Heb. *debir;* here the inner room of the temple; elsewhere called the Most Holy Place, v. 16

5:6 The **Sidonians** were skilled timber workers who are later called Phoenicians.

6:1–38 It is interesting to note that the **temple** was built some 400 years after the tabernacle and stood for about 400 years before being destroyed in 586 B.C. It took approximately 30,000 Israelites and 150,000 Canaanites only seven years to complete the construction of the temple.

6:1 Even though the meaning of this verse is in dispute, it still provides a chronological anchor to give us a general perspective as to the chronological relationship of biblical events. The exact date of this verse cannot be established because there is uncertainty as to when the beginning of the reign of Solomon is to be dated. **The fourth year of Solomon's reign** is regarded by many to be about 960 B.C. In that case the Exodus could have occurred about 1440 B.C.

6:2 A cubit was approximately 18 inches; therefore, the temple was about 90 feet long by 30 feet wide by 45 feet tall. These dimensions exactly doubled those of the tabernacle of Moses.

support beams would not be fastened
into the walls of the [1]temple.
7 And [a]the temple, when it was being
built, was built with stone finished at
the quarry, so that no hammer or chisel
or any iron tool was heard in the temple while it was being built.
8 The doorway for the [1]middle story
was on the right side of the temple.
They went up by stairs to the middle
story, and from the middle to the third.
9 [a]So he built the [1]temple and finished it, and he paneled the temple
with beams and boards of cedar.
10 And he built side chambers against
the entire temple, each five cubits high;
they were attached to the temple with
cedar beams.
11 Then the word of the LORD came to
Solomon, saying:
12 "*Concerning* this [1]temple which you
are building, [a]if you walk in My statutes, execute My judgments, keep all
My commandments, and walk in them,
then I will perform My [2]word with you,
[b]which I spoke to your father David.
13 "And [a]I will dwell among the children of Israel, and will not [b]forsake My
people Israel."
14 So Solomon built the temple and
finished it.
15 And he built the inside walls of the
temple with cedar boards; from the
floor of the temple to the ceiling he
paneled the inside with wood; and he
covered the floor of the temple with
planks of cypress.
16 Then he built the twenty-cubit room
at the rear of the temple, from floor to
ceiling, with cedar boards; he built *it*
inside as the inner sanctuary, as the
[a]Most Holy *Place*.
17 And in front of it the temple sanctuary was forty cubits *long*.
18 The inside of the temple was cedar,
carved with ornamental buds and open
flowers. All *was* cedar; there was no
stone *to be* seen.
19 And he prepared the [1]inner sanctuary inside the temple, to set the ark of
the covenant of the LORD there.
20 The inner sanctuary *was* twenty cubits long, twenty cubits wide, and
twenty cubits high. He overlaid it with
pure gold, and overlaid the altar of cedar.
21 So Solomon overlaid the inside of
the temple with pure gold. He stretched
gold chains across the front of the inner sanctuary, and overlaid it with
gold.

6 [1]Lit. *house*
7 [a]Ex. 20:25; Deut. 27:5, 6
8 [1]So with MT, Vg.; LXX *upper story;* Tg. *ground story*
9 [a]1 Kin. 6:14, 38 [1]Lit. *house*
12 [a]1 Kin. 2:4; 9:4 [b][2 Sam. 7:13; 1 Chr. 22:10] [1]Lit. *house* [2]*promise*
13 [a]Ex. 25:8; Lev. 26:11; [2 Cor. 6:16; Rev. 21:3] [b][Deut. 31:6]
16 [a]Ex. 26:33; Lev. 16:2; 1 Kin. 8:6; 2 Chr. 3:8; Ezek. 45:3; Heb. 9:3
19 [1]The Most Holy Place
22 [a]Ex. 30:1, 3, 6
23 [a]Ex. 37:7–9; 2 Chr. 3:10–12
27 [a]Ex. 25:20; 37:9; 1 Kin. 8:7; 2 Chr. 5:8 [1]Lit. *house*
29 [a]Ex. 36:8, 35
31 [1]Or *five-sided*
33 [1]*temple* [2]Or *four-sided*
34 [a]Ezek. 41:23–25
36 [a]1 Kin. 7:12; Jer. 36:10
37 [a]1 Kin. 6:1

22 The whole temple he overlaid with
gold, until he had finished all the temple; also he overlaid with gold [a]the entire altar that *was* by the inner sanctuary.
23 Inside the inner sanctuary [a]he made
two cherubim *of* olive wood, *each* ten
cubits high.
24 One wing of the cherub *was* five
cubits, and the other wing of the
cherub five cubits: ten cubits from
the tip of one wing to the tip of the
other.
25 And the other cherub *was* ten cubits; both cherubim *were* of the same
size and shape.
26 The height of one cherub *was* ten
cubits, and so *was* the other cherub.
27 Then he set the cherubim inside the
inner [1]room; and [a]they stretched out
the wings of the cherubim so that the
wing of the one touched *one* wall, and
the wing of the other cherub touched
the other wall. And their wings touched each other in the middle of the
room.
28 Also he overlaid the cherubim with
gold.
29 Then he carved all the walls of the
temple all around, both the inner and
outer *sanctuaries,* with carved [a]fig-
ures of cherubim, palm trees, and open
flowers.
30 And the floor of the temple he overlaid with gold, both the inner and outer
sanctuaries.
31 For the entrance of the inner sanctuary he made doors *of* olive wood; the
lintel *and* doorposts *were* [1]one-fifth *of
the wall.*
32 The two doors *were of* olive wood;
and he carved on them figures of cherubim, palm trees, and open flowers,
and overlaid *them* with gold; and he
spread gold on the cherubim and on
the palm trees.
33 So for the door of the [1]sanctuary
he also made doorposts *of* olive wood,
[2]one-fourth *of the wall.*
34 And the two doors *were of* cypress
wood; [a]two panels *comprised* one folding door, and two panels *comprised* the
other folding door.
35 Then he carved cherubim, palm
trees, and open flowers *on them,* and
overlaid *them* with gold applied evenly
on the carved work.
36 And he built the [a]inner court with
three rows of hewn stone and a row
of cedar beams.
37 [a]In the fourth year the foundation

6:13 Here the Lord explains the reason for the temple: God wanted to dwell among His people.

of the house of the LORD was laid, in
the month of [1]Ziv.
38 And in the eleventh year, in the
month of [1]Bul, which is the eighth
month, the house was finished in all
its details and according to all its plans.
So he was [a]seven years in building it.

Solomon's Other Buildings

7 But Solomon took [a]thirteen years
to build his own house; so he finished all his house.
2 He also built the [a]House of the Forest of Lebanon; its length *was* [1]one
hundred cubits, its width [2]fifty cubits,
and its height thirty cubits, with four
rows of cedar pillars, and cedar beams
on the pillars.
3 And *it was* paneled with cedar
above the beams that *were* on forty-
five pillars, fifteen *to* a row.
4 *There were* windows *with beveled
frames in* three rows, and window *was*
opposite window *in* three tiers.
5 And all the doorways and doorposts
had rectangular frames; and window
was opposite window *in* three tiers.
6 He also made the Hall of Pillars: its
length *was* fifty cubits, and its width
thirty cubits; and in front of them *was*
a portico with pillars, and a canopy
was in front of them.
7 Then he made a hall for the throne,
the Hall of Judgment, where he might
judge; and *it was* paneled with cedar
from floor to [1]ceiling.
8 And the house where he dwelt *had*
another court inside the hall, of like
workmanship. Solomon also made a
house like this hall for Pharaoh's
daughter, [a]whom he had taken *as wife.*
9 All these *were of* costly stones cut
to size, trimmed with saws, inside and
out, from the foundation to the eaves,
and also on the outside to the great
court.
10 The foundation *was of* costly
stones, large stones, some ten cubits
and some eight cubits.
11 And above *were* costly stones,
hewn to size, and cedar wood.
12 The great court *was* enclosed with
three rows of hewn stones and a row
of cedar beams. So were the [a]inner
court of the house of the LORD [b]and
the vestibule of the temple.

Hiram the Craftsman

13 Now King Solomon sent and
brought [1]Huram from Tyre.
14 [a]He *was* the son of a widow from
the tribe of Naphtali, and [b]his father
was a man of Tyre, a bronze worker;
[c]he was filled with wisdom and understanding and skill in working with all
kinds of bronze work. So he came to
King Solomon and did all his work.

The Bronze Pillars for the Temple

15 And he [1]cast [a]two pillars of bronze,
each one eighteen cubits high, and a
line of twelve cubits measured the circumference of each.
16 Then he made two capitals *of* cast
bronze, to set on the tops of the pillars.
The height of one capital *was* five cubits, and the height of the other capital
was five cubits.
17 *He made* a lattice network, with
wreaths of chainwork, for the capitals
which *were* on top of the pillars: seven
chains for one capital and seven for the
other capital.
18 So he made the pillars, and two
rows of pomegranates above the network all around to cover the capitals
that *were* on top; and thus he did for
the other capital.
19 The capitals which *were* on top of
the pillars in the hall *were* in the shape
of lilies, four cubits.
20 The capitals on the two pillars also
had pomegranates above, by the con-
vex surface which *was* next to the network; and there *were* [a]two hundred
such pomegranates in rows on each of
the capitals all around.
21 [a]Then he set up the pillars by the
vestibule of the temple; he set up the
pillar on the right and called its name
[1]Jachin, and he set up the pillar on the
left and called its name [2]Boaz.
22 The tops of the pillars were in the
shape of lilies. So the work of the pillars was finished.

37 [1]Or *Ayyar,* April or May
38 [a]2 Sam. 7:13; 1 Kin. 5:5; 6:1; 8:19 [1]Or *Heshvan,* October or November

CHAPTER 7

1 [a]1 Kin. 3:1; 9:10; 2 Chr. 8:1
2 [a]1 Kin. 10:17, 21; 2 Chr. 9:16 [1]About 150 feet [2]About 75 feet
7 [1]Lit. *floor* of the upper level
8 [a]1 Kin. 3:1; 9:24; 11:1; 2 Chr. 8:11
12 [a]1 Kin. 6:36 [b]John 10:23; Acts 3:11
13 [1]Heb. *Hiram;* cf. 2 Chr. 2:13, 14
14 [a]2 Chr. 2:14 [b]2 Chr. 4:16 [c]Ex. 31:3; 36:1
15 [a]2 Kin. 25:17; 2 Chr. 3:15; 4:12; Jer. 52:21 [1]*fashioned*
20 [a]2 Chr. 3:16; 4:13; Jer. 52:23
21 [a]2 Chr. 3:17 [1]Lit. *He Shall Establish* [2]Lit. *In It Is Strength*

7:1–8 In addition to the temple, Solomon built a royal palace. It consisted of **the House of the Forest of Lebanon** (v. 2), the **Hall of Pillars** (v. 6), the **Hall of Judgment** (v. 7), his own personal residence (v. 8), and a residence for Pharaoh's daughter (v. 8). According to the Jewish historian Josephus, these were not separate buildings, but sections of a single palace.

7:9–12 The building materials and style of architecture for Solomon's palace were very similar to the temple's.

7:13, 14 Huram: This is a variant spelling for the Hebrew name "Hiram," an artisan, not to be confused with Hiram, the king of Tyre (5:1).

7:18–22 Two freestanding pillars or monuments, **Jachin** and **Boaz** were constructed to mark the entrance to the temple. This is characteristic of Phoenician structures and suggests that both the temple and Solomon's palace reflected ancient Phoenician architecture.

The Sea and the Oxen

23 And he made [a]the Sea of cast bronze, ten cubits from one brim to the other; *it was* completely round. Its height *was* five cubits, and a line of thirty cubits measured its circumference.

24 Below its brim *were* ornamental buds encircling it all around, ten to a cubit, [a]all the way around the Sea. The ornamental buds *were* cast in two rows when it was cast.

25 It stood on [a]twelve oxen: three looking toward the north, three looking toward the west, three looking toward the south, and three looking toward the east; the Sea *was set* upon them, and all their back parts *pointed* inward.

26 It *was* a handbreadth thick; and its brim was shaped like the brim of a cup, *like* a lily blossom. It contained [1]two thousand baths.

The Carts and the Lavers

27 He also made ten [1]carts of bronze; four cubits *was* the length of each cart, four cubits its width, and three cubits its height.

28 And this *was* the design of the carts: They had panels, and the panels *were* between frames;

29 on the panels that *were* between the frames *were* lions, oxen, and cherubim. And on the frames *was* a pedestal on top. Below the lions and oxen *were* wreaths of plaited work.

30 Every cart had four bronze wheels and axles of bronze, and its four feet had supports. Under the laver *were* supports of cast *bronze* beside each wreath.

31 Its opening inside the crown at the top *was* one cubit in diameter; and the opening *was* round, shaped *like* a pedestal, one and a half cubits in outside diameter; and also on the opening *were* engravings, but the panels were square, not round.

32 Under the panels *were* the four wheels, and the axles of the wheels *were joined* to the cart. The height of a wheel *was* one and a half cubits.

33 The workmanship of the wheels *was* like the workmanship of a chariot wheel; their axle pins, their rims, their spokes, and their hubs *were* all of cast *bronze*.

34 And *there were* four supports at the four corners of each cart; its supports *were* part of the cart itself.

35 On the top of the cart, at the height of half a cubit, *it was* perfectly round. And on the top of the cart, its flanges and its panels *were* of the same casting.

36 On the plates of its flanges and on its panels he engraved cherubim, lions, and palm trees, wherever there was a clear space on each, with wreaths all around.

37 Thus he made the ten carts. All of them were of [1]the same mold, one measure, *and* one shape.

38 Then [a]he made ten lavers of bronze; each laver contained [1]forty baths, *and* each laver *was* four cubits. On each of the ten carts *was* a laver.

39 And he put five carts on the right side of the house, and five on the left side of the house. He set the Sea on the right side of the house, toward the southeast.

Furnishings of the Temple

40 [a]Huram[1] made the lavers and the shovels and the bowls. So Huram finished doing all the work that he was to do for King Solomon *for* the house of the LORD:

41 the two pillars, the *two* bowl-shaped capitals that *were* on top of the two pillars; the two [a]networks covering the two bowl-shaped capitals which *were* on top of the pillars;

42 [a]four hundred pomegranates for the two networks (two rows of pomegranates for each network, to cover the two bowl-shaped capitals that *were* on top of the pillars);

43 the ten carts, and ten lavers on the carts;

44 one Sea, and twelve oxen under the Sea;

45 [a]the pots, the shovels, and the bowls. All these articles which [1]Huram made for King Solomon *for* the house of the LORD *were of* burnished bronze.

46 [a]In the plain of Jordan the king had them cast in clay molds, between [b]Succoth and [c]Zaretan.

47 And Solomon did not weigh all the articles, because *there were* so many; the weight of the bronze was not [a]determined.

48 Thus Solomon had all the fur-

23 [a]2 Kin. 25:13; 2 Chr. 4:2; Jer. 52:17
24 [a]2 Chr. 4:3
25 [a]2 Chr. 4:4, 5; Jer. 52:20
26 [1]About 12,000 gallons; *three thousand*, 2 Chr. 4:5
27 [1]Or *stands*
37 [1]*one*
38 [a]Ex. 30:18; 2 Chr. 4:6 [1]About 240 gallons
40 [a]2 Chr. 4:11—5:1 [1]Heb. *Hiram;* cf. 2 Chr. 2:13, 14
41 [a]1 Kin. 7:17, 18
42 [a]1 Kin. 7:20
45 [a]Ex. 27:3; 2 Chr. 4:16 [1]Heb. *Hiram;* cf. 2 Chr. 2:13, 14
46 [a]2 Chr. 4:17 [b]Gen. 33:17; Josh. 13:27 [c]Josh. 3:16
47 [a]1 Chr. 22:3, 14

7:23–26 Sea of cast bronze: This was probably some type of reservoir to hold the great amount of water needed for lavers and for worship in the temple.

7:27–39 These verses describe the **carts** constructed to transport the water from the **Sea** of cast bronze to various stations in the temple.

7:48 The **table** may have been one large one, with nine others (2 Chr. 4:8). The **showbread** was a holy or

nishings made for the house of the LORD: [a]the altar of gold, and [b]the table of gold on which *was* [c]the showbread;

49 the lampstands of pure gold, five on the right *side* and five on the left in front of the inner sanctuary, with the flowers and the lamps and the wick-trimmers of gold;

50 the basins, the trimmers, the bowls, the ladles, and the [1]censers of pure gold; and the hinges of gold, *both* for the doors of the inner room (the Most Holy *Place*) *and* for the doors of the main hall of the temple.

51 So all the work that King Solomon had done for the house of the LORD was finished; and Solomon brought in the things [a]which his father David had dedicated: the silver and the gold and the furnishings. He put them in the treasuries of the house of the LORD.

The Ark Brought into the Temple

8 Now [a]Solomon assembled the elders of Israel and all the heads of the *tribes, the chief fathers of the children of Israel, to King Solomon in Jerusalem, [b]that they might bring [c]up the ark of the covenant of the LORD from the City of David, which *is* Zion.

2 Therefore all the men of Israel assembled with King Solomon at the [a]feast in the month of [1]Ethanim, which *is* the seventh month.

3 So all the elders of Israel came, [a]and the priests took up the ark.

4 Then they brought up the ark of the LORD, [a]the [1]tabernacle of meeting, and all the holy furnishings that *were* in the tabernacle. The priests and the Levites brought them up.

5 Also King Solomon, and all the *congregation of Israel who were assembled with him, *were* with him before the ark, [a]sacrificing sheep and oxen that could not be counted or numbered for multitude.

6 Then the priests [a]brought in the ark of the covenant of the LORD to [b]its place, into the inner sanctuary of the temple, to the Most Holy *Place,* [c]under the wings of the cherubim.

7 For the cherubim spread *their* two wings over the place of the ark, and the cherubim overshadowed the ark and its poles.

8 The poles [a]extended so that the [1]ends of the poles could be seen from the holy *place,* in front of the inner sanctuary; but they could not be seen from outside. And they are there to this day.

9 [a]Nothing *was* in the ark [b]except the two tablets of stone which Moses [c]put there at Horeb, [d]when the LORD made *a covenant* with the children of Israel, when they came out of the land of Egypt.

10 And it came to pass, when the priests came out of the holy *place,* that the cloud [a]filled the house of the LORD,

11 so that the priests could not continue ministering because of the cloud; for the [a]glory of the LORD filled the house of the LORD.

12 [a]Then Solomon spoke:

"The LORD said He would dwell
[b]in the dark cloud.

13 [a]I have surely built You an exalted house,
[b]And a place for You to dwell in forever."

Solomon's Speech at Completion of the Work

14 Then the king turned around and [a]blessed the whole assembly of Israel, while all the assembly of Israel was standing.

15 And he said: [a]"Blessed *be* the LORD God of Israel, who [b]spoke with His mouth to my father David, and with His hand has fulfilled *it,* saying,

16 'Since the day that I brought My people Israel out of Egypt, I have *chosen no city from any tribe of Israel *in which* to build a house, that [a]My name might be there; but I chose [b]David to be over My people Israel.'

48 [a]Ex. 37:25, 26; 2 Chr. 4:8 [b]Ex. 37:10, 11 [c]Lev. 24:5–8
50 [1]*firepans*
51 [a]2 Sam. 8:11

CHAPTER 8

1 [a]2 Chr. 5:2–14 [b]2 Sam. 6:12–17 [c]2 Sam. 5:7; 6:12, 16 *See WW at Ex. 38:22.
2 [a]Lev. 23:34 [1]Or *Tishri,* September or October
3 [a]Num. 4:15; 7:9
4 [a]2 Chr. 1:3 [1]*tent*
5 [a]2 Sam. 6:13 *See WW at Josh. 22:17.
6 [a]2 Sam. 6:17 [b]1 Kin. 6:19 [c]1 Kin. 6:27
8 [a]Ex. 25:13–15; 37:4, 5 [1]*heads*
9 [a]Ex. 25:21 [b]Deut. 10:5 [c]Ex. 24:7, 8; 40:20 [d]Ex. 34:27, 28
10 [a]Ex. 40:34, 35
11 [a]2 Chr. 7:1, 2
12 [a]2 Chr. 6:1 [b]Ps. 18:11; 97:2
13 [a]2 Sam. 7:13 [b]Ps. 132:14
14 [a]2 Sam. 6:18
15 [a]Luke 1:68 [b]2 Sam. 7:2, 12, 13, 25
16 [a]1 Kin. 8:29 [b]2 Sam. 7:8 *See WW at 1 Kin. 11:34.

---

consecrated bread placed in the tabernacle (Ex. 25:23–30) or the temple (2 Chr. 13:11; 29:18) every Sabbath (1 Chr. 9:32) to symbolize God's continual presence and His provision for His people. The 12 loaves of bread symbolized the 12 tribes of the nation of Israel. The showbread was a reminder to them that God's presence is more essential than one's daily bread, and that they were to depend on God to provide for their spiritual and physical needs.

7:49 The tabernacle of Moses had one large lampstand, whereas the temple had 10 smaller lampstands.

8:2 The dedication of the temple coincided with the Feast of Tabernacles, about 11 months after its completion (6:38).

8:9 The rod of Aaron and the pot of manna, which had been kept in the ark (Heb. 9:4), were no longer there. They were lost or stolen (1 Sam. 6:19).

8:10, 11 The **cloud** that **filled the house of the LORD** (v. 10), the **glory of the LORD** (v. 11), is taken by some as a reference to the Holy Spirit. For further insight, see the reference to 2 Chr. 5:13, 14 in Introduction to 2 Chronicles: The Holy Spirit at Work. **The priests could not continue ministering** (v. 11): Evidently they were in some way incapacitated because of the presence of the Lord.

8:12–21 **Solomon** explained to the people why the cloud filled the temple (v. 10) and why he had built it for the Lord.

17 "Now [a]it was in the heart of my father David to build a [1]temple for the
name of the LORD God of Israel.
18 [a]"But the LORD said to my father
David, 'Whereas it was in your heart
to build a temple for My name, you did
well that it was in your heart.
19 'Nevertheless [a]you shall not build
the temple, but your son who will come
from your body, he shall build the temple for My name.'
20 "So the LORD has fulfilled His word
which He spoke; and I have [1]filled the
position of my father David, and sit on
the throne of Israel, [a]as the LORD promised; and I have built a temple for the
name of the LORD God of Israel.
21 "And there I have made a place for
the ark, in which *is* [a]the covenant of
the LORD which He made with our fathers, when He brought them out of the
land of Egypt."

Solomon's Prayer of Dedication

22 Then Solomon stood before [a]the altar of the LORD in the presence of all
the assembly of Israel, and [b]spread out
his hands toward heaven;
23 and he said: "LORD God of Israel,
[a]*there is* no God in **heaven** above or
on earth below like You, [b]who keep
Your covenant and mercy with Your
servants who [c]walk before You with
all their hearts.

WORD WEALTH

8:23 heaven, *shamayim* (shah-*my*-yeem); Strong's #8064: Sky, skies; heaven, heavens. The word *shamayim* is plural in form, because the Hebrews knew the great expanse above the Earth (the heavens) to be immeasurably vast, and its stars to be uncountable (Jer. 33:22). In the heavens, the dwelling place of God is located. However, even such an expanse does not hold God in, for Solomon stated, "Behold, heaven and the heaven of heavens cannot contain You. How much less this temple which I have built!" (2 Chr. 6:18). Since God spoke "from heaven" (Ex. 20:22), and is "in heaven" (Eccl. 5:2), Jews naturally came to say "heaven" as a euphemism for "God." Thus, "the kingdom of heaven" in Matt. is called "the kingdom of God" in other Gospels.

24 "You have kept what You promised
Your servant David my father; You
have both spoken with Your mouth
and fulfilled *it* with Your hand, as *it*
is this day.
25 "Therefore, LORD God of Israel, now
keep what You promised Your servant
David my father, saying, [a]'You shall
not fail to have a man sit before Me
on the throne of Israel, only if your
sons take heed to their way, that they
walk before Me as you have walked
before Me.'
26 [a]"And now I pray, O God of Israel,
let Your word come true, which You
have spoken to Your servant David my
father.
27 "But [a]will God indeed dwell on the 3
earth? Behold, heaven and the [b]heaven
of heavens cannot contain You. How
much less this temple which I have
built!
28 "Yet regard the *prayer of Your servant and his supplication, O LORD my
God, and listen to the cry and the
prayer which Your servant is praying
before You today:
29 "that Your eyes may be open toward this [1]temple night and day, toward the place of which You said,
[a]'My name shall be [b]there,' that You
may hear the prayer which Your servant makes [c]toward this place.
30 [a]"And may You hear the supplication of Your servant and of Your people Israel, when they pray toward this
place. Hear in heaven Your dwelling
place; and when You hear, forgive.
31 "When anyone sins against his
neighbor, and is forced to take [a]an
oath, and comes *and* takes an oath before Your altar in this temple,
32 "then hear in heaven, and act, and
judge Your servants, [a]condemning the
*wicked, bringing his way on his head,
and justifying the righteous by giving
him according to his righteousness.
33 [a]"When Your people Israel are defeated before an enemy because they

17 [a]2 Sam. 7:2, 3; 1 Chr. 17:1, 2 [1]Lit. *house,* and so in vv. 18–20
18 [a]2 Chr. 6:8, 9
19 [a]2 Sam. 7:5, 12, 13; 1 Kin. 5:3, 5; 6:38; 1 Chr. 17:11, 12; 22:8–10; 2 Chr. 6:2
20 [a]1 Chr. 28:5, 6 [1]*risen in the place of*
21 [a]Deut. 31:26; 1 Kin. 8:9
22 [a]1 Kin. 8:54; 2 Chr. 6:12 [b]Ex. 9:33; Ezra 9:5
23 [a]Ex. 15:11; 2 Sam. 7:22 [b][Deut. 7:9; Neh. 1:5; Dan. 9:4] [c][Gen. 17:1; 1 Kin. 3:6]; 2 Kin. 20:3
25 [a]2 Sam. 7:12, 16; 1 Kin. 2:4; 9:5
26 [a]2 Sam. 7:25
27 [a][2 Chr. 2:6; Is. 66:1; Acts 7:49; 17:24] [b]2 Cor. 12:2
28 *See WW at 2 Chr. 6:20.
29 [a]Deut. 12:11 [b]1 Kin. 9:3; 2 Chr. 7:15 [c]Dan. 6:10 [1]Lit. *house*
30 [a]Neh. 1:6
31 [a]Ex. 22:8–11
32 [a]Deut. 25:1 *See WW at Prov. 10:16.
33 [a]Lev. 26:17; Deut. 28:25

8:22–53 Much can be learned about prayer from Solomon's prayer. First, Solomon begins his prayer with praise and worship (vv. 22–25). Second, he acknowledges his unworthiness to be in God's presence (vv. 26–30). Third, Solomon requests forgiveness for Israel's sins against their neighbors (vv. 31, 32), for sins that caused defeat by enemies (vv. 33, 34), for sins that caused drought (vv. 35, 36), and for sins that resulted in other misfortunes (vv. 37–40). Fourth, he asks the Lord to be merciful to foreigners who fear God (vv. 41–43). Fifth, Solomon prays that God will grant them victory in battle (vv. 44, 45). And sixth, the king seeks God for their future restoration when they fail (vv. 46–53).

8:22 Solomon . . . spread out his hands toward heaven: He lifted his hands to praise and give thanks to the Lord. The lifting of hands in Scripture is a frequent physical expression of worship to God.

8:27 See section 3 of Truth-In-Action at the end of 1 Kin.

have sinned against You, and [b]when
they turn back to You and confess
Your name, and *pray and make supplication to You in this temple,
34 "then hear in heaven, and forgive
the sin of Your people Israel, and bring
them back to the land which You gave
to their [a]fathers.
35 [a]"When the heavens are shut up
and there is no rain because they have
sinned against You, when they pray toward this place and confess Your
name, and turn from their sin because
You afflict them,
36 "then hear in heaven, and forgive
the sin of Your servants, Your people
Israel, that You may [a]teach them
[b]the good way in which they should
walk; and send rain on Your land
which You have given to Your people
as an inheritance.
37 [a]"When there is famine in the land,
pestilence *or* blight *or* mildew, locusts
or grasshoppers; when their enemy besieges them in the land of their [1]cities;
whatever plague or whatever sickness
there is;
38 "whatever prayer, whatever supplication is made by anyone, *or* by all
Your people Israel, when each one
knows the plague of his own heart, and
spreads out his hands toward this temple:
4 39 "then hear in heaven Your dwelling
place, and forgive, and act, and give
to everyone according to all his ways,
whose heart You know (for You alone
[a]know the hearts of all the sons of
men),
40 [a]"that they may fear You all the
days that they live in the land which
You gave to our fathers.
41 "Moreover, concerning a foreigner,
who *is* not of Your people Israel, but
has come from a far country for Your
name's sake
42 "(for they will hear of Your great
name and Your [a]strong hand and Your
outstretched arm), when he comes and
prays toward this temple,
43 "hear in heaven Your dwelling
place, and do according to all for which
the foreigner calls to You, [a]that all peoples of the earth may know Your name
and [b]fear You, as *do* Your people Israel, and that they may know that this
temple which I have built is called by
Your name.
44 "When Your people go out to battle
against their enemy, wherever You
send them, and when they pray to the
LORD toward the city which You have
chosen and the temple which I have
built for Your name,
45 "then hear in heaven their prayer
and their supplication, and maintain
their [1]cause.
46 "When they sin against You [a](for 7
there is no one who does not sin), and
You become angry with them and deliver them to the enemy, and they take
them captive [b]to the land of the enemy,
far or near;
47 [a]"*yet* when they [1]come to themselves in the land where they were carried captive, and repent, and make supplication to You in the land of those
who took them captive, [b]saying, 'We
have sinned and done wrong, we have
committed wickedness';
48 "and *when* they [a]return to You with
all their heart and with all their soul
in the land of their enemies who led
them away captive, and [b]pray to You
toward their land which You gave to
their fathers, the city which You have
chosen and the temple which I have
built for Your name:
49 "then hear in heaven Your dwelling
place their prayer and their supplication, and maintain their [1]cause,
50 "and forgive Your people who have
sinned against You, and all their transgressions which they have transgressed against You; and [a]grant them
*compassion before those who took
them captive, that they may have compassion on them
51 "(for [a]they *are* Your people and
Your inheritance, whom You brought
out of Egypt, [b]out of the iron furnace),
52 [a]"that Your eyes may be *open to
the supplication of Your servant and
the supplication of Your people Israel,
to listen to them whenever they call to
You.
53 "For You separated them from
among all the peoples of the earth *to
be* Your inheritance, [a]as You spoke
by Your servant Moses, when You
brought our fathers out of Egypt, O
Lord GOD."

Solomon Blesses the Assembly

54 [a]And so it was, when Solomon had
finished praying all this prayer and
supplication to the LORD, that he arose

33 [b]Lev. 26:39, 40 *See WW at Job 42:10. **34** [a][Lev. 26:40–42; Deut. 30:1–3] **35** [a]Lev. 26:19; Deut. 28:23 **36** [a]Ps. 25:4; 27:11; 94:12 [b]1 Sam. 12:23 **37** [a]Lev. 26:16, 25, 26; Deut. 28:21, 22, 27, 38, 42, 52 [1]Lit. *gates* **39** [a][1 Sam. 16:7; 1 Chr. 28:9; Jer. 17:10]; Acts 1:24 **40** [a][Ps. 130:4] **42** [a]Ex. 13:3; Deut. 3:24 **43** [a][Ex. 9:16; 1 Sam. 17:46; 2 Kin. 19:19] [b]Ps. 102:15 **45** [1]*justice* **46** [a]2 Chr. 6:36; Ps. 130:3; Prov. 20:9; Eccl. 7:20; [Rom. 3:23; 1 John 1:8, 10] [b]Lev. 26:34, 44; Deut. 28:36, 64; 2 Kin. 17:6, 18; 25:21 **47** [a][Lev. 26:40–42]; Neh. 9:2 [b]Ezra 9:6, 7; Neh. 1:6; Ps. 106:6; Dan. 9:5 [1]Lit. *bring back to their heart* **48** [a]Jer. 29:12–14 [b]Dan. 6:10; Jon. 2:4 **49** [1]*justice* **50** [a][2 Chr. 30:9]; Ezra 7:6; Ps. 106:46; Acts 7:10 *See WW at Hos. 2:23. **51** [a]Ex. 32:11, 12; Deut. 9:26–29; Neh. 1:10; [Rom. 11:28, 29] [b]Deut. 4:20; Jer. 11:4 **52** [a]1 Kin. 8:29 *See WW at Jer. 40:4. **53** [a]Ex. 19:5, 6 **54** [a]2 Chr. 7:1

8:39, 40 See section 4 of Truth-In-Action at the end of 1 Kin.
8:46 See section 7 of Truth-In-Action at the end of 1 Kin.

8:54 Here is one of the clearest pictures in the Bible showing the posture of an intercessor, **kneeling on his knees with his hands spread up to heaven.**

from before the altar of the LORD, from
kneeling on his knees with his hands
spread up to heaven.
55 Then he stood [a]and blessed all the
assembly of Israel with a loud voice,
saying:
56 "Blessed *be* the LORD, who has
given [a]rest[1] to His people Israel, according to all that He promised.
[b]There has not failed one word of all
His good promise, which He promised
through His servant Moses.
57 "May the LORD our God be with us,
as He was with our fathers. [a]May He
not leave us nor forsake us,
58 "that He may [a]incline our hearts to
Himself, to walk in all His ways, and
to keep His commandments and His
statutes and His judgments, which He
commanded our fathers.
59 "And may these words of mine,
with which I have made supplication
before the LORD, be near the LORD our
God day and night, that He may maintain the cause of His servant and the
cause of His people Israel, as each day
may require,
60 [a]"that all the peoples of the earth
may know that [b]the LORD *is* God; *there
is* no other.
5 61 "Let your [a]heart therefore be
[1]loyal to the LORD our God, to walk in
His statutes and keep His commandments, as at this day."

Solomon Dedicates the Temple

62 Then [a]the king and all Israel with
him *offered sacrifices before the
LORD.
63 And Solomon offered a sacrifice of
peace offerings, which he offered to
the LORD, twenty-two thousand bulls
and one hundred and twenty thousand
sheep. So the king and all the children
of Israel dedicated the house of the
LORD.
64 On [a]the same day the king consecrated the middle of the court that *was*
in front of the house of the LORD; for
there he offered burnt offerings, grain
offerings, and the fat of the peace offerings, because the [b]bronze altar that
was before the LORD *was* too small to
receive the burnt offerings, the grain
offerings, and the fat of the peace offerings.
65 At that time Solomon held [a]a feast,
and all Israel with him, a great assem-

55 [a]2 Sam. 6:18
56 [a]1 Chr. 22:18 [b]Deut. 12:10 [1]*peace*
57 [a]Deut. 31:6
58 [a]Ps. 119:36
60 [a]1 Sam. 17:46 [b]Deut. 4:35, 39
61 [a]Deut. 18:13 [1]Lit. *at peace with*
62 [a]2 Chr. 7:4–10 *See WW at Deut. 16:2.
64 [a]2 Chr. 7:7 [b]2 Chr. 4:1
65 [a]Lev. 23:34 [b]Num. 34:8 [c]Gen. 15:18 [d]2 Chr. 7:8
66 [a]2 Chr. 7:9 [1]*thanked* *See WW at 2 Chr. 7:10.

CHAPTER 9

1 [a]2 Chr. 7:11 [b]1 Kin. 7:1 [c]2 Chr. 8:6
2 [a]1 Kin. 3:5; 11:9
3 [a]Ps. 10:17 [b]1 Kin. 8:29 [c]Deut. 11:12
4 [a]Gen. 17:1 [b]1 Kin. 11:4, 6; 15:5 [c]1 Kin. 8:61
5 [a]2 Sam. 7:12, 16
6 [a]2 Sam. 7:14–16 [1]*turn back*
7 [a][Lev. 18:24–29] [b][Jer. 7:4–14] [c]Ps. 44:14 [1]*destroy* *See WW at Prov. 1:6.
8 [a]2 Chr. 7:21 [b][Deut. 29:24–26]

bly from [b]the entrance of Hamath to
[c]the Brook of Egypt, before the LORD
our God, [d]seven days and seven *more*
days—fourteen days.
66 [a]On the eighth day he sent the people away; and they [1]blessed the king,
and went to their tents *joyful and glad
of heart for all the good that the LORD
had done for His servant David, and
for Israel His people.

God's Second Appearance to Solomon

9 And [a]it came to pass, when Solomon had finished building the
house of the LORD [b]and the king's
house, and [c]all Solomon's desire which
he wanted to do,
2 that the LORD appeared to Solomon
the second time, [a]as He had appeared
to him at Gibeon.
3 And the LORD said to him: [a]"I have
heard your prayer and your supplication that you have made before Me; I
have consecrated this house which you
have built [b]to put My name there forever, [c]and My eyes and My heart will
be there perpetually.
4 "Now if you [a]walk before Me
[b]as your father David walked, in integrity of heart and in uprightness, to do
according to all that I have commanded you, *and* if you [c]keep My statutes and My judgments,
5 "then I will establish the throne of
your kingdom over Israel forever,
[a]as I promised David your father, saying, 'You shall not fail to have a man
on the throne of Israel.'
6 [a]"*But* if you or your sons at all
[1]turn from following Me, and do not
keep My commandments *and* My statutes which I have set before you, but
go and serve other gods and worship
them,
7 [a]"then I will [1]cut off Israel from the
land which I have given them; and this
house which I have consecrated
[b]for My name I will cast out of My
sight. [c]Israel will be a *proverb and a
byword among all peoples.
8 "And *as for* [a]this house, *which* is
exalted, everyone who passes by it will
be astonished and will hiss, and say,
[b]'Why has the LORD done thus to this
land and to this house?'
9 "Then they will answer, 'Because
they forsook the LORD their God, who
brought their fathers out of the land

8:61 See section 5 of Truth-In-Action at the end of 1 Kin.
9:1–9 In the second appearance to Solomon (v. 2), the Lord promises the king an everlasting dynasty (v. 5). However, this promise is conditional upon Solomon and his sons walking in **integrity** and **uprightness** before the Lord (vv. 4, 6–9). This is a reaffirmation of the Davidic covenant.

of Egypt, and have embraced other
gods, and worshiped them and served
them; therefore the LORD has brought
all this [a]calamity on them.' "

Solomon and Hiram Exchange Gifts

10 Now [a]it happened at the end of
twenty years, when Solomon had built
the two houses, the house of the LORD
and the king's house
11 [a](Hiram the king of Tyre had supplied Solomon with cedar and cypress
and gold, as much as he desired), *that*
King Solomon then gave Hiram twenty
cities in the land of Galilee.
12 Then Hiram went from Tyre to see
the cities which Solomon had given
him, but they did not please him.
13 So he said, "What *kind of* cities *are*
these which you have given me, my
brother?" [a]And he called them the land
of [1]Cabul, as they are to this day.
14 Then Hiram sent the king one hundred and twenty talents of gold.

Solomon's Additional Achievements

15 And this *is* the reason for [a]the labor
force which King Solomon raised: to
build the house of the LORD, his own
house, [1]the [b]Millo, the wall of Jerusalem, [c]Hazor, [d]Megiddo, and [e]Gezer.
16 (Pharaoh king of Egypt had gone
up and taken Gezer and burned it with
fire, [a]had killed the Canaanites who
dwelt in the city, and had given it *as*
a dowry to his daughter, Solomon's
wife.)
17 And Solomon built Gezer, Lower
[a]Beth Horon,
18 [a]Baalath, and Tadmor in the wilderness, in the land *of Judah,*
19 all the storage cities that Solomon
had, cities for [a]his chariots and cities
for his [b]cavalry, and whatever Solomon [c]desired to build in Jerusalem, in
Lebanon, and in all the land of his dominion.
20 [a]All the people *who were* left of the
Amorites, Hittites, Perizzites, Hivites,
and Jebusites, who *were* not of the children of Israel—
21 that is, their descendants [a]who
were left in the land after them,
[b]whom the children of Israel had not
been able to destroy completely—
[c]from these Solomon raised [d]forced labor, as it is to this day.
22 But of the children of Israel Solomon [a]made no forced laborers, because they *were* men of war and his
servants: his officers, his captains,
commanders of his chariots, and his
cavalry.
23 Others *were* chiefs of the officials
who *were* over Solomon's work:
[a]five hundred and fifty, who ruled over
the people who did the work.
24 But [a]Pharaoh's daughter came up
from the City of David to [b]her house
which [1]*Solomon* had built for her.
[c]Then he built the Millo.
25 [a]Now three times a year Solomon
offered burnt offerings and peace offerings on the altar which he had built
for the LORD, and he burned incense
with them *on the altar* that *was* before
the LORD. So he finished the temple.
26 [a]King Solomon also built a fleet of
ships at [b]Ezion Geber, which *is* near
[1]Elath on the shore of the Red Sea, in
the land of Edom.
27 [a]Then Hiram sent his servants with
the fleet, seamen who knew the sea,
to work with the servants of Solomon.
28 And they went to [a]Ophir, and acquired four hundred and twenty talents
of gold from there, and brought *it* to
King Solomon.

The Queen of Sheba's Praise of Solomon

10 Now when the [a]queen of Sheba
heard of the fame of Solomon
concerning the name of the LORD, she
came [b]to test him with hard questions.
2 She came to Jerusalem with a very
great [1]retinue, with camels that bore
spices, very much gold, and precious
stones; and when she came to Solomon, she spoke with him about all that
was in her heart.
3 So Solomon answered all her questions; there was nothing [1]so difficult
for the king that he could not explain
it to her.
4 And when the queen of Sheba had
seen all the wisdom of Solomon, the
house that he had built,
5 the food on his table, the seating of

9 [a][Deut. 29:25–28]
10 [a]1 Kin. 6:37, 38; 7:1; 2 Chr. 8:1
11 [a]1 Kin. 5:1
13 [a]Josh. 19:27 [1]Lit. *Good for Nothing*
15 [a]1 Kin. 5:13 [b]2 Sam. 5:9; 1 Kin. 9:24 [c]Josh. 11:1; 19:36 [d]Josh. 17:11 [e]Josh. 16:10 [1]Lit. *The Landfill*
16 [a]Josh. 16:10; Judg. 1:29
17 [a]Josh. 10:10; 16:3; 21:22; 2 Chr. 8:5
18 [a]Josh. 19:44; 2 Chr. 8:4
19 [a]1 Kin. 10:26; 2 Chr. 1:14 [b]1 Kin. 4:26 [c]1 Kin. 9:1
20 [a]2 Chr. 8:7
21 [a]Judg. 1:21–36; 3:1 [b]Josh. 15:63; 17:12, 13 [c]Judg. 1:28, 35 [d]Ezra 2:55, 58; Neh. 7:57
22 [a][Lev. 25:39]
23 [a]2 Chr. 8:10
24 [a]1 Kin. 3:1 [b]1 Kin. 7:8 [c]2 Sam. 5:9; 1 Kin. 11:27; 2 Chr. 32:5 [1]Lit. *he;* cf. 2 Chr. 8:11
25 [a]Ex. 23:14–17; Deut. 16:16; 2 Chr. 8:12, 13
26 [a]2 Chr. 8:17, 18 [b]Num. 33:35; Deut. 2:8; 1 Kin. 22:48 [1]Heb. *Eloth*
27 [a]1 Kin. 5:6, 9; 10:11
28 [a]Job 22:24

CHAPTER 10

1 [a]2 Chr. 9:1; Matt. 12:42; Luke 11:31 [b]Judg. 14:12; Ps. 49:4; Prov. 1:6
2 [1]*company*
3 [1]*too*

9:25 The **three times a year** were probably the Passover and Feast of Unleavened Bread, the Feast of Harvest (sometimes called the Feast of Weeks or Pentecost), and the Feast of Tabernacles (also called Ingathering).

10:1 **Sheba** was a rather mountainous country approximately 1,200 miles from Jerusalem. Sheba may have been the land of the Sabeans (Job 1:15; Ezek. 23:42; Joel 3:8), and is identified as modern Yemen.

10:5 **There was no more spirit in her:** The queen of Sheba was breathless with amazement at Solomon's wealth, wisdom, and organization. Not only did she marvel at the lavish manner of the temple ceremonies, but observed that

his servants, the service of his waiters
and their apparel, his cupbearers,
[a]and his entryway by which he went
up to the house of the LORD, there was
no more spirit in her.
6 Then she said to the king: "It was
a true report which I heard in my own
land about your words and your wisdom.
7 "However I did not believe the
words until I came and saw with my
own eyes; and indeed the half was not
told me. Your wisdom and prosperity
exceed the fame of which I heard.
8 [a]"Happy *are* your men and happy
are these your servants, who stand
*continually before you *and* hear your
wisdom!
9 [a]"Blessed be the LORD your God,
who [b]delighted in you, setting you on
the throne of Israel! Because the LORD
has loved Israel forever, therefore He
made you king, [c]to do justice and righteousness."
10 Then she [a]gave the king one hundred and twenty talents of gold, spices
in great quantity, and precious stones.
There never again came such abundance of spices as the queen of Sheba
gave to King Solomon.
11 [a]Also, the ships of Hiram, which
brought gold from Ophir, brought
great *quantities* of [1]almug wood and
precious stones from Ophir.
12 [a]And the king made [1]steps of the
almug wood for the house of the LORD
and for the king's house, also harps
and stringed instruments for *singers.
There never again came such [b]almug
wood, nor has the like been seen to this
day.
13 Now King Solomon gave the queen
of Sheba all she desired, whatever
she asked, besides what Solomon
had given her according to the royal
generosity. So she turned and went
to her own country, she and her servants.

Solomon's Great Wealth

14 The weight of gold that came to Solomon yearly was six hundred and
sixty-six talents of gold,
15 besides *that* from the [a]traveling
merchants, from the income of traders,
[b]from all the kings of Arabia, and from
the governors of the country.
16 And King Solomon made two hundred large shields *of* hammered gold;
six hundred *shekels* of gold went into
each shield.
17 He also *made* [a]three hundred
shields *of* hammered gold; three minas
of gold went into each shield. The king
put them in the [b]House of the Forest
of Lebanon.
18 [a]Moreover the king made a great
throne of ivory, and overlaid it with
pure gold.
19 The throne had six *steps, and the
top of the throne *was* round at the
back; *there were* armrests on either
side of the place of the seat, and two
lions stood beside the armrests.
20 Twelve lions stood there, one on
each side of the six steps; nothing like
this had been made for any *other* kingdom.
21 [a]All King Solomon's drinking vessels *were* gold, and all the vessels of
the House of the Forest of Lebanon
were pure gold. Not *one was* silver, for
this was *accounted as nothing in the
days of Solomon.
22 For the king had [a]merchant[1] ships
at sea with the fleet of Hiram. Once
every three years the merchant [b]ships
came bringing gold, silver, ivory, apes,
and [2]monkeys.
23 So [a]King Solomon surpassed all the
kings of the earth in riches and wisdom.
24 Now all the earth sought the presence of Solomon to hear his wisdom,
which God had put in his heart.
25 Each man brought his present: articles of silver and gold, garments, armor, spices, horses, and mules, at a set
rate year by year.
26 [a]And Solomon [b]gathered chariots
and horsemen; he had one thousand
four hundred chariots and twelve thousand horsemen, whom he [1]stationed in
the chariot cities and with the king at
Jerusalem.
27 [a]The king made silver *as common*
in Jerusalem as stones, and he made

5 [a]1 Chr. 26:16; 2 Chr. 9:4
8 [a]Prov. 8:34 *See WW at Ex. 28:30.
9 [a]1 Kin. 5:7 [b]2 Sam. 22:20 [c]2 Sam. 8:15; Ps. 72:2; [Prov. 8:15]
10 [a]Ps. 72:10, 15
11 [a]1 Kin. 9:27, 28; Job 22:24 [1]*algum,* 2 Chr. 9:10, 11
12 [a]2 Chr. 9:11 [b]2 Chr. 9:10 [1]Or *supports* *See WW at Judg. 5:3.
15 [a]2 Chr. 1:16 [b]2 Chr. 9:24; Ps. 72:10
17 [a]1 Kin. 14:26 [b]1 Kin. 7:2
18 [a]1 Kin. 10:22; 2 Chr. 9:17; Ps. 45:8
19 *See WW at Amos 9:6.
21 [a]2 Chr. 9:20 *See WW at Gen. 15:6.
22 [a]Gen. 10:4; 2 Chr. 20:36 [b]1 Kin. 9:26–28; 22:48; Ps. 72:10 [1]Lit. *ships of Tarshish,* deep-sea vessels [2]Or *peacocks*
23 [a]1 Kin. 3:12, 13; 4:30; 2 Chr. 1:12
26 [a]1 Kin. 4:26; 2 Chr. 1:14; 9:25 [b][Deut. 17:16]; 1 Kin. 9:19 [1]So with LXX, Syr., Tg., Vg. (cf. 2 Chr. 9:25); MT *led*
27 [a][Deut. 17:17]; 2 Chr. 1:15–17

even insignificant aspects of Solomon's household and public affairs were in such order that his wives and servants were happy (v. 8).

10:9 It is likely that the queen of Sheba was a pagan, and yet even she realized that the Lord was the source of all of Solomon's blessings.

10:10 One hundred and twenty talents of gold would be over 4 tons.

10:14, 15 The annual income of gold would have been about 25 tons, aside from the taxes from both traveling caravans (the **merchants** and **traders**) and state monopolies (the **kings** and **governors**).

10:23, 24 God had raised this insignificant group of people to the pinnacle of political and economic power.

10:26, 28, 29 Though Solomon was wealthy and wise, we can observe here one of the seeds of his downfall. The Lord had instructed His people in the Mosaic Law (Deut. 17:16) not to multiply horses.

cedar trees as abundant as the sycamores which *are* in the lowland.
28 [a]Also Solomon had horses imported from Egypt and Keveh; the
king's merchants bought them in Keveh at the *current* price.
29 Now a chariot that was imported
from Egypt cost six hundred *shekels*
of silver, and a horse one hundred and
fifty; [a]and [1]thus, through their agents,
they exported *them* to all the kings of
the Hittites and the kings of Syria.

Solomon's Heart Turns from the LORD

5 **11** But [a]King Solomon loved
[b]many foreign women, as well
as the daughter of Pharaoh: women of
the Moabites, Ammonites, Edomites,
Sidonians, *and* Hittites—
2 from the nations of whom the LORD
had said to the children of Israel,
[a]"You shall not intermarry with them,
nor they with you. Surely they will turn
away your hearts after their gods."
Solomon clung to these in love.
3 And he had seven hundred wives,
princesses, and three hundred concubines; and his wives turned away his
heart.
4 For it was so, when Solomon was
old, [a]that his wives turned his heart after other gods; and his [b]heart was not
[1]loyal to the LORD his God, [c]as *was* the
heart of his father David.
5 For Solomon went after [a]Ashtoreth
the goddess of the Sidonians, and after
[b]Milcom[1] the abomination of the [c]Am-
monites.
6 Solomon did evil in the sight of the
LORD, and did not fully follow the LORD,
as *did* his father David.
7 [a]Then Solomon built a [1]high place
for [b]Chemosh the abomination of
Moab, on [c]the hill that *is* east of Jerusalem, and for Molech the abomination
of the people of Ammon.
8 And he did likewise for all his foreign wives, who burned incense and
sacrificed to their gods.
9 So the LORD became angry with Solomon, because his heart had turned
from the LORD God of Israel, [a]who had
appeared to him twice,
10 and [a]had commanded him concerning this thing, that he should not go
after other gods; but he did not keep
what the LORD had commanded.
11 Therefore the LORD said to Solomon, "Because you have done this,
and have not kept My covenant and
My statutes, which I have commanded
you, [a]I will surely tear the kingdom
away from you and give it to your
[b]servant.
12 "Nevertheless I will not do it in your
days, for the sake of your father David;
I will tear it out of the hand of your
son.
13 [a]"However I will not tear away the
whole kingdom; I will give [b]one tribe
to your son [c]for the sake of My servant
David, and for the sake of Jerusalem
[d]which I have chosen."

Adversaries of Solomon

14 Now the LORD [a]raised up an adversary against Solomon, Hadad the
Edomite; he *was* a descendant of the
king in Edom.
15 [a]For it happened, when David was
in Edom, and Joab the commander of
the army had gone up to bury the slain,
[b]after he had killed every male in
Edom
16 (because for six months Joab *remained there with all Israel, until he
had cut down every male in Edom),
17 that Hadad fled to go to Egypt, he
and certain Edomites of his father's
servants with him. Hadad *was* still a
little child.
18 Then they arose from Midian and
came to Paran; and they took men with
them from Paran and came to Egypt,
to Pharaoh king of Egypt, who gave
him a house, apportioned food for him,
and gave him land.
19 And Hadad found great favor in the
sight of Pharaoh, so that he gave him
as wife the sister of his own wife, that
is, the sister of Queen Tahpenes.
20 Then the sister of Tahpenes bore

28 [a][Deut. 17:16]; 2 Chr. 1:16; 9:28
29 [a]Josh. 1:4; 2 Kin. 7:6, 7 [1]Lit. *by their hands*

CHAPTER 11

1 [a][Neh. 13:26] [b][Deut. 17:17]; 1 Kin. 3:1
2 [a]Ex. 34:16; [Deut. 7:3, 4]
4 [a][Deut. 17:17; Neh. 13:26] [b]1 Kin. 8:61 [c]1 Kin. 9:4 [1]Lit. *at peace with*
5 [a]Judg. 2:13; 1 Kin. 11:33 [b][Lev. 20:2–5] [c]2 Kin. 23:13 [1]Or *Molech*
7 [a]Num. 33:52 [b]Num. 21:29; Judg. 11:24 [c]2 Kin. 23:13 [1]A place for pagan worship
9 [a]1 Kin. 3:5; 9:2
10 [a]1 Kin. 6:12; 9:6, 7
11 [a]1 Kin. 11:31; 12:15, 16 [b]1 Kin. 11:31, 37
13 [a]2 Sam. 7:15; 1 Chr. 17:13; Ps. 89:33 [b]1 Kin. 12:20 [c]2 Sam. 7:15, 16 [d]Deut. 12:11; 1 Kin. 9:3; 14:21
14 [a]1 Chr. 5:26
15 [a]2 Sam. 8:14; 1 Chr. 18:12, 13 [b]Num. 24:18, 19; [Deut. 20:13]
16 *See WW at Lam. 5:19.

11:1–8 See section 5 of Truth-In-Action at the end of 1 Kin.

11:1–4 The greatest kingdom of the known world began to crumble, not from external opposition, but from internal weakness. Not only was Solomon prohibited from multiplying horses (see note on 10:26, 28, 29), but it was also forbidden for him to marry many wives (Deut. 17:17). The reason for this restriction was that pagan wives would lead God's people into idolatry. As God had warned, so it happened.

11:5–7 Ashtoreth was the Canaanite goddess of fertility whose worship involved not only sexual rites, but astrology. The worship of **Milcom** or **Molech** included human sacrifices, especially of children. The worship of **Chemosh** was equally cruel and also centered in astrology. For an explanation of a **high place,** see note on 3:2–4.

11:9–13 Even in the midst of judgment, God shows mercy by promising not to take the kingdom from Solomon in his lifetime (v. 12) and by assuring him that his son will reign over one tribe (v. 13).

11:14–25 In addition to the internal weakness, the Lord now brings external opposition by raising up two adversaries: **Hadad the Edomite** (vv. 14–22) and **Rezon . . . of Zobah** (vv. 23–25).

him Genubath his son, whom Tahpenes weaned in Pharaoh's house. And
Genubath was in Pharaoh's household
among the sons of Pharaoh.
21 [a]So when Hadad heard in Egypt
that David [1]rested with his fathers, and
that Joab the commander of the army
was dead, Hadad said to Pharaoh,
[2]"Let me depart, that I may go to my
own country."
22 Then Pharaoh said to him, "But
what have you lacked with me, that
suddenly you seek to go to your own
country?" So he answered, "Nothing,
but do let me go anyway."
23 And God raised up *another* adversary against him, Rezon the son of
Eliadah, who had fled from his lord,
[a]Hadadezer king of Zobah.
24 So he gathered men to him and became captain over a band *of raiders,*
[a]when David killed those *of Zobah.*
And they went to Damascus and dwelt
there, and reigned in Damascus.
25 He was an adversary of Israel all
the days of Solomon (besides the trouble that Hadad *caused*); and he abhorred Israel, and reigned over Syria.

Jeroboam's Rebellion

26 Then Solomon's servant, [a]Jero-
boam the son of Nebat, an Ephraimite
from Zereda, whose mother's name
was Zeruah, a widow, [b]also [c]rebelled
against the king.
27 And this *is* what caused him to rebel
against the king: [a]Solomon had built
the Millo *and* [1]repaired the *damages
to the City of David his father.
28 The man Jeroboam *was* a mighty
man of valor; and Solomon, seeing that
the young man was [a]industrious, made
him the officer over all the labor force
of the house of Joseph.
29 Now it happened at that time, when
Jeroboam went out of Jerusalem, that
the prophet [a]Ahijah the Shilonite met
him on the way; and he had clothed
himself with a new garment, and the
two *were* alone in the field.
30 Then Ahijah took hold of the new
garment that *was* on him, and [a]tore it
into twelve pieces.
31 And he said to Jeroboam, "Take for
yourself ten pieces, for [a]thus says the
LORD, the God of Israel: 'Behold, I will
tear the kingdom out of the hand of
Solomon and will give ten tribes to you
32 '(but he shall have one tribe for the
sake of My servant David, and for the
sake of Jerusalem, the city which I
have chosen out of all the tribes of Israel),
33 [a]'because [1]they have forsaken Me,
and worshiped Ashtoreth the goddess
of the Sidonians, Chemosh the god of
the Moabites, and Milcom the god of
the people of Ammon, and have not
walked in My ways to do *what is* right
in My eyes and *keep* My statutes and
My judgments, as *did* his father David.
34 'However I will not take the whole
kingdom out of his hand, because I
have made him ruler all the days of
his life for the sake of My servant David, whom I **chose** because he kept My
commandments and My statutes.

> **WORD WEALTH**
>
> **11:34 chose,** *bachar* (bah-*char*); Strong's #977: To choose, select, elect; to determine to have one in particular. *Bachar* describes the kind of choosing that is made when more than one item is examined, with only one (or a few) being selected. *Bachar* is used primarily with the idea of God's making significant choices. In this reference, God chose David to be ruler over Israel. The right of God to choose whomever He wishes is well established in Scripture. He chose Abraham to pioneer, Moses to instruct, Israel to bring salvation to the world, and He chose believers before the world began (Eph. 1:4).

35 'But [a]I will take the kingdom out of
his son's hand and give it to you—ten
tribes.
36 'And to his son I will give one tribe,
that [a]My servant David may always
have a lamp before Me in Jerusalem,
the city which I have chosen for Myself, to put My name there.

21 [a]1 Kin. 2:10, 34 [1]Died and joined his ancestors [2]Lit. *Send me away*
23 [a]2 Sam. 8:3; 10:16
24 [a]2 Sam. 8:3; 10:8, 18
26 [a]1 Kin. 12:2 [b]1 Kin. 11:11; 2 Chr. 13:6 [c]2 Sam. 20:21
27 [a]1 Kin. 9:15, 24 [1]Lit. *closed up the breaches* *See WW at Ezek. 22:30.
28 [a][Prov. 22:29]
29 [a]1 Kin. 12:15; 14:2; 2 Chr. 9:29
30 [a]1 Sam. 15:27, 28; 24:5
31 [a]1 Kin. 11:11, 13
33 [a]1 Sam. 7:3; 1 Kin. 11:5–8 [1]So with MT, Tg.; LXX, Syr., Vg. *he has*
35 [a]1 Kin. 12:16, 17
36 [a][1 Kin. 15:4; 2 Kin. 8:19]

11:26–28 The most dangerous adversary the Lord raised up against Solomon was **Jeroboam,** for he led a revolt from within. Jeroboam would later lead 10 of the tribes of Israel in a rebellion against Solomon's successor Rehoboam, and he became the first king of the northern kingdom known as "Israel" (ch. 12).

11:29–39 In an illustrated prophecy, **Ahijah** tears a new garment into 12 pieces (v. 30) to give a visible demonstration of how God would tear the kingdom from Solomon. 10 pieces (vv. 31, 35) were given to Jeroboam and represented the 10 northern tribes (the Israel in v. 37, 38). Two pieces would be left for Solomon's son and represented the tribes of Judah and Benjamin. Benjamin was assimilated into Judah, so the two were often regarded as **one tribe** (vv. 33, 36) called "Judah" (see note on 12:20).

11:36 This is an illuminating commentary on the fact that God will honor His promises to a person, even beyond his lifetime on this Earth. Though David was gone, God honored His commitment to him.

37 'So I will take you, and you shall
reign over all your heart desires, and
you shall be king over Israel.
38 'Then it shall be, if you heed all that
I command you, walk in My ways, and
do *what is* right in My sight, to keep
My statutes and My commandments,
as My servant David did, then [a]I will
be with you and [b]build for you an
enduring house, as I built for David,
and will give Israel to you.
39 'And I will afflict the descendants
of David because of this, but not forever.' "
40 Solomon therefore sought to kill
Jeroboam. But Jeroboam arose and
fled to Egypt, to [a]Shishak king of
Egypt, and was in Egypt until the death
of Solomon.

Death of Solomon

41 Now [a]the rest of the acts of Solomon, all that he did, and his wisdom,
are they not written in the book of the
acts of Solomon?
42 [a]And the period that Solomon
reigned in Jerusalem over all Israel
was forty years.
43 [a]Then Solomon [1]rested with his fathers, and was buried in the City of David his father. And Rehoboam his son
reigned in his [b]place.

The Revolt Against Rehoboam

12 And [a]Rehoboam went to [b]She-
chem, for all Israel had gone to
Shechem to make him king.
2 So it happened, when [a]Jeroboam
the son of Nebat heard *it* (he was still
in [b]Egypt, for he had fled from the
presence of King Solomon and had
been dwelling in Egypt),
3 that they sent and called him. Then
Jeroboam and the whole assembly of
Israel came and spoke to Rehoboam,
saying,
4 "Your father made our [a]yoke
[1]heavy; now therefore, lighten the
burdensome service of your father, and
his heavy yoke which he put on us, and
we will serve you."
5 So he said to them, "Depart *for*
three days, then come back to me."
And the people departed.
6 Then King Rehoboam consulted the 6
elders who stood before his father Solomon while he still lived, and he said,
"How do you advise *me* to answer
these people?"
7 And they spoke to him, saying,
[a]"If you will be a servant to these people today, and serve them, and answer
them, and speak good words to them,
then they will be your servants forever."
8 But he rejected the advice which the
elders had given him, and consulted
the young men who had grown up with
him, who stood before him.
9 And he said to them, "What advice
do you give? How should we answer
this people who have spoken to me,
saying, 'Lighten the yoke which your
father put on us'?"
10 Then the young men who had
grown up with him spoke to him, saying, "Thus you should speak to this
people who have spoken to you, saying, 'Your father made our yoke heavy,
but you make *it* lighter on us'—thus
you shall say to them: 'My little *finger*
shall be thicker than my father's waist!
11 'And now, whereas my father put
a heavy yoke on you, I will add to your
yoke; my father *chastised you with
whips, but I will chastise you with
[1]scourges!' "
12 So Jeroboam and all the people
came to Rehoboam the third day, as
the king had directed, saying, "Come
back to me the third day."
13 Then the king answered the people
[1]roughly, and rejected the advice
which the elders had given him;
14 and he spoke to them according to
the advice of the young men, saying,
"My father made your yoke heavy, but
I will add to your yoke; my father chastised you with whips, but I will chastise
you with [1]scourges!"
15 So the king did not listen to the people; for [a]the turn *of events* was from
the LORD, that He might fulfill His
word, which the LORD had [b]spoken by
Ahijah the Shilonite to Jeroboam the
son of Nebat.
16 Now when all Israel saw that the

38 [a]Deut. 31:8; Josh. 1:5 [b]2 Sam. 7:11, 27
40 [a]1 Kin. 11:17; 14:25; 2 Chr. 12:2–9
41 [a]2 Chr. 9:29
42 [a]2 Chr. 9:30
43 [a]1 Kin. 2:10; 2 Chr. 9:31 [b]1 Kin. 14:21; 2 Chr. 10:1 [1]Died and joined his ancestors

CHAPTER 12

1 [a]2 Chr. 10:1 [b]Judg. 9:6
2 [a]1 Kin. 11:26 [b]1 Kin. 11:40
4 [a]1 Sam. 8:11–18; 1 Kin. 4:7; 5:13–15 [1]*hard*
7 [a]2 Chr. 10:7; [Prov. 15:1]
11 [1]Scourges with points or barbs, lit. *scorpions* *See WW at Jer. 10:24.
13 [1]*harshly*
14 [1]Lit. *scorpions*
15 [a]Deut. 2:30; Judg. 14:4; 1 Kin. 12:24; 2 Chr. 10:15 [b]1 Kin. 11:11, 29, 31

11:40 Solomon, the man who began so humbly by asking for wisdom, now engages in an insane attempt to kill the one to whom the Lord has chosen to give the kingdom that Solomon had forfeited.

12:2–4 The leaders of the northern tribes sent for Jeroboam to come and be their spokesman. Sometime during Rehoboam's coronation proceedings, he articulated to Rehoboam the people's plea for lower taxes.

12:6–11 See section 6 of Truth-In-Action at the end of 1 Kin.

12:15 One of the mysteries of Scripture is how God works through men to accomplish His purposes. Here the self-seeking interests of Rehoboam were used by the Lord to fulfill His promise through the prophet **Ahijah** (11:29–39).

12:16 The negotiations having failed, the revolt continued. The cry **To your tents** was the cue for the 10 northern tribes to disperse.

king did not listen to them, the people
answered the king, saying:

[a]"What share have we in David?
We have no inheritance in the son
of Jesse.
To your tents, O Israel!
Now, see to your own house,
O David!"

So Israel departed to their tents.
17 But Rehoboam reigned over [a]the
children of Israel who dwelt in the cities of Judah.
18 Then King Rehoboam [a]sent Adoram, who *was* in charge of the revenue;
but all Israel stoned him with stones,
and he died. Therefore King Rehoboam mounted his chariot in haste to
flee to Jerusalem.
19 So [a]Israel has been in rebellion
against the house of David to this day.
20 Now it came to pass when all Israel
heard that Jeroboam had come back,
they sent for him and called him to the
congregation, and made him king over
all [a]Israel. There was none who followed the house of David, but the tribe
of Judah [b]only.
21 And when [a]Rehoboam came to Jerusalem, he assembled all the house of
Judah with the tribe of [b]Benjamin, one
hundred and eighty thousand chosen
men who were warriors, to fight
against the house of Israel, that he
might restore the kingdom to Rehoboam the son of Solomon.
22 But [a]the word of God came to Shemaiah the man of God, saying,
23 "Speak to Rehoboam the son of Solomon, king of Judah, to all the house
of Judah and Benjamin, and to the rest
of the people, saying,

16 [a]2 Sam. 20:1
17 [a]1 Kin. 11:13, 36; 2 Chr. 11:14–17
18 [a]1 Kin. 4:6; 5:14
19 [a]2 Kin. 17:21
20 [a]2 Kin. 17:21 [b]1 Kin. 11:13, 32, 36
21 [a]2 Chr. 11:1–4 [b]2 Sam. 19:17
22 [a]2 Chr. 11:2; 12:5–7
24 [a]1 Kin. 12:15
25 [a]Gen. 12:6; Judg. 9:45–49; 1 Kin. 12:1 [b]Gen. 32:30, 31; Judg. 8:8, 17 [1]*fortified*
27 [a][Deut. 12:5–7, 14]
28 [a]2 Kin. 10:29; 17:16; [Hos. 8:4–7] [b]Ex. 32:4, 8
29 [a]Gen. 28:19 [b]Judg. 18:26–31
30 [a]1 Kin. 13:34; 2 Kin. 17:21
31 [a][Num. 3:10; 17:1–11]; Judg. 17:5; 1 Kin. 13:33; 2 Kin. 17:32; 2 Chr. 11:14, 15 [1]Lit. *a house;* cf. 1 Kin. 13:32, lit. *houses*
32 [a]Lev. 23:33, 34; Num. 29:12; 1 Kin. 8:2, 5 [1]*instituted*

24 'Thus says the LORD: "You shall not
go up nor fight against your brethren
the children of Israel. Let every man
return to his house, [a]for this thing is
from Me." ' " Therefore they obeyed
the word of the LORD, and turned back,
according to the word of the LORD.

Jeroboam's Gold Calves

25 Then Jeroboam [a]built[1] Shechem in
the mountains of Ephraim, and dwelt
there. Also he went out from there and
built [b]Penuel.
26 And Jeroboam said in his heart,
"Now the kingdom may return to the
house of David:
27 "If these people [a]go up to offer sacrifices in the house of the LORD at Jerusalem, then the heart of this people will
turn back to their lord, Rehoboam king
of Judah, and they will kill me and go
back to Rehoboam king of Judah."
28 Therefore the king asked advice, 6
[a]made two calves of gold, and said to
the people, "It is too much for you to
go up to Jerusalem. [b]Here are your
gods, O Israel, which brought you up
from the land of Egypt!"
29 And he set up one in [a]Bethel, and
the other he put in [b]Dan.
30 Now this thing became [a]a sin, for
the people went *to worship* before the
one as far as Dan.
31 He made [1]shrines on the high
places, [a]and made priests from every
class of people, who were not of the
sons of Levi.
32 Jeroboam [1]ordained a feast on the
fifteenth day of the eighth month, like
[a]the feast that *was* in Judah, and offered sacrifices on the altar. So he did
at Bethel, sacrificing to the calves that

12:17 The northern tribes had not yet made Jeroboam king; they were simply refusing to submit to **Rehoboam.** The only Israelites over whom Rehoboam exercised control were the ones in the cities of **Judah.**

12:18 Rehoboam attempted to enforce his oppressive tactics in the north, but this resulted in the death of his ambassador, **Adoram,** and he barely escaped with his own life.

12:20 From this point the kingdom remained divided until the downfall of Israel in 722 B.C. Subsequent to this, Kings refers to the northern kingdom as **Israel** and the southern kingdom as **Judah,** though it was later supplemented by Levites, Benjamites, and others of the 10 tribes.

12:25 It is possible that Jeroboam chose **Shechem** as his capital for a political reason, since this was where Rehoboam had been crowned (v. 1). **Penuel** was east of the Jordan River, and was probably fortified to give protection from the Gileadites who were loyal to David (2:7; 2 Sam. 17:27–29; 19:31–39).

12:26–33 Instead of trusting the Lord to establish his reign as promised (11:38, 39), Jeroboam became fearful that he would lose the people and resorted to methods of sinful manipulation. He set up new worship centers to rival Jerusalem (vv. 27–30), ordained his own priesthood (vv. 31, 32), and instituted a new festival as a counterfeit of Judah's feast (vv. 32, 33). Jeroboam made **two calves of gold** (v. 28) and placed one at **Bethel** and the other at **Dan** (vv. 28–31), so that people would have places of worship and not return to Jerusalem (vv. 26, 27). Since v. 28 includes a quote from Ex. 32:4, Jeroboam's statement may be intended to imply that these two calves of gold were the same as the golden calf made by Aaron. In light of the fact that some of the pagan gods were portrayed as standing on bulls or calves to symbolize their strength, another possibility is that Jeroboam made the two calves as a pedestal on which the God of Israel was to be enthroned. In either case, this new form of worship resulted in unprecedented idolatry (14:9).

12:28 See section 6 of Truth-In-Action at the end of 1 Kin.

12:32 **Jeroboam** ordained a counterfeit **feast** like **the feast that *was* in Judah.** There were three fall festivals that occurred in their seventh month (Tishri, October-November) and marked the end of the agricultural year. The Feast of

he had made. [b]And at Bethel he installed the priests of the high places which he had made.

33 So he made offerings on the altar which he had made at Bethel on the fifteenth day of the eighth month, in the month which he had [a]devised in his own heart. And he [1]ordained a feast for the children of Israel, and offered sacrifices on the altar and [b]burned incense.

The Message of the Man of God

13 And behold, [a]a man of God went from Judah to Bethel [1]by the word of the LORD, [b]and Jeroboam stood by the altar to burn incense.

2 Then he cried out against the altar [1]by the word of the LORD, and said, "O altar, altar! Thus says the LORD: 'Behold, a child, [a]Josiah by name, shall be born to the house of David; and on you he shall sacrifice the priests of the high places who burn incense on you, and men's bones shall be [b]burned on you.' "

3 And he gave [a]a *sign the same day, saying, "This *is* the sign which the LORD has spoken: Surely the altar shall split apart, and the ashes on it shall be poured out."

4 So it came to pass when King Jeroboam heard the saying of the man of God, who cried out against the altar in Bethel, that he stretched out his hand from the altar, saying, "Arrest him!" Then his hand, which he stretched out toward him, withered, so that he could not pull it back to himself.

5 The altar also was split apart, and the ashes poured out from the altar, according to the sign which the man of God had given by the word of the LORD.

6 Then the king answered and said to the man of God, "Please [a]entreat the favor of the LORD your God, and pray for me, that my hand may be *restored to me." So the man of God entreated the LORD, and the king's hand was restored to him, and became as before.

7 Then the king said to the man of God, "Come home with me and refresh yourself, and [a]I will give you a reward."

8 But the man of God said to the king, [a]"If you were to give me half your house, I would not go in with you; nor would I eat bread nor drink water in this place.

9 "For so it was commanded me by the word of the LORD, saying, [a]'You shall not eat bread, nor drink water, nor return by the same way you came.' "

10 So he went another way and did not return by the way he came to Bethel.

Death of the Man of God

11 Now an [a]old prophet dwelt in Bethel, and his [1]sons came and told him all the works that the man of God had done that day in Bethel; they also told their father the words which he had spoken to the king.

12 And their father said to them, "Which way did he go?" For his sons [1]had seen which way the man of God went who came from Judah.

13 Then he said to his sons, "Saddle the donkey for me." So they saddled the donkey for him; and he rode on it,

14 and went after the man of God, and found him sitting under an oak. Then he said to him, "*Are* you the man of God who came from Judah?" And he said, "I *am*."

15 Then he said to him, "Come home with me and eat bread."

16 And he said, [a]"I cannot return with you nor go in with you; neither can I eat bread nor drink water with you in this place.

17 "For [1]I have been told [a]by the word

32 [b]Amos 7:10–13
33 [a]Num. 15:39 [b]1 Kin. 13:1 [1]*instituted*

CHAPTER 13

1 [a]2 Kin. 23:17 [b]1 Kin. 12:32, 33 [1]*at the LORD's command*
2 [a]2 Kin. 23:15, 16 [b][Lev. 26:30] [1]*at the LORD's command*
3 [a]Ex. 4:1–5; Judg. 6:17; Is. 7:14; 38:7; John 2:18; 1 Cor. 1:22 *See WW at Zech. 3:8.
6 [a]Ex. 8:8; 9:28; 10:17; Num. 21:7; Jer. 37:3; Acts 8:24; [James 5:16] *See WW at Ruth 4:15.
7 [a]1 Sam. 9:7; 2 Kin. 5:15
8 [a]Num. 22:18; 24:13; 1 Kin. 13:16, 17
9 [a][1 Cor. 5:11]
11 [a]1 Kin. 13:25 [1]Lit. *son*
12 [1]LXX, Syr., Tg., Vg. *showed him*
16 [a]1 Kin. 13:8, 9
17 [a]1 Kin. 20:35; 1 Thess. 4:15 [1]Lit. *a command came to me by*

Trumpets was on the first day of the month (Lev. 23:23–25; Num. 29:1–6), the Day of Atonement on the tenth day (Lev. 23:26–32; Num. 29:7–11), and the Feast of Tabernacles on the fifteenth day (Lev. 23:33–43; Num. 29:12–39). Jeroboam was apparently trying to provide an alternative to one or more of these feasts. That this new **feast** was to be held on **the fifteenth day of the eighth month** may indicate that Jeroboam was trying to counterfeit the Feast of Tabernacles, since it began on the fifteenth day of the seventh month (Lev. 23:34).

13:1, 2 The prophecy by this unnamed **man of God** against Jeroboam is truly remarkable, since it names and describes the actions of **Josiah** almost 300 years before this king comes on the scene.

13:3 To illustrate that God was not pleased with the idolatry that resulted from the influence of Jeroboam, and to give a sign affirming the prophecy about Josiah, Jeroboam's altar would **split apart.**

13:4 Since the hand symbolized authority, the withering of Jeroboam's hand demonstrated the superiority of God's authority.

13:6 Some think that Jeroboam betrays the sinful condition of his heart when he refers to the Lord not as "my God" but as **your God.** However, in light of the use of the phrase in 2:3 and Gen. 27:20, this may not necessarily be so.

13:8 To eat bread or **drink water** implied the giving of approval.

13:11–19 The incident of the seduction of the man of God, though somewhat confusing, serves to portray how even this man of God had been affected by the evil influence of Jeroboam.

of the LORD, 'You shall not eat bread
nor drink water there, nor return by
going the way you came.'"
18 He said to him, "I too *am* a prophet
as you *are*, and an angel spoke to me
by the word of the LORD, saying, 'Bring
him back with you to your house, that
he may eat bread and drink water.'"
(He was lying to him.)
19 So he went back with him, and ate
bread in his house, and drank water.
20 Now it happened, as they sat at the
table, that the word of the LORD came
to the prophet who had brought him
back;
21 and he cried out to the man of God
who came from Judah, saying, "Thus
says the LORD: 'Because you have disobeyed the word of the LORD, and have
not kept the commandment which the
LORD your God commanded you,
22 'but you came back, ate bread, and
drank water in the [a]place of which *the
LORD* said to you, "Eat no bread and
drink no water," your corpse shall not
come to the tomb of your fathers.'"
23 So it was, after he had eaten bread
and after he had drunk, that he saddled
the donkey for him, the prophet whom
he had brought back.
24 When he was gone, [a]a lion met him
on the road and killed him. And his
corpse was thrown on the road, and
the donkey stood by it. The lion also
stood by the corpse.
25 And there, men passed by and saw
the corpse thrown on the road, and the
lion standing by the corpse. Then they
went and told *it* in the city where the
old prophet dwelt.
26 Now when the prophet who had
brought him back from the way heard
it, he said, "It *is* the man of God who
was disobedient to the word of the
LORD. Therefore the LORD has delivered him to the lion, which has torn
him and killed him, according to the
word of the LORD which He spoke to
him."
27 And he spoke to his sons, saying,
"Saddle the donkey for me." So they
saddled *it*.
28 Then he went and found his corpse
thrown on the road, and the donkey
and the lion standing by the corpse.
The lion had not eaten the corpse nor
torn the donkey.
29 And the prophet took up the corpse
of the man of God, laid it on the donkey, and brought it back. So the old
prophet came to the city to mourn, and
to bury him.
30 Then he laid the corpse in his own
tomb; and they mourned over him, *saying*, [a]"Alas, my brother!"
31 So it was, after he had buried him,
that he spoke to his sons, saying,
"When I am dead, then bury me in the
tomb where the man of God *is* buried;
[a]lay my bones beside his bones.
32 [a]"For the [1]saying which he cried out
by the word of the LORD against the
altar in Bethel, and against all the
[2]shrines on the high places which *are*
in the cities of [b]Samaria, will surely
come to pass."
33 [a]After this event Jeroboam did not
turn from his evil way, but again he
made priests from every class of people for the *high places; whoever
wished, he consecrated him, and he became *one* of the priests of the high
places.
34 [a]And this thing was the sin of the 6
house of Jeroboam, so as [b]to exterminate and destroy *it* from the face of the
earth.

Judgment on the House of Jeroboam

14 At that time Abijah the son of
Jeroboam became sick.
2 And Jeroboam said to his wife,
"Please arise, and disguise yourself,
that they may not recognize you as the
wife of Jeroboam, and go to *Shiloh.
Indeed, Ahijah the prophet *is* there,
who told me that [a]*I would be* king over
this people.
3 [a]"Also take [1]with you ten loaves,
some cakes, and a jar of honey, and
go to him; he will tell you what will
become of the child."
4 And Jeroboam's wife did so; she
arose [a]and went to Shiloh, and came
to the house of Ahijah. But Ahijah
could not see, for his eyes were [1]glazed
by reason of his age.
5 Now the LORD had said to Ahijah,
"Here is the wife of Jeroboam, coming

22 [a]1 Kin. 13:9
24 [a]1 Kin. 20:36
30 [a]Jer. 22:18
31 [a]Ruth 1:17; 2 Kin. 23:17, 18
32 [a]1 Kin. 13:2; 2 Kin. 23:16, 19 [b]1 Kin. 16:24; John 4:5; Acts 8:14 [1]Lit. *word* [2]Lit. *houses*
33 [a]1 Kin. 12:31, 32; 2 Chr. 11:15; 13:9 *See WW at Ezek. 6:3.
34 [a]1 Kin. 12:30; 2 Kin. 17:21 [b][1 Kin. 14:10; 15:29, 30]

CHAPTER 14

2 [a]1 Kin. 11:29–31 *See WW at Gen. 49:10.
3 [a]1 Sam. 9:7, 8; 1 Kin. 13:7; 2 Kin. 4:42 [1]Lit. *in your hand*
4 [a]1 Kin. 11:29 [1]Lit. *set*

13:20–32 Why did God deal so harshly with the man of God and not the prophet, when both were disobedient? Perhaps it was because the sin of the man of God would have brought doubt upon the prophecy he had just given and would have impinged on God's reliability. This explains the actions of the older prophet in vv. 31, 32.
13:32 Samaria would become the capital city of the 10 northern tribes (16:23, 24). **The cities of Samaria** then is a designation for the whole territory of the nation Israel.
13:33, 34 Even after this incident with the man of God, Jeroboam still **did not turn from his evil way.** Not only had Jeroboam ordained his own priesthood (12:31; 13:33), but now he made himself ***one* of the priests of the high places.** For this final act of apostasy, God would **exterminate and destroy** the house of Jeroboam.
13:34 See section 6 of Truth-In-Action at the end of 1 Kin.

to ask you something about her son,
for he *is* sick. Thus and thus you shall
say to her; for it will be, when she
comes in, that she will pretend *to be*
another *woman.*"
6 And so it was, when Ahijah heard
the sound of her footsteps as she came
through the door, he said, "Come in,
wife of Jeroboam. Why do you pretend
to be another *person*? For I *have been*
sent to you *with* bad *news.*
7 "Go, tell Jeroboam, 'Thus says the
LORD God of Israel: [a]"Because I exalted
you from among the people, and made
you ruler over My people Israel,
8 "and [a]tore the kingdom away from
the house of David, and gave it to you;
and *yet* you have not been as My servant David, [b]who kept My commandments and who followed Me with all
his heart, to do only *what was* right
in My eyes;
9 "but you have done more evil than
all who were before you, [a]for you have
gone and made for yourself other gods
and molded images to provoke Me to
anger, and [b]have cast Me behind your
back—
10 "therefore behold! [a]I will bring disaster on the house of Jeroboam, and
[b]will cut off from Jeroboam every male
in Israel, [c]bond and free; I will take
away the remnant of the house of Jeroboam, as one takes away refuse until
it is all gone.
11 "The dogs shall eat [a]whoever belongs to Jeroboam and dies in the city,
and the birds of the air shall eat whoever dies in the field; for the LORD has
spoken!"'
12 "Arise therefore, go to your own
house. [a]When your feet enter the city,
the child shall die.
13 "And all Israel shall mourn for him
and bury him, for he is the only one
of Jeroboam who shall [1]come to the
grave, because in him [a]there is found
something good toward the LORD God
of Israel in the house of Jeroboam.
14 [a]"Moreover the LORD will raise up
for Himself a king over Israel who shall
cut off the house of Jeroboam; [1]this is
the day. What? Even now!
15 "For the LORD will strike Israel, as
a reed is shaken in the water. He will
[a]uproot Israel from this [b]good land
which He gave to their fathers, and will
scatter them [c]beyond [1]the River, [d]be-
cause they have made their [2]wooden
images, provoking the LORD to anger.
16 "And He will give Israel up because
of the sins of Jeroboam, [a]who sinned
and who made Israel sin."
17 Then Jeroboam's wife arose and departed, and came to [a]Tirzah. [b]When
she came to the threshold of the house,
the child died.
18 And they buried him; and all Israel
mourned for him, [a]according to the
word of the LORD which He spoke
through His servant Ahijah the
prophet.

Death of Jeroboam

19 Now the rest of the acts of Jeroboam, how he [a]made war and how he
*reigned, indeed they *are* written in the
book of the chronicles of the kings of
Israel.
20 The period that Jeroboam reigned
was twenty-two years. So he rested
with his fathers. Then [a]Nadab his son
reigned in his place.

Rehoboam Reigns in Judah

21 And Rehoboam the son of Solomon
reigned in Judah. [a]Rehoboam *was*
forty-one years old when he became
king. He reigned seventeen years in Jerusalem, the city [b]which the LORD had
chosen out of all the tribes of Israel,
to put His name there. [c]His mother's

7 [a]2 Sam. 12:7, 8; 1 Kin. 16:2
8 [a]1 Kin. 11:31 [b]1 Kin. 11:33, 38; 15:5
9 [a]1 Kin. 12:28; 2 Chr. 11:15 [b]2 Chr. 29:6; Neh. 9:26; Ps. 50:17
10 [a]1 Kin. 15:29 [b]1 Kin. 21:21; 2 Kin. 9:8 [c]Deut. 32:36; 2 Kin. 14:26
11 [a]1 Kin. 16:4; 21:24
12 [a]1 Kin. 14:17
13 [a]2 Chr. 12:12; 19:3 [1]Be buried
14 [a]1 Kin. 15:27–29 [1]Or *this day and from now on*
15 [a]Deut. 29:28; 2 Kin. 17:6; Ps. 52:5 [b][Josh. 23:15, 16] [c]2 Kin. 15:29 [d][Ex. 34:13, 14; Deut. 12:3] [1]The Euphrates [2]Heb. *Asherim,* Canaanite deities
16 [a]1 Kin. 12:30; 13:34; 15:30, 34; 16:2
17 [a]1 Kin. 15:21, 33; 16:6, 8, 15, 23; Song 6:4 [b]1 Kin. 14:12
18 [a]1 Kin. 14:13
19 [a]1 Kin. 14:30; 2 Chr. 13:2–20 *See WW at 2 Sam. 8:15.
20 [a]1 Kin. 15:25
21 [a]2 Chr. 12:13 [b]1 Kin. 11:32, 36 [c]1 Kin. 14:31

14:13–18 According to the prophecy of Ahijah, all the male descendants of Jeroboam would die and be unburied (14:10, 11). The exception to this was Abijah (14:1, 13). Abijah *received an honorable burial* (v. 18) **because in him there is found something good toward the LORD God of Israel** (v. 13). What this "something good" refers to is unclear. Perhaps Abijah had not been corrupted since he was still a child (vv. 3, 12, 17).

14:14 This predicts the actions of Baasha against Nadab in 15:27–29.

14:15 Ahijah's prophecy points toward the captivity of Israel by Assyria in 722 B.C.

14:17 Jeroboam had moved from Shechem (12:25) to **Tirzah.** Tirzah was the capital city of the northern kingdom until Israel's sixth king, Omri, built Samaria and made it the seat of government (16:23, 24).

14:19 The book of the chronicles of the kings of Israel: This is not to be confused with the OT books of 1 and 2 Chr., which were written much later than 1 and 2 Kin. (compare "Date" in the introductions to 1 Kin., 2 Kin., 1 Chr., and 2 Chr.). From the time of David, several individuals acted as recorders of the events experienced by God's people in the kingdom period (4:3; 2 Sam. 8:16; 20:24; 2 Kin. 18:18, 37; 2 Chr. 34:8). Such historical documents would have been kept in the royal archives. These records were probably a source for 1 and 2 Kin., since such chronicles are mentioned 32 times in 1 Kin. 14:19—2 Kin. 24:5. The author then was guided by the Holy Spirit to select and record the events found in 1 and 2 Kin.

14:21–28 Under **Rehoboam,** the southern kingdom of Judah was not doing any better than Israel to the north. Their sinful state made them no match for the invasion of **Shishak** of Egypt (which 2 Chr. 12 regards as divine retribution).

name *was* Naamah, an Ammonitess.

22 [a]Now Judah did evil in the sight of the LORD, and they [b]provoked Him to jealousy with their sins which they committed, more than all that their fathers had done.

23 For they also built for themselves [a]high[1] places, [b]*sacred* pillars, and [c]wooden images on every high hill and [d]under every green tree.

24 [a]And there were also [1]perverted persons in the land. They did according to all the [b]abominations of the nations which the LORD had cast out before the children of [c]Israel.

25 [a]It happened in the fifth year of King Rehoboam *that* Shishak king of Egypt came up against Jerusalem.

26 [a]And he took away the treasures of the house of the LORD and the treasures of the king's house; he took away everything. He also took away all the gold shields [b]which Solomon had made.

27 Then King Rehoboam made bronze shields in their place, and [1]committed *them* to the hands of the captains of the [2]guard, who guarded the doorway of the king's house.

28 And whenever the king entered the house of the LORD, the guards carried them, then brought them back into the guardroom.

29 [a]Now the rest of the acts of Rehoboam, and all that he did, *are* they not written in the book of the chronicles of the kings of Judah?

30 And there was [a]war between Rehoboam and Jeroboam all *their* days.

31 [a]So Rehoboam [1]rested with his fathers, and was buried with his fathers in the City of David. [b]His mother's name *was* Naamah, an Ammonitess. Then [c]Abijam[2] his son reigned in his place.

Abijam Reigns in Judah

15 [a]In the eighteenth year of King Jeroboam the son of Nebat, Abijam became king over Judah.

2 He reigned three years in Jerusalem. [a]His mother's name *was* [b]Maachah the granddaughter of [c]Abishalom.

3 And he walked in all the sins of his 6
father, which he had done before him; [a]his heart was not [1]loyal to the LORD his God, as was the heart of his father David.

4 Nevertheless [a]for David's sake the LORD his God gave him a lamp in Jerusalem, by setting up his son after him and by establishing Jerusalem;

5 because David [a]did *what was* right in the eyes of the LORD, and had not turned aside from anything that He commanded him all the days of his life, [b]except in the matter of Uriah the Hittite.

6 [a]And there was war between [1]Rehoboam and Jeroboam all the days of his life.

7 [a]Now the rest of the acts of Abijam, and all that he did, *are* they not written in the book of the chronicles of the kings of Judah? And there was war between Abijam and Jeroboam.

8 [a]So Abijam [1]rested with his fathers, and they buried him in the City of David. Then Asa his son reigned in his place.

Asa Reigns in Judah

9 In the twentieth year of Jeroboam king of Israel, Asa became king over Judah.

10 And he reigned forty-one years in Jerusalem. His grandmother's name *was* Maachah the granddaughter of Abishalom.

11 [a]Asa did *what was* right in the eyes 6
of the LORD, as *did* his father David.

12 [a]And he banished the [1]perverted persons from the land, and removed all the idols that his fathers had made.

13 Also he removed [a]Maachah his grandmother from *being* queen mother, because she had made an obscene image of [1]Asherah. And Asa cut down her obscene image and [b]burned *it* by the Brook Kidron.

14 [a]But the [1]high places were not removed. Nevertheless Asa's [b]heart was loyal to the LORD all his days.

22 [a]2 Chr. 12:1, 14 [b]Deut. 32:21 **23** [a]Deut. 12:2 [b][Deut. 16:22] [c][2 Kin. 17:9, 10] [d]Is. 57:5 [1]Places for pagan worship **24** [a]Deut. 23:17 [b]Deut. 20:18 [c][Deut. 9:4, 5] [1]Heb. *qadesh,* one practicing sodomy and prostitution in religious rituals **25** [a]1 Kin. 11:40 **26** [a]2 Chr. 12:9–11 [b]1 Kin. 10:17 **27** [1]*entrusted* [2]Lit. *runners* **29** [a]2 Chr. 12:15, 16 **30** [a]1 Kin. 12:21–24; 15:6 **31** [a]2 Chr. 12:16 [b]1 Kin. 14:21 [c]2 Chr. 12:16 [1]Died and joined his ancestors [2]*Abijah,* 2 Chr. 12:16

CHAPTER 15

1 [a]2 Chr. 13:1 **2** [a]2 Chr. 11:20–22 [b]2 Chr. 13:2 [c]2 Chr. 11:21

3 [a]Ps. 119:80 [1]Lit. *at peace with* **4** [a]2 Sam. 21:17 **5** [a]1 Kin. 9:4; 14:8 [b]2 Sam. 11:3, 15–17; 12:9, 10 **6** [a]1 Kin. 14:30 [1]So with MT, LXX, Tg., Vg.; some Heb. mss., Syr. *Abijam* **7** [a]2 Chr. 13:2–22 **8** [a]2 Chr. 14:1 [1]Died and joined his ancestors **11** [a]2 Chr. 14:2 **12** [a]1 Kin. 14:24; 22:46 [1]Heb. *qedeshim,* those practicing sodomy and prostitution in religious rituals

13 [a]2 Chr. 15:16–18 [b]Ex. 32:20 [1]A Canaanite goddess **14** [a]1 Kin. 3:2; 22:43 [b]1 Kin. 8:61; 15:3 [1]Places for pagan worship

14:29 The chronicles: See note on v. 19.

15:1–8 The second king in the southern kingdom was **Abijam.** He did little better than his father Rehoboam, yet God remained faithful to His promise to David by letting this descendant rule Judah.

15:3 See section 6 of Truth-In-Action at the end of 1 Kin.

15:9–24 Asa, the third king of Judah, was a refreshing contrast. Of the 20 regents who reigned in the south, Asa was the first of only eight good kings. Asa was a reformer and promptly set out to purge the land of idolatry (v. 12). Though Kings tells us that **Asa's heart was loyal to the LORD all his days** (v. 14), Chronicles explains that in his later years he departed from his total devotion to God (2 Chr. 16).

15:11 See section 6 of Truth-In-Action at the end of 1 Kin.

15 He also brought into the house of
the LORD the things which his father
[a]had dedicated, and the things which
he himself had dedicated: silver and
gold and utensils.
16 Now there was war between Asa
and Baasha king of Israel all their
days.
17 And [a]Baasha king of Israel came up
against Judah, and built [b]Ramah,
[c]that he might let none go out or come
in to Asa king of Judah.
18 Then Asa took all the silver and
gold *that was* left in the treasuries of
the house of the LORD and the treasuries of the king's house, and delivered
them into the hand of his servants. And
King Asa sent them to [a]Ben-Hadad the
son of Tabrimmon, the son of Hezion,
king of Syria, who dwelt in [b]Damas-
cus, saying,
19 "*Let there be* a treaty between you
and me, as there was between my father and your father. See, I have sent
you a present of silver and gold. Come
and break your treaty with Baasha
king of Israel, so that he will withdraw
from me."
20 So Ben-Hadad heeded King Asa,
and [a]sent the captains of his armies
against the cities of Israel. He attacked
[b]Ijon, [c]Dan, [d]Abel Beth Maachah, and
all Chinneroth, with all the land of
Naphtali.
21 Now it happened, when Baasha
heard *it,* that he stopped building Ramah, and remained in [a]Tirzah.
22 [a]Then King Asa made a proclamation throughout all Judah; none *was*
exempted. And they took away the
stones and timber of Ramah, which Baasha had used for building; and with
them King Asa built [b]Geba of Benjamin, and [c]Mizpah.
23 The rest of all the acts of Asa, all
his might, all that he did, and the cities
which he built, *are* they not written in
the book of the chronicles of the kings
of Judah? But [a]in the time of his old
age he was diseased in his feet.
24 So Asa [1]rested with his fathers,
and was buried with his fathers in
the City of David his father. [a]Then
[b]Jehoshaphat his son reigned in his
place.

15 [a]1 Kin. 7:51 **17** [a]2 Chr. 16:1–6 [b]Josh. 18:25; 1 Kin. 15:21, 22 [c]1 Kin. 12:26–29 **18** [a]2 Kin. 12:17, 18; 2 Chr. 16:2 [b]Gen. 14:15; 1 Kin. 11:23, 24 **20** [a]1 Kin. 20:1 [b]2 Kin. 15:29 [c]Judg. 18:29; 1 Kin. 12:29 [d]2 Sam. 20:14, 15 **21** [a]1 Kin. 14:17; 16:15–18 **22** [a]2 Chr. 16:6 [b]Josh. 21:17 [c]Josh. 18:26 **23** [a]2 Chr. 16:11–14 **24** [a]2 Chr. 17:1 [b]1 Kin. 22:41–44; Matt. 1:8 [1]Died and joined his ancestors

25 [a]1 Kin. 14:20 **26** [a]1 Kin. 12:28–33; 14:16 **27** [a]1 Kin. 14:14 [b]Josh. 19:44; 21:23; 1 Kin. 16:15 **29** [a]1 Kin. 14:10–14 *See WW at Ps. 150:6. **30** [a]1 Kin. 14:9, 16 **32** [a]1 Kin. 15:16 **34** [a]1 Kin. 13:33; 14:16

CHAPTER 16

1 [a]1 Kin. 16:7; 2 Chr. 19:2; 20:34 [b]2 Chr. 16:7–10 [c]1 Kin. 15:27 **2** [a]1 Sam. 2:8; 1 Kin. 14:7 [b]1 Kin. 12:25–33; 15:34

Nadab Reigns in Israel

25 Now [a]Nadab the son of Jeroboam
became king over Israel in the second
year of Asa king of Judah, and he
reigned over Israel two years.
26 And he did evil in the sight of the
LORD, and walked in the way of his father, and in [a]his sin by which he had
made Israel sin.
27 [a]Then Baasha the son of Ahijah,
of the house of Issachar, conspired
against him. And Baasha killed him at
[b]Gibbethon, which *belonged* to the
Philistines, while Nadab and all Israel
laid siege to Gibbethon.
28 Baasha killed him in the third year
of Asa king of Judah, and reigned in
his place.
29 And it was so, when he became
king, *that* he killed all the house of Jeroboam. He did not leave to Jeroboam
anyone that *breathed, until he had destroyed him, according to [a]the word of
the LORD which He had spoken by His
servant Ahijah the Shilonite,
30 [a]because of the sins of Jeroboam,
which he had sinned and by which
he had made Israel sin, because of
his provocation with which he had
provoked the LORD God of Israel to
anger.
31 Now the rest of the acts of Nadab,
and all that he did, *are* they not written
in the book of the chronicles of the
kings of Israel?
32 [a]And there was war between Asa
and Baasha king of Israel all their
days.

Baasha Reigns in Israel

33 In the third year of Asa king of Judah, Baasha the son of Ahijah became
king over all Israel in Tirzah, and
reigned twenty-four years.
34 He did evil in the sight of the LORD,
and walked in [a]the way of Jeroboam,
and in his sin by which he had made
Israel sin.

16

Then the word of the LORD came
to [a]Jehu the son of [b]Hanani,
against [c]Baasha, saying:
2 [a]"Inasmuch as I lifted you out of the
dust and made you ruler over My people Israel, and [b]you have walked in the

---

15:18 Ben-Hadad: There were three kings of Damascus in Syria whose names were Ben-Hadad, and all are referred to in Scripture. Ben-Hadad I is mentioned here. His son, Ben-Hadad II, was unsuccessful in his war against King Ahab, and was smothered to death by Hazael (20:1–43; 2 Kin. 7; 8). The third Ben-Hadad was the son of Hazael (2 Kin. 13:24).

15:25–34 Nadab was the second king in Israel, but after two years he was assassinated by **Baasha** in fulfillment of Ahijah's prophecy (14:14). This ended Jeroboam's dynasty. However, as the third king of Israel, Baasha was just as sinful as his two predecessors.

16:1–7 These verses record the prophecy of **Jehu . . . against Baasha,** and although we do not know how it happened, these words were fulfilled (v. 4).

way of Jeroboam, and have made My
people Israel sin, to provoke Me to
anger with their sins,

WORD WEALTH

16:2 anger, *cha'as* (*kah*-ahs); Strong's #3707: To grieve, exasperate, vex, provoke, make angry. This word portrays the kind of anger that results from repeated irritation, and not the anger that suddenly explodes for no apparent reason. Thus *cha'as* is closer to "exasperation" than to "wrath." The verb *cha'as* is usually translated "provoke to anger."

3 "surely I will [a]take[1] away the posterity of Baasha and the posterity of
his house, and I will make your house
like [b]the house of Jeroboam the son
of Nebat.
4 "The dogs shall eat [a]whoever belongs to Baasha and dies in the city,
and the birds of the air shall eat whoever dies in the fields."
5 Now the rest of the acts of Baasha,
what he did, and his might, [a]*are* they
not written in the book of the chronicles of the kings of Israel?
6 So Baasha [1]rested with his fathers
and was buried in [a]Tirzah. Then Elah
his son reigned in his place.
7 And also the word of the LORD came
by the prophet [a]Jehu the son of Hanani
against Baasha and his house, because
of all the evil that he did in the sight
of the LORD in provoking Him to anger
with the work of his hands, in being
like the house of Jeroboam, and because [b]he killed them.

Elah Reigns in Israel

8 In the twenty-sixth year of Asa king
of Judah, Elah the son of Baasha became king over Israel, *and reigned* two
years in Tirzah.
9 [a]Now his servant Zimri, commander of half *his* chariots, conspired
against him as he was in Tirzah drinking himself drunk in the house of Arza,
[b]steward[1] of *his* house in Tirzah.
10 And Zimri went in and struck him
and killed him in the twenty-seventh
year of Asa king of Judah, and reigned
in his place.
11 Then it came to pass, when he began to reign, as soon as he was seated
on his throne, *that* he killed all the
household of Baasha; he [a]did not leave
him one male, neither of his relatives
nor of his friends.
12 Thus Zimri destroyed all the household of Baasha, [a]according to the word
of the LORD, which He spoke against
Baasha by Jehu the prophet,
13 for all the sins of Baasha and the
sins of Elah his son, by which they had
sinned and by which they had made
Israel sin, in provoking the LORD God
of Israel to anger [a]with their [1]idols.
14 Now the rest of the acts of Elah, and
all that he did, *are* they not written in
the book of the chronicles of the kings
of Israel?

Zimri Reigns in Israel

15 In the twenty-seventh year of Asa
king of Judah, Zimri had reigned in
Tirzah seven days. And the people
were encamped [a]against Gibbethon,
which *belonged* to the Philistines.
16 Now the people *who were* encamped heard it said, "Zimri has conspired and also has killed the king."
So all Israel made Omri, the commander of the army, king over Israel
that day in the camp.
17 Then Omri and all Israel with him
went up from Gibbethon, and they besieged Tirzah.
18 And it happened, when Zimri saw
that the city was [1]taken, that he went
into the citadel of the king's house and
burned the king's house [2]down upon
himself with fire, and died,
19 because of the sins which he had
committed in doing evil in the sight of
the LORD, [a]in walking in the [b]way of
Jeroboam, and in his sin which he had
committed to make Israel sin.
20 Now the rest of the acts of Zimri,
and the treason he committed, *are* they
not written in the book of the chronicles of the kings of Israel?

Omri Reigns in Israel

21 Then the people of Israel were divided into two parts: half of the people
followed Tibni the son of Ginath, to

3 [a]1 Kin. 16:11; 21:21 [b]1 Kin. 14:10; 15:29 [1]*consume*
4 [a]1 Kin. 14:11; 21:24
5 [a]2 Chr. 16:11
6 [a]1 Kin. 14:17; 15:21 [1]Died and joined his ancestors
7 [a]1 Kin. 16:1 [b]1 Kin. 15:27, 29
9 [a]2 Kin. 9:30–33 [b]Gen. 24:2; 39:4; 1 Kin. 18:3 [1]Lit. *who was over the house*
11 [a]1 Sam. 25:22
12 [a]1 Kin. 16:3
13 [a]Deut. 32:21; 1 Sam. 12:21; [Is. 41:29; Jon. 2:8; 1 Cor. 8:4; 10:19] [1]Lit. *vanities*
15 [a]1 Kin. 15:27
18 [1]*captured* [2]Lit. *over him*
19 [a]1 Kin. 15:26, 34 [b]1 Kin. 12:25–33

16:8–14 The fourth king in the northern kingdom was **Elah the son of Baasha.** He reigned as an evil king for almost two years, and one day when Elah was drunk he was murdered by **Zimri.** Zimri then proceeded to dispose of all the survivors of the house of Baasha. This fulfilled Jehu's prophecy (16:3) and ended Baasha's dynasty.

16:15–20 **Zimri** was Israel's fifth king, but he only reigned for seven days. When the people discovered what he had done to Elah, they selected **Omri** as their captain and rebelled. Zimri feared being taken, so he committed suicide as he burned the palace down.

16:21–28 With the vacuum of Zimri's death, half of the people of Israel followed **Omri** and half followed **Tibni.** However, Omri took quick action and did away with Tibni.

make him king, and half followed Omri.

22 But the people who followed Omri prevailed over the people who followed Tibni the son of Ginath. So Tibni died and Omri reigned.

23 In the thirty-first year of Asa king of Judah, Omri became king over Israel, *and reigned* twelve years. Six years he reigned in [a]Tirzah.

24 And he bought the hill of Samaria from Shemer for two talents of silver; then he built on the hill, and called the name of the city which he built, [a]Samaria,[1] after the name of Shemer, *owner of the hill.

25 [a]Omri did *evil in the eyes of the LORD, and did worse than all who *were* before him.

26 For he [a]walked in all the ways of Jeroboam the son of Nebat, and in his sin by which he had made Israel sin, provoking the LORD God of Israel to anger with their [b]idols.[1]

27 Now the rest of the acts of Omri which he did, and the might that he showed, *are* they not written in the book of the chronicles of the kings of Israel?

28 So Omri rested with his fathers and was buried in Samaria. Then Ahab his son reigned in his place.

Ahab Reigns in Israel

29 In the thirty-eighth year of Asa king of Judah, Ahab the son of Omri became king over Israel; and Ahab the son of Omri reigned over Israel in Samaria twenty-two years.

30 Now Ahab the son of Omri did evil in the sight of the LORD, more than all who *were* before him.

31 And it came to pass, as though it had been a trivial thing for him to walk in the sins of Jeroboam the son of Nebat, [a]that he took as wife Jezebel the daughter of Ethbaal, king of the [b]Sidonians; [c]and he went and served Baal and worshiped him.

32 Then he set up an altar for Baal in [a]the temple of Baal, which he had built in Samaria.

33 [a]And Ahab made a [1]wooden image. Ahab [b]did more to provoke the LORD God of Israel to anger than all the kings of Israel who were before him.

34 In his days Hiel of Bethel built Jericho. He laid its foundation [1]with Abiram his firstborn, and with his youngest *son* Segub he set up its gates, [a]according to the word of the LORD, which He had spoken through Joshua the son of Nun.

Elijah Proclaims a Drought

17 And Elijah the Tishbite, of the [a]inhabitants of Gilead, said to Ahab, [b]"*As* the LORD God of Israel lives, [c]before whom I stand, [d]there shall not be dew nor rain [e]these years, except at my word." 8

2 Then the word of the LORD came to him, saying,

3 "Get away from here and turn eastward, and hide by the Brook Cherith, which flows into the Jordan.

4 "And it will be *that* you shall drink from the brook, and I have commanded the [a]ravens to feed you there."

5 So he went and did according to the word of the LORD, for he went and stayed by the Brook Cherith, which flows into the Jordan.

6 The ravens brought him bread and meat in the morning, and bread and meat in the evening; and he drank from the brook.

7 And it happened after a while that the brook dried up, because there had been no rain in the land.

23 [a]1 Kin. 15:21; 2 Kin. 15:14
24 [a]1 Kin. 13:32; 2 Kin. 17:24; John 4:4 [1]Heb. *Shomeron* *See WW at Mic. 4:13.
25 [a]Mic. 6:16 *See WW at Ps. 5:4.
26 [a]1 Kin. 16:19 [b]1 Kin. 16:13 [1]Lit. *vanities*
31 [a]Deut. 7:3 [b]Judg. 18:7; 1 Kin. 11:1–5 [c]1 Kin. 21:25, 26; 2 Kin. 10:18; 17:16
32 [a]2 Kin. 10:21, 26, 27
33 [a]2 Kin. 13:6 [b]1 Kin. 14:9; 16:29, 30; 21:25 [1]Heb. *Asherah,* a Canaanite goddess
34 [a]Josh. 6:26 [1]At the cost of the life of

CHAPTER 17

1 [a]Judg. 12:4 [b]1 Kin. 18:10; 22:14; 2 Kin. 3:14; 5:20 [c]Deut. 10:8 [d]1 Kin. 18:1; James 5:17 [e]Luke 4:25
4 [a]Job 38:41

Omri, as the sixth king in the north, perpetuated Jeroboam's apostasy. See note on v. 24.

16:24 Samaria: Omri's most noteworthy accomplishment was building the new capital city Samaria. Shechem was *the capital of the 10 northern tribes* for a brief time (12:25), then Jeroboam moved it to Tirzah (14:17) where it remained until Omri moved it to Samaria. The location of Samaria was almost impregnable and withstood vicious assaults (2 Kin. 6:24, 25) until it was finally captured by the Assyrians in 722 B.C. (2 Kin. 17). Samaria was repopulated by foreigners (2 Kin. 17:24) who brought idolatrous practices with them. The intermarriage of these foreigners with the native Jews created a mixed race known as Samaritans, who were hated by full-blooded Jews at the time of Jesus (John 4:1–10).

16:29–34 Asa came to reign in Judah when Jeroboam was still on the throne in Israel. He continued his reign in the south, while the north was ruled by the kings Nadab, Baasha, Elah, Zimri, and Omri. Asa was still ruling when **Ahab,** the seventh and worst king (v. 33) of Israel came to reign.

16:31 He took as wife Jezebel: This wife was a zealous participant in the worship of **Baal.** Ahab's marriage to her led to the official endorsement of this immoral and idolatrous worship.

17:1–9 See section 8 of Truth-In-Action at the end of 1 Kin.

17:1 God answered Israel's worst king by raising up one of the greatest and most powerful prophets in the OT, **Elijah the Tishbite.** The Tishbite means that he was from the city Tishbe in **Gilead.** The significance of the prophecy of no rain becomes apparent when we understand that those who worshiped Baal believed that Baal controlled the rain. In effect, Elijah cut to the heart of Baalism and challenged their so-called god, proclaiming that the **LORD God of Israel** controlled the weather.

17:3 The location of **Cherith** is unknown. Evidently this area was not under the jurisdiction of Ahab.

Elijah and the Widow

8 Then the word of the LORD came to
him, saying,
9 "Arise, go to [a]Zarephath, which *belongs* to [b]Sidon, and dwell there. See,
I have commanded a widow there to
*provide for you."
10 So he arose and went to Zarephath.
And when he came to the gate of the
city, indeed a widow *was* there gathering sticks. And he called to her and
said, "Please bring me a little water in
a cup, that I may drink."
11 And as she was going to get *it*, he
called to her and said, "Please bring
me a morsel of bread in your hand."
12 So she said, "As the LORD your God
lives, I do not have bread, only a handful of flour in a bin, and a little oil in
a [1]jar; and see, I *am* gathering a couple
of sticks that I may go in and prepare
it for myself and my son, that we may
eat it, and [a]die."
13 And Elijah said to her, "Do not
*fear; go *and* do as you have said, but
make me a small cake from it first, and
bring *it* to me; and afterward make
some for yourself and your son.
14 "For thus says the LORD God of Israel: 'The bin of flour shall not be used
up, nor shall the jar of oil run dry, until
the day the LORD sends rain on the
earth.' "
15 So she went away and did according to the word of Elijah; and she and
he and her household ate for *many*
days.
16 The bin of flour was not used up,
nor did the jar of oil run dry, according
to the word of the LORD which He
spoke by Elijah.

KINGDOM DYNAMICS

17:8–16 You Must Give God an Opportunity, SEED FAITH. This episode teaches us to invite God to work by His unlimited power within our limited circumstances and resources. Two important principles for our giving are illustrated by this passage of Scripture.

First, we must give something out of our need. That is the kind of giving that involves our faith. This woman had a need for herself and her family, but she gave to sustain the ministry and life of God's prophet, Elijah. Then God multiplied her giving back to her.

Second, this woman gave first. Her giving activated the miracle supply of God flowing back into her life. For perhaps as long as three years God multiplied her seed sown.

Your giving causes something to happen according to God's eternal principles of seedtime and harvest. There is an old saying that bears repeating: "Without God, you cannot; without you, God will not." God has already given from His side. Now we must step out in our giving to Him. Doing so will release His flow of provision on our Earth-side of things. Sow! Give Him something to multiply!

(Ex. 15:26/2 Chr. 25:9) O.R.

Elijah Revives the Widow's Son

17 Now it happened after these things
that the son of the woman who owned
the house became sick. And his sickness was so [1]serious that [2]there was
no breath left in him.
18 So she said to Elijah, [a]"What have
I to do with you, O man of God? Have
you come to me to bring my sin to remembrance, and to kill my son?"
19 And he said to her, "Give me your
son." So he took him out of her arms
and carried him to the upper room
where he was staying, and laid him on
his own bed.
20 Then he cried out to the LORD
and said, "O LORD my God, have You
also brought tragedy on the widow
with whom I lodge, by killing her
son?"
21 [a]And he stretched himself out on
the child three times, and cried out to
the LORD and said, "O LORD my God, I
pray, let this child's soul come back to
him."
22 Then the LORD heard the voice of
Elijah; and the soul of the child came
back to him, and he [a]revived.
23 And Elijah took the child and
brought him down from the upper
room into the house, and gave him to
his mother. And Elijah said, "See, your
son lives!"
24 Then the woman said to Elijah,
"Now by this [a]I know that you *are* a

9 [a]Obad. 20; Luke 4:25, 26 [b]2 Sam. 24:6 *See WW at Ps. 55:22.
12 [a]Deut. 28:23, 24 [1]Lit. *pitcher or water jar*
13 *See WW at Ex. 1:17.

17 [1]*severe* [2]He died.
18 [a]Luke 5:8
21 [a]2 Kin. 4:34, 35; Acts 20:10
22 [a]Luke 7:14, 15; Heb. 11:35
24 [a]John 2:11; 3:2; 16:30

17:8–15 Zarephath, *a city on the Mediterranean coast in* Phoenicia, was the location of the first miracle of Elijah. **A widow** who was nearly without foodstuffs was asked to give her last food to Elijah. If she did, God would give her an unfailing provision. The woman overcame her fear, responded in faith, and God was faithful to His promise.
17:17–24 The second miracle of Elijah was to restore to life the dead son of the widow of Zarephath. Some skeptics have said that the boy was not really dead, but only unconscious. However, from vv. 18, 20, 22, and 23 it is very clear that the youth was dead. Kings includes these incidents of ch. 17 to demonstrate that the Lord God of Israel is more powerful than Baal.

man of God, *and* that the word of the
LORD in your mouth *is* the truth."

Elijah's Message to Ahab

18 And it came to pass *after*
[a]many days that the word of the
LORD came to Elijah, in the third year,
saying, "Go, present yourself to Ahab,
and [b]I will send rain on the earth."
2 So Elijah went to present himself
to Ahab; and *there was* a severe famine in Samaria.
3 And Ahab had called Obadiah, who
was [1]in charge of *his* house. (Now Obadiah feared the LORD greatly.
4 For so it was, while Jezebel [1]mas-
sacred the prophets of the LORD, that
Obadiah had taken one hundred
prophets and hidden them, fifty to a
cave, and had fed them with bread and
water.)
5 And Ahab had said to Obadiah, "Go
into the land to all the springs of water
and to all the brooks; perhaps we may
find grass to keep the horses and mules
alive, so that we will not have to kill
any livestock."
6 So they divided the land between
them to explore it; Ahab went one way
by himself, and Obadiah went another
way by himself.
7 Now as Obadiah was on his way,
suddenly Elijah met him; and he
[a]recognized him, and fell on his face,
and said, "*Is* that you, my lord Elijah?"
8 And he answered him, "*It is* I. Go,
tell your master, 'Elijah *is here.*' "
9 So he said, "How have I sinned, that
you are delivering your servant into
the hand of Ahab, to kill me?
10 "*As* the LORD your God lives, there
is no nation or kingdom where my
master has not sent someone to hunt
for you; and when they said, '*He is* not
here,' he took an oath from the kingdom or nation that they could not find
you.
11 "And now you say, 'Go, tell your
master, "Elijah *is here*" '!
12 "And it shall come to pass, *as soon
as* I am gone from you, that [a]the Spirit
of the LORD will carry you to a place I
do not know; so when I go and tell
Ahab, and he cannot find you, he will
kill me. But I your servant have feared
the LORD from my youth.
13 "Was it not reported to my lord
what I did when Jezebel killed the
prophets of the LORD, how I hid one
hundred men of the LORD's prophets,
fifty to a cave, and fed them with bread
and water?
14 "And now you say, 'Go, tell your
master, "Elijah *is here.*" ' He will kill
me!"
15 Then Elijah said, "*As* the LORD of
hosts lives, before whom I stand, I will
surely present myself to him today."
16 So Obadiah went to meet Ahab, and
told him; and Ahab went to meet Elijah.
17 Then it happened, when Ahab saw
Elijah, that Ahab said to him, [a]"*Is that*
you, O [b]troubler of Israel?"
18 And he answered, "I have not troubled Israel, but you and your father's
house *have,* [a]in that you have forsaken
the commandments of the LORD and
have followed the Baals.
19 "Now therefore, send *and* gather all
Israel to me on [a]Mount Carmel, the
four hundred and fifty prophets of
Baal, [b]and the four hundred prophets
of [1]Asherah, who [2]eat at Jezebel's table."

Elijah's Mount Carmel Victory

20 So Ahab sent for all the children of
Israel, and [a]gathered the prophets together on Mount Carmel.
21 And Elijah came to all the people,
and said, [a]"How long will you falter
between two opinions? If the LORD *is*
God, follow Him; but if Baal, [b]follow

CHAPTER 18
1 [a]1 Kin. 17:1; Luke 4:25; James 5:17 [b]Deut. 28:12
3 [1]Lit. *over the house*
4 [1]Lit. *cut off*
7 [a]2 Kin. 1:6–8
12 [a]2 Kin. 2:16; Ezek. 3:12, 14; Matt. 4:1; Acts 8:39
17 [a]1 Kin. 21:20 [b]Josh. 7:25; Acts 16:20
18 [a]1 Kin. 16:30–33; [2 Chr. 15:2]
19 [a]Josh. 19:26; 2 Kin. 2:25 [b]1 Kin. 16:33 [1]A Canaanite goddess [2]Are provided for by Jezebel
20 [a]1 Kin. 22:6
21 [a]2 Kin. 17:41; [Matt. 6:24] [b]Josh. 24:15

18:1–46 After nearly three years of drought, the looming question of whether it was the Lord God of Israel or Baal who controlled the rain was about to be answered in a contest on Mt. Carmel.

18:3 The **Obadiah** mentioned here was certainly a believer in the Lord, but he is not the prophet Obadiah who authored the biblical book by that name.

18:12 The Spirit: This is the only direct reference to the Holy Spirit in the Book of 1 Kings. Apparently the Holy Spirit sometimes transported Elijah from one location to another (see 2 Kin. 2:16). Philip has a similar experience in Acts 8:39, 40. For further insights on the Holy Spirit in the kingdom period, see "The Holy Spirit at Work" in introductions to 1 Kin., 2 Kin., 1 Chr., and 2 Chr.

18:17, 18 Elijah was quick to clear the record. The drought was not his fault; instead it had resulted from Ahab's failure to acknowledge the Lord and his allowing himself and all Israel to be seduced into Baal worship by Jezebel.

18:19 Elijah was calling for a showdown between their god and the Lord. All Israel was to observe the contest between Elijah and the prophets who were cared for and protected by Jezebel. **Baal** was the chief male deity of the Canaanites and Phoenicians. He symbolized the productive forces of nature. **Asherah** was the wife of Baal in Canaanite mythology.

18:20 The contest was to take place on **Mount Carmel,** a prominent peak in a range of mountains stretching southeast from the coast of the Mediterranean Sea. On this mountain Canaanites built sanctuaries to pagan weather deities. This was the ideal place for a confrontation to show the superiority of the Lord over Baal.

18:21 The classic challenge of Elijah, **How long will you**

him." But the people answered him not
a word.
22 Then Elijah said to the people,
[a]"I alone am left a prophet of the LORD;
[b]but Baal's prophets *are* four hundred
and fifty men.
23 "Therefore let them give us two
bulls; and let them choose one bull for
themselves, cut it in pieces, and lay *it*
on the wood, but put no fire *under it;*
and I will prepare the other bull, and
lay *it* on the wood, but put no fire *under*
it.
24 "Then you call on the name of your
gods, and I will call on the name of
the LORD; and the God who [a]answers
by fire, He is God." So all the people
answered and said, [1]"It is well spoken."
25 Now Elijah said to the prophets of
Baal, "Choose one bull for yourselves
and prepare *it* first, for you *are* many;
and call on the name of your god, but
put no fire *under it.*"
26 So they took the bull which was
given them, and they prepared *it,* and
called on the name of Baal from morning even till noon, saying, "O Baal,
[1]hear us!" But *there was* [a]no voice; no
one answered. Then they [2]leaped
about the altar which they had made.
27 And so it was, at noon, that Elijah
mocked them and said, "Cry [1]aloud,
for he *is* a god; either he is meditating,
or he is busy, or he is on a journey, *or*
perhaps he is sleeping and must be
awakened."
28 So they cried aloud, and [a]cut themselves, as was their custom, with
[1]knives and lances, until the blood
gushed out on them.
29 And when midday was past, [a]they
prophesied until the *time* of the offering of the *evening* sacrifice. But *there*
was [b]no voice; no one answered, no
one paid attention.
30 Then Elijah said to all the people,
"Come near to me." So all the people
came near to him. [a]And he repaired
the altar of the LORD *that was* broken
down.
31 And Elijah took twelve stones, according to the number of the tribes of
the sons of Jacob, to whom the word

22 [a]1 Kin. 19:10, 14 [b]1 Kin. 18:19
24 [a]1 Kin. 18:38; 1 Chr. 21:26 [1]Lit. *The word is good*
26 [a]Ps. 115:5; Jer. 10:5; [1 Cor. 8:4] [1]*answer* [2]Lit. *limped about, leaped in dancing around*
27 [1]*with a loud voice*
28 [a][Lev. 19:28; Deut. 14:1] [1]*swords*
29 [a]Ex. 29:39, 41 [b]1 Kin. 18:26
30 [a]1 Kin. 19:10, 14; 2 Chr. 33:16
31 [a]Gen. 32:28; 35:10; 2 Kin. 17:34
32 [a][Ex. 20:25; Col. 3:17]
33 [a]Gen. 22:9; Lev. 1:6–8 [b]Judg. 6:20
35 [a]1 Kin. 18:32, 38
36 [a]Gen. 28:13; Ex. 3:6; 4:5; [Matt. 22:32] [b]1 Kin. 8:43; 2 Kin. 19:19 [c]Num. 16:28
38 [a]Gen. 15:17; Lev. 9:24; 10:1, 2; Judg. 6:21; 2 Kin. 1:12; 1 Chr. 21:26; 2 Chr. 7:1; Job 1:16
39 [a]1 Kin. 18:21, 24
40 [a]2 Kin. 10:25 [b]Judg. 4:7; 5:21 [c][Deut. 13:5; 18:20]
42 [a]James 5:17, 18 *See WW at Ex. 19:20.

of the LORD had come, saying, [a]"Israel
shall be your name."
32 Then with the stones he built an altar [a]in the name of the LORD; and he
made a trench around the altar large
enough to hold two seahs of seed.
33 And he [a]put the wood in order, cut
the bull in pieces, and laid *it* on the
wood, and said, "Fill four waterpots
with water, and [b]pour *it* on the burnt
sacrifice and on the wood."
34 Then he said, "Do *it* a second time,"
and they did *it* a second time; and he
said, "Do *it* a third time," and they did
it a third time.
35 So the water ran all around the altar; and he also filled [a]the trench with
water.
36 And it came to pass, at *the time* of
the offering of the *evening* sacrifice,
that Elijah the prophet came near and
said, "LORD [a]God of Abraham, Isaac,
and Israel, [b]let it be known this day
that You *are* God in Israel and I *am*
Your servant, and *that* [c]I have done
all these things at Your word.
37 "Hear me, O LORD, hear me, that
this people may know that You *are* the
LORD God, and *that* You have turned
their hearts back *to You* again."
38 Then [a]the fire of the LORD fell and
consumed the burnt sacrifice, and the
wood and the stones and the dust, and
it licked up the water that *was* in the
trench.
39 Now when all the people saw *it,*
they fell on their faces; and they said,
[a]"The LORD, He *is* God! The LORD, He
is God!"
40 And Elijah said to them, [a]"Seize the
prophets of Baal! Do not let one of
them escape!" So they seized them;
and Elijah brought them down to the
Brook [b]Kishon and [c]executed them
there.

The Drought Ends

41 Then Elijah said to Ahab, "Go up,
eat and drink; for *there is* the sound
of abundance of rain."
42 So Ahab *went up to eat and drink.
And Elijah went up to the top of Carmel; [a]then he bowed down on the

falter, betrays the double-mindedness of the people. They must follow the Lord wholeheartedly or not at all.

18:22 By human reasoning, the odds of 450 to 1 would be nearly impossible. Yet nothing is impossible with the Lord God of Israel!

18:26–29 The prophets of Baal had spent six hours crying out to their god with no response.

18:36 The time of the ***evening* sacrifice** was about 3:00 P.M.

18:41–45 Much can be learned about prayer from observing Elijah: First, even though we have a promise for God's provision, we are not to stop praying for its fulfillment (v. 41). Second, we see one of the postures of prayer as we read that **he bowed down on the ground, and put his face between his knees** (v. 42). Third, we learn the importance of persistence in prayer as we read that Elijah prayed **seven times** (v. 43). And fourth, we understand the necessity of faith as we pray by realizing that Elijah believed

ground, and put his face between his
knees,
43 and said to his servant, "Go up now,
look toward the sea." So he went up
and looked, and said, "*There is* nothing." And seven times he said, "Go
again."
44 Then it came to pass the seventh
time, that he said, "There is a cloud,
as small as a man's hand, rising out
of the sea!" So he said, "Go up, say to
Ahab, [1]'Prepare *your chariot,* and go
down before the rain stops you.' "
45 Now it happened in the meantime
that the sky became black with clouds
and wind, and there was a heavy rain.
So Ahab rode away and went to Jezreel.
46 Then the [a]hand of the LORD came
upon Elijah; and he [b]girded[1] up his
loins and ran ahead of Ahab to the entrance of Jezreel.

Elijah Escapes from Jezebel

19 And Ahab told Jezebel all that
Elijah had done, also how he
had [a]executed all the prophets with the
sword.
2 Then Jezebel sent a messenger to
Elijah, saying, [a]"So let the gods do *to
me,* and more also, if I do not make
your life as the life of one of them by
tomorrow about this time."
3 And when he saw *that,* he arose
and ran for his life, and went to Beersheba, which *belongs* to Judah, and left
his servant there.
4 But he himself went a day's journey
into the wilderness, and came and sat
down under a [1]broom tree. And he
[a]prayed* that he might die, and said,
"It is enough! Now, LORD, take my life,
for I *am* no better than my fathers!"
5 Then as he lay and slept under a
broom tree, suddenly an [1]angel
touched him, and said to him, "Arise
and eat."
6 Then he looked, and there by his
head *was* a cake baked on [1]coals, and
a jar of water. So he ate and drank,
and lay down again.
7 And the [1]angel of the LORD came
back the second time, and touched
him, and said, "Arise *and* eat, because
the journey *is* too great for you."
8 So he arose, and ate and drank; and
he went in the strength of that food
forty days and [a]forty nights as far as
[b]Horeb, the mountain of God.
9 And there he went into a cave, and
spent the night in that place; and behold, the word of the LORD *came* to
him, and He said to him, "What are
you doing here, Elijah?"
10 So he said, [a]"I have been very
[b]zealous* for the LORD God of hosts;
for the children of Israel have forsaken
Your covenant, torn down Your altars,
and [c]killed Your prophets with the
sword. [d]I alone am left; and they seek
to take my life."

God's Revelation to Elijah

11 Then He said, "Go out, and stand
[a]on the mountain before the LORD."
And behold, the LORD [b]passed by, and
[c]a great and strong wind tore into the
mountains and broke the rocks in
pieces before the LORD, *but* the LORD
was not in the wind; and after the wind
an earthquake, *but* the LORD *was* not
in the earthquake;
12 and after the earthquake a fire, *but*
the LORD *was* not in the fire; and after
the fire [1]a still small voice.
13 So it was, when Elijah heard *it,* that
[a]he wrapped his face in his mantle and
went out and stood in the entrance of
the cave. [b]Suddenly a voice *came* to
him, and said, "What are you doing
here, Elijah?"
14 [a]And he said, "I have been very
zealous for the LORD God of hosts; because the children of Israel have

44 [1]Lit. *Bind* or *Harness*
46 [a]2 Kin. 3:15; Is. 8:11; Ezek. 3:14 [b]2 Kin. 4:29; 9:1; Jer. 1:17; 1 Pet. 1:13 [1]Tucked the skirts of his robe in his belt in preparation for quick travel

CHAPTER 19

1 [a]1 Kin. 18:40
2 [a]Ruth 1:17; 1 Kin. 20:10; 2 Kin. 6:31
4 [a]Num. 11:15; Jer. 20:14–18; Jon. 4:3, 8 [1]*juniper* *See WW at Ps. 122:6.
5 [1]Or *Angel*
6 [1]*hot stones*
7 [1]Or *Angel*
8 [a]Ex. 24:18; 34:28; Deut. 9:9–11, 18; Matt. 4:2 [b]Ex. 3:1; 4:27
10 [a]Rom. 11:3 [b]Num. 25:11, 13; Ps. 69:9 [c]1 Kin. 18:4 [d]1 Kin. 18:22; Rom. 11:3 *See WW at Zech. 8:2.
11 [a]Ex. 19:20; 24:12, 18 [b]Ex. 33:21, 22 [c]Ezek. 1:4; 37:7
12 [1]*a delicate whispering voice*
13 [a]Ex. 3:6; Is. 6:2 [b]1 Kin. 19:9
14 [a]1 Kin. 19:10

---

his prayer was answered before the answer actually came (vv. 44, 45). James 5:17, 18 explains that the prayer of a Christian can be as effective as the prayer of Elijah.

18:45 The coming of the rain was the final proof that Baal was impotent and that the Lord God of Israel was supreme.

18:46 Elijah was divinely empowered by **the hand of the LORD** to outrun Ahab's chariot from Carmel to Jezreel, a distance of approximately 25 miles. The phrase "the hand of the LORD" is a formula that refers to the divine inspiration of the prophets and probably is an indirect reference to the Holy Spirit (compare 2 Kin. 3:15 and Ezek. 1:3 with 1 Sam. 10:6, 10 and 19:20, 23). Here Elijah was supernaturally strengthened by the Spirit of God to do a miraculous feat. Read Judg. 14:6, 9 and 15:14 for similar accounts. For more on the work of the Holy Spirit in 1 Kin., see note on 18:12.

19:1–3 Elijah had just challenged and defeated 450 prophets of Baal, as well as confronted Ahab himself. Evidently **Jezebel** had not been present on Mt. Carmel, and now just one threat from her sent Elijah running. He ran to **Beersheba,** which is the southernmost city in the southern kingdom of Judah.

19:4 Elijah was so despondent that he wanted to die.

19:8 Mt. **Horeb** is a variant name for Mt. Sinai, and was about 200 miles from Beersheba. Elijah was going to the very place where the Lord had revealed Himself to Moses and the children of Israel.

19:11, 12 The Lord did not reveal Himself to Elijah in the spectacular ways by which He had shown Himself to Moses. To this discouraged, despondent old prophet, God responds in gentleness.

19:14–18 To the Lord's inquiry, Elijah retorts with self-pity. Instead of rebuking him, the Lord gently pulls him from his

forsaken Your covenant, torn down
Your altars, and killed Your prophets
with the sword. I alone am left; and
they seek to take my life."
15 Then the LORD said to him: "Go, return on your way to the Wilderness of
Damascus; [a]and when you arrive,
anoint Hazael *as* king over Syria.
16 "Also you shall anoint [a]Jehu the
son of Nimshi *as* king over Israel. And
[b]Elisha the son of Shaphat of Abel Meholah you shall anoint *as* prophet in
your place.

15 [a]2 Kin. 8:8–15
16 [a]2 Kin. 9:1–10 [b]1 Kin. 19:19–21; 2 Kin. 2:9–15
17 [a]2 Kin. 8:12; 13:3, 22 [b]2 Kin. 9:14—10:28 [c][Hos. 6:5]
18 [a]Rom. 11:4 [b]Hos. 13:2

17 [a]"It shall be *that* whoever escapes
the sword of Hazael, Jehu will [b]kill;
and whoever escapes the sword of
Jehu, [c]Elisha will kill.
18 [a]"Yet I have reserved seven thousand in Israel, all whose knees have
not bowed to Baal, [b]and every mouth
that has not kissed him."

Elisha Follows Elijah

19 So he departed from there, and
found Elisha the son of Shaphat, who

---

despair by giving him three new assignments (vv. 15, 16) and by assuring him that he is not alone (v. 18). Indeed, there were 7,000 others. God has always had a remnant (see Paul's use of vv. 10, 14 in Rom. 11:3).

19:19 That **he was with the twelfth** means that there were 12 teams of oxen plowing, and Elisha was driving the twelfth

Elijah and Elisha. Elijah's victory on Mt. Carmel ended with the slaying of 450 prophets of Baal (1 Kin. 18:20–40). His ministry spanned Canaan from the Brook Cherith near his birthplace (1 Kin. 17:1–7) to Zarephath where he performed the miracle that sustained the widow and her son, and to as far south as Mt. Horeb in the Sinai Peninsula. In Samaria Elijah denounced King Ahab's injustice against Naboth of Jezreel (1 Kin. 21:17–29). Near Jericho Elijah separated the waters of the Jordan River to cross over and subsequently was carried to heaven in a chariot of fire (2 Kin. 2:1–12).

Elisha healed Naaman of leprosy in the Jordan River (2 Kin. 5:1–19) and led the blinded Syrians to their defeat at Samaria (2 Kin. 6:8–23). In Damascus, Elisha prophesied the death of King Ben-Hadad of Syria and the succession of Hazael as king of Syria.

was plowing *with* twelve yoke *of oxen*
before him, and he was with the
twelfth. Then Elijah passed by him and
threw his [a]mantle on him.
20 And he left the oxen and ran after
Elijah, and said, [a]"Please let me kiss
my father and my mother, and *then* I
will follow you." And he said to him,
"Go back again, for what have I done
to you?"
21 So *Elisha* turned back from him,
and took a yoke of oxen and slaughtered them and [a]boiled their flesh, using the oxen's equipment, and gave it
to the people, and they ate. Then he
arose and followed Elijah, and became
his *servant.

Ahab Defeats the Syrians

20 Now [a]Ben-Hadad the king of
Syria gathered all his forces together; thirty-two kings *were* with him,
with horses and chariots. And he went
up and besieged [b]Samaria, and made
war against it.
2 Then he sent messengers into the
city to Ahab king of Israel, and said
to him, "Thus says Ben-Hadad:
3 'Your silver and your gold *are* mine;
your loveliest wives and children are
mine.' "
4 And the king of Israel answered and
said, "My lord, O king, just as you say,
I and all that I have *are* yours."
5 Then the messengers came back
and said, "Thus speaks Ben-Hadad,
saying, 'Indeed I have sent to you, saying, "You shall deliver to me your silver and your gold, your wives and your
children";
6 'but I will send my servants to you
tomorrow about this time, and they
shall search your house and the houses
of your servants. And it shall be, *that*
whatever is [1]pleasant in your eyes,
they will put in their hands and take
it.' "
7 So the king of Israel called all the
elders of the land, and said, "Notice,
please, and see how this *man* seeks
trouble, for he sent to me for my wives,
my children, my silver, and my gold;
and I did not deny him."
8 And all the elders and all the people
said to him, "Do not **listen** or consent."

WORD WEALTH

20:8 listen, *shama'* (shah-*mah*); Strong's #8085: To hear; to listen, consider, pay attention; to listen carefully and intelligently, to obey. The word conveys a sense of intensity. The most famous reference containing *shama'* is Deut. 6:4, which states, *"Sh'ma Yisrael!* Hear, O Israel! The LORD our God, the LORD *is* one!" These words are called the *Sh'ma,* which is the central creed of Judaism. Moses was calling Israel to listen attentively and very carefully with a mind to obey what God would say. The verb *shama'* also appears in the name *Shmuel* (Samuel), "Heard of God." Samuel was so named after his mother asked for a son, and the Lord listened to her (1 Sam. 3:20).

9 Therefore he said to the messengers
of Ben-Hadad, "Tell my lord the king,
'All that you sent for to your servant
the first time I will do, but this thing I
cannot do.' " And the messengers departed and brought back word to him.
10 Then Ben-Hadad sent to him and
said, [a]"The gods do so to me, and more
also, if enough dust is left of Samaria
for a handful for each of the people
[1]who follow me."
11 So the king of Israel answered and
said, "Tell *him,* 'Let not the one who
puts on *his armor* [a]boast like the one
who takes *it off.*' "
12 And it happened when *Ben-Hadad*
heard this message, as he and the kings
were [a]drinking at the [1]command post,
that he said to his servants, "Get
ready." And they got ready to attack
the city.
13 Suddenly a prophet approached
Ahab king of Israel, saying, "Thus says
the LORD: 'Have you seen all this great

19 [a]1 Sam. 28:14; 2 Kin. 2:8, 13, 14
20 [a][Matt. 8:21, 22; Luke 9:61, 62]; Acts 20:37
21 [a]2 Sam. 24:22 *See WW at 1 Chr. 15:2.

CHAPTER 20

1 [a]1 Kin. 15:18, 20; 2 Kin. 6:24 [b]1 Kin. 16:24; 2 Kin. 6:24
6 [1]*pleasing*
10 [a]1 Kin. 19:2; 2 Kin. 6:31 [1]Lit. *at my feet*
11 [a]Prov. 27:1; [Eccl. 7:8]
12 [a]1 Kin. 20:16 [1]Lit. *booths* or *shelters*

team. That Elijah **threw his mantle on him** symbolized that he was electing Elisha to receive the authority and power of his office (see v. 16).

19:20, 21 The phrase **Go back again, for what have I done to you?** is Elijah's approval that it is appropriate to say farewell to his family. Elisha uses the animals and implements of his former livelihood to host a farewell celebration. From this point on he does not turn back.

20:1 Ben-Hadad: See note on 15:18 about the three Ben-Hadads in Scripture.

20:10 Ben-Hadad threatens to destroy Israel totally in a life-jeopardizing oath where he boasts of parceling off Samaria to his followers. When Ben-Hadad refers to his gods, he is implying this is not just a contest of military strategy, but a test of the stronger deity.

20:11 Ahab's answer to the threat of Ben-Hadad means that Ben-Hadad should not boast of victory when he has not yet won the battle. He calls Ben-Hadad's bluff, inviting him to attack, or if not, to quit intimidating Israel.

20:12–22 At the word of the Lord, through a prophet, **Ahab** attacked the drunken **Ben-Hadad** and won an initial victory. However, the prophet warned Ahab that the Syrians would regroup and attack (v. 22). That Ahab heeded the voice of a prophet of God is an indication that there were some lasting effects to Elijah's victory on Mt. Carmel.

multitude? Behold, [a]I will deliver it into
your hand today, and you shall know
that I *am* the LORD.' "
14 So Ahab said, "By whom?" And he
said, "Thus says the LORD: 'By the
young leaders of the provinces.' " Then
he said, "Who will set the battle in order?" And he answered, "You."
15 Then he mustered the young leaders of the provinces, and there were
two hundred and thirty-two; and after
them he mustered all the people, all the
children of Israel—seven thousand.
16 So they went out at noon. Meanwhile Ben-Hadad and the thirty-two
kings helping him were [a]getting drunk
at the command post.
17 The young leaders of the provinces
went out first. And Ben-Hadad sent out
a patrol, and they told him, saying,
"Men are coming out of Samaria!"
18 So he said, "If they have come out
for peace, take them alive; and if they
have come out for war, take them
alive."
19 Then these young leaders of the
provinces went out of the city with the
army which followed them.
20 And each one killed his man; so the
Syrians fled, and Israel pursued them;
and Ben-Hadad the king of Syria escaped on a horse with the cavalry.
21 Then the king of Israel went out and
attacked the horses and chariots, and
killed the Syrians with a great slaughter.
22 And the prophet came to the king
of Israel and said to him, "Go,
strengthen yourself; take note, and see
what you should do, [a]for [1]in the spring
of the year the king of Syria will come
up against you."

The Syrians Again Defeated

23 Then the servants of the king of
Syria said to him, "Their gods *are* gods
of the hills. Therefore they were stronger than we; but if we fight against
them in the plain, surely we will be
stronger than they.
24 "So do this thing: Dismiss the kings,
each from his position, and put captains in their [1]places;
25 "and you shall muster an army like
the army [1]that you have lost, horse for
horse and chariot for chariot. Then we
will fight against them in the plain;
surely we will be stronger than they."
And he listened to their voice and did
so.
26 So it was, in the spring of the year,
that Ben-Hadad mustered the Syrians
and went up to [a]Aphek to fight against
Israel.
27 And the children of Israel were
mustered and given provisions, and
they went against them. Now the children of Israel encamped before them
like two little flocks of goats, while the
Syrians filled the [a]countryside.
28 Then a [a]man of God came and
spoke to the king of Israel, and said,
"Thus says the LORD: 'Because the Syrians have said, "The LORD *is* God of
the hills, but He *is* not God of the valleys," therefore [b]I will deliver all this
great multitude into your hand, and
you shall know that I *am* the LORD.' "
29 And they encamped opposite each
other for seven days. So it was that on
the seventh day the battle was joined;
and the children of Israel killed one
hundred thousand foot soldiers *of* the
Syrians in one day.
30 But the rest fled to Aphek, into the
city; then a wall fell on twenty-seven
thousand of the men *who were* left.
And Ben-Hadad fled and went into the
city, into an inner chamber.

Ahab's Treaty with Ben-Hadad

31 Then his servants said to him,
"Look now, we have heard that the
kings of the house of Israel *are* merciful kings. Please, let us [a]put sackcloth
around our waists and ropes around
our heads, and go out to the king of
Israel; perhaps he will spare your life."
32 So they wore sackcloth around
their waists and *put* ropes around their
heads, and came to the king of Israel
and said, "Your servant Ben-Hadad
says, 'Please let me live.' " And he said,
"*Is* he still alive? He *is* my brother."
33 Now the men were watching closely
to see whether *any sign of mercy would
come* from him; and they quickly
grasped *at this word* and said, "Your
brother Ben-Hadad." So he said, "Go,
bring him." Then Ben-Hadad came out
to him; and he had him come up into
the chariot.
34 So *Ben-Hadad* said to him, [a]"The
cities which my father took from your

13 [a]1 Kin. 20:28
16 [a]1 Kin. 16:9; 20:12; [Prov. 20:1]
22 [a]2 Sam. 11:1; 1 Kin. 20:26 [1]Lit. *at the return*
24 [1]*positions*
25 [1]Lit. *that fell from you*
26 [a]Josh. 13:4; 2 Kin. 13:17
27 [a]Judg. 6:3–5; 1 Sam. 13:5–8
28 [a]1 Kin. 17:18 [b]1 Kin. 20:13
31 [a]Gen. 37:34; 2 Sam. 3:31
34 [a]1 Kin. 15:20

20:23 The Syrians assumed they had lost because they were not fighting in the dominant territory of their deity. They were not just challenging the Israelites, but asserting that their gods were more powerful than the God of Israel.

20:28 The LORD affirms that He will give Ahab the victory over the **Syrians** since they had spoken against Him.

20:31–34 Ahab unwisely spared Ben-Hadad, an action that is reminiscent of Saul's sparing King Agag (1 Sam. 15:9).

father I will restore; and you may set
up marketplaces for yourself in Damascus,
as my father did in Samaria."
Then *Ahab said,* "I will send you away
with this treaty." So he made a treaty
with him and sent him away.

Ahab Condemned

35 Now a certain man of [a]the sons of
the prophets said to his neighbor
[b]by the word of the LORD, "Strike me,
please." And the man refused to strike
him.
36 Then he said to him, "Because you
have not obeyed the voice of the LORD,
surely, as soon as you depart from me,
a lion shall kill you." And as soon as
he left him, [a]a lion found him and
killed him.
37 And he found another man, and
said, "Strike me, please." So the man
struck him, inflicting a wound.
38 Then the prophet departed and
waited for the king by the road, and
disguised himself with a bandage over
his eyes.
39 Now [a]as the king passed by, he
cried out to the king and said, "Your
servant went out into the midst of the
battle; and there, a man came over and
brought a man to me, and said, 'Guard
this man; if by any means he is missing,
[b]your life shall be for his life, or
else you shall [1]pay a talent of silver.'
40 "While your servant was busy here
and there, he was gone." Then the king
of Israel said to him, "So *shall* your
judgment *be;* you yourself have decided
it."
41 And he hastened to take the bandage
away from his eyes; and the king
of Israel recognized him as one of the
prophets.
42 Then he said to him, "Thus says the
LORD: [a]'Because you have let slip out
of *your* hand a man whom I appointed
to utter destruction, therefore your life
shall go for his life, and your people
for his people.' "
43 So the king of Israel [a]went to his
house sullen and displeased, and came
to Samaria.

Naboth Is Murdered for His Vineyard

21 And it came to pass after these
things *that* Naboth the Jezreelite
had a vineyard which *was* in
[a]Jezreel, next to the palace of Ahab
king of Samaria.
2 So Ahab spoke to Naboth, saying,
"Give me your [a]vineyard, that I may
have it for a vegetable garden, because
it *is* near, next to my house; and for it
I will give you a vineyard better than
it. *Or,* if it seems good to you, I will
give you its worth in money."
3 But Naboth said to Ahab, "The
LORD forbid [a]that I should give the inheritance
of my fathers to you!"
4 So Ahab went into his house sullen
and displeased because of the word
which Naboth the Jezreelite had spoken
to him; for he had said, "I will not
give you the inheritance of my fathers."
And he lay down on his bed,
and turned away his face, and would
eat no food.
5 But [a]Jezebel his wife came to him,
and said to him, "Why is your spirit
so sullen that you eat no food?"
6 He said to her, "Because I spoke to
Naboth the Jezreelite, and said to him,
'Give me your vineyard for money; or
else, if it pleases you, I will give you
another vineyard for it.' And he answered,
'I will not give you my vineyard.' "
7 Then Jezebel his wife said to
him, "You now exercise authority
over Israel! Arise, eat food, and let
your heart be cheerful; I will give you
the vineyard of Naboth the Jezreelite."
8 And she wrote letters in Ahab's
name, sealed *them* with his seal, and
sent the letters to the elders and the
nobles who *were* dwelling in the city
with Naboth.
9 She wrote in the letters, saying,

> Proclaim a *fast, and seat Naboth
> [1]with high honor among the
> people;
> 10 and seat two men, scoundrels,
> before him to bear witness
> against him, saying, "You have
> [a]blasphemed God and the king."
> *Then* take him out, and [b]stone
> him, that he may die.

11 So the men of his city, the elders
and nobles who were inhabitants of his
city, did as Jezebel had sent to them,

35 [a]2 Kin. 2:3, 5, 7, 15 [b]1 Kin. 13:17, 18
36 [a]1 Kin. 13:24
39 [a]2 Sam. 12:1 [b]2 Kin. 10:24 [1]Lit. *weigh*
42 [a]1 Kin. 22:31–37
43 [a]1 Kin. 21:4

CHAPTER 21

1 [a]Judg. 6:33; 1 Kin. 18:45, 46
2 [a]1 Sam. 8:14
3 [a][Lev. 25:23; Num. 36:7; Ezek. 46:18]
5 [a]1 Kin. 19:1, 2
9 [1]Lit. *at the head* *See WW at Jon. 3:5.
10 [a][Ex. 22:28; Lev. 24:15, 16]; Acts 6:11 [b][Lev. 24:14]

20:35–43 Ahab's act of sparing Ben-Hadad is denounced by the Lord in an illustrated message by one of the prophets.

21:1–3 According to the Mosaic Law, ancestral property was to remain in the family and not to be sold. Therefore, Ahab and Jezebel were not just expressing interest in something they wanted, but were displaying open contempt for God's laws.

21:4, 5 **Ahab** behaved more like a spoiled child than a king of Israel.

as it *was* written in the letters which she had sent to them.

12 [a]They proclaimed a fast, and seated Naboth with high honor among the people.

13 And two men, scoundrels, came in and sat before him; and the scoundrels [a]witnessed against him, against Naboth, in the presence of the people, saying, "Naboth has blasphemed God and the king!" [b]Then they took him outside the city and stoned him with stones, so that he died.

14 Then they sent to Jezebel, saying, "Naboth has been stoned and is dead."

15 And it came to pass, when Jezebel heard that Naboth had been stoned and was dead, that Jezebel said to Ahab, "Arise, take possession of the vineyard of Naboth the Jezreelite, which he refused to give you for money; for Naboth is not alive, but dead."

16 So it was, when Ahab heard that Naboth was dead, that Ahab got up and went down to take possession of the vineyard of Naboth the Jezreelite.

The LORD *Condemns Ahab*

17 [a]Then the word of the LORD came to [b]Elijah the Tishbite, saying,

18 "Arise, go down to meet Ahab king of Israel, [a]who *lives* in Samaria. There *he is,* in the vineyard of Naboth, where he has gone down to take possession of it.

19 "You shall speak to him, saying, 'Thus says the LORD: "Have you murdered and also taken possession?"' And you shall speak to him, saying, 'Thus says the LORD: [a]"In the place where dogs licked the blood of Naboth, dogs shall lick your blood, even yours."'"

20 So Ahab said to Elijah, [a]"Have you found me, O my enemy?" And he answered, "I have found *you,* because [b]you have sold yourself to do evil in the sight of the LORD:

21 'Behold, [a]I will bring calamity on you. I will take away your [b]posterity, and will cut off from Ahab [c]every male in Israel, both [d]bond and free.

22 'I will make your house like the house of [a]Jeroboam the son of Nebat, and like the house of [b]Baasha the son of Ahijah, because of the provocation with which you have provoked *Me* to anger, and made Israel sin.'

23 "And [a]concerning Jezebel the LORD also spoke, saying, 'The dogs shall eat Jezebel by the [1]wall of Jezreel.'

24 "The dogs shall eat [a]whoever belongs to Ahab and dies in the city, and the birds of the air shall eat whoever dies in the field."

25 But [a]there was no one like Ahab who sold himself to do wickedness in the sight of the LORD, [b]because Jezebel his wife [1]stirred him up.

26 And he behaved very abominably in following idols, according to all [a]*that* the Amorites had done, whom the LORD had cast out before the children of Israel.

27 So it was, when Ahab heard those words, that he tore his clothes and [a]put sackcloth on his body, and fasted and lay in sackcloth, and went about mourning.

28 And the word of the LORD came to Elijah the Tishbite, saying,

29 "See how Ahab has humbled himself before Me? Because he [a]has humbled himself before Me, I will not bring the calamity in his days. [b]In the days of his son I will bring the calamity on his house."

Micaiah Warns Ahab

22 Now three years passed without war between Syria and Israel.

2 Then it came to pass, in the third year, that [a]Jehoshaphat the king of Judah went down to *visit* the king of Israel.

3 And the king of Israel said to his servants, "Do you know that [a]Ramoth in Gilead *is* ours, but we hesitate to take it out of the hand of the king of Syria?"

4 So he said to Jehoshaphat, "Will

12 [a]Is. 58:4
13 [a][Ex. 20:16; 23:1, 7] [b]2 Kin. 9:26; 2 Chr. 24:21; Acts 7:58, 59; Heb. 11:37
17 [a][Ps. 9:12] [b]1 Kin. 19:1
18 [a]1 Kin. 13:32; 2 Chr. 22:9
19 [a]1 Kin. 22:38; 2 Kin. 9:26
20 [a]1 Kin. 18:17 [b]1 Kin. 21:25; 2 Kin. 17:17; [Rom. 7:14]
21 [a]1 Kin. 14:10; 2 Kin. 9:8 [b]2 Kin. 10:10 [c]1 Sam. 25:22 [d]1 Kin. 14:10
22 [a]1 Kin. 15:29 [b]1 Kin. 16:3, 11
23 [a]2 Kin. 9:10, 30–37 [1]So with MT, LXX; some Heb. mss., Syr., Tg., Vg. *plot of ground* instead of *wall* (cf. 2 Kin. 9:36)
24 [a]1 Kin. 14:11; 16:4
25 [a]1 Kin. 16:30–33; 21:20 [b]1 Kin. 16:31 [1]*incited him*
26 [a]Gen. 15:16; [Lev. 18:25–30]; 2 Kin. 21:11
27 [a]Gen. 37:34; 2 Sam. 3:31; 2 Kin. 6:30
29 [a][2 Kin. 22:19] [b]2 Kin. 9:25; 10:11, 17

CHAPTER 22
2 [a]1 Kin. 15:24; 2 Chr. 18:2
3 [a]Deut. 4:43; Josh. 21:38; 1 Kin. 4:13

21:13 There were **two men** because the law specified that there must be at least two witnesses to condemn a person (Deut. 17:6, 7). They **stoned** Naboth because that was the penalty for cursing God (Lev. 24:16).

21:19 *Though Ahab had not actually* **murdered** Naboth, he and Jezebel were the guilty parties for they had instigated his death.

21:25 This verse sums up the crux of the trouble in Israel. **Ahab** sold himself out to evil because he was incited by **Jezebel,** as the incident with Naboth so aptly illustrates. For this, God would judge them and their descendants.

21:27–29 The judgment had been pronounced, yet God responds in kindness even to one so wicked as Ahab when he humbles himself and repents. God would be merciful and not let the calamity happen in Ahab's lifetime. Though God postpones the consequences of Ahab's sin, He does not negate the punishment.

22:1–4 Ahab enlists the support of **Jehoshaphat** in his struggle with Syria. Jehoshaphat's son Jehoram had married Ahab's daughter Athaliah. In ch. 15, we saw Asa reigning in Judah, during the reign of Ahab in the north; now Jehoshaphat had succeeded to the throne in the south.

you go with me to fight at Ramoth
Gilead?" Jehoshaphat said to the king of
Israel, [a]"I *am* as you *are,* my people
as your people, my horses as your
horses."
5 Also Jehoshaphat said to the king
of Israel, [a]"Please inquire for the word
of the LORD today."
6 Then the king of Israel [a]gathered
[1]the prophets together, about four hundred men, and said to them, "Shall I
go against Ramoth Gilead to fight, or
shall I refrain?" So they said, "Go up,
for the Lord will deliver *it* into the
hand of the king."
7 And [a]Jehoshaphat said, "*Is there*
not still a prophet of the LORD here,
that we may inquire of [1]Him?"
8 So the king of Israel said to Jehoshaphat, "*There is* still one man, Micaiah the son of Imlah, by whom we
may inquire of the LORD; but I hate
him, because he does not prophesy
good concerning me, but evil." And Jehoshaphat said, "Let not the king say
such things!"
9 Then the king of Israel called an officer and said, "Bring Micaiah the son
of Imlah quickly!"
10 The king of Israel and Jehoshaphat
the king of Judah, having put on *their*
robes, sat each on his throne, at a
threshing floor at the entrance of the
gate of Samaria; and all the prophets
prophesied before them.
11 Now Zedekiah the son of Chenaanah had made [a]horns of iron for
himself; and he said, "Thus says the
LORD: 'With these you shall [b]gore the
Syrians until they are destroyed.' "
12 And all the prophets prophesied so,
saying, "Go up to Ramoth Gilead and
prosper, for the LORD will deliver *it* into
the king's hand."
13 Then the messenger who had gone
to call Micaiah spoke to him, saying,
"Now listen, the words of the prophets
with one accord encourage the king.
Please, let your word be like the word

4 [a]2 Kin. 3:7
5 [a]2 Kin. 3:11
6 [a]1 Kin. 18:19 [1]The false prophets
7 [a]2 Kin. 3:11 [1]Or *him*
11 [a]Zech. 1:18–21 [b]Deut. 33:17

14 [a]Num. 22:38; 24:13
17 [a]Num. 27:17; 1 Kin. 22:34–36; 2 Chr. 18:16; Matt. 9:36; Mark 6:34
19 [a]Is. 6:1; Ezek. 1:26–28; Dan. 7:9 [b]Job 1:6; 2:1; Ps. 103:20; Dan. 7:10; Zech. 1:10; [Matt. 18:10; Heb. 1:7, 14]
22 [a]Judg. 9:23; 1 Sam. 16:14; 18:10; 19:9; Job 12:16; [Ezek. 14:9; 2 Thess. 2:11]
23 [a][Ezek. 14:9]
24 [a]Jer. 20:2

of one of them, and speak encouragement."
14 And Micaiah said, "*As* the LORD 6
lives, [a]whatever the LORD says to me,
that I will speak."
15 Then he came to the king; and the
king said to him, "Micaiah, shall we
go to war against Ramoth Gilead, or
shall we refrain?" And he answered
him, "Go and prosper, for the LORD will
deliver *it* into the hand of the king!"
16 So the king said to him, "How many
times shall I make you swear that you
tell me nothing but the truth in the
name of the LORD?"
17 Then he said, "I saw all Israel
[a]scattered on the mountains, as sheep
that have no shepherd. And the LORD
said, 'These have no master. Let each
return to his house in peace.' "
18 And the king of Israel said to Jehoshaphat, "Did I not tell you he would
not prophesy good concerning me, but
evil?"
19 Then *Micaiah* said, "Therefore hear
the word of the LORD: [a]I saw the LORD
sitting on His throne, [b]and all the host
of heaven standing by, on His right
hand and on His left.
20 "And the LORD said, 'Who will persuade Ahab to go up, that he may fall
at Ramoth Gilead?' So one spoke in
this manner, and another spoke in that
manner.
21 "Then a spirit came forward and
stood before the LORD, and said, 'I will
persuade him.'
22 "The LORD said to him, 'In what
way?' So he said, 'I will go out and be
a lying spirit in the mouth of all his
prophets.' And the LORD said, [a]'You
shall persuade *him,* and also prevail.
Go out and do so.'
23 [a]"Therefore look! The LORD has put
a lying spirit in the mouth of all these
prophets of yours, and the LORD has
declared disaster against you."
24 Now Zedekiah the son of Chenaanah went near and [a]struck Micaiah

22:5–8 Jehoshaphat wisely insists on divine counsel before he engages in a battle, yet he is hesitant about the advice of Ahab's prophets, discerning that they are only interested in saying what Ahab wants to hear. This is confirmed by Ahab's contempt for **Micaiah.**

22:11, 12 Before Micaiah arrived, an optimistic prophecy was given by **Zedekiah** confirming the word by Ahab's prophets.

22:14–28 See section 6 of Truth-In-Action at the end of 1 Kin.

22:15–23 **Micaiah,** in an encounter very reminiscent of Elijah's on Mt. Carmel, stands alone and speaks the **truth.** Ahab, Jehoshaphat, and the prophets wanted to believe a lie more than they really wanted the Lord's will. God is not the father of lies; the Devil is (John 8:44). So God permitted an evil spirit to accomplish what Satan is always intent on doing.

22:17 Jesus uses this picture of **sheep that have no shepherd** in Mark 6:34.

22:24, 25 A slap in the face was a horrible insult. Zedekiah's response implies that he believed his own prophecy to be genuine and not a lie. The **spirit from the LORD** probably refers to the lying spirit in vv. 22, 23 because "spirit" is not capitalized. However, in the original Hebrew there are no capital or lowercase distinctions. Therefore, some take "the spirit from the LORD" as a reference to the Spirit of the Lord who enabled the prophets to prophesy (1 Sam. 10:6, 10; 19:20, 23). In the first interpretation, **Zedekiah** would be taunting **Micaiah,** asking him to tell him which way the lying spirit went, if he could indeed see it. In the second, Zedekiah

on the cheek, and said, [b]"Which way
did the spirit from the LORD go from
me to speak to you?"
25 And Micaiah said, "Indeed, you
shall see on that day when you go into
an [a]inner chamber to hide!"
26 So the king of Israel said, "Take
Micaiah, and return him to Amon the
governor of the city and to Joash the
king's son;
27 "and say, 'Thus says the king: "Put
this *fellow* in [a]prison, and feed him
with bread of affliction and water of
affliction, until I come in peace." ' "
28 But Micaiah said, "If you ever return in peace, [a]the LORD has not spoken by me." And he said, "Take heed,
all you people!"

Ahab Dies in Battle

29 So the king of Israel and Jehoshaphat the king of Judah went up to Ramoth Gilead.
30 And the king of Israel said to Jehoshaphat, "I will disguise myself and
go into battle; but you put on your
robes." So the king of Israel [a]disguised
himself and went into battle.
31 Now the [a]king of Syria had commanded the thirty-two [b]captains of his
chariots, saying, "Fight with no one
small or great, but only with the king
of Israel."
32 So it was, when the captains of the
chariots saw Jehoshaphat, that they
said, "Surely it *is* the king of Israel!"
Therefore they turned aside to fight
against him, and Jehoshaphat [a]cried
out.
33 And it happened, when the captains
of the chariots saw that it *was* not the
king of Israel, that they turned back
from pursuing him.
34 Now a *certain* man drew a bow at
random, and struck the king of Israel
between the joints of his armor. So he
said to the driver of his chariot, "Turn
around and take me out of the battle,
for I am wounded."
35 The battle increased that day; and
the king was propped up in his chariot,
facing the Syrians, and died at evening.
The blood ran out from the wound onto
the floor of the chariot.
36 Then, as the sun was going down,
a shout went throughout the army, say-

24 [b]2 Chr. 18:23
25 [a]1 Kin. 20:30
27 [a]2 Chr. 16:10; 18:25–27
28 [a]Num. 16:29; Deut. 18:20–22
30 [a]2 Chr. 35:22
31 [a]1 Kin. 20:1 [b]1 Kin. 20:24; 2 Chr. 18:30
32 [a]2 Chr. 18:31
38 [a]1 Kin. 21:19 [1]Tg., Syr. *they washed his armor*
39 [a]Ps. 45:8; Amos 3:15
40 [a]2 Kin. 1:2, 18 [1]Died and joined his ancestors
41 [a]2 Chr. 20:31
43 [a]2 Chr. 17:3; 20:32, 33 [b]1 Kin. 14:23; 15:14; 2 Kin. 12:3
44 [a]2 Chr. 19:2 [b]2 Chr. 18:1
45 [a]2 Chr. 20:34
46 [a]Gen. 19:5; Deut. 23:17; 1 Kin. 14:24; 15:12; 2 Kin. 23:7; Jude 7 [1]Heb. *qadesh*, one practicing sodomy and prostitution in religious rituals
47 [a]2 Sam. 8:14; 2 Kin. 3:9; 8:20
48 [a]2 Chr. 20:35–37 [b]1 Kin. 10:22 [c]1 Kin. 9:28 [d]2 Chr. 20:37 [e]1 Kin. 9:26 [1]Or *ships of Tarshish*

ing, "Every man to his city, and every
man to his own country!"
37 So the king died, and was brought
to Samaria. And they buried the king
in Samaria.
38 Then *someone* washed the chariot
at a pool in Samaria, and the dogs
licked up his blood while [1]the harlots
bathed, according [a]to the word of the
LORD which He had spoken.
39 Now the rest of the acts of Ahab,
and all that he did, [a]the ivory house
which he built and all the cities that
he built, *are* they not written in the
book of the chronicles of the kings of
Israel?
40 So Ahab [1]rested with his fathers.
Then [a]Ahaziah his son reigned in his
place.

Jehoshaphat Reigns in Judah

41 [a]Jehoshaphat the son of Asa had
become king over Judah in the fourth
year of Ahab king of Israel.
42 Jehoshaphat *was* thirty-five years
old when he became king, and he
reigned twenty-five years in Jerusalem. His mother's name *was* Azubah
the daughter of Shilhi.
43 And [a]he walked in all the ways of
his father Asa. He did not turn aside
from them, doing *what was* right in
the eyes of the LORD. Nevertheless
[b]the high places were not taken away,
for the people offered sacrifices
and burned incense on the high
places.
44 Also [a]Jehoshaphat made [b]peace
with the king of Israel.
45 Now the rest of the acts of Jehoshaphat, the might that he showed,
and how he made war, *are* they not
written [a]in the book of the chronicles
of the kings of Judah?
46 [a]And the rest of the [1]perverted persons, who remained in the days of
his father Asa, he banished from the
land.
47 [a]*There was* then no king in Edom,
only a deputy of the king.
48 [a]Jehoshaphat [b]made [1]merchant
ships to go to [c]Ophir for gold; [d]but they
never sailed, for the ships were
wrecked at [e]Ezion Geber.
49 Then Ahaziah the son of Ahab said
to Jehoshaphat, "Let my servants go

---

would be affirming his belief that he was inspired by the Spirit of God, and would be asking Micaiah to prove his ability to tell that the prophecy of Zedekiah and the other prophets was not divinely inspired. In either case, only time would tell who was correct (v. 25).

22:41–50 Kings now explains how **Jehoshaphat** had begun to reign in the southern kingdom. As Judah's fourth ruler, Jehoshaphat was a godly king like **his father Asa.** For more information on Jehoshaphat's noteworthy achievements, see 2 Chr. 17—19.

with your servants in the ships." But
Jehoshaphat would not.
50 And [a]Jehoshaphat [1]rested with his
fathers, and was buried with his fathers in the City of David his father.
Then Jehoram his son reigned in his
place.

Ahaziah Reigns in Israel

51 [a]Ahaziah the son of Ahab became
king over Israel in Samaria in the
seventeenth year of Jehoshaphat king
of Judah, and reigned two years over
Israel.
52 He did evil in the sight of the LORD,
and [a]walked in the way of his father
and in the way of his mother and in
the way of Jeroboam the son of Nebat,
who had made Israel sin;
53 for [a]he served Baal and worshiped
him, and provoked the LORD God of Israel to anger, [b]according[1] to all that
his father had done.

50 [a]2 Chr. 21:1 [1]Died and joined his ancestors
51 [a]1 Kin. 22:40
52 [a]1 Kin. 15:26; 21:25
53 [a]Judg. 2:11 [b]1 Kin. 16:30–32 [1]In the same way that

22:51–53 Shifting back to the north, 1 Kin. ends by explaining that **Ahaziah,** the son of Ahab and Jezebel, had become the eighth king in Israel. The book concludes on the sad note that Ahaziah was as wicked as his parents.

TRUTH-IN-ACTION through 1 KINGS

Letting the LIFE of the Holy Spirit Bring Faith's Works Alive in You!

Truth 1 Kings Teaches	Text	**Action** 1 Kings Invites
1 Guidelines for Growing in Godliness The godly person has confidence that God cares about his character, faithfulness, and integrity and that He rewards those who walk faithfully with Him.	1:29 2:3	**Remember** and **carry out** vows and promises you make. **Be assured** the Lord has heard and will enable you to do so. **Remember** that the Lord prospers and grants success to those who walk in His ways.
2 Steps to Holiness Holiness implies a life that is separate from the world. Taking even small steps across this line too easily makes room for greater compromise.	3:3	**Avoid** even small compromises in holiness, purity, and worship. **Understand** that even the slightest deviations from what you know to be right may eventually become major transgressions.
3 Steps in Developing Humility Humility refuses to promote or exalt itself, trusting the Lord to bring advancement. It quickly acknowledges the Lord when anything it does is recognized, knowing that all accomplishments are realized through God.	1:5, 29 8:27	**Avoid** self-promotion. **Rely** upon the Lord to bring promotion to you. **Remember:** He who exalts himself will be humbled (see Matt. 23:12). **Be aware** that your life is only a conduit for or a reflection of God's life. **Know** that even the greatest thing you build will manifest only a small facet of God's glory.
4 Keys to Wise Living God is the only source of true wisdom, and He promises to give it to anyone who asks for it. Wisdom begins with the fear of the Lord and finds its fulfillment in love for others.	3:7–14 3:16–28 8:39, 40	**Do not presume** to know how to do what the Lord has called you to do. **Cleave** to the Lord. **Depend** upon him for wisdom. **Choose to believe** that God will give wisdom to all who ask for it (see James 1:5). **Be assured** that only God knows the hearts of men; we cannot. **Allow** this to cause you to reverence God.

Truth 1 Kings Teaches	Text	**Action** 1 Kings Invites
5 Steps to Dynamic Devotion Make no mistake about it: God gives special recognition to those whose hearts are wholly His. To believe that casual devotion to God is as blessed as whole-hearted devotion is self-deception.	8:61 11:1–8	**Be assured** that the Lord's promises are for those whose hearts are fully committed to Him and His ways. **Examine** yourself for any lukewarmness you need to confess. **Be very careful** not to let those for whom you have affection lead you away from full devotion to the Lord.
6 Lessons for Leaders God's leaders serve Him on the people's behalf, not vice versa. Confusion on this point has caused many a tragedy among God's people. The kings who sought to please the people rather than God opened the way for great sin and received a bad report. What an important lesson in a day when popularity has become such an idol to many! God's leaders are encouraged to follow His Word closely and to be careful regarding other sources of advice.	12:6–11 12:28; 13:34; 22:14–28 15:3, 11	Leaders, **be wise** and **seek counsel** from other seasoned and fruitful leaders. **Avoid** the exclusive counsel of untried leaders who have borne little fruit. Leaders, **be faithful** to God's Word. What you say may not always be popular, but it must measure up to the standards of Scripture. Otherwise, your ministry may promote idolatry. Leaders, **pattern your lives** and ministries after leaders who have God's approval and follow His Word closely. **Avoid** patterns that, although successful by worldly standards, contradict God's Word.
7 Steps to Dealing with Sin Deception begins when we forget that all of us are inclined to sin.	8:46	**Be assured** that there is no one who does not sin. **Let God search your heart daily** to guard you against sin, which you might not notice.
8 Key Lessons in Faith Believe that where the Lord leads, He feeds. Where He guides, He provides. Faith does not let a threat of privation alter the course the Lord has set.	17:1–9	**Do not allow** the threat of reduced income to cause you to disobey the Lord's direction for your life. **Choose to believe** that the Lord knows how to care for His servants.

The Second Book of the
KINGS

Author: Unknown, Attributed to Jeremiah
Date: Uncertain, Probably Between 560 B.C. and 538 B.C.
Theme: Lessons from the Ruin of Israel and Judah
Key Words: King, House, Prophet

Author Second Kings was originally the second half of one book which included 1 and 2 Kings (see "Content" below). This work must have been compiled sometime after the capture of Judah by the Babylonians in 586 B.C. (see ch. 25). It seems to have been the product of one author, who was an eyewitness to the fall of Jerusalem. Though the authorship cannot be known with certainty, several suggestions have been made. Some have nominated Ezra as the compiler, while others point to Isaiah as the editor. Compare 18:19, 20 with Isaiah 36—39. A number of scholars say that the writer of 2 Kings was an unknown prophet or some Jewish captive in Babylon at about 550 B.C. Because Josephus (a prominent Jewish historian of the first century A.D.) ascribes Kings to "the prophets," many have abandoned the search for a specific author. However, the most probable position is that the prophet Jeremiah was author of 1 and 2 Kings. Early Jewish tradition of the Talmud states that Jeremiah wrote Kings. This famous prophet preached in Jerusalem before and after its fall, and chapters 24 and 25 appear in Jeremiah 39—42; 52. The contents of all but the last appendix (25:27–30) could have been written by Jeremiah, and the final verses added by one of Jeremiah's disciples.

Date Though the precise date for the composition of 1 and 2 Kings is uncertain, it is believed to have come into its final compilation sometime in the late sixth century B.C. The last event recorded in 2 Kings is the release of King Jehoiachin of Judah from imprisonment in Babylon. Since Jehoiachin was imprisoned in 597 B.C. (see 24:8–17) and released thirty-seven years later (see 25:27), then Kings must have been written after 560 B.C. to include this information. It is almost certain that the writer of Kings would have mentioned something as significant as the fall of Babylon to Persia in 538 B.C. had he known of these events. Since there is no mention of this prominent event in Kings, it is then concluded that 1 and 2 Kings probably was written before 538 B.C. Therefore the date of 1 and 2 Kings is fixed between 560 and 538 B.C., though some of the events recorded in these books occurred many years earlier.

Background The events covered in 2 Kings span a period of almost three hundred years. Second Kings records the turbulent experiences of God's people from the reign of Ahaziah (the ninth king in the northern kingdom of Israel) around 853 B.C., through the fall of Israel to Assyria in 722 B.C., through the fall of Jerusalem and the deportation of Judah to Babylon in 586 B.C., and ends with the release of King Jehoiachin in 560 B.C. This was a difficult period in the history of God's people, a time of great change and upheaval. There was struggle from within and pressure from without. The result was a dark moment in the history of God's people: the collapse and eventual captivity of both nations.

Occasion and Purpose Contemplating the horror of the exile of God's people, the author compiles 1 and 2 Kings to answer the looming question of why both the northern kingdom of Israel and the southern kingdom of Judah had been taken captive. He writes with a prophetic message, showing that this punishment by captivity to foreign pagan nations was the inevitable consequence of the persistent violation of God's covenant with them. Kings was written to cause the exiles to reflect on their history and return to the Lord. Perhaps this prophetic perspective is one reason why it was included in the "earlier prophets" in the Hebrew Bible.

Content First and 2 Kings were originally one unbroken book, which formed a sequel to 1 and 2 Samuel. The composers of the Greek Old Testament (the Septuagint, or LXX) divided the work into "3 and 4 Kingdoms" (1 and 2 Sam. were "1 and 2 Kingdoms"). The title "Kings" is derived from Jerome's Latin translation (the Vulgate) and is appropriate because of the emphasis of these books on the kings who reigned during these centuries.

The Book of 2 Kings takes up recording the historical events of God's people where the Book of 1 Kings leaves off. However, 2 Kings is more than just a compilation of the politically important or socially significant happenings in Israel and Judah. In fact, it is not as detailed a history as might be expected (three hundred years in only twenty-five chapters). Instead, 2 Kings is a selective history, one with a theological purpose. Therefore, the author selects and emphasizes the people and events that are morally and religiously significant. Second Kings presents God as the Lord of history. From history, this book establishes God's providential working in and through the lives of His people for His redemptive purpose. It demonstrates the necessity of obedience to God's covenant and the painful consequence of disobedience. Therefore, the Book of 2 Kings is not to be viewed as mere history, but as theology and lessons from history.

Second Kings picks up the tragic history of the "divided kingdom" with Ahaziah on the throne of Israel, while Jehoshaphat is ruling in Judah. As with 1 Kings, the narrative is difficult to follow. The author switches back and forth between the northern kingdom of Israel and the southern kingdom of Judah, tracing their histories simultaneously. There were nineteen regents in Israel, all of them bad. In Judah, there were twenty rulers, only eight of them good. Second Kings records the last ten kings in Israel, and the last sixteen rulers in Judah. Some of these twenty-six regents are only mentioned in a few verses, while whole chapters are devoted to others.

Major attention is directed to those who either serve as a model of uprightness, or to those who illustrate why these nations eventually collapsed.

Personal Application The message of 2 Kings is as relevant today as when it was written. God still controls human affairs. The nation, leader, or person who responds to and obeys the Lord will enjoy the benefits of their relationship with Him. Those who refuse and rebel will experience God's discipline. Though people are sinful, God is the author of redemption, and He graciously forgives those who will repent and return to Him.

Christ Revealed The failure of the prophets, priests, and kings of God's people points to the necessity of the advent of Christ. Christ Himself would be the ideal combination of these three offices. As a Prophet, Christ's word far surpasses that of the great prophet Elijah (Matt. 17:1–5). Many of the miracles of Jesus were reminiscent of the wonders God did through Elijah and Elisha in 2 Kings. In addition, Christ is a Priest superior to any of those recorded in Kings (Heb. 7:22–27). Especially, 2 Kings vividly illustrates the need for Christ as our reigning King. When asked if He was King of the Jews, Jesus affirmed that He was (Matt. 27:11). However, Christ is a King greater than their greatest king (Matt. 12:42). The reign of each of the twenty-six rulers came to an end, but Christ will reign on the throne of David forever (1 Chr. 17:14; Is. 9:6), for He is "KING OF KINGS AND LORD OF LORDS" (Rev. 19:16). For a further study of allusions to Christ during the time of 2 Kings, read Introduction to 2 Chronicles: Christ Revealed.

The Holy Spirit at Work The words of the prophets in 2:16 indicate that the Holy Spirit (the "Spirit of the LORD") sometimes transported Elijah from one location to another (see 1 Kin. 18:12). This is not unlike Acts 8:39, 40, where Philip is described as having a similar experience.

There is an indirect reference to the Holy Spirit in the phrase "spirit of Elijah" found in 2:9, 15 (see the text and note on 1 Kin. 2:9–16). Here Elisha is seeking to receive the same empowerment Elijah had in order to carry on Elijah's prophetic ministry. The energizing spirit or power that enabled Elijah to prophesy was the Spirit of God (see 1 Sam. 10:6, 10 and 19:20, 23). Second Kings 2:9–16 then provides an interesting Old Testament parallel to Acts 1:4–9 and 2:1–4. Elijah went into heaven, Elisha sought the promise of empowerment to carry on his master's ministry, and he received it. In a similar way, Jesus ascended, the disciples awaited the promise, and the Holy Spirit descended to empower them to carry on the work that their Lord began.

A final allusion to the Holy Spirit in 2 Kings is in 3:15. Here the "hand of the LORD" came upon Elisha, enabling him to prophesy to King Jehoshaphat. The formula "hand of the LORD" referred to the divine inspiration for prophets (see Ezek. 1:3), which as noted above, is the Spirit of God. That prophecy is a manifestation of the Holy Spirit is confirmed in 1 Corinthians 12:7–11.

For more on the Holy Spirit in the kingdom period, read Introduction to 1 Kings: The Holy Spirit at Work and Introduction to 2 Chronicles: The Holy Spirit at Work.

Outline of 2 Kings

I. The divided kingdom 1:1—17:41

A. The reign of Ahaziah in Israel 1:1–18
B. The reign of Jehoram in Israel 2:1—8:15
C. The reign of Jehoram in Judah 8:16–24
D. The reign of Ahaziah in Judah 8:25—9:29
E. The reign of Jehu in Israel 9:30—10:36
F. The reign of Queen Athaliah in Judah 11:1–16
G. The reign of Joash in Judah 11:17—12:21
H. The reign of Jehoahaz in Israel 13:1–9
I. The reign of Jehoash in Israel 13:10–25
J. The reign of Amaziah in Judah 14:1–22
K. The reign of Jeroboam II in Israel 14:23–29
L. The reign of Azariah in Judah 15:1–7
M. The reigns of Zechariah, Shallum, Menahem, Pekahiah, and Pekah in Israel 15:8–31
N. The reign of Jotham in Judah 15:32–38
O. The reign of Ahaz in Judah 16:1–20
P. The reign of Hoshea in Israel 17:1–5
Q. The captivity of Israel to Assyria 17:6–41

II. The kingdom of Judah alone 18:1—25:30

A. The reign of Hezekiah 18:1—20:21
B. The reign of Manasseh 21:1–18
C. The reign of Amon 21:19–26
D. The reign of Josiah 22:1—23:30
E. The reign of Jehoahaz 23:31–34
F. The reign of Jehoiakim 23:35—24:7
G. The reign of Jehoiachin 24:8–16
H. The reign of Zedekiah 24:17–20
I. The fall of Jerusalem 25:1–7
J. The captivity of Judah to Babylon 25:8–26
K. The release of Jehoiachin 25:27–30

God Judges Ahaziah

MOAB [a]rebelled against Israel
[b]after the death of Ahab.
2 Now [a]Ahaziah fell through the lattice of his upper room in Samaria, and
was injured; so he sent messengers and
said to them, "Go, inquire of [b]Baal-
Zebub,[1] the god of [c]Ekron, whether I
shall recover from this injury."
3 But the [1]angel of the LORD said to
Elijah the Tishbite, "Arise, go up to
meet the messengers of the king of Samaria, and say to them, '*Is it* because
there is no God in Israel *that* you are
going to inquire of Baal-Zebub, the god
of Ekron?'
4 "Now therefore, thus says the LORD:
'You shall not come down from the bed
to which you have gone up, but you
shall surely die.' " So Elijah departed.
5 And when the messengers returned
to [1]him, he said to them, "Why have
you come back?"
6 So they said to him, "A man came
up to meet us, and said to us, 'Go, return to the king who sent you, and say
to him, "Thus says the LORD: '*Is it* because *there is* no God in Israel *that* you
are sending to inquire of Baal-Zebub,
the god of Ekron? Therefore you shall
not come down from the bed to which
you have gone up, but you shall surely
die.' " ' "
7 Then he said to them, "What kind
of man *was it* who came up to meet
you and told you these words?"
8 So they answered him, [a]"A hairy
man wearing a leather belt around his
waist." And he said, [b]"It *is* Elijah the
Tishbite."
9 Then the king sent to him a captain

CHAPTER 1
1 [a]2 Sam. 8:2 [b]2 Kin. 3:5
2 [a]1 Kin. 22:40 [b]2 Kin. 1:3, 6, 16; Matt. 10:25; Mark 3:22 [c]1 Sam. 5:10 [1]Lit. *Lord of Flies*
3 [1]Or *Angel*
5 [1]Ahaziah
8 [a]Zech. 13:4; Matt. 3:4; Mark 1:6 [b]1 Kin. 18:7

1:1, 2 2 Kin. picks up where 1 Kin. leaves off, since they were originally one scroll. **Ahaziah** was the eighth ruler in *the northern kingdom of Israel. He had fallen* through the **lattice** that covered the window in his upper room and sustained a severe injury. Ahaziah, as evil and idolatrous as his father Ahab and his mother Jezebel, attempted to consult the local fertility god **Baal-Zebub** concerning his injury.

1:3–17 Elijah, last mentioned in 1 Kin. 21, now appears to confront Ahaziah with his sin. He sent Ahaziah's delegation back and ridiculed him for his idolatry. When Ahaziah attempted to have him seized, Elijah miraculously called down fire to destroy his would-be captors. The penalty for Ahaziah's sin was that he would not recover from his injury. Some have taken exception to Elijah's action here, citing Luke 9:51–56. However, in Luke, the action of the disciples was offensive, while Elijah's action was defensive and an act of God's judgment.

of fifty with his fifty men. So he went
up to him; and there he was, sitting on
the top of a hill. And he spoke to him:
"Man of God, the king has said, 'Come
down!' "
10 So Elijah answered and said to the
captain of fifty, "If I *am* a man of God,
then [a]let fire come down from *heaven
and consume you and your fifty men."
And fire came down from heaven and
consumed him and his fifty.
11 Then he sent to him another captain
of fifty with his fifty men. And he answered and said to him: "Man of God,
thus has the king said, 'Come down
quickly!' "
12 So Elijah answered and said to
them, "If I *am* a man of God, let fire
come down from heaven and consume
you and your fifty men." And the fire
of God came down from heaven and
consumed him and his fifty.
13 Again, he sent a third captain of
fifty with his fifty men. And the third
captain of fifty went up, and came and
[1]fell on his knees before Elijah, and
pleaded with him, and said to him:
"Man of God, please let my life and
the life of these fifty servants of yours
[a]be precious in your sight.
14 "Look, fire has come down from
heaven and burned up the first two
captains of fifties with their fifties. But
let my life now be precious in your
sight."
15 And the [1]angel of the LORD said to
Elijah, "Go down with him; do not be
afraid of him." So he arose and went
down with him to the king.
16 Then he said to him, "Thus says the
LORD: 'Because you have sent messengers to inquire of Baal-Zebub, the god
of Ekron, *is it* because *there is* no God
in Israel to inquire of His word? Therefore you shall not come down from the
bed to which you have gone up, but
you shall surely die.' "
17 So *Ahaziah* died according to the
word of the LORD which Elijah had spoken. Because he had no son, [a]Jehoram[1]
became king in his place, in the second
year of Jehoram the son of Jehoshaphat, king of Judah.
18 Now the rest of the acts of Ahaziah
which he did, *are* they not written in
the book of the chronicles of the kings
of Israel?

Elijah Ascends to Heaven

2 And it came to pass, when the LORD 5
was about to [a]take up Elijah into
heaven by a whirlwind, that Elijah
went with [b]Elisha from Gilgal.
2 Then Elijah said to Elisha, [a]"Stay
here, please, for the LORD has sent me
on to Bethel." But Elisha said, "*As* the
LORD lives, and [b]*as* your soul lives, I
will not leave you!" So they went down
to Bethel.
3 Now [a]the sons of the prophets who
were at Bethel came out to Elisha, and
said to him, "Do you know that the
LORD will take away your master
[1]from over you today?" And he said,
"Yes, I know; keep silent!"
4 Then Elijah said to him, "Elisha,
stay here, please, for the LORD has sent
me on to Jericho." But he said, "*As* the
LORD lives, and *as* your soul lives, I will
not leave you!" So they came to Jericho.
5 Now the sons of the prophets who
were at Jericho came to Elisha and said
to him, "Do you know that the LORD
will take away your master from over
you today?" So he answered, "Yes, I
know; keep silent!"
6 Then Elijah said to him, "Stay here,
please, for the LORD has sent me on to
the Jordan." But he said, "*As* the LORD
lives, and *as* your soul lives, I will not
leave you!" So the two of them went
on.
7 And fifty men of the sons of the
prophets went and stood facing *them*
at a distance, while the two of them
stood by the Jordan.
8 Now Elijah took his mantle, rolled
it up, and struck the *water; and
[a]it was divided this way and that, so
that the two of them crossed over on
dry [b]ground.
9 And so it was, when they had 6
crossed over, that Elijah said to Elisha,
"Ask! What may I do for you, before I

10 [a]1 Kin. 18:36–38; Luke 9:54 *See WW at 1 Kin. 8:23.
13 [a]1 Sam. 26:21; Ps. 72:14 [1]Lit. *bowed down*
15 [1]Or *Angel*
17 [a]1 Kin. 22:50; 2 Kin. 8:16; Matt. 1:8 [1]The son of Ahab king of Israel, 2 Kin. 3:1

CHAPTER 2

1 [a]Gen. 5:24; [Heb. 11:5] [b]1 Kin. 19:16–21
2 [a]Ruth 1:15, 16 [b]1 Sam. 1:26; 2 Kin. 2:4, 6; 4:30
3 [a]1 Kin. 20:35; 2 Kin. 2:5, 7, 15; 4:1, 38; 9:1 [1]Lit. *from your head*
8 [a]Ex. 14:21, 22; Josh. 3:16; 2 Kin. 2:14 [b]Josh. 3:17 *See WW at Is. 43:2.

1:17 Both Jehoshaphat and Ahab had sons named **Jehoram.** These men were brothers-in-law (see note on 1 Kin. 22:1–4).
2:1–15 See section 5 of Truth-In-Action at the end of 2 Kin.
2:1 Gilgal was east of Jericho, near the Jordan River.
2:2–6 Somehow **Elisha** had learned that **Elijah** would soon be departing this Earth, and he was determined to follow him until the end. Elijah had called Elisha to take up his office (see note on 1 Kin. 19:19). Elisha was determined to follow him since a dying person would often pronounce blessings on others (see Gen. 49), and Elisha did not want to miss his moment of opportunity. Elisha's commitment was tested three times by Elijah. **Sons of the prophets** here implies that they were members of a prophetic order, not that they were physical descendants of prophets.
2:8 The dividing of the Jordan was Elijah's last prophetic sign.
2:9 See section 6 of Truth-In-Action at the end of 2 Kin.
2:9–16 Elisha requests of Elijah one last thing, a **double portion** of Elijah's **spirit.** Since the double portion was the

am taken away from you?" Elisha said, "Please let a double portion of your *spirit be upon me."

10 So he said, "You have asked a hard thing. *Nevertheless,* if you see me *when I am* taken from you, it shall be so for you; but if not, it shall not be so."

11 Then it happened, as they continued on and talked, that suddenly [a]a chariot of fire *appeared* with horses of fire, and separated the two of them; and Elijah [b]went up by a whirlwind into heaven.

12 And Elisha saw *it,* and he cried out, [a]"My father, my father, the chariot of Israel and its horsemen!" So he saw him no more. And he took hold of his own clothes and tore them into two pieces.

13 He also took up the mantle of Elijah that had fallen from him, and went back and stood by the bank of the Jordan.

14 Then he took the mantle of Elijah that had fallen from him, and struck the water, and said, "Where *is* the LORD God of Elijah?" And when he also had struck the water, [a]it was divided this way and that; and Elisha crossed over.

15 Now when the sons of the prophets who *were* [a]from[1] Jericho saw him, they said, "The spirit of Elijah rests on Elisha." And they came to meet him, and bowed to the ground before him.

16 Then they said to him, "Look now, there are fifty strong men with your servants. Please let them go and search for your master, [a]lest perhaps the Spirit of the LORD has taken him up and cast him upon some mountain or into some valley." And he said, "You shall not send anyone."

17 But when they urged him till he was [a]ashamed,* he said, "Send *them!*" Therefore they sent fifty men, and they searched for three days but did not find him.

18 And when they came back to him, for he had stayed in Jericho, he said to them, "Did I not say to you, 'Do not go'?"

Elisha Performs Miracles

19 Then the men of the city said to Elisha, "Please notice, the situation of this city *is* pleasant, as my lord sees; but the water *is* bad, and the ground barren."

20 And he said, "Bring me a new bowl, and put salt in it." So they brought *it* to him.

21 Then he went out to the source of the water, and [a]cast in the salt there, and said, "Thus says the LORD: 'I have [1]healed this water; from it there shall be no more death or barrenness.' "

22 So the water remains [a]healed to this day, according to the word of Elisha which he spoke.

23 Then he went up from there to 5
Bethel; and as he was going up the road, some youths came from the city and mocked him, and said to him, "Go up, you baldhead! Go up, you baldhead!"

24 So he turned around and looked at them, and [a]pronounced a curse on them in the name of the LORD. And two female bears came out of the woods and mauled forty-two of the youths.

25 Then he went from there to [a]Mount Carmel, and from there he returned to Samaria.

Moab Rebels Against Israel

3 Now [a]Jehoram the son of Ahab became king over Israel at Samaria

9 *See WW at 2 Sam. 23:2. **11** [a]2 Kin. 6:17; Ps. 104:4 [b]Gen. 5:24; Heb. 11:5 **12** [a]2 Kin. 13:14 **14** [a]2 Kin. 2:8 **15** [a]2 Kin. 2:7 [1]*Or at Jericho opposite him saw* **16** [a]1 Kin. 18:12; Ezek. 8:3; Acts 8:39 **17** [a]2 Kin. 8:11 *See WW at Ezek. 16:63.

21 [a]Ex. 15:25, 26; 2 Kin. 4:41; 6:6; John 9:6 [1]*purified* **22** [a]Ezek. 47:8, 9 **24** [a]Deut. 27:13–26 **25** [a]1 Kin. 18:19, 20; 2 Kin. 4:25

CHAPTER 3

1 [a]2 Kin. 1:17

privilege of the firstborn (see Deut. 21:17), it has been suggested that Elisha is asking to be Elijah's successor. Yet this is more than just a petition to be Elijah's successor, because that had already been established (see 1 Kin. 19:16–21). Elisha realized that he did not have the capability to fulfill the awesome responsibility of carrying on Elijah's work. As Elijah's successor, Elisha applies the principle of the firstborn to ask for a spiritual inheritance. This is described as the **spirit of Elijah** (vv. 9, 15), and is either an indirect or direct reference to the Holy Spirit. The Hebrew word for "spirit" has a wide range of meaning (it can refer to the human spirit, the Holy Spirit, an evil spirit, a prophetic gift, or even the wind). Here it probably refers to the energizing power of the prophetic spirit that characterized the life of Elijah. The Holy Spirit is the author of Elijah's prophetic gift (see 1 Sam. 10:6, 10; 19:20, 23) and the energizing power of his ministry (see the text and notes of 1 Kin. 18:12 and 18:46). For more on the Holy Spirit, see Introduction to 2 Kings: The Holy Spirit at Work.

2:11 According to the biblical record, only Enoch (Gen. 5:24) and Elijah went directly to the Lord without having to die.

2:12 Tearing clothing symbolized mourning; Elisha and the people of God had just lost one of their spiritual heroes.

2:13 The prophet's **mantle** was a symbol of the authority he had been given by God.

2:14–22 Elisha duplicated the dividing of the Jordan and now he purified the water at a city believed to be Jericho.

2:16 Spirit: See note on 1 Kin. 18:12.

2:23–25 See section 5 of Truth-In-Action at the end of 2 Kin.

2:23, 24 On the surface, these verses seem to portray Elisha as ruthless. However, on the basis of the language and culture of that day, the word **youths** implies that they were probably idolatrous young men and not innocent boys. Further, their mocking **Go up** is likely a reference to the translation of Elijah. In effect, they were expressing contempt against the God of Elijah and Elisha and were promptly judged.

3:1–5 After Jehoram (1:17) began to reign as Israel's ninth king, **Mesha king of Moab** refused to pay him tribute. Moab

in the eighteenth year of Jehoshaphat
king of Judah, and reigned twelve
years.
2 And he did evil in the sight of the
LORD, but not like his father and
mother; for he put away the *sacred* pillar of Baal [a]that his father had made.
3 Nevertheless he persisted in [a]the
sins of Jeroboam the son of Nebat, who
had made Israel sin; he did not depart
from them.
4 Now Mesha king of Moab was a
sheepbreeder, and he [a]regularly paid
the king of Israel one hundred thousand [b]lambs and the wool of one hundred thousand rams.
5 But it happened, when [a]Ahab died,
that the king of Moab rebelled against
the king of Israel.
6 So King Jehoram went out of Samaria at that time and mustered all Israel.
7 Then he went and sent to Jehoshaphat king of Judah, saying, "The king
of Moab has rebelled against me. Will
you go with me to fight against Moab?"
And he said, "I will go up; [a]I *am* as
you *are*, my people as your people, my
horses as your horses."
8 Then he said, "Which way shall we
go up?" And he answered, "By way of
the Wilderness of Edom."
9 So the king of Israel went with the
king of Judah and the king of Edom,
and they marched on that roundabout
route seven days; and there was no water for the army, nor for the animals
that followed them.
10 And the king of Israel said, "Alas!
For the LORD has called these three
kings together to deliver them into the
hand of Moab."
11 But [a]Jehoshaphat said, "*Is there* no
prophet of the LORD here, that we may
inquire of the LORD by him?" So one
of the servants of the king of Israel answered and said, "Elisha the son of
Shaphat *is* here, who [b]poured[1] water
on the hands of Elijah."
12 And Jehoshaphat said, "The word
of the LORD is with him." So the king
of Israel and Jehoshaphat and the king
of Edom [a]went down to him.
13 Then Elisha said to the king of Israel, [a]"What have I to do with you?
[b]Go to [c]the prophets of your father and
the [d]prophets of your mother." But the
king of Israel said to him, "No, for the
LORD has called these three kings *together* to deliver them into the hand
of Moab."
14 And Elisha said, [a]"*As* the LORD of
hosts lives, before whom I stand, surely
were it not that I regard the presence
of Jehoshaphat king of Judah, I would
not look at you, nor see you.
15 "But now bring me [a]a musician."
Then it happened, when the musician
[b]played, that [c]the hand of the LORD
came upon him.
16 And he said, "Thus says the LORD:
[a]'Make this valley full of [1]ditches.'
17 "For thus says the LORD: 'You shall
not see wind, nor shall you see rain;
yet that valley shall be filled with water, so that you, your cattle, and your
animals may drink.'
18 "And this is a simple matter in the
sight of the LORD; He will also deliver
the Moabites into your hand.
19 "Also you shall attack every fortified city and every choice city, and
shall cut down every good tree, and
stop up every spring of water, and ruin
every good piece of land with stones."
20 Now it happened in the morning,
when [a]the grain offering was offered,
that suddenly water came by way of
Edom, and the land was filled with water.
21 And when all the Moabites heard
that the kings had come up to fight
against them, all who were able to bear
arms and older were [1]gathered; and
they stood at the border.
22 Then they rose up early in the
morning, and the sun was shining on
the water; and the Moabites saw the
water on the other side *as* red as blood.
23 And they said, "This is blood; the
kings have surely struck swords and
have killed one another; now therefore, Moab, to the spoil!"
24 So when they came to the camp of
Israel, Israel rose up and attacked the
Moabites, so that they fled before
them; and they entered *their* land, killing the Moabites.
25 Then they destroyed the cities, and
each man threw a stone on every good

2 [a]1 Kin. 16:31, 32 **3** [a]1 Kin. 12:28–32 **4** [a]2 Sam. 8:2 [b]Is. 16:1, 2 **5** [a]2 Kin. 1:1 **7** [a]1 Kin. 22:4 **11** [a]1 Kin. 22:7 [b]1 Kin. 19:21; [John 13:4, 5, 13, 14] [1]*Was the personal servant of* **12** [a]2 Kin. 2:25 **13** [a][Ezek. 14:3] [b]Judg. 10:14; Ruth 1:15 [c]1 Kin. 22:6–11 [d]1 Kin. 18:19
14 [a]1 Kin. 17:1; 2 Kin. 5:16 **15** [a]1 Sam. 10:5 [b]1 Sam. 16:16, 23; 1 Chr. 25:1 [c]Ezek. 1:3; 3:14, 22; 8:1 **16** [a]Jer. 14:3 [1]*water canals* **20** [a]Ex. 29:39, 40 **21** [1]*summoned*

was a son of Lot (Gen. 19:37), and his descendants became neighbors of Israel and lived on the eastern border of the Dead Sea. These people had been subjugated by Omri and were paying tribute to the kings of Israel.
3:6–25 Jehoram mustered the help of **Jehoshaphat king of Judah** and **the king of Edom** to subdue Mesha, but they marched into a barren area with no water. Through the assistance of **Elisha,** the Lord miraculously provided water and gave them victory over the **Moabites.**
3:15 The phrase **the hand of the LORD** was a formula referring to the divine inspiration of the prophets (see Ezek. 1:3). The Spirit of God was the One who enabled the prophets to prophesy (1 Sam. 10:6, 10; 19:20, 23; 2 Chr. 12:18; 15:1; 20:14; 24:20). See Introduction to 2 Kings: The Holy Spirit at Work.

piece of land and filled it; and they
stopped up all the springs of water and
cut down all the good trees. But they
left the stones of [a]Kir Haraseth *intact.*
However the slingers surrounded and
attacked it.
26 And when the king of Moab saw
that the battle was too fierce for him,
he took with him seven hundred men
who drew swords, to break through to
the king of Edom, but they could not.
27 Then [a]he took his eldest son who
would have reigned in his place, and
offered him *as* a burnt offering upon
the wall; and there was great [1]indig-
nation against Israel. [b]So they departed
from him and returned to *their own*
land.

Elisha and the Widow's Oil

3 **4** A certain woman of the wives of
[a]the sons of the prophets cried out
to Elisha, saying, "Your servant my
husband is dead, and you know that
your servant feared the LORD. And the
creditor is coming [b]to take my two
sons to be his slaves."
2 So Elisha said to her, "What shall
I do for you? Tell me, what do you have
in the *house?" And she said, "Your
maidservant has nothing in the house
but a jar of oil."
3 Then he said, "Go, borrow vessels
from everywhere, from all your neighbors—empty vessels; [a]do not gather
just a few.
4 "And when you have come in, you
shall shut the door behind you and
your sons; then pour it into all those
vessels, and set aside the full ones."
5 So she went from him and shut the
door behind her and her sons, who
brought *the vessels* to her; and she
poured *it* out.
6 Now it came to pass, when the vessels were full, that she said to her son,
"Bring me another vessel." And he
said to her, "*There is* not another vessel." So the oil ceased.

25 [a]Is. 16:7, 11; Jer. 48:31, 36
27 [a][Deut. 18:10; Amos 2:1; Mic. 6:7] [b]2 Kin. 8:20 [1]*wrath*

CHAPTER 4

1 [a]1 Kin. 20:35; 2 Kin. 2:3 [b][Lev. 25:39–41, 48]; 1 Sam. 22:2; Neh. 5:2–5; Matt. 18:25
2 *See WW at 2 Sam. 7:11.
3 [a]2 Kin. 3:16

8 [a]Josh. 19:18 [1]Lit. *great* [2]Lit. *laid hold on him*
10 [1]Or *a small walled upper chamber*
12 [a]2 Kin. 4:29–31; 5:20–27; 8:4, 5
16 [a]2 Kin. 4:28 [1]Lit. *About this season, as the time of life*

7 Then she came and told the man of
God. And he said, "Go, sell the oil and
pay your debt; and you *and* your sons
live on the rest."

Elisha Raises the Shunammite's Son

8 Now it happened one day that Elisha went to [a]Shunem, where there *was*
a [1]notable woman, and she [2]persuaded
him to eat some food. So it was, as often as he passed by, he would turn in
there to eat some food.
9 And she said to her husband, "Look
now, I know that this *is* a holy man of
God, who passes by us regularly.
10 "Please, let us make [1]a small upper
room on the wall; and let us put a bed
for him there, and a table and a chair
and a lampstand; so it will be, whenever he comes to us, he can turn in
there."
11 And it happened one day that he
came there, and he turned in to the upper room and lay down there.
12 Then he said to [a]Gehazi his servant,
"Call this Shunammite woman." When
he had called her, she stood before
him.
13 And he said to him, "Say now to
her, 'Look, you have been concerned
for us with all this care. What *can I*
do for you? Do you want me to speak
on your behalf to the king or to the
commander of the army?'" She answered, "I dwell among my own people."
14 So he said, "What then *is* to be done
for her?" And Gehazi answered, "Actually, she has no son, and her husband
is old."
15 So he said, "Call her." When he had
called her, she stood in the doorway.
16 Then he said, [1]"About this time next
year you shall embrace a son." And
she said, "No, my lord. Man of God,
[a]do not lie to your maidservant!"
17 But the woman conceived, and bore
a son when the appointed time had
come, of which Elisha had told her.

3:26, 27 To Mesha, the defeat in battle was a sign that his god Chemosh was angry with Moab. As a result, Mesha offered his own son in a sacrifice to please his god. **Great indignation against Israel** may mean that Mesha's action was so repulsive that the Israelites broke off their attack, or that the battle suddenly went against Israel. Another possibility is that the Israelites ceased their assault because God was displeased with them in some way.

4:1–7 See section 3 of Truth-In-Action at the end of 2 Kin.

4:1 Jewish historian Josephus explains that this needy woman was the widow of the prophet Obadiah.

4:2 The **jar of oil** was likely olive oil, used for cooking and for fuel.

4:3–7 In the ancient Near East, women were regarded as inferior. But this miracle by Elisha demonstrates God's faithful care and provision for the vulnerable and outcast. The provision was in proportion to the woman's faith and ability to receive.

4:8, 9 In his travels **Elisha** frequently passed through **Shunem,** which was located near Jezreel. In contrast to Obadiah's poor widow (vv. 1–7), this Shunammite was a **notable woman** (implying she was very affluent), and she had a husband.

4:10–17 As God had provided children for Sarah, Rachel, and Hannah, so He miraculously enabled this hospitable woman and her husband to have a son.

18 And the child grew. Now it happened one day that he went out to his
father, to the reapers.
19 And he said to his father, "My head,
my head!" So he said to a servant,
"Carry him to his mother."
20 When he had taken him and
brought him to his mother, he sat on
her knees till noon, and *then* died.
21 And she went up and laid him on
the bed of the man of God, shut *the
door* upon him, and went out.
22 Then she called to her husband, and
said, "Please send me one of the young
men and one of the donkeys, that I
may run to the man of God and come
back."
23 So he said, "Why are you going to
him today? *It is* neither the [a]New
Moon nor the Sabbath." And she said,
[1]"*It is* well."
24 Then she saddled a donkey, and
said to her servant, "Drive, and go forward; do not slacken the pace for me
unless I tell you."
25 And so she departed, and went to
the man of God [a]at Mount Carmel.
So it was, when the man of God saw
her afar off, that he said to his servant Gehazi, "Look, the Shunammite
woman!
26 "Please run now to meet her, and
say to her, '*Is it* well with you? *Is it*
well with your husband? *Is it* well with
the child?' " And she answered, "*It is*
well."
27 Now when she came to the man of
God at the hill, she caught him by the
feet, but Gehazi came near to push her
away. But the man of God said, "Let
her alone; for her soul *is* in deep distress, and the LORD has hidden *it* from
me, and has not told me."
28 So she said, "Did I ask a son of my
lord? [a]Did I not say, 'Do not deceive
me'?"
29 Then he said to Gehazi, [a]"Get[1]
yourself ready, and take my staff in
your hand, and be on your way. If you
meet anyone, [b]do not greet him; and
if anyone greets you, do not answer
him; but [c]lay my staff on the face of
the child."
30 And the mother of the child said,
[a]"*As* the LORD lives, and *as* your soul
lives, I will not [b]leave you." So he
arose and followed her.

23 [a]Num. 10:10; 28:11; 1 Chr. 23:31 [1]Or *It will be well*
25 [a]2 Kin. 2:25
28 [a]2 Kin. 4:16
29 [a]1 Kin. 18:46; 2 Kin. 9:1 [b]Luke 10:4 [c]Ex. 7:19; 14:16; 2 Kin. 2:8, 14; Acts 19:12 [1]Lit. *Gird up your loins.* The skirt of the robe was wrapped around the legs and tucked in the belt to gain freedom of movement.
30 [a]2 Kin. 2:2 [b]2 Kin. 2:4
31 [a]John 11:11
33 [a]2 Kin. 4:4; [Matt. 6:6]; Luke 8:51 [b]1 Kin. 17:20
34 [a]1 Kin. 17:21–23; Acts 20:10
35 [a]1 Kin. 17:21 [b]2 Kin. 8:1, 5
37 [a]1 Kin. 17:23; [Heb. 11:35]
38 [a]2 Kin. 2:1 [b]2 Kin. 8:1 [c]Luke 10:39; Acts 22:3
40 [a]Ex. 10:17
41 [a]Ex. 15:25; 2 Kin. 2:21

31 Now Gehazi went on ahead of them,
and laid the staff on the face of the
child; but *there was* neither voice nor
hearing. Therefore he went back to
meet him, and told him, saying, "The
child has [a]not awakened."
32 When Elisha came into the house,
there was the child, lying dead on his
bed.
33 He [a]went in therefore, shut the door
behind the two of them, [b]and prayed
to the LORD.
34 And he went up and lay on the
child, and put his mouth on his mouth,
his eyes on his eyes, and his hands on
his hands; and [a]he stretched himself
out on the child, and the flesh of the
child became warm.
35 He returned and walked back and
forth in the house, and again went up
[a]and stretched himself out on him;
then [b]the child sneezed seven times,
and the child opened his eyes.
36 And he called Gehazi and said,
"Call this Shunammite woman." So he
called her. And when she came in to
him, he said, "Pick up your son."
37 So she went in, fell at his feet, and
bowed to the ground; then she [a]picked
up her son and went out.

Elisha Purifies the Pot of Stew

38 And Elisha returned to [a]Gilgal, and
there was a [b]famine in the land. Now
the sons of the prophets *were* [c]sitting
before him; and he said to his servant,
"Put on the large pot, and boil stew
for the sons of the prophets."
39 So one went out into the field to 4
gather herbs, and found a wild vine,
and gathered from it a lapful of wild
gourds, and came and sliced *them* into
the pot of stew, though they did not
know *what they were.*
40 Then they served it to the men
to eat. Now it happened, as they were
eating the stew, that they cried out
and said, "Man of God, *there is*
[a]death in the pot!" And they could not
eat *it.*
41 So he said, "Then bring some
flour." And [a]he put *it* into the pot, and
said, "Serve *it* to the people, that they
may eat." And there was nothing
harmful in the pot.

4:18, 19 It is believed that the Shunammite's son died from inflammation of the brain produced by a sunstroke.
4:24–37 The actions of both Elisha and the Shunammite woman in this incident provide illustrations of the importance of faith and persistence.
4:39–41 See section 4 of Truth-In-Action at the end of 2 Kin.
4:40 Death in the pot: The gourds used to make the stew (v. 39) were harmless in small amounts, but in larger dosages they were fatal. Elisha demonstrated the same care for the daily provisions of people as he had witnessed in Elijah (1 Kin. 17:4–6).

Elisha Feeds One Hundred Men

42 Then a man came from [a]Baal Shalisha, [b]and brought the man of God
bread of the firstfruits, twenty loaves
of barley bread, and newly ripened
grain in his knapsack. And he said,
"Give *it* to the people, that they may
eat."
3 43 But his servant said, [a]"What? Shall
I set this before one hundred men?" He
said again, "Give it to the people, that
they may eat; for thus says the LORD:
[b]'They shall eat and have *some* left
over.'"
44 So he set *it* before them; and they
ate [a]and had *some* left over, according
to the word of the LORD.

Naaman's Leprosy Healed

5 Now [a]Naaman, commander of the
army of the king of Syria, was [b]a
great and honorable man in the eyes
of his master, because by him the LORD
had given victory to Syria. He was also
a mighty man of valor, *but* a leper.
2 And the Syrians had gone out
[a]on[1] raids, and had brought back captive a young girl from the land of Israel. She [2]waited on Naaman's wife.
3 Then she said to her mistress, "If
only my master *were* with the prophet
who *is* in Samaria! For he would heal
him of his leprosy."
4 And *Naaman* went in and told his
master, saying, "Thus and thus said the
girl who *is* from the land of Israel."
5 Then the king of Syria said, "Go
now, and I will send a letter to the king
of Israel." So he departed and [a]took
with him ten talents of silver, six thousand *shekels* of gold, and ten changes
of clothing.
6 Then he brought the letter to the
king of Israel, which said,

> Now be advised, when this letter
> comes to you, that I have sent
> Naaman my servant to you, that
> you may heal him of his leprosy.

7 And it happened, when the king of
Israel read the letter, that he tore his
clothes and said, "*Am* I [a]God, to kill
and make alive, that this man sends a
man to me to heal him of his leprosy?
Therefore please consider, and see
how he seeks a quarrel with me."
8 So it was, when Elisha the man of
God heard that the king of Israel had
torn his clothes, that he sent to the
king, saying, "Why have you torn your
clothes? Please let him come to me, and
he shall know that there is a prophet
in Israel."
9 Then Naaman went with his horses
and chariot, and he stood at the door
of Elisha's house.
10 And Elisha sent a messenger to him,
saying, "Go and [a]wash in the Jordan
seven times, and your flesh shall be restored to you, and *you shall* be clean."
11 But Naaman became furious, and
went away and said, "Indeed, I said to
myself, 'He will surely come out *to me,*
and stand and call on the name of the
LORD his God, and wave his hand over
the place, and heal the leprosy.'
12 "*Are* not the [1]Abanah and the Phar-
par, the rivers of Damascus, better
than all the waters of Israel? Could I
not wash in them and be clean?" So
he turned and went away in a rage.
13 And his [a]servants came near and
spoke to him, and said, "My father, *if*
the prophet had told you *to do* something great, would you not have done
it? How much more then, when he says
to you, 'Wash, and be clean'?"
14 So he went down and dipped seven
times in the Jordan, according to the
saying of the man of God; and his
[a]flesh was restored like the flesh of a
little child, and [b]he was clean.
15 And he returned to the man of God,
he and all his aides, and came and
stood before him; and he said, "Indeed,
now I know that *there is* [a]no God in
all the earth, except in Israel; now
therefore, please take [b]a gift from your
servant."

42 [a]1 Sam. 9:4 [b]1 Sam. 9:7; [1 Cor. 9:11; Gal. 6:6]
43 [a]Luke 9:13; John 6:9 [b]Luke 9:17; John 6:11
44 [a]Matt. 14:20; 15:37; John 6:13

CHAPTER 5

1 [a]Luke 4:27 [b]Ex. 11:3
2 [a]2 Kin. 6:23; 13:20 [1]Or *in bands* [2]Served, lit. *was before*
5 [a]1 Sam. 9:8; 2 Kin. 8:8, 9
7 [a][Gen. 30:2; Deut. 32:39; 1 Sam. 2:6]
10 [a]2 Kin. 4:41; John 9:7
12 [1]So with Kt., LXX, Vg.; Qr., Syr., Tg. *Amanah*
13 [a]1 Sam. 28:23
14 [a]2 Kin. 5:10; Job 33:25 [b]Luke 4:27; 5:13
15 [a]Dan. 2:47; 3:29; 6:26, 27 [b]Gen. 33:11

KINGDOM DYNAMICS

5:1–15 Lessons in Sharing Healing Hope, DIVINE HEALING. Naaman the Syrian general was a good man, and apparently his leprosy was not the result of his wrongdoing. Thus, the episode furnishes us with some practical insights

4:42–44 This miracle by Elisha is similar to Jesus' miracle of multiplying the loaves and fish.
4:43, 44 See section 3 of Truth-In-Action at the end of 2 Kin.
5:1 Apparently the Syrians did not quarantine lepers.
5:2, 3 The young girl here provides a poignant picture of the importance of overcoming the fear of people and pointing others to the Lord.
5:7 Jehoram became alarmed at the request of Naaman and the letter from Ben-Hadad, for it appeared that the Syrians were provoking a fight.
5:8–14 The story of Naaman provides a parallel to what happens to those who come to Jesus for salvation.

into God's healing process when the sick person is innocent of known disobedience or action exposing them to their affliction. 1) See the importance of our sharing the hope of God's healing with others. The door to Naaman's healing was opened by a Jewish maid who recommended he seek out the prophet Elisha. Believers do good when they witness to others of both the saving and healing power of Jesus. 2) See how God knows what to deal with in each person. Naaman was instructed to dip seven times in the Jordan River, and this displeased him. His human brashness and hidden pride were surfaced, and his obedience and submission opened the way to health. A similar call may face any of us, as healing often awaits obedient action. For example, Jesus instructed 10 lepers to show themselves to the priest, and they were healed after taking that first step of obedience (Luke 17:12–14). People who have received prayer for healing sometimes give up when they do not see immediate healing, rather than seek God for a possible faith-building step of submission. (See also 2 Kin. 20:1–11.)

(Num. 21:5–9/2 Kin. 20:1–11) N.V.

16 But he said, [a]"*As* the LORD lives, before whom I stand, [b]I will receive nothing." And he urged him to take *it*, but
he refused.
17 So Naaman said, "Then, if not,
please let your servant be given two
mule-loads of earth; for your servant
will no longer offer either burnt offering or sacrifice to other gods, but to
the LORD.
18 "Yet in this thing may the LORD
*pardon your servant: when my master
goes into the temple of Rimmon to worship there, and [a]he leans on my hand,
and I bow down in the temple of Rimmon—when I bow down in the temple
of Rimmon, may the LORD please pardon your servant in this thing."
1 19 Then he said to him, "Go in peace."
So he departed from him a short distance.

Gehazi's Greed

20 But [a]Gehazi, the servant of Elisha
the man of God, said, "Look, my master has spared Naaman this Syrian,
while not receiving from his hands
what he brought; but *as* the LORD lives,
I will run after him and take something
from him."
21 So Gehazi pursued Naaman. When
Naaman saw *him* running after him,
he got down from the chariot to meet
him, and said, "*Is* all well?"
22 And he said, "All *is* [a]well. My master has sent me, saying, 'Indeed, just
now two young men of the sons of the
prophets have come to me from the
mountains of Ephraim. Please give
them a talent of silver and two changes
of garments.' "
23 So Naaman said, "Please, take two
talents." And he urged him, and bound
two talents of silver in two bags, with
two changes of garments, and handed
them to two of his servants; and they
carried *them* on ahead of him.
24 When he came to [1]the citadel, he
took *them* from their hand, and stored
them away in the house; then he let
the men go, and they departed.
25 Now he went in and stood before
his master. Elisha said to him, "Where
did you go, Gehazi?" And he said,
"Your servant did not go anywhere."
26 Then he said to him, "Did not my
heart go *with you* when the man turned
back from his chariot to meet you? *Is*
it [a]time to receive money and to receive clothing, olive groves and vineyards, sheep and oxen, male and female servants?
27 "Therefore the leprosy of Naaman
[a]shall cling to you and your descendants forever." And he went out from
his presence [b]leprous, *as white* as
snow.

The Floating Ax Head

6 And [a]the sons of the prophets said
to Elisha, "See now, the place
where we dwell with you is too small
for us.
2 "Please, let us go to the Jordan, and
let every man take a beam from there,
and let us make there a place where
we may dwell." So he answered, "Go."
3 Then one said, [a]"Please consent to
go with your servants." And he answered, "I will go."
4 So he went with them. And when
they came to the Jordan, they cut down
trees.
5 But as one was cutting down a tree,

16 [a]2 Kin. 3:14 [b]Gen. 14:22, 23; 2 Kin. 5:20, 26; [Matt. 10:8]; Acts 8:18, 20
18 [a]2 Kin. 7:2, 17 *See WW at Ps. 103:3.
20 [a]2 Kin. 4:12; 8:4, 5
22 [a]2 Kin. 4:26
24 [1]Lit. *the hill*
26 [a][Eccl. 3:1, 6]
27 [a][1 Tim. 6:10] [b]Ex. 4:6; Num. 12:10; 2 Kin. 15:5

CHAPTER 6

1 [a]2 Kin. 4:38
3 [a]2 Kin. 5:23

5:18 Rimmon, thought to be a god of rain and thunder, was the local deity of Damascus. Though it was Naaman's responsibility to assist Ben-Hadad in the idolatry of Syria, he sought God's pardon because he recognized that only the Lord was truly God.

5:19–27 See section 1 of Truth-In-Action at the end of 2 Kin.

5:20–27 In contrast to Naaman's liberality, Kings records the greed of **Gehazi.**

the iron *ax head* fell into the water; and
he cried out and said, "Alas, master!
For it was [a]borrowed."
6 So the man of God said, "Where did
it fall?" And he showed him the place.
So [a]he cut off a stick, and threw *it* in
there; and he made the iron float.
7 Therefore he said, "Pick *it* up for
yourself." So he reached out his hand
and took it.

The Blinded Syrians Captured

8 Now the [a]king of Syria was making
war against Israel; and he consulted
with his servants, saying, "My camp
will be in such and such a place."
9 And the man of God sent to the king
of Israel, saying, "Beware that you do
not pass this place, for the Syrians are
coming down there."
10 Then the king of Israel sent *someone* to the place of which the man of
God had told him. Thus he warned
him, and he was watchful there, not
just once or twice.
11 Therefore the heart of the king of
Syria was greatly troubled by this
thing; and he called his servants and
said to them, "Will you not show me
which of us *is* for the king of Israel?"
12 And one of his servants said,
"None, my lord, O king; but Elisha, the
prophet who *is* in Israel, tells the king
of Israel the words that you speak in
your bedroom."
13 So he said, "Go and see where he
is, that I may send and get him." And
it was told him, saying, "Surely *he is*
in [a]Dothan."
14 Therefore he sent horses and chariots and a great army there, and they
came by night and surrounded the city.
15 And when the servant of the man
of God arose early and went out, there
was an army, surrounding the city with
horses and chariots. And his servant
said to him, "Alas, my master! What
shall we do?"
16 So he answered, [a]"Do not fear, for
[b]those who *are* with us *are* more than
those who *are* with them."
17 And Elisha prayed, and said, "LORD,
I pray, open his eyes that he may see."
Then the LORD [a]opened the eyes of the
young man, and he saw. And behold,
the mountain *was* full of [b]horses and
chariots of fire all around Elisha.

5 [a][Ex. 22:14]
6 [a]Ex. 15:25; 2 Kin. 2:21; 4:41
8 [a]2 Kin. 8:28, 29
13 [a]Gen. 37:17
16 [a]Ex. 14:13; 1 Kin. 17:13 [b]2 Chr. 32:7; Ps. 55:18; [Rom. 8:31]
17 [a]Num. 22:31; Luke 24:31 [b]2 Kin. 2:11; Ps. 34:7; 68:17; Zech. 1:8; 6:1–7
18 [a]Gen. 19:11; Acts 13:11
21 [a]2 Kin. 2:12; 5:13; 8:9

KINGDOM DYNAMICS

6:8–17 The Invisible Realm and Victorious Warfare, FAITH'S WARFARE. To believe the impossible one must first see the invisible—the lesson Elisha taught his servant. The text involves war between Israel and Syria, and the prophet Elisha's informing his people of the enemy's tactics through prophetic insight (v. 12). Here is the lesson: Prayer is the key to discerning our adversary's stratagems. Further, the key to dispelling Elisha's servant's panic was his vision being opened to see the invisible. Note these crucial words: "Elisha prayed"! Elisha did not ask God simply to show the servant another miracle; he asked for his servant to see into another dimension. The answer came immediately: "The LORD opened the eyes of the young man, and he saw. And behold, the mountain *was* full of horses and chariots of fire all around Elisha" (v. 17). Seeing into the invisible is a key to victorious praying—discerning spiritual issues from God's perspective rather than man's, seeing the Adversary's attack plan, and perceiving God's angelic strike-force.

(Eph. 6:10–18/Jer. 33:3) D.E.

18 So when *the Syrians* came down to
him, Elisha prayed to the LORD, and
said, "Strike this people, I pray, with
blindness." And [a]He struck them with
blindness according to the word of Elisha.
19 Now Elisha said to them, "This *is*
not the way, nor *is* this the city. Follow
me, and I will bring you to the man
whom you seek." But he led them to
Samaria.
20 So it was, when they had come to
Samaria, that Elisha said, "LORD, open
the eyes of these *men*, that they may
see." And the LORD opened their eyes,
and they saw; and there *they were*, inside Samaria!
21 Now when the king of Israel saw
them, he said to Elisha, "My [a]father,
shall I kill *them*? Shall I kill *them*?"
22 But he answered, "You shall not kill
them. Would you kill those whom you

6:8 The king of Syria was probably Ben-Hadad II (about 860–841 B.C.).
6:9–14 Through his prophetic enablement, Elisha would inform Jehoram of Ben-Hadad's strategy. Therefore, Ben-Hadad sent a great army to capture Elisha. That the army **came by night** betrays that the **Syrians** did not really believe in Elisha's power to anticipate their moves. That Ben-Hadad sent a **great army** indicates that the Syrians were not going to take any chances.
6:15–17 These verses have been a great source of comfort and assurance to believers of all ages. As Rom. 8:31 says, "If God *is* for us, who *can be* against us?"
6:21–23 Such treatment of the enemy demonstrates Israel's confidence in God as their protector and was a move toward establishing peaceful relations between Israel and Syria.

have taken captive with your sword and your bow? [a]Set food and water before them, that they may eat and drink and go to their master."

23 Then he prepared a great feast for them; and after they ate and drank, he sent them away and they went to their master. So [a]the bands of Syrian *raiders* came no more into the land of Israel.

Syria Besieges Samaria in Famine

24 And it happened after this that [a]Ben-Hadad king of Syria gathered all his army, and went up and besieged Samaria.

25 And there was a great [a]famine in Samaria; and indeed they besieged it until a donkey's head was *sold* for eighty *shekels* of silver, and one-fourth of a [1]kab of dove droppings for five *shekels* of silver.

26 Then, as the king of Israel was passing by on the wall, a woman cried out to him, saying, "Help, my lord, O king!"

27 And he said, "If the LORD does not help you, where can I find help for you? From the threshing floor or from the winepress?"

28 Then the king said to her, "What is troubling you?" And she answered, "This woman said to me, 'Give your son, that we may eat him today, and we will eat my son tomorrow.'

29 "So [a]we boiled my son, and ate him. And I said to her on the next day, 'Give your son, that we may eat him'; but she has hidden her son."

30 Now it happened, when the king heard the words of the woman, that he [a]tore his clothes; and as he passed by on the wall, the people looked, and there underneath *he had* sackcloth on his body.

31 Then he said, [a]"God do so to me and more also, if the head of Elisha the son of Shaphat remains on him today!"

32 But Elisha was sitting in his house, and [a]the elders were sitting with him. And *the king* sent a man ahead of him, but before the messenger came to him, he said to the elders, [b]"Do you see how this son of [c]a murderer has sent someone to take away my head? Look, when the messenger comes, shut the door, and hold him fast at the door. *Is* not the sound of his master's feet behind him?"

33 And while he was still talking with them, there was the messenger, coming down to him; and then *the king* said, "Surely this calamity *is* from the LORD; [a]why should I wait for the LORD any longer?"

7 Then Elisha said, *"Hear the word of the LORD. Thus says the LORD: [a]'Tomorrow about this time a [1]seah of fine flour *shall be sold* for a shekel, and two seahs of barley for a shekel, at the gate of Samaria.'"

2 [a]So an officer on whose hand the king leaned answered the man of God and said, "Look, [b]*if* the LORD would make windows in heaven, could this thing be?" And he said, "In fact, you shall see *it* with your eyes, but you shall not eat of it."

The Syrians Flee

3 Now there were four leprous men [a]at the entrance of the gate; and they said to one another, "Why are we sitting here until we die?

4 "If we say, 'We will enter the city,' the famine *is* in the city, and we shall die there. And if we sit here, we die also. Now therefore, come, let us surrender to the [a]army of the Syrians. If they keep us alive, we shall live; and if they kill us, we shall only die."

5 And they rose at twilight to go to the camp of the Syrians; and when they had come to the outskirts of the Syrian camp, to their surprise no one *was* there.

6 For the LORD had caused the army of the Syrians [a]to hear the noise of chariots and the noise of horses—the noise of a great army; so they said to one another, "Look, the king of Israel has hired against us [b]the kings of the Hittites and the kings of the Egyptians to attack us!"

7 Therefore they [a]arose and fled at twilight, and left the camp intact—their tents, their horses, and their donkeys—and they fled for their lives.

8 And when these lepers came to the outskirts of the camp, they went into one tent and ate and drank, and carried from it silver and gold and clothing,

22 [a][Rom. 12:20]
23 [a]2 Kin. 5:2; 6:8, 9
24 [a]1 Kin. 20:1
25 [a]2 Kin. 4:38; 8:1 [1]Approximately 1 pint
29 [a]Lev. 26:27–29; Deut. 28:52–57; Lam. 4:10
30 [a]1 Kin. 21:27
31 [a]Ruth 1:17; 1 Kin. 19:2
32 [a]Ezek. 8:1; 14:1; 20:1 [b]Luke 13:32 [c]1 Kin. 18:4, 13, 14; 21:10, 13
33 [a]Job 2:9

CHAPTER 7

1 [a]2 Kin. 7:18, 19 [1]A third of an ephah, or about 8 gallons *See WW at 1 Kin. 20:8.
2 [a]2 Kin. 5:18; 7:17, 19, 20 [b]Gen. 7:11; Mal. 3:10
3 [a][Lev. 13:45, 46; Num. 5:2–4; 12:10–14]
4 [a]2 Kin. 6:24
6 [a]2 Sam. 5:24; 2 Kin. 19:7; Job 15:21 [b]1 Kin. 10:29
7 [a]Ps. 48:4–6; [Prov. 28:1]

6:24–33 As Israel persisted in their sinfulness, God raised up **Ben-Hadad** (see note on 1 Kin. 15:18 on the three Ben-Hadads in Scripture) as an adversary to drive them to Himself. The famine that resulted from Ben-Hadad's siege was so severe that Israel resorted to cannibalism, and Jehoram blamed Elisha for their difficulty.

7:1 At the height of the famine described in ch. 6, Elisha prophesied that the Lord would soon end the famine.

7:2, 17 The actions of Jehoram's assistant are a powerful illustration of God's attitude toward unbelief.

and went and hid *them;* then they
came back and entered another tent,
and carried *some* from there *also,* and
went and hid *it.*
9 Then they said to one another, "We
are not doing right. This day *is* a day
of good news, and we remain silent. If
we wait until morning light, some
[1]punishment will come upon us. Now
therefore, come, let us go and tell the
king's household."
10 So they went and called to the gatekeepers of the city, and told them,
saying, "We went to the Syrian camp,
and surprisingly no one *was* there, not
a human sound—only horses and donkeys tied, and the tents intact."
11 And the gatekeepers called out, and
they told *it* to the king's household inside.
12 So the king arose in the night and
said to his servants, "Let me now tell
you what the Syrians have done to us.
They know that we *are* [a]hungry; therefore they have gone out of the camp
to [1]hide themselves in the field, saying,
'When they come out of the city, we
shall catch them alive, and get into the
city.' "
13 And one of his servants answered
and said, "Please, let several *men* take
five of the remaining horses which are
left in the city. Look, they *may either
become* like all the multitude of Israel
that are left in it; or indeed, *I say,* they
may become like all the multitude of
Israel left from those who are consumed; so let us send them and see."
14 Therefore they took two chariots
with horses; and the king sent them in
the direction of the Syrian army, saying, "Go and see."
15 And they went after them to the Jordan; and indeed all the road *was* full
of garments and weapons which the
Syrians had thrown away in their
haste. So the messengers returned and
told the king.
16 Then the people went out and plundered the tents of the Syrians. So a
seah of fine flour was *sold* for a shekel,
and two seahs of barley for a shekel,
[a]according to the word of the LORD.
17 Now the king had appointed the officer on whose hand he leaned to have
charge of the gate. But the people trampled him in the gate, and he died, just
[a]*as the man of God had* said, who
spoke when the king came down to
him.
18 So it happened just as the man of
God had spoken to the king, saying,
[a]"Two seahs of barley for a shekel, and
a seah of fine flour for a shekel, shall
be *sold* tomorrow about this time in the
gate of Samaria."
19 Then that officer had answered the
man of God, and said, "Now look, *if*
the LORD would make windows in
heaven, could such a thing be?" And
he had said, "In fact, you shall see *it*
with your eyes, but you shall not eat
of it."
20 And so it happened to him, for the
people trampled him in the gate, and
he died.

The King Restores the Shunammite's Land

8 Then Elisha spoke to the woman
[a]whose son he had restored to life,
saying, "Arise and go, you and your
household, and stay wherever you can;
for the LORD [b]has called for a [c]famine,
and furthermore, it will come upon the
land for seven years."
2 So the woman arose and did according to the saying of the man of
God, and she went with her household
and dwelt in the land of the Philistines
seven years.
3 It came to pass, at the end of seven
years, that the woman returned from
the land of the Philistines; and she
went to make an appeal to the king for
her house and for her land.
4 Then the king talked with [a]Gehazi,
the servant of the man of God, saying,
"Tell me, please, all the great things
Elisha has done."
5 Now it happened, as he was telling
the king how he had restored the dead
to life, that there was the woman
whose son he had [a]restored to life, appealing to the king for her house and
for her land. And Gehazi said, "My
lord, O king, this *is* the woman, and
this *is* her son whom Elisha restored
to life."
6 And when the king asked the
woman, she told him. So the king appointed a certain officer for her, saying, "Restore all that *was* hers, and all
the proceeds of the field from the day
that she left the land until now."

Death of Ben-Hadad

7 Then Elisha went to Damascus, and
[a]Ben-Hadad king of Syria was sick;

9 [1]Calamity
12 [a]2 Kin. 6:24–29 [1]Hide themselves in ambush
16 [a]2 Kin. 7:1
17 [a]2 Kin. 6:32; 7:2
18 [a]2 Kin. 7:1

CHAPTER 8

1 [a]2 Kin. 4:18, 31–35 [b]Ps. 105:16; Hag. 1:11 [c]2 Sam. 21:1; 1 Kin. 18:2; 2 Kin. 4:38; 6:25
4 [a]2 Kin. 4:12; 5:20–27
5 [a]2 Kin. 4:35
7 [a]2 Kin. 6:24

8:7–9 It was a common practice to consult another's god concerning one's fate. See Ahaziah's request in 1:1, 2. So this is not an indication that Ben-Hadad had turned to the Lord.

and it was told him, saying, "The man
of God has come here."
8 And the king said to [a]Hazael,
[b]"Take a present in your hand, and go
to meet the man of God, and [c]inquire
of the LORD by him, saying, 'Shall I recover from this disease?' "
9 So [a]Hazael went to meet him and
took a present with him, of every good
thing of Damascus, forty camel-loads;
and he came and stood before him, and
said, "Your son Ben-Hadad king of
Syria has sent me to you, saying, 'Shall
I recover from this disease?' "
10 And Elisha said to him, "Go, say to
him, 'You shall certainly recover.'
However the LORD has shown me that
[a]he will really die."
11 Then he [1]set his countenance in a
stare until he was ashamed; and the
man of God [a]wept.
12 And Hazael said, "Why is my lord
weeping?" He answered, "Because I
know [a]the evil that you will do to the
children of Israel: Their strongholds
you will set on fire, and their young
men you will kill with the sword; and
you [b]will dash their children, and rip
open their women with child."
13 So Hazael said, "But what [a]*is* your
servant—a dog, that he should do this
gross thing?" And Elisha answered,
[b]"The LORD has shown me that you *will
become* king over Syria."
14 Then he departed from Elisha, and
came to his master, who said to him,
"What did Elisha say to you?" And he
answered, "He told me you would
surely recover."
15 But it happened on the next day that
he took a thick cloth and dipped *it* in
water, and spread *it* over his face so
that he died; and Hazael reigned in his
place.

Jehoram Reigns in Judah

16 Now [a]in the fifth year of Joram the
son of Ahab, king of Israel, Jehoshaphat *having been* king of Judah, [b]Jeho-
ram the son of Jehoshaphat began to
reign as [1]king of Judah.
17 He was [a]thirty-two years old when
he became king, and he reigned eight
years in Jerusalem.
18 And he walked in the way of the
kings of Israel, just as the house of
Ahab had done, for [a]the daughter of
Ahab was his wife; and he did evil in
the sight of the LORD.
19 Yet the LORD would not destroy Judah, for the sake of his servant David,
[a]as He promised him to give a lamp
to him *and* his sons forever.
20 In his days [a]Edom revolted against
Judah's authority, [b]and made a king
over themselves.
21 So [1]Joram went to Zair, and all his
chariots with him. Then he rose by
night and attacked the Edomites who
had surrounded him and the captains
of the chariots; and the troops fled to
their tents.
22 Thus Edom has been in revolt
against Judah's authority to this day.
[a]And Libnah revolted at that time.
23 Now the rest of the acts of [1]Joram,
and all that he did, *are* they not written
in the book of the chronicles of the
kings of Judah?
24 So Joram [1]rested with his fathers,
and was buried with his fathers in the
City of David. Then [a]Ahaziah[2] his son
reigned in his place.

Ahaziah Reigns in Judah

25 In the twelfth year of Joram the son
of Ahab, king of Israel, Ahaziah the
son of Jehoram, king of Judah, began
to reign.
26 Ahaziah *was* [a]twenty-two years old
when he became king, and he reigned
one year in Jerusalem. His mother's
name *was* Athaliah the granddaughter
of Omri, king of Israel.
27 [a]And he walked in the way of the
house of Ahab, and did evil in the sight
of the LORD, like the house of Ahab,
for he *was* the son-in-law of the house
of Ahab.
28 Now he went [a]with Joram the son
of Ahab to war against Hazael king of
Syria at [b]Ramoth Gilead; and the Syrians wounded Joram.
29 Then [a]King Joram went back to
Jezreel to recover from the wounds
which the Syrians had inflicted on him
at [1]Ramah, when he fought against
Hazael king of Syria. [b]And Ahaziah the
son of Jehoram, king of Judah, went

8 [a]1 Kin. 19:15 [b]1 Sam. 9:7; 1 Kin. 14:3; 2 Kin. 5:5 [c]2 Kin. 1:2
9 [a]1 Kin. 19:15
10 [a]2 Kin. 8:15
11 [a]Luke 19:41 [1]*fixed his gaze*
12 [a]2 Kin. 10:32; 12:17; 13:3, 7; Amos 1:3, 4 [b]2 Kin. 15:16; Hos. 13:16; Amos 1:13; Nah. 3:10
13 [a]1 Sam. 17:43; 2 Sam. 9:8 [b]1 Kin. 19:15
16 [a]2 Kin. 1:17; 3:1 [b]2 Chr. 21:3 [1]Co-regent with his father
17 [a]2 Chr. 21:5–10
18 [a]2 Kin. 8:26, 27
19 [a]2 Sam. 7:13; 1 Kin. 11:36; 15:4; 2 Chr. 21:7
20 [a]Gen. 27:40; 2 Chr. 21:8–10 [b]1 Kin. 22:47
21 [1]*Jehoram,* v. 16
22 [a]Josh. 21:13; 2 Kin. 19:8; 2 Chr. 21:10
23 [1]*Jehoram,* v. 16
24 [a]2 Chr. 22:1, 7 [1]Died and joined his ancestors [2]Or *Azariah* or *Jehoahaz*
26 [a]2 Chr. 22:2
27 [a]2 Chr. 22:3, 4
28 [a]2 Chr. 22:5 [b]1 Kin. 22:3, 29
29 [a]2 Kin. 9:15 [b]2 Kin. 9:16; 2 Chr. 22:6, 7 [1]*Ramoth,* v. 28

8:15 Ben-Hadad was suffocated by **Hazael.**

8:16–24 Kings now shifts back to the events in the southern kingdom of Judah. During the reign of Jehoram in Israel, another **Jehoram** (see note on 3:1–5) had become **king of Judah.** He was Judah's fifth ruler and, in contrast to his father Jehoshaphat, Jehoram was a wicked king. Jehoram was greatly influenced by his evil wife Athaliah, the daughter of Jezebel and Ahab.

8:25–29 The sixth king in **Judah** was **Ahaziah** who is not to be confused with the eighth king in Israel. See 1 Kin. 22:51—2 Kin. 1:18. He was also a wicked ruler and, like his father Jehoram, received idolatrous input from Athaliah (see 2 Chr. 22:3).

down to see Joram the son of Ahab in
Jezreel, because he was sick.

Jehu Anointed King of Israel

9 And Elisha the prophet called one
of [a]the sons of the prophets, and
said to him, [b]"Get[1] yourself ready, take
this flask of oil in your hand, [c]and go
to Ramoth Gilead.
2 "Now when you arrive at that place,
look there for Jehu the son of Jehoshaphat, the son of Nimshi, and go in
and make him rise up from among
[a]his associates, and take him to an inner room.
3 "Then [a]take the flask of oil, and
pour *it* on his head, and say, 'Thus says
the LORD: "I have *anointed you king
over Israel." ' Then open the door and
flee, and do not delay."
4 So the young man, the servant of
the prophet, went to Ramoth Gilead.
5 And when he arrived, there *were*
the captains of the army sitting; and
he said, "I have a message for you,
Commander." Jehu said, "For which
one of us?" And he said, "For you,
Commander."
6 Then he arose and went into the
house. And he poured the oil on his
head, and said to him, [a]"Thus says the
LORD God of Israel: 'I have anointed
you king over the people of the LORD,
over Israel.
7 'You shall strike down the house of
Ahab your master, that I may [a]avenge
the blood of My servants the prophets,
and the blood of all the servants of the
LORD, [b]at the hand of Jezebel.
8 'For the whole house of Ahab shall
*perish; and [a]I will cut off from Ahab
all [b]the males in Israel, both [c]bond and
free.
9 'So I will make the house of Ahab
like the house of [a]Jeroboam the son
of Nebat, and like the house of [b]Baasha
the son of Ahijah.
10 [a]'The dogs shall eat Jezebel on the
*plot *of ground* at Jezreel, and *there
shall be* none to bury *her*.' " And he
opened the door and fled.
11 Then Jehu came out to the servants
of his master, and *one* said to him, "*Is*

CHAPTER 9

1 [a]1 Kin. 20:35 [b]2 Kin. 4:29; Jer. 1:17 [c]2 Kin. 8:28, 29 [1]Lit. *Gird up your loins*
2 [a]2 Kin. 9:5, 11
3 [a]1 Kin. 19:16 *See WW at Is. 61:1.
6 [a]1 Sam. 2:7, 8; 1 Kin. 19:16; 2 Kin. 9:3; 2 Chr. 22:7
7 [a][Deut. 32:35, 41] [b]1 Kin. 18:4; 21:15
8 [a]1 Kin. 14:10; 21:21; 2 Kin. 10:17 [b]1 Sam. 25:22 [c]Deut. 32:36; 2 Kin. 14:26 *See WW at Judg. 5:31.
9 [a]1 Kin. 14:10; 15:29; 21:22 [b]1 Kin. 16:3, 11
10 [a]1 Kin. 21:23; 2 Kin. 9:35, 36 *See WW at Zech. 2:12.
11 [a]Jer. 29:26; Hos. 9:7; Mark 3:21; John 10:20; Acts 26:24; [1 Cor. 4:10]
13 [a]Matt. 21:7, 8; Mark 11:7, 8 [1]Lit. *under his feet* *See WW at Amos 9:6.
14 [a]2 Kin. 8:28
15 [a]2 Kin. 8:29 [1]*Jehoram*, v. 24
16 [a]2 Kin. 8:29
17 [1]Are you peaceful?
18 [1]Lit. *Turn behind me*

all well? Why did [a]this madman come
to you?" And he said to them, "You
know the man and his babble."
12 And they said, "A lie! Tell us now."
So he said, "Thus and thus he spoke
to me, saying, 'Thus says the LORD: "I
have anointed you king over Israel." ' "
13 Then each man hastened [a]to take
his garment and put *it* [1]under him on
the top of the *steps; and they blew
trumpets, saying, "Jehu is king!"

Joram of Israel Killed

14 So Jehu the son of Jehoshaphat, the
son of Nimshi, conspired against
[a]Joram. (Now Joram had been defending Ramoth Gilead, he and all Israel, against Hazael king of Syria.
15 But [a]King [1]Joram had returned to
Jezreel to recover from the wounds
which the Syrians had inflicted on him
when he fought with Hazael king of
Syria.) And Jehu said, "If you are so
minded, let no one leave *or* escape
from the city to go and tell *it* in Jezreel."
16 So Jehu rode in a chariot and went
to Jezreel, for Joram was laid up there;
[a]and Ahaziah king of Judah had come
down to see Joram.
17 Now a watchman stood on the
tower in Jezreel, and he saw the company of Jehu as he came, and said, "I
see a company of men." And Joram
said, "Get a horseman and send him
to meet them, and let him say, [1]'*Is it*
peace?' "
18 So the horseman went to meet him,
and said, "Thus says the king: '*Is it*
peace?' " And Jehu said, "What have
you to do with peace? [1]Turn around
and follow me." So the watchman reported, saying, "The messenger went
to them, but is not coming back."
19 Then he sent out a second horseman who came to them, and said,
"Thus says the king: '*Is it* peace?' "
And Jehu answered, "What have you
to do with peace? Turn around and follow me."
20 So the watchman reported, saying,
"He went up to them and is not coming
back; and the driving *is* like the driving

9:1–6 Kings turns northward and relates how Elisha commanded that **Jehu** was to be anointed as tenth **king over . . . Israel.**

9:7–9 As the Lord had destroyed the dynasties of Jeroboam (1 Kin. 14:10), of Baasha (1 Kin. 16:3), and of Zimri (1 Kin. 16:16), so now He would do away with the fourth dynasty of Israel by ending the house of Ahab.

9:10 Jezebel was still alive at this time and was likely the dominant force behind the idolatry in the reigns of Ahaziah and Jehoram.

9:10–20 Jehu's hasty behavior is understandable when we realize that his anointing and acclamation as king amounted to treason. Therefore it was crucial that he get to Jehoram before the news of the rebellion did. **Ramoth Gilead** (v. 14) was about 50 miles from **Jezreel** (v. 16).

of Jehu the son of Nimshi, for he drives
furiously!"
21 Then Joram said, [1]"Make ready."
And his chariot was made ready. Then
[a]Joram king of Israel and Ahaziah
king of Judah went out, each in his
chariot; and they went out to meet
Jehu, and [2]met him [b]on the property
of Naboth the Jezreelite.
22 Now it happened, when Joram saw
Jehu, that he said, "*Is it* peace, Jehu?"
So he answered, "What peace, as
long as the harlotries of your mother
Jezebel and her witchcraft *are* so
many?"
23 Then Joram turned around and fled,
and said to Ahaziah, "Treachery, Ahaziah!"
24 Now Jehu [1]drew his bow with full
strength and shot Jehoram between his
arms; and the arrow came out at his
*heart, and he sank down in his char-
iot.
25 Then *Jehu* said to Bidkar his captain, "Pick *him* up, *and* throw him into
the tract of the field of Naboth the Jezreelite; for remember, when you and I
were riding together behind Ahab his
father, that [a]the LORD laid this [b]burden
upon him:
26 'Surely I saw yesterday the blood
of Naboth and the blood of his sons,'
says the LORD, [a]'and I will repay you
[1]in this plot,' says the LORD. Now therefore, take *and* throw him on the plot
of ground, according to the word of the
LORD."

Ahaziah of Judah Killed

27 But when Ahaziah king of Judah
saw *this,* he fled by the road to [1]Beth
Haggan. So Jehu pursued him, and
said, [2]"Shoot him also in the chariot."
And they shot him at the Ascent of
Gur, which is by Ibleam. Then he fled
to [a]Megiddo, and died there.
28 And his servants carried him in the
chariot to Jerusalem, and buried him
in his tomb with his fathers in the City
of David.
29 In the eleventh year of Joram the
son of Ahab, Ahaziah had become king
over Judah.

21 [a]1 Kin. 19:17; 2 Chr. 22:7 [b]1 Kin. 21:1–14 [1]*Harness up* [2]Lit. *found*
24 [1]Lit. *filled his hand* *See WW at Ps. 37:4.
25 [a]1 Kin. 21:19, 24–29 [b]Is. 13:1
26 [a]1 Kin. 21:13, 19 [1]*on this property*
27 [a]2 Chr. 22:7, 9 [1]Lit. *The Garden House* [2]Lit. *Strike*
30 [a][Jer. 4:30]; Ezek. 23:40
31 [a]1 Kin. 16:9–20; 2 Kin. 9:18–22
34 [a][Ex. 22:28]; 1 Kin. 16:31
36 [a]1 Kin. 21:23
37 [a]Ps. 83:10

CHAPTER 10

1 [1]So with MT, Syr., Tg.; LXX *Samaria;* Vg. *city* [2]*the guardians of*
3 [1]*most upright*

Jezebel's Violent Death

30 Now when Jehu had come to Jezreel, Jezebel heard *of it;* [a]and she
put paint on her eyes and adorned her
head, and looked through a window.
31 Then, as Jehu entered at the gate,
she said, [a]"*Is it* peace, Zimri, murderer
of your master?"
32 And he looked up at the window,
and said, "Who *is* on my side? Who?"
So two *or* three eunuchs looked out at
him.
33 Then he said, "Throw her down."
So they threw her down, and *some* of
her blood spattered on the wall and on
the horses; and he trampled her underfoot.
34 And when he had gone in, he ate
and drank. Then he said, "Go now, see
to this accursed *woman,* and bury her,
for [a]she was a king's daughter."
35 So they went to bury her, but they
found no more of her than the skull
and the feet and the palms of *her*
hands.
36 Therefore they came back and told
him. And he said, "This *is* the word of
the LORD, which He spoke by His servant Elijah the Tishbite, saying, [a]'On
the plot *of ground* at Jezreel dogs
shall eat the flesh of Jezebel;
37 'and the corpse of Jezebel shall be
[a]as refuse on the surface of the field,
in the plot at Jezreel, so that they shall
not say, "Here *lies* Jezebel."' "

Ahab's Seventy Sons Killed

10 Now Ahab had seventy sons in
Samaria. And Jehu wrote and
sent letters to Samaria, to the rulers
of [1]Jezreel, to the elders, and to
[2]those who reared Ahab's *sons,* saying:

2 Now as soon as this letter comes
to you, since your master's sons
are with you, and you have
chariots and horses, a fortified
city also, and weapons,
3 choose the [1]best qualified of your
master's sons, set *him* on his
father's throne, and fight for your
master's house.

9:21–37 Jehu proceeded to initiate the task the Lord had assigned him (vv. 7–10) by executing Jehoram and Jezebel. This fulfilled part of the prophecy that he and his captain Bidkar had heard from Elijah in 1 Kin. 21:17–26. At this time Jehu also executed Ahaziah the king of Judah (vv. 27–29).

10:1–28 Jehu promptly sets out to accomplish God's directive to do away with the house of Ahab (9:7). He executed Ahab's **seventy sons** (his descendants in Samaria), then he killed Ahaziah's forty-two **brothers** (relatives), and finally he exterminated the rest of Ahab's family in Samaria (v. 17). All of this was to avenge the evil done by the fourth dynasty (9:7) and to fulfill Elijah's prophecy. Compare v. 10 with 1 Kin. 21:17–26. Jehu's final strategy was to destroy Baal worship in Israel by trapping and executing the worshipers of Baal and burning their temple (vv. 18–28). His helper **Jehonadab** (vv. 15, 23) is noted in Jer. 35:6.

4 But they were exceedingly afraid,
and said, "Look, [a]two kings could not
[1]stand up to him; how then can we
stand?"
5 And he who *was* in charge of the
house, and he who *was* in charge of
the city, the elders also, and those who
reared *the sons,* sent to Jehu, saying,
"We *are* your servants, we will do all
you tell us; but we will not make anyone king. Do *what is* good in your
sight."
6 Then he wrote a second letter to
them, saying:

> If you *are* for me and will obey
> my voice, take the heads of the
> men, your master's sons, and
> come to me at Jezreel by this time
> tomorrow.

Now the king's sons, seventy persons,
were with the great men of the city,
who were rearing them.
7 So it was, when the letter came to
them, that they took the king's sons
and [a]slaughtered seventy persons, put
their heads in baskets and sent *them*
to him at Jezreel.
8 Then a messenger came and told
him, saying, "They have brought the
heads of the king's sons." And he said,
"Lay them in two heaps at the entrance
of the gate until morning."
9 So it was, in the morning, that he
went out and stood, and said to all the
people, "You *are* righteous. Indeed
[a]I conspired against my master and
killed him; but who killed all these?
10 "Know now that nothing shall
[a]fall to the earth of the word of the
LORD which the LORD spoke concerning the house of Ahab; for the LORD
has done what He spoke [b]by His servant Elijah."
11 So Jehu killed all who remained of
the house of Ahab in Jezreel, and all
his great men and his close acquaintances and his priests, until he left him
none remaining.

Ahaziah's Forty-two Brothers Killed

12 And he arose and departed and
went to Samaria. On the way, at
[1]Beth Eked of the Shepherds,
13 [a]Jehu met with the brothers of Ahaziah king of Judah, and said, "Who *are*
you?" So they answered, "We *are* the
brothers of Ahaziah; we have come
down to greet the sons of the king and
the sons of the queen mother."
14 And he said, "Take them alive!" So
they took them alive, and [a]killed them
at the well of [1]Beth Eked, forty-two
men; and he left none of them.

The Rest of Ahab's Family Killed

15 Now when he departed from there,
he [1]met [a]Jehonadab the son of [b]Re-
chab, *coming* to meet him; and he
greeted him and said to him, "Is your
heart right, as my heart *is* toward your
heart?" And Jehonadab answered, "It
is." *Jehu said,* "If it is, [c]give *me* your
hand." So he gave *him* his hand, and
he took him up to him into the chariot.
16 Then he said, "Come with me, and
see my [a]zeal for the LORD." So they
had him ride in his chariot.
17 And when he came to Samaria,
[a]he killed all who remained to Ahab
in Samaria, till he had destroyed them,
according to the word of the LORD
[b]which He spoke to Elijah.

Worshipers of Baal Killed

18 Then Jehu gathered all the people
together, and said to them, [a]"Ahab
served Baal a little, Jehu will serve him
much.
19 "Now therefore, call to me all the
[a]prophets of Baal, all his servants, and
all his priests. Let no one be missing,
for I have a great sacrifice for Baal.
Whoever is missing shall not live." But
Jehu acted deceptively, with the intent
of destroying the worshipers of Baal.
20 And Jehu said, [1]"Proclaim a solemn
assembly for Baal." So they proclaimed *it.*
21 Then Jehu sent throughout all Israel; and all the worshipers of Baal
came, so that there was not a man left
who did not come. So they came into
the [1]temple of Baal, and the [a]temple
of Baal was full from one end to the
other.
22 And he said to the one in charge
of the wardrobe, "Bring out vestments
for all the worshipers of Baal." So he
brought out vestments for them.
23 Then Jehu and Jehonadab the son
of Rechab went into the temple of Baal,
and said to the worshipers of Baal,
"Search and see that no servants of the
LORD are here with you, but only the
worshipers of Baal."
24 So they went in to offer sacrifices
and burnt offerings. Now Jehu had appointed for himself eighty men on the
outside, and had said, "*If* any of the
men whom I have brought into your
hands escapes, *whoever lets him escape, it shall be* [a]his life for the life of
the other."

4 [a]2 Kin. 9:24, 27 [1]Lit. *stand before*
7 [a]Judg. 9:5; 1 Kin. 21:21; 2 Kin. 11:1
9 [a]2 Kin. 9:14–24
10 [a]1 Sam. 3:19; 1 Kin. 8:56; Jer. 44:28 [b]1 Kin. 21:17–24, 29
12 [1]Or *The Shearing House*
13 [a]2 Chr. 22:8
14 [a]2 Chr. 22:8 [1]Or *The Shearing House*
15 [a]Jer. 35:6 [b]1 Chr. 2:55 [c]Ezra 10:19; Ezek. 17:18 [1]Lit. *found*
16 [a]1 Kin. 19:10
17 [a]2 Kin. 9:8; 2 Chr. 22:8 [b]1 Kin. 21:21, 29
18 [a]1 Kin. 16:31, 32
19 [a]1 Kin. 18:19; 22:6
20 [1]*Consecrate*
21 [a]1 Kin. 16:32; 2 Kin. 11:18 [1]Lit. *house*
24 [a]1 Kin. 20:39

25 Now it happened, as soon as he had made an end of offering the burnt offering, that Jehu said to the guard and to the captains, "Go in *and* kill them; let no one come out!" And they killed them with the edge of the sword; then the guards and the officers threw *them* out, and went into the [1]inner room of the temple of Baal.

26 And they brought the [a]*sacred* pillars out of the temple of Baal and burned them.

27 Then they broke down the *sacred* pillar of Baal, and tore down the [1]temple of Baal and [a]made it a refuse dump to this day.

2 28 Thus Jehu destroyed Baal from Israel.

29 However Jehu did not turn away from the sins of Jeroboam the son of Nebat, who had made Israel sin, *that is,* from [a]the golden calves that *were* at Bethel and Dan.

30 And the LORD [a]said to Jehu, "Because you have done well in doing *what is* right in My sight, *and* have done to the house of Ahab all that *was* in My heart, [b]your sons shall sit on the throne of Israel to the fourth *generation.*"

31 But Jehu [1]took no heed to walk in the law of the LORD God of Israel with all his heart; for he did not depart from [a]the sins of Jeroboam, who had made Israel sin.

Death of Jehu

32 In those days the LORD began to cut off *parts* of Israel; and [a]Hazael conquered them in all the territory of Israel

33 from the Jordan eastward: all the land of Gilead—Gad, Reuben, and Manasseh—from [a]Aroer, which *is* by the River Arnon, including [b]Gilead and Bashan.

34 Now the rest of the acts of Jehu, all that he did, and all his might, *are* they not written in the book of the chronicles of the kings of Israel?

35 So Jehu [1]rested with his fathers, and they buried him in Samaria. Then [a]Jehoahaz his son reigned in his place.

36 And the period that Jehu reigned over Israel in Samaria *was* twenty-eight years.

Athaliah Reigns in Judah

11 When [a]Athaliah [b]the mother of Ahaziah saw that her son was [c]dead, she arose and destroyed all the royal heirs.

2 But [1]Jehosheba, the daughter of King Joram, sister of [a]Ahaziah, took [2]Joash the son of Ahaziah, and stole him away from among the king's sons *who were* being murdered; and they hid him and his nurse in the bedroom, from Athaliah, so that he was not killed.

3 So he was hidden with her in the house of the LORD for six years, while Athaliah reigned over the land.

Joash Crowned King of Judah

4 In [a]the seventh year Jehoiada sent and brought the captains of hundreds—of the bodyguards and the [1]escorts—and brought them into the house of the LORD to him. And he made a covenant with them and took an oath from them in the house of the LORD, and showed them the king's son.

5 Then he commanded them, saying, "This *is* what you shall do: One-third of you who [1]come on duty [a]on the Sabbath shall be keeping watch over the king's house,

6 "one-third *shall be* at the gate of Sur, and one-third at the gate behind the escorts. You shall keep the watch of the house, lest it be broken down.

7 "The two [1]contingents of you who go off duty on the Sabbath shall keep the watch of the house of the LORD for the king.

8 "But you shall surround the king on all sides, every man with his weapons in his hand; and whoever comes within range, let him be put to death. You are to be with the king as he goes out and as he comes in."

9 [a]So the captains of the hundreds did according to all that Jehoiada the priest commanded. Each of them took

25 [1]Lit. *city*
26 [a][Deut. 7:5, 25]; 1 Kin. 14:23; 2 Kin. 3:2
27 [a]Ezra 6:11; Dan. 2:5; 3:29 [1]Lit. *house*
29 [a]1 Kin. 12:28–30; 13:33, 34
30 [a]2 Kin. 9:6, 7 [b]2 Kin. 13:1, 10; 14:23; 15:8, 12
31 [a]1 Kin. 14:16 [1]*was not careful*
32 [a]1 Kin. 19:17; 2 Kin. 8:12; 13:22
33 [a]Deut. 2:36 [b]Amos 1:3–5
35 [a]2 Kin. 13:1 [1]Died and joined his ancestors

CHAPTER 11
1 [a]2 Chr. 22:10 [b]2 Kin. 8:26 [c]2 Kin. 9:27
2 [a]2 Kin. 8:25 [1]*Jehoshabeath,* 2 Chr. 22:11 [2]Or *Jehoash*
4 [a]2 Kin. 12:2; 2 Chr. 23:1 [1]*guards*
5 [a]1 Chr. 9:25 [1]Lit. *enter in*
7 [1]*companies*
9 [a]2 Chr. 23:8

10:28–31 See section 2 of Truth-In-Action at the end of 2 Kin.

10:29–36 Jehu is to be commended for purging Israel of the house of Ahab and its Baal worship. For this, his dynasty would last four generations. Indeed, this fifth dynasty was the longest and most stable of all of Israel's dynasties. However, because Jehu was not fully devoted to the Lord, God disciplined him with territorial losses to Hazael of Syria.

11:1 Kings turns once again to the events in Judah. At the death of her son Ahaziah (10:25–29), **Athaliah** usurped the throne of Judah and attempted to protect her position by destroying the **royal heirs.** Among Judah's rulers, she was the only reigning queen and the strongest proponent of Baal worship.

11:2–20 In God's providence, **Joash** had been concealed from the treachery of Athaliah. Through the skillful and quick organization of the priest **Jehoiada,** Joash was made Judah's eighth ruler and Athaliah was put to death.

his men who were to be on duty on
the Sabbath, with those who were going off duty on the Sabbath, and came
to Jehoiada the priest.
10 And the priest gave the captains of
hundreds the spears and shields which
had belonged to King David, [a]that were
in the temple of the LORD.
11 Then the escorts stood, every man
with his weapons in his hand, all
around the king, from the right [1]side
of the temple to the left side of the temple, by the altar and the house.
12 And he brought out the king's son,
put the crown on him, and *gave him*
the [a]Testimony;[1] they made him king
and anointed him, and they clapped
their hands and said, [b]"Long live the
king!"

Death of Athaliah

13 [a]Now when Athaliah heard the
noise of the escorts *and* the people, she
came to the people *in* the temple of the
LORD.
14 When she looked, there was the
king standing by [a]a pillar according
to custom; and the leaders and the
trumpeters were by the king. All the
people of the land were rejoicing and
blowing trumpets. So Athaliah tore her
clothes and cried out, "Treason! Treason!"
15 And Jehoiada the priest commanded the captains of the hundreds,
the officers of the army, and said to
them, "Take her outside [1]under guard,
and slay with the sword whoever follows her." For the priest had said, "Do
not let her be killed in the house of the
LORD."
16 So they seized her; and she went
by way of the horses' entrance *into* the
king's house, and there she was killed.
17 [a]Then Jehoiada [b]made a covenant
between the LORD, the king, and the
people, that they should be the LORD's
people, and *also* [c]between the king and
the people.
1 18 And all the people of the land went
to the [a]temple of Baal, and tore it
down. They thoroughly [b]broke in
pieces its altars and [1]images, and
[c]killed Mattan the priest of Baal before

10 [a]2 Sam. 8:7; 1 Chr. 18:7
11 [1]Lit. *shoulder*
12 [a]Ex. 25:16; 31:18 [b]1 Sam. 10:24 [1]Law, Ex. 25:16, 21; Deut. 31:9
13 [a]2 Kin. 8:26; 2 Chr. 23:12
14 [a]2 Kin. 23:3; 2 Chr. 34:31
15 [1]Lit. *between ranks*
17 [a]2 Chr. 23:16 [b]Josh. 24:24, 25; 2 Chr. 15:12–15 [c]2 Sam. 5:3
18 [a]2 Kin. 10:26, 27 [b][Deut. 12:3] [c]1 Kin. 18:40; 2 Kin. 10:11 [d]2 Chr. 23:18 [1]Idols [2]Lit. *offices*
21 [a]2 Chr. 24:1–14

CHAPTER 12

1 [a]2 Chr. 24:1 [1]*Joash*, 2 Kin. 11:2ff.
2 [a]2 Kin. 11:4
3 [a]1 Kin. 15:14; 22:43; 2 Kin. 14:4; 15:35 [1]Places for pagan worship
4 [a]2 Kin. 22:4 [b]Ex. 30:13–16 [c]Lev. 27:2–28 [d]Ex. 35:5; 1 Chr. 29:3–9 [1]Lit. *the money coming over* [2]*any man's heart prompts him to bring*
5 [1]Lit. *breaches*
6 [a]2 Chr. 24:5
7 [a]2 Chr. 24:6

the altars. And [d]the priest appointed
[2]officers over the house of the LORD.
19 Then he took the captains of hundreds, the bodyguards, the escorts, and
all the people of the land; and they
brought the king down from the house
of the LORD, and went by way of the
gate of the escorts to the king's house.
Then he sat on the throne of the kings.
20 So all the people of the land rejoiced; and the city was quiet, for they
had slain Athaliah with the sword *in*
the king's house.
21 Jehoash *was* [a]seven years old when
he became king.

Jehoash Repairs the Temple

12 In the seventh year of Jehu,
[a]Jehoash[1] became king, and he
reigned forty years in Jerusalem. His
mother's name *was* Zibiah of Beersheba.
2 Jehoash did *what was* right in the
sight of the LORD all the days in which
[a]Jehoiada the priest instructed him.
3 But [a]the [1]high places were not
taken away; the people still sacrificed
and burned incense on the high places.
4 And Jehoash said to the priests,
[a]"All the money of the dedicated gifts
that are brought into the house of the
LORD—each man's [b]census[1] money,
each man's [c]assessment money—*and*
all the money that [2]a man [d]purposes
in his heart to bring into the house of
the LORD,
5 "let the priests take *it* themselves,
each from his constituency; and let
them repair the [1]damages of the temple, wherever any dilapidation is
found."
6 Now it was so, by the twenty-third
year of King Jehoash, [a]*that* the priests
had not repaired the damages of the
temple.
7 [a]So King Jehoash called Jehoiada
the priest and the *other* priests, and
said to them, "Why have you not repaired the damages of the temple?
Now therefore, do not take *more*
money from your constituency, but deliver it for repairing the damages of the
temple."
8 And the priests agreed that they

11:18 See section 1 of Truth-In-Action at the end of 2 Kin.
11:21 Jehoash is a variant name for Joash (v. 2).
12:1–16 In the years that Jehoash was a youth (11:21 says he was only seven years old when he began to reign), it is apparent that **Jehoiada the priest** served as regent. Under the influence of Jehoiada, a great religious revival ensued and the temple was repaired.
12:2, 3 After the death of Jehoiada, Jehoash drifted from the Lord and even allowed idolatry in Judah (2 Chr. 24). Jehoash followed the advice of certain Judean officials, and as a result he turned from the Lord (2 Chr. 24:17, 18). God sent prophets to warn the nation. When Zechariah (son of the high priest Jehoiada) echoed the prophetic warning, Jehoash had him stoned to death in the temple courtyard (2 Chr. 24:20–22).

would neither receive *more* money
from the people, nor repair the damages of the temple.
9 Then Jehoiada the priest took
[a]a chest, bored a hole in its lid, and
set it beside the **altar,** on the right side
as one comes into the house of the
LORD; and the priests who [1]kept the
door put [b]there all the money brought
into the house of the LORD.

> **WORD WEALTH**
>
> **12:9 altar,** *mizbeach* (meez-*beh*-ahch); Strong's #4196: Altar, place of sacrifice. The root of *mizbeach* is *zabach,* which means "to slay, to sacrifice, to offer an animal." The word *mizbeach* occurs more than 400 times. Altars were of great importance in the lives of Noah and the three patriarchs. In the Levitical system and in Solomon's temple, the altar was the center of daily activity, without which the rest of Israel's worship could not take place. The "altar of sacrifice" was also crucial in God's revelation of true worship for joyful times, such as feasts.

10 So it was, whenever they saw that
there was much money in the chest,
that the king's [a]scribe[1] and the high
priest came up and [2]put it in bags, and
counted the money that was found in
the house of the LORD.
11 Then they gave the money, which
had been apportioned, into the hands
of those who did the work, who had
the oversight of the house of the LORD;
and they [1]paid it out to the carpenters
and builders who worked on the house
of the LORD,
12 and to masons and stonecutters,
and for buying timber and hewn stone,
to [a]repair the damage of the house of
the LORD, and for all that was paid out
to repair the temple.
6 13 However [a]there were not made for
the house of the LORD basins of silver,
trimmers, sprinkling-bowls, trumpets,
any articles of gold or articles of silver,
from the money brought into the house
of the LORD.
14 But they gave that to the workmen,
and they repaired the house of the
LORD with it.
15 Moreover [a]they did not require an
account from the men into whose hand
they delivered the money to be paid
to workmen, for they dealt *faithfully.
16 [a]The money from the trespass offerings and the money from the sin offerings was not brought into the house
of the LORD. [b]It belonged to the priests.

Hazael Threatens Jerusalem

17 [a]Hazael king of Syria went up and
fought against Gath, and took it; then
[b]Hazael set his face to [1]go up to Jerusalem.
18 And Jehoash king of Judah [a]took
all the sacred things that his fathers,
Jehoshaphat and Jehoram and Ahaziah, kings of Judah, had dedicated,
and his own sacred things, and all the
gold found in the treasuries of the
house of the LORD and in the king's
house, and sent *them* to Hazael king
of Syria. Then he went away from Jerusalem.

Death of Joash

19 Now the rest of the acts of [1]Joash,
and all that he did, *are* they not written
in the book of the chronicles of the
kings of Judah?
20 And [a]his servants arose and formed
a conspiracy, and killed Joash in the
house of [1]the Millo, which goes down
to Silla.
21 For [1]Jozachar the son of Shimeath
and Jehozabad the son of [2]Shomer, his
servants, struck him. So he died, and
they buried him with his fathers in the

9 [a]2 Chr. 23:1; 24:8 [b]Mark 12:41; Luke 21:1 [1]*guarded at the door*
10 [a]2 Sam. 8:17; 2 Kin. 19:2; 22:3, 4, 12 [1]*secretary* [2]*tied it up*
11 [1]Lit. *weighed*
12 [a]2 Kin. 22:5, 6
13 [a]2 Chr. 24:14
15 [a]2 Kin. 22:7; [1 Cor. 4:2]; 2 Cor. 8:20 *See WW at Prov. 28:20.
16 [a][Lev. 5:15, 18] [b][Lev. 7:7; Num. 18:9]
17 [a]2 Kin. 8:12 [b]2 Chr. 24:23 [1]Advance upon
18 [a]1 Kin. 15:18; 2 Kin. 16:8; 18:15, 16
19 [1]*Jehoash,* vv. 1–18
20 [a]2 Kin. 14:5; 2 Chr. 24:25 [1]Lit. *The Landfill*
21 [1]*Zabad,* 2 Chr. 24:26 [2]*Shimrith,* 2 Chr. 24:26

12:13–16 See section 6 of Truth-In-Action at the end of 2 Kin.

12:17, 18 Because of the failure in Jehoash's later years, God permitted Hazael's forces to assault Jerusalem (see 2 Chr. 24:23, 24). Tragically, Jehoash gave some of the temple treasuries and valuables to pay Hazael for withdrawing his forces.

12:20, 21 There are discrepancies between this verse and the parallel account in 2 Chr. 24:25, 26. The first conspirator here is identified as **Jozachar,** whereas in 2 Chr. 24:26 he is named Zabad. The name in 2 Chr. should be Zachar, the abbreviated name for Jozachar (as Joash is for Jehoash), but was miscopied as Zabad. This would be easy to do since the Hebrew letters in those names closely resemble each other.

Another discrepancy is that the parent of **Jehozabad** is recorded here as **Shomer,** but as Shimrith in 2 Chr. 24:26. Apparently a copyist incorrectly recorded the name Shimrith, which is the feminine counterpart to the masculine name Shomer.

A third slight variation in these two accounts is that here they **killed Joash in the house of the Millo,** whereas in 2 Chr. 24:25 it states they killed him on his bed. In this case, the account of 2 Chr. 24 serves as a supplement to this one, clarifying that Joash was murdered while sleeping in the house of the Millo. A final discrepancy is that here Joash is buried **with his fathers in the City of David,** whereas 2 Chr. 24:25 says that they did not bury him in the tombs of the kings. The account in 2 Chr. 24 again supplements this one to clarify that even though he was buried with his fathers, Joash was not buried in the tombs of the kings.

City of David. Then [a]Amaziah his son
reigned in his place.

Jehoahaz Reigns in Israel

13 In the twenty-third year of
[a]Joash[1] the son of Ahaziah,
king of Judah, [b]Jehoahaz the son of
Jehu became king over Israel in Samaria, *and reigned* seventeen years.
2 And he did evil in the sight of the
LORD, and followed the [a]sins of Jeroboam the son of Nebat, who had made
Israel sin. He did not [1]depart from
them.
3 Then [a]the anger of the LORD was
aroused against Israel, and He delivered them into the hand of [b]Hazael
king of Syria, and into the hand of
[c]Ben-Hadad the son of Hazael, all *their*
days.
4 So Jehoahaz [a]pleaded with the
LORD, and the LORD listened to him; for
[b]He saw the oppression of Israel, because the king of Syria oppressed
them.
5 [a]Then the LORD gave Israel a deliverer, so that they escaped from under the hand of the Syrians; and the
children of Israel dwelt in their tents
as before.
6 Nevertheless they did not depart
from the sins of the house of Jeroboam,
who had made Israel sin, *but* walked
in them; [a]and the [1]wooden image also
remained in Samaria.
7 For He left of the army of Jehoahaz
only fifty horsemen, ten chariots, and
ten thousand foot soldiers; for the king
of Syria had destroyed them [a]and
made them [b]like the dust at threshing.
8 Now the rest of the acts of Jehoahaz, all that he did, and his might, *are*
they not written in the book of the
chronicles of the kings of Israel?
9 So Jehoahaz [1]rested with his fathers, and they buried him in Samaria.
Then [2]Joash his son reigned in his
place.

21 [a]2 Chr. 24:27

CHAPTER 13

1 [a]2 Kin. 12:1 [b]2 Kin. 10:35 [1]*Jehoash,* 2 Kin. 12:1–18
2 [a]1 Kin. 12:26–33 [1]Lit. *turn*
3 [a]Judg. 2:14 [b]2 Kin. 8:12 [c]Amos 1:4
4 [a][Ps. 78:34] [b][Ex. 3:7, 9; Judg. 2:18]; 2 Kin. 14:26
5 [a]2 Kin. 13:25; 14:25, 27; Neh. 9:27
6 [a]1 Kin. 16:33 [1]Heb. *Asherah,* a Canaanite goddess
7 [a]2 Kin. 10:32 [b][Amos 1:3]
9 [1]Died and joined his ancestors [2]Or *Jehoash*
10 [1]*Joash,* v. 9
12 [a]2 Kin. 14:8–15 [b]2 Kin. 13:14–19, 25 [c]2 Kin. 14:9; 2 Chr. 25:17–25
13 [a]2 Kin. 14:16 [1]Died and joined his ancestors
14 [a]2 Kin. 2:12
17 [a]1 Kin. 20:26

Jehoash Reigns in Israel

10 In the thirty-seventh year of Joash
king of Judah, [1]Jehoash the son of Jehoahaz became king over Israel in Samaria, *and reigned* sixteen years.
11 And he did evil in the sight of the
LORD. He did not depart from all the
sins of Jeroboam the son of Nebat, who
made Israel sin, *but* walked in them.
12 [a]Now the rest of the acts of Joash,
[b]all that he did, and [c]his might with
which he fought against Amaziah king
of Judah, *are* they not written in the
book of the chronicles of the kings of
Israel?
13 So Joash [a]rested[1] with his fathers.
Then Jeroboam sat on his throne. And
Joash was buried in Samaria with the
kings of Israel.

Death of Elisha

14 Elisha had become sick with the illness of which he would die. Then
Joash the king of Israel came down to
him, and wept over his face, and said,
"O my father, my father, [a]the chariots
of Israel and their horsemen!"
15 And Elisha said to him, "Take a
bow and some arrows." So he took
himself a bow and some arrows.
16 Then he said to the king of Israel,
"Put your hand on the bow." So he put
his hand *on it,* and Elisha put his hands
on the king's hands.
17 And he said, "Open the east window"; and he opened *it.* Then Elisha
said, "Shoot"; and he shot. And he
said, "The arrow of the LORD's deliverance and the arrow of deliverance from
Syria; for you must strike the Syrians
at [a]Aphek till you have destroyed
them."
18 Then he said, "Take the arrows";
so he took *them.* And he said to the
king of Israel, "Strike the ground"; so
he struck three times, and stopped.
19 And the man of God was angry with
him, and said, "You should have struck
five or six times; then you would have

13:1–9 The scenery shifts again to Israel where, following the death of Jehu, his son **Jehoahaz** had become king. He was the eleventh of 19 evil kings in the northern kingdom. Jehoahaz permitted idolatry to flourish, so that the Lord allowed Hazael and later Ben-Hadad III of Syria to oppress Israel. Under the oppression, Jehoahaz temporarily repented, but Israel went right back to idolatry.

13:5 The **deliverer** God raised up was Assyria, which threatened Syria so that they broke off their oppression of Israel in order to protect their own interests.

13:9–13 Jehoahaz was succeeded by his son **Jehoash** (or **Joash**). He was the twelfth king in Israel and is not to be confused with the eighth king of Judah with the same name.

13:14–21 It is ironic that **Elisha,** the great giant of faith who had done so many miracles in his lifetime (and even one after his death, see vv. 21, 22), would die from **illness.** There is an element of mystery in the ministry of the miraculous. See note on 2 Tim. 4:20. Before he died, Elisha extended to King Jehoahaz an opportunity to participate in an enacted prophecy that symbolized his future victories over the Syrians. Jehoahaz would not be victorious as he could have been, because he lacked faith and was unwilling to do enthusiastically something that may have seemed foolish to him.

struck Syria till you had destroyed *it!*
[a]But now you will strike Syria *only*
three times."
20 Then Elisha [1]died, and they buried
him. And the [a]*raiding* bands from
Moab invaded the land in the spring
of the year.
21 So it was, as they were burying a
man, that suddenly they spied a band
of raiders; and they put the man in the
tomb of Elisha; and when the man was
let down and touched the bones of
Elisha, he revived and stood on his
feet.

Israel Recaptures Cities from Syria

22 And [a]Hazael king of Syria oppressed Israel all the days of Jehoahaz.
23 But the LORD was [a]gracious* to
them, had compassion on them, and
[b]regarded them, [c]because of His covenant with Abraham, Isaac, and Jacob,
and would not yet destroy them or cast
them from His presence.
24 Now Hazael king of Syria died.
Then Ben-Hadad his son reigned in his
place.
25 And [1]Jehoash the son of Jehoahaz
recaptured from the hand of Ben-
Hadad, the son of Hazael, the cities
which he had taken out of the hand
of Jehoahaz his father by war. [a]Three
times Joash defeated him and recaptured the cities of Israel.

Amaziah Reigns in Judah

14 In [a]the second year of Joash the
son of Jehoahaz, king of Israel,
[b]Amaziah the son of Joash, king of Judah, became king.
2 He was twenty-five years old when
he became king, and he reigned
twenty-nine years in Jerusalem. His
mother's name was Jehoaddan of Jerusalem.
3 And he did *what was* right in the
sight of the LORD, yet not like his father
David; he did everything [a]as his father
Joash had done.
4 [a]However the [1]high places were not
taken away, and the people still sacrificed and burned incense on the high
places.
5 Now it happened, as soon as the
kingdom was established in his hand,
that he executed his servants [a]who had
murdered his father the king.
6 But the children of the murderers
he did not execute, according to what
is written in the Book of the Law of
Moses, in which the LORD commanded,
saying, [a]"Fathers shall not be put to
death for their children, nor shall children be put to death for their fathers;
but a person shall be put to death for
his own sin."
7 [a]He killed ten thousand Edomites
in [b]the Valley of Salt, and took [1]Sela
by war, [c]and called its name Joktheel
to this day.
8 [a]Then Amaziah sent messengers to
[1]Jehoash the son of Jehoahaz, the son
of Jehu, king of Israel, saying, "Come,
let us face one another *in battle.*"
9 And Jehoash king of Israel sent to
Amaziah king of Judah, saying,
[a]"The thistle that *was* in Lebanon sent
to the [b]cedar that *was* in Lebanon, saying, 'Give your daughter to my son as
wife'; and a wild beast that *was* in
Lebanon passed by and trampled the
thistle.
10 "You have indeed defeated Edom,
and [a]your heart has [1]lifted you up.
Glory *in that,* and stay at home; for
why should you meddle with trouble
so that you fall—you and Judah with
you?"
11 But Amaziah would not heed.
Therefore Jehoash king of Israel went
out; so he and Amaziah king of Judah
faced one another at [a]Beth Shemesh,
which *belongs* to Judah.
12 And Judah was defeated by Israel,
and every man fled to his tent.
13 Then Jehoash king of Israel captured Amaziah king of Judah, the son
of Jehoash, the son of Ahaziah, at Beth
Shemesh; and he went to Jerusalem,
and broke down the wall of Jerusalem
from [a]the Gate of Ephraim to [b]the Corner Gate—[1]four hundred cubits.
14 And he took all [a]the gold and silver,
all the articles that were found in the
house of the LORD and in the treasuries
of the king's house, and hostages, and
returned to Samaria.
15 [a]Now the rest of the acts of Jehoash
which he did—his might, and how he
fought with Amaziah king of Judah—

19 [a]2 Kin. 13:25
20 [a]2 Kin. 3:5; 24:2 [1]Having prophesied at least 55 years
22 [a]2 Kin. 8:12, 13
23 [a]2 Kin. 14:27 [b][Ex. 2:24, 25] [c]Gen. 13:16, 17; 17:2–7; Ex. 32:13 *See WW at Mal. 1:9.
25 [a]2 Kin. 13:18, 19 [1]*Joash,* vv. 12–14, 25

CHAPTER 14

1 [a]2 Kin. 13:10 [b]2 Chr. 25:1, 2
3 [a]2 Kin. 12:2
4 [a]2 Kin. 12:3 [1]Places for pagan worship
5 [a]2 Kin. 12:20
6 [a]Deut. 24:16; [Jer. 31:30; Ezek. 18:4, 20]
7 [a]2 Chr. 25:5–16 [b]2 Sam. 8:13; 1 Chr. 18:12; Ps. 60:title [c]Josh. 15:38 [1]Lit. *The Rock;* the city of Petra
8 [a]2 Chr. 25:17, 18 [1]*Joash,* 2 Kin. 13:9, 12–14, 25; 2 Chr. 25:17ff.
9 [a]Judg. 9:8–15 [b]1 Kin. 4:33
10 [a]Deut. 8:14; 2 Chr. 32:25; [Ezek. 28:2, 5, 17; Hab. 2:4] [1]Made you proud
11 [a]Josh. 19:38; 21:16
13 [a]Neh. 8:16; 12:39 [b]Jer. 31:38; Zech. 14:10 [1]About 600 feet
14 [a]1 Kin. 7:51; 2 Kin. 12:18; 16:8
15 [a]2 Kin. 13:12, 13

13:25 As Elisha had prophesied (v. 19), three times Jehoahaz was victorious over Syria.

14:1–9 Kings now returns to the events in Judah. After the death of Jehoash, his son **Amaziah** became the ninth ruler of the southern kingdom. He was one of Judah's more aggressive rulers and restored some of its prestige. He executed the ones who had murdered his father (vv. 5, 6) and won a memorable battle against Edom (v. 7). The **Valley of Salt** is a plain at the south end of the Dead Sea. **Sela,** renamed **Joktheel,** is the famous Petra. A stronghold carved out of sheer rock, it served as Edom's capital city. In later years Amaziah became overconfident and instigated a war with Israel in which he was defeated (vv. 8–19).

are they not written in the book of the
chronicles of the kings of Israel?
16 So Jehoash [1]rested with his fathers,
and was buried in Samaria with the
kings of Israel. Then Jeroboam his son
reigned in his place.
17 [a]Amaziah the son of Joash, king of
Judah, lived fifteen years after the
death of Jehoash the son of Jehoahaz,
king of Israel.
18 Now the rest of the acts of Amaziah,
are they not written in the book of the
chronicles of the kings of Judah?
19 And [a]they formed a conspiracy
against him in Jerusalem, and he fled
to [b]Lachish; but they sent after him to
Lachish and killed him there.
20 Then they brought him on horses,
and he was buried at Jerusalem with
his fathers in the City of David.
21 And all the people of Judah took
[a]Azariah,[1] who *was* sixteen years old,
and made him king instead of his father Amaziah.
22 He built [a]Elath[1] and restored it to
Judah, after [2]the king rested with his
fathers.

Jeroboam II Reigns in Israel

23 In the fifteenth year of Amaziah the
son of Joash, king of Judah, Jeroboam
the son of Joash, king of Israel, became
king in Samaria, *and reigned* forty-one
years.
24 And he did evil in the sight of the
LORD; he did not depart from all the
[a]sins of Jeroboam the son of Nebat,
who had made Israel sin.
25 He [a]restored the [1]territory of Israel
[b]from the entrance of Hamath to
[c]the[2] Sea of the Arabah, according to
the word of the LORD God of Israel,
which He had spoken through His servant [d]Jonah the son of Amittai, the
prophet who *was* from [e]Gath Hepher.
26 For the LORD [a]saw *that* the affliction of Israel *was* very bitter; and
whether bond or free, [b]there was no
helper for Israel.
27 [a]And the LORD did not say that He
would blot out the name of Israel from
under heaven; but He saved them by
the hand of Jeroboam the son of Joash.
28 Now the rest of the acts of Jeroboam, and all that he did—his might,
how he made war, and how he recaptured for Israel, from [a]Damascus and
Hamath, [b]*what had belonged* to Judah—*are* they not written in the book
of the chronicles of the kings of Israel?
29 So Jeroboam [1]rested with his fathers, the kings of Israel. Then [a]Zecha-
riah his son reigned in his place.

Azariah Reigns in Judah

15 In the twenty-seventh year of
Jeroboam king of Israel, [a]Aza-
riah the son of Amaziah, king of Judah,
[b]became king.
2 He was sixteen years old when he
became king, and he reigned fifty-two
years in Jerusalem. His mother's name
was Jecholiah of Jerusalem.
3 And he did *what was* right in the
sight of the LORD, according to all that
his father Amaziah had done,
4 [a]except that the [1]high places were
not removed; the people still sacrificed
and burned incense on the high places.
5 Then the LORD [a]struck the king, so
that he was a leper until the day of his
[b]death; so he [c]dwelt in an isolated
house. And Jotham the king's son *was*
over the *royal* house, judging the people of the land.
6 Now the rest of the acts of Azariah,
and all that he did, *are* they not written
in the book of the chronicles of the
kings of Judah?
7 So Azariah [1]rested with his fathers,
and [a]they buried him with his fathers
in the City of David. Then Jotham his
son reigned in his place.

Zechariah Reigns in Israel

8 In the thirty-eighth year of Azariah
king of Judah, [a]Zechariah the son of
Jeroboam reigned over Israel in Samaria six months.

16 [1]Died and joined his ancestors
17 [a]2 Chr. 25:25–28
19 [a]2 Chr. 25:27 [b]Josh. 10:31
21 [a]2 Kin. 15:13; 2 Chr. 26:1 [1]*Uzziah,* 2 Chr. 26:1ff.; Is. 6:1; etc.
22 [a]1 Kin. 9:26; 2 Kin. 16:6; 2 Chr. 8:17 [1]Heb. *Eloth* [2]Amaziah died and joined his ancestors.
24 [a]1 Kin. 12:26–33
25 [a]2 Kin. 10:32; 13:5, 25 [b]Num. 13:21; 34:8; 1 Kin. 8:65 [c]Deut. 3:17 [d]Jon. 1:1; Matt. 12:39, 40 [e]Josh. 19:13 [1]*border* [2]The Dead Sea
26 [a]Ex. 3:7; 2 Kin. 13:4; Ps. 106:44 [b]Deut. 32:36
27 [a][2 Kin. 13:5, 23]
28 [a]1 Kin. 11:24 [b]2 Sam. 8:6; 1 Kin. 11:24; 2 Chr. 8:3
29 [a]2 Kin. 15:8 [1]Died and joined his ancestors

CHAPTER 15

1 [a]2 Kin. 15:13, 30 [b]2 Kin. 14:21; 2 Chr. 26:1, 3, 4
4 [a]2 Kin. 12:3; 14:4; 15:35 [1]Places for pagan worship
5 [a]2 Chr. 26:19–23; Ps. 78:31 [b]Is. 6:1 [c][Lev. 13:46]; Num. 12:14
7 [a]2 Chr. 26:23 [1]Died and joined his ancestors
8 [a]2 Kin. 14:29

14:23–29 Shifting back to Israel, Kings now explains that the successor of Jehoram was his son **Jeroboam** II. As Israel's thirteenth regent, Jeroboam II was a capable ruler but a poor religious reformer because of his immorality and idolatry.

14:25 Jonah: This is the same prophet Jonah who traveled to the city of Nineveh (Jon. 1:1, 2), and who had a prophetic ministry during the reign of Jeroboam II.

15:1–7 Kings returns to the southern kingdom, describing how **Azariah** had become the tenth ruler in Judah's history. He was one of Judah's more stable kings, beginning his rule at age 16 and reigning 52 years. Azariah is remembered as the "leper-king," because the Lord punished him with leprosy for his toleration of idolatry. He was also known as Uzziah. At Uzziah's death the prophet Isaiah was given a special revelation of God (Is. 6:1).

15:8–16 Shifting back to Israel, Kings records the reign of **Zechariah.** He was the son of Jeroboam II, and served as Israel's fourteenth king. King Zechariah persisted in calf worship, and after he had ruled only six months he was assassinated by **Shallum.** This marked the end of Jehu's dynasty. This fifth of Israel's dynasties was the longest, spanning more than a century and involving five kings.

9 And he did evil in the sight of the LORD, [a]as his fathers had done; he did not depart from the sins of Jeroboam the son of Nebat, who had made Israel sin.
10 Then Shallum the son of Jabesh conspired against him, and [a]struck and killed him in front of the people; and he reigned in his place.
11 Now the rest of the acts of Zechariah, indeed they *are* written in the book of the chronicles of the kings of Israel.
12 This *was* the word of the LORD which He spoke to Jehu, saying, [a]"Your sons shall sit on the throne of Israel to the fourth *generation.*" And so it was.

Shallum Reigns in Israel

13 Shallum the son of Jabesh became king in the thirty-ninth year of [1]Uzziah king of Judah; and he reigned a full month in Samaria.
14 For Menahem the son of Gadi went up from [a]Tirzah, came to Samaria, and struck Shallum the son of Jabesh in Samaria and killed him; and he reigned in his place.
15 Now the rest of the acts of Shallum, and the conspiracy which he [1]led, indeed they *are* written in the book of the chronicles of the kings of Israel.
16 Then from Tirzah, Menahem attacked [a]Tiphsah, all who *were* there, and its territory. Because they did not surrender, therefore he attacked *it.* All [b]the women there who were with child he ripped open.

Menahem Reigns in Israel

17 In the thirty-ninth year of Azariah king of Judah, Menahem the son of Gadi became king over Israel, *and reigned* ten years in Samaria.
18 And he did evil in the sight of the LORD; he did not depart all his days from the sins of Jeroboam the son of Nebat, who had made Israel sin.
19 [a]Pul[1] king of Assyria came against the land; and Menahem gave Pul a thousand talents of silver, that his [2]hand might be with him to [b]strengthen the kingdom under his control.
20 And Menahem [a]exacted[1] the money from Israel, from all the very wealthy, from each man fifty shekels of silver, to give to the king of Assyria. So the king of Assyria turned back, and did not stay there in the land.
21 Now the rest of the acts of Menahem, and all that he did, *are* they not written in the book of the chronicles of the kings of Israel?
22 So Menahem [1]rested with his fathers. Then Pekahiah his son reigned in his place.

Pekahiah Reigns in Israel

23 In the fiftieth year of Azariah king of Judah, Pekahiah the son of

9 [a]2 Kin. 14:24
10 [a]Amos 7:9
12 [a]2 Kin. 10:30
13 [1]*Azariah,* 2 Kin. 14:21ff.; 15:1ff.
14 [a]1 Kin. 14:17; Song 6:4
15 [1]Lit. *conspired*
16 [a]1 Kin. 4:24 [b]2 Kin. 8:12; Hos. 13:16
19 [a]1 Chr. 5:26; Is. 66:19; Hos. 8:9 [b]2 Kin. 14:5 [1]Tiglath-Pileser III, v. 29 [2]Support
20 [a]2 Kin. 23:35 [1]*took*
22 [1]Died and joined his ancestors

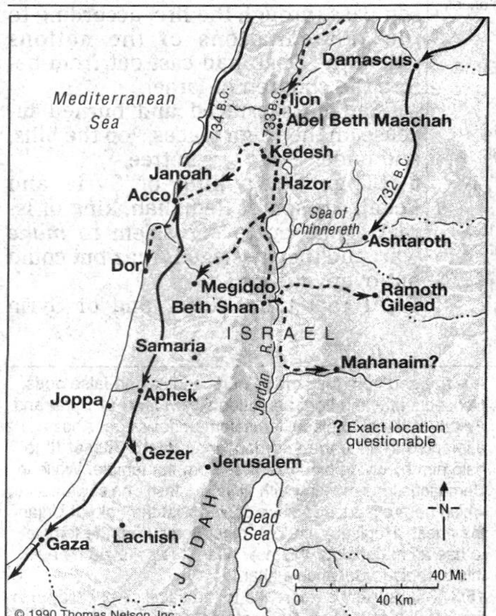

Assyrian Campaigns Against Israel and Judah (734–732 B.C.). From 734 B.C. to 732 B.C. Tiglath-Pileser III mounted one invasion against Judah and two against Israel.

15:13–16 Zechariah's murderer, **Shallum,** reigned as Israel's fifteenth king for just one month, and then he was executed by **Menahem.** Shallum's death marked the end of Israel's sixth dynasty.
15:17–22 **Menahem,** the sixteenth king of Israel, ruled for 10 years. He was dominated by **Pul** (Tiglath-Pileser III), one of Assyria's greatest monarchs. Pul imposed burdensome tributes, forcing Menahem to increase Israel's taxes oppressively.
15:23–26 The son of Menahem, **Pekahiah,** came to the throne as Israel's seventeenth ruler. After he reigned two years, he was murdered by his successor **Pekah,** thus ending the seventh dynasty in Israel.

Menahem became king over Israel in Samaria, *and reigned* two years.

24 And he did evil in the sight of the LORD; he did not depart from the sins of Jeroboam the son of Nebat, who had made Israel sin.

25 Then Pekah the son of Remaliah, an officer of his, conspired against him and [1]killed him in Samaria, in the [a]citadel of the king's house, along with Argob and Arieh; and with him were fifty men of Gilead. He killed him and reigned in his place.

26 Now the rest of the acts of Pekahiah, and all that he did, indeed they *are* written in the book of the chronicles of the kings of Israel.

Pekah Reigns in Israel

27 In the fifty-second year of Azariah king of Judah, [a]Pekah the son of Remaliah became king over Israel in Samaria, *and reigned* twenty years.

28 And he did evil in the sight of the LORD; he did not depart from the sins of Jeroboam the son of Nebat, who had made Israel sin.

29 In the days of Pekah king of Israel, [1]Tiglath-Pileser king of Assyria [a]came and took [b]Ijon, Abel Beth Maachah, Janoah, Kedesh, Hazor, Gilead, and Galilee, all the land of Naphtali; and he [c]carried them captive to Assyria.

30 Then Hoshea the son of Elah led a conspiracy against Pekah the son of Remaliah, and struck and killed him; so he [a]reigned in his place in the twentieth year of Jotham the son of Uzziah.

31 Now the rest of the acts of Pekah, and all that he did, indeed they *are* written in the book of the chronicles of the kings of Israel.

Jotham Reigns in Judah

32 In the second year of Pekah the son of Remaliah, king of Israel, [a]Jotham the son of Uzziah, king of Judah, began to reign.

33 He was twenty-five years old when he became king, and he reigned sixteen years in Jerusalem. His mother's name *was* [1]Jerusha the daughter of Zadok.

34 And he did *what was* right in the sight of the LORD; he did [a]according to all that his father Uzziah had done.

35 [a]However the [1]high places were not removed; the people still sacrificed and burned incense on the high places. [b]He built the Upper Gate of the house of the LORD.

36 Now the rest of the acts of Jotham, and all that he did, *are* they not written in the book of the chronicles of the kings of Judah?

37 In those days the LORD began to send [a]Rezin king of Syria and [b]Pekah the son of Remaliah against Judah.

38 So Jotham [1]rested with his fathers, and was buried with his fathers in the City of David his father. Then Ahaz his son reigned in his place.

Ahaz Reigns in Judah

16 In the seventeenth year of Pekah the son of Remaliah, Ahaz the son of Jotham, king of Judah, began to reign.

2 Ahaz *was* twenty years old when he became king, and he reigned sixteen years in Jerusalem; and he did not do *what was* right in the sight of the LORD his God, as his father David *had done.*

3 But he walked in the way of the kings of Israel; indeed [a]he made his son pass through the fire, according to the [b]abominations of the nations whom the LORD had cast out from before the children of Israel.

4 And he sacrificed and burned incense on the [a]high places, [b]on the hills, and under every green tree.

5 [a]Then Rezin king of Syria and Pekah the son of Remaliah, king of Israel, came up to Jerusalem to *make* war; and they besieged Ahaz but could not overcome *him.*

6 At that time Rezin king of Syria

25 [a]1 Kin. 16:18 [1]Lit. *struck*
27 [a]2 Chr. 28:6; Is. 7:1
29 [a]2 Kin. 16:7, 10; 1 Chr. 5:26 [b]1 Kin. 15:20 [c]2 Kin. 17:6 [1]A later name of *Pul*, v. 19
30 [a]2 Kin. 17:1; [Hos. 10:3, 7, 15]
32 [a]2 Chr. 27:1
33 [1]*Jerushah*, 2 Chr. 27:1
34 [a]2 Kin. 15:3, 4; 2 Chr. 26:4, 5
35 [a]2 Kin. 15:4 [b]2 Chr. 23:20; 27:3 [1]Places for pagan worship
37 [a]2 Kin. 16:5–9; Is. 7:1–17 [b]2 Kin. 15:26, 27
38 [1]Died and joined his ancestors

CHAPTER 16

3 [a][Lev. 18:21]; 2 Kin. 17:17; 2 Chr. 28:3; Ps. 106:37, 38; Is. 1:1 [b][Deut. 12:31]; 2 Kin. 21:2, 11
4 [a]2 Kin. 15:34, 35 [b][Deut. 12:2]; 1 Kin. 14:23
5 [a]2 Kin. 15:37; Is. 7:1, 4

15:27–31 As the eighteenth regent in the north, **Pekah . . . did evil,** and Israel was therefore invaded by **Tiglath-Pileser** III of Assyria. This was the beginning of the end for Israel, as Assyria annexed certain of Israel's territories and took many of its people captive.

15:32–38 In Judah, **Jotham** had ascended to the throne as Judah's eleventh monarch. He was a good king and is noteworthy because he rebuilt the northern gate of the temple. Pekah's demise marked the end of Israel's eighth dynasty.

16:1–20 **Ahaz** became the twelfth ruler in Judah. In contrast to his father Jotham and his grandfather Azariah (or Uzziah), Ahaz turned from the Lord to pursue idols and false gods. Consequently, the Lord permitted **Rezin king of Syria** and **Pekah** of Israel to place Jerusalem under siege. Ahaz attempted to bribe the Assyrian king **Tiglath-Pileser** III to help him by giving him treasures from the temple. While in Damascus for a meeting with Tiglath-Pileser, he saw an altar, which he proceeded to have copied with the help of Urijah the priest. Tragically, he took other items from the temple to use as material for this new altar. It is believed he built this to replace Solomon's altar.

16:3 This is likely a reference to the sacrifice of children in the worship of Molech. See note on 1 Kin. 11:5–7.

[a]captured [1]Elath for Syria, and drove
the men of Judah from Elath. Then the
[2]Edomites went to Elath, and dwell
there to this day.
7 So Ahaz sent messengers to
[a]Tiglath-Pileser[1] king of Assyria, saying, "I *am* your servant and your son.
Come up and *save me from the hand
of the king of Syria and from the hand
of the king of Israel, who rise up
against me."
8 And Ahaz [a]took the silver and gold
that was found in the house of the
LORD, and in the treasuries of the
king's house, and sent *it as* a present
to the king of Assyria.
9 So the king of Assyria heeded him;
for the king of Assyria went up against
[a]Damascus and [b]took it, carried *its
people* captive to [c]Kir, and killed Rezin.
10 Now King Ahaz went to Damascus
to meet Tiglath-Pileser king of Assyria,
and saw an altar that *was* at Damascus; and King Ahaz sent to Urijah the
priest the design of the altar and its
pattern, according to all its workmanship.
11 Then [a]Urijah the priest built an altar according to all that King Ahaz had
sent from Damascus. So Urijah the
priest made *it* before King Ahaz came
back from Damascus.
12 And when the king came back from
Damascus, the king saw the altar; and
[a]the king approached the altar and
made offerings on it.
13 So he burned his burnt offering and
his grain offering; and he poured his
drink offering and sprinkled the blood
of his peace offerings on the altar.
14 He also brought [a]the bronze altar
which *was* before the LORD, from the
front of the [1]temple—from between the
new altar and the house of the LORD—
and put it on the north side of the *new*
altar.
15 Then King Ahaz commanded Urijah the priest, saying, "On the great
new altar burn [a]the morning burnt offering, the evening grain offering, the
king's burnt sacrifice, and his grain offering, with the burnt offering of all the
people of the land, their grain offering,
and their drink offerings; and sprinkle
on it all the blood of the burnt offering
and all the blood of the sacrifice. And
the bronze altar shall be for me to inquire *by.*"
16 Thus did Urijah the priest, according to all that King Ahaz commanded.
17 [a]And King Ahaz cut off [b]the panels
of the carts, and removed the lavers
from them; and he took down [c]the Sea
from the bronze oxen that *were* under
it, and put it on a pavement of stones.
18 Also he removed the Sabbath pavilion which they had built in the temple,
and he removed the king's outer entrance from the house of the LORD, on
account of the king of Assyria.
19 Now the rest of the acts of Ahaz
which he did, *are* they not written in
the book of the chronicles of the kings
of Judah?
20 So Ahaz rested with his fathers, and
[a]was buried with his fathers in the City
of David. Then Hezekiah his son
reigned in his place.

Hoshea Reigns in Israel

17 In the twelfth year of Ahaz king
of Judah, [a]Hoshea the son of
Elah became king of Israel in Samaria,
and he reigned nine years.
2 And he did evil in the sight of the
LORD, but not as the kings of Israel who
were before him.
3 [a]Shalmaneser king of Assyria came
up against him; and Hoshea [b]became
his vassal, and paid him tribute money.
4 And the king of Assyria uncovered
a conspiracy by Hoshea; for he had
sent messengers to So, king of Egypt,
and brought no tribute to the king of
Assyria, as *he had done* year by year.
Therefore the king of Assyria shut him
up, and bound him in prison.

Israel Carried Captive to Assyria

5 Now [a]the king of Assyria went
throughout all the land, and went up
to Samaria and besieged it for three
years.
6 [a]In the ninth year of Hoshea, the
king of Assyria took Samaria and
[b]carried Israel away to Assyria,
[c]and placed them in Halah and by the
Habor, the River of Gozan, and in the
cities of the Medes.
7 For [a]so it was that the children of

6 [a]2 Kin. 14:22; 2 Chr. 26:2 [1]Lit. *Large Tree;* sing. of *Eloth* [2]A few ancient mss. *Syrians*
7 [a]2 Kin. 15:29; 1 Chr. 5:26; 2 Chr. 28:20 [1]A later name of *Pul,* 2 Kin. 15:19 *See WW at Jer. 17:14.
8 [a]2 Kin. 12:17, 18; 2 Chr. 28:21
9 [a]2 Kin. 14:28 [b]Amos 1:5 [c]Is. 22:6; Amos 9:7
11 [a]Is. 8:2
12 [a]2 Chr. 26:16, 19
14 [a]Ex. 27:1, 2; 40:6, 29; 2 Chr. 4:1 [1]Lit. *house*
15 [a]Ex. 29:39–41
17 [a]2 Chr. 28:24 [b]1 Kin. 7:27–29 [c]1 Kin. 7:23–25
20 [a]2 Chr. 28:27

CHAPTER 17

1 [a]2 Kin. 15:30
3 [a]2 Kin. 18:9–12 [b]2 Kin. 24:1
5 [a]2 Kin. 18:9; Hos. 13:16
6 [a]2 Kin. 18:10, 11; Is. 7:7–9; Hos. 1:4; 13:16; Amos 4:2 [b]Lev. 26:32, 33; [Deut. 28:36, 64; 29:27, 28] [c]1 Chr. 5:26
7 [a][Josh. 23:16]

16:17 Sea: See note on 1 Kin. 7:23–26.

17:1 Kings now returns to Israel to record its last king. **Hoshea** was the last of Israel's rulers. He represented the ninth and final dynasty. In its relatively brief history (a little over 200 years), the northern kingdom of Israel had 19 kings with 9 dynasties; and all of its rulers were wicked.

17:6 The Assyrian monarch Shalmaneser (727–722 B.C.) initiated the fall of Samaria, but it is believed that his successor Sargon II (722–705 B.C.) actually seized Samaria and captured its people. Thus, the northern kingdom of Israel ended in approximately 722 B.C. and was taken captive by Assyria.

17:7–15 See section 1 of Truth-In-Action at the end of 2 Kin.

Israel had sinned against the LORD their God, who had brought them up out of the land of Egypt, from under the hand of Pharaoh king of Egypt; and they had [b]feared other gods,
8 and [a]had walked in the statutes of the nations whom the LORD had cast out from before the children of Israel, and of the kings of Israel, which they had made.
9 Also the children of Israel secretly did against the LORD their God things that *were* not right, and they built for themselves [1]high places in all their cities, [a]from watchtower to fortified city.
10 [a]They set up for themselves *sacred* pillars and [b]wooden images[1] [c]on every high hill and under every green tree.
11 There they burned incense on all the high places, like the nations whom the LORD had carried away before them; and they did wicked things to *provoke the LORD to anger,
12 for they served idols, [a]of which the LORD had said to them, [b]"You shall not do this thing."
13 Yet the LORD testified against Israel and against Judah, by all of His [a]prophets, [b]every seer, saying, [c]"Turn from your evil ways, and keep My commandments *and* My statutes, according to all the law which I commanded your fathers, and which I sent to you by My servants the prophets."
14 Nevertheless they would not hear, but [a]stiffened their necks, like the necks of their fathers, who [b]did not believe in the LORD their God.
15 And they [a]rejected His statutes [b]and His covenant that He had made with their fathers, and His testimonies which He had testified against them; they followed [c]idols, [d]became idolaters, and *went* after the nations who *were* all around them, *concerning* whom the LORD had charged them that they should [e]not do like them.
16 So they left all the commandments of the LORD their God, [a]made for themselves a molded image *and* two calves, [b]made a wooden image and worshiped all the [c]host of heaven, [d]and served Baal.
17 [a]And they caused their sons and daughters to pass through the fire, [b]practiced witchcraft and soothsaying, and [c]sold themselves to do evil in the sight of the LORD, to provoke Him to anger.
18 Therefore the LORD was very angry with Israel, and removed them from His sight; there was none left [a]but the tribe of Judah alone.
19 Also [a]Judah did not keep the commandments of the LORD their God, but walked in the statutes of Israel which they made.
20 And the LORD rejected all the descendants of Israel, afflicted them, and [a]delivered them into the hand of plunderers, until He had cast them from His [b]sight.

7 [b]Judg. 6:10
8 [a][Lev. 18:3]
9 [a]2 Kin. 18:8 [1]Places for pagan worship
10 [a]Is. 57:5 [b][Ex. 34:12–14] [c][Deut. 12:2] [1]Heb. *Asherim*, Canaanite deities
11 *See WW at 1 Kin. 16:2.
12 [a][Ex. 20:3–5] [b][Deut. 4:19]
13 [a]Neh. 9:29, 30 [b]1 Sam. 9:9 [c][Jer. 18:11; 25:5; 35:15]
14 [a][Acts 7:51] [b]Deut. 9:23
15 [a]Jer. 44:3 [b]Deut. 29:25 [c]Deut. 32:21 [d][Rom. 1:21–23] [e][Deut. 12:30, 31]
16 [a]1 Kin. 12:28 [b][1 Kin. 14:15] [c][Deut. 4:19] [d]1 Kin. 16:31; 22:53
17 [a]2 Kin. 16:3 [b][Deut. 18:10–12] [c]1 Kin. 21:20
18 [a]1 Kin. 11:13, 32
19 [a]Jer. 3:8
20 [a]2 Kin. 13:3; 15:29 [b]2 Kin. 24:20

17:7–23 Here, with glaring clarity, Kings gives the reason for Israel's fall and captivity. It was the inevitable consequence of their sin. According to the prophet Hosea, Israel's captivity has never ended (Hos. 1:6, 9).

Assyrian Campaigns Against Israel (725 B.C.). In 725 B.C. Shalmaneser V invaded Israel and marched on Samaria. Sargon II took Samaria in 722 B.C.

21 For [a]He tore Israel from the house of David, and [b]they made Jeroboam the son of Nebat king. Then Jeroboam drove Israel from following the LORD, and made them commit a great sin.
22 For the children of Israel walked in all the sins of Jeroboam which he did; they did not depart from them,
23 until the LORD removed Israel out of His sight, [a]as He had said by all His servants the prophets. [b]So Israel was carried away from their own land to Assyria, *as it is* to this day.

Assyria Resettles Samaria

24 [a]Then the king of Assyria brought *people* from Babylon, Cuthah, [b]Ava, Hamath, and from Sepharvaim, and placed *them* in the cities of Samaria instead of the children of Israel; and they took possession of Samaria and dwelt in its cities.
25 And it was so, at the beginning of their dwelling there, *that* they did not fear the LORD; therefore the LORD sent lions among them, which killed *some* of them.
26 So they spoke to the king of Assyria, saying, "The nations whom you have removed and placed in the cities of Samaria do not know the rituals of the God of the land; therefore He has sent lions among them, and indeed, they are killing them because they do not know the rituals of the God of the land."
27 Then the king of Assyria commanded, saying, "Send there one of the priests whom you brought from there; let him go and dwell there, and let him teach them the rituals of the God of the land."
28 Then one of the priests whom they had carried away from Samaria came and dwelt in Bethel, and taught them how they should fear the LORD.
29 However every nation continued to make gods of its own, and put *them* [a]in the shrines on the high places which the Samaritans had made, *every* nation in the cities where they dwelt.
30 The men of [a]Babylon made Succoth Benoth, the men of Cuth made Nergal, the men of Hamath made Ashima,
31 [a]and the Avites made Nibhaz and Tartak; and the Sepharvites [b]burned their children in fire to Adrammelech and Anammelech, the gods of Sepharvaim.
32 So they feared the LORD, [a]and from every class they appointed for themselves priests of the [1]high places, who sacrificed for them in the shrines of the high places.
33 [a]They feared the LORD, yet served their own gods—according to the rituals of the nations from among whom they were carried away.
34 To this day they continue practicing the former rituals; they do not fear the LORD, nor do they follow their statutes or their ordinances, or the law and commandment which the LORD had commanded the children of Jacob, [a]whom He named Israel,
35 with whom the LORD had made a covenant and charged them, saying: [a]"You shall not fear other gods, nor [b]bow down to them nor serve them nor sacrifice to them;
36 "but the LORD, who [a]brought you up from the land of Egypt with great *power and [b]an outstretched arm, [c]Him you shall fear, Him you shall worship, and to Him you shall offer sacrifice.
37 "And the statutes, the ordinances, the law, and the commandment which He wrote for you, [a]you shall be careful to observe forever; you shall not fear other gods.
38 "And the covenant that I have made with you, [a]you shall not forget, nor shall you fear other gods.
39 "But the LORD your God you shall fear; and He will deliver you from the hand of all your enemies."
40 However they did not obey, but they followed their former rituals.
41 [a]So these nations feared the LORD, yet served their carved images; also their children and their children's children have continued doing as their fathers did, even to this day.

Hezekiah Reigns in Judah

18 Now it came to pass in the third year of [a]Hoshea the son of Elah, king of Israel, *that* [b]Hezekiah the son

21 [a]1 Kin. 11:11, 31 [b]1 Kin. 12:20, 28
23 [a]1 Kin. 14:16 [b]2 Kin. 17:6
24 [a]Ezra 4:2, 10 [b]2 Kin. 18:34
29 [a]1 Kin. 12:31; 13:32
30 [a]2 Kin. 17:24
31 [a]Ezra 4:9 [b][Deut. 12:31]
32 [a]1 Kin. 12:31; 13:33 [1]Places for pagan worship
33 [a]Zeph. 1:5
34 [a]Gen. 32:28; 35:10
35 [a]Judg. 6:10 [b][Ex. 20:5]
36 [a]Ex. 14:15–30 [b]Ex. 6:6; 9:15 [c][Deut. 10:20] *See WW at Deut. 8:18.
37 [a]Deut. 5:32
38 [a]Deut. 4:23; 6:12
41 [a]2 Kin. 17:32, 33

CHAPTER 18
1 [a]2 Kin. 17:1 [b]2 Chr. 28:27; 29:1

17:24–41 To prevent resistance, the Assyrians deported the tribes of Israel and mixed them with other minority groups. The intermarriage of Israel with these foreigners resulted in the people known as the **Samaritans** (v. 29). The Samaritans were hated by the people of Judah from the time of Ezra, as also by the Jews during the time of Jesus. See Luke 10:30; John 4:5. The Assyrians allowed Israelite priests to teach the worship of Yahweh. But instead of converting others and securing the Israelites, the attempts of the priests only resulted in syncretism (the merging of different beliefs and practices). Although there were some representatives of Israel who returned to Jerusalem with Zerubbabel, there was never any systematic return of these 10 tribes.

18:1–8 With Israel now out of the picture, Kings turns to record the decline and fall of Judah. Hezekiah has succeeded Ahaz as Judah's thirteenth ruler. He swept into

of Ahaz, king of Judah, began to reign.
2 He was twenty-five years old when
he became king, and he reigned
twenty-nine years in Jerusalem. His
mother's name *was* [a]Abi[1] the daughter
of Zechariah.
3 And he did *what was* right in the
sight of the LORD, according to all that
his father David had done.
6 4 [a]He removed the [1]high* places and
broke the *sacred* pillars, cut down the
[2]wooden image and broke in pieces the
[b]bronze serpent that Moses had made;
for until those days the children of Israel burned incense to it, and called it
[3]Nehushtan.
4 5 He [a]trusted in the LORD God of Israel, [b]so that after him was none like
him among all the kings of Judah, nor
who were before him.
6 For he [a]held fast to the LORD; he did
not depart from following Him, but
kept His commandments, which the
LORD had commanded Moses.
7 The LORD [a]was with him; he [b]pros-
pered wherever he went. And he [c]re-
belled against the king of Assyria
and did not serve him.
8 [a]He [1]subdued the Philistines, as far
as Gaza and its territory, [b]from watchtower to fortified city.
9 Now [a]it came to pass in the fourth
year of King Hezekiah, which *was* the
seventh year of Hoshea the son of Elah,
king of Israel, *that* Shalmaneser king
of Assyria came up against Samaria
and besieged it.

2 [a]Is. 38:5 [1]*Abijah*, 2 Chr. 29:1ff.
4 [a]2 Chr. 31:1 [b]Num. 21:5–9 [1]Places for pagan worship [2]Heb. *Asherah*, a Canaanite goddess [3]Lit. *Bronze Thing*, also similar to Heb. *nahash*, *serpent* *See WW at Ezek. 6:3.
5 [a]2 Kin. 19:10; [Job 13:15; Ps. 13:5] [b]2 Kin. 23:25
6 [a]Deut. 10:20; Josh. 23:8
7 [a][2 Chr. 15:2] [b]Gen. 39:2, 3; 1 Sam. 18:5, 14; Ps. 60:12 [c]2 Kin. 16:7
8 [a]1 Chr. 4:41; 2 Chr. 28:18; Is. 14:29 [b]2 Kin. 17:9 [1]Lit. *struck*
9 [a]2 Kin. 17:3
10 [a]2 Kin. 17:6
11 [a]2 Kin. 17:6; Hos. 1:4; Amos 4:2 [b]1 Chr. 5:26
12 [a]2 Kin. 17:7–18
13 [a]2 Chr. 32:1; Is. 36:1—39:8
15 [a]1 Kin. 15:18, 19; 2 Kin. 12:18; 16:8
16 [1]Lit. *them* *See WW at Hag. 2:15.

10 And at the end of three years they
took it. In the sixth year of Hezekiah,
that *is*, [a]the ninth year of Hoshea king
of Israel, Samaria was taken.
11 [a]Then the king of Assyria carried
Israel away captive to Assyria, and put
them [b]in Halah and by the Habor, the
River of Gozan, and in the cities of the
Medes,
12 because they [a]did not obey the
voice of the LORD their God, but transgressed His covenant *and* all that Moses the servant of the LORD had commanded; and they would neither hear
nor do *them*.
13 And [a]in the fourteenth year of King
Hezekiah, Sennacherib king of Assyria
came up against all the fortified cities
of Judah and took them.
14 Then Hezekiah king of Judah sent
to the king of Assyria at Lachish, saying, "I have done wrong; turn away
from me; whatever you impose on me
I will pay." And the king of Assyria
assessed Hezekiah king of Judah three
hundred talents of silver and thirty talents of gold.
15 So Hezekiah [a]gave *him* all the silver
that was found in the house of the LORD
and in the treasuries of the king's
house.
16 At that time Hezekiah stripped *the*
gold from the doors of the *temple of
the LORD, and *from* the pillars which
Hezekiah king of Judah had overlaid, and gave [1]it to the king of Assyria.

power instigating spiritual reforms on a wide scale. Hezekiah purged Judah of idolatry, as well as restoring and rededicating the temple.

18:1, 13 The comparison of these verses presents a difficult chronological problem. Hezekiah began to reign the **third year of Hoshea** (v. 1). Since Hoshea began to reign about 732 B.C., that would mean Hezekiah began to rule in 729 B.C. It would follow then that **the fourteenth year of King Hezekiah** (v. 13) would be about 710 B.C. However, the invasion of **Sennacherib** (v. 13) can be accurately dated at 701 B.C. The simplest solution to this knotty problem is that Hezekiah was a coregent with his father Ahaz from 729 to 715 B.C. Therefore, Hezekiah began the coregency "in the third year of Hoshea" (v. 1) at 729 B.C., but became sole monarch in 715 B.C. Fourteen years later (701 B.C.), Sennacherib invaded Judah.

18:4 See section 6 of Truth-In-Action at the end of 2 Kin.

18:5–7 See section 4 of Truth-In-Action at the end of 2 Kin.

18:13–37 **Sennacherib** assumed the Assyrian throne after Sargon II. He promptly attacked and pillaged Judah and imposed a weighty tribute on Hezekiah. Following the poor *example of his father* Ahaz (16:8), Hezekiah took treasures from the temple to give to the king of Assyria.

Assyrian Campaign Against Judah (701 B.C.). Sennacherib moved southward along the coastal plains to Lachish and camped against Jerusalem in 701 B.C.

Sennacherib Boasts Against the L*ORD*

17 Then the king of Assyria sent *the* [1]Tartan, *the* [2]Rabsaris, *and the* [3]Rabshakeh from Lachish, with a great army against Jerusalem, to King Hezekiah. And they went up and came to Jerusalem. When they had come up, they went and stood by the [a]aqueduct from the upper pool, [b]which *was* on the highway to the Fuller's Field.

18 And when they had called to the king, [a]Eliakim the son of Hilkiah, who *was* over the household, Shebna the [1]scribe, and Joah the son of Asaph, the recorder, came out to them.

19 Then *the* Rabshakeh said to them, "Say now to Hezekiah, 'Thus says the great king, the king of Assyria: [a]"What confidence *is* this in which you trust?

20 "You speak of *having* plans and power for war; but *they are* [1]mere words. And in whom do you trust, that you rebel against me?

21 [a]"Now look! You are trusting in the staff of this broken reed, Egypt, on which if a man leans, it will go into his hand and pierce it. So *is* Pharaoh king of Egypt to all who trust in him.

22 "But if you say to me, 'We trust in the LORD our God,' *is* it not He [a]whose [1]high places and whose altars Hezekiah has taken away, and said to Judah and Jerusalem, 'You shall worship before this altar in Jerusalem'?" '

23 "Now therefore, I urge you, give a pledge to my master the king of Assyria, and I will give you two thousand horses—if you are able on your part to put riders on them!

24 "How then will you repel one captain of the least of my master's servants, and put your trust in Egypt for chariots and horsemen?

25 "Have I now come up without the LORD against this place to destroy it? The LORD said to me, 'Go up against this land, and destroy it.' "

26 [a]Then Eliakim the son of Hilkiah, Shebna, and Joah said to *the* Rabshakeh, "Please speak to your servants in [b]Aramaic, for we understand *it;* and do not speak to us in [1]Hebrew in the hearing of the people who *are* on the wall."

27 But *the* Rabshakeh said to them, "Has my master sent me to your master and to you to speak these words, and not to the men who sit on the wall, who will eat and drink their own waste with you?"

28 Then *the* Rabshakeh stood and called out with a loud voice in [1]Hebrew, and spoke, saying, "Hear the word of the great king, the king of Assyria!

29 "Thus says the king: [a]'Do not let Hezekiah deceive you, for he shall not be able to deliver you from his hand;

30 'nor let Hezekiah make you trust in the LORD, saying, "The LORD will surely deliver us; this city shall not be given into the hand of the king of Assyria." '

31 "Do not listen to Hezekiah; for thus says the king of Assyria: 'Make *peace* with me [1]by a present and come out to me; and every one of you eat from his own [a]vine and every one from his own fig tree, and every one of you drink the waters of his own cistern;

32 'until I come and take you away to a land like your own land, [a]a land of grain and new wine, a land of bread and vineyards, a land of olive groves and honey, that you may *live and not die. But do not listen to Hezekiah, lest he persuade you, saying, "The LORD will deliver us."

33 [a]'Has any of the gods of the nations at all delivered its land from the hand of the king of Assyria?

34 'Where *are* the gods of [a]Hamath and Arpad? Where *are* the gods of Sepharvaim and Hena and [b]Ivah? Indeed, have they delivered Samaria from my hand?

35 'Who among all the gods of the lands have delivered their countries from my hand, [a]that the LORD should deliver Jerusalem from my hand?' "

36 But the people held their peace and answered him not a word; for the king's commandment was, "Do not answer him."

37 Then Eliakim the son of Hilkiah, who *was* over the household, Shebna the scribe, and Joah the son of Asaph, the recorder, came to Hezekiah [a]with *their* clothes torn, and told him the words of *the* Rabshakeh.

Isaiah Assures Deliverance

19 And [a]so it was, when King Hezekiah heard *it,* that he tore his clothes, covered himself with

17 [a]2 Kin. 20:20 [b]Is. 7:3 [1]A title, probably *Commander in Chief* [2]A title, probably *Chief Officer* [3]A title, probably *Chief of Staff* or *Governor*
18 [a]2 Kin. 19:2; Is. 22:20 [1]*secretary*
19 [a]2 Chr. 32:10; [Ps. 118:8, 9]
20 [1]Lit. *a word of the lips*
21 [a]Is. 30:2–7; Ezek. 29:6, 7
22 [a]2 Kin. 18:4; 2 Chr. 31:1; 32:12 [1]Places for pagan worship
26 [a]Is. 36:11—39:8 [b]Ezra 4:7; Dan. 2:4 [1]Lit. *Judean*
28 [1]Lit. *Judean*
29 [a]2 Chr. 32:15
31 [a]1 Kin. 4:20, 25 [1]By paying tribute
32 [a]Deut. 8:7–9; 11:12 *See WW at Hab. 2:4.
33 [a]2 Kin. 19:12; Is. 10:10, 11
34 [a]2 Kin. 19:13 [b]2 Kin. 17:24
35 [a]Dan. 3:15
37 [a]Is. 33:7

CHAPTER 19

1 [a]2 Kin. 18:13; 2 Chr. 32:20–22; Is. 37:1

18:26 Apparently Hezekiah's ambassadors knew the **Aramaic** language, though this was not the common language of the Jews. However, by the time of Christ, Aramaic was widely used by the Jewish people in Palestine.

19:1 Hezekiah's response to the invasion of Sennacherib was to turn wholeheartedly to the Lord. The tearing of clothes symbolized great grief. **Sackcloth** was coarse clothing made of goat's hair and was a symbol of despair.

[b]sackcloth, and went into the house of
the LORD.
2 Then he sent Eliakim, who *was* over
the household, Shebna the scribe, and
the elders of the priests, covered with
sackcloth, to Isaiah the prophet, the
son of Amoz.
3 And they said to him, "Thus says
Hezekiah: 'This day *is* a day of trouble,
and rebuke, and blasphemy; for the
children have come to birth, but *there
is* no strength to [1]bring them forth.
4 [a]'It may be that the LORD your God
will hear all the words of *the* Rabshakeh, whom his master the king of Assyria has sent to [b]reproach the living
God, and will [c]rebuke the words which
the LORD your God has heard. Therefore lift up *your* *prayer for the remnant that is left.' "
5 So the servants of King Hezekiah
came to Isaiah.
6 [a]And Isaiah said to them, "Thus you
shall say to your master, 'Thus says the
LORD: "Do not be [b]afraid of the words
which you have heard, with which the
[c]servants of the king of Assyria have
blasphemed Me.
7 "Surely I will send [a]a spirit upon
him, and he shall hear a rumor and return to his own land; and I will cause
him to fall by the sword in his own
land." ' "

Sennacherib's Threat and Hezekiah's Prayer

8 Then *the* Rabshakeh returned and
found the king of Assyria warring
against Libnah, for he heard that he
had departed [a]from Lachish.
9 And [a]the king heard concerning
Tirhakah king of Ethiopia, "Look, he
has come out to make war with you."
So he again sent messengers to Hezekiah, saying,
10 "Thus you shall speak to Hezekiah
king of Judah, saying: 'Do not let your
God [a]in whom you trust deceive you,
saying, "Jerusalem shall not be given
into the hand of the king of Assyria."
11 'Look! You have heard what the
kings of Assyria have done to all lands
by utterly destroying them; and shall
you be delivered?
12 [a]'Have the gods of the nations delivered those whom my fathers have destroyed, Gozan and Haran and Rezeph,
and the people of [b]Eden who *were* in
Telassar?
13 [a]'Where *is* the king of Hamath, the
king of Arpad, and the king of the city
of Sepharvaim, Hena, and Ivah?' "
14 [a]And Hezekiah received the letter
from the hand of the messengers, and
read it; and Hezekiah went up to the
house of the LORD, and spread it before
the LORD.
15 Then Hezekiah prayed before the
LORD, and said: "O LORD **God** of Israel,
the One [a]who dwells *between* the
cherubim, [b]You are God, You alone, of
all the kingdoms of the earth. You
have made heaven and earth.

> **WORD WEALTH**
>
> **19:15 God,** *'Elohim* (eh-loh-*heem*); Strong's #430: God; God in His fullness; also "gods," that is to say, the gods of the idolatrous nations. The word *'Elohim* appears more than 2,500 times in the OT. Its first occurrence is in the first verse of the Bible. The majority of times *'Elohim* occurs it refers to God the Creator, but sometimes it refers to heathen gods or idols. Most scholars believe that the root is *'el* or *'elah,* meaning "strong," "mighty." Christians have long maintained that *'Elohim,* which is a plural form in Hebrew, reveals that God has more than one part of His being. We call those distinct parts "the Father," "the Son," and "the Holy Spirit." Nevertheless, we have *one* God, not three gods.

16 [a]"Incline Your ear, O LORD, and
hear; [b]open Your eyes, O LORD, and
see; and hear the words of Sennacherib, [c]which he has sent to reproach
the living God.
17 "Truly, LORD, the kings of Assyria
have laid waste the nations and their
lands,
18 "and have cast their gods into the
fire; for they *were* [a]not gods, but
[b]the work of men's hands—wood and
stone. Therefore they destroyed them.
19 "Now therefore, O LORD our God, I
pray, save us from his hand, [a]that all
the kingdoms of the earth may [b]know
that You *are* the LORD God, You
alone."

1 [b]Ps. 69:11
3 [1]*give birth*
4 [a]2 Sam. 16:12 [b]2 Kin. 18:35 [c]Ps. 50:21 *See WW at 2 Chr. 6:20.
6 [a]Is. 37:6 [b][Ps. 112:7] [c]2 Kin. 18:17
7 [a]2 Kin. 19:35–37; Jer. 51:1
8 [a]2 Kin. 18:14, 17
9 [a]1 Sam. 23:27; Is. 37:9
10 [a]2 Kin. 18:5
12 [a]2 Kin. 18:33, 34 [b]Ezek. 27:23
13 [a]2 Kin. 18:34
14 [a]Is. 37:14
15 [a]Ex. 25:22; Ps. 80:1; Is. 37:16 [b][Is. 44:6]
16 [a]Ps. 31:2; Is. 37:17 [b]1 Kin. 8:29; 2 Chr. 6:40 [c]2 Kin. 19:4
18 [a][Is. 44:9–20; Jer. 10:3–5] [b]Ps. 115:4; Jer. 10:3; [Acts 17:29]
19 [a]Ps. 83:18 [b]1 Kin. 8:42, 43

19:2–5 The great prophet **Isaiah** ministered during these dark days when Jerusalem was under siege. It is also probable that Micah served and wrote his book at about this time.

19:6, 7 The actions of the Assyrians were directed, not only against Judah, but against her God. Therefore, Isaiah prophesies of a divine intervention that will bring deliverance to Judah.

19:8–19 **Hezekiah** is an excellent illustration of what a believer should do when threatened by an enemy. Hezekiah does not react to the threats of Sennacherib, but cries out to the Lord for help.

KINGDOM DYNAMICS

19:8–19 Physical Acts in Warfare Prayer, FAITH'S WARFARE. King Sennacherib wrote a letter suggesting that God could not stand against him. King Hezekiah, upon receiving the letter, took it and spread it out before the Lord in prayer (v. 14). This is one example where a physical act seems to parallel the establishing of spiritual authority in the invisible realm. In other words, a physical act becomes prophetically symbolic of a reality that impacts the invisible as action is being taken in the visible realm.

In Hezekiah's case, a physical act of trust—spreading his case (letter) before the Lord—established a foundation for faith upon which Hezekiah prayed. The king was convinced that God would hear his prayer, and the Lord sent an angel that night who destroyed 185,000 enemy troops (2 Kin. 19:35; Is. 37:14–20, 36).

Other physical acts of people recorded in Scripture include vocal praise and shouting (1 Sam. 4:5, 6; 1 Kin. 1:40), lifting hands and bowing heads (Neh. 8:6), dancing or leaping (Ps. 149:3; Luke 6:23), groaning in prayer (Rom. 8:26; Gal. 4:19), shaking or trembling (Acts 16:29; Heb. 12:21), intense weeping (Ezra 3:13; Lam. 1:16, 20) and many instances of prostration (Ezek. 1:26–28; Matt. 17:6; Acts 9:1–9; 10:9–14). Prompted by faith and motivated by a genuine intensity of prayer-passion, these are more than superstitious actions. They address the invisible as real—and gain victories.

(Acts 4:31–34/James 5:13–18) D.E.

The Word of the LORD *Concerning Sennacherib*

20 Then Isaiah the son of Amoz sent to Hezekiah, saying, "Thus says the LORD God of Israel: [a]'Because you have prayed to Me against Sennacherib king of Assyria, [b]I have heard.'
21 "This *is* the word which the LORD has spoken concerning him:

'The *virgin, [a]the daughter of
Zion,
Has despised you, laughed you to
scorn;
The daughter of Jerusalem
[b]Has shaken *her* head behind your
back!

22 'Whom have you reproached and
blasphemed?
Against whom have you raised
your voice,
And lifted up your eyes on high?
Against [a]the Holy *One* of Israel.
23 [a]By your messengers you have
reproached the Lord,
And said: [b]"By the multitude of
my chariots
I have come up to the height of
the mountains,
To the limits of Lebanon;
I will cut down its tall cedars
And its choice cypress trees;
I will enter the extremity of its
borders,
To its fruitful forest.
24 I have dug and drunk strange
water,
And with the soles of my feet I
have [a]dried up
All the brooks of defense."

25 'Did you not hear long ago
How [a]I made it,
From ancient times that I formed
it?
Now I have brought it to pass,
That [b]you should be
For crushing fortified cities *into*
heaps of ruins.
26 Therefore their inhabitants had
little power;
They were dismayed and
confounded;
They were *as* the grass of the field
And the green herb,
As [a]the grass on the housetops
And *grain* blighted before it is
grown.

27 'But [a]I know your dwelling place,
Your going out and your coming
in,
And your rage against Me.
28 Because your rage against Me
and your tumult
Have come up to My ears,
Therefore [a]I will put My hook in
your nose
And My bridle in your lips,
And I will turn you back
[b]By the way which you came.

29 'This *shall be* a [a]sign to you:

You shall eat this year such as
grows [1]of itself,
And in the second year what
springs from the same;
Also in the third year sow and
reap,
Plant vineyards and eat the fruit
of them.
30 [a]And the remnant who have
escaped of the house of Judah
Shall again take root downward,
And bear fruit upward.
31 For out of Jerusalem shall go a
remnant,

20 [a]Is. 37:21 [b]2 Kin. 20:5; Ps. 65:2 **21** [a]Jer. 14:17; Lam. 2:13 [b]Ps. 22:7, 8 *See WW at Ps. 45:14. **22** [a]Jer. 51:5 **23** [a]2 Kin. 18:17 [b]Ps. 20:7

24 [a]Is. 19:6 **25** [a][Is. 45:7] [b]Is. 10:5, 6 **26** [a]Ps. 129:6 **27** [a]Ps. 139:1–3; Is. 37:28 **28** [a]Job 41:2; Ezek. 29:4; 38:4; Amos 4:2 [b]2 Kin. 19:33, 36 **29** [a]Ex. 3:12; 1 Sam. 2:34; 2 Kin. 20:8, 9; Is. 7:11–14; Luke 2:12 [1]Without cultivation **30** [a]2 Kin. 19:4; 2 Chr. 32:22, 23

And those who escape from
Mount Zion.
[a]The zeal of the LORD [1]of hosts will
do this.'

32 "Therefore thus says the LORD concerning the king of Assyria:

'He shall [a]not come into this city,
Nor shoot an arrow there,
Nor come before it with shield,
Nor build a siege mound against
it.
33 By the way that he came,
By the same shall he return;
And he shall not come into this
city,'
Says the LORD.
34 'For [a]I will [b]defend this city, to
save it
For My own sake and [c]for My
servant David's sake.' "

Sennacherib's Defeat and Death

35 And [a]it came to pass on a certain
night that the [1]angel of the LORD went
out, and killed in the camp of the Assyrians one hundred and eighty-five
thousand; and when *people* arose
early in the morning, there were the
corpses—all dead.
36 So Sennacherib king of Assyria departed and went away, returned *home*,
and remained at [a]Nineveh.
37 Now it came to pass, as he was worshiping in the temple of Nisroch his
god, that his sons [a]Adrammelech and
Sharezer [b]struck him down with the
sword; and they escaped into the land
of Ararat. Then [c]Esarhaddon his son
reigned in his place.

Hezekiah's Life Extended

20 In [a]those days Hezekiah was
sick and near death. And Isaiah
the prophet, the son of Amoz, went to
him and said to him, "Thus says the
LORD: 'Set your house in order, for you
shall die, and not live.' "
2 Then he turned his face toward the
wall, and prayed to the LORD, saying,
3 [a]"Remember now, O LORD, I pray,
how I have walked before You in truth
and with a loyal heart, and have done
what was good in Your sight." And
Hezekiah wept bitterly.
4 And it happened, before Isaiah had
gone out into the middle court, that the
word of the LORD came to him, saying,
5 "Return and tell Hezekiah [a]the
leader of My people, 'Thus says the
LORD, the God of David your father:
[b]"I have heard your prayer, I have seen
[c]your tears; surely I will *heal you. On
the third day you shall go up to the
house of the LORD.
6 "And I will add to your days fifteen
years. I will deliver you and this city
from the hand of the king of Assyria;
and [a]I will defend this city for My own
sake, and for the sake of My servant
David." ' "
7 Then [a]Isaiah said, "Take a lump of
figs." So they took and laid *it* on the
boil, and he recovered.
8 And Hezekiah said to Isaiah,
[a]"What *is* the sign that the LORD will
heal me, and that I shall go up to the
house of the LORD the third day?"
9 Then Isaiah said, [a]"This is the sign
to you from the LORD, that the LORD
will do the thing which He has spoken:
shall the shadow go forward ten *degrees or go backward ten degrees?"
10 And Hezekiah answered, "It is an
easy thing for the shadow to go down
ten [1]degrees; no, but let the shadow go
backward ten degrees."
11 So Isaiah the prophet cried out to
the LORD, and [a]He brought the shadow
ten [1]degrees backward, by which it had
gone down on the sundial of Ahaz.

31 [a]2 Kin. 25:26; Is. 9:7 [1]So with many Heb. mss. and ancient vss. (cf. Is. 37:32); MT omits *of hosts*
32 [a]Is. 8:7–10
34 [a]2 Kin. 20:6; 2 Chr. 32:21 [b]Is. 31:5 [c]1 Kin. 11:12, 13
35 [a]Ex. 12:29; Is. 10:12–19; 37:36; Hos. 1:7 [1]Or *Angel*
36 [a]Gen. 10:11
37 [a]2 Kin. 17:31 [b]2 Kin. 19:7; 2 Chr. 32:21 [c]Ezra 4:2

CHAPTER 20

1 [a]2 Kin. 18:13; 2 Chr. 32:24; Is. 38:1–22
3 [a]2 Kin. 18:3–6; Neh. 13:22
5 [a]1 Sam. 9:16; 10:1 [b]2 Kin. 19:20; Ps. 65:2 [c]Ps. 39:12; 56:8 *See WW at Ex. 15:26.
6 [a]2 Kin. 19:34; 2 Chr. 32:21
7 [a]Is. 38:21
8 [a]Judg. 6:17, 37, 39; Is. 7:11, 14; 38:22
9 [a]Num. 23:19; Is. 38:7, 8 *See WW at Amos 9:6.
10 [1]Lit. *steps*
11 [a]Josh. 10:12–14; Is. 38:8 [1]Lit. *steps*

KINGDOM DYNAMICS

20:1–11 Healing by Miracle or Medicine? DIVINE HEALING. This story of Hezekiah's miraculous healing begins with his being informed by the prophet Isaiah that he will die of his illness. He immediately begins to pray and seek God earnestly, not accepting the fate of death. God's addition of 15 years to his life suggests that prayer in the face of terminal illness is never inappropriate. But Isaiah also directs Hezekiah to apply a poultice

19:35, 36 The deliverance prophesied by Isaiah came in the form of a death **angel** who killed 185,000 Assyrian soldiers.

19:37 Sennacherib was murdered as he worshiped **Nisroch,** an Assyrian god who was depicted on Assyrian monuments as part man and part eagle.

20:1–7 Hezekiah's illness and recovery is a powerful picture of how God responds to the urgent cry of His servants. Persistent prayer and simple obedience resulted in Hezekiah's restoration.

20:8–11 A most unusual and miraculous **sign** was given to **Hezekiah** to assure him of his recovery. A stairway, which acted as a sundial, had been constructed during the reign of **Ahaz.** As evidence that Hezekiah would be healed, God caused **the shadow** on this sundial to **go backward ten degrees** (10 steps). Some have suggested that this miracle somehow compensated for Joshua's long day (Josh. 10:12–14).

of figs to his boil. Some scholars point to the figs as a medical prescription, and attribute the healing power to the poultice. The Bible does not condemn resorting to medical remedies; but, in this case, to think that such a poultice, by itself, could cure a terminal illness seems absurd. God is the Author of all healing benefit, however; and the application of the poultice appears to suggest that human medical aid is never inappropriate either. God alone can heal: He does so by miracle means, by natural means, and by human means. None should be demeaned as unworthy. However, this text clearly shows that Hezekiah's deliverance from death came from God, not man. (See James 5:14–16.)
(2 Kin. 5:1–15/Job 42:10–13) N.V.

The Babylonian Envoys

12 [a]At that time [1]Berodach-Baladan
the son of Baladan, king of Babylon,
sent letters and a present to Hezekiah,
for he heard that Hezekiah had been
sick.
13 And [a]Hezekiah was attentive to
them, and showed them all the house
of his treasures—the silver and gold,
the spices and precious ointment, and
[1]all [2]his armory—all that was found
among his treasures. There was nothing
in his house or in all his dominion
that Hezekiah did not show them.
14 Then Isaiah the prophet went to
King Hezekiah, and said to him, "What
did these men say, and from where did
they come to you?" So Hezekiah said,
"They came from a far country, from
Babylon."
15 And he said, "What have they seen
in your house?" So Hezekiah answered,
[a]"They have seen all that *is*
in my house; there is nothing among
my treasures that I have not shown
them."
16 Then Isaiah said to Hezekiah,
"Hear the word of the LORD:
17 'Behold, the days are coming when
all that *is* in your house, and what your
fathers have accumulated until this
day, [a]shall be carried to Babylon; nothing
shall be left,' says the LORD.
18 'And [a]they shall take away some of
your sons who will [1]descend from you,
whom you will beget; [b]and they shall
be [c]eunuchs in the palace of the king
of Babylon.'"
19 So Hezekiah said to Isaiah, [a]"The
word of the LORD which you have spoken
is good!" For he said, "Will there
not be peace and truth at least in my
days?"

Death of Hezekiah

20 [a]Now the rest of the acts of Hezekiah—all
his might, and how he
[b]made a [c]pool and a [1]tunnel and
[d]brought water into the city—*are* they
not written in the book of the chronicles
of the kings of Judah?
21 So [a]Hezekiah [1]rested with his fathers.
Then Manasseh his son reigned
in his place.

Manasseh Reigns in Judah

21 Manasseh [a]*was* twelve years
old when he became king, and
he reigned fifty-five years in Jerusalem.
His mother's name *was* Hephzibah.
2 And he did evil in the sight of the
LORD, [a]according to the abominations
of the nations whom the LORD had cast
out before the children of Israel.
3 For he rebuilt the [1]high places
[a]which Hezekiah his father had destroyed;
he raised up altars for Baal,
and made a [2]wooden image, [b]as Ahab
king of Israel had done; and he [c]worshiped
all [3]the host of heaven and
served them.
4 [a]He also built altars in the house of
the LORD, of which the LORD had said,
[b]"In Jerusalem I will put My name."
5 And he built altars for all the host
of heaven in the [a]two courts of the
house of the LORD.
6 [a]Also he made his son pass through **1**
the fire, practiced [b]soothsaying, used
witchcraft, and consulted spiritists and
mediums. He did much evil in the sight
of the LORD, to provoke *Him* to anger.
7 He even set a carved image of
[1]Asherah that he had made, in the
[2]house of which the LORD had said to

12 [a]2 Kin. 8:8, 9; 2 Chr. 32:31; Is. 39:1–8 [1]*Merodach-Baladan,* Is. 39:1
13 [a]2 Kin. 16:9; 2 Chr. 32:27, 31 [1]So with many Heb. mss., Syr., Tg.; MT omits *all* [2]Lit. *the house of his armor*
15 [a]2 Kin. 20:13
17 [a]2 Kin. 24:13; 25:13–15; 2 Chr. 36:10; Jer. 27:21, 22; 52:17
18 [a]2 Kin. 24:12; 2 Chr. 33:11 [b]Dan. 1:3–7 [c]Dan. 1:11, 18 [1]*be born from*
19 [a]1 Sam. 3:18
20 [a]2 Chr. 32:32 [b]Neh. 3:16 [c]2 Kin. 18:17; Is. 7:3 [d]2 Chr. 32:3, 30 [1]*aqueduct*
21 [a]2 Kin. 16:20; 2 Chr. 32:33 [1]Died and joined his ancestors

CHAPTER 21

1 [a]2 Chr. 33:1–9
2 [a]2 Kin. 16:3
3 [a]2 Kin. 18:4, 22 [b]1 Kin. 16:31–33 [c][Deut. 4:19; 17:2–5]; 2 Kin. 17:16; 23:5 [1]Places for pagan worship [2]Heb. *Asherah,* a Canaanite goddess [3]The gods of the Assyrians
4 [a]Jer. 7:30; 32:34 [b]1 Kin. 11:13
5 [a]1 Kin. 6:36; 7:12; 2 Kin. 23:12
6 [a][Lev. 18:21; 20:2]; 2 Kin. 16:3; 17:17 [b]Lev. 19:26, 31; [Deut. 18:10–14]; 2 Kin. 17:17
7 [1]A Canaanite goddess [2]Temple

20:12–19 When the Babylonians came on a goodwill visit to Hezekiah, he unwisely showed them all of his treasures. This prompted Isaiah to foretell the coming captivity of Judah by the Babylonians.
20:20 Two crews dug this **tunnel** through solid rock. One group started from the pool of Siloam, the other at the spring of Gihon. The tunnel was a remarkable feat of engineering and can be seen in modern Israel today.
21:1–18 As Judah's fourteenth regent, Hezekiah's son **Manasseh** was its most wicked king. He revived idol worship and desecrated the sacred things of the Lord. He sacrificed his son to Molech (v. 6) and practiced **soothsaying** (divination or foretelling the future). He even went so far as to put an idol of **Asherah** in the temple (v. 7). Being such an evil monarch, it was unfortunate that Manasseh's reign was the longest of all of Judah's rulers (55 years).
21:6 See section 1 of Truth-In-Action at the end of 2 Kin.

David and to Solomon his son, [a]“In
this house and in Jerusalem, which I
have chosen out of all the tribes of Israel, I will put My name forever;
8 [a]“and I will not make the feet of Israel wander anymore from the land
which I gave their fathers—only if they
are careful to do according to all that
I have commanded them, and according to all the law that My servant Moses commanded them.”
9 But they paid no attention, and Manasseh [a]seduced them to do more evil
than the nations whom the LORD had
destroyed before the children of Israel.
10 And the LORD spoke [a]by His servants the prophets, saying,
11 [a]“Because Manasseh king of Judah
has done these abominations ([b]he has
acted more wickedly than all the
[c]Amorites who *were* before him, and
[d]has also made Judah sin with his
idols),
12 “therefore thus says the LORD God
of Israel: ‘Behold, *I* am bringing *such*
calamity upon Jerusalem and Judah,
that whoever hears of it, both [a]his ears
will tingle.
13 ‘And I will stretch over Jerusalem
[a]the measuring line of Samaria and the
plummet of the house of Ahab; [b]I will
wipe Jerusalem as *one* wipes a dish,
wiping *it* and turning *it* upside down.
14 ‘So I will forsake the [a]remnant of
My inheritance and deliver them into
the hand of their enemies; and they
shall become victims of plunder to all
their enemies,
15 ‘because they have done evil in My
sight, and have provoked Me to anger
since the day their fathers came out of
Egypt, even to this day.’ ”
16 [a]Moreover Manasseh shed very
much innocent blood, till he had filled
Jerusalem from one end to another, besides his sin by which he made Judah
sin, in doing evil in the sight of the
LORD.
17 Now [a]the rest of the acts of [b]Manas-
seh—all that he did, and the sin that
he committed—*are* they not written in
the book of the chronicles of the kings
of Judah?
18 So [a]Manasseh [1]rested with his fathers, and was buried in the garden of
his own house, in the garden of Uzza.
Then his son Amon reigned in his
place.

Amon’s Reign and Death

19 [a]Amon *was* twenty-two years old
when he became king, and he reigned
two years in Jerusalem. His mother’s
name *was* Meshullemeth the daughter
of Haruz of Jotbah.
20 And he did evil in the sight of the
LORD, [a]as his father Manasseh had
done.
21 So he walked in all the ways that
his father had walked; and he served
the idols that his father had served, and
worshiped them.
22 He [a]forsook the LORD God of his fathers, and did not walk in the way of
the LORD.
23 [a]Then the servants of Amon [b]con-
spired against him, and killed the king
in his own house.
24 But the people of the land [a]executed
all those who had conspired against
King Amon. Then the people of the
land made his son Josiah king in his
place.
25 Now the rest of the acts of Amon
which he did, *are* they not written in
the book of the chronicles of the kings
of Judah?
26 And he was buried in his tomb in
the garden of Uzza. Then Josiah his
son reigned in his place.

Josiah Reigns in Judah

22 Josiah [a]*was* eight years old
when he became king, and he
reigned thirty-one years in Jerusalem.
His mother’s name *was* Jedidah the
daughter of Adaiah of [b]Bozkath.
2 And he did *what was* right in the
sight of the LORD, and walked in all the
ways of his father David; he [a]did not
turn aside to the right hand or to the
left.

Hilkiah Finds the Book of the Law

3 [a]Now it came to pass, in the eighteenth year of King Josiah, *that* the
king sent Shaphan the scribe, the son
of Azaliah, the son of Meshullam, to
the house of the LORD, saying:
4 “Go up to Hilkiah the high priest,

7 [a]2 Sam. 7:13; 1 Kin. 8:29; 9:3; 2 Kin. 23:27; 2 Chr. 7:12, 16; Jer. 32:34
8 [a]2 Sam. 7:10; [2 Kin. 18:11, 12]
9 [a][Prov. 29:12]
10 [a]2 Kin. 17:13
11 [a]2 Kin. 23:26, 27; 24:3, 4 [b]1 Kin. 21:26 [c]Gen. 15:16 [d]2 Kin. 21:9
12 [a]1 Sam. 3:11; Jer. 19:3
13 [a]Lam. 2:8; Amos 7:7, 8 [b]2 Kin. 22:16–19; 25:4–11
14 [a]Jer. 6:9
16 [a]2 Kin. 24:4
17 [a]2 Chr. 33:11–19 [b]2 Kin. 20:21
18 [a]2 Chr. 33:20 [1]Died and joined his ancestors
19 [a]2 Chr. 33:21–23
20 [a]2 Kin. 21:2–6, 11, 16
22 [a]Judg. 2:12, 13; 1 Kin. 11:33; 1 Chr. 28:9
23 [a]1 Chr. 3:14; 2 Chr. 33:24, 25; Matt. 1:10 [b]2 Kin. 12:20; 14:19
24 [a]2 Kin. 14:5

CHAPTER 22

1 [a]1 Kin. 13:2; 2 Chr. 34:1 [b]Josh. 15:39
2 [a]Deut. 5:32; Josh. 1:7
3 [a]2 Chr. 34:8

21:19–26 Amon was the fifteenth ruler of Judah. He was wicked like his father Manasseh; and after reigning only two years, he was murdered by his servants.

22:1, 2 Judah was blessed with a last great revival under its sixteenth ruler, **Josiah.**

22:3–7 There are some interesting parallels between **Josiah** and Jehoash, Judah’s eighth king. Josiah, like Jehoash, assumed the throne at a young age (eight years old), and proceeded to establish a plan to restore the temple. Like Jehoash, who had the help of the priest Jehoiada, Josiah had the assistance of the priest **Hilkiah.**

that he may count the money which has been [a]brought into the house of the LORD, which [b]the doorkeepers have gathered from the people.
5 "And let them [a]deliver it into the hand of those doing the work, who are the overseers in the house of the LORD; let them give it to those who *are* in the house of the LORD doing the work, to repair the damages of the house—
6 "to carpenters and builders and masons—and to buy timber and hewn stone to repair the house.
7 "However [a]there need be no accounting made with them of the money delivered into their hand, because they deal faithfully."
8 Then Hilkiah the high priest said to Shaphan the scribe, [a]"I have found the Book of the Law in the house of the LORD." And Hilkiah gave the book to Shaphan, and he read it.
9 So Shaphan the scribe went to the king, bringing the king word, saying, "Your servants have [1]gathered the money that was found in the house, and have delivered it into the hand of those who do the work, who oversee the house of the LORD."
10 Then Shaphan the scribe showed the king, saying, "Hilkiah the priest has given me a book." And Shaphan read it before the king.
11 Now it happened, when the king heard the words of the Book of the Law, that he tore his clothes.
12 Then the king commanded Hilkiah the priest, [a]Ahikam the son of Shaphan, [1]Achbor the son of Michaiah, Shaphan the scribe, and Asaiah a servant of the king, saying,
13 "Go, inquire of the LORD for me, for the people and for all Judah, concerning the words of this book that has been found; for great *is* [a]the wrath of the LORD that is aroused against us, because our fathers have not obeyed the words of this book, to do according to all that is written concerning us."
14 So Hilkiah the priest, Ahikam, Achbor, Shaphan, and Asaiah went to Huldah the prophetess, the wife of Shallum the son of [a]Tikvah, the son of Harhas, keeper of the wardrobe. (She dwelt in Jerusalem in the Second Quarter.) And they spoke with her.
15 Then she said to them, "Thus says the LORD God of Israel, 'Tell the man who sent you to Me,
16 "Thus says the LORD: 'Behold, [a]I will bring calamity on this place and on its inhabitants—all the words of the book which the king of Judah has read—
17 [a]'because they have forsaken Me and burned incense to other gods, that they might provoke Me to anger with all the works of their hands. Therefore My wrath shall be aroused against this place and shall not be quenched.' " '
18 "But as for [a]the king of Judah, who sent you to inquire of the LORD, in this manner you shall speak to him, 'Thus says the LORD God of Israel: "*Concerning* the words which you have heard—
19 "because your [a]heart was tender, and you [b]humbled yourself before the LORD when you heard what I spoke against this place and against its inhabitants, that they would become [c]a desolation and [d]a curse, and you tore your clothes and wept before Me, I also have heard *you*," says the LORD.
20 "Surely, therefore, I will [1]gather you to your fathers, and you [a]shall [2]be gathered to your grave in peace; and your eyes shall not see all the calamity which I will bring on this place." ' " So they brought back word to the king.

4 [a]2 Kin. 12:4 [b]2 Kin. 12:9, 10
5 [a]2 Kin. 12:11–14
7 [a]2 Kin. 12:15; [1 Cor. 4:2]
8 [a]Deut. 31:24–26; 2 Chr. 34:14
9 [1]Lit. *poured out*
12 [a]2 Kin. 25:22; Jer. 26:24 [1]*Abdon the son of Micah,* 2 Chr. 34:20
13 [a][Deut. 29:23–28; 31:17, 18]
14 [a]2 Chr. 34:22
16 [a]Deut. 29:27; [Dan. 9:11–14]
17 [a]Deut. 29:25–27; 2 Kin. 21:22
18 [a]2 Chr. 34:26
19 [a]1 Sam. 24:5; [Ps. 51:17; Is. 57:15] [b]Ex. 10:3; 1 Kin. 21:29; [2 Chr. 7:14] [c]Lev. 26:31, 32 [d]Jer. 26:6; 44:22
20 [a]2 Kin. 23:30; [Ps. 37:37; Is. 57:1, 2] [1]Cause you to join your ancestors in death [2]Die a natural death

KINGDOM DYNAMICS

22:3–20 The Woman and Today's Prophetic Possibilities (Huldah), WOMEN. The name "Huldah" is derived from the Hebrew root *cheled,* which means "to glide swiftly." Perhaps Huldah's name reflects her quickness of mind and her ability to swiftly and rightly discern the things of God. In any case, this woman was used by God in this fleeting moment in history to voice His judgment and His prophecy, and to spark one of the greatest national revivals in history. She is a case study of the character and the potential of a woman who today will receive the Holy Spirit's fullness and step (*cont. on next page*)

22:8–10 In the process of repairing the temple, **Hilkiah** discovered the **Book of the Law,** and **Shaphan the scribe** read it before King Josiah. From the reforms of Josiah, it is evident that this book contained much of the contents of the Book of Deuteronomy.

22:11–20 Josiah's reaction to the reading of the Book of the Law was to repent immediately and seek the Lord's will for direction. He was assisted in this pursuit by the prophetess Huldah. Because of Josiah's humble response, God would give the nation peace during the reign of Josiah. Yet the nation of Judah would still experience God's judgment for their prolonged apostasy (see 23:26, 27).

22:14 The prophets Jeremiah (Jer. 1:2), Zephaniah (Zeph. 1:1), and perhaps Nahum and Habakkuk, were ministering in and around Jerusalem at this time.

(cont. from preceding page)
through whatever open door God provides. It is worth observing how Hilkiah the high priest and Shaphan the scribe sought out Huldah for God's word of wisdom (v. 14). Clearly, she had the complete respect and confidence of these men, a lesson in the truth that spiritual influence flows from a spiritual life-style, not merely from the presence of spiritual gifts. Acts 2:17, 18 promises that the church age allows for a proliferation of the Holy Spirit's anointing upon women. Let Huldah's example of respectful, trust-begetting, forthright living teach the grounds for wise and effective spiritual ministry.
(Ruth 1:1—4:4/Esth. 4:1) F.L.

Josiah Restores True Worship

23 Now [a]the king sent them to
gather all the elders of Judah
and Jerusalem to him.
2 The king went up to the house of
the LORD with all the men of Judah,
and with him all the inhabitants of Jerusalem—the priests and the prophets
and all the people, both small and
great. And he [a]read in their hearing
all the words of the Book of the Covenant [b]which had been found in the
house of the LORD.
3 Then the king [a]stood by a pillar and
made a [b]covenant before the LORD, to
follow the LORD and to keep His commandments and His testimonies and
His statutes, with all *his* heart and all
his soul, to perform the words of this
covenant that were written in this
book. And all the people took a stand
for the covenant.
4 And the king commanded Hilkiah
the high priest, the [a]priests of the second order, and the doorkeepers, to
bring [b]out of the temple of the LORD
all the articles that were made for Baal,
for [1]Asherah, and for all [2]the host of
heaven; and he burned them outside
Jerusalem in the fields of Kidron, and
carried their ashes to Bethel.

CHAPTER 23
1 [a]2 Sam. 19:11; 2 Chr. 34:29, 30
2 [a]Deut. 31:10–13 [b]2 Kin. 22:8
3 [a]2 Kin. 11:14 [b]2 Kin. 11:17
4 [a]2 Kin. 25:18; Jer. 52:24 [b]2 Kin. 21:3–7 [1]A Canaanite goddess [2]The gods of the Assyrians
5 [a]2 Kin. 21:3 [1]Of the Zodiac
6 [a]2 Kin. 21:7 [b]Ex. 32:20 [c]2 Chr. 34:4 [1]Heb. *Asherah,* a Canaanite goddess
7 [a]1 Kin. 14:24; 15:12 [b]Ex. 35:25, 26; Ezek. 16:16 [c]Ex. 38:8 [1]Lit. *houses* [2]Heb. *qedeshim,* those practicing sodomy and prostitution in religious rituals
8 [a]Josh. 21:17; 1 Kin. 15:22
9 [a][Ezek. 44:10–14] [b]1 Sam. 2:36
10 [a]Is. 30:33; Jer. 7:31, 32 [b]Josh. 15:8 [c][Lev. 18:21; Deut. 18:10]; Ezek. 23:37–39 [d]2 Kin. 21:6 [1]Kt. *Sons*
11 [1]*given*
12 [a]Jer. 19:13; Zeph. 1:5 [b]2 Kin. 21:5; 2 Chr. 33:5

5 Then he removed the idolatrous
priests whom the kings of Judah had
ordained to burn incense on the high
places in the cities of Judah and in the
places all around Jerusalem, and those
who burned incense to Baal, to the sun,
to the moon, to the [1]constellations, and
to [a]all the host of heaven.
6 And he brought out the [a]wooden[1]
image from the house of the LORD, to
the Brook Kidron outside Jerusalem,
burned it at the Brook Kidron and
ground *it* to [b]ashes, and threw its ashes
on [c]the graves of the common people.
7 Then he tore down the *ritual*
[1]booths [a]of the [2]perverted persons that
were in the house of the LORD, [b]where
the [c]women wove hangings for the
wooden image.
8 And he brought all the priests from
the cities of Judah, and defiled the high
places where the priests had burned incense, from [a]Geba to Beersheba; also
he broke down the high places at the
gates which *were* at the entrance of the
Gate of Joshua the governor of the city,
which *were* to the left of the city gate.
9 [a]Nevertheless the priests of the high
places did not come up to the altar of
the LORD in Jerusalem, [b]but they ate
unleavened bread among their brethren.
10 And he defiled [a]Topheth, which *is*
in [b]the Valley of the [1]Son of Hinnom,
[c]that no man might make his son or
his daughter [d]pass through the fire to
Molech.
11 Then he removed the horses that
the kings of Judah had [1]dedicated to
the sun, at the entrance to the house
of the LORD, by the chamber of Nathan-
Melech, the officer who *was* in the
court; and he burned the chariots of
the sun with fire.
12 The altars that *were* [a]on the roof,
the upper chamber of Ahaz, which the
kings of Judah had made, and the altars which [b]Manasseh had made in the
two courts of the house of the LORD,
the king broke down and pulverized

23:1–3 The first step in Josiah's reform was to call a national assembly to renew Judah's commitment to its covenant with the Lord.

23:4–14 Josiah's next step of reform was to eliminate idolatry. These verses graphically display the horror and degradation that were present in Judah. Idols in the temple (vv. 4–6), idolatrous priests (vv. 5, 8), the practice of sodomy and prostitution in the temple (v. 7), astrology (v. 5), and ritual sacrifices of children (v. 10) were only a part of the wickedness that was propagated by Manasseh and Ammon. Josiah promptly set out to destroy all of this. On **Baal** (v. 4), see note on 1 Kin. 16:31. On **Asherah** (v. 4), see note on 1 Kin. 18:19. **Topheth** (v. 10) was the site where children were sacrificed in the worship of **Molech.** See note on 1 Kin. 11:5. In their worship of the **sun,** they paraded horses with chariots (v. 11). The **altars that *were* on the roof** (v. 12) were used in astrological worship. See Jer. 19:13; 32:29. Because of their wickedness, the Mount of Olives had become known as the **Mount of Corruption** (v. 13). On **Ashtoreth** and **Milcom** (v. 13), see note on 1 Kin. 11:5–7. On **Chemosh** (v. 13), see note on 1 Kin. 11:5–7. Josiah **defiled** the high places with **bones of men** (v. 14), which were regarded as unclean and made the sites unsuitable for worship.

23:8, 9 Josiah brought back all of the Levitical **priests** who served at the **high places.** However, he only permitted them to eat the **unleavened bread** brought to the temple (Lev. 6:9, 10, 16) and did not allow them to serve at the **altar.**

there, and threw their dust into the
Brook Kidron.
13 Then the king defiled the [1]high
places that *were* east of Jerusalem,
which *were* on the [2]south of [3]the Mount
of Corruption, which [a]Solomon king
of Israel had built for Ashtoreth the
abomination of the Sidonians, for Chemosh the abomination of the Moabites,
and for Milcom the abomination of the
people of Ammon.
14 And he [a]broke in pieces the *sacred*
pillars and cut down the wooden images, and filled their places with the
bones of men.
15 Moreover the altar that *was* at
Bethel, *and* the [1]high place [a]which Jeroboam the son of Nebat, who made Israel sin, had made, both that altar and
the high place he broke down; and he
burned the high place *and* crushed *it*
to powder, and burned the wooden image.
16 As Josiah turned, he saw the tombs
that *were* there on the mountain. And
he sent and took the bones out of the
tombs and burned *them* on the altar,
and defiled it according to the [a]word
of the LORD which the man of God
proclaimed, who proclaimed these
words.
17 Then he said, "What gravestone *is*
this that I see?" So the men of the city
told him, "*It is* [a]the tomb of the man
of God who came from Judah and proclaimed these things which you have
done against the altar of Bethel."
18 And he said, "Let him alone; let no
one move his bones." So they let his
bones alone, with the bones of [a]the
prophet who came from Samaria.
19 Now Josiah also took away all the
[1]shrines of the [2]high places that *were*
[a]in the cities of Samaria, which the
kings of Israel had made to provoke
[3]the LORD to anger; and he did to them
according to all the deeds he had done
in Bethel.
20 [a]He [b]executed all the priests of the
[1]high places who *were* there, on the
altars, and [c]burned men's bones
on them; and he returned to Jerusalem.
21 Then the king commanded all the
people, saying, [a]"Keep the Passover to
the LORD your God, [b]as *it is* written in
this Book of the Covenant."
22 [a]Such a Passover surely had never
been held since the days of the judges
who *judged Israel, nor in all the days
of the kings of Israel and the kings of
Judah.
23 But in the eighteenth year of King
Josiah this Passover was held before
the LORD in Jerusalem.
24 Moreover Josiah put away those
who consulted mediums and spiritists,
the household gods and idols, all the
abominations that were seen in the
land of Judah and in Jerusalem, that
he might perform the words of [a]the law
which were written in the book [b]that
Hilkiah the priest found in the house
of the LORD.
25 [a]Now before him there was no king
like him, who turned to the LORD with
all his heart, with all his soul, and with
all his might, according to all the Law
of Moses; nor after him did *any* arise
like him.

Impending Judgment on Judah

26 Nevertheless the LORD did not turn
from the fierceness of His great wrath,
with which His anger was aroused
against Judah, [a]because of all the provocations with which Manasseh had
provoked Him.
27 And the LORD said, "I will also remove Judah from My sight, as [a]I have
removed Israel, and will cast off this
city Jerusalem which I have chosen,
and the house of which I said, [b]'My
name shall be there.'"

Josiah Dies in Battle

28 Now the rest of the acts of Josiah,
and all that he did, *are* they not written
in the book of the chronicles of the
kings of Judah?
29 [a]In his days Pharaoh Necho king of
Egypt went [1]to the aid of the king of
Assyria, to the River Euphrates; and
King Josiah went against him. And
Pharaoh Necho killed him at [b]Megiddo
when he [c]confronted him.
30 [a]Then his servants moved his body
in a chariot from Megiddo, brought
him to Jerusalem, and buried him in
his own tomb. And [b]the people of the
land took Jehoahaz the son of Josiah,
anointed him, and made him king in
his father's place.

13 [a]1 Kin. 11:5–7 [1]Places for pagan worship [2]Lit. *right of* [3]The Mount of Olives
14 [a][Ex. 23:24; Deut. 7:5–25]
15 [a]1 Kin. 12:28–33 [1]A place for pagan worship
16 [a]1 Kin. 13:2
17 [a]1 Kin. 13:1, 30, 31
18 [a]1 Kin. 13:11, 31
19 [a]2 Chr. 34:6, 7 [1]Lit. *houses* [2]Places for pagan worship [3]So with LXX, Syr., Vg.; MT, Tg. omit *the LORD*
20 [a]1 Kin. 13:2 [b][Ex. 22:20]; 1 Kin. 18:40; 2 Kin. 10:25; 11:18 [c]2 Chr. 34:5 [1]Places for pagan worship
21 [a]Num. 9:5; Josh. 5:10; 2 Chr. 35:1 [b]Ex. 12:3; Lev. 23:5; Num. 9:2; Deut. 16:2–8
22 [a]2 Chr. 35:18, 19
*See WW at Judg. 2:18.
24 [a][Lev. 19:31; 20:27]; Deut. 18:11 [b]2 Kin. 22:8
25 [a]2 Kin. 18:5
26 [a]2 Kin. 21:11, 12; 24:3, 4; Jer. 15:4
27 [a]2 Kin. 17:18, 20; 18:11; 21:13 [b]1 Kin. 8:29; 9:3; 2 Kin. 21:4, 7
29 [a]2 Chr. 35:20; Jer. 2:16; 46:2 [b]Judg. 5:19; Zech. 12:11 [c]2 Kin. 14:8 [1]Or *to attack,* Heb. *al* can mean *together with* or *against*
30 [a]2 Chr. 35:24; 2 Kin. 22:20 [b]2 Chr. 36:1–4

23:15–20 Josiah even desecrated Jeroboam's altar (v. 16), and then demolished it (v. 15). He also destroyed the pagan temples (v. 19) and executed the pagan priests (v. 20).
23:21–23 Josiah not only eradicated the bad, but he also established the good. He restored the **Passover** in a way that no other king in **Judah** or Israel had ever done.
23:28–30 Josiah was killed by **Pharaoh Necho** during a battle at **Megiddo** in 608 B.C.

The Reign and Captivity of Jehoahaz

31 [a]Jehoahaz *was* twenty-three years
old when he became king, and he
reigned three months in Jerusalem. His
mother's name *was* [b]Hamutal the
daughter of Jeremiah of Libnah.
32 And he did evil in the sight of the
LORD, according to all that his fathers
had done.
33 Now Pharaoh Necho put him in
prison [a]at Riblah in the land of Hamath, that he might not reign in Jerusalem; and he imposed on the land a tribute of one hundred talents of silver and
a talent of gold.
34 Then [a]Pharaoh Necho made Eliakim the son of Josiah king in place
of his father Josiah, and [b]changed his
name to [c]Jehoiakim. And *Pharaoh*
took Jehoahaz [d]and went to Egypt, and
[1]he died there.

Jehoiakim Reigns in Judah

35 So Jehoiakim gave [a]the silver and
gold to Pharaoh; but he taxed the land
to give money according to the command of Pharaoh; he exacted the silver
and gold from the people of the land,
from every one according to his assessment, to give *it* to Pharaoh Necho.
36 [a]Jehoiakim *was* twenty-five years
old when he became king, and he
reigned eleven years in Jerusalem. His
mother's name *was* Zebudah the
daughter of Pedaiah of Rumah.
37 And he did evil in the sight of the
LORD, according to all that his fathers
had done.

Judah Overrun by Enemies

24 In [a]his days Nebuchadnezzar
king of [b]Babylon came up, and
Jehoiakim became his vassal *for* three
years. Then he turned and rebelled
against him.
2 [a]And the LORD sent against him
raiding [1]bands of Chaldeans, bands of
Syrians, bands of Moabites, and bands
of the people of Ammon; He sent them
against Judah to destroy it, [b]according
to the word of the LORD which He had
spoken by His servants the prophets.
3 Surely at the commandment of the
LORD *this* came upon Judah, to remove
them from His sight [a]because of the
sins of Manasseh, according to all that
he had done,
4 [a]and also because of the innocent
blood that he had shed; for he had
filled Jerusalem with innocent blood,
which the LORD would not pardon.
5 Now the rest of the acts of Jehoiakim, and all that he did, *are* they not
written in the book of the chronicles
of the kings of Judah?
6 [a]So Jehoiakim rested with his fathers. Then Jehoiachin his son reigned
in his place.
7 And [a]the king of Egypt did not
come out of his land anymore, for
[b]the king of Babylon had taken all that
belonged to the king of Egypt from the
Brook of Egypt to the River Euphrates.

The Reign and Captivity of Jehoiachin

8 [a]Jehoiachin[1] *was* eighteen years old
when he became king, and he reigned
in Jerusalem three months. His
mother's name *was* Nehushta the
daughter of Elnathan of Jerusalem.
9 And he did evil in the sight of the
LORD, according to all that his father
had done.
10 [a]At that time the servants of Nebuchadnezzar king of Babylon came up
against Jerusalem, and the city [1]was
besieged.
11 And Nebuchadnezzar king of Babylon came against the city, as his servants were besieging it.
12 [a]Then Jehoiachin king of Judah, his
mother, his servants, his princes, and
his officers went out to the king of
Babylon; and the king of Babylon,
[b]in the eighth year of his reign, took
him prisoner.

31 [a]1 Chr. 3:15; Jer. 22:11 [b]2 Kin. 24:18
33 [a]2 Kin. 25:6; Jer. 52:27
34 [a]2 Chr. 36:4 [b]2 Kin. 24:17; Dan. 1:7 [c]Matt. 1:11 [d]Jer. 22:11, 12; Ezek. 19:3, 4 [1]*Jehoahaz*
35 [a]2 Kin. 23:33
36 [a]2 Chr. 36:5; Jer. 22:18, 19; 26:1

CHAPTER 24

1 [a]2 Chr. 36:6; Jer. 25:1, 9; Dan. 1:1 [b]2 Kin. 20:14
2 [a]Jer. 25:9; 32:28; 35:11; Ezek. 19:8 [b]2 Kin. 20:17; 21:12–14; 23:27 [1]*troops*
3 [a]2 Kin. 21:2, 11; 23:26
4 [a]2 Kin. 21:16
6 [a]2 Chr. 36:6, 8; Jer. 22:18, 19
7 [a]Jer. 37:5–7 [b]Jer. 46:2
8 [a]1 Chr. 3:16; 2 Chr. 36:9 [1]*Jeconiah,* 1 Chr. 3:16; Jer. 24:1; or *Coniah,* Jer. 22:24, 28
10 [a]Dan. 1:1 [1]Lit. *came into siege*
12 [a]Jer. 22:24–30; 24:1; 29:1, 2; Ezek. 17:12 [b]2 Chr. 36:10

23:31–34 Jehoahaz succeeded his father Josiah as Judah's seventeenth ruler. He was the wicked king described by Ezekiel (Ezek. 19:1–9), and he had ruled only 90 days when he was imprisoned by **Pharaoh Necho,** king of Egypt (vv. 29, 33). The **Jeremiah** mentioned in v. 31 was not the famous prophet Jeremiah.

23:34–37 The eighteenth ruler in Judah was **Jehoiakim** (the brother of Jehoahaz). His real name was **Eliakim** (v. 34), and he was only a puppet ruler appointed by **Pharaoh Necho.** He was as evil as his brother and imprisoned the prophet Jeremiah. See Jer. 22:18, 19; 26:20–23 on the reign of Jehoiakim.

24:1–7 During the reign of **Jehoiakim** control of Palestine passed from the Assyrian-Egyptian alliance to that of Babylon. Jeremiah records the decisive battle of Carchemish where Pharaoh Necho was defeated by Nebuchadnezzar of Babylon (Jer. 46:2), which is dated at 605–604 B.C. **Chaldeans** (v. 2) is a variant name for the Babylonians.

24:8–16 Jehoiachin, the son of Jehoiakim, was the nineteenth of Judah's rulers. He had reigned for only three months when **Nebuchadnezzar** and the Babylonians besieged Jerusalem, then took Jehoiachin and the royal family captive. Next, Nebuchadnezzar plundered the temple and the palace, and took many of the inhabitants of Jerusalem captive. The prophet Ezekiel was probably among those taken captive at this time. This incident is dated at 597 B.C. and was the beginning of the end for Judah.

The Captivity of Jerusalem

13 [a]And he carried out from there all
the treasures of the house of the LORD
and the treasures of the king's house,
and he [b]cut in pieces all the articles
of gold which Solomon king of Israel
had made in the temple of the LORD,
[c]as the LORD had said.
14 Also [a]he carried into captivity all
Jerusalem: all the captains and all the
mighty men of valor, [b]ten thousand
captives, and [c]all the craftsmen and
smiths. None remained except [d]the
poorest people of the land.
15 And [a]he carried Jehoiachin captive
to Babylon. The king's mother, the
king's wives, his officers, and the
mighty of the land he carried into captivity from Jerusalem to Babylon.
16 [a]All the valiant men, seven thousand, and craftsmen and smiths, one
thousand, all *who were* strong *and* fit
for war, these the king of Babylon
brought captive to Babylon.

Zedekiah Reigns in Judah

17 Then [a]the king of Babylon made
Mattaniah, [b]*Jehoiachin's*[1] uncle, king
in his place, and [c]changed his name
to Zedekiah.
18 [a]Zedekiah *was* twenty-one years
old when he became king, and
he reigned eleven years in Jerusalem.
His mother's name *was* [b]Hamutal
the daughter of Jeremiah of Libnah.
19 [a]He also did evil in the sight of the
LORD, according to all that Jehoiakim
had done.
20 For because of the anger of the
LORD *this* happened in Jerusalem and
Judah, that He finally cast them out
from His presence. [a]Then Zedekiah rebelled against the king of Babylon.

13 [a]2 Kin. 20:17; Is. 39:6 [b]Dan. 5:2, 3 [c]Jer. 20:5
14 [a]Is. 3:2, 3; Jer. 24:1 [b]2 Kin. 24:16; Jer. 52:28 [c]1 Sam. 13:19 [d]2 Kin. 25:12
15 [a]2 Chr. 36:10; Esth. 2:6; Jer. 22:24–28; Ezek. 17:12
16 [a]Jer. 52:28
17 [a]Jer. 37:1 [b]1 Chr. 3:15; 2 Chr. 36:10 [c]2 Chr. 36:4 [1]Lit. *his*
18 [a]2 Chr. 36:11; Jer. 52:1 [b]2 Kin. 23:31
19 [a]2 Chr. 36:12
20 [a]2 Chr. 36:13; Ezek. 17:15

CHAPTER 25

1 [a]2 Chr. 36:17; Jer. 6:6; 34:2; Ezek. 4:2; 24:1, 2; Hab. 1:6
3 [a]2 Kin. 6:24, 25; Is. 3:1; Jer. 39:2; Lam. 4:9, 10
4 [a]Jer. 39:2 [b]Jer. 39:4–7; Ezek. 12:12 [1]Lit. *he* [2]Or *Arabah*, the Jordan Valley

The Fall and Captivity of Judah

25 Now it came to pass [a]in the
ninth year of his reign, in the
tenth month, on the tenth *day* of the
month, *that* Nebuchadnezzar king of
Babylon and all his army came against
Jerusalem and encamped against it;
and they built a siege wall against it
all around.
2 So the city was besieged until the
eleventh year of King Zedekiah.
3 By the ninth *day* of the [a]*fourth*
month the famine had become so severe in the city that there was no food
for the people of the land.
4 Then [a]the city wall was broken
through, and all the men of war *fled*
at night by way of the gate between
two walls, which was by the king's garden, even though the Chaldeans *were*
still encamped all around against the
city. And [b]*the king*[1] went by way of
the [2]plain.
5 But the army of the Chaldeans pursued the king, and they overtook him

24:17–20 The last ruler of Judah was **Zedekiah.** Like Jehoahaz and Jehoiakim, he was the son of Josiah, making him ***Jehoiachin's* uncle.** His original name was **Mattaniah,** and he is remembered as a wicked ruler who was easily manipulated by others (Jer. 38:5, 24).
25:1–3 After three years of submission to the Babylonians, Zedekiah foolishly rebelled (24:20), resulting in Nebuchadnezzar's final siege of Jerusalem.
25:4–7 In 586 B.C. Jerusalem fell, and the southern kingdom of Judah was taken captive. Judah had 20 kings of the single dynasty of David, but only 8 of these were considered good. Zedekiah was deported, his sons were killed, and then his eyes were put out.

Nebuchadnezzar's Campaigns Against Judah (605–586 B.C.). From 605 B.C. to 586 B.C. Judah suffered repeated Babylonian invasions. The final blow came from the southern approach to Jerusalem.

in the plains of Jericho. All his army
was scattered from him.
6 So they took the king and brought
him up to the king of Babylon [a]at Riblah, and they pronounced judgment on
him.
7 Then they killed the sons of Zedekiah before his eyes, [a]put[1] out the eyes
of Zedekiah, bound him with bronze
fetters, and took him to Babylon.
8 And in the fifth month, [a]on the
seventh *day* of the month (which *was*
[b]the nineteenth year of King Nebuchadnezzar king of Babylon), [c]Nebu-
zaradan the captain of the guard, a servant of the king of Babylon, came to
Jerusalem.
9 [a]He burned the house of the LORD
[b]and the king's house; all the houses
of Jerusalem, that is, all the houses of
the great, [c]he burned with fire.
10 And all the army of the Chaldeans
who *were with* the captain of the guard
[a]broke down the walls of Jerusalem all
around.
11 Then Nebuzaradan the captain of
the guard carried away captive [a]the
rest of the people *who* remained in the
city and the defectors who had deserted to the king of Babylon, with the
rest of the multitude.
12 But the captain of the guard [a]left
some of the poor of the land as vinedressers and farmers.
13 [a]The bronze [b]pillars that *were* in
the house of the LORD, and [c]the carts
and [d]the bronze Sea that *were* in the
house of the LORD, the Chaldeans
broke in pieces, and [e]carried their
bronze to Babylon.
14 They also took away [a]the pots, the
shovels, the trimmers, the spoons, and
all the bronze utensils with which the
priests ministered.
15 The firepans and the basins, the
things of solid gold and solid silver, the
captain of the guard took away.
16 The two pillars, one Sea, and
the carts, which Solomon had made
for the house of the LORD, [a]the bronze
of all these articles was beyond measure.
17 [a]The height of one pillar *was* [1]eigh-
teen cubits, and the capital on it
was of bronze. The height of the capital was three cubits, and the network and pomegranates all around
the capital were all of bronze. The

6 [a]2 Kin. 23:33; Jer. 52:9
7 [a]Jer. 39:7; Ezek. 17:16 [1]*blinded*
8 [a]Jer. 52:12 [b]2 Kin. 24:12 [c]Jer. 39:9
9 [a]2 Kin. 25:13; 2 Chr. 36:19; Ps. 79:1; Jer. 7:14 [b]Jer. 39:8 [c]Jer. 17:27
10 [a]2 Kin. 14:13; Neh. 1:3
11 [a]Is. 1:9; Jer. 5:19; 39:9
12 [a]2 Kin. 24:14; Jer. 39:10; 40:7; 52:16
13 [a]Jer. 52:17 [b]1 Kin. 7:15 [c]1 Kin. 7:27 [d]1 Kin. 7:23 [e]2 Kin. 20:17; Jer. 27:19–22
14 [a]Ex. 27:3; 1 Kin. 7:45
16 [a]1 Kin. 7:47
17 [a]1 Kin. 7:15–22; Jer. 52:21 [1]About 27 feet
18 [a]Jer. 39:9–13; 52:12–16, 24 [b]1 Chr. 6:14; Ezra 7:1 [c]Jer. 21:1; 29:25, 29
19 [a]Esth. 1:14; Jer. 52:25 [1]Lit. *those seeing the king's face*
21 [a]Lev. 26:33; Deut. 28:36, 64; 2 Kin. 23:27
22 [a]2 Kin. 22:12 [b]Is. 1:9; Jer. 40:5
23 [a]Jer. 40:7–9 [1]*Jezaniah*, Jer. 40:8
25 [a]Jer. 41:1–3
26 [a]2 Kin. 19:31; Jer. 43:4–7

second pillar was the same, with a network.
18 [a]And the captain of the guard took
[b]Seraiah the chief priest, [c]Zephaniah
the second priest, and the three doorkeepers.
19 He also took out of the city an officer who had charge of the men of
war, [a]five men of [1]the king's close
associates who were found in the
city, the chief recruiting officer of the
army, who mustered the people of
the land, and sixty men of the people
of the land *who were* found in the
city.
20 So Nebuzaradan, captain of the
guard, took these and brought them to
the king of Babylon at Riblah.
21 Then the king of Babylon struck
them and put them to death at Riblah
in the land of Hamath. [a]Thus Judah
was carried away captive from its own
land.

Gedaliah Made Governor of Judah

22 Then he made Gedaliah the son of
[a]Ahikam, the son of Shaphan, governor over [b]the people who remained in
the land of Judah, whom Nebuchadnezzar king of Babylon had left.
23 Now when all the [a]captains of the
armies, they and *their* men, heard that
the king of Babylon had made Gedaliah governor, they came to Gedaliah
at Mizpah—Ishmael the son of Nethaniah, Johanan the son of Careah,
Seraiah the son of Tanhumeth the
Netophathite, and [1]Jaazaniah the
son of a Maachathite, they and their
men.
24 And Gedaliah took an oath before
them and their men, and said to them,
"Do not be afraid of the servants of
the Chaldeans. Dwell in the land and
serve the king of Babylon, and it shall
be well with you."
25 But [a]it happened in the seventh
month that Ishmael the son of Nethaniah, the son of Elishama, of the royal
family, came with ten men and struck
and killed Gedaliah, the Jews, as well
as the Chaldeans who were with him
at Mizpah.
26 And all the people, small and great,
and the captains of the armies, arose
[a]and went to Egypt; for they were
afraid of the Chaldeans.

25:8–21 The Babylonians burned Jerusalem (vv. 8–12), plundered and destroyed the temple (vv. 13–17), and executed Judah's leaders (vv. 18–21).

25:22–26 The poorest class of people remained in the land (v. 11), and Nebuchadnezzar appointed **Gedaliah** to govern Palestine. Gedaliah ruled efficiently for two months, but was then murdered by **Ishmael** (v. 25).

Jehoiachin Released from Prison

27 [a]Now it came to pass in the thirty-
seventh year of the captivity of Jehoiachin king of Judah, in the twelfth
month, on the twenty-seventh *day* of
the month, *that* [1]Evil-Merodach king
of Babylon, in the year that he began
to reign, [b]released Jehoiachin king of
Judah from prison.
28 He spoke kindly to him, and gave
him a more prominent seat than those
of the kings who *were* with him in Babylon.
29 So Jehoiachin changed from his
prison garments, and he [a]ate [1]bread
regularly before the king all the days
of his life.
30 And as for his [1]provisions, *there
was* a [2]regular ration given him by the
king, a portion for each day, all the
days of his life.

27 [a]2 Kin. 24:12, 15; Jer. 52:31–34 [b]Gen. 40:13, 20 [1]Lit. *Man of Marduk*
29 [a]2 Sam. 9:7 [1]Food
30 [1]Lit. *allowance* [2]Lit. *allowance*

25:27–30 In 562 B.C. **Evil-Merodach** succeeded Nebuchadnezzar as ruler of Babylon. "Evil" was a variant spelling for his name and does not necessarily imply that he was evil. In fact, he changed the Babylonian policy toward the kings of Judah and **released** King **Jehoiachin** in 560 B.C. Thus the Book of 2 Kings ends on a positive note of hope. It was because of God's mercy that the Jews were being favored and because of His kindness that they would eventually be allowed to return to their land (Ezra 1:1–4).

TRUTH-IN-ACTION through 2 KINGS

Letting the LIFE of the Holy Spirit Bring Faith's Works Alive in You!

Truth 2 Kings Teaches	Text	**Action** 2 Kings Invites
1 Steps to Holiness Holiness among God's people brings Him honor. Unholiness dishonors Him. Holiness has two equally important dimensions. We are set apart to God and separated from the world. Just as God cannot be glorified by those who are not fully His, neither can He be glorified by those who are of the world. Therefore, we must live in the world, but we must not live as being of the world. Be careful that a negative focus on external behavior does not blind us to the true nature of unholiness and allow us to be seduced by the world.	5:19–27	**Do not covet** the world's reward for your ministry. **Be wary** lest it become an occasion for sin and judgment for you.
	11:18	**Know** that true repentance involves rooting out anything that distracts from your worship of God. **Eliminate** any vestige of idolatry from your own life.
	17:7–15	**Understand** that God judges His people severely when they persist in the world's ways and standards rather than His. **Reject** any areas where world-mindedness has taken root in you.
	21:6	**Do not practice** abortion! **Reject** and **flee from** the occult!
2 Steps to Dynamic Devotion Hear again the recurring theme of how God wants our hearts to be fully devoted to Him. Even zeal with an undevoted heart does not please Him.	10:28–31	**Be zealous** for God with your whole heart. **Dedicate** your life to Him and to His purposes.
3 Key Lessons in Faith Faith is, in essence, taking God at His Word and His Word at face value. God has limitless supply of resources for all who trust in and obey Him. Fearing that we will not have enough in times of need insults the God who has revealed Himself as *Yahweh-Yireh*, The-Lord-Our-Provider.	4:1–7	**Believe** that God is able to supply your needs, even when you have no idea how. **Know** that God promises to keep His people alive in famine. This applies spiritually, too: God's spiritual resources for you are limitless, even during times of spiritual drought.
	4:43, 44	**Choose to believe** that you will always have enough resources to do the will of God.

Truth 2 Kings Teaches	Text	**Action** 2 Kings Invites
4 Keys to Wise Living The God who is our wisdom and gives freely of His wisdom to those who trust in Him is careful to teach us His ways. He who is wise will never turn from the clear counsel of wisdom in God's Word.	4:39–41 18:5–7	**Know the source** of any teaching you receive or pass on to others. **Always judge teachings** according to God's Word. **Follow the Lord,** and He will grant you spiritual success.
5 Keys to Relating to Authority Relating properly to God's delegated authority is a key to spiritual prosperity.	2:1–15 2:23–25	**Be loyal** to those to whom the Lord assigns you. **Understand** that the Lord will reward such loyalty. **Avoid mocking or criticizing** those God anoints for leadership and ministry. **Understand** that God watches over them to protect them.
6 Lessons for Leaders God places great value upon the leaders He places among His people and wants them to be effective and fruitful in their ministry. Effective leadership flows out of God's anointing. This is also true for those who serve with you under your care. Those in leadership must be careful not to take credit for something that has resulted from God's working in their ministry.	2:9 12:13–16 18:4	Leaders, **believe** that God has a greater anointing for your ministry. **Do not settle** for mediocre effectiveness in your ministry. Leaders, **trust** the Holy Spirit's working in those who serve with you. Leaders, **reject praise and honor God** for works He accomplishes through your ministry. **Teach** those you serve to do the same.

The First Book of the CHRONICLES

Author: Attributed to Ezra
Date: Probably Between 425 and 400 B.C.
Theme: Encouragement and Exhortation from Judah's Spiritual Heritage
Key Words: King, House, David, Jerusalem, Priest

Author First and 2 Chronicles were originally one book (see "Content" below). Since the identity of the author of this work is not stated in either 1 or 2 Chronicles, many have opted to refer to this unknown author simply as "the chronicler." However, Ezra is the most likely candidate for the authorship of Chronicles. The early Jewish tradition of the Talmud affirms that Ezra wrote 1 and 2 Chronicles. Also, the closing verses of 2 Chronicles (2 Chr. 36:22, 23) are repeated as the opening verses of Ezra (see Ezra 1:1–3). Not only does this add to the case for Ezra's authorship of 1 Chronicles, it also may be an indication that 1 and 2 Chronicles and Ezra were once a consecutive work. In addition, 1 and 2 Chronicles and Ezra have similar style, vocabulary, and contents. Ezra was a scribe as well as a priest, and played a significant role in the community of exiles who returned to Jerusalem. Though we cannot be certain, it is reasonable to assume that "the chronicler" was Ezra.

Date Though the precise date for 1 and 2 Chronicles cannot be established, it probably came into its final form sometime toward the end of the fifth century B.C. The last event recorded in the closing verses of 2 Chronicles is the decree of the Persian king Cyrus to allow the Jews to return to Judah. This is dated at 538 B.C. and gives the impression that Chronicles would have been composed shortly after this time. However, the latest person mentioned in 1 and 2 Chronicles is actually Anani of the eighth generation of King Jehoiachin (see 1 Chr. 3:24). Jehoiachin was deported to Babylon in 597 B.C. Depending on how these generations are measured (approximately twenty-five years), Anani's birth would have been sometime between 425 and 400 B.C. Therefore, the date for 1 and 2 Chronicles is between 425 and 400 B.C.

Background The Book of 1 Chronicles covers the period from Adam to the death of David around 971 B.C. This is a remarkable scope of time, since it embraces the same period covered in the first ten books of the Old Testament, Genesis through 2 Samuel. Without the genealogies in 1 Chronicles 1—9, 1 and 2 Chronicles cover roughly the same time period as 1 and 2 Kings. However, the specific background of 1 and 2 Chronicles is the period after the Exile. During this time, the ancient world was under the control of the powerful Persian Empire. All that remained of the glorious kingdom of David and Solomon was the tiny province of Judah. The Persians had replaced the monarchy with a provincial governor. Though God's people had been allowed to return to Jerusalem and rebuild the temple, their situation was far removed from the golden days of David and Solomon.

Occasion and Purpose The return of the exiles from Babylon necessitated the recording of the history of God's people, especially Judah. First Chronicles was written for the dual purpose of providing encouragement and exhortation to those who had returned to Jerusalem. The remnant that was left needed encouragement to keep their faith alive in the midst of difficulty, and they needed hope for the future. The emphasis of Chronicles on their spiritual heritage of David, Solomon, the temple, and the priesthood was a refreshing reminder that God was faithful and He would not forget His promises to David and to His people. Yet 1 Chronicles also served as a strong exhortation to motivate God's people to adhere to the Mosaic covenant and ritual, so that the tragedy of the past would not be repeated.

Comparison with Kings One may question the need for the books of 1 and 2 Chronicles, since the material has already been covered in 1 and 2 Kings and other Old Testament books. However, though the books are similar, they are by no means identical. In the same way that there are four accounts of the life of Christ in Matthew, Mark, Luke, and John, there are two accounts of the history of God's people. Though 1 and 2 Kings and 1 and 2 Chronicles are alike in content, they offer two different historical perspectives. While the Books of Kings were written to those in exile, the Books of Chronicles address the postexilic community. They were written for two different purposes. Compare the "Occasion and Purpose" section of this introduction with the same sections in the introductions to 1 and 2 Kings. Also, Kings and Chronicles have different political perspectives. While Kings embraces both kingdoms, Israel and Judah, Chronicles focuses only on Judah. Finally, Kings and Chronicles differ in their theological perspectives. Kings presents a prophetic outlook, while Chronicles operates from a priestly vantage point. However, Chronicles is like Kings in that it is not mere history, but rather theology in the form of a historical narrative. See Introductions to 1 and 2 Kings: Content.

Content In the original Hebrew Scriptures, 1 and 2 Chronicles formed one book, entitled "Events of the Days." It was divided and renamed "Things Passed Over" by the translators of the Greek Old Testament (the Septuagint, or LXX). The title "Chronicles" derives from Jerome. It is not a continuation of the history of God's people, but a duplication of and a supplement to 1 and 2 Samuel and 1 and 2 Kings.

The united work of 1 and 2 Chronicles can be divided into four main sections. First Chronicles gives genealogies (chs. 1—9) and outlines the reign of David (chs. 10—29). Second Chronicles sets forth the reign of Solomon (chs. 1—9) and traces the reigns of the twenty rulers of Judah (chs. 10—36).

The Book of 1 Chronicles has two main divisions. The first section is nine chapters of genealogies. The genealogies begin with Adam and proceed all the way through the Exile to those who returned to Jerusalem. This section is often passed over as unimportant. However, like the Gospels of Matthew and Luke, the genealogies form a foundation for the account that will follow. First Chronicles is weighted with genealogies to underscore the need for racial and religious purity. The genealogies are selectively compiled to highlight the line of David and the tribe of Levi.

The second part of 1 Chronicles (chs. 10—29) records the events and accomplishments in the life of King David. Chapter 10 serves as a prologue to summarize the reign and death of King Saul. In chapters 11 and 12 David becomes king and secures Jerusalem. The rest of the account of David focuses on the three significant aspects of his reign, namely the bringing of the ark of the covenant to Jerusalem (chs. 13—17), his military exploits (chs. 18—20), and the preparations for the building of the temple (chs. 21—27). The closing two chapters of 1 Chronicles record David's last days.

Personal Application While 1 and 2 Kings draw out the fact of human responsibility, showing that sin leads to defeat, 1 Chronicles accentuates the sovereign deliverance of God. The twin themes of encouragement and exhortation still ring true today. God has been faithful throughout all of history to deliver those who cry out to Him. Chronicles skillfully tells the story of how God was true to His word and kept the promises He had made to His people. This is a great source of encouragement for believers of all ages. God is a promise-making and promise-keeping God who is worthy to be trusted. He is still a God of hope, and His purposes will prevail in the lives of His people. However, 1 Chronicles also exhorts us to learn from the failure of God's people in the past, in order that we might not make the same mistakes (1 Cor. 10:11; Heb. 4:11).

Christ Revealed Christ is foreshadowed in 1 Chronicles in much the same way as He is in 1 Kings (see Introduction to 1 Kings: Christ Revealed). However, in 1 Chronicles, many have seen an allusion to Christ in reference to the temple. First Chronicles 21 (also 2 Sam. 24) explains that as a consequence for sin, a death plague had broken out against Israel. David buys a piece of property from Ornan on which to make a sacrifice that stops the plague. This site on Mount Moriah was the very place where Solomon would build the temple (2 Chr. 3:1). It is possible that this was the very mountain where Abraham was asked to sacrifice his son Isaac (Gen. 22:2). In the New Testament, three times Paul refers to believers as the "temple of God" (1 Cor. 3:16, 17; 6:19; Eph. 2:19–22). It is Christ who has purchased the ground for this spiritual temple. It was His sacrifice that delivered us from death (Rom. 5:12–18; 7:24, 25; 1 John 3:14).

The Holy Spirit at Work There are two clear references to the Holy Spirit in 1 Chronicles. The first is in 12:18, where "the Spirit" came upon or clothed Amasai and enabled him to give an inspired utterance. See Introductions to 1 and 2 Kings: The Holy Spirit at Work. They describe the Holy Spirit's inspiring others to prophesy during the kingdom period. The second reference to the Holy Spirit in 1 Chronicles is in 28:12, which explains that it was through the ministry of "the Spirit" that the plans of the temple were revealed to David.

Outline of 1 Chronicles

I. The roots of God's people	1:1—9:44	II. The reign of King David	10:1—29:30
A. The heritage of the sons of Jacob	1:1—2:2	A. David's affirmation as king	10:1—12:40
B. The heritage of David's line in Judah	2:3—3:24	B. David's acquisition of the ark	13:1—17:27
C. The heritage of the Twelve Tribes	4:1—8:40	C. David's military advances	18:1—20:8
D. The heritage of the remnant	9:1–34	D. David's arrangements for the temple	21:1—27:34
E. The heritage of King Saul in Benjamin	9:35–44	E. David's last announcements	28:1—29:30

The Family of Adam—Seth to Abraham

ADAM,[a] [b]Seth, Enosh,
2 Cainan, Mahalalel, Jared,
3 Enoch, Methuselah, Lamech,
4 [a]Noah,[1] Shem, Ham, and Japheth.
5 [a]The sons of Japheth *were* Gomer,
Magog, Madai, Javan, Tubal, Meshech,
and Tiras.
6 The sons of Gomer *were* Ashkenaz,
[1]Diphath, and Togarmah.
7 The sons of Javan *were* Elishah,
[1]Tarshishah, Kittim, and [2]Rodanim.
8 [a]The sons of Ham *were* Cush,
Mizraim, Put, and Canaan.
9 The sons of Cush *were* Seba, Havilah, [1]Sabta, [2]Raama, and Sabtecha.
The sons of Raama *were* Sheba and
Dedan.
10 Cush [a]begot Nimrod; he began to
be a mighty one on the earth.
11 Mizraim begot Ludim, Anamim, Le-
habim, Naphtuhim,
12 Pathrusim, Casluhim (from whom
came the Philistines and the [a]Caphto-
rim).
13 [a]Canaan begot Sidon, his firstborn,
and Heth;
14 the Jebusite, the Amorite, and the
Girgashite;
15 the Hivite, the Arkite, and the Si-
nite;
16 the Arvadite, the Zemarite, and the
Hamathite.
17 The sons of [a]Shem *were* Elam, Asshur, [b]Arphaxad, Lud, Aram, Uz, Hul,
Gether, and [1]Meshech.
18 Arphaxad begot Shelah, and Shelah
begot Eber.
19 To Eber were born two sons: the
name of one *was* [1]Peleg, for in his
days the [2]earth was divided; and his
brother's name *was* Joktan.
20 [a]Joktan begot Almodad, Sheleph,
Hazarmaveth, Jerah,
21 Hadoram, Uzal, Diklah,
22 [1]Ebal, Abimael, Sheba,
23 Ophir, Havilah, and Jobab. All
these *were* the sons of Joktan.
24 [a]Shem, Arphaxad, Shelah,
25 [a]Eber, Peleg, Reu,
26 Serug, Nahor, Terah,
27 and [a]Abram, who *is* Abraham.
28 [a]The sons of Abraham *were* [b]Isaac
and [c]Ishmael.

The Family of Ishmael

29 These *are* their genealogies: The
[a]firstborn of Ishmael *was* Nebajoth;
then Kedar, Adbeel, Mibsam,
30 Mishma, Dumah, Massa, [1]Hadad,
Tema,

CHAPTER 1

1 [a]Gen. 1:27; 2:7; 5:1, 2, 5 [b]Gen. 4:25, 26; 5:3–9
4 [a]Gen. 5:28—10:1 [1]So with MT, Vg.; LXX adds *the sons of Noah*
5 [a]Gen. 10:2–4
6 [1]*Riphath,* Gen. 10:3
7 [1]*Tarshish,* Gen. 10:4 [2]*Dodanim,* Gen. 10:4
8 [a]Gen. 10:6
9 [1]*Sabtah,* Gen. 10:7 [2]*Raamah,* Gen. 10:7
10 [a]Gen. 10:8–10, 13
12 [a]Deut. 2:23
13 [a]Gen. 9:18, 25–27; 10:15
17 [a]Gen. 10:22–29; 11:10 [b]Luke 3:36 [1]*Mash,* Gen. 10:23
19 [1]Lit. *Division,* Gen. 10:25 [2]Or *land*
20 [a]Gen. 10:26
22 [1]*Obal,* Gen. 10:28
24 [a]Luke 3:34–36
25 [a]Gen. 11:15
27 [a]Gen. 17:5
28 [a]Gen. 21:2, 3 [b]Gen. 21:2 [c]Gen. 16:11, 15
29 [a]Gen. 25:13–16 **30** [1]*Hadar,* Gen. 25:15

1:1—9:44 The first nine chapters of 1 Chr. are an important foundation for the story of the Davidic dynasty of Judah, surveying the genealogy of David reaching back to Adam himself. The chronicler is sometimes selective, including and arranging only the lists and individuals that are relevant to his purpose. Thus he sets the stage for his discussion of the Davidic dynasty in five distinct sections. The first section (1:1—2:2) gives the genealogy from Adam to Jacob and his sons. The second section (2:3—3:24) singles out the tribe of Judah and records its genealogies because it is the line of David. In the third division (4:1—8:40), the genealogies of the remainder of the tribes are recorded, with special attention given to the Levites. The fourth section (9:1–34) outlines the genealogies of the remnant that returned to Jerusalem. The final section (9:35–44) traces the family of King Saul.

1:1–28 This section gives a general list of descendants from **Adam** to **Abraham.** For a closer inspection of these men and their lives, read the text and notes of Gen. 1—24.

1:29–33 Before continuing to record the descendants of Isaac (v. 34), 1 Chr. records other descendants of Abraham. For further information about some of these individuals and their times, read the text and notes of Gen. 21:1—25:11.

31 Jetur, Naphish, and Kedemah.
These *were* the sons of Ishmael.

The Family of Keturah

32 Now [a]the sons born to Keturah,
Abraham's concubine, *were* Zimran,
Jokshan, Medan, Midian, Ishbak, and
Shuah. The sons of Jokshan *were*
Sheba and Dedan.
33 The sons of Midian *were* Ephah,
Epher, Hanoch, Abida, and Eldaah. All
these were the children of Keturah.

The Family of Isaac

34 And [a]Abraham begot Isaac. [b]The
sons of Isaac *were* Esau and Israel.
35 The sons of [a]Esau *were* Eliphaz,
Reuel, Jeush, Jaalam, and Korah.
36 And the sons of Eliphaz *were* Teman, Omar, [1]Zephi, Gatam, *and* Kenaz; and *by* [a]Timna, Amalek.
37 The sons of Reuel *were* Nahath,
Zerah, Shammah, and Mizzah.

The Family of Seir

38 [a]The sons of Seir *were* Lotan, Shobal, Zibeon, Anah, Dishon, Ezer, and
Dishan.
39 And the sons of Lotan *were* Hori
and [1]Homam; Lotan's sister *was*
Timna.
40 The sons of Shobal *were* [1]Alian,
Manahath, Ebal, [2]Shephi, and Onam.
The sons of Zibeon *were* Ajah and
Anah.
41 The son of Anah *was* [a]Dishon. The
sons of Dishon *were* [1]Hamran, Eshban,
Ithran, and Cheran.
42 The sons of Ezer *were* Bilhan, Zaavan, *and* [1]Jaakan. The sons of Dishan
were Uz and Aran.

The Kings of Edom

43 Now these *were* the [a]kings who
reigned in the land of Edom before a
king reigned over the children of Israel: Bela the son of Beor, and the
name of his city was Dinhabah.
44 And when Bela died, Jobab the son
of Zerah of Bozrah reigned in his
place.
45 When Jobab died, Husham of the
land of the Temanites reigned in his
place.
46 And when Husham died, Hadad the
son of Bedad, who [1]attacked Midian in
the field of Moab, reigned in his place.
The name of his city *was* Avith.
47 When Hadad died, Samlah of Masrekah reigned in his place.
48 [a]And when Samlah died, Saul of
Rehoboth-by-the-River reigned in his
place.
49 When Saul died, Baal-Hanan the
son of Achbor reigned in his place.
50 And when Baal-Hanan died, [1]Ha-
dad reigned in his place; and the
name of his city was [2]Pai. His wife's
name was Mehetabel the daughter of
Matred, the daughter of Mezahab.
51 Hadad died also. And the chiefs of
Edom were Chief Timnah, Chief
[1]Aliah, Chief Jetheth,
52 Chief Aholibamah, Chief Elah,
Chief Pinon,
53 Chief Kenaz, Chief Teman, Chief
Mibzar,
54 Chief Magdiel, and Chief Iram.
These *were* the chiefs of Edom.

The Family of Israel

2 These *were* the [a]sons of [1]Israel:
[b]Reuben, Simeon, Levi, Judah, Issachar, Zebulun,
2 Dan, Joseph, Benjamin, Naphtali,
Gad, and Asher.

From Judah to David

3 The sons of [a]Judah *were* Er, Onan,
and Shelah. *These* three were born to
him by the daughter of [b]Shua, the Ca-
naanitess. [c]Er, the firstborn of Judah,
was wicked in the sight of the LORD;
so He killed him.
4 And [a]Tamar, his daughter-in-law,
[b]bore him Perez and Zerah. All the
sons of Judah *were* five.
5 The sons of [a]Perez *were* Hezron
and Hamul.
6 The sons of Zerah *were* [1]Zimri,
[a]Ethan, Heman, Calcol, and [2]Dara—
five of them in all.
7 The son of [a]Carmi *was* [1]Achar, the

32 [a]Gen. 25:1–4 **34** [a]Gen. 21:2 [b]Gen. 25:9, 25, 26, 29; 32:28 **35** [a]Gen. 36:10–19 **36** [a]Gen. 36:12 [1]*Zepho,* Gen. 36:11 **38** [a]Gen. 36:20–28 **39** [1]*Hemam* or *Heman,* Gen. 36:22 **40** [1]*Alvan,* Gen. 36:23 [2]*Shepho,* Gen. 36:23 **41** [a]Gen. 36:25 [1]*Hemdan,* Gen. 36:26 **42** [1]*Akan,* Gen. 36:27 **43** [a]Gen. 36:31–43

46 [1]Lit. *struck* **48** [a]Gen. 36:37 **50** [1]*Hadar,* Gen. 36:39 [2]*Pau,* Gen. 36:39 **51** [1]*Alvah,* Gen. 36:40

CHAPTER 2

1 [a]Gen. 29:32–35; 35:23, 26; 46:8–27 [b]Gen. 29:32; 35:22 [1]*Jacob,* Gen. 32:28 **3** [a]Gen. 38:3–5; 46:12; Num. 26:19 [b]Gen. 38:2 [c]Gen. 38:7 **4** [a]Gen. 38:6 [b]Matt. 1:3 **5** [a]Gen. 46:12; Ruth 4:18 **6** [a]1 Kin. 4:31 [1]*Zabdi,* Josh. 7:1 [2]*Darda,* 1 Kin. 4:31 **7** [a]1 Chr. 4:1 [1]*Achan,* Josh. 7:1

1:34–54 The significant offspring of **Isaac** was **Israel.** But before 1 Chr. records the list of Israel and his sons, it inserts the descendants of Ishmael and **Esau** into the account. To appreciate more fully these people and their world, read the text and notes of Gen. 25—36.

2:1, 2 These 2 verses list the 12 **sons of Israel** (that is, Jacob). These men and some of the events of their lives are recorded in Gen. 29—50.

2:3—3:24 In this section, the chronicler highlights the tribe of **Judah,** for this is the line of David. The life, times, and background of these people are more fully set forth in the first eight books of the OT.

2:3–55 This division outlines the descendants of **Judah** as ancestors of David. For further insights about these people, read the text and notes of Gen. 29—2 Sam. 3.

2:4 See notes on Gen. 38:1–30; Ruth 4:18–22.

troubler of Israel, who transgressed in
the [b]accursed[2] thing.
8 The son of Ethan *was* Azariah.
9 Also the sons of Hezron who were
born to him *were* Jerahmeel, [1]Ram,
and [2]Chelubai.
10 Ram [a]begot Amminadab, and Amminadab begot Nahshon, [b]leader of the
children of Judah;
11 Nahshon begot [1]Salma, and Salma
begot Boaz;
12 Boaz begot Obed, and Obed begot
Jesse;
13 [a]Jesse begot Eliab his firstborn,
Abinadab the second, [1]Shimea the
third,
14 Nethanel the fourth, Raddai the
fifth,
15 Ozem the sixth, *and* David the
[a]seventh.
16 Now their sisters *were* Zeruiah and
Abigail. [a]And the sons of Zeruiah *were*
Abishai, Joab, and Asahel—three.
17 Abigail bore Amasa; and the father
of Amasa *was* [1]Jether the Ishmaelite.

The Family of Hezron

18 Caleb the son of Hezron had children by Azubah, *his* wife, and by Jer-
ioth. Now these were her sons: Jesher,
Shobab, and Ardon.
19 When Azubah died, Caleb [1]took
[a]Ephrath[2] as his wife, who bore him
Hur.
20 And Hur begot Uri, and Uri begot
[a]Bezalel.
21 Now afterward Hezron went in to
the daughter of [a]Machir the father of
Gilead, whom he married when he *was*
sixty years old; and she bore him Segub.
22 Segub begot [a]Jair,[1] who had
twenty-three cities in the land of
Gilead.
23 [a](Geshur and Syria took from them
the towns of Jair, with Kenath and its
towns—sixty towns.) All these *belonged to* the sons of Machir the father
of Gilead.
24 After Hezron died in Caleb Ephrathah, Hezron's wife Abijah bore him
[a]Ashhur the father of Tekoa.

The Family of Jerahmeel

25 The sons of Jerahmeel, the firstborn
of Hezron, *were* Ram, the firstborn,
and Bunah, Oren, Ozem, *and* Ahijah.
26 Jerahmeel had another wife, whose
name was Atarah; she was the mother
of Onam.
27 The sons of Ram, the firstborn of
Jerahmeel, were Maaz, Jamin, and
Eker.
28 The sons of Onam were Shammai
and Jada. The sons of Shammai *were*
Nadab and Abishur.
29 And the name of the wife of Abishur
was Abihail, and she bore him Ahban
and Molid.
30 The sons of Nadab *were* Seled and
Appaim; Seled died without children.
31 The son of Appaim *was* Ishi, the son
of Ishi *was* Sheshan, and [a]Sheshan's
son *was* Ahlai.
32 The sons of Jada, the brother of
Shammai, *were* Jether and Jonathan;
Jether died without children.
33 The sons of Jonathan *were* Peleth
and Zaza. These were the sons of Jerahmeel.
34 Now Sheshan had no sons, only
daughters. And Sheshan had an Egyptian servant whose name *was* Jarha.
35 Sheshan gave his daughter to Jarha
his servant as wife, and she bore him
Attai.
36 Attai begot Nathan, and Nathan begot [a]Zabad;
37 Zabad begot Ephlal, and Ephlal begot [a]Obed;
38 Obed begot Jehu, and Jehu begot
Azariah;
39 Azariah begot Helez, and Helez begot Eleasah;
40 Eleasah begot Sismai, and Sismai
begot Shallum;
41 Shallum begot Jekamiah, and Jekamiah begot Elishama.

The Family of Caleb

42 The descendants of Caleb the
brother of Jerahmeel *were* Mesha, his
firstborn, who was the father of Ziph,
and the sons of Mareshah the father
of Hebron.
43 The sons of Hebron *were* Korah,
Tappuah, Rekem, and Shema.
44 Shema begot Raham the father of
Jorkoam, and Rekem begot Shammai.
45 And the son of Shammai *was* Maon,
and Maon *was* the father of Beth Zur.
46 Ephah, Caleb's concubine, bore
Haran, Moza, and Gazez; and Haran
begot Gazez.
47 And the sons of Jahdai *were* Re-
gem, Jotham, Geshan, Pelet, Ephah,
and Shaaph.

7 [b]Josh. 6:18 [2]*banned* or *devoted*
9 [1]*Aram,* Matt. 1:3, 4 [2]*Caleb,* vv. 18, 42
10 [a]Ruth 4:19–22; Matt. 1:4 [b]Num. 1:7; 2:3
11 [1]*Salmon,* Ruth 4:21; Luke 3:32
13 [a]1 Sam. 16:6 [1]*Shammah,* 1 Sam. 16:9
15 [a]1 Sam. 16:10, 11; 17:12
16 [a]2 Sam. 2:18
17 [1]*Jithra the Israelite,* 2 Sam. 17:25
19 [a]1 Chr. 2:50 [1]Lit. *took to himself* [2]Or *Ephrathah*
20 [a]Ex. 31:2; 38:22
21 [a]Num. 27:1; Judg. 5:14; 1 Chr. 7:14
22 [a]Judg. 10:3 [1]Reckoned to Manasseh through the daughter of Machir, Num. 32:41; Deut. 3:14; 25:5, 6; 1 Kin. 4:13; 1 Chr. 7:14
23 [a]Num. 32:41; Deut. 3:14; Josh. 13:30
24 [a]1 Chr. 4:5
31 [a]1 Chr. 2:34, 35
36 [a]1 Chr. 11:41
37 [a]2 Chr. 23:1

2:12 See the text and notes of Ruth 4:13–17.
2:13–15 See note on 1 Sam. 16:1.
2:25 On **Jerahmeel,** see notes on 1 Sam. 27:10 and 30:26–31.

48 Maachah, Caleb's concubine, bore
Sheber and Tirhanah.
49 She also bore Shaaph the father of
Madmannah, Sheva the father of
Machbenah and the father of Gibea.
And the daughter of Caleb *was* [a]Ach-
sah.[1]
50 These were the descendants of Caleb: The sons of [a]Hur, the firstborn of
[1]Ephrathah, *were* Shobal the father of
[b]Kirjath Jearim,
51 Salma the father of Bethlehem, *and*
Hareph the father of Beth Gader.
52 And Shobal the father of Kirjath
Jearim had descendants: [1]Haroeh, *and*
half of the [2]*families of* Manuhoth.
53 The families of Kirjath Jearim *were*
the Ithrites, the Puthites, the Shumath-
ites, and the Mishraites. From these
came the Zorathites and the Eshtao-
lites.
54 The sons of Salma *were* Bethlehem,
the Netophathites, [1]Atroth Beth Joab,
half of the Manahethites, and the Zo-
rites.
55 And the families of the scribes who
dwelt at Jabez *were* the Tirathites, the
Shimeathites, *and* the Suchathites.
These *were* the [a]Kenites who came
from Hammath, the father of the house
of [b]Rechab.

The Family of David

3 Now these were the sons of David
who were born to him in Hebron:
The firstborn *was* [a]Amnon, by [b]Ahin-
oam the [c]Jezreelitess; the second,
[1]Daniel, by [d]Abigail the Carmelitess;
2 the third, [a]Absalom the son of Maacah, the daughter of Talmai, king of
Geshur; the fourth, [b]Adonijah the son
of Haggith;
3 the fifth, Shephatiah, by Abital; the
sixth, Ithream, by his wife [a]Eglah.
4 *These* six were born to him in Hebron. [a]There he reigned seven years
and six months, and [b]in Jerusalem he
reigned thirty-three years.
5 [a]And these were born to him in Jerusalem: [1]Shimea, Shobab, Nathan,
and [b]Solomon—four by [2]Bathshua the
daughter of [3]Ammiel.
6 Also *there* were Ibhar, [1]Elishama,
[2]Eliphelet,
7 Nogah, Nepheg, Japhia,
8 Elishama, [1]Eliada, and Eliphelet—
[a]nine *in all.*

49 [a]Josh. 15:17 [1]Or *Achsa*
50 [a]1 Chr. 4:4 [b]Josh. 9:17; 18:14 [1]*Ephrath,* v. 19
52 [1]*Reaiah,* 1 Chr. 4:2 [2]Or *Manuhothites,* same as *Manahethites,* v. 54
54 [1]Or *Ataroth of the house of Joab*
55 [a]Judg. 1:16 [b]Jer. 35:2

CHAPTER 3

1 [a]2 Sam. 3:2–5 [b]1 Sam. 25:43 [c]Josh. 15:56 [d]1 Sam. 25:39–42 [1]*Chileab,* 2 Sam. 3:3
2 [a]2 Sam. 13:37; 15:1 [b]1 Kin. 1:5
3 [a]2 Sam. 3:5
4 [a]2 Sam. 2:11 [b]2 Sam. 5:5
5 [a]1 Chr. 14:4–7 [b]2 Sam. 12:24, 25 [1]*Shammua,* 1 Chr. 14:4; 2 Sam. 5:14 [2]*Bathsheba,* 2 Sam. 11:3 [3]*Eliam,* 2 Sam. 11:3
6 [1]*Elishua,* 1 Chr. 14:5; 2 Sam. 5:15 [2]*Elpelet,* 1 Chr. 14:5
8 [a]2 Sam. 5:14–16 [1]*Beeliada,* 1 Chr. 14:7
9 [a]2 Sam. 13:1
10 [a]1 Kin. 11:43 [1]*Abijam,* 1 Kin. 15:1
11 [1]*Jehoram,* 2 Kin. 1:17; 8:16 [2]Or *Azariah* or *Jehoahaz* [3]*Jehoash,* 2 Kin. 12:1
12 [1]*Uzziah,* Is. 6:1
15 [1]*Eliakim,* 2 Kin. 23:34 [2]*Jehoahaz,* 2 Kin. 23:31
16 [a]Matt. 1:11 [1]*Jehoiachin,* 2 Kin. 24:8, or *Coniah,* Jer. 22:24 [2]*Mattaniah,* 2 Kin. 24:17

9 *These were* all the sons of David,
besides the sons of the concubines, and
[a]Tamar their sister.

The Family of Solomon

10 Solomon's son *was* [a]Rehoboam;
[1]Abijah *was* his son, Asa his son, Jehoshaphat his son,
11 [1]Joram his son, [2]Ahaziah his son,
[3]Joash his son,
12 Amaziah his son, [1]Azariah his son,
Jotham his son,
13 Ahaz his son, Hezekiah his son, Manasseh his son,
14 Amon his son, *and* Josiah his
son.
15 The sons of Josiah *were* Johanan
the firstborn, the second [1]Jehoiakim,
the third Zedekiah, and the fourth
[2]Shallum.
16 The sons of [a]Jehoiakim *were* [1]Jeco-
niah his son *and* [2]Zedekiah his
son.

The Family of Jeconiah

17 And the sons of [1]Jeconiah [2]*were* Assir, Shealtiel [a]his son,
18 *and* Malchiram, Pedaiah, Shenaz-
zar, Jecamiah, Hoshama, and Neda-
biah.
19 The sons of Pedaiah *were* Zerubbabel and Shimei. The sons of Zerubbabel *were* Meshullam, Hananiah, Shelomith their sister,
20 and Hashubah, Ohel, Berechiah,
Hasadiah, and Jushab-Hesed—five *in
all.*
21 The sons of Hananiah *were* Pelatiah
and Jeshaiah, the sons of Rephaiah,
the sons of Arnan, the sons of Obadiah,
and the sons of Shechaniah.
22 The son of Shechaniah was Shemaiah. The sons of Shemaiah *were*
[a]Hattush, Igal, Bariah, Neariah, and
Shaphat—six *in all.*
23 The sons of Neariah *were* Elioenai,
Hezekiah, and Azrikam—three *in all.*
24 The sons of Elioenai *were* Hodaviah, Eliashib, Pelaiah, Akkub, Johanan, Delaiah, and Anani—seven *in
all.*

17 [a]Matt. 1:12 [1]*Jehoiachin,* 2 Kin. 24:8, or *Coniah,* Jer. 22:24 [2]Or *the captive were Shealtiel*
22 [a]Ezra 8:2

3:1–16 These verses give a general account of David's dynasty up to the time of the Exile.

3:17–24 Here the chronicler records the royal line of David after the Exile. These verses show that the final compilation of 1 and 2 Chr. was after the Exile.

The Family of Judah

4 The sons of Judah *were* [a]Perez, Hezron, [1]Carmi, Hur, and Shobal.

2 And [1]Reaiah the son of Shobal begot Jahath, and Jahath begot Ahumai and Lahad. These *were* the families of the Zorathites.

3 These *were* the sons *of the father* of Etam: Jezreel, Ishma, and Idbash; and the name of their sister *was* Hazelelponi;

4 and Penuel *was* the father of Gedor, and Ezer *was the* father of Hushah. These *were* the sons of [a]Hur, the firstborn of Ephrathah the father of Bethlehem.

5 And [a]Ashhur the father of Tekoa had two wives, Helah and Naarah.

6 Naarah bore him Ahuzzam, Hepher, Temeni, and Haahashtari. These *were* the sons of Naarah.

7 The sons of Helah *were* Zereth, Zohar, and Ethnan;

8 and Koz begot Anub, Zobebah, and the families of Aharhel the son of Harum.

9 Now Jabez was [a]more honorable than his brothers, and his mother called his name [1]Jabez, saying, "Because I bore *him* in pain."

10 And Jabez called on the God of Israel saying, "Oh, that You would bless me indeed, and enlarge my [1]territory, that Your hand would be with me, and that You would keep *me* from evil, that I may not cause pain!" So God granted him what he *requested.

11 Chelub the brother of [a]Shuhah begot Mehir, who *was* the father of Eshton.

12 And Eshton begot Beth-Rapha, Paseah, and Tehinnah the father of [1]Ir-Nahash. These *were* the men of Rechah.

13 The sons of Kenaz *were* [a]Othniel and Seraiah. The sons of Othniel *were* [1]Hathath,

14 and Meonothai *who* begot Ophrah. Seraiah begot Joab the father of [a]Ge Harashim,[1] for they were craftsmen.

15 The sons of [a]Caleb the son of Jephunneh *were* Iru, Elah, and Naam. The son of Elah *was* [1]Kenaz.

16 The sons of Jehallelel *were* Ziph, Ziphah, Tiria, and Asarel.

17 The sons of Ezrah *were* Jether, Mered, Epher, and Jalon. And [1]*Mered's wife bore* Miriam, Shammai, and Ishbah the father of Eshtemoa.

18 ([1]His wife Jehudijah bore Jered the father of Gedor, Heber the father of Sochoh, and Jekuthiel the father of Zanoah.) And these were the sons of Bithiah the daughter of Pharaoh, whom Mered took.

19 The sons of Hodiah's wife, the sister of Naham, *were* the fathers of Keilah the Garmite and of Eshtemoa the [a]Maachathite.

20 And the sons of Shimon *were* Amnon, Rinnah, Ben-Hanan, and Tilon. And the sons of Ishi *were* Zoheth and Ben-Zoheth.

21 The sons of [a]Shelah [b]the son of Judah *were* Er the father of Lecah, Laadah the father of Mareshah, and the families of the house of the linen workers of the house of Ashbea;

22 also Jokim, the men of Chozeba, and Joash; Saraph, who ruled in Moab, and Jashubi-Lehem. Now the [1]records are ancient.

23 These *were* the potters and those who dwell at [1]Netaim and [2]Gederah; there they dwelt with the king for his work.

The Family of Simeon

24 The [a]sons of Simeon *were* [1]Nemuel, Jamin, [2]Jarib, [3]Zerah, *and* Shaul,

25 Shallum his son, Mibsam his son, and Mishma his son.

26 And the sons of Mishma *were* Hamuel his son, Zacchur his son, and Shimei his son.

27 Shimei had sixteen sons and six daughters; but his brothers did not have many children, [a]nor did any of their families multiply as much as the children of Judah.

28 They dwelt at Beersheba, Moladah, Hazar Shual,

29 [1]Bilhah, Ezem, [2]Tolad,

CHAPTER 4

1 [a]Gen. 38:29; 46:12 [1]*Chelubai,* 1 Chr. 2:9 or *Caleb,* 1 Chr. 2:18
2 [1]*Haroeh,* 1 Chr. 2:52
4 [a]Ex. 31:2; 1 Chr. 2:50
5 [a]1 Chr. 2:24
9 [a]Gen. 34:19 [1]Lit. *He Will Cause Pain*
10 [1]*border* *See WW at Ps. 122:6.
11 [a]Job 8:1
12 [1]Lit. *City of Nahash*
13 [a]Josh. 15:17; Judg. 3:9, 11 [1]LXX, Vg. add *and Meonothai*
14 [a]Neh. 11:35 [1]Lit. *Valley of Craftsmen*
15 [a]Josh. 14:6, 14; 15:13, 17; 1 Chr. 6:56 [1]Or *Uknaz*
17 [1]Lit. *she*
18 [1]Or *His Judean wife*
19 [a]2 Kin. 25:23
21 [a]Gen. 38:11, 14 [b]Gen. 38:1–5; 46:12
22 [1]Lit. *words*
23 [1]Lit. *Plants* [2]Lit. *Hedges*
24 [a]Num. 26:12–14 [1]*Jemuel,* Gen. 46:10; Ex. 6:15; Num. 26:12 [2]*Jachin,* Gen. 46:10; Num. 26:12 [3]*Zohar,* Gen. 46:10; Ex. 6:15
27 [a]Num. 2:9
29 [1]*Balah,* Josh. 19:3 [2]*Eltolad,* Josh. 19:4

4:1—8:40 1 Chr. has recorded descendants from Adam to Jacob's sons (1:1—2:2). The tribe of Judah is emphasized because they were the line of David (2:3—3:24). Now, in the third main section of the family trees in 1 Chr. 1—9, the chronicler records some of the ancestry of the other tribes of Israel. In keeping with its emphasis on the southern kingdom and David, 1 Chr. considers the tribe of Judah first (4:1–23), though Judah was the fourth son of Jacob. In its accounting of the ancestry of the tribes of Israel, Zebulun and Dan are not specifically mentioned. However, the genealogies of the two tribes arising through Joseph—Manasseh and Ephraim—are mentioned (5:23–26; 7:14–29). The tribe of Benjamin is mentioned twice (7:6–12; 8:1–40) to show its significance as the line of King Saul. But the tribe that is given special attention in this section is Levi. More space is given to discussing the Levites than to any other tribe (6:1–81) because 1 Chr. repeatedly accents the temple and worship. The life and times of all these people can be found in Gen. 29—2 Kin. 25, and the Levites are given special attention in the Book of Leviticus.

30 Bethuel, Hormah, Ziklag,
31 Beth Marcaboth, [1]Hazar Susim,
Beth Biri, and at Shaaraim. These *were*
their cities until the reign of David.
32 And their villages *were* [1]Etam, Ain,
Rimmon, Tochen, and Ashan—five cities—
33 and all the villages that *were*
around these cities as far as [1]Baal.
These *were* their dwelling places, and
they maintained their genealogy:
34 Meshobab, Jamlech, and Joshah the
son of Amaziah;
35 Joel, and Jehu the son of Joshi-
biah, the son of Seraiah, the son of
Asiel;
36 Elioenai, Jaakobah, Jeshohaiah,
Asaiah, Adiel, Jesimiel, and Benaiah;
37 Ziza the son of Shiphi, the son of
Allon, the son of Jedaiah, the son of
Shimri, the son of Shemaiah—
38 these mentioned by name *were*
leaders in their families, and their father's house increased greatly.
39 So they went to the entrance of Gedor, as far as the east side of the valley,
to seek pasture for their flocks.
40 And they found rich, good pasture,
and the land *was* broad, quiet, and
peaceful; for some Hamites formerly
lived there.
41 These recorded by name came in
the days of Hezekiah king of Judah;
and they [a]attacked[1] their tents and the
Meunites who were found there, and
[b]utterly destroyed them, as it is to this
day. So they dwelt in their place, because *there was* pasture for their flocks
there.
42 Now *some* of them, five hundred
men of the sons of Simeon, went to
Mount Seir, having as their captains
Pelatiah, Neariah, Rephaiah, and Uzziel, the sons of Ishi.
43 And they [1]defeated [a]the rest of the
Amalekites who had escaped. They
have dwelt there to this day.

The Family of Reuben

5 Now the sons of Reuben the firstborn of Israel—[a]he *was* indeed the
firstborn, but because he [b]defiled his
father's bed, [c]his birthright was given
to the sons of Joseph, the son of Israel,
so that the genealogy is not listed according to the birthright;
2 yet [a]Judah prevailed over his
brothers, and from him *came* a [b]ruler,
although [1]the birthright was Joseph's—
3 the sons of [a]Reuben the firstborn of
Israel were Hanoch, Pallu, Hezron, and
Carmi.

31 [1]*Hazar Susah,* Josh. 19:5
32 [1]*Ether,* Josh. 19:7
33 [1]*Baalath Beer,* Josh. 19:8
41 [a]2 Kin. 18:8 [b]2 Kin. 19:11 [1]Lit. *struck*
43 [a]Ex. 17:14; 1 Sam. 15:8; 30:17 [1]Lit. *struck*

CHAPTER 5

1 [a]Gen. 29:32; 49:3 [b]Gen. 35:22; 49:4 [c]Gen. 48:15, 22
2 [a]Gen. 49:8, 10; Ps. 60:7; 108:8 [b]Mic. 5:2; Matt. 2:6 [1]*the right of the firstborn*
3 [a]Gen. 46:9; Ex. 6:14; Num. 26:5
6 [a]2 Kin. 18:11 [1]Heb. *Tilgath-Pilneser*
7 [a]1 Chr. 5:17
8 [a]Num. 32:34; Josh. 12:2; 13:15, 16
9 [a]Josh. 22:8, 9 [1]*beginning* [2]*increased*
10 [a]Gen. 25:12
11 [a]Num. 26:15–18 [b]Josh. 13:11, 24–28 [c]Deut. 3:10
16 [a]1 Chr. 27:29; Song 2:1; Is. 35:2; 65:10 [1]*open lands*
17 [a]2 Kin. 15:5, 32 [b]2 Kin. 14:16, 28
19 [a]Gen. 25:15; 1 Chr. 1:31
20 [a][1 Chr. 5:22]

4 The sons of Joel *were* Shemaiah his
son, Gog his son, Shimei his son,
5 Micah his son, Reaiah his son, Baal
his son,
6 and Beerah his son, whom [1]Tiglath-
Pileser king of Assyria [a]carried into
captivity. He *was* leader of the Reubenites.
7 And his brethren by their families,
[a]when the genealogy of their generations was registered: the chief, Jeiel,
and Zechariah,
8 and Bela the son of Azaz, the son
of Shema, the son of Joel, who dwelt
in [a]Aroer, as far as Nebo and Baal
Meon.
9 Eastward they settled as far as the
[1]entrance of the wilderness this side of
the River Euphrates, because their cattle had [2]multiplied [a]in the land of
Gilead.
10 Now in the days of Saul they made
war [a]with the Hagrites, who fell by
their hand; and they dwelt in their
tents throughout the entire *area* east
of Gilead.

The Family of Gad

11 And the [a]children of Gad dwelt next
to them in the land of [b]Bashan as far
as [c]Salcah:
12 Joel *was* the chief, Shapham the
next, then Jaanai and Shaphat in Bashan,
13 and their brethren of their father's
house: Michael, Meshullam, Sheba, Jo-
rai, Jachan, Zia, and Eber—seven *in
all.*
14 These *were* the children of Abihail
the son of Huri, the son of Jaroah, the
son of Gilead, the son of Michael, the
son of Jeshishai, the son of Jahdo, the
son of Buz;
15 Ahi the son of Abdiel, the son of
Guni, *was* chief of their father's house.
16 And *the Gadites* dwelt in Gilead, in
Bashan and in its villages, and in all
the [1]common-lands of [a]Sharon within
their borders.
17 All these were registered by genealogies in the days of [a]Jotham king of
Judah, and in the days of [b]Jeroboam
king of Israel.
18 The sons of Reuben, the Gadites,
and half the tribe of Manasseh *had*
forty-four thousand seven hundred and
sixty valiant men, men able to bear
shield and sword, to shoot with the
bow, and skillful in war, who went to
war.
19 They made war with the Hagrites,
[a]Jetur, Naphish, and Nodab.
20 And [a]they were helped against

them, and the Hagrites were delivered
into their hand, and all who *were* with
them, for they [b]cried out to God in the
battle. He [1]heeded their prayer, because they [c]put their trust in Him.
21 Then they took away their livestock—fifty thousand of their camels,
two hundred and fifty thousand of their
sheep, and two thousand of their donkeys—also one hundred thousand of
their men;
22 for many fell dead, because the war
[a]*was* God's. And they dwelt in their
place until [b]the captivity.

The Family of Manasseh (East)

23 So the children of the half-tribe of
Manasseh dwelt in the land. Their
numbers increased from Bashan to
Baal Hermon, that is, to [a]Senir, or
Mount Hermon.
24 These *were* the heads of their fathers' houses: Epher, Ishi, Eliel, Azriel,
Jeremiah, Hodaviah, and Jahdiel. They
were mighty men of valor, famous
men, *and* heads of their fathers'
houses.
25 And they were unfaithful to the God
of their fathers, and [a]played the harlot
after the gods of the peoples of the
land, whom God had destroyed before
them.
26 So the God of Israel *stirred up the
spirit of [a]Pul king of Assyria, that is,
[b]Tiglath-Pileser[1] king of Assyria. He
carried the Reubenites, the Gadites,
and the half-tribe of Manasseh into
captivity. He took them to [c]Halah, Habor, Hara, and the river of Gozan to
this day.

The Family of Levi

6 The sons of Levi *were* [a]Gershon,[1]
Kohath, and Merari.
2 The sons of Kohath *were* Amram,
[a]Izhar, Hebron, and Uzziel.
3 The children of Amram *were*
Aaron, Moses, and Miriam. And the
sons of Aaron *were* [a]Nadab, Abihu, Eleazar, and Ithamar.
4 Eleazar begot Phinehas, *and* Phinehas begot Abishua;
5 Abishua begot Bukki, and Bukki begot Uzzi;
6 Uzzi begot Zerahiah, and Zerahiah
begot Meraioth;
7 Meraioth begot Amariah, and Amariah begot Ahitub;
8 [a]Ahitub begot [b]Zadok, and Zadok
begot Ahimaaz;
9 Ahimaaz begot Azariah, and Azariah begot Johanan;

20 [b]2 Chr. 14:11–13 [c]Ps. 9:10; 20:7, 8; 22:4, 5 [1]Lit. *was entreated for them*
22 [a][Josh. 23:10; 2 Chr. 32:8; Rom. 8:31] [b]2 Kin. 15:29; 17:6
23 [a]Deut. 3:9
25 [a]2 Kin. 17:7
26 [a]2 Kin. 15:19 [b]2 Kin. 15:29 [c]2 Kin. 17:6; 18:11 [1]Heb. *Tilgath-Pilneser*
*See WW at Hag. 1:14.

CHAPTER 6

1 [a]Gen. 46:11; Ex. 6:16; Num. 26:57; 1 Chr. 23:6 [1]Or *Gershom,* v. 16
2 [a]1 Chr. 6:18, 22
3 [a]Lev. 10:1, 2
8 [a]2 Sam. 8:17 [b]2 Sam. 15:27
10 [a]2 Chr. 26:17, 18 [b]1 Kin. 6:1; 2 Chr. 3:1 [1]Lit. *house*
11 [a]Ezra 7:3 [b]2 Chr. 19:11
12 [1]*Meshullam,* 1 Chr. 9:11
14 [a]2 Kin. 25:18–21; Neh. 11:11
15 [a]2 Kin. 25:21
16 [a]Gen. 46:11; Ex. 6:16 [1]Heb. *Gershom,* an alternate spelling for *Gershon,* vv. 1, 17, 20, 43, 62, 71
20 [a]1 Chr. 6:42
21 [1]*Ethan,* v. 42 [2]*Adaiah,* v. 41 [3]*Ethni,* v. 41
22 [a]Num. 16:1 [1]*Izhar,* vv. 2, 18
25 [a]1 Chr. 6:35, 36
26 [1]*Zuph,* v. 35; 1 Sam. 1:1 [2]*Toah,* v. 34
27 [1]*Eliel,* v. 34
28 [1]So with LXX, Syr., Arab.; cf. v. 33 and 1 Sam. 8:2 [2]Heb. *Vasheni*
31 [a]1 Chr. 15:16–22, 27; 16:4–6 [b]2 Sam. 6:17; 1 Kin. 8:4; 1 Chr. 15:25—16:1
33 [1]Lit. *stood with*

10 Johanan begot Azariah (it was he
[a]who ministered as priest in the
[b]temple[1] that Solomon built in Jerusalem);
11 [a]Azariah begot [b]Amariah, and Amariah begot Ahitub;
12 Ahitub begot Zadok, and Zadok begot [1]Shallum;
13 Shallum begot Hilkiah, and Hilkiah
begot Azariah;
14 Azariah begot [a]Seraiah, and Seraiah begot Jehozadak.
15 Jehozadak went *into captivity*
[a]when the LORD carried Judah and Jerusalem into captivity by the hand of
Nebuchadnezzar.
16 The sons of Levi *were* [a]Gershon,[1]
Kohath, and Merari.
17 These are the names of the sons of
Gershon: Libni and Shimei.
18 The sons of Kohath *were* Amram,
Izhar, Hebron, and Uzziel.
19 The sons of Merari *were* Mahli and
Mushi. Now these *are* the families of
the Levites according to their fathers:
20 Of Gershon *were* Libni his son, Jahath his son, [a]Zimmah his son,
21 [1]Joah his son, [2]Iddo his son, Zerah
his son, *and* [3]Jeatherai his son.
22 The sons of Kohath *were* [1]Am-
minadab his son, [a]Korah his son,
Assir his son,
23 Elkanah his son, Ebiasaph his son,
Assir his son,
24 Tahath his son, Uriel his son, Uzziah his son, and Shaul his son.
25 The sons of Elkanah *were* [a]Amasai
and Ahimoth.
26 *As for* Elkanah, the sons of Elkanah
were [1]Zophai his son, [2]Nahath his son,
27 [1]Eliab his son, Jeroham his son, *and*
Elkanah his son.
28 The sons of Samuel *were* [1]*Joel* the
firstborn, and Abijah [2]the second.
29 The sons of Merari *were* Mahli,
Libni his son, Shimei his son, Uzzah
his son,
30 Shimea his son, Haggiah his son,
and Asaiah his son.

Musicians in the House of the LORD

31 Now these are [a]the men whom David appointed over the service of song
in the house of the LORD, after the
[b]ark came to rest.
32 They were ministering with music
before the dwelling place of the tabernacle of meeting, until Solomon had
built the house of the LORD in Jerusalem, and they served in their office according to their order.
33 And these *are* the ones who
[1]ministered with their sons: Of the sons

of the [a]Kohathites *were* Heman the
singer, the son of Joel, the son of Samuel,
34 the son of Elkanah, the son of Jeroham, the son of [1]Eliel, the son of
[2]Toah,
35 the son of Zuph, the son of Elkanah,
the son of Mahath, the son of Amasai,
36 the son of Elkanah, the son of Joel,
the son of Azariah, the son of Zephaniah,
37 the son of Tahath, the son of Assir,
the son of [a]Ebiasaph, the son of Korah,
38 the son of Izhar, the son of Kohath,
the son of Levi, the son of Israel.
39 And his brother [a]Asaph, who stood
at his right hand, *was* Asaph the son
of Berachiah, the son of Shimea,
40 the son of Michael, the son of Ba-
aseiah, the son of Malchijah,
41 the son of [a]Ethni, the son of Zerah,
the son of Adaiah,
42 the son of Ethan, the son of Zimmah, the son of Shimei,
43 the son of Jahath, the son of Gershon, the son of Levi.
44 Their brethren, the sons of Merari,
on the left hand, *were* [1]Ethan the son
of [2]Kishi, the son of Abdi, the son of
Malluch,
45 the son of Hashabiah, the son of
Amaziah, the son of Hilkiah,
46 the son of Amzi, the son of Bani,
the son of Shamer,
47 the son of Mahli, the son of Mushi,
the son of Merari, the son of Levi.
48 And their brethren, the Levites,
were appointed to every [a]kind of service of the tabernacle of the house of
God.

The Family of Aaron

49 [a]But Aaron and his sons offered
sacrifices [b]on the altar of burnt offering and [c]on the altar of incense, for
all the work of the Most Holy *Place*,
and to *make atonement for Israel, according to all that Moses the servant
of God had commanded.
50 Now these *are* the [a]sons of Aaron:
Eleazar his son, Phinehas his son,
Abishua his son,
51 Bukki his son, Uzzi his son, Zerahiah his son,
52 Meraioth his son, Amariah his son,
Ahitub his son,
53 Zadok his son, *and* Ahimaaz his
son.

Dwelling Places of the Levites

54 [a]Now these *are* their dwelling
places throughout their settlements in

33 [a]Num. 26:57
34 [1]*Elihu*, 1 Sam. 1:1 [2]*Tohu*, 1 Sam. 1:1
37 [a]Ex. 6:24
39 [a]2 Chr. 5:12
41 [a]1 Chr. 6:21
44 [1]*Jeduthun*, 1 Chr. 9:16; 25:1, 3, 6; 2 Chr. 35:15; Ps. 62:title [2]Or *Kushaiah*
48 [a]1 Chr. 9:14–34
49 [a]Ex. 28:1; [Num. 18:1–8] [b]Lev. 1:8, 9 [c]Ex. 30:7 *See WW at Num. 15:25.
50 [a]1 Chr. 6:4–8; Ezra 7:5
54 [a]Josh. 21
55 [a]Josh. 14:13; 21:11, 12 [1]*open lands*
56 [a]Josh. 14:13; 15:13
57 [a]Josh. 21:13, 19
58 [1]*Holon*, Josh. 21:15
59 [1]*Ain*, Josh. 21:16
60 [1]*Almon*, Josh. 21:18
61 [a]1 Chr. 6:66–70 [b]Josh. 21:5
63 [a]Josh. 21:7, 34–40
64 [1]*open lands*
66 [a]1 Chr. 6:61
67 [a]Josh. 21:21
68 [a]Josh. 21:22

their territory, for they were *given* by
lot to the sons of Aaron, of the family
of the Kohathites:
55 [a]They gave them Hebron in the
land of Judah, with its surrounding
[1]common-lands.
56 [a]But the fields of the city and its villages they gave to Caleb the son of Jephunneh.
57 And [a]to the sons of Aaron they gave
one of the cities of refuge, Hebron; also
Libnah with its common-lands, Jattir,
Eshtemoa with its common-lands,
58 [1]Hilen with its common-lands, Debir with its common-lands,
59 [1]Ashan with its common-lands, and
Beth Shemesh with its common-lands.
60 And from the tribe of Benjamin:
Geba with its common-lands, [1]Alemeth
with its common-lands, and Anathoth
with its common-lands. All their cities
among their families *were* thirteen.
61 [a]To the rest of the family of the tribe
of the Kohathites *they gave* [b]by lot
ten cities from half the tribe of Manasseh.
62 And to the sons of Gershon,
throughout their families, *they gave*
thirteen cities from the tribe of Issachar, from the tribe of Asher, from the
tribe of Naphtali, and from the tribe
of Manasseh in Bashan.
63 To the sons of Merari, throughout
their families, *they gave* [a]twelve cities
from the tribe of Reuben, from the tribe
of Gad, and from the tribe of Zebulun.
64 So the children of Israel gave *these*
cities with their [1]common-lands to the
Levites.
65 And they gave by lot from the tribe
of the children of Judah, from the tribe
of the children of Simeon, and from the
tribe of the children of Benjamin these
cities which are called by *their* names.
66 Now [a]some of the families of the
sons of Kohath *were given* cities as
their territory from the tribe of
Ephraim.
67 [a]And they gave them *one of* the cities of refuge, Shechem with its
common-lands, in the mountains of
Ephraim, also Gezer with its common-
lands,
68 [a]Jokmeam with its common-lands,
Beth Horon with its common-lands,
69 Aijalon with its common-lands, and
Gath Rimmon with its common-lands.
70 And from the half-tribe of Manasseh: Aner with its common-lands and
Bileam with its common-lands, for the
rest of the family of the sons of Kohath.
71 From the family of the half-tribe of
Manasseh the sons of Gershon *were
given* Golan in Bashan with its

common-lands and [1]Ashtaroth with its common-lands.
72 And from the tribe of Issachar: [1]Kedesh with its common-lands, Daberath with its common-lands,
73 Ramoth with its common-lands, and Anem with its common-lands.
74 And from the tribe of Asher: Mashal with its common-lands, Abdon with its common-lands,
75 Hukok with its common-lands, and Rehob with its common-lands.
76 And from the tribe of Naphtali: Kedesh in Galilee with its common-lands, Hammon with its common-lands, and Kirjathaim with its common-lands.
77 From the tribe of Zebulun the rest of the children of Merari *were given* [1]Rimmon with its common-lands and Tabor with its common-lands.
78 And on the other side of the Jordan, across from Jericho, on the east side of the Jordan, *they were given* from the tribe of Reuben: Bezer in the wilderness with its common-lands, Jahzah with its common-lands,
79 Kedemoth with its common-lands, and Mephaath with its common-lands.
80 And from the tribe of Gad: Ramoth in Gilead with its common-lands, Mahanaim with its common-lands,
81 Heshbon with its common-lands, and Jazer with its common-lands.

The Family of Issachar

7 The sons of Issachar *were* [a]Tola, [1]Puah, [2]Jashub, and Shimron—four *in all.*
2 The sons of Tola *were* Uzzi, Rephaiah, Jeriel, Jahmai, Jibsam, and Shemuel, heads of their father's house. *The sons* of Tola *were* mighty men of valor in their generations; [a]their number in the days of David *was* twenty-two thousand six hundred.
3 The son of Uzzi *was* Izrahiah, and the sons of Izrahiah *were* Michael, Obadiah, Joel, and Ishiah. All five of them *were* chief men.
4 And with them, by their generations, according to their fathers' houses, *were* thirty-six thousand troops ready for war; for they had many wives and sons.
5 Now their brethren among all the families of Issachar *were* mighty men of valor, listed by their genealogies, eighty-seven thousand in all.

The Family of Benjamin

6 *The sons* of [a]Benjamin *were* Bela, Becher, and Jediael—three *in all.*
7 The sons of Bela were Ezbon, Uzzi, Uzziel, Jerimoth, and Iri—five *in all.* They *were* heads of *their* fathers' houses, and they were listed by their genealogies, twenty-two thousand and thirty-four mighty men of valor.
8 The sons of Becher *were* Zemirah, Joash, Eliezer, Elioenai, Omri, Jerimoth, Abijah, Anathoth, and Alemeth. All these *are* the sons of Becher.
9 And they were recorded by genealogy according to their generations, heads of their fathers' houses, twenty thousand two hundred mighty men of valor.
10 The son of Jediael *was* Bilhan, and the sons of Bilhan *were* Jeush, Benjamin, Ehud, Chenaanah, Zethan, Tharshish, and Ahishahar.
11 All these sons of Jediael *were* heads of their fathers' houses; *there were* seventeen thousand two hundred mighty men of valor fit to go out for war *and* battle.
12 [1]Shuppim and [2]Huppim *were* the sons of [3]Ir, *and* Hushim *was* the son of [4]Aher.

The Family of Naphtali

13 The [a]sons of Naphtali *were* [1]Jahziel, Guni, Jezer, and [2]Shallum, the sons of Bilhah.

The Family of Manasseh (West)

14 The [a]descendants of Manasseh: his Syrian concubine bore him [b]Machir the father of Gilead, the father of Asriel.
15 Machir took as his wife *the sister* of [1]Huppim and [2]Shuppim, whose name *was* Maachah. The name of *Gilead's* [3]grandson *was* [a]Zelophehad, but Zelophehad begot only daughters.
16 (Maachah the wife of Machir bore a son, and she called his name Peresh. The name of his brother *was* Sheresh, and his sons *were* Ulam and Rakem.
17 The son of Ulam *was* [a]Bedan.) These *were* the descendants of Gilead the son of Machir, the son of Manasseh.
18 His sister Hammoleketh bore Ishhod, [1]Abiezer, and Mahlah.
19 And the sons of Shemida were Ahian, Shechem, Likhi, and Aniam.

The Family of Ephraim

20 [a]The sons of Ephraim *were* Shuthelah, Bered his son, Tahath his son, Eladah his son, Tahath his son,
21 Zabad his son, Shuthelah his son,

71 [1]*Beeshterah,* Josh. 21:27
72 [1]*Kishon,* Josh. 21:28
77 [1]Heb. *Rimmono,* an alternate spelling of *Rimmon,* 1 Chr. 4:32

CHAPTER 7

1 [a]Num. 26:23–25 [1]*Puvah,* Gen. 46:13 [2]*Job,* Gen. 46:13
2 [a]2 Sam. 24:1–9; 1 Chr. 27:1
6 [a]Gen. 46:21; Num. 26:38–41; 1 Chr. 8:1
12 [1]*Shupham,* Num. 26:39 [2]*Hupham,* Num. 26:39 [3]*Iri,* v. 7 [4]*Ahiram,* Num. 26:38
13 [a]Num. 26:48–50 [1]*Jahzeel,* Gen. 46:24 [2]*Shillem,* Gen. 46:24
14 [a]Num. 26:29–34 [b]1 Chr. 2:21
15 [a]Num. 26:30–33; 27:1 [1]*Hupham,* v. 12; Num. 26:39 [2]*Shupham,* v. 12; Num. 26:39 [3]Lit. *the second*
17 [a]1 Sam. 12:11
18 [1]*Jeezer,* Num. 26:30
20 [a]Num. 26:35–37

and Ezer and Elead. The men of Gath
who were born in *that* land killed *them*
because they came down to take away
their cattle.
22 Then Ephraim their father mourned
many days, and his brethren came to
comfort him.
23 And when he went in to his wife,
she conceived and bore a son; and he
called his name [1]Beriah, because tragedy had come upon his house.
24 Now his daughter *was* Sheerah,
who built Lower and Upper [a]Beth Horon and Uzzen Sheerah;
25 and Rephah *was* his son, *as well* as
Resheph, and Telah his son, Tahan his
son,
26 Laadan his son, Ammihud his son,
[a]Elishama his son,
27 [1]Nun his son, and [a]Joshua his
son.
28 Now their [a]possessions* and dwelling places *were* Bethel and its towns:
to the east [1]Naaran, to the west Gezer
and its towns, and Shechem and its
towns, as far as [2]Ayyah and its towns;
29 and by the borders of the children
of [a]Manasseh *were* Beth Shean and its
towns, Taanach and its towns, [b]Me-
giddo and its towns, Dor and its towns.
In these dwelt the children of Joseph,
the son of Israel.

The Family of Asher

30 [a]The sons of Asher *were* Imnah,
Ishvah, Ishvi, Beriah, and their sister
Serah.
31 The sons of Beriah *were* Heber and
Malchiel, who was the father of [1]Bir-
zaith.
32 And Heber begot Japhlet, [1]Shomer,
[2]Hotham, and their sister Shua.
33 The sons of Japhlet *were* Pasach,
Bimhal, and Ashvath. These *were* the
children of Japhlet.
34 The sons of [a]Shemer *were* Ahi,
Rohgah, Jehubbah, and Aram.
35 And the sons of his brother Helem
were Zophah, Imna, Shelesh, and
Amal.
36 The sons of Zophah *were* Suah,
Harnepher, Shual, Beri, Imrah,
37 Bezer, Hod, Shamma, Shilshah,
[1]Jithran, and Beera.
38 The sons of Jether *were* Jephunneh,
Pispah, and Ara.
39 The sons of Ulla *were* Arah, Haniel,
and Rizia.
40 All these *were* the children of
Asher, heads of *their* fathers' houses,
choice men, mighty men of valor, chief
leaders. And they were recorded by genealogies among the army fit for battle; their number *was* twenty-six thousand.

The Family Tree of King Saul of Benjamin

8 Now Benjamin begot [a]Bela his
firstborn, Ashbel the second,
[1]Aharah the third,
2 Nohah the fourth, and Rapha the
fifth.
3 The sons of Bela *were* [1]Addar, Gera,
Abihud,
4 Abishua, Naaman, Ahoah,
5 Gera, [1]Shephuphan, and Huram.
6 These *are* the sons of Ehud, who
were the heads of the fathers' *houses*
of the inhabitants of [a]Geba, and who
forced them to move to [b]Manahath:
7 Naaman, Ahijah, and Gera who
forced them to move. He begot Uzza
and Ahihud.
8 Also Shaharaim had children in
the country of Moab, after he had
sent away Hushim and Baara his
wives.
9 By Hodesh his wife he begot Jobab,
Zibia, Mesha, Malcam,
10 Jeuz, Sachiah, and Mirmah. These
were his sons, heads of their fathers'
houses.
11 And by Hushim he begot Abitub
and Elpaal.
12 The sons of Elpaal *were* Eber, Mi-
sham, and Shemed, who built Ono and
Lod with its towns;
13 and Beriah and [a]Shema, who *were*
heads of their fathers' *houses* of the
inhabitants of Aijalon, who drove out
the inhabitants of Gath.
14 Ahio, Shashak, Jeremoth,
15 Zebadiah, Arad, Eder,
16 Michael, Ispah, and Joha *were* the
sons of Beriah.
17 Zebadiah, Meshullam, Hizki, Heber,
18 Ishmerai, Jizliah, and Jobab *were*
the sons of Elpaal.
19 Jakim, Zichri, Zabdi,
20 Elienai, Zillethai, Eliel,
21 Adaiah, Beraiah, and Shimrath
were the sons of [1]Shimei.
22 Ishpan, Eber, Eliel,
23 Abdon, Zichri, Hanan,
24 Hananiah, Elam, Antothijah,
25 Iphdeiah, and Penuel *were* the sons
of Shashak.
26 Shamsherai, Shehariah, Athaliah,
27 Jaareshiah, Elijah, and Zichri *were*
the sons of Jeroham.
28 These *were* heads of the fathers'
houses by their generations, chief men.
These dwelt in Jerusalem.
29 Now [1]the father of Gibeon, whose

23 [1]Lit. *In Tragedy*
24 [a]Josh. 16:3, 5; 2 Chr. 8:5
26 [a]Num. 10:22
27 [a]Ex. 17:9, 14; 24:13; 33:11 [1]Heb. *Non*
28 [a]Josh. 16:1–10 [1]*Naarath,* Josh. 16:7 [2]Many Heb. mss., Bg., LXX, Tg., Vg. *Gazza* *See WW at Josh. 22:9.
29 [a]Gen. 41:51; Josh. 17:7 [b]Josh. 17:11
30 [a]Gen. 46:17; Num. 26:44–47
31 [1]Or *Birzavith* or *Birzoth*
32 [1]*Shemer,* 1 Chr. 7:34 [2]*Helem,* 1 Chr. 7:35
34 [a]1 Chr. 7:32
37 [1]*Jether,* v. 38

CHAPTER 8

1 [a]Gen. 46:21; Num. 26:38; 1 Chr. 7:6 [1]*Ahiram,* Num. 26:38
3 [1]*Ard,* Num. 26:40
5 [1]*Shupham,* Num. 26:39, or *Shuppim,* 1 Chr. 7:12
6 [a]1 Chr. 6:60 [b]1 Chr. 2:52
13 [a]1 Chr. 8:21
21 [1]*Shema,* 1 Chr. 7:13
29 [1]*Jeiel,* 1 Chr. 9:35

[a]wife's name *was* Maacah, dwelt at
Gibeon.
30 And his firstborn son *was* Abdon,
then Zur, Kish, Baal, Nadab,
31 Gedor, Ahio, [1]Zecher,
32 and Mikloth, *who* begot [1]Shimeah.
They also dwelt [2]alongside their
[3]relatives in Jerusalem, with their
brethren.
33 [a]Ner[1] begot Kish, Kish begot Saul,
and Saul begot Jonathan, Malchishua,
[2]Abinadab, and [3]Esh-Baal.
34 The son of Jonathan *was* [1]Merib-
Baal, and Merib-Baal begot [a]Micah.
35 The sons of Micah *were* Pithon, Melech, [1]Tarea, and Ahaz.
36 And Ahaz begot [1]Jehoaddah; Jehoaddah begot Alemeth, Azmaveth, and
Zimri; and Zimri begot Moza.
37 Moza begot Binea, [1]Raphah his son,
Eleasah his son, *and* Azel his son.
38 Azel had six sons whose names
were these: Azrikam, Bocheru, Ishmael, Sheariah, Obadiah, and Hanan.
All these *were* the sons of Azel.
39 And the sons of Eshek his brother
were Ulam his firstborn, Jeush the second, and Eliphelet the third.
40 The sons of Ulam were mighty men
of valor—archers. *They* had many sons
and grandsons, one hundred and fifty
in all. These *were* all sons of Benjamin.

1 **9** So [a]all Israel was [1]recorded by genealogies, and indeed, they *were*
inscribed in the book of the kings of
Israel. But Judah was carried away
captive to Babylon because of their
unfaithfulness.
2 [a]And the first inhabitants who
dwelt in their possessions in their cities
were Israelites, priests, Levites, and
[b]the Nethinim.

Dwellers in Jerusalem

3 Now in [a]Jerusalem the children of
Judah dwelt, and some of the children
of Benjamin, and of the children of
Ephraim and Manasseh:
4 Uthai the son of Ammihud, the son
of Omri, the son of Imri, the son of
Bani, of the descendants of Perez, the
son of Judah.
5 Of the Shilonites: Asaiah the firstborn and his sons.
6 Of the sons of Zerah: Jeuel, and
their brethren—six hundred and
ninety.

29 [a]1 Chr. 9:35–38
31 [1]*Zechariah,* 1 Chr. 9:37
32 [1]*Shimeam,* 1 Chr. 9:38 [2]Lit. *opposite* [3]*brethren*
33 [a]1 Sam. 14:51 [1]Also the son of Gibeon, 1 Chr. 9:36, 39 [2]*Jishui,* 1 Sam. 14:49 [3]*Ishbosheth,* 2 Sam. 2:8
34 [a]2 Sam. 9:12 [1]*Mephibosheth,* 2 Sam. 4:4
35 [1]*Tahrea,* 1 Chr. 9:41
36 [1]*Jarah,* 1 Chr. 9:42
37 [1]*Rephaiah,* 1 Chr. 9:43

CHAPTER 9

1 [a]Ezra 2:59 [1]*enrolled*
2 [a]Ezra 2:70; Neh. 7:73 [b]Ezra 2:43; 8:20
3 [a]Neh. 11:1, 2
10 [a]Neh. 11:10–14
11 [a]2 Chr. 31:13; Jer. 20:1 [1]*Seraiah,* Neh. 11:11
13 [1]Lit. *mighty men of strength*
15 [a]Neh. 11:17
16 [a]Neh. 11:17 [b]Neh. 11:17
19 [1]Lit. *thresholds*

7 Of the sons of Benjamin: Sallu the
son of Meshullam, the son of Hodaviah, the son of Hassenuah;
8 Ibneiah the son of Jeroham; Elah
the son of Uzzi, the son of Michri; Meshullam the son of Shephatiah, the son
of Reuel, the son of Ibnijah;
9 and their brethren, according to
their generations—nine hundred and
fifty-six. All these men *were* heads of
a father's *house* in their fathers'
houses.

The Priests at Jerusalem

10 [a]Of the priests: Jedaiah, Jehoiarib,
and Jachin;
11 [1]Azariah the son of Hilkiah, the son
of Meshullam, the son of Zadok, the
son of Meraioth, the son of Ahitub, the
[a]officer over the house of God;
12 Adaiah the son of Jeroham, the son
of Pashur, the son of Malchijah; Ma-
asai the son of Adiel, the son of
Jahzerah, the son of Meshullam, the
son of Meshillemith, the son of Immer;
13 and their brethren, heads of their
fathers' *houses*—one thousand seven
hundred and sixty. *They were* [1]very
able men for the work of the service
of the house of God.

The Levites at Jerusalem

14 Of the Levites: Shemaiah the son of
Hasshub, the son of Azrikam, the son
of Hashabiah, of the sons of Merari;
15 Bakbakkar, Heresh, Galal, and Mattaniah the son of Micah, the son of
[a]Zichri, the son of Asaph;
16 [a]Obadiah the son of [b]Shemaiah, the
son of Galal, the son of Jeduthun; and
Berechiah the son of Asa, the son of
Elkanah, who lived in the villages of
the Netophathites.

The Levite Gatekeepers

17 And the gatekeepers *were* Shallum,
Akkub, Talmon, Ahiman, and their
brethren. Shallum *was* the chief.
18 Until then *they had been* gatekeepers for the camps of the children
of Levi at the King's Gate on the east.
19 Shallum the son of Kore, the son
of Ebiasaph, the son of Korah, and his
brethren, from his father's house, the
Korahites, *were* in charge of the work
of the service, [1]gatekeepers of the tab-

9:1–34 These verses are the climax to the genealogies, outlining the descendants of those who returned to Judah from the Exile. The roots of the remnant have been traced from Adam (1:1) all the way down to their present state in Jerusalem. This section affirms that 1 and 2 Chr. are postexilic works.
9:1 See section 1 of Truth-In-Action at the end of 1 Chr.

ernacle. Their fathers had been keepers of the entrance to the camp of the
LORD.
20 And [a]Phinehas the son of Eleazar
had been the officer over them in time
past; the LORD *was* with him.
21 [a]Zechariah the son of Meshelemiah
was [1]keeper of the door of the tabernacle of meeting.
22 All those chosen as gatekeepers
were two hundred and twelve. [a]They
were recorded by their genealogy, in
their villages. David and Samuel
[b]the *seer had appointed them to their
trusted office.
23 So they and their children *were* in
charge of the gates of the house of the
LORD, the house of the tabernacle, by
assignment.
24 The gatekeepers were assigned to
the four directions: the east, west,
north, and south.
25 And their brethren in their villages
had to come with them from time to
time [a]for seven days.
26 For in this trusted office *were* four
chief gatekeepers; they were Levites.
And they had charge over the chambers and treasuries of the house of
God.
27 And they lodged *all* around the
house of God because [1]they *had* the
[a]responsibility, and they *were* in
charge of opening *it* every morning.

Other Levite Responsibilities

28 Now *some* of them were in charge
of the serving vessels, for they brought
them in and took them out by count.
29 *Some* of them *were* appointed over
the furnishings and over all the implements of the sanctuary, and over the
[a]fine flour and the wine and the oil and
the incense and the spices.
30 And *some* of the sons of the priests
made [a]the ointment of the spices.
31 Mattithiah of the Levites, the firstborn of Shallum the Korahite, had the
trusted office [a]over the things that
were baked in the pans.
32 And some of their brethren of the
sons of the Kohathites [a]*were* in charge
of preparing the showbread for every
Sabbath.
33 These are [a]the singers, heads of the
fathers' *houses* of the Levites, *who
lodged* in the chambers, *and were* free
from other duties; for they were employed in *that* work day and night.
34 These heads of the fathers' *houses*
of the Levites *were* heads throughout
their generations. They dwelt at Jerusalem.

The Family of King Saul

35 Jeiel the father of Gibeon, whose
wife's name *was* [a]Maacah, dwelt at
Gibeon.
36 His firstborn son *was* Abdon, then
Zur, Kish, Baal, Ner, Nadab,
37 Gedor, Ahio, [1]Zechariah, and Mikloth.
38 And Mikloth begot [1]Shimeam. They
also dwelt alongside their relatives in
Jerusalem, with their brethren.
39 [a]Ner begot Kish, Kish begot Saul,
and Saul begot Jonathan, Malchishua,
Abinadab, and Esh-Baal.
40 The son of Jonathan *was* Merib-
Baal, and Merib-Baal begot Micah.
41 The sons of Micah *were* Pithon, Melech, [1]Tahrea, [a]and[2] Ahaz.
42 And Ahaz begot [1]Jarah; Jarah begot Alemeth, Azmaveth, and Zimri;
and Zimri begot Moza;
43 Moza begot Binea, [1]Rephaiah his
son, Eleasah his son, and Azel his son.
44 And Azel had six sons whose names
were these: Azrikam, Bocheru, Ishmael, Sheariah, Obadiah, and Hanan;
these *were* the sons of Azel.

Tragic End of Saul and His Sons

10 Now [a]the Philistines fought
against Israel; and the men of
Israel fled from before the Philistines,
and fell slain on Mount Gilboa.
2 Then the Philistines followed hard
after Saul and his sons. And the Philistines killed Jonathan, [1]Abinadab, and
Malchishua, Saul's sons.
3 The battle became fierce against
Saul. The archers hit him, and he was
wounded by the archers.
4 Then Saul said to his armorbearer,
"Draw your sword, and thrust me
through with it, lest these uncircumcised men come and abuse me." But
his armorbearer would not, for he was
greatly afraid. Therefore Saul took a
sword and fell on it.
5 And when his armorbearer saw that

20 [a]Num. 25:6–13; 31:6 **21** [a]1 Chr. 26:2, 14 [1]*gatekeeper* **22** [a]1 Chr. 26:1, 2 [b]1 Sam. 9:9 *See WW at 1 Sam. 9:9. **25** [a]2 Kin. 11:4–7; 2 Chr. 23:8 **27** [a]1 Chr. 23:30–32 [1]*the watch was committed to them* **29** [a]1 Chr. 23:29 **30** [a]Ex. 30:22–25 **31** [a]Lev. 2:5; 6:21 **32** [a]Lev. 24:5–8 **33** [a]1 Chr. 6:31; 25:1

35 [a]1 Chr. 8:29–32 **37** [1]*Zecher,* 1 Chr. 8:31 **38** [1]*Shimeah,* 1 Chr. 8:32 **39** [a]1 Chr. 8:33–38 **41** [a]1 Chr. 8:35 [1]*Tarea,* 1 Chr. 8:35 [2]So with Arab., Syr., Tg., Vg. (cf. 8:35); MT, LXX omit *and Ahaz* **42** [1]*Jehoaddah,* 1 Chr. 8:36 **43** [1]*Raphah,* 1 Chr. 8:37

CHAPTER 10

1 [a]1 Sam. 31:1, 2 **2** [1]*Jishui,* 1 Sam. 14:49

9:35–44 This section gives an account of the family of King Saul. It sets the stage for the discussion of the beginning of the kingdom under Saul in ch. 10.

10:1–14 The story of the rise and fall of King Saul is more explicitly treated in 1 Sam. 9—31. The emphasis of 1 Chr. is on King David, and so ch. 10 serves only as a general overview of Saul's life. Vv. 13, 14 give a glaring indictment of his failure as king.

Saul was dead, he also fell on his sword and died.
6 So Saul and his three sons died, and all his house died together.
7 And when all the men of Israel who *were* in the valley saw that they had fled and that Saul and his sons were dead, they forsook their cities and fled; then the Philistines came and dwelt in them.
8 So it happened the next day, when the Philistines came to [1]strip the slain, that they found Saul and his sons fallen on Mount Gilboa.
9 And they stripped him and took his head and his armor, and sent word *throughout* the land of the Philistines to proclaim the news *in the temple* of their idols and among the people.
10 [a]Then they put his armor in the [1]temple of their gods, and fastened his head in the temple of Dagon.
11 And when all Jabesh Gilead heard all that the Philistines had done to Saul,
12 all the [a]valiant men arose and took the body of Saul and the bodies of his sons; and they brought them to [b]Jabesh, and buried their bones under the tamarisk tree at Jabesh, and fasted seven days.
1 13 So Saul died for his unfaithfulness which he had [1]committed against the LORD, [a]because he did not keep the word of the LORD, and also because [b]he consulted a medium for guidance.
14 But *he* did not inquire of the LORD; therefore He killed him, and [a]turned the kingdom over to David the son of Jesse.

David Made King over All Israel

11 Then [a]all Israel came together to David at Hebron, saying, "Indeed we *are* your bone and your flesh.
2 "Also, in time past, even when Saul was king, you *were* the one who led Israel out and brought them in; and the LORD your [a]God said to you, 'You shall [b]shepherd My people Israel, and be ruler over My people Israel.'"
3 Therefore all the elders of Israel came to the king at Hebron, and David made a covenant with them at Hebron before the LORD. And [a]they anointed David king over Israel, according to the word of the LORD [1]by [b]Samuel.

8 [1]*plunder*
10 [a]1 Sam. 31:10 [1]Lit. *house*
12 [a]1 Sam. 14:52 [b]2 Sam. 21:12
13 [a]1 Sam. 13:13, 14; 15:22–26 [b][Lev. 19:31; 20:6]; 1 Sam. 28:7 [1]Lit. *transgressed*
14 [a]1 Sam. 15:28; 2 Sam. 3:9, 10; 5:3; 1 Chr. 12:23

CHAPTER 11

1 [a]2 Sam. 5:1
2 [a]1 Sam. 16:1–3; Ps. 78:70–72 [b]2 Sam. 7:7
3 [a]2 Sam. 5:3 [b]1 Sam. 16:1, 4, 12, 13 [1]Lit. *by the hand of Samuel*
4 [a]2 Sam. 5:6 [b]Josh. 15:8, 63; Judg. 1:21; 19:10, 11
6 [1]Lit. *head*
7 [1]*Zion,* 2 Sam. 5:7
8 [1]Lit. *The Landfill* [2]Lit. *revived*
9 [a]2 Sam. 3:1 [b]1 Sam. 16:18
10 [a]2 Sam. 23:8 [b]1 Sam. 16:1, 12
11 [a]1 Chr. 27:2 [b]1 Chr. 12:18 [1]So with Qr.; Kt., LXX, Vg. *the thirty* (cf. 2 Sam. 23:8)
12 [a]1 Chr. 27:4
13 [1]*Ephes Dammim,* 1 Sam. 17:1
14 [1]Lit. *took their stand*
15 [a]2 Sam. 23:13 [b]2 Sam. 5:18; 1 Chr. 14:9 [1]Lit. *Giants*

The City of David

4 And David and all Israel [a]went to Jerusalem, which is Jebus, [b]where the Jebusites *were,* the inhabitants of the land.
5 But the inhabitants of Jebus said to David, "You shall not come in here!" Nevertheless David took the stronghold of Zion (that is, the City of David).
6 Now David said, "Whoever attacks the Jebusites first shall be [1]chief and captain." And Joab the son of Zeruiah went up first, and became chief.
7 Then David dwelt in the stronghold; therefore they called it [1]the City of David.
8 And he built the city around it, from [1]the Millo to the surrounding area. Joab [2]repaired the rest of the city.
9 So David [a]went on and became great, and the LORD of hosts *was* with [b]him.

The Mighty Men of David

10 Now [a]these *were* the heads of the mighty men whom David had, who strengthened themselves with him in his kingdom, with all Israel, to make him king, according to [b]the word of the LORD concerning Israel.
11 And this *is* the number of the mighty men whom David had: [a]Jashobeam the son of a Hachmonite, [b]chief of [1]the captains; he had lifted up his spear against three hundred, killed *by him* at one time.
12 After him *was* Eleazar the son of [a]Dodo, the Ahohite, who *was one* of the three mighty men.
13 He was with David at [1]Pasdammim. Now there the Philistines were gathered for battle, and there was a piece of ground full of barley. So the people fled from the Philistines.
14 But they [1]stationed themselves in the middle of *that* field, defended it, and killed the Philistines. So the LORD brought about a great victory.
15 Now three of the thirty chief men [a]went down to the rock to David, into the cave of Adullam; and the army of the Philistines encamped [b]in the Valley of [1]Rephaim.
16 David *was* then in the stronghold, and the garrison of the Philistines *was* then in Bethlehem.
17 And David said with longing, "Oh,

10:13 See section 1 of Truth-In-Action at the end of 1 Chr.
11:1–9 See the text and notes of 2 Sam. 5:1–7 for more information on David's coronation and the capture of Jerusalem.
11:10–47 See the text and notes on 2 Sam. 23:8–39, where David's special guard is also listed.

that someone would give me a drink
of water from the well of Bethlehem,
which is by the gate!"
18 So the three broke through the
camp of the Philistines, drew water
from the well of Bethlehem that *was*
by the gate, and took *it* and brought
it to David. Nevertheless David would
not drink it, but poured it out to the
LORD.
19 And he said, "Far be it from me, O
my God, that I should do this! Shall I
drink the blood of these men *who have*
put their lives *in jeopardy*? For at the
risk of their lives they brought it."
Therefore he would not drink it. These
things were done by the three mighty
men.
20 [a]Abishai the brother of Joab was
chief of *another* [1]three. He had lifted
up his spear against three hundred
men, killed *them,* and won a name
among *these* three.
21 [a]Of the three he was more honored
than the other two men. Therefore he
became their captain. However he did
not attain to the *first* three.
22 Benaiah was the son of Jehoiada,
the son of a valiant man from Kabzeel,
who [1]had done many deeds. [a]He had
killed two lion-like heroes of Moab.
He also had gone down and killed a
lion in the midst of a pit on a snowy
day.
23 And he killed an Egyptian, a man
of *great* height, [1]five cubits tall. In the
Egyptian's hand *there was* a spear like
a weaver's beam; and he went down
to him with a staff, wrested the spear
out of the Egyptian's hand, and killed
him with his own spear.
24 These *things* Benaiah the son of Jehoiada did, and won a name among
three mighty men.
25 Indeed he was more honored than
the thirty, but he did not attain to the
first three. And David appointed him
over his guard.
26 Also the mighty warriors *were*
[a]Asahel the brother of Joab, Elhanan
the son of Dodo of Bethlehem,
27 [1]Shammoth the Harorite, [a]Helez the
[2]Pelonite,
28 [a]Ira the son of Ikkesh the Tekoite,
[b]Abiezer the Anathothite,
29 [1]Sibbechai the Hushathite, [2]Ilai the
Ahohite,
30 [a]Maharai the Netophathite, [1]Heled
the son of Baanah the Netophathite,
31 [1]Ithai the son of Ribai of Gibeah,
of the sons of Benjamin, [a]Benaiah the
Pirathonite,
32 [1]Hurai of the brooks of Gaash,
[2]Abiel the Arbathite,
33 Azmaveth the [1]Baharumite, Eliahba
the Shaalbonite,
34 the sons of [1]Hashem the Gizonite,
Jonathan the son of Shageh the Hararite,
35 Ahiam the son of [1]Sacar the Hararite, [2]Eliphal the son of [3]Ur,
36 Hepher the Mecherathite, Ahijah
the Pelonite,
37 [1]Hezro the Carmelite, [2]Naarai the
son of Ezbai,
38 Joel the brother of Nathan, Mibhar
the son of Hagri,
39 Zelek the Ammonite, Naharai the
[1]Berothite (the armorbearer of Joab
the son of Zeruiah),
40 Ira the Ithrite, Gareb the Ithrite,
41 [a]Uriah the Hittite, [1]Zabad the son
of Ahlai,
42 Adina the son of Shiza the Reubenite (a chief of the Reubenites) and
thirty with him,
43 Hanan the son of Maachah, Joshaphat the Mithnite,
44 Uzzia the Ashterathite, Shama and
Jeiel the sons of Hotham the Aroerite,
45 Jediael the son of Shimri, and Joha
his brother, the Tizite,
46 Eliel the Mahavite, Jeribai and
Joshaviah the sons of Elnaam, Ithmah
the Moabite,
47 Eliel, Obed, and Jaasiel the Me-
zobaite.

The Growth of David's Army

12 Now [a]these *were* the men who
came to David at [b]Ziklag while
he was still a fugitive from Saul the
son of Kish; and they *were* among the
mighty men, helpers in the war,
2 armed with bows, using both the
right hand and [a]the left in *hurling*
stones and *shooting* arrows with the
bow. *They were* of Benjamin, Saul's
brethren.
3 The chief *was* Ahiezer, then Joash,
the sons of [1]Shemaah the Gibeathite;
Jeziel and Pelet the sons of Azmaveth;
Berachah, and Jehu the Anathothite;
4 Ishmaiah the Gibeonite, a mighty
man among the thirty, and over the
thirty; Jeremiah, Jahaziel, Johanan,
and Jozabad the Gederathite;
5 Eluzai, Jerimoth, Bealiah, Shemariah, and Shephatiah the Haruphite;

20 [a]2 Sam. 23:18; 1 Chr. 18:12 [1]So with MT, LXX, Vg.; Syr. *thirty*
21 [a]2 Sam. 23:19
22 [a]2 Sam. 23:20 [1]*was great in deeds*
23 [1]About 7½ feet
26 [a]2 Sam. 23:24
27 [a]2 Sam. 23:26; 1 Chr. 27:10 [1]*Shammah the Harodite,* 2 Sam. 23:25 [2]*Paltite,* 2 Sam. 23:26
28 [a]1 Chr. 27:9 [b]1 Chr. 27:12
29 [1]*Mebunnai,* 2 Sam. 23:27 [2]*Zalmon,* 2 Sam. 23:28
30 [a]1 Chr. 27:13 [1]*Heleb,* 2 Sam. 23:29, or *Heldai,* 1 Chr. 27:15
31 [a]1 Chr. 27:14 [1]*Ittai,* 2 Sam. 23:29
32 [1]*Hiddai,* 2 Sam. 23:30 [2]*Abi-Albon,* 2 Sam. 23:31
33 [1]*Barhumite,* 2 Sam. 23:31
34 [1]*Jashen,* 2 Sam. 23:32
35 [1]*Sharar,* 2 Sam. 23:33 [2]*Eliphelet,* 2 Sam. 23:34 [3]*Ahasbai,* 2 Sam. 23:34
37 [1]*Hezrai,* 2 Sam. 23:38 [2]*Paarai the Arbite,* 2 Sam. 23:35
39 [1]*Beerothite,* 2 Sam. 23:37
41 [a]2 Sam. 11 [1]The last sixteen are not added in 2 Sam. 23.

CHAPTER 12

1 [a]1 Sam. 27:2 [b]1 Sam. 27:6
2 [a]Judg. 3:15; 20:16
3 [1]Or *Hasmaah*

12:1–22 This chapter contains much that is not recorded in 1 and 2 Sam. It tells of David's supporters from Ziklag, from the tribe of Gad, and how even some of Saul's relatives went over to David's side.

6 Elkanah, Jisshiah, Azarel, Joezer,
and Jashobeam, the Korahites;
7 and Joelah and Zebadiah the sons
of Jeroham of Gedor.
8 *Some* Gadites [1]joined David at the
stronghold in the wilderness, mighty
men of valor, men trained for battle,
who could handle shield and spear,
whose faces *were like* the faces of
lions, and *were* [a]as swift as gazelles
on the mountains:
9 Ezer the first, Obadiah the second,
Eliab the third,
10 Mishmannah the fourth, Jeremiah
the fifth,
11 Attai the sixth, Eliel the seventh,
12 Johanan the eighth, Elzabad the
ninth,
13 Jeremiah the tenth, and Machbanai
the eleventh.
14 These *were* from the sons of Gad,
captains of the army; the least was
over a hundred, and the greatest was
over a [a]thousand.
15 These *are* the ones who crossed the
Jordan in the first month, when it had
overflowed all its [a]banks; and they put
to flight all *those* in the valleys, to the
east and to the west.
16 Then some of the sons of Benjamin
and Judah came to David at the stronghold.
17 And David went out [1]to meet them,
and answered and said to them, "If you
have come peaceably to me to help me,
my heart will be united with you; but
if to betray me to my enemies, since
there is no [2]wrong in my hands, may
the God of our fathers look and bring
judgment."
18 Then the Spirit [1]came upon
[a]Amasai, chief of the captains, *and he
said:*

"*We are* yours, O David;
We *are* on your side, O son of
Jesse!
Peace, peace to you,
And peace to your helpers!
For your God helps you."

So David received them, and made
them captains of the troop.
19 And *some* from Manasseh defected
to David [a]when he was going with the
Philistines to battle against Saul; but
they did not help them, for the lords
of the Philistines sent him away by
agreement, saying, [b]"He may defect to
his master Saul *and endanger* our
heads."
20 When he went to Ziklag, those of
Manasseh who defected to him were
Adnah, Jozabad, Jediael, Michael, Jozabad, Elihu, and Zillethai, captains of
the thousands who *were* from Manasseh.
21 And they helped David against
[a]the bands *of raiders,* for they *were* all
mighty men of valor, and they were
captains in the army.
22 For at *that* time they came to David
day by day to help him, until *it was* a
great army, [a]like the army of God.

David's Army at Hebron

23 Now these *were* the numbers of the
[1]divisions *that were* equipped for war,
and [a]came to David at [b]Hebron to
[c]turn *over* the kingdom of Saul to him,
[d]according to the word of the LORD:
24 of the sons of Judah bearing shield
and spear, six thousand eight hundred
[1]armed for war;
25 of the sons of Simeon, mighty men
of valor fit for war, seven thousand one
hundred;
26 of the sons of Levi four thousand
six hundred;
27 Jehoiada, the leader of the Aaronites, and with him three thousand
seven hundred;
28 [a]Zadok, a young man, a valiant
warrior, and from his father's house
twenty-two captains;
29 of the sons of Benjamin, relatives
of Saul, three thousand (until then
[a]the greatest part of them had remained loyal to the house of Saul);
30 of the sons of Ephraim twenty thousand eight hundred, mighty men of
valor, [1]famous men throughout their
father's house;
31 of the half-tribe of Manasseh eighteen thousand, who were designated
by name to come and make David
king;
32 of the sons of Issachar [a]who had understanding of the times, to know what
Israel ought to do, their chiefs were
two hundred; and all their brethren
were at their command;
33 of Zebulun there were fifty thousand who went out to battle, expert in
war with all weapons of war, [a]stout-

8 [a]2 Sam. 2:18 [1]Lit. *separated themselves to*
14 [a]1 Sam. 18:13
15 [a]Josh. 3:15; 4:18, 19
17 [1]Lit. *before them* [2]Lit. *violence*
18 [a]2 Sam. 17:25 [1]Lit. *clothed*
19 [a]1 Sam. 29:2 [b]1 Sam. 29:4
21 [a]1 Sam. 30:1, 9, 10
22 [a]Gen. 32:2; Josh. 5:13–15
23 [a]2 Sam. 2:1–4 [b]1 Chr. 11:1 [c]1 Chr. 10:14 [d]1 Sam. 16:1–4 [1]Lit. *heads of those*
24 [1]*equipped*
28 [a]2 Sam. 8:17; 1 Chr. 6:8, 53
29 [a]2 Sam. 2:8, 9
30 [1]Lit. *men of names*
32 [a]Esth. 1:13
33 [a]Ps. 12:2; [James 1:8]

12:18 This is the first of several references in 1 Chr. to utterances inspired by the Spirit of God. See also 2 Chr. 15:1; 20:14; 24:20. **The Spirit came upon** literally means "the Spirit clothed Himself with" Amasai. The prophets understood that the source for prophetic inspiration was the Spirit of God (1 Sam. 10:6, 10; 19:20, 23). For more on the Holy Spirit in 1 Chr., see Introduction to 1 Chronicles: The Holy Spirit at Work.

12:23–40 David's troops made him king over all Israel at Hebron.

hearted men who could keep ranks;
34 of Naphtali one thousand captains,
and with them thirty-seven thousand
with shield and spear;
35 of the Danites who could keep battle formation, twenty-eight thousand
six hundred;
36 of Asher, those who could go out
to war, able to keep battle formation,
forty thousand;
37 of the Reubenites and the Gadites
and the half-tribe of Manasseh, from
the other side of the Jordan, one hundred and twenty thousand armed for
battle with every *kind* of weapon of
war.
38 All these men of war, who could
keep ranks, came to Hebron with a
loyal heart, to make David king over
all Israel; and all the rest of Israel *were*
of [a]one mind to make David king.
39 And they were there with David
three days, eating and drinking, for
their brethren had prepared for them.
40 Moreover those who were near to
them, from as far away as Issachar and
Zebulun and Naphtali, were bringing
food on donkeys and camels, on mules
and oxen—provisions of flour and
cakes of figs and cakes of raisins, wine
and oil and oxen and sheep abundantly, for *there was* joy in Israel.

The Ark Brought from Kirjath Jearim

13 Then David consulted with the
[a]captains of thousands and hundreds, *and* with every leader.
2 And David said to all the assembly
of Israel, "If *it seems* good to you, and
if it is of the LORD our God, let us send
out to our brethren everywhere *who
are* [a]left in all the land of Israel, and
with them to the priests and Levites
who are in their cities *and* their
common-lands, that they may gather
together to us;
3 "and let us bring the ark of our God
back to us, [a]for we have not inquired
at it since the days of Saul."
4 Then all the assembly said that they
would do so, for the thing was right
in the eyes of all the people.
5 So [a]David gathered all Israel together, from [b]Shihor in Egypt to as far
as the entrance of Hamath, to bring the
ark of God [c]from Kirjath Jearim.
6 And David and all Israel went up
to [a]Baalah,[1] to Kirjath Jearim, which
belonged to Judah, to bring up from
there the ark of God the LORD, [b]who
dwells *between* the *cherubim, where
His name is proclaimed.
7 So they [1]carried the ark of God 3
[a]on a new cart [b]from the house of
Abinadab, and Uzza and Ahio drove the
cart.
8 Then [a]David and all Israel played
music before God with all *their* might,
with [1]singing, on harps, on stringed instruments, on tambourines, on cymbals, and with trumpets.
9 And when they came to [1]Chidon's
threshing floor, Uzza put out his hand
to hold the ark, for the oxen [2]stumbled.
10 Then the anger of the LORD was
aroused against Uzza, and He struck
him [a]because he put his hand to
the ark; and he [b]died there before
God.
11 And David became angry because
of the LORD's *outbreak against Uzza;
therefore that place is called [1]Perez
Uzza to this day.
12 David was afraid of God that day,
saying, "How can I bring the ark of
God to me?"
13 So David would not move the ark
with him into the City of David, but
took it aside into the house of Obed-
Edom the Gittite.
14 [a]The ark of God remained with the
family of Obed-Edom in his house
three months. And the LORD blessed
[b]the house of Obed-Edom and all that
he had.

David Established at Jerusalem

14 Now [a]Hiram king of Tyre sent
messengers to David, and cedar
trees, with masons and carpenters, to
build him a house.
2 So David knew that the LORD had
established him as king over Israel, for
his kingdom was [a]highly exalted for
the sake of His people Israel.
3 Then David took more wives in Jerusalem, and David begot more sons
and daughters.
4 And [a]these are the names of his
children whom he had in Jerusalem:
[1]Shammua, Shobab, Nathan, Solomon,
5 Ibhar, [1]Elishua, [2]Elpelet,

38 [a]2 Chr. 30:12

CHAPTER 13

1 [a]1 Chr. 11:15; 12:34
2 [a]1 Sam. 31:1; Is. 37:4
3 [a]1 Sam. 7:1, 2
5 [a]1 Sam. 7:5 [b]Josh. 13:3 [c]1 Sam. 6:21; 7:1, 2
6 [a]Josh. 15:9, 60 [b]Ex. 25:22; 1 Sam. 4:4; 2 Kin. 19:15 [1]*Baale Judah,* 2 Sam. 6:2 *See WW at Ex. 25:18.
7 [a]Num. 4:15; 1 Sam. 6:7 [b]1 Sam. 7:1 [1]Lit. *caused the ark of God to ride*
8 [a]2 Sam. 6:5 [1]*songs*
9 [1]*Nachon,* 2 Sam. 6:6 [2]Or *let it go off*
10 [a][Num. 4:15]; 1 Chr. 15:13, 15 [b]Lev. 10:2
11 [1]Lit. *Outburst Against Uzza* *See WW at Ezek. 22:30.
14 [a]2 Sam. 6:11 [b][Gen. 30:27]; 1 Chr. 26:4–8

CHAPTER 14

1 [a]2 Sam. 5:11; 1 Kin. 5:1
2 [a]Num. 24:7
4 [a]1 Chr. 3:5–8 [1]*Shimea,* 1 Chr. 3:5
5 [1]*Elishama,* 1 Chr. 3:6 [2]*Eliphelet,* 1 Chr. 3:6

13:1–14 Read the text and notes of 2 Sam. 6:1–11. In keeping with the chronicler's purpose to write a religious history of the nation, the order of events is sometimes rearranged to make a point. The first attempt to bring the ark to Jerusalem actually occurred later, but 1 Chr. places the incident first in David's reign. This highlights David's desire to restore the worship of Yahweh.
13:7–10 See section 3 of Truth-In-Action at the end of 1 Chr.

6 Nogah, Nepheg, Japhia,
7 Elishama, [1]Beeliada, and Eliphelet.

The Philistines Defeated

8 Now when the Philistines heard
that [a]David had been anointed king
over all Israel, all the Philistines went
up to search for David. And David
heard *of it* and went out against them.
9 Then the Philistines went and made
a raid [a]on the Valley of [1]Rephaim.
10 And David [a]inquired of God, saying, "Shall I go up against the Philistines? Will You deliver them into my
hand?" The LORD said to him, "Go
up, for I will deliver them into your
hand."
11 So they went up to Baal Perazim,
and David defeated them there. Then
David said, "God has broken through
my enemies by my hand like a breakthrough of water." Therefore they
called the name of that place [1]Baal Perazim.
12 And when they left their gods there,
David gave a commandment, and they
were burned with fire.
13 [a]Then the Philistines once again
made a raid on the valley.
14 Therefore David inquired again of
God, and God said to him, "You shall
not go up after them; circle around
them, [a]and come upon them in front
of the mulberry trees.
15 "And it shall be, when you hear a
sound of marching in the tops of the
mulberry trees, then you shall go out
to battle, for God has gone out before
you to strike the camp of the Philistines."
16 So David did as God commanded
him, and they drove back the army of
the Philistines from [1]Gibeon as far as
Gezer.
17 Then [a]the fame of David went out
into all lands, and the LORD [b]brought
the fear of him upon all nations.

The Ark Brought to Jerusalem

15 *David* built houses for himself
in the City of David; and he prepared a place for the ark of God,
[a]and pitched a tent for it.
2 Then David said, "No one may
carry the [a]ark of God but the Levites,
for [b]the LORD has chosen them to carry
the ark of God and to **minister** before
Him forever."

7 [1]*Eliada,* 2 Sam. 5:6; 1 Chr. 3:8
8 [a]2 Sam. 5:17–21
9 [a]Josh. 17:15; 18:16; 1 Chr. 11:15; 14:13 [1]Lit. *Giants*
10 [a]1 Sam. 23:2, 4; 30:8; 2 Sam. 2:1; 5:19, 23; 21:1
11 [1]Lit. *Master of Breakthroughs*
13 [a]2 Sam. 5:22–25
14 [a]2 Sam. 5:23
16 [1]*Geba,* 2 Sam. 5:25
17 [a]Josh. 6:27; 2 Chr. 26:8 [b][Ex. 15:14–16; Deut. 2:25; 11:25]; 2 Chr. 20:29

CHAPTER 15

1 [a]1 Chr. 16:1
2 [a][Num. 4:15]; 2 Sam. 6:1–11 [b]Num. 4:2–15; Deut. 10:8; 31:9

WORD WEALTH

15:2 minister, *sharat* (shah-*raht*); Strong's #8334: To wait on, to serve, to minister, to attend. *Sharat* refers to the tasks to which the closest servants of God or the king are assigned. The priests and Levites in their ministry in the tabernacle and the temple served God. Examples of significant positions of service to important persons include Joseph to Potiphar (Gen. 39:4), Joshua to Moses (Ex. 33:11), and Elisha to Elijah (1 Kin. 19:21). In today's usage the title "minister" conveys austerity and self-authority, while the scriptural use of the term conveys yieldedness, servanthood, and obedience.

3 And David [a]gathered all Israel together at Jerusalem, to bring up the ark
of the LORD to its place, which he had
prepared for it.
4 Then David assembled the children
of Aaron and the Levites:
5 of the sons of Kohath, Uriel the
chief, and one hundred and twenty of
his [1]brethren;
6 of the sons of Merari, Asaiah the
chief, and two hundred and twenty of
his brethren;
7 of the sons of Gershom, Joel the
chief, and one hundred and thirty of
his brethren;
8 of the sons of [a]Elizaphan, Shemaiah
the chief, and two hundred of his brethren;
9 of the sons of [a]Hebron, Eliel the
chief, and eighty of his brethren;
10 of the sons of Uzziel, Amminadab
the chief, and one hundred and twelve
of his brethren.
11 And David called for [a]Zadok and 3
[b]Abiathar the priests, and for the Levites: for Uriel, Asaiah, Joel, Shemaiah,
Eliel, and Amminadab.
12 He said to them, "You *are* the heads
of the fathers' *houses* of the Levites;
[1]sanctify yourselves, you and your
brethren, that you may bring up the
ark of the LORD God of Israel to *the
place* I have prepared for it.
13 "For [a]because you *did* not *do it* the
first *time,* [b]the LORD our God broke out
against us, because we did not consult
Him [1]about the proper order."

3 [a]Ex. 40:20, 21; 2 Sam. 6:12; 1 Kin. 8:1; 1 Chr. 13:5
5 [1]*kinsmen*
8 [a]Ex. 6:22
9 [a]Ex. 6:18
11 [a]2 Sam. 8:17; 15:24–29, 35, 36; 18:19, 22, 27; 19:11; 20:25; 1 Chr. 12:28 [b]1 Sam. 22:20–23; 23:6; 30:7; 1 Kin. 2:22, 26, 27; Mark 2:6
12 [1]*consecrate*
13 [a]2 Sam. 6:3 [b]1 Chr. 13:7–11 [1]*regarding the ordinance*

14:8–17 This account of the defeat of the Philistines when David heard the sound of marching in the mulberry trees is in 2 Sam. 5:17–25.

15:1–29 Read the text and notes of 2 Sam. 6:12–20. About three months after the events of ch. 13 David brought the ark up to Jerusalem.

15:11–15 See section 3 of Truth-In-Action at the end of 1 Chr.

14 So the priests and the Levites
[1]sanctified themselves to bring up the
ark of the LORD God of Israel.
15 And the children of the Levites bore
the ark of God on their shoulders, by
its poles, as [a]Moses had commanded
according to the word of the LORD.
16 Then David spoke to the leaders of
the Levites to appoint their brethren
to be the singers accompanied by instruments of music, stringed instruments, harps, and cymbals, by raising
the voice with resounding joy.
17 So the Levites appointed [a]Heman
the son of Joel; and of his brethren,
[b]Asaph the son of Berechiah; and of
their brethren, the sons of Merari,
[c]Ethan the son of Kushaiah;
18 and with them their brethren of the
second *rank:* Zechariah, [1]Ben, Jaaziel,
Shemiramoth, Jehiel, Unni, Eliab, Benaiah, Maaseiah, Mattithiah, Elipheleh,
Mikneiah, Obed-Edom, and Jeiel, the
gatekeepers;
19 the singers, Heman, Asaph, and
Ethan, *were* to sound the cymbals of
bronze;
20 Zechariah, [1]Aziel, Shemiramoth,
Jehiel, Unni, Eliab, Maaseiah, and Benaiah, with strings according to [a]Ala-
moth;
21 Mattithiah, Elipheleh, Mikneiah,
Obed-Edom, Jeiel, and Azaziah, to direct with harps on the [a]Sheminith;
22 Chenaniah, leader of the Levites,
was *instructor *in charge of* the music,
because he *was* skillful;
23 Berechiah and Elkanah *were* doorkeepers for the ark;
24 Shebaniah, Joshaphat, Nethanel,
Amasai, Zechariah, Benaiah, and Eliezer, the priests, [a]were to blow the trumpets before the ark of God; and [b]Obed-
Edom and Jehiah, doorkeepers for the
ark.
25 So [a]David, the elders of Israel, and
the captains over thousands went to
bring up the ark of the covenant of the
LORD from the house of Obed-Edom
with joy.
26 And so it was, when God helped the
Levites who bore the ark of the covenant of the LORD, that they offered
seven bulls and seven rams.
27 David was clothed with a robe of
fine [a]linen, as were all the Levites who
bore the ark, the singers, and Chenaniah the music master *with* the singers.
David also wore a linen *ephod.
28 [a]Thus all Israel brought up the ark
of the covenant of the LORD with
*shouting and with the sound of the
horn, with trumpets and with cymbals,
making music with stringed instruments and harps.
29 And it happened, [a]*as* the ark of the
covenant of the LORD came to the City
of David, that Michal, Saul's daughter,
looked through a window and saw
King David whirling and playing music; and she despised him in her *heart.

14 [1]*consecrated*
15 [a]Ex. 25:14; Num. 4:15; 7:9
17 [a]1 Chr. 6:33; 25:1 [b]1 Chr. 6:39 [c]1 Chr. 6:44
18 [1]So with MT, Vg.; LXX omits *Ben*
20 [a]Ps. 46:title [1]*Jaaziel,* v. 18
21 [a]Ps. 6:title
22 *See WW at Jer. 10:24.
24 [a][Num. 10:8]; Ps. 81:3 [b]1 Chr. 13:13, 14
25 [a]2 Sam. 6:12, 13; 1 Kin. 8:1
27 [a]1 Sam. 2:18, 28 *See WW at Ex. 35:27.
28 [a]Num. 23:21; Josh. 6:20; 1 Chr. 13:8; Zech. 4:7; 1 Thess. 4:16 *See WW at Ezra 3:11.
29 [a]1 Sam. 18:20, 27; 19:11–17; 2 Sam. 3:13, 14; 6:16, 20–23 *See WW at Ps. 37:4.

CHAPTER 16

1 [a]2 Sam. 6:17; 1 Chr. 15:1
2 [a]1 Kin. 8:14
4 [a]Ps. 38:title; 70:title
5 [a]1 Chr. 15:18
6 *See WW at Ex. 28:30.
7 [a]2 Sam. 22:1; 23:1 [b]Ps. 105:1–15

The Ark Placed in the Tabernacle

16 So [a]they brought the ark of
God, and set it in the midst of
the tabernacle that David had erected
for it. Then they offered burnt offerings
and peace offerings before God.
2 And when David had finished offering the burnt offerings and the peace
offerings, [a]he blessed the people in the
name of the LORD.
3 Then he distributed to everyone of
Israel, both man and woman, to everyone a loaf of bread, a piece *of meat,*
and a cake of raisins.
4 And he appointed some of the Levites to minister before the ark of the
LORD, to [a]commemorate, to thank, and
to praise the LORD God of Israel:
5 Asaph the chief, and next to him
Zechariah, *then* [a]Jeiel, Shemiramoth,
Jehiel, Mattithiah, Eliab, Benaiah, and
Obed-Edom: Jeiel with stringed instruments and harps, but Asaph made music with cymbals;
6 Benaiah and Jahaziel the priests
*regularly *blew* the trumpets before the
ark of the covenant of God.

David's Song of Thanksgiving

7 On that day [a]David [b]first delivered
this psalm into the hand of Asaph and
his brethren, to **thank** the LORD:

WORD WEALTH

16:7 thank, *yadah* (yah-*dah*); Strong's #3034: To revere or worship with extended hands; to praise, give thanks, *(cont. on next page)*

16:1–6 See 2 Sam. 6 (especially v. 17). David placed the ark in the tent he had made, the tabernacle of David. Both the original tent, the tabernacle of Moses, and its altar remained in Gibeon. See 2 Chr. 1:3–6. Emphasizing the importance of the Levites, 1 Chr. details their role in the installation ceremony of the ark, whereas 2 Sam. does not.

16:7–23 This psalm is unique to 1 Chr. and was indicative of the worship, not only at the return of the ark, but also of the daily praise that continued before the Lord (v. 37).

(*cont. from preceding page*)
acknowledge, declare the merits of someone. *Yadah* is an important word for "praise" or "thanks," and occurs more than 100 times in the OT, more than half of these in the Book of Psalms. The origin of this verb is the noun *yad* (hand) which developed into the verb *yadah*, suggesting outstretched hands as a means of worship and thanks. Two important related words are *yehudah* and *todah*. *Yehudah* (Judah) was so named when his mother declared, "Now will I praise [or thank] the LORD" (Gen. 29:35). The word *todah* means "thanks."

8 [a]Oh, give thanks to the LORD!
Call upon His name;
Make known His deeds among the peoples!
9 Sing to Him, sing psalms to Him;
Talk of all His wondrous works!
10 Glory in His holy name;
Let the hearts of those rejoice who seek the LORD!
11 Seek the LORD and His *strength;
Seek His face evermore!
12 Remember His marvelous works which He has done,
His wonders, and the *judgments of His mouth,
13 O seed of Israel His servant,
You children of Jacob, His chosen ones!

14 He *is* the LORD our God;
His [a]judgments *are* in all the earth.
15 Remember His covenant forever,
The word which He commanded, for a thousand generations,
16 *The* [a]*covenant which* He made with Abraham,
And His oath to Isaac,
17 And [a]confirmed it to [b]Jacob for a statute,
To Israel *for* an everlasting covenant,
18 Saying, "To you I will give the land of Canaan
As the allotment of your inheritance,"
19 When you were [a]few in number,
Indeed very few, and strangers in it.

20 When they went from one nation to another,
And from *one* kingdom to another people,
21 He permitted no man to do them wrong;
Yes, He [a]rebuked kings for their sakes,
22 *Saying*, [a]"Do not touch My anointed ones,
And do My prophets no harm." **5**

23 [a]Sing* to the LORD, all the earth;
Proclaim the good news of His salvation from day to day.
24 Declare His glory among the nations,
His wonders among all peoples.

25 For the LORD *is* great and greatly to be praised;
He *is* also to be feared above all gods.
26 For all the gods [a]of the peoples *are* [1]idols,
But the LORD made the heavens.
27 Honor and majesty *are* before Him;
Strength and gladness are in His place.

28 Give to the LORD, O families of the peoples,
Give to the LORD glory and strength.
29 Give to the LORD the glory *due* His name;
Bring an offering, and come before Him.
Oh, *worship the LORD in the beauty of holiness!
30 Tremble before Him, all the earth.
The *world also is firmly established,
It shall not be moved.

31 Let the heavens rejoice, and let the earth be glad;
And let them say among the nations, "The LORD reigns."
32 Let the sea roar, and all its fullness;
Let the field rejoice, and all that *is* in it.
33 Then the [a]trees of the woods shall rejoice before the LORD,
For He is [b]coming to judge the earth.

34 [a]Oh, give thanks to the LORD, for *He is* good!
For His mercy *endures* forever.
35 [a]And say, *"Save us, O God of our salvation;
Gather us together, and deliver us from the Gentiles,

8 [a]1 Chr. 17:19, 20; Ps. 105:1–15
11 *See WW at Jer. 16:19.
12 *See WW at Num. 36:13.
14 [a]Ps. 48:10; [Is. 26:9]
16 [a]Gen. 17:2; 26:3; 28:13; 35:11
17 [a]Gen. 35:11, 12 [b]Gen. 28:10–15
19 [a]Gen. 34:30; Deut. 7:7
21 [a]Gen. 12:17; 20:3; Ex. 7:15–18
22 [a]Gen. 20:7; Ps. 105:15
23 [a]Ps. 96:1–13 *See WW at Judg. 5:3.
26 [a]Lev. 19:4; [1 Cor. 8:5, 6] [1]*worthless things*
29 *See WW at Ps. 99:5.
30 *See WW at Jer. 51:15.
33 [a]Is. 55:12, 13 [b][Joel 3:1–14]; Zech. 14:1–14; [Matt. 25:31–46]
34 [a]2 Chr. 5:13; 7:3; Ezra 3:11; Ps. 106:1; 107:1; 118:1; 136:1; Jer. 33:11
35 [a]Ps. 106:47, 48 *See WW at Jer. 17:14.

16:22 See section 5 of Truth-In-Action at the end of 1 Chr.

To give thanks to Your holy
name,
To *triumph in Your *praise."

36 [a]Blessed *be* the LORD God of Israel
From everlasting to everlasting!

And all [b]the people said, "Amen!" and
praised the LORD.

Regular Worship Maintained

37 So he left [a]Asaph and his brothers
there before the ark of the covenant
of the LORD to minister before the ark
regularly, as every day's work [b]re-
quired;
38 and [a]Obed-Edom with his sixty-
eight brethren, including Obed-Edom
the son of Jeduthun, and Hosah, *to be*
gatekeepers;
39 and Zadok the priest and his brethren the priests, [a]before the tabernacle
of the LORD [b]at the [1]high place that *was*
at Gibeon,
40 to offer burnt offerings to the LORD
on the altar of burnt offering regularly
[a]morning and evening, and *to do* according to all that is written in the Law
of the LORD which He commanded Israel;
41 and with them Heman and Jeduthun and the rest who were chosen,
who were designated by name, to give
thanks to the LORD, [a]because His
mercy *endures* forever;
42 and with them Heman and Jeduthun, to sound aloud with trumpets and
cymbals and the musical instruments
of God. Now the sons of Jeduthun *were*
gatekeepers.
43 [a]Then all the people departed, every
man to his house; and David returned
to bless his house.

God's Covenant with David

17 Now [a]it came to pass, when David was dwelling in his house,
that David said to Nathan the prophet,
"See now, I dwell in a house of cedar,
but the ark of the covenant of the LORD
is under tent curtains."
2 Then Nathan said to David, "Do all
that *is* in your heart, for God *is* with
you."
3 But it happened that night that the
word of God came to Nathan, saying,
4 "Go and tell My servant David,
'Thus says the LORD: "You shall
[a]not build Me a house to dwell in.
5 "For I have not dwelt in a house
since the time that I brought up Israel,
even to this day, but have gone from
tent to tent, and from *one* tabernacle
to another.
6 "Wherever I have moved about
with all Israel, have I ever spoken a
word to any of the judges of Israel,
whom I commanded to shepherd My
people, saying, 'Why have you not
built Me a house of cedar?' " '
7 "Now therefore, thus shall you say
to My servant David, 'Thus says the
LORD of hosts: "I took you [a]from the
sheepfold, from following the sheep, to
be [1]ruler over My people Israel.
8 "And I have been with you wherever you have gone, and have cut off
all your enemies from before you, and
have [1]made you a name like the name
of the great men who *are* on the earth.
9 "Moreover I will appoint a place for
My people Israel, and will [a]plant them,
that they may dwell in a place of their
own and move no more; nor shall the
sons of wickedness oppress them anymore, as previously,
10 "since the time that I commanded
judges *to be* over My people Israel.
Also I will subdue all your enemies.
Furthermore I tell you that the LORD
will build you a [1]house.
11 "And it shall be, when your days
are [a]fulfilled, when you must [1]go *to be*
with your fathers, that I will set up your
[b]seed after you, who will be of your
sons; and I will establish his kingdom.
12 [a]"He shall build Me a house, and I
will establish his throne forever.
13 [a]"I will be his Father, and he shall
be My son; and I will not take My
mercy away from him, [b]as I took *it*
from *him* who was before you.
14 "And [a]I will establish him in My
house and in My kingdom forever; and
his throne shall be established forever." ' "
15 According to all these words and
according to all this *vision, so Nathan
spoke to David.
16 [a]Then King David went in and sat

35 *See WW at Ps. 63:3. • See WW at Ps. 100:4.
36 [a]1 Kin. 8:15, 56; Ps. 72:18 [b]Deut. 27:15; Neh. 8:6
37 [a]1 Chr. 16:4, 5 [b]2 Chr. 8:14; Ezra 3:4
38 [a]1 Chr. 13:14
39 [a]1 Chr. 21:29; 2 Chr. 1:3 [b]1 Kin. 3:4 [1]Place for pagan worship
40 [a][Ex. 29:38–42; Num. 28:3, 4]
41 [a]1 Chr. 25:1–6; 2 Chr. 5:13; 7:3; Ezra 3:11; Jer. 33:11
43 [a]2 Sam. 6:18–20

CHAPTER 17

1 [a]2 Sam. 7:1; 1 Chr. 14:1
4 [a][1 Chr. 28:2, 3]
7 [a]1 Sam. 16:11–13 [1]*leader*
8 [1]*given you prestige*
9 [a][Deut. 30:1–9; Jer. 16:14–16; 23:5–8; 24:6; Ezek. 37:21–27]; Amos 9:14
10 [1]Royal dynasty
11 [a]1 Kin. 2:10; 1 Chr. 29:28 [b]1 Kin. 5:5; 6:12; 8:19–21; [1 Chr. 22:9–13; 28:20]; Matt. 1:6; Luke 3:31 [1]Die and join your ancestors
12 [a]1 Kin. 6:38; 2 Chr. 6:2; [Ps. 89:20–37]
13 [a]2 Sam. 7:14, 15; Matt. 3:17; Mark 1:11; Luke 3:22; 2 Cor. 6:18; Heb. 1:5 [b][1 Sam. 15:23–28]; 1 Chr. 10:14
14 [a]Ps. 89:3, 4; Matt. 19:28; 25:31; [Luke 1:31–33]
15 *See WW at 2 Chr. 32:32.
16 [a]2 Sam. 7:18

16:37–43 Again, it is apparent that there were two sanctuaries for worship, one at Jerusalem and the other at Gibeon. See note on vv. 1–6.

17:1–27 Read the text and notes of 2 Sam. 7.

17:1–15 The prophecy of Nathan includes a promise to David known as the Davidic covenant, pointing to the coming rule of Christ.

17:16–27 David's response to the news that he was not to build the temple is an excellent illustration of how a believer should handle disappointment. Instead of being angry and upset at the Lord, David's reaction was one of humility and thanksgiving. See also 1 Thess. 5:18.

before the LORD; and he said: "Who *am*
I, O LORD God? And what is my house,
that You have brought me this far?
17 "And *yet* this was a small thing in
Your sight, O God; and You have *also*
spoken of Your servant's house for a
great while to come, and have regarded me according to the rank of a
man of high degree, O LORD God.
18 "What more can David *say* to You
for the honor of Your servant? For You
know Your servant.
19 "O LORD, for Your servant's sake,
and according to Your own heart, You
have done all this greatness, in making
known all these great things.
20 "O LORD, *there is* none like You, nor
is there any God besides You, according to all that we have heard with our
ears.
21 [a]"And who *is* like Your people Israel, the one nation on the earth whom
God went to redeem for Himself *as* a
people—to make for Yourself a name
by great and awesome deeds, by driving out nations from before Your people whom You redeemed from Egypt?
22 "For You have made Your people
Israel Your very own people forever;
and You, LORD, have become their
God.
23 "And now, O LORD, the word which
You have spoken concerning Your
servant and concerning his house, *let it*
be established forever, and do as You
have said.
24 "So let it be established, that Your
name may be magnified forever, saying, 'The LORD of hosts, the God of Israel, *is* Israel's God.' And let the house
of Your servant David be established
before You.
25 "For You, O my God, [1]have revealed to Your servant that You will
build him a house. Therefore Your
servant has found it *in his heart* to *pray
before You.
26 "And now, LORD, [1]You are God, and
have promised this goodness to Your
servant.
27 "Now You have been pleased to
bless the house of Your servant, that
it may continue before You forever; for
You have blessed it, O LORD, and *it
shall be* blessed forever."

David's Further Conquests

18 After this [a]it came to pass that
David [1]attacked the Philistines,
subdued them, and took Gath and its
towns from the hand of the Philistines.
2 Then he [1]defeated [a]Moab, and the
Moabites became David's [b]servants,
and brought tribute.
3 And [a]David [1]defeated [2]Hadadezer
king of Zobah *as far as* Hamath, as he
went to establish his power by the
River Euphrates.
4 David took from him one thousand
chariots, [1]seven thousand horsemen,
and twenty thousand foot soldiers.
Also David [2]hamstrung all the chariot
horses, except that he spared enough
of them for one hundred chariots.
5 When the [a]Syrians of Damascus
came to help Hadadezer king of Zobah,
David killed twenty-two thousand of
the Syrians.
6 Then David put *garrisons* in Syria
of Damascus; and the Syrians became
David's servants, *and* brought tribute.
So the LORD preserved David wherever
he went.
7 And David took the shields of gold
that were on the servants of Hadadezer, and brought them to Jerusalem.
8 Also from [1]Tibhath and from
[2]Chun, cities of [3]Hadadezer, David
brought a large amount of [a]bronze,
with which [b]Solomon made the bronze
[4]Sea, the pillars, and the articles of
bronze.
9 Now when [1]Tou king of Hamath
heard that David had [2]defeated all the
army of Hadadezer king of Zobah,
10 he sent [1]Hadoram his son to King
David, to greet him and bless him, because he had fought against Hadadezer
and [2]defeated him (for Hadadezer had
been at war with Tou); and *Hadoram
brought with him* all kinds of [a]articles
of gold, silver, and bronze.
11 King David also dedicated these to
the LORD, along with the silver and
gold that he had brought from all *these*
nations—from Edom, from Moab, from
the [a]people of Ammon, from the
[b]Philistines, and from [c]Amalek.
12 Moreover [a]Abishai the son of
Zeruiah killed [b]eighteen thousand
[1]Edomites in the Valley of Salt.
13 [a]He also put garrisons in Edom, and
all the Edomites became David's
servants. And the LORD preserved
David wherever he went.

David's Administration

14 So David reigned over all Israel,
and administered judgment and justice
to all his people.

21 [a][Deut. 4:6–8, 33–38]; Ps. 147:20
25 [1]Lit. *have uncovered the ear of*
*See WW at Job 42:10.
26 [1]Or *You alone are*

CHAPTER 18

1 [a]2 Sam. 8:1–18 [1]Lit. *struck*
2 [a]2 Sam. 8:2; Zeph. 2:9 [b]Ps. 60:8 [1]Lit. *struck*
3 [a]2 Sam. 8:3 [1]Lit. *struck* [2]Heb. *Hadarezer*
4 [1]*seven hundred,* 2 Sam. 8:4 [2]*crippled*
5 [a]2 Sam. 8:5, 6; 1 Kin. 11:23–25
8 [a]2 Sam. 8:8 [b]1 Kin. 7:15, 23; 2 Chr. 4:12, 15, 16 [1]*Betah,* 2 Sam. 8:8 [2]*Berothai,* 2 Sam. 8:8 [3]Heb. *Hadarezer* [4]Great laver or basin
9 [1]*Toi,* 2 Sam. 8:9, 10 [2]Lit. *struck*
10 [a]2 Sam. 8:10–12 [1]*Joram,* 2 Sam. 8:10 [2]Lit. *struck*
11 [a]2 Sam. 10:14 [b]2 Sam. 5:17–25 [c]2 Sam. 1:1
12 [a]2 Sam. 23:18; 1 Chr. 2:16 [b]2 Sam. 8:13 [1]*Syrians,* 2 Sam. 8:13
13 [a]Gen. 27:29–40; Num. 24:18; 2 Sam. 8:14

18:1–17 For a comparative view of David's conquests and the expansion of his kingdom, read the text and notes of 2 Sam. 8.

15 Joab the son of Zeruiah *was* over the army; Jehoshaphat the son of Ahilud *was* recorder;

16 Zadok the son of Ahitub and [1]Abimelech the son of Abiathar *were* the priests; [2]Shavsha *was* the scribe;

17 [a]Benaiah the son of Jehoiada *was* over the Cherethites and the Pelethites; and David's sons *were* [1]chief ministers at the king's side.

The Ammonites and Syrians Defeated

19 It[a] happened after this that Nahash the king of the people of Ammon died, and his son reigned in his place.

2 Then David said, "I will show kindness to Hanun the son of Nahash, because his father showed kindness to me." So David sent messengers to comfort him concerning his father. And David's servants came to Hanun in the land of the people of Ammon to comfort him.

3 And the princes of the people of Ammon said to Hanun, [1]"Do you think that David really honors your father because he has sent comforters to you? Did his servants not come to you to search and to overthrow and to spy out the land?"

4 Therefore Hanun took David's servants, shaved them, and cut off their garments [1]in the middle, at their [a]buttocks, and sent them away.

5 Then *some* went and told David about the men; and he sent to meet them, because the men were greatly ashamed. And the king said, "Wait at Jericho until your beards have grown, and *then* return."

6 When the people of Ammon saw that they had made themselves repulsive to David, Hanun and the people of Ammon sent a thousand talents of silver to hire for themselves chariots and horsemen from [1]Mesopotamia, from Syrian Maacah, [a]and from [2]Zobah.

7 So they hired for themselves thirty-two thousand chariots, with the king of Maacah and his people, who came and encamped before Medeba. Also the people of Ammon gathered together from their cities, and came to battle.

8 Now when David heard *of it,* he sent Joab and all the army of the mighty men.

9 Then the people of Ammon came out and put themselves in battle array before the gate of the city, and the kings who had come *were* by themselves in the field.

10 When Joab saw that the battle line was against him before and behind, he chose some of Israel's best and put *them* in battle array against the Syrians.

11 And the rest of the people he put under the command of Abishai his brother, and they set *themselves* in battle array against the people of Ammon.

12 Then he said, "If the Syrians are too strong for me, then you shall help me; but if the people of Ammon are too strong for you, then I will help you.

13 "Be of good courage, and let us be strong for our people and for the cities of our God. And may the LORD do *what is* good in His sight."

14 So Joab and the people who *were* with him drew near for the battle against the Syrians, and they fled before him.

15 When the people of Ammon saw that the Syrians were fleeing, they also fled before Abishai his brother, and entered the city. So Joab went to Jerusalem.

16 Now when the Syrians saw that they had been defeated by Israel, they sent messengers and brought the Syrians who were beyond [1]the River, and [2]Shophach the commander of Hadadezer's army *went* before them.

17 When it was told David, he gathered all Israel, crossed over the Jordan and came upon them, and set up in battle array against them. So when David had set up in *battle* array against the Syrians, they fought with him.

18 Then the Syrians fled before Israel; and David killed [1]seven thousand charioteers and forty thousand [2]foot soldiers of the Syrians, and killed Shophach the commander of the army.

19 And when the servants of Hadadezer saw that they were defeated by Israel, they made peace with David and became his servants. So the Syrians were not willing to help the people of Ammon anymore.

Rabbah Is Conquered

20 It[a] happened [1]in the spring of the year, at the time kings go

16 [1]*Ahimelech,* 2 Sam. 8:17 [2]*Seraiah,* 2 Sam. 8:17, or *Shisha,* 1 Kin. 4:3
17 [a]2 Sam. 8:18 [1]Lit. *at the hand of the king*

CHAPTER 19

1 [a]1 Sam. 11:1; 2 Sam. 10:1–19
3 [1]Lit. *In your eyes is David honoring your father because*
4 [a]Is. 20:4 [1]*in half*
6 [a]1 Chr. 18:5, 9 [1]Heb. *Aram Naharaim* [2]*Zoba,* 2 Sam. 10:6
16 [1]The Euphrates [2]*Zoba,* 2 Sam. 10:6, or *Shobach,* 2 Sam. 10:16
18 [1]*seven hundred,* 2 Sam. 10:18 [2]*horsemen,* 2 Sam. 10:18

CHAPTER 20

1 [a]2 Sam. 11:1

19:1–19 Read the text and notes of 2 Sam. 10 for another view of David's victory over the Ammonites and Syrians.

20:1–3 Read the text and notes of 2 Sam. 12:26–31 for information on David's capture of Rabbah.

out *to battle,* that Joab led out the
armed forces and ravaged the country
of the people of Ammon, and came and
besieged Rabbah. But [b]David stayed at
Jerusalem. And [c]Joab defeated Rabbah and overthrew it.
2 Then David [a]took their king's
crown from his *head, and found it to
weigh a talent of gold, and *there were*
precious stones in it. And it was set on
David's head. Also he brought out the
[1]spoil of the city in great abundance.
3 And he brought out the people who
were in it, and [1]put *them* to work with
saws, with iron picks, and with axes.
So David did to all the cities of the people of Ammon. Then David and all the
people returned *to* Jerusalem.

Philistine Giants Destroyed

4 Now it happened afterward [a]that
war broke out at [1]Gezer with the Philistines, at which time [b]Sibbechai the
Hushathite killed [2]Sippai, *who was one*
of the sons of [3]the giant. And they were
subdued.
5 Again there was war with the Philistines, and Elhanan the son of [1]Jair
killed Lahmi the brother of Goliath the
Gittite, the shaft of whose spear *was*
like a weaver's [a]beam.
6 Yet again [a]there was war at Gath,
where there was a man of *great* stature, with twenty-four fingers and toes,
six *on each hand* and six *on each foot;*
and he also was born to [1]the giant.
7 So when he defied Israel, Jonathan
the son of [1]Shimea, David's brother,
killed him.
8 These were born to the giant in
Gath, and they fell by the hand of David and by the hand of his servants.

1 [b]2 Sam. 11:2—12:25 [c]2 Sam. 12:26 [1]Lit. *at the return of the year*
2 [a]2 Sam. 12:30, 31 [1]*plunder* *See WW at Gen. 3:15.
3 [1]LXX *cut them with*
4 [a]2 Sam. 21:18 [b]1 Chr. 11:29 [1]*Gob,* 2 Sam. 21:18 [2]*Saph,* 2 Sam. 21:18 [3]Or *Raphah*
5 [a]1 Sam. 17:7; 1 Chr. 11:23 [1]*Jaare-Oregim,* 2 Sam. 21:19
6 [a]1 Sam. 5:8; 2 Sam. 21:20 [1]Or *Raphah*
7 [1]*Shammah,* 1 Sam. 16:9 or *Shimeah,* 2 Sam. 21:21

CHAPTER 21

1 [a]2 Sam. 24:1–25; Job 1:6 [1]*take a census of* *See WW at Job 1:6.
2 [a]1 Chr. 27:23, 24
6 [a]1 Chr. 27:24 [1]*command*
7 [1]Lit. *it was evil in the eyes of God*
8 [a]2 Sam. 24:10 [b]2 Sam. 12:13
9 [a]1 Sam. 9:9; 2 Kin. 17:13; 1 Chr. 29:29; 2 Chr. 16:7, 10; Is. 30:9, 10; Amos 7:12, 13
10 [a]2 Sam. 24:12–14

The Census of Israel and Judah

21 Now [a]Satan* stood up against
Israel, and moved David to
[1]number Israel.
2 So David said to Joab and to the
leaders of the people, "Go, number Israel from Beersheba to Dan, [a]and
bring the number of them to me that I
may know *it.*"
3 And Joab answered, "May the LORD
make His people a hundred times more
than they are. But, my lord the king,
are they not all my lord's servants?
Why then does my lord require this
thing? Why should he be a cause of
guilt in Israel?"
4 Nevertheless the king's word prevailed against Joab. Therefore Joab departed and went throughout all Israel
and came to Jerusalem.
5 Then Joab gave the sum of the number of the people to David. All Israel
had one million one hundred thousand
men who drew the sword, and Judah
had four hundred and seventy thousand men who drew the sword.
6 [a]But he did not count Levi and Benjamin among them, for the king's
[1]word was abominable to Joab.
7 And [1]God was displeased with this
thing; therefore He struck Israel.
8 So David said to God, [a]"I have
sinned greatly, because I have done
this thing; [b]but now, I pray, take away
the iniquity of Your servant, for I have
done very foolishly."
9 Then the LORD spoke to Gad, David's [a]seer, saying,
10 "Go and tell David, [a]saying, 'Thus
says the LORD: "I offer you three
things; choose one of them for yourself, that I may do *it* to you." ' "

20:1, 2 Between vv. 1 and 2, 2 Sam. inserts the episode in which David commits adultery with Bathsheba (2 Sam. 11:1—12:25).

20:4–8 For a further description of the Philistine giants, see 1 Sam. 17:1–6 and 2 Sam. 21:15–17. The **Jonathan** mentioned in v. 7 was not the son of Saul who was David's friend, but David's nephew, the son of Shimea (or Shammah). See 1 Sam. 16:9.

21:1–30 At this juncture, 1 Chr. passes over a number of events in the life of David and proceeds to the end of his life. The chronicler does not discuss the events of 2 Sam. 13:1—23:7, including David's troubles with Amnon and Tamar, his son Absalom, Ziba, Shimei, and Sheba. Instead, the author moves directly to those incidents that set the stage for building the temple.

21:1 To number Israel: The census of David in this chapter is also recorded in 2 Sam. 24, but there it states that it was because God was angry with Israel (the reason for this is unclear) that He moved David to take the census. The account of the census has been problematic because God does not cause anyone to sin (James 1:13) and because it is not apparent why such a census was wrong (Num. 1:2, 3; 26:2–4). The first problem is clarified by comparing 2 Sam. 24:1 with 1 Chr. 21:1. God did not directly incite David to do something for which He would then turn around and judge him (v. 14); rather, He allowed **Satan** to influence David to do what David probably already had in his heart to do (James 1:14, 15).

This is similar to the times when the Lord allowed Satan to trouble Job (Job 1:12; 2:6) or when He permitted an evil spirit to torment Saul (1 Sam. 16:14). This is one of only three OT references where Satan (literally, "Adversary") is mentioned by name (see also Job 1; 2; Zech. 3:1). The absence of the definite article (the) before "Satan" in v. 1 indicates that the title, which emphasized his role in inciting rebellion against God, had already become a proper name.

Although we are not told why the numbering was evil (v. 7), it was perhaps either an indication that David was trusting more in his military strength than in God's power (see Ps. 20:7) or a violation of God's instruction to Moses on how to conduct a census (see Ex. 30:11–16). The first would be a sin of motive and the second, a sin of method.

11 So Gad came to David and said to
him, "Thus says the LORD: 'Choose for
yourself,
12 [a]'either [1]three years of famine, or
three months to be defeated by your
foes with the sword of your enemies
overtaking *you*, or else for three days
the sword of the LORD—the plague in
the land, with the [2]angel of the LORD
destroying throughout all the territory
of Israel.' Now consider what answer
I should take back to Him who sent
me."
13 And David said to Gad, "I am in
great distress. Please let me fall into
the hand of the LORD, for His [a]mercies
are very great; but do not let me fall
into the hand of man."
14 So the LORD sent a [a]plague upon Israel, and seventy thousand men of Israel fell.
15 And God sent [1]an [a]angel to Jerusalem to destroy it. As [2]he was destroying, the LORD looked and [b]re-
lented of the disaster, and said to the
angel who was destroying, "It is
enough; now restrain [3]your hand."
And the angel of the LORD stood by the
[c]threshing floor of [4]Ornan the Jebusite.
16 Then David lifted his eyes and
[a]saw the *angel of the LORD standing
between earth and *heaven, having in
his hand a drawn sword stretched out
over Jerusalem. So David and the elders, clothed in sackcloth, fell on their
faces.
17 And David said to God, "Was it not
I who commanded the people to be
numbered? I am the one who has
sinned and done evil indeed; but these
[a]sheep, what have they done? Let Your
hand, I pray, O LORD my God, be
against me and my father's house, but
not against Your people that they
should be plagued."
18 Therefore, the [a]angel of the LORD
commanded Gad to say to David that
David should go and erect an altar to
the LORD on the threshing floor of Ornan the Jebusite.
19 So David went up at the word of
Gad, which he had spoken in the name
of the LORD.
20 Now Ornan turned and saw the angel; and his four sons *who were* with
him hid themselves, but Ornan continued threshing wheat.
21 So David came to Ornan, and Ornan looked and saw David. And he
went out from the threshing floor, and
bowed before David with *his* face to
the ground.
22 Then David said to Ornan, [1]"Grant
me the place of *this* threshing floor,
that I may build an altar on it to the
LORD. You shall grant it to me at the
full price, that the plague may be withdrawn from the people."
23 But Ornan said to David, "Take *it*
to yourself, and let my lord the king
do *what is* good in his eyes. Look, I
also give *you* the oxen for burnt offerings, the threshing implements for
wood, and the wheat for the *grain offering; I give *it* all."
24 Then King David said to Ornan,
"No, but I will surely buy *it* for the full
price, for I will not take what is yours
for the LORD, nor offer burnt offerings
with *that which* costs *me* nothing."
25 So [a]David gave Ornan six hundred
shekels of gold by weight for the place.
26 And David built there an altar to the
LORD, and offered burnt offerings and
peace offerings, and called on the
LORD; and [a]He answered him from
heaven by fire on the altar of burnt offering.
27 So the LORD commanded the angel, and he returned his sword to its
sheath.
28 At that time, when David saw that
the LORD had answered him on the
threshing floor of Ornan the Jebusite,
he sacrificed there.
29 [a]For the tabernacle of the LORD and
the altar of the burnt offering, which
Moses had made in the wilderness,
were at that time at the high place in
[b]Gibeon.
30 But David could not go before it to
inquire of God, for he was afraid of the
sword of the angel of the LORD.

David Prepares to Build the Temple

22 Then David said, [a]"This *is* the
house of the LORD God, and
this *is* the altar of burnt offering for
Israel."
2 So David commanded to gather the
[a]aliens who *were* in the land of Israel;
and he appointed masons to [b]cut hewn
stones to build the house of God.

12 [a]2 Sam. 24:13 [1]*seven*, 2 Sam. 24:13 [2]Or *Angel*, and so throughout the chapter
13 [a]Ps. 51:1; 130:4, 7
14 [a]1 Chr. 27:24
15 [a]2 Sam. 24:16 [b]Gen. 6:6 [c]2 Chr. 3:1 [1]Or *the Angel* [2]Or *He* [3]Or *Your* [4]*Araunah*, 2 Sam. 24:16, 18–24
16 [a]Josh. 5:13; 2 Chr. 3:1 *See WW at 2 Chr. 32:21. • See WW at 1 Kin. 8:23.
17 [a]2 Sam. 7:8; Ps. 74:1
18 [a]1 Chr. 21:11, 12; 2 Chr. 3:1

22 [1]Lit. *Give*
23 *See WW at Num. 29:6.
25 [a]2 Sam. 24:24
26 [a]Lev. 9:24; Judg. 6:21; 1 Kin. 18:36–38; 2 Chr. 3:1; 7:1
29 [a]1 Kin. 3:4; 2 Chr. 1:3 [b]1 Chr. 16:39

CHAPTER 22

1 [a]Deut. 12:5; 2 Sam. 24:18; 1 Chr. 21:18, 19, 26, 28; 2 Chr. 3:1
2 [a]1 Kin. 9:20, 21; 2 Chr. 2:17, 18 [b]1 Kin. 5:17, 18

21:25 Six hundred shekels of gold: This is an apparent discrepancy with 2 Sam. 24:24 where the price is 50 shekels of silver. However, the 50 shekels of silver in 2 Sam. 24:24 only paid for the threshing floor (an area about 30 by 60 ft.) and oxen, while the "six hundred shekels of gold" here purchased the entire property.

22:1–19 This chapter has no counterpart in 1 and 2 Sam. It is likely that these events occurred during the brief period when David and Solomon reigned together. See 23:1 and 1 Kin. 1. Though David was not to build the temple, he still did all within his power to make preparation for its construction.

3 And David prepared iron in abundance for the nails of the doors of the
gates and for the joints, and bronze in
abundance [a]beyond measure,
4 and cedar trees in abundance; for
the [a]Sidonians and those from Tyre
brought much cedar wood to David.
5 Now David said, [a]"Solomon my son
is young and inexperienced, and the
house to be built for the LORD *must be*
exceedingly magnificent, famous and
glorious throughout all countries. I will
now make preparation for it." So David made abundant preparations before his death.
6 Then he called for his son Solomon,
and [1]charged him to build a house for
the LORD God of Israel.
7 And David said to Solomon: "My
son, as for me, [a]it was in my mind to
build a house [b]to the name of the LORD
my God;
8 "but the word of the LORD came to
me, saying, [a]'You have shed much
blood and have made great wars; you
shall not build a house for My name,
because you have shed much blood on
the earth in My sight.
9 [a]'Behold, a son shall be born to you,
who shall be a man of rest; and I will
give him [b]rest from all his enemies all
around. His name shall be [1]Solomon,
for I will give peace and quietness to
Israel in his days.
10 [a]'He shall build a house for My
name, and [b]he shall be My son, and I
will be his Father; and I will establish
the throne of his kingdom over Israel
forever.'
11 "Now, my son, may [a]the LORD be
with you; and may you prosper, and
build the house of the LORD your God,
as He has said to you.
12 "Only may the LORD [a]give you wisdom and understanding, and give you
charge concerning Israel, that you may
keep the law of the LORD your God.

3 [a]1 Kin. 7:47; 1 Chr. 22:14
4 [a]1 Kin. 5:6–10
5 [a]1 Kin. 3:7; 1 Chr. 29:1, 2
6 [1]*commanded*
7 [a]2 Sam. 7:1, 2; 1 Kin. 8:17; 1 Chr. 17:1; 28:2 [b]Deut. 12:5, 11
8 [a]2 Sam. 7:5–13; 1 Kin. 5:3; 1 Chr. 28:3
9 [a]1 Chr. 28:5 [b]1 Kin. 4:20, 25; 5:4 [1]Lit. *Peaceful*
10 [a]2 Sam. 7:13; 1 Kin. 5:5; 6:38; 1 Chr. 17:12, 13; 28:6; 2 Chr. 6:2 [b]Heb. 1:5
11 [a]1 Chr. 22:16
12 [a]1 Kin. 3:9–12; 2 Chr. 1:10
13 [a][Josh. 1:7, 8]; 1 Chr. 28:7 [b][Deut. 31:7, 8; Josh. 1:6, 7, 9; 1 Chr. 28:20] [1]*commanded* *See WW at Neh. 9:13.
14 [a]1 Chr. 22:3
16 [a]1 Chr. 22:11
17 [a]1 Chr. 28:1–6
18 [a]Deut. 12:10; Josh. 22:4; 2 Sam. 7:1; [1 Kin. 5:4; 8:56]
19 [a]1 Kin. 8:1–11; 2 Chr. 5:2–14 [b]1 Kin. 5:3

CHAPTER 23

1 [a]1 Kin. 1:33–40; 1 Chr. 28:4, 5

13 [a]"Then you will prosper, if you take
care to fulfill the *statutes and judgments with which the LORD [1]charged
Moses concerning Israel. [b]Be strong
and of good courage; do not fear nor
be dismayed.
14 "Indeed I have taken much trouble
to prepare for the house of the LORD
one hundred thousand talents of gold
and one million talents of silver, and
bronze and iron [a]beyond measure, for
it is so abundant. I have prepared timber and stone also, and you may add
to them.
15 "Moreover *there are* workmen with
you in abundance: woodsmen and
stonecutters, and all types of skillful
men for every kind of work.
16 "Of gold and silver and bronze and
iron *there is* no limit. Arise and begin
working, and [a]the LORD be with you."
17 David also commanded all the
[a]leaders of Israel to help Solomon his
son, *saying,*
18 "*Is* not the LORD your God with you?
[a]And has He *not* given you rest on
every side? For He has given the inhabitants of the land into my hand, and
the land is subdued before the LORD
and before His people.
19 "Now set your heart and your soul 2
to seek the LORD your God. Therefore
arise and build the sanctuary of the
LORD God, to [a]bring the ark of the
covenant of the LORD and the holy articles of God into the house that is to
be built [b]for the name of the LORD."

The Divisions of the Levites

23 So when David was old and full
of days, he made his son
[a]Solomon king over Israel.
2 And he gathered together all the
leaders of Israel, with the priests and
the Levites.

22:3, 14, 16 The statements **beyond measure** (vv. 3, 14) and ***there is* no limit** (v. 16) are helpful in understanding the large figures in 1 and 2 Chr. For example, **one hundred thousand talents of gold** (3,750 tons) and **one million talents of silver** (37,500 tons) would be a total of 41,250 tons of precious metal! To some these amounts appear to be exaggerations. However, the admissions "beyond measure" and "*there is* no limit" imply that David was probably *giving a general* estimation, not an exact calculation. Additionally, other factors such as the standard of measurement may have been different. At any rate, the point of the passage is that God had blessed David with abundant resources for building the temple. If Solomon would seek the Lord (vv. 13, 19), then God would prosper him (vv. 11, 13) and bless his efforts in building the temple.

When comparing the figures in 1 and 2 Chr. with those from parallel passages in 1 and 2 Sam. or 1 and 2 Kin., it is important to remember that the main point of the biblical record is to convey theological truth, not to dispense figures. In the duplicate historical accounts where there are a vast number of figures, the biblical record is almost always in agreement. When there are differences in figures, most can be resolved as copyists' errors (see note on 1 Kin. 4:26), different perspectives of the author (see note on 1 Chr. 21:25), or as rounded estimations (v. 14).

22:19 See section 2 of Truth-In-Action at the end of 1 Chr.

23:1—27:34 The next five chapters record how David organized the religious and civil leaders of his administration.

23:1–32 The Levites had cared for the tabernacle of Moses, and now they would maintain the temple. Therefore, among David's administration, they are mentioned first.

3 Now the Levites were numbered
from the age of [a]thirty years and
above; and the number of individual
*males was thirty-eight thousand.
4 Of these, twenty-four thousand
were to [a]look after the work of the
house of the LORD, six thousand *were*
[b]officers and judges,
5 four thousand *were* gatekeepers,
and four thousand [a]praised the LORD
with *musical* instruments, [b]"which I
made," *said David,* "for giving praise."
6 Also [a]David separated them into
[1]divisions among the sons of Levi: Gershon, Kohath, and Merari.
7 Of the [a]Gershonites: [1]Laadan and
Shimei.
8 The sons of Laadan: the first Jehiel,
then Zetham and Joel—three *in all.*
9 The sons of Shimei: Shelomith, Haziel, and Haran—three *in all.* These
were the heads of the fathers' *houses*
of Laadan.
10 And the sons of Shimei: Jahath,
[1]Zina, Jeush, and Beriah. These *were*
the four sons of Shimei.
11 Jahath was the first and Zizah the
second. But Jeush and Beriah did not
have many sons; therefore they were
assigned as one father's house.
12 [a]The sons of Kohath: Amram,
Izhar, Hebron, and Uzziel—four *in
all.*
13 The sons of [a]Amram: Aaron and
Moses; and [b]Aaron was set apart, he
and his sons forever, that he should
[1]sanctify the most holy things, [c]to burn
incense before the LORD, [d]to minister
to Him, and [e]to give the blessing in His
name forever.
14 Now [a]the sons of Moses the man
of God were reckoned to the tribe of
Levi.
15 [a]The sons of Moses *were* [1]Gershon
and Eliezer.
16 Of the sons of Gershon, [a]Shebuel[1]
was the first.
17 Of the descendants of Eliezer,
[a]Rehabiah was the first. And Eliezer
had no other sons, but the sons of Rehabiah were very many.
18 Of the sons of Izhar, [a]Shelomith
was the first.
19 [a]Of the sons of Hebron, Jeriah *was*
the first, Amariah the second, Jahaziel
the third, and Jekameam the fourth.
20 Of the sons of Uzziel, Michah *was*
the first and Jesshiah the second.

3 [a]Num. 4:1–3 *See WW at Jer. 31:22.
4 [a]2 Chr. 2:2, 18; Ezra 3:8, 9 [b]Deut. 16:18–20
5 [a]1 Chr. 15:16 [b]2 Chr. 29:25–27
6 [a]Ex. 6:16; Num. 26:57; 2 Chr. 8:14 [1]*groups*
7 [a]1 Chr. 26:21 [1]*Libni,* Ex. 6:17
10 [1]LXX, Vg. *Zizah* and v. 11
12 [a]Ex. 6:18
13 [a]Ex. 6:20 [b]Ex. 28:1; Heb. 5:4 [c]Ex. 30:7; 1 Sam. 2:28 [d][Deut. 21:5] [e]Num. 6:23 [1]*consecrate*
14 [a]1 Chr. 26:20–24
15 [a]Ex. 18:3, 4 [1]Heb. *Gershom,* 1 Chr. 6:16
16 [a]1 Chr. 26:24 [1]*Shubael,* 1 Chr. 24:20
17 [a]1 Chr. 26:25
18 [a]1 Chr. 24:22
19 [a]1 Chr. 24:23
21 [a]1 Chr. 24:26 [b]1 Chr. 24:29
22 [a]1 Chr. 24:28 [b]Num. 36:6 [1]*kinsmen*
23 [a]1 Chr. 24:30
24 [a]Num. 10:17, 21 [b]Num. 1:3; Ezra 3:8
25 [a]1 Chr. 22:18
26 [a]Num. 4:5, 15; 7:9; Deut. 10:8
27 [a]2 Sam. 23:1
29 [a]Ex. 25:30 [b]Lev. 6:20 [c]Lev. 2:1, 4 [d]Lev. 2:5, 7 [e]Lev. 19:35
30 *See WW at 1 Chr. 16:7.

21 [a]The sons of Merari *were* Mahli and
Mushi. The sons of Mahli *were* Eleazar
and [b]Kish.
22 And Eleazar died, and [a]had no sons,
but only daughters; and their
[1]brethren, the sons of Kish, [b]took them
as wives.
23 [a]The sons of Mushi *were* Mahli,
Eder, and Jeremoth—three *in all.*
24 These *were* the sons of [a]Levi by
their fathers' houses—the heads of the
fathers' *houses* as they were counted
individually by the number of their
names, who did the work for the
service of the house of the LORD,
from the age of [b]twenty years and
above.
25 For David said, "The LORD God of
Israel [a]has given rest to His people,
that they may dwell in Jerusalem forever";
26 and also to the Levites, "They shall
no longer [a]carry the tabernacle, or any
of the articles for its service."
27 For by the [a]last words of David the
Levites *were* numbered from twenty
years old and above;
28 because their duty *was* to help the
sons of Aaron in the service of the
house of the LORD, in the courts and
in the chambers, in the purifying of all
holy things and the work of the service
of the house of God,
29 both with [a]the showbread and
[b]the fine flour for the grain offering,
with [c]the unleavened cakes and
[d]*what is baked in* the pan, with what
is mixed and with all kinds of [e]mea-
sures and sizes;
30 to stand every morning to *thank
and **praise** the LORD, and likewise at
evening;

WORD WEALTH

23:30 praise, *halal* (hah-*lahl*); Strong's #1984: To praise, to thank; rejoice, boast about someone. *Halal* is the root from which "hallelujah" is formed. The phrase is a command: *hallelu-Jah* (all of you must praise *Jah*). Also derived from *halal* is *tehillah,* or *tehillim* in the plural. A *tehillah* is a praise, a psalm, or a song. The Hebrew title of the Book of Psalms is *Tehillim,* literally "Praises." *Halal* usually conveys the idea of speaking or singing about the glories, virtues, or honor of someone or something.

23:3, 24, 27 The apparent discrepancy between **age of thirty years and above** (v. 3) and **age of twenty years and above** (vv. 24, 27) is easily resolved. "Thirty years and above" (v. 3) was the lower age limit designated for ministry by a Levite (Num. 4:3, 30). David reduced this limit to "age of twenty years and above" (vv. 24, 27). This was not unusual, for Moses himself had decreased the limit to age 25 in Num. 8:24. The age limit was probably lowered to meet with the increased demands of ecclesiastical burden.

31 and at every presentation of a burnt
offering to the LORD [a]on the Sabbaths
and on the New Moons and on the
[b]set[1] feasts, by number according to
the ordinance governing them, regularly before the LORD;
32 and that they should [a]attend to the
[b]needs of the tabernacle of meeting,
the needs of the holy *place,* and the
[c]needs of the sons of Aaron their brethren in the work of the house of the
LORD.

The Divisions of the Priests

24 Now *these are* the divisions of
the sons of Aaron. [a]The sons of
Aaron *were* Nadab, Abihu, Eleazar,
and Ithamar.
2 And [a]Nadab and Abihu died before
their father, and had no children;
therefore Eleazar and Ithamar ministered as priests.
3 Then David with Zadok of the sons
of Eleazar, and [a]Ahimelech of the sons
of Ithamar, divided them according to
the schedule of their service.
4 There were more leaders found of
the sons of Eleazar than of the sons
of Ithamar, and *thus* they were divided.
Among the sons of Eleazar *were* sixteen heads of *their* fathers' houses, and
eight heads of their fathers' houses
among the sons of Ithamar.
5 Thus they were divided by lot, one
group as another, for there were officials of the sanctuary and officials *of
the house* of God, from the sons of Eleazar and from the sons of Ithamar.
6 And the scribe, Shemaiah the son
of Nethanel, *one of* the Levites, wrote
them down before the king, the leaders, Zadok the priest, Ahimelech the
son of Abiathar, and the heads of the
fathers' *houses* of the priests and Levites, one father's house taken for Eleazar and *one* for Ithamar.
7 Now the first lot fell to Jehoiarib,
the second to Jedaiah,
8 the third to Harim, the fourth to
Seorim,
9 the fifth to Malchijah, the sixth to
Mijamin,
10 the seventh to Hakkoz, the eighth
to [a]Abijah,
11 the ninth to Jeshua, the tenth to
Shecaniah,
12 the eleventh to Eliashib, the twelfth
to Jakim,
13 the thirteenth to Huppah, the fourteenth to Jeshebeab,
14 the fifteenth to Bilgah, the sixteenth
to Immer,
15 the seventeenth to Hezir, the eighteenth to [1]Happizzez,
16 the nineteenth to Pethahiah, the
twentieth to [1]Jehezekel,
17 the twenty-first to Jachin, the
twenty-second to Gamul,
18 the twenty-third to Delaiah, the
twenty-fourth to Maaziah.
19 This *was* the schedule of their service [a]for coming into the house of the
LORD according to their ordinance by
the hand of Aaron their father, as the
LORD God of Israel had commanded
him.

Other Levites

20 And the rest of the sons of Levi: of
the sons of Amram, [1]Shubael; of the
sons of Shubael, Jehdeiah.
21 Concerning [a]Rehabiah, of the sons
of Rehabiah, the first *was* Isshiah.
22 Of the Izharites, [1]Shelomoth; of the
sons of Shelomoth, Jahath.
23 Of the sons [1]*of* [a]*Hebron,* Jeriah
[1]*was the first,* Amariah the second, Jahaziel the third, *and* Jekameam the
fourth.
24 *Of* the sons of Uzziel, Michah; of the
sons of Michah, Shamir.
25 The brother of Michah, Isshiah; of
the sons of Isshiah, Zechariah.
26 [a]The sons of Merari *were* Mahli and
Mushi; the son of Jaaziah, Beno.
27 The sons of Merari by Jaaziah *were*
Beno, Shoham, Zaccur, and Ibri.
28 Of Mahli: Eleazar, [a]who had no
sons.
29 Of Kish: the son of Kish, Jerahmeel.
30 Also [a]the sons of Mushi *were* Mahli,
Eder, and Jerimoth. These *were* the
sons of the Levites according to their
fathers' houses.
31 These also cast lots just as their
brothers the sons of Aaron did, in
the presence of King David, Zadok,
Ahimelech, and the heads of the fathers'
houses of the priests and Levites. The
chief fathers *did* just as their younger
brethren.

The Musicians

25 Moreover David and the captains of the army separated for

31 [a]Num. 10:10 [b]Lev. 23:2–4 [1]*appointed feasts*
32 [a]2 Chr. 13:10, 11 [b][Num. 1:53]; 1 Chr. 9:27 [c]Num. 3:6–9, 38

CHAPTER 24

1 [a]Lev. 10:1–6; Num. 26:60, 61; 1 Chr. 6:3
2 [a]Num. 3:1–4; 26:61
3 [a]1 Chr. 18:16
10 [a]Neh. 12:4, 17; Luke 1:5
15 [1]LXX, Vg. *Aphses*
16 [1]MT *Jehezkel*
19 [a]1 Chr. 9:25
20 [1]*Shebuel,* 1 Chr. 23:16
21 [a]1 Chr. 23:17
22 [1]*Shelomith,* 1 Chr. 23:18
23 [a]1 Chr. 23:19; 26:31 [1]Supplied from 23:19 (following some Heb. mss. and LXX mss.)
26 [a]Ex. 6:19; 1 Chr. 23:21
28 [a]1 Chr. 23:22
30 [a]1 Chr. 23:23

24:1–31 Within the Levites there were divisions of priests. The sons of Aaron were divided into 24 groups of priests, each group responsible for the temple sacrifices for 2 weeks each year. Their selection and order for service were chosen by lot (v. 5). Next, all the rest of the Levites were divided in a similar manner to assist in the general temple responsibilities.

25:1–31 Musicians played an important role in David's

the service *some* of the sons of [a]Asaph,
of Heman, and of Jeduthun, who
should prophesy with harps, stringed
instruments, and cymbals. And the
number of the skilled men performing
their service was:
2 Of the sons of Asaph: Zaccur, Joseph, Nethaniah, and [1]Asharelah; the
sons of Asaph *were* [2]under the direction of Asaph, who prophesied according to the order of the king.
3 Of [a]Jeduthun, the sons of Jeduthun:
Gedaliah, [1]Zeri, Jeshaiah, [2]Shimei,
Hashabiah, and Mattithiah, [3]six, under
the direction of their father Jeduthun,
who prophesied with a harp to give
thanks and to praise the LORD.
4 Of Heman, the sons of Heman: Bukkiah, Mattaniah, [1]Uzziel, [2]Shebuel,
[3]Jerimoth, Hananiah, Hanani, Eliathah, Giddalti, Romamti-Ezer, Joshbekashah, Mallothi, Hothir, *and* Mahazioth.
5 All these *were* the sons of Heman
the king's seer in the words of God,
to [1]exalt his [a]horn. For God gave Heman fourteen sons and three daughters.
6 All these *were* under the direction
of their father for the music *in* the
house of the LORD, with cymbals,
stringed instruments, and [a]harps, for
the service of the house of God. Asaph,
Jeduthun, and Heman *were* [b]under the
authority of the king.
7 So the [a]number of them, with their
brethren who were instructed in
the songs of the LORD, all who were
skillful, *was* two hundred and eighty-
eight.
8 And they cast lots for their duty, the
small as well as the great, [a]the teacher
with the student.
9 Now the first lot for Asaph came out
for Joseph; the second for Gedaliah,
him with his brethren and sons, twelve;
10 the third for Zaccur, his sons and
his brethren, twelve;
11 the fourth for [1]Jizri, his sons and
his brethren, twelve;
12 the fifth for Nethaniah, his sons and
his brethren, twelve;
13 the sixth for Bukkiah, his sons and
his brethren, twelve;
14 the seventh for [1]Jesharelah, his
sons and his brethren, twelve;

CHAPTER 25

1 [a]1 Chr. 6:30, 33, 39, 44; 2 Chr. 5:12
2 [1]*Jesharelah*, v. 14 [2]Lit. *at the hands of*
3 [a]1 Chr. 16:41, 42 [1]*Jizri*, v. 11 [2]So with one Heb. ms., LXX mss. [3]Shimei is the sixth, v. 17
4 [1]*Azarel*, v. 18 [2]*Shubael*, v. 20 [3]*Jeremoth*, v. 22
5 [a]1 Chr. 16:42 [1]Increase his power or influence
6 [a]1 Chr. 15:16 [b]1 Chr. 15:19; 25:2
7 [a]1 Chr. 23:5
8 [a]2 Chr. 23:13
11 [1]*Zeri*, v. 3
14 [1]*Asharelah*, v. 2
18 [1]*Uzziel*, v. 4
20 [1]*Shebuel*, v. 4
22 [1]*Jerimoth*, v. 4

CHAPTER 26

1 [a]Ps. 42:title [1]*Shelemiah*, v. 14 [2]*Ebiasaph*, 1 Chr. 6:37; 9:19
2 [a]1 Chr. 9:21
4 [a]1 Chr. 15:18, 21

15 the eighth for Jeshaiah, his sons
and his brethren, twelve;
16 the ninth for Mattaniah, his sons
and his brethren, twelve;
17 the tenth for Shimei, his sons and
his brethren, twelve;
18 the eleventh for [1]Azarel, his sons
and his brethren, twelve;
19 the twelfth for Hashabiah, his sons
and his brethren, twelve;
20 the thirteenth for [1]Shubael, his sons
and his brethren, twelve;
21 the fourteenth for Mattithiah, his
sons and his brethren, twelve;
22 the fifteenth for [1]Jeremoth, his sons
and his brethren, twelve;
23 the sixteenth for Hananiah, his sons
and his brethren, twelve;
24 the seventeenth for Joshbekashah,
his sons and his brethren, twelve;
25 the eighteenth for Hanani, his sons
and his brethren, twelve;
26 the nineteenth for Mallothi, his sons
and his brethren, twelve;
27 the twentieth for Eliathah, his sons
and his brethren, twelve;
28 the twenty-first for Hothir, his sons
and his brethren, twelve;
29 the twenty-second for Giddalti, his
sons and his brethren, twelve;
30 the twenty-third for Mahazioth, his
sons and his brethren, twelve;
31 the twenty-fourth for Romamti-
Ezer, his sons and his brethren, twelve.

The Gatekeepers

26 Concerning the divisions of the
gatekeepers: of the Korahites,
[1]Meshelemiah the son of [a]Kore, of the
sons of [2]Asaph.
2 And the sons of Meshelemiah *were*
[a]Zechariah the firstborn, Jediael the
second, Zebadiah the third, Jathniel
the fourth,
3 Elam the fifth, Jehohanan the sixth,
Eliehoenai the seventh.
4 Moreover the sons of [a]Obed-Edom
were Shemaiah the firstborn, Jehozabad the second, Joah the third, Sacar
the fourth, Nethanel the fifth,
5 Ammiel the sixth, Issachar the seventh, Peulthai the eighth; for God
blessed him.
6 Also to Shemaiah his son were sons
born who governed their fathers'

---

administration, since worship had a high priority for David, and he was himself a skilled musician (1 Sam. 16:14–23; 2 Sam. 22:1). The musicians who played and sang were more than just musicians; they were leaders who prophesied through song (v. 1).

26:1–19 The **gatekeepers,** the next division of David's administration, were apparently third-class priests responsible for the care of the temple ("doorkeepers," 2 Kin. 23:4). This included a variety of tasks, such as guarding the entrance to the temple (9:23–27; 2 Chr. 23:19), protecting the ark (15:23), and overseeing the collection and distribution of monetary offerings (2 Kin. 12:9; 22:14; 2 Chr. 31:14). The gatekeepers had to be Levites (9:26; 15:23; 23:5), and their office could be traced back to the time of Moses (9:26).

houses, because they *were* men of
great ability.
7 The sons of Shemaiah *were* Othni,
Rephael, Obed, and Elzabad, whose
brothers Elihu and Semachiah *were*
able men.
8 All these *were* of the sons of Obed-
Edom, they and their sons and their
brethren, [a]able men with strength for
the work: sixty-two of Obed-Edom.
9 And Meshelemiah had sons and
brethren, eighteen able men.
10 Also [a]Hosah, of the children of Merari, had sons: Shimri the first (for
though he was not the firstborn, his father made him the first),
11 Hilkiah the second, Tebaliah the
third, Zechariah the fourth; all the sons
and brethren of Hosah *were* thirteen.
12 Among these *were* the divisions of
the gatekeepers, among the chief men,
having duties just like their brethren,
to serve in the house of the LORD.
13 And they [a]cast lots for each gate,
the small as well as the great, according to their father's house.
14 The lot for the East *Gate* fell to
[1]Shelemiah. Then they cast lots *for* his
son Zechariah, a wise counselor, and
his lot came out for the North Gate;
15 to Obed-Edom the South Gate, and
to his sons the [1]storehouse.
16 To Shuppim and Hosah *the lot
came out* for the West Gate, with the
Shallecheth Gate on the [a]ascending
highway—watchman opposite watchman.
17 On the east were *six* Levites, on the
north four each day, on the south four
each day, and for the [1]storehouse two
by two.
18 As for the [1]Parbar on the west,
there were four on the highway *and*
two at the Parbar.
19 These were the divisions of the
gatekeepers among the sons of Korah
and among the sons of Merari.

The Treasuries and Other Duties

20 Of the Levites, Ahijah *was* [a]over the
treasuries of the house of God and
over the treasuries of the [b]dedicated[1]
things.
21 The sons of [1]Laadan, the descendants of the Gershonites of Laadan,
heads of their fathers' *houses,* of Laadan *the Gershonite:* [2]Jehieli.
22 The sons of Jehieli, Zetham and
Joel his brother, *were* over the treasuries of the house of the LORD.
23 Of the [a]Amramites, the Izharites,
the Hebronites, and the Uzzielites:
24 [a]Shebuel the son of Gershom, the
son of Moses, *was* overseer of the treasuries.
25 And his brethren by Eliezer *were*
Rehabiah his son, Jeshaiah his son,
Joram his son, Zichri his son, and
[a]Shelomith his son.
26 This Shelomith and his brethren
were over all the treasuries of the dedicated things [a]which King David and
the heads of fathers' *houses,* the captains over thousands and hundreds,
and the captains of the army, had dedicated.
27 Some of the [1]spoils won in battles
they dedicated to maintain the house
of the LORD.
28 And all that Samuel [a]the *seer, Saul
the son of Kish, Abner the son of Ner,
and Joab the son of Zeruiah had dedicated, every dedicated *thing,* was under the hand of Shelomith and his
brethren.
29 Of the Izharites, Chenaniah and his
sons [a]*performed* duties as [b]officials
and judges over Israel outside Jerusalem.
30 Of the Hebronites, [a]Hashabiah and
his brethren, one thousand seven hundred able men, had the oversight of Israel on the west side of the Jordan for
all the business of the LORD, and in the
service of the king.
31 Among the Hebronites, [a]Jerijah
was head of the Hebronites according
to his genealogy of the fathers. In the
fortieth year of the reign of David they
were sought, and there were found
among them capable men [b]at Jazer of
Gilead.
32 And his brethren *were* two thousand seven hundred able men, heads
of fathers' *houses,* whom King David
made officials over the Reubenites, the
Gadites, and the half-tribe of Manasseh, for every matter pertaining to God
and the [a]affairs of the king.

The Military Divisions

27 And the children of Israel, according to their number, the
heads of fathers' *houses,* the captains

8 [a]1 Chr. 9:13
10 [a]1 Chr. 16:38
13 [a]1 Chr. 24:5, 31; 25:8
14 [1]*Meshelemiah,* v. 1
15 [1]Heb. *asuppim*
16 [a]1 Kin. 10:5; 2 Chr. 9:4
17 [1]Heb. *asuppim*
18 [1]Probably a court or colonnade extending west of the temple
20 [a]1 Chr. 9:26 [b]2 Sam. 8:11; 1 Chr. 26:22, 24, 26; 28:12; Ezra 2:69 [1]*holy things*
21 [1]*Libni,* 1 Chr. 6:17 [2]*Jehiel,* 1 Chr. 23:8; 29:8
23 [a]Ex. 6:18; Num. 3:19
24 [a]1 Chr. 23:16
25 [a]1 Chr. 23:18
26 [a]2 Sam. 8:11
27 [1]*plunder*
28 [a]1 Sam. 9:9 *See WW at 1 Sam. 9:9.
29 [a]Neh. 11:16 [b]1 Chr. 23:4
30 [a]1 Chr. 27:17
31 [a]1 Chr. 23:19 [b]Josh. 21:39
32 [a]2 Chr. 19:11

26:20–32 Ahijah (one of the Levites) and his descendants acted as overseers and clerks for the treasuries of the temple. The treasuries included gifts, taxes, and spoils of battle.
27:1–34 1 Chr. now records the military commanders (vv. 1–15), the tribal leaders (vv. 16–24), and the government officials (vv. 25–34) in David's administration. Those mentioned in vv. 26–31 appear to be ones who oversaw the royal estates and were experts in agriculture.

of thousands and hundreds and their
officers, served the king in every matter of the *military* divisions. *These divisions* came in and went out month by
month throughout all the months of the
year, each division *having* twenty-four
thousand.
2 Over the first division for the first
month *was* [a]Jashobeam the son of
Zabdiel, and in his division *were*
twenty-four thousand;
3 *he was* of the children of Perez, and
the chief of all the captains of the army
for the first month.
4 Over the division of the second
month *was* [1]Dodai an Ahohite, and of
his division Mikloth also *was* the
leader; in his division *were* twenty-four
thousand.
5 The third captain of the army for
the third month *was* [a]Benaiah, the son
of Jehoiada the priest, who was chief;
in his division *were* twenty-four thousand.
6 This was the Benaiah *who was*
[a]mighty *among* the thirty, and was
over the thirty; in his division *was* Am-
mizabad his son.
7 The fourth *captain* for the fourth
month *was* [a]Asahel the brother of
Joab, and Zebadiah his son after him;
in his division *were* twenty-four thousand.
8 The fifth *captain* for the fifth month
was [1]Shamhuth the Izrahite; in
his division were twenty-four thousand.
9 The sixth *captain* for the sixth
month *was* [a]Ira the son of Ikkesh the
Tekoite; in his division *were* twenty-
four thousand.
10 The seventh *captain* for the seventh
month *was* [a]Helez the Pelonite, of the
children of Ephraim; in his division
were twenty-four thousand.
11 The eighth *captain* for the eighth
month *was* [a]Sibbechai the Hushathite,
of the Zarhites; in his division *were*
twenty-four thousand.
12 The ninth *captain* for the ninth
month *was* [a]Abiezer the Anathothite,
of the Benjamites; in his division *were*
twenty-four thousand.
13 The tenth *captain* for the tenth
month *was* [a]Maharai the Netophathite,
of the Zarhites; in his division *were*
twenty-four thousand.
14 The eleventh *captain* for the eleventh month *was* [a]Benaiah the Pirathonite, of the children of Ephraim; in
his division *were* twenty-four thousand.
15 The twelfth *captain* for the twelfth
month *was* [1]Heldai the Netophathite,
of Othniel; in his division *were* twenty-
four thousand.

Leaders of Tribes

16 Furthermore, over the tribes of Israel: the officer over the Reubenites
was Eliezer the son of Zichri; over the
Simeonites, Shephatiah the son of Maachah;
17 *over* the Levites, [a]Hashabiah the
son of Kemuel; over the Aaronites, Zadok;
18 *over* Judah, [a]Elihu, *one* of David's
brothers; *over* Issachar, Omri the son
of Michael;
19 *over* Zebulun, Ishmaiah the son of
Obadiah; *over* Naphtali, Jerimoth the
son of Azriel;
20 *over* the children of Ephraim, Hoshea the son of Azaziah; *over* the half-
tribe of Manasseh, Joel the son of Pedaiah;
21 *over* the half-*tribe* of Manasseh in
Gilead, Iddo the son of Zechariah; *over*
Benjamin, Jaasiel the son of Abner;
22 *over* Dan, Azarel the son of Jeroham. These *were* the leaders of the
tribes of Israel.
23 But David did not take the number
of those twenty years old and under,
because [a]the LORD had said He would
multiply Israel like the [b]stars of the
heavens.
24 Joab the son of Zeruiah began a
census, but he did not finish, for
[a]wrath came upon Israel because of
this census; nor was the number recorded in the account of the chronicles
of King David.

Other State Officials

25 And Azmaveth the son of Adiel *was*
over the king's treasuries; and Jehonathan the son of Uzziah was over the
storehouses in the field, in the cities,
in the villages, and in the fortresses.
26 Ezri the son of Chelub was over
those who did the work of the field for
tilling the ground.
27 And Shimei the Ramathite *was* over
the vineyards, and Zabdi the Shiph-
mite was over the produce of the
vineyards for the supply of wine.
28 Baal-Hanan the Gederite was over
the olive trees and the sycamore trees
that *were* in the lowlands, and Joash
was over the store of oil.
29 And Shitrai the Sharonite *was* over
the herds that fed in Sharon, and Shaphat the son of Adlai was over the herds
that were in the valleys.
30 Obil the Ishmaelite *was* over the

CHAPTER 27

2 [a]1 Chr. 11:11
4 [1]Heb. *Dodai,* usually spelled *Dodo,* 2 Sam. 23:9
5 [a]1 Chr. 18:17
6 [a]2 Sam. 23:20–23
7 [a]2 Sam. 23:24; 1 Chr. 11:26
8 [1]*Shammah,* 2 Sam. 23:11, or *Shammoth,* 1 Chr. 11:27
9 [a]1 Chr. 11:28
10 [a]1 Chr. 11:27
11 [a]2 Sam. 21:18; 1 Chr. 11:29; 20:4
12 [a]1 Chr. 11:28
13 [a]2 Sam. 23:28; 1 Chr. 11:30
14 [a]1 Chr. 11:31
15 [1]*Heleb,* 2 Sam. 23:29, or *Heled,* 1 Chr. 11:30
17 [a]1 Chr. 26:30
18 [a]1 Sam. 16:6
23 [a][Deut. 6:3] [b]Gen. 15:5; 22:17; 26:4; Ex. 32:13; Deut. 1:10
24 [a]2 Sam. 24:12–15; 1 Chr. 21:1–7

camels, Jehdeiah the Meronothite *was* over the donkeys,

31 and Jaziz the [a]Hagrite *was* over the flocks. All these *were* the officials over King David's property.

32 Also Jehonathan, David's uncle, *was* a counselor, a wise man, and a [1]scribe; and Jehiel the [2]son of Hachmoni *was* with the king's sons.

33 [a]Ahithophel *was* the king's counselor, and [b]Hushai the Archite *was* the king's companion.

34 After Ahithophel *was* Jehoiada the son of Benaiah, then [a]Abiathar. And the general of the king's army *was* [b]Joab.

Solomon Instructed to Build the Temple

28 Now David assembled at Jerusalem all [a]the leaders of Israel: the officers of the tribes and [b]the captains of the divisions who served the king, the captains over thousands and captains over hundreds, and [c]the stewards over all the substance and [1]possessions of the king and of his sons, with the officials, the valiant men, and all [d]the mighty men of valor.

2 Then King David rose to his feet and said, "Hear me, my brethren and my people: [a]I *had* it in my heart to build a house of rest for the ark of the covenant of the LORD, and for [b]the footstool of our God, and had made preparations to build it.

3 "But God said to me, [a]'You shall not build a house for My name, because you *have been* a man of war and have shed [b]blood.'

4 "However the LORD God of Israel [a]chose me above all the house of my father to be king over Israel forever, for He has chosen [b]Judah *to be* the ruler. And of the house of Judah, [c]the house of my father, and [d]among the sons of my father, He was pleased with me to make *me* king over all Israel.

5 [a]"And of all my sons (for the LORD has given me many sons) [b]He has chosen my son Solomon to sit on the throne of the kingdom of the LORD over Israel.

6 "Now He said to me, 'It is [a]your son Solomon *who* shall build My house and My courts; for I have chosen him *to be* My son, and I will be his Father.

7 'Moreover I will establish his kingdom forever, [a]if he is steadfast to observe My commandments and My judgments, as it is this day.' 2

8 "Now therefore, in the sight of all Israel, the assembly of the LORD, and in the hearing of our God, be careful to seek out all the commandments of the LORD your God, that you may possess this good land, and leave *it* as an inheritance for your children after you forever.

9 "As for you, my son Solomon, [a]know the God of your father, and serve Him [b]with a loyal heart and with a willing mind; for [c]the LORD searches all hearts and understands all the intent of the thoughts. [d]If you seek Him, He will be found by you; but if you forsake Him, He will [e]cast you off *forever.

10 "Consider now, [a]for the LORD has chosen you to build a house for the sanctuary; be strong, and do it."

11 Then David gave his son Solomon [a]the plans for the vestibule, its houses, its treasuries, its upper chambers, its inner chambers, and the place of the mercy seat;

12 and the [a]plans for all that he had by the Spirit, of the courts of the house of the LORD, of all the chambers all around, [b]of the treasuries of the house of God, and of the treasuries for the dedicated things;

13 also for the division of the priests and the [a]Levites, for all the work of the service of the house of the LORD, and for all the articles of service in the house of the LORD.

14 *He gave* gold by weight for *things* of gold, for all articles used in every kind of service; also *silver* for all articles of silver by weight, for all articles used in every kind of service;

15 the weight for the [a]lampstands of gold, and their lamps of gold, by weight for each lampstand and its

31 [a]1 Chr. 5:10
32 [1]*secretary* [2]Or *Hachmonite*
33 [a]2 Sam. 15:12 [b]2 Sam. 15:32–37
34 [a]1 Kin. 1:7 [b]1 Chr. 11:6

CHAPTER 28

1 [a]1 Chr. 27:16 [b]1 Chr. 27:1, 2 [c]1 Chr. 27:25 [d]2 Sam. 23:8–39; 1 Chr. 11:10–47 [1]Or *livestock*
2 [a]2 Sam. 7:2 [b]Ps. 99:5; 132:7; [Is. 66:1]
3 [a]2 Sam. 7:5, 13; 1 Kin. 5:3 [b][1 Chr. 17:4; 22:8]
4 [a]1 Sam. 16:6–13 [b]Gen. 49:8–10; 1 Chr. 5:2; Ps. 60:7 [c]1 Sam. 16:1 [d]1 Sam. 13:14; 16:12, 13; Acts 13:22
5 [a]1 Chr. 3:1–9; 14:3–7; 23:1 [b]1 Chr. 22:9; 29:1
6 [a]2 Sam. 7:13, 14; 1 Kin. 6:38; 1 Chr. 22:9, 10; 2 Chr. 1:9; 6:2
7 [a]1 Chr. 22:13
9 [a][1 Sam. 12:24]; Jer. 9:24; Hos. 4:1; [John 17:3] [b]2 Kin. 20:3 [c][1 Sam. 16:7; 1 Kin. 8:39; 1 Chr. 29:17]; Jer. 11:20; 17:10; 20:12; Rev. 2:23 [d]2 Chr. 15:2; [Jer. 29:13] [e]Deut. 31:17 *See WW at Mic. 4:5.
10 [a]1 Chr. 22:13; 28:6
11 [a]1 Kin. 6:3; 1 Chr. 28:19
12 [a]Ex. 25:40; Heb. 8:5 [b]1 Chr. 26:20, 28
13 [a]1 Chr. 23:6
15 [a]Ex. 25:31–39; 1 Kin. 7:49

28:1–21 The author of 1 Chr. moves directly to the transferring of the government to Solomon, without even mentioning the attempt of Adonijah to become king and the plea of Nathan and Bathsheba on behalf of Solomon. For a fuller account of these events, read the text and notes of 1 Kin. 1 and 2. For the chronicler, Solomon and the temple are significant points in Judah's history. Therefore, 1 Chr. gives David's instructions to Solomon in reference to the temple, while in 1 Kin. they are not included. But 1 Kin. records David's instructions to Solomon concerning Joab and Shimei, whereas 1 Chr. does not. The inclusion or exclusion of such events fits within the author's purpose to order his account of history to make a specific theological point.

28:7–10 See section 2 of Truth-In-Action at the end of 1 Chr.

28:12 For more on **the Spirit,** see Introduction to 1 Chronicles: The Holy Spirit at Work.

lamps; for the lampstands of silver by
weight, for the lampstand and its
lamps, according to the use of each
lampstand.
16 And by weight *he gave* gold for the
tables of the showbread, for each
[a]table, and silver for the tables of silver;
17 also pure gold for the forks, the basins, the pitchers of pure gold, and the
golden bowls—*he gave gold* by weight
for every bowl; and for the silver
bowls, *silver* by weight for every bowl;
18 and refined gold by weight for the
[a]altar of incense, and for the construction of the chariot, that is, the gold
[b]cherubim that spread *their wings* and
overshadowed the ark of the covenant
of the LORD.
19 "All *this,*" *said David,* [a]"the LORD
made me understand in writing, by *His*
hand upon me, all the [1]works of these
plans."
6 20 And David said to his son Solomon,
[a]"Be strong and of good courage, and
do *it;* do not *fear nor be dismayed,
for the LORD God—my God—*will be*
with you. [b]He will not leave you nor
forsake you, until you have finished all
the work for the service of the house
of the LORD.
21 "*Here are* [a]the divisions of the
priests and the Levites for all the service of the house of God; and [b]every
willing craftsman *will be* with you for
all manner of workmanship, for every
kind of service; also the leaders and
all the people *will be* completely at
your command."

16 [a]1 Kin. 7:48
18 [a]Ex. 30:1–10 [b]Ex. 25:18–22; 1 Sam. 4:4; 1 Kin. 6:23
19 [a]Ex. 25:40; 1 Chr. 28:11, 12 [1]*details*
20 [a]Deut. 31:6, 7; [Josh. 1:6–9]; 1 Chr. 22:13 [b]Josh. 1:5; Heb. 13:5 *See WW at Ex. 1:17.
21 [a]1 Chr. 24—26 [b]Ex. 35:25–35; 36:1, 2; 2 Chr. 2:13, 14

CHAPTER 29

1 [a]1 Chr. 28:5 [b]1 Kin. 3:7; 1 Chr. 22:5; Prov. 4:3 [1]Lit. *palace*
2 [a]Is. 54:11, 12; Rev. 21:18
3 *See WW at Deut. 26:18.
4 [a]1 Kin. 9:28
5 [a]2 Chr. 29:31; [2 Cor. 8:5, 12] [1]Lit. *fill his hand*
6 [a]1 Chr. 27:1; 28:1 [b]1 Chr. 27:25–31 [c]Ex. 35:21–35
8 [a]1 Chr. 23:8 [1]Possibly the same as *Jehieli,* 1 Chr. 26:21, 22
9 [a]Ex. 25:2; 1 Kin. 8:61; 2 Cor. 9:7
11 [a]Matt. 6:13; 1 Tim. 1:17; Rev. 5:13

Offerings for Building the Temple

29 Furthermore King David said to
all the assembly: "My son Solomon, whom alone God has [a]chosen, *is*
[b]young and inexperienced; and the
work *is* great, because the [1]temple *is*
not for man but for the LORD God.
2 "Now for the house of my God I
have prepared with all my might: gold
for *things to be made of* gold, silver
for *things of* silver, bronze for *things
of* bronze, iron for *things of* iron, wood
for *things of* wood, [a]onyx stones,
stones to be set, glistening stones of
various colors, all kinds of precious
stones, and marble slabs in abundance.
3 "Moreover, because I have set my
affection on the house of my God, I
have given to the house of my God,
over and above all that I have prepared
for the holy house, my own *special
treasure of gold and silver:
4 "three thousand talents of gold, of
the gold of [a]Ophir, and seven thousand
talents of refined silver, to overlay the
walls of the houses;
5 "the gold for *things of* gold and the
silver for *things of* silver, and for all
kinds of work *to be done* by the hands
of craftsmen. Who *then* is [a]willing to
[1]consecrate himself this day to the
LORD?"
6 Then [a]the leaders of the fathers'
houses, leaders of the tribes of Israel,
the captains of thousands and of hundreds, with [b]the officers over the king's
work, [c]offered willingly.
7 They gave for the work of the house
of God five thousand talents and ten
thousand darics of gold, ten thousand
talents of silver, eighteen thousand talents of bronze, and one hundred thousand talents of iron.
8 And whoever had *precious* stones
gave *them* to the treasury of the house
of the LORD, into the hand of [a]Jehiel[1]
the Gershonite.
9 Then the people rejoiced, for they
had offered willingly, because with a
loyal heart they had [a]offered willingly
to the LORD; and King David also rejoiced greatly.

David's Praise to God

10 Therefore David blessed the LORD
before all the assembly; and David
said:

"Blessed are You, LORD God of
Israel, our Father, forever and
ever.
11 [a]Yours, O LORD, *is* the greatness,
The power and the glory,
The victory and the **majesty;**
For all *that is* in heaven and in
earth *is Yours;*
Yours *is* the kingdom, O LORD,

28:20 See section 6 of Truth-In-Action at the end of 1 Chr.
29:1–9 This section, which is also absent from 1 Kin., provides an illuminating model for giving. First, David gives lavishly from his own resources (vv. 1–5). His example and request caused his leaders also to give (vv. 6–8) so that the people gave willingly and joyfully (v. 9).
29:7 A daric was a Persian coin whose value was measured by weight. **Ten thousand darics** weighed approximately 185 pounds. The offerings of **talents** mentioned here are also valued by weight. Their total value was over 5,000 tons.
29:10 In his characteristic fashion, David lifted a prayer of praise to God (vv. 10–19), which encouraged all of the people to bless the Lord (v. 20). This is one of the grandest prayers in the entire OT and demonstrates why David was described as "a man after God's own heart" (Acts 13:22).

And You are exalted as head over
all.

WORD WEALTH

29:11 majesty, *hod (hoad)*; Strong's #1935: Glory, honor, majesty, beauty, grandeur, excellence in form and appearance. Found in 24 OT references, *hod* refers to whatever or whoever is royally glorious. The word "splendor" may best define *hod.* Here David states that the splendor and glory belong to God. Compare with Jesus' words in Matt. 6:13.

12 [a]Both riches and honor *come* from
You,
And You reign over all.
In Your hand *is* power and might;
In Your hand *it is* to make great
And to give strength to all.

13 "Now therefore, our God,
We thank You
And praise Your glorious name.
4 14 But who *am* I, and who *are* my
people,
That we should be able to offer
so willingly as this?
For all things *come* from You,
And [1]of Your own we have given
You.
15 For [a]we *are* [1]aliens and [2]pilgrims
before You,
As *were* all our fathers;
[b]Our days on earth *are* as a
shadow,
And without hope.

16 "O LORD our God, all this abundance that we have prepared to build You a *house for Your holy name is from Your hand, and *is* all Your own.

KINGDOM DYNAMICS

29:10–16 Human Responsibility, FOUNDATIONS OF THE KINGDOM. No text in the Bible more magnificently declares God's sovereign power: there is no one like the Lord, the Almighty One, whose glory fills the universe. And yet, in the center of this grand anthem of acknowledgment to that towering truth, David asserts that although the kingdom is God's (v. 11), God gives resources that are man's to administrate. V. 14 literally reads, "Everything that exists is from You, and we administrate it from Your hand." God is the fountainhead of all life and power; man is the appointed heir for its management. Ps. 8:6 and 115:16 affirm that while the created universe and the glory of the heavens are God's and God's alone, He has delegated the stewardship of Earth's affairs to mankind. Noble views of God's sovereignty must be balanced with a complementary view of man's duties and redeemed capacities. Neglect of this balance, while seeming to extol God's greatness, can produce apathy or irresponsible attitudes. For example, God does not predestine mismanaged resources, families, politics, and so on, any more than He does human sinning. Man is responsible and accountable for Earth's problems and—reinstated under God—is intended to become the agent for their solution. However, he can only become such by drawing on God's sovereign wisdom, power, and resource, that is, on God's "kingdom." Just as man's sin and fall have damaged the potential partnership between the Creator and His appointed heir to this planet, redemption has set the recovery in motion. Renewed under God, the redeemed may, in fact, partner with God and thereby decisively assist in the reestablishment of God's rule over circumstances and situations on Earth. But this only operates under the divine order within redemption's plan under divine grace and through man's receiving divine power by God's Spirit.
(Gen. 26:1–5; 28:1–22/Matt. 3:1, 2) J.W.H.

17 "I know also, my God, that You
[a]test the heart and [b]have pleasure in
uprightness. As for me, in the uprightness of my heart I have willingly
offered all these *things;* and now with
joy I have seen Your people, who
are present here to offer willingly to
You.
18 "O LORD God of Abraham, Isaac,
and Israel, our fathers, keep this forever in the intent of the thoughts of the
heart of Your people, and fix their
heart toward You.
19 "And [a]give my son Solomon a loyal
heart to keep Your commandments
and Your testimonies and Your statutes, to do all *these things,* and to build
the [1]temple for which [b]I have made
provision."
20 Then David said to all the assembly,
"Now bless the LORD your God." So
all the assembly blessed the LORD God
of their fathers, and bowed their heads
and prostrated themselves before the
LORD and the king.

12 [a]Rom. 11:36
14 [1]Lit. *of Your hand*
15 [a]Lev. 25:23; Ps. 39:12; Heb. 11:13, 14; 1 Pet. 2:11 [b]Job 14:2; Ps. 90:9 [1]*sojourners,* temporary residents [2]*transients,* temporary residents in an even more temporary sense
16 *See WW at 2 Sam. 7:11.
17 [a][1 Sam. 16:7; 1 Chr. 28:9] [b]Prov. 11:20
19 [a][1 Chr. 28:9]; Ps. 72:1 [b]1 Chr. 29:1, 2 [1]Lit. *palace*

29:14 See section 4 of Truth-In-Action at the end of 1 Chr.

Solomon Anointed King

21 And they made sacrifices to the
LORD and offered burnt offerings to the
LORD on the next day: a thousand bulls,
a thousand rams, a thousand lambs,
with their drink offerings, and [a]sac-
rifices in abundance for all Israel.
22 So they ate and drank before the
LORD with great gladness on that day.
And they made Solomon the son of
David king the second time, and
[a]anointed *him* before the LORD *to be*
the leader, and Zadok *to be* priest.
23 Then Solomon sat on the throne of
the LORD as king instead of David his
father, and prospered; and all Israel
obeyed him.
24 All the leaders and the mighty men,
and also all the sons of King David,
[a]submitted[1] themselves to King Solomon.
25 So the LORD exalted Solomon exceedingly in the sight of all Israel, and
[a]bestowed on him *such* royal majesty
as had not been on any king before him
in Israel.

The Close of David's Reign

26 Thus David the son of Jesse reigned
over all Israel.
27 [a]And the period that he reigned
over Israel *was* forty years; [b]seven
years he reigned in Hebron, and thirty-
three *years* he reigned in Jerusalem.
28 So he [a]died in a good old age,
[b]full of days and riches and honor; and
Solomon his *son reigned in his place.
29 Now the acts of King David, first
and last, indeed they *are* written in the
[1]book of Samuel the *seer, in the book
of Nathan the prophet, and in the book
of Gad the seer,
30 with all his reign and his might,
[a]and the events that happened to him,
to Israel, and to all the kingdoms of
the lands.

21 [a]1 Kin. 8:62, 63
22 [a]1 Kin. 1:32–35, 39; 1 Chr. 23:1
24 [a]Eccl. 8:2 [1]Lit. *gave the hand*
25 [a]1 Kin. 3:13; 2 Chr. 1:12; Eccl. 2:9
27 [a]2 Sam. 5:4; 1 Kin. 2:11 [b]2 Sam. 5:5
28 [a]Gen. 25:8 [b]1 Chr. 23:1 *See WW at Gen. 29:32.
29 [1]Lit. *words* *See WW at 1 Sam. 9:9.
30 [a]Dan. 2:21; 4:23, 25

29:21–30 1 Chr. ends on the optimistic notes of the grandeur of Solomon's anointing as king (vv. 21–25) and the honor and dignity of David's death (vv. 26–30).

TRUTH-IN-ACTION through 1 CHRONICLES

Letting the LIFE of the Holy Spirit Bring Faith's Works Alive in You!

Truth 1 Chronicles Teaches	Text	**Action** 1 Chronicles Invites
1 Guidelines for Growing in Godliness Godliness means being faithful to God in all that we do. Faithfulness involves letting God and His Word be our exclusive resource of any knowledge we have about Him, His ways, or spiritual reality. The godly person avoids any contact with the occult.	9:1	**Be warned** that unfaithfulness to God may result in our hearts and minds being taken captive by the world system.
	10:13	**Do not seek out** spiritual information or insight from any spiritual source other than the Holy Spirit or Christ-centered counselors. **Be warned** that doing so can result in serious judgment, even death.
2 Steps to Dynamic Devotion We must never allow anything to become more important to us than our pursuit of God. Even learn to guard against letting the things of God become more important than knowing God Himself.	22:19	**Understand** that God gives you times of peace and rest so that you can devote your heart and soul to seeking Him.
	28:7–10	**Be diligent** in the things God gives you to do. **Serve God** with unswerving devotion. **Understand** that the Lord honors those who honor His Word and seek Him with all their heart.
3 Keys to Wise Living Wisdom counsels us that God's ways are higher than our ways and His thoughts than our thoughts. He knows the best way to do His work.	13:7–10; 15:11–15	**Do not undertake** to do God's work in your own way. **Be warned** that employing human wisdom to accomplish God's work can result in frightening consequences.

Truth 1 Chronicles Teaches	Text	**Action** 1 Chronicles Invites
4 **A Key to Generous Living** Knowing the extent of divine resource frees us to greater generosity.	29:14	**Understand** that all we possess comes from the hand of the Lord.
5 **Key to Relating to Authority** God instructs us in how to relate to Him by instructing us in how to relate properly to those He sends.	16:22	**Know** that God has sworn to protect those He sends to proclaim His Word. **Be careful** how you speak about and treat God's servants.
6 **Lessons for Leaders** God calls His leaders to realize that the work to which they are called is His and He will see to its completion.	28:20	Leaders, **take courage** in the fact that the Lord pledges to be with those He calls until that to which He calls them has been completed.

The Second Book of the CHRONICLES

Author: Attributed to Ezra
Date: Probably Between 425 and 400 B.C.
Theme: Encouragement and Exhortation from Judah's Spiritual Heritage
Key Words: King, House, David, Jerusalem, Priest

Author Since 1 and 2 Chronicles were originally one book (see "Content" below), they are to be considered together in the matter of authorship. The fact that the identity of the author of this united work is not stated in either 1 or 2 Chronicles has led many to refer to this unknown author simply as "the chronicler." However, Ezra is the most likely candidate for the authorship of 1 and 2 Chronicles. The early Jewish tradition of the Talmud affirms that Ezra wrote 1 and 2 Chronicles. Also, the closing verses of Chronicles (2 Chr. 36:22, 23) are repeated as the opening verses of Ezra (see Ezra 1:1–3). Not only does this add to the case for Ezra's authorship of 1 and 2 Chronicles, it also may be an indication that 1 and 2 Chronicles and Ezra were once a consecutive work. In addition, 1 and 2 Chronicles and Ezra have similar style, vocabulary, and contents. Ezra was a scribe as well as a priest, and played a significant role in the community of exiles who returned to Jerusalem. Though we cannot be certain, it is reasonable to assume that "the chronicler" was Ezra.

Date Though the precise date of 1 and 2 Chronicles cannot be established, this unified work probably came into its final form sometime toward the end of the fifth century B.C. The last event recorded in the closing verses of 2 Chronicles is the decree of the Persian king Cyrus to allow the Jews to return to Judah. This is dated at 538 B.C. and gives the impression that 1 and 2 Chronicles would have been composed shortly after this time. However, the latest person mentioned in 1 and 2 Chronicles is actually Anani of the eighth generation of King Jehoiachin (see 1 Chr. 3:24). Jehoiachin was deported to Babylon in 597 B.C. Depending on how these generations are measured (approximately twenty-five years), Anani's birth would have been sometime between 425 and 400 B.C. Therefore, the date for 1 and 2 Chronicles is between 425 and 400 B.C.

Background The Book of 2 Chronicles covers the period from the beginning of the reign of Solomon in 971 B.C. to the end of the Exile around 538 B.C. However, the specific background of 1 and 2 Chronicles is the period after the Exile. During this time, the ancient world was under the control of the powerful Persian Empire. All that remained of the glorious kingdom of David and Solomon was the tiny province of Judah. The Persians had replaced the monarchy with a provincial governor. Though God's people had been allowed to return to Jerusalem and rebuild the temple, their situation was far removed from the golden days of David and Solomon.

Occasion and Purpose The return of the exiles from Babylon necessitated the recording of the history of God's people, especially Judah. Second Chronicles was written for the dual purpose of providing encouragement and exhortation to those who had returned to Jerusalem. The remnant that was left needed encouragement to keep their faith alive in the midst of difficulty, and they needed hope for the future. The emphasis of 2 Chronicles on their spiritual heritage of David, Solomon, the temple, and the priesthood was a refreshing reminder that God was faithful and He would not forget His promises to David and to His people. Yet Chronicles also served as a strong exhortation to motivate God's people to adhere to the Mosaic covenant and ritual, so that the tragedy of the past would not be repeated.

Comparison with Kings One may question the need for the books of 1 and 2 Chronicles, since the material has already been covered in 1 and 2 Kings and other Old Testament books. However, though the books are similar, they are by no means identical. In the same way that there are four accounts of the life of Christ in Matthew, Mark, Luke, and John, there are two accounts of the history of God's people. Though 1 and 2 Kings and 1 and 2 Chronicles are alike in content, they offer two different historical perspectives. While the Books of Kings were written to those in exile, the Books of Chronicles address the postexilic community. They were written for two different purposes. Compare the Introductions to 1 and 2 Kings and 2 Chronicles: Occasion and Purpose. Also, Kings and Chronicles have different political perspectives. While Kings embraces both kingdoms, Israel and Judah, Chronicles focuses only on Judah. Finally, Kings and Chronicles differ in their theological perspectives. Kings presents a prophetic outlook, while Chronicles operates from a priestly vantage point. However, Chronicles is like Kings in that it is not mere history, but rather theology in the form of a historical narrative. See Introductions to 1 and 2 Kings: Content.

Content In the original Hebrew Scriptures, 1 and 2 Chronicles formed one book, entitled "Events of the Days." It was divided and renamed "Things Passed Over" by the translators of the Greek Old Testament (the Septuagint, or LXX). The title "Chronicles" derives from Jerome. It is not a continuation of the history of God's people, but a duplication of and a supplement to 1 and 2 Samuel and 1 and 2 Kings.

Second Chronicles can be divided into two main sections. The first part of 2 Chronicles (chs. 1—9) outlines the reign of King Solomon. The account accents the construction of the temple (chs. 2—7), and the wealth and wisdom of this extraordinary king (chs. 8; 9). However, the narrative ends abruptly and makes no mention of Solomon's failure as is recorded in 1 Kings 11.

The second section of 2 Chronicles consists of chapters 10—36. After the division of the kingdom, 2 Chronicles concentrates almost exclusively on the southern kingdom of Judah and treats the history of the northern kingdom of Israel as incidental. Second Chronicles traces the reigns of Judah's twenty rulers down to Babylon's captivity of Judah in 586 B.C. The book concludes with Cyrus's decree for Judah's release and return (36:22, 23).

Personal Application While 1 and 2 Kings draw out the fact of human responsibility, showing that sin leads to defeat, 2 Chronicles accentuates the sovereign deliverance of God. The twin themes of encouragement and exhortation still ring true today. God has been faithful throughout all of history to deliver those who cry out to Him. Second Chronicles skillfully tells the story of how God was true to His word and kept the promises He had made to His people. This is a great source of encouragement for believers of all ages. God is a promise-making and promise-keeping God who is worthy to be trusted. He is still a God of hope, and His purposes will prevail in the lives of His people. However, 2 Chronicles also exhorts us to learn from the failure of God's people in the past, in order that we might not make the same mistakes (1 Cor. 10:11; Heb. 4:11).

Christ Revealed Christ is foreshadowed in 2 Chronicles in much the same way as He is in 2 Kings (see Introduction to 2 Kings: Christ Revealed). However, in 2 Chronicles, many have seen an allusion to Christ in reference to the temple. First Chronicles 21 (see also 2 Sam. 24) explains that as a consequence for sin, a death plague had broken out against Israel. David buys a piece of property from Ornan on which to make a sacrifice that stops the plague. This site on Mount Moriah was the very place where Solomon would build the temple (3:1). It is possible that this was the very mountain where Abraham was asked to sacrifice his son Isaac (Gen. 22:2). In the New Testament, three times Paul refers to believers as the "temple of God" (1 Cor. 3:16, 17; 6:19; Eph. 2:19–22). It is Christ who has purchased the ground for this spiritual temple. It was His sacrifice that delivered us from death (Rom. 5:12–18; 7:24, 25; 1 John 3:14).

The Holy Spirit at Work There are three clear references to the Holy Spirit in 2 Chronicles. He is referred to as the "Spirit of God" (15:1; 24:20) and the "Spirit of the LORD" (20:14). In these references, the Holy Spirit was active to give inspired utterances through Azariah (15:1), Jahaziel (20:14), and Zechariah (24:20). This work of the Holy Spirit to inspire people to prophesy is similar to His activity in 1 and 2 Samuel and 1 and 2 Kings. See Introductions to 1 and 2 Kings: The Holy Spirit at Work.

Besides these references, many see a picture of the Holy Spirit in 2 Chronicles 5:13, 14 (cf. also 1 Kin. 8:10, 11) at the dedication of the temple. This temple, which was built on a place that was purchased, a place where sacrifice was made for sin, is now filled with the presence of God. In the New Testament, Paul explains that believers are the temple of God, the dwelling place of the Holy Spirit (1 Cor. 3:16; 6:19).

Finally, there is a possible reference to the Holy Spirit in 18:23. This is a parallel reference to 1 Kings 22:24. See note on 1 Kings 22:24.

Outline of 2 Chronicles

I. The reign of King Solomon 1:1—9:31

A. The accession of Solomon as king 1:1–17

B. The achievement of building the temple 2:1—7:22

C. The affluence of Solomon 8:1—9:31

II. The reigns of the kings of Judah 10:1—36:16

A. The reign of Rehoboam 10:1—12:16
B. The reign of Abijah 13:1–22
C. The reign of Asa 14:1—16:14
D. The reign of Jehoshaphat 17:1—20:37
E. The reign of Jehoram 21:1–20
F. The reign of Ahaziah 22:1–9
G. The reign of Queen Athaliah 22:10—23:15
H. The reign of Joash 23:16—24:27
I. The reign of Amaziah 25:1–28
J. The reign of Uzziah 26:1–23
K. The reign of Jotham 27:1–9
L. The reign of Ahaz 28:1–27
M. The reign of Hezekiah 29:1—32:33
N. The reign of Manasseh 33:1–20
O. The reign of Amon 33:21–25
P. The reign of Josiah 34:1—35:27
Q. The reign of Jehoahaz 36:1–3
R. The reign of Jehoiakim 36:4–8
S. The reign of Jehoiachin 36:9, 10
T. The reign of Zedekiah 36:11–16

III. Judah's captivity and return 36:17–23

A. Babylon's captivity of Judah 36:17–21
B. The decree by Cyrus for Judah's return 36:22, 23

Solomon Requests Wisdom

NOW [a]Solomon the son of David
was strengthened in his kingdom,
and [b]the LORD his God *was* with him
and [c]exalted him exceedingly.
2 And Solomon spoke to all Israel, to
[a]the captains of thousands and of hundreds, to the *judges, and to every
leader in all Israel, the heads of the fathers' *houses.*
3 Then Solomon, and all the assembly
with him, went to [1]the high place that
was at [a]Gibeon; for the tabernacle of
meeting with God was there, which
Moses the servant of the LORD had
[b]made in the wilderness.
4 [a]But David had brought up the ark
of God from Kirjath Jearim to *the place*
David had prepared for it, for he had
pitched a tent for it at Jerusalem.
5 Now [a]the bronze altar that [b]Bezalel
the son of Uri, the son of Hur, had
made, [1]he put before the tabernacle of
the LORD; Solomon and the assembly
sought Him *there.*
6 And Solomon went up there to the
bronze altar before the LORD, which
was at the tabernacle of meeting, and
[a]offered a thousand burnt offerings on
it.
7 [a]On that night God appeared to Solomon, and said to him, "Ask! What
shall I give you?"
8 And Solomon said to God: "You
have shown great [a]mercy to David my
father, and have made me [b]king in his
place.
9 "Now, O LORD God, let Your promise to David my father be established,
[a]for You have made me king over a
people like the [b]dust of the earth in
multitude.
10 [a]"Now give me wisdom and knowl- 2
edge, that I may [b]go out and come in
before this people; for who can judge
this great people of Yours?"
11 [a]Then God said to Solomon: "Because this was in your heart, and you
have not asked riches or wealth or
honor or the life of your enemies, nor
have you asked long life—but have
asked wisdom and knowledge for
yourself, that you may judge My
people over whom I have made you
king—
12 "wisdom and knowledge *are*
granted to you; and I will give you
riches and wealth and honor, such as
[a]none of the kings have had who *were*
before you, nor shall any after you
have the like."

CHAPTER 1
1 [a]1 Kin. 2:46 [b]Gen. 39:2 [c]1 Chr. 29:25
2 [a]1 Chr. 27:1–34 *See WW at Judg. 2:18.
3 [a]1 Kin. 3:4 [b]Ex. 25—27; 35:4—36:38 [1]Place for worship
4 [a]2 Sam. 6:2–17
5 [a]Ex. 27:1, 2; 38:1, 2 [b]Ex. 31:2 [1]Some authorities *it was there*
6 [a]1 Kin. 3:4
7 [a]1 Kin. 3:5–14; 9:2
8 [a]Ps. 18:50 [b]1 Chr. 28:5
9 [a]2 Sam. 7:8–16 [b]Gen. 13:16
10 [a]1 Kin. 3:9 [b]Deut. 31:2
11 [a]1 Kin. 3:11–13
12 [a]2 Chr. 9:22

1:1–12 1 and 2 Chr. do not record Solomon's execution of Adonijah, Joab, or Shimei, nor the expulsion of Abiathar. Read the text and notes of 1 Kin. 2:13–46. Instead, the chronicler moves directly from the death of David (1 Chr. 29:26–30) to Solomon's request for **wisdom** (1:1–12). 1 and 2 Chr. were originally one scroll, not two books. For a fuller account of Solomon's request for wisdom and the Lord's response, read the text and notes of 1 Kin. 3:1–15. See also 1 Kin. 3:16–28 for a colorful illustration of the wisdom that God gave Solomon. On vv. 1–6, read the text and notes of 1 Chr. 16:1–6.

1:3–6 According to Deut. 12:13, 14, burnt offerings were only to be offered in "the place where the LORD your God chooses." These verses explain why it was acceptable for **Solomon** to offer **a thousand burnt offerings at Gibeon:** because the **tabernacle** (v. 3) and **the bronze altar** (v. 6) were there.

1:10–12 See section 2 of Truth-In-Action at the end of 2 Chr.

Solomon's Military and Economic Power

13 So Solomon came to Jerusalem from [1]the high place that *was* at Gibeon, from before the tabernacle of meeting, and reigned over Israel.

14 [a]And Solomon gathered chariots and horsemen; he had one thousand four hundred chariots and twelve thousand horsemen, whom he stationed in the chariot cities and with the king in Jerusalem.

15 [a]Also the king made silver and gold as common in Jerusalem as stones, and he made cedars as abundant as the sycamores which *are* in the lowland.

16 [a]And Solomon had horses imported from Egypt and Keveh; the king's merchants bought them in Keveh at the *current* price.

17 They also acquired and imported from Egypt a chariot for six hundred *shekels* of silver, and a horse for one hundred and fifty; thus, [1]through their agents, they exported them to all the kings of the Hittites and the kings of Syria.

Solomon Prepares to Build the Temple

2 Then Solomon [a]determined to *build a temple for the name of the LORD, and a royal house for himself.

2 [a]Solomon selected seventy thousand men to bear burdens, eighty thousand to quarry *stone* in the mountains, and three thousand six hundred to oversee them.

3 Then Solomon sent to [1]Hiram king of Tyre, saying:

[a]As you have dealt with David my father, and sent him cedars to build himself a house to dwell in, *so deal with me.*

4 Behold, [a]I am building a temple for the name of the LORD my God, to dedicate *it* to Him, [b]to burn before Him [1]sweet incense, for [c]the continual showbread, for [d]the burnt offerings morning and evening, on the [e]Sabbaths, on the New Moons, and on the [2]set feasts of the LORD our God. This *is an ordinance* forever to Israel.

5 And the temple which I build *will be* great, for [a]our God is greater than all gods.

6 [a]But who is able to build Him a temple, since heaven and the heaven of heavens cannot contain Him? Who *am* I then, that I should build Him a temple, except to burn sacrifice before Him? 3

13 [1]Place for worship
14 [a]1 Kin. 10:26; 2 Chr. 9:25
15 [a]1 Kin. 10:27; 2 Chr. 9:27; Job 22:24
16 [a]1 Kin. 10:28; 22:36; 2 Chr. 9:28
17 [1]Lit. *by their hands*

CHAPTER 2

1 [a]1 Kin. 5:5 *See WW at Zech. 1:16.
2 [a]1 Kin. 5:15, 16; 2 Chr. 2:18
3 [a]1 Chr. 14:1 [1]Heb. *Huram;* cf. 1 Kin. 5:1
4 [a]2 Chr. 2:1 [b]Ex. 30:7 [c]Ex. 25:30; Lev. 24:8 [d]Ex. 29:38–42 [e]Num. 28:3, 9–11 [1]Lit. *incense of spices* [2]*appointed*
5 [a]Ps. 135:5; [1 Cor. 8:5, 6]
6 [a]1 Kin. 8:27; 2 Chr. 6:18; Is. 66:1

1:13–17 Read the text and notes of 1 Kin. 4 for further details on the prosperity, strength, and wisdom of Solomon's reign.
2:1–18 Read the text and notes of 1 Kin. 5 for a similar description of Solomon's preparations for the building of the **temple.**
2:6 See section 3 of Truth-In-Action at the end of 2 Chr.

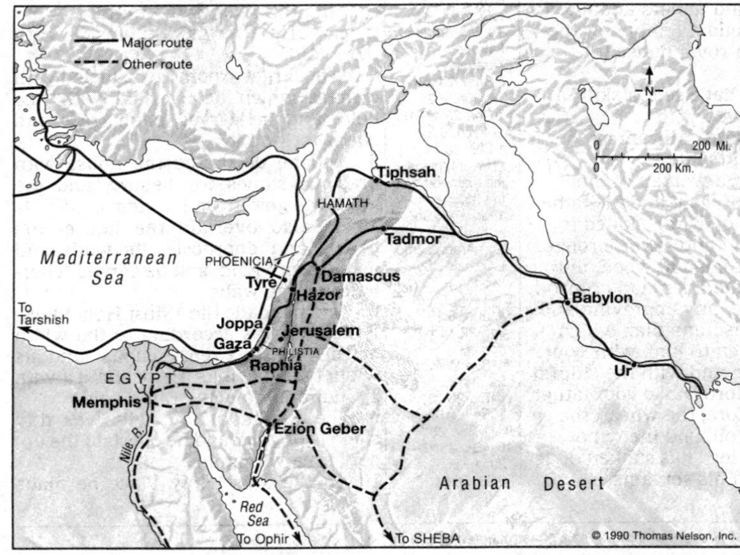

The Spread of Solomon's Fame. Solomon's influence in economic and political affairs was enhanced by the transportation and trade routes that intersected his kingdom.

7 Therefore send me at once a man
skillful to work in gold and silver,
in bronze and iron, in purple and
crimson and blue, who has skill
to engrave with the skillful men
who are with me in Judah and
Jerusalem, [a]whom David my
father provided.
8 [a]Also send me cedar and cypress
and algum logs from Lebanon, for
I know that your servants have
skill to cut timber in Lebanon;
and indeed my servants *will be*
with your servants,
9 to prepare timber for me in
abundance, for the [1]temple which
I am about to build *shall be* great
and wonderful.
10 [a]And indeed I will give to your
servants, the woodsmen who cut
timber, twenty thousand kors of
ground wheat, twenty thousand
kors of barley, twenty thousand
baths of wine, and twenty
thousand baths of oil.

11 Then Hiram king of Tyre answered
in writing, which he sent to Solomon:

[a]Because the LORD loves His
people, He has made you king
over them.

12 [1]Hiram also said:

[a]Blessed *be* the LORD God of
Israel, [b]who made heaven and
earth, for He has given King
David a wise son, endowed with
prudence and understanding,
who will build a temple for the
LORD and a royal house for
himself!
13 And now I have sent a skillful
man, endowed with
understanding, [1]Huram my
[2]master *craftsman*
14 [a](the son of a woman of the
daughters of Dan, and his father
was a man of Tyre), skilled to
work in gold and silver, bronze
and iron, stone and wood, purple
and blue, fine linen and crimson,
and to make any engraving and
to accomplish any plan which
may be given to him, with your
skillful men and with the skillful
men of my lord David your father.
15 Now therefore, the wheat, the
barley, the oil, and the wine
which [a]my lord has spoken of, let
him send to his servants.
16 [a]And we will cut wood from
Lebanon, as much as you need;
we will bring it to you in rafts by
sea to [1]Joppa, and you will carry
it up to Jerusalem.

17 [a]Then Solomon numbered all the
aliens who *were* in the land of Israel,
after the census in which [b]David his
father had numbered them; and there
were found to be one hundred and
fifty-three thousand six hundred.
18 And he made [a]seventy thousand of
them bearers of burdens, eighty thousand stonecutters in the mountain, and
three thousand six hundred overseers
to make the people work.

Solomon Builds the Temple

3 Now [a]Solomon began to build the
house of the LORD at [b]Jerusalem on
Mount Moriah, where [1]*the LORD* had
appeared to his father David, at the
place that David had prepared on
the threshing floor of [c]Ornan[2] the
Jebusite.
2 And he began to build on the second
day of the second month in the fourth
year of his reign.
3 This is the foundation [a]which Solomon laid for building the house of God:
The length *was* sixty cubits (by cubits
according to the former measure) and
the width twenty cubits.
4 And the [a]vestibule that *was* in front
of [1]*the sanctuary* was twenty cubits
long across the width of the house, and
the height *was* [2]one hundred and
twenty. He overlaid the inside with
pure gold.
5 [a]The larger [1]room he [b]paneled with
cypress which he overlaid with fine
gold, and he carved palm trees and
chainwork on it.
6 And he decorated the house with
precious stones for beauty, and the
gold *was* gold from Parvaim.
7 He also overlaid the house—the
beams and doorposts, its walls and
doors—with gold; and he carved *cherubim on the walls.
8 And he made the [a]Most Holy Place.
Its length was according to the width
of the house, twenty cubits, and its
width twenty cubits. He overlaid it with
six hundred talents of fine gold.
9 The weight of the nails *was* fifty
shekels of gold; and he overlaid the upper [a]area with gold.
10 [a]In the Most Holy Place he made

7 [a]1 Chr. 22:15
8 [a]1 Kin. 5:6
9 [1]Lit. *house*
10 [a]1 Kin. 5:11
11 [a]1 Kin. 10:9; 2 Chr. 9:8
12 [a]1 Kin. 5:7 [b]Gen. 1; 2; Acts 4:24; 14:15; Rev. 10:6 [1]Heb. *Huram;* cf. 1 Kin. 5:1
13 [1]*Hiram,* 1 Kin. 7:13 [2]Lit. *father,* 1 Kin. 7:13, 14
14 [a]1 Kin. 7:13, 14
15 [a]2 Chr. 2:10
16 [a]1 Kin. 5:8, 9 [1]Heb. *Japho*
17 [a]1 Kin. 5:13; 2 Chr. 8:7, 8 [b]1 Chr. 22:2
18 [a]2 Chr. 2:2

CHAPTER 3

1 [a]1 Kin. 6:1 [b]Gen. 22:2–14 [c]1 Chr. 21:18; 22:1 [1]Lit. *He,* following MT, Vg.; LXX *the LORD;* Tg. *the Angel of the LORD* [2]*Araunah,* 2 Sam. 24:16
3 [a]1 Kin. 6:2; 1 Chr. 28:11–19
4 [a]1 Kin. 6:3; 1 Chr. 28:11 [1]The holy place, the main room of the temple, 1 Kin. 6:3 [2]So with MT, LXX, Vg.; Arab., some LXX mss., Syr. *twenty*
5 [a]1 Kin. 6:17 [b]1 Kin. 6:15; Jer. 22:14 [1]Lit. *house*
7 *See WW at Ex. 25:18.
8 [a]Ex. 26:33; 1 Kin. 6:16
9 [a]1 Chr. 28:11
10 [a]Ex. 25:18–20; 1 Kin. 6:23–28

3:1–17 A more explicit account of the temple's construction is given in 1 Kin. 6:1–38; 7:15–22.

two cherubim, fashioned by carving,
and overlaid them with gold.
11 The wings of the cherubim *were*
twenty cubits in *overall* length: one
wing *of the one cherub was* five cubits,
touching the wall of the room, and the
other wing *was* five cubits, touching
the wing of the other cherub;
12 *one* wing of the other cherub *was*
five cubits, touching the wall of the
room, and the other wing *also was* five
cubits, touching the wing of the other
cherub.
13 The wings of these cherubim
spanned twenty cubits overall. They
stood on their feet, and they faced inward.
14 And he made the [a]veil of blue, purple, crimson, and fine linen, and wove
cherubim into it.
15 Also he made in front of the [1]temple
[a]two pillars [2]thirty-five cubits [3]high,
and the capital that *was* on the top of
each of *them* was five cubits.
16 He made wreaths of chainwork, as
in the inner sanctuary, and put *them*
on top of the pillars; and he made
[a]one hundred pomegranates, and put
them on the wreaths of chainwork.
17 Then he [a]set up the pillars before
the temple, one on the right hand and
the other on the left; he called the name
of the one on the right hand [1]Jachin,
and the name of the one on the left
[2]Boaz.

Furnishings of the Temple

4 Moreover he made [a]a bronze altar:
twenty cubits was its length,
twenty cubits its width, and ten cubits
its height.
2 [a]Then he made the [1]Sea of cast
bronze, ten cubits from one brim to the
other; *it was* completely round. Its
height *was* five cubits, and a line of
thirty cubits measured its circumference.
3 [a]And under it *was* the likeness of
oxen encircling it all around, ten to a
cubit, all the way around the Sea. The
oxen *were* cast in two rows, when it
was cast.
4 It stood on twelve [a]oxen: three looking toward the north, three looking toward the west, three looking toward
the south, and three looking toward the
east; the Sea *was set* upon them, and
all their back parts *pointed* inward.
5 It *was* a handbreadth thick; and its

14 [a]Ex. 26:31; Matt. 27:51; Heb. 9:3
15 [a]1 Kin. 7:15–20; Jer. 52:21 [1]Lit. *house* [2]*eighteen,* 1 Kin. 7:15; 2 Kin. 25:17; Jer. 52:21 [3]Lit. *long*
16 [a]1 Kin. 7:20
17 [a]1 Kin. 7:21 [1]Lit. *He Shall Establish* [2]Lit. *In It Is Strength*

CHAPTER 4

1 [a]Ex. 27:1, 2; 2 Kin. 16:14; Ezek. 43:13, 16
2 [a]Ex. 30:17–21; 1 Kin. 7:23–26 [1]Great laver or basin
3 [a]1 Kin. 7:24–26
4 [a]1 Kin. 7:25

4:1—5:1 Read the text and notes of 1 Kin. 7:23–51 to gain a better understanding of the furnishings of the temple.

THE PLAN OF SOLOMON'S TEMPLE (3:1)

Solomon constructed the temple on Mt. Moriah, north of the ancient City of David. The temple was built according to plans that David received from the Lord and passed on to Solomon (1 Chr. 28:11–13, 19). The division into a sanctuary and inner sanctuary corresponds to the division of the tabernacle into the holy place and Most Holy Place.

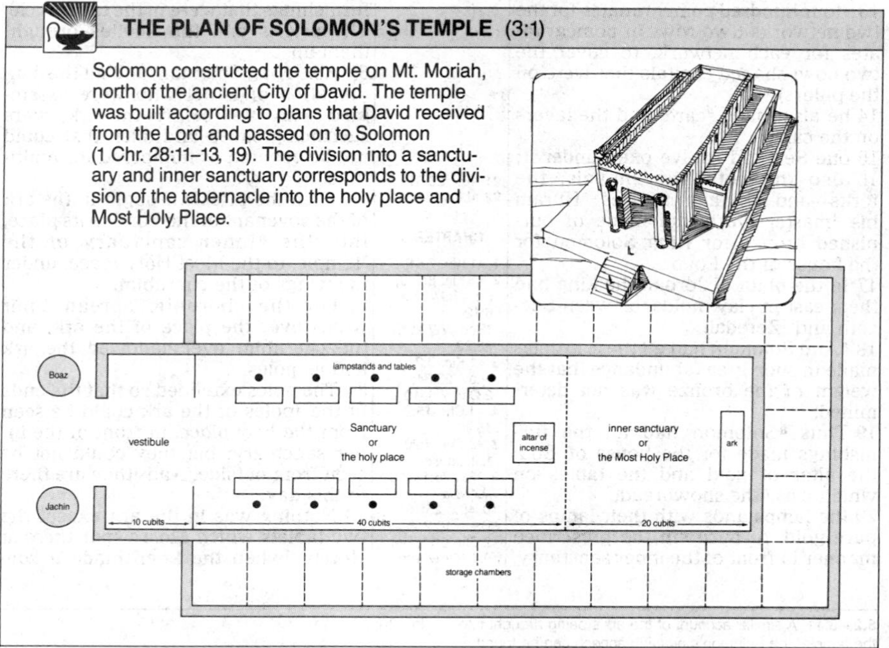

brim was shaped like the brim of a cup,
like a lily blossom. It contained [1]three
thousand baths.
6 He also made [a]ten lavers, and put
five on the right side and five on the
left, to wash in them; such things as
they offered for the burnt offering they
would wash in them, but the [1]Sea *was*
for the [b]priests to wash in.
7 [a]And he made ten lampstands of
gold [b]according to their design, and set
them in the temple, five on the right
side and five on the left.
8 [a]He also made ten tables, and
placed *them* in the temple, five on the
right side and five on the left. And he
made one hundred [b]bowls of gold.
9 Furthermore [a]he made the court of
the priests, and the [b]great court and
doors for the court; and he overlaid
these doors with bronze.
10 [a]He set the Sea on the right side,
toward the southeast.
11 Then [a]Huram made the pots and the
shovels and the bowls. So Huram finished doing the work that he was to
do for King Solomon for the house of
God:
12 the two pillars and [a]the bowl-
shaped capitals *that were* on top of the
two pillars; the two networks covering
the two bowl-shaped capitals which
were on top of the pillars;
13 [a]four hundred pomegranates for the
two networks (two rows of pomegranates for each network, to cover the
two bowl-shaped capitals that *were* on
the pillars);
14 he also made [a]carts and the lavers
on the carts;
15 one Sea and twelve oxen under it;
16 also the pots, the shovels, the
forks—and all their articles [a]Huram
his [1]master *craftsman* made of burnished bronze for King Solomon for
the house of the LORD.
17 In the plain of Jordan the king had
them cast in clay molds, between Succoth and [1]Zeredah.
18 [a]And Solomon had all these articles
made in such great abundance that the
weight of the bronze was not determined.
19 Thus [a]Solomon had all the furnishings made for the house of God:
the altar of gold and the tables on
which *was* [b]the showbread;
20 the lampstands with their lamps of
pure gold, to burn [a]in the prescribed
manner in front of the inner sanctuary,
21 with [a]the flowers and the lamps and
the wick-trimmers of gold, of purest
gold;
22 the trimmers, the bowls, the ladles,
and the censers of pure gold. As for
the entry of the [1]sanctuary, its inner
doors to the Most Holy *Place,* and the
doors of the main hall of the temple,
were gold.

5 So [a]all the work that Solomon had
done for the house of the LORD was
finished; and Solomon brought in the
things which his father David had dedicated: the silver and the gold and all
the furnishings. And he put *them* in the
treasuries of the house of God.

The Ark Brought into the Temple

2 [a]Now Solomon assembled the elders of Israel and all the heads of the
*tribes, the chief fathers of the children
of Israel, in Jerusalem, that they might
bring the ark of the covenant of the
LORD up [b]from the City of David, which
is Zion.
3 [a]Therefore all the men of Israel assembled with the king [b]at the feast,
which *was* in the seventh month.
4 So all the elders of Israel came, and
the [a]Levites took up the ark.
5 Then they brought up the ark, the
tabernacle of meeting, and all the holy
furnishings that *were* in the tabernacle.
The priests and the Levites brought
them up.
6 Also King Solomon, and all the congregation of Israel who were assembled with him before the ark, were
sacrificing sheep and oxen that could
not be counted or numbered for multitude.
7 Then the priests brought in the ark
of the covenant of the LORD to its place,
into the [a]inner sanctuary of the
[1]temple, to the Most Holy *Place,* under
the wings of the cherubim.
8 For the cherubim spread *their*
wings over the place of the ark, and
the cherubim overshadowed the ark
and its poles.
9 The poles extended so that the ends
of the [a]poles of the ark could be seen
from *the holy place,* in front of the inner sanctuary; but they could not be
seen from outside. And [1]they are there
to this day.
10 Nothing was in the ark except the
two tablets which Moses [a]put *there* at
Horeb, [1]when the LORD made *a cov-*

5 [1]About 8,000 gallons; *two thousand,* 1 Kin. 7:26
6 [a]1 Kin. 7:38, 40 [b]Ex. 30:19–21 [1]Great basin
7 [a]1 Kin. 7:49 [b]Ex. 25:31; 1 Chr. 28:12, 19
8 [a]1 Kin. 7:48 [b]1 Chr. 28:17
9 [a]1 Kin. 6:36 [b]2 Kin. 21:5
10 [a]1 Kin. 7:39
11 [a]1 Kin. 7:40–51
12 [a]1 Kin. 7:41
13 [a]1 Kin. 7:20
14 [a]1 Kin. 7:27, 43
16 [a]1 Kin. 7:45; 2 Chr. 2:13 [1]Lit. *father*
17 [1]*Zaretan,* 1 Kin. 7:46
18 [a]1 Kin. 7:47
19 [a]1 Kin. 7:48–50 [b]Ex. 25:30
20 [a]Ex. 27:20, 21
21 [a]Ex. 25:31
22 [1]Lit. *house*

CHAPTER 5

1 [a]1 Kin. 7:51
2 [a]1 Kin. 8:1–9; Ps. 47:9 [b]2 Sam. 6:12 *See WW at Ex. 38:22.
3 [a]1 Kin. 8:2 [b]Lev. 23:34; 2 Chr. 7:8–10
4 [a]1 Chr. 15:2, 15
7 [a]2 Chr. 4:20 [1]Lit. *house*
9 [a]Ex. 25:13–15 [1]Lit. *it is*
10 [a]Ex. 25:16; Deut. 10:2, 5; 2 Chr. 6:11; Heb. 9:4 [1]Or *where*

5:2—6:11 A similar account of the ark's being brought into the temple and Solomon's ensuing speech can be found in 1 Kin. 8:1–21.

enant with the children of Israel, when they had come out of Egypt.

11 And it came to pass when the priests came out of the *Most* Holy *Place* (for all the priests who *were* present had [1]sanctified themselves, without keeping to their [a]divisions),

12 [a]and the Levites *who were* the singers, all those of Asaph and Heman and Jeduthun, with their sons and their brethren, stood at the east end of the altar, clothed in white linen, having cymbals, stringed instruments and harps, [b]and with them one hundred and twenty priests sounding with trumpets—

13 indeed it came to pass, when the trumpeters and singers *were* as one, to make one sound to be heard in *praising and thanking the LORD, and when they lifted up their voice with the trumpets and cymbals and instruments of music, and praised the LORD, *saying*:

[a]"*For He is* good,
For His mercy *endures* forever,"

that the house, the house of the LORD, was filled with a cloud,

KINGDOM DYNAMICS

5:13 Power in Unity of Praise, PRAISE PATHWAY. This text demonstrates the power in unity of praise, thanksgiving, and music: 1) the trumpeters and singers were as one; 2) to make one sound in praise and thanksgiving to the Lord, saying "*For He is* good, for His mercy *endures* [lasts] forever"; 3) the house (temple) was filled with a cloud (the glory of God's presence.)

Remember, even in praise, thanksgiving, and worship, "God is not *the author* of confusion" (1 Cor. 14:33). Anything said or done that draws attention to the praiser/worshiper and away from God, Jesus, and the Holy Spirit needs to be reconsidered.

(Num. 21:16, 17/2 Chr. 20:15–22) C.G.

14 so that the priests could not [1]continue ministering because of the cloud; [a]for the glory of the LORD filled the house of God.

6

Then [a]Solomon spoke:

"The LORD said He would dwell in
the [b]dark cloud.
2 I have surely built You an exalted
house,
And [a]a place for You to dwell in
forever."

Solomon's Speech upon Completion of the Work

3 Then the king turned around and [a]blessed the whole assembly of Israel, while all the assembly of Israel was standing.

4 And he said: "Blessed *be* the LORD God of Israel, who has fulfilled with His hands *what* He spoke with His mouth to my father David, [a]saying,

5 'Since the day that I brought My people out of the land of Egypt, I have chosen no city from any tribe of Israel *in which* to build a house, that My name might be there, nor did I choose any man to be a ruler over My people Israel.

6 [a]'Yet I have chosen Jerusalem, that My name may be there, and I [b]have chosen David to be over My people Israel.'

7 "Now [a]it was in the heart of my father David to build a [1]temple for the name of the LORD God of Israel.

8 "But the LORD said to my father David, 'Whereas it was in your heart to build a temple for My name, you did well in that it was in your heart.

9 'Nevertheless you shall not build the temple, but your son who will come from your body, he shall build the temple for My [a]name.'

10 "So the LORD has fulfilled His word which He spoke, and I have filled the position of my father David, and [a]sit on the throne of Israel, as the LORD promised; and I have built the temple for the name of the LORD God of Israel.

11 "And there I have put the ark, [a]in which *is* the covenant of the LORD which He made with the children of Israel."

Solomon's Prayer of Dedication

12 [a]Then [1]*Solomon* stood before the altar of the LORD in the presence of all the assembly of Israel, and spread out his hands

KINGDOM DYNAMICS

6:12–42; 7:1 God's Holy Fire Falls, PRAYER. When Solomon dedicated the

(*cont. on next page*)

11 [a]1 Chr. 24:1–5 [1]*consecrated* **12** [a]Ex. 32:26; 1 Chr. 25:1–7 [b]1 Chr. 13:8; 15:16, 24 **13** [a]1 Chr. 16:34, 41; 2 Chr. 7:3; Ezra 3:11; Ps. 100:5; 106:1; 136; Jer. 33:11 *See WW at 1 Chr. 23:30. **14** [a]Ex. 40:35; 1 Kin. 8:11; 2 Chr. 7:2; Ezek. 43:5 [1]Lit. *stand to minister*

CHAPTER 6

1 [a]Ex. 19:9; 20:21; 1 Kin. 8:12–21 [b][Lev. 16:2]; Ps. 97:2

2 [a]2 Sam. 7:13; 1 Chr. 17:12; 2 Chr. 7:12 **3** [a]2 Sam. 6:18 **4** [a]1 Chr. 17:5 **6** [a]Deut. 12:5–7; 2 Chr. 12:13; Zech. 2:12 [b]1 Sam. 16:7–13; 1 Chr. 28:4 **7** [a]2 Sam. 7:2; 1 Chr. 17:1; 28:2; Ps. 132:1–5 [1]Lit. *house,* and so in vv. 8–10 **9** [a]1 Chr. 28:3–6 **10** [a]1 Kin. 2:12; 10:9 **11** [a]2 Chr. 5:7–10 **12** [a]1 Kin. 8:22; 2 Chr. 7:7–9 [1]Lit. *he*

5:13, 14 Cloud: This is possibly a reference to the Holy Spirit. Read the text and note of 1 Kin. 8:10, 11, and Introduction to 2 Chronicles: The Holy Spirit at Work.

6:12–42 Much can be learned from Solomon's prayer. Read the text and notes of 1 Kin. 8:22–61 for insights on Solomon's prayer.

(*cont. from preceding page*)
temple, which he had built so God could dwell among His people, he brought before the Lord petitions regarding many situations that would concern Israel in the future: sin, enemies, forgiveness, drought, pestilence, war, captivity, and so on. Each petition was followed by a plea that God would hear Israel's prayers and answer.

When Solomon's petitions ended, God dramatically demonstrated His approval of the temple and His acceptance of Solomon's prayer. A bolt of fire came out of heaven, consuming the sacrifices and burnt offerings. Then the glory of the Lord filled the temple.

There are lessons here for us, for God now dwells in the temples of our hearts (see 1 Cor. 3:16). If we seek Him, He is instantly with us. The moment we lay our choicest gifts upon the altar, His holy fire falls. And whenever we make room for God, He always comes and fills!

(Acts 4:1–37/Acts 12:1–17) L.L.

13 (for Solomon had made a bronze
platform five cubits long, five cubits
wide, and three cubits high, and had
set it in the midst of the court; and he
stood on it, knelt down on his knees
before all the assembly of Israel,
and spread out his hands toward
heaven);
14 and he said: "LORD God of Israel,
[a]*there is* no God in heaven or on earth
like You, who keep *Your* [b]covenant
and mercy with Your servants who
walk before You with all their hearts.
15 [a]"You have kept what You promised Your servant David my father;
You have both spoken with Your
mouth and fulfilled *it* with Your hand,
as *it is* this day.
16 "Therefore, LORD God of Israel, now
keep what You promised Your servant
David my father, saying, [a]'You shall
not fail to have a man sit before Me
on the throne of Israel, [b]only if your
sons take heed to their way, that they
walk in My law as you have walked
before Me.'
17 "And now, O LORD God of Israel,
let Your word come true, which You
have spoken to Your servant David.
18 "But will God indeed dwell with
men on the earth? [a]Behold, heaven and
the heaven of heavens cannot contain
You. How much less this [1]temple
which I have built!
19 "Yet regard the prayer of Your servant and his supplication, O LORD my
God, and listen to the cry and the
prayer which Your servant is praying
before You:

14 [a][Ex. 15:11; Deut. 4:39] [b][Deut. 7:9]
15 [a]1 Chr. 22:9, 10
16 [a]2 Sam. 7:12, 16; 1 Kin. 2:4; 6:12; 2 Chr. 7:18 [b]Ps. 132:12
18 [a][2 Chr. 2:6; Is. 66:1; Acts 7:49] [1]Lit. *house*

20 [a]2 Chr. 7:15 [b]Ps. 5:7; Dan. 6:10
21 [a][Is. 43:25; 44:22; Mic. 7:18]
22 [a]Ex. 22:8–11
23 [a][Job 34:11] *See WW at Prov. 10:16.
24 [a]2 Kin. 21:14, 15
25 *See WW at Ps. 103:3.
26 [a]Deut. 28:23, 24; 1 Kin. 17:1
28 [a]2 Chr. 20:9

20 "that Your eyes may be [a]open toward this temple day and night, toward
the place where *You* said *You would*
put Your name, that You may hear the
prayer which Your servant makes
[b]toward this place.

WORD WEALTH

6:20 prayer, *tephillah* (teh-feel-*lah*); Strong's #8605: Prayer, supplication, intercession. *Tephillah* occurs more than 75 times in the OT, 32 of these in the Psalms. In the present reference, prayer from the temple in Jerusalem was afforded special significance, for day and night God watched over that house of prayer. From *tephillah* comes the word *tephilin,* which refers to the bands wound around the arm of a devout Jew as he prepares for his time of prayer.

21 "And may You hear the supplications of Your servant and of Your people Israel, when they pray toward this
place. Hear from heaven Your dwelling place, and when You hear,
[a]forgive.
22 "If anyone sins against his neighbor, and is forced to take an [a]oath, and
comes *and* takes an oath before Your
altar in this temple,
23 "then hear from heaven, and act,
and judge Your servants, bringing retribution on the *wicked by bringing
his way on his own head, and justifying
the righteous by giving him according
to his [a]righteousness.
24 "Or if Your people Israel are defeated before an [a]enemy because they
have sinned against You, and return
and confess Your name, and pray and
make supplication before You in this
temple,
25 "then hear from heaven and *forgive the sin of Your people Israel, and
bring them back to the land which You
gave to them and their fathers.
26 "When the [a]heavens are shut up
and there is no rain because they have
sinned against You, when they pray toward this place and confess Your
name, and turn from their sin because
You afflict them,
27 "then hear *in* heaven, and forgive
the sin of Your servants, Your people
Israel, that You may teach them the
good way in which they should walk;
and send rain on Your land which You
have given to Your people as an inheritance.
28 "When there [a]is famine in the land,
pestilence or blight or mildew, locusts
or grasshoppers; when their enemies

besiege them in the land of their cities; whatever plague or whatever [b]sickness *there is;*

29 "whatever prayer, whatever supplication is *made* by anyone, or by all Your people Israel, when each one knows his own burden and his own grief, and spreads out his hands to this temple:

30 "then hear from heaven Your dwelling place, and forgive, and give to everyone according to all his ways, whose heart You know (for You alone [a]know the [b]hearts of the sons of men),

31 "that they may fear You, to walk in Your ways as long as they live in the land which You gave to our fathers.

KINGDOM DYNAMICS

6:24–31 The Meaning of "Faith's Confession," FAITH'S CONFESSION. In Solomon's prayer of dedication, he points to the importance of confessing the Lord's name (v. 24). The power-packed word "confess" opens a great truth concerning God's hearing and answering prayers. It is an appropriate word in Christian tradition, historically used to describe a position-in-faith or belief, as, for example, "The Augsburg Confessions." To confess belief is to say, "I openly receive God's promise and choose to take my stand here, humbly, on God's promises and in worship of His Person."

Yadah, the Hebrew word for "confess," contains and supports this idea. Derived from *yad,* meaning "an open or extended hand," the focus is on reaching to take hold of. Just as a closed hand or fist may represent struggle or rebellion, an open hand indicates peace, submitted service or surrender. As Solomon comes with lifted, open hands (v. 12), he comes in peaceful submission to God. *Yadah* also involves worship, with open, extended hands, in a worship-filled confessing of God's faithfulness with thanksgiving and praise. This is the true spirit of the idea of "faith's confession of God's Word": 1) to take a stand on what God says; 2) to speak what is believed with worship and praise; 3) to do so in the humble spirit of faith in God's Person and promise. Such a stance will never be loveless or arrogant, and neither Earth nor hell can successfully protest this confession of faith in heaven's power. (Josh. 6:10/Ps. 19:14) R.H.

32 "Moreover, concerning a foreigner, [a]who is not of Your people Israel, but has come from a far country for the sake of Your great name and Your mighty hand and Your outstretched arm, when they come and pray in this temple;

33 "then hear from heaven Your dwelling place, and do according to all for which the foreigner calls to You, that all peoples of the earth may know Your name and fear You, as *do* Your people Israel, and that they may know that [1]this temple which I have built is called by Your name.

34 "When Your people go out to battle against their enemies, wherever You send them, and when they pray to You toward this city which You have chosen and the temple which I have built for Your name,

35 "then hear from heaven their prayer and their supplication, and maintain their cause.

36 "When they sin against You (for *there is* [a]no one who does not sin), and You become angry with them and deliver them to the enemy, and they take them [b]captive to a land far or near;

37 "*yet* when they [1]come to themselves in the land where they were carried captive, and repent, and make supplication to You in the land of their captivity, saying, 'We have sinned, we have done wrong, and have committed wickedness';

38 "and *when* they return to You with all their heart and with all their soul in the land of their captivity, where they have been carried captive, and pray toward their land which You gave to their fathers, the [a]city which You have chosen, and toward the temple which I have built for Your name:

39 "then hear from heaven Your dwelling place their prayer and their supplications, and maintain their cause, and forgive Your people who have sinned against You.

40 "Now, my God, I pray, let Your eyes be [a]open and *let* Your ears *be* attentive to the prayer *made* in this place.

41 "Now[a] therefore,
Arise, O LORD God, to Your
[b]resting place,
You and the ark of Your
*strength.
Let Your priests, O LORD God, be
clothed with salvation,
And let Your saints [c]rejoice in
goodness.

42 "O LORD God, do not turn away the
face of Your Anointed;
[a]Remember the mercies of Your
servant David."

28 [b][Mic. 6:13] **30** [a][1 Chr. 28:9; Prov. 21:2; 24:12] [b][1 Sam. 16:7] **32** [a]John 12:20; Acts 8:27 **33** [1]Lit. *Your name is called upon this house* **36** [a]Prov. 20:9; Eccl. 7:20; [Rom. 3:9, 19; 5:12; Gal. 3:10]; James 3:2; 1 John 1:8 [b]Deut. 28:63–68 **37** [1]Lit. *bring back to their hearts* **38** [a]Dan. 6:10 **40** [a]2 Chr. 6:20 **41** [a]Ps. 132:8–10, 16 [b]1 Chr. 28:2 [c]Neh. 9:25 *See WW at Jer. 16:19. **42** [a]2 Sam. 7:15; Ps. 89:49; 132:1, 8–10; Is. 55:3

Solomon Dedicates the Temple

7 When [a]Solomon had finished praying, [b]fire came down from heaven and consumed the burnt offering and the sacrifices; and [c]the glory of the LORD filled the [1]temple.

2 [a]And the priests could not enter the house of the LORD, because the glory of the LORD had filled the LORD's house.

3 When all the children of Israel saw how the fire came down, and the glory of the LORD on the temple, they bowed their faces to the ground on the pavement, and worshiped and praised the LORD, *saying:*

[a]"For *He is* good,
[b]For His mercy *endures* forever."

4 [a]Then the king and all the people offered sacrifices before the LORD.

5 King Solomon offered a sacrifice of twenty-two thousand bulls and one hundred and twenty thousand sheep. So the king and all the people dedicated the house of God.

6 [a]And the priests attended to their services; the Levites also with instruments of the music of the LORD, which King David had made to praise the LORD, saying, "For His mercy *endures* forever," whenever David offered praise by their [1]ministry. [b]The priests sounded trumpets opposite them, while all Israel stood.

7 Furthermore [a]Solomon consecrated the middle of the court that *was* in front of the house of the LORD; for there he offered burnt offerings and the fat of the peace offerings, because the bronze altar which Solomon had made was not able to *receive the burnt offerings, the grain offerings, and the fat.

8 [a]At that time Solomon kept the feast seven days, and all Israel with him, a very great assembly [b]from the entrance of Hamath to [c]the[1] Brook of Egypt.

9 And on the eighth day they held a [a]sacred assembly, for they observed the dedication of the altar seven days, and the feast seven days.

10 [a]On the twenty-third day of the seventh month he sent the people away to their tents, **joyful** and glad of heart for the good that the LORD had done for David, for Solomon, and for His people Israel.

WORD WEALTH

7:10 joyful, *sameach* (sah-*meh*-ahch); Strong's #8056: Happy, joyful, cheerful, rejoicing, festive. *Samach* comes from the root *samach,* "to rejoice," "to get happy," or "to be joyful." *Sameach* appears as an adjective 23 times in the Hebrew Bible, and more than 150 times in its verbal form, usually translated "rejoice" or "be glad." *Sameach* is a word that is increasingly being used in Christian circles, as pilgrims return from Israel using the phrase *chag sameach,* which roughly compares to the English phrase "happy holidays," but is literally, "joyous festival."

11 Thus [a]Solomon finished the house of the LORD and the king's house; and Solomon successfully accomplished all that came into his heart to make in the house of the LORD and in his own house.

God's Second Appearance to Solomon

12 Then the LORD [a]appeared to Solomon by night, and said to him: "I have heard your prayer, [b]and have chosen this [c]place for Myself as a house of sacrifice.

13 [a]"When I shut up heaven and there is no rain, or command the locusts to devour the land, or send pestilence among My people,

14 "if My people who are [a]called by 3
My name will [b]humble themselves,
and *pray and seek My face, and turn
from their wicked ways, [c]then I will
hear from heaven, and will *forgive
their sin and *heal their land.

15 "Now [a]My eyes will be open and My ears attentive to prayer *made* in this place.

16 "For now [a]I have chosen and [1]sanctified this house, that My name may be there forever; and [2]My eyes and [3]My heart will be there perpetually.

CHAPTER 7

1 [a]1 Kin. 8:54 [b]Lev. 9:24; Judg. 6:21; 1 Kin. 18:38; 1 Chr. 21:26 [c]1 Kin. 8:10, 11 [1]Lit. *house*
2 [a]2 Chr. 5:14
3 [a]2 Chr. 5:13; Ps. 106:1; 136:1 [b]1 Chr. 16:41; 2 Chr. 20:21
4 [a]1 Kin. 8:62, 63
6 [a]1 Chr. 15:16 [b]2 Chr. 5:12 [1]Lit. *hand*
7 [a]1 Kin. 8:64–66; 9:3 *See WW at Ps. 55:22.
8 [a]1 Kin. 8:65 [b]1 Kin. 4:21, 24; 2 Kin. 14:25 [c]Josh. 13:3 [1]The Shihor, 1 Chr. 13:5
9 [a]Lev. 23:36
10 [a]1 Kin. 8:66
11 [a]1 Kin. 9:1
12 [a]1 Kin. 3:5; 11:9 [b]Deut. 12:5, 11 [c]2 Chr. 6:20
13 [a]Deut. 28:23, 24; 1 Kin. 17:1; 2 Chr. 6:26–28
14 [a]Deut. 28:10; [Is. 43:7] [b]2 Chr. 12:6, 7; [James 4:10] [c]2 Chr. 6:27, 30 *See WW at Job 42:10. • See WW at Ps. 103:3. • See WW at Ex. 15:26.
15 [a]2 Chr. 6:20, 40
16 [a]1 Kin. 9:3; 2 Chr. 6:6 [1]*set apart* [2]My attention [3]My concern

7:1–22 These events are also recorded in 1 Kin. 8:62—9:9.
7:14 See section 3 of Truth-In-Action at the end of 2 Chr.
7:14 This is probably the most well-known and best-loved verse in 2 Chr. In the account of God's second appearance to Solomon in 1 Kin. 9:1–9, this promise is not mentioned. This verse, perhaps more than any other single verse in all Scripture, sets forth the stipulations for Israel to experience God's blessing. It would have special significance to the original recipients, who had actually experienced the truth of the principle God had spoken to Solomon. A twofold condition, with a threefold result, is extended to God's chosen people (those **called by** His **name**). If they will **humble themselves** (turn from their sin) and **seek** His **face** in prayer, then God will **hear, forgive,** and **heal.** God effects His sovereign purposes in concert with the prayers of His children (Phil. 1:9; James 5:16).

17 [a]"As for you, if you walk before Me
as your father David walked, and do
according to all that I have commanded you, and if you keep My statutes and My judgments,
18 "then I will establish the throne of
your kingdom, as I covenanted with
David your father, saying, [a]'You shall
not fail *to have* a man as ruler in Israel.'
19 [a]"But if you turn away and forsake
My statutes and My commandments
which I have set before you, and go
and serve other gods, and worship
them,
20 [a]"then I will uproot them from My
land which I have given them; and this
house which I have [1]sanctified for My
name I will cast out of My sight, and
will make it a *proverb and a [b]byword
among all peoples.
21 "And *as for* [a]this [1]house, which
[2]is exalted, everyone who passes by it
will be [b]astonished and say, [c]'Why has
the LORD done thus to this land and
this house?'
22 "Then they will answer, 'Because
they forsook the LORD God of their fathers, who brought them out of the
land of Egypt, and embraced other
gods, and worshiped them and served
them; therefore He has brought all this
calamity on them.'"

Solomon's Additional Achievements

8 It [a]came to pass at the end of
[b]twenty years, when Solomon had
built the house of the LORD and his own
house,
2 that the cities which [1]Hiram had
given to Solomon, Solomon built them;
and he settled the children of Israel
there.
3 And Solomon went to Hamath Zobah and seized it.
4 [a]He also built Tadmor in the wilderness, and all the storage cities which
he built in [b]Hamath.
5 He built Upper Beth Horon and
[a]Lower Beth Horon, fortified cities
with walls, gates, and bars,
6 also Baalath and all the storage cities that Solomon had, and all the chariot cities and the cities of the cavalry,
and all that Solomon [a]desired to build
in Jerusalem, in Lebanon, and in all
the land of his dominion.
7 [a]All the people *who were* left of the
Hittites, Amorites, Perizzites, Hivites,
and Jebusites, who *were* not of Israel—
8 that is, their descendants who were
left in the land after them, whom the
children of Israel did not destroy—
from these Solomon raised forced labor, as it is to this day.
9 But Solomon did not make the children of Israel [1]servants for his work.
Some *were* men of war, captains of his
officers, captains of his chariots, and
his cavalry.
10 And others *were* chiefs of the officials of King Solomon: [a]two hundred
and fifty, who ruled over the people.
11 Now Solomon [a]brought the daughter of Pharaoh up from the City of David to the house he had built for her,
for he said, "My wife shall not dwell
in the house of David king of Israel,
because *the places* to which the ark of
the LORD has come are holy."
12 Then Solomon offered burnt offerings to the LORD on the altar of the
LORD which he had built before the vestibule,
13 according to the [a]daily rate, offering according to the commandment of
Moses, for the Sabbaths, the New
Moons, and the [b]three appointed
yearly [c]feasts—the Feast of Unleavened Bread, the Feast of Weeks, and
the Feast of Tabernacles.
14 And, according to the [1]order of David his father, he appointed the [a]divi-
sions of the priests for their service,
[b]the Levites for their duties (to praise
and serve before the priests) as the
duty of each day required, and the
[c]gatekeepers by their divisions at each
gate; for so David the man of God had
commanded.
15 They did not depart from the command of the king to the priests and Levites concerning any matter or concerning the [a]treasuries.
16 Now all the work of Solomon was
well-ordered [1]from the day of the foundation of the house of the LORD until
it was finished. So the house of the
LORD was completed.
17 Then Solomon went to [a]Ezion Geber and [1]Elath on the seacoast, in the
land of Edom.
18 [a]And Hiram sent him ships by the
hand of his servants, and servants who
knew the sea. They went with the servants of Solomon to [b]Ophir, and acquired four hundred and fifty talents
of gold from there, and brought it to
King Solomon.

17 [a]1 Kin. 9:4
18 [a]2 Sam. 7:12–16; 1 Kin. 2:4; 2 Chr. 6:16
19 [a]Lev. 26:14, 33; [Deut. 28:15, 36]
20 [a]Deut. 28:63–68; 2 Kin. 25:1–7 [b]Ps. 44:14 [1]*set apart* *See WW at Prov. 1:6.
21 [a]2 Kin. 25:9 [b]2 Chr. 29:8 [c][Deut. 29:24, 25; Jer. 22:8, 9] [1]Temple [2]Or *was*

CHAPTER 8

1 [a]1 Kin. 9:10–14 [b]1 Kin. 6:38—7:1
2 [1]Heb. *Huram,* 2 Chr. 2:3
4 [a]1 Kin. 9:17, 18 [b]1 Chr. 18:3, 9
5 [a]1 Chr. 7:24
6 [a]2 Chr. 7:11
7 [a]Gen. 15:18–21; 1 Kin. 9:20
9 [1]*slaves*
10 [a]1 Kin. 9:23
11 [a]1 Kin. 3:1; 7:8; 9:24; 11:1
13 [a]Ex. 29:38–42; Num. 28:3, 9, 11, 26; 29:1 [b]Ex. 23:14–17; 34:22, 23; Deut. 16:16 [c]Lev. 23:1–44
14 [a]1 Chr. 24:3 [b]1 Chr. 25:1 [c]1 Chr. 9:17; 26:1 [1]*ordinance*
15 [a]1 Chr. 26:20–28
16 [1]So with LXX, Syr., Vg.; MT *as far as*
17 [a]1 Kin. 9:26; 2 Chr. 20:36 [1]Heb. *Eloth,* 2 Kin. 14:22
18 [a]1 Kin. 9:27; 2 Chr. 9:10, 13 [b]1 Chr. 29:4

8:1–18 A parallel account of this chapter is in 1 Kin. 9:1–28. On v. 14, read the text and notes of 1 Chr. 23—26.

The Queen of Sheba's Praise of Solomon

9 Now [a]when the queen of Sheba heard of the fame of Solomon, she came to Jerusalem to test Solomon with hard questions, *having* a very great retinue, camels that bore spices, gold in abundance, and precious stones; and when she came to Solomon, she spoke with him about all that was in her heart.

2 So Solomon answered all her questions; there was nothing so difficult for Solomon that he could not explain it to her.

3 And when the queen of Sheba had seen the *wisdom of Solomon, the house that he had built,

4 the food on his table, the seating of his servants, the service of his waiters and their apparel, his [a]cupbearers and their apparel, and his entryway by which he went up to the house of the LORD, there was no more spirit in her.

5 Then she said to the king: "*It was* a true report which I heard in my own land about your words and your wisdom.

6 "However I did not *believe their words until I came and saw with my own eyes; and indeed the half of the greatness of your wisdom was not told me. You exceed the fame of which I heard.

7 "Happy *are* your men and happy *are* these your servants, who stand continually before you and hear your wisdom!

8 "Blessed be the LORD your God, who delighted in you, setting you on His throne *to be* king for the LORD your God! Because your God has [a]loved Israel, to establish them forever, therefore He made you king over them, to do justice and righteousness."

9 And she gave the king one hundred and twenty talents of gold, spices in great abundance, and precious stones; there never were any spices such as those the queen of Sheba gave to King Solomon.

10 Also, the servants of Hiram and the servants of Solomon, [a]who brought gold from Ophir, brought [1]algum wood and precious stones.

11 And the king made walkways *of* the [1]algum wood for the house of the LORD and for the king's house, also harps and stringed instruments for singers; and there were none such *as these* seen before in the land of Judah.

12 Now King Solomon gave to the queen of Sheba all she desired, whatever she asked, *much more* than she had brought to the king. So she turned and went to her own country, she and her servants.

Solomon's Great Wealth

13 [a]The weight of gold that came to Solomon yearly was six hundred and sixty-six talents of gold,

14 besides *what* the traveling merchants and traders brought. And all the kings of Arabia and governors of the country brought gold and silver to Solomon.

15 And King Solomon made two hundred large shields of hammered gold; six hundred *shekels* of hammered gold went into each shield.

16 *He* also *made* three hundred shields of hammered gold; [1]three hundred *shekels* of gold went into each shield. The king put them in the [a]House of the Forest of Lebanon.

17 Moreover the king made a great throne of ivory, and overlaid it with pure gold.

18 The throne *had* six *steps, with a footstool of gold, *which were* fastened to the throne; there were [1]armrests on either side of the place of the seat, and two lions stood beside the armrests.

19 Twelve lions stood there, one on each side of the six steps; nothing like *this* had been made for any *other* kingdom.

20 All King Solomon's drinking vessels *were* gold, and all the vessels of the House of the Forest of Lebanon *were* pure gold. Not *one was* silver, for this was *accounted as nothing in the days of Solomon.

21 For the king's ships went to [a]Tarshish with the servants of [1]Hiram. Once every three years the [2]merchant ships came, bringing gold, silver, ivory, apes, and [3]monkeys.

22 So King Solomon surpassed all the kings of the earth in riches and wisdom.

23 And all the kings of the earth sought the presence of Solomon to hear his wisdom, which God had put in his heart.

24 Each man brought his present: articles of silver and gold, garments,

CHAPTER 9

1 [a]1 Kin. 10:1; Ps. 72:10; [Matt. 12:42; Luke 11:31]
3 *See WW at Is. 11:2.
4 [a]Neh. 1:11
6 *See WW at 2 Chr. 20:20.
8 [a]Deut. 7:8; 2 Chr. 2:11; [Ps. 44:3]
10 [a]2 Chr. 8:18 [1]*almug*, 1 Kin. 10:11, 12
11 [1]*almug*, 1 Kin. 10:11, 12
13 [a]1 Kin. 10:14–29
16 [a]1 Kin. 7:2 [1]*three minas*, 1 Kin. 10:17
18 [1]Lit. *hands* *See WW at Amos 9:6.
20 *See WW at Gen. 15:6.
21 [a]2 Chr. 20:36, 37; Ps. 72:10 [1]Heb. *Huram*; cf. 1 Kin. 10:22 [2]Lit. *ships of Tarshish*, deep-sea vessels [3]Or *peacocks*

9:1–12 For clarification on the **queen of Sheba**'s visit, read the text and notes of 1 Kin. 10:1–13.

9:13–28 The perspective of the Books of Kings on Solomon's wealth can be found in 1 Kin. 10:14–29.

[a]armor, spices, horses, and mules, at
a set rate year by year.
25 Solomon [a]had four thousand stalls
for horses and chariots, and twelve
thousand horsemen whom he stationed in the chariot cities and with the
king at Jerusalem.
26 [a]So he reigned over all the kings
[b]from [1]the River to the land of the Philistines, as far as the border of Egypt.
27 [a]The king made silver *as common*
in Jerusalem as stones, and he made
cedar trees [b]as abundant as the sycamores which *are* in the lowland.
28 [a]And they brought horses to Solomon from Egypt and from all lands.

Death of Solomon

29 [a]Now the rest of the acts of Solomon, first and last, *are* they not written
in the book of Nathan the prophet, in
the prophecy of [b]Ahijah the Shilonite,
and in the visions of [c]Iddo the seer concerning Jeroboam the son of Nebat?
30 [a]Solomon reigned in Jerusalem
over all Israel forty years.
31 Then Solomon [1]rested with his fathers, and was buried in the City of David his father. And Rehoboam his son
reigned in his place.

The Revolt Against Rehoboam

10 And [a]Rehoboam went to Shechem, for all Israel had gone to
Shechem to make him king.
2 So it happened, when Jeroboam the
son of Nebat heard *it* (he was in Egypt,
[a]where he had fled from the presence
of King Solomon), that Jeroboam returned from Egypt.
3 Then they sent for him and called
him. And Jeroboam and all Israel came
and spoke to Rehoboam, saying,
4 "Your father made our yoke heavy;
now therefore, lighten the burdensome
service of your father and his heavy
yoke which he put on us, and we will
serve you."
5 So he said to them, "Come back to
me after three days." And the people
departed.

24 [a]1 Kin. 20:11
25 [a]Deut. 17:16; 1 Kin. 4:26; 10:26; 2 Chr. 1:14; Is. 2:7
26 [a]1 Kin. 4:21 [b]Gen. 15:18; Ps. 72:8 [1]The Euphrates
27 [a]1 Kin. 10:27 [b]2 Chr. 1:15–17
28 [a]1 Kin. 10:28; 2 Chr. 1:16
29 [a]1 Kin. 11:41 [b]1 Kin. 11:29 [c]2 Chr. 12:15; 13:22
30 [a]1 Kin. 4:21; 11:42, 43; 1 Chr. 29:28
31 [1]Died and joined his ancestors

CHAPTER 10

1 [a]1 Kin. 12:1–20
2 [a]1 Kin. 11:40
8 [a]1 Kin. 12:8–11
11 [1]Scourges with points or barbs, lit. *scorpions*
12 [a]1 Kin. 12:12–14
13 *See WW at Zech. 6:13.
14 [1]So with many Heb. mss., LXX, Syr., Vg. (cf. v. 10; 1 Kin. 12:14); MT / [2]Lit. *scorpions*
15 [a]Judg. 14:4; 1 Chr. 5:22; 2 Chr. 11:4; 22:7 [b]1 Kin. 11:29–39

6 Then King Rehoboam consulted the
elders who stood before his father Solomon while he still lived, saying, "How
do you advise *me* to answer these people?"
7 And they spoke to him, saying, "If
you are kind to these people, and
please them, and speak good words to
them, they will be your servants forever."
8 [a]But he rejected the advice which
the elders had given him, and consulted the young men who had grown
up with him, who stood before him.
9 And he said to them, "What advice
do you give? How should we answer
this people who have spoken to me,
saying, 'Lighten the yoke which your
father put on us'?"
10 Then the young men who had
grown up with him spoke to him, saying, "Thus you should speak to the
people who have spoken to you, saying, 'Your father made our yoke heavy,
but you make *it* lighter on us'—thus
you shall say to them: 'My little *finger* shall be thicker than my father's
waist!
11 'And now, whereas my father put
a heavy yoke on you, I will add to your
yoke; my father chastised you with
whips, but I *will chastise you* with
[1]scourges!'"
12 So [a]Jeroboam and all the people
came to Rehoboam on the third day,
as the king had directed, saying,
"Come back to me the third day."
13 Then the king answered them
roughly. King Rehoboam rejected the
*advice of the elders,
14 and he spoke to them according to
the advice of the young men, saying,
[1]"My father made your yoke heavy,
but I will add to it; my father chastised
you with whips, but I *will chastise you*
with [2]scourges!"
15 So the king did not listen to the people; [a]for the turn *of events* was from
God, that the LORD might fulfill His
[b]word, which He had spoken by the
hand of Ahijah the Shilonite to Jeroboam the son of Nebat.
16 Now when all Israel *saw* that the

9:25 Four thousand stalls: See the note on 1 Kin. 4:26 for the discrepancy with that verse.

9:29–31 The chronicler is again selective in his recording of history, omitting events that are not necessary to his purpose. 1 Kin. records how before his death, Solomon's heart was turned from the Lord. Because of this God raised up Hadad, Rezon, and Jeroboam as adversaries. Read the text and notes of 1 Kin. 11:1–40 for an explanation of these events.

10:1—11:4 These verses begin the last major section of 2 Chr. (see outline), discussing the rulers of the southern kingdom of Judah. 2 Chr. does not record the reigns of the rulers of the northern kingdom of Israel. The author and the people of Judah regarded only the descendants of David as the true kings of Israel. For this reason, 2 Chr. frequently refers to Judah as "Israel," whereas in Kings "Israel" refers to the northern kingdom and "Judah" refers to the southern kingdom. The successor to Solomon was Rehoboam. Read the text and notes of 1 Kin. 12:1–24.

king did not listen to them, the people
answered the king, saying:

"What share have we in David?
We have no inheritance in the son
of Jesse.
Every man to your tents, O Israel!
Now see to your own house, O
David!"

So all Israel departed to their tents.
17 But Rehoboam reigned over the
children of Israel who dwelt in the cities of Judah.
18 Then King Rehoboam sent Hadoram, who *was* in charge of revenue;
but the children of Israel stoned him
with stones, and he died. Therefore
King Rehoboam mounted *his* chariot
in haste to flee to Jerusalem.
19 [a]So Israel has been in rebellion
against the house of David to this day.

11

Now [a]when Rehoboam came to
Jerusalem, he assembled from
the house of Judah and Benjamin one
hundred and eighty thousand chosen
men who were warriors, to fight
against Israel, that he might restore the
kingdom to Rehoboam.
2 But the word of the LORD came
[a]to Shemaiah the man of God, saying,
3 "Speak to Rehoboam the son of Solomon, king of Judah, and to all Israel
in Judah and Benjamin, saying,
4 'Thus says the LORD: "You shall not
go up or fight against your brethren!

19 [a]1 Kin. 12:19

CHAPTER 11

1 [a]1 Kin. 12:21–24
2 [a]1 Chr. 12:5; 2 Chr. 12:15

A Kingdom Divided. The glory of the united kingdom began to fade at the death of Solomon when his son Rehoboam spoke harshly to Jeroboam and those following him. Their response: "Every man to your tents, O Israel! Now, see to your own house, O David!" Rehoboam reigned over Judah to the south, and Jeroboam became king of Israel to the north.

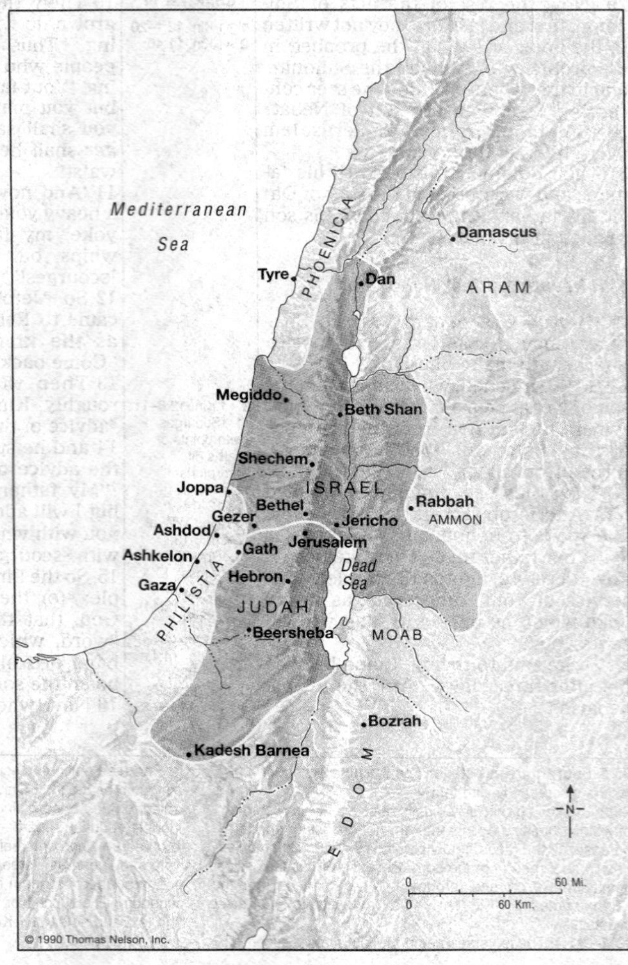

Let every man return to his house, for
this thing is from Me.' ' " Therefore
they obeyed the words of the LORD, and
turned back from attacking Jeroboam.

Rehoboam Fortifies the Cities

5 So Rehoboam dwelt in Jerusalem,
and built cities for defense in Judah.
6 And he built Bethlehem, Etam,
Tekoa,
7 Beth Zur, Sochoh, Adullam,
8 Gath, Mareshah, Ziph,
9 Adoraim, Lachish, Azekah,
10 Zorah, Aijalon, and Hebron, which
are in Judah and Benjamin, fortified
cities.
11 And he fortified the strongholds,
and put captains in them, and stores
of food, oil, and wine.
12 Also in every city *he put* shields and
spears, and made them very strong,
having Judah and Benjamin on his
side.

Priests and Levites Move to Judah

13 And from all their territories the
priests and the Levites who *were* in all
Israel took their stand with him.
14 For the Levites left [a]their common-
lands and their possessions and came
to Judah and Jerusalem, for [b]Jero-
boam and his sons had rejected them
from serving as priests to the LORD.
15 [a]Then he appointed for himself
priests for the [1]high places, for [b]the demons, and [c]the calf idols which he had
made.
16 [a]And [1]after *the Levites left,* those
from all the tribes of Israel, such as set
their heart to seek the LORD God of Israel, [b]came to Jerusalem to sacrifice
to the LORD God of their fathers.
17 So they [a]strengthened the kingdom
of Judah, and made Rehoboam the son
of Solomon strong for three years, because they walked in the way of David
and Solomon for three years.

The Family of Rehoboam

18 Then Rehoboam took for himself as
wife Mahalath the daughter of Jerimoth the son of David, *and of* Abihail
the daughter of [a]Eliah the son of Jesse.
19 And she bore him children: Jeush,
Shamariah, and Zaham.
20 After her he took [a]Maachah the
[1]granddaughter of [b]Absalom; and she
bore him [c]Abijah, Attai, Ziza, and Shelomith.
21 Now Rehoboam loved Maachah the
granddaughter of Absalom more than
all his [a]wives and his concubines; for
he took eighteen wives and sixty concubines, and begot twenty-eight sons
and sixty daughters.
22 And Rehoboam [a]appointed [b]Abijah
the son of Maachah as chief, *to be*
leader among his brothers; for he *intended* to make him king.
23 He dealt wisely, and [1]dispersed
some of his sons throughout all the territories of Judah and Benjamin, to
every [a]fortified city; and he gave them
provisions in abundance. He also
*sought many wives *for them.*

Egypt Attacks Judah

12 Now [a]it came to pass, when Rehoboam had established the
kingdom and had strengthened himself, that [b]he forsook the law of the
LORD, and all Israel along with him.
2 [a]And it happened in the fifth year
of King Rehoboam *that* Shishak king
of Egypt came up against Jerusalem,
because they had transgressed against
the LORD,
3 with twelve hundred chariots, sixty
thousand horsemen, and people without number who came with him out of
Egypt—[a]the Lubim and the Sukkiim
and the Ethiopians.
4 And he took the fortified cities of
Judah and came to Jerusalem.
5 Then [a]Shemaiah the prophet came
to Rehoboam and the leaders of Judah,
who were gathered together in Jerusalem because of Shishak, and said to
them, "Thus says the LORD: 'You have
forsaken Me, and therefore I also have
left you in the hand of Shishak.' "
6 So the leaders of Israel and the king
[a]humbled themselves; and they said,
[b]"The LORD *is* righteous."
7 Now when the LORD saw that they
humbled themselves, [a]the word of the
LORD came to Shemaiah, saying, "They
have humbled themselves; *therefore* I
will not destroy them, but I will grant
them some deliverance. My wrath shall
not be poured out on Jerusalem by the
hand of Shishak.
8 "Nevertheless [a]they will be his servants, that they may distinguish [b]My

14 [a]Num. 35:2–5 [b]1 Kin. 12:28–33; 2 Chr. 13:9
15 [a]1 Kin. 12:31; 13:33; 14:9; [Hos. 13:2] [b][Lev. 17:7; 1 Cor. 10:20] [c]1 Kin. 12:28 [1]Places for pagan worship
16 [a]2 Chr. 14:7 [b]2 Chr. 15:9, 10; 30:11, 18 [1]Lit. *after them*
17 [a]2 Chr. 12:1, 13
18 [a]1 Sam. 16:6
20 [a]2 Chr. 13:2 [b]1 Kin. 15:2 [c]1 Kin. 14:31 [1]Lit. *daughter,* but in the broader sense of granddaughter
21 [a]Deut. 17:17
22 [a]Deut. 21:15–17 [b]2 Chr. 13:1
23 [a]2 Chr. 11:5 [1]*distributed* *See WW at Ps. 122:6.

CHAPTER 12

1 [a]2 Chr. 11:17 [b]1 Kin. 14:22–24
2 [a]1 Kin. 11:40; 14:25
3 [a]2 Chr. 16:8; Nah. 3:9
5 [a]2 Chr. 11:2
6 [a][James 4:10] [b]Ex. 9:27; [Dan. 9:14]
7 [a]1 Kin. 21:28, 29
8 [a]Is. 26:13 [b][Deut. 28:47, 48]

11:5–17 Read the text and notes of 1 Kin. 12:25–33 for an explanation as to why **Rehoboam** strengthened his defenses and why the priests and Levites moved to Judah.

11:18–23 1 Kin. does not list the family of Rehoboam.

12:1–16 Read the text and notes of 1 Kin. 14:21–31.

service from the service of the kingdoms of the nations."
9 [a]So Shishak king of Egypt came up
against Jerusalem, and took away the
treasures of the house of the LORD and
the treasures of the king's house; he
took everything. He also carried away
the gold shields which Solomon had
[b]made.
10 Then King Rehoboam made bronze
shields in their place, and committed
them [a]to the hands of the captains of
the guard, who guarded the doorway
of the king's house.
11 And whenever the king entered the
house of the LORD, the guard would go
and bring them out; then they would
take them back into the guardroom.
12 When he humbled himself, the
wrath of the LORD turned from him, so
as not to destroy *him* completely; and
things also went well in Judah.

The End of Rehoboam's Reign

13 Thus King Rehoboam strengthened
himself in Jerusalem and reigned. Now
[a]Rehoboam *was* forty-one years old
when he became king; and he reigned
seventeen years in Jerusalem, [b]the city
which the LORD had chosen out of all
the tribes of Israel, to put His name
there. His mother's name *was* Naamah,
an [c]Ammonitess.
14 And he did evil, because he did not
prepare his heart to seek the LORD.
15 The acts of Rehoboam, first and
last, *are* they not written in the book
of Shemaiah the prophet, [a]and of Iddo
the seer concerning genealogies?
[b]And *there were* wars between Rehoboam and Jeroboam all their days.
16 So Rehoboam [1]rested with his fathers, and was buried in the City of David. Then [a]Abijah[2] his son reigned in
his place.

Abijah Reigns in Judah

13 In [a]the eighteenth year of King
Jeroboam, Abijah became king
over [b]Judah.
2 He reigned three years in Jerusalem. His mother's name *was* [1]Michaiah
the daughter of Uriel of Gibeah. And
there was war between Abijah and Jeroboam.
3 Abijah set the battle in order with
an army of valiant warriors, four hundred thousand choice men. Jeroboam
also drew up in battle formation
against him with eight hundred thousand choice men, mighty men of valor.
4 Then Abijah stood on Mount
[a]Zemaraim, which *is* in the mountains
of Ephraim, and said, "Hear me, Jeroboam and all Israel:
5 "Should you not know that the
LORD God of Israel [a]gave the dominion
over Israel to David forever, to him and
his sons, [b]by a covenant of salt?
6 "Yet Jeroboam the son of Nebat,
the servant of Solomon the son of David, rose up and [a]rebelled against his
lord.
7 "Then [a]worthless rogues gathered
to him, and strengthened themselves
against Rehoboam the son of Solomon,
when Rehoboam was [b]young and inexperienced and could not withstand
them.
8 "And now you think to withstand
the kingdom of the LORD, which is in
the hand of the sons of David; and you
are a great multitude, and with you are
the gold calves which Jeroboam
[a]made for you as gods.
9 [a]"Have you not cast out the priests
of the LORD, the sons of Aaron, and the
Levites, and made for yourselves
priests, like the peoples of *other* lands,
[b]so that whoever comes to consecrate
himself with a young bull and seven
rams may be a priest of [c]*things that*
are not gods?
10 "But as for us, the LORD *is* our
[a]God, and we have not forsaken Him;
and the priests who minister to the
LORD *are* the sons of Aaron, and the
Levites *attend* to *their* duties.
11 [a]"And they burn to the LORD every
morning and every evening burnt sacrifices and sweet incense; *they* also *set*
the [b]showbread *in order on* the pure
gold table, and the lampstand of gold
with its lamps [c]to burn every evening;
for we keep the command of the LORD
our God, but you have forsaken Him.
12 "Now look, God Himself is with us
as *our* [a]head, [b]and His priests with
sounding trumpets to sound the alarm
against you. O children of Israel, do not
fight against the LORD God of your fathers, for you shall not prosper!"
13 But Jeroboam caused an ambush to
go around behind them; so they were
in front of Judah, and the ambush *was*
behind them.
14 And when Judah looked around, to
their surprise the battle line *was* at

12:9 [a]1 Kin. 14:25, 26 [b]1 Kin. 10:16, 17; 2 Chr. 9:15, 16
10 [a]1 Kin. 14:27
13 [a]1 Kin. 14:21 [b]2 Chr. 6:6 [c]1 Kin. 11:1, 5
15 [a]2 Chr. 9:29; 13:22 [b]1 Kin. 14:30
16 [a]2 Chr. 11:20–22 [1]Died and joined his ancestors [2]*Abijam,* 1 Kin. 14:31

CHAPTER 13

1 [a]1 Kin. 15:1 [b]1 Kin. 12:17
2 [1]*Maachah,* 1 Kin. 15:2; 2 Chr. 11:20, 21
4 [a]Josh. 18:22
5 [a]2 Sam. 7:8–16 [b]Lev. 2:13; Num. 18:19
6 [a]1 Kin. 11:28; 12:20
7 [a]Judg. 9:4 [b]2 Chr. 12:13
8 [a]1 Kin. 12:28; 14:9; 2 Chr. 11:15; [Hos. 8:4–6]
9 [a]2 Chr. 11:13–15 [b]Ex. 29:29–33 [c]Jer. 2:11; 5:7
10 [a]Josh. 24:15
11 [a]Ex. 29:38; 2 Chr. 2:4 [b]Ex. 25:30; Lev. 24:5–9 [c]Ex. 27:20, 21; Lev. 24:2, 3
12 [a]Josh. 5:13–15; [Heb. 2:10] [b][Num. 10:8–10]

13:1–22 In 1 Kin., only eight verses are given to record the reign of **Abijah** (read the text and notes on 1 Kin. 15:1–8). 2 Chr. gives a fuller account to highlight worship and explain the reason for Judah's victory over Jeroboam. **A covenant of salt** (v. 5) refers to a ceremony or ritual that ratified a treaty. As a preservative, salt symbolized faith and loyalty.

both front and rear; and they [a]cried out
to the LORD, and the priests sounded
the trumpets.
15 Then the men of Judah gave a
shout; and as the men of Judah
shouted, it happened that God [a]struck
Jeroboam and all Israel before Abijah
and Judah.
16 And the children of Israel fled before Judah, and God delivered them
into their hand.
17 Then Abijah and his people struck
them with a great slaughter; so five
hundred thousand choice men of Israel
fell slain.
5 18 Thus the children of Israel were
subdued at that time; and the children
of Judah prevailed, [a]because they relied on the LORD God of their fathers.
19 And Abijah pursued Jeroboam and
took cities from him: Bethel with its
villages, Jeshanah with its villages,
and [a]Ephrain[1] with its villages.
20 So Jeroboam did not recover
strength again in the days of Abijah;
and the LORD [a]struck him, and [b]he
died.
21 But Abijah grew mighty, married
fourteen wives, and begot twenty-two
sons and sixteen daughters.
22 Now the rest of the acts of Abijah,
his ways, and his sayings *are* written
in [a]the [1]annals of the prophet Iddo.

14 So Abijah rested with his fathers, and they buried him in
the City of David. Then [a]Asa his son
reigned in his place. In his days the
land was quiet for ten years.

Asa Reigns in Judah

2 Asa did *what was* good and right
in the eyes of the LORD his God,
3 for he removed the altars of the foreign *gods* and [a]the [1]high places, and
[b]broke down the *sacred* pillars [c]and
cut down the wooden images.
7 4 He commanded Judah to [a]seek the
LORD God of their fathers, and to observe the law and the commandment.
5 He also removed the [1]high places
and the incense altars from all the cities of Judah, and the kingdom was
quiet under him.
6 And he built fortified cities in Judah, for the land had rest; he had no

14 [a]Josh. 24:7; 2 Chr. 6:34, 35; 14:11
15 [a]1 Kin. 14:14; 2 Chr. 14:12
18 [a]1 Chr. 5:20; 2 Chr. 14:11; [Ps. 22:5]
19 [a]Josh. 15:9 [1]Or *Ephron*
20 [a]1 Sam. 2:6; 25:38; Acts 12:23 [b]1 Kin. 14:20
22 [a]2 Chr. 9:29 [1]Or *commentary*, Heb. *midrash*

CHAPTER 14

1 [a]1 Kin. 15:8
3 [a]1 Kin. 15:14; 2 Chr. 15:17 [b][Ex. 34:13] [c]1 Kin. 11:7 [1]Places for pagan worship
4 [a][2 Chr. 7:14]
5 [1]Places for pagan worship
6 [a]2 Chr. 15:15
8 [a]1 Chr. 12:2 [b]2 Chr. 13:3 [1]*large shields*
9 [a]2 Chr. 12:2, 3; 16:8 [b]Josh. 15:44
11 [a]Ex. 14:10; 2 Chr. 13:14; [Ps. 22:5] [b][1 Sam. 14:6] [c]1 Sam. 17:45; [Prov. 18:10]
12 [a]2 Chr. 13:15
13 [a]Gen. 10:19; 20:1 [1]*plunder*
14 [a]Gen. 35:5; Deut. 11:25; Josh. 2:9; 2 Chr. 17:10 [1]*plunder*
15 [1]Lit. *struck*

CHAPTER 15

1 [a]Num. 24:2; Judg. 3:10; 2 Chr. 20:14; 24:20

war in those years, because the LORD
had given him [a]rest.
7 Therefore he said to Judah, "Let us
build these cities and make walls
around *them*, and towers, gates, and
bars, *while* the land *is* yet before us,
because we have sought the LORD our
God; we have sought *Him*, and He has
given us rest on every side." So they
built and prospered.
8 And Asa had an army of three hundred thousand from Judah who carried
[1]shields and spears, and from Benjamin two hundred and eighty thousand
men who carried shields and drew
[a]bows; all these *were* mighty men of
[b]valor.
9 [a]Then Zerah the Ethiopian came
out against them with an army of a million men and three hundred chariots,
and he came to [b]Mareshah.
10 So Asa went out against him, and
they set the troops in battle array in
the Valley of Zephathah at Mareshah.
11 And Asa [a]cried out to the LORD his 5
God, and said, "LORD, *it is* [b]nothing for
You to help, whether with many or
with those who have no power; help
us, O LORD our God, for we rest on You,
and [c]in Your name we go against this
multitude. O LORD, You *are* our God;
do not let man prevail against You!"
12 So the LORD [a]struck the Ethiopians
before Asa and Judah, and the Ethiopians fled.
13 And Asa and the people who *were*
with him pursued them to [a]Gerar. So
the Ethiopians were overthrown, and
they could not recover, for they were
broken before the LORD and His army.
And they carried away very much
[1]spoil.
14 Then they defeated all the cities
around Gerar, for [a]the fear of the LORD
came upon them; and they plundered
all the cities, for there was exceedingly
much [1]spoil in them.
15 They also [1]attacked the livestock
enclosures, and carried off sheep and
camels in abundance, and returned to
Jerusalem.

The Reforms of Asa

15 Now [a]the Spirit of God came
upon Azariah the son of Oded.

13:18 See section 5 of Truth-In-Action at the end of 2 Chr.
14:1–15 The reign of **Asa** is condensed in 1 Kin. 15:9–24, yet 2 Chr. gives three chapters to the discussion of Asa's reign. Unique to 2 Chr. is its mention of the battle with **Zerah** (v. 9). Zerah was from Ethiopia and was probably a ruler from Egypt or Arabia. It is noteworthy that Zerah's army is the largest army mentioned in the OT. Consequently, Zerah's defeat was the greatest military victory in Israel's history.
14:4 See section 7 of Truth-In-Action at the end of 2 Chr.
14:11 See section 5 of Truth-In-Action at the end of 2 Chr.
15:1 On **the Spirit of God,** read the text and note of 1 Chr. 12:18.
15:1–19 The reforms of **Asa** are mentioned in 1 Kin. 15:9–24; but the prophecy of **Azariah** (vv. 1–7), which set the

2 2 And he went out [1]to meet Asa, and said to him: "Hear me, Asa, and all Judah and Benjamin. [a]The LORD *is* with you while you are with Him. [b]If you seek Him, He will be found by you; but [c]if you forsake Him, He will forsake you.

3 [a]"For a long time Israel *has been* without the true God, without a [b]teaching priest, and without [c]law;

4 "but [a]when in their trouble they turned to the LORD God of Israel, and sought Him, He was found by them.

5 "And in those times *there was* no peace to the one who went out, nor to the one who came in, but great turmoil *was* on all the inhabitants of the lands.

6 [a]"So nation was [1]destroyed by nation, and city by city, for God troubled them with every adversity.

7 "But you, be strong and do not let your hands be weak, for your work shall be rewarded!"

8 And when Asa heard these words and the prophecy of [1]Oded the prophet, he took courage, and removed the abominable idols from all the land of Judah and Benjamin and from the cities [a]which he had taken in the mountains of Ephraim; and he restored the altar of the LORD that *was* before the vestibule of the LORD.

9 Then he gathered all Judah and Benjamin, and [a]those who dwelt with them from Ephraim, Manasseh, and Simeon, for they came over to him in great numbers from Israel when they saw that the LORD his God was with him.

10 So they gathered together at Jerusalem in the third month, in the fifteenth year of the reign of Asa.

11 [a]And they offered to the LORD [1]at that time seven hundred bulls and seven thousand sheep from the [2]spoil they had brought.

12 Then they [a]entered into a covenant to seek the LORD God of their fathers with all their heart and with all their soul;

13 [a]and whoever would not seek the LORD God of Israel [b]was to be put to death, whether small or great, whether man or woman.

14 Then they took an oath before the LORD with a loud voice, with shouting and trumpets and rams' horns.

15 And all Judah rejoiced at the oath, for they had sworn with all their heart and [a]sought Him with all their soul; and He was found by them, and the LORD gave them [b]rest all around.

16 Also he removed [a]Maachah, the [1]mother of Asa the king, from *being* queen mother, because she had made an obscene image of [2]Asherah; and Asa cut down her obscene image, then crushed and burned *it* by the Brook Kidron.

17 But [a]the [1]high places were not removed from Israel. Nevertheless the heart of Asa was loyal all his days.

18 He also brought into the house of God the things that his father had dedicated and that he himself had dedicated: silver and gold and utensils.

19 And there was no war until the thirty-fifth year of the reign of Asa.

Asa's Treaty with Syria

16 In the thirty-sixth year of the reign of Asa, [a]Baasha king of Israel came up against Judah and built Ramah, [b]that he might let none go out or come in to Asa king of Judah.

2 Then Asa brought silver and gold from the treasuries of the house of the LORD and of the king's house, and sent to Ben-Hadad king of Syria, who dwelt in Damascus, saying,

3 *"Let there be* a treaty between you and me, as there was between my father and your father. See, I have sent you silver and gold; come, break your treaty with Baasha king of Israel, so that he will withdraw from me."

4 So Ben-Hadad heeded King Asa, and sent the captains of his armies against the cities of Israel. They attacked Ijon, Dan, Abel Maim, and all the storage cities of Naphtali.

5 Now it happened, when Baasha heard *it,* that he stopped building Ramah and ceased his work.

6 Then King Asa took all Judah, and they carried away the stones and timber of Ramah, which Baasha had used for building; and with them he built Geba and Mizpah.

Hanani's Message to Asa

7 And at that time [a]Hanani the *seer came to Asa king of Judah, and said to him: [b]"Because you have relied on

2 [a][James 4:8] [b][1 Chr. 28:9]; 2 Chr. 14:4; 33:12, 13; [Jer. 29:13; Matt. 7:7] [c]2 Chr. 24:20 [1]Lit. *before*
3 [a]Hos. 3:4 [b]2 Kin. 12:2 [c]Lev. 10:11; 2 Chr. 17:8, 9
4 [a][Deut. 4:29]
6 [a]Matt. 24:7 [1]Lit. *beaten in pieces*
8 [a]2 Chr. 13:19 [1]So with MT, LXX; Syr., Vg. *Azariah the son of Oded* (cf. v. 1)
9 [a]2 Chr. 11:16
11 [a]2 Chr. 14:13–15 [1]Lit. *in that day* [2]*plunder*
12 [a]2 Kin. 23:3; 2 Chr. 23:16; 34:31; Neh. 10:29
13 [a]Ex. 22:20 [b]Deut. 13:5–15
15 [a]2 Chr. 15:2 [b]2 Chr. 14:7
16 [a]1 Kin. 15:2, 10, 13 [1]Or *grandmother* [2]A Canaanite deity
17 [a]1 Kin. 15:14; 2 Chr. 14:3, 5 [1]Places for pagan worship

CHAPTER 16

1 [a]1 Kin. 15:17–22 [b]2 Chr. 15:9
7 [a]1 Kin. 16:1; 2 Chr. 19:2 [b]2 Chr. 32:8–10; Ps. 118:9; [Is. 31:1; Jer. 17:5] *See WW at 1 Sam. 9:9.

reforms in motion, is not. On **Asherah** (v. 16), see note on 1 Kin. 18:19.

15:2–4 See section 2 of Truth-In-Action at the end of 2 Chr.

16:1–14 Asa's war with **Baasha king of Israel** and the treaty with **Ben-Hadad king of Syria** are both recorded in 1 Kin. 15:9–24. However, neither the prophecy of **Hanani** concerning Asa's demise nor the illness that led to his death are mentioned in 1 Kin. Though he was a good king, in his later years he departed from his dedication to the Lord.

the king of Syria, and have not relied
on the LORD your God, therefore the
army of the king of Syria has escaped
from your hand.
8 "Were [a]the Ethiopians and [b]the Lubim not a huge army with very many
chariots and horsemen? Yet, because
you relied on the LORD, He delivered
them into your [c]hand.
2 9 [a]"For the eyes of the LORD run to
and fro throughout the whole earth, to
show Himself strong on behalf of *those*
whose heart *is* loyal to Him. In this
[b]you have done foolishly; therefore
from now on [c]you shall have wars."
10 Then Asa was angry with the seer,
and [a]put him in prison, for *he was* enraged at him because of this. And Asa
oppressed *some* of the people at that
time.

Illness and Death of Asa

11 [a]Note that the acts of Asa, first and
last, are indeed written in the book of
the kings of Judah and Israel.
12 And in the thirty-ninth year of his
reign, Asa became diseased in his feet,
and his malady was severe; yet in his
disease he [a]did not seek the LORD, but
the physicians.
13 [a]So Asa [1]rested with his fathers; he
died in the forty-first year of his reign.
14 They buried him in his own tomb,
which he had [1]made for himself in the
City of David; and they laid him in the
bed which was filled [a]with spices and
various ingredients prepared in a mixture of ointments. They made [b]a very
great burning for him.

Jehoshaphat Reigns in Judah

17 Then [a]Jehoshaphat his son
reigned in his place, and
strengthened himself against Israel.
2 And he placed troops in all the fortified cities of Judah, and set garrisons
in the land of [a]Judah and in the cities
of Ephraim [b]which Asa his father had
taken.
3 Now the LORD was with Jehoshaphat, because he walked in the former

8 [a]2 Chr. 14:9 [b]2 Chr. 12:3 [c]2 Chr. 13:16, 18
9 [a]Job 34:21; [Prov. 5:21; 15:3; Jer. 16:17; 32:19]; Zech. 4:10 [b]1 Sam. 13:13 [c]1 Kin. 15:32
10 [a]2 Chr. 18:26; Jer. 20:2; Matt. 14:3
11 [a]1 Kin. 15:23, 24; 2 Chr. 14:2
12 [a][Jer. 17:5]
13 [a]1 Kin. 15:24 [1]Died and joined his ancestors
14 [a]Gen. 50:2; Mark 16:1; John 19:39, 40 [b]2 Chr. 21:19; Jer. 34:5 [1]Lit. *dug*

CHAPTER 17

1 [a]1 Kin. 15:24; 2 Chr. 20:31
2 [a]2 Chr. 11:5 [b]2 Chr. 15:8
4 [a]1 Kin. 12:28 [1]LXX *the* LORD *God*
5 [a]1 Sam. 10:27; 1 Kin. 10:25 [b]2 Chr. 18:1
6 [a]1 Kin. 22:43; 2 Chr. 15:17; 19:3; 20:33 [1]Places for pagan worship *See WW at Ezek. 6:3.
7 [a]2 Chr. 15:3; 35:3
9 [a]Deut. 6:4–9; 2 Chr. 35:3; Neh. 8:3, 7
10 [a]Gen. 35:5; 2 Chr. 14:14
11 [a]2 Sam. 8:2; 2 Chr. 9:14; 26:8
16 [a]Judg. 5:2, 9; 1 Chr. 29:9

ways of his father David; he did not
seek the Baals,
4 but sought [1]the God of his father,
and walked in His commandments and
not according to [a]the acts of Israel.
5 Therefore the LORD established the
kingdom in his hand; and all Judah
[a]gave presents to Jehoshaphat, [b]and
he had riches and honor in abundance.
6 And his heart took delight in the
ways of the LORD; moreover [a]he removed the [1]high* places and wooden
images from Judah.
7 Also in the third year of his reign
he sent his leaders, Ben-Hail, Obadiah,
Zechariah, Nethanel, and Michaiah,
[a]to teach in the cities of Judah.
8 And with them *he sent* Levites: Shemaiah, Nethaniah, Zebadiah, Asahel,
Shemiramoth, Jehonathan, Adonijah,
Tobijah, and Tobadonijah—the Levites; and with them Elishama and Jehoram, the priests.
9 [a]So they taught in Judah, and *had* 7
the Book of the Law of the LORD with
them; they went throughout all the cities of Judah and taught the people.
10 And [a]the fear of the LORD fell on
all the kingdoms of the lands that *were*
around Judah, so that they did not
make war against Jehoshaphat.
11 Also *some* of the Philistines
[a]brought Jehoshaphat presents and
silver as tribute; and the Arabians
brought him flocks, seven thousand
seven hundred rams and seven thousand seven hundred male goats.
12 So Jehoshaphat became increasingly powerful, and he built fortresses
and storage cities in Judah.
13 He had much property in the cities
of Judah; and the men of war, mighty
men of valor, *were* in Jerusalem.
14 These *are* their numbers, according
to their fathers' houses. Of Judah, the
captains of thousands: Adnah the captain, and with him three hundred thousand mighty men of valor;
15 and next to him *was* Jehohanan the
captain, and with him two hundred and
eighty thousand;
16 and next to him *was* Amasiah the
son of Zichri, [a]who willingly offered

16:9 See section 2 of Truth-In-Action at the end of 2 Chr.
16:12 The disease in Asa's **feet** is thought to have been gout or gangrene. The **physicians** were probably sorcerers or medicine-men who operated with curses and magic, which is why they should not have been sought. To his shame, Asa is remembered as one who **did not seek the LORD.**
16:14 The **great burning** refers to the burning of spices for burial, not to cremation.
17:1–19 2 Chr. gives a more detailed and systematic account of the reign of **Jehoshaphat** than does 1 Kin. However, 2 Kin. records Jehoshaphat's ill-fated coalition with Ahab's son Jehoram, and the miraculous story of the valley of ditches (2 Kin. 3), whereas 2 Chr. does not. Read the text and notes of 1 Kin. 22:1–50 to compare with 2 Chr. 17—20. As Judah's fourth king, Jehoshaphat was apparently a force to be reckoned with (vv. 2, 10–19) because of his army, fortresses, and holdings. One of his prominent achievements (not noted in 1 Kin.) was his implementing teams of teachers to instruct in the Law (vv. 8, 9).
17:9 See section 7 of Truth-In-Action at the end of 2 Chr.

himself to the LORD, and with him two
hundred thousand mighty men of
valor.
17 Of Benjamin: Eliada a mighty man
of valor, and with him two hundred
thousand men armed with bow and
shield;
18 and next to him *was* Jehozabad,
and with him one hundred and eighty
thousand prepared for war.
19 These *served the king, besides
[a]those the king put in the fortified cities throughout all Judah.

Micaiah Warns Ahab

18 Jehoshaphat [a]had riches and
honor in abundance; and by
marriage he [b]allied himself with
[c]Ahab.
2 [a]After some years he went down to
visit Ahab in Samaria; and Ahab killed
sheep and oxen in abundance for him
and the people who were with him, and
persuaded him to go up *with him* to
Ramoth Gilead.
3 So Ahab king of Israel said to Jehoshaphat king of Judah, "Will you go
with me *against* Ramoth Gilead?" And
he answered him, "I *am* as you *are*,
and my people as your people; *we will
be* with you in the war."
4 Also Jehoshaphat said to the king
of Israel, [a]"Please inquire for the word
of the LORD today."
5 Then the king of Israel gathered the
prophets together, four hundred men,
and said to them, "Shall we go to war
against Ramoth Gilead, or shall I
refrain?" So they said, "Go up, for
God will deliver it into the king's
hand."
6 But Jehoshaphat said, "*Is there* not
still a prophet of the LORD here, that
we may inquire of [a]Him?"[1]
7 7 So the king of Israel said to Jehoshaphat, "*There is* still one man by
whom we may inquire of the LORD; but
I hate him, because he never prophesies good concerning me, but always
evil. He *is* Micaiah the son of Imla."
And Jehoshaphat said, "Let not the
king say such things!"
8 Then the king of Israel called one
of his officers and said, "Bring Micaiah
the son of Imla quickly!"
9 The king of Israel and Jehoshaphat
king of Judah, clothed in *their* robes,
sat each on his throne; and they sat at
a threshing floor at the entrance of the
gate of Samaria; and all the prophets
prophesied before them.
10 Now Zedekiah the son of Chenaanah had made [a]horns of iron for
himself; and he said, "Thus says the
LORD: 'With these you shall gore the
Syrians until they are destroyed.'"
11 And all the prophets prophesied so,
saying, "Go up to Ramoth Gilead and
prosper, for the LORD will deliver *it* into
the king's hand."
12 Then the messenger who had gone
to call Micaiah spoke to him, saying,
"Now listen, the words of the prophets
with one accord encourage the king.
Therefore please let your word be like
the word of one of them, and speak encouragement."
13 And Micaiah said, "*As* the LORD
lives, [a]whatever my God says, that I
will speak."
14 Then he came to the king; and the
king said to him, "Micaiah, shall we
go to war against Ramoth Gilead, or
shall I refrain?" And he said, "Go and
prosper, and they shall be delivered
into your hand!"
15 So the king said to him, "How many
times shall I make you swear that you
tell me nothing but the truth in the
name of the LORD?"
16 Then he said, "I saw all Israel
[a]scattered on the mountains, as sheep
that have no [b]shepherd. And the LORD
said, 'These have no master. Let each
return to his house in peace.'"
17 And the king of Israel said to Jehoshaphat, "Did I not tell you he would
not prophesy good concerning me, but
evil?"
18 Then *Micaiah* said, "Therefore hear
the word of the LORD: I saw the LORD
sitting on His [a]throne, and all the *host
of heaven standing on His right hand
and His left.
19 "And the LORD said, 'Who will persuade Ahab king of Israel to go up, that
he may fall at Ramoth Gilead?' So one
spoke in this manner, and another
spoke in that manner.
20 "Then a [a]spirit came forward and
stood before the LORD, and said, 'I will
persuade him.' The LORD said to him,
'In what way?'
21 "So he said, 'I will go out and be a
lying spirit in the mouth of all his
prophets.' And *the LORD* said, 'You
shall persuade *him* and also prevail; go
out and do so.'
22 "Therefore look! [a]The LORD has put

19 [a]2 Chr. 17:2 *See WW at 1 Chr. 15:2.

CHAPTER 18

1 [a]2 Chr. 17:5 [b]1 Kin. 22:44; 2 Kin. 8:18 [c]1 Kin. 22:40
2 [a][Ex. 23:2]; 1 Kin. 22:2
4 [a]1 Sam. 23:2, 4, 9; 2 Sam. 2:1
6 [a]2 Kin. 3:11 [1]Or *him*
10 [a]Zech. 1:18–21
13 [a]Num. 22:18–20, 35; 23:12, 26; 1 Kin. 22:14
16 [a][Jer. 23:1–8; 31:10] [b]Num. 27:17; 1 Kin. 22:17; [Ezek. 34:5–8]; Matt. 9:36; Mark 6:34
18 [a]Is. 6:1–5; Dan. 7:9, 10 *See WW at Ps. 68:11.
20 [a]Job 1:6; 2 Thess. 2:9
22 [a]Job 12:16, 17; Is. 19:12–14; Ezek. 14:9

18:1—19:3 This section gives an additional perspective on the events recorded in 1 Kin. 22:1–40.

18:7–27 See section 7 of Truth-In-Action at the end of 2 Chr.

18:16 Jesus uses this picture of **sheep that have no shepherd** in Mark 6:34.

a lying spirit in the mouth of these
prophets of yours, and the LORD has
declared disaster against you."
23 Then Zedekiah the son of Chenaanah went near and [a]struck Micaiah
on the cheek, and said, "Which way
did the spirit from the LORD go from
me to speak to you?"
24 And Micaiah said, "Indeed you
shall see on that day when you go into
an inner chamber to hide!"
25 Then the king of Israel said, "Take
Micaiah, and return him to Amon the
governor of the city and to Joash the
king's son;
26 "and say, 'Thus says the king:
[a]"Put this *fellow* in prison, and feed
him with bread of affliction and water
of affliction, until I return in peace." '"
27 But Micaiah said, "If you ever return in peace, the LORD has not spoken
by [a]me." And he said, "Take heed, all
you people!"

Ahab Dies in Battle

28 So the king of Israel and Jehoshaphat the king of Judah went up to Ramoth Gilead.
29 And the king of Israel said to Jehoshaphat, "I will [a]disguise myself and
go into battle; but you put on your
robes." So the king of Israel disguised
himself, and they went into battle.
30 Now the king of Syria had commanded the captains of the chariots
who *were* with him, saying, "Fight with
no one small or great, but only with
the king of Israel."
31 So it was, when the captains of the
chariots saw Jehoshaphat, that they
said, "It *is* the king of Israel!" Therefore they surrounded him to attack; but
Jehoshaphat [a]cried out, and the LORD
helped him, and God diverted them
from him.
32 For so it was, when the captains of
the chariots saw that it was not the
king of Israel, that they turned back
from pursuing him.
33 Now a certain man drew a bow at
random, and struck the king of Israel
between the [1]joints of his armor. So
he said to the driver of his chariot,
"Turn around and take me out of the
battle, for I am wounded."
34 The battle increased that day, and
the king of Israel propped *himself* up
in *his* chariot facing the Syrians until
evening; and about the time of sunset
he died.

19 Then Jehoshaphat the king of
Judah returned safely to his
house in Jerusalem.
2 And Jehu the son of Hanani [a]the 1
seer went out to meet him, and said
to King Jehoshaphat, "Should you help
the wicked and [b]love those who hate
the LORD? Therefore the [c]wrath of the
LORD *is* upon you.
3 "Nevertheless [a]good things are
found in you, in that you have removed
the [1]wooden images from the land, and
have [b]prepared your heart to seek
God."

The Reforms of Jehoshaphat

4 So Jehoshaphat dwelt at Jerusalem;
and he went out again among the people from Beersheba to the mountains
of Ephraim, and brought them back to
the LORD God of their [a]fathers.
5 Then he set [a]judges in the land
throughout all the fortified cities of Judah, city by city,
6 and said to the judges, "Take heed
to what you are doing, for [a]you do not
judge for man but for the LORD,
[b]who *is* with you [1]in the judgment.
7 "Now therefore, let the fear of the
LORD be upon you; take care and do
it, for [a]*there is* no iniquity with the
LORD our God, no [b]partiality, nor taking of bribes."
8 Moreover in Jerusalem, for the
judgment of the LORD and for controversies, Jehoshaphat [a]appointed some
of the Levites and priests, and some
of the chief fathers of Israel, [1]when
they returned to Jerusalem.
9 And he commanded them, saying,
"Thus you shall act [a]in the fear of
the LORD, *faithfully and with a loyal
heart:
10 [a]"Whatever case comes to you from
your brethren who dwell in their cities,
whether of bloodshed or offenses
against law or commandment, against
statutes or ordinances, you shall warn
them, lest they trespass against the
LORD and [b]wrath come upon [c]you and
your brethren. Do this, and you will
not be guilty.
11 "And take notice: [a]Amariah the
chief priest *is* over you [b]in all matters
of the LORD; and Zebadiah the son of
Ishmael, the ruler of the house of

23 [a]Jer. 20:2
26 [a]2 Chr. 16:10
27 [a]Deut. 18:22
29 [a]2 Chr. 35:22
31 [a]2 Chr. 13:14, 15
33 [1]*Or scale armor and the breastplate*

CHAPTER 19

2 [a]1 Kin. 16:1 [b]Ps. 139:21 [c]2 Chr. 32:25
3 [a]2 Chr. 17:4, 6 [b]2 Chr. 30:19 [1]Or *Asherim*, Heb. *Asheroth*
4 [a]2 Chr. 15:8–13
5 [a][Deut. 16:18–20]
6 [a][Deut. 1:17] [b]Ps. 82:1 [1]Lit. *in the matter of the judgment*
7 [a][Deut. 32:4] [b][Deut. 10:17, 18]
8 [a]2 Chr. 17:8 [1]LXX, Vg. *for the inhabitants of Jerusalem*
9 [a][2 Sam. 23:3] *See WW at Prov. 28:20.
10 [a]Deut. 17:8 [b]Num. 16:46 [c][Ezek. 3:18]
11 [a]Ezra 7:3 [b]1 Chr. 26:30

18:23 On **the spirit from the LORD,** read the text and note on 1 Kin. 22:24.
19:2 See section 1 of Truth-In-Action at the end of 2 Chr.

19:4–11 Jehoshaphat not only sent out teachers (17:8, 9), but also established regional courts in individual cities and a central court of appeals in **Jerusalem**.

Judah, for all the king's matters; also
the Levites *will be* officials before you.
Behave courageously, and the LORD
will be [c]with the good."

Ammon, Moab, and Mount Seir
Defeated

20 It happened after this *that* the
people of [a]Moab with the people
of [b]Ammon, and *others* with them besides the [c]Ammonites,[1] came to battle
against Jehoshaphat.
2 Then some came and told Jehoshaphat, saying, "A great multitude
is coming against you from beyond
the sea, from [1]Syria; and they are [a]in
Hazazon Tamar" (which *is* [b]En Gedi).
3 And Jehoshaphat feared, and set
[1]himself to [a]seek the LORD, and [b]pro-
claimed a *fast throughout all Judah.
4 So Judah gathered together to ask
[a]*help* from the LORD; and from all the
cities of Judah they came to seek the
LORD.
5 Then Jehoshaphat stood in the assembly of Judah and Jerusalem, in the
house of the LORD, before the new
court,
6 and said: "O LORD God of our fathers, *are* You not [a]God in heaven, and
[b]do You *not* rule over all the kingdoms
of the nations, and [c]in Your hand *is*
there not power and might, so that no
one is able to withstand You?
7 "*Are* You not [a]our God, *who*
[b]drove out the inhabitants of this land
before Your people Israel, and gave it
to the descendants of Abraham [c]Your
friend forever?
8 "And they dwell in it, and have built
You a sanctuary in it for Your name,
saying,
9 [a]'If disaster comes upon us—sword,
judgment, pestilence, or famine—we
will stand before this temple and in
Your presence (for Your [b]name *is* in
this temple), and cry out to You in our
affliction, and You will hear and save.'
10 "And now, here are the people of
Ammon, Moab, and Mount Seir—
whom You [a]would not let Israel invade
when they came out of the land of
Egypt, but [b]they turned from them and
did not destroy them—
11 "here they are, rewarding us [a]by
coming to throw us out of Your possession which You have given us to
inherit.
12 "O our God, will You not [a]judge
them? For we have no power against
this great multitude that is coming
against us; nor do we know what to
do, but [b]our eyes *are* upon You."
13 Now all Judah, with their little ones,
their wives, and their children, stood
before the LORD.
14 Then [a]the Spirit of the LORD came
upon Jahaziel the son of Zechariah, the
son of Benaiah, the son of Jeiel, the
son of Mattaniah, a Levite of the sons
of Asaph, in the midst of the assembly.
15 And he said, "Listen, all you of Ju- 5
dah and you inhabitants of Jerusalem,
and you, King Jehoshaphat! Thus says
the LORD to you: [a]'Do not be afraid nor
dismayed because of this great multitude, [b]for the battle *is* not yours, but
God's.
16 'Tomorrow go down against them.
They will surely come up by the Ascent
of Ziz, and you will find them at the
end of the [1]brook before the Wilderness of Jeruel.
17 [a]'You will not *need* to fight in this
battle. Position yourselves, stand still
and see the salvation of the LORD, who
is with you, O Judah and Jerusalem!'
Do not *fear or be dismayed; tomorrow
go out against them, [b]for the LORD *is*
with you."
18 And Jehoshaphat [a]bowed his head

11 [c][2 Chr. 15:2; 20:17]

CHAPTER 20

1 [a]1 Chr. 18:2 [b]1 Chr. 19:15 [c]2 Chr. 26:7 [1]So with MT, Vg.; LXX *Meunites* (cf. 2 Chr. 26:7)
2 [a]Gen. 14:7 [b]Josh. 15:62 [1]So with MT, LXX, Vg.; Heb. mss., Old Lat. *Edom*
3 [a]2 Chr. 19:3 [b]Ezra 8:21 [1]Lit. *his face* *See WW at Jon. 3:5.
4 [a]2 Chr. 14:11
6 [a]Deut. 4:39 [b]Dan. 4:17, 25, 32 [c]1 Chr. 29:12
7 [a]Ex. 6:7 [b]Ps. 44:2 [c]Is. 41:8
9 [a]2 Chr. 6:28–30 [b]2 Chr. 6:20
10 [a]Deut. 2:4, 9, 19 [b]Num. 20:21
11 [a]Ps. 83:1–18
12 [a]Judg. 11:27 [b]Ps. 25:15; 121:1, 2; 123:1, 2; 141:8
14 [a]2 Chr. 15:1; 24:20
15 [a][Deut. 1:29, 30; 31:6, 8] [b]1 Sam. 17:47
16 [1]*streambed* or *wadi*
17 [a]Ex. 14:13, 14 [b]Num. 14:9 *See WW at Ex. 1:17.
18 [a]Ex. 4:31

20:1–30 This is probably the most familiar and loved chapter in 2 Chr., for it explains how the Lord grants victory to those who trust in Him. **Jehoshaphat** was facing the greatest external threat of his reign. **A great multitude** (v. 2) of Moabites, Ammonites, and others from Syria were plotting to crush Judah. In the face of these incredible odds, Jehoshaphat humbled himself before the Lord; and the result was the greatest victory he had ever experienced. The promise of the Lord through the prophet **Jahaziel** is a comfort to believers of all ages who face hopeless situations: **Do not be afraid or dismayed . . . for the battle *is* not yours, but God's** (v. 15). However, the account reveals three key elements that put God's people in the place where He could deliver them: 1) fasting (v. 3); 2) prayer (vv. 4–13); and 3) praise (vv. 21, 22).

20:3 Fasting was one of the keys to releasing the deliverance Judah experienced. This was a **proclaimed fast** in which the whole nation participated. Fasting is not a tool by which one manipulates God to accomplish something. Fasting is simply an outward indication of an inward sincerity, evidence of the urgency we feel when praying for special needs. See 1 Sam. 7:6 and Acts 13:2, 3.

20:4–11 A second key that was integral to Judah's deliverance was prayer. The prayer of **Jehoshaphat** here is reminiscent of Solomon's prayer in ch. 6 and in 1 Kin. 8. Perhaps it was based on the promise in 7:14. V. 12 gives the essence of this prayer of helplessness: **For we have no power . . . nor do we know what to do, but our eyes *are* upon You.** The cry of Christians in the darkest night of their experience is: "Lord, I do not know what to do, but I am counting on You."

20:14 Spirit of the LORD: Read the text and note on 1 Chr. 12:18.

20:15–25 See section 5 of Truth-In-Action at the end of 2 Chr.

with *his* face to the ground, and all Judah and the inhabitants of Jerusalem bowed before the LORD, worshiping the LORD.

19 Then the Levites of the children of the Kohathites and of the children of the Korahites stood up to praise the LORD God of Israel with voices loud and high.

4 **20** So they rose early in the morning and went out into the Wilderness of Tekoa; and as they went out, Jehoshaphat stood and said, "Hear me, O Judah and you inhabitants of Jerusalem: [a]**Believe** in the LORD your God, and you shall be established; believe His prophets, and you shall prosper."

WORD WEALTH

20:20 believe, *'aman* (ah-*mahn*); Strong's #539: To be firm, stable, established; also, to be firmly persuaded; to believe solidly. In its causative form *'aman* means "to believe," that is, to "consider trustworthy." This is the word used in Gen. 15:6, when Abraham "believed" in the Lord. Here in 2 Chr. *'aman* appears three times in one verse and could be translated: "Be established in the LORD, . . . and you will be established." From *'aman* comes *'emunah,* "faith." The most famous derivative is "amen," which conveys this idea: "It is solidly, firmly, surely true and verified and established."

21 And when he had consulted with the people, he appointed those who should sing to the LORD, [a]and who should praise the beauty of holiness, as they went out before the army and were saying:

[b]"Praise the LORD,
[c]For His mercy *endures* forever."

4 **22** Now when they began to *sing and to *praise, [a]the LORD set ambushes against the people of Ammon, Moab, and Mount Seir, who had come against Judah; and they were defeated.

KINGDOM DYNAMICS

20:15–22 Powerful Praise Births Victory, PRAISE PATHWAY. Here is a great lesson on the power of praise. Judah was confronted by mortal enemies, Moab and Ammon. The people sought God in prayer and with faith in His Word (20:1–14). Then came the word of the prophet: "Do not be afraid . . . for the battle *is* not yours, but God's" (v. 15).

The victory came in a strange but powerful manner. The Levites stood and praised "the LORD God of Israel with voices loud and high" (v. 19). Then some were actually appointed to sing to the Lord and praise Him in the beauty of holiness. These went before the army, saying: "Praise the LORD, for His mercy *endures* [lasts] forever" (v. 21). The result of this powerful praise was total victory!

(2 Chr. 5:13/Ps. 7:14–17) C.G.

23 For the people of Ammon and Moab stood up against the inhabitants of Mount Seir to utterly kill and destroy *them.* And when they [1]had made an end of the inhabitants of Seir, [a]they helped to destroy one another.

24 So when Judah came to a place overlooking the wilderness, they looked toward the multitude; and there *were* their dead bodies, fallen on the earth. No one had escaped.

25 When Jehoshaphat and his people came to take away their spoil, they found among them an abundance of valuables on the [1]dead bodies, and precious jewelry, which they stripped off for themselves, more than they could carry away; and they were three days gathering the spoil because there was so much.

26 And on the fourth day they assembled in the Valley of [1]Berachah, for there they blessed the LORD; therefore the name of that place was called The Valley of Berachah until this day.

27 Then they returned, every man of Judah and Jerusalem, with Jehoshaphat in front of them, to go back to Jerusalem with joy, for the LORD had [a]made them rejoice over their enemies.

28 So they came to Jerusalem, with stringed instruments and harps and trumpets, to the house of the LORD.

29 And [a]the fear of God was on all the kingdoms of *those* countries when they heard that the LORD had fought against the enemies of Israel.

30 Then the realm of Jehoshaphat was quiet, for his [a]God gave him rest all around.

20 [a]Is. 7:9
21 [a]1 Chr. 16:29; Ps. 29:2; 90:17; 96:9; 110:3 [b]1 Chr. 16:34; Ps. 106:1; 136:1 [c]1 Chr. 16:41; 2 Chr. 5:13
22 [a]Judg. 7:22; 1 Sam. 14:20 *See WW at Ps. 30:5. • See WW at Ps. 100:4.
23 [a]Judg. 7:22; 1 Sam. 14:20 [1]*had finished*
25 [1]A few Heb. mss., Old Lat., Vg. *garments;* LXX *armor*
26 [1]Lit. *Blessing*
27 [a]Neh. 12:43
29 [a]2 Chr. 14:14; 17:10
30 [a]1 Kin. 22:41–43; 2 Chr. 14:6, 7; 15:15; Job 34:29

20:20 See section 4 of Truth-In-Action at the end of 2 Chr.
20:22, 23 These verses highlight the final key in Judah's miraculous deliverance, that of praise (the name **Judah** means "Praise"). As **they began to sing and to praise** God with the expectancy that He would fight for them, their enemies **were defeated.** This activity is not unique to 2 Chr., but has parallels to other OT victories. See Josh. 6:10, 20; Judg. 7:18–22; 2 Kin. 7:3–16; 19:35. Ps. 22:3 explains that God is enthroned in the praises of His people. Whenever and wherever God's people praise Him, He reigns among them and does miraculous things on their behalf.
20:22 See section 4 of Truth-In-Action at the end of 2 Chr.

The End of Jehoshaphat's Reign

31 [a]So Jehoshaphat was king over Judah. *He was* thirty-five years old when
he became king, and he reigned
twenty-five years in Jerusalem. His
mother's name *was* Azubah the daughter of Shilhi.
32 And he walked in the way of his
father [a]Asa, and did not turn aside
from it, doing *what was* right in the
sight of the LORD.
33 Nevertheless [a]the [1]high places were
not taken away, for as yet the people
had not [b]directed their hearts to the
God of their fathers.
34 Now the rest of the acts of Jehoshaphat, first and last, indeed they
are written in the book of Jehu the son
of Hanani, [a]which *is* mentioned in
the book of the kings of Israel.
35 After this [a]Jehoshaphat king of Judah allied himself with Ahaziah king
of Israel, [b]who acted very [c]wickedly.
36 And he allied himself with him
[a]to make ships to go to Tarshish, and
they made the ships in Ezion Geber.
37 But Eliezer the son of Dodavah of
Mareshah prophesied against Jehoshaphat, saying, "Because you have
allied yourself with Ahaziah, the LORD
has destroyed your works." [a]Then the
ships were wrecked, so that they were
not able to go [b]to Tarshish.

Jehoram Reigns in Judah

21 And [a]Jehoshaphat [1]rested with
his fathers, and was buried with
his fathers in the City of David. Then
Jehoram his son reigned in his place.
2 He had brothers, the sons of Jehoshaphat: Azariah, Jehiel, Zechariah,
Azaryahu, Michael, and Shephatiah;
all these *were* the sons of Jehoshaphat
king of Israel.
3 Their father gave them great gifts
of silver and gold and precious things,
with fortified cities in Judah; but he
gave the kingdom to Jehoram, because
he *was* the firstborn.
4 Now when Jehoram [1]was established over the kingdom of his father,
he strengthened himself and killed all
his brothers with the sword, and also
others of the princes of Israel.
5 [a]Jehoram *was* thirty-two years old
when he became king, and he reigned
eight years in Jerusalem.
6 And he walked in the way of the
kings of Israel, just as the house of
Ahab had done, for he had the daughter of [a]Ahab as a wife; and he did evil
in the sight of the LORD.
7 Yet the LORD would not destroy the
house of David, because of the [a]cov-
enant that He had *made with David,
and since He had promised to give
a lamp to him and to his [b]sons for
ever.
8 [a]In his days Edom revolted against
Judah's authority, and made a king
over themselves.
9 So Jehoram went out with his officers, and all his chariots with him.
And he rose by night and attacked the
Edomites who had surrounded him
and the captains of the chariots.
10 Thus Edom has been in revolt
against Judah's authority to this day.
At that time Libnah revolted against
his rule, because he had forsaken the
LORD God of his fathers.
11 Moreover he made [1]high places in
the mountains of Judah, and caused
the inhabitants of Jerusalem to [a]com-
mit harlotry, and led Judah astray.
12 And a letter came to him from Elijah the prophet, saying,

Thus says the LORD God of your
father David:
Because you have not walked in
the ways of Jehoshaphat your
father, or in the ways of Asa king
of Judah,
13 but have walked in the way of the
kings of Israel, and have [a]made
Judah and the inhabitants of
Jerusalem to [b]play the harlot like
the [c]harlotry of the house of
Ahab, and also have [d]killed your
brothers, those of your father's
household, *who were* better than
yourself,
14 behold, the LORD will strike your
people with a serious affliction—
your children, your wives, and all
your possessions;
15 and you *will become* very sick
with a [a]disease of your intestines,
until your intestines come out by
reason of the sickness, day by
day.

31 [a][1 Kin. 22:41–43]
32 [a]2 Chr. 14:2
33 [a]2 Chr. 15:17; 17:6 [b]2 Chr. 12:14; 19:3
[1]Places for pagan worship
34 [a]1 Kin. 16:1, 7
35 [a]2 Chr. 18:1 [b]1 Kin. 22:48–53 [c][2 Chr. 19:2]
36 [a]1 Kin. 9:26; 10:22
37 [a]1 Kin. 22:48 [b]2 Chr. 9:21

CHAPTER 21

1 [a]1 Kin. 22:50 [1]Died and joined his ancestors
4 [1]Lit. *arose*
5 [a]2 Kin. 8:17–22
6 [a]2 Chr. 18:1
7 [a]2 Sam. 7:8–17 [b]1 Kin. 11:36; 2 Kin. 8:19; Ps. 132:11
*See WW at Ex. 34:27.
8 [a]2 Kin. 8:20; 14:7, 10; 2 Chr. 25:14, 19
11 [a][Lev. 20:5] [1]Places for pagan worship
13 [a]2 Chr. 21:11 [b][Ex. 34:15]; Deut. 31:16 [c]1 Kin. 16:31–33; 2 Kin. 9:22 [d]1 Kin. 2:32; 2 Chr. 21:4
15 [a]2 Chr. 21:18, 19

21:1–20 Read the text and notes of 2 Kin. 8:16–24 for a condensed version of the reign of **Jehoram.** He was Judah's fifth king and, because of the evil influence of his wicked wife Athaliah, he unraveled much of the good accomplished by his father **Jehoshaphat.** It is a sad epitaph that no one was sorry that he died (v. 20).

21:12 From 2 Kin. 2:11 and 3:11 it would seem that **Elijah** had been translated either before or during the reign of **Jehoshaphat.**

16 Moreover the [a]LORD [b]stirred* up
against Jehoram the spirit of the Philistines and the [c]Arabians who *were* near
the Ethiopians.
17 And they came up into Judah and
invaded it, and carried away all the
possessions that were found in the
king's house, and also [a]his sons and
his wives, so that there was not a son
left to him except [1]Jehoahaz, the youngest of his sons.
18 After all this the LORD struck him
[a]in his intestines with an incurable disease.
19 Then it happened in the course of
time, after the end of two years, that
his intestines came out because of his
sickness; so he died in severe pain.
And his people made no [1]burning for
him, like [a]the burning for his fathers.
20 He was thirty-two years old when
he became king. He reigned in Jerusalem eight years and, to no one's sorrow, departed. However they buried
him in the City of David, but not in
the tombs of the kings.

Ahaziah Reigns in Judah

22 Then the inhabitants of Jerusalem made [a]Ahaziah his youn-
gest son king in his place, for the raiders who came with the [b]Arabians into
the camp had killed all the [c]older *sons.*
So Ahaziah the son of Jehoram, king
of Judah, reigned.
2 Ahaziah *was* [1]forty-two years old
when he became king, and he reigned
one year in Jerusalem. His mother's
name *was* [a]Athaliah the [2]grand-
daughter of Omri.
3 He also walked in the ways of the
house of Ahab, for his mother advised
him to do wickedly.
4 Therefore he did evil in the sight of
the LORD, like the house of Ahab; for
they were his counselors after the
death of his father, to his destruction.
5 He also followed their advice, and
went with [1]Jehoram the son of Ahab
king of Israel to war against Hazael
king of Syria at Ramoth Gilead; and
the Syrians wounded Joram.
6 [a]Then he returned to Jezreel to recover from the wounds which he had
received at Ramah, when he fought
against Hazael king of Syria. And
[1]Azariah the son of Jehoram, king of
Judah, went down to see Jehoram the
son of Ahab in Jezreel, because he was
sick.
7 His going to Joram [a]was God's occasion for Ahaziah's [1]downfall; for
when he arrived, [b]he went out with
[2]Jehoram against Jehu the son of Nimshi, [c]whom the LORD had *anointed to
[3]cut off the house of Ahab.
8 And it happened, when Jehu was
[a]executing judgment on the house of
Ahab, and [b]found the princes of Judah
and the sons of Ahaziah's brothers
who served Ahaziah, that he killed
them.
9 [a]Then he searched for Ahaziah; and
they caught him (he was hiding in Samaria), and brought him to Jehu. When
they had killed him, they buried him,
"because," they said, "he is the son of
[b]Jehoshaphat, who [c]sought the LORD
with all his heart." So the house of
Ahaziah had no one to assume power
over the kingdom.

Athaliah Reigns in Judah

10 [a]Now when Athaliah the mother of
Ahaziah saw that her son was dead,
she arose and destroyed all the royal
heirs of the house of Judah.
11 But [1]Jehoshabeath, the daughter of
the king, took [a]Joash the son of Ahaziah, and stole him away from among
the king's sons who were being murdered, and put him and his nurse in a
bedroom. So Jehoshabeath, the daughter of King Jehoram, the wife of Jehoiada the priest (for she was the sister
of Ahaziah), hid him from Athaliah so
that she did not kill him.
12 And he was hidden with them in the
house of God for six years, while Athaliah reigned over the land.

Joash Crowned King of Judah

23 In [a]the seventh year [b]Jehoiada
strengthened himself, *and made
a* covenant with the captains of hundreds: Azariah the son of Jeroham, Ishmael the son of Jehohanan, Azariah
the son of [c]Obed, Maaseiah the son of
Adaiah, and Elishaphat the son of
Zichri.
2 And they went throughout Judah

16 [a]2 Chr. 33:11; [Jer. 51:11] [b]1 Kin. 11:14, 23 [c]2 Chr. 17:11 *See WW at Hag. 1:14.
17 [a]2 Chr. 24:7 [1]*Ahaziah* or *Azariah,* 2 Chr. 22:1
18 [a]2 Chr. 13:20; 21:15; Acts 12:23
19 [a]2 Chr. 16:14 [1]Burning of spices

CHAPTER 22

1 [a]2 Chr. 21:17; 22:6 [b]2 Chr. 21:16 [c]2 Chr. 21:17
2 [a]2 Chr. 21:6 [1]*twenty-two,* 2 Kin. 8:26 [2]Lit. *daughter*
5 [1]*Joram,* v. 7; 2 Kin. 8:28
6 [a]2 Kin. 9:15 [1]Heb. mss., LXX, Syr., Vg. *Ahaziah* and 2 Kin. 8:29
7 [a]Judg. 14:4; 1 Kin. 12:15; 2 Chr. 10:15 [b]2 Kin. 9:21–24 [c]2 Kin. 9:6, 7 [1]Lit. *crushing* [2]*Joram,* vv. 5, 7; 2 Kin. 8:28 [3]*destroy* *See WW at Is. 61:1.
8 [a]2 Kin. 9:22–24 [b]2 Kin. 10:10–14; Hos. 1:4
9 [a][2 Kin. 9:27] [b]1 Kin. 15:24 [c]2 Chr. 17:4; 20:3, 4
10 [a]2 Kin. 11:1–3
11 [a]2 Kin. 12:18 [1]*Jehosheba,* 2 Kin. 11:2

CHAPTER 23

1 [a]2 Kin. 11:4 [b]2 Kin. 12:2 [c]1 Chr. 2:37, 38

22:1–9 For an even more abbreviated account of the reign of **Ahaziah,** Judah's sixth king, read the text and notes of 2 Kin. 8:25–29. Ahaziah was killed by **Jehu** when Jehu purged Israel of the descendants of Ahab (see 2 Kin. 9:27–29).

22:10—23:21 Read the text and notes of 2 Kin. 11 for a similar accounting of the usurper **Athaliah** and her overthrow. She was Judah's seventh ruler; **Joash** the rightful heir to the throne was to be Judah's eighth ruler. In keeping with its purpose, 2 Chr. stresses the influence of the priests and the Levites in the placement of Joash.

and gathered the Levites from all the
cities of Judah, and the [a]chief fathers
of Israel, and they came to Jerusalem.
3 Then all the assembly made a covenant with the king in the house of God.
And he said to them, "Behold, the
king's son shall reign, as the LORD has
[a]said of the sons of David.
4 "This *is* what you shall do: One-
third of you [a]entering on the Sabbath,
of the priests and the Levites, *shall be*
keeping watch over the doors;
5 "one-third *shall be* at the king's
house; and one-third at the Gate of the
Foundation. All the people *shall be* in
the courts of the house of the LORD.
6 "But let no one come into the house
of the LORD except the priests and
[a]those of the Levites who serve. They
may go in, for they *are* holy; but all
the people shall keep the watch of the
LORD.
7 "And the Levites shall surround the
king on all sides, every man with his
weapons in his hand; and whoever
comes into the house, let him be put
to death. You are to be with the king
when he comes in and when he goes
out."
8 So the Levites and all Judah did according to all that Jehoiada the priest
commanded. And each man took his
men who were to be on duty on the
Sabbath, with those who were going
off duty on the Sabbath; for Jehoiada
the priest had not dismissed [a]the divisions.
9 And Jehoiada the priest gave to the
captains of hundreds the spears and
the large and small [a]shields which *had
belonged* to King David, that *were* in
the temple of God.
10 Then he set all the people, every
man with his weapon in his hand, from
the right side of the temple to the left
side of the temple, along by the altar
and by the temple, all around the king.
11 And they brought out the king's
son, put the crown on him, [a]*gave him*
the [1]Testimony, and made him king.
Then Jehoiada and his sons anointed
him, and said, "*Long* live the king!"

Death of Athaliah

12 Now when [a]Athaliah heard the
noise of the people running and praising the king, she came to the people
in the temple of the LORD.
13 When she looked, there was the
king standing by his pillar at the entrance; and the leaders and the trumpeters *were* by the king. All the people
of the land were rejoicing and *blowing
trumpets, also the singers with musical
instruments, and [a]those who led in
praise. So Athaliah tore her clothes
and said, [b]"Treason! Treason!"
14 And Jehoiada the priest brought out
the captains of hundreds who were set
over the army, and said to them, "Take
her outside under guard, and slay with
the sword whoever follows her." For
the priest had said, "Do not kill her in
the house of the LORD."
15 So they seized her; and she went
by way of the entrance [a]of the Horse
Gate *into* the king's house, and they
killed her there.
16 Then Jehoiada made a [a]covenant
between himself, the people, and the
king, that they should be the LORD's
people.
17 And all the people went to the
[1]temple of Baal, and tore it down. They
broke in pieces its altars and images,
and [a]killed Mattan the priest of Baal
before the altars.
18 Also Jehoiada appointed the oversight of the house of the LORD to the
hand of the priests, the Levites, whom
David had [a]assigned in the house of
the LORD, to offer the burnt offerings
of the LORD, as *it is* written in the
[b]Law of Moses, with rejoicing and with
singing, *as it was established* by David.
19 And he set the [a]gatekeepers at the
gates of the house of the LORD, so that
no one *who was* in any way unclean
should enter.
20 [a]Then he took the captains of hundreds, the nobles, the governors of the
people, and all the people of the land,
and brought the king down from the
house of the LORD; and they went
through the Upper Gate to the king's
house, and set the king on the throne
of the kingdom.
21 So all the people of the land rejoiced; and the city was quiet, for they
had slain Athaliah with the sword.

Joash Repairs the Temple

24 Joash [a]*was* seven years old
when he became king, and
he reigned forty years in Jerusalem.

2 [a]Ezra 1:5
3 [a]2 Sam. 7:12; 1 Kin. 2:4; 9:5; 2 Chr. 6:16; 7:18; 21:7
4 [a]1 Chr. 9:25
6 [a]1 Chr. 23:28–32
8 [a]1 Chr. 24:1–31
9 [a]2 Sam. 8:7
11 [a]Deut. 17:18 [1]Law, Ex. 25:16, 21; 31:18
12 [a]2 Chr. 22:10
13 [a]1 Chr. 25:6–8 [b]2 Kin. 9:23 *See WW at Ps. 47:1.
15 [a]Neh. 3:28; Jer. 31:40
16 [a]Josh. 24:24, 25; 2 Chr. 15:12–15
17 [a]Deut. 13:6–9; 1 Kin. 18:40 [1]Lit. *house*
18 [a]1 Chr. 23:6, 30, 31; 24:1 [b]Num. 28:2
19 [a]1 Chr. 26:1–19
20 [a]1 Kin. 9:22; 2 Kin. 11:19

CHAPTER 24

1 [a]2 Kin. 11:21; 12:1–15

24:1–27 The great reform of **Joash** with his restoration of the temple, as well as his downfall and death, are also set forth in 2 Kin. 11:21—12:21. However, 2 Kin. does not record how he killed **Zechariah the son of Jehoiada** (vv. 20–22). This incident is one of the great tragedies of Scripture and is referred to in Matt. 23:35.

His mother's name *was* Zibiah of Beersheba.

2 Joash [a]did *what was* right in the sight of the LORD all the days of Jehoiada the priest.

3 And Jehoiada took two wives for him, and he had sons and daughters.

4 Now it happened after this *that* Joash set his heart on repairing the house of the LORD.

5 Then he gathered the priests and the Levites, and said to them, "Go out to the cities of Judah, and [a]gather from all Israel money to repair the house of your God from year to year, and see that you do it quickly." However the Levites did not do it quickly.

6 [a]So the king called Jehoiada the chief *priest*, and said to him, "Why have you not required the Levites to bring in from Judah and from Jerusalem the collection, *according to the commandment* of [b]Moses the servant of the LORD and of the assembly of Israel, for the [c]tabernacle of witness?"

7 For [a]the sons of Athaliah, that wicked woman, had broken into the house of God, and had also presented all the [b]dedicated things of the house of the LORD to the Baals.

8 Then at the king's command [a]they made a chest, and set it outside at the gate of the house of the LORD.

9 And they made a proclamation throughout Judah and Jerusalem to bring to the LORD [a]the collection *that* Moses the servant of God *had imposed* on Israel in the wilderness.

10 Then all the leaders and all the people rejoiced, brought their contributions, and put *them* into the chest until all had given.

11 So it was, at that time, when the chest was brought to the king's official by the hand of the Levites, and [a]when they saw that *there was* much money, that the king's scribe and the high priest's officer came and emptied the chest, and took it and returned it to its place. Thus they did day by day, and gathered money in abundance.

12 The king and Jehoiada gave it to those who did the work of the service of the house of the LORD; and they hired masons and carpenters to [a]repair the house of the LORD, and also those who worked in iron and bronze to restore the house of the LORD.

13 So the workmen labored, and the work was completed by them; they restored the house of God to its original condition and reinforced it.

14 When they had finished, they brought the rest of the money before the king and Jehoiada; [a]they made from it articles for the house of the LORD, articles for serving and offering, spoons and vessels of gold and silver. And they offered burnt offerings in the house of the LORD continually all the days of Jehoiada.

Apostasy of Joash

15 But Jehoiada grew old and was full of days, and he died; *he was* one hundred and thirty years old when he died.

16 And they buried him in the City of David among the kings, because he had done good in Israel, both toward God and His house.

17 Now after the death of Jehoiada the leaders of Judah came and bowed down to the king. And the king listened to them.

18 Therefore they left the house of the LORD God of their fathers, and served [a]wooden images and idols; and [b]wrath came upon Judah and Jerusalem because of their trespass.

19 Yet He [a]sent prophets to them, to bring them back to the LORD; and they testified against them, but they would not listen.

20 Then the *Spirit of God [1]came upon [a]Zechariah the son of Jehoiada the priest, who stood above the people, and said to them, "Thus says God: [b]'Why do you transgress the commandments of the LORD, so that you cannot prosper? [c]Because you have forsaken the LORD, He also has forsaken you.' "

21 So they conspired against him, and at the command of the king they [a]stoned him with stones in the court of the house of the LORD.

22 Thus Joash the king did not remember the kindness which Jehoiada his [1]father had done to him, but killed his son; and as he died, he said, "The LORD look on *it*, and [a]repay!"

Death of Joash

23 So it happened in the spring of the year *that* [a]the army of Syria came up against him; and they came to Judah and Jerusalem, and destroyed all the leaders of the people from among the

2 [a]2 Chr. 26:4, 5
5 [a]2 Kin. 12:4
6 [a]2 Kin. 12:7 [b]Ex. 30:12–16 [c]Num. 1:50; Acts 7:44
7 [a]2 Chr. 21:17 [b]2 Kin. 12:4
8 [a]2 Kin. 12:9
9 [a]2 Chr. 24:6
11 [a]2 Kin. 12:10
12 [a]2 Chr. 30:12
14 [a]2 Kin. 12:13
18 [a]1 Kin. 14:23 [b][Ex. 34:12–14]; Judg. 5:8; 2 Chr. 19:2; 28:13; 29:8; 32:25
19 [a]2 Kin. 17:13; 21:10–15; 2 Chr. 36:15, 16; Jer. 7:25, 26; 25:4
20 [a]Judg. 6:34; Matt. 23:35 [b]Num. 14:41; [Prov. 28:13] [c][2 Chr. 15:2] [1]Lit. *clothed* *See WW at 2 Sam. 23:2.
21 [a][Neh. 9:26]; Matt. 23:35; Acts 7:58, 59
22 [a][Gen. 9:5] [1]Foster father
23 [a]2 Kin. 12:17; Is. 7:2

24:20 Spirit of God: Read the text and note of 1 Chr. 12:18.

people, and sent all their [1]spoil to the
king of Damascus.
24 For the army of the Syrians [a]came
with a small company of men; but the
LORD [b]delivered a very great army into
their hand, because they had forsaken
the LORD God of their fathers. So they
[c]executed judgment against Joash.
25 And when they had withdrawn
from him (for they left him severely
wounded), [a]his own servants conspired against him because of the
blood of the [1]sons of Jehoiada the
priest, and killed him on his bed. So
he died. And they buried him in the
City of David, but they did not bury
him in the tombs of the kings.
26 These are the ones who conspired
against him: [1]Zabad the son of Shimeath the Ammonitess, and Jehozabad the son of [2]Shimrith the Moabitess.
27 Now *concerning* his sons, and
[a]the many oracles about him, and the
repairing of the house of God, indeed
they *are* written in the [1]annals of the
book of the kings. [b]Then Amaziah his
son reigned in his place.

Amaziah Reigns in Judah

25 Amaziah [a]*was* twenty-five
years old *when* he became king,
and he reigned twenty-nine years in Jerusalem. His mother's name *was* Jehoaddan of Jerusalem.
2 And he did *what was* right in the
sight of the LORD, [a]but not with a loyal
heart.
3 [a]Now it happened, as soon as the
kingdom was established for him, that
he executed his servants who had murdered his father the king.
4 However he did not execute their
children, but *did* as *it is* written in the
Law in the Book of Moses, where the
LORD commanded, saying, [a]"The fathers shall not be put to death for their
children, nor shall the children be put
to death for their fathers; but a person
shall die for his own sin."

The War Against Edom

5 Moreover Amaziah gathered Judah
together and set over them captains of
thousands and captains of hundreds,
according to *their* fathers' houses,
throughout all Judah and Benjamin;
and he numbered them [a]from twenty
years old and above, and found them
to be three hundred thousand choice
men, able to go to war, who could handle spear and shield.
6 He also hired one hundred thousand mighty men of valor from Israel
for one hundred talents of silver.
7 But a [a]man of God came to him,
saying, "O king, do not let the army
of Israel go with you, for the LORD *is*
not with Israel—*not with* any of the
children of Ephraim.
8 "But if you go, be gone! Be strong
in battle! *Even so,* God shall make you
fall before the enemy; for God has
[a]power to help and to overthrow."
9 Then Amaziah said to the man of **6**
God, "But what *shall we* do about the
hundred talents which I have given to
the troops of Israel?" And the man of
God answered, [a]"The LORD is able to
give you much more than this."

KINGDOM DYNAMICS

25:9 God Has Unlimited Resources, and the Good News Is That He Makes Them Available to You, SEED FAITH. In man's economy, the law of supply and demand regulates the price paid for goods and services. In times of oversupply, the prices go down; in times of shortage, the prices rise. Man's economy fluctuates with the times and the seasons.

God's economy, however, has no shortages. God's supply always equals our need. He does not want any of His people to have any lack, but rather, to "increase more and more" (see 1 Thess. 4:10–12). Do you think that if you give something to God, you will have less? Not according to God's law of Seed Faith. When you give, you have just put yourself into the position for increase!

We can never outgive God. No matter what we give to Him, He will multiply it back to us in an amount greater than we gave! Our ability to receive the harvest, however, is not automatic. Expecting to receive, not from the person to whom we give, but from God our Source, is an act of our faith also. As a farmboy I learned that to plant means to do something, and receiving the harvest likewise requires doing something! Both are acts of our faith.

(1 Kin. 17:8–16/Matt. 17:19, 20) O.R.

10 So Amaziah discharged the troops
that had come to him from Ephraim,

23 [1]*plunder*
24 [a]Lev. 26:8; [Deut. 32:30]; Is. 30:17 [b]Lev. 26:25; [Deut. 28:25] [c]2 Chr. 22:8; Is. 10:5
25 [a]2 Kin. 12:20, 21; 2 Chr. 25:3 [1]LXX, Vg. *son* and vv. 20–22
26 [1]*Jozachar,* 2 Kin. 12:21 [2]*Shomer,* 2 Kin. 12:21
27 [a]2 Kin. 12:18 [b]2 Kin. 12:21 [1]Or *commentary,* Heb. *midrash*

CHAPTER 25

1 [a]2 Kin. 14:1–6
2 [a]2 Kin. 14:4; 2 Chr. 25:14
3 [a]2 Kin. 14:5; 2 Chr. 24:25
4 [a]Deut. 24:16; 2 Kin. 14:6; Jer. 31:30; [Ezek. 18:20]
5 [a]Num. 1:3
7 [a]2 Chr. 11:2
8 [a]2 Chr. 14:11; 20:6
9 [a][Deut. 8:18]; Prov. 10:22

24:25, 26 Read the note on 1 Kin. 12:20, 21 for a solution to the apparent contradictions between this account and the one in 1 Kin. 12.

25:1–28 Read the text and notes of 2 Kin. 14 for a similar accounting of the reign of **Amaziah.** As the ninth of 20 rulers in Judah, he was a moderately good king. In his later years he succumbed to pride and picked a fight with the northern kingdom of Israel, which led to his eventual demise.

25:9 See section 6 of Truth-In-Action at the end of 2 Chr.

to go back home. Therefore their anger
was greatly aroused against Judah,
and they returned home in great anger.
11 Then Amaziah strengthened himself, and leading his people, he went
to [a]the Valley of Salt and killed ten
thousand of the people of Seir.
12 Also the children of Judah took captive ten thousand alive, brought them
to the top of the rock, and cast them
down from the top of the rock, so that
they all were dashed in pieces.
13 But as for the soldiers of the army
which Amaziah had discharged, so
that they would not go with him to battle, they raided the cities of Judah from
Samaria to Beth Horon, killed three
thousand in them, and took much
[1]spoil.
14 Now it was so, after Amaziah came
from the slaughter of the Edomites,
that [a]he brought the gods of the people
of Seir, set them up *to be* [b]his gods,
and bowed down before them and
burned incense to them.
15 Therefore the anger of the LORD
was aroused against Amaziah, and He
sent him a prophet who said to him,
"Why have you sought [a]the gods of the
people, which [b]could not rescue their
own people from your hand?"
16 So it was, as he talked with him,
that *the king* said to him, "Have we
made you the king's counselor? Cease!
Why should you be killed?" Then the
prophet ceased, and said, "I know that
God has [a]determined to destroy you,
because you have done this and have
not heeded my advice."

Israel Defeats Judah

17 Now [a]Amaziah king of Judah asked
advice and sent to [1]Joash the son of
Jehoahaz, the son of Jehu, king of Israel, saying, "Come, let us face one another *in battle*."
18 And Joash king of Israel sent to
Amaziah king of Judah, saying, "The
thistle that *was* in Lebanon sent to the
cedar that was in Lebanon, saying,
'Give your daughter to my son as wife';
and a wild beast that *was* in Lebanon
passed by and trampled the thistle.
19 "Indeed you say that you have defeated the Edomites, and your heart is
lifted up to [a]boast. Stay at home now;
why should you meddle with trouble,
that you should fall—you and Judah
with you?"
20 But Amaziah would not heed, for
[a]it *came* from God, that He might give
them into the hand *of their enemies*,
because they [b]sought the gods of
Edom.
21 So Joash king of Israel went out;
and he and Amaziah king of Judah
faced one another at [a]Beth Shemesh,
which *belongs* to Judah.
22 And Judah was defeated by Israel,
and every man fled to his tent.
23 Then Joash the king of Israel captured Amaziah king of Judah, the son
of Joash, the son of [a]Jehoahaz, at Beth
Shemesh; and he brought him to Jerusalem, and broke down the wall of Jerusalem from the Gate of Ephraim to
the Corner Gate—four hundred cubits.
24 And *he took* all the gold and silver,
all the articles that were found in the
house of God with [a]Obed-Edom, the
treasures of the king's house, and hostages, and returned to Samaria.

Death of Amaziah

25 [a]Amaziah the son of Joash, king of
Judah, lived fifteen years after the
death of Joash the son of Jehoahaz,
king of Israel.
26 Now the rest of the acts of Amaziah,
from first to last, indeed *are* they not
written in the book of the kings of Judah and Israel?
27 After the time that Amaziah turned
away from following the LORD, they
made a conspiracy against him in Jerusalem, and he fled to Lachish; but they
sent after him to Lachish and killed
him there.
28 Then they brought him on horses
and buried him with his fathers in
[1]the City of Judah.

Uzziah Reigns in Judah

26 Now all the people of Judah
took [1]Uzziah, who *was* sixteen
years old, and made him king instead
of his father Amaziah.
2 He built [1]Elath and restored it to Judah, after the king rested with his fathers.
3 Uzziah *was* sixteen years old when

11 [a]2 Kin. 14:7
13 [1]*plunder*
14 [a]2 Chr. 28:23 [b][Ex. 20:3, 5]
15 [a][Ps. 96:5] [b]2 Chr. 25:11
16 [a][1 Sam. 2:25]
17 [a]2 Kin. 14:8–14 [1]*Jehoash,* 2 Kin. 14:8ff.
19 [a]2 Chr. 26:16; 32:25; [Prov. 16:18]
20 [a]1 Kin. 12:15; 2 Chr. 22:7 [b]2 Chr. 25:14
21 [a]Josh. 19:38
23 [a]2 Chr. 21:17; 22:1, 6
24 [a]1 Chr. 26:15
25 [a]2 Kin. 14:17–22
28 [1]The City of David

CHAPTER 26

1 [1]*Azariah,* 2 Kin. 14:21ff.
2 [1]Heb. *Eloth*

26:1–23 This chapter amplifies the very brief account of **King Uzziah** (or Azariah) in 2 Kin. 15:1–7. As Judah's tenth ruler, Uzziah begins strong and well. He was a resourceful king, taking special care for the livestock (v. 10) and equipping his armies with the latest in military devices (vv. 14, 15). However, his toleration of idolatry and his pride set the stage for his undoing. Uzziah attempted to take the role of a priest (v. 16) and was stricken with **leprosy** (v. 19). This is the king mentioned in Is. 6:1.

he became king, and he reigned fifty-
two years in Jerusalem. His mother's
name was Jecholiah of Jerusalem.
4 And he did *what was* [a]right in the
sight of the LORD, according to all that
his father Amaziah had done.
5 [a]He sought God in the days of Zechariah, who [b]had understanding in the
[1]visions of God; and as long as he
sought the LORD, God made him
[c]prosper.
6 Now he went out and [a]made war
against the Philistines, and broke
down the wall of Gath, the wall of Jab-
neh, and the wall of Ashdod; and he
built cities *around* Ashdod and among
the Philistines.
7 God helped him against [a]the Philistines, against the Arabians who
lived in Gur Baal, and against the
Meunites.
8 Also the Ammonites [a]brought tribute to Uzziah. His fame spread as far
as the entrance of Egypt, for he became
exceedingly strong.
9 And Uzziah built towers in Jerusalem at the [a]Corner Gate, at the Valley
Gate, and at the corner buttress of the
wall; then he *fortified them.
10 Also he built towers in the desert.
He dug many wells, for he had much
livestock, both in the lowlands and in
the plains; *he also had* farmers and
vinedressers in the mountains and in
[1]Carmel, for he loved the soil.
11 Moreover Uzziah had an army of
fighting men who went out to war by
companies, according to the number
on their roll as prepared by Jeiel the
scribe and Maaseiah the officer, under
the hand of Hananiah, *one* of the king's
captains.
12 The total number of [1]chief officers
of the mighty men of valor *was* two
thousand six hundred.
13 And under their authority *was* an
army of three hundred and seven thousand five hundred, that made war with
mighty power, to help the king against
the enemy.
14 Then Uzziah prepared for them, for
the entire army, shields, spears, helmets, body armor, bows, and slings *to
cast* stones.
15 And he made devices in Jerusalem,
invented by [a]skillful men, to be on the
towers and the corners, to shoot arrows and large stones. So his fame
spread far and wide, for he was marvelously helped till he became strong.

4 [a]2 Chr. 24:2
5 [a]2 Chr. 24:2 [b]Gen. 41:15; Dan. 1:17; 10:1 [c][2 Chr. 15:2; 20:20; 31:21] [1]Heb. mss., LXX, Syr., Tg., Arab. *fear*
6 [a]Is. 14:29
7 [a]2 Chr. 21:16
8 [a]2 Sam. 8:2; 2 Chr. 17:11
9 [a]2 Kin. 14:13; 2 Chr. 25:23; Neh. 3:13, 19, 32; Zech. 14:10 *See WW at Josh. 1:9.
10 [1]Or *the fertile fields*
12 [1]Lit. *chief fathers*
15 [a]Ex. 39:3, 8

The Penalty for Uzziah's Pride

16 But [a]when he was strong his heart 3
was [b]lifted up, to *his* destruction, for
he transgressed against the LORD his
God [c]by entering the temple of the
LORD to burn incense on the altar of
incense.
17 So [a]Azariah the priest went in after
him, and with him were eighty priests
of the LORD—valiant men.
18 And they withstood King Uzziah,
and said to him, "*It* [a]*is* not for you, Uzziah, to burn incense to the LORD, but
for the [b]priests, the sons of Aaron, who
are consecrated to burn incense. Get
out of the sanctuary, for you have trespassed! You *shall have* no honor from
the LORD God."
19 Then Uzziah became furious; and
he *had* a censer in his hand to burn
incense. And while he was angry with
the priests, [a]leprosy broke out on his
forehead, before the priests in the
house of the LORD, beside the incense
altar.
20 And Azariah the chief priest and all
the priests looked at him, and there,
on his forehead, he *was* leprous; so
they thrust him out of that place. Indeed he also [a]hurried to get out, because the LORD had struck him.
21 [a]King Uzziah was a leper until the
day of his death. He dwelt in an
[b]isolated house, because he was a
leper; for he was cut off from the house
of the LORD. Then Jotham his son *was*
over the king's house, judging the people of the land.
22 Now the rest of the acts of Uzziah,
from first to last, the prophet [a]Isaiah
the son of Amoz wrote.
23 [a]So Uzziah [1]rested with his fathers,
and they buried him with his fathers
in the field of burial which *belonged*
to the kings, for they said, "He is a
leper." Then Jotham his son reigned
in his place.

Jotham Reigns in Judah

27 Jotham [a]*was* twenty-five years
old when he became king, and
he reigned sixteen years in Jerusalem.
His mother's name *was* [1]Jerushah the
daughter of Zadok.
2 And he did *what was* right in the
sight of the LORD, according to all that
his father Uzziah had done (although
he did not enter the temple of the

16 [a][Deut. 32:15] [b]Deut. 8:14; 2 Chr. 25:19 [c]1 Kin. 13:1–4; 2 Kin. 16:12, 13
17 [a]1 Chr. 6:10
18 [a][Num. 3:10; 16:39, 40; 18:7] [b]Ex. 30:7, 8; Heb. 7:14
19 [a]Lev. 13:42; Num. 12:10; 2 Kin. 5:25–27
20 [a]Esth. 6:12
21 [a]2 Kin. 15:5 [b][Lev. 13:46; Num. 5:2]
22 [a]2 Kin. 20:1; 2 Chr. 32:20, 32; Is. 1:1
23 [a]2 Kin. 15:7; 2 Chr. 21:20; 28:27; Is. 6:1 [1]Died and joined his ancestors

CHAPTER 27

1 [a]2 Kin. 15:32–35 [1]*Jerusha*, 2 Kin. 15:33

26:16 See section 3 of Truth-In-Action at the end of 2 Chr.
27:1–9 A report of **Jotham,** Judah's eleventh ruler, is also found in 2 Kin. 15:32–38. He was a politically astute ruler because he **prepared** [established] **his ways before the LORD** (v. 6), but he allowed for continued religious mixture.

LORD). But still [a]the people acted corruptly.
3 He built the Upper Gate of the house of the LORD, and he built extensively on the wall of [a]Ophel.
4 Moreover he built cities in the mountains of Judah, and in the forests he built fortresses and towers.
5 He also fought with the king of the [a]Ammonites and defeated them. And the people of Ammon gave him in that year one hundred talents of silver, ten thousand kors of wheat, and ten thousand of barley. The people of Ammon paid this to him in the second and third years also.
6 So Jotham became mighty, [a]because he prepared his ways before the LORD his God.
7 Now the rest of the acts of Jotham, and all his wars and his ways, indeed they *are* written in the book of the kings of Israel and Judah.
8 He was twenty-five years old when he became king, and he reigned sixteen years in Jerusalem.
9 [a]So Jotham [1]rested with his fathers, and they buried him in the City of David. Then [b]Ahaz his son reigned in his place.

Ahaz Reigns in Judah

28 Ahaz [a]*was* twenty years old when he became king, and he reigned sixteen years in Jerusalem; and he did not do *what was* right in the sight of the LORD, as his father David *had done*.
2 For he walked in the ways of the kings of Israel, and made [a]molded images for [b]the Baals.
3 He burned incense in [a]the Valley of the Son of Hinnom, and burned [b]his children in the [c]fire, according to the abominations of the nations whom the LORD had [d]cast out before the children of Israel.
4 And he sacrificed and burned incense on the [1]high places, on the hills, and under every green tree.

Syria and Israel Defeat Judah

5 Therefore [a]the LORD his God delivered him into the hand of the king of Syria. They [b]defeated him, and carried away a great multitude of them as captives, and brought *them* to Damascus. Then he was also delivered into the hand of the king of Israel, who defeated him with a great slaughter.
6 For [a]Pekah the son of Remaliah killed one hundred and twenty thousand in Judah in one day, all valiant men, [b]because they had forsaken the LORD God of their fathers.
7 Zichri, a mighty man of Ephraim, killed Maaseiah the king's son, Azrikam the officer over the house, and Elkanah *who was* second to the king.
8 And the children of Israel carried away captive of their [a]brethren two hundred thousand women, sons, and daughters; and they also took away much [1]spoil from them, and brought the spoil to Samaria.

Israel Returns the Captives

9 But a [a]prophet of the LORD was there, whose name *was* Oded; and he went out before the army that came to Samaria, and said to them: "Look, [b]because the LORD God of your fathers was angry with Judah, He has delivered them into your hand; but you have killed them in a rage *that* [c]reaches up to heaven.
10 "And now you propose to force the children of Judah and Jerusalem to be your [a]male and female slaves; *but are* you not also guilty before the LORD your God?
11 "Now hear me, therefore, and return the captives, whom you have taken captive from your brethren, [a]for the fierce wrath of the LORD *is* upon you."
12 Then some of the heads of the children of Ephraim, Azariah the son of Johanan, Berechiah the son of Meshillemoth, Jehizkiah the son of Shallum, and Amasa the son of Hadlai, stood up against those who came from the war,
13 and said to them, "You shall not bring the captives here, for we *already* have offended the LORD. You intend to add to our sins and to our guilt; for our guilt is great, and *there is* fierce wrath against Israel."
14 So the armed men left the captives and the [1]spoil before the leaders and all the assembly.
15 Then the men [a]who were designated by name rose up and took the captives, and from the [1]spoil they clothed all who were naked among them, dressed them and gave them sandals, [b]gave them food and drink,

2 [a]2 Kin. 15:35; Ezek. 20:44; 30:13
3 [a]2 Chr. 33:14; Neh. 3:26
5 [a]2 Chr. 26:8
6 [a]2 Chr. 26:5
9 [a]2 Kin. 15:38 [b]Is. 1:1; Hos. 1:1; Mic. 1:1 [1]Died and joined his ancestors

CHAPTER 28

1 [a]2 Kin. 16:2–4
2 [a]Ex. 34:17; Lev. 19:4 [b]Judg. 2:11
3 [a]Josh. 15:8 [b]2 Kin. 23:10 [c][Lev. 18:21]; 2 Kin. 16:3; 2 Chr. 33:6 [d][Lev. 18:24–30]
4 [1]Places for pagan worship
5 [a][Is. 10:5] [b]2 Kin. 16:5, 6; [2 Chr. 24:24]; Is. 7:1, 17
6 [a]2 Kin. 15:27 [b][2 Chr. 29:8]
8 [a]Deut. 28:25, 41; 2 Chr. 11:4 [1]*plunder*
9 [a]2 Chr. 25:15 [b]Ps. 69:26; [Is. 10:5; 47:6]; Ezek. 25:12, 15; 26:2; Obad. 10; [Zech. 1:15] [c]Ezra 9:6; Rev. 18:5
10 [a][Lev. 25:39, 42, 43, 46]
11 [a]Ps. 78:49; James 2:13
14 [1]*plunder*
15 [a]2 Chr. 28:12 [b][Prov. 25:21, 22; Luke 6:27; Rom. 12:20] [1]*plunder*

28:1–27 Jotham was succeeded by his son **Ahaz,** who was Judah's twelfth ruler. Read the text and notes of 2 Kin. 16 and Is. 7 for more information on the reign of this wicked king. The **king of Syria** mentioned in v. 5 was Rezin.

and anointed them; and they let all the
feeble ones ride on donkeys. So they
brought them to their brethren at Jericho, [c]the city of palm trees. Then they
returned to Samaria.

Assyria Refuses to Help Judah

16 [a]At the same time King Ahaz sent
to the [1]kings of Assyria to help him.
17 For again the [a]Edomites had come,
attacked Judah, and carried away captives.
18 [a]The Philistines also had invaded
the cities of the lowland and of the
South of Judah, and had taken Beth
Shemesh, Aijalon, Gederoth, Sochoh
with its villages, Timnah with its villages, and Gimzo with its villages; and
they dwelt there.
19 For the LORD [1]brought Judah low
because of Ahaz king of [a]Israel, for he
had [b]encouraged moral decline in Judah and had been continually unfaithful to the LORD.
20 Also [a]Tiglath-Pileser[1] king of Assyria came to him and distressed him,
and did not assist him.
21 For Ahaz took part *of the treasures*
from the house of the LORD, from the
house of the king, and from the leaders, and he gave *it* to the king of Assyria; but he did not help him.

Apostasy and Death of Ahaz

22 Now in the time of his distress King
Ahaz became increasingly unfaithful
to the LORD. This *is that* King Ahaz.
[1] 23 For [a]he sacrificed to the gods of Damascus which had defeated him, saying, "Because the gods of the kings of
Syria help them, I will sacrifice to them
[b]that they may help me." But they were
the ruin of him and of all Israel.
24 So Ahaz gathered the articles of the
house of God, cut in pieces the articles
of the house of God, [a]shut up the doors
of the house of the LORD, and made for
himself altars in every corner of Jerusalem.
25 And in every single city of Judah
he made [1]high places to burn incense
to other gods, and provoked to anger
the LORD God of his fathers.
26 [a]Now the rest of his acts and all his
ways, from first to last, indeed they *are*
written in the book of the kings of Judah and Israel.
27 So Ahaz [1]rested with his fathers,
and they buried him in the city, in Jerusalem; but they [a]did not bring him into
the tombs of the kings of Israel. Then
Hezekiah his son reigned in his place.

Hezekiah Reigns in Judah

29 Hezekiah [a]became king *when*
he was twenty-five years old,
and he reigned twenty-nine years in Jerusalem. His mother's name *was*
[1]Abijah the daughter of Zechariah.
2 And he did *what was* right in the
sight of the LORD, according to all that
his father David had done.

Hezekiah Cleanses the Temple

3 In the first year of his reign, in the
first month, he [a]opened the doors of
the house of the LORD and repaired
them.
4 Then he brought in the priests and
the Levites, and gathered them in the
East Square,
5 and said to them: "Hear me, Levites! Now [1]sanctify yourselves, [a]sanc-
tify the house of the LORD God of your
fathers, and carry out the rubbish from
the holy *place*.
6 "For our fathers have trespassed
and done evil in the eyes of the LORD
our God; they have forsaken Him, have
[a]turned their faces away from the
[1]dwelling place of the LORD, and turned
their backs *on Him*.
7 [a]"They have also shut up the doors
of the vestibule, put out the lamps, and
have not burned incense or offered
burnt offerings in the holy *place* to the
God of Israel.
8 "Therefore the [a]wrath of the LORD
fell upon Judah and Jerusalem, and He
has [b]given them up to trouble, to desolation, and to [c]jeering, as you see with
your [d]eyes.
9 "For indeed, because of this [a]our fathers have fallen by the sword; and our
sons, our daughters, and our wives *are*
in captivity.
10 "Now *it is* in my heart to make
[a]a covenant with the LORD God of Israel, that His fierce wrath may turn
away from us.
11 "My sons, do not be negligent now,

15 [c]Deut. 34:3; Judg. 1:16 **16** [a]2 Kin. 16:7 [1]LXX, Syr., Vg. *king* (cf. v. 20) **17** [a]2 Chr. 21:10; Obad. 10–14 **18** [a]2 Chr. 21:16, 17; Ezek. 16:27, 57 **19** [a]2 Kin. 16:2; 2 Chr. 21:2 [b]Ex. 32:25 [1]*humbled Judah* **20** [a]2 Kin. 15:29; 16:7–9; 1 Chr. 5:26 [1]Heb. *Tilgath-Pilneser* **23** [a]2 Chr. 25:14 [b]Jer. 44:17, 18 **24** [a]2 Chr. 29:3, 7 **25** [1]Places for pagan worship **26** [a]2 Kin. 16:19, 20

27 [a]2 Chr. 21:20; 24:25 [1]Died and joined his ancestors

CHAPTER 29

1 [a]2 Kin. 18:1; 2 Chr. 32:22, 33 [1]*Abi*, 2 Kin. 18:2 **3** [a]2 Chr. 28:24; 29:7 **5** [a]1 Chr. 15:12; 2 Chr. 29:15, 34; 35:6 [1]*consecrate* **6** [a][Is. 1:4]; Jer. 2:27; Ezek. 8:16 [1]Temple **7** [a]2 Chr. 28:24 **8** [a]2 Chr. 24:18 [b]2 Chr. 28:5 [c]1 Kin. 9:8; Jer. 18:16; 19:8; 25:9, 18; 29:18 [d]Deut. 28:32 **9** [a]Deut. 28:25; 2 Chr. 28:5–8, 17 **10** [a]2 Chr. 15:12; 23:16

28:23 See section 1 of Truth-In-Action at the end of 2 Chr.

28:24 The **altars** that **Ahaz** built here were to pagan gods, not to the Lord.

29:1–36 The impressive and godly reign of **Hezekiah** is also recorded in 2 Kin. 18—20. The first item on the agenda of this thirteenth ruler of Judah was to cleanse and restore the temple. This vital account is absent from the narrative of 2 Kin., but the chronicler gives a detailed account of these events because they exemplify the reason for Hezekiah's success.

for the LORD has [a]chosen you to stand before Him, to serve Him, and that you should minister to Him and burn incense."

12 Then these Levites arose: [a]Mahath the son of Amasai and Joel the son of Azariah, of the sons of the [b]Kohathites; of the sons of Merari, Kish the son of Abdi and Azariah the son of Jehallelel; of the Gershonites, Joah the son of Zimmah and Eden the son of Joah;

13 of the sons of Elizaphan, Shimri and Jeiel; of the sons of Asaph, Zechariah and Mattaniah;

14 of the sons of Heman, Jehiel and Shimei; and of the sons of Jeduthun, Shemaiah and Uzziel.

15 And they gathered their brethren, [a]sanctified[1] themselves, and went according to the commandment of the king, at the words of the LORD, [b]to cleanse the house of the LORD.

16 Then the priests went into the inner part of the house of the LORD to cleanse *it,* and brought out all the debris that they found in the temple of the LORD to the court of the house of the LORD. And the Levites took *it* out and carried *it* to the Brook [a]Kidron.

17 Now they began to [1]sanctify on the first *day* of the first month, and on the eighth day of the month they came to the vestibule of the LORD. So they sanctified the house of the LORD in eight days, and on the sixteenth day of the first month they finished.

18 Then they went in to King Hezekiah and said, "We have *cleansed all the house of the LORD, the altar of burnt offerings with all its articles, and the table of the showbread with all its articles.

19 "Moreover all the articles which King Ahaz in his reign had [a]cast aside in his transgression we have prepared and [1]sanctified; and there they *are,* before the altar of the LORD."

Hezekiah Restores Temple Worship

20 Then King Hezekiah rose early, gathered the rulers of the city, and went up to the house of the LORD.

21 And they brought seven bulls, seven rams, seven lambs, and seven male goats for a [a]sin* offering for the kingdom, for the sanctuary, and for Judah. Then he commanded the priests, the sons of Aaron, to offer *them* on the altar of the LORD.

22 So they killed the bulls, and the priests received the blood and [a]sprinkled *it* on the altar. Likewise they killed the rams and sprinkled the blood on the altar. They also killed the lambs and sprinkled the blood on the altar.

23 Then they brought out the male goats *for* the sin offering before the king and the assembly, and they laid their [a]hands on them.

24 And the priests killed them; and they presented their blood on the altar as a sin offering [a]to make an atonement for all Israel, for the king commanded *that* the burnt offering and the sin offering *be made* for all Israel.

25 [a]And he stationed the Levites in the house of the LORD with cymbals, with stringed instruments, and with harps, [b]according to the commandment of David, of [c]Gad the king's seer, and of Nathan the prophet; [d]for thus *was* the commandment of the LORD by His prophets.

26 The Levites stood with the instruments [a]of David, and the priests with [b]the trumpets.

27 Then Hezekiah commanded *them* to offer the burnt offering on the altar. And when the burnt offering began, [a]the song of the LORD *also* began, with the trumpets and with the instruments of David king of Israel.

28 So all the assembly worshiped, the singers sang, and the trumpeters sounded; all *this continued* until the burnt offering was finished.

29 And when they had finished offering, [a]the king and all who were present with him bowed and worshiped.

30 Moreover King Hezekiah and the leaders commanded the Levites to sing praise to the LORD with the words of David and of Asaph the seer. So they sang praises with gladness, and they bowed their heads and worshiped.

31 Then Hezekiah answered and said, "Now *that* you have consecrated yourselves to the LORD, come near, and bring sacrifices and [a]thank offerings into the house of the LORD." So the assembly brought in sacrifices and thank offerings, and as many as were of a [b]willing heart *brought* burnt offerings.

32 And the number of the burnt offerings which the assembly brought was seventy bulls, one hundred rams, *and*

11 [a]Num. 3:6; 8:14; 18:2, 6; 2 Chr. 30:16, 17
12 [a]2 Chr. 31:13 [b]Num. 3:19, 20
15 [a]2 Chr. 29:5 [b]1 Chr. 23:28 [1]*consecrated*
16 [a]2 Chr. 15:16; 30:14
17 [1]*consecrate*
18 *See WW at Lev. 14:31.
19 [a]2 Chr. 28:24 [1]*consecrated*
21 [a]Lev. 4:3–14 *See WW at Lev. 9:2.
22 [a]Lev. 8:14, 15, 19, 24; Heb. 9:21
23 [a]Lev. 4:15, 24; 8:14
24 [a]Lev. 14:20
25 [a]1 Chr. 16:4; 25:6 [b]1 Chr. 23:5; 25:1; 2 Chr. 8:14 [c]2 Sam. 24:11 [d]2 Chr. 30:12
26 [a]1 Chr. 23:5; Amos 6:5 [b]Num. 10:8, 10; 1 Chr. 15:24; 16:6; 2 Chr. 5:12
27 [a]2 Chr. 23:18
29 [a]2 Chr. 20:18
31 [a]Lev. 7:12 [b]Ex. 35:5, 22

29:27, 28 An indispensable part of the worship of the Lord was the singing of praises and playing of **instruments** (even loudly, 30:21). This has been true of the worship of God throughout the ages. For further insight on the power of singing, read the text and notes on 20:22, 23.

two hundred lambs; all these *were* for a burnt offering to the LORD.

33 The consecrated things *were* six hundred bulls and three thousand sheep.

34 But the priests were too few, so that they could not skin all the burnt offerings; therefore [a]their brethren the Levites helped them until the work was ended and until the *other* priests had [1]sanctified themselves, [b]for the Levites were [c]more diligent in [d]sanctifying themselves than the priests.

35 Also the burnt offerings *were* in abundance, with [a]the fat of the peace offerings and *with* [b]the drink offerings for *every* burnt offering. So the service of the house of the LORD was set in order.

36 Then Hezekiah and all the people rejoiced that God had prepared the people, since the events took place so suddenly.

Hezekiah Keeps the Passover

30 And Hezekiah sent to all Israel and Judah, and also wrote letters to Ephraim and Manasseh, that they should come to the house of the LORD at Jerusalem, to keep the Passover to the LORD God of Israel.

2 For the king and his leaders and all the assembly in Jerusalem had agreed to keep the Passover in the second [a]month.

3 For they could not keep it [a]at [1]the regular time, [b]because a sufficient number of priests had not consecrated themselves, nor had the people gathered together at Jerusalem.

4 And the matter pleased the king and all the assembly.

5 So they [1]resolved to make a proclamation throughout all Israel, from Beersheba to Dan, that they should come to keep the Passover to the LORD God of Israel at Jerusalem, since they had not done *it* for a long *time* in the *prescribed* manner.

6 Then the [a]runners went throughout all Israel and Judah with the letters from the king and his leaders, and spoke according to the command of the king: "Children of Israel, [b]return to the LORD God of Abraham, Isaac, and Israel; then He will return to the remnant of you who have escaped from the hand of [c]the kings of [d]Assyria.

7 "And do not be [a]like your fathers and your brethren, who trespassed against the LORD God of their fathers, so that He [b]gave them up to [c]desolation, as you see.

8 "Now do not be [a]stiff-necked,[1] as your fathers *were, but* yield yourselves to the LORD; and enter His sanctuary, which He has sanctified forever, and serve the LORD your God, [b]that the fierceness of His wrath may turn away from you.

9 "For if you return to the LORD, your brethren and your children *will be treated* with [a]compassion by those who lead them captive, so that they may come back to this land; for the LORD your God *is* [b]gracious and merciful, and will not turn *His* face from you if you [c]return to Him."

10 So the runners passed from city to city through the country of Ephraim and Manasseh, as far as Zebulun; but [a]they *laughed at them and mocked them.

11 Nevertheless [a]some from Asher, Manasseh, and Zebulun humbled themselves and came to Jerusalem.

12 Also [a]the hand of God was on Judah to give them singleness of heart to obey the command of the king and the leaders, [b]at the word of the LORD.

13 Now many people, a very great assembly, gathered at Jerusalem to keep the Feast of [a]Unleavened Bread in the second month.

14 They arose and took away the [a]altars that *were* in Jerusalem, and they took away all the incense altars and cast *them* into the Brook [b]Kidron.

15 Then they slaughtered the Passover *lambs* on the fourteenth *day* of the second month. The priests and the Levites [1]were [a]ashamed, and [2]sanctified themselves, and brought the burnt offerings to the house of the LORD.

16 They stood in their [a]place [1]according to their custom, according to the Law of Moses the man of God; the priests sprinkled the blood *received* from the hand of the Levites.

17 For *there were* many in the assembly who had not [1]sanctified them-

34 [a]2 Chr. 35:11 [b]2 Chr. 30:3 [c]Ps. 7:10 [d]2 Chr. 29:5 [1]*consecrated*
35 [a]Lev. 3:15, 16 [b]Num. 15:5–10

CHAPTER 30

2 [a]Num. 9:10, 11; 2 Chr. 30:13, 15
3 [a]Ex. 12:6, 18 [b]2 Chr. 29:17, 34 [1]The first month, Lev. 23:5; lit. *that time*
5 [1]*established a decree to*
6 [a]Esth. 8:14; Job 9:25; Jer. 51:31 [b][Jer. 4:1; Joel 2:13] [c]2 Kin. 15:19, 29 [d]2 Chr. 28:20
7 [a]Ezek. 20:18 [b]Is. 1:9 [c]2 Chr. 29:8
8 [a]Ex. 32:9; Deut. 10:16; Acts 7:51 [b]2 Chr. 29:10 [1]Rebellious
9 [a]Ps. 106:46 [b][Ex. 34:6; Mic. 7:18] [c][Is. 55:7]
10 [a]2 Chr. 36:16 *See WW at Eccl. 3:4.
11 [a]2 Chr. 11:16; 30:18, 21
12 [a][2 Cor. 3:5; Phil. 2:13; Heb. 13:20, 21] [b]2 Chr. 29:25
13 [a]Lev. 23:6; Num. 9:11
14 [a]2 Chr. 28:24 [b]2 Chr. 29:16
15 [a]2 Chr. 29:34 [1]*humbled themselves* [2]*set themselves apart*
16 [a]2 Chr. 35:10, 15 [1]Or *in their proper order*
17 [1]*consecrated*

30:1–27 The second item on Hezekiah's agenda for reform was to celebrate the **Passover** with a vigor that had not been seen since the reign of Solomon (v. 26). He even invited the Israelites in the northern kingdom (vv. 5, 6) and extended the festivities another week (v. 23). To understand better the origin and meaning of the Passover, see notes on Ex. 12:1–11. This incident is also omitted by the author of 2 Kin. (2 Kin. 18—20), but for the chronicler this action by **Hezekiah** gives a further reason why he experienced the blessing of the Lord.

selves; [a]therefore the Levites had
charge of the slaughter of the Passover
lambs for everyone *who was* not clean,
to sanctify *them* to the LORD.
18 For a multitude of the people,
[a]many from Ephraim, Manasseh, Issachar, and Zebulun, had not cleansed
themselves, [b]yet they ate the Passover
contrary to what was written. But Hezekiah prayed for them, saying, "May
the good LORD provide atonement for
everyone
19 "*who* [a]prepares his heart to seek
God, the LORD God of his fathers,
though *he is* not *cleansed* according to
the purification of the sanctuary."
20 And the LORD listened to Hezekiah
and healed the people.
21 So the children of Israel who were
present at Jerusalem kept [a]the Feast
of Unleavened Bread seven days with
great gladness; and the Levites and the
priests praised the LORD day by day,
singing to the LORD, accompanied by
loud instruments.
22 And Hezekiah gave encouragement
to all the Levites [a]who taught the good
knowledge of the LORD; and they ate
throughout the *feast seven days, offering peace offerings and [b]making
confession to the LORD God of their fathers.
23 Then the whole *assembly agreed
to keep *the feast* [a]another seven days,
and they kept it *another* seven days
with gladness.
24 For Hezekiah king of Judah [a]gave
to the assembly a thousand bulls and
seven thousand sheep, and the leaders
gave to the assembly a thousand bulls
and ten thousand sheep; and a great
number of priests [b]sanctified[1] themselves.
25 The whole assembly of Judah rejoiced, also the priests and Levites, all
the assembly that came from Israel, the
sojourners [a]who came from the land
of Israel, and those who dwelt in Judah.
26 So there was great joy in Jerusalem,
for since the time of [a]Solomon the son
of David, king of Israel, *there had* been
nothing like this in Jerusalem.
27 Then the priests, the Levites, arose
and [a]blessed the people, and their
voice was heard; and their prayer came
up to [b]His holy dwelling place, to
heaven.

17 [a]2 Chr. 29:34 **18** [a]2 Chr. 30:1, 11, 25 [b]Ex. 12:43–49; [Num. 9:10] **19** [a]2 Chr. 19:3 **21** [a]Ex. 12:15; 13:6; 1 Kin. 8:65 **22** [a][Deut. 33:10]; 2 Chr. 17:9; 35:3 [b]Ezra 10:11 *See WW at Num. 9:2. **23** [a]1 Kin. 8:65; 2 Chr. 35:17, 18 *See WW at Lev. 16:17. **24** [a]2 Chr. 35:7, 8 [b]2 Chr. 29:34 [1]*consecrated* **25** [a]2 Chr. 30:11, 18 **26** [a]2 Chr. 7:8–10 **27** [a]Num. 6:23 [b]Deut. 26:15; Ps. 68:5

CHAPTER 31

1 [a]2 Kin. 18:4 [1]Places for pagan worship *See WW at Josh. 22:9. **2** [a]1 Chr. 23:6; 24:1 [b]1 Chr. 23:30, 31 [1]Temple **3** [a]2 Chr. 35:7 [b]Num. 28:1—29:40 [1]*share* [2]*property* **4** [a]Num. 18:8; 2 Kin. 12:16; Neh. 13:10; Ezek. 44:29 [b]Mal. 2:7 [1]*the portion due* **5** [a]Ex. 22:29; Neh. 13:12 [b][Lev. 27:30]; Deut. 14:28; 26:12, 13 **6** [a][Lev. 27:30]; Deut. 14:28 **10** [a]1 Chr. 6:8, 9 [b][Mal. 3:10]

The Reforms of Hezekiah

31 Now when all this was finished,
all Israel who were present
went out to the cities of Judah and
[a]broke the *sacred* pillars in pieces, cut
down the wooden images, and threw
down the [1]high places and the altars—
from all Judah, Benjamin, Ephraim,
and Manasseh—until they had utterly
destroyed them all. Then all the children of Israel returned to their own cities, every man to his *possession.
2 And Hezekiah appointed [a]the divisions of the priests and the Levites according to their divisions, each man according to his service, the priests and
Levites [b]for burnt offerings and peace
offerings, to serve, to give thanks, and
to praise in the gates of the [1]camp of
the LORD.
3 The king also *appointed* a [1]portion
of his [a]possessions[2] for the burnt offerings: for the morning and evening
burnt offerings, the burnt offerings for
the Sabbaths and the New Moons and
the set feasts, as *it is* written in the
[b]Law of the LORD.
4 Moreover he commanded the people who dwelt in Jerusalem to contribute [a]support[1] for the priests and the
Levites, that they might devote themselves to [b]the Law of the LORD.
5 As soon as the commandment was
circulated, the children of Israel
brought in abundance [a]the firstfruits
of grain and wine, oil and honey, and
of all the produce of the field; and they
brought in abundantly the [b]tithe of everything.
6 And the children of Israel and Judah, who dwelt in the cities of Judah,
brought the tithe of oxen and sheep;
also the [a]tithe of holy things which
were consecrated to the LORD their God
they laid in heaps.
7 In the third month they began laying them in heaps, and they finished
in the seventh month.
8 And when Hezekiah and the leaders
came and saw the heaps, they blessed
the LORD and His people Israel.
9 Then Hezekiah questioned the
priests and the Levites concerning the
heaps.
10 And Azariah the chief priest, from
the [a]house of Zadok, answered him
and said, [b]"Since *the people* began to

30:19 2 Chr. affirms that though proper form is important, it is primarily the attitude of the heart that matters to the Lord.
30:21 The priority and importance of worshiping the Lord with singing is again stressed (see 20:22, 23; 29:27).
31:1–21 Much of this chapter also is not to be found in the account of **Hezekiah** in the Books of Kings (2 Kin. 18—20). That the priests resumed their duties (vv. 2–4, 14–19) and that the people gave tithes and offerings were all part of the reason the reign of Hezekiah was so prosperous.

bring the offerings into the house of the LORD, we have had enough to eat and have plenty left, for the LORD has blessed His people; and what is left *is* this great [c]abundance."

11 Now Hezekiah commanded *them* to prepare [a]rooms[1] in the house of the LORD, and they prepared them.

12 Then they faithfully brought in the offerings, the tithes, and the dedicated things; [a]Cononiah the Levite had charge of them, and Shimei his brother *was* the next.

13 Jehiel, Azaziah, Nahath, Asahel, Jerimoth, Jozabad, Eliel, Ismachiah, Mahath, and Benaiah *were* overseers under the hand of Cononiah and Shimei his brother, at the commandment of Hezekiah the king and Azariah the [a]ruler of the house of God.

14 Kore the son of Imnah the Levite, the keeper of the East Gate, *was* over the [a]freewill offerings to God, to distribute the offerings of the LORD and the most holy things.

15 And under him *were* [a]Eden, Miniamin, Jeshua, Shemaiah, Amariah, and Shecaniah, *his* faithful assistants in [b]the cities of the priests, to distribute [c]allotments to their brethren by divisions, to the great as well as the small.

16 Besides those males from three years old and up who were written in the genealogy, they distributed to everyone who entered the house of the LORD his daily portion for the work of his service, by his division,

17 and to the priests who were written in the genealogy according to their father's house, and to the Levites [a]from twenty years old and up according to their work, by their divisions,

18 and to all who were written in the genealogy—their little ones and their wives, their sons and daughters, the whole company of them—for in their faithfulness they [1]sanctified themselves in holiness.

19 Also for the sons of Aaron the priests, *who were* in [a]the fields of the common-lands of their cities, in every single city, *there were* men who were [b]designated by name to distribute portions to all the males among the priests and to all who were listed by genealogies among the Levites.

20 Thus Hezekiah did throughout all Judah, and he [a]did what *was* good and right and true before the LORD his God.

21 And in every work that he began in the service of the house of God, in the law and in the commandment, to seek his God, he did *it* with all his heart. So he [a]prospered.

Sennacherib Boasts Against the LORD

32 After [a]these deeds of faithfulness, Sennacherib king of Assyria came and entered Judah; he encamped against the fortified cities, thinking to win them over to himself.

2 And when Hezekiah saw that Sennacherib had come, and that his purpose was to make war against Jerusalem,

3 he consulted with his leaders and [1]commanders to stop the water from the springs which *were* outside the city; and they helped him.

4 Thus many people gathered together who stopped all the [a]springs and the brook that ran through the land, saying, "Why should the [1]kings of Assyria come and find much water?"

5 And [a]he strengthened himself, [b]built up all the wall that was broken, raised *it* up to the towers, and *built* another wall outside; also he repaired [1]the [c]Millo *in* the City of David, and made [2]weapons and shields in abundance.

6 Then he set military captains over the people, gathered them together to him in the open square of the city gate, and [a]gave them encouragement, saying,

7 [a]"Be strong and courageous; [b]do not be afraid nor dismayed before the king of Assyria, nor before all the multitude that *is* with him; for [c]*there are* more with us than with him. **5**

8 "With him *is* an [a]arm of flesh; but [b]with us *is* the LORD our God, to help us and to fight our battles." And the people were strengthened by the words of Hezekiah king of Judah.

9 [a]After this Sennacherib king of Assyria sent his servants to Jerusalem (but he and all the forces with him *laid siege* against Lachish), to Hezekiah king of Judah, and to all Judah who *were* in Jerusalem, saying,

10 [a]"Thus says Sennacherib king of

---

10 [c]Ex. 36:5
11 [a]1 Kin. 6:5–8 [1]*storerooms*
12 [a]2 Chr. 35:9; Neh. 13:13
13 [a]1 Chr. 9:11; Jer. 20:1
14 [a]Deut. 23:23; 2 Chr. 35:8
15 [a]2 Chr. 29:12 [b]Josh. 21:1–3, 9 [c]1 Chr. 9:26
17 [a]1 Chr. 23:24, 27
18 [1]*consecrated*
19 [a]Lev. 25:34; Num. 35:1–4 [b]2 Chr. 31:12–15
20 [a]2 Kin. 20:3; 22:2
21 [a]2 Chr. 26:5; 32:30; Ps. 1:3

CHAPTER 32

1 [a]2 Kin. 18:13—19:37; Is. 36:1—37:38
3 [1]Lit. *mighty men*
4 [a]2 Kin. 20:20 [1]So with MT, Vg.; Arab., LXX, Syr. *king*
5 [a]Is. 22:9, 10 [b]2 Kin. 25:4; 2 Chr. 25:23 [c]2 Sam. 5:9; 1 Kin. 9:15, 24; 11:27; 2 Kin. 12:20; 1 Chr. 11:8 [1]Lit. *The Landfill* [2]*javelins*
6 [a]2 Chr. 30:22; Is. 40:2
7 [a][Deut. 31:6] [b]2 Chr. 20:15 [c]2 Kin. 6:16; [Rom. 8:31]
8 [a][Jer. 17:5; 1 John 4:4] [b]Ex. 14:13; [1 Sam. 17:45–47]; 2 Chr. 13:12; 20:17; [Rom. 8:31]
9 [a]2 Kin. 18:17
10 [a]2 Kin. 18:19

31:21 As clearly as any of the proverbs, the author of 2 Chr. outlines in the simplest terms the recipe for success: Seek God with all your heart and you will prosper.

32:1–23 Whereas 2 Chr. focuses its attention more on the reforms of **Hezekiah** (chs. 29—31), 2 Kin. gives more space to record Hezekiah's encounter with and victory over **Sennacherib.** Read the text and notes of 2 Kin. 18:17—19:37.

32:7, 8 See section 5 of Truth-In-Action at the end of 2 Chr.

Assyria: 'In what do you trust, that you
remain under siege in Jerusalem?
11 'Does not Hezekiah persuade you
to give yourselves over to die by famine and by thirst, saying, [a]"The LORD
our God will deliver us from the hand
of the king of Assyria"?
12 [a]'Has not the same Hezekiah taken
away His high places and His altars,
and commanded Judah and Jerusalem,
saying, "You shall worship before one
altar and burn incense on [b]it"?
13 'Do you not know what I and my
fathers have done to all the peoples of
other lands? [a]Were the gods of the nations of those lands in any way able
to deliver their lands out of my hand?
14 'Who *was there* among all the gods
of those nations that my fathers utterly
destroyed that could deliver his people
from my hand, that your God should
be *able to deliver you from my
[a]hand?
15 'Now therefore, [a]do not let Hezekiah deceive you or persuade you like
this, and do not believe him; for no god
of any nation or kingdom was able to
deliver his people from my hand or the
hand of my fathers. How much less will
your God deliver you from my hand?' "
16 Furthermore, his servants spoke
against the LORD God and against His
servant Hezekiah.
17 He also wrote letters to revile the
LORD God of Israel, and to speak
against Him, saying, [a]"As the gods of
the nations of *other* lands have not delivered their people from my hand, so
the God of Hezekiah will not deliver
His people from my [b]hand."
18 [a]Then they called out with a loud
voice in [1]Hebrew to the people of Jerusalem who *were* on the wall, to frighten
them and trouble them, that they might
take the city.
19 And they spoke against the God of
Jerusalem, as against the gods of the
people of the earth—[a]the work of
men's hands.

Sennacherib's Defeat and Death

20 [a]Now because of this King Hezekiah and [b]the prophet Isaiah, the son
of Amoz, prayed and cried out to
heaven.
21 [a]Then the LORD sent an **angel** who
cut down every mighty man of valor,
leader, and captain in the camp of the
king of Assyria. So he returned
[b]shamefaced to his own land. And
when he had gone into the temple of
his god, some of his own offspring
struck him down with the sword there.

WORD WEALTH

32:21 angel, *mal'ach* (mahl-*ahch*); Strong's #4397: A messenger, ambassador; someone dispatched to do a task or relay a message; specifically an "angel" or heavenly messenger from the Lord. Found more than 200 times, *mal'ach* is usually translated "angel" (though often translated "messengers" when referring to human messengers; see Gen. 32:3; 1 Sam. 16:19; 2 Kin. 7:15). Angels, mentioned extensively in the OT, were sent to assist or inform the patriarchs, Balaam, David, the prophet Zechariah, and others. Not all angels are of the "angelic" sort; see Prov. 16:14 (which might have been translated "death angels"), Ps. 78:49, Prov. 17:11. Ps. 104:4 portrays the supernatural qualities (spirit, fire) of the Lord's messengers.

22 Thus the LORD saved Hezekiah and
the inhabitants of Jerusalem from the
hand of Sennacherib the king of Assyria, and from the hand of all *others*,
and [1]guided them on every side.
23 And many brought gifts to the LORD
at Jerusalem, and [a]presents[1] to Hezekiah king of Judah, so that he was
[b]exalted in the sight of all nations
thereafter.

Hezekiah Humbles Himself

24 [a]In those days Hezekiah was sick
and near death, and he prayed to the
LORD; and He spoke to him and gave
him a sign.
25 But Hezekiah [a]did not repay ac- 3
cording to the favor *shown* him, for
[b]his heart was lifted up; [c]therefore
wrath was looming over him and over
Judah and Jerusalem.
26 [a]Then Hezekiah humbled himself
for the pride of his heart, he and the
inhabitants of Jerusalem, so that the
wrath of the LORD did not come upon
them [b]in the days of Hezekiah.

Hezekiah's Wealth and Honor

27 Hezekiah had very great riches and
honor. And he made himself treasuries
for silver, for gold, for precious stones,

11 [a]2 Kin. 18:30
12 [a]2 Kin. 18:22 [b]2 Chr. 31:1, 2
13 [a]2 Kin. 18:33–35
14 [a][Is. 10:5–12] *See WW at Num. 13:30.
15 [a]2 Kin. 18:29
17 [a]2 Kin. 19:9; [1 Cor. 8:5, 6] [b]2 Kin. 19:12; Dan. 3:15
18 [a]2 Kin. 18:28; Ps. 59:6 [1]Lit. *Judean*
19 [a]2 Kin. 19:18; [Ps. 96:5; 115:4–8]
20 [a]2 Kin. 19:15 [b]2 Kin. 19:2
21 [a]2 Kin. 19:35; Is. 10:12–19; Zech. 14:3 [b]Ps. 44:7
22 [1]LXX *gave them rest;* Vg. *gave them treasures*
23 [a]2 Sam. 8:10; 2 Chr. 17:5; 26:8; Ps. 45:12 [b]2 Chr. 1:1 [1]Lit. *precious things*
24 [a]2 Kin. 20:1–11; Is. 38:1–8
25 [a]Ps. 116:12 [b]2 Chr. 26:16; [Hab. 2:4] [c]2 Chr. 24:18
26 [a]Jer. 26:18, 19 [b]2 Kin. 20:19

32:24–26 For a fuller account of Hezekiah's prayer and the unique and miraculous sign of his cure, which happened through the ministry of Isaiah, read the text and notes of 2 Kin. 20:1–11.

32:25 See section 3 of Truth-In-Action at the end of 2 Chr.

for spices, for shields, and for all kinds
of desirable items;
28 storehouses for the harvest of grain,
wine, and oil; and stalls for all kinds
of livestock, and [1]folds for flocks.
29 Moreover he provided cities for
himself, and possessions of flocks and
herds in abundance; for [a]God had
given him very much property.
30 [a]This same Hezekiah also stopped
the water outlet of Upper Gihon, and
[1]brought* the water by tunnel to the
west side of the City of David. Hezekiah [b]prospered in all his works.
31 However, *regarding* the ambassadors of the princes of Babylon, whom
they [a]sent to him to inquire about the
*wonder that was *done* in the land, God
withdrew from him, in order to [b]test*
him, that He might know all *that was*
in his heart.

Death of Hezekiah

32 Now the rest of the acts of Hezekiah, and his goodness, indeed they *are*
written in [a]the **vision** of Isaiah the
prophet, the son of Amoz, *and* in the
[b]book of the kings of Judah and Israel.

> **WORD WEALTH**
>
> **32:32 vision,** *chazon* (cha-*zohn*); Strong's #2377: A prophetic vision, dream, oracle, revelation; especially the kind of revelation that comes through sight, namely a vision from God. This noun occurs 35 times and is from the root *chazah*, "to see, behold, and perceive." *Chazon* is especially used for the revelation which the prophets received. See Is. 1:1; Ezek. 12:27, 28; Dan. 8:1, 2; Obad. 1; Hab. 2:2, 3. The prophets understood God's counsels so clearly because He revealed matters to them by visible means. Prov. 29:18 shows that when a society lacks any revelation from God (divine insight), such a society heads in the direction of anarchy.

33 [a]So Hezekiah [1]rested with his fathers, and they buried him in the upper
tombs of the sons of David; and all Judah and the inhabitants of Jerusalem
[b]honored him at his death. Then Manasseh his son reigned in his place.

Manasseh Reigns in Judah

33 Manasseh [a]*was* twelve years
old when he became king, and
he reigned fifty-five years in Jerusalem.
2 But he did evil in the sight of the
LORD, according to the [a]abominations
of the nations whom the LORD had cast
out before the children of Israel.
3 For he rebuilt the [1]high places
which Hezekiah his father had [a]broken
down; he raised up altars for the Baals,
and [b]made wooden images; and he
worshiped [c]all [2]the host of heaven and
served them.
4 He also built altars in the house of
the LORD, of which the LORD had said,
[a]"In Jerusalem shall My name be forever."
5 And he built altars for all the host
of heaven [a]in the two courts of the
house of the LORD.
6 [a]Also he caused his sons to pass
through the fire in the Valley of the Son
of Hinnom; he practiced [b]soothsaying,
used witchcraft and sorcery, and
[c]consulted mediums and spiritists. He
did much evil in the sight of the LORD,
to provoke Him to anger.
7 [a]He even set a carved image, the
idol which he had made, in the [1]house
of God, of which God had said to David
and to Solomon his son, [b]"In this house
and in Jerusalem, which I have chosen
out of all the tribes of Israel, I will put
My name forever;
8 [a]"and I will not again remove the
foot of Israel from the land which I
have appointed for your fathers—only
if they are careful to do all that I have
commanded them, according to the
whole law and the statutes and the ordinances by the hand of Moses."
9 So Manasseh seduced Judah and
the inhabitants of Jerusalem to do
more evil than the nations whom the
LORD had destroyed before the children of Israel.

Manasseh Restored After Repentance

10 And the LORD spoke to Manasseh
and his people, but they would not
[1]listen.

28 [1]So with LXX, Vg.; Arab., Syr. omit *folds for flocks;* MT *flocks for sheepfolds*
29 [a]1 Chr. 29:12
30 [a]Is. 22:9–11 [b]2 Chr. 31:21 [1]Lit. *brought it straight to* (cf. 2 Kin. 20:20) *See WW at Prov. 3:6.
31 [a]2 Kin. 20:12; Is. 39:1 [b][Deut. 8:2, 16] *See WW at Zech. 3:8. • See WW at Ps. 78:41.
32 [a]Is. 36—39 [b]2 Kin. 18—20
33 [a]1 Kin. 1:21; 2 Kin. 20:21 [b]Ps. 112:6; Prov. 10:7 [1]Died and joined his ancestors

CHAPTER 33

1 [a]2 Kin. 21:1–9
2 [a][Deut. 18:9–12]; 2 Chr. 28:3; [Jer. 15:4]
3 [a]2 Kin. 18:4; 2 Chr. 30:14; 31:1 [b]Deut. 16:21; 2 Kin. 23:5, 6 [c]Deut. 17:3 [1]Places for pagan worship [2]The gods of the Assyrians
4 [a]Deut. 12:11; 1 Kin. 8:29; 9:3; 2 Chr. 6:6; 7:16
5 [a]2 Chr. 4:9
6 [a][Lev. 18:21]; Deut. 18:10; 2 Kin. 23:10; 2 Chr. 28:3; Ezek. 23:37, 39 [b]Deut. 18:11; 2 Kin. 17:17 [c][Lev. 19:31; 20:27]; 2 Kin. 21:6
7 [a]2 Kin. 21:7; 2 Chr. 25:14 [b]Ps. 132:14 [1]Temple
8 [a]2 Sam. 7:10
10 [1]*obey*

32:31 The visit of the **ambassadors of . . . Babylon** is described in greater detail in 2 Kin. 20:12–19. 2 Kin. explains how this incident inspires Isaiah to prophesy about the coming Babylonian captivity. The chronicler shows clearly that God did not approve of Hezekiah's actions but was testing him. Pride, which had nearly cost Hezekiah his life, was surfacing again.

33:1–20 After the reign of King Hezekiah, **Manasseh** came to the throne as the fourteenth of Judah's rulers. Of the 20 rulers in Judah's history, Manasseh was the worst. For further insight on the wickedness of his reign, read the text and notes of 2 Kin. 21:1–18.

33:10–17 The account of Manasseh's change of heart is not mentioned in the description of his reign in 2 Kin. This section demonstrates the amazing grace of the Lord in listening and responding to even the worst of sinners.

11 [a]Therefore the LORD brought upon
them the captains of the army of the
king of Assyria, who took Manasseh
with [1]hooks, [b]bound him with [2]bronze
fetters, and carried him off to Babylon.
12 Now when he was in affliction, he
implored the LORD his God, and
[a]humbled himself greatly before the
God of his fathers,
13 and prayed to Him; and He [a]re-
ceived his entreaty, heard his supplication, and brought him back to Jerusalem into his kingdom. Then Manasseh
[b]knew that the LORD *was* God.
14 After this he built a wall outside the
City of David on the west side of
[a]Gihon, in the valley, as far as the entrance of the Fish Gate; and *it* [b]en-
closed Ophel, and he raised it to a very
great height. Then he put military captains in all the fortified cities of Judah.
15 He took away [a]the foreign gods and
the idol from the house of the LORD,
and all the altars that he had built in
the mount of the house of the LORD and
in Jerusalem; and he cast *them* out of
the city.
16 He also repaired the altar of the
LORD, sacrificed peace offerings and
[a]thank offerings on it, and commanded
Judah to serve the LORD God of Israel.
17 [a]Nevertheless the people still sacrificed on the [1]high places, *but* only to
the LORD their God.

Death of Manasseh

18 Now the rest of the acts of Manasseh, his prayer to his God, and the
words of [a]the seers who spoke to him
in the name of the LORD God of Israel,
indeed they *are written* in the [1]book
of the kings of Israel.
19 Also his prayer and *how God* received his entreaty, and all his sin and
trespass, and the sites where he built
[1]high places and set up wooden images
and carved images, before he was
humbled, indeed they *are* written
among the sayings of [2]Hozai.
20 [a]So Manasseh rested with his fathers, and they buried him in his own
house. Then his son Amon reigned in
his place.

Amon's Reign and Death

21 [a]Amon *was* twenty-two years old
when he became king, and he reigned
two years in Jerusalem.
22 But he did evil in the sight of the
LORD, as his father Manasseh had
done; for Amon sacrificed to all the
carved images which his father Manasseh had made, and served them.
23 And he did not humble himself before the LORD, [a]as his father Manasseh
had humbled himself; but Amon trespassed more and more.
24 [a]Then his servants conspired
against him, and [b]killed him in his own
house.
25 But the people of the land executed
all those who had conspired against
King Amon. Then the people of the
land made his son Josiah king in his
place.

Josiah Reigns in Judah

34 Josiah [a]*was* eight years old
when he became king, and he
reigned thirty-one years in Jerusalem.
2 And he did *what was* right in the
sight of the LORD, and walked in the
ways of his father David; *he* did *not*
turn aside to the right hand or to the
left.
3 For in the eighth year of his reign,
while he was still [a]young, he began to
[b]seek the God of his father David; and
in the twelfth year he began [c]to purge
Judah and Jerusalem [d]of the [1]high
places, the wooden images, the carved
images, and the molded images.
4 [a]They broke down the altars of the
Baals in his presence, and the incense
altars which *were* above them he cut
down; and the wooden images, the
carved images, and the molded images
he broke in pieces, and made dust of
them [b]and scattered *it* on the graves
of those who had sacrificed to them.
5 He also [a]burned the bones of the

11 [a]Deut. 28:36 [b]2 Chr. 36:6; Job 36:8; Ps. 107:10, 11 [1]Nose hooks, 2 Kin. 19:28 [2]*chains*
12 [a]2 Chr. 7:14; 32:26; [1 Pet. 5:6]
13 [a]1 Chr. 5:20; Ezra 8:23 [b]1 Kin. 20:13; Ps. 9:16; Dan. 4:25
14 [a]1 Kin. 1:33 [b]2 Chr. 27:3
15 [a]2 Chr. 33:3, 5, 7
16 [a]Lev. 7:12
17 [a]2 Chr. 32:12 [1]Places for pagan worship
18 [a]1 Sam. 9:9 [1]Lit. *words*
19 [1]Places for pagan worship [2]LXX *the seers*
20 [a]1 Kin. 1:21; 2 Kin. 21:18
21 [a]2 Kin. 21:19–24; 1 Chr. 3:14
23 [a]2 Chr. 33:12, 19
24 [a]2 Kin. 21:23, 24; 2 Chr. 24:25 [b]2 Chr. 25:27

CHAPTER 34

1 [a]2 Kin. 22:1, 2; Jer. 1:2; 3:6
3 [a]Eccl. 12:1 [b]2 Chr. 15:2; [Prov. 8:17] [c]1 Kin. 13:2 [d]2 Chr. 33:17–19, 22 [1]Places for pagan worship
4 [a]Lev. 26:30; 2 Kin. 23:4 [b]2 Kin. 23:6
5 [a]1 Kin. 13:2

However, the damage of Manasseh's wickedness had been done. Though he had changed his heart, the people had not (v. 17).
33:11 When the Assyrians captured foreign dignitaries, they had a cruel custom of humiliating them by driving **hooks** through their noses, much as one would capture an animal.
33:21–25 For a parallel description of Amon's reign, read the text and notes of 2 Kin. 21:19–26. As Judah's fifteenth ruler, **Amon** followed the evil example of **Manasseh** until he was murdered by his servants.
34:1–33 Like 2 Kin., 2 Chr. devotes two chapters to outline the important reign of Judah's sixteenth ruler. Read the text and notes of 2 Kin. 22; 23. In a refreshing contrast to the corruption in the reigns of Manasseh and Amon, **Josiah** was one of Judah's most godly kings. During his reign, idolatry was purged, the temple was repaired, the Book of the Law was found, and worship was restored. Nevertheless, in light of the people's persistent wickedness, all of this was too little and too late to escape the impending judgment (see 2 Kin. 23:26, 27). Josiah's reform was the last ray of light for Judah.

priests on their [b]altars, and cleansed Judah and Jerusalem.

6 And *so he did* in the cities of Manasseh, Ephraim, and Simeon, as far as Naphtali and all around, with [1]axes.

7 When he had broken down the altars and the wooden images, had [a]beaten the carved images into powder, and cut down all the incense altars throughout all the land of Israel, he returned to Jerusalem.

Hilkiah Finds the Book of the Law

8 [a]In the eighteenth year of his reign, when he had purged the land and the [1]temple, he sent [b]Shaphan the son of Azaliah, Maaseiah the [c]governor of the city, and Joah the son of Joahaz the recorder, to repair the *house of the LORD his God.

9 When they came to Hilkiah the high priest, they delivered [a]the money that was brought into the house of God, which the Levites who kept the doors had gathered from the hand of Manasseh and Ephraim, from all the [b]remnant of Israel, from all Judah and Benjamin, and *which* they had brought back to Jerusalem.

10 Then they put *it* in the hand of the foremen who had the oversight of the house of the LORD; and they gave it to the workmen who worked in the house of the LORD, to repair and restore the house.

11 They gave *it* to the craftsmen and builders to buy hewn stone and timber for beams, and to floor the houses which the kings of Judah had destroyed.

12 And the men did the work faithfully. Their overseers *were* Jahath and Obadiah the Levites, of the sons of Merari, and Zechariah and Meshullam, of the sons of the Kohathites, to supervise. *Others of* the Levites, all of whom were skillful with instruments of music,

13 *were* [a]over the burden bearers and *were* overseers of all who did work in any kind of service. [b]And *some* of the Levites *were* scribes, officers, and gatekeepers.

14 Now when they brought out the money that was brought into the house of the LORD, Hilkiah the priest [a]found the Book of the Law of the LORD *given* by Moses.

15 Then Hilkiah answered and said to Shaphan the scribe, "I have found the Book of the Law in the house of the LORD." And Hilkiah gave the [a]book to Shaphan.

5 [b]2 Kin. 23:20
6 [1]Lit. *swords*
7 [a]Deut. 9:21
8 [a]2 Kin. 22:3–20 [b]2 Kin. 25:22 [c]2 Chr. 18:25 [1]Lit. *house* *See WW at 2 Sam. 7:11.
9 [a]2 Kin. 12:4 [b]2 Chr. 30:6
13 [a]2 Chr. 8:10 [b]1 Chr. 23:4, 5
14 [a]2 Kin. 22:8
15 [a]Deut. 31:24, 26
17 [1]Lit. *poured out*
20 [a]Jer. 26:24 [1]*Achbor the son of Michaiah*, 2 Kin. 22:12
21 [a]2 Kin. 17:15–19
22 [1]*Tikvah*, 2 Kin. 22:14 [2]*Harhas*, 2 Kin. 22:14
24 [a]2 Chr. 36:14–20 [b]Deut. 28:15–68
25 *See WW at 1 Kin. 16:2.
27 [a]2 Kin. 22:19; 2 Chr. 12:7; 30:6; 33:12, 13

16 So Shaphan carried the book to the king, bringing the king word, saying, "All that was committed to your servants they are doing.

17 "And they have [1]gathered the money that was found in the house of the LORD, and have delivered it into the hand of the overseers and the workmen."

18 Then Shaphan the scribe told the king, saying, "Hilkiah the priest has given me a book." And Shaphan read it before the king.

19 Thus it happened, when the king heard the words of the Law, that he tore his clothes.

20 Then the king commanded Hilkiah, [a]Ahikam the son of Shaphan, [1]Abdon the son of Micah, Shaphan the scribe, and Asaiah a servant of the king, saying,

21 "Go, inquire of the LORD for me, and for those who are left in Israel and Judah, concerning the words of the book that is found; for great *is* the wrath of the LORD that is poured out on us, because our fathers have not [a]kept the word of the LORD, to do according to all that is written in this book."

22 So Hilkiah and those the king *had appointed* went to Huldah the prophetess, the wife of Shallum the son of [1]Tokhath, the son of [2]Hasrah, keeper of the wardrobe. (She dwelt in Jerusalem in the Second Quarter.) And they spoke to her to that *effect*.

23 Then she answered them, "Thus says the LORD God of Israel, 'Tell the man who sent you to Me,

24 "Thus says the LORD: 'Behold, I will [a]bring calamity on this place and on its inhabitants, all the curses that are written in the [b]book which they have read before the king of Judah,

25 'because they have forsaken Me and burned incense to other gods, that they might *provoke Me to anger with all the works of their hands. Therefore My wrath will be poured out on this place, and not be quenched.' " '

26 "But as for the king of Judah, who sent you to inquire of the LORD, in this manner you shall speak to him, 'Thus says the LORD God of Israel: "*Concerning* the words which you have heard—

27 "because your heart was tender, and you humbled yourself before God when you heard His words against this place and against its inhabitants, and you humbled yourself before Me, and you tore your clothes and wept before Me, I also have heard *you*," says the [a]LORD.

28 "Surely I will gather you to your fa-

thers, and you shall be gathered to
your grave in peace; and your eyes
shall not see all the calamity which I
will bring on this place and its inhabitants." ' " So they brought back word
to the king.

Josiah Restores True Worship

29 [a]Then the king sent and gathered
all the elders of Judah and Jerusalem.
30 The king went up to the house of
the LORD, with all the men of Judah
and the inhabitants of Jerusalem—the
priests and the Levites, and all the people, great and small. And he [a]read in
their hearing all the words of the Book
of the Covenant which had been found
in the house of the LORD.
31 Then the king [a]stood in [b]his place
and made a [c]covenant before the LORD,
to follow the LORD, and to keep His
commandments and His testimonies
and His statutes with all his heart and
all his soul, to perform the words of
the covenant that were written in this
book.
32 And he made all who were present
in Jerusalem and Benjamin take a
stand. So the inhabitants of Jerusalem
did according to the covenant of God,
the God of their fathers.
33 Thus Josiah removed all the [a]abom-
inations from all the country that *belonged* to the children of Israel, and
made all who were present in Israel
[1]diligently serve the LORD their God.
[b]All his days they did not depart from
following the LORD God of their fathers.

Josiah Keeps the Passover

35 Now [a]Josiah kept a Passover to
the LORD in Jerusalem, and they
slaughtered the Passover *lambs* on the
[b]fourteenth *day* of the first month.
2 And he set the priests in their
[a]duties and [b]encouraged them for the
service of the house of the LORD.
3 Then he said to the Levites [a]who
taught all Israel, who were holy to the
LORD: [b]"Put the holy ark [c]in the house
which Solomon the son of David, king
of Israel, built. [d]*It shall* no longer *be*
a burden on *your* shoulders. Now serve
the LORD your God and His people Israel.
4 "Prepare *yourselves* [a]according to
your fathers' [1]houses, according to
your divisions, following the [b]written
instruction of David king of Israel and
the [c]written instruction of Solomon his
son.
5 "And [a]stand in the holy *place* according to the divisions of the fathers'
houses of your brethren the *lay* people,
and *according to* the division of the father's house of the Levites.
6 "So slaughter the Passover *offerings,* [a]consecrate yourselves, and prepare *them* for your brethren, that *they*
may do according to the word of the
LORD by the hand of Moses."
7 Then Josiah [a]gave the *lay* people
lambs and young goats from the flock,
all for Passover *offerings* for all who
were present, to the number of thirty
thousand, as well as three thousand
cattle; these *were* from the king's
[b]possessions.
8 And his [a]leaders gave willingly to
the people, to the priests, and to the
Levites. Hilkiah, Zechariah, and Jehiel,
rulers of the house of God, gave to the
priests for the Passover *offerings* two
thousand six hundred *from the flock,*
and three hundred cattle.
9 Also [a]Conaniah, his brothers Shemaiah and Nethanel, and Hashabiah and
Jeiel and Jozabad, chief of the Levites,
gave to the Levites for Passover *offerings* five thousand *from the flock* and
five hundred cattle.
10 So the service was prepared, and
the priests [a]stood in their places, and
the [b]Levites in their divisions, according to the king's command.
11 And they slaughtered the Passover
offerings; and the priests [a]sprinkled
the blood with their hands, while the
Levites [b]skinned *the animals.*
12 Then they removed the burnt offerings that *they* might give them to the
divisions of the fathers' houses of the
lay people, to offer to the LORD, as *it
is* written [a]in the Book of Moses. And
so *they did* with the cattle.
13 Also they [a]roasted the Passover *offerings* with fire according to the ordinance; but the *other* holy *offerings* they
[b]boiled in pots, in caldrons, and in
pans, and divided *them* quickly among
all the *lay* people.
14 Then afterward they prepared portions for themselves and for the priests,
because the priests, the sons of Aaron,
were busy in offering burnt offerings

29 [a]2 Kin. 23:1–3
30 [a]Neh. 8:1–3
31 [a]2 Chr. 6:13 [b]2 Kin. 11:14; 23:3; 2 Chr. 30:16 [c]2 Chr. 23:16; 29:10
33 [a]1 Kin. 11:5; 2 Chr. 33:2 [b]Jer. 3:10 [1]Lit. *serve to serve*

CHAPTER 35

1 [a]2 Kin. 23:21, 22 [b]Ex. 12:6; Num. 9:3; Ezra 6:19
2 [a]2 Chr. 23:18; Ezra 6:18 [b]2 Chr. 29:5–15
3 [a]Deut. 33:10; 2 Chr. 17:8, 9; Neh. 8:7 [b]2 Chr. 34:14 [c]Ex. 40:21; 2 Chr. 5:7 [d]1 Chr. 23:26
4 [a]1 Chr. 9:10–13 [b]1 Chr. 23—26 [c]2 Chr. 8:14 [1]*households*
5 [a]Ps. 134:1
6 [a]2 Chr. 29:5, 15
7 [a]2 Chr. 30:24 [b]2 Chr. 31:3
8 [a]Num. 7:2
9 [a]2 Chr. 31:12
10 [a]Ezra 6:18; Heb. 9:6 [b]2 Chr. 5:12; 7:6; 8:14, 15; 13:10; 29:25–34
11 [a]Ex. 12:22; 2 Chr. 29:22 [b]2 Chr. 29:34
12 [a]Lev. 3:3; Ezra 6:18
13 [a]Ex. 12:8, 9; Deut. 16:7 [b]1 Sam. 2:13–15

35:1–27 The celebration of the **Passover** was the climax of Josiah's reforms. There had not been a Passover celebration to rival it since **the days of Samuel** (v. 18). For another perspective on this event and on the death of Josiah, read the text and notes of 2 Kin. 23.

and fat until night; therefore the Levites prepared portions for themselves and for the priests, the sons of Aaron.

15 And the singers, the sons of Asaph, *were* in their places, according to the [a]command of David, Asaph, Heman, and Jeduthun the king's seer. Also the gatekeepers [b]were at each gate; they did not have to leave their position, because their brethren the Levites prepared portions for them.

16 So all the service of the LORD was prepared the same day, to keep the Passover and to offer burnt offerings on the altar of the LORD, according to the command of King Josiah.

17 And the children of Israel who were present kept the Passover at that time, and the Feast of [a]Unleavened Bread for seven days.

18 [a]There had been no Passover kept in Israel like that since the days of Samuel the prophet; and none of the kings of Israel had kept such a Passover as Josiah kept, with the priests and the Levites, all Judah and Israel who were present, and the inhabitants of Jerusalem.

19 In the eighteenth year of the reign of Josiah this Passover was kept.

Josiah Dies in Battle

20 [a]After all this, when Josiah had prepared the temple, Necho king of Egypt came up to fight against [b]Carchemish by the Euphrates; and Josiah went out against him.

21 But he sent messengers to him, saying, "What have I to do with you, king of Judah? *I have* not *come* against you this day, but against the house with which I have war; for God commanded me to make haste. Refrain *from meddling with* God, who *is* with me, lest He destroy you."

22 Nevertheless Josiah would not turn his face from him, but [a]disguised himself so that he might fight with him, and did not heed the words of Necho from the mouth of God. So he came to fight in the Valley of Megiddo.

23 And the archers shot King Josiah; and the king said to his servants, "Take me away, for I am severely wounded."

24 [a]His servants therefore took him out of that chariot and put him in the second chariot that he had, and they brought him to Jerusalem. So he died, and was buried in *one of* the tombs of his fathers. And [b]all Judah and Jerusalem mourned for Josiah.

25 Jeremiah also [a]lamented for [b]Josiah. And to this day [c]all the singing men and the singing women speak of Josiah in their lamentations. [d]They made it a custom in Israel; and indeed they *are* written in the Laments.

26 Now the rest of the acts of Josiah and his goodness, according to *what was* written in the Law of the LORD,

27 and his deeds from first to last, indeed they *are* written in the book of the kings of Israel and Judah.

The Reign and Captivity of Jehoahaz

36 Then [a]the people of the land took Jehoahaz the son of Josiah, and made him king in his father's place in Jerusalem.

2 [1]Jehoahaz *was* twenty-three years old when he became king, and he reigned three months in Jerusalem.

3 Now the king of Egypt deposed him at Jerusalem; and he imposed on the land a tribute of one hundred talents of silver and a talent of gold.

4 Then the king of Egypt made [1]*Jehoahaz's* brother Eliakim king over Judah and Jerusalem, and changed his name to Jehoiakim. And Necho took [2]Jehoahaz his brother and carried him off to Egypt.

The Reign and Captivity of Jehoiakim

5 [a]Jehoiakim *was* twenty-five years old when he became king, and he reigned eleven years in Jerusalem. And he did [b]evil in the sight of the LORD his God.

6 [a]Nebuchadnezzar king of Babylon came up against him, and bound him in [1]bronze *fetters* to [b]carry him off to Babylon.

7 [a]Nebuchadnezzar also carried off *some* of the articles from the house of the LORD to Babylon, and put them in his temple at Babylon.

8 Now the rest of the acts of Jehoiakim, the abominations which he did,

15 [a]1 Chr. 25:1–6 [b]1 Chr. 9:17, 18
17 [a]Ex. 12:15; 13:6; 2 Chr. 30:21
18 [a]2 Kin. 23:22, 23
20 [a]2 Kin. 23:29 [b]Is. 10:9; Jer. 46:2
22 [a]1 Kin. 22:30; 2 Chr. 18:29
24 [a]2 Kin. 23:30 [b]1 Kin. 14:18; Zech. 12:11
25 [a]Lam. 4:20 [b]Jer. 22:10, 11 [c]Matt. 9:23 [d]Jer. 22:20

CHAPTER 36

1 [a]2 Kin. 23:30–34
2 [1]MT *Joahaz*
4 [1]Lit. *his* [2]MT *Joahaz*
5 [a]2 Kin. 23:36, 37; 1 Chr. 3:15 [b][Jer. 22:13–19]
6 [a]2 Kin. 24:1; Hab. 1:6 [b][Deut. 29:22–29]; 2 Chr. 33:11; Jer. 36:30 [1]*chains*
7 [a]2 Kin. 24:13; Dan. 1:1, 2

35:22 Megiddo was the site of many famous historical battles and will be the location of the climactic battle of Armageddon (Rev. 16:16).

35:25 It is believed that the prophet **Jeremiah** played a significant role in the reforms of **Josiah,** for this was the time when he carried on his prophetic ministry.

36:1–4 The reign of Judah's seventeenth ruler, **Jehoahaz,** is also set forth in 2 Kin. 23:31–34.

36:5–8 The eighteenth king in Judah was **Jehoiakim.** He began his reign as Egypt's puppet and ended it as Babylon's prisoner. For more information on Jehoiakim's reign as Judah's eighteenth ruler, read the text and notes of 2 Kin. 23:36—24:7.

and what was found against him, indeed they *are* written in the book of
the kings of Israel and Judah. Then
[1]Jehoiachin his son reigned in his
place.

The Reign and Captivity of Jehoiachin

9 [a]Jehoiachin *was* [1]eight years old
when he became king, and he reigned
in Jerusalem three months and ten
days. And he did evil in the sight of
the LORD.
10 At the turn of the year [a]King Nebuchadnezzar summoned *him* and took
him to Babylon, [b]with the costly articles from the house of the LORD,
and made [c]Zedekiah,[1] [2]*Jehoiakim's*
brother, king over Judah and Jerusalem.

Zedekiah Reigns in Judah

11 [a]Zedekiah *was* twenty-one years
old when he became king, and he
reigned eleven years in Jerusalem.
12 He did evil in the sight of the LORD
his God, *and* [a]did not humble himself before Jeremiah the prophet,
who spoke from the mouth of the
LORD.
13 And he also [a]rebelled against King
Nebuchadnezzar, who had made him
swear *an oath* by God; but he [b]stiff-
ened his neck and hardened his
heart against *turning to the LORD God
of Israel.
14 Moreover all the leaders of the
priests and the people transgressed
more and more, *according* to all the
abominations of the nations, and defiled the house of the LORD which He
had consecrated in Jerusalem.

The Fall of Jerusalem

15 [a]And the LORD God of their fathers
sent *warnings* to them by His messengers, rising up early and sending
them, because He had compassion
on His people and on His dwelling
place.
16 But [a]they mocked the messengers
of God, [b]despised His words, and
[c]scoffed at His prophets, until the
[d]wrath of the LORD arose against His
people, till *there was* no *remedy.
17 [a]Therefore He brought against
them the king of the Chaldeans, who
[b]killed their young men with the sword
in the house of their sanctuary, and
had no compassion on young man or
virgin, on the aged or the weak; He
gave *them* all into his hand.
18 [a]And all the articles from the house
of God, great and small, the treasures
of the house of the LORD, and the treasures of the king and of his leaders,
all *these* he took to Babylon.
19 [a]Then they burned the house of
God, broke down the wall of Jerusalem, burned all its palaces with fire,
and destroyed all its precious possessions.
20 And [a]those who escaped from the
sword he carried away to Babylon,
[b]where they became servants to him
and his sons until the rule of the kingdom of Persia,
21 to fulfill the word of the LORD by
the mouth of [a]Jeremiah, until the land
[b]had enjoyed her Sabbaths. As long as
she lay desolate [c]she *kept Sabbath,
to fulfill seventy years.

The Proclamation of Cyrus

22 [a]Now in the first year of Cyrus king
of Persia, that the word of the LORD
by the mouth of [b]Jeremiah might be
fulfilled, the LORD *stirred up the spirit
of [c]Cyrus king of Persia, so that he
made a proclamation throughout all
his kingdom, and also *put it* in writing,
saying,

23 [a]Thus says Cyrus king of Persia:
All the kingdoms of the earth the
LORD God of heaven has given
me. And He has commanded me
to build Him a [1]house at
Jerusalem which is in Judah.
Who *is* among you of all His
people? May the LORD his God *be*
with him, and let him go up!

8 [1]Or *Jeconiah*
9 [a]2 Kin. 24:8–17 [1]Heb. mss., LXX, Syr. *eighteen* and 2 Kin. 24:8
10 [a]2 Kin. 24:10–17 [b]Dan. 1:1, 2 [c]Jer. 37:1 [1]Or *Mattaniah* [2]Lit. *his brother,* 2 Kin. 24:17
11 [a]2 Kin. 24:18–20; Jer. 52:1
12 [a]Jer. 21:3–7; 44:10
13 [a]Jer. 52:3; Ezek. 17:15 [b]2 Kin. 17:14; [2 Chr. 30:8] *See WW at Ruth 4:15.
15 [a]Jer. 7:13; 25:3, 4
16 [a]2 Chr. 30:10; Jer. 5:12, 13 [b][Prov. 1:24–32] [c]Jer. 38:6; Matt. 23:34 [d]2 Chr. 34:25; Ps. 79:5 *See WW at Mal. 4:2.
17 [a]Num. 33:56; Deut. 4:26; 28:49; 2 Kin. 25:1; Ezra 9:7; Is. 3:8 [b]Ps. 74:20
18 [a]2 Kin. 25:13–15; 2 Chr. 36:7, 10
19 [a]2 Kin. 25:9; Ps. 79:1, 7; Is. 1:7, 8; Jer. 52:13
20 [a]2 Kin. 25:11; Jer. 5:19; Mic. 4:10 [b]Jer. 17:4; 27:7
21 [a]Jer. 25:9–12; 27:6–8; 29:10 [b]Lev. 26:34–43; Dan. 9:2 [c]Lev. 25:4, 5 *See WW at Ex. 16:30.
22 [a]Ezra 1:1–3 [b]Jer. 29:10 [c]Is. 44:28; 45:1 *See WW at Hag. 1:14.
23 [a]Ezra 1:2, 3 [1]Temple

36:9, 10 The nineteenth king of Judah was **Jehoiachin.** He began his short rule at age 18 (compare v. 9 with 2 Kin. 24:8). Read the text and notes of 2 Kin. 24:8–16 to discover more about his reign.

36:11–21 The last king of Judah was **Zedekiah.** Further details concerning this king and his reign can be found by reading the text and notes of 2 Kin. 24:18—25:30. In all, Judah had 20 rulers, and only eight of them were good.

36:22, 23 2 Chr. ends on the positive note of the release of Judah from captivity (see the Introduction for a discussion of the dates of these events). God had not forgotten His people. The Lord had punished them, yet He still loved them and had set Himself to do them good (read Jer. 24:4–7). Ironically, God used a pagan ruler to set in motion the release of His people. Note the repetition of these verses in Ezra 1:1–3. The Book of Ezra picks up where 2 Chr. leaves off and continues to record the redemptive work of God in the history of His people.

TRUTH-IN-ACTION through 2 CHRONICLES

Letting the LIFE of the Holy Spirit Bring Faith's Works Alive in You!

Truth 2 Chronicles Teaches	Text	**Action** 2 Chronicles Invites
1 Steps to Holiness Holiness requires that we guard our associations. We must be careful not only to shun unrighteousness and worldliness ourselves, but not to support or participate with others who promote it.	19:2	**Be careful** not to promote the ungodly or to support those whose ways contradict the Scriptures and thus displease the Lord.
	28:23	**Avoid** the evil ethic of expediency. **Do not employ** procedures or practices you suspect of being unethical or ungodly, even if they promise success.
2 Steps to Dynamic Devotion Scripture maintains a consistent testimony that those whose hearts are fully devoted to God are blessed by Him. Partial devotion to God—lukewarmness—inevitably results in spiritual mediocrity and sporadic communion with the Lord.	1:10–12	**Be confident** that God honors those who depend upon His wisdom to carry out the work He has assigned them.
	15:2–4	**Be confident** that if you seek God with all your heart and soul, He will surely be found by you.
	16:9	**Maintain** a heart that is fully committed to the Lord. **Know** that the Lord seeks out such to strengthen them and prosper their works.
3 Steps in Developing Humility The humble person sees himself in the light of his relationship with Almighty God. A truly humble individual regards others more highly than himself because this self-assessment puts others in a better perspective. Also, the humble person is grateful for what he has received from the Lord and not lifted up in pride as a result of success or prosperity.	2:6	**Understand** that God fills the universe. **Know** that nothing we build can contain Him; the best we can do is reflect His glory.
	7:14	**Identify** with the sins of your nation, confessing them as your own. **Repent** and **humble yourself. Seek God's face** to restore His blessing, and **believe** with all your heart that He will.
	26:16;	**Beware** the test of prosperity.
	32:25	**Guard against** pride when you have experienced success. **Be certain,** pride will lead to your downfall. **Repent** if pride is found in you.
4 Key Lessons in Faith Faith is rooted in a trust in God's witness in Scripture as illuminated by His Holy Spirit. Consequently, to grow in faith one must continually choose to receive and believe the witness of Scripture and become loyal to it.	20:20	**Develop** spiritual 20/20 vision: **Choose** to believe the Bible as the absolute Word of God. **Rely upon** its witness to God's nature, character, and promises. **Believe** the words of those who proclaim God's Word. **Trust** prophetic "words" brought by godly men and women.
	20:22	**Employ** and **believe in** praise as a mighty, effectual spiritual weapon.
5 Guidelines to Gaining Victory Exodus 17's revelation of God as "The-Lord-Our-Banner" (that is, "our victory" or "our miracle") forever secures victory for God's people. Victory in spiritual battles comes as we rely upon the Lord to fight on our behalf. This is what it	13:18	**Rely on** the Lord's wisdom, strength and abilities when confronting spiritual opposition. **Be assured** that this is the quickest way to victory.
	14:11; 32:7, 8	**Rely upon** the Lord when the ungodly oppose or persecute you. **Be assured** that man, who is finite, cannot prevail against God.

Truth 2 Chronicles Teaches	Text	**Action** 2 Chronicles Invites
5 means to trust the Lord in battle and stand still to see His deliverance.	20:15–25	**Covet** the presence of the Lord. **Depend** upon His presence when confronting any opposition. **Know** that the battle is not yours, but His. **Trust** the Lord to do your fighting for you.
6 **A Key to Contentment** Contentment results from knowing that the Lord is a ready resource for those who trust in Him.	25:9	**Never allow** finances to determine obedience. **Know** that God will supply all you need to do His will. **Confess** poor stewardship and **accept** God's forgiveness; then **obey.**
7 **Lessons for Leaders** The spiritual leader praised in the Scriptures is faithful to instruct God's people in God's Word, making sure they know it thoroughly and are careful to obey it. God consistently honors those who speak only the message He has put in their mouths.	14:4 17:9 18:7–27	Leaders, **teach** your people to seek the Lord and put His Word into practice. **Trust** that the Lord will cause them to prosper if they do. Leaders, **make sure** that your people are thoroughly taught and well-read in the Scriptures. Leaders, **be steadfast** in speaking only what God has given you to say. **Pursue** the reputation of being someone in whose mouth is the Word of the Lord.

The Book of EZRA

Author: Probably Ezra
Date: 538–457 B.C.
Theme: Exiles' Return to Jerusalem and Temple Reconstruction
Key Words: Build, the Hand of the Lord, the House of God

Author The Book of Ezra, whose name likely means "The Lord Has Helped," derives its title from the chief character of chapters 7—10. We cannot be totally sure whether Ezra himself compiled the book or it was compiled by an unknown editor. The generally accepted conservative view is that Ezra compiled or wrote this book, along with 1 and 2 Chronicles and Nehemiah. The Hebrew Bible recognized Ezra-Nehemiah as a single book.

Ezra himself was a "priest, [a] scribe, expert in the words of the commandments of the LORD" (7:11). He led the second of three groups returning to Jerusalem from Babylon. A devout man, he firmly established the Law (the Pentateuch) as the basis of faith (7:10).

Occasion and Date The events in Ezra cover slightly more than eighty years and fall into two distinct segments. The first segment (chs. 1—6) covers some twenty-three years, dealing with the first postexilic return under Zerubbabel and the reconstruction of the temple.

Following over sixty years in Babylonian captivity, God moves the heart of the ruler of Babylon, King Cyrus of Persia, to issue an edict stating that willing Jews can return to Jerusalem to rebuild the temple and city. A faithful group responds and departs in 538 B.C. under Zerubbabel. Temple construction is begun, but opposition from the non-Jewish inhabitants discourages the people and they cease their work. God then raises up the prophetic ministries of Haggai and Zechariah who call the people to complete the task. Though far less splendid than the previous temple of Solomon, the new temple is completed and dedicated in 515 B.C.

Nearly sixty years later (458 B.C.), another group of exiles returns to Jerusalem under the leadership of Ezra (chs. 7—10). They are sent by the then reigning Persian king, Artaxerxes, with additional monies and valuables to enhance the temple worship. Ezra is also commissioned to appoint leaders in Jerusalem to oversee the people.

Once in Jerusalem, Ezra assumes the ministry of spiritual reformer for what was probably only one year. After that he likely lived as an influential private citizen into the time of Nehemiah. A devout priest, he finds an Israel which has adopted many of the pagan inhabitants' practices; he calls Israel to repentance and to a renewed submission to the Law, even to the point of divorcing their pagan wives.

Content Two major messages emerge from Ezra: God's *faithfulness* and man's *unfaithfulness*.

God had promised through Jeremiah (25:12) that the Babylonian captivity would be limited in duration. In His ordained time, He faithfully keeps this promise and stirs the spirit of King Cyrus of Persia to issue an edict for the exiles to return (1:1–4). He then faithfully provides leadership (Zerubbabel and Ezra), and the exiles are sent off with booty, including items that had been taken from Solomon's temple (1:5–10).

When the people become discouraged because of the enemies' mockings, God faithfully raises up Haggai and Zechariah to encourage the people to complete the task. Their encouragement proves successful (5:1, 2).

Finally, when the people stray from the truths of God's word, He faithfully sends a devout priest who artfully instructs the people in the truth, calling them to confession of sin and repentance from their evil ways (chs. 9; 10).

God's faithfulness is contrasted with the people's unfaithfulness. In spite of their return and divine promises, they allow their enemies to discourage them and they temporarily give up (4:24). Then, having completed their task so they can worship in their own temple (6:16–18), the people become faithless to the commandments of God; an entire generation is raised up whose "iniquities have risen higher than *our* heads" (9:6). However, as noted above, God's faithfulness triumphs in each situation.

Personal Application The messages of Ezra are a constant reminder of how easily God's people can lose heart and their distinctives. God is fulfilling His promises. In spite of this, covenant people easily forget His promises and the moral distinctives that are to characterize "a royal priesthood, a holy nation, His own special people" (1 Pet. 2:9). When this happens God's plans are delayed. Erring saints cannot totally thwart God's sovereign plans, but they can delay or frustrate them. God is greater than we, and He does have ways of transcending our shortcomings. However, He wants us to walk in obedience so that His plans can be fulfilled as originally revealed.

Christ Revealed Ezra himself foreshadows Christ by the life he lives and the roles he fulfills. Three particulars stand out:

1) As one who "had prepared his heart to seek the Law of the LORD, and to do *it*" (7:10), Ezra reminds us of Christ's description of Himself as the One who ardently obeys the Father (John 5:19).

2) As "the priest" (7:11), Ezra foreshadows Christ's role as the "great High Priest" (Heb. 4:14).

3) As the great spiritual reformer who calls Israel to repentance (ch. 10), Ezra typifies Christ's messianic role as the reshaper of Israel's spiritual perspectives, including a call away from dead traditionalism and moral impurity (Matt. 11:20–24; 23).

The Holy Spirit at Work The working of the Holy Spirit in Ezra is clearly seen in the providential moving of God to fulfill His promises. This is indicated by the phrase "the hand of the LORD," which occurs six times.

It would have been by His Spirit that "the LORD stirred up the spirit of Cyrus" (1:1) and "turned the heart of the king of Assyria" (6:22). It would also have been by the Holy Spirit that "Haggai and Zechariah . . . prophesied to the Jews" (5:1).

The work of the Holy Spirit is clearly seen in Ezra's personal life, both in terms of working in him, "Ezra had prepared his heart to seek the Law of the LORD" (7:10), and on his behalf, "the king granted him all his request" (7:6).

Outline of Ezra

I. The return under Zerubbabel **1:1—2:70**
- A. Cyrus proclaims Israel's return 1:1–4
- B. The people prepare to return 1:5–11
- C. The first returnees are named and numbered 2:1–67
- D. The returnees give freely 2:68–70

II. The temple reconstruction process **3:1—6:22**
- A. The altar is built and sacrifices begun 3:1–7
- B. The foundation is laid, amid great praise and sorrow 3:8–13
- C. Enemies discourage the temple project 4:1–5
- D. Bishlam and his associates complain to King Artaxerxes 4:6–16
- E. Artaxerxes orders the work to cease 4:17–24
- F. Tattenai attempts to stop the temple project 5:1–17
- G. Darius assures Tattenai the project is legal 6:1–12
- H. The temple is completed and dedicated 6:13–18
- I. The Passover is celebrated 6:19–22

III. The return under Ezra **7:1—8:36**
- A. Ezra and more exiles depart from Babylon 7:1–10
- B. Artaxerxes writes a letter of support to Ezra 7:11–28
- C. The second group of returnees are named and numbered 8:1–20
- D. The exiles return to Jerusalem 8:21–36

IV. Ezra's reform **9:1—10:44**
- A. Ezra confesses Israel's transgressions 9:1–15
- B. Israel's leaders consent to reform 10:1–44

End of the Babylonian Captivity

CHAPTER 1

1 NOW in the first year of Cyrus king
of Persia, that the word of the
LORD [a]by the mouth of Jeremiah might
be fulfilled, the LORD *stirred up the
spirit of Cyrus king of Persia, [b]so that
he made a proclamation throughout all
his kingdom, and also *put it* in writing,
saying,

2 Thus says Cyrus king of Persia:
All the kingdoms of the earth the
LORD God of heaven has given
me. And He has [a]commanded me
to build Him a [1]house at
Jerusalem which *is* in Judah.
3 Who *is* among you of all His
people? May his God be with him,
and let him go up to Jerusalem
which *is* in Judah, and *build the
house of the LORD God of Israel
[a](He *is* God), which *is* in
Jerusalem.
4 And whoever is left in any place
where he dwells, let the men of
his place help him with silver and
gold, with goods and livestock,
besides the freewill offerings for
the house of God which *is* in
Jerusalem.

5 Then the heads of the fathers'
houses of Judah and Benjamin, and the
priests and the Levites, with all whose

1 [a]2 Chr. 36:22, 23; Jer. 25:12; 29:10 [b]Ezra 5:13, 14; Is. 44:28—45:13 *See WW at Hag. 1:14.
2 [a]Is. 44:28; 45:1, 13 [1]Temple
3 [a]1 Kin. 8:23; 18:39; Is. 37:16; Dan. 6:26 *See WW at Zech. 1:16.

1:1–3 These verses are a virtual repetition of 2 Chr. 36:22, 23, which has given rise to speculation over a common authorship of Chronicles and Ezra.

1:1 See section 1 of Truth-In-Action at the end of Ezra.

1:1 Cyrus was king of Persia from 559 to 530 B.C. This is a reference to 538 B.C., his first year of reigning over Babylon. **That the word of the LORD . . . might be fulfilled** is the underlying explanation of the historical events of this time. **By the mouth of Jeremiah** is probably a reference to Jeremiah's mention of 70 years of Babylonian captivity. If the starting date for the 70 years is the earliest deportation (605 B.C.), 538 marks only 67 years. This shows that either Jeremiah's 70 is not to be taken with strict literalness or that God mercifully shortened the captivity by 3 years.

spirits [a]God [1]had moved, arose to go
up and build the house of the LORD
which *is* in Jerusalem.
6 And all those who *were* around
them [1]encouraged them with articles
of silver and gold, with goods and livestock, and with precious things, besides all *that* was [a]willingly offered.
7 [a]King Cyrus also brought out the
articles of the house of the LORD,
[b]which Nebuchadnezzar had taken
from Jerusalem and put in the [1]temple
of his gods;
8 and Cyrus king of Persia brought
them out by the hand of Mithredath the
treasurer, and counted them out to
[a]Sheshbazzar the prince of Judah.
9 This *is* the number of them: thirty
gold platters, one thousand silver platters, twenty-nine knives,
10 thirty gold basins, four hundred and
ten silver basins of a similar *kind, and*
one thousand other articles.
11 All the articles of gold and silver
were five thousand four hundred. All
these Sheshbazzar took with the captives who were brought from Babylon
to Jerusalem.

5 [a][Phil. 2:13] [1]*stirred up*
6 [a]Ezra 2:68 [1]Lit. *strengthened their hands*
7 [a]Ezra 5:14; 6:5; Dan. 1:2; 5:2, 3 [b]2 Kin. 24:13; 2 Chr. 36:7, 18 [1]Lit. *house*
8 [a]Ezra 5:14, 16

CHAPTER 2

1 [a]Neh. 7:6–73; Jer. 32:15; 50:5; Ezek. 14:22 [b]2 Kin. 24:14–16; 25:11; 2 Chr. 36:20
2 [1]*Azariah,* Neh. 7:7 [2]*Raamiah,* Neh. 7:7 [3]*Mispereth,* Neh. 7:7 [4]*Nehum,* Neh. 7:7
5 [a]Neh. 7:10
6 [a]Neh. 7:11

The Captives Who Returned to Jerusalem

2 Now [a]these *are* the people of the
province who came back from the
captivity, of those who had been carried away, [b]whom Nebuchadnezzar
the king of Babylon had carried away
to Babylon, and who returned to Jerusalem and Judah, everyone to his *own*
city.
2 *Those* who came with Zerubbabel
were Jeshua, Nehemiah, [1]Seraiah,
[2]Reelaiah, Mordecai, Bilshan, [3]Mispar,
Bigvai, [4]Rehum, *and* Baanah. The
number of the men of the people of Israel:
3 the people of Parosh, two thousand
one hundred and seventy-two;
4 the people of Shephatiah, three
hundred and seventy-two;
5 the people of Arah, [a]seven hundred
and seventy-five;
6 the people of [a]Pahath-Moab, of the
people of Jeshua *and* Joab, two thousand eight hundred and twelve;
7 the people of Elam, one thousand
two hundred and fifty-four;

1:8 Sheshbazzar is a mystery figure, mentioned four times in Ezra but nowhere else in the OT. His name is Babylonian, but he is obviously Jewish. **Prince** defines an ambiguous position of authority, which is specified in 5:14 as **governor.**
2:2 Neh. 7:7 adds a twelfth leader, Nahamani, to the Chronicles list. He also has a variation for four of the names, a matter for which there is no uniform explanation among scholars. **Nehemiah** here is not to be confused with the famous Nehemiah of the next OT book, for these are leaders of the return under Zerubbabel.
2:3 This list occurs in Neh. 7 with some variation; the differences in numbers between Ezra and Nehemiah are probably the result of copyists' errors.

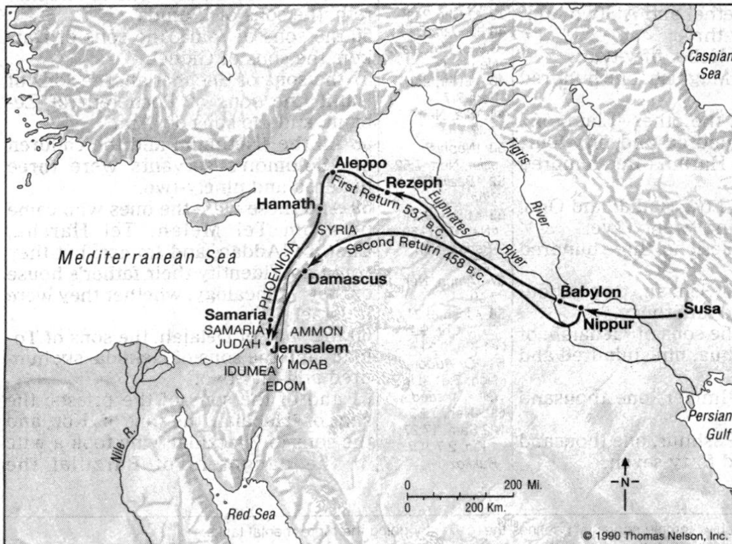

The Return from Exile. When Cyrus the Persian captured Babylon in 539 B.C., the way was opened for captive Judah to begin the return to her homeland. Two major expeditions made the journey, one in 537 B.C. and another in 458 B.C.

8 the people of Zattu, nine hundred
and forty-five;
9 the people of Zaccai, seven hundred
and sixty;
10 the people of [1]Bani, six hundred
and forty-two;
11 the people of Bebai, six hundred
and twenty-three;
12 the people of Azgad, one thousand
two hundred and twenty-two;
13 the people of Adonikam, six hundred and sixty-six;
14 the people of Bigvai, two thousand
and fifty-six;
15 the people of Adin, four hundred
and fifty-four;
16 the people of Ater of Hezekiah,
ninety-eight;
17 the people of Bezai, three hundred
and twenty-three;
18 the people of [1]Jorah, one hundred
and twelve;
19 the people of Hashum, two hundred
and twenty-three;
20 the people of [1]Gibbar, ninety-five;
21 the people of Bethlehem, one hundred and twenty-three;
22 the men of Netophah, fifty-six;
23 the men of Anathoth, one hundred
and twenty-eight;
24 the people of [1]Azmaveth, forty-two;
25 the people of [1]Kirjath Arim, Chephirah, and Beeroth, seven hundred
and forty-three;
26 the people of Ramah and Geba, six
hundred and twenty-one;
27 the men of Michmas, one hundred
and twenty-two;
28 the men of Bethel and Ai, two hundred and twenty-three;
29 the people of Nebo, fifty-two;
30 the people of Magbish, one hundred
and fifty-six;
31 the people of the other [a]Elam, one
thousand two hundred and fifty-four;
32 the people of Harim, three hundred
and twenty;
33 the people of Lod, Hadid, and Ono,
seven hundred and twenty-five;
34 the people of Jericho, three hundred
and forty-five;
35 the people of Senaah, three thousand six hundred and thirty.
36 The priests: the sons of [a]Jedaiah, of
the house of Jeshua, nine hundred and
seventy-three;
37 the sons of [a]Immer, one thousand
and fifty-two;
38 the sons of [a]Pashhur, one thousand
two hundred and forty-seven;
39 the sons of [a]Harim, one thousand
and seventeen.
40 The Levites: the sons of Jeshua and
Kadmiel, of the sons of [1]Hodaviah,
seventy-four.
41 The singers: the sons of Asaph, one
hundred and twenty-eight.
42 The sons of the gatekeepers: the
sons of Shallum, the sons of Ater, the
sons of Talmon, the sons of Akkub,
the sons of Hatita, and the sons of Shobai, one hundred and thirty-nine *in* all.
43 [a]The Nethinim: the sons of Ziha, the
sons of Hasupha, the sons of Tabbaoth,
44 the sons of Keros, the sons of
[1]Siaha, the sons of Padon,
45 the sons of Lebanah, the sons of
Hagabah, the sons of Akkub,
46 the sons of Hagab, the sons of Shalmai, the sons of Hanan,
47 the sons of Giddel, the sons of Gahar, the sons of Reaiah,
48 the sons of Rezin, the sons of Nekoda, the sons of Gazzam,
49 the sons of Uzza, the sons of Paseah, the sons of Besai,
50 the sons of Asnah, the sons of Meunim, the sons of [1]Nephusim,
51 the sons of Bakbuk, the sons of Hakupha, the sons of Harhur,
52 the sons of [1]Bazluth, the sons of Mehida, the sons of Harsha,
53 the sons of Barkos, the sons of Sisera, the sons of Tamah,
54 the sons of Neziah, and the sons of
Hatipha.
55 The sons of [a]Solomon's servants:
the sons of Sotai, the sons of [b]Sophe-
reth, the sons of [1]Peruda,
56 the sons of Jaala, the sons of Darkon, the sons of Giddel,
57 the sons of Shephatiah, the sons of
Hattil, the sons of Pochereth of Zebaim, and the sons of [1]Ami.
58 All the [a]Nethinim and the children
of [b]Solomon's servants were three
hundred and ninety-two.
59 And these *were* the ones who came
up from Tel Melah, Tel Harsha,
Cherub, [1]Addan, and Immer; but they
could not [2]identify their father's house
or their [3]genealogy, whether they *were*
of Israel:
60 the sons of Delaiah, the sons of Tobiah, and the sons of Nekoda, six hundred and fifty-two;
61 and of the sons of the priests: the
sons of [a]Habaiah, the sons of [1]Koz, and
the sons of [b]Barzillai, who took a wife
of the daughters of Barzillai the

10 [1]*Binnui,* Neh. 7:15
18 [1]*Hariph,* Neh. 7:24
20 [1]*Gibeon,* Neh. 7:25
24 [1]*Beth Azmaveth,* Neh. 7:28
25 [1]*Kirjath Jearim,* Neh. 7:29
31 [a]Ezra 2:7
36 [a]1 Chr. 24:7–18
37 [a]1 Chr. 24:14
38 [a]1 Chr. 9:12
39 [a]1 Chr. 24:8
40 [1]*Judah,* Ezra 3:9, or *Hodevah,* Neh. 7:43
43 [a]1 Chr. 9:2; Ezra 7:7
44 [1]*Sia,* Neh. 7:47
50 [1]*Nephishesim,* Neh. 7:52
52 [1]*Bazlith,* Neh. 7:54
55 [a]1 Kin. 9:21 [b]Neh. 7:57–60 [1]*Perida,* Neh. 7:57
57 [1]*Amon,* Neh. 7:59
58 [a]Josh. 9:21, 27; 1 Chr. 9:2 [b]1 Kin. 9:21
59 [1]Or *Addon,* Neh. 7:61 [2]Lit. *tell* [3]Lit. *seed*
61 [a]Neh. 7:63 [b]2 Sam. 17:27; 1 Kin. 2:7 [1]Or *Hakkoz*

2:43 Nethinim (probably "temple servants") defines the lowest rank of temple personnel; they helped the Levites by doing the more menial tasks.

Gileadite, and was called by their
name.
62 These sought their listing *among*
those who were registered by genealogy, but they were not found; [a]there-
fore they *were excluded* from the
priesthood as defiled.
63 And the [1]governor said to them that
they [a]should not eat of the most holy
things till a priest could consult with
the [b]Urim and Thummim.
64 [a]The whole assembly together *was*
forty-two thousand three hundred *and*
sixty,
65 besides their male and female servants, of whom *there were* seven thousand three hundred and thirty-seven;
and they had two hundred men and
women singers.
66 Their horses *were* seven hundred
and thirty-six, their mules two hundred
and forty-five,
67 their camels four hundred and
thirty-five, and *their* donkeys six thousand seven hundred and twenty.
68 [a]*Some* of the heads of the fathers'
houses, when they came to the house
of the LORD which *is* in Jerusalem, offered freely for the house of God, to
erect it in its place:
69 According to their ability, they gave
to the [a]treasury for the work sixty-one
thousand gold drachmas, five thousand minas of silver, and one hundred
priestly garments.
70 [a]So the priests and the Levites,
some of the people, the singers, the
gatekeepers, and the Nethinim, dwelt
in their cities, and all Israel in their cities.

Worship Restored at Jerusalem

3 And when the [a]seventh month had
come, and the children of Israel
were in the cities, the people gathered
together as one man to Jerusalem.
2 Then [1]Jeshua the son of [a]Jozadak[2]
and his brethren the priests, [b]and Zerubbabel the son of [c]Shealtiel and his
brethren, arose and built the *altar of
the God of Israel, to offer burnt offerings on it, as *it is* [d]written in the *Law
of Moses the man of God.
2 3 Though fear *had come* upon them
because of the people of those countries, they set the altar on its [1]bases;
and they offered [a]burnt offerings on it
to the LORD, *both* the morning and evening burnt offerings.
4 [a]They also kept the Feast of Tabernacles, [b]as *it is* written, and [c]*offered*
the daily burnt offerings in the number
required by ordinance for each day.
5 Afterwards *they offered* the [a]regu-
lar burnt offering, and *those* for New
Moons and for all the appointed feasts
of the LORD that were consecrated, and
those of everyone who willingly offered a freewill offering to the LORD.
6 From the first day of the seventh
month they began to offer burnt offerings to the LORD, although the foundation of the *temple of the LORD had not
been laid.
7 They also gave money to the masons and the carpenters, and [a]food,
drink, and oil to the people of Sidon
and Tyre to bring cedar logs from
Lebanon to the sea, to [b]Joppa, [c]accord-
ing to the permission which they had
from Cyrus king of Persia.

Restoration of the Temple Begins

8 Now in the second month of the second year of their coming to the house
of God at Jerusalem, [a]Zerubbabel the
son of Shealtiel, Jeshua the son of
[1]Jozadak, and the rest of their brethren
the priests and the Levites, and all
those who had come out of the captivity to Jerusalem, began *work* [b]and appointed the Levites from twenty years
old and above to oversee the work of
the house of the LORD.
9 Then Jeshua *with* his sons and
brothers, Kadmiel *with* his sons, and
the sons of [1]Judah, arose as one to
oversee those working on the house of
God: the sons of Henadad *with* their
sons and their brethren the Levites.
10 When the builders laid the foundation of the temple of the LORD, [a]the[1]
priests stood in their apparel with
trumpets, and the Levites, the sons of
Asaph, with cymbals, to praise the
LORD, according to the [b]ordinance[2] of
David king of Israel.
11 [a]And they sang responsively,
*praising and giving thanks to the
LORD:

[b]"For *He is* good,
[c]For His mercy *endures* forever
toward Israel."

62 [a]Num. 3:10 **63** [a]Lev. 22:2, 10, 15, 16 [b]Ex. 28:30; Num. 27:21 [1]Heb. *Tirshatha* **64** [a]Neh. 7:66; Is. 10:22 **68** [a]Ezra 1:6; 3:5; Neh. 7:70 **69** [a]1 Chr. 26:20; Ezra 8:25–35 **70** [a]Ezra 6:16, 17; Neh. 7:73

CHAPTER 3

1 [a]Neh. 7:73; 8:1, 2 **2** [a]1 Chr. 6:14, 15; Ezra 4:3; Neh. 12:1, 8; Hag. 1:1; 2:2 [b]Ezra 2:2; 4:2, 3; 5:2 [c]1 Chr. 3:17 [d]Deut. 12:5, 6 [1]Or *Joshua* [2]*Jehozadak,* 1 Chr. 6:14 *See WW at 2 Kin. 12:9. • See WW at Is. 42:21. **3** [a]Num. 28:3 [1]*foundations* **4** [a]Lev. 23:33–43; Neh. 8:14–18; Zech. 14:16 [b]Ex. 23:16 [c]Num. 29:12, 13 **5** [a]Ex. 29:38; Num. 28:3, 11, 19, 26; Ezra 1:4; 2:68; 7:15, 16; 8:28 **6** *See WW at Hag. 2:15. **7** [a]1 Kin. 5:6, 9; 2 Chr. 2:10; Acts 12:20 [b]2 Chr. 2:16; Acts 9:36 [c]Ezra 1:2; 6:3 **8** [a]Ezra 3:2; 4:3 [b]1 Chr. 23:4, 24 [1]*Jehozadak,* 1 Chr. 6:14 **9** [1]*Hodaviah,* Ezra 2:40 **10** [a]1 Chr. 16:5, 6 [b]1 Chr. 6:31; 16:4; 25:1 [1]So with LXX, Syr., Vg.; MT *they stationed the priests* [2]Lit. *hands* **11** [a]Ex. 15:21; 2 Chr. 7:3; Neh. 12:24 [b]1 Chr. 16:34; Ps. 136:1 [c]1 Chr. 16:41; Jer. 33:11 *See WW at 1 Chr. 23:30.

2:63 The Urim and Thummim were sacred lots used to learn God's will.

2:69 Drachma was either a Greek or Persian coin; **mina** was a Babylonian unit for measuring silver.

3:3 See section 2 of Truth-In-Action at the end of Ezra.

3:4 The Feast of Tabernacles is celebrated in the autumn. It is also known as the Feast of Booths, since it commemorates Israel's living in temporary shelters (booths) during the wilderness wanderings. See note on Deut. 16:13.

Then all the people shouted with a **great shout,** when they praised the LORD, because the foundation of the house of the LORD was laid.

WORD WEALTH

3:11 great shout, *teru'ah* (teh-roo-*ah*); Strong's #8643: A shout of joy, a clamor, blast of trumpets; the sounding of an alarm (especially with a trumpet); a cry of jubilee; a victory shout. Occurring 36 times, *teru'ah* is derived from the root verb *ru'a,* "to cry out and shout," whether in alarm or for joy. *Teru'ah* is an ear-piercing, great noise, a sound that cannot be ignored. *Teru'ah* describes the shouting of the Israelites when the ark was returning (2 Sam. 6:15). In Lev. 25:9, *teru'ah* is translated "Jubilee," literally "trumpet of the loud sound." *Teru'ah* is a significant term in Ps.; please refer to Ps. 27:6; 33:3; 47:5; 89:15; 150:5.

12 But many of the priests and Levites
and [a]heads of the fathers' *houses,* *old
men who had seen the first temple,
wept with a loud voice when the foundation of this temple was laid before
their eyes. Yet many shouted aloud for
joy,
13 so that the people could not discern
the noise of the shout of joy from the
noise of the weeping of the people, for
the people shouted with a loud shout,
and the sound was heard afar off.

Resistance to Rebuilding the Temple

4 Now when [a]the [1]adversaries of Judah and Benjamin heard that the
descendants of the captivity were
building the temple of the LORD God
of Israel,
2 they came to Zerubbabel and the
heads of the fathers' *houses,* and said
to them, "Let us build with you, for we
seek your God as you *do;* and we have
sacrificed to Him [a]since the days of
Esarhaddon king of Assyria, who
brought us here."
3 But Zerubbabel and Jeshua and the
rest of the heads of the fathers' *houses*
of Israel said to them, [a]"You may do
nothing with us to build a [1]house for
our God; but we alone will build to the
LORD God of Israel, as [b]King Cyrus the
king of Persia has commanded us."
4 Then [a]the people of the land tried 3
to discourage the people of Judah.
They troubled them in building,
5 and hired counselors against them
to frustrate their purpose all the days
of Cyrus king of Persia, even until the
reign of [a]Darius king of Persia.

Rebuilding of Jerusalem Opposed

6 In the reign of Ahasuerus, in the beginning of his reign, they wrote an accusation against the inhabitants of Judah and Jerusalem.
7 In the days of [a]Artaxerxes also,
[1]Bishlam, Mithredath, Tabel, and the
rest of their companions wrote to Artaxerxes king of Persia; and the letter
was written in [b]Aramaic script, and
translated into the Aramaic language.
8 [1]Rehum the commander and Shimshai the scribe wrote a letter against
Jerusalem to King Artaxerxes in this
fashion:

9 [1]From Rehum the commander,
Shimshai the scribe, and the rest
of their companions—
representatives of [a]the Dinaites,
the Apharsathchites, the
Tarpelites, the people of Persia
and Erech and Babylon and
[2]Shushan, the Dehavites, the
Elamites,
10 [a]and the rest of the nations whom
the great and noble Osnapper
took captive and settled in the
cities of Samaria and the
remainder beyond [1]the River—
[b]and so forth.[2]

11 (This *is* a copy of the letter that they
sent him)

To King Artaxerxes from your
servants, the men *of the region*
beyond the River, [1]and so forth:

12 Let it be known to the king that
the Jews who came up from you

---

12 [a]Ezra 2:68 *See WW at Ps. 119:100.

CHAPTER 4

1 [a]Ezra 4:7–9 [1]*enemies*
2 [a]2 Kin. 17:24; 19:37; Ezra 4:10
3 [a]Neh. 2:20 [b]Ezra 1:1–4 [1]Temple
4 [a]Ezra 3:3
5 [a]Ezra 5:5; 6:1
7 [a]Ezra 7:1, 7, 21 [b]2 Kin. 18:26 [1]Or *in peace*
8 [1]The original language of Ezra 4:8 through 6:18 is Aramaic.
9 [a]2 Kin. 17:30, 31 [1]Lit. *Then* [2]Or *Susa*
10 [a]2 Kin. 17:24; Ezra 4:1 [b]Ezra 4:11, 17; 7:12 [1]The Euphrates [2]Lit. *and now*
11 [1]Lit. *and now*

3:12 The weeping probably results from disappointment over this temple's lack of splendor compared to that of Solomon's temple (see Hag. 2:3).
4:2 Esarhaddon was Assyria's king from 681 to 669 B.C.
4:4, 5 See section 3 of Truth-In-Action at the end of Ezra.
4:5 Cyrus reigned over Babylon from 538 to 530 B.C.; **Darius** reigned from 522 to 486 B.C.
4:6–23 This passage is parenthetical to the narrative. It refers to the later opposition to rebuilding the city's walls. Chronologically it belongs either between chs. 6 and 7 or after the events of Ezra.
4:6 Ahasuerus (his Hebrew name) reigned over Babylon from 486 to 465 B.C. His Greek name is Xerxes.
4:7 Artaxerxes reigned over Babylon from 465 to 423 B.C.
4:8—6:18 This passage and 7:12–26 are written in Aramaic rather than in Hebrew, probably because they preserve an official correspondence with the king.
4:10 Osnapper is Esarhaddon's great-grandson; he reigned from 669 to 627 B.C.

have come to us at Jerusalem, and are building the [a]rebellious and evil city, and are finishing *its* [b]walls and repairing the foundations.
13 Let it now be known to the king that, if this city is built and the walls completed, they will not pay [a]tax, tribute, or custom, and the king's treasury will be diminished.
14 Now because we receive support from the palace, it was not proper for us to see the king's dishonor; therefore we have sent and informed the king,
15 that search may be made in the book of the records of your fathers. And you will find in the book of the records and know that this city *is* a rebellious city, harmful to kings and provinces, and that they have incited sedition within the city in former times, for which cause this city was destroyed.
16 We inform the king that if this city is rebuilt and its walls are completed, the result will be that you will have no dominion beyond the River.

17 The king sent an answer:

To Rehum the commander, *to* Shimshai the scribe, *to* the rest of their companions who dwell in Samaria, and *to* the remainder beyond the River:

Peace, [1]and so forth.

18 The letter which you sent to us has been clearly read before me.
19 And [1]I gave the command, and a search has been made, and it was found that this city in former times has revolted against kings, and rebellion and sedition have been fostered in it.
20 There have also been mighty kings over Jerusalem, who have [a]ruled over all *the region* [b]beyond the River; and tax, tribute, and custom were paid to them.
21 Now [1]give the command to make these men cease, that this city may not be built until the command is given by me.
22 Take heed now that you do not fail to do this. Why should damage increase to the hurt of the kings?

23 Now when the copy of King Artaxerxes' letter *was* read before Rehum, Shimshai the scribe, and their companions, they went up in haste to Jerusalem against the Jews, and by force of arms made them cease.
24 Thus the work of the house of God which *is* at Jerusalem ceased, and it was discontinued until the second year of the reign of Darius king of Persia.

12 [a]2 Chr. 36:13 [b]Ezra 5:3, 9
13 [a]Ezra 4:20; 7:24
17 [1]Lit. *and now*
19 [1]Lit. *by me a decree has been put forth*
20 [a]1 Kin. 4:21; 1 Chr. 18:3; Ps. 72:8 [b]Gen. 15:18; Josh. 1:4
21 [1]*put forth a decree*

Restoration of the Temple Resumed

5 Then the prophet [a]Haggai and [b]Zechariah the son of Iddo, prophets, prophesied to the Jews who *were* in Judah and Jerusalem, in the name of the God of Israel, *who was* over them.
2 So [a]Zerubbabel the son of Shealtiel and Jeshua the son of [1]Jozadak rose up and began to build the house of God which *is* in Jerusalem; and [b]the prophets of God *were* with them, helping them.
3 At the same time [a]Tattenai the governor of *the region* beyond [1]the River and Shethar-Boznai and their companions came to them and spoke thus to them: [b]"Who has commanded you to build this [2]temple and finish this wall?"
4 [a]Then, accordingly, we told them the names of the men who were constructing this building.
5 But [a]the eye of their God was upon the elders of the Jews, so that they could not make them cease till a report could go to Darius. Then a [b]written answer was returned concerning this *matter.*
6 This is a copy of the letter that Tattenai sent:

The governor of *the region* beyond the River, and Shethar-Boznai, [a]and his companions, the Persians who *were in the region* beyond the River, to Darius the king.

7 (They sent a letter to him, in which was written thus)

To Darius the king:

All peace.

8 Let it be known to the king that we went into the province of

CHAPTER 5
1 [a]Hag. 1:1 [b]Zech. 1:1
2 [a]Ezra 3:2; Hag. 1:12 [b]Ezra 6:14; Hag. 2:4 [1]*Jehozadak,* 1 Chr. 6:14
3 [a]Ezra 5:6; 6:6 [b]Ezra 1:3; 5:9 [1]The Euphrates [2]Lit. *house*
4 [a]Ezra 5:10
5 [a]2 Chr. 16:9; Ezra 7:6, 28; Ps. 33:18 [b]Ezra 6:6
6 [a]Ezra 4:7–10

5:1 God often encourages His people by means of prophetic messages. See 1 Cor. 14:3, 31.

Judea, to the [1]temple of the great
God, which is being built with
[2]heavy stones, and timber is
being laid in the walls; and this
work goes on diligently and
prospers in their hands.
9 Then we asked those elders, *and*
spoke thus to them: [a]"Who
commanded you to build this
temple and to finish these walls?"
10 We also asked them their names
to inform you, that we might write
the names of the men who *were*
chief among them.
11 And thus they returned us an
answer, saying: "We are the
servants of the God of heaven and
earth, and we are rebuilding the
[1]temple that was built many years
ago, which a great king of Israel
built [a]and completed.
12 "But [a]because our fathers
provoked the God of heaven to
wrath, He gave them into the
hand of [b]Nebuchadnezzar king of
Babylon, the Chaldean, *who*
destroyed this temple and
[c]carried the people away to
Babylon.
13 "However, in the first year of
[a]Cyrus king of Babylon, King
Cyrus issued a decree to build this
[1]house of God.
14 "Also, [a]the gold and silver
articles of the house of God,
which Nebuchadnezzar had
taken from the temple that *was*
in Jerusalem and carried into the
temple of Babylon—those King
Cyrus took from the temple of
Babylon, and they were given to
[b]one named Sheshbazzar, whom
he had made governor.
15 "And he said to him, 'Take these
articles; go, carry them to the
temple *site* that *is* in Jerusalem,
and let the house of God be
rebuilt on its former site.'
16 "Then the same Sheshbazzar
came *and* [a]laid the foundation of
the house of God which *is* in
Jerusalem; but from that time
even until now it has been under
construction, and [b]it is not
finished."
17 Now therefore, if *it seems* good
to the king, [a]let a search be made
in the king's treasure house,
which *is* there in Babylon,
whether it is *so* that a decree was
issued by King Cyrus to build this

8 [1]Lit. *house* [2]Lit. *stones of rolling,* stones too heavy to be carried
9 [a]Ezra 5:3, 4
11 [a]1 Kin. 6:1, 38 [1]Lit. *house*
12 [a]2 Chr. 34:25; 36:16, 17 [b]2 Kin. 24:2; 25:8–11; 2 Chr. 36:17; Jer. 52:12–15 [c]Jer. 13:19
13 [a]Ezra 1:1 [1]Temple
14 [a]Ezra 1:7, 8; 6:5; Dan. 5:2 [b]Hag. 1:14; 2:2, 21
16 [a]Ezra 3:8–10; Hag. 2:18 [b]Ezra 6:15
17 [a]Ezra 6:1, 2

CHAPTER 6

1 [a]Ezra 5:17 [1]Lit. *house of the scrolls*
2 [a]2 Kin. 17:6 [1]Probably *Ecbatana,* the ancient capital of Media
3 [a]Ezra 1:1; 5:13
4 [a]1 Kin. 6:36 [b]Ezra 3:7
5 [a]Ezra 1:7, 8; 5:14
6 [a]Ezra 5:3, 6
8 [1]Temple

house of God at Jerusalem, and
let the king send us his pleasure
concerning this *matter*.

The Decree of Darius

6 Then King Darius issued a decree, **5**
[a]and a search was made in the
[1]archives, where the treasures were
stored in Babylon.
2 And at [1]Achmetha, in the palace
that *is* in the province of [a]Media, a
scroll was found, and in it a record *was*
written thus:

3 In the first year of King Cyrus,
King Cyrus issued a [a]decree
concerning the house of God at
Jerusalem: "Let the house be
rebuilt, the place where they
offered sacrifices; and let the
foundations of it be firmly laid, its
height sixty cubits *and* its width
sixty cubits,
4 [a]*with* three rows of heavy stones
and one row of new timber. Let
the [b]expenses be paid from the
king's treasury.
5 Also let [a]the gold and silver
articles of the house of God,
which Nebuchadnezzar took
from the temple which *is* in
Jerusalem and brought to
Babylon, be restored and taken
back to the temple which *is* in
Jerusalem, *each* to its place; and
deposit *them* in the house of
God"—
6 [a]Now *therefore,* Tattenai,
governor of *the region* beyond the
River, and Shethar-Boznai, and
your companions the Persians
who *are* beyond the River, keep
yourselves far from there.
7 Let the work of this house of God
alone; let the governor of the
Jews and the elders of the Jews
build this house of God on its site.
8 Moreover I issue a decree *as to*
what you shall do for the elders
of these Jews, for the building of
this [1]house of God: Let the cost
be paid at the king's expense from
taxes *on the region* beyond the
River; this is to be given
immediately to these men, so that
they are not hindered.
9 And whatever they need—young
bulls, rams, and lambs for the
burnt offerings of the God of
heaven, wheat, salt, wine, and oil,

5:14 Zerubbabel followed **Sheshbazzar** as governor.

6:1–12 See section 5 of Truth-In-Action at the end of Ezra.

according to the request of the
priests who *are* in Jerusalem—let
it be given them day by day
without fail,
10 [a]that they may offer sacrifices of
sweet aroma to the God of
heaven, and pray for the life of
the king and his sons.
11 Also I issue a decree that whoever
alters this edict, let a timber be
pulled from his house and
erected, and let him be hanged on
it; [a]and let his house be made a
refuse heap because of this.
12 And may the God who causes His
[a]name to dwell there destroy any
king or people who put their hand
to alter it, or to destroy this
[1]house of God which is in
Jerusalem. I Darius issue a
decree; let it be done diligently.

The Temple Completed and Dedicated

13 Then Tattenai, governor of *the
region* beyond the River, Shethar-
Boznai, and their companions diligently
did according to what King Darius had
sent.
14 [a]So the elders of the Jews built, and
they prospered through the prophesying of Haggai the prophet and Zechariah the son of Iddo. And they built
and finished *it*, according to the commandment of the God of Israel, and
according to the [1]command of [b]Cyrus,
[c]Darius, and [d]Artaxerxes king of Persia.
15 Now the temple was finished on the
third day of the month of Adar, which
was in the sixth year of the reign of
King Darius.
16 Then the children of Israel, the
priests and the Levites and the rest of
the descendants of the captivity, celebrated [a]the dedication of this [1]house
of God with joy.
17 And they [a]offered sacrifices at the
dedication of this house of God, one
hundred bulls, two hundred rams, four
hundred lambs, and as a sin offering
for all Israel twelve male goats, according to the number of the tribes of Israel.
18 They assigned the priests to their
[a]divisions and the Levites to their
[b]divisions, over the service of God in
Jerusalem, [c]as it is written in the Book
of Moses.

The Passover Celebrated

19 [1]And the descendants of the captivity kept the Passover [a]on the fourteenth *day* of the first month.
20 For the priests and the Levites had
[a]purified themselves; all of them *were
ritually* clean. And they [b]slaughtered
the Passover *lambs* for all the descendants of the captivity, for their brethren the priests, and for themselves.
21 Then the children of Israel who had
returned from the captivity ate together with all who had separated
themselves from the [a]filth[1] of the nations of the land in order to seek the
LORD God of Israel.
22 And they kept the [a]Feast of Unleavened Bread seven days with *joy; for
the LORD made them joyful, and
[b]turned the heart [c]of the king of Assyria toward them, to strengthen their
hands in the work of the house of God,
the God of Israel.

The Arrival of Ezra

7 Now after these things, in the reign
of [a]Artaxerxes king of Persia, Ezra
the [b]son of Seraiah, [c]the son of Azariah, the son of [d]Hilkiah,
2 the son of Shallum, the son of Zadok, the son of Ahitub,
3 the son of Amariah, the son of Azariah, the son of Meraioth,
4 the son of Zerahiah, the son of Uzzi,
the son of Bukki,
5 the son of Abishua, the son of
Phinehas, the son of Eleazar, the son of
Aaron the chief priest—
6 this Ezra came up from Babylon;
and he *was* [a]a skilled scribe in the
*Law of Moses, which the LORD God
of Israel had given. The king granted
him all his request, [b]according to the
hand of the LORD his God upon him.
7 [a]*Some* of the children of Israel, the
priests, [b]the Levites, the singers, the
gatekeepers, and [c]the Nethinim came
up to Jerusalem in the seventh year of
King Artaxerxes.

10 [a]Ezra 7:23; [Jer. 29:7; 1 Tim. 2:1, 2]
11 [a]Dan. 2:5; 3:29
12 [a]Deut. 12:5, 11; 1 Kin. 9:3 [1]Temple
14 [a]Ezra 5:1, 2 [b]Ezra 1:1; 5:13; 6:3 [c]Ezra 4:24; 6:12 [d]Ezra 7:1, 11; Neh. 2:1 [1]*decree*
16 [a]1 Kin. 8:63; 2 Chr. 7:5 [1]Temple
17 [a]Ezra 8:35
18 [a]1 Chr. 24:1; 2 Chr. 35:5 [b]1 Chr. 23:6 [c]Num. 3:6; 8:9
19 [a]Ex. 12:6 [1]The Hebrew language resumes in Ezra 6:19 and continues through 7:11.
20 [a]2 Chr. 29:34; 30:15 [b]2 Chr. 35:11
21 [a]Ezra 9:11 [1]*uncleanness*
22 [a]Ex. 12:15; 13:6, 7; 2 Chr. 30:21; 35:17 [b]Ezra 7:27; [Prov. 21:1] [c]2 Kin. 23:29; 2 Chr. 33:11; Ezra 1:1; 6:1 *See WW at 2 Chr. 7:10.

CHAPTER 7

1 [a]Neh. 2:1 [b]1 Chr. 6:14 [c]Jer. 52:24 [d]2 Chr. 35:8
6 [a]Ezra 7:11, 12, 21 [b]Ezra 7:9, 28; 8:22 *See WW at Is. 42:21.
7 [a]Ezra 8:1–14 [b]Ezra 8:15 [c]Ezra 2:43; 8:20

6:14 This is a complete summation of Jerusalem's restoration. The temple was completed under Cyrus and Darius; the walls were completed in Artaxerxes' reign.

6:15 The month of Adar . . . in the sixth year of the reign of King Darius would have been February–March 515 B.C. This was some 72 years after the destruction of Solomon's temple.

6:17 The same temple stood in Jesus' day. It was enlarged and enhanced by Herod the Great and destroyed by Rome in A.D. 70.

6:22 The king of Assyria: A difficult reading since the favor came from the king of Persia. Perhaps "Assyria" was a proverbial term for any foreign ruler.

7:1 Now after these things is almost 60 years later, in 458 B.C.

8 And Ezra came to Jerusalem in the
fifth month, which *was* in the seventh
year of the king.
9 On the first *day* of the first month
he began *his* journey from Babylon,
and on the first *day* of the fifth month
he came to Jerusalem, [a]according to
the good hand of his God upon him.
10 For Ezra had prepared his heart to
[a]seek[1] the Law of the LORD, and to do
it, and to [b]teach *statutes and *ordinances in Israel.

The Letter of Artaxerxes to Ezra

5 11 This *is* a copy of the letter that King
Artaxerxes gave Ezra the priest, the
scribe, expert in the *words of the commandments of the LORD, and of His
statutes to Israel:

12 [1]Artaxerxes, [a]king of kings,

To Ezra the priest, a scribe of the Law of the God of heaven:

Perfect *peace,* [b]and so forth.[2]

13 I issue a decree that all those of the people of Israel and the priests and Levites in my realm, who volunteer to go up to Jerusalem, may go with you.
14 And whereas you are being sent [1]by the king and his [a]seven counselors to inquire concerning Judah and Jerusalem, with regard to the Law of your God which *is* in your hand;
15 and *whereas you are* to carry the silver and gold which the king and his counselors have freely offered to the God of Israel, [a]whose dwelling *is* in Jerusalem;
16 [a]and *whereas* all the silver and gold that you may find in all the province of Babylon, along with the freewill offering of the people and the priests, *are to be* [b]freely offered for the [1]house of their God in Jerusalem—
17 now therefore, be careful to buy with this money bulls, rams, and lambs, with their [a]grain offerings and their drink offerings, and [b]offer them on the altar of the house of your God in Jerusalem.
18 And whatever seems good to you and your brethren to do with the rest of the silver and the gold, do it according to the will of your God.
19 Also the articles that are given to you for the service of the house of your God, deliver in full before the God of Jerusalem.
20 And whatever more may be needed for the house of your God, which you may have occasion to provide, pay *for it* from the king's treasury.
21 And I, *even* I, Artaxerxes the king, issue a decree to all the treasurers who *are in the region* beyond the River, that whatever Ezra the priest, the scribe of the Law of the God of heaven, may require of you, let it be done diligently,
22 up to one hundred talents of silver, one hundred kors of wheat, one hundred baths of wine, one hundred baths of oil, and salt without prescribed limit.
23 Whatever [1]is commanded by the God of heaven, let it diligently be done for the [2]house of the God of heaven. For why should there be wrath against the realm of the king and his sons?
24 Also we inform you that it shall not be lawful to impose tax, tribute, or custom *on* any of the priests, Levites, singers, gatekeepers, Nethinim, or servants of this house of God.
25 And you, Ezra, according to your God-given wisdom, [a]set magistrates and judges who may judge all the people who *are in the region* beyond the River, all such as know the laws of your God; and [b]teach those who do not know *them.*
26 Whoever will not observe the law of your God and the law of the king, let judgment be executed speedily on him, whether *it be* death, or [1]banishment, or confiscation of goods, or imprisonment.

27 [a]Blessed[1] *be* the LORD God of our
fathers, [b]who has put *such a thing* as
this in the king's heart, to beautify the
house of the LORD which *is* in Jerusalem,
28 and [a]has extended mercy to me before the king and his counselors, and
before all the king's mighty princes.

9 [a]Ezra 7:6; Neh. 2:8, 18 **10** [a]Ps. 119:45 [b]Deut. 33:10; Ezra 7:6, 25; Neh. 8:1–8; [Mal. 2:7] [1]Study *See WW at Neh. 9:13. • See WW at Num. 36:13. **11** *See WW at Deut. 1:1. **12** [a]Ezek. 26:7; Dan. 2:37 [b]Ezra 4:10 [1]The original language of Ezra 7:12–26 is Aramaic. [2]Lit. *and now* **14** [a]Esth. 1:14 [1]*from before* **15** [a]2 Chr. 6:2; Ezra 6:12; Ps. 135:21 **16** [a]Ezra 8:25 [b]1 Chr. 29:6, 9 [1]Temple **17** [a]Num. 15:4–13 [b]Deut. 12:5–11

23 [1]Lit. *is from the decree* [2]Temple **25** [a]Ex. 18:21, 22; Deut. 16:18 [b]2 Chr. 17:7; Ezra 7:10; [Mal. 2:7; Col. 1:28] **26** [1]Lit. *rooting out* **27** [a]1 Chr. 29:10 [b]Ezra 6:22; [Prov. 21:1] [1]The Hebrew language resumes in Ezra 7:27. **28** [a]Ezra 9:9

7:10 Ezra's personal devotion and discipline later qualify him to minister as a priest in Jerusalem.

7:11–28 See section 5 of Truth-In-Action at the end of Ezra.

So I was encouraged, as [b]the hand
of the LORD my God *was* upon me; and
I gathered leading men of Israel to go
up with me.

Heads of Families Who Returned with Ezra

8 These *are* the heads of their fathers' *houses,* and *this is* the genealogy of those who went up with me
from Babylon, in the reign of King Artaxerxes:
2 of the sons of Phinehas, Gershom;
of the sons of Ithamar, Daniel; of the
sons of David, [a]Hattush;
3 of the sons of Shecaniah, of the sons
of [a]Parosh, Zechariah; and registered
with him *were* one hundred and fifty
males;
4 of the sons of [a]Pahath-Moab, Eliehoenai the son of Zerahiah, and with
him two hundred males;
5 of [1]the sons of Shechaniah, Ben-
Jahaziel, and with him three hundred
males;
6 of the sons of Adin, Ebed the son
of Jonathan, and with him fifty males;
7 of the sons of Elam, Jeshaiah the
son of Athaliah, and with him seventy
males;
8 of the sons of Shephatiah, Zebadiah
the son of Michael, and with him eighty
males;
9 of the sons of Joab, Obadiah the son
of Jehiel, and with him two hundred
and eighteen males;
10 of [1]the sons of Shelomith, Ben-
Josiphiah, and with him one hundred
and sixty males;
11 of the sons of [a]Bebai, Zechariah the
son of Bebai, and with him twenty-
eight males;
12 of the sons of Azgad, Johanan
[1]the son of Hakkatan, and with him
one hundred and ten males;
13 of the last sons of Adonikam, whose
names *are* these—Eliphelet, Jeiel,
and Shemaiah—and with them sixty
males;
14 also of the sons of Bigvai, Uthai
and [1]Zabbud, and with them seventy
males.

28 [b]Ezra 5:5; 7:6, 9; 8:18

CHAPTER 8

2 [a]1 Chr. 3:22; Ezra 2:68
3 [a]Ezra 2:3
4 [a]Ezra 10:30
5 [1]So with MT, Vg.; LXX *the sons of Zatho, Shechaniah*
10 [1]So with MT, Vg.; LXX *the sons of Banni, Shelomith*
11 [a]Ezra 10:28
12 [1]Or *the youngest son,*
14 [1]Or *Zakkur*

15 [a]Ezra 7:7; 8:2
16 [a]Ezra 10:15
17 [1]Lit. *I put words in their mouths to say* [2]So with Vg.; MT *to Iddo his brother;* LXX *to their brethren*
18 [a]2 Chr. 30:22; Neh. 8:7 *See WW at Ezek. 34:14.
19 [a]Neh. 12:24
20 [a]Ezra 2:43; 7:7
21 [a]1 Sam. 7:6; 2 Chr. 20:3 [b]Lev. 16:29; 23:29; Is. 58:3, 5 [c]Ps. 5:8 *See WW at Jon. 3:5.
22 [a]1 Cor. 9:15 [b]Ezra 7:6, 9, 28 [c][Ps. 33:18, 19; 34:15, 22; Rom. 8:28] [d][Ps. 34:16] [e][2 Chr. 15:2] *See WW at Ezek. 16:63 • See WW at Hos. 5:15.
23 [a][1 Chr. 5:20]; 2 Chr. 33:13; Is. 19:22

Servants for the Temple

15 Now I gathered them by the river 6
that flows to Ahava, and we camped
there three days. And I looked among
the people and the priests, and found
none of the [a]sons of Levi there.
16 Then I sent for Eliezer, Ariel, Shemaiah, Elnathan, Jarib, Elnathan, Nathan, Zechariah, and [a]Meshullam,
leaders; also for Joiarib and Elnathan,
men of understanding.
17 And I gave them a command for
Iddo the chief man at the place Casiphia, and [1]I told them what they
should say to [2]Iddo *and* his brethren
the Nethinim at the place Casiphia—
that they should bring us servants for
the house of our God.
18 Then, by the *good hand of our God
upon us, they [a]brought us a man of understanding, of the sons of Mahli the
son of Levi, the son of Israel, namely
Sherebiah, with his sons and brothers,
eighteen men;
19 and [a]Hashabiah, and with him
Jeshaiah of the sons of Merari, his
brothers and their sons, twenty men;
20 [a]also of the Nethinim, whom David
and the leaders had appointed for the
service of the Levites, two hundred and
twenty Nethinim. All of them were designated by name.

Fasting and Prayer for Protection

21 Then I [a]proclaimed a *fast there at 6
the river of Ahava, that we might
[b]humble ourselves before our God, to
seek from Him the [c]right way for us
and our little ones and all our possessions.
22 For [a]I was *ashamed to request of
the king an escort of soldiers and
horsemen to help us against the enemy
on the road, because we had spoken
to the king, saying, [b]"The hand of our
God *is* upon all those for [c]good who
*seek Him, but His power and His
wrath *are* [d]against all those who
[e]forsake Him."
23 So we fasted and entreated our God
for this, and He [a]answered our prayer.

8:1–14 This listing shows the specific fulfillment of Artaxerxes' decree in 7:13. It gives the return of priests (v. 2), royalty (vv. 2, 3) and common Hebrews (vv. 3–14). The list suggests a group of about 5,000 returned with Ezra.
8:15–36 This provides details of 7:6–9.
8:15–20 See section 6 of Truth-In-Action at the end of Ezra.
8:15–20 Before departing, Ezra has the entourage to camp for three days so he can inspect it. The missing Levites were necessary for priestly duties during the journey and for priestly reinforcements in Jerusalem to handle the planned celebration on arrival. **Ahava** was a large open space near Babylon through which flowed a tributary of the Euphrates River.
8:21–23 See section 6 of Truth-In-Action at the end of Ezra.
8:21 This **fast** demonstrates Ezra's profound faith and dependence on God.
8:22 The hand of our God occurs six times in the explanation of Ezra's return (7:6, 9, 28; 8:18, 22, 31). It is the key to understanding the events, which otherwise might appear to be the results of the kindness of a gracious king and the homeland loyalty of some hearty foreign citizens.

KINGDOM DYNAMICS

8:21–23 Fasting to Spiritual Breakthrough, FAITH'S WARFARE. As the exiled Jews prepared to return to Jerusalem, Ezra called for a nationwide fast (v. 21). The purpose of the fast was threefold: First, they petitioned God to lead them in a "right way." This was the guidance focus of their fast. Second, they petitioned God to protect their little ones. This was the assistance focus of their fast. Finally, they petitioned God to guard their possessions. This was the substance focus of their fast.

Fasting is repeatedly referred to throughout Scripture as a sacrificial form of prayer warfare that produces results available in no other way. This is especially emphasized in the demoniac's deliverance in Christ's day (Mark 9:14–29). Fasting involves a sacrificial denial of necessary nourishment while turning one's attention to seeking God during that denial. The duration of a fast may be as long as 40 days, as in Moses' case (Deut. 9:18–21), or as brief as a portion of a single day, as in Israel's case (2 Sam. 1:11, 12).

(Jer. 29:11–14/Rev. 12:7–11) D.E.

Gifts for the Temple

24 And I separated twelve of the leaders of the priests—Sherebiah, Hashabiah, and ten of their brethren with
them—
25 and weighed out to them [a]the silver, the gold, and the articles, the offering for the house of our God which the king and his counselors and his princes, and all Israel *who were* present, had offered.
26 I weighed into their hand six hundred and fifty talents of silver, silver articles *weighing* one hundred talents, one hundred talents of gold,
27 twenty gold basins *worth* a thousand drachmas, and two vessels of fine polished bronze, precious as gold.
6 28 And I said to them, "You *are* [a]holy[1] to the LORD; the articles *are* [b]holy also; and the silver and the gold *are* a freewill offering to the LORD God of your fathers.
29 "Watch and keep *them* until you weigh *them* before the leaders of the priests and the Levites and [a]heads of the fathers' *houses* of Israel in Jerusalem, *in* the chambers of the house of the LORD."
30 So the priests and the Levites received the silver and the gold and the articles by weight, to bring *them* to Jerusalem to the house of our God.

The Return to Jerusalem

31 Then we departed from the river of Ahava on the twelfth *day* of the first month, to go to Jerusalem. And [a]the hand of our God was upon us, and He delivered us from the hand of the enemy and from ambush along the road.
32 So we [a]came to Jerusalem, and stayed there three days.
33 Now on the fourth day the silver and the gold and the articles were [a]weighed in the house of our God by the hand of Meremoth the son of Uriah the priest, and with him *was* Eleazar the son of Phinehas; with them *were* the Levites, [b]Jozabad the son of Jeshua and Noadiah the son of Binnui,
34 with the number *and* weight of everything. All the weight was written down at that time.
35 The children of those who had been [a]carried away captive, who had come from the captivity, [b]offered burnt offerings to the God of Israel: twelve bulls for all Israel, ninety-six rams, seventy-seven lambs, and twelve male goats *as* a *sin offering. All *this was* a burnt offering to the LORD.
36 And they delivered the king's [a]orders to the king's satraps and the governors *in the region* beyond [1]the River. So they gave support to the people and the [2]house of God.

Intermarriage with Pagans

9 When these things were done, the leaders came to me, saying, "The people of Israel and the priests and the Levites have not [a]separated themselves from the peoples of the lands, [b]with respect to the abominations of the Canaanites, the Hittites, the Perizzites, the Jebusites, the Ammonites, the Moabites, the Egyptians, and the Amorites.
2 "For they have [a]taken some of their daughters *as wives* for themselves and their sons, so that the [b]holy seed is

25 [a]Ezra 7:15, 16
28 [a]Lev. 21:6–9; Deut. 33:8 [b]Lev. 22:2, 3; Num. 4:4, 15, 19, 20
[1]*consecrated*
29 [a]Ezra 4:3
31 [a]Ezra 7:6, 9, 28
32 [a]Neh. 2:11
33 [a]Ezra 8:26, 30 [b]Neh. 11:16
35 [a]Ezra 2:1 [b]Ezra 6:17
*See WW at Lev. 9:2.
36 [a]Ezra 7:21–24
[1]The Euphrates
[2]Temple

CHAPTER 9

1 [a]Ezra 6:21; Neh. 9:2 [b]Deut. 12:30, 31
2 [a]Ex. 34:16; [Deut. 7:3]; Ezra 10:2; Neh. 13:23 [b]Ex. 22:31; [Deut. 7:6]

8:26 A talent weighed about 75 pounds.
8:28–33 See section 6 of Truth-In-Action at the end of Ezra.
9:1–5 Ezra's initial joy at the return is quickly marred when he hears that those who returned under Zerubbabel have disobeyed God's basic commandments (Deut. 7:1–4). His response of grief again reinforces his serious devotion to God.

[c]mixed with the peoples of *those* lands. Indeed, the hand of the leaders and rulers has been foremost in this [1]trespass."

4 3 So when I heard this thing, [a]I tore my garment and my robe, and plucked out some of the hair of my head and beard, and sat down [b]astonished.

4 Then everyone who [a]trembled at the words of the God of Israel assembled to me, because of the transgression of those who had been carried away captive, and I sat astonished until the [b]evening sacrifice.

6 5 At the evening sacrifice I arose from my fasting; and having torn my garment and my robe, I fell on my knees and [a]spread out my hands to the LORD my God.

6 And I said: "O my God, I am too [a]ashamed and humiliated to lift up my face to You, my God; for [b]our *iniquities have risen higher than *our* heads, and our guilt has [c]grown up to the heavens.

7 "Since the days of our fathers to this day [a]we *have been* very guilty, and for our iniquities [b]we, our kings, *and* our priests have been delivered into the hand of the kings of the lands, to the [c]sword, to captivity, to plunder, and to [d]humiliation,[1] as *it is* this day.

8 "And now for a little while grace has been *shown* from the LORD our God, to leave us a remnant to escape, and to give us a peg in His holy place, that our God may [a]enlighten our eyes and give us a measure of revival in our bondage.

9 [a]"For we *were* slaves. [b]Yet our God did not forsake us in our bondage; but [c]He extended mercy to us in the sight of the kings of Persia, to revive us, to repair the house of our God, to rebuild its ruins, and to give us [d]a wall in Judah and Jerusalem.

10 "And now, O our God, what shall we say after this? For we have forsaken Your commandments,

11 "which You commanded by Your servants the prophets, saying, 'The land which you are entering to possess is an unclean land, with the [a]uncleanness of the peoples of the lands, with their abominations which have filled it from one end to another with their impurity.

12 'Now therefore, [a]do not give your daughters as wives for their sons, nor take their daughters to your sons; and [b]never seek their *peace or prosperity, that you may be strong and eat the good of the land, and [c]leave *it* as an inheritance to your children forever.'

13 "And after all that has come upon us for our evil deeds and for our great guilt, since You our God [a]have punished us less than our iniquities *deserve*, and have given us *such* deliverance as this,

14 "should we [a]again break Your commandments, and [b]join in marriage with the people *committing* these abominations? Would You not be [c]angry with us until You had [1]consumed *us*, so that *there would be* no remnant or survivor?

15 "O LORD God of Israel, [a]You *are* righteous, for we are left as a remnant, as *it is* this day. [b]Here we *are* before You, [c]in our guilt, though no one can stand before You because of this!"

2 [c][2 Cor. 6:14] [1]*unfaithfulness* **3** [a]Job 1:20 [b]Ps. 143:4 **4** [a]Ezra 10:3; Is. 66:2 [b]Ex. 29:39 **5** [a]Ex. 9:29 **6** [a]Dan. 9:7, 8 [b]Ps. 38:4 [c]2 Chr. 28:9; [Ezra 9:13, 15]; Rev. 18:5 *See WW at Ps. 130:3. **7** [a]2 Chr. 36:14–17; Ps. 106:6; Dan. 9:5, 6 [b]Deut. 28:36; Neh. 9:30 [c]Deut. 32:25 [d]Dan. 9:7, 8 [1]Lit. *shame of faces* **8** [a]Ps. 34:5 **9** [a]Neh. 9:36; Esth. 7:4 [b]Neh. 9:17; Ps. 136:23 [c]Ezra 7:28 [d]Is. 5:2

11 [a]Ezra 6:21 **12** [a][Ex. 23:32; 34:15, 16; Deut. 7:3, 4]; Ezra 9:2 [b]Deut. 23:6 [c][Prov. 13:22; 20:7] *See WW at Nah. 1:15. **13** [a][Ps. 103:10] **14** [a][John 5:14; 2 Pet. 2:20] [b]Neh. 13:23 [c]Deut. 9:8 [1]*destroyed* **15** [a]Neh. 9:33; Dan. 9:14 [b][Rom. 3:19] [c]1 Cor. 15:17

9:3, 4 See section 4 of Truth-In-Action at the end of Ezra.
9:5–15 See section 6 of Truth-In-Action at the end of Ezra.

9:7 Ezra is concerned that Israel is repeating the sin pattern that had taken her into captivity less than 100 years earlier.

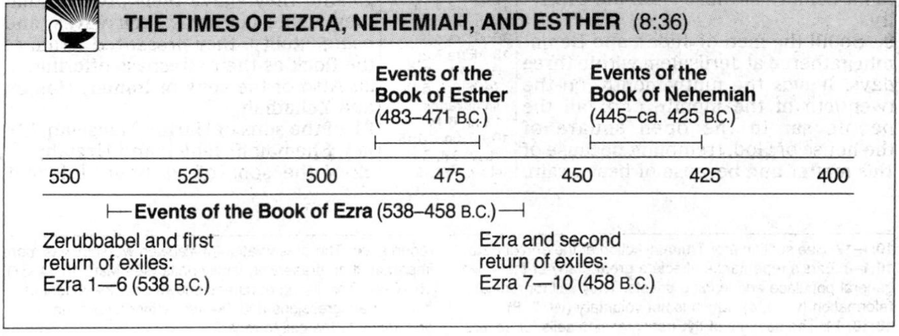

Confession of Improper Marriages

4 **10** Now [a]while Ezra was praying,
and while he was confessing,
weeping, and bowing down [b]before the
house of God, a very large assembly
of men, women, and children gathered
to him from Israel; for the *people wept
very [c]bitterly.
2 And Shechaniah the son of Jehiel,
one of the sons of Elam, spoke up and
said to Ezra, "We have [a]trespassed[1]
against our God, and have taken pagan
wives from the peoples of the land; yet
now there is hope in Israel in spite of
this.
3 "Now therefore, let us make [a]a covenant with our God to put away all
these wives and those who have been
born to them, according to the advice
of my master and of those who [b]trem-
ble at [c]the commandment of our God;
and let it be done according to the
[d]law.
4 "Arise, for *this* matter *is* your *responsibility*. We also *are* with you.
[a]Be of good courage, and do *it*."
5 Then Ezra arose, and made the
leaders of the priests, the Levites, and
all Israel [a]swear* an oath that they
would do according to this word. So
they swore an oath.
6 Then Ezra rose up from before the
house of God, and went into the chamber of Jehohanan the son of Eliashib;
and *when* he came there, he [a]ate no
bread and drank no water, for he
*mourned because of the guilt of those
from the captivity.
7 And they issued a proclamation
throughout Judah and Jerusalem to all
the descendants of the captivity, that
they must gather at Jerusalem,
8 and that whoever would not come
within three days, according to the instructions of the leaders and elders, all
his property would be confiscated, and
he himself would be separated from
the assembly of those from the captivity.
9 So all the men of Judah and Benjamin gathered at Jerusalem within three
days. It *was* the ninth month, on the
twentieth of the month; and [a]all the
people sat in the open square of
the house of God, trembling because of
this matter and because of heavy rain.

CHAPTER 10

1 [a]Dan. 9:4, 20 [b]2 Chr. 20:9 [c]Neh. 8:1–9 *See WW. at Ruth 1:16. **2** [a]Ezra 10:10, 13, 14, 17, 18; Neh. 13:23–27 [1]*been unfaithful to* **3** [a]2 Chr. 34:31 [b]Ezra 9:4 [c]Deut. 7:2, 3 [d]Deut. 24:1, 2 **4** [a]1 Chr. 28:10 **5** [a]Ezra 10:12, 19; Neh. 5:12; 13:25 *See WW at Gen. 26:3. **6** [a]Deut. 9:18 *See WW at Joel 1:9. **9** [a]1 Sam. 12:18; Ezra 9:4; 10:3

10 [1]*acted unfaithfully* [2]Heb. *have caused to dwell or have brought back* **11** [a][Lev. 26:40–42]; Josh. 7:19; [Prov. 28:13] [b]Ezra 10:3 **14** [a]2 Kin. 23:26; 2 Chr. 28:11–13; 29:10; 30:8 *See WW at Is. 33:6. **15** [a]Ezra 8:16; Neh. 3:4 **16** [a]Ezra 4:3 **18** [a]Ezra 5:2; Hag. 1:1, 12; 2:4; Zech. 3:1; 6:11 [1]*Jehozadak,* 1 Chr. 6:14 **19** [a]2 Kin. 10:15 [b]Lev. 6:4, 6 [c]Lev. 5:6, 15

10 Then Ezra the priest stood up and
said to them, "You have [1]transgressed
and [2]have taken pagan wives, adding
to the guilt of Israel.
11 "Now therefore, [a]make confession
to the LORD God of your fathers, and
do His will; [b]separate yourselves from
the peoples of the land, and from the
pagan wives."
12 Then all the assembly answered
and said with a loud voice, "Yes! As
you have said, so we must do.
13 "But *there are* many people; *it is*
the season for heavy rain, and we are
not able to stand outside. Nor *is this*
the work of one or two days, for *there
are* many of us who have transgressed
in this matter.
14 "Please, let the leaders of our entire
assembly stand; and let all those in our
cities who have taken pagan wives
come at appointed *times, together
with the elders and judges of their cities, until [a]the fierce wrath of our God
is turned away from us in this matter."
15 Only Jonathan the son of Asahel
and Jahaziah the son of Tikvah opposed this, and [a]Meshullam and Shabbethai the Levite gave them support.
16 Then the descendants of the captivity did so. And Ezra the priest, *with*
certain [a]heads of the fathers' *households,* were set apart by the fathers'
households, each of them by name; and
they sat down on the first day of the
tenth month to examine the matter.
17 By the first day of the first month
they finished *questioning* all the men
who had taken pagan wives.

Pagan Wives Put Away

18 And among the sons of the priests
who had taken pagan wives *the following* were found of the sons of
[a]Jeshua the son of [1]Jozadak, and his
brothers: Maaseiah, Eliezer, Jarib, and
Gedaliah.
19 And they [a]gave their promise that
they would put away their wives; and
being [b]guilty, *they presented* a ram of
the flock as their [c]trespass offering.
20 Also of the sons of Immer: Hanani
and Zebadiah;
21 of the sons of Harim: Maaseiah, Elijah, Shemaiah, Jehiel, and Uzziah;
22 of the sons of Pashhur: Elioenai,

10:1–17 See section 4 of Truth-In-Action at the end of Ezra.
10:1–8 Ezra's repentance affects a great many of the general populace and leading priests. They call for radical reformation (vv. 3, 4), which is not voluntary (vv. 7, 8).
10:10, 11 The severity of the transgression calls for severe repentance. The preservation of Yahweh worship was more important than preserving family units (see Matt. 10:34–37).
10:18–44 This listing of names shows both the extent of Israel's transgressions and the necessity of thorough obedience to the call to repent.

Maaseiah, Ishmael, Nethanel, Jozabad,
and Elasah.
23 Also of the Levites: Jozabad,
Shimei, Kelaiah (the same *is* Kelita),
Pethahiah, Judah, and Eliezer.
24 Also of the singers: Eliashib; and of
the gatekeepers: Shallum, Telem, and
Uri.
25 And others of Israel: of the [a]sons
of Parosh: Ramiah, Jeziah, Malchiah,
Mijamin, Eleazar, Malchijah, and Benaiah;
26 of the sons of Elam: Mattaniah,
Zechariah, Jehiel, Abdi, Jeremoth, and
Eliah;
27 of the sons of Zattu: Elioenai, Eliashib, Mattaniah, Jeremoth, Zabad,
and Aziza;
28 of the [a]sons of Bebai: Jehohanan,
Hananiah, Zabbai, *and* Athlai;
29 of the sons of Bani: Meshullam,
Malluch, Adaiah, Jashub, Sheal, *and*
[1]Ramoth;
30 of the [a]sons of Pahath-Moab: Adna,
Chelal, Benaiah, Maaseiah, Mattaniah,
Bezalel, Binnui, and Manasseh;
31 *of* the sons of Harim: Eliezer, Ishi-
jah, Malchijah, Shemaiah, Shimeon,
32 Benjamin, Malluch, *and* Shemariah;
33 of the sons of Hashum: Mattenai,
Mattattah, Zabad, Eliphelet, Jeremai,
Manasseh, *and* Shimei;
34 of the sons of Bani: Maadai, Amram, Uel,
35 Benaiah, Bedeiah, [1]Cheluh,
36 Vaniah, Meremoth, Eliashib,
37 Mattaniah, Mattenai, [1]Jaasai,
38 Bani, Binnui, Shimei,
39 Shelemiah, Nathan, Adaiah,
40 Machnadebai, Shashai, Sharai,
41 Azarel, Shelemiah, Shemariah,
42 Shallum, Amariah, *and* Joseph;
43 of the sons of Nebo: Jeiel, Mattithiah, Zabad, Zebina, [1]Jaddai, Joel,
and Benaiah.
44 All these had taken pagan wives,
and *some* of them had wives *by whom*
they had children.

25 [a]Ezra 2:3; 8:3; Neh. 7:8
28 [a]Ezra 8:11
29 [1]Or *Jeremoth*
30 [a]Ezra 8:4
35 [1]Or *Cheluhi* or *Cheluhu*
37 [1]Or *Jaasu*
43 [1]Or *Jaddu*

TRUTH-IN-ACTION through EZRA

Letting the LIFE of the Holy Spirit Bring Faith's Works Alive in You!

Truth Ezra Teaches	Text	**Action** Ezra Invites
1 Knowing God Knowing God is knowing that He honors His Word, even above His name.	1:1	**Be assured** God makes certain that His Word will be fulfilled.
2 A Guideline for Godly Living Godly living is standing up for what you believe even in the face of hostile opposition.	3:3	**Be faithful** to God, and be bold in your faith in Him despite the possible hostility of the world around you. **Remember** that the Lord will honor those who honor Him.
3 Steps to Holiness The holy life is separated from the world and set apart to God.	4:4, 5	**Be advised** that the world seeks to discourage and frustrate the purposes of God's people. **Seek counsel** from God, and **shun** the advice of the ungodly.
4 Steps to Dealing with Sin We must be careful lest we forget the cost of forgiveness. Sin is serious, and we must deal with it seriously! Sin sent God's only Son to the Cross. Let us not forget that God's conditions for forgiveness include our repentance, confession of, and forsaking of our sin.	9:3, 4 10:1–17	**Avoid** becoming calloused to sin. **Let sin disturb you** and bring appropriate remorse. To mourn over sin is to be humbled when recognizing it. Take sin seriously, and **deal** with it thoroughly. **Follow through** with repentance: **Take steps** to right the wrongs sin has brought about. **Do not pervert** forgiveness by continuing in sin.
5 Keys to Relating to Authority The righteous can manifest submission even when facing hostile civil authority. Our faith that God is	6:1–12	**Submit** to all authority, knowing that it comes from God. **Trust** God to work through any authority to which you must respond.

Truth Ezra Teaches	Text	**Action** Ezra Invites
5 sovereign beyond all authority allows the spirit of submission to prevail, knowing God can work beyond all authority to accomplish His will.	7:11–28	**Believe** that God is able to work blessing for His people through civil authority, even when it may be hostile. **Trust** His ability to work His will, even beyond civil government.
6 **Lessons for Leaders** The biblical model for leaders is that of the "servant leader." The servant leader does not boss, dominate, or dictate to God's people. He "goes before" them. To lead as a servant is to "do it first," avoiding the way of the Pharisees who instructed people to do things they themselves would not do. The servant leader asks God's people to do what he himself has established in his own life. This should first be evident in the way he deals with sin and be manifest in his spirit of repentance.	8:15–20 8:21–23 8:28–33 9:5–15	Leaders, **ask** the Lord to send others to help you in your assigned place of ministry. **Do not** try to accomplish the job alone. Leaders, **employ** corporate fasting when you undertake a major project or enter a significant season in your church's life. **Be assured** that God regards the self-humbling that accompanies prayer and fasting. Leaders, **pursue excellence** in your stewardship of material things. **Keep** all financial dealings "in the light"! Leaders, **choose to intercede** for God's people rather than become upset with them. **Identify** with their sin, and **confess** it as your own. Leaders, **learn to lead** in the confession of sin as a model for your people.

The Book of

NEHEMIAH

Author: Nehemiah
Date: Approximately 423 B.C.
Theme: Godly Leadership, Cooperation, Opposition to Success
Key Words: Distress, Praying, Work, the Book, Weeping, Joy, Service

Author The book derives its present title from the main character whose name appears in 1:1. (See "Occasion and Date" below). Our first glimpse of Nehemiah is in his role as cupbearer at the court of Artaxerxes. A cupbearer had a position of great trust as advisor to the king and had the responsibility of keeping the king from being poisoned. While Nehemiah no doubt enjoyed the luxury of the palace, his heart was in Jerusalem, a little city on the far frontier of the empire.

Nehemiah's prayer and fasting, qualities of leadership, powerful eloquence, inspirational organizational skills, confidence in God's purpose, and quick, decisive response to problems qualify him as a great leader and man of God. Most importantly, he shows us a self-sacrificing spirit whose only interest is summed up in his repeated prayer, "Remember me, O my God, for good."

Occasion and Date In the Hebrew Scriptures Nehemiah was originally included with Ezra. Many scholars consider Ezra as the compiler/author of Ezra-Nehemiah, as well as 1 and 2 Chronicles. Though we cannot be sure, it does seem that Nehemiah contributed some of the material in the book bearing his name (chs. 1—7; 11—13).

Jerome, who translated the Bible into Latin, honored Nehemiah by naming the book after him as its main character. Nehemiah means "Yahweh Comforts." The story begins in the Book of Ezra and is completed in Nehemiah. Nehemiah, who twice served as governor of Judea, leaves Persia on his first mission in the twentieth year of Artaxerxes I of Persia, who reigned from 465 until 424 B.C. (2:1). He returns to Persia in the king's thirty-second year (13:6), and he leaves again for Jerusalem "after certain days."

The contents of the book dictate that the work could not have been written until some time after Nehemiah's return from Persia to Jerusalem. Perhaps it was written in its completed form before the death of Artaxerxes I in 424 B.C.; otherwise the death of such a gracious monarch would probably have been mentioned in Nehemiah.

The historical period covered by the books of Ezra and Nehemiah is about 110 years. The period of rebuilding the temple under Zerubbabel, inspired by the preaching of Zechariah and Haggai, was twenty-one years. Sixty years later Ezra brought a revival and proper teaching on temple worship. After thirteen years Nehemiah came to work on the walls. Malachi may also have prophesied during this time. If so, Nehemiah and Malachi worked together to eradicate the evil of the worship of many gods, and they attacked the evil of compromise with the peoples who had been forcibly resettled in the land by the Assyrians approximately two hundred years earlier. They succeeded so well that, during the intertestamental period, the people of God did not return to idolatry. Thus, when the Messiah came, people such as Zacharias and Elizabeth, Mary and Joseph, Simeon, Anna, the shepherds, and others were godly people with whom God would communicate.

Content Nehemiah expresses the practical, everyday side of our faith in God. Ezra had led a spiritual renewal, while Nehemiah was the James of the Old Testament, challenging the people to show their faith by their works.

The first section of the book (chs. 1—7) deals with the wall. Protection from those outside the city was necessary for Judah and Benjamin to remain a people. In the wall-building period, the committed believers under this dynamic leader overcame laziness (4:6), mockery (2:20), conspiracy (3:9), and threats of physical attack (4:17).

The second section of the book (chs. 8—10) addresses the people inside the walls. The covenant was renewed, and the enemies inside the wall were exposed and dealt with very firmly. To lead His people God chose a man whose heart was right and who had a clear perspective on the issues, placed him in the right place at the right time, equipped him with His Spirit, and sent him forth to do exploits.

In the last section (chs. 11—13), the people are restored to obedience to God's Word, as Nehemiah the layman works with Ezra the priest. As governor during this period, Nehemiah used the influence of his office to support Ezra and to lead spiritually. Here is a man who wisely thinks things through in advance of his action ("after serious thought") and a man filled with boldness ("I contended with the nobles").

Personal Application Four lasting principles stand out in Nehemiah. First, compassion is often the springboard of obedience to God's will. Second, cooperation with others is required to carry out God's will. Third, confidence results from fervent prayer and the exposition of the Word of God, which reveals God's will. Fourth, courage will manifest itself as sanctified tenacity in refusing to compromise on the conviction that one is doing God's will.

Christ Revealed Nehemiah, with his associate Ezra, called on the people of God to remember the law. Doing so, he became part of the chain of inspired writers of Holy Scripture who put the people in the hands of the "tutor" (Gal. 3:23, 24) to guard them until Christ should arrive.

While Christ is not directly referred to in Nehemiah, Nehemiah typifies Him by the life he modeled. He was a courageous leader, defying the odds and encouraging the people to do Yahweh's work (2:18), even as Christ defied the people's opposition and encouraged His disciples to endure (John 15:18–27). He was an ardent prayer (2:1–20; 6:9–14), even as Christ was (Luke 6:12). Finally, he was dedicated to God's law (8:9, 10), an important element in Christ's life as well (Matt. 5:17).

The Holy Spirit at Work Since creation, the Holy Spirit has been the executive arm of God on Earth. Elihu spoke the truth when he said to Job, "The Spirit of God has made me" (Job 33:4). The pattern is consistent in that it is the Spirit of God who works to make us all that God desires us to be. Nehemiah 2:18 states, "And I told them of the hand of my God which had been good upon me." The hand of God, His action on Earth, is the Holy Spirit. Ezekiel, a captive in Babylon before the liberation of God's people and their return to Jerusalem, wrote: "I will give you a new heart and put a new spirit within you; I will take the heart of stone out of your flesh and give you a heart of flesh. I will put My Spirit within you and cause you to walk in My statutes, and you will keep My judgments and do *them*. Then you shall dwell in the land that I gave to your fathers; you shall be My people, and I will be your God" (Ezek. 36:26–28). Nehemiah, whose name means "Yahweh Comforts," was clearly an instrument of the Holy Spirit. Under the power of God's Spirit, he certainly modeled the Holy Spirit's workings and became one of the early fulfillments of this remarkable prophecy.

Outline of Nehemiah

I. Nehemiah goes from exile to rebuild the walls of Jerusalem 1:1—7:73
- A. Authority from Artaxerxes I to rebuild the wall 1:1—2:8
- B. Planning the work, motivating and organizing the workers 2:9—3:32
- C. Opposition and defense 4:1–23
- D. Extortion and usury resisted by Nehemiah's godly example 5:1–19
- E. Walls completed in spite of evil plots 6:1—7:3
- F. Reestablishment of Jerusalem's citizens 7:3–73

II. Ezra and Nehemiah work together to establish the people 8:1—10:39
- A. Reading the Bible 8:1–12
- B. Celebration of Feast of Tabernacles 8:13–18
- C. Confession of personal and corporate sin 9:1–37
- D. Commitment to keep the law and support the temple 9:38—10:39

III. True repentance results in righteousness 11:1—13:31
- A. Census of Jerusalem and surrounding villages 11:1—12:26
- B. Dedication of walls and provision for the finances of the temple 12:27—13:3
- C. Nehemiah's second term as governor, including further reforms and a final prayer 13:4–31

Nehemiah Prays for His People

THE words of [a]Nehemiah the son of Hachaliah.
It came to pass in the month of Chislev, *in* the [b]twentieth year, as I was in [c]Shushan[1] the [2]citadel,
2 that [a]Hanani one of my brethren came with men from Judah; and I asked them concerning the Jews who had escaped, who had survived the captivity, and concerning Jerusalem.
3 And they said to me, "The survivors who are left from the captivity in the [a]province *are* there in great distress and [b]reproach. [c]The wall of Jerusalem

CHAPTER 1

1 [a]Neh. 10:1 [b]Neh. 2:1 [c]Esth. 1:1, 2, 5 [1]Or *Susa* [2]Or *fortified palace,* and so elsewhere in the book
2 [a]Neh. 7:2
3 [a]Neh. 7:6 [b]Neh. 2:17 [c]Neh. 2:17

1:1–3 Chislev, *in* the twentieth year (of Artaxerxes I), would be December 446 B.C. The setting is **Shushan,** ancient winter capital of the kings of Persia, located in the southwestern area of present-day Iran. Daniel was here during Belshazzar's reign (Dan. 8:2). Esther, Mordecai, and Haman also were here. In Nehemiah's mind **Shushan** is contrasted with the broken down walls of **Jerusalem,** his ancestral city.

[d]*is* also broken down, and its gates *are*
burned with fire."
1 4 So it was, when I heard these
words, that I sat down and wept, and
mourned *for many* days; I was fasting and praying before the God of
heaven.
5 And I said: "I pray, [a]LORD God of
heaven, O great and [b]awesome God,
[c]*You* who keep *Your* covenant and
mercy with those who *love [1]You and
observe [2]Your commandments,
6 "please let Your ear be attentive
and [a]Your eyes open, that You may
hear the *prayer of Your servant which
I *pray before You now, day and night,
for the children of Israel Your servants,
and [b]confess the sins of the children
of Israel which we have sinned against
You. Both my father's house and I have
sinned.
7 [a]"We have acted very corruptly
against You, and have [b]not kept the
commandments, the statutes, nor the
ordinances which You commanded
Your servant Moses.
8 "Remember, I pray, the word that
You commanded Your servant Moses,
saying, [a]'*If* you [1]are unfaithful, I will
scatter you among the nations;
9 [a]'but *if* you return to Me, and keep
My commandments and do them,
[b]though some of you were cast out to
the farthest part of the heavens, *yet* I
will gather them from there, and bring
them to the place which I have chosen
as a dwelling for My name.'
10 [a]"Now these *are* Your servants
and Your people, whom You have
redeemed by Your great *power, and
by Your strong hand.

3 [d]2 Kin. 25:10
5 [a]Dan. 9:4 [b]Neh. 4:14 [c][Ex. 20:6; 34:6, 7] [1]Lit. *Him* [2]Lit. *His* *See WW at Ps. 97:10.
6 [a]2 Chr. 6:40 [b]Dan. 9:20 *See WW at 2 Chr. 6:20. • See WW at Job 42:10.
7 [a]Dan. 9:5 [b]Deut. 28:15
8 [a]Lev. 26:33 [1]*act treacherously*
9 [a][Deut. 4:29–31; 30:2–5] [b]Deut. 30:4
10 [a]Deut. 9:29 *See WW at Deut. 8:18.
11 [a]Neh. 1:6 [b]Is. 26:8 [c]Neh. 2:1

CHAPTER 2

1 [a]Ezra 7:1 [b]Neh. 1:11 [1]Artaxerxes Longimanus
2 [a]Prov. 15:13 [1]Lit. *very much*

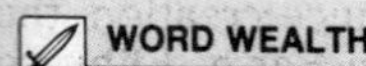

WORD WEALTH

1:10 redeemed, *padah* (pah-*dah*); Strong's #6299: To release, preserve, rescue, deliver, liberate, cut loose, sever; to free; to ransom. This verb occurs about 60 times. It describes how God delivered Israel out of Egyptian bondage (Deut. 7:8) and portrays Israel's rescue from all sin (Ps. 130:8). The "redemption of the firstborn" is another example of the verb's usage; see Ex. 13:15. God pledges to ransom His people from the power of the grave (Hos. 13:14). The phrase "the ransomed of the LORD" (Is. 35:10; 51:11) contains the verb *padah.* Whether the ransom is effected by means of a payment or a miraculous liberation, *padah* speaks of God's desire to free His people.

11 "O Lord, I pray, please [a]let Your ear 3
be attentive to the prayer of Your servant, and to the prayer of Your servants who [b]desire to fear Your name;
and let Your servant prosper this day,
I pray, and grant him mercy in the
sight of this man." For I was the king's
[c]cupbearer.

Nehemiah Sent to Judah

2 And it came to pass in the month
of Nisan, in the twentieth year of
[a]King [1]Artaxerxes, *when* wine *was* before him, that [b]I took the wine and
gave it to the king. Now I had never
been sad in his presence before.
2 Therefore the king said to me,
"Why *is* your face sad, since you *are*
not sick? This *is* nothing but [a]sorrow
of heart." So I became [1]dreadfully
afraid,

1:4–11 See section 1 of Truth-In-Action at the end of Neh.
1:4 His distress over Jerusalem drives Nehemiah to fast and pray.
1:5 Strong intercession is based on awareness of the sovereignty of God, who acts according to His promises (vv. 8, 9) when one confesses sin with true remorse and depends completely on God's mercy.
1:11 See section 3 of Truth-In-Action at the end of Neh.
1:11 The king's cupbearer: God has gone before to put His man in the right place at the right time. The cupbearer was responsible to select and serve the wine, taste it to be sure it was not poisoned, and be a tactful companion to the king. As the latter, he often offered informal counsel and enjoyed the king's confidence.
2:1, 2 Nisan was four months after Chislev (1:1). Nehemiah is afraid to appear sad at an inappropriate time before the king because cupbearers were to hide their emotions for the king's sake. To violate this was punishable by death.

PERSIAN KINGS OF THE RESTORATION, 559–404 B.C. (2:1)

Cyrus	Cambyses	Smerdis	Darius I	Xerxes I (Ahasuerus)	Artaxerxes I	Xerxes II	Darius II
559–530	530–522	522	522–486	(486–465)	465–424	424	423–404

575 550 525 500 475 450 425 400

3 and said to the king, [a]"May the king
live forever! Why should my face not
be sad, when [b]the city, the place of my
fathers' tombs, *lies* waste, and its gates
are burned with [c]fire?"
4 4 Then the king said to me, "What do
you request?" So I [a]prayed to the God
of heaven.
5 And I said to the king, "If it pleases
the king, and if your servant has found
favor in your sight, I ask that you send
me to Judah, to the city of my fathers'
tombs, that I may rebuild it."
6 Then the king said to me (the queen
also sitting beside him), "How long will
your journey be? And when will you
return?" So it pleased the king to send
me; and I set him [a]a time.
7 Furthermore I said to the king, "If
it pleases the king, let letters be given
to me for the [a]governors *of the region*
beyond [1]the River, that they must permit me to pass through till I come to
Judah,
4 8 "and a letter to Asaph the keeper
of the king's forest, that he must give
me timber to make beams for the gates
of the [1]citadel which *pertains* [a]to the
[2]temple, for the city wall, and for the
house that I will occupy." And the king
granted *them* to me [b]according to the
good hand of my God upon me.
9 Then I went to the governors *in the
region* beyond the River, and gave
them the king's letters. Now the king
had sent captains of the army and
horsemen with me.
3 10 When [a]Sanballat the Horonite and
Tobiah the Ammonite [1]official heard
of it, they were deeply disturbed that
a man had come to *seek the well-being of the children of Israel.

Nehemiah Views the Wall of Jerusalem

11 So I [a]came to Jerusalem and was
there three days.
3 12 Then I arose in the night, I and a
few men with me; I told no one what
my God had put in my heart to do at
Jerusalem; nor was there any animal
with me, except the one on which I
rode.
13 And I went out by night [a]through
the Valley Gate to the Serpent Well
and the [1]Refuse Gate, and [2]viewed the
walls of Jerusalem which were
[b]broken down and its gates which
were burned with fire.
14 Then I went on to the [a]Fountain
Gate and to the [b]King's Pool, but *there
was* no room for the animal under me
to pass.
15 So I went up in the night by the
[a]valley,[1] and [2]viewed the wall; then I
turned back and entered by the Valley
Gate, and so returned.
16 And the officials did not know
where I had gone or what I had done;
I had not yet told the Jews, the priests,
the nobles, the officials, or the others
who did the work.
17 Then I said to them, "You see the
distress that we *are* in, how Jerusalem
lies [1]waste, and its gates are burned
with fire. Come and let us *build the
wall of Jerusalem, that we may no
longer be [a]a reproach."
18 And I told them of [a]the hand of
my God which had been good upon
me, and also of the king's words
that he had spoken to me. So they
said, "Let us rise up and build."
Then they [b]set[1] their hands to *this*
good *work.*
19 But when Sanballat the Horonite, 3
Tobiah the Ammonite official, and Geshem the Arab heard *of it,* they
laughed at us and despised us, and
said, "What *is* this thing that you are
doing? [a]Will you rebel against the
king?"
20 So I answered them, and said to
them, "The God of heaven Himself will
prosper us; therefore we His servants
will arise and build, [a]but you have no

3 [a]1 Kin. 1:31; Dan. 2:4; 5:10; 6:6, 21 [b]2 Kin. 25:8–10; 2 Chr. 36:19; Jer. 52:12–14 [c]2 Kin. 24:10; Neh. 1:3
4 [a]Neh. 1:4
6 [a]Neh. 5:14; 13:6
7 [a]Ezra 7:21; 8:36 [1]The Euphrates
8 [a]Neh. 3:7 [b]Ezra 5:5; 7:6, 9, 28; Neh. 2:18 [1]*palace* [2]Lit. *house*
10 [a]Neh. 2:19; 4:1 [1]Lit. *servant* *See WW at Hos. 5:15.
11 [a]Ezra 8:32
13 [a]2 Chr. 26:9; Neh. 3:13 [b]Neh. 1:3; 2:17 [1]*Dung* [2]*examined*
14 [a]Neh. 3:15 [b]2 Kin. 20:20
15 [a]2 Sam. 15:23; Jer. 31:40 [1]*torrent valley, wadi* [2]*examined*
17 [a]Neh. 1:3; Ps. 44:13; 79:4; Jer. 24:9; Ezek. 5:14, 15; 22:4 [1]*desolate* *See WW at Zech. 1:16.
18 [a]Neh. 2:8 [b]2 Sam. 2:7 [1]Lit. *strengthened*
19 [a]Neh. 6:6
20 [a]Ezra 4:3; Neh. 6:16

2:4–6 See section 4 of Truth-In-Action at the end of Neh.
2:6 The queen also sitting beside him indicates the traditional role of the queen, to influence her husband to follow a kinder and gentler way.
2:8 See section 4 of Truth-In-Action at the end of Neh.
2:10 See section 3 of Truth-In-Action at the end of Neh.
2:12–16 See section 3 of Truth-In-Action at the end of Neh.
2:12–16 As a wise leader Nehemiah refrained from sharing his ideas with the people until he had accurately assessed matters, and, no doubt, prayerfully considered the cost.
2:17, 18 After the night of inspection, the true reason for the new governor's term of office comes out. The people recognize God's call on Nehemiah and offer full cooperation.
2:19 See section 3 of Truth-In-Action at the end of Neh.
2:19 Sanballat (whose name is Babylonian and means "Sin [the moon god] Gives Life") was Nehemiah's prime enemy. He loosely aligned himself with Yahwehism, as seen in the Yahwistic names he gave his two sons. **The Horonite** likely means he lived north of Jerusalem in Beth Horon. He was governor of Samaria as late as 408 B.C.

Tobiah (whose name is mysteriously Yahwistic) was an **Ammonite** indicating he was a pagan. He was apparently Sanballat's junior colleague. **Geshem the Arab** was perhaps governor of the Persian province of Arabia, just south of Judah, or he may have been a powerful tribal chieftain living as a nomad near the area's cities, just as the Bedouin do today in the Middle East. Abraham was such a powerful chieftain, able to raise an army sufficient to rescue neighboring kings and their people (Gen. 14).
2:20 Rather than arguing with them, Nehemiah affirms God's sovereignty, stating that these leaders no longer have any civic, legal, or religious rights **in Jerusalem.**

*heritage or right or *memorial in Jerusalem."

Rebuilding the Wall

3 Then [a]Eliashib the high priest rose up with his brethren the priests [b]and built the Sheep Gate; they consecrated it and hung its doors. They built [c]as far as the Tower of [1]the Hundred, *and* consecrated it, then as far as the Tower of [d]Hananel.

2 [1]Next to *Eliashib* [a]the men of Jericho built. And next to them Zaccur the son of Imri built.

3 Also the sons of Hassenaah built [a]the Fish Gate; they laid its beams and [b]hung its doors with its bolts and bars.

4 And next to them [a]Meremoth the son of Urijah, the son of [1]Koz, made repairs. Next to them [b]Meshullam the son of Berechiah, the son of Meshezabel, made repairs. Next to them Zadok the son of Baana made repairs.

6 5 Next to them the Tekoites made repairs; but their nobles did not put their [1]shoulders to [a]the work of their Lord.

6 Moreover Jehoiada the son of Paseah and Meshullam the son of Besodeiah repaired [a]the Old Gate; they laid its beams and hung its doors, with its bolts and bars.

7 And next to them Melatiah the Gibeonite, Jadon the Meronothite, the [a]men of Gibeon and Mizpah, repaired the [b]residence[1] of the governor *of the region* [2]beyond the River.

8 Next to him Uzziel the son of Harhaiah, one of the goldsmiths, made repairs. Also next to him Hananiah, [1]one of the perfumers, made repairs; and they [2]fortified Jerusalem as far as the [a]Broad Wall.

9 And next to them Rephaiah the son of Hur, leader of half the district of Jerusalem, made repairs.

10 Next to them Jedaiah the son of Harumaph made repairs in front of his house. And next to him Hattush the son of Hashabniah made repairs.

11 Malchijah the son of Harim and Hashub the son of Pahath-Moab repaired another section, [a]as well as the Tower of the Ovens.

12 And next to him was Shallum the son of Hallohesh, leader of half the district of Jerusalem; he and his daughters made repairs.

13 Hanun and the inhabitants of Zanoah repaired [a]the Valley Gate. They built it, hung its doors with its bolts and bars, and *repaired* a thousand cubits of the wall as far as [b]the Refuse Gate.

14 Malchijah the son of Rechab, leader of the district of [a]Beth Haccerem, repaired the Refuse Gate; he built it and hung its doors with its bolts and bars.

15 Shallun the son of Col-Hozeh, leader of the district of Mizpah, repaired [a]the Fountain Gate; he built it, covered it, hung its doors with its bolts and bars, and repaired the wall of the Pool of [b]Shelah[1] by the [c]King's Garden, as far as the *stairs that go down from the City of David.

16 After him Nehemiah the son of Azbuk, leader of half the district of Beth Zur, made repairs as far as *the place* in front of the [1]tombs of David, to the [a]man-made pool, and as far as the House of the Mighty.

17 After him the Levites, *under* Rehum the son of Bani, made repairs. Next to him Hashabiah, leader of half the district of Keilah, made repairs for his district.

18 After him their brethren, *under* [1]Bavai the son of Henadad, leader of the *other* half of the district of Keilah, made repairs.

19 And next to him Ezer the son of Jeshua, the leader of Mizpah, repaired another section in front of the Ascent to the Armory at the [a]buttress.[1]

20 After him Baruch the son of [1]Zabbai carefully repaired the other section, from the [2]buttress to the door of the house of Eliashib the high priest.

21 After him Meremoth the son of Urijah, the son of [1]Koz, repaired another section, from the door of the house of Eliashib to the end of the house of Eliashib.

22 And after him the priests, the men of the plain, made repairs.

23 After him Benjamin and Hasshub made repairs opposite their house. After them Azariah the son of Maaseiah,

20 *See WW at Zech. 2:12. • See WW at Ex. 39:7.

CHAPTER 3

1 [a]Neh. 3:20; 12:10; 13:4, 7, 28 [b]John 5:2 [c]Neh. 12:39 [d]Jer. 31:38; Zech. 14:10 [1]Heb. *Hammeah*
2 [a]Ezra 2:34; Neh. 7:36 [1]Lit. *On his hand*
3 [a]2 Chr. 33:14; Neh. 12:39; Zeph. 1:10 [b]Neh. 6:1; 7:1
4 [a]Ezra 8:33 [b]Ezra 10:15 [1]Or *Hakkoz*
5 [a][Judg. 5:23] [1]Lit. *necks*
6 [a]Neh. 12:39
7 [a]Neh. 7:25 [b]Ezra 8:36; Neh. 2:7–9 [1]Lit. *throne* [2]West of the Euphrates
8 [a]Neh. 12:38 [1]Lit. *the son* [2]*restored*
11 [a]Neh. 12:38
13 [a]Neh. 2:13, 15 [b]Neh. 2:13
14 [a]Jer. 6:1
15 [a]Neh. 2:14 [b]Is. 8:6; John 9:7 [c]2 Kin. 25:4 [1]Or *Shiloah* *See WW at Amos 9:6.
16 [a]2 Kin. 20:20; Is. 7:3; 22:11 [1]LXX, Syr., Vg. *tomb*
18 [1]So with MT, Vg.; some Heb. mss., LXX, Syr. *Binnui* (cf. v. 24)
19 [a]2 Chr. 26:9 [1]Lit. *turning*
20 [1]A few Heb. mss., Syr., Vg. *Zaccai* [2]Lit. *turning*
21 [1]Or *Hakkoz*

3:1–32 This chapter reveals a remarkable display of unity. The reconstruction of the walls was a tremendous challenge. Some 40 groups worked simultaneously. On the eastern and southeastern sides a whole new wall had to be constructed, and on the northwest and southwest the older wall needed to be repaired. Archaeologists have found remnants of the new wall, which are 8 feet thick. The successful rebuilding demonstrates Nehemiah's great ability to lead and organize. It also foreshadows unity of purpose and work that is to characterize the church (Phil. 1:27, 28).

3:5 See section 6 of Truth-In-Action at the end of Neh.

3:5 There is no reason given for the resistance by the Tekoite **nobles. Did not put . . . work** seems to indicate a resentment against Nehemiah's leadership.

3:12 Even the **daughters** repaired the wall. Surely this was unusual for the time.

the son of Ananiah, made repairs by
his house.
24 After him [a]Binnui the son of Henadad repaired another section, from the
house of Azariah to [b]the [1]buttress,
even as far as the corner.
25 Palal the son of Uzai *made repairs*
opposite the [1]buttress, and on the
tower which projects from the king's
upper house that *was* by the [a]court of
the prison. After him Pedaiah the son
of Parosh *made repairs.*
26 Moreover [a]the Nethinim who dwelt
in [b]Ophel *made repairs* as far as *the
place* in front of [c]the Water Gate toward the east, and on the projecting
tower.
27 After them the Tekoites repaired
another section, next to the great projecting tower, and as far as the wall
of Ophel.
28 Beyond the [a]Horse Gate the priests
made repairs, each in front of his *own*
house.
29 After them Zadok the son of Immer
made repairs in front of his *own* house.
After him Shemaiah the son of Shechaniah, the keeper of the East Gate, made
repairs.
30 After him Hananiah the son of Shelemiah, and Hanun, the sixth son of Za-
laph, repaired another section. After
him Meshullam the son of Berechiah made repairs in front of his
[1]dwelling.
31 After him Malchijah, [1]one of the
goldsmiths, made repairs as far as the
house of the Nethinim and of the merchants, in front of the [2]Miphkad Gate,
and as far as the upper room at the
corner.
32 And between the upper room at the
corner, as far as the [a]Sheep Gate, the
goldsmiths and the merchants made
repairs.

The Wall Defended Against Enemies

8 **4** But it so happened, [a]when Sanballat heard that we were rebuilding
the wall, that he was furious and very
indignant, and mocked the Jews.
2 And he spoke before his brethren
and the army of Samaria, and said,

24 [a]Ezra 8:33 [b]Neh. 3:19 [1]Lit. *turning*
25 [a]Jer. 32:2; 33:1; 37:21 [1]Lit. *turning*
26 [a]Ezra 2:43; Neh. 11:21 [b]2 Chr. 27:3 [c]Neh. 8:1, 3; 12:37
28 [a]2 Kin. 11:16; 2 Chr. 23:15; Jer. 31:40
30 [1]Lit. *room*
31 [1]Lit. *a son of the goldsmiths* [2]Lit. *Inspection* or *Recruiting*
32 [a]Neh. 3:1; 12:39

CHAPTER 4

1 [a]Neh. 2:10, 19

3 [a]Neh. 2:10, 19
4 [a]Ps. 123:3, 4 [b]Ps. 79:12; Prov. 3:34
5 [a]Ps. 69:27, 28; 109:14, 15; Jer. 18:23 *See WW at 1 Kin. 16:2.
7 [a]Neh. 4:1 [b]Neh. 2:19 [1]Lit. *breaks*
8 [a]Ps. 83:3–5
9 [a][Ps. 50:15]
10 *See WW at Num. 13:30.
13 *See WW at Gen. 12:3.

"What are these feeble Jews doing?
Will they fortify themselves? Will they
offer sacrifices? Will they complete it
in a day? Will they revive the stones
from the heaps of rubbish—*stones* that
are burned?"
3 Now [a]Tobiah the Ammonite *was*
beside him, and he said, "Whatever
they build, if even a fox goes up *on
it,* he will break down their stone
wall."
4 [a]Hear, O our God, for we are despised; [b]turn their reproach on their
own heads, and give them as plunder
to a land of captivity!
5 [a]Do not cover their iniquity, and do
not let their sin be blotted out from before You; for they have *provoked *You*
to anger before the builders.
6 So we built the wall, and the entire
wall was joined together up to half its
height, for the people had a mind to
work.
7 Now it happened, [a]when Sanballat,
Tobiah, [b]the Arabs, the Ammonites,
and the Ashdodites heard that the
walls of Jerusalem were being restored
and the [1]gaps were beginning to be
closed, that they became very angry,
8 and all of them [a]conspired together
to come *and* attack Jerusalem and create confusion.
9 Nevertheless [a]we made our prayer
to our God, and because of them we
set a watch against them day and
night.
10 Then Judah said, "The strength of
the laborers is failing, and *there is* so
much rubbish that we are not *able to
build the wall."
11 And our adversaries said, "They
will neither know nor see anything, till
we come into their midst and kill them
and cause the work to cease."
12 So it was, when the Jews who dwelt
near them came, that they told us ten
times, "From whatever place you turn,
they will be upon us."
13 Therefore I positioned *men* behind
the lower parts of the wall, at the openings; and I set the people according to
their *families, with their swords, their
spears, and their bows.
14 And I looked, and arose and said

4:1–6 See section 8 of Truth-In-Action at the end of Neh.

4:1–5 Ridicule's power is based on peer pressure. Nehemiah was immune because of his service to the peerless One, His God. Nehemiah's prayer may have been influenced by Ps. 109, a calling for judgment on the enemies of God's cause.

4:6 For the project to succeed the people had to combine right attitude with right action.

4:7–9 The threat of armed attack and physical violence cannot stop those whose purpose is more important to them than their lives.

4:10–23 By propaganda and fear-mongering, the enemies try to discourage some whose dedication to the task is waning, but those who are strong for God's purpose redouble their efforts. They add weapons to their assortment of masonry tools.

4:14 Remember the Lord, great and awesome was the exhortation sufficient to produce such single-minded devotion

to the nobles, to the leaders, and to the rest of the people, [a]"Do not be afraid of them. Remember the Lord, [b]great and awesome, and [c]fight for your brethren, your sons, your daughters, your wives, and your houses."

15 And it happened, when our enemies heard that it was known to us, and [a]*that* God had brought their plot to nothing, that all of us returned to the wall, everyone to his work.

16 So it was, from that time on, *that* half of my servants worked at construction, while the other half held the spears, the shields, the bows, and *wore* armor; and the leaders [1]*were* behind all the house of Judah.

8 17 Those who built on the wall, and those who carried burdens, loaded themselves so that with one hand they worked at construction, and with the other held a weapon.

18 Every one of the builders had his sword girded at his side as he built. And the one who *sounded the *trumpet *was* beside me.

19 Then I said to the nobles, the rulers, and the rest of the people, "The work *is* great and extensive, and we are separated far from one another on the wall.

20 "Wherever you hear the sound of the trumpet, rally to us there. [a]Our God will fight for us."

21 So we labored in the work, and half of [1]*the men* held the spears from daybreak until the stars appeared.

22 At the same time I also said to the people, "Let each man and his servant stay at night in Jerusalem, that they may be our guard by night and a working party by day."

23 So neither I, my brethren, my servants, nor the men of the guard who followed me took off our clothes, *except* that everyone took them off for washing.

Nehemiah Deals with Oppression

6 **5** And there was a great [a]outcry of the people and their wives against their [b]Jewish brethren.

2 For there were those who said, "We, our sons, and our daughters *are* many; therefore let us get grain, that we may eat and *live."

3 There were also *some* who said, "We have mortgaged our lands and vineyards and houses, that we might buy grain because of the famine."

4 There were also those who said, "We have borrowed money for the king's tax *on* our lands and vineyards.

5 "Yet now [a]our flesh *is* as the flesh of our brethren, our children as their children; and indeed we [b]are forcing our sons and our daughters to be slaves, and *some* of our daughters have been brought into slavery. *It is* not in our power *to redeem them,* for other men have our lands and vineyards."

6 And I became very angry when I heard their outcry and these words.

7 After serious thought, I rebuked the nobles and rulers, and said to them, [a]"Each of you is [1]exacting usury from his brother." So I [2]called a great assembly against them.

8 And I said to them, "According to our ability we have [a]redeemed our Jewish brethren who were sold to the nations. Now indeed, will you even sell your brethren? Or should they be sold to us?" Then they were silenced and found nothing *to say.*

9 Then I said, "What you are doing *is* not good. Should you not walk [a]in the fear of our God [b]because of the reproach of the nations, our enemies?

10 "I also, *with* my brethren and my servants, am lending them money and grain. Please, let us stop this [1]usury!

11 *"Restore now to them, even this day, their lands, their vineyards, their olive groves, and their houses, also a hundredth of the money and the grain, the new wine and the oil, that you have charged them."

12 So they said, "We will restore *it,* and will require nothing from them; we will do as you say." Then I called the priests, [a]and required an oath from them that they would do according to this promise.

13 Then [a]I shook out [1]the fold of my garment and said, "So may God shake out each man from his house, and from his property, who does not perform this promise. Even thus may he be shaken out and emptied." And all the assembly said, "Amen!" and *praised the LORD. [b]Then the people did according to this promise.

14 [a][Num. 14:9]; Deut. 1:29 [b][Deut. 10:17] [c]2 Sam. 10:12
15 [a]Job 5:12
16 [1]Supported
18 *See WW at Ps. 47:1. • See WW at Hos. 8:1.
20 [a]Ex. 14:14, 25; Deut. 1:30; 3:22; 20:4; Josh. 23:10; 2 Chr. 20:29
21 [1]Lit. *them*

CHAPTER 5

1 [a]Lev. 25:35–37; Neh. 5:7, 8 [b]Deut. 15:7
2 *See WW at Hab. 2:4.
5 [a]Is. 58:7 [b]Ex. 21:7; [Lev. 25:39]
7 [a][Ex. 22:25; Lev. 25:36; Deut. 23:19, 20]; Ezek. 22:12 [1]*charging interest* [2]Lit. *held*
8 [a]Lev. 25:48
9 [a]Lev. 25:36 [b]2 Sam. 12:14; Rom. 2:24; [1 Pet. 2:12]
10 [1]*interest*
11 *See WW at Ruth 4:15.
12 [a]Ezra 10:5; Jer. 34:8, 9
13 [a]Matt. 10:14; Acts 13:51; 18:6 [b]2 Kin. 23:3 [1]Lit. *my lap* *See WW at 1 Chr. 23:30.

---

that they work beyond sunset (Deut. 24:15) until the stars are out. The city wall was 1.5 miles long and approximately 8 feet thick, and represented a prodigious task.

4:17–23 See section 8 of Truth-In-Action at the end of Neh.

5:1–13 See section 6 of Truth-In-Action at the end of Neh.

5:1–13 An economic crisis had struck before Nehemiah's arrival. A famine, along with the need to pay taxes, had forced many families into insolvency. Nehemiah's presence emboldened the dispossessed to cry out for justice. The poor had found a champion for their cause. An exceedingly angry Nehemiah set about to right these wrongs, resulting in the reform of audit policies and the redressing of past excesses.

The Generosity of Nehemiah

14 Moreover, from the time that I was appointed to be their governor in the land of Judah, from the twentieth year [a]until the thirty-second year of King Artaxerxes, twelve years, neither I nor my brothers [b]ate the governor's provisions.

6 15 But the former governors who *were* before me laid burdens on the people, and took from them bread and wine, besides forty shekels of silver. Yes, even their servants bore rule over the people, but [a]I did not do so, because of the [b]fear of God.

16 Indeed, I also continued the [a]work on this wall, and [1]we did not buy any land. All my servants *were* gathered there for the work.

17 And [a]at my table *were* one hundred and fifty Jews and rulers, besides those who came to us from the nations around us.

18 Now *that* [a]which was prepared daily *was* one ox *and* six choice sheep. Also fowl were prepared for me, and once every ten days an abundance of all kinds of wine. Yet in spite of this [b]I did not demand the governor's provisions, because the bondage was heavy on this people.

19 [a]Remember me, my God, for good, *according to* all that I have done for this people.

Conspiracy Against Nehemiah

6 Now it happened [a]when Sanballat, Tobiah, [1]Geshem the Arab, and the rest of our enemies heard that I had rebuilt the wall, and *that* there were no *breaks left in it [b](though at that time I had not hung the doors in the gates),

2 that Sanballat and [1]Geshem [a]sent to me, saying, "Come, let us meet together [2]among the villages in the plain of [b]Ono." But they [c]thought to do me harm.

3 So I sent messengers to them, saying, "I *am* doing a great work, so that I cannot come down. Why should the work cease while I leave it and go down to you?"

4 But they sent me this message four times, and I answered them in the same manner.

5 Then Sanballat sent his servant to me as before, the fifth time, with an *open letter in his hand.

6 In it *was* written:

> It is reported among the nations, and [1]Geshem says, *that* you and the Jews plan to rebel; therefore, according to these rumors, you are rebuilding the wall, [a]that you may be their king.
>
> 7 And you have also appointed prophets to proclaim concerning you at Jerusalem, saying, "*There is* a king in Judah!" Now these matters will be reported to the king. So come, therefore, and let us consult together.

8 Then I sent to him, saying, "No such things as you say are being done, but you invent them in your own heart."

9 For they all *were trying to* make us afraid, saying, "Their hands will be weakened in the work, and it will not be done."

Now therefore, *O God*, strengthen my hands.

10 Afterward I came to the house of Shemaiah the son of Delaiah, the son of Mehetabel, who *was* a secret informer; and he said, "Let us meet together in the house of God, within the [1]temple,* and let us close the doors of the temple, for they are coming to kill you; indeed, at night they will come to kill you."

11 And I said, "Should such a man as I flee? And who *is there* such as I who would go into the temple to save his life? I will not go in!"

12 Then I perceived that God had not 3
sent him at all, but that [a]he pronounced *this* prophecy against me because Tobiah and Sanballat had hired him.

13 For this reason he *was* hired, that I should be afraid and act that way and sin, so *that* they might have *cause* for

14 [a]Neh. 2:1; 13:6 [b][1 Cor. 9:4–15]
15 [a]2 Cor. 11:9; 12:13 [b]Neh. 5:9
16 [a]Neh. 4:1; 6:1 [1]So with MT; LXX, Syr., Vg. *I*
17 [a]2 Sam. 9:7; 1 Kin. 18:19
18 [a]1 Kin. 4:22 [b]Neh. 5:14, 15
19 [a]2 Kin. 20:3; Neh. 13:14, 22, 31

CHAPTER 6

1 [a]Neh. 2:10, 19; 4:1, 7; 13:28 [b]Neh. 3:1, 3 [1]Or *Gashmu* *See WW at Ezek. 22:30.
2 [a]Prov. 26:24, 25 [b]1 Chr. 8:12; Neh. 11:35 [c]Ps. 37:12, 32 [1]Or *Gashmu* [2]Or *in Kephirim*, exact location unknown
5 *See WW at Jer. 40:4.
6 [a]Neh. 2:19 [1]Heb. *Gashmu*
10 [1]Lit. *house* *See WW at Hag. 2:15.
12 [a]Ezek. 13:22

5:14–19 Nehemiah is a man who leads by example. Self-sacrifice is necessary for moral leadership, as Nehemiah shows. Previous governors had lived richly at the taxpayers' expense, but Nehemiah refused to do so. He believed strongly in retribution for evil, as his prayer here and elsewhere indicates.

5:15, 16 See section 6 of Truth-In-Action at the end of Neh.

6:1–14 Opposition arises again. **The Plain of Ono** is 25 miles northwest of Jerusalem. Nehemiah detected a plot on the part of Sanballat and Geshem and wisely refused their offer. Four times Nehemiah was too busy to come. Finally, the opponents saw the strategy. In a fifth letter they charged Nehemiah with planning treason against the king. The invitation of Shemaiah the priest to accept sanctuary in the temple was not an alternative for Nehemiah for two reasons: Since he was not a priest, he could not with impunity enter the Holy Place, and God revealed to him that this was a plot on his life.

6:12 See section 3 of Truth-In-Action at the end of Neh.

an evil report, that they might reproach me.

14 [a]My God, remember Tobiah and Sanballat, according to these their works, and the [b]prophetess Noadiah and the rest of the prophets who would have made me afraid.

The Wall Completed

15 So the wall was finished on the twenty-fifth *day* of Elul, in fifty-two days.

16 And it happened, [a]when all our enemies heard *of it,* and all the nations around us saw *these things,* that they were very disheartened in their own eyes; for [b]they perceived that this work was done by our God.

17 Also in those days the nobles of Judah sent many letters to Tobiah, and *the letters of* Tobiah came to them.

18 For many in Judah were pledged to him, because he was the [a]son-in-law of Shechaniah the son of Arah, and his son Jehohanan had married the daughter of [b]Meshullam the son of Berechiah.

19 Also they reported his good deeds before me, and reported my [1]words to him. Tobiah sent letters to frighten me.

7 Then it was, when the wall was built and I had [a]hung the doors, when the gatekeepers, the singers, and the Levites had been appointed,

6 2 that I gave the charge of Jerusalem to my brother [a]Hanani, and Hananiah the leader [b]of the [1]citadel, for he *was* a faithful man and [c]feared God more than many.

3 And I said to them, "Do not let the gates of Jerusalem be opened until the sun is hot; and while they stand *guard,* let them shut and bar the doors; and appoint guards from among the inhabitants of Jerusalem, one at his watch station and another in front of his own house."

The Captives Who Returned to Jerusalem

4 Now the city *was* large and spacious, but the people in it *were* [a]few, and the houses *were* not rebuilt.

5 Then my God put it into my heart to gather the nobles, the rulers, and the people, that they might be registered by genealogy. And I found a register of the genealogy of those who had come up in the first *return,* and found written in it:

6 [a]These *are* the people of the province who came back from the captivity, of those who had been carried away, whom Nebuchadnezzar the king of Babylon had carried away, and who returned to Jerusalem and Judah, everyone to his city.

7 Those who came with [a]Zerubbabel *were* Jeshua, Nehemiah, [1]Azariah, Raamiah, Nahamani, Mordecai, Bilshan, [2]Mispereth, Bigvai, Nehum, and Baanah.

The number of the men of the people of Israel:

8 the sons of Parosh, two thousand one hundred and seventy-two;

9 the sons of Shephatiah, three hundred and seventy-two;

10 the sons of Arah, six hundred and fifty-two;

11 the sons of Pahath-Moab, of the sons of Jeshua and Joab, two thousand eight hundred and eighteen;

12 the sons of Elam, one thousand two hundred and fifty-four;

13 the sons of Zattu, eight hundred and forty-five;

14 the sons of Zaccai, seven hundred and sixty;

15 the sons of [1]Binnui, six hundred and forty-eight;

16 the sons of Bebai, six hundred and twenty-eight;

17 the sons of Azgad, two thousand three hundred and twenty-two;

18 the sons of Adonikam, six hundred and sixty-seven;

19 the sons of Bigvai, two thousand and sixty-seven;

20 the sons of Adin, six hundred and fifty-five;

14 [a]Neh. 13:29 [b]Ezek. 13:17
16 [a]Neh. 2:10, 20; 4:1, 7; 6:1 [b]Ps. 126:2
18 [a]Neh. 13:4, 28 [b]Ezra 10:15; Neh. 3:4
19 [1]Or *affairs*

CHAPTER 7

1 [a]Neh. 6:1, 15
2 [a]Neh. 1:2 [b]Neh. 2:8; 10:23 [c]Ex. 18:21 [1]*palace*
4 [a]Deut. 4:27
6 [a]Ezra 2:1–70
7 [a]Ezra 5:2; Neh. 12:1, 47; Matt. 1:12, 13 [1]*Seraiah,* Ezra 2:2 [2]*Mispar,* Ezra 2:2
15 [1]*Bani,* Ezra 2:10

6:15–19 Differences exist as to whether the "completion" of the wall refers to the construction and hanging of the gates (compare 6:1 and 7:1) or to the whole of the repairs and construction. In either case, completion was on October 2, 52 days after the project started. Archaeologists are greatly impressed by the size and design of this wall. Even the enemies recognized that God was vitally involved in the process. **Tobiah** and **his son** had married Jerusalem women, apparently from prominent families. Their relatives provided a spy service against Nehemiah within the city.

7:1–73 This is a list similar to the one found in Ezra 2:1–70. See notes on Ezra 2:2, 3.

7:2 See section 6 of Truth-In-Action at the end of Neh.

7:2 Nehemiah, governor of the province of Judah, appointed his **brother Hanani** as governor of **Jerusalem. Hananiah** was made head of the fortress area. Military responsibilities were included along with civic duties. For security purposes 10 percent of the Jews were brought from the outlying areas to reside in the city (11:1). Nehemiah's authority was obviously absolute, except for the king's since resettlement of this many people could not be accomplished by a minor official.

21 the sons of Ater of Hezekiah, ninety-eight;
22 the sons of Hashum, three hundred and twenty-eight;
23 the sons of Bezai, three hundred and twenty-four;
24 the sons of [1]Hariph, one hundred and twelve;
25 the sons of [1]Gibeon, ninety-five;
26 the men of Bethlehem and Netophah, one hundred and eighty-eight;
27 the men of Anathoth, one hundred and twenty-eight;
28 the men of [1]Beth Azmaveth, forty-two;
29 the men of [1]Kirjath Jearim, Chephirah, and Beeroth, seven hundred and forty-three;
30 the men of Ramah and Geba, six hundred and twenty-one;
31 the men of Michmas, one hundred and twenty-two;
32 the men of Bethel and Ai, one hundred and twenty-three;
33 the men of the other Nebo, fifty-two;
34 the sons of the other [a]Elam, one thousand two hundred and fifty-four;
35 the sons of Harim, three hundred and twenty;
36 the sons of Jericho, three hundred and forty-five;
37 the sons of Lod, Hadid, and Ono, seven hundred and twenty-one;
38 the sons of Senaah, three thousand nine hundred and thirty.
39 The priests: the sons of [a]Jedaiah, of the house of Jeshua, nine hundred and seventy-three;
40 the sons of [a]Immer, one thousand and fifty-two;
41 the sons of [a]Pashhur, one thousand two hundred and forty-seven;
42 the sons of [a]Harim, one thousand and seventeen.
43 The Levites: the sons of Jeshua, of Kadmiel, *and* of the sons of [1]Hodevah, seventy-four.
44 The singers: the sons of Asaph, one hundred and forty-eight.
45 The gatekeepers: the sons of Shallum, the sons of Ater, the sons of Talmon, the sons of Akkub, the sons of Hatita, the sons of Shobai, one hundred and thirty-eight.
46 The Nethinim: the sons of Ziha, the sons of Hasupha, the sons of Tabbaoth,
47 the sons of Keros, the sons of [1]Sia, the sons of Padon,
48 the sons of [1]Lebana, the sons of [2]Hagaba, the sons of [3]Salmai,
49 the sons of Hanan, the sons of Giddel, the sons of Gahar,
50 the sons of Reaiah, the sons of Rezin, the sons of Nekoda,
51 the sons of Gazzam, the sons of Uzza, the sons of Paseah,
52 the sons of Besai, the sons of Meunim, the sons of [1]Nephishesim,
53 the sons of Bakbuk, the sons of Hakupha, the sons of Harhur,
54 the sons of [1]Bazlith, the sons of Mehida, the sons of Harsha,
55 the sons of Barkos, the sons of Sisera, the sons of Tamah,
56 the sons of Neziah, and the sons of Hatipha.
57 The sons of Solomon's servants: the sons of Sotai, the sons of Sophereth, the sons of [1]Perida,
58 the sons of Jaala, the sons of Darkon, the sons of Giddel,
59 the sons of Shephatiah, the sons of Hattil, the sons of Pochereth of Zebaim, and the sons of [1]Amon.
60 All the Nethinim, and the sons of Solomon's servants, *were* three hundred and ninety-two.
61 And these *were* the ones who came up from Tel Melah, Tel Harsha, Cherub, [1]Addon, and Immer, but they could not identify their father's house nor their lineage, whether they *were* of Israel:
62 the sons of Delaiah, the sons of Tobiah, the sons of Nekoda, six hundred and forty-two;
63 and of the priests: the sons of Habaiah, the sons of [1]Koz, the sons of Barzillai, who took a wife of the daughters of Barzillai the Gileadite, and was called by their name.
64 These sought their listing *among* those who were registered by genealogy, but it was not found; therefore they were excluded from the priesthood as defiled.
65 And the [1]governor said to them that they should not eat of the most holy things till a priest could consult with the Urim and Thummim.
66 Altogether the whole assembly *was* forty-two thousand three hundred and sixty,
67 besides their male and female servants, of whom *there were* seven thousand three hundred

24 [1]*Jorah,* Ezra 2:18
25 [1]*Gibbar,* Ezra 2:20
28 [1]*Azmaveth,* Ezra 2:24
29 [1]*Kirjath Arim,* Ezra 2:25
34 [a]Neh. 7:12
39 [a]1 Chr. 24:7
40 [a]1 Chr. 9:12
41 [a] Ezra 2:38; 10:22
42 [a]1 Chr. 24:8
43 [1]*Hodaviah,* Ezra 2:40; or *Judah,* Ezra 3:9
47 [1]*Siaha,* Ezra 2:44
48 [1]MT *Lebanah* [2]MT *Hogabah* [3]*Shalmai,* Ezra 2:46; or *Shamlai*
52 [1]*Nephusim,* Ezra 2:50
54 [1]*Bazluth,* Ezra 2:52
57 [1]*Peruda,* Ezra 2:55
59 [1]*Ami,* Ezra 2:57
61 [1]*Addan,* Ezra 2:59
63 [1]Or *Hakkoz*
65 [1]Heb. *Tirshatha*

and thirty-seven; and they had two hundred and forty-five men and women singers.
68 Their horses were seven hundred and thirty-six, their mules two hundred and forty-five,
69 *their* camels four hundred and thirty-five, *and* donkeys six thousand seven hundred and twenty.
70 And some of the heads of the fathers' houses gave to the work. [a]The [1]governor gave to the treasury one thousand gold drachmas, fifty basins, and five hundred and thirty priestly garments.
71 Some of the heads of the fathers' *houses* gave to the treasury of the work [a]twenty thousand gold drachmas, and two thousand two hundred silver minas.
72 And that which the rest of the people gave *was* twenty thousand gold drachmas, two thousand silver minas, and sixty-seven priestly garments.

73 So the priests, the Levites, the gatekeepers, the singers, *some* of the people, the Nethinim, and all Israel dwelt in their cities.

Ezra Reads the Law

[a]When the seventh month came, the children of Israel *were* in their cities.
1 8 Now all [a]the people gathered together as one man in the open
square that *was* [b]in front of the Water
Gate; and they told Ezra the [c]scribe to
bring the Book of the *Law of Moses,
which the LORD had commanded Israel.
2 So Ezra the priest brought [a]the Law
before the assembly of men and
women and all who *could* hear with
understanding [b]on the first day of the
seventh month.
3 Then he [a]read from it in the open
square that *was* in front of the Water
Gate [1]from morning until midday, before the men and women and those
who could understand; and the ears of
all the people *were attentive* to the
Book of the Law.

70 [a]Neh. 8:9 [1]Heb. *Tirshatha*
71 [a]Ezra 2:69
73 [a]Ezra 3:1

CHAPTER 8

1 [a]Ezra 3:1 [b]Neh. 3:26 [c]Ezra 7:6 *See WW at Is. 42:21.
2 [a][Deut. 31:11, 12]; Neh. 8:9 [b]Lev. 23:24; Num. 29:1–6
3 [a]Deut. 31:9–11; 2 Kin. 23:2 [1]Lit. *from the light*
5 [a]Judg. 3:20; 1 Kin. 8:12–14
6 [a]Neh. 5:13; [1 Cor. 14:16] [b]Ps. 28:2; Lam. 3:41; 1 Tim. 2:8 [c]Ex. 4:31; 12:27; 2 Chr. 20:18
7 [a]Lev. 10:11; Deut. 33:10; 2 Chr. 17:7; [Mal. 2:7] [b]Neh. 9:3
9 [a]Ezra 2:63; Neh. 7:65, 70; 10:1 [b]Lev. 23:24; Num. 29:1 [c]Deut. 16:14; Eccl. 3:4 [1]Heb. *Tirshatha* *See WW at Joel 1:9.

4 So Ezra the scribe stood on a platform of wood which they had made for
the purpose; and beside him, at his
right hand, stood Mattithiah, Shema,
Anaiah, Urijah, Hilkiah, and Maaseiah; and at his left hand Pedaiah,
Mishael, Malchijah, Hashum, Hashbadana, Zechariah, *and* Meshullam.
5 And Ezra opened the book in the
sight of all the people, for he was
standing above all the people; and
when he opened it, all the people
[a]stood up.
6 And Ezra blessed the LORD, the
great God. Then all the people [a]answered, "Amen, Amen!" while [b]lifting
up their hands. And they [c]bowed their
heads and worshiped the LORD with
their faces to the ground.
7 Also Jeshua, Bani, Sherebiah, Jamin, Akkub, Shabbethai, Hodijah,
Maaseiah, Kelita, Azariah, Jozabad,
Hanan, Pelaiah, and the Levites,
[a]helped the people to understand the
Law; and the people [b]*stood* in their
place.
8 So they read distinctly from the
book, in the Law of God; and they gave
the sense, and helped *them* to **understand** the reading.

WORD WEALTH

8:8 understand, *bin* (*bean*); Strong's #995. To understand, discern, perceive, grasp, consider, regard; be perceptive, have insight. This verb occurs more than 165 times and refers to that intelligent process of perception, discernment, and understanding, which all human beings possess in varying amounts. For biblical range of meaning in the word *bin,* refer to 1 Sam. 3:8; Ps. 92:5–7; Prov. 24:11, 12; Is. 40:21; Jer. 30:24; Dan. 10:12. From *bin* is derived the noun *binah,* meaning "understanding"; this term occurs 37 times. See Prov. 3:5; 4:5; Is. 11:2; Dan. 10:1. In the present reference, spiritual revival did not come until the people clearly understood the text.

9 [a]And Nehemiah, who *was* the
[1]governor, Ezra the priest *and* scribe,
and the Levites who taught the people
said to all the people, [b]"This day *is*
holy to the LORD your God; [c]do not
*mourn nor weep." For all the people

7:73—10:39 Ch. 8 of Nehemiah seems to fit after Ezra 8. This public assembly took place on the first day of the seventh month. A similar assembly described in Ezra 10 was on the twentieth of the ninth month. The law was read for five or six hours (8:3). Thirteen Levites helped the people understand, moving through the congregation and perhaps translating difficult Hebrew passages into Aramaic, the language of the empire. Nehemiah would stop often to give them an opportunity to resolve questions in their groups. Joy and weeping, sorrow for sin and joy at God's provision, sadness for their backslidings, but joy at the opportunity to know truth, were the mixed emotions that brought a firm decision for renewal.

8:1–6 See section 1 of Truth-In-Action at the end of Neh.

wept, when they heard the words of the Law.

1 10 Then he said to them, "Go your way, eat the fat, drink the sweet, [a]and send portions to those for whom nothing is prepared; for *this* day *is* holy to our Lord. Do not sorrow, for the joy of the LORD is your strength."

11 So the Levites quieted all the people, saying, "Be still, for the day *is* holy; do not be grieved."

12 And all the people went their way to eat and drink, to [a]send portions and rejoice greatly, because they [b]understood the words that were declared to them.

The Feast of Tabernacles

13 Now on the second day the heads of the fathers' *houses* of all the people, with the priests and Levites, were gathered to Ezra the scribe, in order to understand the words of the Law.

14 And they found written in the Law, which the LORD had commanded by Moses, that the children of Israel should dwell in [a]booths[1] during the feast of the seventh month,

15 and [a]that they should announce and proclaim in all their cities and [b]in Jerusalem, saying, "Go out to the mountain, and [c]bring olive branches, branches of oil trees, myrtle branches, palm branches, and branches of leafy trees, to make booths, as *it is* written."

16 Then the people went out and brought *them* and made themselves booths, each one on the [a]roof of his house, or in their courtyards or the courts of the house of God, and in the open square of the [b]Water Gate [c]and in the open square of the Gate of Ephraim.

17 So the whole assembly of those who had returned from the captivity made [1]booths and sat under the booths; for since the days of Joshua the son of Nun until that day the children of Israel had not done so. And there was very [a]great gladness.

18 Also [a]day by day, from the first day until the last day, he read from the Book of the Law of God. And they kept the feast [b]seven days; and on the [c]eighth day *there was* a sacred assembly, according to the *prescribed* manner.

The People Confess Their Sins

9 Now on the twenty-fourth day of [a]this month the children of Israel 5
were assembled with fasting, in sackcloth, [b]and with [1]dust on their heads.

2 Then [a]those of Israelite lineage separated themselves from all foreigners; and they stood and [b]confessed their sins and the *iniquities of their fathers.

3 And they stood up in their place and [a]read from the Book of the Law of the LORD their God *for one*-fourth of the day; and *for another* fourth they confessed and worshiped the LORD their God.

4 Then Jeshua, Bani, Kadmiel, Shebaniah, Bunni, Sherebiah, Bani, *and* Chenani stood on the [1]stairs of the Levites and cried out with a loud voice to the LORD their God.

5 And the Levites, Jeshua, Kadmiel, Bani, Hashabniah, Sherebiah, Hodijah, Shebaniah, *and* Pethahiah, said:

"Stand up *and* bless the LORD your
God
Forever and ever!

"Blessed be [a]Your glorious name,
Which is exalted above all
blessing and *praise!
6 [a]You alone *are* the LORD;
[b]You have made heaven,
[c]The heaven of heavens, with
[d]all their host,
The earth and everything on it,
The seas and all that is in them,
And You [e]preserve them all.
The host of heaven worships You.

7 "You *are* the LORD God,
Who chose [a]Abram,
And brought him out of Ur of the
Chaldeans,
And gave him the name
[b]Abraham;

10 [a][Deut. 26:11–13]; Esth. 9:19, 22; Rev. 11:10
12 [a]Neh. 8:10 [b]Neh. 8:7, 8
14 [a]Lev. 23:34, 40, 42; Deut. 16:13 [1]Temporary shelters
15 [a]Lev. 23:4 [b]Deut. 16:16 [c]Lev. 23:40
16 [a]Deut. 22:8 [b]Neh. 12:37 [c]2 Kin. 14:13; Neh. 12:39
17 [a]2 Chr. 30:21 [1]Temporary shelters
18 [a]Deut. 31:11 [b]Lev. 23:36 [c]Num. 29:35

CHAPTER 9

1 [a]Neh. 8:2 [b]Josh. 7:6; 1 Sam. 4:12; 2 Sam. 1:2; Job 2:12 [1]Lit. *earth on them*
2 [a]Ezra 10:11; Neh. 13:3, 30 [b]Neh. 1:6 *See WW at Ps. 130:3.
3 [a]Neh. 8:7, 8
4 [1]Lit. *ascent*
5 [a]1 Chr. 29:13 *See WW at Ps. 100:4.
6 [a]Deut. 6:4; 2 Kin. 19:15, 19; [Ps. 86:10]; Is. 37:16, 20 [b]Gen. 1:1; Ex. 20:11; Rev. 14:7 [c][Deut. 10:14]; 1 Kin. 8:27 [d]Gen. 2:1 [e][Ps. 36:6]
7 [a]Gen. 11:31 [b]Gen. 17:5

8:10 See section 1 of Truth-In-Action at the end of Neh.

8:13–18 The Feast of Tabernacles (or Feast of Booths) was reinstituted. It was a feast such as Joshua had celebrated. It is still celebrated each fall by Jewish people around the world, from the little leafy booths on a New York City apartment balcony to the massive celebrations in Israel. See Lev. 23:6; Num. 29:35–38; Deut. 31:10–13.

9:1–38 See section 5 of Truth-In-Action at the end of Neh.

9:1–3 A great separation between Israelites and foreigners takes place. All those entering the covenant (the most solemn agreement of which a person is capable) had to be pure.

9:4–37 Some of the Levites prayed to God and exhorted the people. The righteous Lord has created and preserved the world, and the hosts of heaven worship Him. He chose Abram, and the events of Nehemiah's day were the result of God's faithfulness to His covenant relationship with Abram. All of God's dealings with Abram's descendants are recounted and revolve around that covenant.

8 You found his heart [a]faithful
before You,
And made a [b]covenant with him
To give the land of the
Canaanites,
The Hittites, the Amorites,
The Perizzites, the Jebusites,
And the Girgashites—
To give *it* to his descendants.
You [c]have performed Your
words,
For You *are* righteous.

9 "You[a] saw the affliction of our
fathers in Egypt,
And [b]heard their cry by the Red
Sea.
10 You [a]showed *signs and wonders
against Pharaoh,
Against all his servants,
And against all the people of his
land.
For You knew that they [b]acted
[1]proudly against them.
So You [c]made a name for
Yourself, as *it is* this day.
11 [a]And You divided the sea before
them,
So that they went through the
midst of the sea on the dry land;
And their persecutors You threw
into the deep,
[b]As a stone into the mighty waters.
12 Moreover You [a]led them by day
with a cloudy pillar,
And by night with a pillar of fire,
To give them light on the road
Which they should travel.

13 "You[a] came down also on Mount
Sinai,
And spoke with them from
heaven,
And gave them [b]just *ordinances
and true laws,
Good **statutes** and
commandments.

WORD WEALTH

9:13 statutes, *choq* (*choak*); Strong's #2706: An enactment, engraving, inscription, appointment; a written rule, decreed limit, law, custom, decree. This noun refers to a defined boundary, especially when written into law, but sometimes not in written form, as in God's limits for the sea and for rain (Prov. 8:29; Job 28:26). Here *choq* appears with *mitzvah* (commandment or precept), *torah* (instruction or Law), and *mishpat* (judgment or regulation). *Choq* appears about 220 times. In Ps. 119, *choq* occurs 21 times. The messianic decree (*choq*), which the Lord Jesus is destined to declare, is world dominion for God's only begotten Son (Ps. 2:7–9).

14 You made known to them Your
[a]holy Sabbath,
And commanded them precepts,
statutes and laws,
By the hand of Moses Your
servant.
15 You [a]gave them bread from
heaven for their hunger,
And [b]brought them water out of
the rock for their thirst,
And told them to [c]go in to
*possess the land
Which You had [1]sworn to give
them.

16 "But[a] they and our fathers acted
[1]proudly,
[b]Hardened[2] their necks,
And did not heed Your
commandments.
17 They refused to obey, 5
And [a]they were not mindful of
Your wonders
That You did among them.
But they hardened their necks,
And [1]in their rebellion
They appointed [b]a leader
To return to their bondage.
But You *are* God,
Ready to pardon,
[c]Gracious and merciful,
Slow to *anger,
Abundant in kindness,
And did not forsake them.

18 "Even [a]when they made a molded
calf for themselves,
And said, 'This *is* your god
That brought you up out of
Egypt,'
And worked great provocations,
19 Yet in Your [a]manifold mercies
You did not forsake them in the
wilderness.
The [b]pillar of the cloud did not
depart from them by day,
To lead them on the road;
Nor the pillar of fire by night,
To show them light,
And the way they should go.
20 You also gave Your [a]good Spirit
to instruct them,
And did not withhold Your
[b]manna from their mouth,

8 [a]Gen. 15:6; 22:1–3; [James 2:21–23] [b]Gen. 15:18 [c]Josh. 23:14
9 [a]Ex. 2:25; 3:7 [b]Ex. 14:10
10 [a]Ex. 7—14 [b]Ex. 18:11 [c]Jer. 32:20 [1]*presumptuously* or *insolently* *See WW at Ps. 86:17.
11 [a]Ex. 14:20–28 [b]Ex. 15:1, 5
12 [a]Ex. 13:21, 22
13 [a]Ex. 20:1–18 [b][Rom. 7:12] *See WW at Num. 36:13.
14 [a]Gen. 2:3; Ex. 16:23; 20:8; 23:12
15 [a]Ex. 16:14–17; John 6:31 [b]Ex. 17:6; Num. 20:8; [1 Cor. 10:4] [c]Deut. 1:8 [1]Lit. *raised Your hand to* *See WW at Deut. 8:1.
16 [a]Ps. 106:6 [b]Deut. 1:26–33; 31:27; Neh. 9:29 [1]*presumptuously* [2]*Stiffened their necks,* became stubborn
17 [a]Ps. 78:11, 42–45 [b]Num. 14:4; Acts 7:39 [c]Joel 2:13 [1]So with MT, Vg.; LXX *in Egypt* *See WW at Judg. 10:7.
18 [a]Ex. 32:4–8, 31
19 [a]Ps. 106:45 [b]Ex. 13:20–22; 1 Cor. 10:1
20 [a]Num. 11:17 [b]Ex. 16:14–16

9:17 See section 5 of Truth-In-Action at the end of Neh.

And gave them [c]water for their
thirst.
21 [a]Forty years You *sustained them
in the wilderness;
They lacked nothing;
Their [b]clothes did not wear out
And their feet did not swell.

22 "Moreover You gave them
kingdoms and nations,
And divided them into [1]districts.
So they took possession of the
land of [a]Sihon,
[2]The land of the king of Heshbon,
And the land of Og king of
Bashan.
23 You also multiplied [a]their
children as the stars of heaven,
And brought them into the land
Which You had told their fathers
To go in and possess.
24 So [a]the [1]people went in
And possessed the land;
[b]You subdued before them the
inhabitants of the land,
The Canaanites,
And gave them into their hands,
With their kings
And the people of the land,
That they might do with them as
they wished.
25 And they took strong cities and
a [a]rich land,
And possessed [b]houses full of all
goods,
Cisterns *already* dug, vineyards,
olive groves,
And [1]fruit trees in abundance.
So they ate and were filled and
[c]grew fat,
And delighted themselves in Your
great [d]goodness.

26 "Nevertheless they [a]were
disobedient
And rebelled against You,
[b]Cast Your law behind their
backs
And killed Your [c]prophets, who
[1]testified against them
To turn them to Yourself;
And they worked great
provocations.
27 [a]Therefore You delivered them
into the hand of their enemies,
Who oppressed them;
And in the time of their trouble,
When they cried to You,
You [b]heard from heaven;
And according to Your abundant
mercies
[c]You gave them deliverers who
saved them
From the hand of their enemies.

28 "But after they had *rest,
[a]They again did evil before You.
Therefore You left them in the
hand of their enemies,
So that they had dominion over
them;
Yet when they returned and cried
out to You,
You heard from heaven;
And [b]many *times You delivered
them according to Your
mercies,
29 And [1]testified against them, 6
That You might bring them back
to Your law.
Yet they acted [2]proudly,
And did not heed Your
commandments,
But sinned against Your
judgments,
[a]'Which if a *man does, he shall
live by them.'
And they shrugged their
shoulders,
[3]Stiffened their necks,
And would not hear.
30 Yet for many years You had
patience with them,
And [1]testified [a]against them by
Your Spirit [b]in Your prophets.
Yet they would not listen;
[c]Therefore You gave them into the
hand of the peoples of the
lands.
31 Nevertheless in Your great mercy
[a]You did not utterly consume them
nor forsake them;
For You *are* God, gracious and
merciful.

32 "Now therefore, our God,
The great, the [a]mighty, and
awesome God,
Who keeps covenant and mercy:
Do not let all the [1]trouble seem
small before You
That has come upon us,
Our kings and our princes,
Our priests and our prophets,
Our fathers and on all Your
people,
[b]From the days of the kings of
Assyria until this day.
33 However [a]You *are* just in all that
has befallen us;
For You have dealt faithfully,
But [b]we have done wickedly.

20 [c]Ex. 17:6 **21** [a]Deut. 2:7 [b]Deut. 8:4; 29:5 *See WW at Ps. 55:22. **22** [a]Num. 21:21–35 [1]Lit. *corners* [2]So with MT, Vg.; LXX omits *The land of* **23** [a]Gen. 15:5; 22:17; Heb. 11:12 **24** [a]Josh. 1:2–4 [b]Josh. 18:1; [Ps. 44:2, 3] [1]Lit. *sons* **25** [a]Num. 13:27 [b]Deut. 6:11; Josh. 24:13 [c][Deut. 32:15] [d]Hos. 3:5 [1]Lit. *trees for eating* **26** [a]Judg. 2:11 [b]1 Kin. 14:9; Ps. 50:17 [c]1 Kin. 18:4; 19:10; Matt. 23:37; Acts 7:52 [1]*admonished* or *warned them* **27** [a]Judg. 2:14; Ps. 106:41 [b]Ps. 106:44 [c]Judg. 2:18

28 [a]Judg. 3:12 [b]Ps. 106:43 *See WW at Ex. 33:14. • See WW at Is. 33:6. **29** [a]Lev. 18:5; Rom. 10:5; [Gal. 3:12] [1]*admonished them* [2]*presumptuously* [3]Became stubborn *See WW at Gen. 1:26. **30** [a]2 Kin. 17:13–18; 2 Chr. 36:11–20; Jer. 7:25 [b][Acts 7:51]; 1 Pet. 1:11 [c]Is. 5:5 [1]*admonished* or *warned them* **31** [a]Jer. 4:27; [Rom. 11:2–5] **32** [a][Ex. 34:6, 7] [b]2 Kin. 15:19; 17:3–6; Ezra 4:2, 10 [1]*hardship* **33** [a]Ps. 119:137; [Dan. 9:14] [b]Ps. 106:6; [Dan. 9:5, 6, 8]

9:29 See section 6 of Truth-In-Action at the end of Neh.

34 Neither our kings nor our princes,
Our priests nor our fathers,
Have kept Your law,
Nor heeded Your commandments
and Your testimonies,
With which You testified against
them.
35 For they have [a]not served You in
their kingdom,
Or in the many good *things* that
You gave them,
Or in the large and rich land
which You set before them;
Nor did they turn from their
wicked works.

36 "Here [a]we *are,* servants today!
And the land that You gave to our
fathers,
To eat its fruit and its bounty,
Here we *are,* servants in it!
37 And [a]it yields much increase to
the kings
You have set over us,
Because of our sins;
Also they have [b]dominion over
our bodies and our cattle
At their *pleasure;
And we *are* in great distress.

38 "And because of all this,
We [a]make a sure *covenant* and
*write *it;*
Our leaders, our Levites, *and* our
priests [b]seal *it.*"

The People Who Sealed the Covenant

10 Now those who placed *their*
seal on *the document were:*
Nehemiah the [1]governor, [a]the son
of Hacaliah, and Zedekiah,
2 [a]Seraiah, Azariah, Jeremiah,
3 Pashhur, Amariah, Malchijah,
4 Hattush, Shebaniah, Malluch,
5 Harim, Meremoth, Obadiah,
6 Daniel, Ginnethon, Baruch,
7 Meshullam, Abijah, Mijamin,
8 Maaziah, Bilgai, *and* Shemaiah.
These *were* the priests.
9 The Levites: Jeshua the son of
Azaniah, Binnui of the sons of
Henadad, *and* Kadmiel.
10 Their brethren: Shebaniah,
Hodijah, Kelita, Pelaiah, Hanan,
11 Micha, Rehob, Hashabiah,
12 Zaccur, Sherebiah, Shebaniah,
13 Hodijah, Bani, *and* Beninu.
14 The leaders of the people:
[a]Parosh, Pahath-Moab, Elam,
Zattu, Bani,
15 Bunni, Azgad, Bebai,
16 Adonijah, Bigvai, Adin,
17 Ater, Hezekiah, Azzur,
18 Hodijah, Hashum, Bezai,
19 Hariph, Anathoth, Nebai,
20 Magpiash, Meshullam, Hezir,
21 Meshezabel, Zadok, Jaddua,
22 Pelatiah, Hanan, Anaiah,
23 Hoshea, Hananiah, Hasshub,
24 Hallohesh, Pilha, Shobek,
25 Rehum, Hashabnah, Maaseiah,
26 Ahijah, Hanan, Anan,
27 Malluch, Harim, *and* Baanah.

The Covenant That Was Sealed

28 [a]Now the rest of the people—the
priests, the Levites, the gatekeepers,
the singers, the Nethinim, [b]and all
those who had separated themselves
from the peoples of the lands to the
*Law of God, their wives, their sons,
and their daughters, everyone who had
knowledge and understanding—
29 these joined with their brethren,
their nobles, [a]and entered into a curse
and an oath [b]to walk in God's Law,
which was given by Moses the servant
of God, and to observe and do all the
commandments of the LORD our Lord,
and His ordinances and His statutes:
30 We would not give [a]our daughters
as wives to the peoples of the land, nor
take their daughters for our sons;
31 [a]*if* the peoples of the land brought
[1]wares or any grain to sell on the Sabbath day, we would not buy it from
them on the Sabbath, or on a holy day;
and we would forego the [b]seventh
year's *produce* and the [c]exacting[2] of
every debt.
32 Also we made ordinances for ourselves, to exact from ourselves yearly
[a]one-third of a shekel for the service
of the house of our God:
33 for [a]the showbread, for the regular
grain offering, for the [b]regular burnt
offering of the Sabbaths, the New
Moons, and the set feasts; for the holy
things, for the *sin offerings to *make
atonement for Israel, and all the work
of the house of our God.

35 [a]Deut. 28:47 **36** [a]Deut. 28:48; Ezra 9:9 **37** [a]Deut. 28:33, 51 [b]Deut. 28:48 *See WW at Deut. 33:23. **38** [a]2 Kin. 23:3; 2 Chr. 29:10; Ezra 10:3 [b]Neh. 10:1 *See WW at Deut. 31.9.

CHAPTER 10

1 [a]Neh. 1:1 [1]Heb. *Tirshatha* **2** [a]Neh. 12:1–21 **14** [a]Ezra 2:3 **28** [a]Ezra 2:36–43 [b]Ezra 9:1; Neh. 13:3 *See WW at Is. 42:21. **29** [a]Deut. 29:12; Neh. 5:12; Ps. 119:106 [b]2 Kin. 23:3; 2 Chr. 34:31 **30** [a]Ex. 34:16; Deut. 7:3; [Ezra 9:12] **31** [a]Ex. 20:10; Lev. 23:3; Deut. 5:12 [b]Ex. 23:10, 11; Lev. 25:4; Jer. 34:14 [c][Deut. 15:1, 2]; Neh. 5:12 [1]*merchandise* [2]*collection* **32** [a]Ex. 30:11–16; 38:25, 26; 2 Chr. 24:6, 9; Matt. 17:24 **33** [a]Lev. 24:5; 2 Chr. 2:4 [b]Num. 28; 29 *See WW at Lev. 9:2. • See WW at Num. 15:25.

9:38—10:39 God's people enter into a covenant with Him. Areas needing change were pointed out, such as mixed marriages, keeping the Sabbath, offerings, tithes, and proper care of the temple. Initially there were 21 priests, 17 Levites, and 44 leaders of the people, along with Nehemiah and Zedekiah (probably Nehemiah's assistant) who voluntarily bind themselves to a renewed pledge to walk in God's law. Most of these names are also on other lists in Ezra and Nehemiah. In 10:28 it seems that virtually everyone followed their leaders in a solemn oath to follow the Law.

10:32 One-third of a shekel was a new tax, designed to regulate a steady income for the sanctuary.

34 We cast lots among the priests, the
Levites, and the people, [a]for *bringing*
the wood offering into the house of our
God, according to our fathers' houses,
at the appointed times year by year,
to burn on the *altar of the LORD our
God [b]as *it is* written in the Law.
35 And *we made ordinances* [a]to bring
the firstfruits of our ground and the
firstfruits of all fruit of all trees, year
by year, to the house of the LORD;
36 to bring the [a]firstborn of our sons
and our cattle, as *it is* written in the
Law, and the firstborn of our herds and
our flocks, to the house of our God, to
the priests who minister in the house
of our God;
37 [a]to bring the firstfruits of our
dough, our offerings, the fruit from all
kinds of trees, *the* new wine and oil,
to the priests, to the storerooms of
the [1]house of our God; and to bring
[b]the tithes of our land to the Levites,
for the Levites should receive the tithes
in all our farming communities.
38 And the priest, the descendant of
Aaron, shall be with the Levites
[a]when the Levites receive tithes; and
the Levites shall bring up a tenth of
the tithes to the house of our God, to
[b]the rooms of the storehouse.
39 For the children of Israel and the
children of Levi [a]shall bring the offering of the grain, of the new wine and
the oil, to the storerooms where the articles of the sanctuary *are, where* the
priests who minister and the gatekeepers [b]and the singers *are;* and we
will not [c]neglect the house of our God.

The People Dwelling in Jerusalem

11 Now the leaders of the people
dwelt at Jerusalem; the rest of
the people cast lots to bring one out
of ten to dwell in Jerusalem, [a]the holy
city, and nine-tenths *were to dwell* in
other cities.
2 And the people blessed all the men
who [a]willingly offered themselves to
dwell at Jerusalem.
3 [a]These *are* the heads of the province who dwelt in Jerusalem. (But in
the cities of Judah everyone dwelt in
his own *possession in their cities—
Israelites, priests, Levites, [b]Nethinim,
and [c]descendants of Solomon's servants.)
4 Also [a]in Jerusalem dwelt *some* of
the children of Judah and of the children of Benjamin.
The children of Judah: Athaiah the
son of Uzziah, the son of Zechariah,
the son of Amariah, the son of Shephatiah, the son of Mahalalel, of the children of [b]Perez;
5 and Maaseiah the son of Baruch,
the son of Col-Hozeh, the son of Ha-
zaiah, the son of Adaiah, the son of
Joiarib, the son of Zechariah, the son
of Shiloni.
6 All the sons of Perez who dwelt at
Jerusalem *were* four hundred and
sixty-eight valiant men.
7 And these are the sons of Benjamin:
Sallu the son of Meshullam, the son of
Joed, the son of Pedaiah, the son of
Kolaiah, the son of Maaseiah, the son
of Ithiel, the son of Jeshaiah;
8 and after him Gabbai *and* Sallai,
nine hundred and twenty-eight.
9 Joel the son of Zichri *was* their
overseer, and Judah the son of [1]Se-
nuah *was* second over the city.
10 [a]Of the priests: Jedaiah the son of
Joiarib, and Jachin;
11 Seraiah the son of Hilkiah, the son
of Meshullam, the son of Zadok, the
son of Meraioth, the son of Ahitub, *was*
the leader of the house of God.
12 Their brethren who did the work of
the house *were* eight hundred and
twenty-two; and Adaiah the son of Jeroham, the son of Pelaliah, the son of
Amzi, the son of Zechariah, the son of
Pashhur, the son of Malchijah,
13 and his brethren, heads of the fathers' *houses, were* two hundred and
forty-two; and Amashai the son of Azarel, the son of Ahzai, the son of Meshillemoth, the son of Immer,
14 and their brethren, mighty men of
valor, *were* one hundred and twenty-
eight. Their overseer *was* Zabdiel
[1]the son of *one of* the great men.
15 Also of the Levites: Shemaiah the
son of Hasshub, the son of Azrikam,
the son of Hashabiah, the son of Bunni;
16 [a]Shabbethai and [b]Jozabad, of the
heads of the Levites, *had* the oversight
of [c]the business outside of the [1]house
of God;
17 Mattaniah the son of [1]Micha, the
son of Zabdi, the son of Asaph, the
leader *who* began the thanksgiving
with prayer; Bakbukiah, the second
among his brethren; and Abda the son
of Shammua, the son of Galal, the son
of Jeduthun.
18 All the Levites in [a]the holy city *were*
two hundred and eighty-four.
19 Moreover the gatekeepers, Akkub,

34 [a]Neh. 13:31; [Is. 40:16] [b]Lev. 6:12
*See WW at 2 Kin. 12:9.
35 [a]Ex. 23:19; 34:26; Lev. 19:23; Num. 18:12; Deut. 26:1, 2
36 [a]Ex. 13:2, 12, 13; Lev. 27:26, 27; Num. 18:15, 16
37 [a]Lev. 23:17; Num. 15:19; 18:12; Deut. 18:4; 26:2 [b]Lev. 27:30; Num. 18:21; Mal. 3:10
[1]Temple
38 [a]Num. 18:26 [b]1 Chr. 9:26; 2 Chr. 31:11
39 [a]Deut. 12:6, 11; 2 Chr. 31:12; Neh. 13:12 [b]Neh. 13:10, 11 [c][Heb. 10:25]

CHAPTER 11

1 [a]Neh. 10:18; Matt. 4:5; 5:35; 27:53
2 [a]Judg. 5:9; 2 Chr. 17:16
3 [a]1 Chr. 9:2, 3 [b]Ezra 2:43 [c]Ezra 2:55
*See WW at Josh. 22:9.
4 [a]1 Chr. 9:3 [b]Gen. 38:29

9 [1]Or *Hassenuah*
10 [a]1 Chr. 9:10
14 [1]Or *the son of Haggedolim*
16 [a]Ezra 10:15 [b]Ezra 8:33 [c]1 Chr. 26:29 [1]Temple
17 [1]Or *Michah*
18 [a]Neh. 11:1

11:1–24 The account returns to Nehemiah's central role and the success of his repopulation program.

Talmon, and their brethren who kept the gates, *were* one hundred and seventy-two.

20 And the rest of Israel, of the priests *and* Levites, *were* in all the cities of Judah, everyone in his inheritance.

21 [a]But the Nethinim dwelt in Ophel. And Ziha and Gishpa *were* over the Nethinim.

22 Also the overseer of the Levites at Jerusalem *was* Uzzi the son of Bani, the son of Hashabiah, the son of Mattaniah, the son of Micha, of the sons of Asaph, the singers in charge of the [1]service of the [2]house of God.

23 For [a]*it was* the king's command concerning them that a [1]certain portion should be for the singers, a quota day by day.

24 Pethahiah the son of Meshezabel, of the children of [a]Zerah the son of Judah, *was* [b]the[1] king's deputy in all matters concerning the people.

The People Dwelling Outside Jerusalem

25 And as for the villages with their fields, *some* of the children of Judah dwelt in [a]Kirjath Arba and its villages, Dibon and its villages, Jekabzeel and its villages;

26 in Jeshua, Moladah, Beth Pelet,

27 Hazar Shual, and Beersheba and its villages;

28 in Ziklag and Meconah and its villages;

29 in En Rimmon, Zorah, Jarmuth,

30 Zanoah, Adullam, and their villages; in Lachish and its fields; in Azekah and its villages. They dwelt from Beersheba to the Valley of Hinnom.

31 Also the children of Benjamin from Geba *dwelt* in Michmash, Aija, and Bethel, and their villages;

32 in Anathoth, Nob, Ananiah;

33 in Hazor, Ramah, Gittaim;

34 in Hadid, Zeboim, Neballat;

35 in Lod, Ono, *and* [a]the Valley of Craftsmen.

36 Some of the Judean divisions of Levites *were* in Benjamin.

The Priests and Levites

12 Now these *are* the [a]priests and the Levites who came up with [b]Zerubbabel the son of Shealtiel, and Jeshua: [c]Seraiah, Jeremiah, Ezra,

2 Amariah, [1]Malluch, Hattush,

3 [1]Shechaniah, [2]Rehum, [3]Meremoth,

4 Iddo, [1]Ginnethoi, [a]Abijah,

5 [1]Mijamin, [2]Maadiah, Bilgah,

6 Shemaiah, Joiarib, Jedaiah,

7 [1]Sallu, Amok, Hilkiah, *and* Jedaiah.

These *were* the heads of the priests and their brethren in the days of [a]Jeshua.

8 Moreover the Levites *were* Jeshua, Binnui, Kadmiel, Sherebiah, Judah, *and* Mattaniah [a]*who led* the thanksgiving *psalms,* he and his brethren.

9 Also Bakbukiah and Unni, their brethren, *stood* across from them in *their* duties.

10 Jeshua begot Joiakim, Joiakim begot Eliashib, Eliashib begot Joiada,

11 Joiada begot Jonathan, and Jonathan begot Jaddua.

12 Now in the days of Joiakim, the priests, the [a]heads of the fathers' *houses were:* of Seraiah, Meraiah; of Jeremiah, Hananiah;

13 of Ezra, Meshullam; of Amariah, Jehohanan;

14 of [1]Melichu, Jonathan; of [2]Shebaniah, Joseph;

15 of [1]Harim, Adna; of [2]Meraioth, Helkai;

16 of Iddo, Zechariah; of Ginnethon, Meshullam;

17 of Abijah, Zichri; *the son* of [1]Minjamin; of [2]Moadiah, Piltai;

18 of Bilgah, Shammua; of Shemaiah, Jehonathan;

19 of Joiarib, Mattenai; of Jedaiah, Uzzi;

20 of [1]Sallai, Kallai; of Amok, Eber;

21 of Hilkiah, Hashabiah; *and* of Jedaiah, Nethanel.

22 During the reign of Darius the Persian, a record *was also kept* of the Levites and priests *who had been* [a]heads of their fathers' *houses* in the days of Eliashib, Joiada, Johanan, and Jaddua.

23 The sons of Levi, the heads of the fathers' *houses* until the days of Johanan the son of Eliashib, *were* written in the book of the [a]chronicles.

24 And the heads of the Levites *were* Hashabiah, Sherebiah, and Jeshua the son of Kadmiel, with their brothers across from them, to [a]praise *and* give thanks, [b]group[1] alternating with group, [c]according to the command of David the man of God.

21 [a]2 Chr. 27:3; Neh. 3:26
22 [1]*work* [2]*Temple*
23 [a]Ezra 6:8, 9; 7:20 [1]*fixed share*
24 [a]Gen. 38:30 [b]1 Chr. 18:17 [1]Lit. *at the king's hand*
25 [a]Josh. 14:15
35 [a]1 Chr. 4:14

CHAPTER 12

1 [a]Ezra 2:1, 2; 7:7 [b]Neh. 7:7; Matt. 1:12, 13 [c]Neh. 10:2–8
2 [1]*Melichu,* v. 14
3 [1]*Shebaniah,* v. 14 [2]*Harim,* v. 15 [3]*Meraioth,* v. 15
4 [a]Luke 1:5 [1]*Ginnethon,* v. 16
5 [1]*Minjamin,* v. 17 [2]*Moadiah,* v. 17
7 [a]Ezra 3:2; Hag. 1:1; Zech. 3:1 [1]*Sallai,* v. 20
8 [a]Neh. 11:17
12 [a]Neh. 7:70, 71; 8:13; 11:13
14 [1]*Malluch,* v. 2 [2]*Shechaniah,* v. 3
15 [1]*Rehum,* v. 3 [2]*Meremoth,* v. 3
17 [1]*Mijamin,* v. 5 [2]*Maadiah,* v. 5
20 [1]*Sallu,* v. 7
22 [a]1 Chr. 24:6
23 [a]1 Chr. 9:14–22
24 [a]Neh. 11:17 [b]Ezra 3:11 [c]1 Chr. 23—26 [1]Lit. *watch by watch*

11:21 Nethinim were temple servants (janitors, maintenance, repair).

11:24 Pethahiah was the Jewish ambassador to the Persian court. Perhaps he served as political watchdog for the regime, appointed by Persia to report Nehemiah and Ezra's activities.

11:25–36 These were communities outside of Jerusalem in Judah and Benjamin.

12:1–26 These were lists of priests and Levites from the original return until the time of writing.

25 Mattaniah, Bakbukiah, Obadiah, Meshullam, Talmon, and Akkub *were* gatekeepers keeping the watch at the storerooms of the gates.

26 These *lived* in the days of Joiakim the son of Jeshua, the son of [1]Jozadak, and in the days of Nehemiah [a]the governor, and of Ezra the priest, [b]the scribe.

Nehemiah Dedicates the Wall

[1] 27 Now at [a]the dedication of the wall of Jerusalem they sought out the Levites in all their places, to bring them to Jerusalem to celebrate the dedication with gladness, [b]both with thanksgivings and singing, *with* cymbals and stringed instruments and harps.

28 And the sons of the singers gathered together from the countryside around Jerusalem, from the [a]villages of the Netophathites,

29 from the house of Gilgal, and from the fields of Geba and Azmaveth; for the singers had built themselves villages all around Jerusalem.

30 Then the priests and Levites [a]purified themselves, and purified the people, the gates, and the wall.

31 So I brought the leaders of Judah up on the wall, and appointed two large thanksgiving choirs. [a]*One* went to the right hand on the wall [b]toward the Refuse Gate.

32 After them went Hoshaiah and half of the leaders of Judah,

33 and Azariah, Ezra, Meshullam,

34 Judah, Benjamin, Shemaiah, Jeremiah,

35 and some of the priests' sons [a]with trumpets—Zechariah the son of Jonathan, the son of Shemaiah, the son of Mattaniah, the son of Michaiah, the son of Zaccur, the son of Asaph,

36 and his brethren, Shemaiah, Azarel, Milalai, Gilalai, Maai, Nethanel, Judah, *and* Hanani, with [a]the musical [b]instruments of David the man of God. Ezra the scribe *went* before them.

37 [a]By the Fountain Gate, in front of them, they went up [b]the *stairs of the [c]City of David, on the stairway of the wall, beyond the house of David, as far as [d]the Water Gate eastward.

38 [a]The other thanksgiving choir went the opposite *way,* and I *was* behind them with half of the people on the wall, going past the [b]Tower of the Ovens as far as [c]the Broad Wall,

39 [a]and above the Gate of Ephraim, above [b]the Old Gate, above [c]the Fish Gate, [d]the Tower of Hananel, the Tower of [1]the Hundred, as far as [e]the Sheep Gate; and they stopped by [f]the Gate of the Prison.

40 So the two thanksgiving choirs stood in the house of God, likewise I and the half of the rulers with me;

41 and the priests, Eliakim, Maaseiah, [1]Minjamin, Michaiah, Elioenai, Zechariah, *and* Hananiah, with trumpets;

42 also Maaseiah, Shemaiah, Eleazar, Uzzi, Jehohanan, Malchijah, Elam, and Ezer. The singers [1]sang loudly with Jezrahiah the director.

43 Also that day they *offered great sacrifices, and rejoiced, for God had made them rejoice with great joy; the women and the children also rejoiced, so that the joy of Jerusalem was heard [a]afar off.

Temple Responsibilities

44 [a]And at the same time some were appointed over the rooms of the storehouse for the offerings, the firstfruits, and the [b]tithes, to gather into them from the fields of the cities the portions specified by the Law for the priests and Levites; for Judah rejoiced over the priests and Levites who [1]ministered.

45 Both the singers and the gatekeepers kept the charge of their God and the charge of the purification, [a]according to the command of David *and* Solomon his son.

46 For in the days of David [a]and Asaph of old *there were* chiefs of the singers, and songs of praise and thanksgiving to God.

47 In the days of Zerubbabel and in the days of Nehemiah all Israel gave the portions for the singers and the gatekeepers, a portion for [a]each day. [b]They also [1]consecrated *holy things* for the Levites, [c]and the Levites consecrated *them* for the children of Aaron.

Principles of Separation

13 On that day [a]they read from the Book of Moses in the hearing of

26 [a]Neh. 8:9 [b]Ezra 7:6, 11 [1]*Jehozadak,* 1 Chr. 6:14
27 [a]Deut. 20:5; Neh. 7:1; Ps. 30:title [b]1 Chr. 25:6; 2 Chr. 5:13; 7:6
28 [a]1 Chr. 9:16
30 [a]Ezra 6:20; Neh. 13:22, 30
31 [a]Neh. 12:38 [b]Neh. 2:13; 3:13
35 [a]Num. 10:2, 8
36 [a]1 Chr. 23:5 [b]2 Chr. 29:26, 27
37 [a]Neh. 2:14; 3:15 [b]Neh. 3:15 [c]2 Sam. 5:7–9 [d]Neh. 3:26; 8:1, 3, 16 *See WW at Amos 9:6.
38 [a]Neh. 12:31 [b]Neh. 3:11 [c]Neh. 3:8
39 [a]2 Kin. 14:13; Neh. 8:16 [b]Neh. 3:6 [c]Neh. 3:3 [d]Neh. 3:1 [e]Neh. 3:32 [f]Jer. 32:2 [1]Heb. *Hammeah*
41 [1]Or *Mijamin,* v. 5
42 [1]Lit. *made their voice to be heard*
43 [a]Ezra 3:13 *See WW at Deut. 16:2.
44 [a]2 Chr. 31:11, 12; Neh. 13:5, 12, 13 [b]Neh. 10:37–39 [1]Lit. *stood*
45 [a]1 Chr. 25; 26
46 [a]1 Chr. 25:1; 2 Chr. 29:30
47 [a]Neh. 11:23 [b]Num. 18:21, 24 [c]Num. 18:26 [1]*set apart*

CHAPTER 13

1 [a][Deut. 31:11, 12]; 2 Kin. 23:2; Neh. 8:3, 8; 9:3; Is. 34:16

12:27–43 See section 1 of Truth-In-Action at the end of Neh.
12:27–43 Note the double procession for the dedication service. Ezra's procession traveled around Jerusalem counterclockwise and Nehemiah's clockwise, coming together at the temple square. The contributions of the priest and the governor were both honored in this unique way.
12:44–47 Support of the priests and Levites was generous because they had ministered well.
13:1–3 Syncretism (a meshing of various religions) had been the source of much trouble for Israel. Now action was taken to ensure that never again would the remnant turn aside to add other gods to their worship of Yahweh.

the people, and in it was found written
[b]that no Ammonite or Moabite should
ever come into the assembly of God,
2 because they had not met the children of Israel with bread and water,
but [a]hired Balaam against them to
curse them. [b]However, our God turned
the curse into a blessing.
3 So it was, when they had heard the
Law, [a]that they separated all the mixed
multitude from Israel.

The Reforms of Nehemiah

2 4 Now before this, [a]Eliashib the
priest, having authority over the storerooms of the house of our God, *was*
allied with [b]Tobiah.
5 And he had prepared for him a
large room, [a]where previously they
had stored the grain offerings, the
frankincense, the articles, the tithes of
grain, the new wine and oil, [b]which
were commanded *to be given* to the Levites and singers and gatekeepers, and
the offerings for the priests.
6 But during all this I was not in Jerusalem, [a]for in the thirty-second year of
Artaxerxes king of Babylon I had returned to the king. Then after certain
days I obtained leave from the king,
7 and I came to Jerusalem and discovered the evil that Eliashib had done for
Tobiah, in [a]preparing a room for him
in the courts of the [1]house of God.
8 And it grieved me bitterly; therefore
I threw all the household goods of Tobiah out of the room.
9 Then I commanded them to
[a]cleanse* the rooms; and I brought
back into them the articles of the house
of God, with the grain offering and the
frankincense.
7 10 I also realized that the portions for
the Levites had [a]not been given *them;*
for each of the Levites and the singers
who did the work had gone back to
[b]his field.
11 So [a]I contended with the rulers, and
said, [b]"Why is the house of God forsaken?" And I gathered them together
and set them in their place.
12 [a]Then all Judah brought the tithe
of the grain and the new wine and the
oil to the storehouse.
13 [a]And I appointed as treasurers over
the storehouse Shelemiah the priest
and Zadok the scribe, and of the Levites, Pedaiah; and next to them *was*
Hanan the son of Zaccur, the son of
Mattaniah; for they were considered
[b]faithful, and their task *was* to distribute to their brethren.
14 [a]Remember* me, O my God, concerning this, and do not wipe out my
good deeds that I have done for the
house of my God, and for its services!
15 In those days I saw *people* in Judah
treading wine presses [a]on the Sabbath,
and bringing in sheaves, and loading
donkeys with wine, grapes, figs, and
all *kinds of* burdens, [b]which they
brought into Jerusalem on the Sabbath
day. And I warned *them* about the day
on which they were selling provisions.
16 Men of Tyre dwelt there also, who
brought in fish and all kinds of goods,
and sold *them* on the Sabbath to the
children of Judah, and in Jerusalem.
17 Then I contended with the nobles
of Judah, and said to them, "What evil
thing *is* this that you do, by which you
profane the Sabbath day?
18 [a]"Did not your fathers do thus, and
did not our God bring all this disaster
on us and on this city? Yet you bring
added wrath on Israel by profaning the
Sabbath."
19 So it was, at the gates of Jerusalem,
as it [a]began to be dark before the Sabbath, that I commanded the gates to
be shut, and charged that they must
not be opened till after the Sabbath.
[b]Then I posted *some* of my servants
at the gates, *so that* no burdens would
be brought in on the Sabbath day.
20 Now the merchants and sellers of
all kinds of [1]wares [2]lodged outside Jerusalem once or twice.
21 Then I warned them, and said to
them, "Why do you spend the night
[1]around the wall? If you do *so* again,
I will lay hands on you!" From that
time on they came no *more* on the Sabbath.
22 And I commanded the Levites that

1 [b]Deut. 23:3, 4
2 [a]Num. 22:5; Josh. 24:9, 10 [b]Num. 23:1; 24:10; Deut. 23:5
3 [a]Neh. 9:2; 10:28
4 [a]Neh. 12:10 [b]Neh. 2:10; 4:3; 6:1
5 [a]Neh. 12:44 [b]Num. 18:21, 24
6 [a]Neh. 5:14–16
7 [a]Neh. 13:1, 5 [1]Temple
9 [a]2 Chr. 29:5, 15, 16 *See WW at Lev. 14:31.
10 [a]Neh. 10:37; Mal. 3:8 [b]Num. 35:2
11 [a]Neh. 13:17, 25 [b]Neh. 10:39
12 [a]Neh. 10:38; 12:44
13 [a]2 Chr. 31:12 [b]1 Cor. 4:2
14 [a]Neh. 5:19; 13:22, 31 *See WW at Is. 62:6.
15 [a][Ex. 20:10] [b]Neh. 10:31; [Jer. 17:21]
18 [a]Ezra 9:13; [Jer. 17:21]
19 [a]Lev. 23:32 [b]Jer. 17:21, 22
20 [1]*merchandise* [2]*spent the night*
21 [1]Lit. *before*

13:4–9 See section 2 of Truth-In-Action at the end of Neh.
13:4–9 It is hard to imagine the audacity of Tobiah. As soon as Nehemiah left for Persia, Tobiah had dared to move into a room in the temple! Upon his return a very perturbed Nehemiah ejects Tobiah with his furniture.
13:10–14 The Levites had been scattered during the years because of inadequate financial support. Now the tithes were paid. Malachi presents this message clearly in the days following Nehemiah (Mal. 3:8–12). Nehemiah sacrificed a great deal in order to minister to his people, but he seems quite sure that God is not in any man's debt. He prays three times in this chapter that God will remember him and reward him for his good deeds.
13:10–13 See section 7 of Truth-In-Action at the end of Neh.
13:15–22 Thirty years had passed since Ezra's initial ministry concerning the Sabbath, and people had begun to violate the day during Nehemiah's second term as governor. Nehemiah's warning was that the same sins would produce the same dire results.

[a]they should cleanse themselves, and
that they should go and guard the
gates, to sanctify the Sabbath day.
Remember me, O my God, *concerning* this also, and spare me according
to the greatness of Your mercy!
2 23 In those days I also saw Jews *who*
[a]had married women of [b]Ashdod, Ammon, *and* Moab.
24 And half of their children spoke the
language of Ashdod, and could not
speak the language of Judah, but spoke
according to the language of one or the
other people.
25 So I [a]contended with them and
[1]cursed* them, struck some of them
and pulled out their hair, and made
them [b]swear by God, *saying*, "You
shall not give your daughters as wives
to their sons, nor take their daughters
for your sons or yourselves.
26 [a]"Did not Solomon king of Israel
sin by these things? Yet among many
nations there was no king like him,
[b]who was beloved of his God; and God
made him king over all Israel. [c]Never-
theless pagan women caused even
him to sin.
27 "Should we then hear of your doing
all this great evil, [a]transgressing
against our God by marrying pagan
women?"
28 And *one* of the sons [a]of Joiada, the
son of Eliashib the high priest, *was* a
son-in-law of [b]Sanballat the Horonite;
therefore I drove him from me.
29 [a]Remember them, O my God, because they have defiled the priesthood
and [b]the covenant of the priesthood
and the Levites.
30 [a]Thus I cleansed them of everything
pagan. I also [b]assigned duties to the
priests and the Levites, each to his service,
31 and *to bringing* [a]the wood offering
and the firstfruits at appointed times.
[b]Remember me, O my God, for
good!

22 [a]1 Chr. 15:12; Neh. 12:30 **23** [a][Ex. 34:16; Deut. 7:3, 4]; Ezra 9:2; Neh. 10:30 [b]Neh. 4:7 **25** [a]Prov. 28:4 [b]Ezra 10:5; Neh. 10:29, 30 [1]*pronounced them cursed* *See WW at Jer. 8:11. **26** [a]1 Kin. 11:1, 2 [b]2 Sam. 12:24, 25 [c]1 Kin. 11:4–8 **27** [a][Ezra 10:2]; Neh. 13:23 **28** [a]Neh. 12:10, 12 [b]Neh. 4:1, 7; 6:1, 2 **29** [a]Neh. 6:14 [b]Mal. 2:4, 11, 12 **30** [a]Neh. 10:30 [b]Neh. 12:1 **31** [a]Neh. 10:34 [b]Neh. 13:14, 22

13:23–29 We are not told that Nehemiah dissolved existing interfaith marriages, but he did rebuke them forcefully. Deut. 7:3 was vigorously enforced for all future marriages. See note on Ezra 10:10, 11.

13:23–27 See section 2 of Truth-In-Action at the end of Neh.

13:30, 31 This is a recapitulation of reforms in which Nehemiah shows that he has fulfilled his calling. His satisfaction with the results is seen in his final prayer in which he rests his case, making no additional requests for rewards.

TRUTH-IN-ACTION through NEHEMIAH

Letting the LIFE of the Holy Spirit Bring Faith's Works Alive in You!

Truth Nehemiah Teaches	Text	**Action** Nehemiah Invites
1 Guidelines for Growing in Godliness Living God's way means making God's priorities our priorities, realizing that they often are different from ours. God still accomplishes all things through His Word. Therefore, the Scriptures are a guide for ordering our lives according to God's will. Understanding and obeying them brings joy. They also teach us to acknowledge God's hand in all of our success.	1:4–11	**Make** the welfare of God's people a higher priority than your own welfare. **Understand** that a general sin of God's people is yours to confess, too.
	8:1–6	**Give place** to the public reading of Scripture as a source of understanding and encouragement.
	8:10	**Cultivate** and **promote** the joy of the Lord among God's people as a powerful source of spiritual strength.
	12:27–43	**Observe** the regular celebration of holy success and spiritual progress. **Dedicate** your works to the Lord, knowing it is He who gives all success and progress.
2 Steps to Holiness True holiness is active and dynamic, not passive and static. We must actively remove the ways of the world from our lives.	13:4–9	**Be willing to root out** worldly ways where they have become established in the life of the church. **Reject** carnal compromises.
	13:23–27	**Refuse** evil alliances. **Do not marry** an unbeliever.
3 Keys to Wise Living Wisdom knows that the Lord is the source of any spiritual advance-	1:11	**Understand** and **believe** that success and favor with men comes from the Lord.

Truth Nehemiah Teaches	Text	**Action** Nehemiah Invites
3 ment. It is also aware that no such progress will go unopposed, but will incur spiritual opposition, sometimes expressed through human agency. Therefore, act with discernment. The wise will discern the true origin of many verbal attacks as an assault motivated by our spiritual adversary.	2:12–16 2:19 2:10 6:12	**Understand** that wisdom involves searching out a matter before making any decisions or decrees. **Postpone** informing others until you have ascertained the mind of the Lord. **Expect** and **do not be surprised or dismayed** at hostility when you undertake to do the will of God. **Be aware** that any favor shown to God's people will anger our spiritual adversary. **Discern** that much human enmity is spiritually motivated. **Discern** and **reject** negative prophecy from malignant sources.
4 Key Lessons in Faith Faith takes God at His word. Do not question His promises. Through faith, we can speak confidently, praising Him for promises that will bring success.	2:4–6 2:8	**Pray** that your responses in demanding situations will be from the Lord. **Do not answer** impetuously or presumptuously. **Express** gratitude for all success and favor.
5 Steps to Dealing with Sin Much sin is corporate. We must deal with such sin together and believe that God is faithful to forgive corporate sins.	9:1–38 9:17	**Allow for** the public, corporate confession of sin when necessary. **Teach** and **believe** that God is gracious and forgiving when confessing and repenting of sin.
6 Lessons for Leaders Leaders must insure the welfare of the church. They must lead the way so that everyone carries a fair share of the work and no one puts his own interests above those of others. Leaders are servants, providing examples of obedience and diligence to God's people. Only those who live this way should be entrusted with leadership responsibility.	3:5 5:1–13 5:15, 16 7:2 9:29	Leaders, **note** and **reprove** those who, due to their position or privilege, will not serve. Leaders, **reprove** those who ignore the welfare of others, pursuing instead personal gain. **Champion** the cause of the poor and needy. Leaders, **do not lord it over** others. Rather, **devote yourself** to working diligently. Leaders, **honor** men of integrity who fear the Lord. **Entrust** such with leadership responsibility. Leaders, **understand** and **teach** that righteous living is obedient to the will of God as revealed in the Scriptures.
7 Keys to Generous Living We must be generous toward God's work first, making the care of His servants a high priority.	13:10–13	**Insure** that God's servants are adequately cared for. **Avoid** any tendency to neglect the work of God in favor of personal concerns or selfish ambitions.
8 Guidelines to Gaining Victory Spiritual victory comes through faith that God fights for us. We can ignore the insults of those opposed to us and trust God for victory.	4:1–6 4:17–23	**Ignore** the reproaches and insults of those who oppose your pursuit of God's will. **Trust** God's justice and faithfulness. **Realize** that all spiritual ministry involves spiritual warfare. **Be prepared** for battle, **quick to aid** those who are under spiritual attack.

The Book of ESTHER

Author: Unknown
Date: Shortly After 465 B.C.
Theme: Teamwork That Shaped a Nation
Key Words: Humility, Interdependence, The Fear of God

Author While the name of the author is unknown, the book was written by a Jew, who was familiar with Persian customs and words. Mordecai or Ezra may have been the writer.

Background and Date The Book of Esther is a graphic narrative, which relates how God's people were preserved from ruin during the fifth century B.C.

The book takes its name from the beautiful, orphaned Jewess who became the queen of the Persian king Ahasuerus. He is generally believed to have been King Xerxes I who succeeded Darius I in 485 B.C. and ruled for twenty years over 127 provinces from India to Ethiopia. He lived in the Persian capital of Shushan. At this time a number of Jews were still in Babylon under Persian rule, even though they had been free to return to Jerusalem (Ezra 1; 2) for over fifty years. The story takes place over a period of four years, starting in the third year of Xerxes' reign.

Content Esther is a study in the survival of God's people amidst hostility. Haman, the king's second in command, wants the Jews destroyed. He manipulates the king to call for their execution. Esther is brought on the scene and is used by God to save her people. Haman is hanged; and Mordecai, a leader to the Jews in the Persian Empire, becomes prime minister. The Feast of Purim is then instituted to mark their deliverance.

A unique feature of Esther is that the name of God is not mentioned. However, the imprint of God and His ways are obvious throughout, especially in the lives of Esther and Mordecai. From a human perspective, Esther and Mordecai were two of the most unlikely people to be chosen to play major roles in shaping a nation. He was a Jewish Benjamite exile; she was his adopted, orphaned cousin (2:7). Esther's spiritual maturity is seen in her knowing to wait for God's timing to make her request to save her people and to denounce Haman (5:6–8; 7:3–6). Mordecai also demonstrates a maturity to seek God for timing and direction. As a result, he knew the right time for Esther to disclose her identity as a Jew (2:10). These obviously divinely controlled restraints proved to be crucial (6:1–14; 7:9, 10) and testify to the book's spiritual base.

Finally, both Esther and Mordecai feared God, not men. Regardless of the consequences, Mordecai refused to pay homage to Haman. Esther risked her life for the sake of her people by going to the king without being summoned. Their mission was always to save the life that the enemy planned to destroy (2:21–23; 4:1–17; 7:1–6; 8:3–6). As a result, they led a nation into freedom, were honored by the king and given greater authority, privileges, and responsibilities.

Personal Application One of the main purposes of the Book of Esther is to show us from the lives of Esther and Mordecai a classic example of successful teamwork. Their relationship vividly portrays the unity that the Lord Jesus prayed for His disciples to experience (John 17). The success of their individual roles, even their very survival, depended entirely upon their unity. Esther also shows how God destroys those who try to harm His people. From this we are reminded that He is faithful to destroy Satan and that His sovereign purposes ultimately prevail.

Christ Revealed Queen Esther is similar to Jesus in several ways. She lived in submission, dependence, and obedience to her God-given authorities Mordecai and King Ahasuerus even as the Lord Jesus, during His earthly ministry, lived in total submission, dependence, and obedience to His Father God.

Esther also fully identified herself with her people and fasted for three days as she interceded to God on their behalf (4:16). Hebrews 2:17 tells us that "in all things He [Jesus] had to be made like *His* brethren, that He might be a merciful and faithful High Priest." As such, He both fasted and prayed for His own (Matt. 4:2; John 17:20).

Third, Esther gave up her right to live in order to save the nation from certain death. For this she was exalted by the king. In like fashion Jesus gave up His life that a world of sinners might be saved from eternal death and was highly exalted by God (Phil. 2:5–11).

The Holy Spirit at Work Although the Holy Spirit is not mentioned directly, it is His work that produced in both Esther and Mordecai the deep level of humility, leading to their mutual love and loyalty (see Rom. 5:5).

The Holy Spirit also directed and energized Esther to fast for her nation and to call her people to do the same (see Rom. 8:26, 27).

Outline of Esther

I. A new queen chosen **1:1—2:17**
- A. King Ahasuerus displays his power and holds a feast 1:1–8
- B. Queen Vashti is deposed 1:9–22
- C. Esther is chosen to be queen 2:1–18

II. The king's life saved **2:19–23**
- A. Mordecai uncovers a conspiracy 2:19–21
- B. Esther informs the king 2:22, 23

III. A plot against the Jews formed **3:1—4:17**
- A. Haman plots to destroy the Jews 3:1–15
- B. Mordecai persuades Esther to intervene 4:1–14
- C. Esther solicits Mordecai's help 4:15–17

IV. Mordecai exalted **5:1—6:14**
- A. Esther plans a banquet 5:1–8
- B. Haman plots to destroy Mordecai 5:9–14
- C. Haman is forced to honor Mordecai 6:1–14

V. Haman hanged **7:1–10**
- A. Esther discloses her identity and exposes Haman 7:1–6
- B. Haman is hanged on gallows prepared for Mordecai 7:7–10

VI. The Jews saved 8:1—9:17
- A. Esther brings her request to the king 8:1–6
- B. The king issues a decree on behalf of the Jews 8:7–17
- C. The Jews defeat their enemies 9:1–17

VII. The Feast of Purim established 9:18—10:3
- A. The Jews celebrate the first Purim 9:18–32
- B. The king advances Mordecai 10:1–3

The King Dethrones Queen Vashti

NOW it came to pass in the days
of [a]Ahasuerus[1] (this *was* the
Ahasuerus who *reigned [b]over one
hundred and twenty-seven provinces,
[c]from India to Ethiopia),
2 in those days when King Ahasuerus
[a]sat on the throne of his kingdom,
which *was* in [b]Shushan[1] the [2]citadel,
3 *that* in the third year of his reign
he [a]made a feast for all his officials and
servants—the powers of Persia and
Media, the nobles, and the princes of
the provinces *being* before him—
4 when he showed the riches of his
glorious kingdom and the splendor of
his excellent majesty for many days,
one hundred and eighty days *in all.*
5 And when these days were completed, the king made a feast lasting
seven days for all the people who were
present in [1]Shushan the [2]citadel, from
great to small, in the court of the garden of the king's palace.
6 *There were* white and blue linen
curtains fastened with cords of fine
linen and purple on silver rods and
marble pillars; *and the* [a]couches *were*
of gold and silver on a *mosaic* pavement of alabaster, turquoise, and white
and black marble.
7 And they served drinks in golden
vessels, each vessel being different
from the other, with royal wine in
abundance, [a]according to the [1]gener-
osity of the king.
8 In accordance with the law, the
drinking was not compulsory; for so
the king had ordered all the officers
of his household, that they should do
according to each man's pleasure.
9 Queen Vashti also made a feast for
the women *in* the royal palace which
belonged to King Ahasuerus.
10 On the seventh day, when the heart
of the king was merry with wine, he
commanded Mehuman, Biztha, [a]Har-
bona, Bigtha, Abagtha, Zethar, and
Carcas, seven eunuchs who served in
the presence of King Ahasuerus,
11 to bring Queen Vashti before the
king, *wearing* her royal crown, in order
to show her *beauty to the people and
the officials, for she *was* beautiful to
behold.
12 But Queen Vashti refused to come
at the king's command *brought* by *his*
eunuchs; therefore the king was furious, and his anger burned within him.
13 Then the king said to the [a]wise men
[b]who understood the *times (for this
was the king's manner toward all who
knew law and justice,
14 those closest to him *being* Car-
shena, Shethar, Admatha, Tarshish,
Meres, Marsena, and Memucan, the
[a]seven princes of Persia and Media,
[b]who had access to the king's presence, *and* who [1]ranked highest in the
kingdom):
15 "What *shall we* do to Queen Vashti,
according to law, because she did not
obey the command of King Ahasuerus
brought to her by the eunuchs?"
16 And Memucan answered before the
king and the princes: "Queen Vashti
has not only wronged the king, but also
all the princes, and all the people who
are in all the provinces of King Ahasuerus.
17 "For the queen's behavior will 4
become known to all women, so that
they will [a]despise their husbands in

CHAPTER 1

1 [a]Ezra 4:6; Dan. 9:1 [b]Esth. 8:9 [c]Dan. 6:1 [1]Generally identified with Xerxes I (485–464 B.C.) *See WW at 2 Sam. 8:15.
2 [a]1 Kin. 1:46 [b]Neh. 1:1; Dan. 8:2 [1]Or *Susa* [2]Or *fortified palace,* and so elsewhere in the book
3 [a]Gen. 40:20; Esth. 2:18
5 [1]Or *Susa* [2]*palace*
6 [a]Esth. 7:8; Ezek. 23:41; Amos 2:8; 6:4
7 [a]Esth. 2:18 [1]Lit. *hand*
10 [a]Esth. 7:9
11 *See WW at Ezek. 28:12.
13 [a]Jer. 10:7; Dan. 2:12; Matt. 2:1 [b]1 Chr. 12:32 *See WW at Is. 33:6.
14 [a]Ezra 7:14 [b]2 Kin. 25:19; [Matt. 18:10] [1]Lit. *sat in first place*
17 [a][Eph. 5:33]

1:1 Ahasuerus: See Introduction to Esther: Background and Date.

1:3 The third year was 482 B.C. **A feast** was a special 180-day banquet (v. 4). **Persia:** An ancient world empire that flourished from 539 to 331 B.C. **Media:** The ancient name for modern northwest Iran; it was the most important province of Persia. The customs and laws of the Medes were combined with those of the Persians, and many Medes were given positions of responsibility.

1:5 The 180-day feast was followed by a 7-day feast in the palace, which Shushan's males were allowed to attend.

1:10 Eunuchs: Trustworthy court officers, personal attendants to both sexes. Some were military officials or governors.

1:13 Wise men who understood the times: Men skilled in the law.

1:17, 18 See section 4 of Truth-In-Action at the end of Esth.

1:17 Leadership involves both responsibilities and influence. In her rebellion, **Vashti** ignores her responsibility to her authority **King Ahasuerus**. His advisors fear that, because of Vashti's position, other women may follow her example.

their eyes, when they report, 'King Ahasuerus commanded Queen Vashti to be brought in before him, but she did not come.'

18 "This very day the *noble* ladies of Persia and Media will say to all the king's officials that they have heard of the behavior of the queen. Thus *there will be* excessive contempt and wrath.

19 "If it pleases the king, let a royal [1]decree go out from him, and let it be recorded in the laws of the Persians and the Medes, so that it will [a]not [2]be altered, that Vashti shall come no more before King Ahasuerus; and let the king give her royal position to another who is better than she.

20 "When the king's decree which he will make is proclaimed throughout all his empire (for it is great), all wives will [a]honor their husbands, both great and small."

21 And the reply pleased the king and the princes, and the king did according to the word of Memucan.

22 Then he sent letters to all the king's provinces, [a]to each province in its own script, and to every people in their own language, that each man should [b]be master in his own house, and speak in the language of his own people.

Esther Becomes Queen

2 After these things, when the wrath of King Ahasuerus subsided, he remembered Vashti, [a]what she had done, and what had been decreed against her.

2 Then the king's servants who attended him said: "Let beautiful young virgins be sought for the king;

3 "and let the king appoint officers in all the provinces of his kingdom, that they may gather all the beautiful young virgins to [1]Shushan the [2]citadel, into the women's quarters, under the custody of [3]Hegai the king's eunuch, custodian of the women. And let beauty preparations be given *them.*

4 "Then let the young woman who pleases the king be queen instead of Vashti." This thing pleased the king, and he did so.

5 In [1]Shushan the [2]citadel there was a certain Jew whose name *was* Mordecai the son of Jair, the son of Shimei, the son of [a]Kish, a Benjamite.

6 [a]*Kish*[1] had been carried away from Jerusalem with the captives who had been captured with [2]Jeconiah king of Judah, whom Nebuchadnezzar the king of Babylon had carried away.

7 And *Mordecai* had brought up Hadassah, that *is,* Esther, [a]his uncle's daughter, for she had neither father nor mother. The young woman *was* lovely and beautiful. When her father and mother died, Mordecai took her as his own daughter.

8 So it was, when the king's command and decree were heard, and when many young women were [a]gathered at [1]Shushan the [2]citadel, *under* the custody of Hegai, that Esther also was taken to the king's palace, into the care of Hegai the custodian of the women.

9 Now the young woman pleased him, and she obtained his favor; so he readily gave [a]beauty preparations to her, besides [1]her allowance. Then seven choice maidservants were provided for her from the king's palace, and he moved her and her maidservants to the best *place* in the house of the women.

10 [a]Esther had not [1]revealed her people or family, for Mordecai had charged her not to reveal *it.*

11 And every day Mordecai paced in front of the court of the women's quarters, to learn of Esther's welfare and what was happening to her.

12 Each young woman's turn came to go in to King Ahasuerus after she had completed twelve months' preparation, according to the regulations for the women, for thus were the days of their preparation apportioned: six months with oil of myrrh, and six months with

19 [a]Esth. 8:8; Dan. 6:8 [1]Lit. *word* [2]*pass away*
20 [a][Eph. 5:33; Col. 3:18; 1 Pet. 3:1]
22 [a]Esth. 3:12; 8:9 [b][Eph. 5:22–24; 1 Tim. 2:12]

CHAPTER 2

1 [a]Esth. 1:19, 20
3 [1]Or *Susa* [2]*palace* [3]Heb. *Hege*
5 [a]1 Sam. 9:1 [1]Or *Susa* [2]*palace*
6 [a]2 Kin. 24:14, 15; 2 Chr. 36:10, 20; Jer. 24:1 [1]Lit. *Who* [2]*Jehoiachin,* 2 Kin. 24:6
7 [a]Esth. 2:15
8 [a]Esth. 2:3 [1]Or *Susa* [2]*palace*
9 [a]Esth. 2:3, 12 [1]Lit. *her portions*
10 [a]Esth. 2:20 [1]Revealed the identity of

1:19 Laws . . . not be altered: According to the Persians and the Medes their law was unchangeable. Even the king was powerless to alter it.

2:6 The captives: Those Jews taken from Jerusalem to Babylon in 586 B.C.

2:7 Hadassah: "Myrtle." **Esther:** "Star." Probably Mordecai renamed her when he adopted her.

2:8, 9 Esther is well trained, well adjusted socially, and spiritually prepared. This is evident from the favor she receives from her superiors at the palace. **Beauty preparations:** See note on v. 12. **Her allowance** consists of numerous dietary delicacies.

2:10 Although Esther is catapulted out of obscurity into a totally different environment, she continues to obey Mordecai's instructions. He wanted to protect her from the possibility of anti-Semitic reactions.

2:11 Mordecai continues to discharge his responsibility and care of Esther although she is physically removed from him.

2:12 Preparations for beautifying women: Persian law required that Esther be attractive physically. This required **twelve months' preparation,** with costly ointments. But in order for her to fulfill God's purposes, she needed to be equally prepared spiritually. She is a wonderful example of godly womanhood as described in 1 Pet. 3:1–4.

perfumes and preparations for beautifying women.
13 Thus *prepared, each* young woman
went to the king, and she was given
whatever she desired to take with her
from the women's quarters to the
king's palace.
14 In the evening she went, and in the
morning she returned to the second
house of the women, to the custody of
Shaashgaz, the king's eunuch who
kept the concubines. She would not go
in to the king again unless the king delighted in her and called for her by
name.
15 Now when the turn came for Esther
[a]the daughter of Abihail the uncle of
Mordecai, who had taken her as his
daughter, to go in to the king, she requested nothing but what Hegai the
king's eunuch, the custodian of the
women, advised. And Esther [b]obtained
favor in the sight of all who saw her.
16 So Esther was taken to King
Ahasuerus, into his royal palace, in the
tenth month, which *is* the month of Te-
beth, in the seventh year of his reign.
17 The king loved Esther more than all
the *other* women, and she obtained
*grace and favor in his sight more than
all the *virgins; so he set the royal
[a]crown upon her head and made her
queen instead of Vashti.
18 Then the king [a]made a great feast,
the Feast of Esther, for all his officials
and servants; and he proclaimed a holiday in the provinces and gave gifts according to the [1]generosity of a king.

Mordecai Discovers a Plot

19 When virgins were gathered together a second time, Mordecai sat
within the king's gate.
20 [a]*Now* Esther had not revealed her
family and her people, just as Mordecai
had charged her, for Esther obeyed the
command of Mordecai as when she
was brought up by him.
21 In those days, while Mordecai sat
within the king's gate, two of the king's
eunuchs, [1]Bigthan and Teresh, doorkeepers, became furious and sought to
lay hands on King Ahasuerus.
22 So the matter became known to
Mordecai, [a]who told Queen Esther,
and Esther informed the king in Mordecai's name.
23 And when an inquiry was made into
the matter, it was confirmed, and both
were hanged on a gallows; and it was
written in [a]the book of the chronicles
in the presence of the king.

15 [a]Esth. 2:7; 9:29 [b]Esth. 5:2, 8
17 [a]Esth. 1:11 *See WW at Zech. 12:10. • See WW at Ps. 45:14.
18 [a]Esth. 1:3 [1]Lit. *hand*
20 [a]Esth. 2:10; [Prov. 22:6]
21 [1]*Bigthana,* Esth. 6:2
22 [a]Esth. 6:1, 2
23 [a]Esth. 6:1

Haman's Conspiracy Against the Jews

3 After these things King Ahasuerus
promoted Haman, the son of Hammedatha the [a]Agagite, and [b]advanced
him and set his seat above all the
princes who *were* with him.
2 And all the king's servants who 1
were [a]within the king's gate bowed
and paid homage to Haman, for so the
king had commanded concerning him.
But Mordecai [b]would not bow or pay
homage.
3 Then the king's servants who *were*
within the king's gate said to Mordecai,
"Why do you transgress the [a]king's
command?"
4 Now it happened, when they spoke
to him daily and he would not listen
to them, that they told *it* to Haman, to
see whether Mordecai's words would
stand; for *Mordecai* had told them that
he *was* a Jew.
5 When Haman saw that Mordecai
[a]did not bow or pay him homage, Haman was [b]filled with wrath.
6 But he disdained to lay hands on
Mordecai alone, for they had told him
of the people of Mordecai. Instead, Haman [a]sought to destroy all the Jews
who *were* throughout the whole kingdom of Ahasuerus—the people of Mordecai.
7 In the first month, which is the
month of Nisan, in the twelfth year of
King Ahasuerus, [a]they cast Pur (that
is, the lot), before Haman [1]to determine
the day and the [2]month, [3]until *it fell*
on the twelfth *month,* which *is* the
month of Adar.

CHAPTER 3

1 [a]Num. 24:7; 1 Sam. 15:8 [b]Esth. 5:11
2 [a]Esth. 2:19, 21; 5:9 [b]Esth. 3:5; Ps. 15:4
3 [a]Esth. 3:2
5 [a]Esth. 3:2; 5:9 [b]Dan. 3:19
6 [a]Ps. 83:4; [Rev. 12:1–17]
7 [a]Esth. 9:24–26 [1]Lit. *from day to day and month to month* [2]LXX adds *to destroy the people of Mordecai in one day;* Vg. adds *the nation of the Jews should be destroyed* [3]So with MT, Vg.; LXX *and the lot fell on the fourteenth of the month*

2:13 Whatever she desired . . . from the women's quarters refers to jewelry and clothes.
2:19 A second time may have the sense of restating events prior to vv. 17, 18. **The king's gate** was where important legal and business transactions took place.
2:20 Esther is learning that God links lives according to His sovereign purpose. When God gave her prominence as the queen, with the king as a new authority over her, she still recognized Mordecai's authority. God's linkings come in different categories for different purposes.
2:22, 23 Their teamwork saves the king's life and his enemies are destroyed. Events significant in the history of the kingdom were recorded **in the book of the chronicles,** not to be confused with the OT books 1 and 2 Chr.
3:1 After these things indicates an indefinite period of as much as five years. **Haman** is **advanced** (promoted) to a high executive position.
3:2 See section 1 of Truth-In-Action at the end of Esth.
3:7 They cast . . . the lot, likely to determine the best day to carry out Haman's plans.

1 8 Then Haman said to King Ahasuerus, "There is a certain people scattered and dispersed among the people
in all the provinces of your kingdom;
[a]their laws *are* different from all *other*
people's, and they do not keep the
king's laws. Therefore it *is* not fitting
for the king to let them remain.
9 "If it pleases the king, let *a decree*
be written that they be destroyed, and
I will pay ten thousand talents of silver
into the hands of those who do the
work, to bring *it* into the king's treasuries."
10 So the king [a]took [b]his signet ring
from his hand and gave it to Haman,
the son of Hammedatha the Agagite,
the [c]enemy of the Jews.
11 And the king said to Haman, "The
money and the people *are* given to you,
to do with them as seems good to you."
12 [a]Then the king's scribes were called
on the thirteenth day of the first month,
and *a decree* was written according to
all that Haman commanded—to the
king's satraps, to the governors who
were over each province, to the officials of all people, to every province
[b]according to its script, and to every
people in their language. [c]In the name
of King Ahasuerus it was written, and
sealed with the king's signet ring.
13 And the letters were [a]sent by couriers into all the king's provinces, to destroy, to kill, and to annihilate all the
Jews, both young and old, little children and women, [b]in one day, on the
thirteenth *day* of the twelfth *month*,
which *is* the month of Adar, and
[c]to plunder their [1]possessions.
14 [a]A copy of the document was to be
issued as law in every province, being
published for all people, that they
should be ready for that day.
15 The couriers went out, hastened by
the king's command; and the decree
was proclaimed in [1]Shushan the
[2]citadel. So the king and Haman sat
down to drink, but [a]the city of Shushan
was [3]perplexed.

Esther Agrees to Help the Jews

4 When Mordecai learned all that
had happened, [1]he [a]tore his clothes
and put on sackcloth [b]and ashes, and
went out into the midst of the city. He
[c]cried out with a loud and bitter cry.

KINGDOM DYNAMICS

4:1 Rising to Meet Your Destiny (Esther), WOMEN. Esther was a Jewish orphan—a virtual nonentity, raised by her cousin, Mordecai, and with no particular promise. But the account contained in this book unfolds the way God opens destiny to any person who will keep His priorities. Even in the presence of recognition, success, wealth, and luxury—an environment many may covet, but which has so often proven destructive to spiritual commitment—Esther retained her sense of perspective and integrity.

Esther's Hebrew name was "Hadassah," which means "Myrtle," referring to the well-known and beautiful evergreen shrub. She reflected the myrtle in her courage and obedience, which clearly did not wither, even when she faced death! In Persian "Esther" means "Star"; again Esther's beauty, grace, and character shone, bright and unwavering, against the darkness threatening the Jewish people.

Note: 1) Esther's response to Mordecai's call to recognize God's providence in her placement: She believed God, not her beauty, had put her on the throne (4:14). 2) Her respect for the power of prayer and fasting: She recognized the reality of the spiritual realm and the Holy Spirit's resources (4:16). 3) Her unswerving will to lay down her own life for others and her practical good sense and patience in pursuing her enterprise (ch. 5).

(2 Kin. 22:3–20/Luke 1:26–56) F.L.

2 He went as far as the front of the
king's gate, for no one *might* enter the
king's gate clothed with sackcloth.
3 And in every province where the
king's command and decree arrived,
there was great mourning among the
Jews, with *fasting, weeping, and wailing; and many lay in sackcloth and
ashes.
4 So Esther's maids and eunuchs
came and told her, and the queen was
deeply distressed. Then she sent garments to clothe Mordecai and take his
sackcloth away from him, but he would
not accept *them*.
5 Then Esther called Hathach, *one* of
the king's eunuchs whom he had appointed to attend her, and she gave him

8 [a]Ezra 4:12–15; Acts 16:20, 21
10 [a]Gen. 41:42 [b]Esth. 8:2, 8 [c]Esth. 7:6
12 [a]Esth. 8:9 [b]Esth. 1:22 [c]1 Kin. 21:8; Esth. 8:8–10
13 [a]2 Chr. 30:6; Esth. 8:10, 14 [b]Esth. 8:12 [c]Esth. 8:11; 9:10 [1]LXX adds the text of the letter here
14 [a]Esth. 8:13, 14
15 [a]Esth. 8:15; [Prov. 29:2] [1]Or *Susa* [2]*palace* [3]*in confusion*

CHAPTER 4

1 [a]2 Sam. 1:11; Esth. 3:8–10; Jon. 3:5, 6 [b]Josh. 7:6; Ezek. 27:30 [c]Gen. 27:34 [1]Lit. *Mordecai*

3 *See WW at Jon. 3:5.

3:8–15 See section 1 of Truth-In-Action at the end of Esth.
3:10 When the king gave **his signet ring to Haman,** it was a sign of his delegating full royal authority.
3:12 There are three levels of Persian authorities here. **Satraps** were rulers over provinces, **governors** were their assisting leaders over the province or individual cities within them, and **officials** were tribal chieftains.
3:13 Haman's plan (vv. 5–9) is to be carried out 11 months later.
4:1 Tearing clothes and putting on **sackcloth** (a black coarse cloth usually made of goat's hair) and **ashes** was a sign of mourning for personal or national disaster.

a command concerning Mordecai, to
learn what and why this *was*.
6 So Hathach went out to Mordecai
in the city square that *was* in front of
the king's gate.
7 And Mordecai told him all that had
happened to him, and [a]the sum of
money that Haman had promised to
pay into the king's treasuries to destroy the Jews.
8 He also gave him [a]a copy of the
written decree for their destruction,
which was given at [1]Shushan, that he
might show it to Esther and explain it
to her, and that he might command her
to go in to the king to make supplication to him and plead before him for
her people.
9 So Hathach returned and told Esther the words of Mordecai.
10 Then Esther spoke to Hathach, and
gave him a command for Mordecai:
11 "All the king's servants and the
people of the king's provinces know
that any man or woman who goes into
[a]the inner court to the king, who has
not been called, [b]*he has* but one law:
put *all* to death, except the one [c]to
whom the king holds out the golden
scepter, that he may *live. Yet I myself
have not been [d]called to go in to the
king these thirty days."
2 12 So they told Mordecai Esther's
words.
13 And Mordecai told *them* to answer
Esther: "Do not think in your heart
that you will escape in the king's palace any more than all the other Jews.
14 "For if you remain completely silent
at this time, relief and deliverance will
arise for the Jews from another place,
but you and your father's house will
perish. Yet who knows whether you
have come to the kingdom for *such* a
time as this?"
15 Then Esther told *them* to reply to
Mordecai:
16 "Go, gather all the Jews who are
present in [1]Shushan, and fast for me;
neither eat nor drink for [a]three days,
night or day. My maids and I will fast
likewise. And so I will go to the king,
which *is* against the law; [b]and if I *perish, I perish!"
17 So Mordecai went his way and did
according to all that Esther commanded [1]him.

Esther's Banquet

5 Now it happened [a]on the third day
that Esther put on *her* royal *robes*
and stood in [b]the inner court of the
king's palace, across from the king's
house, while the king sat on his royal
throne in the royal house, facing the
entrance of the [1]house.
2 So it was, when the king saw Queen
Esther standing in the court, *that*
[a]she found favor in his sight, and
[b]the king held out to Esther the golden
scepter that *was* in his hand. Then Esther went near and touched the top of
the scepter.
3 And the king said to her, "What do
you wish, Queen Esther? What *is* your
request? [a]It shall be given to you—up
to half the kingdom!"
4 So Esther answered, "If it pleases
the king, let the king and Haman come
today to the banquet that I have prepared for him."
5 Then the king said, "Bring Haman
quickly, that he may do as Esther has
said." So the king and Haman went
to the banquet that Esther had prepared.
6 At the banquet of wine [a]the king
said to Esther, [b]"What *is* your petition?
It shall be granted you. What *is* your
request, up to half the kingdom? It
shall be done!"
7 Then Esther answered and said,
"My petition and request *is this:*
8 "If I have found favor in the sight
of the king, and if it pleases the king
to grant my petition and [1]fulfill my request, then let the king and Haman
come to the [a]banquet which I will prepare for them, and tomorrow I will do
as the king has said."

7 [a]Esth. 3:9
8 [a]Esth. 3:14, 15 [1]Or *Susa*
11 [a]Esth. 5:1; 6:4 [b]Dan. 2:9 [c]Esth. 5:2; 8:4 [d]Esth. 2:14 *See WW at Hab. 2:4.
16 [a]Esth. 5:1 [b]Gen. 43:14 [1]Or *Susa* *See WW at Judg. 5:31.
17 [1]LXX adds a prayer of Mordecai here

CHAPTER 5

1 [a]Esth. 4:16 [b]Esth. 4:11; 6:4 [1]LXX adds many extra details in vv. 1, 2
2 [a][Prov. 21:1] [b]Esth. 4:11; 8:4
3 [a]Esth. 7:2; Mark 6:23
6 [a]Esth. 7:2 [b]Esth. 9:12
8 [a]Esth. 6:14 [1]Lit. *to do*

4:12–14 See section 2 of Truth-In-Action at the end of Esth.
4:13, 14 After hearing Esther say in effect "If I do as you say, I could die" (v. 11), Mordecai's response is profound. It means "You will die anyway. If you are silent, you may miss the main opportunity, purpose, and privilege for being where God has put you in relation to this nation."
4:16 Esther's response is the ultimate commitment to Mordecai and her people, the condemned Jews. In essence, she says, "You do your part to help me; and I will do what you have said, even if I die doing it." Fasting, especially when accompanied by prayer, is a sign of intensity of desire related to a desperate need (Jon. 3:5–8).
5:2 The **scepter** was the rod (often ornate) of a ruler, symbolizing his power. When the king extends the scepter, he offers entrance and favor. When Esther touches the top of the scepter, she gratefully acknowledges her acceptance of the king's proffered grace. We can petition our God and King in prayer on the basis of His invitation to us (see Heb. 4:16).
5:6 See note on 7:2.
5:8 Esther is being used wisely and shrewdly by God (see Matt. 10:16). She understands the importance of waiting for God's timing before making her request (see Eccl. 8:5, 6).

Haman's Plot Against Mordecai

9 So Haman went out that day [a]joyful* and with a glad heart; but when Haman saw Mordecai in the king's gate, and [b]that he did not stand or tremble before him, he was filled with indignation against Mordecai.

10 Nevertheless Haman [a]restrained himself and went home, and he sent and called for his friends and his wife Zeresh.

11 Then Haman told them of his great riches, [a]the multitude of his children, everything in which the king had promoted him, and how he had [b]advanced him above the officials and servants of the king.

12 Moreover Haman said, "Besides, Queen Esther invited no one but me to come in with the king to the banquet that she prepared; and tomorrow I am again invited by her, along with the king.

13 "Yet all this avails me nothing, so long as I see Mordecai the Jew sitting at the king's gate."

14 Then his wife Zeresh and all his friends said to him, "Let a [a]gallows[1] be made, [2]fifty cubits high, and in the morning [b]suggest to the king that Mordecai be hanged on it; then go merrily with the king to the banquet." And the thing pleased Haman; so he had [c]the gallows made.

The King Honors Mordecai

3 **6** That night [1]the king could not sleep. So one was commanded to bring [a]the book of the *records of the chronicles; and they were read before the king.

2 And it was found written that Mordecai had told of [1]Bigthana and Teresh, two of the king's eunuchs, the doorkeepers who had sought to lay hands on King Ahasuerus.

3 Then the king said, "What honor or dignity has been bestowed on Mordecai for this?" And the king's servants who attended him said, "Nothing has been done for him."

4 So the king said, "Who *is* in the court?" Now Haman had *just* entered [a]the outer court of the king's palace [b]to suggest that the king hang Mordecai on the gallows that he had prepared for him.

5 The king's servants said to him, "Haman is there, standing in the court." And the king said, "Let him come in."

6 So Haman came in, and the king asked him, "What shall be done for the man whom the king *delights to honor?" Now Haman thought in his heart, "Whom would the king delight to honor more than [a]me?"

7 And Haman answered the king, "*For* the man whom the king delights to honor,

8 "let a royal robe be brought which the king has worn, and [a]a horse on which the king has ridden, which has a royal [1]crest placed on its head.

9 "Then let this robe and horse be delivered to the hand of one of the king's most noble princes, that he may array the man whom the king delights to honor. Then [1]parade him on horseback through the city square, [a]and proclaim before him: 'Thus shall it be done to the man whom the king delights to honor!' "

10 Then the king said to Haman, "Hurry, take the robe and the horse, as you have suggested, and do so for Mordecai the Jew who sits within the king's gate! Leave nothing undone of all that you have spoken."

11 So Haman took the robe and the horse, arrayed Mordecai and led him on horseback through the city square, and proclaimed before him, "Thus shall it be done to the man whom the king delights to honor!"

12 Afterward Mordecai went back to the king's gate. But Haman [a]hurried to his house, mourning [b]and with his head covered.

13 When Haman told his wife Zeresh and all his friends everything that had happened to him, his wise men and his wife Zeresh said to him, "If Mordecai, before whom you have begun to fall, is of Jewish descent, you will not *prevail against [a]him but will surely fall before him."

14 While they *were* still talking with him, the king's eunuchs came, and has-

9 [a][Job 20:5; Luke 6:25] [b]Esth. 3:5 *See WW at 2 Chr. 7:10. **10** [a]2 Sam. 13:22 **11** [a]Esth. 9:7–10 [b]Esth. 3:1 **14** [a]Esth. 7:9 [b]Esth. 6:4 [c]Esth. 7:10 [1]Lit. *tree or wood* [2]About 75 feet

CHAPTER 6

1 [a]Esth. 2:23; 10:2 [1]Lit. *the king's sleep fled away* *See WW at Ex. 39:7. **2** [1]*Bigthan*, Esth. 2:21

4 [a]Esth. 5:1 [b]Esth. 5:14 **6** [a][Prov. 16:18; 18:12] *See WW at Ps. 112:1. **8** [a]1 Kin. 1:33 [1]*crown* **9** [a]Gen. 41:43 [1]Lit. *cause him to ride* **12** [a]2 Chr. 26:20 [b]2 Sam. 15:30; Jer. 14:3, 4 **13** [a][Gen. 12:3]; Zech. 2:8 *See WW at Num. 13:30.

5:14 Fifty cubits high was about 75 feet; Haman wanted the hanging to be an obvious public humiliation.

6:1–11 See section 3 of Truth-In-Action at the end of Esth.

6:1 God sovereignly intervenes, showing that He has numerous ways to see that His will is carried out for His obedient children (see Job 42:2; Ps. 57:2).

6:2 Doorkeepers guarded the entrance to a city, to a public building, or to a rich man's house.

6:11 God causes **Mordecai** to be honored because he has proved by his actions that he fears God, not man.

6:12 Back to the king's gate: Mordecai has the humility of heart to know that regardless of how prominent he has become, he needs to remain in close touch with Esther.

tened to bring Haman to [a]the banquet
which Esther had prepared.

Haman Hanged Instead of Mordecai

7 So the king and Haman went to
dine with Queen Esther.
2 And on the second day, [a]at the banquet of wine, the king again said to Esther, "What *is* your petition, Queen Esther? It shall be granted you. And what
is your request, up to half the kingdom? It shall be done!"
3 Then Queen Esther answered and
said, "If I have found favor in your
sight, O king, and if it pleases the king,
let my life be given me at my petition,
and my people at my request.
4 "For we have been [a]sold, my people
and I, to be destroyed, to be killed, and
to be annihilated. Had we been sold as
[b]male and female slaves, I would have
held my tongue, although the enemy
could never compensate for the king's
loss."
5 So King Ahasuerus answered and
said to Queen Esther, "Who is he, and
where is he, who would dare presume
in his heart to do such a thing?"
6 And Esther said, "The adversary
and [a]enemy *is* this wicked Haman!" So
Haman was terrified before the king
and queen.
7 Then the king arose in his wrath
from the banquet of wine *and went*
into the palace garden; but Haman
stood before Queen Esther, pleading
for his life, for he saw that evil was
determined against him by the king.
8 When the king returned from the
palace garden to the place of the banquet of wine, Haman had fallen across
[a]the couch where Esther *was*. Then the
king said, "Will he also assault the
queen while I *am* in the house?" As
the word left the king's mouth, they
[b]covered Haman's face.
9 Now [a]Harbonah, one of the eunuchs, said to the king, "Look! [b]The
[1]gallows, fifty cubits high, which Haman made for Mordecai, who spoke
[c]good on the king's behalf, is standing
at the house of Haman." Then the king
said, "Hang him on it!"
10 So [a]they [b]hanged Haman on the
gallows that he had prepared for Mordecai. Then the king's wrath subsided.

Esther Saves the Jews

8 On that day King Ahasuerus gave
Queen Esther the house of Haman,
the [a]enemy of the Jews. And Mordecai
came before the king, for Esther had
told [b]how he *was related* to her.
2 So the king took off [a]his signet ring,
which he had taken from Haman, and
gave it to Mordecai; and Esther appointed Mordecai over the house of
Haman.
3 Now Esther spoke again to the king,
fell down at his feet, and implored him
with tears to counteract the evil of Haman the Agagite, and the scheme
which he had devised against the Jews.
4 And [a]the king held out the golden
scepter toward Esther. So Esther arose
and stood before the king,
5 and said, "If it pleases the king, and
if I have found favor in his sight and
the thing *seems* *right to the king
and I am pleasing in his eyes, let it be
written to revoke the [a]letters devised
by Haman, the son of Hammedatha the
Agagite, which he wrote to annihilate
the Jews who *are* in all the king's provinces.
6 "For how can I endure to see
[a]the evil that will come to my people?
Or how can I endure to see the destruction of my countrymen?"
7 Then King Ahasuerus said to Queen
Esther and Mordecai the Jew, "Indeed,
[a]I have given Esther the house of Haman, and they have hanged him on the
gallows because he *tried to* lay his
hand on the Jews.
8 "You yourselves write *a decree* concerning the Jews, [1]as you please, in the
king's name, and seal *it* with the king's
signet ring; for whatever is written in
the king's name and sealed with the

14 [a]Esth. 5:8

CHAPTER 7

2 [a]Esth. 5:6
4 [a]Esth. 3:9; 4:7 [b]Deut. 28:68
6 [a]Esth. 3:10
8 [a]Esth. 1:6 [b]Job 9:24
9 [a]Esth. 1:10 [b]Esth. 5:14; [Ps. 7:16; Prov. 11:5, 6] [c]Esth. 6:2 [1]Lit. *tree* or *wood*
10 [a][Ps. 7:16; 94:23; Prov. 11:5, 6] [b]Ps. 37:35, 36; Dan. 6:24

CHAPTER 8

1 [a]Esth. 7:6 [b]Esth. 2:7, 15
2 [a]Esth. 3:10
4 [a]Esth. 4:11; 5:2
5 [a]Esth. 3:13 *See WW at Eccl. 11:6.
6 [a]Neh. 2:3; Esth. 7:4; 9:1
7 [a]Esth. 8:1; Prov. 13:22
8 [1]Lit. *as is good in your eyes*

7:2 The second day refers to the day of the second banquet. **The banquet of wine** was the time after the meal when the guests relaxed over wine.
7:4 Although the enemy . . . king's loss refers to Haman's inability to make up for the loss of revenue from the Jews' taxes.
7:8 Haman's anxiety causes him to violate palace etiquette by being too close to **the couch** on which Esther reclined to eat. **They covered Haman's face** as a sign of his being condemned to death.
7:10 Though ironic, this verse reinforces a key truth of Esther: God sovereignly destroys His enemies.
8:1 The house of Haman includes his property and family.
8:2 Mordecai receives Haman's position and property.
8:3–6 Haman is dead, but the problem of the irreversible decree remains. Though aware of the problem facing Ahasuerus, Esther appeals for mercy and, in doing so, risks her life again. She valued her life in the same way the apostle Paul valued his (Acts 20:24; Phil. 1:20).
8:7–12 Ahasuerus deals with the problem by authorizing Mordecai to **write *a decree* . . . in the king's name.** The decree states that the Jews can legally fight back if assaulted.

king's signet ring [a]no one can revoke."

9 [a]So the king's scribes were called at that time, in the third month, which *is* the month of Sivan, on the twenty-third *day;* and it was written, according to all that Mordecai commanded, to the Jews, the satraps, the governors, and the princes of the provinces [b]from India to Ethiopia, one hundred and twenty-seven provinces *in all,* to every province [c]in its own script, to every people in their own language, and to the Jews in their own script and language.

10 [a]And he wrote in the name of King Ahasuerus, sealed *it* with the king's signet ring, and sent letters by couriers on horseback, riding on royal horses [1]bred from swift steeds.

11 By these letters the king permitted the Jews who *were* in every city to [a]gather together and protect their lives—to [b]destroy, kill, and annihilate all the forces of any people or province that would assault them, *both* little children and women, and to plunder their possessions,

12 [a]on one day in all the provinces of King Ahasuerus, on the thirteenth *day* of the twelfth month, which *is* the month of [1]Adar.

13 [a]A copy of the document was to be issued as a decree in every province and published for all people, so that the Jews would be ready on that day to avenge themselves on their enemies.

14 The couriers who rode on royal horses went out, hastened and pressed on by the king's command. And the decree was issued in [1]Shushan the [2]citadel.

15 So Mordecai went out from the presence of the king in royal apparel of [1]blue and white, with a great crown of gold and a garment of fine linen and purple; and [a]the city of [2]Shushan rejoiced and was glad.

16 The Jews had [a]light and gladness, joy and honor.

2 17 And in every province and city, wherever the king's command and decree came, the Jews had joy and gladness, a feast [a]and a holiday. Then many of the people of the land [b]became Jews, because [c]fear of the Jews fell upon them.

8 [a]Esth. 1:19; Dan. 6:8, 12, 15
9 [a]Esth. 3:12 [b]Esth. 1:1 [c]Esth. 1:22; 3:12
10 [a]1 Kin. 21:8; Esth. 3:12, 13 [1]Lit. *sons of the swift horses*
11 [a]Esth. 9:2 [b]Esth. 9:10, 15, 16
12 [a]Esth. 3:13; 9:1 [1]LXX adds the text of the letter here
13 [a]Esth. 3:14, 15
14 [1]Or *Susa* [2]*palace*
15 [a]Esth. 3:15; Prov. 29:2 [1]*violet* [2]Or *Susa*
16 [a]Ps. 97:11; 112:4
17 [a]1 Sam. 25:8; Esth. 9:19 [b]Ps. 18:43 [c]Gen. 35:5; Ex. 15:16; Deut. 2:25; 11:25; 1 Chr. 14:17; Esth. 9:2

CHAPTER 9

1 [a]Esth. 8:12 [b]Esth. 3:13 [c]2 Sam. 22:41
2 [a]Esth. 8:11; 9:15–18 [b]Ps. 71:13, 14 [c]Esth. 8:17
4 [a]2 Sam. 3:1; 1 Chr. 11:9; [Prov. 4:18]
6 [a]Esth. 1:2; 3:15; 4:16 [1]Or *Susa* [2]*palace*
10 [a]Esth. 5:11; 9:7–10; Job 18:19; 27:13–15; Ps. 21:10 [b]Esth. 8:11 [1]*spoil*
11 [1]Or *Susa* [2]*palace* [3]Lit. *came*
12 [a]Esth. 5:6; 7:2

The Jews Destroy Their Tormentors

9 Now [a]in the twelfth month, that *is,* the month of Adar, on the thirteenth day, [b]*the time* came for the king's command and his decree to be executed. On the day that the enemies of the Jews had hoped to overpower them, the opposite occurred, in that the Jews themselves [c]overpowered those who hated them.

2 The Jews [a]gathered together in their cities throughout all the provinces of King Ahasuerus to lay hands on those who [b]sought their harm. And no one could withstand them, [c]because fear of them fell upon all people.

3 And all the officials of the provinces, the satraps, the governors, and all those doing the king's work, helped the Jews, because the fear of Mordecai fell upon them.

4 For Mordecai *was* great in the king's palace, and his fame spread throughout all the provinces; for this man Mordecai [a]became increasingly prominent.

5 Thus the Jews defeated all their enemies with the stroke of the sword, with slaughter and destruction, and did what they pleased with those who hated them.

6 And in [a]Shushan[1] the [2]citadel the Jews killed and destroyed five hundred men.

7 Also Parshandatha, Dalphon, Aspatha,

8 Poratha, Adalia, Aridatha,

9 Parmashta, Arisai, Aridai, and Vajezatha—

10 [a]the ten sons of Haman the son of Hammedatha, the enemy of the Jews—they killed; [b]but they did not lay a hand on the [1]plunder.

11 On that day the number of those who were killed in [1]Shushan the [2]citadel [3]was brought to the king.

12 And the king said to Queen Esther, "The Jews have killed and destroyed five hundred men in Shushan the citadel, and the ten sons of Haman. What have they done in the rest of the king's provinces? Now [a]what *is* your petition? It shall be granted to you. Or what *is* your further request? It shall be done."

13 Then Esther said, "If it pleases the

8:9 Haman's law had stood 70 days, symbolic of the 70 years of Babylonian captivity.
8:16, 17 This is a fourfold reversal of the distresses in 4:3.
8:17 See section 2 of Truth-In-Action at the end of Esth.
9:1–17 The Jews had nearly nine months to prepare for their defense (see 8:9). When the day of Haman's decree arrives (see 3:13), they are well prepared to defend, as indicated by the large numbers the Jews killed.
9:12 Further request: Esther is rewarded for fearing God and not men, for intense intercession, for being willing to sacrifice her life for others, and for fulfilling the conditions of biblical unity. God promises the same reward to those who fulfill the same conditions (see John 15:7).

king, let it be granted to the Jews who
are in Shushan to do again tomorrow
[a]according to today's decree, and let
Haman's ten sons [b]be hanged on the
gallows."
14 So the king commanded this to be
done; the decree was issued in Shushan, and they hanged Haman's ten
sons.
15 And the Jews who *were* in
[1]Shushan [a]gathered together again on
the fourteenth day of the month of
Adar and killed three hundred men at
Shushan; [b]but they did not lay a hand
on the plunder.
16 The remainder of the Jews in the
king's provinces [a]gathered together
and protected their lives, had rest from
their enemies, and killed seventy-five
thousand of their enemies; [b]but they
did not lay a hand on the plunder.
17 *This was* on the thirteenth *day of
the month of Adar. And on the fourteenth of [1]*the month* they rested and
made it a day of feasting and gladness.

The Feast of Purim

18 But the Jews who *were* at [1]Shushan
assembled together [a]on the thirteenth
day, as well as on the fourteenth; and
on the fifteenth of [2]*the month* they
rested, and made it a day of feasting
and gladness.
19 Therefore the Jews of the villages
who dwelt in the unwalled towns celebrated the fourteenth day of the month
of Adar [a]*with* gladness and feasting,
[b]as a holiday, and for [c]sending
presents to one another.
20 And Mordecai wrote these things
and sent letters to all the Jews, near
and far, who *were* in all the provinces
of King Ahasuerus,
21 to establish among them that they
should celebrate yearly the fourteenth
and fifteenth days of the month of
Adar,
22 as the days on which the Jews had
rest from their enemies, as the month
which was turned from sorrow to joy
for them, and from mourning to a holiday; that they should make them days
of feasting and joy, of [a]sending
presents to one another and gifts to the
[b]poor.
23 So the Jews accepted the custom

13 [a]Esth. 8:11; 9:15 [b]2 Sam. 21:6, 9
15 [a]Esth. 8:11; 9:2 [b]Esth. 9:10 [1]Or *Susa*
16 [a]Esth. 9:2 [b]Esth. 8:11
17 [1]Lit. *it* *See WW at Zeph. 1:7.
18 [a]Esth. 9:11, 15 [1]Or *Susa* [2]Lit. *it*
19 [a]Deut. 16:11, 14 [b]Esth. 8:16, 17 [c]Neh. 8:10, 12; Esth. 9:22
22 [a]Neh. 8:10; Esth. 9:19 [b][Deut. 15:7–11]; Job 29:16
24 [a]Esth. 3:6, 7; 9:26
25 [a]Esth. 7:4–10; 8:3; 9:13, 14 [b]Esth. 7:10 [1]Lit. *she* or *it* [2]Lit. *his*
26 [a]Esth. 9:20 [1]Lit. *Lot* *See WW at Jer. 33:3.
27 [a]Esth. 8:17; [Is. 56:3, 6]; Zech. 2:11
28 *See WW at Gen. 12:3.
29 [a]Esth. 2:15

which they had begun, as Mordecai
had written to them,
24 because Haman, the son of Hammedatha the Agagite, the enemy of all the
Jews, [a]had plotted against the Jews to
annihilate them, and had cast Pur (that
is, the lot), to consume them and destroy them;
25 but [a]when [1]*Esther* came before the
king, he commanded by letter that
[2]this wicked plot which *Haman* had devised against the Jews should [b]return
on his own head, and that he and his
sons should be hanged on the gallows.
26 So they *called these days Purim,
after the name [1]Pur. Therefore, because of all the words of [a]this letter,
what they had seen concerning this
matter, and what had happened to
them,
27 the Jews established and imposed
it upon themselves and their descendants and all who would [a]join them,
that without fail they should celebrate
these two days every year, according
to the written *instructions* and according to the *prescribed* time,
28 *that* these days *should be* remembered and kept throughout every **generation,** every *family, every province,
and every city, that these days of Purim
should not fail *to be observed* among
the Jews, and *that* the memory of them
should not perish among their descendants.

WORD WEALTH

9:28 generation, *dor* (*doar*); Strong's #1755: A generation; an age; a revolution of time; a life span, or some portion of one's lifetime. This noun occurs about 160 times. From the verb *dur,* "to dwell," or "to circle," *dor* describes what a generation is: a coming full circle in life (whether from birth to death or from the time one is conceived until he himself produces offspring). Thus *dor* does not represent a fixed number of years. God's design that "one generation shall praise Your works to another" (Ps. 145:4) may be accomplished by fathers who teach their children, or by the writers of Scripture, who keep praising God's deeds to each generation of believers (Ps. 78:5–8).

29 Then Queen Esther, [a]the daughter
of Abihail, with Mordecai the Jew,

9:18–32 The commemorative feast is to last two days in honor of the extra day of fighting in **Shushan.** A happy feast that includes giving gifts, much celebrating, and the reading of the Book of Esther, **Purim** is celebrated annually a month before Passover.

wrote with full authority to confirm
this [b]second letter about Purim.
30 And *Mordecai* sent letters to all the
Jews, to [a]the one hundred and twenty-
seven provinces of the kingdom of
Ahasuerus, *with* words of peace and
truth,
31 to confirm these days of Purim at
their *appointed* time, as Mordecai the
Jew and Queen Esther had prescribed
for them, and as they had decreed for
themselves and their descendants concerning matters of their [a]fasting and
lamenting.
32 So the decree of Esther confirmed
these matters of Purim, and it was written in the book.

29 [b]Esth. 8:10; 9:20, 21
30 [a]Esth. 1:1
31 [a]Esth. 4:3, 16

CHAPTER 10

1 [a]Gen. 10:5; Ps. 72:10; Is. 11:11; 24:15
2 [a]Esth. 8:15; 9:4 [b]Esth. 6:1 [1]Lit. *made him great*
3 [a]Gen. 41:40, 43, 44; 2 Chr. 28:7 [b]Neh. 2:10; Ps. 122:8, 9 [1]Lit. *seed.* LXX, Vg. add a dream of Mordecai here; Vg. adds six more chapters

Mordecai's Advancement

10 And King Ahasuerus imposed
tribute on the land and *on*
[a]the islands of the sea.
2 Now all the acts of his power and
his might, and the account of the greatness of Mordecai, [a]to which the king
[1]advanced him, *are* they not written in
the book of the [b]chronicles of the kings
of Media and Persia?
3 For Mordecai the Jew *was* [a]second 2
to King Ahasuerus, and was great
among the Jews and well received by
the multitude of his brethren, [b]seeking
the good of his people and speaking
peace to all his [1]countrymen.

10:1 Ahasuerus's imposition of forced labor throughout his kingdom is specified to emphasize his power, a power obviously great, and yet not as great as God's power working through Esther and Mordecai. Their wills are yielded to Him, their hearts are humble, their unity is remarkable, and their God is victorious.

10:3 See section 2 of Truth-In-Action at the end of Esth.

TRUTH-IN-ACTION through ESTHER

Letting the LIFE of the Holy Spirit Bring Faith's Works Alive in You!

Truth Esther Teaches	Text	**Action** Esther Invites
1 Steps to Holiness Holy living realizes that inordinate honor or fawning and flattering to gain favor can be a form of idolatry. But wisdom also teaches that not showing such deference may incur the anger of those who expect it.	3:2 3:8–15	**Be careful** that you worship no one but the Lord. **Understand** that showing undue honor or currying favor can be a form of worship. **Be aware** that pursuing holiness and not living like others around you may incur the hatred and hostility of unbelievers.
2 Keys to Wise Living The wise man seeks to "discern the seasons and know what men ought to do." He uses God's favor, not as an opportunity to further selfish ambition, but as an occasion to serve His purpose.	8:17 4:12–14; 10:3	**Know** that God grants seasons of favor for His people in order to extend His kingdom. **Do not employ** such seasons for personal benefit. **Realize** that God places people in high positions to advance His purposes. **Always employ** any advantaged position for the welfare of God's people.
3 A Key Lesson in Faith The man of faith will not seek recognition because he knows that God sees and rewards.	6:1–11	**Know** that God will not forget your acts of righteousness. **Believe** that He will reward them openly in His time.
4 A Lesson for Leaders The astute leader knows that his life is the most powerful sermon he will ever preach.	1:17, 18	Leaders, **live** what you speak.

The Book of JOB

Author: Uncertain; Perhaps Moses or Solomon
Date: Unspecified (Fifteenth–Second Century B.C.)
Theme: The Suffering of the Godly and the Sovereignty of God
Key Words: Sin, Righteousness

Author The authorship of Job is uncertain. Some scholars attribute this book to Moses. Others attribute it to one of the ancient wise men whose works can be found in Proverbs and Ecclesiastes, perhaps even to Solomon himself.

Date The manners, customs, and general life-style of Job are from the patriarchal period (about 2000–1800 B.C.). Scholars differ, however, regarding when it was compiled, as its writing was an obvious recording of a long-standing oral tradition. Those who attribute it to Moses opt for a fifteenth century B.C. date. Others opt for as late as the second century B.C. Most conservatives assign it to the Solomonic era, the mid-tenth century B.C.

Background Scripture itself attests that Job was a real person. He is referred to in Ezekiel 14:14 and James 5:11. Job was a Gentile, is thought to have been a descendant of Nahor, Abraham's brother, and knew God by the name of "Shaddai"—the Almighty. (There are 30 references to Shaddai in the Book of Job.) Job was a wealthy man living a seminomadic life-style.

Content The Book of Job has been called "a dramatic poem framed in an epic story" (J. Sidlow Baxter). Chapters 1 and 2 are a prologue, which give the setting of the story. Satan presents himself, with the sons of God, and challenges the piety of Job, stating, "Does Job fear God for nothing?" (1:9). He goes on to suggest that were everything to be taken away, Job would curse God. God gives Satan permission to try Job's faith by stripping him of his wealth, his family, and finally, his health. Yet, "Job did not sin with his lips" (2:10). Job is then visited by three friends—Eliphaz the Temanite, Bildad the Shuhite, and Zophar the Naamathite, who are so overwhelmed by Job's deplorable condition that they sit in silence with Job for seven days.

The bulk of the book is taken up with three dialogues between Job and Eliphaz, Job and Bildad, and Job and Zophar, followed by Elihu's challenge to Job. The four men seek to answer the question, "Why does Job suffer?" Eliphaz, basing his answer on experience, states that Job suffers because he has sinned. He argues that those who sin are punished. Since Job is suffering, obviously he has sinned. Bildad, resting his authority on tradition, suggests that Job is a hypocrite. He, too, takes the inferential approach and says that since trouble has come, Job must have sinned. "If you *were* pure and upright, surely now He would awake for you" (8:6). Zophar condemns Job for verbosity, presumption, and sinfulness, concluding that Job is getting less than what he deserves: "Know therefore that God exacts from you *less* than your iniquity *deserves*" (11:6).

The three men come to the same basic conclusion: suffering is the direct outcome of sin, and wickedness is always punished. They argue that one can ascertain God's favor or disfavor toward a person by looking at his material prosperity or adversity. They falsely make the assumption that people can comprehend the ways of God without taking into account the fact that divine retribution and blessing may extend beyond this present life.

In his replies to his friends, Job maintains his innocence, stating that experience proves that both the godly and ungodly suffer and both enjoy prosperity. He laments his deplorable condition and tremendous losses, venting his anger at them for accusing him rather than bringing him comfort.

After the three friends have concluded, a younger man named Elihu confronts Job, who chooses not to respond to his accusations. Elihu's argument is: God is greater than any human being; therefore, a person has no right or authority to require an explanation of Him. He argues that some things that God does are humanly incomprehensible. At the same time, Elihu suggests that God will speak if we will listen. His emphasis is on the attitude of the sufferer, that is, an attitude of humility allows God to intervene. This is the core of his message: instead of learning from his suffering, Job has the same attitude toward God as do the ungodly, and this is why judgment still afflicts him. Elihu's appeal to Job is: 1) to have faith in God Himself rather than to demand an explanation; 2) to change his attitude to one of humility.

It should not be concluded that all the objections of Job's friends represent other than the view of God contemporary to their times. As the revelation of God's nature has unfolded through history and the Scriptures, we find that some of their views have been shown as incomplete. This, of course, does not make the text less than inspired, but gives us a Holy Spirit-inspired report of the incidents as they occurred.

When the four have concluded, God answers Job out of a whirlwind. His response does not attempt to explain Job's sufferings, but by a series of interrogations, He seeks to humble Job. As we review the whirlwind address we come to three conclusions regarding Job's suffering: 1) Job was not meant to know the explanation of his sufferings. Some things about human suffering God cannot possibly explain to us at the time without destroying the very purpose they were designed to fulfill. 2) God is involved in human affairs: Job and his grief meant enough to God to cause Him to speak. 3) God's purpose also was to bring Job to the end of his own self-righteousness, self-vindication, and self-wisdom, so he could find his all in God.

Personal Application The Book of Job teaches several lessons: 1) God is sovereign. We cannot understand His workings by rational thinking alone; faith must rest in God's love and our knowledge of Him. Sovereignty means that God is all-powerful; He knows all, He is everywhere present, and His decision is final (Jer. 10:10; Dan. 4:17). God is the author of all the power of the universe. 2) We understand ourselves and our lives in direct relationship to our understanding of the character and workings of God. When we understand that God's will toward us is good (John 10:10), that God cares and communicates His caring to His children—as He did to Job—this changes everything. Faith must have a resting place. When deep suffering threatens the foundations of faith, as was the case with Job, an assault on our faith can destroy us unless we are firmly rooted in these truths. 3) In times of tragedy we face the temptation of making God our adversary instead of our advocate. With Job of old, we can focus on declaring our innocence and questioning the justice of God, or we can bow in humility and wait for God to reveal Himself and His purposes to us. 4) The struggle of faith is a personal one. We each enter the crucible of life alone; we must test the mettle of our faith in God against uncontrollable forces and win our individual victories. There will be times when family and friends may be taken from us and we must stand alone.

Christ Revealed There is no direct reference to Christ in the Book of Job; however, Job may be seen as a type of Christ. Job suffered greatly and was humbled and stripped of all he had, but in the end he was restored and became the intercessor for his friends. Christ emptied Himself, taking on Himself human form. He suffered, was persecuted for a time by men and demons, seemed forsaken by God, and became an intercessor. The greatest difference between Christ and Job is that Christ chose to empty Himself, whereas Job's abasement came about through circumstances beyond his control.

The Book of James directs the reader's attention to the patience and endurance of Job. James states that, as God's intention toward Job was good, so our Lord's intention toward us is good (5:11).

The Holy Spirit at Work Elihu, in his debate with Job, makes three significant statements about the role of the Holy Spirit in the relationship of people to God. In 32:8 he declares that a person's understanding is not due to his age or station in life, but rather is a result of the operation of the Spirit of God. The Spirit then is the Author of wisdom, endowing one with the capacity to know and making sense out of life for him. Thus knowledge and wisdom are the Spirit's gift to men.

The Spirit of God is also the Source of life itself (33:4). Apart from the direct influence of the Spirit, man as we know him would not have come into existence. From the original creation it was so, and continues to be so. Elihu states that his own existence witnesses to the life-giving power of the Spirit. The Spirit of God is the Spirit of life.

Because the Spirit gives life and wisdom to man, He is also essential to the very continuation of the human race. If God should turn His attention elsewhere, if He should withdraw His life-giving Spirit from this world, then human history would come to an end (34:14, 15). Elihu's point is that God is neither capricious nor selfish. Because He cares for man, He constantly sustains him by the abundant flow of His Spirit. Thus the Holy Spirit in the Book of Job is the Creator and Sustainer of life, and He gives meaning and rationality to life.

Outline of Job

Introduction	**1:1—2:13**
A. Job has both wealth and piety	1:1–5
B. Satan challenges Job's character	1:6–12
C. Satan destroys Job's property and children	1:13–22
D. Satan attacks Job's health	2:1–8
E. Job's wife responds	2:9, 10
F. Job's friends visit	2:11–13
I. Dialogues between Job and his three friends	**3:1—26:14**
A. Job's outcry of despair	3:1–26
B. First dialogue	4:1—14:22
C. Second dialogue	15:1—21:34
D. Third dialogue	22:1—26:14
II. Job's final address to his friends	**27:1—31:40**
III. Elihu's challenge to Job	**32:1—37:24**
IV. God's address from the whirlwind	**38:1—41:34**
V. Job's response	**42:1–6**
VI. Closing historical section	**42:7–17**

Job and His Family in Uz

THERE was a man [a]in the land of
Uz, whose name *was* [b]Job; and that
man was [c]blameless and upright, and
one who [d]feared God and [1]shunned
evil.
2 And seven sons and three daughters were born to him.
3 Also, his possessions were seven
thousand sheep, three thousand camels, five hundred yoke of oxen, five
hundred female donkeys, and a very
large household, so that this man was
the greatest of all the [1]people of the
East.
4 And his sons would go and feast *in
their* houses, each on his *appointed*
day, and would send and invite their
three sisters to eat and drink with
them.
5 So it was, when the days of feasting
had run their course, that Job would
send and [1]sanctify them, and he would
rise early in the morning [a]and offer
burnt offerings *according to* the number of them all. For Job said, "It may
be that my *sons have sinned and
[b]cursed[2] God in their hearts." Thus Job
did regularly.

CHAPTER 1

1 [a]1 Chr. 1:17 [b]Ezek. 14:14, 20; James 5:11 [c]Gen. 6:9; 17:1; [Deut. 18:13] [d][Prov. 16:6] [1]Lit. *turned away from*
3 [1]Lit. *sons*
5 [a]Gen. 8:20; [Job 42:8] [b]1 Kin. 21:10, 13 [1]*consecrate* [2]Lit. *blessed,* but in an evil sense; cf. Job 1:11; 2:5, 9 *See WW at Gen. 29:32.
6 [a]Job 2:1 [1]Lit. *the Adversary* *See WW at Zeph. 1:7.
7 [1]Lit. *the Adversary*

Satan Attacks Job's Character

6 Now [a]there was a *day when the 1
sons of God came to present themselves before the LORD, and [1]**Satan** also
came among them.

WORD WEALTH

1:6 Satan, *satan* (sah-*tahn*); Strong's #7854: An opponent, or the Opponent; the hater; the accuser; adversary, enemy; one who resists, obstructs, and hinders whatever is good. *Satan* comes from the verb which means "to be an opponent," or "to withstand." As a noun, *satan* can describe any "opponent" (2 Sam. 19:21, 22). However, when the form *ha-satan* (the Adversary) occurs, the translation is usually "Satan," not his name, but his accurate description: hateful enemy. Since Satan is the Hater, he is all the more opposed to God, who is love (see 1 John 3:10–15; 4:7, 8). Mankind did not witness Satan's beginning, but by God's design shall see his end, one of ceaseless torment and humiliation (see Is. 14:12–20; Ezek. 28:16–19; Rev. 20:10).

7 And the LORD said to [1]Satan, "From
where do you come?" So Satan answered the LORD and said, "From

1:1 This is not a parable but an account of a real man who was acknowledged by man and God to be **blameless and upright.**

1:6—2:7 Satan's interviews with God tell us that 1) Satan is accountable to God (1:6), since he came to present himself to God; 2) Satan's mind is an open book to God—God's questions are asked to compel Satan to confess; 3) Satan is behind the evils that curse the Earth (2:7); 4) he is neither omnipresent nor omniscient; 5) he can do nothing without divine permission (1:10); 6) when God gives permission to Satan, He sets definite limits on his power.

1:6–12 See section 1 of Truth-In-Action at the end of Job.

1:6 Sons of God is the same phrase that occurs in Gen. 6:2. Here, however, its meaning is clearly that of celestial beings or angels God created as His servants. **Satan** is among them. He appears as "the Adversary" to disturb God's kingdom by causing trouble. See note on 1 Chr. 21:1 for further information on Satan in the OT.

[a]going to and fro on the earth, and
from walking back and forth on it."
8 Then the LORD said to Satan, "Have
you [1]considered My servant Job, that
there is none like him on the earth, a
blameless and upright man, one who
fears God and [2]shuns evil?"
9 So Satan answered the LORD and
said, "Does Job fear God for nothing?
10 [a]"Have You not [1]made a hedge
around him, around his household, and
around all that he has on every side?
[b]You have blessed the work of his
hands, and his possessions have increased in the land.
11 [a]"But now, stretch out Your hand
and touch all that he has, and he will
surely [b]curse[1] You to Your face!"
12 And the LORD said to Satan, "Behold, all that he has *is* in your [1]power;
only do not lay a hand on his *person*."
So Satan went out from the presence
of the LORD.

Job Loses His Property and Children

13 Now there was a day [a]when his
sons and daughters *were* eating and
drinking wine in their oldest brother's
house;
14 and a messenger came to Job and
said, "The oxen were plowing and the
donkeys feeding beside them,
15 "when the [1]Sabeans [2]raided *them*
and took them away—indeed they
have killed the servants with the edge
of the sword; and I alone have escaped
to tell you!"
16 While he *was* still speaking, another also came and said, "The fire of
God fell from heaven and burned up
the sheep and the servants, and
[1]consumed them; and I alone have escaped to tell you!"
17 While he *was* still speaking, another also came and said, "The Chaldeans formed three bands, raided the
camels and took them away, yes, and
killed the servants with the edge of the
sword; and I alone have escaped to tell
you!"
18 While he *was* still speaking, another also came and said, [a]"Your sons
and daughters *were* eating and drink-

7 [a][1 Pet. 5:8]
8 [1]Lit. *set your heart on* [2]Lit. *turns away from*
10 [a]Job 29:2–6; Ps. 34:7; Is. 5:2 [b][Ps. 128:1, 2; Prov. 10:22] [1]Protected him
11 [a]Job 2:5; 19:21 [b]Is. 8:21; Mal. 3:13, 14 [1]Lit. *bless,* but in an evil sense; cf. Job 1:5
12 [1]Lit. *hand*
13 [a][Eccl. 9:12]
15 [1]Lit. *Sheba,* cf. Job 6:19 [2]Lit. *fell upon*
16 [1]*destroyed*
18 [a]Job 1:4, 13
19 [1]LXX omits *across*
20 [a]Gen. 37:29, 34; Josh. 7:6; Ezra 9:3 [b][1 Pet. 5:6]
21 [a][Ps. 49:17; Eccl. 5:15]; 1 Tim. 6:7 [b]Eccl. 5:19; [James 1:17] [c]Gen. 31:16; [1 Sam. 2:6] [d]Eph. 5:20; [1 Thess. 5:18]
22 [a]Job 2:10

CHAPTER 2

1 [a]Job 1:6–8 *See WW at Job 1:6.
2 [a]Job 1:7
3 [a]Job 1:1, 8 [b]Job 27:5, 6 [c]Job 9:17 [1]Lit. *consume*
5 [a]Job 1:11 [b]Job 19:20 [1]Lit. *bless,* but in an evil sense; cf. Job 1:5
6 [a]Job 1:12

ing wine in their oldest brother's
house,
19 "and suddenly a great wind came
from [1]across the wilderness and struck
the four corners of the house, and it
fell on the young people, and they are
dead; and I alone have escaped to tell
you!"
20 Then Job arose, [a]tore his robe, and
shaved his head; and he [b]fell to the
ground and worshiped.
21 And he said:

[a]"Naked I came from my mother's
womb,
And naked shall I return there.
The LORD [b]gave, and the LORD has
[c]taken away;
[d]Blessed be the name of the LORD."

22 [a]In all this Job did not sin nor 4
charge God with wrong.

Satan Attacks Job's Health

2 Again [a]there was a day when the 3
sons of God came to present themselves before the LORD, and *Satan
came also among them to present himself before the LORD.
2 And the LORD said to Satan, "From
where do you come?" So [a]Satan answered the LORD and said, "From going
to and fro on the earth, and from walking back and forth on it."
3 Then the LORD said to Satan, "Have 1
you considered My servant Job, that
there is none like him on the earth,
[a]a blameless and upright man, one
who fears God and shuns evil? And
still he [b]holds fast to his integrity, although you incited Me against him,
[c]to [1]destroy him without cause."
4 So Satan answered the LORD and
said, "Skin for skin! Yes, all that a man
has he will give for his life.
5 [a]"But stretch out Your hand now,
and touch his [b]bone and his flesh, and
he will surely [1]curse You to Your
face!"
6 [a]And the LORD said to Satan, "Behold, he *is* in your hand, but spare his
life."
7 So Satan went out from the pres-

1:8 Job is declared by God Himself to be **blameless and upright,** and yet he is tried—not because of his unrighteousness but in spite of his righteousness. His trial was to establish his righteousness, as well as to give him deeper insight into his relationship with God and a greater understanding of his own nature. While Satan's goal was to prove Job to be a sinner, God's goal was to establish forever the sincerity of Job's faith. God does not allow trials to see if we will fail; He allows trials to strengthen our faith. The trial is, in fact, a statement of God's faith in our faithfulness and integrity.

1:9 For nothing means "without reason." He is implying that Job's good deeds spring from selfish motives of being blessed and protected by God.

1:22 See section 4 of Truth-In-Action at the end of Job.

2:1 See section 3 of Truth-In-Action at the end of Job.

2:3–6 See section 1 of Truth-In-Action at the end of Job.

2:7 Painful boils: A similar description is given in Deut.

ence of the LORD, and struck Job with
painful boils [a]from the sole of his foot
to the crown of his head.
8 And he took for himself a potsherd
with which to scrape himself [a]while he
sat in the midst of the ashes.
9 Then his wife said to him, "Do you
still hold fast to your integrity? [1]Curse
God and die!"
10 But he said to her, "You speak as
one of the foolish women speaks.
[a]Shall we indeed accept good from
God, and shall we not accept adversity?" [b]In all this Job did not [c]sin with
his lips.

Job's Three Friends

11 Now when Job's three friends heard
of all this adversity that had come upon
him, each one came from his own
place—Eliphaz the [a]Temanite, Bildad
the [b]Shuhite, and Zophar the Naamathite. For they had made an appointment together to come [c]and mourn
with him, and to comfort him.
12 And when they raised their eyes
from afar, and did not recognize him,
they lifted their voices and wept; and
each one tore his robe and [a]sprinkled
dust on his head toward heaven.
13 So they sat down with him on the
ground [a]seven days and seven nights,
and no one spoke a word to him, for
they saw that *his* grief was very great.

Job Deplores His Birth

3 After this Job opened his mouth
and cursed the day of his *birth.*
2 And Job [1]spoke, and said:

3 "May[a] the day *perish on which I
was born,
And the night *in which* it was
said,
'A *male child is conceived.'
4 May that day be darkness;
May God above not seek it,
Nor the light shine upon it.
5 May darkness and [a]the shadow
of death claim it;
May a cloud settle on it;
May the blackness of the day
terrify it.
6 *As for* that night, may darkness
seize it;
May it not [1]rejoice among the
days of the year,
May it not come into the number
of the months.
7 Oh, may that night be barren!
May no joyful shout come into it!
8 May those curse it who curse the
day,
Those [a]who are ready to arouse
Leviathan.
9 May the stars of its morning be
dark;
May it look for light, but *have*
none,
And not see the [1]dawning of the
day;
10 Because it did not shut up the
doors of my *mother's* womb,
Nor hide *sorrow from my eyes.

11 "Why[a] did I not die at birth?
Why did I *not* [1]perish when I
came from the womb?
12 [a]Why did the knees receive me?
Or why the breasts, that I should
nurse?
13 For now I would have lain still
and been quiet,
I would have been asleep;
Then I would have been at rest
14 With kings and counselors of the
earth,
Who [a]built ruins for themselves,
15 Or with princes who had gold,
Who filled their houses *with*
silver;
16 Or *why* was I not hidden
[a]like a stillborn child,
Like infants who never saw light?
17 There the *wicked cease *from*
troubling,
And there the [1]weary are at
[a]rest.

7 [a]Is. 1:6
8 [a]Job 42:6; Jer. 6:26; Ezek. 27:30; Jon. 3:6; Matt. 11:21
9 [1]Lit. *Bless,* but in an evil sense; cf. Job 1:5
10 [a]Job 1:21, 22; [Heb. 12:6; James 5:10, 11] [b]Job 1:22; [James 1:12] [c]Ps. 39:1
11 [a]Gen. 36:11; 1 Chr. 1:36; Job 6:19; Jer. 49:7; Obad. 9 [b]Gen. 25:2; 1 Chr. 1:32 [c]Job 42:11; Rom. 12:15
12 [a]Josh. 7:6; Neh. 9:1; Lam. 2:10; Ezek. 27:30
13 [a]Gen. 50:10; Ezek. 3:15

CHAPTER 3

2 [1]Lit. *answered*
3 [a]Job 10:18, 19; Jer. 20:14–18 *See WW at Judg. 5:31. • See WW at Jer. 31:22.
5 [a]Job 10:21, 22; Jer. 13:16; Amos 5:8
6 [1]LXX, Syr., Tg., Vg. *be joined*
8 [a]Jer. 9:17
9 [1]*eyelids of the dawn*
10 *See WW at Job 5:7.
11 [a]Job 10:18, 19 [1]*expire*
12 [a]Gen. 30:3
14 [a]Job 15:28; Is. 58:12
16 [a]Ps. 58:8
17 [a]Job 17:16 [1]Lit. *weary of strength* *See WW at Prov. 10:16.

28:35 and Lev. 13:18, and may refer to elephantiasis, a disease resulting in extreme pain and disfigurement. The disease appears to have come upon Job suddenly and to have covered his body quickly.

2:8 There is no indication that isolation was imposed on Job; however, he had removed himself already to **the midst of the ashes** in mourning for his children.

2:9, 10 At this point, Job's wife displays her lack of spiritual insight and sympathy for her husband's condition. Astonished at Job's continued integrity and steadfast faith, she taunts him. Tormented though he is, Job expresses a genuine faith in God.

2:11 Friends is a term used for those showing a solemn, covenant relationship. The **three** had a sincere desire to share his grief and ease his pain. Teman was in northern Edom. Shuah was on the Middle Euphrates, below the mouth of the Khabur River. Naamah was between Beirut and Damascus.

3:2–26 With a curse (vv. 3–13) and lament (vv. 14–26), Job pours out a torrent of pain and bitterness, seeing himself as the object of God's anger. He longs for inner rest. He does not curse God, as Satan had wanted him to do; he does, however, curse his conception and birth. This outburst could also be read as an appeal for concern and sympathy from his friends.

3:8 Leviathan: See note on 40:6—41:34.

18 *There* the prisoners [1]rest together;
[a]They do not hear the voice of the oppressor.
19 The small and great are there,
And the servant *is* free from his *master.

20 "Why[a] is light given to him who is in misery,
And life to the [b]bitter of soul,
21 Who [a]long[1] for death, but it does not *come*,
And search for it more than [b]hidden treasures;
22 Who rejoice exceedingly,
And are glad when they can find the [a]grave?
23 *Why is light given* to a man whose way is hidden,
[a]And whom God has hedged in?
24 For my sighing comes before [1]I eat,
And my groanings pour out like water.
5 25 For the thing I greatly [a]feared* has come upon me,
And what I dreaded has happened to me.
26 I am not at ease, nor am I quiet;
I have no rest, for trouble comes."

Eliphaz: Job Has Sinned

4 Then Eliphaz the Temanite answered and said:

2 "*If* one attempts a word with you, will you become weary?
But who can withhold himself from speaking?
3 Surely you have instructed many,
And you [a]have strengthened weak hands.
4 Your words have upheld him who was stumbling,
And you [a]have strengthened the [1]feeble knees;
5 But now it comes upon you, and you are weary;
It touches you, and you are troubled.
6 *Is* not [a]your reverence [b]your confidence?
And the integrity of your ways your *hope?

7 "Remember now, [a]who *ever* perished being innocent?
Or where were the upright *ever* cut off?
8 Even as I have seen,
[a]Those who plow *iniquity
And sow trouble reap the same.
9 By the blast of God they perish,
And by the breath of His anger they are consumed.
10 The roaring of the lion,
The voice of the fierce lion,
And [a]the teeth of the young lions are broken.
11 [a]The old lion perishes for lack of prey,
And the cubs of the lioness are scattered.

12 "Now a word was secretly brought to me,
And my ear received a whisper of it.
13 [a]In disquieting thoughts from the visions of the night,
When deep sleep falls on men,
14 Fear came upon me, and [a]trembling,
Which made all my bones shake.
15 Then a spirit passed before my face;
The hair on my body stood up.
16 It stood still,
But I could not discern its appearance.
A form *was* before my eyes;
There was silence;
Then I heard a voice *saying*:
17 'Can a **mortal** be more righteous than God? 3
Can a man be more pure than his Maker?

18 [a]Job 39:7 [1]*are at ease*
19 *See WW at Mic. 4:13.
20 [a]Jer. 20:18 [b]2 Kin. 4:27
21 [a]Rev. 9:6 [b]Prov. 2:4 [1]Lit. *wait*
22 [a]Job 7:15, 16
23 [a]Job 19:8; Ps. 88:8; Lam. 3:7
24 [1]Lit. *my bread*
25 [a][Job 9:28; 30:15] *See WW at Hos. 3:5.

CHAPTER 4

3 [a]Is. 35:3
4 [a]Is. 35:3 [1]Lit. *bending*
6 [a]Job 1:1 [b]Prov. 3:26 *See WW at Hos. 2:15.
7 [a][Job 8:20; 36:6, 7; Ps. 37:25]
8 [a][Job 15:31, 35; Prov. 22:8; Hos. 10:13; Gal. 6:7] *See WW at Prov. 22:8.
10 [a]Job 5:15; Ps. 58:6
11 [a]Job 29:17; Ps. 34:10
13 [a]Job 33:15
14 [a]Hab. 3:16

3:25 See section 5 of Truth-In-Action at the end of Job.
3:25 It is unnecessary to construe that Job's fears were responsible for producing his dilemma. The preceding narrative makes clear that Satan's initiative brought the tragedy about, not Job's uncertainties or fears (1:6–12; 2:1–7). Job does, however, acknowledge his human fears, a common disposition of our humanity. His fears do not reflect on his understanding of God's nature, but on his knowledge of life's unpredictability.
4:1 This begins a three-cycle dialogue between Job and his friends. Each gives a speech and Job responds. The first cycle allows each friend to express his position. Although faulty in their diagnoses, each presses Job to seek God in order to enjoy prosperity once again. On the truth contained in their speeches, see Introduction to Job: Content.
4:1—5:27 Eliphaz's position (see Introduction to Job: Content) is based on the assumption that everyone commits error. He firmly propagates the principle of retribution (4:7–21), noting that God always is compassionate to deliver His sons from sorrow (5:9–26). Therefore, Job is being reproved, reaping his own just punishment (4:7). However, his counsel is wrong.
4:13 Eliphaz speaks in proverbs, parables, hymns, and exhortations; here he speaks from information gained in dreams and **visions**.
4:17 See section 3 of Truth-In-Action at the end of Job.

WORD WEALTH

4:17 mortal, *'enosh* (eh-*noash*); Strong's #582: A man, a mortal; man in his frailty, limitation, and imperfection. Derived from the verb *'anash, 'enosh* means "to be frail, sick, weak, and sad." *'Enosh* is one of the four primary Hebrew words for man. If *'adam* is man as a species, *'ish* is man as an individual citizen, and *geber* is man at the height of his manly power, then *'enosh* is man as a basically weak creature. *'Enosh* occurs more than 550 times in the OT and often is simply an alternate term for *'adam.* Yet sometimes the original connotation persists, such as in the question in Ps. 8:4, "What is man [*'enosh*] that You are mindful of him?" In Dan. 7:13, the Aramaic equivalent *bar'enash* (Son of Man) is a messianic term. The Lord Jesus repeatedly called Himself "the Son of Man." He identified with the human race in its weaknesses, yet rises to a position of everlasting strength.

18 If He [a]puts no trust in His
servants,
If He charges His angels with
error,
19 How much more those who dwell
in houses of clay,
Whose foundation is in the dust,
Who are crushed before a moth?
20 [a]They are broken in pieces from
morning till evening;
They perish forever, with no one
regarding.
21 Does not their own excellence go
away?
They die, even without wisdom.'

Eliphaz: Job Is Chastened by God

5 "Call out now;
Is there anyone who will answer
you?
And to which of the holy ones will
you turn?
2 2 For wrath kills a foolish man,
And envy slays a simple one.
3 [a]I have seen the foolish taking
root,
But suddenly I cursed his
dwelling place.
4 His sons are [a]far from safety,
They are crushed in the gate,
And [b]*there is* no deliverer.
5 Because the hungry eat up his
harvest,
[1]Taking it even from the thorns,
[2]And a snare snatches their
[3]substance.
6 For affliction does not come from
the dust,
Nor does trouble spring from the
ground;
7 Yet man is [a]born to [1]**trouble,** 4
As the sparks fly upward.

WORD WEALTH

5:7 trouble, *'amal* (ah-*mahl*); Strong's #5999: Sorrow, labor, toil, grief, pain, trouble, misery, fatigue, exhaustion. This noun occurs 56 times in the OT. Its root is the verb *'amal,* "to labor or toil to the point of exhaustion." The verb is used in Ps. 127:1, which pictures the exhausted state of workers who are trying to build God's house without God's cooperation. When Joseph finally obtained happiness after his family's betrayal, his unhappy position as a servant, and his unfair imprisonment, he said, "God has made me forget all my toil and all my father's house" (Gen. 41:51), referring to his anguish, grief, and pain.

8 "But as for me, I would seek God,
And to God I would commit my
cause—
9 Who does great things, and
unsearchable,
Marvelous things without
number.
10 [a]He gives rain on the *earth,
And sends *waters on the
fields.
11 [a]He sets on high those who are
lowly,
And those who mourn are lifted
to safety.
12 [a]He frustrates the devices of the
crafty,
So that their hands cannot carry
out their plans.
13 He catches the [a]wise in their own
craftiness,
And the counsel of the cunning
comes quickly upon them.
14 They meet with darkness in the
daytime,
And grope at noontime as in the
night.
15 But [a]He saves the needy from the
sword,
From the mouth of the mighty,
And from their hand.
16 [a]So the poor have hope,
And injustice shuts her mouth.

18 [a]Job 15:15
20 [a]Ps. 90:5, 6

CHAPTER 5

3 [a][Ps. 37:35, 36]; Jer. 12:1–3
4 [a]Ps. 119:155 [b]Ps. 109:12
5 [1]LXX *They shall not be taken from evil men;* Vg. *And the armed man shall take him by violence* [2]LXX *The might shall draw them off;* Vg. *And the thirsty shall drink up their riches* [3]*wealth*
7 [a]Job 14:1 [1]*labor*
10 [a][Job 36:27–29; 37:6–11; 38:26] *See WW at Ex. 32:13. • See WW at Is. 43:2.
11 [a]Ps. 113:7
12 [a]Neh. 4:15
13 [a][Job 37:24; 1 Cor. 3:19]
15 [a]Job 4:10, 11; Ps. 35:10
16 [a]1 Sam. 2:8; Ps. 107:41, 42

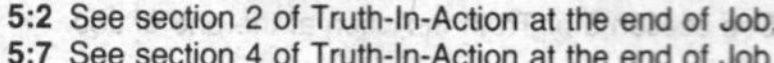

5:2 See section 2 of Truth-In-Action at the end of Job.
5:7 See section 4 of Truth-In-Action at the end of Job.
5:13 Paul quotes this verse in 1 Cor. 3:19 to show that God's wisdom is far superior to human wisdom.

2 17 "Behold,[a] happy *is* the man whom
God corrects;
Therefore do not *despise the
chastening of the Almighty.
18 [a]For He bruises, but He binds up;
He wounds, but His hands make
whole.
19 [a]He shall deliver you in six
troubles,
Yes, in seven [b]no evil shall touch
you.
20 [a]In famine He shall redeem you
from death,
And in war from the [1]power of
the sword.
5 21 [a]You shall be hidden from the
scourge of the tongue,
And you shall not be afraid of
destruction when it comes.
22 You shall *laugh at destruction
and famine,
And [a]you shall not be afraid of
the [b]beasts of the earth.
23 [a]For you shall have a covenant
with the stones of the field,
And the beasts of the field shall
be at peace with you.
24 You shall know that your tent *is*
in peace;
You shall visit your dwelling and
find nothing amiss.
25 You shall also know that
[a]your descendants *shall be*
many,
And your offspring [b]like the grass
of the earth.
26 [a]You shall come to the grave at a
full age,
As a sheaf of grain ripens in its
season.
27 Behold, this we have [a]searched
out;
It *is* true.
Hear it, and know for yourself."

Job: My Complaint Is Just

6

Then Job answered and said:
2 "Oh, that my grief were fully
weighed,
And my calamity laid with it on
the scales!
3 For then it would be heavier than
the sand of the sea—
Therefore my words have been
rash.
4 [a]For the arrows of the Almighty
are within me;
My spirit drinks in their poison;
[b]The terrors of God are arrayed
[c]against me.
5 Does the [a]wild donkey bray when
it has grass,
Or does the ox low over its
fodder?
6 Can flavorless food be eaten
without salt?
Or is there *any* taste in the white
of an egg?
7 My soul refuses to touch them;
They *are* as loathsome food to me.

8 "Oh, that I might have my request,
That God would grant *me* the
thing that I long for!
9 That it would please God to crush
me,
That He would loose His hand
and [a]cut me off!
10 Then I would still have comfort;
Though in anguish I would exult,
He will not spare;
For [a]I have not concealed the
words of [b]the Holy One.

11 "What strength do I have, that I
should *hope?
And what *is* my end, that I should
prolong my life?
12 *Is* my strength the strength of
stones?
Or is my flesh bronze?
13 *Is* my help not within me?
And is success driven from me?

14 "To[a] him who is [1]afflicted,
kindness *should be shown* by
his friend,
Even though he forsakes the fear
of the Almighty.
15 [a]My brothers have dealt
deceitfully like a brook,
[b]Like the streams of the brooks
that *pass away,
16 Which are dark because of the
ice,
And into which the snow
vanishes.
17 When it is warm, they cease to
flow;
When it is hot, they vanish from
their place.
18 The paths of their way turn aside,
They go nowhere and perish.

17 [a]Ps. 94:12; [Prov. 3:11, 12; Heb. 12:5, 6; Rev. 3:19] *See WW at Amos 2:4. **18** [a][Deut. 32:39; 1 Sam. 2:6, 7]; Is. 30:26; Hos. 6:1 **19** [a]Ps. 34:19; 91:3; [1 Cor. 10:13] [b]Ps. 91:10; [Prov. 24:16] **20** [a]Ps. 33:19, 20; 37:19 [1]Lit. *hand* **21** [a]Job 5:15; Ps. 31:20 **22** [a]Ps. 91:13; Is. 11:9; 35:9; 65:25; Ezek. 34:25 [b]Hos. 2:18 *See WW at Eccl. 3:4. **23** [a]Ps. 91:12 **25** [a]Ps. 112:2 [b]Ps. 72:16 **26** [a][Prov. 9:11; 10:27] **27** [a]Ps. 111:2

CHAPTER 6

4 [a]Job 16:13; Ps. 38:2 [b]Ps. 88:15, 16 [c]Job 30:15 **5** [a]Job 39:5–8 **9** [a]Num. 11:15; 1 Kin. 19:4; Job 7:16; 9:21; 10:1 **10** [a]Acts 20:20 [b][Lev. 19:2; Is. 57:15] **11** *See WW at Mic. 7:7. **14** [a][Prov. 17:17] [1]Or *despairing* **15** [a]Ps. 38:11 [b]Jer. 15:18 *See WW at Josh. 3:4.

5:17 See section 2 of Truth-In-Action at the end of Job.
5:21 See section 5 of Truth-In-Action at the end of Job.
6:1—7:21 Job's first response is a lengthy lament in which he justifies his laments by directing attention to the depth of his suffering. He expresses his disappointment at receiving this bitter, unwarranted attack by his friends (ch. 6), and his viewpoint that God is his cruel persecutor (ch. 7). He begins to channel his hurt away from self-pity to anger and begins to seek relief in this life.

19 The caravans of [a]Tema look,
The travelers of [b]Sheba hope for them.
20 They are [a]disappointed[1] because they were confident;
They come there and are confused.
21 For now [a]you are nothing,
You see terror and [b]are afraid.
22 Did I ever say, 'Bring *something* to me'?
Or, 'Offer a bribe for me from your wealth'?
23 Or, 'Deliver me from the enemy's hand'?
Or, 'Redeem me from the hand of oppressors'?

24 "Teach* me, and I will hold my tongue;
Cause me to understand wherein I have erred.
25 How forceful are right words!
But what does your arguing prove?
26 Do you intend to rebuke *my* words,
And the speeches of a desperate one, *which are* as wind?
27 Yes, you overwhelm the fatherless,
And you [a]undermine your friend.
28 Now therefore, be pleased to look at me;
For I would never lie to your face.
29 [a]Yield now, let there be no injustice!
Yes, concede, my [b]righteousness [1]still stands!
30 Is there injustice on my tongue?
Cannot my [1]taste discern the unsavory?

Job: My Suffering Is Comfortless

7 "*Is there* not [a]a time of hard service for man on earth?
Are not his days also like the days of a hired man?
2 Like a servant who [1]earnestly desires the shade,
And like a hired man who eagerly looks for his wages,
3 So I have been allotted [a]months of futility,
And wearisome nights have been appointed to me.
4 [a]When I lie down, I say, 'When shall I arise,
And the night be ended?'
For I have had my fill of tossing till dawn.
5 My flesh is [a]caked with worms and dust,
My skin is cracked and breaks out afresh.

6 "My[a] days are swifter than a weaver's shuttle,
And are spent without hope.
7 Oh, remember that [a]my life *is* a breath!
My eye will never again see good.
8 [a]The eye of him who sees me will see me no *more;*
While your *eyes* are upon me, I shall no longer *be.*
9 *As* the cloud disappears and vanishes away,
So [a]he who goes down to the grave does not come up.
10 He shall never return to his house,
[a]Nor shall his place know him anymore.

11 "Therefore I will [a]not restrain my mouth;
I will speak in the anguish of my spirit;
I will [b]complain in the bitterness of my soul.
12 *Am* I a sea, or a sea serpent,
That You set a guard over me?
13 [a]When I say, 'My bed will comfort me,
My couch will ease my complaint,'
14 Then You scare me with dreams
And terrify me with visions,
15 So that my soul chooses strangling
And death rather than [1]my body.
16 [a]I loathe *my life;*
I would not live forever.
[b]Let me alone,
For [c]my days *are but* [1]a breath.

17 "What[a] *is* man, that You should exalt him, **1**
That You should set Your heart on him,
18 That You should [1]visit him every morning,
And test him every moment?
19 How long?
Will You not look away from me,
And let me alone till I swallow my saliva?

19 [a]Gen. 25:15; Is. 21:14; Jer. 25:23 [b]1 Kin. 10:1; Ps. 72:10; Ezek. 27:22, 23 **20** [a]Jer. 14:3 [1]Lit. *ashamed* **21** [a]Job 13:4 [b]Ps. 38:11 **24** *See WW at Ps. 32:8. **27** [a]Ps. 57:6 **29** [a]Job 17:10 [b]Job 27:5, 6; 34:5 [1]Lit. *is in it* **30** [1]*palate*

CHAPTER 7

1 [a][Job 14:5, 13, 14]; Ps. 39:4 **2** [1]Lit. *pants for* **3** [a][Job 15:31] **4** [a]Deut. 28:67; Job 7:13, 14 **5** [a]Is. 14:11 **6** [a]Job 9:25; 16:22; 17:11; Is. 38:12; [James 4:14] **7** [a]Job 7:16; Ps. 78:39; 89:47 **8** [a]Job 8:18; 20:9 **9** [a]2 Sam. 12:23 **10** [a]Ps. 103:16 **11** [a]Ps. 39:1, 9 [b]1 Sam. 1:10 **13** [a]Job 9:27 **15** [1]Lit. *my bones* **16** [a]Job 10:1 [b]Job 14:6 [c]Ps. 62:9 [1]Without substance, futile **17** [a]Job 22:2; Ps. 8:4; 144:3; Heb. 2:6 **18** [1]*attend to*

7:17, 18 See section 1 of Truth-In-Action at the end of Job.

20 Have I sinned?
What have I done to You,
[a]O watcher of men?
Why [b]have You set me as Your target,
So that I am a burden [1]to myself?
21 Why then do You not pardon my transgression,
And take away my iniquity?
For now I will lie down in the dust,
And You will seek me diligently,
But I *will* no longer *be*."

Bildad: Job Should Repent

8 Then Bildad the Shuhite answered and said:

2 "How long will you speak these *things*,
And the words of your mouth *be like* a strong wind?
3 [a]Does God subvert *judgment?
Or does the *Almighty pervert justice?
4 If [a]your sons have sinned against Him,
He has cast them away [1]for their transgression.
5 [a]If you would earnestly seek God
And make your supplication to the Almighty,
6 If you *were* pure and upright,
Surely now He would [1]awake for you,
And prosper your rightful dwelling place.
7 Though your beginning was small,
Yet your latter end would [a]increase abundantly.

8 "For[a] inquire, please, of the former age,
And consider the things discovered by their fathers;
9 For [a]we *were born* yesterday, and know [1]nothing,
Because our days on earth *are* a shadow.
10 Will they not teach you and tell you,
And utter words from their heart?

11 "Can the papyrus grow up without a marsh?
Can the reeds flourish without water?
12 [a]While it *is* yet green *and* not cut down,
It withers before any *other* plant.
13 So *are* the paths of all who [a]forget God;
And the hope of the [b]hypocrite shall perish,
14 Whose confidence shall be cut off,
And whose trust *is* [1]a spider's web.
15 [a]He leans on his house, but it does not stand.
He holds it fast, but it does not endure.
16 He grows green in the sun,
And his branches spread out in his garden.
17 His roots wrap around the rock heap,
And look for a place in the stones.
18 [a]If he is destroyed from his place,
Then *it* will deny him, *saying*, 'I have not seen you.'

19 "Behold, this is the joy of His way,
And [a]out of the earth others will grow.
20 Behold, [a]God will not [1]cast away the blameless,
Nor will He uphold the evildoers.
21 He will yet *fill your mouth with laughing,
And your lips with [1]rejoicing.
22 Those who hate you will be [a]clothed with shame,
And the dwelling place of the wicked [1]will come to nothing."

Job: There Is No Mediator

9 Then Job answered and said:

2 "Truly I know *it is* so,
But how can a [a]man be [b]righteous before God?
3 If one wished to [1]contend with Him,
He could not answer Him one time out of a thousand.

20 [a]Ps. 36:6 [b]Ps. 21:12 [1]So with MT, Tg., Vg.; LXX, Jewish tradition *to You*

CHAPTER 8

3 [a]Gen. 18:25; [Deut. 32:4; 2 Chr. 19:7; Job 34:10, 12; 36:23; 37:23]; Rom. 3:5 *See WW at Num. 36:13. • See WW at Ps. 91:1.
4 [a]Job 1:5, 18, 19 [1]Lit. *into the hand of their transgression*
5 [a][Job 5:17–27; 11:13]
6 [1]*arise*
7 [a]Job 42:12
8 [a]Deut. 4:32; 32:7; Job 15:18; 20:4
9 [a]Gen. 47:9; [1 Chr. 29:15]; Job 7:6; [Ps. 39:5; 102:11; 144:4] [1]Lit. *not*
12 [a]Ps. 129:6
13 [a]Ps. 9:17 [b]Job 11:20; 18:14; 27:8; Ps. 112:10; [Prov. 10:28]
14 [1]Lit. *a spider's house*
15 [a]Job 8:22; 27:18; Ps. 49:11
18 [a]Job 7:10
19 [a]Ps. 113:7
20 [a]Job 4:7 [1]*reject*
21 [1]Lit. *shouts of joy* *See WW at Jer. 23:24.
22 [a]Ps. 35:26; 109:29 [1]Lit. *will not be*

CHAPTER 9

2 [a][Job 4:17; 15:14–16; Ps. 143:2; Rom. 3:20] [b][Hab. 2:4; Rom. 1:17; Gal. 3:11; Heb. 10:38]
3 [1]*argue*

3

8:1–22 Bildad's premise (Introduction to Job: Content) is that all God's ways are just (v. 3). A champion of tradition, he will allow for no variation of his orthodox doctrine of retribution: the righteous are blessed and the wicked punished. He does, however, desire Job's restoration (vv. 21, 22).

9:1—10:22 Job's response is one of a quest (ch. 9) to which he adds another lament (ch. 10). Frustrated, he jumps from topic to topic. Job again affirms his innocence, describing his suffering, which continues even though God, who is omniscient, surely knows he is innocent. He also speaks of his helplessness in doing battle with God, with no hope of victory. He closes this section by lamenting his birth and praying that he be granted a brief respite from his torment before dying and suffering further torment. His despairing picture of God at this point is that of One who has absolute power, who destroys the innocent and the guilty, a God against whom man is powerless to defend himself.

9:2 See section 3 of Truth-In-Action at the end of Job.

4 [a]*God is* wise in heart and mighty
in strength.
Who has hardened *himself*
against Him and prospered?
5 He removes the mountains, and
they do not know
When He overturns them in His
anger;
6 He [a]shakes the earth out of its
place,
And its [b]pillars tremble;
7 He commands the sun, and it does
not rise;
He seals off the stars;
8 [a]He alone spreads out the heavens,
And [1]treads* on the [2]waves of the
sea;
9 [a]He made [1]the Bear, Orion, and
the Pleiades,
And the chambers of the south;
10 [a]He does great things past finding
out,
Yes, *wonders without number.
11 [a]If He goes by me, I do not see
Him;
If He moves past, I do not
perceive Him;
12 [a]If He takes away, [1]who can
hinder Him?
Who can say to Him, 'What are
You doing?'
13 God will not withdraw His anger,
[a]The allies of [1]the proud lie
prostrate beneath Him.

14 "How then can I answer Him,
And choose my words *to reason*
with Him?
15 [a]For though I were righteous, I
could not answer Him;
I would beg mercy of my Judge.
16 If I called and He answered me,
I would not *believe that He was
listening to my voice.
17 For He crushes me with a
tempest,
And multiplies my wounds
[a]without cause.
18 He will not allow me to catch my
breath,
But fills me with bitterness.
19 If *it is a matter* of strength,
indeed *He is* strong;
And if of justice, who will appoint
my day *in court?*
20 Though I were righteous, my own
mouth would condemn me;
Though I *were* blameless, it
would prove me perverse.

21 "I am blameless, yet I do not know
myself;
I despise my life.
22 It *is* all one *thing;*
Therefore I say, [a]'He destroys the
blameless and the *wicked.'
23 If the scourge slays suddenly,
He laughs at the plight of the
innocent.
24 The earth is given into the hand
of the wicked.
He covers the faces of its judges.
If it is not *He,* who else could it
be?

25 "Now [a]my days are swifter than a
runner;
They flee away, they see no good.
26 They pass by like [1]swift ships,
[a]Like an eagle swooping on its
prey.
27 [a]If I say, 'I will forget my
complaint,
I will put off my sad face and wear
a smile,'
28 [a]I am afraid of all my sufferings;
I know that You [b]will not hold me
innocent.
29 *If* I am condemned,
Why then do I labor in vain?
30 [a]If I wash myself with snow water,
And cleanse my hands with
[1]soap,
31 Yet You will plunge me into the
pit,
And my own clothes will
[1]abhor me.

32 "For [a]*He is* not a man, as I *am,*
That I may answer Him,
And that we should go to court
together.
33 [a]Nor is there any mediator
between us,
Who may lay his hand on us both.
34 [a]Let Him take His rod away from
me,
And do not let dread of Him
terrify me.
35 *Then* I would speak and not fear
Him,
But it is not so with me.

Job: I Would Plead with God

10

"My [a]soul loathes my life;
I will [1]give free course to my
complaint,

4 [a]Job 36:5
6 [a]Is. 2:19, 21; Hag. 2:6; Heb. 12:26 [b]Job 26:11
8 [a]Gen. 1:6; Job 37:18; Ps. 104:2, 3; Is. 40:22 [1]*walks* [2]Lit. *heights* *See WW at Deut. 11:25.
9 [a]Gen. 1:16; Job 38:31; Amos 5:8 [1]Heb. *Ash, Kesil,* and *Kimah*
10 [a]Job 5:9 *See WW at Judg. 13:19.
11 [a][Job 23:8, 9; 35:14]
12 [a][Is. 45:9; Dan. 4:35; Rom. 9:20] [1]Lit. *who can turn Him back?*
13 [a]Job 26:12 [1]Heb. *rahab*
15 [a]Job 10:15; 23:1–7
16 *See WW at 2 Chr. 20:20.
17 [a]Job 2:3
22 [a][Eccl. 9:2, 3]; Ezek. 21:3 *See WW at Prov. 10:16.
25 [a]Job 7:6, 7
26 [a]Job 39:29; Hab. 1:8 [1]Lit. *ships of reeds*
27 [a]Job 7:13
28 [a]Ps. 119:120 [b]Ex. 20:7
30 [a][Jer. 2:22] [1]*lye*
31 [1]*loathe*
32 [a]Eccl. 6:10; [Is. 45:9; Jer. 49:19; Rom. 9:20]
33 [a][1 Sam. 2:25]; Job 9:19; Is. 1:18
34 [a]Job 13:20, 21; Ps. 39:10

CHAPTER 10
1 [a]1 Kin. 19:4; Job 7:16; Jon. 4:3 [1]Lit. *leave on myself*

9:9 This verse reflects ancient astronomy. The **Bear** is likely Ursa Major. The **Pleiades** refers to a cluster of seven stars, also mentioned in Amos 5:8.
9:10–12 See section 1 of Truth-In-Action at the end of Job.
9:33–35 See section 1 of Truth-In-Action at the end of Job.
9:33 Job's desire for **any mediator** reflects his desire for any help possible to restore his relationship with God.

[b]I will speak in the bitterness of
my soul.
2 I will say to God, 'Do not
condemn me;
Show me why You contend with
me.
3 *Does it* seem good to You that
You should oppress,
That You should despise the work
of Your hands,
And smile on the counsel of the
wicked?
4 Do You have eyes of flesh?
Or [a]do You see as man sees?
5 *Are* Your days like the days of a
*mortal man?
Are Your years like the days of
a mighty man,
6 That You should seek for my
iniquity
And search out my sin,
7 Although You know that I am not
wicked,
And *there is* no one who can
deliver from Your hand?

8 'Your[a] hands have made me and
fashioned me,
An intricate unity;
Yet You would [b]destroy me.
9 *Remember, I pray, [a]that You have
made me like clay.
And will You turn me into dust
again?
10 [a]Did You not pour me out like
milk,
And curdle me like cheese,
11 Clothe me with skin and flesh,
And knit me together with bones
and sinews?
12 You have granted me life and
favor,
And Your care has **preserved** my
spirit.

WORD WEALTH

10:12 preserved, *shamar* (shah-*mar*); Strong's #8104: To guard, keep, protect, preserve; watch over, care for, safekeep occurs about 450 times in the OT. *Shamar* first appears in Gen. 2:15, where Adam was to tend and keep the Garden of Eden. People are told to guard the covenant, the Sabbath, or the commandments (Gen. 17:9; Ex. 31:14; Deut. 28:9). The participle *shomer* means "guardian," or "he who watches," that is, a watchman or shepherd. The Lord is called "*shomer Yisrael,*" the "One who guards Israel"; this Keeper never slumbers and never sleeps, but is always on duty (Ps. 121:4).

13 'And these *things* You have
hidden in Your heart;
I know that this *was* with You:
14 If I sin, then [a]You mark me,
And will not *acquit me of my
iniquity.
15 If I am wicked, [a]woe to me;
[b]Even *if* I am righteous, I [1]cannot
lift up my head.
I am full of disgrace;
[c]See my misery!
16 If *my head* is exalted,
[a]You hunt me like a fierce lion,
And again You show Yourself
awesome against me.
17 You renew Your witnesses
against me,
And increase Your indignation
toward me;
Changes and war are *ever* with
me.

18 'Why[a] then have You brought me
out of the womb?
Oh, that I had perished and no eye
had seen me!
19 I would have been as though I had
not been.
I would have been carried from
the womb to the grave.
20 [a]Are not my days few?
Cease! [b]Leave me alone, that I
may take a little comfort,
21 Before I go *to the place from
which* I shall not return,
[a]To the land of darkness [b]and the
shadow of death,
22 A land as dark as darkness *itself,*
As the shadow of death, without
any order,
Where even the light *is* like
darkness.' "

Zophar Urges Job to Repent

11 Then Zophar the Naamathite
answered and said:

2 "Should not the multitude of words
be answered?

1 [b]Job 7:11
4 [a][1 Sam. 16:7; Job 28:24; 34:21]
5 *See WW at Job 4:17.
8 [a]Job 10:3; Ps. 119:73 [b][Job 9:22]
9 [a]Gen. 2:7; Job 33:6 *See WW at Is. 62:6.
10 [a][Ps. 139:14–16]
14 [a]Job 7:20; Ps. 139:1 *See WW at Num. 14:18.
15 [a]Job 10:7; Is. 3:11 [b][Job 9:12, 15] [c]Ps. 25:18 [1]Lit. *will not*
16 [a]Is. 38:13; Lam. 3:10; Hos. 13:7
18 [a]Job 3:11–13
20 [a]Ps. 39:5 [b]Job 7:16, 19
21 [a]Ps. 88:12 [b]Ps. 23:4

11:1–20 Zophar addresses Job even more violently (vv. 1–4), calling on God in His wisdom to convince Job of his guilt and need of repentance (vv. 5–12). He adds that Job's suffering is justified. One is either a repentant worshiper or an arrogant sinner. Job is the latter, and he needs to drop his claim to innocence. Zophar declares that his words are **pure,** that is, based on reasoned theology. He concludes that repentance is the only way for Job to escape his present suffering and eternal damnation as well (vv. 13–20).

And should [1]a man full of talk be vindicated?
3 Should your empty talk make men [1]hold their peace?
And when you mock, should no one rebuke you?
4 For you have said,
[a]'My doctrine *is* pure,
And I am clean in your eyes.'
5 But oh, that God would speak,
And open His lips against you,
6 That He would show you the secrets of *wisdom!
For *they would* double *your* prudence.
Know therefore that [a]God [1]exacts from you
Less than your iniquity *deserves.*

7 "Can[a] you search out the deep things of God?
Can you find out the limits of the Almighty?
8 *They are* higher than heaven—what can you do?
Deeper than [1]Sheol— what can you know?
9 Their measure *is* longer than the earth
And broader than the sea.

10 "If[a] He passes by, imprisons, and gathers *to judgment,*
Then who can [1]hinder Him?
11 For [a]He knows deceitful men;
He sees wickedness also.
Will He not then consider *it?*
12 For an [a]empty-headed man will be wise,
When a wild donkey's colt is born a man.

13 "If you would [a]prepare your heart,
And [b]stretch out your hands toward Him;
14 If *iniquity *were* in your hand, *and you* put it far away,
And [a]would not let wickedness *dwell in your tents;
15 [a]Then surely you could lift up your face without spot;
Yes, you could be steadfast, and not fear;
16 Because you would [a]forget *your* misery,
And remember *it* as waters *that have* passed away,
17 And *your* life [a]would be brighter than noonday.
Though you were dark, you would be like the morning.
18 And you would be secure, because there is hope;
Yes, you would dig *around you, and* [a]take your rest in safety.
19 You would also lie down, and no one would make *you* afraid;
Yes, many would court your favor.
20 But [a]the eyes of the wicked will fail,
And they shall not escape,
And [b]their hope—[1]loss of life!"

Job Answers His Critics

12 Then Job answered and said:

2 "No doubt you *are* the people,
And wisdom will die with you!
3 But I have [1]understanding as well as you;
I *am* not [a]inferior to you.
Indeed, who does not *know* such things as these?

4 "I[a] am one *mocked by his friends,
Who [b]called on God, and He answered him,
The just and blameless *who is* ridiculed.
5 A [1]lamp is despised in the thought of one who is at ease;
It is made ready for [a]those whose feet slip.
6 [a]The tents of robbers prosper,
And those who provoke God are secure—
In what God provides by His hand.

7 "But now ask the beasts, and they will teach you;
And the birds of the air, and they will tell you;
8 Or speak to the earth, and it will teach you;
And the fish of the sea will explain to you.
9 Who among all these does not know

CHAPTER 11

2 [1]Lit. *a man of lips* **3** [1]*be silent* **4** [a]Job 6:30 **6** [a][Ezra 9:13] [1]Lit. *forgets some of your iniquity for you* *See WW at Is. 11:2. **7** [a]Job 33:12, 13; 36:26; [Eccl. 3:11; Rom. 11:33] **8** [1]The abode of the dead **10** [a]Job 9:12; [Rev. 3:7] [1]*restrain* **11** [a][Ps. 10:14] **12** [a][Ps. 39:5]; Rom. 1:22 **13** [a][1 Sam. 7:3] [b]Ps. 88:9 **14** [a]Ps. 101:3 *See WW at Prov. 22:8. • See WW at Num. 10:12. **15** [a]Job 22:26; Ps. 119:6; [1 John 3:21] **16** [a]Is. 65:16 **17** [a]Ps. 37:6; Prov. 4:18; Is. 58:8, 10 **18** [a]Lev. 26:5, 6; Ps. 3:5; Prov. 3:24 **20** [a]Lev. 26:16; Deut. 28:65; Job 17:5 [b]Job 18:14; [Prov. 11:7] [1]Lit. *the breathing out of life*

CHAPTER 12

3 [a]Job 13:2 [1]Lit. *a heart* **4** [a]Job 21:3 [b]Ps. 91:15 *See WW at Eccl. 3:4. **5** [a]Prov. 14:2 [1]Or *disaster* **6** [a][Job 9:24; 21:6–16; Ps. 73:12; Jer. 12:1; Mal. 3:15]

12:1—14:22 Job turns on his friends with energy that matches their attacks, maintaining his innocence and wisdom while including himself among a morally corrupt society (12:1—13:17). Telling them that he knows as much as they know, and that their teachings are false, Job reaffirms his faith in God and makes two requests (13:21); 1) that God not withdraw from him; 2) that the dread of God not cause him to be overcome by fear. He searches for a cause—perhaps a sin of his youth—that may have brought about his suffering. In his melancholic discourse, Job still represents God as tyrannical and capricious in His dealings with mankind, petitioning God to try his case before the heavenly tribunal (13:18—14:22).

That the hand of the LORD has
done this,
10 [a]In whose hand *is* the [1]life of every
living thing,
And the [b]breath of [2]all
mankind?
11 Does not the ear test words
And the [1]mouth *taste its food?
4 12 Wisdom *is* with aged men,
And with [1]length of days,
understanding.

13 "With Him *are* [a]wisdom and
strength,
He has counsel and
understanding.
4 14 If [a]He breaks *a thing* down, it
cannot be rebuilt;
If He imprisons a man, there can
be no release.
15 If He [a]withholds the waters, they
dry up;
If He [b]sends them out, they
overwhelm the earth.
16 With Him *are* *strength and
prudence.
The deceived and the deceiver *are*
His.
17 He leads counselors away
plundered,
And makes fools of the judges.
18 He loosens the bonds of kings,
And binds their waist with a
belt.
19 He leads [1]princes away
plundered,
And overthrows the mighty.
20 [a]He deprives the trusted ones of
speech,
And takes away the discernment
of the elders.
21 [a]He pours contempt on princes,
And [1]disarms the mighty.
22 He [a]uncovers deep things out of
darkness,
And brings the shadow of death
to light.
23 [a]He makes nations great, and
destroys them;
He [1]enlarges nations, and guides
them.
24 He takes away the
[1]understanding of the chiefs of
the people of the earth,
And [a]makes them wander in a
pathless wilderness.
25 [a]They grope in the dark without
light,
And He makes them [b]stagger like
a drunken *man*.

10 [a][Acts 17:28] [b]Job 27:3; 33:4 [1]Or *soul* [2]Lit. *all flesh of men*
11 [1]*palate* *See WW at Ps. 34:8.
12 [1]Long life
13 [a]Job 9:4; 36:5
14 [a]Job 11:10; Is. 25:2
15 [a]Deut. 11:17; [1 Kin. 8:35, 36] [b]Gen. 7:11–24
16 *See WW at Jer. 16:19.
19 [1]Lit. *priests*, but not in a technical sense
20 [a]Job 32:9
21 [a][Job 34:19]; Ps. 107:40; [Dan. 2:21] [1]*loosens the belt of*
22 [a]Dan. 2:22; [1 Cor. 4:5]
23 [a]Is. 9:3; 26:15 [1]Lit. *spreads out*
24 [a]Ps. 107:4 [1]Lit. *heart*
25 [a]Job 5:14; 15:30; 18:18 [b]Ps. 107:27

CHAPTER 13

1 *See WW at Neh. 8:8.
2 [a]Job 12:3
3 [a]Job 23:3; 31:35
4 [a]Job 6:21; [Jer. 23:32]
5 [a]Job 13:13; 21:5; Prov. 17:28
7 [a]Job 27:4; 36:4 [1]*unrighteously*
9 *See WW at Job 4:17.
11 [1]Lit. *exaltation*
13 [1]*Be silent*
14 [a]Job 18:4
15 [a]Ps. 23:4; [Prov. 14:32] [b]Job 27:5 *See WW at Mic. 7:7.
16 [a]Job 8:13
18 [a][Rom. 8:34]
19 [a]Job 7:21; 10:8; Is. 50:8

13 "Behold, my eye has seen all
this,
My ear has heard and
*understood it.
2 [a]What you know, I also know;
I *am* not inferior to you.
3 [a]But I would speak to the
Almighty,
And I desire to reason with
God.
4 But you forgers of lies,
[a]You *are* all worthless physicians.
5 Oh, that you would be silent,
And [a]it would be your wisdom!
6 Now hear my reasoning,
And heed the pleadings of my
lips.
7 [a]Will you speak [1]wickedly for
God,
And talk deceitfully for Him?
8 Will you show partiality for
Him?
Will you contend for God?
9 Will it be well when He searches
you out?
Or can you mock Him as one
mocks a *man?
10 He will surely rebuke you
If you secretly show partiality.
11 Will not His [1]excellence make
you afraid,
And the dread of Him fall upon
you?
12 Your platitudes *are* proverbs of
ashes,
Your defenses are defenses of
clay.

13 "Hold[1] your peace with me, and let
me speak,
Then let come on me what *may!*
14 Why [a]do I take my flesh in my
teeth,
And put my life in my hands?
15 [a]Though He slay me, yet will I 5
*trust Him.
[b]Even so, I will defend my own
ways before Him.
16 He also *shall* be my salvation,
For a [a]hypocrite could not come
before Him.
17 Listen carefully to my speech,
And to my declaration with your
ears.
18 See now, I have prepared *my*
case,
I know that I shall be [a]vindicated.
19 [a]Who *is* he *who* will contend with
me?
If now I hold my tongue, I perish.

12:12 See section 4 of Truth-In-Action at the end of Job.
12:14 See section 4 of Truth-In-Action at the end of Job.
13:15 See section 5 of Truth-In-Action at the end of Job.

Job's Despondent Prayer

20 "Only[a] two *things* do not do to me,
Then I will not hide myself from You:
21 [a]Withdraw Your hand far from me,
And let not the dread of You make me afraid.
22 Then call, and I will [a]answer;
Or let me speak, then You respond to me.
23 How many *are* my *iniquities and sins?
Make me know my transgression and my sin.
24 [a]Why do You hide Your face,
And [b]regard me as Your enemy?
25 [a]Will You frighten a leaf driven to and fro?
And will You pursue dry stubble?
26 For You write bitter things against me,
And [a]make me inherit the iniquities of my youth.
27 [a]You put my feet in the stocks,
And watch closely all my paths.
You [1]set a limit for the [2]soles of my feet.

28 "*Man*[1] decays like a rotten thing,
Like a garment that is moth-eaten.

14

[4] "Man* *who is* born of woman
Is of few days and [a]full of [1]trouble.
2 [a]He comes forth like a flower and fades away;
He flees like a shadow and does not continue.
3 And [a]do You open Your eyes on such a one,
And [b]bring [1]me to judgment with Yourself?
4 Who [a]can bring a clean *thing* out of an *unclean?
No one!
5 [a]Since his days *are* determined,
The number of his months *is* with You;
You have appointed his limits, so that he cannot pass.
6 [a]Look away from him that he may [1]rest,
Till [b]like a hired man he finishes his day.

7 "For there is hope for a tree,
If it is cut down, that it will sprout again,
And that its tender shoots will not cease.
8 Though its root may grow old in the earth,
And its stump may die in the ground,
9 *Yet* at the scent of water it will bud
And bring forth branches like a plant.
10 But man dies and [1]is laid away;
Indeed he [2]breathes his last
And where *is* [a]he?
11 *As* water disappears from the sea,
And a river becomes parched and dries up,
12 So man lies down and does not rise.
[a]Till the heavens *are* no more,
They will not awake
Nor be roused from their sleep.

13 "Oh, that You would hide me in the *grave,
That You would conceal me until Your wrath is past,
That You would appoint me a set time, and remember me!
14 If a man dies, shall he live *again?*
All the days of my hard service [a]I will wait,
Till my change comes.
15 [a]You shall call, and I will answer You;
You shall desire the work of Your hands.
16 For now [a]You number my steps,
But do not watch over my sin.
17 [a]My transgression *is* sealed up in a bag,
And You [1]cover my iniquity.

18 "But *as* a mountain falls *and* crumbles away,
And *as* a rock is moved from its place;
19 *As* water wears away stones,
And as torrents wash away the soil of the earth;
So You destroy the hope of man.
20 You prevail forever against him, and he passes on;
You change his countenance and send him away.
21 His sons come to honor, and [a]he does not know *it;*
They are brought low, and he does not perceive *it.*
22 But his flesh will be in pain over it,
And his soul will *mourn over it."

20 [a]Job 9:34
21 [a]Job 9:34; Ps. 39:10
22 [a]Job 9:16; 14:15
23 *See WW at Ps. 130:3.
24 [a][Deut. 32:20]; Ps. 13:1 [b]Lam. 2:5
25 [a]Is. 42:3
26 [a]Job 20:11
27 [a]Job 33:11 [1]Lit. *inscribe a print* [2]Lit. *roots*
28 [1]Lit. *He*

CHAPTER 14

1 [a]Job 5:7; Eccl. 2:23 [1]*turmoil* *See WW at Gen. 1:26.
2 [a]Job 8:9; Ps. 90:5, 6, 9; 102:11; 103:15; 144:4; Is. 40:6; James 1:10, 11; 1 Pet. 1:24
3 [a]Ps. 8:4; 144:3 [b][Ps. 143:2] [1]LXX, Syr., Vg. *him*
4 [a][Job 15:14; 25:4; Ps. 51:2, 5, 10; John 3:6; Rom. 5:12; Eph. 2:3] *See WW at Lev. 10:10.
5 [a]Job 7:1; 21:21; Heb. 9:27
6 [a]Job 7:16, 19; Ps. 39:13 [b]Job 7:1 [1]Lit. *cease*
10 [a]Job 10:21, 22 [1]*lies prostrate* [2]*expires*
12 [a]Ps. 102:25, 26; [Is. 51:6; 65:17; 66:22]; Acts 3:21; [2 Pet. 3:7, 10, 11; Rev. 20:11; 21:1]
13 *See WW at Hos. 13:14.
14 [a]Job 13:15
15 [a]Job 13:22
16 [a]Job 10:6, 14; 13:27; 31:4; 34:21; Ps. 56:8; 139:1–3; Prov. 5:21; [Jer. 32:19]
17 [a]Deut. 32:32–34 [1]Lit. *plaster over*
21 [a]Eccl. 9:5; Is. 63:16
22 *See WW at Joel 1:9.

14:1, 2 See section 4 of Truth-In-Action at the end of Job.

Eliphaz Accuses Job of Folly

15 Then [a]Eliphaz the Temanite answered and said:

2 "Should a wise man answer with empty *knowledge,
And fill [1]himself with the east wind?
3 Should he reason with unprofitable talk,
Or by speeches with which he can do no good?
4 Yes, you cast off fear,
And restrain [1]prayer before God.
5 For your iniquity teaches your mouth,
And you choose the tongue of the crafty.
6 [a]Your own mouth condemns you, and not I;
Yes, your own lips testify against you.

7 "*Are* you the first man *who* was born?
[a]Or were you made before the hills?
8 [a]Have you heard the counsel of God?
Do you limit wisdom to yourself?
9 [a]What do you know that we do not know?
What do you understand that *is* not in us?
10 [a]Both the gray-haired and the aged *are* among us,
Much older than your father.
11 *Are* the consolations of God too small for you,
And the word *spoken* [1]gently with you?
12 Why does your heart carry you away,
And [1]what do your eyes wink at,
13 That you turn your spirit against God,
And let *such* words go out of your mouth?

3 14 "What[a] *is* man, that he could be pure?
And *he who is* born of a woman, that he could be righteous?
15 [a]If *God* puts no trust in His saints,
And the heavens are not pure in His sight,
16 [a]How much less man, *who is* abominable and filthy,
[b]Who drinks iniquity like water!

17 "I will tell you, hear me;
What I have seen I will declare,
18 What wise men have told,
Not hiding *anything received* [a]from their fathers,
19 To whom alone the [1]land was given,
And [a]no alien passed among them:
20 The wicked man writhes with pain all *his* days,
[a]And the number of years is hidden from the oppressor.
21 [1]Dreadful sounds *are* in his ears;
[a]In prosperity the destroyer comes upon him.
22 He does not believe that he will [a]return from darkness,
For a sword is waiting for him.
23 He [a]wanders about for bread, *saying,* 'Where *is it?*'
He knows [b]that a day of darkness is ready at his hand.
24 Trouble and anguish make him afraid;
They overpower him, like a king ready for [1]battle.
25 For he stretches out his hand against God,
And acts defiantly against the Almighty,
26 Running stubbornly against Him
With his strong, embossed shield.

27 "Though[a] he has covered his face with his fatness,
And made *his* waist heavy with fat,
28 He dwells in desolate cities,
In houses which no one inhabits,
Which are destined to become ruins.
29 He will not be rich,
Nor will his wealth [a]continue,
Nor will his possessions overspread the earth.
30 He will not depart from darkness;
The flame will dry out his branches,
And [a]by the breath of His mouth he will go away.
31 Let him not [a]trust in futile *things,* deceiving himself,

CHAPTER 15

1 [a]Job 4:1
2 [1]Lit. *his belly* *See WW at Mal. 2:7.
4 [1]*meditation* or *complaint*
6 [a]Job 9:20; [Luke 19:22]
7 [a]Job 38:4, 21; Ps. 90:2; Prov. 8:25
8 [a]Job 29:4; Rom. 11:34; [1 Cor. 2:11]
9 [a]Job 12:3; 13:2
10 [a]Job 8:8–10; 12:12; 32:6, 7
11 [1]Or *a secret thing*
12 [1]Or *why do your eyes flash*
14 [a]Job 14:4; Prov. 20:9; [Eccl. 7:20; 1 John 1:8, 10]
15 [a]Job 4:18; 25:5
16 [a]Job 4:19; Ps. 14:3; 53:3 [b]Job 34:7; Prov. 19:28
18 [a]Job 8:8; 20:4
19 [a]Joel 3:17 [1]Or *earth*
20 [a]Ps. 90:12
21 [a]Job 20:21; 1 Thess. 5:3 [1]*Terrifying*
22 [a]Job 14:10–12
23 [a]Ps. 59:15; 109:10 [b]Job 18:12
24 [1]*attack*
27 [a]Ps. 17:10; 73:7; 119:70
29 [a]Job 20:28; 27:16, 17
30 [a]Job 4:9
31 [a]Job 35:13; Is. 59:4

15:1–35 Eliphaz rejects Job's claim to being innocent and wise (vv. 2–16) and reminds him of the woes of the wicked (vv. 17–35). He is severely reprimanding, warning Job of the dire consequences of such stubbornness. He offers no consolation.

15:1 This begins the second cycle of speeches in which Job's friends become increasingly impatient in their attempt to establish his serious sin. They beg him to repent; he refuses, convinced of his innocence.

15:14, 15 Eliphaz rightly instructs in the doctrine of inherent sin and moral weakness.

15:14 See section 3 of Truth-In-Action at the end of Job.

For futility will be his reward.
32 It will be accomplished [a]before
his time,
And his branch will not be green.
33 He will shake off his unripe grape
like a vine,
And cast off his blossom like an
olive tree.
34 For the company of hypocrites
will be barren,
And fire will consume the tents
of bribery.
35 [a]They conceive trouble and bring
forth futility;
Their womb prepares deceit."

Job Reproaches His Pitiless Friends

16 Then Job answered and said:

2 "I have heard many such things;
[a]Miserable[1] comforters *are* you
all!
3 Shall [1]words of wind have an
end?
Or what provokes you that you
answer?
4 I also could speak as you *do,*
If your soul were in my soul's
place.
I could heap up words against
you,
And [a]shake my *head at you;
5 *But* I would strengthen you with
my mouth,
And the comfort of my lips would
relieve *your grief.*

6 "Though I speak, my grief is not
relieved;
And *if* I remain silent, how am I
eased?
7 But now He has [a]worn me out;
You [b]have made desolate all my
company.
8 You have shriveled me up,
And it is a [a]witness *against me;*
My leanness rises up against me
And bears witness to my face.
9 [a]He tears *me* in His wrath, and
hates me;
He gnashes at me with His teeth;
[b]My adversary sharpens His gaze
on me.
10 They [a]gape at me with their
mouth,

32 [a]Job 22:16; Ps. 55:23; Eccl. 7:17
35 [a]Ps. 7:14; Is. 59:4; [Hos. 10:13]

CHAPTER 16

2 [a]Job 13:4; 21:34 [1]*Troublesome*
3 [1]Empty words
4 [a]Ps. 22:7; 109:25; Lam. 2:15; Zeph. 2:15; Matt. 27:39 *See WW at Gen. 3:15.
7 [a]Job 7:3 [b]Job 16:20; 19:13–15
8 [a]Job 10:17
9 [a]Job 10:16, 17; 19:11; Hos. 6:1 [b]Job 13:24; 33:10
10 [a]Ps. 22:13; 35:21 [b]Is. 50:6; Lam. 3:30; Mic. 5:1; Matt. 26:67; Mark 14:65; Luke 22:63; Acts 23:2
11 [a]Job 1:15, 17
12 [a]Job 9:17 [b]Job 7:20; Lam. 3:12
13 [1]Lit. *kidneys*
14 [1]Vg. *giant* *See WW at Ezek. 22:30.
15 [a]Job 30:19; Ps. 7:5 [1]Lit. *horn*
16 [1]Lit. *red*
18 [a]Job 27:9; [Ps. 66:18]
19 [a]Gen. 31:50; Rom. 1:9; Phil. 1:8; 1 Thess. 2:5
21 [a]Job 31:35; Eccl. 6:10; [Is. 45:9; Rom. 9:20] [1]*friend*
22 [a]Job 10:21; Eccl. 12:5

CHAPTER 17

1 [a]Ps. 88:3, 4
2 [a]1 Sam. 1:6; Job 12:4; 17:6; 30:1, 9; 34:7 [1]Lit. *lodge*

They [b]strike me reproachfully on
the cheek,
They gather together against me.
11 God [a]has delivered me to the
ungodly,
And turned me over to the hands
of the wicked.
12 I was at ease, but He has
[a]shattered me;
He also has taken *me* by my neck,
and shaken me to pieces;
He has [b]set me up for His target,
13 His archers surround me.
He pierces my [1]heart and does not
pity;
He pours out my gall on the
ground.
14 He breaks me with *wound upon
wound;
He runs at me like a [1]warrior.

15 "I have sewn sackcloth over my
skin,
And [a]laid my [1]head in the dust.
16 My face is [1]flushed from weeping,
And on my eyelids *is* the shadow
of death;
17 Although no violence *is* in my
hands,
And my prayer *is* pure.

18 "O earth, do not cover my blood,
And [a]let my cry have no *resting*
place!
19 Surely even now [a]my witness *is* **1**
in heaven,
And my evidence *is* on high.
20 My friends scorn me;
My eyes pour out *tears* to God.
21 [a]Oh, that one might plead for a
man with God,
As a man *pleads* for his
[1]neighbor!
22 For when a few years are
finished,
I shall [a]go the way of no return.

Job Prays for Relief

17 "My spirit is broken,
My days are extinguished,
[a]The grave *is ready* for me.
2 *Are* not mockers with me?
And does not my eye [1]dwell on
their [a]provocation?

16:1—17:16 Despairing of ever receiving any comfort from his friends and sure that they are not open to receiving his statements (16:1–6), Job's fourth response appeals to God to verify his innocence (16:18—17:16). Not only has God allowed this suffering to come to him, but now He has also caused him to be ridiculed by his friends. As his friends exaggerated his guilt, so Job, who is not totally free of self-righteousness, exaggerates his innocence. Even as his pain wears on him, Job sees in God his hope for future justification (17:10–16).

16:19–22 See section 1 of Truth-In-Action at the end of Job.

3 "Now put down a pledge for me
with Yourself.
Who *is* he *who* [a]will shake hands
with me?
4 For You have hidden their heart
from [a]understanding;
Therefore You will not exalt
them.
5 He who speaks flattery to *his*
friends,
Even the eyes of his children will
[a]fail.

6 "But He has made me [a]a byword
of the people,
And I have become one in whose
face men spit.
7 [a]My eye has also grown dim
because of sorrow,
And all my members *are* like
shadows.
8 Upright *men* are astonished at
this,
And the innocent *stirs himself up
against the hypocrite.
9 Yet the righteous will hold to his
[a]way,
And he who has [b]clean hands will
be stronger and stronger.

10 "But please, [a]come back again,
[1]all of you,
For I shall not find *one* wise *man*
among you.
11 [a]My days are past,
My purposes are broken off,
Even the [1]thoughts of my heart.
12 They change the night into day;
'The light *is* near,' *they say,* in the
face of darkness.
13 If I *wait *for* the grave *as* my
house,
If I make my bed in the darkness,
14 If I say to corruption, 'You *are* my
father,'
And to the worm, 'You *are* my
mother and my sister,'
15 Where then *is* my [a]hope?
As for my hope, who can see
it?
16 *Will* they go down [a]to the gates
of [1]Sheol?
Shall *we have* [b]rest together in
the dust?"

Bildad: The Wicked Are Punished

18 Then [a]Bildad the Shuhite answered and said:

2 "How long *till* you put an end to
words?
Gain understanding, and
afterward we will speak.
3 Why are we counted [a]as beasts,
And regarded as stupid in your
sight?
4 [a]You[1] who tear yourself in
anger,
Shall the earth be forsaken for
you?
Or shall the rock be removed
from its place?

5 "The[a] light of the wicked indeed
goes out,
And the flame of his fire does not
shine.
6 The light is dark in his tent,
[a]And his lamp beside him is put
out.
7 The steps of his strength are
shortened,
And [a]his own counsel casts him
down.
8 For [a]he is cast into a net by his
own feet,
And he walks into a snare.
9 The net takes *him* by the heel,
And [a]a snare lays hold of him.
10 A noose *is* hidden for him on the
ground,
And a trap for him in the road.
11 [a]Terrors frighten him on every
side,
And drive him to his feet.
12 His strength is starved,
And [a]destruction *is* ready at his
side.
13 It devours patches of his skin;
The firstborn of death devours his
[1]limbs.
14 He is uprooted from [a]the shelter
of his tent,
And they parade him before the
king of terrors.
15 They dwell in his tent *who are*
none of his;
Brimstone is scattered on his
dwelling.
16 [a]His roots are dried out below,
And his branch withers above.
17 [a]The memory of him perishes from
the earth,
And he has no name [1]among the
renowned.
18 [1]He is driven from light into
darkness,
And chased out of the *world.

3 [a]Prov. 6:1; 17:18; 22:26 **4** [a]Job 12:20; 32:9 **5** [a]Job 11:20 **6** [a]Job 30:9 **7** [a]Ps. 6:7; 31:9 **8** *See WW at Hag. 1:14. **9** [a]Prov. 4:18 [b]Ps. 24:4 **10** [a]Job 6:29 [1]So with some Heb. mss., LXX, Syr., Vg.; MT, Tg. *all of them* **11** [a]Job 7:6 [1]*desires* **13** *See WW at Lam. 3:25. **15** [a]Job 7:6; 13:15; 14:19; 19:10 **16** [a]Jon. 2:6 [b]Job 3:17–19; 21:33 [1]The abode of the dead

CHAPTER 18

1 [a]Job 8:1

3 [a]Ps. 73:22 **4** [a]Job 13:14 [1]Lit. *one who tears his soul* **5** [a]Job 21:17; Prov. 13:9; 20:20; 24:20 **6** [a]Job 21:17; Ps. 18:28 **7** [a]Job 5:12, 13; 15:6 **8** [a]Job 22:10; Ps. 9:15; 35:8; Is. 24:17, 18 **9** [a]Job 5:5 **11** [a]Job 20:25; Jer. 6:25 **12** [a]Job 15:23 **13** [1]*parts* **14** [a]Job 11:20 **16** [a]Job 29:19 **17** [a]Job 24:20; [Ps. 34:16]; Prov. 10:7 [1]Lit. *before the outside,* i.e., the distinguished or famous **18** [1]Or *They drive him* *See WW at Jer. 51:15.

18:1–21 In his second address to Job, Bildad again sharply rebukes Job, referring to his words as ravings (vv. 2–4), and predicts that Job, as a hardened sinner, will surely see destruction if he does not repent (vv. 5–21). His picture is bleak and hopeless, painted with vivid metaphors.

19 [a]He has neither son nor posterity
among his people,
Nor any remaining in his
dwellings.
20 Those [1]in the west are astonished
[a]at his day,
As those [2]in the east are
frightened.
21 Surely such *are* the dwellings of
the wicked,
And this *is* the place *of him who*
[a]does not know God."

Job Trusts in His Redeemer

19 Then Job answered and said:
2 "How long will you torment my
soul,
And break me in pieces with
words?
3 These ten times you have
[1]reproached me;
You are not *ashamed *that* you
[2]have wronged me.
4 And if indeed I have erred,
My error remains with me.
5 If indeed you [a]exalt *yourselves*
against me,
And plead my disgrace against
me,
6 Know then that [a]God has
wronged me,
And has surrounded me with His
net.

7 "If I cry out concerning [1]wrong, I
am not heard.
If I cry aloud, *there is* no justice.
8 [a]He has [1]fenced up my way, so
that I cannot pass;
And He has set darkness in my
paths.
9 [a]He has stripped me of my glory,
And taken the crown *from* my
head.
10 He breaks me down on every
side,
And I am gone;
My [a]hope He has uprooted like a
tree.
11 He has also kindled His wrath
against me,
And [a]He counts me as *one of* His
enemies.
12 His troops come together
And build up their road against
me;
They encamp all around my tent.

13 "He[a] has removed my brothers far
from me,
And my acquaintances are
completely estranged from me.
14 My relatives have failed,
And my close friends have
forgotten me.
15 Those who *dwell in my house,
and my maidservants,
Count me as a stranger;
I am an alien in their sight.
16 I call my servant, but he gives no
answer;
I beg him with my mouth.
17 My breath is offensive to my wife,
And I am [1]repulsive to the
children of my own body.
18 Even [a]young children despise me;
I arise, and they speak against
me.
19 [a]All my close friends abhor me,
And those whom I love have
turned against me.
20 [a]My bone clings to my skin and
to my flesh,
And I have escaped by the skin
of my teeth.

21 "Have pity on me, have pity on me,
O you my friends,
For the hand of God has struck
me!
22 Why do you [a]persecute me as
God *does,*
And are not satisfied with my
flesh?

23 "Oh, that my words were written!
Oh, that they were inscribed in a
book!
24 That they were engraved on a
rock
With an iron pen and lead,
*forever!
25 For I know *that* my Redeemer
lives,
And He shall stand at last on the
earth;
26 And after my skin is [1]destroyed,
this *I know,*
That [a]in my **flesh** I shall see
God,

18:19 [a]Job 27:14, 15; Is. 14:22
20 [a]Ps. 37:13; Jer. 50:27; Obad. 12 [1]Lit. *who came after* [2]Lit. *who have gone before*
21 [a]Jer. 9:3; 1 Thess. 4:5

CHAPTER 19

3 [1]*shamed or disgraced* [2]A Jewish tradition *make yourselves strange to me* *See WW at Ezek. 16:63.
5 [a]Ps. 35:26; 38:16; 55:12, 13
6 [a]Job 16:11
7 [1]*violence*
8 [a]Job 3:23; Ps. 88:8; Lam. 3:7, 9 [1]*walled off my way*
9 [a]Job 12:17, 19; Ps. 89:44
10 [a]Job 17:14–16
11 [a]Job 13:24; 33:10
13 [a]Job 16:20; Ps. 31:11; 38:11; 69:8; 88:8, 18
15 *See WW at Jer. 42:17.
17 [1]Lit. *strange*
18 [a]2 Kin. 2:23; Job 17:6
19 [a]Ps. 38:11; 55:12, 13
20 [a]Job 16:8; 33:21; Ps. 102:5; Lam. 4:8
22 [a]Job 13:24, 25; 16:11; 19:6; Ps. 69:26
24 *See WW at Mic. 4:5.
26 [a][Ps. 17:15]; Matt. 5:8; 1 Cor. 13:12; [1 John 3:2] [1]Lit. *struck off*

19:1–29 Job's fifth response makes an appeal for pity from the friends who have become his tormentors (vv. 1–6). Although hope of recovery seems to be dying, and he has great complaints against God's brutal treatment of him (vv. 7–20), Job states his enduring hope that in the end he will be vindicated by God his Redeemer (vv. 25–27). He concludes with a warning to his friends (vv. 28, 29).
19:25, 26 This is one of the OT's greatest prophetic affirmations of an anticipated **Redeemer**/Savior who will bring hope of a literal, physical resurrection to redeemed mankind (see 1 Cor. 15:35–49).

WORD WEALTH

19:26 flesh, *basar* (bah-*sar*); Strong's #1320: Flesh, body, human being. *Kol basar,* "all flesh," means all humanity together. *Basar* refers to the human body, and in some instances, to the bodies of animals as well. Occasionally, *basar* means "meat," that is, the cooked or uncooked pieces of animal flesh, as in Num. 11:33. The first occurrence of *basar* is in Gen. 2:21, where God closed up the sleeping man's "flesh" after extracting one rib. The simplest meaning is "the visible part of man or animal," that is, the skin, muscle, flesh, and so on.

27 Whom I shall see for myself,
And my eyes shall behold, and not another.
How my [1]heart yearns within me!
28 If you should say, 'How shall we persecute him?'—
Since the root of the matter is found in me,
29 Be afraid of the sword for yourselves;
For wrath *brings* the punishment of the sword,
That you may know *there is* a judgment."

Zophar's Sermon on the Wicked Man

20 Then [a]Zophar the Naamathite answered and said:

2 "Therefore my anxious thoughts make me answer,
Because of the turmoil within me.
3 I have heard the rebuke [1]that reproaches me,
And the spirit of my understanding causes me to answer.

4 "Do you *not* know this of [a]old,
Since man was placed on earth,
5 [a]That the triumphing of the wicked is short,
And the joy of the hypocrite is *but* for a [b]moment?
6 [a]Though his haughtiness mounts up to the heavens,
And his head reaches to the clouds,
7 *Yet* he will perish forever like his own refuse;
Those who have seen him will say, 'Where is he?'
8 He will fly away [a]like a dream, and not be found;
Yes, he [b]will be chased away like a vision of the night.
9 The eye *that* saw him will *see him* no more,
Nor will his place behold him anymore.
10 His children will seek the favor of the poor,
And his hands will restore his wealth.
11 His bones are full of [a]his youthful vigor,
[b]But it will lie down with him in the dust.

12 "Though evil is sweet in his mouth,
And he hides it under his tongue,
13 *Though* he spares it and does not forsake it,
But still keeps it in his [1]mouth,
14 *Yet* his food in his stomach turns sour;
It becomes cobra venom within him.
15 He swallows down riches
And vomits them up again;
God casts them out of his belly.
16 He will suck the poison of cobras;
The viper's tongue will slay him.
17 He will not see [a]the streams,
The rivers flowing with honey and cream.
18 He will restore that for which he labored,
And will not swallow *it* down;
From the proceeds of business
He will get no enjoyment.
19 For he has [1]oppressed *and* forsaken the poor,
He has violently seized a house which he did not build.

20 "Because[a] he knows no quietness in his [1]heart,
He will not save anything he desires.
21 Nothing is left for him to eat;
Therefore his well-being will not last.
22 In his self-sufficiency he will be in distress;
Every hand of [1]misery will come against him.
23 *When* he is about to fill his stomach,

27 [1]Lit. *kidneys*

CHAPTER 20

1 [a]Job 11:1
3 [1]Lit. *of my insulting correction*
4 [a]Job 8:8; 15:10
5 [a]Ps. 37:35, 36 [b][Job 8:13; 13:16; 15:34; 27:8]
6 [a]Is. 14:13, 14
8 [a]Ps. 73:20; 90:5 [b]Job 18:18; 27:21–23
11 [a]Job 13:26 [b]Job 21:26
13 [1]Lit. *palate*
17 [a]Ps. 36:8; Jer. 17:8
19 [1]*crushed*
20 [a]Eccl. 5:13–15 [1]Lit. *belly*
22 [1]Or *the wretched* or *sufferer*

20:1–29 Zophar speaks again, this time about the devastating end of the wicked person and the hypocrite, including Job in those categories (vv. 4–29). Zophar is narrow-minded and legalistic, with no mercy for Job. He does not know how to answer Job's questions and is indignant at Job's accusations toward his friends (vv. 1–3).

God will cast on him the fury of His wrath,
And will rain it on him while he is eating.
24 [a]He will flee from the iron weapon;
A bronze bow will pierce him through.
25 It is drawn, and comes out of the body;
Yes, [a]the glittering *point comes* out of his [1]gall.
[b]Terrors *come* upon him;
26 Total darkness *is* reserved for his treasures.
[a]An unfanned fire will consume him;
It shall go ill with him who is left in his tent.
27 The heavens will *reveal his iniquity,
And the earth will rise up against him.
28 The increase of his house will depart,
And his goods will flow away in the day of His [a]wrath.
29 [a]This *is* the portion from God for a wicked man,
The heritage appointed to him by God."

Job's Discourse on the Wicked

21 Then Job answered and said:
2 "Listen* carefully to my speech,
And let this be your [1]consolation.
3 Bear with me that I may speak,
And after I have spoken, keep [a]mocking.

4 "As for me, *is* my complaint against man?
And if *it were,* why should I not be impatient?
5 Look at me and be astonished;
[a]Put *your* hand over *your* mouth.
6 Even when I remember I am terrified,
And trembling takes hold of my flesh.
7 [a]Why do the wicked live *and* become old,
Yes, become mighty in power?
8 Their descendants are established with them in their sight,
And their offspring before their eyes.
9 Their houses *are* safe from fear,
[a]Neither *is* [1]the rod of God upon them.
10 Their bull breeds without failure;
Their cow calves [a]without miscarriage.
11 They send forth their little ones like a flock,
And their children dance.
12 They sing to the tambourine and harp,
And rejoice to the sound of the flute.
13 They [a]spend their days in wealth,
And [1]in a moment go down to the [2]grave.
14 [a]Yet they say to God, 'Depart from us,
For we do not desire the knowledge of Your ways.
15 [a]Who *is* the Almighty, that we should serve Him?
And [b]what profit do we have if we pray to Him?'
16 Indeed [1]their prosperity *is* not in their hand;
[a]The counsel of the wicked is far from me.

17 "How often is the lamp of the wicked put out?
How often does their destruction come upon them,
The sorrows *God* [a]distributes in His anger?
18 [a]They are like straw before the wind,
And like chaff that a storm [1]carries away.
19 *They say,* 'God [1]lays up [2]one's iniquity [a]for his children';
Let Him recompense him, that he may know *it.*
20 Let his eyes see his destruction,
And [a]let him drink of the wrath of the Almighty.
21 For what does he care about his household after him,
When the number of his months is cut in half?

22 "Can[a] *anyone* teach God knowledge,
Since He judges those on high?
23 One dies in his full strength,
Being wholly at ease and secure;
24 His [1]pails are full of milk,
And the marrow of his bones is moist.

---

24 [a]Is. 24:18; Amos 5:19
25 [a]Job 16:13 [b]Job 18:11, 14 [1]Gallbladder
26 [a]Ps. 21:9
27 *See WW at Amos 3:7.
28 [a]Job 20:15; 21:30
29 [a]Job 27:13; 31:2, 3

CHAPTER 21

2 [1]*comfort* *See WW at 1 Kin. 20:8.
3 [a]Job 16:10
5 [a]Judg. 18:19; Job 13:5; 29:9; 40:4
7 [a]Job 12:6; Ps. 17:10, 14; 73:3, 12; [Jer. 12:1]; Hab. 1:13, 16
9 [a]Ps. 73:5 [1]The rod of God's chastisement
10 [a]Ex. 23:26
13 [a]Job 21:23; 36:11 [1]Without lingering [2]Or *Sheol*
14 [a]Job 22:17
15 [a]Ex. 5:2; Job 22:17; 34:9 [b]Job 35:3; Mal. 3:14
16 [a]Job 22:18; Ps. 1:1; Prov. 1:10 [1]Lit. *their goal*
17 [a][Job 31:2, 3; Luke 12:46]
18 [a]Ps. 1:4; 35:5; Is. 17:13; Hos. 13:3 [1]*steals away*
19 [a][Ex. 20:5]; Jer. 31:29; Ezek. 18:2 [1]*stores up* [2]Lit. *his*
20 [a]Ps. 75:8; Is. 51:17; Jer. 25:15; Rev. 14:10; 19:15
22 [a]Job 35:11; 36:22; [Is. 40:13; 45:9; Rom. 11:34; 1 Cor. 2:16]
24 [1]LXX, Vg. *bowels;* Syr. *sides;* Tg. *breasts*

21:1–34 Job appeals for a hearing (vv. 1–6) to challenge their oversimplified doctrine of retribution (vv. 7–33). He again confirms his own innocence; calamity falls on the just and unjust, a truth that history confirms. Sometimes the ungodly prosper throughout life while the godly know little except want. Here the subject moves from a focus on Job specifically to the larger question of the suffering of the godly. Thus Job challenges the major theological view of the day.

25 Another man dies in the
bitterness of his soul,
Never having eaten with
pleasure.
26 They [a]lie down alike in the dust,
And worms cover them.

27 "Look, I know your thoughts,
And the schemes *with which* you
would wrong me.
28 For you say,
'Where *is* the house of the prince?
And where *is* [1]the tent,
The *dwelling place of the
wicked?'
29 Have you not asked those who
travel the road?
And do you not know their signs?
30 [a]For the wicked are reserved for
the day of doom;
They shall be brought out on the
day of wrath.
31 Who condemns his way to his
face?
And who repays him *for what* he
has done?
32 Yet he shall be brought to the
grave,
And a vigil kept over the tomb.
33 The clods of the valley shall be
sweet to him;
[a]Everyone shall follow him,
As countless *have gone* before
him.
34 How then can you comfort me
with empty words,
Since [1]falsehood remains in your
answers?"

Eliphaz Accuses Job of Wickedness

22 Then [a]Eliphaz the Temanite answered and said:

2 "Can[a] a man be profitable to God,
Though he who is wise may be
profitable to himself?
3 *Is it* any pleasure to the Almighty
that you are righteous?
Or *is it* gain *to Him* that you make
your ways blameless?

4 "Is it because of your fear of Him
that He corrects you,
And enters into judgment with
you?
5 *Is* not your wickedness great,
And your iniquity without end?

26 [a]Job 3:13; 20:11; Eccl. 9:2
28 [1]Vg. omits *the tent*
*See WW at Is. 32:18.
30 [a]Job 20:29; [Prov. 16:4; 2 Pet. 2:9]
33 [a]Heb. 9:27
34 [1]*faithlessness*

CHAPTER 22

1 [a]Job 4:1; 15:1; 42:9
2 [a]Job 35:7; [Ps. 16:2; Luke 17:10]
6 [a][Ex. 22:26, 27]; Deut. 24:6, 10, 17; Job 24:3, 9; Ezek. 18:16
7 [a]Deut. 15:7; Job 31:17; Is. 58:7; Ezek. 18:7; Matt. 25:42
8 [1]Lit. *man of arm*
9 [1]Lit. *arms*
11 [a]Job 38:34; Ps. 69:1, 2; 124:5; Lam. 3:54
13 [a]Ps. 73:11
14 [a]Ps. 139:11, 12
16 [a]Job 14:19; 15:32; Ps. 90:5; Is. 28:2; Matt. 7:26, 27
17 [a]Job 21:14, 15 [1]LXX, Syr. *us*
19 [a]Ps. 52:6; 58:10; 107:42
20 [1]LXX *substance is*

6 For you have [a]taken pledges from
your brother for no reason,
And stripped the naked of their
clothing.
7 You have not given the weary
water to drink,
And you [a]have withheld bread
from the hungry.
8 But the [1]mighty man possessed
the land,
And the honorable man dwelt in
it.
9 You have sent widows away
empty,
And the [1]strength of the
fatherless was crushed.
10 Therefore snares *are* all around
you,
And sudden fear troubles you,
11 Or darkness *so that* you cannot
see;
And an abundance of [a]water
covers you.

12 "Is not God in the height of
heaven?
And see the highest stars, how
lofty they are!
13 And you say, [a]'What does God
know?
Can He judge through the deep
darkness?
14 [a]Thick clouds cover Him, so that
He cannot see,
And He walks above the circle of
heaven.'
15 Will you keep to the old way
Which wicked men have trod,
16 Who [a]were cut down before their
time,
Whose foundations were swept
away by a flood?
17 [a]They said to God, 'Depart from
us!
What can the Almighty do to
[1]them?'
18 Yet He filled their houses with
good *things;*
But the counsel of the wicked is
far from me.

19 "The[a] righteous see *it* and are
glad,
And the innocent laugh at them:
20 'Surely our [1]adversaries are cut
down,
And the fire consumes their
remnant.'

22:1–30 Only Eliphaz and Bildad participate in this final cycle. Disregarding Job's previous argument, Eliphaz charges Job with specific sins (vv. 1–11) and appeals to him to repent (vv. 21–30). Then he will be forgiven and have his prosperity restored. What may seem to be a beautiful call to repentance is, in fact, another accusation against Job. Eliphaz appears to be intent on theological arguments; his comfort has turned to condemnation, accusing Job of practical atheism.

21 "Now acquaint yourself with Him,
 and [a]be at peace;
 Thereby good will come to you.
22 Receive, please, [a]instruction from
 His mouth,
 And [b]lay up His words in your
 heart.
23 If you return to the *Almighty,
 you will be built up;
 You will remove iniquity far from
 your tents.
24 Then you will [a]lay your gold in
 the dust,
 And the *gold* of Ophir among the
 stones of the brooks.
25 Yes, the Almighty will be your
 [1]gold
 And your precious silver;
26 For then you will have your
 [a]delight in the Almighty,
 And lift up your face to God.
27 [a]You will make your prayer to
 Him,
 He will hear you,
 And you will pay your vows.
28 You will also declare a thing,
 And it will be established for you;
 So light will shine on your ways.
29 When they cast *you* down, and
 you say, 'Exaltation *will come!*'
 Then [a]He will save the humble
 person.
30 He will *even* deliver one who is
 not innocent;
 Yes, he will be delivered by the
 purity of your hands."

Job Proclaims God's Righteous Judgments

23

Then Job answered and said:

2 "Even today my [a]complaint is
 bitter;
 [1]My hand is listless because of my
 groaning.
3 [a]Oh, that I knew where I might
 find Him,
 That I might come to His seat!
4 I would present *my* case before
 Him,
 And fill my mouth with
 arguments.
5 I would know the words *which* He
 would answer me,
 And understand what He would
 say to me.
6 [a]Would He contend with me in His
 great *power?
 No! But He would take *note* of
 me.
7 There the upright could reason
 with Him,
 And I would be delivered forever
 from my Judge.

8 "Look,[a] I go forward, but He is not
 there,
 And backward, but I cannot
 perceive Him;
9 When He works on the left hand,
 I cannot behold *Him;*
 When He turns to the right hand,
 I cannot see *Him.*
10 But [a]He knows the way that I
 take; 4
 When [b]He has tested me, I shall
 come forth as gold.
11 [a]My foot has held fast to His steps;
 I have kept His way and not
 turned aside.
12 I have not departed from the
 [a]commandment of His lips;
 [b]I have treasured the words of His
 mouth
 More than my [1]necessary *food.*

13 "But He *is* unique, and who can
 make Him change?
 And *whatever* [a]His soul desires,
 that He does.
14 For He performs *what is*
 [a]appointed for me,
 And many such *things are* with
 Him.
15 Therefore I am terrified at His
 presence;
 When I consider *this,* I am *afraid
 of Him.
16 For God [a]made my heart weak,
 And the Almighty terrifies me;
17 Because I was not [a]cut off
 [1]from the presence of darkness,
 And He did *not* hide deep
 darkness from my face.

Job Complains of Violence on the Earth

24

"*Since* [a]times* are not hidden
 from the Almighty,
 Why do those who know Him see
 not His [b]days?

21 [a][Ps. 34:10]; Is. 27:5
22 [a]Job 6:10; 23:12; Prov. 2:6 [b][Ps. 119:11]
23 *See WW at Ps. 91:1.
24 [a]2 Chr. 1:15
25 [1]Ancient vss. suggest *defense;* MT *gold,* as in v. 24
26 [a]Job 27:10; Ps. 37:4; Is. 58:14
27 [a]Job 11:13; 33:26; [Is. 58:9–11]
29 [a]Job 5:11; [Matt. 23:12; James 4:6; 1 Pet. 5:5]

CHAPTER 23

2 [a]Job 7:11 [1]So with MT, Tg., Vg.; LXX, Syr. *His*
3 [a]Job 13:3, 18; 16:21; 31:35
6 [a]Is. 57:16 *See WW at Deut. 8:18.
8 [a]Job 9:11; 35:14
10 [a][Ps. 1:6; 139:1–3] [b][Ps. 17:3; 66:10; James 1:12]
11 [a]Job 31:7; Ps. 17:5
12 [a]Job 6:10; 22:22 [b]Ps. 44:18 [1]Lit. *appointed portion*
13 [a][Ps. 115:3]
14 [a][1 Thess. 3:2–4]
15 *See WW at Hos. 3:5.
16 [a]Ps. 22:14
17 [a]Job 10:18, 19 [1]Or *by* or *before*

CHAPTER 24

1 [a][Acts 1:7] [b][Is. 2:12]; Jer. 46:10; [Obad. 15]; Zeph. 1:7 *See WW at Is. 33:6.

23:1–17 Job's seventh response ignores his friends, focusing his case toward God. He repeats his longing for God and affirms God's righteousness. He confidently believes that, if he could find God, He **would take *note*** of him (v. 6).

23:10 See section 4 of Truth-In-Action at the end of Job.

24:1–25 Continuing his soliloquy, Job complains against the violence God permits to occur in the Earth, such as the oppression of the innocent and the persecution of the defenseless by evildoers. He calls attention to the murderer and adulterer who perform their deeds in secret and seem to escape speedy judgment; in fact, it appears that God

2 "*Some* remove [a]landmarks;
They seize flocks violently and
*feed *on them;*
3 They drive away the donkey of
the fatherless;
They [a]take the widow's ox as a
pledge.
4 They push the *needy off the
road;
All the [a]poor of the land are
forced to hide.
5 Indeed, *like* wild donkeys in the
desert,
They go out to their work,
searching for food.
The wilderness *yields* food for
them *and* for *their* children.
6 They gather their fodder in the
field
And glean in the vineyard of the
wicked.
7 They [a]spend the night naked,
without clothing,
And have no covering in the cold.
8 They are wet with the showers of
the mountains,
And [a]huddle around the rock for
want of *shelter.

9 "*Some* snatch the fatherless from
the breast,
And take a pledge from the *poor.
10 They cause *the poor* to go naked,
without [a]clothing;
And they take away the sheaves
from the hungry.
11 They press out oil within their
walls,
And tread winepresses, yet suffer
thirst.
12 The dying groan in the city,
And the souls of the wounded cry
out;
Yet God does not charge *them*
with wrong.

13 "There are those who rebel against
the light;
They do not know its ways
Nor abide in its paths.
14 [a]The murderer rises with the light;
He kills the poor and needy;
And in the night he is like a thief.
15 [a]The eye of the adulterer waits for
the twilight,
[b]Saying, 'No eye will see me';
And he [1]disguises *his* face.
16 In the dark they break into houses

2 [a][Deut. 19:14; 27:17]; Prov. 22:28; 23:10; Hos. 5:10 *See WW at Is. 40:11.
3 [a][Deut. 24:6, 10, 12, 17]; Job 22:6, 9
4 [a]Job 29:16; Prov. 28:28 *See WW at Ps. 70:5.
7 [a]Ex. 22:26, 27; [Deut. 24:12, 13]; Job 22:6; [James 2:15, 16]
8 [a]Lam. 4:5 *See WW at Prov. 14:26.
9 *See WW at Ps. 40:17.
10 [a]Job 31:19
14 [a]Ps. 10:8
15 [a]Prov. 7:7–10 [b]Ps. 10:11 [1]Lit. *puts a covering on his face*

16 [a][John 3:20]
19 [1]Lit. *seize* [2]Or *Sheol*
20 [a]Job 18:17; Ps. 34:16; Prov. 10:7
21 [1]Lit. *feeds on*
23 [a]Ps. 11:4; [Prov. 15:3]
24 [1]Lit. *gathered up*

CHAPTER 25

1 [a]Job 8:1; 18:1

Which they marked for
themselves in the daytime;
[a]They do not know the light.
17 For the morning is the same to
them as the shadow of death;
If *someone* recognizes *them,*
They are in the terrors of the
shadow of death.

18 "They *should be* swift on the face
of the waters,
Their portion *should be* cursed in
the earth,
So that no *one would* turn into
the way of their vineyards.
19 As drought and heat [1]consume
the snow waters,
So [2]the grave *consumes those
who* have sinned.
20 The womb *should* forget him,
The worm *should* feed sweetly on
him;
[a]He *should* be remembered no
more,
And wickedness *should* be
broken like a tree.
21 For he [1]preys on the barren *who*
do not bear,
And does no good for the widow.

22 "But *God* draws the mighty away
with His power;
He rises up, but no *man* is sure
of life.
23 He gives them security, and they
rely *on it;*
Yet [a]His eyes *are* on their ways.
24 They are exalted for a little while,
Then they are gone.
They are brought low;
They are [1]taken out of the way
like all *others;*
They dry out like the heads of
grain.

25 "Now if *it is* not *so,* who will prove
me a liar,
And make my speech worth
nothing?"

Bildad: How Can Man Be Righteous?

25 Then [a]Bildad the Shuhite answered and said:

2 "Dominion and fear *belong* to
Him;

grants them security. It appears his own suffering has made him more sensitive to evil and general human suffering. Essentially, Job debates the age-old questions: How can a righteous God allow the ungodly to prosper? And, why is there such a long delay in their punishment?

25:1–6 In his final statement to Job, Bildad asserts: 1) man cannot argue with God; 2) no man can say he is pure before God. It is unthinkable that God would grant Job a hearing.

He makes peace in His high places.
3 [1]Is there any number to His armies?
Upon whom does [a]His light not rise?
3 4 [a]How then can *man be righteous before God?
Or how can he be [b]pure *who is* born of a woman?
5 If even the moon does not shine,
And the stars are not pure in His [a]sight,
6 How much less man, *who is* [a]a maggot,
And a son of man, *who is* a worm?"

Job: Man's Frailty and God's Majesty

26 But Job answered and said:
2 "How have you helped *him who is* without power?
How have you saved the arm *that has* no strength?
3 How have you counseled *one who has* no wisdom?
And *how* have you declared sound advice to many?
4 To whom have you uttered words?
And whose spirit came from you?

5 "The dead tremble,
Those under the waters and those inhabiting them.
6 [a]Sheol *is* naked before Him,
And Destruction has no covering.
7 [a]He stretches out the north over empty space;
He hangs the earth on *nothing.
8 [a]He binds up the water in His thick clouds,
Yet the clouds [1]are not broken under it.
9 He covers the face of *His* throne,
And spreads His cloud over it.
10 [a]He drew a circular horizon on the face of the waters,
At the boundary of light and darkness.
11 The pillars of heaven tremble,
And are [1]astonished at His rebuke.
12 [a]He stirs up the sea with His power,
And by His understanding He breaks up [1]the storm.

3 [a]James 1:17 [1]Can His armies be counted?
4 [a]Job 4:17; 15:14; Ps. 130:3; 143:2 [b][Job 14:4] *See WW at Job 4:17.
5 [a]Job 15:15
6 [a]Ps. 22:6

CHAPTER 26

6 [a][Ps. 139:8]; Prov. 15:11; [Heb. 4:13]
7 [a]Job 9:8; Ps. 24:2; 104:2 *See WW at Is. 45:18.
8 [a]Job 37:11; Prov. 30:4 [1]*do not break*
10 [a][Job 38:1–11]; Ps. 33:7; 104:9; Prov. 8:29; Jer. 5:22
11 [1]*amazed*
12 [a]Ex. 14:21; Job 9:13; Is. 51:15; [Jer. 31:35] [1]Heb. *rahab*
13 [a][Job 9:8]; Ps. 33:6 [b]Is. 27:1

CHAPTER 27

2 [a]Job 34:5
5 [a]Job 2:9; 13:15
6 [a]Job 2:3; 33:9 [b]Acts 24:16 [1]*reprove*
8 [a]Matt. 16:26; Luke 12:20
9 [a]Job 35:12, 13; Ps. 18:41; Prov. 1:28; 28:9; [Is. 1:15]; Jer. 14:12; Ezek. 8:18; [Mic. 3:4; John 9:31; James 4:3]
10 [a]Job 22:26, 27; [Ps. 37:4; Is. 58:14]
11 [1]Or *by*
13 [a]Job 20:29

13 [a]By His Spirit He adorned the heavens;
His hand pierced [b]the fleeing serpent.
14 Indeed these *are* the mere edges of His ways,
And how small a whisper we hear of Him!
But the thunder of His power who can understand?"

Job Maintains His Integrity

27 Moreover Job continued his discourse, and said:
2 "*As* God lives, [a]*who* has taken away my justice,
And the Almighty, *who* has made my soul bitter,
3 As long as my breath *is* in me,
And the breath of God in my nostrils,
4 My lips will not speak wickedness,
Nor my tongue utter deceit.
5 Far be it from me
That I should say you are right;
Till I die [a]I will not put away my integrity from me.
6 My righteousness I [a]hold fast, and will not let it go;
[b]My heart shall not [1]reproach *me* as long as I live.

7 "May my enemy be like the wicked,
And he who rises up against me like the unrighteous.
8 [a]For what is the hope of the hypocrite,
Though he may gain *much,*
If God takes away his life?
9 [a]Will God hear his cry
When trouble comes upon him?
10 [a]Will he delight himself in the Almighty?
Will he always call on God?

11 "I will teach you [1]about the hand of God;
What *is* with the Almighty I will not conceal.
12 Surely all of you have seen *it;*
Why then do you behave with complete nonsense?

13 "This[a] is the portion of a wicked man with God,

25:4 See section 3 of Truth-In-Action at the end of Job.
26:1–14 Job turns to reflect on God's great power. He is exasperated with his counselors.
26:6 Destruction can also be translated "Abaddon," a metaphoric name for the grave (Ps. 88:11).
27:1–23 Job continues with a statement of his innocence and his belief that the ungodly eventually will be punished, for God is just and merciful.

And the heritage of oppressors,
received from the Almighty:
14 [a]If his children are multiplied, *it is* for the sword;
And his offspring shall not be
*satisfied with bread.
15 Those who survive him shall be
buried in death,
And [a]their[1] widows shall not
weep,
16 Though he heaps up silver like
dust,
And piles up clothing like clay—
17 He may pile *it* up, but [a]the just
will wear *it*,
And the innocent will divide the
silver.
18 He builds his house like a
[1]moth,
[a]Like a [2]booth *which* a watchman
makes.
19 The rich man will lie down,
[1]But not be gathered *up;*
He opens his eyes,
And he *is* [a]no more.
20 [a]Terrors overtake him like a flood;
A tempest steals him away in the
night.
21 The east wind carries him away,
and he is gone;
It sweeps him out of his place.
22 It hurls against him and does not
[a]spare;
He flees desperately from its
[1]power.
23 *Men* shall clap their hands at him,
And shall hiss him out of his
place.

Job's Discourse on Wisdom

28 "Surely there is a mine for
silver,
And a place *where* gold is refined.
2 Iron is taken from the [1]earth,
And copper *is* smelted *from* ore.
3 *Man* puts an end to darkness,
And searches every recess
For ore in the darkness and the
shadow of death.
4 He breaks open a shaft away
from people;
In places forgotten by feet
They hang far away from men;
They swing to and fro.
5 *As for* the earth, from it comes
bread,
But underneath it is turned up as
by fire;
6 Its stones *are* the source of
sapphires,
And it contains gold dust.
7 *That* path no bird knows,
Nor has the falcon's eye seen it.
8 The [1]proud lions have not
trodden it,
Nor has the fierce lion passed
over it.
9 He puts his hand on the flint;
He overturns the mountains
[1]at the roots.
10 He cuts out channels in the rocks,
And his eye sees every precious
thing.
11 He dams up the streams from
trickling;
What is hidden he brings forth to
light.

12 "But[a] where can wisdom be found?
And where *is* the place of
understanding?
13 Man does not know its [a]value,
Nor is it found in the land of the
living.
14 [a]The deep says, '*It is* not in me';
And the sea says, '*It is* not with
me.'
15 It [a]cannot be purchased for gold,
Nor can silver be weighed *for* its
price.
16 It cannot be valued in the gold of
Ophir,
In precious onyx or sapphire.
17 Neither [a]gold nor crystal can
equal it,
Nor can it be exchanged for
[1]jewelry of fine gold.
18 No mention shall be made of
[1]coral or quartz,
For the price of wisdom *is* above
[a]rubies.
19 The topaz of Ethiopia cannot
equal it,
Nor can it be valued in pure
[a]gold.

20 "From[a] where then does wisdom
come?
And where *is* the place of
understanding?
21 It is hidden from the eyes of all
living,
And concealed from the birds of
the [1]air.
22 [a]Destruction[1] and Death say,
'We have heard a report about it
with our ears.'

14 [a]Deut. 28:41; Esth. 9:10; Hos. 9:13 *See WW at Amos 4:8. **15** [a]Ps. 78:64 [1]Lit. *his* **17** [a]Prov. 28:8; [Eccl. 2:26] **18** [a]Is. 1:8; Lam. 2:6 [1]So with MT, Vg.; LXX, Syr. *spider* (cf. 8:14); Tg. *decay* [2]Temporary shelter **19** [a]Job 7:8, 21; 20:7 [1]So with MT, Tg.; LXX, Syr. *But shall not add* (i.e., do it again); Vg. *But take away nothing* **20** [a]Job 18:11 **22** [a]Jer. 13:14; Ezek. 5:11; 24:14 [1]Lit. *hand*

CHAPTER 28

2 [1]Lit. *dust* **8** [1]Lit. *sons of pride,* figurative of the great lions **9** [1]At the base **12** [a]Eccl. 7:24 **13** [a]Prov. 3:15 **14** [a]Job 28:22 **15** [a]Prov. 3:13–15; 8:10, 11, 19 **17** [a]Prov. 8:10; 16:16 [1]*vessels* **18** [a]Prov. 3:15; 8:11 [1]Heb. *ramoth* **19** [a]Prov. 8:19 **20** [a]Job 28:12; [Ps. 111:10; Prov. 1:7; 9:10] **21** [1]*heaven* **22** [a]Job 28:14 [1]Heb. *Abaddon*

28:1–28 In this discourse on wisdom, Job affirms that only true wisdom brings well-being. This wisdom lies in God who alone can resolve the unanswerable questions of life. Man's solution is to find peace through submission to divine authority. This hymn is a bridge to the next speeches and reiterates to Job's friends the fact that he does understand the ways of God and His wisdom.

28:16 The location of **Ophir** is unknown.

23 God understands its way,
And He knows its place.
24 For He looks to the ends of the earth,
And [a]sees under the whole heavens,
25 [a]To establish a weight for the wind,
And apportion the waters by measure.
26 When He [a]made a law for the rain,
And a path for the thunderbolt,
27 Then He saw [1]*wisdom* and declared it;
He prepared it, indeed, He searched it out.
28 And to man He said,
'Behold, [a]the fear of the Lord, that *is* wisdom,
And to depart from evil *is* understanding.' "

Job's Summary Defense

29 Job further continued his discourse, and said:

2 "Oh, that I were as *in* months [a]past,
As *in* the days *when* God [b]watched* over me;
3 [a]When His lamp shone upon my head,
And when by His light I walked *through* darkness;
4 Just as I was in the days of my prime,
When [a]the friendly counsel of God *was* over my tent;
5 When the Almighty *was* yet with me,
When my children *were* around me;
6 When [a]my steps were bathed with [1]cream,
And [b]the rock poured out rivers of oil for me!

7 "When I went out to the gate by the city,
When I took my seat in the open square,
8 The young men saw me and hid,
And the aged arose *and* stood;
9 The princes refrained from talking,
And [a]put *their* hand on their mouth;
10 The voice of nobles was hushed,
And their [a]tongue stuck to the roof of their mouth.
11 When the ear heard, then it *blessed me,
And when the eye saw, then it approved me;
12 Because [a]I delivered the poor who cried out,
The fatherless and *the one who* had no helper.
13 The blessing of a perishing *man* came upon me,
And I caused the widow's heart to sing for joy.
14 [a]I put on righteousness, and it clothed me;
My justice *was* like a robe and a turban.
15 I *was* [a]eyes to the blind,
And I *was* feet to the lame.
16 I *was* a father to the poor,
And [a]I searched out the case *that* I did not know.
17 I broke [a]the fangs of the wicked,
And plucked the victim from his teeth.

18 "Then I said, [a]'I shall die in my nest,
And multiply *my* days as the sand.
19 [a]My root *is* spread out [b]to the waters,
And the dew lies all night on my branch.
20 My glory *is* fresh within me,
And my [a]bow is renewed in my hand.'

21 "*Men* listened to me and *waited,
And kept silence for my counsel.
22 After my words they did not speak again,
And my speech *settled on them *as dew.*
23 They waited for me *as* for the rain,

24 [a][Ps. 11:4; 33:13, 14; 66:7; Prov. 15:3]
25 [a]Ps. 135:7
26 [a]Job 37:3; 38:25
27 [1]Lit. *it*
28 [a][Deut. 4:6; Ps. 111:10; Prov. 1:7; 9:10; Eccl. 12:13]

CHAPTER 29

2 [a]Job 1:1–5 [b]Job 1:10 *See WW at Job 10:12.
3 [a]Job 18:6
4 [a]Job 15:8; [Ps. 25:14; Prov. 3:32]
6 [a]Gen. 49:11; Deut. 32:14; Job 20:17 [b]Deut. 32:13; Ps. 81:16 [1]So with ancient vss. and a few Heb. mss. (cf. Job 20:17); MT *wrath*
9 [a]Job 21:5
10 [a]Ps. 137:6
11 *See WW at Prov. 31:28.
12 [a]Job 31:16–23; [Ps. 72:12; Prov. 21:13; 24:11]
14 [a]Deut. 24:13; Job 27:5, 6; Ps. 132:9; [Is. 59:17; 61:10; Eph. 6:14]
15 [a]Num. 10:31
16 [a]Prov. 29:7
17 [a]Ps. 58:6; Prov. 30:14
18 [a]Ps. 30:6
19 [a]Job 18:16 [b]Ps. 1:3; [Jer. 17:7, 8]
20 [a]Gen. 49:24; Ps. 18:34
21 *See WW at Mic. 7:7.
22 *See WW at Ezek. 21:2.

29:1—31:40 As he closes his defense, Job again states his argument that his suffering is not due to his sin but has some deeper reason, which only God knows. Job reviews his former prosperity (29:1–10); he states that this prosperity was a direct result of his life-style of piety and benevolence (29:11–17); he speaks of his former expectation that this prosperity would continue until his death (29:18–25). Job directs attention to the disdain he now suffers from men in contrast to the high honor he received formerly (30:1–15). He recognizes his present miserable state and considers all his hopes for the future to be lost.

Continuing his vow of innocence, Job states that He has not given himself over to lust (31:1–4) and that he has been upright in all his doings, acting in justice and kindness toward all men (31:5–23). Job closes his discourse by again saying that he is guilty of no hypocrisy, either outwardly or secretly in his heart (31:24–40). This is his firmest vow of innocence. Now with disciplined thinking, he is seeking God for answers.

And they opened their mouth
wide *as* for [a]the spring rain.
24 *If* I mocked at them, they did not
believe *it*,
And the light of my countenance
they did not cast down.
25 I chose the way for them, and sat
as chief;
So I dwelt as a king in the army,
As one *who* comforts mourners.

30 "But now they mock at me, *men*
[1]younger than I,
Whose fathers I disdained to put
with the dogs of my flock.
2 Indeed, what *profit* is the strength
of their hands to me?
Their vigor has perished.
3 *They are* gaunt from want and
famine,
Fleeing late to the wilderness,
desolate and waste,
4 Who pluck [1]mallow by the
bushes,
And broom tree roots *for* their
food.
5 They were driven out from among
men,
They shouted at them as *at* a
thief.
6 *They had* to live in the clefts of
the [1]valleys,
In [2]caves of the earth and the
rocks.
7 Among the bushes they brayed,
Under the nettles they nestled.
8 *They were* sons of fools,
Yes, sons of vile men;
They were scourged from the
land.

9 "And[a] now I am their taunting
song;
Yes, I am their byword.
10 They abhor me, they keep far
from me;
They do not hesitate [a]to spit in
my face.
11 Because [a]He has loosed [1]my
bowstring and afflicted me,
They have cast off restraint
before me.
12 At *my* right *hand* the rabble
arises;
They push away my feet,
And [a]they raise against me their
ways of destruction.
13 They break up my path,
They promote my calamity;
They have no helper.
14 They come as broad breakers;
Under the ruinous storm they
*roll along.
15 Terrors are turned upon me;
They pursue my honor as the
wind,
And my prosperity has passed
like a cloud.

16 "And[a] now my *soul is [b]poured out
because of my *plight;*
The days of affliction take hold
of me.
17 My bones are pierced in me at
night,
And my gnawing pains take no
rest.
18 By great force my garment is
disfigured;
It binds me about as the collar of
my coat.
19 He has cast me into the mire,
And I have become like dust and
ashes.

20 "I [a]cry out to You, but You do not
answer me;
I stand up, and You regard me.
21 *But* You have become cruel to
me;
With the strength of Your hand
You [a]oppose me.
22 You lift me up to the wind and
cause me to ride *on it;*
You spoil my success.
23 For I know *that* You will bring
me *to* death,
And *to* the house [a]appointed for
all living.

24 "Surely He would not stretch out
His hand against a heap of
ruins,
If they cry out when He destroys
it.
25 [a]Have I not wept for him who was
in trouble?
Has *not* my soul grieved for the
poor?
26 [a]But when I looked for good, evil
came *to me;*
And when I waited for light, then
came darkness.
27 [1]My heart is in turmoil and cannot
rest;
Days of affliction confront me.
28 [a]I go about mourning, but not in
the sun;
I stand up in the assembly *and* cry
out for help.
29 [a]I am a brother of jackals,
And a companion of ostriches.
30 [a]My skin grows black and falls
from me;
[b]My bones burn with fever.
31 My harp is *turned* to mourning,
And my flute to the voice of those
who weep.

23 [a][Zech. 10:1]

CHAPTER 30

1 [1]Lit. *of fewer days*
4 [1]A plant of the salty marshes
6 [1]*wadis* [2]Lit. *holes*
9 [a]Job 17:6; Ps. 69:12; Lam. 3:14, 63
10 [a]Num. 12:14; Deut. 25:9; Job 17:6; Is. 50:6; Matt. 26:67; 27:30
11 [a]Job 12:18 [1]So with MT, Syr., Tg.; LXX, Vg. *His*
12 [a]Job 19:12
14 *See WW at Prov. 16:3.
16 [a]Ps. 42:4 [b]Ps. 22:14; Is. 53:12 *See WW at Prov. 10:3.
20 [a]Job 19:7
21 [a]Job 10:3; 16:9, 14; 19:6, 22
23 [a][Heb. 9:27]
25 [a]Ps. 35:13, 14; Rom. 12:15
26 [a]Job 3:25, 26; Jer. 8:15
27 [1]*I seethe inside*
28 [a]Job 30:31; Ps. 38:6; 42:9; 43:2
29 [a]Ps. 44:19; 102:6; Mic. 1:8
30 [a]Ps. 119:83; Lam. 4:8; 5:10 [b]Ps. 102:3

6 31 "I have made a covenant with my eyes;
Why then should I [1]look upon a [a]young woman?
2 For what *is* the [a]allotment of God from above,
And the inheritance of the Almighty from on high?
3 *Is* it not destruction for the wicked,
And disaster for the workers of *iniquity?
4 [a]Does He not see my ways,
And count all my steps?

5 "If I have walked with falsehood,
Or if my foot has hastened to deceit,
6 [1]Let me be weighed on honest scales,
That God may know my [a]integrity.
7 If my step has turned from the way,
Or [a]my heart walked after my eyes,
Or if any spot adheres to my hands,
8 *Then* [a]let me sow, and another eat;
Yes, let my harvest be [1]rooted out.

9 "If my heart has been enticed by a woman,
Or *if* I have lurked at my neighbor's door,
10 *Then* let my wife grind for [a]another,
And let others bow down over her.
11 For that *would be* wickedness;
Yes, [a]it *would be* iniquity *deserving of* judgment.
12 For that *would be* a fire *that* consumes to destruction,
And would root out all my increase.

13 "If I have [a]despised* the cause of my male or female servant
When they complained against me,
14 What then shall I do when [a]God rises up?
When He punishes, how shall I answer Him?
1 15 [a]Did not He who made me in the womb make them?
Did not the same One fashion us in the womb?

CHAPTER 31

1 [a][Matt. 5:28] [1]*look intently* or *gaze*
2 [a]Job 20:29
3 *See WW at Prov. 22:8.
4 [a][2 Chr. 16:9]; Job 24:23; 28:24; 34:21; 36:7; [Prov. 5:21; 15:3; Jer. 32:19]
6 [a]Job 23:10; 27:5, 6 [1]Lit. *Let Him weigh me*
7 [a]Num. 15:39; [Eccl. 11:9]; Ezek. 6:9; [Matt. 5:29]
8 [a]Lev. 26:16; Deut. 28:30, 38; Job 20:18; Mic. 6:15 [1]*uprooted*
10 [a]Deut. 28:30; 2 Sam. 12:11; Jer. 8:10
11 [a]Gen. 38:24; [Lev. 20:10; Deut. 22:22]; Job 31:28
13 [a][Deut. 24:14, 15] *See WW at Amos 2:4.
14 [a][Ps. 44:21]
15 [a]Job 34:19; Prov. 14:31; 22:2; [Mal. 2:10]
16 [a]Job 29:12
18 [1]Lit. *her*
20 [a][Deut. 24:13] [1]Lit. *loins*
21 [a]Job 22:9
23 [a]Is. 13:6
24 [a][Matt. 6:19, 20; Mark 10:23–25]
25 [a]Job 1:3, 10; Ps. 62:10
26 [a][Deut. 4:19; 17:3]; Ezek. 8:16 [1]Lit. *light*
29 [a][Prov. 17:5; 24:17]; Obad. 12
30 [a][Matt. 5:44] [1]Or *life*

16 "If I have kept the poor from *their* desire,
Or caused the eyes of the widow to [a]fail,
17 Or eaten my morsel by myself,
So that the fatherless could not eat of it
18 (But from my youth I reared him as a father,
And from my mother's womb I guided [1]*the widow*);
19 If I have seen anyone perish for lack of clothing,
Or any poor *man* without covering;
20 If his [1]heart has not [a]blessed me,
And *if* he was *not* warmed with the fleece of my sheep;
21 If I have raised my hand [a]against the fatherless,
When I saw I had help in the gate;
22 *Then* let my arm fall from my shoulder,
Let my arm be torn from the socket.
23 For [a]destruction *from* God *is* a terror to me,
And because of His magnificence I cannot endure.

24 "If[a] I have made gold my hope,
Or said to fine gold, '*You are* my confidence';
25 [a]If I have rejoiced because my wealth *was* great,
And because my hand had gained much;
26 [a]If I have observed the [1]sun when it shines,
Or the moon moving *in* brightness,
27 So that my heart has been secretly enticed,
And my mouth has kissed my hand;
28 This also *would be* an iniquity *deserving of* judgment,
For I would have denied God *who is* above.

29 "If[a] I have rejoiced at the destruction of him who hated me,
Or lifted myself up when evil found him
30 [a](Indeed I have not allowed my mouth to sin
By asking for a curse on his [1]soul);
31 If the men of my tent have not said,

31:1–40 See section 6 of Truth-In-Action at the end of Job. **31:15** See section 1 of Truth-In-Action at the end of Job.

'Who is there that has not been
satisfied with his meat?'
32 [a](*But* no sojourner had to lodge in
the street,
For I have opened my doors to the
[1]traveler);
33 If I have covered my
transgressions [a]as[1] Adam,
By hiding my iniquity in my
bosom,
34 Because I feared the great
[a]multitude,
And dreaded the contempt of
families,
So that I kept silence
And did not go out of the door—
35 [a]Oh, that I had one to hear me!
Here is my mark.
Oh, [b]*that* the Almighty would
answer me,
That my [1]Prosecutor had written
a book!
36 Surely I would carry it on my
shoulder,
And bind it on me *like* a crown;
37 I would declare to Him the
number of my steps;
Like a prince I would approach
Him.

38 "If my land cries out against me,
And its furrows weep together;
39 If [a]I have eaten its [1]fruit without
money,
Or [b]caused its owners to lose
their lives;
40 *Then* let [a]thistles grow instead of
wheat,
And weeds instead of barley."

The words of Job are ended.

Elihu Contradicts Job's Friends

32 So these three men ceased answering Job, because he *was*
[a]righteous in his own eyes.
2 Then the wrath of Elihu, the son of
Barachel the [a]Buzite, of the family of
Ram, was aroused against Job; his
wrath was aroused because he [b]justified himself rather than God.
3 Also against his three friends his
wrath was aroused, because they had
found no answer, and *yet* had condemned Job.
4 Now because they *were* years older
than he, Elihu had waited [1]to speak to
Job.
5 When Elihu saw that *there was* no
answer in the mouth of these three
men, his wrath was aroused.
6 So Elihu, the son of Barachel the
Buzite, answered and said:

"I *am* [a]young in years, and you *are*
very old;
Therefore I was afraid,
And dared not declare my
opinion to you.
7 I said, [1]'Age should speak,
And multitude of years should
teach wisdom.'
8 But *there is* a spirit in man,
And [a]the breath of the Almighty
gives him understanding.
9 [a]Great[1] men are not *always* wise,
Nor do the aged *always*
understand justice.

10 "Therefore I say, 'Listen to me,
I also will declare my opinion.'
11 Indeed I waited for your words,
I listened to your reasonings,
while you searched out what to
say.
12 I paid close attention to you;
And surely not one of you
convinced Job,
Or answered his words—
13 [a]Lest you say,
'We have found wisdom';
God will vanquish him, not man.
14 Now he has not [1]directed *his*
words against me;
So I will not answer him with
your words.

15 "They are dismayed and answer
no more;
Words escape them.
16 And I have waited, because they
did not speak,
Because they stood still *and*
answered no more.
17 I also will answer my part,
I too will declare my opinion.
18 For I am full of words;
The spirit within me compels me.
19 Indeed my [1]belly *is* like wine *that*
has no [2]vent;
It is ready to burst like new
wineskins.

32 [a]Gen. 19:2, 3 [1]So with LXX, Syr., Tg., Vg.; MT *road* **33** [a]Gen. 3:10; [Prov. 28:13] [1]Or *as men do* **34** [a]Ex. 23:2 **35** [a]Job 19:7; 30:20, 24, 28 [b]Job 13:22, 24; 33:10 [1]Lit. *Accuser* **39** [a]Job 24:6, 10–12; [James 5:4] [b]1 Kin. 21:19 [1]Lit. *strength* **40** [a]Gen. 3:18

CHAPTER 32

1 [a]Job 6:29; 31:6; 33:9 **2** [a]Gen. 22:21 [b]Job 27:5, 6 **4** [1]Vg. *till Job had spoken* **6** [a]Lev. 19:32 **7** [1]Lit. *Days, i.e., years* **8** [a]1 Kin. 3:12; 4:29; [Job 35:11; 38:36; Prov. 2:6; Eccl. 2:26; Dan. 1:17; 2:21; Matt. 11:25; James 1:5] **9** [a][1 Cor. 1:26] [1]Or *Men of many years* **13** [a][Jer. 9:23; 1 Cor. 1:29] **14** [1]*ordered* **19** [1]*bosom* [2]*opening*

32:1–22 Elihu, who up to this point has remained silent (possibly because he is younger than the three friends), addresses Job. He is from Buz, which makes him either an Aramean or an Edomite. Elihu is angry at the three men because they have not discovered the reason for Job's suffering, ***yet*** have **condemned Job;** and he is angry at Job because of his self-righteousness (**he justified himself rather than God**). He begins his first speech with a lengthy apology (vv. 6–22).

20 I will speak, that I may find relief;
I must open my lips and answer.
21 Let me not, I pray, show partiality
to anyone;
Nor let me flatter any man.
22 For I do not know how to flatter,
Else my Maker would soon take
me [a]away.

Elihu Contradicts Job

33 "But please, Job, hear my
speech,
And listen to all my words.
2 Now, I open my mouth;
My tongue speaks in my mouth.
3 My words *come* from my upright
heart;
My lips utter pure knowledge.
4 [a]The *Spirit of God has made me,
And the *breath of the Almighty
gives me life.
5 If you can answer me,
Set *your words* in order before
me;
Take your stand.
6 [a]Truly I *am* [1]as your spokesman
before God;
I also have been formed out of
clay.
7 [a]Surely no fear of me will terrify
you,
Nor will my hand be heavy on
you.

8 "Surely you have spoken [1]in my
hearing,
And I have heard the sound of
your words, *saying,*
9 'I[a] *am* pure, without
transgression;
I *am* innocent, and *there is* no
iniquity in me.
10 Yet He finds occasions against
me,
[a]He counts me as His enemy;
11 [a]He puts my feet in the stocks,
He watches all my paths.'

12 "Look, *in* this you are not
righteous.
I will answer you,
For God is greater than man.
13 Why do you [a]contend with Him?
For He does not give an
accounting of any of His words.
14 [a]For God may speak in one way,
or in another,

22 [a]Job 27:8

CHAPTER 33

4 [a][Gen. 2:7]; Job 32:8 *See WW at 2 Sam. 23:2. • See WW at Ps. 150:6.
6 [a]Job 4:19 [1]Lit. *as your mouth*
7 [a]Job 9:34
8 [1]Lit. *in my ears*
9 [a]Job 10:7
10 [a]Job 13:24; 16:9
11 [a]Job 13:27; 19:8
13 [a]Job 40:2; [Is. 45:9]
14 [a]Job 33:29; 40:5; Ps. 62:11
15 [a][Num. 12:6]
16 [a][Job 36:10, 15]
18 [1]Lit. *passing*
19 [a]Job 30:17
20 [a]Ps. 107:18 [b]Job 3:24; 6:7 [1]*desirable*
24 [1]*an atonement*
27 [a][2 Sam. 12:13; Prov. 28:13; Luke 15:21; 1 John 1:9] [b][Rom. 6:21]
28 [a]Is. 38:17 [1]Kt. *my* [2]Kt. *my*

Yet man does not perceive it.
15 [a]In a dream, in a vision of the
night,
When deep sleep falls upon men,
While slumbering on their beds,
16 [a]Then He opens the ears of men,
And seals their instruction.
17 In order to turn man *from his*
deed,
And conceal pride from man,
18 He keeps back his soul from the
Pit,
And his life from [1]perishing by
the sword.

19 "*Man* is also chastened with pain
on his [a]bed,
And with strong *pain* in many of
his bones,
20 [a]So that his life abhors [b]bread,
And his soul [1]succulent food.
21 His flesh wastes away from
sight,
And his bones stick out *which*
once were not seen.
22 Yes, his soul draws near the Pit,
And his life to the executioners.

23 "If there is a messenger for him,
A mediator, one among a
thousand,
To show man His uprightness,
24 Then He is gracious to him, and
says,
'Deliver him from going down to
the Pit;
I have found [1]a ransom';
25 His flesh shall be young like a
child's,
He shall return to the days of his
youth.
26 He shall pray to God, and He will
delight in him,
He shall see His face with joy,
For He restores to man His
righteousness.
27 Then he looks at men and
[a]says,
'I have sinned, and perverted *what*
was right,
And it [b]did not profit me.'
28 He will [a]redeem [1]his soul from
going down to the Pit,
And [2]his life shall see the light.

29 "Behold, God works all these
things,

33:1–33 Following further apology (vv. 1–7), Elihu argues that God has a higher purpose in Job's suffering (vv. 8–30). God's purpose is not to exact retribution from Job, but to discipline him to keep Job from wrongdoing, either real or potential. He invites Job to respond (vv. 31–33). In vv. 12, 13, Elihu makes the point that God is greater than we are, and no one has the right to require an explanation from Him for what occurs. Some things done by God remain incomprehensible to man. Yet, Elihu says, we can hear God speaking if only we will listen (vv. 14–16).

Twice, *in fact*, three *times* with a
man,
30 [a]To bring back his soul from the
Pit,
That he may be enlightened with
the light of life.

31 "Give ear, Job, listen to me;
Hold your peace, and I will speak.
32 If you have anything to say,
answer me;
Speak, for I desire to justify you.
33 If not, [a]listen to me;
[1]Hold your peace, and I will teach
you wisdom."

Elihu Proclaims God's Justice

34 Elihu further answered and
said:

2 "Hear my words, you wise *men;*
Give ear to me, you who have
knowledge.
3 [a]For the ear tests words
As the palate *tastes food.
4 Let us choose justice for
ourselves;
Let us know among ourselves
what *is* good.

5 "For Job has said, [a]'I am righteous,
But [b]God has taken away my
justice;
6 [a]Should I lie concerning my right?
My [1]wound *is* incurable, *though*
I am without transgression.'
7 What man *is* like Job,
[a]*Who* drinks [1]scorn like water,
8 Who goes in company with the
workers of iniquity,
And walks with wicked men?
9 For [a]he has said, 'It profits a man
nothing
That he should delight in God.'

1 **10** "Therefore listen to me, you
[1]men of understanding:
[a]Far be it from God *to do*
wickedness,
And *from* the Almighty to *commit*
iniquity.
11 [a]For He repays man *according to*
his work,
And makes man to find a reward
according to *his* way.
12 Surely God will never do
wickedly,
Nor will the Almighty [a]pervert
justice.

13 Who gave Him charge over the
earth?
Or who appointed *Him over* the
whole world?
14 If He should set His heart on it,
If He should [a]gather to Himself
His Spirit and His *breath,
15 [a]All flesh would perish together,
And man would return to dust.

16 "If *you have* understanding, hear
this;
Listen to the sound of my words:
17 [a]Should one who hates justice
govern?
Will you [b]condemn *Him who is*
most just?
18 [a]*Is it fitting* to say to a king, '*You*
are worthless,'
And to nobles, '*You are* wicked'?
19 Yet He [a]is not partial to princes,
Nor does He regard the rich more
than the poor;
For [b]they *are* all the work of His
hands.
20 In a moment they die, [a]in the
middle of the night;
The people are shaken and pass
away;
The mighty are taken away
without a hand.

21 "For[a] His eyes *are* on the ways of
man,
And He sees all his steps.
22 [a]There is no darkness nor shadow
of death
Where the workers of iniquity
may hide themselves.
23 For He need not further consider
a man,
That he should go before God in
judgment.
24 [a]He breaks in pieces mighty men
without inquiry,
And sets others in their place.
25 Therefore He knows their
works;
He overthrows *them* in the night,
And they are crushed.
26 He strikes them as wicked *men*
In the open sight of others,
27 Because they [a]turned back from
Him,
And [b]would not consider any of
His ways,
28 So that they [a]caused the cry of
the poor to come to Him;
For He [b]hears the cry of the
afflicted.

30 [a]Ps. 56:13 **33** [a]Ps. 34:11 [1]*Keep silent*

CHAPTER 34

3 [a]Job 6:30; 12:11 *See WW at Ps. 34:8. **5** [a]Job 13:18; 33:9 [b]Job 27:2 **6** [a]Job 6:4; 9:17 [1]Lit. *arrow* **7** [a]Job 15:16 [1]*derision* **9** [a]Mal. 3:14 **10** [a][Gen. 18:25; Deut. 32:4; 2 Chr. 19:7]; Job 8:3; 36:23; Ps. 92:15; Rom. 9:14 [1]*men of heart* **11** [a]Job 34:25; Ps. 62:12; [Prov. 24:12; Jer. 32:19]; Ezek. 33:20; [Matt. 16:27]; Rom. 2:6; [2 Cor. 5:10; Rev. 22:12] **12** [a]Job 8:3 **14** [a]Job 12:10; Ps. 104:29; [Eccl. 12:7] *See WW at Ps. 150:6. **15** [a][Gen. 3:19]; Job 10:9; [Eccl. 12:7] **17** [a]2 Sam. 23:3; Job 34:30 [b]Job 40:8 **18** [a]Ex. 22:28 **19** [a][Deut. 10:17; Acts 10:34; Rom. 2:11, 12] [b]Job 31:15 **20** [a]Ex. 12:29; Job 34:25; 36:20 **21** [a][2 Chr. 16:9]; Job 31:4; Ps. 34:15; [Prov. 5:21; 15:3; Jer. 16:17; 32:19] **22** [a][Ps. 139:11, 12; Amos 9:2, 3] **24** [a]Job 12:19; [Dan. 2:21] **27** [a]1 Sam. 15:11 [b]Ps. 28:5; Is. 5:12 **28** [a]Job 35:9; James 5:4 [b][Ex. 22:23]; Job 22:27

34:1–37 Elihu continues. He is not a friend seeking to comfort, but he is a young, developing sage attempting to offer new insight while the others are waiting to hear from God. Here he defends God's righteous dealings and begs Job not to harden his heart to God's educational discipline.
34:10–12 See section 1 of Truth-In-Action at the end of Job.

29 When He gives quietness, who
then can make trouble?
And when He hides *His* face, who
then can see Him,
Whether *it is* against a nation or
a man alone?—
30 That the hypocrite should not
*reign,
Lest the people be ensnared.

31 "For has *anyone* said to God,
'I have borne *chastening;*
I will offend no more;
32 Teach me *what* I do not see;
If I have done iniquity, I will do
no more'?
33 Should He repay *it* according to
your *terms,*
Just because you disavow it?
You must choose, and not I;
Therefore speak what you know.

34 "Men of understanding say to
me,
Wise men who listen to me:
35 'Job[a] speaks without knowledge,
His words *are* without wisdom.'
36 Oh, that Job were tried to the
utmost,
Because *his* answers *are like*
those of wicked men!
37 For he adds [a]rebellion to his sin;
He claps *his hands* among us,
And multiplies his words against
God."

Elihu Condemns Self-Righteousness

35 Moreover Elihu answered and said:

2 "Do you think this is right?
Do you say,
'My righteousness is more than
God's'?
3 For [a]you say,
'What advantage will it be to You?
What profit shall I have, more
than *if* I had sinned?'

4 "I will answer you,
And [a]your companions with you.
5 [a]Look to the heavens and see;
And behold the clouds—
They are higher than you.
6 If you sin, what do you
accomplish [a]against Him?

30 *See WW at 2 Sam. 8:15. **35** [a]Job 35:16; 38:2 **37** [a]Job 7:11; 10:1

CHAPTER 35

3 [a]Job 21:15; 34:9 **4** [a]Job 34:8 **5** [a]Gen. 15:5; [Job 22:12; Ps. 8:3] **6** [a]Job 7:20; [Prov. 8:36; Jer. 7:19] *See WW at Ezek. 18:31.

7 [a]Job 22:2; Ps. 16:2; Prov. 9:12; [Luke 17:10]; Rom. 11:35 **9** [a]Job 34:28 **10** [a]Is. 51:13 [b]Job 8:21; Ps. 42:8; 77:6; 149:5; Acts 16:25 **11** [a]Job 36:22; Ps. 94:12; [Is. 48:17]; Jer. 32:33; [1 Cor. 2:13] **12** [a]Prov. 1:28 **13** [a]Job 27:9; [Prov. 15:29; Is. 1:15]; Jer. 11:11; [Mic. 3:4] **14** [a]Job 9:11 [b][Ps. 37:5, 6] **15** [a]Ps. 89:32 **16** [a]Job 34:35; 38:2

Or, *if* your *transgressions are
multiplied, what do you do to
Him?
7 [a]If you are righteous, what do you
give Him?
Or what does He receive from
your hand?
8 Your wickedness affects a man
such as you,
And your righteousness a son of
man.

9 "Because[a] of the multitude of
oppressions they cry out;
They cry out for help because of
the arm of the mighty.
10 But no one says, [a]'Where *is* God
my Maker,
[b]Who gives songs in the night,
11 Who [a]teaches us more than the
beasts of the earth,
And makes us wiser than the
birds of heaven?'
12 [a]There they cry out, but He does
not answer,
Because of the pride of evil
men.
13 [a]Surely God will not listen to
empty *talk,*
Nor will the Almighty regard it.
14 [a]Although you say you do not see
Him,
Yet justice *is* before Him, and
[b]you must wait for Him.
15 And now, because He has not
[a]punished in His anger,
Nor taken much notice of folly,
16 [a]Therefore Job opens his mouth in
vain;
He multiplies words without
knowledge."

Elihu Proclaims God's Goodness

36 Elihu also proceeded and said:

2 "Bear with me a little, and I will
show you
That *there are* yet words to speak
on God's behalf.
3 I will fetch my knowledge from
afar;
I will ascribe righteousness to my
Maker.
4 For truly my words *are* not false;
One who is perfect in knowledge
is with you.

35:1–16 Here Elihu openly condemns Job for his folly in maintaining innocence and charging God. He views Job as quite arrogant.

36:1—37:24 In his concluding speech, Elihu emphasizes God's awesome power in order to establish that no one is ever justified in disputing Him. He appeals to nature as proof of God's power and wisdom. His summons to Job is, **Fear Him** (37:24). His main contribution lies in turning the focus toward educational, rather than retributive, suffering.

5 "Behold, God *is* mighty, but despises *no one;*
[a]*He is* mighty in strength [1]of understanding.
6 He does not preserve the life of the wicked,
But gives justice to the [a]oppressed.
7 [a]He does not withdraw His eyes from the righteous;
But [b]*they are* on the throne with kings,
For He has seated them forever,
And they are exalted.
[4] 8 And [a]if *they are* bound in [1]fetters,
Held in the cords of affliction,
9 Then He tells them their work and their transgressions—
That they have acted [1]defiantly.
10 [a]He also opens their ear to [1]instruction,
And commands that they turn from iniquity.
11 If they obey and serve *Him,*
They shall [a]spend their days in prosperity,
And their years in pleasures.
12 But if they do not obey,
They shall perish by the sword,
And they shall die [1]without [a]knowledge.

13 "But the hypocrites in heart [a]store up wrath;
They do not cry for help when He binds them.
14 [a]They[1] die in youth,
And their life *ends* among the [2]perverted persons.
15 He delivers the poor in their affliction,
And opens their ears in oppression.

16 "Indeed He would have brought you out of dire distress,
[a]*Into* a broad place where *there is* no restraint;
And [b]what is set on your table *would be* full of [c]richness.
17 But you are filled with the judgment due the [a]wicked;
Judgment and justice take hold *of you.*
18 Because *there is* wrath, *beware* lest He take you away with *one* blow;
For [a]a large ransom would not help you avoid *it.*
19 [a]Will your riches,
Or all the mighty forces,
Keep you from distress?
20 Do not desire the night,
When people are cut off in their place.
21 Take heed, [a]do not turn to iniquity,
For [b]you have chosen this rather than affliction.

22 "Behold, God is exalted by His power;
Who teaches like Him?
23 [a]Who has assigned Him His way,
Or who has said, 'You have done [b]wrong'?

Elihu Proclaims God's Majesty

24 "Remember to [a]magnify His work,
Of which men have sung.
25 Everyone has seen it;
Man looks on *it* from afar.

26 "Behold, God *is* great, and we [a]do not know *Him;*
[b]Nor can the number of His years *be* discovered.
27 For He [a]draws up drops of water,
Which distill as rain from the mist,
28 [a]Which the clouds drop down
And pour abundantly on man.
29 Indeed, can *anyone* understand the spreading of clouds,
The thunder from His canopy?
30 Look, He [a]scatters His light upon it,
And covers the depths of the sea.
31 For [a]by these He *judges the peoples;
He [b]gives food in abundance.
32 [a]He covers *His* hands with lightning,
And commands it to [1]strike.
33 [a]His thunder declares it,
The cattle also, concerning [1]the rising *storm.*

37 "At this also my heart trembles,
And leaps from its place.
2 Hear attentively the thunder of His voice,
And the rumbling *that* comes from His mouth.
3 He *sends it forth under the whole heaven,
His [1]lightning to the ends of the earth.
4 After it [a]a voice roars;

CHAPTER 36

5 [a]Job 12:13, 16; 37:23; [Ps. 99:2–5] [1]*of heart*
6 [a]Job 5:15
7 [a][Ps. 33:18; 34:15] [b]Job 5:11; Ps. 113:8
8 [a]Ps. 107:10 [1]*chains*
9 [1]*proudly*
10 [a]Job 33:16; 36:15 [1]*discipline*
11 [a]Job 21:13; [Is. 1:19, 20]
12 [a]Job 4:21 [1]MT *as one without knowledge*
13 [a][Rom. 2:5]
14 [a]Ps. 55:23 [1]Lit. *Their soul dies* [2]Heb. *qedeshim,* those practicing sodomy or prostitution in religious rituals
16 [a]Ps. 18:19; 31:8; 118:5 [b]Ps. 23:5 [c]Ps. 36:8
17 [a]Job 22:5, 10, 11
18 [a]Ps. 49:7
19 [a][Prov. 11:4]
21 [a]Job 36:10; [Ps. 31:6; 66:18] [b]Job 36:8, 15; [Heb. 11:25]
23 [a]Job 34:13; [Is. 40:13, 14] [b][Deut. 32:4]; Job 8:3
24 [a][Ps. 92:5; Rev. 15:3]
26 [a]Job 11:7–9; 37:23; [1 Cor. 13:12] [b]Job 10:5; [Ps. 90:2; 102:24, 27]; Heb. 1:12
27 [a]Job 5:10; 37:6, 11; 38:28; Ps. 147:8
28 [a][Prov. 3:20]
30 [a]Job 37:3
31 [a][Acts 14:17] [b]Gen. 9:3; Ps. 104:14, 15 *See WW at Deut. 32:36.
32 [a]Ps. 147:8 [1]*strike the mark*
33 [a]1 Kin. 18:41; Job 37:2 [1]Lit. *what is rising*

CHAPTER 37

3 [1]Or *light* *See WW at Prov. 3:6.
4 [a]Ps. 29:3

36:8–12 See section 4 of Truth-In-Action at the end of Job.

He thunders with His majestic voice,
And He does not restrain them when His voice is heard.
5 God thunders marvelously with His voice;
[a]He does great things which we cannot comprehend.
6 For [a]He says to the snow, 'Fall *on* the earth';
Likewise to the [1]gentle rain and the heavy rain of His strength.
7 He seals the hand of every man,
[a]That [b]all men may know His work.
8 The beasts [a]go into dens,
And remain in their lairs.
9 From the chamber *of the south* comes the whirlwind,
And cold from the scattering winds *of the north.*
10 [a]By the *breath of God ice is given,
And the broad waters are frozen.
11 Also with moisture He saturates the thick clouds;
He scatters His [1]bright clouds.
12 And they swirl about, being turned by His guidance,
That they may [a]do whatever He commands them
On the face of [1]the whole earth.
13 [a]He causes it to come,
Whether for [1]correction,
Or [b]for His land,
Or [c]for mercy.

14 "Listen to this, O Job;
Stand still and [a]consider the wondrous works of God.
15 Do you know when God [1]dispatches them,
And causes the light of His cloud to shine?
16 [a]Do you know how the clouds are balanced,
Those wondrous works of [b]Him who is perfect in knowledge?
17 Why *are* your garments hot,
When He quiets the earth by the south *wind?*
18 With Him, have you [a]spread out the [b]skies,
Strong as a cast metal mirror?

5 [a]Job 5:9; 9:10; 36:26; Rev. 15:3
6 [a]Ps. 147:16, 17 [1]Lit. *shower of rain*
7 [a]Ps. 109:27 [b]Ps. 19:3, 4
8 [a]Job 38:40; Ps. 104:21, 22
10 [a]Job 38:29, 30; Ps. 147:17, 18 *See WW at Ps. 150:6.
11 [1]*clouds of light*
12 [a]Job 36:32; Ps. 148:8 [1]Lit. *the world of the earth*
13 [a]Ex. 9:18, 23; 1 Sam. 12:18, 19 [b]Job 38:26, 27 [c]1 Kin. 18:41–46 [1]Lit. *a rod*
14 [a]Ps. 111:2
15 [1]*places them*
16 [a]Job 36:29 [b]Job 36:4
18 [a]Gen. 1:6; [Is. 44:24] [b]Job 9:8; Ps. 104:2; [Is. 45:12; Jer. 10:12; Zech. 12:1]

23 [a][Job 11:7, 8; Rom. 11:33, 34; 1 Tim. 6:16] [b][Job 9:4; 36:5]
24 [a][Matt. 10:28] [b][Job 5:13; Matt. 11:25]; 1 Cor. 1:26

CHAPTER 38

1 [a]Ex. 19:16; Job 40:6
2 [a]Job 34:35; 42:3 [b]1 Tim. 1:7
3 [a]Job 40:7 [1]Lit. *gird up your loins like*
4 [a]Job 15:7; Ps. 104:5
5 [1]*measuring line*
7 [a]Job 1:6

19 "Teach us what we should say to Him,
For we can prepare nothing because of the darkness.
20 Should He be told that I *wish to* speak?
If a man were to speak, surely he would be swallowed up.
21 Even now *men* cannot look at the light *when it is* bright in the skies,
When the wind has passed and cleared them.
22 He comes from the north *as* golden *splendor;*
With God *is* awesome majesty.
23 *As for* the Almighty, [a]we cannot find Him;
[b]*He is* excellent in power,
In judgment and abundant justice;
He does not oppress.
24 Therefore men [a]fear Him;
He shows no partiality to any *who are* [b]wise of heart."

The LORD Reveals His Omnipotence to Job

38 Then the LORD answered Job [a]out of the whirlwind, and said: **1**

2 "Who[a] *is* this who darkens counsel
By [b]words without knowledge?
3 [a]Now [1]prepare yourself like a man;
I will question you, and you shall answer Me.

4 "Where[a] were you when I laid the foundations of the earth?
Tell *Me,* if you have understanding.
5 Who determined its measurements?
Surely you know!
Or who stretched the [1]line upon it?
6 To what were its foundations fastened?
Or who laid its cornerstone,
7 When the morning stars sang together,
And all [a]the sons of God shouted for joy?

38:1—42:6 The arguments of the four men are all silenced by the voice of God answering out of the whirlwind. God challenges Job by comparing His omnipotence with Job's impotence. He does this by describing the greatness of the Earth (38:1–18), the complexity of the heavens (38:19–38), and His awesome design of the creatures of the Earth (38:39—39:30). God then directly challenges Job to question Him (40:1, 2).

38:1—40:2 God is convincing Job that He created the Earth and rules it justly and compassionately. Though Lord of all, He cares for Job more than for animals.

38:1—39:30 See section 1 of Truth-In-Action at the end of Job.

8 "Or[a] *who* shut in the sea with doors,
When it burst forth *and* issued from the womb;
9 When I made the clouds its garment,
And thick darkness its swaddling band;
10 When [a]I fixed My limit for it,
And set bars and doors;
11 When I said,
'This far you may come, but no farther,
And here your proud waves [a]must stop!'

12 "Have you [a]commanded the morning since your days *began,*
And caused the dawn to know its place,
13 That it might take hold of the ends of the earth,
And [a]the wicked be shaken out of it?
14 It takes on form like clay *under* a seal,
And stands out like a garment.
15 From the wicked their [a]light is withheld,
And [b]the [1]upraised arm is broken.

16 "Have you [a]entered the springs of the sea?
Or have you walked in search of the depths?
17 Have [a]the gates of death been [1]revealed to you?
Or have you seen the doors of the shadow of death?
18 Have you comprehended the breadth of the earth?
Tell *Me,* if you know all this.

19 "Where *is* the way *to* the dwelling of light?
And darkness, where *is* its place,
20 That you may take it to its territory,
That you may know the paths *to* its home?
21 Do you know *it,* because you were born then,
Or *because* the number of your days *is* great?

22 "Have you entered [a]the treasury of snow,
Or have you seen the treasury of hail,
23 [a]Which I have reserved for the time of trouble,
For the day of battle and war?
24 By what way is light [1]diffused,
Or the east wind scattered over the earth?

25 "Who [a]has divided a channel for the overflowing *water,*
Or a path for the thunderbolt,
26 To cause it to rain on a land *where there is* no one,
A wilderness in which *there is* no man;
27 [a]To satisfy the desolate waste,
And cause to spring forth the growth of tender grass?
28 [a]Has the rain a father?
Or who has begotten the drops of dew?
29 From whose womb comes the ice?
And the [a]frost of heaven, who gives it birth?
30 The waters harden like stone,
And the surface of the deep is [a]frozen.[1]

31 "Can you bind the cluster of the [a]Pleiades,[1]
Or loose the belt of Orion?
32 Can you bring out [1]Mazzaroth in its season?
Or can you guide [2]the Great Bear with its cubs?
33 Do you know [a]the ordinances of the heavens?
Can you set their dominion over the earth?

34 "Can you lift up your voice to the clouds,
That an abundance of water may cover you?
35 Can you send out lightnings, that they may go,
And say to you, 'Here we *are!*'?
36 [a]Who has put wisdom in [1]the mind?
Or who has given understanding to the heart?
37 Who can number the clouds by wisdom?
Or who can pour out the bottles of heaven,
38 When the dust hardens in clumps,
And the clods cling together?

39 "Can[a] you hunt the prey for the lion,
Or satisfy the appetite of the young lions,
40 When they crouch in *their* dens,
Or lurk in their lairs to lie in wait?
41 [a]Who provides food for the raven,
When its young ones cry to God,
And wander about for lack of food?

8 [a]Gen. 1:9; Ps. 33:7; 104:9; Prov. 8:29; [Jer. 5:22]
10 [a]Job 26:10
11 [a][Ps. 89:9; 93:4]
12 [a][Ps. 74:16; 148:5]
13 [a]Job 34:25; Ps. 104:35
15 [a]Job 18:5; [Prov. 13:9] [b][Num. 15:30]; Ps. 10:15; 37:17 [1]Lit. *high*
16 [a][Ps. 77:19]; Prov. 8:24
17 [a]Ps. 9:13 [1]Lit. *opened*
22 [a]Ps. 135:7
23 [a]Ex. 9:18; Josh. 10:11; Is. 30:30; Ezek. 13:11, 13; Rev. 16:21
24 [1]Lit. *divided*
25 [a]Job 28:26
27 [a]Ps. 104:13, 14; 107:35
28 [a]Job 36:27, 28; [Ps. 147:8; Jer. 14:22]
29 [a][Job 37:10]; Ps. 147:16, 17
30 [a][Job 37:10] [1]Lit. *imprisoned*
31 [a]Job 9:9; Amos 5:8 [1]Or *the Seven Stars*
32 [1]Lit. *Constellations* [2]Or *Arcturus*
33 [a][Ps. 148:6]; Jer. 31:35, 36
36 [a][Job 9:4; 32:8; Ps. 51:6; Eccl. 2:26; James 1:5] [1]Lit. *the inward parts*
39 [a]Ps. 104:21
41 [a]Ps. 147:9; [Matt. 6:26; Luke 12:24]

39 "Do you know the time when the wild [a]mountain goats bear young?
Or can you mark when [b]the deer gives birth?
2 Can you number the months *that* they fulfill?
Or do you know the time when they bear young?
3 They bow down,
They bring forth their young,
They deliver their [1]offspring.
4 Their young ones are healthy,
They grow strong with grain;
They depart and do not return to them.

5 "Who set the wild donkey free?
Who loosed the bonds of the [1]onager,
6 [a]Whose home I have made the wilderness,
And the [1]barren land his dwelling?
7 He scorns the tumult of the city;
He does not heed the shouts of the driver.
8 The range of the mountains *is* his pasture,
And he searches after [a]every green thing.

9 "Will the [a]wild ox be willing to serve you?
Will he bed by your manger?
10 Can you bind the wild ox in the furrow with ropes?
Or will he plow the valleys behind you?
11 Will you trust him because his strength *is* great?
Or will you leave your labor to him?
12 Will you trust him to bring home your [1]grain,
And gather it to your threshing floor?

13 "The wings of the ostrich wave proudly,
But are her wings and pinions *like the* kindly stork's?
14 For she leaves her eggs on the ground,
And warms them in the dust;
15 She forgets that a foot may crush them,
Or that a wild beast may break them.
16 She [a]treats her young harshly, as though *they were* not hers;
Her labor is in vain, without [1]concern,
17 Because God deprived her of wisdom,
And did not [a]endow her with understanding.
18 When she lifts herself on high,
She scorns the horse and its rider.

19 "Have you given the horse strength?
Have you clothed his neck with [1]thunder?
20 Can you [1]frighten him like a locust?
His *majestic snorting strikes terror.
21 He paws in the valley, and rejoices in *his* strength;
[a]He gallops into the clash of arms.
22 He mocks at fear, and is not frightened;
Nor does he turn back from the sword.
23 The quiver rattles against him,
The glittering spear and javelin.
24 He devours the distance with fierceness and rage;
Nor does he come to a halt because the trumpet *has* sounded.
25 At *the blast of* the trumpet he says, 'Aha!'
He smells the battle from afar,
The thunder of captains and *shouting.

26 "Does the hawk fly by your wisdom,
And spread its wings toward the south?
27 Does the [a]eagle mount up at your command,
And [b]make its nest on high?
28 On the rock it dwells and resides,
On the crag of the rock and the stronghold.
29 From there it spies out the prey;
Its eyes observe from afar.
30 Its young ones suck up blood;
And [a]where the slain *are*, there it *is*."

40 Moreover the LORD [a]answered Job, and said:
2 "Shall [a]the one who contends with the Almighty correct *Him*?
He who [b]rebukes God, let him answer it."

CHAPTER 39
1 [a]Deut. 14:5; 1 Sam. 24:2; Ps. 104:18 [b]Ps. 29:9
3 [1]Lit. *pangs*
5 [1]A species of wild donkey
6 [a]Job 24:5; Jer. 2:24; Hos. 8:9 [1]Lit. *salt land*
8 [a]Gen. 1:29
9 [a]Num. 23:22; Deut. 33:17; Ps. 22:21; 29:6; 92:10; Is. 34:7
12 [1]Lit. *seed*
16 [a]Lam. 4:3 [1]Lit. *fear*
17 [a]Job 35:11
19 [1]Or *a mane*
20 [1]*make him spring* *See WW at 1 Chr. 29:11.
21 [a]Jer. 8:6
25 *See WW at Ezra 3:11.
27 [a]Prov. 30:18, 19 [b]Jer. 49:16; Obad. 4
30 [a]Matt. 24:28; Luke 17:37

CHAPTER 40
1 [a]Job 38:1
2 [a]Job 9:3; 10:2; 33:13 [b]Job 13:3; 23:4

Job's Response to God

3 Then Job answered the LORD and
said:

3 4 "Behold,[a] I am vile;
What shall I answer You?
[b]I lay my hand over my mouth.
5 Once I have spoken, but I will not answer;
Yes, twice, but I will proceed no further."

God's Challenge to Job

6 [a]Then the LORD answered Job out
of the whirlwind, and said:

7 "Now[a] [1]prepare yourself like a man;
[b]I will question you, and you shall answer Me:

8 "Would[a] you indeed [1]annul My judgment?
Would you condemn Me that you may be justified?
9 Have you an arm like God?
Or can you thunder with [a]a voice like His?
10 [a]Then adorn yourself *with* majesty and splendor,
And array yourself with *glory and beauty.
11 Disperse the rage of your wrath;
Look on everyone *who is* proud, and *humble him.
12 Look on everyone *who is* [a]proud, *and* bring him low;
Tread down the wicked in their place.
13 Hide them in the dust together,
Bind their faces in hidden *darkness.*
14 Then I will also confess to you
That your own right hand can save you.

15 "Look now at the [1]behemoth, which I made *along* with you;
He eats grass like an ox.
16 See now, his strength *is* in his hips,
And his power *is* in his stomach muscles.
17 He moves his tail like a cedar;
The sinews of his thighs are tightly knit.
18 His bones *are like* beams of bronze,
His ribs like bars of iron.
19 He *is* the first of the [a]ways of God;
Only He who made him can bring near His sword.
20 Surely the mountains [a]yield food for him,
And all the beasts of the field play there.
21 He lies under the lotus trees,
In a covert of reeds and marsh.
22 The lotus trees cover him *with* their shade;
The willows by the brook surround him.
23 Indeed the river may rage,
Yet he is not disturbed;
He is confident, though the Jordan gushes into his mouth,
24 *Though* he takes it in his eyes,
Or one pierces *his* nose with a snare.

41 "Can you draw out [a]Leviathan[1] with a hook,
Or *snare* his tongue with a line *which* you lower?
2 Can you [a]put a reed through his nose,
Or pierce his jaw with a [1]hook?
3 Will he make many supplications to you?
Will he speak softly to you?
4 Will he make a covenant with you?
Will you take him as a servant forever?
5 Will you play with him as *with* a bird,
Or will you leash him for your maidens?
6 Will *your* companions [1]make a banquet of him?
Will they apportion him among the merchants?
7 Can you fill his skin with harpoons,
Or his head with fishing spears?

4 [a]Ezra 9:6; Job 42:6 [b]Job 29:9; Ps. 39:9
6 [a]Job 38:1
7 [a]Job 38:3 [b]Job 42:4 [1]Lit. *gird up your loins*
8 [a]Job 16:11; 19:6; [Ps. 51:4; Rom. 3:4] [1]*nullify*
9 [a]Job 37:4; [Ps. 29:3, 4]
10 [a]Ps. 93:1; 104:1
*See WW at 1 Chr. 29:11.
11 *See WW at Jer. 13:18.
12 [a]1 Sam. 2:7; [Is. 2:12; 13:11]; Dan. 4:37
15 [1]A large animal, exact identity unknown
19 [a]Job 26:14
20 [a]Ps. 104:14

CHAPTER 41

1 [a]Ps. 74:14; 104:26; Is. 27:1 [1]A large sea creature, exact identity unknown
2 [a]2 Kin. 19:38; Is. 37:29 [1]*thorn*
6 [1]Or *bargain over him*

40:3–5 Job's response is not unlike that of Isaiah who, when confronted with the holiness of God, sees himself as totally sinful and unable to stand before God (Is. 6). When he comes face-to-face with God, Job also comes face-to-face with his own self-righteousness. Stripped of all he had and confronted by God's holiness, he sees himself as proud and expresses his shame.

40:4, 5 See section 3 of Truth-In-Action at the end of Job.

40:6—41:34 God begins this second statement with a rebuke of Job's presumption of His injustice. God then compares Job's weakness with certain creatures of the Earth, including the **behemoth** (perhaps "hippopotamus," 40:15–24), and the **Leviathan** (perhaps "crocodile," 41:1–34), whom He masters. As Master over these creatures, He is certainly Master over forces behind Job's problems. Job must relinquish his complaint of God's injustice and submit to His lordship.

8 Lay your hand on him;
Remember the battle—
Never do it again!
9 Indeed, *any* hope of *overcoming* him is false;
Shall *one not* be overwhelmed at the sight of him?
10 No one *is so* fierce that he would dare *stir him up.
Who then is able to stand against Me?
11 [a]Who has preceded Me, that I should pay *him?*
[b]Everything under heaven is Mine.

12 "I will not [1]conceal his limbs,
His mighty power, or his graceful proportions.
13 Who can [1]remove his outer coat?
Who can approach *him* with a double bridle?
14 Who can open the doors of his face,
With his terrible teeth all around?
15 *His* rows of [1]scales are *his* pride,
Shut up tightly *as with* a seal;
16 One is so near another
That no air can come between them;
17 They are joined one to another,
They stick together and cannot be parted.
18 His sneezings flash forth light,
And his eyes *are* like the eyelids of the morning.
19 Out of his mouth go burning lights;
Sparks of fire shoot out.
20 Smoke goes out of his nostrils,
As *from* a boiling pot and burning rushes.
21 His breath kindles coals,
And a flame goes out of his mouth.
22 Strength dwells in his neck,
And [1]sorrow dances before him.
23 The folds of his flesh are joined together;
They are firm on him and cannot be moved.
24 His heart is as hard as stone,
Even as hard as the lower *millstone.*
25 When he raises himself up, the mighty are afraid;
Because of his crashings they [1]are beside themselves.
26 *Though* the sword reaches him, it cannot avail;
Nor does spear, dart, or javelin.
27 He regards iron as straw,
And bronze as rotten wood.
28 The arrow cannot make him flee;
Slingstones become like stubble to him.
29 Darts are regarded as straw;
He laughs at the threat of javelins.
30 His undersides *are* like sharp potsherds;
He spreads pointed *marks* in the mire.
31 He makes the deep boil like a pot;
He makes the sea like a pot of ointment.
32 He leaves a shining wake behind him;
One would think the deep had white hair.
33 On earth there is nothing like him,
Which is made without fear.
34 He beholds every high *thing;*
He *is* king over all the children of pride."

Job's Repentance and Restoration

42 Then Job answered the LORD and said:

2 "I know that You [a]can do everything,
And that no purpose *of Yours* can be withheld from You.
3 *You asked,* [a]'Who *is* this who hides counsel without knowledge?'
Therefore I have uttered what I did not understand,
[b]Things too wonderful for me, which I did not know.
4 Listen, please, and let me speak; **3**
You said, [a]'I will question you, and you shall answer Me.'

5 "I have [a]heard of You by the hearing of the ear,
But now my eye sees You.
6 Therefore I [a]abhor[1] *myself,*
And repent in dust and ashes."

7 And so it was, after the LORD had
spoken these words to Job, that the
LORD said to Eliphaz the Temanite,

10 *See WW at Hag. 1:14.
11 [a][Rom. 11:35] [b]Ex. 19:5; [Deut. 10:14; Job 9:5–10; 26:6–14]; Ps. 24:1; 50:12; 1 Cor. 10:26, 28
12 [1]Lit. *keep silent about*
13 [1]Lit. *take off the face of his garment*
15 [1]Lit. *shields*
22 [1]*despair*
25 [1]Or *purify themselves*

CHAPTER 42

2 [a]Gen. 18:14; [Matt. 19:26; Mark 10:27; 14:36; Luke 18:27]
3 [a]Job 38:2 [b]Ps. 40:5; 131:1; 139:6
4 [a]Job 38:3; 40:7
5 [a]Job 26:14; [Rom. 10:17]
6 [a]Ezra 9:6; Job 40:4 [1]*despise*

42:1–6 Job responds in humility. He compares his former knowledge of God, which has come from others—**the hearing of the ear**—with his present knowledge, which is superior because it has come directly—**now my eye sees.** He sees God differently because of personal revelation.
42:4–6 See section 3 of Truth-In-Action at the end of Job.

42:7–9 God then vindicates Job before his three friends—Eliphaz, Bildad, and Zophar—by rebuking them and instructing them to bring offerings to Job who, acting as their priest, will sacrifice to God for them. Then God declares His affirmation of Job (**I will accept him**), because Job had spoken what was right. God is more tolerant of Job's faith

"My wrath is aroused against you and
your two friends, for you have not spoken of Me *what is* right, as My servant
Job *has.*
8 "Now therefore, take for yourselves
[a]seven bulls and seven rams, [b]go to My
servant Job, and offer up for yourselves a burnt offering; and My servant
Job shall [c]pray for you. For I will accept [1]him, lest I deal with you *according to your* folly; because you have not
spoken of Me *what is* right, as My servant Job *has.*"
9 So Eliphaz the Temanite and Bildad
the Shuhite *and* Zophar the Naamathite went and did as the LORD commanded them; for the LORD had
[1]accepted Job.
10 [a]And the LORD [1]restored Job's
losses when he **prayed** for his friends.
Indeed the LORD gave Job [b]twice as
much as he had before.

WORD WEALTH

42:10 prayed, *palal* (pah-*lahl*); Strong's #6419: To pray, entreat, intercede, make supplication. This verb occurs more than 80 times. *Palal* speaks of prayer as intercession, asking someone with more power and wisdom to intervene in behalf of the one praying. For example, Hannah prayed for a son (1 Sam. 1:12); Hezekiah prayed for an extension of his life (Is. 38:2, 3); and Jonah prayed from within the fish's belly (Jon. 2:1–9). Furthermore, *palal* is found in the promise of 2 Chr. 7:14, "If My people . . . will humble themselves, and pray . . . I will hear from heaven." See other intercessory examples of *palal* in Gen. 20:7, 17; Num. 11:2; and 1 Sam. 12:23.

KINGDOM DYNAMICS

42:10–12 Biblical Definition, RESTORATION. This text gives the biblical definition of restoration. The entire concept of "The Holy Spirit and Restoration" is developed in the study article, that begins on page 2012.

(Acts 3:19–21/Gen. 3:21) J.R.

11 Then [a]all his brothers, all his sisters, and all those who had been his
acquaintances before, came to him and
ate food with him in his house; and
they consoled him and comforted him
for all the adversity that the LORD had
brought upon him. Each one gave him
a piece of silver and each a ring of gold.
12 Now the LORD blessed [a]the latter
days of Job more than his beginning;
for he had [b]fourteen thousand sheep,
six thousand camels, one thousand
yoke of oxen, and one thousand female
donkeys.
13 [a]He also had seven sons and three
daughters.

KINGDOM DYNAMICS

42:10–13 Job's Affliction and Total Recovery, DIVINE HEALING. Some point to Job to prove that sickness is God's will for many people. It is true that God permitted Job's illness to show Satan that Job would not turn from his Lord in the face of adversity. However, it is important to see that the affliction was a direct work of the Devil (2:2). Further, illness was only one of Job's adversities. When God later healed him and restored all his losses two times over, the Hebrew text literally refers to his recovery as a return from captivity; an evidence that all his restoration was a driving back of evil; a recovering of something that had been "captured from him" (42:10). This complex case, however, requires the additional acknowledgment that Job's healing appears to coincide with repentance for his attitude. Ch. 29 seems to reveal that Job was extremely self-centered, and he repented later (see 42:5, 6). Job's changed attitude and God's restoring are linked.

Before we philosophize about "God's will" in sicknesses, we would be wise to note how God corrected Job's friends who had argued that his afflictions were a judgment from God (42:7–9). But Job's spirit of forgiveness toward his friends became pivotal for his own well-being and for theirs.

(2 Kin. 20:1–11/Ps. 91:9, 10) N.V.

14 And he called the name of the first
[1]Jemimah, the name of the second
[2]Keziah, and the name of the third
[3]Keren-Happuch.
15 In all the land were found no
women *so* beautiful as the daughters
of Job; and their father gave them an
inheritance among their *brothers.
16 After this Job [a]lived one hundred
and forty years, and saw his children
and grandchildren *for* four *generations.
17 So Job died, old and [a]full of days.

8 [a]Num. 23:1 [b][Matt. 5:24] [c]Gen. 20:17; [James 5:15, 16; 1 John 5:16] [1]Lit. *his face*
9 [1]Lit. *lifted up the face of Job*
10 [a]Deut. 30:3; Ps. 14:7; 85:1–3; 126:1 [b]Is. 40:2 [1]Lit. *turned the captivity of Job,* what was captured from Job
11 [a]Job 19:13
12 [a]Job 1:10; 8:7; James 5:11 [b]Job 1:3
13 [a]Job 1:2
14 [1]Lit. *Handsome as the Day* [2]*Cassia,* a fragrance [3]Lit. *The Horn of Color* or *The Colorful Ray*
15 *See WW at Ps. 133:1.
16 [a]Job 5:26; Prov. 3:16 *See WW at Esth. 9:28.
17 [a]Gen. 15:15; 25:8; Job 5:26

searching for answers than the three friends had been. God clearly states that what the three friends had said about Him was wrong, but He is silent in regard to Elihu. God neither affirms, acknowledges, rebukes, nor responds to him. This underscores the theme of the Book of Job: God is sovereign, and His ways are past finding out.

42:10–17 Job is fully reconciled with God. He has shown that he serves God from a pure heart, solely because he loves Yahweh. Satan was wrong. His restored prosperity proves that a love relationship with God secures abundant life (see John 10:10).

TRUTH-IN-ACTION through JOB

Letting the LIFE of the Holy Spirit Bring Faith's Works Alive in You!

Truth Job Teaches	Text	**Action** Job Invites
1 Steps to Knowing God and His Ways Knowing that God has sovereign control as Creator and Sustainer of both the physical and spiritual universe must govern the way we think. God is intimately involved with our lives in a way that eludes our grasp. Any wisdom that leads to truth comes from Him. The only way any man can know and understand God is by specific revelation. Understanding God's true nature will lead us to a hope in redemption and eternal life. [NOTE: See occasional foreshadowings of Christ in the discourses of Job and his friends.]	1:6–12 2:3–6 7:17, 18 9:10–12 9:33–35; 16:19–22 31:15 34:10–12 38:1—39:30	**Choose to trust** God's absolute sovereignty in any adversity. **Understand** that while God may allow us to be tested, He sets strict limits on the tests. **Believe** that the Lord examines all your ways. **Know** that God's works are often unfathomable by the human mind. **Understand** that Christ is our Advocate with the Father (see 1 John 2:1). **Know** our case is hopeless without Him. **Understand** that God is the Creator of all men. **Understand** that God is totally righteous in what He renders to man and totally free from wrongdoing. **Know** and **Understand** God as Creator and Sustainer of the Universe. **Learn** that He, not you, determines what is right.
2 Guidelines for Growing in Godliness Godliness will result from a true knowledge of God. Godly living rejects evil attitudes and looks for God in every circumstance.	5:2 5:17	**Avoid** resentment, unforgiveness, and envy. **Believe** that they are self-destructive attitudes. **Embrace** the Lord's correction. **Consider** it a blessing. **Know** that it evidences the Lord's love for you.
3 Steps in Developing Humility The true knowledge of God leads to humility. Humility is not the self-deprecation with which many of us are often acquainted. Rather, it is the refusal to trust oneself for fulfillment of needs, looking instead to the Lord.	4:17; 9:2; 15:14; 25:4 2:1; 42:4–6 40:4, 5	**Understand** that man's own righteousness is a vain hope. **Believe** that only Christ's imputed righteousness can allow us to stand before God. **Diligently avoid** any form of self-righteousness. **Understand** that it makes one unteachable and unshapable in God's hand. **Humble** yourself regularly in the presence of the Lord. **Do not be hasty** to reply against God.
4 Keys to Wise Living The wise person lives in view of what he knows to be true about God, the world, and himself. His approach to God is humble and self-effacing, refusing to accuse God of any wrongdoing in adversities. Therefore, the wise man is able to patiently embrace and endure suffering, knowing that God's loving hand will prevail beyond it. Also, the wise man knows that although we are to seek to live	1:22 5:7 12:12 12:14 14:1, 2	**Understand** that to accuse God of any wrongdoing is the sin of blasphemy. **Refuse** to question any of God's workings. **Do not be surprised** at trouble. **Know** and **accept** that it is part of human life, which faith overcomes. **Recognize** the value of the wisdom of those older than you. **Resolve** yourself to the fact that God is the final word in all matters. **Understand** the transitory and trouble-filled nature of human life.

Truth Job Teaches	Text	**Action** Job Invites
4 righteously, our righteousness cannot earn God's favor: grace is a gift, not a debt.	23:10 36:8–12	**Understand** that adversity is a fire by which God is seeking to purify your life. **Discern** whether present adversity, opposition, or restraint is part of the Lord's discipline. **Agree** quickly with His correction and repent.
5 **Key Lessons in Faith** Fear is the converse of faith: it is believing what God says is not true. God commands us not to be afraid. Faith is able to trust God and not act out of fear.	3:25 5:21 13:15	**Know** and **understand** that fear shows lack of faith in God and His promises. **Rely** on the Lord's protection against verbal attacks and **do not fear** them. **Believe** that God honors faith that is stronger than death.
6 **Keys to Moral Purity** Impurity may result from a failure to make a commitment to moral purity.	31:1–40	**Commit** yourself to moral purity. **Keep** your eyes, hands, and body pure from sin.

The Book of PSALMS

Authors: David, Asaph, Sons of Korah, and Others
Date: 1000–300 B.C.
Theme: Communion with God in Prayer and Praise
Key Words: Rejoice, Mercy (Lovingkindness), Praise, Enemies, Lord, Righteousness

Author The Book of Psalms is a compilation of several ancient collections of Hebrew songs and poetry for use in congregational worship, as well as in private devotion. In some collections the ancient compilers gathered together mostly David's superb songs. In others they drew from a variety of authors such as Moses, Asaph, Heman, the sons of Korah, Solomon, Ethan, and Jeduthun. Many are from unnamed sources. Jewish scholars called these "orphan psalms."

Date The individual psalms may have been written at dates extending from the Exodus to the restoration after the Babylonian exile. But the small collections seem to have been gathered at specific periods in Israel's history: the reign of King David (1 Chr. 23:5), the rule of Hezekiah (2 Chr. 29:30), and during the leadership of Ezra and Nehemiah (Neh. 12:24). This collection process helps explain the duplication of some psalms. For example, Psalm 14 is similar to Psalm 53.

The Book of Psalms was edited in its present form with several variations by the time the Greek Septuagint was translated from the Hebrew, a few centuries before Christ's advent.

The Ugaritic texts, when contrasted with the more recent Dead Sea Scrolls, show that the imagery, style, and parallelisms of some of the psalms reflect a very ancient Canaanite style and vocabulary. The Book of Psalms, then, reflects the worship, devotional life, and religious sentiment of approximately one thousand years of Israel's history.

Content The Hebrew title of this book, *Sepher Tehillim*, means "Book of Praises." The Greek titles, *Psalmoi* or *Psalterion*, denote a poem that is to be accompanied by a stringed instrument. However, the Psalter contains more than temple songs and hymns of praise. It includes elegies, laments, personal and national prayers, petitions, meditations, instructions, historical anthems, and acrostic tributes to noble themes.

In its final form in our canon of Scripture, the Book of Psalms is subdivided into five smaller books. Each book is a compilation of several ancient collections of songs and poems. A fitting doxology has been placed at the end of each book by its editors. In Book One (Ps. 1—41) most of the songs are attributed to David. Book

Two (Ps. 42—72) is a collection of songs by, of, or for the sons of Korah, Asaph, David, and Solomon, with four anonymously written. Book Three (Ps. 73—89) is marked by a large collection of Asaph's songs. He was King David's choirmaster (1 Chr. 16:4–7). Although most psalms in Book Four (Ps. 90—106) are without given authors, Moses, David, and Solomon are contributors. More of David's songs are found in Book Five (Ps. 107—150). The series of songs called the Egyptian Hallel (Ps. 113—118) is found here as well. The final songs (Ps. 146—150) in Book Five are known as the "Great Hallel" series. Each song begins and ends with the Hebrew exclamation of praise, "Hallelujah!"

Informative subheadings are found at the beginning of many of the psalms. The Hebrew preposition used in many of the subheadings can be translated three ways: "to," "for," and "of." That is, "dedicated to," "for the use of," and "belonging to." Those subheadings describing the historical occasion of the psalm all deal with the life of David. Psalms 7, 34, 52, 54, 56, 57, 59, and 142 refer to events during David's troublesome relationship with Saul; and Psalms 3, 18, 51, 60, and 63 cover the period when David reigned over both Judah and Israel.

Other subheadings preceding psalms refer to the musical instruments that are to accompany them; to the appropriate tune or melody; to which part of the choir is to lead (for example, soprano, tenor, bass); or to what type of psalm it is (for example, meditation, prayer). Some of the meanings of these liturgical and musical notations are unknown to us today.

Hebrew Poetry Instead of a rhyming of sounds, Hebrew poetry and song are marked by parallelism, or rhyming of thoughts. Most parallelisms are couplets that state synonymous thoughts in each line (36:5). Others are antithetic, where the second line states the negative of the preceding line (20:8). There are also constructive or synthetic couplets, which tend to add to, or build on to, a thought (19:8, 9). A few parallelisms are causal, revealing the justification for the first line (31:21). Sometimes parallelism involves three lines (1:1), four lines (33:2, 3), or more.

Personal Application The New Testament apostles frequently used references from the Book of Psalms as texts for teaching Christian doctrine. The forgiveness of sins by grace, the faithfulness of God, the sinfulness of all men (Jew and Gentile), the inclusion of Gentiles in the church, the existence of angels, and the appropriate conduct of saints, are all doctrines reinforced by quotations from the Psalms.

Also, throughout the centuries the Psalms have been a source of personal inspiration and spiritual strength. In the course of dealing with the adversities of life, people are often frustrated by not being able to express adequately their emotional pain or mental anguish. The Psalms release us from that frustration. With emotionally drenched complaints, humble confessions, desperate pleas, penitent prayers, or screams of pain, the writers of the Psalms skillfully expose and express the yearnings of our deepest thoughts. This use of the Psalms is often the first step toward our own deliverance. By song and Spirit they comfort the lonely, strengthen the weary, bind the brokenhearted, and turn the eyes of the downcast up toward their Creator. Hope returns, faith is renewed, and life again becomes bearable.

The Psalms also have a rich history of liturgical and congregational use. King David organized choirs and orchestras, and appointed skilled conductors and composers to lead the worship (1 Chr. 25). He not only composed many psalms himself, but he invented musical instruments (1 Chr. 23:5). Fifty-five psalms are specifically addressed to the "Chief Musician," or worship leader.

This orchestrated worship was continued in Solomon's temple, although at different periods of Israel's history the worship passed through seasons of misuse and abuse. See 2 Chr. 7:6; 29:25–30; Amos 5:23. With the destruction of the second temple in A.D. 70 and the cessation of animal sacrifices, the singing of psalms along with Scripture reading took a place of increasing importance in synagogue worship services.

The first Christian churches comprised mainly Jewish people, so it was natural that they incorporate the singing of psalms, hymns, and spiritual songs into their worship (Col. 3:16). Throughout the centuries, in most of the major Christian denominations, hymnbooks composed mostly of psalms set to cultural music patterns have been used in congregational singing. In modern times, churches continue to draw from the Book of Psalms for songs of worship. The worship the Christian church has adopted incorporates not only the lyrics and instruments of the Psalms, but involves clapping (47:1), lifting up hands (141:2), bowing (95:6), standing (134:1), shouting (47:1), and dancing (149:3).

Christ Revealed Approximately half of the Old Testament references to the Messiah quoted by New Testament writers are from the Book of Psalms. The apostles saw prophetic reference in this book to Christ's birth (Acts 13:33), His lineage (Matt. 22:42, 43), His zeal (John 2:17), His teaching by parables (Matt. 13:35), His rejection (Matt. 21:42), His priesthood (Heb. 5:6), His betrayal by Judas (John 13:18), His vicarious suffering (Rom. 15:3), His triumphant resurrection (Acts 2:25–28), ascension (Acts 2:34), and reign (1 Cor. 15:27), as well as many other aspects of His ministry.

Some of the prophetic references to Christ are typical, that is, symbolic shadows of future realities. Other references are direct prophetic statements. Either way, the interpretation of these psalms as messianic is verified by Jesus' own words in Luke 24:44, where He declared that the Psalms spoke concerning Him.

The Holy Spirit at Work The Book of Psalms, and the principles of worship they reflect, minister to the soul of man and to the heart of God because they are the product of the work of the Holy Spirit. David, the major contributor to the Book of Psalms, was anointed by the Holy Spirit (1 Sam. 16:13). Not only was this anointing for kingship, but it was for the office of a prophet (Acts 2:30); and the prophetic statements he recorded were by the power of the Holy Spirit (Luke 24:44; Acts 1:16). In fact, the lyrics of his songs were composed by the inspiration of the Spirit (2 Sam. 23:1, 2), as were his plans for appointing chief musicians and choirs with their accompanying orchestras (1 Chr. 28:12, 13).

Thus the Psalms are unique and vastly different from the works of secular composers. Both may reflect the depths of agony experienced by the tormented human spirit, with all its pathos, and express the rapturous joy of the freed soul, yet the Psalms move to a higher plane by the creative anointing of the Holy Spirit.

Specific statements show that the Holy Spirit is at work in creating life (104:30); that He faithfully accompanies the believer (139:7); that He guides and instructs (143:10); that He sustains the penitent (51:11, 12); and that He interacts with the rebellious (106:33).

Outline of Psalms

I. Book One	**1:1—41:13**
A. Introductory songs	1:1—2:12
B. Songs of David	3:1—41:12
C. Doxology	41:13
II. Book Two	**42:1—72:20**
A. Songs of the sons of Korah	42:1—49:20
B. Song of Asaph	50:1–23
C. Songs of David	51:1—71:24
D. Song of Solomon	72:1–17
E. Doxology	72:18, 19
F. Concluding verse	72:20
III. Book Three	**73:1—89:52**
A. Songs of Asaph	73:1—83:18
B. Songs of the sons of Korah	84:1—85:13
C. Song of David	86:1–17
D. Songs of the sons of Korah	87:1—88:18
E. Song of Ethan	89:1–51
F. Doxology	89:52
IV. Book Four	**90:1—106:48**
A. Song of Moses	90:1–17
B. Anonymous songs	91:1—92:15
C. "The Lord Reigns" songs	93:1—100:5
D. Songs of David	101:1–8; 103:1–22
E. Anonymous songs	102:1–28; 104:1—106:47
F. Doxology	106:48
V. Book Five	**107:1—150:6**
A. Thanksgiving song	107:1–43
B. Songs of David	108:1—110:7
C. Egyptian Hallel	111:1—118:29
D. Alphabetic song on the law	119:1–176
E. Songs of ascents	120:1—134:3
F. Anonymous songs	135:1—137:9
G. Songs of David	138:1—145:21
H. "Praise the Lord" songs	146:1—149:9
I. Doxology	150:1–6

BOOK ONE
Psalms 1–41

PSALM 1

The Way of the Righteous and the End of the Ungodly

3 BLESSED [a]*is* the man
Who walks not in the *counsel of the [1]ungodly,
Nor stands in the path of sinners,
[b]Nor sits in the seat of the scornful;
4 2 But [a]his delight *is* in the law of the LORD,
[b]And in His law he [1]**meditates** day and night.
3 He shall be like a tree
[a]Planted by the [1]rivers of water,
That brings forth its fruit in its season,
Whose leaf also shall not wither;
And whatever he does shall [b]prosper.

PSALM 1
1 [a]Prov. 4:14 [b]Ps. 26:4, 5; Jer. 15:17 [1]*wicked* *See WW at Zech. 6:13.
2 [a]Ps. 119:14, 16, 35 [b][Josh. 1:8] [1]*ponders* by talking to himself
3 [a][Ps. 92:12–14]; Jer. 17:8; Ezek. 19:10 [b]Gen. 39:2, 3, 23; Ps. 128:2 [1]*channels*

WORD WEALTH

1:2 meditates, *hagah* (hah-*gah*); Strong's #1897: To reflect; to moan, to mutter; to ponder; to make a quiet sound such as sighing; to meditate or contemplate something as one repeats the words. *Hagah* represents something quite unlike the English "meditation," which may be a mental exercise only. In Hebrew thought, to meditate upon the Scriptures is to quietly repeat them in a soft, droning sound, while utterly abandoning outside distractions. From this tradition comes a specialized type of Jewish prayer called "davening," that is, reciting texts, praying intense prayers, or getting lost in communion with God while bowing or rocking back and forth. Evi-
(cont. on next page)

1:1 See section 3 of Truth-In-Action following Ps. 41.
1:1 Blessed is the word that not only begins this psalm, but in it lies the essence of what is promised to those who read and meditate on all the psalms. In the Hebrew it is plural (blessings) and is equivalent to the Greek word for "blessed" or "happy" (Matt. 5:3). The friends one chooses determine to a large extent one's destiny and success in life; godly **counsel** is a prerequisite for prosperity (v. 3) in its broadest sense.
1:2 See section 4 of Truth-In-Action following Ps. 41.
1:2 Law (Hebrew *torah*) connotes more than written laws; it is the revealed life-style of God's chosen people.

(cont. from preceding page)
dently this dynamic form of meditation-prayer goes back to David's time.

KINGDOM DYNAMICS

1:1–3 Responsible Commitment in God's Prosperity Plan, GOD'S PROSPERITY. "Whatever he does shall prosper." This includes everything: your family, your children, your marriage, your business, your ministry, your job, and your health. It means God intends what He says: everything shall prosper.

However, no promise of God is without responsible action to be taken on our part. No one will prosper until he starts doing what God says. Many people want the promised results without responsible commitment, but none of us will ever gain anything truly worthwhile in just an instant.

The truly worthwhile takes time to develop. Do not expect God's answers to leap to your schedule. Remember, His answers occur when you put His word into action. Just as a period of intensive study precedes a college degree, so through patient pursuit of His promise may we wait for the word of God to mature in our lives.

(John 10:10/Luke 12:15) F.P.

4 The ungodly *are* not so,
But *are* [a]like the chaff which the
wind drives away.
5 Therefore the ungodly shall not
stand in the judgment,
Nor sinners in the *congregation
of the righteous.

6 For [a]the LORD knows the way of
the righteous,
But the way of the ungodly shall
*perish.

PSALM 2

The Messiah's Triumph and Kingdom

WHY [a]do the [1]nations [2]rage,
And the people plot a [3]vain thing?
2 The kings of the earth set
themselves,
And the [a]rulers take counsel
together,
Against the LORD and against His
[b]Anointed,[1]* *saying*,
3 "Let [a]us break Their bonds in
pieces
And cast away Their cords from
us."

4 He who sits in the heavens
[a]shall *laugh;
The LORD shall hold them in
derision.
5 Then He shall speak to them in
His wrath,
And distress them in His deep
displeasure:
6 "Yet I have [1]set My King
[2]On My holy hill of Zion."

7 "I will declare the [1]decree:
The LORD has said to Me,
[a]'You *are* My Son,
Today I have begotten You.
8 Ask of Me, and I will give *You*
The nations *for* Your inheritance,
And the ends of the earth *for* Your
*possession.

KINGDOM DYNAMICS

2:8 God's Promise to His Messiah, WORLD EVANGELISM. This great messianic psalm discloses the heart of God toward His own Son. "Ask of Me . . . I will give *You* the nations *for* Your inheritance." This conversation introduces an amazing declaration, that all the nations of the world are intended to come under the aegis of His Son's rule. However, the qualifier is, "Ask." In John 17, through His High Priestly Prayer, Jesus does exactly this (John 17:1–26). However, His request involves our response. We must unite (John 17:21) and we must receive the authority "manifest" in God's name and glory, which Jesus, as the Interceding Messiah of Ps. 2, has conferred upon us—His church. In this name we pray, and by this glory we triumph—receiving the inheritance of nations as God has promised. (*/Prov. 24:11, 12) G.C.

9 [a]You shall [1]break them with a rod
of iron;

4 [a]Job 21:18; Ps. 35:5; Is. 17:13
5 *See WW at Josh. 22:17.
6 [a]Ps. 37:18; [Nah. 1:7; John 10:14; 2 Tim. 2:19] *See WW at Judg. 5:31.

PSALM 2

1 [a]Acts 4:25, 26 [1]*Gentiles* [2]*throng tumultuously* [3]*worthless or empty*
2 [a][Matt. 12:14; 26:3, 4, 59–66; 27:1, 2; Mark 3:6; 11:18] [b][John 1:41] [1]Christ, Commissioned One, Heb. *Messiah* *See WW at Dan. 9:25.
3 [a]Luke 19:14
4 [a]Ps. 37:13 *See WW at Eccl. 3:4.
6 [1]Lit. *installed* [2]Lit. *Upon Zion, the hill of My holiness*
7 [a]Matt. 3:17; Mark 1:1, 11; Luke 3:22; John 1:18; Acts 13:33; [Heb. 1:5; 5:5] [1]Or *decree of the LORD: He said to Me*
8 *See WW at Josh. 22:9.
9 [a]Ps. 89:23; 110:5, 6; [Rev. 2:26, 27; 12:5; 19:15] [1]So with MT, Tg.; LXX, Syr., Vg. *rule* (cf. Rev. 2:27)

1:4 Chaff, the empty husks of grain, has no weighty substance to stabilize it, but is easily blown by winds of adversity.
2:1–12 This is a messianic psalm in which **nations** and **kings** are warned to serve God because ultimate judgment has been entrusted to Christ. It is applied to Christ at least five times in the NT.
2:1 Vain thing is a rebellion without a chance of success.
2:2 The English word "Messiah" is a transliteration of the Hebrew word here translated **Anointed.** The anointed one here is probably a king of Israel, who prophetically is a type of Christ, the true Anointed One (Acts 4:27).
2:6–9 God is speaking in v. 6, and then the enthroned **King** states the **decree** of God in vv. 7–9.
2:7 Jesus was always conscious that He was the **Son** of God (John 5:18–20), and it was this declaration that caused the Jewish elders to crucify Him (Matt. 26:63–66).
2:8 Matthew records that Jesus recognized this power in His commissioning the disciples to make disciples of all the **nations** (Matt. 28:18–20).

You shall dash them to pieces like
a potter's vessel.' "

10 Now therefore, be wise, O kings;
Be instructed, you judges of the
earth.

11 Serve the LORD with fear,
And *rejoice with trembling.

2 12 [1]Kiss the Son, lest [2]He be angry,
And you perish *in* the way,
When [a]His wrath is kindled but
a little.
[b]Blessed *are* all those who *put
their trust in Him.

PSALM 3

The LORD Helps His Troubled People

A **Psalm** of David [a]when he fled from Absalom his son.

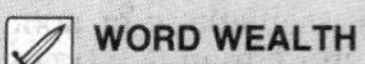

WORD WEALTH

3:title psalm, *mizmor* (meez-*mohr*); Strong's #4210: An instrumental song; a song with words accompanied by musical instruments. *Mizmor* comes from the verb *zamar,* which means "to play or make music while singing, to sing psalms, sing forth praises." The definitive aspect of a *mizmor* is that it requires musical instruments. It is possible to sing songs (*shirim*) without instruments, or to speak praises (*tehillim*) without any musical accompaniment, but it is not possible to fulfill the many biblical commands (as 98:5; Is. 12:5) that use the verb *zamar,* unless instruments are employed. The beauty of musical instruments as a part of worship was greatly developed by King David.

LORD, how they have increased who
trouble me!
Many *are* they who rise up
against me.

2 Many *are* they who say of me,
"*There is* no help for him in God."
Selah

3 But You, O LORD, *are* [a]a shield
[1]for me,
My glory and [b]the One who lifts
up my head.

4 I cried to the LORD with my voice,
And [a]He heard me from His
[b]holy hill. Selah

5 [a]I lay down and slept;
I awoke, for the LORD sustained
me.

6 [a]I will not be afraid of ten
thousands of people
Who have set *themselves* against
me all around.

7 Arise, O LORD;
Save me, O my God!
[a]For You have struck all my
enemies on the cheekbone;
You have broken the teeth of the
ungodly.

8 [a]Salvation *belongs* to the LORD.
Your blessing *is* upon Your
*people. Selah

PSALM 4

The Safety of the Faithful

To the [1]Chief Musician. With stringed instruments. A *Psalm of David.

HEAR me when I call, O *God of
my righteousness!
You have relieved me in *my*
distress;
[1]Have mercy on me, and hear my
*prayer.

2 How long, O you sons of men,
Will you turn my glory to shame?
How long will you love
worthlessness
And seek falsehood? Selah

3 But know that [a]the LORD has
[1]set apart for Himself him who
is godly;

2:11 *See WW at Hab. 3:18.
2:12 [a][Rev. 6:16, 17] [b][Ps. 5:11; 34:22] [1]LXX, Vg. *Embrace discipline;* Tg. *Receive instruction* [2]LXX *the LORD* *See WW at Zeph. 3:12.

PSALM 3

title [a]2 Sam. 15:13–17
3 [a]Ps. 5:12; 28:7 [b]Ps. 9:13; 27:6 [1]Lit. *around*
4 [a]Ps. 4:3; 34:4 [b]Ps. 2:6; 15:1; 43:3
5 [a]Lev. 26:6; Ps. 4:8; Prov. 3:24
6 [a]Ps. 23:4; 27:3
7 [a]Job 16:10
8 [a]Ps. 28:8; 35:3; [Is. 43:11] *See WW at Ruth 1:16.

PSALM 4

title [1]*Choir Director* *See WW at Ps. 3:title.
1 [1]*Be gracious to me* *See WW at 2 Kin. 19:15. See WW at 2 Chr. 6:20.
3 [a][2 Tim. 2:19] [1]Many Heb. mss., LXX, Tg., Vg. *made wonderful*

2:12 See section 2 of Truth-In-Action following Ps. 41.
2:12 Kiss is a sign of submission (1 Kin. 19:18); thus "do homage" is the meaning here.
3:1, 2 The repetition of **many** reveals the traumatic feeling David experienced when his nation turned against him. **Increased** is the same root word used in 2 Sam. 15:12 to describe the growth of rebellion.
3:2 Selah (meaning obscure) is perhaps a musical notation similar to *forte,* or perhaps it denotes an instrumental interlude. It occurs mainly in Davidic psalms (71 times).
3:3 Shield was a common symbol for God's protection, first revealed to Abraham (Gen. 15:1). **Lifts . . . head:** David's head was bowed low in humiliation as he left Jerusalem in a hurry (2 Sam. 15:30).
3:4 The **holy hill** refers to the location of the ark of the presence of God (2 Sam. 15:25). **Heard:** That is, heard and answered with help.
3:5 Slept: Loss of sleep because of anxiety from all kinds of pressures is overcome, now as then, by relating to the Lord in prayer (Phil. 4:6).
3:6 Thousands: Many of the people of Israel followed Absalom in revolt (2 Sam. 15:12, 13), but victory was not dependent on numbers (1 Sam. 14:6).
3:7 To break **teeth** means to render powerless.
3:8 This phrase about **salvation** is David's answer to the mockery of v. 2 where "help" is the same word in Hebrew.
4:2 God is speaking in this verse. **Worthlessness** and **falsehood** are words used repeatedly in the OT to describe idols (Is. 41:29). See Rom. 1:23.

The LORD will *hear when I call
to Him.

4 [a]Be[1] angry, and do not sin.
[b]Meditate within your heart on
your bed, and be still. Selah

5 *Offer [a]the sacrifices of
righteousness,
And [b]put your trust in the LORD.

6 *There are* many who say,
"Who will show us *any* good?"
[a]LORD, lift up the light of Your
countenance upon us.

7 You have put [a]gladness in my
heart,
More than in the season that their
grain and wine increased.

8 [a]I will both lie down in *peace, and
sleep;
[b]For You alone, O LORD, make me
dwell in safety.

PSALM 5

A Prayer for Guidance

To the Chief Musician. With [1]flutes. A *Psalm of David.

GIVE [a]ear to my words, O LORD,
Consider my [1]meditation.

2 Give heed to the voice of my cry,
My King and my God,
For to You I will *pray.

3 My voice You shall hear in the
morning, O LORD;
[a]In the morning I will direct *it* to
You,
And I will look up.

KINGDOM DYNAMICS

5:1–3 Patterns in Prayer and Spiritual Breakthrough, FAITH'S WARFARE. In this text David builds a case for consistency and order in daily prayer. The repetition of the phrase "in the morning" justifies an alternate translation: "morning by morning." Also significant is the psalmist's selection of the Hebrew word *'arak* ("direct") in his declaration that he would "direct" his petitions to God daily. *'Arak* is most frequently used in Moses' writings in reference to the priests "setting in order" the sacrifices to be brought to the Lord each day (Ex. 40:4); also to describe an army being "set in array" in preparation for battle (Judg. 20:20–22). Such usage indicates an "ordered strategy" has been prepared for battle. These definitions connote the thought that David's "direct" prayer speaks of a well-thought-out order to his prayers, a daily prayer strategy with purpose and meaning.

(Ezek. 22:30/Acts 4:31–34) D.E.

4 For You *are* not a God who takes
pleasure in wickedness,
Nor shall **evil** [1]dwell with You.

WORD WEALTH

5:4 evil, *ra'* (*rah*); Strong's #7451: Something bad, evil; badness, tragedy, trouble, distress, wickedness, something of poor quality. *Ra'* occurs more than 600 times in the OT. *Ra'* means "badness," but not necessarily evil in the sense of something being inherently wicked, insidious, morally rotten, and so forth. Malnourished cows are described as "evil in appearance" (Gen. 41:27), that is "bad looking." In other references, evil is contrasted with good (Gen. 2:17) and is to be hated (Ps. 97:10).

5 The [a]boastful shall not [b]stand in
Your sight;
You hate all workers of *iniquity.

6 You shall destroy those who
speak falsehood;
The LORD abhors the
[a]bloodthirsty and deceitful
man.

7 But as for me, I will come into
Your house in the multitude of
Your mercy;
In fear of You I will worship
toward [1]Your holy *temple.

8 [a]Lead me, O LORD, in Your
righteousness because of my
enemies;
*Make Your way straight before
my face.

3 *See WW at 1 Kin. 20:8.
4 [a][Ps. 119:11; Eph. 4:26] [b]Ps. 77:6 [1]Lit. *Tremble* or *Be agitated*
5 [a]Deut. 33:19; Ps. 51:19 [b]Ps. 37:3, 5; 62:8 *See WW at Deut. 16:2.
6 [a]Num. 6:26; Ps. 80:3, 7, 19
7 [a]Ps. 97:11, 12; Is. 9:3; Acts 14:17
8 [a]Job 11:19; Ps. 3:5 [b][Lev. 25:18]; Deut. 12:10 *See WW at Nah. 1:15.

PSALM 5

title [1]Heb. *nehiloth* *See WW at Ps. 3:title.
1 [a]Ps. 4:1 [1]Lit. *groaning*
2 *See WW at Job 42:10.
3 [a]Ps. 55:17; 88:13
4 [1]Lit. *sojourn*
5 [a][Hab. 1:13] [b]Ps. 1:5 *See WW at Prov. 22:8.
6 [a]Ps. 55:23
7 [1]Lit. *the temple of Your holiness* *See WW at Hag. 2:15.
8 [a]Ps. 25:4, 5; 27:11; 31:3 *See WW at Prov. 3:6.

4:4 See section 2 of Truth-In-Action following Ps. 41.
4:4 Angry: That is, in expressing feelings about immediate distress, do not sin against God (Eph. 4:26). **Be still:** Maintain trust, and God will come through (v. 8).
4:6 Lift . . . countenance means "to look favorably on us."
4:7 The satisfaction derived from materialistic success never comes close to the abundance of **gladness** in knowing God's presence. See Luke 12:15.
4:8 Sleep: This verse closes the psalm like the fading notes of a lullaby. The **LORD alone** is the true basis for a peaceful mind (John 14:27).
5:1 The Lord considers not only words, but also the inner motives of the heart. **Meditation** may include "sighs" since the Hebrew word means a dull tone or low sound.
5:3 See section 4 of Truth-In-Action following Ps. 41.
5:3 Look up refers to waiting for the answer to his prayer.
5:4 A comparison of **God** with the deities worshiped by surrounding nations makes us appreciate the One we worship.
5:7 See section 4 of Truth-In-Action following Ps. 41.
5:7 Worship toward is "bow down toward" in Hebrew. The **temple** here is possibly the tabernacle at Nob a few miles north of Jerusalem (1 Sam. 1:9).

9 For *there is* no [1]faithfulness in
their mouth;
Their inward part *is* destruction;
[a]Their throat *is* an open tomb;
They flatter with their tongue.
10 Pronounce them guilty, O God!
Let them fall by their own
counsels;
Cast them out in the multitude of
their transgressions,
For they have rebelled against
You.

11 But let all those rejoice who *put
their trust in You;
Let them *ever shout for joy,
because You [1]defend them;
Let those also who love Your
name
Be joyful in You.
12 For You, O LORD, will *bless the
*righteous;
With *favor You will surround
him as *with* a shield.

PSALM 6

A Prayer of Faith in Time of Distress

To the Chief Musician. With stringed instruments. [a]On [1]an eight-stringed harp. A *Psalm of David.

O LORD, [a]do not rebuke me in Your
*anger,
Nor chasten me in Your hot
displeasure.
2 Have mercy on me, O LORD, for I
am weak;
O LORD, [a]heal* me, for my bones
are troubled.
3 My soul also is greatly [a]troubled;
But You, O LORD—how long?

4 Return, O LORD, deliver me!
Oh, save me for Your mercies'
sake!

9 [a]Rom. 3:13 [1]*uprightness*
11 [1]*protect*, lit. *cover*. *See WW at Zeph. 3:12. • See WW at Ps. 136:1.
12 *See WW at Ps. 145:2. • See WW at Lam. 1:18. • See WW at Deut. 33:23.

PSALM 6

title [a]Ps. 12:title [1]Heb. *sheminith* *See WW at Ps. 3:title.
1 [a]Ps. 38:1; 118:18; [Jer. 10:24] *See WW at Judg. 10:7.
2 [a]Ps. 41:4; 147:3; [Hos. 6:1] *See WW at Ex. 15:26.
3 [a]Ps. 88:3; John 12:27
5 [a]Ps. 30:9; 88:10–12; 115:17; [Eccl. 9:10]; Is. 38:18 *See WW at Hos. 13:14.
6 [1]Or *Every night*
7 [a]Job 17:7; Ps. 31:9
8 [a][Matt. 25:41] [b]Ps. 3:4; 28:6

PSALM 7

title [a]Hab. 3:1 [b]2 Sam. 16 [1]Heb. *Shiggaion*
1 [a]Ps. 31:15 *See WW at Zeph. 3:12.
2 [a]Ps. 57:4; Is. 38:13 [b]Ps. 50:22
3 [a]2 Sam. 16:7 [b]1 Sam. 24:11

5 [a]For in death *there is* no
remembrance of You;
In the *grave who will give You
thanks?

6 I am weary with my groaning;
[1]All night I make my bed swim;
I drench my couch with my tears.
7 [a]My eye wastes away because of
grief;
It grows old because of all my
enemies.

8 [a]Depart from me, all you workers
of iniquity;
For the LORD has [b]heard the voice
of my weeping.
9 The LORD has heard my
supplication;
The LORD will receive my prayer.
10 Let all my enemies be ashamed
and greatly troubled;
Let them turn back *and* be
ashamed suddenly.

PSALM 7

Prayer and Praise for Deliverance from Enemies

A [a]Meditation[1] of David, which he sang to the LORD [b]concerning the words of Cush, a Benjamite.

O LORD my God, in You I *put my
trust;
[a]Save me from all those who
persecute me;
And deliver me,
2 [a]Lest they tear me like a lion,
[b]Rending *me* in pieces, while *there
is* none to deliver.

3 O LORD my God, [a]if I have done
this:
If there is [b]iniquity in my hands,
4 If I have repaid evil to him who
was at peace with me,

5:9 This is quoted by Paul to show that Jews as well as Gentiles have sinned and need a Savior (Rom. 3:13). **An open tomb** was considered extremely unclean by Jewish law (Num. 19:11).
5:12 That God is a **shield** was first revealed to Abraham (Gen. 15:1), though here the reference is to a larger one able to guard the whole body.
6:1–10 Do not rebuke: Though not in all cases is sickness the consequence of sin, yet when it is, the pain can be instrumental in bringing the sinner face-to-face with God (1 Cor. 11:30).
6:2, 3 David's troubled body **greatly troubled** his soul, showing the effect sickness can have on the moods and attitudes of the mind. **Soul:** This was quoted by Jesus as He headed toward crucifixion (John 12:27).
6:2 Bones are mentioned repeatedly in the Psalms as a symbol for the health of the whole body.
6:5 The **grave** (Hebrew *she'ol*) was thought to be a place of gloomy darkness. David's information on the spirit world was incomplete, but later Christ shed light on it (2 Tim. 1:10).
6:7, 8 As vultures gather around a wounded prey, so **enemies** gather to rejoice over the calamities of the struggling and take advantage of any weaknesses.
6:9, 10 Prayer is seen as the prescription that not only heals the body, but strengthens the weakened soul, so that the villains are the ones who become **greatly troubled** and must flee.
7:1 Persecute: Pursue. This is one of several psalms of David regarding his flight from Saul and his men, the Benjamites.
7:3 If I have done this refers to Cush's false accusations against David.
7:4 Repaid evil: Just the opposite was true! David had shown good to those who were his enemies (1 Sam. 24:1–22; 26:1–25).

Or [a]have plundered my enemy without cause,
5 Let the enemy pursue me and overtake *me;*
Yes, let him trample my life to the earth,
And lay my honor in the dust. Selah

6 Arise, O LORD, in Your anger;
[a]Lift Yourself up because of the rage of my enemies;
[b]Rise up [1]for me *to* the judgment You have commanded!
7 So the congregation of the peoples shall surround You;
For their sakes, therefore, return on high.
8 The LORD shall judge the peoples;
[a]Judge me, O LORD, [b]according to my righteousness,
And according to my integrity within me.

9 Oh, let the wickedness of the wicked *come to an end,
But establish the just;
[a]For the righteous God tests the hearts and [1]minds.
10 [1]My defense *is* of God,
Who saves the [a]upright in heart.

11 God *is* a just judge,
And God is angry *with the wicked* every day.
12 If he does not turn back,
He will [a]sharpen His sword;
He bends His bow and makes it ready.
13 He also prepares for Himself instruments of death;
He makes His arrows into fiery shafts.

3 14 [a]Behold, *the wicked* brings forth iniquity;
Yes, he conceives trouble and brings forth falsehood.
15 He made a pit and dug it out,
[a]And has fallen into the ditch *which* he made.
16 [a]His trouble shall return upon his own head,
And his violent dealing shall come down on [1]his own crown.

17 I will praise the LORD according to His righteousness,
And will sing praise to the name of the LORD Most High.

4 [a]1 Sam. 24:7; 26:9
6 [a]Ps. 94:2 [b]Ps. 35:23; 44:23 [1]So with MT, Tg., Vg.; LXX *O LORD my God*
8 [a]Ps. 26:1; 35:24; 43:1 [b]Ps. 18:20; 35:24
9 [a][1 Sam. 16:7] [1]Lit. *kidneys,* the most secret part of man *See WW at Ps. 138:8.
10 [a]Ps. 97:10, 11; 125:4 [1]Lit. *My shield is upon God*
12 [a]Deut. 32:41
14 [a]Job 15:35; Is. 59:4; [James 1:15]
15 [a][Job 4:8]; Ps. 57:6
16 [a]Esth. 9:25; Ps. 140:9 [1]The crown of his own head

PSALM 8

title [1]Heb. *Al Gittith*
1 [a]Ps. 148:13 [b]Ps. 113:4 *See WW at Deut. 18:5. • See WW at 1 Chr. 29:11.

KINGDOM DYNAMICS

7:14–17 Praise Stops the Advancement of Wickedness, PRAISE PATHWAY. This short passage contains two truths about praise.

First, praise is the answer when wickedness and iniquity come against the believer. Temptation to sin and live wickedly will soon disappear in the face of sincere, powerful, and audible praise. This will bring the glorious presence of Jesus, driving out the desire to identify with the sinful act and/or thought.

Second, in v. 17 the writer declares, "I will praise the LORD." Praise is an act of the will. It is not merely an exuberance overflowing with words, but a self-induced declaration of thanksgiving—a sacrifice. The praiser chooses to praise.

Learn this about praise: 1) Do not wait until all conditions and circumstances are favorable, but 2) offer a thanksgiving of praise because God is worthy and it is right. (See also Is. 12:1–3 and Jer. 33:11.)

(2 Chr. 20:15–22/Ps. 18:3) C.G.

PSALM 8

The Glory of the LORD in Creation

To the Chief Musician. [1]On the instrument of Gath. A Psalm of David.

O LORD, our Lord,
How [a]excellent *is* Your *name in all the earth,
Who have [b]set Your *glory above the heavens!

7:6 Although in reality God never sleeps, the psalmist prays for Him to **rise up.** Describing God in human terms is common in the Psalms. **Because of** can be translated "against."
7:8 David's **integrity** is the foundation on which he stands in his pleadings with God.
7:9 Minds: The human conscience.
7:11–17 The writer turns from his own distress to the general teaching on God's dealings with wickedness.
7:12 Turn back in Hebrew is the same as "repentance" in the NT. If a sinner does not turn back in repentance, God will bring judgment.
7:14–16 Pit: This is David's picturesque way of illustrating the principle, you reap what you sow!
7:14 See section 3 of Truth-In-Action following Ps. 41.
7:17 This closing verse sets forth one of the main reasons we have for praising God: His attribute of **righteousness. Sing praise:** Worship is often best expressed in lofty song. **LORD Most High** is the Hebrew *Yahweh 'Elyon,* the Jewish covenant name of God, combined with the supreme title for God, familiar to Jews and Canaanites alike.
8:1–9 This psalm of David is a nature psalm showing the littleness of physical **man** and the greatness of God. Although man is minuscule in relation to the immense universe, he is, nonetheless, the pinnacle of creation and the object of God's watchful care.
8:1 LORD our Lord: This is the personal name of God, combined with the title meaning "Master, Sovereign."

2 [a]Out of the mouth of babes and
nursing infants
You have [1]ordained *strength,
Because of Your enemies,
That You may silence [b]the enemy
and the avenger.

3 When I [a]consider Your heavens,
the work of Your fingers,
The moon and the stars, which
You have ordained,
4 [a]What is *man that You are
mindful of him,
And the son of man that You
[b]visit[1] him?
5 For You have made him a little
lower than [1]the angels,
And You have crowned him with
*glory and **honor.**

WORD WEALTH

8:5 honor, *hadar* (hah-*dar*); Strong's #1926: Splendor, honor, glory, adornment, magnificence, beauty. This noun comes from the verb *hadar,* "to honor, to glorify, to make splendid." *Hadar* speaks of the splendor that belongs to God, to His creation, to His kingdom, and to man made in God's image. The biblical view of man is higher and more worth-affirming than any of the alternate views; in this reference God has actually crowned man with splendor in spite of his smallness relative to the vast heavens! Another well-known use of *hadar* is in the phrase "the beauty of holiness" (96:9; 110:3). The splendor of holiness is a greater beauty than even the glory of nature.

6 [a]You have made him to have
dominion over the works of
Your *hands;
[b]You have put all *things* under his
feet,
7 All sheep and oxen—
Even the beasts of the field,
8 The birds of the air,
And the fish of the sea
That pass through the paths of the
seas.

2 [a]Matt. 21:16; [1 Cor. 1:27] [b]Ps. 44:16 [1]*established* *See WW at Jer. 16:19.
3 [a]Ps. 111:2
4 [a]Job 7:17, 18; [Heb. 2:6–8] [b][Job 10:12] [1]*give attention to* or *care for* *See WW at Job 4:17.
5 [1]Heb. *Elohim, God;* LXX, Syr., Tg., Jewish tradition *angels* *See WW at Is. 60:1.
6 [a][Gen. 1:26, 28] [b][1 Cor. 15:27; Eph. 1:22; Heb. 2:8] *See WW at Josh. 4:24.
9 [a]Ps. 8:1

PSALM 9

title [1]Heb. *Muth Labben*
2 [a]Ps. 5:11; 104:34 [b][Ps. 83:18; 92:1] *See WW at Gen. 14:18.

KINGDOM DYNAMICS

8:4–8 Man's Dominion over Creation, HUMAN WORTH. Not only was man intrinsically distinct from the rest of creation, he was given authority over the Earth and everything upon it. Man was made to rule (v. 6). Our ability to exercise authority over the Earth is dependent on our willingness to submit to, serve, and obey the living God who holds authority over us. Our authority over the Earth makes us accountable for the Earth. The mineral resources of the Earth, the Earth's water and air, the species of animal life beneath and upon the Earth (and in the waters of the Earth) should all be the concern of every government and individual. Can we allow to pass from the Earth forms of life, which the Creator has placed here and committed to our care? Do we dare to pollute and corrupt God's creation? "For everyone to whom much is given, from him much will be required" (Luke 12:48).

(Gen. 1:26–28/Gen. 3:17) C.B.

9 [a]O LORD, our Lord,
How excellent *is* Your name in all
the earth!

PSALM 9

Prayer and Thanksgiving for the LORD's Righteous Judgments

To the Chief Musician. To *the tune of* [1]"Death of the Son." A Psalm of David.

I WILL praise *You,* O LORD, with my
whole heart;
I will tell of all Your marvelous
works.
2 I will be glad and [a]rejoice in You;
I will sing praise to Your name,
[b]O *Most High.

3 When my enemies turn back,
They shall fall and perish at Your
presence.

8:2 Babes: Jesus plucked the first phrase of this verse and used it to justify young people praising Him as Messiah (Matt. 21:16). The Septuagint, or Greek Bible, from which Jesus quoted, considered the Hebrew word here rendered **strength** to be better translated "praise."
8:3 Heavens: No scientific discovery by astronomer (v. 3) or biologist (vv. 7, 8) negates the unique significance and value of human beings as created beings.
8:4 Man, son of man (Hebrew *'enosh, ben 'adam;* man in weakness, man in origin, that is, from earth). "Son of Man" is a title applied to the Messiah in the NT, and the author of Hebrews applied this passage to Jesus specifically (Heb. 2:6), as did Paul (1 Cor. 15:27).
8:5 Human beings were **made . . . a little lower than the angels,** not evolved a little higher than apes. There is a distinct separateness of man and animal. **Angels** (Hebrew *'elohim*) is used in the OT to mean God, gods, or supernatural beings. The Greek Septuagint translates it as angels, as does the author of Heb. (Heb. 2:7).
8:6 Dominion: This parallels the description of the first Adam in Gen. 1:26, 28.
9:1—10:18 Ps. 9 and 10 form an alphabetical (acrostic) poem with the words beginning each stanza corresponding to the letters of the Hebrew alphabet. The Greek and Vulgate Bibles count these as only one psalm, although Ps. 9 deals with corrupt nations outside Israel, and Ps. 10 deals with corruption in the nation of Israel.
9:3 Perish: Judgment on wicked nations has occurred

4 For You have maintained my
right and my cause;
You sat on the throne judging in
righteousness.
5 You have rebuked the [1]nations,
You have destroyed the wicked;
You have [a]blotted out their name
forever and *ever.

6 O enemy, destructions are
finished forever!
And you have destroyed cities;
Even their memory has [a]perished.
7 [a]But the LORD shall endure
forever;
He has prepared His throne for
judgment.
8 [a]He shall *judge the *world in
righteousness,
And He shall administer
judgment for the peoples in
uprightness.

9 The LORD also will be a [a]refuge[1]
for the oppressed,
A refuge in *times of trouble.
5 10 And those who [a]know Your name
will put their trust in You;
For You, LORD, have not forsaken
those who seek You.

11 Sing praises to the LORD, who
dwells in Zion!
[a]Declare His deeds among the
people.
12 [a]When He avenges blood, He
remembers them;
He does not forget the cry of the
[1]humble.

13 Have mercy on me, O LORD!
Consider my trouble from those
who hate me,
You who lift me up from the gates
of death,
14 That I may tell of all Your *praise

5 [a]Prov. 10:7 [1]*Gentiles* *See WW at Mic. 4:5.
6 [a][Ps. 34:16]
7 [a]Ps. 102:12, 26; Heb. 1:11
8 [a][Ps. 96:13; 98:9; Acts 17:31] *See WW at Deut. 32:36. • See WW at Jer. 51:15.
9 [a]Ps. 32:7; 46:1; 91:2 [1]Lit. *secure height* *See WW at Is. 33:6.
10 [a]Ps. 91:14
11 [a]Ps. 66:16; 107:22
12 [a][Gen. 9:5; Ps. 72:14] [1]*afflicted*
14 [a]Ps. 13:5; 20:5; 35:9 [1]Jerusalem *See WW at Ps. 100:4.
15 [a]Ps. 7:15, 16 [1]*Gentiles*
16 [a]Ex. 7:5 [b]Ps. 92:3 [1]Heb. *Higgaion*
17 [a]Job 8:13; Ps. 50:22 [1]*Gentiles*
18 [a]Ps. 9:12; 12:5 [b][Ps. 62:5; 71:5]; Prov. 23:18 *See WW at Ps. 70:5. • See WW at Hos. 2:15.
19 [1]*Gentiles*
20 [1]*Gentiles* *See WW at Is. 8:13.

PSALM 10

2 [a]Ps. 7:16; 9:16 [1]*hotly pursues* *See WW at Ps. 40:17.
3 [a]Ps. 49:6; 94:3, 4

In the gates of [1]the daughter of
Zion.
I will [a]rejoice in Your salvation.

15 [a]The [1]nations have sunk down in
the pit *which* they made;
In the net which they hid, their
own foot is caught.
16 The LORD is [a]known *by* the
judgment He executes;
The wicked is snared in the work
of his own hands.
[b]Meditation.[1] Selah

17 The wicked shall be turned into
hell,
And all the [1]nations [a]that forget
God.
18 [a]For the *needy shall not always
be forgotten;
[b]The *expectation of the poor shall
not perish forever.

19 Arise, O LORD,
Do not let man prevail;
Let the [1]nations be judged in Your
sight.
20 Put them in *fear, O LORD,
That the [1]nations may know
themselves *to be but* men.
Selah

PSALM 10

A Song of Confidence in God's Triumph over Evil

WHY do You stand afar off,
O LORD?
Why do You hide in times of
trouble?
2 The wicked in *his* pride
[1]persecutes the *poor;
[a]Let them be caught in the plots
which they have devised.

3 For the wicked [a]boasts of his
heart's desire;

throughout Israel's history and will culminate in the final Judgment Day. See note on Obad. 15.

9:5 To have the family **name,** or tribal name, lost to succeeding generations was considered by ancient cultures to be a horrible event. Its preservation was highly guarded.

9:8 Judge: This is underscored by Paul on the Areopagus (Mars' Hill) in Acts 17:31.

9:10 See section 5 of Truth-In-Action following Ps. 41.

9:10 Name is a poetic symbol for the total person and personality it represents. Here it stands for the reliable character of God.

9:13, 14 Gates were the public gathering places of ancient times, both of the living and the dead. The two **gates** are vividly contrasted here. **Death** (Hebrew *she'ol*): The thought of the place of the dead being like a walled city with gates is carried into the NT (Matt. 16:18), where the Greek *hades* is equivalent.

9:16 Meditation: The Hebrew for this word (*higgaion*) is hard to translate but seems to have the thought of a solemn or harmonious sound (92:3).

9:17, 18 Hell is the same word translated "death" (Hebrew *she'ol*) in v. 13. The thought is that the wicked nations will be destroyed, brought to the grave, for God will not let them continually oppress the **poor.**

10:1–18 Combined with Ps. 9, this would be an alphabetic (acrostic) poem (though lacking in parts), in which the stanzas begin with successive letters of the Hebrew alphabet.

10:1 Stand afar: The psalmist, like others in distress, at first speaks from his own pain. Because he hurts, he feels that God is distant. See Job 13:24.

10:2 This verse begins a long list describing the despicable conduct of the **wicked** in this heartless, morally bankrupt society.

[1]He [b]blesses the greedy *and*
renounces the LORD.
4 The wicked in his proud
countenance does not seek
God;
[1]God *is* in none of his [a]thoughts.

5 His ways [1]are always prospering;
Your judgments *are* far above,
out of his sight;
As for all his enemies, he sneers
at them.
6 [a]He has said in his heart, "I shall
not be moved;
[b]I shall never be in adversity."
7 [a]His mouth is full of cursing and
[b]deceit and oppression;
Under his tongue *is* trouble and
iniquity.

8 He sits in the lurking places of the
villages;
In the secret places he murders
the innocent;
His eyes are secretly fixed on the
helpless.
9 He lies in wait secretly, as a lion
in his den;
He lies in wait to catch the poor;
He catches the poor when he
draws him into his net.
10 So [1]he crouches, he lies low,
That the helpless may fall by his
[2]strength.
11 He has said in his heart,
"God has forgotten;
He hides His face;
He will never see."

12 Arise, O LORD!
O God, [a]lift up Your hand!
Do not forget the [b]humble.
13 Why do the wicked renounce
God?
He has said in his heart,
"You will not require *an account.*"

14 But You have [a]seen, for You
observe trouble and grief,
To repay *it* by Your hand.
The helpless [b]commits[1] himself to
You;
[c]You are the helper of the
fatherless.
15 Break the arm of the wicked and
the evil *man;*
Seek out his wickedness *until*
You find none.

16 [a]The LORD *is* King forever and
ever;
The nations have perished out of
His land.
17 LORD, You have heard the desire
of the humble;
You will prepare their heart;
You will cause Your ear to hear,
18 To [1]do justice to the fatherless
and the oppressed,
That the *man of the earth may
[2]oppress no more.

3 [b]Prov. 28:4 [1]Or *The greedy man curses and spurns the LORD*
4 [a]Ps. 14:1; 36:1 [1]Or *All his thoughts are, "There is no God."*
5 [1]Lit. *are strong*
6 [a]Ps. 49:11; [Eccl. 8:11] [b]Rev. 18:7
7 [a][Rom. 3:14] [b]Ps. 55:10, 11
10 [1]Or *he is crushed, is bowed* [2]Or *mighty ones*
12 [a]Ps. 17:7; 94:2; Mic. 5:9 [b]Ps. 9:12
14 [a][Ps. 11:4] [b][2 Tim. 1:12] [c]Ps. 68:5; Hos. 14:3 [1]Lit. *leaves,* entrusts
16 [a]Ps. 29:10
18 [1]*vindicate* [2]*terrify* *See WW at Job 4:17.

PSALM 11

Faith in the LORD's Righteousness

To the Chief Musician. A Psalm of David.

IN [a]the LORD I put my trust;
How can you say to my soul,
"Flee *as* a bird to your mountain"?
2 For look! [a]The wicked bend *their*
bow,
They make ready their arrow on
the string,
That they may shoot [1]secretly at
the upright in heart.
3 [a]If the foundations are destroyed,
What can the righteous do?

4 The LORD *is* in His holy temple,
The LORD's [a]throne *is* in *heaven;
[b]His eyes behold,
His eyelids test the sons of men.
5 The LORD [a]tests the righteous,
But the wicked and the one who
loves violence His soul hates.
6 Upon the wicked He will rain
coals;
Fire and brimstone and a burning
wind
[a]*Shall be* [1]the portion of their cup.

PSALM 11
1 [a]Ps. 56:11
2 [a]Ps. 64:3, 4 [1]Lit. *in darkness*
3 [a]Ps. 82:5; 87:1; 119:152
4 [a]Ps. 2:4; [Is. 66:1]; Matt. 5:34; 23:22; [Acts 7:49]; Rev. 4:2 [b][Ps. 33:18; 34:15, 16] *See WW at 1 Kin. 8:23.
5 [a]Gen. 22:1; [James 1:12]
6 [a]1 Sam. 1:4; Ps. 75:8; Ezek. 38:22 [1]Their allotted portion or serving

10:4 See section 2 of Truth-In-Action following Ps. 41.
10:4 None of his thoughts: The secularization of any nation, with its removal of any mention of **God** in its schools, businesses, or politics, is a step toward its ultimate downfall and judgment.
10:7 This verse is quoted by Paul to show that both Jews and Gentiles have **deceit,** and all need a Savior (Rom. 3:14).
10:11–15 See section 1 of Truth-In-Action following Ps. 41.
10:14 Your hand: There are times when the wicked cannot be restrained by the righteous in society. Trust in God for ultimate justice becomes the only hope.
10:18 The man of the earth is contrasted with the Deliverer of all who are oppressed in John 3:31.
11:1–3 Though David would like to get away from it all and **flee** from his troubles, it is impossible because he is surrounded by his enemies and circumstances.
11:4, 5 It is a **test of the righteous** person's patience and faith when he sees **wicked** men committing injustice. The LORD waits momentarily to see who will remain loyal to just ways.
11:6 Brimstone is sulfur and is often associated with judgment (Gen. 19:24). The **cup** represents dire experiences one must face. See Matt. 26:39, where Jesus had to drink a bitter cup, awareness of His own approaching sacrificial death.

7 For the LORD *is* righteous,
He [a]loves righteousness;
[1]His countenance beholds the upright.

PSALM 12

Man's Treachery and God's Constancy

To the Chief Musician. [a]On [1]an eight-stringed harp. A *Psalm of David.

HELP,[1] LORD, for the godly man [a]ceases!*
For the faithful disappear from among the sons of men.
2 [a]They speak idly everyone with his neighbor;
With flattering lips *and* [1]a double heart they speak.

3 May the LORD [1]cut off all flattering lips,
And the tongue that speaks [2]proud things,
4 Who have said,
"With our tongue we will prevail;
Our lips *are* our own;
Who *is* lord over us?"

5 "For the oppression of the poor, for the sighing of the needy,
Now I will arise," says the LORD;
"I will set *him* in the safety for which he yearns."

5 6 The *words of the LORD *are* [a]pure words,
Like silver *tried in a furnace of earth,
Purified seven times.
7 You shall keep them, O LORD,
You shall preserve them from this generation forever.

8 The wicked prowl on every side,
When vileness is exalted among the sons of men.

PSALM 13

Trust in the Salvation of the LORD

To the Chief Musician. A Psalm of David.

HOW long, O LORD? Will You forget me forever?
[a]How long will You hide Your face from me?
2 How long shall I take counsel in my soul,
Having sorrow in my heart daily?
How long will my enemy be exalted over me?

3 Consider *and* hear me, O LORD my God;
[a]Enlighten my eyes,
[b]Lest I sleep the *sleep of* death;
4 Lest my enemy say,
"I have prevailed against him";
Lest those who trouble me rejoice when I am moved.

5 But I have trusted in Your mercy;
My heart shall rejoice in Your salvation.
6 I will *sing to the LORD,
Because He has dealt bountifully with me.

PSALM 14

Folly of the Godless, and God's Final Triumph

To the Chief Musician. A Psalm of David.

THE [a]fool has said in his heart,
"*There is* no God."
They are corrupt,

11:7 [a]Ps. 33:5; 45:7 [1]Or *The upright beholds His countenance*

PSALM 12

title [a]Ps. 6:title [1]Heb. *sheminith* *See WW at Ps. 3:title.
1 [a][Is. 57:1]; Mic. 7:2 [1]*Save* *See WW at Ps. 138:8.
2 [a]Ps. 10:7; 41:6 [1]An inconsistent mind
3 [1]*destroy* [2]*great*
6 [a]2 Sam. 22:31; Ps. 18:30; 119:140; Prov. 30:5 *See WW at 2 Sam. 22:31. • See WW at Zech. 13:9.

PSALM 13

1 [a]Job 13:24; Ps. 89:46
3 [a]1 Sam. 14:29; Ezra 9:8; Job 33:30; Ps. 18:28 [b]Jer. 51:39
6 *See WW at Judg. 5:3.

PSALM 14

1 [a]Ps. 10:4; 53:1

11:7 Beholds: The reward of a good man is face-to-face fellowship with God in heaven.
12:1 Help: It is a sad state of affairs when godly men have no influence in their community.
12:2–4 Speak idly: Idle gossip and scandalous rumors are contrary to godly conduct.
12:5 Disrespect for authority and self-will (v. 4) are not merely matters of independence; they lead to excesses and unaccountable behavior resulting in the **oppression** of others.
12:6, 7 God will speak up for the poor; we have the assurance of His **words.**
12:6 See section 5 of Truth-In-Action following Ps. 41.
12:8 Wicked prowl: Crimes increase in cities where immorality is promoted or flaunted by civic leaders, elected officials, or media personalities.
13:1–6 The feeling of being forgotten is addressed in this song.
13:3 Enlighten: That is, restore the sparkle in my eye—the sign of vitality. **Sleep** does not refer to unconsciousness after **death,** but rather it is a description of death from the viewpoint of the mourners.
13:6 Sing: No matter how distressed when the psalm began, David ends with a song of praise.
14:1–7 This psalm is in essence the same as Ps. 53, except that here *Yahweh* (**LORD**) is used as the name of God along with *'Elohim* (**God**). This duplication shows that the Israelites had several smaller collections of psalms, much as we have many different hymnals in our churches containing some of the same songs.
14:1–3 The **fool** is not someone of diminished intellectual capacity, nor a court jester, but one who makes an intellectual decision to choose moral perversion as a lifestyle. The Hebrew word for "fool" (*nabal*) is also the name of a man who opposed David and died foolishly, so this song may have grown out of that encounter (1 Sam. 25). These verses are quoted by the apostle Paul to show that Jews also are corrupt and in need of a Savior (Rom. 3:10), just as Gentiles are.

They have done abominable
works,
There is none who does good.

2 [a]The LORD looks down from
heaven upon the children of
men,
To see if there are any who
understand, who seek God.
3 [a]They have all turned aside,
They have together become
corrupt;
There is none who does *good,
No, not one.

4 Have all the workers of iniquity
no knowledge,
Who eat up my people *as* they eat
bread,
And [a]do not call on the LORD?
5 There they are in great *fear,
For God *is* with the *generation
of the righteous.
6 You shame the counsel of the
poor,
But the LORD *is* his [a]refuge.

7 [a]Oh,[1] that the salvation of Israel
would come out of Zion!
[b]When the LORD brings back
[2]the captivity of His people,
Let Jacob rejoice *and* Israel be
glad.

PSALM 15

The Character of Those Who May Dwell with the LORD

A Psalm of David.

1 LORD, [a]who may [1]abide in Your
tabernacle?
Who may *dwell in Your holy
hill?

2 He who walks uprightly,
And works righteousness,
And speaks the [a]truth in his
heart;
3 He *who* [a]does not backbite with
his tongue,
Nor does evil to his neighbor,
[b]Nor does he [1]take up a
reproach against his friend;

KINGDOM DYNAMICS

15:3 To Get Closer to God, Love Others, BROTHERLY LOVE. In Ps. 15, David is asking God the necessary qualifications to abide in His tabernacle (v. 1). God's reply emphasizes that to "abide" in God's presence and purpose first requires a will to exhibit a strong relationship with others. To expect to have a strong relationship with God, determine to conduct life in right relationship with others! God tells David 1) to speak kindly of his neighbors; 2) never to gossip or say anything to destroy another's reputation; 3) to do nothing to hurt another person in any way. 4) Finally, God warns David not to "reproach" his neighbor. "Reproach" (Hebrew *cherpah*) means "blame, discredit, disgrace, or shame." If the OT teaches that one desiring to get closer to God must prioritize love toward others, the NT commandment "Love your neighbor as yourself" (Rom. 13:9) is surely vital to our relationship with the heavenly Father today.

(Lev. 19:34/Ps. 86:5) D.S.

4 [a]In whose eyes a vile person is
despised,
But he honors those who fear
the LORD;
He *who* [b]swears to his own hurt
and does not change;
5 He *who* does not put out his
money at usury,
Nor does he take a bribe
against the innocent.

He who does these *things*
[a]shall never be moved.

2

PSALM 16

The Hope of the Faithful, and the Messiah's Victory

A [a]Michtam of David.

1 PRESERVE[1] me, O God, for in You
I put my trust.

14:2 [a]Ps. 33:13, 14; 102:19; Rom. 3:11
3 [a]Rom. 3:12 *See WW at Ezek. 34:14.
4 [a]Ps. 79:6; Is. 64:7; Jer. 10:25; Amos 8:4; Mic. 3:3
5 *See WW at Hos. 3:5. • See WW at Esth. 9:28.
6 [a]Ps. 9:9; 40:17; 46:1; 142:5
7 [a]Ps. 53:6; [Rom. 11:25–27] [b]Deut. 30:3; Job 42:10 [1]Lit. *Who will give out of Zion the salvation of Israel?* [2]Or *His captive people*

PSALM 15
1 [a]Ps. 24:3–5 [1]*sojourn* *See WW at Num. 10:12.
2 [a]Zech. 8:16; [Eph. 4:25]
3 [a][Lev. 19:16–18] [b]Ex. 23:1 [1]*receive*
4 [a]Esth. 3:2 [b]Lev. 5:4
5 [a]2 Pet. 1:10

PSALM 16
title [a]Ps. 56—60
1 [1]*Watch over*

14:4–6 Eat up my people: Vile men do not just wander in their own moral darkness; they attack the people of the light as well.
14:4 All heathen, as well as civilized men, have evidence and **knowledge** that there is a higher moral Agent governing this universe (Rom. 1:20).
14:7 Brings back the captivity means "restores them to prosperity again" (Job 42:10). **Jacob** is symbolic for the whole nation of **Israel.** Ultimate deliverance is a motive to praise God and to **rejoice!**
15:1 Who: This same question is posed in 24:3 where the list may be considered supplementary to this list. The **tabernacle** and the **holy hill** refer to the resting place of the ark of the covenant where the presence of God was, and where worshipers assembled.
15:4 See section 2 of Truth-In-Action following Ps. 41.
15:4 Swears refers to a man's giving his word on a business deal that turns into a deficit, but in which he still keeps his word.
15:5 Usury: The Levitical law prohibited demanding interest on loans to the poor (Lev. 25:36). The man who conducts himself by these guidelines in vv. 2–5 will not **be moved** from the glorious presence of God.
16:title Michtam: Six psalms (16; 56—60), as well as the

2 *O my soul,* you have said to the LORD,
"You *are* my Lord,
[a]My goodness is nothing apart from You."
3 As for the saints who *are* on the earth,
"They are the excellent ones, in [a]whom is all my delight."

4 Their sorrows shall be multiplied who hasten *after* another *god;*
Their drink offerings of [a]blood I will not offer,
[b]Nor take up their names on my lips.

5 O LORD, *You are* the portion of my *inheritance and my cup;
You [1]maintain my lot.
6 The lines have fallen to me in pleasant *places;*
Yes, I have a good inheritance.

7 I will bless the LORD who has given me counsel;
My [1]heart also instructs me in the night seasons.
8 [a]I have set the LORD always before me;
Because *He is* at my right hand I shall not be moved.

9 Therefore my heart is glad, and my glory rejoices;
My *flesh also will [1]rest *in hope.
10 [a]For You will not leave my soul in [1]Sheol,
Nor will You allow Your Holy One to [2]see corruption.

KINGDOM DYNAMICS

16:10 "Declared to Be the Son of God with Power," MESSIAH'S COMING. The apostles clearly recognized this verse as forecasting the resurrection of Jesus. Peter quotes this verse in his sermon on the Day of Pentecost (Acts 2:27), and Paul quotes this verse in his early preaching at Antioch of Pisidia (Acts 13:35).

The sufficiency of Christ's work of atonement is declared in the Resurrection (Rom. 6; 2 Tim. 1:10; Heb. 2:9–18; 1 Pet. 2:18), and by the Resurrection Jesus was "declared *to be* the Son of God with power" (Rom. 1:4). He has completed the work He came to do and has ascended to the right hand of the Father. Now we look forward in hope, for having broken the power of death, He has introduced the promise of eternal life to all who receive Him as Messiah (John 6:40).

(Is. 53:1–12/John 14:1–3) J.H.

2 [a]Job 35:7
3 [a]Ps. 119:63
4 [a]Ps. 106:37, 38 [b][Ex. 23:13]; Josh. 23:7
5 [1]Lit. *uphold* *See WW at Zech. 2:12.
7 [1]Mind, lit. *kidneys*
8 [a][Acts 2:25–28]
9 [1]Or *dwell securely* *See WW at Job 19:26. • See WW at Deut. 33:12.
10 [a]Ps. 49:15; 86:13; Acts 2:31, 32; Heb. 13:20 [1]The abode of the dead [2]*undergo*
11 [a]Ps. 139:24; [Matt. 7:14]

11 You will show me the [a]path of life;
In Your presence *is* fullness of joy;
At Your right hand *are* pleasures forevermore.

PSALM 17

Prayer with Confidence in Final Salvation

A Prayer of David.

HEAR a just cause, O LORD,
Attend to my cry;
Give ear to my prayer *which is* not from deceitful lips.
2 Let my vindication come from Your presence;
Let Your eyes look on the things that are upright.

3 You have tested my heart; **7**
You have visited *me* in the night;
[a]You have [1]tried* me and have found [2]nothing;
I have purposed that my mouth shall not [b]transgress.
4 Concerning the works of men,
By the word of Your lips,
I have kept away from the paths of the destroyer.
5 [a]Uphold my steps in Your paths,
That my footsteps may not slip.

PSALM 17
3 [a]Job 23:10; Ps. 66:10; Zech. 13:9; [1 Pet. 1:7] [b]Ps. 39:1 [1]*examined* [2]Nothing evil *See WW at Zech. 13:9.
5 [a]Job 23:11; Ps. 44:18; 119:133

psalm of Hezekiah in Is. 38:9–20, are so designated, yet the meaning of *Michtam* is obscure. It seems to refer to deliverance from death.

16:2 The first **LORD** is the name of God (Hebrew *Yahweh*); the second **Lord** is a title meaning "Ruler, Master" (Hebrew *'adonai*). Thus, **You have said to [Yahweh], "You *are* my [Master]."**

16:5, 6 Lot and **lines** refer poetically to the division of the Promised Land by Joshua, which climaxed the fulfillment of God's promises (Josh. 21:43–45). God is as special to the psalmist as this **inheritance** of land (**portion**).

16:9 Glory is a poetic expression for the soul, the glorious part of a man.

16:10, 11 Sheol is the domain of the dead. David not only expresses his faith that death will not separate him from God (Rom. 8:38, 39); but also, he prophetically declares that the **Holy One** (Jesus) will be resurrected from the dead, bodily, without **corruption** (decay). This was the exuberant announcement of Peter on the Day of Pentecost (Acts 2:25–31).

17:1 Hear a just cause resembles the words of an accused man as his own lawyer, setting the mood for this prayer of David.

17:3 See section 7 of Truth-In-Action following Ps. 41.

17:3 Tried has reference to being in a refiner's crucible and found not to have any impurities or dross.

6 [a]I have called upon You, for You
will hear me, O God;
Incline Your ear to me, *and* hear
my speech.
7 Show Your marvelous
lovingkindness by Your right
hand,
O You who [1]save those who trust
in You
From those who rise up *against*
them.
8 Keep me as the [1]apple of Your
eye;
Hide me under the shadow of
Your wings,
9 From the wicked who oppress
me,
From my deadly enemies who
surround me.

10 They have closed up their
[a]fat *hearts;*
With their mouths they [b]speak
proudly.
11 They have now surrounded us in
our steps;
They have set their eyes,
crouching down to the earth,
12 As a lion is eager to tear his
prey,
And like a young lion lurking in
secret places.

13 Arise, O LORD,
Confront him, cast him down;
Deliver my life from the wicked
with Your sword,
14 With Your hand from men,
O LORD,
From men of the world *who have*
their portion in *this* life,
And whose belly You fill with
Your hidden treasure.
They are satisfied with children,
And leave the rest of their
possession for their babes.

15 As for me, [a]I will see Your face
in righteousness;
[b]I shall be satisfied when I
[c]awake in Your likeness.

6 [a]Ps. 86:7; 116:2
7 [1]*deliver*
8 [1]*pupil*
10 [a]Ezek. 16:49 [b][1 Sam. 2:3]
15 [a][1 John 3:2] [b]Ps. 4:6, 7; 16:11 [c][Is. 26:19]

PSALM 18

title [a]Ps. 36:title [b]2 Sam. 22
1 [a]Ps. 144:1
2 [a]Heb. 2:13 [1]Lit. *rock* [2]Strength *See WW at Ezek. 29:21.
3 [a]Ps. 76:4; Rev. 5:12
4 [a]Ps. 116:3 [1]Lit. *Belial*

PSALM 18

God the Sovereign Savior

To the Chief Musician. A Psalm of David [a]the servant of the LORD, who spoke to the LORD the words of [b]this song on the day that the LORD delivered him from the hand of all his enemies and from the hand of Saul. And he said:

I [a]WILL love You, O LORD, my
strength.
2 The LORD is my rock and my
fortress and my deliverer;
My God, my [1]strength, [a]in whom
I will trust;
My shield and the [2]horn* of my
salvation, my stronghold.
3 I will call upon the LORD,
[a]*who is worthy* to be praised;
So shall I be saved from my
enemies.

KINGDOM DYNAMICS

18:3 Praise Spotlights God, PRAISE PATHWAY. Here is the most basic reason for our praise to God: He is "*worthy* to be praised [Hebrew *halal,* "praise with a loud voice"]." The most primitive meaning of *halal* is "to cause to shine." Thus, with our praise, we are throwing the spotlight on our God who is worthy and deserves to be praised and glorified. The more we put the spotlight on Him, the more He causes us to shine. Modern medicine attests to the value of bringing a depressed person into a brightly lighted room, acknowledging that light greatly helps to heal their depression. How much more will praise introduce the light of God and bring us into the joy of the Lord.

(Ps. 7:14–17/Ps. 22:3, 4) C.G.

4 [a]The pangs of death surrounded
me,
And the floods of [1]ungodliness
made me afraid.
5 The sorrows of Sheol surrounded
me;
The snares of death confronted
me.
6 In my distress I called upon the
LORD,
And cried out to my God; 7

17:7 Lovingkindness (Hebrew *chesed*): To obtain justice and protection David appeals not only to his own innocence and integrity, but also he appeals to God's character, compassion, and covenant faithfulness.
17:8 The phrase concerning the **eye** is drawn from Deut. 32:10 and refers to sight, which is greatly cherished and diligently protected.
17:9 The incident with Saul in 1 Sam. 23:26 is an example of the **enemies who surround** David.
17:10 Fat *hearts* refers to wanton luxury (James 5:5).
17:14 Portion: The wicked **men** are those who are earthly minded, sensual, materialistic (Phil. 3:19), and who are so gorged that they have an abundance to **leave** to their **children**.
17:15 Likeness: This may have been a verse the apostle John had in mind when he wrote of the future resurrection and its rewards for those who were mistreated in this present life (1 John 3:2).
18:1–50 This psalm is a repeat of the song recorded in 2 Sam. 22 and is the longest psalm in Book One.
18:6 See section 7 of Truth-In-Action following Ps. 41.

He heard my voice from His temple,
And my cry came before Him, *even* to His ears.

7 [a]Then the earth shook and trembled;
The foundations of the hills also quaked and were shaken,
Because He was angry.
8 Smoke *went up from His nostrils,
And devouring fire from His mouth;
Coals were kindled by it.
9 [a]He bowed the heavens also, and came down
With darkness under His feet.
10 [a]And He rode upon a cherub, and flew;
[b]He flew upon the wings of the wind.
11 He made darkness His secret place;
[a]His canopy around Him *was* dark waters
And thick clouds of the skies.
12 [a]From the brightness before Him,
His thick clouds passed with hailstones and coals of fire.

13 The LORD thundered from heaven,
And the Most High uttered [a]His voice,
[1]Hailstones and coals of fire.
14 [a]He sent out His arrows and scattered [1]the foe,
Lightnings in abundance, and He vanquished them.
15 Then the channels of the sea were seen,
The foundations of the world were uncovered
At Your rebuke, O LORD,
At the blast of the breath of Your nostrils.

16 [a]He sent from above, He took me;
He drew me out of many waters.
17 He delivered me from my strong enemy,
From those who hated me,
For they were too strong for me.
18 They confronted me in the day of my calamity,
But the LORD was my support.

7 [a]Acts 4:31
8 *See WW at Ex. 19:20.
9 [a]Ps. 144:5
10 [a]Ps. 80:1; 99:1 [b][Ps. 104:3]
11 [a]Ps. 97:2
12 [a]Ps. 97:3; 140:10; Hab. 3:11
13 [a][Ps. 29:3–9; 104:7] [1]So with MT, Tg., Vg.; a few Heb. mss., LXX omit *Hailstones and coals of fire*
14 [a]Josh. 10:10; Ps. 144:6; Is. 30:30; Hab. 3:11 [1]Lit. *them*
16 [a]Ps. 144:7
19 [a]Ps. 4:1; 31:8; 118:5
20 [a]1 Sam. 24:19; [Job 33:26]; Ps. 7:8
23 [1]*with*
24 [a]1 Sam. 26:23; Ps. 18:20
25 [a][1 Kin. 8:32; Ps. 62:12]; Matt. 5:7
26 [a][Lev. 26:23–28]; Prov. 3:34
27 [a][Ps. 101:5]; Prov. 6:17
28 [a]1 Kin. 15:4; Job 18:6; [Ps. 119:105]
29 [1]Or *run through*
30 [a][Deut. 32:4]; Rev. 15:3 [b]Ps. 12:6; 119:140; [Prov. 30:5] [c][Ps. 17:7] [1]Lit. *refined* *See WW at 2 Sam. 22:31.
31 [a][Deut. 32:31, 39; 1 Sam. 2:2; Ps. 86:8–10; Is. 45:5]
32 [a][Ps. 91:2] *See WW at Zech. 4:6.

19 [a]He also brought me out into a broad place;
He delivered me because He delighted in me.

20 [a]The LORD rewarded me according to my righteousness;
According to the cleanness of my hands
He has recompensed me.
21 For I have kept the ways of the LORD,
And have not wickedly departed from my God.
22 For all His judgments *were* before me,
And I did not put away His statutes from me.
23 I was also blameless [1]before Him,
And I kept myself from my iniquity.
24 [a]Therefore the LORD has recompensed me according to my righteousness,
According to the cleanness of my hands in His sight.

25 [a]With the merciful You will show Yourself merciful;
With a blameless man You will show Yourself blameless;
26 With the pure You will show Yourself pure;
And [a]with the devious You will show Yourself shrewd.
27 For You will save the humble people,
But will bring down [a]haughty looks.

28 [a]For You will light my lamp;
The LORD my God will enlighten my darkness.
29 For by You I can [1]run against a troop,
By my God I can leap over a wall.
30 *As for* God, [a]His way *is* perfect;
[b]The *word of the LORD is [1]proven;
He *is* a shield [c]to all who trust in Him.

31 [a]For who *is* God, except the LORD?
And who *is* a rock, except our God?
32 *It is* God who [a]arms me with *strength,
And makes my way perfect.

18:7–15 Shook and trembled: David waxes eloquent with a group of colorful verses, comparing God's intervention on his behalf to spectacular cataclysms in nature.
18:20 My righteousness: These are not statements of arrogance, but declarations of innocence and integrity, undeserving of the ill-treatment received from Saul.
18:25–27 Merciful: Jesus reinforced these moral guidelines in the Sermon on the Mount (Matt. 5:7, 8).

33 [a]He makes my feet like the *feet of* deer,
And [b]sets me on my *high places.
34 [a]He teaches my hands to make war,
So that my arms can bend a bow of bronze.

35 You have also given me the shield of Your salvation;
Your right hand has held me up,
Your gentleness has made me great.
36 You enlarged my path under me,
[a]So my feet did not slip.

37 I have pursued my enemies and overtaken them;
Neither did I turn back again till they were destroyed.
38 I have wounded them,
So that they could not rise;
They have fallen under my feet.
39 For You have armed me with *strength for the battle;
You have [1]subdued under me those who rose up against me.
40 You have also given me the necks of my enemies,
So that I destroyed those who hated me.
41 They cried out, but *there was* none to save;
[a]*Even* to the LORD, but He did not answer them.
42 Then I beat them as fine as the dust before the wind;
I [a]cast them out like dirt in the streets.

43 You have delivered me from the strivings of the people;
[a]You have made me the head of the [1]nations;
[b]A people I have not known shall *serve me.
44 As soon as they hear of me they obey me;
The foreigners [1]submit to me.
45 [a]The foreigners fade away,
And come frightened from their hideouts.

46 The LORD lives!
Blessed *be* my Rock!
Let the God of my salvation be **exalted.**

WORD WEALTH

18:46 exalted, *rum* (*room*); Strong's #7311: To elevate, raise, bring up, exalt, lift up, hold up, extol; to make high and powerful. Since God is in the highest, and is the Most High (*'El 'Elyon*), He cannot be higher than He is already; however, He can be raised and exalted in our understanding of Him. Related to *rum* are the words *'Abram* (Abram) and *terumah.* Abram's name means "Father of Height," that is, "Exalted Father," or "Man of Stature." *Terumah* means "heave offering," a gift that evidently was tossed upward while being offered.

47 *It is* God who avenges me,
[a]And subdues the peoples under me;
48 He delivers me from my enemies.
[a]You also lift me up above those who rise against me;
You have delivered me from the violent man.
49 [a]Therefore I will *give thanks to You, O LORD, among the [1]Gentiles,
And sing praises to Your name.

50 [a]Great deliverance He gives to His king,
And shows mercy to His anointed,
To David and his [1]descendants forevermore.

PSALM 19

The Perfect Revelation of the LORD

To the Chief Musician. A Psalm of David.

THE [a]heavens declare the *glory of God;
And the [b]firmament[1] shows [2]His handiwork.
2 Day unto day utters speech,
And night unto night reveals *knowledge.
3 *There is* no speech nor language
Where their voice is not heard.
4 [a]Their [1]line has gone out through all the earth,

33 [a]2 Sam. 2:18; Hab. 3:19 [b]Deut. 32:13; 33:29 *See WW at Ezek. 6:3.
34 [a]Ps. 144:1
36 [a]Ps. 66:9; Prov. 4:12
39 [1]Lit. *caused to bow* *See WW at Zech. 4:6.
41 [a]Job 27:9; Prov. 1:28; Is. 1:15; Ezek. 8:18; Zech. 7:13
42 [a]Zech. 10:5
43 [a]2 Sam. 8; Ps. 89:27 [b]Is. 52:15 [1]*Gentiles* *See WW at Ps. 100:2.
44 [1]*feign submission*
45 [a]Mic. 7:17
47 [a]Ps. 47:3
48 [a]Ps. 27:6; 59:1
49 [a]2 Sam. 22:50; Rom. 15:9 [1]*nations* *See WW at 1 Chr. 16:7.
50 [a]2 Sam. 7:12; Ps. 21:1; 144:10 [1]Lit. *seed*

PSALM 19

1 [a]Is. 40:22; [Rom. 1:19, 20] [b]Gen. 1:6, 7 [1]*expanse* of heaven [2]*the work of His hands* *See WW at Is. 60:1.
2 *See WW at Mal. 2:7.
4 [a]Rom. 10:18 [1]LXX, Syr., Vg. *sound;* Tg. *business*

18:42 Beat: The total physical conquest pictured here was a part of the Old Covenant era and is not to be construed as an example for conduct under the New Covenant of Christ and His spiritual kingdom (Matt. 5:43, 44).
18:49 This was quoted by the apostle Paul in Rom. 15:9 to show that Christ came to be the Savior both of the Jews and the **Gentiles.**
19:1–14 This psalm appropriately unites the two ways God has revealed Himself to man: by general revelation in His creation (vv. 1–6; Rom. 1:19, 20), and by specific revelation in His inspired Word (vv. 7–14; Heb. 1:1).
19:1 The **firmament** is the stretched-out expanse of the sky.
19:4 Has gone out: The apostle Paul used this verse to show that the Jews have known the word of truth; but, having

And their words to the end of the
*world.

In them He has set a [2]tabernacle
for the sun,
5 Which *is* like a bridegroom
coming out of his chamber,
[a]*And* *rejoices like a strong man
to run its race.
6 Its rising *is* from one end of
heaven,
And its circuit to the other end;
And there is nothing hidden from
its heat.

4 7 [a]The law of the LORD *is* perfect,
[1]converting the soul;
The testimony of the LORD *is* sure,
making [b]wise the simple;

KINGDOM DYNAMICS

19:7 The Complete Trustworthiness of the Bible, THE WORD OF GOD. That the "law of the LORD *is* perfect," is direct reference to the absolute, complete, and entire trustworthiness of the Holy Scriptures, which constitute the Bible. The Word of God is perfect in its accuracy and sure in its dependability. Two terms are generally used to describe these features of God's Word: 1) Inerrant (perfect) means that, in the original copies of each manuscript written by each Bible book's respective author, there was nothing mistaken or tinged with error. (Further, the excellence of the Holy Spirit's protection of the Scriptures over the centuries, has insured that the copies delivered into our hands from generations past, is essentially the same. Even literary critics who claim no faith in the truth of the Bible, attest to its being the most completely reliable of any book transmitted from antiquity, in terms of its actually remaining unchanged and dependably accurate.) 2) Infallible refers to the fact that the Bible is unfailing as an absolutely trustworthy guide for our faith (belief in God) and practice (life and behavior). This is so because God is true (John 3:33; 17:3), because His Word reveals His truth (John 17:17), and because God cannot lie (Num. 23:19; Titus 1:2; Heb. 6:18).
(2 Tim. 3:16/Prov. 30:5, 6) J.W.H.

4 [2]*tent* *See WW at Jer. 51:15.
5 [a]Eccl. 1:5 *See WW at Is. 64:5.
7 [a]Ps. 111:7; [Rom. 7:12] [b]Ps. 119:130 [1]*restoring*
10 [a]Ps. 119:72, 127; Prov. 8:10, 11, 19 [1]*honey in the combs*
12 [a][Ps. 51:1, 2] *See WW at Neh. 8:8. • See WW at Num. 14:18.
13 [a]Num. 15:30 [b]Ps. 119:133; [Rom. 6:12–14] [1]Or *much*
14 [a]Ps. 51:15 [b]Ps. 31:5; Is. 47:4 [1]Lit. *rock* *See WW at Ps. 37:4.

8 The statutes of the LORD *are* right,
rejoicing the heart;
The commandment of the LORD *is*
pure, enlightening the eyes;
9 The fear of the LORD *is* clean,
enduring forever;
The judgments of the LORD *are*
true *and* righteous altogether.
10 More to be desired *are they* than
[a]gold,
Yea, than much fine gold;
Sweeter also than honey and the
[1]honeycomb.
11 Moreover by them Your servant
is warned,
And in keeping them *there is*
great reward.

12 Who can *understand *his* errors? 6
[a]Cleanse* me from secret *faults*.
13 Keep back Your servant also
from [a]presumptuous *sins;*
Let them not have [b]dominion
over me.
Then I shall be blameless,
And I shall be innocent of
[1]great transgression.

14 [a]Let the words of my mouth and 2
the meditation of my *heart
Be acceptable in Your sight,
O LORD, my [1]strength and my
[b]Redeemer.

KINGDOM DYNAMICS

19:14 "Acceptable" Speech Before God, FAITH'S CONFESSION. This oft-quoted verse attests to the importance and desirability of our words and thoughts being consistent with God's Word and will. The text literally says, "Let what I speak and what my heart murmurs to itself be a delight to You, Lord." Clearly, the acceptability of our words in God's sight is dependent upon their being consistent with what our hearts feel or think. The truth of this text urges us to always speak the kind of words that confirm what we believe or think in our hearts about God, His love, and His power. If we believe, yet contradict that belief with careless words from our mouth, it is not acceptable in God's sight. Remember the lesson

heard it, they refused to obey it, with the result that a door has been opened to the Gentiles to hear the gospel (Rom. 10:18).

19:6 Circuit: David describes the rotation of the Earth from the viewpoint of a man on Earth and is not teaching that the sun revolves around the Earth. By comparison, we use words like "sunrise" and "sunset" to describe the Earth's rotation, when technically the sun does neither.

19:7–11 See section 4 of Truth-In-Action following Ps. 41.

19:7 The general revelation about God was introduced by using the nonspecific name for God (Hebrew *'El*, v. 1); but the specific revelation is marked by the revealed name of God (Hebrew *Yahweh*) translated in vv. 7–9 six times as LORD.

19:12–14 Cleanse me: The correct reaction to seeing and hearing God's revelations is personal introspection (James 1:21–25).

19:12, 13 See section 6 of Truth-In-Action following Ps. 41.

19:14 See section 2 of Truth-In-Action following Ps. 41.

of Cain's sacrifice (Gen. 4:1–7): what is unacceptable is not only faithless and fruitless; it may also become deadly.
(2 Chr. 6:24–31/Prov. 16:23, 24) R.H.

PSALM 20

The Assurance of God's Saving Work

To the Chief Musician. A Psalm of David.

MAY the LORD answer you in the
day of trouble;
May the name of the God of Jacob
[1]defend you;
2 May He send you help from the
sanctuary,
And strengthen you out of Zion;
3 May He remember all your
offerings,
And accept your burnt sacrifice.
Selah

4 May He grant you according to
your heart's *desire*,
And [a]fulfill all your [1]purpose.
5 We will rejoice in your salvation,
And in the name of our God we
will set up *our* banners!
May the LORD fulfill all your
petitions.

6 Now I know that the LORD saves
His [1]anointed;
He will answer him from His holy
heaven
With the saving strength of His
right hand.

7 Some *trust* in chariots, and some
in [a]horses;
But we will remember the name
of the LORD our God.
8 They have bowed down and
fallen;
But we have risen and stand
upright.

9 Save, LORD!
May the King answer us when we
call.

PSALM 20

1 [1]Lit. *set you on high*
4 [a]Ps. 21:2 [1]*counsel*
6 [1]Commissioned one, Heb. *messiah*
7 [a]Deut. 20:1; Ps. 33:16, 17; Prov. 21:31; Is. 31:1

PSALM 21

1 *See WW at 2 Chr. 7:10. • See WW at Hab. 3:18.
2 [a]2 Sam. 7:26–29
4 [a]Ps. 61:5, 6; 133:3 *See WW at Mic. 4:5.
6 [a]Ps. 16:11; 45:7 [1]Lit. *joyful with gladness*
7 [1]*shaken* *See WW at Gen. 14:18.
10 [1]Lit. *seed*

PSALM 21

Joy in the Salvation of the LORD

To the Chief Musician. A Psalm of David.

THE king *shall have joy in Your
strength, O LORD;
And in Your salvation how
greatly shall he *rejoice!
2 You have given him his heart's
desire,
And have not withheld the
[a]request of his lips. Selah

3 For You meet him with the
blessings of goodness;
You set a crown of pure gold
upon his head.
4 [a]He asked life from You, *and* You
gave *it* to him—
Length of days forever and
*ever.
5 His glory *is* great in Your
salvation;
Honor and majesty You have
placed upon him.
6 For You have made him most
blessed forever;
[a]You have made him [1]exceedingly
glad with Your presence.
7 For the king trusts in the LORD,
And through the mercy of the
*Most High he shall not be
[1]moved.

8 Your hand will find all Your
enemies;
Your right hand will find those
who hate You.
9 You shall make them as a fiery
oven in the time of Your anger;
The LORD shall swallow them up
in His wrath,
And the fire shall devour them.
10 Their offspring You shall destroy
from the earth,
And their [1]descendants from
among the sons of men.
11 For they intended evil against
You;

20:1–9 Trouble: This psalm may have been a typical congregational prayer used with sacrifices offered just before going to war.
20:1 The God of Jacob refers to the fact that God delivered Jacob in times of distress (Gen. 35:3).
20:6 Now I know is a statement of faith that prayer is heard.
20:7 Advanced nations used **chariots** and **horses** in warfare, whereas the Israelites had a more primitive arsenal—thus the total reliance on the LORD for victory. Later Solomon acquired a number of chariots and horses (1 Kin. 10:26–29), contrary to the Law (Deut. 17:16).
20:9 Or as the Septuagint Greek version translates: "O LORD, save the king, hear us when we call."
21:1–13 This psalm seems to be a thankful praise for victory in response to the previous pleas in Ps. 20. Some commentators, as well as Jewish rabbis, see here a prophetic type of **king** Messiah (Jesus) ascending in victory.
21:3 For example, after victory over the Ammonites, David received the royal **crown** of the conquered king (2 Sam. 12:30).
21:7 Most High is a title for God (Hebrew *'Elyon*).
21:8 Will find means "will seek out the fleeing or retreating enemy."
21:9 Fiery oven: God's judgment is often described as **fire** (Mal. 4:1), and it is declared that this will be the means of bringing the final Judgment Day to a conclusion (2 Pet. 3:7).
21:10 Offspring: Having no one to carry on the family name was considered a great curse in Middle Eastern culture.

They devised a plot *which* they
are not able *to* [a]*perform.*
12 Therefore You will make them
turn their back;
You will make ready *Your arrows*
on Your string toward their
faces.

13 Be *exalted, O LORD, in Your own
strength!
We will sing and praise Your
power.

PSALM 22

The Suffering, Praise, and Posterity of the Messiah

To the Chief Musician. Set to [1]"The Deer of the Dawn." A Psalm of David.

MY [a]God, My God, why have You
forsaken Me?
Why are You so far from helping
Me,
And from the words of My
groaning?

KINGDOM DYNAMICS

22:1–31 Details of Messiah's Death, MESSIAH'S COMING. Within this psalm are many prophecies that were fulfilled in the death of Jesus; let us look at four. First, the ridicule of the people is predicted (vv. 7, 8). The same expressions of ridicule were actually spoken by the chief priests at the Cross (Matt. 27:36–44). Second, v. 16 specifically predicts that His hands and feet would be pierced. This was fulfilled at the death of Jesus (see John 20:25). Further, the casting of lots for Jesus' clothing (John 19:23, 24) was prophesied in v. 18. But perhaps the most significant statement in the entire psalm is v. 1, which Jesus quoted from the Cross (Matt. 27:46). In that word we see God Himself turning away from His beloved Son who is bearing the sin of the world. Jesus is bearing man's judgment, not only the judgment of death but also the judgment of separation from God. At that moment Jesus is experiencing the darkest moment of His life, and He bore it—for us.

(Ps. 41:9/Is. 53:1–12) J.H.

11 [a]Ps. 2:1–4
13 *See WW at Ps. 18:46.

PSALM 22

title [1]Heb. *Aijeleth Hashahar*
1 [a][Matt. 27:46; Mark 15:34]

3 [a]Deut. 10:21; Ps. 148:14
*See WW at Lev. 19:2.

2 O My God, I cry in the daytime,
but You do not hear;
And in the night season, and am
not silent.

3 But You *are* *holy,
Enthroned in the [a]praises of
Israel.
4 Our fathers trusted in You;
They trusted, and You delivered
them.

KINGDOM DYNAMICS

22:3, 4 Praise, the Pathway to God's Presence, PRAISE PATHWAY. Unquestionably, one of the most remarkable and exciting things about honest and sincere praise is taught here: Praise will bring the presence of God. Although God is everywhere present, there is a distinct manifestation of His rule, which enters the environment of praise. Here is the remedy for times when you feel alone, deserted, or depressed. Praise! However simply, compose your song and testimony of God's goodness in your life. The result: God enters! His presence will live (take up residence) in our lives. The word "inhabit" (Hebrew *yawshab*) means "to sit down, to remain, to settle, or marry." In other words, God does not merely visit us when we praise Him, but His presence abides with us and we partner with Him in a growing relationship. Let this truth create faith and trust, and lead to deliverance from satanic harassments, torment, or bondage. Notice how this text ties three words together: "praises," "trusted," and "delivered"!

(Ps. 18:3/Ps. 47:7) C.G.

KINGDOM DYNAMICS

22:3 "Establishing" God's Throne, WORSHIP AND THE KINGDOM. The Psalms were the praise hymnal of the early church, and as such are laden with principles fully applicable for NT living today. Few principles are more essential to our understanding than this one: the presence of God's kingdom power is directly related to the practice of God's praise. The verb "enthroned" indicates that wherever God's people exalt His name, He is ready to manifest His kingdom's power in the way most appropriate to the situation, as His rule is invited to invade our setting.

22:1–31 This psalm is quoted frequently in the NT Gospels with reference to the crucifixion of Jesus. It parallels the Suffering Servant theme of Is. 53.

22:1 My God, My God: While on the Cross, the tortured Jesus cried out these words (Matt. 27:46; Mark 15:34). Hell is total separation from God as a punishment for unrepented sin, a state of being **forsaken**. Jesus went through this hell experience in our place for our sins, so we will not have to.

22:3 Since God is **enthroned in the praises,** worship is the key to entering fully into His presence. The concept here is that praise releases God's glory, thus bringing to the worshipers actualized responses of His kingly reign. His enthroned responses through the Holy Spirit can take many forms, such as prophecy, healings, miracles, affirmation to individual hearts, a call to reverential silence and awe, conviction of sin, and salvation of sinners. This verse should be a guiding goal for all personal and corporate worship times.

It is this fact that properly leads many to conclude that in a very real way, praise prepares a specific and present place for God among His people. Some have chosen the term "establish His throne" to describe this "enthroning" of God in our midst by our worshiping and praising welcome. God awaits the prayerful and praise-filled worship of His people as an entry point for His kingdom to "come"—to enter, that His "will be done" in human circumstances. (See Luke 11:2–4 and Ps. 93:2.) We do not manipulate God, but align ourselves with the great kingdom truth: His is the power, ours is the privilege (and responsibility) to welcome Him into our world—our private, present world or the circumstances of our society.

(Ex. 19:5–7/Ps. 93:2) J.W.H.

5 They cried to You, and were delivered;
[a]They trusted in You, and were not ashamed.

6 But I *am* [a]a worm, and no man;
[b]A reproach of men, and despised by the people.
7 [a]All those who see Me ridicule Me;
They [1]shoot out the lip, they shake the head, *saying*,
8 "He[a] [1]trusted in the LORD, let Him rescue Him;
[b]Let Him deliver Him, since He delights in Him!"

9 [a]But You *are* He who took Me out of the womb;
You made Me trust *while* on My mother's breasts.
10 I was cast upon You from birth.
From My mother's womb
[a]You *have been* My God.
11 Be not far from Me,
For trouble *is* near;
For *there is* none to help.

12 [a]Many bulls have surrounded Me;
Strong *bulls* of [b]Bashan have encircled Me.
13 [a]They [1]gape at Me *with* their mouths,
Like a raging and *roaring lion.

14 I am poured out like water,
[a]And all My bones are out of joint;
My heart is like wax;
It has melted [1]within Me.
15 [a]My strength is dried up like a potsherd,
And [b]My tongue clings to My jaws;
You have brought Me to the dust of death.

16 For dogs have surrounded Me;
The congregation of the wicked has enclosed Me.
[a]They[1] pierced My hands and My feet;
17 I can count all My bones.
[a]They look *and* stare at Me.
18 [a]They divide My garments among them,
And for My clothing they cast lots.

19 But You, O LORD, do not be far from Me;
O My Strength, hasten to help Me!
20 Deliver Me from the sword,
[a]My[1] precious *life* from the power of the dog.
21 [a]Save* Me from the lion's mouth
And from the horns of the wild oxen!

[b]You have answered Me.

22 [a]I will declare Your name to [b]My *brethren;
In the midst of the assembly I will *praise You.
23 [a]You who fear the LORD, praise Him!
All you [1]descendants of Jacob, glorify Him,
And fear Him, all you offspring of Israel!
24 For He has not despised nor abhorred the affliction of the afflicted;
Nor has He hidden His face from Him;
But [a]when He cried to Him, He heard.

5 [a]Is. 49:23
6 [a]Is. 41:14 [b][Is. 53:3]
7 [a]Matt. 27:39 [1]Show contempt with their mouth
8 [a]Matt. 27:43 [b]Ps. 91:14 [1]LXX, Syr., Vg. *hoped;* Tg. *praised*
9 [a][Ps. 71:5, 6]
10 [a][Is. 46:3; 49:1]
12 [a]Ps. 22:21; 68:30 [b]Deut. 32:14
13 [a]Job 16:10 [1]Lit. *have opened their mouths at Me* *See WW at Joel 3:16.
14 [a]Dan. 5:6 [1]Lit. *in the midst of My bowels*
15 [a]Prov. 17:22 [b]John 19:28
16 [a]Matt. 27:35 [1]So with some Heb. mss., LXX, Syr., Vg.; MT *Like a lion* instead of *They pierced*
17 [a]Luke 23:27, 35
18 [a]Matt. 27:35
20 [a]Ps. 35:17 [1]Lit. *My only one*
21 [a]2 Tim. 4:17 [b]Is. 34:7 *See WW at Jer. 17:14.
22 [a]Heb. 2:12 [b][Rom. 8:29] *See WW at Ps. 133:1. • See WW at 1 Chr. 23:30.
23 [a]Ps. 135:19, 20 [1]Lit. *seed*
24 [a]Heb. 5:7

22:8 The jeers of the mocking crowd at the Cross for God to **deliver** Jesus are found in Matt. 27:40–43.
22:12, 13 Bashan is a grain-growing region east of the Sea of Galilee, ideal for raising cattle. **Bulls** with horns are fearsome when charging a victim, as are hungry **lions** tearing their prey.
22:16 Dogs refers generally to all types of evil men. The piercing was literally fulfilled when Jesus was crucified (John 20:25–27).
22:18 Clothing: This is quoted in all four Gospels concerning Christ's robe being gambled for by the soldiers who carried out the Crucifixion.
22:21 You have answered Me: The resurrection of Jesus was an answer to His prayer and to the agonizing prayer of every sin-laden human soul.
22:22 The NT equivalent for the OT **assembly** is the "church," which Christ calls His "brethren" (Heb. 2:11, 12).

25 [a]My praise *shall be* of You in the great assembly;
[b]I will pay My vows before those who fear Him.
26 The poor shall eat and be *satisfied;
Those who seek Him will praise the LORD.
Let your heart live forever!

27 All the ends of the world
Shall remember and turn to the LORD,
And all the families of the [1]nations
Shall worship before [2]You.
28 [a]For the kingdom *is* the LORD's,
And He rules over the nations.

29 [a]All the prosperous of the earth
Shall eat and worship;
[b]All those who go down to [1]the dust
Shall bow before Him,
Even he who cannot keep himself alive.

30 A posterity shall serve Him.
It will be recounted of the Lord to the *next* generation,
31 They will come and declare His righteousness to a people who will be born,
That He has done *this.*

25 [a]Ps. 35:18; 40:9, 10 [b]Ps. 61:8; Eccl. 5:4 **26** *See WW at Amos 4:8. **27** [1]*Gentiles* [2]So with MT, LXX, Tg.; Arab., Syr., Vg. *Him* **28** [a][Ps. 47:7]; Obad. 21; [Zech. 14:9]; Matt. 6:13 **29** [a]Ps. 17:10; 45:12; Hab. 1:16 [b]Ps. 28:1; [Is. 26:19] [1]Death

PSALM 23

1 [a]Ps. 78:52; 80:1; [Is. 40:11]; Ezek. 34:11, 12; [John 10:11; 1 Pet. 2:25; Rev. 7:16, 17] [b][Ps. 34:9, 10; Phil. 4:19] [1]*lack*

PSALM 23

The LORD the Shepherd of His People

A Psalm of David.

THE LORD *is* [a]my shepherd;
[b]I shall not [1]want. 5

22:27 When one remembers, one brings to mind and then acts upon the thought.

22:29 This is reflected in Phil. 2:9–11, where it is said every knee **shall bow before** the Lord of all.

23:1–6 See section 5 of Truth-In-Action following Ps. 41.

23:1–6 This refreshing pastoral psalm reflects absolute trust

THE CHRIST OF THE PSALMS

Psalm	Portrayal	Fulfilled
2:7	The Son of God	Matthew 3:17
8:2	Praised by children	Matthew 21:15, 16
8:6	Ruler of all	Hebrews 2:8
16:10	Rises from death	Matthew 28:7
22:1	Forsaken by God	Matthew 27:46
22:7, 8	Derided by enemies	Luke 23:35
22:16	Hands and feet pierced	John 20:27
22:18	Lots cast for clothes	Matthew 27:35, 36
34:20	Bones unbroken	John 19:32, 33, 36
35:11	Accused by false witnesses	Mark 14:57
35:19	Hated without cause	John 15:25
40:7, 8	Delights in God's will	Hebrews 10:7
41:9	Betrayed by a friend	Luke 22:47
45:6	The eternal King	Hebrews 1:8
68:18	Ascends to heaven	Acts 1:9–11
69:9	Zealous for God's house	John 2:17
69:21	Given vinegar and gall	Matthew 27:34
109:4	Prays for enemies	Luke 23:34
109:8	His betrayer replaced	Acts 1:20
110:1	Rules over His enemies	Matthew 22:44
110:4	A priest forever	Hebrews 5:6
118:22	The chief stone of God's building	Matthew 21:42
118:26	Comes in the name of the Lord	Matthew 21:9

2 [a]He makes me to lie down in
[1]green pastures;
[b]He leads me beside the [2]still
*waters.
3 He restores my *soul;
[a]He leads me in the paths of
righteousness
For His name's sake.

4 Yea, though I walk through the
valley of [a]the shadow of death,
[b]I will *fear no *evil;
[c]For You *are* with me;
Your rod and Your staff, they
comfort me.

WORD WEALTH

23:4 comfort, *nacham* (nah-*chahm*); Strong's #5162: To comfort, console, extend compassion, sigh with one who is grieving; to repent. *Nacham* originally may have meant "to breathe intensely because of deep emotion." In some references, the word is translated "repent," the idea being that regret causes deep sighing. In its sense of comfort, *nacham* does not describe casual sympathy, but rather deep empathy. It is like "weeping with those who weep," or actually "sighing with those who sigh." From *nacham* are derived the names "Nahum" ("Comforting") and Nehemiah ("Comfort of Yahweh").

5 You [a]prepare a table before me
in the presence of my enemies;
You [b]anoint my head with oil;
My cup runs over.
6 Surely goodness and mercy shall
follow me
All the days of my life;
And I will [1]dwell in the *house of
the LORD
[2]Forever.

2 [a]Ps. 65:11–13; Ezek. 34:14 [b][Rev. 7:17] [1]Lit. *pastures of tender grass* [2]Lit. *waters of rest* *See WW at Is. 43:2.
3 [a]Ps. 5:8; 31:3; Prov. 8:20 *See WW at Prov. 10:3.
4 [a]Job 3:5; 10:21, 22; 24:17; Ps. 44:19 [b][Ps. 3:6; 27:1] [c]Ps. 16:8; [Is. 43:2] *See WW at Ex. 1:17. • See WW at Ps. 5:4.
5 [a]Ps. 104:15 [b]Ps. 92:10; Luke 7:46
6 [1]So with LXX, Syr., Tg., Vg.; MT *return* [2]Or *To the end of my days,* lit. *For length of days* *See WW at 2 Sam. 7:11.

PSALM 24

1 [a]1 Cor. 10:26, 28 *See WW at Ex. 32:13.
2 [a]Ps. 89:11 [1]Lit. *rivers*
3 [a]Ps. 15:1–5 *See WW at Ex. 19:20.
4 [a][Job 17:9]; Ps. 26:6 [b]Ps. 51:10; 73:1; [Matt. 5:8] [c]Ps. 15:4
6 [a]Ps. 27:4, 8
7 [a]Ps. 118:20; Is. 26:2 [b]Ps. 29:2, 9; 97:6; Hag. 2:7; Acts 7:2; [1 Cor. 2:8]
8 [a]Rev. 19:13–16

PSALM 24

The King of Glory and His Kingdom

A Psalm of David.

THE [a]earth* *is* the LORD's, and all its
fullness,
The world and those who dwell
therein.
2 For He has [a]founded it upon the
seas,
And established it upon the
[1]waters.

3 [a]Who may *ascend into the hill of
the LORD?
Or who may stand in His holy
place?
4 He who has [a]clean hands and
[b]a pure heart,
Who has not lifted up his soul to
an idol,
Nor [c]sworn deceitfully.
5 He shall receive blessing from the
LORD,
And righteousness from the God
of his salvation.
6 This *is* Jacob, the generation of
those who [a]seek Him,
Who seek Your face. Selah

7 [a]Lift up your heads, O you gates!
And be lifted up, you everlasting
doors!
[b]And the King of glory shall come
in.
8 Who *is* this King of glory?
The LORD strong and mighty,
The LORD mighty in [a]battle.
9 Lift up your heads, O you gates!
Lift up, you everlasting doors!
And the King of glory shall come
in.

and peaceful confidence in God. It is divided into two metaphors: the Shepherd (vv. 1–4) and the Host (vv. 5, 6).
23:1 Jesus is the good **shepherd** who went one step beyond David's list of provisions—He gave His life for the sheep (John 10:11).
23:3 Daily restoration of the anxious, weary **soul** is a major human need (2 Cor. 4:16).
23:4 The key to provision is the *presence* of God (Josh. 1:5–9). This awesome thought causes the psalmist to change from mere statements (He . . .) to spontaneous heavenward praise (**You *are* with me**).
23:5 Of the two kinds of **oil,** the priestly anointing oil and the Oriental perfumed oil, this is the latter. This act shows favor and excellent hospitality.
23:6 Mercy (Hebrew *chesed*) is the unfailing, steadfast covenant love of God. This lovingkindness is similar to the NT word "grace" (John 1:16, 17).
24:1–10 Some scholars consider this psalm to be a joining of two smaller poems: vv. 1–6 and vv. 7–10. The first one is similar to Ps. 15. These were probably written when the ark was brought to Jerusalem by David.
24:1 The apostle Paul quoted this in 1 Cor. 10:26, 28 to show that all foods were created and "owned" by the Lord, and therefore fully available to His creatures for sustenance.
24:3 Who: This same question is asked in 15:1 and in Is. 33:14–17, with a variety of answers given. Even though every person is the Lord's creation (v. 1), only certain ones are allowed in His presence.
24:4, 5 Clean hands: Those who can enter into the presence of God are those who have conducted their daily business with integrity. External religiosity is meaningless without inward holiness and practical ethics.
24:6 Or translated, "Who seek Your face, O God of Jacob" (Greek Septuagint), or "Who seek Your face, as Jacob did" (see Gen. 32:22–30).
24:7 While the holy congregation waits inside, the **King** with His procession approaches the gate and asks entry.
24:8 The doorkeeper within asks **who** He is, and the response is shouted back. The password gains Him immediate entry.
24:9, 10 For emphasis the poet repeats the words of the herald of the **King**.

10 Who is this King of glory?
The LORD of hosts,
He *is* the King of glory. Selah

PSALM 25

A Plea for Deliverance and Forgiveness

A Psalm of David.

TO [a]You, O LORD, I lift up my
soul.
2 O my God, I [a]trust in You;
Let me not be *ashamed;
[b]Let not my enemies triumph over
me.
3 Indeed, let no one who [1]waits* on
You be ashamed;
Let those be ashamed who deal
treacherously without cause.

4 [a]Show me Your ways, O LORD;
Teach me Your paths.
5 Lead me in Your **truth** and *teach
me,
For You *are* the God of my
salvation;
On You I wait all the day.

WORD WEALTH

25:5 truth, *'emet* (*eh*-met); Strong's #571: Certainty, stability, truth, rightness, trustworthiness. *'Emet* derives from the verb *'aman,* meaning "to be firm, permanent, and established." *'Emet* conveys a sense of dependability, firmness, and reliability. Truth is therefore something upon which a person may confidently stake his life. David prayed that God's truth would continually preserve him (40:11). Scripture speaks of "men of truth" (Ex. 18:21), the "law of truth" (Mal. 2:6), and especially the "true God [or God of truth]" (Jer. 10:10). Curiously, *'emet* is spelled with the first, middle, and last letters of the Hebrew alphabet; thus the rabbis concluded that truth upholds the first and the last of God's creation, and everything in between!

PSALM 25

1 [a]Ps. 86:4; 143:8
2 [a]Ps. 34:8 [b]Ps. 13:4; 41:11 *See WW at Ezek. 16:63.
3 [1]Waits for You in faith *See WW at Lam. 3:25.
4 [a]Ex. 33:13; Ps. 5:8; 27:11; 86:11; 119:27; 143:8
5 *See WW at Is. 48:17.
6 [a]Ps. 103:17; 106:1
7 [a]Job 13:26; [Jer. 3:25] [b]Ps. 51:1 *See WW at Is. 62:6.
8 *See WW at Ps. 32:8.
11 [a]Ps. 31:3; 79:9; 109:21; 143:11
12 [a][Ps. 25:8; 37:23] [1]Or *he*
13 [a][Prov. 19:23] [b]Ps. 37:11; 69:36; Matt. 5:5 [1]Lit. *goodness*
14 [a][Prov. 3:32; John 7:17]
15 [a][Ps. 123:2; 141:8] [1]Lit. *bring out*
16 [a]Ps. 69:16 [1]*lonely*
18 [a]2 Sam. 16:12; Ps. 31:7 *See WW at Job 5:7.

6 Remember, O LORD, [a]Your tender
mercies and Your
lovingkindnesses,
For they *are* from of old.
7 Do not *remember [a]the sins of my
youth, nor my transgressions;
[b]According to Your mercy
remember me,
For Your goodness' sake, O LORD.

8 Good and upright *is* the LORD;
Therefore He *teaches sinners in
the way.
9 The humble He guides in justice,
And the humble He teaches His
way.
10 All the paths of the LORD *are*
mercy and truth,
To such as keep His covenant and
His testimonies.
11 [a]For Your name's sake, O LORD,
Pardon my iniquity, for it *is* great.

12 Who *is* the man that fears the
LORD?
[a]Him shall [1]He teach in the way
[1]He chooses.
13 [a]He himself shall dwell in
[1]prosperity,
And [b]his descendants shall
inherit the earth.
14 [a]The secret of the LORD *is* with
those who fear Him,
And He will show them His
covenant.
15 [a]My eyes *are* ever toward the
LORD,
For He shall [1]pluck my feet out
of the net.

16 [a]Turn Yourself to me, and have
mercy on me,
For I *am* [1]desolate and afflicted.
17 The troubles of my heart have
enlarged;
Bring me out of my distresses!
18 [a]Look on my affliction and my
*pain,
And forgive all my sins.

24:10 LORD of hosts (Hebrew *Yahweh Sabaoth*): The Captain of all the angelic armies (Luke 2:13), of the armies of Israel (Josh. 5:14), of all the hosts of nations (Jer. 3:19), in fact, of everything in heaven and Earth (Gen. 2:1)!
25:1–22 Although not complete, this is an alphabetical (acrostic) psalm, with the first word of each verse beginning with successive letters of the Hebrew alphabet.
25:5 Salvation here primarily means immediate deliverance from adversity.
25:7 See section 6 of Truth-In-Action following Ps. 41.
25:8–10 Good and upright: The penitent writer enters into worship in the middle of his prayer.
25:8 The Hebrew word for **sinners** means "someone who misses the mark or loses his way," so the mention of **the way** throughout is a subtle play on words with deep significance.
25:12–14 Four benefits result when the man who has lost his way returns, out of **fear** (reverent respect), to the way of mercy and truth.
25:12 Or translate, "in the way that He should choose."
25:14 God reveals His **secret** counsel in close friendships, as He did to Abraham who feared the LORD (Gen. 18:17–19), and as He did to the apostles (John 15:15).
25:15 Net is a common Hebrew symbol for dangers laid out by an enemy.
25:16 Desolate and afflicted are literally "alone and poor."
25:18 David realizes that inward **sins** make the soul more susceptible to attacks from the enemy without.

19 Consider my enemies, for they are many;
And they hate me with [1]cruel hatred.
20 Keep my soul, and deliver me;
Let me not be ashamed, for I put my trust in You.
21 Let integrity and uprightness preserve me,
For I wait for You.

22 [a]Redeem Israel, O God,
Out of all their troubles!

PSALM 26

A Prayer for Divine Scrutiny and Redemption

A Psalm of David.

[5] VINDICATE [a]me, O LORD,
For I have [b]walked in my integrity.
[c]I have also trusted in the LORD;
I shall not slip.
2 [a]Examine me, O LORD, and [1]prove me;
*Try my mind and my heart.
3 For Your lovingkindness *is* before my eyes,
And [a]I have walked in Your truth.
4 I have not [a]sat with idolatrous mortals,
Nor will I go in with hypocrites.
5 I have [a]hated the assembly of evildoers,
And will not sit with the wicked.

6 I will wash my hands in innocence;
So I will go about Your altar, O LORD,
7 That I may proclaim with the voice of thanksgiving,
And tell of all Your wondrous works.
8 LORD, [a]I have loved the habitation of Your house,
And the place [1]where Your glory dwells.
9 [a]Do[1] not gather my soul with sinners,
Nor my life with bloodthirsty men,
10 In whose hands *is* a sinister scheme,
And whose right hand is full of [a]bribes.

11 But as for me, I will walk in my integrity;
Redeem me and be merciful to me.
12 [a]My foot stands in an even place;
In the congregations I will bless the LORD.

PSALM 27

An Exuberant Declaration of Faith

A Psalm of David.

THE LORD *is* my [a]light and my salvation;
Whom shall I fear?
The [b]LORD *is* the strength of my life;
Of whom shall I be *afraid?
2 When the wicked came against me
To [a]eat[1] up my flesh,
My enemies and foes,
They stumbled and fell.
3 [a]Though an army may encamp against me,
My heart shall not fear;
Though war may rise against me,
In this I *will be* confident.

4 [a]One* *thing* I have *desired of the LORD, [4]
That will I seek:
That I may [b]dwell in the house of the LORD
All the days of my life,
To behold the [1]beauty of the LORD,
And to inquire in His temple.
5 For [a]in the time of trouble
He shall hide me in His pavilion;

19 [1]*violent hatred* **22** [a][Ps. 130:8]

PSALM 26

1 [a]Ps. 7:8 [b]2 Kin. 20:3; [Prov. 20:7] [c][Ps. 13:5; 28:7] **2** [a]Ps. 17:3; 139:23 [1]*test me* *See WW at Zech. 13:9. **3** [a]2 Kin. 20:3; Ps. 86:11 **4** [a]Ps. 1:1; Jer. 15:17 **5** [a]Ps. 31:6; 139:21 **8** [a]Ps. 27:4; 84:1–4, 10 [1]Lit. *of the tabernacle of Your glory*

9 [a]Ps. 28:3 [1]*Do not take away* **10** [a]1 Sam. 8:3 **12** [a]Ps. 40:2

PSALM 27

1 [a]Ps. 18:28; 84:11; [Is. 60:19, 20; Mic. 7:8] [b]Ex. 15:2; Ps. 62:7; 118:14; Is. 12:2; 33:2 *See WW at Hos. 3:5. **2** [a]Ps. 14:4 [1]*devour* **3** [a]Ps. 3:6 **4** [a]Ps. 26:8; 65:4 [b]Luke 2:37 [1]*delightfulness* *See WW at Deut. 6:4. • See WW at Ps. 122:6. **5** [a]Ps. 31:20; 91:1

25:22 King David's problems are his kingdom's problems as well; thus he pleads for **Israel,** too. **Redeem** here means to deliver from physical bondage primarily, but verses such as these may have a spiritual application from the NT perspective.

26:1 See section 5 of Truth-In-Action following Ps. 41.

26:1 The psalmist's trust in the LORD sets the mood of this plea apart from that of the self-righteous Pharisee of Luke 18:11–14.

26:2 Mind is literally "kidneys," a symbol for the conscience.

26:6 Wash my hands: This is a seemingly ancient ceremony or oath (Deut. 21:6, 7) that was also performed by Pontius Pilate at Jesus' trial (Matt. 27:24). See Ps. 73:13.

26:8 I have loved: This gives us a glimpse into the reason David was a delight to the heart of God. When love for the **house** of God is a high priority in one's life, God responds with His own unfailing love ("mercy," v. 11).

26:10 Bribes: That power corrupts and absolute power corrupts absolutely is well documented in the history of world governments. It takes a real man of valor to stand with "integrity" (v. 11).

27:4 See section 4 of Truth-In-Action following Ps. 41.

27:4 This desire of David gives us a key to understanding why he was a "man after God's heart," and so beloved and blessed by Him.

In the secret place of His
tabernacle
He shall hide me;
He shall [b]set me high upon a
rock.

6 And now [a]my head shall be
[1]lifted up above my enemies all
around me;
Therefore I will *offer sacrifices
of [2]joy in His tabernacle;
I will sing, yes, I will *sing praises
to the LORD.

7 Hear, O LORD, *when* I cry with my
voice!
Have mercy also upon me, and
answer me.
8 *When You said,* "Seek My face,"
My heart said to You, "Your face,
LORD, I will *seek."
9 [a]Do not hide Your face from
me;
Do not turn Your servant away
in anger;
You have been my help;
Do not leave me nor forsake me,
O God of my salvation.
10 [a]When my father and my mother
forsake me,
Then the LORD will take care of
me.

11 [a]Teach me Your way, O LORD,
And lead me in a smooth path,
because of my enemies.
12 Do not deliver me to the will of
my adversaries;
For [a]false witnesses have risen
against me,
And such as breathe out violence.
13 *I would have lost heart,* unless I
had *believed
That I would see the goodness of
the LORD
[a]In the land of the living.

14 [a]Wait[1] on the LORD;
Be of good courage,
And He shall strengthen your
heart;
Wait, I say, on the LORD!

5 [b]Ps. 40:2
6 [a]Ps. 3:3 [1]Lifted up in honor [2]*joyous shouts* *See WW at Deut. 16:2. • See WW at Ps. 149:3.
8 *See WW at Hos. 5:15.
9 [a]Ps. 69:17; 143:7
10 [a]Is. 49:15
11 [a]Ps. 25:4; 86:11; 119:33
12 [a]Deut. 19:18; Ps. 35:11; Matt. 26:60; Mark 14:56; John 19:33
13 [a]Job 28:13; Ps. 52:5; 116:9; 142:5; Is. 38:11; Jer. 11:19; Ezek. 26:20 *See WW at 2 Chr. 20:20.
14 [a]Ps. 25:3; 37:34; 40:1; 62:5; 130:5; Prov. 20:22; Is. 25:9; [Hab. 2:3] [1]Wait in faith

PSALM 28

1 [a]Ps. 35:22; 39:12; 83:1 [b]Ps. 88:4; 143:7; Prov. 1:12
2 [a]Ps. 5:7 [b]Ps. 138:2
3 [a]Ps. 12:2; 55:21; 62:4; Jer. 9:8 [1]*drag*
4 [a][Ps. 62:12]; 2 Tim. 4:14; [Rev. 18:6; 22:12]
5 [a]Is. 5:12
7 [a]Ps. 18:2; 59:17 [b]Ps. 13:5; 112:7
8 [a]Ps. 20:6 [1]So with MT, Tg.; LXX, Syr., Vg. *the strength of His people* [2]Commissioned one, Heb. *messiah* *See WW at Dan. 9:25.
9 [a][Deut. 9:29; 32:9; 1 Kin. 8:51; Ps. 33:12]; 106:40

PSALM 28

Rejoicing in Answered Prayer

A Psalm of David.

TO You I will cry, O LORD my Rock:
[a]Do not be silent to me,
[b]Lest, if You *are* silent to me,
I become like those who go down
to the pit.
2 Hear the voice of my
supplications
When I cry to You,
[a]When I lift up my hands
[b]toward Your holy sanctuary.

3 Do not [1]take me away with the
wicked
And with the workers of iniquity,
[a]Who speak peace to their
neighbors,
But evil *is* in their hearts.
4 [a]Give them according to their
deeds,
And according to the wickedness
of their endeavors;
Give them according to the work
of their hands;
Render to them what they
deserve.
5 Because [a]they do not regard the
works of the LORD,
Nor the operation of His hands,
He shall destroy them
And not build them up.

6 Blessed *be* the LORD,
Because He has heard the voice
of my supplications!
7 The LORD *is* [a]my strength and my
shield;
My heart [b]trusted in Him, and I
am helped;
Therefore my heart greatly
rejoices,
And with my song I will praise
Him.

8 The LORD *is* [1]their strength,
And He *is* the [a]saving refuge of
His [2]anointed.*
9 Save Your people,
And bless [a]Your inheritance;

27:7–14 After the praise in the first half of this psalm, the topic swings to prayer, ending with the statement revealing the key to victorious living: **Wait on the LORD.**
27:10 This is the psalmist's way of saying tnat God is more concerned about our welfare than even one's cherished **father** and **mother** could ever be. God's love transcends parental love. This is more of a "proverbial statement," and is not to be understood as if David's parents forsook him.
28:1 Rock is a symbol of God, emphasizing His protecting and sheltering characteristics.
28:6–9 Blessed: The order of prayer and praise is the reverse of that found in the previous psalm; but either way, both should be considered necessary ingredients in talks with God.
28:6 He has heard is probably a statement of faith, for praise often does have this element of faith in it (Mark 11:24).
28:7 Song: Not just thoughts of thankfulness, but actually verbalizing praise is appropriate when God graciously intervenes in one's life.

Shepherd them also,
[b]And bear them up forever.

PSALM 29

Praise to God in His Holiness and Majesty

A Psalm of David.

[4] GIVE[1] [a]unto the LORD, O you mighty ones,
Give unto the LORD glory and strength.
2 [1]Give unto the LORD the glory [2]due to His name;
*Worship the LORD in [a]the [3]beauty of holiness.

3 The voice of the LORD *is* over the waters;
[a]The God of glory thunders;
The LORD *is* over many waters.
4 The voice of the LORD *is* powerful;
The voice of the LORD *is* full of majesty.

5 The voice of the LORD breaks [a]the cedars,
Yes, the LORD splinters the cedars of Lebanon.
6 [a]He makes them also skip like a calf,
Lebanon and [b]Sirion like a young wild ox.
7 The voice of the LORD [1]divides the flames of fire.

8 The voice of the LORD shakes the wilderness;
The LORD shakes the Wilderness of [a]Kadesh.
9 The voice of the LORD makes the [a]deer give birth,
And strips the forests bare;
And in His temple everyone says, "Glory!"

10 The [a]LORD sat *enthroned* at the Flood,
And [b]the LORD sits as King forever.
11 [a]The LORD will give strength to His people;
The LORD will bless His people with peace.

PSALM 30

The Blessedness of Answered Prayer

A Psalm. A Song [a]at the dedication of the house of David.

I WILL extol You, O LORD, for You have [a]lifted me up,
And have not let my foes [b]rejoice over me.
2 O LORD my God, I cried out to You,
And You [a]healed me.
3 O LORD, [a]You brought my soul up from the grave;
You have kept me alive, [1]that I should not go down to the pit.

4 [a]Sing praise to the LORD, you saints of His,
And give thanks at the remembrance of [1]His holy name.
5 For [a]His anger *is but for* a moment,
[b]His favor *is for* life;
Weeping may endure for a night,
But [1]**joy** *comes* in the morning.

WORD WEALTH

30:5 joy, *rinnah* (ree-*nah*); Strong's #7440: A shout of rejoicing; shouting; loud cheering in triumph; singing. *Rinnah* describes the kind of joyful shouting at the time of a great victory. In Prov. 11:10, *rinnah* describes the jubilation of the righteous when the wicked are

(*cont. on next page*)

9 [b]Deut. 1:31; Is. 63:9

PSALM 29

1 [a]1 Chr. 16:28, 29 [1]*Ascribe*
2 [a]2 Chr. 20:21; Ps. 110:3 [1]*Ascribe* [2]Lit. *of His name* [3]*majesty* *See WW at Ps. 99:5.
3 [a][Job 37:4, 5]; Ps. 18:13; Acts 7:2
5 [a]Judg. 9:15; 1 Kin. 5:6; Ps. 104:16; Is. 2:13; 14:8
6 [a]Ps. 114:4 [b]Deut. 3:9
7 [1]*stirs up*, lit. *hews out*
8 [a]Num. 13:26
9 [a]Job 39:1
10 [a]Gen. 6:17; Job 38:8, 25 [b]Ps. 10:16
11 [a]Ps. 28:8; 68:35; [Is. 40:29]

PSALM 30

title [a]Deut. 20:5
1 [a]Ps. 28:9 [b]Ps. 25:2
2 [a]Ps. 6:2; 103:3; [Is. 53:5]
3 [a]Ps. 86:13 [1]So with Qr., Tg.; Kt., LXX, Syr., Vg. *from those who descend to the pit*
4 [a]Ps. 97:12 [1]Or *His holiness*
5 [a]Ps. 103:9; Is. 26:20; 54:7, 8 [b]Ps. 63:3 [1]*a shout of joy*

29:1, 2 See section 4 of Truth-In-Action following Ps. 41.
29:3 In the following description of a storm there is no evidence of superstitious fears as in pagan cultures (Jon. 1:4–6), nor is God equated *with* the storm and thunder as polytheistic religions depict; but here God is above and **over** nature, commanding it with His spoken Word as at the Creation (Gen. 1).
29:6 Skip: Poetically the psalmist refers to an earthquake, or thunderous quake, in the **Lebanon** mountain range and at **Sirion** (Mt. Hermon), which splinters the biggest of trees, the mighty cedars, as if they were matchsticks.
29:7 This psalm traditionally is recited in synagogues on the Day of Pentecost and refers to the phenomena that occurred in Acts 2:1–4: wind and divided **flames of fire.**
29:9 The thunder makes the **deer give birth** prematurely. But in the **temple** of God there is a vantage point where all in safety and security can see the awesome power of God and respond with applauding shouts of **glory.**
29:11 The God who controls storms is also the God who restores **peace.**
30:1–12 Formal dedication ceremonies with appropriate speeches were common in Israel's history (Deut. 20:5; Ezra 6:16). Which house of David (see Ps. title) this song commemorates is uncertain (2 Sam. 24; 1 Chr. 22).
30:2, 3 Healed: This may have reference to the plague in 1 Chr. 21. An immediate prayer of repentance saved him and Israel; covering sin would have been fatal.
30:5 Life equals lifetime. The plague lasted all day, so the **night** was full of weeping. **Endure** literally means "lodge as a guest." This verse gives good examples of contrasting parallelism common in Hebrew poems.

(*cont. from preceding page*) eliminated. Zeph. 3:17 literally says that God will dance over His beloved people with singing or a shout of joy. *Rinnah* may best be illustrated by the testimony of the redeemed, returning to Zion from captivity. *Rinnah* is the word for both singing and joy.

6 Now in my prosperity I said,
"I shall never be [1]moved."
7 LORD, by Your favor You have made my mountain stand strong;
[a]You hid Your face, *and* I was troubled.

8 I cried out to You, O LORD;
And to the LORD I made supplication:
9 "What profit *is there* in my blood,
When I go down to the pit?
[a]Will the dust praise You?
Will it declare Your truth?
10 Hear, O LORD, and have mercy on me;
LORD, be my helper!"

11 [a]You have turned for me my mourning into dancing;
You have put off [1]my sackcloth and clothed me with gladness,
12 To the end that *my* [1]glory may sing praise to You and not be silent.
O LORD my God, I will give thanks to You forever.

PSALM 31

The LORD a Fortress in Adversity

To the Chief Musician. A *Psalm of David.

IN [a]You, O LORD, I [1]put my trust;
Let me never be ashamed;
Deliver me in Your righteousness.
2 [a]Bow down Your ear to me,
Deliver me speedily;
Be my rock of [1]refuge,
A [2]fortress of defense to save me.

3 [a]For You *are* my rock and my fortress;
Therefore, [b]for Your name's sake,
Lead me and guide me.
4 Pull me out of the net which they have secretly laid for me,
For You *are* my strength.
5 [a]Into Your hand I commit my spirit;
You have *redeemed me, O LORD God of [b]truth.

6 I have hated those [a]who regard useless idols;
But I trust in the LORD.
7 I will be glad and rejoice in Your mercy,
For You have considered my trouble;
You have [a]known my soul in [1]adversities,
8 And have not [a]shut[1] me up into the hand of the enemy;
[b]You have set my feet in a wide place.

9 Have mercy on me, O LORD, for I am in trouble;
[a]My eye wastes away with grief,
Yes, my soul and my [1]body!
10 For my life is spent with grief,
And my years with sighing;
My strength fails because of my iniquity,
And my bones waste away.
11 [a]I am a [1]reproach among all my enemies,
But [b]especially among my neighbors,
And *am* repulsive to my acquaintances;
[c]Those who see me outside flee from me.
12 [a]I am forgotten like a dead man, out of mind;
I am like a [1]broken vessel.
13 [a]For I hear the slander of many;
[b]Fear *is* on every side;
While they [c]take counsel together against me,
They scheme to take away my life.

14 But as for me, I trust in You, O LORD;

6 [1]*shaken* **7** [a][Deut. 31:17; Ps. 104:29; 143:7] **9** [a][Ps. 6:5] **11** [a]Eccl. 3:4; Is. 61:3; Jer. 31:4 [1]The sackcloth of my mourning **12** [1]*soul*

PSALM 31

title *See WW at Ps. 3:title. **1** [a]Ps. 22:5 [1]*have taken refuge* **2** [a]Ps. 17:6; 71:2; 86:1; 102:2 [1]*strength* [2]Lit. *house of fortresses* **3** [a][Ps. 18:2] [b]Ps. 23:3; 25:11

5 [a]Luke 23:46 [b][Deut. 32:4]; Ps. 71:22 *See WW at Neh. 1:10. **6** [a]Jon. 2:8 **7** [a][John 10:27] [1]*troubles* **8** [a][Deut. 32:30]; Ps. 37:33 [b][Ps. 4:1; 18:19] [1]*given me over* **9** [a]Ps. 6:7 [1]Lit. *belly* **11** [a][Is. 53:4] [b]Job 19:13; Ps. 38:11; 88:8, 18 [c]Ps. 64:8 [1]*despised thing* **12** [a]Ps. 88:4, 5 [1]Lit. *perishing* **13** [a]Ps. 50:20; Jer. 20:10 [b]Lam. 2:22 [c]Ps. 62:4; Matt. 27:1

30:6 Never be moved: This haughty attitude may be the motive behind the forbidden census of 1 Chr. 21:1–3. High numbers of army recruits gave a false sense of security (Deut. 8:17). See Dan. 4:30.

30:9, 10 What profit: David describes his time of grief and pleads for **mercy** (see 73:23–26).

30:11 David describes the results of his prayer. As mourners today often wear black, mourners in David's time wore **sackcloth.**

30:12 Glory is a poetic equivalent for the word "soul," the glorious part of man. Ps. 7:5 has it translated as "honor." See 16:9 where by parallelism it is equated with "heart."

31:1 This psalm depicts the soul of man in **trust,** through times of tears and turmoil, on to triumph (v. 19). See 1 John 5:4.

31:5 Commit: Jesus quoted this statement of utmost trust as He died on the Cross (Luke 23:46).

31:9–13 The topic shifts to pleas for deliverance from unwarranted persecution and **trouble,** which seem to follow the righteous (John 17:14, 15).

I say, "You *are* my God."
15 My times *are* in Your [a]hand;
Deliver me from the hand of my enemies,
And from those who persecute me.
16 [a]Make Your face shine upon Your servant;
Save me for Your mercies' sake.
17 [a]Do not let me be ashamed,
O LORD, for I have called upon You;
Let the wicked be ashamed;
[b]Let them be silent in the grave.
18 [a]Let the lying lips be put to silence,
Which [b]speak insolent things proudly and contemptuously against the righteous.

19 [a]Oh, how **great** *is* Your goodness,
Which You have laid up for those who fear You,
Which You have prepared for those who trust in You
In the presence of the sons of men!

WORD WEALTH

31:19 great, *rab* (*rahv*); Strong's #7227: Great, abundant, many, large in number; of major importance; chief, weighty, significant, noble, princely. *Rab* appears more than 400 times in the OT. It is derived from the verb *rabab,* "to become numerous or great." The title *rabbi* is a derivative of *rab.* While *rabbi* has been defined as "my teacher," a more exact explanation is that it means "my great one" (full of knowledge) or "my master" (great instructor). Thus our Lord did not allow His followers to be called by this lofty title: He stressed that we can have but one *Rabbi,* and that must be the Messiah only (Matt. 23:8).

20 [a]You shall hide them in the secret place of Your presence
From the plots of man;
[b]You shall keep them secretly in a [1]pavilion
From the strife of tongues.

21 Blessed *be* the LORD,
For [a]He has shown me His marvelous kindness in a [1]strong city!

15 [a][Job 14:5; 24:1] **16** [a]Ps. 4:6; 80:3 **17** [a]Ps. 25:2, 20 [b][1 Sam. 2:9]; Ps. 94:17; 115:17 **18** [a]Ps. 109:2; 120:2 [b][1 Sam. 2:3]; Ps. 94:4; [Jude 15] **19** [a]Ps. 145:7; [Rom. 2:4; 11:22] **20** [a][Ps. 27:5; 32:7] [b]Job 5:21 [1]*shelter* **21** [a][Ps. 17:7] [1]*fortified*

24 [a][Ps. 27:14] *See WW at Mic. 7:7.

22 For I said in my haste,
"I am cut off from before Your eyes";
Nevertheless You heard the voice of my supplications
When I cried out to You.

23 Oh, love the LORD, all you His saints!
For the LORD preserves the faithful,
And fully repays the proud person.
24 [a]Be of good courage,
And He shall strengthen your heart,
All you who *hope in the LORD.

PSALM 32

The Joy of Forgiveness

A Psalm of David. A [1]Contemplation.

BLESSED *is he whose* [a]transgression *is* forgiven, 6
Whose sin *is* covered.
2 Blessed *is* the man to whom the LORD [a]does not [1]impute iniquity,
And [b]in whose spirit *there is* no deceit.

3 When I kept silent, my bones grew old
Through my groaning all the day long.
4 For day and night Your [a]hand was heavy upon me;
My vitality was turned into the drought of summer. Selah
5 I acknowledged my sin to You,
And my iniquity I have not hidden.
[a]I said, "I will confess my transgressions to the LORD,"
And You forgave the iniquity of my sin. Selah

6 [a]For this cause everyone who is godly shall [b]pray to You
In a time when You may be found;
Surely in a flood of great waters
They shall not come near him.

PSALM 32

title [1]Heb. *Maschil* **1** [a][Ps. 85:2; 103:3]; Rom. 4:7, 8 **2** [a][2 Cor. 5:19] [b]John 1:47 [1]*charge his account with* **4** [a]1 Sam. 5:6; Ps. 38:2; 39:10 **5** [a]2 Sam. 12:13; Ps. 38:18; [Prov. 28:13; 1 John 1:9] **6** [a][1 Tim. 1:16] [b]Ps. 69:13; Is. 55:6

31:15 The eye of faith sees that both troublesome **times** and times of triumph are in God's **hand**.
31:19 That God has **laid up** goodness (rewards) for those who **fear** and **trust** Him is confirmed by Jesus in Matt. 5:11, 12.
32:1–5 See section 6 of Truth-In-Action following Ps. 41.
32:1, 2 The apostle Paul used these verses to describe the happy state of the man whose sin is forgiven by the grace of God, not by struggling to keep the works of the Law (Rom. 4:6–8). **Transgression** means rebellion; **sin** is missing the mark; **iniquity** is moral depravity; and there is also **deceit.** Sins are **forgiven** (literally, lifted away), **covered,** and not imputed (literally, erased from the record), so that the spirit of man is totally righteous in God's eyes.
32:3 Groaning: Complaining, instead of confessing, results in physical and emotional repercussions.

7 [a]You *are* my hiding place;
You shall preserve me from trouble;
You shall surround me with [b]songs of deliverance. Selah

8 I will instruct you and **teach** you in the way you should go;
I will guide you with My eye.

WORD WEALTH

32:8 teach, *yarah* (yah-*rah*); Strong's #3384: To instruct, direct, teach; to point, shoot, aim, throw, cast in a straight manner. The primary meaning of *yarah* is "to shoot straight," or "to direct the flow" of something. Hence a derivative of *yarah* is *yoreh,* "rain." *Moreh* is another derivative, and means "teacher," one who aims and throws his directives in a straight way, one who points out the truth. The most important Bible word derived from *yarah* is *Torah,* which refers to the Law. Although *Torah* is often translated as "Law," its meaning is "instruction, teaching." The Law of Moses is actually the instruction Moses received from God for Israel.

9 Do not be like the [a]horse *or* like the mule,
Which have no understanding,
Which must be harnessed with bit and bridle,
Else they will not come near you.

10 [a]Many sorrows *shall be* to the wicked;
But [b]he who trusts in the LORD, mercy shall surround him.
11 [a]Be glad in the LORD and rejoice, you righteous;
And shout for joy, all *you* upright in heart!

PSALM 33

The Sovereignty of the LORD in Creation and History

REJOICE [a]in the LORD, O you righteous!
For praise from the upright is beautiful.
2 Praise the LORD with the harp;
[1]Make* melody to Him with an instrument of ten strings.
3 Sing to Him a new song;
Play skillfully with a shout of joy.

4 For the word of the LORD *is* right,
And all His work *is done* in truth.
5 He loves righteousness and justice;
The earth is full of the goodness of the LORD.

6 [a]By the word of the LORD the heavens were made,
And all the [b]host of them [c]by the breath of His mouth.
7 [a]He gathers the waters of the sea together [1]as a heap;
He lays up the deep in storehouses.

8 Let all the earth fear the LORD;
Let all the inhabitants of the world stand in awe of Him.
9 For [a]He spoke, and it was *done;*
He commanded, and it stood fast.

10 [a]The LORD brings the counsel of the nations to nothing;
He makes the plans of the peoples of no effect.
11 [a]The counsel of the LORD stands forever,
The plans of His heart to all generations.
12 Blessed *is* the nation whose God *is* the LORD,
The people He has [a]chosen as His own inheritance.

13 [a]The LORD looks from heaven;
He sees all the sons of men.
14 From the place of His dwelling He looks
On all the inhabitants of the earth;
15 He fashions their hearts individually;
[a]He [1]considers all their works.

7 [a]Ps. 9:9 [b]Ex. 15:1; Judg. 5:1; [Ps. 40:3]
9 [a]Prov. 26:3
10 [a]Ps. 16:4; [Prov. 13:21; Rom. 2:9] [b][Ps. 5:11, 12]; Prov. 16:20
11 [a]Ps. 64:10; 68:3; 97:12

PSALM 33

1 [a]Ps. 32:11; 97:12; Phil. 3:1; 4:4
2 [1]Lit. *Sing to Him* *See WW at Ps. 149:3.
6 [a]Gen. 1:6, 7; Ps. 148:5; [Heb. 11:3; 2 Pet. 3:5] [b]Gen. 2:1 [c][Job 26:13]
7 [a]Gen. 1:9; Job 26:10; 38:8 [1]LXX, Tg., Vg. *in a vessel*
9 [a]Gen. 1:3; Ps. 148:5
10 [a][Ps. 2:1–3]; Is. 8:10; 19:3
11 [a][Job 23:13; Prov. 19:21]
12 [a][Ex. 19:5; Deut. 7:6]; Ps. 28:9
13 [a]Job 28:24; [Ps. 14:2]
15 [a][2 Chr. 16:9]; Job 34:21; [Jer. 32:19] [1]*understands*

33:3 A new song, which occurs six times in the Psalms, most likely parallels Paul's "spiritual songs" (Eph. 5:19; Col. 3:16). As such, it is a fresh, spontaneous expression of worship and praise sung to God from the hearts of dedicated worshipers. Both the words and the melody are often spontaneously created. According to 1 Cor. 14:15, the new song can be in one's native language or in tongues. **Joy** is vital to true worship.

33:5 Goodness (Hebrew *chesed*) is also translated "unfailing love," "lovingkindness," "steadfast covenant love," and "mercy." See notes on 17:7 and 23:6.

33:6 The **heavens** (universe) did not evolve, but were created by the **word** of God. No scientific fact supports the evolutionary model of origins.

33:11 Counsel: That is, the whole program for mankind in history.

33:12 The people who have such a sense of security by knowing that the Creator of the universe, the Sovereign over nations, has specifically **chosen** them as **His** very **own people,** can be called no less than **blessed.** See note on 1:1 and 1 Pet. 2:9.

16 [a]No king *is* saved by the multitude
of an army;
A mighty man is not delivered by
great strength.
17 [a]A horse *is* a [1]vain hope for safety;
Neither shall it deliver *any* by its
great *strength.

18 [a]Behold, the eye of the LORD *is* on
those who fear Him,
On those who hope in His mercy,
19 To deliver their soul from death,
And [a]to keep them alive in
famine.

20 Our soul waits for the LORD;
He *is* our help and our shield.
21 For our heart shall rejoice in
Him,
Because we have trusted in His
holy name.
22 Let Your mercy, O LORD, be upon
us,
Just as we hope in You.

PSALM 34

The Happiness of Those Who Trust in God

A Psalm of David [a]when he pretended madness before Abimelech, who drove him away, and he departed.

I WILL [a]bless the LORD at all times;
His praise *shall* *continually *be* in
my mouth.
2 My soul shall make its boast in
the LORD;
The humble shall hear *of it* and
be glad.
3 Oh, magnify the LORD with me,
And let us exalt His name
together.

4 I [a]sought the LORD, and He heard
me,
And delivered me from all my
fears.
5 They looked to Him and were
radiant,
And their faces were not
ashamed.
6 This poor man cried out, and the
LORD heard *him*,
And saved him out of all his
troubles.

16 [a]Ps. 44:6; 60:11; [Jer. 9:23, 24]
17 [a][Ps. 20:7; 147:10; Prov. 21:31] [1]*false* *See WW at Zech. 4:6.
18 [a][Job 36:7]; Ps. 32:8; 34:15; [1 Pet. 3:12]
19 [a]Job 5:20; Ps. 37:19

PSALM 34

title [a]1 Sam. 21:10–15
1 [a][Eph. 5:20; 1 Thess. 5:18] *See WW at Ex. 28:30.
4 [a][2 Chr. 15:2; Ps. 9:10; Matt. 7:7; Luke 11:9]
7 [a][Ps. 91:11]; Dan. 6:22 [b]2 Kin. 6:17 [1]Or *Angel* *See WW at 2 Chr. 32:21.
8 [a]Ps. 119:103; [Heb. 6:5]; 1 Pet. 2:3 [b]Ps. 2:12 *See WW at Jer. 31:22.
9 [1]*lack*
10 [a][Ps. 84:11]
11 [a]Ps. 32:8
12 [a][1 Pet. 3:10–12]
13 [a][Eph. 4:25]
14 [a]Ps. 37:27; Is. 1:16, 17 [b][Rom. 14:19; Heb. 12:14]
15 [a]Job 36:7; [Ps. 33:18]
16 [a]Lev. 17:10; Jer. 44:11; Amos 9:4 [b]Job 18:17; Ps. 9:6; 109:15; [Prov. 10:7] [1]*destroy*
17 [a]Ps. 34:6; 145:19

7 [a]The [1]angel* of the LORD [b]encamps
all around those who fear Him,
And delivers them.

8 Oh, [a]taste and see that the LORD
is good;
[b]Blessed *is* the *man *who* trusts in
Him!

WORD WEALTH

34:8 taste, *ta'am* (*tah*-ahm); Strong's #2938: To taste, eat; discern, perceive; to evaluate. This verb refers to the testing of good by means of the sense of taste. From the primary sense of physical tasting, *ta'am* developed into the idea of evaluative sampling of things other than food. *Ta'am* as a noun came to refer to "discernment," that is, the capacity to choose and delight in good things. Prov. speaks of a woman who lacks "taste" (11:22), and a woman with good taste, who "perceives" (*ta'am*) that her merchandise is of a high quality (31:18).

9 Oh, fear the LORD, you His saints!
There is no [1]want to those who
fear Him.
10 The young lions lack and suffer
hunger;
[a]But those who seek the LORD shall
not lack any good *thing*.

11 Come, you children, listen to me;
[a]I will teach you the fear of the
LORD.
12 [a]Who *is* the man *who* desires life, 7
And loves *many* days, that he
may see good?
13 Keep your tongue from evil,
And your lips from speaking
[a]deceit.
14 [a]Depart from evil and do good;
[b]Seek peace and pursue it.

15 [a]The eyes of the LORD *are* on the
righteous,
And His ears *are open* to their cry.
16 [a]The face of the LORD *is* against
those who do evil,
[b]To [1]cut off the remembrance of
them from the earth.

17 *The righteous* cry out, and
[a]the LORD hears,

33:17 That is, a war **horse,** which pagan armies relied on for victories.
34:title Abimelech may have been a title or another name for King Achish of Gath (1 Sam. 21:10–15).
34:1–22 One of the psalms most quoted in the NT, this is an alphabetical poem—though imperfect in parts—with each verse beginning with a successive letter of the Hebrew alphabet.
34:7 Angel: For other examples of the ministry of angels, see 2 Kin. 6:16, 17; Dan. 3:24, 25.
34:8 This same metaphor of tasting was used by Peter in calling inquirers to examine the wonders of God (1 Pet. 2:3).
34:12–16 This is quoted by the apostle Peter in his practical letter to Christian believers (1 Pet. 3:10–12).
34:12–14 See section 7 of Truth-In-Action following Ps. 41.
34:13 See the admonition on the **tongue** in James 1:26.

And delivers them out of all their troubles.
18 [a]The LORD *is* near [b]to those who have a broken heart,
And saves such as [1]have a contrite spirit.

19 [a]Many *are* the afflictions of the righteous,
[b]But the LORD delivers him out of them all.
20 He guards all his bones;
[a]Not one of them is broken.
21 [a]Evil shall slay the wicked,
And those who hate the righteous shall be [1]condemned.
22 The LORD [a]redeems the soul of His servants,
And none of those who trust in Him shall be condemned.

PSALM 35

The LORD the Avenger of His People

A Psalm of David.

PLEAD[1] *my cause,* O LORD, with those who strive with me;
Fight against those who fight against me.
2 Take hold of shield and [1]buckler,
And stand up for my help.
3 Also draw out the spear,
And stop those who pursue me.
Say to my soul,
"I *am* your salvation."

4 [a]Let those be put to shame and brought to dishonor
Who seek after my life;
Let those be [b]turned back and brought to confusion
Who plot my hurt.
5 [a]Let them be like chaff before the wind,
And let the [1]angel of the LORD chase *them.*
6 Let their way be [a]dark and slippery,
And let the angel of the LORD pursue them.
7 For without cause they have [a]hidden their net for me *in* a pit,
Which they have dug without cause for my life.
8 [1]Let [a]destruction come upon him unexpectedly,
And let his net that he has hidden catch himself;
Into that very destruction let him fall.
9 And my soul shall be joyful in the LORD;
It shall *rejoice in His salvation.
10 [a]All my bones shall say,
"LORD, [b]who *is* like You,
Delivering the poor from him who is too strong for him,
Yes, the poor and the needy from him who plunders him?"

11 Fierce witnesses rise up;
They ask me *things* that I do not know.
12 [a]They reward me evil for good,
To the sorrow of my soul.
13 But as for me, [a]when they were sick,
My clothing *was* sackcloth;
I humbled myself with *fasting;
And my prayer would return to my own [1]heart.
14 I paced about as though *he were* my *friend *or* brother;
I bowed down [1]heavily, as one who mourns *for his* mother.

15 But in my [1]adversity they rejoiced
And gathered together;
Attackers gathered against me,
And I did not know *it;*
They tore *at me* and did not cease;
16 With ungodly mockers at feasts
They gnashed at me with their teeth.

17 Lord, how long will You [a]look on?
Rescue me from their destructions,
My precious *life* from the lions.
18 I will give You thanks in the great assembly;
I will praise You among [1]many people.

---

18 [a][Ps. 145:18] [b]Ps. 51:17; [Is. 57:15] [1]*are crushed in spirit*
19 [a]Prov. 24:16 [b]Ps. 34:4, 6, 17
20 [a]John 19:33, 36
21 [a]Ps. 94:23; 140:11; Prov. 24:16 [1]*held guilty*
22 [a]1 Kin. 1:29

PSALM 35

1 [1]*Contend for me*
2 [1]A small shield
4 [a]Ps. 40:14, 15; 70:2, 3 [b]Ps. 129:5
5 [a]Job 21:18; Ps. 83:13; Is. 29:5 [1]Or *Angel*
6 [a]Ps. 73:18; Jer. 23:12
7 [a]Ps. 9:15
8 [a][Ps. 55:23]; Is. 47:11; [1 Thess. 5:3] [1]Lit. *Let destruction he does not know come upon him,*
9 *See WW at Is. 64:5.
10 [a]Ps. 51:8 [b][Ex. 15:11]; Ps. 71:19; 86:8; [Mic. 7:18]
12 [a]Ps. 38:20; 109:5; Jer. 18:20; John 10:32
13 [a]Job 30:25 [1]Lit. *bosom* *See WW at Jon. 3:5.
14 [1]*in mourning* *See WW at Prov. 17:17.
15 [1]*limping, stumbling*
17 [a]Ps. 13:1; [Hab. 1:13]
18 [1]*a mighty*

34:19 Paul applied this to his being persecuted in Asia Minor (2 Tim. 3:11, 12), and then adds that all Christians will suffer **afflictions.**

34:20 This was prophetic of Jesus on the Cross because none of **his bones** were **broken** (John 19:36). The Passover lamb, which is a type of Christ, was not to have its bones broken (Ex. 12:46).

35:1–28 This psalm eloquently expresses the frustration of one whose mind is tortured by the sufferings of injustice.

35:9 Instead of becoming isolated with bitterness and resentment, the psalmist shows that in all such circumstances the soul can be **joyful** by turning to the **LORD.**

35:13–15 Sackcloth is a garment of mourning and a sign of sympathy and concern for those suffering. David was, in return, shown ingratitude and betrayal.

35:16 Gnashed means David's reputation was ripped to shreds by unjust slander.

19 [a]Let them not rejoice over me who
are wrongfully my enemies;
Nor let them wink with the eye
who hate me without a cause.
20 For they do not speak peace,
But they devise deceitful matters
Against *the* quiet ones in the land.
21 They also opened their mouth
wide against me,
And said, "Aha, aha!
Our eyes have seen *it*."

22 *This* You have seen, O LORD;
Do not keep silence.
O Lord, do not be far from me.
23 Stir up Yourself, and awake to my
vindication,
To my cause, my God and my
Lord.
24 Vindicate me, O LORD my God,
according to Your
righteousness;
And let them not rejoice over me.
25 Let them not say in their hearts,
"Ah, so we would have it!"
Let them not say, "We have
swallowed him up."

26 Let them be ashamed and
brought to mutual confusion
Who rejoice at my hurt;
Let them be [a]clothed with shame
and dishonor
Who exalt themselves against me.

27 [a]Let them shout for joy and be
glad,
Who favor my righteous cause;
And let them say continually,
"Let the LORD be magnified,
Who has pleasure in the
prosperity of His servant."

KINGDOM DYNAMICS

35:27 Happy, Holy, Healthy, and at Peace, GOD'S PROSPERITY. God is pleased when His servants prosper! The Hebrew word, translated here as "prosperity," is laden with meaning: "safety, wellness, happiness, healthiness, peacefulness." In fact, this word usually is translated "peace"; when your needs are met, you are at peace. Moreover, if God is pleased with the prosperity of servants, what must He be with the prosperity of His own children—those who are purchased by the blood of Jesus and adopted as His own? Think how thrilled God must be when we—His own children—prosper in every aspect of our lives. (3 John 2/Mark 10:17–27) F.P.

28 And my tongue shall speak of
Your righteousness
And of Your praise all the day
long.

19 [a]Ps. 69:4; 109:3; Lam. 3:52; [John 15:25]
26 [a]Ps. 109:29
27 [a]Rom. 12:15

PSALM 36

Man's Wickedness and God's Perfections

To the Chief Musician. A Psalm of David the servant of the LORD.

AN oracle within my heart
concerning the transgression of
the wicked:
[a]*There is* no fear of God before his
eyes.
2 For he flatters himself in his own
eyes,
When he finds out his iniquity
and when he hates.
3 The words of his mouth *are*
wickedness and deceit;
[a]He has ceased to be *wise *and* to
do good.
4 [a]He devises wickedness on his
bed;
He sets himself [b]in a way *that is*
not good;
He does not [1]abhor [c]evil. 2

5 Your mercy, O LORD, *is* in the
heavens;
Your *faithfulness *reaches* to the
clouds.
6 Your righteousness *is* like the
[1]great mountains;
[a]Your judgments *are* a great deep;
O LORD, You preserve man and
beast.

7 How precious *is* Your
lovingkindness, O God!
Therefore the children of men
[a]put their trust under the
shadow of Your wings.

PSALM 36
1 [a]Rom. 3:18
3 [a]Ps. 94:8; Jer. 4:22 *See WW at Jer. 3:15.
4 [a]Prov. 4:16; [Mic. 2:1] [b]Is. 65:2 [c][Ps. 52:3; Rom. 12:9] [1]*reject, loathe*
5 *See WW at Prov. 28:20.
6 [a]Job 11:8; Ps. 77:19; [Rom. 11:33] [1]Lit. *mountains of God*
7 [a]Ruth 2:12; Ps. 17:8; 57:1; 91:4

35:23 David's Son, Jesus, who was also falsely accused, uttered a similar plea for **vindication** (John 17:1), and also warned of judgment on those who rejoiced (v. 26) at His mistreatment (Matt. 23:34–36).
36:1–4 This **oracle** is a concise description of the soul totally given over to sin.
36:1 Transgression: Paul quoted this to show that Jews were sinners as well as Gentiles, and that both need a Savior (Rom. 3:18).
36:4 See section 2 of Truth-In-Action following Ps. 41.
36:5–12 In stark contrast to the wicked, the character of the **LORD** is depicted.
36:7 Lovingkindness (Hebrew *chesed*) is also translated "steadfast love," "mercy," "goodness," "unfailing love," and is equivalent to the NT "grace." See note on 33:5.

8 [a]They are abundantly satisfied
with the fullness of Your
house,
And You give them drink from
[b]the river of Your pleasures.
9 [a]For with You *is* the fountain of
life;
[b]In Your light we see light.

10 Oh, continue Your
lovingkindness to those who
know You,
And Your righteousness to the
upright in heart.
11 Let not the foot of pride come
against me,
And let not the hand of the
wicked drive me away.
12 There the workers of iniquity
have fallen;
They have been cast down and
are not able to rise.

PSALM 37

The Heritage of the Righteous and the Calamity of the Wicked

A Psalm of David.

Do[a] not fret because of evildoers,
Nor be envious of the workers of
iniquity.
2 For they shall soon be cut down
[a]like the grass,
And wither as the green herb.

3 Trust in the LORD, and do good;
Dwell in the land, and feed on His
faithfulness.
4 [a]Delight yourself also in the LORD,
And He shall give you the desires
of your [b]**heart.**

WORD WEALTH

37:4 heart, *leb* (*lehv*); Strong's #3820: Heart, intellect, awareness, mind, inner person, inner feelings, deepest thoughts, inner self. As in English, the Hebrew concept of "heart" encompasses both the physical organ (2 Kin. 9:24) and a person's inner yearnings (Ps. 37:4). Perhaps the noblest occurrence of *leb* is Deut. 6:5, commanding Israel to love the Lord "with all your heart" (Jesus laid great emphasis on this sentence; see Mark 12:29, 30). Jer. 17:9 states that the human heart can be the most deceitful thing in the world, but v. 10 shows that the Lord is still able to sort out and analyze what lies within the heart.

8 [a]Ps. 63:5; 65:4; Is. 25:6; Jer. 31:12–14 [b]Ps. 46:4; Rev. 22:1
9 [a][Jer. 2:13; John 4:10, 14] [b][1 Pet. 2:9]

PSALM 37

1 [a]Ps. 73:3; [Prov. 23:17; 24:19]
2 [a]Job 14:2; Ps. 90:5, 6; 92:7; James 1:11
4 [a]Job 22:26; Ps. 94:19; Is. 58:14 [b]Ps. 21:2; 145:19; [Matt. 7:7, 8]
5 [a][Ps. 55:22; Prov. 16:3; 1 Pet. 5:7] [1]Lit. *Roll off onto* *See WW at Prov. 16:3.
6 [a]Job 11:17; [Is. 58:8, 10]
7 [a]Ps. 40:1; 62:5; [Lam. 3:26] [b][Ps. 73:3–12]
8 [a][Eph. 4:26] [b]Ps. 73:3
9 [a]Ps. 25:13; Prov. 2:21; [Is. 57:13; 60:21; Matt. 5:5] [1]*destroyed* *See WW at Deut. 8:1. • See WW at Ex. 32:13.
10 [a][Heb. 10:37] [b]Job 7:10; Ps. 37:35, 36
11 [a][Matt. 5:5]
12 [a]Ps. 35:16
13 [a]Ps. 2:4; 59:8 [b]1 Sam. 26:10; Job 18:20 *See WW at Eccl. 3:4.
16 [a]Prov. 15:16; 16:8; [1 Tim. 6:6]

5 [a]Commit[1]* your way to the LORD, **5**
Trust also in Him,
And He shall bring *it* to pass.
6 [a]He shall bring forth your
righteousness as the light,
And your justice as the noonday.

7 Rest in the LORD, [a]and wait
patiently for Him;
Do not fret because of him who
[b]prospers in his way,
Because of the man who brings
wicked schemes to pass.
8 [a]Cease from anger, and forsake
wrath;
[b]Do not fret—*it* only *causes* harm.

9 For evildoers shall be [1]cut off;
But those who wait on the LORD,
They shall [a]inherit* the *earth.
10 For [a]yet a little while and the
wicked *shall be* no *more;*
Indeed, [b]you will look carefully
for his place,
But it *shall be* no *more.*
11 [a]But the meek shall inherit the
earth,
And shall delight themselves in
the abundance of peace.

12 The wicked plots against the just,
[a]And gnashes at him with his
teeth.
13 [a]The Lord *laughs at him,
For He sees that [b]his day is
coming.
14 The wicked have drawn the
sword
And have bent their bow,
To cast down the poor and needy,
To slay those who are of upright
conduct.
15 Their sword shall enter their own
heart,
And their bows shall be broken.

16 [a]A little that a righteous man has
Is better than the riches of many
wicked.

36:9 This **light** is further revealed in Jesus (John 8:12).
37:1–40 This is an alphabetic psalm (acrostic) where each *pair of lines begins with successive* letters of the Hebrew alphabet. It is written to men, rather than to God, and contrasts the life-style of the wicked and deceitful with the righteous and forgiven.
37:3 Eight times the thought **dwell in the land,** or inherit the land, is mentioned, showing to the righteous Jews that their future is secure.
37:5 See section 5 of Truth-In-Action following Ps. 41.
37:7 The believer who waits **patiently** for the timing of God has nothing to fear or be envious about.
37:11 See Jesus' application of this in the kingdom of God where the **meek** reign (Matt. 5:5).
37:14 God keeps a record of the economic inequities in nations and of the oppression of the **poor,** and there will be a day of reckoning (Mark 10:23–31).

17 For the arms of the wicked shall be broken,
But the LORD upholds the righteous.

18 The LORD knows the days of the upright,
And their inheritance shall be forever.
19 They shall not be ashamed in the evil time,
And in the days of famine they shall be satisfied.
20 But the wicked shall perish;
And the enemies of the LORD,
Like the splendor of the meadows, shall vanish.
Into smoke they shall vanish away.

21 The wicked borrows and does not repay,
But [a]the righteous shows mercy and gives.
22 [a]For *those* blessed by Him shall inherit the earth,
But *those* cursed by Him shall be [1]cut off.

23 [a]The steps of a *good* man are [1]ordered by the LORD,
And He delights in his way.
24 [a]Though he fall, he shall not be utterly cast down;
For the LORD upholds *him with* His hand.

25 I have been young, and *now* am old;
Yet I have not seen the righteous forsaken,
Nor his descendants begging bread.
26 [a]*He is* [1]ever merciful, and lends;
And his descendants *are* blessed.

27 Depart from evil, and do good;
And dwell forevermore.
28 For the LORD loves justice,
And does not forsake His saints;
They are preserved forever,
But the descendants of the wicked shall be cut off.
29 [a]The righteous shall inherit the land,
And dwell in it forever.

30 [a]The mouth of the righteous speaks *wisdom,
And his tongue talks of justice.
31 The law of his God *is* in his heart;
None of his steps shall [1]slide.

32 The wicked [a]watches* the righteous,
And seeks to slay him.
33 The LORD [a]will not leave him in his hand,
Nor condemn him when he is judged.

34 [a]Wait on the LORD,
And keep His way,
And He shall exalt you to inherit the land;
When the wicked are cut off, you shall see *it*.
35 I have seen the wicked in great power,
And spreading himself like a native green tree.
36 Yet [1]he passed away, and behold, he *was* no *more;*
Indeed I sought him, but he could not be found.

37 Mark the blameless *man,* and observe the upright;
For the future of *that* man *is* peace.
38 [a]But the transgressors shall be destroyed together;
The future of the wicked shall be cut off.

39 But the salvation of the righteous *is* from the LORD;
He is their strength [a]in the time of trouble.
40 And [a]the LORD shall help them and deliver them;
He shall deliver them from the wicked,
And save them,
[b]Because they trust in Him.

PSALM 38

Prayer in Time of Chastening

A Psalm of David. [a]To bring to remembrance.

O LORD, do not [a]rebuke me in Your wrath,
Nor chasten me in Your hot displeasure!
2 For Your arrows pierce me deeply,
And Your hand presses me down.

21 [a]Ps. 112:5, 9 **22** [a][Prov. 3:33] [1]*destroyed* **23** [a][1 Sam. 2:9]; Ps. 40:2; 66:9; 119:5 [1]*established* **24** [a]Prov. 24:16 **26** [a][Deut. 15:8]; Ps. 37:21 [1]Lit. *all the day* **29** [a]Ps. 37:9; Prov. 2:21 **30** [a][Matt. 12:35] *See WW at Is. 11:2.

31 [1]*slip* **32** [a]Ps. 10:8; 17:11 *See WW at Hos. 9:8. **33** [a]Ps. 31:8; [2 Pet. 2:9] **34** [a]Ps. 27:14; 37:9 **36** [1]So with MT, LXX, Tg.; Syr., Vg. *I passed by* **38** [a][Ps. 1:4–6; 37:20, 28] **39** [a]Ps. 9:9; 37:19 **40** [a]Ps. 22:4; Is. 31:5; Dan. 3:17; 6:23 [b]1 Chr. 5:20; Ps. 34:22

PSALM 38

title [a]Ps. 70:title **1** [a]Ps. 6:1

37:40 The primary thought of this psalm is **trust** in God to bring about economic justice in His time.
38:1–22 According to this psalm's title, prayer brings man to God's "remembrance." The word does not imply forgetfulness, but the bringing to mind so decisive action will be taken on behalf of someone (1 Sam. 1:19).

3 *There is* no soundness in my flesh
Because of Your anger,
Nor *any* health in my bones
Because of my sin.
4 For my *iniquities have gone over
my head;
Like a heavy burden they are too
heavy for me.
5 My wounds are foul *and* festering
Because of my foolishness.

6 I am [1]troubled, I am bowed down
greatly;
I go mourning all the day long.
7 For my loins are full of
inflammation,
And *there is* no soundness in my
flesh.
8 I am feeble and severely broken;
I groan because of the turmoil of
my heart.

9 Lord, all my desire *is* before You;
And my sighing is not hidden
from You.
10 My heart pants, my strength fails
me;
As for the light of my eyes, it also
has gone from me.

11 My loved ones and my friends
[a]stand aloof from my plague,
And my relatives stand afar off.
12 Those also who seek my life lay
snares *for me;*
Those who seek my hurt speak of
destruction,
And plan deception all the day
long.

13 But I, like a deaf *man,* do not
hear;
And *I am* like a mute *who* does
not open his mouth.
14 Thus I am like a man who does
not hear,
And in whose mouth *is* no
response.

15 For [1]in You, O LORD, [a]I hope;
You will [2]hear, O Lord my God.
16 For I said, *"Hear me,* lest they
rejoice over me,
Lest, when my foot slips, they
exalt *themselves* against me."

4 *See WW at Ps. 130:3.
6 [1]Lit. *bent down*
11 [a]Ps. 31:11; 88:18
15 [a][Ps. 39:7] [1]*I wait for You, O* LORD [2]*answer*

17 [a]For I *am* ready to fall,
And my sorrow *is* continually
before me.
18 For I will [a]declare my iniquity;
I will be [b]in [1]anguish over my sin.
19 But my enemies *are* vigorous, *and*
they are strong;
And those who hate me
wrongfully have multiplied.
20 Those also [a]who render evil for
good,
They are my adversaries, because
I follow *what is* good.

21 Do not forsake me, O LORD;
O my God, [a]be not far from me!
22 Make haste to help me,
O Lord, my salvation!

PSALM 39

Prayer for Wisdom and Forgiveness

To the Chief Musician. To Jeduthun. A Psalm of David.

I SAID, "I will guard my ways,
Lest I sin with my [a]tongue;
I will restrain my mouth with a
muzzle,
While the wicked are before me."
2 [a]I was mute with silence,
I held my peace *even* from good;
And my sorrow was stirred up.
3 My heart was hot within me;
While I was [1]musing, the fire
burned.
Then I spoke with my tongue:

4 "LORD, [a]make me to know my end,
And what *is* the measure of my
days,
That I may know how frail I *am.*
5 Indeed, You have made my days
as handbreadths,
And my age *is* as nothing before
You;
Certainly every man at his best
state *is* but [a]vapor. Selah
6 Surely every man walks about
like a shadow;
Surely they [1]busy themselves in
vain;
He heaps up *riches,*
And does not know who will
gather them.

17 [a]Ps. 51:3
18 [a]Ps. 32:5 [b][2 Cor. 7:9, 10] [1]*anxiety*
20 [a]Ps. 35:12
21 [a]Ps. 22:19; 35:22

PSALM 39

1 [a]Job 2:10; Ps. 34:13; [James 3:5–12]
2 [a]Ps. 38:13
3 [1]*meditating*
4 [a]Ps. 90:12; 119:84
5 [a]Ps. 62:9; [Eccl. 6:12]
6 [1]*make an uproar for nothing*

38:3–8 Not all sickness is the result of **sin,** but sometimes it is (1 Cor. 11:30).
38:16 Instead of restoring the penitent sinner (Gal. 6:1), acquaintances often turn **against** him, forgetting they too are not immune to failure.
39:title This psalm was to be given **to the Chief Musician** in the temple, **Jeduthun,** to incorporate into worship (1 Chr. 16:41).
39:1–6 Thinking about the pain and injustices of life often arouses indignation (v. 3, **hot**), and when these bring one to death's door he realizes how fleeting life is (v. 5, **vapor**). See James 4:14.

7 "And now, Lord, what do I wait for?
My [a]hope *is* in You.
8 Deliver me from all my transgressions;
Do not make me [a]the reproach of the foolish.
9 [a]I was mute, I did not open my mouth,
Because it was [b]You who did *it*.
10 [a]Remove Your plague from me;
I am consumed by the blow of Your hand.
11 When with rebukes You *correct man for iniquity,
You make his beauty [a]melt away like a moth;
Surely every man *is* vapor. Selah

12 "Hear my prayer, O LORD,
And give ear to my cry;
Do not be silent at my tears;
For I *am* a stranger with You,
A sojourner, [a]as all my fathers *were*.
13 [a]Remove Your gaze from me, that I may regain strength,
Before I go away and [b]am no more."

7 [a]Ps. 38:15 8 [a]Ps. 44:13; 79:4; 119:22 9 [a]Ps. 39:2 [b]2 Sam. 16:10; Job 2:10 10 [a]Job 9:34; 13:21 11 [a]Job 13:28; [Ps. 90:7]; Is. 50:9 *See WW at Jer. 10:24. 12 [a]Gen. 47:9; Lev. 25:23; 1 Chr. 29:15; Ps. 119:19; Heb. 11:13; 1 Pet. 2:11 13 [a]Job 7:19; 10:20, 21; 14:6; Ps. 102:24 [b][Job 14:10]

PSALM 40

Faith Persevering in Trial

To the Chief Musician. A Psalm of David.

I [a]WAITED patiently for the LORD;
And He inclined to me,
And heard my cry.
2 He also brought me up out of a horrible pit,
Out of [a]the miry clay,
And [b]set my feet upon a rock,
And established my steps.
3 [a]He has put a new song in my mouth—
Praise to our God;
Many will see *it* and fear,
And will trust in the LORD.

4 [a]Blessed *is* that man who makes the LORD his trust,
And does not respect the proud, nor such as turn aside to lies.
5 [a]Many, O LORD my God, *are* Your wonderful works
Which You have done;
[b]And Your thoughts toward us
Cannot be recounted to You in order;
If I would declare and speak *of them*,
They are more than can be numbered.

6 [a]Sacrifice and *offering You did not desire; 4
My ears You have opened.
Burnt offering and sin offering
You did not require.
7 Then I said, "Behold, I come;
In the scroll of the book *it is* written of me.
8 [a]I *delight to do Your *will, O my God,
And Your *law *is* [b]within my heart."
9 [a]I have proclaimed the good news of righteousness
In the great assembly;
Indeed, [b]I do not restrain my lips,
O LORD, You Yourself know.
10 [a]I have not hidden Your righteousness within my *heart;
I have declared Your *faithfulness and Your salvation;
I have not concealed Your lovingkindness and Your truth
From the great assembly.

11 Do not withhold Your tender mercies from me, O LORD;
[a]Let Your lovingkindness and Your truth continually preserve me.
12 For innumerable evils have surrounded me;
[a]My iniquities have overtaken me, so that I am not able to look up;
They are more than the hairs of my head;
Therefore my heart fails me.

13 [a]Be pleased, O LORD, to deliver me;
O LORD, make haste to help me!
14 [a]Let them be ashamed and brought to mutual confusion
Who seek to destroy my [1]life;
Let them be driven backward and brought to dishonor

PSALM 40

1 [a]Ps. 25:5; 27:14; 37:7 2 [a]Ps. 69:2, 14; Jer. 38:6 [b]Ps. 27:5 3 [a]Ps. 32:7; 33:3 4 [a]Ps. 34:8; 84:12 5 [a]Job 9:10 [b]Ps. 139:17; [Is. 55:8] 6 [a][1 Sam. 15:22]; Ps. 51:16; Is. 1:11; [Jer. 6:20; 7:22, 23]; Amos 5:22; [Mic. 6:6–8; Heb. 10:5–9] *See WW at Num. 29:6. 8 [a][Matt. 26:39; John 4:34; 6:38]; Heb. 10:7 [b][Ps. 37:31; Jer. 31:33; 2 Cor. 3:3] *See WW at Ps. 112:1. • See WW at Deut. 33:23. • See WW at Is. 42:21. 9 [a]Ps. 22:22, 25 [b]Ps. 119:13 10 [a]Acts 20:20, 27 *See WW at Ps. 37:4. • See WW at Prov. 28:20. 11 [a]Ps. 61:7; Prov. 20:28 12 [a]Ps. 38:4; 65:3 13 [a]Ps. 70:1 14 [a]Ps. 35:4, 26; 70:2; 71:13 [1]Lit. *soul*

39:12 Being a **stranger** and **sojourner,** he is therefore totally dependent on the hospitality and provision of God in whose land he resides.

40:4 Respect literally means "has not turned to," that is, for help or companionship.

40:6–8 See section 4 of Truth-In-Action following Ps. 41.

40:6–8 The author of Heb. applies these verses to Jesus, showing that His once-for-all offering of Himself on the Cross was to replace the **sacrifice burnt** year after year (Heb. 10:5–9).

Who wish me evil.
15 Let them be [a]confounded because of their shame,
Who say to me, "Aha, aha!"

16 [a]Let all those who seek You
*rejoice and be glad in You;
Let such as love Your salvation
[b]say continually,
"The LORD be magnified!"
17 [a]But I *am* **poor** and needy;
[b]*Yet* the LORD thinks upon me.
You *are* my help and my deliverer;
Do not delay, O my God.

WORD WEALTH

40:17 poor, *'ani* (ah-*nee*); Strong's #6041: Poor, afflicted, needy; lowly, humble; low in status. *'Ani* may refer to the person whose outward condition makes him poor, afflicted, or depressed. It may also refer to the person who inwardly is lowly, humble, and absolutely not self-exalting. God maintains the cause of these afflicted (140:12). In Is. 61:1, God commissions the Messiah to preach the good news specifically to the poor. To be of a lowly status is neither a crime nor an indication of lack of faith, as the testimony of the heroes of faith amply demonstrates (see Heb. 11:36–40).

PSALM 41

The Blessing and Suffering of the Godly

To the Chief Musician. A Psalm of David.

BLESSED *is* he who considers the [1]poor;
The LORD will deliver him in time of trouble.
2 The LORD will *preserve him and keep him alive,
And he will be *blessed on the earth;
[a]You will not deliver him to the will of his enemies.
3 The LORD will strengthen him on his bed of illness;
You will [1]sustain him on his sickbed.

15 [a]Ps. 73:19
16 [a]Ps. 70:4 [b]Ps. 35:27 *See WW at Is. 64:5.
17 [a]Ps. 70:5; 86:1; 109:22 [b]Ps. 40:5; 1 Pet. 5:7

PSALM 41

1 [1]*helpless* or *powerless*
2 [a]Ps. 27:12 *See WW at Job 10:12. • See WW at Prov. 31:28.
3 [1]*restore*
4 [a]Ps. 6:2; 103:3; 147:3 *See WW at Ex. 15:26.
6 [1]*empty words*
7 [1]*plot*
8 [1]Lit. *A thing of Belial*
9 [a]2 Sam. 15:12; Job 19:13, 19 [b]Ps. 55:12–14, 20; Jer. 20:10; Obad. 7; [Mic. 7:5]; Matt. 26:14–16, 21–25, 47–50; John 13:18, 21–30; Acts 1:16, 17 [1]*Acted as a traitor*

4 I said, "LORD, be merciful to me;
[a]Heal* my soul, for I have sinned against You."
5 My enemies speak evil of me:
"When will he die, and his name perish?"
6 And if he comes to see *me,* he speaks [1]lies;
His heart gathers iniquity to itself;
When he goes out, he tells *it.*
7 All who hate me whisper together against me;
Against me they [1]devise my hurt.
8 "An[1] evil disease," *they say,*
"clings to him.
And *now* that he lies down, he will rise up no more."
9 [a]Even my own familiar friend in whom I trusted,
[b]Who ate my bread,
Has [1]lifted up *his* heel against me.

KINGDOM DYNAMICS

41:9; Zech. 11:12, 13 Detailed Account of the Betrayal of the Messiah, MESSIAH'S COMING. David, who wrote Ps. 41, lived about 500 years before Zechariah; and Zechariah lived more than 500 years before Christ. Yet the words of these two men form a single prophecy, which was fulfilled in detail. David prophesied that a trusted friend would be the Lord's betrayer; and Judas Iscariot, one of the Twelve, betrayed Him (Matt. 26:14–16; Luke 22:1–6). Zechariah went even further, specifying the amount that would be paid to the traitor, predicting that it would be cast into the house of the Lord, and stating that it would be used to buy a potter's field. Every point was fulfilled in detail: The chief priests gave Judas 30 pieces of silver (Matt. 26:15); Judas, in remorse, returned the money and threw it down in the temple (Matt. 27:5); and the priests used the money to buy a potter's field (Matt. 27:6–10). The detailed fulfillment of this prophecy is truly a testimony to God's sovereign working in the affairs of men.

(Zech. 9:9/Ps. 22:1–31) J.H.

10 But You, O LORD, be merciful to me, and raise me up,

40:17 Remember, it is the great king of Israel who is saying **I am poor.** That is the true humility that is required when coming into the presence of God (see 1 Pet. 5:6, 7).

41:1–13 This psalm and Ps. 55 and 109 describe betrayal by friends and are quoted in the NT with reference to Judas Iscariot (Luke 22:21–23).

41:1 Poor: That is, poor in health, the weak and gaunt (Gen. 41:19).

41:4 The sin of David, which resulted in the chaos about to be described, may have been his affair with Bathsheba (2 Sam. 12:9–14).

41:9 The **friend** referred to may have been David's cabinet member Ahithophel (2 Sam. 17:23). We note similarities between Ahithophel and Judas, who **ate** the Passover **bread** with Christ before he betrayed Him (John 13:1). Both Ahithophel and Judas hanged themselves after their acts of betrayal.

That I may repay them.
11 By this I know that You are well pleased with me,
Because my enemy does not triumph over me.
12 As for me, You uphold me in my integrity,
And [a]set me before Your face forever.

13 [a]Blessed *be* the LORD God of Israel
From everlasting to everlasting!
Amen and Amen.

12 a[Job 36:7; Ps. 21:6; 34:15] 13 aPs. 72:18, 19; 89:52; 106:48; 150:6

41:10 Repay is in the sense of bringing the enemies to justice. As king, David was obligated to do so.
41:13 This verse is the closing doxology of Book One and is not an integral part of the psalm. **Amen** is from the Hebrew root word for "true" or "faithful," and in the NT its equivalent is often translated "truly."

TRUTH-IN-ACTION through PSALMS (Book One: Psalms 1—41)

Letting the LIFE of the Holy Spirit Bring Faith's Works Alive in You!

Truth Psalms Teaches	Text	**Action** Psalms Invites
1 A Step to Knowing God Knowing and believing that God is omniscient will keep us from trying to hide from Him.	10:11–15	**Understand** that God sees and knows all things. **Believe** that nothing you do is hidden from Him.
2 Guidelines for Growing in Godliness Godly living is radically different from the way we learned to live while in the world. It offends our fleshly, sinful nature. Therefore, because godliness is unnatural to us, we must have the supernatural assistance of the Holy Spirit. Godly living requires radical change in our speech, conduct, and thinking.	2:12	**Honor** the Lord Jesus Christ in your speech and conduct.
	4:4	**Refuse** to respond out of anger. **Sleep on it** and **give time** for righteous reflection.
	10:4	**Let God fill** your thoughts and thus **avoid** wickedness.
	15:4	**Honor** commitments and your word even when it is costly to do so.
	19:14	**Speak** and **think** only in ways that you know please the Lord.
	36:4	**Understand** that righteousness actively rejects wrongdoing.
3 Steps to Holiness Holy people not only live in a manner distinct from the world, but also disallow the world's value system to have control in their lives. If we give place to the world, we will receive the results that ungodly living anticipates.	1:1	**Do not conduct your life** as the world does, **do not participate** in questionable activities, and **do not be cynical. Live distinctly** from the world as God's own people.
	7:14	**Understand** that allowing evil to develop in your heart will result in disillusionment and bring unnecessary trouble into your life.
4 Steps to Dynamic Devotion Consistently spending time with God effects permanent change in our lives. Insincere attempts at this result in half-hearted devotion. Those who make their devotion to God their highest priority are those whose lives know true, heart-felt devotion.	1:2	**Practice** regular Bible meditation. **Delight** in the Scriptures and **let them** be your guide.
	5:3	**Seek** the Lord in the morning. **Wait** on Him expectantly to speak to your heart and spirit.
	5:7	**Prioritize** private and corporate worship.
	19:7–11	**Thank** God daily that He has revealed Himself, His will and His promises to you in His Word.
	27:4	**Make** time with God and His people your high priority and your delight.
	29:1, 2	**Testify** regularly to God's goodness in your life.

Truth Psalms Teaches	Text	**Action** Psalms Invites
	40:6–8	**Choose** to live a life of disciplined obedience as God's servant.
5 Key Lessons in Faith God's people must actively, consciously trust that God's Word is true and that He always acts in accordance with it. Every situation we encounter is an opportunity to choose to trust God rather than our own inclinations. Faith involves an element of risk, but always yields the richest dividends.	9:10	**Choose to believe** that the Lord will never forsake you when you trust Him.
	12:6	**Know** that the Word of God has been proven to be absolutely trustworthy.
	23:1–6	**Expect** Jesus' shepherding care. **Know** that He will keep you from want, protect you, and restore your life.
	26:1	**Believe** the Lord for your vindication, not seeking it yourself.
	37:5	**Consciously commit** all your plans to the Lord daily. **Do not presume** His help if it is uninvited.
6 Steps to Dealing with Sin Dealing properly with sin involves the courage to allow the Word of God and the Spirit of God to examine your heart and mind. Covering up sin and trying to hide it results in distress and usually greater sin. Agree with God about sinful behavior, turn from it, and God's gracious forgiveness will cover it.	19:12, 13	**Receive** examination and correction from the Word of God. **Understand** that doing so will keep you from sin.
	25:7	**Confess** and **turn from** sin and rebellion. **Receive** God's forgiveness. **Understand** God forgets as well.
	32:1–5	**Acknowledge** and **confess** sin. **Understand** that God desires to forgive and restore you, but **do not** take God's forgiveness lightly.
7 How to Tame the Tongue Few sins exist that do not somehow involve the tongue. Righteous speech results from discipline and choice. Too easily do we speak too much, too hastily, and too freely. Choosing to speak much less and more carefully will result in less sinning.	17:3	**Choose** to speak only that which is righteous. **Commit** yourself to godly conversation.
	18:6	**Do not** grumble and complain when in distress or trouble. **Cry** out to God. **Trust** that He will hear and answer.
	34:12–14	**Guard carefully** your speech. **Know** that righteous speech carries with it the promise of long life.

BOOK TWO
Psalms 42–72

PSALM 42

Yearning for God in the Midst of Distresses

To the Chief Musician. A [1]Contemplation of the sons of Korah.

2 AS the deer [1]pants for the water brooks,
So pants my *soul for You, O God.

2 [a]My soul thirsts for God, for the [b]living God.
When shall I come and [1]appear before God?
3 [a]My tears have been my food day and night,
While they continually say to me,
[b]"Where *is* your God?"
4 When I remember these *things,*
[a]I pour out my soul within me.

PSALM 42

title [1]Heb. *Maschil*
1 [1]Lit. *longs for* *See WW at Prov. 10:3.
2 [a]Ps. 63:1; 84:2; 143:6 [b]1 Thess. 1:9 [1]So with MT, Vg.; some Heb. mss., LXX, Syr., Tg. *I see the face of God*
3 [a]Ps. 80:5; 102:9 [b]Ps. 79:10; 115:2
4 [a]Job 30:16

42:1–11 Many consider Ps. 42 and 43 to be one psalm since the refrains of 42:5, 11 are the same as 43:5, and Ps. 43 has no title. These two psalms may be messianic since Christ also was "exiled" to Perea (v. 6; Mark 10:1), and was delivered to the Gentiles (43:1; Mark 10:32–34).

42:1, 2 See section 2 of Truth-In-Action following Ps. 72.

42:2 That is, **appear** in person at the temple sanctuary to worship again.

For I used to go with the multitude;
[b]I went with them to the house of God,
With the voice of *joy and praise,
With a multitude that *kept a pilgrim feast.

5 [a]Why are you [1]cast down, O my soul?
And *why* are you disquieted within me?
[b]Hope in God, for I shall yet praise Him
[2]*For* the help of His countenance.

6 [1]O my God, my soul is cast down within me;
Therefore I will remember You from the land of the Jordan,
And from the heights of Hermon,
From [2]the Hill Mizar.
7 Deep calls unto deep at the noise of Your waterfalls;
[a]All Your waves and billows have gone over me.
8 The LORD will [a]command His lovingkindness in the daytime,
And [b]in the night His song *shall be* with me—
A prayer to the God of my life.

9 I will say to God my Rock,
[a]"Why have You forgotten me?
Why do I go mourning because of the oppression of the enemy?"
10 *As* with a [1]breaking of my bones,
My enemies [2]reproach me,
[a]While they say to me all day long,
"Where *is* your God?"

11 [a]Why are you cast down, O my soul?
And why are you disquieted within me?
Hope in God;
For I shall yet praise Him,
The [1]help of my countenance and my God.

4 [b]Ps. 55:14; 122:1; Is. 30:29 *See WW at Ps. 30:5. • See WW at Ex. 23:14. 5 [a]Ps. 42:11; 43:5 [b]Ps. 71:14; Lam. 3:24 [1]Lit. *bowed down* [2]So with MT, Tg.; a few Heb. mss., LXX, Syr., Vg. *The help of my countenance, my God* 6 [1]So with MT, Tg.; a few Heb. mss., LXX, Syr., Vg. put *my God* at the end of v. 5 [2]Or *Mount* 7 [a]Ps. 69:1, 2; 88:7; Jon. 2:3 8 [a]Deut. 28:8 [b]Job 35:10; Ps. 149:5 9 [a]Ps. 38:6 10 [a]Ps. 42:3; Joel 2:17; Mic. 7:10 [1]Lit. *shattering* [2]*revile* 11 [a]Ps. 43:5 [1]Lit. *salvation*

PSALM 43

1 [a][Ps. 26:1; 35:24] [b]1 Sam. 24:15; Ps. 35:1 2 [a]Ps. 42:9 3 [a][Ps. 40:11] [b]Ps. 3:4 [1]*dwelling places* *See WW at Ps. 25:5. 5 [a]Ps. 42:5, 11 [1]Lit. *salvation*

PSALM 44

title [a]Ps. 42:title [1]Heb. *Maschil*

PSALM 43

Prayer to God in Time of Trouble

VINDICATE [a]me, O God,
And [b]plead my cause against an ungodly nation;
Oh, deliver me from the deceitful and unjust man!
2 For You *are* the God of my strength;
Why do You cast me off?
[a]Why do I go mourning because of the oppression of the enemy?

3 [a]Oh, send out Your light and Your *truth! 4
Let them lead me;
Let them bring me to [b]Your holy hill
And to Your [1]tabernacle.
4 Then I will go to the altar of God,
To God my exceeding joy;
And on the harp I will praise You,
O God, my God.

5 [a]Why are you cast down, O my soul?
And why are you disquieted within me?
Hope in God;
For I shall yet praise Him,
The [1]help of my countenance and my God.

PSALM 44

Redemption Remembered in Present Dishonor

To the Chief Musician. A [a]Contemplation[1] of the sons of Korah.

WE have heard with our ears, O God,

42:4 If corporate worship and fellowship was such a time of **joy** and **praise** in OT times, how much more festive should they be with the advent of Christ and His glorious gospel (Phil. 4:4)?
42:5 The spirit of faith here addresses the **soul cast down,** taking its eyes off the circumstance and looking to God.
42:6 The land of Jordan is the mountainous strip of land east of the Jordan River, called Perea in the NT, where Jesus stayed because the religious leaders in Jerusalem desired to kill Him.
42:9 Forgotten: The subjective feelings of distress war against the facts of faith, and they are strengthened by the embarrassing questions of the enemies.
42:11 The ultimate course of action in any distress is to **hope** to the end, no matter how bleak the outcome appears to be.
43:1–5 Some ancient manuscripts join Ps. 42 and 43, though the Greek Septuagint lists them as two separate psalms, since this is the only psalm in Book Two without a title. In some traditional churches 43:1 is sung as the introit on Passion Sunday, recalling the last trip of Jesus to Jerusalem to stand trial.
43:2 Why is repeated from 42:9.
43:3, 4 Tabernacle: The return to corporate worship in the sanctuary of God's presence is the heart's desire of true believers of every age.
43:3 See section 4 of Truth-In-Action following Ps. 72.
43:5 These words described the agonizing **soul** of Jesus in the garden of betrayal (Matt. 26:38).
44:1–26 We have heard: This lament expresses the

[a]Our fathers have told us,
The deeds You did in their days,
In days of old:
2 [a]You drove out the [1]nations with Your hand,
But them You planted;
You afflicted the peoples, and cast them out.
3 3 For [a]they did not gain possession of the land by their own sword,
Nor did their own arm save them;
But it was Your right hand, Your arm, and the light of Your countenance,
[b]Because You favored them.

4 [a]You are my King, [1]O God;
[2]Command victories for Jacob.
5 Through You [a]we will push down our enemies;
Through Your name we will trample those who rise up against us.
6 For [a]I will not trust in my bow,
Nor shall my sword save me.
7 But You have saved us from our enemies,
And have put to shame those who hated us.
8 [a]In God we boast all day long,
And praise Your name forever. Selah

9 But [a]You have cast *us* off and put us to shame,
And You do not go out with our armies.
10 You make us [a]turn back from the enemy,
And those who hate us have taken [1]spoil for themselves.
11 [a]You have given us up like sheep *intended* for food,
And have [b]scattered us among the nations.
12 [a]You sell Your people for *next to* nothing,
And are not enriched by selling them.

13 [a]You make us a reproach to our neighbors,
A scorn and a derision to those all around us.
14 [a]You make us a byword among the nations,
[b]A shaking of the head among the peoples.
15 My dishonor *is* continually before me,
And the shame of my face has covered me,
16 Because of the voice of him who reproaches and reviles,
[a]Because of the enemy and the avenger.

17 [a]All this has come upon us;
But we have not forgotten You,
Nor have we dealt falsely with Your covenant.
18 Our heart has not turned back,
[a]Nor have our steps departed from Your way;
19 But You have severely broken us in [a]the place of jackals,
And covered us [b]with the shadow of death.

20 If we had forgotten the name of our God,
Or [a]stretched[1] out our hands to a foreign god,
21 [a]Would not God search this out?
For He knows the secrets of the heart.
22 [a]Yet for Your sake we are killed all day long; 2
We are accounted as sheep for the slaughter.

23 [a]Awake! Why do You sleep, O Lord?
Arise! Do not cast *us* off forever.
24 [a]Why do You hide Your face,
And forget our affliction and our oppression?
25 For [a]our soul is bowed down to the [1]dust;
Our body clings to the ground.
26 Arise for our help,
And redeem us for Your mercies' sake.

1 [a][Ex. 12:26, 27; Deut. 6:20]; Judg. 6:13; Ps. 78:3 **2** [a]Ex. 15:17; 2 Sam. 7:10; Jer. 24:6; Amos 9:15 [1]*Gentiles, heathen* **3** [a][Deut. 8:17, 18]; Josh. 24:12 [b][Deut. 4:37; 7:7, 8] **4** [a][Ps. 74:12] [1]So with MT, Tg.; LXX, Vg. *and my God* [2]So with MT, Tg.; LXX, Syr., Vg. *Who commands* **5** [a]Deut. 33:17; [Dan. 8:4] **6** [a][1 Sam. 17:47]; Ps. 33:16; [Hos. 1:7] **8** [a]Ps. 34:2; [Jer. 9:24] **9** [a]Ps. 60:1 **10** [a]Lev. 26:17; Josh. 7:8, 12; Ps. 89:43 [1]*plunder* **11** [a]Ps. 44:22; Rom. 8:36 [b]Lev. 26:33; Deut. 4:27; 28:64; Ps. 106:27; Ezek. 20:23 **12** [a]Is. 52:3, 4; Jer. 15:13 **13** [a]Ps. 79:4; 80:6; Jer. 24:9

14 [a]Deut. 28:37 [b]Job 16:4 **16** [a]Ps. 8:2 **17** [a]Dan. 9:13 **18** [a]Job 23:11 **19** [a]Is. 34:13 [b][Ps. 23:4] **20** [a][Deut. 6:14] [1]Worshiped **21** [a]Job 31:14; [Ps. 139:1, 2; Jer. 17:10] **22** [a]Rom. 8:36 **23** [a]Ps. 7:6 **24** [a]Job 13:24 **25** [a]Ps. 119:25 [1]Ground, in humiliation

consternation of those who suffer defeat at the hands of evil men without apparent reason. See Heb. 11:32–40 for the NT answer to this dilemma.

44:3–8 See section 3 of Truth-In-Action following Ps. 72.

44:3 Own arm: The Israelites were *outnumbered* (Deut. 4:38), poorly armed (Deut. 20:1), and without walled strongholds (Deut. 9:1) when they conquered the Promised Land.

44:17–21 Dealt falsely: The psalmist is not suffering for any sins he has committed; he has a clear conscience.

44:22 See section 2 of Truth-In-Action following Ps. 72.

44:22 The apostle Paul, with NT insight, consoles believers with the truth that although many are **killed,** none are ever separated from God and His love (Rom. 8:36–39).

44:23–26 Awake and **arise** stress the urgency of the psalmist's need. These verses are echoed in the martyrs' complaint of Rev. 6:9–11.

44:24 To **forget** in Hebrew thought is to be "inactive," just as to remember is to "acknowledge a situation and respond accordingly" (Eccl. 12:1). According to NT revelation, justice delayed is not justice denied (2 Tim. 2:12).

PSALM 45

The Glories of the Messiah and His Bride

To the Chief Musician. [a]Set to [1]"The Lilies." A [2]Contemplation of the sons of Korah. A Song of Love.

MY heart is overflowing with a
good theme;
I recite my composition
concerning the King;
My tongue *is* the pen of a
[1]ready writer.

2 You are fairer than the sons of
men;
[a]Grace is poured upon Your
lips;
Therefore God has blessed You
forever.
3 [1]Gird Your [a]sword upon *Your*
thigh, [b]O Mighty One,
With Your [c]glory and Your
majesty.
4 [a]And in Your majesty ride
prosperously because of truth,
humility, *and* righteousness;
And Your right hand shall teach
You awesome things.
5 Your arrows *are* sharp in the
heart of the King's enemies;
The peoples fall under You.

6 [a]Your throne, O God, *is* forever
and ever;
A [b]scepter of righteousness *is* the
scepter of Your kingdom.
7 You love righteousness and hate
wickedness;
Therefore God, Your God, has
[a]anointed You
With the oil of [b]gladness more
than Your companions.
8 All Your garments are [a]scented
with myrrh and aloes *and*
cassia,
Out of the ivory palaces, by which
they have made You glad.
9 [a]Kings' daughters *are* among Your
honorable women;
[b]At Your right hand stands the
queen in gold from Ophir.

10 Listen, O daughter,
Consider and incline your ear;
[a]Forget your own people also, and
your father's house;
11 So the King will greatly desire
your *beauty;
[a]Because He *is* your Lord, worship
Him.
12 And the daughter of Tyre *will*
come with a gift;
[a]The rich among the people will
seek your favor.

13 The royal daughter *is* all glorious
within *the palace;*
Her clothing *is* woven with gold.
14 [a]She shall be brought to the King
in robes of many colors;
The **virgins,** her companions who
follow her, shall be brought to
You.

WORD WEALTH

45:14 virgins, *betulah* (beh-too-*lah*); Strong's #1330: A virgin; a maiden, a damsel, a grown-up young woman of marriageable age; a fiancee; a newly married bride. *Betulah* is not the only Hebrew word to describe a maiden, a virgin, or a mature young woman; *'almah* also describes a young woman or "lass." Both words come from roots that connote "separation." Nevertheless, *betulah* is used to describe an unfaithful or wayward young woman (Jer. 18:13–15). In Deut. 22:17, *betulah* refers to physical virginity. Generally, the term refers to the vitality and strength of a young woman in a certain age group, whether she is an unmarried maiden or a recently married bride.

15 With gladness and rejoicing they
shall be brought;
They shall enter the King's
palace.

16 Instead of Your fathers shall be
Your sons,
[a]Whom You shall make princes in
all the earth.
17 [a]I will make Your name to be **1**
remembered in all generations;

PSALM 45

title [a]Ps. 69:title [1]Heb. *Shoshannim* [2]Heb. *Maschil*
1 [1]*skillful*
2 [a]Luke 4:22
3 [a][Is. 49:2; Heb. 4:12]; Rev. 1:16 [b][Is. 9:6] [c]Jude 25 [1]*Belt on*
4 [a]Rev. 6:2
6 [a][Ps. 93:2]; Heb. 1:8, 9 [b][Num. 24:17]
7 [a]Ps. 2:2 [b]Ps. 21:6; Heb. 1:8, 9
8 [a]Song 1:12, 13
9 [a]Song 6:8 [b]1 Kin. 2:19
10 [a]Deut. 21:13; Ruth 1:16, 17
11 [a]Ps. 95:6; [Is. 54:5] *See WW at Ezek. 28:12.
12 [a]Is. 49:23
14 [a]Song 1:4
16 [a][1 Pet. 2:9; Rev. 1:6; 20:6]
17 [a]Mal. 1:11

45:1–17 My heart: This emotional wedding song prefigures prophetically the relationship of Christ and His bride, the church (Eph. 5:32). Ancient rabbis have applied it to the Messiah and His majesty.
45:6, 7 The writer of Heb. applies these verses to Jesus, the Son of God (Heb. 1:8, 9). "Messiah" represents the Hebrew word for one who is **anointed.**
45:9 That is, there stands the "soon-to-be" **queen.**
45:10 Forget means more than leaving parents as in Gen. 2:24. The bride of a king was often from another nation, and so she had to break with her own culture to marry, just as Christians now must forsake marriage to worldly things in order to be part of the bride of Christ.
45:12 The daughter of Tyre represents the inhabitants of the richest commercial city in OT times. Those who become the bride of Christ also receive gifts (Mark 10:29, 30).
45:15 Gladness: Likewise, believers experience excitement and joy in meeting with Christ. See Deut. 28:47.
45:16 Sons: The pain of leaving the old culture is lost in the joyous expectation of seeing future generations—one's own children—reigning with Christ (Eph. 2:6).
45:17 See section 1 of Truth-In-Action following Ps. 72.

Therefore the people shall praise
You forever and ever.

PSALM 46

God the Refuge of His People and Conqueror of the Nations

To the Chief Musician. A Psalm of the sons of Korah. A Song [a]for Alamoth.

GOD *is* our [a]refuge* and *strength,
[b]A[1] very present help in trouble.
2 Therefore we will not fear,
Even though the earth be removed,
And though the mountains be carried into the [1]midst of the sea;
3 [a]*Though* its waters roar *and* be troubled,
Though the mountains shake with its swelling. Selah

4 *There is* a [a]river whose streams shall make glad the [b]city of God,
The holy *place* of the [1]tabernacle of the Most High.
5 God *is* [a]in the midst of her, she shall not be [1]moved;
God shall help her, just [2]at the break of dawn.
6 [a]The nations raged, the kingdoms were moved;
He uttered His voice, the earth melted.

7 The [a]LORD of hosts *is* with us;
The God of Jacob *is* our refuge. Selah

8 Come, behold the works of the LORD,
Who has made desolations in the earth.
9 [a]He makes wars cease to the end of the earth;
[b]He breaks the bow and cuts the spear in two;
[c]He burns the chariot in the fire.

10 Be still, and know that I *am* God; **2**
[a]I will be exalted among the nations,
I will be exalted in the earth!

11 The LORD of hosts *is* with us;
The God of Jacob *is* our refuge. Selah

PSALM 47

Praise to God, the Ruler of the Earth

To the Chief Musician. A *Psalm of the sons of Korah.

OH, **clap** your hands, all you peoples! **2**
Shout to God with the voice of triumph!

> **WORD WEALTH**
>
> **47:1 clap,** *taqa'* (tah-*kah*); Strong's #8628: To clatter, clang, sound, blow (trumpets), clap, strike. This verb occurs more than 65 times. "Strike" may be the truest one-word definition; "sound" is also a possibility. *Taqa'* describes pitching a tent or fastening a nail, probably due to the striking of the hammer used for both tasks. In other references, *taqa'* describes blowing a trumpet or sounding an alarm. Thus *taqa'* indicates energy and enthusiasm. Here all nations are commanded to clap their hands and shout triumphantly to God. Formalistic religion seeks to discourage this kind of worship, although God has built into the human being an almost instinctive urge to clap and shout when victory is experienced.

2 For the LORD Most High *is* awesome;

PSALM 46
title [a]1 Chr. 15:20
1 [a]Ps. 62:7, 8 [b][Deut. 4:7; Ps. 145:18] [1]*An abundantly available help* *See WW at Prov. 14:26. • See WW at Jer. 16:19.
2 [1]Lit. *heart*
3 [a][Ps. 93:3, 4]
4 [a][Ezek. 47:1–12] [b]Ps. 48:1, 8; Is. 60:14 [1]*dwelling places*
5 [a][Deut. 23:14; Is. 12:6]; Ezek. 43:7; Hos. 11:9; [Joel 2:27; Zeph. 3:15; Zech. 2:5, 10, 11; 8:3] [1]*shaken* [2]Lit. *at the turning of the morning*
6 [a]Ps. 2:1, 2
7 [a]Num. 14:9; 2 Chr. 13:12
9 [a]Is. 2:4 [b]Ps. 76:3 [c]Ezek. 39:9
10 [a][Is. 2:11, 17]

PSALM 47
title *See WW at Ps. 3:title.

46:title Alamoth means "Maidens," that is, soprano voices. Some scholars feel this is a subscript of Ps. 45, which speaks of the marriage of a royal princess. See Hab. 3:19 for this kind of subscript.
46:1 Present help means a help that has been found to be reliable, or proven to be a reliable stronghold in the past, so that any future calamity is no reason to fear.
46:2 Jesus was so confident of God's being with man that He taught faith could remove **mountains . . . into the midst of the sea** (Matt. 21:21).
46:4 *In contrast to the raging environment there is a peaceful* **river** of supply in God's sanctuary that produces life.
46:7 LORD of hosts (Hebrew *Yahweh Sabaoth*) is a phrase common to the era of the Hebrew kings and was used by Hannah in 1 Sam. 1:11.
46:8 Desolations is more appropriately "astonishingly terrific events," such as destroying evil or overcoming wicked armies.
46:10, 11 Be still: This is not a call for "silent" worship. V. 10 is the voice of God addressing the wicked warring nations with a warning. In other words, "Cease and desist; it is I, God, who will be exalted in victory; you do not have a chance of winning."
46:10 See section 2 of Truth-In-Action following Ps. 72.
47:1–9 Clap your hands: This psalm was used in celebration of the New Year by later Jews with the thought that God would rule over the nations in the coming year. Christians have often applied this psalm prophetically to the Ascension because Jesus came to Israel, obtained our inheritance (Eph. 1:18), and **has gone up** (Acts 1:9, 10).
47:1–7 See section 2 of Truth-In-Action following Ps. 72.
47:2 Christ is not only King of the Jews (John 19:19), but **King over all the earth** and her kings (1 Tim. 6:15).

He is a great [a]King over all the earth.
3 [a]He will subdue the peoples under us,
And the nations under our feet.
4 He will choose our [a]inheritance for us,
The excellence of Jacob whom He loves. Selah

5 [a]God has gone up with a *shout,
The LORD with the sound of a trumpet.
6 *Sing praises to God, sing praises!
Sing praises to our King, sing praises!
7 [a]For God *is* the King of all the earth;
[b]Sing praises with *understanding.

KINGDOM DYNAMICS

47:7 Sing Praises with Understanding, PRAISE PATHWAY. The word "understanding" (Hebrew *sakal,* "prudent or cautious, and hence, intelligent") is linked to wisdom and prosperity. Prov. 21:16 provides contrast to such understanding: "A man who wanders from the way of understanding will rest in the assembly of the dead." But when we "sing praises with understanding," we are giving testimony to God's love for us and our love for Him. Life results instead of death. Others, listening to us praise God, hear testimony of our salvation and our joyful relationship with Him, which often leads to their own salvation.

(Ps. 22:3, 4/Ps. 50:22, 23) C.G.

8 [a]God reigns over the nations;
God [b]sits on His [c]holy throne.
9 The princes of the people have gathered together,
[a]The people of the God of Abraham.
[b]For the shields of the earth *belong* to God;
He is greatly exalted.

2 [a]Deut. 7:21; Neh. 1:5; Ps. 76:12 **3** [a]Ps. 18:47 **4** [a][1 Pet. 1:4] **5** [a]Ps. 68:24, 25 *See WW at Ezra 3:11. **6** *See WW at Ps. 149:3. **7** [a]Zech. 14:9 [b]1 Cor. 14:15 *See WW at Jer. 3:15. **8** [a]1 Chr. 16:31 [b]Ps. 97:2 [c]Ps. 48:1 **9** [a][Rom. 4:11, 12] [b][Ps. 89:18]

PSALM 48

The Glory of God in Zion

A Song. A Psalm of the sons of Korah.

GREAT *is* the LORD, and greatly to be praised
In the [a]city of our God,
In His holy mountain.
2 [a]Beautiful in [1]elevation,
The joy of the whole earth,
Is Mount Zion *on* the sides of the north,
The city of the *great King.
3 God *is* in her palaces;
He is known as her refuge.

4 For behold, [a]the kings assembled,
They passed by together.
5 They saw *it, and* so they marveled;
They were troubled, they hastened away.
6 Fear [a]took hold of them there,
And pain, as of a woman in birth pangs,
7 *As when* You break the [a]ships of Tarshish
With an east wind.

8 As we have heard,
So we have seen
In the city of the LORD of hosts,
In the city of our God:
God will [a]establish it forever. Selah

9 We have thought, O God, on
[a]Your lovingkindness,
In the midst of Your temple.
10 According to [a]Your name, O God,
So *is* Your praise to the ends of the earth;
Your right hand is full of righteousness.
11 Let Mount Zion rejoice,
Let the daughters of Judah be glad,
Because of Your judgments.

PSALM 48

1 [a]Ps. 46:4; 87:3; Matt. 5:35 **2** [a]Ps. 50:2 [1]*height* *See WW at Ps. 31:19. **4** [a]2 Sam. 10:6, 14 **6** [a]Ex. 15:15 **7** [a]1 Kin. 10:22; Ezek. 27:25 **8** [a][Ps. 87:5; Is. 2:2]; Mic. 4:1 **9** [a]Ps. 26:3 **10** [a][Deut. 28:58]; Josh. 7:9; Mal. 1:11

47:4 The **inheritance** is not merely land, but all the promises to Abraham, which includes the gospel of Jesus (Gal. 3:16–18). See Col. 1:12.
47:5 God has gone up in victory (Heb. 12:2), after having first come down to accomplish salvation (Phil. 2:6–10). Christ will return in like manner with the **shout** and the **trumpet** (1 Thess. 4:16).
47:7 Understanding (Hebrew *maskil*) is used in the title for several psalms and is thought to mean "instructive" or "contemplative." See 1 Cor. 14:15 for the NT application of this phrase.
47:8 The NT affirms that Jesus is seated upon this **throne** (Heb. 8:1).
47:9 Shields, from an ancient Hebrew word (Gen. 15:1), is symbolic for protective rulers who all are under God's dominion (Eph. 1:20, 21).
48:2 The city of **Zion,** which was the center of Jewish worship, is a prophetic type of the NT church (Heb. 12:22) established throughout the **whole earth.** This psalm is often read on Whitsunday in celebration of the church's birthday. Jesus affirmed that the **great King** is God (Matt. 5:35). The glorious temple was located in the **north** (northeastern) part of Mt. Zion.
48:4–6 Sennacherib **hastened away** from his defeat (2 Kin. 19:36).
48:6 A woman in birth pangs is a metaphor commonly used in Hebrew literature to show sudden calamity (1 Thess. 5:3).
48:7 The ships of Tarshish were sturdy, ore-bearing vessels used throughout the Mediterranean Sea.

12 Walk about Zion,
And go all around her.
Count her towers;
13 Mark well her bulwarks;
Consider her palaces;
That you may [a]tell *it* to the
generation following.
14 For this *is* God,
Our God forever and ever;
[a]He will be our guide
[1]*Even* to death.

PSALM 49

The Confidence of the Foolish

To the Chief Musician. A Psalm of the sons of Korah.

HEAR this, all peoples;
Give ear, all inhabitants of the
world,
2 Both low and high,
Rich and poor together.
3 My mouth shall speak wisdom,
And the meditation of my heart
shall give understanding.
4 I will incline my ear to a proverb;
I will disclose my [1]dark saying on
the harp.

5 Why should I fear in the days of
evil,
When the iniquity at my heels
surrounds me?
6 Those who [a]trust in their wealth
And boast in the multitude of
their riches,
7 None *of them* can by any means
redeem *his* brother,
Nor [a]give to God a ransom for
him—
8 For [a]the redemption of their souls
is costly,
And it shall cease forever—
9 That he should continue to live
eternally,
And [a]not [1]see the Pit.
10 For he sees wise men die;
Likewise the fool and the
senseless person perish,
And leave their wealth to others.
11 [1]Their inner thought *is that* their
houses *will last* forever,
Their *dwelling places to all
generations;
They [a]call *their* lands after their
own names.
12 Nevertheless man, *though* in
honor, does not [1]remain;
He is like the beasts *that* perish.

13 This is the way of those who *are*
[a]foolish,
And of their posterity who
approve their sayings. Selah
14 Like sheep they are laid in the
grave;
Death shall feed on them;
[a]The upright shall have dominion
over them in the morning;
[b]And their beauty shall be
consumed in [1]the grave, far
from their dwelling.
15 But God [a]will redeem my soul
from the power of [1]the *grave,
For He shall [b]receive me. Selah
16 Do not be afraid when one
becomes rich,
When the glory of his house is
increased;
17 For when he dies he shall carry
nothing away;
His glory shall not descend after
him.
18 Though while he lives [a]he blesses
himself
(For *men* will praise you when
you do well for yourself),
19 He shall go to the generation of
his fathers;
They shall never see [a]light.[1]
20 A man *who is* in honor, yet does
not understand,
[a]Is like the beasts *that* perish.

13 [a][Ps. 78:5–7]
14 [a]Is. 58:11 [1]So with MT, Syr.; LXX, Vg. *Forever*

PSALM 49

4 [1]*riddle*
6 [a]Job 31:24; Ps. 52:7; [Prov. 11:28; Mark 10:23, 24]
7 [a]Job 36:18, 19
8 [a][Matt. 16:26]
9 [a]Ps. 89:48 [1]*experience corruption*
11 [a]Gen. 4:17; Deut. 3:14 [1]LXX, Syr., Tg., Vg. *Their graves shall be their houses forever* *See WW at Is. 32:18.
12 [1]So with MT, Tg.; LXX, Syr., Vg. *understand* (cf. v. 20)
13 [a][Luke 12:20]
14 [a]Ps. 47:3; [Dan. 7:18; 1 Cor. 6:2; Rev. 2:26] [b]Job 4:21 [1]Or *Sheol*
15 [a][Hos. 13:4]; Mark 16:6, 7; Acts 2:31, 32 [b]Ps. 73:24 [1]Or *Sheol* *See WW at Hos. 13:14.
18 [a]Deut. 29:19; Luke 12:19
19 [a]Job 33:30 [1]The light of life
20 [a]Eccl. 3:19

48:12–14 That **God** is a mighty fortress with **bulwarks** (strong walls) never failing is the theme of Christian hymns written in many eras.
48:14 To death: The Greek Septuagint version reads "unto eternity"; the Hebrew is difficult to translate.
49:1–20 Hear this: This psalm gives hope to the "have-nots" when the "haves" are taking advantage of them (v. 5). The same problem is dealt with in Ps. 37 and 73.
49:2 Mentioning two extremes, such as **rich** and **poor,** is a common Hebrew poetic way of including the extremes *and everything in between.*
49:3 Wisdom and **understanding** are intensive plurals in Hebrew, implying "deep insight."
49:4 On the harp: This psalm is to be regarded as a hymn containing deep theological insight.
49:6 See Christ's teaching in Luke 12:16–21 on this subject.
49:7–9 None: Even with modern medicine, when it comes time even for a Christian to die, no amount of money can stop death. The last part of v. 8 could read, "and riches can never suffice."
49:14, 15 Riches in this life do not have the final word; **God** has yet to speak and issue appropriate recompense. **Receive** is the same verb used of Enoch in Gen. 5:24. Sadducees and Pharisees at the time of Christ debated whether verses like these meant resurrection (Acts 23:6).
49:16, 17 Glory is symbolic for wealth with its high social status.
49:17 Dies: Death is the great equalizer of rich and poor alike. See 1 Tim. 6:7.
49:19 That is, the foolish rich man shall die just as certainly as **his fathers** before him died.
49:20 The wealthy who live without godly principles will die without godly comforts as **beasts** do.

PSALM 50

God the Righteous Judge

A Psalm of Asaph.

1 THE [a]Mighty One, God the LORD,
Has spoken and called the earth
From the rising of the sun to its going down.
2 Out of Zion, the perfection of *beauty,
[a]God will shine forth.
3 Our God shall come, and shall not keep silent;
[a]A fire shall devour before Him,
And it shall be very tempestuous all around Him.

4 [a]He shall call to the heavens from above,
And to the earth, that He may judge His people:
5 "Gather [a]My saints together to Me,
[b]Those who have [1]made a covenant with Me by sacrifice."
6 Let the [a]heavens declare His righteousness,
For [b]God Himself *is* Judge. Selah

7 "Hear, O My people, and I will speak,
O Israel, and I will testify against you;
[a]I *am* God, your God!
8 [a]I will not [1]rebuke you [b]for your sacrifices
Or your burnt offerings,
Which are continually before Me.
9 [a]I will not take a bull from your house,
Nor goats out of your folds.
10 For every beast of the forest *is* Mine,
And the cattle on a thousand hills.
11 I know all the birds of the mountains,
And the wild beasts of the field *are* Mine.

12 "If I were hungry, I would not tell you;
[a]For the world *is* Mine, and all its fullness.
13 [a]Will I eat the flesh of bulls,
Or drink the blood of goats?
14 [a]Offer to God *thanksgiving,
And [b]pay your vows to the Most High.
15 [a]Call upon Me in the day of trouble;
I will deliver you, and you shall glorify Me."

16 But to the wicked God says:
"What *right* have you to declare My statutes,
Or take My covenant in your mouth,
17 [a]Seeing you hate *instruction
And cast My words behind you?
18 When you saw a thief, you [a]consented[1] with him,
And have been a [b]partaker with adulterers.
19 You give your mouth to evil,
And [a]your tongue frames deceit.
20 You sit *and* speak against your brother;
You slander your own mother's son.
21 These *things* you have done, and I kept silent;
[a]You thought that I was altogether like you;
But I will rebuke you,
And [b]set *them* in order before your eyes.

22 "Now consider this, you who [a]forget God,
Lest I tear *you* in pieces,
And *there be* none to deliver:
23 Whoever offers praise glorifies Me;
And [a]to him who orders *his* conduct *aright*
I will show the salvation of God."

PSALM 50

1 [a]Is. 9:6
2 [a]Deut. 33:2; Ps. 80:1 *See WW at Ezek. 28:12.
3 [a]Lev. 10:2; Num. 16:35; [Ps. 97:3]
4 [a]Deut. 4:26; 31:28; 32:1; Is. 1:2
5 [a]Deut. 33:3 [b]Ex. 24:7 [1]Lit. *cut*
6 [a][Ps. 97:6] [b]Ps. 75:7
7 [a]Ex. 20:2
8 [a]Jer. 7:22 [b]Is. 1:11; [Hos. 6:6] [1]*reprove*
9 [a]Ps. 69:31
12 [a]Ex. 19:5; [Deut. 10:14; Job 41:11]; 1 Cor. 10:26
13 [a][Ps. 51:15–17]
14 [a]Hos. 14:2; Heb. 13:15 [b]Num. 30:2; Deut. 23:21 *See WW at Ps. 95:2.
15 [a]Job 22:27; [Zech. 13:9]
17 [a]Neh. 9:26; Rom. 2:21 *See WW at Prov. 4:13.
18 [a][Rom. 1:32] [b]1 Tim. 5:22 [1]LXX, Syr., Tg., Vg. *ran*
19 [a]Ps. 52:2
21 [a][Rom. 2:4] [b][Ps. 90:8]
22 [a][Job 8:13]
23 [a]Gal. 6:16

50:title Asaph was one of David's skilled musicians who played the cymbals (1 Chr. 15:17–19) and who wrote psalms (2 Chr. 29:30).

50:1 The Mighty One, God the LORD in Hebrew are *'El, 'Elohim,* and *Yahweh,* and emphasize His strength, His sublime nature, and His unchanging character. **Earth** means "all its inhabitants," who are witnesses of what is to be said.

50:4 Heavens . . . earth: This all-inclusive phrase is common in Hebrew religious literature (Deut. 4:39).

50:6, 7 The witnesses have been called, the **Judge** is announced, the summons is given (v. 7); and now indictments and verdicts will be announced ("set . . . in order," v. 21).

50:9–13 Bull: The writer separates the Israelite symbolic, sacrificial ritual from the heathen concept that pagan gods thrived on sacrifices.

50:10 Thousands may describe **the cattle,** not the number of **hills.** That is, "cattle by the thousands on the hill."

50:14 Heartfelt **thanksgiving,** not primarily the ritualistic thank-offering sacrifice (Lev. 7:12), is meant here. The sacrifices, like the tithe, are instituted to show that everything belongs to God.

50:17–20 The instructions referred to here are the eighth, seventh, and ninth commandments of the Decalogue (Ex. 20:14–16).

50:21 That is, God has ruled on the indictments, and has **set** forth His verdicts of guilty.

50:22 The judgment is tempered with mercy: a space of time to **consider** their ways and repent.

50:23 Salvation: Those who respond by restoring pure worship are saved from impending judgment.

KINGDOM DYNAMICS

50:22, 23 Praise, the Road to Success, PRAISE PATHWAY. This whole chapter relates God's power, majesty, and glory, and is summed up in these closing verses, which apply to us as well as to the people of Israel. If we leave God out of our lives and live in rebellion, destruction follows. In contrast, the simple road to success is set forth: 1) Offer praise, and we glorify God. The focus of praise is directed toward God, but in His wisdom we are the ultimate beneficiaries. 2) We receive power to order our conduct; thus, our life-style comes into obedience to God. 3) Result: We receive a revelation (understanding)—that is, insight into God's salvation. Our praise becomes a vehicle for God to come to us and to minister through us.

(Ps. 47:7/Ps. 63:1–5) C.G.

PSALM 51

A Prayer of Repentance

To the Chief Musician. A *Psalm of David [a]when Nathan the prophet went to him, after he had gone in to Bathsheba.

5 HAVE mercy upon me, O God,
According to Your lovingkindness;
According to the multitude of Your tender mercies,
[a]Blot out my transgressions.
2 [a]Wash me thoroughly from my iniquity,
And cleanse me from my *sin.

3 For I acknowledge my transgressions,
And my sin *is* always before me.
4 [a]Against You, You only, have I sinned,
And done *this* evil [b]in Your sight—
[c]That You may be found just [1]when You speak,
And blameless when You judge.

5 [a]Behold, I was brought forth in iniquity,
And in sin my mother conceived me.
6 Behold, You desire *truth in the inward parts,
And in the hidden *part* You will make me to know wisdom.

7 [a]Purge me with hyssop, and I shall be clean;
Wash me, and I shall be [b]whiter than snow.
8 Make me hear joy and gladness,
That the bones You have broken [a]may *rejoice.
9 Hide Your face from my sins,
And blot out all my iniquities.

10 [a]Create* in me a clean heart, O God, 4
And renew a steadfast *spirit within me.
11 Do not cast me away from Your presence,
And do not take Your [a]Holy Spirit from me.

12 Restore to me the joy of Your salvation,
And uphold me *by Your* [a]generous Spirit.
13 *Then* I will *teach transgressors Your ways,
And sinners shall be converted to You.

14 Deliver me from the guilt of bloodshed, O God,
The God of my salvation,
And my tongue shall sing aloud of Your righteousness.
15 O Lord, *open my lips,
And my mouth shall show forth Your praise.
16 For [a]You do not desire sacrifice, or else I would give *it;*
You do not delight in burnt offering.
17 [a]The sacrifices of God *are* a broken spirit,
A broken and a contrite heart—
These, O God, You will not despise.

18 Do good in Your good *pleasure to Zion;
Build the walls of Jerusalem.
19 Then You shall be pleased with [a]the sacrifices of righteousness,

PSALM 51

title [a]2 Sam. 12:1 *See WW at Ps. 3:title.
1 [a][Is. 43:25; 44:22; Acts 3:19; Col. 2:14]
2 [a]Jer. 33:8; Ezek. 36:33; [Heb. 9:14; 1 John 1:7, 9] *See WW at Lev. 9:2.
4 [a]2 Sam. 12:13 [b][Luke 5:21] [c]Rom. 3:4 [1]LXX, Tg., Vg. *in Your words*
5 [a][Job 14:4; Ps. 58:3; John 3:6; Rom. 5:12]
6 *See WW at Ps. 25:5.
7 [a]Ex. 12:22; Lev. 14:4; Num. 19:18; Heb. 9:19 [b][Is. 1:18]
8 [a][Matt. 5:4] *See WW at Hab. 3:18.
10 [a][Ezek. 18:31; Eph. 2:10] *See WW at Gen. 1:1. • See WW at 2 Sam. 23:2.
11 [a][Luke 11:13]
12 [a][2 Cor. 3:17]
13 *See WW at Is. 48:17.
15 *See WW at Jer. 40:4.
16 [a][1 Sam. 15:22]; Ps. 50:8–14; [Mic. 6:6–8]
17 [a]Ps. 34:18; [Is. 57:15]; 66:2
18 *See WW at Deut. 33:23.
19 [a]Ps. 4:5

51:1–19 *See section 5 of Truth-In-Action following Ps. 72.*
51:4 This is quoted in Rom. 3:4 to show the righteousness of God in all His ways.
51:7 Hyssop was an herb associated with cleansing and purification (Num. 19:6) and is used here symbolically of cleansing the soul. The Hebrew word for **wash** is not the one used for the simple cleaning of a dish in water, but rather the washing of clothes by beating and pounding. David wanted a thorough cleansing from the sin nature.
51:10 See section 4 of Truth-In-Action following Ps. 72.
51:16, 17 Ritual **sacrifice,** or any other external religiosity, without a change of attitude in the inner **spirit,** falls short of true repentance.

With burnt offering and whole
burnt offering;
Then they shall offer bulls on
Your altar.

 **KINGDOM DYNAMICS**

51:1–19 David Asks for Joy and God's Presence, PRAYER. David's prayer of repentance remains on record as a tear-stained testimony of his brokenness before God and as instruction for all others who sin. His repentance did not stem from fear of punishment or concern of future success. He repented for having violated God Himself, His Person and His nature. David cried out, not just for pardon, but for purity; not just for acquittal, but for acceptance; not just for comfort, but for complete cleansing—whatever the cost. Although his heart was crushed by his shame and sorrow over sin, he knew the great breadth of God's mercy. See how, once his sins are confessed, forgiven, and purged, David dares to ask for God's choicest gifts: joy, restoration, God's presence, His Holy Spirit. Then he humbly offers himself to be used as an instrument to show forth God's praise and to teach other transgressors. This psalm evidences that God accepted that offer.

(John 4:34/Gen. 18:17–33*) L.L.

PSALM 52

The End of the Wicked and the Peace of the Godly

To the Chief Musician. A [1]Contemplation of David [a]when Doeg the Edomite went and [b]told Saul, and said to him, "David has gone to the house of Ahimelech."

WHY do you boast in evil, O mighty
man?
The goodness of God *endures*
continually.
2 Your tongue devises destruction,
Like a sharp razor, working
deceitfully.
3 You love evil more than good,
Lying rather than speaking
righteousness. Selah
4 You love all devouring words,
You deceitful tongue.
5 God shall likewise destroy you
forever;
He shall take you away, and
pluck you out of *your* dwelling
place,
And uproot you from the land of
the living. Selah
6 The righteous also shall see and
fear,
And shall *laugh at him, *saying,*
7 "Here is the man *who* did not make
God his strength,
But trusted in the abundance of
his riches,
And strengthened himself in his
[1]wickedness."
8 But I *am* [a]like a green olive tree
in the house of God;
I trust in the mercy of God forever
and ever.
9 I will praise You forever,
Because You have done *it;*
And in the presence of Your
saints
I will wait on Your name, for *it*
[1]*is* good.

PSALM 52
title [a]1 Sam. 22:9 [b]Ezek. 22:9 [1]Heb. *Maschil*
6 *See WW at Eccl. 3:4.
7 [1]Lit. *desire,* in evil sense
8 [a]Jer. 11:16
9 [1]Or *has a good reputation*

PSALM 53

Folly of the Godless, and the Restoration of Israel

To the Chief Musician. Set to "Mahalath." A [1]Contemplation of David.

THE [a]fool has said in his heart,
"*There is* no God."
They are corrupt, and have done
abominable iniquity;
[b]*There is* none who does good.

2 God looks down from heaven
upon the children of men,
To see if there are *any* who
understand, who [a]seek God.
3 Every one of them has turned
aside;
They have together become
corrupt;
There is none who does good,
No, not one. 3

4 Have the workers of iniquity
[a]no knowledge,

PSALM 53
title [1]Heb. *Maschil*
1 [a]Ps. 10:4 [b]Rom. 3:10–12
2 [a][2 Chr. 15:2]
4 [a]Jer. 4:22

52:2 The loose **tongue** of Doeg resulted in the slaughter of innocent godly priests (1 Sam. 22:9–23).
52:8 Tree: That is, like a tree planted in the *courtyard* of the temple area. Symbolically, he is as a part of God's beautiful landscape.
53:1–6 This psalm is essentially the same as Ps. 14, except that *'Elohim* is used instead of *Yahweh* for the name of **God.** This shows the hymnbook compilation process in ancient times.
53:1 Corrupt is a word first used in Gen. 6:5 to describe the wickedness before the Flood.
53:3 See section 3 of Truth-In-Action following Ps. 72.
53:4 Eat up: Wicked people do not passively carry on their own business in darkness; they attack the people of light as well (Matt. 12:30).

Who eat up my people *as* they eat bread,
And do not call upon God?
5 [a]There they are in great *fear
Where no fear was,
For God has scattered the bones of him who encamps against you;
You have put *them* to shame,
Because God has despised them.

6 [a]Oh, that the salvation of Israel would come out of Zion!
When God brings back [1]the captivity of His people,
Let Jacob rejoice *and* Israel be glad.

PSALM 54

Answered Prayer for Deliverance from Adversaries

To the Chief Musician. With [1]stringed instruments. A [2]Contemplation of David [a]when the Ziphites went and said to Saul, "Is David not hiding with us?"

SAVE me, O God, by Your name,
And *vindicate me by Your strength.
2 Hear my *prayer, O God;
Give ear to the words of my mouth.
3 For strangers have risen up against me,
And oppressors have sought after my life;
They have not set God before them. Selah

4 Behold, God *is* my helper;
The Lord *is* with those who [1]uphold my life.
5 He will repay my enemies for their evil.
[1]Cut them off in Your [2]truth.

6 I will freely sacrifice to You;
I will praise Your name, O LORD, for *it is* good.
7 For He has delivered me out of all trouble;
[a]And my eye has seen *its desire* upon my enemies.

PSALM 55

Trust in God Concerning the Treachery of Friends

To the Chief Musician. With [1]stringed instruments. A [2]Contemplation of David.

GIVE ear to my prayer, O God,
And do not hide Yourself from my supplication.
2 Attend to me, and hear me;
I [a]am[1] restless in my complaint, and moan noisily,
3 Because of the voice of the enemy,
Because of the oppression of the wicked;
[a]For they bring down trouble upon me,
And in wrath they hate me.

4 [a]My heart is severely pained within me,
And the terrors of death have fallen upon me.
5 Fearfulness and trembling have come upon me,
And horror has overwhelmed me.
6 So I said, "Oh, that I had wings like a dove!
I would fly away and be at rest.
7 Indeed, I would wander far off,
And remain in the wilderness. Selah
8 I would hasten my escape
From the windy storm *and* tempest."

9 Destroy, O Lord, *and* divide their [1]tongues,
For I have seen [a]violence and strife in the city.
10 Day and night they go around it on its walls;
[a]Iniquity and trouble *are* also in the midst of it.
11 Destruction *is* in its midst;
[a]Oppression and deceit do not depart from its streets.

12 [a]For *it is* not an enemy *who* reproaches me;
Then I could bear *it*.
Nor *is it* one *who* hates me who has [b]exalted *himself* against me;
Then I could hide from him.

5 [a]Lev. 26:17, 36; Prov. 28:1 *See WW at Hos. 3:5. **6** [a]Ps. 14:7 [1]Or *His captive people*

PSALM 54

title [a]1 Sam. 23:19 [1]Heb. *neginoth* [2]Heb. *Maschil* **1** *See WW at Deut. 32:36. **2** *See WW at 2 Chr. 6:20. **4** [1]*sustain my soul* **5** [1]*Destroy them* [2]Or *faithfulness* **7** [a]Ps. 59:10

PSALM 55

title [1]Heb. *neginoth* [2]Heb. *Maschil* **2** [a]Is. 38:14; 59:11; Ezek. 7:16 [1]*wander* **3** [a]2 Sam. 16:7, 8 **4** [a]Ps. 116:3 **9** [a]Jer. 6:7 [1]*speech,* their counsel **10** [a]Ps. 10:7 **11** [a]Ps. 10:7 **12** [a]Ps. 41:9 [b]Ps. 35:26; 38:16

53:5 *Past deliverances, where* **God** *had reduced the proud* to **fear** and the haughty to **shame,** give the psalmist hope for future deliverance (v. 6).
54:1 The **name** of God, which represents His covenant-keeping character, is also the NT Christian's basis for hope (Acts 3:16).
54:7 **Eye:** That is, David has hope because he has seen victory over his **enemies** in the past.
55:6 **Dove:** The desire to run from problems is a common trait of all mankind, but confidence in God allows us to face difficulties (v. 16).
55:12–15 One of the deepest hurts is betrayal by a seemingly spiritual **companion** (v. 13), Ahithophel (2 Sam. 15:31). See Jesus' attitude toward such a man in Mark 14:21.

13 But *it was* you, a *man my equal,
[a]My companion and my acquaintance.
14 We took sweet counsel together,
And [a]walked to the house of God in the throng.

15 Let death seize them;
Let them [a]go down alive into [1]hell,
For wickedness *is* in their dwellings *and* among them.

16 As for me, I will call upon God,
And the LORD shall save me.
17 [a]Evening and morning and at noon
I will pray, and cry aloud,
And He shall hear my voice.
18 He has redeemed my soul in peace from the battle *that was* against me,
For [a]there were many against me.
19 God will hear, and afflict them,
[a]Even He who abides from of old. Selah
Because they do not change,
Therefore they do not fear God.

20 He has [a]put forth his hands against those who [b]were at peace with him;
He has broken his [1]covenant.
21 [a]*The words* of his mouth were smoother than butter,
But war *was* in his heart;
His words were softer than oil,
Yet they *were* drawn swords.

4 22 [a]Cast your burden on the LORD,
And [b]He shall **sustain** you;
He shall never permit the righteous to be [1]moved.

WORD WEALTH

55:22 sustain, *chul* (*kool*); Strong's #3557: To maintain, nourish, provide food, bear, hold up, protect, support, defend; to supply the means necessary for living. Occurring nearly 40 times, *chul* primarily suggests "to measure out a provision of food," that is, "to provide." In some references *chul* means "to contain," "to receive," or "to hold" (see 1 Kin. 7:26; 2 Chr. 7:7; Jer. 2:13). In Gen. 50:21, Joseph pledges to provide for his brothers and their little children. In the present reference, God will support, nourish, and provide for any person who acknowledges that the burden of cruel treatment (v. 21) is one that only the Lord can handle.

23 But You, O God, shall bring them down to the pit of destruction;
[a]Bloodthirsty and deceitful men
[b]shall not live out half their days;
But I will trust in You.

13 [a]2 Sam. 15:12 *See WW at Job 4:17.
14 [a]Ps. 42:4
15 [a]Num. 16:30, 33 [1]Or *Sheol*
17 [a]Dan. 6:10; Luke 18:1; Acts 3:1; 10:3, 30
18 [a]2 Chr. 32:7, 8
19 [a][Deut. 33:27]
20 [a]Acts 12:1 [b]Ps. 7:4 [1]*treaty*
21 [a]Ps. 28:3; 57:4; [Prov. 5:3, 4; 12:18]
22 [a][Ps. 37:5; Matt. 6:25–34; Luke 12:22–31; 1 Pet. 5:7] [b]Ps. 37:24 [1]*shaken*
23 [a]Ps. 5:6 [b]Prov. 10:27

PSALM 56

Prayer for Relief from Tormentors

To the Chief Musician. Set to [1]"The Silent Dove in Distant Lands." A Michtam of David when the [a]Philistines captured him in Gath.

BE [a]merciful to me, O God, for man would swallow me up;
Fighting all day he oppresses me.
2 My enemies would [a]hound *me* all day,
For *there are* many who fight against me, O Most High.

3 Whenever I am afraid, 4
I will trust in You.
4 In God (I will praise His word),
In God I have put my trust;
[a]I will not fear.
What can flesh do to me?

5 All day they twist my words;
All their thoughts *are* against me for evil.
6 They gather together,
They hide, they mark my steps,
When they *lie in wait for my life.
7 Shall they escape by iniquity?
In anger cast down the peoples, O God!

8 You number my wanderings;
Put my tears into Your bottle;
[a]*Are they* not in Your book?
9 When I cry out *to You,*
Then my enemies will turn back;
This I know, because [a]God *is* for me.
10 In God (I will praise *His* word), 4

PSALM 56
title [a]1 Sam. 21:11 [1]Heb. *Jonath Elem Rechokim*
1 [a]Ps. 57:1
2 [a]Ps. 57:3
4 [a]Ps. 118:6; Is. 31:3; [Heb. 13:6]
6 *See WW at Lam. 3:25.
8 [a][Mal. 3:16]
9 [a][Ps. 118:6; Rom. 8:31]

55:17 The Hebrew day started at **evening,** so this list is in the correct order for praying all day long.
55:22 See section 4 of Truth-In-Action following Ps. 72.
55:22 Cast your burden is reflected in Peter's admonition in 1 Pet. 5:7.
56:title The Silent Dove may be a subscript for the preceding psalm; it fits the topic there (55:6).
56:1 Swallow: This psalm may refer to the time David was harassed in the Philistine city of Gath (v. 6) after he had fled there from Saul (v. 2). See 1 Sam. 21:10–15.
56:3, 4 See section 4 of Truth-In-Action following Ps. 72.
56:8 The idea of God's keeping a record in a **book** is found in Ex. 32:32 and is confirmed in the NT (Luke 10:20).
56:10, 11 See section 4 of Truth-In-Action following Ps. 72.

In the LORD (I will praise *His* word),
11 In God I have put my trust;
I will not be afraid.
What can man do to me?

12 Vows *made* to You *are binding* upon me, O God;
I will render praises to You,
13 [a]For You have delivered my soul from death.
Have You not *kept* my feet from falling,
That I may walk before God
In the [b]light of the living?

PSALM 57

Prayer for Safety from Enemies

To the Chief Musician. Set to [1]"Do Not Destroy." A Michtam of David [a]when he fled from Saul into the cave.

BE merciful to me, O God, be merciful to me!
For my soul trusts in You;
[a]And in the shadow of Your wings
I will make my refuge,
[b]Until *these* calamities have passed by.

2 I will cry out to God Most High,
To God [a]who *performs *all things* for me.
3 [a]He shall send from heaven and save me;
He reproaches the one who [1]would swallow me up. Selah
God [b]shall send forth His mercy and His truth.

4 My soul *is* among lions;
I lie *among* the sons of men
Who are set on fire,
[a]Whose teeth *are* spears and arrows,
And their tongue a sharp sword.
5 [a]Be exalted, O God, above the heavens;
Let Your glory *be* above all the earth.

6 [a]They have prepared a net for my steps;
My soul is bowed down;
They have dug a pit before me;
Into the midst of it they *themselves* have fallen. Selah

7 [a]My heart is steadfast, O God, my heart is steadfast;
I will sing and give praise.
8 Awake, [a]my glory!
Awake, lute and harp!
I will awaken the dawn.

9 [a]I will praise You, O Lord, among the peoples;
I will sing to You among the [1]nations.
10 [a]For Your mercy reaches unto the heavens,
And Your truth unto the clouds.

11 [a]Be exalted, O God, above the heavens;
Let Your glory *be* above all the earth.

PSALM 58

The Just Judgment of the Wicked

To the Chief Musician. Set to [1]"Do Not Destroy." A Michtam of David.

DO you indeed speak righteousness, you silent ones?
Do you judge uprightly, you sons of men?
2 No, in heart you work wickedness;
You weigh out the violence of your hands in the earth.

3 [a]The wicked are estranged from the womb;
They go astray as soon as they are born, speaking lies.
4 [a]Their poison *is* like the poison of a serpent;
They are like the deaf cobra *that* stops its ear,
5 Which will not [a]heed the voice of charmers,
Charming ever so skillfully.

6 [a]Break[1] their teeth in their mouth, O God!

---

13 [a]Ps. 116:8, 9 [b]Job 33:30

PSALM 57

title [a]1 Sam. 22:1 [1]Heb. *Al Tashcheth*
1 [a]Ruth 2:12; Ps. 17:8; 63:7 [b]Is. 26:20
2 [a][Ps. 138:8] *See WW at Ps. 138:8.
3 [a]Ps. 144:5, 7 [b]Ps. 43:3 [1]*snaps at* or *hounds me*, or *crushes me*
4 [a]Prov. 30:14
5 [a]Ps. 108:5
6 [a]Ps. 9:15
7 [a]Ps. 108:1–5
8 [a]Ps. 16:9
9 [a]Ps. 108:3 [1]*Gentiles*
10 [a]Ps. 103:11
11 [a]Ps. 57:5

PSALM 58

title [1]Heb. *Al Tashcheth*
3 [a][Ps. 53:3; Is. 48:8]
4 [a]Eccl. 10:11
5 [a]Jer. 8:17
6 [a]Job 4:10 [1]*Break away*

56:11 This **trust** in God's watchful care is reaffirmed in Heb. 13:6.
57:1–11 A refrain in vv. 5 and 11 divides this psalm into two sections: a plea for protection and praise for providence.
57:7–11 This section appears in 108:1–5 of Book Five, thus showing something of how the Book of Psalms was compiled.
57:8 **My glory** is a poetic expression for "my soul."
58:1–11 This strongly worded psalm is not a personal vendetta, but a call for the cleansing of corruption among the judges and in the justice system of Israel. See Deut. 1:16, 17.
58:2 Justice is symbolically pictured as a balance of scales weighing justice impartially. These judges, however, tipped the scales with unjust **violence**.

Break out the fangs of the young
lions, O LORD!
7 [a]Let them flow away as waters
which run continually;
When he bends *his bow,*
Let his arrows be as if cut in
pieces.
8 *Let them be* like a snail which
melts away as it goes,
[a]*Like* a stillborn child of a woman,
that they may not see the sun.

9 Before your [a]pots can feel *the*
burning thorns,
He shall take them away
[b]as with a whirlwind,
As in His living and burning
wrath.
10 The righteous shall rejoice when
he sees the [a]vengeance;
[b]He shall wash his feet in the blood
of the wicked,
11 [a]So that men will say,
"Surely *there is* a reward for the
righteous;
Surely He is God who [b]judges in
the earth."

7 [a]Josh. 2:11; 7:5; Ps. 112:10; Is. 13:7; Ezek. 21:7
8 [a]Job 3:16
9 [a]Ps. 118:12; Eccl. 7:6 [b]Job 27:21; Prov. 10:25
10 [a][Deut. 32:43]; Jer. 11:20 [b]Ps. 68:23
11 [a]Ps. 92:15; Prov. 11:18; [2 Cor. 5:10] [b]Ps. 50:6; 75:7

PSALM 59

The Assured Judgment of the Wicked

To the Chief Musician. Set to [1]"Do Not Destroy." A Michtam of David [a]when Saul sent men, and they watched the house in order to kill him.

DELIVER me from my enemies,
O my God;
[1]Defend me from those who rise
up against me.
2 Deliver me from the workers of
iniquity,
And save me from bloodthirsty
men.

3 For look, they lie in wait for my
life;
[a]The mighty gather against me,
Not *for* my transgression nor *for*
my sin, O LORD.
4 They run and prepare themselves
through no fault *of mine.*

[a]Awake to help me, and behold!
5 You therefore, O LORD God of
hosts, the God of Israel,
Awake to punish all the [1]nations;
Do not be merciful to any wicked
transgressors. Selah

6 [a]At evening they return,
They growl like a dog,
And go all around the city.
7 Indeed, they belch with their
mouth;
[a]Swords *are* in their lips;
For *they say,* [b]"Who hears?"

8 But [a]You, O LORD, shall *laugh at
them;
You shall have all the [1]nations in
derision.
9 I will wait for You, O You
[1]his Strength;
[a]For God *is* my [2]defense.
10 [1]My God of mercy shall [a]come to
meet me;
God shall let [b]me see *my desire*
on my enemies.

11 Do not slay them, lest my people
forget;
Scatter them by Your power,
And bring them down,
O Lord our shield.
12 [a]*For* the sin of their mouth *and* the
words of their lips,
Let them even be taken in their
pride,
And for the cursing and lying
which they speak.
13 [a]Consume *them* in wrath,
consume *them,*
That they *may* not *be;*
And [b]let them know that God
rules in Jacob
To the ends of the earth. Selah

14 And [a]at evening they return,
They growl like a dog,
And go all around the city.
15 They [a]wander up and down for
food,
And [1]howl if they are not
satisfied.

16 But I will sing of Your power; **2**
Yes, I will sing aloud of Your
mercy in the morning;
For You have been my defense
And refuge in the day of my
trouble.

PSALM 59
title [a]1 Sam. 19:11 [1]Heb. *Al Tashcheth*
1 [1]Lit. *Set me on high*
3 [a]Ps. 56:6
4 [a]Ps. 35:23
5 [1]*Gentiles*
6 [a]Ps. 59:14
7 [a]Ps. 57:4; Prov. 12:18 [b]Job 22:13; Ps. 10:11
8 [a]Prov. 1:26 [1]*Gentiles* *See WW at Eccl. 3:4.
9 [a][Ps. 62:2] [1]So with MT, Syr.; some Heb. mss., LXX, Tg., Vg. *my Strength* [2]Lit. *fortress*
10 [a]Ps. 21:3 [b]Ps. 54:7 [1]So with Qr.; some Heb. mss., LXX, Vg. *My God, His mercy;* Kt., some Heb. mss., Tg. *O God, my mercy;* Syr. *O God, Your mercy*
12 [a]Prov. 12:13
13 [a]Ps. 104:35 [b]Ps. 83:18
14 [a]Ps. 59:6
15 [a]Job 15:23 [1]So with LXX, Vg.; MT, Syr., Tg. *spend the night*

58:11 The chief Judge of the most high supreme court is **God,** before whom lesser judges will all stand to give account.
59:3 Lie in wait: The story of David's escape with Michal's help is found in 1 Sam. 19:10–17.
59:6–9 At evening: This section and vv. 14–17 are similar and read like choruses in the two stanzas of this song of faith.
59:9 Though chased from his home, David took refuge in a more secure High Tower (literally translated here as **defense**).
59:16, 17 See section 2 of Truth-In-Action following Ps. 72.

17 To You, [a]O my Strength, I will
sing praises;
For God *is* my defense,
My God of mercy.

PSALM 60

Urgent Prayer for the Restored Favor of God

To the Chief Musician. [a]Set to [1]"Lily of the Testimony." A Michtam of David. For teaching. [b]When he fought against Mesopotamia and Syria of Zobah, and Joab returned and killed twelve thousand Edomites in the Valley of Salt.

O GOD, [a]You have cast us off;
You have broken us down;
You have been displeased;
Oh, restore us again!
2 You have made the earth tremble;
You have broken it;
[a]Heal its breaches, for it is
shaking.
3 [a]You have shown Your people
hard things;
[b]You have made us drink the wine
of [1]confusion.

4 [a]You have given a banner to those
who fear You,
That it may be displayed because
of the truth. Selah
5 [a]That Your beloved may be
delivered,
Save *with* Your right hand, and
hear me.

6 God has [a]spoken in His holiness:
"I will rejoice;
I will [b]divide [c]Shechem
And measure out [d]the Valley of
Succoth.
7 Gilead *is* Mine, and Manasseh *is*
Mine;
[a]Ephraim also *is* the [1]helmet for
My head;
[b]Judah *is* My lawgiver.
8 [a]Moab *is* My washpot;
[b]Over Edom I will cast My shoe;
[c]Philistia, shout in triumph
because of Me."

9 Who will bring me *to* the strong
city?
Who will lead me to Edom?
10 *Is it* not You, O God, [a]*who* cast
us off?
And You, O God, *who* did
[b]not go out with our armies?
11 Give us help from trouble,
[a]For the help of man *is* useless.
12 Through God [a]we will do
valiantly,
For *it is* He *who* shall tread down
our enemies.

PSALM 61

Assurance of God's Eternal Protection

To the Chief Musician. On [1]a stringed instrument. A Psalm of David.

HEAR my cry, O God;
Attend to my prayer.
2 From the end of the earth I will
cry to You,
When my heart is overwhelmed;
Lead me to the rock *that* is higher
than I.

3 For You have been a shelter for
me,
[a]A strong tower from the enemy.
4 I will abide in Your [1]tabernacle
forever;
[a]I will trust in the shelter of Your
wings. Selah

5 For You, O God, have heard my
vows;
You have given *me* the heritage
of those who fear Your name.
6 You will prolong the king's life,
His years as many generations.
7 He shall abide before God
forever.
Oh, prepare mercy [a]and truth,
which may [1]preserve him!

8 So I will *sing praise to Your
name forever,
That I may daily perform my
vows.

PSALM 62

A Calm Resolve to Wait for the Salvation of God

To the Chief Musician. To [a]Jeduthun. A Psalm of David.

TRULY [a]my soul silently *waits* for
God;

---

17 [a]Ps. 18:1

PSALM 60

title [a]Ps. 80 [b]2 Sam. 8:3, 13; 1 Chr. 18:3 [1]Heb. *Shushan Eduth*
1 [a]Ps. 44:9
2 [a][2 Chr. 7:14]; Is. 30:26
3 [a]Ps. 71:20 [b]Is. 51:17, 22; Jer. 25:15 [1]*staggering*
4 [a]Ps. 20:5; Is. 5:26; 11:12; 13:2
5 [a]Ps. 108:6–13
6 [a]Ps. 89:35 [b]Josh. 1:6 [c]Gen. 12:6 [d]Josh. 13:27
7 [a]Deut. 33:17 [b][Gen. 49:10] [1]Lit. *protection*
8 [a]2 Sam. 8:2 [b]2 Sam. 8:14; Ps. 108:9 [c]2 Sam. 8:1
10 [a]Ps. 108:11 [b]Josh. 7:12
11 [a]Ps. 118:8; 146:3
12 [a]Num. 24:18

PSALM 61

title [1]Heb. *neginah*
3 [a]Prov. 18:10
4 [a]Ps. 91:4 [1]*tent*
7 [a]Ps. 40:11 [1]Lit. *guard* or *keep*
8 *See WW at Ps. 149:3.

PSALM 62

title [a]1 Chr. 25:1
1 [a]Ps. 33:20

60:4 The **banner** was a rallying point for the defense of the **truth** that Israel possessed in the midst of a pagan world of ignorance.
60:5–12 These verses also appear in 108:6–13.
60:6 **In His holiness** is a phrase introducing a prophetic message (Amos 4:2), which reaffirms Israel's possession of the land, as well as Israel's victories over adjoining lands.
61:1–8 This picturesque psalm uses four metaphors to represent God as a **shelter:** a high **rock** (v. 2), a fortified **tower** (v. 3), a pitched tent (v. 4), and a mother hen with outstretched **wings** (v. 4).
62:1–12 So confident and assured is the psalmist of God's

From Him *comes* my salvation.
2 He only *is* my rock and my salvation;
He is my [1]defense;
I shall not be greatly [a]moved.[2]

3 How long will you attack a *man?
You shall be slain, all of you,
[a]Like a leaning wall and a tottering fence.
4 They only consult to cast *him* down from his high position;
They [a]delight in lies;
They bless with their mouth,
But they curse inwardly. Selah

5 My soul, wait silently for God alone,
For my [1]expectation *is* from Him.
6 He only *is* my rock and my salvation;
He is my defense;
I shall not be [1]moved.
7 [a]In God *is* my salvation and my glory;
The rock of my strength,
And my *refuge, *is* in God.

8 Trust in Him at all times, you people;
[a]Pour out your heart before Him;
God *is* a refuge for us. Selah

9 [a]Surely men of low degree *are* [1]a vapor,
Men of high degree *are* a lie;
If they are weighed on the scales,
They *are* altogether *lighter* than vapor.
10 Do not trust in oppression,
Nor vainly hope in robbery;
[a]If riches increase,
Do not set *your* heart *on them.*

11 God has spoken once,
Twice I have heard this:
That power *belongs* to God.
1 12 Also to You, O Lord, *belongs* mercy;
For [a]You [1]render to each one according to his work.

2 [a]Ps. 55:22 [1]*strong tower* [2]*shaken*
3 [a]Is. 30:13 *See WW at Is. 32:2.
4 [a]Ps. 28:3
5 [1]*hope*
6 [1]*shaken*
7 [a][Jer. 3:23] *See WW at Prov. 14:26.
8 [a]1 Sam. 1:15; Ps. 42:4; Lam. 2:19
9 [a]Job 7:16; Ps. 39:5; Is. 40:17 [1]*vanity*
10 [a]Job 31:25; [Mark 10:24; Luke 12:15; 1 Tim. 6:10]
12 [a][Matt. 16:27]; Rom. 2:6; 1 Cor. 3:8 [1]*reward*

PSALM 63

title [a]1 Sam. 22:5
1 [a]Ps. 42:2; [Matt. 5:6]
2 [a]Ps. 27:4
3 [a]Ps. 138:2
4 [a]Ps. 28:2; 143:6
5 [1]Lit. *fat* [2]Abundance

PSALM 63

Joy in the Fellowship of God

A Psalm of David [a]when he was in the wilderness of Judah.

O GOD, You *are* my God; 2
Early will I seek You;
[a]My soul thirsts for You;
My flesh longs for You
In a dry and thirsty land
Where there is no water.
2 So I have looked for You in the sanctuary,
To see [a]Your power and Your glory.

3 [a]Because Your lovingkindness *is* better than life,
My lips shall **praise** You.
4 Thus I will bless You while I live;
I will [a]lift up my hands in Your name.
5 My soul shall be satisfied as with [1]marrow and [2]fatness,
And my mouth shall praise *You* with joyful lips.

WORD WEALTH

63:3 praise, *shabach* (shah-*vahch*); Strong's #7623: To commend, praise; to adore; to glory in something; to still, quiet, or pacify someone. *Shabach* goes in two directions, "praising" and "calming." The verb occurs 11 times in the OT, 8 of these having to do with speaking words of praise. The other 3 references speak either about calming the tumultuous sea (65:7; 89:9) or about hushing up things within one's heart (Prov. 29:11). There appears to be a connection between "praising with words" and "soothing with words," as any aggrieved individual offered words of honor can testify.

KINGDOM DYNAMICS

63:1–5 Praise Releases Blessings and Satisfaction, PRAISE PATHWAY. This classic passage teaches how expressed praise releases the blessings of praise. Notice, this is not a silent prayer: "My

(cont. on next page)

justice that six times he repeats the thought of **only, surely,** and **truly.**
62:9 Status or rank carries no weight on the **scales** of justice in God's eyes.
62:11, 12 Jesus adds the "kingdom" and the "glory" to this list of things that belong to God (Matt. 6:13).
62:12 See section 1 of Truth-In-Action following Ps. 72.
62:12 Work: This idea of accountability is underscored in Rom. 2:6 and in Rev. 22:12.
63:1, 2 See section 2 of Truth-In-Action following Ps. 72.
63:1 The second word for **God** in Hebrew is *'El,* "the Strong One," a title appropriate when the worshiper is feeling weak and exhausted. **Thirsty land:** David draws upon symbols from the natural environment of the wilderness in which he was hiding from Absalom (2 Sam. 15:23). See Matt. 5:6.
63:2–6 The psalmist is totally involved in this worshipful hymn to God: eyes (**see,** v. 2), **lips** (v. 3), **hands** (v. 4), **soul** (v. 5), **mouth** (v. 5), and mind (**meditate,** v. 6); as such, he serves as an example of the true worshiper.

(*cont. from preceding page*)
mouth shall praise You with joyful lips." And look at the fruit: 1) "O God, You *are* my God" (affirmed relationship); 2) "Early will I seek You" (clear priorities); 3) "My soul thirsts . . . My flesh longs for You" (deep intensity); 4) "I have looked for You in the sanctuary, to see Your power and glory" (desire for corporate involvement); 5) "Because Your lovingkindness *is* better than life, my lips shall praise You" (appropriate gratitude); 6) Result: "My soul [the real me] shall be satisfied as with marrow and fatness" (personal needs met).
(Ps. 50:22, 23/Ps. 71:14) C.G.

6 When [a]I remember You on my bed,
I *meditate on You in the *night* watches.
7 Because You have been my help,
Therefore in the shadow of Your wings I will rejoice.
8 My soul follows close behind You;
Your right hand upholds me.

9 But those *who* seek my life, to destroy *it*,
Shall go into the lower parts of the earth.
10 They shall [1]fall by the sword;
They shall be [2]a portion for jackals.

11 But the king shall rejoice in God;
[a]Everyone who swears by Him shall glory;
But the mouth of those who speak lies shall be stopped.

6 [a]Ps. 42:8 *See WW at Ps. 1:2.
10 [1]Lit. *pour him out by the hand of the sword* [2]Prey
11 [a]Deut. 6:13; [Is. 45:23; 65:16]

PSALM 64

Oppressed by the Wicked but Rejoicing in the LORD

To the Chief Musician. A Psalm of David.

■1 HEAR my voice, O God, in my [1]meditation;
Preserve my life from fear of the enemy.
2 Hide me from the secret plots of the wicked,
From the rebellion of the workers of iniquity,
3 Who sharpen their tongue like a sword,
[a]And bend *their bows to shoot* their arrows—bitter words,
4 That they may shoot in secret at the blameless;
Suddenly they shoot at him and do not fear.

5 They encourage themselves *in* an evil matter;
They talk of laying snares secretly;
[a]They say, "Who will see them?"
6 They devise iniquities:
"We have perfected a shrewd scheme."
Both the inward thought and the heart of man are deep.

7 But God shall shoot at them *with* an arrow;
Suddenly they shall be wounded.
8 So He will make them stumble over their own tongue;
[a]All who see them shall flee away.
9 All men shall fear,
And shall [a]declare the work of God;
For they shall wisely consider His doing.

10 [a]The righteous shall be glad in the LORD, and trust in Him.
And all the upright in heart shall glory.

PSALM 64
1 [1]*complaint*
3 [a]Ps. 58:7
5 [a]Ps. 10:11; 59:7
8 [a]Ps. 31:11
9 [a]Jer. 50:28; 51:10
10 [a]Job 22:19; Ps. 32:11

PSALM 65

Praise to God for His Salvation and Providence

To the Chief Musician. A Psalm of David. A Song.

PRAISE is awaiting You, O God, in Zion;
And to You the [1]vow shall be performed.
2 O You who hear prayer,
[a]To You all flesh will come.
3 Iniquities prevail against me;
As for our transgressions,
You will [a]provide atonement for them.

4 [a]Blessed *is the man* You [b]choose,
And cause to approach *You*,

PSALM 65
1 [1]A promised deed
2 [a][Is. 66:23]
3 [a]Ps. 51:2; 79:9; Is. 6:7; [Heb. 9:14; 1 John 1:7, 9]
4 [a]Ps. 33:12 [b]Ps. 4:3

64:1–10 Hear my voice: This psalm may refer to the kind of incident occurring when David's chief counselor turned against him (2 Sam. 15:12, 31).
64:1 See section 1 of Truth-In-Action following Ps. 72.
64:8 So also Ahithophel **stumbled** when his counsel against David backfired (2 Sam. 17:23).
64:9 Note the contrast between the secret counsel of evil (v. 2) and the open declaration of God's works.
65:1–13 Praise is elicited in this psalm by recognizing God's dealings in individual lives (v. 3), in divine communion (v. 4), in the affairs of nations (v. 8), and in nature (vv. 9–13).

That he may dwell in Your courts.
[c]We shall be satisfied with the goodness of Your house,
Of Your holy temple.

5 *By* awesome deeds in righteousness You will answer us,
O God of our salvation,
You who are the confidence of all the ends of the earth,
And of the far-off seas;
6 Who established the mountains by His strength,
[a]*Being* clothed with power;
7 [a]You who *still the noise of the seas,
The noise of their waves,
[b]And the tumult of the peoples.
8 They also who dwell in the farthest parts are afraid of Your signs;
You make the outgoings of the morning and evening [1]rejoice.

9 You [1]visit the earth and [a]water it,
You greatly enrich it;
[b]The river of God is full of water;
You provide their grain,
For so You have prepared it.
10 You water its ridges abundantly,
You settle its furrows;
You make it soft with showers,
You bless its growth.

11 You crown the year with Your goodness,
And Your paths drip *with* abundance.
12 They drop *on* the pastures of the wilderness,
And the little hills rejoice on every side.
13 The pastures are clothed with flocks;
[a]The valleys also are covered with grain;
They shout for joy, they also sing.

PSALM 66

Praise to God for His Awesome Works

To the Chief Musician. A Song. A Psalm.

MAKE [a]a joyful shout to God, all the earth!

4 [c]Ps. 36:8
6 [a]Ps. 93:1
7 [a]Matt. 8:26 [b]Is. 17:12, 13
*See WW at Ps. 63:3.
8 [1]*shout for joy*
9 [a][Deut. 11:12]; Jer. 5:24 [b]Ps. 46:4; 104:13; 147:8 [1]*give attention to*
13 [a]Is. 44:23; 55:12

PSALM 66

1 [a]Ps. 100:1
3 [a]Ps. 65:5 [b]Ps. 18:44
4 [a]Ps. 117:1; Zech. 14:16
6 [a]Ex. 14:21 [b]Josh. 3:14–16
9 [1]*slip*
10 [a]Job 23:10; Ps. 17:3 [b][Is. 48:10; Zech. 13:9; Mal. 3:3; 1 Pet. 1:7]
*See WW at Zech. 13:9.
11 [a]Lam. 1:13; Ezek. 12:13
12 [a]Is. 51:23 [b]Is. 43:2 [1]*abundance*
13 [a]Ps. 100:4; 116:14, 17–19 [b][Eccl. 5:4] [1]Promised deeds

2 Sing out the honor of His name;
Make His praise glorious.
3 Say to God,
"How [a]awesome are Your works!
[b]Through the greatness of Your power
Your enemies shall submit themselves to You.
4 [a]All the earth shall worship You
And sing praises to You;
They shall sing praises *to* Your name." Selah

5 Come and see the works of God;
He is awesome *in His* doing toward the sons of men.
6 [a]He turned the sea into dry *land;*
[b]They went through the river on foot.
There we will rejoice in Him.
7 He rules by His power forever;
His eyes observe the nations;
Do not let the rebellious exalt themselves. Selah

8 Oh, bless our God, you peoples!
And make the voice of His praise to be heard,
9 Who keeps our soul among the living,
And does not allow our feet to [1]be moved.
10 For [a]You, O God, have tested us;
[b]You have *refined us as silver is refined.
11 [a]You brought us into the net;
You laid affliction on our backs.
12 [a]You have caused men to ride over our heads;
[b]We went through fire and through water;
But You brought us out to [1]rich *fulfillment.*

13 [a]I will go into Your house with burnt offerings;
[b]I will pay You my [1]vows,
14 Which my lips have uttered
And my mouth has spoken when I was in trouble.
15 I will offer You burnt sacrifices of fat animals,
With the sweet aroma of rams;
I will offer bulls with goats. Selah

65:8–13 Earth: God's existence, as well as His sustaining role, are clearly evident in the ecological balance of nature (Acts 14:17).

65:11 Undoubtedly, this psalm was sung at the Harvest Festival at the end of the agricultural **year.**

66:1–20 The **joyful shout** of corporate worship is heard in vv. 1–12, while vv. 13–20 are the praises of a personal testimony.

66:10 Tested: This thought is echoed in 1 Pet. 1:7 where suffering is seen to have value in the process of discipline and maturation.

16 Come *and* hear, all you who fear God,
And I will declare what He has done for my soul.
17 I cried to Him with my mouth,
And He was [1]extolled with my tongue.
6 18 [a]If I regard iniquity in my heart,
The Lord will not hear.
19 *But* certainly God [a]has heard *me;*
He has attended to the voice of my prayer.

20 Blessed *be* God,
Who has not turned away my prayer,
Nor His mercy from me!

PSALM 67

An Invocation and a Doxology

To the Chief Musician. On [1]stringed instruments. A Psalm. A Song.

GOD be merciful to us and bless us,
And [a]cause His face to shine upon us, Selah
2 That [a]Your way may be known on earth,
[b]Your salvation among all nations.

3 Let the peoples praise You, O God;
Let all the peoples praise You.
4 Oh, let the nations be glad and sing for joy!
For [a]You shall judge the people righteously,
And govern the nations on earth. Selah

5 Let the peoples praise You, O God;
Let all the peoples praise You.
6 [a]*Then* the earth shall [1]yield her increase;
God, our own God, shall bless us.
7 God shall bless us,
And all the ends of the earth shall fear Him.

17 [1]*praised*
18 [a]Job 27:9; [Prov. 15:29; 28:9]; Is. 1:15; [John 9:31; James 4:3]
19 [a]Ps. 116:1, 2

PSALM 67

title [1]Heb. *neginoth*
1 [a]Num. 6:25
2 [a]Acts 18:25 [b]Is. 52:10; Titus 2:11
4 [a][Ps. 96:10, 13; 98:9]
6 [a]Lev. 26:4; Ps. 85:12; [Ezek. 34:27]; Zech. 8:12 [1]*give her produce*

PSALM 68

1 [a]Num. 10:35
2 [a][Is. 9:18]; Hos. 13:3 [b]Ps. 97:5; Mic. 1:4
3 [a]Ps. 32:11
4 [a]Deut. 33:26 [b][Ex. 6:3] [1]*Praise* [2]MT *deserts;* Tg. *heavens* (cf. v. 34 and Is. 19:1) [3]Lit. LORD, a shortened Heb. form *See WW at Is. 12:2.
5 [a][Ps. 10:14, 18; 146:9]
6 [a]Ps. 107:4–7 [b]Acts 12:6–11 [c]Ps. 107:34

PSALM 68

The Glory of God in His Goodness to Israel

To the Chief Musician. A Psalm of David. A Song.

LET [a]God arise,
Let His enemies be scattered;
Let those also who hate Him flee before Him.
2 [a]As smoke is driven away,
So drive *them* away;
[b]As wax melts before the fire,
So let the wicked perish at the presence of God.
3 But [a]let the righteous be glad;
Let them rejoice before God;
Yes, let them rejoice exceedingly.

4 Sing to God, sing praises to His name;
[a]Extol[1] Him who rides on the [2]clouds,
[b]By His name [3]YAH,*
And rejoice before Him.

5 [a]A **father** of the fatherless, a defender of widows,
Is God in His holy habitation.
6 [a]God sets the solitary in families;
[b]He brings out those who are bound into prosperity;
But [c]the rebellious dwell in a dry *land.*

WORD WEALTH

68:5 father, *'ab* (*ahv*); Strong's #1: Father; forefather; producer of a certain thing. A very simple word, *'ab* is supposed to be one of the first words a baby can speak. The Aramaic form of *'ab* is *'abba,* which has become common in modern Hebrew as the word Israeli children use for "daddy." Jesus applied this toddler's word to His divine Father (Mark 14:36). The Holy Spirit teaches us to call God *"Abba"* (Rom. 8:15). *'Ab* is found in many compound names in the Bible; for example, *'Abraham* (Abraham), "Father of a Multitude"; *'Abimelech* (Abimelech), "My Father Is King"; *Yoab* (Joab), "Yahweh Is a Father"; and *'Abshalom* (Absalom), "Father of Peace." Sometimes *'ab* does not mean physical father so much as it does archi-

66:18 See section 6 of Truth-In-Action following Ps. 72.
67:1 *This psalm begins with the priestly blessing of* Num. 6:24–26 where the shining **face** is equivalent to our modern "smile of approval."
67:3, 4 It is evident here that God's intent never was just for one race, but for all **peoples** and **nations** to know and enjoy Him.
68:1 Let God arise: David begins his psalm with the marching cry of Moses (Num. 10:35), and then follows it with several other ancient battle hymns.
68:4 One who **rides on the clouds:** Archaeological discoveries of ancient writings found in Ugarit (Syria) also portray their gods in this way. **YAH** is the short form of *Yahweh,* the covenant **name** of God.
68:5, 6 David believes that defense of the defenseless is the motive for warfare.

tect, builder, creator, and the one who causes something to be. Hence, a "father of evil" is someone who produces evil. Jesus described Satan as the "father of lies." *'Ab* as "creator" and "producer" is applied to the Lord Jesus who is *'abi-'ad,* the "Everlasting Father," or more literally, the "Father of Eternity" (Is. 9:6).

KINGDOM DYNAMICS

68:5, 6 Divine Appointment Places People in Families, FAMILY ORDER. We sometimes speak about difficult circumstances into which people are born as "an accident of birth." Viewed from a divine perspective, however, our placement in a human family is no accident at all: it is a divine appointment. "God sets the solitary in families." Indeed, the protection and care that one receives in a family is so essential to human life that God says He will personally intervene on behalf of widows and orphans who lose the normal protection of a husband and father. When we are tempted to complain about our family, or suppose that our birth-circumstance would be better somewhere else, we need to regain this divine perspective. This is not to become passive or fatalistic about one's situation, nor is it to say this will cause an escape from sorrow or suffering. Nevertheless, we are reminded that the ultimate well-being of our human families rests upon the promise and care of our Father in heaven and that His sovereign and loving purpose will intervene for our benefit.

(Matt. 19:1–9/Hos. 11:1, 3, 4) L.C.

7 O God, [a]when You went out
before Your people,
When You marched through the
wilderness, Selah
8 The earth shook;
The heavens also *dropped *rain*
at the presence of God;
Sinai itself *was moved* at the
presence of God, the God of
Israel.
9 [a]You, O God, sent a plentiful
rain,
Whereby You confirmed Your
inheritance,
When it was weary.
10 Your congregation dwelt in it;
[a]You, O God, provided from Your
goodness for the poor.

11 The Lord gave the word;
*Great *was* the [1]**company** of those
who proclaimed *it:*

7 [a]Ex. 13:21; [Hab. 3:13]
8 *See WW at Ezek. 21:2.
9 [a]Lev. 26:4; Deut. 11:11; Job 5:10; Ezek. 34:26
10 [a]Deut. 26:5; Ps. 74:19
11 [1]*host* *See WW at Ps. 31:19.

12 [a]Num. 31:8; Josh. 10:16; Judg. 5:19 [1]*plunder*
13 [a]Ps. 81:6 [b]Ps. 105:37 [1]Or *saddlebags*
14 [a]Josh. 10:10
16 [a][Deut. 12:5]; 1 Kin. 9:3 [1]Lit. *stare*
17 [a]Deut. 33:2; Dan. 7:10
18 [a]Mark 16:19; Acts 1:9; Eph. 4:8; Phil. 2:9; Col. 3:1; Heb. 1:3 [b]Judg. 5:12 [c]Acts 2:4, 33; 10:44–46; [1 Cor. 12:4–11; Eph. 4:7–12] [d][1 Tim. 1:13] [e]Ps. 78:60

WORD WEALTH

68:11 company, ***tsaba'*** **(tsah-*vah*);** Strong's #6635: An army, a company, host, battalion, throng; a division of soldiers. This noun pictures a great mass of people or things. *Tsaba'* appears more than 425 times in the OT. The hosts (armies) of heaven are the innumerable heavenly bodies, which God has created (Gen. 2:1; Ps. 33:6). A title by which God is frequently known is "the LORD of hosts," *Yahweh tsaba'ot* (in English this is sometimes inadequately spelled "Lord Sabaoth"). The Lord of hosts is the God of the armies of Israel, who also has great spiritual armies at His command (see Rev. 19:14).

12 "Kings[a] of armies flee, they flee,
And she who remains at home
divides the [1]spoil.
13 [a]Though you lie down among the
[1]sheepfolds,
[b]*You will be* like the wings of a
dove covered with silver,
And her feathers with yellow
gold."
14 [a]When the Almighty scattered
kings in it,
It was *white* as snow in Zalmon.

15 A mountain of God *is* the
mountain of Bashan;
A mountain *of many* peaks *is* the
mountain of Bashan.
16 Why do you [1]fume with envy, you
mountains of *many* peaks?
[a]*This is* the mountain *which* God
desires to dwell in;
Yes, the LORD will dwell *in it*
forever.

17 [a]The chariots of God *are* twenty
thousand,
Even thousands of thousands;
The Lord is among them *as in*
Sinai, in the Holy *Place.*
18 [a]You have ascended on high,
[b]You have led captivity captive;
[c]You have received gifts among
men,
Even *from* [d]the rebellious,
[e]That the LORD God might dwell
there.

19 Blessed *be* the Lord,
Who daily loads us *with benefits,*
The God of our salvation! Selah

68:7–10 You went out: David extracts this section from Deborah's battle song (Judg. 5:4, 5).
68:18 Ascended: Paul quotes the wording about this grand march of triumph and applies it to Christ's triumph after the Cross (Eph. 4:8).

20 Our God *is* the God of salvation;
And [a]to GOD the Lord *belong*
escapes from death.

21 But [a]God will wound the head of
His enemies,
[b]The hairy scalp of the one who
still goes on in his trespasses.
22 The Lord said, "I will bring
[a]back from Bashan,
I will bring *them* back [b]from the
depths of the sea,
23 [a]That [1]your foot may crush *them*
in blood,
[b]And the tongues of your dogs
may have their portion from
your enemies."

24 They have seen Your [1]procession,
O God,
The procession of my God, my
King, into the sanctuary.
25 [a]The singers went before, the
players on instruments
followed after;
Among *them were* the maidens
playing timbrels.
26 Bless God in the congregations,
The Lord, from [a]the fountain of
Israel.
27 [a]There *is* little Benjamin, their
leader,
The princes of Judah *and* their
[1]company,
The princes of Zebulun *and* the
princes of Naphtali.

28 [1]Your God has [a]commanded your
strength;
Strengthen, O God, what You
have done for us.
29 Because of Your temple at
Jerusalem,
[a]Kings will bring presents to
You.
30 Rebuke the beasts of the reeds,
[a]The herd of bulls with the calves
of the peoples,
Till everyone [b]submits himself
with pieces of silver.
Scatter the peoples *who* delight in
war.
31 [a]Envoys will come out of Egypt;
[b]Ethiopia will quickly [c]stretch out
her hands to God.

32 Sing to God, you [a]kingdoms of
the earth;
Oh, sing praises to the Lord,
Selah

33 To Him [a]who rides on the heaven
of heavens, *which were* of old!
Indeed, He sends out His voice,
a [b]mighty voice.
34 [a]Ascribe strength to God;
His excellence *is* over Israel,
And His strength *is* in the clouds.
35 O God, [a]*You are* more awesome
than Your holy places.
The God of Israel *is* He who gives
strength and power to *His*
people.

Blessed *be* God!

PSALM 69

An Urgent Plea for Help in Trouble

To the Chief Musician. Set to [1]"The Lilies." A Psalm of David.

SAVE me, O God!
For [a]the waters have come up to
my [1]neck.
2 [a]I sink in deep mire,
Where *there is* no standing;
I have come into deep waters,
Where the floods overflow me.
3 [a]I am weary with my crying;
My throat is dry;
[b]My eyes fail while I wait for my
God.

4 Those who [a]hate me without a
cause
Are more than the hairs of my
head;
They are mighty who would
destroy me,
Being my enemies wrongfully;
Though I have stolen nothing,
I *still* must restore *it*.

5 O God, You know my foolishness;
And my sins are not hidden from
You.
6 Let not those who [1]wait for You,
O Lord GOD of hosts, be
ashamed because of me;
Let not those who seek You be
[2]confounded because of me,
O God of Israel.
7 Because for Your sake I have
borne reproach;
Shame has covered my face.
8 [a]I have become a stranger to my
brothers,
And an alien to my mother's
children;

20 [a][Deut. 32:39] **21** [a]Hab. 3:13 [b]Ps. 55:23 **22** [a]Num. 21:33; Deut. 30:1–9; Amos 9:1–3 [b]Ex. 14:22 **23** [a]Ps. 58:10 [b]1 Kin. 21:19; Jer. 15:3 [1]LXX, Syr., Tg., Vg. *you may dip your foot* **24** [1]Lit. *goings* **25** [a]1 Chr. 13:8 **26** [a]Deut. 33:28; Is. 48:1 **27** [a]Judg. 5:14; 1 Sam. 9:21 [1]*throng* **28** [a]Ps. 42:8; Is. 26:12 [1]LXX, Syr., Tg., Vg. *Command, O God* **29** [a]1 Kin. 10:10, 25; 2 Chr. 32:23; Ps. 45:12; 72:10; Is. 18:7 **30** [a]Ps. 22:12 [b]2 Sam. 8:2 **31** [a]Is. 19:19–23 [b]Is. 45:14; Zeph. 3:10 [c]Ps. 44:20 **32** [a][Ps. 67:3, 4]

33 [a]Deut. 33:26; Ps. 18:10 [b]Ps. 46:6; Is. 30:30 **34** [a]Ps. 29:1 **35** [a]Ps. 76:12

PSALM 69

title [1]Heb. *Shoshannim* **1** [a]Job 22:11; Jon. 2:5 [1]Lit. *soul* **2** [a]Ps. 40:2 **3** [a]Ps. 6:6 [b]Deut. 28:32; Ps. 119:82, 123; Is. 38:14 **4** [a]Ps. 35:19; John 15:25 **6** [1]Wait in faith [2]*dishonored* **8** [a]Is. 53:3; Mark 3:21; Luke 8:19; John 7:3–5

68:24–27 The **procession** is a victory parade after a battle. See Ex. 15:20, 21.

69:4 Jesus applies this phrase about **hate** to those who rejected Him (John 15:25).

1 9 [a]Because zeal for Your house has eaten me up,
[b]And the reproaches of those who reproach You have fallen on me.
10 When I wept *and chastened* my soul with fasting,
That became my reproach.
11 I also [1]made sackcloth my garment;
I became a *byword to them.
12 Those who [1]sit in the gate speak against me,
And I *am* the song of the [a]drunkards.

13 But as for me, my prayer *is* to You,
O LORD, *in* the acceptable time;
O God, in the multitude of Your mercy,
Hear me in the truth of Your salvation.
14 Deliver me out of the mire,
And let me not sink;
Let me be delivered from those who hate me,
And out of the deep waters.
15 Let not the floodwater overflow me,
Nor let the deep swallow me up;
And let not the pit shut its mouth on me.

16 Hear me, O LORD, for Your lovingkindness *is* good;
Turn to me according to the multitude of Your tender mercies.
17 And do not hide Your face from Your servant,
For I am in trouble;
Hear me speedily.
18 Draw near to my soul, *and* redeem it;
Deliver me because of my enemies.

19 You know [a]my reproach, my shame, and my dishonor;
My adversaries *are* all before You.
20 Reproach has broken my heart,
And I am full of [1]heaviness;
[a]I looked *for someone* to take pity, but *there was* none;
And for [b]comforters, but I found none.
21 They also gave me gall for my food,
[a]And for my thirst they gave me vinegar to drink.

22 [a]Let their table become a snare before them,
And their well-being a trap.
23 [a]Let their eyes be darkened, so that they do not see;
And make their loins shake continually.
24 [a]Pour out Your indignation upon them,
And let Your wrathful anger take hold of them.
25 [a]Let their dwelling place be desolate;
Let no one live in their tents.
26 For they persecute the *ones* [a]You have struck,
And talk of the grief of those You have wounded.
27 [a]Add iniquity to their iniquity,
[b]And let them not come into Your righteousness.
28 Let them [a]be blotted out of the book of the living,
[b]And not be written with the righteous.

29 But I *am* poor and sorrowful;
Let Your salvation, O God, set me up on high.
30 [a]I will praise the name of God with a song,
And will magnify Him with *thanksgiving.
31 [a]*This* also shall please the LORD better than an ox *or* bull,
Which has horns and hooves.
32 [a]The humble shall see *this and* be glad;
And you who seek God, [b]your hearts shall live.
33 For the LORD hears the poor,
And does not despise [a]His prisoners.

34 [a]Let heaven and earth praise Him,
The seas [b]and everything that moves in them.
35 [a]For God will save Zion
And build the cities of Judah,

9 [a]John 2:17 [b]Rom. 15:3
11 [1]Symbolic of sorrow *See WW at Prov. 1:6.
12 [a]Job 30:9 [1]Sit as judges
19 [a]Ps. 22:6, 7; Heb. 12:2
20 [a]Is. 63:5 [b]Job 16:2 [1]Lit. *sickness*
21 [a]Matt. 27:34, 48; Mark 15:23, 36; Luke 23:36; John 19:28–30
22 [a]Rom. 11:9, 10
23 [a]Is. 6:9, 10
24 [a][1 Thess. 2:16; Jer. 10:25]
25 [a]Matt. 23:38; Luke 13:35; Acts 1:20
26 [a][Is. 53:4; 1 Pet. 2:24]
27 [a]Neh. 4:5; [Rom. 1:28] [b][Is. 26:10]
28 [a][Ex. 32:32]; Phil. 4:3; [Rev. 3:5; 13:8] [b]Ezek. 13:9; Luke 10:20; Heb. 12:23
30 [a][Ps. 28:7] *See WW at Ps. 95:2.
31 [a]Ps. 50:13, 14, 23; 51:16
32 [a]Ps. 34:2 [b]Ps. 22:26
33 [a][Ps. 68:6]; Eph. 3:1
34 [a]Ps. 96:11; Is. 44:23; 49:13 [b]Is. 55:12
35 [a]Ps. 51:18; Is. 44:26

69:9 See section 1 of Truth-In-Action following Ps. 72.
69:9 These words about **zeal** are used to describe Jesus' passion for cleansing the temple of commercialism (John 2:17). Relieving the **reproaches** of others was also exemplified in Christ's life (Rom. 15:3).
69:21 According to Matt. 27:34, **gall** and "sour wine" (**vinegar**) were offered to Jesus during the agony of His crucifixion.
69:25 Judas, who betrayed Jesus, prophetically becomes the object of these curses, including the desolation of his habitation (Acts 1:16–20).

That they may dwell there and
possess it.
36 Also, [a]the [1]descendants of His
servants shall inherit it,
And those who love His name
shall dwell in it.

PSALM 70

Prayer for Relief from Adversaries

To the Chief Musician. *A Psalm* of David. [a]To bring to remembrance.

MAKE *haste,* [a]O God, to deliver me!
Make haste to help me, O LORD!

2 [a]Let them be ashamed and
confounded
Who seek my life;
Let them be [1]turned back and
confused
Who desire my hurt.
3 [a]Let them be turned back because
of their shame,
Who say, [1]"Aha, aha!"

4 Let all those who seek You
*rejoice and be glad in You;
And let those who love Your
salvation say continually,
"Let God be magnified!"

5 [a]But I *am* poor and **needy;**
[b]Make haste to me, O God!
You *are* my help and my
deliverer;
O LORD, do not delay.

> **WORD WEALTH**
>
> **70:5 needy,** *'ebyon* (ehv-*yoan*); Strong's #34: One in need; a destitute, lacking, or poor individual. This adjective occurs about 60 times in the OT. In the Law, God required that the poor should be treated justly (Ex. 23:6). The prophets strongly denounced those who crush or oppress needy persons (Amos 4:1; Ezek. 22:29–31). God is the special Protector of the needy (Is. 25:4). Jesus noted, "The poor have the gospel preached to them" (Matt. 11:5). Thus one of the earliest groups of Jewish followers of Jesus adopted the name "Ebionites" (*'ebyon-ites*), that is, "the poor ones." They delighted in the fact that their needy state prepared them to see the riches of the gospel and the treasure that is the Lord Jesus.

36 [a]Ps. 102:28 [1]Lit. *seed*

PSALM 70

title [a]Ps. 38:title
1 [a]Ps. 40:13–17
2 [a]Ps. 35:4, 26 [1]So with MT, LXX, Tg., Vg.; some Heb. mss., Syr. *appalled* (cf. 40:15)
3 [a]Ps. 40:15 [1]An expression of scorn
4 *See WW at Is. 64:5.
5 [a]Ps. 72:12, 13 [b]Ps. 141:1

PSALM 71

1 [a]Ps. 25:2, 3
2 [a]Ps. 31:1 [b]Ps. 17:6
3 [a]Ps. 31:2, 3 [b]Ps. 44:4 [1]Lit. *rock of refuge* or *rock of habitation*
4 [a]Ps. 140:1, 3
5 [a]Jer. 14:8; 17:7, 13, 17; 50:7 *See WW at Hos. 2:15.
6 [a]Ps. 22:9, 10; Is. 46:3 [1]*sustained from the womb* *See WW at Ex. 28:30.
7 [a]Is. 8:18; Zech. 3:8; 1 Cor. 4:9 *See WW at Zech. 3:8. • See WW at Prov. 14:26.
8 [a]Ps. 35:28 *See WW at Jer. 23:24.
10 [a]2 Sam. 17:1
12 [a]Ps. 35:22 [b]Ps. 70:1
13 [1]*ashamed*

PSALM 71

God the Rock of Salvation

IN [a]You, O LORD, I put my trust;
Let me never be put to shame.
2 [a]Deliver me in Your
righteousness, and cause me to
escape;
[b]Incline Your ear to me, and save
me.
3 [a]Be my [1]strong refuge,
To which I may resort
continually;
You have given the
[b]commandment to save me,
For You *are* my rock and my
fortress.

4 [a]Deliver me, O my God, out of the
hand of the wicked,
Out of the hand of the
unrighteous and cruel man.
5 For You are [a]my *hope, O Lord
GOD;
You are my trust from my youth.
6 [a]By You I have been [1]upheld from
birth;
You are He who took me out of
my mother's womb.
My praise *shall be* *continually of
You.

7 [a]I have become as a *wonder to
many,
But You *are* my strong *refuge.
8 Let [a]my mouth be *filled *with*
Your praise
And with Your glory all the day.

9 Do not cast me off in the time of
old age;
Do not forsake me when my
strength fails.
10 For my enemies speak against
me;
And those who lie in wait for my
life [a]take counsel together,
11 Saying, "God has forsaken him;
Pursue and take him, for *there is*
none to deliver *him.*"

12 [a]O God, do not be far from me;
O my God, [b]make haste to help
me!
13 Let them be [1]confounded *and*
consumed
Who are adversaries of my life;

70:1–5 This psalm repeats 40:13–17.

71:1–24 I put my trust: This psalm is a personal testimony of a devout old man (v. 9) who has memorized Scripture, as is evident by his frequent quotations here.

71:8–24 His repetitious use of words, such as **mouth, praise, mention, declare, sing, lips, tongue,** emphasizes the fact that praise is to be expressed openly in the congregation, and not only as quiet thoughts in a secluded garden of meditation.

Let them be covered *with*
reproach and dishonor
Who seek my hurt.

14 But I will hope continually,
And will praise You yet more and
more.

KINGDOM DYNAMICS

71:14 Creative Praise Stays Lively, PRAISE PATHWAY. Here the psalmist makes a commitment: "I . . . will praise You [God] yet more and more." The idea expressed is beautiful, saying, "I will find fresh and new ways to express my praise toward God." This does not mean to abandon the old ways but to become as creative in our praises to God as God is creative in meeting our needs. Thus we will not fall prey to careless praise, which becomes dull and boring and ends in merely mouthing phrases. God wants us to be creative.

(Ps. 63:1–5/Ps. 145:4) C.G.

15 My mouth shall tell of Your
righteousness
And Your salvation all the day,
For I do not know *their* limits.
16 I will go in the strength of the
Lord GOD;
I will make mention of Your
righteousness, of Yours only.

17 O God, You have taught me from
my [a]youth;
And to this *day* I declare Your
wondrous works.
18 Now also [a]when *I am* old and
grayheaded,
O God, do not forsake me,
Until I declare Your strength to
this generation,
Your power to everyone *who* is
to come.

19 Also [a]Your righteousness, O God,
is [1]very high,
You who have done great
things;
[b]O God, who *is* like You?
20 [a]*You,* who have shown me great
and severe troubles,
[b]Shall revive me again,
And bring me up again from the
depths of the earth.
21 You shall increase my greatness,
And comfort me on every side.

22 Also [a]with the lute I will praise
You—
And Your faithfulness, O my God!
To You I will *sing with the harp,
O [b]Holy One of Israel.
23 My lips shall greatly rejoice when
I sing to You,
And [a]my soul, which You have
redeemed.
24 My tongue also shall talk of Your
righteousness all the day long;
For they are confounded,
For they are brought to shame
Who seek my hurt.

PSALM 72

Glory and Universality of the Messiah's Reign

A Psalm [a]of Solomon.

GIVE the king Your judgments,
O God,
And Your righteousness to the
king's Son.
2 [a]He will judge Your people with
righteousness,
And Your poor with justice.
3 [a]The mountains will bring peace
to the people,
And the little hills, by
righteousness.
4 [a]He will bring justice to the poor
of the people;
He will save the children of the
needy,
And will [1]break in pieces the
oppressor.

5 [1]They shall fear You
[a]As long as the sun and moon
endure,
Throughout all generations.
6 [a]He shall come down like rain
upon the grass before mowing,
Like showers *that* water the
earth.
7 In His days the righteous shall
flourish,
[a]And abundance of peace,
Until the moon is no more.

8 [a]He shall have dominion also from
sea to sea,
And from the River to the ends
of the earth.
9 [a]Those who dwell in the

17 [a]Deut. 4:5; 6:7 **18** [a][Is. 46:4] **19** [a]Deut. 3:24; Ps. 57:10 [b]Ps. 35:10 [1]*great,* lit. *to the height* of heaven **20** [a]Ps. 60:3 [b]Hos. 6:1, 2

22 [a]Ps. 92:1–3 [b]2 Kin. 19:22; Is. 1:4 *See WW at Ps. 149:3. **23** [a]Ps. 103:4

PSALM 72

title [a]Ps. 127:title **2** [a][Is. 9:7; 11:2–5; 32:1] **3** [a]Ps. 85:10 **4** [a]Is. 11:4 [1]*crush* **5** [a]Ps. 72:7, 17; 89:36 [1]So with MT, Tg.; LXX, Vg. *They shall continue* **6** [a]Deut. 32:2; 2 Sam. 23:4; Hos. 6:3 **7** [a]Is. 2:4 **8** [a]Ex. 23:31; [Is. 9:6; Zech. 9:10] **9** [a]Ps. 74:14; Is. 23:13

71:20 All of life, the good times and the **troubles,** are in God's providence.
71:22 Holy One of Israel is a most reverent title for God, used frequently by Isaiah in his prophecies (see Is. 5:19).

72:title While 1,005 songs are said to have been written by **Solomon** (1 Kin. 4:32), only two are ascribed to him in the Book of Psalms: 72 and 127.

wilderness will bow before Him,
[b]And His enemies will lick the dust.
10 [a]The kings of Tarshish and of the isles
Will bring presents;
The kings of Sheba and Seba
Will offer gifts.
11 [a]Yes, all kings shall fall down before Him;
All nations shall *serve Him.

12 For He [a]will deliver the *needy when he cries,
The poor also, and *him* who has no helper.
13 He will spare the poor and needy,
And will save the souls of the needy.
14 He will redeem their life from oppression and violence;
And [a]precious shall be their *blood in His sight.

15 And He shall live;
And the gold of [a]Sheba will be given to Him;
Prayer also will be made for Him continually,
And daily He shall be praised.

16 There will be an abundance of grain in the earth,
On the top of the mountains;
Its fruit shall wave like Lebanon;
[a]And *those* of the city shall flourish like grass of the earth.

17 [a]His name shall endure forever;
His name shall continue as long as the sun.
And [b]*men* shall be *blessed in Him;
[c]All nations shall call Him blessed.

18 [a]Blessed *be* the LORD God, the God of Israel,
[b]Who only does wondrous things!
19 And [a]blessed *be* His glorious name forever!
[b]And let the whole earth be filled *with* His glory.
Amen and Amen.

20 The prayers of David the son of Jesse are ended.

9 [b]Is. 49:23; Mic. 7:17
10 [a]1 Kin. 10:2; 2 Chr. 9:21
11 [a]Is. 49:23
*See WW at Ps. 100:2.
12 [a]Job 29:12
*See WW at Ps. 70:5.
14 [a]1 Sam. 26:21; [Ps. 116:15]
*See WW at Lev. 17:11.
15 [a]Is. 60:6
16 [a]1 Kin. 4:20
17 [a][Ps. 89:36]
[b][Gen. 12:3]
[c]Luke 1:48
*See WW at Prov. 31:28.
18 [a]1 Chr. 29:10
[b]Ex. 15:11; Job 5:9
19 [a][Neh. 9:5]
[b]Num. 14:21; Hab. 2:14

72:12–14 It is the duty of governments, whether monarchical or democratic, to be public servants and to help **the poor and needy.**
72:15 Prayer for governments is enjoined in the NT as well (1 Tim. 2:1–3), and is vital for peace in the affairs of men.
72:18, 19 Blessed: These two verses are a closing doxology for Book Two. See note on 1:1.
72:20 This subscription is to be taken as an ending of a previous smaller collection of psalms now incorporated into Book Two, for though most of the psalms in Book Two are David's, some are not. There are more of David's psalms in the remaining books within this Psalter.

TRUTH-IN-ACTION through PSALMS (Book Two: Psalms 42—72)

Letting the LIFE of the Holy Spirit Bring Faith's Works Alive in You!

Truth Psalms Teaches	Text	**Action** Psalms Invites
1 Guidelines for Growing in Godliness Those who choose to live godly lives will not go unrewarded and will look for opportunities to share with others what God is doing in and through them.	62:12	**Understand** and **know** that God will reward everyone according to his deeds.
	64:1; 69:9	**Voice** any complaints to God alone. **Be zealous** that the purposes of God be fulfilled in and through the church.
	45:17	**Be faithful** to bear witness to Jesus Christ as Lord and Savior.
2 Steps to Dynamic Devotion Worship and its biblically prescribed forms are an *important* part of our devotion to God. Unwisely, we often neglect certain unfamiliar elements of worship. God is remarkably present with those who worship Him as He asks. Also, in prayer	42:1, 2; 63:1, 2	**Cultivate** a conscious hunger and thirst for God. **Anticipate** that this will result in more time with Him.
	59:16, 17	**Sing** to God in your times alone with Him.
	47:1–7	**Practice** joyful and vocal worship. **Do not despise** hearty applause directed toward the Father.

Truth Psalms Teaches	Text	**Action** Psalms Invites
2 we often forget to spend as much time listening as we do speaking to God. This is all the more amazing when we remember with whom we are communing when we pray.	46:10 44:22	**Understand** that knowing God involves experiencing regular times of silent waiting and expectant quietude. **Offer** your life to God daily as a living sacrifice. **Consider** yourself dead to personal ambition.
3 **Keys to Wise Living** Wise individuals reject man's testimony about himself. Much confusion has been generated among God's people because they have accepted a mere humanistic belief in man's intrinsic goodness. As a result, many have stumbled because they trusted only in man and not in God.	53:3 44:3–8	**Accept** God's testimony about man's basic nature. **Understand** the impact of sin on every human being. **Understand** that it is not the hand, mind, or strength of the flesh that brings spiritual victory. **Be assured** that victory comes from the Lord alone.
4 **Key Lessons in Faith** Faith is a conscious choice to act on what God says is true, not some passive response of the Christian to his circumstances. Like everything else, faith requires practice to grow and become strong. Faith comes from God's Word illumined by the Holy Spirit and is released through acts of obedience. Faith requires a singleness of commitment that draws us from doubt and wavering.	56:3, 4, 10, 11 55:22 51:10 43:3	When you are tempted to be afraid, **choose to trust** the Lord as an act of your will, not as a response to your emotions. **Practice** a determined, praise-filled refusal to be afraid. **Quickly release** concerns and worries to the Father who wants to carry them for you. **Beseech** the Lord to work in you a singleness of purpose in heart. **Ask** Him for a spirit that endures and stands fast on the truth you know. **Expect** God's Spirit illuminating the Scriptures to give you clear guidance every day.
5 **Necessity of Humility** The unbroken, proud, and arrogant spirit is not pleasing to God. In order to commune with God, we must be humbled, acknowledging our sin and our need for cleansing by Him.	51:1–19	**Understand** that the spirit of humility opens the pathway to fullness of joy.
6 **Steps to Dealing with Sin** Dealing with sin begins by understanding that sin originates in the heart.	66:18	**Avoid** nullifying your prayers by planning, harboring, or entertaining sin or wickedness in your heart.

BOOK THREE
Psalms 73–89

PSALM 73

The Tragedy of the Wicked, and the Blessedness of Trust in God

A Psalm of [a]Asaph.

TRULY God *is* good to Israel,
To such as are pure in heart.
2 But as for me, my feet had almost stumbled;
My steps had nearly [a]slipped.
3 [a]For I *was* *envious of the boastful,
When I saw the prosperity of the [b]wicked.

4 For *there are* no [1]pangs in their death,
But their strength *is* firm.
5 [a]They *are* not in *trouble *as other* men,
Nor are they plagued like *other* men.
6 Therefore pride serves as their necklace;
Violence covers them [a]*like* a garment.
7 [a]Their [1]eyes bulge with abundance;
They have more than heart could wish.
8 [a]They scoff and speak wickedly *concerning* oppression;
They [b]speak [1]loftily.
9 They set their mouth [a]against the heavens,
And their tongue walks through the earth.

10 Therefore his people return here,
[a]And waters of a full *cup* are drained by them.
11 And they say, [a]"How does God know?
And is there knowledge in the Most High?"
12 Behold, these *are* the ungodly,
Who are always at ease;
They increase *in* riches.
13 Surely I have [1]cleansed my heart *in* [a]vain,
And washed my hands in innocence.
14 For all day long I have been plagued,
And chastened every morning.

15 If I had said, "I will speak thus,"
Behold, I would have been untrue to the generation of Your children.
16 When I thought *how* to understand this, **2**
It *was* [1]too painful for me—
17 Until I went into the sanctuary of God;
Then I understood their [a]end.

18 Surely [a]You set them in slippery places;
You cast them down to destruction.
19 Oh, how they are *brought* to desolation, as in a moment!
They are utterly consumed with terrors.
20 As a *dream when *one* awakes,
So, Lord, when You awake,
You shall despise their image.

21 Thus my heart was grieved, **2**
And I was [1]vexed in my mind.
22 [a]I *was* so foolish and ignorant;
I was *like* a beast before You.
23 Nevertheless I *am* continually with You;
You hold *me* by my right hand.
24 [a]You will guide me with Your counsel,
And afterward receive me *to* glory.

25 [a]Whom have I in heaven *but* You?
And *there is* none upon earth *that* I desire besides You.
26 [a]My flesh and my heart fail;
But God *is* the [1]strength of my heart and my [b]portion*
forever.

27 For indeed, [a]those who are far from You shall perish;
You have destroyed all those who [1]desert You for harlotry.
28 But *it is* good for me to [a]draw near to God;
I have put my trust in the Lord GOD,
That I may [b]declare all Your works.

PSALM 73
title [a]Ps. 50:title
2 [a]Job 12:5
3 [a]Ps. 37:1, 7; [Prov. 23:17] [b]Job 21:5–16; Jer. 12:1 *See WW at Zech. 8:2.
4 [1]*pains*
5 [a]Job 21:9 *See WW at Job 5:7.
6 [a]Ps. 109:18
7 [a]Job 15:27; Jer. 5:28 [1]Tg. *face bulges;* LXX, Syr., Vg. *iniquity bulges*
8 [a]Ps. 53:1 [b]2 Pet. 2:18; Jude 16 [1]Proudly
9 [a]Rev. 13:6
10 [a][Ps. 75:8]
11 [a]Job 22:13
13 [a]Job 21:15; 35:3; Mal. 3:14 [1]*kept my heart pure in vain*
16 [1]*troublesome in my eyes*
17 [a][Ps. 37:38; 55:23]
18 [a]Ps. 35:6
20 *See WW at Joel 2:28.
21 [1]Lit. *pierced in my kidneys*
22 [a]Ps. 92:6
24 [a]Ps. 32:8; 48:14; Is. 58:11
25 [a][Phil. 3:8]
26 [a]Ps. 84:2 [b]Ps. 16:5 [1]Lit. *rock* *See WW at Zech. 2:12.
27 [a][Ps. 119:155] [1]Are unfaithful to You
28 [a][Heb. 10:22; James 4:8] [b]Ps. 116:10; 2 Cor. 4:13

73:4, 5 No pangs: Bitterness often hinders the mind from thinking clearly and tempts it to make sweeping generalizations that are not completely accurate, such as the one here.

73:15 He kept his nagging doubts to himself, instead of dragging his family and **children** down with him.

73:16, 17 See section 2 of Truth-In-Action following Ps. 89.

73:21, 22 See section 2 of Truth-In-Action following Ps. 89.

PSALM 74

A Plea for Relief from Oppressors

A [1]Contemplation of Asaph.

O GOD, why have You cast *us* off
forever?
Why does Your anger smoke
against the sheep of Your
pasture?
2 Remember Your congregation,
which You have purchased of
old,
The tribe of Your inheritance,
which You have *redeemed—
This Mount Zion where You have
dwelt.
3 Lift up Your feet to the perpetual
desolations.
The enemy has damaged
everything in the sanctuary.
4 [a]Your enemies *roar in the midst
of Your meeting place;
[b]They set up their banners *for*
signs.
5 They seem like men who lift up
Axes among the thick trees.
6 And now they break down its
carved work, all at once,
With axes and hammers.
7 They have set fire to Your
sanctuary;
They have defiled the dwelling
place of Your name to the
ground.
8 [a]They said in their hearts,
"Let us [1]destroy them
altogether."
They have burned up all the
meeting places of God in the
land.

4 9 We do not see our signs;
[a]*There is* no longer any prophet;
Nor *is there* any among us who
knows how long.
10 O God, how long will the
adversary [1]reproach?
Will the enemy blaspheme Your
name forever?
11 [a]Why do You withdraw Your
hand, even Your right hand?
Take it out of Your bosom and
destroy *them*.
12 For [a]God *is* my King from of
old,
Working salvation in the midst of
the earth.
13 [a]You divided the sea by Your
strength;
You broke the heads of the
[1]sea serpents in the waters.
14 You broke the heads of
[1]Leviathan in pieces,
And gave him *as* food to the
people inhabiting the
wilderness.
15 [a]You broke open the fountain and
the flood;
[b]You dried up mighty rivers.
16 The day *is* Yours, the night also
is [a]Yours;
[b]You have prepared the light and
the sun.
17 You have [a]set all the borders of
the earth;
[b]You have made summer and
winter.

18 Remember this, *that* the enemy
has reproached, O LORD,
And *that* a foolish people has
blasphemed Your name.
19 Oh, do not deliver the life of
Your turtledove to the wild
beast!
Do not forget the life of Your poor
forever.
20 [a]Have respect to the covenant;
For the [1]dark places of the earth
are full of the [2]haunts of
[3]cruelty.
21 Oh, do not let the oppressed
return ashamed!
Let the poor and *needy praise
Your name.

22 Arise, O God, plead Your own
cause;
Remember how the foolish man
[1]reproaches You daily.
23 Do not forget the voice of Your
enemies;
The tumult of those who rise up
against You increases
continually.

PSALM 74

title [1]Heb. *Maschil*
2 *See WW at Is. 52:9.
4 [a]Lam. 2:7 [b]Num. 2:2 *See WW at Joel 3:16.
8 [a]Ps. 83:4 [1]*oppress*
9 [a]1 Sam. 3:1; Lam. 2:9; Ezek. 7:26; Amos 8:11
10 [1]*revile*
11 [a]Lam. 2:3
12 [a]Ps. 44:4
13 [a]Ex. 14:21 [1]*sea monsters*
14 [1]A large sea creature of unknown identity
15 [a]Ex. 17:5, 6; Num. 20:11; Ps. 105:41; Is. 48:21 [b]Ex. 14:21, 22; Josh. 2:10; 3:13
16 [a]Job 38:12 [b]Gen. 1:14–18
17 [a]Deut. 32:8; Acts 17:26 [b]Gen. 8:22
20 [a]Gen. 17:7, 8; Lev. 26:44, 45 [1]*hiding places* [2]*homes* [3]*violence*
21 *See WW at Ps. 70:5.
22 [1]*reviles* or *taunts*

74:title This prayer was not written by **Asaph** since its subject matter refers to a later era, but belongs to his "school" of composers.
74:1 God's **anger** in the OT is often symbolized by aspects of fire: **smoke** (v. 1), kindled (106:40), consuming fire (Deut. 4:24).
74:7 Burning of the **sanctuary** by Nebuzaradan of Babylon is recorded in 2 Kin. 25:9.
74:9 See section 4 of Truth-In-Action following Ps. 89.
74:13–17 The repetition of **You,** the personal pronoun, emphasizes that God, and no other, is capable of these mighty acts.
74:14 Leviathan is a symbol for the oppressive rulers of Egypt (Ezek. 29:3). Beasts often represented nations. **People** is translated by some as "beasts" agreeing with Ezek. 32:4.
74:18 Foolish here and in v. 22 refers to pagan and godless people, not just uneducated people.

PSALM 75

Thanksgiving for God's Righteous Judgment

To the Chief Musician. Set to [a]"Do[1] Not Destroy." A Psalm of Asaph. A Song.

WE *give thanks to You, O God, we give thanks!
For Your wondrous works declare *that* Your name is near.

2 "When I choose the [1]proper time,
I will judge uprightly.
3 The earth and all its inhabitants are dissolved;
I set up its pillars firmly. Selah

4 "I said to the boastful, 'Do not deal boastfully,'
And to the wicked, [a]'Do not [1]lift up the horn.
5 Do not lift up your horn on high;
Do *not* speak with [1]a stiff neck.' "
4 6 For exaltation *comes* neither from the east
Nor from the west nor from the south.
7 But [a]God *is* the *Judge:
[b]He puts down one,
And exalts another.
8 For [a]in the hand of the LORD *there is* a cup,
And the wine is red;
It is fully mixed, and He pours it out;
Surely its dregs shall all the wicked of the earth
Drain *and* drink down.

9 But I will declare forever,
I will sing praises to the God of Jacob.

10 "All[a] the [1]horns of the wicked I will also cut off,
But [b]the horns of the righteous shall be [c]exalted."*

PSALM 76

The Majesty of God in Judgment

To the Chief Musician. On [1]stringed instruments. A Psalm of Asaph. A Song.

IN [a]Judah God *is* known;
His name *is* great in Israel.
2 In [1]Salem also is His tabernacle,
And His dwelling place in Zion.
3 There He broke the arrows of the bow,
The shield and sword of battle. Selah

4 You *are* more glorious and excellent
[a]*Than* the mountains of prey.
5 [a]The stouthearted were plundered;
[b]They [1]have sunk into their sleep;
And none of the *mighty men have found the use of their hands.
6 [a]At Your rebuke, O God of Jacob,
Both the chariot and horse were cast into a dead sleep.

7 You, Yourself, *are* to be feared;
And [a]who may stand in Your presence
When once You are angry?
8 [a]You caused judgment to be heard from heaven;
[b]The earth feared and was still,
9 When God [a]arose to judgment,
To deliver all the oppressed of the earth. Selah

10 [a]Surely the wrath of man shall praise You;
With the remainder of wrath You shall gird Yourself.

11 [a]Make vows to the LORD your God, and pay *them;* 3
[b]Let all who are around Him bring presents to Him who ought to be *feared.
12 He shall cut off the spirit of princes;
[a]*He is* awesome to the kings of the earth.

PSALM 77

The Consoling Memory of God's Redemptive Works

To the Chief Musician. [a]To Jeduthun. A Psalm of Asaph.

I CRIED out to God with my voice—
To God with my voice;
And He gave ear to me.

PSALM 75
title [a]Ps. 57:title [1]Heb. *Al Tashcheth*
1 *See WW at 1 Chr. 16:7.
2 [1]*appointed*
4 [a][1 Sam. 2:3]; Ps. 94:4 [1]Raise the head proudly like a horned animal
5 [1]Insolent pride
7 [a]Ps. 50:6 [b]1 Sam. 2:7; Ps. 147:6; Dan. 2:21 *See WW at Judg. 2:18.
8 [a]Job 21:20; Ps. 60:3; Jer. 25:15; Rev. 14:10; 16:19
10 [a]Ps. 101:8; Jer. 48:25 [b]Ps. 89:17; 148:14 [c]1 Sam. 2:1 [1]Strength *See WW at Ps. 18:46.

PSALM 76
title [1]Heb. *neginoth*
1 [a]Ps. 48:1, 3
2 [1]Jerusalem
4 [a]Ezek. 38:12
5 [a]Is. 10:12; 46:12 [b]Ps. 13:3 [1]Lit. *have slumbered their sleep* *See WW at Zech. 4:6.
6 [a]Ex. 15:1–21; Ezek. 39:20; Nah. 2:13; Zech. 12:4
7 [a][Ezra 9:15; Nah. 1:6; Mal. 3:2; Rev. 6:17]
8 [a]Ex. 19:9 [b]1 Chr. 16:30; 2 Chr. 20:29
9 [a][Ps. 9:7–9]
10 [a]Ex. 9:16; Rom. 9:17
11 [a][Eccl. 5:4–6] [b]2 Chr. 32:22, 23 *See WW at Is. 8:13.
12 [a]Ps. 68:35

PSALM 77
title [a]Ps. 39:title

75:5–7 This theme of **exaltation** by way of humility runs throughout the Bible, *from the mouth of Samuel's* mother (1 Sam. 2:8) to the heart of Mary, the mother of Jesus (Luke 1:52).
75:5 Horn here and in v. 10 is symbolic of power, and so may have the thought of not bullying people in a climb to the top. See Luke 14:11 for Jesus' comment.
75:6, 7 See section 4 of Truth-In-Action following Ps. 89.
75:8 Red wine is fermented and foaming, hence intoxicating. Instead of prominence, the wicked will find a place with the drunkards.
76:1–12 This victory song, written after the **Asaph** tradition, may refer to the confrontation between Israel and Sennacherib (2 Kin. 19:35).
76:5, 6 Sleep is a euphemism for death.
76:11 See section 3 of Truth-In-Action following Ps. 89.

2 In the day of my trouble I sought
the Lord;
My hand was stretched out in the
night without ceasing;
My soul refused to be comforted.
3 I remembered God, and was
troubled;
I complained, and my spirit was
overwhelmed. Selah

4 You hold my eyelids *open;*
I am so troubled that I cannot
speak.
5 I have considered the days of old,
The years of ancient times.
6 I call to remembrance my song in
the night;
I meditate within my heart,
And my spirit [1]makes diligent
search.

7 Will the Lord cast off forever?
And will He be favorable no
more?
8 Has His mercy ceased forever?
Has *His* [a]promise *failed
[1]forevermore?
9 Has God forgotten to be gracious?
Has He in anger shut up His
tender mercies? Selah

6 10 And I said, "This *is* my [1]anguish;
But I will remember the years of
the right hand of the *Most
High."
11 I will remember the works of the
*LORD;
Surely I will remember Your
wonders of old.
12 I will also *meditate on all Your
work,
And talk of Your deeds.
13 Your way, O God, *is* in [1]the
[a]sanctuary;
Who *is* so great a God as *our*
God?
14 You *are* the God who does
wonders;
You have declared Your strength
among the peoples.
15 You have with *Your* arm
redeemed Your people,
The sons of Jacob and Joseph.
Selah

16 The waters saw You, O God;
The waters saw You, they were
[a]afraid;
The depths also trembled.
17 The clouds poured out water;
The skies sent out a sound;
Your arrows also flashed about.
18 The voice of Your thunder *was* in
the whirlwind;
The lightnings lit up the world;
The earth trembled and shook.
19 Your way *was* in the sea,
Your path in the great waters,
And Your footsteps were not
known.
20 You led Your people like a flock
By the hand of Moses and Aaron.

PSALM 78

God's Kindness to Rebellious Israel

A [a]Contemplation[1] of Asaph.

GIVE ear, O my people, *to* my law;
Incline your ears to the words of
my mouth.
2 I will open my mouth in a
[a]parable;
I will utter [1]dark sayings of old,
3 Which we have heard and known,
And our fathers have told us.
4 [a]We will not hide *them* from their 2
children,
[b]Telling to the generation to come
the praises of the LORD,
And His strength and His
wonderful works that He has
done.

5 For [a]He established a testimony
in Jacob,
And appointed a law in Israel,
Which He commanded our
fathers,
That [b]they should make them
known to their children;
6 [a]That the generation to come
might know *them,*
The children *who* would be born,
That they may arise and declare
them to their children,
7 That they may set their hope in
God,

6 [1]*ponders diligently*
8 [a][2 Pet. 3:8, 9] [1]Lit. *unto generation and generation* *See WW at Ps. 138:8.
10 [1]Lit. *infirmity* *See WW at Gen. 14:18.
11 *See WW at Is. 12:2.
12 *See WW at Ps. 1:2.
13 [a]Ps. 73:17 [1]Or *holiness*
16 [a]Ex. 14:21; Hab. 3:8, 10

PSALM 78

title [a]Ps. 74:title [1]Heb. *Maschil*
2 [a]Matt. 13:34, 35 [1]*obscure sayings* or *riddles*
4 [a]Ex. 12:26, 27; Deut. 4:9; 6:7; Job 15:18; Is. 38:19; Joel 1:3 [b]Ex. 13:8, 14
5 [a]Ps. 147:19 [b]Deut. 4:9; 11:19
6 [a]Ps. 102:18

77:4 Eyelids *open:* He is so disturbed he cannot sleep.
77:7–9 Forever: The six rhetorical questions about God's watchful care are answered by remembering that God has faithfully guided Israel through troublesome times before (vv. 15, 20).
77:10–20 See section 6 of Truth-In-Action following Ps. 89.
77:10 Right hand: This often-used symbol in Asaphic psalms represents God's ability to respond in powerful acts (73:23; 74:11; 78:54).
78:2 This is quoted by Matthew regarding Jesus' use of parables (Matt. 13:35). It is the same Hebrew word (*mashal*) translated "proverb" in the Book of Proverbs, and it means "comparison."
78:4–8 See section 2 of Truth-In-Action following Ps. 89.
78:4–8 Parents' passing along the faith to **their children** is extremely important. The primary source for religious instruction must always be the **fathers.**

And not forget the works of God,
But keep His commandments;
8 And [a]may not be like their fathers,
[b]A stubborn and rebellious generation,
A generation [c]*that* did not [1]set its heart aright,
And whose spirit was not faithful to God.

9 The children of Ephraim, *being* armed *and* [1]carrying bows,
Turned back in the day of battle.
10 [a]They did not keep the covenant of God;
They refused to walk in His law,
11 And [a]forgot His works
And His wonders that He had shown them.

12 [a]Marvelous things He did in the sight of their fathers,
In the land of Egypt, [b]*in* the field of Zoan.
13 [a]He divided the sea and caused them to pass through;
And [b]He made the *waters stand up like a heap.
14 [a]In the daytime also He led them with the cloud,
And all the night with a light of fire.
15 [a]He split the rocks in the wilderness,
And gave *them* drink in abundance like the depths.
16 He also brought [a]streams out of the rock,
And caused waters to run down like rivers.

17 But they sinned even more against Him
By [a]rebelling against the Most High in the wilderness.
18 And [a]they *tested God in their heart
By asking for the food of their fancy.
19 [a]Yes, they spoke against God:
They said, "Can God prepare a table in the wilderness?
20 [a]Behold, He struck the rock,
So that the waters gushed out,
And the streams overflowed.
Can He give bread also?
Can He provide meat for His people?"

8 [a]2 Kin. 17:14; 2 Chr. 30:7; Ezek. 20:18 [b]Ex. 32:9; Deut. 9:7, 24; 31:27; Judg. 2:19; Is. 30:9 [c]Job 11:13; Ps. 78:37 [1]Lit. *prepare its heart*
9 [1]Lit. *bow shooters*
10 [a]2 Kin. 17:15
11 [a]Ps. 106:13
12 [a]Ex. 7—12 [b]Num. 13:22; Is. 19:11; 30:4; Ezek. 30:14
13 [a]Ex. 14:21 [b]Ex. 15:8 *See WW at Is. 43:2.
14 [a]Ex. 13:21
15 [a]Ex. 17:6; Num. 20:11; Is. 48:21; [1 Cor. 10:4]
16 [a]Num. 20:8, 10, 11
17 [a]Deut. 9:22; Is. 63:10; Heb. 3:16
18 [a]Ex. 16:2 *See WW at Ps. 78:41.
19 [a]Ex. 16:3; Num. 11:4; 20:3; 21:5
20 [a]Num. 20:11

21 [a]Num. 11:1
22 [a]Deut. 1:32; 9:23; [Heb. 3:18]
23 [a]Gen. 7:11; [Mal. 3:10]
24 [a]Ex. 16:4 [b]John 6:31 [1]Lit. *grain*
25 [1]*satiation*
26 [a]Num. 11:31
29 [a]Num. 11:19, 20
30 [a]Num. 11:33 [1]Lit. *separated*
32 [a]Num. 14:16, 17 [b]Num. 14:11; Ps. 78:11, 22
33 [a]Num. 14:29, 35
34 [a]Num. 21:7; [Hos. 5:15]
35 [a][Deut. 32:4, 15] [b][Ex. 15:13]; Deut. 7:8; Is. 41:14; 44:6; 63:9
36 [a]Ex. 24:7, 8; Ezek. 33:31

21 Therefore the LORD heard *this*
And [a]was furious;
So a fire was kindled against Jacob,
And anger also came up against Israel,
22 Because they [a]did not believe in God,
And did not trust in His salvation.
23 Yet He had commanded the clouds above,
[a]And opened the doors of heaven,
24 [a]Had rained down manna on them to eat,
And given them of the [1]bread of [b]heaven.
25 Men ate angels' food;
He sent them food to [1]the full.
26 [a]He caused an east wind to blow in the heavens;
And by His power He brought in the south wind.
27 He also rained meat on them like the dust,
Feathered fowl like the sand of the seas;
28 And He let *them* fall in the midst of their camp,
All around their dwellings.
29 [a]So they ate and were well filled,
For He gave them their own desire.
30 They were not [1]deprived of their craving;
But [a]while their food *was* still in their mouths,
31 The wrath of God came against them,
And slew the stoutest of them,
And struck down the choice *men* of Israel.

32 In spite of this [a]they still sinned,
And [b]did not believe in His wondrous works.
33 [a]Therefore their days He consumed in futility,
And their years in fear.
34 [a]When He slew them, then they sought Him;
And they returned and sought earnestly for God.
35 Then they remembered that [a]God *was* their rock,
And the Most High God [b]their Redeemer.
36 Nevertheless they [a]flattered Him with their mouth,

78:9 The author seems to be more favorable to Judah, a southern tribe (vv. 67, 68), than to **Ephraim,** a northern tribe, implying that this was written after the kingdom of Israel was divided by Jeroboam's rebellion.

78:25 Angels' food is, literally, "bread of the mighty."

And they lied to Him with their
tongue;
37 For their heart was not steadfast
with Him,
Nor were they faithful in His
covenant.
38 [a]But He, *being* full of [b]compassion,
forgave *their* iniquity,
And did not destroy *them*.
Yes, many a time [c]He turned His
anger away,
And [d]did not stir up all His wrath;
39 For [a]He remembered [b]that they
were but flesh,
[c]A breath that passes away and
does not come again.

40 How often they [a]provoked[1] Him
in the wilderness,
And grieved Him in the desert!
41 Yes, [a]again and again they
tempted God,
And limited the Holy One of
Israel.

WORD WEALTH

78:41 tempted, *nasah* (nah-*sah*); Strong's #5254: To put to the test; to try, prove, tempt. This verb occurs less than 40 times in the OT. The basic idea is to put someone to the test to see how he will respond, as in 1 Kin. 10:1. Abraham was tested by God (Gen. 22:1) to the utmost degree. David called for God to test his mind and heart, confident that he would pass this test (Ps. 26:2, 3). It is God's privilege to test man; it is not man's right to test God. In this reference, the wilderness generation insulted and grieved the Lord by tempting and limiting Him, as if to test His patience or His power.

42 They did not remember His
[1]power:
The day when He redeemed them
from the enemy,
43 When He worked His signs in
Egypt,
And His wonders in the field of
Zoan;
44 [a]Turned their rivers into blood,
And their streams, that they could
not drink.
45 [a]He sent swarms of flies among
them, which devoured them,
And [b]frogs, which destroyed
them.
46 He also gave their crops to the
caterpillar,
And their labor to the [a]locust.
47 [a]He destroyed their vines with
hail,
And their sycamore trees with
frost.
48 He also gave up their [a]cattle to
the hail,
And their flocks to fiery
[1]lightning.
49 He cast on them the fierceness of
His anger,
Wrath, indignation, and trouble,
By sending angels of destruction
among them.
50 He made a path for His anger;
He did not spare their soul from
death,
But gave [1]their life over to the
plague,
51 And destroyed all the [a]firstborn
in Egypt,
The first of *their* strength in the
tents of Ham.
52 But He [a]made His own people go
forth like sheep,
And guided them in the
wilderness like a flock;
53 And He [a]led them on *safely, so
that they did not fear;
But the sea [b]overwhelmed their
enemies.
54 And He brought them to His
[a]holy border,
This mountain [b]*which* His right
hand had acquired.
55 [a]He also drove out the nations
before them,
[b]Allotted them an inheritance by
[1]survey,
And made the tribes of Israel
dwell in their tents.

56 [a]Yet they *tested and provoked the
*Most High God,
And did not keep His testimonies,
57 But [a]turned back and acted
unfaithfully like their fathers;
They were turned aside [b]like a
deceitful bow.
58 [a]For they *provoked Him to anger
with their [b]high* places,
And moved Him to jealousy with
their carved images.
59 When God heard *this*, He was
furious,
And greatly abhorred Israel,
60 [a]So that He forsook the tabernacle
of *Shiloh,
The tent He had placed among
men,

38 [a][Num. 14:18–20] [b]Ex. 34:6 [c][Is. 48:9] [d]1 Kin. 21:29
39 [a]Job 10:9; Ps. 103:14–16 [b]John 3:6 [c][Job 7:7, 16; James 4:14]
40 [a]Ps. 95:8–10; [Eph. 4:30]; Heb. 3:16 [1]*rebelled against Him*
41 [a]Num. 14:22; Deut. 6:16
42 [1]Lit. *hand*
44 [a]Ex. 7:20
45 [a]Ex. 8:24 [b]Ex. 8:6
46 [a]Ex. 10:14
47 [a]Ex. 9:23–25
48 [a]Ex. 9:19 [1]*lightning bolts*
50 [1]Or *their beasts*
51 [a]Ex. 12:29, 30
52 [a]Ps. 77:20
53 [a]Ex. 14:19, 20 [b]Ex. 14:27, 28 *See WW at Deut. 33:12.
54 [a]Ex. 15:17 [b]Ps. 44:3
55 [a]Josh. 11:16–23; Ps. 44:2 [b]Josh. 13:7; 19:51; 23:4 [1]*surveyed measurement,* lit. *measuring cord*
56 [a]Judg. 2:11–13 *See WW at Ps. 78:41. • See WW at Gen. 14:18.
57 [a]Ezek. 20:27, 28 [b]Hos. 7:16
58 [a]Deut. 32:16, 21; Judg. 2:12; 1 Kin. 14:9; Is. 65:3 [b]Deut. 12:2 *See WW at 1 Kin. 16:2. • See WW at Ezek. 6:3.
60 [a]1 Sam. 4:11; Jer. 7:12–14; 26:6–9 *See WW at Gen. 49:10.

78:51 Ham was a son of Noah and ancestor of Egyptian peoples (Gen. 10:6).
78:60 After the conquest of the Promised Land, the tabernacle that had accompanied Israel in their wilderness journey was set up at **Shiloh**, approximately 35 miles northeast of Jerusalem.

61 [a]And delivered His strength into
captivity,
And His glory into the enemy's
hand.
62 [a]He also gave His people over to
the sword,
And was furious with His
inheritance.
63 The fire consumed their young
men,
And [a]their maidens were not
given in marriage.
64 [a]Their priests fell by the sword,
And [b]their widows made no
lamentation.

65 Then the Lord awoke as *from*
sleep,
[a]Like a mighty man who shouts
because of wine.
66 And [a]He beat back His enemies;
He put them to a perpetual
reproach.

67 Moreover He rejected the tent of
Joseph,
And did not choose the tribe of
Ephraim,
68 But chose the tribe of Judah,
Mount Zion [a]which He loved.
69 And He built His [a]sanctuary like
the heights,
Like the earth which He has
established forever.
70 [a]He also *chose David His servant,
And took him from the
sheepfolds;
71 From following [a]the ewes that
had young He brought him,
[b]To *shepherd Jacob His people,
And Israel His inheritance.
72 So he shepherded them according
to the [a]integrity of his heart,
And guided them by the
skillfulness of his hands.

PSALM 79

A Dirge and a Prayer for Israel, Destroyed by Enemies

A Psalm of Asaph.

O GOD, the [1]nations have come into
[a]Your inheritance;
Your holy temple they have
defiled;
[b]They have laid Jerusalem
[2]in heaps.
2 [a]The dead bodies of Your servants
They have given *as* food for the
birds of the heavens,
The flesh of Your saints to the
beasts of the earth.
3 Their blood they have shed like
water all around Jerusalem,
And *there was* no one to bury
them.
4 We have become a reproach to
our [a]neighbors,
A scorn and derision to those who
are around us.

5 [a]How long, LORD?
Will You be angry forever?
Will Your [b]jealousy burn like
fire?
6 [a]Pour out Your wrath on the
[1]nations that [b]do not know
You,
And on the kingdoms that
[c]do not call on Your name.
7 For they have devoured Jacob,
And laid waste his dwelling place.

8 [a]Oh, do not *remember [1]former
*iniquities against us!
Let Your tender mercies come
speedily to meet us,
For we have been brought very
low.
9 Help us, O God of our salvation, **1**
For the glory of Your name;
And deliver us, and provide
atonement for our sins,
[a]For Your name's sake!
10 [a]Why should the [1]nations say,
"Where *is* their God?"
Let there be known among the
nations in our sight
The avenging of the blood of Your
servants *which has been* shed.

11 Let [a]the groaning of the prisoner
come before You;
According to the greatness of
Your [1]power
Preserve those who are appointed
to die;
12 And return to our neighbors
[a]sevenfold into their bosom

61 [a]Judg. 18:30 **62** [a]Judg. 20:21; 1 Sam. 4:10 **63** [a]Jer. 7:34; 16:9; 25:10 **64** [a]1 Sam. 4:17; 22:18 [b]Job 27:15; Ezek. 24:23 **65** [a]Is. 42:13 **66** [a]1 Sam. 5:6 **68** [a][Ps. 87:2] **69** [a]1 Kin. 6:1–38 **70** [a]1 Sam. 16:11, 12; 2 Sam. 7:8 *See WW at 1 Kin. 11:34. **71** [a]2 Sam. 7:8; [Is. 40:11] [b]2 Sam. 5:2; 1 Chr. 11:2 *See WW at Is. 40:11. **72** [a]1 Kin. 9:4

PSALM 79

1 [a]Ps. 74:2 [b]2 Kin. 25:9, 10; 2 Chr. 36:17–19; Jer. 26:18; 52:12–14; Mic. 3:12 [1]*Gentiles* [2]*in ruins*

2 [a]Deut. 28:26; Jer. 7:33; 19:7; 34:20 **4** [a]Ps. 44:13; [Dan. 9:16] **5** [a]Ps. 74:1, 9 [b][Zeph. 3:8] **6** [a]Jer. 10:25; [Zeph. 3:8] [b]Is. 45:4, 5; 1 Thess. 4:5; [2 Thess. 1:8] [c]Ps. 53:4 [1]*Gentiles* **8** [a]Is. 64:9 [1]Or *against us the iniquities of those who were before us* *See WW at Is. 62:6. • See WW at Ps. 130:3. **9** [a]Jer. 14:7, 21 **10** [a]Ps. 42:10 [1]*Gentiles* **11** [a]Ps. 102:20 [1]Lit. *arm* **12** [a]Gen. 4:15; Lev. 26:21; Prov. 6:31; Is. 30:26

78:71 References to a **shepherd** or his work, here and in Ps. 77, 79, and 80, gave rise to the name for these Asaphic psalms as "Shepherd Psalms."

79:1–13 Nations have come: This psalm belongs to the Asaphic school of song writers, and was written after Jerusalem was destroyed by the Babylonians in 597–587 B.C.

79:2 Birds: This verse brings to bear the prophecy of Jeremiah (Jer. 19:7).

79:6 Wrath: Jeremiah utters this same curse in Jer. 10:25. Many other verses in this psalm are quotes from other psalms.

79:9 See section 1 of Truth-In-Action following Ps. 89.

[b]Their reproach with which they
have reproached You, O Lord.

13 So [a]we, Your people and sheep
of Your pasture,
Will give You thanks forever;
[b]We will show forth Your praise
to all generations.

PSALM 80

Prayer for Israel's Restoration

To the Chief Musician. [a]Set to [1]"The Lilies."
A [2]Testimony of Asaph. A Psalm.

GIVE ear, O Shepherd of Israel,
[a]You who lead Joseph [b]like a
flock;
You who dwell *between* the
cherubim, [c]shine forth!
2 Before [a]Ephraim, Benjamin, and
Manasseh,
Stir up Your strength,
And come *and* save us!

3 [a]Restore us, O God;
[b]Cause Your face to shine,
And we shall be saved!

4 O LORD God of hosts,
[a]How long will You be angry
Against the prayer of Your
people?
5 [a]You have fed them with the bread
of tears,
And given them tears to drink in
great measure.
6 You have made us a strife to our
neighbors,
And our enemies laugh among
themselves.

7 Restore us, O God of hosts;
Cause Your face to shine,
And we shall be saved!

8 You have brought [a]a vine out of
Egypt;
[b]You have cast out the [1]nations,
and planted it.
9 You prepared *room* for it,
And caused it to take deep
root,
And it filled the land.

12 [b]Ps. 74:10, 18, 22
13 [a]Ps. 74:1; 95:7 [b]Is. 43:21

PSALM 80

title [a]Ps. 45:title [1]Heb. *Shoshannim* [2]Heb. *Eduth*
1 [a][Ex. 25:20–22]; 1 Sam. 4:4; 2 Sam. 6:2 [b]Ps. 77:20 [c]Deut. 33:2
2 [a]Ps. 78:9, 67
3 [a]Lam. 5:21 [b]Num. 6:25; Ps. 4:6
4 [a]Ps. 79:5
5 [a]Ps. 42:3; Is. 30:20
8 [a][Is. 5:1, 7]; Jer. 2:21; Ezek. 15:6; 17:6; 19:10 [b]Ps. 44:2; Acts 7:45 [1]*Gentiles*
10 [a]Lev. 23:40 [1]Lit. *cedars of God*
11 [1]The Mediterranean [2]The Euphrates
12 [a]Is. 5:5; Nah. 2:2 [1]*walls* or *fences*
14 [a]Is. 63:15
15 [a][Is. 49:5]
16 [a][Ps. 39:11]
17 [a]Ps. 89:21

PSALM 81

title [a]Ps. 8:title [1]Heb. *Al Gittith*

10 The hills were covered with its
shadow,
And the [1]mighty cedars with its
[a]boughs.
11 She sent out her boughs to
[1]the Sea,
And her branches to [2]the River.

12 Why have You [a]broken down her
[1]hedges,
So that all who pass by the way
pluck her *fruit?*
13 The boar out of the woods
uproots it,
And the wild beast of the field
devours it.

14 Return, we beseech You, O God
of hosts;
[a]Look down from heaven and see,
And visit this vine
15 And the vineyard which Your
right hand has planted,
And the branch *that* You made
strong [a]for Yourself.
16 *It is* burned with fire, *it is* cut
down;
[a]They perish at the rebuke of Your
countenance.
17 [a]Let Your hand be upon the man
of Your right hand,
Upon the son of man *whom* You
made strong for Yourself.
18 Then we will not turn back from
You;
Revive us, and we will call upon
Your name.

19 Restore us, O LORD God of hosts;
Cause Your face to shine,
And we shall be saved!

PSALM 81

An Appeal for Israel's Repentance

To the Chief Musician. [a]On[1] an instrument of
Gath. A Psalm of Asaph.

SING aloud to God our strength;
Make a joyful shout to the God
of Jacob.
2 Raise a song and strike the
timbrel,
The pleasant harp with the lute.

80:1, 2 God is pictured as sitting on the mercy seat over the ark of the covenant, which was placed between two **cherubim** (1 Chr. 13:6). The three tribes mentioned followed next to the ark when Israel journeyed (Num. 2:17–24).
80:3 To shine is similar to our modern expression "to smile on us." This refrain is repeated in vv. 7 and 19, with the name of **God** (Hebrew *'Elohim, 'Elohim Sabaoth, Yahweh 'Elohim Sabaoth*) intensified each time.
80:7 Hosts is used to mean armies of men or angels.
80:11 Sea to **River** are symbols for the western and eastern boundaries of the nation of Israel.
80:18 Revive us: This prayer is based on the prayer concerning restoration voiced by Solomon (1 Kin. 8:33, 34).
81:1–5 This song was for the New Year and the Feast of Tabernacles in the autumn. Its first five verses are an introduction to an oration in which God speaks personally in the last 11 verses.

3 *Blow the trumpet at the time of
the New Moon,
At the full moon, on our solemn
feast day.
4 For [a]this *is* a statute for Israel,
A law of the God of Jacob.
5 This He established in Joseph *as*
a testimony,
When He went throughout the
land of Egypt,
[a]*Where* I heard a language I did
not understand.

6 "I removed his shoulder from the
burden;
His hands were freed from the
baskets.
7 [a]You called in trouble, and I
delivered you;
[b]I answered you in the secret place
of thunder;
I [c]tested you at the waters of
[1]Meribah. Selah

8 "Hear,[a] O My people, and I will
admonish you!
O Israel, if you will listen to
Me!
9 There shall be no [a]foreign god
among you;
Nor shall you worship any
foreign god.
10 [a]I *am* the LORD your God,
Who brought you out of the land
of Egypt;
[b]Open your mouth wide, and I will
*fill it.

11 "But My people would not heed My
voice,
And Israel would *have* [a]none of
Me.
12 [a]So I gave them over to [1]their own
stubborn heart,
To walk in their own counsels.

7 13 "Oh,[a] that My people would listen
to Me,
That Israel would walk in My
ways!
14 I would soon subdue their
enemies,
And turn My hand against their
adversaries.
15 [a]The haters of the LORD would
pretend submission to Him,
But their [1]fate would endure
forever.
16 He would [a]have fed them also
with [1]the finest of wheat;
And with honey [b]from the rock I
would have satisfied you."

PSALM 82

A Plea for Justice

A Psalm of Asaph.

GOD [a]stands in the *congregation
of [1]the mighty;
He judges among [b]the [2]gods.
2 How long will you judge unjustly,
And [a]show partiality to the
wicked? Selah
3 [1]Defend the poor and fatherless; 2
Do justice to the afflicted and
[a]needy.
4 Deliver the poor and needy;
Free *them* from the hand of the
wicked.

5 They do not know, nor do they
understand;
They walk about in darkness;
All the [a]foundations of the earth
are [1]unstable.

6 I said, [a]"You *are* [1]gods,
And all of you *are* children of the
Most High.
7 But you shall die like men,
And fall like one of the princes."

8 Arise, O God, judge the earth;
[a]For You shall inherit all nations.

PSALM 83

Prayer to Frustrate Conspiracy Against Israel

A Song. A Psalm of Asaph.

DO[a] not keep silent, O God!
Do not hold Your peace,

3 *See WW at Ps. 47:1.
4 [a]Lev. 23:24; Num. 10:10
5 [a]Deut. 28:49; Ps. 114:1; Jer. 5:15
7 [a]Ex. 2:23; 14:10; Ps. 50:15 [b]Ex. 19:19; 20:18 [c]Ex. 17:6, 7; Num. 20:13 [1]Lit. *Strife* or *Contention*
8 [a][Ps. 50:7]
9 [a][Ex. 20:3; Deut. 5:7; 32:12]; Ps. 44:20; [Is. 43:12]
10 [a]Ex. 20:2; Deut. 5:6 [b]Ps. 103:5 *See WW at Jer. 23:24.
11 [a]Ex. 32:1; Deut. 32:15
12 [a][Job 8:4; Acts 7:42; Rom. 1:24, 26] [1]*the dictates of their heart*
13 [a][Deut. 5:29; Is. 48:18]
15 [a]Rom. 1:30 [1]Lit. *time*
16 [a]Deut. 32:14 [b]Job 29:6 [1]Lit. *fat of wheat*

PSALM 82

1 [a][2 Chr. 19:6; Eccl. 5:8] [b]Ps. 82:6 [1]Heb. *El*, lit. *God* [2]Judges; Heb. *elohim*, lit. *mighty ones* or *gods* *See WW at Josh. 22:17.
2 [a][Deut. 1:17]; Prov. 18:5
3 [a][Deut. 24:17; Is. 11:4; Jer. 22:16] [1]*Vindicate*
5 [a]Ps. 11:3 [1]*moved*
6 [a]John 10:34 [1]Judges; Heb. *elohim*, lit. *mighty ones* or *gods*
8 [a]Ps. 2:8; [Rev. 11:15]

PSALM 83

1 [a]Ps. 28:1

81:3 The **trumpet** (Hebrew *shophar*) is a ram's horn. The **New Moon** was the beginning of the festival, and the **full moon** was its ending (the first day and the fifteenth day of the month, respectively). **Solemn,** as an adjective, is not in the Hebrew text. It should read simply "festival day," a time of happiness and joy.
81:6–16 This is a short version of the first half of the song of Moses in Deut. 32.
81:13–16 See section 7 of Truth-In-Action following Ps. 89.
82:1–8 This short psalm is a vindictive pronouncement against corrupt judges. **Gods:** In Canaanite culture, the heads of clans, tribes, or city-kings were highly venerated by following generations and often received the title of "gods."
82:3, 4 See section 2 of Truth-In-Action following Ps. 89.
82:6 This is quoted by Jesus in John 10:34 to defend His claim to sonship. Since all the Jewish leaders were called **gods, . . . children of the Most High,** certainly Jesus should be allowed the title of Son of God. It is also fitting that Jesus uses this psalm, which speaks of the corruption in leadership, since many religious leaders were corrupt at that time in history (Matt. 23). See note on John 10:34.

And do not be still, O God!
2 For behold, [a]Your enemies make a [1]tumult;
And those who hate You have [2]lifted up their head.
3 They have taken crafty counsel against Your people,
And consulted together [a]against Your sheltered ones.
4 They have said, "Come, and [a]let us cut them off from *being* a nation,
That the name of Israel may be remembered no more."

5 For they have consulted together with one [1]consent;
They [2]form a confederacy against You:
6 [a]The tents of Edom and the Ishmaelites;
Moab and the Hagrites;
7 Gebal, Ammon, and Amalek;
Philistia with the inhabitants of Tyre;
8 Assyria also has joined with them;
They have helped the children of Lot. Selah

9 Deal with them as *with* [a]Midian,
As *with* [b]Sisera,
As *with* Jabin at the Brook Kishon,
10 Who perished at En Dor,
[a]*Who* became *as* refuse on the earth.
11 Make their nobles like [a]Oreb and like Zeeb,
Yes, all their princes like [b]Zebah and Zalmunna,
12 Who said, "Let us take for ourselves
The pastures of God for a possession."

13 [a]O my God, make them like the whirling dust,
[b]Like the chaff before the wind!
14 As the fire burns the woods,
And as the flame [a]sets the mountains on fire,
15 So pursue them with Your tempest,
And frighten them with Your storm.
16 Fill their faces with shame,
That they may seek Your name, O LORD.
17 Let them be [1]confounded and dismayed *forever;
Yes, let them be put to shame and perish,
18 [a]That they may know that You, whose [b]name alone *is* the LORD,
Are [c]the Most High over all the earth.

2 [a]Ps. 81:15; Is. 17:12; Acts 4:25 [1]*uproar* [2]Exalted themselves
3 [a][Ps. 27:5]
4 [a]Esth. 3:6, 9; Jer. 11:19; 31:36
5 [1]Lit. *heart* [2]Lit. *cut a covenant*
6 [a]2 Chr. 20:1, 10, 11
9 [a]Num. 31:7; Judg. 7:22 [b]Judg. 4:15–24; 5:20, 21
10 [a]Zeph. 1:17
11 [a]Judg. 7:25 [b]Judg. 8:12–21
13 [a]Is. 17:13 [b]Job 21:18; Ps. 35:5; Is. 40:24; Jer. 13:24
14 [a]Ex. 19:18; Deut. 32:22
17 [1]*ashamed* *See WW at Mic. 4:5.
18 [a]Ps. 59:13 [b]Ex. 6:3 [c][Ps. 92:8]

PSALM 84

The Blessedness of Dwelling in the House of God

To the Chief Musician. [a]On[1] an instrument of Gath. A Psalm of the sons of Korah.

HOW [a]lovely [1]*is* Your tabernacle, O LORD of hosts!
2 [a]My soul longs, yes, even faints
For the courts of the LORD;
My heart and my flesh cry out for the living God.

3 Even the sparrow has found a home,
And the swallow a nest for herself,
Where she may lay her young—
Even Your altars, O LORD of hosts,
My King and my God.
4 Blessed *are* those who dwell in Your [a]house;
They will still be praising You. Selah

5 Blessed *is* the man whose strength *is* in You, 5
Whose heart *is* set on pilgrimage.
6 *As they* pass through the Valley [a]of [1]Baca,

PSALM 84
title [a]Ps. 8:title [1]Heb. *Al Gittith*
1 [a]Ps. 27:4; 46:4, 5 [1]*are Your dwellings*
2 [a]Ps. 42:1, 2
4 [a][Ps. 65:4]
6 [a]2 Sam. 5:22–25 [1]Lit. *Weeping*

83:6, 7 The list of small nations from **Edom** to **Amalek** were located on the eastern border of Israel; **Philistia** was southwest and **Tyre** northwest.
83:8 Assyria eventually became a much larger militaristic nation and was situated far northeast of Israel (modern Iraq). **The children of Lot** refers back to Moab and Ammon.
83:9–12 Deal with them: The psalmist recalls past victories of Israel recorded in Judg. 4, 5, 7, and 8, led by Deborah and Gideon.
83:18 The LORD (Hebrew *Yahweh*) is the sacred name of God, whose significance was revealed first to Moses (Ex. 6:2).
84:2 Just as the nation **longs** for the autumn rain at the end of a parched summer, so also the pilgrims coming to the Feast of Tabernacles in Jerusalem thirst for fellowship with **God** in the temple.
84:3 The worshiper, poetically, is envious of the **sparrow** who has free access, at any time, to the temple courtyard.
84:5 See section 5 of Truth-In-Action following Ps. 89.
84:6, 7 Baca is a type of balsam plant that can survive in dry conditions. The **Valley of Baca** is thought by some scholars to be the same as the Valley of Rephaim (2 Sam. 5:22–24). **The rain** is the early rain that begins to fall in the autumn and gives new life to sprouting plants and **strength** to men.

They make it a spring;
The rain also covers it with
[2]pools.
7 They go [a]from *strength to
strength;
[1]*Each one* [b]appears before God in
Zion.

8 O LORD God of hosts, hear my
prayer;
Give ear, O God of Jacob! Selah
9 [a]O God, behold our shield,
And look upon the face of Your
[1]anointed.*

10 For a day in Your courts *is* better
than a thousand.
I would rather [1]be a doorkeeper
in the house of my God
Than dwell in the tents of
wickedness.
11 For the LORD God *is* [a]a sun and
[b]shield;
The LORD will give *grace and
glory;
[c]No good *thing* will He withhold
From those who walk uprightly.

12 O LORD of hosts,
[a]Blessed *is* the man who trusts in
You!

PSALM 85

Prayer that the LORD Will Restore Favor to the Land

To the Chief Musician. A Psalm [a]of the sons of Korah.

LORD, You have been favorable to
Your land;
You have [a]brought back the
captivity of Jacob.
2 You have forgiven the iniquity of
Your people;
You have covered all their sin.
Selah
3 You have taken away all Your
wrath;
You have turned from the
fierceness of Your anger.

4 [a]Restore us, O God of our
salvation,
And cause Your anger toward us
to cease.

6 [2]Or *blessings*
7 [a]Prov. 4:18; Is. 40:31; John 1:16; 2 Cor. 3:18 [b]Ex. 34:23; Deut. 16:16 [1]LXX, Syr., Vg. *The God of gods shall be seen* *See WW at Zech. 4:6.
9 [a]Gen. 15:1 [1]Commissioned one, Heb. *messiah* *See WW at Dan. 9:25.
10 [1]*stand at the threshold*
11 [a]Is. 60:19, 20; Mal. 4:2; Rev. 21:23 [b]Gen. 15:1 [c]Ps. 34:9, 10 *See WW at Zech. 12:10.
12 [a][Ps. 2:12; 40:4]

PSALM 85

title [a]Ps. 42:title
1 [a]Ezra 1:11—2:1; Ps. 14:7; Jer. 30:18; 31:23; Ezek. 39:25; Hos. 6:11; Joel 3:1
4 [a]Ps. 80:3, 7
5 [a]Ps. 79:5
6 [a]Hab. 3:2
8 [1]*foolishness*
9 [a]Is. 46:13 [b]Hag. 2:7; Zech. 2:5; [John 1:14]
10 [a]Ps. 72:3; [Is. 32:17]; Luke 2:14
12 [a][Ps. 84:11; James 1:17]

PSALM 86

2 [1]Lit. *soul* *See WW at Job 10:12.
4 [a]Ps. 25:1; 143:8 [1]*Make glad*

5 [a]Will You be angry with us
forever?
Will You prolong Your anger to
all generations?
6 Will You not [a]revive us again,
That Your people may rejoice in
You?
7 Show us Your mercy, LORD,
And grant us Your salvation.

8 I will hear what God the LORD will
speak,
For He will speak peace
To His people and to His saints;
But let them not turn back to
[1]folly.
9 Surely [a]His salvation *is* near to
those who fear Him,
[b]That glory may dwell in our land.

10 Mercy and truth have met
together;
[a]Righteousness and peace have
kissed.
11 Truth shall spring out of the
earth,
And righteousness shall look
down from heaven.
12 [a]Yes, the LORD will give *what is*
good;
And our land will yield its
increase.
13 Righteousness will go before
Him,
And shall make His footsteps *our*
pathway.

PSALM 86

Prayer for Mercy, with Meditation on the Excellencies of the LORD

A Prayer of David.

BOW down Your ear, O LORD, hear
me;
For I *am* poor and needy.
2 *Preserve my [1]life, for I *am* holy;
You are my God;
Save Your servant who trusts in
You!
3 Be merciful to me, O Lord,
For I cry to You all day long.
4 [1]Rejoice the soul of Your servant,
[a]For to You, O Lord, I lift up my
soul.

84:10 Doorkeeper *means, literally,* "*stand at the door.*"
85:1 It may be that this poem of gratitude was written after the Babylonian **captivity.**
85:4 There was still work to be done when the exiles returned, thus the prayer to **restore** (Neh. 1:3).
85:8 I will hear introduces a response from **God** (Hab. 2:1). Today as then He speaks **peace** (John 14:27). **Folly** is not simply foolishness, but is used in the OT to mean evil, wickedness, and idolatry.
86:1–17 This is the only psalm in Book Three attributed to David, and it is unique in that David used the title *'Adonai* (Sovereign **Lord**) seven times, preferring it more often than *Yahweh,* the name of God.

5 For [a]You, Lord, *are* good, and
ready to forgive,
And abundant in mercy to all
those who call upon You.

KINGDOM DYNAMICS

86:5 Abundantly Forgiven, Abundantly Forgive, BROTHERLY LOVE. These words are basic, yet their impact is intended to be life-changing at both points: 1) in our receiving God's love and merciful forgiveness and 2) in our giving it just as we have received it. Two virtues—goodness and forgiveness—are attributes birthed by our heavenly Father and expected to be found in our own lives. He expects us to be like Him—to stand ready to forgive our brother's transgressions in the same abundance of mercy He shows. "Abundant" is from the Hebrew *rab,* meaning "aboundingly, exceedingly." God does not want us to portion out our mercy and forgiveness with teaspoons. He is looking for people who portion out their forgiveness and mercy with huge, unlimiting shovels.
(Ps. 15:3/Matt. 5:44) D.S.

6 Give ear, O LORD, to my prayer;
And attend to the voice of my
supplications.
7 In the day of my trouble I will call
upon You,
For You will answer me.

8 [a]Among the gods *there is* none like
You, O Lord;
Nor *are there any works* like
Your works.
9 All nations whom You have made
Shall come and worship before
You, O Lord,
And shall glorify Your name.
10 For You *are* great, and [a]do
wondrous things;
[b]You alone *are* God.

3 11 [a]Teach* me Your way, O LORD;
I will walk in Your truth;
[1]Unite my heart to fear Your
name.
12 I will praise You, O Lord my God,
with all my heart,
And I will glorify Your name
forevermore.
13 For great *is* Your mercy toward
me,
And You have delivered my soul
from the depths of [1]Sheol.

5 [a]Ps. 130:7; 145:9; [Joel 2:13]
8 [a][Ex. 15:11]; 2 Sam. 7:22; 1 Kin. 8:23; Ps. 89:6; Jer. 10:6
10 [a][Ex. 15:11] [b]Deut. 6:4; Is. 37:16; Mark 12:29; 1 Cor. 8:4
11 [a]Ps. 27:11; 143:8 [1]Give me singleness of heart *See WW at Ps. 32:8.
13 [1]The abode of the dead

14 O God, the proud have risen
against me,
And a mob of violent *men* have
sought my life,
And have not set You before
them.
15 But [a]You, O Lord, *are* a God full
of compassion, and gracious,
Longsuffering and abundant in
mercy and truth.

16 Oh, turn to me, and have mercy
on me!
Give Your strength to Your
servant,
And save the son of Your
maidservant.
17 Show me a **sign** for good,
That those who hate me may see
it and be ashamed,
Because You, LORD, have helped
me and comforted me.

WORD WEALTH

86:17 sign, *'ot (oat);* Strong's #226: A sign, token, visible illustration, portent, ensign, signpost; a miracle, a mighty deed or event. This noun occurs 78 times in the OT. The rainbow (Gen. 9:12–17), circumcision (Gen. 17:11), and the blood of the Passover lamb (Ex. 12:13) are visible illustrations of something that cannot be seen, that is, an agreement between God and His people. God struck Egypt 10 times; these miraculous events are called "signs" (Ex. 10:2). In this reference, David prays for a miracle, a token, or some sort of signboard, which his enemies can read loud and clear.

PSALM 87

The Glories of the City of God

A Psalm of the sons of Korah. A Song.

HIS foundation *is* in the holy
mountains.
2 [a]The LORD loves the gates of Zion
More than all the *dwellings of
Jacob.
3 [a]Glorious things are spoken of
you,
O city of God! Selah

4 "I will make mention of [1]Rahab
and Babylon to those who
know Me;

15 [a]Ex. 34:6; [Ps. 86:5]

PSALM 87

2 [a]Ps. 78:67, 68 *See WW at Is. 32:18.
3 [a]Is. 60:1
4 [1]Egypt

86:8 These **gods** are idols and myths that pagans call gods. David is not acquiescing to polytheism (1 Cor. 8:5, 6).
86:11 See section 3 of Truth-In-Action following Ps. 89.
86:11 Unite: That is, do not let the **heart** have many allegiances or distractions.
87:2 The **gates** are symbolic of security and strength. See Matt. 16:18 where the gates of hell do not prevail against the church.

Behold, O Philistia and Tyre, with Ethiopia:
'This *one* was born there.'"

5 And of Zion it will be said,
"This *one* and that *one* were born in her;
And the Most High Himself shall establish her."
6 The LORD will record,
When He [a]registers the peoples:
"This *one* was born there." Selah

7 Both the singers and the players on instruments *say,*
"All my springs *are* in you."

PSALM 88

A Prayer for Help in Despondency

A Song. A Psalm of the sons of Korah. To the Chief Musician. Set to "Mahalath Leannoth." A [1]Contemplation of [a]Heman the Ezrahite.

O LORD, [a]God of my salvation,
I have cried out day and night before You.
2 Let my prayer come before You;
[1]Incline Your ear to my cry.

3 For my soul is full of troubles,
And my life [a]draws near to the grave.
4 I am counted with those who [a]go[1] down to the pit;
[b]I am like a man *who has* no strength,
5 [1]Adrift among the dead,
Like the slain who lie in the grave,
Whom You remember no more,
And who are cut off from Your hand.

6 You have laid me in the lowest pit,
In darkness, in the depths.
7 Your wrath lies heavy upon me,
And You have afflicted *me* with all [a]Your waves. Selah
8 [a]You have [1]put away my acquaintances far from me;
You have made me an abomination to them;
[b]I *am* shut up, and I cannot get out;
9 My eye wastes away because of affliction.

[a]LORD, I have called daily upon You;
I have stretched out my hands to You.
10 Will You work wonders for the dead?
Shall [1]the dead arise *and* praise You? Selah
11 Shall Your lovingkindness be declared in the grave?
Or Your faithfulness in the place of destruction?
12 Shall Your wonders be known in the dark?
And Your righteousness in the land of forgetfulness?

13 But to You I have cried out, O LORD,
And in the morning my prayer comes before You.
14 LORD, why do You cast off my soul?
Why do You hide Your face from me?
15 I *have been* afflicted and ready to die from *my* youth;
I suffer Your terrors;
I am distraught.
16 Your fierce wrath has gone over me;
Your terrors have [1]cut me off.
17 They came around me all day long like water;
They engulfed me altogether.
18 [a]Loved one and friend You have put far from me,
And my acquaintances into darkness.

PSALM 89

Remembering the Covenant with David, and Sorrow for Lost Blessings

A [1]Contemplation of [a]Ethan the Ezrahite.

I WILL sing of the mercies of the LORD forever;
With my mouth will I make

6 [a]Is. 4:3

PSALM 88

title [a]1 Kin. 4:31; 1 Chr. 2:6 [1]Heb. *Maschil*
1 [a]Ps. 27:9; [Luke 18:7]
2 [1]Listen to
3 [a]Ps. 107:18
4 [a][Ps. 28:1] [b]Ps. 31:12 [1]Die
5 [1]Lit. *Free*
7 [a]Ps. 42:7
8 [a]Job 19:13, 19; Ps. 31:11; 142:4 [b]Lam. 3:7 [1]*taken away my friends*
9 [a]Ps. 86:3
10 [1]*shades, ghosts*
16 [1]*destroyed me*
18 [a]Job 19:13; Ps. 31:11; 38:11

PSALM 89

title [a]1 Kin. 4:31 [1]Heb. *Maschil*

87:6 Registers: See Heb. 12:23 where the church of the firstborn is registered in heaven.
88:title Some translate **Mahalath Leannoth** in the title as "in sickness or suffering" and **Ezrahite** as meaning "native-born." This is possibly a poem by the sons of Korah for Heman (1 Kin. 4:31), who was gravely ill with what may have been leprosy.
88:4 The **pit** is literally a cistern, used here as a symbol for the grave.
88:10–12 Dead: The soul overcome with bereavement often does not have the same perspective as the eye of faith.
88:13 Although oppressed, the psalmist remains persistent in **prayer** (vv. 1, 2, 9, 13). See Luke 18:7 for God's response to such persistence.
89:1–52 This is a messianic psalm reaffirming the Davidic covenant in which his Seed will reign. It shows that God is able to rescue His promise from the depths of the grave, if necessary, to fulfill it.

known Your *faithfulness to all generations.
2 For I have said, "Mercy shall be built up forever;
[a]Your faithfulness You shall establish in the very heavens."

3 "I[a] have *made a covenant with My chosen,
I have [b]sworn to My servant David:
4 'Your seed I will establish forever,
And build up your throne
[a]to all generations.'" Selah

5 And [a]the heavens will praise Your wonders, O LORD;
Your faithfulness also in the assembly of the saints.
6 [a]For who in the heavens can be compared to the LORD?
Who among the sons of the mighty can be likened to the LORD?
7 [a]God is greatly to be feared in the assembly of the saints,
And to be held in reverence by all *those* around Him.
8 O *LORD God of hosts,
Who *is* mighty like You, O LORD?
Your faithfulness also surrounds You.
9 [a]You rule the raging of the sea;
When its waves rise, You *still them.
10 [a]You have broken [1]Rahab in pieces, as one who is slain;
You have scattered Your enemies with Your mighty arm.

11 [a]The heavens *are* Yours, the earth also *is* Yours;
The world and all its fullness, You have founded them.
12 The north and the south, You have created them;
[a]Tabor and [b]Hermon rejoice in Your name.
13 You have a mighty arm;
Strong is Your hand, *and* high is Your right hand.
14 Righteousness and justice *are* the foundation of Your throne;
Mercy and truth go before Your face.

1 *See WW at Prov. 28:20.
2 [a][Ps. 119:89, 90]
3 [a]1 Kin. 8:16 [b]2 Sam. 7:11; 1 Chr. 17:10–12 *See WW at Ex. 34:27.
4 [a][2 Sam. 7:13; Is. 9:7; Luke 1:33]
5 [a][Ps. 19:1]
6 [a]Ps. 86:8; 113:5
7 [a]Ps. 76:7, 11
8 *See WW at Is. 12:2.
9 [a]Ps. 65:7; 93:3, 4; 107:29 *See WW at Ps. 63:3.
10 [a]Ex. 14:26–28; Ps. 87:4; Is. 30:7; 51:9 [1]Egypt
11 [a][Gen. 1:1; 1 Chr. 29:11]
12 [a]Josh. 19:22; Judg. 4:6; Jer. 46:18 [b]Deut. 3:8; Josh. 11:17; 12:1; Song 4:8
15 [a]Lev. 23:24; Num. 10:10; Ps. 98:6
17 [a]Ps. 75:10; 92:10; 132:17 [1]Strength
18 *See WW at Lev. 19:2.
19 [a]1 Kin. 11:34 [1]So with many Heb. mss.; MT, LXX, Tg., Vg. *holy ones* *See WW at 2 Chr. 32:32.
20 [a]1 Sam. 13:14; 16:1–12; Acts 13:22 *See WW at Is. 61:1.
21 [a]Ps. 80:17
22 [1]*Or exact usury from him*
25 [a]Ps. 72:8
26 [a]2 Sam. 7:14; [1 Chr. 22:10]; Jer. 3:19 [b]2 Sam. 22:47 *See WW at Ps. 68:5.
27 [a]Ex. 4:22; Ps. 2:7; Jer. 31:9; [Col. 1:15, 18] [b]Num. 24:7; [Ps. 72:11]; Rev. 19:16
28 [a]Is. 55:3

15 Blessed *are* the people who know the [a]joyful sound!
They walk, O LORD, in the light of Your countenance.
16 In Your name they rejoice all day long,
And in Your righteousness they are exalted.
17 For You *are* the glory of their strength,
And in Your favor our [1]horn is [a]exalted.
18 For our shield *belongs* to the LORD,
And our king to the *Holy One of Israel.

19 Then You spoke in a *vision to Your [1]holy one,
And said: "I have given help to *one who is* mighty;
I have exalted one [a]chosen from the people.
20 [a]I have found My servant David;
With My holy oil I have *anointed him,
21 [a]With whom My hand shall be established;
Also My arm shall strengthen him.
22 The enemy shall not [1]outwit him,
Nor the son of wickedness afflict him.
23 I will beat down his foes before his face,
And plague those who hate him.

24 "But My faithfulness and My mercy *shall be* with him,
And in My name his horn shall be exalted.
25 Also I will [a]set his hand over the sea,
And his right hand over the rivers.
26 He shall cry to Me, 'You *are* [a]my *Father,
My God, and [b]the rock of my salvation.'
27 Also I will make him [a]*My* firstborn,
[b]The highest of the kings of the earth.
28 [a]My mercy I will keep for him forever,

89:10 Rahab is another name for Egypt, one of Israel's old **enemies.**
89:12 Tabor and Hermon are mountains that are personified as rejoicing as part of God's creation.
89:15 Blessed: Those who have learned to worship in joy enter into God's presence and find happiness.
89:17 The parallel structure of this verse shows that **horn** is a metaphor for **strength.**
89:20 Paul refers to this verse, with its messianic hope, in Acts 13:22, 23 (**I have found**).
89:26 My Father were words constantly on Jesus' lips (see Matt. 11:27).
89:27 This verse is applied to Christ, who was the **firstborn** from the dead by the Resurrection (Col. 1:15–18).

And My covenant shall stand firm with him.
29 His seed also I will make *to endure* forever,
[a]And his throne [b]as the days of heaven.

30 "If[a] his sons [b]forsake My law
And do not walk in My judgments,
31 If they [1]break My statutes
And do not keep My commandments,
32 Then I will punish their transgression with the rod,
And their iniquity with stripes.
33 [a]Nevertheless My lovingkindness I will not [1]utterly take from him,
Nor [2]allow My faithfulness to fail.
34 My covenant I will not break,
Nor [a]alter the word that has gone out of My lips.
35 Once I have sworn [a]by My holiness;
I will not lie to David:
36 [a]His seed shall endure forever,
And his throne [b]as the sun before Me;
37 It shall be established forever like the moon,
Even *like* the faithful witness in the sky." Selah

38 But You have [a]cast off and [b]abhorred,[1]
You have been furious with Your [2]anointed.*
39 You have renounced the covenant of Your servant;
[a]You have [1]profaned his crown *by casting it* to the ground.
40 You have broken down all his hedges;
You have brought his [1]strongholds to ruin.

29 [a][1 Kin. 2:4; Is. 9:7]; Jer. 33:17 [b]Deut. 11:21
30 [a][2 Sam. 7:14] [b]Ps. 119:53
31 [1]*profane*
33 [a]2 Sam. 7:14, 15 [1]Lit. *break off* [2]Lit. *deal falsely with My faithfulness*
34 [a][Num. 23:19]; Jer. 33:20–22
35 [a][1 Sam. 15:29]; Amos 4:2; [Titus 1:2]
36 [a][Luke 1:33] [b]Ps. 72:17
38 [a][1 Chr. 28:9] [b]Deut. 32:19 [1]*rejected* [2]Commissioned one, Heb. *messiah* *See WW at Dan. 9:25.
39 [a]Ps. 74:7; Lam. 5:16 [1]*defiled*
40 [1]*fortresses*
41 [a]Ps. 80:12
44 [1]*splendor* or *brightness*
47 [a]Ps. 90:9 [b]Ps. 62:9
48 [a][Eccl. 3:19] [1]*experience death* [2]Or *Sheol*
49 [a][2 Sam. 7:15]; Jer. 30:9; Ezek. 34:23 [b]Ps. 54:5
50 [a]Ps. 69:9, 19
51 [a]Ps. 74:10, 18, 22 [1]Commissioned one, Heb. *messiah*
52 [a]Ps. 41:13

41 All who pass by the way [a]plunder him;
He is a reproach to his neighbors.
42 You have exalted the right hand of his adversaries;
You have made all his enemies rejoice.
43 You have also turned back the edge of his sword,
And have not sustained him in the battle.
44 You have made his [1]glory cease,
And cast his throne down to the ground.
45 The days of his youth You have shortened;
You have covered him with shame. Selah

46 How long, LORD?
Will You hide Yourself forever?
Will Your wrath burn like fire?
47 Remember how short my time [a]is;
For what [b]futility have You created all the children of men?
48 What man can live and not [1]see [a]death?
Can he deliver his life from the power of [2]the grave? Selah

49 Lord, where *are* Your former lovingkindnesses,
Which You [a]swore to David [b]in Your truth?
50 Remember, Lord, the reproach of Your servants—
[a]*How* I bear in my bosom *the reproach of* all the many peoples,
51 [a]With which Your enemies have reproached, O LORD,
With which they have reproached the footsteps of Your [1]anointed.

52 [a]Blessed *be* the LORD forevermore!
Amen and Amen.

89:38 Cast off: That there is a deeper fulfillment than the immediate circumstances of the Israelite poet is evidenced by his bewilderment in vv. 38–51 at the crown's being cast off.
89:45 The emotional struggle and inner turmoil may prophetically reflect the rejection and dishonor shown to Christ with its **reproach** (v. 41), shortening of His life, and seeming loss of all hope of reigning.
89:49 Truth, in Hebrew, is steadfastness.
89:52 This doxology closes the collection of psalms called Book Three.

TRUTH-IN-ACTION through PSALMS (Book Three: Psalms 73—89)

Letting the LIFE of the Holy Spirit Bring Faith's Works Alive in You!

Truth Psalms Teaches	Text	**Action** Psalms Invites
1 A Step to Knowing God's Ways We must know that God honors His name and will see to it that it is exalted.	79:9	**Understand** that God saves and blesses His people because of His name, that is, His honor, and not because of their works of righteousness.
2 Guidelines for Growing in Godliness Godliness adopts God's concerns for the widow, the orphan, the alien, the poor, and the needy because these are foremost in His heart as is care and training of our children. Also, the godly person resorts to God when troubled, rather than to the arm of the flesh.	82:3, 4	**Understand** that God prioritizes ministry to the destitute, poor, and needy. **Do not fail** to help them when it is in your power to do so.
	78:4–8	**Do not fail** to teach your children and train them up in the way of the Lord.
	73:21, 22	**Avoid** letting a grieved heart become an embittered spirit.
	73:16, 17	When bewildered, **spend time** in God's presence to gain proper understanding and perspective.
3 Steps to Dynamic Devotion God desires the hearts of all of us to be fully and singly devoted to Him. It takes commitment to develop such a devotion: One must continue to choose God above all else.	86:11	**Seek God** continually for an undivided heart and the fear of the Lord.
	76:11	**Understand** that vows are an acceptable and biblical means to making spiritual advances in difficult areas.
4 Keys to Wise Living Growing in wisdom means learning to discern the times by applying the principles of God's Word. It also means refusing to seek for the honor that can only come from God.	75:6, 7	**Know** that all promotion or exaltation comes from the Lord.
	74:9	**Understand** that when we reject God's way, the blessing and guidance of His Spirit may be withdrawn, leaving us in spiritual drought.
5 Steps in Developing Humility The humble person, acknowledging his need for continual growth, never develops an unteachable spirit.	84:5	**Set your heart** on pilgrimage: **Humble yourself** and **accept** that you will "never arrive," that is, never stop needing to learn and grow.
6 A Key Lesson in Faith Never underestimate the power of personal testimony in persuading men to take bolder steps in faith.	77:10–20	**Think about** and **testify to** God's mighty workings among His people in order to encourage them and build their faith.
7 Guidelines to Gaining Victory We can be our own worst enemies in the fight for spiritual victory. Even stronger than any external opposition we face may be negative influences in our own lives.	81:13–16	**Pray for release** from disobedient and stubborn attitudes that hinder God's hand in granting you spiritual victory.

BOOK FOUR
Psalms 90–106

PSALM 90

The Eternity of God, and Man's Frailty

A Prayer [a]of Moses the man of God.

LORD, [a]You have been our
[1]dwelling place in all
generations.
2 [a]Before the mountains were
brought forth,
Or ever You [1]had formed the
earth and the world,
Even from everlasting to
everlasting, You *are* God.

3 You turn man to destruction,
And say, [a]"Return, O children of
men."
4 [a]For a thousand years in Your
sight
Are like yesterday when it is
past,
And *like* a watch in the night.
5 You carry them away *like* a flood;
[a]*They are* like a sleep.
In the morning [b]they are like
grass *which* grows up:
6 In the morning it flourishes and
grows up;
In the evening it is cut down and
withers.

7 For we have been consumed by
Your anger,
And by Your wrath we are
terrified.
8 [a]You have set our iniquities before
You,
Our [b]secret *sins* in the light of
Your countenance.
9 For all our days have passed
away in Your wrath;
We finish our years like a sigh.
10 The days of our lives *are* seventy
years;
And if by reason of strength *they*
are eighty years,
Yet their boast *is* only labor and
sorrow;
For it is soon cut off, and we fly
away.
11 Who knows the power of Your
anger?
For as the fear of You, *so is* Your
wrath.
12 [a]So teach *us* to number our
days,
That we may gain a heart of
wisdom.

3

13 Return, O LORD!
How long?
And [a]have compassion on Your
servants.
14 Oh, satisfy us early with Your
mercy,
[a]That we may rejoice and be glad
all our days!
15 Make us glad according to the
days *in which* You have
afflicted us,
The years *in which* we have seen
evil.
16 Let [a]Your work appear to Your
servants,
And Your *glory to their children.
17 [a]And let the beauty of the LORD our
God be upon us,
And [b]establish the work of our
hands for us;
Yes, establish the work of our
hands.

PSALM 91

Safety of Abiding in the Presence of God

HE [a]who dwells in the secret place
of the Most High
Shall abide [b]under the shadow of
the **Almighty.**

PSALM 90
title [a]Deut. 33:1
1 [a][Deut. 33:27; Ezek. 11:16] [1]LXX, Tg., Vg. *refuge*
2 [a]Job 15:7; [Prov. 8:25, 26] [1]Lit. *gave birth to*
3 [a]Gen. 3:19; Job 34:14, 15
4 [a]2 Pet. 3:8
5 [a]Ps. 73:20 [b]Is. 40:6
8 [a]Ps. 50:21; [Jer. 16:17] [b]Ps. 19:12; [Eccl. 12:14]
12 [a]Deut. 32:29; Ps. 39:4
13 [a]Ex. 32:12; Deut. 32:36
14 [a]Ps. 85:6
16 [a][Deut. 32:4]; Hab. 3:2
*See WW at Ps. 8:5.
17 [a]Ps. 27:4 [b]Is. 26:12

PSALM 91
1 [a]Ps. 27:5; 31:20; 32:7 [b]Ps. 17:8; Is. 25:4; 32:2

90:1–17 This psalm begins a series of Sabbath songs (Ps. 90—99) intended for public worship.
90:2 Moses mentions the infinity of **God** by comparison, to give a point of reference to this psalm's main topic: life's brevity.
90:3 Destruction: That is, man returns to dust (Gen. 3:19).
90:4 Hebrew time was divided into watches, which consisted of three hours each (see Judg. 7:19).
90:5 Three metaphors underline the brevity of life stated in the previous verse: a sudden flash **flood, sleep** with no awareness of time, and withered **grass.**
90:8 Sins: The fallen nature of man is the ultimate reason for life's brevity. See Rom. 6:23.
90:10 If one's life is extended 10 years, it merely contains more **labor** and **sorrow** and flies away like a forgotten dream (Job 20:8).
90:11 Anger is a divine response to the irresponsible use of time by men. We should consider with **fear** our accountability to God for all our actions in this life.
90:12 See section 3 of Truth-In-Action following Ps. 106.
90:13–17 Contemplation of this topic drives the psalmist to his knees in prayer.
90:13 The **LORD** respects a man's contrition and repentance and will show **compassion.**
90:14 Early: In the morning. That is, "Let there be a new day of mercy."
90:16 Work: Acts of mercy and salvation. See Deut. 32:4.
90:17 Beauty: Pleasantness, sweetness, or delight.
91:1, 2 There are three titles for **God** in these verses besides the personal name of **the LORD** (*Yahweh*): *'Elyon* (**the Most High**), *Shaddai* (**the Almighty**), and *'Elohim* (here meaning "the Sublime God").

WORD WEALTH

91:1 Almighty, *shadday* (shad-*dye*); Strong's #7706: All-powerful; when it appears as *'El Shadday,* it is "God Almighty." This name occurs about 50 times in the OT. It was a name by which God was known to the patriarchs (Gen. 17:1; Ex. 6:3). Some scholars trace its origin to the verb *shadad,* meaning "mighty, unconquerable." Others relate its origin to the Akkadian word for "mountain," indicating God's greatness, strength, or His everlasting nature. Another explanation is that *Shadday* is a compound of the particle *sheh* (which or who) and *day* (sufficient). *Sheh-day* or *Shadday* is therefore the all-sufficient God, eternally capable of being all that His people need.

2 [a]I will say of the LORD, "*He is* my
*refuge and my fortress;
My God, in Him I will trust."

3 Surely [a]He shall deliver you from
the snare of the [1]fowler
And from the perilous pestilence.
4 [a]He shall cover you with His
feathers,
And under His wings you shall
*take refuge;
His truth *shall be your* shield and
[1]buckler.
5 [a]You shall not be afraid of the
terror by night,
Nor of the arrow *that* flies by day,
6 *Nor* of the pestilence *that* walks
in darkness,
Nor of the destruction *that* lays
waste at noonday.

7 A thousand may fall at your side,
And ten thousand at your right
hand;
But it shall not come near you.
8 Only [a]with your eyes shall you
look,
And see the reward of the wicked.

4 9 Because you have made the LORD,
who is [a]my refuge,
Even the *Most High, [b]your
dwelling place,
10 [a]No *evil shall befall you,
Nor shall any plague come near
your dwelling;

2 [a]Ps. 142:5 *See WW at Prov. 14:26. **3** [a]Ps. 124:7; Prov. 6:5 [1]One who catches birds in a trap or snare **4** [a]Ps. 17:8 [1]A small shield *See WW at Zeph. 3:12. **5** [a][Job 5:19; Ps. 112:7; Is. 43:2] **8** [a]Ps. 37:34; Mal. 1:5 **9** [a]Ps. 91:2 [b]Ps. 90:1 *See WW at Gen. 14:18. **10** [a][Prov. 12:21] *See WW at Ps. 5:4.

KINGDOM DYNAMICS

91:9, 10 A Promise of Divinely Protected Health, DIVINE HEALING. This passage promises protection from sickness as a blessing of the redeemed life. The word "plague" (Hebrew *nehgah*) is used of something "inflicted" on a body, and specifically was used to refer to "spots of leprosy." Here the Lord describes an abiding defense against "inflicted" disease, but the promise is conditioned upon making the Lord our true refuge and habitation. How can we do this? Two Hebrew words in v. 9 give us the answer. The word *makhseh,* translated "refuge," means "a shelter," "a place of trust," and derives from the root *khawsaw,* meaning "to flee for protection," "to confide in." *Maween,* translated "dwelling place," indicates "a retreat." It comes from the root *'onah,* which describes the security of intimately "dwelling together as in marriage." These key words elaborate a principle. When we make the Lord our refuge and habitation by trusting Him—taking our cares, fears and needs to Him; by seeking His counsel, spending times of refreshing with Him; and by loving Him and walking closely with Him through every day, we enter into a sheltered place of promise regarding health. This truth safeguards against making prayer for healing only a recourse for emergencies, though some do, in sickness or emergency, find repentance and renewed fellowship with God and discover His mercy.

(Job 42:10–13/Ps. 103:3) N.V.

11 [a]For He shall give His *angels
charge over you,
To keep you in all your ways.
12 In *their* hands they shall
[1]bear you up,
[a]Lest you [2]dash your foot against
a stone.

11 [a]Ps. 34:7; Matt. 4:6; Luke 4:10; [Heb. 1:14] *See WW at 2 Chr. 32:21. **12** [a]Matt. 4:6; Luke 4:11 [1]*lift* [2]*strike*

KINGDOM DYNAMICS

91:11, 12 Guardian Angels Watch Over Us, ANGELS. Each of us has our own private guardian angels. Dr. Billy Graham, observing the plural in this text, concluded that each believer must have at least two angels whose assigned duty it is to protect them. Ps. 91:4 speaks of God "covering us with His feathers" and

(*cont. on next page*)

91:3–13 Deliver: Ancient Jewish commentators considered these verses descriptive of demonic attacks. Demonology was a large part of Hebrew theology at the time of Christ's advent (Matt. 9:34). It was mentioned in the Great Commission (Mark 16:15–18).
91:3 Pestilence: Attacks that come like a plague. The metaphor is significant to the Hebrews since plagues of locusts and disease were common in the Middle East (Joel 1:4).
91:9–13 See section 4 of Truth-In-Action following Ps. 106.
91:11, 12 This was quoted by Satan to mislead Jesus in His wilderness temptation by attempting to coax Him into irresponsible behavior (Matt. 4:6).

(*cont. from preceding page*)
mentions that we are under His "wings." Since God has no feathers or wings, some have suggested that these feathers and wings speak of our guardian angels' wings, which protectively cover us to keep us from falling, getting lost, or stumbling into unknown dangers in the unseen realm of the spirit.
(Acts 8:26/Ex. 3:2, 4) M.H.

13 You shall *tread upon the lion and the cobra,
The young lion and the serpent you shall trample underfoot.

14 "Because he has set his love upon Me, therefore I will deliver him;
I will [1]set him on high, because he has [a]known My name.
15 He shall [a]call upon Me, and I will answer him;
I *will be* [b]with him in trouble;
I will deliver him and honor him.
16 With [1]long life I will satisfy him,
And show him My salvation."

13 *See WW at Deut. 11:25.
14 [a][Ps. 9:10] [1]*exalt him*
15 [a]Job 12:4; Ps. 50:15 [b]Is. 43:2
16 [1]Lit. *length of days*

PSALM 92

Praise to the LORD *for His Love and Faithfulness*

A *Psalm. A Song for the Sabbath day.

It is [a]good to give thanks to the LORD,
And to sing praises to Your name, O Most High;
2 To [a]declare Your lovingkindness in the morning,
And Your faithfulness every night,
3 [a]On an instrument of ten strings,
On the lute,
And on the harp,
With harmonious sound.
4 For You, LORD, have made me glad through Your work;
I will triumph in the works of Your hands.

5 [a]O LORD, how great are Your works!
[b]Your thoughts are very deep.
6 [a]A senseless man does not know,
Nor does a fool understand this.
7 When [a]the wicked [1]spring up like grass,
And when all the workers of iniquity flourish,
It is that they may be destroyed forever.

8 [a]But You, LORD, *are* on high forevermore.
9 For behold, Your enemies, O LORD,
For behold, Your enemies shall perish;
All the workers of iniquity shall [a]be scattered.

10 But [a]my [1]horn* You have exalted like a wild ox;
I have been [b]anointed with fresh oil.
11 [a]My eye also has seen *my desire* on my enemies;
My ears hear *my desire* on the wicked
Who rise up against me.

12 [a]The righteous shall flourish like a palm tree,
He shall grow like a cedar in Lebanon.
13 Those who are planted in the house of the LORD
Shall flourish in the courts of our God.
14 They shall still bear fruit in old age;
They shall be [1]fresh and [2]flourishing,
15 To declare that the LORD is upright;
[a]*He is* my rock, and [b]*there is* no unrighteousness in Him.

PSALM 92
title *See WW at Ps. 3:title.
1 [a]Ps. 147:1
2 [a]Ps. 89:1
3 [a]1 Chr. 23:5
5 [a]Ps. 40:5; [Rev. 15:3] [b]Ps. 139:17, 18; [Is. 28:29; Rom. 11:33, 34]
6 [a]Ps. 73:22
7 [a]Job 12:6; Ps. 37:1, 2; Jer. 12:1, 2; [Mal. 3:15] [1]*sprout*
8 [a][Ps. 83:18]
9 [a]Ps. 68:1
10 [a]Ps. 89:17 [b]Ps. 23:5 [1]Strength *See WW at Ezek. 29:21.
11 [a]Ps. 54:7
12 [a]Num. 24:6; Ps. 52:8; Jer. 17:8; Hos. 14:5, 6
14 [1]Full of oil or sap, lit. *fat* [2]*green*
15 [a][Deut. 32:4] [b][Rom. 9:14]

PSALM 93

The Eternal Reign of the LORD

THE [a]LORD *reigns, He is clothed with majesty;
The LORD is clothed,

PSALM 93
1 [a]Ps. 96:10 *See WW at 2 Sam. 8:15.

91:13 See Luke 10:19 and Rom. 16:20.
91:14–16 Because: God, in this section, responds to the psalmist. The best prayer is dialogue, not monologue.
91:15 Although the psalmist (and reader) are not promised total immunity from calamities, the Lord assures him that *He will be* present with those who **call upon** Him and that He **will deliver and honor** them.
92:2 Every **morning** and **every night** animal sacrifices were offered with praise under the Mosaic system.
92:3 The use of **instruments** in worship services has the full sanction of the teaching of Scripture.
92:6 In OT writings, the **fool** is not merely a simpleton but a decadent sinner.
92:9 Be scattered (literally, "shall scatter themselves"): Evil, by its very nature, disintegrates because of its weaknesses and then self-destructs.
92:10 The **horn** is a symbol for strength and positions of prominence and security.
93:1–5 The thought of this royal poem is that after other things are swept away by **floods** of adversity (v. 3), hostile nations, or evil powers, the **LORD** remains **established** (v. 2), and His Word stands **sure** (v. 5).

[b]He has girded Himself with strength.
Surely the world is established, so that it cannot be [1]moved.
2 [a]Your throne *is* established from of old;
You *are* from everlasting.

KINGDOM DYNAMICS

93:2 Inviting God's Rule, WORSHIP AND THE KINGDOM. "Your throne is established from of old." The notion that kingdom advance "establishes" God's throne needs clearer understanding. It is foolish to think man could add to or diminish the power or glory of God's kingdom rule. However, it is equally unwise to overlook the responsible place the redeemed have been given. We are to welcome the kingdom and administrate situations on Earth by inviting the overarching might of God's Spirit to move into difficult or impossible circumstances and transform them. This is done by praise: "In everything [not "for" everything] give thanks [fill the situation with praise], for this is God's will for you" (1 Thess. 5:17). Thus we welcome the overruling power of God's presence into any situation we face. Pray, "Your kingdom come, Your will be done—Here." Then, set up a place for God's throne to enter by filling your life's settings with praise. As Gideon's trumpeters (Judg. 7:17–22) and Jehoshaphat's choir (2 Chr. 20:20–22) confounded their enemies and paved the way for the victory the Lord said He would give, so praise brings the same entry of the King's kingdom today.

(Ps. 22:3/Rev. 1:5, 6) J.W.H.

3 The floods have [1]lifted up, O LORD,
The floods have lifted up their voice;
The floods lift up their waves.
4 [a]The LORD on high *is* mightier
Than the noise of many waters,
Than the mighty waves of the sea.

5 Your testimonies are very sure;
Holiness adorns Your house,
O LORD, [1]forever.

PSALM 94

God the Refuge of the Righteous

O LORD God, [a]to whom vengeance belongs—
O God, to whom vengeance belongs, shine forth!
2 Rise up, O [a]Judge of the earth;
[1]Render punishment to the proud.
3 LORD, [a]how long will the wicked,
How long will the wicked triumph?

4 They [a]utter speech, *and* speak insolent things;
All the workers of iniquity boast in themselves.
5 They break in pieces Your people, O LORD,
And afflict Your heritage.
6 They slay the widow and the stranger,
And murder the fatherless.
7 [a]Yet they say, "The LORD does not see,
Nor does the God of Jacob [1]understand."

8 Understand, you senseless among the people;
And *you* fools, when will you be wise?
9 [a]He who planted the ear, shall He not hear?
He who formed the eye, shall He not see?
10 He who [1]instructs the [2]nations, shall He not correct,
He who teaches man knowledge?
11 The LORD [a]knows the thoughts of man,
That they *are* futile.

12 Blessed *is* the man whom You [a]instruct, O LORD, 3
And *teach out of Your law,
13 That You may give him [1]rest from the days of adversity,
Until the pit is dug for the wicked.
14 For the LORD will not [1]cast off His people,
Nor will He forsake His inheritance.
15 But judgment will return to righteousness,
And all the upright in heart will follow it.

16 Who will rise up for me against the evildoers?
Who will stand up for me against the workers of iniquity?

1 [b]Ps. 65:6 [1]shaken
2 [a]Ps. 45:6; [Lam. 5:19]
3 [1]*raised up*
4 [a]Ps. 65:7
5 [1]Lit. *for length of days*

PSALM 94

1 [a]Deut. 32:35; [Is. 35:4; Nah. 1:2; Rom. 12:19]
2 [a][Gen. 18:25] [1]*Repay with*
3 [a][Job 20:5]
4 [a]Ps. 31:18; Jude 15
7 [a]Job 22:13; Ps. 10:11 [1]*pay attention*
9 [a][Ex. 4:11; Prov. 20:12]
10 [1]*disciplines* [2]*Gentiles*
11 [a]Job 11:11; 1 Cor. 3:20
12 [a][Deut. 8:5; Job 5:17; Ps. 119:71; Prov. 3:11, 12; Heb. 12:5, 6] *See WW at Is. 48:17.
13 [1]*relief*
14 [1]*abandon*

93:5 That God's **house** (temple) is one of **holiness** is reaffirmed by Paul in 1 Cor. 3:17.
94:1–23 In this petition for help, the **people** as a nation (v. 5) cry out in vv. 1–15, and an individual **soul** (v. 17) cries out in vv. 16–23.
94:12–15 See section 3 of Truth-In-Action following Ps. 106.
94:15 Judgment (justice) delayed is *not* justice denied from God's perspective.

17 Unless the LORD *had been* my help,
My soul would soon have settled in silence.
18 If I say, "My foot slips,"
Your mercy, O LORD, will hold me up.
4 19 In the multitude of my anxieties within me,
Your comforts delight my soul.

20 Shall [a]the throne of iniquity, which devises evil by law,
Have fellowship with You?
21 They gather together against the life of the righteous,
And condemn [a]innocent blood.
22 But the LORD has been my defense,
And my God the rock of my *refuge.
23 He has brought on them their own iniquity,
And shall [1]cut them off in their own wickedness;
The LORD our God shall cut them off.

PSALM 95

A Call to Worship and Obedience

OH come, let us sing to the LORD!
Let us shout joyfully to the Rock of our salvation.
2 Let us come before His presence with **thanksgiving;**
Let us shout joyfully to Him with [a]psalms.

WORD WEALTH

95:2 thanksgiving, ***todah*** **(toh-*dah*);** Strong's #8426: Thanks, thanksgiving, adoration, praise. This word is derived from the verb *yadah,* "to give thanks, to praise." The root of *yadah* is *yad,* "hand." Thus, to thank or praise God is "to lift or extend one's hands" in thanks to Him. *Todah* appears more than 30 times in the OT, a dozen of these in the Psalms (50:23; 100:4). *Todah* is translated "sacrifice of praise" in Jer. 33:11.

3 For [a]the LORD *is* the great God,
And the great King above all gods.
4 [1]In His hand *are* the deep places of the earth;
The heights of the hills *are* His also.
5 [a]The sea *is* His, for He made it;
And His hands formed the dry *land.*

6 Oh come, let us *worship and bow down; 2
Let [a]us kneel before the LORD our Maker.
7 For He *is* our God,
And [a]we *are* the people of His pasture,
And the sheep [1]of His hand.

[b]Today, if you will hear His voice:
8 "Do not harden your hearts, as in the [1]rebellion,
[a]As *in* the day of [2]trial in the wilderness,
9 When [a]your fathers *tested Me;
They tried Me, though they [b]saw My work.
10 For [a]forty years I was [1]grieved with *that* generation,
And said, 'It *is* a people who go astray in their hearts,
And they do not know My ways.'
11 So [a]I swore in My wrath,
'They shall not enter My *rest.' "

PSALM 96

A Song of Praise to God Coming in Judgment

OH, [a]sing* to the LORD a new song!
Sing to the LORD, all the earth.
2 Sing to the LORD, bless His name;
Proclaim the good news of His salvation from day to day.
3 Declare His *glory among the [1]nations,
His *wonders among all peoples.

4 For [a]the LORD *is* great and [b]greatly to be praised;
[c]He *is* to be feared above all gods.

---

20 [a]Amos 6:3 **21** [a][Ex. 23:7]; Ps. 106:38; [Prov. 17:15]; Matt. 27:4 **22** *See WW at Prov. 14:26. **23** [1]*destroy them*

PSALM 95

2 [a]Eph. 5:19; James 5:13
3 [a][Ps. 96:4; 1 Cor. 8:5, 6] **4** [1]In His possession **5** [a]Gen. 1:9, 10; Jon. 1:9 **6** [a]2 Chr. 6:13; Dan. 6:10; [Phil. 2:10] *See WW at Ps. 99:5. **7** [a]Ps. 79:13 [b]Heb. 3:7–11, 15; 4:7 [1]Under His care **8** [a]Ex. 17:2–7; Num. 20:13 [1]Or *Meribah,* lit. *Strife, Contention* [2]Or *Massah,* lit. *Trial, Testing* **9** [a]Ps. 78:18; [1 Cor. 10:9] [b]Num. 14:22 *See WW at Ps. 78:41. **10** [a]Acts 7:36; 13:18; Heb. 3:10, 17 [1]*disgusted* **11** [a]Num. 14:23, 28–30; Deut. 1:35; Heb. 4:3, 5 *See WW at Is. 28:12.

PSALM 96

1 [a]1 Chr. 16:23–33 *See WW at Judg. 5:3. **3** [1]*Gentiles* *See WW at Is. 60:1. • See WW at Judg. 13:19. **4** [a]Ps. 145:3 [b]Ps. 18:3 [c]Ps. 95:3

94:16, 17 For good men to keep **silence** in the passing of unjust law (v. *20*) *is unconscionable (Matt.* 5:13).
94:19 See section 4 of Truth-In-Action following Ps. 106.
95:2, 6 An important key to entering into the **presence** of God is to come humbly with abundant praise.
95:6–11 See section 2 of Truth-In-Action following Ps. 106.
95:9 See Ex. 17:7 where "Massah" and "Meribah" mean "Tempted" and "Contention."
95:11 The satisfying result of being in God's presence by means of praise is **rest.** Grumbling, complaining, and unbelief destroy that rest (Heb. 3:7–15).
96:1–13 This psalm is included in the jubilant praise King David offered when he brought the ark of the covenant to Jerusalem (1 Chr. 16:23–33).
96:4, 5 **Idols:** The root of this word means "worthless"; all the gods are worthless, but **the LORD** (*Yahweh*) is **great.**

5 For [a]all the gods of the peoples *are* idols,
[b]But the LORD made the heavens.
6 Honor and *majesty *are* before Him;
Strength and [a]beauty *are* in His sanctuary.

7 [a]Give[1] to the LORD, O families of the peoples,
Give to the LORD glory and strength.
8 [1]Give to the LORD the glory *due* His name;
Bring an offering, and come into His courts.
9 Oh, worship the LORD [a]in the beauty of holiness!
Tremble before Him, all the earth.

10 Say among the [1]nations,
[a]"The LORD reigns;
The world also is firmly established,
It shall not be [2]moved;
[b]He shall judge the peoples righteously."

11 [a]Let the heavens rejoice, and let the earth be glad;
[b]Let the sea roar, and [1]all its fullness;
12 Let the field be joyful, and all that *is* in it.
Then all the trees of the woods will rejoice before the LORD.
13 For He is coming, for He is coming to judge the earth.
[a]He shall judge the world with righteousness,
And the peoples with His truth.

PSALM 97

A Song of Praise to the Sovereign LORD

THE LORD [a]reigns;
Let the earth rejoice;
Let the multitude of [1]isles be glad!

2 [a]Clouds and darkness surround Him;
[b]Righteousness and justice *are* the foundation of His throne.
3 [a]A fire goes before Him,
And burns up His enemies round about.
4 [a]His lightnings light the world;
The earth sees and trembles.
5 [a]The mountains melt like wax at the presence of the LORD,
At the presence of the Lord of the whole earth.
6 [a]The heavens declare His righteousness,
And all the peoples see His glory.

7 [a]Let all be put to shame who serve carved images,
Who boast of idols.
[b]Worship Him, all *you* gods.
8 Zion hears and is glad,
And the daughters of Judah rejoice
Because of Your judgments, O LORD.
9 For You, LORD, *are* [a]most high above all the earth;
[b]You are exalted far above all gods.

10 You who **love** the LORD, [a]hate evil!
[b]He preserves the souls of His saints;
[c]He delivers them out of the hand of the wicked.

WORD WEALTH

97:10 love, *'ahab* (ah-*hahv*); Strong's #157: To love, to have affection for someone; to like, to be a friend. *'Ahab* is remarkably similar to the English word "love" in that its range of meanings covers the same ideas. *'Ahab* can refer to loving God, loving one's friend, romantic love, love of ideals, love of pleasures, and so on. The participial form, *'oheb,* refers to a friend or lover. The first mention of love in the Bible is in Gen. 22:2, where Abraham loved his son Isaac.

11 [a]Light is sown for the righteous,
And gladness for the upright in heart.
12 [a]Rejoice in the LORD, you righteous,
[b]And give thanks [1]at the remembrance of [2]His holy name.

5 [a]1 Chr. 16:26; [Jer. 10:11] [b]Ps. 115:15; Is. 42:5
6 [a]Ps. 29:2 *See WW at Ps. 8:5.
7 [a]1 Chr. 16:28, 29; Ps. 29:1, 2 [1]*Ascribe*
8 [1]*Ascribe*
9 [a]1 Chr. 16:29; 2 Chr. 20:21; Ps. 29:2
10 [a]Ps. 93:1; 97:1; [Rev. 11:15; 19:6] [b]Ps. 67:4 [1]*Gentiles* [2]*shaken*
11 [a]Ps. 69:34; Is. 49:13 [b]Ps. 98:7 [1]*all that is in it*
13 [a][Rev. 19:11]

PSALM 97

1 [a][Ps. 96:10] [1]Or *coastlands*
2 [a]Ex. 19:9; Deut. 4:11; 1 Kin. 8:12; Ps. 18:11 [b][Ps. 89:14]
3 [a]Ps. 18:8; Dan. 7:10; Hab. 3:5
4 [a]Ex. 19:18
5 [a]Ps. 46:6; Amos 9:5; Mic. 1:4; Nah. 1:5
6 [a]Ps. 19:1
7 [a][Ex. 20:4] [b][Heb. 1:6]
9 [a]Ps. 83:18 [b]Ex. 18:11; Ps. 95:3; 96:4
10 [a][Ps. 34:14; Prov. 8:13; Amos 5:15; Rom. 12:9] [b]Ps. 31:23; 145:20; Prov. 2:8 [c]Ps. 37:40; Jer. 15:21; Dan. 3:28
11 [a]Job 22:28; Ps. 112:4; Prov. 4:18
12 [a]Ps. 33:1 [b]Ps. 30:4 [1]Or *for the memory* [2]Or *His holiness*

96:13 The apostle Paul confirms this link of judgment with **righteousness** and adds that Jesus will be the Judge (Acts 17:31).
97:3–6 The imagery depicted here is taken from the account in Ex. 19 when God appeared to Moses with the Law.
97:3 God as **fire** is used by the author of Heb. to encourage endurance in the Christian walk (Heb. 12:29).
97:7 ***You gods:*** The songwriter is not condescending to polytheism, but is exalting the Lord above everything men may call gods (96:5). See an example of such supremacy in 1 Sam. 5:3.

PSALM 98

A Song of Praise to the LORD *for His Salvation and Judgment*

A *Psalm.

OH, [a]sing to the LORD a new song!
For He has [b]done marvelous things;
His right hand and His holy arm have gained Him the victory.
2 [a]The LORD has made known His salvation;
[b]His righteousness He has revealed in the sight of the [1]nations.
3 He has remembered His mercy and His faithfulness to the house of Israel;
[a]All the ends of the earth have seen the salvation of our God.

4 Shout joyfully to the LORD, all the earth;
Break forth in song, rejoice, and *sing praises.
5 Sing to the LORD with the harp,
With the harp and the sound of a psalm,
6 With trumpets and the sound of a horn;
Shout joyfully before the LORD, the King.

7 Let the sea roar, and all its fullness,
The world and those who dwell in it;
8 Let the rivers clap *their* hands;
Let the hills be joyful together before the LORD,
9 [a]For He is coming to judge the earth.
With righteousness He shall judge the world,
And the peoples with [1]equity.

PSALM 99

Praise to the LORD *for His Holiness*

THE LORD reigns;
Let the peoples tremble!
[a]He dwells *between* the *cherubim;
Let the earth be [1]moved!
2 The LORD *is* great in Zion,
And He *is* *high above all the peoples.
3 Let them praise Your great and awesome name—
[1]He *is* holy.

4 The King's strength also loves justice;
You have established equity;
You have executed justice and righteousness in Jacob.
5 Exalt the LORD our God,
And **worship** at His footstool—
He *is* holy.

WORD WEALTH

99:5 worship, ***shachah*** (shah-*chah*); Strong's #7812: To bow, to stoop; to bow down before someone as an act of submission or reverence; to worship; to fall or bow down when paying homage to God. The primary meaning is "to make oneself low." In the present reference, *shachah* is used in contrast to exaltation: exalt the Lord (lift Him up high) and worship (bow yourselves down low before Him) at the place of His feet.

6 Moses and Aaron were among His priests,
And Samuel was among those who [a]called upon His name;
They called upon the LORD, and He answered them.
7 He spoke to them in the cloudy pillar;
They kept His testimonies and the [1]ordinance He gave them.

8 You answered them, O LORD our God;
You were to them God-Who-Forgives,
Though You took vengeance on their deeds.
9 Exalt the LORD our God,
And worship at His holy hill;
For the LORD our God *is* holy.

PSALM 98

title *See WW at Ps. 3:title.
1 [a]Ps. 33:3; Is. 42:10 [b]Ex. 15:11; Ps. 77:14
2 [a]Is. 52:10; [Luke 1:77; 2:30, 31] [b]Is. 62:2; Rom. 3:25 [1]*Gentiles*
3 [a][Is. 49:6]; Luke 3:6; [Acts 13:47; 28:28]
4 *See WW at Ps. 149:3.
9 [a][Ps. 96:10, 13] [1]*uprightness*

PSALM 99

1 [a]Ex. 25:22; 1 Sam. 4:4; Ps. 80:1 [1]*shaken* *See WW at Ex. 25:18.
2 *See WW at Ps. 18:46.
3 [1]Or *It*
6 [a]1 Sam. 7:9; 12:18
7 [1]*statute*

98:1–9 This **song** of victory begins and ends with the same phrases as Ps. 96, *and here it celebrates* God's merciful restoration. In these expanding stanzas, **Israel** (vv. 1–3), all the people of the **earth** (vv. 4–6), and then all of nature (vv. 7–9) are exhorted to join in praise.

99:1–9 This hymn to holiness is marked by three stanzas, each of which ends with a declaration that God ***is* holy** (vv. 3, 5, 9).

99:1 He dwells: God spoke to Moses and the high priests from the mercy seat on top of the ark of the covenant which was between two winged **cherubim** (Ex. 25:18–22).

99:8 Though **God forgives,** there are consequences of sin, lest man forget how offensive it is to God and how harmful it is to mankind (Ex. 34:6, 7).

99:9 The **holy hill** is the temple mount in Jerusalem.

PSALM 100

A Song of Praise for the LORD's Faithfulness to His People

[a]A Psalm of Thanksgiving.

MAKE [a]a joyful shout to the LORD,
[1]all you lands!
2 **Serve** the LORD with gladness;
Come before His presence with singing.

WORD WEALTH

100:2 serve, *'abad* (ah-*vahd*); Strong's #5647: To work for, serve, do labor for someone; to be a servant; to worship. From this verbal root comes *'ebed,* "servant," "slave," or "laborer." "Servant" is generally someone who acts at the bidding of a superior. The most significant bearer of this designation is the messianic "Servant of the Lord" in Is. *'Abad* appears in several names, among which are Obed-Edom ("Servant of Edom"), Abed-Nego ("Servant of Nego"), and Obadiah ("Servant of Yah"). Ps. 35:27 illustrates how much God values and is kindly disposed to His servants. Unlike human overlords and masters, God is deeply concerned with the total well-being of each of His servants.

3 Know that the LORD, He *is* God;
[a]*It is* He *who* has made us, and [1]not we ourselves;
[b]*We are* His people and the sheep of His pasture.

4 [a]Enter into His gates with *thanksgiving,
And into His courts with **praise.**
Be thankful to Him, *and* bless His name.

WORD WEALTH

100:4 praise, *tehillah* (te-hil-*lah*, or in the plural, te-hil-*lim*); Strong's #8416: A celebration, a lauding of someone praiseworthy; the praise or exaltation of God; praises, songs of admiration. The noun *tehillah* comes from the verb *halal,* which means "to praise, celebrate, and laud." The Hebrew title of the Book of Psalms is *Tehillim,* literally the Book of Praises.

PSALM 100
title [a]Ps. 145:title
1 [a]Ps. 95:1 [1]Lit. *all the earth*
3 [a]Job 10:3, 8; Ps. 119:73; 139:13, 14; [Eph. 2:10] [b]Ps. 95:7; [Is. 40:11]; Ezek. 34:30, 31 [1]So with Kt., LXX, Vg.; Qr., many Heb. mss., Tg. *we are His*
4 [a]Ps. 66:13; 116:17–19 *See WW at Ps. 95:2.
5 [a]Ps. 136:1

PSALM 101
1 *See WW at Ps. 149:3.
2 [a]1 Kin. 11:4 [1]*blameless*
3 [a]Ps. 97:10 [b]Josh. 23:6 [1]*worthless*
4 [a][Ps. 119:115]
5 [a]Prov. 6:17
6 [1]*blameless*
7 [1]Lit. *be established*

The Book of Psalms was actually the Psalter or songbook for worship events in the temple in Jerusalem. Suitable for prayer or recitation, but especially designed for singing, the Psalms provide the means for eager hearts to express their praises to Israel's Holy One.

5 For the LORD *is* good;
[a]His mercy *is* everlasting,
And His truth *endures* to all generations.

PSALM 101

Promised Faithfulness to the LORD

A Psalm of David.

I WILL sing of mercy and justice;
To You, O LORD, I will *sing praises.

2 I will behave wisely in a [1]perfect way.
Oh, when will You come to me?
I will [a]walk within my house with a perfect heart.

3 I will set nothing [1]wicked before my eyes; 5
[a]I hate the work of those [b]who fall away;
It shall not cling to me.
4 A perverse heart shall depart from me;
I will not [a]know wickedness.

5 Whoever secretly slanders his neighbor,
Him I will destroy;
[a]The one who has a haughty look and a proud heart,
Him I will not endure.

6 My eyes *shall be* on the faithful of the land,
That they may dwell with me;
He who walks in a [1]perfect way,
He shall serve me.
7 He who works deceit shall not dwell within my house;
He who tells lies shall not [1]continue in my presence.

100:1–5 This poetic gem sets forth a key to a successful spiritual life: entering into God's presence by means of dynamic **praise,** which includes **singing, gladness, thanksgiving,** and worship.
100:3 Not we ourselves: or translate, "and we are His." "Not" and "His" sound alike in Hebrew.
100:4 Arrogant intrusion into the **courts** of the King of the universe is inappropriate.
100:5 For: The summons to praise is based on these three valid reasons.
101:1–8 An "oath of office" is what some consider an appropriate summary for this psalm of David, for it deals with the way an official should **behave** (v. 2).
101:3 See section 5 of Truth-In-Action following Ps. 106.
101:3 Wicked: The Hebrew word is *belial.*

8 [a]Early I will destroy all the wicked
of the land,
That I may cut off all the evildoers
[b]from the city of the LORD.

PSALM 102

The LORD's Eternal Love

A Prayer of the afflicted, [a]when he is overwhelmed and pours out his complaint before the LORD.

HEAR my prayer, O LORD,
And let my cry come to You.
2 [a]Do not hide Your face from me
in the day of my trouble;
Incline Your ear to me;
In the day that I call, answer me
speedily.

3 For my days [1]are [a]consumed like
smoke,
And my bones are burned like a
hearth.
4 My heart is stricken and withered
like grass,
So that I forget to eat my bread.
5 Because of the sound of my
groaning
My bones cling to my [1]skin.
6 I am like a pelican of the
wilderness;
I am like an owl of the desert.
7 I lie awake,
And am like a sparrow alone on
the housetop.

8 My enemies reproach me all day
long;
Those who deride me swear an
oath against me.
9 For I have eaten ashes like bread,
And mingled my drink with
weeping,
10 Because of Your indignation and
Your wrath;
For You have lifted me up and
cast me away.
11 My days *are* like a shadow that
lengthens,
And I wither away like grass.

12 But You, O LORD, shall endure
forever,
And the remembrance of Your
name to all generations.

8 [a][Ps. 75:10]; Jer. 21:12 [b]Ps. 48:2, 8

PSALM 102

title [a]Ps. 61:2
2 [a]Ps. 27:9; 69:17
3 [a]James 4:14 [1]Lit. *end in*
5 [1]*flesh*
15 [a]1 Kin. 8:43 [1]*Gentiles*
16 [a][Is. 60:1, 2] *See WW at Zech. 1:16.
17 [a]Neh. 1:6; Ps. 22:24
18 [a]Deut. 31:19; [Rom. 15:4; 1 Cor. 10:11] [b]Ps. 22:31
19 [a]Deut. 26:15; Ps. 14:2
20 [a]Ps. 79:11 *See WW at Jer. 40:4.
21 [a]Ps. 22:22 *See WW at Ps. 100:4.
22 [a][Is. 2:2, 3; 49:22, 23; 60:3]; Zech. 8:20–23
23 [a]Job 21:21
24 [a][Ps. 39:13]; Is. 38:10 [b]Job 36:26; [Ps. 90:2]; Hab. 1:12
25 [a][Gen. 1:1; Neh. 9:6; Heb. 1:10–12]
26 [a]Is. 34:4; 51:6; Matt. 24:35; [2 Pet. 3:7, 10–12]; Rev. 20:11 [1]*continue*

13 You will arise *and* have mercy on
Zion;
For the time to favor her,
Yes, the set time, has come.
14 For Your servants take pleasure
in her stones,
And show favor to her dust.
15 So the [1]nations shall [a]fear the
name of the LORD,
And all the kings of the earth
Your glory.
16 For the LORD shall *build up Zion;
[a]He shall appear in His glory.
17 [a]He shall regard the prayer of the
destitute,
And shall not despise their
prayer.

18 This will be [a]written for the
generation to come,
That [b]a people yet to be created
may praise the LORD.
19 For He [a]looked down from the
height of His sanctuary;
From heaven the LORD viewed the
earth,
20 [a]To hear the groaning of the
prisoner,
To *release those appointed to
death,
21 To [a]declare the name of the LORD
in Zion,
And His *praise in Jerusalem,
22 [a]When the peoples are gathered
together,
And the kingdoms, to serve the
LORD.

23 He weakened my strength in the
way;
He [a]shortened my days.
24 [a]I said, "O my God,
Do not take me away in the midst
of my days;
[b]Your years *are* throughout all
generations.
25 [a]Of old You laid the foundation of
the earth,
And the heavens *are* the work of
Your hands.
26 [a]They will perish, but You will
[1]endure;
Yes, they will all grow old like a
garment;
Like a cloak You will change
them,

101:8 Early: Late in his life, as well, King David gave to Solomon instructions for dealing with evil men in **the city** (1 Kin. 2:5–9). Only in the "New Jerusalem" will this principle be fully carried out (Rev. 21:27).

102:11 Grass is a common biblical symbol for life's fleeting moments (James 1:10, 11).

102:18 Paul the apostle leaned heavily on the idea that OT writings were **written** for the benefit of the **generation to come** (Rom. 15:4; 1 Cor. 10:11).

102:25–27 You laid the foundation: This is quoted by the writer of Heb. to show the permanence of Jesus, the Son of God, over the angels (Heb. 1:10–12).

And they will be changed.
27 But [a]You *are* the same,
And Your years will have no end.
28 [a]The children of Your servants will continue,
And their descendants will be established before You."

27 [a][Is. 41:4; 43:10; Mal. 3:6; Heb. 13:8]; James 1:17
28 [a]Ps. 69:36

PSALM 103

Praise for the LORD'S *Mercies*

A Psalm of David.

BLESS [a]the LORD, O my soul;
And all that is within me, *bless*
His holy name!
4 2 *Bless the LORD, O my soul,
And forget not all His benefits:
3 [a]Who **forgives** all your iniquities,
Who [b]heals all your diseases,

WORD WEALTH

103:3 forgives, *salach* (sah-*lahch*); Strong's #5545: To forgive, pardon; spare someone; to relieve someone of the burden of their offense. This verb and its derivatives occur 50 times in the OT. In every occurrence God does the forgiving; never does *salach* represent a man's forgiving anyone. This alone explains the shock of Jesus' listeners when they heard Him say "your sins are forgiven" (Luke 5:20). They responded, "Who can forgive sins but God alone?" (Luke 5:21). These scribes knew that forgiveness is God's prerogative. In Is. 55:7, *salach* is intensified by a helping verb: "He will abundantly pardon." Jer. 33:8 proclaims God's eagerness to forgive His people.

KINGDOM DYNAMICS

103:3 God's Saving and Healing Benefit, DIVINE HEALING. This is a definite OT promise of bodily healing based upon the character of Yahweh as the Healer. It is clear that the dimension of healing promised here is specifically to include physical wholeness. The text reinforces the healing covenant, since the Hebrew word *tachawloo* (diseases) is from the same root (*chawlah*) as the word for "disease" in Ex. 15:26 (*makhaleh*). Further, the words for "heal" are the same in both passages (Hebrew *rapha'*), the distinct meaning involving the idea of mending or curing. The two texts form a strong bond (Deut. 19:15; 2 Cor. 13:1). These two verses bear witness from the OT that the Lord not only forgives iniquities; He heals our diseases. If under the former covenant bodily healing was pointedly included with the Father's many other benefits, we can rejoice and rest in faith. The New Covenant "glory" exceeds everything of the Old (2 Cor. 3:7–11), and we can be certain that God, in Christ, has made a complete provision for the well-being of our total person.

(Ps. 91:9, 10/Ps. 107:20) N.V.

PSALM 103
1 [a]Ps. 104:1, 35
2 *See WW at Ps. 145:2.
3 [a]Ps. 130:8; Is. 33:24 [b][Ex. 15:26]; Ps. 147:3; [Is. 53:5]; Jer. 17:14

4 Who *redeems your life from destruction,
[a]Who crowns you with lovingkindness and tender mercies,
5 Who satisfies your mouth with good *things,*
So that [a]your youth is renewed like the eagle's.

6 The LORD executes righteousness
And justice for all who are oppressed.
7 [a]He made known His ways to Moses,
His acts to the children of Israel.
8 [a]The LORD *is* merciful and gracious,
Slow to *anger, and abounding in mercy.
9 [a]He will not always strive *with us,*
Nor will He keep *His anger* forever.
10 [a]He has not dealt with us according to our sins,
Nor punished us according to our iniquities.

11 For as the heavens are high above the earth,
So great is His mercy toward those who fear Him;
12 As far as the east is from the west,
So far has He [a]removed our *transgressions from us.
13 [a]As a *father *pities *his* children,
So the LORD pities those who fear Him.
14 For He [1]knows our frame;
He remembers that we *are* dust.

15 *As for* man, [a]his days *are* like grass;
As a flower of the field, so he flourishes.

4 [a][Ps. 5:12] *See WW at Is. 52:9.
5 [a][Is. 40:31]
7 [a]Ex. 33:12–17; Ps. 147:19
8 [a][Ex. 34:6, 7; Num. 14:18]; Deut. 5:10; Neh. 9:17; Ps. 86:15; Jer. 32:18; Jon. 4:2; James 5:11 *See WW at Judg. 10:7.
9 [a][Ps. 30:5; Is. 57:16]; Jer. 3:5; [Mic. 7:18]
10 [a][Ezra 9:13; Lam. 3:22]
12 [a][2 Sam. 12:13; Is. 38:17; 43:25; Zech. 3:9; Heb. 9:26] *See WW at Ezek. 18:31.
13 [a]Mal. 3:17 *See WW at Ps. 68:5. • See WW at Hos. 2:23.
14 [1]Understands our constitution
15 [a]Is. 40:6–8; James 1:10, 11; 1 Pet. 1:24

103:2–5 See section 4 of Truth-In-Action following Ps. 106.
103:8 See Ex. 34:6. David has studied the Law faithfully, and it has become second nature for him to incorporate quotes about God's **merciful and gracious** character from it into his own songs.
103:13 In contrast to the vastness of the merciful dealings of God, David returns to emphasize the closeness and sensitive intimacy of God in His fatherly role.
103:14 That man's **frame** (literally, "form") is **dust** refers to creation (Gen. 2:7).
103:15 Grass is a common metaphor used in the Bible for life's brevity. See Is. 40:6–8.

16 [a]For the wind passes over it, and
it is [1]gone,
And [b]its place remembers it no
more.
17 But the mercy of the LORD *is* from
everlasting to everlasting
On those who fear Him,
And His righteousness to
children's children,
18 [a]To such as keep His *covenant,
And to those who remember
His commandments to do
them.

19 The LORD has established His
throne in heaven,
And [a]His kingdom rules over all.

20 [a]Bless the LORD, you His angels,
Who excel in strength, who
[b]do His word,
Heeding the voice of His word.
21 Bless the LORD, all *you* His hosts,
[a]*You* [1]ministers of His, who do His
pleasure.

KINGDOM DYNAMICS

103:20, 21 Fivefold Ministry of Angels, ANGELS. These verses show God's purpose for angels. Angels exist to serve God in five ways: 1) to "bless the LORD" (in worship and service); 2) to "do His word" (concerning activities on Earth); 3) to heed the voice of God's word (as it is spoken through the saints on Earth); 4) to minister on God's behalf (as described in Heb. 1:14); and 5) to do God's pleasure (as His hosts are at His direction). (*/Judg. 13:6) M.H.

22 Bless the LORD, all His works,
In all places of His dominion.

Bless the LORD, O my soul!

PSALM 104

Praise to the Sovereign LORD for His Creation and Providence

BLESS [a]the LORD, O my soul!

O LORD my God, You are very
great:
You are clothed with honor and
majesty,
2 Who cover *Yourself* with light as
with a garment,
Who stretch out the heavens like
a curtain.

3 [a]He lays the beams of His upper
chambers in the waters,
Who makes the clouds His
chariot,
Who walks on the wings of the
wind,
4 Who makes His angels spirits,
His [1]ministers* a flame of fire.

5 *You who* [1]laid the foundations of
the earth,
So *that* it should not be moved
forever,
6 You [a]covered it with the deep as
with a garment;
The waters stood above the
mountains.
7 At Your rebuke they fled;
At the voice of Your thunder they
hastened away.
8 [1]They went up over the mountains;
They went down into the valleys,
To the place which You founded
for them.
9 You have [a]set a boundary that
they may not pass over,
[b]That they may not return to cover
the earth.

10 He sends the springs into the
valleys;
They flow among the hills.
11 They give drink to every beast of
the field;
The wild donkeys quench their
thirst.
12 By them the birds of the heavens
have their home;
They sing among the branches.
13 [a]He waters the hills from His
upper chambers;
The earth is satisfied with
[b]the fruit of Your works.

14 [a]He causes the grass to grow for
the cattle,
And vegetation for the service of
man,

16 [a][Is. 40:7] [b]Job 7:10 [1]*not* **18** [a][Deut. 7:9]; Ps. 25:10 *See WW at Gen. 17:7. **19** [a][Ps. 47:2; Dan. 4:17, 25] **20** [a]Ps. 148:2 [b][Matt. 6:10] **21** [a][Heb. 1:14] [1]*servants*

PSALM 104

1 [a]Ps. 103:1

3 [a][Amos 9:6] **4** [1]*servants* *See WW at 1 Chr. 15:2. **5** [1]Lit. *founded the earth upon her bases* **6** [a]Gen. 1:6 **8** [1]Or *The mountains rose up; the valleys sank down* **9** [a]Job 26:10; Ps. 33:7; [Jer. 5:22] [b]Gen. 9:11–15 **13** [a]Ps. 147:8 [b]Jer. 10:13 **14** [a]Gen. 1:29

103:19–22 This song of gratitude began in the sickroom of despair and ends in the **throne** *room of divine splendor.*
104:1–35 Bless the LORD: In this creation hymn the composer draws upon common observations of nature that other nations, such as Egypt, also took note of, with one exception: the psalmist attributes them all to the correct source of creation, the Lord (v. 24). See the Egyptian poem, Hymn to Aton (14th century B.C.), and John 1:3.
104:4 This is quoted in Heb. 1:7 to show that angels are created beings inferior to Jesus.
104:5–9 The Earth was originally covered with **waters** which receded to allow dry land to appear (Gen. 1:2).
104:12 That the **birds** and other animals are sustained by the intricate design of the Lord is reemphasized in the NT (Matt. 6:26) to inspire our faith to look to God for our daily provision.

That he may bring forth [b]food
from the earth,
15 And [a]wine *that* makes glad the
heart of man,
Oil to make *his* face shine,
And bread *which* strengthens
man's heart.
16 The trees of the LORD are full *of
sap,*
The cedars of Lebanon which He
planted,
17 Where the birds make their
nests;
The stork has her home in the fir
trees.
18 The high hills *are* for the wild
goats;
The cliffs are a *refuge for the
[a]rock[1] badgers.

19 [a]He appointed the moon for
*seasons;
The [b]sun knows its going down.
20 [a]You make darkness, and it is
night,
In which all the beasts of the
forest creep about.
21 [a]The young lions *roar after their
prey,
And seek their food from God.
22 *When* the sun rises, they gather
together
And lie down in their dens.
23 Man goes out to [a]his work
And to his labor until the evening.

24 [a]O LORD, how manifold are Your
works!
In wisdom You have made them
all.
The earth is full of Your
[b]possessions—
25 This great and wide sea,
In which *are* innumerable
teeming things,
Living things both small and
great.
26 There the ships sail about;
There is that [a]Leviathan[1]
Which You have [2]made to play
there.

27 [a]These all wait for You,
That You may give *them* their
food in due season.

14 [b]Job 28:5
15 [a]Judg. 9:13; Ps. 23:5; Prov. 31:6; Eccl. 10:19
18 [a]Lev. 11:5 [1]*rock hyraxes* *See WW at Prov. 14:26.
19 [a]Gen. 1:14 [b]Job 38:12; Ps. 19:6 *See WW at Num. 9:2.
20 [a][Ps. 74:16; Is. 45:7]
21 [a]Job 38:39 *See WW at Joel 3:16.
23 [a]Gen. 3:19
24 [a]Ps. 40:5; Prov. 3:19; [Jer. 10:12]; 51:15 [b]Ps. 65:9
26 [a]Job 41:1; Is. 27:1 [1]A large sea creature of unknown identity [2]Lit. *formed*
27 [a]Job 36:31; Ps. 136:25
29 [a]Job 34:15; [Eccl. 12:7]
30 [a]Is. 32:15 *See WW at Gen. 1:1.
31 [a]Gen. 1:31; Prov. 8:31
32 [a]Hab. 3:10 [b]Ex. 19:18; Ps. 144:5
33 [a]Ps. 63:4
34 [a]Ps. 19:14
35 [a]Ps. 37:38 [1]Heb. *Hallelujah* *See WW at 1 Chr. 23:30.

PSALM 105

1 [a]1 Chr. 16:8–22, 34; Ps. 106:1; Is. 12:4 [b]Ps. 145:12
2 [a]Ps. 119:27
4 [a]Ps. 27:8
5 [a]Ps. 77:11

28 *What* You give them they gather
in;
You open Your hand, they are
filled with good.
29 You hide Your face, they are
troubled;
[a]You take away their breath, they
die and return to their dust.
30 [a]You send forth Your Spirit, they
are *created;
And You renew the face of the
earth.

31 May the glory of the LORD endure
forever;
May the LORD [a]rejoice in His
works.
32 He looks on the earth, and it
[a]trembles;
[b]He touches the hills, and they
smoke.

33 [a]I will sing to the LORD as long as
I live;
I will sing praise to my God while
I have my being.
34 May my [a]meditation be sweet to 5
Him;
I will be glad in the LORD.
35 May [a]sinners be consumed from
the earth,
And the wicked be no more.

Bless the LORD, O my soul!
[1]Praise* the LORD!

PSALM 105

The Eternal Faithfulness of the LORD

OH, [a]give thanks to the LORD!
Call upon His name;
[b]Make known His deeds among
the peoples!
2 Sing to Him, sing psalms to Him;
[a]Talk of all His wondrous works!
3 Glory in His holy name;
Let the hearts of those rejoice
who seek the LORD!
4 Seek the LORD and His strength;
[a]Seek His face evermore!
5 [a]Remember His marvelous works
which He has done,
His wonders, and the judgments
of His mouth,

104:15 Wine, olive **oil,** and **bread** (wheat) are the three main staples of Israel, and this list is repeated throughout the OT.
104:24 God is not part of nature as pagans conceived their gods to be. He is above nature and separate from it, just as a worker is distinct from his **works.**
104:34 See section 5 of Truth-In-Action following Ps. 106.
105:1–45 His deeds: This song and the next one (Ps. 106) relate a brief history of the rise of the Israelite nation from Abraham (v. 6).
105:1–15 Give thanks: This stanza parallels the song David prepared for Asaph and the musicians when the ark of the covenant was brought to Jerusalem (1 Chr. 16:8–22).

6 O seed of Abraham His servant,
You children of Jacob, His chosen
ones!

7 He *is* the LORD our God;
[a]His judgments *are* in all the earth.
8 He [a]remembers His covenant
forever,
The word *which* He commanded,
for a thousand generations,
9 [a]*The covenant* which He made
with Abraham,
And His oath to Isaac,
10 And confirmed it to Jacob for a
statute,
To Israel *as* an everlasting
covenant,
11 Saying, [a]"To you I will give the
land of Canaan
As the allotment of your
inheritance,"
12 [a]When they were few in number,
Indeed very few, [b]and strangers
in it.

13 When they went from one nation
to another,
From *one* kingdom to another
people,
14 [a]He permitted no one to do them
wrong;
Yes, [b]He rebuked kings for their
sakes,
15 *Saying,* "Do not touch My
anointed ones,
And do My *prophets no harm."

16 Moreover [a]He called for a famine
in the land;
He destroyed all the [b]provision of
bread.
17 [a]He sent a man before them—
Joseph—*who* [b]was sold as a
slave.
18 [a]They hurt his feet with fetters,
[1]He was laid in irons.
19 Until the time that his word came
to pass,
[a]The word of the LORD tested him.
20 [a]The king sent and *released him,
The ruler of the people let him go
free.
21 [a]He made him lord of his house,
And ruler of all his possessions,
22 To [1]bind his princes at his
pleasure,
And teach his elders wisdom.

23 [a]Israel also came into Egypt,
And Jacob dwelt [b]in the land of
Ham.
24 [a]He increased His people greatly,
And made them stronger than
their enemies.
25 [a]He turned their heart to hate His
people,
To deal craftily with His servants.

26 [a]He sent Moses His servant,
And Aaron whom He had chosen.
27 They [a]performed His signs
among them,
And *wonders in the land of Ham.
28 He sent darkness, and made *it*
dark;
And they did not rebel against His
word.
29 [a]He turned their waters into blood,
And killed their fish.
30 [a]Their land abounded with frogs,
Even in the chambers of their
kings.
31 [a]He spoke, and there came swarms
of flies,
And lice in all their territory.
32 [a]He gave them hail for rain,
And flaming fire in their land.
33 [a]He struck their vines also, and
their fig trees,
And splintered the trees of their
territory.
34 [a]He spoke, and locusts came,
Young locusts without number,
35 And ate up all the vegetation in
their land,
And devoured the fruit of their
ground.
36 [a]He also [1]destroyed all the
firstborn in their land,
[b]The first of all their strength.

37 [a]He also brought them out with
silver and gold,
And *there was* none feeble
among His tribes.
38 [a]Egypt was glad when they
departed,
For the fear of them had fallen
upon them.
39 [a]He spread a cloud for a covering,
And fire to give light in the night.
40 [a]*The people* asked, and He
brought quail,
And [b]satisfied them with the
bread of heaven.

7 [a][Is. 26:9] **8** [a]Luke 1:72 **9** [a]Gen. 17:2; Luke 1:73; [Gal. 3:17]; Heb. 6:17 **11** [a]Gen. 13:15; 15:18 **12** [a]Gen. 34:30; [Deut. 7:7] [b]Gen. 23:4; Heb. 11:9 **14** [a]Gen. 35:5 [b]Gen. 12:17 **15** *See WW at 1 Sam. 3:20. **16** [a]Gen. 41:54 [b]Lev. 26:26; Is. 3:1; Ezek. 4:16 **17** [a][Gen. 45:5] [b]Gen. 37:28, 36; Acts 7:9 **18** [a]Gen. 40:15 [1]*His soul came into iron* **19** [a]Gen. 39:11–21; 41:25, 42, 43 **20** [a]Gen. 41:14 *See WW at Jer. 40:4. **21** [a]Gen. 41:40–44 **22** [1]Bind as prisoners

23 [a]Gen. 46:6; Acts 7:15 [b]Ps. 78:51 **24** [a]Ex. 1:7, 9 **25** [a]Ex. 1:8–10; 4:21 **26** [a]Ex. 3:10; 4:12–15 **27** [a]Ex. 7—12; Ps. 78:43 *See WW at Zech. 3:8. **29** [a]Ex. 7:20, 21; Ps. 78:44 **30** [a]Ex. 8:6 **31** [a]Ex. 8:16, 17 **32** [a]Ex. 9:23–25 **33** [a]Ps. 78:47 **34** [a]Ex. 10:4 **36** [a]Ex. 12:29; 13:15; Ps. 135:8; 136:10 [b]Gen. 49:3 [1]Lit. *struck down* **37** [a]Ex. 12:35, 36 **38** [a]Ex. 12:33 **39** [a]Ex. 13:21; Neh. 9:12; Ps. 78:14; Is. 4:5 **40** [a]Ex. 16:12 [b]Ps. 78:24

105:7 He and **His** are repeated at least 49 times in this work, emphasizing God's providence in Israel's history.
105:15 Do not touch: This command refers to the stories of Sarah (Gen. 12:17) and Rebekah (Gen. 26:8–11).
105:19 Tested refers to the years of character development Joseph experienced (Gen. 39—41) before his childhood dreams of promotion finally came true (Gen. 37:5–11).
105:22 Wisdom: That is, how to store up food for a seven-year famine in Egypt.

41 [a]He opened the rock, and water
gushed out;
It ran in the dry places *like* a river.

42 For He remembered [a]His holy
promise,
And Abraham His servant.
43 He brought out His people with
joy,
His chosen ones with [1]gladness.
44 [a]He gave them the lands of the
[1]Gentiles,
And they inherited the *labor of
the nations,
45 [a]That they might observe His
statutes
And keep His laws.

[1]Praise the LORD!

PSALM 106

Joy in Forgiveness of Israel's Sins

PRAISE[1] the LORD!

[a]Oh, give thanks to the LORD, for
He is good!
For His mercy *endures* forever.

2 Who can [1]utter the mighty acts
of the LORD?
Who can declare all His praise?
3 Blessed *are* those who keep
justice,
And [1]he who [a]does righteousness
at [b]all times!

4 [a]Remember me, O LORD, with the
*favor *You have toward* Your
people.
Oh, visit me with Your salvation,
5 That I may see the benefit of Your
chosen ones,
That I may rejoice in the gladness
of Your nation,
That I may glory with [1]Your
inheritance.

6 [a]We have sinned with our fathers,
We have committed iniquity,
We have done wickedly.
7 Our fathers in Egypt did not
*understand Your wonders;
They did not remember the
multitude of Your mercies,

41 [a]Ex. 17:6; Num. 20:11; Ps. 78:15; 114:8; Is. 48:21; [1 Cor. 10:4]
42 [a]Gen. 15:13, 14; Ps. 105:8
43 [1]*a joyful shout*
44 [a]Josh. 11:16–23; 13:7; Ps. 78:55 [1]*nations* *See WW at Job 5:7.
45 [a][Deut. 4:1, 40] [1]Heb. *Hallelujah*

PSALM 106

1 [a]1 Chr. 16:34, 41 [1]Heb. *Hallelujah*
2 [1]*express*
3 [a]Ps. 15:2 [b][Gal. 6:9] [1]LXX, Syr., Tg., Vg. *those who do*
4 [a]Ps. 119:132 *See WW at Deut. 33:23.
5 [1]The people of Your inheritance
6 [a]1 Kin. 8:47; [Ezra 9:7; Neh. 1:7; Jer. 3:25; Dan. 9:5]
7 [a]Ex. 14:11, 12 *See WW at Jer. 3:15.
8 [a]Ex. 9:16
9 [a]Ex. 14:21; Ps. 18:15; Is. 51:10; Nah. 1:4 [b]Is. 63:11–13
10 [a]Ex. 14:30
11 [a]Ex. 14:27, 28; 15:5
12 [a]Ex. 15:1–21
13 [a]Ex. 15:24; 16:2; 17:2
14 [a]Num. 11:4; 1 Cor. 10:6 *See WW at Ps. 78:41.
15 [a]Num. 11:31 [b]Is. 10:16
16 [a]Num. 16:1–3
17 [a]Num. 16:31, 32; Deut. 11:6
18 [a]Num. 16:35, 46
19 [a]Ex. 32:1–4; Deut. 9:8; Acts 7:41
20 [a]Jer. 2:11; Rom. 1:23
23 [a]Ex. 32:10; Deut. 9:19 [b]Ezek. 22:30

[a]But rebelled by the sea—the Red
Sea.

8 Nevertheless He saved them for
His name's sake,
[a]That He might make His mighty
power known.
9 [a]He rebuked the Red Sea also, and
it dried up;
So [b]He led them through the
depths,
As through the wilderness.
10 He [a]saved them from the hand of
him who hated *them,*
And redeemed them from the
hand of the enemy.
11 [a]The waters covered their
enemies;
There was not one of them left.
12 [a]Then they believed His words;
They sang His praise.

13 [a]They soon forgot His works;
They did not wait for His counsel,
14 [a]But lusted exceedingly in the
wilderness,
And *tested God in the desert.
15 [a]And He gave them their request,
But [b]sent leanness into their soul.

16 When [a]they envied Moses in the
camp,
And Aaron the saint of the LORD,
17 [a]The earth opened up and
swallowed Dathan,
And covered the faction of
Abiram.
18 [a]A fire was kindled in their
company;
The flame burned up the wicked.

19 [a]They made a calf in Horeb,
And worshiped the molded
image.
20 Thus [a]they changed their glory
Into the image of an ox that eats
grass.
21 They forgot God their Savior,
Who had done great things in
Egypt,
22 Wondrous works in the land of
Ham,
Awesome things by the Red Sea.
23 [a]Therefore He said that He would 1
destroy them,
Had not Moses His chosen one
[b]stood before Him in the
breach,

106:1–48 Ps. 106 continues the history of the preceding psalm with a marked difference: it realistically portrays the sins of the nation down to its destruction by Babylon.
106:6 Sinned: This section begins a narrative of seven occasions of Israel's rebellion against God in the wilderness journey. See 1 Cor. 10:5, 6 for an application.
106:20 Paul's stinging appraisal of mankind's changing **their glory** contains this verse (Rom. 1:23).
106:23 See section 1 of Truth-In-Action following Ps. 106.

To turn away His wrath, lest He
destroy *them.*

24 Then they *despised [a]the pleasant
land;
They [b]did not believe His word,
25 [a]But complained in their tents,
And did not heed the voice of the
LORD.
26 [a]Therefore He raised up His hand
in an oath against them,
[b]To [1]overthrow them in the
wilderness,
27 [a]To [1]overthrow their descendants
among the [2]nations,
And to scatter them in the lands.

28 [a]They joined themselves also to
Baal of Peor,
And ate sacrifices [1]made to the
dead.
29 Thus they provoked *Him* to anger
with their deeds,
And the plague broke out among
them.
30 [a]Then Phinehas stood up and
intervened,
And the plague was stopped.
31 And that was accounted to him
[a]for righteousness
To all generations forevermore.

32 [a]They angered *Him* also at the
waters of [1]strife,
[b]So that it went ill with Moses on
account of them;
33 [a]Because they rebelled against His
Spirit,
So that he spoke rashly with his
lips.

34 [a]They did not destroy the peoples,
[b]Concerning whom the LORD had
commanded them,
35 [a]But they mingled with the
Gentiles
And learned their works;
36 [a]They served their idols,
[b]Which became a snare to them.
37 [a]They even sacrificed their sons
And their daughters to [b]demons,
38 And shed innocent blood,
The blood of their sons and
daughters,
Whom they sacrificed to the idols
of Canaan;
And [a]the land was polluted with
blood.
39 Thus they [1]were [a]defiled by their
own works,
And [b]played[2] the harlot by their
own deeds.

40 Therefore [a]the wrath of the LORD
was kindled against His people,
So that He abhorred [b]His own
inheritance.
41 And [a]He gave them into the hand
of the Gentiles,
And those who hated them ruled
over them.
42 Their enemies also oppressed
them,
And they were brought into
subjection under their hand.
43 [a]Many times He delivered them;
But they rebelled in their counsel,
And were brought low for their
iniquity.

44 Nevertheless He regarded their
affliction,
When [a]He heard their cry;
45 [a]And for their sake He
remembered His covenant,
And [b]relented [c]according to the
multitude of His mercies.
46 [a]He also made them to be pitied
By all those who carried them
away captive.

47 [a]Save us, O LORD our God,
And gather us from among the
Gentiles,
To give thanks to Your holy
name,
To *triumph in Your praise.

24 [a]Deut. 8:7 [b][Heb. 3:18, 19] *See WW at Amos 2:4. **25** [a]Num. 14:2, 27 **26** [a]Ezek. 20:15, 16 [b]Num. 14:28–30 [1]*make them fall* **27** [a]Lev. 26:33 [1]*make their descendants fall also* [2]*Gentiles* **28** [a]Hos. 9:10 [1]*offered* **30** [a]Num. 25:7, 8 **31** [a]Num. 25:11–13 **32** [a]Num. 20:3–13 [b]Deut. 1:37; 3:26 [1]Or *Meribah* **33** [a]Num. 20:3, 10 **34** [a]Judg. 1:21 [b][Deut. 7:2, 16] **35** [a]Judg. 3:5, 6 **36** [a]Judg. 2:12 [b]Deut. 7:16 **37** [a]2 Kin. 16:3; 17:17 [b][Lev. 17:7]

38 [a][Num. 35:33] **39** [a]Ezek. 20:18 [b][Lev. 17:7] [1]*became unclean* [2]Were unfaithful **40** [a]Judg. 2:14 [b][Deut. 9:29; 32:9] **41** [a]Judg. 2:14 **43** [a]Judg. 2:16 **44** [a]Judg. 3:9; 6:7; 10:10 **45** [a][Lev. 26:41, 42] [b]Judg. 2:18 [c]Ps. 69:16 **46** [a]Ezra 9:9 **47** [a]1 Chr. 16:35, 36 *See WW at Ps. 63:3.

WORD WEALTH

106:47 Gentiles, *goyim* (go-*yeem*); Strong's #1471: Nations, heathen, peoples, Gentiles. This is the plural form of goy, which means "nation" or "Gentile." Generally *goy* designates a defined group of people viewed from outside the

106:28 Baal is a title for any of the many Canaanite gods. **Peor** is probably one of the hill shrines where a baal was worshiped. ***Joined themselves*** refers to the immorality that Israel committed with the baal cult prostitutes (1 Cor. 6:16–20).

106:34–39 Gentiles: The disobedience of Israel continued even in the Promised Land by their adapting to the customs of the corrupt nations there—the worst of which was child sacrifice.

106:37 The existence of **demons** is confirmed by Paul (1 Cor. 10:20).

106:43 Many times refers to the era of the judges when God repeatedly raised up deliverers for Israel.

106:47 Gather us: The psalmist is writing during the era after the Babylonian captivity when Jews are scattered throughout the Middle East.

group. Although *goy* occasionally refers to Israel, usually Israel is sharply contrasted with the *goyim*. It was prophesied that Israel was not to be reckoned among the nations, but rather was to dwell alone (Num. 23:9). This does not mean that there is no ethnic or racial continuity among Jacob's descendants; it does mean that Israel is not merely one more "nation," but rather a people uniquely known as the Lord's inheritance.

48 [a]Blessed *be* the LORD God of Israel
From everlasting to everlasting!
And let all the people say,
"Amen!"
[1]Praise the LORD!

48 [a]Ps. 41:13
[1]Heb. *Hallelujah*

106:48 Blessed: This verse serves as a doxology for Book Four, the fourth collection of ancient psalms.

TRUTH-IN-ACTION through PSALMS (Book Four: Psalms 90—106)

Letting the LIFE of the Holy Spirit Bring Faith's Works Alive in You!

Truth Psalms Teaches	Text	**Action** Psalms Invites
1 A Guideline for Godliness Fervent intercession for the church is a mark of a godly person.	106:23	**Intercede** for God's people to bring repentance and avert judgment.
2 Showing Respect for God Humble postures in worship should reflect a humble attitude of heart.	95:6–11	**Humble yourself** before the Lord through bowing and kneeling in worship. **Open your heart** to Him and to His will.
3 Keys to Wise Living The wise person gratefully receives God's teaching and discipline. He also turns away from procrastination and other time-wasters.	94:12–15 90:12	**Expect** and **be grateful** for the Lord's discipline. **Know** it is His instruction, leading to patience and righteousness. **Use time wisely. Understand** that squandering time is throwing away a part of your life.
4 Key Lessons in Faith Faith is a forward focus on God, His Word, and His promises. But faith also looks back at the blessings of God to gain strength. Faith allows us to flee confidently to God when in trouble and to abide in Him for protection.	103:2–5 94:19 91:9–13	**Rehearse** periodically all of God's blessings as a source of encouragement and faith. **Look** to the Lord for consolation when you have anxiety about anything. **Abide** in Christ, **set your affection** on Him, and **acknowledge** Him in all you do. **Rest** in His protection and salvation.
5 Steps to Holiness As holy people it is better not to stare at or meditate on things that are inappropriate to a life separated to the Lord and His purposes.	101:3 104:34	**Guard** your eyes zealously. Your inner life is affected by the things you focus on. **Dwell** only on things that are pleasing to the Lord.

BOOK FIVE
Psalms 107–150

PSALM 107
Thanksgiving to the LORD for His Great Works of Deliverance

OH, [a]give thanks to the LORD, for *He is* good!
For His [1]mercy *endures* forever.
2 Let the *redeemed of the LORD say *so*,
Whom He has redeemed from the hand of the enemy,
3 And [a]gathered out of the lands,
From the east and from the west,
From the north and from the south.

4 They wandered in [a]the wilderness in a desolate way;
They found no city to dwell in.
5 Hungry and thirsty,
Their soul fainted in them.
6 [a]Then they cried out to the LORD in their trouble,
And He delivered them out of their distresses.
7 And He led them forth by the [a]right way,
That they might go to a city for a dwelling place.
8 [a]Oh, that *men* would give thanks to the LORD *for* His goodness,
And *for* His *wonderful works to the children of men!
9 For [a]He satisfies the longing soul,
And fills the hungry soul with goodness.

10 Those who [a]sat in darkness and in the shadow of death,
[b]Bound[1] in affliction and irons—
11 Because they [a]rebelled against the words of God,
And [1]despised [b]the counsel of the *Most High,
12 Therefore He brought down their heart with *labor;
They fell down, and *there was* [a]none to help.
13 Then they cried out to the LORD in their trouble,
And He saved them out of their distresses.
14 [a]He brought them out of darkness and the shadow of death,
And broke their chains in pieces.
15 Oh, that *men* would give thanks to the LORD *for* His goodness,
And *for* His wonderful works to the children of men!
16 For He has [a]broken the gates of bronze,
And cut the bars of iron in two.

17 Fools, [a]because of their transgression,
And because of their iniquities, were afflicted.
18 [a]Their soul abhorred all manner of food,
And they [b]drew near to the gates of death.
19 Then they cried out to the LORD in their trouble,
And He saved them out of their distresses.
20 [a]He sent His word and [b]healed them,
And [c]delivered *them* from their destructions.

KINGDOM DYNAMICS

107:20 Deliverance from Our "Destructions," DIVINE HEALING. In this psalm, sickness is the punishment for transgression. To transgress is to willfully violate known boundaries of obedience. The punishment, then, is not so much a direct action of God's will as an indirect result of our having violated the blessings within the boundaries of His will, and thus having exposed ourselves to the judgments outside it. However, deliverance may come with genuine repentance. Too often people do not call upon God until calamity strikes. Storms come upon us all; sudden difficulty or severe sickness may arrest us from our unperceived or willful spiritual decline. But the text implies that if the Lord is sought with a contrite heart, crying for deliverance, the calamity may be reversed and result in both spiritual and physical healing. The Lord will hear such a cry; and when He does, He heals us with "His word" (v. 20). (A beautiful example of this is seen in Jesus' healing of the centurion's servant in Matt. 8:8.)

(Ps. 103:3/Is. 53:4, 5) N.V.

21 Oh, that *men* would give thanks to the LORD *for* His goodness,
And *for* His wonderful works to the children of men!
22 [a]Let them sacrifice the sacrifices of *thanksgiving, **3**

PSALM 107

1 [a]1 Chr. 16:34; Ps. 106:1; Jer. 33:11 [1]Heb. same as *goodness*, vv. 8, 15, 21, 31, and *lovingkindness*, v. 43
2 *See WW at Is. 52:9.
3 [a]Is. 43:5, 6; Jer. 29:14; 31:8–10; [Ezek. 39:27, 28]
4 [a]Num. 14:33; 32:13; [Deut. 2:7; 32:10]; Josh. 5:6; 14:10
6 [a]Ps. 50:15; [Hos. 5:15]
7 [a]Ezra 8:21; Ps. 5:8; Jer. 31:9
8 [a]Ps. 107:15, 21 *See WW at Judg. 13:19.
9 [a][Ps. 34:10; Luke 1:53]
10 [a][Is. 42:7; Mic. 7:8; Luke 1:79] [b]Job 36:8 [1]*Prisoners*
11 [a]Lam. 3:42 [b][Ps. 73:24] [1]*scorned* *See WW at Gen. 14:18.
12 [a]Ps. 22:11 *See WW at Job 5:7.
14 [a]Ps. 68:6
16 [a]Is. 45:1, 2
17 [a][Is. 65:6, 7; Jer. 30:14, 15]; Lam. 3:39; Ezek. 24:23
18 [a]Job 33:20 [b]Job 33:22
20 [a]Matt. 8:8 [b]2 Kin. 20:5; Ps. 30:2 [c]Job 33:28, 30
22 [a]Lev. 7:12; Ps. 50:14; Heb. 13:15 *See WW at Ps. 95:2.

107:1–43 This psalm of deliverance features a refrain found in vv. 1, 8, 15, 21, and 31.
107:22 See section 3 of Truth-In-Action following Ps. 150.
107:22 Thank offerings were a kind of peace offering that an Israelite could **sacrifice** out of gratitude (Lev. 7:11–15); but this verse may also refer to the verbal sacrifices of worship and praise (Heb. 13:15).

And [b]declare His works with
[1]rejoicing.*

23 Those who go down to the sea in ships,
Who do business on great waters,
24 They see the works of the LORD,
And His wonders in the deep.
25 For He commands and [a]raises the stormy wind,
Which lifts up the waves of the sea.
26 They mount up to the heavens,
They go down again to the depths;
[a]Their soul melts because of trouble.
27 They reel to and fro, and stagger like a drunken man,
And [1]are at their wits' end.
28 Then they cry out to the LORD in their trouble,
And He brings them out of their distresses.
29 [a]He calms the storm,
So that its waves are still.
30 Then they are glad because they are quiet;
So He guides them to their desired haven.
31 [a]Oh, that *men* would give thanks to the LORD *for* His goodness,
And *for* His wonderful works to the children of men!
32 Let them exalt Him also [a]in the assembly of the people,
And praise Him in the company of the elders.

33 He [a]turns rivers into a wilderness,
And the watersprings into dry ground;
34 A [a]fruitful land into [1]barrenness,
For the wickedness of those who dwell in it.
35 [a]He turns a wilderness into pools of water,
And dry land into watersprings.
36 There He makes the hungry dwell,
That they may establish a city for a dwelling place,
37 And sow fields and plant vineyards,
That they may yield a fruitful harvest.
38 [a]He also blesses them, and they multiply greatly;
And He does not let their cattle [b]decrease.

39 When they are [a]diminished and brought low
Through oppression, affliction and sorrow,
40 [a]He pours contempt on princes,
And causes them to wander in the *wilderness *where there is* no way;
41 [a]Yet He sets the poor on high, far from affliction,
And [b]makes *their* *families like a flock.
42 [a]The righteous see *it* and rejoice,
And all [b]iniquity stops its mouth.

43 [a]Whoever *is* wise will observe these *things*,
And they will understand the lovingkindness of the LORD.

22 [b]Ps. 9:11 [1]*joyful singing* *See WW at Ps. 30:5.
25 [a]Jon. 1:4
26 [a]Ps. 22:14
27 [1]Lit. *all their wisdom is swallowed up*
29 [a]Ps. 89:9; Matt. 8:26; Luke 8:24
31 [a]Ps. 107:8, 15, 21
32 [a]Ps. 22:22, 25
33 [a]1 Kin. 17:1, 7; Is. 50:2
34 [a]Gen. 13:10; Deut. 29:23 [1]Lit. *a salty waste*
35 [a]Ps. 114:8; [Is. 41:17, 18]
38 [a]Gen. 12:2; 17:16, 20 [b]Ex. 1:7; [Deut. 7:14]
39 [a]2 Kin. 10:32
40 [a]Job 12:21, 24 *See WW at Is. 45:18.
41 [a]1 Sam. 2:8; [Ps. 113:7, 8] [b]Ps. 78:52 *See WW at Gen. 12:3.
42 [a]Job 5:15, 16 [b]Job 5:16; Ps. 63:11; [Rom. 3:19]
43 [a]Ps. 64:9; Jer. 9:12; [Hos. 14:9]

PSALM 108

Assurance of God's Victory over Enemies

A Song. A *Psalm of David.

O [a]GOD, my heart is steadfast;
I will sing and give praise, even with my glory.
2 [a]Awake, lute and harp!
I will awaken the dawn.
3 I will praise You, O LORD, among the peoples,
And I will sing praises to You among the nations.
4 For Your mercy *is* great above the [1]heavens,
And Your truth *reaches* to the clouds.

5 [a]Be exalted, O God, above the heavens,
And Your glory above all the earth;
6 [a]That Your beloved may be delivered,
Save *with* Your right hand, and [1]hear me.

7 God has spoken in His holiness:
"I will rejoice;
I will divide Shechem
And measure out the Valley of Succoth.

PSALM 108
title *See WW at Ps. 3:title.
1 [a]Ps. 57:7–11
2 [a]Ps. 57:8–11
4 [1]*skies*
5 [a]Ps. 57:5, 11
6 [a]Ps. 60:5–12 [1]Lit. *answer*

107:26 Soul melts is another way of saying that courage is gone.
107:41 Setting **the poor on high** resembles the praise of Mary's Magnificat (Luke 1:51–53).

108:1–13 "A Song. A Psalm" (see 108:title): This psalm is a combination of verses from 57:7–11 and 60:5–12, exhibiting clearly the Psalter's character as a collected body of songs.

8 Gilead *is* Mine; Manasseh *is* Mine;
Ephraim also *is* the [1]helmet for My head;
[a]Judah *is* My lawgiver.
9 Moab *is* My washpot;
Over Edom I will cast My shoe;
Over Philistia I will triumph."

10 [a]Who will bring me *into* the strong city?
Who will lead me to Edom?
11 *Is it* not *You*, O God, *who* cast us off?
And *You*, O God, *who* did not go out with our armies?
12 Give us help from trouble,
For the help of man is useless.
13 [a]Through God we will do valiantly,
For *it is* He *who* shall tread down our enemies.

PSALM 109

Plea for Judgment of False Accusers

To the Chief Musician. A Psalm of David.

Do[a] not keep silent,
O God of my praise!
2 For the mouth of the wicked and the mouth of the deceitful
Have opened against me;
They have spoken against me with a [a]lying tongue.
3 They have also surrounded me with words of hatred,
And fought against me [a]without a cause.
4 In return for my love they are my accusers,
But I *give myself to* prayer.
5 Thus [a]they have rewarded me evil for good,
And hatred for my love.

6 Set a wicked man over him,
And let [a]an [1]accuser* stand at his right hand.
7 When he is judged, let him be found guilty,
And [a]let his prayer become sin.
8 Let his days be [a]few,
And [b]let another take his office.
9 [a]Let his children be fatherless,
And his wife a widow.
10 Let his children [1]continually be vagabonds, and beg;
Let them [2]seek *their bread* also from their desolate places.

11 [a]Let the creditor seize all that he has,
And let strangers plunder his labor.
12 Let there be none to extend mercy to him,
Nor let there be any to favor his fatherless children.
13 [a]Let his [1]posterity be cut off,
And in the generation following let their [b]name be blotted out.

14 [a]Let the iniquity of his fathers be remembered before the LORD,
And let not the *sin of his mother [b]be blotted out.
15 Let them be continually before the LORD,
That He may [a]cut off the memory of them from the earth;
16 Because he did not remember to show mercy,
But persecuted the poor and needy man,
That he might even slay the [a]broken in heart.
17 [a]As he loved cursing, so let it come to him;
As he did not delight in blessing, so let it be far from him.
18 As he clothed himself with cursing as with his garment,
So let it [a]enter his body like water,
And like oil into his bones.
19 Let it be to him like the garment which covers him,
And for a belt with which he girds himself continually.
20 *Let* this *be* the LORD's reward to my accusers,
And to those who speak evil against my person.

21 But You, O GOD the Lord,
Deal with me for Your name's sake;
Because Your mercy *is* good, deliver me.
22 For I *am* *poor and needy,
And my heart is wounded within me.
23 I am gone [a]like a shadow when it lengthens;
I am shaken off like a locust.
24 My [a]knees are weak through fasting,
And my flesh is feeble from lack of fatness.

8 [a][Gen. 49:10] [1]Lit. *protection*
10 [a]Ps. 60:9
13 [a]Ps. 60:12

PSALM 109

1 [a]Ps. 83:1
2 [a]Ps. 27:12
3 [a]Ps. 35:7; 69:4; John 15:25
5 [a]Ps. 35:7, 12; 38:20; Prov. 17:13
6 [a]Zech. 3:1 [1]Heb. *satan* *See WW at Job 1:6.
7 [a][Prov. 28:9]
8 [a][Ps. 55:23]; John 17:12 [b]Ps. 69:25; Acts 1:20
9 [a]Ex. 22:24
10 [1]*wander continuously* [2]So with MT, Tg.; LXX, Vg. *be cast out*
11 [a]Neh. 5:7; Job 5:5; 18:9
13 [a]Job 18:19; Ps. 37:28 [b]Prov. 10:7 [1]*descendants be destroyed*
14 [a][Ex. 20:5; Num. 14:18]; Is. 65:6; [Jer. 32:18] [b]Neh. 4:5; Jer. 18:23 *See WW at Lev. 9:2.
15 [a]Job 18:17; [Ps. 34:16]
16 [a][Ps. 34:18]
17 [a]Prov. 14:14; [Matt. 7:2]
18 [a]Num. 5:22
22 *See WW at Ps. 40:17.
23 [a]Ps. 102:11
24 [a]Heb. 12:12

109:6 Accuser is literally "Satan," but is often translated "adversary," or "accuser," as here (1 Pet. 5:8; Rev. 12:10).
109:8 His days: This wording was applied by the apostles to the greatest of traitors, Judas Iscariot, after his death (Acts 1:20).

25 I also have become [a]a reproach
to them;
When they look at me, [b]they
shake their heads.

26 Help me, O LORD my God!
Oh, save me according to Your
mercy,
27 [a]That they may know that this *is*
Your hand—
That You, LORD, have done it!
28 [a]Let them curse, but You bless;
When they arise, let them be
ashamed,
But let [b]Your servant rejoice.
29 [a]Let my accusers be clothed with
shame,
And let them cover themselves
with their own disgrace as with
a mantle.

30 I will greatly praise the LORD with
my mouth;
Yes, [a]I will praise Him among the
multitude.
31 For [a]He shall stand at the right
hand of the poor,
To save *him* from those [1]who
condemn him.

PSALM 110

Announcement of the Messiah's Reign

A Psalm of David.

THE [a]LORD said to my Lord,
"Sit at My right hand,
Till I make Your enemies Your
[b]footstool."
2 The LORD shall send the rod of
Your strength [a]out of Zion.
[b]Rule in the midst of Your
enemies!

3 [a]Your people *shall be* volunteers
In the day of Your power;
[b]In the *beauties of holiness, from
the womb of the morning,
You have the dew of Your youth.
4 The LORD has sworn
And [a]will not relent,
"You *are* a [b]priest forever
According to the order of
[c]Melchizedek."

5 The Lord *is* [a]at Your right hand;
He shall [1]execute kings [b]in the
day of His wrath.
6 He shall judge among the nations,
He shall fill *the places* with dead
bodies,
[a]He shall [1]execute the heads of
many countries.
7 He shall drink of the brook by the
wayside;
[a]Therefore He shall lift up the
head.

PSALM 111

Praise to God for His Faithfulness and Justice

PRAISE[1] the LORD!

[a]I will praise the LORD with *my*
whole heart,
In the assembly of the upright and
in the congregation.

2 [a]The works of the LORD *are* great,
[b]Studied by all who have pleasure
in them.
3 His work *is* [a]honorable and
glorious,
And His righteousness endures
forever.
4 He has made His wonderful
works to be remembered;
[a]The LORD *is* gracious and full of
compassion.

---

25 [a]Ps. 22:7; Jer. 18:16; Lam. 2:15 [b]Matt. 27:39; Mark 15:29
27 [a]Job 37:7
28 [a]2 Sam. 6:11, 12 [b]Is. 65:14
29 [a]Job 8:22; Ps. 35:26
30 [a]Ps. 35:18; 111:1
31 [a][Ps. 16:8] [1]Lit. *judging his soul*

PSALM 110

1 [a]Matt. 22:44; Mark 12:36; 16:19; Luke 20:42, 43; Acts 2:34, 35; Col. 3:1; Heb. 1:13 [b][1 Cor. 15:25; Eph. 1:22]
2 [a][Rom. 11:26, 27] [b][Ps. 2:9; Dan. 7:13, 14]
3 [a]Judg. 5:2; Neh. 11:2 [b]1 Chr. 16:29; Ps. 96:9 *See WW at Ps. 8:5.
4 [a][Num. 23:19] [b][Zech. 6:13] [c][Heb. 5:6, 10; 6:20]
5 [a][Ps. 16:8] [b]Ps. 2:5, 12; [Rom. 2:5; Rev. 6:17] [1]Lit. *break kings in pieces*
6 [a]Ps. 68:21 [1]Lit. *break in pieces*
7 [a][Is. 53:12]

PSALM 111

1 [a]Ps. 35:18 [1]Heb. *Hallelujah*
2 [a]Ps. 92:5 [b]Ps. 143:5
3 [a]Ps. 145:4, 5
4 [a][Ps. 86:5]

109:25 Heads: The bystanders reviled Christ on the Cross and shook their heads in contempt (Matt. 27:39).
110:1–7 The LORD: This psalm is considered by Jews and Christians alike to be messianic, and this interpretation is confirmed by Jesus' own use of it to prove His deity (Luke 20:42).
110:1 My Lord: That is, the Lord of the universe (*Yahweh*) told David's Lord (*'Adonai*, the Messiah) to rejoice. Many NT writers quote this verse. The word **said** is a unique word which only refers to inspired prophetic utterances. For **footstool** see Josh. 10:24, 25.
110:2 Rod is another word for the royal scepter, a symbol of power. **Rule:** As Paul showed in 1 Cor. 15:25, Christ is ruling now among enemies.
110:3 Similar to 2 Sam. 23:4, this is a picturesque description of a new king rising to the throne.
110:4 Clearly the offices of the Messiah as King and **priest** are revealed here, since Christ constantly intercedes for man, as the NT affirms by quoting this verse (Heb. 7:21–25). The **Melchizedek** priesthood is considered superior to the Aaronic one (Heb. 7:3–28), since Abraham paid tithes to Melchizedek (Gen. 14:18–20).
110:5–7 These verses are addressed to God (*Yahweh*) talking about the work of the **Lord** Jesus (*'Adonai*).
110:5 One aspect of the **wrath** of Jesus is shown in the judgment predicted in Matt. 23—25.
110:7 Drink: That is, after the judgment, or battle, he is refreshed as if drinking from a cool **brook.**
111:1–10 This is an acrostic poem of 22 lines, each beginning with successive letters of the Hebrew alphabet. Vv. 9 and 10 contain three lines each, while the other verses contain two each. In Hebrew each of the lines usually contains just three words.
111:1 Praise: This is a fitting psalm for **congregational** worship since it carries out the intent, stated here, of praising God for His works and His character.

5 He has given food to those who fear Him;
He will ever be mindful of His covenant.
6 He has declared to His people the power of His works,
In giving them the [1]heritage of the nations.

7 The works of His hands *are* [a]verity[1] and justice;
All His precepts *are* sure.
8 [a]They stand fast forever and ever,
And are [b]done in truth and uprightness.
9 [a]He has sent redemption to His people;
He has commanded His covenant forever:
[b]Holy and awesome *is* His name.

1 10 [a]The fear of the LORD *is* the beginning of wisdom;
A good understanding have all those who do *His commandments.*
His praise endures forever.

PSALM 112

The Blessed State of the Righteous

PRAISE[1] the LORD!

Blessed *is* the man *who* fears the LORD,
Who [a]**delights** greatly in His commandments.

WORD WEALTH

112:1 delights, *chafets* (chah-*fayts*); Strong's #2654: To be delighted in something; to take pleasure in; to be bent or inclined toward; to cherish; to be favorably disposed toward someone; to love and desire. From *chafets* comes the noun *chefets,* "delight" or "pleasure." A well-known biblical name derived from this word is "Hephzibah" (literally "My Delight Is in Her"), a prophetic name for the land of Israel (Is. 62:4), for God will find His people and His land a delight, that is, very attractive in His view. Here a blessed individual finds God's commandments pleasurable, attractive, delightful, pleasing, and desirable.

6 [1]*inheritance*
7 [a][Rev. 15:3] [1]*truth*
8 [a]Is. 40:8; Matt. 5:18 [b][Rev. 15:3]
9 [a]Luke 1:68 [b]Luke 1:49
10 [a]Job 28:28; [Prov. 1:7; 9:10]; Eccl. 12:13

PSALM 112

1 [a]Ps. 128:1 [1]Heb. *Hallelujah*
2 [a][Ps. 102:28] *See WW at Esth. 9:28.
3 [a]Prov. 3:16; 8:18; [Matt. 6:33] [1]*stands*
4 [a]Job 11:17; Ps. 97:11
5 [a]Ps. 37:26; [Luke 6:35] [b][Eph. 5:15; Col. 4:5]
6 [a]Prov. 10:7
7 [a][Prov. 1:33]
8 [a]Heb. 13:9 [b][Ps. 27:1; 56:11]; Prov. 1:33; 3:24; [Is. 12:2] [c]Ps. 59:10
9 [1]Strength

2 [a]His descendants will be mighty on earth; 1
The *generation of the upright will be blessed.
3 [a]Wealth and riches *will be* in his house,
And his righteousness [1]endures forever.
4 [a]Unto the upright there arises light in the darkness;
He is gracious, and full of compassion, and righteous.
5 [a]A good man deals graciously and lends;
He will guide his affairs [b]with discretion.
6 Surely he will never be shaken;
[a]The righteous will be in everlasting remembrance.
7 [a]He will not be afraid of evil tidings;
His heart is steadfast, trusting in the LORD.
8 His [a]heart *is* established;
[b]He will not be afraid,
Until he [c]sees *his desire* upon his enemies.

9 He has dispersed abroad,
He has given to the poor;
His righteousness endures forever;
His [1]horn will be exalted with honor.
10 The wicked will see *it* and be grieved;
He will gnash his teeth and melt away;
The desire of the wicked shall perish.

111:5 The **food** is either a reference to manna, a supernatural bread that sustained Israel in the wilderness wandering, or a reference to the Passover meal.
111:6 Heritage is a reference to the land of Canaan given to Israel.
111:9 Redemption recalls the redeeming of Israel from Egyptian slavery, and the **covenant** *is the Mosaic one given at Mt. Sinai.*
111:10 See section 1 of Truth-In-Action following Ps. 150.
112:1–10 This is an acrostic poem of 22 lines, each line beginning with successive letters of the Hebrew alphabet. While Ps. 111, also acrostic, celebrates the holy God, this reveres the holy man.
112:1 Blessed (Hebrew *'esher*) means happy, and is equivalent to the Greek *makarios* of Matt. 5:3.
112:2 See section 1 of Truth-In-Action following Ps. 150.
112:3 This statement about **wealth** must be balanced with 37:16 and stories of men like Job and Paul who suffered financial setbacks (2 Cor. 11:23–30). Consideration of **riches** laid up in heaven gives this a proper perspective.
112:9 Dispersed: This is quoted by Paul in 2 Cor. 9:9 to encourage Christian charity. **Horn** is an OT symbol for prominence and social standing.
112:10 Grieved: Remorse for not choosing the charitable path in life, though more demanding at times, is the consequence that awaits the wicked (Luke 13:24–28).

PSALM 113

The Majesty and Condescension of God

PRAISE[1] the LORD!

[a]Praise, O servants of the LORD,
Praise the name of the LORD!
2 [a]Blessed be the name of the LORD
From this time forth and forevermore!
3 [a]From the rising of the sun to its going down
The LORD's name *is* to be praised.

4 The LORD *is* [a]high above all nations,
[b]His glory above the heavens.
5 [a]Who *is* like the LORD our God,
Who dwells on high,
6 [a]Who *humbles Himself to behold
The things that are in the heavens and in the earth?

7 [a]He raises the poor out of the dust,
And lifts the [b]needy out of the ash heap,
8 That He may [a]seat *him* with princes—
With the princes of His people.
9 [a]He grants the [1]barren woman a home,
Like a *joyful mother of children.

Praise the LORD!

PSALM 114

The Power of God in His Deliverance of Israel

WHEN [a]Israel went out of Egypt,
The house of Jacob [b]from a people [1]of strange language,
2 [a]Judah became His sanctuary,
And Israel His dominion.

3 [a]The sea saw *it* and fled;
[b]Jordan turned back.
4 [a]The mountains skipped like rams,
The little hills like lambs.
5 [a]What ails you, O sea, that you fled?
O Jordan, *that* you turned back?
6 O mountains, *that* you skipped like rams?
O little hills, like lambs?

7 Tremble, O earth, at the presence of the Lord,
At the presence of the God of Jacob,
8 [a]Who turned the rock *into* a pool of water,
The flint into a fountain of waters.

PSALM 115

The Futility of Idols and the Trustworthiness of God

NOT [a]unto us, O LORD, not unto us,
But to Your name give glory,
Because of Your mercy,
Because of Your truth.
2 Why should the [1]Gentiles say,
[a]"So where *is* their God?"

3 [a]But our God *is* in heaven;
He does whatever He pleases.
4 [a]Their idols *are* silver and gold,
The work of men's hands.
5 They have mouths, but they do not speak;
Eyes they have, but they do not see;
6 They have ears, but they do not hear;
Noses they have, but they do not smell;
7 They have hands, but they do not handle;
Feet they have, but they do not walk;

2

PSALM 113
1 [a]Ps. 135:1 [1]Heb. *Hallelujah*
2 [a][Dan. 2:20]
3 [a]Is. 59:19; Mal. 1:11
4 [a]Ps. 97:9; 99:2 [b][Ps. 8:1]
5 [a]Ps. 89:6; [Is. 57:15]
6 [a][Ps. 11:4; Is. 57:15] *See WW at Jer. 13:18.
7 [a]1 Sam. 2:8; Ps. 107:41 [b]Ps. 72:12
8 [a][Job 36:7]
9 [a]1 Sam. 2:5; Is. 54:1 [1]*childless* *See WW at 2 Chr. 7:10.

PSALM 114
1 [a]Ex. 12:51; 13:3 [b]Ps. 81:5 [1]*who spoke unintelligibly*
2 [a]Ex. 6:7; 19:6; 25:8; 29:45, 46; Deut. 27:9
3 [a]Ex. 14:21; Ps. 77:16 [b]Josh. 3:13–16
4 [a]Ex. 19:18; Judg. 5:5; Ps. 29:6; Hab. 3:6
5 [a]Hab. 3:8
8 [a]Ex. 17:6; Num. 20:11; Ps. 107:35

PSALM 115
1 [a][Is. 48:11]; Ezek. 36:32
2 [a]Ps. 42:3, 10 [1]*nations*
3 [a][1 Chr. 16:26]
4 [a]Deut. 4:28; 2 Kin. 19:18; Is. 37:19; 44:10, 20; Jer. 10:3

113:1–9 Praise: This and the following Hallel songs were sung in two parts (113—114 and 115—118) in every dwelling where the Passover was celebrated. It was the singing of the second part that is referred to in Matt. 26:30, just before the crucifixion of Jesus.
113:6 Humbles Himself: The marvelous condescension of God goes beyond beholding, and unfolds further in the incarnation and crucifixion of Jesus (Phil. 2:5–8). The deist postulating God's aloofness is thereby dealt a mortal blow.
113:7–9 Raises the poor: These verses are lifted from Hannah's prayer in 1 Sam. 2:5, 8. **Dust** and **ash heap** are symbols of the lowest shame and deepest poverty (1 Kin. 16:2).
114:1–8 This reference to **Egypt** gives the Egyptian Hallel group of psalms (113—118) their name. OT faith was based on specific historical events, not on mythology that characterized other national religions.
114:3 In a capsule the psalmist describes the history of the exodus from slavery by crossing the Red Sea and passing through the **Jordan** River on dry ground (Ex. 14:16; Josh. 3:17).
114:4 Skipped refers to the shaking and quaking of Mt. Sinai when the Law was given to Moses (Ex. 19:18).
114:8 The miracle of the **rock** producing water is found in Ex. 17:6, and the **flint** refers to the event of Num. 20:11. See Deut. 8:15.
115:2–8 See section 2 of Truth-In-Action following Ps. 150.
115:3–8 The contrast between the spiritual **God** who reigns omnisciently and omnipotently, and the metallic **idols** who are limited to the space of a carved object, is so telling that it makes idolatry absurd. See Isaiah's further mockery in Is. 44:12–20.

Nor do they mutter through their throat.
8 [a]Those who make them are like them;
So is everyone who trusts in them.

9 [a]O Israel, trust in the LORD;
[b]He *is* their help and their shield.
10 O house of Aaron, trust in the LORD;
He *is* their help and their shield.
11 You who fear the LORD, trust in the LORD;
He *is* their help and their shield.

12 The LORD [1]has been mindful of *us;*
He will bless us;
He will bless the house of Israel;
He will bless the house of Aaron.
13 [a]He will bless those who fear the LORD,
Both small and great.

14 May the LORD give you increase more and more,
You and your children.
15 *May* you *be* [a]blessed by the LORD,
[b]Who made heaven and earth.

16 The heaven, *even* the heavens, *are* the LORD's;
But the earth He has given to the children of men.
17 [a]The dead do not praise the LORD,
Nor any who go down into silence.
18 [a]But we will bless the LORD
From this time forth and forevermore.

Praise the LORD!

PSALM 116

Thanksgiving for Deliverance from Death

I [a]LOVE the LORD, because He has heard
My voice *and* my supplications.
2 Because He has inclined His ear to me,
Therefore I will call *upon Him* as long as I live.

3 [a]The [1]pains of death surrounded me,
And the [2]pangs of Sheol [3]laid hold of me;
I found trouble and sorrow.
4 Then I called upon the name of the LORD:
"O LORD, I implore You, deliver my soul!"

5 [a]Gracious *is* the LORD, and [b]righteous;
Yes, our God *is* merciful.
6 The LORD preserves the simple;
I was brought low, and He saved me.
7 Return to your [a]rest, O my soul,
For [b]the LORD has dealt bountifully with you.

8 [a]For You have delivered my soul from death,
My eyes from tears,
And my feet from falling.
9 I will walk before the LORD
[a]In the land of the living.
10 [a]I *believed, therefore I spoke,
"I am greatly afflicted."
11 [a]I said in my haste,
[b]"All men *are* liars."

12 What shall I render to the LORD
For all His benefits toward me?
13 I will take up the cup of salvation,
And call upon the name of the LORD.
14 [a]I will pay my vows to the LORD
Now in the presence of all His people.

15 [a]Precious in the sight of the LORD
Is the death of His saints.

16 O LORD, truly [a]I *am* Your servant;
I *am* Your servant, [b]the son of Your maidservant;
You have loosed my bonds.

---

8 [a]Ps. 135:18; Is. 44:9–11
9 [a]Ps. 118:2, 3 [b]Ps. 33:20
12 [1]*has remembered us*
13 [a]Ps. 128:1, 4
15 [a][Gen. 14:19] [b]Gen. 1:1; Acts 14:15; Rev. 14:7
17 [a]Ps. 6:5; 88:10–12; [Is. 38:18]
18 [a]Ps. 113:2; Dan. 2:20

PSALM 116

1 [a]Ps. 18:1
3 [a]Ps. 18:4–6 [1]Lit. *cords* [2]*distresses* [3]Lit. *found me*
5 [a][Ps. 103:8] [b][Ezra 9:15]; Neh. 9:8; [Ps. 119:137; 145:17; Jer. 12:1; Dan. 9:14]
7 [a][Jer. 6:16; Matt. 11:29] [b]Ps. 13:6
8 [a]Ps. 56:13
9 [a]Ps. 27:13
10 [a]2 Cor. 4:13 *See WW at 2 Chr. 20:20.
11 [a]Ps. 31:22 [b]Rom. 3:4
14 [a]Ps. 116:18
15 [a]Ps. 72:14; [Rev. 14:13]
16 [a]Ps. 119:125; 143:12 [b]Ps. 86:16

115:8 Like them: The root word for idol is "worthless"; so then, their worshipers become worthless (Jer. 2:5) and corrupt individuals (2 Kin. 17:15–17).
115:12–15 *The switch from* **us** *to* **you** *may indicate the* congregational use of this psalm where the speaking alternates between the minister (priest) and the congregation.
115:17 From the perspective of physical life on Earth, it seems the **dead** are silent; but from the viewpoint of the spirit world, the dead are fully alive (Matt. 22:32). Ps. 16:9, 10 balances this statement of v. 17.
116:1 I love the LORD is the exact response God's heart desires as a result of God's interventions in our lives. It fulfills the royal law (Matt. 22:37, 38) and is a perfect "thank You." **He has heard:** This psalm highlights the joy of answered prayer, here most probably a healing from a terminal illness (vv. 3, 6, 8, 15).
116:10 I believed: Paul took this psalm of "near-death" and applied it to faith-believing ministers who were near death's door because of persecution (2 Cor. 4:12, 13).

17 I will offer to You [a]the sacrifice of *thanksgiving,
And will call upon the name of the LORD.
18 I will pay my vows to the LORD
Now in the presence of all His people,
19 In the [a]courts of the LORD's house,
In the midst of you, O Jerusalem.

[1]Praise the LORD!

PSALM 117

Let All Peoples Praise the LORD

PRAISE [a]the LORD, all you Gentiles!
[1]Laud* Him, all you peoples!
2 For His merciful kindness is great toward us,
And [a]the truth of the LORD *endures* forever.

Praise the *LORD!

PSALM 118

Praise to God for His Everlasting Mercy

OH, [a]give thanks to the LORD, for *He is* good!
[b]For His mercy *endures* forever.

2 [a]Let Israel now say,
"His mercy *endures* forever."
3 Let the house of Aaron now say,
"His mercy *endures* forever."
4 Let those who fear the LORD now say,
"His mercy *endures* forever."

5 [a]I called on the LORD in distress;
The LORD answered me *and* [b]*set me* in a broad place.
6 [a]The LORD *is* on my side;
I will not fear.
What can man do to me?
7 [a]The LORD is for me among those who help me;
Therefore [b]I shall see *my desire* on those who hate me.

17 [a]Lev. 7:12; Ps. 50:14; 107:22 *See WW at Ps. 95:2.
19 [a]Ps. 96:8 [1]Heb. *Hallelujah*

PSALM 117

1 [a]Rom. 15:11 [1]*Praise* *See WW at Ps. 63:3.
2 [a][Ps. 100:5] *See WW at Is. 12:2.

PSALM 118

1 [a]1 Chr. 16:8, 34; Jer. 33:11 [b]2 Chr. 5:13; 7:3; Ezra 3:11; [Ps. 136:1–26]
2 [a][Ps. 115:9]
5 [a]Ps. 120:1 [b]Ps. 18:19
6 [a]Ps. 27:1; 56:9; [Rom. 8:31; Heb. 13:6]
7 [a]Ps. 54:4 [b]Ps. 59:10

8 [a]2 Chr. 32:7, 8; Ps. 40:4; Is. 31:1, 3; 57:13; Jer. 17:5
9 [a]Ps. 146:3
11 [a]Ps. 88:17
12 [a]Deut. 1:44 [b]Eccl. 7:6; Nah. 1:10 [1]*cut them off*
14 [a]Ex. 15:2; Is. 12:2
15 *See WW at Ps. 30:5.
16 [a]Ex. 15:6
17 [a][Ps. 6:5]; Hab. 1:12 [b]Ps. 73:28
18 [a]Ps. 73:14; Jer. 31:18; [1 Cor. 11:32]; 2 Cor. 6:9 [1]*disciplined*
19 [a]Is. 26:2
20 [a]Ps. 24:7 [b]Is. 35:8; [Rev. 21:27; 22:14, 15]
21 [a]Ps. 116:1

8 [a]*It is* better to trust in the LORD
Than to put confidence in man.
9 [a]*It is* better to trust in the LORD
Than to put confidence in princes.

10 All nations surrounded me,
But in the name of the LORD I will destroy them.
11 They [a]surrounded me,
Yes, they surrounded me;
But in the name of the LORD I will destroy them.
12 They surrounded me [a]like bees;
They were quenched [b]like a fire of thorns;
For in the name of the LORD I will [1]destroy them.
13 You pushed me violently, that I might fall,
But the LORD helped me.
14 [a]The LORD *is* my strength and song,
And He has become my salvation.

15 The voice of *rejoicing and salvation
Is in the tents of the righteous;
The right hand of the LORD does valiantly.
16 [a]The right hand of the LORD is exalted;
The right hand of the LORD does valiantly.
17 [a]I shall not die, but live,
And [b]declare the works of the LORD.
18 The LORD has [a]chastened[1] me severely,
But He has not given me over to death.

19 [a]Open to me the gates of righteousness;
I will go through them,
And I will praise the LORD.
20 [a]This is the gate of the LORD,
[b]Through which the righteous shall enter.

21 I will praise You,
For You have [a]answered me,
And have become my salvation.

117:1 Though short, this call to worship finds its place in Paul's theology which included **Gentiles** in God's eternal plan (Rom. 15:11).
117:2 Powerful motivations for **praise** are God's mercy (Hebrew *chesed*) and steadfast **truth**. These two attributes of God are constant themes from one end of the Bible (Gen. 24:27) to the other (John 1:17).
118:1 **Mercy** (Hebrew *chesed*) is often translated "steadfast love," "unfailing love," or "lovingkindness" and is equivalent to the NT "grace."
118:6 **My side:** This was used as a text in the NT to remind Christians of God's faithful provision of the necessities of life (Heb. 13:5, 6).
118:19, 20 These statements about entering **gates** set the mood for the crowd's use of vv. 25, 26 as praise when Jesus made His public Triumphal Entry into Jerusalem (Mark 11:1–11).

22 [a]The stone *which* the builders
rejected
Has become the chief
cornerstone.
23 [1]This was the LORD's doing;
It *is* marvelous in our eyes.
24 This *is* the day the LORD has
made;
We will rejoice and be glad in it.

25 Save now, I pray, O LORD;
O LORD, I pray, send now
prosperity.
26 [a]Blessed *is* he who comes in the
name of the LORD!
We have blessed you from the
house of the LORD.
27 God *is* the LORD,
And He has given us [a]light;
Bind the sacrifice with cords to
the horns of the *altar.
28 You *are* my God, and I will praise
You;
[a]*You are* my God, I will exalt You.

29 Oh, give thanks to the LORD, for
He is good!
For His mercy *endures* forever.

PSALM 119

Meditations on the Excellencies of the Word of God

א ALEPH

BLESSED *are* the [1]undefiled in the
way,
[a]Who walk in the *law of the LORD!
2 Blessed *are* those who keep His
testimonies,
Who seek Him with the [a]whole
heart!
3 [a]They also do no iniquity;
They walk in His ways.
4 You have commanded *us*
To keep Your *precepts
diligently.
5 Oh, that my ways were directed
To keep Your statutes!
6 [a]Then I would not be ashamed,
When I look into all Your
commandments.
7 I will praise You with uprightness
of heart,
When I learn Your righteous
judgments.
8 I will keep Your statutes;
Oh, do not forsake me utterly!

ב BETH

9 How can a young man cleanse his
way?
By taking heed according to Your
word.
10 With my whole heart I have
[a]sought You;
Oh, let me not wander from Your
commandments!
11 [a]Your *word I have hidden in my
heart,
That I might not sin against You.
12 Blessed *are* You, O LORD!
Teach me Your statutes.
13 With my lips I have [a]declared
All the judgments of Your mouth.
14 I have rejoiced in the way of Your
testimonies,
As *much as* in all riches.
15 I will meditate on Your **precepts**,
And [1]contemplate Your ways.

22 [a]Matt. 21:42; Mark 12:10, 11; Luke 20:17; Acts 4:11; [Eph. 2:20; 1 Pet. 2:7, 8] **23** [1]Lit. *This is from the LORD* **26** [a]Matt. 21:9; 23:39; Mark 11:9; Luke 13:35; 19:38 **27** [a]Esth. 8:16; [1 Pet. 2:9] *See WW at 2 Kin. 12:9. **28** [a]Ex. 15:2; Is. 25:1

PSALM 119

1 [a]Ps. 128:1; [Ezek. 11:20; 18:17]; Mic. 4:2 [1]*blameless* *See WW at Is. 42:21. **2** [a]Deut. 6:5; 10:12; 11:13; 13:3 **3** [a][1 John 3:9; 5:18] **4** *See WW at Ps. 119:15.

6 [a]Job 22:26 **10** [a]2 Chr. 15:15 **11** [a]Ps. 37:31; Luke 2:19 *See WW at 2 Sam. 22:31. **13** [a]Ps. 34:11 **15** [1]*look into*

WORD WEALTH

119:15 precepts, *piqud* (pee-*kood*); Strong's #6490: A commandment, a precept, statute, mandate; something appointed or authorized by God. This word comes from the root verb *paqad,* "to appoint, oversee, take account, or allocate." The verb contains a strong sense of "counting" and "numbering" one's charges (those for which one is responsible). *Piqud* occurs 24 times, all in Ps. (21 are found in Ps. 119; the remainder are located in 19:8; 103:18; 111:7). The Lord's *piqudim* are His appointed statutes, mandates, numbered precepts, and His authorized, listed commandments.

118:22, 23 These verses are quoted five times in the NT as applied to Jesus' being **rejected** by the Jewish leadership (1 Pet. 2:7). Rejection is a hard thing for anyone to experience, but it is **marvelous** when God turns it around for good.

118:25 The shouts of **Save now** (Hebrew *hosanna*) were a recognition by the NT crowd that Jesus is the **LORD** who *can save—He is God* (*vv. 25–27;* Matt. 21:9).

118:27 Horns are stone outcroppings extending from each corner of the sacrificial altars.

119:1–176 Aleph (heading before v. 1): This skillfully written psalm is an alphabetic (acrostic) masterpiece divided into 22 stanzas with eight couplets in each stanza. All the couplets in the first stanza begin with the first letter of the Hebrew alphabet, *'aleph;* the couplets in the second stanza begin with the second letter, *beth;* and so on, to the end of the poem.

The sublime topic adroitly presented is the divine revelation variously called "the Law," "commandments," "testimonies," "statutes," "precepts," "judgments," "word," "ordinances," and "way." This seems to be an expansion of 19:7–11.

119:1 Blessed (happy) sets the theme for the entire poem: the key to happiness is doing the will of God revealed in His Word.

119:9 See section 1 of Truth-In-Action following Ps. 150.

119:11 See section 3 of Truth-In-Action following Ps. 150.

16 I will [a]delight myself in Your
statutes;
I will not forget Your *word.

ג GIMEL

17 [a]Deal bountifully with Your
servant,
That I may live and keep Your
word.

[4] 18 Open my eyes, that I may see
Wondrous things from Your
law.

19 [a]I *am* a stranger in the earth;
Do not hide Your commandments
from me.

20 [a]My soul [1]breaks with longing
For Your judgments at all times.

21 You rebuke the proud—the
cursed,
Who stray from Your
commandments.

22 [a]Remove from me reproach and
contempt,
For I have kept Your testimonies.

[3] 23 Princes also sit *and* speak against
me,
But Your servant meditates on
Your *statutes.

24 Your testimonies also *are* my
delight
And my counselors.

ד DALETH

25 [a]My soul clings to the dust;
[b]Revive me according to Your
word.

26 I have declared my ways, and
You answered me;
[a]Teach me Your statutes.

[4] 27 Make me *understand the way of
Your *precepts;
So [a]shall I meditate on Your
wonderful works.

28 [a]My soul [1]melts from [2]heaviness;
Strengthen me according to Your
word.

29 Remove from me the way of
lying,
And grant me Your law
*graciously.

30 I have *chosen the way of truth;
Your judgments I have laid *before
me.*

31 I cling to Your testimonies;
O LORD, do not put me to shame!

32 I will run the course of Your
commandments,
For You shall [a]enlarge my
heart.

ה HE

33 [a]Teach* me, O LORD, the way of
Your statutes,
And I shall keep it *to* the end.

34 [a]Give me understanding, and I
shall keep Your law;
Indeed, I shall observe it with *my*
whole heart.

35 Make me *walk in the path of
Your **commandments,**
For I *delight in it.

WORD WEALTH

119:35 commandments, *mitsvah,* plural *mitsvot* (mits-*vah,* mits-*voht*); Strong's #4687: Command, ordinance, precept, law; a charge; an order; a directive. *Mitsvah* is derived from the verb *tsavah,* "to command, charge, or appoint" something. *Tsavah* may have involved "marking down" orders since one of its derivatives (*tsiyun*) means "signpost" (Ezek. 39:15). God marked down the commandments, which He gave Israel upon stone tablets. *Mitsvah* occurs 180 times in the OT, 43 times in Deut., 22 times in Ps. 119, honoring God's multifaceted instructions to His servants. While *mitsvah* sometimes describes a king's "orders" (2 Chr. 8:14), it most often refers to God's commands. The term *Bar Mitsvah* ("Son of the Commandment") marks the coming of age for a young Jewish male who accepts his duties relating to the Law of Moses.

36 [1]Incline my heart to Your
testimonies,
And not to [a]covetousness. [2]

37 [a]Turn[1] away my eyes from
[b]looking at worthless things,
And revive me in [2]Your way.

38 [a]Establish Your word to Your
servant,
Who *is devoted* to fearing You.

39 Turn away my reproach which I
dread,
For Your judgments *are* good.

40 Behold, I long for Your *precepts;
Revive me in Your righteousness.

ו WAW

41 Let Your mercies come also to
me, O LORD—
Your salvation according to Your
word.

42 So shall I have an answer for him
who [1]reproaches me,
For I trust in Your word.

16 [a]Ps. 1:2 *See WW at Deut. 1:1. **17** [a]Ps. 116:7 **19** [a]Gen. 47:9; Lev. 25:23; 1 Chr. 29:15; Ps. 39:12; Heb. 11:13 **20** [a]Ps. 42:1, 2; 63:1; 84:2 [1]*is crushed* **22** [a]Ps. 39:8 **23** *See WW at Neh. 9:13. **25** [a]Ps. 44:25 [b]Ps. 143:11 **26** [a]Ps. 25:4; 27:11; 86:11 **27** [a]Ps. 145:5, 6 *See WW at Neh. 8:8. • See WW at Ps. 119:15. **28** [a]Ps. 107:26 [1]Lit. *drops* [2]*grief* **29** *See WW at Mal. 1:9. **30** *See WW at 1 Kin. 11:34. **32** [a]1 Kin. 4:29; Is. 60:5; 2 Cor. 6:11, 13

33 [a][Matt. 10:22; Rev. 2:26] *See WW at Ps. 32:8. **34** [a][Prov. 2:6; James 1:5] **35** *See WW at Deut. 11:25. • See WW at Ps. 112:1. **36** [a]Ezek. 33:31; [Mark 7:20–23]; Luke 12:15; [Heb. 13:5] [1]Cause me to long for **37** [a]Is. 33:15 [b]Prov. 23:5 [1]Lit. *Cause my eyes to pass away from* [2]So with MT, LXX, Vg.; Tg. *Your words* **38** [a]2 Sam. 7:25 **40** *See WW at Ps. 119:15. **42** [1]*taunts*

119:18 See section 4 of Truth-In-Action following Ps. 150.
119:23, 24 See section 3 of Truth-In-Action following Ps. 150.
119:27 See section 4 of Truth-In-Action following Ps. 150.
119:36 See section 2 of Truth-In-Action following Ps. 150.

43 And take not the word of truth
utterly out of my mouth,
For I have hoped in Your
ordinances.
44 So shall I keep Your law
continually,
Forever and ever.
45 And I will walk [1]at [a]liberty,
For I seek Your precepts.
46 [a]I will speak of Your testimonies
also before kings,
And will not be ashamed.
47 And I will delight myself in Your
commandments,
Which I love.
48 My hands also I will lift up to
Your commandments,
Which I love,
And I will meditate on Your
statutes.

ז ZAYIN

49 Remember the word to Your
servant,
Upon which You have caused me
to hope.
50 This *is* my [a]comfort in my
affliction,
For Your word has given me life.
51 The proud have me in great
derision,
Yet I do not turn aside from Your
law.
52 I remembered Your judgments of
old, O LORD,
And have comforted myself.
53 [a]Indignation has taken hold of me
Because of the wicked, who
forsake Your law.
54 Your statutes have been my songs
In the house of my pilgrimage.
55 [a]I remember Your name in the
night, O LORD,
And I keep Your law.
1 56 This has become mine,
Because I kept Your *precepts.

ח HETH

57 [a]*You are* my portion, O LORD;
I have said that I would keep Your
words.
58 I entreated Your favor with *my*
whole heart;
Be merciful to me according to
Your word.
59 I [a]thought about my ways,
And turned my feet to Your
testimonies.
60 I made haste, and did not delay
To keep Your commandments.

45 [a]Prov. 4:12 [1]Lit. *in a wide place*
46 [a]Ps. 138:1; Matt. 10:18; Acts 26
50 [a]Job 6:10; [Rom. 15:4]
53 [a]Ex. 32:19; Ezra 9:3; Neh. 13:25
55 [a]Ps. 63:6
56 *See WW at Ps. 119:15.
57 [a]Num. 18:20; Ps. 16:5; Jer. 10:16; Lam. 3:24
59 [a]Mark 14:72; Luke 15:17
62 [a]Acts 16:25
64 [a]Ps. 33:5
66 [a]Phil. 1:9
67 [a]Prov. 3:11; Jer. 31:18, 19; [Heb. 12:5–11]
68 [a]Ps. 106:1; 107:1; [Matt. 19:17]
69 [a]Job 13:4; Ps. 109:2 [1]Lit. *smeared me with a lie*
70 [a]Deut. 32:15; Job 15:27; Ps. 17:10; Is. 6:10; Jer. 5:28; Acts 28:27 [1]Insensible
72 [a]Ps. 19:10; Prov. 8:10, 11, 19

61 The cords of the wicked have
bound me,
But I have not forgotten Your
law.
62 [a]At midnight I will rise to give
thanks to You,
Because of Your righteous
judgments.
63 I *am* a **companion** of all who fear
You,
And of those who keep Your
precepts.

WORD WEALTH

119:63 companion, *chaber* (chah-*vehr*); Strong's #2270: A friend, companion, partner, associate; someone joined together or knit together with another person. *Chaber* comes from the verb *chabar,* "to join together, fellowship, associate with." The plural *chaberim* refers to "friends" who are closely bonded together in love or in a common purpose. In this reference, the psalmist states, "I am a friend of anyone and everyone who reveres the Lord," or to greatly paraphrase it, "Any friend of God's is a friend of mine."

64 [a]The earth, O LORD, is full of Your
mercy;
Teach me Your statutes.

ט TETH

65 You have dealt well with Your
servant,
O LORD, according to Your word.
66 Teach me good judgment and
[a]knowledge,
For I believe Your
commandments.
67 Before I was [a]afflicted I went
astray,
But now I keep Your word.
68 You *are* [a]good, and do good;
Teach me Your statutes.
69 The proud have [a]forged[1] a lie
against me,
But I will keep Your precepts
with *my* whole heart.
70 [a]Their heart is [1]as fat as grease,
But I delight in Your law.
71 *It is* good for me that I have been 6
afflicted,
That I may learn Your statutes.
72 [a]The law of Your mouth *is* better
to me
Than thousands of *coins of* gold
and silver.

119:56 See section 1 of Truth-In-Action following Ps. 150.
119:70 Grease: That is, they are as dull or senseless as a bucket of lard.
119:71 See section 6 of Truth-In-Action following Ps. 150.

י YOD

73 [a]Your hands have made me and
fashioned me;
Give me understanding, that I
may learn Your
commandments.
74 [a]Those who fear You will be glad
when they see me,
Because I have hoped in Your
word.
75 I know, O LORD, [a]that Your
judgments *are* [1]right,
And *that* in faithfulness You have
afflicted me.
76 Let, I *pray, Your merciful
kindness be for my *comfort,
According to Your word to Your
servant.
77 Let Your tender mercies come to
me, that I may live;
For Your law *is* my delight.
78 Let the proud [a]be ashamed,
For they treated me wrongfully
with falsehood;
But I will meditate on Your
*precepts.
79 Let those who fear You turn to
me,
Those who know Your
testimonies.
80 Let my heart be blameless
regarding Your statutes,
That I may not be *ashamed.

כ KAPH

81 [a]My soul faints for Your salvation,
But I hope in Your word.
82 My eyes fail *from searching* Your
word,
Saying, "When will You comfort
me?"
83 For [a]I have become like a
wineskin in smoke,
Yet I do not forget Your statutes.
84 [a]How many *are* the days of Your
servant?
[b]When will You execute judgment
on those who persecute me?
85 [a]The proud have dug pits for me,
Which *is* not according to Your
law.
86 All Your commandments *are*
*faithful;
They persecute me [a]wrongfully;
Help me!
87 They almost made an end of me
on earth,
But I did not forsake Your
precepts.
88 Revive me according to Your
lovingkindness,
So that I may keep the testimony
of Your mouth.

ל LAMED

89 [a]Forever, O LORD,
Your word [1]is settled in heaven.
90 Your faithfulness *endures* to all
generations;
You established the earth, and it
[1]abides.
91 They continue this day according
to [a]Your ordinances,
For all *are* Your servants.

KINGDOM DYNAMICS

119:89–91 The Authority of God's Word over Our Lives, THE WORD OF GOD. This text asserts the all-encompassing, absolutely authoritative Word of God as unchangingly secured in heaven, noting: 1) The timelessness of God's rule by His Word. Though times and seasons change, though social customs, human opinions, and philosophical viewpoints vary, they have no effect on the constancy or authority of God's Word. 2) God is faithful in applying the power, promise, and blessing of His Word, along with its requirements of justice and judgment (v. 91). Just as He spoke and the Earth was created and is sustained, so He has spoken regarding His laws for living. The relativism of human thought does not affect His authority or standards. 3) While creation abides by His Word (responding as His "servants," v. 90), man is often a study in contrast to this submission to the Creator's authority. However, whatever our past rebellion, upon coming to Christ, a practical reinstatement of God's Word as the governing principle for all our life is to take place. Not only does Jesus conclusively declare this (John 8:47), but Paul notes that to respond otherwise is to compromise the level of life to which we have been called (1 Cor. 2:13–16). As "spiritual" people we are to refuse the "natural" inclinations of fallen men. As we hear and yield to the authority of God's Word, we verify that we are no longer dominated by the world's spirit of error (1 John 4:6).

(1 Pet. 1:23/Deut. 8:3) J.W.H.

92 Unless Your law *had been* my
delight,
I would then have perished in my
affliction.
93 I will never forget Your precepts,
For by them You have given me
life.
94 I *am* Yours, save me;
For I have sought Your precepts.

73 [a]Job 10:8; 31:15; [Ps. 139:15, 16]
74 [a]Ps. 34:2
75 [a][Heb. 12:10] [1]Lit. *righteous*
76 *See WW at Ps. 122:6. • See WW at Ps. 23:4.
78 [a]Ps. 25:3 *See WW at Ps. 119:15.
80 *See WW at Ezek. 16:63.
81 [a]Ps. 73:26; 84:2
83 [a]Job 30:30
84 [a]Ps. 39:4 [b]Rev. 6:10
85 [a]Ps. 35:7; Prov. 16:27; Jer. 18:22
86 [a]Ps. 35:19 *See WW at Prov. 28:20.
89 [a]Ps. 89:2; Is. 40:8; Matt. 24:35; [1 Pet. 1:25] [1]Lit. *stands firm*
90 [1]Lit. *stands*
91 [a]Jer. 33:25

119:83 In smoke: Or, he is old and wrinkled, perhaps aged prematurely.

95 The wicked wait for me to
destroy me,
But I will [1]consider Your
testimonies.
96 [a]I have seen the consummation of
all perfection,
But Your commandment *is*
exceedingly broad.

מ MEM

97 Oh, how I *love Your law!
[a]It *is* my meditation all the day.
98 You, through Your
commandments, make me
[a]wiser than my enemies;
For they *are* ever with me.
99 I have more *understanding than
all my teachers,
[a]For Your testimonies *are* my
meditation.
100 [a]I understand more than the
[1]**ancients,**
Because I keep Your precepts.

WORD WEALTH

119:100 ancients, *zaqen* (zah-*kayn*); Strong's #2205: An elder, old man, aged person. The verb means "to become old." *Zaqan* means "beard," something that grows with age. Older persons are respected in Scripture because their experience in life has brought them wisdom. Hence, the elders who accompanied Moses (Ex. 24:9–14) or counseled kings (1 Kin. 12:6–8) were older, mature men. In this reference, the psalmist has been schooled by the Lord to such a degree that he knows much more than the old men know (see also v. 99). Young and old should equally hear from God in the outpouring of the Holy Spirit (Joel 2:28).

101 I have restrained my feet from
every evil way,
That I may keep Your word.
102 I have not departed from Your
judgments,
For You Yourself have taught
me.
103 [a]How sweet are Your words to
my taste,
Sweeter than honey to my
mouth!
104 Through Your *precepts I get
understanding;
Therefore I hate every false way.

נ NUN

2 105 [a]Your word *is* a lamp to my feet
And a light to my path.

95 [1]*give attention to*
96 [a]Matt. 5:18
97 [a]Ps. 1:2
*See WW at Ps. 97:10.
98 [a]Deut. 4:6
99 [a][2 Tim. 3:15]
*See WW at Jer. 3:15.
100 [a][Job 32:7–9] [1]*aged*
103 [a]Ps. 19:10; Prov. 8:11
104 *See WW at Ps. 119:15.
105 [a]Prov. 6:23

KINGDOM DYNAMICS

119:105 God's Word and Practical, Fruitful Living, THE WORD OF GOD. We are all inexperienced in too much of life to be without a guide. God's Word is that guide. The whole of Ps. 119 unfolds manifold features of God's Word, showing how dynamically it will assist us in life's most practical circumstances. But no single verse focuses this more clearly than v. 105, which shows how God's Word lights the way, giving direction for each step ("to my feet") and giving wisdom for long-range plans ("to my path"). Joshua links the regular application of God's Word to life as the most certain way to both success and prosperity in living (Josh. 1:8). Further, Ps. 119:130 notes the wisdom God's Word gives to the "simple" (Hebrew *pethawee*), a truth specifically pointing toward the avoidance of making decisions based on human delusion or outright senselessness. Also, Prov. 6:23 reminds us that the "reproofs" or corrections the Bible gives are as much a part of the "light" it provides as any positive or confirming direction we find therein. Let God's Word guide, correct, instruct, lead, teach, and confirm. Do not hasten ahead without it—ever.

(Deut. 8:3/1 Cor. 3:1–5) J.W.H.

106 [a]I have sworn and confirmed
That I will keep Your righteous
judgments.
107 I am afflicted very much;
Revive me, O LORD, according to
Your word.
108 Accept, I pray, [a]the freewill
offerings of my mouth,
O LORD,
And teach me Your judgments.
109 [a]My life *is* continually [1]in my
hand,
Yet I do not forget Your law.
110 [a]The wicked have laid a snare for
me,
Yet I have not strayed from Your
precepts.
111 [a]Your testimonies I have taken as
a [1]heritage forever,
For they *are* the rejoicing of my
heart.
112 I have inclined my heart to
perform Your statutes
Forever, to the very end.

ס SAMEK

113 I hate the [1]double-minded,
But I love Your law.

106 [a]Neh. 10:29
108 [a]Hos. 14:2; Heb. 13:15
109 [a]Judg. 12:3; Job 13:14 [1]*In danger*
110 [a]Ps. 140:5
111 [a]Deut. 33:4 [1]*inheritance*
113 [1]Lit. *divided in heart or mind*

119:99, 100 Secular **teachers** and **ancients** are of little value in comparison to the wisdom of God's Word.
119:105 See section 2 of Truth-In-Action following Ps. 150.

119:108 The **freewill offerings** are a reference to praise (Heb. 13:15).

114 [a]You *are* my hiding place and my shield;
I hope in Your word.
115 [a]Depart from me, you evildoers,
For I will keep the commandments of my God!
116 Uphold me according to Your word, that I may live;
And do not let me [a]be ashamed of my hope.
117 [1]Hold me up, and I shall be safe,
And I shall observe Your statutes continually.
118 You reject all those who stray from Your statutes,
For their deceit *is* falsehood.
119 You [1]put away all the wicked of the earth [a]*like* [2]dross;
Therefore I love Your testimonies.
120 [a]My flesh trembles for fear of You,
And I am afraid of Your judgments.

ע AYIN

121 I have done justice and righteousness;
Do not leave me to my oppressors.
122 Be [a]surety[1] for Your servant for good;
Do not let the proud oppress me.
123 My eyes fail *from seeking* Your salvation
And Your righteous word.
124 Deal with Your servant according to Your mercy,
And teach me Your statutes.
125 [a]I *am* Your servant;
Give me understanding,
That I may *know Your testimonies.
126 *It is* time for *You* to act, O LORD,
For they have [1]regarded Your law as void.
127 [a]Therefore I love Your commandments
More than gold, yes, than fine gold!
4 128 Therefore all *Your* *precepts *concerning* all *things*
I consider *to be* right;
I hate every false way.

פ PE

129 Your testimonies are wonderful;
Therefore my soul keeps them.
130 The entrance of Your words gives light; **2**
[a]It gives understanding to the [b]simple.
131 I opened my mouth and [a]panted,
For I longed for Your commandments.
132 [a]Look upon me and be merciful to me,
[b]As Your custom *is* toward those who love Your name.
133 [a]Direct my steps by Your word,
And [b]let no iniquity have dominion over me.
134 [a]Redeem me from the oppression of man,
That I may keep Your *precepts.
135 [a]Make Your face shine upon Your servant,
And teach me Your statutes.
136 [a]Rivers of water run down from my eyes,
Because *men* do not keep Your law.

צ TSADDE

137 [a]Righteous *are* You, O LORD,
And upright *are* Your judgments.
138 [a]Your testimonies, *which* You have commanded,
Are righteous and very faithful.
139 [a]My zeal has [1]consumed me,
Because my enemies have forgotten Your words.
140 [a]Your word *is* very [1]pure;
Therefore Your servant loves it.
141 I *am* small and despised,
Yet I do not forget Your precepts.
142 Your righteousness *is* an everlasting righteousness,
And Your law *is* [a]truth.
143 Trouble and anguish have [1]overtaken me,
Yet Your commandments *are* my delights.
144 The righteousness of Your testimonies *is* everlasting;
Give me understanding, and I shall live.

ק QOPH

145 I cry out with *my* whole heart;
Hear me, O LORD!
I will keep Your statutes.
146 I cry out to You;

114 [a][Ps. 32:7] **115** [a]Ps. 6:8; Matt. 7:23 **116** [a]Ps. 25:2; [Rom. 5:5; 9:33; 10:11; Phil. 1:20] **117** [1]*Uphold me* **119** [a]Is. 1:22, 25; Ezek. 22:18, 19 [1]*destroy*, lit. *cause to cease* [2]*slag* or *refuse* **120** [a]Job 4:14; Hab. 3:16 **122** [a]Job 17:3; Heb. 7:22 [1]*guaranty* **125** [a]Ps. 116:16 *See WW at Ex. 3:7. **126** [1]*broken Your law* **127** [a]Ps. 19:10 **128** *See WW at Ps. 119:15.

130 [a]Prov. 6:23 [b][Ps. 19:7]; Prov. 1:4 **131** [a]Ps. 42:1 **132** [a]Ps. 106:4 [b]Ps. 51:1; [2 Thess. 1:6] **133** [a]Ps. 17:5 [b][Ps. 19:13; Rom. 6:12] **134** [a]Luke 1:74 *See WW at Ps. 119:15. **135** [a]Num. 6:25; Ps. 4:6 **136** [a]Jer. 9:1, 18; 14:17; Lam. 3:48; Ezek. 9:4 **137** [a]Ezra 9:15; Neh. 9:33; Jer. 12:1; Lam. 1:18; Dan. 9:7, 14 **138** [a][Ps. 19:7–9] **139** [a]Ps. 69:9; John 2:17 [1]*put an end to* **140** [a]Ps. 12:6 [1]Lit. *refined* or *tried* **142** [a][Ps. 19:9; John 17:17] **143** [1]Lit. *found*

119:127 Fine gold is pure, like 24-karat gold.
119:128 See section 4 of Truth-In-Action following Ps. 150.
119:130 See section 2 of Truth-In-Action following Ps. 150.
119:130 Entrance is literally "opening"; that is, their exposition gives **light** or direction in life.

*Save me, and I will keep Your testimonies.
147 [a]I rise before the dawning of the morning,
And cry for help;
I hope in Your word.
148 [a]My eyes are awake through the *night* watches,
That I may meditate on Your word.
149 Hear my voice according to Your lovingkindness;
O LORD, revive me according to Your justice.
150 They draw near who follow after wickedness;
They are far from Your law.
151 You *are* [a]near, O LORD,
And all Your commandments *are* truth.
152 Concerning Your testimonies,
I have known of old that You have founded them [a]forever.

ר RESH

153 [a]Consider my affliction and deliver me,
For I do not forget Your law.
154 [a]Plead my cause and redeem me;
Revive me according to Your word.
155 Salvation *is* far from the wicked,
For they do not seek Your statutes.
156 [1]Great *are* Your tender mercies, O LORD;
Revive me according to Your judgments.
157 Many *are* my persecutors and my enemies,
Yet I do not [a]turn from Your testimonies.
158 I see the treacherous, and [a]am disgusted,
Because they do not keep Your word.
159 Consider how I love Your *precepts;
Revive me, O LORD, according to Your lovingkindness.
160 The entirety of Your word *is* truth,
And every one of Your righteous judgments *endures* forever.

ש SHIN

161 [a]Princes persecute me without a cause,
But my heart stands in awe of Your word.

146 *See WW at Jer. 17:14.
147 [a]Ps. 5:3
148 [a]Ps. 63:1, 6
151 [a][Ps. 145:18]; Is. 50:8
152 [a]Luke 21:33
153 [a]Lam. 5:1
154 [a]1 Sam. 24:15; Mic. 7:9
156 [1]Or *Many*
157 [a]Ps. 44:18
158 [a]Ezek. 9:4
159 *See WW at Ps. 119:15.
161 [a]1 Sam. 24:11; 26:18

162 I rejoice at Your word
As one who finds great treasure.
163 I hate and abhor lying,
But I love Your law.
164 Seven times a day I praise You,
Because of Your righteous judgments.
165 [a]Great* peace have those who love Your law,
And [1]nothing causes them to stumble.
166 [a]LORD, I hope for Your salvation,
And I do Your commandments.
167 My soul keeps Your testimonies,
And I love them exceedingly.
168 I keep Your precepts and Your testimonies,
[a]For all my ways *are* before You.

ת TAU

169 Let my cry come before You, O LORD;
[a]Give me understanding according to Your word.
170 Let my [1]supplication come before You;
Deliver me according to Your word.
171 [a]My lips shall utter praise,
For You teach me Your statutes.
172 My tongue shall speak of Your word,
For all Your commandments *are* righteousness.
173 Let Your hand become my help,
For [a]I have chosen Your *precepts.
174 [a]I long for Your salvation, O LORD,
And [b]Your *law *is* my delight.
175 Let my soul *live, and it shall praise You;
And let Your judgments help me.
176 [a]I have gone astray like a lost sheep;
Seek Your servant,
For I do not forget Your *commandments.

165 [a]Prov. 3:2; [Is. 26:3; 32:17] [1]Lit. *they have no stumbling block* *See WW at Ps. 31:19.
166 [a]Gen. 49:18
168 [a]Job 24:23; Prov. 5:21
169 [a]Ps. 119:27, 144
170 [1]Prayer of supplication
171 [a]Ps. 119:7
173 [a]Josh. 24:22; Luke 10:42 *See WW at Ps. 119:15.
174 [a]Ps. 119:166 [b]Ps. 119:16, 24 *See WW at Is. 42:21.
175 *See WW at Hab. 2:4.
176 [a][Is. 53:6]; Jer. 50:6; Matt. 18:12; Luke 15:4; [1 Pet. 2:25] *See WW at Ps. 119:35.

PSALM 120

Plea for Relief from Bitter Foes

A Song of Ascents.

IN [a]my distress I cried to the LORD,
And He heard me.
2 Deliver my soul, O LORD, from lying lips
And from a deceitful tongue.

PSALM 120
1 [a]Jon. 2:2

120:1–7 This psalm and Ps. 121—134 are probably those sung by pilgrims ascending the hills to Jerusalem for the yearly feasts (122:4). See title: "A Song of Ascents."

3 What shall be given to you,
Or what shall be done to you,
You false tongue?
4 Sharp arrows of the [1]warrior,
With coals of the broom tree!

5 Woe is me, that I dwell in
[a]Meshech,
[b]*That* I *dwell among the tents of
Kedar!
6 My soul has dwelt too long
With one who hates peace.
7 I *am for* peace;
But when I speak, they *are* for
war.

PSALM 121

God the Help of Those Who Seek Him

A Song of Ascents.

I [a]WILL lift up my eyes to the hills—
From whence comes my help?
2 [a]My help *comes* from the LORD,
Who made heaven and earth.

3 [a]He will not allow your foot to
[1]be moved;
[b]He who keeps you will not
slumber.
4 Behold, He who keeps Israel
Shall neither slumber nor sleep.

5 The LORD *is* your [1]keeper;
The LORD *is* [a]your shade
[b]at your right hand.
6 [a]The sun shall not strike you by
day,
Nor the moon by night.

7 The LORD shall [1]preserve* you
from all evil;
He shall [a]preserve your soul.
8 The LORD shall [a]preserve[1] your
going out and your coming in
From this time forth, and even
forevermore.

PSALM 122

The Joy of Going to the House of the LORD

A Song of Ascents. Of David.

I WAS glad when they said to me,
[a]"Let us go into the house of the
LORD."
2 Our feet have been standing
Within your gates, O Jerusalem!

3 Jerusalem is built
As a city that is [a]compact
together,
4 [a]Where the tribes go up,
The tribes of the LORD,
[1]To [b]the Testimony of Israel,
To give thanks to the name of the
LORD.
5 [a]For thrones are set there for
judgment,
The thrones of the house of
David.

6 [a]**Pray** for the peace of Jerusalem:
"May they prosper who love you.

WORD WEALTH

122:6 pray, *sha'al* (shah-*ahl*); Strong's #7592: To ask, inquire, request, pray, desire, wish for, demand. *Sha'al* is not the usual Hebrew word for "pray," but it has the suggestion of "asking for" or "inquiring about" something. In this psalm for (*cont. on next page*)

---

4 [1]*mighty one*
5 [a]Gen. 10:2; 1 Chr. 1:5; Ezek. 27:13; 38:2, 3; 39:1 [b]Gen. 25:13; Is. 21:16; 60:7; Jer. 2:10; 49:28; Ezek. 27:21 *See WW at Num. 10:12.

PSALM 121

1 [a][Jer. 3:23]
2 [a][Ps. 124:8]
3 [a]1 Sam. 2:9; Prov. 3:23, 26 [b][Ps. 127:1; Prov. 24:12]; Is. 27:3 [1]*slip*
5 [a]Is. 25:4 [b]Ps. 16:8 [1]*protector*
6 [a]Ps. 91:5; Is. 49:10; Jon. 4:8; Rev. 7:16
7 [a]Ps. 41:2 [1]*keep* *See WW at Job 10:12.
8 [a]Deut. 28:6; [Prov. 2:8; 3:6] [1]*keep*

PSALM 122

1 [a][Is. 2:3; Mic. 4:2]; Zech. 8:21
3 [a]2 Sam. 5:9
4 [a]Ex. 23:17; Deut. 16:16 [b]Ex. 16:34 [1]Or *As a testimony to*
5 [a]Deut. 17:8; 2 Chr. 19:8
6 [a]Ps. 51:18

120:3, 4 Arrows: This is another way of saying the slanderers will reap what they sow. **The broom tree** is a thorny brushwood preferred for kindling because it produces a long, hot fire; so, lying lips will themselves be burned (see Prov. 16:27).

120:5, 6 Meshech and **Kedar** symbolically stand for warlike tribes around Israel. The intent is, "Though I stand for **peace,** I am surrounded by men of hate."

121:1 The **hills** that the writer sees are the hills of Zion and Jerusalem, the OT symbol for the dwelling place of God that He chose as the central place of OT worship (Deut. 12:5).

121:2 The Creator of **heaven** and **earth** is also its Guardian and Caretaker. This refutes the philosophy of transcendentalism or deism, where God is said to be remote (Col. 1:17).

121:3 The Hebrew word for **keeps** (preserves) is used six times in this song, dramatically emphasizing the care of God (see Jude 24).

121:6 The **sun** and **moon** represent 24-hour protection.

121:7 The saint is preserved, not in the sense that he will never suffer adversity, but that he will go through adversity and come out a winner.

121:8 The keeping power of God sustains until the very coming of **the LORD** Jesus Christ (1 Thess. 5:23).

122:1–9 House: Although the center of worship is not now just one city as in this OT setting, but rather many local churches (John 4:21), yet we can learn from this psalm great respect for the things of God: worship, revelation, unity, and justice.

122:1 Glad: Since OT congregational worship was so exciting, how much more joyous ought worship in the NT church to be, now that the full gospel of Jesus has been revealed.

122:3–5 That is, the psalmist rejoices in the fact that the **Testimony** (the revealed Mosaic Law) for maintaining an orderly society is the unique possession of Israel, and that it is being administered by the fair and just rulings of King **David** and his administrators.

122:6 There is a poetic play on words here, since **Jerusalem** means "City of Peace." His prayer is that the city will live up to its name. **Peace** (Hebrew *shalom*) is a comprehensive word that includes welfare, health, prosperity, and happiness, not just the absence of strife.

(*cont. from preceding page*)
the sake of God's people and for the sake of the Lord's house (vv. 8, 9) we are instructed to seek Jerusalem's good, that is, to inquire earnestly about its welfare, pray for its peace, and ask with true concern about its condition. From *sha'al* comes the proper name *Sha'ul* (Saul), meaning "Asked For" or "Requested," that is to say, a wanted child.

KINGDOM DYNAMICS

122:6 Prophecy and the Future of Israel, PROPHECY. Theologically, there are two different positions concerning what may be expected with regard to the future of Israel. The difference centers on the question: Does Israel, as the ancient people of God, still hold a preferred place in His economy, or have they lost that place through unbelief?

Many see a continuing and distinctive role for Israel in God's plans until the end of time. These believe that Rom. 9—11 indicates that a restoration of Israel will take place ("all Israel will be saved," Rom. 11:26), and that the church needs to recognize its Jewish roots ("The root supports you," Rom. 11:18). This view, however, may also allow for a fulfillment of some OT promises and blessings in individual believers and through the church. The church is to demonstrate what it means to enjoy the full blessing of God so that Israel will be encouraged to return to the One who loves them eternally.

Others, however, have seen the church replacing Israel in the plan of God because the majority of the Jewish people refused to accept Jesus as Messiah. Thus the blessings and promises addressed to Israel may now only rightly be applied to the church. From this view, the modern State of Israel and the Jewish people are simply the same as all other nations and ethnic groups, and God will not deal with them differently than He will with any other peoples.

(Obad. 15/Rom. 11:19–24) J.W.H.

7 Peace be within your walls,
Prosperity within your palaces."
8 For the sake of my brethren and companions,
I will now say, "Peace *be* within you."
9 Because of the house of the LORD our God
I will [a]seek your good.

PSALM 123

Prayer for Relief from Contempt

A Song of Ascents.

UNTO You [a]I lift up my eyes,
O You [b]who dwell in the heavens.
2 Behold, as the eyes of servants *look* to the hand of their masters,
As the eyes of a maid to the hand of her mistress,
[a]So our eyes *look* to the LORD our God,
Until He has mercy on us.

3 Have mercy on us, O LORD, have mercy on us!
For we are exceedingly filled with contempt.
4 Our soul is exceedingly filled
With the scorn of those who are at ease,
With the contempt of the proud.

PSALM 124

The LORD the Defense of His People

A Song of Ascents. Of David.

"IF it had not been the LORD who was on our [a]side,"
[b]Let Israel now say—
2 "If it had not been the LORD who was on our side,
When men rose up against us,
3 Then they would have [a]swallowed us alive,
When their wrath was kindled against us;
4 Then the waters would have overwhelmed us,
The stream would have [1]gone over our soul;
5 Then the swollen waters
Would have [1]gone over our soul."

6 Blessed *be* the LORD,
Who has not given us *as* prey to their teeth.

9 [a]Neh. 2:10; Esth. 10:3

PSALM 123

1 [a]Ps. 121:1; 141:8 [b]Ps. 2:4; 11:4; 115:3
2 [a]Ps. 25:15

PSALM 124

1 [a]Ps. 118:6; [Rom. 8:31] [b]Ps. 129:1
3 [a]Num. 16:30; Ps. 56:1, 2; 57:3; Prov. 1:12
4 [1]*swept over*
5 [1]*swept over*

122:9 The main attraction in OT Jerusalem, and in the spiritual Jerusalem (Gal. 4:26), was the **house** of worship where the presence of **God** was.

123:1–4 Just as Jesus looked up to heaven in recognition of His source of supply (John 17:1), and as Stephen looked steadfastly into heaven for comfort during persecution (Acts 7:55), so the psalmist sets an example for us in looking to **God** as a helping **hand.**

123:4 Words of **scorn** and **contempt** often hurt our feelings more than the pain of a flesh wound.

124:1–8 With three metaphors the beleaguered psalmist describes his enemies: beasts who would have **swallowed** (devoured) him (v. 3), floods of **swollen waters** (v. 5), and **fowlers** (bird-hunters) (v. 7). But the Creator of nature also controls nature and is his **help** (v. 8).

7 [a]Our soul has escaped [b]as a bird
from the snare of the [1]fowlers;
The snare is broken, and we have
escaped.
8 [a]Our help *is* in the name of the
LORD,
[b]Who made heaven and earth.

PSALM 125

The LORD *the Strength of His People*

A Song of Ascents.

THOSE who trust in the LORD
Are like Mount Zion,
Which cannot be moved, *but*
abides forever.
2 As the mountains surround
Jerusalem,
So the LORD surrounds His people
From this time forth and forever.

3 For [a]the scepter of wickedness
shall not rest
On the land allotted to the
righteous,
Lest the righteous reach out their
hands to iniquity.

4 Do good, O LORD, to *those who
are* good,
And to *those who are* upright in
their hearts.

5 As for such as turn aside to their
[a]crooked ways,
The LORD shall lead them away
With the workers of iniquity.

[b]Peace *be* upon Israel!

PSALM 126

A Joyful Return to Zion

A Song of Ascents.

WHEN [a]the LORD brought back
[1]the captivity of Zion,
[b]We were like those who dream.
2 Then [a]our mouth was filled with
laughter,
And our tongue with *singing.
Then they said among the
[1]nations,
"The LORD has done great things
for them."
3 The LORD has done great things
for us,
And we are glad.

4 Bring back our captivity, O LORD,
As the streams in the South.

5 [a]Those who *sow in tears 1
Shall reap in *joy.
6 He who continually goes
[1]forth weeping,
Bearing [2]seed for sowing,
Shall doubtless come again
[3]with [a]rejoicing,
Bringing his sheaves *with him.*

7 [a]Ps. 91:3 [b]Prov. 6:5; Hos. 9:8 [1]Persons who catch birds in a trap or snare
8 [a][Ps. 121:2] [b]Gen. 1:1; Ps. 134:3

PSALM 125

3 [a]Prov. 22:8; Is. 14:5
5 [a]Prov. 2:15; Is. 59:8 [b]Ps. 128:6; [Gal. 6:16]

PSALM 126

1 [a]Ps. 85:1; Jer. 29:14; Hos. 6:11; Joel 3:1 [b]Acts 12:9 [1]Those of the captivity
2 [a]Job 8:21 [1]*Gentiles*
*See WW at Ps. 30:5.
5 [a]Is. 35:10; 51:11; 61:7; Jer. 31:9; [Gal. 6:9] *See WW at Hos. 10:12. • See WW at Ps. 30:5.
6 [a]Is. 61:3 [1]*to and fro* [2]Lit. *a bag of seed for sowing* [3]*with shouts of joy*

PSALM 127

1 [a][Ps. 121:3–5] *See WW at Jer. 1:12.

KINGDOM DYNAMICS

126:5, 6 Tears and Brokenness in Victorious Warfare, FAITH'S WARFARE. Tears in Scripture play a unique role in spiritual breakthrough. Here we discover that the planting of seeds accompanied by a spirit of brokenness will not only bring a spiritual harvest of results, but will leave the sower with a spirit of rejoicing in the process. This passage, along with numerous others in Scripture regarding a spirit of brokenness, pictures a variety of purposes and functions related to what might be termed "the ministry of tears," a ministry Charles H. Spurgeon defined as "liquid prayer." First, there are tears of sorrow or suffering (2 Kin. 20:5). Second, there are tears of joy (Gen. 33:4). Third, there are tears of compassion (John 11:35). Fourth, there are tears of desperation (Esth. 4:1, 3). Fifth, there are tears of travail, or giving birth (Is. 42:14). Sixth, there are tears of repentance (Joel 2:12, 13). Passion in spiritual warfare is clearly needed.

(Num. 10:1–10/Eph. 6:10–18*) D.E.

PSALM 127

Laboring and Prospering with the LORD

A Song of Ascents. Of Solomon.

UNLESS the LORD builds the house, 2
They labor in vain who build it;
Unless [a]the LORD guards the city,
The watchman *stays awake in
vain.

125:1 Mount Zion is a symbol of security.
125:2 Jerusalem is situated in a mountain range running north and south, parallel to and west of the Jordan River.
126:1–6 This gleeful song refers to the return of the Jews from the Babylonian **captivity** after 70 years in exile (Ezra 1:1–3). Three metaphors are used to express the overwhelming joy of coming home: a pleasant **dream** (v. 1), the refreshing water of **streams** in the southern desert area (v. 4), and harvesttime festivities (v. 6).
126:5, 6 See section 1 of Truth-In-Action following Ps. 150.
127:1–5 Of the 1,005 songs of **Solomon** only this one and Ps. 72 are attributed to him in the Book of Psalms (1 Kin. 4:32).
127:1, 2 See section 2 of Truth-In-Action following Ps. 150.

2 *It is* vain for you to rise up early,
To sit up late,
To [a]eat the bread of sorrows;
For so He gives His beloved sleep.

3 Behold, [a]children *are* a heritage from the LORD,
[b]The fruit of the womb *is* a [c]reward.
4 Like arrows in the hand of a warrior,
So *are* the children of one's youth.
5 [a]Happy *is* the man who has his quiver full of them;
[b]They shall not be ashamed,
But shall speak with their enemies in the gate.

KINGDOM DYNAMICS

127:3–5 Loving and Caring for Children Honors God, FAMILY ORDER. God's covenant with Adam and Eve contained two interdependent provisions: descendants and dominion. Two people alone could not take dominion of the Earth. It would require descendants.

For believers, having children is a response to the command, "Be fruitful and multiply; fill the earth and subdue it" (Gen. 1:28). In this psalm, children are called "a heritage from the LORD." This means that children belong to God; they are "ours" only in a secondary sense. God gives children to parents, as a man entrusts his fortune to his heirs. Jesus wants us not to despise "one of these little ones," and He holds up their faith in God as an example for adults (Matt. 18:1–5, 10).

When a couple enters into marriage, they make themselves available to love, serve, and sacrifice for the next generation. To love and care for children is one of the principal ways that we honor God and share in building His kingdom.

(Hos. 11:1, 3, 4/Eph. 6:4) L.C.

PSALM 128

Blessings of Those Who Fear the LORD

A Song of Ascents.

BLESSED [a]*is* every one who fears the LORD,
Who walks in His ways.

2 [a]When you eat the [1]labor of your hands,
You *shall be* happy, and *it shall be* [b]well with you.
3 Your wife *shall be* [a]like a fruitful vine
In the very heart of your house,
Your [b]children [c]like olive plants
All around your table.
4 Behold, thus shall the man be blessed
Who fears the LORD.

5 [a]The LORD bless you out of Zion,
And may you see the good of Jerusalem
All the days of your life.
6 Yes, may you [a]see your children's children.

[b]Peace *be* upon Israel!

PSALM 129

Song of Victory over Zion's Enemies

A Song of Ascents.

"MANY a time they have [a]afflicted[1] me from [b]my youth,"
[c]Let Israel now say—
2 "Many a time they have afflicted me from my youth;
Yet they have not prevailed against me.
3 The plowers plowed on my back;
They made their furrows long."
4 The LORD *is* righteous;
He has cut in pieces the cords of the wicked.

5 Let all those who hate Zion
Be put to shame and turned back.
6 Let them be as the [a]grass *on* the housetops,
Which withers before it grows up,
7 With which the reaper does not fill his hand,
Nor he who binds sheaves, his [1]arms.
8 Neither let those who pass by them say,
[a]"The blessing of the LORD *be* upon you;
We bless you in the name of the LORD!"

2 [a][Gen. 3:17, 19] **3** [a][Gen. 33:5; Josh. 24:3, 4; Ps. 113:9] [b]Deut. 7:13; 28:4; Is. 13:18 [c][Ps. 113:9] **5** [a]Ps. 128:2, 3 [b]Job 5:4; Prov. 27:11

PSALM 128

1 [a]Ps. 119:1 **2** [a]Is. 3:10 [b]Deut. 4:40 [1]Fruit of the labor **3** [a]Ezek. 19:10 [b]Ps. 127:3–5 [c]Ps. 52:8; 144:12 **5** [a]Ps. 134:3 **6** [a]Gen. 48:11; 50:23; Job 42:16; Ps. 103:17; [Prov. 17:6] [b]Ps. 125:5

PSALM 129

1 [a][Jer. 1:19; 15:20]; Matt. 16:18; 2 Cor. 4:8, 9 [b]Ezek. 23:3; Hos. 2:15 [c]Ps. 124:1 [1]*persecuted* **6** [a]Ps. 37:2 **7** [1]*arms full,* lit. *bosom* **8** [a]Ruth 2:4

127:2 Sorrows (anxiety): This verse is a condensed way of saying what Jesus taught in Matt. 6:25–34 about worrying.
127:3–5 This section concerning **children** must be taken spiritually as well as biologically in light of NT revelation. See Phil. 2:19–22 for an example of a spiritual son.
128:1–6 The benedictions here are all based on a too-often overlooked element of worship: the fear of the Lord (v. 1).
129:1 Youth: That is, from its early beginning in history as a nation.
129:6 That is, **grass** that has sprouted in the gutters or corners where dirt has collected on the flat roof and quickly withers in the sun's heat.

PSALM 130

Waiting for the Redemption of the LORD

A Song of Ascents.

OUT [a]of the depths I have cried to
You, O LORD;
2 Lord, hear my voice!
Let Your ears be attentive
To the voice of my supplications.

3 [a]If You, LORD, should [1]mark
iniquities,
O Lord, who could [b]stand?

WORD WEALTH

130:3 iniquities, *'avon* (ah-*voan*); Strong's #5771: Evil, fault, sin, iniquity, guilt, blame; moral illness, perversion, crookedness. *'Avon* is derived from *'avah,* to "bend" or "distort." Thus iniquity is the "evil bent" within human beings, or the "crooked" direction or "warped" deeds of sinners. *'Avon* occurs more than 220 times in the OT. Its first mention is in Gen. 4:13, where Cain finally understands the enormity of his deed and states, "My punishment [iniquity] is greater than I can bear." Knowing that iniquity is something too heavy to be borhe by fallen humanity, God promised that His Suffering Servant would bear the iniquities of His people (Is. 53:11; *'avon* also appears in vv. 5, 6).

4 But *there is* [a]forgiveness with
You,
That [b]You may be feared.

5 [a]I *wait for the LORD, my soul
waits,
And [b]in His word I do hope.
6 [a]My soul *waits* for the Lord
More than those who watch for
the morning—
Yes, more than those who watch
for the morning.

7 [a]O Israel, hope in the LORD;
For [b]with the LORD *there is*
*mercy,
And with Him *is* abundant
redemption.

PSALM 130

1 [a]Lam. 3:55
3 [a][Ps. 143:2] [b][Nah. 1:6; Mal. 3:2]; Rev. 6:17 [1]*take note of*
4 [a][Ex. 34:7; Neh. 9:17; Ps. 86:5; Is. 55:7; Dan. 9:9] [b][1 Kin. 8:39, 40; Jer. 33:8, 9]
5 [a][Ps. 27:14] [b]Ps. 119:81 *See WW at Lam. 3:25.
6 [a]Ps. 119:147
7 [a]Ps. 131:3 [b][Ps. 86:5, 15; Is. 55:7] *See WW at Mic. 6:8.
8 [a][Ps. 103:3, 4]; Luke 1:68; Titus 2:14

PSALM 131

1 [a]Jer. 45:5; [Rom. 12:16] [1]Proud [2]Arrogant [3]Lit. *walk in* [4]*difficult*
2 [a][Matt. 18:3; 1 Cor. 14:20]
3 [a][Ps. 130:7]

PSALM 132

2 [a]Ps. 65:1 [b]Gen. 49:24; Is. 49:26; 60:16
4 [a]Prov. 6:4
5 [a]1 Kin. 8:17; 1 Chr. 22:7; Ps. 26:8; Acts 7:46
6 [a]1 Sam. 17:12 [b]1 Sam. 7:1 [c]1 Chr. 13:5 [1]Heb. *Jaar,* lit. *Woods*
7 [a]Ps. 5:7; 99:5
8 [a]Num. 10:35

8 And [a]He shall redeem Israel
From all his iniquities.

PSALM 131

Simple Trust in the LORD

A Song of Ascents. Of David.

LORD, my heart is not [1]haughty,
Nor my eyes [2]lofty.
[a]Neither do I [3]concern myself with
great matters,
Nor with things too [4]profound for
me.

2 Surely I have calmed and quieted 3
my soul,
[a]Like a weaned child with his
mother;
Like a weaned child *is* my soul
within me.

3 [a]O Israel, hope in the LORD
From this time forth and forever.

PSALM 132

The Eternal Dwelling of God in Zion

A Song of Ascents.

LORD, remember David
And all his afflictions;
2 How he swore to the LORD,
[a]*And* vowed to [b]the Mighty One
of Jacob:
3 "Surely I will not go into the
chamber of my house,
Or go up to the comfort of my
bed;
4 I will [a]not give sleep to my eyes
Or slumber to my eyelids,
5 Until I [a]find a place for the LORD,
A dwelling place for the Mighty
One of Jacob."

6 Behold, we heard of it [a]in
Ephrathah;
[b]We found it [c]in the fields of
[1]the woods.
7 Let us go into His tabernacle;
[a]Let us worship at His footstool.
8 [a]Arise, O LORD, to Your resting
place,

130:1–8 This example of true repentance begins with a cry to be delivered **out of the depths** of a sinful life-style (v. 1) and ends with the assurance that God will **redeem** him, literally, "out of" **all his iniquities** (v. 8).
130:8 The emphasis is on **He** (literally "He Himself"). God, in Christ Jesus, fulfilled that hope (Matt. 1:21).
131:1 Nor . . . lofty: This attitude of humility is underlined by Paul (Rom. 12:16). The only description Jesus gave of Himself is "gentle and lowly in heart," that is, humble (Matt. 11:29).
131:2 See section 3 of Truth-In-Action following Ps. 150.
131:2 The kingdom of God, which is basically righteousness, peace, and joy, can be entered by a trusting, humble **child** (Matt. 18:3)—in fact, only by one who is like a child.
132:5 That is, **find a place** where the ark of the covenant could be placed—a magnificent temple.
132:6 Woods: The ark of the covenant had been located at Kirjath Jearim ("City of Forests") before David brought it to Jerusalem (1 Sam. 7:1, 2).
132:8 Arise was the ancient word for moving the **ark** (Num. 10:35, 36).

You and [b]the ark of Your
strength.
9 Let Your priests [a]be clothed with
righteousness,
And let Your saints shout for joy.

10 For Your servant David's sake,
Do not turn away the face of Your
[1]Anointed.

11 [a]The LORD has sworn *in* truth to
David;
He will not turn from it:
"I will set upon your throne
[b]the [1]fruit of your body.
12 If your sons will keep My
covenant
And My testimony which I shall
teach them,
Their sons also shall sit upon your
throne forevermore."

13 [a]For the LORD has chosen Zion;
He has desired *it* for His
[1]dwelling place:
14 "This[a] *is* My *resting place forever;
Here I will dwell, for I have
desired it.
15 [a]I will abundantly bless her
[1]provision;
I will satisfy her poor with bread.
16 [a]I will also clothe her priests with
salvation,
[b]And her saints shall shout aloud
for joy.
17 [a]There I will make the [1]horn* of
David grow;
[b]I will prepare a lamp for My
[2]Anointed.
18 His enemies I will [a]clothe with
shame,
But upon Himself His crown shall
flourish."

PSALM 133

Blessed Unity of the People of God

A Song of Ascents. Of David.

1 BEHOLD, how good and how
pleasant *it is*
For [a]**brethren** to dwell together in
unity!

8 [b]Ps. 78:61
9 [a]Job 29:14
10 [1]Commissioned One, Heb. *Messiah*
11 [a][Ps. 89:3, 4, 33; 110:4] [b]2 Sam. 7:12; [1 Kin. 8:25; 2 Chr. 6:16; Luke 1:69; Acts 2:30] [1]*offspring*
13 [a][Ps. 48:1, 2] [1]*home*
14 [a]Ps. 68:16; Matt. 23:21 *See WW at Is. 28:12.
15 [a]Ps. 147:14 [1]*supply of food*
16 [a]2 Chr. 6:41; Ps. 132:9; 149:4 [b]1 Sam. 4:5; Hos. 11:12
17 [a]Ezek. 29:21; Luke 1:69 [b]1 Kin. 11:36; 15:4; 2 Kin. 8:19; 2 Chr. 21:7; Ps. 18:28 [1]Government [2]Heb. *Messiah* *See WW at Ezek. 29:21.
18 [a]Job 8:22; Ps. 35:26

PSALM 133

1 [a]Gen. 13:8; Heb. 13:1
3 [a]Deut. 4:48 [b]Lev. 25:21; Deut. 28:8; Ps. 42:8

PSALM 134

2 [a][1 Tim. 2:8]

WORD WEALTH

133:1 brethren, *'ach* (*ahch*); Strong's #251: Brother, especially an immediate relative, but also any fellowman; countryman, companion. *'Ach* occurs more than 740 times in the OT. Gen. 4:9 illustrates the narrowest usage of *'ach,* referring to sons of the same two parents. Is. 41:6, 7 presents the wider usage of *'ach,* speaking of the neighbors or fellow workers of craftsmen.

2 *It is* like the precious oil upon the
head,
Running down on the beard,
The beard of Aaron,
Running down on the edge of his
garments.
3 *It is* like the dew of [a]Hermon,
Descending upon the mountains
of Zion;
For [b]there the LORD commanded
the blessing—
Life forevermore.

PSALM 134

Praising the LORD in His House at Night

A Song of Ascents.

BEHOLD, bless the LORD,
All *you* servants of the LORD,
Who by night stand in the house
of the LORD!
2 [a]Lift up your hands *in* the
sanctuary,
And bless the LORD.

3 The LORD who made heaven and
earth
Bless you from Zion!

PSALM 135

Praise to God in Creation and Redemption

PRAISE the LORD!

Praise the name of the LORD;

132:11 This was quoted by Peter on the Day of Pentecost, confirming the resurrection of Jesus and His ascension to the **throne** of **David** (Acts 2:30).
133:1–3 Two similes are used by David to describe the joy of **brethren** literally "sitting together" in **unity:** aromatic anointing perfume and refreshing mountain **dew.** See John 17:23 for NT affirmation of this necessary congregational ingredient.
133:1 See section 1 of Truth-In-Action following Ps. 150.
133:3 Mt. **Hermon** is located on the northern border of Israel.
134:2 Uplifted hands are an integral part of both Jewish and Christian worship (1 Tim. 2:8).
134:3 The last of the Songs of Ascents fittingly closes with a benediction and blessing on the pilgrims who have traveled to Jerusalem for the feasts. The full form of blessing is found in Num. 6:24–27.
135:1 Servants: That is, the Levitical priests and temple

[a]Praise *Him,* O you servants of the LORD!
2 [a]You who stand in the house of the LORD,
In [b]the courts of the house of our God,
3 Praise the LORD, for [a]the LORD *is* good;
Sing praises to His name,
[b]for *it is* pleasant.
4 For [a]the LORD has chosen Jacob for Himself,
Israel for His [1]special* treasure.

5 For I know that [a]the LORD *is* great,
And our Lord *is* above all gods.
6 [a]Whatever the LORD pleases He does,
In heaven and in earth,
In the seas and in all deep places.
7 [a]He causes the [1]vapors to ascend from the ends of the earth;
[b]He makes lightning for the rain;
He brings the wind out of His [c]treasuries.

8 [a]He [1]destroyed the firstborn of Egypt,
[2]Both of man and beast.
9 [a]He sent *signs and wonders into the midst of you, O Egypt,
[b]Upon Pharaoh and all his servants.
10 [a]He defeated many nations
And slew mighty kings—
11 Sihon king of the Amorites,
Og king of Bashan,
And [a]all the kingdoms of Canaan—
12 [a]And gave their land *as* a [1]heritage,
A heritage to Israel His people.

13 [a]Your name, O LORD, *endures* forever,
Your fame, O LORD, throughout all generations.
14 [a]For the LORD will judge His people,
And He will have compassion on His servants.

15 [a]The idols of the nations *are* silver and gold,
The work of men's hands.
16 They have mouths, but they do not speak;
Eyes they have, but they do not see;
17 They have ears, but they do not hear;
Nor is there *any* breath in their mouths.
18 Those who make them are like them;
So is everyone who trusts in them.

19 [a]Bless the LORD, O house of Israel!
Bless the LORD, O house of Aaron!
20 Bless the LORD, O house of Levi!
You who fear the LORD, bless the LORD!
21 Blessed be the LORD [a]out of Zion,
Who dwells in Jerusalem!

Praise the LORD!

PSALM 136

Thanksgiving to God for His Enduring Mercy

OH, [a]give thanks to the LORD, for *He is* good!
[b]For His mercy *endures* **forever.**

> **WORD WEALTH**
>
> **136:1 forever,** *'olam* (oh-*lahm*); Strong's #5769: Eternity; the ages; infinity; the universe, the world. Derived from the verb *'alam* ("veil from sight" or "conceal"), *'olam* refers to that infinite and everlasting expanse God has created. It is both an unending expanse of space (universe) and time (eternity), indicating the limitless dimensions in which God's sovereignty is displayed. The word sometimes refers to the remotely distant past (93:2) and sometimes to the remotely distant future (Jer. 25:5). God is called *'El 'Olam,* "the Everlasting God" (Gen. 21:33; Is. 40:28). As God is eternal, so is His mercy *le-'olam,* that is, "unto the forever."

2 Oh, give thanks to [a]the God of gods!

PSALM 135

1 [a]Ps. 113:1 **2** [a]Luke 2:37 [b]Ps. 116:19 **3** [a][Ps. 119:68] [b]Ps. 147:1 **4** [a][Ex. 19:5]; Mal. 3:17; [Titus 2:14; 1 Pet. 2:9] [1]*precious possession* *See WW at Deut. 26:18. **5** [a]Ps. 95:3; 97:9 **6** [a]Ps. 115:3 **7** [a]Jer. 10:13 [b]Job 28:25, 26; 38:24–28 [c]Jer. 51:16 [1]Water vapor **8** [a]Ex. 12:12; Ps. 78:51 [1]Lit. *struck down* [2]Lit. *From man to beast* **9** [a]Ex. 7:10; Deut. 6:22; Ps. 78:43 [b]Ps. 136:15 *See WW at Ps. 86:17. **10** [a]Num. 21:24; Ps. 136:17 **11** [a]Josh. 12:7–24 **12** [a]Ps. 78:55; 136:21, 22 [1]*inheritance* **13** [a][Ex. 3:15; Ps. 102:12] **14** [a]Deut. 32:36 **15** [a][Ps. 115:4–8] **19** [a][Ps. 115:9] **21** [a]Ps. 134:3

PSALM 136

1 [a]Ps. 106:1 [b]1 Chr. 16:34; Jer. 33:11 **2** [a][Deut. 10:17]

workers or, as vv. 19, 20 state, the houses of Aaron and Levi.
135:4 Jacob, the ancestor of the 12 tribes, is symbolic of the whole nation of **Israel.**
135:14 Will judge: That is, God will defend them against wicked prosecutors and accusers.
135:15–21 Idols: This section is borrowed from 115:4–13.
135:21 Praise the LORD is the Hebrew word "Hallelujah."
136:1 Endures: The literal meaning is "because forever is His mercy." **Mercy** (Hebrew *chesed*) is also translated "lovingkindness," "unfailing love," or "steadfast covenant love," and is similar to the NT word "grace." God's love (mercy) is repeated line by line in this poem.
136:2 Gods: That is, those false idols that men ignorantly call "gods" (135:15–18). The psalmist is not advocating polytheism, with **God** as supreme over many lesser **gods** (Deut. 10:17).

For His mercy *endures* forever.
3 Oh, give thanks to the Lord of lords!
For His mercy *endures* forever:

4 To Him [a]who alone does great wonders,
For His mercy *endures* forever;
5 [a]To Him who by wisdom made the heavens,
For His mercy *endures* forever;
6 [a]To Him who laid out the earth above the waters,
For His mercy *endures* forever;
7 [a]To Him who made great lights,
For His mercy *endures* forever—
8 [a]The sun to rule by day,
For His mercy *endures* forever;
9 The moon and stars to rule by night,
For His mercy *endures* forever.

10 [a]To Him who struck Egypt in their firstborn,
For His mercy *endures* forever;
11 [a]And brought out Israel from among them,
For His mercy *endures* forever;
12 [a]With a strong hand, and with [1]an outstretched arm,
For His mercy *endures* forever;
13 [a]To Him who divided the Red Sea in two,
For His mercy *endures* forever;
14 And made Israel pass through the midst of it,
For His mercy *endures* forever;
15 [a]But overthrew Pharaoh and his army in the Red Sea,
For His mercy *endures* forever;
16 [a]To Him who led His people through the wilderness,
For His mercy *endures* forever;
17 [a]To Him who struck down great kings,
For His mercy *endures* forever;
18 [a]And slew famous kings,
For His mercy *endures* forever—
19 [a]Sihon king of the Amorites,
For His mercy *endures* forever;
20 [a]And Og king of Bashan,
For His mercy *endures* forever—
21 [a]And gave their land as a [1]heritage,
For His mercy *endures* forever;
22 A heritage to Israel His servant,
For His mercy *endures* forever.

23 Who [a]remembered us in our lowly state,
For His mercy *endures* forever;
24 And [a]rescued us from our enemies,
For His mercy *endures* forever;
25 [a]Who gives food to all flesh,
For His mercy *endures* forever.

26 Oh, give thanks to the God of heaven!
For His mercy *endures* forever.

4 [a]Deut. 6:22; Job 9:10; Ps. 72:18
5 [a]Gen. 1:1, 6–8; Prov. 3:19; Jer. 51:15
6 [a]Gen. 1:9; Ps. 24:2; [Is. 42:5]; Jer. 10:12
7 [a]Gen. 1:14–18
8 [a]Gen. 1:16
10 [a]Ex. 12:29; Ps. 135:8
11 [a]Ex. 12:51; 13:3, 16
12 [a]Ex. 6:6; Deut. 4:34; 5:15; 7:19; 9:29; 11:2; 2 Kin. 17:36; 2 Chr. 6:32; Jer. 32:17 [1]Mighty power
13 [a]Ex. 14:21
15 [a]Ex. 14:27
16 [a]Ex. 13:18; 15:22; Deut. 8:15
17 [a]Ps. 135:10–12
18 [a]Deut. 29:7
19 [a]Num. 21:21
20 [a]Num. 21:33
21 [a]Josh. 12:1 [1]*inheritance*
23 [a]Gen. 8:1; Deut. 32:36; Ps. 113:7
24 [a]Ps. 44:7
25 [a]Ps. 104:27; 145:15

PSALM 137

Longing for Zion in a Foreign Land

BY the rivers of Babylon,
There we sat down, yea, we wept
When we remembered Zion.
2 We hung our harps
Upon the willows in the midst of it.
3 For there those who carried us away captive asked of us a song,
And those who [a]plundered us *requested* mirth,
Saying, "Sing us *one* of the songs of Zion!"

4 How shall we sing the LORD's song
In a foreign land?
5 If I forget you, O Jerusalem,
Let my right hand forget *its skill!*
6 If I do not remember you,
Let my [a]tongue cling to the roof of my mouth—
If I do not exalt Jerusalem
Above my chief joy.

7 Remember, O LORD, against [a]the sons of Edom
The day of Jerusalem,
Who said, [1]"Raze *it,* raze *it,*
To its very foundation!"

PSALM 137
3 [a]Ps. 79:1
6 [a]Job 29:10; Ps. 22:15; Ezek. 3:26
7 [a]Jer. 49:7–22; Lam. 4:21; Ezek. 25:12–14; 35:2; Amos 1:11; Obad. 10–14 [1]Lit. *Make bare*

137:1 Babylon was situated on a plain, which had little rainfall, and was dependent on its intricate system of **rivers** and man-made canals for its supply of water.
137:2 Though song-writing came to a standstill and the **harps** hung **upon the willows,** by God's restoring power the Jews were able to sing again in their own land. This is evidenced by the fact that most of the songs of the fourth and fifth books in the Psalter were written during the period of the second temple after the Exile.
137:4 The thought is that Zion's **song** is for worship, not for mere entertainment.
137:5, 6 Hand . . . *skill:* That is, the ability to play instruments; **tongue . . . mouth:** That is, cease being able to sing.
137:7 Edom gloated over the misfortunes of Israel (Ezek. 35:1–15).

8 O daughter of Babylon, [a]who are
to be destroyed,
Happy the one [b]who repays you
as you have served us!
9 Happy the one who takes and
[a]dashes
Your little ones against the rock!

PSALM 138

The LORD's Goodness to the Faithful

A *Psalm* of David.

I WILL *praise You with my whole
heart;
[a]Before the gods I will sing praises
to You.
2 [a]I will worship [b]toward Your holy
temple,
And praise Your name
For Your lovingkindness and
Your truth;
For You have [c]magnified Your
*word above all Your name.
3 In the day when I cried out, You
answered me,
And made me bold *with* strength
in my soul.

4 [a]All the kings of the earth shall
praise You, O LORD,
When they hear the words of
Your mouth.
5 Yes, they shall sing of the ways
of the LORD,
For great *is* the glory of the LORD.
6 [a]Though the LORD *is* on high,
Yet [b]He regards the lowly;
But the proud He knows from
afar.

7 [a]Though I walk in the midst of
trouble, You will revive me;
You will stretch out Your hand
Against the wrath of my enemies,
And Your right hand will save
me.
5 8 [a]The LORD will [1]**perfect** *that which*
concerns me;
Your mercy, O LORD, *endures*
forever;
[b]Do not forsake the works of Your
hands.

8 [a]Is. 13:1–6; 47:1 [b]Jer. 50:15; Rev. 18:6
9 [a]2 Kin. 8:12; Is. 13:16; Hos. 13:16; Nah. 3:10

PSALM 138

1 [a]Ps. 119:46 *See WW at 1 Chr. 16:7.
2 [a]Ps. 28:2 [b]1 Kin. 8:29 [c]Is. 42:21 *See WW at 2 Sam. 22:31.
4 [a]Ps. 102:15
6 [a][Ps. 113:4–7] [b]Prov. 3:34; [Is. 57:15]; Luke 1:48; [James 4:6; 1 Pet. 5:5]
7 [a][Ps. 23:3, 4]
8 [a]Ps. 57:2; [Phil. 1:6] [b]Job 10:3, 8 [1]*complete*

PSALM 139

1 [a]Ps. 17:3; Jer. 12:3
2 [a]2 Kin. 19:27 [b]Is. 66:18; Matt. 9:4
3 [a]Job 14:16; 31:4 [1]Lit. *winnow*
4 [a][Heb. 4:13]
5 [1]*enclosed*
6 [a]Job 42:3; Ps. 40:5
7 [a][Jer. 23:24; Amos 9:2–4] *See WW at 2 Sam. 23:2.
8 [a][Amos 9:2–4] [b][Job 26:6; Prov. 15:11] [1]Or *Sheol*

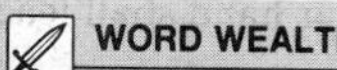
WORD WEALTH

138:8 perfect, *gamar* (gah-*mar*); Strong's #1584: To end, finish, accomplish, perfect; to come to an end, cease; to perform, fulfill. This verb occurs five times in the OT. Three times it refers to something or someone being cut off or brought to an end (7:9; 12:1; 77:8). Twice it refers to the completing, finishing, and perfecting of God's work in one's life (57:2; 138:8). These two references are OT parallels to Phil. 1:6. The idea is that God begins to work out His purposes in the life of His servant and continues His work until it is absolutely and completely done.

PSALM 139

God's Perfect Knowledge of Man

For the Chief Musician. A Psalm of David.

O LORD, [a]You have searched me
and known *me.*
2 [a]You know my sitting down and
my rising up;
You [b]understand my thought afar
off.
3 [a]You [1]comprehend my path and
my lying down,
And are acquainted with all my
ways.
4 For *there is* not a word on my
tongue,
But behold, O LORD, [a]You know
it altogether.
5 You have [1]hedged me behind and
before,
And laid Your hand upon me.
6 [a]*Such* knowledge *is* too wonderful
for me;
It is high, I cannot *attain* it.

7 [a]Where can I go from Your 5
*Spirit?
Or where can I flee from Your
presence?
8 [a]If I ascend into heaven, You *are*
there;
[b]If I make my bed in [1]hell, behold,
You *are there.*
9 *If* I take the wings of the morning,
And dwell in the uttermost parts
of the sea,

137:8, 9 Little ones: These are the same atrocities the Jews suffered, and the psalmist is advocating "an eye for an eye."
138:1, 2 Before the gods: The wording of these two verses strongly suggests the psalmist is in a foreign, idolatrous land (Dan. 6:10).
138:8 See section 5 of Truth-In-Action following Ps. 150.
138:8 This thought that God **will perfect** (fulfill) all of His promises and purposes in a man's life is confirmed by Paul (Phil. 1:6) and Peter (1 Pet. 5:10).
139:1–24 In four stanzas of six verses each the psalmist displays with sublime beauty the attributes of God: omniscience (vv. 1–6), omnipresence (vv. 7–12), omnipotence (vv. 13–18); and then he bursts out with a keen sense of responsibility and awareness of sin.
139:7 See section 5 of Truth-In-Action following Ps. 150.
139:8 Hell is *she'ol* (Hebrew), the underworld; hence, from the heights to the depths God is there.
139:9 Morning is poetic for east, and **uttermost parts** is the west; so, from east to west God is there!

10 Even there Your hand shall lead me,
And Your right hand shall hold me.
11 If I say, "Surely the darkness shall [1]fall on me,"
Even the night shall be light about me;
12 Indeed, [a]the darkness [1]shall not hide from You,
But the night shines as the day;
The darkness and the light *are* both alike *to You*.

13 For You formed my inward parts;
You [1]covered me in my mother's womb.

KINGDOM DYNAMICS

139:13 17. Is Abortion Wrong? SPIRITUAL ANSWERS. For the answer to this and other probing questions about God and the power life in His kingdom, see the study article "Spiritual Answers to Hard Questions," which begins on page 1996. P.R.

14 I will praise You, for [1]I am fearfully *and* wonderfully made;
*Marvelous are Your works,
And *that* my soul knows very well.
15 [a]My [1]frame was not hidden from You,
When I was made in secret,
And skillfully wrought in the lowest parts of the earth.
16 Your eyes saw my substance, being yet unformed.
And in Your book they all were written,
The days fashioned for me,
When *as yet there were* none of them.

17 [a]How precious also are Your thoughts to me, O God!
How great is the sum of them!

11 [1]Vg., Symmachus *cover*
12 [a]Job 26:6; 34:22; [Dan. 2:22; Heb. 4:13] [1]Lit. *is not dark*
13 [1]*wove*
14 [1]So with MT, Tg.; LXX, Syr., Vg. *You are fearfully wonderful* *See WW at Judg. 13:19.
15 [a]Job 10:8, 9; Eccl. 11:5 [1]Lit. *bones were*
17 [a][Ps. 40:5; Rom. 11:33]
19 [a][Is. 11:4] [b]Ps. 119:115 [1]Lit. *men of bloodshed*
20 [a]Jude 15 [1]LXX, Vg. *They take your cities in vain*
21 [a]2 Chr. 19:2
22 [1]*complete*
23 [a]Job 31:6; Ps. 26:2
24 [a]Ps. 5:8; 143:10

PSALM 140

2 [a]Ps. 56:6
3 [a]Ps. 58:4; Rom. 3:13; James 3:8
4 [a]Ps. 71:4

18 *If* I should count them, they would be more in number than the sand;
When I awake, I am still with You.

19 Oh, that You would [a]slay the wicked, O God!
[b]Depart from me, therefore, you [1]bloodthirsty men.
20 For they [a]speak against You wickedly;
[1]Your enemies take *Your name* in vain.
21 [a]Do I not hate them, O LORD, who hate You?
And do I not loathe those who rise up against You?
22 I hate them with [1]perfect hatred;
I count them my enemies.

23 [a]Search me, O God, and know my heart; **3**
Try me, and know my anxieties;
24 And see if *there is any* wicked way in me,
And [a]lead me in the way everlasting.

PSALM 140

Prayer for Deliverance from Evil Men

To the Chief Musician. A Psalm of David.

DELIVER me, O LORD, from evil men;
Preserve me from violent men,
2 Who plan evil things in *their* hearts;
[a]They continually gather together *for* war.
3 They sharpen their tongues like a serpent;
The [a]poison of asps *is* under their lips. Selah
4 [a]Keep me, O LORD, from the hands of the wicked;
Preserve me from violent men,
Who have purposed to make my steps stumble.

139:13–15 Covered is better translated "interwoven." That is, the white bones, blue veins, and red arteries are all woven together. The thought is repeated in v. 15 where **wrought** means "embroidered with various colors."
139:15 Earth is a metaphor for the "womb," which is **secret** or **hidden from** view, dark and mysterious.
139:16 Substance . . . unformed is language used for clay not yet formed into a pot, or a skein of thread not yet unrolled and woven (Ezek. 27:24). Here it is applied to the fetus of a human life.
139:19–22 An understanding of life includes the awareness of evil men in the population of God's creation who spoil its beauty.
139:23, 24 David's previous statements are softened somewhat by his recognition that wickedness may be lurking in the recesses of his heart as well. Self-judgment is better than vengeance (Rom. 2:1–16).
139:23 See section 3 of Truth-In-Action following Ps. 150.
140:1–13 This psalm laments persecution, not by pagan enemies, but by evil men in Israel.
140:2 The wars daily plotted are the kind described in James 4:1 as arising from greedy and covetous men within the nation, not from foreign conquerors.
140:3 Tongues: Paul, who was also slandered, used this verse to show that Jews, as well as Gentiles, are guilty of sin and need a Savior (Rom. 3:8–13).

5 The proud have hidden a
[a]snare for me, and cords;
They have spread a net by the
wayside;
They have set traps for me.
Selah

6 I said to the LORD: "You *are* my
God;
Hear the voice of my
supplications, O LORD.
7 O GOD the Lord, the strength of
my salvation,
You have [1]covered my head in the
day of battle.
8 Do not grant, O LORD, the desires
of the wicked;
Do not further his *wicked*
scheme,
[a]*Lest* they be exalted. Selah

9 "*As for* the head of those who
surround me,
Let the evil of their lips cover
them;
10 [a]Let burning coals fall upon them;
Let them be cast into the fire,
Into deep pits, that they rise not
up again.
11 Let not a slanderer be established
in the earth;
Let evil hunt the violent man to
overthrow *him*."

12 I know that the LORD will
[a]maintain
The cause of the afflicted,
And justice for the poor.
13 Surely the righteous shall give
thanks to Your name;
The upright shall dwell in Your
presence.

PSALM 141

Prayer for Safekeeping from Wickedness

A Psalm of David.

LORD, I cry out to You;
Make haste to me!
Give ear to my voice when I cry
out to You.
2 Let my prayer be set before You
[a]*as* incense,
[b]The lifting up of my hands *as*
[c]the evening sacrifice.

3 Set a guard, O LORD, over my
[a]mouth;
Keep watch over the door of my
lips.
4 Do not incline my heart to any
evil thing,
To practice wicked works
With men who work iniquity;
[a]And do not let me eat of their
delicacies.

5 [a]Let the righteous strike me;
It shall be a kindness.
And let him rebuke me;
It shall be as excellent oil;
Let my head not refuse it.

For still my prayer *is* against the
deeds of the wicked.
6 Their judges are overthrown by
the sides of the [1]cliff,
And they hear my words, for they
are sweet.
7 Our bones are scattered at the
mouth of the grave,
As when one plows and breaks
up the earth.

8 But [a]my eyes *are* upon You,
O GOD the Lord;
In You I take refuge;
[1]Do not leave my soul
destitute.
9 Keep me from [a]the snares they
have laid for me,
And from the traps of the workers
of iniquity.
10 [a]Let the wicked fall into their own
nets,
While I escape safely.

5 [a]Ps. 35:7; Jer. 18:22
7 [1]*sheltered*
8 [a]Deut. 32:27
10 [a]Ps. 11:6
12 [a]1 Kin. 8:45; Ps. 9:4

PSALM 141

2 [a][Ex. 30:8]; Luke 1:10; [Rev. 5:8; 8:3, 4] [b]Ps. 134:2; [1 Tim. 2:8] [c]Ex. 29:39, 41; 1 Kin. 18:29, 36; Dan. 9:21
3 [a][Prov. 13:3; 21:23]
4 [a]Prov. 23:6
5 [a][Prov. 9:8; Eccl. 7:5; Gal. 6:1]
6 [1]*rock*
8 [a]2 Chr. 20:12; Ps. 25:15 [1]Lit. *Do not make my soul bare*
9 [a]Ps. 119:110
10 [a]Ps. 35:8

140:9 Their lips: Evil often self-destructs, so vengeance and vindictiveness are not warranted.
140:10 If the **fire** of judgment does not consume the wicked, the **pits** of water will drown them.
140:12, 13 Amid all the political reshuffling **the LORD** still reigns in **justice,** and this is another reason to praise.
141:2 The **incense** used in rituals was made with fragrant frankincense (Lev. 2:2). Two lambs were sacrificed daily by the priests, one in the morning and one as an **evening sacrifice** (Num. 28:1–8). These statements of David are hints of the coming NT spiritual worship replacing physical offerings. See Heb. 13:15; Rev. 8:3, 4.
141:4 David recognizes that carnal propensities within and cultural pressures without lead to **iniquity. Delicacies** are those foods that taste good but are forbidden by Mosaic Law. They symbolize any sinful pleasure.
141:5 Rebuke: Being accountable to fellow believers is an important check and balance against moral lapse.
141:6, 7 Bones: The Hebrew is obscure in vv. 5–7. The thought seems to be that the wicked eventually will be judged, and they will discover that David's **words** were true. V. 7 is a quote from the wicked who have been judged.
141:8 Leave . . . destitute means "Do not let me die," as in Is. 53:12.

PSALM 142

A Plea for Relief from Persecutors

A [a]Contemplation[1] of David. A Prayer [b]when he was in the cave.

I CRY out to the LORD with my voice;
With my voice to the LORD I make my supplication.
2 I pour out my complaint before Him;
I declare before Him my trouble.

3 When my spirit [1]was [a]overwhelmed within me,
Then You knew my path.
In the way in which I walk
They have secretly [b]set a snare for me.
4 Look on *my* right hand and see,
For *there is* no one who acknowledges me;
Refuge has failed me;
No one cares for my soul.

5 I cried out to You, O LORD:
I said, "You *are* my refuge,
My portion in the land of the living.
6 [1]Attend to my cry,
For I am brought very low;
Deliver me from my persecutors,
For they are stronger than I.
7 Bring my soul out of prison,
That I may [a]praise Your name;
The righteous shall surround me,
For You shall deal bountifully with me."

PSALM 143

An Earnest Appeal for Guidance and Deliverance

A Psalm of David.

HEAR my prayer, O LORD,
Give ear to my supplications!
In Your faithfulness answer me,
And in Your righteousness.
2 Do not enter into judgment with Your servant,
[a]For in Your sight no one living is righteous.
3 For the enemy has persecuted my soul;
He has crushed my life to the ground;
He has made me dwell in [1]darkness,
Like those who have long been dead.
4 [a]Therefore my spirit is overwhelmed within me;
My heart within me is distressed.

5 [a]I remember the days of old;
I *meditate on all Your works;
I [1]muse on the work of Your hands.
6 I spread out my hands to You;
[a]My soul *longs* for You like a thirsty land. Selah

7 Answer me speedily, O LORD;
My spirit fails!
Do not hide Your face from me,
[a]Lest I [1]be like those who [2]go down into the pit.
8 Cause me to hear Your lovingkindness [a]in the morning,
For in You do I trust;
[b]Cause me to know the way in which I should walk,
For [c]I lift up my soul to You.

9 Deliver me, O LORD, from my enemies;
[1]In You I take shelter.
10 [a]Teach* me to do Your will,
For You *are* my God;
[b]Your Spirit *is* good.
Lead me in [c]the land of uprightness.

11 [a]Revive me, O LORD, for Your name's sake!
For Your righteousness' sake bring my soul out of trouble.
12 In Your mercy [a]cut[1] off my enemies,
And destroy all those who afflict my soul;
For I *am* Your servant.

PSALM 142
title [a]Ps. 32:title [b]1 Sam. 22:1; Ps. 57:title [1]Heb. *Maschil*
3 [a]Ps. 77:3 [b]Ps. 141:9 [1]Lit. *fainted*
6 [1]*Give heed*
7 [a]Ps. 34:1, 2

PSALM 143
2 [a][Ex. 34:7]; Job 4:17; 9:2; 25:4; Ps. 130:3; Eccl. 7:20; [Rom. 3:20–23; Gal. 2:16]
3 [1]*dark places*
4 [a]Ps. 77:3
5 [a]Ps. 77:5, 10, 11 [1]*ponder* *See WW at Ps. 1:2.
6 [a]Ps. 63:1
7 [a]Ps. 28:1 [1]*become* [2]Die
8 [a]Ps. 46:5 [b]Ps. 5:8 [c]Ps. 25:1
9 [1]LXX, Vg. *To You I flee*
10 [a]Ps. 25:4, 5 [b]Neh. 9:20 [c]Is. 26:10 *See WW at Is. 48:17.
11 [a]Ps. 119:25
12 [a]Ps. 54:5 [1]*put an end to*

4

142:title The **cave** referred to in this title may be Adullam (1 Sam. 22) or En Gedi (1 Sam. 24).
142:1, 2 These two verses are an example of four-line parallelism in Hebrew poetry.
142:2 Verbalizing one's distraught feelings is the first step *toward recovery*.
142:4, 5 When forsaken by all others, or seemingly forsaken, the Lord remains as a faithful **refuge.** And in due time the righteous (v. 7) will rally around.
142:5 **Portion** is "inheritance." **Land of the living** implies "as long as I live."
142:7 Though a literal **prison** cannot be ruled out, David probably refers figuratively to circumstances that closed in on him, thus paralleling the next phrase **shall surround.** In other words, "Though now hemmed in by evil, I shall be encompassed by good."
143:1–12 The Greek Septuagint translation adds a reference in the title to Absalom's rebellion against his father, King David (2 Sam. 15).
143:5 **Remember:** Faith is increased by rehearsing the Word, which recalls previous divine encounters (Rom. 10:17).
143:10 See section 4 of Truth-In-Action following Ps. 150.
143:11, 12 Or, "You will revive me" (see 138:7).

PSALM 144

A Song to the LORD *Who Preserves and Prospers His People*

A Psalm of David.

BLESSED *be* the LORD my Rock,
[a]Who trains my hands for war,
And my fingers for battle—
2 My lovingkindness and my fortress,
My high tower and my deliverer,
My shield and *the One* in whom I take refuge,
Who subdues [1]my people under me.

3 [a]LORD, what *is* man, that You take knowledge of him?
Or the son of *man, that You are *mindful of him?
4 [a]Man is like a breath;
[b]His days *are* like a *passing shadow.

5 [a]Bow down Your heavens, O LORD, and come down;
[b]Touch the mountains, and they shall smoke.
6 [a]Flash forth lightning and scatter them;
Shoot out Your arrows and destroy them.
7 Stretch out Your hand from above;
Rescue me and deliver me out of great waters,
From the hand of foreigners,
8 Whose mouth [a]speaks [1]lying words,
And whose right hand *is* a right hand of falsehood.

9 I will [a]sing* a new song to You, O God;
On a harp of ten strings I will *sing praises to You,
10 *The One* who gives [1]salvation to kings,
[a]Who delivers David His servant
From the deadly sword.
11 Rescue me and deliver me from the hand of foreigners,
Whose mouth speaks lying words,
And whose right hand *is* a right hand of falsehood—
12 That our sons *may be* [a]as plants grown up in their youth;
That our daughters *may be* as [1]pillars,
Sculptured in palace style;
13 *That* our barns *may be* full,
Supplying all kinds of produce;
That our sheep may bring forth thousands
And ten thousands in our fields;
14 *That* our oxen *may be* well laden;
That there be no [1]breaking in or going out;
That there be no outcry in our streets.
15 [a]Happy *are* the people who are in such a state;
Happy *are* the people whose God *is* the LORD!

PSALM 144
1 [a]2 Sam. 22:35; Ps. 18:34
2 [1]So with MT, LXX, Vg.; Syr., Tg. *the peoples* (cf. 18:47)
3 [a]Job 7:17; Ps. 8:4; Heb. 2:6 *See WW at Job 4:17. • See WW at Gen. 15:6.
4 [a]Ps. 39:11 [b]Job 8:9; 14:2; Ps. 102:11 *See WW at Josh. 3:4.
5 [a]Ps. 18:9; Is. 64:1 [b]Ps. 104:32
6 [a]Ps. 18:13, 14
8 [a]Ps. 12:2 [1]*empty* or *worthless*
9 [a]Ps. 33:2, 3; 40:3 *See WW at Judg. 5:3. • See WW at Ps. 149:3.
10 [a]Ps. 18:50 [1]*deliverance*
12 [a]Ps. 128:3 [1]*corner pillars*
14 [1]Lit. *breach*
15 [a]Deut. 33:29; [Ps. 33:12; Jer. 17:7]

PSALM 145

A Song of God's Majesty and Love

[a]A Praise of David.

I WILL [1]extol You, my God, O King;
And I will bless Your name forever and ever.
2 Every day I will **bless** You,
And I will praise Your name forever and ever.

PSALM 145
title [a]Ps. 100:title
1 [1]*praise*

WORD WEALTH

145:2 bless, *barach* (bah-*rahch*); Strong's #1288: To bless; to salute, congratulate, thank, praise; to kneel down. *Barach* is the root word from which *baruch* ("blessed one") and *barachah* ("blessing") are derived. *Berech,* "knee," is probably the source of those words. In OT times, one got down on his knees when preparing to speak or receive *(cont. on next page)*

144:1–7 The first seven verses borrow many phrases from Ps. 18.
144:1 This battle song reflects David's reliance upon God for victory in **war,** which was necessary to preserve the caretakers of God's oracles, the nation of Israel.
144:9 A "singing soldier" seems a contradiction of terms to those uninstructed in spiritual realities; but the enlightened know of its necessity and importance.
144:11 Right hand may refer to the use of hands in swearing oaths or making alliances. The harassment against the returning Jews in later history by Tobiah is an example of such deceit (Neh. 6:12–14).
144:12–14 The purpose of David's wars was ultimately peaceful commerce.
144:12 Pillars: Ornate cornerstones, or decorative cornices, which are symbols of majestic beauty.
144:15 When Israel had **the LORD** as their Captain of Hosts, they were assured of victory in war and subsequent peaceful existence (Josh. 5:14).
145:1–21 This acrostic (alphabetic) poem contains 22 couplets beginning with successive letters of the Hebrew alphabet. It covers nearly every aspect of verbal praise (**extol, bless, praise, declare, meditate, speak, utter, sing, make known**), thus justifying the use of *tehillah* (Hebrew for "praise hymn") as its title.

(*cont. from preceding page*)
words of blessing, whether to God in heaven, or to the king on his throne. From God's side, He is the Blesser, the One who gives the capacity for living a full, rich life. The first action of God the Creator to the newly created man and woman was to bless them (Gen. 1:28). The Aaronic Benediction (Num. 6:22–27) epitomizes God's promise of blessing to His people. In Jewish worship, God is frequently called *ha-Qodesh baruch hu,* or literally, "the Holy One, blessed is He!"

3 [a]Great *is* the LORD, and greatly to
be praised;
And [b]His greatness *is*
[1]unsearchable.

4 [a]One generation shall *praise Your
works to another,
And shall declare Your mighty
acts.

KINGDOM DYNAMICS

145:4 Teach Your Children Praise, PRAISE PATHWAY. This verse emphasizes the importance of passing on the praise of God from one generation to another. Praise is to be taught to our children. The Bible enjoins us to raise a generation of praisers. We must not merely "suppose" that children will grow up and desire God. We must be careful. Whatever we possess of God's blessing and revelation can be lost in one generation. We must consistently praise Him and we must also teach (by example, as well as by words), so our children and our children's children will do the same.
(Ps. 71:14/Ps. 150:1–6) C.G.

5 [1]I will meditate on the glorious
*splendor of Your majesty,
And [2]on Your wondrous works.
6 *Men* shall speak of the might of
Your awesome acts,
And I will declare Your greatness.
7 They shall [1]utter the memory of
Your great goodness,
And shall sing of Your
righteousness.

8 [a]The LORD *is* gracious and full of
compassion,
Slow to anger and great in mercy.
9 [a]The LORD *is* good to all,
And His tender mercies *are* over
all His works.

10 [a]All Your works shall praise You,
O LORD,
And Your saints shall bless You.
11 They shall speak of the glory of
Your kingdom,
And talk of Your power,
12 To make known to the sons of
men His mighty acts,
And the glorious majesty of His
kingdom.
13 [a]Your kingdom *is* an everlasting
kingdom,
And Your dominion *endures*
throughout all [1]generations.

14 The LORD upholds all who fall,
And [a]raises up all *who are* bowed
down.
15 [a]The eyes of all look expectantly
to You,
And [b]You give them their food in
due season.
16 You open Your hand
[a]And satisfy the desire of every
living thing.

17 The LORD *is* righteous in all His
ways,
Gracious in all His works.
18 [a]The LORD *is* near to all who call
upon Him,
To all who call upon Him
[b]in truth.
19 He will fulfill the desire of those
who fear Him;
He also will hear their cry and
save them.
20 [a]The LORD preserves all who *love
Him,
But all the wicked He will
destroy.
21 My mouth shall speak the praise
of the LORD,
And all flesh shall bless His holy
name
Forever and *ever.

PSALM 146

The Happiness of Those Whose Help Is the LORD

PRAISE[1] the LORD!

[a]Praise the LORD, O my soul!

3 [a][Ps. 147:5] [b]Job 5:9; 9:10; 11:7; Is. 40:28; [Rom. 11:33] [1]Beyond our understanding
4 [a]Is. 38:19 *See WW at Ps. 63:3.
5 [1]So with MT, Tg.; DSS, LXX, Syr., Vg. *They* [2]Lit. *on the words of Your wondrous works* *See WW at Ps. 8:5.
7 [1]*eagerly utter,* lit. *bubble forth*
8 [a][Ex. 34:6, 7; Num. 14:18]; Ps. 86:5, 15
9 [a][Ps. 100:5]; Jer. 33:11; Nah. 1:7; [Matt. 19:17; Mark 10:18]

10 [a]Ps. 19:1
13 [a]Dan. 2:44; 4:3; [1 Tim. 1:17; 2 Pet. 1:11] [1]So with MT, Tg.; DSS, LXX, Syr., Vg. add *The LORD is faithful in all His words, and holy in all His works*
14 [a]Ps. 146:8
15 [a]Ps. 104:27 [b]Ps. 136:25
16 [a]Ps. 104:21, 28
18 [a][Deut. 4:7] [b][John 4:24]
20 [a][Ps. 31:23] *See WW at Ps. 97:10.
21 *See WW at Mic. 4:5.

PSALM 146
1 [a]Ps. 103:1 [1]Heb. *Hallelujah*

145:4 God's **works** and **acts** are mentioned eight times in this short song and are a major reason for praise to God.
145:8 This verse is quoted in Jon. 4:2 and Neh. 9:17.
145:14 That is, **bowed down** with toil, disease, or poverty.
145:15 The ultimate source is always God; that is why Jesus lifted His **eyes** heavenward when blessing His food (Luke 9:16).
145:21 Not only does the psalmist's mouth **praise** God, but **all flesh,** Jew and Gentile, is to enter into praise and prayer unceasingly (1 Thess. 5:17).
146:1–10 This psalm contrasts the wisdom of those who hope in the eternal kingship of the Lord and His benevolent

2 [a]While I live I will praise the LORD;
I will sing praises to my God
while I have my being.

3 [a]Do not put your trust in princes,
Nor in [1]a son of man, in whom
there is no [2]help.
4 [a]His spirit departs, he returns to
his earth;
In that very day [b]his plans perish.

5 [a]Happy *is he* who *has* the God of
Jacob for his help,
Whose hope *is* in the LORD his
God,
6 [a]Who made heaven and earth,
The sea, and all that *is* in them;
Who keeps truth forever,
7 [a]Who executes justice for the
oppressed,
[b]Who gives food to the hungry.
[c]The LORD gives freedom to the
prisoners.

8 [a]The LORD opens *the eyes of* the
blind;
[b]The LORD raises those who are
bowed down;
The LORD loves the righteous.
9 [a]The LORD watches over the
strangers;
He relieves the fatherless and
widow;
[b]But the way of the wicked He
[1]turns upside down.

10 [a]The LORD shall *reign forever—
Your God, O Zion, to all
generations.

Praise the LORD!

PSALM 147

Praise to God for His Word and Providence

PRAISE[1] the LORD!
For [a]*it is* good to sing praises to
our God;
[b]For *it is* pleasant, *and* [c]praise is
beautiful.

2 The LORD [a]builds up Jerusalem;
[b]He gathers together the outcasts
of Israel.
3 [a]He heals the brokenhearted
And binds up their [1]wounds.
4 [a]He counts the number of the
stars;
He calls them all by name.
5 [a]Great *is* our Lord, and [b]mighty in
*power;
[c]His understanding *is* infinite.
6 [a]The LORD lifts up the humble;
He casts the wicked down to the
ground.

7 Sing to the LORD with
thanksgiving;
Sing praises on the harp to our
God,
8 [a]Who covers the heavens with
clouds,
Who prepares rain for the earth,
Who makes grass to grow on the
mountains.
9 [a]He gives to the beast its food,
And [b]to the young ravens that
cry.

10 [a]He does not delight in the
strength of the horse;
He takes no pleasure in the legs
of a man.
11 The LORD takes pleasure in those
who fear Him,
In those who hope in His mercy.

12 *Praise the LORD, O Jerusalem!
Praise your God, O Zion!
13 For He has strengthened the bars
of your gates;
He has blessed your children
within you.
14 [a]He makes peace *in* your borders,
And [b]fills you with [1]the finest
wheat.

15 [a]He sends out His command *to the*
earth;
His word runs very swiftly.
16 [a]He gives snow like wool;
He scatters the frost like ashes;

2 [a]Ps. 104:33
3 [a][Is. 2:22] [1]A human being [2]*salvation*
4 [a][Eccl. 12:7] [b][Ps. 33:10; 1 Cor. 2:6]
5 [a]Jer. 17:7
6 [a]Gen. 1:1; Ex. 20:11; Acts 4:24; Rev. 14:7
7 [a]Ps. 103:6 [b]Ps. 107:9 [c]Ps. 107:10; Is. 61:1
8 [a]Matt. 9:30; [John 9:7, 32, 33] [b]Luke 13:13
9 [a]Deut. 10:18; Ps. 68:5 [b]Ps. 147:6 [1]Lit. *makes crooked*
10 [a]Ex. 15:18; Ps. 10:16; [Rev. 11:15] *See WW at 2 Sam. 8:15.

PSALM 147

1 [a]Ps. 92:1 [b]Ps. 135:3 [c]Ps. 33:1 [1]Heb. *Hallelujah*
2 [a]Ps. 102:16 [b]Deut. 30:3; Is. 11:12; 56:8; Ezek. 39:28
3 [a][Ps. 51:17]; Is. 61:1; Luke 4:18 [1]Lit. *sorrows*
4 [a]Is. 40:26
5 [a]Ps. 48:1 [b]Nah. 1:3 [c]Is. 40:28 *See WW at Deut. 8:18.
6 [a]Ps. 146:8, 9
8 [a]Job 38:26; Ps. 104:13
9 [a]Job 38:41 [b][Matt. 6:26]
10 [a]Ps. 33:16, 17
12 *See WW at Ps. 63:3.
14 [a]Is. 54:13; 60:17, 18 [b]Ps. 132:15 [1]Lit. *fat of wheat*
15 [a][Ps. 107:20]
16 [a]Job 37:6

justice (vv. 5–10) with the folly of those who trust in mortal rulers (vv. 1–4).

146:3 Princes: The temporary nature of governments, foreign alliances, and political policies is well known in the experience of any nation's history (see 1 Cor. 2:6).

146:4 Perish does not mean extinction of **spirit** or soul-sleep, but rather that one's purposes and **plans** come to a halt.

146:6 Truth connotes being truthful in keeping promises and, thus God's faithfulness in maintaining His role as Sustainer of the universe (Col. 1:17).

146:7–9 The social agenda listed here was the heart and soul of Jesus' ministry to the needy during His First Advent.

147:1 Praise is a **good, pleasant,** and **beautiful** response to the many blessings of God.

147:10, 11 Those saints who pause to recognize the compassionate acts of God, and who stand in awe of those deeds, are a **pleasure** to the heart of God. Some say the reference here is to a war **horse** and foot soldiers, and that God controls the outcome of battle in favor of His people (Job 39:19–25).

147:13 Bolts and **bars** held the wooden slats of the **gates** together (Neh. 3:3).

17 He casts out His hail like
[1]morsels;
Who can stand before His cold?
18 [a]He sends out His word and melts
them;
He causes His wind to blow, *and*
the waters flow.

19 [a]He declares His word to Jacob,
[b]His statutes and His judgments to
Israel.
20 [a]He has not dealt thus with any
nation;
And *as for His* judgments, they
have not known them.

[1]Praise the LORD!

PSALM 148

Praise to the LORD from Creation

PRAISE[1] the LORD!

Praise the LORD from the heavens;
Praise Him in the heights!
2 Praise Him, all His angels;
Praise Him, all His hosts!
3 Praise Him, sun and moon;
Praise Him, all you stars of light!
4 Praise Him, [a]you heavens of
heavens,
And [b]you waters above the
heavens!

5 Let them praise the name of the
LORD,
For [a]He commanded and they
were created.
6 [a]He also established them forever
and ever;
He made a decree which shall not
pass away.

7 Praise the LORD from the earth,
[a]You great sea creatures and all
the depths;
8 Fire and hail, snow and clouds;
Stormy wind, fulfilling His word;
9 [a]Mountains and all hills;
Fruitful trees and all cedars;
10 Beasts and all cattle;
Creeping things and flying fowl;
11 Kings of the earth and all peoples;
Princes and all judges of the
earth;
12 Both young men and maidens;
Old men and children.

13 Let them praise the name of the
LORD,
For His [a]name alone is exalted;
His *glory *is* above the earth and
heaven.
14 And He [a]has exalted the
[1]horn of His people,
The praise of [b]all His saints—
Of the children of Israel,
[c]A people near to Him.

[2]Praise the LORD!

PSALM 149

Praise to God for His Salvation and Judgment

PRAISE[1] the LORD!

[a]Sing to the LORD a new song,
And His praise in the assembly
of saints.

2 Let Israel rejoice in their Maker;
Let the children of Zion be joyful
in their [a]King.
3 [a]Let them praise His name with
the dance;
Let them **sing praises** to Him with
the timbrel and harp.

17 [1]*fragments* of food
18 [a]Job 37:10
19 [a]Deut. 33:4; Ps. 103:7 [b]Mal. 4:4
20 [a]Deut. 4:32–34; [Rom. 3:1, 2] [1]Heb. *Hallelujah*

PSALM 148

1 [1]Heb. *Hallelujah*
4 [a]Deut. 10:14; 1 Kin. 8:27; [Neh. 9:6] [b]Gen. 1:7
5 [a]Gen. 1:1, 6
6 [a]Ps. 89:37; [Jer. 31:35, 36; 33:20, 25]
7 [a]Is. 43:20
9 [a]Is. 44:23; 49:13
13 [a]Ps. 8:1 *See WW at 1 Chr. 29:11.
14 [a]1 Sam. 2:1; Ps. 75:10 [b]Ps. 149:9 [c]Lev. 10:3; Eph. 2:17 [1]Strength or dominion [2]Heb. *Hallelujah*

PSALM 149

1 [a]Ps. 33:3 [1]Heb. *Hallelujah*
2 [a]Judg. 8:23; Zech. 9:9; Matt. 21:5
3 [a]Ex. 15:20; Ps. 81:2

149:3 sing praises, *zamar* (zah-*mar*); Strong's #2167: To make music, sing praises; to sing songs accompanied by musical instruments. *Zamar* occurs more than 45 times, mostly in Ps. There seems to be a special affinity between *zamar* and stringed instruments. The most important derivative of *zamar* is *mizmor* (a psalm, or song accompanied by instruments). Musical instruments are an integral part of praise and worship.

148:1–14 This psalm is divided into two sections. Vv. 1–4 call for the **heavens** and all that is in them to praise the Lord, with the reasons stated in vv. 5, 6: the Lord is the great Creator and Sustainer of them. Vv. 7–12 command **praise** in unison **from the earth** and all its inhabitants for the reasons given in vv. 13, 14: the Lord controls their destiny.
148:3 Sun and moon: Nature praises God here by the poet's technique of personification.
148:13 That is, praise His **name** and all it represents in respect to God's essence, character, and power.
148:14 Exalting **the horn** is symbolic for raising up a country and enduing it with power and respectability in the community of nations. God is not aloof from His creation or creatures; He is near to them, and they are **near to Him.**
149:1–9 There are two groups of verses: one deals with **praise** (vv. 1–4) and the other with **judgment** (vv. 5–9). Through the linking of these two concepts, this psalm teaches us that there is tremendous power in worship and praise. Of the mighty spiritual weapons given believers, worship and praise are chief among them. They enthrone God to deal directly with our spiritual enemies (see note on 22:3).

4 For [a]the LORD takes pleasure in
His people;
[b]He will beautify the [1]humble with
salvation.

5 Let the saints be joyful in glory;
Let them [a]sing aloud on their
beds.
6 *Let* the high praises of God *be* in
their mouth,
And [a]a two-edged sword in their
hand,
7 To execute vengeance on the
nations,
And punishments on the peoples;
8 To bind their kings with chains,
And their nobles with fetters of
iron;
9 [a]To execute on them the written
judgment—
[b]This *honor have all His saints.

[1]Praise the LORD!

4 [a]Ps. 35:27 [b]Ps. 132:16; Is. 61:3 [1]*meek*
5 [a]Job 35:10
6 [a]Heb. 4:12; Rev. 1:16
9 [a]Deut. 7:1, 2; Ezek. 28:26 [b]Ps. 148:14; 1 Cor. 6:2 [1]Heb. *Hallelujah* *See WW at Ps. 8:5.

PSALM 150

Let All Things Praise the LORD

PRAISE[a1] the LORD!

Praise God in His sanctuary;
Praise Him in His mighty
[2]firmament!

2 Praise Him for His mighty acts;
Praise Him according to His
excellent [a]greatness!

3 Praise Him with the sound of the
[1]trumpet;*
Praise Him with the lute and
harp!
4 Praise Him with the timbrel and
dance;
Praise Him with stringed
instruments and flutes!
5 Praise Him with loud cymbals;
Praise Him with clashing
cymbals!

6 Let everything that has **breath**
praise the LORD.

[1]Praise the LORD!

PSALM 150

1 [a]Ps. 145:5, 6 [1]Heb. *Hallelujah* [2]*expanse* of heaven
2 [a]Deut. 3:24
3 [1]*cornet* *See WW at Hos. 8:1.
6 [1]Heb. *Hallelujah*

WORD WEALTH

150:6 breath, *neshamah* (ne-sha-*mah*); Strong's #5397: Breath, breath of life, breathing person, living soul. This word first appears in Gen. 2:7, where God breathed into man's nostrils the *nishmat chayim,* "breath of life," and man became a living being. This is the tender account of how man took his first breath, aided entirely by the Creator, who shared His own breath with him. God literally taught man how to breathe. The psalmist here counsels everyone and everything that has *neshamah* (breath) to praise the Lord.

KINGDOM DYNAMICS

150:1–6 A Mighty Appeal to Praise, PRAISE PATHWAY. The Psalms conclude with a mighty appeal to praise the Lord. Some psalms are desperate cries, some filled with thanksgiving, and some have theologically or historically based instructions to "praise the LORD" for His own Person, holiness, power, or goodness. But the climax is a command to praise the Lord. We are to praise God 1) in His sanctuary—that is, His earthly temple and throughout His created universe and 2) for His mighty acts and according to His excellent greatness. Then a list of instruments and ways to praise follows. This list is not exhaustive but demonstrates how creative our praise is to be. Finally, in case even one person feels less than inclined to praise Him, the instruction is clear: If you have God's gift of life-breath, you should praise Him. Hallelujah! (Ps. 145:4/Is. 61:3) C.G.

149:6 This statement may be drawing from the OT historical event of sending the singers and Levites out to battle with the Israelite soldiers (2 Chr. 20:21, 22). Human strength, without acknowledging God's might, does not win spiritual battles either.
149:7–9 The literal enemies mentioned here find their NT counterparts in Paul's list of Eph. 6:12 and in the generalized works of the Devil (disease, poverty, demonization, and so on). All these enemies can be countered in a worshiper's life by God's reign released through heartfelt worship and praise.
150:1–6 This whole psalm serves as the doxology, not only for Book Five, but for the whole Book of Psalms.
150:1 This verse instructs us where to worship: indoors and outdoors.
150:2 This verse tells us why we are to worship: because of God's **mighty** deeds and His **excellent** character.
150:3–5 Vv. 3–5 inform us on how to worship: with variety in symphonic rhapsody.
150:6 We are first told in this verse who is to worship: **everything** that breathes. Then it closes by restating the object of worship: **the LORD** (*Yahweh*). The final commentary is that every living thing should "praise the LORD" (Hebrew "Hallelujah").

TRUTH-IN-ACTION through PSALMS (Book Five: Psalms 107—150)

Letting the LIFE of the Holy Spirit Bring Faith's Works Alive in You!

Truth Psalms Teaches	Text	**Action** Psalms Invites
1 Guidelines for Growing in Godliness By living your life according to the Scriptures and its instructions you will grow in godliness.	133:1	**Strive** for the unity of the church in all you do.
	126:5, 6	**Sow** to righteousness through deeds of righteous obedience for a rich harvest.
	119:56	**Practice** obedience to God's Word. **Understand** that it's the key to further understanding.
	119:9	**Order** all your life according to God's Word as the key to purity.
	111:10; 112:2	**Seek God** and **cultivate** the fear of the Lord; doing so leads to wisdom and results in great blessing.
2 Steps to Holiness Holiness involves trusting the Lord and not the world, most often requiring that we make a choice for the former and against the latter. The line between the two is drawn finer and closer to the Lord the longer we walk with Him.	115:2–8	**Do not put your trust** in things you have built for security. **Know** that God calls this idolatry.
	119:105, 130	**Seek** illumination from God's eternal Word and not from man's finite wisdom.
	119:36	**Set** your affections on doing God's word rather than on personal gain.
	127:1, 2	**Know** that employing your skills for the Lord is futile without His presence and anointing upon them.
3 Steps to Dynamic Devotion God wants our hearts, not just our verbal allegiance, and He desires that our affections be wholly His. Developing the disciplined practices that lead to this kind of life must be a high priority. This requires that we reorder our priorities accordingly.	139:23	**Daily ask** the Lord to search and know your heart.
	131:2	**Give yourself** to secluded times of quiet and stillness as a regular part of your devotion to God.
	119:23, 24	**Regularly meditate** on the Scriptures in order to plumb their depths.
	119:11	**Diligently practice** Scripture memorization, training your heart to avoid sin.
	107:22	**Employ** praise songs as a vehicle of personal gratitude.
4 Keys to Wise Living Only the life lived in the light of God's Word is lived wisely. For this reason, our study of the Bible must be constantly accompanied with the petition that God will give us wisdom and understanding through our study so that we can learn to live in a way that pleases Him.	143:10	**Ask** the Lord to teach you and lead you in the performing of His will.
	119:128	**Take your stand** on the rightness of God's Word. **Understand** that evil is that which disregards God's instruction.
	119:27	**Seek knowledge** but, most of all, **gain understanding. Know** that practical understanding is more important than mere knowledge.
	119:18	Daily **ask** God to open your heart and mind through the ministry of the Holy Spirit to the message of the Scriptures.

Truth Psalms Teaches	Text	**Action** Psalms Invites
5 Key Lessons in Faith God wants us to take Him at His Word and to take His Word at its face value. The truth therein is available through no other source. We must receive and believe them to benefit from them.	139:7 138:8	**Be consoled** in the truth that God is always and everywhere present. **Be assured** that if you continue in Him, the Lord will most certainly fulfill His purpose for you.
6 God Is True to His Word God is consistent and unchanging. His nature is reflected in His law.	119:71	Even in your afflictions, **recognize** that God is true to His Word. You can **depend** on Him.

TRUTH-IN-ACTION through PSALMS (A Summary)

Letting the LIFE of the Holy Spirit Bring Faith's Works Alive in You!

Editorial Note: In addition to the truths covered in each of the five book divisions of Psalms, a number of other directives are frequently repeated. This brief summary focuses on some of them.

Truth Psalms Teaches	**Action** Psalms Invites
Worship the Lord Worship means to ascribe worth to something or someone through speech and conduct. Worship addresses God directly, expressing reverence for His nature, character attributes, and power, and grateful praise for all He is and does.	a. **Worship** the Lord with all your heart and mind. **Rehearse** His attributes consciously. **Recount** how who God is affects you and is changing you. **Avoid worshiping** mindlessly or by rote or becoming passive in worship. **Give yourself** wholeheartedly to it. b. **Employ** singing, both with the spirit and with the understanding, using speaking, bowing, kneeling, dancing, corporate applause, and instrumental music to enhance expression of worship.
Praise the Lord To praise the Lord means to speak well of God with exuberance and enthusiasm to others and/or to Him because of what He has done. "Praise the Lord!" (Hebrew *Hallelujah!*) is a command to extol God's virtues and exalt Him because of His mighty acts. A praise gathering is a celebration of God's mighty power and purpose.	a. **Praise God** with a loud and enthusiastic voice. **Clap** your hands and **shout joyfully** to the Lord. **Participate** in processions of praise. **Speak** and **sing praise** to God. **Involve** such physical expressions as raising hands, dancing, applause, and kneeling. b. **Discipline** yourself to praise God for every benefit He provides. **Be disciplined** in corporate praise. **Be careful** to submit to leadership in praise services, not letting praise degenerate into fleshly enthusiasm.
Trust in the Lord Trust is the belief in and reliance on the integrity, strength, ability, surety of a person or thing. To trust in the Lord is to believe Him, (that is, to take Him at His word) and to believe absolutely that what He says is true.	a. **Trust** in the Lord and not in yourself. b. **Trust** in the Lord and not your wealth for financial security. c. **Trust** in the Lord and not in your physical strength or your nation's military prowess for protection. d. **Trust** in the Lord and not in political power or connections. e. **Trust** in the Lord and not in things you have built.

Truth Psalms Teaches	**Action** Psalms Invites
Thanksgiving The psalmists call for constant verbal expression of heartfelt gratitude to God for all of His benefits and gifts to man.	a. **Give thanks** to God, first of all, for who He is. b. **Give thanks** to God for all that He has given you. c. **Give thanks** to God for His lovingkindness and mercy. d. **Give thanks** to God for His protection. e. **Give thanks** to God for His guidance. f. **Give thanks** to God for all His mighty acts. g. **Give thanks** to God that His purposes will prevail.
Proclaim As one of their major themes, the psalmists call God's people to declare openly His goodness, lovingkindness, and mercy to them and to the nations.	a. **Proclaim** God's love, mercy, and forgiveness to all of Israel. b. **Proclaim** God's truth and justice to all the nations. c. **Proclaim** His righteousness. d. **Proclaim** His mighty acts. e. **Proclaim** all that He has done. f. **Proclaim** His salvation, day after day!
Rely upon God's Protection The psalmists encourage the people to turn to God and rely upon Him rather than on themselves, and their own strength in times of trouble.	a. **Rely upon God** when confronted by any enemy. b. **Rely upon God** whenever you are in any kind of distress. c. **Rely upon God** in times of natural calamity. d. **Rely upon God** in times of political crisis. e. **Rely upon God** when confronted with sickness or physical weakness.

The Book of PROVERBS

Author: Solomon, with Portions by Agur and King Lemuel

Date: About 950 B.C., with Portions About 720 B.C.

Theme: Universal Principles for Living

Key Words: Wisdom, Knowledge, Understanding, Instruction, the Fear of the Lord

Author Solomon, king of Israel, was the son of David and Bathsheba. He reigned for forty years, from 970 to 930 B.C., taking the throne at about twenty years of age.

No doubt influenced by the psalm-writing of his father, Solomon has left us more books than any other Old Testament writer except Moses. It seems probable that his Song of Solomon was written when he was a young romantic, his Proverbs when he was mature and at the height of his powers, and his Ecclesiastes when he had become more aged, more inclined to philosophical conclusions, and perhaps more cynical. His strengths were not on the battlefield, but in the realm of the mind: meditation, planning, negotiation, and organization.

Solomon's reputation for wisdom springs not only from its practical results, as in the case of the dispute over a baby (1 Kin. 3:16–27), but also from the direct statements of Scripture. In 1 Kings 3:12 God says, "There has not been anyone like you before you, nor shall any like you arise after you." In 1 Kings 4:31 he is called "wiser than all men," with names of other wise men cited in specific comparison.

Of Agur and King Lemuel (30:1; 31:1) we know nothing except that, by their names, they were not Israelites. Wisdom is universal, not national.

Date Since the Book of Proverbs is a compilation, its writing was spread over a period of years, with the main work probably centered about 950 B.C. Chapters 25 through 29 are identified as copied by "Hezekiah's men," which places the copying at about 720 B.C., though the material itself was by Solomon, perhaps in a separate document found in Hezekiah's time.

Background Under Solomon's leadership Israel reached its greatest geographical extent and enjoyed the least violence of the entire kingdom period. "Peaceful," the meaning of his name, describes Solomon's reign. And peace, with wisdom, brought unprecedented prosperity to the nation, which became a cause of wonder and admiration to the queen of Sheba (1 Kin. 10:6–9) and to the other rulers of the time.

Wise sayings, like music or other art forms, tend to blossom in such a time, then endure through succeeding generations.

Content The Book of Proverbs is not just a collection of sayings, but a collection of collections. Its unifying thought or theme is, "The fear of the LORD *is* the beginning of wisdom" (9:10), appearing in another form as, "The fear of the LORD *is* the beginning [or principal part] of knowledge" (1:7). Coming through the diversity of examples time and again are such truths as these:

1. Wisdom (the ability to judge and act according to God's directives) is the most valuable of assets.
2. Wisdom is available to anyone, but the price is high.
3. Wisdom originates in God, not self, and comes by attention to instruction.
4. Wisdom and righteousness go together. It is good to be wise, and it is wise to be good.
5. Evil men suffer the consequences of their evil deeds.
6. The simple, the fool, the lazy, the ignorant, the proud, the profligate, the sinful are never to be admired.

Many powerful contrasts are found again and again. Antithesis helps to clarify the meaning of key words. Among the ideas set in vivid contrast with each other are:

Wisdom versus Folly
Righteousness versus Wickedness
Good versus Evil
Life versus Death
Prosperity versus Poverty
Honor versus Dishonor
Permanence versus Transience
Truth versus Falsehood
Industry versus Indolence
Friend versus Enemy
Prudence versus Rashness
Fidelity versus Adultery
Peace versus Violence
Goodwill versus Anger
God versus Man

Personal Application The wisdom contained in the Book of Proverbs is as meaningful today as when it was written. Yet it is neither a prosperity pamphlet nor a "how to succeed" handbook in the worldly sense. It tells rather how to order one's values, which leads to character, which leads to wholeness, which leads to satisfaction. It warns of the pitfalls along the way, and declares the folly of *not* developing the fear of the Lord. Because the thirty-one-chapter book contains so much that is worth daily meditation and is relevant for every era, many Bible readers have found it desirable to read a chapter a day, thus covering the entire book every month.

Christ Revealed No direct references to Christ, prophetic or typological, are especially conspicuous in the Book of Proverbs. In fact, the personification of Wisdom is normally feminine throughout. Nevertheless some passages (such as 8:23–31) seem an unmistakable description of Jesus Christ, who was "in the beginning with God" (John 1:2), is "the wisdom of God" (1 Cor. 1:24), and "became for us wisdom" (1 Cor. 1:30).

Certainly the book performs a powerful service in whetting the human appetite for wisdom and understanding, a hunger that can only be fully satisfied in Christ.

Proverbs, much like the Mosaic Law, describes an ideal, an aspiration, a longing for perfection. Yet even Solomon himself was not perfectly wise, or he would not have so flagrantly disobeyed and thus displeased God (1 Kin. 11:9–11). Only later, in Jesus Christ, came the full example of all that Proverbs extols, the One "in whom are hidden all the treasures of wisdom" (Col. 2:3).

Point by point, the qualities of wisdom are the qualities of the Christ. Obedience to God, right behavior, patience, reliability, humility, diligence, the perception of things as they really are—all these, plus love, are perfectly illustrated in the Savior.

The Holy Spirit at Work The Holy Spirit is not mentioned directly in the Book of Proverbs. But Wisdom refers to her spirit (1:23), which of course is the Spirit of God. In fact, a main point of the book is that wisdom apart from God is impossible, so in that sense His Spirit is prominent throughout. However the dominant word translated "spirit" in the book is almost always with the meaning of "attitude," or "demeanor," never implying a personality.

In our era, a time of the special work of the Holy Spirit, it is the Spirit who helps us mine the riches of the Proverbs, rather than Proverbs helping us understand the Spirit. It has been said of the Old and New Testaments, "The New is in the Old concealed; the Old is in the New revealed."

In the case of the Book of Proverbs, the Holy Spirit in the New Testament demonstrates how the wisdom of this book (which comes only through righteousness) is made achievable.

Unique Features The book is different from all others in the Bible in these respects:

1. It gives clear internal evidence of multiple authorship. This is deduced or implied in some other Bible books, but never revealed so plainly as in Proverbs.

2. It also shows clear internal evidence of having been put together over the amazing span of about 250 years, since Hezekiah, mentioned in 25:1, lived about that long after King Solomon. Other books (Genesis, for example) may cover long *historical* spans of time, but none of them so clearly indicate the span of their *composition.*

Outline of Proverbs

I. Introduction **1:1–7**
- A. Title, purpose and introduction 1:1–6
- B. Theme or motto 1:7

II. A father's warnings and Wisdom's admonitions **1:8—8:36**
- A. A father's warnings, part one 1:8–19
- B. Wisdom's admonitions, part one 1:20–33
- C. A father's warnings, part two 2:1—7:27
- D. Wisdom's admonitions, part two 8:1–36

III. The way of wisdom versus the way of folly **9:1–18**

IV. Solomon's proverbs and sayings of the wise **10:1—29:27**
- A. Solomon's proverbs—first collection 10:1—22:16

The Beginning of Knowledge

THE [a]proverbs of Solomon the son of David, king of Israel:

2 To know wisdom and instruction,
To [1]perceive the words of understanding,
3 To receive the *instruction of wisdom,
Justice, judgment, and equity;
4 To give prudence to the [a]simple,
To the young man knowledge and discretion—
5 [a]A wise *man* will hear and increase learning,
And a man of understanding will [1]attain wise counsel,
6 To understand a **proverb** and an enigma,
The words of the wise and their [a]riddles.

WORD WEALTH

1:6 proverb, *mashal* (mah-*shahl*); Strong's #4912: Proverb, parable, maxim, adage; a simile or allegory; an object lesson or illustration. This noun comes from the verb *mashal,* "to compare; to be similar." Based on the Book of Proverbs, it might appear that a proverb is a short saying containing a nugget of truth. Yet OT evidence shows it has broader uses. Balaam's long discourse is termed a *mashal* (Num. 23:7—24:24). In other references, *mashal* suggests a taunt, a byword, or an illustration. In still others, it suggests a person or a nation out of which God has made an example. Compare 1 Kin. 9:7 with Ps. 69:11.

7 [a]The fear of the LORD *is* the beginning of *knowledge,
But fools despise wisdom and instruction.

Shun Evil Counsel

8 [a]My son, hear the instruction of your *father,
And do not forsake the law of your mother;
9 For they *will be* a [a]graceful ornament on your head,
And chains about your neck.
10 My son, if sinners entice you,
[a]Do not consent.
11 If they say, "Come with us,
Let us [a]lie in wait to *shed* blood;
Let us lurk secretly for the innocent without cause;
12 Let us swallow them alive like [1]Sheol,
And whole, [a]like those who go down to the Pit;

CHAPTER 1

1 [a]1 Kin. 4:32; Prov. 10:1; 25:1; Eccl. 12:9
2 [1]*understand* or *discern*
3 *See WW at Prov. 4:13.
4 [a]Prov. 9:4
5 [a]Prov. 9:9 [1]*acquire*
6 [a]Num. 12:8; Ps. 78:2; Dan. 8:23
7 [a]Job 28:28; Ps. 111:10; Prov. 9:10; 15:33; [Eccl. 12:13] *See WW at Mal. 2:7.
8 [a]Prov. 4:1 *See WW at Ps. 68:5.
9 [a]Prov. 3:22
10 [a]Gen. 39:7–10; Deut. 13:8; Ps. 50:18; [Eph. 5:11]
11 [a]Prov. 12:6; Jer. 5:26
12 [a]Ps. 28:1 [1]Or *the grave*

1:1 Here is immediate identification of the book with its principal author. However, the meaning is not that all the proverbs are original with Solomon. He was anthologist as well as author. In 1 Kin. 4:32 we read that he "spoke" 3,000 proverbs. In Eccl. he calls himself "the Preacher" (Eccl. 1:1). As such, he no doubt collected and quoted useful expressions—just as a modern preacher might quote a poem or a powerful metaphor. The proverbs are his, not just because he composed most of them, but because he collected and used them. (See note on 22:17.)
1:2–6 The *purposes* of the proverbs are listed; however, grammatically, this whole passage could be the title of the book.
1:2 Wisdom: See Introduction to Proverbs: Content.
1:7 The fear of the LORD: Expressed in many ways, this is the theme repeated throughout the book as the key, the means, the secret of obtaining genuine wisdom. It is not the terror of a tyrant, but the kind of awe and respect which will lead to obedience to Him who is the wisest of all. ***But* fools:** Stark and immediate contrast is one of the strongest ways the writer makes his point. In Solomon's time this balancing or doubling of a true statement by following up with its opposite was an expected and satisfying literary device.
1:8, 9 Receiving parental instruction is not to be a burden or an annoyance, but an enhancement, a means of increased attractiveness, like jewelry joyfully worn.
1:10–19 Here is the first warning passage. Quoting what sinners (vicious men) may say is a practical way of preparing a son to resist their suggestions. But the son has the choice to make.

13 We shall find all *kinds* of precious
[1]possessions,
We shall fill our houses with
[2]spoil;
14 Cast in your lot among us,
Let us all have one purse"—
15 My son, [a]do not walk in the way
with them,
[b]Keep your foot from their path;
16 [a]For their feet run to evil,
And they make haste to shed
blood.
17 Surely, in [1]vain the net is spread
In the sight of any [2]bird;
18 But they lie in wait for their *own*
blood,
They lurk secretly for their *own*
lives.
19 [a]So *are* the ways of everyone who
is greedy for gain;
It takes away the life of its
owners.

The Call of Wisdom

20 [a]Wisdom calls aloud [1]outside;
She raises her voice in the open
squares.
21 She cries out in the [1]chief
concourses,
At the openings of the gates in the
city
She speaks her words:
22 "How long, you [1]simple ones, will
you love [2]simplicity?
For scorners delight in their
scorning,
And fools hate knowledge.
23 Turn at my rebuke;
Surely [a]I will pour out my spirit
on you;
I will make my words known to
you.
24 [a]Because I have called and you
refused,
I have stretched out my *hand
and no one regarded,
25 Because you [a]disdained all my
counsel,
And would have none of my
rebuke,
26 [a]I also will *laugh at your
calamity;
I will mock when your terror
comes,
27 When [a]your terror comes like a
storm,
And your destruction comes like
a whirlwind,
When distress and anguish come
upon you.

28 "Then[a] they will call on me, but I
will not answer;
They will seek me diligently, but
they will not find me.
29 Because they [a]hated knowledge
And did not [b]choose the fear of
the LORD,
30 [a]They would have none of my
counsel
And despised my every rebuke.
31 Therefore [a]they shall eat the fruit
of their own way,
And be filled to the full with their
own fancies.
32 For the [1]turning* away of the
simple will slay them,
And the complacency of fools will
destroy them;
33 But whoever listens to me will
dwell [a]safely,*
And [b]will be [1]secure, without fear
of evil."

The Value of Wisdom

2 My son, if you receive my words, **1**
And [a]treasure my commands
within you,
2 So that you incline your ear to
wisdom,
And apply your heart to
understanding;
3 Yes, if you cry out for
discernment,
And lift up your voice for
understanding,
4 [a]If you seek her as silver, **2**
And search for her as *for* hidden
treasures;
5 [a]Then you will *understand the
fear of the LORD,
And find the knowledge of God.
6 [a]For the LORD gives wisdom;
From His mouth *come* knowledge
and understanding;
7 He stores up sound wisdom for
the upright;
[a]*He is* a shield to those who walk
uprightly;
8 He guards the paths of justice,
And [a]preserves the way of His
saints.

13 [1]Lit. *wealth* [2]*plunder*
15 [a]Ps. 1:1 [b]Ps. 119:101
16 [a][Is. 59:7]
17 [1]*futility* [2]Lit. *lord of the wing*
19 [a][1 Tim. 6:10]
20 [a][John 7:37] [1]*in the street*
21 [1]LXX, Syr., Tg. *top of the walls;* Vg. *the head of multitudes*
22 [1]*naive* [2]*naivete*
23 [a]Joel 2:28
24 [a]Jer. 7:13 *See WW at Josh. 4:24.
25 [a]Luke 7:30
26 [a]Ps. 2:4 *See WW at Eccl. 3:4.
27 [a][Prov. 10:24, 25]
28 [a]Is. 1:15
29 [a]Job 21:14 [b]Ps. 119:173
30 [a]Ps. 81:11
31 [a]Job 4:8
32 [1]*wayward-ness* *See WW at Jer. 5:6.
33 [a]Prov. 3:24–26 [b]Ps. 112:7 [1]*at ease* *See WW at Deut. 33:12.

CHAPTER 2

1 [a][Prov. 4:21]
4 [a][Prov. 3:14]
5 [a][James 1:5, 6] *See WW at Neh. 8:8.
6 [a]1 Kin. 3:9, 12
7 [a][Ps. 84:11]
8 [a][1 Sam. 2:9]

1:20, 21 Wisdom calls: An "it" becomes a "she," and is not only personified, but characterized as a *communicating* person, not a cold abstraction.

1:22–33 The direct quotation adds to the reality of Wisdom as a caring personality. Her tone contains scolding, but her promise is specific and encouraging (v. 33).

2:1–9 Three "ifs" (vv. 1, 3, 4) fulfilled will lead to the glorious treasures of understanding (v. 4) and the knowledge of God (v. 5).

2:1–6 See section 1 of Truth-In-Action at the end of Prov.

2:4–6 See section 2 of Truth-In-Action at the end of Prov.

9 Then you will understand
righteousness and justice,
Equity *and* every good path.

10 When wisdom enters your heart,
And knowledge is pleasant to
your soul,
11 Discretion will *preserve you;
[a]Understanding will keep you,
12 To deliver you from the way of
evil,
From the man who speaks
perverse things,
13 From those who leave the paths
of uprightness
To [a]walk in the ways of darkness;
14 [a]Who rejoice in doing evil,
And delight in the perversity of
the wicked;
15 [a]Whose ways *are* crooked,
And *who are* devious in their
paths;
16 To deliver you from [a]the immoral
woman,
[b]From the seductress *who* flatters
with her words,
17 Who forsakes the companion of
her youth,
And forgets the covenant of her
God.
18 For [a]her house [1]leads down to
death,
And her paths to the dead;
19 None who go to her return,
Nor do they [1]regain the paths of
life—
20 So you may walk in the way of
goodness,
And keep *to* the paths of
*righteousness.
21 For the upright will dwell in the
[a]land,
And the blameless will remain in
it;
22 But the wicked will be [1]cut off
from the [2]earth,
And the unfaithful will be
uprooted from it.

Guidance for the Young

3 My *son, do not forget my law,
[a]But let your heart keep my
commands;
2 For length of days and long life
And [a]peace they will add to you.

3 Let not mercy and *truth forsake
you;
[a]Bind them around your neck,
[b]Write* them on the tablet of your
*heart,
4 [a]*And* so find favor and [1]high
esteem
In the sight of God and man.

5 [a]Trust in the LORD with all your
heart, **2**
[b]And lean not on your own
understanding;
6 [a]In all your ways acknowledge
Him,
And He shall [1]**direct** your paths.

11 [a]Prov. 4:6; 6:22 *See WW at Job 10:12.
13 [a]Ps. 82:5; Prov. 4:19; [John 3:19, 20]
14 [a]Prov. 10:23; Jer. 11:15; [Rom. 1:32]
15 [a]Ps. 125:5; [Prov. 21:8]
16 [a]Prov. 5:20; 6:24; 7:5 [b]Prov. 5:3
18 [a]Prov. 7:27 [1]*sinks*
19 [1]Lit. *reach*
20 *See WW at Lam. 1:18.
21 [a]Ps. 37:3
22 [1]*destroyed* [2]*land*

CHAPTER 3

1 [a]Deut. 8:1 *See WW at Gen. 29:32.
2 [a]Ps. 119:165; Prov. 4:10
3 [a]Ex. 13:9; Deut. 6:8; Prov. 6:21 [b]Prov. 7:3; Jer. 17:1; [2 Cor. 3:3] *See WW at Ps. 25:5. • See WW at Deut. 31:9. • See WW at Ps. 37:4.
4 [a]1 Sam. 2:26; Luke 2:52; Rom. 14:18 [1]Lit. *good understanding*
5 [a][Ps. 37:3, 5]; Prov. 22:19 [b]Prov. 23:4; [Jer. 9:23, 24]
6 [a][1 Chr. 28:9]; Prov. 16:3; [Phil. 4:6; James 1:5] [1]Or *make smooth* or *straight*

WORD WEALTH

3:6 direct, *yashar* (yah-*shar*); Strong's #3474: To be straight, right, upright, pleasing, good. *Yashar* appears in an intensive form here and means to "make straight and right." God will "straighten out" the path of His devoted, trusting servants. From this verb comes the noun *yosher,* "uprightness" (Ps. 119:7). Job is described as blameless and upright (Job 1:1). God's promise to Cyrus was that the crooked places would be made straight (Is. 45:2). Finally, from *yashar* comes the poetical name "Jeshurun" ("Upright One"), a name always applied to Israel as God's righteous nation (Deut. 33:5; Is. 44:2).

KINGDOM DYNAMICS

3:5, 6 Intimacy and Spiritual Breakthrough, FAITH'S WARFARE. Two words in this passage are especially significant—the words "ways" and "acknowledge."

The word "ways" (Hebrew *derek*) means "a road, a course, or a mode of action." It suggests specific opportunities a person may encounter on a recurring basis. The most common "segment of opportunity" we experience regularly is each new day. It is as if this passage suggests that in all our "days" we should acknowledge God, and in so doing He will direct our paths.

Of equal significance is the word "ac-

2:10–19 Vv. 10 and 11 give the condition for escape from the list of threats represented by vv. 12–19, which comprise wicked males (vv. 12–15) and wicked females (vv. 16–19).
2:20–22 Reminiscent of the contrasts of Ps. 1 regarding the blessed man versus the ungodly, here the benefits of the righteous are followed with the dire end of the wicked (v. 22).
3:1 The Law (Torah), the Jewish name for the Pentateuch, and meaning basically "teaching," is the foundation of righteousness. The expression "*my* law," assuming it is still the parent speaking, implies the more personal principles of the household—close to those of God, but with detailed application.
3:3 Bind them . . . write them: Mercy and truth are to be considered constant and valuable equipment, never left behind.
3:5, 6 See section 2 of Truth-In-Action at the end of Prov.
3:5 Lean: "Support yourself" expresses the thought.
3:6 Acknowledge: This suggests being fully aware of and in fellowship with Him.

knowledge" (Hebrew *yada'*). Elsewhere *yada'* is translated "know," meaning to know by observation, investigation, reflection, or firsthand experience. But the highest level of *yada'* is in "direct, intimate contact." This refers to life-giving intimacy, as in marriage. Applied to a spiritual context, it suggests an intimacy with God in prayer that conceives and births blessings and victories. Joined to our Prov. text, we might conclude that if in all our "days" we maintain *yada'* (direct, intimate contact with God), God promises to direct our paths toward fruitful, life-begetting endeavors.

(Jer. 33:3/Acts 6:1–4) D.E.

7 Do not be wise in your own
[a]eyes;
Fear the LORD and depart from
*evil.
8 It will be health to your [1]flesh,
And [a]strength[2] to your bones.

4 9 [a]Honor the LORD with your
possessions,
And with the firstfruits of all your
increase;
10 [a]So your barns will *be filled with
plenty,
And your vats will overflow with
new wine.

11 [a]My son, do not *despise the
chastening of the LORD,
Nor detest His correction;
12 For whom the LORD loves He
corrects,
[a]Just as a father the son *in whom*
he delights.

1 13 [a]Happy *is* the man *who* finds
wisdom,
And the man *who* gains
understanding;
14 [a]For her proceeds *are* better than
the profits of silver,
And her gain than fine gold.
15 She *is* more precious than rubies,
And [a]all the things you may
desire cannot compare with
her.

7 [a]Rom. 12:16 *See WW at Ps. 5:4.
8 [a]Job 21:24 [1]Body, lit. *navel* [2]Lit. *drink*
9 [a]Ex. 22:29; Deut. 26:2; [Mal. 3:10]
10 [a]Deut. 28:8 *See WW at Jer. 23:24.
11 [a]Job 5:17; Ps. 94:12; Heb. 12:5, 6; Rev. 3:19 *See WW at Amos 2:4.
12 [a]Deut. 8:5; Prov. 13:24
13 [a]Prov. 8:32, 34, 35
14 [a]Job 28:13
15 [a]Matt. 13:44
16 [a]Prov. 8:18; [1 Tim. 4:8]
17 [a][Matt. 11:29]
18 [a]Gen. 2:9; Prov. 11:30; 13:12; 15:4; Rev. 2:7 [1]*hold her fast*
19 [a]Ps. 104:24; Prov. 8:27
20 [a]Gen. 7:11
23 [a][Ps. 37:24; 91:11, 12]; Prov. 10:9
24 *See WW at Hos. 3:5.
25 [a]Ps. 91:5; 1 Pet. 3:14
27 [a]Rom. 13:7; [Gal. 6:10] [1]Lit. *its owners*
28 [a]Lev. 19:13; Deut. 24:15

16 [a]Length of days *is* in her right
hand,
In her left hand riches and honor.
17 [a]Her ways *are* ways of
pleasantness,
And all her paths *are* peace.
18 She *is* [a]a tree of life to those who
take hold of her,
And happy *are all* who [1]retain
her.

19 [a]The LORD by wisdom founded the
earth;
By understanding He established
the heavens;
20 By His knowledge the depths
were [a]broken up,
And clouds drop down the dew.

21 My son, let them not depart from 1
your eyes—
Keep sound wisdom and
discretion;
22 So they will be life to your soul
And grace to your neck.
23 [a]Then you will walk safely in your
way,
And your foot will not stumble.
24 When you lie down, you will not
be *afraid;
Yes, you will lie down and your
sleep will be sweet.
25 [a]Do not be afraid of sudden terror,
Nor of trouble from the wicked
when it comes;
26 For the LORD will be your
confidence,
And will keep your foot from
being caught.

27 [a]Do not withhold good from 4
[1]those to whom it is due,
When it is in the power of your
hand to do *so*.
28 [a]Do not say to your neighbor,
"Go, and come back,
And tomorrow I will give *it*,"
When *you have* it with you.
29 Do not devise evil against your
neighbor,
For he dwells by you for safety's
sake.

3:9, 10 That righteousness brings reward, repeatedly stated in Prov. and many other Scriptures, is not a mechanical guarantee of cause and effect. Rather, like sowing and reaping, it is a general law built into the nature of God's world. Exceptions may occur, at least temporarily, but they do not change the inexorable principles of the universe. Here is reality.
3:9 See section 4 of Truth-In-Action at the end of Prov.
3:11, 12 Despise . . . detest: The meaning is to reject or shrink from. Correction, hard as it is, proves God's love and concern.
3:13–18 See section 1 of Truth-In-Action at the end of Prov.
3:14 Proceeds: The use of a term ordinarily used for merchandising or profit declares wisdom is worth more than commerce.
3:16–18 A compact (and only partial) list of things wisdom offers: longevity, wealth, recognition, enjoyment, peace, vitality, and happiness.
3:19, 20 Wisdom is not just God's possession, but His tool.
3:21–26 See section 1 of Truth-In-Action at the end of Prov.
3:22–26 Wisdom offers security from many dangers.
3:27–30 Neighborly honesty is a practical application of wisdom.
3:27, 28 See section 4 of Truth-In-Action at the end of Prov.

30 [a]Do not strive with a man without cause,
If he has done you no harm.

31 [a]Do not *envy the oppressor,
And choose none of his ways;
32 For the perverse *person is* an abomination to the LORD,
[a]But His secret counsel *is* with the upright.
33 [a]The curse of the LORD *is* on the house of the wicked,
But [b]He blesses the home of the just.
34 [a]Surely He scorns the scornful,
But gives grace to the humble.
35 The wise shall inherit glory,
But shame shall be the legacy of fools.

Security in Wisdom

4 Hear, [a]*my* children, the *instruction of a father,
And give attention to *know understanding;
2 For I give you good doctrine:
Do not forsake my law.
3 When I was my father's son,
[a]Tender and the *only one in the sight of my mother,
4 [a]He also taught me, and said to me:
"Let your heart retain my words;
[b]Keep my commands, and live.
1 5 [a]Get wisdom! Get understanding!
Do not forget, nor turn away from the words of my mouth.
6 Do not forsake her, and she will *preserve you;
[a]Love her, and she will keep you.
7 [a]Wisdom *is* the principal thing;
Therefore get wisdom.
And in all your getting, get understanding.
8 [a]Exalt her, and she will promote you;
She will bring you honor, when you embrace her.
9 She will place on your head [a]an ornament of grace;
A crown of glory she will deliver to you."
10 Hear, my son, and receive my sayings,
[a]And the years of your life will be many.
11 I have [a]taught you in the way of wisdom;
I have led you in right paths.
12 When you walk, [a]your steps will not be hindered,
[b]And when you run, you will not stumble.
13 Take firm hold of **instruction,** do not let go;
Keep her, for she *is* your life.

WORD WEALTH

4:13 instruction, *musar* (moo-*sar*); Strong's #4148: Correction, chastisement, instruction, discipline; an admonition, rebuke, or warning. *Musar* comes from the verb *yasar*, "to reform, chastise, discipline, instruct." *Musar* appears 50 times in the OT, 30 of these in Prov. *Musar* is broad enough to encompass chastening by words and by punishments (1:3; 22:15). Is. 53:5 states, "The chastisement for our peace was upon Him, and by His stripes we are healed." In Prov. 3:11, we are urged not to "despise the chastening of the LORD," nor to grow weary of His correction. A wicked man may even "die for lack of instruction" (Prov. 5:23). Thus *musar* includes all forms of discipline intended to lead to a transformed life.

14 [a]Do not enter the path of the wicked,
And do not walk in the way of evil.
15 Avoid it, do not travel on it;
Turn away from it and pass on.
16 [a]For they do not sleep unless they have done evil;
And their sleep is [1]taken away unless they make *someone* fall.
17 For they eat the bread of wickedness,
And drink the wine of violence.
18 [a]But the path of the just [b]*is* like the shining [1]sun,
That shines ever brighter unto the perfect day.
19 [a]The way of the wicked *is* like darkness;
They do not know what makes them stumble.

30 [a]Prov. 26:17; [Rom. 12:18]
31 [a]Ps. 37:1; Prov. 24:1 *See WW at Zech. 8:2.
32 [a]Ps. 25:14
33 [a]Lev. 26:14, 16; Deut. 11:28; Zech. 5:3, 4; Mal. 2:2 [b]Job 8:6; Ps. 1:3
34 [a]James 4:6; 1 Pet. 5:5

CHAPTER 4

1 [a]Ps. 34:11; Prov. 1:8 *See WW at Prov. 4:13. • See WW at Ex. 3:7.
3 [a]1 Chr. 29:1 *See WW at Gen. 22:2.
4 [a]1 Chr. 28:9; Eph. 6:4 [b]Prov. 7:2
5 [a]Prov. 2:2, 3
6 [a]2 Thess. 2:10 *See WW at Job 10:12.
7 [a]Prov. 3:13, 14; Matt. 13:44
8 [a]1 Sam. 2:30
9 [a]Prov. 3:22
10 [a]Prov. 3:2
11 [a]1 Sam. 12:23
12 [a]Job 18:7; Ps. 18:36 [b][Ps. 91:11]; Prov. 3:23
14 [a]Ps. 1:1; Prov. 1:15
16 [a]Ps. 36:4; Mic. 2:1 [1]Lit. *robbed*
18 [a]Is. 26:7; Matt. 5:14, 45; Phil. 2:15 [b]2 Sam. 23:4 [1]Lit. *light*
19 [a]1 Sam. 2:9; [Job 18:5, 6]; Prov. 2:13; [Is. 59:9, 10; Jer. 23:12]; John 12:35

3:31–35 God curses the wicked, but blesses the righteous.
4:1–9 The advising father quotes his own advising father. Wise counsel is a heritage to be perpetuated. What is passed on is not just a collection of adages for good behavior, but a basic yearning for wisdom.
4:5–9 See section 1 of Truth-In-Action at the end of Prov.
4:12–15 A strong, rapid succession of verbs, mostly negative imperatives, warns the son.
4:16, 17 They: The wicked are literally addicted to evil. It becomes as natural to them as sleeping, eating, and drinking.
4:18 The just: Here, sandwiched between the ways of the wicked, his destiny shines with ever-rising promise.

20 My son, give attention to my words;
Incline your ear to my sayings.
21 Do not let them depart from your eyes;
Keep them in the midst of your heart;
22 For they *are* life to those who find them,
And *health to all their flesh.
23 Keep your heart with all diligence,
For out of it *spring* the issues of [a]life.
24 Put away from you a [1]deceitful mouth,
And put perverse lips far from you.
25 Let your eyes look straight ahead,
And your eyelids look *right before you.
26 Ponder the path of your [a]feet,
And let all your ways be established.
27 Do not turn to the right or the left;
Remove your foot from evil.

The Peril of Adultery

5 My son, pay attention to my wisdom;
[1]Lend your ear to my understanding,
2 That you may [1]preserve discretion,
And your lips [a]may keep knowledge.
3 [a]For the lips of [1]an immoral woman *drip honey,
And her mouth *is* [b]smoother than oil;
4 But in the end she is bitter as wormwood,
Sharp as a two-edged sword.
5 Her feet go down to death,
[a]Her steps lay hold of [1]hell.
6 Lest you ponder *her* path of life—
Her ways are unstable;
You do not know *them*.

7 Therefore hear me now, *my* children,
And do not depart from the words of my mouth.
8 Remove your way far from her,
And do not go near the door of her house,
9 Lest you give your [1]honor* to others,
And your years to the cruel *one;*
10 Lest aliens be filled with your [1]wealth,
And your labors *go* to the house of a foreigner;
11 And you mourn at last,
When your flesh and your body are consumed,
12 And say:
"How I have hated instruction,
And my heart despised correction!
13 I have not obeyed the voice of my teachers,
Nor inclined my ear to those who instructed me!
14 I was on the verge of total ruin,
In the midst of the assembly and congregation."

15 Drink water from your own cistern,
And running water from your own well.
16 Should your fountains be dispersed abroad,
[1]Streams of water in the streets?
17 Let them be only your own,
And not for strangers with you.
18 Let your fountain be blessed,
And rejoice with [a]the wife of your youth.
19 [a]*As a* loving deer and a graceful doe,
Let her breasts satisfy you at all times;
And always be [1]enraptured with her love.
20 For why should you, my son, be enraptured by [a]an immoral woman,
And be embraced in the arms of a seductress?

21 [a]For the ways of *man *are* before the eyes of the LORD,
And He [1]ponders all his paths.
22 [a]His own iniquities entrap the wicked *man*,

22 *See WW at Mal. 4:2. **23** [a][Matt. 12:34; 15:18, 19; Mark 7:21; Luke 6:45] **24** [1]*devious* **25** *See WW at Prov. 3:6. **26** [a]Prov. 5:21; Heb. 12:13

CHAPTER 5

1 [1]Lit. *Bow* **2** [a]Mal. 2:7 [1]*appreciate good judgment* **3** [a]Prov. 2:16 [b]Ps. 55:21 [1]Lit. *a strange* *See WW at Ezek. 21:2. **5** [a]Prov. 7:27 [1]Or *Sheol*

9 [1]*vigor* *See WW at 1 Chr. 29:11. **10** [1]Lit. *strength* **16** [1]*Channels* **18** [a]Deut. 24:5; Eccl. 9:9; Mal. 2:14 **19** [a]Song 2:9 [1]Lit. *intoxicated* **20** [a]Prov. 2:16 **21** [a]2 Chr. 16:9; Job 31:4; 34:21; Prov. 15:3; Jer. 16:17; 32:19; Hos. 7:2; Heb. 4:13 [1]*observes*, lit. *weighs* *See WW at Is. 32:2. **22** [a]Num. 32:23; Ps. 9:5; Prov. 1:31; Is. 3:11

4:20–22 Three verses here, plus two at 5:1, 2, and one at 5:7, intersperse at intervals the call to remember the *importance* of the truth being given.
4:23 Keep your heart: Value and protect your mind, emotions, and will. How Solomon would have profited by following his own advice!
4:24–27 Mouth, lips, eyes, and feet are physical symbols for communication, attention, and behavior.
5:3–6, 8 The stark picture of the seductress ends with a warning.
5:9–14 To ignore the warning of v. 8 brings remorse and misery.
5:15–20 First with metaphor (**water, fountains, streams**), then with literal description, faithfulness in marriage is called for.
5:21–23 Never hidden from God, the sinner comes to a pitiful end.

And he is caught in the cords of
his sin.
23 [a]He shall die for lack of
instruction,
And in the greatness of his folly
he shall go astray.

Dangerous Promises

6 My son, [a]if you become [1]surety
for your friend,
If you have [2]shaken hands in
pledge for a stranger,
2 You are snared by the words of
your mouth;
You are taken by the words of
your mouth.
3 So do this, my son, and deliver
yourself;
For you have come into the hand
of your friend:
Go and humble yourself;
Plead with your friend.
4 [a]Give no sleep to your eyes,
Nor slumber to your eyelids.
5 Deliver yourself like a gazelle
from the hand *of the hunter,*
And like a bird from the hand of
the [1]fowler.

The Folly of Indolence

4 6 [a]Go to the ant, you sluggard!
Consider her ways and be wise,
7 Which, having no [1]captain,
Overseer or ruler,
8 Provides her [1]supplies in the
summer,
And gathers her food in the
harvest.
9 [a]How long will you [1]slumber,
O sluggard?
When will you rise from your
sleep?
10 A little sleep, a little slumber,
A little folding of the hands to
sleep—

23 [a]Job 4:21
CHAPTER 6
1 [a]Prov. 11:15 [1]*guaranty* or *collateral* [2]Lit. *struck*
4 [a]Ps. 132:4
5 [1]One who catches birds in a trap or snare
6 [a]Job 12:7
7 [1]Lit. *leader*
8 [1]Lit. *bread*
9 [a]Prov. 24:33, 34 [1]Lit. *lie down*
11 [a]Prov. 10:4
13 [a]Job 15:12; Ps. 35:19; Prov. 10:10 [1]*gives signals,* lit. *scrapes*
14 [a]Prov. 3:29; Mic. 2:1 [b]Prov. 6:19
15 [a]Prov. 24:22; Is. 30:13; 1 Thess. 5:3 [b]Jer. 19:11 [c]2 Chr. 36:16 *See WW at Mal. 4:2.
16 [1]Lit. *His soul*
17 [a]Ps. 101:5; Prov. 21:4 [b]Ps. 120:2; Prov. 12:22 [c]Deut. 19:10; Prov. 28:17; Is. 1:15 [1]Lit. *Haughty eyes*
18 [a]Gen. 6:5; Ps. 36:4; Prov. 24:2; Jer. 18:18; Mark 14:1, 43–46 [b]2 Kin. 5:20–27; Is. 59:7; Rom. 3:15
19 [a]Ps. 27:12; Prov. 19:5, 9; Matt. 26:59–66 [b]Prov. 6:14; 1 Cor. 1:11–13; [Jude 3, 4, 16–19]
20 [a]Eph. 6:1
21 [a]Prov. 3:3 *See WW at Ex. 28:30.
22 [a][Prov. 3:23] [b]Prov. 2:11 [1]Lit. *it*

11 [a]So shall your poverty come on
you like a prowler,
And your need like an armed
man.

The Wicked Man

12 A worthless person, a wicked
man,
Walks with a perverse mouth;
13 [a]He winks with his eyes,
He [1]shuffles his feet,
He points with his fingers;
14 Perversity *is* in his heart,
[a]He devises evil continually,
[b]He sows discord.
15 Therefore his calamity shall come
[a]suddenly;
Suddenly he shall [b]be broken
[c]without *remedy.

16 These six *things* the LORD hates,
Yes, seven *are* an abomination to
[1]Him:
17 [a]A[1] proud look,
[b]A lying tongue,
[c]Hands that shed innocent blood,
18 [a]A heart that devises wicked
plans,
[b]Feet that are swift in running to
evil,
19 [a]A false witness *who* speaks lies,
And one who [b]sows discord
among brethren.

Beware of Adultery

20 [a]My son, keep your father's
command,
And do not forsake the law of
your mother.
21 [a]Bind them *continually upon your
heart;
Tie them around your neck.
22 [a]When you roam, [1]they will lead
you;
When you sleep, [b]they will keep
you;

6:1–5 The warning against entanglement (by guaranteeing what one cannot control) rings with the urgency and reality of true life experience—the writer's or his son's.

6:6–11 See section 4 of Truth-In-Action at the end of Prov.

6:6–11 The industrious insect's instinct shames lazy humanity! Prov. condemns the sluggard's passivity, lack of initiative, the habit of procrastination, obliviousness to the dire results, and lack of discipline. Note also 10:26; 13:4; 24:30–34.

6:12 Worthless: The word is literally "of Belial," signifying both worthlessness and wickedness, appropriate since a great theme of the book is that wickedness is really of no value to anyone. Belial is most commonly used elsewhere in Scripture to represent wicked *men* (for example, see marginal note on 1 Sam. 2:12).

6:13, 14 Winks . . . shuffles . . . points: These are the tools of innuendo with which one sows discord. Sowing discord is the climactic item in the citation of things God hates (vv. 17–19).

6:16 Six . . . seven is a metaphoric device to indicate the list is not intended to be exhaustive.

6:17 Lying tongue: Here is untruthfulness as an innate trait of personality, speaking with no care nor regard for veracity. Compare with **false witness** (v. 19), which implies deliberate perjury to injure another person. Thus both forms of falsehood are on the list of what is abhorrent. And worse than either is he who sows discord.

6:20–23 Again (as previously at 4:20–22; 5:1, 2, 7; and later at 7:1–4, 24) comes the appeal to take seriously what parents have taught: that there is guidance (v. 22), light (v. 23), and life (v. 23) in commandments and corrections.

And *when* you awake, they will
speak with you.
23 [a]For the commandment *is* a lamp,
And the law a light;
Reproofs of instruction *are* the
way of life,
24 [a]To keep you from the evil woman,
From the flattering tongue of a
seductress.
25 [a]Do not lust after her *beauty in
your heart,
Nor let her allure you with her
eyelids.
26 For [a]by means of a harlot
A man is reduced to a crust of
bread;
[b]And [1]an adulteress will [c]prey
upon his precious life.
27 Can a man take fire to his bosom,
And his clothes not be burned?
28 Can one walk on hot coals,
And his feet not be seared?
29 So *is* he who goes in to his
neighbor's wife;
Whoever touches her shall not be
innocent.

30 *People* do not despise a thief
If he steals to satisfy himself
when he is starving.
31 Yet *when* he is found, [a]he must
restore sevenfold;
He may have to give up all the
substance of his house.
32 Whoever commits adultery with
a woman [a]lacks understanding;
He *who* does so destroys his own
soul.
33 Wounds and dishonor he will get,
And his reproach will not be
wiped away.
34 For [a]jealousy *is* a husband's fury;
Therefore he will not spare in the
day of vengeance.
35 He will [1]accept no recompense,
Nor will he be appeased though
you give many gifts.

7 My son, keep my words,
And [a]treasure my commands
within you.
2 [a]Keep my commands and live,

23 [a]Ps. 19:8; 2 Pet. 1:19
24 [a]Prov. 2:16
25 [a]Matt. 5:28 *See WW at Ezek. 28:12.
26 [a]Prov. 29:3 [b]Gen. 39:14 [c]Ezek. 13:18 [1]Wife of another, lit. *a man's wife*
31 [a]Ex. 22:1–4
32 [a]Prov. 7:7
34 [a]Prov. 27:4; Song 8:6
35 [1]Lit. *lift up the face of any*

CHAPTER 7

1 [a]Prov. 2:1
2 [a]Lev. 18:5; Prov. 4:4; [Is. 55:3] [b]Deut. 32:10; Ps. 17:8; Zech. 2:8
3 [a]Deut. 6:8; Prov. 6:21
5 [a]Prov. 2:16; 5:3
7 [a][Prov. 6:32; 9:4, 16] [1]Lit. *sons* [2]*lacking*
9 [a]Job 24:15
11 [a]Prov. 9:13; 1 Tim. 5:13 [b]Titus 2:5
13 [1]*shameless*
16 [a]Is. 19:9; Ezek. 27:7

[b]And my law as the apple of your
eye.
3 [a]Bind them on your fingers;
Write them on the tablet of your
heart.
4 Say to wisdom, "You *are* my
sister,"
And call understanding *your*
nearest kin,
5 [a]That they may keep you from the
immoral woman,
From the seductress *who* flatters
with her words.

The Crafty Harlot

6 For at the window of my house
I looked through my lattice,
7 And saw among the simple,
I perceived among the [1]youths,
A young man [a]devoid[2] of
understanding,
8 Passing along the street near her
corner;
And he took the path to her house
9 [a]In the twilight, in the evening,
In the black and dark night.

10 And there a woman met him,
With the attire of a harlot, and a
crafty heart.
11 [a]She *was* loud and rebellious,
[b]Her feet would not stay at home.
12 At times *she was* outside, at times
in the open square,
Lurking at every corner.
13 So she caught him and kissed
him;
With an [1]impudent face she said
to him:
14 "*I have* peace offerings with me;
Today I have paid my vows.
15 So I came out to meet you,
Diligently to seek your face,
And I have found you.
16 I have spread my bed with
tapestry,
Colored coverings of [a]Egyptian
linen.
17 I have perfumed my bed
With myrrh, aloes, and
cinnamon.

6:24–35 This lengthy and eloquent appeal against adultery is based on the results that are likely to follow the act: poverty (v. 26), scorn (v. 33), and angry retribution (vv. 34, 35). The adulterer is worse than a thief (v. 30), ignorant (v. 32), and self-destructive (v. 32).

7:6–23 Here is the short, sad story of a typical visit to a harlot, ending in death—either literal or figurative. The "immoral woman" of 5:3, 20 is probably a loose, married woman. The "evil woman" of 6:24 can be a harlot (6:26) or a neighbor's wife (6:29). The **harlot** of 7:10 is clearly a brazen professional in manner, if not in full-time occupation. She has a husband (v. 19), but dresses like a harlot (v. 10). She does not seek money for her affections, but gets her satisfaction directly in the wickedness of destroying her prey.

7:14 Peace offerings . . . paid my vows: Obedient to the letter of some minor (and easy) parts of the Law, the immoral woman would celebrate a religious occasion by abandonment to gross carnality. Thus may formal, ceremonial religion observe a kind of mechanical piety while blind or rebellious to larger issues. Jesus roundly condemned the neglect of "weightier *matters*" (Matt. 23:23).

18 Come, let us take our fill of love
until morning;
Let us delight ourselves with love.
19 For [1]my husband *is* not at home;
He has gone on a long journey;
20 He has taken a bag of money
[1]with him,
And will come home [2]on the
appointed day."

21 [1]With [a]her enticing speech she
caused him to yield,
[b]With her flattering lips she
[2]seduced him.
22 Immediately he went after her, as
an ox goes to the slaughter,
Or [1]as a fool to the correction of
the [2]stocks,
23 Till an arrow struck his liver.
[a]As a bird hastens to the snare,
He did not know it [1]*would cost*
his life.

24 Now therefore, listen to me, *my*
children;
Pay attention to the words of my
mouth:
25 Do not let your heart turn aside
to her ways,
Do not stray into her paths;
26 For she has cast down many
wounded,
And [a]all who were slain by her
were strong *men*.
27 [a]Her house *is* the way to [1]hell,
Descending to the chambers of
death.

The Excellence of Wisdom

8 Does not [a]wisdom cry out,
And understanding lift up her
voice?
2 She takes her stand on the top of
the [1]high hill,
Beside the way, where the paths
meet.
3 She cries out by the gates, at the
entry of the city,
At the entrance of the doors:
4 "To you, O men, I call,

19 [1]Lit. *the man*
20 [1]Lit. *in his hand* [2]*at the full moon*
21 [a]Prov. 5:3 [b]Ps. 12:2 [1]*By the greatness of her words* [2]*compelled*
22 [1]LXX, Syr., Tg. *as a dog to bonds;* Vg. *as a lamb . . . to bonds* [2]*shackles*
23 [a]Eccl. 9:12 [1]Lit. *is for*
26 [a]Neh. 13:26
27 [a]Prov. 2:18; 5:5; 9:18; [1 Cor. 6:9, 10; Rev. 22:15] [1]Or *Sheol*

CHAPTER 8

1 [a]Prov. 1:20, 21; 9:3; [1 Cor. 1:24]
2 [1]Lit. *heights*

5 [1]*naive*
6 [a]Prov. 22:20
11 [a]Job 28:15; Ps. 19:10; 119:127; Prov. 3:14, 15; 4:5, 7; 16:16
13 [a]Prov. 3:7; 16:6 [b]1 Sam. 2:3; [Prov. 16:17, 18; Is. 13:11] [c]Prov. 4:24
14 [a]Eccl. 7:19; 9:16
15 [a]2 Chr. 1:10; Prov. 29:4; Dan. 2:21; [Matt. 28:18]; Rom. 13:1 *See WW at 2 Sam. 8:15.
16 [1]MT, Syr., Tg., Vg. *righteousness;* LXX, Bg., some mss. and editions *earth*
17 [a]1 Sam. 2:30; [Ps. 91:14]; Prov. 4:6; [John 14:21] [b]Prov. 2:4, 5; John 7:37; James 1:5 *See WW at Ps. 97:10.
18 [a]Prov. 3:16; [Matt. 6:33]

And my voice *is* to the sons of
men.
5 O you [1]simple ones, understand
prudence,
And you fools, be of an
understanding heart.
6 Listen, for I will speak of
[a]excellent things,
And from the opening of my lips
will come right things;
7 For my mouth will speak truth;
Wickedness *is* an abomination to
my lips.
8 All the words of my mouth *are*
with righteousness;
Nothing crooked or perverse *is* in
them.
9 They *are* all plain to him who
understands,
And right to those who find
knowledge.
10 Receive my instruction, and not
silver,
And knowledge rather than
choice gold;
11 [a]For wisdom *is* better than rubies,
And all the things one may desire
cannot be compared with her.

12 "I, wisdom, dwell with prudence, 1
And find out knowledge *and*
discretion.
13 [a]The fear of the LORD *is* to hate
evil;
[b]Pride and arrogance and the evil
way
And [c]the perverse mouth I hate.
14 Counsel *is* mine, and sound
wisdom;
I *am* understanding, [a]I have
strength.
15 [a]By me kings *reign,
And rulers decree justice.
16 By me princes rule, and nobles,
All the judges of [1]the earth.
17 [a]I *love those who love me,
And [b]those who seek me
diligently will find me.
18 [a]Riches and honor *are* with me,
Enduring riches and
righteousness.

7:22, 23 Ox . . . fool . . . bird: He who yields to seduction is as hopelessly naive as these simple-minded creatures, no matter how strong (v. 26).
8:1–3 Wisdom, far from hiding herself and defying discovery, makes her appeal from the high place, the crossroads, and the city entrance—most conspicuous sites. Compare with the similar list in 1:20, 21.
8:4–36 The personification of wisdom as a very desirable woman gives her the opportunity to woo attention in competition (and extreme contrast) with the evil woman of ch. 7.
8:4–9 Men . . . sons of men: The appeal is to all humanity: To the **simple** (v. 5), the **fools** (v. 5), and **him who understands** (v. 9).
8:10, 11 Silver . . . gold . . . rubies: Wisdom should be chosen over any of these (a threefold comparison repeated from 3:14, 15), the most precious physical objects mentioned in the Bible.
8:12–21 See section 1 of Truth-In-Action at the end of Prov.
8:13 Fear of the LORD, here equated with hating evil, is elsewhere equated with wisdom (9:10) and knowledge (1:7); therefore wisdom and knowledge are the hating of evil.
8:15–21 The products of wisdom include rulership (v. 15), **justice** (v. 15), **riches, honor,** and **righteousness** (v. 18).

19 My fruit *is* better than gold, yes,
than fine gold,
And my revenue than choice
silver.
20 I [1]traverse the way of
righteousness,
In the midst of the paths of
justice,
21 That I may cause those who love
me to inherit wealth,
That I may fill their treasuries.

22 "The[a] LORD possessed me at the
beginning of His way,
Before His works of old.
23 [a]I have been established from
everlasting,
From the beginning, before there
was ever an earth.
24 When *there were* no depths I was
brought forth,
When *there were* no fountains
abounding with water.
25 [a]Before the mountains were
settled,
Before the hills, I was brought
forth;
26 While as yet He had not made the
earth or the [1]fields,
Or the [2]primal dust of the *world.
27 When He prepared the heavens,
I *was* there,
When He drew a circle on the face
of the deep,
28 When He established the clouds
above,
When He strengthened the
fountains of the deep,
29 [a]When He assigned to the sea its
limit,
So that the waters would not
transgress His command,
When [b]He marked out the
foundations of the earth,
30 [a]Then I was beside Him *as*
[1]a master craftsman;
[b]And I was daily *His* delight,
Rejoicing always before Him,
31 Rejoicing in His inhabited world,
And [a]my delight *was* with the
sons of men.

32 "Now therefore, listen to me, *my*
children,
For [a]blessed *are those who* keep
my ways.
33 Hear instruction and be wise,
And do not disdain *it*.
34 [a]Blessed is the *man who listens
to me,
*Watching daily at my gates,
Waiting at the posts of my doors.
35 For whoever finds me finds life,
And [a]obtains *favor from the
LORD;
36 But he who sins against me
[a]wrongs his own soul;
All those who hate me love
death."

The Way of Wisdom

9 Wisdom has [a]built her house,
She has hewn out her seven
pillars;
2 [a]She has slaughtered her meat,
[b]She has mixed her wine,
She has also [1]furnished her table.
3 She has sent out her maidens,
She cries out from the highest
places of the city,
4 "Whoever[a] *is* simple, let him turn
in here!"
As for him who lacks
understanding, she says to him,
5 "Come,[a] eat of my bread
And drink of the wine I have
mixed.
6 Forsake foolishness and live,
And go in the way of
understanding.

7 "He who corrects a scoffer gets
shame for himself,
And he who rebukes a wicked
man only harms himself. **3**
8 [a]Do not correct a scoffer, lest he
hate you;
[b]Rebuke a wise *man*, and he will
love you.
9 Give *instruction* to a wise *man*,
and he will be still wiser;
Teach a just *man*, [a]and he will
increase in learning.

10 "The[a] fear of the LORD *is* the
beginning of wisdom,
And the knowledge of the *Holy
One *is* understanding. **1**

---

20 [1]*walk about on* **22** [a]Job 28:26–28; Ps. 104:24; Prov. 3:19; [John 1:1] **23** [a][Ps. 2:6] **25** [a]Job 15:7, 8 **26** [1]*outer places* [2]Lit. *beginning of the dust* *See WW at Jer. 51:15. **29** [a]Gen. 1:9, 10; Job 38:8–11; Ps. 33:7; 104:9; Jer. 5:22 [b]Job 28:4, 6; Ps. 104:5 **30** [a][John 1:1–3, 18] [b][Matt. 3:17] [1]A Jewish tradition *one brought up* **31** [a]Ps. 16:3; John 13:1

32 [a]Ps. 119:1, 2; 128:1; Prov. 29:18; Luke 11:28 **34** [a]Prov. 3:13, 18 *See WW at Gen. 1:26. • See WW at Jer. 1:12. **35** [a]Prov. 3:4; 12:2; [John 17:3] *See WW at Deut. 33:23. **36** [a]Prov. 20:2

CHAPTER 9

1 [a][Matt. 16:18; 1 Cor. 3:9, 10; Eph. 2:20–22; 1 Pet. 2:5] **2** [a]Matt. 22:4 [b]Prov. 23:30 [1]*arranged* **4** [a]Ps. 19:7 **5** [a]Song 5:1; Is. 55:1; [John 6:27] **8** [a]Prov. 15:12; Matt. 7:6 [b]Ps. 141:5; Prov. 10:8 **9** [a][Matt. 13:12] **10** [a]Job 28:28; Ps. 111:10; Prov. 1:7 *See WW at Lev. 19:2.

8:21 Wealth refers more specifically to monetary gain than does the more general "riches" (v. 18).
8:22–31 Eloquently, but without arrogance, Wisdom makes the point that she is as eternal as God Himself, since she is a quality and a pre-Creation possession of God.
8:32 Now therefore argues that Wisdom should be listened to because of her ancient and special place in God's plan.
8:34, 35 More benefits of wisdom are: blessing, **life,** and **favor.**
8:36 The benefits of Wisdom are clearer because of the sad contrast with the condition of those who reject her.
9:7–11 Samples of wise sayings exemplify the practical perceptions available, a display case of chosen nuggets to prove wisdom is worthwhile.
9:7–9 See section 3 of Truth-In-Action at the end of Prov.
9:10 See section 1 of Truth-In-Action at the end of Prov.

11 [a]For by me your days will be multiplied,
And years of life will be added to you.
12 [a]If you are wise, you are wise for yourself,
And *if* you scoff, you will bear *it* alone."

The Way of Folly

13 [a]A foolish woman is [1]clamorous;
She is simple, and knows nothing.
14 For she sits at the door of her house,
On a seat [a]*by* the highest places of the city,
15 To call to those who pass by,
Who go straight on their way:
16 "Whoever[a] *is* [1]simple, let him turn in here";
And *as for* him who lacks understanding, she says to him,
17 "Stolen[a] water is sweet,
And bread *eaten* in secret is pleasant."
18 But he does not know that
[a]the dead *are* there,
That her guests *are* in the depths of [1]hell.

Wise Sayings of Solomon

10 The proverbs of [a]Solomon:
[b]A wise son makes a glad father,
But a foolish son *is* the grief of his mother.

2 [a]Treasures of wickedness profit nothing,
[b]But righteousness delivers from death.
3 [a]The LORD will not allow the righteous **soul** to famish,
But He casts away the desire of the wicked.

11 [a]Prov. 3:2, 16
12 [a]Job 35:6, 7; Prov. 16:26
13 [a]Prov. 7:11 [1]*boisterous*
14 [a]Prov. 9:3
16 [a]Prov. 7:7, 8 [1]*naive*
17 [a]Prov. 20:17
18 [a]Prov. 2:18; 7:27 [1]Or *Sheol*

CHAPTER 10

1 [a]Prov. 1:1; 25:1 [b]Prov. 15:20; 17:21, 25; 19:13; 29:3, 15
2 [a]Ps. 49:7; Prov. 11:4; 21:6; Ezek. 7:19; [Luke 12:19, 20] [b]Dan. 4:27
3 [a]Ps. 34:9, 10; 37:25; Prov. 28:25; [Matt. 6:33]

4 [a]Prov. 19:15 [b]Prov. 12:24; 13:4; 21:5
5 [a]Prov. 6:8 [b]Prov. 19:26
7 [a]Ps. 112:6; Eccl. 8:10

WORD WEALTH

10:3 soul, *nephesh* (*neh*-fesh); Strong's #5315: A life, a living being; soul, self, person, mind, personality; inner desires and feelings. This noun, occurring more than 750 times, is a highly significant Bible term. "Soul" is the word usually chosen in translations for *nephesh,* but "heart," "person," "life," and "mind" are occasionally best suited to a particular context. Unlike the English word "soul," which usually describes only the inner person and is contrasted with the outer person, *nephesh* describes the whole person as a unit, that is a life, a living creation. The first five occurrences of *nephesh* (Gen. 1:20, 21, 24, 30; 2:7) illustrate that the scope of the word is broad enough to include animals as living, breathing creatures, as well as human beings. In Ex. 1:5, 70 "persons" came down to Egypt. God's being or person (self, desires, life) is described as a soul; *nephesh* is used concerning God in Jer. 5:9 ("Shall I not avenge Myself [My soul]?") and Amos 6:8 ("The Lord GOD has sworn by Himself [His soul]").

4 [a]He who has a slack hand becomes poor, **4**
But [b]the hand of the diligent makes rich.
5 He who gathers in [a]summer *is* a wise son;
He who sleeps in harvest *is*
[b]a son who causes shame.

6 Blessings *are* on the head of the righteous,
But violence covers the mouth of the wicked.
7 [a]The memory of the righteous *is* blessed,
But the name of the wicked will rot.

9:12 If you . . . you . . . alone: The individual has the choice; he controls his own fate.
9:13–18 Brief clauses summarize all the preceding appeals of folly, ending with a deadly warning.
10:1—22:16 Proverbs of Solomon: What follows (to 22:16) is a collection of what are almost certainly Solomon's own original sayings, not merely sayings collected by him from other sources. Whereas the book has to this point been mostly an argument for the importance of godly wisdom, interspersed with strong moral warnings (as against adultery in chs. 5; 6; 7; 9), it now turns to a recitation of important practical truths about many aspects of life, each truth standing more or less alone, like a gem with beauty of its own.

Literary note: Again and again the individual truth is presented in the form of a couplet, not of rhyme but of meaning. The second part of each saying generally takes one of these forms: 1) a contrasted or opposite truth; 2) a companion or parallel truth; 3) a simile which clarifies the truth; 4) a refinement or further detailing of the truth.

Frequently several proverbs dealing with the same or a similar subject are grouped together, becoming a miniature lesson on the particular topic.
10:1 Father . . . mother: Both the gladness and the grief are felt by both parents. The allocation of gladness to father and grief to mother here, besides the poetic balance it contains, may suggest each is more likely to be *visible* in the parent mentioned. Actions of one member of a family inevitably affect all members.
10:4, 5 See section 4 of Truth-In-Action at the end of Prov.
10:4 A clear teaching about industry versus laziness: the one brings riches, the other poverty.
10:5 For the second time wisdom is shown to include planning ahead (see 6:8).

3 8 The wise in heart will receive commands,
[a]But [1]a prating fool will [2]fall.

9 [a]He who walks with integrity walks securely,
But he who perverts his ways will become known.

10 He who winks with the eye causes trouble,
But a prating fool will fall.

11 The mouth of the righteous *is* a well of life,
But violence covers the mouth of the wicked.

12 Hatred stirs up strife,
But [a]love covers all sins.

13 Wisdom is found on the lips of him who has understanding,
But [a]a rod *is* for the back of him who [1]is devoid of understanding.

4 14 Wise *people* store up knowledge,
But [a]the mouth of the foolish *is* near destruction.

15 The [a]rich man's wealth *is* his strong city;
The destruction of the poor *is* their poverty.

16 The labor of the righteous *leads* to [a]life,
The wages of the **wicked** to sin.

WORD WEALTH

10:16 wicked, *rasha'* (rah-*shah*); Strong's #7563: Wicked, wrong, violently disrupted, godless, lawless, guilty, condemned, punishable; vicious, unrighteous, sinful. This noun occurs more than 250 times. It comes from the verb *rasha'* "to be guilty," "wicked," "condemned." Some sense of violent internal disturbance may be conveyed (as if to say that a man is wicked because of unresolved inner turmoil). Often the wicked are contrasted with the righteous, as here and in Gen. 18:23, where Abraham knew that God regarded these two groups of people as requiring separate treatment. *Rasha'* occurs almost 80 times in Prov. (see, for example, 12:10; 15:29; 25:26). In 12:10, we read of a wicked man so far gone that even his "tender mercies" seem cruel.

8 [a]Prov. 10:10 [1]Lit. *the foolish of lips* [2]*be thrust down* or *ruined*
9 [a][Ps. 23:4; Prov. 3:23; 28:18; Is. 33:15, 16]
12 [a]Prov. 17:9; [1 Cor. 13:4–7; James 5:20]; 1 Pet. 4:8
13 [a]Prov. 26:3 [1]Lit. *lacks heart*
14 [a]Prov. 18:7
15 [a]Job 31:24; Ps. 52:7; Prov. 18:11; [1 Tim. 6:17]
16 [a]Prov. 6:23
17 [1]*leads* *See WW at Prov. 4:13.
18 [a]Prov. 26:24 [b]Ps. 15:3; 101:5
19 [a]Job 11:2; [Prov. 18:21]; Eccl. 5:3 [b]Prov. 17:27; [James 1:19; 3:2] *See WW at Jer. 3:15.
21 [1]Lit. *heart*
22 [a]Gen. 24:35; 26:12; Deut. 8:18; Ps. 37:22; Prov. 8:21
23 [a]Prov. 2:14; 15:21
24 [a]Job 15:21; Prov. 1:27; Is. 66:4 [b]Ps. 145:19; Prov. 15:8; Matt. 5:6; [1 John 5:14, 15]
25 [a]Ps. 37:9, 10 [b]Ps. 15:5; Prov. 12:3; Matt. 7:24, 25
27 [a]Prov. 9:11 [b]Job 15:32
28 [a]Job 8:13 *See WW at Judg. 5:31.

17 He who keeps *instruction *is in* the way of life,
But he who refuses correction [1]goes astray.

18 Whoever [a]hides hatred *has* lying lips,
And [b]whoever spreads slander *is* a fool.

19 [a]In the multitude of words sin is not lacking,
But [b]he who restrains his lips *is* *wise.

20 The tongue of the righteous *is* choice silver;
The heart of the wicked *is worth* little.

21 The lips of the righteous feed many,
But fools die for lack of [1]wisdom.

22 [a]The blessing of the LORD makes *one* rich,
And He adds no sorrow with it.

23 [a]To do evil *is* like sport to a fool,
But a man of understanding has wisdom.

24 [a]The fear of the wicked will come upon him,
And [b]the desire of the righteous will be granted.

25 When the whirlwind passes by, [a]the wicked *is* no *more*,
But [b]the righteous *has* an everlasting foundation.

26 As vinegar to the teeth and smoke to the eyes,
So *is* the lazy *man* to those who send him.

27 [a]The fear of the LORD prolongs days,
But [b]the years of the wicked will be shortened.

28 The hope of the righteous *will be* gladness,
But the [a]expectation of the wicked will *perish.

10:8 See section 3 of Truth-In-Action at the end of Prov.
10:10 He who winks . . . causes trouble because he merely hints at what he should say frankly. **But a prating fool will fall:** Speech that is too frank or lacks insight is dangerous. See notes on 6:12–15.
10:11 Violence covers the mouth: What the wicked say is not heard or heeded; their violence nullifies it.
10:14 See section 4 of Truth-In-Action at the end of Prov.
10:19, 22 Wordiness brings evil with it, but divine blessing is undiluted.
10:26 A lazy employee is not only unproductive, but irritating.

29 The way of the LORD *is* strength
for the upright,
But [a]destruction *will come* to the
workers of iniquity.

30 [a]The righteous will never be
removed,
But the wicked will not inhabit
the [1]earth.
31 [a]The mouth of the righteous brings
forth wisdom,
But the perverse tongue will be
cut out.
32 The lips of the righteous know
what is acceptable,
But the mouth of the wicked *what*
is perverse.

11 [a]Dishonest[1] scales *are* an
abomination to the LORD,
But a [2]just weight *is* His delight.

2 When pride comes, then comes
[a]shame;
But with the humble *is* wisdom.

3 The integrity of the upright will
guide [a]them,
But the perversity of the
unfaithful will destroy them.
4 [a]Riches do not profit in the day of
wrath,
But [b]righteousness delivers from
death.
5 The righteousness of the
blameless will [1]direct* his way
aright,
But the wicked will fall by his
own [a]wickedness.
6 The righteousness of the upright
will deliver them,
But the unfaithful will be caught
by *their* lust.

7 When a wicked man dies, *his*
expectation will [a]perish,
And the hope of the unjust
perishes.
8 [a]The righteous is delivered from
trouble,
And it comes to the wicked
instead.
9 The hypocrite with *his* mouth
destroys his neighbor,
But through knowledge the
righteous will be delivered.
10 [a]When it goes well with the
righteous, the city *rejoices;
And when the wicked perish,
there is jubilation.
11 By the blessing of the upright the
city is [a]exalted,*
But it is overthrown by the mouth
of the wicked.

12 He who [1]is devoid of wisdom
despises his neighbor,
But a man of understanding holds
his peace.

13 [a]A talebearer reveals secrets,
But he who is of a faithful spirit
[b]conceals a matter.

14 [a]Where *there is* no counsel, the
people fall;
But in the multitude of counselors
there is safety.

15 He who is [a]surety[1] for a stranger
will suffer,
But one who hates [2]being surety
is secure.

16 A gracious woman retains honor,
But ruthless *men* retain riches.
17 [a]The merciful man does good for
his own soul,
But *he who is* cruel troubles his
own flesh.
18 The wicked *man* does deceptive
work,
But [a]he who sows righteousness
will have a sure reward.
19 As righteousness *leads* to
[a]life,
So he who pursues evil *pursues*
it to his own [b]death.
20 Those who are of a perverse heart
are an abomination to the LORD,
But *the* blameless in their ways
are His delight.
21 [a]*Though they join* [1]forces, the
wicked will not go unpunished;
But [b]the posterity of the righteous
will be delivered.

22 *As* a ring of gold in a swine's
snout,
So is a lovely woman who lacks
[1]discretion.

23 The desire of the righteous *is* only
good,
But the expectation of the wicked
[a]*is* wrath.

29 [a]Ps. 1:6
30 [a]Ps. 37:22; Prov. 2:21 [1]*land*
31 [a]Ps. 37:30; Prov. 10:13

CHAPTER 11

1 [a]Lev. 19:35, 36; Deut. 25:13–16; Prov. 20:10, 23; Mic. 6:11 [1]*deceptive* [2]Lit. *perfect stone*
2 [a]Prov. 16:18; 18:12; 29:23
3 [a]Prov. 13:6
4 [a]Prov. 10:2; Ezek. 7:19; Zeph. 1:18 [b]Gen. 7:1
5 [a]Prov. 5:22 [1]Or *make smooth* or *straight* *See WW at Prov. 3:6.
7 [a]Prov. 10:28
8 [a]Prov. 21:18
10 [a]Prov. 28:12 *See WW at Ps. 30:5.
11 [a]Prov. 14:34 *See WW at Ps. 18:46.
12 [1]Lit. *lacks heart*
13 [a]Lev. 19:16; Prov. 20:19; 1 Tim. 5:13 [b]Prov. 19:11
14 [a]1 Kin. 12:1
15 [a]Prov. 6:1, 2 [1]*guaranty* [2]*those pledging guaranty*, lit. *those who strike hands*
17 [a][Matt. 5:7; 25:34–36]
18 [a]Hos. 10:12; [Gal. 6:8, 9]; James 3:18
19 [a]Prov. 10:16; 12:28 [b]Prov. 21:16; [Rom. 6:23; James 1:15]
21 [a]Prov. 16:5 [b]Ps. 112:2; Prov. 14:26 [1]Lit. *hand to hand*
22 [1]*taste*
23 [a]Prov. 10:28; Rom. 2:8, 9

10:32 Lips . . . know: Utterance (expression) is tightly linked to perception.
11:3–8 In the long view, retribution is sure and appropriate.
11:10, 11 City: Righteousness is good citizenship, appreciated by a civilized population.
11:20, 21 The wicked not only bring trouble on themselves by natural law, but by the wrath of God.

24 There is *one* who [a]scatters, yet
increases more;
And there is *one* who withholds
more than is right,
But it *leads* to poverty.
25 [a]The generous soul will be made
rich,
[b]And he who waters will also be
watered himself.
26 The people will curse [a]him who
withholds grain,
But [b]blessing *will be* on the head
of him who sells *it*.
27 He who earnestly seeks good
[1]finds favor,
[a]But trouble will come to him who
seeks *evil*.
28 [a]He who trusts in his riches will
fall,
But [b]the righteous will flourish
like foliage.
29 He who troubles his own house
[a]will inherit the wind,
And the fool *will be* [b]servant to
the wise of heart.
30 The fruit of the righteous *is a* tree
of life,
And [a]he who [1]wins souls *is* wise.
31 [a]If the righteous will be
[1]recompensed on the earth,
How much more the ungodly and
the sinner.

12

Whoever loves instruction
loves knowledge,
But he who hates correction *is*
stupid.
2 A good *man* obtains *favor from
the LORD,
But a man of wicked intentions
He will condemn.
3 A man is not established by
wickedness,
But the [a]root of the righteous
cannot be moved.
4 [a]An[1] excellent wife *is* the crown
of her *husband,
But she who *causes shame *is*
[b]like rottenness in his bones.
5 The thoughts of the righteous *are*
right,
But the counsels of the wicked
are deceitful.
6 [a]The words of the wicked *are,* "Lie
in wait for blood,"
[b]But the mouth of the upright will
deliver them.
7 [a]The wicked are overthrown and
are no more,
But the house of the righteous will
stand.
8 A man will be commended
according to his wisdom,
[a]But he who is of a perverse heart
will be despised.
9 [a]Better *is the one* who is [1]slighted
but has a servant,
Than he who honors himself but
lacks bread.
10 [a]A righteous *man* regards the life
of his animal,
But the tender mercies of the
wicked *are* cruel.
11 [a]He who [1]tills his land will be
*satisfied with [b]bread,
But he who follows [2]frivolity
[c]*is* devoid of [3]understanding.
12 The wicked covet the catch of evil
men,
But the root of the righteous
yields *fruit*.
13 [a]The wicked is ensnared by the
transgression of *his* lips,
[b]But the righteous will come
through trouble.
14 [a]A man will be satisfied with good
by the fruit of *his* mouth,
[b]And the recompense of a man's
hands will be rendered to him.
15 [a]The way of a fool *is* right in his
own eyes,
But he who heeds counsel *is* wise.
16 [a]A fool's wrath is known at once,
But a prudent *man* covers shame.
17 [a]He *who* speaks truth declares
righteousness,

24 [a]Ps. 112:9; Prov. 13:7; 19:17
25 [a]Prov. 3:9, 10; [2 Cor. 9:6, 7] [b][Matt. 5:7]
26 [a]Amos 8:5, 6 [b]Job 29:13
27 [a]Esth. 7:10; Ps. 7:15, 16; 57:6 [1]Lit. *seeks*
28 [a]Job 31:24 [b]Ps. 1:3; Jer. 17:8
29 [a]Eccl. 5:16 [b]Prov. 14:19
30 [a]Prov. 14:25; [Dan. 12:3; 1 Cor. 9:19–22; James 5:20] [1]Lit. *takes,* in the sense of *brings,* cf. 1 Sam. 16:11
31 [a]Jer. 25:29 [1]*rewarded*

CHAPTER 12

2 *See WW at Deut. 33:23.
3 [a][Prov. 10:25]
4 [a]Prov. 31:23; 1 Cor. 11:7 [b]Prov. 14:30; Hab. 3:16 [1]Lit. *A wife of valor* *See WW at Hos. 2:8. • See WW at Ezek. 16:63.
6 [a]Prov. 1:11, 18 [b]Prov. 14:3
7 [a]Ps. 37:35–37; Prov. 11:21; Matt. 7:24–27
8 [a]1 Sam. 25:17; Prov. 18:3
9 [a]Prov. 13:7 [1]*lightly esteemed*
10 [a]Deut. 25:4
11 [a]Gen. 3:19 [b]Prov. 28:19 [c]Prov. 6:32 [1]*works or cultivates* [2]Lit. *vain things* [3]Lit. *heart* *See WW at Amos 4:8.
13 [a]Prov. 18:7 [b][2 Pet. 2:9]
14 [a]Prov. 13:2; 15:23; 18:20 [b]Job 34:11; Prov. 1:31; 24:12; [Is. 3:10, 11]; Hos. 4:9
15 [a]Prov. 3:7; Luke 18:11
16 [a]Prov. 11:13; 29:11
17 [a]Prov. 14:5

11:24–26 Generosity prospers a person; stinginess impoverishes.
11:30 Fruit . . . souls: The wise will harvest not just the temporal, but also the eternal (souls).
12:9 Standard of living counts for more in the practical world than a touchy sense of honor.
12:10 A righteous man is sensitive enough to care about the welfare of animals (a rare concern in that era), but a wicked man, even when sensitive, is still cruel (to human beings).
12:14 Mouth . . . hands: Each yields a product, which—good or bad—is the reward of the speaker or the worker.
12:17–22 Words, powerful implements, can do good or harm, please or displease God, depending upon their wisdom and truth.

But a false witness, deceit.
18 [a]There is one who speaks like the piercings of a sword,
But the tongue of the wise *promotes* health.
19 The truthful lip shall be established forever,
[a]But a lying tongue *is* but for a moment.
20 Deceit is in the heart of those who devise evil,
But counselors of peace have joy.
21 [a]No grave [1]trouble will overtake the righteous,
But the wicked shall be filled with evil.
22 [a]Lying lips *are* an abomination to the LORD,
But those who deal truthfully *are* His delight.

23 [a]A prudent man conceals knowledge,
But the heart of fools proclaims foolishness.

24 [a]The hand of the diligent will rule,
But the lazy *man* will be put to forced labor.

25 [a]Anxiety in the heart of man causes depression,
But [b]a good word makes it glad.

26 The righteous should choose his friends carefully,
For the way of the wicked leads them astray.
27 The lazy *man* does not roast what he took in hunting,
But diligence *is* man's precious possession.

28 In the way of righteousness *is* life,
And in *its* pathway *there is* no death.

13

A wise son *heeds* his father's instruction,
[a]But a scoffer does not listen to rebuke.

2 [a]A man shall eat well by the fruit of *his* mouth,
But the soul of the unfaithful feeds on violence.
3 [a]He who guards his mouth preserves his life,
But he who opens wide his lips shall have destruction.

4 [a]The soul of a lazy *man* desires, and *has* nothing;
But the soul of the diligent shall be made rich.

5 A righteous *man* hates lying,
But a wicked *man* is loathsome and comes to shame.
6 [a]Righteousness guards *him whose* way is blameless,
But wickedness overthrows the sinner.

7 [a]There is one who makes himself rich, yet *has* nothing;
And one who makes himself poor, yet *has* great riches.

8 The ransom of a man's life *is* his riches,
But the poor does not hear rebuke.

9 The light of the righteous rejoices,
[a]But the lamp of the wicked will be put out.

10 By pride comes nothing but [a]strife,
But with the well-advised *is* wisdom.

11 [a]Wealth *gained by* dishonesty will be diminished,
But he who gathers by labor will increase.

12 Hope deferred makes the heart sick,
But [a]*when* the desire comes, *it is* a tree of life.

13 He who [a]despises the word will be destroyed,
But he who fears the commandment will be rewarded.
14 [a]The law of the wise *is* a fountain of life,
To turn *one* away from [b]the snares of death.

15 Good understanding [1]gains [a]favor,
But the way of the unfaithful *is* hard.

18 [a]Ps. 57:4; Prov. 4:22; 15:4 **19** [a][Ps. 52:4, 5]; Prov. 19:9 **21** [a]Ps. 91:10; Prov. 1:33; 1 Pet. 3:13 [1]*harm* **22** [a]Prov. 6:17; 11:20; Rev. 22:15 **23** [a]Prov. 13:16 **24** [a]Prov. 10:4 **25** [a]Prov. 15:13 [b]Is. 50:4

CHAPTER 13

1 [a]Is. 28:14, 15 **2** [a]Prov. 12:14 **3** [a]Ps. 39:1; Prov. 21:23; [James 3:2] **4** [a]Prov. 10:4 **6** [a]Prov. 11:3, 5, 6 **7** [a][Prov. 11:24; 12:9; Luke 12:20, 21] **9** [a]Job 18:5, 6; 21:17; Prov. 24:20 **10** [a]Prov. 10:12 **11** [a]Prov. 10:2; 20:21 **12** [a]Prov. 13:19 **13** [a]Num. 15:31; 2 Chr. 36:16; Is. 5:24 **14** [a]Prov. 6:22; 10:11; 14:27 [b]2 Sam. 22:6 **15** [a]Ps. 111:10; Prov. 3:4 [1]*gives*

12:26 Even the righteous is in danger if he consorts with evil companions.
12:27 The initial energy of hunting is nullified if one is too lazy to cook the game.
13:7 Greediness is counterproductive; generosity enriches—in one way or another.

16 [a]Every prudent *man* acts with knowledge,
But a fool lays open *his* folly.

17 A wicked messenger falls into trouble,
But [a]a faithful ambassador *brings* health.

3 18 Poverty and shame *will come* to him who [1]disdains correction,
But [a]he who regards a rebuke will be honored.

19 A desire accomplished is sweet to the soul,
But *it is* an abomination to fools to depart from evil.

20 He who walks with wise *men* will be wise,
But the companion of fools will be destroyed.

21 [a]Evil pursues sinners,
But to the righteous, good shall be repaid.

22 A good *man* leaves an inheritance to his children's children,
But [a]the wealth of the sinner is stored up for the righteous.

23 [a]Much food *is in* the [1]fallow *ground* of the poor,
And for lack of justice there is [2]waste.

5 24 [a]He who spares his rod hates his son,
But he who loves him disciplines him [1]promptly.

KINGDOM DYNAMICS

13:24 Corrective Discipline for the Rebellious, FAMILY ORDER. Discipline is the other side of teaching. A child with a teachable spirit will still need thorough explanation, much patience, opportunity to try and experiment, including the right to fail and to learn by failure. A child, however, who is caught up in willful disobedience (Prov. 29:15), rebellion (1 Sam. 15:23), or stubborn foolishness (Prov. 22:15), closes off effective teaching and disrupts the harmony of the family. God's answer to this is firm and loving discipline.

The Bible makes a clear distinction between discipline and physical abuse. Discipline may be painful but not injurious. We are never to inflict harm on a child (Prov. 23:13), but at times pain may be a part of effective correction. God describes Himself as a strict disciplinarian. Although He always disciplines us out of love and for our own benefit, His correction may cause us pain (Heb. 12:5–11). Likewise, God requires that parents properly correct their children. Even a child's eternal destiny can hinge upon the godly discipline provided by parents (Prov. 23:14).

(Eph. 6:4/Rom. 15:5–7) L.C.

25 [a]The righteous eats to the satisfying of his soul,
But the stomach of the wicked shall be in want.

14

The wise woman builds her *house,
But the foolish pulls it down with her hands.

2 He who walks in his uprightness fears the LORD,
[a]But *he who is* perverse in his ways despises Him.

3 In the mouth of a fool *is* a rod of pride, 2
[a]But the lips of the wise will preserve them.

4 Where no oxen *are*, the [1]trough *is* clean;
But much increase *comes* by the strength of an ox.

5 A [a]faithful witness does not lie,
But a false witness will utter [b]lies.

6 A scoffer seeks wisdom and does not *find it*,
But [a]knowledge *is* easy to him who understands.

16 [a]Prov. 12:23
17 [a]Prov. 25:13
18 [a]Prov. 15:5, 31, 32 [1]Lit. *ignores*
21 [a]Ps. 32:10; Is. 47:11
22 [a]Job 27:16, 17; Prov. 28:8; [Eccl. 2:26]
23 [a]Prov. 12:11 [1]*uncultivated* [2]Lit. *what is swept away*
24 [a]Prov. 19:18 [1]*early*
25 [a]Ps. 34:10; Prov. 10:3

CHAPTER 14

1 *See WW at 2 Sam. 7:11.
2 [a][Rom. 2:4]
3 [a]Prov. 12:6
4 [1]*manger* or *feed trough*
5 [a]Rev. 1:5; 3:14 [b]Ex. 23:1; Deut. 19:16; Prov. 6:19; 12:17
6 [a]Prov. 8:9; 17:24

13:18 See section 3 of Truth-In-Action at the end of Prov.
13:22 A good person can expect his foresight to bless his posterity; a sinner unwittingly accumulates what will eventually go to the righteous.
13:23 The poor suffer through the unrealized potential of their resources; injustice sweeps away the possessions of the poor.
13:24 See section 5 of Truth-In-Action at the end of Prov.
13:24 See note on 23:13, 14.
14:1 Construction or demolition—the distinction between the wise or the foolish woman. Here is one of the very rare proverbs about *feminine* behavior. **Her hands** symbolize her own actions or behavior. She destroys herself and her family.
14:3 See section 2 of Truth-In-Action at the end of Prov.
14:4 Where there is no action, there are no problems. To have power (the ox) one must sometimes put up with the clutter that comes with it.

7 Go from the presence of a foolish man,
When you do not perceive *in him* the lips of [a]knowledge.
8 The wisdom of the prudent *is* to understand his way,
But the folly of fools *is* deceit.

9 [a]Fools mock at [1]sin,
But among the upright *there is* favor.

10 The heart knows its own bitterness,
And a stranger does not share its joy.

11 [a]The house of the wicked will be overthrown,
But the tent of the upright will flourish.

12 [a]There is a way *that seems* right to a man,
But [b]its end *is* the way of [c]death.

13 Even in laughter the heart may sorrow,
And [a]the end of mirth *may be* grief.

14 The backslider in heart will be [a]filled with his own ways,
But a good man *will be satisfied* [1]from [b]above.

15 The simple believes every word,
But the prudent considers well his steps.
16 [a]A wise *man* fears and departs from evil,
But a fool rages and is self-confident.
17 A quick-tempered *man* acts foolishly,
And a man of wicked intentions is hated.
18 The simple inherit folly,
But the prudent are crowned with knowledge.
19 The evil will bow before the good,
And the wicked at the gates of the righteous.

20 [a]The poor *man* is hated even by his own neighbor,
But [1]the rich *has* many [b]friends.
21 He who despises his neighbor sins;
[a]But he who has mercy on the poor, happy *is* he.

22 Do they not go astray who devise evil?
But mercy and truth *belong* to those who devise good.

23 In all labor there is profit,
But [1]idle chatter *leads* only to poverty.

24 The crown of the wise is their riches,
But the foolishness of fools *is* folly.

25 A true witness [1]delivers [a]souls,
But a deceitful *witness* speaks lies.

26 In the fear of the LORD *there is* strong confidence,
And His children will have a place of **refuge.**

WORD WEALTH

14:26 refuge, *machseh* (mahch-*seh*); Strong's #4268: A shelter, refuge, protection, fortress; a hope; a place of trust; a shelter from storm. This noun occurs 20 times in the OT, more than half of these in Ps. See especially Ps. 46:1; 61:3; 91:2, 9; 142:5. *Machseh* is translated "trust" in Ps. 73:28, where the psalmist has put his trust in the Lord (that is, he made the Lord his trustworthy place of shelter). In Is. 25:4, God is described as a "refuge" from the storm and a "shade" from the heat, illustrating the "sheltering from the elements" often contained in *machseh.* In the present reference, a fortress is suggested.

27 [a]The fear of the LORD *is* a fountain of life,
To turn *one* away from the snares of death.

28 In a multitude of people *is* a king's honor,
But in the lack of people *is* the downfall of a prince.

7 [a]Prov. 23:9 **9** [a]Prov. 10:23 [1]Lit. *guilt* **11** [a]Job 8:15 **12** [a]Prov. 16:25 [b]Rom. 6:21 [c]Prov. 12:15 **13** [a]Prov. 5:4; Eccl. 2:1, 2 **14** [a]Prov. 1:31; 12:15 [b]Prov. 13:2; 18:20 [1]Lit. *from above himself* **16** [a]Job 28:28; Ps. 34:14; Prov. 22:3 **20** [a]Prov. 19:7 [b]Prov. 19:4 [1]Lit. *many are the lovers of the rich* **21** [a]Ps. 112:9; [Prov. 19:17] **23** [1]Lit. *talk of the lips* **25** [a][Ezek. 3:18–21] [1]*saves lives* **27** [a]Prov. 13:14

14:10 Inner pain and happiness are very private matters, not fully understood by others.
14:13 Outward appearance does not always portray the true feelings of the heart.
14:20, 21 Human nature defers to the rich for the sake of favors, but caring for the poor will reward with happiness.
14:23 In the battle of values, industrious work wins over mere talk.
14:28 Without followers, leadership is meaningless.

29 [a]*He who is* slow to wrath has great understanding,
But *he who is* [1]impulsive exalts folly.

30 A sound heart *is* life to the body,
But [a]envy *is* [b]rottenness to the bones.

31 [a]He who oppresses the poor reproaches [b]his Maker,
But he who honors Him has mercy on the needy.

32 The wicked is banished in his wickedness,
But [a]the righteous has a refuge in his death.

33 Wisdom rests in the heart of him who has understanding,
But [a]*what is* in the heart of fools is made known.

34 Righteousness exalts a [a]nation,
But *sin *is* a [1]reproach to *any* people.

35 [a]The king's favor *is* toward a wise servant,
But his wrath *is against* him who causes shame.

15

A [a]soft answer turns away wrath,
But [b]a harsh word stirs up *anger.
2 The tongue of the wise uses knowledge rightly,
[a]But the mouth of fools pours forth foolishness.

3 [a]The eyes of the LORD *are* in every place,
Keeping watch on the evil and the good.

4 A [1]wholesome tongue *is* a tree of life,
But perverseness in it breaks the spirit.

5 [a]A fool despises his father's instruction,
[b]But he who [1]receives correction is prudent.

6 *In* the house of the righteous *there is* much treasure,
But in the revenue of the wicked is trouble.

7 The lips of the wise [1]disperse knowledge,
But the heart of the fool *does* not *do* so.

8 [a]The sacrifice of the wicked *is* an abomination to the LORD,
But the *prayer of the upright *is* His delight.
9 The way of the wicked *is* an abomination to the LORD,
But He loves him who [a]follows righteousness.

10 [a]Harsh discipline *is* for him who forsakes the way,
And [b]he who hates correction will die.

11 [a]Hell[1] and [2]Destruction *are* before the LORD;
So how much more [b]the hearts of the sons of men.

12 [a]A scoffer does not love one who corrects him,
Nor will he go to the wise.

13 [a]A merry heart makes a cheerful [1]countenance,
But [b]by sorrow of the heart the spirit is broken.

14 The heart of him who has understanding seeks knowledge,
But the mouth of fools feeds on foolishness.

15 All the days of the afflicted *are* evil,
[a]But he who is of a merry heart *has* a continual feast.

16 [a]Better *is* a little with the fear of the LORD,
Than great treasure with trouble.
17 [a]Better *is* a dinner of [1]herbs where love is,
Than a fatted calf with hatred.

29 [a]Prov. 16:32; 19:11; Eccl. 7:9; James 1:19 [1]Lit. *short of spirit*
30 [a]Ps. 112:10 [b]Prov. 12:4; Hab. 3:16
31 [a]Prov. 17:5; Matt. 25:40; 1 John 3:17 [b][Job 31:15; Prov. 22:2]
32 [a]Gen. 49:18; Job 13:15; [Ps. 16:11; 73:24]; 2 Cor. 1:9; 5:8; [2 Tim. 4:18]
33 [a]Prov. 12:16
34 [a]Prov. 11:11 [1]*shame* or *disgrace* *See WW at Lev. 9:2.
35 [a]Matt. 24:45–47

CHAPTER 15

1 [a]Prov. 25:15 [b]1 Sam. 25:10 *See WW at Judg. 10:7.
2 [a]Prov. 12:23
3 [a]2 Chr. 16:9; Job 34:21; Prov. 5:21; Jer. 16:17; 32:19; Zech. 4:10; Heb. 4:13
4 [1]Lit. *healing*
5 [a]Prov. 10:1 [b]Prov. 13:18 [1]Lit. *keeps*
7 [1]*spread*
8 [a]Prov. 21:27; Eccl. 5:1; Is. 1:11; Jer. 6:20; Mic. 6:7 *See WW at 2 Chr. 6:20.
9 [a]Prov. 21:21
10 [a]1 Kin. 22:8 [b]Prov. 5:12
11 [a]Job 26:6; Ps. 139:8 [b]1 Sam. 16:7; 2 Chr. 6:30; Ps. 44:21; Acts 1:24 [1]Or *Sheol* [2]Heb. *Abaddon*
12 [a]Prov. 13:1; Amos 5:10; 2 Tim. 4:3
13 [a]Prov. 12:25 [b]Prov. 17:22 [1]*face*
15 [a]Prov. 17:22
16 [a]Ps. 37:16; Prov. 16:8; Eccl. 4:6; 1 Tim. 6:6
17 [a]Prov. 17:1 [1]Or *vegetables*

14:30 Sound heart: A tranquil mind brings good physical health; envy of others ruins it. Attitude and health are perceived as related, even in this early time.
14:34 There is such a thing as corporate righteousness, which brings corporate benefit.
15:3 Keeping watch: An omniscient God not only sees, but keeps account.
15:8 Sacrifice: A *gift* to God is unacceptable if from an evil heart. **Prayer:** A *request* to God brings Him pleasure if from a righteous heart.
15:11 Hell and Destruction: If the horrors of the invisible world are plain to God, He certainly sees also the hidden thoughts of men.
15:15 Life is miserable when one is in pain, a banquet when one is joyful.
15:16, 17 Peace of mind and family affection are worth more than money or gourmet food.

18 [a]A wrathful man stirs up strife,
But *he who is* slow to anger allays
contention.

19 [a]The way of the lazy *man is* like
a hedge of thorns,
But the way of the upright *is* a
highway.

20 [a]A wise son makes a father glad,
But a foolish man despises his
mother.

21 [a]Folly *is* joy *to him who is* destitute
of [1]discernment,
[b]But a man of understanding
walks *uprightly.

22 [a]Without counsel, plans go awry,
But in the multitude of counselors
they are established.

2 23 A man has joy by the answer of
his mouth,
And [a]a word *spoken* [1]in due
season, how good *it is!*

24 [a]The way of life *winds* upward for
the wise,
That he may [b]turn away from
[1]hell below.

25 [a]The LORD will destroy the house
of the proud,
But [b]He will establish the
boundary of the widow.

26 [a]The thoughts of the wicked *are*
an abomination to the LORD,
[b]But *the words* of the pure *are*
pleasant.

27 [a]He who is greedy for gain
troubles his own house,
But he who hates bribes will live.

28 The heart of the righteous
[a]studies how to answer,
But the mouth of the wicked
pours forth evil.

29 [a]The LORD *is* far from the wicked,
But [b]He hears the prayer of the
righteous.

30 The light of the eyes rejoices the
heart,
And a good report makes the
bones [1]healthy.

18 [a]Prov. 26:21
19 [a]Prov. 22:5
20 [a]Prov. 10:1
21 [a]Prov. 10:23 [b]Eph. 5:15 [1]Lit. *heart* *See WW at Prov. 3:6.
22 [a]Prov. 11:14
23 [a]Prov. 25:11; Is. 50:4 [1]Lit. *in its time*
24 [a]Phil. 3:20; [Col. 3:1, 2] [b]Prov. 14:16 [1]Or *Sheol*
25 [a]Prov. 12:7; Is. 2:11 [b]Ps. 68:5, 6
26 [a]Prov. 6:16, 18 [b]Ps. 37:30
27 [a]Is. 5:8; [Jer. 17:11]
28 [a]1 Pet. 3:15
29 [a]Ps. 10:1; 34:16 [b]Ps. 145:18; [James 5:16]
30 [1]Lit. *fat*
33 [a]Prov. 1:7 [b]Prov. 18:12

CHAPTER 16

1 [a]Jer. 10:23 [b]Matt. 10:19 [1]*plans*
2 [a]Prov. 21:2
3 [a]Ps. 37:5; Prov. 3:6; [1 Pet. 5:7] [1]Lit. *Roll*
4 [a]Is. 43:7; Rom. 11:36 [b]Job 21:30; [Rom. 9:22] [1]Lit. *evil*
5 [a]Prov. 6:17; 8:13 [1]Lit. *hand to hand*
6 [a]Dan. 4:27; Luke 11:41 [b]Prov. 8:13; 14:16

31 The ear that hears the rebukes of
life
Will abide among the wise.

32 He who disdains instruction
despises his own soul,
But he who heeds rebuke gets
understanding.

33 [a]The fear of the LORD *is* the
instruction of wisdom,
And [b]before honor *is* humility.

16

The [a]preparations[1] of the heart
belong to man,
[b]But the answer of the tongue *is*
from the LORD.

2 All the ways of a man *are* pure
in his own [a]eyes,
But the LORD weighs the spirits.

3 [a]**Commit**[1] your works to the LORD,
And your thoughts will be
established.

WORD WEALTH

16:3 commit, *galal* (gah-*lahl*); Strong's #1556: To roll, roll down, roll away, remove. In Gen. 29:3, *galal* refers to rolling the stone from the well's mouth. In Josh. 5:9, the reproach of Egypt is rolled off from Israel. In this text, the reader is encouraged to roll his works into God's care (see also Ps. 37:5). The picture is of a camel, burdened with a heavy load; when the load is to be removed, the camel kneels down, tilts far to one side, and the load rolls off. From *galal* numerous words are derived, among which are *galgal* ("wheel" or "whirlwind"), *galil* (Galilee, literally, "Circuit" or "District"), *gulgolet* (Golgotha, "Skull" or "Head"), and *megillah* ("scroll").

4 The [a]LORD has made all for
Himself,
[b]Yes, even the wicked for the day
of [1]doom.

5 [a]Everyone proud in heart *is* an
abomination to the LORD;
Though they join [1]forces, none
will go unpunished.

6 [a]In mercy and truth
Atonement is provided for
iniquity;
And [b]by the fear of the LORD *one*
departs from evil.

7 When a man's ways please the
LORD,

15:23 See section 2 of Truth-In-Action at the end of Prov.
15:23 Word in season: Here is praise of the concept of the proverb itself!
15:25 God defends the helpless.
15:31–33 Learning must come before recognition.
16:3 If one turns over to the Lord what he plans to do, his life purposes will come to fruition.

He makes even his enemies to be
at peace with him.

8 [a]Better *is* a little with
righteousness,
Than vast revenues without
justice.

9 [a]A man's heart plans his way,
[b]But the LORD directs his steps.

10 Divination *is* on the lips of the
king;
His mouth must not transgress in
judgment.
11 [a]Honest weights and scales *are* the
LORD's;
All the weights in the bag *are* His
[1]work.
12 *It is* an abomination for kings to
commit wickedness,
For [a]a throne is established by
righteousness.
13 [a]Righteous lips *are* the delight of
kings,
And they love him who speaks
what is right.
14 As messengers of death *is* the
king's wrath,
But a wise man will [a]appease it.
15 In the light of the king's face *is*
life,
And his *favor *is* like a [a]cloud of
the latter rain.

16 [a]How much better to get *wisdom
than gold!
And to get understanding is to be
chosen rather than silver.

17 The highway of the upright *is* to
depart from evil;
He who keeps his way preserves
his soul.

18 Pride *goes* before destruction,
And a haughty spirit before
[1]a fall.
19 Better *to be* of a humble spirit
with the lowly,
Than to divide the [1]spoil with the
proud.

20 He who heeds the word wisely
will find good,
And whoever [a]trusts in the LORD,
happy *is* he.

21 The wise in heart will be called
prudent,
And sweetness of the lips
increases learning.

22 Understanding *is* a wellspring of
life to him who has it.
But the correction of fools *is* folly.

23 The heart of the wise teaches his
mouth,
And adds learning to his lips.

24 Pleasant words *are like* a
honeycomb,
Sweetness to the soul and health
to the bones.

KINGDOM DYNAMICS

16:23, 24 Wise Words Bring Health, FAITH'S CONFESSION. This text reveals what God's wisdom (His Word) has taught our hearts: those truths and promises are to influence our speech—to transmit that learning to our lips. The Word in our hearts is to teach or control our speech and conduct. The "sweetness" and "health" such speech promotes are desirable, whether in our human relationships or in the release of divine grace in our daily living. It leads the believer to an overcoming, victorious life, through a consistent acknowledgment of the power and might of God with both mouth and manner.

(Ps. 19:14/Matt. 15:7–9) R.H.

25 There is a way *that seems* right
to a man,
But its end *is* the way of [a]death.

26 The person who labors, labors for
himself,
For his *hungry* mouth drives
[a]him *on.*

27 [1]An ungodly man digs up evil,
And *it is* on his lips like a burning
[a]fire.
28 A perverse man sows strife,
And [a]a whisperer separates the
best of friends.
29 A violent man entices his
neighbor,
And leads him in a way *that is*
not good.
30 He winks his eye to devise
perverse things;
He [1]purses his lips *and* brings
about evil.

31 [a]The silver-haired head *is* a crown
of glory,

8 [a]Ps. 37:16; Prov. 15:16
9 [a]Prov. 19:21 [b]Ps. 37:23; Prov. 20:24; Jer. 10:23
11 [a]Lev. 19:36 [1]*concern*
12 [a]Prov. 25:5
13 [a]Prov. 14:35
14 [a]Prov. 25:15
15 [a]Zech. 10:1 *See WW at Deut. 33:23.
16 [a]Prov. 8:10, 11, 19 *See WW at Is. 11:2.
18 [1]*stumbling*
19 [1]*plunder*
20 [a]Ps. 34:8; Jer. 17:7
25 [a]Prov. 14:12
26 [a][Eccl. 6:7; John 6:35]
27 [a][James 3:6] [1]Lit. *A man of Belial*
28 [a]Prov. 17:9
30 [1]Lit. *compresses*
31 [a]Prov. 20:29

16:10–15 One in authority (such as a king) has great power, but also great responsibility to wield it wisely.
16:24 See section 4 of Truth-In-Action at the end of Prov.
16:26 Self-interest is the great universal motive.
16:31 Age is an honor, if reached in righteousness.

If it is found in the way of
righteousness.

32 [a]*He who is* slow to anger *is* better
than the mighty,
And he who rules his spirit than
he who takes a city.

33 The lot is cast into the lap,
But its every decision *is* from the
LORD.

17 Better *is* [a]a dry morsel with
quietness,
Than a house full of [1]feasting
with strife.

2 A wise servant will rule over
[a]a son who causes shame,
And will share an inheritance
among the brothers.

3 The refining pot *is* for silver and
the furnace for gold,
[a]But the LORD tests the hearts.

4 An evildoer gives heed to false
lips;
A liar listens eagerly to a
[1]spiteful tongue.

5 [a]He who mocks the poor
reproaches his Maker;
[b]He who is glad at calamity will
not go unpunished.

6 [a]Children's children *are* the crown
of old men,
And the glory of children *is* their
father.

7 Excellent speech is not becoming
to a fool,
Much less lying lips to a prince.

8 A present *is* a precious stone in
the eyes of its possessor;
Wherever he turns, he prospers.

9 [a]He who covers a transgression
seeks love,
But [b]he who repeats a matter
separates friends.

10 [a]Rebuke is more effective for a
wise *man*
Than a hundred blows on a fool. 3

11 An evil *man* seeks only rebellion;
Therefore a cruel messenger will
be sent against him.

12 Let a man meet [a]a bear robbed
of her cubs,
Rather than a fool in his folly.

13 Whoever [a]rewards evil for good,
Evil will not depart from his
house.

14 The beginning of strife *is like*
releasing water;
Therefore [a]stop contention before
a quarrel starts.

15 [a]He who justifies the wicked, and
he who condemns the just,
Both of them alike *are* an
abomination to the LORD.

16 Why *is there* in the hand of a fool
the purchase price of wisdom,
Since *he has* no heart *for it?*

17 [a]A **friend** loves at all times,
And a brother is born for
adversity.

WORD WEALTH

17:17 friend, *re'a* (*ray*-ah); Strong's #7453: Friend, companion, neighbor, fellowman; a familiar person. This noun occurs more than 180 times. Its root is the verb *ra'ah,* "associate with," "be a friend of." The present reference is a prescription for a healthy friendship: a friend should love at all times. The responsibility to one's neighbor (*re'a*) is outlined in Ps. 101:5; Prov. 24:28; Zech. 8:17.

18 [a]A man devoid of [1]understanding
[2]shakes hands in a pledge, 4

32 [a]Prov. 14:29; 19:11

CHAPTER 17

1 [a]Prov. 15:17 [1]Or *sacrificial meals*
2 [a]Prov. 10:5
3 [a]1 Chr. 29:17; Ps. 26:2; Prov. 15:11; Jer. 17:10; [Mal. 3:3]
4 [1]Lit. *destructive*
5 [a]Prov. 14:31 [b]Job 31:29; Prov. 24:17; Obad. 12; 1 Cor. 13:6
6 [a][Ps. 127:3; 128:3]
9 [a][Prov. 10:12; 1 Cor. 13:5–7; James 5:20] [b]Prov. 16:28
10 [a]Prov. 10:17; [Mic. 7:9]
12 [a]2 Sam. 17:8; Hos. 13:8
13 [a]Ps. 109:4, 5; Jer. 18:20; Rom. 12:17; 1 Thess. 5:15; [1 Pet. 3:9]
14 [a][Prov. 20:3; 1 Thess. 4:11]
15 [a]Ex. 23:7; Prov. 24:24; Is. 5:23
17 [a]Ruth 1:16; Prov. 18:24
18 [a]Prov. 6:1 [1]Lit. *heart* [2]Lit. *strikes the hands*

16:32 Self-discipline is more important—and more difficult—than physical prowess.
16:33 God can exercise control in all things.
17:3 As precious metals are purified by heat, so God purifies hearts by adversity.
17:6 *It is natural to be proud of* ancestry and posterity.
17:8 Present: Here it means something given in expectation of a favor, virtually a bribe. It is unfortunate that often the **possessor,** the one giving the bribe, **prospers** in his evil deeds.
17:10 See section 3 of Truth-In-Action at the end of Prov.
17:12 No angry animal is as dangerous as a **fool.** A "fool" is someone who either denies the reality of God (Ps. 14:1) or refuses to obey His commands (Prov. 10:8). His ways are to be avoided. Some characteristics of a fool in Prov. are: he slanders (10:18); he enjoys doing evil (10:23); he brings trouble to his family (11:29); he is unsubmissive to counsel (12:15); and he is easily annoyed (12:16). See also 14:16; 17:10, 16, 21; 18:2.
17:14 Triggering an argument is like turning on a faucet. It is better to leave it closed.
17:17 Friendship is at its best, not in prosperity, but in time of trouble.
17:18 See section 4 of Truth-In-Action at the end of Prov.

And becomes [3]surety for his
friend.

19 He who loves transgression loves
strife,
And [a]he who exalts his gate seeks
destruction.

20 He who has a [1]deceitful heart
finds no good,
And he who has [a]a perverse
tongue falls into evil.

21 He who begets a scoffer *does so*
to his sorrow,
And the father of a fool has no
*joy.

22 A [a]merry heart [1]does good, *like*
medicine,
But a broken spirit dries the
bones.

23 A wicked *man* accepts a bribe
[1]behind the back
To pervert the ways of justice.

24 [a]Wisdom *is* in the sight of him who
has understanding,
But the eyes of a fool *are* on the
ends of the earth.

25 A [a]foolish son *is* a grief to his
father,
And bitterness to her who bore
him.

26 Also, to punish the righteous *is*
not good,
Nor to strike princes for *their*
uprightness.

4 27 [a]He who has knowledge spares his
words,
And a man of understanding is of
a calm spirit.
28 [a]Even a fool is counted wise when
he holds his peace;
When he shuts his lips, *he is*
considered perceptive.

18

A man who isolates himself
seeks his own desire;
He rages against all [1]wise
judgment.

18 [3]*guaranty* or *collateral*
19 [a]Prov. 16:18
20 [a]James 3:8 [1]*crooked*
21 *See WW at 2 Chr. 7:10.
22 [a]Prov. 12:25; 15:13, 15 [1]Or *makes medicine even better*
23 [1]Under cover, lit. *from the bosom*
24 [a]Eccl. 2:14
25 [a]Prov. 10:1; 15:20; 19:13
27 [a]Prov. 10:19; James 1:19
28 [a]Job 13:5

CHAPTER 18

1 [1]*sound wisdom*

2 [a]Eccl. 10:3 *See WW at Ps. 112:1.
4 [a]Prov. 10:11 [b][James 3:17]
5 [a]Lev. 19:15; Deut. 1:17; 16:19; Ps. 82:2; Prov. 17:15
7 [a]Ps. 64:8; 140:9; Prov. 10:14 [b]Eccl. 10:12
8 [a]Prov. 12:18 [1]*gossip* or *slanderer* [2]A Jewish tradition *wounds* [3]Lit. *rooms of the belly*
10 [a]2 Sam. 22:2, 3, 33; Ps. 18:2; 61:3; 91:2; 144:2 [1]*secure*, lit. *set on high*
12 [a]Prov. 15:33; 16:18
14 *See WW at 2 Sam. 23:2. • See WW at Ps. 55:22.

2 A fool *has no delight in
understanding,
But in expressing his [a]own heart.

3 When the wicked comes,
contempt comes also;
And with dishonor *comes*
reproach.

4 [a]The words of a man's mouth *are*
deep waters;
[b]The wellspring of wisdom *is* a
flowing brook.

5 *It is* not good to show partiality
to the wicked,
Or to overthrow the righteous in
[a]judgment.

6 A fool's lips enter into contention,
And his mouth calls for blows.
7 [a]A fool's mouth *is* his destruction,
And his lips *are* the snare of his
[b]soul.
8 [a]The words of a [1]talebearer *are*
like [2]tasty trifles,
And they go down into the
[3]inmost body.

9 He who is slothful in his work
Is a brother to him who is a great
destroyer.

10 The name of the LORD *is* a strong
[a]tower;
The righteous run to it and are
[1]safe.
11 The rich man's wealth *is* his
strong city,
And like a high wall in his own
esteem.

12 [a]Before destruction the heart of a
man is haughty,
And before honor *is* humility.

13 He who answers a matter before
he hears *it*,
It *is* folly and shame to him.

14 The *spirit of a man will *sustain
him in sickness,
But who can bear a broken spirit?

17:19 Exalts his gate: Glorifies his position.
17:22 Merry heart does good: Though the Bible contains much humor, it rarely comments about it. Here is forthright praise of one's capacity to laugh.
17:27, 28 See section 4 of Truth-In-Action at the end of Prov.
17:28 It is usually in *talking* that foolishness is revealed. It is good judgment to be silent.
18:1 One who cuts himself off from others will soon be out of step with everyone.
18:8 Tasty trifles: Refers to how gossip is relished by the gossiper himself. He feeds on his own malicious words.
18:9 Laziness destroys by wiping out what could have been accomplished, losing both time and opportunity.
18:10 Strong tower: The name of the Lord protects not only by strength, but by height. **Safe** here implies "lifted out of reach."
18:13 Do not jump to conclusions.
18:14 A broken spirit is one's personhood which has been crushed by life's difficulties. It is often accompanied by

15 The heart of the prudent acquires
knowledge,
And the ear of the wise seeks
knowledge.

16 [a]A man's gift makes room for him,
And brings him before great men.

17 The first *one* to plead his cause
seems right,
Until his neighbor comes and
examines him.

18 Casting [a]lots causes contentions
to cease,
And keeps the mighty apart.

19 A brother offended *is harder to
win* than a strong city,
And contentions *are* like the bars
of a castle.

20 [a]A man's stomach shall be
satisfied from the fruit of his
mouth;
From the produce of his lips he
shall be filled.

21 [a]Death and life *are* in the power
of the tongue,
And those who love it will eat its
fruit.

22 [a]*He who* finds a wife finds a good
thing,
And obtains favor from the LORD.

23 The poor *man* uses entreaties,
But the rich answers [a]roughly.

24 A man *who has* friends [1]must
himself be friendly,
[a]But there is a friend *who* sticks
closer than a brother.

19 Better [a]*is* the poor who walks
in his integrity
Than *one who is* perverse in his
lips, and is a fool.

2 Also it is not good *for* a soul *to
be* without knowledge,
And he sins who hastens with *his*
feet.

3 The foolishness of a man twists
his way,
And his heart frets against the
LORD.

4 [a]Wealth makes many friends,
But the poor is separated from his
friend.

5 A [a]false witness will not go
unpunished,
And *he who* speaks lies will not
escape.

6 Many entreat the favor of the
nobility,
And every man *is* a friend to one
who gives gifts.

7 [a]All the brothers of the poor hate
him;
How much more do his friends go
[b]far from him!
He may pursue *them with* words,
yet they [1]abandon *him*.

8 He who gets [1]wisdom loves his
own soul;
He who keeps understanding
[a]will find good.

9 A false witness will not go
unpunished,
And *he who* speaks lies shall
perish.

10 Luxury is not fitting for a fool,
Much less [a]for a servant to rule
over princes.

11 [a]The discretion of a man makes
him slow to anger,
[b]And his glory *is* to overlook a
transgression.

12 [a]The king's wrath *is* like the
roaring of a lion,
But his favor *is* [b]like dew on the
grass.

13 [a]A foolish son *is* the ruin of his
father,
[b]And the contentions of a wife *are*
a continual [1]dripping.

14 [a]Houses and riches *are* an
inheritance from fathers,
But [b]a prudent wife *is* from the
LORD.

15 [a]Laziness casts *one* into a deep
sleep,
And an idle person will [b]suffer
hunger.

16 [a]Gen. 32:20, 21; 1 Sam. 25:27; Prov. 17:8; 21:14
18 [a][Prov. 16:33]
20 [a]Prov. 12:14; 14:14
21 [a]Prov. 12:13; 13:3; Matt. 12:37
22 [a]Gen. 2:18; [Prov. 12:4; 19:14]
23 [a]James 2:3, 6
24 [a]Prov. 17:17; [John 15:14, 15] [1]So with Gr. mss., Syr., Tg., Vg.; MT *may come to ruin*

CHAPTER 19
1 [a]Prov. 28:6
4 [a]Prov. 14:20
5 [a]Ex. 23:1; Deut. 19:16–19; Prov. 6:19; 21:28
7 [a]Prov. 14:20 [b]Ps. 38:11 [1]Lit. *are not*
8 [a]Prov. 16:20 [1]Lit. *heart*
10 [a]Prov. 30:21, 22
11 [a]James 1:19 [b]Prov. 16:32; [Matt. 5:44]; Eph. 4:32; Col. 3:13
12 [a]Prov. 16:14 [b]Gen. 27:28; Deut. 33:28; Ps. 133:3; Hos. 14:5; Mic. 5:7
13 [a]Prov. 10:1 [b]Prov. 21:9, 19 [1]Irritation
14 [a]2 Cor. 12:14 [b]Prov. 18:22
15 [a]Prov. 6:9 [b]Prov. 10:4

depression (15:13; 17:22). Healing such wounded personalities is part of Jesus' ministry (Luke 4:18).
18:16 Gift makes room: This gift is not a bribe, but an asset or talent which opens the way.
18:21 A person's life largely reflects the fruit of his tongue. To speak **life** is to speak God's perspective on any issue of life; to speak **death** is to declare life's negatives, to declare defeat, or complain constantly.
19:4, 6, 7 The rich and powerful easily attract company, but the fact is noted with derision.

16 [a]He who keeps the commandment
keeps his soul,
But he who [1]is careless of his
ways will die.

17 [a]He who has pity on the poor lends
to the LORD,
And He will pay back what he has
given.

5 18 [a]Chasten your son while there is
hope,
And do not set your heart
[1]on his destruction.

19 *A man of* great wrath will suffer
punishment;
For if you rescue *him,* you will
have to do it again.

20 Listen to counsel and receive
instruction,
That you may be wise [a]in your
latter days.

21 There are many plans in a man's
heart,
[a]Nevertheless the LORD's
counsel—that will stand.

22 What is desired in a man is
[1]kindness,
And a poor man is better than a
liar.

23 [a]The fear of the LORD *leads* to life,
And *he who has it* will abide in
satisfaction;
He will not be visited with evil.

24 [a]A lazy *man* buries his hand in the
[1]bowl,
And will not so much as bring it
to his mouth again.

25 Strike a scoffer, and the simple
[a]will become wary;
[b]Rebuke one who has
understanding, *and* he will
discern knowledge.

26 He who mistreats *his* father *and*
chases away *his* mother
Is [a]a son who causes shame and
brings reproach.

27 Cease listening to *instruction,
my son,
And you will stray from the
words of knowledge.

28 A [1]disreputable witness scorns
justice,
And [a]the mouth of the wicked
devours iniquity.

29 Judgments are prepared for
scoffers,
[a]And beatings for the backs of
fools.

20

Wine [a]*is* a mocker,
Strong drink *is* a brawler,
And whoever is led astray by it
is not wise.

2 The [1]wrath of a king *is* like the
roaring of a lion;
Whoever provokes him to anger
sins *against* his own life.

3 [a]*It is* honorable for a man to stop
striving,
Since any fool can start a quarrel.

4 [a]The lazy *man* will not plow
because of winter;
[b]He will beg during harvest and
have nothing.

5 Counsel in the heart of man *is like*
deep water,
But a man of understanding will
draw it out.

6 Most men will proclaim each his
own [1]goodness,
But who can find a faithful man?

7 [a]The righteous *man* walks in his
integrity;
[b]His children *are* blessed after
him.

8 A king who sits on the throne of
judgment
Scatters all evil with his eyes.

9 [a]Who can say, "I have made my
heart clean,
I am pure from my sin"?

10 [a]Diverse weights *and* diverse
measures,
They *are* both alike, an
abomination to the LORD.

16 [a]Prov. 13:13; 16:17; Luke 10:28; 11:28 [1]Is reckless, lit. *despises*
17 [a]Deut. 15:7, 8; Job 23:12, 13; Prov. 28:27; Eccl. 11:1; Matt. 10:42; 25:40; [2 Cor. 9:6–8]; Heb. 6:10
18 [a]Prov. 13:24 [1]Lit. *to put him to death;* a Jewish tradition *on his crying*
20 [a]Ps. 37:37
21 [a]Ps. 33:10, 11; Prov. 16:9; Is. 46:10; Heb. 6:17
22 [1]Lit. *lovingkindness*
23 [a]Prov. 14:27; [1 Tim. 4:8]
24 [a]Prov. 15:19 [1]LXX, Syr. *bosom;* Tg., Vg. *armpit*
25 [a]Deut. 13:11 [b]Prov. 9:8
26 [a]Prov. 17:2
27 *See WW at Prov. 4:13.
28 [a]Job 15:16 [1]Lit. *witness of Belial, worthless witness*
29 [a]Prov. 26:3

CHAPTER 20

1 [a]Gen. 9:21; Prov. 23:29–35; Is. 28:7; Hos. 4:11
2 [1]Lit. *fear* or *terror,* produced by the king's wrath
3 [a]Prov. 17:14
4 [a]Prov. 10:4 [b]Prov. 19:15
6 [1]Lit. *mercy*
7 [a]2 Cor. 1:12 [b]Ps. 37:26
9 [a][1 Kin. 8:46; 2 Chr. 6:36]; Job 9:30, 31; 14:4; [Ps. 51:5; Eccl. 7:20; Rom. 3:9; 1 John 1:8]
10 [a]Deut. 25:13

19:17 Here is perhaps the clearest identification of God Himself with the plight of the poor. The help they are given becomes God's own debt to the giver.
19:18 See section 5 of Truth-In-Action at the end of Prov.
19:18 See note on 23:13, 14.
19:19 Temper is a weakness prone to repetition.
19:24 The ultimate sloth: a man too lazy to eat!
20:3 A peacemaker is better than a troublemaker.
20:8 **With his eyes:** Clear perception of fact is the talent that defeats injustice in the courtroom.

11 Even a child is [a]known by his deeds,
Whether what he does *is* pure and right.

12 [a]The hearing ear and the seeing eye,
The LORD has made them both.

13 [a]Do not love sleep, lest you come to poverty;
Open your eyes, *and* you will be satisfied with bread.

14 "*It is* [1]good for nothing," cries the buyer;
But when he has gone his way, then he boasts.

2 15 There is gold and a multitude of rubies,
But [a]the lips of knowledge *are* a precious jewel.

16 [a]Take the garment of one who is surety *for* a stranger,
And hold it as a pledge *when it* is for a seductress.

17 [a]Bread gained by deceit *is* sweet to a man,
But afterward his mouth will be filled with gravel.

18 [a]Plans are established by counsel;
[b]By wise counsel wage war.

19 [a]He who goes about *as* a talebearer reveals secrets;
Therefore do not associate with one [b]who flatters with his lips.

20 [a]Whoever curses his father or his mother,
[b]His lamp will be put out in deep darkness.

21 [a]An inheritance gained hastily at the beginning
[b]Will not be blessed at the end.

22 [a]Do not say, "I will [1]recompense evil";
[b]Wait* for the LORD, and He will save you.

23 Diverse weights *are* an abomination to the LORD,
And dishonest scales *are* not good.

24 A man's steps *are* of the LORD;
How then can a man understand his own way?

25 *It is* a snare for a man to devote rashly *something as* holy,
And afterward to reconsider *his* vows.

26 [a]A wise king sifts out the wicked,
And brings the threshing wheel over them.

27 [a]The spirit of a man *is* the lamp of the LORD,
Searching all the [1]inner depths of his heart.

28 [a]Mercy and truth preserve the king,
And by [1]lovingkindness he upholds his throne.

29 The glory of young men *is* their strength,
And [a]the splendor of old men *is* their gray head.

30 Blows that hurt cleanse away evil,
As *do* stripes the [1]inner depths of the heart.

21

The king's heart *is* in the hand of the LORD,
Like the [1]rivers of water;
He turns it wherever He wishes.

2 [a]Every way of a man *is* right in his own eyes,
[b]But the LORD weighs the hearts.

3 [a]To do righteousness and justice
Is more acceptable to the LORD than sacrifice.

4 [a]A haughty look, a proud heart,
And the [1]plowing of the wicked *are* sin.

5 [a]The plans of the diligent *lead* surely to plenty,
But *those of* everyone *who is* hasty, surely to poverty.

6 [a]Getting treasures by a lying tongue

11 [a]Matt. 7:16
12 [a]Ex. 4:11; Ps. 94:9
13 [a]Rom. 12:11
14 [1]Lit. *evil, evil*
15 [a][Job 28:12–19; Prov. 3:13–15]
16 [a]Prov. 22:26
17 [a]Prov. 9:17
18 [a]Prov. 24:6 [b]Luke 14:31
19 [a]Prov. 11:13 [b]Rom. 16:18
20 [a]Ex. 21:17; Lev. 20:9; Prov. 30:11; Matt. 15:4 [b]Job 18:5, 6; Prov. 24:20
21 [a]Prov. 28:20 [b]Hab. 2:6
22 [a][Deut. 32:35]; Prov. 17:13; 24:29; [Rom. 12:17–19]; 1 Thess. 5:15; [1 Pet. 3:9] [b]2 Sam. 16:12 [1]*repay* *See WW at Lam. 3:25.
26 [a]Ps. 101:8
27 [a]1 Cor. 2:11 [1]Lit. *rooms of the belly*
28 [a]Ps. 101:1; Prov. 21:21 [1]*mercy*
29 [a]Prov. 16:31
30 [1]Lit. *rooms of the belly*

CHAPTER 21
1 [1]*channels*
2 [a]Prov. 16:2 [b]Prov. 24:12; Luke 16:15
3 [a]1 Sam. 15:22; Prov. 15:8; Is. 1:11, 16, 17; Hos. 6:6; [Mic. 6:7, 8]
4 [a]Prov. 6:17 [1]Or *lamp*
5 [a]Prov. 10:4
6 [a]2 Pet. 2:3

20:14 A bargainer belittles merchandise at the moment of purchase but later gloats over its value.
20:15 See section 2 of Truth-In-Action at the end of Prov.
20:27 Lamp of the LORD: Man's spirit (more than soul or body) is God's contact point, through which He illumines man and shows him his own true nature.
21:1 Turns it: God can steer a government.
21:2 Any person justifies his behavior, but God considers also his motives.

[1]*Is* the fleeting fantasy of those
who seek death.

7 The violence of the wicked will
[1]destroy them,
Because they refuse to do justice.

8 The way of [1]a guilty man *is*
perverse;
But *as for* the pure, his work *is*
right.

9 Better to dwell in a corner of a
housetop,
Than in a house shared with
[a]a contentious woman.

10 [a]The soul of the wicked desires
evil;
His neighbor finds no favor in his
eyes.

11 When the scoffer is punished, the
simple is made wise;
But when the [a]wise is instructed,
he receives knowledge.

12 The righteous *God* wisely
considers the house of the
wicked,
Overthrowing the wicked for
their wickedness.

13 [a]Whoever shuts his ears to the cry
of the poor
Will also cry himself and not be
heard.

14 A gift in secret pacifies anger,
And a bribe [1]behind the back,
strong wrath.

15 *It is* a joy for the just to do justice,
But destruction *will come* to the
workers of iniquity.

16 A man who wanders from the
way of *understanding
Will rest in the assembly of the
[a]dead.

17 He who loves pleasure *will be* a
poor man;
He who loves wine and oil will
not be rich.

18 The wicked *shall be* a ransom for
the righteous,
And the unfaithful for the upright.

19 Better to dwell [1]in the wilderness,
Than with a contentious and
angry woman.

20 [a]*There is* desirable treasure,
And oil in the dwelling of the
wise,
But a foolish man squanders it.

21 [a]He who follows righteousness
and mercy
Finds life, righteousness and
honor.

22 A [a]wise *man* [1]scales the city of
the mighty,
And brings down the trusted
*stronghold.

23 [a]Whoever guards his mouth and
tongue
Keeps his soul from troubles.

24 A proud *and* haughty *man*—
"Scoffer" *is* his name;
He acts with arrogant pride.

25 The [a]desire of the lazy *man* kills
him,
For his hands refuse to labor.

26 He covets greedily all day long,
But the righteous [a]gives and does
not spare.

27 [a]The sacrifice of the wicked *is* an
abomination;
How much more *when* he brings
it with wicked intent!

28 A false witness shall perish,
But the man who hears *him* will
speak endlessly.

29 A wicked man hardens his face,
But *as for* the upright, he
[1]establishes his way.

30 [a]*There is* no wisdom or
understanding
Or counsel against the LORD.

31 The horse *is* prepared for the day
of battle,
But [a]deliverance *is* of the LORD.

22

A [a]*good* name is to be *chosen
rather than *great riches,
Loving favor rather than silver
and gold.

2 The [a]rich and the poor have this
in common,

6 [1]LXX *Pursue vanity on the snares of death;* Vg. *Is vain and foolish, and shall stumble on the snares of death;* Tg. *They shall be destroyed, and they shall fall who seek death*
7 [1]Lit. *drag them away*
8 [1]Or *The way of a man is perverse and strange;*
9 [a]Prov. 19:13
10 [a]James 4:5
11 [a]Prov. 19:25
13 [a][Matt. 7:2; 18:30–34]; James 2:13; 1 John 3:17
14 [1]Under cover, lit. *in the bosom*
16 [a]Ps. 49:14
*See WW at Jer. 3:15.
19 [1]Lit. *in the land of the desert*
20 [a]Ps. 112:3; Prov. 8:21
21 [a]Prov. 15:9; Matt. 5:6; [Rom. 2:7]; 1 Cor. 15:58
22 [a]2 Sam. 5:6–9; Prov. 24:5; Eccl. 7:19; 9:15, 16
[1]Climbs over the walls of
*See WW at Jer. 16:19.
23 [a]Prov. 12:13; 13:3; 18:21; [James 3:2]
25 [a]Prov. 13:4
26 [a][Prov. 22:9; Eph. 4:28]
27 [a]Prov. 15:8; Is. 66:3; Jer. 6:20; Amos 5:22
29 [1]Qr., LXX *understands*
30 [a]Is. 8:9, 10; [Jer. 9:23, 24]; Acts 5:39; 1 Cor. 3:19, 20
31 [a]Ps. 3:8; Jer. 3:23; [1 Cor. 15:57]

CHAPTER 22

1 [a][Prov. 10:7]; Eccl. 7:1
*See WW at 1 Kin. 11:34. • See WW at Ps. 31:19.
2 [a]Prov. 29:13

21:9 See note on 25:24.
21:18 **Ransom:** That which is given up to secure what is more valuable. The wicked and unfaithful are expendable when compared to the righteous and the upright.
21:28 The damaging results of a lie continue even after the liar is dead.

The [b]LORD *is* the maker of them
all.

3 A prudent *man* foresees evil and
hides himself,
But the simple pass on and are
[a]punished.

4 By humility *and* the fear of the
LORD
Are riches and honor and life.

5 Thorns *and* snares *are* in the way
of the perverse;
He who guards his soul will be
far from them.

5 6 [a]Train up a child in the way he
should go,
[1]And when he is old he will not
depart from it.

7 The [a]rich rules over the poor,
And the borrower *is* servant to
the lender.

8 He who sows iniquity will reap
[a]**sorrow,**[1]
And the rod of his anger will fail.

WORD WEALTH

22:8 sorrow *'aven* (*ah*-ven); Strong's #205: Exhaustion, affliction, wickedness, iniquity, unrighteousness; sorrow, mourning; emptiness; idolatry. *'Aven* occurs about 85 times. In Hebrew there is such a link between evil and its certain ill effects, that *'aven* can easily involve both meanings. *'Aven* is one of several Hebrew words in which sin and penalty are inextricably yoked.

9 [a]He who has a [1]generous eye will
be [b]blessed,
For he gives of his bread to the
poor.

10 [a]Cast out the scoffer, and
contention will leave;
Yes, strife and reproach will
cease.

11 [a]He who loves purity of heart
And has grace on his lips,
The king *will be* his friend.

12 The eyes of the LORD preserve
knowledge,
But He overthrows the words of
the faithless.

13 [a]The lazy *man* says, "*There is* a
lion outside!
I shall be slain in the streets!"

14 [a]The mouth of an immoral woman
is a deep pit;
[b]He who is abhorred by the LORD
will fall there.

15 Foolishness *is* bound up in the
heart of a child;
[a]The rod of correction will drive
it far from him.

16 He who oppresses the poor to
increase his *riches,*
And he who gives to the rich, *will*
surely *come* to poverty.

Sayings of the Wise

17 Incline your ear and hear the
words of the wise, 2
And apply your heart to my
knowledge;
18 For *it is* a pleasant thing if you
keep them within you;
Let them all be fixed upon your
lips,
19 So that your trust may be in the
LORD;
I have instructed you today, even
you.
20 Have I not written to you
excellent things
Of counsels and knowledge,
21 [a]That I may make you know the
certainty of the words of truth,

2 [b]Job 31:15; [Prov. 14:31]
3 [a]Prov. 27:12; Is. 26:20
6 [a]Eph. 6:4; 2 Tim. 3:15 [1]*Even*
7 [a]Prov. 18:23; James 2:6
8 [a]Job 4:8 [1]*trouble*
9 [a]2 Cor. 9:6 [b][Prov. 19:17] [1]Lit. *good*
10 [a]Ps. 101:5
11 [a]Ps. 101:6
13 [a]Prov. 26:13
14 [a]Prov. 2:16; 5:3; 7:5 [b]Eccl. 7:26
15 [a]Prov. 13:24; 23:13, 14
21 [a]Luke 1:3, 4

22:6 See section 5 of Truth-In-Action at the end of Prov.
22:6 Train up has the idea of a parent graciously investing in a child whatever wisdom, love, nurture, and discipline is needed for him to become fully committed to God. It presupposes the emotional and spiritual maturity of the parent to do so. **In the way he should go** is to do the training according to the unique personality, gifts, and aspirations of the child. It also means to train the child to avoid whatever natural tendencies he might have that would prevent total commitment to God (for example, a weak will, a lack of discipline, a susceptibility to depression). Hence, the promise is that proper development insures the child will stay committed to God.
22:13 Laziness invents bizarre excuses (see 26:13).
22:15 See note on 23:13, 14.
22:17–21 See section 2 of Truth-In-Action at the end of Prov.
22:17 The wise: Probably means a number of wise men whose sayings follow, though the use of "I" (vv. 19, 20, 21) gives a personal touch. The first person introduction may be by Solomon himself, or by whoever is the first "wise man" cited.

Literary note: This collection of sayings (through 24:22) is marked by several noteworthy differences from what has gone before: 1) Its proverbs are not nearly so uniform in following the couplet format (see note on 10:1). 2) The grammatical structure uses longer, more complex constructions, and includes explanations more often. 3) Nevertheless, meanings are often more cryptic and hard to grasp. 4) There is much greater use of rhetorical questions and imperative commands.

[b]That you may answer words of truth
To those who [1]send to you?

22 Do not rob the [a]poor because he *is* poor,
Nor oppress the afflicted at the gate;
23 [a]For the LORD will plead their cause,
And plunder the soul of those who plunder them.

24 Make no friendship with an angry man,
And with a [a]furious man do not go,
25 Lest you learn his ways
And set a snare for your soul.

26 [a]Do not be one of those who [1]shakes hands in a pledge,
One of those who is [2]surety for debts;
27 If you have nothing *with which* to pay,
Why should he take away your bed from under you?

28 [a]Do not remove the ancient [1]landmark
Which your fathers have set.

29 Do you see a man *who* [1]excels in his work?
He will stand before kings;
He will not stand before [2]unknown *men*.

4 23 When you sit down to eat with a ruler,
Consider carefully what *is* before you;
2 And put a knife to your throat
If you *are* a man given to appetite.
3 Do not desire his delicacies,
For they *are* deceptive food.

4 [a]Do not overwork to be rich;
[b]Because of your own understanding, cease!
5 [1]Will you set your eyes on that which is not?
For *riches* certainly make themselves wings;
They fly away like an eagle *toward* heaven.

6 Do not eat the bread of [a]a[1] miser,
Nor desire his delicacies;
7 For as he thinks in his heart, so *is* he.
"Eat and drink!" [a]he says to you,
But his heart is not with you.
8 The morsel you have eaten, you will vomit up,
And waste your pleasant words.

9 [a]Do not speak in the hearing of a fool,
For he will despise the wisdom of your words.

10 Do not remove the ancient [1]landmark,
Nor enter the fields of the fatherless;
11 [a]For their Redeemer *is* mighty;
He will plead their cause against you.

12 Apply your heart to instruction,
And your ears to words of knowledge.

13 [a]Do not withhold correction from a child,
For *if* you beat him with a rod, he will not die.
14 You shall beat him with a rod,
And deliver his soul from [1]hell.

15 My son, if your heart is wise,
My heart will rejoice—indeed, I myself;
16 Yes, my [1]inmost being will rejoice
When your lips speak right things.

17 [a]Do not let your heart envy sinners,
But [b]*be zealous* for the fear of the LORD all the day;
18 [a]For surely there is a [1]hereafter,
And your hope will not be cut off.

21 [b]Prov. 25:13; 1 Pet. 3:15 [1]Or *send you*
22 [a]Ex. 23:6; Job 31:16–21; Zech. 7:10
23 [a]1 Sam. 24:12; Ps. 12:5; 140:12
24 [a]Prov. 29:22
26 [a]Prov. 11:15 [1]Lit. *strikes* [2]*guaranty*
28 [a]Deut. 19:14; 27:17; Job 24:2; Prov. 23:10 [1]*boundary*
29 [1]*is prompt in his business* [2]*obscure*

CHAPTER 23

4 [a][Prov. 28:20; Matt. 6:19; 1 Tim. 6:9, 10; Heb. 13:5] [b]Rom. 12:16
5 [1]Lit. *Will you cause your eyes to fly upon it and it is not?*
6 [a]Deut. 15:9; Prov. 28:22 [1]Lit. *one who has an evil eye*
7 [a]Prov. 12:2
9 [a]Prov. 9:8; Matt. 7:6
10 [1]*boundary*
11 [a]Prov. 22:23
13 [a]Prov. 13:24
14 [1]Or *Sheol*
16 [1]Lit. *kidneys*
17 [a]Ps. 37:1; Prov. 24:1, 19 [b]Prov. 28:14
18 [a][Ps. 37:37] [1]Future, lit. *latter end*

22:28 Respect the boundaries of tradition—behavioral as well as geographical.
22:29 Unknown men: The destiny of the diligent is not the company of the obscure and insignificant.
23:1–3 See section 4 of Truth-In-Action at the end of Prov.
23:1–3 Control yourself when offered unaccustomed luxuries—for appearance' sake as well as for your health.
23:13, 14 Beat him with a rod means to spank a child with one's hand or an instrument of sufficient strength so as to cause pain but not injury. The Bible teaches that spanking is to stem from an attitude of love and patience (Heb. 12:3–6), is necessary because of Adamic foolishness in children (Prov. 22:15), can come too late in a child's life to be effective (19:18), and is a necessary part of nurturing spiritual development (v. 14).
23:15–28 Again come warnings specifically for a son. He should beware of envying sinners and of consorting with drunkards, gluttons, and harlots. On the positive side, he should fear the Lord, give attention to his parents, value the truth, and gladden the family.
23:17, 18 Hereafter: The fact of eternity should motivate one to **fear of the LORD.**

4 19 Hear, my son, and be wise;
And guide your heart in the way.
20 [a]Do not mix with winebibbers,
Or with gluttonous eaters of meat;
21 For the drunkard and the glutton will come to poverty,
And drowsiness will clothe *a man* with rags.

22 [a]Listen to your father who begot you,
And do not despise your mother when she is old.

23 [a]Buy the truth, and do not sell *it*,
Also wisdom and instruction and understanding.

24 [a]The father of the righteous will greatly *rejoice,
And he who begets a wise *child* will delight in him.
25 Let your *father and your mother be glad,
And let her who bore you rejoice.

4 26 My son, give me your heart,
And let your eyes observe my ways.
27 [a]For a harlot *is* a deep pit,
And a seductress *is* a narrow well.
28 [a]She also lies in wait as *for* a victim,
And increases the unfaithful among men.

4 29 [a]Who has woe?
Who has sorrow?
Who has contentions?
Who has complaints?
Who has wounds without cause?
Who [b]has redness of eyes?
30 [a]Those who linger long at the wine,
Those who go in search of [b]mixed wine.
31 Do not look on the wine when it is red,
When it sparkles in the cup,
When it [1]swirls around smoothly;
32 At the last it bites like a serpent,
And stings like a viper.
33 Your eyes will see strange things,
And your heart will utter perverse things.

20 [a]Prov. 20:1; 23:29, 30; Is. 5:22; Matt. 24:49; [Luke 21:34]; Rom. 13:13; [Eph. 5:18]
22 [a]Prov. 1:8; Eph. 6:1
23 [a]Prov. 4:7; 18:15; [Matt. 13:44]
24 [a]Prov. 10:1 *See WW at 2 Chr. 7:10.
25 *See WW at Ps. 68:5.
27 [a]Prov. 22:14
28 [a]Prov. 7:12; Eccl. 7:26
29 [a]Is. 5:11, 22 [b]Gen. 49:12
30 [a]1 Sam. 25:36; Prov. 20:1; 21:17; Is. 5:11; 28:7; [Eph. 5:18] [b]Ps. 75:8
31 [1]*goes around*
34 [1]Lit. *heart*
35 [a]Prov. 27:22; Jer. 5:3 [b]Eph. 4:19

CHAPTER 24

1 [a]Ps. 1:1; 37:1; Prov. 23:17
5 [a]Prov. 21:22; Eccl. 9:16 *See WW at Jer. 31:22.
6 [a]Luke 14:31
7 [a]Ps. 10:5; Prov. 14:6
8 [a]Prov. 6:14; 14:22; Rom. 1:30 [1]Lit. *master of evil plots*
10 [a]Deut. 20:8; Job 4:5; Jer. 51:46; Heb. 12:3
11 [a]Ps. 82:4; Is. 58:6, 7; 1 John 3:16
12 [a]1 Sam. 16:7; Prov. 21:2

34 Yes, you will be like one who lies down in the [1]midst of the sea,
Or like one who lies at the top of the mast, *saying:*
35 "They[a] have struck me, *but* I was not hurt;
They have beaten me, but I did not feel *it.*
When shall [b]I awake, that I may seek another *drink?*"

24 Do not be [a]envious of evil men,
Nor desire to be with them;
2 For their heart devises violence,
And their lips talk of troublemaking.

3 Through wisdom a house is built,
And by understanding it is established;
4 By knowledge the rooms are filled
With all precious and pleasant riches.

5 [a]A wise *man *is* strong,
Yes, a man of knowledge increases strength;
6 [a]For by wise counsel you will wage your own war,
And in a multitude of counselors *there is* safety.

7 [a]Wisdom *is* too lofty for a fool;
He does not open his mouth in the gate.

8 He who [a]plots to do evil
Will be called a [1]schemer.
9 The devising of foolishness *is* sin,
And the scoffer *is* an abomination to men.

10 *If* you [a]faint in the day of adversity,
Your strength *is* small.

11 [a]Deliver *those who* are drawn toward death,
And hold back *those* stumbling to the slaughter.
12 If you say, "Surely we did not know this,"
Does not [a]He who weighs the hearts consider *it?*

23:19–21 See section 4 of Truth-In-Action at the end of Prov.
23:26–28 See section 4 of Truth-In-Action at the end of Prov.
23:29–35 See section 4 of Truth-In-Action at the end of Prov.
23:29–35 Here is a brief essay against alcohol abuse. Wine is described as dangerous as a snake (v. 32), producing hallucinations (v. 33), bad language (v. 33), and insensitivity (vv. 34, 35).
24:6 Your own war: Each of us has his own battles to fight, and needs wise and frequent advice to fight them well.
24:10 Strength is not measured in good times, but in bad.
24:11, 12 Presented here with evangelistic fervor is our obligation to rescue the ignorant headed for destruction. God will not accept our excuses.

He who keeps your soul, does He
not know *it?*
And will He *not* render to *each*
man [b]according to his deeds?

KINGDOM DYNAMICS

24:11, 12 Committed Action to Our Generation, WORLD EVANGELISM. There are just two groups of people in the world: those who have heard the gospel and those who have not. If those who have heard (and believed) refuse to tell those who have not heard, God will render to each according "to his deeds." Sobering! We are responsible to our generation. While people often debate over those who have died without hearing the gospel, this passage reveals the soul-stirring importance of seeking those who are alive and have not heard! A practical guideline from Acts 13:36 can teach us: "David . . . served his generation by the will of God." We cannot go back to the last generation, nor can we reach the next generation, but we can serve this one. The only generation God expects us to be vitally concerned about is our own!
(Ps. 2:8/Is. 40:8–11) G.C.

2 13 My son, [a]eat honey because *it is*
good,
And the honeycomb *which is*
sweet to your taste;
14 [a]So *shall* the knowledge of wisdom
be to your soul;
If you have found *it,* there is a
[1]prospect,
And your hope will not be cut
off.
15 Do not lie in wait, O wicked *man,*
against the dwelling of the
righteous;
Do not plunder his resting place;
16 [a]For a righteous *man* may fall
seven times
And rise again,
[b]But the wicked shall fall by
calamity.
17 [a]Do not rejoice when your enemy
falls,
And do not let your heart be glad
when he stumbles;
18 Lest the LORD see *it,* and
[1]it displease Him,

12 [b]Job 34:11; Ps. 62:12; Rev. 2:23; 22:12
13 [a]Ps. 19:10; 119:103; Prov. 25:16; Song 5:1
14 [a]Ps. 19:10; 58:11; Prov. 23:18 [1]Lit. *latter end*
16 [a]Job 5:19; [Ps. 34:19; 37:24; Mic. 7:8] [b]Esth. 7:10; Amos 5:2
17 [a]Job 31:29; Ps. 35:15, 19; [Prov. 17:5]; Obad. 12
18 [1]Lit. *it be evil in His eyes*
19 [a]Ps. 37:1
21 [a][Rom. 13:7; 1 Pet. 2:17]
23 [a]Lev. 19:15; Deut. 1:17; 16:19; [John 7:24] [1]Lit. *recognize faces*
24 [a]Prov. 17:15; Is. 5:23
25 [a]Prov. 28:23
27 [a]1 Kin. 5:17; Prov. 27:23–27
28 [a]Lev. 6:2, 3; 19:11; Eph. 4:25 [1]LXX, Vg. *Do not deceive*
29 [a][Prov. 20:22; Matt. 5:39–44; Rom. 12:17–19]

And He turn away His wrath from
him.
19 [a]Do not fret because of evildoers,
Nor be envious of the wicked;
20 For there will be no prospect for
the evil *man;*
The lamp of the wicked will be
put out.
21 My son, [a]fear the LORD and the
king;
Do not associate with those given
to change;
22 For their calamity will rise
suddenly,
And who knows the ruin those
two can bring?

Further Sayings of the Wise

23 These *things* also *belong* to the
wise:

[a]*It is* not good to [1]show partiality
in judgment.
24 [a]He who says to the wicked, "You
are righteous,"
Him the people will curse;
Nations will abhor him.
25 But those who rebuke *the wicked*
will have [a]delight,
And a good blessing will come
upon them.
26 He who gives a right answer
kisses the lips.
27 [a]Prepare your outside work,
Make it fit for yourself in the
field;
And afterward build your house.
28 [a]Do not be a witness against your
neighbor without cause,
[1]For would you deceive with your
lips?
29 [a]Do not say, "I will do to him just
as he has done to me;
I will render to the man according
to his work."
30 I went by the field of the lazy
man,
And by the vineyard of the man
devoid of understanding;

24:13, 14 See section 2 of Truth-In-Action at the end of Prov.
24:16 Falling is not fatal, except to the wicked.
24:17, 18 God may see one's gloating over another's mistakes as punishment enough for the sinner.
24:21, 22 Revolution against God or government is dangerous, for both are powerful.
24:23–34 Here is another brief collection of wise men's sayings, similar in style to the preceding group.
24:26 Kisses the lips: Brings pleasure.
24:27 First give attention to what is productive, then to what is comfortable.
24:28, 29 Avoid vindictiveness against a neighbor, whether he deserves it or not.
24:30–34 Observation of a lazy man's farm makes vivid the tragedy of idleness. See note on 6:6–11.

31 And there it was, [a]all overgrown
with thorns;
Its surface was covered with
nettles;
Its stone wall was broken down.
32 When I saw *it*, I considered *it*
well;
I looked on *it and* received
*instruction:
33 [a]A little sleep, a little slumber,
A little folding of the hands to
rest;
34 [a]So shall your poverty come *like*
[1]a prowler,
And your need like [2]an armed
man.

Further Wise Sayings of Solomon

25 These[a] also *are* proverbs of Solomon which the men of Hezekiah king of Judah copied:

2 [a]*It is* the glory of God to conceal
a matter,
But the glory of kings *is* to search
out a matter.

3 *As* the heavens for height and the
earth for depth,
So the heart of kings *is*
unsearchable.

4 [a]Take away the dross from silver,
And it will go to the silversmith
for jewelry.
5 Take away the wicked from
before the king,
And his throne will be established
in [a]righteousness.

6 Do not exalt yourself in the
presence of the king,
And do not stand in the place of
the great;
7 [a]For *it is* better that he say to you,
"Come up here,"
Than that you should be put
lower in the presence of the
prince,
Whom your eyes have seen.

8 [a]Do not go hastily to [1]court;
For what will you do in the end,
When your neighbor has put you
to shame?
9 [a]Debate your case with your
neighbor,
And do not disclose the secret to
another;
10 Lest he who hears *it* expose your
shame,
And [1]your reputation be ruined.

11 A word fitly [a]spoken *is like* apples
of gold
In settings of silver.
12 *Like* an earring of gold and an
ornament of fine gold
Is a wise rebuker to an obedient
ear.

13 [a]Like the cold of snow in time of
harvest
Is a faithful messenger to those
who send him,
For he refreshes the soul of his
masters.

14 [a]Whoever falsely boasts of giving
Is like [b]clouds and wind without
rain.

15 [a]By long forbearance a ruler is
persuaded,
And a gentle tongue breaks a
bone.

16 Have you found honey?
Eat only *as much as you need,
Lest you be filled with it and
vomit.

17 Seldom set foot in your
neighbor's house,
Lest he become weary of you and
hate you.

18 [a]A man who bears false witness
against his neighbor
Is like a club, a sword, and a sharp
arrow.

31 [a]Gen. 3:18 **32** *See WW at Prov. 4:13. **33** [a]Prov. 6:9, 10 **34** [a]Prov. 6:9–11 [1]Lit. *one who walks about* [2]Lit. *a man with a shield*

CHAPTER 25

1 [a]1 Kin. 4:32 **2** [a]Deut. 29:29; Rom. 11:33 **4** [a]2 Tim. 2:21 **5** [a]Prov. 16:12; 20:8 **7** [a]Luke 14:7–11

8 [a]Prov. 17:14; Matt. 5:25 [1]Lit. *contend or bring a lawsuit* **9** [a][Matt. 18:15] **10** [1]*the evil report concerning you not pass away* **11** [a]Prov. 15:23; Is. 50:4 **13** [a]Prov. 13:17 **14** [a]Prov. 20:6 [b]Jude 12 **15** [a]Prov. 15:1 **16** *See WW at Mal. 3:10. **18** [a]Ps. 57:4; Prov. 12:18

25:1—29:27 Again we read the crisp, terse style of Solomon himself, in a collection of his sayings copied by Hezekiah's men. This must have been done about 720 B.C., when the writing had already survived more than 200 years, but we have no clue as to the source or history of the document from which these scribes copied. Many of the proverbs in this group are more pungent and stinging than the others. It seems likely that at least some of these are among Solomon's later sayings, when his skill at pithy comment was well honed. Nevertheless numerous thoughts in chs. 25 and 26 are also found (sometimes in the same words) in the earlier collection of Solomon's proverbs (10:1—22:16). Except for a few passages (such as 27:23–27) the thoughts are highly compressed, each expressed in a single verse.

25:2 Conceal . . . search out: Man always feels the need to find out; God never does, as He already knows.

25:4, 5 The wicked are blemishes to any kingdom.

25:6, 7 It is better to start with a humble place and be invited higher, a truth Jesus quotes in essence in Luke 14:7–11.

25:13 Time of harvest: What is normally a time of perspiring labor is alleviated by the unexpected refreshment of cooling snow. Just as pleasing is the work of a good envoy.

25:16 There is such a thing as too much, even of something good.

19 Confidence in an unfaithful *man*
in time of trouble
Is like a bad tooth and a foot out
of joint.

20 *Like* one who takes away a
garment in cold weather,
And like vinegar on soda,
Is one who [a]sings* songs to a
heavy heart.

21 [a]If your enemy is hungry, give him
bread to eat;
And if he is thirsty, give him
water to drink;
22 For *so* you will heap coals of fire
on his head,
[a]And the LORD will reward you.

23 The north wind brings forth rain,
And [a]a backbiting tongue an
angry countenance.

24 [a]*It is* better to dwell in a corner
of a housetop,
Than in a house shared with a
contentious woman.

25 *As* cold water to a weary *soul,
So *is* [a]good news from a far
country.

26 A righteous *man* who falters
before the wicked
Is like a murky spring and a
[1]polluted well.

27 *It is* not good to eat much honey;
So [a]to seek one's own glory *is not*
glory.

28 [a]Whoever *has* no rule over his own
spirit
Is like a city broken down,
without walls.

26

As snow in summer [a]and rain
in harvest,
So honor is not fitting for a fool.

2 Like a flitting sparrow, like a
flying swallow,
So [a]a curse without cause shall
not alight.

3 [a]A whip for the horse,
A bridle for the donkey,
And a rod for the fool's back.
4 Do not answer a fool according
to his folly,
Lest you also be like him.
5 [a]Answer a fool according to his
folly,
Lest he be wise in his own eyes.
6 He who sends a message by the
hand of a fool
Cuts off *his own* feet *and* drinks
violence.
7 *Like* the legs of the lame that
hang limp
Is a proverb in the mouth of fools.
8 Like one who binds a stone in a
sling
Is he who gives honor to a fool.
9 *Like* a thorn *that* goes into the
hand of a drunkard
Is a proverb in the mouth of fools.
10 [1]The great *God* who formed
everything
Gives the fool *his* hire and the
transgressor *his* wages.
11 [a]As a dog returns to his own vomit,
[b]*So* a fool repeats his folly.
12 [a]Do you see a man wise in his own
eyes?
There is more *hope for a fool
than for him.

13 The lazy *man* says, "*There is* a
lion in the road!
A fierce lion *is* in the [1]streets!"
14 *As* a door turns on its hinges,
So *does* the lazy *man* on his bed.
15 The [a]lazy *man* buries his hand in
the [1]bowl;
It wearies him to bring it back to
his mouth.
16 The lazy *man is* wiser in his own
eyes
Than seven men who can answer
sensibly.

17 He who passes by *and* meddles
in a quarrel not his own
Is like one who takes a dog by the
ears.

18 Like a madman who throws
firebrands, arrows, and death,

20 [a]Dan. 6:18 *See WW at Judg. 5:3.
21 [a]Ex. 23:4, 5; 2 Kin. 6:22; 2 Chr. 28:15; Matt. 5:44; Rom. 12:20
22 [a]2 Sam. 16:12; [Matt. 6:4, 6]
23 [a]Ps. 101:5
24 [a]Prov. 19:13
25 [a]Prov. 15:30 *See WW at Prov. 10:3.
26 [1]*ruined*
27 [a]Prov. 27:2; [Luke 14:11]
28 [a]Prov. 16:32

CHAPTER 26
1 [a]1 Sam. 12:17
2 [a]Num. 23:8; Deut. 23:5; 2 Sam. 16:12
3 [a]Ps. 32:9; Prov. 19:29
5 [a]Matt. 16:1–4; Rom. 12:16
10 [1]Heb. difficult in v. 10; ancient and modern translators differ greatly
11 [a]2 Pet. 2:22 [b]Ex. 8:15
12 [a]Prov. 29:20; Luke 18:11, 12; [Rev. 3:17] *See WW at Hos. 2:15.
13 [1]Or *plazas, squares*
15 [a]Prov. 19:24 [1]LXX, Syr. *bosom;* Tg., Vg. *armpit*

25:19 The pain is both acute and chronic.
25:20 The jarring inappropriateness of these two similes shows the same kind of thinking as, "To everything there is . . . a time" (Eccl. 3:1). The protest is against that which is unsuitable and in bad taste.
25:24 This is an example of Proverbs' teachings on a controlled tongue. **Contentious** means "quarrelsome."
25:26 A righteous *man* who falters: One who is basically good becomes contaminated when he is indecisive in the face of temptation. His ability to serve is marred.
25:28 As a river is a swamp if it lacks the discipline of banks, so (in terms of the time) a city without walls is no city. And a man out of control (with no self-imposed limits) is no man.
26:4, 5 These apparently contradictory proverbs are compatible if we recognize that each teaches a separate truth. If you imitate the style of a fool, you are one yourself; but if you respond to him as you would to a wise man, he will think himself one.
26:6–11, 17–19, 23 Here is a vivid list of incongruities, things that should normally never be together.

19 *Is* the man *who* deceives his neighbor,
And says, [a]"I was only joking!"

20 Where *there is* no wood, the fire goes out;
And where *there is* no [1]talebearer, strife ceases.
21 [a]*As* charcoal *is* to burning coals, and wood to fire,
So *is* a contentious man to kindle strife.
22 The words of a [1]talebearer *are* like [2]tasty trifles,
And they go down into the [3]inmost body.

23 Fervent lips with a wicked heart
Are like earthenware covered with silver dross.

24 He who hates, disguises *it* with his lips,
And lays up deceit within himself;
25 [a]When [1]he speaks kindly, do not believe him,
For *there are* seven abominations in his heart;
26 *Though his* hatred is covered by deceit,
His wickedness will be revealed before the assembly.

27 [a]Whoever digs a pit will fall into it,
And he who *rolls a stone will have it roll back on him.

28 A lying tongue hates *those who are* crushed by it,
And a flattering mouth works [a]ruin.

27 Do[a] not boast about tomorrow,
For you do not know what a day may bring forth.

2 [a]Let another man *praise you, and not your own mouth;
A stranger, and not your own lips.

3 A stone *is* heavy and sand *is* weighty,
But a fool's wrath *is* heavier than both of them.

4 Wrath *is* cruel and anger a torrent,
But [a]who *is* able to stand before jealousy?

5 [a]Open rebuke *is* better
Than love carefully concealed.

6 Faithful *are* the wounds of a friend,
But the kisses of an enemy *are* [a]deceitful.

7 A satisfied soul [1]loathes the honeycomb,
But to a hungry soul every bitter thing *is* sweet.

8 Like a bird that wanders from its nest
Is a man who wanders from his place.

9 Ointment and perfume delight the heart,
And the sweetness of a man's friend *gives delight* by [1]hearty *counsel.

10 Do not forsake your own friend or your father's friend,
Nor go to your brother's house in the day of your calamity;
[a]Better *is* a neighbor nearby than a brother far away.

11 My son, be wise, and make my heart glad,
[a]That I may answer him who reproaches me.

12 A prudent *man* foresees evil *and* hides himself;
The simple pass on *and* are [a]punished.

13 Take the garment of him who is surety for a stranger,
And hold it in pledge *when* he is surety for a seductress.

14 He who blesses his friend with a loud voice, rising early in the morning,
It will be counted a curse to him.

15 A [a]continual dripping on a very rainy day
And a contentious woman are alike;

19 [a]Eph. 5:4 **20** [1]*gossip* or *slanderer*, lit. *whisperer* **21** [a]Prov. 15:18 **22** [1]*gossip* or *slanderer* [2]A Jewish tradition *wounds* [3]Lit. *rooms of the belly* **25** [a]Ps. 28:3; Prov. 26:23; Jer. 9:8 [1]Lit. *his voice is gracious* **27** [a]Esth. 7:10; Ps. 7:15; Prov. 28:10; Eccl. 10:8 *See WW at Prov. 16:3. **28** [a]Prov. 29:5

CHAPTER 27

1 [a]Luke 12:19–21; James 4:13–16 **2** [a]Prov. 25:27; 2 Cor. 10:12, 18; 12:11 *See WW at 1 Chr. 23:30. **4** [a]Prov. 6:34; 1 John 3:12 **5** [a][Prov. 28:23]; Gal. 2:14 **6** [a]Matt. 26:49 **7** [1]*tramples on* **9** [1]Lit. *counsel of the soul* *See WW at Zech. 6:13. **10** [a]Prov. 17:17; 18:24 **11** [a]Prov. 10:1; 23:15–26 **12** [a]Prov. 22:3 **15** [a]Prov. 19:13

27:1—29:27 Stylistic note: These three chapters collect some of the strongest, most penetrating thoughts of the book, and with little repetition of previous material. They are not sorted or organized by subject; each idea stands complete, jewel-like, on its own.

27:6 Tough love is better than flattering hypocrisy.

27:12 We would say, "Discretion is the better part of valor."

16 Whoever [1]restrains her restrains
the wind,
And grasps oil with his right
hand.

17 *As* iron sharpens iron,
So a man sharpens the
countenance of his friend.

18 [a]Whoever [1]keeps the fig tree will
eat its fruit;
So he who waits on his master
will be honored.

19 As in water face *reflects* face,
So a man's heart *reveals* the man.

20 [a]Hell[1] and [2]Destruction are never
full;
So [b]the eyes of man are never
satisfied.

21 [a]The refining pot *is* for silver and
the furnace for gold,
And a man *is valued* by what
others say of him.

22 [a]Though you grind a fool in a
mortar with a pestle along with
crushed grain,
Yet his foolishness will not
depart from him.

23 Be diligent to know the state of
your [a]flocks,
And attend to your herds;
24 For riches *are* not forever,
Nor does a crown *endure* to all
*generations.
25 [a]*When* the hay is removed, and the
tender grass shows itself,
And the herbs of the mountains
are gathered in,
26 The lambs *will provide* your
clothing,
And the goats the price of a field;
27 *You shall have* *enough goats'
milk for your food,
For the food of your household,
And the nourishment of your
maidservants.

28

The [a]wicked flee when no one
pursues,
But the righteous are bold as a
lion.

2 Because of the transgression of a
land, many *are* its princes;
But by a man of understanding
and knowledge
Right will be prolonged.

3 [a]A poor man who oppresses the
poor
Is like a driving rain [1]which
leaves no food.

4 [a]Those who forsake the law praise
the wicked,
[b]But such as keep the law contend
with them.

5 [a]Evil men do not understand
justice,
But [b]those who seek the LORD
understand all.

6 Better *is* the poor who walks in
his integrity
Than one perverse *in his* ways,
though he *be* rich.

7 Whoever keeps the law *is* a
discerning son,
But a companion of gluttons
shames his father.

8 One who increases his
possessions by usury and
extortion
Gathers it for him who will pity
the poor.

9 One who turns away his ear from
hearing the law,
[a]Even his prayer *is* an
abomination.

10 [a]Whoever causes the upright to go
astray in an evil way,
He himself will fall into his own
pit;
[b]But the blameless will inherit
good.

11 The rich man *is* wise in his own
eyes,
But the poor who has
understanding searches him
out.

12 When the righteous rejoice, *there
is* great [a]glory;
But when the wicked arise, men
[1]hide themselves.

16 [1]Lit. *hides*
18 [a]2 Kin. 18:31; Song 8:12; Is. 36:16; [1 Cor. 3:8; 9:7–13]; 2 Tim. 2:6 [1]*protects* or *tends*
20 [a]Prov. 30:15, 16; Hab. 2:5 [b]Eccl. 1:8; 4:8 [1]Or *Sheol* [2]Heb. *Abaddon*
21 [a]Prov. 17:3
22 [a]Prov. 23:35; 26:11; Jer. 5:3
23 [a]Prov. 24:27
24 *See WW at Esth. 9:28.
25 [a]Ps. 104:14
27 *See WW at Mal. 3:10.

CHAPTER 28

1 [a]Lev. 26:17, 36; Ps. 53:5
3 [a]Matt. 18:28 [1]Lit. *and there is no bread*
4 [a]Ps. 49:18; Rom. 1:32 [b]1 Kin. 18:18; Neh. 13:11, 15; Matt. 3:7; 14:4; Eph. 5:11
5 [a]Ps. 92:6; Is. 6:9; 44:18 [b]Ps. 119:100; Prov. 2:9; John 17:17; 1 Cor. 2:15; [1 John 2:20, 27]
9 [a]Ps. 66:18; 109:7; Prov. 15:8
10 [a]Ps. 7:15; Prov. 26:27 [b][Matt. 6:33; Heb. 6:12; 1 Pet. 3:9]
12 [a]Prov. 11:10; 29:2 [1]Lit. *will be searched for*

27:21 You are genuine if you can survive the comments of acquaintances.
27:22 Solomon's pessimism considers foolishness almost indestructible.
27:23–27 A rare (for this section) multi-verse essay praises the wisdom of planning ahead.
28:8 Gathers it for him: This echoes the truth of 13:22, that in God's long accounts the world's resources end up in the hands of the righteous.

13 [a]He who covers his sins will not
prosper,
But whoever confesses and
forsakes *them* will have mercy.

14 Happy *is* the man who is always
*reverent,
But he who hardens his heart will
fall into calamity.

15 [a]*Like* a roaring lion and a charging
bear
[b]*Is* a wicked ruler over poor
people.

16 A ruler who lacks understanding
is a great [a]oppressor,
But he who hates covetousness
will prolong *his* days.

17 [a]A man burdened with bloodshed
will flee into a pit;
Let no one help him.

18 Whoever walks blamelessly will
be [1]saved,
But *he who is* perverse *in his* ways
will suddenly fall.

19 [a]He who tills his land will have
plenty of bread,
But he who follows frivolity will
have poverty enough!

20 A **faithful** man will abound with
blessings,
[a]But he who hastens to be rich will
not go unpunished.

WORD WEALTH

28:20 faithful, *'emunah* (eh-moo-*nah*); Strong's #530: Firmness, stability, faithfulness, fidelity, conscientiousness, steadiness, certainty; that which is permanent, enduring, steadfast. *'Emunah* comes from the root *'aman,* "to be firm, sure, established, and steady." "Amen," derived from this same root, means, "It is firmly, truly so!" *'Emunah* occurs 49 times. It is often translated "faithfulness" or "truth," as truth is considered something ultimately certain, stable, and unchangingly fixed. This word appears in Hab. 2:4, the great verse so influential to NT thought and Reformation history: "The just shall live by his *'emunah,*" that is, his firmness, steadiness, and solid belief.

13 [a]Ps. 32:3–5; 1 John 1:8–10 **14** *See WW at Hos. 3:5. **15** [a]Prov. 19:12; 1 Pet. 5:8 [b]Ex. 1:14; Prov. 29:2; Matt. 2:16 **16** [a]Eccl. 10:16; Is. 3:12 **17** [a]Gen. 9:6 **18** [1]*delivered* **19** [a]Prov. 12:11; 20:13 **20** [a]Prov. 13:11; 20:21; 23:4; 1 Tim. 6:9

21 [a]Prov. 18:5 [b]Ezek. 13:19 [1]Lit. *recognize faces* **22** [a]Prov. 21:5 **23** [a]Prov. 27:5, 6 **24** [a]Prov. 18:9 *See WW at Ps. 119:63. **25** [a]Prov. 13:10 [b]Prov. 29:25; 1 Tim. 6:6 **26** [a]Prov. 3:5 **27** [a]Deut. 15:7; Prov. 19:17; 22:9 **28** [a]Job 24:4

CHAPTER 29

1 [a]2 Chr. 36:16; Prov. 6:15 *See WW at Mal. 4:2. **2** [a]Esth. 8:15; Prov. 28:12 [b]Esth. 4:3 [1]*become great*

21 [a]To [1]show partiality *is* not good,
[b]Because for a piece of bread a
man will transgress.

22 A man with an evil eye hastens
after riches,
And does not consider that
[a]poverty will come upon him.

23 [a]He who rebukes a man will find
more favor afterward
Than he who flatters with the
tongue.

24 Whoever robs his father or his
mother,
And says, "*It is* no
transgression,"
The same [a]*is* *companion to a
destroyer.

25 [a]He who is of a proud heart stirs
up strife,
[b]But he who trusts in the LORD will
be prospered.

26 He who [a]trusts in his own heart
is a fool,
But whoever walks wisely will be
delivered.

27 [a]He who gives to the poor will not
lack,
But he who hides his eyes will
have many curses.

28 When the wicked arise, [a]men
hide themselves;
But when they perish, the
righteous increase.

29 He[a] who is often rebuked, *and*
hardens *his* neck,
Will suddenly be destroyed, and
that without *remedy.

2 When the righteous [1]are in
authority, the [a]people rejoice;
But when a wicked *man* rules,
[b]the people groan.

3 Whoever loves wisdom makes his
father rejoice,
But a companion of harlots
wastes *his* wealth.

4 The king establishes the land by
justice,
But he who receives bribes
overthrows it.

28:13 Will have mercy (that is, receive mercy): Confession will prompt mercy from mankind as well as from God.
28:23 More favor afterward: Honesty, though painful, wins the long-term reward.
28:28 The righteous may have to cycle between quiescence and activity, but his persistence brings success.

5 A man who [a]flatters his neighbor
Spreads a net for his feet.

6 By transgression an evil man is snared,
But the righteous sings and rejoices.

7 The righteous [a]considers the cause of the poor,
But the wicked does not understand *such* knowledge.

8 Scoffers [a]set a city aflame,
But wise *men* turn away wrath.

9 *If* a wise man contends with a foolish man,
[a]Whether *the fool* rages or *laughs, *there is* no peace.

10 [a]The bloodthirsty hate the blameless,
But the upright seek his [1]well-being.

11 A fool vents all his [a]feelings,[1]
But a wise *man* *holds them back.

12 If a ruler pays attention to lies,
All his servants *become* wicked.

13 The poor *man* and the oppressor have this in common:
[a]The LORD gives light to the eyes of both.

14 The king who judges the [a]poor with truth,
His throne will be established *forever.

15 The rod and rebuke give [a]wisdom,
But a child left *to himself* brings shame to his mother.

16 When the wicked are multiplied, transgression increases;
But the righteous will see their [a]fall.

17 *Correct your son, and he will *give you rest;
Yes, he will give delight to your soul.

18 [a]Where *there is* no [1]revelation, the people cast off restraint;
But [b]happy *is* he who keeps the law.

19 A servant will not be *corrected by mere words;
For though he understands, he will not respond.

20 Do you see a man hasty in his words?
[a]*There is* more *hope for a fool than for him.

21 He who pampers his servant from childhood
Will have him as a son in the end.

22 [a]An angry man stirs up strife,
And a furious man abounds in transgression.

23 [a]A man's pride will *bring him low,
But the humble in spirit will retain honor.

24 Whoever is a partner with a thief hates his own life;
[a]He [1]swears to tell the truth, but reveals nothing.

25 [a]The fear of man brings a snare,
But whoever trusts in the LORD shall be [1]safe.

26 [a]Many seek the ruler's [1]favor,
But justice for man *comes* from the LORD.

27 An unjust man *is* an abomination to the righteous,
And *he who is* upright in the way *is* an abomination to the wicked.

The Wisdom of Agur

30 The words of Agur the son of Jakeh, *his* utterance. This man declared to Ithiel—to Ithiel and Ucal:

5 [a]Prov. 26:28 **7** [a]Job 29:16; Ps. 41:1; Prov. 31:8, 9 **8** [a]Prov. 11:11 **9** [a]Matt. 11:17 *See WW at Eccl. 3:4. **10** [a]Gen. 4:5–8; 1 John 3:12 [1]Lit. *soul* or *life* **11** [a]Prov. 14:33 [1]Lit. *spirit* *See WW at Ps. 63:3. **13** [a][Matt. 5:45] **14** [a]Ps. 72:4; Is. 11:4 *See WW at Mic. 4:5. **15** [a]Prov. 22:15 **16** [a]Ps. 37:34; Prov. 21:12 **17** *See WW at Jer. 10:24. • See WW at Ex. 33:14.

18 [a]1 Sam. 3:1; Ps. 74:9; Amos 8:11, 12 [b]Prov. 8:32; John 13:17 [1]*prophetic vision* **19** *See WW at Jer. 10:24. **20** [a]Prov. 26:12 *See WW at Hos. 2:15. **22** [a]Prov. 26:21 **23** [a]Job 22:29; Prov. 15:33; 18:12; Is. 66:2; Dan. 4:30; Matt. 23:12; Luke 14:11; 18:14; Acts 12:23; [James 4:6–10; 1 Pet. 5:5, 6] *See WW at Jer. 13:18. **24** [a]Lev. 5:1 [1]Lit. *hears the adjuration* or *oath* **25** [a]Gen. 12:12; 20:2; Luke 12:4; John 12:42, 43 [1]*secure,* lit. *set on high* **26** [a]Ps. 20:9 [1]Lit. *face*

29:18 See WW at 2 Chr. 32:32.
29:21 Will have him as a son: Solomon unwittingly predicts the succession of his servant Jeroboam to the throne, usurping (though in God's plan) the place of a son.
29:26 In what are almost his final words in the book, Solomon acknowledges as a ruler that his fairness in judgment is from God, the boon he had sought at the beginning of his reign (1 Kin. 3:9).
29:27 Each kind of person appreciates only those like himself.
30:1–33 Authorship note: Agur's identity is unknown; but his style, often different from (and not repetitive of) the rest of the book, carries equal truth with power and vivid images. His comments are not those of a philosopher shut away, but of a keen eye and a perceptive mind, interpreting his first-hand observations of nature and humankind.

2 [a]Surely I *am* more stupid than *any* man,
And do not have the understanding of a man.
3 I neither learned wisdom
Nor have [a]knowledge of the Holy One.

4 [a]Who has ascended into heaven, or descended?
[b]Who has gathered the wind in His fists?
Who has bound the waters in a garment?
Who has established all the ends of the earth?
What *is* His name, and what *is* His Son's name,
If you know?

5 [a]Every *word of God *is* [1]pure;
[b]He *is* a shield to those who put their *trust in Him.
6 [a]Do not add to His words,
Lest He rebuke you, and you be found a liar.

KINGDOM DYNAMICS

30:5, 6 The Content of God's Word Is Completed, THE WORD OF GOD. The word "canon" is the term used to describe the completed number of the books of the Bible—the closed canon of the 66 books of the Holy Scriptures. It is derived from ancient words meaning "measuring stick," and is applied here to designate those books that meet the requirements of being acknowledged as divinely inspired.

The Bible warns against either adding to or subtracting from its contents. Rev. 22:18 makes a conclusive statement, positional in God's providence and wisdom, at the Bible's end. While it refers directly to the Book of Revelation, most Bible scholars also provide a finalizing footnote on this subject: "Add to or subtract from the Bible at your own risk." (A classic study of the judgment for "taking away" from God's Word is seen in Jer. 36:20–32.)

In this regard, we are wise to understand terms. When we refer to the "revelation of the Scriptures," it is important that we distinguish this consummate order of divine revelation from any other use of the term, however sacred. There are many today who do not know the difference between a "revelation" (an insight or an idea that may be of God, of man, or of the Devil) and the revelation of God, which is in the closed canon of the Scriptures.

Because there are many books that claim to be divinely given, a casual or gullible attitude toward them can result in confusion and eventual destruction. It is interesting to note that even in Jesus' time, several books held by some today to be intended for the OT were in existence then. Yet, in the 64 times Jesus quotes from the OT, not once does He quote from any of those books. The Bible is complete, completely trustworthy, and sufficient to completely answer anything we need to know for eternal salvation or practical wisdom concerning our relationships, morality, character, or conduct. (Ps. 19:7/Luke 16:17) J.W.H.

CHAPTER 30

2 [a]Ps. 73:22; Prov. 12:1
3 [a][Prov. 9:10]
4 [a][Ps. 68:18; John 3:13] [b]Job 38:4; Ps. 104:3; Is. 40:12
5 [a]Ps. 12:6; 19:8; 119:140 [b]Ps. 18:30; 84:11; 115:9–11 [1]*tested, refined, found pure* *See WW at 2 Sam. 22:31. • See WW at Zeph. 3:12.
6 [a]Deut. 4:2; 12:32; Rev. 22:18
8 [a]Job 23:12; Matt. 6:11; [Phil. 4:19]
9 [a]Deut. 8:12–14; Neh. 9:25, 26; Hos. 13:6
10 *See WW at Mic. 4:13. • See WW at Lev. 4:13.
11 [a]Ex. 21:17; Prov. 20:20
12 [a][Prov. 16:2]; Is. 65:5; Luke 18:11; [Titus 1:15, 16]
13 [a]Ps. 131:1; Prov. 6:17; Is. 2:11; 5:15 [1]*In arrogance*
14 [a]Job 29:17; Ps. 52:2 [b]Ps. 14:4; Amos 8:4

7 Two *things* I request of You
(Deprive me not before I die):
8 Remove falsehood and lies far from me;
Give me neither poverty nor riches—
[a]Feed me with the food allotted to me;
9 [a]Lest I be full and deny *You,*
And say, "Who *is* the LORD?"
Or lest I be poor and steal,
And profane the name of my God.

10 Do not malign a servant to his *master,
Lest he curse you, and you be found *guilty.

11 *There is* a generation *that* curses its [a]father,
And does not bless its mother.
12 *There is* a generation [a]*that is* pure in its own eyes,
Yet is not washed from its filthiness.
13 *There is* a generation—oh, how [a]lofty are their eyes!
And their eyelids are [1]lifted up.
14 [a]*There is* a generation whose teeth *are like* swords,
And whose fangs *are like* knives,
[b]To devour the poor from off the earth,
And the needy from *among* men.

15 The leech has two daughters—
Give *and* Give!

There are three *things that* are never satisfied,

Agur loves balance and also lists of things that lead to climax. As elsewhere in the book, the **three . . . four** (vv. 15, 18, 21, 29) is a rhetorical means of indicating that the lists are not intended to be exhaustive of their respective subjects. His lists are: 1) the insatiable (vv. 15, 16); 2) the mysterious (vv. 18, 19); 3) the insufferable (vv. 21–23); 4) the weak but wise (vv. 24–28); 5) the majestic (vv. 29–31).
30:8, 9 This prayer of a pious man alerts us to certain realities that can easily tempt us away from God. **The food alloted to me** refers to daily needs (see Matt. 6:11).

Four never say, "Enough!":
16 [a]The[1] *grave,
The barren womb,
The earth *that* is not satisfied with water—
And the fire never says, "Enough!"

17 [a]The eye *that* mocks *his* father,
And scorns obedience to *his* mother,
The ravens of the valley will pick it out,
And the young eagles will eat it.

18 There are three *things which* are too *wonderful for me,
Yes, four *which* I do not understand:
19 The way of an eagle in the air,
The way of a serpent on a rock,
The way of a ship in the [1]midst of the sea,
And the way of a man with a virgin.

20 This *is* the way of an adulterous woman:
She eats and wipes her mouth,
And says, "I have done no wickedness."

21 For three *things* the earth is perturbed,
Yes, for four it cannot bear up:
22 [a]For a servant when he reigns,
A fool when he is filled with food,
23 A [1]hateful *woman* when she is married,
And a maidservant who succeeds her mistress.

24 There are four *things which* are little on the earth,
But they *are* exceedingly wise:
25 [a]The ants *are* a people not strong,
Yet they prepare their food in the summer;
26 [a]The [1]rock badgers are a feeble folk,
Yet they make their homes in the crags;
27 The locusts have no king,
Yet they all advance in ranks;
28 The [1]spider skillfully grasps with its hands,
And it is in kings' palaces.

29 There are three *things which* are majestic in pace,
Yes, four *which* are stately in walk:
30 A lion, *which is* mighty among beasts
And does not turn away from any;
31 A [1]greyhound,
A male goat also,
And [2]a king *whose* troops *are* with him.

32 If you have been foolish in exalting yourself,
Or if you have devised evil,
[a]*put your* hand on *your* mouth.
33 For *as* the churning of milk produces butter,
And wringing the nose produces blood,
So the forcing of wrath produces strife.

The Words of King Lemuel's Mother

31 The words of King Lemuel, the utterance which his mother taught him:

2 What, my son?
And what, son of my womb?
And what, [a]son of my vows?
3 [a]Do not give your *strength to women,
Nor your ways [b]to that which destroys kings.

16 [a]Prov. 27:20; Hab. 2:5 [1]Or *Sheol* *See WW at Hos. 13:14. **17** [a]Gen. 9:22; Lev. 20:9; Prov. 20:20 **18** *See WW at Judg. 13:19. **19** [1]Lit. *heart* **22** [a]Prov. 19:10; Eccl. 10:7 **23** [1]Or *hated* **25** [a]Prov. 6:6

26 [a]Lev. 11:5; Ps. 104:18 [1]*rock hyraxes* **28** [1]Or *lizard* **31** [1]Or perhaps *strutting rooster,* lit. *girded of waist* [2]A Jewish tradition *a king against whom there is no uprising* **32** [a]Job 21:5; 40:4; Mic. 7:16

CHAPTER 31

2 [a]Is. 49:15 **3** [a]Prov. 5:9 [b]Deut. 17:17; 1 Kin. 11:1; Neh. 13:26; Prov. 7:26; Hos. 4:11 *See WW at Zech. 4:6.

30:24–28 Ants . . . rock badgers . . . locusts . . . spider: The identified characteristics of these creatures summarize the teaching of the entire book. The ants demonstrate foresight; the rock badgers, security; the locusts, cooperation with others; the spider, usefulness (in eliminating less desirable insects). The alternate reading for spider, "lizard," would be even stronger, as lizards are recognized even today in many cultures to be useful inhabitants of the home (or the palace) because they keep other vermin away. The wise person has all these same qualities.

30:33 A high level of anger will quite predictably result in conflict—by words or violence.

31:1–31 Authorship note: As with Agur, we do not know the identity of **King Lemuel.** He does not appear among the kings of Judah or Israel. His place in the book is earned, not by position, king or not (there were many in surrounding kingdoms), but by the self-evident wisdom of his observations. Yet he is perhaps only a secondary author, as his words were what **his mother taught him.**

31:2–9 The threefold warning against womanizing (v. 3), drinking (vv. 4–7), and injustice (vv. 8, 9) is specifically for a ruler, not just for the general population (see v. 4). For example, Lemuel has been exhorted not merely to abstain from oppressing the poor and needy and condemned, but to speak up on their behalf.

The broad concept is that one in authority must measure to higher standards than the mere average, a principle Solomon violated flamboyantly by his collection of horses, wives, and gold. Whether Lemuel and his mother knew the God of Israel or not, they were in tune with His will for kingly restraint. Solomon has quoted his father (4:4); Lemuel quotes his mother (31:1). Wisdom is not sexist.

4 [a]*It is* not for kings, O Lemuel,
It is not for kings to drink wine,
Nor for princes intoxicating drink;
5 [a]Lest they drink and forget the law,
And pervert the justice of all [1]the afflicted.
6 [a]Give strong drink to him who is perishing,
And wine to those who are bitter of heart.
7 Let him drink and forget his poverty,
And remember his *misery no more.

8 [a]Open your mouth for the speechless,
In the cause of all *who are* [1]appointed to die.
9 Open your mouth, [a]judge righteously,
And [b]plead the cause of the poor and *needy.

The Virtuous Wife

10 [a]Who[1] can find a [2]virtuous wife?
For her worth *is* far above rubies.
11 The heart of her *husband safely trusts her;
So he will have no lack of gain.
12 She does him good and not evil
All the days of her life.
13 She seeks wool and flax,
And willingly works with her hands.
14 She is like the merchant ships,
She brings her food from afar.
15 [a]She also rises while it is yet night,
And [b]provides food for her household,
And a portion for her maidservants.
16 She considers a field and buys it;
From [1]her profits she plants a vineyard.
17 She girds herself with strength,
And strengthens her arms.
18 She *perceives that her merchandise *is* good,
And her lamp does not go out by night.

4 [a]Eccl. 10:17
5 [a]Hos. 4:11 [1]Lit. *sons of affliction*
6 [a]Ps. 104:15
7 *See WW at Job 5:7.
8 [a]Job 29:15, 16; Ps. 82 [1]Lit. *sons of passing away*
9 [a]Lev. 19:15; Deut. 1:16 [b]Job 29:12; Is. 1:17; Jer. 22:16 *See WW at Ps. 70:5.
10 [a]Ruth 3:11; Prov. 12:4; 19:14 [1]Vv. 10–31 are an alphabetic acrostic in Hebrew; cf. Ps. 119 [2]Lit. *a wife of valor,* in the sense of all forms of excellence
11 *See WW at Hos. 2:8.
15 [a]Prov. 20:13; Rom. 12:11 [b]Luke 12:42
16 [1]Lit. *the fruit of her hands*
18 *See WW at Ps. 34:8.
20 [a]Deut. 15:11; Job 31:16–20; Prov. 22:9; Rom. 12:13; Eph. 4:28; Heb. 13:16 *See WW at Ps. 40:17.
23 [a]Prov. 12:4
25 *See WW at Ps. 8:5.

19 She stretches out her hands to the distaff,
And her hand holds the spindle.
20 [a]She extends her hand to the *poor,
Yes, she reaches out her hands to the needy.
21 She is not afraid of snow for her household,
For all her household *is* clothed with scarlet.
22 She makes tapestry for herself;
Her clothing *is* fine linen and purple.
23 [a]Her husband is known in the gates,
When he sits among the elders of the land.
24 She makes linen garments and sells *them,*
And supplies sashes for the merchants.
25 Strength and *honor *are* her clothing;
She shall rejoice in time to come.
26 She opens her mouth with wisdom,
And on her tongue *is* the law of kindness.
27 She watches over the ways of her household,
And does not eat the bread of idleness.
28 Her children rise up and call her **blessed;**
Her husband *also,* and he praises her:

WORD WEALTH

31:28 blessed, *'ashar* (ah-*shar*); Strong's #833: Happy, blessed, prosperous, successful, straight, right, contented. Its original meaning is "be straight." Note the use of the word in Gen. 30:13; Leah gave birth to a son and said, "I am happy, for the daughters will call me blessed." She named this son "Asher" (from *'ashar*), meaning "Happy One." Both the Messiah and the nation of Israel will be called "blessed" (*'ashar*) by the whole world: "*Men* shall be blessed in Him; all nations shall call Him blessed" (Ps. 72:17). "And all nations will call you blessed, for you will be a delightful land" (Mal. 3:12).

31:10–31 That the description of the virtuous woman is a continuation of the thoughts of Lemuel's mother is much more likely than that it is about or by Bathsheba, Solomon's own mother. Neither Solomon nor Bathsheba would have been likely to write v. 11, after the foul murder of her first husband, Uriah (2 Sam. 11:15).

Devotional note: The high standard for womanhood, apparently drawn not by some romantic male, but by one who was herself a virtuous woman, presents an inspiring goal. The cultural details of her specific tasks are different in our era, but the principles are timeless.

Stylistic note: Vv. 10–31 (22 verses) are in the form of an acrostic poem, each verse beginning with a different character from the 22 letters of the Hebrew alphabet. Together they make up an artistic paean of praise for the ideal married woman.

29 "Many daughters have done well,
But you excel them all."
30 Charm *is* deceitful and *beauty *is* passing,
But a woman *who* fears the LORD, she shall be praised.
31 Give her of the fruit of her hands,
And let her own works praise her in the gates.

30 *See WW at Ezek. 28:12.

TRUTH-IN-ACTION through PROVERBS

Letting the LIFE of the Holy Spirit Bring Faith's Works Alive in You!

EDITOR'S NOTE: Most books in the Bible are historical narrative, didactic discourse, apocalyptic prose, or poetic prayers or reflections. The Book of Proverbs, on the other hand, is largely loosely related aphorisms, each calling for meditation and requiring faithful application. One can understand most often how to put each into action with minimal reflection. In the following, we describe the five most dominant themes of the wisdom of Prov. Next we present a digest of the most often repeated imperatives of the book. The selected texts are just a small sampling of the wealth of wisdom you will find in these chapters.

Truth Proverbs Teaches	Text	**Action** Proverbs Invites
1 Attaining Wisdom and Gaining Understanding "Wisdom *is* the principal thing; *Therefore* get wisdom. And in all your getting, get understanding" (4:7) exhorts Solomon. Wisdom is knowing the truth and how to apply it to any given situation; understanding is knowledge seasoned and modified by wisdom and insight. The words "wisdom" or "wise" and "understanding" occur over 140 times in Prov.	4:5–9	**Prioritize** wisdom. **Seek after** and **cherish** understanding. **Accept** that knowledge without wisdom and understanding is futile.
	9:10	**Pursue** the fear of the Lord, reproofs, instruction, advice and humility. **Know** that from these come wisdom and understanding.
	2:1–6	**Apply** your heart, **pay attention** and **turn** your ear to wisdom and understanding. **Understand** that you must embrace them both, not just know about them.
	3:13–18, 21–26; 8:12–21	**Embrace** wisdom and **follow after** understanding. **Know** that patience, discernment, favor, prosperity, safety, and other benefits will result.
2 Acquiring Knowledge The knowledge of Prov. consists of more than information, facts, and sense data. It is knowledge that begins with the fear of the Lord and is therefore godly knowledge that always includes Him as the primary factor. Because of its divine source, it comes with understanding implicit in it.	2:4–6; 24:13, 14	**Seek out** knowledge. **Cherish** it as a valued possession when you have found it.
	3:5, 6; 22:17–21	**Study** God's Word and **listen** to the Holy Spirit. **Believe** God's prophets. **Understand** that these are the true sources of godly knowledge.
	14:3; 15:23; 20:15	**Be prudent** in how you give out knowledge. **Do not stray** from the words of knowledge. **Share** your knowledge with restraint, and do not let it become a source of pride.
3 Loving Instruction and Heeding Reproof Discipline involves both instruction and exercise designed to train in	9:7–9; 17:10	**Embrace** the discipline of instruction and heed reproofs gladly. **Realize** that man is inclined to turn away from both.

Truth Proverbs Teaches	Text	**Action** Proverbs Invites
3 proper conduct or action. Punishment may also be inflicted as a means of correction.	10:8; 13:18	**Follow** instruction diligently. **Accept** the correction of reproof. **Value** their lessons. **Seek** after both instruction and reproof.
4 **The Wise vs. the Fool** Prov. presents two categories of people: the wise or prudent and the fool, scoffer, or mocker. The former seeks wisdom and loves instruction; the latter neglects discipline and spurns reproof. Also, each can be characterized by his response to parental and other authority, the former bringing joy and delight, the latter bringing shame, disgrace, and sadness. Prov. exhorts its reader to become wise and despise the foolish and his folly.	10:14; 16:24; 17:27, 28 6:6–11 3:9, 27, 28; 10:4, 5; 17:18; 23:1–3, 19–21, 26–28, 29–35	**Be careful** in what you say. **Measure** every word. **Do not speak** unless it is important that you do so. **Speak** only in order to build up and strengthen. **Be diligent** in all your work. **Avoid** any form of laziness. **Serve** those to whom your lot assigns you with gladness. **Seek** to please those under or for whom you work. **Be frugal** in your handling of money. **Practice** good stewardship. **Avoid being** either a spendthrift or a miser. **Learn** the proper investment of time and substance. **Do not consume** unnecessarily. **Use, do not abuse** the things God gives you. **Avoid** drunkenness, excessiveness, and immoral sexual conduct.
5 **The Proper Discipline of Children** Perhaps biblical wisdom most significantly challenges our modern philosophies and practices of child-rearing.	22:6 13:24; 19:18	**Train** children to honor authority, obey, and follow instruction. **Discourage** rebellion, stubbornness, and disobedience. **Practice** consistent discipline and corporal correction in rearing children. **Recognize** that children are trained to obedience by these.

The Book of ECCLESIASTES

Author: Traditionally Solomon, but May Be the Work of a Teacher Who Calls Himself *Qoheleth,* Otherwise Unknown to Us

Date: Traditionally, Near Solomon's Death (About 931 B.C.), Though Many Consider It Much Later

Theme: A Quest for Something of True Value in This Life

Key Words: Profit, Vanity, Under the Sun, Grasping After Wind

Author and Date The name *Ecclesiastes* is derived from the Greek word *ekklesia* ("assembly") and means "One Who Addresses an Assembly." The Hebrew word so represented is *qoheleth,* which means "One Who Convenes an Assembly," thus often being rendered "Teacher" or "Preacher" in English versions.

Ecclesiastes is generally credited to Solomon (about 971 to 931 B.C.), written in his old age. The rather pessimistic tone that pervades the book would be in keeping with Solomon's spiritual state at the time (see 1 Kin. 11). Although not mentioned in 1 Kings, Solomon must have come to his senses before his death, repented, and turned back to God. Ecclesiastes 1:1, "The words of the Preacher, the son of David, king in Jerusalem," seems to point to Solomon. Scattered throughout the book are allusions to Solomon's wisdom (1:16), wealth (2:8), servants (2:7), pleasures (2:3), and building activities (2:4–6).

Because of the problems posed by an apostate Solomon writing Holy Scripture and because some of the language in Ecclesiastes belongs to a period much later in Israel's history, some scholars believe the book may have had its origin in the time of Ezra (about 450 B.C.).

Background The book evinces a time when traditional solutions to life's great questions, particularly the meaning of life, have lost their relevance for the author. Rather than respond to such questions with citations from Scripture, the Preacher introduces a methodology that is predicated on observation and induction. Wisdom, when found in the other wisdom literature of the Bible (Job, Proverbs, and certain psalms), is a synonym for virtue and piety; its antithesis, folly, thus becomes "wickedness." In the Book of Ecclesiastes, the word "wisdom" is sometimes used in this manner when dealing with the conventional Israelite interpretation of wisdom (as in 7:1—8:9; 10:1—11:6). But in the opening chapter (1:12–18) the author deals with wisdom that is a process of pure thought, more like Greek philosophy, the enduring worth of which he questions. While never disputing the existence of God who has given meaning to His creation, the Preacher nevertheless determines to seek out that meaning through his own experience and observation so that he may personally verify it and pass it down to his disciples.

Content The Book of Ecclesiastes gives every evidence of being a carefully composed literary essay that must be grasped as a totality before it can be understood in part. The content of the book is defined by nearly identical verses (1:2; 12:8), which circumscribe the book by anticipating and by summarizing the conclusions of the author. The theme is set forth in 1:3: "What profit has a man from all his labor in which he toils under the sun [that is, in this life]?" Or, can true wisdom be found by a human being apart from revelation from God?

The Preacher's quest is for some sort of fixed, unchanging value ("profit") that can be found in this life ("under the sun") that can serve as a basis for proper living. The Hebrew word translated "profit" is *yitron* (1:3), and may also be translated "gain, value." "Vanity" is a key word in the book, translating the Hebrew *hebel* (literally, "breath"), thus indicating what is mortal, transitory, and of no permanence. As he tries each of the avenues proposed by humanity to achieve the value being sought, he finds them elusive ("grasping for the wind") and fleeting, transitory ("vanity").

The "wisdom" of 1:12–18 is found bankrupt of real value. Neither is the answer to be found in pleasure, in wealth, in great accomplishments (2:1–11), in a doctrine of retribution (2:12–17), or in materialism (2:18–26).

If neither accomplishments nor things are *yitron*, what then should be one's attitude toward them, seeing they have no permanent value? The answer introduces the secondary theme of the book: one should enjoy both life and the things with which God has blessed him (3:11, 12; 5:18–20; 9:7–10), remembering that in the end God will judge him for the way this is done (11:7–10).

Even human life itself, in any secular, humanistic sense, cannot be the *yitron* the Preacher seeks. The interplay of death and life is also a subordinate theme for the book.

But returning to the Preacher's grand quest: is it destined to conclude (12:8), as it began (1:2), on a note of despair? The Preacher's constant probing of all existence for meaning shows him to be an optimist, not a pessimist, and his failure to discover any absolute, abiding value in this life ("under the sun") does not mean his quest is a failure. Instead, he finds himself compelled (by his observation that God placed order in the universe at the time of its creation, 3:1–14) to seek the value he seeks in the world to come (not "under the sun" but "above the sun," so to speak). Although he does not specifically state it as such, the logic that undergirds his entire quest compels him to find the only real *yitron* in the fear (reverence) and obedience of God (11:7—12:7). This is affirmed in the epilogue: reverence for God and keeping His commandments are the whole duty of mankind (12:13). This duty must be carried out in full knowledge that, while there is no real justice to be had in this life, God will eventually judge all that is and set it right (11:9; 12:14). On this profound note the book concludes.

Personal Application

Too often Christians in the modern church find themselves passive intellectually, accepting almost anything they are taught or simply challenging a doctrine on the basis of how it feels instead of looking to see whether it has a biblical foundation. The Preacher's challenge finds a parallel in the apostle Paul's words to the Ephesian Christians not to be "tossed to and fro and carried about with every wind of doctrine" (Eph. 4:14). With the privilege of interpreting the Scriptures for oneself, clearly established by Luther and the Reformers, comes the obligation to "search the Scriptures" (John 5:39) and see what they really say.

The determination of the Preacher to find what is of real value in this life should be a challenge for any true believer in Jesus Christ, "the way, the truth, and the life" (John 14:6). The Preacher's failure to find real value in earthly things and comfortable life-styles challenges the Christian who lives in this age of greed and materialism to concentrate on the things that are above (Col. 3:1) and not to glorify greed and possessions.

Christ Revealed

Although the Book of Ecclesiastes contains no direct or typological prophecies of Jesus Christ, it anticipates a number of teachings of Him who was the fulfillment of the Law and the Prophets (Matt. 5:17). While Jesus said little about wisdom, Paul had much to say about the wisdom given by God (Rom. 11:33) contrasted to the wisdom of this world with its human limitations (1 Cor. 1:17; 3:19; 2 Cor. 1:12).

In Matthew 6:19–21 Jesus warned against seeking wealth in this life, urging instead that it be sought in the next, a perspective that echoes the Preacher's indictment of materialism in 2:1–11, 18–26; 4:4–6; 5:8–14. The stress Jesus laid on heaven likewise mirrors the Preacher's despair of finding true value "under the sun" (in this life). The conclusion to which the Preacher is driven, that true value lies only in reverence and obedience to God (12:13), mirrors the teachings of Jesus that one's values should be first determined by a proper attitude toward God (Matt. 22:37, quoting Deut. 6:5) and then a proper attitude toward one's fellow human beings (Matt. 22:39, quoting Lev. 19:18).

The Holy Spirit at Work

All references to "spirit" in Ecclesiastes are to the life-force that animates the human or the animal (see 3:18–21). The book nevertheless anticipates some of the problems faced by the apostle Paul in the implementation of spiritual gifts in 1 Corinthians 12—14. People who believe that God speaks to them through the Holy Spirit in dreams and visions (Joel 2:28–32; Acts 2:17–21) would do well to heed the wise advice of the Preacher that not every dream is the voice of God (5:3). Paul seems to have a caution like this in mind for the revelatory gifts of tongues and prophecy in 1 Corinthians 14:29, when he advises an orderly manifestation followed by a judgment on the utterance by the assembly. Likewise, the Preacher's stress on reverence and obedience to God parallel Paul's concern for the edification of the church (1 Cor. 14:5). True spiritual gifts—genuine manifestations of miraculous utterance or deed—will be used in a spirit of reverence for the glory of God through Christ and for the edification of the believer.

Outline of Ecclesiastes

I. Prologue **1:1, 2**
- A. Identification of the book 1:1
- B. Summary of the Preacher's investigations 1:2

II. Statement of the problem **1:3–1[illegible]**
- A. Statement of the problem: Can true value be found in this life? 1:3
- B. Exposition of the problem: A refutation of humanistic solutions 1:4–11

III. Attempts at solutions to the problem **1:12—2:26**
- A. The refutation of pure reason: Human wisdom alone is useless 1:12–18
- B. The failure of hedonism: Pleasure in itself is meaningless 2:1–11
- C. The failure of retribution: The wise and the fool face a common end 2:12–17
- D. The failure of materialism 2:18–26

IV. Developing the theme **3:1—6:12**
- A. Uselessness in man's efforts to change the created order 3:1–15
- B. Uselessness in an equal end for unequal creatures 3:16–22
- C. Uselessness in an oppressed life 4:1–3
- D. Uselessness of envy 4:4–6
- E. Uselessness in being alone 4:7–12
- F. Uselessness in a hereditary monarchy 4:13–16
- G. Uselessness in pretense in formal religion 5:1–7
- H. Uselessness in materialistic values systems 5:8–14
- I. Uselessness in leaving products of one's labor behind at death
- J. Uselessness in the futility of a deprived life 20
- K. Uselessness in the determinism of nature 6.

V. Practical wisdom and its uses **7:1**
- A. Moralizing proverbs about life and death, good and evil 7:1
- B. Wisdom and its applications 7:11–
- C. Miscellaneous wise observations 7:23—8
- D. Wisdom in the king's court 8:2–

VI. A return to the theme **8:10—9:1[illegible]**
- A. Uselessness in the failure of retribution (again) 8:10—9:12
- B. Uselessness in the fickle nature of man (again) 9:13–18

VII. More on wisdom and its uses **10:1—11:6**

VIII. The only value is to fear God and obey Him **11:7—12:7**
- A. The first summary of the conclusions drawn 11:7–10
- B. The second summary: the allegory of old age and death 12:1–7

IX. Epilogue: confirmation of the conclusion **12:8–14**
- A. Summary of the Preacher's conclusions 12:8
- B. Summary of the Preacher's conclusions by a disciple 12:9–14

The Vanity of Life

THE words of the Preacher, the *son of David, [a]king in Jerusalem.

2 "Vanity[a][1] of vanities," says the Preacher;
"Vanity of vanities, [b]all *is* vanity."

3 [a]What profit has a man from all his *labor
In which he [1]toils under the sun?
4 *One* *generation passes away, and *another* generation comes;
[a]But the earth abides forever.
5 [a]The sun also rises, and the sun goes down,
And [1]hastens to the place where it arose.
6 [a]The wind goes toward the south,
And turns around to the north;
The wind whirls about continually,
And comes again on its circuit.
7 [a]All the rivers run into the sea,
Yet the sea *is* not full;
To the place from which the rivers come,
There they return again.
8 All things *are* [1]full of labor;
Man cannot express *it*.
[a]The eye is not *satisfied with seeing,
Nor the ear filled with hearing.

9 [a]That which has been *is* what will be,
That which *is* done is what will be done,
And *there is* nothing new under the sun.
4 10 Is there anything of which it may be said,
"See, this *is* new"?
It has already been in ancient times before us.

CHAPTER 1
1 [a]Prov. 1:1 *See WW at Gen. 29:32.
2 [a]Ps. 39:5, 6; 62:9; 144:4; Eccl. 12:8 [b][Rom. 8:20, 21] [1]Or *Absurdity, Frustration, Futility, Nonsense;* and so throughout the book
3 [a]Eccl. 2:22; 3:9 [1]*labors* *See WW at Job 5:7.
4 [a]Ps. 104:5; 119:90 *See WW at Esth. 9:28.
5 [a]Ps. 19:4–6 [1]Is eager for, lit. *panting*
6 [a]Eccl. 11:5; John 3:8
7 [a][Ps. 104:8, 9; Jer. 5:22]
8 [a]Prov. 27:20; Eccl. 4:8 [1]*wearisome* *See WW at Amos 4:8.
9 [a]Eccl. 3:15
11 [a]Eccl. 2:16
13 [a][Eccl. 7:25; 8:16, 17] [b]Gen. 3:19; Eccl. 3:10 [1]Or *afflicted*
15 [a]Eccl. 7:13
16 [a]1 Kin. 3:12, 13; Eccl. 2:9 [1]Lit. *seen*
17 [a]Eccl. 2:3, 12; 7:23, 25; [1 Thess. 5:21]
18 [a]Eccl. 12:12

CHAPTER 2
1 [a]Luke 12:19 [b]Prov. 14:13; [Eccl. 7:4; 8:15] [1]*gladness*

11 *There is* [a]no remembrance of former *things*,
Nor will there be any remembrance of *things* that are to come
By *those* who will come after.

The Grief of Wisdom

12 I, the Preacher, was king over Israel
in Jerusalem.
13 And I set my heart to seek and
[a]search out by wisdom concerning all
that is done under heaven; [b]this burdensome
task God has given to the
sons of man, by which they may be
[1]exercised.
14 I have seen all the works that are
done under the sun; and indeed, all *is*
vanity and grasping for the wind.

15 [a]*What is* crooked cannot be made straight,
And what is lacking cannot be numbered.

16 I communed with my heart, saying,
"Look, I have attained greatness, and
have gained [a]more wisdom than all
who were before me in Jerusalem. My
heart has [1]understood great wisdom
and knowledge."
17 [a]And I set my heart to know wisdom
and to know madness and folly.
I perceived that this also is grasping
for the wind.

18 For [a]in much wisdom *is* much grief,
And he who increases knowledge increases sorrow.

The Vanity of Pleasure

2 I said [a]in my heart, "Come now, I 3
will test you with [b]mirth;[1]

1:2 Vanity of vanities: Or, "utterly meaningless, useless" (literally "Breath of breaths!" meaning "a most useless thing"). The metaphor "breath" points to what is transitory and impermanent, as will "the wind" later in the chapter (v. 14). The wording in 12:8 is nearly identical; 1:2 thus sets forth the beginning and 12:8 the conclusion of the Preacher's quest.
1:3 Here is the true theme of the book. What gives genuine value (*yitron*) to existence? Can that factor be found in the present life? The question posed by the Preacher explains why everything is useless: there is no gain, no profit, no abiding value to man from his labor in this life. **Under the sun:** In the Preacher's terms this is more a synonym for "in this life" than "on this planet."
1:4 Man is born and dies, but the world seems not to notice.
1:5–7 The sun, wind, and rivers behave exactly as they always have since time began, independent of man's enterprise.
1:9–11 The writer finds a weariness in the inability of human effort to introduce any lasting change into the world.
1:10, 11 See section 4 of Truth-In-Action at the end of Eccl.
1:12–18 The Preacher now turns his attention to the problem and recounts his efforts to solve it.
1:13 Wisdom: The Preacher uses the word "wisdom" in an unconventional manner here. Normally, "wisdom" in biblical wisdom literature means piety, godliness, and virtue. But here human wisdom is meant, perhaps along the lines of Greek philosophy, where truth is sought solely by means of the intellect. **Burdensome task . . . by which they may be exercised:** Or "an unhappy task God has given people with which to be busied."
1:14 All man's labor is useless; it cannot remedy the ills of the world. It is like trying to catch the wind in one's fist.
1:15 The fallacy of human wisdom as an ultimate value: it cannot repair what is defective nor supply what is lacking.
1:18 The second fallacy of wisdom as an ultimate value: it has brought the Preacher only grief. So wisdom and knowledge are vanity, too!

therefore enjoy pleasure"; but surely,
[c]this also *was* vanity.
2 I said of laughter—"Madness!"; and
of mirth, "What does it accomplish?"
3 [a]I searched in my heart *how* [1]to
gratify my flesh with wine, while guiding my heart with wisdom, and how
to lay hold on folly, till I might see what
was [b]good for the sons of men to do
under heaven all the days of their
lives.
4 I made my works great, I built myself [a]houses, and planted myself vineyards.
5 I made myself gardens and orchards, and I planted all *kinds* of fruit
trees in them.
6 I made myself water pools from
which to [1]water the growing trees of
the grove.
7 I acquired male and female servants, and had [1]servants born in my
house. Yes, I had greater possessions
of herds and flocks than all who were
in Jerusalem before me.
8 [a]I also gathered for myself silver
and gold and the *special treasures of
kings and of the provinces. I acquired
male and female singers, the delights
of the sons of men, *and* [1]musical instruments of all kinds.
9 [a]So I became great and [1]excelled
[b]more than all who were before me in
Jerusalem. Also my wisdom remained
with me.

10 Whatever my eyes *desired I did
not keep from them.
I did not withhold my heart from
any pleasure,
For my heart rejoiced in all my
labor;
And [a]this was my [1]reward from
all my labor.
11 Then I looked on all the works
that my hands had done
And on the labor in which I had
toiled;
And indeed all *was* [a]vanity and
grasping for the wind.
There was no profit under the
sun.

The End of the Wise and the Fool

12 Then I turned myself to consider 3
wisdom [a]and madness and
folly;
For what *can* the man *do* who
succeeds the king?—
Only what he has already
[b]done.
13 Then I saw that wisdom [a]excels
folly
As light excels darkness.
14 [a]The wise man's eyes *are* in his
head,
But the fool walks in darkness.
Yet I myself perceived
That [b]the same event happens to
them all.

15 So I said in my heart,
"As it happens to the fool,
It also happens to me,
And why was I then more wise?"
Then I said in my heart,
"This also *is* vanity."
16 For *there is* [a]no more
remembrance of the wise than
of the fool forever,
Since all that now *is* will be
forgotten in the days to
come.
And how does a wise *man* die?
As the fool!

17 Therefore I hated life because the 3
work that was done under the sun *was*
distressing to me, for all *is* vanity and
grasping for the wind.
18 Then I hated all my labor in which
I had toiled under the sun, because

1 [c]Eccl. 1:2
3 [a]Eccl. 1:17 [b][Eccl. 3:12, 13; 5:18; 6:12] [1]Lit. *to draw my flesh*
4 [a]1 Kin. 7:1–12
6 [1]*irrigate*
7 [1]Lit. *sons of my house*
8 [a]1 Kin. 9:28; 10:10, 14, 21 [1]Exact meaning unknown *See WW at Deut. 26:18.
9 [a]Eccl. 1:16 [b]2 Chr. 9:22 [1]Lit. *increased*
10 [a]Eccl. 3:22; 5:18; 9:9 [1]Lit. *portion* *See WW at Ps. 122:6.
11 [a]Eccl. 1:3, 14
12 [a]Eccl. 1:17; 7:25 [b]Eccl. 1:9
13 [a]Eccl. 7:11, 14, 19; 9:18; 10:10
14 [a]Prov. 17:24; Eccl. 8:1 [b]Ps. 49:10; Eccl. 9:2, 3, 11
16 [a]Eccl. 1:11; 4:16

2:1–11 See section 3 of Truth-In-Action at the end of Eccl.
2:3 The Preacher wants to make it quite clear that his pursuit of pleasure was an intellectual one, not one of base passion. His goal was to ask if engaging in an orgy of pleasure for its own sake is something worthwhile for humans.
2:8 Musical instruments: The Hebrew term is uncertain, possibly meaning "many concubines."
2:10 In this passage (vv. 1–11), the Preacher has tried to sate his restless spirit in pleasure. He has tried wine (v. 3), construction projects and planting vineyards (v. 4), gardens and orchards (v. 5), and irrigation projects (v. 6); he has acquired many servants and livestock (v. 7), wealth and concubines (v. 8).
2:11 When he reflects on his works, he realizes that they are worthless. Pleasure satisfies only for the moment and shares the same defect as human wisdom: it accomplishes nothing (v. 2; see notes on 1:15, 18).
2:12–16 See section 3 of Truth-In-Action at the end of Eccl.
2:12 The Preacher here turns to the doctrine of retribution, that God will balance the scales somehow to compensate for life's inequalities. Perhaps this is the value he seeks.
2:13, 14 Wisdom is of far greater value than foolishness, because the wise man realizes what he is doing, but the fool blunders along like a blind man. See also 4:13, 14; 10:12–14.
2:14–16 The Preacher realizes that both wise and fool are destined to death. The value he seeks, therefore, cannot lie in any hope of retribution in this life.
2:17–23 See section 3 of Truth-In-Action at the end of Eccl.
2:17 If wisdom does not guarantee him justice, then all the effort exerted in becoming wise accomplishes nothing.
2:18, 19 Not only do wealth and pleasure accomplish nothing (vv. 1–11), but the Preacher cannot take it with him at death. And because he cannot know whether his heir will be wise or a fool, leaving his wealth behind yields the Preacher little comfort.

[a]I must leave it to the man who will
come after me.
19 And who knows whether he will be
wise or a fool? Yet he will rule over
all my labor in which I toiled and in
which I have shown myself wise under
the sun. This also *is* vanity.
20 Therefore I turned my heart and despaired of all the labor in which I had
toiled under the sun.
21 For there is a man whose labor *is*
with wisdom, knowledge, and skill; yet
he must leave his [1]heritage to a man
who has not labored for it. This also
is vanity and a great evil.
22 [a]For what has man for all his labor,
and for the striving of his heart with
which he has toiled under the sun?
23 For all his days *are* [a]sorrowful, and
his work burdensome; even in the
night his heart takes no rest. This also
is vanity.
2 24 [a]Nothing *is* better for a man *than*
that he should eat and drink, and *that*
his soul should enjoy good in his labor.
This also, I saw, was from the hand of
God.
25 For who can eat, or who can have
enjoyment, [1]more than I?
26 For *God* gives [a]wisdom and knowledge and joy to a man who *is* good in
His sight; but to the sinner He gives
the work of gathering and collecting,
that [b]he may give to *him who is* good
before God. This also *is* vanity and
grasping for the wind.

Everything Has Its Time

3 To everything *there is* a season,
A [a]time* for every purpose under
heaven:

2 A time [1]to be born,
And [a]a time to die;
A time to plant,
And a time to pluck *what is*
planted;
3 A time to kill,
And a time to *heal;
A time to break down,
And a time to build up;

18 [a]Ps. 49:10
21 [1]Lit. *portion*
22 [a]Eccl. 1:3; 3:9
23 [a]Job 5:7; 14:1
24 [a]Eccl. 3:12, 13, 22; Is. 56:12; Luke 12:19; 1 Cor. 15:32; [1 Tim. 6:17]
25 [1]So with MT, Tg., Vg.; some Heb. mss., LXX, Syr. *without Him*
26 [a]Job 32:8; Prov. 2:6; James 1:5 [b]Job 27:16, 17; Prov. 28:8

CHAPTER 3

1 [a]Eccl. 3:17; 8:6 *See WW at Is. 33:6.
2 [a]Job 14:5; Heb. 9:27 [1]Lit. *to bear*
3 *See WW at Ex. 15:26.
4 [a]Rom. 12:15
5 [a]Joel 2:16; 1 Cor. 7:5
7 [a]Amos 5:13 [b]Prov. 25:11
8 [a]Prov. 13:5; Luke 14:26
9 [a]Eccl. 1:3
10 [a]Eccl. 1:13
11 [a]Job 5:9; Eccl. 7:23; 8:17; Rom. 11:33
12 [a]Eccl. 2:3, 24

4 A time to [a]weep,
And a time to **laugh;**
A time to mourn,
And a time to dance;

WORD WEALTH

3:4 laugh, *sachaq* (sah-*chahk*); Strong's #7832: To laugh; to rejoice; to play; to be amused about something; to mock, tease, ridicule, or laugh at something. While *sachaq* primarily means "to laugh," it occasionally means "to play," whether as exuberant, leaping animals (Job 40:20), or as persons do when dancing, laughing, and playing music during a celebration (2 Sam. 6:5, 21). In its negative sense, *sachaq* refers to the behavior of rowdy, mocking crowds who come together to ridicule someone for sport and entertainment, as in Jer. 15:17. *Sachaq* is the root of the name "Isaac," "He Causes Laughter" (Gen. 21:5–7).

5 A time to cast away stones,
And a time to gather stones;
[a]A time to embrace,
And a time to refrain from
embracing;
6 A time to gain,
And a time to lose;
A time to keep,
And a time to throw away;
7 A time to tear,
And a time to sew;
[a]A time to keep silence,
And a time to [b]speak;
8 A time to love,
And a time to [a]hate;
A time of war,
And a time of peace.

The God-Given Task

9 [a]What profit has the worker from
that in which he labors?
10 [a]I have seen the God-given task
with which the sons of men are to be
occupied.
11 He has made everything beautiful 4
in its time. Also He has put eternity in
their hearts, except that [a]no one can
find out the work that God does from
beginning to end.
12 I know that nothing *is* [a]better for

2:20–23 This impasse brings the Preacher to despair: why should he leave the fruit of his labor to one who has not worked for it and who does not deserve it?
2:24–26 See section 2 of Truth-In-Action at the end of Eccl.
2:24, 25 If he cannot take it with him and is uncertain as to how his heirs would treat it, one should enjoy what he has while he is alive. Enjoyment of what one has as a blessing from God is an important secondary theme of the book; it will reappear frequently (see list of references in the note on 5:18–20).
3:1 If retribution fails as a value, perhaps there exists some mystical cosmic order that grants meaning to life, for each thing has its proper time or cycle.
3:9 Man, when faced with this determinism, is helpless to control it or change it.
3:10, 11 When God created the world, He pronounced it very good (Gen. 1:31). Since the Preacher cannot improve on the created order, the best thing for man is to acknowledge it by enjoying life, once again returning to the same conclusion he arrived at in 2:24, 25 (see note there).
3:11 See section 4 of Truth-In-Action at the end of Eccl.
3:12, 13 Everything has been placed on the Earth for man's benefit and should be received with thanks.

them than to rejoice, and to do good in their lives,
13 and also that [a]every man should eat and drink and enjoy the good of all his labor—it *is* the gift of God.

14 I know that whatever God does,
It shall be forever.
[a]Nothing can be added to it,
And nothing taken from it.
God does *it,* that men should fear
before Him.
15 [a]That which is has already been,
And what is to be has already
been;
And God [1]requires an account of
[2]what is past.

Injustice Seems to Prevail

16 Moreover [a]I saw under the sun:

In the place of [1]judgment,
Wickedness *was* there;
And *in* the place of
righteousness,
[2]Iniquity *was* there.

17 I said in my heart,

[a]"God shall judge the righteous and
the wicked,
For *there is* a time there for every
[1]purpose and for every work."

18 I said in my heart, "Concerning the condition of the sons of men, God tests them, that they may see that they themselves are *like* animals."
19 [a]For what happens to the sons of men also happens to animals; one thing befalls them: as one dies, so dies the other. Surely, they all have one breath; man has no advantage over animals, for all *is* vanity.
20 All go to one place: [a]all are from the dust, and all return to dust.
21 [a]Who[1] knows the spirit of the sons of men, which goes upward, and the spirit of the animal, which goes down to the earth?
22 [a]So I perceived that nothing *is* better than that a man should rejoice in his own works, for [b]that *is* his [1]heritage. [c]For who can bring him to see what will happen after him?

4 Then I returned and considered all the [a]oppression that is done under the sun:

And look! The tears of the
oppressed,
But they have no comforter—
[1]On the side of their oppressors
there is power,
But they have no comforter.
2 [a]Therefore I *praised the dead who
were already dead,
More than the living who are still
alive.
3 [a]Yet, better than both *is he* who
has never existed,
Who has not seen the evil work
that is done under the sun.

The Vanity of Selfish Toil

4 Again, I saw that for all toil and every skillful work a man is envied by his neighbor. This also *is* vanity and grasping for the wind.

5 [a]The fool folds his *hands
And consumes his own flesh.
6 [a]Better a handful *with* quietness
Than both hands full, *together
with* toil and grasping for the
wind.

7 Then I returned, and I saw vanity under the sun:

8 There is one alone, without
[1]companion:

13 [a]Eccl. 2:24
14 [a]James 1:17
15 [a]Eccl. 1:9 [1]Lit. *seeks* [2]*what is pursued*
16 [a]Eccl. 5:8 [1]*justice* [2]*Wickedness*
17 [a]Gen. 18:25; Ps. 96:13; Eccl. 11:9; [Matt. 16:27; Rom. 2:6–10; 2 Cor. 5:10; 2 Thess. 1:6–9] [1]*desire*
19 [a]Ps. 49:12, 20; 73:22; [Eccl. 2:16]
20 [a]Gen. 3:19; Ps. 103:14
21 [a]Eccl. 12:7 [1]LXX, Syr., Tg., Vg. *Who knows whether the spirit . . . goes upward, and whether . . . goes downward to the earth?*
22 [a]Eccl. 2:24; 5:18 [b]Eccl. 2:10 [c]Eccl. 6:12; 8:7 [1]*portion or lot*

CHAPTER 4

1 [a]Job 35:9; Ps. 12:5; Eccl. 3:16; 5:8; Is. 5:7 [1]Lit. *At the hand*
2 [a]Job 3:17, 18 *See WW at Ps. 63:3.
3 [a]Job 3:11–22; Eccl. 6:3; Luke 23:29
5 [a]Prov. 6:10; 24:33 *See WW at Josh. 4:24.
6 [a]Prov. 15:16, 17; 16:8
8 [1]Lit. *a second*

3:14, 15 Man, in attempting to change the cycles of nature, (creation), is actually attempting to change the order God has established. But this is not a power allotted to man, and God will call him into account for his actions in this.
3:14 See section 1 of Truth-In-Action at the end of Eccl.
3:16 Perhaps human courts can dispense the justice that nature lacks. But, alas, because human wickedness makes human judgment perverse, any expectation of justice by human agencies in this life is unfounded.
3:17 While the Preacher never reasons from tradition or revelation, his belief in God and in a natural order that is good (see note on vv. 10, 11) drives him to conclude that God will judge the world in an appropriate time, if not in this life. He will return to this in 11:9.
3:18–21 The Preacher returns to his observations on equal ends for unequal creatures. Both men and beasts die the same death and go to the same place (the grave).
3:22 See section 2 of Truth-In-Action at the end of Eccl.
3:22 Again, the secondary theme: enjoy life (see note on 2:24, 25).
4:1 The Preacher considers those in the world who suffer oppression. In a statement brimming with passion, he finds the oppressed have **no comforter** (champion) and power lies on the side of **their oppressors.** Because of these two factors, the oppressed have no hope (see 5:8, 9).
4:2, 3 The Preacher concludes that the dead are better off than the oppressed who are still alive. If all life can offer is oppression, it is better not to have been born. Yet this outburst of passionate empathy is not the Preacher's final verdict on the value of human life (see note on 9:4).
4:5, 6 **The fool** destroys himself by his idleness. Another minor theme that runs throughout the book is that work in moderation is good and adds to the dignity of the person. But if it is overwhelming and dominates his life, it is futile: for a little with peace is better than much in turmoil.
4:8 When one labors alone, without an heir to whom he

He has neither son nor brother.
Yet *there is* no end to all his labors,
Nor is his [a]eye satisfied with riches.
But [b]*he never asks,*
"For whom do I toil and deprive myself of [c]good?"
This also *is* vanity and a [2]grave misfortune.

The Value of a Friend

9 Two *are* better than one,
Because they have a good reward for their labor.
10 For if they fall, one will lift up his companion.
But woe to him *who is* alone when he falls,
For *he has* no one to help him up.
11 Again, if two lie down together, they will keep warm;
But how can one be warm *alone?*
12 Though one may be overpowered by another, two can withstand him.
And a threefold cord is not quickly broken.

Popularity Passes Away

4 13 Better a poor and wise youth
Than an old and foolish king who will be admonished no more.
14 For he comes out of prison to be king,
Although [1]he was born poor in his kingdom.

8 [a]Prov. 27:20; Eccl. 5:10; [1 John 2:16] [b]Ps. 39:6 [c]Eccl. 2:18–21 [2]Lit. *evil task*
14 [1]The youth
16 [1]Lit. *to all before whom he was to be*

CHAPTER 5

1 [a]Ex. 3:5; Is. 1:12 [b][1 Sam. 15:22]; Ps. 50:8; Prov. 15:8; 21:27; [Hos. 6:6]
2 [a]Prov. 20:25 [b]Prov. 10:19; Matt. 6:7
3 [a]Prov. 10:19
4 [a]Num. 30:2; Deut. 23:21–23; Ps. 50:14; 76:11 [b]Ps. 66:13, 14
5 [a]Prov. 20:25; Acts 5:4
6 [a]Prov. 6:2 [b]1 Cor. 11:10

15 I saw all the living who walk under the sun;
They were with the second youth who stands in his place.
16 *There was* no end of all the people [1]over whom he was made king;
Yet those who come afterward will not rejoice in him.
Surely this also *is* vanity and grasping for the wind.

Fear God, Keep Your Vows

5 Walk [a]prudently when you go to 7
the house of God; and draw near
to hear rather [b]than to give the sacrifice of fools, for they do not know that
they do evil.

2 Do not be [a]rash with your mouth,
And let not your heart utter anything hastily before God.
For God *is* in heaven, and you on earth;
Therefore let your words [b]be few.
3 For a dream comes through much activity,
And [a]a fool's voice *is known* by *his* many words.

4 [a]When you make a vow to God, 7
do not delay to [b]pay it;
For *He has* no pleasure in fools.
Pay what you have vowed—
5 [a]Better not to vow than to vow and not pay.

6 Do not let your [a]mouth cause your
flesh to sin, [b]nor say before the mes-

can leave his wealth, he deprives himself for nothing. He is better off to take a little time to enjoy what he has rather than being consumed with making more.

4:9, 10 Two *are* better than one, for a joint investment often has a better foundation of capital and thus a better chance of success. If the one partner succeeds, the other may share in the fruits of his labor. If he fails, he has his partner to help him.

4:11 Although the image may refer to lonely travelers who huddle together to stay warm in the cool nights of Palestine, the image of husband and wife is too obvious to ignore. A married couple are the "two" that are ordained by God (Gen. 2:23, 24), the divine manner of facing the problems of the world.

4:12 If v. 11 is a portrait of travelers, when they find themselves set on by robbers, each will come to the aid of the other. And if there be three, they are all but invincible. On the other hand, if v. 11 refers to a husband and wife facing the world together, they become even stronger if they have a child (heir).

4:13–16 See section 4 of Truth-In-Action at the end of Eccl.

4:13 Wisdom does have some value: a wise young beggar is better than an old **foolish king.**

4:14 This is a difficult verse, turning on the interpretation of the Hebrew idiom behind **although.** The sense seems to be that a youth, like David of old, though born to a poor family, may come, if he is wise, from confinement to the throne.

4:15, 16 The child who became king (v. 14), as well as his successor (his own natural child), will be forgotten. So a hereditary monarchy is not a genuine value either, because it places rank by birth ahead of merit and leadership.

5:1–3 See section 7 of Truth-In-Action at the end of Eccl.

5:1 Draw near to hear: It is better to obey God's precepts than **to give the sacrifice of fools** (that is, sacrifices to atone for hasty words).

5:2 Comparing v. 1 and v. 4, it would seem that the rashness that the Preacher has in mind is that which must be atoned for by sacrifice or results in a hasty vow that often cannot be paid. Jesus warns against rash vows in Matt. 5:33–37.

5:3 Activity: The Hebrew word (*'inyan*) might also be translated "concern." Dreams are often the products of natural anxieties, cares, and concerns, with little meaning behind them. Even so, the words of a fool are many, with little meaning behind them.

5:4–7 See section 7 of Truth-In-Action at the end of Eccl.

5:6 Do not permit your mouth to make rash vows that you cannot keep and thus cause yourself to sin (see James 1:26).

senger *of God* that it *was* an error. Why
should God be angry at your [1]excuse
and destroy the work of your hands?
7 For in the multitude of dreams and
many words *there is* also vanity. But
[a]fear God.

The Vanity of Gain and Honor

8 If you [a]see the oppression of the
poor, and the violent [1]perversion of
justice and righteousness in a province, do not marvel at the matter; for
[b]high official watches over high official, and higher officials are over
them.
9 Moreover the profit of the land is
for all; *even* the king is served from
the field.

5 10 He who loves silver will not be
satisfied with silver;
Nor he who loves abundance,
with increase.
This also *is* vanity.

5 11 When goods increase,
They increase who eat them;
So what profit have the owners
Except to see *them* with their
eyes?

12 The sleep of a laboring man *is*
sweet,
Whether he eats little or much;
But the abundance of the rich will
not permit him to sleep.

13 [a]There is a severe evil *which* I have
seen under the sun:
Riches kept for their owner to his
hurt.
14 But those riches perish through
[1]misfortune;
When he begets a son, *there is*
nothing in his hand.

15 [a]As he came from his mother's
womb, naked shall he return,
To go as he came;
And he shall take nothing from
his labor
Which he may carry away in his
hand.

16 And this also *is* a severe evil—
Just exactly as he came, so shall
he go.
And [a]what profit has he [b]who has
labored for the wind?
17 All his days [a]he also eats in
darkness,
And *he has* much sorrow and
sickness and anger.

18 Here is what I have seen: [a]*It is* good 3
and fitting *for one* to eat and drink, and
to enjoy the good of all his labor in
which he toils under the sun all the
days of his life which God gives him;
[b]for it *is* his [1]heritage.
19 As for [a]every man to whom God has 5
given riches and wealth, and given him
power to eat of it, to receive his [1]her-
itage and rejoice in his labor—this *is*
the [b]gift of God.
20 For he will not dwell unduly on the
days of his life, because God keeps *him*
busy with the joy of his heart.

6 There[a] is an evil which I have seen 3
under the sun, and it *is* common
among men:
2 A *man to whom God has given
riches and wealth and honor, [a]so that
he lacks nothing for himself of all he
desires; [b]yet God does not give him
power to eat of it, but a foreigner consumes it. This *is* vanity, and it *is* an
evil [1]affliction.
3 If a man begets a hundred *children*
and lives many years, so that the days
of his years are many, but his soul is

6 [1]Lit. *voice*
7 [a][Eccl. 12:13]
8 [a]Eccl. 3:16 [b][Ps. 12:5; 58:11; 82:1] [1]*wresting*
13 [a]Eccl. 6:1, 2
14 [1]Lit. *bad business*
15 [a]Job 1:21; Ps. 49:17; 1 Tim. 6:7
16 [a]Eccl. 1:3 [b]Prov. 11:29
17 [a]Ps. 127:2
18 [a]Eccl. 2:24; 3:12, 13; [1 Tim. 6:17] [b]Eccl. 2:10; 3:22 [1]Lit. *portion*
19 [a][Eccl. 6:2] [b]Eccl. 2:24; 3:13 [1]Lit. *portion*

CHAPTER 6

1 [a]Eccl. 5:13
2 [a]Job 21:10; Ps. 17:14; 73:7 [b]Luke 12:20 [1]*disease* *See WW at Is. 32:2.

When the temple messenger comes to collect what you have vowed, do not try to excuse yourself from the debt on grounds that you made the vow in error.
5:7 Multitude of dreams . . . words . . . vanity: The line could be translated, "For many useless things and words [come] in an abundance of dreams."
5:8, 9 These are transition verses. They say: 1) oppression is not a worthy thing, yet is a common one; 2) government is often a chain of exploitative practices; 3) all share in the increase of the land through rake-offs in taxes and fees; 4) the king gets most of all, since he is at the top of the chain (see 4:1–3). The Preacher is not returning to the subject of oppression; instead, he is about to embark on a discussion of the failure of materialistic values.
5:10 See section 5 of Truth-In-Action at the end of Eccl.
5:10 Wealth and material gain *do* not and *can*not satisfy. All human systems of economics, whether Marxist, socialist, or capitalist, are predicated on materialism, and thus are futile.
5:11–15 The more material gain, the more one finds himself beset by things that deplete it. One can take nothing of his substance with him when he departs this life. So then, all his labor is useless. God has given man His blessing in material form, and it is man's duty to enjoy these blessings and be content with them in moderation.
5:11 See section 5 of Truth-In-Action at the end of Eccl.
5:18–20 See section 3 of Truth-In-Action at the end of Eccl.
5:18–20 Once again the Preacher returns to the secondary theme of the book: though one cannot discover an absolute, ultimate value by his efforts in this life, he should at least receive what God has given him with thanks and enjoy it. This theme (seen already in 2:20–25; 3:10, 11, 22; 5:11–15) will appear again in 6:1, 2, 9 and 9:7–12.
5:19 See section 5 of Truth-In-Action at the end of Eccl.
6:1, 2 See section 3 of Truth-In-Action at the end of Eccl.
6:1, 2 There is futility in not partaking of one's own substance.
6:3–6 A stillborn child is better than a person who has not tasted of his own labors and thus has deprived himself for nothing.

not satisfied with goodness, or [a]indeed
he has no burial, I say *that* [b]a [1]stillborn
child *is* better than he—
4 for it comes in vanity and departs
in darkness, and its name is covered
with darkness.
5 Though it has not seen the sun or
known *anything,* this has more rest
than that man,
6 even if he lives a thousand years
twice—but has not seen goodness. Do
not all go to one [a]place?

7 [a]All the labor of man *is* for his
mouth,
And yet the soul is not satisfied.
8 For what more has the wise *man*
than the fool?
What does the poor man have,
Who knows *how* to walk before
the living?
9 Better *is* [1]the [a]sight of the eyes
than the wandering of [2]desire.
This also *is* vanity and grasping
for the wind.

10 Whatever one is, he has been
named [a]already,
For it is known that he *is* man;
[b]And he cannot contend with Him
who is mightier than he.
11 Since there are many things that
increase vanity,
How *is* man the better?

12 For who knows what *is* good for
man in life, [1]all the days of his [2]vain
life which he passes like [a]a shadow?
[b]Who can tell a man what will happen
after him under the sun?

The Value of Practical Wisdom

4 **7** A [a]good name *is* better than
precious ointment,
And the day of death than the day
of one's [b]birth;

3 [a]2 Kin. 9:35; Is. 14:19, 20; Jer. 22:19 [b]Job 3:16; Ps. 58:8; Eccl. 4:3 [1]Or *miscarriage*
6 [a]Eccl. 2:14, 15
7 [a]Prov. 16:26
9 [a]Eccl. 11:9 [1]What the eyes see [2]Lit. *soul*
10 [a]Eccl. 1:9; 3:15 [b]Job 9:32; Is. 45:9; Jer. 49:19
12 [a]Ps. 102:11; James 4:14 [b]Ps. 39:6; Eccl. 3:22 [1]Lit. *the number of the days* [2]*futile*

CHAPTER 7

1 [a]Prov. 22:1 [b]Eccl. 4:2
2 [a][Ps. 90:12]
3 [a][2 Cor. 7:10] [1]*Vexation* or *Grief* [2]*well* or *pleasing*
5 [a]Ps. 141:5; [Prov. 13:18; 15:31, 32] [1]*listen to*
6 [a]Eccl. 2:2 [1]Lit. *sound*
7 [a]Ex. 23:8; Deut. 16:19; [Prov. 17:8, 23] [1]*destroys*
8 [a]Prov. 14:29; Gal. 5:22; Eph. 4:2
9 [a]Prov. 14:17; James 1:19
11 [a]Eccl. 11:7
12 [a]Eccl. 9:18 [1]A protective shade, lit. *shadow*

2 Better to go to the house of
mourning
Than to go to the house of
feasting,
For that *is* the end of all men;
And the living will take *it* to
[a]heart.
3 [1]Sorrow *is* better than laughter,
[a]For by a sad countenance the
heart is made [2]better.
4 The heart of the wise *is* in the
house of mourning,
But the heart of fools *is* in the
house of mirth.

5 [a]*It is* better to [1]hear the rebuke of
the wise
Than for a man to hear the song
of fools.
6 [a]For like the [1]crackling of thorns
under a pot,
So *is* the laughter of the fool.
This also is vanity.
7 Surely oppression destroys a wise
man's reason,
[a]And a bribe [1]debases the heart.

8 The end of a thing *is* better than 2
its beginning;
[a]The patient in spirit *is* better than
the proud in spirit.
9 [a]Do not hasten in your spirit to be
angry,
For anger rests in the bosom of
fools.
10 Do not say,
"Why were the former days better
than these?"
For you do not inquire wisely
concerning this.

11 Wisdom *is* good with an
inheritance,
And profitable [a]to those who see
the sun.
12 For wisdom *is* [1]a [a]defense *as*
money *is* a defense,

6:7 Materialism alone is not sufficient (see notes on 5:8, 9; 5:10; 5:11–15).

6:8, 9 It is best to be content with what one has (**the sight of the eyes**). This keeps one's appetite from roving (from coveting).

6:10 See note on 1:9–11.

6:12 See 5:15–17; 6:1–9.

7:1—8:9 While human wisdom is not the ultimate value (*yitron*), it has a relative value that makes it superior to foolishness (2:13, 14). In this section and in 10:1—11:6 the Preacher lists a number of wise sayings and observations that do not directly contribute to his quest, but rather tell how one can best carry out the secondary theme (enjoyment of life: see note on 5:18–20) by using wisdom.

7:1–4 See section 4 of Truth-In-Action at the end of Eccl.

7:1–4 The Preacher returns to his point that death is superior to life (see note on 4:2). But this time he speaks, not of one's own death, but of experiencing the death of another. Confronting one's own mortality at the funeral of another should make one live a wiser, more sober life, since he himself will eventually die.

7:5, 6 The song (praise) and mirth of fools is mindless and meaningless. How much better is well-intended constructive criticism from a wise man, even if it hurts to receive it!

7:7 Oppression: Or, "the oppressor." **Bribe debases:** Bribery is a way of life in many places even today; but when it occurs, it brings with it the corruption of morals, especially in a court of law (Ex. 23:8).

7:8, 9 See section 2 of Truth-In-Action at the end of Eccl.

7:10 The "good old days" reside only in memories—in part real, in part fantasy.

7:11, 12 While both wisdom and money may provide protection, the advantage to wisdom is that it gives life (see note on 8:1).

But the [2]excellence of
*knowledge *is that* wisdom
gives [b]life to those who have it.

13 Consider the work of God;
For [a]who can make straight what
He has made crooked?
14 [a]In the day of prosperity be joyful,
But in the day of adversity
consider:
Surely God has appointed the one
[1]as well as the other,
So that man can find out nothing
that will come after him.

3 **15** I have seen everything in my days
of vanity:

[a]There is a just *man* who perishes
in his righteousness,
And there is a wicked *man* who
prolongs *life* in his wickedness.

16 [a]Do not be overly righteous,
[b]Nor be overly wise:
Why should you destroy
yourself?
17 Do not be overly wicked,
Nor be foolish:
[a]Why should you die before your
time?
18 *It is* good that you grasp this,
And also not remove your hand
from the other;
For he who [a]fears God will
[1]escape them all.

19 [a]Wisdom strengthens the wise
More than ten rulers of the city.

20 [a]For *there is* not a just man on
earth who does good
And does not sin.

21 Also do not take to heart
everything people say,
Lest you hear your servant
cursing you.
22 For many times, also, your own
heart has known
That even you have *cursed
others.

23 All this I have [1]proved by
wisdom.
[a]I said, "I will be wise";
But it *was* far from me.
24 [a]As for that which is far off and
[b]exceedingly deep,
Who can find it out?
25 [a]I applied my heart to know,
To search and seek out wisdom
and the reason *of things*,
To know the wickedness of folly,
Even of foolishness *and* madness.
26 [a]And I find more bitter than death
The woman whose heart *is* snares
and nets,
Whose hands *are* fetters.
[1]He who pleases God shall escape
from her,
But the sinner shall be trapped by
her.

27 "Here is what I have found," says
[a]the Preacher,
"*Adding* one thing to the other to
find out the reason,
28 Which my soul still seeks but I
cannot find:
[a]One man among a thousand I
have found,
But a woman among all these I
have not found.
29 Truly, this only I have found:
[a]That God made man upright,
But [b]they have sought out many
schemes."

8

Who *is* like a wise *man?*
And who knows the
interpretation of a thing?

12 [b]Prov. 3:18 [2]*advantage* or *profit* *See WW at Mal. 2:7. **13** [a]Job 12:14 **14** [a]Deut. 28:47 [1]*alongside* **15** [a]Eccl. 8:12–14 **16** [a]Prov. 25:16; Phil. 3:6 [b]Rom. 12:3 **17** [a]Job 15:32; Ps. 55:23 **18** [a]Eccl. 3:14; 5:7; 8:12, 13 [1]Lit. *come forth from all of them* **19** [a]Prov. 21:22; Eccl. 9:13–18 **20** [a]1 Kin. 8:46; 2 Chr. 6:36; Prov. 20:9; Rom. 3:23; 1 John 1:8

22 *See WW at Jer. 8:11. **23** [a]Rom. 1:22 [1]*tested* **24** [a]Job 28:12; 1 Tim. 6:16 [b]Rom. 11:33 **25** [a]Eccl. 1:17 **26** [a]Prov. 5:3, 4 [1]Lit. *He who is good before God* **27** [a]Eccl. 1:1, 2 **28** [a]Job 33:23 **29** [a]Gen. 1:27 [b]Gen. 3:6, 7

7:13 See note on 1:15.
7:14 God has permitted life to consist of both good and evil so that man cannot independently determine what the future holds for him. This then is an indirect warning to those who considered prosperity as a sure mark of God's blessing and poverty as God's curse upon wickedness.
7:15–18 See section 3 of Truth-In-Action at the end of Eccl.
7:15 The righteous were traditionally said to have a long life (Ex. 20:12; Deut. 4:40; Ps. 91:16; Prov. 3:2, 16; 4:10), and the wicked a short one (Ps. 37:10; 55:23; 58:3–9; 73:18). But the Preacher has seen the opposite circumstances often enough and warns that one's life-style is no guarantee of one's life span.
7:16–18 A fanatical zeal for religion or a privately defined "righteousness" can lead to an early death, especially if it erupts into physical conflict. On the other hand, a wicked life of sin and debauchery clearly leads to an early death.
7:20 This is the reason for frustration in being overly righteous: no one is innocent from having done evil. Paul might have quoted these words when making his case for the universal sinfulness of humanity (Rom. 3:10–20).
7:21, 22 If you have belittled others, you may expect them to belittle you. But do not pay too much attention to it. It is human nature (v. 20) and is to be expected.
7:23, 24 The Preacher repeats his resolution to dedicate himself to wisdom, but he finds true wisdom beyond his natural abilities. An important aspect of the theme appears here, for while the Preacher classes himself among the wise, *true* wisdom, the abiding value (*yitron*) he has been seeking, remains out of his reach and cannot be acquired by his efforts.
7:25 See note on 2:3.
7:27–29 The point is not that men are more virtuous than women, but that, while God created humanity upright, both men and women have defiled themselves (see also Job 5:7). As a result, there are none who are without blame.
8:1 One advantage to wisdom over other alternatives is the dignity and strength it gives a person (see note on 7:12).

[a]A man's wisdom makes his face
shine,
And [b]the [1]sternness of his face is
changed.

Obey Authorities for God's Sake

2 I *say,* "Keep the king's commandment [a]for the sake of your oath to God.
3 [a]"Do not be hasty to go from his
presence. Do not take your stand for
an evil thing, for he does whatever
pleases him."

4 Where the word of a king *is, there*
is power;
And [a]who may say to him, "What
are you doing?"
2 5 He who keeps his command will
experience nothing harmful;
And a wise man's heart [1]discerns
both time and judgment,
6 Because [a]for every matter there
is a time and judgment,
Though the misery of man
[1]increases greatly.
7 [a]For he does not know what will
happen;
So who can tell him when it will
occur?
6 8 [a]No one has power over the spirit
to retain the spirit,
And no one has power in the day
of death.
There is [b]no release from that
war,
And wickedness will not deliver
those who are given to it.

9 All this I have seen, and applied my
heart to every work that is done under
the sun: *There is* a time in which one
man rules over another to his own hurt.

Death Comes to All

10 Then I saw the wicked buried, who
had come and gone from the place of
*holiness, and they were [a]forgotten[1] in
the city where they had so done. This
also *is* vanity.
11 [a]Because the sentence against an **6**
evil work is not executed speedily,
therefore the heart of the sons of men
is fully set in them to do evil.
12 [a]Though a sinner does evil a hundred *times,* and his *days* are prolonged,
yet I surely know that [b]it will be well
with those who fear God, who fear before Him.
13 But it will not be well with the
wicked; nor will he prolong *his* days,
which are as a shadow, because he
does not fear before God.
14 There is a vanity which occurs on
earth, that there are just *men* to whom
it [a]happens according to the work of
the wicked; again, there are wicked
men to whom it happens according to
the work of the [b]righteous. I said that
this also *is* vanity.
15 [a]So I *commended enjoyment, because a man has nothing better under
the sun than to eat, drink, and be
merry; for this will remain with him
in his labor *all* the days of his life which
God gives him under the sun.
16 When I applied my heart to know
wisdom and to see the business that
is done on earth, even though one sees
no sleep day or night,
17 then I saw all the work of God, that

CHAPTER 8
1 [a]Prov. 4:8, 9; Acts 6:15 [b]Deut. 28:50 [1]Lit. *strength*
2 [a]Ex. 22:11; 2 Sam. 21:7; 1 Chr. 29:24; Ezek. 17:18; [Rom. 13:5]
3 [a]Eccl. 10:4
4 [a]1 Sam. 13:11, 13; Job 34:18
5 [1]Lit. *knows*
6 [a]Eccl. 3:1, 17 [1]*is great upon him*
7 [a]Prov. 24:22; Eccl. 6:12
8 [a]Ps. 49:6, 7; Job 14:5 [b]Deut. 20:5–8
10 [a]Eccl. 2:16; 9:5 [1]Some Heb. mss., LXX, Vg. *praised* *See WW at Lev. 19:2.
11 [a]Ps. 10:6; 50:21; Is. 26:10
12 [a]Is. 65:20; [Rom. 2:5–7] [b][Deut. 4:40; Ps. 37:11, 18, 19; Prov. 1:32, 33; Is. 3:10; Matt. 25:34, 41]
14 [a]Ps. 73:14 [b]Eccl. 2:14; 7:15; 9:1–3
15 [a]Eccl. 2:24 *See WW at Ps. 63:3.

8:2 The Preacher advises his disciples to be diligent to keep the commands of the king because they had sworn an oath of loyalty to do so.
8:3 The Hebrew of the first line of this verse is difficult. It could mean: Do not leave the king's presence in anger or in some other hasty fashion. **Do not take your stand:** That is, Do not persist in a losing argument.
8:4 When the king wields power merely by a **word,** who can challenge his *actions?*
8:5, 6 *See section* 2 of Truth-In-Action at the end of Eccl.
8:6 Though the misery of a man increases greatly: The expression may refer to the man's own misfortune about which he has come to see the king, in which case he is urged to be patient and make his plea when the king is ready to hear it. It is also possible that it is the king's bad temper that is in view, in which case the man is encouraged not to make an inappropriate response.
8:7 The man at court can predict neither the king's humor nor his actions.
8:8 See section 6 of Truth-In-Action at the end of Eccl.
8:8 Examples of other things man cannot control or predict: 1) man cannot force the spirit to stay in his body, keeping his body alive when it is his time to die; 2) he cannot postpone death; 3) he cannot avoid service in time of war; and 4) he cannot use wickedness to save himself, for it ensnares him.
8:9 The Preacher's final remark on despotism and its evils: without accountability to others one will sooner or later inflict damage on himself, as well as on those he rules.
8:10 The holy place is probably the temple in Jerusalem. The point is that just as the wisdom of tne wise man is forgotten, so the wickedness of the evil man is forgotten. And the world is little better or worse for either of them.
8:11 See section 6 of Truth-In-Action at the end of Eccl.
8:11 When justice is not quickly executed, the deterrent aspect of the sentence is diminished.
8:12, 13 The Preacher recites the conventional doctrine of retribution.
8:14 Retribution does not hold up; there are gross violations of this ideal. There are righteous men whose end is like the wicked (who die young) and wicked ones whose end is like those who do righteous deeds (who live long).
8:15 Man should enjoy life (see note on 5:18–20).
8:16, 17 God's works, among them the meaning of life, cannot be fathomed by the human intellect, even if one labors on the task day and night.

[a]a man cannot find out the work that is done under the sun. For though a man labors to discover *it,* yet he will not find *it;* moreover, though a wise *man* attempts to know *it,* he will not be able to find *it.*

9 For I [1]considered all this in my heart, so that I could declare it all: [a]that the righteous and the wise and their works *are* in the hand of God. People know neither love nor hatred *by* anything *they see* before them.

2 [a]All things *come* alike to all:

One event *happens* to the
righteous and the wicked;
To the [1]good, the clean, and the
*unclean;
To him who sacrifices and him
who does not sacrifice.
As is the good, so *is* the sinner;
He who takes an oath as *he* who
fears an oath.

3 This *is* an evil in all that is done under the sun: that one thing *happens* to
all. Truly the hearts of the sons of men
are full of evil; madness *is* in their
hearts while they live, and after that
they go to the dead.
4 But for him who is joined to all the
living there is hope, for a living dog is
better than a dead lion.

5 For the living know that they will
die;
But [a]the dead know nothing,
And they have no more reward,
For [b]the memory of them is
forgotten.
6 Also their love, their hatred, and
their envy have now perished;
Nevermore will they have a share
In anything done under the sun.

2 7 Go, [a]eat your bread with joy,
And drink your wine with a
merry heart;
For God has already accepted
your works.
8 Let your garments always be
white,
And let your head lack no oil.

9 [1]Live joyfully with the wife whom
you love all the days of your vain life
which He has given you under the sun,
all your days of vanity; [a]for that *is* your
portion in life, and in the labor which
you perform under the sun.
10 [a]Whatever your hand finds to do,
do *it* with your [b]might; for *there is* no
work or device or knowledge or
wisdom in the *grave where you are
going.
11 I returned [a]and saw under the sun
that—

The race *is* not to the swift,
Nor the battle to the strong,
Nor bread to the wise,
Nor riches to men of
understanding,
Nor favor to men of skill;
But time and [b]chance happen to
them all.
12 For [a]man also does not know his
time:
Like fish taken in a cruel net,
Like birds caught in a snare,
So the sons of men *are* [b]snared
in an evil time,
When it falls suddenly upon
them.

Wisdom Superior to Folly

13 This wisdom I have also seen under
the sun, and it *seemed* great to me:
14 [a]*There was* a little city with few
men in it; and a great king came
against it, besieged it, and built great
[1]snares around it.
15 Now there was found in it a poor
wise man, and he by his wisdom delivered the city. Yet no one remembered
that same poor man.
16 Then I said:

"Wisdom *is* better than [a]strength.
Nevertheless [b]the poor man's
wisdom *is* despised,
And his words are not heard.
17 Words of the wise, *spoken*
quietly, *should be* heard
Rather than the shout of a ruler
of fools.
18 Wisdom *is* better than weapons
of war;
But [a]one* sinner destroys much
good."

17 [a]Job 5:9; Ps. 73:16; Eccl. 3:11; Rom. 11:33

CHAPTER 9

1 [a]Deut. 33:3; Job 12:10; Eccl. 8:14 [1]Lit. *put*
2 [a]Gen. 3:17–19; Job 21:7; Ps. 73:3, 12, 13; Mal. 3:15 [1]LXX, Syr., Vg. *good and bad,* *See WW at Lev. 10:10.
5 [a]Job 14:21; Is. 63:16 [b]Job 7:8–10; Eccl. 1:11; 2:16; 8:10; Is. 26:14
7 [a]Eccl. 8:15
9 [a]Eccl. 2:10 [1]Lit. *See life*
10 [a][Col. 3:17] [b]Rom. 12:11; Col. 3:23 *See WW at Hos. 13:14.
11 [a]Jer. 9:23; Amos 2:14, 15 [b]1 Sam. 6:9
12 [a]Eccl. 8:7 [b]Prov. 29:6; Luke 12:20, 39; 17:26; 1 Thess. 5:3
14 [a]2 Sam. 20:16–22 [1]LXX, Syr., Vg. *bulwarks*
16 [a]Eccl. 7:12, 19 [b]Mark 6:2, 3
18 [a]Josh. 7:1–26; 2 Kin. 21:2–17 *See WW at Deut. 6:4.

9:1 The future is unknown to mere mortals.
9:2, 3 The Preacher returns to a previous subject: one fate awaits all men, whatever their status. Thus retribution as an eternal verity is a failure. ***He who fears an oath:*** The one against whom the oath has been sworn.
9:4 Life is better than death because the living have hope.
9:7–10 See section 2 of Truth-In-Action at the end of Eccl.
9:11, 12 Again the Preacher returns to the common end for all. Since the only thing in life that is certain is death, enjoy life while you have it.
9:13–18 Men are vain because they forget the good deeds of the wise man as they earlier forgot the evil done by the wicked (8:10).

10 Dead[1] flies [2]putrefy the
perfumer's ointment,
And cause it to give off a foul
odor;
So does a little folly to one
respected for wisdom *and*
honor.
2 A wise man's heart *is* at his right
hand,
But a fool's heart at his left.
3 Even when a fool walks along the
way,
He lacks wisdom,
[a]And he shows everyone *that* he
is a fool.
4 If the spirit of the ruler rises
against you,
[a]Do not leave your post;
For [b]conciliation[1] pacifies great
offenses.

5 There is an evil I have seen under
the sun,
As an error proceeding from the
ruler:
6 [a]Folly is set in [1]great dignity,
While the rich sit in a lowly place.
7 I have seen servants [a]on horses,
While princes walk on the ground
like servants.

8 [a]He who digs a pit will fall into it,
And whoever breaks through a
wall will be bitten by a serpent.
9 He who quarries stones may be
hurt by them,
And he who splits wood may be
endangered by it.
10 If the ax is dull,
And one does not sharpen the
edge,
Then he must use more *strength;
But wisdom [1]brings* success.

CHAPTER 10

1 [1]Lit. *Flies of death* [2]Tg., Vg. omit *putrefy* **3** [a]Prov. 13:16; 18:2 **4** [a]Eccl. 8:3 [b]1 Sam. 25:24–33; Prov. 25:15 [1]Lit. *healing, health* **6** [a]Esth. 3:1 [1]*exalted positions* **7** [a]Prov. 19:10; 30:22 **8** [a]Ps. 7:15; Prov. 26:27 **10** [1]Lit. *is a successful advantage* *See WW at Zech. 4:6. • See WW at Eccl. 11:6.

11 [a]Ps. 58:4, 5; Jer. 8:17 [1]Lit. *master of the tongue* **12** [a]Prov. 10:32; Luke 4:22 [b]Prov. 10:14; Eccl. 4:5 **14** [a][Prov. 15:2]; Eccl. 5:3 [b]Eccl. 3:22; 8:7 **16** [a]Is. 3:4, 5; 5:11 **17** [a]Prov. 31:4; Is. 5:11 **18** [a]Prov. 24:30–34 [1]Lit. *rafters sink* **19** [a]Judg. 9:13; Ps. 104:15; Eccl. 2:3 **20** [a]Ex. 22:28; Acts 23:5

11 A serpent may bite [a]when *it is* not
charmed;
The [1]babbler is no different.
12 [a]The words of a wise man's mouth
are gracious,
But [b]the lips of a fool shall
swallow him up;
13 The words of his mouth begin
with foolishness,
And the end of his talk *is* raving
madness.
14 [a]A fool also multiplies words.
No man knows what is to be;
Who can tell him [b]what will be
after him?
15 The labor of fools wearies them,
For they do not even know how
to go to the city!

16 [a]Woe to you, O land, when your
king *is* a child,
And your princes feast in the
morning!
17 Blessed *are* you, O land, when
your king *is* the son of nobles,
And your [a]princes feast at the
proper time—
For strength and not for
drunkenness!
18 Because of laziness the [1]building
decays,
And [a]through idleness of hands
the house leaks.
19 A feast is made for laughter,
And [a]wine makes merry;
But money answers everything.

20 [a]Do not curse the king, even in
your thought;
Do not curse the rich, even in
your bedroom;
For a bird of the air may carry
your voice,

10:1—11:6 The Preacher returns to his discussion of traditional wisdom and its uses that were broken off in 8:10. It is difficult to divide this portion of the book into sections, since each verse or two appears to treat a different subject.
10:1 People always seem more ready to notice your bad points than your good ones.
10:2 Right . . . left: Good and evil as the ancient world saw them.
10:3 Walks along the way: Even in the casual affairs of life, the fool (the wicked man) cannot disguise his true nature.
10:4 When you encounter a difficult situation in the king's presence, do not panic. Keep calm and see it through (see note on 8:3).
10:5–7 From corrupted power come corrupt appointments: fools in high positions, **rich** (that is, wise) men in low ones; **servants** on horseback and **princes** on foot.
10:8, 9 The one who plots evil will eventually feel its effects.
10:10 The wise person gets the job done much more quickly and efficiently than the fool who is compared to a **dull ax.**
10:12–14 Once again the Preacher shows the superiority of the wise man over the **fool**: the fool simply babbles on, unaware he is damaging himself by his speech (see note on 2:13, 14).
10:15 Go to the city: That is, get along in life.
10:16 Child: The Hebrew term means "boy"; it is the same word translated "young men" in 1 Kin. 12:8, 10 where it describes the brash counselors consulted by Rehoboam, even though they were probably about 40 years old. Thus, the term is used in a derogatory manner to denote someone without wisdom and good judgment. **Feast in the morning:** If feasting were done in the "proper time—for strength and not for drunkenness," that is, in the evening, the land would be blessed (v. 17). But feasting in the morning points to drunkenness, which would result in a mismanaged government and economy.
10:19 Money answers everything: The Preacher has just stated the purpose for the **feast** (**laughter**) and **wine** (**makes merry**). Money, on the other hand, can be spent or invested, and the one who has it always retains options that are automatically forfeited by the person who has spent all his cash.

And a bird in flight may tell the
matter.

The Value of Diligence

11 Cast your bread [a]upon the
waters,
[b]For you will find it after many
days.
2 [a]Give a serving [b]to seven, and also
to eight,
[c]For you do not know what evil
will be on the earth.

3 If the clouds are full of rain,
They empty *themselves* upon the
earth;
And if a tree falls to the south or
the north,
In the place where the tree falls,
there it shall lie.
4 He who observes the wind will
not sow,
And he who regards the clouds
will not reap.

5 As [a]you do not know what *is* the
way of the [1]wind,
[b]*Or* how the bones *grow* in the
womb of her who is with child,
So you do not know the works of
God who makes everything.
6 In the morning *sow your seed,
And in the evening do not
withhold your hand;
For you do not know which will
prosper,
Either this or that,
Or whether both alike *will be*
good.

WORD WEALTH

11:6 prosper, *chashar* (kah-*shar*); Strong's #3787: To be right, successful, proper, correct; to be correctly aligned with certain requirements. *Chashar* occurs 3 times in the OT: in this reference; in 10:10, "bring success"; and in Esth. 8:5, where the queen presents her request on condition that it "seem right" to the king. *Chashar* thus describes whatever is right, fitting, and proper; furthermore, something will prosper and be successful simply because of its "rightness." Its postbiblical derivative *kosher* means that food is properly prepared according to Jewish dietary laws derived from Scripture and rabbinic specifications.

7 Truly the light is sweet,
And *it is* pleasant for the eyes
[a]to behold the sun;
8 But if a man lives many years
And [a]rejoices in them all,
Yet let him [b]remember the days
of darkness,
For they will be many.
All that is coming *is* vanity.

Seek God in Early Life

9 Rejoice, O young man, in your
youth,
And let your heart cheer you in
the days of your youth;
[a]Walk in the [1]ways of your heart,
And [2]in the sight of your eyes;
But know that for all these
[b]God will bring you into judgment.
10 Therefore remove [1]sorrow from
your heart,
And [a]put away evil from your
flesh,
[b]For childhood and [2]youth *are*
vanity.

12 *Remember[a] now your Creator **1**
in the days of your youth,
Before the [1]difficult days come,
And the years draw near
[b]when you say,
"I have no pleasure in them":
2 While the sun and the light,

CHAPTER 11

1 [a]Is. 32:20 [b][Deut. 15:10; Prov. 19:17; Matt. 10:42; 2 Cor. 9:8; Gal. 6:9, 10; Heb. 6:10] **2** [a]Ps. 112:9; Matt. 5:42; Luke 6:30; [1 Tim. 6:18, 19] [b]Mic. 5:5 [c]Eph. 5:16 **5** [a]John 3:8 [b]Ps. 139:14 [1]Or *spirit* **6** *See WW at Hos. 10:12. **7** [a]Eccl. 7:11 **8** [a]Eccl. 9:7 [b]Eccl. 12:1 **9** [a]Num. 15:39; Job 31:7; Eccl. 2:10 [b]Eccl. 3:17; 12:14; [Rom. 14:10] [1]Impulses [2]As you see to be best **10** [a]2 Cor. 7:1; 2 Tim. 2:22 [b]Ps. 39:5 [1]*vexation* [2]Prime of life

CHAPTER 12

1 [a]2 Chr. 34:3; Prov. 22:6; Lam. 3:27 [b]2 Sam. 19:35 [1]Lit. *evil* *See WW at Is. 62:6.

11:1 Cast your bread upon the waters: Invest your money; do not simply hoard it.
11:2 Give a serving to seven: Be generous with your wealth; or, if tied to v. 1, be diverse in your investments. In either case, the **evil** that **will be on the earth** speaks of times of hardship when one needs friends and secure investments.
11:3–6 The Preacher advises against delaying because of a greedy desire to invest at the ideal time in order to realize the last bit of profit. Rather, sow your seed **in the morning,** that is, make diversified investments while you are young.
11:7–10 Here the entire mood of the book changes and the first summary of the conclusion occurs. See the Outline. The Preacher has failed to find anything of lasting value "under the sun" (in this life), since life itself is **vanity** (transitory and impermanent, v. 8; see note on 1:2). Thus he is driven to two conclusions: 1) in this life the best thing to do is to enjoy the blessings of God (see note on 5:18–20); and 2) any absolute value must transcend this life, finding itself rooted in the justice of God (v. 9). Knowing that God will judge all things should motivate us to lead moral lives (v. 10) even in the course of enjoying the things with which He has blessed us.
12:1–7 The second summary of the conclusion is presented in the form of an allegory on old age (vv. 2–5) and death (vv. 6, 7), designed to show how fleeting life is and why we should remember God while we are young (v. 1).
12:1 See section 1 of Truth-In-Action at the end of Eccl.
12:2 Darkened . . . clouds: Darkness speaks of the clouding of vision that frequently accompanies old age. Clouds probably refer to the depression into which old people often sink.

The moon and the stars,
Are not darkened,
And the clouds do not return after
the rain;
3 In the day when the keepers of
the house tremble,
And the strong men bow down;
When the grinders cease because
they are few,
And those that look through the
windows grow dim;
4 When the doors are shut in the
streets,
And the sound of grinding is low;
When one rises up at the sound
of a bird,
And all [a]the daughters of music
are brought low.
5 Also they are afraid of height,
And of terrors in the way;
When the almond tree blossoms,
The grasshopper is a burden,
And desire fails.
For man goes to [a]his eternal
home,
And [b]the mourners go about the
streets.

6 *Remember your Creator* before
the silver cord is [1]loosed,
Or the golden bowl is broken,
Or the pitcher shattered at the
fountain,
Or the wheel broken at the well.
7 [a]Then the dust will return to the
earth as it was,
[b]And the spirit will return to God
[c]who gave it.

8 "Vanity[a] of vanities," says the
Preacher,
"All *is* vanity."

The Whole Duty of Man

9 And moreover, because the
Preacher was wise, he still taught the
people knowledge; yes, he pondered
and sought out *and* [a]set[1] in order many
proverbs.
10 The Preacher sought to find
[1]acceptable words; and *what was* written *was* upright—words of truth.
11 The words of the wise are like
goads, and the words of [1]scholars are
like well-driven nails, given by one
Shepherd.
12 And further, my son, be admon- **2**
ished by these. Of making many books
there is no end, and [a]much study *is*
wearisome to the flesh.
13 Let us hear the conclusion of the
whole matter:

[a]Fear God and keep His
commandments,
For this is man's all.
14 For [a]God will bring every work
into judgment,
Including every secret thing,
Whether good or evil.

4 [a]2 Sam. 19:35
5 [a]Job 17:13 [b]Gen. 50:10; Jer. 9:17
6 [1]So with Qr., Tg.; Kt. *removed;* LXX, Vg. *broken*
7 [a]Gen. 3:19; Job 34:15; Ps. 90:3 [b]Eccl. 3:21 [c]Num. 16:22; 27:16; Job 34:14; Is. 57:16; Zech. 12:1
8 [a]Ps. 62:9
9 [a]1 Kin. 4:32 [1]*arranged*
10 [1]Lit. *delightful*
11 [1]Lit. *masters of assemblies*
12 [a]Eccl. 1:18
13 [a][Deut. 6:2; 10:12]; Mic. 6:8
14 [a]Eccl. 11:9; Matt. 12:36; [Acts 17:30, 31; Rom. 2:16; 1 Cor. 4:5; 2 Cor. 5:10]

12:3 Keepers of the house tremble: The hands of the aged, which "keep" (take care of) the **house** (the body), **tremble. Grinders cease:** A loss of teeth normally accompanies increasing age, especially in the ancient world where there was no real dental care.

12:4 The picture painted here is of an elderly person who seldom goes out, eats little, is easily awakened by trivial noises, and whose hearing is failing.

12:5 Elderly people are generally frightened of heights because their balance and depth perception are no longer reliable. **Almond tree blossoms:** The blossoms of the almond tree are white, and so is the hair of the aged. Grasshopper . . . burden: Either 1) something as light as a grasshopper is a burden; or 2) the grasshopper is a burden to himself when he is about to die, portraying an aged person to whom movement is painful.

12:6 Death is here pictured as the loosing of a silver cord, the breaking of a golden bowl, or the shattering of a pitcher at the well.

12:7 The picture of death given here as the separation of **the spirit** (breath) from the body is paralleled by 3:21; 8:8; Job 34:14, 15; Ps. 104:29 and, as such, forms a picture antithetical to that of the creation of human life described in Gen. 2:7; Ezek. 37:9, 10.

12:8 See note on 1:2.

12:9–14 These verses, like 1:1, 2 are written in the third person, showing the work of a disciple who arranged the book of the Preacher's work in its present form. The disciple wants the reader to understand the importance of his teacher's work (vv. 9–11), after which he adds a summary in his own words, probably quoting his teacher in vv. 12–14, in order to make certain that the reader really has understood the point being made. Although the increase of books and human knowledge will never cease, human wisdom yields values that are limited and transitory (see notes on 1:13–18) and thus brings weariness. By contrast, reverence for God and the obedience that is its natural outgrowth are literally **man's all,** a term that stands in sharp contrast to the things of this world that are found to be "vanity." Those things will pass away, but one's relationship with God will stand at the time when He judges the Earth (v. 14). Was, then, the Preacher's quest futile? By no means. It showed clearly where one's priorities should lie: not in the things of this life, but in God.

12:12–14 See section 2 of Truth-In-Action at the end of Eccl.

TRUTH-IN-ACTION through ECCLESIASTES

Letting the LIFE of the Holy Spirit Bring Faith's Works Alive in You!

Truth Ecclesiastes Teaches	Text	**Action** Ecclesiastes Invites
1 Knowing God and His Ways We are to revere God as the Creator who works everything perfectly after the counsel of His own will.	3:14	**Believe** that everything God does is perfect.
	12:1	**Establish** your relationship with God while you are young, before the evils of life harden your heart.
2 Guidelines for Growing in Godliness The "Preacher" counsels his readers toward godly living. We are to live with a view to the futility and vanity of a life spent without reference to God. Much of the energy we spend trying to accomplish various tasks ends up "sowing to the wind." The life lived in fidelity and integrity is the only one that has any real meaning.	2:24–26	**Seek to please God** in all you do.
	3:22	**Endeavor** to find enjoyment in your work and daily life.
	7:8, 9	**Avoid** rashness or hastiness. **Know** that God is never in a hurry. **Make no important decisions** with an agitated spirit.
	8:5, 6	**Determine** to obey those who have the rule over you. **Believe** that you will know how and when to accomplish the assigned task.
	9:7–10	**Conduct** a Spirit-filled life. **Honor** marital fidelity. **Serve** the Lord with all your might.
	12:12–14	**Do not attempt** to substitute scholarship for obedience. **Cultivate** the fear of the Lord.
3 Keys to Wise Living The "Preacher" says that if you know God and seek to live your life before Him in a way that pleases Him, you will be living wisely. Wise living involves learning to assess the relative value of choices one might make. The wise individual chooses those things that have lasting value. Often the wisest choices will not be those that are apparently best by the world's standards.	2:1–11	**Understand** that the pursuit of pleasure for its own sake is a vain pursuit.
	2:12–16	**Understand** that a life lived strictly for the sake of wisdom is futile.
	2:17–23	**Recognize** that dedication to work as its own reward is a vain pursuit.
	5:18–20	**Get into work** you really enjoy and for which you can be grateful. **Understand** that to toil without enjoyment is vain and meaningless.
	6:1, 2	**Understand** that to work so hard that you cannot enjoy the fruit of your labors is foolishness. **Beware** workaholism!
	7:15–18	**Avoid** taking extreme positions unnecessarily.
4 Steps in Developing Humility One message in Eccl. comes through loud and clear: Walk gently and humbly before the Lord. "God *is* in heaven, and you on earth." The more we know about God, the more humble we will be. The humble person recognizes his own limitations and accepts them.	1:10, 11	**Accept** and **recognize** that human understanding of history is partial and distorted. **Know** that the facts mankind has forgotten could change your perspective entirely.
	3:11	**Accept** your limitations. **Know** that you cannot comprehend eternity. **Learn to accept** God's perfect timing.
	4:13–16	**Understand** that the pursuit of personal ambition is vain and futile.
	7:1–4	**Be mindful** of your mortality. **Let bereavement bring** you times of sober self-assessment.

Truth Ecclesiastes Teaches	Text	**Action** Ecclesiastes Invites
5 Keys to Handling Money Being a righteous steward of worldly wealth flows out of a godly perspective with regard to money. Money is a servant to utilize, not a god to serve. One's motives in acquiring and using money are the determining factors.	5:10 5:11 5:19	**Consider** and **understand** that wealth is intrinsically elusive. **Understand** that wealth is by its very nature deceptive. **Know** the difference between wealth that has been sought and wealth that has come from the hand of God. **Understand** that the latter has no curse associated with it.
6 Steps to Dealing with Sin The wise person understands that to willfully practice sin is to become its slave, and to delay in dealing with sin appropriately is to promote it.	8:8 8:11	**Understand** that you are the slave of any wickedness that you practice (see Rom. 6:16). **Carry out** any discipline you determine is necessary without delay, because delay may foster wrongdoing.
7 How to Tame the Tongue When we speak, we must be aware that the Lord hears every word we say. Presumptuous speech displeases the Lord and can bring discipline.	5:1–3 5:4–7	**Be quick** to listen and **slow** to speak. **Cultivate** humility and **learn** to walk softly before the Lord. **Do not speak presumptuously** of spiritual commitment or endeavor. **Cultivate** reverence for the Lord.

The Song of SOLOMON

Author: Attributed to Solomon
Date: Solomon Reigned 970–930 B.C.
Theme: The Quest for Authentic Love
Key Words: Love, Garden, Mother's House

Author Solomon's authorship is disputed, but the glory of Solomonic symbolism is essential to the Song. Jesus referred twice to Solomon's glory and wisdom (Matt. 6:29; 12:42). As David's royal son, Solomon had a unique place in covenant history (2 Sam. 7:12, 13). His two birth names, which symbolize peace (Solomon) and love (Jedidiah), readily apply to the Song (2 Sam. 12:24, 25; 1 Chr. 22:9). Solomon's glorious kingdom was like a restoration of the Garden of Eden (1 Kin. 4:20–34), and the temple and palace he built embody the truths of the tabernacle and the conquest of the Promised Land (1 Kin. 6; 7). Solomon is perfectly cast as the personified blessings of covenant love since he appears in the Song with all of his regal perfection (1:2–4; 5:10–16).

Occasion and Date Though the Song does not supply precise background information, Solomon reigned over Israel from 970 to 930 B.C. Similar language and ideals are also found in David's temple prayer for Solomon and for the people at Solomon's enthronement (1 Chr. 29).

Purpose "Love" is the key word in the Song. This love, presenting the passionate desire between a man and a woman, King Solomon and the Shulamite, celebrates the joyous potential of marriage in light of sworn covenant principles. The basis for all human love should be covenant love, the master metaphor of the Bible. This covenant love is also the basis of the relationship between God and man; therefore, the Song applies properly to both marriage and to covenant history. The Shulamite therefore personifies the wife in an ideal marriage and the covenant people and their history in the Promised Land under the blessings of royal Solomonic love.

Characteristics The Song is the best of all songs, a literary work of art and a theological masterpiece. In the second century one of the greatest Jewish rabbis, Akiba ben Joseph, said, "In the entire world there is nothing to equal the day on which the Song of Songs was given to Israel." The Song itself is like its favorite fruit, pomegranates, alive with color and full of seeds. Quite unlike any other biblical book, it merits special consideration as a biblical archetype which presents anew the basic realities of man's relationships. The Song employs symbolic language to express timeless truths, much like the Book of Revelation.

Content The Song contains portraits of the Shulamite woman along with a full array of her garden products. These should be taken both as poetic parallels of marital love and as covenant blessings of the people in their land.

Clear directions are given in the discovery of covenant blessings, "Follow in the footsteps of the flock" (1:8). Footsteps here is literally "heelprints," and may be an allusion to Jacob, the national father whose name connotes "a heel." Jacob's shepherd role and his lifelong struggle for the blessing of God and man are cited as the biblical norm for God's people (Hos. 12:3–6, 12, 13). He was born grasping his brother's heel, a congenital manipulator. He was "disjointed" with deception at the core of his being as illustrated by his limp at Mahanaim (Gen. 32). He was forced to live outside the land under the threat of an angry brother. He returned to the land after twenty years with a faulty family foundation. Deception, lack of love, jealousy, anger, and love for hire (for mandrakes) went into the shaky substructure. The very names of the Twelve Tribes show the need for a new family history.

The Shulamite relives and rewrites that history. She does the memorial dance to Mahanaim (6:13; see Gen. 32:2). When she finds the one she loves she holds him and will not let him go (3:4; see Gen. 32:26). Fragrant mandrakes grow in her fields (7:11–13; see Gen. 30:14). When the daughters see her, they call her blessed or happy (6:9; see Gen. 30:13). In the Shulamite the corrupt family tree of Israel bears "pleasant *fruits*," the very best (7:13; see Deut. 33:13–17). The covenant blessings that had gone awry are redeemed.

These same incidents can be seen as portraits of marital love as well. In this respect it is her husband whom she holds and will not let go (3:4). It is her husband who praises her beauty (6:4–10), and it is a royal wedding procession and the bride and groom's rejoicing in one another that are portrayed in 3:6—5:1.

Personal Application The Song is a constant goad to drifting marriages with its challenge to seek for openness, growth, and joyous relationship. It also makes an excellent premarital manual. As a biblical archetype it can bring healing to the core of our being with its hope of covenant love as it reshapes our marriages. Its portrayal of the covenant love relationship also has application to the covenant love relationship enjoyed by God's church. In this regard, the Song can be rich in symbolism but should not be read as an arbitrary allegory with mysterious meanings supplied by the whim of the reader; rather, any such personal application of one's love relationship with Christ should be interpreted with solid application, using *obvious* biblical parallels.

Christ Revealed In the Song of Solomon, as in other parts of the Bible, the Garden of Eden, the Promised Land, the tabernacle with its ark of the covenant, the temple of Solomon, the new heavens and the new earth are all related to Jesus Christ, so it is not a matter of merely choosing a few verses that prophesy of Christ. The very essence of covenant history and covenant love is reproduced in Him (Luke 24:27; 2 Cor. 1:20).

The Holy Spirit at Work According to Romans 5:5, "the love of God has been poured out in our hearts by the Holy Spirit." On the basis of Jesus Christ, the Holy Spirit is the bond and the binding power of love. The joyous oneness revealed in the Song is inconceivable apart from the Holy Spirit. The very form of the book as song and symbol is especially adapted to the Spirit, for He Himself uses dreams, picture-language, and singing (Acts 2:17; Eph. 5:18, 19). A subtle wordplay based on the divine "breathing" of the breath of life (the Holy Spirit, Ps. 104:29, 30) in Genesis 2:7 seems to surface in the Song. It shows up in the "break" or breathing of the day (2:17; 4:6), in the "blowing" of the wind on the Shulamite's garden (4:16), and surprisingly in the fragrant scent and fruit of the apple tree (7:8).

Outline of Song of Solomon

I. Opening scenes **1:1—2:7**
- A. Remembering the love of the king with the good name 1:1–4
- B. The dark but lovely vineyard keeper 1:5, 6
- C. Finding love in the footsteps of the flock 1:7, 8
- D. Removing the marks of slavery 1:9–11
- E. The language of love 1:12–17
- F. The thorn and the tree 2:1–6
- G. The first sworn charge 2:7

II. The quest for openness **2:8—3:5**
- A. Beginning the quest 2:8–15
- B. The joy of love in the cool of the day 2:16, 17
- C. The determined search for the primal goal 3:1–4
- D. The second sworn charge 3:5

III. The quest for mutuality **3:6—5:8**
- A. The royal wedding carriage of covenant love 3:6–11
- B. Getting acquainted with the Shulamite 4:1–7
- C. A view of the land from the top of Mount Hermon 4:8
- D. Intimate union life in a shared garden banquet 4:9—5:1
- E. The fall of the Shulamite 5:2–7
- F. The third sworn charge 5:8

IV. The quest for oneness **5:9—8:4**
- A. Getting acquainted with Solomon 5:9—6:3
- B. The Shulamite's triumphant glory 6:4–10
- C. The Shulamite's noble people 6:11, 12
- D. The memorial dance to Mahanaim 6:13—7:9
- E. The initiation of a new love as equals 7:9—8:3
- F. The fourth sworn charge 8:4

V. Closing scenes with summary achievements **8:5–14**
- A. Achieving the primal goal 8:5
- B. Achieving authentic love 8:6, 7
- C. Achieving motherhood and peace 8:8–10
- D. Achieving a vineyard equal to Solomon's 8:11, 12
- E. Achieving the inheritance 8:13, 14

THE [a]song of songs, which *is* Solomon's.

The Banquet

THE [1]SHULAMITE

[1] 2 Let him kiss me with the kisses
of his mouth—
[a]For [2]your love *is* better than wine.
3 Because of the fragrance of your
good ointments,
Your name *is* ointment poured
forth;
Therefore the virgins love you.
4 [a]Draw me away!

THE DAUGHTERS OF JERUSALEM

[b]We will run after [1]you.

THE SHULAMITE

The king [c]has brought me into his
chambers.

CHAPTER 1

1 [a]1 Kin. 4:32
2 [a]Song 4:10 [1]A Palestinian young woman, Song 6:13. The speaker and audience are identified according to the number, gender, and person of the Hebrew words. Occasionally the identity is not certain. [2]Masc. sing.: the Beloved

4 [a]Hos. 11:4 [b]Phil. 3:12–14 [c]Ps. 45:14, 15 [1]Masc. sing.: the Beloved

1:1 The Shulamite: It will be most helpful to carefully note the NKJV insertions as to who is speaking.
1:2–4 See section 1 of Truth-In-Action at the end of Song.
1:2–4 This scene reveals awakened desire for intimate life with the king because of his surpassing excellence, illustrating that love is a passionate desire for union life. The love of this fragrant **king** is twice **good** (the word "good" appears twice in Hebrew in its plural form).

THE DAUGHTERS OF JERUSALEM

We will be glad and rejoice in
[2]you.

We will remember [3]your love
more than wine.

THE SHULAMITE

Rightly do they *love [3]you.

5 I *am* dark, but lovely,
O daughters of Jerusalem,
Like the tents of Kedar,
Like the curtains of Solomon.
6 Do not look upon me, because I
am dark,
Because the sun has [1]tanned me.
My mother's sons were angry
with me;
They made me the keeper of the
vineyards,
But my own [a]vineyard I have not
kept.

(TO HER BELOVED)

2 7 Tell me, O you whom I love,
Where you feed *your flock,*
Where you make *it* rest at noon.
For why should I be as one who
[1]veils herself
By the flocks of your
*companions?

THE BELOVED

2 8 If you do not know, [a]O fairest
among women,
[1]Follow in the footsteps of the
flock,
And feed your little goats
Beside the shepherds' tents.

4 [2]Fem. sing.: the Shulamite [3]Masc. sing.: the Beloved *See WW at Ps. 97:10.
6 [a]Song 8:11, 12 [1]Lit. *looked upon me*
7 [1]LXX, Syr., Vg. *wanders* *See WW at Ps. 119:63.
8 [a]Song 5:9 [1]Lit. *Go out*

9 [a]Song 2:2, 10, 13; 4:1, 7; John 15:14 [b]2 Chr. 1:16
10 [a]Ezek. 16:11
11 [1]Fem. sing.: the Shulamite
12 [1]*perfume*
15 [a]Song 4:1; 5:12 [1]*my companion, friend*
16 [a]Song 5:10–16 [1]*couch*

9 I have compared you, [a]my love,
[b]To my filly among Pharaoh's
chariots.
10 [a]Your cheeks are lovely with
ornaments,
Your neck with chains *of gold.*

THE DAUGHTERS OF JERUSALEM

11 We will make [1]you ornaments of
gold
With studs of silver.

THE SHULAMITE

12 While the king *is* at his table,
My [1]spikenard sends forth its
fragrance.
13 A bundle of myrrh *is* my beloved
to me,
That lies all night between my
breasts.
14 My beloved *is* to me a cluster of
henna *blooms*
In the vineyards of En Gedi.

THE BELOVED

15 [a]Behold, you *are* fair, [1]my love!
Behold, you *are* fair!
You *have* dove's eyes.

THE SHULAMITE

16 Behold, you *are* [a]handsome, my
beloved!
Yes, pleasant!
Also our [1]bed *is* green.
17 The beams of our houses *are*
cedar,
And our rafters of fir.

2 I *am* the rose of Sharon,
And the lily of the valleys.

1:5, 6 Dark denotes a ruddy color from sunburning. **But lovely** is her courageous and proud response to the **daughters of Jerusalem** who were staring with the implication that her coloring was some natural defect of her beauty. She was exposed to **the sun** because of the anger of her **mother's sons.** Human anger is the directly destructive opposite of the blessings of covenant love, and usually disguises hatred against God. The Shulamite's family is characterized by burning anger.
1:7 See section 2 of Truth-In-Action at the end of Song.
1:7 The Shulamite shuns being **one who veils herself.** This best describes the isolation of a leper who dwells alone, outside the camp, in contrast to the community's shared life of covenant love. Shared covenant love is crucial for curing "leprosy-loneliness." This is perhaps why Jesus specifically sent the disciples to the "lost sheep of the house of Israel" with a command to "cleanse the lepers" (Matt. 10:6–8).
1:8 See section 2 of Truth-In-Action at the end of Song.
1:8 The footsteps of the flock are literally "heelprints," from which Jacob gets his name (Gen. 25:23–26). All the patriarchs of Israel were shepherds, and Jacob's shepherd role is a norm for the nation (Hos. 12:12, 13). Her beloved is therefore telling her to look to history for the cure to aloneness.
1:12–17 This brief series of loving responses models communication and shows the inherent dialogue of love. **En Gedi** is a beautiful oasis alongside the Dead Sea, where David refused to harm Saul. The language of love ends all hostile and divisive communication, for it speaks out of a shared life and magnifies oneness: **our bed, our houses, our rafters.**
2:1–6 The pronoun in v. 5 is emphatic: this means *me, I am* lovesick! Love is a life-and-death issue, a personal matter; without the love of the other, one is alone and incomplete, love-starved. The **banner** over the **banqueting** house joyously signals that love has the proper place, the necessary provisions, and the triumphant power to respond.

THE BELOVED

2 Like a lily among thorns,
So is my love among the daughters.

THE SHULAMITE

3 Like an apple tree among the trees of the woods,
So *is* my beloved among the sons.
I sat down in his shade with great delight,
And [a]his fruit *was* sweet to my taste.

THE SHULAMITE TO THE DAUGHTERS OF JERUSALEM

4 He brought me to the [1]banqueting house,
And his banner over me *was* love.
5 Sustain me with cakes of raisins,
Refresh me with apples,
For I *am* lovesick.

6 [a]His left hand *is* under my head,
And his right hand embraces me.
1 7 [a]I [1]charge you, O daughters of Jerusalem,
By the gazelles or by the does of the field,
Do not stir up nor awaken love
Until it pleases.

The Beloved's Request

THE SHULAMITE

8 The voice of my beloved!
Behold, he comes
Leaping upon the mountains,
Skipping upon the hills.
9 [a]My beloved is like a gazelle or a young stag.
Behold, he stands behind our wall;
He is looking through the windows,
Gazing through the lattice.

CHAPTER 2
3 [a]Song 4:16; Rev. 22:1, 2
4 [1]Lit. *house of wine*
6 [a]Song 8:3
7 [a]Song 3:5; 8:4 [1]*adjure*
9 [a]Prov. 6:5; Song 2:17
14 [a]Song 5:2 [b]Song 8:13 [1]Lit. *appearance*
15 [a]Ps. 80:13; Ezek. 13:4; Luke 13:32
16 [a]Song 6:3
17 [a]Song 4:6 [b]Song 8:14 [1]Lit. *Separation*

10 My beloved spoke, and said to me:
"Rise up, my love, my fair one,
And come away.
11 For lo, the winter is past,
The rain is over *and* gone.
12 The flowers appear on the earth;
The time of singing has come,
And the voice of the turtledove
Is heard in our land.
13 The fig tree puts forth her green figs,
And the vines *with* the tender grapes
Give a good smell.
Rise up, my love, my fair one,
And come away!

14 "O my [a]dove, in the clefts of the rock, 2
In the secret *places* of the cliff,
Let me see your [1]face,
[b]Let me hear your voice;
For your voice *is* sweet,
And your face *is* lovely."

HER BROTHERS

15 Catch us [a]the foxes,
The little foxes that spoil the vines,
For our vines *have* tender grapes.

THE SHULAMITE

16 [a]My beloved *is* mine, and I *am* his.
He feeds *his flock* among the lilies.

(TO HER BELOVED)

17 [a]Until the day breaks
And the shadows flee away,
Turn, my beloved,
And be [b]like a gazelle
Or a young stag
Upon the mountains of [1]Bether.

2:7 See section 1 of Truth-In-Action at the end of Song.
2:7 This charge appears four times with variations and provides an overall outline for the Song (v. 7; 3:5; 5:8; 8:4). The urgent message is that unauthorized **love** is not to be stirred up or awakened. In other words, there is no true love without self-restraint and ethical responsibility. In these charges love appears as a person; it has its own laws and operates by independent rights as natural as the laws of nature. These sworn principles are illustrated by **the gazelles** and **does of the field,** magnificent fugitive animals never meant to be tamed. They belong in the wild, following their own inner laws of joyous unbounded freedom.
2:8–15 Love can bound over **mountains,** but it cannot leap over the **wall** of the **beloved**; it is strong but never uses force. She must come out from behind her wall and willingly venture into the openness of springtime. There are no giants in **our land,** but there are **little foxes,** like unbelief, resistance, and hardness of heart (Num. 13; 14). Hardness of heart is the great enemy of love, since everything depends on receptivity and openness.
2:14, 15 See section 2 of Truth-In-Action at the end of Song.
2:16, 17 The Song frequently inserts a series of similar joyous relational statements (vv. 6, 16, 17; 4:6; 6:2, 3; 7:10; 8:3, 14). They affirm the truth of oneness and acknowledge the need for mutual nurturing.

A Troubled Night

THE SHULAMITE

3 By [a]night on my bed I sought the
one I love;
I sought him, but I did not find
him.
2 "I will rise now," *I said,*
"And go about the city;
In the streets and in the squares
I will seek the one I love."
I sought him, but I did not find
him.
3 [a]The watchmen who go about the
city found me;
I said,
"Have you seen the one I love?"
4 Scarcely had I passed by them,
When I found the one I love.
I held him and would not let him
go,
Until I had brought him to the
[a]house of my mother,
And into the [1]chamber of her who
conceived me.
1 5 [a]I [1]charge you, O daughters of
Jerusalem,
By the gazelles or by the does of
the field,
Do not *stir up nor awaken love
Until it pleases.

The Coming of Solomon

THE SHULAMITE

6 [a]Who *is* this coming out of the
wilderness
Like pillars of smoke,
Perfumed with myrrh and
frankincense,
With all the merchant's fragrant
powders?
7 Behold, it *is* Solomon's couch,
With sixty valiant men around it,
Of the valiant of Israel.
8 They all hold swords,
Being expert in war.
Every man *has* his sword on his
thigh
Because of fear in the night.
9 Of the wood of Lebanon
Solomon the King
Made himself a [1]palanquin:
10 He made its pillars *of* silver,
Its support *of* gold,
Its seat *of* purple,
Its interior paved *with* love
By the daughters of Jerusalem.
11 Go forth, O daughters of Zion,
And see King Solomon with the
crown
With which his mother crowned
him
On the day of his wedding,
The day of the gladness of his
heart.

THE BELOVED

4 Behold, [a]you *are* fair, my love! 3
Behold, you *are* fair!
You *have* dove's eyes behind your
veil.
Your hair *is* like a [b]flock of goats,
Going down from Mount Gilead.
2 [a]Your teeth *are* like a flock of
shorn *sheep*
Which have come up from the
washing,
Every one of which bears twins,
And none *is* [1]barren among them.
3 Your lips *are* like a strand of
scarlet,
And your mouth is lovely.
[a]Your temples behind your veil
Are like a piece of pomegranate.
4 [a]Your neck *is* like the tower of
David,
Built [b]for an armory,
On which hang a thousand
[1]bucklers,
All shields of mighty men.
5 [a]Your two breasts *are* like two
fawns,
Twins of a gazelle,
Which feed among the lilies.

CHAPTER 3

1 [a]Is. 26:9
3 [a]Song 5:7; Is. 21:6–8, 11, 12
4 [a]Song 8:2 [1]*room*
5 [a]Song 2:7; 8:4 [1]*adjure* *See WW at Hag. 1:14.
6 [a]Song 8:5
9 [1]A portable enclosed chair

CHAPTER 4

1 [a]Song 1:15; 5:12 [b]Song 6:5
2 [a]Song 6:6 [1]*bereaved*
3 [a]Song 6:7
4 [a]Song 7:4 [b]Neh. 3:19 [1]Small shields
5 [a]Prov. 5:19; Song 7:3

3:1–5 The Shulamite is disappointed that her beloved has not appeared and is having a troubled night's sleep. She finally decides to **rise** and **seek the one** she loves.
3:5 See section 1 of Truth-In-Action at the end of Song.
3:6–11 The interpretation of this section is diverse among scholars. Most see it as the approach of her beloved, even portraying their **wedding.** In this case the **palanquin** would be a type of royal wedding bed, which formed part of the regal cavalcade characterizing wedding processions prior to the destruction of the second temple.

Apart from its interpretive difficulties, covenant love principles between God and Israel seem clear. The route of the palanquin out of the wilderness to **Zion** follows the redemptive journey of the ark of the covenant. The opening question (v. 6) recalls the first appearance of God's glory in the giving of the manna (Ex. 16:10–15). The fragrant **smoke** resembles the pillar of the guiding cloud and the altar of incense (Ex. 13:21; 30:34–38).
4:1–7 See section 3 of Truth-In-Action at the end of Song.
4:1–7 This portrait of the Shulamite mingles ancient poetic imagery with covenant blessings, picturing a fruitful and perfected covenant people in full possession of the Promised Land. Mt. Gilead, across the Jordan, is an *expanded* land and includes the rest of the tribes of Israel (Num. 32).

6 [a]Until the day breaks
And the shadows flee away,
I will go my way to the mountain of myrrh
And to the hill of frankincense.

7 [a]You *are* all fair, my love,
And *there is* no spot in you.
8 Come with me from Lebanon, *my* spouse,
With me from Lebanon.
Look from the top of Amana,
From the top of Senir [a]and Hermon,
From the lions' dens,
From the mountains of the leopards.

9 You have ravished my heart,
My sister, *my* spouse;
You have ravished my heart
With one *look* of your eyes,
With one link of your necklace.
10 How fair is your love,
My sister, *my* spouse!
[a]How much better than wine is your love,
And the [1]scent of your perfumes
Than all spices!
11 Your lips, O *my* spouse,
Drip as the honeycomb;
[a]Honey and milk *are* under your tongue;
And the fragrance of your garments
Is [b]like the fragrance of Lebanon.

12 A garden [1]enclosed
Is my sister, *my* spouse,
A spring shut up,
A fountain sealed.
13 Your plants *are* an orchard of pomegranates
With pleasant fruits,
Fragrant henna with spikenard,
14 Spikenard and saffron,
Calamus and cinnamon,
With all trees of frankincense,
Myrrh and aloes,
With all the chief spices—
15 A fountain of gardens,
A well of [a]living waters,
And streams from Lebanon.

THE SHULAMITE

16 Awake, O north *wind*,
And come, O south!
Blow upon my garden,
That its spices may flow out.
[a]Let my beloved come to his garden
And eat its pleasant [b]fruits.

THE BELOVED

5 I [a]have come to my garden, my [b]sister, *my* spouse; 3
I have gathered my myrrh with my spice;
[c]I have eaten my honeycomb with my honey;
I have drunk my wine with my milk.

(TO HIS FRIENDS)

Eat, O [d]friends!
Drink, yes, drink deeply,
O beloved ones!

The Shulamite's Troubled Evening

THE SHULAMITE

2 I sleep, but my heart is awake;
It is the voice of my beloved!
[a]He knocks, *saying*,
"Open for me, my sister, [1]my love,
My dove, my perfect one;
For my head is covered with dew,
My [2]locks with the drops of the night."

3 I have taken off my robe;
How can I put it on *again?*
I have washed my feet;

6 [a]Song 2:17
7 [a]Song 1:15; Eph. 5:27
8 [a]Deut. 3:9; 1 Chr. 5:23; Ezek. 27:5
10 [a]Song 1:2, 4 [1]*fragrance*
11 [a]Prov. 24:13, 14; Song 5:1 [b]Gen. 27:27; Hos. 14:6, 7
12 [1]*locked* or *barred*
15 [a]Zech. 14:8; John 4:10; 7:38
16 [a]Song 5:1 [b]Song 7:13

CHAPTER 5

1 [a]Song 4:16 [b]Song 4:9 [c]Song 4:11 [d]Luke 15:7, 10; John 3:29
2 [a]Rev. 3:20 [1]*my companion, friend* [2]*curls* or *hair*

4:8 All the mountain scenes in the Song are positive; this is not an invitation to leave **Lebanon** but an invitation to tour *through* Lebanon and **look** around from its highest peaks to view the entire Promised Land.
4:9—5:1 Man's deepest need is to experience the oneness of authentic love in a dependable relationship. The endearing terms **sister** and **spouse,** used of the Shulamite, depict an enduring mutuality and permanent oneness. She is not a **garden enclosed** locking him out, but a private protected garden for royal use into which she invites her **beloved** to enter. The Shulamite, along with all her choice products, is now his. Together as friends and lovers they share the satisfying common meal with encouragement and approval (5:1).
5:1 See section 3 of Truth-In-Action at the end of Song.
5:2–7 The Shulamite has a troubled dream in which she sees her beloved leaving her (**had turned away *and* was gone**). The reason for his departure is her delayed response, which is attributed to the removal of her two garments, making her unpresentable. She herself had **taken off** one of the garments, symbolizing her own independent actions. She then goes looking for him and is seen by **the watchmen** who mistake her for a harlot and violently remove her second garment, a **veil** (likely an outer garment worn over her dress). This symbolizes the removal of her authority. Her **beloved** is her only hope; but where has he gone, and when will he return? Her independent action and the violent action of others then have caused her loss.

How can I [1]defile them?
4 My beloved put his hand
By the [1]latch *of the door,*
And my heart yearned for him.
5 I arose to open for my beloved,
And my hands dripped *with* myrrh,
My fingers with liquid myrrh,
On the handles of the lock.

6 I opened for my beloved,
But my beloved had turned away *and* was gone.
My [1]heart leaped up when he spoke.
[a]I sought him, but I could not find him;
I called him, but he gave me no answer.
7 [a]The watchmen who went about the city found me.
They struck me, they wounded me;
The keepers of the walls
Took my veil away from me.
8 I charge you, O daughters of Jerusalem,
If you find my beloved,
That you tell him I *am* lovesick!

THE DAUGHTERS OF JERUSALEM

9 What *is* your beloved
More than *another* beloved,
[a]O fairest among women?
What *is* your beloved
More than *another* beloved,
That you so [1]charge us?

THE SHULAMITE

10 My beloved *is* white and ruddy,
[1]Chief among ten thousand.
11 His head *is like* the finest gold;
His locks *are* wavy,
And black as a raven.
12 [a]His eyes *are* like doves
By the rivers of waters,
Washed with milk,
And [1]fitly set.
13 His cheeks *are* like a bed of spices,
Banks of scented herbs.
His lips *are* lilies,
*Dripping liquid myrrh.
14 His hands *are* rods of gold
Set with beryl.
His body *is* carved ivory
Inlaid *with* sapphires.
15 His legs *are* pillars of marble
Set on bases of fine gold.
His countenance *is* like Lebanon,
Excellent as the cedars.
16 His mouth *is* most sweet,
Yes, he *is* altogether lovely.
This *is* my beloved,
And this *is* my *friend,
O daughters of Jerusalem!

THE DAUGHTERS OF JERUSALEM

6 Where has your beloved gone,
[a]O fairest among women?
Where has your beloved turned aside,
That we may seek him with you?

THE SHULAMITE

2 My beloved has gone to his [a]garden,
To the beds of spices,
To feed *his flock* in the gardens,
And to gather lilies.
3 [a]I *am* my beloved's,
And my beloved *is* mine.
He feeds *his flock* among the lilies.

Praise of the Shulamite's Beauty

THE BELOVED

4 O my love, you *are as* beautiful as Tirzah, **3**
Lovely as Jerusalem,
Awesome as *an army* with banners!
5 Turn your eyes away from me,
For they have [1]overcome me.
Your hair *is* [a]like a flock of goats
Going down from Gilead.
6 [a]Your teeth *are* like a flock of sheep
Which have come up from the washing;
Every one bears twins,
And none *is* [1]barren among them.
7 [a]Like a piece of pomegranate

3 [1]*dirty*
4 [1]*opening*
6 [a]Song 3:1 [1]Lit. *soul*
7 [a]Song 3:3
9 [a]Song 1:8; 6:1 [1]*adjure*
10 [1]*Distinguished*
12 [a]Song 1:15; 4:1 [1]*sitting in a setting*
13 *See WW at Ezek. 21:2.
16 *See WW at Prov. 17:17.

CHAPTER 6

1 [a]Song 1:8; 5:9
2 [a]Song 4:16; 5:1
3 [a]Song 2:16; 7:10
5 [a]Song 4:1 [1]*overwhelmed*
6 [a]Song 4:2 [1]*bereaved*
7 [a]Song 4:3

5:9—6:3 Solomon's glory rightly represents the regal perfections of love. He is like his father David, **ruddy,** altogether lovely, and memorialized by the number **ten thousand** (1 Sam. 16:12; 18:7). He is unequaled in dependability, endurance, strength, and value; but he is no hard, cold metallic man. For the Shulamite her **beloved** is beyond compare (5:9).

6:4–10 This happy scene exalts the Shulamite's beautiful queenly power and records her glorious impression. Her two capital cities, **Tirzah** (the first capital of the northern kingdom) and **Jerusalem,** manifest her lovely majesty. Everyone—**queens, concubines, virgins,** and **daughters**—praises the Shulamite because she personifies them.

6:4–9 See section 3 of Truth-In-Action at the end of Song.

Are your temples behind your veil.

8 There are sixty queens
And eighty concubines,
And [a]virgins without number.
9 My dove, my [a]perfect one,
Is the only one,
The only one of her mother,
The favorite of the one who bore her.
The daughters saw her
And called her *blessed,
The queens and the concubines,
And they praised her.

10 Who is she who looks forth as the morning,
Fair as the moon,
Clear as the sun,
[a]Awesome as *an army* with banners?

THE SHULAMITE

11 I went down to the garden of nuts
To see the verdure of the valley,
[a]To see whether the vine had budded
And the pomegranates had bloomed.
12 Before I was even aware,
My soul had made me
As the chariots of [1]my noble people.

THE BELOVED AND HIS FRIENDS

13 *Return, return, O Shulamite;
Return, return, that we may look upon you!

THE SHULAMITE

What would you see in the Shulamite—
As it were, the dance of [1]the two camps?

8 [a]Song 1:3
9 [a]Song 2:14; 5:2 *See WW at Prov. 31:28.
10 [a]Song 6:4
11 [a]Song 7:12
12 [1]Heb. *Ammi Nadib*
13 [1]Heb. *Mahanaim* *See WW at Ruth 4:15.

CHAPTER 7

1 [a]Ps. 45:13 *See WW at Josh. 4:24.
2 [1]Lit. *mixed* or *spiced drink*
3 [a]Song 4:5
4 [a]Song 4:4
8 [1]Lit. *nose*

Expressions of Praise

THE BELOVED

7 How beautiful are your feet in sandals,
[a]O prince's daughter!
The curves of your thighs *are* like jewels,
The work of the *hands of a skillful workman.
2 Your navel *is* a rounded goblet;
It lacks no [1]blended beverage.
Your waist *is* a heap of wheat
Set about with lilies.
3 [a]Your two breasts *are* like two fawns,
Twins of a gazelle.
4 [a]Your neck *is* like an ivory tower,
Your eyes *like* the pools in Heshbon
By the gate of Bath Rabbim.
Your nose *is* like the tower of Lebanon
Which looks toward Damascus.
5 Your head *crowns* you like *Mount* Carmel,
And the hair of your head *is* like purple;
A king *is* held captive by *your* tresses.

6 How fair and how pleasant you are,
O love, with your delights!
7 This stature of yours is like a palm tree,
And your breasts *like* its clusters.
8 I said, "I will go up to the palm tree,
I will take hold of its branches."
Let now your breasts be like clusters of the vine,
The fragrance of your [1]breath like apples,
9 And the roof of your mouth like the best wine.

6:11, 12 The chariots identify her **noble people,** *Ammi Nadib. Nadib* is a royal person of true nobility, a prince with freedom and liberality.

6:13—7:9 This section deals with Solomon's attempt to resecure the Shulamite's wandering love. His ardent call to **return, return** is given against the backdrop of the wandering of God's covenant people, a backdrop to which he alludes in his reference to Mahanaim, **the two camps.** Mahanaim is the memorial name of a supreme event in covenant history (Gen. 32). It marked the return of the national family to the land (6:13; see Gen. 32:9; Hos. 14:1). Here Jacob received his new name, "Israel," "Prince with God," God's name joined to Jacob's. Mahanaim magnified grace and truth by contrasting the unworthy smallness of Jacob in his departure from the land, with only a staff, with his massive fruitful return as two companies (Gen. 32:9, 10; Amos 7:2, 5).

7:4 Heshbon was the ancient capital of Sihon, about 20 miles east of the Dead Sea. It was known for its lush reservoirs. **Bath Rabbim** is unknown today. **The tower of Lebanon** was a famous and beautiful projecting tower in an unspecified city near the eastern slopes of Hermon. **Nose** here may be a reference to her face.

7:7 Palm tree implies life-giving water (Ex. 15:27).

7:9—8:3 The Song moves from openness to mutuality and now oneness. Everything is new: new growth, new **pleasant** ***fruits,*** a new **spiced wine,** a vital new relationship, and a new manner of love.

THE SHULAMITE

The wine goes *down* smoothly for
my beloved,
[1]Moving gently the [2]lips of
sleepers.
3 10 [a]I *am* my beloved's,
And [b]his desire *is* toward me.

11 Come, my beloved,
Let us go forth to the field;
Let us lodge in the villages.
12 Let us get up early to the
vineyards;
Let us [a]see if the vine has budded,
Whether the grape blossoms are
open,
And the pomegranates are in
bloom.
There I will give you my love.
13 The [a]mandrakes give off a
fragrance,
And at our gates [b]*are* pleasant
fruits,
All manner, new and old,
Which I have laid up for you, my
beloved.

8 Oh, that you were like my
brother,
Who nursed at my mother's
breasts!
If I should find you outside,
I would kiss you;
I would not be despised.
2 I would lead you *and* bring
you
Into the [a]house of my mother,
She *who* used to instruct me.
I would cause you to drink of
[b]spiced wine,
Of the juice of my pomegranate.

(TO THE DAUGHTERS OF JERUSALEM)

3 [a]His left hand *is* under my head,
And his right hand embraces
me.
1 4 [a]I charge you, O daughters of
Jerusalem,
Do not stir up nor awaken love
Until it pleases.

9 [1]*Gliding over* [2]LXX, Syr., Vg. *lips and teeth.*
10 [a]Song 2:16; 6:3 [b]Ps. 45:11
12 [a]Song 6:11
13 [a]Gen. 30:14 [b]Song 2:3; 4:13, 16; Matt. 13:52

CHAPTER 8

2 [a]Song 3:4 [b]Prov. 9:2
3 [a]Song 2:6
4 [a]Song 2:7; 3:5

5 [a]Song 3:6
6 [a]Is. 49:16; Jer. 22:24; Hag. 2:23 [b]Prov. 6:34, 35 [1]*severe,* lit. *hard* [2]Or *Sheol* [3]Lit. *A flame of* YAH, poetic form of *YHWH, the* LORD *See WW at Hos. 13:14.
7 [a]Prov. 6:35
8 [a]Ezek. 23:33

Love Renewed in Lebanon

A RELATIVE

5 [a]Who *is* this coming up from the
wilderness,
Leaning upon her beloved?

I awakened you under the apple
tree.
There your mother brought you
forth;
There she *who* bore you brought
you forth.

THE SHULAMITE TO HER BELOVED

6 [a]Set me as a seal upon your heart, 2
As a seal upon your arm;
For love *is as* strong as death,
[b]Jealousy *as* [1]cruel as [2]the *grave;
Its flames *are* flames of fire,
[3]A most vehement flame.

7 Many waters cannot quench love,
Nor can the floods drown it.
[a]If a man would give for love
All the wealth of his house,
It would be utterly despised.

THE SHULAMITE'S BROTHERS

8 [a]We have a little sister, 1
And she has no breasts.
What shall we do for our sister
In the day when she is spoken
for?
9 If she *is* a wall,
We will build upon her
A battlement of silver;
And if she *is* a door,
We will enclose her
With boards of cedar.

THE SHULAMITE

10 I *am* a wall, 1
And my breasts like towers;
Then I became in his eyes
As one who found peace.
11 Solomon had a vineyard at Baal
Hamon;

7:10–13 See section 3 of Truth-In-Action at the end of Song.
8:4 See section 1 of Truth-In-Action at the end of Song.
8:5 The couple come, not dependently **leaning,** but clinging, joined equally. Love has worked its awakening power.
8:6, 7 See section 2 of Truth-In-Action at the end of Song.
8:6, 7 A **seal** represents a person and his authoritative power, somewhat like a signature. As Solomon's seal, the Shulamite identifies with his love and represents it.
8:8–10 The Shulamite's house is a protective towerlike palace built into the city wall. Her **breasts** have developed into a nurturing life source. She is a **wall,** not a door, mature with integrity and protective of others. The Shulamite has found motherhood and peace, and she models marriageability for all "little sisters."
8:8, 9 See section 1 of Truth-In-Action at the end of Song.
8:10–12 See section 1 of Truth-In-Action at the end of Song.
8:11, 12 Solomon's vineyards were priceless, as the **thousand silver coins** prove (Is. 7:23). Now the Shulamite's **own vineyard** is before her; she is the sole owner, and it

[a]He leased the vineyard to
keepers;
Everyone was to bring for its
fruit
A thousand silver coins.

(TO SOLOMON)

12 My own vineyard *is* before me.
You, O Solomon, *may have* a
thousand,
And those who tend its fruit two
hundred.

THE BELOVED

13 You who dwell in the gardens,
The *companions listen for your
voice—
[a]Let me hear it!

THE SHULAMITE

14 [a]Make[1] haste, my beloved,
And [b]be like a gazelle
Or a young stag
On the mountains of spices.

11 [a]Matt. 21:33
13 [a]Song 2:14 *See WW at Ps. 119:63.
14 [a]Rev. 22:17, 20 [b]Song 2:7, 9, 17 [1]*Hurry*, lit. *Flee*

equals Solomon's. As the free and full owner, she will return the vineyard to its Solomonic source and give the owner's portion, the thousand, back to Solomon himself. She owns everything and gives everything away. She has therefore proven to her brothers that she is capable of handling relationships and temptations.

8:13, 14 The unending kingdom of love with its **mountains of spices** awaits lovers.

TRUTH-IN-ACTION through SONG OF SOLOMON

Letting the LIFE of the Holy Spirit Bring Faith's Works Alive in You!

EDITOR'S NOTE: The Song of Solomon is often interpreted as an allegory of the love of Yahweh for Israel or of Jesus for His bride, the church. However, the grammatical-historical approach to exegesis interprets the Song simply as one of the finest examples of ancient, Oriental love poetry. The Hebrew culture celebrated the sexual relationship experienced between a man and a woman within the sanctity of marriage as an exquisitely beautiful gift from our Creator.

Minimal research into Oriental and Semitic symbology will yield rich dividends and help bring this book alive for the reader.

Truth the Song Teaches	Text	**Action** the Song Invites
1 Keys to Moral Purity Maintaining sexual purity until marriage is a key to establishing a strong Christian marriage. In view of the prevailing social acceptance of sexually immoral behavior, it is of great importance that God's holy people renounce impurity and make a renewed effort to rebuild commitment to moral purity in the church.	1:2–4	**Understand** that physical desires for your spouse are entirely appropriate.
	2:7	**Refuse** any sexual involvement before marriage, . . . **Knowing** it diminishes sexual fulfillment within marriage.
	3:5	. . . **Knowing** it compromises necessary objectivity in important premarital evaluations and decisions.
	8:4	. . . **Knowing** it seriously weakens a couple's ability to make necessary sexual adjustments within marriage.
	8:8, 9	Christian families: **Get involved** in the development of your children's sexual morality. **Encourage** and **support** their sexual purity and virginity. **Build defenses** against attempts to seduce them away from sexual righteousness.
	8:10–12	**Value** virginity very highly! **Do not ever discredit** the inestimable value of being able to present to your new spouse your body and soul, wholly undefiled and kept pure for him/her.

Truth the Song Teaches	Text	**Action** the Song Invites
2 Advice to Dating Couples Using courtship to maximum advantage minimizes difficulties in marriage. Many couples enter marriage unprepared to deal with the things they will face. Though brief and indirect, the advice given by Solomon and the Shulamite should be heeded by those preparing for marriage.	1:7	**Understand** that it is of the utmost importance that we learn to know and accept our intended spouse as he/she is. **Accept** as wrong thinking any hidden plans to change that person.
	1:8	**Know** it is better not to follow through with plans for marriage than to marry one you cannot accept as he/she is.
	2:14, 15	**Take time** to identify and resolve potential problems to your marriage. **Face** them honestly and candidly.
	8:6, 7	**Determine** to build a strong, unbreakable commitment to each other in your marriage.
3 Keys to an Enduring Marriage Successful marriages result from the disciplined practices that have been proven through the centuries by countless couples whose love and commitment grew stronger and more passionate. Today when the cultural environment wars against the Christian marriage—seeking to redefine, dilute, and delude our understanding of God's institution—recovering these dynamic principles is essential. God's Word is, of course, the place to start looking. And where better than God's love song?	4:1–7	Marriage partners: **Learn** the lost art of verbal lovemaking. **Learn** to speak words of love that caress your mate's soul.
	5:1	**Understand** and **believe** that the Lord continues to view the sexual relationship within the sanctity of marriage as "very good" and to bless it.
	6:4–9	Throughout marriage **extol** your spouse's virtues above those of others.
	7:10–13	**Set aside** regular, periodic times away with your spouse to **refresh** and **renew** the romance in your marriage.

The Book of ISAIAH

Author: Isaiah
Date: About 700–690 B.C.
Theme: Salvation
Key Ideas: Judgment of Sin, Messianic Promise
Key Words: Salvation, Redeemer, Righteousness, Peace, Comfort

Author The first verse of this book names its author as Isaiah, the son of Amoz. The name "Isaiah" means "Yahweh Is Salvation." The vision and prophecy are claimed four times by Isaiah; his name is mentioned an additional twelve times in the book. His name also occurs twelve times in 2 Kings and four times in 2 Chronicles.

The Book of Isaiah is directly quoted twenty-one times in the New Testament and attributed in each case to the prophet Isaiah. Some scholars who have difficulty with detailed prophetic prediction of future events have denied to Isaiah the authorship of chapters 40—66. They term this section Second Isaiah and insist that since these chapters deal with events that took place long after Isaiah's day, such as the Babylonian captivity of Judah, the return from Exile, and the rise of Cyrus, the Persian ruler who mandated the return from Exile (45:1), they were written later and attached to Isaiah.

If divine inspiration of Scripture and the possibility of the supernatural are accepted, however, one should have no difficulty with the unity of authorship of Isaiah. After all, Isaiah and other prophets of his time prophesied events in the life of Jesus that happened seven hundred years later. Furthermore, critics overlook the fact that Isaiah had access to the Book of Deuteronomy, which predicted both a captivity and a return from exile (Deut. 29; 30). If the mention of Cyrus (44:28; 45:1) is a stumbling block, what about Bethlehem, Jesus' birthplace, named and predicted by Micah, a contemporary of Isaiah (Mic. 5:2)?

Other arguments favor single authorship: 1) key words and phrases are equally distributed throughout Isaiah; 2) references to landscape and local coloring are also uniform. The greater beauty in style of Hebrew poetry in the latter chapters of Isaiah can be explained by the change in subject matter from judgment and entreaty to comfort and assurance. In any case, as clearly likely as it is that Isaiah was written via one penman, contending for this position is not intended to impugn the sincerity of any with contrary opinion.

Date The prophet states that he prophesied during the reigns of "Uzziah, Jotham, Ahaz, *and* Hezekiah, kings of Judah" (1:1). Some accept his call to the prophetic office as being in the year that King Uzziah died, which was about 740 B.C. (6:1, 8). It is likely, however, he began during the last decade of Uzziah's reign. Since Isaiah mentions the death of the Assyrian king, Sennacherib, who died about 680 B.C. (37:37, 38), he must have outlived Hezekiah by a few years. Tradition has it that Isaiah was martyred during the reign of Manasseh, Hezekiah's son. Many believe that the clause "sawn in two" in Hebrews 11:37 is a reference to Isaiah's death. The first part of the book may have been written in Isaiah's earlier years, the latter chapters after his retirement from public life.

If Isaiah began prophesying about 750 B.C., his ministry may have briefly overlapped those of Amos and Hosea in Israel, as well as that of Micah in Judah.

Background Isaiah prophesied at the most crucial period in the history of Judah and Israel. Both the southern and northern kingdoms had experienced nearly a half-century of increasing prosperity and power. Israel, ruled by Jeroboam and six other minor kings, had succumbed to pagan worship; Judah, under Uzziah, Jotham, and Hezekiah, had maintained an outward conformity to orthodoxy, but had gradually fallen into serious moral and spiritual decline (3:8–26). Secret places of pagan worship were tolerated; the wealthy oppressed the poor; the women neglected their families in the quest of carnal pleasure; many of the priests and prophets became drunken men-pleasers (5:7–12, 18–23; 22:12–14). While there would come one more revival in Judah under King Josiah (640–609 B.C.), it was clear to Isaiah that the covenant recorded by Moses in Deuteronomy 30:11–20 had been so completely violated that judgment and captivity were inevitable for Judah, even as it was for Israel.

Isaiah entered his ministry at about the time of the founding of Rome and the first Olympic games of the Greeks. European powers were not quite ready for wide conquest, but several Asian powers were looking beyond their borders. Assyria particularly was poised for conquest to the south and to the west. The prophet, who was a student of world affairs, could see the conflict that was imminent. Assyria took Samaria in 721 B.C.

Purpose One of Isaiah's purposes was to declare God's displeasure with and judgment upon sin in Judah, Israel, and the surrounding nations. Almost all the Hebrew words for sin are employed by the prophet. A parallel purpose was to endeavor to turn God's people away from disobedience in order to avert disaster, a purpose that was only partially successful. Perhaps the greatest purpose, however, was to lay a foundation of hope and promise for the faithful remnant of God's people. Thus the book is full of promises of restoration and redemption, of the certain advent of the Messiah, of salvation for all the nations, and of the triumph of God's purposes in spite of intervals of suffering.

Personal Application No Old Testament book, with the possible exception of the Psalms, speaks more powerfully and appropriately to the modern-day church than the Book of Isaiah. Isaiah has been called both the "messianic prophet" and the "evangelical prophet." He prophesied for all future ages, predicting both the first and second advents of Christ. His very name means "Salvation," a salvation not only for those of his day, but also a salvation of the peoples of the nations for all time. This salvation issues from a Savior or Redeemer who has provided a ransom; it is always a vicarious salvation by grace.

The prophetic time frame of Isaiah will not close until the Son of David rules over His kingdom of peace (2:1–5; 11:1–9; 42:1–4; 61:1–11; 65:17–25; 66:22, 23).

Isaiah speaks as powerfully to our day as he did to the society of his day. He focused a spotlight of holiness upon the sordid sins of Israel; he summoned his contemporaries to cease from their social injustice, their quest for carnal indulgence, their trust in the arm of flesh, and their hypocritical pretense of orthodox religion. He also warned of the consequences of judgment if sin continued.

Christ Revealed

After His resurrection Jesus walked with two of His disciples and "expounded to them in all the Scriptures the things concerning Himself" (Luke 24:27). To do so He must have drawn heavily from the Book of Isaiah, because seventeen chapters of Isaiah contain prophetic references to Christ.

Christ is spoken of as the "LORD," "Branch of the LORD," "Immanuel," "Wonderful, Counselor," "Mighty God," "Everlasting Father," "Prince of Peace," "Rod of Jesse," "Cornerstone," "King," "Shepherd," "Servant of Yahweh," "Elect One," "Lamb of God," "Leader and Commander," "Redeemer," and "Anointed One."

Chapter 53 is the greatest single Old Testament chapter prophesying the Messiah's atoning work. No text in either Testament more completely sets forth the purpose of Christ's vicarious death on the Cross than this chapter. It is directly quoted nine or ten times by New Testament writers: 52:15 (Rom. 15:21); 53:1 (John 12:38; Rom. 10:16); 53:4 (Matt. 8:17); 53:5 (Rom. 4:25; 1 Pet. 2:24); 53:7, 8 (Acts 8:32, 33); 53:9 (1 Pet. 2:22); 53:10 (1 Cor. 15:3, 4); 53:12 (Luke 22:37). There are also many New Testament fulfillments of details in chapter 53 in addition to the direct quotations.

The Holy Spirit at Work

The Holy Spirit is mentioned specifically fifteen times in the Book of Isaiah, not counting references to the Spirit's power, effect, or influence without mention of His name. There are three general categories under which the work of the Holy Spirit may be described:

1. The Spirit's anointing upon the Messiah to empower Him for His rule and administration as King on the throne of David (11:1–12); as the suffering Servant of the Lord who will heal, liberate, enlighten, and bring justice to the nations (42:1–9); as the Anointed One (Messiah) in both His advents (61:1–3; Luke 4:17–21).

2. The Spirit's outpouring upon Israel to give them success in their rehabilitation after the pattern of the Exodus (44:1–5; 63:1–5), to protect them from their enemies (59:19), and to preserve Israel in covenant relationship with Yahweh (59:21). However, Israel must be careful not to rebel and grieve the Holy Spirit (63:10; Eph. 4:30).

3. The Spirit's operation at Creation and in the preservation of nature (40:13; see also 48:16).

The Lord Jesus, whose earthly ministry was carried out in the power and anointing of the Holy Spirit, as Isaiah has prophesied, promised to pour out His Spirit upon the church to empower it for ministry in the fulfillment of the Great Commission.

Outline of Isaiah

I. Prophecy of denunciation and invitation (Part One) 1:1—35:10

- A. Messages of judgment and promise 1:1—6:13
  1. An indictment of rebellion, call to repent 1:1–31
  2. Future glory, punishment for perversion 2:1—4:1
  3. Branch of the Lord 4:2–6
  4. Song of the vineyard, and assorted woes 5:1–30
  5. The prophet, his vision, and call 6:1–13
- B. Messages concerning Immanuel 7:1—12:6
  1. Invasion against Ahaz, Yahweh's sign: a Child's birth 7:1–25
  2. Assyria, the Lord's instrument 8:1–22
  3. A great light, God's Wonderful Child 9:1–7
  4. God's judgment upon Israel and Assyria 9:8—10:19
  5. The remnant of Jacob, Branch of Jesse 10:20—11:16
  6. Songs of praise to the Lord 12:1–6
- C. Messages of judgment upon the nations 13:1—24:23
- D. Messages of judgment, praise, promise 25:1—27:13
  1. The Lord's deliverance, the kingdom age 25:1–12
  2. The Rock of Ages and the resurrection 26:1–21
  3. Doom of oppressors, Israel restored 27:1–13
- E. Woes to unbelievers and immoral in Israel 28:1—33:24
  1. Woe to drunkards and scoffers 28:1–29
  2. Woe to hypocrites in Zion 29:1–24
  3. Woes to those who trust in Egypt 30:1—31:9
  4. About the coming King and His reign of peace, mingled with assorted woes 32:1—33:24
- F. Summary 34:1—35:10
  1. Judgments upon ungodly nations 34:1–17
  2. Joy and blessing to God's people 35:1–10

II. God's dealing with Hezekiah 36:1—39:8

- A. God's deliverance of Judah 36:1—37:38
- B. God's healing of Hezekiah 38:1–22
- C. God's censure of Hezekiah 39:1–8

III. Prophecy of comfort and peace (Part Two) 40:1—66:24

- A. The assurance of comfort and peace 40:1—48:22
  1. The greatness of Yahweh the Comforter 40:1–31
  2. His challenge to the nations and Israel 41:1–29
  3. Yahweh's servants: Christ and Israel 42:1–25
  4. Yahweh's gracious redemption 43:1—44:5
  5. Yahweh's indictment of idolatry 44:6–23
  6. Yahweh's using Cyrus as a deliverer 44:24—45:25
  7. Yahweh and idols contrasted 46:1–13
  8. Yahweh's judgment upon Babylon 47:1–15
  9. Yahweh's rebuke to Israel followed by promise 48:1–22
- B. The Lord's Servant, the Author of comfort and peace 49:1—57:21
  1. The Servant's restoration of Israel and light to the nations 49:1–26
  2. The disobedience of Israel and the obedience of the Servant 50:1–11
  3. Yahweh's remnant encouraged to listen 51:1—52:12
  4. The Servant's triumph through vicarious suffering 52:13—53:12
  5. The resulting restoration of Israel 54:1–17
  6. God's grace and peace toward repentant sinners 55:1—56:8
  7. The rebuke of false leaders and idolatrous backsliders 56:9—57:21

C. The realization of comfort and peace 58:1—66:24
1. False and true worship compared 58:1–14
2. Israel's sin and God's Redeemer 59:1–21
3. The well-being and peace of the redeemed of the Lord 60:1–22
4. The Spirit-anointed Redeemer who brings the kingdom of peace 61:1—62:12
5. God's vengeance and Israel's prayer for deliverance 63:1—64:12
6. God's answer to prayer and Israel's future hope 65:1—66:24

THE [a]vision* of Isaiah the son of Amoz, which he saw concerning Judah and Jerusalem in the [b]days of Uzziah, Jotham, Ahaz, *and* Hezekiah, kings of Judah.

The Wickedness of Judah

2 [a]Hear, O heavens, and give ear, O earth!
For the LORD has spoken:
"I have nourished and brought up children,
And they have rebelled against Me;
3 [a]The ox knows its owner
And the donkey its master's [1]crib;
But Israel [b]does not know,
My people do not [2]consider."

4 Alas, sinful nation,
A people [1]laden with iniquity,
[a]A [2]brood of evildoers,
Children who are corrupters!
They have forsaken the LORD,
They have provoked to anger
The Holy One of Israel,
They have turned away backward.

5 [a]Why should you be stricken again?
You will revolt more and more.
The whole head is sick,
And the whole heart faints.
6 From the sole of the foot even to the head,
There is no soundness in it,
But wounds and bruises and putrefying sores;
They have not been closed or bound up,
Or soothed with ointment.

7 [a]Your country *is* desolate,
Your cities *are* burned with fire;
Strangers devour your land in your presence;
And *it is* desolate, as overthrown by strangers.
8 So the daughter of Zion is left
[a]as a [1]booth in a vineyard,
As a hut in a garden of cucumbers,
[b]As a besieged city.
9 [a]Unless the LORD of hosts
Had left to us a very small remnant,
We would have become like [b]Sodom,

CHAPTER 1

1 [a]Num. 12:6 [b]2 Chr. 26—32 *See WW at 2 Chr. 32:32.
2 [a]Jer. 2:12
3 [a]Jer. 8:7 [b]Jer. 9:3, 6 [1]*manger or feed trough* [2]*understand*
4 [a]Is. 57:3, 4; Matt. 3:7 [1]Lit. *heavy, weighed down* [2]*offspring, seed*
5 [a]Jer. 5:3
7 [a]Deut. 28:51, 52; 2 Chr. 36:19
8 [a]Job 27:18 [b]Jer. 4:17 [1]*shelter*
9 [a]2 Kin. 25:11, 22; Lam. 3:22 [b]Gen. 19:24; Rom. 9:29

1:1 Vision: A Hebrew word usually meaning divine revelation of truth. Isaiah's prophecy was revealed to him by God. Vision describes the content of all 66 chapters, arranged in acts and scenes like a play. **Isaiah** means "Yahweh Is Salvation." He is the greatest of the OT prophets and the most quoted in the NT. **Amoz** is not the minor prophet with a similar name. A Jewish tradition makes Amoz an uncle of King Uzziah. If true, the tradition would make Isaiah a cousin of the king. Isaiah certainly had free access to the palace. **Uzziah:** Isaiah's prophetic career spanned the reigns of Uzziah (791–740 B.C.), Jotham (740–736), Ahaz (736–716), and Hezekiah (716–687).
1:2 Hear, O heavens: Like Moses, Isaiah calls upon both heaven and Earth to witness his indictment of spiritually bankrupt Judah (see Deut. 32:1). **Rebelled:** Speaking as a disappointed Father, God diagnosed the problem and its effects on the relationship. Sin is basically rebellion.
1:3 The ox . . . the donkey: Note the poetic style of this book. Isaiah wrote in a Hebrew poetic style called parallelism, in which ideas are repeated in other words, and often one idea is contrasted with another. Isaiah also used many figures of speech. **Israel:** Some scholars feel his focal point in vv. 3–7 is the northern kingdom; it is more likely that Israel here represents Judah (v. 1).
1:4 To be **sinful** is to miss the mark. Judah as a nation had completely missed the mark of obedience to Yahweh's will. **Holy One of Israel** is the prophet's favorite name for the Lord, occurring 26 times. To a sinful nation God revealed Himself as the "Holy One." He has not changed (1 Pet. 1:15; 2:9).
1:5 The whole head is sick is a picture of total depravity.
1:7 Your country *is* desolate: Sin and rebellion had brought disaster upon their formerly fruitful land.
1:8, 9 The daughter of Zion is a personification of Jerusalem and its inhabitants. **A booth in a vineyard** was constructed for the man guarding the ripening fruit from theft. The booth was left after the guard was no longer needed. When God leaves Judah, she will be just as lonely and dreary as the abandoned booth. **Remnant:** Some will remain faithful in Judah.

We would have been made like
Gomorrah.

10 Hear the word of the LORD,
You rulers [a]of Sodom;
Give ear to the law of our God,
You people of Gomorrah:
11 "To what purpose *is* the multitude
of your [a]sacrifices to Me?"
Says the LORD.
"I have had enough of burnt
offerings of rams
And the fat of fed cattle.
I do not *delight in the blood of
bulls,
Or of lambs or goats.

KINGDOM DYNAMICS

1:11 The Issue of Blood Is Right Relationship, THE BLOOD. The ultimate issue in blood sacrifice is the attitude of the heart. To be acceptable, the sacrifice must represent sincere devotion. Isaiah stated that God had had more than enough of animals that were insincerely offered. Indeed God's holiness required the blood for cleansing, but right relationship was the ultimate goal of His covenant. David reflected this understanding in Ps. 51 when he stated that God's delight was not in animal sacrifices but rather in a broken and contrite spirit. Right relationship, not mere ceremony and sacrifice, is the goal of God's covenant-making activity. Therefore, sacrifices without a sincere desire for relationship with God pervert the real purpose of the sacrificial system and are unacceptable to God.
(Gen. 4:1–10/Heb. 9:12) C.S.

12 "When you come [a]to appear before
Me,
Who has required this from your
hand,
To trample My courts?
13 Bring no more [a]futile[1] sacrifices;
Incense is an abomination to Me.
The New Moons, the Sabbaths,
and [b]the calling of assemblies—
I cannot endure iniquity and the
sacred meeting.

10 [a]Deut. 32:32 **11** [a][1 Sam. 15:22] *See WW at Ps. 112:1. **12** [a]Ex. 23:17 **13** [a]Matt. 15:9 [b]Joel 1:14 [1]*worthless*

14 [a]Num. 28:11 [b]Lam. 2:6 **15** [a]Prov. 1:28 [b]Ps. 66:18; Is. 59:1–3; Mic. 3:4 [1]Pray [2]*bloodshed* **16** [a]Jer. 4:14 [b]Rom. 12:9 **17** [1]Some ancient vss. *the oppressed* [2]*Vindicate* **18** [a]Is. 43:26; Mic. 6:2 [b]Ps. 51:7; [Is. 43:25]; Rev. 7:14 **20** [a]Is. 40:5; 58:14; Mic. 4:4; [Titus 1:2] **21** [a]Is. 57:3–9; Jer. 2:20 [b]Mic. 3:1–3 [1]Unfaithful **22** [a]Jer. 6:28 **23** [a]Hos. 9:15 [b]Prov. 29:24 *See WW at Ps. 119:63.

14 Your [a]New Moons and your
[b]appointed feasts
My soul hates;
They are a trouble to Me,
I am weary of bearing *them.*
15 [a]When you [1]spread out your
hands,
I will hide My eyes from you;
[b]Even though you make many
prayers,
I will not hear.
Your hands are full of [2]blood.

16 "Wash[a] yourselves, make 5
yourselves clean;
Put away the evil of your doings
from before My eyes.
[b]Cease to do evil,
17 Learn to do good;
Seek justice,
Rebuke [1]the oppressor;
[2]Defend the fatherless,
Plead for the widow.

18 "Come now, and let us [a]reason 5
together,"
Says the LORD,
"Though your sins are like scarlet,
[b]They shall be as white as snow;
Though they are red like crimson,
They shall be as wool.
19 If you are willing and obedient,
You shall eat the good of the land;
20 But if you refuse and rebel,
You shall be devoured by the
sword";
[a]For the mouth of the LORD has
spoken.

The Degenerate City

21 [a]How the faithful city has become
a [1]harlot!
It was full of justice;
Righteousness lodged in it,
But now [b]murderers.
22 [a]Your silver has become dross,
Your wine mixed with water.
23 [a]Your princes *are* rebellious,
And [b]companions* of thieves;

1:11–15 To what purpose *is* the multitude of your sacrifices?: Sacrifice had been God's ordained way of approach to Him for forgiveness of sin. Isaiah is not opposing sacrifice, prayer, corporate worship, and blood atonement. He is only condemning their empty-hearted sacrifice and soulless worship, which was not accompanied with social justice and true devotion. **Burnt offerings:** See notes on Lev. 1:3, 4.
1:13 The New Moons were sacred celebrations at the beginning of the lunar month.
1:16, 17 Wash yourselves: The only hope for Judah to approach God was with genuine repentance and the institution of social **justice**. See Introduction to Isaiah: Background.
1:16, 17 See section 5 of Truth-In-Action at the end of Is.
1:18–20 See section 5 of Truth-In-Action at the end of Is.
1:18–20 Come . . . let us reason together: Isaiah declares that God is willing to cleanse and forgive if Judah will come back to Him and submit to His holy provision. God is gracious and forgiving, but sinful people must choose between obedience and judgment.
1:21–23 Harlot: Instead of being a city where the people were drawn to God, Jerusalem had become a seductress to evil and idolatry.

[c]Everyone loves bribes,
And follows after rewards.
They [d]do not defend the fatherless,
Nor does the cause of the widow come before them.

24 Therefore the Lord says,
The LORD of hosts, the Mighty One of Israel,
"Ah, [a]I will [1]rid Myself of My adversaries,
And [2]take vengeance on My enemies.
25 I will turn My hand against you,
And [a]thoroughly[1] *purge away your dross,
And take away all your alloy.
26 I will restore your judges
[a]as at the first,
And your counselors as at the beginning.
Afterward [b]you shall be called the city of righteousness, the faithful city."

27 Zion shall be redeemed with justice,
And her [1]penitents with righteousness.
28 The [a]destruction of transgressors and of sinners *shall be* together,
And those who forsake the LORD shall be consumed.
29 For [1]they shall be ashamed of the [2]terebinth trees
Which you have desired;
And you shall be embarrassed because of the gardens
Which you have chosen.
30 For you shall be as a terebinth whose leaf fades,
And as a garden that has no water.
31 [a]The strong shall be as tinder,
And the work of it as a spark;
Both will burn together,
And no one shall [b]quench *them*.

23 [c]Jer. 22:17 [d]Is. 10:2; Jer. 5:28; Ezek. 22:7; Zech. 7:10
24 [a]Deut. 28:63 [1]*be relieved of* [2]*avenge Myself*
25 [a]Is. 48:10; Ezek. 22:19–22; Mal. 3:3 [1]*refine with lye* *See WW at Zech. 13:9.
26 [a]Jer. 33:7–11 [b]Is. 33:5; Zech. 8:3
27 [1]Lit. *returners*
28 [a]Job 31:3; Ps. 9:5; [Is. 66:24; 2 Thess. 1:8, 9]
29 [1]So with MT, LXX, Vg.; some Heb. mss., Tg. *you* [2]Sites of pagan worship
31 [a]Ezek. 32:21 [b]Is. 66:24; Matt. 3:12; Mark 9:43

The Future House of God

2 The word that Isaiah the son of Amoz saw concerning Judah and Jerusalem.

2 Now [a]it shall come to pass
[b]in the latter days
[c]*That* the mountain of the LORD's house
Shall be established on the top of the mountains,
And shall be exalted above the hills;
And all nations shall flow to it.
3 Many people shall come and say,
[a]"Come, and let us go up to the mountain of the LORD,
To the house of the God of Jacob;
He will teach us His ways,
And we shall walk in His paths."
[b]For out of Zion shall go forth the law,
And the word of the LORD from Jerusalem.
4 He shall judge between the nations,
And rebuke many people;
They shall beat their swords into plowshares,
And their spears into pruning [1]hooks;
Nation shall not lift up sword against nation,
Neither shall they learn war anymore.

The Day of the LORD

5 O house of Jacob, come and let us [a]walk
In the light of the LORD.

6 For You have forsaken Your people, the house of Jacob,
Because they are filled [a]with eastern ways;
They *are* [b]soothsayers like the Philistines,

CHAPTER 2

2 [a]Mic. 4:1 [b]Gen. 49:1 [c]Ps. 68:15
3 [a]Jer. 50:5; [Zech. 8:21–23; 14:16–21] [b]Luke 24:47
4 [1]*knives*
5 [a]Eph. 5:8
6 [a]Num. 23:7 [b]Deut. 18:14

1:24–26 God will take unilateral action; the appeal of vv. 18–20 was apparently unheeded so He must judge. But He will also restore. The three names of God here, **Lord, LORD of hosts,** and **Mighty One of Israel,** are all names of power and authority by which He will **purge** and transform Jerusalem into a **city of righteousness**.

1:27–31 Transgressors are those whose sin is motivated by rebellion. The city can be made a righteous city only after such rebels are destroyed. **Gardens** were open-air places of pagan worship.

2:1 Word that Isaiah saw: A revelation from God to Isaiah's inner eye of spiritual perception, not a natural talent enhanced. V. 1 introduces chs. 2—5.

2:2–4 This passage is almost identical to Mic. 4:1–3. The cessation of war and a universal divine rule as the future hope were and are so important that God revealed this eloquent passage to both prophets. The language here is messianic, applying in part to the church age, in part to the Millennium and the world to come. See notes on Obad. 15 and Mic. 4:1–5.

2:5 Let us walk in the light: The hope of God's final resolution of all ills casts a great light on the present. See note on Mic. 4:5.

2:6–9 Abandoned: So disobedient and idolatrous had the majority in Judah become that God must abandon them through judgment. See note on Ezra 10:1–22. The prophet urged the Lord **not** to **forgive them,** for they were beyond remedy.

[c]And they [1]are pleased with the
children of foreigners.
7 [a]Their land is also full of silver and
gold,
And there is no end to their
treasures;
Their land is also full of horses,
And there is no end to their
chariots.
8 [a]Their land is also full of idols;
They worship the work of their
own hands,
That which their own fingers
have made.
9 People bow down,
And each man *humbles himself;
Therefore do not forgive them.

10 [a]Enter into the rock, and hide in
the dust,
From the terror of the LORD
And the *glory of His majesty.
11 The [1]lofty looks of man shall be
[a]humbled,*
The haughtiness of men shall be
bowed down,
And the LORD alone shall be
exalted [b]in that day.

12 For the day of the LORD of hosts
Shall come upon everything
proud and lofty,
Upon everything lifted up—
And it shall be brought low—
13 Upon all [a]the cedars of Lebanon
that are high and lifted up,
And upon all the oaks of Bashan;
14 [a]Upon all the high mountains,
And upon all the hills *that are*
lifted up;
15 Upon every high tower,
And upon every fortified wall;
16 [a]Upon all the ships of Tarshish,
And upon all the beautiful sloops.
17 The [1]loftiness of man shall be
bowed down,
And the haughtiness of men shall
be brought low;
The LORD alone will be exalted in
that day,
18 But the idols [1]He shall utterly
abolish.

6 [c]Ps. 106:35 [1]Or *clap, shake hands to make bargains with the children*
7 [a]Deut. 17:16
8 [a]Jer. 2:28
9 *See WW at Jer. 13:18.
10 [a]Rev. 6:15, 16 *See WW at Ps. 8:5.
11 [a]Prov. 16:5 [b]Hos. 2:16 [1]*proud* *See WW at Jer. 13:18.
13 [a]Zech. 11:1, 2
14 [a]Is. 30:25
16 [a]1 Kin. 10:22
17 [1]*pride*
18 [1]Or *shall utterly vanish*
19 [a]Hos. 10:8 [b][2 Thess. 1:9] [c]Hag. 2:6, 7 [1]Lit. *dust* *See WW at Ps. 8:5.
21 *See WW at Ps. 8:5.
22 [a]Jer. 17:5 [b]Job 27:3 [1]Lit. *Cease yourselves from the man* [2]Lit. *in what is he to be esteemed* *See WW at Gen. 15:6.

CHAPTER 3

1 [a]Jer. 37:21 [b]Lev. 26:26 [1]Every support *See WW at Mic. 4:13.
2 [a]2 Kin. 24:14 *See WW at Ps. 119:100.
3 [1]Eminent looking men
4 [a]Eccl. 10:16 [1]*boys* [2]Or *capricious ones*

19 They shall go into the [a]holes of
the rocks,
And into the caves of the
[1]earth,
[b]From the terror of the LORD
And the *glory of His majesty,
When He arises [c]to shake the
earth mightily.

20 In that day a man will cast away
his idols of silver
And his idols of gold,
Which they made, *each* for
himself to worship,
To the moles and bats,
21 To go into the clefts of the rocks,
And into the crags of the rugged
rocks,
From the terror of the LORD
And the *glory of His majesty,
When He arises to shake the
earth mightily.

22 [a]Sever[1] yourselves from such a
man,
Whose [b]breath *is* in his nostrils;
For [2]of what *account is he?

Judgment on Judah and Jerusalem

3 For behold, the *Lord, the LORD
of hosts,
[a]Takes away from Jerusalem and
from Judah
[b]The[1] stock and the store,
The whole supply of bread and
the whole supply of water;
2 [a]The mighty man and the man of
war,
The judge and the prophet,
And the diviner and the *elder;
3 The captain of fifty and the
[1]honorable man,
The counselor and the skillful
artisan,
And the expert enchanter.

4 "I will give [a]children[1] *to be* their
princes,
And [2]babes shall rule over them.
5 The people will be oppressed,

2:10–22 This passage blends Judah's historical judgment (586 B.C.) with that of God's general judgments in history, culminating with His final judgment on **the day of the LORD.** See note on Obad. 15. The major point is man's self-exaltation (**haughtiness**) rather than his exaltation of God.
2:10 Enter into the rock: Isaiah taunts the doomed idolaters to find a hiding place.
2:13 Cedars of Lebanon . . . oaks of Bashan are metaphors for kings and commanders.
2:14 High mountains . . . hills are figures of speech for nations and cities.
2:15 High tower . . . fortified wall represent military fortresses.
2:16 Ships of Tarshish . . . beautiful sloops signify human commerce and humanistic civilization. Everything lifted up in defiance of God's rule will be brought low. All idols will be found useless (v. 20).
2:20 That day: See note on Obad. 15.
3:1–12 Isaiah returns to the Lord's 586 B.C. judgment on **Judah**.
3:2–7 In this time of chaos all thoughtful people will refuse leadership; only the infantile, immature, and weak will attempt to rule.

Every one by another and every one by his neighbor;
The child will be insolent toward the [1]elder,
And the [2]base toward the honorable."
6 When a man takes hold of his brother
In the house of his father, *saying,*
"You have clothing;
You be our ruler,
And *let* these ruins *be* under your [1]power,"
7 In that day he will protest, saying,
"I cannot cure *your* ills,
For in my house *is* neither food nor clothing;
Do not make me a ruler of the people."

8 For [a]Jerusalem stumbled,
And Judah is fallen,
Because their tongue and their doings
Are against the LORD,
To provoke the eyes of His glory.
9 The look on their countenance witnesses against them,
And they declare their *sin as [a]Sodom;
They do not hide *it.*
Woe to their soul!
For they have brought evil upon themselves.

10 "Say to the righteous [a]that *it shall be* well *with them,*
[b]For they shall eat the fruit of their doings.
11 Woe to the wicked! [a]*It shall be* ill *with him,*
For the reward of his hands shall be [1]given him.
12 *As for* My people, children *are* their oppressors,
And women rule over them.
O My people! [a]Those who lead you [1]cause *you* to err,
And destroy the way of your paths."

Oppression and Luxury Condemned

13 The LORD stands up [a]to [1]plead,
And stands to *judge the people.
14 The LORD will enter into judgment
With the *elders of His people
And His princes:
"For you have [1]eaten up [a]the vineyard;
The plunder of the poor *is* in your houses.
15 What do you mean by [a]crushing My people
And grinding the faces of the poor?"
Says the Lord GOD of hosts.

16 Moreover the LORD says:

"Because the daughters of Zion are haughty,
And walk with [1]outstretched necks
And [2]wanton eyes,
Walking and [3]mincing *as* they go,
Making a jingling with their feet,
17 Therefore the Lord will strike with [a]a scab
The crown of the head of the daughters of Zion,
And the LORD will [b]uncover their secret parts."

18 In that day the Lord will take away the finery:
The jingling anklets, the [1]scarves, and the [a]crescents;
19 The pendants, the bracelets, and the veils;
20 The headdresses, the leg ornaments, and the headbands;
The perfume boxes, the charms,
21 and the rings;
The nose jewels,
22 the festal apparel, and the mantles;
The outer garments, the purses,
23 and the mirrors;
The fine linen, the turbans, and the robes.

24 And so it shall be:

Instead of a sweet smell there will be a stench;
Instead of a sash, a rope;
Instead of well-set hair, [a]baldness;
Instead of a rich robe, a girding of sackcloth;

5 [1]*aged* [2]*despised, lightly esteemed*
6 [1]Lit. *hand*
8 [a]2 Chr. 36:16, 17; Mic. 3:12
9 [a]Gen. 13:13; Is. 1:10–15
*See WW at Lev. 9:2.
10 [a][Deut. 28:1–14; Eccl. 8:12; Is. 54:17] [b]Ps. 128:2
11 [a][Ps. 11:6; Eccl. 8:12, 13] [1]*done to him*
12 [a]Is. 9:16 [1]*lead you astray*
13 [a]Is. 66:16; Hos. 4:1; Mic. 6:2 [1]*contend, plead His case*
*See WW at Deut. 32:36.
14 [a]Matt. 21:33 [1]*burned*
*See WW at Ps. 119:100.
15 [a]Mic. 3:2, 3
16 [1]Head held high [2]*seductive, ogling* [3]*tripping or skipping*
17 [a]Deut. 28:27 [b]Jer. 13:22
18 [a]Judg. 8:21, 26 [1]*headbands*
24 [a]Is. 22:12; Ezek. 27:31; Amos 8:10

3:8, 9 His glory: Man is created for the glory of God (43:7). God will not share His glory with haughty men (42:8).
3:10, 11 Righteous . . . wicked: In time of judgment it will be ill for the wicked but well for the righteous. Each will be rewarded accordingly.
3:13–15 When men eliminate God and His laws from their economy, every level of society suffers, **the poor** most of all (see Lev. 19:13).
3:16—4:1 When women turn away from God as those in Judah did, the picture is tragic. Constantly flirting women show disrespect for the marriage vows. These flirtatious women who lightly esteemed their marriages will see their husbands killed **in war.** With a ratio of **seven women** for **one man,** women would be willing to earn their **own food and . . . apparel** in order to acquire the respectability of marriage.

And [1]branding instead of *beauty.
25 Your men shall fall by the sword,
And your [1]mighty in the war.

26 [a]Her gates shall lament and *mourn,
And she *being* desolate [b]shall sit on the ground.

4 And [a]in that day seven women shall take hold of *one *man, saying,
"We will [b]eat our own food and wear our own apparel;
Only let us be called by your name,
To take away [c]our reproach."

The Renewal of Zion

2 In that day [a]the Branch of the LORD shall be beautiful and glorious;
And the fruit of the earth *shall be* excellent and appealing
For those of Israel who have escaped.

3 And it shall come to pass that *he
who is* left in Zion and remains in Jerusalem [a]will be called holy—everyone
who is [b]recorded among the living in
Jerusalem.

KINGDOM DYNAMICS

4:2, 3 Restoration of the God-Image, RESTORATION. This text prophesies the restoration of the "God-Image" in man, or His divine nature and family tie with man. The entire concept of "The Holy Spirit and Restoration" is developed in the study article that begins on page 2012.
(Acts 15:16–18/Rev. 19:7–9) J.R.

4 When [a]the Lord has washed away
the filth of the daughters of Zion, and
purged the [1]blood of Jerusalem from
her midst, by the spirit of judgment and
by the spirit of burning,
5 then the LORD will create above
every dwelling place of Mount Zion,
and above her assemblies, [a]a cloud and
smoke by day and [b]the shining of a
flaming fire by night. For over all the
glory there *will be* a [1]covering.
6 And there will be a tabernacle for
shade in the daytime from the heat,
[a]for a *place of refuge, and for a shelter
from storm and rain.

24 [1]*burning scar* *See WW at Ezek. 28:12.
25 [1]Lit. *strength*
26 [a]Jer. 14:2; Lam. 1:4 [b]Lam. 2:10 *See WW at Joel 1:9.

CHAPTER 4

1 [a]Is. 2:11, 17 [b]2 Thess. 3:12 [c]Luke 1:25 *See WW at Deut. 6:4. • See WW at Is. 32:2.
2 [a]Is. 12:1–6; [Jer. 23:5]; Zech. 3:8
3 [a]Is. 60:21 [b]Phil. 4:3
4 [a]Mal. 3:2, 3 [1]*bloodshed*
5 [a]Ex. 13:21, 22; Num. 9:15–23 [b]Zech. 2:5 [1]*canopy*
6 [a]Ps. 27:5; Is. 25:4 *See WW at Prov. 14:26.

CHAPTER 5

1 [a]Ps. 80:8; Jer. 2:21; Matt. 21:33; Mark 12:1; Luke 20:9 [1]Lit. *In a horn, the son of fatness*
2 [a]Deut. 32:6 [1]Lit. *hewed out*
3 [a][Rom. 3:4]
4 [a]2 Chr. 36:15, 16; Jer. 2:5; 7:25, 26; Mic. 6:3; Matt. 23:37
5 [a]2 Chr. 36:19; Ps. 80:12; 89:40, 41
6 [a]2 Chr. 36:19–21 [b]Is. 7:19–25; Jer. 25:11 [1]*hoed*

God's Disappointing Vineyard

5 Now let me sing to my Well-beloved
A song of my Beloved [a]regarding His vineyard:

My Well-beloved has a vineyard
[1]On a very fruitful hill.
2 He dug it up and cleared out its stones,
And planted it with the choicest vine.
He built a tower in its midst,
And also [1]made a winepress in it;
[a]So He expected *it* to bring forth *good* grapes,
But it brought forth wild grapes.

3 "And now, O inhabitants of Jerusalem and men of Judah,
[a]Judge, please, between Me and My vineyard.
4 What more could have been done to My vineyard
That I have not done in [a]it?
Why then, when I expected *it* to bring forth *good* grapes,
Did it bring forth wild grapes?
5 And now, please let Me tell you what I will do to My vineyard:
[a]I will take away its hedge, and it shall be burned;
And break down its wall, and it shall be trampled down.
6 I will lay it [a]waste;
It shall not be pruned or [1]dug,
But there shall come up briers and [b]thorns.
I will also command the clouds
That they rain no rain on it."

4:2–4 Branch of the LORD: This term in Isaiah and the other prophets refers to the coming Messiah (see 11:1; 53:2; Jer. 23:5; 33:15; and note on Zech. 3:8). Only when He rules will all the evils described in ch. 3 be cleansed away.
4:5, 6 These verses describe the conditions of protection, guidance, and divine glory that prevailed during the wilderness journeys of Israel (Ex. 40:34–38). The memory of these conditions is celebrated yearly at the Feast of Tabernacles. These conditions will be restored and greatly enhanced by the Messiah. See note on vv. 2–4.
5:1 This beautiful "Song of the Vineyard" is an example of the sublime poetic style of Isaiah, unexcelled anywhere in literature. In this allegory the **Well-beloved** or **Beloved** represents Yahweh, and the **vineyard** represents Israel and Judah (v. 7).
5:2 *Good* grapes: God expected Israel and Judah to be an obedient, holy, witnessing people.
5:3, 4 Wild grapes: The people produced bigotry, injustice, and idolatry instead of a witness to the nations; they did this in spite of God's abundant love and care.
5:5 Trampled down: In judgment God will permit pagan invaders to trample down His people's fair Land of Promise. Israel fell to Assyria in 721 B.C.; Judah fell to Babylon in 586 B.C.

7 For the vineyard of the LORD
of hosts *is* the house of
Israel,
And the men of Judah are His
pleasant plant.
He looked for justice, but behold,
oppression;
For righteousness, but behold,
[1]a cry *for help.*

Impending Judgment on Excesses

8 Woe to those who [1]join [a]house to
house;
They add field to field,
Till *there is* no place
Where they may dwell alone in
the midst of the land!
9 [a]In my hearing the LORD of hosts
said,
"Truly, many houses shall be
desolate,
Great and beautiful ones, without
inhabitant.
10 For ten acres of vineyard shall
yield one [a]bath,[1]
And a homer of seed shall yield
one [2]ephah."

11 [a]Woe to those who rise early in the
morning,
That they may [1]follow
intoxicating drink;
Who continue until night, *till*
wine inflames them!
5 12 [a]The harp and the strings,
The tambourine and flute,
And wine are in their feasts;
But [b]they do not regard the work
of the LORD,
Nor consider the operation of His
hands.

13 [a]Therefore my people have gone
into captivity,
Because *they have* no
[b]knowledge;
Their honorable men *are*
famished,
And their multitude dried up with
thirst.
14 Therefore Sheol has enlarged
itself
And opened its mouth beyond
measure;
Their glory and their multitude
and their pomp,
And he who is jubilant, shall
descend into it.
15 People shall be brought down,
[a]Each man shall be *humbled,
And the eyes of the lofty shall be
humbled.
16 But the LORD of hosts shall be
[a]exalted in judgment,
And God who is holy shall be
hallowed in righteousness.
17 Then the lambs shall feed in their
pasture,
And in the waste places of
[a]the [1]fat ones strangers shall
eat.

18 Woe to those who [1]draw iniquity
with cords of [2]vanity,
And sin as if with a cart rope;
19 [a]That say, "Let Him make speed
and hasten His work,
That we may see *it;*
And let the *counsel of the Holy
One of Israel draw near and
come,
That we may know *it.*"

20 Woe to those who call *evil *good,
and good evil;
Who put darkness for light, and
light for darkness;
Who put bitter for sweet, and
sweet for bitter!

21 Woe to *those who are* [a]wise in
their own eyes,
And prudent in their own sight!

22 Woe to men mighty at drinking
wine,
Woe to men *valiant for mixing
intoxicating drink,
23 Who [a]justify the wicked for a
bribe,
And take away justice from the
righteous man!

24 Therefore, [a]as the [1]fire devours
the stubble,
And the flame consumes the
chaff,
So [b]their root will be as
rottenness,

7 [1]*wailing*
8 [a]Jer. 22:13–17; Mic. 2:2; Hab. 2:9–12 [1]Accumulate houses
9 [a]Is. 22:14
10 [a]Ezek. 45:11 [1]1 bath = 1/10 homer [2]1 homer = 1/10 ephah
11 [a]Prov. 23:29, 30; Eccl. 10:16, 17; Is. 5:22 [1]*pursue*
12 [a]Amos 6:5 [b]Job 34:27; Ps. 28:5
13 [a]2 Kin. 24:14–16 [b]Is. 1:3; 27:11; Hos. 4:6
15 [a]Is. 2:9, 11 *See WW at Jer. 13:18.
16 [a]Is. 2:11
17 [a]Is. 10:16 [1]Lit. *fatlings,* rich ones
18 [1]*drag* [2]*emptiness* or *falsehood*
19 [a]Jer. 17:15; Amos 5:18 *See WW at Zech. 6:13.
20 *See WW at Ps. 5:4. • See WW at Ezek. 34:14.
21 [a]Prov. 3:7; Rom. 1:22; 12:16; [1 Cor. 3:18–20]
22 *See WW at Zech. 4:6.
23 [a]Ex. 23:8; Prov. 17:15; Is. 1:23; Mic. 3:11; 7:3
24 [a]Ex. 15:7 [b]Job 18:16 [1]Lit. *tongue of fire*

5:7 Justice . . . oppression . . . righteousness . . . cry: In Hebrew this is a play on words with each pair of words having a similar sound. A possible English rendering might be: "He looked for justice, but behold, injustice; for equity, but behold, iniquity."
5:8–30 In these verses **woe** is pronounced six times upon Israel and Judah, suggesting a funeral setting. Their sins are specified: 1) covetousness and self-indulgence (vv. 8, 10); 2) drunken revelry (v. 11, 12); 3) defiant vanity (vv. 18, 19); 4) moral subversion (v. 20); 5) inordinate pride (v. 21); 6) perverted justice (vv. 22, 23). As a result of these perversions God will call for a foreign nation that will invade, devastate, and carry them away captive.
5:12 See section 5 of Truth-In-Action at the end of Is.
5:18 The rulers of Israel and Judah are so attached to sin that they drag it with them wherever they go.

And their blossom will ascend
like dust;
Because they have rejected the
law of the LORD of hosts,
And despised the word of the
Holy One of Israel.
25 [a]Therefore the anger of the LORD
is aroused against His people;
He has stretched out His hand
against them
And stricken them,
And [b]the hills trembled.
Their carcasses *were* as refuse in
the midst of the streets.

[c]For all this His anger is not turned
away,
But His hand *is* stretched out
still.

26 [a]He will lift up a banner to the
nations from afar,
And will [b]whistle to them from
[c]the end of the earth;
Surely [d]they shall come with
speed, swiftly.
27 No one will be weary or stumble
among them,
No one will slumber or sleep;
Nor [a]will the belt on their loins
be loosed,
Nor the strap of their sandals be
broken;
28 [a]Whose arrows *are* sharp,
And all their bows bent;
Their horses' hooves will
[1]seem like flint,
And their wheels like a
whirlwind.
29 Their roaring *will be* like a lion,
They will *roar like young lions;
Yes, they will roar
And lay hold of the prey;
They will carry *it* away safely,
And no one will deliver.
30 In that day they will roar against
them
Like the roaring of the sea.
And if *one* [a]looks to the land,
Behold, darkness *and* [1]sorrow;
And the light is darkened by the
clouds.

25 [a]2 Kin. 22:13, 17; Is. 66:15 [b]Ps. 18:7; Is. 64:3; Jer. 4:24; Nah. 1:5 [c]Is. 9:12, 17; Jer. 4:8; Dan. 9:16 **26** [a]Is. 11:10, 12 [b]Is. 7:18; Zech. 10:8 [c]Mal. 1:11 [d]Joel 2:7 **27** [a]Dan. 5:6 **28** [a]Jer. 5:16 [1]Lit. *be regarded as* **29** *See WW at Joel 3:16. **30** [a]Is. 8:22; Jer. 4:23–28; Joel 2:10; Luke 21:25, 26 [1]*distress*

CHAPTER 6

1 [a]2 Kin. 15:7; 2 Chr. 26:23; Is. 1:1 [b]John 12:41; Rev. 4:2, 3; 20:11 **2** [a]Ezek. 1:11 **3** [a]Rev. 4:8 [b]Num. 14:21; Ps. 72:19 *See WW at Lev. 19:2. • See WW at Ex. 32:13.

Isaiah Called to Be a Prophet

6 In the year that [a]King Uzziah died,
I [b]saw the Lord sitting on a throne,
high and lifted up, and the train of His
robe filled the temple.
2 Above it stood **seraphim;** each one
had six wings: with two he covered his
face, [a]with two he covered his feet, and
with two he flew.

WORD WEALTH

6:2 seraphim, *seraphim,* plural of *seraph* (seh-rah-*feem;* seh-*rahf*); Strong's #8314: A burning, fiery, gliding, angelic being; also a fire-colored, agile, gliding desert creature, presumably a fiery serpent. The root is the verb *seraph,* "to set on fire, to burn." Accordingly, the *seraphim* may be angels of a fiery color or appearance, or flamelike in motion or clearness. Only in Is. 6:2, 6 does the word appear as "seraphim"; in all the remaining five occurrences (Num. 21:6, 8; Deut. 8:15; Is. 14:29; 30:6), it is translated "fiery serpents" and appears along with scorpions and vipers. Perhaps the color or motion of the earthly fiery serpents resembles that of the fiery angels.

KINGDOM DYNAMICS

6:2 Seraphim, ANGELS. The ministry of the seraphim is closely related to the throne and the praises of God. They are seen constantly glorifying God—extolling His nature and attributes, and apparently supervising heaven's worship. It is possible the seraphim are the praising angels of Ps. 148:2 though they are not specifically identified as such. Whereas cherubim are positioned beside and around the throne of God (Ps. 99:1; Rev. 4:6), the six-winged seraphim are seen as hovering above the throne as they minister in worship.

(Heb. 1:14/Gen. 3:24) M.H.

3 And one cried to another and said:

[a]"Holy,* holy, holy *is* the LORD of
hosts;
[b]The whole *earth *is* full of His
glory!"

6:1 Uzziah died: The date usually given for his death is 740 B.C. The history of Uzziah is found in 2 Kin. and 2 Chr. (see marginal references). **Saw the Lord:** John states that no man has ever seen God (John 1:18); according to John 12:41 Isaiah saw the glory of Christ and Yahweh, much as Moses did. See notes on Ex. 33:19–23; 34:6, 7. The word used for Lord here is *Adonai,* which means "Supreme Lord and Master" (see Rev. 4:2).
6:2 Seraphim are literally "burning ones," here angelic beings represented as winged. **Covered his face:** Out of respect for God's glory. **Covered his feet:** Or body, in modesty. **He flew:** Giving instant obedience.
6:3 Holy, holy, holy: A praise to God for revealing His innermost nature. The Hebrew word for "holy" here means "separated," "unapproachable." However, there can be relationship because the Lord takes the initiative to provide a Mediator. **LORD of hosts:** A title for Yahweh used over 50 times by Isaiah and more than 200 times in the OT, it signifies He is the Deliverer surrounded by hosts of heavenly power. **Glory** is that aspect of God's character that emphasizes His greatness and authority.

4 And the posts of the door were shaken by the voice of him who cried out, and the house was filled with smoke.

2 5 So I said:

"Woe *is* me, for I am [1]undone!
Because I *am* a man of [a]unclean* lips,
And I dwell in the midst of a people of unclean lips;
For my eyes have seen the King,
The LORD of hosts."

6 Then one of the *seraphim flew to me, having in his hand a live coal *which* he had taken with the tongs from [a]the *altar.
7 And he [a]touched my mouth *with it,* and said:

"Behold, this has touched your lips;
Your iniquity is taken away,
And your sin [1]purged."*

8 Also I heard the voice of the Lord, saying:

"Whom shall I send,
And who will go for [a]Us?"

Then I said, "Here *am* I! Send me."
9 And He said, "Go, and [a]tell this people:

'Keep on hearing, but do not understand;
Keep on seeing, but do not perceive.'

KINGDOM DYNAMICS

6:8, 9 Call of God, LEADER TRAITS. One of the tasks of the Holy Spirit is to call godly leaders in the kingdom. All men and women are "called" to God (Rom. 8:28, 30); yet only a few respond (Matt. 7:13, 14; 22:14; John 15:16). Leaders, however, experience a different kind of call and are called in different ways. 1) Many are called sovereignly. Moses was singled out by God who spoke to him from a burning bush (Ex. 3:1—4:17). The child Samuel was called while he was asleep (1 Sam. 3:1–18). Young Isaiah was worshiping in the temple when called by God (Is. 6:1–9). 2) Others are called through men. Samuel went to David and anointed him with oil (1 Sam. 16:1–13). Paul instructed Titus to appoint elders in the churches of Crete (Titus 1:5). There is a difference between being a "man of God"—as all are called to be, and being "God's man"—one called to leadership.
(*/Matt. 16:13–20) J.B.

5 [a]Ex. 6:12, 30 [1]*destroyed, cut off* *See WW at Lev. 10:10. 6 [a]Rev. 8:3 *See WW at Is. 6:2. • See WW at 2 Kin. 12:9. 7 [a]Jer. 1:9; Dan. 10:16 [1]*atoned for* *See WW at Num. 15:25. 8 [a]Gen. 1:26 9 [a]Is. 43:8; Matt. 13:14; Mark 4:12; Luke 8:10; John 12:40; Acts 28:26; Rom. 11:8
10 [a]Ps. 119:70; Mark 6:1–6; Acts 7:51; Rom. 10:1–4 [b]Jer. 5:21 *See WW at 1 Kin. 20:8. 11 [a]Mic. 3:12 12 [a]2 Kin. 25:21; Is. 5:9 13 [a]Deut. 7:6; Ezra 9:2

CHAPTER 7
1 [a]2 Chr. 28 [b]2 Kin. 16:5, 9 [1]*conquer it*

10 "Make [a]the heart of this people dull,
And their ears heavy,
And shut their eyes;
[b]Lest they see with their eyes,
And *hear with their ears,
And understand with their heart,
And return and be healed."

11 Then I said, "Lord, how long?" And He answered:

[a]"Until the cities are laid waste and without inhabitant,
The houses are without a man,
The land is utterly desolate,
12 [a]The LORD has removed men far away,
And the forsaken places *are* many in the midst of the land.
13 But yet a tenth *will be* in it,
And will return and be for consuming,
As a terebinth tree or as an oak,
Whose stump *remains* when it is cut down.
So [a]the holy seed *shall be* its stump."

Isaiah Sent to King Ahaz

7 Now it came to pass in the days of [a]Ahaz the son of Jotham, the son of Uzziah, king of Judah, *that* Rezin king of Syria and Pekah the son of Remaliah, king of Israel, went up to Jerusalem to *make* war against [b]it, but could not [1]prevail against it.

6:4, 5 Woe *is* me: Having delivered six woes in ch. 5, the prophet adds a seventh upon himself as a representative of the wayward nation. They have **unclean lips,** unclean natures which express themselves in inappropriate speech.
6:5–7 See section 2 of Truth-In-Action at the end of Is.
6:6, 7 This is part of the vision's symbolism. Isaiah was not physically **touched. Taken away:** Literally, "cut off." A sinful man in the presence of the Holy One is doomed, but God took the initiative to provide atonement and cleansing because Isaiah was contrite.
6:8 Us: See note on Gen. 1:26. **Send me:** The prophet enlightened, cleansed, and called is ready to volunteer for the crucible of prophetic ministry.
6:9, 10 The prophet is given no reason to expect a positive response. God knew the nation was now almost beyond remedy, as it would be in the day of Jesus. See note on Mark 4:12.
6:11–13 A tenth (remnant) will return from captivity. A mere **stump** of the tree will ultimately be left to sprout again as God's **holy seed**. See note on Zeph. 2:7.
7:1 Ahaz was the ungodly and idolatrous grandson of **Uzziah. Rezin** and **Pekah** formed a coalition to make war against **Judah** in 734 B.C. (2 Kin. 16). They wanted Judah to strengthen their coalition against Assyria.

2 And it was told to the house of David, saying, "Syria's forces are [1]de-
ployed in Ephraim." So his heart and
the heart of his people were moved as
the trees of the woods are moved with
the wind.
3 Then the LORD said to Isaiah, "Go
out now to meet Ahaz, you and [1]Shear-
Jashub your son, at the end of the
aqueduct from the upper pool, on the
highway to the Fuller's Field,
4 "and say to him: [1]'Take heed, and
[2]be [a]quiet; do not fear or be fainthearted for these two stubs of smoking
firebrands, for the fierce anger of
Rezin and Syria, and the son of Remaliah.
5 'Because Syria, Ephraim, and the
son of Remaliah have plotted evil
against you, saying,
6 "Let us go up against Judah and
[1]trouble it, and let us make a gap in
its wall for ourselves, and set a king
over them, the son of Tabel"—
7 'thus says the Lord GOD:

[a]"It shall not stand,
Nor shall it come to pass.
8 [a]For the head of Syria *is*
Damascus,
And the head of Damascus *is*
Rezin.
Within sixty-five years Ephraim
will be [1]broken,
So that it will not *be* a people.
9 The head of Ephraim *is* Samaria,
And the head of Samaria *is*
Remaliah's son.
[a]If you will not *believe,
Surely you shall not be
established." ' "

2 [1]Lit. *settled upon*
3 [1]Lit. *A Remnant Shall Return*
4 [a]Ex. 14:13; Is. 30:15; Lam. 3:26 [1]*Be careful* [2]*be calm*
6 [1]*cause a sickening dread*
7 [a]2 Kin. 16:5; Is. 8:10; Acts 4:25, 26
8 [a]2 Sam. 8:6; 2 Kin. 17:6 [1]Lit. *shattered*
9 [a]2 Chr. 20:20; Is. 5:24 *See WW at 2 Chr. 20:20.
11 [a]Matt. 12:38 [1]Lit. *make the request deep or make it high above* *See WW at 2 Kin. 19:15.
12 *See WW at Ps. 78:41.
14 [a]Matt. 1:23; Luke 1:31; John 1:45; Rev. 12:5 [b][Is. 9:6] [c]Is. 8:8, 10 [1]Lit. *God-With-Us* *See WW at Ps. 86:17.

The Immanuel Prophecy

10 Moreover the LORD spoke again to
Ahaz, saying,
11 [a]"Ask a sign for yourself from the
LORD your *God; [1]ask it either in the
depth or in the height above."
12 But Ahaz said, "I will not ask, nor
will I *test the LORD!"
13 Then he said, "Hear now, O house
of David! *Is it* a small thing for you to
weary men, but will you weary my God
also?
14 "Therefore the Lord Himself will
give you a *sign: [a]Behold, the virgin
shall conceive and bear [b]a Son, and
shall call His name [c]Immanuel.[1]

KINGDOM DYNAMICS

7:14 Christ Birthed by a Young, Virgin Woman, MESSIAH'S COMING. The prophecy of the Virgin Birth has been a source of considerable controversy due to the use of the Hebrew word *'almah,* which can be translated "young woman," as well as "virgin." Isaiah used *'almah* under the inspiration of the Spirit, because the Lord was making a dual prophecy in this passage. The Lord was giving the sign of a child to King Ahaz, and the conception and birth of that child is recorded in ch. 8. But the Holy Spirit was also speaking of the Messiah who would come, and that Child would literally be born of a virgin. The fact that Christ was virgin-born is indisputable from Matthew and Luke's use of the Greek word *parthenos,* which definitely means "virgin" (Matt. 1:23; Luke 1:27).
(Is. 9:6/Mic. 5:2, 4, 5) J.H.

7:2 House of David: The royal court. Because Ahaz, who ruled on the Davidic throne, had no faith in Yahweh, the hearts of the whole court shook **as the trees . . . moved with the wind.**
7:3, 4 God sent **Isaiah** to assure **Ahaz** that He would protect Judah and the throne of David against invasion. **Shear-Jashub,** "A Remnant Shall Return," was the name given to Isaiah's son as a prophecy. In spite of judgment upon the unbelieving majority in Judah, a remnant would always be faithful to secure God's messianic promises to Abraham. See *note on* 6:11–13.
7:4 Two stubs: The kings of **Syria** and Israel, who seemed like firebrands, would both die shortly. Pekah was assassinated in 732 B.C. **Rezin** was killed the same year by Tiglath-Pileser III of Assyria.
7:6 The son of Tabel, otherwise unknown, was the coalition's intended king.
7:8 Sixty-five years: A period after which the northern kingdom of Israel, called **Ephraim** after the largest of the 10 tribes, would cease to exist. The date is difficult to calculate as Israel fell 13 years later. It may refer to the extensive depopulation of Israel under Assyria's Esarhaddon (680–669 B.C.).
7:10, 11 Sign: A miracle in the sky or on the Earth to assure King Ahaz that God will fulfill His promises.
7:12 Test the LORD: A hypocritical answer. **Ahaz** did not want to trust God. The sign would not be tempting God in this case, because God was offering it.
7:14 This prophetic **sign** was given to Ahaz as an assurance of Judah's hope in the midst of adversity. It therefore had an immediate, historical fulfillment. Its usage in the NT shows that it also has a messianic fulfillment. The Hebrew word for **virgin** (*'almah*) means either a "virgin" or a "young woman" of marriageable age. Isaiah's readers could have understood it to be either. Messianically, it irrefutably refers to the Virgin Mary (Matt. 1:23; Luke 1:27), where the Greek *parthenos* (virgin) removes any question. The optional form of the Hebrew word was essential for the prophecy to serve the dual situation, relating both to the Messiah's birth in the future and to a more immediate birth in the kingly line. A **Son** to Isaiah's readers would have been an unidentified heir from Ahaz's house, perhaps his son Hezekiah. Messianically, it was fulfilled in Jesus Christ. **Immanuel** ("God-With-Us") was the title given to assure God's participation in bringing about deliverance from the Syrian and Israelite coalition; messianically, it became a key name marking Christ's incarnation.

15 "Curds and honey He shall eat, that
He may know to refuse the evil and
choose the good.
16 [a]"For before the Child shall know
to refuse the evil and choose the good,
the land that you dread will be forsaken by [b]both her kings.
17 [a]"The LORD will bring the king of
Assyria upon you and your people and
your father's house—days that have
not come since the day that [b]Ephraim
departed from Judah."

18 And it shall come to pass in that
day
That the LORD [a]will whistle for
the fly
That *is* in the farthest part of the
rivers of Egypt,
And for the bee that *is* in the land
of Assyria.
19 They will come, and all of them
will rest
In the desolate valleys and in
[a]the clefts of the rocks,
And on all thorns and in all
pastures.

20 In the same day the Lord will
shave with a [a]hired [b]razor,
With those from beyond [1]the
River, with the king of Assyria,
The head and the hair of the legs,
And will also remove the beard.

21 It shall be in that day
That a man will keep alive a
young cow and two sheep;
22 So it shall be, from the abundance
of milk they give,
That he will eat curds;
For curds and honey everyone
will eat who is left in the land.

16 [a]Is. 8:4 [b]2 Kin. 15:30
17 [a]2 Chr. 28:19, 20; Is. 8:7, 8; 10:5, 6 [b]1 Kin. 12:16
18 [a]Is. 5:26
19 [a]Is. 2:19; Jer. 16:16
20 [a]Is. 10:5, 15 [b]2 Kin. 16:7; 2 Chr. 28:20 [1]The Euphrates
23 [a]Is. 5:6

CHAPTER 8

1 [a]Is. 30:8; Hab. 2:2 [1]Lit. *Speed the Spoil, Hasten the Booty*
2 [a]2 Kin. 16:10
4 [a]2 Kin. 17:6; Is. 7:16 [b]2 Kin. 15:29 [1]*knows how* [2]*plunder* *See WW at Ps. 68:5.
6 [a]John 9:7 *See WW at Is. 43:2.

23 It shall happen in that day,
That wherever there could be a
thousand vines
Worth a thousand *shekels* of
silver,
[a]It will be for briers and thorns.
24 With arrows and bows men will
come there,
Because all the land will become
briers and thorns.

25 And to any hill which could be
dug with the hoe,
You will not go there for fear of
briers and thorns;
But it will become a range for
oxen
And a place for sheep to roam.

Assyria Will Invade the Land

8 Moreover the LORD said to me,
"Take a large scroll, and [a]write on
it with a man's pen concerning [1]Maher-
Shalal-Hash-Baz.
2 "And I will take for Myself faithful
witnesses to record, [a]Uriah the priest
and Zechariah the son of Jeberechiah."
3 Then I went to the prophetess, and
she conceived and bore a son. Then the
LORD said to me, "Call his name
Maher-Shalal-Hash-Baz;
4 [a]"for before the child [1]shall have
knowledge to cry 'My *father' and 'My
mother,' [b]the riches of Damascus and
the [2]spoil of Samaria will be taken
away before the king of Assyria."
5 The LORD also spoke to me again,
saying:

6 "Inasmuch as these people refused
The *waters of [a]Shiloah that flow
softly,

7:15 Curds and honey, foods for a weaned child, symbolize the ability from a young age to discern likes (**the good**) and dislikes (**the evil**). This shows righteous ability to rule. This part of the prophecy is not applied to Jesus in the NT.
7:16 The short duration of the coalition (see note on v. 4) is indicated by stating that **before the Child** is old enough to make decisions, **the land** of the two **kings** will be devastated. The present crisis will not last long.
7:17 While God promised that **Assyria** would aid **Judah** against the coalition, she will also be an instrument of judgment against Judah. **Days that have not . . . Judah** indicates the disaster will be greater than any since the civil war in 930 B.C. (1 Kin. 11:26—14:20). Jerusalem suffered Assyrian attacks in 714 and 701 B.C.
7:18–25 The invasion is vividly portrayed. Ahaz had hoped for total relief; instead, **the LORD will whistle** for invading armies from central Africa and the upper Euphrates (**the fly . . . the bee**).
7:18 That day usually refers to God's eschatological judgment. See note on Obad. 15. Here it refers to the Assyrian invasion, a historical inbreaking of His judgment.
7:20 Shave . . . razor was a mark of dishonor applied to slaves.
7:21, 22 Curds and honey here symbolize foods of deprivation.
7:23–25 Judah will no longer be a prosperous "land of milk and honey."
8:1–4 Isaiah returns to the judgment against Syria and Israel. See note on 7:3, 4. Through a prophetic biography, **the LORD** emphasizes that Assyria will end the siege against Judah.
8:2 Two **witnesses** are required by the Law (Deut. 17:6). **Uriah** was likely the chief **priest** (2 Kin. 16:10–16) and **Zechariah** King Ahaz's father-in-law (2 Kin. 18:2), representing the highest leadership.
8:3 I went often described sexual union (Gen. 16:4), making **the prophetess** Isaiah's wife. The **son**'s **name** was a prophecy that Assyria would soon plunder Syria and Israel, Judah's enemies.
8:6–10 These people (Israel) were faced with an alternative: peaceful coexistence with Assyria (**waters . . . flow softly**) or the rebellion of **Rezin** and Pekah. Their choice

And rejoice [b]in Rezin and in
Remaliah's son;
7 Now therefore, behold, the Lord
brings up over them
The waters of [1]the River, strong
and mighty—
The king of Assyria and all his
glory;
He will [2]go up over all his
channels
And go over all his banks.
8 He will pass through Judah,
He will overflow and pass
over,
[a]He will reach up to the neck;
And the stretching out of his
wings
Will [1]fill the breadth of Your land,
O [b]Immanuel.[2]

9 "Be[a] shattered, O you peoples, and
be broken in pieces!
Give ear, all you from far
countries.
Gird yourselves, but be broken in
pieces;
Gird yourselves, but be broken in
pieces.
10 [a]Take counsel together, but it will
come to nothing;
Speak the word, [b]but it will not
stand,
[c]For [1]God *is* with us."

Fear God, Heed His Word

11 For the LORD spoke thus to me with
[1]a strong hand, and instructed me that
I should not walk in the way of this
people, saying:

4 12 "Do not say, 'A conspiracy,'
Concerning all that this people
call a conspiracy,
Nor be afraid of their [1]threats,*
nor be [2]troubled.
13 The LORD of hosts, Him you shall
hallow;
Let Him *be* your **fear,**
And *let* Him *be* your dread.

6 [b]Is. 7:1, 2
7 [1]The Euphrates [2]Overflow
8 [a]Is. 30:28 [b]Is. 7:14; Matt. 1:23 [1]Lit. *be the fullness of* [2]Lit. *God-With-Us*
9 [a]Joel 3:9
10 [a]Is. 7:7; Acts 5:38 [b]Is. 7:14 [c]Rom. 8:31 [1]Heb. *Immanuel*
11 [1]Mighty power
12 [1]Lit. *fear* or *terror* [2]Lit. *in dread* *See WW at Is. 8:13.

WORD WEALTH

8:13 fear, *morah* (moh-*rah*); Strong's #4172: Fear, reverence, terror, awe; an object of fear, respect, or reverence. *Morah* is derived from *yare'*, "to be afraid of, to fear, to reverence." *Morah* occurs a dozen times in the OT, beginning with Gen. 9:2, which speaks of the fear and dread Noah's descendants would inspire in all animals after the Flood. The Lord also inspires fear, as in Ps. 76:11. In the present reference, Isaiah is admonished never to fear human threats, but to let God alone be the object of his reverential fear.

14 [a]He will be as a [1]sanctuary,
But [b]a stone of stumbling and a
rock of [2]offense
To both the houses of Israel,
As a trap and a snare to the
inhabitants of Jerusalem.
15 And many among them shall
[a]stumble;
They shall fall and be broken,
Be snared and [1]taken."

16 Bind up the testimony,
Seal the law among my disciples.
17 And I will wait on the LORD,
Who [a]hides His face from the
house of Jacob;
And I [b]will hope in Him.
18 [a]Here am I and the children whom
the LORD has given me!
We [b]*are* for signs and wonders
in Israel
From the LORD of hosts,
Who *dwells in Mount Zion.

19 And when they say to you, [a]"Seek 1
those who are mediums and wizards,
[b]who whisper and *mutter," should not
a people seek their God? *Should they*
[c]*seek* the dead on behalf of the living?
20 [a]To the law and to the testimony!
If they do not speak according to this
word, *it is* because [b]*there*[1] *is* no light
in them.
21 They will pass through it hard-
pressed and hungry; and it shall hap-

14 [a]Is. 4:6; 25:4; Ezek. 11:16 [b]Luke 2:34; 20:17; Rom. 9:33; 1 Pet. 2:8 [1]*holy abode* [2]*stumbling over*
15 [a]Matt. 21:44 [1]*captured*
17 [a]Deut. 31:17; Is. 54:8 [b]Hab. 2:3
18 [a]Heb. 2:13 [b]Ps. 71:7 *See WW at Num. 10:12.
19 [a]1 Sam. 28:8 [b]Is. 29:4 [c]Ps. 106:28 *See WW at Ps. 1:2.
20 [a]Is. 1:10; 8:16; Luke 16:29 [b]Is. 8:22; Mic. 3:6 [1]Or *they have no dawn*

of the latter was against God's providence, bringing judgment (v. 7).
8:6 Shiloah: A reference to the healing pool of Siloam in Jerusalem, typical of God's counsel as contrasted with the waters of the Euphrates. Because Judah rejected God's healing word, they would receive Assyria's fury.
8:9, 10 God *is* with us: The Hebrew word is *Immanuel*. In spite of His judgment, God warns the nations—even those, such as Assyria, which were used as instruments of judgment—that the Hebrews are His people and their future is in His control.
8:11–15 God assures Isaiah that He is in all these events, in spite of the fact an enemy is used to judge His people. Such seemed to the people to be **a conspiracy;** in fact, it was the plan of **the LORD of hosts**. See note on 6:3.
8:12–15 See section 4 of Truth-In-Action at the end of Is.
8:14 The houses of Israel: Both kingdoms.
8:16–18 There will be an interval of some 13 years before Isaiah's words are fulfilled. In the meantime he must hold his prophetic ground, in spite of the people's derision that identified him with heathen spiritualists (v. 19).
8:19, 20 See section 1 of Truth-In-Action at the end of Is.
8:20 The Judahites mockingly appeal for a "real" prophet who rightly declares the truths of **the law** and **the testimony.**

pen, when they are hungry, that they
will be enraged and [a]curse [1]their king
and their God, and look upward.
22 Then they will look to the earth, and
see trouble and darkness, gloom of anguish; and *they will be* driven into
darkness.

The Government of the Promised Son

9 Nevertheless [a]the gloom *will* not
be upon her who *is* distressed,
As when at [b]first He lightly
esteemed
The land of Zebulun and the land
of Naphtali,
And [c]afterward more heavily
oppressed *her*,
By the way of the sea, beyond the
Jordan,
In Galilee of the Gentiles.

2 [a]The people who walked in
darkness
Have seen a great light;
Those who dwelt in the land of
the shadow of death,
Upon them a light has shined.

3 You have multiplied the nation
And [1]increased its joy;
They *rejoice before You
According to the joy of harvest,
As *men* *rejoice [a]when they
divide the spoil.
4 For You have broken the yoke of
his burden
And the staff of his shoulder,
The rod of his oppressor,
As in the day of [a]Midian.
5 For every warrior's [1]sandal from
the noisy battle,
And garments *rolled in blood,
[a]Will be used for burning *and* fuel
[2]of fire.

21 [a]Rev. 16:11 [1]Or *by their king and by their God*

CHAPTER 9

1 [a]Is. 8:22 [b]2 Kin. 15:29; 2 Chr. 16:4 [c]Matt. 4:13–16
2 [a]Matt. 4:16; Luke 1:79; 2 Cor. 4:6; Eph. 5:8
3 [a]Judg. 5:30 [1]So with Qr., Tg.; Kt., Vg. *not increased joy;* LXX *Most of the people You brought down in Your joy* *See WW at 2 Chr. 7:10. • See WW at Hab. 3:18.
4 [a]Judg. 7:22
5 [a]Is. 66:15 [1]*boot* [2]*for the fire* *See WW at Prov. 16:3.

6 [a][Is. 7:14; Luke 2:11]; John 1:45 [b]Luke 2:7; [John 3:16; 1 John 4:9] [c][Matt. 28:18; 1 Cor. 15:25]; Rev. 12:5 [d]Judg. 13:18 [e]Titus 2:13 [f]Eph. 2:14 *See WW at Jer. 33:3.
7 [a]Dan. 2:44; Matt. 1:1, 6; Luke 1:32, 33; John 7:42 [b]Is. 37:32 *See WW at Ps. 136:1.

6 [a]For unto us a Child is born,
Unto us a [b]Son is given;
And [c]the government will be
upon His shoulder.
And His name will be *called
[d]Wonderful, Counselor, [e]Mighty
God,
Everlasting Father, [f]Prince of
Peace.

KINGDOM DYNAMICS

9:6 Messiah's Becoming a Man, MESSIAH'S COMING. In this scripture we have one of the most beautifully poetic promises of the Messiah's coming reign. Yearly we recite this verse and hear it sung as we celebrate Christmas. Yet this verse also contains a reference to one of the great, incomprehensible truths in the Bible: the Incarnation—"a Child is born, . . . a Son is given." God would become a man. A newborn baby would be called "Mighty God, Everlasting Father." We can accept that truth by faith, but we cannot fully grasp what it meant for the Second Person of the Godhead to shed His eternal state and put on flesh. But Paul tells us that He took the form of a servant and came as a man. "Therefore God also has highly exalted Him and given Him the name which is above every name" (Phil. 2:7, 9).

(Deut. 18:18, 19/Is. 7:14) J.H.

7 Of the increase of *His* government
and peace
[a]*There will be* no end,
Upon the throne of David and
over His kingdom,
To order it and establish it with
judgment and justice
From that time forward, even
*forever.
The [b]zeal of the LORD of hosts will
perform this.

9:1–7 Shifting away from **gloom** (8:19–22), Isaiah prophesies bright hope. God is in control and will turn things around for His faithful. Although the historical reference is not specified, the NT identifies this section with Christ and His reign. See marginal references.
9:1, 2 Zebulun . . . Naphtali: These are principal cities of **Galilee** captured by Assyria. Although Galilee was held in contempt (2 Kin. 15:29), the promised Christ would dwell there as a source of **light** to **the Gentiles** (Matt. 4:14–16).
9:3–7 You refers to God who has increased the nation's **joy** in sending the miracle Child, Immanuel. His reign will eventually bring freedom from enemy domination (vv. 4, 5) and the universal rulership of the house of **David** (vv. 6, 7). The NT indicates that the final fulfillment of these promises awaits Christ's return. See note on Obad. 15.
9:6, 7 The fourfold name and attributes of the **Child** (Messiah) who shall be born to reign forever **upon the throne of David** are given. **Wonderful, Counselor** (see 28:29) is likely one name that expresses His ability as a political guide and leader. He is the living Word, the infallible source of guidance, the inexhaustible wisdom, the Truth, and the Way. On Him will rest **the government** (the entitlement to rule). **Mighty God:** The Child is God incarnate, the omnipotent One. The word translated "Mighty" has the additional meaning of "hero." The Lord is the infinite Hero of His people, the Divine Warrior who has triumphed over sin and death. **Everlasting Father** expresses Christ's fatherly care. The name is not in conflict with that of the First Person of the Trinity. Jesus said to Philip, "He who has seen Me has seen the Father" (John 14:9). "Everlasting" can also mean "everywhere present"; He has the divine attributes of both eternity and omnipresence as He rules upon the throne of David and within the hearts of the redeemed. **Prince of Peace:** His reign will be characterized by *shalom,* health, well-being, prosperity, happiness, and cessation of enmity. The NT states this required His triumph over Satan. **Kingdom:** See The Kingdom of God: The Message of the Kingdom and Conflict and the Kingdom.

The Punishment of Samaria

8 The Lord sent a word against
[a]Jacob,
And it has fallen on Israel.
9 All the people will know—
Ephraim and the inhabitant of
Samaria—
Who say in pride and arrogance
of heart:
10 "The bricks have fallen down,
But we will rebuild with hewn
stones;
The sycamores are cut down,
But we will replace *them* with
cedars."
11 Therefore the LORD shall set up
The adversaries of Rezin against
him,
And spur his enemies on,
12 The Syrians before and the
Philistines behind;
And they shall devour Israel with
an open mouth.

For all this His anger is not turned
away,
But His hand *is* [1]stretched out
still.

13 For the people do not turn to Him
who strikes them,
Nor do they seek the LORD of
hosts.
14 Therefore the LORD will cut off
head and tail from Israel,
Palm branch and bulrush
[a]in one day.
15 The *elder and honorable, he *is*
the head;
The prophet who teaches lies, he
is the tail.
16 For [a]the leaders of this people
cause *them* to err,
And *those who are* led by them
are destroyed.
17 Therefore the Lord [a]will *have no
joy in their young men,
Nor have mercy on their
fatherless and widows;
For everyone *is* a hypocrite and
an evildoer,
And every mouth speaks
[1]folly.

[b]For all this His anger is not turned
away,
But His hand *is* stretched out still.

18 For wickedness [a]burns as the fire;
It shall devour the briers and
thorns,
And kindle in the thickets of the
forest;
They shall mount up *like* rising
smoke.
19 Through the wrath of the LORD of
hosts
[a]The land is burned up,
And the people shall be as fuel
for the fire;
[b]No man shall spare his brother.
20 And he shall [1]snatch on the right
hand
And be hungry;
He shall devour on the left hand
[a]And not be *satisfied;
[b]Every man shall eat the flesh of
his own arm.
21 Manasseh *shall devour* Ephraim,
and Ephraim Manasseh;
Together they *shall be* [a]against
Judah.

[b]For all this His anger is not turned
away,
But His hand *is* stretched out still.

10 "Woe to those who [a]decree
unrighteous decrees,
Who write misfortune,
Which they have prescribed
2 To rob the needy of justice,
And to take what is right from the
poor of My people,
That widows may be their prey,
And *that* they may rob the
fatherless.
3 [a]What will you do in [b]the day of
punishment,
And in the desolation *which* will
come from [c]afar?
To whom will you flee for help?
And where will you leave your
glory?
4 Without Me they shall bow down
among the [a]prisoners,
And they shall fall [1]among the
slain."

[b]For all this His anger is not turned
away,
But His hand *is* stretched out still.

8 [a]Gen. 32:28 **12** [1]In judgment **14** [a]Rev. 18:8 **15** *See WW at Ps. 119:100. **16** [a]Is. 3:12; Mic. 3:1, 5, 9; Matt. 15:14 **17** [a]Ps. 147:10 [b]Is. 5:25 [1]*foolishness* *See WW at 2 Chr. 7:10.

18 [a]Ps. 83:14; [Is. 1:7; 10:17]; Nah. 1:10; Mal. 4:1 **19** [a]Is. 8:22 [b]Mic. 7:2, 6 **20** [a]Lev. 26:26 [b]Jer. 19:9 [1]*slice off* or *tear* *See WW at Amos 4:8. **21** [a]2 Chr. 28:6, 8; Is. 11:13 [b]Is. 9:12, 17

CHAPTER 10

1 [a]Ps. 58:2 **3** [a]Job 31:14 [b]Is. 13:6; Jer. 9:9; Hos. 9:7; Luke 19:44 [c]Is. 5:26 **4** [a]Is. 24:22 [b]Is. 5:25 [1]Lit. *under*

9:8—10:4 These verses describe God's judgment upon **Israel,** also termed **Ephraim,** whose capital was **Samaria.** The idolatrous 10 northern tribes that broke away from Judah will end their history sadly by a failed conspiracy **against Judah**. See note on 7:1. The 10 tribes were betrayed by their kings, prophets, and priests (vv. 15, 16).

9:8 A word refers to a courtroom verdict. **Jacob** is **Israel,** the northern kingdom.

9:11, 12 See notes on 7:1–4; 8:1–4.

9:21 There will be internal dissension in Israel as well as war **against Judah.** See note on 7:1–4.

10:1–4 God's judgment will not be averted. The sin and social injustices are too great. See note on 5:7.

Arrogant Assyria Also Judged

5 "Woe to Assyria, [a]the rod of My anger
And the staff in whose hand is My indignation.
6 I will send him against [a]an ungodly nation,
And against the people of My wrath
I will [b]give him charge,
To seize the spoil, to take the prey,
And to tread them down like the mire of the streets.
7 [a]Yet he does not mean so,
Nor does his heart think so;
But *it is* in his heart to destroy,
And cut off not a few nations.
8 [a]For he says,
'*Are* not my princes altogether kings?
9 *Is* not [a]Calno [b]like Carchemish?
Is not Hamath like Arpad?
Is not Samaria [c]like Damascus?
10 As my hand has found the kingdoms of the idols,
Whose carved images excelled those of Jerusalem and Samaria,
11 As I have done to Samaria and her idols,
Shall I not do also to Jerusalem and her idols?' "

12 Therefore it shall come to pass,
when the Lord has [1]performed all His
work [a]on Mount Zion and on Jerusalem, *that He will say,* [b]"I will punish
the fruit of the arrogant heart of the
king of Assyria, and the glory of his
haughty looks."
13 [a]For he says:

"By the strength of my hand I have done *it,*
And by my wisdom, for I am prudent;
Also I have removed the boundaries of the people,
And have robbed their treasuries;
So I have put down the inhabitants like a [1]valiant *man.*
14 [a]My hand has found like a nest the riches of the people,
And as one gathers eggs *that are* left,
I have gathered all the earth;
And there was no one who moved *his* wing,
Nor opened *his* mouth with even a peep."

15 Shall [a]the ax boast itself against him who chops with it?
Or shall the saw *exalt itself against him who saws with it?
As if a rod could wield *itself* against those who lift it up,
Or as if a staff could lift up, *as if it were* not wood!
16 Therefore the Lord, the [1]Lord of hosts,
Will send leanness among his fat ones;
And under his glory
He will kindle a burning
Like the burning of a fire.
17 So the Light of Israel will be for a fire,
And his Holy One for a flame;
[a]It will burn and devour
His thorns and his briers in one day.
18 And it will consume the glory of his forest and of [a]his fruitful field,
Both soul and body;
And they will be as when a sick man wastes away.
19 Then the rest of the trees of his forest
Will be so few in number
That a child may write them.

The Returning Remnant of Israel

20 And it shall come to pass in that day
That the remnant of Israel,
And such as have escaped of the house of Jacob,
[a]Will never again depend on him who [1]defeated them,
But will depend on the LORD, the Holy One of Israel, in *truth.

5 [a]Jer. 51:20 **6** [a]Is. 9:17 [b]2 Kin. 17:6; Jer. 34:22 **7** [a]Gen. 50:20; Mic. 4:11, 12; Acts 2:23, 24 **8** [a]2 Kin. 19:10 **9** [a]Gen. 10:10; Amos 6:2 [b]2 Chr. 35:20 [c]2 Kin. 16:9 **12** [a]2 Kin. 19:31; Is. 28:21 [b]2 Kin. 19:35; 2 Chr. 32:21; Jer. 50:18 [1]*completed* **13** [a][2 Kin. 19:22–24]; Is. 37:24–27; Ezek. 28:4; Dan. 4:30 [1]*mighty*

14 [a]Job 31:25 **15** [a]Jer. 51:20 *See WW at Ps. 18:46. **16** [1]So with Bg.; MT, DSS *YHWH* (*the* LORD) **17** [a]Is. 9:18 **18** [a]2 Kin. 19:23 **20** [a]2 Kin. 16:7 [1]Lit. *struck* *See WW at Ps. 25:5.

10:5–11 When God's people became incurably corrupt, He often used **Assyria** and other pagan nations to apply the *punishment*. This did not spare them their own judgment, however.
10:7, 8 Assyria, likely unaware of being used by Yahweh, became egotistical and given to excessive violence.
10:9 Calno . . . Arpad refers to Assyria's victories in Syrian territories. **Samaria** refers to their 733 B.C. invasion in which Pekah was murdered (2 Kin. 15:29).
10:10 The Assyrians considered the Syrian **idols** (gods) greater than the God of the Hebrews.
10:11 See note on 7:17.
10:12–19 See notes on vv. 5–11 and vv. 7, 8. The arrogant spirit of **Assyria** has been confirmed by archaeological discoveries of tablets recording these very conquests.
10:20–23 Remnant: In spite of God's judgments against His disobedient people, they will never be totally destroyed; a faithful remnant will always be preserved to keep alive the testimony of divine truth and the hope of the coming Messiah. See note on Zeph. 2:7.

21 The remnant will return, the
remnant of Jacob,
To the [a]Mighty God.
22 [a]For though your people, O Israel,
be as the sand of the sea,
[b]A remnant of them will return;
The destruction decreed shall
overflow with righteousness.
23 [a]For the Lord GOD of hosts
Will make a determined end
In the midst of all the land.

24 Therefore thus says the Lord GOD
of hosts: "O My people, who dwell in
Zion, [a]do not be afraid of the Assyrian.
He shall strike you with a rod and lift
up his staff against you, in the manner
of [b]Egypt.
25 "For yet a very little while [a]and the
indignation will cease, as will My anger in their destruction."
26 And the LORD of hosts will [1]stir* up
[a]a scourge for him like the slaughter
of [b]Midian at the rock of Oreb; [c]*as* His
rod was on the sea, so will He lift it
up in the manner of Egypt.

27 It shall come to pass in that day
That his burden will be taken
away from your shoulder,
And his yoke from your neck,
And the yoke will be destroyed
because of [a]the anointing oil.

28 He has come to Aiath,
He has passed Migron;
At Michmash he has attended to
his equipment.
29 They have gone [1]along [a]the
ridge,
They have taken up lodging at
Geba.
Ramah is afraid,
[b]Gibeah of Saul has fled.
30 [1]Lift up your voice,
O daughter [a]of Gallim!
Cause it to be heard as far as
[b]Laish—
[2]O poor Anathoth!
31 [a]Madmenah has fled,
The inhabitants of Gebim seek
refuge.
32 As yet he will remain [a]at Nob that
day;
He will [b]shake his fist at the
mount of [c]the daughter of Zion,
The hill of Jerusalem.

33 Behold, the Lord,
The LORD of hosts,
Will lop off the bough with terror;
[a]Those of high stature *will be*
hewn down,
And the haughty will be humbled.
34 He will cut down the thickets of
the forest with iron,
And Lebanon will fall by the
Mighty One.

The Reign of Jesse's Offspring

11 There [a]shall come forth a
[1]Rod from the [2]stem of
[b]Jesse,
And [c]a Branch shall [3]grow out of
his roots.
2 [a]The Spirit of the LORD shall *rest
upon Him,
The Spirit of **wisdom** and
understanding,
The Spirit of counsel and might,
The Spirit of *knowledge and of
the fear of the LORD.

21 [a][Is. 9:6]
22 [a]Rom. 9:27, 28 [b]Is. 6:13
23 [a]Is. 28:22; Dan. 9:27; Rom. 9:28
24 [a]Is. 7:4; 12:2 [b]Ex. 14
25 [a]Is. 10:5; 26:20; Dan. 11:36
26 [a]2 Kin. 19:35 [b]Judg. 7:25; Is. 9:4 [c]Ex. 14:26, 27 [1]*arouse* *See WW at Hag. 1:14.
27 [a]Ps. 105:15; [1 John 2:20]
29 [a]1 Sam. 13:23 [b]1 Sam. 11:4 [1]Or *over the pass*
30 [a]1 Sam. 25:44 [b]Judg. 18:7 [1]Or *Cry shrilly* [2]So with MT, Tg., Vg.; LXX, Syr. *Listen to her, O Anathoth*
31 [a]Josh. 15:31
32 [a]1 Sam. 21:1; Neh. 11:32 [b]Is. 13:2 [c]Is. 37:22
33 [a]Is. 37:24, 36–38; Ezek. 31:3; Amos 2:9

CHAPTER 11

1 [a][Zech. 6:12]; Rev. 5:5 [b][Is. 9:7; 11:10]; Matt. 1:5; [Acts 13:23] [c]Is. 4:2 [1]*Shoot* [2]*stock* or *trunk* [3]*be fruitful*
2 [a][Is. 42:1; 48:16; 61:1; Matt. 3:16]; Mark 1:10; Luke 3:22; [John 1:32] *See WW at Ex. 33:14. • See WW at Mal. 2:7.

WORD WEALTH

11:2 wisdom, *chochmah* (choach-*mah*); Strong's #2451: Wisdom; wiseness; skillfulness, whether in the artistic sense (craftsmanship) or the moral sense (skills for living correctly). This noun occurs about 150 times. It is found in all sections of the OT, but is mentioned extensively in Job, Prov., and Eccl. Biblical wisdom

(*cont. on next page*)

10:24–27 Here God is encouraging the remnant of Israel not to fear **the Assyrian,** for in due time He will again deliver His faithful as He did under Moses (v. 24) and Gideon (v. 26; see Judg. 7:25). **The anointing oil:** Prophets, priests, and kings were initiated into office by the anointing with oil, symbolic of the inner working of the Holy Spirit. Since God's blessing comes upon His people when the kings, priests, and prophets are faithful in their functions, Isaiah prophesies of **that day** when woes would end, revival would come and these offices would properly function again. See note on Obad. 15.

10:28–32 These verses mention a string of cities in the pathway of the Assyrian invasion.

10:34 Lebanon refers to a territory on the slopes of Mt. Hermon to the north of Israel.

11:1–10 Isaiah again speaks a message of future hope centered in a God-ordained Davidic ruler and His reign. See 7:14–16 and 9:1–7. Again, it is best to see the fulfillment as ultimately messianic with some initial fulfillment in Hezekiah. See note on 7:14.

11:1 Stem presupposes the difficulties that have befallen the Davidic throne since the kingdom divided. From this same damaged root system (10:33, 34) will emerge fresh life in a new ruler, symbolically called a **Rod** and **Branch.** Rev. 5:5 terms Christ "the Root of David."

11:2 The Spirit of the LORD gives the king his skills to rule, a truth clearly seen in Christ's ministry (Luke 4:14). The Holy Spirit is mentioned by Isaiah more than by any other prophet. The attributes of the Spirit's anointing here suggest the names of the miracle Child. See note on 9:6, 7. The seven distinct ministries of the Holy Spirit mentioned—exalting the Lord's rule, **wisdom, understanding, counsel, might, knowledge, fear** (reverence)—are thought by some to be the OT counter reference to Rev. 4:5, revealing multiplicity of expression in the Holy Spirit's workings.

(cont. from preceding page)
unites God, the Source of all understanding, with daily life, where the principles of right living are put into practice. Therefore, one is exhorted to make God the starting point in any quest for wisdom (Ps. 111:10) and to seek wisdom above all else if he would live successfully (Prov. 4:5–9). The present reference shows that wisdom is a permanent characteristic of the Messiah; compare 1 Cor. 1:24.

3 His delight *is* in the fear of the
LORD,
And He shall not judge by the
sight of His eyes,
Nor decide by the hearing of His
ears;
4 But [a]with righteousness He shall
judge the poor,
And decide with equity for the
meek of the earth;
He shall [b]strike the earth with the
rod of His mouth,
And with the breath of His lips
He shall slay the wicked.
5 Righteousness shall be the belt of
His loins,
And faithfulness the belt of His
waist.

6 "The[a] wolf also shall dwell with
the lamb,
The leopard shall lie down with
the young goat,
The calf and the young lion and
the fatling together;
And a little child shall lead them.
7 The cow and the bear shall graze;
Their young ones shall lie down
together;
And the lion shall eat straw like
the ox.
8 The nursing child shall play by
the cobra's hole,
And the weaned child shall put
his hand in the viper's den.
9 [a]They shall not hurt nor destroy
in all My holy mountain,
For [b]the earth shall be full of the
knowledge of the LORD
As the waters cover the sea.

4 [a]Rev. 19:11 [b]Job 4:9; Is. 30:28, 33; Mal. 4:6; 2 Thess. 2:8
6 [a]Hos. 2:18
9 [a]Job 5:23; Is. 65:25; Ezek. 34:25; Hos. 2:18 [b]Ps. 98:2, 3; Is. 45:6; Hab. 2:14
10 [a]Is. 2:11 [b]Is. 11:1; Rom. 15:12 [c]Is. 27:12, 13 [d]Rom. 15:10 *See WW at Is. 28:12.
11 [a]Is. 19:23–25; Hos. 11:11; Zech. 10:10 [1]Or *coastlands*
12 [a]John 7:35 [1]*gather* [2]Lit. *wings*
13 [a]Is. 9:21; Jer. 3:18; Ezek. 37:16, 17, 22; Hos. 1:11
14 [a]Is. 63:1; Dan. 11:41; Joel 3:19; Amos 9:12 [1]Lit. *sons*
15 [a]Is. 50:2; 51:10, 11; Zech. 10:10, 11 [1]So with MT, Vg.; LXX, Syr., Tg. *dry up* [2]The Euphrates [3]Lit. *in sandals* *See WW at Deut. 11:25.
16 [a]Is. 19:23

10 "And[a] in that day [b]there shall be
a Root of Jesse,
Who shall stand as a [c]banner to
the people;
For the [d]Gentiles shall seek Him,
And His *resting place shall be
glorious."

11 It shall come to pass in that day
That the Lord shall set His hand
again the second time
To recover the remnant of His
people who are left,
[a]From Assyria and Egypt,
From Pathros and Cush,
From Elam and Shinar,
From Hamath and the [1]islands of
the sea.

12 He will set up a banner for the
nations,
And will [1]assemble the outcasts
of Israel,
And gather together [a]the
dispersed of Judah
From the four [2]corners of the
earth.
13 Also [a]the envy of Ephraim shall
depart,
And the adversaries of Judah
shall be cut off;
Ephraim shall not envy Judah,
And Judah shall not harass
Ephraim.
14 But they shall fly down upon the
shoulder of the Philistines
toward the west;
Together they shall plunder the
[1]people of the East;
[a]They shall lay their hand on
Edom and Moab;
And the people of Ammon shall
obey them.
15 The LORD [a]will utterly [1]destroy
the tongue of the Sea of Egypt;
With His mighty wind He will
shake His fist over [2]the River,
And strike it in the seven streams,
And make *men* *cross over
[3]dry-shod.
16 [a]There will be a highway for the
remnant of His people

11:4 He shall strike . . . the wicked: Christ's first coming accomplished this in the spiritual realm (Col. 2:15). He will consummate it literally and spiritually at the end of this age (Rev. 19:11–16; 20:11–15).
11:6–9 This symbolic picture of perfected, pastoral tranquillity stems from **the earth**'s being **full of the knowledge of the LORD**. Such conditions imply God's redeemed and recreated world, conditions that will be foreshadowed in the millennial interlude (Rev. 20:1–4; 21:1—22:5).
11:10 That day: See note on Obad. 15. **Root of Jesse:** See note on v. 1. **Gentiles:** The Messiah's kingdom will include the redeemed of all nations who will gather to His **banner**.
11:11, 12 Recover the remnant: See notes on Zeph. 2:7, 9. **Pathros** is Upper Egypt. **Cush** is the Sudan. **Elam** lies east of Mesopotamia. **Shinar** is the Euphrates Delta. **Islands . . . sea** are Mediterranean and Aegean coastlands. These places represent **the four corners of the earth.**
11:13–16 See notes on Zeph. 1:2–6 and 2:4–15. **The tongue of the Sea of Egypt** is likely the upper end of the Gulf of Suez.

Who will be left from Assyria,
[b]As it was for Israel
In the day that he came up from
the land of Egypt.

A Hymn of Praise

12 And [a]in that day you will say:
"O LORD, I will *praise You;
Though You were angry with me,
Your anger is turned away, and
You comfort me.
2 Behold, God *is* my salvation,
I will trust and not be afraid;
[a]'For [b]YAH, the LORD, *is* my
*strength and song;
He also has become my
salvation.'"

WORD WEALTH

12:2 YAH, *Yah (yah)*; Strong's #3050: The shorter form of the Lord's holy name *Yahweh,* or Jehovah. This contracted form of the name of the Lord God appears 50 times in the OT. Of these 50 occurrences, 44 are found in Ps.; the remaining 6 are found in Ex. and Is. Many of the references in Ps. involve the compound word *Hallelu-Yah,* translated "Praise the LORD"; the word literally means "You must all praise Yah!" This word has spread from Hebrew into many languages and is a beautiful expression suitable for joyous worship.

3 Therefore with joy you will draw
[a]water
From the wells of salvation.

4 And in that day you will say:

[a]"Praise the LORD, call upon His
name;
[b]Declare His deeds among the
peoples,
Make mention that His [c]name is
exalted.
5 [a]Sing* to the LORD,
For He has done excellent things;
This *is* known in all the earth.
6 [a]Cry out and shout, O inhabitant
of Zion,
For great *is* [b]the Holy One of
Israel in your midst!"

Proclamation Against Babylon

13 The [a]burden[1] against Babylon
which Isaiah the son of Amoz
saw.

2 "Lift[a] up a banner [b]on the high
mountain,
*Raise your voice to them;
[c]Wave your hand, that they may
enter the gates of the nobles.
3 I have commanded My [1]sanctified
ones;
I have also called [a]My mighty
ones for My anger—
Those who [b]rejoice in My
exaltation."

4 The [a]noise of a multitude in the
mountains,
Like that of *many people!
A tumultuous noise of the
kingdoms of nations gathered
together!
The LORD of hosts musters
The army for battle.
5 They come from a far country,
From the end of heaven—
The [a]LORD and His [1]weapons of
indignation,
To destroy the whole [b]land.

16 [b]Ex. 14:29

CHAPTER 12

1 [a]Is. 2:11 *See WW at 1 Chr. 16:7. **2** [a]Ps. 83:18 [b]Ex. 15:2; Ps. 118:14 *See WW at Jer. 16:19. **3** [a][John 4:10, 14; 7:37, 38] **4** [a]1 Chr. 16:8; Ps. 105:1 [b]Ps. 145:4–6 [c]Ps. 34:3 **5** [a]Ex. 15:1; Ps. 98:1; Is. 24:14; 42:10, 11; 44:23 *See WW at Ps. 149:3. **6** [a]Is. 52:9; 54:1; Zeph. 3:14, 15 [b]Ps. 89:18

CHAPTER 13

1 [a]Jer. 50; 51; Matt. 1:11; Rev. 14:8 [1]*oracle, prophecy* **2** [a]Is. 18:3 [b]Jer. 51:25 [c]Is. 10:32 *See WW at Ps. 18:46. **3** [a]Joel 3:11 [b]Ps. 149:2 [1]*consecrated* or *set apart* **4** [a]Is. 17:12; Joel 3:14 *See WW at Ps. 31:19. **5** [a]Is. 42:13 [b]Is. 24:1; 34:2 [1]Or *instruments*

12:1–6 A hymn of **praise** composed to celebrate the hope of the glorious reign of **the Holy One of Israel.** The mention of **that day** (see note on Obad. 15) and the complete cessation of God's **anger** (see 10:25) make this hymn messianic. It therefore goes beyond postexilic Israel and anticipates the fullness of messianic **salvation.**
12:2 Song connotes energy or vitality experienced through praise.
12:3 Wells of salvation: A reference to the enjoyment of God's bountiful blessings through the Anointed One of David's house.
12:4 Praise here means to "lift up your hands" in adoration to **the LORD.**
13:1—23:18 A series of judgments called "burdens" against the **nations** surrounding Israel. Yahweh is not the God of Israel alone, but the Creator and Lord of all nations. See notes on Zeph. 1:2–6 and 2:4–15. Their judgment is actually part of the bigger picture of the destruction of evil and consummation of God's reign as part of **the day of the LORD.** See note on Obad. 15.
13:1–22 Babylon was the capital of the ancient Babylonian Empire. Babylonian myth says it was built by the god Marduk. Its proud and accomplished history spanned from about 2300 B.C. to 325 B.C. when it fell into insignificance after the collapse of Alexander the Great's empire. The OT saw this decline as God's judgment for her destruction of Jerusalem. See Rev. 18:1—19:10 for Babylon's symbolism in the NT. See also notes on Jer. 50.
13:2, 3 The judgment oracles begin with the summons of unidentified troops (**sanctified ones, mighty ones**). These may be heavenly armies, indicating that the ensuing earthly judgment battles are reflections of spiritual warfare. See note on Rev. 12:1–17. The various oracles will therefore vacillate between judgment against specific nations and the whole Earth (v. 5). **Sanctified** here has no moral connotation, but means "chosen for a special purpose."
13:4, 5 The kingdoms of nations: God's spiritual armies (see note on vv. 2, 3) fight through literal nations on the earthly scene. **The LORD of hosts:** See note on 6:3. **The whole land** likely refers to the whole world.

6 Wail, [a]for the day of the LORD *is*
at hand!
[b]It will come as destruction from
the *Almighty.
7 Therefore all hands will be limp,
Every man's heart will melt,
8 And they will be afraid.
[a]Pangs[1] and sorrows will take hold
of *them;*
They will be in pain as a woman
in childbirth;
They will be amazed at one
another;
Their faces *will be like* flames.

9 Behold, [a]the day of the LORD
comes,
Cruel, with both wrath and fierce
anger,
To lay the land desolate;
And He will destroy [b]its sinners
from it.
10 For the stars of heaven and their
constellations
Will not give their light;
The sun will be [a]darkened in its
going forth,
And the moon will not cause its
light to shine.

11 "I will [a]punish the *world for *its*
evil,
And the wicked for their iniquity;
[b]I will halt the arrogance of the
proud,
And will lay low the haughtiness
of the [1]terrible.
12 I will make a *mortal more rare
than fine gold,
A man more than the golden
wedge of Ophir.
13 [a]Therefore I will shake the
heavens,
And the earth will move out of
her place,
In the wrath of the LORD of hosts
And in [b]the day of His fierce
anger.
14 It shall be as the hunted gazelle,
And as a sheep that no man
[1]takes up;
[a]Every man will turn to his own
people,
And everyone will flee to his
own land.
15 Everyone who is found will be
thrust through,

6 [a]Is. 2:12; Ezek. 30:3; Amos 5:18; Zeph. 1:7; Rev. 6:17 [b]Is. 10:25; Job 31:23; Joel 1:15 *See WW at Ps. 91:1.
8 [a]Ps. 48:6 [1]*Sharp pains*
9 [a]Mal. 4:1 [b]Ps. 104:35; Prov. 2:22
10 [a]Is. 24:21–23; Ezek. 32:7; Joel 2:31; Matt. 24:29; Mark 13:24; Luke 21:25
11 [a]Is. 26:21 [b][Is. 2:17] [1]Or *tyrants* *See WW at Jer. 51:15.
12 *See WW at Job 4:17.
13 [a]Is. 34:4; 51:6; Hag. 2:6 [b]Ps. 110:5; Lam. 1:12
14 [a]Jer. 50:16; 51:9 [1]*gathers*
16 [a]Ps. 137:8, 9; Is. 13:18; 14:21; Hos. 10:14; Nah. 3:10 [b]Zech. 14:2
17 [a]Is. 21:2; Jer. 51:11, 28; Dan. 5:28, 31 [1]*esteem*
19 [a]Is. 14:4; Dan. 4:30; Rev. 18:11–16, 19, 21 [b]Gen. 19:24; Deut. 29:23; Jer. 50:40; Amos 4:11
20 [a]Jer. 50:3 *See WW at Esth. 9:28.
21 [a]Is. 34:11–15; Zeph. 2:14; Rev. 18:2 [1]Or *howling creatures*
22 [a]Jer. 51:33

CHAPTER 14

1 [a]Ps. 102:13; Is. 49:13, 15; 54:7, 8 [b]Is. 41:8, 9; Zech. 1:17; 2:12 [c]Is. 60:4, 5, 10
2 [a]Is. 49:22; 60:9; 66:20

And everyone who is captured
will fall by the sword.
16 Their children also will be
[a]dashed to pieces before their
eyes;
Their houses will be plundered
And their wives [b]ravished.

17 "Behold,[a] I will stir up the Medes
against them,
Who will not [1]regard silver;
And *as for* gold, they will not
delight in it.
18 Also *their* bows will dash the
young men to pieces,
And they will have no pity on the
fruit of the womb;
Their eye will not spare children.
19 [a]And Babylon, the glory of
kingdoms,
The beauty of the Chaldeans'
pride,
Will be as when God overthrew
[b]Sodom and Gomorrah.
20 [a]It will never be inhabited,
Nor will it be settled from
*generation to generation;
Nor will the Arabian pitch tents
there,
Nor will the shepherds make their
sheepfolds there.
21 [a]But wild beasts of the desert will
lie there,
And their houses will be full of
[1]owls;
Ostriches will dwell there,
And wild goats will caper there.
22 The hyenas will howl in their
citadels,
And jackals in their pleasant
palaces.
[a]Her time *is* near to come,
And her days will not be
prolonged."

Mercy on Jacob

14 For the LORD [a]will have mercy
on Jacob, and [b]will still choose
Israel, and settle them in their own
land. [c]The strangers will be joined with
them, and they will cling to the house
of Jacob.
2 Then people will take them [a]and
bring them to their place, and the
house of Israel will possess them for
servants and maids in the land of the

13:6–16 The judgment against Babylon (v. 19) is but part of God's larger judgment against evil. Such prophetic judgments find fulfillment in numerous activities in history, especially in the advancement of God's spiritual rule through the church. The references here will culminate with the consummation of Christ's kingdom. See note on Obad. 15.

13:17–22 God's historical destruction of **Babylon** will be at the hands of **the Medes**. See note on vv. 1–22.

14:1–3 Choose Israel: Israel would return from Babylon to their own land to continue being Yahweh's instrument. See notes on Zeph. 2:7, 9.

LORD; they will take them captive whose captives they were, [b]and rule over their oppressors.

Fall of the King of Babylon

3 It shall come to pass in the day the LORD gives you rest from your sorrow, and from your fear and the hard bondage in which you were made to serve,
4 that you [a]will take up this *proverb against the king of Babylon, and say:

"How the oppressor has ceased,
The [b]golden[1] city ceased!
5 The LORD has broken [a]the staff of the wicked,
The scepter of the rulers;
6 He who struck the people in wrath with a continual stroke,
He who ruled the nations in anger,
Is persecuted *and* no one hinders.
7 The whole earth is at rest *and* quiet;
They break forth into singing.
8 [a]Indeed the cypress trees rejoice over you,
And the cedars of Lebanon,
Saying, 'Since you [1]were cut down,
No woodsman has come up against us.'

9 "Hell[a1] from beneath is excited about you,
To meet *you* at your coming;
It stirs up the dead for you,
All the chief ones of the earth;
It has raised up from their thrones
All the kings of the nations.
10 They all shall [a]speak and say to you:
'Have you also become as weak as we?
Have you become like us?
11 Your pomp is brought down to Sheol,
And the sound of your stringed instruments;
The maggot is spread under you,
And worms cover you.'

2 [b]Is. 60:14
4 [a]Is. 13:19; Hab. 2:6 [b]Rev. 18:16 [1]Or *insolent* *See WW at Prov. 1:6.
5 [a]Ps. 125:3
8 [a]Is. 55:12; Ezek. 31:16 [1]*have lain down*
9 [a]Ezek. 32:21 [1]Or *Sheol*
10 [a]Ezek. 32:21
12 [a]Is. 34:4; Luke 10:18; [Rev. 12:7–9] [1]Lit. *Day Star*
13 [a]Ezek. 28:2; Matt. 11:23 [b]Dan. 8:10; 2 Thess. 2:4 [c]Ezek. 28:14 [d]Ps. 48:2
14 [a]Is. 47:8; 2 Thess. 2:4 *See WW at Gen. 14:18.
15 [a]Ezek. 28:8; Matt. 11:23; Luke 10:15 [1]Lit. *recesses*
17 [1]Would not release

The Fall of Lucifer

12 "How[a] you are fallen from heaven, 2
O [1]Lucifer, son of the morning!
How you are cut down to the ground,
You who weakened the nations!
13 For you have said in your heart:
[a]'I will ascend into heaven,
[b]I will exalt my throne above the stars of God;
I will also sit on the [c]mount of the congregation
[d]On the farthest sides of the north;
14 I will ascend above the heights of the clouds,
[a]I will be like the *Most High.'

KINGDOM DYNAMICS

14:12–14 Lucifer, ANGELS. Satan was once an angel called Lucifer, who, in love with his own beauty, fell into pride and self-centeredness. His rebellion manifests in five "I will" statements addressed against God (vv. 13, 14). With five utterances he declares he will take the place of the Most High God. But vv. 15–20 reveal that God has the last word, as the Most High makes five responses: "Satan, you will 1) be thrown into hell; 2) be gazed upon (that is, made a spectacle); 3) be talked about (mocked, scorned); 4) be cast out of your grave like a carcass; and 5) be alone." God's "last word" on Satan is still applicable to any challenge he attempts to bring against any of the people of God.

(Jude 9/Luke 16:22) M.H.

15 Yet you [a]shall be brought down to Sheol,
To the [1]lowest depths of the Pit.

16 "Those who see you will gaze at you,
And consider you, *saying:*
'*Is* this the man who made the earth tremble,
Who shook kingdoms,
17 Who made the world as a wilderness
And destroyed its cities,
Who [1]did not open the house of his prisoners?'

14:4–11 Proverb: After Israel's restoration this taunting song will be sung against Babylon. Again, these verses have multiple application. **The king of Babylon** symbolizes not only a specific, yet unidentified, Babylonian ruler (perhaps Sargon) but all evil and its rulers. God's people (Rev. 14:8; 17:5; 18:10, 21), through whom He reigns in victory, will taunt their enemies throughout history.
14:12–21 See section 2 of Truth-In-Action at the end of Is.
14:12–21 Lucifer, son of the morning: These verses also have a double application. They are still part of the proverb against the king of Babylon. The language, however, shows that he is a type of Satan. Lucifer means "Light Bearer." The basic sin was that of unchecked personal ambition, desiring to be equal to or above **God**. With reference to Satan, it is best not to press every detail but instead to grasp the symbolic intent. (See note on Ezek. 28:11–19.) In vv. 13–15 **I will** occurs five times. Satan's fall was occasioned by two things: pride that presumed to supplant God's rule with his own, and self-will that asserted independence from the Most High.

18 "All the kings of the nations,
All of them, sleep in glory,
Everyone in his own house;
19 But you are cast out of your grave
Like an [1]abominable branch,
Like the garment of those who are slain,
[2]Thrust through with a sword,
Who go down to the stones of the pit,
Like a corpse trodden underfoot.
20 You will not be joined with them in burial,
Because you have destroyed your land
And slain your people.
[a]The brood of evildoers shall never be named.
21 Prepare slaughter for his children
[a]Because of the iniquity of their fathers,
Lest they rise up and possess the land,
And fill the face of the world with cities."

Babylon Destroyed

22 "For I will rise up against them," says the LORD of hosts,
"And cut off from Babylon
[a]the name and [b]remnant,
[c]And offspring and posterity," says the LORD.
23 "I will also make it a possession for the [a]porcupine,
And marshes of muddy water;
I will sweep it with the broom of destruction," says the LORD of hosts.

Assyria Destroyed

24 The LORD of hosts has sworn, saying,
"Surely, as I have thought, so it shall come to pass,
And as I have purposed, *so* it shall [a]stand:
25 That I will break the [a]Assyrian in My land,
And on My mountains tread him underfoot.
Then [b]his yoke shall be removed from them,
And his burden removed from their shoulders.
26 This *is* the [a]purpose that is purposed against the whole earth,
And this *is* the hand that is stretched out over all the nations.
27 For the LORD of hosts has [a]purposed,
And who will annul *it?*
His hand *is* stretched out,
And who will turn it back?"

Philistia Destroyed

28 This is the [1]burden which came in
the year that [a]King Ahaz died.

29 "Do not rejoice, all you of Philistia,
[a]Because the rod that struck you is broken;
For out of the serpent's roots will come forth a viper,
[b]And its offspring *will be* a *fiery flying serpent.
30 The firstborn of the poor will feed,
And the *needy will lie down in *safety;
I will kill your roots with famine,
And it will slay your remnant.
31 Wail, O gate! Cry, O city!
All you of Philistia *are* dissolved;
For smoke will come from the north,
And no one *will be* alone in his [1]appointed times."

32 What will they answer the messengers of the nation?
That [a]the LORD has founded Zion,
And [b]the poor of His people shall take refuge in it.

Proclamation Against Moab

15

The [a]burden[1] against Moab.
Because in the night [b]Ar of
[c]Moab is laid waste

19 [1]*despised* [2]*Pierced*
20 [a]Job 18:19; Ps. 21:10; 109:13; Is. 1:4; 31:2
21 [a]Ex. 20:5; Lev. 26:39; Is. 13:16; Matt. 23:35
22 [a]Prov. 10:7; Is. 26:14; Jer. 51:62 [b]1 Kin. 14:10 [c]Job 18:19; Is. 47:9
23 [a]Is. 34:11; Zeph. 2:14
24 [a]Is. 43:13
25 [a]Mic. 5:5, 6; Zeph. 2:13 [b]Is. 10:27; Nah. 1:13
26 [a]Is. 23:9; Zeph. 3:6, 8
27 [a]2 Chr. 20:6; Job 9:12; 23:13; Ps. 33:11; Prov. 19:21; 21:30; Is. 43:13; Dan. 4:31, 35
28 [a]2 Kin. 16:20; 2 Chr. 28:27 [1]*oracle, prophecy*
29 [a]2 Chr. 26:6 [b]2 Kin. 18:8 *See WW at Is. 6:2.
30 *See WW at Ps. 70:5. • See WW at Deut. 33:12.
31 [1]Or *ranks*
32 [a]Ps. 87:1, 5 [b]Zech. 11:11

CHAPTER 15

1 [a]2 Kin. 3:4 [b]Deut. 2:9; Num. 21:28 [c]Is. 15:1—16:14; Jer. 25:21; 48:1–47; Amos 2:1–3; Zeph. 2:8–11 [1]*oracle, prophecy*

14:24–27 The record of the historical fulfillment of this prophecy is found in 37:21–38. See also notes on 10:5–11 and 10:7, 8.
14:28 King Ahaz died about 716 B.C.
14:29–32 Philistia: The Philistines apparently offered a coalition against Assyria. Isaiah had warned against any such foreign alliances. Therefore God used Assyria (**the north**) to judge Philistia.
14:29 The rod and **serpent's roots** refer to Shalmaneser V, the Assyrian king who received tribute from Israel and finally led the initial siege against Samaria in 722 B.C. **The viper . . . flying serpent** was Sargon II, Shalmaneser's successor who finished the siege.
15:1—16:14 Burden against Moab: Another judgment oracle. See note on 13:1—23:18. Moab was a son of Lot by an incestuous relationship with a daughter (Gen. 19:37). The Moabites had been a constant thorn in the side of Israel. Their destruction is due to pride (16:6–8) and false worship (16:9–12). There is no indication who destroyed Moab nor when this happened. Extrabiblical accounts attribute it to a 715 B.C. invasion by a nomadic tribe from the east.
15:1 Ar was a major district in **Moab. Kir** was its capital.

And destroyed,
Because in the night Kir of Moab
is laid waste
And destroyed,
2 He has gone up to the [1]temple and
Dibon,
To the *high places to weep.
Moab will wail over Nebo and
over Medeba;
[a]On all their heads *will be*
baldness,
And every beard cut off.
3 In their streets they will clothe
themselves with sackcloth;
On the tops of their houses
And in their streets
Everyone will wail, [a]weeping
bitterly.
4 Heshbon and Elealeh will cry out,
Their voice shall be heard as far
as [a]Jahaz;
Therefore the [1]armed soldiers of
Moab will cry out;
His life will be burdensome to
him.

5 "My[a] heart will cry out for
Moab;
His fugitives *shall flee* to Zoar,
Like [1]a three-year-old heifer.
For [b]by the Ascent of Luhith
They will go up with weeping;
For in the way of Horonaim
They will raise up a cry of
destruction,
6 For the waters [a]of Nimrim will be
desolate,
For the green grass has withered
away;
The grass fails, there is nothing
green.
7 Therefore the abundance they
have gained,
And what they have laid up,
They will carry away to the Brook
of the Willows.
8 For the cry has gone all around
the borders of Moab,
Its wailing to Eglaim
And its wailing to Beer Elim.
9 For the waters of [1]Dimon will be
full of blood;
Because I will bring more upon
[1]Dimon,

2 [a]Lev. 21:5; Jer. 48:37 [1]Heb. *bayith (house)* *See WW at Ezek. 6:3.
3 [a]Jer. 48:38
4 [a]Num. 21:28; 32:3; Jer. 48:34 [1]So with MT, Tg., Vg.; LXX, Syr. *loins*
5 [a]Is. 16:11; Jer. 48:31 [b]Jer. 48:5 [1]Or *The Third Eglath,* an unknown city, Jer. 48:34
6 [a]Num. 32:36
9 [a]2 Kin. 17:25; Jer. 50:17 [1]So with MT, Tg.; DSS, Vg. *Dibon;* LXX *Rimon*

CHAPTER 16

1 [a]2 Kin. 3:4; Ezra 7:17 [b]2 Kin. 14:7; Is. 42:11 [1]Lit. *Rock*
2 [a]Prov. 27:8 [b]Num. 21:13
4 [1]*devastator* *See WW at Jer. 42:17.
5 [a][Is. 9:6, 7; 32:1; 55:4; Dan. 7:14; Mic. 4:7; Luke 1:33; Rev. 11:15] [b]Ps. 72:2 [c]Is. 9:7 *See WW at Mic. 6:8.
6 [a]Jer. 48:29; Amos 2:1; Obad. 3, 4; Zeph. 2:8, 10 [b]Is. 28:15 [1]Lit. *vain talk*
7 [a]Jer. 48:20 [b]2 Kin. 3:25; Jer. 48:31
8 [a]Is. 24:7 [b]Is. 16:9 *See WW at Hos. 2:8.

[a]Lions upon him who escapes
from Moab,
And on the remnant of the land."

Moab Destroyed

16 Send [a]the lamb to the ruler of
the land,
[b]From [1]Sela to the wilderness,
To the mount of the daughter of
Zion.
2 For it shall be as a [a]wandering
bird thrown out of the nest;
So shall be the daughters of Moab
at the fords of the [b]Arnon.

3 "Take counsel, execute judgment;
Make your shadow like the night
in the middle of the day;
Hide the outcasts,
Do not betray him who escapes.
4 Let My outcasts *dwell with you,
O Moab;
Be a shelter to them from the face
of the [1]spoiler.
For the extortioner is at an end,
Devastation ceases,
The oppressors are consumed out
of the land.
5 In *mercy [a]the throne will be
established;
And One will sit on it in truth, in
the tabernacle of David,
[b]Judging and seeking justice and
hastening [c]righteousness."

6 We have heard of the [a]pride of
Moab—
He is very proud—
Of his haughtiness and his pride
and his wrath;
[b]*But* his [1]lies *shall* not *be* so.
7 Therefore Moab shall [a]wail for
Moab;
Everyone shall wail.
For the foundations [b]of Kir
Hareseth you shall mourn;
Surely *they are* stricken.
8 For [a]the fields of Heshbon
languish,
And [b]the vine of Sibmah;
The *lords of the nations have
broken down its choice plants,

15:2 The oracle presents a remarkable list of Moabite cities east of the Dead Sea, inhabited during Moab's 1,000-year history. **Baldness . . . beard cut off:** See note on 7:20.
15:5 God's mercy, in tension with His righteous judgment, causes His **heart** to **cry out** amid the judgment of sinful **Moab.**
16:1–5 **The land** is Judah. The Edomites entreat Judah's help in accepting her refugees (**outcasts**). The entreaty is made with a **lamb,** symbolic of the thousands King Mesha of Moab once sent in tribute (2 Kin. 3:4). Judah is sympathetic, and Moab again becomes her vassal (2 Sam. 8:2), under **One . . . of David** (v. 5).
16:1 **Sela** was likely Petra in modern Jordan.
16:5 **Tabernacle of David:** The household of David. It is a possible reference to the rule of Hezekiah, but more likely it is a prophecy of the messianic rulership of the throne of David. See Amos 9:11, 12; Acts 15:16, 17.

Which have reached to Jazer
And wandered through the
wilderness.
Her branches are stretched
out,
They are gone over the [c]sea.
9 Therefore I will bewail the vine
of Sibmah,
With the weeping of Jazer;
I will drench you with my tears,
[a]O Heshbon and Elealeh;
For [1]battle cries have fallen
Over your summer fruits and
your harvest.

10 [a]Gladness is taken away,
And joy from the plentiful field;
In the vineyards there will be no
singing,
Nor will there be shouting;
No *treaders will tread out wine
in the presses;
I have made their shouting
cease.
11 Therefore [a]my [1]heart shall
resound like a harp for Moab,
And my inner being for [2]Kir
Heres.

12 And it shall come to pass,
When it is seen that Moab is
weary on [a]the high place,
That he will come to his
sanctuary to *pray;
But he will not prevail.

13 This *is* the word which the LORD has
spoken concerning Moab since that
time.
14 But now the LORD has spoken, saying, "Within three years, [a]as the years
of a hired man, the glory of Moab will
be despised with all that great multitude, and the remnant *will be* very
small *and* feeble."

Proclamation Against Syria and Israel

17

The [a]burden[1] against Damascus.

"Behold, Damascus will cease
from *being* a city,
And it will be a ruinous heap.
2 [1]The cities of [a]Aroer *are* forsaken;
They will be for flocks
Which lie down, and [b]no one will
make *them* afraid.
3 [a]The fortress also will cease from
Ephraim,
The kingdom from Damascus,
And the remnant of Syria;
They will be as the glory of the
children of Israel,"
Says the LORD of hosts.

4 "In that day it shall come to pass
That the glory of Jacob will
[1]wane,
And [a]the fatness of his flesh grow
lean.
5 [a]It shall be as when the harvester
gathers the grain,
And reaps the heads with his
arm;
It shall be as he who gathers
heads of grain
In the Valley of Rephaim.
6 [a]Yet gleaning grapes will be left
in it,
Like the shaking of an olive
tree,
Two *or* three olives at the top of
the uppermost bough,
Four *or* five in its most fruitful
branches,"
Says the LORD God of Israel.

7 In that day a man will [a]look to
his Maker,
And his eyes will have respect for
the Holy One of Israel.
8 He will not look to the altars,
The work of his hands;
He will not respect what his
[a]fingers have made,
Nor the [1]wooden images nor the
incense altars.

9 In that day his strong cities will
be as a forsaken [1]bough
And [2]an uppermost branch,
Which they left because of the
children of Israel;
And there will be desolation.

8 [c]Jer. 48:32
9 [a]Is. 15:4 [1]Or *shouting has*
10 [a]Is. 24:8; Jer. 48:33 *See WW at Deut. 11:25.
11 [a]Is. 15:5; 63:15; Jer. 48:36; Hos. 11:8; Phil. 2:1 [1]Lit. *belly* [2]*Kir Hareseth,* v. 7
12 [a]Is. 15:2 *See WW at Job 42:10.
14 [a]Job 7:1; 14:6; Is. 21:16

CHAPTER 17

1 [a]Gen. 14:15; 15:2; 2 Kin. 16:9; Jer. 49:23; Amos 1:3–5; Zech. 9:1; Acts 9:2 [1]*oracle, prophecy*
2 [a]Num. 32:34 [b]Jer. 7:33 [1]So with MT, Vg.; LXX *It shall be forsaken forever;* Tg. *Its cities shall be forsaken and desolate*
3 [a]Is. 7:16; 8:4
4 [a]Is. 10:16 [1]*fade*
5 [a]Is. 17:11; Jer. 51:33; Joel 3:13; Matt. 13:30
6 [a]Deut. 4:27; Is. 24:13; Obad. 5
7 [a]Is. 10:20; Hos. 3:5; Mic. 7:7
8 [a]Is. 2:8; 31:7 [1]Heb. *Asherim,* Canaanite deities
9 [1]LXX *Hivites;* Tg. *laid waste;* Vg. *as the plows* [2]LXX *Amorites;* Tg. *in ruins;* Vg. *corn*

16:14 Isaiah's prophecy was given shortly before its fulfillment. Though God judged them (v. 13), His mercy saved a Moabite **remnant.**

17:1–8 Damascus was (and is) the capital of **Syria.** Syria, together with **Ephraim (Israel)**, would be destroyed utterly because of their attack upon Judah and Jerusalem. Syria was invaded by Assyria in 732 B.C., at which time the northern section of Israel was taken. In 721 B.C. Israel was completely defeated and carried away captive, except for a small remnant of the faithful who would turn wholeheartedly to God and away from all idolatry (vv. 7, 8). See note on 8:1–4.

17:1 Burden: See note on 13:1—23:18.

17:3 The glory . . . Israel is irony. They will be judged with **the remnant of Syria.**

17:9–14 Most scholars see this section as referring to Judah. **His strong cities** were likely those abandoned during the coalition's invasion in 734 B.C. See note on 7:1. This did not, however, press Judah to Yahweh; she therefore will suffer judgment, too. See note on 7:17.

10 Because you have forgotten
[a]the God of your salvation,
And have not been mindful of the
Rock of your [1]stronghold,
Therefore you will plant pleasant
plants
And set out foreign seedlings;
11 In the day you will make your
plant to grow,
And in the morning you will make
your seed to flourish;
But the harvest *will be* a heap of
ruins
In the day of grief and desperate
sorrow.

12 Woe to the multitude of many
people
Who make a noise [a]like the roar
of the seas,
And to the rushing of nations
That make a rushing like the
rushing of mighty waters!
13 The nations will rush like the
rushing of many waters;
But *God* will [a]rebuke them and
they will flee far away,
And [b]be chased like the chaff
of the mountains before the
wind,
Like a rolling thing before the
whirlwind.
14 Then behold, at eventide, trouble!
And before the morning, he *is* no
more.
This *is* the portion of those who
plunder us,
And the lot of those who rob
us.

Proclamation Against Ethiopia

18 Woe [a]to the land shadowed
with buzzing wings,
Which *is* beyond the rivers of
[1]Ethiopia,
2 Which sends ambassadors by
sea,
Even in vessels of reed on the
waters, *saying,*
"Go, swift messengers, to a nation
tall and smooth *of skin,*
To a people terrible from their
beginning onward,
A nation powerful and treading
down,
Whose land the rivers divide."

3 All inhabitants of the world and
dwellers on the earth:
[a]When he lifts up a banner on the
mountains, you see *it;*
And when he blows a trumpet,
you hear *it.*
4 For so the LORD said to me,
"I will take My rest,
And I will [1]look from My dwelling
place
Like clear heat in sunshine,
Like a cloud of dew in the heat
of harvest."
5 For before the harvest, when the
bud is perfect
And the sour grape is ripening in
the flower,
He will both cut off the sprigs
with pruning hooks
And take away *and* cut down the
branches.
6 They will be left together for the
mountain birds of prey
And for the beasts of the earth;
The birds of prey will summer on
them,
And all the beasts of the earth will
winter on them.

7 In that time [a]a present will be
brought to the LORD of hosts
[1]From a people tall and smooth *of
skin,*
And from a people terrible from
their beginning onward,
A nation powerful and treading
down,
Whose land the rivers divide—
To the place of the name of the
LORD of hosts,
To Mount Zion.

10 [a]Ps. 68:19; Is. 51:13 [1]*refuge*
12 [a]Is. 5:30; Jer. 6:23; Ezek. 43:2; Luke 21:25
13 [a]Ps. 9:5; Is. 41:11 [b]Ps. 83:13; Hos. 13:3

CHAPTER 18

1 [a]2 Kin. 19:9; Is. 20:4, 5; Ezek. 30:4, 5, 9; Zeph. 2:12; 3:10 [1]Heb. *Cush*
3 [a]Is. 5:26
4 [1]*watch*
7 [a]Ps. 68:31; 72:10; Is. 16:1; Zeph. 3:10; Mal. 1:11; Acts 8:27–38 [1]So with DSS, LXX, Vg.; MT omits *From;* Tg. *To*

17:10 Rock of your stronghold: The fatal defect of man is forgetting the God of his salvation, who is the only sure foundation for life (see 26:4; Deut. 32:4, 15, 18).

17:13, 14 The nations (Assyria) will be limited in their judgment of Judah; and they, too, will be judged. See note on 10:5–11.

18:1–7 Ethiopia is another name for Cush, located just south of Egypt. Ham was said to be its father (Gen. 10:6). Ethiopia was a strong country able to dominate Egypt for 60 years, beginning in 715 B.C. Ethiopia offered an alliance with Hezekiah against Assyria, but the Lord had warned against any alliance with either Ethiopia or Egypt. They were defeated by Assyria.

18:1 Buzzing wings refers either to the tsetse fly of the upper Nile Valley or to sailboats.

18:2 The oracle is occasioned by the arrival of Ethiopia's **ambassadors** in about 715 B.C., offering an alliance. They are simultaneously met by Judean **messengers** going to Ethiopia. See note on vv. 1–7.

18:4–6 God warns Hezekiah that He has no intention of intervening in the attack against Assyria, so Hezekiah should not align with Ethiopia. As a matter of fact, Ethiopia is heading for disaster.

18:7 From should probably be omitted (see marginal reading). The Assyrians will offer the Ethiopians as **a present . . . to the LORD.**

Proclamation Against Egypt

19 The [a]burden[1] against Egypt.

Behold, the LORD [b]rides on a swift cloud,
And will come into Egypt;
[c]The idols of Egypt will [2]totter at His presence,
And the heart of Egypt will melt in its midst.

2 "I will [a]set Egyptians against Egyptians;
Everyone will fight against his brother,
And everyone against his neighbor,
City against city, kingdom against kingdom.
3 The spirit of Egypt will fail in its midst;
I will destroy their counsel,
And they will [a]consult the idols and the charmers,
The mediums and the sorcerers.
4 And the Egyptians I will give
[a]Into the hand of a cruel master,
And a fierce king will rule over them,"
Says the Lord, the LORD of hosts.

5 [a]The waters will fail from the sea,
And the river will be wasted and dried up.
6 The rivers will turn foul;
The brooks [a]of defense will be emptied and dried up;
The reeds and rushes will wither.
7 The papyrus reeds by [1]the River, by the mouth of the River,
And everything sown by the River,
Will wither, be driven away, and be no more.
8 The fishermen also will mourn;
All those will lament who cast hooks into the River,
And they will languish who spread nets on the waters.
9 Moreover those who work in [a]fine flax
And those who weave fine fabric will be ashamed;
10 And its foundations will be broken.
All who make wages *will be* troubled of soul.

11 Surely the princes of [a]Zoan *are* fools;
Pharaoh's wise counselors give foolish counsel.
[b]How do you say to Pharaoh, "I *am* the son of the wise,
The son of ancient kings?"
12 [a]Where *are* they?
Where are your wise men?
Let them tell you now,
And let them know what the LORD of hosts has [b]purposed against Egypt.
13 The princes of Zoan have become fools;
[a]The princes of [1]Noph are deceived;
They have also [2]deluded Egypt,
Those who are the [3]mainstay of its tribes.
14 The LORD has mingled [a]a perverse spirit in her midst;
And they have caused Egypt to err in all her work,
As a drunken man staggers in his vomit.
15 Neither will there be *any* work for Egypt,
Which [a]the head or tail,
Palm branch or bulrush, may do.

16 In that day Egypt will [a]be like
women, and will be afraid and *fear
because of the waving of the hand of
the LORD of hosts, [b]which He waves
over it.
17 And the land of Judah will be a terror to Egypt; everyone who makes
mention of it will be afraid in himself,
because of the counsel of the LORD of
hosts which He has [a]determined
against it.

CHAPTER 19

1 [a]Jer. 9:25, 26; Ezek. 29:1—30:19; Joel 3:19 [b]Ps. 18:10; 104:3; Matt. 26:64; Rev. 1:7 [c]Ex. 12:12; Jer. 43:12 [1]*oracle, prophecy* [2]Lit. *shake*
2 [a]Judg. 7:22; 1 Sam. 14:16, 20; 2 Chr. 20:23; Matt. 10:21, 36
3 [a]1 Chr. 10:13; Is. 8:19; 47:12; Dan. 2:2
4 [a]Is. 20:4; Jer. 46:26; Ezek. 29:19
5 [a]Is. 50:2; Jer. 51:36; Ezek. 30:12
6 [a]2 Kin. 19:24
7 [1]The Nile
9 [a]1 Kin. 10:28; Prov. 7:16; Ezek. 27:7
11 [a]Num. 13:22; Ps. 78:12, 43; Is. 30:4 [b]Gen. 41:38, 39; 1 Kin. 4:29, 30; Acts 7:22
12 [a]1 Cor. 1:20 [b]Ps. 33:11
13 [a]Jer. 2:16; Ezek. 30:13 [1]Ancient Memphis [2]Lit. *caused to stagger* [3]*cornerstone*
14 [a]1 Kin. 22:22; Is. 29:10
15 [a]Is. 9:14–16
16 [a]Jer. 51:30; Nah. 3:13 [b]Is. 11:15 *See WW at Hos. 3:5.
17 [a]Is. 14:24; Dan. 4:35

19:1–17 Burden against Egypt: Among the nations surrounding Israel that God will judge is Egypt, the old enemy of God's people. See note on 13:1—23:18. Often the Lord warned Israel against trusting in the arm of Egypt. The reference here is to the Ethiopian takeover in 711 B.C., arranged by God to judge Egypt. It lasted 60 years.
19:2 Egyptians against Egyptians: God orchestrated inner strife and civil war, giving the Ethiopians easier access to the throne.
19:4 Cruel master likely refers to the Ethiopian Shabaka.
19:5–10 Waters will fail: Since Egypt depends upon **the** [Nile] **River** for sustenance, God will allow its failure in order to bring great disaster to all forms of livelihood. God controls nature, so all people are dependent upon Him.
19:11–15 Wise men: In their distress, nations are prone to look to political advisors for direction instead of to God; yet such men are wise **counselors** only if they trust God. **Zoan** was an Egyptian delta city near Israel. **Noph** often served as Egypt's northern capital. Both were political centers.
19:16–22 These verses describe a time when **Egypt** will turn to Yahweh and experience salvation. The section begins with the phrase **in that day,** which often refers to the times of the Messiah. See note on Obad. 15. This section then refers to a future reality.

Egypt, Assyria, and Israel Blessed

18 In that day five cities in the land of Egypt will [a]speak the language of Canaan and [b]swear by the LORD of hosts; one will be called the City of [1]Destruction.

19 In that day [a]there will be an altar to the LORD in the midst of the land of Egypt, and a pillar to the [b]LORD at its border.

20 And [a]it will be for a sign and for a witness to the LORD of hosts in the land of Egypt; for they will cry to the LORD because of the oppressors, and He will send them a [b]Savior and a Mighty One, and He will deliver them.

21 Then the LORD will be known to Egypt, and the Egyptians will [a]know the LORD in that day, and [b]will make sacrifice and offering; yes, they will make a vow to the LORD and perform *it*.

22 And the LORD will strike Egypt, He will strike and [a]heal *it;* they will return to the LORD, and He will be entreated by them and heal them.

23 In that day [a]there will be a highway from Egypt to Assyria, and the Assyrian will come into Egypt and the Egyptian into Assyria, and the Egyptians will [b]serve with the Assyrians.

24 In that day Israel will be one of three with Egypt and Assyria—a blessing in the midst of the land,

25 whom the LORD of hosts shall bless, saying, *"Blessed *is* Egypt My people, and Assyria [a]the work of My hands, and Israel My inheritance."

The Sign Against Egypt and Ethiopia

20 In the year that [a]Tartan[1] came to Ashdod, when Sargon the king of Assyria sent him, and he fought against Ashdod and took it,

2 at the same time the LORD spoke by Isaiah the son of Amoz, saying, "Go, and remove [a]the sackcloth from your [1]body, and take your sandals off your feet." And he did so, [b]walking naked and barefoot.

3 Then the LORD said, "Just as My servant Isaiah has walked naked and barefoot three years [a]*for* a sign and a *wonder against Egypt and Ethiopia,

4 "so shall the [a]king of Assyria lead away the Egyptians as prisoners and the Ethiopians as captives, young and old, naked and barefoot, [b]with their buttocks uncovered, to the shame of Egypt.

5 [a]"Then they shall be afraid and ashamed of Ethiopia their expectation and Egypt their glory.

6 "And the inhabitant of this territory will say in that day, 'Surely such *is* our expectation, wherever we flee for [a]help to be delivered from the king of Assyria; and how shall we escape?' "

The Fall of Babylon Proclaimed

21 The [1]burden against the Wilderness of the Sea.

As [a]whirlwinds in the South pass through,
So it comes from the desert, from a terrible land.

2 A distressing vision is declared to me;
[a]The treacherous dealer deals treacherously,
And the plunderer plunders.
[b]Go up, O Elam!
Besiege, O Media!
All its sighing I have made to cease.

3 Therefore [a]my loins are *filled with pain;
[b]Pangs have taken hold of me, like the pangs of a woman in labor.
I was [1]distressed when *I* heard *it;*
I was dismayed when *I* saw *it*.

4 My heart wavered, fearfulness frightened me;
[a]The night for which I longed He turned into fear for me.

18 [a]Zeph. 3:9 [b]Is. 45:23 [1]Some Heb. mss., Arab., DSS, Tg., Vg. *Sun;* LXX *Asedek,* lit. *Righteousness*
19 [a]Ex. 24:4 [b]Ps. 68:31
20 [a]Josh. 4:20; 22:27 [b]Is. 43:11
21 [a][Is. 2:3, 4; 11:9] [b]Mal. 1:11
22 [a]Deut. 32:39
23 [a]Is. 11:16; 35:8; 49:11; 62:10 [b]Is. 27:13
25 [a]Is. 29:23 *See WW at Ps. 145:2.

CHAPTER 20

1 [a]2 Kin. 18:17 [1]Or *the Commander in Chief*
2 [a]Zech. 13:4 [b]1 Sam. 19:24 [1]Lit. *loins*
3 [a]Is. 8:18 *See WW at Zech. 3:8.
4 [a]Is. 19:4 [b]Jer. 13:22
5 [a]2 Kin. 18:21
6 [a]Is. 30:5, 7

CHAPTER 21

1 [a]Zech. 9:14 [1]*oracle, prophecy*
2 [a]Is. 33:1 [b]Jer. 49:34
3 [a]Is. 15:5; 16:11 [b]Is. 13:8 [1]Lit. *bowed* *See WW at Jer. 23:24.
4 [a]Deut. 28:67

19:23–25 These verses also refer to future blessings in God's consummated kingdom. **Egypt** and **Assyria,** typical of all Gentile peoples, and **Israel** will all experience one salvation through the Messiah.

20:1–6 This chapter describes another experience of Isaiah (see note on 8:1–4) in order to reinforce symbolically the message to **Egypt and Ethiopia** of impending invasion by **Assyria,** and to Israel that she was not to place confidence in an alliance with Egypt.

20:1 The year is apparently 711 B.C.

20:2, 3 Sackcloth was a mourner's outer garment. **Naked** means without his outer garment, wearing only a simple tunic. **Three years:** 714–711 B.C.

20:4 Their buttocks uncovered referred to prisoners' being led captive, wearing only simple tunics.

21:1–10 Babylon (**Wilderness of the Sea**) suffered a series of setbacks between 710 and 703 B.C. See note on 13:1–22. Here news arrives in Jerusalem of Babylon's 703 B.C. defeat by Sennacherib of Assyria. This terrorizes Jerusalem, who fears she is next (see chs. 36; 37; 2 Kin. 18; 19; 2 Chr. 32:1–23).

21:1 The South is the Negev.

21:2 Elam . . . Media are references to the Medes and Persians, who somehow participated with Assyria.

21:3–10 Isaiah's emotional response identified with Jerusalem's at the thought of what **Babylon**'s fall might mean. See note on vv. 1–10.

5 [a]Prepare the table,
Set a watchman in the tower,
Eat and drink.
Arise, you princes,
Anoint the shield!

6 For thus has the Lord said to me:
"Go, set a *watchman,
Let him declare what he sees."
7 And he saw a chariot *with* a pair
of horsemen,
A chariot of donkeys, *and* a
chariot of camels,
And he listened earnestly with
great care.
8 [1]Then he cried, "A lion, my Lord!
I stand *continually on the
[a]watchtower in the daytime;
I have sat at my post every night.
9 And look, here comes a chariot
of men *with* a pair of
horsemen!"
Then he answered and said,
[a]"Babylon is fallen, is fallen!
And [b]all the carved images of her
gods
He has broken to the ground."

10 [a]Oh, my threshing and the grain
of my floor!
That which I have heard from the
LORD of hosts,
The God of Israel,
I have declared to you.

Proclamation Against Edom

11 [a]The [1]burden against Dumah.

He calls to me out of [b]Seir,
"Watchman, what of the night?
Watchman, what of the night?"
12 The watchman said,
"The morning comes, and also the
night.
If you will inquire, inquire;
Return! Come back!"

Proclamation Against Arabia

13 [a]The [1]burden against Arabia.

In the forest in Arabia you will
lodge,

5 [a]Jer. 51:39; Dan. 5:5
6 *See WW at Hos. 9:8.
8 [a]Hab. 2:1 [1]DSS *Then the observer cried, "My Lord!* *See WW at Ex. 28:30.
9 [a]Is. 13:19; 47:5, 9; 48:14; Jer. 51:8; Dan. 5:28, 31; Rev. 14:8; 18:2 [b]Is. 46:1; Jer. 50:2; 51:44
10 [a]Jer. 51:33; Mic. 4:13
11 [a]Gen. 25:14; 1 Chr. 1:30; Josh. 15:52 [b]Gen. 32:3; Jer. 49:7; Ezek. 35:2; Obad. 1 [1]*oracle, prophecy*
13 [a]Jer. 25:24; 49:28 [b]Gen. 10:7; 1 Chr. 1:9, 32; Jer. 25:23; Ezek. 27:15 [1]*oracle, prophecy*
16 [a]Is. 16:14 [b]Ps. 120:5; Song 1:5; Is. 42:11; 60:7; Ezek. 27:21

CHAPTER 22

1 [1]*oracle, prophecy*
2 [a]Is. 32:13 [1]*boisterous*
4 [a]Jer. 4:19
5 [a]Is. 37:3 [b]Lam. 1:5; 2:2
6 [a]Jer. 49:35

O you traveling companies
[b]of Dedanites.
14 O inhabitants of the land of Tema,
Bring water to him who is thirsty;
With their bread they met him
who fled.
15 For they fled from the swords,
from the drawn sword,
From the bent bow, and from the
distress of war.

16 For thus the LORD has said to me:
"Within a year, [a]according to the year
of a hired man, all the glory of [b]Kedar
will fail;
17 "and the remainder of the number
of archers, the mighty men of the people of Kedar, will be diminished; for
the LORD God of Israel has spoken *it*."

Proclamation Against Jerusalem

22 The [1]burden against the Valley
of Vision.

What ails you now, that you have
all gone up to the housetops,
2 You who are full of noise,
A [1]tumultuous city, [a]a joyous
city?
Your slain *men are* not slain with
the sword,
Nor dead in battle.
3 All your rulers have fled together;
They are captured by the archers.
All who are found in you are
bound together;
They have fled from afar.
4 Therefore I said, "Look away
from me,
[a]I will weep bitterly;
Do not labor to comfort me
Because of the plundering of the
daughter of my people."

5 [a]For *it is* a day of trouble and
treading down and perplexity
[b]By the Lord GOD of hosts
In the Valley of Vision—
Breaking down the walls
And of crying to the mountain.
6 [a]Elam bore the quiver
With chariots of men *and*
horsemen,

21:11, 12 Burden against Dumah is a reference to Edom, the land of Esau (Gen. 32:3). See note on Obad. 10, 11.
21:13–16 Dedanites . . . Kedar were tribes of **Arabia. Tema** was an important oasis city in Arabia. Arabia would be invaded by the Assyrians; for years various Arabians had battled Israel.
22:1–14 This judgment **against the Valley of Vision** (Jerusalem) deals with Sennacherib's 701 B.C. invasion. See notes on 7:17 and 21:1–10.
22:2–4 Isaiah is overwhelmed (v. 4) at the bravado of Jerusalem (v. 2). As yet none have died, but the military policies will fail (vv. 2, 3).
22:5–7 While Hezekiah was himself a godly king, most of the people were still unchanged from the days of Ahaz. God would permit an invasion by Assyria that would not succeed totally, but would bring great damage to Judah and Jerusalem. See note on 7:17. **Elam . . . Kir:** Sennacherib had mustered an international army.

And [b]Kir uncovered the shield.
7 It shall come to pass *that* your
choicest valleys
Shall be full of chariots,
And the horsemen shall set
themselves in array at the gate.

8 [a]He removed the [1]protection of
Judah.
You looked in that day to the
armor [b]of the House of the
Forest;
9 [a]You also saw the [1]damage to the
city of David,
That it was great;
And you gathered together the
waters of the lower pool.
10 You numbered the houses of
Jerusalem,
And the houses you broke down
To fortify the wall.
11 [a]You also made a reservoir
between the two walls
For the water of the old [b]pool.
But you did not look to its Maker,
Nor did you have respect for Him
who fashioned it long ago.

12 And in that day the Lord GOD of
hosts
[a]Called for weeping and for
mourning,
[b]For baldness and for girding with
sackcloth.
13 But instead, joy and gladness,
Slaying oxen and killing sheep,
Eating meat and [a]drinking wine:
[b]"Let us eat and drink, for
tomorrow we die!"

14 [a]Then it was revealed in my
hearing by the LORD of hosts,
"Surely for this iniquity there
[b]will be no atonement for you,
Even to your death," says the
Lord GOD of hosts.

The Judgment on Shebna

15 Thus says the Lord GOD of hosts:

"Go, proceed to this steward,
To [a]Shebna, who *is* over the
house, *and say:*

6 [b]Is. 15:1
8 [a]2 Kin. 18:15, 16 [b]1 Kin. 7:2; 10:17 [1]Lit. *covering*
9 [a]2 Kin. 20:20; 2 Chr. 32:4; Neh. 3:16 [1]Lit. *breaches* in the city walls
11 [a]Neh. 3:16 [b]2 Kin. 20:20; 2 Chr. 32:3, 4
12 [a]Is. 32:11; Joel 1:13; 2:17 [b]Ezra 9:3; Is. 15:2; Mic. 1:16
13 [a]Is. 5:11, 22; 28:7, 8; Luke 17:26–29 [b]Is. 56:12; 1 Cor. 15:32
14 [a]Is. 5:9 [b]1 Sam. 3:14; Ezek. 24:13
15 [a]2 Kin. 18:37; Is. 36:3

16 'What have you here, and whom
have you here,
That you have hewn a sepulcher
here,
As he [a]who hews himself a
sepulcher on high,
Who carves a tomb for himself in
a rock?
17 Indeed, the LORD will throw you
away violently,
O mighty man,
[a]And will surely seize you.
18 He will surely turn violently and
toss you like a ball
Into a large country;
There you shall die, and there
[a]your glorious chariots
Shall be the shame of your
master's house.
19 So I will drive you out of your
office,
And from your position [1]he will
pull you down.

20 'Then it shall be in that day,
That I will call My servant
[a]Eliakim the son of Hilkiah;
21 I will clothe him with your robe
And strengthen him with your
belt;
I will commit your responsibility
into his hand.
He shall be a father to the
inhabitants of Jerusalem
And to the house of Judah.
22 The key of the house of David
I will lay on his [a]shoulder;
So he shall [b]open, and no one
shall shut;
And he shall shut, and no one
shall open.
23 I will fasten him *as* [a]a peg in a
secure place,
And he will become a glorious
throne to his father's house.

24 'They will hang on him all the glory
of his father's house, the offspring and
the posterity, all vessels of small quantity, from the cups to all the pitchers.
25 'In that day,' says the LORD of hosts,
'the peg that is fastened in the secure
place will be removed and be cut down

16 [a]2 Sam. 18:18; 2 Chr. 16:14; Matt. 27:60
17 [a]Esth. 7:8
18 [a]Is. 2:7
19 [1]LXX omits *he will pull you down;* Syr., Tg., Vg. *I will pull you down*
20 [a]2 Kin. 18:18; Is. 36:3, 22; 37:2
22 [a]Is. 9:6 [b]Job 12:14; Rev. 3:7
23 [a]Ezra 9:8; Zech. 10:4

22:8–14 2 Chr. 32 records the construction of Hezekiah's tunnel (vv. 9, 11) as a wise move to foil Sennacherib's plan to poison Jerusalem's water. Chronicles also records Jerusalem's military efforts as responsible actions. Isaiah, however, gives insight into their **iniquity;** they lacked dependence on God in all they were doing (**you did not look to its Maker**). Hezekiah did later turn to God (2 Kin. 18:17—19:37).
22:8 The House of the Forest was a storehouse for arms.
22:11 The old pool is the pool of Siloam.

22:15–19 Shebna was the king's chamberlain and treasurer (**steward,** 36:3; 37:2) on whom judgment fell because of his lack of trust in God (vv. 13, 16).
22:20–25 Eliakim was successor to Shebna and served as **a father** [advisor] **. . . of Jerusalem**. Eliakim was a type of Christ (vv. 22, 23); what is said of him is said of Christ in Rev. 3:7. **Peg:** Successors to Eliakim would not be as faithful as he. As pegs they would not hold; therefore, they **will be removed**.

and fall, and the burden that *was* on it will be cut off; for the LORD has spoken.' "

Proclamation Against Tyre

23 The [a]burden[1] against Tyre.

Wail, you ships of Tarshish!
For it is laid waste,
So that there is no house, no
harbor;
From the land of [2]Cyprus it is
*revealed to them.

2 Be still, you inhabitants of the
coastland,
You merchants of Sidon,
[1]Whom those who cross the sea
have filled.
3 And on great waters the grain of
Shihor,
The harvest of [1]the River, *is* her
revenue;
And [a]she is a marketplace for the
nations.

4 Be *ashamed, O Sidon;
For the sea has spoken,
The strength of the sea, saying,
"I do not labor, nor bring forth
children;
Neither do I rear young men,
Nor bring up virgins."
5 [a]When the report *reaches* Egypt,
They also will be in agony at the
report of Tyre.

6 Cross over to Tarshish;
Wail, you inhabitants of the
coastland!
7 *Is* this your [a]joyous *city,*
Whose antiquity *is* from ancient
days,
Whose feet carried her far off to
dwell?

CHAPTER 23

1 [a]Jer. 25:22; 47:4; Ezek. 26—28; Amos 1:9; Zech. 9:2, 4 [1]*oracle, prophecy* [2]Heb. *Kittim,* western lands, especially Cyprus *See WW at Amos 3:7.
2 [1]So with MT, Vg.; LXX, Tg. *Passing over the water;* DSS *Your messengers passing over the sea*
3 [a]Ezek. 27:3–23 [1]The Nile
4 *See WW at Ezek. 16:63.
5 [a]Is. 19:16
7 [a]Is. 22:2; 32:13
8 [a]Ezek. 28:2, 12
9 [a]Is. 14:26 [b]Job 40:11, 12; Is. 13:11; 24:4; Dan. 4:37 [1]*pollute*
10 [1]The Nile [2]*restraint,* lit. *belt*
11 [a]Zech. 9:2–4
12 [a]Ezek. 26:13, 14; Rev. 18:22
13 [a]Is. 47:1 [b]Ps. 72:9
14 [a]Ezek. 27:25–30

8 Who has taken this counsel
against Tyre, [a]the crowning
city,
Whose merchants *are* princes,
Whose traders *are* the honorable
of the earth?
9 The LORD of hosts has [a]purposed
it,
To [1]bring to dishonor the
[b]pride of all glory,
To bring into contempt all the
honorable of the earth.

10 Overflow through your land like
[1]the River,
O daughter of Tarshish;
There is no more [2]strength.
11 He stretched out His hand over
the sea,
He shook the kingdoms;
The LORD has given a
commandment [a]against
Canaan
To destroy its strongholds.
12 And He said, "You will rejoice no
more,
O you oppressed virgin daughter
of Sidon.
Arise, [a]cross over to Cyprus;
There also you will have no rest."

13 Behold, the land of the
[a]Chaldeans,
This people *which* was not;
Assyria founded it for [b]wild
beasts of the desert.
They set up its towers,
They raised up its palaces,
And brought it to ruin.

14 [a]Wail, you ships of Tarshish!
For your strength is laid waste.

15 Now it shall come to pass in that
day that Tyre will be forgotten seventy
years, according to the days of one

23:1–18 Burden against Tyre: This is the last of the judgments against foreign nations. See note on 13:1—23:18. Tyre, a seaport, is another name for Phoenicia, the leading maritime power of Isaiah's day. Their empire extended as far as the coast of North Africa, perhaps even to Spain. Phoenicians invented the alphabet, evidence of an advanced civilization; however, their religion was abominable. They worshiped Baal and Ashtoreth, the deities that the Tyrian Jezebel brought into Israel, and which Elijah withstood and humiliated on Mt. Carmel.

Ezek. 28, also directed against Tyre, makes clear that the reason for the wrath of God lay primarily in their idolatrous pride (v. 9), as evidenced by their king. See notes on Ezek. 28:2 and 28:11–19. This particular section is likely prophesying its 667 B.C. loss of Mediterranean dominance by an invasion of Esarhaddon of Assyria.

23:1 Tarshish was a Phoenician city of unknown location, thought to be in Spain, Cyprus, or on the northern coast of Africa.

23:2 Sidon was the sister city to Tyre located on the coast about 20 miles north of Tyre. Tyre and Sidon were conquered by Babylon in 572 B.C. after a long siege. The fortified island city of Tyre withstood the attack, but was completely destroyed by Alexander in 332 B.C.

23:9 The LORD of hosts: See note on 6:3.

23:11 Against Canaan . . . its strongholds: A second reason for Tyre's judgment (see note on vv. 1–18) was to further destroy heathen influence in Canaan, much of which the Phoenicians propagated (see Judg. 3:3).

23:13 The Chaldeans (Babylonians) are given as an example of an unsuccessful defiance of Assyria. See note on 21:1–10.

23:15–18 Tyre will have a future following Esarhaddon's attack. She did in fact recover enough to withstand a siege

king. At the end of seventy years it will happen to Tyre as *in* the song of the harlot:

16 "Take a harp, go about the city,
You forgotten harlot;
Make sweet melody, sing many songs,
That you may be remembered."

17 And it shall be, at the end of seventy years, that the LORD will deal with Tyre. She will return to her hire, and [a]commit fornication with all the kingdoms of the world on the face of the earth.
18 Her gain and her pay [a]will be set apart for the LORD; it will not be treasured nor laid up, for her gain will be for those who dwell before the LORD, to eat sufficiently, and for [1]fine clothing.

Impending Judgment on the Earth

24 Behold, the LORD makes the earth empty and makes it waste,
Distorts its surface
And scatters abroad its inhabitants.
2 And it shall be:
As with the people, so with the [a]priest;
As with the servant, so with his *master;
As with the maid, so with her mistress;
[b]As with the buyer, so with the seller;
As with the lender, so with the borrower;
As with the creditor, so with the debtor.
3 The land shall be entirely emptied and utterly plundered,
For the LORD has spoken this word.
4 The earth mourns *and* fades away,
The world languishes *and* fades away;
The [a]haughty[1] people of the earth languish.
5 [a]The earth is also defiled under its inhabitants,
Because they have [b]transgressed the laws,
Changed the ordinance,
Broken the [c]everlasting covenant.
6 Therefore [a]the curse has devoured the earth,
And those who dwell in it are [1]desolate.
Therefore the inhabitants of the earth are [b]burned,
And few men *are* left.

7 [a]The new wine fails, the vine languishes,
All the merry-hearted sigh.
8 The mirth [a]of the tambourine ceases,
The noise of the jubilant ends,
The joy of the harp ceases.
9 They shall not drink wine with a song;
Strong drink is bitter to those who drink it.
10 The city of confusion is broken down;
Every house is shut up, so that none may go in.
11 *There is* a cry for wine in the streets,
All joy is darkened,
The mirth of the land is gone.
12 In the city desolation is left,
And the gate is stricken with destruction.

17 [a]Rev. 17:2
18 [a]Ex. 28:36; Zech. 14:20, 21 [1]*choice*

CHAPTER 24

2 [a]Hos. 4:9 [b]Ezek. 7:12, 13 *See WW at Mic. 4:13.
4 [a]Is. 25:11 [1]*proud*
5 [a]Gen. 3:17; Num. 35:33; Is. 9:17; 10:6 [b]Is. 59:12 [c]1 Chr. 16:14–19; Ps. 105:7–12
6 [a]Mal. 4:6 [b]Is. 9:19 [1]Or *held guilty*
7 [a]Is. 16:8–10; Joel 1:10, 12
8 [a]Is. 5:12, 14; Jer. 7:34; 16:9; 25:10; Ezek. 26:13; Hos. 2:11; Rev. 18:22

by Nebuchadnezzar for 13 years (585 to 572 B.C.). **Seventy years** is a round number referring to an extended period of time.

Her future will be one of a seductive influence on international trade, as well as a contribution to Israel's temple life (Tyre supplied cedar logs for the second temple, Ezra 3:7). Jesus visited Tyre's territory (Matt. 15:21), and Paul found disciples there at the end of his third missionary journey (Acts 21:3–5).

24:1—27:13 This section is difficult and scholars are divided on its meanings. It is generally referred to as "Isaiah's Apocalypse." Following the lengthy section on the judgments of the nations, this section concerns itself with how God will consummate His reign over evil. It is best, therefore, not to try to pinpoint specific historical events in the chapters. In addition to prophecies about what God will do, there are hymns of praise and thanksgiving. As apocalyptic literature, much of the language is figurative. See note on Mic. 4:1–5.

24:1–6 The apocalyptic section opens with a picture of universal judgment for man's sinfulness. The sin of mankind is clearly defined and summed up in the clause **broken the everlasting covenant.** There are many covenants made in the OT, but they all point forward to the covenant fulfilled by the atoning death of Christ on the Cross. The ultimate cause of this wrath of God, therefore, is rejection of the gracious offer of salvation made in the gospel of Christ Jesus.

It is not clear what form the devastation will take. The imagery suggests drought and possible earthquakes. Such judgments have happened throughout human history and will be climaxed during the time before Christ's return, often referred to as the Great Tribulation.

24:7–13 The devastation will include the cessation of festivities (vv. 7–9), followed by total judgment upon the world's confused society (vv. 10–13). Again, the language is symbolic.

13 When it shall be thus in the midst
of the land among the people,
[a]*It shall be* like the shaking of an
olive tree,
Like the gleaning of grapes when
the vintage is done.

14 They shall lift up their voice, they
shall sing;
For the majesty of the LORD
They shall cry aloud from the sea.
15 Therefore [a]glorify the LORD in the
dawning light,
[b]The name of the LORD God of
Israel in the coastlands of the
sea.
16 From the ends of the earth we
have heard songs:
"Glory to the righteous!"
But I said, [1]"I am ruined, ruined!
Woe to me!
[a]The treacherous dealers have
dealt treacherously,
Indeed, the treacherous dealers
have dealt very treacherously."

17 [a]Fear and the pit and the snare
Are upon you, O inhabitant of the
earth.
18 And it shall be
That he who flees from the noise
of the fear
Shall fall into the pit,
And he who comes up from the
midst of the pit
Shall be [1]caught in the snare;
For [a]the windows from on high
are open,
And [b]the foundations of the earth
are shaken.

19 [a]The earth is violently broken,
The earth is split open,
The earth is shaken exceedingly.
20 The earth shall [a]reel[1] to and fro
like a drunkard,
And shall totter like a hut;
Its transgression shall be heavy
upon it,
And it will fall, and not rise again.

21 It shall come to pass in that day
That the LORD will punish on high
the host of exalted ones,
And on the earth [a]the kings of the
earth.
22 They will be gathered together,
As prisoners are gathered in the
[1]pit,
And will be shut up in the prison;
After many days they will be
punished.
23 Then the [a]moon will be disgraced
And the sun ashamed;
For the LORD of hosts will
[b]reign
On [c]Mount Zion and in Jerusalem
And before His *elders,
gloriously.

Praise to God

25 O LORD, You *are* my God.
[a]I will exalt You,
I will praise Your name,
[b]For You have done wonderful
things;
[c]*Your* counsels of old *are*
*faithfulness *and* truth.
2 For You have made [a]a city a ruin,
A fortified city a ruin,
A palace of foreigners to be a city
no more;
It will never be rebuilt.
3 Therefore the strong people will
[a]glorify You;
The city of the [1]terrible nations
will fear You.
4 For You have been a strength to
the poor,
A strength to the needy in his
distress,
[a]A *refuge from the storm,
A shade from the heat;
For the blast of the terrible ones
is as a storm *against* the wall.
5 You will reduce the noise of
aliens,
As heat in a dry place;
As heat in the shadow of a cloud,
The song of the terrible ones will
be [1]diminished.

6 And in [a]this mountain
[b]The LORD of hosts will make for
[c]all people

13 [a][Is. 17:5, 6; 27:12] **15** [a]Is. 25:3 [b]Mal. 1:11 **16** [a]Is. 21:2; 33:1; Jer. 3:20; 5:11 [1]Lit. *Leanness to me, leanness to me* **17** [a]Jer. 48:43; Amos 5:19 **18** [a]Gen. 7:11 [b]Ps. 18:7; 46:2; Is. 2:19, 21; 13:13 [1]Lit. *taken* **19** [a]Jer. 4:23 **20** [a]Is. 19:14; 24:1; 28:7 [1]*stagger*

21 [a]Ps. 76:12 **22** [1]*dungeon* **23** [a]Is. 13:10; 60:19; Ezek. 32:7; Joel 2:31; 3:15 [b]Rev. 19:4, 6 [c][Heb. 12:22] *See WW at Ps. 119:100.

CHAPTER 25

1 [a]Ex. 15:2 [b]Ps. 98:1 [c]Num. 23:19 *See WW at Prov. 28:20. **2** [a]Is. 21:9; 23:13; Jer. 51:37 **3** [a]Is. 24:15; Rev. 11:13 [1]*terrifying* **4** [a]Is. 4:6 *See WW at Prov. 14:26. **5** [1]*humbled* **6** [a][Is. 2:2–4; 56:7] [b]Prov. 9:2; Matt. 22:4 [c][Dan. 7:14; Matt. 8:11]

24:14–20 Unidentified voices praise God for righteousness in the judgment (vv. 14–16), followed by a reiteration of the violent judgment (vv. 16–20). John refers to this same principle (Rev. 11:15–18).
24:21–23 That day: See note on Obad. 15. **The LORD of hosts will reign:** See note on Rev. 19:6–10.
25:1–12 A chapter of **praise,** which will be sung by God's righteous throughout history, regardless of judgment. "I" is not Isaiah, but all God's redeemed, especially those of the final apocalyptic scene.
25:2 City is symbolic language for urban life. It should not be identified with one particular city, ancient or future.
25:3–5 At the final judgment **all people** will honor God and stand in awe of His achievement.
25:6–8 In this mountain refers to Mt. Zion and is part of the symbolism that depicts God as being honored at an international **feast** that He has made. Some see here a reference to the marriage supper of the Lamb (Rev. 19:9). **Swallow up death** is borrowed by the apostle Paul to describe the effect of the resurrection (1 Cor. 15:54). As a result of this final victory over death, the Lord will **wipe away tears** (Rev. 21:4).

A feast of [1]choice pieces,
A feast of [2]wines on the lees,
Of fat things full of marrow,
Of well-refined wines on the lees.
7 And He will destroy on this mountain
The surface of the covering cast over all people,
And [a]the veil that is spread over all nations.
8 He will [a]swallow up death forever,
And the Lord GOD will [b]wipe away tears from all faces;
The rebuke of His people
He will take away from all the earth;
For the LORD has spoken.

9 And it will be said in that day:
"Behold, this *is* our God;
[a]We have waited for Him, and He will save us.
This *is* the LORD;
We have waited for Him;
[b]We will be glad and rejoice in His salvation."

10 For on this mountain the hand of the LORD will rest,
And [a]Moab shall be trampled down under Him,
As straw is trampled down for the refuse heap.
11 And He will spread out His hands in their midst
As a swimmer reaches out to swim,
And He will bring down their [a]pride
Together with the trickery of their hands.
12 The [a]fortress of the high fort of your walls
He will bring down, lay low,
And bring to the ground, down to the dust.

6 [1]Lit. *fat things* [2]*wines matured on the sediment*
7 [a]2 Cor. 3:15; [Eph. 4:18]
8 [a][Hos. 13:14; 1 Cor. 15:54; Rev. 20:14] [b]Is. 30:19; Rev. 7:17; 21:4
9 [a]Gen. 49:18; Is. 8:17; 26:8; [Titus 2:13] [b]Ps. 20:5
10 [a]Is. 16:14; Jer. 48:1–47; Ezek. 25:8–11; Amos 2:1–3; Zeph. 2:9
11 [a]Is. 24:4; 26:5
12 [a]Is. 26:5

CHAPTER 26
1 [a]Is. 2:11; 12:1 [b]Is. 60:18
2 [a]Ps. 118:19, 20 [1]Or *remains faithful*
3 [a]Is. 57:19; [Phil. 4:6, 7]
4 [a]Is. 12:2; 45:17 [1]Or *Rock of Ages* *See WW at Mic. 4:5. • See WW at Is. 12:2.
5 [a]Is. 25:11, 12 [1]*low*
6 [1]*trample*
7 [a]Ps. 37:23 [1]Or *make level*
8 [a]Is. 64:5 [b]Is. 25:9; 33:2
9 [a]Ps. 63:6; Song 3:1; Is. 50:10; Luke 6:12 *See WW at Num. 36:13.
10 [a]Eccl. 8:12; [Rom. 2:4] [b]Ps. 143:10

A Song of Salvation

26 In [a]that day this song will be sung in the land of Judah:

"We have a strong city;
[b]*God* will appoint salvation *for* walls and bulwarks.
2 [a]Open the gates,
That the righteous nation which [1]keeps the truth may enter in.
3 You will keep *him* in perfect [a]peace,
Whose mind *is* stayed *on You,*
Because he trusts in You.
4 Trust in the LORD *forever,
[a]For in *YAH, the LORD, *is* [1]everlasting strength.
5 For He brings [1]down those who dwell on high,
[a]The lofty city;
He lays it low,
He lays it low to the ground,
He brings it down to the dust.
6 The foot shall [1]tread it down—
The feet of the poor
And the steps of the needy."

7 The way of the just *is* uprightness;
[a]O Most Upright,
You [1]weigh the path of the just.
8 Yes, [a]in the way of Your judgments,
O LORD, we have [b]waited for You;
The desire of *our* soul *is* for Your name
And for the remembrance of You.
9 [a]With my soul I have desired You in the night,
Yes, by my spirit within me I will seek You early;
For when Your *judgments *are* in the earth,
The inhabitants of the world will learn righteousness.

10 [a]Let grace be shown to the wicked,
Yet he will not learn righteousness;
In [b]the land of uprightness he will deal unjustly,

25:9–12 This passage consists of three loosely associated units. V. 9 is a thanksgiving for God's salvation. **Moab,** representative of all unbelieving nations, will not enjoy the salvation (vv. 10, 11); and all military activity will cease with God's complete salvation (v. 12).
26:1–21 Continues the **song** of praise begun in the previous chapter. **In that day** again marks it as apocalyptic. See note on Obad. 15.
26:1 The **strong city** is Jerusalem, which symbolizes the **salvation** of God's people.
26:3 Perfect peace is expressed in Hebrew by *shalom, shalom,* a Hebrew method of putting great emphasis on a word. **You will keep *him* in** everything the word *shalom* implies: health, happiness, well-being, peace. The word translated **mind** is not the usual Hebrew word, but rather is a word meaning "creative imagination." Isaiah's thought is that he whose creative imagination, the seat of plans and ideas, is firmly founded on the eternal Lord, will enjoy *shalom* in all its implications.
26:5 The lofty city: See note on 25:2.
26:7–9 God's **judgments** are a vital part of teaching **righteousness** to the unredeemed.
26:10–15 A lament over experiences under the domination of their captors, an awakening to the futility of the way of unbelief and a praise to the Lord for His longsuffering.

And will not behold the majesty
of the LORD.
11 LORD, *when* Your hand is lifted
up, [a]they will not see.
But they will see and be ashamed
For [1]*their* envy of people;
Yes, the fire of Your enemies
shall devour them.

12 LORD, You will establish peace for
us,
For You have also done all our
works [1]in us.
13 O LORD our God, [a]masters besides
You
Have had dominion over us;
But by You only we make
mention of Your name.
14 *They are* dead, they will not *live;
They are deceased, they will not
rise.
Therefore You have punished and
destroyed them,
And made all their memory to
[a]perish.
15 You have increased the nation,
O LORD,
You have [a]increased the nation;
You are glorified;
You have expanded all the
[1]borders of the land.

16 LORD, [a]in trouble they have
visited You,
They poured out a prayer *when*
Your chastening *was* upon
them.
17 As [a]a woman with child
Is in pain and cries out in her
[1]pangs,
When she draws near the time of
her delivery,
So have we been in Your sight,
O LORD.
18 We have been with child, we have
been in pain;
We have, as it were, [1]brought
forth wind;
We have not accomplished any
deliverance in the earth,
Nor have [a]the inhabitants of the
world fallen.

11 [a]Job 34:27; Ps. 28:5; Is. 5:12 [1]Or *Your zeal for the people*
12 [1]Or *for us*
13 [a]2 Chr. 12:8
14 [a]Eccl. 9:5; Is. 14:22 *See WW at Hab. 2:4.
15 [a]Is. 9:3 [1]Or *ends*
16 [a]Is. 37:3; Hos. 5:15
17 [a]Is. 13:8; [John 16:21] [1]*sharp pains*
18 [a]Ps. 17:14 [1]*given birth to*
19 [a]Is. 25:8; [Ezek. 37:1–14] [b][Dan. 12:2]; Hos. 13:14 [1]So with MT, Vg.; Syr., Tg. *their dead bodies;* LXX *those in the tombs*
20 [a]Ex. 12:22, 23; [Ps. 91:1, 4] [b][Ps. 30:5; Is. 54:7, 8; 2 Cor. 4:17]
21 [a]Mic. 1:3; [Jude 14] [1]Or *bloodshed*

CHAPTER 27

1 [a]Gen. 3:1; Ps. 74:13, 14; Rev. 12:9, 15 [b]Is. 51:9; Ezek. 29:3; 32:2
2 [a]Is. 5:1 [b]Ps. 80:8; Is. 5:7; Jer. 2:21 [1]So with MT (Kittel's *Biblia Hebraica*), Bg., Vg.; MT (*Biblia Hebraica Stuttgartensia*), some Heb. mss., LXX *delight;* Tg. *choice vineyard*
3 [a]1 Sam. 2:9; Ps. 121:4, 5; Is. 31:5; [John 10:28]
4 [a]2 Sam. 23:6; Is. 9:18
5 [a]Is. 25:4

19 [a]Your dead shall live;
Together with [1]my dead body
they shall arise.
[b]Awake and sing, you who dwell
in dust;
For your dew *is like* the dew of
herbs,
And the earth shall cast out the
dead.

Take Refuge from the Coming Judgment

20 Come, my people, [a]enter your
chambers,
And shut your doors behind you;
Hide yourself, as it were,
[b]for a little moment,
Until the indignation is past.
21 For behold, the LORD [a]comes out
of His place
To punish the inhabitants of the
earth for their iniquity;
The earth will also disclose her
[1]blood,
And will no more cover her slain.

27 In that day the LORD with His
severe sword, great and
strong,
Will punish Leviathan the fleeing
serpent,
[a]Leviathan that twisted serpent;
And He will slay [b]the reptile that
is in the sea.

The Restoration of Israel

2 In that day [a]sing to her,
[b]"A vineyard of [1]red wine!
3 [a]I, the LORD, keep it,
I water it every moment;
Lest any hurt it,
I keep it night and day.
4 Fury *is* not in Me.
Who would set [a]briers *and* thorns
Against Me in battle?
I would go through them,
I would burn them together.
5 Or let him take hold [a]of My
strength,

26:16–18 Expresses regret over failure to be a vessel for God and a faithful witness to the nations.
26:19 Dead shall live: The resurrection of the righteous dead affirms the hope of eternal life. See also note on 25:6–8.
26:20, 21 These verses give a word of hope to the faithful remnant awaiting God's action. See note on 24:1—27:13.
27:1–13 The final chapter of "Isaiah's Apocalypse" (see note on 24:1—27:13) contains two separate eschatological scenes: God's final overthrow of evil (v. 1) and His future dealings with Israel, including a retrospective look at the judgment of the northern kingdom (vv. 2–13).
27:1 Leviathan is the name of a creature of chaos in ancient mythology, which is used by Isaiah as a type of God's enemies who were incited by Satan (Rev. 12:9). It thus personifies evil, which God will ultimately **slay**.
27:2–11 Again **Israel** is compared to a **vineyard,** but unlike the vineyard in 5:1–7, this one will be fruitful (v. 6), because idolatry will be purged by the judgment of exile (v. 9). **Struck Israel:** God disciplined the northern kingdom, but His dealing with Israel will differ from the way He deals with the nations that He permits to strike Israel. They will perish; Israel will be purged and redeemed.

...ay [b]make peace with
...e shall make peace with
...e."

6 Those who come He shall cause
[a]to take root in Jacob;
Israel shall blossom and bud,
And fill the face of the world with
fruit.

7 [a]Has He struck [1]Israel as He struck
those who struck him?
Or has He been slain according
to the slaughter of those who
were slain by Him?
8 [a]In measure, by sending it away,
You contended with it.
[b]He removes *it* by His rough wind
In the day of the east wind.
9 Therefore by this the iniquity of
Jacob will be covered;
And this *is* all the fruit of taking
away his sin:
When he makes all the stones of
the altar
Like chalkstones that are beaten
to dust,
[1]Wooden images and incense
altars shall not stand.

10 Yet the fortified city *will be*
[a]desolate,
The habitation forsaken and left
like a wilderness;
There the calf will feed, and there
it will lie down
And consume its branches.
11 When its boughs are withered,
they will be broken off;
The women come *and* set them on
fire.
For [a]it *is* a people of no
understanding;
Therefore He who made them will
[b]not have mercy on them,
And [c]He who formed them will
show them no favor.

12 And it shall come to pass in that
day
That the LORD will thresh,
From the channel of [1]the River to
the Brook of Egypt;
And you will be [a]gathered one by
one,
O you children of Israel.

13 [a]So it shall be in that day:
[b]The great *trumpet will be blown;
They will come, who are about to
perish in the land of Assyria,
And they who are outcasts in the
land of [c]Egypt,
And shall [d]worship* the LORD in
the holy mount at Jerusalem.

Woe to Ephraim and Jerusalem

28 Woe to the crown of pride, to
the drunkards of Ephraim,
Whose glorious beauty *is* a fading
flower
Which *is* at the head of the
[1]verdant valleys,
To those who are overcome with
wine!
2 Behold, the Lord has a mighty
and strong one,
[a]Like a tempest of hail and a
destroying storm,
Like a flood of mighty waters
overflowing,
Who will bring *them* down to the
earth with *His* hand.
3 The crown of pride, the
drunkards of Ephraim,
Will be trampled underfoot;
4 And the glorious beauty is a
fading flower
Which *is* at the head of the
[1]verdant valley,
Like the first fruit before the
summer,
Which an observer sees;
He eats it up while it is still in his
hand.

5 In that day the LORD of hosts
will be
For a crown of glory and a
diadem of beauty
To the remnant of His people,
6 For a spirit of justice to him who
sits in judgment,

5 [b]Job 22:21; Is. 26:3, 12; [Rom. 5:1; 2 Cor. 5:20]
6 [a]Is. 37:31; Hos. 14:5, 6
7 [a]Is. 10:12, 17; 30:30–33 [1]Lit. *him*
8 [a]Job 23:6; Ps. 6:1; Jer. 10:24; 30:11; 46:28; [1 Cor. 10:13] [b][Ps. 78:38]
9 [1]Heb. *Asherim,* Canaanite deities
10 [a]Is. 5:6, 17; 32:14; Jer. 26:18
11 [a]Deut. 32:28; Is. 1:3 [b]Is. 9:17 [c]Deut. 32:18; Is. 43:1, 7; 44:2, 21, 24
12 [a][Is. 11:11; 56:8] [1]The Euphrates
13 [a]Is. 2:11 [b]Lev. 25:9; 1 Chr. 15:24; Matt. 24:31; Rev. 11:15 [c]Is. 19:21, 22 [d][Is. 2:3]; Zech. 14:16; [Heb. 12:22] *See WW at Hos. 8:1. • See WW at Ps. 99:5.

CHAPTER 28

1 [1]Lit. *valleys of fatness*
2 [a]Is. 30:30; Ezek. 13:11
4 [1]Lit. *valley of fatness*

27:12, 13 Gathered: There will be a regathering of a remnant, not only from **Assyria** and **Egypt,** but at last from all nations. **Israel** and **Jerusalem:** See note on Zech. 8:1–17.
28:1—33:24 This passage returns to the latter part of Hezekiah's reign and the struggles with Sennacherib. The main theme is Judah's struggle with Assyria and the temptation to look to Egypt for support. See notes on 7:17 and 19:1–17.
28:1–13 Though concerned with Judah, Isaiah begins with a backward look at the miserable last decade of **Ephraim,** the northern 10 tribes. Their leaders and prominent people had become like **drunkards,** refusing to listen to Yahweh's warnings. Hence, they fell in 722 B.C. to Shalmaneser, the **strong one** (v. 2).
28:3 Crown of pride: Israel gloried in the beauty of their capital city Samaria, and in the riches and luxury of their wealth.
28:5 That day: See note on Obad. 15. **Remnant:** See notes on Zeph. 2:7, 9.

And for strength to those who
turn back the battle at the gate.

7 But they also [a]have erred through wine,
And through intoxicating drink are out of the way;
[b]The priest and the prophet have erred through intoxicating drink,
They are swallowed up by wine,
They are out of the way through intoxicating drink;
They err in vision, they stumble *in* judgment.
8 For all tables are full of vomit *and* filth;
No place *is clean.*

9 "Whom[a] will he teach knowledge?
And whom will he make to understand the message?
Those *just* weaned from milk?
Those *just* drawn from the breasts?
10 [a]For precept *must be* upon precept, precept upon precept,
Line upon line, line upon line,
Here a little, there a little."

11 For with [a]stammering lips and another tongue
He will speak to this people,
12 To whom He said, "This *is* the [a]**rest** *with which*
You may cause the weary to rest,"
And, "This *is* the refreshing";
Yet they would not hear.

WORD WEALTH

28:12 rest, *menuchah* (meh-noo-*chah*); Strong's #4496: Resting place; place of stillness, repose, consolation, peace, rest; a quiet place; also the condition of restfulness. *Menuchah* is derived from *nuach,* a verb meaning "to rest, soothe, settle down, comfort." Because Noah's parents foresaw comfort through his life (Gen. 5:29), they named him "Noah," which comes from this root. Is. 28:12 states, "This is the resting place; let the weary rest!" *Menuchah* is greatly soothing, comforting, and settling, as in Ps. 23:2, "He leads me beside the waters of *menuchah* [the waters of quietness]." Compare Num. 10:33, where it refers to the resting place the Israelites were searching to find. See also Ps. 132:14; Is. 11:10.

KINGDOM DYNAMICS

28:11, 12 Speaking with Tongues Prophesied, SPIRITUAL GIFTS. Isaiah's prediction regarding speaking in various languages—known and unknown—was said by the apostle Paul to be a prophecy fulfilled in the church. An elaboration of this and related themes appears in the study article on page 2018, "Holy Spirit Gifts and Power."

(*/John 14:16, 17) P.W.

13 But the word of the LORD was to them,
"Precept upon precept, precept upon precept,
Line upon line, line upon line,
Here a little, there a little,"
That they might go and fall backward, and be broken
And snared and caught.

14 Therefore hear the word of the LORD, you scornful men,
Who rule this people who *are* in Jerusalem,
15 Because you have said, "We have made a covenant with death,
And with Sheol we are in agreement.
When the overflowing scourge passes through,
It will not come to us,
[a]For we have made lies our *refuge,
And under falsehood we have hidden ourselves."

A Cornerstone in Zion

16 Therefore thus says the Lord GOD:

"Behold, I lay in Zion [a]a stone for a foundation,

7 [a]Prov. 20:1; Is. 5:11, 22; Hos. 4:11 [b]Is. 56:10, 12 **9** [a]Jer. 6:10 **10** [a][2 Chr. 36:15; Neh. 9:30; Jer. 25:3, 4; 35:15; 44:4] **11** [a]Is. 33:19; 1 Cor. 14:21 **12** [a]Is. 30:15; Jer. 6:16; [Matt. 11:28, 29] **15** [a]Is. 9:15; Ezek. 13:22; Amos 2:4 *See WW at Prov. 14:26. **16** [a]Gen. 49:24; Ps. 118:22; Is. 8:14, 15; Matt. 21:42; Mark 12:10; Luke 20:17; Acts 4:11; Rom. 9:33; 10:11; Eph. 2:20; 1 Pet. 2:6–8

28:9–13 The self-indulgent leaders despised the prophecies of Isaiah and ridiculed him with gibberish, implying that he was lecturing them with baby talk. **Stammering lips:** For *their irreverence and stubbornness, God would send against* them a foreign invader (Assyria) whose language would seem to them like gibberish; since they refused God's instruction through the prophets, a foreign conqueror would speak judgment to them in **another tongue** (Assyrian). Paul quotes this passage in 1 Cor. 14:21 to explain that one use of the NT gifts of tongues and interpretation is that of a sign of warning to unbelievers. See note on 1 Cor. 14:21–25.

28:14, 15 From Israel's example God makes application to Judah. They lacked faith in Yahweh, so they had made foreign alliances that they believed would protect them from **death;** but their ally, Egypt, would be a refuge of lies.

28:16–22 God reiterates to Judah that they should trust His actions. He has been consistently at work for years **in Zion;** His intent now, as for centuries past and future, is to work through the Davidic dynasty, **a sure foundation.** Though Hezekiah could have been the immediate focus of the prophecy, he was but a type of Christ, man's proven security (**a tried stone,** 1 Pet. 2:6).

A tried stone, a precious
cornerstone, a sure foundation;
Whoever believes will not act
hastily.
17 Also I will make justice the
measuring line,
And righteousness the plummet;
The hail will sweep away the
refuge of lies,
And the waters will overflow the
hiding place.
18 Your covenant with death will be
annulled,
And your agreement with Sheol
will not stand;
When the overflowing scourge
passes through,
Then you will be trampled down
by it.
19 As often as it goes out it will take
you;
For morning by morning it will
pass over,
And by day and by night;
It will be a terror just to
understand the report."

20 For the bed is too short to stretch
out *on*,
And the covering so narrow
that one cannot wrap himself *in*
it.
21 For the LORD will rise up as *at*
Mount [a]Perazim,
He will be angry as in the Valley
of [b]Gibeon—
That He may do His work,
[c]His awesome work,
And bring to pass His act, His
[1]unusual act.
22 Now therefore, do not be
mockers,
Lest your bonds be made strong;
For I have heard from the Lord
GOD of hosts,
[a]A [1]destruction determined even
upon the whole earth.

Listen to the Teaching of God

23 Give ear and hear my voice,
Listen and hear my speech.
24 Does the plowman keep plowing
all day to sow?
Does he keep turning his soil and
breaking the clods?
25 When he has leveled its surface,
Does he not sow the black
cummin
And scatter the cummin,
Plant the wheat in rows,
The barley in the appointed place,
And the [1]spelt in its place?
26 For He instructs him in right
judgment,
His God teaches him.

27 For the black cummin is not
threshed with a threshing
sledge,
Nor is a cartwheel rolled over the
cummin;
But the black cummin is beaten
out with a stick,
And the cummin with a rod.
28 Bread *flour* must be ground;
Therefore he does not thresh it
forever,
Break *it with* his cartwheel,
Or crush it *with* his horsemen.
29 This also comes from the LORD of
hosts,
[a]*Who* is wonderful in counsel *and*
excellent in [1]guidance.

Woe to Jerusalem

29 "Woe [a]to [1]Ariel, to Ariel, the
city [b]*where* David dwelt!
Add year to year;
Let feasts come around.
2 Yet I will distress Ariel;
There shall be heaviness and
sorrow,
And it shall be to Me as Ariel.
3 I will encamp against you all
around,
I will lay siege against you with
a mound,
And I will raise siegeworks
against you.
4 You shall be brought down,
You shall speak out of the
ground;
Your speech shall be low, out of
the dust;
Your voice shall be like a
medium's, [a]out of the ground;

21 [a]2 Sam. 5:20; 1 Chr. 14:11 [b]Josh. 10:10, 12; 2 Sam. 5:25; 1 Chr. 14:16 [c][Lam. 3:33; Luke 19:41–44] [1]Lit. *foreign*
22 [a]Is. 10:22; Dan. 9:27 [1]Lit. *complete end*
25 [1]*rye*
29 [a]Ps. 92:5; Is. 9:6; Jer. 32:19 [1]*sound wisdom*

CHAPTER 29

1 [a]Ezek. 24:6, 9 [b]2 Sam. 5:9 [1]Jerusalem, lit. *Lion of God*
4 [a]Is. 8:19

28:20 The bed is too short: Total reliance on mere human initiative and endeavor will leave us uncovered.
28:21 Mount Perazim . . . Gibeon: Perhaps a reference to God's routing the Philistines through David at Baal Perazim (2 Sam. 5).
28:23–29 Just as God **instructs the plowman** in matters of agriculture, so He is willing to instruct each nation's leaders (v. 29). If allowed, the Lord will use just the right strategy at exactly the right time to accomplish His purposes and bring repentance and redemption.
29:1–8 Ariel means either "Lion of God" (see marginal note) or "Altar of Burnt Offering." Because the implied altar was in the temple in Jerusalem, Ariel was a symbolic name for Jerusalem. In the hour of judgment (v. 6), though once like a strong lion, she would be like an altar of burnt offering (v. 2). The verses once again give divine insight into Sennacherib's invasion. See note on 7:17.

And your speech shall whisper
out of the dust.

5 "Moreover the multitude of your
[a]foes
Shall be like fine dust,
And the multitude of the terrible
ones
Like [b]chaff that passes away;
Yes, it shall be [c]in an instant,
suddenly.
6 [a]You will be punished by the LORD
of hosts
With thunder and [b]earthquake
and great noise,
With storm and tempest
And the flame of devouring fire.
7 [a]The multitude of all the nations
who fight against [1]Ariel,
Even all who fight against her and
her fortress,
And distress her,
Shall be [b]as a dream of a night
vision.
8 [a]It shall even be as when a hungry
man dreams,
And look—he eats;
But he awakes, and his soul is still
empty;
Or as when a thirsty man dreams,
And look—he drinks;
But he awakes, and indeed *he is*
faint,
And his soul still craves:
So the multitude of all the nations
shall be,
Who fight against Mount Zion."

The Blindness of Disobedience

9 Pause and wonder!
Blind yourselves and be blind!
[a]They are drunk, [b]but not with
wine;
They stagger, but not with
intoxicating drink.
10 For [a]the LORD has poured out on
you
The spirit of deep sleep,
And has [b]closed your eyes,
namely, the prophets;
And He has covered your heads,
namely, [c]the seers.

5 [a]Is. 25:5 [b]Job 21:18; Is. 17:13 [c]Is. 30:13; 47:11; 1 Thess. 5:3
6 [a]Is. 28:2; 30:30 [b]1 Sam. 2:10; Zech. 14:4; Matt. 24:7; Mark 13:8; Luke 21:11; Rev. 16:18, 19
7 [a]Is. 37:36; Mic. 4:11, 12; Zech. 12:9 [b]Job 20:8 [1]Jerusalem
8 [a]Ps. 73:20
9 [a]Is. 28:7, 8 [b]Is. 51:21
10 [a]Ps. 69:23; Is. 6:9, 10; Mic. 3:6; Rom. 11:8 [b]Ps. 69:23; Is. 6:10 [c]1 Sam. 9:9; Is. 44:18; Mic. 3:6; [2 Thess. 2:9–12]
11 [a]Is. 8:16 [b]Dan. 12:4, 9; [Matt. 13:11–16]; Rev. 5:1–5, 9 [1]*scroll*
12 [1]Lit. *does not know books*
13 [a]Ps. 78:36; Ezek. 33:31; Matt. 15:8, 9; Mark 7:6, 7 [b]Col. 2:22
14 [a]Is. 6:9, 10; 28:21; Hab. 1:5 [b]Is. 44:25; Jer. 49:7; Obad. 8; 1 Cor. 1:19 *See WW at Judg. 13:19.
15 [a]Is. 30:1 [b]Ps. 10:11; 94:7; Is. 47:10; Ezek. 8:12; Mal. 2:17
16 [a]Is. 45:9; Jer. 18:1–6; [Rom. 9:19–21]
17 [a]Is. 32:15

11 The whole vision has become to you
like the words of a [1]book [a]that is
sealed, which *men* deliver to one who
is literate, saying, "Read this, please."
[b]And he says, "I cannot, for it *is*
sealed."
12 Then the book is delivered to one
who [1]is illiterate, saying, "Read this,
please." And he says, "I am not literate."
13 Therefore the Lord said: 3

[a]"Inasmuch as these people draw
near with their mouths
And honor Me [b]with their lips,
But have removed their hearts far
from Me,
And their fear toward Me is
taught by the commandment of
men,
14 [a]Therefore, behold, I will again *do
a marvelous work
Among this people,
A marvelous work and a wonder;
[b]For the wisdom of their wise *men*
shall perish,
And the understanding of their
prudent *men* shall be hidden."

15 [a]Woe to those who seek deep to
hide their counsel far from the
LORD,
And their works are in the dark;
[b]They say, "Who sees us?" and,
"Who knows us?"
16 Surely you have things turned
around!
Shall the potter be esteemed as
the clay;
For shall the [a]thing made say of
him who made it,
"He did not make me"?
Or shall the thing formed say of
him who formed it,
"He has no understanding"?

Future Recovery of Wisdom

17 *Is* it not yet a very little while
Till [a]Lebanon shall be turned into
a fruitful field,
And the fruitful field be esteemed
as a forest?

29:5–8 Israel would be punished by an Assyrian invasion in 701 B.C., yet Assyria would gain nothing permanent by the conquest. She, in turn, would be torn by inner strife and be finally conquered by Babylon, which, in turn, would suffer the same fate. See note on 10:5–11.
29:9–16 Blind . . . drunk: A spiritual stupor characterized those in Judah who were rejecting the word of God. They had only a lip-service religion, denying God's sovereign role. Because they have rejected divine counsel, God will make His **book** of true wisdom a closed book. Jesus (Matt. 15:8, 9) quotes v. 13 in reference to the Israel of His day. Paul alludes to v. 16 (Rom. 9:19–21) to prove God's supremacy and sovereign actions in history.
29:13, 14 See section 3 of Truth-In-Action at the end of Is.
29:17–24 Deaf . . . hear . . . blind . . . see: Blindness and deafness will not persist (v. 18), for one day Israel will see, hear, and **learn doctrine** (v. 24). **Lebanon,** famed for its great trees, symbolizes restored fertility to the Earth as part of the **understanding.** The passage is eschatological. See note on Obad. 15.

18 [a]In that day the deaf shall hear the words of the book,
And the eyes of the blind shall see out of obscurity and out of darkness.
19 [a]The humble also shall increase *their* joy in the LORD,
And [b]the poor among men shall *rejoice
In the Holy One of Israel.
20 For the [1]terrible one is brought to nothing,
[a]The scornful one is consumed,
And all who [b]watch for *iniquity are cut off—
21 Who make a man an offender by a word,
And [a]lay a snare for him who reproves in the gate,
And turn aside the just [b]by empty words.

22 Therefore thus says the LORD, [a]who
redeemed Abraham, concerning the
house of Jacob:

"Jacob shall not now be [b]ashamed,
Nor shall his face now grow pale;
23 But when he sees his children,
[a]The work of My hands, in his midst,
They will hallow My name,
And hallow the Holy One of Jacob,
And fear the God of Israel.
24 These also [a]who erred in spirit will come to understanding,
And those who complained will learn doctrine."

Futile Confidence in Egypt

30 "Woe to the rebellious children," says the LORD,
[a]"Who take counsel, but not of Me,
And who [1]devise plans, but not of My Spirit,
[b]That they may add sin to sin;
2 [a]Who walk to go down to Egypt,
And [b]have not asked My advice,
To strengthen themselves in the strength of Pharaoh,
And to trust in the shadow of Egypt!
3 [a]Therefore the strength of Pharaoh
Shall be your shame,
And trust in the shadow of Egypt
Shall be *your* humiliation.
4 For his princes were at [a]Zoan,
And his ambassadors came to Hanes.
5 [a]They were all ashamed of a people *who* could not benefit them,
Or be help or benefit,
But a shame and also a reproach."

6 [a]The [1]burden against the beasts of
the South.

Through a land of trouble and anguish,
From which *came* the lioness and lion,
[b]The viper and *fiery flying serpent,
They will carry their riches on the backs of young donkeys,
And their treasures on the humps of camels,
To a people *who* shall not profit;
7 [a]For the Egyptians shall help in vain and to no purpose.
Therefore I have called her
[1]Rahab-Hem-Shebeth.

A Rebellious People

8 Now go, [a]write it before them on a tablet,
And note it on a scroll,
That it may be for time to come,
Forever and ever:
9 That [a]this *is* a rebellious people,
Lying children,
Children *who* will not hear the law of the LORD;
10 [a]Who say to the *seers, "Do not see,"
And to the prophets, "Do not prophesy to us right things;
[b]Speak to us smooth things, prophesy deceits.
11 Get out of the way,
Turn aside from the path,
Cause the Holy One of Israel
To cease from before us."

18 [a]Is. 35:5; Matt. 11:5; Mark 7:37
19 [a][Ps. 25:9; 37:11; Is. 11:4; 61:1; Matt. 5:5; 11:29] [b]Is. 14:30; [Matt. 5:3; 11:5; James 2:5] *See WW at Hab. 3:18.
20 [a]Is. 28:14 [b]Is. 59:4; Mic. 2:1 [1]*terrifying* *See WW at Prov. 22:8.
21 [a]Amos 5:10, 12 [b]Prov. 28:21
22 [a]Josh. 24:3 [b]Is. 45:17
23 [a][Is. 45:11; 49:20–26; Eph. 2:10]
24 [a]Is. 28:7

CHAPTER 30

1 [a]Is. 29:15 [b]Deut. 29:19 [1]Lit. *weave a web*
2 [a]Is. 31:1; Jer. 43:7 [b]Num. 27:21; Josh. 9:14; 1 Kin. 22:7; Jer. 21:2; 42:2, 20
3 [a]Is. 20:5; Jer. 37:5, 7
4 [a]Is. 19:11
5 [a]Jer. 2:36
6 [a]Is. 57:9; Hos. 8:9; 12:1 [b]Deut. 8:15; Is. 14:29 [1]*oracle, prophecy* *See WW at Is. 6:2.
7 [a]Jer. 37:7 [1]Lit. *Rahab Sits Idle*
8 [a]Hab. 2:2
9 [a]Deut. 32:20; Is. 1:2, 4; 65:2
10 [a]Is. 5:20; Jer. 11:21; Amos 2:12; Mic. 2:6 [b]1 Kin. 22:8, 13; Jer. 6:14; 23:17, 26; Ezek. 13:7; Mic. 2:11; Rom. 16:18; 2 Tim. 4:3, 4 *See WW at 1 Sam. 9:9.

30:1–33 Counsel ... but not of My Spirit: This chapter is a struggle between **the LORD** and Judah's leaders who were bent on seeking foreign alliances (here with **Egypt**) as a protection against **Assyria.** They rejected divine guidance, grieving the Holy Spirit. Egypt was not a guardian, only a **shadow.** See note on 20:1–6.

30:1, 2 See section 1 of Truth-In-Action at the end of Is.

30:4, 5 Hezekiah's **ambassadors** to Egypt (**Zoan ... Hanes**) ultimately learned Egypt **could not benefit them.** See note on 19:11–15.

30:6, 7 Burden: See note on 13:1—23:18. Egypt's caravans in **the South** (the Negev) will be of no **help.** Here called **Rahab** (an alternate name for Leviathan; see note on 27:1), Egypt can only "sit idle" (**Hem-Shebeth;** see marginal note).

12 Therefore thus says the Holy One of Israel:

"Because you [a]despise* this word,
And trust in oppression and perversity,
And rely on them,
13 Therefore this iniquity shall be to you
[a]Like a *breach ready to fall,
A bulge in a high wall,
Whose breaking [b]comes suddenly, in an instant.
14 And [a]He shall break it like the breaking of the potter's vessel,
Which is broken in pieces;
He shall not spare.
So there shall not be found among its fragments
[1]A shard to take fire from the hearth,
Or to take water from the cistern."

15 For thus says the Lord GOD, the Holy One of Israel:

[a]"In returning and rest you shall be saved;
In quietness and confidence shall be your strength."
[b]But you would not,
16 And you said, "No, for we will flee on horses"—
Therefore you shall flee!
And, "We will ride on swift *horses*"—
Therefore those who pursue you shall be swift!

17 [a]One thousand *shall flee* at the threat of one,
At the threat of five you shall flee,
Till you are left as a [1]pole on top of a mountain
And as a banner on a hill.

God Will Be Gracious

18 Therefore the LORD will wait, that He may *be [a]gracious to you;
And therefore He will be *exalted, that He may have mercy on you.
For the LORD *is* a God of justice;
[b]Blessed *are* all those who [c]wait for Him.

19 For the people [a]shall dwell in Zion at Jerusalem;
You shall [b]weep no more.
He will be very gracious to you at the sound of your cry;
When He hears it, He will [c]answer you.
20 And *though* the Lord gives you
[a]The bread of adversity and the water of [1]affliction,
Yet [b]your teachers will not be moved into a corner anymore,
But your eyes shall see your teachers.
21 Your ears shall hear a word behind you, saying,
"This *is* the way, walk in it,"
Whenever you [a]turn to the right hand
Or whenever you turn to the left.
22 [a]You will also defile the covering of your images of silver,
And the ornament of your molded images of gold.
You will throw them away as an unclean thing;
[b]You will say to them, "Get away!"

23 [a]Then He will give the rain for your seed
With which you sow the ground,
And bread of the increase of the earth;
It will be [1]fat and plentiful.
In that day your cattle will feed
In large pastures.
24 Likewise the oxen and the young donkeys that work the ground
Will eat cured fodder,
Which has been winnowed with the shovel and fan.
25 There will be [a]on every high mountain
And on every high hill
Rivers *and* streams of waters,
In the day of the [b]great slaughter,
When the towers fall.
26 Moreover [a]the light of the moon will be as the light of the sun,
And the light of the sun will be sevenfold,
As the light of seven days,
In the day that the LORD binds up the bruise of His people
And heals the stroke of their wound.

12 [a]Lev. 26:43; Num. 15:31; Prov. 1:30; 13:13; Is. 5:24; Ezek. 20:13, 16, 24; Amos 2:4 *See WW at Amos 2:4. **13** [a]1 Kin. 20:30; Ps. 62:3, 4; Is. 58:12 [b]Is. 29:5 *See WW at Ezek. 22:30. **14** [a]Ps. 2:9; Jer. 19:11 [1]A piece of broken pottery **15** [a]Ps. 116:7; Is. 7:4; 28:12 [b]Matt. 23:37 **17** [a]Lev. 26:36; Deut. 28:25; 32:30; Josh. 23:10; [Prov. 28:1] [1]A tree stripped of branches **18** [a]Is. 33:2 [b]Ps. 2:12; 34:8; Prov. 16:20; Jer. 17:7 [c]Is. 26:8 *See WW at Mal. 1:9. • See WW at Ps. 18:46.

19 [a]Is. 65:9; [Ezek. 37:25, 28] [b]Is. 25:8 [c]Ps. 50:15; Is. 65:24; [Matt. 7:7–11] **20** [a]1 Kin. 22:27; Ps. 127:2 [b]Ps. 74:9; Amos 8:11 [1]*oppression* **21** [a]Josh. 1:7 **22** [a]2 Chr. 31:1; Is. 2:20; 31:7 [b]Hos. 14:8 **23** [a][Matt. 6:33]; 1 Tim. 6:8 [1]*rich* **25** [a]Is. 2:14, 15 [b]Is. 2:10–21; 34:2 **26** [a][Is. 60:19, 20; Rev. 21:23; 22:5]

30:12–17 Judah's trust in the **swift horses** of Egypt (v. 16) rather than in God (v. 15) would result in their being left alone **as a pole on top of a mountain** (v. 17).

30:18–26 Be gracious to you: In spite of judgments, **the LORD** is eager to bless His people. The day will come when the people will hear **teachers** like Isaiah and walk in divine guidance. As a result idolatry will be abandoned and true worship embraced. In that day all nature (vv. 23–26) will cooperate and God's glory will outshine **the sun.** See note on 29:17–24.

Judgment on Assyria

27 Behold, the name of the LORD
comes from afar,
Burning *with* His anger,
And *His* burden *is* heavy;
His lips are full of indignation,
And His tongue like a devouring
fire.
28 [a]His breath is like an overflowing
stream,
[b]Which reaches up to the neck,
To sift the nations with the sieve
of futility;
And *there shall be* [c]a bridle in the
jaws of the people,
Causing *them* to err.

29 You shall have a song
As in the night *when* a holy
festival is kept,
And gladness of heart as when
one goes with a flute,
To come into [a]the mountain of the
LORD,
To [1]the Mighty One of Israel.
30 [a]The LORD will cause His glorious
voice to be heard,
And show the descent of His arm,
With the indignation of *His* anger
And the flame of a devouring
fire,
With scattering, tempest,
[b]and hailstones.
31 For [a]through the voice of the
LORD
Assyria will be [1]beaten down,
As He strikes with the [b]rod.
32 And *in* every place where the staff
of punishment passes,
Which the LORD lays on him,
It will be with tambourines and
harps;
And in battles of [a]brandishing He
will fight with it.
33 [a]For Tophet *was* established of
old,
Yes, for the king it is prepared.
He has made *it* deep and large;
Its pyre *is* fire with much wood;
The *breath of the LORD, like a
stream of brimstone,
Kindles it.

28 [a]Is. 11:4; 2 Thess. 2:8 [b]Is. 8:8 [c]2 Kin. 19:28; Is. 37:29
29 [a][Is. 2:3] [1]Lit. *the Rock*
30 [a]Is. 29:6 [b]Is. 28:2
31 [a]Is. 14:25; 37:36 [b]Is. 10:5, 24 [1]Lit. *shattered*
32 [a]Is. 11:15
33 [a]2 Kin. 23:10; Jer. 7:31
*See WW at Ps. 150:6.

CHAPTER 31

1 [a]Is. 30:1, 2 [b]Deut. 17:16; Ps. 20:7; Is. 2:7; 30:16 [c]Is. 9:13; Dan. 9:13; Amos 5:4–8
2 [a]Num. 23:19; Jer. 44:29 [1]*retract*
3 [a]Is. 20:6
4 [a]Num. 24:9; Hos. 11:10; Amos 3:8
5 [a]Deut. 32:11; Ps. 91:4
6 [a]Hos. 9:9

The Folly of Not Trusting God

31 Woe to those [a]who go down to **1**
Egypt for help,
And [b]rely on horses,
Who trust in chariots because
they are many,
And in horsemen because they
are very strong,
But who do not look to the Holy
One of Israel,
[c]Nor seek the LORD!
2 Yet He also *is* wise and will bring
disaster,
And [a]will not [1]call back His
words,
But will arise against the house
of evildoers,
And against the help of those who
work iniquity.
3 Now the Egyptians *are* men, and
not God;
And their horses are flesh, and
not spirit.
When the LORD stretches out His
hand,
Both he who helps will fall,
And he who is helped will fall
down;
They all will perish [a]together.

God Will Deliver Jerusalem

4 For thus the LORD has spoken to me:

[a]"As a lion roars,
And a young lion over his prey
(When a multitude of shepherds
is summoned against him,
He will not be afraid of their voice
Nor be disturbed by their noise),
So the LORD of hosts will come
down
To fight for Mount Zion and for
its hill.
5 [a]Like birds flying about,
So will the LORD of hosts defend
Jerusalem.
Defending, He will also deliver *it;*
Passing over, He will preserve *it.*"

6 Return *to Him* against whom the
children of Israel have [a]deeply revolted.

30:27–33 In preparation for that day, God will visit with indignation the enemies of Israel, including **Assyria,** the present foe. See note on Zech. 12:1–9. **Tophet:** A place in the Valley of Hinnom where sacrifices, including children, were offered to the god Moloch; it suggests a funeral pyre and symbolizes that the foreign king would be dead by God's **breath** of judgment.

31:1–9 Woe to those who go down to Egypt: Continues the Lord's warning to Judah against an alliance with Egypt, which showed distrust of **the Holy One of Israel**. See note on 30:1–33.

31:1–3 See section 1 of Truth-In-Action at the end of Is.

31:4–9 Again, God will not forsake His people forever; there shall be restoration. See note on 30:18–26. Two metaphors are used for the Lord's defense of **Jerusalem.** He will come as an irresistible **lion** (v. 4), perhaps a reference to the Lion of the tribe of Judah, and as **birds flying** over His city. **In that day** they will throw away their **idols; then Assyria,** a type of all Judah's enemies, will be devoured. See note on 30:27–33.

7 For in that day every man shall
[a]throw away his idols of silver and his
idols of gold—[b]sin, which your own
hands have made for yourselves.

8 "Then Assyria shall [a]fall by a
sword not of man,
And a sword not of mankind shall
[b]devour him.
But he shall flee from the sword,
And his young men shall become
forced labor.
9 [a]He shall cross over to his
stronghold for fear,
And his princes shall be afraid of
the banner,"
Says the LORD,
Whose fire *is* in Zion
And whose furnace *is* in
Jerusalem.

A Reign of Righteousness

32 Behold, [a]a king will *reign in
righteousness,
And princes will rule with justice.
2 A **man** will be as a hiding place
from the wind,
And [a]a [1]cover from the tempest,
As rivers of water in a dry place,
As the shadow of a great rock in
a weary land.

WORD WEALTH

32:2 man, *'ish* (*eesh*); Strong's #376: A man, a husband, a male, an individual person. This is one of the four main Hebrew words for "man" in the OT. Unlike the generic term *'adam,* which means "human," *'ish* portrays maleness and so is logically paired with its feminine form, *'ishah,* "wife" or "woman." In Gen. 2:23, Adam says, "She shall be called *'ishah* because out of *'ish* she has been taken." *'Ish* often conveys a sense of nobility, dignity, strength, and especially social standing, as does the word "gentleman"; as in Ps. 62:9, *bnay 'adam,* "sons of men," is translated "men of low degree," whereas *bnay 'ish,* "sons of men," is translated "men of high degree." It is also used with another noun to describe a person; as *'ish 'Elohim,* or "man of God"; other such phrases include "man of blood," "man of the field," "man of words."

7 [a]Is. 2:20; 30:22 [b]1 Kin. 12:30
8 [a]2 Kin. 19:35, 36 [b]Is. 37:36
9 [a]Is. 37:37

CHAPTER 32

1 [a]Ps. 45:1 *See WW at 2 Sam. 8:15.
2 [a]Is. 4:6 [1]*shelter*

3 [a]Is. 29:18; 35:5
4 [a]Is. 29:24 [1]*hasty*
5 [1]*noble*
6 [a]Prov. 24:7–9
7 [a]Jer. 5:26–28; Mic. 7:3
8 [1]*noble*
9 [a]Is. 47:8; Amos 6:1; Zeph. 2:15 *See WW at 2 Sam. 22:31.

3 [a]The eyes of those who see will not
be dim,
And the ears of those who hear
will listen.
4 Also the heart of the [1]rash will
[a]understand knowledge,
And the tongue of the stammerers
will be ready to speak plainly.

5 The foolish person will no longer
be called [1]generous,
Nor the miser said *to be*
bountiful;
6 For the foolish person will speak
foolishness,
And his heart will work [a]iniquity:
To practice ungodliness,
To utter error against the LORD,
To keep the hungry unsatisfied,
And he will cause the drink of the
thirsty to fail.
7 Also the schemes of the schemer
are evil;
He devises wicked plans
To destroy the poor with
[a]lying words,
Even when the needy speaks
justice.
8 But a [1]generous man devises
generous things,
And by generosity he shall stand.

Consequences of Complacency

9 Rise up, you women [a]who are at
ease,
Hear my voice;
You complacent daughters,
Give ear to my *speech.
10 In a year and *some* days
You will be troubled, you
complacent women;
For the vintage will fail,
The gathering will not come.
11 Tremble, you *women* who are at
ease;
Be troubled, you complacent
ones;
Strip yourselves, make
yourselves bare,
And gird *sackcloth* on *your*
waists.

12 People shall mourn upon their
breasts

32:1–8 *This civics lesson describes leaders reigning* **in righteousness,** an obvious contrast to the current leaders. The ideal pictured makes the passage messianic, describing Christ's current reign in the spiritual dimension and His physical reign during the Millennium (Rev. 20:1–6).

32:1, 2 Princes are likely the royal sons of the court (see Rev. 20:4). When properly ruling they protect society (v. 2).

32:3–8 Not only were the leaders at fault, but the public was imperceptive in allowing its deficient leaders to rule. Their social maladies will be reversed with the reign of the righteous King.

32:9–15 Complacent daughters: The lack of perception of vv. 3–8 is exemplified in Isaiah's interaction with a group of **women.** They perceive peace when God's Spirit has identified turmoil.

32:10 Disaster will strike by the end of the agricultural year.

For the pleasant fields, for the fruitful vine.
13 [a]On the land of my people will come up thorns *and* briers,
Yes, on all the happy homes *in* [b]the joyous city;
14 [a]Because the palaces will be forsaken,
The bustling city will be deserted.
The forts and towers will become lairs forever,
A joy of wild donkeys, a pasture of flocks—
15 Until [a]the Spirit is poured upon us from on high,
And [b]the wilderness becomes a fruitful field,
And the fruitful field is counted as a forest.

The Peace of God's Reign

16 Then justice will dwell in the wilderness,
And righteousness *remain in the fruitful field.
17 [a]The work of righteousness will be peace,
And the effect of righteousness, quietness and assurance forever.
18 My people will dwell in a peaceful habitation,
In secure **dwellings,** and in quiet [a]resting places,

WORD WEALTH

32:18 dwellings, *mishchan* (meesh-*kahn*); Strong's #4908: A tabernacle, a dwelling place; a place of residence, a habitation. *Mishchan* appears more than 130 times in the OT, nearly 100 of these in Ex.—Num., for the tabernacle at Shiloh, and even the dwelling places of the wicked (Ps. 78:60; Job 18:21). The root of *mishchan* is *shachan,* meaning "to dwell, reside, remain, abide, stay." Thus, *mishchan* means literally "place of dwelling." Also from the root *shachan* is *Shekinah,* or "abiding presence and glory" of the Lord. *Shekinah* is not found in the OT, but comes from later Jewish writings.

19 [a]Though hail comes down [b]on the forest,
And the city is brought low in humiliation.

13 [a]Is. 7:23–25; Hos. 9:6 [b]Is. 22:2
14 [a]Is. 27:10
15 [a][Is. 11:2]; Ezek. 39:29; [Joel 2:28] [b]Ps. 107:35; Is. 29:17
16 *See WW at Lam. 5:19.
17 [a]Ps. 119:165; Is. 2:4; Rom. 14:17; James 3:18
18 [a]Is. 11:10; 14:3; 30:15; [Hos. 2:18–23; Zech. 2:5; 3:10]
19 [a]Is. 30:30 [b]Zech. 11:2
20 [a][Eccl. 11:1]; Is. 30:23, 24

CHAPTER 33

1 [a]Is. 21:2; Hab. 2:8 [b]Rev. 13:10 [c]Is. 10:12; 14:25; 31:8
2 [a]Is. 25:9; 26:8 [1]LXX omits *their;* Syr., Tg., Vg. *our* *See WW at Mal. 1:9.
3 [a]Is. 17:13
5 [a]Ps. 97:9

20 Blessed *are* you who sow beside all waters,
Who send out freely the feet of [a]the ox and the donkey.

A Prayer in Deep Distress

33 Woe to you [a]who plunder, though you *have* not *been* plundered;
And you who deal treacherously, though they have not dealt treacherously with you!
[b]When you cease plundering,
You will be [c]plundered;
When you make an end of dealing treacherously,
They will deal treacherously with you.

2 O LORD, *be gracious to us;
[a]We have waited for You.
Be [1]their arm every morning,
Our salvation also in the time of trouble.
3 At the noise of the tumult the people [a]shall flee;
When You lift Yourself up, the nations shall be scattered;
4 And Your plunder shall be gathered
Like the gathering of the caterpillar;
As the running to and fro of locusts,
He shall run upon them.

5 [a]The LORD is exalted, for He dwells on high;
He has filled Zion with justice and righteousness.
6 Wisdom and knowledge will be the stability of your **times,**
And the strength of salvation;
The fear of the LORD *is* His treasure.

WORD WEALTH

33:6 times, *'et* (*eht*); Strong's #6256: A particular time; season, age, occasion, or some period of time; current times. Unlike *'olam,* which refers to a vast expanse of time, *'et* is used to describe a small space of time. *'Et* can be a season, such as Passover season, rainy season, harvest season (see 2 Chr. 35:17; Jer. 51:33; Zech. 10:1). It may refer to a portion of a lifetime, "time of old age" (Ps. 71:9).
(*cont. on next page*)

32:15 Until the Spirit . . . on high: See note on 29:17–24.
32:16–20 See note on 11:6–9.
33:1–6 You who plunder is likely a reference to Sennacherib, king of Assyria, who had betrayed and plundered Judah, although some identify "you" as Babylon. He in turn would **be plundered** and destroyed because of Jerusalem's trust in Yahweh (vv. 5, 6). See notes on 10:5–11 and 22:8–14.

(cont. from preceding page)
(See also "time of trouble," "time of love," and "evil time," Ps. 37:39; Ezek. 16:8; Amos 5:13.) *'Et* occurs 290 times. The present reference speaks of the stabilizing force God will provide to the believers, even in the midst of the uncertain times of this present age (see vv. 2–5 for context).

7 Surely their valiant ones shall cry
outside,
[a]The ambassadors of peace shall
weep bitterly.
8 [a]The highways lie waste,
The traveling man ceases.
[b]He has broken the covenant,
[1]He has *despised the [2]cities,
He regards no *man.
9 [a]The earth mourns *and* languishes,
Lebanon is shamed *and*
shriveled;
Sharon is like a wilderness,
And Bashan and Carmel shake
off *their fruits.*

Impending Judgment on Zion

10 "Now[a] I will rise," says the LORD;
"Now I will be exalted,
Now I will lift Myself up.
11 [a]You shall conceive chaff,
You shall bring forth stubble;
Your breath, *as* fire, shall devour
you.
12 And the people shall be *like* the
burnings of lime;
[a]*Like* thorns cut up they shall be
burned in the fire.
13 Hear, [a]you *who are* afar off, what
I have done;
And you *who are* near,
acknowledge My might."

14 The sinners in Zion are afraid;
Fearfulness has seized the
hypocrites:
"Who among us shall *dwell with
the devouring [a]fire?
Who among us shall dwell with
everlasting burnings?"
15 He who [a]walks righteously and
speaks uprightly,
He who despises the gain of
oppressions,
Who gestures with his hands,
refusing bribes,
Who stops his ears from hearing
of bloodshed,
And [b]shuts his eyes from seeing
evil:
16 He will dwell on [1]high;
His place of defense *will be* the
fortress of rocks;
Bread will be given him,
His water *will be* sure.

The Land of the Majestic King

17 Your eyes will see the King in His
[a]beauty;*
They will see the land that is very
far off.
18 Your heart will *meditate on
terror:
[a]"Where *is* the scribe?
Where *is* he who weighs?
Where *is* he who counts the
towers?"
19 [a]You will not see a fierce people,
[b]A people of obscure speech,
beyond perception,
Of a [1]stammering tongue *that you*
cannot understand.

20 [a]Look upon Zion, the city of our
appointed feasts;
Your eyes will see [b]Jerusalem, a
quiet home,
A tabernacle *that* will not be
taken down;
[c]Not one of [d]its stakes will ever
be removed,
Nor will any of its cords be
broken.
21 But there the majestic LORD *will
be* for us
A place of broad rivers *and*
streams,
In which no [1]galley with oars will
sail,
Nor majestic ships pass by
22 (For the LORD *is* our [a]Judge,
The LORD *is* our [b]Lawgiver,
[c]The LORD *is* our King;
He will save us);
23 Your tackle is loosed,
They could not strengthen their
mast,
They could not spread the sail.

7 [a]2 Kin. 18:18, 37 **8** [a]Judg. 5:6 [b]2 Kin. 18:13–17 [1]Tg. *They have been removed from their cities* [2]So with MT, Vg.; DSS *witnesses;* LXX omits *cities* *See WW at Amos 2:4. • See WW at Job 4:17. **9** [a]Is. 24:4 **10** [a]Ps. 12:5; Is. 2:19, 21 **11** [a][Ps. 7:14; Is. 26:18; 59:4; James 1:15] **12** [a]Is. 9:18 **13** [a]Ps. 48:10; Is. 49:1 **14** [a]Is. 30:27, 30; Heb. 12:29 *See WW at Jer. 42:17. **15** [a]Ps. 15:2; 24:3, 4; Is. 58:6–11 [b]Ps. 119:37

16 [1]Lit. *heights* **17** [a]Ps. 27:4 *See WW at Ezek. 28:12. **18** [a]1 Cor. 1:20 *See WW at Ps. 1:2. **19** [a]2 Kin. 19:32 [b]Deut. 28:49, 50; Is. 28:11; Jer. 5:15 [1]Unintelligible speech **20** [a]Ps. 48:12 [b]Ps. 46:5; 125:1; Is. 32:18 [c]Is. 37:33 [d]Is. 54:2 **21** [1]*ship* **22** [a][Acts 10:42] [b]Is. 1:10; 51:4, 7; James 4:12 [c]Ps. 89:18; Is. 25:9; 35:4; Zech. 9:9

33:7–13 Yahweh will triumph in spite of widespread devastation by the Assyrians of the whole area from **Bashan** (east of the Jordan) to **Carmel** and **Lebanon** (on the seacoast).
33:14–24 Who will endure **the devouring fire** of testing? The righteous (v. 15) who will also see **the King in His beauty,** a prophecy with messianic overtones. In Judah's God-given victory, the Assyrian officials that domineered for a while and spoke in **obscure** [foreign] **speech** will be removed. **Jerusalem** (**Zion**) is likened to the **tabernacle** in the wilderness, but its **stakes** and **cords** in the coming quiet time will never be disturbed as **the LORD** dwells permanently among His people. Though historically referring to Jerusalem's recovery from Assyrian invasion, the section is also eschatological. See note on Zech. 8:1–17.
33:21 Galley with oars: No ship of war will successfully invade.

Then the prey of great plunder is divided;
The lame take the prey.
24 And the inhabitant will not say, "I am sick";
[a]The people who dwell in it *will be* forgiven *their* iniquity.

Judgment on the Nations

34 Come [a]near, you nations, to hear;
And heed, you people!
[b]Let the earth hear, and all that is in it,
The *world and all things that come forth from it.
2 For the indignation of the LORD *is* against all nations,
And *His* fury against all their armies;
He has utterly destroyed them,
He has given them over to the [a]slaughter.
3 Also their slain shall be thrown out;
[a]Their stench shall rise from their corpses,
And the mountains shall be melted with their blood.
4 [a]All the *host of heaven shall be dissolved,
And the heavens shall be *rolled up like a scroll;
[b]All their host shall fall down
As the leaf falls from the vine,
And as [c]*fruit* falling from a fig tree.

5 "For [a]My sword shall be bathed in heaven;
Indeed it [b]shall come down on Edom,
And on the people of My curse, for judgment.
6 The [a]sword of the LORD is filled with blood,
It is made [1]overflowing with fatness,
With the blood of lambs and goats,
With the fat of the kidneys of rams.
For [b]the LORD has a sacrifice in Bozrah,
And a great slaughter in the land of Edom.
7 The wild oxen shall come down with them,
And the young bulls with the mighty bulls;
Their land shall be soaked with blood,
And their dust [1]saturated with fatness."

8 For *it is* the day of the LORD's [a]vengeance,
The year of recompense for the cause of Zion.
9 [a]Its streams shall be turned into pitch,
And its dust into brimstone;
Its land shall become burning pitch.
10 It shall not be quenched night or day;
[a]Its smoke shall ascend forever.
[b]From generation to generation it shall lie waste;
No one shall pass through it forever and ever.
11 [a]But the [1]pelican and the [2]porcupine shall possess it,
Also the owl and the raven shall dwell in it.
And [b]He shall stretch out over it
The line of confusion and the stones of emptiness.
12 They shall call its nobles to the kingdom,
But none *shall be* there, and all its princes shall be nothing.

13 And [a]thorns shall come up in its palaces,
Nettles and brambles in its fortresses;
[b]It shall be a habitation of jackals,
A courtyard for ostriches.
14 The wild beasts of the desert shall also meet with the [1]jackals,
And the wild goat shall bleat to its companion;
Also [2]the night creature shall rest there,

24 [a]Is. 40:2; Jer. 50:20; Mic. 7:18, 19; 1 John 1:7–9

CHAPTER 34

1 [a]Ps. 49:1; Is. 41:1; 43:9 [b]Deut. 32:1; Is. 1:2 *See WW at Jer. 51:15.
2 [a]Is. 13:5
3 [a]Joel 2:20; Amos 4:10
4 [a]Ps. 102:26; Is. 13:13; Ezek. 32:7, 8; Joel 2:31; Matt. 24:29; 2 Pet. 3:10 [b]Is. 14:12 [c]Rev. 6:12–14 *See WW at Ps. 68:11. • See WW at Prov. 16:3.
5 [a]Deut. 32:41, 42; Jer. 46:10; Ezek. 21:3–5 [b]Is. 63:1; Jer. 49:7, 8, 20; Ezek. 25:12–14; 35:1–15; Amos 1:11, 12; Obad. 1–14; Mal. 1:4
6 [a]Is. 66:16 [b]Zeph. 1:7 [1]Lit. *fat*
7 [1]Lit. *made fat*
8 [a]Is. 63:4
9 [a]Deut. 29:23; Ps. 11:6; Is. 30:33
10 [a]Rev. 14:11; 18:18; 19:3 [b]Is. 13:20–22; 24:1; 34:10–15; Mal. 1:3, 4
11 [a]Is. 14:23; Zeph. 2:14; Rev. 18:2 [b]2 Kin. 21:13; Lam. 2:8 [1]Or *owl* [2]Or *hedgehog*
13 [a]Is. 32:13; Hos. 9:6 [b]Is. 13:21
14 [1]Lit. *howling creatures* [2]Heb. *lilith*

34:1—35:10 Isaiah continues to alternate between woe and judgment upon the rebellious (ch. 34) and promises of peace and blessing for the faithful (ch. 35). Because the prophecies are apocalyptic, much of the language is symbolic.
34:1–17 Nations: See note on 13:1—23:18.
34:5 Edom: A land southeast of the Dead Sea inhabited by the descendants of Esau; it included the land of Mt. Seir, its highest peak, and Sela (Petra), its capital city. Edom, almost always Israel's enemy, who rejoiced at the fall of Jerusalem, is symbolic of all evil and hostile nations. See note on Obad. 10, 11.
34:6 Bozrah: A chief city in Edom (Idumea); its name means "Impenetrable," and it is a symbol of evil's pride. The destruction of rebellious nations, of which Edom and Bozrah are symbols, will be so complete that it is typified by the barrenness of a land of thorns and wild animals (vv. 13–15).

And find for herself a place of
rest.
15 There the arrow snake shall make
her nest and lay *eggs*
And hatch, and gather *them*
under her shadow;
There also shall the hawks be
gathered,
Every one with her mate.

16 "Search from [a]the book of the
LORD, and read:
Not one of these shall fail;
Not one shall lack her mate.
For My mouth has commanded it,
and His Spirit has gathered
them.
17 He has cast the lot for them,
And His hand has divided it
among them with a measuring
line.
They shall possess it forever;
From generation to generation
they shall dwell in it."

The Future Glory of Zion

35 The [a]wilderness and the
[1]wasteland shall *be glad for
them,
And the [b]desert[2] shall rejoice and
blossom as the rose;
2 [a]It shall blossom abundantly and
rejoice,
Even with joy and singing.
The glory of Lebanon shall be
given to it,
The excellence of Carmel and
Sharon.
They shall see the [b]glory of the
LORD,
The excellency of our God.

3 [a]Strengthen* the [1]weak hands,
And make firm the [2]feeble knees.
4 Say to those *who are* fearful-
hearted,
"Be strong, do not *fear!
Behold, your God will come *with*
[a]vengeance,
With the recompense of God;
He will come and [b]save you."

16 [a][Mal. 3:16]

CHAPTER 35

1 [a]Is. 32:15; 55:12 [b]Is. 41:19; 51:3 [1]*desert* [2]Heb. *arabah* *See WW at Is. 64:5.
2 [a]Is. 32:15 [b]Is. 40:5
3 [a]Job 4:3, 4; Heb. 12:12 [1]Lit. *sinking* [2]*tottering or stumbling* *See WW at Josh. 1:9.
4 [a]Is. 34:8 [b]Ps. 145:19; Is. 33:22 *See WW at Ex. 1:17.
5 [a]Is. 29:18; Matt. 9:27; John 9:6, 7 [b][Matt. 11:5]
6 [a]Matt. 11:5; 15:30; John 5:8, 9; Acts 8:7 [b]Is. 32:4; Matt. 9:32; 12:22 [c]Is. 41:18; [John 7:38]
7 [a]Is. 34:13
8 [a]Is. 19:23 [b]Is. 52:1; Joel 3:17; [Matt. 7:13, 14]; 1 Pet. 1:15, 16; Rev. 21:27
9 [a]Lev. 26:6; [Is. 11:7, 9]; Ezek. 34:25 *See WW at Is. 52:9.
10 [a]Is. 51:11 [b]Is. 25:8; 30:19; 65:19; [Rev. 7:17; 21:4] *See WW at Neh. 1:10.

CHAPTER 36

1 [a]2 Kin. 18:13, 17; 2 Chr. 32:1

5 Then the [a]eyes of the blind shall
be opened,
And [b]the ears of the deaf shall be
unstopped.
6 Then the [a]lame shall leap like a
deer,
And the [b]tongue of the dumb
sing.
For [c]waters shall burst forth in
the wilderness,
And streams in the desert.
7 The parched ground shall become
a pool,
And the thirsty land springs of
water;
In [a]the habitation of jackals,
where each lay,
There shall be grass with reeds
and rushes.

8 A [a]highway shall be there, and a
road,
And it shall be called the
Highway of Holiness.
[b]The unclean shall not pass over
it,
But it *shall be* for others.
Whoever walks the road,
although a fool,
Shall not go astray.
9 [a]No lion shall be there,
Nor shall *any* ravenous beast go
up on it;
It shall not be found there.
But the *redeemed shall walk
there,
10 And the [a]ransomed* of the LORD
shall return,
And come to Zion with singing,
With everlasting joy on their
heads.
They shall obtain joy and
gladness,
And [b]sorrow and sighing shall
flee away.

Sennacherib Boasts Against the LORD

36 Now [a]it came to pass in the
fourteenth year of King Hezekiah *that* Sennacherib king of Assyria

34:16, 17 The book likely refers to similar sections earlier in Isaiah. **Cast the lot** means Yahweh has irrevocably ordained the judgment symbolized by the wild animals' inhabitation.

35:1–10 After the judgments are consummated, God will reign in righteousness and peace. This section is again messianic, fulfilled in stages by the ministry of Christ. See notes on 32:1–8 and Obad. 15.

35:2 The beauty of the messianic reign is likened to that of **Lebanon, Carmel,** and **Sharon,** the beauty spots of Israel. See note on 29:17–24.

35:3 Heb. 12:12 quotes this verse as part of a Christian's response to God's discipline process. This again shows the multifaceted application of such messianic promises. See note on vv. 1–10.

35:8–10 Holiness is a basic attribute of Yahweh. Isaiah refers to the Lord 26 times as the "Holy One of Israel." Those who share in God's holiness by justification through Christ will **walk** the **Highway** of Holiness with **joy and gladness.**

36:1—39:8 A near verbatim repeat of 2 Kin. 18:17—20:19. The section forms a link between Isaiah's woe section (chs. 1—35) and his comfort section (chs. 40—66). It also serves

came up against all the fortified cities
of Judah and took them.

KINGDOM DYNAMICS

36:1—37:40 God Intervenes with Power, PRAYER. Hezekiah's being threatened with destruction by Sennacherib's army reminds us that even the righteous are often overtaken by trouble. The Assyrian monarch invaded Judah, took 46 fortified cities, carried away 200,000 people, and shut up Hezekiah in Jerusalem like a bird in a cage. But note how Isaiah and Hezekiah went to prayer, their anguish over Sennacherib's blasphemy of God's name rising above their anxiety for Jerusalem (37:16, 17).

Consider the magnitude of the crisis. If Sennacherib had taken Jerusalem, the Jews could have ceased to exist as a nation. The messianic promise of God's kingdom's eventually triumphing on Earth was in the balance. But when Hezekiah and Isaiah prayed, God intervened with a demonstration of supernatural power that proved to Assyria that He was God indeed (37:36). From that point on, Assyria, which had enjoyed a two-century span of conquests, began its decline—a lesson in the power of prayer to 1) face troublesome times and 2) break evil powers.

(Josh. 10:12–14/Ezek. 22:30) L.L.

2 Then the king of Assyria sent *the*
[1]Rabshakeh with a great army from
Lachish to King Hezekiah at Jerusalem. And he stood by the aqueduct
from the upper pool, on the highway
to the Fuller's Field.
3 And [a]Eliakim the son of Hilkiah,
who was over the household, [b]Shebna
the scribe, and Joah the son of Asaph,
the recorder, came out to him.
4 [a]Then *the* Rabshakeh said to them,
"Say now to Hezekiah, 'Thus says the
great king, the king of Assyria: "What
confidence is this in which you trust?
5 "I say you speak of having plans
and power for war; but *they are*
[1]mere words. Now in whom do you
trust, that you rebel against me?
6 "Look! You are trusting in the
[a]staff of this broken reed, Egypt, on
which if a man leans, it will go into
his hand and pierce it. So *is* Pharaoh
king of Egypt to all who [b]trust in him.
7 "But if you say to me, 'We trust in
the LORD our God,' *is it* not He whose
high places and whose altars Hezekiah
has taken away, and said to Judah and
Jerusalem, 'You shall worship before
this altar'?" '
8 "Now therefore, I urge you, give a
pledge to my master the king of Assyria, and I will give you two thousand
horses—if you are *able on your part
to put riders on them!
9 "How then will you repel one captain of the least of my master's servants, and put your trust in Egypt for
chariots and horsemen?
10 "Have I now come up without the
LORD against this land to destroy it?
The LORD said to me, 'Go up against
this land, and destroy it.' "
11 Then Eliakim, Shebna, and Joah
said to *the* Rabshakeh, "Please speak
to your servants in Aramaic, for we understand *it;* and do not speak to us in
[1]Hebrew in the hearing of the people
who *are* on the wall."
12 But *the* Rabshakeh said, "Has my
master sent me to your master and to
you to speak these words, and not to
the men who sit on the wall, who will
eat and drink their own waste with
you?"
13 Then *the* Rabshakeh stood and
called out with a loud voice in Hebrew,
and said, "Hear the words of the great
king, the king of Assyria!
14 "Thus says the king: 'Do not let

2 [1]A title, probably *Chief of Staff* or *Governor*
3 [a]Is. 22:20 [b]Is. 22:15
4 [a]2 Kin. 18:19
5 [1]Lit. *a word of the lips*
6 [a]Ezek. 29:6 [b]Ps. 146:3; Is. 30:3, 5, 7
8 *See WW at Num. 13:30.
11 [1]Lit. *Judean*

as a transition in Judah's history from the dominance of Assyria to the role of Babylon.

The historical setting is the ill-fated invasion of Jerusalem by Sennacherib in 701 B.C. The chapters are written in prose, except for a prophetic utterance by Isaiah and King Hezekiah's poem of praise. See notes on 22:5–7 and 2 Kin. 18:13–37.

36:1 Fourteenth year: See note on 2 Kin. 18:1, 13.

36:2 Rabshakeh: This Aramaic word is not a name but a title, meaning "cupbearer," "field marshal," or "Chief of Staff" (marginal note). **Lachish** was a fortified city of Judah 30 miles southwest of Jerusalem.

36:4–6 What confidence is this? Judah under Ahaz had made an alliance with and paid tribute to Assyria. Because of fear of invasion by Assyria, Hezekiah, along with leaders of other nations, had wrongly made an alliance with **Egypt.** Sennacherib invaded to put down the rebellion. See note on 30:1–33.

36:7–10 Hezekiah had destroyed the places of idol worship in Jerusalem (2 Chr. 29; 30). Following the reform, zealous Judahites moved throughout the countryside destroying other places of worship (2 Chr. 31:1). The Rabshakeh deridingly suggests **Hezekiah** may have even had them destroy places of Yahweh worship (v. 7). Furthermore, because the people of Judah had been guilty of worship at these shrines, he argues that **the LORD** told him to **destroy** Judah. He is, in part, correct. See notes on ch. 30.

36:11–20 Rabshakeh made his threats **in Hebrew** rather than **in Aramaic,** the diplomatic language, in order to intimidate the soldiers **on the wall.** He casts doubt on Hezekiah's integrity and then recalls Assyria's seemingly endless military victories. His **boast** against the very Lord he claimed to represent (v. 10) will be his downfall.

Hamath and **Arpad** were cities of Syria, which fell to Assyria between 740 and 722 B.C. **Sepharvaim** was a city of unknown location.

Hezekiah deceive you, for he will not
be able to deliver you;
15 'nor let Hezekiah make you trust in
the LORD, saying, "The LORD will surely
deliver us; this city will not be given
into the hand of the king of Assyria." '
16 "Do not listen to Hezekiah; for thus
says the king of Assyria: 'Make *peace*
with me *by a* present and come out to
me; [a]and every one of you eat from his
own vine and every one from his own
fig tree, and every one of you drink the
waters of his own cistern;
17 'until I come and take you away to
a land like your own land, a land of
grain and new wine, a land of bread
and vineyards.
18 '*Beware* lest Hezekiah persuade
you, saying, "The LORD will deliver
us." Has any one of the [a]gods of the
nations delivered its land from the
hand of the king of Assyria?
19 'Where *are* the gods of Hamath and
Arpad? Where *are* the gods of Sepharvaim? Indeed, have they delivered
[a]Samaria from my hand?
20 'Who among all the gods of these
lands have delivered their countries
from my hand, that the LORD should
deliver Jerusalem from my hand?' "
21 But they [1]held their peace and answered him not a word; for the king's
commandment was, "Do not answer
him."
22 Then Eliakim the son of Hilkiah,
who *was* over the household, Shebna
the scribe, and Joah the son of Asaph,
the recorder, came to Hezekiah with
their clothes torn, and told him the
words of *the* Rabshakeh.

Isaiah Assures Deliverance

37 And [a]so it was, when King Hezekiah heard *it,* that he tore his
clothes, covered himself with sackcloth, and went into the house of the
LORD.
2 Then he sent Eliakim, who *was* over
the household, Shebna the scribe, and
the elders of the priests, covered with
sackcloth, to Isaiah the *prophet, the
son of Amoz.
3 And they said to him, "Thus says
Hezekiah: 'This day *is* a day of [a]trouble
and rebuke and [1]blasphemy; for the
children have come to birth, but *there*
is no strength to bring them forth.
4 'It may be that the LORD your God
will hear the words of *the* Rabshakeh,
whom his master the king of Assyria
has sent to [a]reproach the living God,
and will rebuke the words which the
LORD your God has heard. Therefore
lift up *your* prayer for the remnant that
is left.' "
5 So the servants of King Hezekiah
came to Isaiah.
6 And Isaiah said to them, "Thus you
shall say to your master, 'Thus says the
LORD: "Do not be afraid of the words
which you have heard, with which the
servants of the king of Assyria have
blasphemed Me.
7 "Surely I will send a spirit upon
him, and he shall hear a rumor and return to his own land; and I will cause
him to fall by the sword in his own
land." ' "

Sennacherib's Threat and Hezekiah's Prayer

8 Then *the* Rabshakeh returned, and
found the king of Assyria warring
against Libnah, for he heard that he
had departed from Lachish.
9 And the king heard concerning Tirhakah king of Ethiopia, "He has come
out to make war with you." So when
he heard *it,* he sent messengers to Hezekiah, saying,
10 "Thus you shall speak to Hezekiah
king of Judah, saying: 'Do not let your
God in whom you trust deceive you,
saying, "Jerusalem shall not be given
into the hand of the king of Assyria."
11 'Look! You have heard what the
kings of Assyria have done to all lands
by utterly destroying them; and shall
you be delivered?
12 'Have the [a]gods of the nations delivered those whom my fathers have destroyed, Gozan and Haran and Rezeph,
and the people of Eden who *were* in
Telassar?
13 'Where *is* the king of [a]Hamath, the
king of Arpad, and the king of the city
of Sepharvaim, Hena, and Ivah?' "
14 And Hezekiah received the letter

16 [a]1 Kin. 4:25; Mic. 4:4; Zech. 3:10
18 [a]2 Kin. 19:12; Is. 37:12
19 [a]2 Kin. 17:6
21 [1]*were silent*

CHAPTER 37

1 [a]2 Kin. 19:1–37; Is. 37:1–38
2 *See WW at 1 Sam. 3:20.
3 [a]Is. 22:5; 26:16; 33:2 [1]*contempt*
4 [a]Is. 36:15, 18, 20
12 [a]Is. 36:18, 19
13 [a]Is. 49:23

36:22 ***Torn clothes*** *were a symbol of humility and repentance, like sackcloth.*
37:1–7 House of the LORD: ***The*** **Rabshakeh** relied upon threat, ridicule, and **blasphemy** to subdue Judah. **Hezekiah** went to the house of the Lord, and inquired of Isaiah. See notes on 2 Kin. 19:8–19; 19:35, 36.
37:8–13 Lachish (see note on 36:2) has apparently fallen. Sennacherib moved to destroy **Libnah,** another Judean city, when he heard Egypt had entered battle to help **Jerusalem** (**Tirhakah . . . Ethiopia**). This prompts a letter **to Hezekiah** with content similar to the verbal threat made by ***the*** **Rabshakeh**. See note on 36:11–20.
37:12, 13 Assyria had destroyed numerous Mesopotamian cities and their **gods.**
37:14–20 See note on vv. 1–7.

from the hand of the messengers, and
read it; and Hezekiah went up to the
house of the LORD, and spread it before
the LORD.
15 Then Hezekiah prayed to the LORD,
saying:
16 "O LORD of hosts, God of Israel, *the*
One who dwells *between* the *cherubim, You *are* God, You [a]alone, of all
the kingdoms of the earth. You have
made heaven and earth.
17 [a]"Incline Your ear, O LORD, and
hear; open Your eyes, O LORD, and see;
and [b]hear all the words of Sennacherib, which he has sent to reproach
the living God.
18 "Truly, LORD, the kings of Assyria
have laid waste all the nations and
their [a]lands,
19 "and have cast their gods into the
fire; for they *were* [a]not gods, but the
work of men's hands—wood and stone.
Therefore they destroyed them.
20 "Now therefore, O LORD our God,
[a]save us from his hand, that all the
kingdoms of the earth may [b]know that
You *are* the LORD, You alone."

The Word of the LORD Concerning Sennacherib

21 Then Isaiah the son of Amoz sent
to Hezekiah, saying, "Thus says the
LORD God of Israel, 'Because you have
prayed to Me against Sennacherib king
of Assyria,
22 'this *is* the word which the LORD has
spoken concerning him:

"The *virgin, the daughter of Zion,
Has despised you, laughed you to
scorn;
The daughter of Jerusalem
Has shaken *her* head behind your
back!

23 "Whom have you reproached and
blasphemed?
Against whom have you raised
your voice,
And lifted up your eyes on high?
Against the Holy One of Israel.
24 By your servants you have
reproached the Lord,
And said, 'By the multitude of my
chariots
I have come up to the height of
the mountains,
To the limits of Lebanon;
I will cut down its tall cedars
And its choice cypress trees;
I will enter its farthest height,
To its fruitful forest.
25 I have dug and drunk water,
And with the soles of my feet I
have dried up
All the brooks of [1]defense.'

26 "Did you not hear [a]long ago
How I made it,
From ancient times that I formed
it?
Now I have brought it to pass,
That you should be
For crushing fortified cities *into*
heaps of ruins.
27 Therefore their inhabitants *had*
little power;
They were dismayed and
confounded;
They were *as* the grass of the field
And the green herb,
As the grass on the housetops
And *grain* blighted before it is
grown.

28 "But I know your dwelling place,
Your going out and your coming
in,
And your rage against Me.
29 Because your rage against Me
and your tumult
Have come up to My ears,
Therefore [a]I will put My hook in
your nose
And My bridle in your lips,
And I will [b]turn you back
By the way which you came." '

30 "This *shall be* a sign to you:

You shall eat this year such as
grows of itself,
And the second year what springs
from the same;
Also in the third year sow and
reap,
Plant vineyards and eat the fruit
of them.
31 And the remnant who have
escaped of the house of Judah
Shall again take root downward,
And bear fruit upward.
32 For out of Jerusalem shall go a
remnant,

16 [a]Is. 43:10, 11 *See WW at Ex. 25:18.
17 [a]2 Chr. 6:40; Ps. 17:6; Dan. 9:18 [b]Ps. 74:22
18 [a]2 Kin. 15:29; 16:9; 17:6, 24; 1 Chr. 5:26
19 [a]Is. 40:19, 20
20 [a]Is. 33:22 [b]Ps. 83:18
22 *See WW at Ps. 45:14.

25 [1]Or perhaps *Egypt*
26 [a]Is. 25:1; 40:21; 45:21
29 [a]2 Kin. 19:35–37; 2 Chr. 32:21; Is. 30:28; Ezek. 38:4 [b]Ezek. 38:4; 39:2

37:21–29 Through **Isaiah, the LORD** speaks concerning **Sennacherib.** See notes on 10:5–11 and 10:7, 8.
37:26 From ancient times reflects the doctrine of the sovereignty of God. Nations may glory in their conquests, as did Assyria, but it is God who uses them as His instruments.
37:30–32 The Lord now addresses His message to King Hezekiah. He offers **a sign** that Judeans would survive the siege as a testimony to His faithfulness.

And those who escape from
Mount Zion.
The [a]zeal of the LORD of hosts will
do this.

33 "Therefore thus says the LORD concerning the king of Assyria:

'He shall not come into this city,
Nor shoot an arrow there,
Nor come before it with shield,
Nor build a siege mound against
it.
34 By the way that he came,
By the same shall he return;
And he shall not come into this
city,'
Says the LORD.
35 'For I will [a]defend this city, to
save it
For My own sake and for My
servant [b]David's sake.' "

Sennacherib's Defeat and Death

36 Then the [a]angel[1] of the LORD went
out, and [2]killed in the camp of the Assyrians one hundred and eighty-five
thousand; and when *people* arose early
in the morning, there were the
corpses—all dead.
37 So Sennacherib king of Assyria departed and went away, returned *home*,
and remained at Nineveh.
38 Now it came to pass, as he was worshiping in the house of Nisroch his god,
that his sons Adrammelech and Sharezer struck him down with the sword;
and they escaped into the land of Ararat. Then [a]Esarhaddon his son reigned
in his place.

Hezekiah's Life Extended

38 In [a]those days Hezekiah was
sick and near death. And Isaiah
the prophet, the son of Amoz, went to
him and said to him, "Thus says the
LORD: [b]'Set your house in order, for
you shall die and not live.' "
2 Then Hezekiah turned his face toward the wall, and *prayed to the LORD,
3 and said, [a]"Remember* now, O
LORD, I pray, how I have walked before
You in truth and with a [1]loyal heart,
and have done *what is* good in Your

32 [a]2 Kin. 19:31; Is. 9:7; 59:17; Joel 2:18; Zech. 1:14
35 [a]2 Kin. 20:6; Is. 31:5; 38:6 [b]1 Kin. 11:13
36 [a]2 Kin. 19:35; Is. 10:12, 33, 34 [1]Or *Angel* [2]Lit. *struck*
38 [a]Ezra 4:2

CHAPTER 38

1 [a]2 Kin. 20:1–6, 9–11; 2 Chr. 32:24; Is. 38:1–8 [b]2 Sam. 17:23
2 *See WW at Job 42:10.
3 [a]Neh. 13:14 [b]2 Kin. 18:5, 6; Ps. 26:3 [1]*whole or peaceful* *See WW at Is. 62:6.
5 *See WW at 2 Chr. 6:20.
6 [a]2 Kin. 19:35–37; 2 Chr. 32:21; Is. 31:5; 37:35
7 [a]Judg. 6:17, 21, 36–40; 2 Kin. 20:8; Is. 7:11
11 [a]Ps. 27:13; 116:9 [1]Heb. YAH, YAH [2]LXX omits *among the inhabitants of the world* [3]So with some Heb. mss.; MT, Vg. *rest;* Tg. *land* *See WW at Gen. 1:26.
12 [a]Job 7:6
14 [a]Is. 59:11; Ezek. 7:16; Nah. 2:7 [1]So with Bg.; MT, DSS *Lord* [2]*Be my surety*

[b]sight." And Hezekiah wept bitterly.
4 And the word of the LORD came to
Isaiah, saying,
5 "Go and tell Hezekiah, 'Thus says
the LORD, the God of David your father:
"I have heard your *prayer, I have seen
your tears; surely I will add to your
days fifteen years.
6 "I will deliver you and this city from
the hand of the king of Assyria, and
[a]I will defend this city." '
7 "And this *is* [a]the sign to you from
the LORD, that the LORD will do this
thing which He has spoken:
8 "Behold, I will bring the shadow on
the sundial, which has gone down with
the sun on the sundial of Ahaz, ten degrees backward." So the sun returned
ten degrees on the dial by which it had
gone down.
9 This is the writing of Hezekiah king
of Judah, when he had been sick and
had recovered from his sickness:

10 I said,
"In the prime of my life
I shall go to the gates of Sheol;
I am deprived of the remainder
of my years."
11 I said,
"I shall not see [1]YAH,
The LORD [a]in the land of the
living;
I shall observe *man no more
[2]among the inhabitants of
[3]the world.
12 [a]My life span is gone,
Taken from me like a shepherd's
tent;
I have cut off my life like a
weaver.
He cuts me off from the loom;
From day until night You make
an end of me.
13 I have considered until morning—
Like a lion,
So He breaks all my bones;
From day until night You make
an end of me.
14 Like a crane *or* a swallow, so I
chattered;
[a]I mourned like a dove;
My eyes fail *from looking*
upward.
O [1]LORD, I am oppressed;
[2]Undertake for me!

37:33–35 The LORD prophesies the failure of the Assyrian invasion of Jerusalem. Sennacherib's defeat was the result of earnest prayer by Hezekiah.
37:36–38 See notes on 2 Kin. 19:35, 36 and 19:37.
38:1–22 Ch. 38 is the account of the life-threatening illness of King Hezekiah and his miraculous healing in answer to prayer. See note on 2 Kin. 20:1–7.
38:8 See note on 2 Kin. 20:8–11.
38:9–20 These verses express Hezekiah's reaction to the thought of being doomed to death. He appeals to God for help. When he receives it, he evaluates the meaning of life in terms of worshiping God. Doing so, he exemplifies the NT believer's attitude at being rescued from death and given eternal life.

15 "What shall I say?
[1]He has both spoken to me,
And He Himself has done *it.*
I shall walk carefully all my years
[a]In the bitterness of my soul.
16 O Lord, by these *things men* live;
And in all these *things is* the life
of my spirit;
So You will restore me and make
me live.
17 Indeed *it was* for *my own* peace
That I had great bitterness;
But You have lovingly *delivered*
my soul from the pit of
corruption,
For You have cast all my sins
behind Your back.
18 For [a]Sheol cannot thank You,
Death cannot *praise You;
Those who go down to the pit
cannot hope for Your truth.
19 The living, the living man, he
shall praise You,
As I *do* this day;
[a]The father shall make known
Your truth to the children.

20 "The LORD *was ready* to save me;
Therefore we will sing my songs
with stringed instruments
All the days of our life, in the
house of the LORD."

21 Now [a]Isaiah had said, "Let them
take a lump of figs, and apply *it* as a
poultice on the boil, and he shall recover."
22 And [a]Hezekiah had said, "What *is*
the sign that I shall go up to the house
of the LORD?"

The Babylonian Envoys

39 At [a]that time [1]Merodach-
Baladan the son of Baladan,
king of Babylon, sent letters and a present to Hezekiah, for he heard that he
had been sick and had recovered.

15 [a]Job 7:11; 10:1; Is. 38:17 [1]So with MT, Vg.; DSS, Tg. *And shall I say to Him;* LXX omits first half of this verse
18 [a]Ps. 6:5; 30:9; 88:11; 115:17; [Eccl. 9:10] *See WW at 1 Chr. 16:7.
19 [a]Deut. 4:9; 6:7; Ps. 78:3, 4
21 [a]2 Kin. 20:7
22 [a]2 Kin. 20:8

CHAPTER 39

1 [a]2 Kin. 20:12–19; 2 Chr. 32:31; Is. 39:1–8 [1]*Berodach-Baladan,* 2 Kin. 20:12
2 [a]2 Chr. 32:25, 31; Job 31:25
3 [a]Deut. 28:49; Jer. 5:15 *See WW at 1 Sam. 3:20.
6 [a]2 Kin. 24:13; 25:13–15; Jer. 20:5
7 [a]Dan. 1:1–7
8 [a]1 Sam. 3:18

CHAPTER 40

1 *See WW at Ruth 1:16.
2 [1]Lit. *to the heart of* *See WW at Ps. 130:3.

2 [a]And Hezekiah was pleased with
them, and showed them the house of
his treasures—the silver and gold, the
spices and precious ointment, and all
his armory—all that was found among
his treasures. There was nothing in his
house or in all his dominion that Hezekiah did not show them.
3 Then Isaiah the *prophet went to
King Hezekiah, and said to him, "What
did these men say, and from where did
they come to you?" So Hezekiah said,
"They came to me from a [a]far country,
from Babylon."
4 And he said, "What have they seen
in your house?" So Hezekiah answered, "They have seen all that *is* in
my house; there is nothing among
my treasures that I have not shown
them."
5 Then Isaiah said to Hezekiah,
"Hear the word of the LORD of hosts:
6 'Behold, the days are coming
[a]when all that *is* in your house, and
what your fathers have accumulated
until this day, shall be carried to Babylon; nothing shall be left,' says the
LORD.
7 'And they shall take away *some* of
your [a]sons who will descend from you,
whom you will beget; and they shall
be eunuchs in the palace of the king
of Babylon.'"
8 So Hezekiah said to Isaiah, [a]"The
word of the LORD which you have spoken *is* good!" For he said, "At least
there will be peace and truth in my
days."

God's People Are Comforted

40 "Comfort, yes, comfort My
*people!"
Says your God.
2 "Speak [1]comfort to Jerusalem, and
cry out to her,
That her warfare is ended,
That her *iniquity is pardoned;

38:15–20 ***It was for my own peace:*** God's promise of healing brought joyful relief to the king; his spirit was totally revived.
38:21 God chose to miraculously heal Hezekiah through a simple medical procedure (see John 9:6–15). It is not clear why a simple **boil** was nearly fatal (v. 1).
39:1–8 This chapter recounts Hezekiah's great diplomatic blunder. Because of pride in wealth and military might, he showed the Babylonian envoys all the treasures and arms of Judah. **Isaiah** rebuked **Hezekiah** and predicted that one day **Babylon** would carry away all the wealth along with the people themselves. The prophecy was fulfilled 100 years later, exactly according to Isaiah's prediction. Instead of repentance for prideful error, the king merely remarked that he, at least, would have **peace** during his reign. See note on 2 Kin. 20:12–19.
39:1 Merodach-Baladan means "The God Marduk Has Given an Heir." He died about 695 B.C.
40:1 Comfort My people: Ch. 40 is transitional, paving the way for the remainder of the Book of Isaiah. Chs. 1—39 dealt predominantly with burdens of judgment against disobedient Judah, Israel, and the pagan nations. Beginning with ch. 40 Isaiah prophesies Jacob/Israel' s return from captivity and deals primarily with comfort, peace, the Messiah's advent, and His future reign. Some scholars see in the change of subject matter a change in authorship also. This is not likely. See Introduction to Isaiah: Author.
40:2 Jerusalem . . . her warfare is ended clearly marks a change of Jerusalem's status from previous chapters. Isaiah is speaking from the standpoint of her fall in 587 B.C., although that will not happen for over 100 years. See note on 39:1–8.

[a]For she has received from the
LORD's hand
Double for all her sins."

3 [a]The voice of one crying in the
wilderness:
[b]"Prepare the way of the LORD;
[c]Make* straight [1]in the desert
A highway for our God.
4 Every valley shall be exalted
And every mountain and hill
*brought low;
[a]The crooked places shall be made
[1]straight
And the rough places smooth;
5 The [a]glory* of the LORD shall be
*revealed,
And all flesh shall see *it* together;
For the mouth of the LORD has
spoken."

6 The voice said, "Cry out!"
And [1]he said, "What shall I cry?"

[a]"All *flesh *is* grass,
And all its loveliness *is* like the
flower of the field.
7 The grass withers, the flower
fades,
Because the breath of the LORD
blows upon it;
Surely the people *are* grass.
8 The grass withers, the flower
fades,
But [a]the word of our God stands
forever."

9 O Zion,
You who bring good tidings,
Get up into the high mountain;
O Jerusalem,
You who bring good tidings,
Lift up your voice with strength,
Lift *it* up, be not afraid;
Say to the cities of Judah,
"Behold your God!"

10 Behold, the Lord GOD shall come
[1]with a strong *hand,*
And [a]His arm shall rule for Him;
Behold, [b]His reward *is* with Him,
And His [2]work before Him.
11 He will [a]**feed** His flock like a
shepherd;
He will gather the lambs with His
arm,
And carry *them* in His bosom,
And gently lead those who are
with young.

2 [a]Is. 61:7
3 [a]Matt. 3:3; Mark 1:3; Luke 3:4–6; John 1:23 [b][Mal. 3:1; 4:5, 6] [c]Ps. 68:4 [1]So with MT, Tg., Vg.; LXX omits *in the desert* *See WW at Prov. 3:6.
4 [a]Is. 45:2 [1]Or *a plain* *See WW at Jer. 13:18.
5 [a]Is. 35:2 *See WW at Is. 60:1. • See WW at Amos 3:7.
6 [a]Job 14:2; James 1:10; 1 Pet. 1:24, 25 [1]So with MT, Tg.; DSS, LXX, Vg. *I* *See WW at Job 19:26.
8 [a][John 12:34]
10 [a]Is. 59:16, 18 [b]Is. 62:11; Rev. 22:12 [1]*in strength* [2]*recompense*
11 [a]Jer. 31:10; [Ezek. 34:23, 31]; Mic. 5:4; [John 10:11, 14–16; Heb. 13:20; 1 Pet. 2:25]

WORD WEALTH

40:11 feed, *ra'ah* (rah-*ah*); Strong's #7462: To shepherd, feed, tend; to pasture; to cause one's herd or flock to graze. *Ra'ah* has to do with tending and caring for one's animals, particularly by providing them with good pasture. This verb occurs more than 170 times in the OT. David's early duty to feed his father's flocks (1 Sam. 17:15) is followed by his later task of shepherding the heavenly Father's flock, Israel (Ps. 78:71). The participial form of *ra'ah* is *ro'eh,* "shepherd, tender of sheep, caretaker." *Ro'eh* appears in "The LORD *is* my shepherd; I shall not want" (Ps. 23:1). See also "Shepherd of Israel" in Ps. 80:1. Ezek. 34:23 and Mic. 5:4 describe the Messiah's responsibility as one of feeding and shepherding.

KINGDOM DYNAMICS

40:8–11 Spread the Good Tidings—Fearlessly, WORLD EVANGELISM. The prophet declares the eternal reminder: "The word of our God stands forever," and then anticipates the spread of that word. The world needs a sound foundation upon which to build life, just as surely as it needs a sure salvation to redeem it. "Zion"—the people of God—have that word and are privileged to bring these "good tidings"—the pleasant, happy, and wholesome news of life now and hope forever. Thus 1) "Lift up your voice" (v. 9). The message is to proclaim good tidings, for nothing will happen until that declaration is made. 2) "Be not afraid" (v. 9); for God will manifest Himself as the proclaimer says, "Behold your God!" (v. 9). 3) Our message of One who has strength to rule ("a strong *hand*") and a reward to give ("*is* with Him," v. 10) will be confirmed. Answering our call to spread "good tidings," we are wise to be fearlessly obedient, believing God to confirm His word (Mark 16:20). Jesus tells of the servant who buried his talent, saying, "I was afraid!" Let God's perfect love and powerful promise cast out fears, and speak "Behold" to those He allows us to address with His Good News. He will confirm His word with proving power.

(Prov. 24:11, 12/Matt. 13:37, 38) G.C.

40:3–5 God is pictured as returning to Jerusalem from the Arabah. Jerusalem's judgment had called for His departure. See note on Ezek. 10:1–22. Matt. 3:3 applies v. 3 to John the Baptist's heralding of Christ. This clearly indicates that God's ultimate return is through the Messiah, to a very different Jerusalem. See notes on Ezek. 40:1—48:35; Gal. 6:16; Rev. 21:2.

40:6–11 All flesh refers to Babylon who shall also fall, allowing the remnant to return. See note on 21:1–10. The verses also apply to mankind's frailty in general and God's reign through the Messiah.

12 [a]Who has measured the [1]waters in
the hollow of His hand,
Measured heaven with a
[2]span
And calculated the dust of the
earth in a measure?
Weighed the mountains in scales
And the hills in a balance?
13 [a]Who has directed the Spirit of the
LORD,
Or *as* His counselor has taught
Him?
14 With whom did He take counsel,
and *who* instructed Him,
And [a]taught Him in the path of
justice?
Who taught Him knowledge,
And showed Him the way of
understanding?

15 Behold, the nations *are* as a drop
in a bucket,
And are counted as the small dust
on the scales;
Look, He lifts up the isles as a
very little thing.
16 And Lebanon *is* not *sufficient to
burn,
Nor its beasts sufficient for a
burnt offering.
17 All nations before Him *are* as
[a]nothing,
And [b]they are counted by Him
less than nothing and
worthless.

18 To whom then will you [a]liken
God?
Or what likeness will you
compare to Him?
19 [a]The workman molds an image,
The goldsmith overspreads it
with gold,
And the silversmith casts silver
chains.
20 Whoever *is* too impoverished for
such [1]a contribution
Chooses a tree *that* will not rot;
He seeks for himself a skillful
workman
[a]To prepare a carved image *that*
will not totter.

12 [a]Prov. 30:4 [1]So with MT, LXX, Vg.; DSS adds *of the sea;* Tg. adds *of the world* [2]A span = ½ cubit, 9 inches; or the width of His hand
13 [a]Job 21:22; Rom. 11:34; [1 Cor. 2:16]
14 [a]Job 36:22, 23
16 *See WW at Mal. 3:10.
17 [a]Dan. 4:35 [b]Ps. 62:9
18 [a]Ex. 8:10; 15:11; 1 Sam. 2:2; Is. 46:5; [Mic. 7:18]; Acts 17:29
19 [a]Ps. 115:4–8; Is. 41:7; 44:10; Hab. 2:18, 19
20 [a]1 Sam. 5:3, 4; Is. 41:7; 46:7; Jer. 10:3 [1]*an offering*
21 [a]Ps. 19:1; Is. 37:26; Acts 14:17; Rom. 1:19
22 [a]Job 9:8; Ps. 104:2; Is. 42:5; 44:24; Jer. 10:12 [b]Job 36:29; Ps. 19:4
23 [a]Job 12:21; Ps. 107:40; Is. 34:12; [1 Cor. 1:26–29] [1]*reduces*
25 [a][Deut. 4:15]; Is. 40:18; [John 14:9; Col. 1:15]
26 [a]Ps. 147:4
27 [a]Is. 54:7, 8

21 [a]Have you not known?
Have you not heard?
Has it not been told you from the
beginning?
Have you not understood from
the foundations of the earth?
22 *It is* He who sits above the circle
of the earth,
And its inhabitants *are* like
grasshoppers,
Who [a]stretches out the heavens
like a curtain,
And spreads them out like a
[b]tent to dwell in.
23 He [1]brings the [a]princes to
nothing;
He makes the judges of the earth
useless.

24 Scarcely shall they be planted,
Scarcely shall they be sown,
Scarcely shall their stock take
root in the earth,
When He will also blow on them,
And they will wither,
And the whirlwind will take them
away like stubble.

25 "To[a] whom then will you liken Me,
Or *to whom* shall I be equal?"
says the Holy One.
26 Lift up your eyes on high,
And see who has created these
things,
Who brings out their host by
number;
[a]He calls them all by name,
By the greatness of His might
And the strength of *His* power;
Not one is missing.

27 [a]Why do you say, O Jacob,
And speak, O Israel:
"My way is hidden from the LORD,
And my just claim is passed over
by my God"?
28 Have you not known?
Have you not heard?
The everlasting God, the LORD,
The Creator of the ends of the
earth,
Neither faints nor is weary.

40:12–31 Isaiah describes aspects of God's greatness, sovereignty, and future strategy for the world. They develop the idea of God's ultimate return to Jerusalem through the reign of the Messiah.

40:12–14 Measured the waters: God's omnipotence in the Creation and His infinite knowledge. See note on Job 36:1—37:24.

40:15–17 Nations . . . a drop in a bucket: A statement of the sovereignty of God over all nations. See note on 13:1—23:18.

40:18–20 Molds an image: Isaiah mocks the fact that man thinks God's greatness can be captured in **a carved image.** This is the essence of the Second Commandment (Ex. 20:4–6).

40:27–31 My way is hidden: A proper understanding of God's dealings in life comes only by knowing His perspective and ways. This calls for great patience (v. 31). **Wait on the LORD** means to go about the routines of life with a fervent, patient hope that He will consummate His rule in His time; He *will* deal with evil. Such an inner attitude gives one **strength** to **mount up** above the moment, with vigor to go on. See Rom. 8:18–30.

[a]His understanding is
unsearchable.
29 He gives *power to the weak,
And to *those who have* no might
He increases strength.
30 Even the youths shall faint and
be weary,
And the young men shall utterly
fall,
31 But those who [a]wait* on the LORD
[b]Shall renew *their* strength;
They shall mount up with wings
like eagles,
They shall run and not be weary,
They shall walk and not faint.

Israel Assured of God's Help

41 "Keep [a]silence before Me,
O coastlands,
And let the people renew *their*
strength!
Let them come near, then let them
speak;
Let us [b]come near together for
judgment.

2 "Who raised up one [a]from the
east?
Who in righteousness called him
to His feet?
Who [b]gave the nations before
him,
And made *him* rule over kings?
Who gave *them* as the dust *to* his
sword,
As driven stubble to his bow?
3 Who pursued them, *and* passed
[1]safely
By the way *that* he had not gone
with his feet?
4 [a]Who has performed and done *it,*
Calling the generations from the
beginning?
'I, the LORD, am [b]the first;
And with the last I *am* [c]He.' "

5 The coastlands saw *it* and feared,
The ends of the earth were afraid;
They drew near and came.

6 [a]Everyone helped his neighbor,
And said to his brother,
[1]"Be of good courage!"
7 [a]So the craftsman encouraged the
[b]goldsmith;[1]
He who smooths *with* the
hammer *inspired* him who
strikes the anvil,
Saying, [2]"It *is* ready for the
soldering";
Then he fastened it with pegs,
[c]*That* it might not totter.

8 "But you, Israel, *are* My servant,
Jacob whom I have [a]chosen,
The descendants of Abraham My
[b]friend.
9 *You* whom I have taken from the
ends of the earth,
And called from its farthest
regions,
And said to you,
'You *are* My servant,
I have chosen you and have not
cast you away:
10 [a]Fear not, [b]for I *am* with you;
Be not dismayed, for I *am* your
God.
I will strengthen you,
Yes, I will help you,
I will uphold you with My
righteous right hand.'

11 "Behold, all those who were
incensed against you
Shall be [a]ashamed and disgraced;
They shall be as nothing,
And those who strive with you
shall perish.
12 You shall seek them and not find
them—
[1]Those who contended with
you.
Those who war against you
Shall be as nothing,
As a nonexistent thing.
13 For I, the LORD your God, will
hold your right hand,
Saying to you, 'Fear not, I will
help you.'

28 [a]Ps. 147:5; Eccl. 11:5; Rom. 11:33
29 *See WW at Deut. 8:18.
31 [a]Is. 30:15; 49:23 [b][Job 17:9]; Ps. 103:5; [2 Cor. 4:8–10, 16] *See WW at Lam. 3:25.

CHAPTER 41

1 [a]Hab. 2:20; Zech. 2:13 [b]Is. 1:18
2 [a]Is. 46:11 [b]Gen. 14:14; Is. 45:1, 13
3 [1]Lit. *in peace*
4 [a]Is. 41:26 [b]Rev. 1:8, 17; 22:13 [c]Is. 43:10; 44:6
6 [a]Is. 40:19 [1]Lit. *Be strong*
7 [a]Is. 44:13 [b]Is. 40:19 [c]Is. 40:20 [1]*refiner* [2]Or *The soldering is good*
8 [a]Deut. 7:6; 10:15; Ps. 135:4; [Is. 43:1] [b]2 Chr. 20:7; James 2:23
10 [a]Is. 41:13, 14; 43:5 [b][Deut. 31:6]
11 [a]Ex. 23:22; Is. 45:24; 60:12; Zech. 12:3
12 [1]Lit. *Men of your strife*

40:29–31 See section 4 of Truth-In-Action at the end of Is.
41:1–20 This section is a type of trial scene. Israel had complained against God's care (40:27); He now counters that idea by showing that her interests are in mind as He sovereignly controls nations.
41:1 ***Coastlands:*** *Philistia and Phoenicia*, called as witnesses to the speech.
41:2, 3 One from the east: A reference to Cyrus, the successful Persian conqueror who would decree the release of Judah from captivity. God is behind his success. **By the way . . . his feet:** A master statesman, Cyrus won many victories through diplomacy, never having to travel personally to many areas to war.
41:4 God in His sovereign rule had foreordained Persia under Cyrus to be one of the great Gentile world powers and the emancipator of Judah.
41:5–7 The coastlands tremble with fear at the supremacy and sovereignty of God and resort vainly to their golden images.
41:8–13 My servant: Israel is called the servant of Yahweh as God reassures them of their special status as **descendants of Abraham.** They are to be His instrument of divine revelation, witness to the nations, and lineage of the Messiah (43:10; 44:1, 8, 21; 45:4; 48:20). Isaiah's use of "servant" develops Israel as a type of Christ, the ultimate Servant (42:1; 49:5; 50:4–10; 52:13; 53:11).

14 "Fear not, you [a]worm Jacob,
You men of Israel!
I will help you," says the LORD
And your Redeemer, the Holy One of Israel.
15 "Behold, [a]I will make you into a new threshing sledge with sharp teeth;
You shall thresh the mountains and beat *them* small,
And make the hills like chaff.
16 You shall [a]winnow them, the wind shall carry them away,
And the whirlwind shall scatter them;
You shall rejoice in the LORD,
And [b]glory in the Holy One of Israel.

17 "The poor and needy seek water, but *there is* none,
Their tongues fail for thirst.
I, the LORD, will hear them;
I, the God of Israel, will not [a]forsake them.
18 I will open [a]rivers in desolate heights,
And fountains in the midst of the valleys;
I will make the [b]wilderness a pool of water,
And the dry land springs of water.
19 I will plant in the wilderness the cedar and the acacia tree,
The myrtle and the oil tree;
I will set in the [a]desert the cypress tree *and* the pine
And the box tree together,
20 [a]That they may see and *know,
And consider and understand together,
That the hand of the LORD has done this,
And the Holy One of Israel has *created it.

The Futility of Idols

21 "Present your case," says the LORD.
"Bring forth your strong *reasons*," says the [a]King of Jacob.
22 "Let[a] them bring forth and show us what will happen;
Let them show the [b]former things, what they *were*,
That we may [1]consider them,
And know the latter end of them;
Or declare to us things to come.
23 [a]Show the things that are to come hereafter,
That we may know that you *are* gods;
Yes, [b]do good or do evil,
That we may be dismayed and see *it* together.
24 Indeed [a]you *are* nothing,
And your work *is* nothing;
He who chooses you *is* an abomination.

25 "I have raised up one from the north,
And he shall come;
From the [1]rising of the sun [a]he shall call on My name;
[b]And he shall come against princes as *though* mortar,
As the potter treads clay.
26 [a]Who has declared from the beginning, that we may know?
And former times, that we may say, '*He is* righteous'?
Surely *there is* no one who shows,
Surely *there is* no one who declares,
Surely *there is* no one who hears your words.
27 [a]The first time [b]*I said* to Zion,
'Look, there they are!'
And I will give to Jerusalem one who brings good tidings.
28 [a]For I looked, and *there was* no man;
I looked among them, but *there was* no counselor,
Who, when I asked of them, could answer a word.
29 [a]Indeed they *are* all [1]worthless;
Their works *are* nothing;
Their molded images *are* wind and confusion.

The Servant of the LORD

42 "Behold! [a]My Servant whom I uphold,

14 [a]Job 25:6; Ps. 22:6 **15** [a]Mic. 4:13; Hab. 3:12; [2 Cor. 10:4] **16** [a]Jer. 51:2 [b]Is. 45:25 **17** [a]Ps. 94:14; Rom. 11:2 **18** [a]Is. 35:6, 7; 43:19; 44:3 [b]Ps. 107:35 **19** [a]Is. 35:1 **20** [a]Job 12:9; Is. 66:14 *See WW at Ex. 3:7. • See WW at Gen. 1:1. **21** [a]Is. 43:15 **22** [a]Is. 45:21 [b]Is. 43:9 [1]Lit. *set our heart on them*

23 [a]Is. 42:9; 44:7, 8; 45:3; [John 13:19] [b]Jer. 10:5 **24** [a]Ps. 115:8; Is. 44:9; [Rom. 3:10–20; 1 Cor. 8:4] **25** [a]Ezra 1:2 [b]Is. 41:2; Jer. 50:3 [1]East **26** [a]Is. 43:9 **27** [a]Is. 41:4 [b]Is. 40:9; Nah. 1:15 **28** [a]Is. 63:5 **29** [a]Is. 41:24 [1]So with MT, Vg.; DSS, Syr., Tg. *nothing;* LXX omits first line

CHAPTER 42

1 [a]Is. 43:10; 49:3, 6; Matt. 12:18; [Phil. 2:7]

41:14–16 You worm Jacob: Israel is called a worm, a symbol of weakness, but Yahweh will make His servant into a **threshing sledge,** an instrument that in His hands will pulverize **the mountains,** her current difficulties. The verses are a call to expect deliverance as the people **rejoice in the LORD.**

41:17–20 Will not forsake: See notes on 10:20–23 and 29:17–24.

41:21—42:13 God challenges the false **gods** to deal with the future (41:21–29) and returns to another significant role of His **servant** in history (42:1–13).

41:21–24 Declare to us things to come: God, who through His prophets often predicted the future, challenges the idolatrous **gods** to produce any true prophecy of the future.

41:25–29 One from the north: See note on vv. 2, 3. Isaiah predicts the coming of Cyrus, which none of the **worthless** wizards of the pagan nations could do.

42:1–4 Behold! My Servant: Israel was previously called

My [1]Elect One *in whom* My soul
[b]delights!
[c]I have put My Spirit upon Him;
He will bring forth justice to the
*Gentiles.
2 He will not cry out, nor raise *His*
voice,
Nor cause His voice to be heard
in the street.
3 A bruised reed He will not break,
And [1]smoking flax He will not
[2]quench;
He will bring forth justice for
truth.
4 He will not fail nor be
discouraged,
Till He has established justice in
the earth;
[a]And the coastlands shall wait for
His law."

5 Thus says God the LORD,
[a]Who created the heavens and
stretched them out,
Who spread forth the earth and
that which comes from it,
[b]Who gives *breath to the people
on it,
And spirit to those who walk on
it:
6 "I,[a] the LORD, have called You in
righteousness,
And will hold Your hand;
I will keep You [b]and give You as
a covenant to the people,
As [c]a light to the Gentiles,
7 [a]To open blind eyes,
To [b]bring out prisoners from the
prison,
Those who sit in [c]darkness from
the prison house.
8 I *am* the LORD, that *is* My name;
And My [a]glory I will not give to
another,
Nor My praise to carved images.
9 Behold, the former things have
come to pass,
And new things I declare;

1 [b]Matt. 3:17; 17:5; Mark 1:11; Luke 3:22; Eph. 1:6 [c][Is. 11:2]; Matt. 3:16; [Luke 4:18, 19, 21]; John 3:34 [1]*Chosen* *See WW at Ps. 106:47.
3 [1]*dimly burning* [2]*extinguish*
4 [a][Gen. 49:10]
5 [a]Is. 44:24; Zech. 12:1 [b]Job 12:10; 33:4; Is. 57:16; Dan. 5:23; Acts 17:25 *See WW at Ps. 150:6.
6 [a]Is. 43:1 [b]Is. 49:8 [c]Is. 49:6; Luke 2:32; [Acts 10:45; 13:47; Gal. 3:14]
7 [a]Is. 35:5 [b]Is. 61:1; Luke 4:18; [2 Tim. 2:26; Heb. 2:14] [c]Is. 9:2
8 [a]Ex. 20:3–5; Is. 48:11
10 [a]Ps. 33:3; 40:3; 98:1 [b]Ps. 107:23 [1]Lit. *its fullness* *See WW at Judg. 5:3.
13 [a]Is. 31:4 *See WW at Hag. 1:14.
14 [1]*childbirth*

Before they spring forth I tell you
of them."

Praise to the LORD

10 [a]Sing* to the LORD a new song,
And His praise from the ends of
the earth,
[b]You who go down to the sea, and
[1]all that is in it,
You coastlands and you
inhabitants of them!
11 Let the wilderness and its cities
lift up *their voice,*
The villages *that* Kedar inhabits.
Let the inhabitants of Sela sing,
Let them shout from the top of the
mountains.
12 Let them give glory to the LORD,
And declare His praise in the
coastlands.
13 The LORD shall go forth like a
mighty man;
He shall *stir up *His* zeal like a
man of war.
He shall cry out, [a]yes, shout
aloud;
He shall prevail against His
enemies.

Promise of the LORD's Help

14 "I have held My peace a long time,
I have been still and restrained
Myself.
Now I will cry like a woman in
[1]labor,
I will pant and gasp at once.
15 I will lay waste the mountains and
hills,
And dry up all their vegetation;
I will make the rivers coastlands,
And I will dry up the pools.
16 I will bring the blind by a way
they did not know;
I will lead them in paths they have
not known.
I will make darkness light before
them,

God's servant. See note on 41:8–13. The Servant here appears to be someone different. The NT's use of v. 1 (Matt. 3:17; 12:18–21; 17:5) marks the section as clearly messianic, fulfilled in Christ. As such, it is the first of four "Servant Songs" depicting Christ (see also 49:1–6; 50:4–9; 52:13—53:12). Acts 3:13 says, "The God of Abraham . . . glorified His Servant Jesus." Historically, some scholars interpret Cyrus to be the servant, fulfilling the role of a type of Christ. See note on vv. 5–9.

Isaiah prophesies that Christ will **bring forth justice** to the nations without violence; He will encourage **the bruised;** He will not give up until His work is done.

I have put My Spirit: The Servant will accomplish His intended mission through the power of the Holy Spirit. See Luke 4:14.

42:5–9 I, the LORD have called You: Considerable controversy surrounds the interpretation of this section. Many scholars feel it is independent of vv. 1–4 and refers to Cyrus. See note on 41:2, 3. Others see it as a continuation of vv. 1–4, further describing the Messiah's ministry. The latter is more probable, with **the people** (v. 6) being mankind. **The former things . . . pass** refers to the events leading up to Cyrus's decree that Israel could return to Jerusalem.

42:10–13 The accomplishments of the Servant call for a **new song** of **praise to the LORD. Kedar** is a tribe in the northern Arabian Desert. **Sela** is likely Petra.

42:14–25 Isaiah now shifts focal points. **My servant** (v. 19) here is Israel/Judah; the section is a lament looking back on the disobedience that led to God's judging **anger.** The fundamental problem leading to the judgments was **trust in carved images** (v. 17). See note on 7:17.

And crooked places straight.
These things I will do for them,
And not forsake them.
17 They shall be [a]turned back,
They shall be greatly ashamed,
Who trust in carved images,
Who say to the molded images,
'You *are* our gods.'

18 "Hear, you deaf;
And look, you blind, that you may see.
19 [a]Who *is* blind but My servant,
Or deaf as My messenger *whom* I send?
Who *is* blind as *he who is* perfect,
And blind as the LORD's servant?
20 Seeing many things, [a]but you do not observe;
Opening the ears, but he does not hear."

Israel's Obstinate Disobedience

21 The LORD is well pleased for His righteousness' sake;
He will exalt the **law** and make *it* honorable.

WORD WEALTH

42:21 law, *torah* (toh-*rah*); Strong's #8451: Instruction, teaching, direction, Law, precept. This noun occurs 217 times in the OT. Usually *torah* refers to the Law of Moses, or a portion of the Law. Sometimes *torah* refers to the rules or instructions of a human parent, or of some other wise person (Prov. 1:8; 3:1; 13:14). The root of *torah* is *yarah,* meaning "to shoot, to cast down in a straight manner, to direct, to rain down." The idea is that God's instructions to Israel (the Torah) were given to them in a straightforward, direct manner. For Israel the new covenant, by the power of the Spirit of God, will cause the Torah to be written in their hearts (Jer. 31:33, 34; Ezek. 36:25, 26).

22 But this *is* a people robbed and plundered;
All of them are [1]snared in holes,
And they are hidden in prison houses;
They are for prey, and no one delivers;
For plunder, and no one says, "Restore!"

17 [a]Ps. 97:7; Is. 1:29; 44:11; 45:16
19 [a]Is. 43:8; Ezek. 12:2; [John 9:39, 41]
20 [a]Rom. 2:21
22 [1]Or *trapped in caves*
24 [a]Is. 65:2
25 [a]2 Kin. 25:9 [b]Is. 1:3; 5:13; Hos. 7:9 [c]Is. 29:13

CHAPTER 43

1 [a]Is. 43:5; 44:6 [b]Is. 42:6; 45:4
2 [a][Ps. 66:12; 91:3] [b][Deut. 31:6]; Jer. 30:11 [c]Dan. 3:25

23 Who among you will give ear to this?
Who will listen and hear for the time to come?
24 Who gave Jacob for plunder, and Israel to the robbers?
Was it not the LORD,
He against whom we have sinned?
[a]For they would not walk in His ways,
Nor were they obedient to His law.
25 Therefore He has poured on him the fury of His anger
And the strength of battle;
[a]It has set him on fire all around,
[b]Yet he did not know;
And it burned him,
Yet he did not take *it* to [c]heart.

The Redeemer of Israel

43 But now, thus says the LORD, who created you, O Jacob,
And He who formed you, O Israel:
"Fear not, [a]for I have redeemed you;
[b]I have called *you* by your name;
You *are* Mine.
2 [a]When you pass through the **waters,** [b]I *will be* with you;
And through the rivers, they shall not overflow you.
When you [c]walk through the fire, you shall not be burned,
Nor shall the flame scorch you.

WORD WEALTH

43:2 waters, *mayim* (*my*-yeem); Strong's #4325: Water; waters, floods, seas. *Mayim* is the Hebrew word for "water," but is always in the plural: "waters." *Mayim* appears 570 times in the OT and has a wide range of use. It occurs as a metaphor for the raging heathen, the chaotic, stormy seas at creation, and vast nations (or seas of people). See Ps. 32:6; 33:7; 46:3; Jer. 46:7, 8. Most significantly, *mayim* speaks of life, sustenance, fertility, blessing, and refreshing. See Ps. 23:2; Is. 12:3; 32:2; 55:1; 58:11; Jer. 17:8.

3 For I *am* the LORD your God,
The Holy One of Israel, your Savior;

42:23—43:7 See section 4 of Truth-In-Action at the end of Is.

43:1–21 I have redeemed you: Here is assurance of God's providential care for His people and of their redemption from captivity. The words "redeemer," "redeem," and "redemption" are common to Isaiah and hark back to God's deliverance from Egypt.

43:3 God somehow spoke to Cyrus, promising him large sections of Africa in exchange for his part in restoring Jerusalem.

[a]I gave Egypt for your ransom,
Ethiopia and Seba in your place.
4 Since you were precious in My sight,
You have been honored,
And I have [a]loved you;
Therefore I will give men for you,
And people for your life.
5 [a]Fear not, for I *am* with you;
I will bring your descendants from the east,
And [b]gather you from the west;
6 I will say to the [a]north, 'Give them up!'
And to the south, 'Do not keep them back!'
Bring My sons from afar,
And My daughters from the ends of the earth—
7 Everyone who is [a]called by My name,
Whom [b]I have *created for My glory;
I have formed him, yes, I have made him."

8 [a]Bring out the blind people who have eyes,
And the [b]deaf who have ears.
9 Let all the nations be gathered together,
And let the people be assembled.
[a]Who among them can declare this,
And show us former things?
Let them bring out their witnesses, that they may be justified;
Or let them hear and say, "*It is* truth."
10 "You[a] *are* My witnesses," says the LORD,
[b]"And My servant whom I have chosen,
That you may know and [c]believe* Me,
And *understand that I *am* He.
Before Me there was no God formed,
Nor shall there be after Me.
11 I, *even* I, [a]*am* the LORD,
And besides Me *there is* no savior.
12 I have declared and saved,
I have proclaimed,
And *there was* no [a]foreign *god* among you;

3 [a][Prov. 11:8; 21:18]
4 [a]Is. 63:9
5 [a]Is. 41:10; 44:2; Jer. 30:10; 46:27, 28 [b]Is. 54:7
6 [a]Is. 49:12
7 [a]Is. 63:19; James 2:7 [b]Ps. 100:3; Is. 29:23; [John 3:2, 3; 2 Cor. 5:17; Eph. 2:10]
*See WW at Gen. 1:1.
8 [a]Is. 6:9; 42:19; Ezek. 12:2 [b]Is. 29:18
9 [a]Is. 41:21, 22, 26
10 [a]Is. 44:8 [b]Is. 55:4 [c]Is. 41:4; 44:6
*See WW at 2 Chr. 20:20. • See WW at Neh. 8:8.
11 [a]Is. 45:21; Hos. 13:4
12 [a]Deut. 32:16; Ps. 81:9 [b]Is. 44:8
13 [a]Ps. 90:2; Is. 48:16 [b]Job 9:12; Is. 14:27
15 [a]Is. 41:20, 21
16 [a]Ex. 14:16, 21, 22; Ps. 77:19; Is. 51:10 [b]Josh. 3:13
17 [a]Ex. 14:4–9, 25
18 [a]Jer. 16:14
19 [a]Is. 42:9; 48:6; [2 Cor. 5:17; Rev. 21:5] [b]Ex. 17:6; Num. 20:11; Deut. 8:15; Ps. 78:16; Is. 35:1, 6
20 [a]Is. 48:21
21 [a]Ps. 102:18; Is. 42:12; [Luke 1:74, 75; Eph. 1:5, 6; 1 Pet. 2:9] [b]Jer. 13:11
*See WW at Ps. 100:4.

[b]Therefore you *are* My witnesses,"
Says the LORD, "that I *am* God.
13 [a]Indeed before the day *was*, I *am* He;
And *there is* no one who can deliver out of My hand;
I work, and who will [b]reverse it?"

14 Thus says the LORD, your Redeemer,
The Holy One of Israel:
"For your sake I will send to Babylon,
And bring them all down as fugitives—
The Chaldeans, who rejoice in their ships.
15 I *am* the LORD, your Holy One,
The Creator of Israel, your [a]King."

16 Thus says the LORD, who [a]makes a way in the sea
And a [b]path through the mighty waters,
17 Who [a]brings forth the chariot and horse,
The army and the power
(They shall lie down together, they shall not rise;
They are extinguished, they are quenched like a wick):
18 "Do[a] not remember the former things,
Nor consider the things of old.
19 Behold, I will do a [a]new thing,
Now it shall spring forth;
Shall you not know it?
[b]I will even make a road in the wilderness
And rivers in the desert.
20 The beast of the field will honor Me,
The jackals and the ostriches,
Because [a]I give waters in the wilderness
And rivers in the desert,
To give drink to My people, My chosen.
21 [a]This people I have formed for Myself;
They shall declare My [b]praise.*

Pleading with Unfaithful Israel

22 "But you have not called upon Me, O Jacob;

43:4 God providentially controlled Persia and Egypt to fulfill His destiny for Israel. See also vv. 14, 15.
43:5, 6 In addition to the return from Babylon, these verses likely point to God's gathering of His remnant throughout history. See notes on Zeph. 2:7 and 2:9.
43:16–21 Judah is called upon to forget when she struggled to be a nation among nations (1 Sam. 8:5, 20). God has a new destiny. **A new thing is this people** being built through the historical processes of the captivity and return.
43:22–28 You have not called upon Me, O Jacob: Israel

And you [a]have been weary of Me,
O Israel.
23 [a]You have not brought Me the
sheep for your burnt offerings,
Nor have you honored Me with
your sacrifices.
I have not caused you to *serve
with grain offerings,
Nor wearied you with incense.
24 You have bought Me no sweet
cane with money,
Nor have you satisfied Me with
the fat of your sacrifices;
But you have burdened Me with
your sins,
You have [a]wearied Me with your
iniquities.

25 "I, *even* I, *am* He who [a]blots out
your *transgressions [b]for My
own sake;
[c]And I will not remember your
sins.
26 Put Me in remembrance;
Let us contend together;
State your *case*, that you may be
[1]acquitted.
27 Your first father sinned,
And your [1]mediators have
transgressed against Me.
28 Therefore I will profane the
princes of the sanctuary;
[a]I will give Jacob to the curse,
And Israel to reproaches.

22 [a]Mic. 6:3; Mal. 1:13; 3:14
23 [a]Amos 5:25 *See WW at Ps. 100:2.
24 [a]Ps. 95:10; Is. 1:14; 7:13; Ezek. 6:9; Mal. 2:17
25 [a]Is. 44:22; Jer. 50:20; [Acts 3:19] [b]Ezek. 36:22 [c]Is. 1:18; Jer. 31:34 *See WW at Ezek. 18:31.
26 [1]*justified*
27 [1]*interpreters*
28 [a]Ps. 79:4; Jer. 24:9; Dan. 9:11; Zech. 8:13

God's Blessing on Israel

44 "Yet hear now, O Jacob My
servant,
And Israel whom I have chosen.
2 Thus says the LORD who made
you
And formed you from the womb,
who will help you:
'Fear not, O Jacob My servant;
And you, Jeshurun, whom I have
chosen.
3 For I will pour water on him who
is thirsty,
And floods on the dry ground;
I will pour My Spirit on your
descendants,
And My blessing on your
offspring;
4 They will spring up among the
grass
Like willows by the
watercourses.'
5 One will say, 'I *am* the LORD's';
Another will call *himself* by the
name of Jacob;
Another will write *with* his hand,
'The LORD's,'
And name *himself* by the name
of Israel.

There Is No Other God

6 "Thus says the LORD, the King of
Israel,
And his Redeemer, the LORD of
hosts:
[a]'I *am* the First and I *am* the Last;
Besides Me *there is* no God.
7 And [a]who can proclaim as I do?
Then let him declare it and set it
in order for Me,
Since I appointed the ancient
people.
And the things that are coming
and shall come,
Let them show these to them.
8 Do not fear, nor be afraid;
[a]Have I not told you from that
time, and declared *it*?
[b]You *are* My witnesses.
Is there a God besides Me?
Indeed [c]*there is* no other Rock;
I know not *one*.' "

Idolatry Is Foolishness

9 [a]Those who make an image, all of
them *are* useless,
And their precious things shall
not profit;
They *are* their own witnesses;
[b]They neither see nor know, that
they may be ashamed.
10 Who would form a god or mold
an image
[a]*That* profits him nothing?
11 Surely all his companions would
be [a]ashamed;

CHAPTER 44

6 [a]Is. 41:4; [Rev. 1:8, 17; 22:13]
7 [a]Is. 41:4, 22, 26
8 [a]Is. 41:22 [b]Is. 43:10, 12 [c]Deut. 4:35; 32:39; 1 Sam. 2:2; 2 Sam. 22:32; Is. 45:5; Joel 2:27
9 [a]Is. 41:24 [b]Ps. 115:4
10 [a]Is. 41:29; Jer. 10:5; Hab. 2:18; Acts 19:26
11 [a]Ps. 97:7; Is. 1:29; 42:17

had not yet been fully reformed; though many duties are lacking, still there is assurance that the **transgressions** will be blotted out. Her future will be different from her past.
43:23 Burnt offerings: See notes on Lev. 1:3, 4. **Grain offerings:** See note on Lev. 2:1.
43:24 Sweet cane was one of the ingredients in the holy anointing oil (Ex. 30:23).
43:25–28 Your first father was likely Jacob. **Your mediators** were Moses, Aaron, and their successors. **The princes** were the leaders of the Jerusalem priesthood. **I will profane** means God will take away their priestly status.
44:1–5 Reproach (43:22–28) turns to promise of blessing. See note on 41:8–13. **Jeshurun:** A poetic term of endearment applied to Israel (see Deut. 33:5).
44:6–20 The prophet voices another warning against idolatry. This section shows the absurdity of idolatry as compared with the worship of the one true, dependable God, Yahweh, the **Rock** (v. 8). See notes on 40:18–20 and 41:5–7.

And the workmen, they *are* mere men.
Let them all be gathered together,
Let them stand up;
Yet they shall fear,
They shall be ashamed together.

12 [a]The blacksmith with the tongs works one in the coals,
Fashions it with hammers,
And works it with the strength of his arms.
Even so, he is hungry, and his strength fails;
He drinks no water and is faint.

13 The craftsman stretches out *his* rule,
He marks one out with chalk;
He fashions it with a plane,
He marks it out with the compass,
And makes it like the figure of a man,
According to the beauty of a man, that it may *remain in the house.
14 He cuts down cedars for himself,
And takes the cypress and the oak;
He [1]secures *it* for himself among the trees of the forest.
He plants a pine, and the rain nourishes *it*.

15 Then it shall be for a man to burn,
For he will take some of it and warm himself;
Yes, he kindles *it* and bakes bread;
Indeed he makes a god and worships *it;*
He makes it a carved image, and falls down to it.
16 He burns half of it in the fire;
With this half he eats meat;
He roasts a roast, and is satisfied.
He even warms *himself* and says,
"Ah! I am warm,
I have seen the fire."
17 And the rest of it he makes into a god,
His carved image.
He falls down before it and worships *it,*
Prays to it and says,
"Deliver me, for you *are* my god!"

18 [a]They do not know nor understand;
For [b]He has [1]shut their eyes, so that they cannot see,
And their hearts, so that they cannot [c]understand.
19 And no one [a]considers in his heart,
Nor *is there* knowledge nor understanding to say,
"I have burned half of it in the fire,
Yes, I have also baked bread on its coals;
I have roasted meat and eaten *it;*
And shall I make the rest of it an abomination?
Shall I fall down before a block of wood?"
20 He feeds on ashes;
[a]A deceived heart has turned him aside;
And he cannot deliver his soul,
Nor say, "*Is there* not a [b]lie in my right hand?"

Israel Is Not Forgotten

21 "Remember these, O Jacob,
And Israel, for you *are* My servant;
I have formed you, you *are* My servant;
O Israel, you will not be [a]forgotten by Me!
22 [a]I have blotted out, like a thick cloud, your transgressions,
And like a cloud, your sins.
*Return to Me, for [b]I have redeemed you."

23 [a]Sing, O heavens, for the LORD has done *it!*
Shout, you lower parts of the earth;
Break forth into singing, you mountains,
O forest, and every tree in it!
For the LORD has redeemed Jacob,
And [b]glorified Himself in Israel.

Judah Will Be Restored

24 Thus says the LORD, [a]your Redeemer,
And [b]He who formed you from the womb:
"I *am* the LORD, who makes all *things,*
[c]Who stretches out the heavens [1]all alone,
Who spreads abroad the earth by Myself;
25 Who [a]frustrates the signs [b]of the babblers,

12 [a]Is. 40:19; Jer. 10:3–5
13 *See WW at Lam. 5:19.
14 [1]Lit. *appropriates*
18 [a]Is. 45:20 [b][Ps. 81:12]; Is. 6:9, 10; 29:10; 2 Thess. 2:11 [c]Jer. 10:14 [1]Lit. *smeared over*
19 [a]Is. 46:8
20 [a]Job 15:31; Hos. 4:12; Rom. 1:21, 22; 2 Thess. 2:11; 2 Tim. 3:13 [b]Is. 57:11; 59:3, 4, 13; Rom. 1:25
21 [a]Is. 49:15
22 [a]Is. 43:25 [b]Is. 43:1; 1 Cor. 6:20; [1 Pet. 1:18, 19] *See WW at Ruth 4:15.
23 [a]Ps. 69:34; Is. 42:10; 49:13; Jer. 51:48; Rev. 18:20 [b]Is. 49:3; 60:21
24 [a]Is. 43:14 [b]Is. 43:1 [c]Job 9:8 [1]By Himself
25 [a]Is. 47:13 [b]Jer. 50:36

44:21–23 See note on 43:1–21.

And drives diviners mad;
Who turns wise men backward,
[c]And makes their knowledge foolishness;
26 [a]Who confirms the word of His servant,
And performs the counsel of His messengers;
Who says to Jerusalem, 'You shall be inhabited,'
To the cities of Judah, 'You shall be *built,'
And I will raise up her waste places;
27 [a]Who says to the deep, 'Be dry!
And I will dry up your rivers';
28 Who says of [a]Cyrus, '*He is* My shepherd,
And he shall perform all My pleasure,
Saying to Jerusalem, [b]"You shall be built,"
And to the *temple, "Your foundation shall be laid." '

Cyrus, God's Instrument

45 "Thus says the LORD to His anointed,
To [a]Cyrus, whose [b]right hand I have [1]held—
[c]To subdue nations before him
And [d]loose the armor of kings,
To open before him the double doors,
So that the gates will not be shut:
2 'I will go before you
[a]And[1] *make the [2]crooked places straight;
[b]I will break in pieces the gates of bronze
And cut the bars of iron.
3 I will give you the treasures of darkness
And hidden riches of secret places,
[a]That you may know that I, the LORD,
Who [b]call *you* by your name,
Am the God of Israel.
4 For [a]Jacob My servant's sake,
And Israel My elect,
I have even called you by your name;
I have named you, though you have not known Me.
5 I [a]*am* the LORD, and [b]*there is* no other;
There is no God besides Me.
[c]I will gird you, though you have not known Me,
6 [a]That they may [b]know from the rising of the sun to its setting
That *there is* none besides Me.
I *am* the LORD, and *there is* no other;
7 I form the light and create darkness,
I make peace and [a]create calamity;
I, the LORD, do all these *things*.'

8 "Rain[a] down, you heavens, from above,
And let the skies pour down righteousness;
Let the earth open, let them bring forth salvation,
And let righteousness spring up together.
I, the LORD, have created it.

9 "Woe to him who strives with [a]his Maker!
Let the potsherd *strive* with the potsherds of the earth!
[b]Shall the clay say to him who forms it, 'What are you making?'
Or shall your handiwork *say*, 'He has no hands'?
10 Woe to him who says to *his* father, 'What are you begetting?'
Or to the woman, 'What have you brought forth?' "

11 Thus says the LORD,
The Holy One of Israel, and his Maker:
[a]"Ask Me of things to come concerning [b]My sons;
And concerning [c]the work of My hands, you command Me.
12 [a]I have made the earth,
And [b]created man on it.
I—My hands—stretched out the heavens,

25 [c]2 Sam. 15:31; Job 5:12–14; Ps. 33:10; Is. 29:14; Jer. 51:57; 1 Cor. 1:20, 27
26 [a]Zech. 1:6; Matt. 5:18 *See WW at Zech. 1:16.
27 [a]Jer. 50:38; 51:36
28 [a]2 Chr. 36:22; Ezra 1:1; Is. 45:13 [b]Ezra 6:7 *See WW at Hag. 2:15.

CHAPTER 45

1 [a]Is. 44:28 [b]Ps. 73:23; Is. 41:13 [c]Dan. 5:30 [d]Job 12:21; Is. 45:5 [1]*strengthened* or *sustained*
2 [a]Is. 40:4 [b]Ps. 107:16 [1]Tg. *I will trample down the walls;* Vg. *I will humble the great ones of the earth* [2]DSS, LXX *mountains* *See WW at Prov. 3:6.
3 [a]Is. 41:23 [b]Ex. 33:12
4 [a]Is. 44:1
5 [a]Deut. 4:35; 32:39; Is. 44:8 [b]Is. 45:14, 18 [c]Ps. 18:32
6 [a]Ps. 102:15; Is. 37:20; Mal. 1:11 [b][Is. 11:9; 52:10]
7 [a]Is. 31:2; 47:11; Amos 3:6
8 [a]Ps. 85:11
9 [a]Is. 64:8 [b]Jer. 18:6; Rom. 9:20, 21
11 [a]Is. 8:19 [b]Jer. 31:9 [c]Is. 29:23; 60:21; 64:8
12 [a]Is. 42:5; Jer. 27:5 [b]Gen. 1:26

44:28 Cyrus: See note on 41:2, 3.

45:1–13 Isaiah continues with Cyrus. See note on 41:2, 3. Cyrus is said to be **anointed** in the sense that God chose him for a special mission. God, through Isaiah, called Cyrus **by name** 100 years before his time to prove to the Persian king that He, Yahweh, was the only true **God**. Note the confession of Cyrus in Ezra 1:3. Josephus says that Cyrus released Israel when he was shown the prophecy of Is. 45.

Some modern scholars reject Isaiah's authorship of this part of the book on the grounds that a prediction of Cyrus by name would be an impossibility. Those who believe in the supernatural character of prophecy and the divine inspiration of the Scriptures have no problem with this or other prophetic predictions. See Introduction to Isaiah: Author.

45:3 The treasures of darkness were Egyptian booty and control of Egyptian trade routes.

And [c]all their host I have
commanded.
13 [a]I have raised him up in
righteousness,
And I will [1]direct all his
ways;
He shall [b]build My city
And let My exiles go free,
[c]Not for price nor reward,"
Says the LORD of hosts.

The LORD, the Only Savior

14 Thus says the LORD:

[a]"The labor of Egypt and
merchandise of Cush
And of the Sabeans, men of
stature,
Shall come over to you, and they
shall be yours;
They shall walk behind you,
They shall come over [b]in chains;
And they shall bow down to
you.
They will make supplication to
you, *saying,* [c]'Surely God *is*
in you,
And *there is* no other;
[d]*There is* no other God.'"

15 Truly You *are* God, [a]who hide
Yourself,
O God of Israel, the Savior!
16 They shall be [a]ashamed
And also disgraced, all of
them;
They shall go in confusion
together,
Who are makers of idols.
17 [a]*But* Israel shall be *saved by the
LORD
With an [b]everlasting salvation;
You shall not be ashamed or
[c]disgraced
Forever and ever.

18 For thus says the LORD,
[a]Who created the heavens,
Who is God,
Who formed the earth and made
it,
Who has established it,
Who did not create it [1]**in vain,**
Who formed it to be [b]inhabited:
[c]"I *am* the LORD, and *there is* no
other.

12 [c]Gen. 2:1; Neh. 9:6
13 [a]Is. 41:2 [b]2 Chr. 36:22; Is. 44:28 [c][Rom. 3:24] [1]*Or make all his ways straight*
14 [a]Ps. 68:31; 72:10, 11; Is. 14:1; 49:23; 60:9, 10, 14, 16; Zech. 8:22, 23 [b]Ps. 149:8 [c]Jer. 16:19; Zech. 8:20–23; 1 Cor. 14:25 [d]Is. 45:5
15 [a]Ps. 44:24; Is. 57:17
16 [a]Is. 44:11
17 [a]Is. 26:4; [Rom. 11:26] [b]Is. 51:6 [c]Is. 29:22 *See WW at Jer. 17:14.
18 [a]Is. 42:5 [b]Gen. 1:26; Ps. 115:16; Acts 17:26 [c]Is. 45:5 [1]*Or empty, a waste*
19 [a]Deut. 30:11 [b]Ps. 19:8; Is. 45:23; 63:1 [1]*Or in a waste place* *See WW at Hos. 5:15.
20 [a]Is. 44:9; 46:7; Jer. 10:5
21 [a]Is. 41:22; 43:9 [b]Is. 44:8
22 [a]Ps. 22:27; 65:5
23 [a]Gen. 22:16; Is. 62:8; [Heb. 6:13] [b]Rom. 14:11; [Phil. 2:10] [c]Deut. 6:13; Ps. 63:11; Is. 19:18; 65:16

WORD WEALTH

45:18 in vain, *tohu* (*toh*-hoo); Strong's #8414: A formless, chaotic mess, a waste, a worthless thing, emptiness and desolation, for no purpose, for nothing. This word first occurs in Gen. 1:2, "The earth was without form [*tohu*], and void [*bohu*]." *Tohu* and its rhyming synonym *bohu* are coupled to describe a scene of disorder, confusion, and lack of arrangement. However, the Lord brought order out of chaos, as Gen. (and our present Earth) testifies. Elsewhere *tohu* refers to a howling waste, a trackless wilderness, a scene of utter disarray, desolation, and barrenness. *Tohu* suggests "sheer emptiness" as opposed to order and balance.

19 I have not spoken in [a]secret,
In a dark place of the earth;
I did not say to the seed of Jacob,
'Seek* Me [1]in vain';
[b]I, the LORD, speak righteousness,
I declare things that are right.

20 "Assemble yourselves and come;
Draw near together,
You *who have* escaped from the
nations.
[a]They have no knowledge,
Who carry the wood of their
carved image,
And pray to a god *that* cannot
save.
21 Tell and bring forth *your case;*
Yes, let them take counsel
together.
[a]Who has declared this from
ancient time?
Who has told it from that time?
Have not I, the LORD?
[b]And *there is* no other God besides
Me,
A just God and a Savior;
There is none besides Me.

22 "Look to Me, and be saved,
[a]All you ends of the earth!
For I *am* God, and *there is* no
other.
23 [a]I have sworn by Myself;
The word has gone out of My
mouth *in* righteousness,
And shall not return,
That to Me every [b]knee shall bow,
[c]Every tongue shall take an oath.
24 He shall say,

45:14–25 This is a dialogue between God and Cyrus. It again affirms that God's goals are being accomplished through him (**God *is* in you**). See note on 41:2, 3.
45:14 Egypt, Cush (south of Egypt), and southwestern Arabia (**Sabeans**) were to be subdued; and the prisoners would somehow acknowledge Yahweh's working through Cyrus.
45:23 Every knee shall bow: Quoted by Paul in Phil. 2:10, 11 as being fulfilled through Christ at the end of this age.

[1]'Surely in the LORD I have
[a]righteousness and strength.
To Him *men* shall come,
And [b]all shall be ashamed
Who are incensed against
Him.
25 [a]In the LORD all the descendants
of Israel
Shall be justified, and [b]shall
glory.' "

Dead Idols and the Living God

46 Bel [a]bows down, Nebo stoops;
Their idols were on the beasts
and on the cattle.
Your carriages *were* heavily
loaded,
[b]A burden to the weary *beast.*
2 They stoop, they bow down
together;
They could not deliver the
burden,
[a]But have themselves gone into
captivity.

3 "Listen to Me, O house of Jacob,
And all the remnant of the house
of Israel,
[a]Who have been upheld *by Me*
from [1]birth,
Who have been carried from the
womb:
4 Even to *your* old age, [a]I *am*
He,
And *even* to gray hairs [b]I will
carry *you!*
I have made, and I will bear;
Even I will carry, and will deliver
you.

5 "To[a] whom will you liken Me, and
make *Me* equal
And compare Me, that we should
be alike?
6 [a]They lavish gold out of the bag,
And weigh silver on the scales;
They hire a [b]goldsmith, and he
makes it a god;
They prostrate themselves, yes,
they worship.
7 [a]They bear it on the shoulder, they
carry it

24 [a]Is. 54:17; [Jer. 23:5; 1 Cor. 1:30] [b]Is. 41:11 [1]Or *Only in the LORD are all righteousness and strength*
25 [a]Is. 45:17 [b]1 Cor. 1:31

CHAPTER 46

1 [a]Is. 21:9; Jer. 50:2 [b]Jer. 10:5
2 [a]Judg. 18:17, 18, 24; 2 Sam. 5:21; Jer. 48:7; Hos. 10:5, 6
3 [a]Deut. 32:11; Ps. 71:6; Is. 63:9 [1]Lit. *the belly*
4 [a]Mal. 3:6 [b]Ps. 48:14
5 [a]Is. 40:18, 25
6 [a]Is. 40:19; 41:6; Jer. 10:4 [b]Is. 44:12
7 [a]Is. 45:20; 46:1; Jer. 10:5 [b]Is. 45:20
8 [a]Is. 44:19 [1]*be men,* take courage
9 [a]Deut. 32:7; Is. 42:9; 65:17 [b]Is. 45:5, 21
10 [a]Is. 45:21; 48:3 [b]Ps. 33:11; Prov. 19:21; 21:30; Is. 14:24; 25:1; Acts 5:39; Heb. 6:17
11 [a]Is. 41:2, 25 [b]Is. 44:28 [c]Num. 23:19
12 [a]Ps. 76:5; Is. 48:4; Zech. 7:11, 12; Mal. 3:13 [b][Rom. 10:3]
13 [a][Rom. 1:17] [b]Hab. 2:3 [c]Is. 62:11; Joel 3:17; [1 Pet. 2:6] [1]*delay*

CHAPTER 47

1 [a]Jer. 48:18 [b]Is. 3:26 [c]Is. 14:18–23; Jer. 25:12; 50:1–51:64 [1]*dainty*

And set it in its place, and it
stands;
From its place it shall not move.
Though [b]*one* cries out to it, yet it
cannot answer
Nor save him out of his trouble.

8 "Remember this, and [1]show
yourselves men;
[a]Recall to mind, O you
transgressors.
9 [a]Remember the former things of
old,
For I *am* God, and [b]*there is* no
other;
I am God, and *there is* none like
Me,
10 [a]Declaring the end from the
beginning,
And from ancient times *things*
that are not *yet* done,
Saying, [b]'My counsel shall
stand,
And I will do all My pleasure,'
11 Calling a bird of prey [a]from the
east,
The man [b]who executes My
counsel, from a far country.
Indeed [c]I have spoken *it;*
I will also bring it to pass.
I have purposed *it;*
I will also do it.

12 "Listen to Me, you [a]stubborn-
hearted,
[b]Who *are* far from righteousness:
13 [a]I bring My righteousness near, it
shall not be far off;
My salvation [b]shall not [1]linger.
And I will place [c]salvation in
Zion,
For Israel My glory.

The Humiliation of Babylon

47 "Come [a]down and [b]sit in the
dust,
O virgin daughter of [c]Babylon;
Sit on the ground without a
throne,
O daughter of the Chaldeans!
For you shall no more be called
Tender and [1]delicate.

46:1–13 This is a chapter of two major contrasts: idols, which must be supported as opposed to Yahweh, who supports Israel (vv. 1–7); God's plan to use Cyrus to restore Jerusalem and Israel's stubbornness in approving the plan (vv. 8–13).

46:1 Bel and **Nebo** were gods of Babylon. Israel needed to see their futility as a warning to avoid these false gods with which they would be surrounded during their captivity in Babylon.

46:3, 4 From birth refers to the days of Abraham. ***Your old age*** refers to the Judah of Isaiah's day.

46:11 A bird of prey is a reference to Cyrus who would restore Jerusalem.

47:1–15 Another message of judgment against **Babylon** for idolatry, sorcery, self-indulgence, arrogance, and cruelty to God's people, particularly to the elderly. See notes on 13:1–22 and 14:4–11.

47:1 Virgin daughter of Babylon: The city is called a virgin because her walls had never been breached, but her virginity would be ended by Cyrus.

2 [a]Take the millstones and grind
meal.
Remove your veil,
Take off the skirt,
Uncover the thigh,
*Pass through the rivers.
3 [a]Your nakedness shall be
uncovered,
Yes, your shame will be seen;
[b]I will take vengeance,
And I will not arbitrate with a
man."

4 *As for* [a]our Redeemer, the LORD
of *hosts *is* His name,
The Holy One of Israel.

5 "Sit in [a]silence, and go into
darkness,
O daughter of the Chaldeans;
[b]For you shall no longer be called
The Lady of Kingdoms.
6 [a]I was angry with My people;
[b]I have profaned My inheritance,
And given them into your hand.
You showed them no mercy;
[c]On the *elderly you laid your
yoke very heavily.
7 And you said, 'I shall be [a]a lady
forever,'
So that you did not [b]take these
things to heart,
[c]Nor remember the latter end of
them.

8 "Therefore hear this now, *you who
are* given to pleasures,
Who dwell securely,
Who say in your heart,
'I *am,* and *there is* no one else
besides me;
I shall not sit *as* a widow,
Nor shall I know the loss of
children';
9 But these two *things* shall come
to you
[a]In a moment, in one day:
The loss of children, and
widowhood.
They shall come upon you in their
fullness
Because of the multitude of your
sorceries,
For the great abundance of your
enchantments.

10 "For you have trusted in your
wickedness;
You have said, 'No one [a]sees me';
Your wisdom and your
knowledge have [1]warped you;
And you have said in your heart,
'I *am,* and *there is* no one else
besides me.'
11 Therefore evil shall come upon
you;
You shall not know from where
it arises.
And trouble shall fall upon you;
You will not be able [1]to put it off.
And [a]desolation shall come upon
you [b]suddenly,
Which you shall not know.

12 "Stand now with your
enchantments
And the multitude of your
sorceries,
In which you have labored from
your youth—
Perhaps you will be able to profit,
Perhaps you will prevail.
13 [a]You are wearied in the multitude
of your counsels;
Let now [b]the[1] astrologers, the
stargazers,
And [2]the monthly
prognosticators
Stand up and save you
From what shall come upon you.
14 Behold, they shall be [a]as stubble,
The fire shall [b]burn them;
They shall not deliver themselves
From the power of the flame;
It shall not *be* a coal to be warmed
by,
Nor a fire to sit before!
15 Thus shall they be to you
With whom you have labored,
[a]Your merchants from your youth;
They shall wander each one to his
[1]quarter.
No one shall save you.

Israel Refined for God's Glory

48 "Hear this, O house of Jacob,
Who are called by the name of
Israel,
And have come forth from the
wellsprings of Judah;

2 [a]Ex. 11:5; Jer. 25:10 *See WW at Josh. 3:4.
3 [a]Is. 3:17; 20:4 [b][Rom. 12:19]
4 [a]Jer. 50:34 *See WW at Ps. 68:11.
5 [a]1 Sam. 2:9 [b]Is. 13:19; [Dan. 2:37]; Rev. 17:18
6 [a]2 Sam. 24:14 [b]Is. 43:28 [c]Deut. 28:49, 50 *See WW at Ps. 119:100.
7 [a]Rev. 18:7 [b]Is. 42:25; 46:8 [c]Deut. 32:29; Jer. 5:31; Ezek. 7:2, 3
9 [a]Ps. 73:19; 1 Thess. 5:3; Rev. 18:8
10 [a]Is. 29:15; Ezek. 8:12; 9:9 [1]*led you astray*
11 [a]Is. 13:6; Jer. 51:8, 43; Luke 17:27; 1 Thess. 5:3 [b]Is. 29:5 [1]Lit. *to cover it* or *atone for it*
13 [a]Is. 57:10 [b]Is. 8:19; 44:25; 47:9; Dan. 2:2, 10 [1]Lit. *viewers of the heavens* [2]Lit. *those giving knowledge for new moons*
14 [a]Is. 5:24; Nah. 1:10; Mal. 4:1 [b][Is. 10:17]; Jer. 51:58
15 [a]Rev. 18:11 [1]*own side* or *way*

47:2 Babylon is likened to a slave who will have to earn her way.
47:4 The LORD of hosts: See note on 6:3.
47:5 The Lady of Kingdoms: Babylon's destruction is portrayed in terms of a dethroned queen. Although Cyrus's 539 B.C. invasion did not annihilate Babylon, it was substantially destroyed.
47:6–15 See notes on 10:5–11 and 10:7, 8.
47:13 The monthly prognosticators divided the heavens into segments to study the movement of stars and planets so as to predict Earth's events. Present-day zodiacal maps derive from them.
48:1–11 An indictment against **Israel** for idolatry, obstinacy, and hypocrisy. Israel went through the motions of true worship; but, scorning the true prophet, she trusted more in her secret idols and will need refining through captivity.

Who swear by the name of the
LORD,
And make mention of the God of
Israel,
But [a]not in truth or in
righteousness;
2 For they call themselves [a]after the
holy city,
And [b]lean on the God of Israel;
The LORD of hosts *is* His name:

3 "I have [a]declared the former
things from the beginning;
They went forth from My mouth,
and I caused them to hear it.
Suddenly I did *them,* [b]and they
came to pass.
4 Because I knew that you *were*
[1]obstinate,
And [a]your neck *was* an iron
sinew,
And your brow bronze,
5 Even from the beginning I have
declared *it* to you;
Before it came to pass I
proclaimed *it* to you,
Lest you should say, 'My idol has
done them,
And my carved image and my
molded image
Have commanded them.'

6 "You have heard;
See all this.
And will you not declare *it?*
I have made you hear new things
from this time,
Even hidden things, and you did
not know them.
7 They are created now and not
from the beginning;
And before this day you have not
heard them,
Lest you should say, 'Of course I
knew them.'
8 Surely you did not hear,
Surely you did not know;
Surely from long ago your ear
was not opened.
For I knew that you would deal
very treacherously,
And were called [a]a transgressor
from the womb.

9 "For[a] My name's sake [b]I will
[1]defer My anger,
And *for* My praise I will restrain
it from you,
So that I do not cut you off.

10 Behold, [a]I have refined you, but
not as silver;
I have tested you in the [b]furnace
of affliction.
11 For My own sake, for My own
sake, I will do *it;*
For [a]how should *My name* be
profaned?
And [b]I will not give My glory to
another.

God's Ancient Plan to Redeem Israel

12 "Listen to Me, O Jacob,
And Israel, My called:
I *am* He, [a]I *am* the [b]First,
I *am* also the Last.
13 Indeed [a]My hand has laid the
foundation of the earth,
And My right hand has stretched
out the heavens;
When [b]I call to them,
They stand up together.

14 "All of you, assemble yourselves,
and hear!
Who among them has declared
these *things?*
[a]The LORD loves him;
[b]He shall do His pleasure on
Babylon,
And His arm *shall be against* the
Chaldeans.
15 I, *even* I, have spoken;
Yes, [a]I have called him,
I have brought him, and his way
will prosper.

16 "Come near to Me, hear this:
[a]I have not spoken in secret from
the beginning;
From the time that it was, I *was*
there.
And now [b]the Lord GOD and His
Spirit
[1]Have sent Me."

17 Thus says [a]the LORD, your
Redeemer,
The Holy One of Israel:
"I *am* the LORD your God,
Who **teaches** you to profit,
[b]Who leads you by the way you
should go.

WORD WEALTH

48:17 teaches, *lamad* (lah-*mahd*); Strong's #3925: To instruct, train; prod, *(cont. on next page)*

CHAPTER 48

1 [a]Is. 58:2; Jer. 4:2; 5:2
2 [a]Is. 52:1; 64:10 [b]Is. 10:20; Jer. 7:4; 21:2; Mic. 3:11; Rom. 2:17
3 [a]Is. 44:7, 8; 46:10 [b]Josh. 21:45; Is. 42:9
4 [a]Ex. 32:9; Deut. 31:27; Ezek. 2:4; 3:7 [1]Heb. *hard*
8 [a]Deut. 9:7, 24; Ps. 58:3; Is. 46:3, 8
9 [a]Ps. 79:9; 106:8; Is. 43:25; Ezek. 20:9, 14, 22, 44 [b][Neh. 9:30, 31]; Ps. 78:38; Is. 30:18; 65:8 [1]*delay*
10 [a]Ps. 66:10; Jer. 9:7 [b]Deut. 4:20; 1 Kin. 8:51; Jer. 11:4
11 [a]Lev. 22:2, 32; Deut. 32:26, 27; Ezek. 20:9 [b]Is. 42:8
12 [a]Deut. 32:39 [b]Is. 44:6; [Rev. 22:13]
13 [a]Ex. 20:11; Ps. 102:25; Is. 42:5; 45:12, 18; Heb. 1:10–12 [b]Is. 40:26
14 [a]Is. 45:1 [b]Is. 44:28; 47:1–15
15 [a]Is. 45:1, 2
16 [a]Is. 45:19 [b]Is. 61:1; Zech. 2:8, 9, 11 [1]Heb. verb is sing.; or *Has sent Me and His Spirit*
17 [a]Is. 43:14 [b]Ps. 32:8; Is. 49:9, 10

48:12–16 God speaks again to **Israel,** confirming His choice of Cyrus. See note on 47:1.
48:16 The Lord GOD and His Spirit: See note on 11:2. **Have sent Me** has been subject to much debate. Most scholars feel that this is Cyrus, affirming God's empowering of him. Others see it as God's affirming the work of the Trinity through Cyrus.

(*cont. from preceding page*)
goad; teach; to cause someone to learn. The origin of the verb may be traced to the goading of cattle. Similarly, teaching and learning are attained through a great variety of goading, by memorable events, techniques, or lessons. From *lamad* comes *talmid, melammed,* and *Talmud,* being respectively, "scholar," "student," and the "Book of Rabbinic Learning."

18 [a]Oh, that you had heeded My commandments!
[b]Then your peace would have been like a river,
And your righteousness like the waves of the sea.
19 [a]Your descendants also would have been like the sand,
And the offspring of your body like the grains of sand;
His name would not have been cut off
Nor destroyed from before Me."

20 [a]Go forth from Babylon!
Flee from the Chaldeans!
With a voice of *singing,
Declare, proclaim this,
Utter it to the end of the earth;
Say, "The LORD has [b]redeemed His servant Jacob!"
21 And they [a]did not thirst
When He led them through the deserts;
He [b]caused the waters to flow from the rock for them;
He also split the rock, and the waters gushed out.

22 "*There*[a] *is* no peace," says the LORD, "for the wicked."

The Servant, the Light to the Gentiles

49 "Listen, [a]O coastlands, to Me,
And take heed, you peoples from afar!
[b]The LORD has called Me from the womb;
From the [1]matrix of My mother
He has made mention of My name.
2 And He has made [a]My mouth like a sharp sword;
[b]In the shadow of His hand He has hidden Me,
And made Me [c]a polished shaft;
In His quiver He has hidden Me."

3 "And He said to me,
[a]'You *are* My servant, O Israel,
[b]In whom I will be glorified.'
4 [a]Then I said, 'I have labored in vain,
I have spent my strength *for nothing and in vain;
Yet surely my [1]just reward *is* with the LORD,
And my [2]work with my God.'"

5 "And now the LORD says,
Who formed Me from the womb *to be* His Servant,
To bring Jacob back to Him,
So that Israel [a]is [1]gathered to Him
(For I shall be glorious in the eyes of the LORD,
And My God shall be My strength),
6 Indeed He says,
'It is too small a thing that You should be My Servant
To raise up the tribes of Jacob,
And to restore the preserved ones of Israel;
I will also give You as a [a]light to the Gentiles,
That You should be My salvation to the ends of the earth.'"

7 Thus says the LORD,
The Redeemer of Israel, [1]their Holy One,

18 [a]Deut. 5:29; Ps. 81:13 [b]Deut. 28:1–14; Ps. 119:165; Is. 32:16–18; 66:12
19 [a]Gen. 22:17; Is. 10:22; 44:3, 4; 54:3; Jer. 33:22; Hos. 1:10
20 [a]Jer. 50:8; 51:6, 45; Zech. 2:6, 7; Rev. 18:4 [b][Ex. 19:4–6] *See WW at Ps. 30:5.
21 [a][Is. 41:17, 18] [b]Ex. 17:6; Ps. 105:41
22 [a][Is. 57:21]

CHAPTER 49

1 [a]Is. 41:1 [b]Jer. 1:5; Matt. 1:20; Luke 1:35; John 1:14; 10:36 [1]Lit. *inward parts*
2 [a]Is. 11:4; Hos. 6:5; [Heb. 4:12]; Rev. 1:16; 2:12 [b]Is. 51:16 [c]Ps. 45:5
3 [a][Is. 41:8; 42:1; Zech. 3:8] [b]Is. 44:23; Matt. 12:18; [John 13:31, 32; 14:13; 15:8; 17:4; Eph. 1:6]
4 [a][Ezek. 3:19] [1]*justice* [2]*recompense* *See WW at Is. 45:18.
5 [a]Matt. 23:37; [Rom. 11:25–29] [1]Qr., DSS, LXX *gathered to Him;* Kt. *not gathered*
6 [a]Is. 42:6; 51:4; [Luke 2:32]; Acts 13:47; [Gal. 3:14]
7 [1]Lit. *his* or *its*

48:18 Oh, that you had heeded My commandments: God had promised comfort and peace to Israel (the theme of chs. 40—66), but His people persisted in disobedience. Had they obeyed, **Your peace would have been like a river.** Nonetheless, they will be delivered from Babylon (v. 20).
49:1–6 The second of the **Servant** Songs. See note on 42:1–4.
49:3 My servant . . . Israel: See note on 41:8–13.
49:4 Isaiah prophetically portrays Christ's inner frustration at the apparent lack of results in His ministry. The NT is relatively silent in this regard. It is alluded to, however, in His lament over Jerusalem (Matt. 23:37–39).
49:5 Israel is gathered to Him: See notes on Zeph. 2:7 and Gal. 6:16.
49:6 A light to the Gentiles is alluded to by Simeon in his blessing of the child Jesus (Luke 2:32).
49:7–13 Isaiah continues with the Servant's involvement in Israel's return from Babylon. Most scholars see **the Servant** (v. 7) two ways: 1) historically, as Darius, and 2) prophetically, as a type of Christ. Each one would have a role in facilitating Israel's return at different times in history to come. It is also apparent that the specifics of this restoration look beyond the postexilic return to Christ's care for His church throughout this age. See John 10:1–30 and Luke 4:18, 19.
49:7 Him whom man despises: Darius I, a spear-bearer to Cambyses who was only remotely related to royalty, was thought an unlikely candidate for the Persian throne. Christ, his antetype, was also despised (Luke 10:10).

[a]To Him [2]whom man despises,
To Him whom the nation abhors,
To the Servant of rulers:
[b]"Kings shall see and arise,
Princes also shall worship,
Because of the LORD who is faithful,
The Holy One of Israel;
And He has chosen You."

8 Thus says the LORD:

"In an [a]acceptable[1] time I have heard You,
And in the day of salvation I have helped You;
I will [2]preserve You [b]and give You
As a covenant to the people,
To restore the earth,
To cause them to inherit the desolate [3]heritages;
9 That You may say [a]to the prisoners, 'Go forth,'
To those who *are* in darkness, 'Show yourselves.'

"They shall *feed along the roads,
And their pastures *shall be* on all desolate heights.
10 They shall neither [a]hunger nor thirst,
[b]Neither heat nor sun shall strike them;
For He who has mercy on them [c]will lead them,
Even by the springs of water He will guide them.
11 [a]I will make each of My mountains a road,
And My highways shall be elevated.
12 Surely [a]these shall come from afar;
Look! Those from the north and the west,
And these from the land of Sinim."

13 [a]Sing, O heavens!
Be joyful, O earth!
And break out in singing, O mountains!
For the LORD has *comforted His people,
And will have mercy on His afflicted.

God Will Remember Zion

14 [a]But Zion said, "The LORD has forsaken me,
And my Lord has forgotten me."
15 "Can[a] a woman forget her nursing child,
[1]And not have compassion on the son of her womb?
Surely they may forget,
[b]Yet I will not forget you.
16 See, [a]I have inscribed you on the palms *of My hands;*
Your walls *are* continually before Me.
17 Your [1]sons shall make haste;
Your destroyers and those who laid you waste
Shall go away from you.
18 [a]Lift up your eyes, look around and see;
All these gather together *and* come to you.
As I live," says the LORD,
"You shall surely clothe yourselves with them all [b]as an ornament,
And bind them *on you* as a bride *does.*

19 "For your waste and desolate places,
And the land of your destruction,
[a]Will even now be too small for the inhabitants;
And those who swallowed you up will be far away.
20 [a]The children you will have,
[b]After you have lost the others,
Will say again in your ears,
'The place *is* too small for me;
Give me a place where I may dwell.'
21 Then you will say in your heart,
'Who has begotten these for me,
Since I have lost my children and am desolate,
A captive, and wandering to and fro?
And who has brought these up?
There I was, left alone;
But these, where *were* they?' "

22 [a]Thus says the Lord GOD:

"Behold, I will lift My hand in an oath to the nations,

7 [a][Ps. 22:6; Is. 53:3; Matt. 26:67; 27:41]; Mark 15:29; Luke 23:35 [b][Is. 52:15] [2]Lit. *who is despised of soul*
8 [a]Ps. 69:13; 2 Cor. 6:2 [b]Is. 42:6 [1]*favorable* [2]*keep* [3]*inheritances*
9 [a]Is. 61:1; Zech. 9:12; Luke 4:18 *See WW at Is. 40:11.
10 [a]Is. 33:16; 48:21; Rev. 7:16 [b]Ps. 121:6 [c]Ps. 23:2; Is. 40:11; 48:17
11 [a]Is. 40:4
12 [a]Is. 43:5, 6
13 [a]Is. 44:23 *See WW at Ps. 23:4.
14 [a]Is. 40:27
15 [a]Ps. 103:13; Mal. 3:17 [b]Rom. 11:29 [1]Lit. *From having compassion*
16 [a]Ex. 13:9; Song 8:6; Hag. 2:23
17 [1]DSS, LXX, Tg., Vg. *builders*
18 [a]Is. 60:4; John 4:35 [b]Prov. 17:6
19 [a]Is. 54:1, 2; Zech. 10:10
20 [a]Is. 60:4 [b][Matt. 3:9; Rom. 11:11]
22 [a]Is. 60:4

49:8 Some scholars feel similar words were previously spoken to Cyrus. See note on 42:5–9.
49:11 My highways: See note on 35:8–10.
49:12 Sinim is likely Aswan in Egypt.
49:14–26 The LORD has forsaken me: Israel complains of being forsaken, but the Lord promises to inscribe them on His hands. He will overcome Israel's destroyer, clothe Israel in ornaments, multiply her numbers, and cause the nations to help her. He will indeed be her Savior and Redeemer. See notes on 43:1–21; 43:5, 6; Obad. 15.

And set up My [1]standard for the peoples;
They shall bring your sons in *their* [2]arms,
And your daughters shall be carried on *their* shoulders;
23 [a]Kings shall be your foster fathers,
And their queens your nursing mothers;
They shall bow down to you with *their* faces to the earth,
And [b]lick up the dust of your feet.
Then you will know that I *am* the LORD,
[c]For they shall not be ashamed who wait for Me."

24 [a]Shall the prey be taken from the mighty,
Or the captives [1]of the righteous be delivered?

25 But thus says the LORD:

"Even the captives of the mighty shall be taken away,
And the prey of the terrible be delivered;
For I will contend with him who contends with you,
And I will save your children.
26 I will [a]feed those who oppress you with their own flesh,
And they shall be drunk with their own [b]blood as with sweet wine.
All flesh [c]shall know
That I, the LORD, *am* your Savior,
And your Redeemer, the Mighty One of Jacob."

The Servant, Israel's Hope

50

Thus says the LORD:
"Where *is* [a]the certificate of your mother's divorce,
Whom I have put away?
Or which of My [b]creditors *is it* to whom I have sold you?
For your iniquities [c]you have sold yourselves,
And for your transgressions your mother has been put away.
2 Why, when I came, *was there* no man?
Why, when I called, *was there* none to answer?
Is My hand shortened at all that it cannot redeem?
Or have I no power to deliver?
Indeed with My [a]rebuke I dry up the sea,
I make the rivers a wilderness;
Their fish stink because *there is* no water,
And die of thirst.
3 [a]I clothe the heavens with blackness,
[b]And I make sackcloth their covering."

4 "The[a] Lord GOD has given Me
The tongue of the learned,
That I should know how to speak
A word in season to *him who is* [b]weary.
He awakens Me morning by morning,
He awakens My ear
To hear as the learned.
5 The Lord GOD [a]has opened My ear;
And I was not [b]rebellious,
Nor did I turn away.
6 [a]I gave My back to those who struck *Me,*
And [b]My cheeks to those who plucked out the beard;
I did not hide My face from shame and [c]spitting.

7 "For the Lord GOD will help Me;
Therefore I will not be disgraced;
Therefore [a]I have set My face like a flint,
And I know that I will not be ashamed.
8 [a]*He is* near who justifies Me;
Who will contend with Me?
Let us stand together.
Who *is* [1]My adversary?
Let him come near Me.
9 Surely the Lord GOD will help Me;
Who *is* he *who* will condemn Me?
[a]Indeed they will all grow old like a garment;
[b]The moth will eat them up.

22 [1]*banner* [2]Lit. *bosom*
23 [a]Ps. 72:11; Is. 52:15 [b]Ps. 72:9; Mic. 7:17 [c]Ps. 34:22; [Rom. 5:5]
24 [a]Matt. 12:29; Luke 11:21, 22 [1]So with MT, Tg.; DSS, Syr., Vg. *of the mighty;* LXX *unjustly*
26 [a]Is. 9:20 [b]Rev. 14:20 [c]Ps. 9:16; Is. 60:16

CHAPTER 50

1 [a]Deut. 24:1; Jer. 3:8 [b]Deut. 32:30; 2 Kin. 4:1; Neh. 5:5 [c]Is. 52:3
2 [a]Ps. 106:9; Nah. 1:4
3 [a]Ex. 10:21 [b]Is. 13:10; Rev. 6:12
4 [a]Ex. 4:11 [b]Matt. 11:28
5 [a]Ps. 40:6; Is. 35:5 [b]Matt. 26:39; Mark 14:36; Luke 22:42; John 8:29; 14:31; 15:10; Acts 26:19; [Phil. 2:8; Heb. 5:8; 10:7]
6 [a]Matt. 27:26; John 18:22 [b]Matt. 26:67; 27:30; Mark 14:65; 15:19 [c]Lam. 3:30
7 [a]Ezek. 3:8, 9; Luke 9:51
8 [a]Acts 2:24; [Rom. 8:32–34] [1]Lit. *master of My judgment*
9 [a]Job 13:28; Ps. 102:26; Heb. 1:11 [b]Is. 51:6, 8

50:1–3 God continues to deal with the complaint that He has forsaken Israel.
50:4–9 The third Servant Song. See note on 42:1–4. Historically, many see this unidentified Servant as Zerubbabel, in his postexilic leadership and teaching roles, another type of Christ.
50:4, 5 One of the gifts **GOD** gave the Servant (Christ) was **the tongue of the learned,** the ability to deliver effectively the message He was given (see John 7:46). **Not rebellious** defines His submission to God's strategy (see Matt. 26:39).
50:6 This is a clear prophecy of Christ's vicarious suffering. Matthew alludes to this verse three times (26:67; 27:26, 30). See note on 53:4.
50:7–9 The Servant turns to a note of triumph, seeing Himself as having won a great legal battle with God's **help**. Luke alludes to the flintlike steadfastness of Christ's devotion (Luke 9:51).

10 "Who among you fears the LORD?
Who obeys the voice of His
Servant?
Who [a]walks in darkness
And has no light?
[b]Let him trust in the name of the
LORD
And rely upon his God.
11 Look, all you who kindle a fire,
Who encircle *yourselves* with
sparks:
Walk in the light of your fire and
in the sparks you have
kindled—
[a]This you shall have from My
hand:
You shall lie down [b]in torment.

The LORD Comforts Zion

51 "Listen to Me, [a]you who
[1]follow after righteousness,
You who seek the LORD:
Look to the rock *from which* you
were hewn,
And to the hole of the pit *from
which* you were dug.
2 [a]Look to Abraham your father,
And to Sarah *who* bore you;
[b]For I called him alone,
And [c]blessed him and increased
him."

3 For the LORD will [a]comfort*
Zion,
He will comfort all her waste
places;
He will make her wilderness like
Eden,
And her desert [b]like the garden
of the LORD;
Joy and gladness will be found in
it,
*Thanksgiving and the voice of
melody.

4 "Listen to Me, My people;
And give ear to Me, O My nation:
[a]For *law will proceed from Me,
And I will make My justice rest
[b]As a light of the peoples.
5 [a]My righteousness *is* near,
My salvation has gone forth,
[b]And My arms will judge the
peoples;
[c]The coastlands will *wait upon
Me,
And [d]on My arm they will trust.
6 [a]Lift up your eyes to the heavens,
And look on the earth beneath.
For [b]the heavens will vanish
away like smoke,
[c]The earth will grow old like a
garment,
And those who dwell in it will die
in like manner;
But My salvation will be
[d]forever,
And My righteousness will not be
[1]abolished.

7 "Listen to Me, you who know
righteousness,
You people [a]in whose heart *is* My
law:
[b]Do not fear the reproach of
men,
Nor be afraid of their insults.
8 For [a]the moth will eat them up
like a garment,
And the worm will eat them like
wool;
But My righteousness will be
forever,
And My salvation from
generation to generation."

9 [a]Awake, awake, [b]put on strength,
O arm of the LORD!
Awake [c]as in the ancient days,
In the generations of old.
[d]*Are* You not *the arm* that cut
[e]Rahab apart,
And wounded the [f]serpent?

10 *Are* You not *the One* who
[a]dried up the sea,
The waters of the great deep;
That made the depths of the sea
a road
For the redeemed to cross over?
11 So [a]the ransomed of the LORD
shall return,
And come to Zion with *singing,
With everlasting joy on their
heads.

10 [a]Ps. 23:4 [b]2 Chr. 20:20 **11** [a][John 9:39] [b]Ps. 16:4

CHAPTER 51

1 [a][Rom. 9:30–32] [1]*pursue* **2** [a]Rom. 4:1–3; Heb. 11:11 [b]Gen. 12:1 [c]Gen. 24:35; Deut. 1:10; Ezek. 33:24 **3** [a]Is. 40:1; 52:9; Ps. 102:13 [b]Gen. 13:10; Joel 2:3 *See WW at Ps. 23:4. • See WW at Ps. 95:2. **4** [a]Is. 2:3 [b]Is. 42:6 *See WW at Is. 42:21. **5** [a]Is. 46:13 [b]Ps. 67:4 [c]Is. 60:9 [d][Rom. 1:16] *See WW at Mic. 7:7. **6** [a]Is. 40:26 [b]Ps. 102:25, 26; Is. 13:13; 34:4; Matt. 24:35; Heb. 1:10–12; 2 Pet. 3:10 [c]Is. 24:19, 20; 50:9; Heb. 1:10–12 [d]Is. 45:17 [1]*broken* **7** [a]Ps. 37:31; Jer. 31:33; [Heb. 10:16] [b]Is. 25:8; 54:4; [Matt. 5:11, 12; 10:28; Acts 5:41] **8** [a]Is. 50:9 **9** [a]Ps. 44:23 [b]Ps. 93:1 [c]Ps. 44:1 [d]Job 26:12; Ps. 89:10; Is. 30:7 [e]Ps. 87:4 [f]Ps. 74:13; Is. 27:1 **10** [a]Ex. 14:21; Is. 63:11–13 **11** [a]Is. 35:10; Jer. 31:11, 12 *See WW at Ps. 30:5.

50:10, 11 Let him trust is an exhortation to trust in Yahweh's Servant; the other option is to ignore Him, in which case one will ultimately **lie down in torment**.

51:1–8 Look to the rock: The Lord challenges Israel to return in thought to her origin as the seed of **Abraham,** chosen to bring blessing to all the nations. Through Israel as God's witness, the world will enjoy **salvation** and **righteousness** (v. 6). See note on 40:1. Historically, this was prophesied for the postexilic remnant under Zerubbabel.

In the broadest application, these truths apply to the Christian, the descendant of Abraham in Christ. See notes on 35:1–10 and Gal. 6:16.

51:9–16 The **arm of the LORD** that brought Israel through the Red Sea will also deliver her from Babylonian captivity and restore her in **Zion.** The Lord who spoke the heaven and Earth into being now speaks to Israel: **You are My people.** See note on 41:8–13.

51:9 Rahab . . . the serpent is a reference to the same personage. See note on 30:6, 7.

51:11 See note on 35:8–10.

They shall obtain joy and
gladness;
Sorrow and sighing shall flee
away.

12 "I, *even* I, *am* He [a]who comforts
you.
Who *are* you that you should be
afraid
[b]Of a man *who* will die,
And of the son of a man *who* will
be made [c]like grass?
13 And [a]you forget the LORD your
Maker,
[b]Who stretched out the heavens
And laid the foundations of the
earth;
You have feared continually
every day
Because of the fury of the
oppressor,
When *he has* prepared to destroy.
[c]And where *is* the fury of the
oppressor?
14 The captive exile hastens, that he
may be loosed,
[a]That he should not die in the pit,
And that his bread should not fail.
15 But I *am* the LORD your God,
Who [a]divided the sea whose
waves roared—
The LORD of hosts *is* His name.
16 And [a]I have put My words in your
mouth;
[b]I have covered you with the
shadow of My hand,
[c]That I may [1]plant the heavens,
Lay the foundations of the earth,
And say to Zion, 'You *are* My
people.'"

God's Fury Removed

17 [a]Awake, awake!
Stand up, O Jerusalem,
You who [b]have drunk at the hand
of the LORD
The cup of His fury;
You have drunk the dregs of the
cup of trembling,
And drained *it* out.
18 *There is* no one to guide her
Among all the sons she has
brought forth;
Nor *is there any* who takes her
by the hand
Among all the sons she has
brought up.

12 [a]2 Cor. 1:3 [b]Ps. 118:6; Is. 2:22 [c]Is. 40:6, 7; James 1:10; 1 Pet. 1:24
13 [a]Deut. 6:12; 8:11; Is. 17:10; Jer. 2:32 [b]Ps. 104:2 [c]Job 20:7
14 [a]Zech. 9:11
15 [a]Job 26:12
16 [a]Deut. 18:18; Is. 59:21; John 3:34 [b]Ex. 33:22; Is. 49:2 [c]Is. 65:17 [1]*establish*
17 [a]Is. 52:1 [b]Job 21:20; Is. 29:9; Jer. 25:15; Rev. 14:10; 16:19
19 [a]Is. 47:9 [b]Amos 7:2
20 [a]Lam. 2:11
21 [a]Lam. 3:15
22 [a]Is. 3:12, 13; 49:25; Jer. 50:34
23 [a]Is. 14:2; Jer. 25:17, 26–28; Zech. 12:2 [1]Lit. *your soul*

CHAPTER 52

1 [a]Neh. 11:1; Is. 48:2; 64:10; Zech. 14:20, 21; Matt. 4:5; [Rev. 21:2–27]
2 [a]Is. 3:26 [b]Is. 9:4; 10:27; 14:25; Zech. 2:7
3 [a]Ps. 44:12; Jer. 15:13 [b]Is. 45:13

19 [a]These two *things* have come to
you;
Who will be sorry for you?—
Desolation and destruction,
famine and sword—
[b]By whom will I comfort you?
20 [a]Your sons have fainted,
They lie at the head of all the
streets,
Like an antelope in a net;
They are full of the fury of the
LORD,
The rebuke of your God.

21 Therefore please hear this, you
afflicted,
And drunk [a]but not with wine.
22 Thus says your Lord,
The LORD and your God,
Who [a]pleads the cause of His
people:
"See, I have taken out of your hand
The cup of trembling,
The dregs of the cup of My fury;
You shall no longer drink it.
23 [a]But I will put it into the hand of
those who afflict you,
Who have said to [1]you,
'Lie down, that we may walk over
you.'
And you have laid your body like
the ground,
And as the street, for those who
walk over."

God Redeems Jerusalem

52 Awake, awake!
Put on your strength, O Zion;
Put on your beautiful garments,
O Jerusalem, the holy city!
For the uncircumcised [a]and the
unclean
Shall no longer come to you.
2 [a]Shake yourself from the dust,
arise;
Sit down, O Jerusalem!
[b]Loose yourself from the bonds of
your neck,
O captive daughter of Zion!

3 For thus says the LORD:

[a]"You have sold yourselves for
nothing,
And you shall be redeemed
[b]without money."

51:13 The oppressor refers historically to the Babylonian Empire.
52:1, 2 Awake, . . . O Zion: See note on 51:17–23.
52:3–12 Another celebration of God's anticipated coming to the **waste places of Jerusalem.** Its fulfillment is twofold: the return from Babylonian captivity, and **the salvation of our God** in Christ. This latter is seen in Isaiah's use of **that day.** See note on Obad. 15.

4 For thus says the Lord GOD:
"My people went down at first
Into [a]Egypt to [1]dwell there;
Then the Assyrian oppressed
them without cause.
5 Now therefore, what have I here,"
says the LORD,
"That My people are taken away
for nothing?
Those who rule over them
[1]Make them wail," says the LORD,
"And My name *is* [a]blasphemed
continually every day.
6 Therefore My people shall know
My name;
Therefore *they shall know* in that
day
That I *am* He who speaks:
'Behold, *it is* I.' "

7 [a]How beautiful upon the
mountains
Are the feet of him who brings
good news,
Who proclaims peace,
Who brings glad tidings of *good
things,
Who proclaims salvation,
Who says to Zion,
[b]"Your God reigns!"
8 Your watchmen shall lift up *their*
voices,
With their voices they shall sing
together;
For they shall see eye to eye
When the LORD brings back Zion.
9 Break forth into joy, sing
together,
You waste places of Jerusalem!
For the LORD has comforted His
people,
He has **redeemed** Jerusalem.

WORD WEALTH

52:9 redeemed, *ga'al* (gah-*ahl*); Strong's #1350: Ransom, redeem, repurchase; to set free by avenging or repaying. *Ga'al* refers to the custom of buying back something a person has lost through helplessness, poverty, or violence. Furthermore, the one who does the redeeming is often a close relative who is in a stronger position and buys back the lost property on behalf of his weaker relative. Ps. 72 is universally understood as speaking of the Messiah; v. 14 states "He will redeem [*ga'al*] the life of the needy from oppression and violence." In Is. 52:9, God redeems Jerusalem, buying it back from its oppressors on behalf of His people. The biblical view of redemption is extremely wide, for God has pledged to redeem the whole creation, which currently groans in bondage (Rom. 8:20–23).

10 [a]The LORD has [1]made bare His
holy arm
In the eyes of [b]all the nations;
And all the ends of the earth shall
see
The salvation of our God.

11 [a]Depart! Depart! Go out from
there,
Touch no unclean *thing;*
Go out from the midst of her,
[b]Be clean,
You who bear the vessels of the
LORD.
12 For [a]you shall not go out with
haste,
Nor go by flight;
[b]For the LORD will go before you,
[c]And the God of Israel *will be* your
rear guard.

The Sin-Bearing Servant

13 Behold, [a]My Servant shall
[1]deal prudently;
[b]He shall be exalted and [2]extolled
and be very high.
14 Just as many were astonished at
you,
So His [a]visage[1] was marred more
than any man,

4 [a]Gen. 46:6 [1]As resident aliens
5 [a]Ezek. 36:20, 23; Rom. 2:24 [1]DSS *Mock;* LXX *Marvel and wail;* Tg. *Boast themselves;* Vg. *Treat them unjustly*
7 [a]Is. 40:9; 61:1; Nah. 1:15; Rom. 10:15; Eph. 6:15 [b]Ps. 93:1; Is. 24:23 *See WW at Ezek. 34:14.
10 [a]Ps. 98:1–3 [b]Luke 3:6 [1]Revealed His power
11 [a]Is. 48:20; Jer. 50:8; Zech. 2:6, 7; 2 Cor. 6:17 [b]Lev. 22:2; [Is. 1:16]
12 [a]Ex. 12:11, 33; Deut. 16:3 [b]Mic. 2:13 [c]Ex. 14:19, 20; Is. 58:8
13 [a]Is. 42:1 [b]Is. 57:15; Phil. 2:9 [1]*prosper* [2]Lit. *be lifted up*
14 [a]Ps. 22:6, 7; Matt. 26:67; 27:30; John 19:3 [1]*appearance*

52:4 The Assyrian oppressed: See notes on 7:17 and 10:7, 8.
52:7 Beautiful upon the mountains: God will overthrow Babylon. Darius, the Lord's chosen instrument, has established his authority and will decree restoration **to Zion.** Let the watchman climb the mountains and proclaim this good news, **Your God reigns!** Paul quotes this verse in Rom. 10:15 with direct reference to preaching the gospel.
52:10 Made bare His holy arm: This is a colloquialism meaning "God will roll up His sleeves" and use His sword to redeem His people in the sight of **all the nations.**
52:13—53:12 Behold My Servant: This is the final Servant Song: See note on 42:1–4. It is one of the greatest passages in the Bible, the mountain peak of Isaiah's book, the most sublime messianic prophecy in the OT, relating so many features of Jesus Christ's redemptive work.

The song concerns the enemies' killing of the Servant (Messiah) (53:4, 5), who astonishingly is restored to life by Yahweh (53:10). All His suffering and His death are for others' sins (53:5).

Some commentators, looking for a historical figure to fulfill this role as a type of Christ, see the servant here again as Zerubbabel. See note on 50:4–9. Based on the fact that he "mysteriously" disappears from Scripture prior to the dedication of the second temple, some scholars see in this text that he was beaten and murdered.
52:13 Exalted . . . very high: After the utmost suffering, the **Servant** will be highly exalted (see Phil. 2:6–11).
52:14 Marred more than any man: The suffering and physical disfigurement of the Servant would be unparalleled. The crown of thorns precedes the crown of glory (see John 12:23–25).

And His form more than the sons
of men;
15 [a]So shall He [1]sprinkle many
nations.
Kings shall shut their mouths at
Him;
For [b]what had not been told them
they shall see,
And what they had not heard they
shall consider.

53 Who [a]has believed our report?
And to whom has the arm of
the LORD been *revealed?

KINGDOM DYNAMICS

53:1–12 Purposes of the Crucifixion, Atonement, and Abundant Life, MESSIAH'S COMING. This is the best-known prophecy of the Crucifixion in the Bible, and both Matthew (Matt. 8:17) and Peter (1 Pet. 2:24) quote from it. Writing eight centuries before Christ, Isaiah made incredibly accurate statements concerning the facts of the Crucifixion; but more importantly, he spoke of the purpose of the Cross.

In Christ's suffering and death, He bore more than our sins. The penalty for sin is death, but Christ did not need to suffer as He did to provide atonement. This chapter tells us why He suffered: He suffered to bear our griefs and sorrows (v. 4), and He suffered for our peace and healing (v. 5).

Surely atonement for sin is our greatest need; yet God, sending His Son to suffer and die, provided more than an escape from judgment; He provided for abundant life beginning today (see John 10:10). (Ps. 22:1–31/Ps. 16:10) J.H.

2 For He shall grow up before Him
as a tender plant,
And as a root out of dry
ground.
He has no [1]form or [2]comeliness;
And when we see Him,
There is no [3]beauty that we
should desire Him.
3 [a]He is despised and [1]rejected by
men,
A Man of [2]sorrows and
[b]acquainted with [3]grief.
And we hid, as it were, *our* faces
from Him;
He was despised, and [c]we did not
esteem Him.

4 Surely [a]He has borne our 5
[1]griefs
And carried our [2]sorrows;
Yet we [3]esteemed Him stricken,
[4]Smitten by God, and afflicted.
5 But He *was* [a]wounded[1] for our
*transgressions,
He was [2]bruised for our
iniquities;
The chastisement for our peace
was upon Him,
And by His [b]stripes[3] we are
healed.

15 [a]Num. 19:18–21; Ezek. 36:25 [b]Rom. 15:21; [Eph. 3:5, 9]; 1 Pet. 1:2 [1]Or *startle*

CHAPTER 53

1 [a]John 12:38; Rom. 10:16 *See WW at Amos 3:7.
2 [1]Stately form [2]*splendor* [3]Lit. *appearance*
3 [a]Ps. 22:6; [Is. 49:7; Matt. 27:30, 31; Luke 18:31–33; 23:18] [b][Heb. 4:15] [c][John 1:10, 11] [1]Or *forsaken* [2]Lit. *pains* [3]Lit. *sickness*
4 [a][Matt. 8:17; Heb. 9:28; 1 Pet. 2:24] [1]Lit. *sicknesses* [2]Lit. *pains* [3]*reckoned* [4]*Struck down*
5 [a][Is. 53:10; Rom. 4:25; 1 Cor. 15:3, 4] [b][1 Pet. 2:24, 25] [1]Or *pierced through* [2]*crushed* [3]Blows that cut in *See WW at Ezek. 18:31.

KINGDOM DYNAMICS

53:4, 5 Healing Prophesied Through Christ's Atonement, DIVINE HEALING. Is. 53 clearly teaches that bodily healing is included in the atoning work of Christ, His suffering, and His Cross. The Hebrew words for "griefs" and "sorrows" (v. 4) specifically mean physical affliction. This is verified in the fact that Matt. 8:17 says this Is. text is being exemplarily fulfilled in Jesus' healing people of human sickness and other physical need.

Further, that the words "borne" and "carried" refer to Jesus' atoning work on the Cross is made clear by the fact that they are the same words used to describe Christ's bearing our sins (see v. 11; also 1 Pet. 2:24). These texts unequivocally link the grounds of provision for both our salvation and our healing to the atoning work of Calvary. Neither is automatically appropriated however; for each provision—a soul's eternal salvation or a person's temporal, physical healing—must be received by faith. Christ's work on the Cross makes each possible: simple faith receives each as we choose.

Incidentally, a few contend that Isaiah's prophecy about sickness was fulfilled completely by the one-day healings described by Matt. 8:17. A close look, however, will show that the word "ful-

52:15 Sprinkle many nations: The Servant's atoning sacrifice will cleanse many Gentiles and cause even **kings** to be astounded at the result of suffering.
53:2 A root out of dry ground expresses the obscurity of *the Messiah's origin.* See note on 11:1. **No form . . . desire Him** laments His death. Jesus' trial and crucifixion were nothing to desire.
53:3 Acquainted with grief: To be our perfect High Priest, Christ Jesus had to know our griefs by experience. See notes on Heb. 2:14, 15 and 4:15. **Despised:** See note on 49:7.
53:4–12 See section 5 of Truth-In-Action at the end of Is.
53:4 Has borne . . . carried: These verbs mean "to take upon oneself," or "to carry as a burden," obvious references to vicarious suffering. The remainder of the chapter speaks of the Servant's vicarious suffering. **Grief . . . sorrows:** These nouns have reference to sicknesses, both spiritual and physical. See note on Matt. 8:17. **Smitten by God:** The Servant's suffering is part of God's providential plan.
53:5 Transgressions . . . iniquities are literally wickedness and rebellion. **Our:** The pronoun is emphatic; He suffered not for Himself but for mankind's sins and sicknesses (v. 6). **Stripes . . . healed:** Peter sees this as referring to Christ on the Cross. See note on 1 Pet. 2:24, 25.

fill" often applies to an action that extends throughout the whole church age. (See Is. 42:1–4; Matt. 12:14–17.)
(Ps. 107:20/Matt. 4:23–25) N.V.

6 All we like sheep have gone
astray;
We have turned, every one, to his
own way;
And the LORD [1]has laid on Him
the iniquity of us all.

7 He was oppressed and He was
afflicted,
Yet [a]He opened not His mouth;
[b]He was led as a lamb to the
slaughter,
And as a sheep before its shearers
is silent,
So He opened not His mouth.
8 He was [a]taken from [1]prison and
from judgment,
And who will declare His
generation?
For [b]He was cut off from the land
of the living;
For the transgressions of My
people He was stricken.
9 [a]And [1]they made His grave with
the wicked—
But with the rich at His death,
Because He had done no violence,
Nor *was any* [b]deceit in His mouth.

10 Yet it pleased the LORD to
[1]bruise Him;
He has put *Him* to grief.
When You make His soul
[a]an offering for sin,
He shall see *His* seed, He shall
prolong *His* days,
And the pleasure of the LORD
shall prosper in His hand.
11 [1]He shall see the labor of His soul,
and be satisfied.
By His *knowledge [a]My
*righteous [b]Servant shall
[c]justify many,
For He shall bear their iniquities.
12 [a]Therefore I will divide Him a
portion with the great,

6 [1]Lit. *has caused to land on Him*
7 [a]Matt. 26:63; 27:12–14 [b]Acts 8:32, 33
8 [a]Luke 23:1–25 [b][Dan. 9:26] [1]*confinement*
9 [a]Matt. 27:57–60 [b]1 Pet. 2:22 [1]Lit. *he* or *He*
10 [a][2 Cor. 5:21] [1]*crush*
11 [a][1 John 2:1] [b]Is. 42:1 [c][Rom. 5:15–18] [1]So with MT, Tg., Vg.; DSS, LXX *From the labor of His soul He shall see light* *See WW at Mal. 2:7. • See WW at Lam. 1:18.
12 [a]Ps. 2:8

53:7 Opened not His mouth is a statement of the Servant's complete submission. Philip the evangelist expounded this verse to the Ethiopian eunuch, leading him to Christ (see Acts 8:32).
53:8, 9 He had done no violence depicts the sinlessness of Christ in spite of the fact He suffered great injustice (v. 8). **The rich . . . death** prophesies Christ's decent and honorable burial in the tomb of Joseph of Arimathea (Matt. 27:57–60).
53:10 Offering for sin: Christ's death on the Cross was the infinite sin offering, the only offering that could atone for the sins of mankind. See note on v. 4. **Prolong *His* days** is paradoxical in light of the Servant's death. It is an obvious reference to Christ's resurrection. ***His* seed** are His redeemed.
53:11 Justify many: By bearing man's iniquities, Christ obtains a righteous standing before God for all who personally accept His atonement. See Rom. 5:1.
53:12 Made intercession here means more than prayer. It is a summary statement meaning that Christ gave Himself completely on behalf of mankind. **I will divide . . . the strong** is symbolic language denoting Yahweh's **reward** of Christ for His faithfulness. See note on 52:13.

THE SUFFERING SERVANT (53:12)

Jesus understood His mission and work as the fulfillment of Isaiah's Suffering Servant.

The Prophecy	The Fulfillment
He will be exalted (52:13)	Philippians 2:9
He will be disfigured by suffering (52:14; 53:2)	Mark 15:17, 19
He will make a blood atonement (52:15)	1 Peter 1:2
He will be widely rejected (53:1, 3)	John 12:37, 38
He will bear our sins and sorrows (53:4, 5)	Romans 4:25; 1 Peter 2:24, 25
He will be our substitute (53:6, 8)	2 Corinthians 5:21
He will voluntarily accept our guilt and punishment (53:7, 8)	John 10:11; 19:30
He will be buried in a rich man's tomb (53:9)	John 19:38–42
He will save us who believe in Him (53:10, 11)	John 3:16; Acts 16:31
He will die on behalf of transgressors (53:12)	Mark 15:27, 28; Luke 22:37

[b]And He shall divide the [1]spoil
with the strong,
Because He [c]poured out His soul
unto death,
And He was [d]numbered with the
transgressors,
And He bore the sin of many,
And [e]made* intercession for the
transgressors.

A Perpetual Covenant of Peace

54 "Sing, O [a]barren,
You *who* have not borne!
Break forth into *singing, and cry
aloud,
You *who* have not labored with
child!
For more *are* the children of the
desolate
Than the children of the married
woman," says the LORD.
2 "Enlarge[a] the place of your
tent,
And let them stretch out the
curtains of your dwellings;
Do not spare;
Lengthen your cords,
And strengthen your stakes.
3 For you shall expand to the right
and to the left,
And your descendants will
[a]inherit the nations,
And make the desolate cities
inhabited.

4 "Do[a] not fear, for you will not be
ashamed;
Neither be disgraced, for you will
not be put to shame;
For you will forget the shame of
your youth,
And will not remember the
reproach of your widowhood
anymore.
5 [a]For your Maker *is* your husband,
The LORD of hosts *is* His name;
And your Redeemer *is* the Holy
One of Israel;
He is called [b]the God of the whole
earth.

12 [b]Col. 2:15 [c]Is. 50:6; [Rom. 3:25] [d]Matt. 27:38; Mark 15:28; Luke 22:37; 2 Cor. 5:21 [e]Luke 23:34 [1]*plunder* *See WW at Jer. 27:18

CHAPTER 54

1 [a]Gal. 4:27 *See WW at Ps. 30:5.
2 [a]Is. 49:19, 20
3 [a]Is. 14:2; 49:22, 23; 60:9
4 [a]Is. 41:10
5 [a]Jer. 3:14; Hos. 2:19 [b]Zech. 14:9; Rom. 3:29

KINGDOM DYNAMICS

54:5 The Husband, Protector and Provider, FAMILY ORDER. God reveals Himself by the title husband to disclose how deeply He loves His people and how effectively He cares for them. In so doing, He unveils an important dimension of human family life with particular reference to husbands: a husband is to love and take care of his wife and children. God is a Protector and a Provider. Husbands who open themselves to God's direction will find both the inspiration and the power to be those things for their families, for those attributes of God's being will flow into and fill their lives.
(1 Cor. 7:3, 4/Mal. 2:13, 14, 16) L.C.

6 For the LORD [a]has called you
Like a woman forsaken and
grieved in spirit,
Like a youthful wife when you
were refused,"
Says your God.
7 "For[a] a mere moment I have
forsaken you,
But with great mercies [b]I will
gather you.
8 With a little wrath I hid My face
from you for a moment;
[a]But with everlasting kindness
I will *have mercy on
you,"
Says the LORD, your Redeemer.

9 "For this *is* like the waters of
[a]Noah to Me;
For as I have sworn
That the waters of Noah would no
longer cover the earth,
So have I sworn
That I would not be angry with
[b]you, nor rebuke you.
10 For [a]the mountains shall depart
And the hills be removed,
[b]But My kindness shall not depart
from you,
Nor shall My covenant of peace
be removed,"
Says the LORD, who has mercy on
you.

6 [a]Is. 62:4
7 [a]Ps. 30:5; Is. 26:20; 60:10; 2 Cor. 4:17 [b][Is. 43:5; 56:8]
8 [a]Is. 55:3; Jer. 31:3 *See WW at Hos. 2:23.
9 [a]Gen. 8:21; 9:11; [2 Pet. 3:6, 7] [b]Is. 12:1; Ezek. 39:29
10 [a]Ps. 46:2; Is. 51:6; Matt. 5:18 [b]2 Sam. 23:5; Ps. 89:33, 34; Is. 55:3; 59:21; 61:8

54:1–10 Historically, these verses prophesy Jerusalem's restoration under Darius. Again future prosperity is promised in response to Israel's complaint of being **forsaken.** See note on 49:14–26. In type this passage also teaches how Christians overcome the trauma of grief and the barren areas of life.

54:1 The good news of the atoning work and exaltation of the Servant is followed by a command to the **barren** woman (Israel) to prepare for expansion of Yahweh's covenant family. Israel in captivity is compared to a barren woman, an object of **disappointment** and scorn in the ancient world. **To sing** in the face of such a state would be a cruel act, were it not for the power of song. Isaiah's word is to deal with the barrenness through worship, to enthrone God in song in order to release His miraculous provision. See note on Ps. 22:3.

54:2 This amplifies v. 1. As an act of faith, the yet barren exiles are to make provision for God's expansion (v. 3).

54:4 The shame of your youth is a reference to the bondage in Egypt. **The reproach of your widowhood** is a reference to the Babylonian captivity.

54:7 I will gather you: See note on Zeph. 2:7.

11 "O you afflicted one,
Tossed with tempest, *and* not comforted,
Behold, I will lay your stones with [a]colorful gems,
And lay your foundations with sapphires.
12 I will make your pinnacles of rubies,
Your gates of crystal,
And all your walls of precious stones.
13 All your children *shall be* [a]taught by the LORD,
And [b]great *shall be* the peace of your children.
14 In righteousness you shall be established;
You shall be far from oppression, for you shall not fear;
And from terror, for it shall not come near you.
15 Indeed they shall surely assemble, *but* not because of Me.
Whoever assembles against you shall [a]fall for your sake.
16 "Behold, I have created the blacksmith
Who blows the coals in the fire,
Who brings forth an [1]instrument for his work;
And I have created the [2]spoiler to destroy.
17 No weapon formed against you shall [a]prosper,
And every tongue *which* rises against you in judgment
You shall condemn.
This *is* the heritage of the servants of the LORD,
[b]And their righteousness *is* from Me,"
Says the LORD.

An Invitation to Abundant Life

[3] 55 "Ho! [a]Everyone who thirsts,
Come to the waters;
And you who have no money,
[b]Come, buy and eat.
Yes, come, buy wine and milk
Without money and without price.
2 Why do you [1]spend money for *what is* not bread,
And your wages for *what* does not satisfy?
Listen carefully to Me, and eat *what is* good,
And let your soul delight itself in abundance.
3 Incline your ear, and [a]come to Me.
Hear, and your soul shall live;
[b]And I will make an everlasting covenant with you—
The [c]sure mercies of David.
4 Indeed I have given him *as* [a]a witness to the people,
[b]A leader and commander for the people.
5 [a]Surely you shall call a nation you do not know,
[b]And nations *who* do not know you shall run to you,
Because of the LORD your God,
And the Holy One of Israel;
[c]For He has glorified you."

6 [a]Seek the LORD while He may be [b]found,
Call upon Him while He is near.
7 [a]Let the [1]wicked forsake his way,
And the unrighteous man [b]his thoughts;
Let him return to the LORD,
[c]And He will have mercy on him;
And to our God,
For He will abundantly *pardon.
8 "For[a] My thoughts *are* not your thoughts,
Nor *are* your ways My ways,"
says the LORD.
9 "For[a] *as* the heavens are higher than the earth,
So are My ways higher than your ways,
And My thoughts than your thoughts.

11 [a]1 Chr. 29:2; Job 28:16; Rev. 21:18, 19
13 [a]Jer. 31:34; [John 6:45; 1 Cor. 2:10]; 1 Thess. 4:9; [1 John 2:20] [b]Ps. 119:165
15 [a]Is. 41:11–16
16 [1]Or *weapon* [2]*destroyer*
17 [a]Is. 17:12–14; 29:8 [b]Is. 45:24, 25; 54:14

CHAPTER 55

1 [a][Matt. 5:6; John 4:14; 7:37; Rev. 21:6; 22:17] [b][Matt. 13:44; Rev. 3:18]
2 [1]Lit. *weigh out silver*
3 [a]Matt. 11:28 [b]Is. 54:8; 61:8; Jer. 32:40 [c]2 Sam. 7:8; Ps. 89:28; [Acts 13:34]
4 [a][John 18:37; Rev. 1:5] [b][Jer. 30:9; Ezek. 34:23; Dan. 9:25]
5 [a]Is. 52:15; Eph. 2:11, 12 [b]Is. 60:5 [c]Is. 60:9
6 [a]Matt. 5:25; 25:11; John 7:34; 8:21; 2 Cor. 6:2; [Heb. 3:13] [b]Ps. 32:6; Is. 49:8
7 [a]Is. 1:16 [b]Is. 59:7; Zech. 8:17 [c]Ps. 130:7; Jer. 3:12 [1]Lit. *man of iniquity* *See WW at Ps. 103:3.
8 [a]2 Sam. 7:19
9 [a]Ps. 103:11

54:11–17 This section is best interpreted eschatologically. See note on Ezek. 40:1—48:35.
54:17 This *is* the heritage: Though Yahweh's people must await the world to come for the consummation of this promise, it is also applicable now. God does foil evil plots and accusations against His people.
55:1–5 See section 3 of Truth-In-Action at the end of Is.
55:1–5 Yahweh addresses the exiles. He summons them to detach themselves from Babylon's influences (v. 2) that they may enjoy His gracious, abundant meal (true satisfaction in Him as returnees to Jerusalem).
55:1 Have no money: God's abundant life is free.
55:3 The sure mercies of David defines God's **covenant** in terms of God's acts of faithfulness to David. Paul applied this to life in Christ (Acts 13:34).
55:4 A witness to the people: A new Leader will assume David's role. This is a reference to Christ (see Rev. 1:5); Isaiah still has the Servant in view.
55:6–13 In anticipation of the restoration of His people, Yahweh calls Israel to repent (vv. 6, 7). He addresses any who doubt that He is about to move by reminding them that His plans transcend man's; man cannot always accurately read God's **ways** (vv. 8, 9); nothing can stop His decrees (vv. 11–13).

4 10 "For [a]as the rain comes down, and
the snow from heaven,
And do not return there,
But water the earth,
And make it bring forth and bud,
That it may give seed to the
*sower
And bread to the eater,
11 [a]So shall My word be that goes
forth from My mouth;
It shall not return to Me [1]void,
But it shall accomplish what I
please,
And it shall [b]prosper *in the thing*
for which I sent it.

KINGDOM DYNAMICS

55:10, 11 God's Word, Evangelism, and Expansion, THE WORD OF GOD. Evangelism (the spreading of the Good News) and expansion (the enlarging of life's potential under God) both multiply by the "seed" of God's Word. Jesus described the Word as "seed" also (Luke 8:11), the source of all saving life and growth possibilities transmitted from the Father to mankind. All increase of life within His love comes by His Word, as human response gives place for His blessing. When received, God's word of promise will never be barren. The power in His Word will always fulfill the promise of His Word. We never need wonder how faith is developed or how fruitfulness is realized. Faith comes by "hearing" God's Word (Rom. 10:17), that is, by receiving it wholeheartedly and humbly. Fruitfulness is the guaranteed by-product—whether for the salvation of a lost soul or the provision of a disciple's need—God's Word cannot be barren or fruitless: His own life-power is within it!
(James 1:23–25/2 Tim. 2:15) J.W.H.

12 "For[a] you shall go out with joy,
And be led out with peace;
The mountains and the hills
Shall [b]break forth into singing
before you,
And [c]all the trees of the field shall
clap *their* hands.
13 [a]Instead of [b]the thorn shall come
up the cypress tree,
And instead of the brier shall
come up the myrtle tree;
And it shall be to the LORD
[c]for a name,
For an everlasting sign *that* shall
not be cut off."

10 [a]Deut. 32:2 *See WW at Hos. 10:12.
11 [a]Is. 45:23; Matt. 24:35 [b]Is. 46:9–11 [1]*empty, without fruit*
12 [a]Is. 35:10 [b]Ps. 98:8 [c]1 Chr. 16:33
13 [a]Is. 41:19 [b]Mic. 7:4 [c]Jer. 13:11

Salvation for the Gentiles

56 Thus says the LORD:
"Keep justice, and do
righteousness,
[a]For My salvation *is* about to
come,
And My righteousness to be
revealed.
2 Blessed *is* the man *who* does this,
And the son of man *who* lays hold
on it;
[a]Who keeps from defiling the
Sabbath,
And keeps his hand from doing
any evil."

3 Do not let [a]the son of the
foreigner
Who has joined himself to the
LORD
Speak, saying,
"The LORD has utterly separated
me from His people";
Nor let the [b]eunuch say,
"Here I am, a dry tree."
4 For thus says the LORD:
"To the eunuchs who keep My
Sabbaths,
And choose what pleases Me,
And hold fast My covenant,
5 Even to them I will give in
[a]My house
And within My walls a place
[b]and a name
Better than that of sons and
daughters;
I will give [1]them an everlasting
name
That shall not be cut off.
6 "Also the sons of the foreigner
Who join themselves to the LORD,
to serve Him,

CHAPTER 56

1 [a]Is. 46:13; Matt. 3:2; 4:17; Rom. 13:11, 12
2 [a]Ex. 20:8–11; 31:13–17; Is. 58:13; Jer. 17:21, 22; Ezek. 20:12, 20
3 [a]Is. 14:1; [Eph. 2:12–19] [b]Deut. 23:1; Jer. 38:7; Acts 8:27
5 [a]1 Tim. 3:15 [b][1 John 3:1, 2] [1]Lit. *him*

55:10, 11 See section 4 of Truth-In-Action at the end of Is.
55:11 God's promises and plans (**words**) are as sure of fulfillment as the fact that it rains and snows (v. 10).
55:12, 13 These verses symbolically depict creation's joy at God's redemptive action. Fulfilled in part in the postexilic return, the verses are ultimately messianic and eschatological. They depict cosmic joy at the reign of Christ (see Luke 2:13, 14) as well as prophesy the world to come when "creation itself also will be delivered from the bondage of corruption" (Rom. 8:21).
56:1–8 A prophecy that God's **salvation** will include people of all nations. After the return from Babylon, there were many Gentile proselytes to Judaism. In the reign of the Messiah, Jews and Gentiles worship God together (see Eph. 2:11–22).
56:2 Son of man is mankind. **Who keeps . . . the Sabbath** symbolizes the entire process of repentance and a desire to walk with Yahweh.
56:3 The eunuch symbolizes all those the Law prohibited from worshiping with God's people. See Lev. 21:20.
56:5 Better than . . . daughters: See Matt. 8:5–12.

And to *love the name of the
LORD, to be His servants—
Everyone who keeps from
defiling the Sabbath,
And holds fast My covenant—
7 Even them I will [a]bring to My
holy mountain,
And *make them joyful in My
[b]house of prayer.
[c]Their burnt offerings and their
sacrifices
Will be [d]accepted on My altar;
For [e]My house shall be called a
house of prayer [f]for all
nations."
8 The Lord GOD, [a]who gathers the
outcasts of Israel, says,
[b]"Yet I will gather to him
Others besides those who are
gathered to him."

Israel's Irresponsible Leaders

9 [a]All you beasts of the field, come
to devour,
All you beasts in the forest.
10 His *watchmen *are* [a]blind,
They are all ignorant;
[b]They *are* all dumb dogs,
They cannot bark;
[1]Sleeping, lying down, loving to
slumber.
11 Yes, *they are* [a]greedy[1] dogs
Which [b]never[2] have enough.
And they *are* shepherds
Who cannot understand;
They all look to their own way,
Every one for his own gain,
From his *own* territory.
12 "Come," *one says,* "I will bring
wine,
And we will fill ourselves with
intoxicating [a]drink;
[b]Tomorrow will be [c]as today,
And much more abundant."

Israel's Futile Idolatry

57 The righteous perishes,
And no man takes *it* to heart;
[a]Merciful men *are* taken away,
[b]While no one considers
That the righteous is taken away
from [1]evil.

6 *See WW at Ps. 97:10
7 [a][Is. 2:2, 3; 60:11] [b]Mark 11:17 [c][Rom. 12:1] [d]Is. 60:7 [e]Matt. 21:13 [f][Mal. 1:11] *See WW at 2 Chr. 7:10.
8 [a]Is. 11:12; 27:12; 54:7 [b][John 10:16]
9 [a]Jer. 12:9
10 [a]Matt. 15:14 [b]Phil. 3:2 [1]Or *Dreaming* *See WW at Hos. 9:8.
11 [a][Mic. 3:5, 11] [b]Ezek. 34:2–10 [1]Lit. *strong of soul* [2]Lit. *do not know satisfaction*
12 [a]Is. 28:7 [b]Luke 12:19 [c]2 Pet. 3:4

CHAPTER 57

1 [a]Ps. 12:1 [b]1 Kin. 14:13 [1]Lit. *the face of evil*

2 [a]2 Chr. 16:14
3 [a]Matt. 16:4
5 [a]2 Kin. 16:4 [b]Jer. 7:31
6 [a]Jer. 3:9 [b]Jer. 5:9, 29; 9:9
7 [a]Ezek. 16:16 [b]Ezek. 23:41
8 [a]Ezek. 16:26 [1]Lit. *cut* [2]Lit. *hand,* a euphemism *See WW at Ex. 34:27.
9 [a]Hos. 7:11 [b]Ezek. 23:16, 40

2 He shall enter into peace;
They shall rest in [a]their beds,
Each one walking *in* his
uprightness.

3 "But come here,
[a]You sons of the sorceress,
You offspring of the adulterer and
the harlot!
4 Whom do you ridicule?
Against whom do you make a
wide mouth
And stick out the tongue?
Are you not children of
transgression,
Offspring of falsehood,
5 Inflaming yourselves with gods
[a]under every green tree,
[b]Slaying the children in the
valleys,
Under the clefts of the rocks?
6 Among the smooth [a]*stones* of the
stream
Is your portion;
They, they, *are* your lot!
Even to them you have poured a
drink offering,
You have offered a grain offering.
Should I receive comfort in
[b]these?

7 "On[a] a lofty and high mountain
You have set [b]your bed;
Even there you went up
To offer sacrifice.
8 Also behind the doors and their
posts
You have set up your
remembrance;
For you have uncovered yourself
to those other than Me,
And have gone up to them;
You have enlarged your bed
And [1]made* *a covenant* with
them;
[a]You have loved their bed,
Where you saw *their* [2]nudity.
9 [a]You went to the king with
ointment,
And increased your perfumes;
You sent your [b]messengers far
off,
And *even* descended to Sheol.

56:9–12 This is likely a prophetic indictment against the sinful leadership (**watchmen . . . shepherds**) of postexilic Jerusalem. They are characterized by much the same attitude as the preexilic leaders. See note on Ezra 9:7.
57:1–13 Continues the thought of 56:9–12, with an emphasis on the general populace. A disciplined Israel is still guilty of all the forms of idolatry and pagan sacrifice that characterized preexilic times. In their spiritual adultery, they have no fear of God nor inclination to repent. See note on Ezra 9:1–5 and Introduction to Ezra: Content.
57:4 The idolaters were mocking and making rude gestures of contempt to the faithful remnant.
57:5 Slaying the children refers to child sacrifice to Molech. See note on Jer. 32:35.
57:9, 10 Descended to Sheol refers to the low estate into which they have fallen. They are seen as serving Satan. Nonetheless, they did not repent (v. 10).

10 You are wearied in the length of your way;
[a]*Yet* you did not say, 'There is no hope.'
You have found the life of your hand;
Therefore you were not grieved.

11 "And [a]of whom have you been afraid, or feared,
That you have lied
And not remembered Me,
Nor taken *it* to your heart?
Is it not because [b]I have [1]held My peace from of old
That you do not fear Me?
12 I will declare your righteousness
And your works,
For they will not profit you.
13 When you cry out,
Let your collection *of idols* deliver you.
But the wind will carry them all away,
A breath will take *them.*
But he who *puts his trust in Me
shall possess the land,
And shall inherit My holy mountain."

Healing for the Backslider

14 And one shall say,
[a]"Heap it up! Heap it up!
Prepare the way,
Take the stumbling block out of the way of My people."

15 For thus says the High and Lofty One
Who inhabits eternity, [a]whose name *is* *Holy:
[b]"I dwell in the high and holy *place,*
[c]With him *who* has a contrite and humble spirit,
[d]To revive the spirit of the humble,
And to revive the heart of the contrite ones.
16 [a]For I will not contend forever,
Nor will I always be angry;
For the spirit would fail before Me,
And the souls [b]*which* I have made.

10 [a]Jer. 2:25; 18:12
11 [a]Prov. 29:25; Is. 51:12, 13 [b]Ps. 50:21; Eccl. 8:11; Is. 42:14 [1]*remained silent*
13 *See WW at Zeph. 3:12.
14 [a]Is. 40:3; 62:10; Jer. 18:15
15 [a]Job 6:10; Luke 1:49 [b]Ps. 68:35; Zech. 2:13 [c]Ps. 34:18; 51:17; Is. 66:2 [d]Ps. 147:3; Is. 61:1–3 *See WW at Lev. 19:2.
16 [a]Ps. 85:5; 103:9; [Mic. 7:18] [b]Num. 16:22; Job 34:14; Heb. 12:9
17 [a]Is. 2:7; 56:11; Jer. 6:13 [b]Is. 8:17; 45:15; 59:2 [c]Is. 9:13 [1]Or *turning back*
18 [a]Jer. 3:22 [b]Is. 61:2 *See WW at Ex. 15:26.
19 [a]Is. 6:7; 51:16; 59:21; Heb. 13:15 [b]Acts 2:39; Eph. 2:17
20 [a]Job 15:20; Prov. 4:16; Jude 13
21 [a]Is. 48:22

CHAPTER 58

1 [a]Mic. 3:8 [1]*do not hold back*
3 [a]Mal. 3:13–18; Luke 18:12 [b]Lev. 16:29; 23:27 [1]Lit. *drive hard* *See WW at Jon. 3:5.
4 [a]1 Kin. 21:9

17 For the iniquity of [a]his covetousness
I was angry and struck him;
[b]I hid and was angry,
[c]And he went on [1]backsliding in the way of his heart.
18 I have seen his ways, and
[a]will *heal him;
I will also lead him,
And restore comforts to him
And to [b]his mourners.

19 "I create [a]the fruit of the lips:
Peace, peace [b]to *him who is* far off and to *him who is* near,"
Says the LORD,
"And I will heal him."
20 [a]But the wicked *are* like the troubled sea,
When it cannot rest,
Whose waters cast up mire and dirt.

21 "*There*[a] *is* no peace,"
Says my God, "for the wicked."

Fasting that Pleases God

58 "Cry aloud, [1]spare not;
Lift up your voice like a trumpet;
[a]Tell My people their transgression,
And the house of Jacob their sins.
2 Yet they seek Me daily,
And delight to know My ways,
As a nation that did righteousness,
And did not forsake the ordinance of their God.
They ask of Me the ordinances of justice;
They take delight in approaching God.
3 'Why[a] have we *fasted,' *they say,*
'and You have not seen?
Why have we [b]afflicted our souls,
and You take no notice?'

"In fact, in the day of your fast you find pleasure,
And [1]exploit all your laborers.
4 [a]Indeed you fast for strife and debate,

57:11 From of old: They have taken advantage of God's longsuffering and the fact He did not totally annihilate them "on the spot."
57:14–21 A contrite . . . spirit: God will have mercy and forgive those who repent with a contrite **heart;** He greatly desires to be at **peace** with His wayward family, but there can be **no peace for the wicked** and unrepentant.
58:1–5 Israel has yet another **transgression,** that of defective worship, particularly the wrong concept of fasting. Israel worshiped and sacrificed with regularity, but their works belied their religion. Their ostentatious self-denial was really selfish. They were ignoring the real needs.

Some see this as a word to Judah in Isaiah's day. See note on 1:11–15. Others see it as a prophetic word to the returned exiles during their first decade of return.
58:4 Their **fast** days turned into times of physical strife.

And to strike with the fist of
wickedness.
You will not fast as *you do* this
day,
To make your voice heard on
high.
5 Is [a]it a fast that I have chosen,
[b]A day for a man to afflict his soul?
Is it to bow down his head like a
bulrush,
And [c]to spread out sackcloth and
ashes?
Would you call this a fast,
And an acceptable day to the
LORD?

6 "*Is* this not the fast that I have
chosen:
To [a]loose the bonds of
wickedness,
[b]To undo the [1]heavy burdens,
[c]To let the oppressed go free,
And that you break every yoke?
7 *Is it* not [a]to share your bread with
the hungry,
And that you bring to your house
the *poor who are [1]cast out;
[b]When you see the naked, that you
cover him,
And not hide yourself from
[c]your own flesh?
8 [a]Then your light shall break forth
like the morning,
Your healing shall spring forth
speedily,
And your righteousness shall go
before you;
[b]The glory of the LORD shall be
your rear guard.
9 Then you shall call, and the LORD
will answer;
You shall cry, and He will say,
'Here I *am*.'

"If you take away the yoke from
your midst,
The [1]pointing of the finger, and
[a]speaking wickedness,
10 *If* you extend your soul to the
hungry
And satisfy the afflicted soul,
Then your light shall dawn in the
darkness,
And your [1]darkness shall *be* as
the noonday.

5 [a]Zech. 7:5 [b]Lev. 16:29 [c]Esth. 4:3; Job 2:8; Dan. 9:3
6 [a]Luke 4:18, 19 [b]Neh. 5:10–12 [c]Jer. 34:9 [1]Lit. *bonds of the yoke*
7 [a]Ezek. 18:7; Matt. 25:35 [b]Job 31:19–22; James 2:14–17 [c]Gen. 29:14; Neh. 5:5 [1]*wandering* *See WW at Ps. 40:17.
8 [a]Job 11:17 [b]Ex. 14:19; Is. 52:12
9 [a]Ps. 12:2; Is. 59:13 [1]Lit. *sending out of*
10 [1]Or *gloom*
12 [a]Is. 61:4 [1]Lit. *Paths* *See WW at Ezek. 22:30. • See WW at Ruth 4:15.
13 [a]Ex. 31:16, 17; 35:2, 3; Is. 56:2, 4, 6; Jer. 17:21–27
14 [a]Job 22:26; Is. 61:10 [b]Deut. 32:13; 33:29; Is. 33:16; Hab. 3:19 [c]Is. 1:20; 40:5; Mic. 4:4

CHAPTER 59

1 [a]Num. 11:23; Is. 50:2; Jer. 32:17

11 The LORD will guide you
continually,
And satisfy your soul in drought,
And strengthen your bones;
You shall be like a watered
garden,
And like a spring of water, whose
waters do not fail.
12 Those from among you
[a]Shall build the old waste places;
You shall raise up the
foundations of many
generations;
And you shall be called the
Repairer of the *Breach,
The *Restorer of [1]Streets to
Dwell In.

13 "If [a]you turn away your foot from
the Sabbath,
From doing your pleasure on My
holy day,
And call the Sabbath a delight,
The holy *day* of the LORD
honorable,
And shall honor Him, not doing
your own ways,
Nor finding your own pleasure,
Nor speaking *your own* words,
14 [a]Then you shall delight yourself in
the LORD;
And I will cause you to [b]ride on
the high hills of the earth,
And feed you with the heritage of
Jacob your father.
[c]The mouth of the LORD has
spoken."

KINGDOM DYNAMICS

58:1–14 Repentance in Restoration, RESTORATION. The whole text of Is. 58 emphasizes the place of repentance in restoration. The entire concept of "The Holy Spirit and Restoration" is developed in the study article that begins on page 2012.

(Heb. 12:26, 27/Acts 15:16–18) J.R.

Separated from God

59 Behold, the LORD's hand is not 5
[a]shortened,
That it cannot save;
Nor His ear heavy,
That it cannot hear.

58:6–14 The fast that I have chosen: The Lord clarifies the meaning of true fasting for Israel. She must cease to oppress the poor and must observe **the Sabbath** with pure and joyful worship. See note on 56:2. Then the Lord will give **light, healing,** and full restoration.

58:9 The yoke refers to all forms of political, economic, and social injustice. **The pointing . . . finger** refers to falsely accusing people with fear tactics. **Speaking wickedness** refers to stirring up trouble.

58:12 Most scholars see this as a promise of the redevelopment of a postexilic Jerusalem if the previous conditions are met.

59:1–15 See section 5 of Truth-In-Action at the end of Is.

59:1–8 Another indictment against violence, deception, and injustice, with the result that Israel had no **peace**. See notes on 58:1–5 and 58:6–14.

2 But your iniquities have
separated you from your God;
And your sins have hidden *His*
face from you,
So that He will [a]not hear.
3 For [a]your hands are defiled with
[1]blood,
And your fingers with iniquity;
Your lips have spoken lies,
Your tongue has *muttered
perversity.

4 No one calls for justice,
Nor does *any* plead for truth.
They trust in [a]empty words and
speak lies;
[b]They conceive [1]evil and bring
forth iniquity.
5 They hatch vipers' eggs and
weave the spider's web;
He who eats of their eggs dies,
And *from* that which is crushed
a viper breaks out.

6 [a]Their webs will not become
garments,
Nor will they cover themselves
with their works;
Their works *are* works of
iniquity,
And the act of violence *is* in their
hands.
7 [a]Their feet run to evil,
And they make haste to shed
[b]innocent blood;
[c]Their thoughts *are* thoughts of
iniquity;
Wasting and [d]destruction *are* in
their paths.
8 The way of [a]peace they have not
known,
And *there is* no justice in their
ways;
[b]They have made themselves
crooked paths;
Whoever takes that way shall not
know peace.

Sin Confessed

9 Therefore justice is far from us,
Nor does righteousness overtake
us;
[a]We look for light, but there is
darkness!
For brightness, *but* we walk in
blackness!
10 [a]We grope for the wall like the
blind,
And we grope as if *we had* no
eyes;
We stumble at noonday as at
twilight;
We are as dead *men* in desolate
places.
11 We all growl like bears,
And [a]moan sadly like doves;
We look for justice, but *there is*
none;
For salvation, *but* it is far from
us.
12 For our [a]transgressions are
multiplied before You,
And our sins testify against us;
For our transgressions *are* with
us,
And *as for* our iniquities, we
know them:
13 In transgressing and lying against
the LORD,
And departing from our God,
Speaking oppression and revolt,
Conceiving and uttering [a]from
the heart words of falsehood.
14 Justice is turned back,
And righteousness stands afar
off;
For truth is fallen in the street,
And equity cannot enter.
15 So truth fails,
And he *who* departs from evil
makes himself a [a]prey.

The Redeemer of Zion

Then the LORD saw *it,* and
[1]it displeased Him
That *there was* no justice.
16 [a]He saw that *there was* no man,
And [b]wondered that *there was* no
*intercessor;
[c]Therefore His own arm brought
salvation for Him;
And His own righteousness, it
sustained Him.
17 [a]For He put on righteousness as a
breastplate,
And a helmet of salvation on His
*head;

2 [a]Is. 1:15
3 [a]Is. 1:15, 21; Jer. 2:30, 34; Ezek. 7:23; Hos. 4:2 [1]*bloodshed* *See WW at Ps. 1:2.
4 [a]Is. 30:12; Jer. 7:4 [b]Job 15:35; Ps. 7:14; Is. 33:11 [1]*trouble*
6 [a]Job 8:14
7 [a]Prov. 1:16; Rom. 3:15 [b]Prov. 6:17 [c]Is. 55:7 [d]Rom. 3:16, 17
8 [a]Is. 57:20, 21 [b]Ps. 125:5; Prov. 2:15
9 [a]Jer. 8:15
10 [a]Deut. 28:29; Job 5:14; Amos 8:9
11 [a]Is. 38:14; Ezek. 7:16
12 [a]Is. 24:5; 58:1
13 [a]Matt. 12:34
15 [a]Is. 5:23; 10:2; 29:21; 32:7 [1]Lit. *it was evil in His eyes*
16 [a]Is. 41:28; 63:5; 64:7; Ezek. 22:30 [b]Mark 6:6 [c]Ps. 98:1; Is. 63:5 *See WW at Jer. 27:18.
17 [a]Eph. 6:14, 17; 1 Thess. 5:8 *See WW at Gen. 3:15.

59:9–15 The prophet here takes up a lament for the benighted nation submerged in injustice, oppression, and falsehood. However, beginning with v. 12, he voices an awareness and confession that the people are beginning to recognize they have created their own problems.
59:16–21 His own arm brought salvation: Finding no human **intercessor** qualified to represent fallen Israel, **the LORD** provides His own **salvation**. He clothes Himself in the armor of a soldier to deal with enemies and the unrepentant. Then He brings redemption to the penitent in Zion. The section is messianic, referring to the salvation wrought by Christ. Historically, it was partially fulfilled through the redemptive actions of the Persian emperor, Artaxerxes I (465–423 B.C.).
59:16 No intercessor: See note on Ezek. 22:30.

He put on the garments of
vengeance for clothing,
And was clad with zeal as a
cloak.
18 [a]According to *their* deeds,
accordingly He will repay,
Fury to His adversaries,
Recompense to His enemies;
The coastlands He will fully
repay.
19 [a]So shall they fear
The name of the LORD from the
west,
And His glory from the rising of
the sun;
When the enemy comes in
[b]like a flood,
The Spirit of the LORD will lift up
a standard against him.

20 "The[a] Redeemer will come to Zion,
And to those who turn from
transgression in Jacob,"
Says the LORD.

21 "As[a] for Me," says the LORD, "this
is My covenant with them: My Spirit
who *is* upon you, and My words which
I have put in your mouth, shall not depart from your mouth, nor from the
mouth of your descendants, nor from
the mouth of your descendants' descendants," says the LORD, "from
this time and forevermore."

18 [a]Is. 63:6; Rom. 2:6
19 [a]Ps. 113:3; Mal. 1:11 [b]Rev. 12:15
20 [a]Rom. 11:26
21 [a][Heb. 8:10; 10:16]

CHAPTER 60
1 [a]Eph. 5:14 [b]Mal. 4:2

The Gentiles Bless Zion

60 Arise, [a]shine;
For your light has come!
And [b]the **glory** of the LORD is
risen upon you.

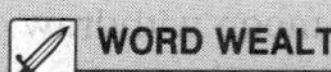

WORD WEALTH

60:1 glory, *chabod* (kah-*vohd*); Strong's #3519: Weightiness; that which is substantial or heavy; glory, honor, splendor, power, wealth, authority, magnificence, fame, dignity, riches, and excellency. The root of *chabod* is *chabad,* "to be heavy, glorious, notable," or "to be renowned." In the OT, "heaviness" represented honor and substance, while "lightness" was equated with vanity, instability, temporariness, and emptiness (see Judg. 9:4; Zeph. 3:4). *Chabod* is God's glory, not only His honor, renown, and majesty, but also His visible splendor, which filled Solomon's temple and will someday fill the Earth (1 Kin. 8:11; Num. 14:21). From *chabod* are derived the names "Jochebed" ("Yahweh Is Glory") and Ichabod ("Where Is the Glory?").

2 For behold, the darkness shall
cover the earth,
And deep darkness the people;
But the LORD will arise over
you,
And His glory will be seen upon
you.
3 The [a]Gentiles shall come to your
light,
And kings to the brightness of
your rising.

4 "Lift[a] up your eyes all around, and
see:
They all gather together,
[b]they come to you;
Your sons shall come from afar,
And your daughters shall be
nursed at *your* side.
5 Then you shall see and become
radiant,
And your heart shall swell with
joy;
Because [a]the abundance of the
sea shall be turned to you,
The wealth of the Gentiles shall
come to you.
6 The multitude of camels shall
cover your *land,*
The dromedaries of Midian and
[a]Ephah;
All those from [b]Sheba shall come;
They shall bring [c]gold and
incense,
And they shall proclaim the
praises of the LORD.
7 All the flocks of [a]Kedar shall be
gathered together to you,

3 [a]Is. 49:6, 23; Rev. 21:24
4 [a]Is. 49:18 [b]Is. 49:20–22
5 [a][Rom. 11:25–27]
6 [a]Gen. 25:4 [b]Gen. 25:3; Ps. 72:10 [c]Is. 61:6; Matt. 2:11
7 [a]Gen. 25:13

59:19 When the enemy . . . against him: God's people are assured their enemies will be met with the irresistible power of His **Spirit**. For the work of the Spirit in the life of the Redeemer, see note on 11:2.

59:20 Redeemer: The word used implies redemption secured by an atoning sacrifice.

59:21 My Spirit: A promise of the Spirit's power to rest upon the true prophets and spokesmen in Israel. Joel 2:28, 29 prophesied that the Spirit would be poured out in the last days upon all flesh, which Peter said is fulfilled in the church (Acts 2:16–21).

60:1–22 While these glowing prophetic promises of restoration would bring hope to **Israel** in captivity, the fullest unfolding is messianic and eschatological. See notes on 32:1–8 and Obad. 15.

60:3 The Gentiles: See note on 56:1–8.

60:5 The wealth of the Gentiles: This was partially fulfilled in the material assistance provided by Persia during the return to the land in 538 B.C.

60:6, 7 Midian, Ephah, Sheba, Kedar, and **Nebaioth** were cities of the Arabian Desert. **Glorify the house of My glory:** The Gentile wealth brought from the above cities would be for the adorning of the second temple (see Ezra 1:5–11).

The rams of Nebaioth shall
*minister to you;
They shall ascend with
[b]acceptance on My altar,
And [c]I will glorify the house of
My glory.

8 "Who *are* these *who* fly like a
cloud,
And like doves to their roosts?
9 [a]Surely the coastlands shall wait
for Me;
And the ships of Tarshish *will*
come first,
[b]To bring your sons from afar,
[c]Their silver and their gold with
them,
To the name of the LORD your
God,
And to the Holy One of Israel,
[d]Because He has glorified you.

10 "The[a] sons of foreigners shall
build up your walls,
[b]And their kings shall minister to
you;
For [c]in My wrath I struck you,
[d]But in My *favor I have had
mercy on you.
11 Therefore your gates [a]shall be
open continually;
They shall not be shut day or
night,
That *men* may bring to you the
wealth of the Gentiles,
And their kings in procession.
12 [a]For the nation and kingdom
which will not serve you shall
perish,
And *those* nations shall be utterly
ruined.

13 "The[a] glory of Lebanon shall come
to you,
The cypress, the pine, and the box
tree together,
To beautify the place of My
sanctuary;
And I will make [b]the place of My
feet glorious.
14 Also the sons of those who
afflicted you
Shall come [a]bowing to you,
And all those who despised you
shall [b]fall prostrate at the soles
of your feet;
And they shall call you The City
of the LORD,
[c]Zion of the Holy One of Israel.

7 [b]Is. 56:7 [c]Is. 60:13; Hag. 2:7, 9 *See WW at 1 Chr. 15:2.
9 [a]Ps. 72:10 [b][Gal. 4:26] [c]Jer. 3:17 [d]Is. 55:5
10 [a]Is. 14:1, 2; 61:5; Zech. 6:15 [b]Is. 49:23; Rev. 21:24 [c]Is. 57:17 [d]Is. 54:7, 8 *See WW at Deut. 33:23.
11 [a]Is. 26:2; 60:18; 62:10; Rev. 21:25, 26
12 [a]Is. 14:2; Zech. 14:17; Matt. 21:44
13 [a]Is. 35:2 [b]1 Chr. 28:2; Ps. 132:7
14 [a]Is. 45:14 [b]Is. 49:23; Rev. 3:9 [c][Heb. 12:22; Rev. 14:1]
16 [a]Is. 49:23 [b]Is. 43:3
18 [a]Is. 26:1 [1]*devastation* *See WW at Ps. 100:4.
19 [a]Rev. 21:23; 22:5 [b]Is. 41:16; 45:25; Zech. 2:5
20 [a]Amos 8:9
21 [a]Is. 52:1; Rev. 21:27 [b]Ps. 37:11; Matt. 5:5 [c]Is. 61:3; [Matt. 15:13; John 15:2] [d]Is. 29:23; [Eph. 2:10] *See WW at Deut. 8:1.
22 [a]Matt. 13:31, 32

15 "Whereas you have been forsaken
and hated,
So that no one went through *you,*
I will make you an eternal
excellence,
A joy of many generations.
16 You shall drink the milk of the
Gentiles,
[a]And milk the breast of kings;
You shall know that [b]I, the LORD,
am your Savior
And your Redeemer, the Mighty
One of Jacob.

17 "Instead of bronze I will bring
gold,
Instead of iron I will bring silver,
Instead of wood, bronze,
And instead of stones, iron.
I will also make your officers
peace,
And your magistrates
righteousness.
18 Violence shall no longer be heard
in your land,
Neither [1]wasting nor destruction
within your borders;
But you shall call [a]your walls
Salvation,
And your gates *Praise.

God the Glory of His People

19 "The [a]sun shall no longer be your
light by day,
Nor for brightness shall the moon
give light to you;
But the LORD will be to you an
everlasting light,
And [b]your God your glory.
20 [a]Your sun shall no longer go
down,
Nor shall your moon withdraw
itself;
For the LORD will be your
everlasting light,
And the days of your mourning
shall be ended.
21 [a]Also your people *shall* all *be*
righteous;
[b]They shall *inherit the land
forever,
[c]The branch of My planting,
[d]The work of My hands,
That I may be glorified.
22 [a]A little one shall become a
thousand,
And a small one a strong nation.

60:13 Cypress, pine, and **box** were woods for the construction of the second temple.
60:16 You shall drink the milk of the Gentiles, and milk the breast of kings are metaphors describing the support in vv. 5–13.
60:17–22 The descriptions in this section are unquestionably eschatological. See note on Ezek. 40:1—48:35.

I, the LORD, will hasten it in its
time."

The Good News of Salvation

61 "The [a]Spirit of the Lord GOD *is*
upon Me,
Because the LORD [b]has
anointed Me
To preach good tidings to the
poor;
He has sent Me [c]to [1]heal the
brokenhearted,
To proclaim [d]liberty* to the
captives,
And the opening of the prison to
those who are bound;

WORD WEALTH

61:1 anointed, *mashach* (mah-*shahch*); Strong's #4886: To anoint, to rub with oil, especially in order to consecrate someone or something. Appearing almost 70 times, *mashach* refers to the custom of rubbing or smearing with sacred oil to consecrate holy persons or holy things. Priests (Lev. 8:12; 16:32) and kings (2 Sam. 2:4; 5:3; 1 Kin. 1:39) in particular were installed in their offices by anointing. In Ex. 40:9–14, the tabernacle was to be anointed, as well as the altar, the laver, and the high priest's sons. The most important derivative of *mashach* is *mashiyach* (Messiah), "anointed one." As Jesus was and is the promised Anointed One, His title came to be "Jesus the Messiah." Messiah was translated into Greek as *Christos*, thus His designation, "Jesus Christ."

2 [a]To proclaim the acceptable year
of the LORD,
And [b]the day of vengeance of our
God;
[c]To comfort all who mourn,
3 To [1]console those who mourn in
Zion,
[a]To give them beauty for ashes,
The oil of joy for mourning,
The garment of praise for the
spirit of heaviness;

CHAPTER 61

1 [a]Is. 11:2; Matt. 3:17; Luke 4:18, 19; John 1:32; 3:34 [b]Ps. 45:7; Matt. 11:5; Luke 7:22 [c]Ps. 147:3 [d]Is. 42:7; [Acts 10:43] [1]Lit. *bind up* *See WW at Lev. 25:10.
2 [a]Lev. 25:9 [b]Is. 34:8; Mal. 4:1, 3; [2 Thess. 1:7] [c]Is. 57:18; Jer. 31:13; Matt. 5:4
3 [a]Ps. 30:11 [b]Is. 60:21; [Jer. 17:7, 8] [c][John 15:8] [1]Lit. *appoint*

4 [a]Is. 49:8; 58:12; Ezek. 36:33; Amos 9:14
5 [a][Eph. 2:12]
6 [a]Ex. 19:6 [b]Is. 60:5, 11 *See WW at 1 Chr. 15:2.
7 [a]Is. 40:2; Zech. 9:12

That they may be called trees of
righteousness,
[b]The planting of the LORD,
[c]that He may be glorified."

KINGDOM DYNAMICS

61:3 The Glorious Garment of Praise, PRAISE PATHWAY. The Hebrew root for "garment" (*'atah*) shows praise as more than a piece of clothing casually thrown over our shoulders. It literally teaches us "to wrap" or "cover" ourselves—that the garment of praise is to leave no openings through which hostile elements can penetrate. This garment of praise repels and replaces the heavy spirit. This special message of instruction and hope is for those oppressed by fear or doubt. "Put on" this garment. A warm coat from our closet only resists the cold wind when it is "put on." When distressed, be dressed—with praise! Act according to God's Word!
(Ps. 150:1–6/Matt. 21:16) C.G.

4 And they shall [a]rebuild the old
ruins,
They shall raise up the former
desolations,
And they shall repair the ruined
cities,
The desolations of many
generations.
5 [a]Strangers shall stand and feed
your flocks,
And the sons of the foreigner
Shall be your plowmen and your
vinedressers.
6 [a]But you shall be named the
priests of the LORD,
They shall call you the *servants
of our God.
[b]You shall eat the riches of the
Gentiles,
And in their glory you shall boast.
7 [a]Instead of your shame *you shall
have* double *honor*,
And *instead of* confusion they
shall rejoice in their portion.
Therefore in their land they shall
possess double;
Everlasting joy shall be theirs.

61:1–11 This section describes the ministry of God's **anointed** as a healer and messenger of freedom and comfort (vv. 1–3). See note on v. 1. It also describes what God's ministry means to the nations (vv. 4–7). All this is due to God's covenant promises (vv. 8–11). Historically, some scholars see the anointed as Ezra. See Introduction to Ezra: Christ Revealed.

61:1 Jesus quoted this verse and part of v. 2 in the synagogue at Nazareth (Luke 4:17–20). He affirmed that it depicts the essence of His ministry. It also describes the basic ministry He passed on to His church. See note on Matt. 10:1, 2.

61:2 The day of vengeance belongs to Christ's Second Coming. See note on Obad. 15.

61:3 The symbolism here depicts festive joy as part of the Messiah's reign. **The spirit of heaviness** refers to discouragement. It is to be replaced by an abundant life (**the garment of praise**). Many see in this text the power of worship-filled praise to cast off oppressive works of darkness.

61:4–7 Sons of the foreigner: A continued promise that **the Gentiles** would honor and serve God's purposes and that God's people would always supply **priests** for the nations. See note on 1 Pet. 2:9, 10.

8 "For [a]I, the LORD, love justice;
[b]I hate robbery [1]for burnt offering;
I will direct their work in truth,
[c]And will make with them an everlasting *covenant.
9 Their descendants shall be known among the Gentiles,
And their offspring among the people.
All who see them shall acknowledge them,
[a]That they *are* the posterity *whom* the LORD has blessed."

10 [a]I will greatly *rejoice in the LORD,
My soul shall *be joyful in my God;
For [b]He has clothed me with the garments of salvation,
He has covered me with the robe of righteousness,
[c]As a bridegroom decks *himself* with ornaments,
And as a bride adorns *herself* with her jewels.
11 For as the earth brings forth its bud,
As the garden causes the things that are sown in it to spring forth,
So the Lord GOD will cause [a]righteousness and [b]praise to spring forth before all the nations.

Assurance of Zion's Salvation

62 For Zion's sake I will not [1]hold My peace,
And for Jerusalem's sake I will not rest,
Until her righteousness goes forth as brightness,
And her salvation as a lamp *that* burns.
2 [a]The Gentiles shall see your righteousness,
And all [b]kings your glory.
[c]You shall be called by a new name,
Which the mouth of the LORD will name.
3 You shall also be [a]a crown of glory
In the *hand of the LORD,
And a royal diadem
In the hand of your God.
4 [a]You shall no longer be termed [b]Forsaken,[1]
Nor shall your land any more be termed [c]Desolate;[2]
But you shall be called [3]Hephzibah, and your land [4]Beulah;
For the LORD delights in you,
And your land shall be married.
5 For *as* a young man marries a virgin,
So shall your sons marry you;
And *as* the bridegroom rejoices over the bride,
[a]*So* shall your God *rejoice over you.

6 [a]I have set watchmen on your walls, O Jerusalem;
They shall [1]never hold their peace day or night.
You who [2]**make mention** of the LORD, do not keep silent,

WORD WEALTH

62:6 make mention, *zachar* (zah-*char*); Strong's #2142: To remember, bring into mind, recollect; also, to mention, meditate upon, mark down, record, recall, and retain in one's thoughts. To remember something or someone is to approve of, to acknowledge, and to treat as a matter of importance, whereas to forget something or someone is to dismiss or abandon as unimportant. God remembered Noah, Abraham, Rachel, and His covenant (Gen. 8:1; 19:29; 30:22; Ex. 2:24). In the new covenant, God promises to never again remember Israel's sin (Jer. 31:34).

7 And give Him no rest till He establishes
And till He makes Jerusalem [a]a praise in the earth.

8 The LORD has sworn by His right hand
And by the arm of His strength:
"Surely I will no longer [a]give your grain
As food for your enemies;
And the sons of the foreigner shall not drink your new wine,
For which you have labored.
9 But those who have gathered it shall eat it,
And praise the LORD;
Those who have brought it together shall drink it [a]in My holy courts."

8 [a]Ps. 11:7 [b]Is. 1:11, 13 [c]Gen. 17:7; Ps. 105:10; Is. 55:3; Jer. 32:40 [1]Or *in* *See WW at Gen. 17:7. **9** [a]Is. 65:23 **10** [a]Hab. 3:18 [b]Ps. 132:9, 16 [c]Is. 49:18; Rev. 21:2 *See WW at Is. 64:5. • See WW at Hab. 3:18. **11** [a]Ps. 72:3; 85:11 [b]Is. 60:18; 62:7

CHAPTER 62

1 [1]*keep silent* **2** [a]Is. 60:3 [b]Ps. 102:15, 16; 138:4, 5; 148:11, 13 [c]Is. 62:4, 12; 65:15 **3** [a]Is. 28:5; Zech. 9:16; 1 Thess. 2:19 *See WW at Josh. 4:24. **4** [a]Hos. 1:10; 1 Pet. 2:10 [b]Is. 49:14; 54:6, 7 [c]Is. 54:1 [1]Heb. *Azubah* [2]Heb. *Shemamah* [3]Lit. *My Delight Is in Her* [4]Lit. *Married*

5 [a]Is. 65:19 *See WW at Is. 64:5. **6** [a]Is. 52:8; Jer. 6:17; Ezek. 3:17; 33:7 [1]*not be silent* [2]*remember* **7** [a]Is. 60:18; 61:11; Jer. 33:9; Zeph. 3:19, 20 **8** [a]Lev. 26:16; Deut. 28:31, 33; Judg. 6:3–6; Is. 1:7; Jer. 5:17 **9** [a]Deut. 12:12; 14:23, 26

61:10, 11 An unidentified speaker announces the personal benefits of the ministry of the Anointed (vv. 1–3). **Righteousness** connotes deliverance.
62:1–12 The description of **Zion**'s restoration continues. See notes on 60:1–22 and 61:4–7.
62:1–5 See section 3 of Truth-In-Action at the end of Is.
62:6, 7 God's restoration will include **watchmen** of prayer.

10 Go through,
Go through the gates!
[a]Prepare the way for the people;
Build up,
Build up the highway!
Take out the stones,
[b]Lift up a banner for the peoples!

11 Indeed the LORD has proclaimed
To the end of the world:
[a]"Say to the daughter of Zion,
'Surely your salvation is coming;
Behold, His [b]reward *is* with
Him,
And His [1]work before Him.' "
12 And they shall call them The Holy
People,
The Redeemed of the LORD;
And you shall be called Sought
Out,
A City Not Forsaken.

The LORD in Judgment and Salvation

63 Who *is* this who comes from
Edom,
With dyed garments from
Bozrah,
This *One who is* [1]glorious in His
apparel,
Traveling in the greatness of His
strength?—

"I who speak in righteousness,
mighty to save."

2 Why [a]*is* Your apparel red,
And Your garments like one who
treads in the winepress?

3 "I have [a]trodden the winepress
alone,
And from the peoples no one *was*
with Me.
For I have trodden them in My
anger,
And trampled them in My fury;
Their blood is sprinkled upon My
garments,
And I have stained all My robes.

10 [a]Is. 40:3; 57:14 [b]Is. 11:12
11 [a]Zech. 9:9; Matt. 21:5; John 12:15 [b]Is. 40:10; [Rev. 22:12] [1]*recompense*

CHAPTER 63

1 [1]Or *adorned*
2 [a][Rev. 19:13, 15]
3 [a]Lam. 1:15; Rev. 14:19, 20; 19:15

4 [a]Is. 34:8; 35:4; 61:2; Jer. 51:6 *See WW at Is. 52:9.
5 [a]Is. 41:28; 59:16 [b][John 16:32] [c]Ps. 98:1; Is. 59:16
9 [a]Judg. 10:16 [b]Ex. 14:19 [c]Deut. 7:7 [d]Ex. 19:4 [1]Kt., LXX, Syr. *not afflicted*
10 [a]Ex. 15:24 [b]Num. 14:11; Ps. 78:40; Acts 7:51; 1 Cor. 10:1–11 [c]Ex. 23:21; Ps. 106:40

4 For the [a]day of vengeance *is* in
My heart,
And the year of My *redeemed
has come.
5 [a]I looked, but [b]*there was* no one
to help,
And I wondered
That *there was* no one to uphold;
Therefore My own [c]arm brought
salvation for Me;
And My own fury, it sustained
Me.
6 I have trodden down the peoples
in My anger,
Made them drunk in My fury,
And brought down their strength
to the earth."

God's Mercy Remembered

7 I will mention the
lovingkindnesses of the LORD
And the praises of the LORD,
According to all that the LORD has
bestowed on us,
And the great goodness toward
the house of Israel,
Which He has bestowed on them
according to His mercies,
According to the multitude of His
lovingkindnesses.
8 For He said, "Surely they *are* My
people,
Children *who* will not lie."
So He became their Savior.
9 [a]In all their affliction He was
[1]afflicted,
[b]And the Angel of His Presence
saved them;
[c]In His love and in His pity He
redeemed them;
And [d]He bore them and carried
them
All the days of old.
10 But they [a]rebelled and [b]grieved
His Holy Spirit;
[c]So He turned Himself against
them as an enemy,
And He fought against them.

62:12 A City Not Forsaken: God's people, forsaken during the captivity, would again become **Sought Out.**

63:1–6 This section has no OT parallel. It symbolically depicts Yahweh in bloodstained garments, returning from annihilating the enemies of His people. The initial messianic fulfillment is noted in Matt. 12:22–29 and Col. 2:15; its consummation is found in Rev. 19:11–21.

63:1 Edom was a territory southeast of the Dead Sea, inhabited by the descendants of Esau; the name "Edom" means "Red." That nation was usually in conflict with Judah, and Edom became a symbol of wicked nations. See note on Obad. 10, 11. **Bozrah** was a city of Edom whose name means "Grape Gathering."

63:3 Winepress is a play on the Hebrew meaning of "Bozrah."

63:4 The day of vengeance: See note on 61:2.

63:5 See note on 59:16–21.

63:7–19 These verses consist of a sermon-prayer by Isaiah for his nation's restoration, but particularly for the faithful remnant whom he calls **Your servants**. Its basis is a memorializing of God's Exodus deeds.

63:9 The Angel of His Presence refers to God's Presence (Ex. 33:15).

63:10–14 His Holy Spirit: These verses list three references to the work of the Holy Spirit in Israel's exodus from Egypt, a work of saving, guiding, and giving rest.

11 Then he [a]remembered the days of old,
Moses *and* his people, *saying:*
"Where *is* He who [b]brought them up out of the sea
With the [1]shepherd of His flock?
[c]Where *is* He who put His Holy Spirit within them,
12 Who led *them* by the right hand of Moses,
[a]With His glorious arm,
[b]Dividing the water before them
To make for Himself an everlasting name,
13 [a]Who led them through the deep,
As a horse in the wilderness,
That they might not stumble?"

14 As a beast goes down into the valley,
And the Spirit of the LORD causes him to *rest,
So You lead Your people,
[a]To make Yourself a glorious name.

A Prayer of Penitence

15 [a]Look down from heaven,
And see [b]from Your habitation, holy and glorious.
Where *are* Your zeal and Your strength,
The yearning [c]of Your heart and Your mercies toward me?
Are they restrained?
16 [a]Doubtless You *are* our *Father,
Though Abraham [b]was ignorant of us,
And Israel does not acknowledge us.
You, O LORD, *are* our Father;
Our Redeemer from Everlasting *is* Your name.
17 O LORD, why have You [a]made us stray from Your ways,
And hardened our heart from Your fear?
Return for Your servants' sake,
The tribes of Your inheritance.
18 [a]Your holy people have possessed *it* but a little while;
[b]Our adversaries have trodden down Your sanctuary.
19 We have become *like* those of old, over whom You never ruled,
Those who were never called by Your name.

64 Oh, that You would [1]rend the heavens!
That You would come down!
That the mountains might shake at Your [a]presence—
2 As fire burns brushwood,
As fire causes water to boil—
To make Your name known to Your adversaries,
That the nations may tremble at Your presence!
3 When [a]You did awesome things *for which* we did not look,
You came down,
The mountains shook at Your presence.
4 For since the beginning of the world
[a]*Men* have not heard nor perceived by the ear,
Nor has the eye seen any God besides You,
Who acts for the one who waits for Him.
5 You meet him who **rejoices** and does righteousness,
Who remembers You in Your ways.
You are indeed angry, for we have sinned—
[a]In these ways we continue;
And we need to be saved.

WORD WEALTH

64:5 rejoices, ***sus*** **(soos);** Strong's #7797: To rejoice, be glad, be greatly happy. *Sus* is one of several Hebrew words for "rejoice." It occurs 27 times, appearing in such well-loved references as Ps. 40:16; Is. 35:1; 62:5; Zeph. 3:17. From this verb is derived *sason,* a noun meaning "joy, rejoicing, gladness." *Sason* is quite evident in Esth. 8:16; Ps. 45:7; Is. 12:3; 61:3; Jer. 31:13. These verses describe a rejoicing that is the complete antithesis of mourning; it is a pervasive, irresistible joy.

6 But we are all like an unclean *thing,*
And all [a]our righteousnesses *are* like [1]filthy rags;
We all [b]fade as a leaf,

11 [a]Ps. 106:44, 45 [b]Ex. 14:30 [c]Num. 11:17, 25, 29; Hag. 2:5 [1]MT, Vg. *shepherds*
12 [a]Ex. 15:6 [b]Ex. 14:21, 22; Josh. 3:16; Is. 11:15; 51:10
13 [a]Ps. 106:9
14 [a]2 Sam. 7:23 *See WW at Ex. 33:14.
15 [a]Deut. 26:15; Ps. 80:14 [b]Ps. 33:14 [c]Jer. 31:20; Hos. 11:8
16 [a]Deut. 32:6 [b]Job 14:21 *See WW at Ps. 68:5.
17 [a]Is. 6:9, 10; John 12:40
18 [a]Deut. 7:6 [b]Ps. 74:3–7; Is. 64:11

CHAPTER 64

1 [a]Ex. 19:18; Ps. 18:9; 144:5; Mic. 1:3, 4; [Hab. 3:13] [1]*tear open*
3 [a]Ex. 34:10
4 [a]Ps. 31:19
5 [a]Mal. 3:6
6 [a][Phil. 3:9] [b]Ps. 90:5, 6; Is.1:30 [1]Lit. *a filthy garment*

63:16 Israel refers to Jacob.
63:17 Why have You made . . . Your fear? likely represents the view of the exiles. It is obviously theologically incorrect.
64:1–12 A continuation of the prayer of Isaiah, here praying that God would **come down** in Earth-shaking manifestation to punish **the nations** and to save **Zion** as would a **Father**.
64:4 Paul alludes to this verse in 1 Cor. 2:9 to support the fact that sinful **man** is ignorant of what God has accomplished in Christ.
64:6 Righteousness . . . filthy rags: Sin and guilt have left the Israelites like soiled underclothes.

And our iniquities, like the wind,
Have taken us away.
7 And *there is* no one who calls on
Your name,
Who *stirs himself up to take hold
of You;
For You have hidden Your face
from us,
And have [1]consumed us because
of our iniquities.

8 But now, O LORD,
You *are* our Father;
We *are* the clay, and You our
[a]potter;
And all we *are* the work of Your
hand.
9 Do not be furious, O LORD,
Nor remember iniquity forever;
Indeed, please look—we all *are*
Your people!
10 Your holy cities are a wilderness,
Zion is a wilderness,
Jerusalem a desolation.
11 Our holy and beautiful [1]temple,
Where our fathers *praised You,
Is burned up with fire;
And all [a]our pleasant things
[2]are laid waste.
12 [a]Will You restrain Yourself
because of these *things,*
O LORD?
[b]Will You [1]hold Your peace, and
afflict us very severely?

The Righteousness of God's Judgment

65 "I was [a]sought by *those who* did
not ask *for Me;*
I was found by *those who* did not
*seek Me.
I said, 'Here I am, here I am,'
To a nation *that* [b]was not called
by My name.
2 [a]I have stretched out My hands all
day long to a [b]rebellious
people,
Who [c]walk in a way *that is* not
good,
According to their own thoughts;

7 [1]Lit. *caused us to melt* *See WW at Hag. 1:14.
8 [a]Is. 29:16; 45:9; Jer. 18:6; [Rom. 9:20, 21]
11 [a]Ezek. 24:21 [1]Lit. *house* [2]*have become a ruin* *See WW at 1 Chr. 23:30.
12 [a]Is. 42:14 [b]Ps. 83:1 [1]*keep silent*

CHAPTER 65

1 [a]Rom. 9:24; 10:20 [b]Is. 63:19 *See WW at Hos. 5:15.
2 [a]Rom. 10:21 [b]Is. 1:2, 23 [c]Is. 42:24
3 [a]Deut. 32:21 [b]Is. 1:29 *See WW at 1 Kin. 16:2.
4 [a]Deut. 18:11 [b]Lev. 11:7; Is. 66:17 [1]Unclean meats, Lev. 7:18; 19:7 *See WW at Lam. 5:19.
5 [a]Matt. 9:11; Luke 7:39; 18:9–12 [1]Cause My wrath to smoke
6 [a]Deut. 32:34 [b]Ps. 50:3 [c]Ps. 79:12
7 [a]Ex. 20:5 [b]Ezek. 18:6 [c]Is. 57:7; Ezek. 20:27, 28
8 [a]Joel 2:14 [b]Is. 1:9; Amos 9:8, 9
9 [a]Matt. 24:22
10 [a]Is. 33:9 [b]Josh. 7:24; Hos. 2:15 [c]Is. 55:6

3 A people [a]who *provoke Me to
anger continually to My face;
[b]Who sacrifice in gardens,
And burn incense on altars of
brick;
4 [a]Who *sit among the graves,
And spend the night in the tombs;
[b]Who eat swine's flesh,
And the broth of [1]abominable
things is *in* their vessels;
5 [a]Who say, 'Keep to yourself,
Do not come near me,
For I am holier than you!'
These [1]*are* smoke in My nostrils,
A fire that burns all the day.
6 "Behold, [a]*it is* written before Me:
[b]I will not keep silence, [c]but will
repay—
Even repay into their bosom—
7 Your iniquities and [a]the iniquities
of your fathers together,"
Says the LORD,
[b]"Who have burned incense on the
mountains
[c]And blasphemed Me on the hills;
Therefore I will measure their
former work into their bosom."
8 Thus says the LORD:

"As the new wine is found in the
cluster,
And *one* says, 'Do not destroy it,
For [a]a blessing *is* in it,'
So will I do for My servants' sake,
That I may not destroy them
[b]all.
9 I will bring forth descendants
from Jacob,
And from Judah an heir of My
mountains;
My [a]elect shall inherit it,
And My servants shall dwell
there.
10 [a]Sharon shall be a fold of flocks,
And [b]the Valley of Achor a place
for herds to lie down,
For My people who have
[c]sought Me.

64:8 Clay, and . . . potter: This metaphor points to the sovereignty of God who molds the individual, the nations, and the history of mankind.
64:10, 11 Prophetically, Isaiah describes Jerusalem and the temple in ruin and desolation following the captivity over 100 years later. See note on 45:1–13.
65:1–16 Best seen as God's response to the sermon-prayer of 63:7—64:12. It explains His decisions (vv. 1–10), reaffirms His judgment (vv. 11, 12), and contrasts His treatment of His faithful **servants** with His treatment of idolatrous sinners (vv. 13–16).
65:1, 2 Here I am pitifully pictures God reaching out **to a rebellious people**. In Rom. 10:20, 21, Paul sees God calling here to two different peoples, the Gentiles (v. 1) and Israel (v. 2).
65:3–7 Provoke Me is a terrible indictment against Israel for pagan idolatry, disgusting heathen practices, and blasphemous insolence.
65:8–10 My servants is addressed to the faithful remnant who were not guilty of idol worship. See note on vv. 13–16. **Jacob** and **Judah** represent all 12 tribes of Israel: Jacob refers to the 10 northern tribes and Judah refers to the 2 southern tribes. Both will be represented in the faithful remnant. **Sharon** and the **Valley of Achor** were 2 productive regions that His **elect shall inherit**. See notes on Zeph. 2:7, 9.

11 "But you *are* those who forsake the
LORD,
Who forget [a]My holy mountain,
Who prepare [b]a table for
[1]Gad,
And who furnish a drink offering
for [2]Meni.
12 Therefore I will number you for
the sword,
And you shall all bow down to the
slaughter;
[a]Because, when I called, you did
not answer;
When I spoke, you did not hear,
But did evil before My eyes,
And chose *that* in which I do not
delight."

13 Therefore thus says the Lord GOD:

"Behold, My servants shall eat,
But you shall be hungry;
Behold, My servants shall drink,
But you shall be thirsty;
Behold, My servants shall rejoice,
But you shall be ashamed;
14 Behold, My servants shall sing for
joy of heart,
But you shall cry for sorrow of
heart,
And [a]wail for [1]grief of spirit.
15 You shall leave your name
[a]as a curse to [b]My chosen;
For the Lord GOD will slay you,
And [c]call His servants by another
name;
16 [a]So that he who blesses himself in
the earth
Shall bless himself in the God of
truth;
And [b]he who swears in the
earth
Shall swear by the God of truth;
Because the former troubles are
forgotten,
And because they are hidden
from My eyes.

The Glorious New Creation

17 "For behold, I create [a]new heavens
and a new earth;

11 [a]Is. 56:7 [b]Ezek. 23:41; [1 Cor. 10:21] [1]Lit. *Troop* or *Fortune;* a pagan deity [2]Lit. *Number* or *Destiny;* a pagan deity
12 [a]2 Chr. 36:15, 16; Prov. 1:24; Is. 41:28; 50:2; 66:4; Jer. 7:13
14 [a]Matt. 8:12; Luke 13:28 [1]Or *a broken spirit*
15 [a]Jer. 29:22; Zech. 8:13 [b]Is. 65:9, 22 [c][Acts 11:26]
16 [a]Ps. 72:17; Jer. 4:2 [b]Deut. 6:13; Zeph. 1:5
17 [a]Is. 51:16; 66:22; [2 Pet. 3:13]; Rev. 21:1 [1]Lit. *come upon the heart*

And the former shall not be
remembered or [1]come to mind.
18 But be glad and rejoice forever in
what I create;
For behold, I create Jerusalem *as*
a rejoicing,
And her people a joy.
19 [a]I will rejoice in Jerusalem,
And joy in My people;
The [b]voice of weeping shall no
longer be heard in her,
Nor the voice of crying.

20 "No more shall an infant from
there *live but a few* days,
Nor an old man who has not
fulfilled his days;
For the child shall die one
hundred years old,
[a]But the sinner *being* one hundred
years old shall be accursed.
21 [a]They shall build houses and
inhabit *them;*
They shall plant vineyards and
eat their fruit.
22 They shall not build and another
inhabit;
They shall not plant and
[a]another eat;
For [b]as the days of a tree, *so shall
be* the days of My people,
And [c]My elect shall long enjoy
the work of their hands.
23 They shall not labor in vain,
[a]Nor bring forth children for
trouble;
For [b]they *shall be* the
descendants of the blessed of
the LORD,
And their offspring with them.

24 "It shall come to pass
That [a]before they call, I will
answer;
And while they are still speaking,
I will [b]hear.
25 The [a]wolf and the lamb shall
*feed together,
The lion shall eat straw like the
ox,
[b]And dust *shall be* the serpent's
food.

19 [a]Is. 62:4, 5 [b]Is. 35:10; 51:11; Rev. 7:17; 21:4
20 [a]Eccl. 8:12, 13; Is. 3:11; 22:14
21 [a]Ezek. 28:26; 45:4; Hos. 11:11; Amos 9:14
22 [a]Is. 62:8, 9 [b]Ps. 92:12 [c]Is. 65:9, 15
23 [a]Hos. 9:12 [b]Is. 61:9; [Jer. 32:38, 39; Acts 2:39]
24 [a]Ps. 91:15; Is. 58:9 [b]Is. 30:19; Dan. 9:20–23
25 [a]Is. 11:6–9 [b]Gen. 3:14; Mic. 7:17 *See WW at Is. 40:11.

65:11 Gad and **Meni** are pagan deities worshiped by the rebellious in Israel, whose "fortune" and "destiny" would be **the sword.**

65:13–16 God speaks and draws a contrast between the *destiny of His* **servants** and the unfaithful in Israel: the servants will receive blessing and joy; the rebellious will receive shame, sorrow, and the curse of death.

65:17—66:4 A description of God's new world for His new city. Since life expectancy and animal nature are transformed, this obviously is eschatological. See note on Ezek. 40:1—48:35.

65:17–19 See notes on Rev. 21.

65:20 One hundred years stands for "a long life." **An infant** enjoying longevity is seen as a sign of God's favor, a symbol of endless life in the consummated order.

65:21–25 These conditions will likely begin during the Millennium. See Rev. 20:4–6.

65:25 This verse depicts proverbial opposites, emphasizing the different order of the Millennium and world to come. **Dust *shall be* . . . food,** an obvious allusion to the curse of Gen. 3:14, refers contextually to a reversal of the Fall's effects. It does not, however, prophesy Satan's redemption.

They shall not hurt nor destroy
in all My holy mountain,"
Says the LORD.

True Worship and False

66 Thus says the LORD:
[a]"Heaven *is* My throne,
And earth *is* My footstool.
Where *is* the house that you will
build Me?
And where *is* the place of My
*rest?
2 For all those *things* My hand has
made,
And all those *things* exist,"
Says the LORD.
[a]"But on this *one* will I look:
[b]On *him who is* poor and of a
contrite spirit,
And who trembles at My word.

3 "He[a] who kills a bull *is as if* he
slays a man;
He who sacrifices a lamb, *as if* he
[b]breaks a dog's neck;
He who offers a grain offering, *as
if he offers* swine's blood;
He who burns incense, *as if* he
blesses an idol.
Just as they have chosen their
own ways,
And their soul delights in their
abominations,
4 So will I *choose their delusions,
And bring their fears on them;
[a]Because, when I called, no one
answered,
When I spoke they did not hear;
But they did evil before My
eyes,
And chose *that* in which I do not
delight."

The LORD Vindicates Zion

5 Hear the word of the LORD,
You who tremble at His word:
"Your *brethren who [a]hated you,
Who cast you out for My name's
sake, said,
[b]'Let the LORD be glorified,
That [c]we may see your joy.'
But they shall be ashamed."

6 The sound of noise from the city!
A voice from the temple!
The voice of the LORD,
Who fully repays His enemies!

7 "Before she was in labor, she gave
birth;
Before her pain came,
She delivered a male child.
8 Who has heard such a thing?
Who has seen such things?
Shall the earth be made to give
birth in one day?
Or shall a nation be born at once?
For as soon as Zion was in labor,
She gave birth to her children.
9 Shall I bring to the time of birth,
and not cause delivery?" says
the LORD.
"Shall I who cause delivery shut
up *the womb?*" says your God.
10 "Rejoice with Jerusalem,
And be glad with her, all you who
love her;
Rejoice for joy with her, all you
who *mourn for her;
11 That you may feed and be
satisfied
With the consolation of her
bosom,
That you may drink deeply and
be delighted
With the abundance of her
glory."

12 For thus says the LORD:

"Behold, [a]I will extend *peace to
her like a river,
And the glory of the Gentiles like
a flowing stream.
Then you shall [b]feed;
On *her* sides shall you be
[c]carried,
And be dandled on *her* knees.
13 As one whom his mother
comforts,
So I will [a]comfort you;
And you shall be comforted in
Jerusalem."

CHAPTER 66

1 [a]1 Kin. 8:27; 2 Chr. 6:18; Ps. 11:4; Matt. 5:34; Acts 17:24 *See WW at Is. 28:12.
2 [a]Ps. 34:18; [Is. 57:15; 61:1; Matt. 5:3, 4; Luke 18:13, 14] [b]Ps. 34:18; 51:17
3 [a][Is. 1:10–17; 58:1–7; Mic. 6:7, 8] [b]Deut. 23:18
4 [a]Prov. 1:24; Is. 65:12; Jer. 7:13 *See WW at 1 Kin. 11:34.
5 [a]Ps. 38:20; Is. 60:15; [Luke 6:22, 23] [b]Is. 5:19 [c][2 Thess. 1:10; Titus 2:13] *See WW at Ps. 133:1.
10 *See WW at Joel 1:9.
12 [a]Is. 48:18; 60:5 [b]Is. 60:16 [c]Is. 49:22; 60:4 *See WW at Nah. 1:15.
13 [a]Is. 51:3; [2 Cor. 1:3, 4]

66:1, 2 Heaven *is* My throne and earth *is* My footstool: Stephen quoted this passage (Acts 7:49, 50) as proof that God's NT plan is to live in human beings and not in man-made temples.

66:3, 4 These verses again denounce all religious ritualism that is not accompanied with reverence, justice, and sincerity. See note on 1:11–15.

66:5–24 The book closes by noting that God's revealed strategies for the future of His people have been successfully concluded, but it took great power and determination to arrive at **the new heavens and the new earth** (v. 22).

66:5–9 Isaiah again prophesies Jerusalem's rebuilding. God shall restore and when He does, He will do it quickly. Historically, this was fulfilled in Nehemiah's taking only two years to complete the wall that had lain in ruin for over 100 years. See note on 35:1–10 for a secondary application.

66:5 Let the LORD . . . joy is a taunt of the idolatrous against the faithful, mocking their assurance that God is on their side. See note on 65:13–16.

The Reign and Indignation of God

14 When you see *this,* your heart
shall rejoice,
And [a]your bones shall flourish
like grass;
The hand of the LORD shall be
known to His servants,
And *His* indignation to His
enemies.
15 [a]For behold, the LORD will come
with fire
And with His chariots, like a
whirlwind,
To render His anger with fury,
And His rebuke with flames of
fire.
16 For by fire and by [a]His sword
The LORD will judge all flesh;
And the slain of the LORD shall
be [b]many.

17 "Those[a] who sanctify themselves
and purify themselves,
To go to the gardens
[1]After an *idol* in the midst,
Eating swine's flesh and the
abomination and the mouse,
Shall [2]be consumed together,"
says the LORD.

18 "For I *know* their works and their
[a]thoughts. It shall be that I will [b]gather
all nations and tongues; and they shall
come and see My glory.
19 [a]"I will set a sign among them; and
those among them who escape I will
send to the nations: *to* Tarshish and
[1]Pul and Lud, who draw the bow, and
Tubal and Javan, *to* the coastlands afar
off who have not heard My fame nor
seen My *glory. [b]And they shall declare My glory among the *Gentiles.
20 "Then they shall [a]bring all your
brethren [b]for an *offering to the LORD
out of all nations, on horses and in
chariots and in litters, on mules and
on camels, to My holy mountain Jerusalem," says the LORD, "as the children
of Israel bring an offering in a clean
vessel into the house of the LORD.
21 "And I will also take some of them
for [a]priests *and* Levites," says the
LORD.

22 "For as [a]the new heavens and the
new earth
Which I will make shall remain
before Me," says the LORD,
"So shall your descendants and
your name remain.
23 And [a]it shall come to pass
That from one New Moon to
another,
And from one Sabbath to
another,
[b]All flesh shall come to *worship
before Me," says the LORD.

24 "And they shall go forth and look
Upon the corpses of the men
Who have transgressed against
Me.
For their [a]worm does not die,
And their fire is not quenched.
They shall be an abhorrence to all
flesh."

14 [a]Ezek. 37:1
15 [a]Is. 9:5; [2 Thess. 1:8]
16 [a]Is. 27:1 [b]Is. 34:6
17 [a]Is. 65:3–8 [1]Lit. *After one* [2]*come to an end*
18 [a]Is. 59:7 [b]Is. 45:22–25; Jer. 3:17
19 [a]Luke 2:34 [b]Mal. 1:11 [1]So with MT, Tg.; LXX *Put* (cf. Jer. 46:9) *See WW at Is. 60:1. • See WW at Ps. 106:47.
20 [a]Is. 49:22 [b]Is. 18:7; [Rom. 15:16] *See WW at Num. 29:6.
21 [a]Ex. 19:6; Is. 61:6; 1 Pet. 2:9; Rev. 1:6
22 [a]Is. 65:17; Heb. 12:26, 27; 2 Pet. 3:13; Rev. 21:1
23 [a]Zech. 14:16 [b]Zech. 14:17–21 *See WW at Ps. 99:5.
24 [a]Is. 14:11; Mark 9:44, 46, 48

66:14–17 See note on 63:1–6.
66:17 This is a description of various pagan rites. It symbolizes the idolatry of some postexilic returnees as well as the evil of man's heart in general.
66:18–21 God in His sovereign grace will cause salvation to reach **all nations.** See note on 61:4–7.
66:19 Tarshish, Pul, Lud, Tubal, and **Javan** represent lands from Spain to Greece; they symbolize **the nations.**
66:22–24 The Book of Isaiah ends with the prophet's characteristic twofold focus: the obedient enjoying the Lord's consummated peace and comfort, and the disobedient suffering undying judgment. See notes on Rev. 21.

TRUTH-IN-ACTION through ISAIAH

Letting the LIFE of the Holy Spirit Bring Faith's Works Alive in You!

Truth Isaiah Teaches	Text	**Action** Isaiah Invites
1 Steps to Holiness God's people have often gotten in trouble by employing unholy means *toward holy ends and thinking* about holy things in an unholy way. The ends do not justify the means. Unholy methodology leads to unholy alliances that can become our undoing.	8:19, 20	**Reject** spiritual counsel from anyone who does not speak according to the Word of God. **Avoid** any form of the occult or spiritism.
	30:1, 2	**Be wary** of plans or relationships God has not ordained and, therefore, will not bless. **Seek the Lord** for wisdom in making plans and entering covenantal relationships.

Truth Isaiah Teaches	Text	**Action** Isaiah Invites
	31:1–3	**Employ** only God's methods to do God's work.
2 Steps in Developing Humility Humility is essential to righteous, Christ-like behavior. Humility and meekness are Spirit-engendered characteristics in the mature believer. Their opposites, pride and arrogance, have a diabolical source. Humility refuses to promote its own interests, but looks out, rather, for the interests of others.	6:5–7 14:12–21	**Humble** yourself in the presence of the Lord. **Understand** this is the only way to be cleansed and gain a clear perspective on your call to ministry. **Beware of** selfish ambition that sets itself above God and pride that takes glory from God. **Understand** that they are the hallmarks of Satan's rebellion through which he became God's enemy.
3 Steps to Dynamic Devotion God wants His people to be fully devoted to Him. We cannot feign devotion: God knows our hearts and knows whether what we say has integrity. This is the best reason to pursue worship with a whole heart. We are to seek God's face continually, expressing our wholehearted devotion to Him.	29:13, 14 55:1–5 62:1–5	**Realize** that God only honors worship that is accompanied by genuine obedience and heartfelt adoration. **Know** that insincere worship can result in diminished wisdom and understanding. **Hunger** and **thirst** after the knowledge of the Lord (see Phil. 3:10–13) and not after the perishable things this world offers. **Continually pray** for a fresh moving of the Holy Spirit and revival.
4 Key Lessons in Faith Faith takes God at His word when circumstances seem to deny the truth of His promises. Our ability to endure to the end will depend upon our allowing the Holy Spirit to train us in this kind of faith.	8:12–15 40:29–31 42:23—43:7 55:10, 11	**Believe** that the Lord is your refuge, and **overcome** worldly fear that threatens in times of major crisis. **Understand** that spiritual strength comes from waiting upon the Lord. **Trust** that God knows how to protect His righteous ones from the judgment and wrath He pours out upon others. **Choose to believe** that God's Word is the most powerful force in the universe and **act** accordingly.
5 Steps to Dealing with Sin We may believe that if we sin, we will be immediately aware of it; but sin is subtle, and our hearts may not perceive or acknowledge our guilt. So those most in need of repentance and cleansing may have no awareness of their spiritual state. Therefore, we must continually examine ourselves before the Lord, asking Him to enlighten our hearts to any unacknowledged sin and to cleanse us of all unrighteousness.	1:16, 17 1:18–20 5:12 53:4–12 59:1–15	**Understand** that when we disagree with God's agenda, we must repent and change our way of thinking. **Understand** that repentance and obedience are reasonable to a willing and obedient heart, but folly to one with a resistant and rebellious attitude. **Celebrate** the Lord's goodness ahead of turning to amusement and entertainment. **Judge** any such tendencies in yourself and repent. **Believe** that your sins and iniquities were placed on Jesus, the sinless Lamb of God. **Choose** to forgive others' sins against you. **Know** that God often does not answer our prayers because our own sin and iniquity prevents it. **Allow** unanswered prayer to become an occasion for soul-searching and possible repentance.

The Book of JEREMIAH

Author: Jeremiah
Date: 626–586 B.C.
Theme: Failure to Repent Will Lead to Destruction
Key Words: Repentance, Restoration

Author Jeremiah, son of Hilkiah, was a prophet from the priestly town of Anathoth and perhaps was descended from Abiathar. The meaning of his name is uncertain, but "Yahweh Exalts" and "Yahweh Throws" are possibilities. More is known about the personal life of this prophet than any other in the Old Testament because he has given us so many glimpses into his thinking, concerns, and frustrations.

Jeremiah was commanded not to marry or have children to illustrate his message that judgment was pending and that the next generation would be swept away. His closest friend and associate was his scribe Baruch. Other than this he had few friends. Only Ahikam, Ahikam's son Gedaliah, and Ebed-Melech seem to qualify. Partly, this was because of the message of doom proclaimed by Jeremiah, a message contrary to the hope of the people and one that included a suggestion of surrender to the Babylonians. In spite of his message of doom, his scathing rebuke of the leaders, and contempt for idolatry, his heart ached for his people because he knew that Israel's salvation could not be divorced from faith in God and a right covenantal relationship expressed by obedience.

Date Jeremiah prophesied to Judah during the reigns of Josiah, Jehoiakim, Jehoiachin, and Zedekiah. His call is dated at 626 B.C., and his ministry continued until a short time after the fall of Jerusalem in 586 B.C. The prophet Zephaniah preceded Jeremiah slightly, and Nahum, Habakkuk, and Obadiah were contemporaries. Ezekiel was a younger contemporary who prophesied in Babylon from 593 to 571 B.C.

Background Jeremiah began his ministry in the reign of Josiah, a good king who temporarily delayed God's judgment promised because of the frightful rule of Manasseh. Events were changing rapidly in the Near East. Josiah had begun a reform, which included destruction of pagan high places throughout Judah and Samaria. The reform, however, had little lasting effect on the people. Ashurbanipal, the last great Assyrian king, died in 627 B.C. Assyria was weakening, Josiah was expanding his territory to the north, and Babylon under Nabopolassar, and Egypt under Necho, were trying to assert their authority over Judah.

In 609 B.C., Josiah was killed at Megiddo when he attempted to prevent Pharaoh Necho from going to the aid of the Assyrian remnant. Three sons of Josiah (Jehoahaz, Jehoiakim, and Zedekiah) and a grandson (Jehoiachin) followed him on the throne. Jeremiah saw the folly of the political policy of these kings and warned them of God's plan for Judah, but none of them heeded the warning. Jehoiakim was openly hostile to Jeremiah and destroyed one scroll sent by Jeremiah by cutting off a few columns at a time and throwing them into the fire. Zedekiah was a weak and vacillating ruler, at times seeking Jeremiah's advice, but at other times allowing Jeremiah's enemies to mistreat and imprison him.

Content The book consists mainly of a short introduction (1:1–3), a collection of oracles against Judah and Jerusalem which Jeremiah dictated to his scribe Baruch (1:4—20:18), oracles against foreign nations (25:15–38; chs. 46—51), events written about Jeremiah in the third person, probably by Baruch (chs. 26—45), and a historical appendix (ch. 52), which is almost identical to 2 Kings 24 and 25. The prophecies in the book are not in chronological order.

Jeremiah had a compassionate heart for his people and prayed for them even when the Lord told him not to do so. Yet he condemned the rulers, the priests, and false prophets for leading the people astray. He also attacked the people for their idolatry and proclaimed severe judgment unless the people repented. Because he knew God's intentions, he advocated surrender to the Babylonians and wrote to those already in exile to settle down and live normal lives. For his preaching he was branded a traitor by many. Jeremiah, however, had their best interest at heart. He knew that unless God's covenant was honored, the nation would be destroyed. God was also interested in individuals and their relationship to Him. Like Ezekiel, he stressed individual responsibility.

Jeremiah was just a youth when he was called to carry a severe message of doom to his people. He attempted to avoid this task but was unable to remain silent. The people had become so corrupt under Manasseh that God must bring an end to the nation. Defeated and taken into exile, they would reflect on what had happened to them and why. Then, after proper chastisement and repentance, God would bring a remnant back to Judah, punish the nations who had punished them, and fulfill His old covenants with Israel, David, and the Levites. And He would give them a new covenant and write His law on their hearts. David's throne would again be established, and faithful priests would serve them.

The oracles against foreign nations illustrate the sovereignty of God over the whole world. All nations belong to Him and all must answer to Him for their conduct.

Literary Features Jeremiah uses many literary styles and devices. His book is the longest in the Bible, and while some chapters are written in prose, most are poetic in form. His poetry is as beautiful and lyrical as any in Scripture. He effectively makes use of repetition, such as the phrase "by the sword, by the famine, and by the pestilence" (14:12 and note), the threefold "earth, earth, earth" (22:19) and "the temple of the LORD" (7:4), and words such as "a hissing" (18:16). Symbolism occurs in the use of the linen sash (13:1), the potter's earthen flask (19:1), and the bonds and yokes (27:2). Cryptograms are used in 25:26 and 51:1, 41. Jeremiah is a keen observer of plants and animals (2:21, 23). He has given us many beautiful phrases (2:13; 7:11; 8:20, 22; 31:29, 33).

Personal Application Jeremiah saw that religion was essentially a moral and spiritual relationship with God, a relationship that required the devotion of each individual. Each person is responsible for his or her own sin. The new covenant (31:27–40) is the spiritual bond between God and the individual. This is a new and unconditional covenant that involves God's writing the Law on human hearts, the forgiving of iniquity, and the remembering of sin no more. All this was fulfilled in the incarnation of Christ and in the gospel He preached.

Much of the message of Jeremiah is relevant because it is timeless. Sin always must be punished, but true repentance brings restoration. Our idolatry, which consists of such things as wealth, talent, or position, is called by new names, but the sin is the same, and the remedy is the same. God calls for obedience to His commands in a pure covenantal relationship. Sin requires repentance and restoration; obedience leads to blessing and joy.

Christ Revealed Through his action and attitude Jeremiah portrays a life-style similar to that of Jesus, and for this reason he may be called a type of Christ in the Old Testament. He showed great compassion for his people and wept over them. He suffered much at their hands, but he forgave them. Jeremiah is one of the most Christlike personalities in the Old Testament.

Several passages from Jeremiah are alluded to by Jesus in His teaching: "Has this house, which is called by My name, become a den of thieves in your eyes?" (7:11; Matt. 21:13); "Who have eyes and see not, and who have ears and hear not" (5:21; Mark 8:18); "Then you will find rest for your souls" (6:16; Matt. 11:29); "My people have been lost sheep" (50:6; Matt. 10:6).

The Holy Spirit at Work A symbol of the Holy Spirit is fire. God assured Jeremiah, "I will make My words in your mouth fire" (5:14). At one point Jeremiah wanted to stop mentioning God, but "*His word* was in my heart like a burning fire shut up in my bones; I was weary of holding *it* back, and I could not" (20:9). Today we would call this the work of the Holy Spirit in Jeremiah.

Apart from the normal work of inspiring the prophet and revealing God's message to him, the Holy Spirit is the One to carry out the promise of a new covenant that will put God's law in the minds of His people and write it on their hearts. The external commands of the old covenant will now be internalized, and the believer will have the power to conform in every respect to the moral law of God. The knowledge of God will be universal, and other peoples will be included in God's blessing. Under the old covenant forgiveness was promised, but now forgiveness comes with the promise that God will remember their sin no more.

Outline of Jeremiah

I. Call of Jeremiah **1:1–19**
II. Collection of discourses **2:1—33:26**
- A. Earliest oracles 2:1—6:30
- B. Temple sermon and cultic abuses 7:1—8:3
- C. Miscellaneous materials 8:4—10:25
- D. Events in Jeremiah's life 11:1—13:27
- E. Drought and other catastrophes 14:1—15:21
- F. Warnings and promises 16:1—17:18
- G. Keep the Sabbath day holy 17:19–27
- H. Lessons from the potter 18:1—20:18

I. Oracles against kings, prophets, and people 21:1—24:10
J. The Babylonian Exile 25:1—29:32
K. The book of consolation 30:1—33:26

III. Historical appendix 34:1—35:19
A. Warning to Zedekiah 34:1–7
B. Manumission of slaves revoked 34:8–22
C. The symbol of the Rechabites 35:1–19

IV. Trials and sufferings of Jeremiah 36:1—45:5
A. Jehoiakim and the scrolls 36:1–32
B. Siege and fall of Jerusalem 37:1—40:6
C. Gedaliah and his assassination 40:7—41:18
D. The flight to Egypt 42:1—43:7
E. Jeremiah in Egypt 43:8—44:30
F. Oracle to Baruch 45:1–5

V. Oracles against foreign nations 46:1—51:64
A. Against Egypt 46:1–28
B. Against the Philistines 47:1–7
C. Against Moab 48:1–47
D. Against the Ammonites 49:1–6
E. Against Edom 49:7–22
F. Against Damascus 49:23–27
G. Against Kedar and Hazor 49:28–33
H. Against Elam 49:34–39
I. Against Babylon 50:1—51:64

VI. Historical appendix 52:1–34
A. Zedekiah's reign 52:1–3
B. Siege and fall of Jerusalem 52:4–27
C. Summary of three deportations 52:28–30
D. Release of Jehoiachin from prison 52:31–34

THE words of Jeremiah the son of
Hilkiah, of the priests who *were*
[a]in Anathoth in the land of Benjamin,
2 to whom the word of the LORD came
in the days of [a]Josiah the son of Amon,
king of Judah, [b]in the thirteenth year
of his reign.
3 It came also in the days of [a]Jehoia-
kim the son of Josiah, king of Judah,
[b]until the end of the eleventh year of
Zedekiah the son of Josiah, king of Judah, [c]until the carrying away of Jerusalem captive [d]in the fifth month.

The Prophet Is Called

4 Then the word of the LORD came to
me, saying:

5 "Before I [a]formed you in the womb
[b]I knew you;
Before you were born I
[c]sanctified[1] you;
I [2]ordained you a prophet to the
nations."

6 Then said I: 1

[a]"Ah, Lord GOD!
Behold, I cannot speak, for I *am*
a youth."

7 But the LORD said to me:

"Do not say, 'I *am* a youth,'
For you shall go to all to whom I
send you,
And [a]whatever I command you,
you shall speak.
8 [a]Do not be afraid of their faces,
For [b]I *am* with you to deliver
you," says the LORD.

9 Then the LORD put forth His hand 4
and [a]touched my mouth, and the LORD
said to me:

CHAPTER 1
1 [a]Josh. 21:18
2 [a]2 Kin. 21:24 [b]Jer. 25:3
3 [a]2 Kin. 23:34 [b]Jer. 39:2 [c]Jer. 52:12 [d]2 Kin. 25:8
5 [a]Is. 49:1, 5 [b]Ex. 33:12 [c][Luke 1:15] [1]*set you apart* [2]*appointed*
6 [a]Ex. 4:10; 6:12, 30
7 [a]Num. 22:20, 38
8 [a]Ezek. 2:6; 3:9 [b]Ex. 3:12
9 [a]Is. 6:7

1:1 Son of Hilkiah: Used to distinguish this Jeremiah from several other men of the same name, two of whom were his contemporaries (35:3; 52:1). **Priests:** Like Ezekiel, who was his younger contemporary, Jeremiah was both a prophet and priest. **Anathoth:** A city located about 3 miles northeast of Jerusalem in the territory of Benjamin and the birthplace of Jeremiah. God instructed him to redeem a field in that city (32:7–9).

1:2 Word of the LORD: A favorite expression of Jeremiah, used more than 50 times. **Josiah** was the last good king of Judah, and Jeremiah's ministry began in Josiah's **thirteenth year** (626 B.C.).

1:3 Jehoiakim: The throne name of the second son of Josiah to rule. His brother Jehoahaz II was deposed by Pharaoh Necho, and Jehoiakim was appointed to rule in his place. **The eleventh year of Zedekiah,** a third son of Josiah and the last king of Judah, was 587 or 586 B.C. **Fifth month:** The month Ab (July-August).

1:5 God's sovereignty is shown in that He **formed, sanctified** (set apart), and **ordained** (appointed) Jeremiah to be a **prophet** (one who is called) and to be His spokesman **to the nations** (Assyria, Babylon, Egypt, Judah, and others).

1:6–8 See section 1 of Truth-In-Action at the end of Jer.

1:6–8 I cannot speak: Like Moses (Ex. 3:4), Jeremiah claimed inadequacy and inexperience (**a youth**), but God's support and presence (**I *am* with you**) will overcome Jeremiah's deficiency.

1:9, 10 See section 4 of Truth-In-Action at the end of Jer.

1:9 Touched my mouth: Compare the experience of Isaiah (see Is. 6:7).

"Behold, I have [b]put My *words in
your mouth.
10 [a]See, I have this day set you over
the nations and over the
kingdoms,
To [b]root out and to pull down,
To destroy and to throw down,
To build and to plant."

4 11 Moreover the word of the LORD
came to me, saying, "Jeremiah, what
do you see?" And I said, "I see a
[1]branch of an almond tree."
12 Then the LORD said to me, "You
have seen well, for I am [1]**ready** to perform My word."

WORD WEALTH

1:12 ready, *shaqad* (shah-*kahd*); Strong's #8245: Watching, waking, hastening, anticipating; to be sleepless, alert, vigilant; on the lookout; to care for watchfully. This verb occurs 12 times, including Ps. 127:1: "Unless the LORD guards the city, the watchman stays awake in vain." In Jer. 31:28, God promises to watch over His people with an intent to build and to plant. The present reference may best be understood by noting the linguistic connection between "waking" (*shaqad*) and "almond" (*shaqed*) in Hebrew. The almond is considered the "waker" in Hebrew thought, because it, of all trees, blossoms early, watching diligently for the opportunity to bloom. Thus, in vv. 11, 12, the linking of the vision of an almond branch and its interpretation is clear.

13 And the word of the LORD came to
me the second time, saying, "What do
you see?" And I said, "I see [a]a boiling
pot, and it is facing away from the
north."
14 Then the LORD said to me:

"Out of the [a]north calamity shall
break forth
On all the inhabitants of the land.
15 For behold, I am [a]calling
All the families of the kingdoms
of the north," says the LORD;

9 [b]Ex. 4:11–16; Deut. 18:18; Is. 51:16 *See WW at Deut. 1:1
10 [a]1 Kin. 19:17 [b]Jer. 18:7–10; Ezek. 22:18; [2 Cor. 10:4, 5]
11 [1]Lit. *rod*
12 [1]Lit. *watching*
13 [a]Ezek. 11:3; 24:3
14 [a]Jer. 6:1
15 [a]Jer. 6:22; 25:9 [b]Is. 22:7; Jer. 39:3
16 [a]Deut. 28:20; Jer. 17:13 [b]Is. 65:3, 4; Jer. 7:9 [c]Is. 37:19; Jer. 2:28
17 [a]1 Kin. 18:46; 2 Kin. 4:29; Job 38:3; Luke 12:35; [1 Pet. 1:13] [b]Ezek. 2:6
18 [a]Is. 50:7; Jer. 6:27; 15:20

CHAPTER 2

2 [a]Ezek. 16:8; Hos. 2:15 [b]Deut. 2:7; Jer. 2:6 [1]*followed*
3 [a][Ex. 19:5, 6; Deut. 7:6; 14:2]

"They shall come and [b]each one
set his throne
At the entrance of the gates of
Jerusalem,
Against all its walls all around,
And against all the cities of
Judah.
16 I will utter My judgments
Against them concerning all their
wickedness,
Because [a]they have forsaken Me,
Burned [b]incense to other gods,
And worshiped the works of their
own [c]hands.

17 "Therefore [a]prepare yourself and 5
arise,
And speak to them all that I
command you.
[b]Do not be dismayed before their
faces,
Lest I dismay you before them.
18 For behold, I have made you this
day
[a]A fortified city and an iron pillar,
And bronze walls against the
whole land—
Against the kings of Judah,
Against its princes,
Against its priests,
And against the people of the
land.
19 They will fight against you,
But they shall not prevail against
you.
For I *am* with you," says the
LORD, "to deliver you."

God's Case Against Israel

2 Moreover the word of the LORD
came to me, saying,
2 "Go and cry in the hearing of Jerusalem, saying, 'Thus says the LORD:

"I remember you,
The kindness of your [a]youth,
The love of your betrothal,
[b]When you [1]went after Me in the
wilderness,
In a land not sown.
3 [a]Israel *was* holiness to the LORD,

1:10 God's word is a dynamic and creative force that will accomplish His purpose (see Is. 55:10, 11). Jeremiah repeatedly uses the verbs **to root out** and **to pull down, to destroy** and **to throw down, to build** and **to plant** (see 18:7–9; 24:6; 31:28; 42:10).

1:11, 12 See section 4 of Truth-In-Action at the end of Jer.

1:13, 14 A second vision is a **boiling pot** (judgment and calamity) **from the north,** since most of the invaders of Israel and Judah came from that direction.

1:15, 16 The Babylonians are the major instrument used by God to punish His enemies (see Hab. 1:6), and they did set up a **throne** in the middle gate of Jerusalem (39:3). Judgment will come because of the broken covenant (**they have forsaken Me**) and idolatry.

1:17–19 See section 5 of Truth-In-Action at the end of Jer.

1:17 Prepare yourself: Literally "gird your loins," that is, arrange your clothing for activity. For similar action, see Ex. 12:11 and 1 Kin. 18:46.

2:2 Kindness: The Hebrew word conveys the concept of covenant loyalty, love, and faithfulness. **Betrothal:** The Sinai covenant is compared to a marriage vow, and God is called Israel's husband (see Is. 54:5; Ezek. 16:1–14; Hos. 2:16).

2:3 Holiness: As in 1:5 the basic idea is to be set apart **to the LORD.**

[b]The firstfruits of His increase.
[c]All that devour him will offend;
Disaster will [d]come upon them,"
says the LORD.' "

4 Hear the word of the LORD, O house of Jacob and all the families of the house of Israel.
5 Thus says the LORD:

[a]"What injustice have your fathers found in Me,
That they have gone far from Me,
[b]Have followed [1]idols,
And have become idolaters?
6 Neither did they say, 'Where *is* the LORD,
Who [a]brought us up out of the land of Egypt,
Who led us through [b]the wilderness,
Through a land of deserts and pits,
Through a land of drought and the shadow of death,
Through a land that no one crossed
And where no one dwelt?'
7 I brought you into [a]a bountiful country,
To eat its fruit and its goodness.
But when you entered, you [b]defiled My land
And made My heritage an abomination.
8 The priests did not say, 'Where *is* the LORD?'
And those who handle the [a]law did not know Me;
The rulers also transgressed against Me;
[b]The prophets prophesied by Baal,
And walked after *things that* do not profit.

9 "Therefore [a]I will yet [1]bring charges against you," says the LORD,
"And against your children's children I will bring charges.
10 For pass beyond the coasts of [1]Cyprus and see,
Send to [2]Kedar and consider diligently,
And see if there has been such *a* [a]*thing.*
11 [a]Has a nation changed *its* gods,
Which *are* [b]not gods?
[c]But My people have changed their Glory
For *what* does not profit.
12 Be astonished, O heavens, at this,
And be horribly afraid;
Be very desolate," says the LORD.
13 "For My people have committed two evils:
They have forsaken Me, the [a]fountain of living *waters,
And hewn themselves cisterns—broken cisterns that can hold no water.

14 "*Is* Israel [a]a servant?
Is he a homeborn *slave?*
Why is he plundered?
15 [a]The young lions roared at him, *and* growled;
They made his land waste;
His cities are burned, without inhabitant.
16 Also the people of [1]Noph and [a]Tahpanhes
Have [2]broken the crown of your head.
17 [a]Have you not brought this on yourself,
In that you have forsaken the LORD your God
When [b]He led you in the way?
18 And now why take [a]the road to Egypt,
To drink the waters of [b]Sihor?
Or why take the road to [c]Assyria,
To drink the waters of [1]the River?
19 Your own wickedness will [a]correct you,

3 [b]James 1:18; Rev. 14:4 [c]Jer. 12:14 [d]Gen. 12:3; Is. 41:11; Jer. 30:15, 16; 50:7
5 [a]Is. 5:4; Mic. 6:3 [b]2 Kin. 17:15; Jer. 8:19; [Jon. 2:8]; Rom. 1:21 [1]*vanities* or *futilities*
6 [a]Ex. 20:2; Is. 63:11 [b]Deut. 8:15; 32:10
7 [a]Num. 13:27 [b]Num. 35:33; Is. 24:5; Hos. 4:3
8 [a]Rom. 2:20 [b]Jer. 23:13
9 [a]Jer. 2:35; Ezek. 20:35, 36; Mic. 6:2 [1]*contend with*
10 [a]Jer. 18:13 [1]Heb. *Kittim,* representative of western cultures [2]In northern Arabian desert, representative of eastern cultures
11 [a]Mic. 4:5 [b]Ps. 115:4; Is. 37:19 [c]Ps. 106:20; Rom. 1:23
13 [a]Ps. 36:9; Jer. 17:13; [John 4:14] *See WW at Is. 43:2.
14 [a][Ex. 4:22]
15 [a]Is. 1:7; Jer. 50:17
16 [a]2 Kin. 23:29–37; Jer. 43:7–9 [1]Memphis in ancient Egypt [2]Or *grazed*
17 [a]Jer. 4:18 [b]Deut. 32:10
18 [a]Is. 30:1–3 [b]Josh. 13:3 [c]Hos. 5:13 [1]The Euphrates
19 [a]Is. 3:9; Jer. 4:18; Hos. 5:5

2:6, 7 The Exodus from Egypt, wilderness wanderings, and conquest of the land are mentioned as part of God's grace and mercy, but Israel **defiled** the land, making it ceremonially unclean by her action (see 3:1, 2, 9).

2:8 Those responsible for leading—the **priests, rulers,** and **prophets**—were all disobedient because they failed to consult the **LORD**.

2:9–13 Such folly had not been seen in any culture, neither in **Cyprus** (representing the Western cultures) nor in **Kedar** (a site in northern Arabia representing the Eastern cultures), that is, the folly of a people forsaking **living waters,** which only God can supply (see 17:13; Ps. 36:9; Is. 55:1; John 4:10–14) for **cisterns** that leak. The ability to make cisterns watertight by the use of plaster enabled the Israelites to settle where no natural water supply was available.

2:15 Lions: Used figuratively of the Assyrians who **made his land waste** and **burned** his cities.

2:16 Noph: Memphis, capital of ancient lower (northern) Egypt. **Tahpanhes:** Egyptian border fortress, also known as Baal Zephon (Greek Daphnai, modern Tell Deforeh), in the eastern delta region about 27 miles south-southwest of modern Port Said. **Broken:** More likely "grazed," in the sense that the head is shaved, which brought disgrace.

2:18 History shows Israel's tendency to seek help alternately from Assyria and Egypt. **Sihor:** More properly Shihor, the easternmost branch of the Nile River, which flows into the Mediterranean Sea near Pelusium. Perhaps it forms the southwest limit of the territory of Israel (see Josh. 13:3). The term is Egyptian and means "Waters of Horus." **The River** is the Euphrates.

And your *backslidings will
rebuke you.
Know therefore and see that *it is*
an evil and bitter *thing*
That you have forsaken the LORD
your God,
And the [1]fear of Me *is* not in you,"
Says the Lord GOD of hosts.

20 "For of old I have [a]broken your
yoke *and* burst your bonds;
And [b]you said, 'I will not
[1]transgress,'
When [c]on every high hill and
under every green tree
You lay down, [d]playing the
harlot.
21 Yet I had [a]planted you a noble
vine, a seed of highest quality.
How then have you turned before
Me
Into [b]the degenerate plant of an
alien vine?
22 For though you wash yourself
with lye, and use much soap,
Yet your iniquity is [a]marked[1]
before Me," says the Lord GOD.

23 "How[a] can you say, 'I am not
[1]polluted,
I have not gone after the Baals'?
See your way in the valley;
Know what you have done:
You are a swift dromedary
breaking loose in her ways,
24 A wild donkey used to the
wilderness,
That sniffs at the wind in her
desire;
In her time of mating, who can
turn her away?
All those who seek her will not
weary themselves;
In her month they will find
her.
25 Withhold your foot from being
unshod, and your throat from
thirst.
But you said, [a]'There is no hope.
No! For I have loved [b]aliens, and
after them I will go.'

26 "As the thief is ashamed when he
is found out,
So is the house of Israel ashamed;
They and their kings and their
princes, and their priests and
their [a]prophets,
27 Saying to a tree, 'You *are* my
father,'
And to a [a]stone, 'You gave birth
to me.'
For they have turned *their* back
to Me, and not *their* face.
But in the time of their [b]trouble
They will say, 'Arise and save us.'
28 But [a]where *are* your gods that
you have made for yourselves?
Let them arise,
If they [b]can save you in the time
of your [1]trouble;
For [c]*according to* the number of
your cities
Are your gods, O Judah.

29 "Why will you plead with Me?
You all have transgressed against
Me," says the LORD.
30 "In vain I have [a]chastened your
children;
They [b]received no correction.
Your sword has [c]devoured your
prophets
Like a destroying lion.

31 "O *generation, see the word of the
LORD!
Have I been a wilderness to
Israel,
Or a land of darkness?
Why do My people say, 'We
[1]are lords;
[a]We will come no more to You'?

19 [1]*dread* *See WW at Jer. 5:6. **20** [a]Lev. 26:13 [b]Ex. 19:8; Josh. 24:18; Judg. 10:16; 1 Sam. 12:10 [c]Deut. 12:2; Is. 57:5, 7; Jer. 3:6 [d]Ex. 34:15 [1]Kt. *serve* **21** [a]Ex. 15:17; Ps. 44:2; 80:8; Is. 5:2 [b]Deut. 32:32; Is. 5:4 **22** [a]Job 14:16, 17; Jer. 17:1, 2; Hos. 13:12 [1]*stained* **23** [a]Prov. 30:12 [1]*defiled*

25 [a]Is. 57:10; Jer. 18:12 [b]Jer. 3:13 **26** [a]Is. 28:7; Jer. 5:31 **27** [a]Jer. 3:9 [b]Judg. 10:10; Is. 26:16; Hos. 5:15 **28** [a]Deut. 32:37; Judg. 10:14 [b]Is. 45:20 [c]2 Kin. 17:30, 31; Jer. 11:13 [1]Or *evil* **30** [a]Is. 9:13 [b]Is. 1:5; Jer. 5:3; 7:28 [c]Neh. 9:26; Jer. 26:20–24; Acts 7:52; 1 Thess. 2:15 **31** [a]Deut. 32:15; Jer. 2:20, 25 [1]*have dominion* *See WW at Esth. 9:28.

2:20—3:5 Jeremiah uses numerous figures of speech to portray the rebellion of Judah: a stubborn ox (v. 20), a wild **vine** (v. 21), a stain that will not wash out (v. 22), a **dromedary** and **wild donkey** in heat (vv. 23, 24), and a **thief** (v. 26).

2:20 Although Judah has sworn to keep the commands of the Lord who freed her from her **yoke** and **bonds,** she has offered sacrifices where the pagans worship on **every high hill and under every green tree**. In doing this she has committed spiritual adultery like a **harlot**.

2:21 God had planted Judah as **a noble vine** (a Sorek vine *bore red grapes of highest quality*) but she has become **degenerate** (see Is. 5:1–7).

2:22 Lye and **soap** are mineral and vegetable alkali respectively. Judah's **iniquity** can be taken away only by repentance, never by soap.

2:23 The valley: Probably the Hinnom Valley where infants were sacrificed to the pagan god Molech. The **dromedary** here is a young she-camel galloping aimlessly.

2:24 The **wild donkey** was free and untameable (see Job 39:5–8) and was **used to the wilderness**. **Sniffs at the wind** indicates active searching. Her lovers will not need to find her; she will find them.

2:25 Withhold your foot has the implication of not wearing out the shoes running after **aliens,** either foreign gods or people or both.

2:26 The thief is ashamed when he is caught, not so much because he has been doing wrong, but that **he is found out**. For the rulers involved, see v. 8.

2:27 The **tree** (or Asherah) and **stone** (or sacred pillar) were used in pagan cult practices. The Israelites were ordered to destroy them (Deut. 12:2, 3), but much of the time they joined in their use (Judg. 2:11–15).

2:30 Sword has devoured your prophets: An example is 26:20–23. See also Neh. 9:26; Matt. 23:35.

32 Can a *virgin forget her
ornaments,
Or a bride her attire?
Yet My people [a]have forgotten
Me days without number.

33 "Why do you beautify your way to
seek love?
Therefore you have also taught
The wicked women your ways.
34 Also on your skirts is found
[a]The blood of the lives of the poor
innocents.
I have not found it by [1]secret
search,
But plainly on all these things.
35 [a]Yet you say, 'Because I am
innocent,
Surely His anger shall turn from
me.'
Behold, [b]I will plead My case
against you,
[c]Because you say, 'I have not
sinned.'
36 [a]Why do you gad about so much
to change your way?
Also [b]you shall be ashamed of
Egypt [c]as you were ashamed of
Assyria.
37 Indeed you will go forth from him
With your hands on [a]your head;
For the LORD has rejected your
trusted allies,
And you will [b]not prosper by
them.

Israel Is Shameless

3 "They say, 'If a man divorces his
wife,
And she goes from him
And becomes another man's,
[a]May he return to her again?'
Would not that [b]land be greatly
polluted?
But you have [c]played the harlot
with many lovers;
[d]Yet return to Me," says the LORD.

32 [a]Ps. 106:21; Is. 17:10; Jer. 3:21; 13:25; Hos. 8:14 *See WW at Ps. 45:14. **34** [a]2 Kin. 21:16; 24:4; Ps. 106:38; Jer. 7:6; 19:4 [1]*digging* **35** [a]Jer. 2:23, 29; Mal. 2:17; 3:8 [b]Jer. 2:9 [c][Prov. 28:13; 1 John 1:8, 10] **36** [a]Jer. 31:22; Hos. 5:13; 12:1 [b]Is. 30:3 [c]2 Chr. 28:16 **37** [a]2 Sam. 13:19; Jer. 14:3, 4 [b]Jer. 37:7–10

CHAPTER 3

1 [a]Deut. 24:1–4 [b]Jer. 2:7 [c]Jer. 2:20; Ezek. 16:26 [d]Jer. 4:1; [Zech. 1:3]

2 [a]Deut. 12:2; Jer. 2:20; 3:21; 7:29 [b]Prov. 23:28 [c]Jer. 2:7 [1]Kt. *been violated* **3** [a]Lev. 26:19; Jer. 14:3–6 [b]Zeph. 3:5 **4** [a]Ps. 71:17; Prov. 2:17 [b]Jer. 2:2; Hos. 2:15 **5** [a]Ps. 103:9; [Is. 57:16]; Jer. 3:12 **6** [a]Jer. 7:24 [b]Jer. 2:20 *See WW at Jer. 5:6. **7** [a]2 Kin. 17:13 [b]Jer. 3:11; Ezek. 16:47, 48 **8** [a]Ezek. 23:9 [b]2 Kin. 17:6; Is. 50:1 [c]Ezek. 23:11 *See WW at Jer. 5:6. **9** [a]Jer. 2:7

2 "Lift up your eyes to [a]the desolate
heights and see:
Where have you not [1]lain *with
men?*
[b]By the road you have sat for them
Like an Arabian in the
wilderness;
[c]And you have polluted the land
With your harlotries and your
wickedness.
3 Therefore the [a]showers have
been withheld,
And there has been no latter rain.
You have had a [b]harlot's
forehead;
You refuse to be ashamed.
4 Will you not from this time cry
to Me,
'My Father, You *are* [a]the guide of
[b]my youth?
5 [a]Will He remain angry forever?
Will He keep it to the end?'
Behold, you have spoken and
done evil things,
As you were able."

A Call to Repentance

6 The LORD said also to me in the days
of Josiah the king: "Have you seen
what [a]backsliding* Israel has done?
She has [b]gone up on every high mountain and under every green tree, and
there played the harlot.
7 [a]"And I said, after she had done all
these *things,* 'Return to Me.' But she
did not return. And her treacherous
[b]sister Judah saw it.
8 "Then I saw that [a]for all the causes
for which *backsliding Israel had committed adultery, I had [b]put her away
and given her a certificate of divorce;
[c]yet her treacherous sister Judah did
not fear, but went and played the harlot also.
9 "So it came to pass, through her casual harlotry, that she [a]defiled the land

2:32 Forget: Contrast v. 2 where God remembers (see 18:15).
2:36 Egypt and **Assyria:** See vv. 15–18.
2:37 Hands on your head: Ancient reliefs depict captives with their hands tied together above their heads. **Trusted allies:** Assyria and Egypt.
3:1 Deut. 24:1–4 forbids a husband from taking back his divorced wife if she has married another man. Judah has **played the harlot** on such a scale that the land itself is **polluted** (see Lev. 18:25, 27, where the land is defiled by the action of the people).
3:1 Yet return to Me: Rather to be taken as a question: "Will you return to Me?"
3:2 Desolate heights: Sites of pagan idolatry. **By the road you have sat** recalls the action of Tamar (Gen. 38:14), and its connection with harlotry is spelled out by Ezekiel (Ezek. 16:25).
3:3 As a part of God's remedial punishment, **showers have been withheld** (see 14:1–6; Amos 4:7). **The latter rain** is the spring rain (see Joel 2:23).
3:4 My Father: The title of God as Father is much rarer in the OT than in the NT. See v. 19; Ps. 2:7; 89:26; Is. 63:16; 64:8; Mal. 2:10.
3:6 Backsliding Israel: A reference to the northern kingdom of Israel (Samaria, destroyed by Assyria in 722 B.C.).
3:7 Her treacherous sister: The southern kingdom of Judah.
3:8 Put her away is a reference to the Exile, a literal enactment of the **divorce** proceedings, which included the giving of a **certificate** (see Deut. 24:1).
3:9 Committed adultery with stones and trees: Worship of pagan gods. See note on 2:27.

and committed adultery with [b]stones
and trees.
10 "And yet for all this her treacherous sister Judah has not turned to Me
[a]with her whole heart, but in pretense," says the LORD.
11 Then the LORD said to me, [a]"Backsliding* Israel has shown herself more
righteous than treacherous Judah.
12 "Go and proclaim these words toward [a]the north, and say:

'Return, backsliding Israel,' says
the LORD;
'I will not cause My anger to fall
on you.
For I *am* [b]merciful,' says the
LORD;
'I will not remain angry forever.
13 [a]Only acknowledge your iniquity,
That you have transgressed
against the LORD your God,
And have [b]scattered your
[1]charms
To [c]alien deities [d]under every
green tree,
And you have not obeyed My
voice,' says the LORD.

14 "Return, O backsliding children,"
says the LORD; [a]"for I am married to
you. I will take you, [b]one from a city
and two from a family, and I will bring
you to [c]Zion.
15 "And I will give you [a]shepherds according to My heart, who will [b]feed*
you with knowledge and **understanding.**

WORD WEALTH

3:15 understanding, *sachal* (sah-*chahl*); Strong's #7919: To be wise, behave wisely; to understand, be instructed; to wisely consider; to be prudent and intelligent. *Sachal* describes the complex, intelligent thinking process that occurs when one observes, ponders, reasons, learns, and reaches a conclusion. The word is occasionally translated "prosper." In 1 Kin. 2:3, David urged Solomon to be obedient to God's instructions so that he could prosper (literally, "do wisely") in everything he undertook. A derivative of *sachal* is *maschil,* "to give instruction, to make wise and skillful." Thirteen instructive psalms are titled *"Maschil"* (NKJV, "Contemplation"). The *maschil* psalms (32; 42; 44; 45; 52; 53; 54; 55; 74; 78; 88; 89; 142) are designed to make the reader wise.

16 "Then it shall come to pass, when
you are multiplied and [a]increased in
the land in those days," says the LORD,
"that they will say no more, 'The ark
of the covenant of the LORD.' [b]It shall
not come to mind, nor shall they remember it, nor shall they visit *it,* nor
shall it be made anymore.
17 "At that time Jerusalem shall be
called The Throne of the LORD, and all
the nations shall be gathered to it,
[a]to the name of the LORD, to Jerusalem.
No more shall they [b]follow[1] the dictates of their evil hearts.
18 "In those days [a]the house of Judah
shall walk with the house of Israel, and
they shall come together out of the
land of [b]the north to [c]the land that I
have given as an inheritance to your
fathers.
19 "But I said:

'How can I put you among the
children
And give you [a]a pleasant land,
A beautiful heritage of the hosts
of nations?'

"And I said:

'You shall call Me, [b]"My Father,"
And not turn away from Me.'
20 Surely, *as* a wife treacherously
departs from her [1]husband,
So [a]have you dealt treacherously
with Me,
O house of Israel," says the LORD.

21 A voice was heard on [a]the
desolate heights,

9 [b]Is. 57:6; Jer. 2:27
10 [a]Jer. 12:2; Hos. 7:14
11 [a]Ezek. 16:51, 52
*See WW at Jer. 5:6.
12 [a]2 Kin. 17:6 [b]Ps. 86:15; Jer. 12:15; 31:20; 33:26
13 [a]Lev. 26:40; Deut. 30:1, 2; [Prov. 28:13; 1 John 1:9] [b]Ezek. 16:15 [c]Jer. 2:25 [d]Deut. 12:2 [1]Lit. *ways*
14 [a]Jer. 31:32; Hos. 2:19, 20 [b]Jer. 31:6 [c][Rom. 11:5]
15 [a]Jer. 23:4; 31:10; [Ezek. 34:23]; Eph. 4:11 [b]Acts 20:28
*See WW at Is. 40:11.
16 [a]Is. 49:19; Jer. 23:3 [b]Is. 65:17
17 [a]Is. 60:9 [b]Deut. 29:19; Jer. 7:24 [1]*walk after the stubbornness* or *imagination*
18 [a]Is. 11:13; Jer. 50:4; Ezek. 37:16–22; Hos. 1:11 [b]Jer. 31:8 [c]Amos 9:15
19 [a]Ps. 106:24 [b]Is. 63:16; Jer. 3:4
20 [a]Is. 48:8 [1]Lit. *companion*
21 [a]Is. 15:2

3:10 Pretense: Judah's response to the reform instituted by Josiah was superficial and insincere.
3:11 More righteous: Judah had the example of Israel, her "elder" sister, but this did not deter her from going the same way (see v. 8).
3:12 North: The direction in which Israel went into captivity.
3:14 Married to you: The root of this verb is *ba'al,* "to be husband or ruler." Instead of treating God as their husband, His people ran after "the Baals" (2:23; see 31:32). **One . . . two:** The remnant (see Is. 10:20–22).
3:15 Shepherds: Rulers (see 2:8). **According to My heart:** Like David (see 1 Sam. 13:14).
3:16 In those days: The period when these and other prophecies will come to pass, best seen as the messianic age (v. 18). See note on Obad. 15. **The ark of the covenant** symbolized God's presence among His people (see 1 Sam. 4:3, 7). When the Messiah is present, the symbol is no longer relevant. **They:** Israel.
3:18 Judah and **Israel** will once again be united in the land. See note on Ezek. 37:15–28.
3:19 My Father: See v. 4. The image changes from a husband-wife relationship to that of father-son, but switches back again in the next verse.
3:20 Wife treacherously departs: Spelled out in detail in Hos. 1—3.
3:21 The combined **voice** of prophet and people who are

Weeping *and* supplications of the children of Israel.
For they have perverted their way;
They have forgotten the LORD their God.

22 "Return, you backsliding children,
And I will [a]heal your *backslidings."

"Indeed we do come to You,
For You are the LORD our God.
23 [a]Truly, in vain *is salvation hoped for* from the hills,
And from the multitude of mountains;
[b]Truly, in the LORD our God
Is the salvation of Israel.
24 [a]For shame has devoured
The labor of our fathers from our youth—
Their flocks and their herds,
Their sons and their daughters.
25 We lie down in our shame,
And our [1]reproach covers us.
[a]For we have sinned against the LORD our God,
We and our fathers,
From our youth even to this day,
And [b]have not obeyed the voice of the LORD our God."

4 "If you will return, O Israel," says the LORD,
[a]"Return to Me;
And if you will put away your abominations out of My sight,
Then you shall not be moved.
2 [a]And you shall swear, 'The LORD lives,'
[b]In *truth, in [1]judgment, and in righteousness;
[c]The nations shall *bless themselves in Him,
And in Him they shall [d]glory."

3 For thus says the LORD to the men of Judah and Jerusalem:

[a]"Break up your [1]fallow ground,
And [b]do not *sow among thorns.
4 [a]Circumcise yourselves to the LORD,
And take away the foreskins of your hearts,
You men of Judah and inhabitants of Jerusalem,
Lest My fury come forth like fire,
And burn so that no one can quench *it*,
Because of the evil of your doings."

An Imminent Invasion

5 Declare in Judah and proclaim in Jerusalem, and say:

[a]"Blow* the *trumpet in the land;
Cry, 'Gather together,'
And say, [b]'Assemble yourselves,
And let us go into the fortified cities.'
6 Set up the [1]standard toward Zion.
Take refuge! Do not delay!
For I will bring disaster from the [a]north,
And great destruction."

7 [a]The lion has come up from his thicket,
And [b]the destroyer of nations is on his way.
He has gone forth from his place
[c]To make your land desolate.
Your cities will be laid waste,
Without inhabitant.
8 For this, [a]clothe yourself with sackcloth,
Lament and wail.
For the fierce anger of the LORD
Has not turned back from us.

22 [a]Hos. 6:1; 14:4 *See WW at Jer. 5:6. **23** [a]Ps. 121:1, 2 [b]Ps. 3:8 **24** [a]Hos. 9:10 **25** [a]Ezra 9:6, 7 [b]Jer. 22:21 [1]*disgrace*

CHAPTER 4

1 [a]Joel 2:12 **2** [a]Deut. 10:20 [b]Zech. 8:8 [c][Gen. 22:18] [d]1 Cor. 1:31 [1]*justice* *See WW at Ps. 25:5. • See WW at Ps. 145:2.

3 [a]Hos. 10:12 [b]Matt. 13:7 [1]*untilled* *See WW at Hos. 10:12. **4** [a]Deut. 10:16; 30:6 **5** [a]Hos. 8:1 [b]Jer. 8:14 *See WW at Ps. 47:1. • See WW at Hos. 8:1. **6** [a]Jer. 1:13–15; 6:1, 22; 50:17 [1]*banner* **7** [a]Dan. 7:4 [b]Jer. 25:9 [c]Is. 1:7; 6:11 **8** [a]Is. 22:12

weeping and confessing their sin as expressed in vv. 22–25. **Desolate heights:** See v. 2.

3:22 Return: The Hebrew root occurs many times in this prophecy (3:6—4:4) and is used as a pun here, since **return, backsliding,** and **backslidings** are all variations of the same root.

3:25 From our youth: Historically, the period of the judges. In view is the corporate personality of Israel.

4:1–4 God's reply to the people's confession. Blessing awaits if repentance is genuine and sincere, but fury like a fire awaits if the repentance is deception.

4:2 In truth, in judgment, and in righteousness emphasize the quality of genuine repentance.

4:3 The first image used by Jeremiah is taken from agriculture. Judah is to **break up** the **fallow ground,** that is, prepare it for planting (see Hos. 10:12). She must also be careful where she sows and avoid thorns (see Matt. 13:7, 22).

4:4 A second image taken from the religious practice. The people are told to **circumcise** the **foreskins of your hearts,** a reference to spiritual preparedness and inner change, not mere outward conformity.

4:5 Trumpet: Used to warn the inhabitants of danger. **Fortified cities:** People living in the open country would flee to the nearest walled city to protect themselves from the invader.

4:6 Set up the standard: A flag raised on a pole signaled danger and the place for assembly. **Disaster from the north:** The Babylonians will come from the north and bring **great destruction** (see 1:14).

4:7 Lion: A metaphor for Nebuchadnezzar, king of Babylon (see 2:15 where lions are a symbol of Assyrians).

4:8 Sackcloth was worn to express grief, mourning, and repentance.

9 "And it shall come to pass in that
day," says the LORD,
"*That* the heart of the king shall
*perish,
And the heart of the princes;
The priests shall be astonished,
And the prophets shall wonder."

10 Then I said, "Ah, Lord GOD!
[a]Surely You have greatly deceived
this people and Jerusalem,
[b]Saying, 'You shall have peace,'
Whereas the sword reaches to the
[1]heart."

11 At that time it will be said
To this people and to Jerusalem,
[a]"A dry wind of the desolate heights
blows in the wilderness
Toward the daughter of My
people—
Not to fan or to cleanse—
12 A wind too strong for these will
come for Me;
Now [a]I will also speak judgment
against them."

13 "Behold, he shall come up like
clouds,
And [a]his chariots like a
whirlwind.
[b]His horses are swifter than
eagles.
Woe to us, for we are plundered!"

14 O Jerusalem, [a]wash your heart
from wickedness,
That you may be saved.
How long shall your evil thoughts
lodge within you?
15 For a voice declares [a]from Dan
And proclaims [1]affliction* from
Mount Ephraim:
16 "Make mention to the nations,
Yes, proclaim against Jerusalem,
That watchers come from a
[a]far country
And raise their voice against the
cities of Judah.

17 [a]Like keepers of a field they are
against her all around,
Because she has been rebellious
against Me," says the LORD.
18 "Your[a] ways and your doings
Have procured these *things* for
you.
This *is* your wickedness,
Because it is bitter,
Because it reaches to your heart."

Sorrow for the Doomed Nation

19 O my [a]soul, my soul!
I am pained in my very heart!
My heart makes a noise in me;
I cannot hold my peace,
Because you have heard, O my
soul,
The sound of the trumpet,
The alarm of war.
20 [a]Destruction upon destruction is
cried,
For the whole land is plundered.
Suddenly [b]my tents are
plundered,
And my curtains in a moment.
21 How long will I see the [1]standard,
And hear the sound of the
trumpet?

22 "For My people *are* foolish,
They have not known Me.
They *are* [1]silly children,
And they have no understanding.
[a]They *are* wise to do evil,
But to do good they have no
knowledge."

23 [a]I beheld the earth, and indeed *it*
was [b]without form, and void;
And the heavens, they *had* no
light.
24 [a]I beheld the mountains, and
indeed they trembled,
And all the hills moved back and
forth.
25 I beheld, and indeed *there was* no
man,

9 *See WW at Judg. 5:31 **10** [a]2 Kin. 25:10–12; Ezek. 14:9; 2 Thess. 2:11 [b]Jer. 5:12; 14:13 [1]Lit. *soul* **11** [a]Jer. 51:1; Ezek. 17:10; Hos. 13:15 **12** [a]Jer. 1:16 **13** [a]Is. 5:28 [b]Deut. 28:49; Lam. 4:19; Hos. 8:1; Hab. 1:8 **14** [a]Prov. 1:22; Is. 1:16; Jer. 13:27; James 4:8 **15** [a]Jer. 8:16; 50:17 [1]Or *wickedness* *See WW at Prov. 22:8. **16** [a]Is. 39:3; Jer. 5:15
17 [a]2 Kin. 25:1, 4 **18** [a]Ps. 107:17; Is. 50:1; Jer. 2:17, 19 **19** [a]2 Kin. 25:11; 2 Chr. 36:20; Is. 15:5; 16:11; 21:3; 22:4; Jer. 9:1, 10; 20:9 **20** [a]Ps. 42:7; Ezek. 7:26 [b]Jer. 10:20 **21** [1]*banner* **22** [a]Jer. 9:3; 13:23; Rom. 16:19; 1 Cor. 14:20 [1]*foolish* **23** [a]Is. 24:19 [b]Gen. 1:2 **24** [a]Is. 5:25; Jer. 10:10; Ezek. 38:20

4:10 You have greatly deceived: Through false prophets, purporting to speak for God, the people have been led astray. They falsely preached **peace** (see 14:13; 23:17).
4:11 Dry wind: The khamsin or sirocco, a dry, hot, devastating wind blowing from the desert.
4:12 A wind too strong: A gentle breeze from the Mediterranean was used to fan (winnow, a process of separating chaff from grain) or to cleanse (blow dust from the grain).
4:15 Dan was the northern border of Israel, while **Mount Ephraim** was only a few miles from Jerusalem. This may indicate the rapid pace of the enemy (see v. 13).
4:16 Far country: Babylon (see Is. 39:3).
4:19–26 A personal lament expressing the agony that Jeremiah feels at the destruction of his people.
4:21 Standard and **trumpet:** See vv. 5, 6.
4:22 God speaks: See Is. 1:3; Hos. 4:1.
4:23–26 This short poem is tied together by the literary device of repetition. **I beheld** occurs at the beginning of each verse.
4:23 Without form, and void: This phrase is used only here and in Gen. 1:2. Jeremiah sees his land in ruins. His vision expresses the awesome extent of the destruction brought by the Babylonians in judgment on Judah, a cosmic cataclysm and a return to the primeval chaos. **No light:** Conditions before the first day of creation (see Gen. 1:2, 3).
4:25 No man: See Gen. 2:5. The work of creation is undone.

And [a]all the birds of the heavens
had fled.
26 I beheld, and indeed the fruitful
land *was* a [a]wilderness,
And all its cities were broken
down
At the presence of the LORD,
By His fierce anger.

27 For thus says the LORD:

"The whole land shall be desolate;
[a]Yet I will not make a full end.
28 For this [a]shall the earth *mourn,
And [b]the heavens above be black,
Because I have spoken.
I have [c]purposed and [d]will not
relent,
Nor will I turn back from it.
29 The whole city shall flee from the
noise of the horsemen and
bowmen.
They shall go into thickets and
climb up on the rocks.
Every city *shall be* forsaken,
And not a man shall dwell in it.

30 "And *when* you *are* plundered,
What will you do?
Though you clothe yourself with
crimson,
Though you adorn *yourself* with
ornaments of gold,
[a]Though you enlarge your eyes
with paint,
In vain you will make yourself
fair;
[b]*Your* lovers will *despise you;
They will seek your life.

31 "For I have heard a voice as of a
woman in [1]labor,
The anguish as of her who brings
forth her first child,
The voice of the daughter of Zion
bewailing herself;
She [a]spreads her hands, *saying,*
'Woe *is* me now, for my soul is
[2]weary
Because of murderers!'

The Justice of God's Judgment

5 "Run to and fro through the streets
of Jerusalem;
See now and know;
And seek in her open places
[a]If you can find a *man,
[b]If there is *anyone* who executes
[1]judgment,
Who seeks the truth,
[c]And I will pardon her.
2 [a]Though they say, '*As* [b]the LORD
lives,'
Surely they [c]swear falsely."

3 O LORD, *are* not [a]Your eyes on the
truth?
You have [b]stricken them,
But they have not grieved;
You have consumed them,
But [c]they have refused to receive
correction.
They have made their faces
harder than rock;
They have refused to return.

4 Therefore I said, "Surely these
are poor.
They are foolish;
For [a]they do not know the way
of the LORD,
The judgment of their God.
5 I will go to the great men and
speak to them,
For [a]they have known the way of
the LORD,
The judgment of their God."
But these have altogether
[b]broken the yoke
And burst the bonds.
6 Therefore [a]a lion from the forest
shall slay them,

25 [a]Jer. 9:10; 12:4; Zeph. 1:3
26 [a]Jer. 9:10
27 [a]Jer. 5:10, 18; 30:11; 46:28
28 [a]Jer. 12:4, 11; 14:2; Hos. 4:3 [b]Is. 5:30; 50:3; Joel 2:30, 31 [c]Is. 46:10, 11; [Dan. 4:35] [d][Num. 23:19]; Jer. 7:16; 23:30; 30:24 *See WW at Joel 1:9.
30 [a]2 Kin. 9:30; Ezek. 23:40 [b]Jer. 22:20, 22; Lam. 1:2, 19; Ezek. 23:9, 10, 22 *See WW at Amos 2:4.
31 [a]Is. 1:15; Lam. 1:17 [1]*childbirth* [2]*faint*

CHAPTER 5

1 [a]Ezek. 22:30 [b]Gen. 18:23–32 [c]Gen. 18:26 [1]*justice* *See WW at Is. 32:2.
2 [a]Is. 48:1; Titus 1:16 [b]Jer. 4:2 [c]Jer. 7:9
3 [a]2 Kin. 25:1; [2 Chr. 16:9; Jer. 16:17] [b]Is. 1:5; 9:13; Jer. 2:30 [c]Is. 9:13; Jer. 7:28; Zeph. 3:2
4 [a]Is. 27:11; Jer. 8:7; Hos. 4:6
5 [a]Mic. 3:1 [b]Ex. 32:25; Ps. 2:3; Jer. 2:20
6 [a]Jer. 4:7

4:27 Not make a full end: God's judgment is tempered by mercy (see 5:10, 18; 30:11; 46:28).
4:28 Will not relent: Repentance brings mercy, but judgment is sure unless His people repent (see 18:8).
4:30, 31 Jeremiah personifies Judah and Jerusalem, first as a prostitute (v. 30), then as a woman **in labor** (v. 31).
4:30 Paint: Antimony, a black powder used to make the eyes seem larger and more glamorous (**fair**). See 2 Kin. 9:30; Ezek. 23:40.
5:1–6 Jeremiah is told to **run to and fro through the streets of Jerusalem** to try to locate anyone who **executes judgment**. If such a **man** is found, God will forgive the inhabitants. Jeremiah starts with the **poor** (the little people), but is unsuccessful (v. 4). He then goes to the **great men** (the leaders), but fares no better. All have **broken the yoke,** that is, rebelled (2:20), and so God will send wild beasts to punish them.
5:1 A man: Hyperbole used to illustrate the wickedness of the city of Jerusalem. If one man **seeks the truth,** God will pardon the city (see Gen. 18:32). **Judgment** and **truth** describe righteousness.
5:2 *As* the LORD lives: See 4:2. **Swear falsely:** Perjury (see Lev. 19:12). The same concept is expressed by the phrase "take the name of the LORD your God in vain" (Ex. 20:7).
5:3 See section 1 of Truth-In-Action at the end of Jer.
5:3 Your eyes: Used to express God's sovereign awareness of all that transpires (see Judg. 2:11; Job. 36:7; Ps. 33:18). **Faces harder than rock:** A vivid expression for rebellion.
5:6 Wild animals are considered instruments of God's judgment. See Lev. 26:22; 2 Kin. 17:25, 26; Ezek. 14:15.

[b]A wolf of the deserts shall destroy
them;
[c]A leopard will watch over their
cities.
Everyone who goes out from
there shall be torn in pieces,
Because their *transgressions are
many;
Their **backslidings** have
increased.

WORD WEALTH

5:6 backslidings, *meshubah* (meh-shoo-*vah*); Strong's #4878: Turning back, turning away; defecting; faithlessness, apostasy, disloyalty; reverting, backsliding. This noun is found 12 times in the OT, 9 times in Jer. alone. The 3 other references are Prov. 1:32; Hos. 11:7; 14:4. The root word is *shub,* a verb which means to "turn, return, or repent." If repentance is a "turning around," backsliding is a "turning back," or "turning away" from God. God gave a merciful invitation to the backslider in Jer. 3:12–15, 22. In this latter verse, God regards backsliding as a condition that requires healing.

7 "How shall I pardon you for this?
Your children have forsaken Me
And [a]sworn by *those* [b]*that are*
not gods.
[c]When I had fed them to the full,
Then they committed adultery
And assembled themselves by
troops in the harlots' houses.
8 [a]They were *like* well-fed lusty
stallions;
Every one neighed after his
neighbor's wife.
9 Shall I not punish *them* for these
things?" says the LORD.
"And shall I not [a]avenge Myself on
such a nation as this?

10 "Go up on her walls and destroy,
But do not [1]make a [a]complete
end.
Take away her branches,
For they *are* not the LORD's.
11 For [a]the house of Israel and the
house of Judah
Have dealt very treacherously
with Me," says the LORD.

12 [a]They have lied about the LORD,
And said, [b]"*It is* not He.
[c]Neither will [1]evil come upon us,
Nor shall we see sword or famine.
13 And the prophets become wind,
For the word *is* not in them.
Thus shall it be done to them."

14 Therefore thus says the LORD God
of hosts:

"Because you speak this word,
[a]Behold, I will make My words in
your mouth fire,
And this people wood,
And it shall devour them.
15 Behold, I will bring a [a]nation
against you [b]from afar,
O house of Israel," says the LORD.
"It *is* a mighty nation,
It *is* an ancient nation,
A nation whose language you do
not know,
Nor can you understand what
they say.
16 Their quiver *is* like an open tomb;
They *are* all mighty men.
17 And they shall eat up your
[a]harvest and your bread,
Which your sons and daughters
should eat.
They shall eat up your flocks and
your herds;
They shall eat up your vines and
your fig trees;
They shall destroy your fortified
cities,
In which you trust, with the
sword.

18 "Nevertheless in those days," says
the LORD, "I [a]will not [1]make a complete
end of you.
19 "And it will be when you say,
[a]'Why does the LORD our God do all
these *things* to us?' then you shall answer them, 'Just as you have [b]forsaken
Me and served foreign gods in your
land, so [c]you shall serve aliens in a
land *that is* not yours.'

20 "Declare this in the house of Jacob
And proclaim it in Judah, saying,
21 'Hear this now, O [a]foolish people,
Without [1]understanding,
Who have eyes and see not,
And who have ears and hear not:
22 [a]Do you not fear Me?' says the
LORD.

6 [b]Ps. 104:20; Ezek. 22:27; Hab. 1:8; Zeph. 3:3 [c]Hos. 13:7 *See WW at Ezek. 18:31. **7** [a]Josh. 23:7; Jer. 12:16; Zeph. 1:5 [b]Deut. 32:21; Jer. 2:11; Gal. 4:8 [c]Deut. 32:15 **8** [a]Jer. 13:27; 29:23; Ezek. 22:11 **9** [a]Jer. 9:9 **10** [a]Jer. 4:27 [1]*completely destroy* **11** [a]Jer. 3:6, 7, 20 **12** [a]2 Chr. 36:16; Jer. 4:10 [b]Is. 28:15; 47:8; Jer. 23:17 [c]Jer. 14:13 [1]*disaster* **14** [a]Is. 24:6; Jer. 1:9; 23:29; Hos. 6:5; Zech. 1:6 **15** [a]Deut. 28:49; Is. 5:26; Jer. 1:15; 6:22 [b]Is. 39:3; Jer. 4:16 **17** [a]Lev. 26:16; Deut. 28:31, 33; Jer. 8:16; 50:7, 17 **18** [a]Jer. 30:11; Amos 9:8 [1]*completely destroy* **19** [a]Deut. 29:24–29; 1 Kin. 9:8, 9; Jer. 13:22; 16:10–13 [b]Jer. 1:16; 2:13 [c]Deut. 28:48; Jer. 16:13 **21** [a]Is. 6:9; Jer. 6:10; Ezek. 12:2; Matt. 13:14; John 12:40; Acts 28:26; Rom. 11:8 [1]Lit. *heart* **22** [a]Deut. 28:58; Ps. 119:120; Jer. 2:19; 10:7; [Rev. 15:4]

5:7–9 Idolatry is portrayed as flagrant adultery, like **stallions** neighing after the wives of others. God promises punishment for such action.
5:12, 13 The false prophets have **lied about the LORD,** and they contradict the message of Jeremiah by saying, **Neither will evil come upon us**. See note on 4:10.
5:14–17 Failure to repent brings a **mighty nation,** the Babylonians, to **eat** the produce of the land and to **destroy**.
5:14 The words of Jeremiah will be like **fire** to **devour,** in contrast to the **wind** (v. 13) of the false prophets.
5:21 Eyes and ears: See Is. 6:10.

'Will you not tremble at My presence,
Who have placed the sand as the [b]bound of the sea,
By a perpetual decree, that it cannot pass beyond it?
And though its waves toss to and fro,
Yet they cannot prevail;
Though they roar, yet they cannot pass over it.
23 But this people has a defiant and rebellious heart;
They have revolted and departed.
24 They do not say in their heart,
"Let us now fear the LORD our God,
[a]Who gives rain, both the [b]former and the latter, in its season.
[c]He reserves for us the appointed weeks of the harvest."
25 [a]Your *iniquities have turned these *things* away,
And your sins have withheld good from you.

26 'For among My people are found wicked *men;*
They [a]lie in wait as one who sets snares;
They set a trap;
They catch men.
27 As a cage is full of birds,
So their houses *are* full of deceit.
Therefore they have become great and grown rich.
28 They have grown [a]fat, they are sleek;
Yes, they [1]surpass the deeds of the wicked;
They do not plead [b]the cause,
The cause of the fatherless;
[c]Yet they prosper,
And the right of the needy they do not defend.

22 [b]Job 26:10
24 [a]Ps. 147:8; Jer. 14:22; [Matt. 5:45]; Acts 14:17 [b]Deut. 11:14; Joel 2:23; James 5:7 [c][Gen. 8:22]
25 [a]Jer. 3:3 *See WW at Ps. 130:3.
26 [a]Ps. 10:9; Prov. 1:11; Jer. 18:22; Hab. 1:15
28 [a]Deut. 32:15 [b]Is. 1:23; Jer. 7:6; 22:3; Zech. 7:10 [c]Job 12:6; Ps. 73:12 [1]Or *pass over* or *overlook*
29 [a]Jer. 5:9; Mal. 3:5
30 [a]Jer. 23:14; Hos. 6:10; 2 Tim. 4:3
31 [a]Jer. 14:14; Ezek. 13:6 [b]Mic. 2:11

CHAPTER 6

1 [a]Neh. 3:14 [b]Jer. 4:6
3 [a]2 Kin. 25:1–4; Jer. 4:17; 12:10
4 [a]Jer. 51:27; Joel 3:9 [b]Jer. 15:8; Zeph. 2:4

29 [a]Shall I not punish *them* for these *things?*' says the LORD.
'Shall I not avenge Myself on such a nation as this?'

30 "An astonishing and [a]horrible thing
Has been committed in the land:
31 The prophets prophesy [a]falsely, 2
And the priests rule by their *own* power;
And My people [b]love *to have it* so.
But what will you do in the end?

Impending Destruction from the North

6 "O you children of Benjamin,
Gather yourselves to flee from the midst of Jerusalem!
Blow the trumpet in Tekoa,
And set up a signal-fire in [a]Beth Haccerem;
[b]For disaster appears out of the north,
And great destruction.
2 I have likened the daughter of Zion
To a lovely and delicate woman.
3 The [a]shepherds with their flocks shall come to her.
They shall pitch *their* tents against her all around.
Each one shall pasture in his own place."

4 "Prepare[a] war against her;
Arise, and let us go up [b]at noon.
Woe to us, for the day goes away,
For the shadows of the evening are lengthening.
5 Arise, and let us go by night,
And let us destroy her palaces."

6 For thus has the LORD of hosts said:

5:24 Rain, both the former and the latter: See 3:3. **Appointed weeks:** The seven weeks from Passover to Pentecost.
5:26–30 Wicked men have caught the defenseless in cages like birds, and contrary to "orthodox" theology, the wicked have prospered. They have denied the rights of others in order to amass wealth for themselves. This is only a temporary situation, however, because the Lord will avenge Himself on them.
5:27 Deceit: The wealth they have accumulated by their dishonest schemes.
5:28 The **fatherless** and the **needy** are used as standards by which deeds are measured. Kings and all others have an obligation to the destitute and suffering ones because God desires it (see 22:16; Deut. 10:18; James 1:27).
5:30 Astonishing and **horrible** describe the acceptance by the people of the ministry of false prophets and wicked priests; they actually desire to continue this farce (see 6:13–15).
5:31 See section 2 of Truth-In-Action at the end of Jer.
6:1 In 4:6 the people are encouraged to flee to Jerusalem for refuge. Now, they are warned **to flee** from **Jerusalem** because no place will be safe from the invaders. **Benjamin** was the tribal territory just north of Jerusalem. **Tekoa** was 12 miles south of Jerusalem. **Beth Haccerem** is modern Ramat Rahel, 2 miles south of Jerusalem. **Blow** and "Tekoa" are a wordplay; the words sound similar in Hebrew. **Set up** and **signal-fire** are also a wordplay for the same reason.
6:3 Shepherds with their flocks are rulers with their troops.
6:4, 5 The invaders are speaking.
6:4 Prepare: The root of this word in Hebrew is the same as "consecrate" (see Joel 3:9; Mic. 3:5). Preparation included religious ritual (see 1 Sam. 21:4, 5). **Noon:** Chosen as an element of surprise since the attack normally began in the morning.
6:5 Night: Indicates the eagerness of the soldiers since most fighting stopped at sundown.
6:6 Preparation for a siege included the cutting of **trees** and the building of a **mound** or siege ramps.

"Cut down trees,
And build a mound against
Jerusalem.
This *is* the city to be punished.
She *is* full of oppression in her
midst.
7 [a]As a fountain [1]wells up with
water,
So she wells up with her
wickedness.
[b]Violence and plundering are
heard in her.
Before Me *continually *are*
[2]grief and wounds.
8 Be instructed, O Jerusalem,
Lest [a]My soul depart from you;
Lest I make you desolate,
A land not inhabited."

9 Thus says the LORD of hosts:

"They shall thoroughly glean as a
vine the remnant of Israel;
As a grape-gatherer, put your
hand back into the branches."

2 10 To whom shall I speak and give
warning,
That they may hear?
Indeed their [a]ear *is*
uncircumcised,
And they cannot give heed.
Behold, [b]the word of the LORD is
a reproach to them;
They have no delight in it.
11 Therefore I am full of the fury of
the LORD.
[a]I am weary of holding *it* in.
"I will pour it out [b]on the children
outside,
And on the assembly of young
men together;
For even the husband shall be
taken with the wife,
The aged with *him who is* full of
days.
12 And [a]their houses shall be turned
over to others,
Fields and wives together;
For I will stretch out My hand
Against the inhabitants of the
land," says the LORD.
13 "Because from the least of them
even to the greatest of them,
Everyone *is* given to
[a]covetousness;
And from the prophet even to the
[b]priest,
Everyone deals falsely.
14 They have also [a]healed the
[1]hurt of My people [2]slightly,*
[b]Saying, 'Peace, peace!'
When *there is* no peace.
15 Were they [a]ashamed when they
had committed abomination?
No! They were not at all
*ashamed;
Nor did they know how to blush.
Therefore they shall fall among
those who fall;
At the time I punish them,
They shall be cast down," says
the LORD.

16 Thus says the LORD: 4

"Stand in the ways and see,
And ask for the [a]old paths, where
the good way *is*,
And walk in it;
Then you will find [b]rest for your
souls.
But they said, 'We will not walk
in it.'
17 Also, I set [a]watchmen over you,
saying,
[b]'Listen to the sound of the
trumpet!'
But they said, 'We will not listen.'
18 Therefore hear, you nations,
And know, O congregation, what
is among them.
19 [a]Hear, O earth!
Behold, I will certainly bring
[b]calamity on this people—
[c]The fruit of their thoughts,
Because they have not heeded My
words

7 [a]Is. 57:20 [b]Ps. 55:9 [1]*gushes* [2]*sickness* *See WW at Ex. 28:30.
8 [a]Ezek. 23:18; Hos. 9:12
10 [a]Ex. 6:12; Jer. 5:21; 7:26; [Acts 7:51] [b]Jer. 8:9; 20:8
11 [a]Jer. 20:9 [b]Jer. 9:21
12 [a]Deut. 28:30; Jer. 8:10; 38:22
13 [a]Is. 56:11; Jer. 8:10; 22:17 [b]Jer. 5:31; 23:11; Mic. 3:5, 11
14 [a]Jer. 8:11–15; Ezek. 13:10 [b]Jer. 4:10; 23:17 [1]Lit. *crushing* [2]*Superficially* *See WW at Jer. 8:11.
15 [a]Jer. 3:3; 8:12 *See WW at Ezek. 16:63.
16 [a]Is. 8:20; Jer. 18:15; Mal. 4:4; Luke 16:29 [b]Matt. 11:29
17 [a]Is. 21:11; 58:1; Jer. 25:4; Ezek. 3:17; Hab. 2:1 [b]Deut. 4:1
19 [a]Is. 1:2 [b]Jer. 19:3, 15 [c]Prov. 1:31

6:9 Glean: See Is. 17:5, 6 and note on Ruth 2:1. **Remnant:** A very important concept in the prophetic material (see 11:23; 23:3; 31:7; 40:11, 15; 42:2, 15, 19; 43:5; 44:12, 14, 28; and note on Zeph. 2:7).
6:10–15 The prophet speaks. He alternates between speaking the wrath of God and showing compassion and concern. Here wrath predominates.
6:10 See section 2 of Truth-In-Action at the end of Jer.
6:11 Fury (see 25:15) comes on all; **children, young men, husband, wife,** and the **aged**.
6:12–15 Repeated with slight variation in 8:10–12.
6:12 The figure of an **outstretched arm** occurs several times (21:5; 27:5; 32:17, 21) and is used of God's power to deliver (Ex. 6:6), to punish (21:5), and here to destroy (see 15:6).
6:14 The **peace** expressed by the false prophets was absence of war or calamity, a concept far removed from the OT *shalom,* which emphasizes wholeness or soundness. True peace involves complete fellowship with God and right relations with others. It has more to do with character and attitude than outward circumstances.
6:16–23 The Lord speaks and admonishes His people to walk in the **old paths** of righteousness, but in their stubbornness they refuse.
6:16 See section 4 of Truth-In-Action at the end of Jer.
6:17 Watchmen: One of the terms used for true prophets. See notes on Ezek. 3:17; 33:1–9; Hab. 2:1.

Nor My law, but rejected it.
20 [a]For what purpose to Me
Comes frankincense [b]from Sheba,
And [c]sweet cane from a far country?
[d]Your burnt offerings *are* not acceptable,
Nor your sacrifices sweet to Me."

21 Therefore thus says the LORD:

"Behold, I will lay stumbling blocks before this people,
And the fathers and the sons together shall fall on them.
The neighbor and his *friend shall perish."

22 Thus says the LORD:

"Behold, a people comes from the [a]north country,
And a great nation will be raised from the farthest parts of the earth.
23 They will lay hold on bow and spear;
They *are* cruel and have no mercy;
Their voice [a]roars like the sea;
And they ride on horses,
As men of war set in array against you, O daughter of Zion."

24 We have heard the report of it;
Our hands grow feeble.
[a]Anguish has taken hold of us,
Pain as of a woman in [1]labor.
25 Do not go out into the field,
Nor walk by the way.
Because of the sword of the enemy,
Fear *is* on every side.
26 O daughter of my people,
[a]Dress in sackcloth
[b]And roll about in ashes!
[c]Make mourning *as for* an *only son, most bitter lamentation;
For the plunderer will suddenly come upon us.

27 "I have set you *as* an assayer *and* [a]a fortress among My people,
That you may know and test their way.
28 [a]They *are* all stubborn rebels, [b]walking as slanderers.
They are [c]bronze and iron,
They *are* all corrupters;
29 The bellows blow fiercely,
The lead is consumed by the fire;
The smelter *refines in vain,
For the wicked are not drawn off.
30 *People* will call them [a]rejected silver,
Because the LORD has rejected them."

20 [a]Ps. 40:6; 50:7–9; Is. 1:11; 66:3; Amos 5:21; Mic. 6:6, 7 [b]Is. 60:6 [c]Is. 43:24 [d]Jer. 7:21–23
21 *See WW at Prov. 17:17.
22 [a]Jer. 1:15; 10:22; 50:41–43
23 [a]Is. 5:30
24 [a]Jer. 4:31; 13:21; 49:24 [1]*childbirth*
26 [a]Jer. 4:8 [b]Jer. 25:34; Mic. 1:10 [c]Amos 8:10; [Zech. 12:10] *See WW at Gen. 22:2.
27 [a]Jer. 1:18
28 [a]Jer. 5:23 [b]Jer. 9:4 [c]Ezek. 22:18
29 *See WW at Zech. 13:9.
30 [a]Is. 1:22; Jer. 7:29

Trusting in Lying Words

7 The word that came to Jeremiah
from the LORD, saying,
2 [a]"Stand in the gate of the LORD's
house, and proclaim there this word,
and say, 'Hear the word of the LORD,
all *you of* Judah who enter in at these
gates to worship the LORD!' "
3 Thus says the LORD of hosts, the
God of Israel: [a]"Amend your ways and
your doings, and I will cause you to
dwell in this place.
4 [a]"Do not trust in these lying words,
saying, 'The *temple of the LORD, the
temple of the LORD, the temple of the
LORD *are* these.'

CHAPTER 7

2 [a]Jer. 17:19; 26:2
3 [a]Jer. 4:1; 18:11; 26:13
4 [a]Jer. 7:8; Mic. 3:11 *See WW at Hag. 2:15.

6:20 Outward conformity to religious ritual is not enough. This point is stressed as well by the eighth-century prophets (see Is. 1:10–17; Amos 5:21–24; Mic. 6:6–8). **Sheba:** A site in Arabia known for its spice trade (Is. 60:6). **Sweet cane:** Calamus, an aromatic reed (see Ex. 30:23; Song 4:14; Is. 43:24).
6:21 To put **stumbling blocks** before the blind was forbidden by Lev. 19:14. Judah's spiritual blindness has created the nation's own stumbling blocks, the Babylonians.
6:22–24 Repeated with slight variation in 50:41–43; but there "Babylon" is substituted for **Zion,** and "the king of Babylon" for **we have heard.**
6:24–26 Jeremiah speaks to or for the people.
6:25 Fear *is* on every side: A favorite expression of Jeremiah to indicate all-encompassing danger (20:10; 46:5; 49:29).
6:26 Sackcloth and **ashes** are used as symbols of **mourning** (see note on 4:8).
6:27–30 God speaks to Jeremiah and assigns him the task of testing the people as an **assayer** tests metals. See 9:7; Is. 1:25; Mal. 3:2, 3.
6:27 A fortress: Better understood as "precious metals."
6:28 Bronze and iron: Compared to silver and gold these are base metals.
6:29, 30 The process for refining silver employed the addition of lead to the ore. The **lead** was **consumed** as the alloys were **drawn off**. Here the process fails because the silver ore has too many impurities. The people, then, are **rejected silver**.
7:1—8:3 This temple sermon is a denunciation of an unholy and corrupt standard of living by people who held that the city of Jerusalem was inviolable because of the physical presence of the temple (7:4). This belief was based on an incident over a hundred years earlier when Isaiah prophesied that the Assyrian king Sennacherib would not take the city (Is. 37:6, 7, 29). But times have changed, and God's will now is that this city and temple shall be destroyed (Jer. 7:14) unless the people repent and amend their ways (7:3).
7:4 The threefold repetition of the phrase **the temple of the LORD** is a literary device used for emphasis (see 22:29; 23:30–32; Is. 6:3). The mere recitation of the phrase is trusting in **lying words,** since God's protection and blessing can come only through right living.

5 "For if you thoroughly amend your
ways and your doings, if you thoroughly [a]execute [1]judgment between a
man and his neighbor,
6 "*if* you do not oppress the stranger,
the fatherless, and the widow, and do
not shed innocent blood in this place,
[a]or walk after other gods to your hurt,
7 [a]"then I will cause you to *dwell in
this place, in [b]the land that I gave to
your fathers forever and ever.
8 "Behold, you trust in [a]lying words
that cannot profit.
9 [a]"Will you steal, murder, commit
adultery, swear falsely, burn incense
to Baal, and [b]walk after other gods
whom you do not know,
10 [a]"and *then* come and stand before
Me in this house [b]which is *called by
My name, and say, 'We are delivered
to do all these abominations'?
11 "Has [a]this house, which is called by
My name, become a [b]den of thieves in
your eyes? Behold, I, even I, have seen
it," says the LORD.
12 "But go now to [a]My place which
was in Shiloh, [b]where I set My name
at the first, and see [c]what I did to it
because of the wickedness of My people Israel.
13 "And now, because you have done
all these works," says the LORD, "and
I spoke to you, [a]rising up early and
speaking, but you did not hear, and I
[b]called you, but you did not answer,
14 "therefore I will do to the house
which is called by My name, in which
you trust, and to this place which I
gave to you and your fathers, as I have
done to [a]Shiloh.*
15 "And I will cast you out of My sight,
[a]as I have cast out all your brethren—
[b]the whole posterity of Ephraim.
16 "Therefore [a]do not pray for this
people, nor lift up a cry or prayer for
them, nor *make intercession to Me;
[b]for I will not hear you.
17 "Do you not see what they do in the
cities of Judah and in the streets of Jerusalem?
18 [a]"The children gather wood, the fathers kindle the fire, and the women
knead dough, to make cakes for the
queen of heaven; and *they* [b]pour out
drink offerings to other gods, that they
may provoke Me to anger.
19 [a]"Do they provoke Me to anger?"
says the LORD. "*Do they* not *provoke*
themselves, to the shame of their own
faces?"
20 Therefore thus says the Lord GOD:
"Behold, My anger and My fury will
be poured out on this place—on man
and on beast, on the trees of the field
and on the fruit of the ground. And it
will burn and not be quenched."
21 Thus says the LORD of hosts, the
God of Israel: [a]"Add your burnt offerings to your sacrifices and eat meat.
22 [a]"For I did not speak to your fathers, or command them in the day that
I brought them out of the land of Egypt,
concerning burnt offerings or sacrifices.
23 "But this is what I commanded
them, saying, [a]'Obey My voice, and
[b]I will be your God, and you shall be
My people. And walk in all the ways
that I have commanded you, that it
may be well with you.'
24 [a]"Yet they did not obey or incline
their ear, but [b]followed[1] the counsels
and the [2]dictates of their evil hearts,
and [c]went[3] backward and not forward.
25 "Since the day that your fathers
came out of the land of Egypt until this

5 [a]Jer. 21:12; 22:3 [1]*justice*
6 [a]Deut. 6:14, 15
7 [a]Deut. 4:40 [b]Jer. 3:18 *See WW at Num. 10:12.
8 [a]Jer. 5:31; 14:13, 14
9 [a]1 Kin. 18:21 [b]Ex. 20:3
10 [a]Ezek. 23:39 [b]Jer. 7:11, 14; 32:34; 34:15 *See WW at Jer. 33:3.
11 [a]Is. 56:7 [b]Matt. 21:13
12 [a]Josh. 18:1 [b]Deut. 12:11 [c]1 Sam. 4:10
13 [a]2 Chr. 36:15 [b]Prov. 1:24
14 [a]1 Sam. 4:10, 11 *See WW at Gen. 49:10.
15 [a]2 Kin. 17:23 [b]Ps. 78:67
16 [a]Ex. 32:10 Jer. 11:14 [b]Jer. 15:1 *See WW at Jer. 27:18.
18 [a]Jer. 44:17 [b]Jer. 19:13
19 [a]Deut. 32:16, 21
21 [a]Jer. 6:20
22 [a][Hos. 6:6]
23 [a]Deut. 6:3 [b][Ex. 19:5, 6]
24 [a]Ps. 81:11 [b]Deut. 29:19 [c]Jer. 32:33 [1]*walked in* [2]*stubbornness* or *imagination* [3]Lit. *they were*

7:5 The conduct necessary for God's blessing involves **judgment** (or justice) with one another.
7:6 The care of **the stranger, the fatherless, and the widow** is an essential ingredient in God's social order. This concern is stressed often in Scripture (see Deut. 16:11, 14; 24:19–21; 26:12, 13; 27:19; Job 31:16; Ps. 94:6; Is. 1:17; James 1:17). The practice of true religion today includes a social concern for all people.
7:11 Mere formal attendance at God's **house** is also condemned by Jesus. See Matt. 21:13; Mark 11:17; Luke 19:46.
7:12 **Shiloh** was where the ark of the covenant was kept in the days of the judges (1 Sam. 4:3). When the ark was captured by the Philistines, it was not returned to Shiloh, and in the time of Jeremiah the city was in ruins.
7:13 ***Rising up early:*** *This idiom carries the connotation* of "earnestly and persistently" or "again and again" (see v. 25; 11:7; 25:3, 4; 26:5; 29:19; 32:33; 35:14, 15; 44:4).
7:15 **Whole posterity of Ephraim:** All the inhabitants of the northern kingdom of Israel were **cast out** (sent into exile) in 722 B.C.
7:16 Perhaps the events of ch. 26 belong between vv. 15 and 16. Jeremiah is commanded not to **pray for this people** as a prophet normally would (see 27:18; Ex. 32:31, 32; 1 Sam. 12:23). There is virtually no hope for this people because of their consistent rebellion. Jeremiah, however, did pray for them on occasion (see 18:20).
7:18 The whole family participates in the worship of **the queen of heaven,** the Babylonian goddess Ishtar. **Drink offerings** are provided for other gods as well.
7:20 The sin of the people corrupts and brings judgment not only on themselves but on all of creation. See 5:17; Rom. 8:20–22.
7:21–23 These verses are not a rejection of OT sacrifices, but they do emphasize that **sacrifices** are worthless without proper heart attitude (see 6:20 and note; 1 Sam. 15:22, 23; Ps. 40:6–8; Amos 5:24). God's command was, **Obey My voice**.
7:25, 26 Obeying the Lord, not concern for ritual matters, should be Israel's main focus. In their present condition they might as well eat the burnt offerings themselves. **Daily rising up early and sending:** Again and again God sent the prophets (see v. 13).

day, I have even [a]sent to you all My servants the prophets, daily rising up early and sending *them*.

26 [a]"Yet they did not obey Me or incline their ear, but [b]stiffened their neck. [c]They did worse than their fathers.

27 "Therefore [a]you shall speak all these words to them, but they will not obey you. You shall also call to them, but they will not answer you.

Judgment on Obscene Religion

2 **28** "So you shall say to them, 'This *is* a nation that does not obey the voice of the LORD their God [a]nor receive correction. [b]Truth has perished and has been cut off from their mouth.

29 [a]'Cut off your hair and cast *it* away, and take up a lamentation on the desolate heights; for the LORD has rejected and forsaken the generation of His wrath.'

30 "For the children of Judah have done evil in My sight," says the LORD. [a]"They have set their abominations in the house which is called by My name, to [1]pollute it.

31 "And they have built the [a]high places of Tophet, which *is* in the Valley of the Son of Hinnom, to [b]burn their sons and their daughters in the fire, [c]which I did not command, nor did it come into My heart.

32 "Therefore behold, [a]the days are coming," says the LORD, "when it will no more be called Tophet, or the Valley of the Son of Hinnom, but the Valley of Slaughter; [b]for they will bury in Tophet until there is no room.

33 "The [a]corpses of this people will be food for the birds of the heaven and for the beasts of the earth. And no one will frighten *them away*.

34 "Then I will cause to [a]cease from the cities of Judah and from the streets of Jerusalem the voice of mirth and the voice of gladness, the voice of the bridegroom and the voice of the bride. For [b]the land shall be desolate.

8 "At that time," says the LORD, "they shall bring out the bones of the kings of Judah, and the bones of its princes, and the bones of the priests, and the bones of the prophets, and the bones of the inhabitants of Jerusalem, out of their graves.

2 "They shall spread them before the sun and the moon and all the host of heaven, which they have loved and which they have served and after which they have walked, which they have sought and [a]which they have worshiped. They shall not be gathered [b]nor buried; they shall be like refuse on the face of the earth.

3 "Then [a]death shall be chosen rather than life by all the [1]residue of those who remain of this evil family, who remain in all the places where I have driven them," says the LORD of hosts.

The Peril of False Teaching

4 "Moreover you shall say to them, 'Thus says the LORD:

"Will they fall and not rise?
Will one turn away and not return?
5 Why has this people [a]slidden back,
Jerusalem, in a perpetual *backsliding?
[b]They hold fast to deceit,
[c]They refuse to return.
6 [a]I listened and heard,
But they do not speak aright.
[b]No man repented of his wickedness,
Saying, 'What have I done?'
Everyone turned to his own course,
As the horse rushes into the battle.

7 "Even [a]the stork in the heavens
Knows her appointed times;
And the turtledove, the swift, and the swallow
Observe the *time of their coming.
But [b]My people do not know the judgment of the LORD.

8 "How can you say, 'We *are* wise,
[a]And the *law of the LORD *is* with us'?

25 [a]2 Chr. 36:15 **26** [a]Jer. 11:8 [b]Neh. 9:17 [c]Jer. 16:12 **27** [a]Ezek. 2:7 **28** [a]Jer. 5:3 [b]Jer. 9:3 **29** [a]Mic. 1:16 **30** [a]Dan. 9:27; 11:31 [1]*defile* **31** [a]2 Kin. 23:10 [b]Ps. 106:38 [c]Deut. 17:3 **32** [a]Jer. 19:6 [b]2 Kin. 23:10 **33** [a]Jer. 9:22; 19:11 **34** [a]Is. 24:7, 8 [b]Lev. 26:33

CHAPTER 8

2 [a]2 Kin. 23:5 [b]Jer. 22:19 **3** [a]Rev. 9:6 [1]*remnant* **5** [a]Jer. 7:24 [b]Jer. 9:6 [c]Jer. 5:3 *See WW at Jer. 5:6. **6** [a]Ps. 14:2 [b]Mic. 7:2 **7** [a]Song 2:12 [b]Jer. 5:4; 9:3 *See WW at Is. 33:6. **8** [a]Rom. 2:17 *See WW at Is. 42:21.

7:28 See section 2 of Truth-In-Action at the end of Jer.

7:29 Cut off your hair: A sign of mourning. See Job 1:20; Mic. 1:16.

7:31 Tophet: A "high place" in the Valley of Hinnom, just outside of Jerusalem, where children were sacrificed to the heathen god Molech. Jeremiah predicts it will become a cemetery (v. 32; 19:6, 11–14).

7:34 Repeated with slight variation in 16:9 (see 25:10 and contrast 33:10, 11).

8:1 Bring out the bones: An act of sacrilege and disgrace for those whose bones are exposed. See 2 Kin. 23:16, 18; Amos 2:1.

8:4–7 Israel is completely indifferent to God's Word. The birds know and understand their divine destiny, but God's people do not know (see Is. 1:2, 3).

8:8, 9 Having failed to understand the written **law of the LORD,** the **wise men** now reject the spoken **word of the LORD** through the prophets. The **scribe** administered the law.

Look, the false pen of the scribe
certainly works falsehood.
9 [a]The wise men are ashamed,
They are dismayed and taken.
Behold, they have rejected the
word of the LORD;
So [b]what wisdom do they have?

KINGDOM DYNAMICS

8:8, 9 Man's Futile Efforts at Self-Restoration, RESTORATION. Jer. 8—10 demonstrates man's futile efforts at self-restoration. The entire concept of "The Holy Spirit and Restoration" is developed in the study article that begins on page 2012.

(Gen. 41:42, 43/Ezek. 34:1–10) J.R.

10 Therefore [a]I will give their wives
to others,
And their fields to those who will
inherit *them;*
Because from the least even to the
greatest
Everyone is given to
[b]covetousness;
From the prophet even to the
priest
Everyone deals falsely.
11 For they have [a]healed the hurt of
the daughter of My people
[1]**slightly,**
Saying, [b]'Peace, peace!'
When *there is* no peace.

WORD WEALTH

8:11 slightly, *qalal* (kah-*lahl*); Strong's #7043: In a superficial or light manner; easy, trifling; having very little weight; also, cursing, reviling, making light of someone; ridiculing another person. *Qalal* occurs 82 times. For examples of its use as "curse" or "make light of someone," see Gen. 12:3; 2 Sam. 16:13; Ezek. 22:7. For examples of its use in reference to matters that are considered "light," or of relatively small weight, see 1 Kin. 12:9; 2 Kin. 20:10; Is. 49:6. In the present reference, Israel's spiritual leaders superficially tended to the deep wounds of the people.

12 Were they [a]ashamed when they
had committed abomination?

9 [a]Is. 19:11; Jer. 6:15; [1 Cor. 1:27] [b]Is. 44:25; Jer. 4:22
10 [a]Deut. 28:30; Amos 5:11; Zeph. 1:13 [b]Is. 56:11; 57:17; Jer. 6:13
11 [a]Jer. 6:14 [b]Ezek. 13:10 [1]Superficially
12 [a]Ps. 52:1, 7; Is. 3:9; Jer. 3:3; 6:15; Zeph. 3:5
13 [a]Jer. 5:17; 7:20; Joel 1:17 [b]Matt. 21:19; Luke 13:6 [c]Deut. 28:39, 40 [1]Or *take them away*
14 [a]Jer. 4:5 [b]Deut. 29:18; Ps. 69:21; Jer. 9:15; Lam. 3:19; Matt. 27:34 [1]Bitter or poisonous water
15 [a]Jer. 14:19 *See WW at Lam. 3:25.
16 [a]Judg. 18:29; Jer. 4:15 [b]Jer. 47:3
17 [a]Ps. 58:4, 5

No! They were not at all ashamed,
Nor did they know how to blush.
Therefore they shall fall among
those who fall;
In the time of their punishment
They shall be cast down," says
the LORD.

13 "I will surely [1]consume them,"
says the LORD.
"No grapes *shall be* [a]on the vine,
Nor figs on the [b]fig tree,
And the leaf shall fade;
And *the things* I have given them
shall [c]pass away from
them." ' "

14 "Why do we sit still?
[a]Assemble yourselves,
And let us enter the fortified
cities,
And let us be silent there.
For the LORD our God has put us
to silence
And given us [b]water[1] of gall to
drink,
Because we have sinned against
the LORD.

15 "*We* [a]looked* for peace, but no
good *came;*
And for a time of health, and
there was trouble!
16 The snorting of His horses was
heard from [a]Dan.
The whole land trembled at the
sound of the neighing of His
[b]strong ones;
For they have come and devoured
the land and all that is in it,
The city and those who dwell in
it."

17 "For behold, I will send serpents
among you,
Vipers which cannot be
[a]charmed,
And they shall bite you," says the
LORD.

The Prophet Mourns for the People

18 I would comfort myself in sorrow;
My heart *is* faint in me.
19 Listen! The voice,

8:10–12 See 6:12–15.
8:13—9:25 This passage *is read in synagogues* each year on the ninth day of Abib (March–April) to commemorate the destruction of the temple by the Babylonians in 586 B.C. and by the Romans in A.D. 70.
8:13–15 Judah is like an unfruitful **vine** or **fig tree** which has no **grapes** or **figs** (individual people) and is destined for destruction. They flee to the **fortified cities** to find refuge, but they are not safe.
8:15 Repeated with slight variation in 14:19.
8:16 Dan was in the extreme north and would be the first to experience the enemy's advance.
8:18—9:2 The prophet mourns for his people, some of whom are in exile in a **far country**. The people are perplexed; the **LORD** is in **Zion,** but they have been defeated.

The cry of the daughter of my
people
From [a]a far country:
"*Is* not the LORD in Zion?
Is not her King in her?"

"Why have they *provoked Me to
anger
With their carved images—
With foreign idols?"

20 "The harvest is past,
The summer is ended,
And we are not saved!"

21 [a]For the hurt of the daughter of my
people I am hurt.
I am [b]mourning;
Astonishment has taken hold of
me.
22 *Is there* no [a]balm in Gilead,
Is there no physician there?
Why then is there no recovery
For the health of the daughter of
my people?

9 Oh, [a]that my *head were waters,
And my eyes a fountain of tears,
That I might weep day and night
For the slain of the daughter of
my people!
2 Oh, that I had in the wilderness
A lodging place for travelers;
That I might leave my people,
And go from them!
For [a]they *are* all adulterers,
An assembly of treacherous men.

3 "And *like* their bow [a]they have
bent their tongues *for* lies.
They are not valiant for the truth
on the earth.
For they proceed from [b]evil to
evil,
And they [c]do not know Me," says
the LORD.
4 "Everyone[a] take heed to his
[1]neighbor,
And do not trust any brother;
For every brother will utterly
supplant,
And every neighbor will [b]walk
with slanderers.
5 Everyone will [a]deceive his
neighbor,
And will not speak the truth;

19 [a]Is. 39:3; Jer. 5:15
*See WW at 1 Kin. 16:2.
21 [a]Jer. 9:1 [b]Jer. 14:2; Joel 2:6; Nah. 2:10
22 [a]Gen. 37:25; Jer. 46:11

CHAPTER 9

1 [a]Is. 22:4; Jer. 10:19; Lam. 2:18
*See WW at Gen. 3:15.
2 [a]Jer. 5:7, 8; 23:10; Hos. 4:2
3 [a]Ps. 64:3; Is. 59:4; Jer. 9:8; Hos. 4:1, 2 [b]Jer. 4:22; 13:23 [c]Judg. 2:10; 1 Sam. 2:12; Jer. 4:22; Hos. 4:1; 1 Cor. 15:34
4 [a]Ps. 12:2; Prov. 26:24, 25; Jer. 9:8; Mic. 7:5, 6 [b]Ps. 15:3; Prov. 10:18; Jer. 6:28 [1]*friend*
5 [a]Ps. 36:3, 4; Is. 59:4
7 [a]Is. 1:25; Jer. 6:27; Mal. 3:3 [b]Hos. 11:8 [1]*test*
*See WW at Zech. 13:9.
8 [a]Ps. 12:2 [b]Ps. 55:21 [1]Inwardly he [2]*sets his ambush*
9 [a]Is. 1:24; Jer. 5:9, 29
10 [a]Jer. 4:26; Hos. 4:3 [b]Jer. 4:25; Hos. 4:3 [1]Or *pastures*
11 [a]Is. 25:2; Jer. 19:3, 8; 26:9 [b]Is. 13:22; 34:13
12 [a]Ps. 107:43; Is. 42:23; Hos. 14:9
*See WW at Neh. 8:8.
13 [a]Jer. 3:25; 7:24
14 [a]Jer. 7:24; 11:8; Rom. 1:21–24 [1]*stubbornness* or *imagination*

They have taught their tongue to
speak lies;
They weary themselves to
commit iniquity.
6 Your dwelling place *is* in the
midst of deceit;
Through deceit they refuse to
know Me," says the LORD.

7 Therefore thus says the LORD of
hosts:

"Behold, [a]I will *refine them and
[1]try them;
[b]For how shall I deal with the
daughter of My people?
8 Their tongue *is* an arrow shot out;
It speaks [a]deceit;
One speaks [b]peaceably to his
neighbor with his mouth,
But [1]in his heart he [2]lies in wait.
9 [a]Shall I not punish them for these
things?" says the LORD.
"Shall I not avenge Myself on such
a nation as this?"

10 I will take up a weeping and
wailing for the mountains,
And [a]for the [1]dwelling places of
the wilderness a lamentation,
Because they are burned up,
So that no one can pass through;
Nor can *men* hear the voice of the
cattle.
[b]Both the birds of the heavens and
the beasts have fled;
They are gone.

11 "I will make Jerusalem [a]a heap of
ruins, [b]a den of jackals.
I will make the cities of Judah
desolate, without an
inhabitant."

12 [a]Who *is* the wise man who may *understand this? And *who is he* to whom
the mouth of the LORD has spoken, that
he may declare it? Why does the land
perish *and* burn up like a wilderness,
so that no one can pass through?
13 And the LORD said, "Because they
have forsaken My law which I set before them, and have [a]not obeyed My
voice, nor walked according to it,
14 "but they have [a]walked according
to the [1]dictates of their own hearts and

8:22 Balm in Gilead: The area of Gilead in Transjordan was an important source for spice and balm (see Gen. 37:25), but the wound of Judah is incurable (but see 30:17).
9:1 Jeremiah is called the "weeping prophet" from verses such as this.
9:2 Jeremiah would like to get as far away from the sinful people as possible.
9:3 The LORD speaks. He describes the breakdown of personal relationships (vv. 3–6, 8) and promises to **refine, try,** and **punish** His people (vv. 7, 9; 6:27–30).
9:11 A den of jackals: A frequent figure in Jer. (10:22; 14:6; 49:33; 51:37), and Is. (13:22; 34:13; 35:7; 43:20).

after the Baals, [b]which their fathers taught them,"
15 therefore thus says the LORD of hosts, the God of Israel: "Behold, I will [a]feed them, this people, [b]with wormwood, and give them [1]water of gall to drink.
16 "I will [a]scatter them also among the Gentiles, whom neither they nor their fathers have known. [b]And I will send a sword after them until I have consumed them."

The People Mourn in Judgment

17 Thus says the LORD of hosts:

"Consider and call for [a]the
mourning women,
That they may come;
And send for skillful wailing
women,
That they may come.
18 Let them make haste
And take up a wailing for us,
That [a]our eyes may run with
tears,
And our eyelids gush with
water.
19 For a voice of wailing is heard
from Zion:
'How we are plundered!
We are greatly ashamed,
Because we have forsaken the
land,
Because we have been cast out of
[a]our dwellings.' "

20 Yet hear the word of the LORD,
O women,
And let your ear receive the word
of His mouth;
*Teach your daughters wailing,
And everyone her neighbor a
lamentation.
21 For death has come through our
windows,
Has entered our palaces,
To kill off [a]the children—
[1]*no longer to be* outside!
And the young men— [2]*no longer*
on the streets!

14 [b]Gal. 1:14; 1 Pet. 1:18 **15** [a]Ps. 80:5 [b]Deut. 29:18; Jer. 8:14; 23:15; Lam. 3:15 [1]Bitter or poisonous water **16** [a]Lev. 26:33; Deut. 28:64; Jer. 15:2–4 [b]Lev. 26:33; Jer. 44:27; Ezek. 5:2 **17** [a]2 Chr. 35:25; Job 3:8; Eccl. 12:5; Amos 5:16; Matt. 9:23 **18** [a]Is. 22:4; Jer. 9:1; 14:17 **19** [a]Lev. 18:28 **20** *See WW at Is. 48:17. **21** [a]2 Chr. 36:17; Jer. 6:11; 18:21; Ezek. 9:5, 6 [1]Lit. *from outside* [2]Lit. *from the square*

22 [a]Ps. 83:10; Is. 5:25; Jer. 8:1, 2 **23** [a][Eccl. 9:11; Is. 47:10]; Ezek. 28:3–7 [b]Ps. 33:16–18 **24** [a]Ps. 20:7; 44:8; Is. 41:16; Jer. 4:2; 1 Cor. 1:31; 2 Cor. 10:17; [Gal. 6:14] [b]Is. 61:8; Mic. 7:18 [1]*justice* *See WW at Ps. 112:1. **25** [a][Jer. 4:4; Rom. 2:28, 29] **26** [a]Jer. 25:23 [b]Lev. 26:41; Jer. 4:4; 6:10; Ezek. 44:7; [Rom. 2:28]

CHAPTER 10

2 [a][Lev. 18:3; 20:23; Deut. 12:30] **3** [a]Is. 40:19; 45:20 [1]Lit. *vanity*

22 Speak, "Thus says the LORD:

'Even the carcasses of men shall
fall [a]as refuse on the open field,
Like cuttings after the harvester,
And no one shall gather *them*.' "

23 Thus says the LORD: 3

[a]"Let not the wise *man* glory in his
wisdom,
Let not the mighty *man* glory in
his [b]might,
Nor let the rich *man* glory in his
riches;
24 But [a]let him who glories glory in
this,
That he understands and knows
Me,
That I *am* the LORD, exercising
lovingkindness, [1]judgment, and
righteousness in the earth.
[b]For in these I *delight," says the
LORD.

25 "Behold, the days are coming," says
the LORD, "that [a]I will punish all *who*
are circumcised with the uncircumcised—
26 "Egypt, Judah, Edom, the people of
Ammon, Moab, and all *who are* in the
[a]farthest corners, who dwell in the wilderness. For all *these* nations *are* uncircumcised, and all the house of Israel
are [b]uncircumcised in the heart."

Idols and the True God

10 Hear the word which the LORD speaks to you, O house of Israel.
2 Thus says the LORD:

[a]"Do not learn the way of the
Gentiles;
Do not be dismayed at the signs
of heaven,
For the Gentiles are dismayed at
them.
3 For the customs of the peoples *are*
[1]futile;
For [a]*one* cuts a tree from the
forest,

9:17–19 Professional **mourning women** (see 2 Sam. 14:2; Matt. 9:23; John 11:31, 33) were a part of the funeral ceremonies. Their task was to evoke proper lamentation for the bereaved. Even now their voice is **heard from Zion**.

9:20, 21 Jeremiah tells the women to instruct their daughters how to wail because so great will be the number of dead that their services will be required.

9:23, 24 See section 3 of Truth-In-Action at the end of Jer.

9:23, 24 The only true reality is to understand and know God. All else is transitory, including **wisdom, might,** and **riches**.

10:1–16 In this part of his temple sermon, Jeremiah contrasts idols and **the LORD,** alternating back and forth. Idols and their worshipers are condemned in vv. 2–5, 8, 9, 11, 14, 15; God is praised in vv. 6, 7, 10, 12, 13, 16. See Is. 40:18–20; 41:7; 44:9–20; 46:5–7.

10:3–5 Objects made by the hands of men are impotent to help, for they cannot **do evil** or **good**. They must be fastened in place, **they cannot speak,** and **they must be carried**. See Ps. 115:4–7; 135:15–18.

The work of the hands of the
workman, with the ax.
4 They decorate it with silver and
gold;
They [a]fasten it with nails and
hammers
So that it will not topple.
5 They *are* upright, like a palm tree,
And [a]they cannot speak;
They must be [b]carried,
Because they cannot go *by*
themselves.
Do not be afraid of them,
For [c]they cannot do evil,
Nor can they do any good."

6 Inasmuch as *there is* none
[a]like You, O LORD
(You *are* great, and Your name
is great in might),
7 [a]Who would not fear You, O King
of the nations?
For this is Your rightful due.
For [b]among all the wise *men* of
the nations,
And in all their kingdoms,
There is none like You.
8 But they are altogether [a]dull-
hearted and foolish;
A wooden idol *is* a [1]worthless
doctrine.
9 Silver is beaten into plates;
It is brought from Tarshish,
And [a]gold from Uphaz,
The work of the craftsman
And of the hands of the
metalsmith;
Blue and purple *are* their
clothing;
They *are* all [b]the work of skillful
men.
10 But the LORD *is* the true God;
He *is* [a]the living God and the
[b]everlasting King.
At His wrath the earth will
tremble,
And the nations will not be able
to endure His indignation.

11 Thus you shall say to them: [a]"The
gods that have not made the heavens
and the earth [b]shall perish from the
earth and from under these heavens."

12 He [a]has made the earth by His
power,
He has [b]established the *world by
His wisdom,
And [c]has stretched out the
heavens at His discretion.
13 [a]When He utters His voice,
There is a [1]multitude of waters in
the heavens:
[b]"And He causes the vapors to
ascend from the ends of the
earth.
He makes lightning for the rain,
He brings the wind out of His
treasuries."

14 [a]Everyone is [b]dull-hearted,
without knowledge;
[c]Every metalsmith is put to shame
by an image;
[d]For his molded image *is*
falsehood,
And *there is* no breath in them.
15 They *are* futile, a work of errors;
In the time of their punishment
they shall perish.
16 [a]The Portion of Jacob *is* not like
them,
For He *is* the Maker of all *things,*
And [b]Israel *is* the tribe of His
inheritance;
[c]The LORD of hosts *is* His name.

The Coming Captivity of Judah

17 [a]Gather up your wares from the
land,
O [1]inhabitant of the fortress!

18 For thus says the LORD:

"Behold, I will [a]throw out at this
time
The inhabitants of the land,
And will distress them,
[b]That they may find *it so.*"

19 [a]Woe is me for my hurt!
My wound is severe.
But I say, [b]"Truly this *is* an
infirmity,
And [c]I must bear it."
20 [a]My tent is plundered,
And all my cords are broken;
My children have gone from
me,
And they *are* [b]no more.

4 [a]Is. 41:7
5 [a]Ps. 115:5; Is. 46:7; Jer. 10:5; 1 Cor. 12:2 [b]Ps. 115:7; Is. 46:1, 7 [c]Is. 41:23, 24
6 [a]Ex. 15:11; Deut. 33:26; Ps. 86:8, 10; Is. 46:5–9; Jer. 10:16
7 [a]Jer. 5:22; Rev. 15:4 [b]Ps. 89:6
8 [a]Ps. 115:8; Hab. 2:18 [1]*vain teaching*
9 [a]Dan. 10:5 [b]Ps. 115:4
10 [a]1 Tim. 6:17 [b]Ps. 10:16
11 [a]Ps. 96:5 [b]Is. 2:18; Zeph. 2:11
12 [a]Gen. 1:1, 6, 7; Jer. 51:15 [b]Ps. 93:1 [c]Job 9:8; Ps. 104:2; Is. 40:22
*See WW at Jer. 51:15.
13 [a]Job 38:34 [b]Ps. 135:7 [1]Or *noise*
14 [a]Jer. 51:17 [b]Prov. 30:2 [c]Is. 42:17; 44:11 [d]Hab. 2:18
16 [a]Ps. 16:5; Jer. 51:19; Lam. 3:24 [b]Deut. 32:9; Ps. 74:2 [c]Is. 47:4
17 [a]Jer. 6:1 [1]Or *you who dwell under siege*
18 [a]1 Sam. 25:29; 2 Chr. 36:20 [b]Ezek. 6:10
19 [a]Jer. 8:21 [b]Ps. 77:10 [c]Mic. 7:9
20 [a]Jer. 4:20; Lam. 2:4 [b]Jer. 31:15; Lam. 1:5

10:6, 7 In contrast to the impotent idols, God is unique. There is **none** (no god) like Him. He is more than a tribal deity confined to a geographical area, for He is **King of the nations,** King over all.
10:9 **Silver** came from **Tarshish** (see Ezek. 27:12). **Uphaz** is mentioned only here and Dan. 10:5. Its location is unknown.
10:12–16 Repeated with slight variation in 51:15–19.
10:17–22 Punishment and exile are near, so God tells the people to **gather up** their belongings.
10:19, 20 Jeremiah bemoans his own fate and that of his countrymen. His **children** are the inhabitants of Judah and Jerusalem, since he himself never married or had children (16:2).

There is no one to pitch my tent
anymore,
Or set up my curtains.

21 For the shepherds have become
dull-hearted,
And have not sought the LORD;
Therefore they shall not prosper,
And all their flocks shall be
[a]scattered.
22 Behold, the noise of the report has
come,
And a great commotion out of the
[a]north country,
To make the cities of Judah
desolate, a [b]den of jackals.

23 O LORD, I know the [a]way of man
is not in himself;
It is not in man who walks to
direct his own steps.
24 O LORD, [a]**correct** me, but with
justice;
Not in Your anger, lest You bring
me to nothing.

WORD WEALTH

10:24 correct, *yasar* (yah-*sar*); Strong's #3256: To chasten, correct, instruct; to reform someone. This verb refers to the discipline and correction necessary to moral training. Moses told Israel in Deut. 8:5, that "as a man chastens his son, so the LORD your God chastens you." Some individuals cannot be corrected by words alone (Prov. 29:19). *Yasar* may involve tough measures, as with whips (1 Kin. 12:11), or teaching technique by itself, as in the case of the music director who instructed the Levitical musicians (1 Chr. 15:22). From *yasar* is derived the noun *musar,* "instruction."

25 [a]Pour out Your fury on the
Gentiles, [b]who do not know
You,
And on the families who do not
call on Your name;
For they have eaten up Jacob,
[c]Devoured him and consumed
him,
And made his dwelling place
desolate.

21 [a]Jer. 23:2 **22** [a]Jer. 5:15 [b]Jer. 9:11 **23** [a]Prov. 16:1; 20:24 **24** [a]Ps. 6:1; 38:1; Jer. 30:11 **25** [a]Ps. 79:6, 7; Zeph. 3:8 [b]Job 18:21; 1 Thess. 4:5; [2 Thess. 1:8] [c]Jer. 8:16

CHAPTER 11

3 [a]Deut. 27:26; [Jer. 17:5]; Gal. 3:10 **4** [a]Deut. 4:20; 1 Kin. 8:51 [b]Lev. 26:3; Deut. 11:27; Jer. 7:23 **5** [a]Ex. 13:5; Deut. 7:12; Ps. 105:9; Jer. 32:22 [b]Ex. 3:8 [1]Heb. *Amen* **6** [a]Deut. 17:19; [Rom. 2:13]; James 1:22 **7** [a]Jer. 35:15 **8** [a]Jer. 7:26 [b]Jer. 13:10 [1]*walked in the stubbornness* or *imagination* **9** [a]Ezek. 22:25; Hos. 6:9 **10** [a]1 Sam. 15:11; Jer. 3:10, 11; Ezek. 20:18

The Broken Covenant

11 The word that came to Jeremiah
from the LORD, saying,
2 "Hear the words of this covenant,
and speak to the men of Judah and to
the inhabitants of Jerusalem;
3 "and say to them, 'Thus says the
LORD God of Israel: [a]"Cursed *is* the
man who does not obey the words of
this covenant
4 "which I commanded your fathers
in the day I brought them out of the
land of Egypt, [a]from the iron furnace,
saying, [b]'Obey My voice, and do according to all that I command you; so
shall you be My people, and I will be
your God,'
5 "that I may establish the [a]oath
which I have sworn to your fathers, to
give them [b]'a land flowing with milk
and honey,' as *it is* this day." ' " And I
answered and said, [1]"So be it, LORD."
6 Then the LORD said to me, "Proclaim all these words in the cities of
Judah and in the streets of Jerusalem,
saying: 'Hear the words of this covenant [a]and do them.
7 'For I earnestly exhorted your fathers in the day I brought them up out
of the land of Egypt, until this day,
[a]rising early and exhorting, saying,
"Obey My voice."
8 [a]'Yet they did not obey or incline
their ear, but [b]everyone [1]followed the
dictates of his evil heart; therefore I
will bring upon them all the words of
this covenant, which I commanded
them to do, but *which* they have not
done.' "
9 And the LORD said to me, [a]"A conspiracy has been found among the men
of Judah and among the inhabitants of
Jerusalem.
10 "They have turned back to [a]the iniquities of their forefathers who refused
to hear My words, and they have gone
after other gods to serve them; the
house of Israel and the house of Judah
have broken My covenant which I
made with their fathers."
11 Therefore thus says the LORD: "Behold, I will surely bring calamity on

10:21 The **shepherds** are the rulers, and the **flocks** are the people.
10:23–25 Jeremiah yields to God's program of judgment, but he prays for divine **justice**.
10:25 *Repeated with slight variation in* Ps. 79:6, 7.
11:1—13:27 Failure of the people of Judah to keep the stipulations of the covenant leads to their exile from the land. This section is autobiographical in style and consists basically of a conversation between God and Jeremiah.
11:1–17 Jeremiah is enjoined by God to **proclaim** the **words** of the covenant in the streets of Jerusalem and exhort the people to **do them** (v. 6). Their fathers did not listen even though God exhorted them again and again (v. 7). As a result of disobedience, God will now bring the penalty contained in the covenant (v. 8).
11:3 Cursed *is* the man: See Deut. 27:15–26, where "cursed *is* the one" occurs at the beginning of each verse. According to Deut. 28, blessings come upon those who diligently obey the commandments (vv. 1–14), and curses come on those who do not obey (vv. 15–68).
11:9 Conspiracy: Probably opposition to the reform of Josiah is meant.

them which they will not be able to
[1]escape; and [a]though they cry out to
Me, I will not listen to them.
12 "Then the cities of Judah and the
inhabitants of Jerusalem will go and
[a]cry out to the gods to whom they offer
incense, but they will not save them
at all in the time of their trouble.
13 "For *according to* the number of
your [a]cities were your gods, O Judah;
and *according to* the number of the
streets of Jerusalem you have set up
altars to *that* shameful thing, altars to
burn incense to Baal.
14 "So [a]do not pray for this people, or
lift up a cry or prayer for them; for I
will not hear *them* in the time that they
cry out to Me because of their trouble.

15 "What[a] has My beloved to do in
My house,
Having [b]done lewd deeds with
many?
And [c]the holy flesh has passed
from you.
When you do evil, then you
[d]rejoice.
16 The LORD called your name,
[a]Green Olive Tree, Lovely *and* of
Good Fruit.
With the noise of a great tumult
He has kindled fire on it,
And its branches are broken.

17 "For the LORD of hosts, [a]who
planted you, has pronounced doom
against you for the evil of the house
of Israel and of the house of Judah,
which they have done against themselves to provoke Me to anger in offering incense to Baal."

Jeremiah's Life Threatened

18 Now the LORD gave me knowledge
of it, and I know *it;* for You showed
me their doings.
19 But I *was* like a docile lamb brought
to the slaughter; and I did not know
that they had devised schemes against
me, *saying,* "Let us destroy the tree
with its fruit, [a]and let us cut him off
from [b]the land of the living, that his
name may be remembered no more."

20 But, O LORD of hosts,
You who judge righteously,
[a]Testing the [1]mind and the heart,
Let me see Your [b]vengeance on
them,
For to You I have revealed my
cause.

21 "Therefore thus says the LORD concerning the men of [a]Anathoth who
seek your life, saying, [b]'Do not prophesy in the name of the LORD, lest you
die by our hand'—
22 "therefore thus says the LORD of
hosts: 'Behold, I will punish them. The
young men shall die by the sword, their
sons and their daughters shall [a]die by
famine;
23 'and there shall be no remnant of
them, for I will bring catastrophe on
the men of Anathoth, *even* [a]the year
of their punishment.' "

Jeremiah's Question

12 *Righteous [a]*are* You, O LORD,
when I plead with You;
Yet let me talk with You about
Your judgments.
[b]Why does the way of the *wicked
prosper?
Why are those happy who deal so
treacherously?
2 You have planted them, yes, they
have taken root;
They grow, yes, they bear fruit.
[a]You *are* near in their mouth
But far from their [1]mind.
3 But You, O LORD, [a]know me;
You have seen me,
And You have [b]tested my heart
toward You.

11 [a]Ps. 18:41; Prov. 1:28; Is. 1:15; Jer. 14:12; Ezek. 8:18; Mic. 3:4; Zech. 7:13 [1]Lit. *go out*
12 [a]Deut. 32:37; Jer. 44:17
13 [a]2 Kin. 23:13; Jer. 2:28
14 [a]Ex. 32:10; Jer. 7:16; 14:11; [1 John 5:16]
15 [a]Ps. 50:16 [b]Ezek. 16:25 [c][Titus 1:15] [d]Prov. 2:14
16 [a]Ps. 52:8; [Rom. 11:17]
17 [a]Is. 5:2; Jer. 2:21; 12:2
19 [a]Ps. 83:4; Jer. 18:18 [b]Ps. 27:13
20 [a]1 Sam. 16:7; 1 Chr. 28:9; Ps. 7:9 [b]Jer. 15:15 [1]Most secret parts, lit. *kidneys*
21 [a]Jer. 1:1; 12:5, 6 [b]Is. 30:10; Amos 2:12; Mic. 2:6
22 [a]Jer. 9:21
23 [a]Jer. 23:12; Hos. 9:7; Mic. 7:4

CHAPTER 12

1 [a]Ezra 9:15; Ps. 51:4; Jer. 11:20 [b]Job 12:6; Jer. 5:27, 28; Hab. 1:4; Mal. 3:15 *See WW at Lam. 1:18. • See WW at Prov. 10:16.
2 [a]Is. 29:13; Ezek. 33:31; Matt. 15:8; Mark 7:6 [1]Most secret parts, lit. *kidneys*
3 [a]Ps. 17:3 [b]Ps. 7:9; 11:5; Jer. 11:20

11:14 Again Jeremiah is told **not** to **pray** for this people (see 7:16; 14:11).

11:17 This **doom** was fulfilled when the Babylonians destroyed Jerusalem in 586 B.C.

11:18–23 The first of Jeremiah's six personal laments or "confessions"; the others are 12:1–6; 15:10–21; 17:14–18; 18:18–23; 20:7–18.

11:18 Gave me knowledge: Jeremiah's life was threatened by the men of Anathoth (vv. 21, 23; 12:6), his own family and friends.

11:19 Lamb brought to the slaughter: A tame pet lamb such as is described in 2 Sam. 12:3. As it does not suspect it is being led to the slaughter, Jeremiah had no suspicion that his own people were planning his death (see 12:6; Is. 53:7).

12:1–6 The second of Jeremiah's laments (see note on 11:18–23). Jeremiah is displeased with the prosperity of the wicked and demands that they be cut off. God reproves him for his impatience and tells him that the present situation is merely preparation for a more demanding future.

12:1 Wicked prosper: The question of the prosperity of the wicked (why does God not take action) is a popular theme (see Job 21:7–15; Ps. 73:3–12; Hab. 1:2–4). No definitive answer is given, but always it is clear God has all things under control. Ultimately, the wicked will perish (vv. 7–13), and God's righteousness will be vindicated. The attitude of the believer should be to let God be in complete control, especially of one's own life (see Job 42:2; Hab. 3:17–19).

Pull them out like sheep for the
slaughter,
And prepare them for [c]the day of
slaughter.
4 How long will [a]the land mourn,
And the herbs of every field
wither?
[b]The beasts and birds are
consumed,
[c]For the wickedness of those who
dwell there,
Because they said, "He will not
see our final end."

The LORD Answers Jeremiah

5 "If you have run with the footmen,
and they have wearied you,
Then how can you contend with
horses?
And *if* in the land of peace,
In which you trusted, *they*
wearied you,
Then how will you do in
[a]the [1]floodplain of the Jordan?
6 For even [a]your brothers, the
house of your father,
Even they have dealt
treacherously with you;
Yes, they have called [1]a multitude
after you.
[b]Do not believe them,
Even though they speak [2]smooth
words to you.

7 "I have forsaken My house, I have
left My heritage;
I have given the dearly beloved
of My soul into the hand of her
enemies.
8 My heritage is to Me like a lion
in the forest;
It cries out against Me;
Therefore I have [a]hated it.
9 My [1]heritage *is* to Me *like* a
speckled vulture;
The vultures all around *are*
against her.
Come, assemble all the beasts of
the field,
[a]Bring them to devour!

3 [c]Jer. 17:18; 50:27; James 5:5
4 [a]Jer. 23:10; Hos. 4:3 [b]Jer. 9:10; Hos. 4:3; Hab. 3:17 [c]Ps. 107:34
5 [a]Josh. 3:15; 1 Chr. 12:15 [1]Or *thicket*
6 [a]Gen. 37:4–11; Job 6:15; Ps. 69:8; Jer. 9:4, 5 [b]Ps. 12:2; Prov. 26:25 [1]Or *abundantly* [2]Lit. *good*
8 [a]Hos. 9:15; Amos 6:8
9 [a]Lev. 26:22 [1]*inheritance*
10 [a]Jer. 6:3; 23:1 [b]Ps. 80:8–16; Is. 5:1–7 [c]Is. 63:18 [1]Lit. *shepherds* or *pastors* [2]*desired portion* of land
11 [a]Jer. 10:22; 22:6 [b]Is. 42:25
13 [a]Lev. 26:16; Deut. 28:38; Mic. 6:15; Hag. 1:6 [1]Or *strained*
14 [a]Jer. 2:3; 50:11, 12; Zech. 2:8 [b]Deut. 30:3; Ps. 106:47; Is. 11:11–16; Jer. 32:37
15 [a]Jer. 31:20; Lam. 3:32; Ezek. 28:25 [b]Amos 9:14 *See WW at Hos. 2:23.
16 [a][Jer. 4:2]; Zeph. 1:5 [b][Eph. 2:20, 21; 1 Pet. 2:5]
17 [a]Ps. 2:8–12; Is. 60:12

10 "Many [a]rulers[1] have destroyed
[b]My vineyard,
They have [c]trodden My portion
underfoot;
They have made My [2]pleasant
portion a desolate wilderness.
11 They have made it [a]desolate;
Desolate, it mourns to Me;
The whole land is made desolate,
Because [b]no one takes *it* to heart.
12 The plunderers have come
On all the desolate heights in the
wilderness,
For the sword of the LORD shall
devour
From *one* end of the land to the
other end of the land;
No flesh shall have peace.
13 [a]They have sown wheat but
reaped thorns;
They have [1]put themselves to
pain *but* do not profit.
But be ashamed of your harvest
Because of the fierce anger of the
LORD."

14 Thus says the LORD: "Against all
My evil neighbors who [a]touch the inheritance which I have caused My people Israel to inherit—behold, I will
[b]pluck them out of their land and pluck
out the house of Judah from among
them.
15 [a]"Then it shall be, after I have
plucked them out, that I will return and
*have compassion on them [b]and bring
them back, everyone to his heritage
and everyone to his land.
16 "And it shall be, if they will learn
carefully the ways of My people,
[a]to swear by My name, 'As the LORD
lives,' as they taught My people to
swear by Baal, then they shall be
[b]established in the midst of My people.
17 "But if they do not [a]obey, I will utterly pluck up and destroy that nation,"
says the LORD.

Symbol of the Linen Sash

13 Thus the LORD said to me: "Go
and get yourself a linen sash,

12:5 God warns Jeremiah that his troubles will increase.
12:7–13 God laments that He must take such action against His **house** and **heritage** (the land and people) by bringing her enemies (the Babylonians). God speaks of His people in several figures: **dearly beloved of My soul, lion, speckled vulture, vineyard**.
12:14–17 Judah's neighbors will also go into exile, but if they are converted (16:19–21) God will establish them in the midst of His restored people; otherwise, He will destroy them.
13:1–11 The **linen sash** is the first of the symbolic acts Jeremiah used to convey God's word to the people. Linen is the material used for priestly garments (Ezek. 44:17, 18) and symbolizes Israel as a holy people, a "kingdom of priests" (see Ex. 19:6). The sash, as an emblem of Israel, speaks of the intimate relationship of God to His covenant people (v. 11).
13:1 Sash: A belt in oriental cultures indicates status, as "black belt" is used for achievement in the martial arts. **Do not put it in water:** Symbolic of Judah's sinful pride, the belt was not to be washed (v. 9).

and put it [1]around your waist, but do
not put it in water."
2 So I got a [1]sash according to the
word of the LORD, and put *it* around
my waist.
3 And the word of the LORD came to
me the second time, saying,
4 "Take the [1]sash that you acquired,
which *is* [2]around your waist, and arise,
go to the [3]Euphrates, and hide it there
in a hole in the rock."
5 So I went and hid it by the Euphrates, as the LORD commanded me.
6 Now it came to pass after many
days that the LORD said to me, "Arise,
go to the Euphrates, and take from
there the sash which I commanded you
to hide there."
7 Then I went to the Euphrates and
dug, and I took the [1]sash from the place
where I had hidden it; and there was
the sash, ruined. It was profitable for
nothing.
8 Then the word of the LORD came to
me, saying,
9 "Thus says the LORD: 'In this manner [a]I will ruin the pride of Judah and
the *great [b]pride of Jerusalem.
10 'This evil people, who [a]refuse to
hear My words, who [b]follow[1] the dictates of their hearts, and walk after
other gods to serve them and worship
them, shall be just like this sash which
is profitable for nothing.
11 'For as the sash clings to the waist
of a man, so I have caused the whole
house of Israel and the whole house
of Judah to cling to Me,' says the LORD,
'that [a]they may become My people,
[b]for renown, for *praise, and for
[c]glory; but they would [d]not hear.'

Symbol of the Wine Bottles

12 "Therefore you shall speak to them
this word: 'Thus says the LORD God of
Israel: "Every bottle shall be filled with
wine." ' And they will say to you, 'Do
we not certainly know that every bottle
will be filled with wine?'
13 "Then you shall say to them, 'Thus
says the LORD: "Behold, I will *fill all
the inhabitants of this land—even the
kings who sit on David's throne, the
priests, the prophets, and all the inhabitants of Jerusalem—[a]with drunkenness!
14 "And [a]I will dash them [1]one against
another, even the fathers and the sons
together," says the LORD. "I will not
pity nor spare nor have mercy, but will
destroy them." ' "

Pride Precedes Captivity

15 Hear and give ear:
Do not be proud,
For the LORD has spoken.
16 [a]Give glory to the LORD your God
Before He causes [b]darkness,
And before your feet stumble
On the dark mountains,
And while you are [c]looking for
light,
He turns it into [d]the shadow of
death
And makes *it* dense darkness.
17 But if you will not hear it,
My soul will [a]weep in secret for
your pride;
My eyes will weep bitterly
And run down with tears,
Because the LORD's flock has been
taken captive.

18 Say to [a]the king and to the queen
mother,
"**Humble** yourselves;
Sit down,
For your rule shall collapse, the
crown of your glory."

WORD WEALTH

13:18 humble, *shaphel* (shah-*fail*); Strong's #8213: To make low, depress, sink, lower, debase, set in a lower place, lay low, descend, humble, abase. *Shaphel* occurs 29 times and is generally translated "humble," "bring down," or "make low." *Shaphel* is illustrated by Is. 2:11; 5:15. Notice the irony of Prov. 29:23, "A man's pride will bring him low, but the humble in spirit will retain honor." In Ps. 113:6, God, who dwells on high, humbles Himself to watch what is occurring in heaven and on Earth. The most important derivative of *shaphel* is *shephelah,* "low country," or "low hills and plains," referring to the rolling hill country west of the Judean mountains.

CHAPTER 13
1 [1]Lit. *upon your loins*
2 [1]*waistband*
4 [1]*waistband* [2]Lit. *upon your loins* [3]Heb. *Perath*
7 [1]*waistband*
9 [a]Lev. 26:19 [b][Is. 2:10–17; 23:9]; Zeph. 3:11 *See WW at Ps. 31:19.
10 [a]Jer. 16:12 [b]Jer. 7:24; 16:12 [1]*walk in the stubbornness* or *imagination*
11 [a][Ex. 19:5, 6; Deut. 32:10, 11] [b]Jer. 33:9 [c]Is. 43:21 [d]Ps. 81:11; Jer. 7:13, 24, 26 *See WW at Ps. 100:4.
13 [a]Ps. 60:3; 75:8; Is. 51:17; 63:6; Jer. 25:27; 51:7, 57 *See WW at Jer. 23:24.
14 [a]2 Chr. 36:17; Ps. 2:9; Is. 9:20, 21; Jer. 19:9–11 [1]Lit. *a man against his brother*
16 [a]Josh. 7:19; Ps. 96:8; Mal. 2:2 [b]Is. 5:30; 8:22; Amos 8:9 [c]Is. 59:9 [d]Ps. 44:19; Jer. 2:6
17 [a]Ps. 119:136; Jer. 9:1; 14:17; Luke 19:41, 42
18 [a]2 Kin. 24:12; Jer. 22:26

13:6–9 Euphrates: On the basis of location, some suggest Jeremiah's experience is only a symbolic vision, or a parable because he would hardly have made two trips to the Euphrates River hundreds of miles away. Perhaps the reference is to Parah (Josh. 18:23) which is 3 miles northwest of Anathoth. The geographical destination is less important than the message that the sash is **ruined** (v. 7), and so God will **ruin the pride of Judah and the great pride of Jerusalem** (v. 9).

13:12–14 Jeremiah uses a familiar saying (v. 12) and the imagery of **drunkenness** (v. 13) to describe divine punishment for Jerusalem. Drunkenness will rob them of their ability to act, and then God will smash them like the bottles.

13:18 The **king** is probably Jehoiachin, and the **queen mother** is Nehushta (2 Kin. 24:8, 15).

19 The cities of the South shall be
shut up,
And no one shall open *them;*
Judah shall be carried away
captive, all of it;
It shall be wholly carried away
captive.

20 Lift up your eyes and see
Those who come from the
[a]north.
Where *is* the flock *that* was given
to you,
Your beautiful sheep?
21 What will you say when He
punishes you?
For you have taught them
To be chieftains, to be head over
you.
Will not [a]pangs seize you,
Like a woman in [1]labor?
22 And if you say in your heart,
[a]"Why have these things come
upon me?"
For the greatness of your iniquity
[b]Your skirts have been uncovered,
Your heels [1]made bare.
23 Can the Ethiopian change his
skin or the leopard its spots?
Then may you also do good who
are accustomed to do evil.

24 "Therefore I will [a]scatter them
[b]like stubble
That passes away by the wind of
the wilderness.
25 [a]This is your lot,
The portion of your measures
from Me," says the LORD,
"Because you have forgotten Me
And trusted in [b]falsehood.
26 Therefore [a]I will uncover your
skirts over your face,
That your shame may appear.
27 I have seen your adulteries
And your *lustful* [a]neighings,
The lewdness of your harlotry,
Your abominations [b]on the hills
in the fields.
Woe to you, O Jerusalem!
Will you still not be *made
clean?"

Sword, Famine, and Pestilence

14 The word of the LORD that came to Jeremiah concerning the droughts.

2 "Judah mourns,
And [a]her gates languish;
They [b]mourn for the land,
And [c]the cry of Jerusalem has
gone up.
3 Their nobles have sent their lads
for water;
They went to the cisterns *and*
found no water.
They returned with their vessels
empty;
They were [a]ashamed and
confounded
[b]And covered their heads.
4 Because the ground is parched,
For there was [a]no rain in the
land,
The plowmen were ashamed;
They covered their heads.
5 Yes, the deer also gave birth in
the field,
But [1]left because there was no
grass.
6 And [a]the wild donkeys stood in
the desolate heights;
They sniffed at the wind like
jackals;
Their eyes failed because *there
was* no grass."

7 O LORD, though our iniquities
testify against us,
Do it [a]for Your name's sake;
For our *backslidings are many,
We have sinned against You.
8 [a]O the Hope of Israel, his Savior
in time of trouble,
Why should You be like a
stranger in the land,
And like a traveler *who* turns
aside to tarry for a night?
9 Why should You be like a man
astonished,
Like a mighty one [a]*who* cannot
save?
Yet You, O LORD, [b]*are* in our
midst,
And we are called by Your name;
Do not leave us!

10 Thus says the LORD to this people:

[a]"Thus they have loved to wander;
They have not restrained their
feet.
Therefore the LORD does not
accept them;

20 [a]Jer. 10:22; 46:20
21 [a]Jer. 6:24 [1]*childbirth*
22 [a]Jer. 16:10 [b]Is. 47:2; Ezek. 16:37; Nah. 3:5 [1]Lit. *suffer violence*
24 [a]Lev. 26:33; Jer. 9:16; Ezek. 5:2, 12 [b]Ps. 1:4; Hos. 13:3
25 [a]Job 20:29; Ps. 11:6; Matt. 24:51 [b]Jer. 10:14
26 [a]Lam. 1:8; Ezek. 16:37; Hos. 2:10
27 [a]Jer. 5:7, 8 [b]Is. 65:7; Jer. 2:20; Ezek. 6:13 *See WW at Lev. 14:31.

CHAPTER 14

2 [a]2 Kin. 25:3; Is. 3:26 [b]Jer. 8:21 [c]1 Sam. 5:12; Jer. 11:11; 46:12; Zech. 7:13
3 [a]Job 6:20; Ps. 40:14 [b]2 Sam. 15:30
4 [a]Jer. 3:3; Ezek. 22:24
5 [1]*abandoned her young*
6 [a]Job 39:5, 6; Jer. 2:24
7 [a]Ps. 25:11; Jer. 14:21 *See WW at Jer. 5:6.
8 [a]Jer. 17:13
9 [a]Is. 59:1 [b]Ex. 29:45; Lev. 26:11; Ps. 46:5; Jer. 8:19
10 [a]Jer. 2:23–25

13:20–27 *Jeremiah describes the events relating to the invasion* (vv. 20–23), and God states the reason for the action (vv. 24–27). Jerusalem is personified as a woman, and because of her shamelessness (**iniquity,** v. 22) she will experience shame (**skirts . . . uncovered** and **heels made bare**).

13:23 A rhetorical question demanding a negative answer.

14:1—15:21 These prophecies were given during a period of severe drought, which affected life in the city (v. 3), country (v. 4), and open fields (vv. 5, 6), so no class of people or animal was exempt.

14:10–12 God's response is not favorable because the

[b]He will remember their iniquity now,
And punish their sins."

11 Then the LORD said to me, [a]"Do not
pray for this people, for *their* good.
12 [a]"When they fast, I will not hear
their cry; and [b]when they offer burnt
offering and grain offering, I will not
accept them. But [c]I will consume them
by the sword, by the famine, and by
the pestilence."
13 [a]Then I said, "Ah, Lord GOD! Behold, the prophets say to them, 'You
shall not see the sword, nor shall you
have famine, but I will give you
[1]assured [b]peace in this place.'"
14 And the LORD said to me, [a]"The
prophets prophesy lies in My name.
[b]I have not sent them, commanded
them, nor spoken to them; they prophesy to you a false vision, [1]divination,
a worthless thing, and the [c]deceit of
their heart.
15 "Therefore thus says the LORD concerning the prophets who prophesy in
My name, whom I did not send,
[a]and who say, 'Sword and famine shall
not be in this land'—'By sword and
famine those prophets shall be consumed!
16 'And the people to whom they
prophesy shall be cast out in the streets
of Jerusalem because of the famine
and the sword; [a]they will have no one
to bury them—them nor their wives,
their sons nor their daughters—for I
will pour their wickedness on them.'
17 "Therefore you shall say this word
to them:

[a]'Let my eyes flow with tears night and day,
And let them not cease;
[b]For the *virgin daughter of my people
Has been broken with a mighty stroke, with a very severe blow.
18 If I go out to [a]the field,
Then behold, those slain with the sword!
And if I enter the city,
Then behold, those sick from famine!
Yes, both prophet and [b]priest go about in a land they do not know.'"

10 [b]Hos. 8:13
11 [a]Ex. 32:10
12 [a]Ezek. 8:18 [b]Jer. 6:20 [c]Jer. 9:16
13 [a]Jer. 4:10 [b]Jer. 8:11; 23:17 [1]*true*
14 [a]Jer. 27:10 [b]Jer. 29:8, 9 [c]Jer. 23:16 [1]Telling the future by signs and omens
15 [a]Ezek. 14:10
16 [a]Ps. 79:2, 3
17 [a]Jer. 9:1; 13:17 [b]Jer. 8:21 *See WW at Ps. 45:14.
18 [a]Ezek. 7:15 [b]Jer. 23:11
19 [a]Lam. 5:22 [b]Jer. 15:18 [c]Jer. 8:15 *See WW at Mal. 4:2.
20 [a]Jer. 3:25 [b]Dan. 9:8
21 [a]Ps. 106:45
22 [a]Zech. 10:1 [b]Deut. 32:21 [c]Jer. 5:24 [d]Ps. 135:7

CHAPTER 15

1 [a]Ezek. 14:14 [b]Ex. 32:11–14 [c]1 Sam. 7:9 [1]Lit. *soul was not toward*
2 [a]Zech. 11:9 [b]Jer. 9:16; 16:13
3 [a]Ezek. 14:21

The People Plead for Mercy

19 [a]Have You utterly rejected Judah?
Has Your soul loathed Zion?
Why have You stricken us so that [b]*there is* no *healing for us?
[c]We looked for peace, but *there was* no good;
And for the time of healing, and there was trouble.
20 We acknowledge, O LORD, our wickedness
And the iniquity of our [a]fathers,
For [b]we have sinned against You.
21 Do not abhor *us*, for Your name's sake;
Do not disgrace the throne of Your glory.
[a]Remember, do not break Your covenant with us.
22 [a]Are there any among [b]the idols of the nations that can cause [c]rain?
Or can the heavens give showers?
[d]*Are* You not He, O LORD our God?
Therefore we will wait for You,
Since You have made all these.

The LORD Will Not Relent

15 Then the LORD said to me,
[a]"*Even* if [b]Moses and [c]Samuel
stood before Me, My [1]mind *would* not
be favorable toward this people. Cast
them out of My sight, and let them go
forth.
2 "And it shall be, if they say to you,
'Where should we go?' then you shall
tell them, 'Thus says the LORD:

[a]"Such as *are* for death, to death;
And such as *are* for the sword, to the sword;
And such as *are* for the famine, to the famine;
And such as *are* for the [b]captivity, to the captivity."'

3 "And I will [a]appoint over them four
forms *of destruction*," says the LORD:

people refuse to repent, and they **wander** after false gods. Jeremiah is instructed **not** to **pray** for the people (see 7:16; 11:14). Offerings and fasting will be of no avail either (see note on 6:20).

14:12 The threefold punishment **by the sword, by the famine, and by the pestilence** occurs 15 times in Jer., and is part of the curses for disobeying God (Lev. 26:25, 26).

14:14–18 God denies He has commissioned the lying prophets. Their message has come from themselves, and what they say will not happen. **Sword and famine** will rebound on them for their punishment. The people to whom they prophesy will share the same fate; the sword will take those in the field, and famine will take those in the city.

14:14–16 See section 1 of Truth-In-Action at the end of Jer.

15:1–9 The Lord will not relent and stresses that their sin is so great that even the intercession of Moses and Samuel (Ex. 32:11–14, 30–34; Num. 14:13–23; 1 Sam. 7:5–9; 12:19–25; Ps. 99:6–8) would be ineffective.

15:3, 4 Promised in Deut. 28:25, 26.

"the sword to slay, the dogs to drag, [b]the birds of the heavens and the beasts of the earth to devour and destroy.
4 "I will hand them over to [a]trouble, to all kingdoms of the earth, because of [b]Manasseh the son of Hezekiah, king of Judah, for what he did in Jerusalem.

5 "For who will have pity on you,
O Jerusalem?
Or who will bemoan you?
Or who will turn aside to ask how
you are doing?
6 [a]You have forsaken Me," says the
LORD,
"You have [b]gone backward.
Therefore I will stretch out My
hand against you and destroy
you;
[c]I am [1]weary of relenting!
7 And I will winnow them with a
winnowing fan in the gates of
the land;
I will [a]bereave *them* of children;
I will destroy My people,
Since they [b]do not return from
their ways.
8 Their widows will be increased to
Me more than the sand of the
seas;
I will bring against them,
Against the mother of the young
men,
A plunderer at noonday;
I will cause anguish and terror to
fall on them [a]suddenly.
9 "She[a] languishes who has borne
seven;
She has breathed her last;
[b]Her sun has gone down
While *it was* yet day;
She has been ashamed and
confounded.
And the remnant of them I will
deliver to the sword
Before their enemies," says the
LORD.

3 [b]Jer. 7:33
4 [a]Deut. 28:25 [b]2 Kin. 24:3, 4
6 [a]Jer. 2:13 [b]Is. 1:4; Jer. 7:24 [c]Jer. 20:16; Zech. 8:14 [1]*tired*
7 [a]Jer. 18:21; Hos. 9:12–16 [b]Is. 9:13; Jer. 5:3; Amos 4:10, 11
8 [a]Is. 29:5
9 [a]1 Sam. 2:5; Is. 47:9 [b]Jer. 6:4; Amos 8:9
10 [a]Job 3:1; Jer. 20:14 [1]*Or land*
11 [a]Jer. 40:4, 5
13 [a]Ps. 44:12; Is. 52:3
14 [a]Deut. 28:36, 64; Jer. 16:13 [b]Deut. 32:22; Ps. 21:9; Jer. 17:4 [1]So with MT, Vg.; LXX, Syr., Tg. *cause you to serve* (cf. 17:4)
15 [a]Jer. 12:3 [b]Jer. 20:12 [c]Ps. 69:7–9; Jer. 20:8 [1]*attend to*
16 [a]Ezek. 3:1, 3; Rev. 10:9 [b][Job 23:12; Ps. 119:72]
17 [a]Ps. 26:4, 5

Jeremiah's Dejection

10 [a]Woe is me, my mother,
That you have borne me,
A man of strife and a man of
contention to the whole [1]earth!
I have neither lent for interest,
Nor have men lent to me for
interest.
Every one of them curses me.

11 The LORD said:

"Surely it will be well with your
remnant;
Surely I will cause [a]the enemy to
intercede with you
In the time of adversity and in the
time of affliction.
12 Can anyone break iron,
The northern iron and the
bronze?
13 Your wealth and your treasures
I will give as [a]plunder without
price,
Because of all your sins,
Throughout your territories.
14 And I will [1]make *you* cross over
with your enemies
[a]Into a land *which* you do not
know;
For a [b]fire is kindled in My anger,
Which shall burn upon you."

15 O LORD, [a]You know;
Remember me and [1]visit me,
And [b]take vengeance for me on
my persecutors.
In Your enduring patience, do not
take me away.
Know that [c]for Your sake I have
suffered rebuke.
16 Your words were found, and I
[a]ate them,
And [b]Your word was to me the
joy and rejoicing of my heart;
For I am called by Your name,
O LORD God of hosts.
17 [a]I did not sit in the assembly of the
mockers,
Nor did I rejoice;

15:4 Manasseh: Considered the worst king in the history of Judah (2 Kin. 21:1–11, 16), his sins are primarily responsible for Judah's demise. See 2 Kin. 21:12–15; 23:26, 27; 24:3, 4.
15:6 Stretch out My hand: See note on 6:12. **Weary of relenting:** Anthropomorphic language. From a human point of view it appears God changes His mind, but we must recognize that many of the prophetic pronouncements are conditional. God *will punish unless the people* respond. He gives them every opportunity to avert the promised judgment.
15:7 Winnow: A process whereby the chaff and straw are removed from the grain by tossing it into the air in the afternoon breeze. The wind carries the lighter material away. See note on Ruth 3:2. The winnowing process is a figure of judgment in 51:2; Prov. 20:26; Is. 41:16.
15:9 A blessed and favored mother is one **who has borne seven** sons.
15:10–21 Jeremiah's third personal lament. See note on 11:18–23. Pointing to his rejection (v. 10) and the faithful discharge of his duty (vv. 16, 17), Jeremiah cries out at the anguish this has brought him and charges God with failing him in his hour of need (v. 18).
15:10 See 20:14, 15; Job 3:3–10.
15:11 It will be well with your remnant: Can also be translated, "I will strengthen you for good," or, "I will free you for good." God encourages Jeremiah.
15:12 A rhetorical question expecting a negative answer. **Iron** is a symbol of strength.
15:17 Sat alone: Jeremiah did not marry. See note on 16:2.

I sat alone because of Your
hand,
For You have filled me with
indignation.
18 Why is my [a]pain perpetual
And my wound incurable,
Which refuses to be healed?
Will You surely be to me
[b]like an unreliable stream,
As waters *that* [1]fail?

The LORD *Reassures Jeremiah*

5 19 Therefore thus says the LORD:

[a]"If you return,
Then I will bring you back;
You shall [b]stand before Me;
If you [c]take out the precious from
the vile,
You shall be as My mouth.
Let them return to you,
But you must not return to
them.
20 And I will make you to this people
a fortified bronze [a]wall;
And they will fight against you,
But [b]they shall not prevail against
you;
For I *am* with you to save you
And deliver you," says the
LORD.
21 "I will deliver you from the hand
of the wicked,
And I will *redeem you from the
grip of the terrible."

Jeremiah's Life-Style and Message

16 The word of the LORD also came
to me, saying,
2 "You shall not take a wife, nor shall
you have sons or daughters in this
place."
3 For thus says the LORD concerning the sons and daughters who are
born in this place, and concerning their
mothers who bore them and their fathers who begot them in this land:
4 "They shall die [a]gruesome deaths;
they shall not be [b]lamented nor shall
they be [c]buried, *but* they shall be
[d]like refuse on the face of the earth.
They shall be consumed by the sword
and by famine, and their [e]corpses shall
be meat for the birds of heaven and
for the beasts of the earth."
5 For thus says the LORD: [a]"Do not
enter the house of mourning, nor go
to lament or bemoan them; for I have
taken away My peace from this people," says the LORD, "lovingkindness
and mercies.
6 "Both the great and the small shall
die in this land. They shall not be buried; [a]neither shall men lament for
them, [b]cut themselves, nor [c]make
themselves bald for them.
7 "Nor shall *men* break *bread* in
mourning for them, to comfort them
for the dead; nor shall *men* give them
the cup of consolation to [a]drink for
their father or their mother.
8 "Also you shall not go into the
house of feasting to sit with them, to
eat and drink."
9 For thus says the LORD of hosts, the
God of Israel: "Behold, [a]I will cause
to cease from this place, before your
eyes and in your days, the voice of
[1]mirth and the voice of gladness, the
voice of the bridegroom and the voice
of the bride.
10 "And it shall be, when you show
this people all these words, and they
say to you, [a]'Why has the LORD pronounced all this great disaster against
us? Or what *is* our iniquity? Or what
is our sin that we have committed
against the LORD our God?'
11 "then you shall say to them, [a]'Because your fathers have forsaken Me,'
says the LORD; 'they have walked after
other gods and have served them and
worshiped them, and have forsaken
Me and not kept My law.
12 'And you have done [a]worse than
your fathers, for behold, [b]each one
[1]follows the dictates of his own evil
heart, so that no one listens to Me.
13 [a]'Therefore I will cast you out of
this land [b]into a land that you do not
know, neither you nor your fathers;
and there you shall serve other gods
day and night, where I will not show
you favor.'

18 [a]Job 34:6; Jer. 10:19; 30:15; Mic. 1:9 [b]Job 6:15 [1]Or *cannot be trusted*
19 [a]Jer. 4:1; Zech. 3:7 [b]1 Kin. 17:1; Jer. 15:1 [c]Jer. 6:29; Ezek. 22:26; 44:23
20 [a]Jer. 1:18; 6:27; Ezek. 3:9 [b]Ps. 46:7; Is. 41:10; Jer. 1:8, 19; 20:11; 37:21; 38:13; 39:11, 12
21 *See WW at Neh. 1:10.

CHAPTER 16

4 [a]Jer. 15:2 [b]Jer. 22:18; 25:33 [c]Jer. 14:16; 19:11 [d]Ps. 83:10; Jer. 8:2; 9:22 [e]Ps. 79:2; Is. 18:6; Jer. 7:33; 34:20
5 [a]Ezek. 24:17, 22, 23
6 [a]Jer. 22:18 [b]Lev. 19:28; Deut. 14:1; Jer. 41:5; 47:5 [c]Is. 22:12; Jer. 7:29
7 [a]Prov. 31:6
9 [a]Is. 24:7, 8; Jer. 7:34; 25:10; Ezek. 26:13; Hos. 2:11; Rev. 18:23 [1]*rejoicing*
10 [a]Deut. 29:24; 1 Kin. 9:8; Jer. 5:19
11 [a]Deut. 29:25; 1 Kin. 9:9; 2 Chr. 7:22; Neh. 9:26–29; Jer. 22:9
12 [a]Jer. 7:26 [b]Jer. 3:17; 18:12 [1]*walks after the stubbornness or imagination*
13 [a]Deut. 4:26; 28:36, 63 [b]Jer. 15:14

15:18 Two rhetorical questions; one directed to his own condition, the other concerned with God's reliability. An **unreliable stream** is the wadi that is dry most of the year (see Job 6:15; but contrast 2:13 and 17:13).
15:19–21 See section 5 of Truth-In-Action at the end of Jer.
16:1–13 Special instructions are given to Jeremiah concerning his life-style and message.
16:2 As a sign of the impending doom coming upon Judah, Jeremiah was forbidden to take a wife or have children.
16:5–7 Instructions concerning contact with the dead. See Ezek. 24:16, 17, 22, 23.
16:6 According to the Law (Lev. 19:28; 21:5; Deut. 14:1), the Israelites were forbidden to **cut themselves** or **make themselves bald,** customs prevalent in surrounding pagan cultures.
16:7 Food was normally given to mourners. See Ezek. 24:17, 22; Hos. 9:4.
16:8, 9 Jeremiah was to avoid festive celebrations as well as funerals.
16:9 See note on 7:34.

God Will Restore Israel

14 "Therefore behold, the [a]days are
coming," says the LORD, "that it shall
no more be said, 'The LORD lives who
brought up the children of Israel from
the land of Egypt,'
15 "but, 'The LORD lives who brought
up the children of Israel from the land
of the [a]north and from all the lands
where He had driven them.' For
[b]I will bring them back into their land
which I gave to their fathers.
16 "Behold, I will send for many
[a]fishermen," says the LORD, "and they
shall fish them; and afterward I will
send for many hunters, and they shall
hunt them from every mountain and
every hill, and out of the holes of the
rocks.
17 "For My [a]eyes *are* on all their ways;
they are not hidden from My face, nor
is their iniquity hidden from My eyes.
18 "And first I will repay [a]double for
their iniquity and their sin, because
[b]they have defiled My land; they have
filled My inheritance with the carcasses of their detestable and abominable idols."

19 O LORD, [a]my **strength** and my
fortress,
[b]My refuge in the day of affliction,
The Gentiles shall come to You
From the ends of the earth and
say,
"Surely our fathers have inherited
lies,
Worthlessness and [c]unprofitable
things."
20 Will a man make gods for
himself,
[a]Which *are* not gods?

21 "Therefore behold, I will this once
cause them to know,
I will cause them to know
My hand and My might;
And they shall know that
[a]My name *is* the LORD.

WORD WEALTH

16:19 strength, *'oz* (*oaz*); Strong's #5797: Strength, power, security. This noun comes from the verb *'azaz,* "to be firm and strong." Here Jeremiah's description of his God has a poetic quality in Hebrew: *'Uzi u-Ma'uzi* (my strength and my fortress). *'Oz* occurs approximately 100 times in the OT, often in well-loved verses (see Ps. 8:2; 46:1; 63:2; Is. 12:2). David danced joyfully before the Lord with all his strength (2 Sam. 6:14). Ps. 105:4 sagely counsels us to "seek the LORD and His strength."

14 [a]Is. 43:18; Jer. 23:7, 8; [Ezek. 37:21–25]
15 [a]Jer. 3:18 [b]Jer. 24:6; 30:3; 32:37
16 [a]Amos 4:2; Hab. 1:15
17 [a]2 Chr. 16:9; Job 34:21; Ps. 90:8; Prov. 5:21; Jer. 23:24; 32:19; Zech. 4:10; [Luke 12:2; 1 Cor. 4:5]; Heb. 4:13
18 [a]Is. 40:2; Jer. 17:18; Rev. 18:6 [b][Ezek. 43:7]
19 [a]Ps. 18:1, 2; Is. 25:4 [b]Jer. 17:17 [c]Is. 44:10
20 [a]Ps. 115:4–8; Is. 37:19; Jer. 2:11; 5:7; Hos. 8:4–6; Gal. 4:8
21 [a]Ex. 15:3; Ps. 83:18; Is. 43:3; Jer. 33:2; Amos 5:8

CHAPTER 17
1 [a]Jer. 2:22 [b]Job 19:24 [c]Prov. 3:3; 7:3; Is. 49:16; 2 Cor. 3:3
2 [a]Judg. 3:7 [1]Heb. *Asherim,* Canaanite deities
4 [a]Jer. 16:13 [b]Is. 5:25; Jer. 15:14
5 [a]Ps. 146:3; Is. 30:1, 2; 31:1 [b]Is. 31:3 [1]Lit. *arm* *See WW at Jer. 31:22.
6 [a]Jer. 48:6 [b]Job 20:17 [c]Deut. 29:23; Job 39:6

Judah's Sin and Punishment

17 "The sin of Judah *is* [a]written
with a [b]pen of iron;
With the point of a diamond *it is*
[c]engraved
On the tablet of their heart,
And on the horns of your altars,
2 While their children remember
Their altars and their [a]wooden[1]
images
By the green trees on the high
hills.
3 O My mountain in the field,
I will give as plunder your wealth,
all your treasures,
And your high places of sin
within all your borders.
4 And you, even yourself,
Shall let go of your heritage
which I gave you;
And I will cause you to serve your
enemies
In [a]the land which you do not
know;
For [b]you have kindled a fire in
My anger *which* shall burn
forever."

5 Thus says the LORD:

[a]"Cursed *is* the *man who trusts in
man
And makes [b]flesh his [1]strength,
Whose heart departs from the
LORD.
6 For he shall be [a]like a shrub in
the desert,
And [b]shall not see when good
comes,
But shall inhabit the parched
places in the wilderness,
[c]*In* a salt land *which is* not
inhabited.

16:14, 15 Repeated with slight variation in 23:7, 8. Hope and reassurance appear in the midst of punishment and destruction, for Israel's homecoming is promised as a new exodus from the lands where God has dispersed them.
16:16 The **fishermen** and **hunters** are the conquerors.
16:19, 20 A ray of hope for Gentiles who will turn to God when they realize the worthlessness of their idols. God will teach them, and they will know His name.

17:1–4 The **sin of Judah** is indelibly written with a **pen of iron** (an instrument used to inscribe permanent records on stone) or a **diamond**-tipped stylus. Their sins are so grievous they are written permanently **on the tablet of their heart, and on the horns of your altars** as a constant reminder to God, and they are not atoned for.
17:3 My mountain: Mt. Zion where the temple is located.

7 "Blessed[a] *is* the man who trusts in
the LORD,
And whose hope is the LORD.
8 For he shall be [a]like a tree planted
by the waters,
Which spreads out its roots by the
river,
And will not [1]fear when heat
comes;
But its leaf will be green,
And will not be anxious in the
year of drought,
Nor will cease from yielding fruit.

9 "The [a]heart* *is* deceitful above all
things,
And [1]desperately wicked;
Who can know it?
10 I, the LORD, [a]search the heart,
I test the [1]mind,
[b]Even to give every man according
to his ways,
According to the fruit of his
doings.

11 "*As* a partridge that [1]broods but
does not hatch,
So is he who gets riches, but not
by right;
It [a]will leave him in the midst of
his days,
And at his end he will be
[b]a fool."

12 A glorious high throne from the
beginning
Is the place of our sanctuary.
13 O LORD, [a]the hope of Israel,
[b]All who forsake You shall be
ashamed.

"Those who depart from Me
Shall be [c]written in the earth,
Because they have forsaken the
LORD,
The [d]fountain of living waters."

Jeremiah Prays for Deliverance

14 Heal me, O LORD, and I shall be
healed;

7 [a]Ps. 2:12; 34:8; 125:1; 146:5; Prov. 16:20; [Is. 30:18]; Jer. 39:18
8 [a]Job 8:16; [Ps. 1:3; Ezek. 31:3–9] [1]Qr., Tg. *see*
9 [a][Eccl. 9:3]; Matt. 15:19; [Mark 7:21, 22] [1]Or *incurably sick*
*See WW at Ps. 37:4.
10 [a]1 Sam. 16:7; 1 Chr. 28:9; Ps. 7:9; 139:23, 24; Prov. 17:3; Jer. 11:20; 20:12; Rom. 8:27; Rev. 2:23 [b]Ps. 62:12; Jer. 32:19; Rom. 2:6 [1]Most secret parts, lit. *kidneys*
11 [a]Ps. 55:23 [b]Luke 12:20 [1]Sits on eggs
13 [a]Jer. 14:8 [b][Ps. 73:27; Is. 1:28] [c]Luke 10:20 [d]Jer. 2:13
14 [a]Deut. 10:21; Ps. 109:1
15 [a]Is. 5:19; Ezek. 12:22; 2 Pet. 3:4
16 [a]Jer. 1:4–12
17 [a]Jer. 16:19; Nah. 1:7
18 [a]Ps. 35:4; 70:2; Jer. 15:10; 18:18 [b]Ps. 25:2 [c]Jer. 11:20 [1]Lit. *crush*
20 [a]Ps. 49:1, 2; Jer. 19:3, 4

Save me, and I shall be saved,
For [a]You *are* my praise.

WORD WEALTH

17:14 save, *yasha'* (yah-*shah*); Strong's #3467: To rescue, save, defend; to free, preserve, avenge, deliver, help. The verb, found more than 200 times throughout the OT, is a one-word description of God's response to the needs of humanity. God chose a form of this verb to be His Son's name: *Yeshua,* meaning "He Shall Save." See Matt. 1:21. The original thought of *yasha'* was "to release," "to open wide." Our Deliverer is the One who opened wide the gates of captivity, released and rescued us, and continually defends and preserves us.

15 Indeed they say to me,
[a]"Where *is* the word of the LORD?
Let it come now!"
16 As for me, [a]I have not hurried
away from *being* a shepherd
who follows You,
Nor have I desired the woeful
day;
You know what came out of my
lips;
It was right there before You.
17 Do not be a terror to me;
[a]You *are* my hope in the day of
doom.
18 [a]Let them be ashamed who
persecute me,
But [b]do not let me be put to
shame;
Let them be dismayed,
But do not let me be dismayed.
Bring on them the day of doom,
And [c]destroy[1] them with double
destruction!

Hallow the Sabbath Day

19 Thus the LORD said to me: "Go and
stand in the gate of the children of the
people, by which the kings of Judah
come in and by which they go out, and
in all the gates of Jerusalem;
20 "and say to them, [a]'Hear the word

17:9, 10 The **heart** is the inner self, which thinks, feels, and acts. It is central to man (see Prov. 4:23), but it is **deceitful** and **wicked**.
17:11 A proverb expressing the folly of gaining wealth by dishonest means. Jeremiah continues to expose deception.
17:13 Written in the earth: Perhaps Jesus had this verse in mind when He stooped down and wrote on the ground (John 8:6, 8). **Fountain of living waters:** See note on 2:9–13.
17:14–18 Jeremiah's fourth personal lament (see note on 11:18–23). Dejected because of his opponent's taunts, Jeremiah prays for healing.
17:15 The accusation is that he is a false prophet because his words have not come to pass (see Deut. 18:21, 22).
17:16 Shepherd: A symbol of leadership, which Jeremiah exercised as a prophet (see Ezek. 34:2, 12).
17:19–27 A discourse concerning **the Sabbath,** which stresses one of the commandments easily monitored. Failure to observe the Sabbath is indicative of the sinful response of the people toward all of God's laws. This commandment was basic to the whole structure of worship because it was instituted as part of creation (Gen. 2:2, 3; Ex. 20:11) and was a sign of God's relationship with Israel (Ex. 31:13–17; Ezek. 20:12).

of the LORD, you kings of Judah, and
all Judah, and all the inhabitants of Jerusalem, who enter by these gates.
21 'Thus says the LORD: [a]"Take heed
to yourselves, and bear no burden on
the Sabbath day, nor bring *it* in by the
gates of Jerusalem;
22 "nor carry a burden out of your
houses on the Sabbath day, nor do any
work, but hallow the Sabbath day, as
I [a]commanded your fathers.
23 [a]"But they did not obey nor incline
their ear, but [1]made their neck stiff,
that they might not hear nor receive
*instruction.
24 "And it shall be, [a]if you heed Me
carefully," says the LORD, "to bring no
burden through the gates of this city
on the [b]Sabbath day, but hallow the
Sabbath day, to do no work in it,
25 [a]"then shall enter the gates of this
city kings and princes *sitting on the
throne of David, riding in chariots and
on horses, they and their princes, accompanied by the men of Judah and
the inhabitants of Jerusalem; and this
city shall remain forever.
26 "And they shall come from the cities of Judah and from [a]the places
around Jerusalem, from the land of
Benjamin and from [b]the [1]lowland,
from the mountains and from [c]the
[2]South, bringing burnt offerings and
sacrifices, grain offerings and incense,
bringing [d]sacrifices of praise to the
house of the LORD.
27 "But if you will not heed Me to hallow the Sabbath day, such as not carrying a burden when entering the gates
of Jerusalem on the Sabbath day, then
[a]I will kindle a fire in its gates, [b]and
it shall devour the palaces of Jerusalem, and it shall not be [c]quenched." ' "

The Potter and the Clay

18 The word which came to Jeremiah from the LORD, saying:
2 "Arise and go down to the potter's
*house, and there I will cause you to
hear My words."
3 Then I went down to the potter's
house, and there he was, making something at the [1]wheel.
4 And the vessel that he [1]made of clay
was [2]marred in the hand of the potter;
so he made it again into another vessel,
as it seemed good to the potter to
make.
5 Then the word of the LORD came to
me, saying:
6 "O house of Israel, [a]can I not do
with you as this potter?" says the LORD.
"Look, [b]as the clay *is* in the potter's
hand, so *are* you in My hand, O house
of Israel!
7 "The instant I speak concerning a
nation and concerning a kingdom, to
[a]pluck up, to pull down, and to destroy
it,
8 [a]"if that nation against whom I
have spoken turns from its evil,
[b]I will relent of the disaster that I
thought to bring upon it.
9 "And the instant I speak concerning
a nation and concerning a kingdom, to
build and to plant *it*,
10 "if it does evil in My sight so that
it does not obey My voice, then I will
relent concerning the good with which
I said I would benefit it.
11 "Now therefore, speak to the men
of Judah and to the inhabitants of Jerusalem, saying, 'Thus says the LORD:
"Behold, I am fashioning a disaster
and devising a plan against you.
[a]Return now every one from his evil
way, and make your ways and your doings [b]good." ' "

God's Warning Rejected

12 And they said, [a]"That is hopeless!
So we will walk according to our own
plans, and we will every one [1]obey the
[b]dictates[2] of his evil heart."
13 Therefore thus says the LORD:

[a]"Ask now among the Gentiles,
Who has heard such things?
The virgin of Israel has done
[b]a very horrible thing.

21 [a]Neh. 13:19
22 [a]Ex. 20:8; 31:13
23 [a]Jer. 7:24, 26 [1]Were stubborn *See WW at Prov. 4:13.
24 [a]Jer. 11:4; 26:3 [b]Ex. 16:23–30; 20:8–10
25 [a]Jer. 22:4 *See WW at Lam. 5:19.
26 [a]Jer. 33:13 [b]Zech. 7:7 [c]Judg. 1:9 [d]Ps. 107:22; 116:17 [1]Heb. *shephelah* [2]Heb. *Negev*
27 [a]Lam. 4:11 [b]2 Kin. 25:9 [c]Jer. 7:20

CHAPTER 18

2 *See WW at 2 Sam. 7:11.
3 [1]Potter's wheel
4 [1]*was making* [2]*ruined*
6 [a]Rom. 9:20, 21 [b]Is. 64:8
7 [a]Jer. 1:10
8 [a][Ezek. 18:21; 33:11] [b]Jer. 26:3
11 [a]2 Kin. 17:13 [b]Jer. 7:3–7
12 [a]Jer. 2:25 [b]Jer. 3:17; 23:17 [1]Lit. *do* [2]*stubbornness* or *imagination*
13 [a]Jer. 2:10, 11 [b]Jer. 5:30

18:1—20:18 This section, based on Jeremiah's experience at the potter's house, contains examples of all the literary styles found in the book: biography, prose discourses, poetic oracles, and laments.
18:1–23 Jeremiah visits the potter's house at God's command. There he learns that the potter sometimes rejected some of the pots, perhaps because of poor quality. So God is sovereign over His people Judah. What the potter makes depends on the quality of the clay; what God makes of His people depends on their response. The clay can frustrate the potter's intention and make him alter the vessel. As the quality of the clay limits what the potter can do with it, so the quality of a people limits what God will do with them.
18:4 Marred: Represents the same Hebrew word used of the linen sash in 13:7, where it is translated "ruined." The clay was not suitable for the potter's design. **As it seemed good:** He could make something else from the clay, but not the originally intended vessel.
18:7–10 The Lord limits His sovereign action on the basis of the response of the people (see 4:28). For the verbs **to pluck up, to pull down,** and so on, see note on 1:10.
18:13–17 See note on 2:9–13. A poetic commentary on v. 12.

14 Will *a man* [1]leave the snow water of Lebanon,
Which comes from the rock of the field?
Will the cold flowing waters be forsaken for strange waters?

15 "Because My people have forgotten [a]Me,
They have burned incense to worthless idols.
And they have caused themselves to stumble in their ways,
From the [b]ancient paths,
To walk in pathways and not on a highway,
16 To make their land [a]desolate *and* a perpetual [b]hissing;
Everyone who passes by it will be astonished
And shake his head.
17 [a]I will scatter them [b]as with an east wind before the enemy;
[c]I will [1]show them the back and not the face
In the day of their calamity."

Jeremiah Persecuted

18 Then they said, [a]"Come and let us
devise plans against Jeremiah; [b]for the
law shall not perish from the priest, nor
counsel from the wise, nor the word
from the prophet. Come and let us attack him with the tongue, and let us
not give heed to any of his words."

19 Give heed to me, O LORD,
And listen to the voice of those who contend with me!
20 [a]Shall evil be repaid for good?
For they have [b]dug a pit for my life.
Remember that I [c]stood before You
To speak good [1]for them,
To turn away Your wrath from them.
21 Therefore [a]deliver up their children to the famine,
And pour out their *blood*
By the force of the sword;
Let their wives *become* widows
And [b]bereaved of their children.
Let their men be put to death,
Their young men *be* slain
By the sword in battle.
22 Let a cry be heard from their houses,
When You bring a troop suddenly upon them;
For they have dug a pit to take me,
And hidden snares for my feet.
23 Yet, LORD, You know all their counsel
Which is against me, to slay *me*.
[a]Provide no atonement for their iniquity,
Nor blot out their sin from Your sight;
But let them be overthrown before You.
Deal *thus* with them
In the time of Your [b]anger.

The Sign of the Broken Flask

19 Thus says the LORD: "Go and get
a potter's earthen flask, and
take some of the *elders of the people
and some of the elders of the priests.
2 "And go out to [a]the Valley of the
Son of Hinnom, which *is* by the
entry of the Potsherd Gate; and proclaim there the words that I will tell
you,
3 [a]"and say, 'Hear the word of the
LORD, O kings of Judah and inhabitants
of Jerusalem. Thus says the LORD of
hosts, the God of Israel: "Behold, I will
bring such a catastrophe on this place,
that whoever hears of it, his ears will
[b]tingle.
4 "Because they [a]have forsaken Me
and made this an alien place, because
they have burned incense in it to other

14 [1]*forsake*
15 [a]Jer. 2:13, 32 [b]Jer. 6:16
16 [a]Jer. 19:8 [b]1 Kin. 9:8; Lam. 2:15; Mic. 6:16
17 [a]Jer. 13:24 [b]Ps. 48:7 [c]Jer. 2:27 [1]So with LXX, Syr., Tg., Vg.; MT *look them in*
18 [a]Jer. 11:19 [b]Lev. 10:11; Mal. 2:7; [John 7:48]
20 [a]Ps. 109:4 [b]Ps. 35:7; 57:6; Jer. 5:26 [c]Jer. 14:7—15:1 [1]*concerning*
21 [a]Ps. 109:9–20; Jer. 11:22; 14:16 [b]Jer. 15:7, 8; Ezek. 22:25
23 [a]Neh. 4:5; Ps. 35:14; 109:14; Is. 2:9; Jer. 11:20 [b]Jer. 7:20

CHAPTER 19

1 *See WW at Ps. 119:100.
2 [a]Josh. 15:8; 2 Kin. 23:10; Jer. 7:31; 32:35
3 [a]Jer. 17:20 [b]1 Sam. 3:11; 2 Kin. 21:12
4 [a]Deut. 28:20; Is. 65:11; Jer. 2:13, 17, 19; 15:6; 17:13

18:14 Cold flowing waters come from the region of Mt. Hermon, a part of which is the source of the Jordan River.
18:16 Hissing was done to express shock, scorn, ridicule, or derision. The word in Hebrew is onomatopoeic and sounds like "shriek" in English (see 19:8; 25:9, 18; 29:18; 51:37). **Shake his head:** This was a gesture showing scorn or derision (see 48:27; Job 16:4; Ps. 44:14; 109:25; Matt. 27:39, "wagging").
18:17 East wind: The dry, hot wind from the desert (see 4:11).
18:18–23 Jeremiah's fifth lament (see note on 11:18–23). Unidentified persons plot against Jeremiah because of his attacks on the leaders (see 2:8; 5:5; 25:34–36). Jeremiah asks that his persecutors be completely destroyed.
18:18 Responsibility for the **law** was assigned to the **priest**.
18:20 Jeremiah suggests that at one time he interceded with God to **turn away . . . wrath** from them. Now they are repaying **evil** for good.
19:1–15 Jeremiah is commanded to take an **earthen flask,** to go with witnesses to the **Valley** near the **Potsherd Gate** (later called the Refuse Gate, Neh. 2:13), and there to deliver a symbolic message to the people. Unlike the clay vessel of ch. 18, this flask is not pliable and cannot be reworked. If it is not suitable for the task, it can only be destroyed.
19:1 Elders: Include lay and religious leaders.
19:2 For the **Valley of the Son of Hinnom,** see note on 7:31.
19:3 Ears will tingle: An expression found also in 1 Sam. 3:11; 2 Kin. 21:12.
19:6 Tophet: See note on 7:31, 32.

gods whom neither they, their fathers,
nor the kings of Judah have known,
and have filled this place with [b]the
blood of the innocents
5 [a]"(they have also built the *high
places of Baal, to burn their sons with
fire *for* burnt offerings to Baal, [b]which
I did not command or speak, nor did
it come into My mind),
6 "therefore behold, the days are
coming," says the LORD, "that this
place shall no more be called Tophet
or [a]the Valley of the Son of Hinnom,
but the Valley of Slaughter.
7 "And I will make void the counsel
of Judah and Jerusalem in this place,
[a]and I will cause them to fall by the
sword before their enemies and by the
hands of those who seek their lives;
their [b]corpses I will give as meat for
the birds of the heaven and for the
beasts of the earth.
8 "I will make this city [a]desolate and
a hissing; everyone who passes by it
will be astonished and hiss because of
all its plagues.
9 "And I will cause them to eat the
[a]flesh of their sons and the flesh of
their daughters, and everyone shall eat
the flesh of his friend in the siege and
in the desperation with which their enemies and those who seek their lives
shall drive them to despair." '
10 [a]"Then you shall break the flask in
the sight of the men who go with you,
11 "and say to them, 'Thus says the
LORD of hosts: [a]"Even so I will break
this people and this city, as *one* breaks
a potter's vessel, which cannot be
[1]made whole again; and they shall
[b]bury *them* in Tophet till *there is* no
place to bury.
12 "Thus I will do to this place," says
the LORD, "and to its inhabitants, and
make this city like Tophet.
13 "And the houses of Jerusalem and
the houses of the kings of Judah shall
be defiled [a]like the place of Tophet, because of all the houses on whose
[b]roofs they have burned incense to all
the host of heaven, and [c]poured out
drink offerings to other gods." ' "
14 Then Jeremiah came from Tophet,
where the LORD had sent him to
prophesy; and he stood in [a]the court
of the Lord's house and said to all the
people,
15 "Thus says the LORD of hosts, the
God of Israel: 'Behold, I will bring on
this city and on all her towns all the
doom that I have pronounced against
it, because [a]they have stiffened their
necks that they might not hear My
words.' "

The Word of God to Pashhur

20 Now [a]Pashhur the son of
[b]Immer, the priest who *was* also
chief governor in the house of the
LORD, heard that Jeremiah prophesied
these things.
2 Then Pashhur struck Jeremiah the
prophet, and put him in the stocks that
were in the high [a]gate of Benjamin,
which *was* by the house of the LORD.
3 And it happened on the next day
that Pashhur brought Jeremiah out of
the stocks. Then Jeremiah said to him,
"The LORD has not called your name
Pashhur, but [1]Magor-Missabib.
4 "For thus says the LORD: 'Behold, I
will make you a terror to yourself and
to all your friends; and they shall fall
by the sword of their enemies, and
your eyes shall see *it*. I will [a]give all
Judah into the hand of the king of Babylon, and he shall carry them captive
to Babylon and slay them with the
sword.
5 'Moreover I [a]will deliver all the
wealth of this city, all its produce, and
all its precious things; all the treasures
of the kings of Judah I will give into
the hand of their enemies, who will
plunder them, seize them, and [b]carry
them to Babylon.

4 [b]2 Kin. 21:12; Jer. 2:34; 7:6
5 [a]Num. 22:41; Jer. 7:31; 32:35 [b]Lev. 18:21; 2 Kin. 17:17; Ps. 106:37, 38 *See WW at Ezek. 6:3.
6 [a]Josh. 15:8; Jer. 7:32
7 [a]Lev. 26:17; Deut. 28:25; Jer. 15:2, 9 [b]Ps. 79:2; Jer. 7:33; 16:4; 34:20
8 [a]Jer. 18:16; 49:13; 50:13
9 [a]Lev. 26:29; Deut. 28:53, 55; Is. 9:20; Lam. 4:10; Ezek. 5:10
10 [a]Jer. 51:63, 64
11 [a]Ps. 2:9; Is. 30:14; Jer. 13:14; Lam. 4:2; Rev. 2:27 [b]Jer. 7:32 [1]*restored*
13 [a]2 Kin. 23:10; Ps. 74:7; 79:1; Jer. 52:13; Ezek. 7:21, 22 [b]2 Kin. 23:12; Jer. 32:29; Zeph. 1:5 [c]Jer. 7:18; Ezek. 20:28
14 [a]2 Chr. 20:5; Jer. 26:2–8
15 [a]Neh. 9:17, 29; Jer. 7:26; 17:23

CHAPTER 20

1 [a]Ezra 2:37, 38 [b]1 Chr. 24:14
2 [a]Jer. 37:13; Zech. 14:10
3 [1]Lit. *Fear on Every Side*
4 [a]Jer. 21:4–10
5 [a]2 Kin. 20:17; 2 Chr. 36:10; Jer. 3:24; 27:21, 22 [b]Is. 39:6

19:8 Hissing: See note on 18:16.
19:9 Eat the flesh: A part of the covenant curse for disobedience (Lev. 26:29; Deut. 28:53–57). During the siege by the Babylonians in 586 B.C. this curse was fulfilled (see Lam. 2:20; 4:10; Ezek. 5:10). The siege of Samaria by Syria resulted in the same behavior (see 2 Kin. 6:28, 29) as did the siege of Jerusalem by the Romans in A.D. 70.
19:10–13 The symbolic action of breaking **the flask** breaks the people as well. Egyptians and Hittites have left evidence of this procedure. For Jeremiah it was the setting in motion of God's word.
19:13 King Josiah **defiled . . . Tophet** (see 2 Kin. 23:10).
20:1–6 Reaction of **Pashhur** to Jeremiah's symbolic act is immediate, but his opposition to God's word earns him a new name, symbolic of the fate he will suffer.
20:1 Pashhur the son of Immer is to be distinguished from other men of the same name (see 21:1; 38:1). **Chief governor:** Charged with maintaining order in the temple, he dealt with the troublemakers (see 29:26).
20:2 The first time the title **prophet** is used for Jeremiah, but it is used again in 25:2 and then frequently after 28:5. This is also the first of many recorded physical acts of violence against Jeremiah.
20:3, 4 Magor-Missabib: "Fear on Every Side" is the new name of Pashhur (v. 10; 6:25), and this is the fate of all Judah who will either go **captive to Babylon** or fall by **the sword.**
20:5 Fulfilled with the capture of Jerusalem by Nebuchadnezzar in 597 B.C. (see 2 Kin. 24:13) and in 586 B.C. (see 52:17–23; 2 Kin. 25:13–17).

6 'And you, Pashhur, and all who
dwell in your house, shall go into captivity. You shall go to Babylon, and there you shall die, and be buried there, you and all your friends, to whom you have [a]prophesied lies.' "

Jeremiah's Unpopular Ministry

7 O LORD, You [1]induced me, and I was persuaded;
[a]You are *stronger than I, and have prevailed.
[b]I am [2]in derision daily;
Everyone mocks me.
8 For when I spoke, I cried out;
[a]I shouted, "Violence and plunder!"
Because the word of the LORD was made to me
A reproach and a derision daily.
9 Then I said, "I will not make mention of Him,
Nor speak anymore in His name."
But *His word* was in my heart like a [a]burning fire
Shut up in my bones;
I was weary of holding *it* back,
And [b]I could not.
10 [a]For I heard many [1]mocking:
"Fear on every side!"
"Report," *they say*, "and we will report it!"
[b]All my acquaintances watched for my stumbling, *saying*,
"Perhaps he can be induced;
Then we will prevail against him,
And we will take our revenge on him."

11 But the LORD *is* [a]with me as a mighty, awesome One.
Therefore my persecutors will stumble, and will not [b]prevail.
They will be greatly ashamed, for they will not prosper.
Their [c]everlasting confusion will never be forgotten.

6 [a]Jer. 14:13–15; Lam. 2:14
7 [a]Jer. 1:6, 7 [b]Job 12:4; Lam. 3:14 [1]*enticed* or *persuaded* [2]Lit. *a laughingstock all the day* *See WW at Josh. 1:9.
8 [a]Jer. 6:7
9 [a]Job 32:18–20; Ps. 39:3; Jer. 4:19; 23:9; [Ezek. 3:14]; Acts 4:20 [b]Job 32:18; Jer. 6:11; Acts 18:5
10 [a]Ps. 31:13 [b]Job 19:19; Ps. 41:9; 55:13, 14; Luke 11:53, 54 [1]*slandering*
11 [a]Jer. 1:18, 19 [b]Jer. 15:20; 17:18 [c]Jer. 23:40
12 [a]Ps. 7:9; 11:5; 17:3; 139:23; [Jer. 11:20; 17:10] [b]Ps. 54:7; 59:10; Jer. 15:15 [1]Most secret parts, lit. *kidneys*
13 [a]Ps. 35:9, 10; 109:30, 31 *See WW at Judg. 5:3.
14 [a]Job 3:3; Jer. 15:10
16 [a]Gen. 19:25 [b]Jer. 18:22 *See WW at Ezra 3:11.
17 [a]Job 3:10, 11
18 [a]Job 3:20; Jer. 15:10 [b]Lam. 3:1 [1]*toil* *See WW at Job 5:7.

CHAPTER 21

1 [a]2 Kin. 24:17, 18; Jer. 32:1–3; 37:1; 52:1–3 [b]1 Chr. 9:12; Jer. 38:1 [c]2 Kin. 25:18; Jer. 29:25; 37:3

12 But, O LORD of hosts,
You who [a]test the righteous,
And see the [1]mind and heart,
[b]Let me see Your vengeance on them;
For I have pleaded my cause before You.

13 *Sing to the LORD! Praise the LORD!
For [a]He has delivered the life of the poor
From the hand of evildoers.

14 [a]Cursed *be* the day in which I was born!
Let the day not be blessed in which my mother bore me!
15 Let the man *be* cursed
Who brought news to my father, saying,
"A male child has been born to you!"
Making him very glad.
16 And let that man be like the cities
Which the LORD [a]overthrew, and did not relent;
Let him [b]hear the cry in the morning
And the *shouting at noon,
17 [a]Because he did not kill me from the womb,
That my mother might have been my grave,
And her womb always enlarged *with me*.
18 [a]Why did I come forth from the womb to [b]see [1]labor* and sorrow,
That my days should be consumed with shame?

Jerusalem's Doom Is Sealed

21 The word which came to Jeremiah from the LORD when
[a]King Zedekiah sent to him [b]Pashhur
the son of Melchiah, and [c]Zephaniah
the son of Maaseiah, the priest, saying,

20:6 Probably fulfilled with the first captivity in 597 B.C.
20:7–18 In this sixth and final lament (see note on 11:18–23) Jeremiah expresses deep anguish in the midst of persecution and comes very close to blasphemy in the language he uses to address God. The prophetic office has brought Jeremiah nothing but abuse and derision (v. 10), and in spite of a desire to stop speaking in His name, he cannot stop. The lament ends on a positive note of trust and praise (v. 13). But from the height of praise, Jeremiah sinks to the depths of despair (vv. 14–18). Caught between the divine call he cannot evade, and the rejection and persecution by the people and the betrayal by friends, he curses the day he was born. His agony of spirit is unrestrained and his choice of words is sublime.
20:7 Induced me: Seduced (see Ex. 22:16; Judg. 16:5) or deceived (see 2 Sam. 3:25), a very strong word verging on blasphemy (see v. 10). **Persuaded:** Jeremiah feels God used undue force (see 1:7, 8).
20:10 Fear on every side: See note on v. 3.
20:13 From the time of Amos (2:6) **poor** and "righteous" were synonymous.
20:14 Cursed be the day: See Job 3:3.
20:16 Cities which the LORD overthrew: Sodom and Gomorrah.
21:1—24:10 Jeremiah denounces Judah's leadership (21:1—23:8), false prophets (23:9–40), and sinful people (24:1–10). For the rest of the book the material is arranged by subject matter rather than chronologically as the first 20 chapters are arranged.
21:1—23:8 Judah's leaders, who have the greater responsibility for the conduct of the nation, are the first to be denounced. The context is similar to 37:1–10, but the

2 [a]"Please inquire of the LORD for us,
for [1]Nebuchadnezzar king of Babylon
makes war against us. Perhaps the
LORD will deal with us according to all
His *wonderful works, that *the king*
may go away from us."
3 Then Jeremiah said to them, "Thus
you shall say to Zedekiah,
4 'Thus says the LORD God of Israel:
"Behold, I will turn back the weapons
of war that *are* in your hands, with
which you fight against the king of
Babylon and the [1]Chaldeans who besiege you outside the walls; and
[a]I will assemble them in the midst of
this city.
5 "I [a]Myself will fight against you
with an [b]outstretched hand and with
a strong arm, even in anger and fury
and great wrath.
6 "I will strike the inhabitants of this
city, both man and beast; they shall die
of a great pestilence.
7 "And afterward," says the LORD,
[a]"I will deliver Zedekiah king of Judah, his servants and the people, and
such as are left in this city from the
pestilence and the sword and the famine, into the hand of Nebuchadnezzar
king of Babylon, into the hand of their
enemies, and into the hand of those
who seek their life; and he shall strike
them with the edge of the sword.
[b]He shall not spare them, or have pity
or mercy." '
8 "Now you shall say to this people,
'Thus says the LORD: "Behold, [a]I set before you the way of life and the way
of death.
9 "He who [a]remains in this city shall
die by the sword, by famine, and by
pestilence; but he who goes out and
[1]defects to the Chaldeans who besiege
you, he shall [b]live, and his life shall
be as a prize to him.
10 "For I have [a]set My face against this
city for adversity and not for good,"
says the LORD. [b]"It shall be given into
the hand of the king of Babylon, and
he shall [c]burn it with fire." '

Message to the House of David

11 "And concerning the house of the
king of Judah, *say,* 'Hear the word of
the LORD,
12 'O house of David! Thus says the
LORD:

[a]"Execute[1] judgment [b]in the
morning;
And deliver *him who is* plundered
Out of the hand of the oppressor,
Lest My fury go forth like fire
And burn so that no one can
quench *it,*
Because of the evil of your doings.

13 "Behold, [a]I *am* against you,
O [1]inhabitant of the valley,
And rock of the plain," says the
LORD,
"Who say, [b]'Who shall come down
against us?
Or who shall enter our
dwellings?'
14 But I will punish you according
to the [a]fruit of your [1]doings,"
says the LORD;
"I will kindle a fire in its forest,
And [b]it shall devour all things
around it." ' "

22 Thus says the LORD: "Go down
to the house of the king of Judah, and there speak this word,
2 "and say, [a]'Hear the word of the
LORD, O king of Judah, you who sit on
the throne of David, you and your servants and your people who enter these
gates!
3 'Thus says the LORD: [a]"Execute[1]
judgment and righteousness, and deliver the plundered out of the hand of
the oppressor. Do no wrong and do no
violence to the stranger, the [b]father-

2 [a]Jer. 37:3, 7 [1]Heb. *Nebuchadrezzar,* and so elsewhere in the book *See WW at Judg. 13:19. **4** [a]Is. 13:4 [1]Or *Babylonians,* and so elsewhere in the book **5** [a]Is. 63:10 [b]Ex. 6:6 **7** [a]Jer. 37:17; 39:5; 52:9 [b]2 Chr. 36:17 **8** [a]Deut. 30:15, 19 **9** [a]Jer. 38:2 [b]Jer. 39:18 [1]Lit. *falls away to* **10** [a]Amos 9:4 [b]Jer. 38:3 [c]Jer. 34:2, 22; 37:10
12 [a]Zech. 7:9 [b]Ps. 101:8 [1]*Dispense justice* **13** [a][Ezek. 13:8] [b]Jer. 49:4 [1]*dweller* **14** [a]Is. 3:10, 11 [b]2 Chr. 36:19 [1]*deeds*

CHAPTER 22

2 [a]Jer. 17:20 **3** [a]Jer. 21:12 [b]Jer. 7:6 [1]*Dispense justice*

---

delegation sent by the king is different. The events described take place late in the reign of Zedekiah, perhaps 589 or 588 B.C.

21:1 Pashhur the son of Melchiah: See 38:1. To be distinguished from the Pashhur of 20:1–6, although the similarity in names may account for the placing of ch. 21 after ch. 20. **Zephaniah the son of Maaseiah:** See 29:25, 29; 37:3. Zephaniah was later executed by Nebuchadnezzar at Riblah (52:24, 27).

21:2 Inquire of the LORD: See Gen. 25:22; 1 Kin. 22:5; 2 Kin. 1:2. In each case *information* is sought. ***Nebuchadnezzar:*** Greatest king (605–562 B.C.) of the Neo-Babylonian Empire. **Wonderful works:** Zedekiah wanted a miraculous intervention of God as in the time of Hezekiah (Is. 37:36).

21:4 Originally **Chaldeans** designated the people of southern Babylonia, but during the reign of Nebuchadnezzar II (see v. 2) the term was synonymous with Babylonians.

21:5 Outstretched hand: See note on 6:12.

21:7 I will deliver Zedekiah: A prophecy fulfilled in 52:8–11, 24–27. **The pestilence and the sword and the famines:** See note on 14:12.

21:8–10 The two days are alluded to in 6:16 (see Deut. 30:15). Here the alternative is surrender and live, or stay in the city and die. Most of the people will choose the wrong way. In any event, Jerusalem will be destroyed.

21:11–14 The king is to **execute judgment** (see 5:28; 22:3); if he fails this task he will be punished.

21:13 Valley stands for Jerusalem, which is surrounded by valleys on three sides. The **rock of the plain** is Mt. Zion.

22:2 O king of Judah: Probably Zedekiah.

less, or the widow, nor shed innocent
blood in this place.
4 "For if you indeed do this thing,
[a]then shall enter the gates of this
house, riding on horses and in chariots,
accompanied by servants and people,
kings who sit on the throne of
David.
5 "But if you will not [1]hear these
words, [a]I *swear by Myself," says the
LORD, "that this house shall become a
desolation." ' "
6 For thus says the LORD to the house
of the king of Judah:

"You *are* [a]Gilead to Me,
The head of Lebanon;
Yet I surely will make you a
wilderness,
Cities *which* are not inhabited.
7 I will prepare destroyers against
you,
Everyone with his weapons;
They shall cut down [a]your choice
cedars
[b]And cast *them* into the fire.

8 "And many nations will pass by this
city; and everyone will say to his
neighbor, [a]'Why has the LORD done so
to this great city?'
9 "Then they will answer, [a]'Because
they have forsaken the covenant of the
LORD their God, and worshiped other
gods and served them.' "

10 Weep not for [a]the dead, nor
bemoan him;
Weep bitterly for him [b]who goes
away,
For he shall return no more,
Nor see his native country.

Message to the Sons of Josiah

11 For thus says the LORD concerning
[a]Shallum[1] the son of Josiah, king of
Judah, who reigned instead of Josiah
his father, [b]who went from this place:
"He shall not return here anymore,
12 "but he shall die in the place where
they have led him captive, and shall
see this land no more.

13 "Woe[a] to him who builds his house
by unrighteousness
And his [1]chambers by injustice,
[b]*Who* uses his neighbor's service
without wages
And gives him nothing for his
work,
14 Who says, 'I will build myself a
wide house with spacious
[1]chambers,
And cut out windows for it,
Paneling *it* with cedar
And painting *it* with vermilion.'

15 "Shall you reign because you
enclose *yourself* in cedar?
Did not your father eat and drink,
And do justice and
righteousness?
Then [a]*it was* well with him.
16 He [1]judged the cause of the poor
and *needy;
Then *it was* well.
Was not this knowing Me?" says
the LORD.
17 "Yet[a] your eyes and your heart *are*
for nothing but your
covetousness,
For shedding innocent blood,
And practicing oppression and
violence."

18 Therefore thus says the LORD concerning Jehoiakim the son of Josiah,
king of Judah:

[a]"They shall not lament for him,
Saying, [b]'Alas, my brother!' or
'Alas, my sister!'
They shall not lament for him,
Saying, 'Alas, master!' or 'Alas,
his *glory!'
19 [a]He shall be buried with the burial
of a donkey,
Dragged and cast out beyond the
gates of Jerusalem.

20 "Go up to Lebanon, and cry out,
And lift up your voice in Bashan;
Cry from Abarim,
For all your lovers are destroyed.
21 I spoke to you in your prosperity,
But you said, 'I will not hear.'

4 [a]Jer. 17:25
5 [a]Matt. 23:38; Heb. 6:13, 17 [1]Obey *See WW at Gen. 26:3.
6 [a]Gen. 37:25; Num. 32:1; Song 4:1
7 [a]Is. 37:24 [b]Jer. 21:14
8 [a]Deut. 29:24–26; 1 Kin. 9:8, 9; 2 Chr. 7:20–22; Jer. 16:10
9 [a]2 Kin. 22:17; 2 Chr. 34:25; Jer. 11:3
10 [a]2 Kin. 22:20 [b]Jer. 14:17; 22:11; Lam. 3:48
11 [a]1 Chr. 3:15 [b]2 Kin. 23:34; 2 Chr. 36:4; Ezek. 19:4 [1]Or *Jehoahaz*
13 [a]2 Kin. 23:35; Jer. 17:11; Ezek. 22:13 [b]Lev. 19:13; Deut. 24:14, 15; Mic. 3:10; Hab. 2:9; James 5:4 [1]Lit. *roof chambers, upper chambers*
14 [1]Lit. *roof chambers, upper chambers*
15 [a]2 Kin. 23:25; Ps. 128:2; Is. 3:10; Jer. 7:23; 42:6
16 [1]Defended *See WW at Ps. 70:5.
17 [a]Jer. 6:13; 8:10; Ezek. 19:6; [Luke 12:15–20]
18 [a]Jer. 16:4, 6 [b]1 Kin. 13:30 *See WW at 1 Chr. 29:11.
19 [a]1 Kin. 21:23, 24; 2 Chr. 36:6; Jer. 36:30; Dan. 1:2

22:6 Gilead and **Lebanon** were famous for forests.
22:8, 9 Similar to 1 Kin. 9:8, 9.
22:10 The dead is Josiah; **him who goes away** is Jehoahaz, a son of Josiah whom Pharaoh Necho took to Egypt in 609 B.C. He never returned (see vv. 11, 12).
22:13–19 Jeremiah bitterly denounces Jehoiakim who has enlarged and embellished his house (v. 14) by unjust means (v. 13), contrasts this action with that of his father Josiah (vv. 15, 16), and condemns Jehoiakim for conduct unbecoming a king. With biting irony Jeremiah suggests he qualifies as king because of luxurious surroundings rather than because of just administration. Jehoiakim, who was addressed in the third person (vv. 13, 14) and second person (vv. 15, 17), is now fully identified (v. 18), and his ignominious death is described (vv. 18, 19).
22:19 Burial of a donkey: No burial at all. See 36:30 and 2 Kin. 24:6, where no burial is mentioned.
22:20 Lebanon, Bashan, and **Abarim** are all mountains; the **lovers** are allies of Judah.

[a]This *has been* your manner from
your youth,
That you did not obey My voice.
22 The wind shall eat up all
[a]your [1]rulers,
And your lovers shall go into
captivity;
Surely then you will be ashamed
and humiliated
For all your wickedness.
23 O inhabitant of Lebanon,
Making your nest in the cedars,
How *gracious will you be when
pangs come upon you,
Like [a]the pain of a woman in
[1]labor?

Message to Coniah

24 "*As* I live," says the LORD, [a]"though
[1]Coniah the son of Jehoiakim, king of
Judah, [b]were the [2]signet on My right
hand, yet I would pluck you off;
25 [a]"and I will give you into the hand
of those who seek your life, and into
the hand *of those* whose face you
fear—the hand of Nebuchadnezzar
king of Babylon and the hand of the
[1]Chaldeans.
26 [a]"So I will cast you out, and your
mother who bore you, into another
country where you were not born; and
there you shall die.
27 "But to the land to which they desire to return, there they shall not return.

28 "Is this man [1]Coniah a despised,
broken idol—
[a]A vessel in which *is* no pleasure?
Why are they cast out, he and his
descendants,
And cast into a land which they
do not know?
29 [a]O earth, earth, earth,
Hear the word of the LORD!
30 Thus says the LORD:
'Write this man down as
[a]childless,
A man *who* shall not prosper in
his days;
For [b]none of his descendants
shall prosper,
Sitting on the throne of David,
And ruling anymore in Judah.' "

The Branch of Righteousness

23 "Woe [a]to the shepherds who destroy and scatter the sheep of
My pasture!" says the LORD.
2 Therefore thus says the LORD God
of Israel against the shepherds who
feed My people: "You have scattered
My flock, driven them away, and not
attended to them. [a]Behold, I will attend
to you for the evil of your doings," says
the LORD.
3 "But [a]I will gather the remnant of
My flock out of all countries where I
have driven them, and bring them back
to their folds; and they shall be fruitful
and increase.
4 "I will set up [a]shepherds over them
who will feed them; and they shall fear
no more, nor be dismayed, nor shall
they be lacking," says the LORD.

5 "Behold, [a]*the* days are coming,"
says the LORD,
"That I will raise to David a
Branch of righteousness;
A King shall reign and [1]prosper,
[b]And execute [2]judgment and
righteousness in the [3]earth.
6 [a]In His days Judah will be saved,
And Israel [b]will dwell safely;
Now [c]this *is* His name by which
He will be called:

[1]THE LORD OUR
RIGHTEOUSNESS.

7 "Therefore, behold, [a]*the* days are
coming," says the LORD, "that they
shall no longer say, 'As the LORD lives
who brought up the children of Israel
from the land of Egypt,'
8 "but, 'As the LORD lives who

21 [a]Jer. 3:24, 25; 32:30
22 [a]Jer. 23:1 [1]Lit. *shepherds*
23 [a]Jer. 6:24 [1]*childbirth* *See WW at Mal. 1:9.
24 [a]2 Kin. 24:6, 8 [b]Hag. 2:23 [1]Or *Jeconiah* or *Jehoiachin* [2]*signet ring*
25 [a]Jer. 34:20 [1]Or *Babylonians*
26 [a]2 Kin. 24:15
28 [a]Hos. 8:8 [1]See note at v. 24
29 [a]Deut. 32:1
30 [a]Matt. 1:12 [b]Jer. 36:30

CHAPTER 23

1 [a]Jer. 10:21
2 [a]Ex. 32:34
3 [a]Jer. 32:37
4 [a]Jer. 3:15
5 [a]Jer. 33:14 [b]Ps. 72:2 [1]*act wisely* [2]*justice* [3]*land*
6 [a]Zech. 14:11 [b]Jer. 32:37 [c][1 Cor. 1:30] [1]Heb. *YHWH Tsidkenu*
7 [a]Jer. 16:14

22:24–30 A prophecy concerning Jehoiachin (or Coniah) which was fulfilled in 24:1; 29:2. Jehoiachin was exiled to Babylon by Nebuchadnezzar in 597 B.C., but was later freed by Evil-Merodach (2 Kin. 25:27–30).
22:24 Signet on My right hand: A symbol of authority; the curse was apparently reversed in Hag. 2:23.
22:26 Mother who bore you: Nehushta (see 13:18; 2 Kin. 24:8). Fulfilled in 2 Kin. 24:15.
22:29 Earth, earth, earth: Literary device for emphasis. See note on 7:4.
22:30 Childless: Jehoiachin had at least seven children (1 Chr. 3:17, 18), but none sat **on the throne of David**. His grandson Zerubbabel was governor of Judah. Jehoiachin was the last legitimate king of Judah until the birth of Jesus Christ. Jesus' line is traced through Jehoiachin (or Jeconiah, Matt. 1:11–16) to show His legal right to the throne of David.
23:1–8 A messianic oracle. After denouncing the **shepherds who destroy** (v. 12), God promises to **gather the remnant, bring them back** (vv. 3, 4, 7, 8), and raise up **a Branch of righteousness** who will be a true Davidic **King** (vv. 5, 6). See notes on Ezek. 34:11–16, 23.
23:5 *The* days are coming: See 16:14; 31:27. The phrase is used of the messianic era. **Branch** is a messianic title. See notes on Zech. 3:8 and Obad. 15.
23:6 THE LORD OUR RIGHTEOUSNESS: A play on the name of Zedekiah. Although Zedekiah did not live up to the meaning of his name, "The Lord Is My Righteousness," the Messiah, Jesus, was righteousness in all He did (see v. 5).
23:7, 8 Repeated with slight variation in 16:14, 15.

brought up and led the descendants of the house of Israel from the north country [a]and from all the countries where I had driven them.' And they shall dwell in their own [b]land."

False Prophets and Empty Oracles

9 My heart within me is broken
Because of the prophets;
[a]All my bones shake.
I am like a drunken man,
And like a man whom wine has overcome,
Because of the LORD,
And because of His holy words.
10 For [a]the land is full of adulterers;
For [b]because of a curse the land mourns.
[c]The pleasant places of the wilderness are dried up.
Their course of life is evil,
And their might *is* not right.

11 "For [a]both prophet and priest are profane;
Yes, [b]in My house I have found their wickedness," says the LORD.
12 "Therefore[a] their way shall be to them
Like slippery *ways;*
In the darkness they shall be driven on
And fall in them;
For I [b]will bring disaster on them,
The year of their punishment,"
says the LORD.
13 "And I have seen [1]folly in the prophets of Samaria:
[a]They prophesied by Baal
And [b]caused My people Israel to err.
14 Also I have seen a horrible thing in the prophets of Jerusalem:
[a]They commit adultery and walk in lies;
They also [b]strengthen the hands of evildoers,
So that no one turns back from his wickedness.
All of them are like [c]Sodom to Me,
And her inhabitants like Gomorrah.

8 [a]Is. 43:5, 6; Ezek. 34:13; Amos 9:14, 15 [b]Gen. 12:7; Jer. 16:14, 15; 31:8 **9** [a]Jer. 8:18; Hab. 3:16 **10** [a]Jer. 9:2 [b]Hos. 4:2; Mal. 3:5 [c]Ps. 107:34; Jer. 9:10 **11** [a]Jer. 6:13; Zeph. 3:4 [b]Jer. 7:30; 32:34; Ezek. 8:11; 23:39 **12** [a]Ps. 35:6; [Prov. 4:19]; Jer. 13:16 [b]Jer. 11:23 **13** [a]1 Kin. 18:18–21; Jer. 2:8 [b]Is. 9:16 [1]Lit. *distastefulness* **14** [a]Jer. 29:23 [b]Jer. 23:22; Ezek. 13:22, 23 [c]Gen. 18:20; Deut. 32:32; Is. 1:9, 10

15 [a]Deut. 29:18; Jer. 9:15 [1]Or *Pollution* **16** [a]Jer. 14:14; Ezek. 13:3, 6 **17** [a]Jer. 8:11; Ezek. 13:10; Zech. 10:2 [b]Deut. 29:19; Jer. 3:17 [c]Jer. 5:12; Amos 9:10; Mic. 3:11 [1]*stubbornness* or *imagination* *See WW at Nah. 1:15. **18** [a]Job 15:8, 9; [Jer. 23:22; 1 Cor. 2:16] **19** [a]Jer. 25:32; 30:23; Amos 1:14 **20** [a]2 Kin. 23:26, 27; Jer. 30:24 [b]Gen. 49:1 **21** [a]Jer. 14:14; 23:32; 27:15

15 "Therefore thus says the LORD of hosts concerning the prophets:

'Behold, I will feed them with [a]wormwood,
And make them drink the water of gall;
For from the prophets of Jerusalem
[1]Profaneness has gone out into all the land.' "

16 Thus says the LORD of hosts:

"Do not listen to the words of the prophets who prophesy to you.
They make you worthless;
[a]They speak a vision of their own heart,
Not from the mouth of the LORD.
17 They continually say to those who despise Me,
'The LORD has said, [a]"You shall have *peace" ';
And *to* everyone who [b]walks according to the [1]dictates of his own heart, they say,
[c]'No evil shall come upon you.' "

18 For [a]who has stood in the counsel of the LORD,
And has perceived and heard His word?
Who has marked His word and heard *it?*
19 Behold, a [a]whirlwind of the LORD has gone forth in fury—
A violent whirlwind!
It will fall violently on the head of the wicked.
20 The [a]anger of the LORD will not turn back
Until He has executed and performed the thoughts of His heart.
[b]In the latter days you will understand it perfectly.

21 "I[a] have not sent these prophets, yet they ran.
I have not spoken to them, yet they prophesied.
22 But if they had stood in My counsel,

23:9–40 The denunciation of false prophets (2:8; 5:31; 6:13–15) is the theme of these verses. Jeremiah seemed to be most at odds with those members of society who bore the title "prophet," and in this section he gives us reasons for his opposition and hostility to them.

23:9 Heart within me is broken: Jeremiah is disturbed in his mind; he is shocked at what he sees.

23:13, 14 Compared to **the prophets of Samaria,** who were considered apostate, **the prophets** of Judah are worse, for they flagrantly sin and, by their actions, fail to turn people from wickedness. The people are as bad as those God destroyed in **Sodom** and **Gomorrah** (see 20:16; Gen. 19:24).

23:16–22 The message of the prophets is as perverse as their actions. They preach **peace,** when anyone **who has stood in the counsel of the LORD,** as Jeremiah has, knows that condemnation of the wicked is God's word for the day.

23:19, 20 Repeated with minor variations in 30:23, 24.

And had caused My people to
hear My words,
Then they would have [a]turned
them from their evil way
And from the evil of their doings.

23 "*Am* I a God near at hand," says
the LORD,
"And not a God afar off?
24 Can anyone [a]hide himself in
secret places,
So I shall not see him?" says the
LORD;
[b]"Do I not **fill** heaven and earth?"
says the LORD.

> **WORD WEALTH**
>
> **23:24 fill,** *male'* (mah-*lay*); Strong's #4390: To fill, fill up, be full; to fulfill. *Male'* is the source of Hebrew words relating to fullness and fulfillment: filling something up to the brim (2 Kin. 4:6); causing something to be thoroughly saturated (as was Naphtali, "full" of the blessings of the Lord, Deut. 33:23); fulfilling one's word, that is, to declare that one will do something, and then to do it (1 Kin. 2:27). God promises to fill all the Earth with awareness of His glory (Num. 14:21; Hab. 2:14). *Male'* is the word used in the OT to describe being filled with the Spirit of God (Ex. 31:3; Mic. 3:8).

5 25 "I have heard what the prophets
have said who prophesy lies in My
name, saying, 'I have dreamed, I have
dreamed!'
26 "How long will *this* be in the heart
of the prophets who prophesy lies? Indeed *they are* prophets of the deceit
of their own heart,
27 "who try to make My people forget
My name by their dreams which everyone tells his neighbor, [a]as their fathers
forgot My name for Baal.

28 "The prophet who has a *dream,
let him tell a dream;
And he who has My word, let him
speak My word faithfully.
What *is* the chaff to the wheat?"
says the LORD.
29 "*Is* not My word like a [a]fire?" says
the LORD,
"And like a hammer *that* breaks
the rock in pieces?

30 "Therefore behold, [a]I *am* against
the prophets," says the LORD, "who
steal My words every one from his
neighbor.
31 "Behold, I *am* [a]against the prophets," says the LORD, "who use their
tongues and say, 'He says.'
32 "Behold, I *am* against those who
prophesy false dreams," says the LORD,
"and tell them, and cause My people
to err by their [a]lies and by [b]their recklessness. Yet I did not send them or
command them; therefore they shall
not [c]profit this people at all," says the
LORD.
33 "So when these people or the
prophet or the priest ask you, saying,
'What is [a]the [1]oracle of the LORD?' you
shall then say to them, [2]'What oracle?'
I will even forsake you," says the
LORD.
34 "And *as for* the prophet and the
priest and the people who say, 'The
[1]oracle of the LORD!' I will even punish
that man and his house.
35 "Thus every one of you shall say
to his neighbor, and every one to his
brother, 'What has the LORD answered?' and, 'What has the LORD spoken?'
36 "And the [1]oracle of the LORD you
shall mention no more. For every
man's word will be his oracle, for you
have [a]perverted the words of the living
God, the LORD of hosts, our God.
37 "Thus you shall say to the prophet,
'What has the LORD answered you?'
and, 'What has the LORD spoken?'
38 "But since you say, 'The [1]oracle of
the LORD!' therefore thus says the
LORD: 'Because you say this word,
"The oracle of the LORD!" and I have
sent to you, saying, "Do not say, 'The
oracle of the LORD!' "
39 'therefore behold, I, even I, [a]will utterly forget you and forsake you, and
the city that I gave you and your fathers, and *will cast you* out of My presence.
40 'And I will bring [a]an everlasting reproach upon you, and a perpetual

22 [a]Jer. 25:5
24 [a][Ps. 139:7]; Amos 9:2, 3 [b][1 Kin. 8:27]; Ps. 139:7
27 [a]Judg. 3:7
28 *See WW at Joel 2:28.
29 [a]Jer. 5:14
30 [a]Deut. 18:20; Ps. 34:16; Jer. 14:14, 15; Ezek. 13:8, 9
31 [a]Ezek. 13:9
32 [a]Jer. 20:6; 27:10; Lam. 2:14; 3:37 [b]Zeph. 3:4 [c]Jer. 7:8; Lam. 2:14
33 [a]Is. 13:1; Nah. 1:1; Hab. 1:1; Zech. 9:1; Mal. 1:1 [1]*burden, prophecy* [2]LXX, Tg., Vg. *'You are the burden.'*
34 [1]*burden, prophecy*
36 [a]Deut. 4:2 [1]*burden, prophecy*
38 [1]*burden, prophecy*
39 [a]Hos. 4:6
40 [a]Jer. 20:11; Ezek. 5:14, 15

23:23–32 God is both transcendent and immanent and is aware of the prophets' deception of the people by false revelations through dreams. Usually God spoke to His prophets *directly* (1:4–10; Is. 8:1) or in a vision (1:11, 13; Is. 6:1), but dreams also were valid (31:26). Jeremiah rebukes the prophets for putting forth their own words as God's word, or repeating the words of others as a divine revelation from God.

23:25–27 See section 5 of Truth-In-Action at the end of Jer.

23:33 Oracle: Or "burden." There may be a wordplay. The oracle (lifting up of the voice) was a burden (lifting something physically) placed upon the prophet until the message was delivered, and the effect of the message was a "burden" for the people. On the other hand, the "burden" of the Lord is that the people are a "burden."

23:39 Forget: A pun on the word "oracle" (vv. 33, 34, 36, 38); the Hebrew words have similar sounds.

[b]shame, which shall not be forgotten.' "

The Sign of Two Baskets of Figs

24 The [a]LORD showed me, and
there were two baskets of figs
set before the temple of the LORD, after
Nebuchadnezzar [b]king of Babylon had
carried away captive [c]Jeconiah the son
of Jehoiakim, king of Judah, and the
princes of Judah with the craftsmen
and smiths, from Jerusalem, and had
brought them to Babylon.
2 One basket *had* very good figs, like
the figs *that are* first ripe; and the other
basket *had* very bad figs which could
not be eaten, they were so [a]bad.
3 Then the LORD said to me, "What
do you see, Jeremiah?" And I said,
"Figs, the good figs, very good; and the
bad, very bad, which cannot be eaten,
they are so bad."
4 Again the word of the LORD came
to me, saying,
5 "Thus says the LORD, the God of Israel: 'Like these good figs, so will I
[1]acknowledge those who are carried
away captive from Judah, whom I have
sent out of this place for *their own*
good, into the land of the Chaldeans.
6 'For I will set My eyes on them for
good, and [a]I will bring them back to
this land; [b]I will build them and not
pull *them* down, and I will plant them
and not pluck *them* up.
7 'Then I will give them [a]a heart to
know Me, that I *am* the LORD; and they
shall be [b]My people, and I will be their
God, for they shall return to Me
[c]with their whole heart.
8 'And as the bad [a]figs which cannot
be eaten, they are so bad'—surely thus
says the LORD—'so will I give up Zedekiah the king of Judah, his princes, the
[b]residue of Jerusalem who remain in
this land, and [c]those who dwell in the
land of Egypt.
9 'I will deliver them to [a]trouble into
all the kingdoms of the earth, for *their*
harm, [b]*to be* a reproach and a *byword, a taunt and a curse, in all places
where I shall drive them.
10 'And I will send the sword, the famine, and the pestilence among them, till
they are [1]consumed from the land that
I gave to them and their fathers.' "

Seventy Years of Desolation

25 The word that came to Jeremiah
concerning all the people of Judah, [a]in the fourth year of [b]Jehoiakim
the son of Josiah, king of Judah (which
was the first year of Nebuchadnezzar
king of Babylon),
2 which Jeremiah the prophet spoke
to all the people of Judah and to all
the inhabitants of Jerusalem, saying:
3 [a]"From the thirteenth year of Josiah
the son of Amon, king of Judah, even
to this day, this *is* the twenty-third year
in which the word of the LORD has
come to me; and I have spoken to you,
rising early and speaking, [b]but you
have not listened.
4 "And the LORD has sent to you all
His servants the prophets, [a]rising early
and sending *them,* but you have not
listened nor inclined your ear to hear.
5 "They said, [a]'Repent now everyone
of his evil way and his evil doings, and
dwell in the land that the LORD has
given to you and your fathers forever
and ever.
6 'Do not go after other gods to serve
them and worship them, and do not
provoke Me to anger with the works
of your hands; and I will not harm you.'
7 "Yet you have not listened to Me,"
says the LORD, "that you might [a]pro-
voke Me to anger with the works of
your hands to your own hurt.
8 "Therefore thus says the LORD of
hosts: 'Because you have not heard My
words,
9 'behold, I will send and take [a]all the
families of the north,' says the LORD,

40 [b]Mic. 3:5–7

CHAPTER 24

1 [a]Amos 7:1, 4; 8:1 [b]2 Kin. 24:12–16; 2 Chr. 36:10 [c]Jer. 22:24–28; 29:2
2 [a]Is. 5:4, 7; Jer. 29:17
5 [1]*regard*
6 [a]Jer. 12:15; 29:10; Ezek. 11:17 [b]Jer. 32:41; 33:7; 42:10
7 [a][Deut. 30:6; Jer. 32:39; Ezek. 11:19; 36:26, 27] [b]Is. 51:16; Jer. 30:22; 31:33; 32:38; Ezek. 14:11; Zech. 8:8; [Heb. 8:10] [c]1 Sam. 7:3; Ps. 119:2; Jer. 29:13
8 [a]Jer. 29:17 [b]Jer. 39:9 [c]Jer. 44:1, 26–30
9 [a]Deut. 28:25, 37; 1 Kin. 9:7; 2 Chr. 7:20; Jer. 15:4; 29:18; 34:17 [b]Ps. 44:13, 14
*See WW at Prov. 1:6.
10 [1]*destroyed*

CHAPTER 25

1 [a]Jer. 36:1 [b]2 Kin. 24:1, 2; 2 Chr. 36:4–6; Dan. 1:1, 2
3 [a]Jer. 1:2 [b]Jer. 7:13; 11:7, 8, 10
4 [a]Jer. 7:13, 25
5 [a]2 Kin. 17:13; [Is. 55:6, 7]; Jer. 18:11; Ezek. 18:30; [Jon. 3:8–10]
7 [a]Deut. 32:21; Jer. 7:19; 32:30
9 [a]Jer. 1:15

24:1–10 Using a vision of **two baskets of figs,** God divides the people into two parts. The **good figs** are those whom Nebuchadnezzar exiled in 597 B.C., including Jehoiachin, the princes, craftsmen, and metalsmiths (vv. 1, 5). The **bad figs** are those who remained in the land (v. 8). The exiles will be restored to the land (vv. 6, 7; 29:10–14; Ezek. 11:14–20) and will prosper, but **Zedekiah** and those now in the land will be destroyed (vv. 8–10; 29:15–19).
24:6 See note on Ezek. 11:17–20.
24:10 The sword, the famine, and the pestilence: See note on 14:12.
25:1–38 The chapter divides into two sections: vv. 1–14 serve as a conclusion to the judgment on Judah with a prediction of 70 years (a lifetime) of desolation; and vv. 15–38 serve as an introduction to the prophecies against the nations (especially chs. 46–51).
25:1–14 Jeremiah recalls 23 years of preaching to the people to repent, but they have refused to listen. Therefore God will use Nebuchadnezzar as His instrument of punishment, the people will go into exile for 70 years, and then the king of Babylon himself will be punished.
25:1 The **fourth year of Jehoiakim** and the **first year of Nebuchadnezzar,** 605 B.C., is the year Nebuchadnezzar defeated Necho of Egypt at Carchemish.
25:3 Thirteenth year: This was 626 B.C. The 23 years include 19 under Josiah and 4 under Jehoiakim. **Rising early:** See note on 7:13.
25:9 Families of the north: Babylon and her allies. **My servant:** God's instrument of judgment, just as Cyrus is called "shepherd" in Is. 44:28. **A hissing:** See note on 18:16.

'and Nebuchadnezzar the king of Babylon, [b]My servant, and will bring them
against this land, against its inhabitants, and against these nations all
around, and will utterly destroy them,
and [c]make them an astonishment, a
hissing, and perpetual desolations.
10 'Moreover I will [1]take from them
the [a]voice of mirth and the voice of
gladness, the voice of the bridegroom
and the voice of the bride, [b]the sound
of the millstones and the light of the
lamp.
11 'And this whole land shall be a desolation *and* an astonishment, and these
nations shall serve the king of Babylon
seventy [a]years.
12 'Then it will come to pass, [a]when
[1]seventy years are completed, *that* I
will punish the king of Babylon and
that nation, the land of the Chaldeans,
for their iniquity,' says the LORD;
[b]'and I will make it a perpetual desolation.
13 'So I will bring on that land all My
words which I have pronounced
against it, all that is written in this
book, which Jeremiah has prophesied
concerning all the nations.
14 [a]'(For many nations [b]and great
kings shall [c]be served by them also;
[d]and I will repay them according to
their deeds and according to the works
of their own hands.)' "

Judgment on the Nations

15 For thus says the LORD God of Israel
to me: "Take this [a]wine cup of [1]fury
from My hand, and cause all the nations, to whom I send you, to drink it.
16 "And [a]they will drink and stagger
and go mad because of the sword that
I will send among them."
17 Then I took the cup from the LORD's
hand, and made all the nations drink,
to whom the LORD had sent me:
18 Jerusalem and the cities of Judah,

9 [b]Is. 45:1 [c]Jer. 18:16
10 [a]Rev. 18:23 [b]Eccl. 12:4 [1]Lit. *cause to perish from them*
11 [a]Jer. 29:10
12 [a]Ezra 1:1 [b]Is. 13:20 [1]Beginning circa 605 B.C. (2 Kin. 24:1) and ending circa 536 B.C. (Ezra 1:1)
14 [a]Jer. 50:9; 51:27, 28 [b]Jer. 51:27 [c]Jer. 27:7 [d]Jer. 50:29; 51:6, 24
15 [a]Rev. 14:10 [1]*wrath*
16 [a]Nah. 3:11
18 [a]Jer. 25:9, 11 [b]Jer. 24:9
20 [a]Job 1:1 [b]Jer. 47:1–7 [c]Is. 20:1
21 [a]Jer. 49:7
22 [a]Jer. 47:4 [b]Jer. 49:23
23 [a]Jer. 49:7, 8
24 [a]Ezek. 30:5
25 [a]Jer. 49:34 [b]Jer. 51:11, 28
26 [a]Jer. 50:9 [1]A code word for Babylon, Jer. 51:41
27 [a]Hab. 2:16 [b]Is. 63:6
29 [a]Ezek. 9:6 [b]Dan. 9:18 [c]Ezek. 38:21

its kings and its princes, to make them
[a]a desolation, an astonishment, a hissing, and [b]a curse, as *it is* this day;
19 Pharaoh king of Egypt, his servants, his princes, and all his people;
20 all the mixed multitude, all the
kings of [a]the land of Uz, all the kings
of the land of the [b]Philistines (namely,
Ashkelon, Gaza, Ekron, and [c]the remnant of Ashdod);
21 [a]Edom, Moab, and the people of
Ammon;
22 all the kings of [a]Tyre, all the kings
of Sidon, and the kings of the coastlands which *are* across the [b]sea;
23 [a]Dedan, Tema, Buz, and all *who are*
in the farthest corners;
24 all the kings of Arabia and all the
kings of the [a]mixed multitude who
dwell in the desert;
25 all the kings of Zimri, all the kings
of [a]Elam, and all the kings of the
[b]Medes;
26 [a]all the kings of the north, far and
near, one with another; and all the
kingdoms of the world which *are* on
the face of the earth. Also the king of
[1]Sheshach shall drink after them.
27 "Therefore you shall say to them,
'Thus says the LORD of hosts, the God
of Israel: [a]"Drink, [b]be drunk, and
vomit! Fall and rise no more, because
of the sword which I will send among
you." '
28 "And it shall be, if they refuse to
take the cup from your hand to drink,
then you shall say to them, 'Thus says
the LORD of hosts: "You shall certainly
drink!
29 "For behold, [a]I begin to bring calamity on the city [b]which is called by
My name, and should you be utterly
unpunished? You shall not be unpunished, for [c]I will call for a sword on
all the inhabitants of the earth," says
the LORD of hosts.'
30 "Therefore prophesy against them
all these words, and say to them:

25:11 Seventy years: A round number signifying a lifetime and generally coordinated with 538 B.C., the year the Jews were allowed to return home from the Babylonian exile. See note on Ezra. 1:1.

25:15–38 Jeremiah is commanded to take the **wine cup of fury** from God's hand and to cause all the nations **to drink it** as punishment for their transgressions (see Amos 1:3—3:2). Judah, God's own people, will be judged first, followed by the rest of the nations beginning with Egypt and *ending with Sheshach* (or Babylon). Basically the same nations appear in chs. 46—51.

25:15 Cup: Symbolic of wrath and judgment. See v. 28; 49:12; 51:7; Is. 51:17; Ezek. 23:31–34; Rev. 14:10; 16:19.

25:18 Hissing: See note on 18:16.

25:19 Egypt: See 46:2–28.

25:21 Edom: See 49:7–22. **Moab:** See 48:1–47. **Ammon:** See 49:1–6.

25:22 Tyre and **Sidon:** See 47:4.

25:23 Dedan and **Tema:** See 49:7, 8.

25:24 Arabia: See 49:28–33.

25:25 Elam: See 49:34–39. **Medes:** See 51:11, 28.

25:26 Sheshach is a cryptogram for Babylon. This is a literary device known as "atbash," where the last consonant of the Hebrew alphabet is substituted for the first, the next-to-last for the second, and so on. See 51:41.

25:30, 31 The judgment is described in various conventional figures: **Roar** and **utter His voice** (see Joel 3:16; Amos 1:2), **tread the grapes** (see Job 24:11; Is. 16:10; 63:1–6), **has a controversy** (a courtroom scene, see Hos. 4:1; 12:2;

'The LORD will [a]roar* from on
high,
And utter His voice from
[b]His holy habitation;
He will roar mightily against
[c]His fold.
He will give [d]a shout, as those
who tread *the grapes,*
Against all the inhabitants of the
earth.
31 A noise will come to the ends of
the earth—
For the LORD has [a]a controversy
with the nations;
[b]He will plead His case with all
flesh.
He will give those *who are* wicked
to the sword,' says the LORD."

32 Thus says the LORD of hosts:

"Behold, disaster shall go forth
From nation to nation,
And [a]a great whirlwind shall be
raised up
From the farthest parts of the
earth.

33 [a]"And at that day the slain of the
LORD shall be from *one* end of the earth
even to the *other* end of the earth. They
shall not be [b]lamented, [c]or gathered,
or buried; they shall become refuse on
the ground.

34 "Wail,[a] shepherds, and cry!
Roll about *in the ashes,*
You leaders of the flock!
For the days of your slaughter
and your dispersions are
fulfilled;
You shall fall like a precious
vessel.
35 And the shepherds will have no
[1]way to flee,
Nor the leaders of the flock to
escape.
36 A voice of the cry of the
shepherds,
And a wailing of the leaders to
the flock *will be heard.*
For the LORD has plundered their
pasture,

30 [a]Is. 42:13; Joel 3:16; Amos 1:2 [b]Ps. 11:4 [c]1 Kin. 9.3; Ps. 132:14 [d]Is. 16:9; Jer. 48:33 *See WW at Joel 3:16. **31** [a]Hos. 4:1; Mic. 6:2 [b]Is. 66:16; Joel 3:2 **32** [a]Jer. 23:19; 30:23 **33** [a]Is. 34:2, 3; 66:16 [b]Jer. 16:4, 6; Ezek. 39:4, 17 [c]Ps. 79:3; Jer. 8:2; Rev. 11:9 **34** [a]Jer. 4:8; 6:26; Ezek. 27:30 **35** [1]Or *refuge*

CHAPTER 26

2 [a]2 Chr. 24:20, 21; Jer. 19:14 [b]Deut. 4:2; Jer. 43:1; Ezek. 3:10; Matt. 28:20; [Rev. 22:19] [c]Acts 20:27 *See WW at Ps. 99:5. **3** [a]Is. 1:16–19; Jer. 36:3–7 [b]Jer. 18:8; Jon. 3:9 **4** [a]Lev. 26:14, 15; Deut. 28:15; 1 Kin. 9:6; Is. 1:20; Jer. 17:27; 22:5 **5** [a]Jer. 25:4; 29:19 **6** [a]1 Sam. 4:10, 11; Ps. 78:60; Jer. 7:12, 14 [b]2 Kin. 22:19; Is. 65:15; Jer. 24:9 *See WW at Gen. 49:10. **9** [a]Jer. 9:11

37 And the peaceful dwellings are
cut down
Because of the fierce anger of the
LORD.
38 He has left His lair like the lion;
For their land is desolate
Because of the fierceness of the
Oppressor,
And because of His fierce anger."

Jeremiah Saved from Death

26 In the beginning of the reign of
Jehoiakim the son of Josiah,
king of Judah, this word came from the
LORD, saying,
2 "Thus says the LORD: 'Stand in
[a]the court of the LORD's house, and
speak to all the cities of Judah, which
come to *worship *in* the LORD's house,
[b]all the words that I command you to
speak to them. [c]Do not diminish a
word.
3 [a]'Perhaps everyone will listen and
turn from his evil way, that I may
[b]relent concerning the calamity which
I purpose to bring on them because of
the evil of their doings.'
4 "And you shall say to them, 'Thus
says the LORD: [a]"If you will not listen
to Me, to walk in My law which I have
set before you,
5 "to heed the words of My servants
the prophets [a]whom I sent to you, both
rising up early and sending *them* (but
you have not heeded),
6 "then I will make this house like
[a]Shiloh,* and will make this city
[b]a curse to all the nations of the
earth." ' "
7 So the priests and the prophets and
all the people heard Jeremiah speaking
these words in the house of the LORD.
8 Now it happened, when Jeremiah
had made an end of speaking all that
the LORD had commanded *him* to speak
to all the people, that the priests and
the prophets and all the people seized
him, saying, "You will surely die!
9 "Why have you prophesied in the
name of the LORD, saying, 'This house
shall be like Shiloh, and this city shall
be [a]desolate, without an inhabitant'?"

Mic. 6:2), and **sword** (see 5:12; 12:12; Ex. 5:3; Deut. 32:25; Is. 1:20).
25:32 Great whirlwind: The judgment of God in the form of the Babylonian army.
25:33 That day: See note on Obad. 15.
25:34–38 The rulers (**shepherds** and **leaders**) of the nations are dismayed and in confusion because of God's fierce anger.
26:1–24 This temple sermon and its results may be related to the events of chs. 7—10.
26:1 In the beginning of the reign of Jehoiakim: Perhaps 609 B.C.
26:6 Shiloh: See note on 7:12.
26:7–24 The arrest of Jeremiah is the result of his controversy with false **prophets** and corrupt **priests,** for they would be severely affected by a destroyed temple. The **princes of Judah,** who had responsibility for legal decisions, took their places **in the entry of the New Gate** to hear the charges (v. 10). After hearing Jeremiah's defense (vv. 12–15), the princes decided in his favor (v. 16).

And all the people were gathered
against Jeremiah in the house of the
LORD.
10 When the princes of Judah heard
these things, they came up from the
king's house to the house of the LORD
and sat down in the entry of the New
Gate of the LORD's *house.*
11 And the priests and the prophets
spoke to the princes and all the people,
saying, [1]"This man deserves to [a]die!
For he has prophesied against this city,
as you have heard with your ears."
12 Then Jeremiah spoke to all the
princes and all the people, saying:
"The LORD sent me to prophesy against
this house and against this city with
all the words that you have heard.
13 "Now therefore, [a]amend your ways
and your doings, and obey the voice
of the LORD your God; then the LORD
will relent concerning the doom that
He has pronounced against you.
14 "As for me, here [a]I am, in your
hand; do with me as seems good and
[1]proper to you.
15 "But know for certain that if you
put me to death, you will surely bring
innocent blood on yourselves, on this
city, and on its inhabitants; for truly
the LORD has sent me to you to speak
all these words in your hearing."
16 So the princes and all the people
said to the priests and the prophets,
"This man does not deserve to die. For
he has spoken to us in the name of the
LORD our God."
17 [a]Then certain of the elders of the
land rose up and spoke to all the assembly of the people, saying:
18 [a]"Micah of Moresheth prophesied
in the days of Hezekiah king of Judah,
and spoke to all the people of Judah,
saying, 'Thus says the LORD of hosts:

[b]"Zion shall be plowed *like* a field,
Jerusalem shall become [c]heaps of ruins,
And the mountain of the [1]temple
Like the [2]bare hills of the forest." '

19 "Did Hezekiah king of Judah and
all Judah ever put him to death?
[a]Did he not fear the LORD and [b]seek
the LORD's favor? And the LORD
[c]relented concerning the doom which
He had pronounced against them.
[d]But we are doing great evil against
ourselves."
20 Now there was also a man who
prophesied in the name of the LORD,
Urijah the son of Shemaiah of Kirjath
Jearim, who prophesied against this
city and against this land according to
all the words of Jeremiah.
21 And when Jehoiakim the king, with
all his mighty men and all the princes,
heard his words, the king sought to put
him to death; but when Urijah heard
it, he was afraid and fled, and went to
Egypt.
22 Then Jehoiakim the king sent men
to Egypt: Elnathan the son of Achbor,
and *other* men *who went* with him to
Egypt.
23 And they brought Urijah from
Egypt and brought him to Jehoiakim
the king, who killed him with the
sword and cast his dead body into the
graves of the [1]common people.
24 Nevertheless [a]the hand of Ahikam
the son of Shaphan was with Jeremiah,
so that they should not give him into
the hand of the people to put him to
death.

Symbol of the Bonds and Yokes

27 In[1] the beginning of the reign
of [2]Jehoiakim the son of Josiah,
[a]king of Judah, this word came to Jeremiah from the LORD, saying,
2 "Thus says the LORD to me: 'Make

11 [a]Jer. 38:4 [1]Lit. *A judgment of death to this man*
13 [a]Jer. 7:3; [Joel 2:13]; Jon. 3:8
14 [a]Jer. 38:5 [1]*right*
17 [a]Acts 5:34
18 [a]Mic. 1:1 [b]Mic. 3:12 [c]Neh. 4:2; Ps. 79:1; Jer. 9:11 [1]Lit. *house* [2]Lit. *high places*
19 [a]2 Chr. 32:26; Is. 37:1, 4, 15–20 [b]2 Kin. 20:1–19 [c]Ex. 32:14; 2 Sam. 24:16; Jer. 18:8 [d][Acts 5:39]
23 [1]Lit. *sons of the people*
24 [a]2 Kin. 22:12–14; Jer. 39:14; 40:5–7

CHAPTER 27
1 [a]Jer. 27:3, 12, 20; 28:1 [1]LXX omits v. 1. [2]So with MT, Tg., Vg.; some Heb. mss., Arab., Syr. *Zedekiah* (cf. 27:3, 12; 28:1)

26:18 Micah of Moresheth: This passage is quoted verbatim from Mic. 3:12, the only such time one prophet quotes another and gives the source.
26:19 Because **Hezekiah** repented and prayed, the Lord delivered the city of Jerusalem in 701 B.C.
26:20–23 The example of **Urijah,** a contemporary of Jeremiah, is used to show the personal danger Jeremiah faced. Urijah was extradited from **Egypt** and executed by **Jehoiakim,** a vivid contrast to the attitude toward Micah by the good king Hezekiah. His execution, *however,* is not unique in the prophetic tradition (see 2 Chr. 24:20–22; Matt. 23:29–31).
26:22 Elnathan: See 36:12, 25. One of Jehoiakim's high officials.
26:24 Ahikam the son of Shaphan: An official of Josiah (2 Kin. 22:12) and the father of Gedaliah, the governor of Judah after the destruction of Jerusalem in 586 B.C. (see 40:5), who also helped Jeremiah (39:14).
27:1—28:17 The message of Jeremiah to the nations (vv. 2–11) and to King Zedekiah (vv. 3, 12–15) is to submit to the yoke of the king of Babylon (vv. 2, 11, 12), for the nations have been given to Nebuchadnezzar (v. 6), and any rebellion is contrary to God's will (v. 8). Jeremiah also addresses the people (vv. 16–22) and declares that prophets who proclaim another message are lying (v. 14), and God has not sent them (v. 15).
27:1 In the beginning of the reign of Jehoiakim: See 26:1. But v. 3 mentions Zedekiah who would be king later. So probably 593 B.C. is meant, and this is supported by 28:1.
27:2 Bonds and yokes: Similar to the device worn by draft animals, the yoke was a symbol of political submission.

for yourselves bonds and yokes, [a]and put them on your neck,
3 'and send them to the king of Edom, the king of Moab, the king of the Ammonites, the king of Tyre, and the king of Sidon, by the hand of the messengers who come to Jerusalem to Zedekiah king of Judah.
4 'And command them to say to their masters, "Thus says the LORD of hosts, the God of Israel—thus you shall say to your masters:
5 [a]'I have made the earth, the man and the beast that *are* on the ground, by My great power and by My outstretched arm, and [b]have given it to whom it seemed proper to Me.
6 [a]'And now I have given all these lands into the hand of Nebuchadnezzar the king of Babylon, [b]My servant; and [c]the beasts of the field I have also given him to serve him.
7 [a]'So all nations shall serve him and his son and his son's son, [b]until the time of his land comes; [c]and then many nations and great kings shall make him serve them.
8 'And it shall be, *that* the nation and kingdom which will not serve Nebuchadnezzar the king of Babylon, and which will not put its neck under the yoke of the king of Babylon, that nation I will punish,' says the LORD, 'with the sword, the famine, and the pestilence, until I have consumed them by his hand.
9 'Therefore do not listen to your prophets, your diviners, your [1]dreamers, your soothsayers, or your sorcerers, who speak to you, saying, "You shall not serve the king of Babylon."
10 'For they prophesy a [a]lie to you, to remove you far from your land; and I will drive you out, and you will perish.
11 'But the nations that bring their necks under the yoke of the king of Babylon and serve him, I will let them remain in their own land,' says the LORD, 'and they shall till it and dwell in it.' " ' "
12 I also spoke to [a]Zedekiah king of Judah according to all these words, saying, "Bring your necks under the yoke of the king of Babylon, and serve him and his people, and live!
13 [a]"Why will you die, you and your people, by the sword, by the famine, and by the pestilence, as the LORD has spoken against the nation that will not serve the king of Babylon?
14 "Therefore [a]do not listen to the words of the prophets who speak to you, saying, 'You shall not serve the king of Babylon,' for they prophesy [b]a lie to you;
15 "for I have [a]not sent them," says the LORD, "yet they prophesy a lie in My name, that I may drive you out, and that you may perish, you and the prophets who prophesy to you."
16 Also I spoke to the priests and to all this people, saying, "Thus says the LORD: 'Do not listen to the words of your prophets who prophesy to you, saying, "Behold, [a]the vessels of the LORD's house will now shortly be brought back from Babylon"; for they prophesy a lie to you.
17 'Do not listen to them; serve the king of Babylon, and live! Why should this city be laid waste?
18 'But if they *are* prophets, and if the word of the LORD is with them, let them now **make intercession** to the LORD of hosts, that the vessels which are left in the house of the LORD, *in* the house of the king of Judah, and at Jerusalem, do not go to Babylon.'

2 [a]Jer. 28:10, 12; Ezek. 4:1; 12:3; 24:3
5 [a]Ps. 115:15; 146:6; Is. 45:12 [b]Deut. 9:29; Ps. 115:16; Jer. 32:17; Dan. 4:17, 25, 32
6 [a]Jer. 28:14 [b]Jer. 25:9; 43:10; Ezek. 29:18, 20 [c]Jer. 28:14; Dan. 2:38
7 [a]2 Chr. 36:20 [b]Jer. 25:12; 50:27; [Dan. 5:26]; Zech. 2:8, 9 [c]Jer. 25:14
9 [1]Lit. *dreams*
10 [a]Jer. 23:16, 32; 28:15
12 [a]Jer. 28:1; 38:17
13 [a][Prov. 8:36]; Jer. 27:8; 38:23; [Ezek. 18:31]
14 [a]Jer. 23:16 [b]Jer. 14:14; 23:21; 29:8, 9; Ezek. 13:22
15 [a]Jer. 23:21; 29:9
16 [a]2 Kin. 24:13; 2 Chr. 36:7, 10; Jer. 28:3; Dan. 1:2

WORD WEALTH

27:18 make intercession, *paga'* (pah-*gah*); Strong's #6293: To reach; to meet someone; to pressure or urge someone strongly; to meet up with a person; encounter, entreat; to assail with urgent petitions. This verb occurs 46 times. In some passages it is translated "meet," as in Josh. 2:16. In Josh. 19:27, *paga'* refers to the extent to which a tribal boundary is reached. Sometimes the verb refers to "falling upon" someone in battle, that is, to meet up with the enemy with hostile intent (1 Kin. 2:29). *Paga'* is also (*cont. on next page*)

27:3 The nations mentioned are neighbors of Judah: **Edom, Moab,** and **Ammon** to the south and east; **Tyre** and **Sidon** to the north. Rebellion was probably the subject under discussion.

27:7 Three generations of rulers are promised; then the end comes for Babylon.

27:8 The sword, the famine, and the pestilence: See note on 14:12.

27:9 The **prophets** are false prophets; **diviners, soothsayers,** and **sorcerers** were prohibited in Israel (see Lev. 19:26; Deut. 18:10, 11); **dreamers** could include both prophets and diviners (see 23:25–28; 29:8).

27:16 Shortly be brought back: Jeremiah had suggested a 70-year stay in Babylon (25:11; 29:10), so this emphasis by the prophets contradicted his message (see 28:1–3).

27:18–22 Jeremiah suggests that if they are true prophets they should intercede with the Lord for Judah, so that those vessels still left in the temple may remain, for Jeremiah's message is that all will be carried to Babylon.

(*cont. from preceding page*)
translated "make intercession," the idea being that a supplicant catches up with a superior, and reaches him with an urgent request. Thus, intercession involves reaching God, meeting God, and entreating Him for His favor.

19 "For thus says the LORD of hosts [a]concerning the pillars, concerning the Sea, concerning the carts, and concerning the remainder of the vessels that remain in this city,
20 "which Nebuchadnezzar king of Babylon did not take, when he carried away [a]captive Jeconiah the son of Jehoiakim, king of Judah, from Jerusalem to Babylon, and all the nobles of Judah and Jerusalem—
21 "yes, thus says the LORD of hosts, the God of Israel, concerning the [a]vessels that remain in the house of the LORD, and in the house of the king of Judah and of Jerusalem:
22 'They shall be [a]carried to Babylon, and there they shall be until the day that I [b]visit them,' says the LORD. 'Then [c]I will bring them up and restore them to this place.' "

Hananiah's Falsehood and Doom

28 And [a]it happened in the same year, at the beginning of the reign of Zedekiah king of Judah, in the [b]fourth year *and* in the fifth month, *that* Hananiah the son of [c]Azur the prophet, who *was* from Gibeon, spoke to me in the house of the LORD in the presence of the priests and of all the people, saying,
2 "Thus speaks the LORD of hosts, the God of Israel, saying: 'I have broken [a]the yoke of the king of Babylon.
3 [a]'Within two full years I will bring back to this place all the vessels of the LORD's house, that Nebuchadnezzar king of Babylon [b]took away from this place and carried to Babylon.
4 'And I will bring back to this place [1]Jeconiah the son of Jehoiakim, king of Judah, with all the captives of Judah who went to Babylon,' says the LORD, 'for I will break the yoke of the king of Babylon.' "
5 Then the *prophet Jeremiah spoke to the prophet Hananiah in the presence of the priests and in the presence of all the people who stood in the house of the LORD,
6 and the prophet Jeremiah said, [a]"Amen! The LORD do so; the LORD perform your words which you have prophesied, to bring back the vessels of the LORD's house and all who were carried away captive, from Babylon to this place.
7 "Nevertheless hear now this word that I speak in your hearing and in the hearing of all the people:
8 "The prophets who have been before me and before you of old prophesied against many countries and great kingdoms—of war and disaster and pestilence.
9 "As for [a]the prophet who prophesies of [b]peace, when the word of the prophet comes to pass, the prophet will be known *as* one whom the LORD has truly sent."
10 Then Hananiah the prophet took the [a]yoke off the prophet Jeremiah's neck and broke it.
11 And Hananiah spoke in the presence of all the people, saying, "Thus says the LORD: 'Even so I will break the yoke of Nebuchadnezzar king of Babylon [a]from the neck of all nations within the space of two full years.' " And the prophet Jeremiah went his way.
12 Now the word of the LORD came to Jeremiah, after Hananiah the prophet had broken the yoke from the neck of the prophet Jeremiah, saying,
13 "Go and tell Hananiah, saying, 'Thus says the LORD: "You have broken the yokes of wood, but you have made in their place yokes of iron."
14 'For thus says the LORD of hosts, the God of Israel: [a]"I have put a yoke of iron on the neck of all these nations, that they may serve Nebuchadnezzar king of Babylon; and they shall serve him. [b]I have given him the beasts of the field also." ' "

19 [a]1 Kin. 7:15; 2 Kin. 25:13–17; Jer. 52:17, 20, 21
20 [a]2 Kin. 24:14, 15; 2 Chr. 36:10, 18; Jer. 24:1
21 [a]Jer. 20:5
22 [a]2 Kin. 25:13; 2 Chr. 36:18 [b]2 Chr. 36:21; Jer. 29:10; 32:5 [c]Ezra 1:7; 7:19

CHAPTER 28

1 [a]Jer. 27:1 [b]Jer. 51:59 [c]Ezek. 11:1
2 [a]Jer. 27:12
3 [a]Jer. 27:16 [b]2 Kin. 24:13; Dan. 1:2
4 [1]*Jehoiachin,* 2 Kin. 24:12
5 *See WW at 1 Sam. 3:20.
6 [a]1 Kin. 1:36; Ps. 41:13; Jer. 11:5
9 [a]Deut. 18:22 [b]Jer. 23:17; Ezek. 13:10, 16
10 [a]Jer. 27:2
11 [a]Jer. 27:7
14 [a]Deut. 28:48; Jer. 27:7, 8 [b]Jer. 27:6

27:22 The day: See note on Obad. 15.
28:1–17 As **Jeremiah** confronts **the prophet Hananiah,** the people are faced with a dilemma: How can one tell a false prophet from a true prophet? Hananiah uses the formula ***Thus speaks the LORD* of hosts, the God of Israel** (v. 2; 29:4), and he may have been sincere. Jeremiah would like to believe Hananiah's message (v. 6), but it was not in the tradition of the prophets of old (v. 8). Prophet now contradicted prophet. Only the fulfillment of the event would show who spoke the truth (see v. 9; Deut. 18:21, 22).
28:2 The yoke: See note on 27:2.
28:10 Yoke off the prophet: See 27:2. A symbolic act of breaking the yoke is performed by Hananiah.
28:11 Jeremiah **went his way** for he had no immediate reply for Hananiah.
28:13 Yokes of wood . . . yokes of iron: Submission becomes servitude.
28:14 Beasts of the field: Complete control of man and animal is given to Nebuchadnezzar (see 27:6).

15 Then the prophet Jeremiah said to
Hananiah the prophet, "Hear now,
Hananiah, the LORD has not sent you,
but [a]you make this people trust in a
[b]lie.
16 "Therefore thus says the LORD: 'Behold, I will cast you from the face of
the earth. This year you shall [a]die, because you have taught [b]rebellion
against the LORD.' "
17 So Hananiah the prophet died the
same year in the seventh month.

Jeremiah's Letter to the Captives

29 Now these *are* the words of the
letter that Jeremiah the prophet
sent from Jerusalem to the remainder
of the elders who were [a]carried away
captive—to the priests, the prophets,
and all the people whom Nebuchadnezzar had carried away captive from
Jerusalem to Babylon.
2 (This happened after [a]Jeconiah[1] the
king, the [b]queen mother, the [2]eunuchs,
the princes of Judah and Jerusalem,
the craftsmen, and the smiths had departed from Jerusalem.)
3 *The letter was sent* by the hand of
Elasah the son of [a]Shaphan, and Gemariah the son of Hilkiah, whom Zedekiah king of Judah sent to Babylon, to
Nebuchadnezzar king of Babylon, saying,

4 Thus says the LORD of hosts, the
God of Israel, to all who were
carried away captive, whom I
have caused to be carried away
from Jerusalem to Babylon:
5 Build houses and dwell *in them;*
plant gardens and eat their fruit.
6 Take wives and beget sons and
daughters; and take wives for
your sons and give your
daughters to husbands, so that
they may bear sons and
daughters—that you may be
increased there, and not
diminished.
7 And seek the peace of the city
where I have caused you to be
carried away captive, [a]and pray
to the LORD for it; for in its peace
you will have peace.
8 For thus says the LORD of hosts,
the God of Israel: Do not let your
prophets and your diviners who
are in your midst [a]deceive you,
nor listen to your dreams which
you cause to be dreamed.
9 For they prophesy [a]falsely to you
in My name; I have not sent them,
says the LORD.
10 For thus says the LORD: After 4
[a]seventy years are completed at
Babylon, I will visit you and
perform My good word toward
you, and cause you to [b]return to
this place.
11 For I know the thoughts that I
think toward you, says the LORD,
thoughts of peace and not of evil,
to give you a future and a hope.
12 Then you will [a]call upon Me and
go and pray to Me, and I will
[b]listen to you.
13 And [a]you will seek Me and find
Me, when you search for Me
[b]with all your heart.
14 [a]I will be found by you, says the
LORD, and I will bring you back
from your captivity; [b]I will gather
you from all the nations and from
all the places where I have driven
you, says the LORD, and I will
bring you to the place from which
I cause you to be carried away
captive.

15 [a]Jer. 20:6; 29:31; Lam. 2:14; Ezek. 13:22; Zech. 13:3 [b]Jer. 27:10; 29:9
16 [a]Jer. 20:6 [b]Deut. 13:5; Jer. 29:32

CHAPTER 29

1 [a]Jer. 27:20
2 [a]2 Kin. 24:12–16; 2 Chr. 36:9, 10; Jer. 22:24–28 [b]2 Kin. 24:12, 15; Jer. 13:18 [1]*Jehoiachin,* 2 Kin. 24:12; 2 Chr. 36:10 [2]*Or officers*
3 [a]2 Chr. 34:8
7 [a]Ezra 6:10; Neh. 1:4–11; Dan. 9:16; 1 Tim. 2:2
8 [a]Jer. 14:14; 23:21; 27:14, 15; Eph. 5:6
9 [a]Jer. 28:15; 37:19
10 [a]2 Chr. 36:21–23; Ezra 1:1–4; Jer. 25:12; 27:22; Dan. 9:2; Zech. 7:5 [b][Jer. 24:6, 7]; Zeph. 2:7
12 [a]Ps. 50:15; Jer. 33:3; Dan. 9:3 [b]Ps. 145:19
13 [a]Lev. 26:39–42; Deut. 30:1–3 [b]1 Chr. 22:19; 2 Chr. 22:9; Jer. 24:7
14 [a][Deut. 4:7]; Ps. 32:6; 46:1; [Is. 55:6, 7]; Jer. 24:7 [b]Is. 43:5, 6; Jer. 23:8; 32:37

KINGDOM DYNAMICS

29:11–14 Seeking God and Spiritual Warfare, FAITH'S WARFARE. Throughout Scripture we find repeated references to God's people seeking after Him. Implied in these passages is a quest for God that includes a level of intensity beyond what might be termed ordinary prayer. The word "search" along with the phrase "with all your heart" suggests an earnestness that borders on desperation. The word "search" (Hebrew *darash*) suggests a "following after," or close pursuit of a desired objective; it also implies a (*cont. on next page*)

28:16 This year: A short-term prediction that will attest the trustworthiness of the Word (see v. 9; Deut. 18:21, 22). **Taught rebellion:** See 29:32. Rebellious activity by the prophet was punishable by death (see Deut. 13:5; 18:20).
28:17 Seventh month: Two months later **Hananiah** died.
29:1–32 Jeremiah writes a letter to the exiles of 597 B.C. (vv. 4–23) and then deals with the false prophet **Shemaiah** (vv. 24–32). The exiles were being misled by messages of a speedy return.
29:2 See notes on 13:18 and 24:1–10.
29:3 ***Letter was sent:*** Conveniently and safely carried by diplomatic means.
29:4 I have caused: The Exile was the doing of the Lord.
29:5 The same verbs (**build** and **plant**) as in the call of Jeremiah (1:10), but here used in a literal sense.
29:7 Pray to the LORD for it: A totally new concept to pray for the well-being of their captors.
29:8 Prophets and **diviners:** See note on 27:9.
29:10–20 See section 4 of Truth-In-Action at the end of Jer.
29:10 Seventy years: See note on 25:11.
29:11–14 See notes on Ezra 1:1 and Zech. 10:9.

(*cont. from preceding page*)
diligence in the searching process. In 2 Chr. 15:2, Azariah promises the Lord will be with His people if they "seek" (*darash*) after Him—another indicator of God's emphasis on intensity and diligence in prayer.
(James 5:13–18/Ezra 8:21–23) D.E.

15 Because you have said, "The
LORD has raised up prophets for
us in Babylon"—
16 [a]therefore thus says the LORD
concerning the king who sits on
the throne of David, concerning
all the people who dwell in this
city, and concerning your
brethren who have not gone out
with you into captivity—
17 thus says the LORD of hosts:
Behold, I will send on them the
sword, the famine, and the
pestilence, and will make them
like [a]rotten figs that cannot be
eaten, they are so bad.
18 And I will pursue them with the
sword, with famine, and with
pestilence; and I [a]will deliver
them to trouble among all the
kingdoms of the earth—to be
[b]a curse, an astonishment, a
hissing, and a reproach among all
the nations where I have driven
them,
19 because they have not heeded My
words, says the LORD, which
[a]I sent to them by My servants
the prophets, rising up early and
sending *them;* neither would you
heed, says the LORD.
20 Therefore hear the word of the
LORD, all you of the captivity,
whom I have sent from Jerusalem
to Babylon.
21 Thus says the LORD of hosts, the
God of Israel, concerning Ahab
the *son of Kolaiah, and Zedekiah
the son of Maaseiah, who
prophesy a [a]lie to you in My
name: Behold, I will deliver them
into the hand of Nebuchadnezzar
king of Babylon, and he shall slay
them before your eyes.
22 [a]And because of them a curse

16 [a]Jer. 38:2, 3, 17–23
17 [a]Jer. 24:3, 8–10
18 [a]Deut. 28:25; 2 Chr. 29:8; Jer. 15:4; 24:9; 34:17; Ezek. 12:15 [b]Jer. 26:6; 42:18
19 [a]Jer. 25:4; 26:5; 35:15
21 [a]Jer. 14:14, 15; Lam. 2:14; 2 Pet. 2:1
*See WW at Gen. 29:32.
22 [a]Gen. 48:20; Is. 65:15 [b]Dan. 3:6, 21
23 [a]Jer. 23:14 [b][Prov. 5:21; Jer. 16:17]; Mal. 3:5; [Heb. 4:13]
25 [a]2 Kin. 25:18; Jer. 21:1
26 [a]Jer. 20:1 [b]2 Kin. 9:11; Hos. 9:7; Mark 3:21; John 10:20; Acts 26:24; [2 Cor. 5:13] [c]Jer. 20:1, 2; Acts 16:24
31 [a]Jer. 28:15 [b]Ezek. 13:8–16, 22, 23

shall be taken up by all the
captivity of Judah who *are* in
Babylon, saying, "The LORD make
you like Zedekiah and Ahab,
[b]whom the king of Babylon
roasted in the fire";
23 because [a]they have done
disgraceful things in Israel, have
committed adultery with their
neighbors' wives, and have
spoken lying words in My name,
which I have not commanded
them. Indeed I [b]know, and *am* a
witness, says the LORD.

24 You shall also speak to Shemaiah
the Nehelamite, saying,
25 Thus speaks the LORD of hosts,
the God of Israel, saying: You
have sent letters in your name to
all the people who *are* at
Jerusalem, [a]to Zephaniah the son
of Maaseiah the priest, and to all
the priests, saying,
26 "The LORD has made you priest
instead of Jehoiada the priest, so
that there should be [a]officers *in*
the house of the LORD over every
man *who* is [b]demented and
considers himself a prophet, that
you should [c]put him in prison and
in the stocks.
27 Now therefore, why have you not
rebuked Jeremiah of Anathoth
who makes himself a prophet to
you?
28 For he has sent to us *in* Babylon,
saying, 'This *captivity is* long;
build houses and dwell *in them,*
and plant gardens and eat their
fruit.' "
29 Now Zephaniah the priest read
this letter in the hearing of
Jeremiah the prophet.
30 Then the word of the LORD came
to Jeremiah, saying:
31 Send to all those in captivity,
saying, Thus says the LORD
concerning Shemaiah the
Nehelamite: Because Shemaiah
has prophesied to you, [a]and I
have not sent him, and he has
caused you to trust in a [b]lie—
32 therefore thus says the LORD:
Behold, I will punish Shemaiah

29:21 Ahab and **Zedekiah** were false prophets in Babylon (see v. 22).
29:22 Roasted in the fire: A form of execution in Babylon (see Dan. 3:6, 24).
29:24–32 Judgment of **Shemaiah,** a false prophet (v. 31) who wrote letters to the inhabitants of Jerusalem and to the priest **Zephaniah** (v. 25) requesting that he rebuke Jeremiah (v. 27). The letter is given verbatim (vv. 26–28) and contains a quote from the letter Jeremiah wrote to Babylon (see v. 5).
29:26 *Who* is demented: Prophetic behavior sometimes caused questions concerning mental stability.
29:31, 32 The word of the Lord to **Shemaiah** is similar to that against Hananiah (see 28:15, 16).
29:32 Taught rebellion: See note on 28:16.

the Nehelamite and his [1]family:
he shall not have anyone to dwell
among this people, nor shall he
see the good that I will do for My
people, says the LORD, [a]because
he has taught rebellion against
the LORD.

Restoration of Israel and Judah

30 The word that came to Jeremiah
from the LORD, saying,
2 "Thus speaks the LORD God of Israel, saying: 'Write in a book for yourself all the words that I have spoken
to you.
3 'For behold, the days are coming,'
says the LORD, 'that [a]I will bring back
from captivity My people Israel and Judah,' says the LORD. [b]'And I will cause
them to return to the land that I gave
to their fathers, and they shall *possess
it.' "
4 Now these *are* the words that the
LORD spoke concerning Israel and Judah.
5 "For thus says the LORD:

'We have heard a voice of
trembling,
Of [1]fear, and not of peace.
6 Ask now, and see,
Whether a [1]man is ever in
[2]labor with child?
So why do I see every man *with*
his hands on his loins
[a]Like a woman in labor,
And all faces turned pale?
7 [a]Alas! For that day *is* great,
[b]So that none *is* like it;
And it *is* the time of Jacob's
trouble,
But he shall be saved out of it.

8 'For it shall come to pass in that
day,'
Says the LORD of hosts,
'*That* I will break his yoke from
your neck,
And will burst your bonds;

32 [a]Jer. 28:16 [1]*descendants*, lit. *seed*

CHAPTER 30

3 [a]Ps. 53:6; Jer. 29:14; 30:18; 32:44; Ezek. 39:25; Amos 9:14; Zeph. 3:20 [b]Jer. 16:15; Ezek. 20:42; 36:24 *See WW at Deut. 8:1.
5 [1]*dread*
6 [a]Jer. 4:31; 6:24 [1]Lit. *male can give birth* [2]*childbirth*
7 [a][Is. 2:12]; Hos. 1:11; Joel 2:11; Amos 5:18; Zeph. 1:14 [b]Lam. 1:12; Dan. 9:12; 12:1
9 [a]Is. 55:3; Ezek. 34:23; 37:24; Hos. 3:5 [b][Luke 1:69; Acts 2:30; 13:23] *See WW at Ps. 100:2.
10 [a]Is. 41:13; 43:5; 44:2; Jer. 46:27, 28 [b]Jer. 3:18
11 [a][Is. 43:2–5] [b]Amos 9:8 [c]Jer. 4:27; 46:27, 28 [d]Ps. 6:1; Is. 27:8; Jer. 10:24; 46:28 *See WW at Jer. 10:24.
12 [a]2 Chr. 36:16; Jer. 15:18
13 [a]Jer. 8:22 *See WW at Deut. 32:36.
14 [a]Jer. 22:20, 22; Lam. 1:2 [b]Job 13:24; 16:9; 19:11 [c]Job 30:21 [d]Jer. 5:6
15 [a]Jer. 15:18

Foreigners shall no more enslave
them.
9 But they shall *serve the LORD
their God,
And [a]David their king,
Whom I will [b]raise up for them.

10 'Therefore [a]do not fear, O My
servant Jacob,' says the LORD,
'Nor be dismayed, O Israel;
For behold, I will save you from
afar,
And your seed [b]from the land of
their captivity.
Jacob shall return, have rest and
be quiet,
And no one shall make *him*
afraid.
11 For I *am* with [a]you,' says the
LORD, 'to save you;
[b]Though I make a full end of all
nations where I have scattered
you,
[c]Yet I will not make a complete
end of you.
But I will *correct you [d]in justice,
And will not let you go altogether
unpunished.'

12 "For thus says the LORD:

[a]'Your affliction *is* incurable,
Your wound *is* severe.
13 *There is* no one to *plead your
cause,
That you may be bound up;
[a]You have no healing medicines.
14 [a]All your lovers have forgotten
you;
They do not seek you;
For I have wounded you with the
wound [b]of an enemy,
With the chastisement [c]of a cruel
one,
For the multitude of your
iniquities,
[d]*Because* your sins have
increased.
15 Why [a]do you cry about your
affliction?

30:1—33:26 Written just before the destruction of Jerusalem (see 32:1), this book of consolation is a long-sustained prophecy on the future restoration of both Israel (the northern kingdom) and Judah (the southern kingdom). For its fulfillment see note on Zeph. 2:7, 9.

30:2 Write in a book: Most prophecy was originally given orally and only later written down. On another occasion Jeremiah was told to write his prophecy because he was unable to deliver the message in person (see 36:2, 4, 32; 45:1). The intent here is to preserve the prophecy for future generations.

30:6 Woman in labor: A symbol of anguish.

30:7 Time of Jacob's trouble: A description of the Day of the Lord (see note on Obad. 15) and called "a time of trouble" in Dan. 12:1. Jacob is an alternate name for Israel.

30:8 That day: The day when the event will take place, when God intervenes in the affairs of men and nations. It was generally viewed as a time when Israel would be exalted above the other nations, but Amos and Isaiah warn that it will be a day of darkness and gloom. It is thus often used in an eschatological sense, the ushering in of the final events and the establishment of God's kingdom on Earth. See note on Obad. 15.

30:9 David their king is the Messiah, the descendant of David.

30:12–17 Though her wound seems to be incurable (v. 12) because of the multitude of her iniquities (v. 15), Israel will be healed (v. 17) and her oppressors plundered (v. 16).

Your sorrow *is* incurable.
Because of the multitude of your iniquities,
Because your sins have increased,
I have done these things to you.

16 'Therefore all those who devour you [a]shall be devoured;
And all your adversaries, every one of them, shall go into [b]captivity;
Those who plunder you shall become [c]plunder,
And all who prey upon you I will make a [d]prey.
17 [a]For I will restore health to you
And heal you of your wounds,'
says the LORD,
'Because they called you an outcast *saying:*
"This *is* Zion;
No one seeks her." '

18 "Thus says the LORD:

'Behold, I will bring back the captivity of Jacob's tents,
And [a]have mercy on his *dwelling places;
The city shall be built upon its own [1]mound,
And the palace shall *remain according to its own plan.
19 Then [a]out of them shall proceed *thanksgiving
And the voice of those who make merry;
[b]I will multiply them, and they shall not diminish;
I will also glorify them, and they shall not be small.
20 Their children also shall be [a]as before,
And their *congregation shall be established before Me;
And I will punish all who oppress them.
21 Their nobles shall be from among them,
[a]And their governor shall come from their midst;
Then I will [b]cause him to draw near,
And he shall approach Me;
For who *is* this who pledged his heart to approach Me?' says the LORD.
22 'You shall be [a]My people,
And I will be your God.' "

23 Behold, the [a]whirlwind of the LORD
Goes forth with fury,
A [1]continuing whirlwind;
It will fall violently on the head of the wicked.
24 The fierce anger of the LORD will not return until He has done it,
And until He has performed the intents of His heart.

[a]In the latter days you will consider it.

16 [a]Ex. 23:22; Is. 41:11; Jer. 10:25 [b]Is. 14:2; Joel 3:8 [c]Is. 33:1; Ezek. 39:10 [d]Jer. 2:3
17 [a]Ex. 15:26; Ps. 107:20; Is. 30:26; Jer. 33:6
18 [a]Ps. 102:13 [1]*ruins* *See WW at Is. 32:18. • See WW at Lam. 5:19.
19 [a]Ps. 126:1, 2; Is. 51:11; Jer. 31:4; Zeph. 3:14 [b]Is. 49:19–21; Jer. 23:3; 33:22; Zech. 10:8 *See WW at Ps. 95:2.
20 [a]Is. 1:26 *See WW at Josh. 22:17.
21 [a]Gen. 49:10 [b]Num. 16:5; Ps. 65:4
22 [a]Ex. 6:7; Jer. 32:38; Ezek. 36:28; Hos. 2:23; Zech. 13:9
23 [a]Jer. 23:19, 20; 25:32 [1]Or *sweeping*
24 [a]Gen. 49:1

CHAPTER 31

1 [a]Jer. 30:24 [b]Jer. 30:22 *See WW at Gen. 12:3.
2 [a]Ex. 33:14; Num. 10:33; Deut. 1:33; Josh. 1:13; Ps. 95:11; Is. 63:14
3 [a]Deut. 4:37; 7:8; Mal. 1:2 [b]Is. 43:4; Rom. 11:28 [c]Hos. 11:4 [1]Lit. *from afar* *See WW at Ps. 97:10.
4 [a]Jer. 33:7

The Remnant of Israel Saved

31 "At [a]the same time," says the LORD, [b]"I will be the God of all the *families of Israel, and they shall be My people."
2 Thus says the LORD:

"The people who survived the sword
Found grace in the wilderness—
Israel, when [a]I went to give him rest."

3 The LORD has appeared [1]of old to me, *saying:*
"Yes, [a]I have *loved you with [b]an everlasting love;
Therefore with lovingkindness I have [c]drawn you.
4 Again [a]I will build you, and you shall be rebuilt,

30:18 Its own mound: Cities were frequently rebuilt on the ruins of previous sites and thus formed the typical flat-topped hills called "tells." The tell was a man-made mound built up by the accumulation of the debris of many successive layers of occupation.

30:21 Governor shall come from their midst: The reference is first of all to the Jewish rulers immediately after the Exile, but the Targum reads "Messiah," and so it is ultimately Jesus Christ who fulfills this *promise. He combined in Himself the* dual roles of Priest and King, and in this capacity has the legitimate right to approach God. For an unauthorized person to approach God meant death (see Ex. 19:21).

31:1–40 Restoration continues with messages directed to **all God's people** (v. 1): the northern kingdom, now restored (vv. 2–22); the southern kingdom, now restored (vv. 23–26); and the combined nations of Israel and Judah (vv. 27–40). See note on 30:1—33:26.

31:1 All the families of Israel: The 12 tribes; emphasizes the inclusiveness of the term "Israel."

31:2–6 Using vocabulary from the Exodus account (**found grace,** Ex. 33:12–17) and the concept of release from bondage, Jeremiah speaks of the return as a new exodus (see 23:7, 8). The people will be restored to their land (vv. 4, 5) and will again make pilgrimages to Zion (v. 6).

31:2 The people who survived the sword: The righteous remnant (see v. 7 and note on 6:9) who will return from exile.

31:3 Lovingkindness: See note on 2:2.

O virgin of Israel!
You shall again be adorned with your [b]tambourines,
And shall go forth in the dances of those who rejoice.
5 [a]You shall yet plant vines on the mountains of Samaria;
The planters shall plant and [1]eat *them* as ordinary food.
6 For there shall be a day
When the watchmen will cry on Mount Ephraim,
[a]'Arise, and let us go up *to* Zion,
To the LORD our God.' "

7 For thus says the LORD:

[a]"Sing with gladness for Jacob,
And shout among the chief of the nations;
Proclaim, give praise, and say,
'O LORD, save Your people,
The remnant of Israel!'
8 Behold, I will bring them
[a]from the north country,
And [b]gather them from the ends of the earth,
Among them the blind and the lame,
The woman with child
And the one who labors with child, together;
A great throng shall return there.
9 [a]They shall come with weeping,
And with supplications I will lead them.
I will cause them to walk
[b]by the rivers of waters,
In a *straight way in which they shall not stumble;
For I am a *Father to Israel,
And Ephraim *is* My [c]firstborn.

10 "Hear the word of the LORD, O nations,
And declare *it* in the [1]isles afar off, and say,
'He who scattered Israel [a]will gather him,
And keep him as a shepherd *does* his flock.'
11 For [a]the LORD has redeemed Jacob,
And ransomed him [b]from the hand of one stronger than he.
12 Therefore they shall come and sing in [a]the height of Zion,
Streaming to [b]the goodness of the LORD—
For wheat and new wine and oil,
For the young of the flock and the herd;
Their souls shall be like a [c]well-watered garden,
[d]And they shall sorrow no more at all.

13 "Then shall the virgin rejoice in the dance,
And the young men and the old, together;
For I will turn their mourning to joy,
Will *comfort them,
And make them rejoice rather than sorrow.
14 I will [1]satiate the soul of the priests with abundance,
And My people shall be *satisfied with My goodness, says the LORD."

Mercy on Ephraim

15 Thus says the LORD:

[a]"A voice was heard in [b]Ramah,
Lamentation *and* bitter [c]weeping,
Rachel weeping for her children,
Refusing to be comforted for her children,
Because [d]they *are* no more."

16 Thus says the LORD:

"Refrain your voice from [a]weeping,
And your eyes from tears;
For your work shall be rewarded, says the LORD,
And they shall come back from the land of the enemy.
17 There is [a]hope* in your future, says the LORD,
That *your* children shall come back to their own border.

18 "I have surely heard Ephraim bemoaning himself:

4 [b]Ex. 15:20; Judg. 11:34; Ps. 149:3
5 [a]Ps. 107:37; Is. 65:21; Ezek. 28:26; Amos 9:14 [1]Lit. *treat them as common*
6 [a][Is. 2:3; Jer. 31:12; 50:4, 5; Mic. 4:2]
7 [a]Is. 12:5, 6
8 [a]Jer. 3:12, 18; 23:8 [b]Deut. 30:4; Is. 43:6; Ezek. 20:34, 41; 34:13
9 [a][Ps. 126:5; Jer. 50:4] [b]Is. 35:8; 43:19; 49:10, 11 [c]Ex. 4:22 *See WW at Prov. 3:6. • See WW at Ps. 68:5.
10 [a]Is. 40:11; Ezek. 34:12–14 [1]Or *coastlands*
11 [a]Is. 44:23; 48:20; Jer. 15:21; 50:19 [b]Is. 49:24
12 [a]Ezek. 17:23 [b]Hos. 3:5 [c]Is. 58:11 [d]Is. 35:10; 65:19; [John 16:22; Rev. 21:4]
13 *See WW at Ps. 23:4.
14 [1]Fill to the full *See WW at Amos 4:8.
15 [a]Matt. 2:17, 18 [b]Josh. 18:25; Judg. 4:5; Is. 10:29; Jer. 40:1 [c]Gen. 37:35 [d]Jer. 10:20
16 [a][Is. 25:8; 30:19]
17 [a]Jer. 29:11 *See WW at Hos. 2:15.

31:6 Let us go up *to* Zion: From the time of Jeroboam the people in the northern kingdom worshiped at rival shrines; now they will return to the one place God set His name.

31:15–22 Rachel, mother of Joseph and Benjamin (see Gen. 30:22–24; 35:16–20), laments for her children (the northern tribes who are going into exile, 722 B.C.). V. 15 is quoted in Matt. 2:18 to express grief over the slaughter of innocent babies, but here it introduces the hope of restoration and joy.

31:18–21 The first step in repentance for **Ephraim** (a synonym for Israel) is confession and a **turning** to God (see 3:22–25; Hos. 6:1–3). To prevent a return to the old ways, Ephraim is encouraged to **set up signposts** (31:21) and remember the way that led to punishment.

'You have [a]chastised me, and I
was chastised,
Like an untrained bull;
[b]Restore me, and I will return,
For You *are* the LORD my God.
19 Surely, [a]after my turning, I
repented;
And after I was instructed, I
struck myself on the thigh;
I was [b]ashamed, yes, even
humiliated,
Because I bore the reproach of my
youth.'
20 *Is* Ephraim My dear son?
Is he a pleasant child?
For though I spoke against him,
I earnestly remember him still;
[a]Therefore My [1]heart yearns for
him;
[b]I will surely have mercy on him,
says the LORD.

21 "Set up signposts,
Make landmarks;
[a]Set your heart toward the
highway,
The way in *which* you went.
[1]Turn back, O virgin of Israel,
Turn back to these your cities.
22 How long will you [a]gad about,
O you [b]backsliding daughter?
For the LORD has *created a new
thing in the earth—
A woman shall encompass a
man."

WORD WEALTH

31:22 man, *geber* (*geh*-vehr); Strong's #1397: A champion, hero, warrior, mighty man; a man in all his strength. *Geber* is one of the four outstanding words for "man" in the OT. This word describes a man of strength or bravery, and is derived from the verb *gabar,* "to be strong." An intensive form of *geber* is *gibbor,* meaning "champion" or "mighty man of valor," as in Judg. 6:12. The word also appears in the phrase *'El Gibbor* ("the Mighty God"), which might be translated "God the Champion"; this title appears in Is. 9:6 in reference to the Messiah.

18 [a]Job 5:17; Ps. 94:12 [b]Ps. 80:3, 7, 19; Jer. 17:4; Lam. 5:21; [Acts 3:26] **19** [a]Deut. 30:2 [b]Ezek. 36:31; [Zech. 12:10] **20** [a]Gen. 43:30; Deut. 32:36; Judg. 10:16; Is. 63:15; Hos. 11:8 [b]Is. 57:18; Jer. 3:12; 12:15; [Hos. 14:4]; Mic. 7:18 [1]Lit. *inward parts* **21** [a]Jer. 50:5 [1]Or *Return* **22** [a]Jer. 2:18, 23, 36 [b]Jer. 3:6, 8, 11, 12, 14, 22 *See WW at Gen. 1:1.

23 [a]Ps. 122:5–8; Is. 1:26 [b][Zech. 8:3] **24** [a]Jer. 33:12 **25** [1]*fully satisfied* **26** [a]Prov. 3:24 **27** [a]Ezek. 36:9–11; Hos. 2:23 **28** [a]Jer. 44:27; Dan. 9:14 [b]Jer. 1:10; 18:7 [c]Jer. 24:6 *See WW at Jer. 1:12. **29** [a]Lam. 5:7; Ezek. 18:2, 3 **30** [a]Deut. 24:16; 2 Chr. 25:4; Is. 3:11; [Ezek. 18:4, 20; Gal. 6:5, 7] **31** [a]Jer. 32:40; 33:14; Ezek. 37:26; Heb. 8:8–12; 10:16, 17 *See WW at Gen. 17:7.

Future Prosperity of Judah

23 Thus says the LORD of hosts, the
God of Israel: "They shall again use
this speech in the land of Judah and
in its cities, when I bring back their
captivity: [a]'The LORD bless you, O
home of justice, *and* [b]mountain of holiness!'
24 "And there shall dwell in Judah itself, and [a]in all its cities together, farmers and those going out with flocks.
25 "For I have [1]satiated the weary soul,
and I have replenished every sorrowful
soul."
26 After this I awoke and looked
around, and my sleep was [a]sweet to
me.
27 "Behold, the days are coming, says
the LORD, that [a]I will sow the house of
Israel and the house of Judah with the
seed of man and the seed of beast.
28 "And it shall come to pass, *that* as
I have [a]watched* over them [b]to pluck
up, to break down, to throw down, to
destroy, and to afflict, so I will watch
over them [c]to build and to plant, says
the LORD.
29 [a]"In those days they shall say no
more:

'The fathers have eaten sour
grapes,
And the children's teeth are set
on edge.'

30 [a]"But every one shall die for his
own iniquity; every man who eats the
sour grapes, his teeth shall be set on
edge.

A New Covenant

31 "Behold, the [a]days are coming, says
the LORD, when I will make a new *cov-

31:22 A woman shall encompass a man: Perhaps the idea that the woman shall protect the man, a reversal of the usual (see Is. 11:6–9). The meaning is unclear.
31:23–40 Restoration will include normalization of life, a return to the days of prosperity and peace, but also a new covenant that will enable the people to serve God in spirit and in truth.
31:26 I awoke: Jeremiah had apparently been asleep and received this message (30:3—31:25) in a dream. See note on 23:23–32.
31:28 To pluck up: See note on 1:10.
31:29, 30 Individual responsibility is stressed by the quotation of an old proverb repeated in Ezek. 18:2. Apparently people had misinterpreted the intent of some Scriptures (Ex. 20:5; Num. 14:18), so that they excused their own sinful behavior and blamed God's judgment on their predecessors. Corporate or collective responsibility is an important theme in the OT (Josh. 7:24, 25); but Jeremiah and Ezekiel both stress that the calamity about to fall on Jerusalem is due to the sin of those then living, not on their ancestors.
31:31–34 The heart of Jeremiah's prophecy is the **new covenant** that God will make with His people, forgiving their sins (v. 34), putting His **law in their minds** and writing **it on their hearts** so that all of them will know Him. The passage is quoted in its entirety in the NT (Heb. 8:8–12; 10:16, 17). This is clearly a messianic prophecy referring to the church age.

enant with the house of Israel and with
the house of Judah—
32 "not according to the covenant that
I *made with their fathers in the day
that [a]I took them by the hand to lead
them out of the land of Egypt, My covenant which they broke, [1]though I was
a husband to them, says the LORD.
33 [a]"But this *is* the covenant that I will
make with the house of Israel after
those days, says the LORD: [b]I will put
My law in their minds, and *write it
on their [1]hearts; [c]and I will be their
*God, and they shall be My *people.
3 34 "No more shall every man teach his
neighbor, and every man his brother,
saying, *'Know the LORD,' for [a]they all
shall know Me, from the least of them
to the greatest of them, says the LORD.
For [b]I will *forgive their iniquity, and
their sin I will remember no more."

35 Thus says the LORD,
[a]Who gives the sun for a light by
day,
The ordinances of the moon and
the stars for a light by night,
Who disturbs [b]the sea,
And its waves roar
[c](The LORD of hosts *is* His name):

36 "If [a]those ordinances depart
From before Me, says the LORD,
Then the seed of Israel shall also
cease
From being a nation before Me
forever."

37 Thus says the LORD:

[a]"If heaven above can be measured,
And the foundations of the earth
searched out beneath,
I will also [b]cast off all the seed
of Israel
For all that they have done, says
the LORD.

38 "Behold, the days are coming, says
the LORD, that the city shall be built
for the LORD [a]from the Tower of Hananel to the Corner Gate.
39 [a]"The surveyor's line shall again
extend straight forward over the hill
Gareb; then it shall turn toward Goath.
40 "And the whole valley of the dead
bodies and of the ashes, and all the
fields as far as the Brook Kidron,
[a]to the corner of the Horse Gate toward
the east, [b]*shall be* holy to the LORD. It
shall not be plucked up or thrown
down anymore forever."

Jeremiah Buys a Field

32 The word that came to Jeremiah
from the LORD [a]in the tenth year
of Zedekiah king of Judah, which was
the eighteenth year of Nebuchadnezzar.
2 For then the king of Babylon's army
besieged Jerusalem, and Jeremiah the
prophet was shut up [a]in the court of
the prison, which *was in* the king of
Judah's house.
3 For Zedekiah king of Judah had
shut him up, saying, "Why do you
[a]prophesy and say, 'Thus says the
LORD: [b]"Behold, I will give this city into
the hand of the king of Babylon, and
he shall take it;
4 "and Zedekiah king of Judah
[a]shall not escape from the hand of the
Chaldeans, but shall surely be delivered into the hand of the king of Babylon, and shall speak with him [1]face
to face, and see him [b]eye to eye;
5 "then he shall [a]lead Zedekiah to
Babylon, and there he shall be [b]until I
visit him," says the LORD; [c]"though you
fight with the Chaldeans, you shall not
succeed" '?"
6 And Jeremiah said, "The word of
the LORD came to me, saying,
7 'Behold, Hanamel the son of Shallum your uncle will come to you, saying, "Buy my field which *is* in Anathoth, for the [a]right of redemption *is*
yours to buy *it*." '
8 "Then Hanamel my uncle's son
came to me in the court of the prison
according to the word of the LORD, and
said to me, 'Please buy my field that
is in Anathoth, which *is* in the country
of Benjamin; for the right of inheritance *is* yours, and the redemption
yours; buy *it* for yourself.' Then I knew
that this was the word of the LORD.

32 [a]Deut. 1:31 [1]So with MT, Tg., Vg.; LXX, Syr. *and I turned away from them* *See WW at Ex. 34:27.
33 [a]Jer. 32:40 [b]Ps. 40:8 [c]Jer. 24:7; 30:22; 32:38 [1]Lit. *inward parts* *See WW at Deut. 31:9. • See WW at 2 Kin. 19:15. • See WW at Ruth 1:16.
34 [a][John 6:45] [b][Rom. 11:27] *See WW at Ex. 3:7. • See WW at Ps. 103:3.
35 [a]Gen. 1:14–18 [b]Is. 51:15 [c]Jer. 10:16
36 [a]Ps. 148:6
37 [a]Jer. 33:22 [b][Rom. 11:2–5, 26, 27]
38 [a]Zech. 14:10
39 [a]Zech. 2:1, 2
40 [a]Neh. 3:28 [b][Joel 3:17]

CHAPTER 32

1 [a]Jer. 39:1, 2
2 [a]Jer. 33:1; 37:21; 39:14
3 [a]Jer. 26:8, 9 [b]Jer. 21:3–7; 34:2
4 [a]Jer. 34:3; 38:18, 23; 39:5; 52:9 [b]Jer. 39:5 [1]Lit. *mouth to mouth*
5 [a]Ezek. 12:12, 13 [b]Jer. 27:22 [c]Jer. 21:4; 33:5
7 [a]Ruth 4:4

31:31 Will make: Literally "cut" (see Gen. 15:10; note on Jer. 34:18). In light of Heb. 8, **the house of Israel . . . Judah** is to a large degree the church. See note on Gal. 6:16.
31:32 I was a husband: See note on 3:14.
31:33 In their minds is to internalize the law, while **on their hearts** gives them an effective control for living.
31:34 See section 3 of Truth-In-Action at the end of Jer.
32:1–44 Jeremiah buys a field in **Anathoth** from his cousin **Hanamel** as a sign that God will restore His people to the land, and fields will again be bought and sold.
32:1 The **tenth** and **eighteenth year** is 587 B.C., while Jerusalem was under siege, but before it was destroyed.
32:2, 3 Jeremiah was imprisoned by Zedekiah (37:21) and remained **shut up in the court of the prison** until Jerusalem fell (38:13, 28; 39:14).
32:3–5 See 21:3–7; 34:2–5; 37:17. For fulfillment see 52:7–14.
32:7 Anathoth: Hometown of Jeremiah (see 1:1). **Right of redemption:** Not only a right but an obligation (see Lev. 25:23–25; Ruth 4:3, 4).

9 "So I bought the field from Hanamel, the son of my uncle who *was* in
Anathoth, and [a]weighed *out to* him the
money—seventeen shekels of silver.
10 "And I signed the [1]deed and sealed
it, took witnesses, and weighed the
money on the scales.
11 "So I took the purchase deed, *both*
that which was sealed *according* to the
law and custom, and that which was
open;
12 "and I gave the purchase deed to
[a]Baruch the son of Neriah, son of Mahseiah, in the presence of Hanamel my
uncle's *son,* and in the presence of the
[b]witnesses who signed the purchase
deed, before all the Jews who sat in
the court of the prison.
13 "Then I charged [a]Baruch before
them, saying,
14 'Thus says the LORD of hosts, the
God of Israel: "Take these deeds, both
this purchase deed which is sealed and
this deed which is open, and put them
in an earthen vessel, that they may last
many days."
15 'For thus says the LORD of hosts, the
God of Israel: "Houses and fields and
vineyards shall be [a]possessed again in
this land." '

Jeremiah Prays for Understanding

16 "Now when I had delivered the purchase deed to Baruch the son of Neriah, I prayed to the LORD, saying:
17 'Ah, Lord GOD! Behold, [a]You have
made the *heavens and the earth by
Your great power and outstretched
arm. [b]There is nothing too [1]hard for
You.
18 '*You* show [a]lovingkindness to thousands, and repay the iniquity of the fathers into the bosom of their children
after them—the Great, [b]the Mighty
God, whose name *is* [c]the LORD of hosts.
19 '*You are* [a]great in counsel and
mighty in [1]work, for Your [b]eyes *are*
open to all the ways of the sons of men,
[c]to give everyone according to his
ways and according to the fruit of his
doings.
20 'You have set signs and wonders in
the land of Egypt, to this day, and in
Israel and among *other* men; and You
have made Yourself [a]a name, as it is
this day.
21 'You [a]have brought Your people Israel out of the land of Egypt with signs
and wonders, with a strong hand and
an outstretched arm, and with great
terror;
22 'You have given them this land, of
which You swore to their fathers to
give them—[a]"a land flowing with milk
and honey."
23 'And they came in and took possession of it, but [a]they have not obeyed
Your voice or walked in Your law.
They have done nothing of all that You
commanded them to do; therefore You
have caused all this calamity to come
upon them.
24 'Look, the siege mounds! They have
come to the city to take it; and the city
has been given into the hand of the
Chaldeans who fight against it, because of [a]the sword and famine and
pestilence. What You have spoken has
happened; there You see *it!*
25 'And You have said to me, O Lord
GOD, "Buy the field for money, and
take witnesses"!—yet the city has
been given into the hand of the Chaldeans.' "

God's Assurance of the People's Return

26 Then the word of the LORD came to
Jeremiah, saying,
27 "Behold, I *am* the LORD, the [a]God
of all *flesh. Is there anything too hard
for Me?
28 "Therefore thus says the LORD: 'Behold, I will give this city into the hand

9 [a]Gen. 23:16; Zech. 11:12
10 [1]Lit. *book*
12 [a]Jer. 36:4 [b]Is. 8:2
13 [a]Jer. 36:4
15 [a]Ezra 2:1; [Jer. 31:5, 12, 14]; Amos 9:14, 15; Zech. 3:10
17 [a]2 Kin. 19:15; Ps. 102:25; Is. 40:26–29; Jer. 27:5 [b]Gen. 18:14; Jer. 32:27; Zech. 8:6; Matt. 19:26; Mark 10:27; Luke 18:27 [1]*difficult* *See WW at 1 Kin. 8:23.
18 [a]Ex. 20:6; 34:7; Deut. 5:9, 10 [b]Ps. 50:1; [Is. 9:6]; Jer. 20:11 [c]Jer. 10:16
19 [a]Is. 28:29 [b]Job 34:21; Ps. 33:13; Prov. 5:21; Jer. 16:17 [c]Ps. 62:12; Jer. 17:10; [Matt. 16:27; John 5:29] [1]*deed*
20 [a]Ex. 9:16; 1 Chr. 17:21; Is. 63:12; Jer. 13:11; Dan. 9:15
21 [a]Ex. 6:6; 2 Sam. 7:23; 1 Chr. 17:21; Ps. 136:11, 12
22 [a]Ex. 3:8, 17; Deut. 1:8; Ps. 105:9–11; Jer. 11:5
23 [a][Neh. 9:26]; Jer. 11:8; [Dan. 9:10–14]
24 [a]Jer. 14:12; Ezek. 14:21
27 [a][Num. 16:22] *See WW at Job 19:26.

32:9–14 One of the most detailed accounts of a business transaction in the Bible. For another, see Gen. 23:1–16.
32:9 Seventeen shekels of silver: About 7 ounces by weight. Coins were not yet common.
32:10 Deed: A copy of the transaction written on papyrus was rolled up and **sealed** to prevent anyone from tampering with it. The **open** copy was readily available for anyone to see.
32:12 Baruch: Jeremiah's scribe and friend (see 36:4; 43:3; 45:1).
32:14 The documents were placed in an **earthen vessel** for preservation. Such deeds have been found at Elephantine in southern Egypt and in the desert area near the Dead Sea.
32:15 This verse contains the basic theme of this chapter, and Jeremiah's deed would give him title to the land when conditions were again normal.
32:16–25 A prayer of Jeremiah expressing God's omnipotence, omniscience, and wonders for Israel, but in view of the present circumstances of siege, asking why he should buy the field at all.
32:17 Outstreteched arm: See note on 6:12. **There is nothing too hard for You:** See Gen. 18:14; Luke 1:34–37.
32:24 Sword and famine and pestilence: See note on 14:12.
32:26–44 In His answer to Jeremiah, God assures the prophet that He is a God for whom nothing is impossible. He then cites the present situation (vv. 26–29), recalls Israel's idolatry from their youth (vv. 30–35), His intention to punish the sinful inhabitants of Jerusalem **by the sword, by the famine, and by the pestilence** (v. 36), and finally promises restoration to the land (vv. 37–44).

of the Chaldeans, into the hand of
Nebuchadnezzar king of Babylon, and
he shall take it.
29 'And the Chaldeans who fight
against this city shall come and
[a]set fire to this city and burn it, with
the houses [b]on whose roofs they have
offered incense to Baal and poured out
drink offerings to other gods, to provoke Me to anger;
30 'because the children of Israel and
the children of Judah [a]have done only
evil before Me from their youth. For
the children of Israel have provoked
Me only to anger with the work of their
hands,' says the LORD.
31 'For this city has been to Me *a prov-*
ocation of My anger and My fury from
the day that they built it, even to this
day; [a]so I will remove it from before
My face
32 'because of all the evil of the children of Israel and the children of Judah, which they have done to provoke
Me to anger—[a]they, their kings, their
princes, their priests, [b]their prophets,
the men of Judah, and the inhabitants
of Jerusalem.
33 'And they have turned to Me the
[a]back, and not the face; though I
taught them, [b]rising up early and
teaching *them*, yet they have not listened to receive instruction.
34 'But they [a]set their abominations in
[1]the house which is called by My name,
to defile it.
35 'And they built the high places of
Baal which *are* in the Valley of the Son
of Hinnom, to [a]cause their sons and
their daughters to pass through *the fire*
to [b]Molech, [c]which I did not command
them, nor did it come into My mind
that they should do this abomination,
to cause Judah to sin.'
36 "Now therefore, thus says the LORD,
the God of Israel, concerning this city
of which you say, 'It shall be delivered
into the hand of the king of Babylon
by the sword, by the famine, and by
the pestilence':
37 'Behold, I will [a]gather them out of
all countries where I have driven them
in My anger, in My fury, and in great
wrath; I will bring them back to this
place, and I will cause them [b]to dwell
*safely.

29 [a]2 Chr. 36:19; Jer. 21:10; 37:8, 10; 52:13 [b]Jer. 19:13
30 [a]Deut. 9:7–12; Is. 63:10; Jer. 2:7; 3:25; 7:22–26; Ezek. 20:28
31 [a]2 Kin. 23:27; 24:3; Jer. 27:10
32 [a]Ezra 9:7; Is. 1:4, 6; Dan. 9:8 [b]Jer. 23:14
33 [a]Jer. 2:27; 7:24 [b]Jer. 7:13
34 [a]2 Kin. 21:1–7; Jer. 7:10–12, 30; 23:11; Ezek. 8:5, 6 [1]The temple
35 [a]2 Chr. 28:2, 3; 33:6; Jer. 7:31; 19:5 [b]Lev. 18:21; 1 Kin. 11:33; 2 Kin. 23:10; Acts 7:43 [c]Jer. 7:31
37 [a]Deut. 30:3; Jer. 23:3; 29:14; 31:10; 50:19; Ezek. 37:21 [b]Jer. 33:16 *See WW at Deut. 33:12.
38 [a][Jer. 24:7; 30:22; 31:33]
39 [a][Jer. 24:7; Ezek. 11:19] *See WW at Deut. 6:4.
40 [a]Is. 55:3; Jer. 31:31; Ezek. 37:26 [b]Deut. 31:6, 8; [Ezek. 39:29; Jer. 31:33]
41 [a]Deut. 30:9; Is. 62:5; 65:19; Zeph. 3:17 [b]Jer. 24:6; 31:28; Amos 9:15 [1]*truly*
42 [a]Jer. 31:28; Zech. 8:14, 15
43 [a]Jer. 33:10
44 [a]Jer. 17:26 [b]Jer. 33:7, 11 [1]Heb. *shephelah* [2]Heb. *Negev*

CHAPTER 33

1 [a]Jer. 32:2, 3
2 [a]Is. 37:26 [b]Ex. 15:3; [Jer. 10:16]; Amos 5:8; 9:6 [1]Heb. *YHWH*
3 [a]Ps. 91:15; [Is. 55:6, 7]; Jer. 29:12 [1]*inaccessible*

38 'They shall be [a]My people, and I
will be their God;
39 'then I will [a]give them *one heart
and one way, that they may fear Me
forever, for the good of them and their
children after them.
40 'And [a]I will make an everlasting
covenant with them, that I will not turn
away from doing them good; but
[b]I will put My fear in their hearts so
that they will not depart from Me.
41 'Yes, [a]I will rejoice over them to do
them good, and [b]I will [1]assuredly plant
them in this land, with all My heart and
with all My soul.'
42 "For thus says the LORD: [a]'Just as I
have brought all this great calamity on
this people, so I will bring on them all
the good that I have promised them.
43 'And fields will be bought in this
land [a]of which you say, "*It is* desolate,
without man or beast; it has been given
into the hand of the Chaldeans."
44 'Men will buy fields for money, sign
deeds and seal *them*, and take witnesses, in [a]the land of Benjamin, in the
places around Jerusalem, in the cities
of Judah, in the cities of the mountains,
in the cities of the [1]lowland, and in the
cities of the [2]South; for [b]I will cause
their captives to return,' says the
LORD."

Excellence of the Restored Nation

33 Moreover the word of the LORD
came to Jeremiah a second
time, while he was still [a]shut up in the
court of the prison, saying,
2 "Thus says the LORD [a]who made it,
the LORD who formed it to establish it
[b](the[1] LORD *is* His name):
3 [a]'**Call** to Me, and I will answer you,
and show you great and [1]mighty
things, which you do not know.'

WORD WEALTH

33:3 call, *qara'* (kah-*rah*); Strong's #7121: To call out to someone; cry out; to address someone; to shout, or speak out, to proclaim. *Qara'* often describes calling out loudly in an attempt to get someone's attention (Is. 58:1), or for calling upon the Lord or upon His name.

(*cont. on next page*)

32:33 Rising up early: See note on 7:13.
32:35 Molech was the god of the Ammonites. See 49:1, 3 where the text translates "Milcom"; Lev. 18:21; 20:2–5.
32:43, 44 The gesture of Jeremiah in buying his cousin's field was symbolic of normal conditions that would prevail after the Exile when **fields will be bought** (see v. 15; 33:10, 12).
33:1–26 Two additional sayings are joined to the book of consolation. Vv. 1–13 are linked by the opening phrase (see 32:2) and further develop the theme of 32:15. The final section (vv. 14–26) is a commentary on 23:5, 6.
33:3 The positive assurance from God is that if we will **call** on Him, He **will answer** us in ways that will astound us. See Ps. 4:3; 18:6; Matt. 7:7.

(cont. from preceding page)
(See Is. 55:6; Joel 2:32). Sometimes *qara'* means "to name something," that is, to call it by its name, as God did when He called the light Day and the darkness Night (Gen. 1:5). Similarly, *qara'* involves the naming of places, holidays, or children; for example, Leah praised the Lord for the birth of her son, and "called his name Judah" (Gen. 29:35). Compare Gen. 21:31; Esth. 9:26. *Qara'* appears more than 700 times in the Bible.

KINGDOM DYNAMICS

33:3 Divine Revelation and Spiritual Warfare, FAITH'S WARFARE. God promised Jeremiah that if he would call to Him, not only would He answer him, but He would reveal to him "great and mighty things" that could not otherwise be known. The word "mighty" (Hebrew *batsar*) is better rendered "isolated" or "inaccessible." The suggestion is that God would give Jeremiah "revelational insight," revealing things that otherwise would be inaccessible or isolated.

Such "revelational insight" always has been essential for a clear understanding of victorious spiritual warfare. One cannot pray effectively without insight into how to pray, as well as into what things God truly longs for us to seek after in prayer.

(2 Kin. 6:8–17/Prov. 3:5, 6) D.E.

4 "For thus says the LORD, the God
of Israel, concerning the houses of this
city and the houses of the kings of Judah, which have been pulled down *to*
fortify against [a]the siege mounds and
the sword:
5 'They come to fight with the Chaldeans, but *only* to [a]fill their places with
the dead bodies of men whom I will
slay in My anger and My fury, all for
whose wickedness I have hidden My
face from this city.
6 'Behold, [a]I will bring it health and
*healing; I will heal them and *reveal
to them the abundance of peace and
truth.
7 'And [a]I will cause the captives of
Judah and the captives of Israel to return, and will rebuild those places
[b]as at the first.
8 'I will [a]cleanse them from all their
iniquity by which they have sinned
against Me, and I will pardon all their
iniquities by which they have sinned
and by which they have transgressed
against Me.
9 [a]'Then it shall be to Me a name of
joy, a praise, and an honor before all
nations of the earth, who shall hear all
the good that I do to them; they shall
[b]fear* and tremble for all the goodness
and all the prosperity that I provide for
it.'
10 "Thus says the LORD: 'Again there
shall be heard in this place—[a]of which
you say, "It *is* desolate, without man
and without beast"—in the cities of Judah, in the streets of Jerusalem that are
desolate, without man and without inhabitant and without beast,
11 'the [a]voice of joy and the voice of
gladness, the voice of the bridegroom
and the voice of the bride, the voice
of those who will say:

[b]"Praise* the LORD of hosts,
For the LORD *is* good,
For His *mercy *endures*
*forever"—

and of those *who will* bring [c]the sacrifice of praise into the house of the
LORD. For I will cause the captives of
the land to return as at the first,' says
the LORD.
12 "Thus says the LORD of hosts:
[a]'In this place which is desolate, without man and without beast, and in all
its cities, there shall again be a dwelling place of shepherds causing *their*
flocks to lie down.
13 [a]'In the cities of the mountains, in
the cities of the lowland, in the cities
of the South, in the land of Benjamin, in the places around Jerusalem,
and in the cities of Judah, the flocks
shall again [b]pass under the hands
of him who counts *them*,' says the
LORD.
14 [a]'Behold, the days are coming,' says
the LORD, 'that [b]I will perform that
good thing which I have promised to
the house of Israel and to the house
of Judah:

4 [a]Is. 22:10; Jer. 32:24; Ezek. 4:2; 21:22; Hab. 1:10
5 [a]2 Kin. 23:14; Jer. 21:4–7; 32:5
6 [a]Jer. 30:17; Hos. 6:1 *See WW at Mal. 4:2. • See WW at Amos 3:7.
7 [a]Ps. 85:1; Jer. 30:3; 32:44; Amos 9:14 [b]Is. 1:26; Jer. 24:6; 30:20; 31:4, 28; 42:10; Amos 9:14, 15
8 [a]Ps. 51:2; Is. 44:22; Jer. 50:20; Ezek. 36:25, 33; Mic. 7:18, 19; Zech. 13:1; [Heb. 9:11–14]
9 [a]Is. 62:7; Jer. 13:11 [b]Is. 60:5 *See WW at Hos. 3:5.
10 [a]Jer. 32:43
11 [a]Jer. 7:34; 16:9; 25:10; Rev. 18:23 [b]1 Chr. 16:8; 2 Chr. 5:13; Ezra 3:11; Ps. 136:1; Is. 12:4 [c]Lev. 7:12; Ps. 107:22; 116:17; Heb. 13:15 *See WW at 1 Chr. 16:7. • See WW at Mic. 6:8. • See WW at Ps. 136:1.
12 [a]Is. 65:10; [Jer. 31:24; 50:19; Ezek. 34:12–15; Zeph. 2:6, 7]
13 [a]Jer. 17:26; 32:44 [b]Lev. 27:32; [Luke 15:4]
14 [a]Jer. 23:5; 31:27, 31 [b]Is. 32:1; Jer. 29:10; 32:42; Ezek. 34:23–25; Hag. 2:6–9

33:4 The **houses** of the people and king were often demolished to secure material for strengthening the walls of the city or to allow easier troop movement within the city. **Siege mounds** were built by the enemy to bring instruments of war up to the city's walls.

33:6–13 After punishment and repentance will come **healing** (see 3:22; 30:17), the captives will **return** (v. 7) and be cleansed of sin (v. 8), and the city will be **a name of joy, a praise, and an honor before all nations**. See note on 30:1—33:26.

33:11 The reversal of previous statements of judgment (see 7:34; 16:9; 25:10).

33:14–26 The words of 23:5, 6 are repeated with slight variation in vv. 15, 16, and enlarged upon in vv. 17, 18 to include the covenant with Levi as well. Having introduced the subject of the covenant, God illustrates the permanence of His covenant with David and Levi.

15 'In those days and at that time
I will cause to grow up to David
A [a]Branch of righteousness;
He shall execute judgment and
righteousness in the earth.
16 In those days Judah will be
*saved,
And Jerusalem will dwell safely.
And this *is the name* by which she
will be called:

[1]THE LORD OUR
RIGHTEOUSNESS.'

17 "For thus says the LORD: 'David
shall never [a]lack a man to sit on the
throne of the house of Israel;
18 'nor shall the [a]priests, the Levites,
lack a man to [b]offer burnt offerings before Me, to [1]kindle grain offerings, and
to sacrifice continually.' "

The Permanence of God's Covenant

19 And the word of the LORD came to
Jeremiah, saying,
20 "Thus says the LORD: 'If you can
break My covenant with the day and
My covenant with the night, so that
there will not be day and night in their
season,
21 'then [a]My covenant may also be
broken with David My servant, so that
he shall not have a son to reign on his
throne, and with the Levites, the
priests, My *ministers.
22 'As [a]the host of heaven cannot be
numbered, nor the sand of the sea measured, so will I [b]multiply the descendants of David My servant and the
[c]Levites who minister to Me.' "
23 Moreover the word of the LORD
came to Jeremiah, saying,
24 "Have you not considered what
these people have spoken, saying, 'The
two families which the LORD has chosen, He has also cast them off'? Thus
they have [a]despised My people, as if
they should no more be a nation before
them.
25 "Thus says the LORD: 'If [a]My cov-

15 [a]Is. 4:2; 11:1; Jer. 23:5; Zech. 3:8; 6:12, 13
16 [1]Heb. *YHWH Tsidkenu;* cf. Jer. 23:5, 6
*See WW at Jer. 17:14.
17 [a]2 Sam. 7:16; 1 Kin. 2:4; Ps. 89:29; [Luke 1:32]
18 [a]Num. 3:5–10; Deut. 18:1; 24:8; Josh. 3:3; Ezek. 44:15 [b][Rom. 12:1; 15:16; 1 Pet. 2:5, 9; Rev. 1:6] [1]*burn*
21 [a]2 Sam. 23:5; 2 Chr. 7:18; 21:7; Ps. 89:34
*See WW at 1 Chr. 15:2.
22 [a]Gen. 15:5; 22:17; Jer. 31:37 [b]Jer. 30:19; Ezek. 36:10, 11 [c]Is. 66:21; Jer. 33:18
24 [a]Neh. 4:2–4; Esth. 3:6–8; Ps. 44:13, 14; 83:4; Ezek. 36:2
25 [a]Gen. 8:22; Jer. 33:20 [b]Ps. 74:16; 104:19
26 [a]Jer. 31:37 [b]Rom. 11:1, 2

CHAPTER 34

1 [a]2 Kin. 25:1; Jer. 32:1, 2; 39:1; 52:4 [b]Jer. 1:15; 25:9; Dan. 2:37, 38
2 [a]2 Chr. 36:11, 12; Jer. 22:1, 2; 37:1, 2 [b]2 Kin. 25:9; Jer. 21:10; 32:3, 28
3 [a]2 Kin. 25:4, 5; Jer. 21:7; 52:7–11 [b]2 Kin. 25:6, 7; Jer. 32:4; 39:5, 6 [1]Lit. *mouth to mouth*
5 [a]2 Chr. 16:14; 21:19 [b]Dan. 2:46 [c]Jer. 22:18
7 [a]2 Kin. 18:13; 19:8; 2 Chr. 11:5, 9

enant *is* not with day and night, *and if*
I have not [b]appointed the ordinances
of heaven and earth,
26 [a]'then I will [b]cast away the descendants of Jacob and David My servant,
so that I will not take *any* of his descendants *to be* rulers over the descendants
of Abraham, Isaac, and Jacob. For I
will cause their captives to return, and
will have mercy on them.' "

Zedekiah Warned by God

34 The word which came to Jeremiah from the LORD, [a]when
Nebuchadnezzar king of Babylon and
all his army, [b]all the kingdoms of the
earth under his dominion, and all the
people, fought against Jerusalem and
all its cities, saying,
2 "Thus says the LORD, the God of Israel: 'Go and [a]speak to Zedekiah king
of Judah and tell him, "Thus says the
LORD: 'Behold, [b]I will give this city into
the hand of the king of Babylon, and
he shall burn it with fire.
3 'And [a]you shall not escape from his
hand, but shall surely be taken and delivered into his hand; your eyes shall
see the eyes of the king of Babylon,
he shall speak with you [b]face[1] to face,
and you shall go to Babylon.' " '
4 "Yet hear the word of the LORD, O
Zedekiah king of Judah! Thus says the
LORD concerning you: 'You shall not
die by the sword.
5 'You shall die in peace; as in
[a]the ceremonies of your fathers, the
former kings who were before you,
[b]so they shall burn incense for you and
[c]lament for you, *saying,* "Alas, lord!"
For I have pronounced the word, says
the LORD.' "
6 Then Jeremiah the prophet spoke
all these words to Zedekiah king of Judah in Jerusalem,
7 when the king of Babylon's army
fought against Jerusalem and all the
cities of Judah that were left, against
Lachish and Azekah; for *only* [a]these

33:17 David shall never lack a man indicates the permanence of the Davidic dynasty. Though there may not always be someone ruling on the throne of Judah, his line will continue and eventually exercise permanent and enduring sovereignty. The angel Gabriel made it clear to Mary that Jesus was the fulfillment of this covenant (Luke 1:32).

33:20 My covenant with the day: See v. 25; Gen. 1:14–18; 8:22.

34:1—35:19 This historical appendix brings to a close the first major division of the book (chs. 2—35).

34:1–7 While the city of Jerusalem was under siege (588 B.C.) and most of the fortified cities of Judah had fallen, **Zedekiah** is assured that he will be captured by the Babylonians but will have a peaceful death and proper funeral rites. A darker picture is given in 21:1–10, and the treatment of Zedekiah is described in 52:8–11.

34:1 The kingdom of **Nebuchadnezzar** was extensive, and he controlled an army made up of many nations (Ezek. 26:7).

34:3 Face to face: Fulfilled in 39:4–7.

34:7 Lachish and **Azekah** were both fortified by Rehoboam, son of Solomon. Lachish, 44 kilometers (27 miles) southwest of Jerusalem, was destroyed by Sennacherib in 701 B.C., and was now under siege by Nebuchadnezzar. An ostracon, dating to this period and found at the site, mentions both Lachish and Azekah. Azekah is situated 17 kilometers (10½ miles) northwest of Lachish and about 29 kilometers (18½ miles) west of Jerusalem.

fortified cities remained of the cities of Judah.

Treacherous Treatment of Slaves

8 *This is* the word that came to Jeremiah from the LORD, after King Zedekiah had made a covenant with all the people who *were* at Jerusalem to proclaim [a]liberty* to them:
9 [a]that every man should set free his male and female slave—a Hebrew man or woman—[b]that no one should keep a Jewish brother in bondage.
10 Now when all the princes and all the people, who had entered into the covenant, heard that everyone should set free his male and female slaves, that no one should keep them in bondage anymore, they obeyed and let *them* go.
11 But afterward they changed their minds and made the male and female slaves return, whom they had set free, and brought them into subjection as male and female slaves.
12 Therefore the word of the LORD came to Jeremiah from the LORD, saying,
13 "Thus says the LORD, the God of Israel: 'I made a [a]covenant with your fathers in the day that I brought them out of the land of Egypt, out of the house of bondage, saying,
14 "At the end of [a]seven years let every man set free his Hebrew brother, who [1]has been sold to him; and when he has served you six years, you shall let him go free from you." But your fathers did not obey Me nor incline their ear.
15 'Then you [1]recently turned and did what was right in My sight—every man proclaiming liberty to his neighbor; and you [a]made a covenant before Me [b]in the house which is called by My name.
16 'Then you turned around and [a]profaned My name, and every one of you brought back his male and female slaves, whom you had set at liberty, at their pleasure, and brought them back into subjection, to be your male and female slaves.'
17 "Therefore thus says the LORD: 'You have not obeyed Me in proclaiming liberty, every one to his brother and every one to his neighbor. [a]Behold, I proclaim liberty to you,' says the LORD—[b]'to the sword, to pestilence, and to famine! And I will deliver you to [c]trouble among all the kingdoms of the earth.
18 'And I will give the men who have transgressed My covenant, who have not performed the words of the covenant which they made before Me, when [a]they cut the calf in two and passed between the parts of it—
19 'the princes of Judah, the princes of Jerusalem, the [1]eunuchs, the priests, and all the people of the land who passed between the parts of the calf—
20 'I will [a]give them into the hand of their enemies and into the hand of those who seek their life. Their [b]dead bodies shall be for meat for the birds of the heaven and the beasts of the earth.
21 'And I will give Zedekiah king of Judah and his princes into the hand of their enemies, into the hand of those who seek their life, and into the hand of the king of Babylon's army [a]which has gone back from you.
22 [a]'Behold, I will command,' says the LORD, 'and cause them to return to this city. They will fight against it [b]and take it and burn it with fire; and [c]I will make the cities of Judah a desolation without inhabitant.' "

The Obedient Rechabites

35 The word which came to Jeremiah from the LORD in the days of Jehoiakim the son of Josiah, king of Judah, saying,

8 [a]Ex. 21:2; Lev. 25:10; Neh. 5:1–13; Is. 58:6; Jer. 34:14, 17 *See WW at Lev. 25:10.
9 [a]Neh. 5:11 [b]Lev. 25:39–46
13 [a]Ex. 24:3, 7, 8; Deut. 5:2, 3, 27; Jer. 31:32
14 [a]Ex. 21:2; 23:10; Deut. 15:12; 1 Kin. 9:22 [1]Or *sold himself*
15 [a]2 Kin. 23:3; Neh. 10:29 [b]Jer. 7:10 [1]Lit. *today*
16 [a]Ex. 20:7; Lev. 19:12
17 [a]Lev. 26:34, 35; Esth. 7:10; Dan. 6:24; [Matt. 7:2; Gal. 6:7]; James 2:13 [b]Jer. 32:24, 36 [c]Deut. 28:25, 64; Jer. 29:18
18 [a]Gen. 15:10, 17
19 [1]Or *officers*
20 [a]2 Kin. 25:19–21; Jer. 22:25 [b]Deut. 28:26; 1 Sam. 17:44, 46; 1 Kin. 14:11; 16:4; Ps. 79:2; Jer. 7:33; 16:4; 19:7
21 [a]Jer. 37:5–11; 39:4–7
22 [a]Jer. 37:8, 10 [b]Jer. 38:3; 39:1, 2, 8; 52:7, 13 [c]Jer. 9:11; 44:2, 6

34:8–22 Presumably the dire situation of the city under siege led to a searching of heart by the people, and many concluded that they had not acted properly toward their Hebrew slaves. The slaves were freed, but later when conditions improved (perhaps the temporary withdrawal of the Babylonian forces to face the Egyptian army, see 37:5), many changed their minds and took back their slaves.
34:8 Proclaim liberty: See Lev. 25:10 and note on Lev. 25:1–55.
34:9 Male and female slave: A Hebrew should be freed after six years of labor (Ex. 21:2–11).
34:18 Cut the calf in two and passed between the parts of it: The words **make** and **cut** come from the same root. To "make a covenant" often involved an oath that called down curses on the person if he failed to keep the covenant (see Gen. 31:44–53; Ruth 1:17; 1 Sam. 25:22) and that was symbolized by cutting an animal in two and walking between the halves (see Gen. 15:10, 17).
34:21 Which has gone back from you: The temporary withdrawal of the Babylonian forces to confront the Egyptian army (see 37:5).
35:1–9 The Rechabites were a nomadic religious order founded by Jonadab son of Rechab during the ninth century B.C. (see 2 Kin. 10:15, 23). They refrained from living in houses or using any product from the grapevine. For 250 years they had maintained the life-style imposed upon them by their founder. After Jeremiah invites the Rechabites to drink wine and they refuse (vv. 1–11), he addresses the people and contrasts their disobedience to God's commands with the Rechabites' faithfulness to the commands of their

2 "Go to the house of the [a]Rechabites,
speak to them, and bring them into the
house of the LORD, into one of [b]the
chambers, and give them wine to
drink."
3 Then I took Jaazaniah the son of
Jeremiah, the son of Habazziniah, his
brothers and all his sons, and the
whole house of the Rechabites,
4 and I brought them into the house
of the LORD, into the chamber of the
sons of Hanan the son of Igdaliah, a
man of God, which *was* by the chamber of the princes, above the chamber
of Maaseiah the son of Shallum,
[a]the keeper of the [1]door.
5 Then I set before the sons of the
house of the Rechabites bowls full of
wine, and cups; and I said to them,
"Drink wine."
6 But they said, "We will drink no
wine, for [a]Jonadab the son of Rechab,
our father, commanded us, saying,
'You shall drink [b]no wine, you nor
your sons, forever.
7 'You shall not build a house, sow
seed, plant a vineyard, nor have *any
of these;* but all your days you shall
dwell in tents, [a]that you may live many
days in the land where you are sojourners.'
8 "Thus we have [a]obeyed the voice
of Jonadab the son of Rechab, our father, in all that he charged us, to drink
no wine all our days, we, our wives,
our sons, or our daughters,
9 "nor to build ourselves houses to
dwell in; nor do we have vineyard,
field, or seed.
10 "But we have dwelt in tents, and
have obeyed and done according to all
that Jonadab our father commanded
us.
11 "But it came to pass, when Nebuchadnezzar king of Babylon came up
into the land, that we said, 'Come, let
us [a]go to Jerusalem for fear of the
army of the Chaldeans and for fear of
the army of the Syrians.' So we dwell
at Jerusalem."
12 Then came the word of the LORD to
Jeremiah, saying,
13 "Thus says the LORD of hosts, the
God of Israel: 'Go and tell the men of
Judah and the inhabitants of Jerusalem, "Will you not [a]receive *instruction to [1]obey My words?" says the
LORD.
14 "The words of Jonadab the son of
Rechab, which he commanded his
sons, not to drink wine, are performed;
for to this day they drink none, and
obey their father's commandment.
[a]But although I have spoken to you,
[b]rising early and speaking, you did not
[1]obey Me.
15 "I have also sent to you all My
[a]servants the prophets, rising up early
and sending *them,* saying, [b]'Turn now
everyone from his evil way, amend
your doings, and do not go after other
gods to serve them; then you will
[c]dwell in the land which I have given
you and your fathers.' But you have
not inclined your ear, nor obeyed
Me.
16 "Surely the sons of Jonadab the son
of Rechab have performed the commandment of their [a]father, which he
commanded them, but this people has
not obeyed Me." '
17 "Therefore thus says the LORD God
of hosts, the God of Israel: 'Behold, I
will bring on Judah and on all the
inhabitants of Jerusalem all the doom
that I have pronounced against them;
[a]because I have spoken to them but
they have not heard, and I have called
to them but they have not answered.' "
18 And Jeremiah said to the house of
the Rechabites, "Thus says the LORD
of hosts, the God of Israel: 'Because
you have obeyed the commandment of
Jonadab your father, and kept all his
precepts and done according to all that
he commanded you,
19 'therefore thus says the LORD of
hosts, the God of Israel: "Jonadab the
son of Rechab shall not lack a man to
[a]stand before Me forever." ' "

The Scroll Read in the Temple

36 Now it came to pass in the
[a]fourth year of Jehoiakim the
son of Josiah, king of Judah, *that* this
word came to Jeremiah from the LORD,
saying:

CHAPTER 35

2 [a]2 Sam. 4:2; 2 Kin. 10:15; 1 Chr. 2:55 [b]1 Kin. 6:5, 8; 1 Chr. 9:26, 33
4 [a]2 Kin. 12:9; 25:18; 1 Chr. 9:18, 19 [1]Lit. *threshold*
6 [a]2 Kin. 10:15, 23 [b]Lev. 10:9; Num. 6:2–4; Judg. 13:7, 14; Prov. 31:4; Ezek. 44:21; Luke 1:15
7 [a]Ex. 20:12; Eph. 6:2, 3
8 [a][Prov. 1:8, 9; 4:1, 2, 10; 6:20; Eph. 6:1; Col. 3:20]
11 [a]Jer. 4:5–7; 8:14
13 [a][Is. 28:9–12]; Jer. 6:10; 17:23; 32:33 [1]*listen to* *See WW at Prov. 4:13.
14 [a]2 Chr. 36:15 [b]Jer. 7:13; 25:3 [1]*listen to*
15 [a]Jer. 26:4, 5; 29:19 [b][Is. 1:16, 17]; Jer. 18:11; 25:5, 6; [Ezek. 18:30–32]; Acts 26:20 [c]Jer. 7:7; 25:5, 6
16 [a][Heb. 12:9]
17 [a]Prov. 1:24; Is. 65:12; 66:4; Jer. 7:13
19 [a][Ex. 20:12]; Jer. 15:19; [Luke 21:36; Eph. 6:2, 3]

CHAPTER 36

1 [a]2 Kin. 24:1; 2 Chr. 36:5–7; Jer. 25:1, 3; 45:1; Dan. 1:1

human ancestor (vv. 12–17). He closes the chapter with an address to the Rechabites and promises continued existence for their faithfulness.

35:1 In the days of Jehoiakin: The mention of Babylonian (Chaldean) and Syrian armies (v. 11) suggests a date of 601 B.C.

35:2 House of the Rechabites: See v. 18. Since the Rechabites were nomadic and disdained houses, the use of "house" here means "members of a clan or community."

35:7 The prohibition against drinking wine was accompanied also by a command not to **build a house, sow seed,** or **plant a vineyard.** All of these were, to them, symbols of an agrarian and urban culture, which endangered the purity of the worship of the Lord.

35:14 Rising early: See note on 7:13.

36:1—45:5 The trials, suffering, and persecution of Jeremiah.

36:1 Fourth year: 605 B.C. See 25:1; 46:2.

2 "Take a [a]scroll of a book and
[b]write* on it all the words that I have
spoken to you against Israel, against
Judah, and against [c]all the nations,
from the day I spoke to you, from the
days of [d]Josiah even to this day.
3 "It [a]may be that the house of Judah
will hear all the adversities which I
purpose to bring upon them, that
everyone may [b]turn from his evil way,
that I may forgive their iniquity and
their sin."
4 Then Jeremiah [a]called Baruch the
son of Neriah; and [b]Baruch wrote on
a scroll of a book, [1]at the instruction
of Jeremiah, all the words of the LORD
which He had spoken to him.
5 And Jeremiah commanded Baruch,
saying, "I *am* confined, I cannot go into
the house of the LORD.
6 "You go, therefore, and read from
the scroll which you have written
[1]at my instruction, the words of the
LORD, in the hearing of the people in
the LORD's house on [a]the day of fasting.
And you shall also read them in the
hearing of all Judah who come from
their cities.
7 "It may be that they will present
their supplication before the LORD, and
everyone will turn from his evil way.
For great *is* the anger and the fury that
the LORD has pronounced against this
people."
8 And Baruch the son of Neriah did
according to all that Jeremiah the
prophet commanded him, reading
from the book the words of the LORD
in the LORD's house.
9 Now it came to pass in the fifth year
of Jehoiakim the son of Josiah, king
of Judah, in the ninth month, *that* they
proclaimed a *fast before the LORD to
all the people in Jerusalem, and to all
the people who came from the cities
of Judah to Jerusalem.
10 Then Baruch read from the book
the words of Jeremiah in the house of
the LORD, in the chamber of Gemariah
the son of Shaphan the scribe, in the
upper court at the [a]entry of the New
Gate of the LORD's house, in the
[1]hearing of all the people.

The Scroll Read in the Palace

11 When Michaiah the son of Gemariah, the son of Shaphan, heard all the
words of the LORD from the book,
12 he then went down to the king's
house, into the scribe's chamber; and
there all the princes were sitting—
[a]Elishama the scribe, Delaiah the son
of Shemaiah, [b]Elnathan the son of
Achbor, Gemariah the son of Shaphan, Zedekiah the son of Hananiah,
and all the princes.
13 Then Michaiah declared to them all
the words that he had heard when
Baruch read the book in the hearing
of the people.
14 Therefore all the princes sent Jehudi the son of Nethaniah, the son
of Shelemiah, the son of Cushi, to Baruch, saying, "Take in your hand the
scroll from which you have read in the
hearing of the people, and come."
So Baruch the son of Neriah took the
scroll in his hand and came to
them.
15 And they said to him, "Sit down
now, and read it in our hearing." So
Baruch read *it* in their hearing.
16 Now it happened, when they had
heard all the words, that they looked
in fear from one to another, and said
to Baruch, "We will surely tell the king
of all these words."
17 And they asked Baruch, saying,
"Tell us now, how did you write all
these words—[1]at his instruction?"
18 So Baruch answered them, "He proclaimed with his mouth all these words
to me, and I wrote *them* with ink in
the book."
19 Then the princes said to Baruch,
"Go and hide, you and Jeremiah; and
let no one know where you are."

2 [a]Is. 8:1; Ezek. 2:9; Zech. 5:1 [b]Jer. 30:2; Hab. 2:2 [c]Jer. 25:15 [d]Jer. 25:3 *See WW at Deut. 31:9.
3 [a]Jer. 26:3; Ezek. 12:3 [b][Deut. 30:2, 8; 1 Sam. 7:3]; Is. 55:7; Jer. 18:8; Jon. 3:8
4 [a]Jer. 32:12 [b]Jer. 45:1 [1]Lit. *from Jeremiah's mouth*
6 [a]Lev. 16:29; 23:27–32; Acts 27:9 [1]Lit. *from my mouth*
9 *See WW at Jon. 3:5.
10 [a]Jer. 26:10 [1]Lit. *ears*
12 [a]Jer. 41:1 [b]Jer. 26:22
17 [1]Lit. *with his mouth*

36:2 Scroll: See note on 30:2.
36:3 A theme emphasized again and again is that if the people repent and turn from their evil way, then God will relent and not bring the evil He has promised. Most often when God deals with His people, punishment is meant to be remedial, not punitive. Eventually, however, when God's mercy and grace are constantly rejected, judgment must fall.
36:4 Baruch: See note on 32:12. This verse indicates that Baruch was responsible for the written text of Jeremiah, and he may have been the editor for the final text.
36:5 I *am* confined: Why Jeremiah was barred from the temple is unknown, but it may be because of his previous ministry at the temple (see 7:2–15; 20:1, 2; 26:2–6).
36:6 The day of fasting: Large crowds would be at the temple on a day of fasting. The fast was proclaimed in times of emergency and was not a fixed event (see v. 9).
36:9 The **fifth year** and **ninth month** is December 604 B.C.
36:10 Shaphan the scribe: A friend of Jeremiah (see 26:24; 29:3; 2 Kin. 22:3) and father of Ahikam, Elasah, and Gemariah.
36:11–19 After **Michaiah** heard **Baruch** read **the scroll** and asked him to read it again to some nobles, they were impressed and wanted to inform Jehoiakim. Sensing an unfavorable response from the king, they suggested **Jeremiah** and Baruch go into hiding.
36:11 Elnathan: See note on 26:22.
36:18 This is the only time **ink** is mentioned in the OT.

The King Destroys Jeremiah's Scroll

20 And they went to the king, into the
court; but they stored the scroll in the
chamber of Elishama the scribe, and
told all the words in the hearing of the
king.
21 So the king sent Jehudi to bring the
scroll, and he took it from Elishama
the scribe's chamber. And Jehudi read
it in the hearing of the king and in the
hearing of all the princes who stood
beside the king.
22 Now the king was sitting in [a]the
winter house in the ninth month, with
a fire burning on the hearth before him.
23 And it happened, when Jehudi had
read three or four columns, *that the
king* cut it with the scribe's knife and
cast *it* into the fire that *was* on the
hearth, until all the scroll was consumed in the fire that *was* on the
hearth.
24 Yet they were [a]not afraid, nor did
they [b]tear their garments, the king nor
any of his servants who heard all these
words.
25 Nevertheless Elnathan, Delaiah,
and Gemariah *implored the king not
to burn the scroll; but he would not listen to them.
26 And the king commanded Jerahmeel [1]the king's son, Seraiah the son
of Azriel, and Shelemiah the son of Ab-
deel, to seize Baruch the scribe and
Jeremiah the prophet, but the LORD hid
them.

Jeremiah Rewrites the Scroll

27 Now after the king had burned the
scroll with the words which Baruch
had written [1]at the instruction of Jeremiah, the word of the LORD came to
Jeremiah, saying:
28 "Take yet another scroll, and write
on it all the former words that were
in the first scroll which Jehoiakim the
king of Judah has burned.
29 "And you shall say to Jehoiakim
king of Judah, 'Thus says the LORD:
"You have burned this scroll, saying,
[a]'Why have you written in it that the
king of Babylon will certainly come
and destroy this land, and cause man
and beast to [b]cease from here?'"
30 'Therefore thus says the LORD concerning Jehoiakim king of Judah:
[a]"He shall have no one to sit on the
throne of David, and his dead body
shall be [b]cast out to the heat of the day
and the frost of the night.
31 "I will punish him, his [1]family, and
his servants for their iniquity; and I
will bring on them, on the inhabitants
of Jerusalem, and on the men of Judah
all the doom that I have pronounced
against them; but they did not
heed."'"
32 Then Jeremiah took another scroll
and gave it to Baruch the scribe, the
son of Neriah, who wrote on it [1]at the
instruction of Jeremiah all the words
of the book which Jehoiakim king of
Judah had burned in the fire. And besides, there were added to them many
similar words.

Zedekiah's Vain Hope

37 Now King [a]Zedekiah the son of
Josiah reigned instead of Coniah the son of Jehoiakim, whom
Nebuchadnezzar king of Babylon
made king in the land of Judah.
2 [a]But neither he nor his servants nor
the people of the land gave heed to the
words of the LORD which He spoke by
the prophet Jeremiah.
3 And Zedekiah the king sent Jehucal
the son of Shelemiah, and [a]Zephaniah
the son of Maaseiah, the priest, to the
prophet Jeremiah, saying, [b]"Pray now
to the LORD our God for us."
4 Now Jeremiah was coming and going among the people, for they had not
yet put him in prison.
5 Then [a]Pharaoh's army came up
from Egypt; and when the Chaldeans
who were besieging Jerusalem heard
news of them, they departed from Jerusalem.
6 Then the word of the LORD came to
the prophet Jeremiah, saying,

22 [a]Judg. 3:20; Amos 3:15
24 [a][Ps. 36:1]; Jer. 36:16 [b]Gen. 37:29, 34; 2 Sam. 1:11; 1 Kin. 21:27; 2 Kin. 19:1, 2; 22:11; Is. 36:22; 37:1; Jon. 3:6
25 *See WW at Jer. 27:18.
26 [1]Or *son of Hammelech*
27 [1]Lit. *from Jeremiah's mouth*
29 [a]Jer. 32:3 [b]Jer. 25:9–11; 26:9
30 [a]Jer. 22:30 [b]Jer. 22:19
31 [1]Lit. *seed*
32 [1]Lit. *from Jeremiah's mouth*

CHAPTER 37

1 [a]2 Kin. 24:17; 1 Chr. 3:15; 2 Chr. 36:10; Jer. 22:24
2 [a]2 Kin. 24:19, 20; 2 Chr. 36:12–16; [Prov. 29:12]
3 [a]Jer. 21:1, 2; 29:25; 52:24 [b]1 Kin. 13:6; Jer. 42:2; Acts 8:24
5 [a]2 Kin. 24:7; Jer. 37:7; Ezek. 17:15

36:20–26 Being informed about the content of the scroll, the king ordered it brought and read. After every three or four columns were read, the king cut them off and burned them.

36:23 In stark contrast with the action of King Josiah, who tore his garments when he heard the Word of God read (2 Kin. 22:11—23:3; 23:21–24), Jehoiakim tore the scroll and tried to destroy God's Word.

36:27–32 After the destruction of the scroll by **Jehoiakim,** Jeremiah is instructed to **take yet another scroll** and write **all the former words** with additional comments for Jehoiakim.

36:30 No one to sit on the throne of David: His son Jehoiachin ruled only 3 months and was taken captive to Babylon (see 2 Kin. 24:8, 12, 15). **Body shall be cast out:** His punishment because he cast the scroll into the fire (v. 23; 22:18, 19).

37:1 Zedekiah was the third son of Josiah to reign as king. His appointment fulfilled the prophecy of 36:30 concerning Jehoiakim, his brother.

37:3 Pray now: See 21:1; 34:21, 22. The request may have been to make the temporary reprieve (v. 5) permanent.

7 "Thus says the LORD, the God of Israel, 'Thus you shall say to the king of Judah, [a]who sent you to Me to inquire of Me: "Behold, Pharaoh's army which has come up to help you will return to Egypt, to their own land.

8 [a]"And the Chaldeans shall come back and fight against this city, and take it and burn it with fire." '

9 "Thus says the LORD: 'Do not deceive yourselves, saying, "The Chaldeans will surely depart from us," for they will not depart.

10 [a]'For though you had defeated the whole army of the Chaldeans who fight against you, and there remained *only* wounded men among them, they would rise up, every man in his tent, and burn the city with fire.' "

Jeremiah Imprisoned

11 And it happened, when the army of the Chaldeans left *the siege* of Jerusalem for fear of Pharaoh's army,

12 that Jeremiah went out of Jerusalem to go into the land of Benjamin to claim his property there among the people.

13 And when he was in the Gate of Benjamin, a captain of the guard *was* there whose name *was* Irijah the son of Shelemiah, the son of Hananiah; and he seized Jeremiah the prophet, saying, "You are defecting to the Chaldeans!"

14 Then Jeremiah said, [1]"False! I am not defecting to the Chaldeans." But he did not listen to him. So Irijah seized Jeremiah and brought him to the princes.

15 Therefore the princes were angry with Jeremiah, and they struck him [a]and put him in prison in the [b]house of Jonathan the scribe. For they had made that the prison.

5 16 When Jeremiah entered [a]the dungeon and the cells, and Jeremiah had remained there many days,

17 then Zedekiah the king sent and took him *out*. The king asked him secretly in his house, and said, "Is there *any* word from the LORD?" And Jeremiah said, "There is." Then he said, "You shall be [a]delivered into the hand of the king of Babylon!"

18 Moreover Jeremiah said to King Zedekiah, "What offense have I committed against you, against your servants, or against this people, that you have put me in prison?

19 "Where now *are* your prophets who prophesied to you, saying, 'The king of Babylon will not come against you or against this land'?

20 "Therefore please hear now, O my lord the king. Please, let my petition be accepted before you, and do not make me return to the house of Jonathan the scribe, lest I die there."

21 Then Zedekiah the king commanded that they should commit Jeremiah [a]to the court of the prison, and that they should give him daily a piece of bread from the bakers' street, [b]until all the bread in the city was gone. Thus Jeremiah remained in the court of the prison.

Jeremiah in the Dungeon

38 Now Shephatiah the son of Mattan, Gedaliah the son of Pashhur, [a]Jucal[1] the son of Shelemiah, and [b]Pashhur the son of Malchiah [c]heard the words that Jeremiah had spoken to all the people, saying,

2 "Thus says the LORD: [a]'He who remains in this city shall die by the sword, by famine, and by pestilence; but he who goes over to the Chaldeans shall live; his life shall be as a prize to him, and he shall live.'

3 "Thus says the LORD: [a]'This city shall surely be [b]given into the hand of the king of Babylon's army, which shall take it.' "

4 Therefore the princes said to the king, "Please, [a]let this man be put to death, for thus he [1]weakens the hands of the men of war who remain in this city, and the hands of all the people,

7 [a]Is. 36:6; Jer. 21:2; Ezek. 17:17
8 [a]2 Chr. 36:19; Jer. 34:22
10 [a]Lev. 26:36–38; Is. 30:17; Jer. 21:4, 5
14 [1]*a lie*
15 [a]Jer. 20:2; [Matt. 21:35] [b]Gen. 39:20; 2 Chr. 16:10; 18:26; Jer. 38:26; Acts 5:18
16 [a]Jer. 38:6
17 [a]2 Kin. 25:4–7; Jer. 21:7; Ezek. 12:12, 13; 17:19–21
21 [a]Jer. 32:2; 38:13, 28 [b]2 Kin. 25:3; Jer. 38:9; 52:6

CHAPTER 38

1 [a]Jer. 37:3 [b]Jer. 21:1 [c]Jer. 21:8 [1]*Jehucal*, Jer. 37:3
2 [a]Jer. 21:9
3 [a]Jer. 21:10; 32:3 [b]Jer. 34:2
4 [a]Jer. 26:11 [1]Is discouraging

37:7 Pharaoh's army was defeated by Nebuchadnezzar (see Ezek. 30:21–26) and did **return to Egypt**.

37:11–21 While attempting to leave Jerusalem **to claim his property** during a brief lifting of the siege (v. 12), Jeremiah was **seized** (v. 13) and **put . . . in prison** (v. 15).

37:13 You are *defecting:* *The charge of* **Irijah** was justified *because* Jeremiah had advocated surrender to the Babylonians (21:9; 38:2) and many had already defected (38:19; 39:9; 52:15).

37:15 They struck him: See note on 20:2.

37:16 See section 5 of Truth-In-Action at the end of Jer.

37:16 The dungeon and the cells: The place of confinement was an underground dungeon, probably converted from a cistern.

37:17–21 The king secretly interviewed Jeremiah to find support for his revolt, but he was disappointed (see 21:1). He did, however, change Jeremiah's place of imprisonment (v. 21; 32:2) and provided him with food until the city fell.

38:1–13 Jeremiah continually advocated surrender, and this was seen as dangerous to the pro-Egyptian counselors **Gedaliah, Jucal** (Jehucal of 37:3), and **Pashhur** (21:1), who asked the king to **put** him **to death**. Jeremiah was placed in a cistern and left to die, but was rescued by **Ebed-Melech,** a royal official (eunuch) to the king.

by speaking such words to them. For
this man does not seek the [2]welfare of
this people, but their harm."
5 Then Zedekiah the king said,
"Look, he *is* in your hand. For the king
can *do* nothing against you."
6 [a]So they took Jeremiah and cast
him into the dungeon of Malchiah
[1]the king's son, which *was* in the court
of the prison, and they let Jeremiah
down with ropes. And in the dungeon
there was no water, but mire. So Jeremiah sank in the mire.
7 [a]Now Ebed-Melech the Ethiopian,
one of the [1]eunuchs, who was in the
king's house, heard that they had put
Jeremiah in the dungeon. When the
king was sitting at the Gate of Benjamin,
8 Ebed-Melech went out of the king's
house and spoke to the king, saying:
9 "My lord the king, these men have
done evil in all that they have done to
Jeremiah the prophet, whom they have
cast into the dungeon, and he is likely
to die from hunger in the place where
he is. For *there is* [a]no more bread in
the city."
10 Then the king commanded Ebed-
Melech the Ethiopian, saying, "Take
from here thirty men with you, and lift
Jeremiah the prophet out of the dungeon before he dies."
11 So Ebed-Melech took the men with
him and went into the house of the king
under the treasury, and took from
there old clothes and old rags, and let
them down by ropes into the dungeon
to Jeremiah.
12 Then Ebed-Melech the Ethiopian
said to Jeremiah, "Please put these old
clothes and rags under your armpits,
under the ropes." And Jeremiah did so.
13 So they pulled Jeremiah up with
ropes and lifted him out of the dungeon. And Jeremiah remained [a]in the
court of the prison.

Zedekiah's Fears and Jeremiah's Advice

14 Then Zedekiah the king sent and
had Jeremiah the prophet brought to
him at the third entrance of the house
of the LORD. And the king said to Jeremiah, "I will [a]ask you something. Hide
nothing from me."
15 Jeremiah said to Zedekiah, "If I declare *it* to you, will you not surely put
me to death? And if I give you advice,
you will not listen to me."
16 So Zedekiah the king swore secretly to Jeremiah, saying, "*As* the
LORD lives, [a]who made our very souls,
I will not put you to death, nor will I
give you into the hand of these men
who seek your life."
17 Then Jeremiah said to Zedekiah,
"Thus says the LORD, the God of hosts,
the God of Israel: 'If you surely
[a]surrender[1] [b]to the king of Babylon's
princes, then your soul shall live; this
city shall not be burned with fire, and
you and your house shall live.
18 'But if you do not [1]surrender to the
king of Babylon's princes, then this
city shall be given into the hand of the
Chaldeans; they shall burn it with fire,
and [a]you shall not escape from their
hand.'"
19 And Zedekiah the king said to Jeremiah, "I am afraid of the Jews who
have [a]defected to the Chaldeans, lest
they deliver me into their hand, and
they [b]abuse me."
20 But Jeremiah said, "They shall not
deliver *you*. Please, obey the voice of
the LORD which I speak to you. So it
shall be [a]well with you, and your soul
shall live.
21 "But if you refuse to [1]surrender, this
is the word that the LORD has shown
me:
22 'Now behold, all the [a]women who
are left in the king of Judah's house
shall be surrendered to the king of Babylon's princes, and those *women* shall
say:

"Your close friends have [1]set upon
you
And prevailed against you;
Your feet have sunk in the mire,
And they have [2]turned away
again."

23 'So they shall surrender all your
wives and [a]children to the Chaldeans.
[b]You shall not escape from their hand,
but shall be taken by the hand of the
king of Babylon. And you shall cause
this city to be burned with fire.'"
24 Then Zedekiah said to Jeremiah,

4 [2]Well-being; lit. *peace*
6 [a]Jer. 37:21; Lam. 3:55 [1]Or *son of Hammelech*
7 [a]Jer. 39:16 [1]Or *officers*
9 [a]Jer. 37:21
13 [a]Neh. 3:25; Jer. 37:21; Acts 23:35; 24:27; 28:16, 30
14 [a]Jer. 21:1, 2; 37:17
16 [a]Num. 16:22; Is. 57:16; Zech. 12:1; [Acts 17:25, 28]
17 [a]2 Kin. 24:12 [b]Jer. 39:3 [1]Lit. *go out*
18 [a]Jer. 32:4; 34:3 [1]Lit. *go out*
19 [a]Jer. 39:9 [b]1 Sam. 31:4
20 [a]Jer. 40:9
21 [1]Lit. *go out*
22 [a]Jer. 8:10 [1]Or *misled* [2]Deserted you
23 [a]Jer. 39:6; 41:10 [b]Jer. 39:5

38:7 The king was sitting at the Gate of Benjamin to hear complaints and to litigate cases. This **gave Ebed-Melech** access; he had a complaint.

38:9 For *there is* no more bread: But compare 37:21. If there were no more bread, taking Jeremiah from the cistern would not have helped him much.

38:10 Thirty reads "3" in some Hebrew manuscripts. If 30 is correct, perhaps they were needed for protection.

38:14–28 Zedekiah again **sent** for **Jeremiah,** who still advocated surrender. Zedekiah was afraid of those who had already defected and afraid of his court officials, so he continued to vacillate in his decision.

"Let no one know of these words, and
you shall not die.
25 "But if the princes hear that I have
talked with you, and they come to you
and say to you, 'Declare to us now
what you have said to the king, and
also what the king said to you; do not
hide *it* from us, and we will not put
you to death,'
26 "then you shall say to them, [a]'I presented my request before the king, that
he would not make me return [b]to Jonathan's house to die there.' "
27 Then all the princes came to Jeremiah and asked him. And he told them
according to all these words that the
king had commanded. So they stopped
speaking with him, for the conversation had not been heard.
28 Now [a]Jeremiah remained in the
court of the prison until the day that
Jerusalem was taken. And he was
there when Jerusalem was taken.

The Fall of Jerusalem

39 In the [a]ninth year of Zedekiah
king of Judah, in the tenth
month, Nebuchadnezzar king of Babylon and all his army came against Jerusalem, and besieged it.
2 In the [a]eleventh year of Zedekiah,
in the fourth month, on the ninth
day of the month, the [1]city was penetrated.
3 [a]Then all the princes of the king of
Babylon came in and sat in the Middle
Gate: Nergal-Sharezer, Samgar-Nebo,
Sarsechim, [1]Rabsaris, Nergal-Sarezer,
[2]Rabmag, with the rest of the princes
of the king of Babylon.
4 [a]So it was, when Zedekiah the king
of Judah and all the men of war saw
them, that they fled and went out of
the city by night, by way of the king's
garden, by the gate between the two
walls. And he went out by way of the
[1]plain.
5 But the Chaldean army pursued
them and [a]overtook Zedekiah in the
plains of Jericho. And when they had
captured him, they brought him up to
Nebuchadnezzar king of Babylon, to
[b]Riblah in the land of Hamath, where
he pronounced judgment on him.
6 Then the king of Babylon killed the
sons of Zedekiah before his [a]eyes in
Riblah; the king of Babylon also killed
all the [b]nobles of Judah.
7 Moreover [a]he put out Zedekiah's
eyes, and bound him with bronze
[1]fetters to carry him off to Babylon.
8 [a]And the Chaldeans burned the
king's house and the houses of the people with [b]fire, and broke down the
[c]walls of Jerusalem.
9 [a]Then Nebuzaradan the captain of
the guard carried away captive to Babylon the remnant of the people who remained in the city and those who
[b]defected to him, with the rest of the
people who remained.
10 But Nebuzaradan the captain of the
guard left in the land of Judah the
[a]poor people, who had nothing, and
gave them vineyards and fields [1]at the
same time.

Jeremiah Goes Free

11 Now Nebuchadnezzar king of Babylon gave charge concerning Jeremiah
to Nebuzaradan the captain of the
guard, saying,
12 "Take him and look after him, and
do him no [a]harm; but do to him just
as he says to you."
13 So Nebuzaradan the captain of the
guard sent Nebushasban, Rabsaris,
Nergal-Sharezer, Rabmag, and all the
king of Babylon's chief officers;
14 then they sent *someone* [a]to take Jeremiah from the court of the prison, and
committed him [b]to Gedaliah the son of
[c]Ahikam, the son of Shaphan, that he
should take him home. So he dwelt
among the people.
15 Meanwhile the word of the LORD
had come to Jeremiah while he was
shut up in the court of the prison, saying,
16 "Go and speak to [a]Ebed-Melech the
Ethiopian, saying, 'Thus says the LORD
of hosts, the God of Israel: "Behold,
[b]I will bring My words upon this city
for adversity and not for good, and

26 [a]Jer. 37:20 [b]Jer. 37:15
28 [a][Ps. 23:4]; Jer. 37:21; 39:14

CHAPTER 39

1 [a]2 Kin. 25:1–12; Jer. 52:4; Ezek. 24:1, 2
2 [a]Jer. 1:3 [1]*city wall was breached*
3 [a]Jer. 1:15; 38:17 [1]A title, probably *Chief Officer;* also v. 13 [2]A title, probably *Troop Commander;* also v. 13
4 [a]2 Kin. 25:4; Is. 30:16; Jer. 52:7; Amos 2:14 [1]Or *Arabah;* the Jordan Valley
5 [a]Jer. 21:7; 32:4; 38:18, 23 [b]2 Kin. 23:33; Jer. 52:9, 26, 27
6 [a]Deut. 28:34 [b]Jer. 34:19–21
7 [a]2 Kin. 25:7; Jer. 52:11; Ezek. 12:13 [1]*chains*
8 [a]2 Kin. 25:9; Jer. 38:18; 52:13 [b]Jer. 21:10 [c]2 Kin. 25:10; Neh. 1:3; Jer. 52:14
9 [a]2 Kin. 25:8, 11, 12, 20 [b]Jer. 38:19
10 [a]Jer. 40:7 [1]Lit. *on that day*
12 [a]Jer. 1:18, 19; 15:20, 21
14 [a]Jer. 38:28 [b]Jer. 40:5 [c]2 Kin. 22:12, 14; 2 Chr. 34:20; Jer. 26:24
16 [a]Jer. 38:7, 12 [b]Jer. 21:10; [Dan. 9:12; Zech. 1:6]

39:1 The **ninth year** and **tenth month** was January 15, 588 B.C. (see 52:4; 2 Kin. 25:1).
39:2 The city fell on July 18, 586 B.C. (see 52:5, 6; 2 Kin. 25:2, 3). *Some scholars, using a different calculation,* place the fall of Jerusalem in 587 B.C.
39:3 The Babylonian officers constituted a military court or government. There are only three men named: **Nergal-Sharezer** of **Samgar-Nebo, Sarsechim** the **Rabsaris,** and **Nergal-Sarezer** the **Rabmag** (Nergal-Sharezer, v. 13). A contemporary Babylonian inscription cites Nergal-Sharezer as governor of Sin-magir (Samgar). "Rabsaris" is a title, a high official. "Rabmag" is a high officer of some kind.
39:4 Plain: The Arabah, a broad valley extending from the Dead Sea to the Red Sea. Jericho is a major city in the Arabah.
39:5 Riblah in the land of Hamath: A city on the Orontes River in Syria, 56 kilometers (35 miles) northeast of Baalbek and south of Kadesh (see 52:9; 2 Kin. 25:6).
39:13 See note on v. 3.
39:14 Gedaliah the son of Ahikam: See note on 26:24.

they shall be *performed* in that day before you.
17 "But I will deliver you in that day,"
says the LORD, "and you shall not be
given into the hand of the men of
whom you *are* afraid.
18 "For I will surely deliver you, and
you shall not fall by the sword; but
[a]your life shall be as a prize to you,
[b]because you have put your trust in
Me," says the LORD.' "

Jeremiah with Gedaliah the Governor

40 The word that came to Jeremiah
from the LORD [a]after Nebuzaradan the captain of the guard had let
him go from Ramah, when he had
taken him bound in chains among all
who were carried away captive from
Jerusalem and Judah, who were carried away captive to Babylon.
2 And the captain of the guard took
Jeremiah and [a]said to him: "The LORD
your God has pronounced this doom
on this place.
3 "Now the LORD has brought *it,* and
has done just as He said. [a]Because you
people have sinned against the LORD,
and not obeyed His voice, therefore
this thing has come upon you.
4 "And now look, I **free** you this day
from the chains that [1]*were* on your
hand. [a]If it seems good to you to come
with me to Babylon, come, and I will
look after you. But if it seems wrong
for you to come with me to Babylon,
remain here. See, [b]all the land *is* before
you; wherever it seems good and convenient for you to go, go there."

WORD WEALTH

40:4 free, *patach* (pah-*tahch*); Strong's #6605: To open, open wide, loosen; set free, release, untie, unshackle, liberate. This verb occurs about 150 times. Often referring to opening one's hand, eyes, or mouth, or opening a book, door, gate, or window, occasionally, *patach* means "to free or loose" (Ps. 102:20). The related noun *petach,* "door," "gate" or "entrance," is applied to the door of the tabernacle and the entrance to a house, cave, or city. Hos. 2:15 promises that the Valley of *Achor* (trouble) will be renamed the door of hope, or *petach tiqvah.* In the present reference, great freedom was granted to Jeremiah through the release from all his chains.

5 Now while Jeremiah had not yet
gone back, *Nebuzaradan said,* "Go
back to [a]Gedaliah the son of Ahikam,
the son of Shaphan, [b]whom the king
of Babylon has made governor over the
cities of Judah, and dwell with him
among the people. Or go wherever it
seems convenient for you to go." So
the captain of the guard gave him rations and a gift and let him go.
6 [a]Then Jeremiah went to Gedaliah
the son of Ahikam, to [b]Mizpah, and
dwelt with him among the people who
were left in the land.
7 [a]And when all the captains of the
armies who *were* in the fields, they and
their men, heard that the king of Babylon had made Gedaliah the son of
Ahikam governor in the land, and had
committed to him men, women, children, and [b]the poorest of the land who
had not been carried away captive to
Babylon,
8 then they came to Gedaliah at Mizpah—[a]Ishmael the son of Nethaniah,
[b]Johanan and Jonathan the sons of Kareah, Seraiah the son of Tanhumeth,
the sons of Ephai the Netophathite, and [c]Jezaniah[1] the son of a
[d]Maachathite, they and their men.
9 And Gedaliah the son of Ahikam,
the son of Shaphan, took an oath before them and their men, saying, "Do
not be *afraid to serve the Chaldeans.
Dwell in the land and *serve the king
of Babylon, and it shall be [a]well with
you.
10 "As for me, I will indeed dwell at
Mizpah and serve the Chaldeans who
come to us. But you, gather wine and
summer fruit and oil, put *them* in your
vessels, and dwell in your cities that
you have taken."
11 Likewise, when all the Jews who
were in Moab, among the Ammonites,
in Edom, and who *were* in all the countries, heard that the king of Babylon
had left a remnant of Judah, and that
he had set over them Gedaliah the son
of Ahikam, the son of Shaphan,
12 then all the Jews [a]returned out of
all places where they had been driven,
and came to the land of Judah, to
Gedaliah at Mizpah, and gathered
wine and summer fruit in abundance.
13 Moreover Johanan the son of Kareah and all the captains of the forces
that *were* in the fields came to Gedaliah at Mizpah,

18 [a]Jer. 21:9; 45:5 [b]1 Chr. 5:20; Ps. 37:40; [Jer. 17:7, 8]

CHAPTER 40

1 [a]Jer. 39:9, 11
2 [a]Jer. 50:7
3 [a]Deut. 29:24, 25; Jer. 50:7; Dan. 9:11; [Rom. 2:5]
4 [a]Jer. 39:12 [b]Gen. 20:15 [1]Or *are*
5 [a]Jer. 39:14 [b]2 Kin. 25:22; Jer. 41:10
6 [a]Jer. 39:14 [b]Judg. 20:1; 1 Sam. 7:5; 2 Chr. 16:6
7 [a]2 Kin. 25:23, 24 [b]Jer. 39:10
8 [a]Jer. 41:1–10 [b]Jer. 41:11; 43:2 [c]Jer. 42:1 [d]Deut. 3:14; Josh. 12:5; 2 Sam. 10:6 [1]*Jaazaniah,* 2 Kin. 25:23
9 [a]Jer. 27:11; 38:17–20 *See WW at Ex. 1:17. • See WW at Ps. 100:2.
12 [a]Jer. 43:5

40:6 Mizpah: A city 12 kilometers (7 miles) north of Jerusalem on the Benjamin plateau near Geba and Ramah, it became the capital of Judah for a short time after the destruction of Jerusalem.

40:10 Gather wine and summer fruit and oil: Grapes, figs, and olives are part of the summer fruit, usually harvested in August and September.

14 and said to him, [1]"Do you certainly
know that [a]Baalis the king of the Ammonites
has sent Ishmael the son of
Nethaniah to murder you?" But Gedaliah
the son of Ahikam did not *believe
them.
15 Then Johanan the son of Kareah
spoke secretly to Gedaliah in Mizpah,
saying, "Let me go, please, and I will
kill Ishmael the son of Nethaniah, and
no one will know *it*. Why should he
murder you, so that all the Jews who
are gathered to you would be scattered,
and the [a]remnant in Judah perish?"
16 But Gedaliah the son of Ahikam
said to Johanan the son of Kareah,
"You shall not do this thing, for you
speak falsely concerning Ishmael."

Insurrection Against Gedaliah

41 Now it came to pass in the seventh
month [a]*that* Ishmael the
son of Nethaniah, the son of Elishama,
of the royal [1]family and of the officers
of the king, came with ten men to Gedaliah
the son of Ahikam, at [b]Mizpah.
And there they ate bread together in
Mizpah.
2 Then Ishmael the son of Nethaniah,
and the ten men who were with him,
arose and [a]struck Gedaliah the son of
[b]Ahikam, the son of Shaphan, with the
sword, and killed him whom the king
of Babylon had made [c]governor over
the land.
3 Ishmael also struck down all the
Jews who were with him, *that is*, with
Gedaliah at Mizpah, and the Chaldeans
who were found there, the men
of war.
4 And it happened, on the second day
after he had killed Gedaliah, when as
yet no one knew *it*,
5 that certain men came from Shechem,
from Shiloh, and from Samaria,
eighty men [a]with their beards shaved
and their clothes torn, having cut themselves,
with *offerings and incense in
their hand, to bring *them* to [b]the house
of the LORD.
6 Now Ishmael the son of Nethaniah
went out from Mizpah to meet them,
weeping as he went along; and it happened
as he met them that he said to
them, "Come to Gedaliah the son of
Ahikam!"
7 So it was, when they came into the
midst of the city, that Ishmael the son
of Nethaniah [a]killed them *and cast
them* into the midst of a [1]pit, he and
the men who were with him.
8 But ten men were found among
them who said to Ishmael, "Do not kill
us, for we have treasures of wheat, barley,
oil, and honey in the field." So he
desisted and did not kill them among
their brethren.
9 Now the [1]pit into which Ishmael
had cast all the dead bodies of the men
whom he had slain, because of Gedaliah,
was [a]the same one Asa the king
had made for fear of Baasha king of
Israel. Ishmael the son of Nethaniah
filled it with *the* slain.
10 Then Ishmael carried away captive
all the [a]rest of the people who *were* in
Mizpah, [b]the king's daughters and all
the people who remained in Mizpah,
[c]whom Nebuzaradan the captain of the
guard had committed to Gedaliah the
son of Ahikam. And Ishmael the son
of Nethaniah carried them away captive
and departed to go over to [d]the
Ammonites.
11 But when [a]Johanan the son of Kareah
and all the captains of the forces
that *were* with him heard of all the evil
that Ishmael the son of Nethaniah had
done,
12 they took all the men and went to
fight with Ishmael the son of Nethaniah;
and they found him by [a]the great
pool that *is* in Gibeon.
13 So it was, when all the people who
were with Ishmael saw Johanan the
son of Kareah, and all the captains of
the forces who *were* with him, that
they were glad.
14 Then all the people whom Ishmael
had carried away captive from Mizpah
turned around and came back, and
went to Johanan the son of Kareah.
15 But Ishmael the son of Nethaniah
escaped from Johanan with eight men
and went to the Ammonites.
16 Then Johanan the son of Kareah,
and all the captains of the forces that
were with him, took from Mizpah all
the [a]rest of the people whom he had

14 [a]Jer. 41:10 [1]Or *Certainly you know that* *See WW at 2 Chr. 20:20. **15** [a]Jer. 42:2

CHAPTER 41

1 [a]2 Kin. 25:25 [b]Jer. 40:6, 10 [1]Lit. *seed*
2 [a]2 Sam. 3:27; 20:9, 10; 2 Kin. 25:25; Ps. 41:9; 109:5; John 13:18 [b]Jer. 26:24 [c]Jer. 40:5
5 [a]Lev. 19:27, 28; Deut. 14:1; Is. 15:2 [b]1 Sam. 1:7; 2 Kin. 25:9; Neh. 10:34, 35 *See WW at Num. 29:6.
7 [a]Ps. 55:23; Is. 59:7; Ezek. 22:27; 33:24, 26 [1]Or *cistern*
9 [a]1 Kin. 15:22; 2 Chr. 16:6 [1]Or *cistern*
10 [a]Jer. 40:11, 12 [b]Jer. 43:6 [c]Jer. 40:7 [d]Jer. 40:14
11 [a]Jer. 40:7, 8, 13–16
12 [a]2 Sam. 2:13
16 [a]Jer. 40:11, 12; 43:4–7

41:1–3 See 2 Kin. 25:25.
41:1 In the **seventh *month*,** *just* two months after the fall of Jerusalem, Gedaliah was assassinated. Since the year is not given, this can only be an assumption; and some think the events related need a much longer time, perhaps even several years. **Ate bread together:** A host was duty bound by customary law to protect his guests, and the guests were obligated to reciprocate in good faith (see Gen. 19:2–8; Judg. 19:22–24). This breach of etiquette is cited in other places (see Judg. 4:21; 2 Sam. 13:28, 29; and perhaps Ps. 41:9).
41:7 A pit: A cistern was a handy place to dispose of bodies.
41:9 Asa the king had made: As part of the fortification against Baasha, Asa dug cisterns to provide water during the time of siege.
41:12 The great pool that *is* in Gibeon: Perhaps the same pool mentioned in 2 Sam. 2:13.

recovered from Ishmael the son of
Nethaniah after he had murdered Gedaliah the son of Ahikam—the mighty
men of war and the women and the
children and the eunuchs, whom he
had brought back from Gibeon.
17 And they departed and dwelt in the
habitation of [a]Chimham, which is near
Bethlehem, as they went on their way
to [b]Egypt,
18 because of the Chaldeans; for they
were afraid of them, because Ishmael
the son of Nethaniah had murdered
Gedaliah the son of Ahikam, [a]whom
the king of Babylon had made governor in the land.

The Flight to Egypt Forbidden

42 Now all the captains of the
forces, [a]Johanan the son of Kareah, Jezaniah the son of Hoshaiah,
and all the people, from the least to the
greatest, came near
2 and said to Jeremiah the prophet,
[a]"Please, let our petition be acceptable
to you, and [b]pray for us to the LORD
your God, for all this remnant (since
we are left *but* [c]a few of many, as you
can see),
3 "that the LORD your God may show
us [a]the way in which we should walk
and the thing we should do."
4 Then Jeremiah the prophet said to
them, "I have heard. Indeed, I will pray
to the LORD your God according to your
words, and it shall be, *that* [a]whatever
the LORD answers you, I will declare
it to you. I will [b]keep nothing back
from you."
5 So they said to Jeremiah, [a]"Let the
LORD be a true and faithful witness between us, if we do not do according to
everything which the LORD your God
sends us by you.
6 "Whether *it is* [1]pleasing or [2]dis-
pleasing, we will [a]obey the voice of
the LORD our God to whom we send
you, [b]that it may be well with us when
we obey the voice of the LORD our
God."
7 And it happened after ten days that
the word of the LORD came to Jeremiah.
8 Then he called Johanan the son of
Kareah, all the captains of the forces
which *were* with him, and all the people from the least even to the greatest,
9 and said to them, "Thus says the

17 [a]2 Sam. 19:37, 38 [b]Jer. 43:7
18 [a]Jer. 40:5

CHAPTER 42

1 [a]Jer. 40:8, 13; 41:11
2 [a]Jer. 15:11 [b]Ex. 8:28; 1 Sam. 7:8; 12:19; 1 Kin. 13:6; Is. 37:4; Jer. 37:3; Acts 8:24; [James 5:16] [c]Lev. 26:22; Deut. 28:62; Is. 1:9; Lam. 1:1
3 [a]Ezra 8:21
4 [a]1 Kin. 22:14; Jer. 23:28 [b]1 Sam. 3:17, 18; Ps. 40:10; Acts 20:20
5 [a]Gen. 31:50; Judg. 11:10; Jer. 43:2; Mic. 1:2; Mal. 2:14; 3:5
6 [a]Ex. 24:7; Deut. 5:27; Josh. 24:24 [b]Deut. 5:29, 33; 6:3; Jer. 7:23 [1]Lit. *good* [2]Lit. *evil*
10 [a]Jer. 24:6; 31:28; 33:7; Ezek. 36:36 [b]Deut. 32:36; [Jer. 18:8]
11 [a]Num. 14:9; 2 Chr. 32:7, 8; Is. 8:9, 10; 43:2, 5; Jer. 1:19; 15:20; Rom. 8:31
12 [a]Neh. 1:11; Ps. 106:46; Prov. 16:7
13 [a]Jer. 44:16
14 [a]Is. 31:1; Jer. 41:17; 43:7
15 [a]Deut. 17:16; Jer. 44:12–14 [b]Luke 9:51 [1]Or *surely*
16 [a]Jer. 44:13, 27; Ezek. 11:8; Amos 9:1–4
17 [a]Jer. 44:14, 28

LORD, the God of Israel, to whom you
sent me to present your petition before
Him:
10 'If you will still remain in this land,
then [a]I will build you and not pull *you*
down, and I will plant you and not
pluck *you* up. For I [b]relent concerning
the disaster that I have brought upon
you.
11 'Do not be afraid of the king of Babylon, of whom you are afraid; do not
be afraid of him,' says the LORD,
[a]'for I *am* with you, to save you and
deliver you from his hand.
12 'And [a]I will show you mercy, that
he may have mercy on you and cause
you to return to your own land.'
13 "But if [a]you say, 'We will not dwell
in this land,' disobeying the voice of
the LORD your God,
14 "saying, 'No, but we will go to the
land of [a]Egypt where we shall see no
war, nor hear the sound of the trumpet,
nor be hungry for bread, and there we
will dwell'—
15 "Then hear now the word of the
LORD, O remnant of Judah! Thus says
the LORD of hosts, the God of Israel:
'If you [a]wholly[1] set [b]your faces to enter
Egypt, and go to dwell there,
16 'then it shall be *that* the [a]sword
which you feared shall overtake you
there in the land of Egypt; the famine
of which you were afraid shall follow
close after you there *in* Egypt; and
there you shall die.
17 'So shall it be with all the men who
set their faces to go to Egypt to **dwell**
there. They shall die by the sword, by
famine, and by pestilence. And [a]none
of them shall remain or escape from
the disaster that I will bring upon
them.'

WORD WEALTH

42:17 dwell, *gur* (*goor*); Strong's #1481: To lodge somewhere, to temporarily reside; to dwell as a stranger among other people; to sojourn; to be a guest or alien in a particular land. *Gur* means to have a temporary resident's status. Here Jeremiah warns his countrymen to avoid plans to lodge temporarily in Egypt, for this would meet with tragic failure. From *gur* comes the noun *ger*, "stranger, alien, resident foreigner." This word occurs about 90 times, mostly in the Law of (*cont. on next page*)

42:1 Jezaniah the son of Hoshaiah: Perhaps the same as Jezaniah (40:8) and Azariah (43:2).

42:5, 6 The remnant promised to **obey the voice of the LORD,** whatever it might be. But, as it conflicted with what they had already decided to do, they rejected the word of God through Jeremiah.

42:10 See 1:10; 31:28.

42:16 The sword: See note on 43:11.

(cont. from preceding page)
Moses, where God repeatedly outlines the rights of "alien" residents. Ex. 23:9 indicates the empathy His people were to feel toward sojourners. Note also David's perceptive and humble words in 1 Chr. 29:15.

18 "For thus says the LORD of hosts,
the God of Israel: 'As My anger and
My fury have been [a]poured out on the
inhabitants of Jerusalem, so will My
fury be poured out on you when you
enter Egypt. And [b]you shall be an oath,
an astonishment, a curse, and a reproach;
and you shall see this place no
more.'
19 "The LORD has said concerning you,
O remnant of Judah, [a]'Do not go to
Egypt!' Know certainly that I have
[1]admonished you this day.
20 "For you [1]were hypocrites in your
hearts when you sent me to the LORD
your God, saying, 'Pray for us to the
LORD our God, and according to all that
the LORD your God says, so declare to
us and we will do *it*.'
21 "And I have this day declared *it* to
you, but you have [a]not obeyed the
voice of the LORD your God, or anything
which He has sent you by me.
22 "Now therefore, know certainly
that you [a]shall die by the sword, by
famine, and by pestilence in the place
where you desire to go to dwell."

Jeremiah Taken to Egypt

43 Now it happened, when Jeremiah
had stopped speaking to
all the people all the [a]words of the
LORD their God, for which the LORD
their God had sent him to them, all
these words,
5 2 [a]that Azariah the son of Hoshaiah,
Johanan the son of Kareah, and all the
proud men spoke, saying to Jeremiah,
"You speak falsely! The LORD our God
has not sent you to say, 'Do not go to
Egypt to dwell there.'
3 "But [a]Baruch the son of Neriah has
[1]set you against us, to deliver us into
the hand of the Chaldeans, that they
may put us to death or carry us away
captive to Babylon."

18 [a]2 Chr. 36:16–19; Jer. 7:20 [b]Deut. 29:21; Is. 65:15; Jer. 18:16; 24:9; 26:6; 29:18, 22; 44:12
19 [a]Deut. 17:16; Is. 30:1–7 [1]*warned*
20 [1]Lit. *used deceit against your souls*
21 [a]Is. 30:1–7
22 [a]Jer. 42:17; Ezek. 6:11

CHAPTER 43
1 [a]Jer. 42:9–18
2 [a]Jer. 42:1
3 [a]Jer. 36:4; 45:1 [1]Or *incited*

4 [a]2 Kin. 25:26
5 [a]Jer. 40:11, 12 *See WW at Jer. 42:17.
6 [a]Jer. 41:10 [b]Jer. 39:10; 40:7
7 [a]Jer. 42:19 [b]Jer. 2:16; 44:1
8 [a]Jer. 44:1–30
9 [1]Or *mortar*
10 [a]Jer. 25:9; 27:6; Ezek. 29:18; 20
11 [a]Is. 19:1–25; Jer. 25:15–19; 44:13; 46:1, 2, 13–26; Ezek. 29:19, 20 [b]Jer. 15:2; Zech. 11:9
12 [a]Ex. 12:12; Is. 19:1; Jer. 46:25; Ezek. 30:13 [1]So with MT, Tg.; LXX, Syr., Vg. *He*
13 [1]Lit. *House of the Sun,* ancient On, later called Heliopolis

4 So Johanan the son of Kareah, all
the captains of the forces, and all the
people would [a]not obey the voice of
the LORD, to remain in the land of Judah.
5 But Johanan the son of Kareah and
all the captains of the forces took
[a]all the remnant of Judah who had returned
to *dwell in the land of Judah,
from all nations where they had been
driven—
6 men, women, children, [a]the king's
daughters, [b]and every person whom
Nebuzaradan the captain of the guard
had left with Gedaliah the son of Ahikam,
the son of Shaphan, and Jeremiah
the prophet and Baruch the son
of Neriah.
7 [a]So they went to the land of Egypt,
for they did not obey the voice of the
LORD. And they went as far as [b]Tahpanhes.
8 Then the [a]word of the LORD came
to Jeremiah in Tahpanhes, saying,
9 "Take large stones in your hand,
and hide them in the sight of the men
of Judah, in the [1]clay in the brick courtyard
which *is* at the entrance to Pharaoh's
house in Tahpanhes;
10 "and say to them, 'Thus says the
LORD of hosts, the God of Israel: "Behold,
I will send and bring Nebuchadnezzar
the king of Babylon, [a]My servant,
and will set his throne above
these stones that I have hidden. And
he will spread his royal pavilion over
them.
11 [a]"When he comes, he shall strike
the land of Egypt *and deliver* to death
[b]*those appointed* for death, and to captivity
those appointed for captivity,
and to the sword *those appointed* for
the sword.
12 [1]"I will kindle a fire in the houses
of [a]the gods of Egypt, and he shall burn
them and carry them away captive.
And he shall array himself with the
land of Egypt, as a shepherd puts on
his garment, and he shall go out from
there in peace.
13 "He shall also break the *sacred* pillars
of [1]Beth Shemesh that *are* in the
land of Egypt; and the houses of the
gods of the Egyptians he shall burn
with fire." ' "

42:20 You were hypocrites: The Hebrew verb means to make a mistake, and the *intent is* that they have "made a *grave* error at the risk of their lives." The mistake was to promise absolute obedience to God's word in the hope that He would grant them their desire.
43:2–7 See section 5 of Truth-In-Action at the end of Jer.
43:7 Tahpanhes: See note on 2:16.
43:10, 11 A text in the British Museum confirms a punitive expedition by Nebuchadnezzar against Pharaoh Amasis of Egypt in 568 or 567 B.C. (see Ezek. 29:17–20).
43:13 Sacred pillars were obelisks, for which Heliopolis was famous.
43:13 Beth Shemesh: The temple of the sun in Egypt. Heliopolis (On), near Memphis, is meant, not the Beth Shemesh in Judah.

Israelites Will Be Punished in Egypt

44 The word that came to Jeremiah
concerning all the Jews who
dwell in the land of Egypt, who dwell
at [a]Migdol, at [b]Tahpanhes, at [c]Noph,[1]
and in the country of [d]Pathros, saying,
2 "Thus says the LORD of hosts, the
God of Israel: 'You have seen all the
calamity that I have brought on Jerusalem and on all the cities of Judah; and
behold, this day they *are* [a]a desolation,
and no one dwells in them,
3 'because of their wickedness which
they have committed to provoke Me to
anger, in that they went [a]to burn incense *and* to [b]serve other gods whom
they did not know, they nor you nor
your fathers.
4 'However [a]I have sent to you all My
servants the prophets, rising early and
sending *them*, saying, "Oh, do not do
this abominable thing that I hate!"
5 'But they did not listen or incline
their ear to turn from their wickedness,
to burn no incense to other gods.
6 'So My fury and My anger were
poured out and kindled in the cities of
Judah and in the streets of Jerusalem;
and they [1]are wasted *and* desolate, as
it is this day.'
7 "Now therefore, thus says the LORD,
the God of hosts, the God of Israel:
'Why do you commit *this* great evil
[a]against yourselves, to cut off from you
man and woman, child and infant, out
of Judah, leaving none to remain,
8 'in that you [a]provoke Me to wrath
with the works of your hands, burning
incense to other gods in the land of
Egypt where you have gone to dwell,
that you may cut yourselves off and be
[b]a curse and a reproach among all the
nations of the earth?
9 'Have you forgotten the wickedness
of your fathers, the wickedness of the
kings of Judah, the wickedness of their
wives, your own wickedness, and the
wickedness of your wives, which they
committed in the land of Judah and in
the streets of Jerusalem?
10 'They have not been [a]humbled,[1] to
this day, nor have they [b]feared; they
have not walked in My law or in My
statutes that I set before you and your
fathers.'
11 "Therefore thus says the LORD of
hosts, the God of Israel: 'Behold,
[a]I will set My face against you for catastrophe and for [1]cutting off all Judah.
12 'And I will take the remnant of Judah who have set their faces to go into
the land of Egypt to *dwell there, and
[a]they shall all be consumed *and* fall in
the land of Egypt. They shall be consumed by the sword *and* by famine.
They shall die, from the least to the
greatest, by the sword and by famine;
and [b]they shall be an oath, an astonishment, a curse and a reproach!
13 [a]'For I will punish those who dwell
in the land of Egypt, as I have punished
Jerusalem, by the sword, by famine,
and by pestilence,
14 'so that none of the remnant of Judah who have gone into the land of
Egypt to dwell there shall escape or
survive, lest they return to the land of
Judah, to which they [a]desire[1] to return
and dwell. For [b]none shall return except those who escape.'"
15 Then all the men who knew that
their wives had burned incense to
other gods, with all the women who
stood by, a great multitude, and all the
people who dwelt in the land of Egypt,
in Pathros, answered Jeremiah, saying:
16 "*As for* the word that you have spoken to us in the name of the LORD,
[a]we will not listen to you!
17 "But we will certainly do [a]whatever
has gone out of our own mouth, to burn
incense to the [b]queen of heaven and
pour out drink offerings to her, as we
have done, we and our fathers, our
kings and our princes, in the cities of
Judah and in the streets of Jerusalem.
For *then* we had plenty of [1]food, were
well-off, and saw no trouble.
18 "But since we stopped burning incense to the queen of heaven and pouring out drink offerings to her, we have
lacked everything and have been consumed by the sword and by famine."
19 *The women also said,* [a]"And when

CHAPTER 44

1 [a]Ex. 14:2; Jer. 46:14 [b]Jer. 43:7; Ezek. 30:18 [c]Is. 19:13; Jer. 2:16; 46:14; Ezek. 30:13, 16; Hos. 9:6 [d]Is. 11:11; Ezek. 29:14; 30:14 [1]Ancient Memphis
2 [a]Is. 6:11; Jer. 4:7; 9:11; 34:22; Mic. 3:12
3 [a]Jer. 19:4 [b]Deut. 13:6; 32:17
4 [a]2 Chr. 36:15; Jer. 7:25; 25:4; 26:5; 29:19; Zech. 7:7
6 [1]Or *became a ruin*
7 [a]Num. 16:38; Jer. 7:19; [Ezek. 33:11]; Hab. 2:10
8 [a]2 Kin. 17:15–17; Jer. 25:6, 7; 44:3; 1 Cor. 10:21, 22 [b]1 Kin. 9:7, 8; 2 Chr. 7:20; Jer. 42:18
10 [a]2 Chr. 36:12; Jer. 6:15; 8:12; Dan. 5:22 [b][Prov. 28:14] [1]Lit. *crushed*
11 [a]Lev. 17:10; 20:5, 6; Jer. 21:10; Amos 9:4 [1]*destroying*
12 [a]Jer. 42:15–17, 22 [b]Is. 65:15; Jer. 42:18 *See WW at Jer. 42:17.
13 [a]Jer. 43:11
14 [a]Jer. 22:26, 27 [b][Is. 4:2; 10:20]; Jer. 44:28; [Rom. 9:27] [1]Lit. *lift up their soul*
16 [a]Jer. 6:16
17 [a]Num. 30:12; Deut. 23:23; Judg. 11:36 [b]2 Kin. 17:16; Jer. 7:18 [1]Lit. *bread*
19 [a]Jer. 7:18

44:1 All the Jews would include the party led by Azariah and Johanan as well as many who had been deported earlier (see 2 Kin. 23:34). Jewish colonies existed at an early period throughout Egypt. **Migdol:** A site in northeastern Egypt whose precise location is uncertain (see 46:14). **Noph** is the Hebrew name for Memphis, on the western bank of the Nile south of Cairo. **Pathros** is Hebrew for Upper (southern) Egypt, roughly the area between Cairo and Aswan (see v. 15).

44:8 Works of your hands: Idols.

44:17 Queen of heaven: See note on 7:18.

44:18 We have lacked everything: The reform of Josiah (2 Kin. 23:4–14) put an end to their worship of Ishtar and was seen by them as a factor that led to the nation's downfall. Since that time they have experienced nothing but calamity. They reason, therefore, that the failure to worship Ishtar has caused the calamity. See vv. 21–23 for a contrary opinion.

44:19 Husbands' *permission:* Any action or vow by a married woman needed the consent of her husband to be valid. See v. 25; Num. 30:10–15.

we burned incense to the queen of
heaven and poured out drink offerings
to her, did we make cakes for her, to
worship her, and pour out drink offerings to her without our husbands' *permission?*"
20 Then Jeremiah spoke to all the people—the men, the women, and all the
people who had given him *that* answer—saying:
21 "The incense that you burned in the
cities of Judah and in the streets of Jerusalem, you and your fathers, your
kings and your princes, and the people
of the land, did not the LORD remember
them, and did it *not* come into His
mind?
22 "So the LORD could no longer bear
it, because of the evil of your doings
and because of the abominations
which you committed. Therefore your
land is a desolation, an astonishment,
a curse, and without an inhabitant,
[a]as *it is* this day.
23 "Because you have burned incense
and because you have sinned against
the LORD, and have not obeyed the
voice of the LORD or walked in His law,
in His statutes or in His testimonies,
[a]therefore this calamity has happened
to you, as *at* this day."
24 Moreover Jeremiah said to all the
people and to all the women, "Hear the
word of the LORD, all Judah who *are*
in the land of Egypt!
25 "Thus says the LORD of hosts, the
God of Israel, saying: 'You and your
wives have spoken with your mouths
and fulfilled with your hands, saying, "We will surely keep our vows
that we have made, to burn incense
to the queen of heaven and pour out
drink offerings to her." You will surely
keep your vows and perform your
vows!'
26 "Therefore hear the word of the
LORD, all Judah who dwell in the land
of Egypt: 'Behold, [a]I have sworn by My
[b]great name,' says the LORD, 'that
[c]My name shall no more be named in
the mouth of any man of Judah in all
the land of Egypt, saying, "The Lord
GOD lives."
27 'Behold, I will *watch over them for
adversity and not for good. And all the
men of Judah who *are* in the land of
Egypt [a]shall be consumed by the sword
and by famine, until there is an end
to them.
28 'Yet [a]a small number who escape
the sword shall return from the land
of Egypt to the land of Judah; and all
the remnant of Judah, who have gone
to the land of Egypt to dwell there,
shall know whose words will stand,
Mine or theirs.
29 'And this *shall be* a sign to you,'
says the LORD, 'that I will punish you
in this place, that you may know that
My words will surely [a]stand against
you for adversity.'
30 "Thus says the LORD: 'Behold,
[a]I will give Pharaoh Hophra king of
Egypt into the hand of his enemies and
into the hand of those who seek his
life, as I gave [b]Zedekiah king of Judah
into the hand of Nebuchadnezzar king
of Babylon, his enemy who sought his
life.'"

Assurance to Baruch

45 The [a]word that Jeremiah the
prophet spoke to [b]Baruch the
son of Neriah, when he had written
these words in a book [1]at the instruction of Jeremiah, in the [c]fourth year
of Jehoiakim the son of Josiah, king
of Judah, saying,
2 "Thus says the LORD, the God of Israel, to you, O Baruch:
3 'You said, "Woe is me now! For the
LORD has added grief to my sorrow. I
[a]fainted in my sighing, and I find no
*rest."'
4 "Thus you shall say to him, 'Thus
says the LORD: "Behold, [a]what I have
built I will break down, and what I
have planted I will pluck up, that is,
this whole land.
5 "And do you seek great things for
yourself? Do not seek *them;* for behold, [a]I will bring adversity on all
flesh," says the LORD. "But I will give
your [b]life to you as a prize in all places,
wherever you go."'"

22 [a]Jer. 25:11, 18, 38
23 [a]1 Kin. 9:9; Neh. 13:18; Jer. 44:2; Dan. 9:11, 12
26 [a]Gen. 22:16; Deut. 32:40, 41; Jer. 22:5; Amos 6:8; Heb. 6:13 [b]Jer. 10:6 [c]Neh. 9:5; Ps. 50:16; Ezek. 20:39
27 [a]Jer. 1:10; 31:28; Ezek. 7:6 *See WW at Jer. 1:12.
28 [a]Is. 10:19; 27:12, 13
29 [a][Ps. 33:11]
30 [a]Jer. 46:25, 26; Ezek. 29:3; 30:21 [b]2 Kin. 25:4–7; Jer. 39:5

CHAPTER 45

1 [a]Jer. 36:1, 4, 32 [b]Jer. 32:12, 16; 43:3 [c]Jer. 25:1; 36:1; 46:2 [1]Lit. *from Jeremiah's mouth*
3 [a]Ps. 6:6; 69:3; [2 Cor. 4:1, 16; Gal. 6:9] *See WW at Is. 28:12.
4 [a]Is. 5:5; Jer. 1:10; 11:17; 18:7–10; 31:28
5 [a]Jer. 25:17–26 [b]Jer. 21:9; 38:2; 39:18

44:21–23 Jeremiah contends that calamity has come upon Judah precisely because the incense was offered in *idolatrous worship,* and God **could no longer bear *it*** (v. 22). Jeremiah's interpretation of the calamity is diametrically opposed to that of the people.

44:25 You will surely keep your vows: Spoken in irony.

44:27 I will watch: See note on 1:1–12.

44:30 Pharaoh Hophra, or Apries, ruled Egypt from 589 to 570 B.C., but lost his life in a power struggle with Ahmosis II (Amasis), a former court official.

45:1–5 In despair, and overcome by the difficulties he faced, **Baruch** is told by God not to **seek great things** for himself but to be grateful that he will escape with his life. No hint is given as to why Baruch was so dejected. It is clear, however, that Baruch was a part of the overall plan of God to bring destruction on the nation and that he should be content to play his part.

Judgment on Egypt

46 The word of the LORD which
came to Jeremiah the prophet
against [a]the *nations.
2 Against [a]Egypt.
[b]Concerning the army of Pharaoh
Necho, king of Egypt, which was by
the River Euphrates in Carchemish,
and which Nebuchadnezzar king of
Babylon [c]defeated in the [d]fourth year
of Jehoiakim the son of Josiah, king
of Judah:

3 "Order[1] the [2]buckler and shield,
And draw near to battle!
4 Harness the horses,
And mount up, you horsemen!
Stand forth with *your* helmets,
Polish the spears,
[a]Put on the armor!
5 Why have I seen them dismayed
and turned back?
Their mighty ones are beaten
down;
They have speedily fled,
And did not look back,
For [a]fear *was* all around," says
the LORD.
6 "Do not let the swift flee away,
Nor the mighty man escape;
They will [a]stumble and fall
Toward the north, by the River
Euphrates.

7 "Who *is* this coming up [a]like a
flood,
Whose waters move like the
rivers?
8 Egypt rises up like a flood,
And *its* waters move like the
rivers;
And he says, 'I will go up *and*
cover the earth,
I will destroy the city and its
inhabitants.'
9 Come up, O horses, and rage,
O chariots!
And let the mighty men come
forth:
[1]The Ethiopians and [2]the Libyans
who handle the shield,
And the Lydians [a]who handle *and*
bend the bow.
10 For this *is* [a]the day of the Lord
GOD of hosts,
A day of vengeance,
That He may avenge Himself on
His adversaries.
[b]The sword shall devour;
It shall be [1]satiated and made
drunk with their blood;
For the Lord GOD of hosts
[c]has a sacrifice
In the north country by the River
Euphrates.

11 "Go[a] up to Gilead and take balm,
[b]O virgin, the daughter of Egypt;
In vain you will use many
medicines;
[c]You shall not be cured.
12 The nations have heard of your
[a]shame,
And your cry has filled the land;
For the mighty man has stumbled
against the mighty;
They both have fallen together."

Babylonia Will Strike Egypt

13 The word that the LORD spoke to
Jeremiah the prophet, how Nebuchadnezzar king of Babylon would come
and [a]strike the land of Egypt.

14 "Declare in Egypt, and proclaim in
[a]Migdol;
Proclaim in [1]Noph and in
[b]Tahpanhes;
Say, 'Stand fast and prepare
yourselves,
For the sword devours all around
you.'
15 Why are your valiant *men* swept
away?
They did not stand
Because the LORD drove them
away.
16 He made many fall;
Yes, [a]one fell upon another.
And they said, 'Arise!
[b]Let us go back to our own people
And to the land of our nativity
From the oppressing sword.'
17 They cried there,

CHAPTER 46
1 [a]Jer. 25:15 *See WW at Ps. 106:47.
2 [a]Jer. 25:17–19; Ezek.29:2—32:32 [b]2 Kin. 23:33–35 [c]2 Kin. 23:29; 24:7; 2 Chr. 35:20 [d]Jer. 45:1
3 [1]*Set in order* [2]A small shield
4 [a]Is. 21:5; Jer. 51:11, 12; Joel 3:9; Nah. 2:1; 3:14
5 [a]Jer. 49:29
6 [a]Jer. 46:12, 16; Dan. 11:19
7 [a]Is. 8:7, 8; Jer. 47:2; Dan. 11:22
9 [a]Is. 66:19 [1]Heb. *Cush* [2]Heb. *Put*
10 [a]Is. 13:6; Joel 1:15 [b]Deut. 32:42; Is. 31:8; Jer. 12:12 [c]Is. 34:6; Zeph. 1:7; Ezek. 39:17 [1]Filled to the full
11 [a]Jer. 8:22 [b]Is. 47:1; Jer. 31:4, 21 [c]Ezek. 30:21
12 [a]Jer. 2:36; Nah. 3:8–10
13 [a]Is. 19:1; Jer. 43:10, 11; Ezek. 29:1–21
14 [a]Jer. 44:1 [b]Ezek. 30:18 [1]Ancient Memphis
16 [a]Lev. 26:36, 37; Jer. 46:6 [b]Jer. 51:9

46:1—51:64 Prophecies against foreign nations (see Is. 13—23; Ezek. 25—32; and note on Amos 1:3—2:3). The prophecies begin with **Egypt** and end with **Babylon,** in a general west to east direction. They show God's sovereignty over all nations.
46:1–12 Describes the defeat of the Egyptians at the battle of Carchemish.
46:2 Against Egypt: See Is. 19; 20; Ezek. 29; 32. **Pharaoh Necho** ruled Egypt 610–595 B.C. One of the most important battles of the ancient world was fought at **Carchemish** (see 2 Chr. 35:20; Is. 10:9), for Egypt was defeated by **Nebuchadnezzar** and lost her influence in Syro-Palestine. The **fourth year** was 605 B.C.
46:7–10 Like the Nile River, Egypt expected to inundate the lands to the north. The **day of the LORD,** however, led to Egypt's defeat and humiliation. See note on Obad. 15.
46:11, 12 Gilead was known for its medicinal **balm** (see 8:22), but the wound of Egypt is incurable.
46:14 For these cities, see note on 44:1.
46:17 But a noise: In Is. 30:7 Egypt is called Rahab-Hem-Shebeth, "Rahab, the Do-Nothing." Jeremiah expresses the same sentiment, indicating Egypt has missed her opportunity

'Pharaoh, king of Egypt, *is but* a noise.
He has passed by the appointed time!'

18 "*As* I live," says the King,
[a]Whose name *is* the LORD of hosts,
"Surely as Tabor *is* among the mountains
And as Carmel by the sea, *so* he shall come.
19 O [a]you daughter dwelling in Egypt,
Prepare yourself [b]to go into captivity!
For [1]Noph shall be waste and desolate, without inhabitant.

20 "Egypt *is* a very pretty [a]heifer,
But destruction comes, it comes [b]from the north.
21 Also her mercenaries are in her midst like [1]fat bulls,
For they also are turned back,
They have fled away together.
They did not stand,
For [a]the day of their calamity had come upon them,
The time of their punishment.
22 [a]Her noise shall go like a serpent,
For they shall march with an army
And come against her with axes,
Like those who chop wood.

23 "They shall [a]cut down her forest," says the LORD,
"Though it cannot be searched,
Because they *are* innumerable,
And more numerous than [b]grasshoppers.
24 The daughter of Egypt shall be ashamed;
She shall be delivered into the hand
Of [a]the people of the north."

25 The LORD of hosts, the God of Israel,
says: "Behold, I will bring punishment
on [1]Amon of [a]No,[2] and Pharaoh and
Egypt, [b]with their gods and their
kings—Pharaoh and those who [c]trust
in him.
26 [a]"And I will deliver them into the
hand of those who seek their lives, into
the hand of Nebuchadnezzar king of
Babylon and the hand of his servants.
[b]Afterward it shall be inhabited as in
the days of old," says the LORD.

18 [a]Is. 47:4; Jer. 48:15; Mal. 1:14 **19** [a]Jer. 48:18 [b]Is. 20:4 [1]Ancient Memphis **20** [a]Hos. 10:11 [b]Jer. 1:14 **21** [a][Ps. 37:13]; Jer. 50:27 [1]Lit. *calves of the stall* **22** [a][Is. 29:4] **23** [a]Is. 10:34 [b]Judg. 6:5; 7:12; Joel 2:25 **24** [a]Jer. 1:15 **25** [a]Ezek. 30:14–16; Nah. 3:8 [b]Ex. 12:12; Jer. 43:12, 13; Ezek. 30:13; Zeph. 2:11 [c]Is. 30:1–5; 31:1–3 [1]A sun god [2]Ancient Thebes **26** [a]Jer. 44:30; Ezek. 32:11 [b]Ezek. 29:8–14

God Will Preserve Israel

27 "But[a] do not fear, O My servant Jacob,
And do not be dismayed, O Israel!
For behold, I will [b]save you from afar,
And your offspring from the land of their captivity;
Jacob shall return, have rest and be at ease;
No one shall make *him* afraid.
28 Do not fear, O Jacob My servant," says the LORD,
"For I *am* with you;
For I will make a complete end of all the nations
To which I have driven you,
But I will not make [a]a complete end of you.
I will rightly [b]correct* you,
For I will not leave you wholly unpunished."

27 [a]Is. 41:13, 14; 43:5; 44:2; Jer. 30:10, 11 [b]Is. 11:11; Jer. 23:3, 4; Mic. 7:12 **28** [a]Jer. 10:24; Amos 9:8, 9 [b]Jer. 30:11 *See WW at Jer. 10:24.

Judgment on Philistia

47

The word of the LORD that came
to Jeremiah the prophet
[a]against the Philistines, [b]before Pharaoh attacked Gaza.
2 Thus says the LORD:

"Behold, [a]waters rise [b]out of the north,
And shall be an overflowing flood;
They shall overflow the land and all that is in it,
The city and those who dwell within;
Then the men shall cry,
And all the inhabitants of the land shall wail.
3 At the [a]noise of the stamping hooves of his strong horses,
At the rushing of his chariots,
At the rumbling of his wheels,

CHAPTER 47

1 [a]Is. 14:29–31; Ezek. 25:15–17; Zeph. 2:4, 5; Zech. 9:6 [b]Amos 1:6 **2** [a]Is. 8:7, 8; Jer. 46:7, 8 [b]Jer. 1:14 **3** [a]Judg. 5:22; Jer. 8:16; Nah. 3:2

because she failed to do anything when Nebuchadnezzar was called back to Babylon on the death of his father.
46:18 ***Tabor** and **Carmel*** in northern Israel are prominent mountains, and both give the impression of grandeur because of insignificant surroundings. In the same way Nebuchadnezzar will tower over the Egyptians.
46:20 Egypt is described as a **pretty heifer,** but **destruction** (perhaps a "gadfly," something that nips or pinches) comes from the north (Babylon). Compare the use of fly and bee (Is. 7:18) or hornets (Ex. 23:28).
46:22 The **serpent** was used by the pharaohs as a symbol of authority.
47:1–7 Other prophets also spoke **against the Philistines** (see Is. 14:28–32; Ezek. 25:15–17; Amos 1:6–8; Zeph. 2:4–7). Along with Tyre and Sidon, the Philistines were condemned for selling Israelites into slavery (see Joel 3:4–6; Amos 1:6–10).

The fathers will not look back for
their children,
[1]Lacking courage,
4 Because of the day that comes to
plunder all the [a]Philistines,
To cut off from [b]Tyre and Sidon
every helper who remains;
For the LORD shall plunder the
Philistines,
[c]The remnant of the country of
[d]Caphtor.[1]
5 [a]Baldness has come upon Gaza,
[b]Ashkelon is cut off
With the remnant of their valley.
How long will you cut yourself?

6 "O you [a]sword of the LORD,
How long until you are quiet?
Put yourself up into your
scabbard,
Rest and be still!
7 How can [1]it be quiet,
Seeing the LORD has [a]given it a
charge
Against Ashkelon and against the
seashore?
There He has [b]appointed it."

Judgment on Moab

48 Against [a]Moab.
Thus says the LORD of hosts,
the God of Israel:

"Woe to [b]Nebo!
For it is plundered,
[c]Kirjathaim is shamed *and* taken;
[1]The high stronghold is shamed
and dismayed—
2 [a]No more praise of Moab.
In [b]Heshbon they have devised
evil against her:
'Come, and let us cut her off as a
nation.'
You also shall be cut down,
O [c]Madmen![1]
The sword shall pursue you;
3 A voice of crying *shall be* from
[a]Horonaim:
'Plundering and great
destruction!'
4 "Moab is destroyed;
[1]Her little ones have caused a cry
to be heard;
5 [a]For in the Ascent of Luhith they
ascend with continual weeping;
For in the descent of Horonaim
the enemies have heard a cry
of destruction.

6 "Flee, save your lives!
And be like [1]the [a]juniper in the
wilderness.
7 For because you have trusted in
your works and your
[a]treasures,
You also shall be taken.
And [b]Chemosh shall go forth into
captivity,
His [c]priests and his princes
together.
8 And [a]the plunderer shall come
against every city;
No one shall escape.
The valley also shall perish,
And the plain shall be destroyed,
As the LORD has spoken.

9 "Give[a] wings to Moab,
That she may flee and get away;
For her cities shall be desolate,
Without any to dwell in them.
10 [a]Cursed *is* he who does the work 5
of the LORD deceitfully,
And cursed *is* he who keeps back
his sword from blood.

11 "Moab has been at ease from
[1]his youth;
He [a]has settled on his dregs,
And has not been emptied from
vessel to vessel,
Nor has he gone into captivity.
Therefore his taste remained in
him,
And his scent has not changed.

12 "Therefore behold, the days are
coming," says the LORD,
"That I shall send him [1]wine
workers
Who will tip him over
And empty his vessels
And break the bottles.
13 Moab shall be ashamed of
[a]Chemosh,
As the house of Israel [b]was
ashamed of [c]Bethel, their
confidence.

14 "How can you say, [a]'We *are*
mighty
And strong men for the war'?

3 [1]Lit. *From sinking hands* **4** [a]Is. 14:29–31 [b]Jer. 25:22 [c]Ezek. 25:16 [d]Gen. 10:14 [1]Crete **5** [a]Mic. 1:16 [b]Jer. 25:20 **6** [a]Ezek.21:3–5 **7** [a]Ezek. 14:17 [b]Mic. 6:9 [1]Lit. *you*

CHAPTER 48

1 [a]Is. 15:1—16:14; 25:10 [b]Is. 15:2 [c]Num. 32:37 [1]Heb. *Misgab* **2** [a]Is. 16:14 [b]Jer. 49:3 [c]Is. 10:31 [1]A city of Moab **3** [a]Is. 15:5 **4** [1]So with MT, Tg., Vg.; LXX *Proclaim it in Zoar* **5** [a]Is. 15:5

6 [a]Jer. 17:6 [1]Or *Aroer,* a city of Moab **7** [a]Jer. 9:23 [b]Jer. 48:13 [c]Jer. 49:3 **8** [a]Jer. 6:26 **9** [a]Ps. 55:6 **10** [a]1 Sam. 15:3, 9 **11** [a]Zeph. 1:12 [1]Heb. uses masc. and fem. pronouns interchangeably in this chapter. **12** [1]Lit. *tippers* of wine bottles **13** [a]1 Kin. 11:7 [b]Hos. 10:6 [c]1 Kin. 12:29; 13:32–34 **14** [a]Is. 16:6

48:1–47 Other prophets also spoke **against Moab** (see Is. 15, 16; Ezek. 25:8–11; Amos 2:1–3; Zeph. 2:8–11). According to Josephus (*Antiquities* 10.9.7), this prophecy of destruction for Moab was carried out in the twenty-third year of the reign of Nebuchadnezzar.
48:10–12 See section 5 of Truth-In-Action at the end of Jer.

48:11–13 Moab is likened to wine left to improve with age (see Is. 25:6). However, **wine workers** (the approaching Babylonian army) will **empty his vessels and break the bottles**. **Chemosh:** The god of Moab (see vv. 7, 46; Judg. 11:24; 1 Kin. 11:7, 33; 2 Kin. 23:13).

15 Moab is plundered and gone up
from her cities;
Her chosen young men have
[a]gone down to the slaughter,"
says [b]the King,
Whose name *is* the LORD of hosts.

16 "The calamity of Moab *is* near at
hand,
And his affliction comes quickly.
17 Bemoan him, all you who are
around him;
And all you who know his name,
Say, [a]'How the strong staff is
broken,
The beautiful rod!'

18 "O [a]daughter inhabiting [b]Dibon,
Come down from *your* glory,
And sit in thirst;
For the plunderer of Moab has
come against you,
He has destroyed your
strongholds.
19 O inhabitant of [a]Aroer,
[b]Stand by the way and watch;
Ask him who flees
And her who escapes;
Say, 'What has happened?'
20 Moab is shamed, for he is broken
down.
[a]Wail and cry!
Tell it in [b]Arnon, that Moab is
plundered.

21 "And judgment has come on the
plain country:
On Holon and Jahzah and
Mephaath,
22 On Dibon and Nebo and Beth
Diblathaim,
23 On Kirjathaim and Beth Gamul
and Beth Meon,
24 On [a]Kerioth and Bozrah,
On all the cities of the land of
Moab,
Far or near.
25 [a]The [1]horn* of Moab is cut off,
And his [b]arm is broken," says the
LORD.

26 "Make[a] him drunk,
Because he exalted *himself*
against the LORD.
Moab shall wallow in his vomit,
And he shall also be in derision.
27 For [a]was not Israel a derision to
you?
[b]*Was he* found among thieves?
For whenever you speak of him,
You shake *your head in* [c]scorn.

15 [a][Is. 40:30, 31]; Jer. 50:27 [b]Jer. 46:18; 51:57; Mal. 1:14
17 [a]Is. 9:4; 14:4, 5
18 [a]Is. 47:1 [b]Num. 21:30; Josh. 13:9, 17; Is. 15:2; Jer. 48:22
19 [a]Deut. 2:36; Josh. 12:2; Is. 17:2 [b]1 Sam. 4:13, 14, 16
20 [a]Is. 16:7 [b]Num. 21:13
24 [a]Jer. 48:41; Amos 2:2
25 [a]Ps. 75:10; Zech. 1:19–21 [b]Ezek. 30:21 [1]Strength *See WW at Ezek. 29:21.
26 [a]Jer. 25:15
27 [a]Zeph. 2:8 [b]Jer. 2:26 [c]Lam. 2:15; [Mic. 7:8–10]

28 [a]Ps. 55:6, 7 [b]Song 2:14
29 [a]Is. 16:6; Zeph. 2:8, 10 [b]Jer. 49:16
30 [a]Is. 16:6; Jer. 50:36 [1]*idle talk*
31 [a]Is. 15:5; 16:7, 11 [1]So with DSS, LXX, Vg.; MT *He*
32 [a]Is. 16:8, 9 [b]Num. 21:32; Is. 16:10
33 [a]Is. 16:10; Jer. 25:10; Joel 1:12 [1]*cease*
34 [a]Is. 15:4–6 [b]Num. 32:3, 37 [c]Is. 15:5, 6 [1]Or *The Third Eglath,* an unknown city, Is. 15:5
35 [a]Is. 15:2; 16:12 [1]Places for pagan worship
36 [a]Is. 15:5; 16:11 [b]Is. 15:7
37 [a]Is. 15:2, 3; Jer. 16:6; 41:5; 47:5

28 You who dwell in Moab,
Leave the cities and [a]dwell in the
rock,
And be like [b]the dove *which*
makes her nest
In the sides of the cave's mouth.

29 "We have heard the [a]pride of
Moab
(He *is* exceedingly proud),
Of his loftiness and arrogance
and [b]pride,
And of the haughtiness of his
heart."

30 "I know his wrath," says the LORD,
"But it *is* not right;
[a]His [1]lies have made nothing right.
31 Therefore [a]I will wail for Moab,
And I will cry out for all Moab;
[1]I will mourn for the men of Kir
Heres.
32 [a]O vine of Sibmah! I will weep for
you with the weeping of [b]Jazer.
Your plants have gone over the
sea,
They reach to the sea of Jazer.
The plunderer has fallen on your
summer fruit and your vintage.
33 [a]Joy and gladness are taken
From the plentiful field
And from the land of Moab;
I have caused wine to [1]fail from
the winepresses;
No one will tread with joyous
shouting—
Not joyous shouting!

34 "From[a] the cry of Heshbon to
[b]Elealeh and to Jahaz
They have uttered their voice,
[c]From Zoar to Horonaim,
Like [1]a three-year-old heifer;
For the waters of Nimrim also
shall be desolate.

35 "Moreover," says the LORD,
"I will cause to cease in Moab
[a]The one who offers *sacrifices* in
the [1]high places
And burns incense to his gods.
36 Therefore [a]My heart shall wail
like flutes for Moab,
And like flutes My heart shall
wail
For the men of Kir Heres.
Therefore [b]the riches they have
acquired have perished.

37 "For [a]every head *shall be* bald, and
every beard clipped;

48:26, 27 Moab is brought low because of his attitude toward Israel; as he ridiculed Israel, so he will be ridiculed.

48:37 Various signs of mourning are mentioned (see Is. 15:2, 3).

On all the hands *shall be* cuts, and
[b]on the loins sackcloth—
38 A general lamentation
On all the [a]housetops of Moab,
And in its streets;
For I have [b]broken Moab like a
vessel in which *is* no pleasure,"
says the LORD.
39 "They shall wail:
'How she is broken down!
How Moab has turned her back
with shame!'
So Moab shall be a derision
And a dismay to all those about
her."

40 For thus says the LORD:

"Behold, [a]one shall fly like an
eagle,
And [b]spread his wings over
Moab.
41 Kerioth is taken,
And the strongholds are
surprised;
[a]The mighty men's hearts in Moab
on that day shall be
Like the heart of a woman in birth
pangs.
42 And Moab shall be destroyed
[a]as a people,
Because he exalted *himself*
against the LORD.
43 [a]Fear and the pit and the snare
shall be upon you,
O inhabitant of Moab," says the
LORD.
44 "He who flees from the fear shall
fall into the pit,
And he who gets out of the pit
shall be caught in the [a]snare.
For upon Moab, upon it [b]I will
bring
The year of their punishment,"
says the LORD.

45 "Those who fled stood under the
shadow of Heshbon
Because of exhaustion.
But [a]a fire shall come out of
Heshbon,
A flame from the midst of
[b]Sihon,
And [c]shall devour the brow of
Moab,
The crown of the head of the sons
of tumult.
46 [a]Woe to you, O Moab!
The people of Chemosh perish;
For your sons have been taken
captive,
And your daughters captive.
47 "Yet I will bring back the captives
of Moab
[a]In the latter days," says the LORD.

Thus far *is* the judgment of Moab.

Judgment on Ammon

49 Against the [a]Ammonites.
Thus says the LORD:

"Has Israel no sons?
Has he no heir?
Why *then* does [1]Milcom inherit
[b]Gad,
And his people dwell in its cities?
2 [a]Therefore behold, the days are
coming," says the LORD,
"That I will cause to be heard an
alarm of war
In [b]Rabbah of the Ammonites;
It shall be a desolate mound,
And her [1]villages shall be burned
with fire.
Then Israel shall take possession
of his inheritance," says the
LORD.

3 "Wail, O [a]Heshbon, for Ai is
plundered!
Cry, you daughters of Rabbah,
[b]Gird yourselves with sackcloth!
Lament and run to and fro by the
walls;
For [1]Milcom shall go into
captivity
With his [c]priests and his princes
together.
4 Why [a]do you boast in the valleys,
[1]Your flowing valley,
O [b]backsliding daughter?
Who trusted in her [c]treasures,
[d]*saying,*
'Who will come against me?'
5 Behold, I will bring fear upon
you,"
Says the Lord GOD of hosts,

37 [b]Gen. 37:34; Is. 15:3; 20:2
38 [a]Is. 15:3 [b]Jer. 22:28
40 [a]Deut. 28:49; Jer. 49:22; Hos. 8:1; Hab. 1:8 [b]Is. 8:8
41 [a]Is. 13:8; 21:3; Jer. 30:6; Mic. 4:9, 10
42 [a]Ps. 83:4; Jer. 48:2
43 [a]Is. 24:17, 18; Lam. 3:47
44 [a]1 Kin. 19:17; Is. 24:18; Amos 5:19 [b]Jer. 11:23
45 [a]Num. 21:28, 29 [b]Num. 21:21, 26; Ps. 135:11 [c]Num. 24:17
46 [a]Num. 21:29
47 [a]Jer. 49:6, 39

CHAPTER 49

1 [a]Deut. 23:3, 4; 2 Chr. 20:1; Jer. 25:21; Ezek. 21:28–32; 25:1–7 [b]Amos 1:13–15; Zeph. 2:8–11 [1]Heb. *Malcam,* lit. *their king;* an Ammonite god, 1 Kin. 11:5; *Molech,* Lev. 18:21
2 [a]Amos 1:13–15 [b]Ezek. 25:5 [1]Lit. *daughters*
3 [a]Jer. 48:2 [b]Is. 32:11; Jer. 48:37 [c]Jer. 48:7 [1]See v. 1
4 [a]Jer. 9:23 [b]Jer. 3:14 [c]Jer. 48:7 [d]Jer. 21:13 [1]Lit. *Your valley is flowing*

48:40, 41 Similar to 49:22 where it is applied to Edom.
48:45 The **fire** and **flame** against Moab are first mentioned in Num. 21:28.
48:47 After a devastating punishment, God will have mercy and **bring back the captives of Moab in the latter days.** This mercy is probably shown because Moab, like Ammon, was descended from Lot, the nephew of Abraham (see Gen. 19:30–38). The precise time of fulfillment of this prophecy is not clear.
49:1–6 Other prophets also spoke **against the Ammonites**. See Ezek. 25:1–7; Amos 1:13–15; Zeph. 2:8–11.
49:1 Milcom, chief god of the Ammonites (v. 3; 1 Kin. 11:5, 33), is also called Molech (1 Kin. 11:7).

"From all those who are around you;
You shall be driven out, everyone headlong,
And no one will gather those who wander off.
6 But [a]afterward I will bring back
The captives of the people of Ammon," says the LORD.

Judgment on Edom

7 [a]Against Edom.
Thus says the LORD of hosts:

[b]"*Is* wisdom no more in Teman?
[c]Has *counsel perished from the prudent?
Has their wisdom [d]vanished?
8 Flee, turn back, dwell in the depths, O inhabitants of [a]Dedan!
For I will bring the calamity of Esau upon him,
The time *that* I will punish him.
9 [a]If grape gatherers came to you,
Would they not leave *some* gleaning grapes?
If thieves by night,
Would they not destroy until they have *enough?
10 [a]But I have made Esau bare;
I have uncovered his secret places,
And he shall not be *able to hide himself.
His descendants are plundered,
His brethren and his neighbors,
And [b]he *is* no more.
11 Leave your fatherless children,
I will preserve *them* alive;
And let your widows trust in Me."

12 For thus says the LORD: "Behold,
[a]those whose judgment *was* not to
drink of the cup have assuredly drunk.
And *are* you the one who will altogether go unpunished? You shall not
go unpunished, but you shall surely
drink *of it*.
13 "For [a]I have sworn by Myself," says
the LORD, "that [b]Bozrah shall become
a desolation, a reproach, a [1]waste, and
a curse. And all its cities shall be perpetual [2]wastes."

6 [a]Jer. 48:47 **7** [a]Gen. 25:30; 32:3; Is. 34:5, 6; Jer. 25:21; Ezek. 25:12–14; 35:1–15; Joel 3:19; Amos 1:11, 12; Obad. 1–9, 15, 16 [b]Gen. 36:11; Job 2:11 [c]Is. 19:11 [d]Jer. 8:9 *See WW at Zech. 6:13. **8** [a]Is. 21:13; Jer. 25:23 **9** [a]Obad. 5, 6 *See WW at Mal. 3:10. **10** [a]Obad. 5, 6; Mal. 1:3 [b]Is. 17:14 *See WW at Num. 13:30. **12** [a]Jer. 25:29; Obad. 16 **13** [a]Gen. 22:16; Is. 45:23; Jer. 44:26; Amos 6:8 [b]Gen. 36:33; 1 Chr. 1:44; Is. 34:6; 63:1; Amos 1:12 [1]*ruin* [2]*ruins*

14 [a]I have heard a message from the LORD,
And an ambassador has been sent to the nations:
"Gather together, come against her,
And rise up to battle!

15 "For indeed, I will make you small among nations,
Despised among men.
16 Your fierceness has deceived you,
The [a]pride of your heart,
O you who dwell in the clefts of the rock,
Who hold the height of the hill!
[b]Though you make your [c]nest as high as the eagle,
[d]I will bring you down from there," says the LORD.

17 "Edom also shall be an astonishment;
[a]Everyone who goes by it will be astonished
And will hiss at all its plagues.
18 [a]As in the overthrow of Sodom and Gomorrah
And their neighbors," says the LORD,
"No one shall remain there,
Nor shall a son of man *dwell in it.

19 "Behold,[a] he shall come up like a lion from [b]the [1]floodplain of the Jordan
Against the dwelling place of the strong;
But I will suddenly make him run away from her.
And who *is* a chosen *man that* I may appoint over her?
For [c]who *is* like Me?
Who will arraign Me?
And [d]who *is* that shepherd
Who will withstand Me?"

20 [a]Therefore hear the counsel of the LORD that He has taken against Edom,
And His purposes that He has proposed against the inhabitants of Teman:
Surely the least of the flock shall [1]draw them out;

14 [a]Obad. 1–4 **16** [a]Jer. 48:29 [b]Obad. 3, 4 [c]Job 39:27; Is. 14:13–15 [d]Amos 9:2 **17** [a]Jer. 18:16; 49:13; 50:13; Ezek. 35:7 **18** [a]Gen. 19:24, 25; Deut. 29:23; Jer. 50:40; Amos 4:11; Zeph. 2:9 *See WW at Jer. 42:17. **19** [a]Jer. 50:44 [b]Josh. 3:15; Jer. 12:5 [c]Ex. 15:11; Is. 46:9 [d]Job 41:10 [1]Or *thicket* **20** [a]Is. 14:24, 27; Jer. 50:45 [1]Or *drag them away*

49:6 Ammon is promised restoration after destruction. See note on 48:47.

49:7–22 Other prophets also spoke **against Edom**. See Is. 21:11, 12; Ezek. 25:12–14; Amos 1:11, 12; and notes on Obad. 1–16.

49:13 **Bozrah** and "grape-gatherers" (v. 9) have the same Hebrew root.

49:14–16 Parallel to Obad. 1–4.

49:18 Repeated with slight variation in 50:40.

49:19–21 Repeated with slight variation and applied against Babylon in 50:44–46.

Surely He shall make their
dwelling places desolate with
them.
21 [a]The earth shakes at the noise of
their fall;
At the cry its noise is heard at the
Red Sea.
22 Behold, [a]He shall come up and fly
like the eagle,
And spread His wings over
Bozrah;
The heart of the mighty men of
Edom in that day shall be
Like the heart of a woman in birth
pangs.

Judgment on Damascus

23 [a]Against Damascus.

[b]"Hamath and Arpad are shamed,
For they have heard bad news.
They are fainthearted;
[c]*There is* [1]trouble on the sea;
It cannot be quiet.
24 Damascus has grown feeble;
She turns to flee,
And fear has seized *her*.
[a]Anguish and sorrows have taken
her like a woman in [1]labor.
25 Why is [a]the city of praise not
deserted, the city of My joy?
26 [a]Therefore her young men shall
fall in her streets,
And all the men of war shall be
cut off in that day," says the
LORD of hosts.
27 "I[a] will kindle a fire in the wall of
Damascus,
And it shall consume the palaces
of Ben-Hadad."

Judgment on Kedar and Hazor

28 [a]Against Kedar and against the
kingdoms of Hazor, which Nebuchadnezzar king of Babylon shall strike.
Thus says the LORD:

"Arise, go up to Kedar,
And devastate [b]the men of the
East!
29 Their [a]tents and their flocks they
shall take away.
They shall take for themselves
their curtains,
All their vessels and their camels;
And they shall cry out to them,
[b]'Fear *is* on every side!'

30 "Flee, get far away! Dwell in the
depths,
O inhabitants of Hazor!" says the
LORD.
"For Nebuchadnezzar king of
Babylon has taken counsel
against you,
And has conceived a plan against
you.

31 "Arise, go up to [a]the wealthy
nation that dwells securely,"
says the LORD,
"Which has neither gates nor bars,
[b]Dwelling alone.
32 Their camels shall be for booty,
And the multitude of their cattle
for plunder.
I will [a]scatter to all winds those
[1]in the farthest corners,
And I will bring their calamity
from all its sides," says the
LORD.
33 "Hazor [a]shall be a dwelling for
jackals, a desolation forever;
No one shall reside there,
Nor son of man dwell in it."

Judgment on Elam

34 The word of the LORD that came to
Jeremiah the prophet against [a]Elam, in
the [b]beginning of the reign of Zedekiah
king of Judah, saying,
35 "Thus says the LORD of hosts:

'Behold, I will break [a]the
[1]bow of Elam,
The foremost of their might.
36 Against Elam I will bring the four
winds
From the four quarters of heaven,
And scatter them toward all those
winds;
There shall be no nations where
the outcasts of Elam will not go.
37 For I will cause Elam to be
dismayed before their enemies
And before those who seek their
life.
[a]I will bring disaster upon them,
My fierce anger,' says the LORD;

21 [a]Jer. 50:46; Ezek. 26:15, 18 **22** [a]Jer. 48:40, 41 **23** [a]Is. 17:1–3; Amos 1:3, 5; Zech. 9:1, 2 [b]Jer. 39:5; Zech. 9:2 [c][Is. 57:20] [1]*anxiety* **24** [a]Is. 13:8; Jer. 4:31; 6:24; 48:21 [1]*childbirth* **25** [a]Jer. 33:9 **26** [a]Jer. 50:30; Amos 4:10 **27** [a]Amos 1:4 **28** [a]Gen. 25:13; Ps. 120:5; Is. 21:16, 17; Jer. 2:10; Ezek. 27:21 [b]Judg. 6:3; Job 1:3 **29** [a]Ps. 120:5 [b]Jer. 46:5

31 [a]Ezek. 38:11 [b]Num. 23:9; Deut. 33:28; Mic. 7:16 **32** [a]Ezek. 5:10 [1]Lit. *cut off at the corner,* Jer. 9:26; 25:23 **33** [a]Jer. 9:11; 10:22; Zeph. 2:9, 12–15; Mal. 1:3 **34** [a]Gen. 10:22; Jer. 25:25; Ezek. 32:24; Dan. 8:2 [b]2 Kin. 24:17, 18; Jer. 28:1 **35** [a]Ps. 46:9; Is. 22:6 [1]Power **37** [a]Jer. 9:16

49:22 Similar to 48:40, 41 where applied to Moab.
49:23–27 Other prophets also spoke **against Damascus** (see Is. 17:1–3 and note on Amos 1:3–5).
49:26 Repeated exactly (except for the name of God) in 50:30.
49:28–33 **Hazor** is a center of Arab occupation, not to be confused with the city north of the Sea of Galilee.
49:31 **Neither gates nor bars** implies open settlements characteristic of nomadic people.
49:34–39 Other prophets also spoke **against Elam**. See Is. 11:11; 21:2; 22:6; Ezek. 32:24.

'And I will send the sword after
them
Until I have consumed them.
38 I will [a]set My throne in Elam,
And will destroy from there the
king and the princes,' says the
LORD.

39 'But it shall come to pass
[a]in the latter days:
I will bring back the captives of
Elam,' says the LORD."

Judgment on Babylon and Babylonia

50 The word that the LORD spoke
[a]against Babylon *and* against
the land of the Chaldeans by Jeremiah
the prophet.

2 "Declare among the nations,
Proclaim, and [1]set up a standard;
Proclaim—do not conceal *it*—
Say, 'Babylon is [a]taken, [b]Bel is
shamed.
[2]Merodach is broken in pieces;
[c]Her idols are humiliated,
Her images are broken in pieces.'
3 [a]For out of the north [b]a nation
comes up against her,
Which shall make her land
desolate,
And no one shall dwell therein.
They shall [1]move, they shall
depart,
Both man and beast.

4 "In those days and in that time,"
says the LORD,
"The children of Israel shall come,
[a]They and the children of Judah
together;
[b]With continual weeping they
shall come,
[c]And seek the LORD their God.
5 They shall ask the way to Zion,
With their faces toward it, *saying,*
'Come and let us join ourselves to
the LORD
In [a]a perpetual covenant
That will not be forgotten.'

6 "My people have been [a]lost
sheep.
Their shepherds have led them
[b]astray;
They have turned them away *on*
[c]the mountains.
They have gone from mountain to
hill;
They have forgotten their resting
place.
7 All who found them have
[a]devoured them;
And [b]their adversaries said,
[c]'We have not offended,
Because they have sinned against
the LORD, [d]the habitation of
justice,
The LORD, [e]the hope of their
fathers.'

8 "Move[a] from the midst of Babylon,
Go out of the land of the
Chaldeans;
And be like the [1]rams before the
flocks.
9 [a]For behold, I will raise and cause
to come up against Babylon
An *assembly of great nations
from the north country,
And they shall array themselves
against her;
From there she shall be captured.
Their arrows *shall be* like *those*
of [1]an expert warrior;
[b]None shall return in vain.
10 And Chaldea shall become
plunder;
[a]All who plunder her shall be
satisfied," says the LORD.

11 "Because[a] you were glad, because
you rejoiced,
You destroyers of My heritage,
Because you have grown fat
[b]like a heifer threshing grain,
And you [1]bellow like bulls,
12 Your mother shall be deeply
ashamed;
She who bore you shall be
ashamed.
Behold, the least of the nations
shall be a [a]wilderness,
A dry land and a desert.
13 Because of the wrath of the
LORD
She shall not be inhabited,

38 [a]Jer. 43:10
39 [a]Jer. 48:47

CHAPTER 50

1 [a]Gen. 10:10; 11:9; 2 Kin. 17:24; Is. 13:1; 47:1; Dan. 1:1; Rev. 14:8
2 [a]Is. 21:9 [b]Is. 46:1; Jer. 51:44 [c]Jer. 43:12, 13 [1]*lift* [2]Or *Marduk;* a Babylonian god
3 [a]Jer. 51:48; Dan. 5:30, 31 [b]Is. 13:17, 18, 20 [1]Or *wander*
4 [a]Ezra 2:1; Is. 11:12, 13; Jer. 3:18; 31:31; 33:7; Hos. 1:11 [b]Ezra 3:12, 13; [Ps. 126:5]; Jer. 31:9; [Zech. 12:10] [c]Hos. 3:5
5 [a]Jer. 31:31
6 [a]Is. 53:6; [Ezek. 34:15, 16]; Matt. 9:36; 10:6; 1 Pet. 2:25 [b]Jer. 23:1; Ezek. 34:2 [c][Jer. 2:20; 3:6, 23]
7 [a]Ps. 79:7 [b]Jer. 40:2, 3; Zech. 11:5 [c]Jer. 2:3; Dan. 9:16 [d][Ps. 90:1; 91:1] [e]Ps. 22:4; Jer. 14:8; 17:13
8 [a]Is. 48:20; Jer. 51:6, 45; Zech. 2:6, 7; [Rev. 18:4] [1]*male goats*
9 [a]Jer. 15:14; 51:27 [b]2 Sam. 1:22 [1]So with some Heb. mss., LXX, Syr.; MT, Tg., Vg. *a warrior who makes childless*
*See WW at Lev. 16:17.
10 [a][Rev. 17:16]
11 [a]Is. 47:6 [b]Hos. 10:11 [1]Or *neigh like steeds*
12 [a]Jer. 51:43

49:39 A hope of future restoration is mentioned for Elam as it was for Moab (48:47) and Ammon (49:6). On its fulfillment, *see note on 48:47.*

50:1—51:64 The other prophet to speak **against Babylon** is Isaiah (Is. 13:1—14:23; 21:1–9; 47:1–15; 48:14). In this lengthy oracle Jeremiah proclaims judgment against Babylon and restoration for exiled Israel.

50:2 The first of three summons given to rally people against Babylon (see 50:29; 51:27). **Merodach** (or Marduk) was the chief god of Babylon, and **Bel** was a title of Marduk. The Hebrew for **her images** is a word meaning "little dung balls," a derogatory reference frequently applied to foreign gods, and a special favorite of Ezekiel who uses it about 40 times. See notes on Zeph. 2:4–15 and Obad. 15.

50:4–7 A message of hope for the return and restoration of Israel and Judah interposed in the oracle against Babylon. See also vv. 33, 34; 51:5–10; and note on 30:1—33:26.

[a]But she shall be wholly desolate.
[b]Everyone who goes by Babylon
shall be horrified
And hiss at all her plagues.

14 "Put[a] yourselves in array against
Babylon all around,
All you who bend the bow;
Shoot at her, spare no arrows,
For she has sinned against the
LORD.
15 Shout against her all around;
She has [a]given her hand,
Her foundations have fallen,
[b]Her walls are thrown down;
For [c]it *is* the vengeance of the
LORD.
Take vengeance on her.
As she has done, so do to her.
16 Cut off the *sower from Babylon,
And him who handles the sickle
at harvest time.
For fear of the oppressing sword
[a]Everyone shall turn to his own
people,
And everyone shall flee to his
own land.

17 "Israel *is* like [a]scattered sheep;
[b]The lions have driven *him* away.
First [c]the king of Assyria
devoured him;
Now at last this
[d]Nebuchadnezzar king of
Babylon has broken his bones."

18 Therefore thus says the LORD of
hosts, the God of Israel:

"Behold, I will punish the king of
Babylon and his land,
As I have punished the king of
[a]Assyria.
19 [a]But I will bring back Israel to his
home,
And he shall feed on Carmel and
Bashan;
His soul shall be satisfied on
Mount Ephraim and Gilead.
20 In those days and in that time,"
says the LORD,
[a]"The iniquity of Israel shall be
sought, but *there shall be* none;
And the sins of Judah, but they
shall not be found;
For I will pardon those [b]whom I
preserve.

21 "Go up against the land of
Merathaim, against it,
And against the inhabitants of
[a]Pekod.
[1]Waste and utterly destroy them,"
says the LORD,
"And do [b]according to all that I
have commanded you.
22 [a]A sound of battle *is* in the land,
And of great destruction.
23 How [a]the hammer of the whole
earth has been cut apart and
broken!
How Babylon has become a
desolation among the nations!
I have laid a snare for you;
24 You have indeed been [a]trapped,
O Babylon,
And you were not aware;
You have been found and also
caught,
Because you have [b]contended
against the LORD.
25 The LORD has opened His armory,
And has brought out [a]the
weapons of His indignation;
For this *is* the work of the Lord
GOD of hosts
In the land of the Chaldeans.
26 Come against her from the
farthest border;
Open her storehouses;
Cast her up as heaps of ruins,
And destroy her utterly;
Let nothing of her be left.
27 Slay all her [a]bulls,
Let them go down to the
slaughter.
Woe to them!
For their day has come, the time
of [b]their punishment.
28 The voice of those who flee and
escape from the land of
Babylon
[a]Declares in Zion the vengeance
of the LORD our God,
The vengeance of His temple.

29 "Call together the archers against
Babylon.
All you who bend the bow,
encamp against it all around;
Let none of them [1]escape.
[a]Repay her according to her work;
According to all she has done, do
to her;
[b]For she has been proud against
the LORD,

13 [a]Jer. 25:12 [b]Jer. 49:17
14 [a]Jer. 51:2
15 [a]1 Chr. 29:24; 2 Chr. 30:8; Lam. 5:6; Ezek. 17:18 [b]Jer. 51:58 [c]Jer. 51:6, 11
16 [a]Is. 13:14; Jer. 51:9 *See WW at Hos. 10:12.
17 [a]2 Kin. 24:10, 14 [b]Jer. 2:15 [c]2 Kin. 15:29; 17:6; 18:9–13 [d]2 Kin. 24:10–14; 25:1–7
18 [a]Is. 10:12; Ezek. 31:3, 11, 12; Nah. 3:7, 18, 19
19 [a]Is. 65:10; Jer. 33:12; Ezek. 34:13
20 [a]Num. 23:21; Is. 43:25; [Jer. 31:34; Mic. 7:19] [b]Is. 1:9
21 [a]Ezek. 23:23 [b]2 Sam. 16:11; 2 Kin. 18:25; 2 Chr. 36:23; Is. 10:6; 44:28; 48:14 [1]Or *Attack with the sword*
22 [a]Jer. 51:54
23 [a]Is. 14:6; Jer. 51:20–24
24 [a]Jer. 51:8, 31; Dan. 5:30 [b][Is. 45:9]
25 [a]Is. 13:5
27 [a]Ps. 22:12; Is. 34:7; Jer. 46:21 [b]Ps. 37:13; Jer. 48:44; Ezek. 7:7
28 [a]Ps. 149:6–9; Jer. 51:10
29 [a]Ps. 137:8; Jer. 51:56; [2 Thess. 1:6]; Rev. 18:6 [b][Is. 47:10] [1]Qr., some Heb. mss., LXX, Tg. add *to her*

50:17–20 A second comment about Israel's restoration (see vv. 4–7), which includes a pardon for the sins of the people.
50:21 Puns are frequently used by the prophets, and here there are two plays on names. **Merathaim** ("Land of Double Rebellion"): A name for southern Babylonia, from the Hebrew root meaning "to rebel." **Pekod** ("Punishment"): The name of a tribe, from a Hebrew root meaning "to punish."
50:29 A second summons **against Babylon.** See note on v. 2. **Repay them:** An idea expressed in 25:14.

Against the Holy One of Israel.
30 [a]Therefore her young men shall fall in the streets,
And all her men of war shall be cut off in that day," says the LORD.
31 "Behold, I *am* against you,
O most haughty one!" says the Lord GOD of hosts;
"For your day has come,
[1]The time *that* I will punish you.
32 The most [a]proud shall stumble and fall,
And no one will raise him up;
[b]I will kindle a fire in his cities,
And it will devour all around him."

33 Thus says the LORD of hosts:

"The children of Israel *were* oppressed,
Along with the children of Judah;
All who took them captive have held them fast;
They have refused to let them go.
34 [a]Their Redeemer *is* strong;
[b]The LORD of hosts *is* His name.
He will thoroughly plead their [c]case,
That He may give rest to the land,
And disquiet the inhabitants of Babylon.

35 "A sword *is* against the Chaldeans," says the LORD,
"Against the inhabitants of Babylon,
And [a]against her princes and [b]her wise men.
36 A sword *is* [a]against the soothsayers, and they will be fools.
A sword *is* against her mighty men, and they will be dismayed.
37 A sword *is* against their horses,
Against their chariots,
And against all [a]the mixed peoples who *are* in her midst;
And [b]they will become like women.
A sword *is* against her treasures, and they will be robbed.
38 [a]A [1]drought *is* against her waters, and they will be dried up.
For it *is* the land of carved images,
And they are insane with *their* idols.

39 "Therefore[a] the wild desert beasts shall dwell *there* with the jackals,
And the ostriches shall dwell in it.
[b]It shall be inhabited no more forever,
Nor shall it be dwelt in from generation to generation.
40 [a]As God overthrew Sodom and Gomorrah
And their neighbors," says the LORD,
"*So* no one shall reside there,
Nor son of man [b]dwell in it.

41 "Behold,[a] a people shall come from the north,
And a great nation and many kings
Shall be raised up from the ends of the earth.
42 [a]They shall hold the bow and the lance;
[b]They *are* cruel and shall not show mercy.
[c]Their voice shall roar like the sea;
They shall ride on horses,
Set in array, like a man for the battle,
Against you, O daughter of Babylon.

43 "The king of Babylon has [a]heard the report about them,
And his hands grow feeble;
Anguish has taken hold of him,
Pangs as of a woman in [b]childbirth.

44 "Behold,[a] he shall come up like a lion from the [1]floodplain of the Jordan
Against the dwelling place of the strong;
But I will make them suddenly run away from her.
And who *is* a chosen *man that* I may appoint over her?
For who *is* like Me?
Who will arraign Me?

30 [a]Is. 13:18; Jer. 49:26; 51:4 **31** [1]So with MT, Tg.; LXX, Vg. *The time of your punishment* **32** [a]Is. 26:5; Mal. 4:1 [b]Jer. 21:14 **34** [a]Prov. 23:11; Is. 43:14; Jer. 15:21; 31:11; Rev. 18:8 [b]Is. 47:4 [c]Jer. 51:36; Mic. 7:9 **35** [a]Dan. 5:30 [b]Is. 47:13; Jer. 51:57 **36** [a]Is. 44:25; Jer. 48:30 **37** [a]Jer. 25:20; Ezek. 30:5 [b]Jer. 51:30; Nah. 3:13 **38** [a]Is. 44:27; Jer. 51:36; Rev. 16:12 [1]So with MT, Tg., Vg.; Syr. *sword;* LXX omits *A drought is*

39 [a]Is. 13:21, 22; 34:14; Jer. 51:37; Rev. 18:2 [b]Is. 13:20; Jer. 25:12 **40** [a]Gen. 19:24, 25; Is. 13:19; Jer. 49:18; [Luke 17:28–30]; 2 Pet. 2:6; Jude 7 [b]Is. 13:20 **41** [a]Is. 13:2–5; Jer. 6:22; 25:14; 51:27 **42** [a]Jer. 6:23 [b]Is. 13:18 [c]Is. 5:30 **43** [a]Jer. 51:31 [b]Jer. 6:24 **44** [a]Jer. 49:19–21 [1]Or *thicket*

50:33, 34 Assurance that the **Redeemer** of Israel ***is* strong** and will deliver His people. See note on Ezek. 34:23.
50:35–37 An oracle of a **sword . . . against the Chaldeans,** a reversal of her role in Ezek. 21, where Babylon is the sword.
50:38–40 Babylon will dry up like a **desert,** and only wild animals will live there.
50:41–46 Babylon, once the dreaded foe from the north, now stands in dread of another foe from the north. Directed here to the king of Babylon, vv. 41–43 are repeated with slight variation from 6:22–24, where the daughter of Zion is addressed. Vv. 44–46, directed to the Chaldeans, are repeated with slight variation from 49:19–21, where Edom is addressed.

And [b]who *is* that shepherd
Who will withstand Me?"

45 Therefore hear [a]the counsel of the LORD that He has taken against Babylon,
And His [b]purposes that He has proposed against the land of the Chaldeans:
[c]Surely the least of the flock shall draw them out;
Surely He will make their dwelling place desolate with them.
46 [a]At the noise of the taking of Babylon
The earth trembles,
And the cry is heard among the nations.

The Utter Destruction of Babylon

51 Thus says the LORD:
"Behold, I will raise up against [a]Babylon,
Against those who dwell in [1]Leb Kamai,
[b]A destroying wind.
2 And I will send [a]winnowers to Babylon,
Who shall winnow her and empty her land.
[b]For in the day of doom
They shall be against her all around.
3 Against *her* [a]let the archer bend his bow,
And lift himself up against *her* in his armor.
Do not spare her young men;
[b]Utterly destroy all her army.
4 Thus the slain shall fall in the land of the Chaldeans,
[a]And *those* thrust through in her streets.
5 For Israel is [a]not forsaken, nor Judah,
By his God, the LORD of hosts,
Though their land was filled with sin against the Holy One of Israel."

6 [a]Flee from the midst of Babylon,
And every one save his life!
Do not be cut off in her iniquity,
For [b]this *is* the time of the LORD's vengeance;
[c]He shall recompense her.

44 [b]Job 41:10; Jer. 49:19 **45** [a][Ps. 33:11; Is. 14:24]; Jer. 51:10, 11 [b]Jer. 51:29 [c]Jer. 49:19, 20 **46** [a]Rev. 18:9

CHAPTER 51

1 [a]Is. 47:1; Jer. 50:1 [b]2 Kin. 19:7; Jer. 4:11; Hos. 13:15 [1]Lit. *The Midst of Those Who Rise Up Against Me;* a code word for Chaldea, Babylonia **2** [a]Is. 41:16; Jer. 15:7; Matt. 3:12 [b]Jer. 50:14 **3** [a]Jer. 50:14, 29 [b]Jer. 50:21 **4** [a]Jer. 49:26; 50:30, 37 **5** [a][Is. 54:7, 8; Jer. 33:24–26; 46:28] **6** [a]Jer. 50:8; Rev. 18:4 [b]Jer. 50:15 [c]Jer. 25:14

7 [a]Jer. 25:15; Hab. 2:16; Rev. 17:4 [b]Rev. 14:8 [c]Jer. 25:16 **8** [a]Is. 21:9; Jer. 50:2; Rev. 14:8; 18:2 [b][Is. 48:20]; Rev. 18:9, 11, 19 [c]Jer. 46:11 **9** [a]Is. 13:14; Jer. 46:16; 50:16 [b]Ezra 9:6; Rev. 18:5 **10** [a]Ps. 37:6; Mic. 7:9 [b][Is. 40:2]; Jer. 50:28 **11** [a]Jer. 46:4, 9; Joel 3:9, 10 [b]Is. 13:17 [c]Jer. 50:45 [d]Jer. 50:28 [1]*Polish the arrows!* **12** [a]Nah. 2:1; 3:14 **13** [a]Rev. 17:1, 15 **14** [a]Jer. 49:13; Amos 6:8 [b]Jer. 51:27; Nah. 3:15 [c]Jer. 50:15 **15** [a]Gen. 1:1, 6; Jer. 10:12–16 [b]Job 9:8; Ps. 104:2; Is. 40:22

7 [a]Babylon *was* a golden cup in the LORD's hand,
That made all the earth drunk.
[b]The nations drank her wine;
Therefore the nations [c]are deranged.
8 Babylon has suddenly [a]fallen and been destroyed.
[b]Wail for her!
[c]Take balm for her pain;
Perhaps she may be healed.

9 We would have healed Babylon,
But she is not healed.
Forsake her, and [a]let us go everyone to his own country;
[b]For her judgment reaches to heaven and is lifted up to the skies.
10 The LORD has [a]revealed our righteousness.
Come and let us [b]declare in Zion the work of the LORD our God.

11 [a]Make[1] the arrows bright!
Gather the shields!
[b]The LORD has raised up the spirit of the kings of the Medes.
[c]For His plan *is* against Babylon to destroy it,
Because it *is* [d]the vengeance of the LORD,
The vengeance for His temple.
12 [a]Set up the standard on the walls of Babylon;
Make the guard strong,
Set up the watchmen,
Prepare the ambushes.
For the LORD has both devised and done
What He spoke against the inhabitants of Babylon.
13 [a]O you who dwell by many waters,
Abundant in treasures,
Your end has come,
The measure of your covetousness.
14 [a]The LORD of hosts has sworn by Himself:
"Surely I will fill you with men, [b]as with locusts,
And they shall lift [c]up a shout against you."

15 [a]He has made the earth by His power;
He has established the **world** by His wisdom,
And [b]stretched out the heaven by His understanding.

51:1 Leb Kamai is an "atbash" (see note on 25:26) for Chaldea.

51:15–19 Repeated with slight variation from 10:12–16. The name "Israel" does not occur in the Hebrew of v. 19.

WORD WEALTH

51:15 world, *tebel* (teh-*vel*); Strong's #8398: The fruitful Earth; the globe, the world, the dry land; Earth's substantial material (land); also the entire world (that is, all its inhabitants). *Tebel* occurs 36 times. God formed or established the world. See 1 Sam. 2:8. The primary idea is land in general, or inhabited world (Prov. 8:31). The root of *tebel* is *yabal,* "to bring," which may imply earth that produces.

16 When He utters *His* voice—
There is a multitude of waters in the heavens:
[a]"He causes the vapors to ascend from the ends of the earth;
He makes lightnings for the rain;
He brings the wind out of His treasuries."

17 [a]Everyone is dull-hearted, without knowledge;
Every metalsmith is put to shame by the carved image;
[b]For his molded image *is* falsehood,
And *there is* no breath in them.
18 They *are* futile, a work of errors;
In the time of their punishment they shall perish.
19 The *Portion of Jacob *is* not like them,
For He *is* the Maker of all things;
And *Israel is* the tribe of His inheritance.
The LORD of hosts *is* His name.

20 "You[a] *are* My battle-ax *and* weapons of war:
For with you I will break the nation in pieces;
With you I will destroy kingdoms;
21 With you I will break in pieces the horse and its rider;
With you I will break in pieces the chariot and its rider;
22 With you also I will break in pieces man and woman;
With you I will break in pieces [a]old and young;
With you I will break in pieces the young man and the maiden;
23 With you also I will break in pieces the shepherd and his flock;
With you I will break in pieces the farmer and his yoke of oxen;
And with you I will break in pieces governors and rulers.

24 "And[a] I will repay Babylon
And all the inhabitants of Chaldea
For all the evil they have done
In Zion in your sight," says the LORD.

25 "Behold, I *am* against you,
[a]O destroying mountain,
Who destroys all the earth," says the LORD.
"And I will stretch out My hand against you,
*Roll you down from the rocks,
[b]And make you a burnt mountain.
26 They shall not take from you a stone for a corner
Nor a stone for a foundation,
[a]But you shall be desolate forever," says the LORD.

27 [a]Set up a banner in the land,
Blow the trumpet among the nations!
[b]Prepare the nations against her,
Call [c]the kingdoms together against her:
Ararat, Minni, and Ashkenaz.
Appoint a general against her;
Cause the horses to come up like the bristling locusts.
28 Prepare against her the nations,
With the kings of the Medes,
Its governors and all its rulers,
All the land of his dominion.
29 And the land will tremble and sorrow;
For every [a]purpose of the LORD shall be performed against Babylon,
[b]To make the land of Babylon a desolation without inhabitant.
30 The mighty men of Babylon have ceased fighting,
They have remained in their strongholds;
Their might has failed,
[a]They became *like* women;
They have burned her dwelling places,
[b]The bars of her *gate* are broken.

16 [a]Ps. 135:7; Jer. 10:13 **17** [a][Is. 44:18–20]; Jer. 10:14 [b]Jer. 50:2 **19** *See WW at Zech. 2:12. **20** [a]Is. 10:5, 15; Jer. 50:23 **22** [a]2 Chr. 36:17; Is. 13:15, 16
24 [a]Jer. 50:15, 29 **25** [a]Is. 13:2; Zech. 4:7 [b]Rev. 8:8 *See WW at Prov. 16:3. **26** [a]Jer. 50:26, 40 **27** [a]Is. 13:2; Jer. 50:2; 51:12 [b]Jer. 25:14 [c]Jer. 50:41, 42 **29** [a]Jer. 50:45 [b]Is. 13:19, 20; 47:11; Jer. 50:13; 51:26, 43 **30** [a]Is. 19:16; Jer. 48:41 [b]Is. 45:1, 2; Lam. 2:9; Amos 1:5; Nah. 3:13

51:20–23 Use of repetition as a literary device by Jeremiah. Babylon is described as a hammer, an instrument used by God to carry out His punishment.
51:24 Even though **Babylon** was the instrument in the hand of God, she will fall as did Assyria (Is. 10:5, 15) because of her arrogance.
51:27 The third summons against Babylon. See note on 50:2.

31 [a]One runner will run to meet another,
And one messenger to meet another,
To show the king of Babylon that his city is taken on *all* sides;
32 [a]The passages are blocked,
The reeds they have burned with fire,
And the men of war are terrified.

33 For thus says the LORD of hosts, the God of Israel:

"The daughter of Babylon *is* [a]like a threshing floor
When [b]*it is* time to thresh her;
Yet a little while
[c]And the time of her harvest will come."

34 "Nebuchadnezzar the king of Babylon
Has [a]devoured me, he has crushed me;
He has made me an [b]empty vessel,
He has swallowed me up like a monster;
He has filled his stomach with my delicacies,
He has spit me out.
35 Let the violence *done* to me and my flesh *be* upon Babylon,"
The inhabitant of Zion will say;
"And my blood be upon the inhabitants of Chaldea!"
Jerusalem will say.

36 Therefore thus says the LORD:

"Behold, [a]I will plead your case and take vengeance for you.
[b]I will dry up her sea and make her springs dry.
37 [a]Babylon shall become a heap,
A dwelling place for jackals,
[b]An astonishment and a hissing,
Without an inhabitant.
38 They shall roar together like lions,
They shall growl like lions' whelps.
39 In their excitement I will prepare their feasts;
[a]I will make them drunk,
That they may rejoice,

31 [a]Jer. 50:24
32 [a]Jer. 50:38
33 [a]Is. 21:10; Dan. 2:35; Amos 1:3; Mic. 4:13 [b]Is. 41:15; Hab. 3:12 [c]Is. 17:15; Hos. 6:11; Joel 3:13; Rev. 14:15
34 [a]Jer. 50:17 [b]Is. 24:1–3
36 [a][Ps. 140:12]; Jer. 50:34 [b]Jer. 50:38
37 [a]Is. 13:22; Jer. 50:39; [Rev. 18:2] [b]Jer. 25:9, 11
39 [a]Jer. 51:57
41 [a]Jer. 25:26 [b]Is. 13:19; Jer. 49:25; [Dan. 4:30] [1]A code word for *Babylon,* Jer. 25:26
42 [a]Is. 8:7, 8; Jer. 51:55; Dan. 9:26
43 [a]Jer. 50:39, 40 [b]Is. 13:20
44 [a]Jer. 50:2; Is. 46:1 [b]Jer. 50:15 [1]A Babylonian god
45 [a]Is. 48:20; [Jer. 50:8, 28; 51:6; Rev. 18:4] [1]Lit. *his soul*
46 [a]2 Kin. 19:7; Is. 13:3–5
48 [a]Is. 44:23; 48:20; 49:13; Rev. 18:20 [b]Jer. 50:3, 41

And sleep a perpetual sleep
And not awake," says the LORD.
40 "I will bring them down
Like lambs to the slaughter,
Like rams with male goats.

41 "Oh, how [a]Sheshach[1] is taken!
Oh, how [b]the praise of the whole earth is seized!
How Babylon has become desolate among the nations!
42 [a]The sea has come up over Babylon;
She is covered with the multitude of its waves.
43 [a]Her cities are a desolation,
A dry land and a wilderness,
A land where [b]no one dwells,
Through which no son of man passes.
44 I will punish [a]Bel[1] in Babylon,
And I will bring out of his mouth what he has swallowed;
And the nations shall not stream to him anymore.
Yes, [b]the wall of Babylon shall fall.

45 "My[a] people, go out of the midst of her!
And let everyone deliver [1]himself from the fierce anger of the LORD.
46 And lest your heart faint,
And you fear [a]for the rumor that *will be* heard in the land
(A rumor will come *one* year,
And after that, in *another* year
A rumor *will come,*
And violence in the land,
Ruler against ruler),
47 Therefore behold, the days are coming
That I will bring judgment on the carved images of Babylon;
Her whole land shall be ashamed,
And all her slain shall fall in her midst.
48 Then [a]the heavens and the earth and all that *is* in them
Shall sing joyously over Babylon;
[b]For the plunderers shall come to her from the north," says the LORD.

49 As Babylon *has caused* the slain of Israel to fall,

51:34–40 The deliverance of Jerusalem will be miraculous, but Babylon will be destroyed (see note on 50:4–7), **become a heap** (v. 37), **a dwelling place for jackals** (see note on 9:11), **an astonishment and a hissing** (see note on 18:16).
51:41 Sheshach: An "atbash" cipher. See note on 25:26.
51:44 Punish Bel: The defeat of Babylon will also be the defeat of her god. God will **bring out of his mouth what he has swallowed,** that is, the captive people, idols and images, and the loot taken from conquered lands.

So at Babylon the slain of all the
earth shall fall.
50 [a]You who have escaped the sword,
Get away! Do not stand still!
[b]Remember the LORD afar off,
And let Jerusalem come to your
mind.

51 [a]We are ashamed because we have
heard reproach.
Shame has covered our faces,
For strangers [b]have come into the
[1]sanctuaries of the LORD's
house.

52 "Therefore behold, the days are
coming," says the LORD,
"That I will bring judgment on her
carved images,
And throughout all her land the
wounded shall groan.
53 [a]Though Babylon were to
[1]mount up to heaven,
And though she were to fortify
the height of her strength,
Yet from Me plunderers would
come to her," says the LORD.

54 [a]The sound of a cry *comes* from
Babylon,
And great destruction from the
land of the Chaldeans,
55 Because the LORD is plundering
Babylon
And silencing her loud voice,
Though her waves roar like great
waters,
And the noise of their voice is
uttered,
56 Because the plunderer comes
against her, against Babylon,
And her mighty men are taken.
Every one of their bows is
broken;
[a]For the LORD *is* the God of
recompense,
He will surely repay.

57 "And I will make drunk
Her princes and [a]wise men,
Her governors, her deputies, and
her mighty men.
And they shall sleep a perpetual
sleep
And not awake," says [b]the King,
Whose name *is* the LORD of hosts.

58 Thus says the LORD of hosts:

"The broad walls of Babylon shall
be utterly [a]broken,[1]
And her high gates shall be
burned with fire;
[b]The people will labor in vain,
And the nations, because of the
fire;
And they shall be weary."

Jeremiah's Command to Seraiah

59 The word which Jeremiah the
prophet commanded Seraiah the son
of [a]Neriah, the son of Mahseiah, when
he went with Zedekiah the king of Judah to Babylon in the fourth year of
his reign. And Seraiah *was* the quarter-
master.
60 So Jeremiah [a]wrote in a book all
the evil that would come upon Babylon, all these words that are written
against Babylon.
61 And Jeremiah said to Seraiah,
"When you arrive in Babylon and see
it, and read all these words,
62 "then you shall say, 'O LORD, You
have spoken against this place to cut
it off, so that [a]none shall *remain in
it, neither man nor beast, but it shall
be desolate forever.'
63 "Now it shall be, when you have finished reading this book, [a]*that* you
shall tie a stone to it and throw it out
into the Euphrates.
64 "Then you shall say, 'Thus Babylon
shall sink and not rise from the catastrophe that I will bring upon her. And
they shall be weary.' " Thus far *are* the
words of Jeremiah.

The Fall of Jerusalem Reviewed

52 Zedekiah *was* [a]twenty-one
years old when he became king,
and he reigned eleven years in Jerusalem. His mother's name *was* Hamutal
the daughter of Jeremiah of [b]Libnah.
2 He also did evil in the sight of the
LORD, according to all that Jehoiakim
had done.
3 For because of the anger of the
LORD *this* happened in Jerusalem and
Judah, till He finally cast them out
from His presence. Then Zedekiah
[a]rebelled against the king of Babylon.
4 Now it came to pass in the [a]ninth
year of his reign, in the tenth month,
on the tenth *day* of the month, *that*

50 [a]Jer. 44:28 [b][Deut. 4:29–31]; Ezek. 6:9
51 [a]Ps. 44:15; 79:4 [b]Ps. 74:3–8; Jer. 52:13; Lam. 1:10 [1]*holy places*
53 [a]Gen. 11:4; Job 20:6; [Ps. 139:8–10; Is. 14:12–14]; Jer. 49:16; Amos 9:2; Obad. 4 [1]*ascend*
54 [a]Jer. 50:22
56 [a]Ps. 94:1; Jer. 50:29
57 [a]Jer. 50:35 [b]Jer. 46:18; 48:15
58 [a]Jer. 50:15 [b]Hab. 2:13 [1]Lit. *laid utterly bare*
59 [a]Jer. 32:12
60 [a]Is. 30:8; Jer. 36:2
62 [a]Is. 13:20; 14:22, 23; Jer. 50:3, 39 *See WW at Lam. 5:19.
63 [a]Jer. 19:10, 11; Rev. 18:21

CHAPTER 52
1 [a]2 Kin. 24:18; 2 Chr. 36:11 [b]Josh. 10:29; 2 Kin. 8:22; Is. 37:8
3 [a]2 Chr. 36:13
4 [a]2 Kin. 25:1; Jer. 39:1; Ezek. 24:1, 2; Zech. 8:19

51:59–64 A prose conclusion to the book and especially to the prophecy concerning **Babylon. Seraiah,** Baruch's brother, was to take the written message against Babylon to that city, read it, tie a stone to it, and throw it into the **Euphrates** River. The city of Babylon would sink as the book had sunk.
52:1–27 A historical appendix to the book. Very close parallel to 2 Kin. 24:18—25:21.

Nebuchadnezzar king of Babylon and all his army came against Jerusalem and encamped against it; and *they* built a siege wall against it all around.

5 So the city was besieged until the eleventh year of King Zedekiah.

6 By the fourth month, on the ninth day of the month, the famine had become so severe in the city that there was no food for the people of the land.

7 Then the city wall was broken through, and all the men of war fled and went out of the city at night by way of the gate between the two walls, which *was* by the king's garden, even though the Chaldeans *were* near the city all around. And they went by way of the [1]plain.

8 But the army of the Chaldeans pursued the king, and they overtook Zedekiah in the plains of Jericho. All his army was scattered from him.

9 [a]So they took the king and brought him up to the king of Babylon at Riblah in the land of Hamath, and he pronounced judgment on him.

10 [a]Then the king of Babylon killed the sons of Zedekiah before his eyes. And he killed all the princes of Judah in Riblah.

11 He also [a]put out the eyes of Zedekiah; and the king of Babylon bound him in [1]bronze fetters, took him to Babylon, and put him in prison till the day of his death.

The Temple and City Plundered and Burned

12 [a]Now in the fifth month, on the tenth *day* of the month ([b]which *was* the nineteenth year of King Nebuchadnezzar king of Babylon), [c]Nebuzaradan, the captain of the guard, *who* served the king of Babylon, came to Jerusalem.

13 He burned the house of the LORD and the king's house; all the houses of Jerusalem, that is, all the houses of the great, he burned with fire.

14 And all the army of the Chaldeans who *were* with the captain of the guard broke down all the walls of Jerusalem all around.

15 [a]Then Nebuzaradan the captain of the guard carried away captive *some* of the poor people, the rest of the people who remained in the city, the defectors who had deserted to the king of Babylon, and the rest of the craftsmen.

16 But Nebuzaradan the captain of the guard left *some* of the poor of the land as vinedressers and farmers.

17 [a]The [b]bronze pillars that *were* in the house of the LORD, and the carts and the bronze Sea that *were* in the house of the LORD, the Chaldeans broke in pieces, and carried all their bronze to Babylon.

18 They also took away [a]the pots, the shovels, the trimmers, the [1]bowls, the spoons, and all the bronze utensils with which the priests ministered.

19 The basins, the firepans, the bowls, the pots, the lampstands, the spoons, and the cups, whatever *was* solid gold and whatever *was* solid silver, the captain of the guard took away.

20 The two pillars, one Sea, the twelve bronze bulls which *were* under *it, and* the carts, which King Solomon had made for the house of the LORD—[a]the bronze of all these articles was beyond measure.

21 Now *concerning* the [a]pillars: the height of one pillar *was* eighteen [1]cubits, a measuring line of twelve cubits could measure its circumference, and its thickness *was* [2]four fingers; *it was* hollow.

22 A capital of bronze *was* on it; and the height of one capital *was* five cubits, with a network and pomegranates all around the capital, all of bronze. The second pillar, with pomegranates was the same.

23 There were ninety-six pomegranates on the sides; [a]all the pomegranates, all around on the network, *were* one hundred.

The People Taken Captive to Babylonia

24 [a]The captain of the guard took Seraiah the chief priest, [b]Zephaniah the second priest, and the three doorkeepers.

25 He also took out of the city an [1]officer who had charge of the men of war, seven men of the king's close associates who were found in the city, the principal scribe of the army who mustered the people of the land, and sixty men of the people of the land who were found in the midst of the city.

26 And Nebuzaradan the captain of the guard took these and brought them to the king of Babylon at Riblah.

27 Then the king of Babylon struck them and put them to death at Riblah in the land of Hamath. Thus Judah was carried away captive from its own land.

28 [a]These *are* the people whom Nebuchadnezzar carried away captive:

7 [1]Or *Arabah;* the Jordan Valley
9 [a]2 Kin. 25:6; Jer. 32:4; 39:5
10 [a]Ezek. 12:13
11 [a]Ezek. 12:13 [1]*shackles*
12 [a]2 Kin. 25:8–21 [b]Jer. 52:29 [c]Jer. 39:9
15 [a]Jer. 39:9
17 [a]Jer. 27:19 [b]1 Kin. 7:15, 23, 27, 50
18 [a]Ex. 27:3; 1 Kin. 7:40, 45; 2 Kin. 25:14 [1]*basins*
20 [a]1 Kin. 7:47; 2 Kin. 25:16
21 [a]1 Kin. 7:15; 2 Kin. 25:17; 2 Chr. 3:15 [1]18 inches each [2]3 inches
23 [a]1 Kin. 7:20
24 [a]2 Kin. 25:18; 1 Chr. 6:14; Ezra 7:1 [b]Jer. 21:1; 29:25
25 [1]Lit. *eunuch*
28 [a]2 Kin. 24:2

[b]in the seventh year, [c]three thousand
and twenty-three Jews;
29 [a]in the eighteenth year of Nebuchadnezzar he carried away captive
from Jerusalem eight hundred and
thirty-two persons;
30 in the twenty-third year of Nebuchadnezzar, Nebuzaradan the captain
of the guard carried away captive of
the Jews seven hundred and forty-five
persons. All the persons *were* four
thousand six hundred.

Jehoiachin Released from Prison

31 [a]Now it came to pass in the thirty-
seventh year of the captivity of Jehoiachin king of Judah, in the twelfth
month, on the twenty-fifth *day* of the
month, *that* [1]Evil-Merodach king of
Babylon, in the first *year* of his reign,
[b]lifted[2] up the head of Jehoiachin king
of Judah and brought him out of
prison.
32 And he spoke kindly to him and
gave him a more prominent seat than
those of the kings who *were* with him
in Babylon.
33 So [1]Jehoiachin changed from his
prison garments, [a]and he ate bread
regularly before the king all the days
of his life.
34 And as for his provisions, there was
a regular ration given him by the king
of Babylon, a portion for each day until
the day of his death, all the days of
his life.

28 [b]2 Kin. 24:12 [c]2 Kin. 24:14 **29** [a]2 Kin. 25:11; Jer. 39:9 **31** [a]2 Kin. 25:27–30 [b]Gen. 40:13, 20; Ps. 3:3; 27:6 [1]Or *Awil-Marduk;* lit. *The Man of Marduk* [2]Showed favor to

33 [a]2 Sam. 9:7, 13; 1 Kin. 2:7 [1]Lit. *he*

52:30–34 Very close parallel to 2 Kin. 25:27–30. Jer. 52:34 adds **until the day of his death** (see v. 11), probably a contrast between the fate of Zedekiah who remained in prison until he died, and Jehoiachin who was freed from prison.

TRUTH-IN-ACTION through JEREMIAH

Letting the LIFE of the Holy Spirit Bring Faith's Works Alive in You!

Truth Jeremiah Teaches	Text	**Action** Jeremiah Invites
1 Guidelines for Growing in Godliness The godly person learns to perceive his life from God's standpoint. He is teachable and adjusts his way as the Lord instructs. He is careful to avoid presumption in all he says and does.	1:6–8	**Seek to understand** that the Lord's calling on your life is based on His power and not simply on your natural abilities. **Believe** that God will empower you to do all that He demands.
	5:3	**Learn** that responsiveness to the Lord's correction or discipline keeps the heart soft and helps you to hear God's voice clearly.
	14:14–16	**Be absolutely certain** God has spoken before saying "the Lord told me," and **do not speak** presumptuously in His name.
2 Keys to Wise Living The wise individual accepts God's testimony about human inclination to sin. He judges himself by the Word of God, rather than by the flattering words of those around him.	5:31	**Be cautioned** at how people naturally incline to follow carnal leadership due to shortsightedness.
	6:10	**Open** your ears to God's Word, even when it is not pleasant to you.
	7:28	**Realize** that receiving correction results in the ability to discern the truth of a matter.
3 Steps to Dynamic Devotion The goal of single-minded devotion is to know God. Remember that the final judgment will be measured ultimately by how much we have come to know the Lord and allowed Him to live through us.	9:23, 24	**Define** your life and service by your desire to know God.
	31:34	**Understand** that the focus of the New Covenant is a people who know their God. **See** how God defines eternal life in terms of the substance of your relationship with Him.

Truth Jeremiah Teaches	Text	**Action** Jeremiah Invites
4 Key Lessons in Faith A person of faith takes God at His Word and realizes that God is committed to His Word. He knows that God honors His Word above His name and has settled in his heart that God intends to bring His Word to fulfillment. He remains confident in God's promises and takes His warnings seriously.	1:9, 10	**Believe** that God's Word is sovereign over the nations and all of history.
	1:11, 12	**Rest** in the confidence that God is always working to fulfill His Word.
	6:16	**Evaluate** any "new" teaching, and **stay close** to the plain meaning of God's Word. **Be assured** that you cannot improve on the Bible.
	29:10–20	**Remember** that God intends good for His people to give them hope.
5 Lessons for Leaders Those God calls to leadership among His people must be willing servants of His Word. God creates, builds faith, and governs through His Word. But the Bible tells us that we must have our minds renewed. Without this transformation, we "follow the devices and desires of our own hearts." Leaders must face this fact and remain faithful, not being too concerned about how popular they are.	1:17–19	Leaders, **believe** that the Lord is the strong defense of all those He commissions and sends to proclaim His Word. **Have courage** when facing opposition for preaching the truth of God's Word.
	37:16	Leaders, **bear in mind** that God's servants have often been persecuted for faithfully proclaiming God's Word without compromise.
	43:2–7; 15:19–21	Leaders, **do not compromise** the truth due to disfavor or **alter** God's Word to appease men. **Trust** that the Lord protects those He sends to speak His word.
	23:25–27	Teachers, **know** that the Lord will not hold anyone guiltless who speaks his own opinions in the Lord's name.
	48:10–12	Leaders, **stand fast** in faithfully preaching the full counsel of God.

The Book of LAMENTATIONS

Author: Probably Jeremiah
Date: 587 B.C.
Theme: Suffering as Punishment for Sin
Key Words: Hardship, Sorrow, Sin, Prayer

Name of the Book As was their custom, the Jews used the first word of the book as its title, and it originally became known as *'ekah,* "How!" This word was commonly used to mean something like "Alas!" Compare its use in 2:1; 4:1; and Isaiah 1:21. Some also referred to the book as *qinot* or "lamentations," however, and this is how we arrived at the English title.

Author The author is not named, but traditions long before Christ claim that Jeremiah wrote it. Some scholars have doubted this and point to a number of differences between the use of poetic style, words, and expressions in this book and those used in the Book of Jeremiah, as well as to certain differences in emphasis. However, the prophet was known to compose laments (2 Chr. 35:25), and there is an even more impressive array of similarities, as we shall see when we examine the text. The differences, therefore, could simply be due to the different circumstances under which Lamentations was written.

Historical Background The Judahites had been able to think of themselves only as God's chosen race. As such, they felt that they would always experience good things. God had made covenants of blessing with them, but these were conditional. Blatant disobedience would mean that the pleasurable aspects of blessing would be replaced by punishment. The fulfillment of the promises of blessing could always skip a few generations of disobedient Israelites.

The books of 2 Kings and 2 Chronicles describe the moral decline of the kingdom of Judah (in spite of prophetic warnings) that would lead to its defeat and captivity (see 2:17). When King Zedekiah rebelled against the Babylonians, to whom Judah was subject, Nebuchadnezzar came against Jerusalem (2 Kin. 24:20). While he was besieging it, the people inside were starving. When he breached the wall, Zedekiah and the soldiers managed to escape (2 Kin. 25:4). But they were soon taken captive. Nebuzaradan, Nebuchadnezzar's official, destroyed most of Jerusalem, burned the temple, and carried all but the poorest people into exile (2 Kin. 25:8–12).

The poems of this book seem to have been composed during and after the time in which all this was happening. These poems are especially heartrending when they contrast the former blessings and strengths of Judah with the chaos and suffering their sin had brought on them (see note on 1:7). The chosen, favored people had lost everything and were in a hopeless position. Everything of significance had been destroyed. But the poems also describe the ministry of Jeremiah, sent again as a prophet to speak about the changed circumstances of God's people. He helped them to give the necessary expression to their grief and to comfort them in it. He also encouraged them to think about the hand of God on them in punishment and helped them to submit penitently to the judgment they deserved until it had passed (3:28–33). Only after the people were completely humbled would they be able to think of restoration.

Structure Laments were typically composed as poetry in the ancient world. Jeremiah had already written some (see Jer. 7:29; 9:10, 19), and so had other prophets. See Ezek. 19:1–14; Amos 5:1–3. But this book contains the longest and best known of such poems. There are five poems. The first four are acrostics, or poems in which each stanza begins with a successive letter of the Hebrew alphabet. These were probably acknowledged as special artistic achievements in those days. A number of the Psalms are acrostics. See Psalms 25, 34, 37, and 119. This device may have assisted memorization, but it also seems to indicate here that the poet was expressing all his feelings from *Aleph* to *Tau*, or as we would say, from *A* to *Z*. He was working through every grief, hurt, and fear, and was opening up completely to both man and God.

The fifth poem is not an acrostic, probably because it is a personal prayer, which could have made the material unsuitable for the acrostic form.

There is little systematic arrangement of subject matter throughout the book as a whole, except for a possible climax in chapter 3 and a progressive conclusion in the final two chapters. But this is, after all, the nature of grief. It waxes and wanes, goes away, and returns again unexpectedly.

Themes Lamentations features six major themes, all linked with the concept of suffering:

1. **Their Suffering Was the Result of Their Sin.** This strong theme is acknowledged in each chapter (as in 1:5; 2:14; 3:42; 4:13; 5:16). By the time the poems were written, this was obviously fully accepted. Even the Babylonians acknowledged the fact (Jer. 40:3). They knew that their suffering had not come upon them by chance. It was due to the wrath of God provoked by their sin (2:1). He was dealing with their spiritual condition, and they were supposed to take it personally.
2. **Their Suffering Was Seen as Coming from God Rather Than from Men.** The Babylonians were no more than an instrument in His hands. The fact that He was the ultimate cause is brought out throughout the book. No less than forty-four verses refer to this fact—an average of 1 out of every 3.5 verses. A few examples are 1:13, 15; 2:1, 4; 3:1, 37, 38.
3. **Their Suffering Could Direct Them Toward God.** The prophet is constantly conscious of God, of His purposes, and of His dealings with His people. There is no indication here of suffering resulting in a total abandonment of God or an eradication of His principles from their minds.
4. **Suffering, Tears, and Prayer Belong Together.** They were encouraged to pour out their hearts to God, to weep before Him, and to tell Him all the details of their pain, grief, and frustration.

Each chapter, except chapter 4, ends with a prayer. But then the whole of chapter 5 is a prayer, as though making up for this lack. The prayers are both detailed (2:20, 21; 5:1–10) and emotional (1:20, 21; 3:48–51). They contain the language of grief and repentance (1:20; 3:40–42), and are an indication that it is entirely appropriate to pray like this when the occasion demands it.

5. **Prayer Should Always Look for Some Ray of Hope.** It should never be completely given over to sorrow. After the detailed descriptions of suffering and sorrow in the first two and one-half chapters, a new understanding seems to surface in 3:21–24. Here the poet speaks about hope, and about God's mercies, compassion, and faithfulness. It was a realization that a manifestation of God's discipline did not mean that His love had ceased. When the discipline had accomplished His purpose, the circumstances would change (3:31, 32). God may have been using Babylon, but that did not mean that they were His elect or that He favored their cruel methods (3:34–36). The future held a vindication of Israel over their enemies (3:58–66).
6. **Their Responsibility Was to Submit to Their Sufferings Patiently.** Their sorrow had to be accepted in patience, with the realization that it would end when God's will had been accomplished (3:26–32).

Personal Application

This book has a great deal to say to us today:

1. The best way to survive grief is to express it. It needs to be shared with others and with God. There is a therapeutic value in working through each aspect of sorrow.
2. The destruction of Jerusalem and the lessons God taught His people were so significant that the Jews started reading this book at an annual service to commemorate the destruction of Jerusalem. They did not want the painful experience to be forgotten. Defeats as well as victories need to be remembered. If the church would commemorate some of its failures, for which God has had to discipline it, these failures would be less likely to be repeated.
3. When Christians have received much blessing and enlightenment from God, and then turn their backs on Him, it is an extremely serious matter. Privileges do not protect us either from responsibility or from discipline. They increase our responsibility and our culpability, and deserve more serious discipline. This is particularly true of church leaders.
4. To what extent does God punish His people for their sins today? Christ's death for us and His resurrection have certainly redeemed us. We do not bear retributive punishment for any sin we commit, since Christ has suffered in our place. We are living under a different covenant than did the Jews of 587 B.C. Even unbelievers are not normally punished for their sins until the next life (2 Pet. 2:4–10). But both believers and unbelievers sometimes have to suffer the consequences of past sins, such as drug addiction, drunkenness, and murder. And God often allows suffering in our lives to discipline us (Heb. 12:3–17). Through it we learn to obey Him and become stronger Christians (vv. 9, 12, 13).

Another consideration is church discipline. Christians who turn their backs on God should undergo some discipline in their home church. God sometimes disciplines people Himself by allowing suffering (1 Cor. 5:1–6) and even death (Acts 5:1–11). The main purpose of discipline, however, is restoration (2 Cor. 2:5–8). Even though we are not retributively punished for our sins, God will sometimes allow us to suffer when we have sinned in order to restore us to fellowship with Him. We need to submit to what God is doing and attempt to learn from the experience. If it is God's discipline, it will last as long as is necessary. There is no quick-fix solution to some of these problems and no easy way out. Discipline will direct us to God, drive us to prayer, and bring us into submission. We need it.

5. Of course, not all suffering is the result of God's discipline. Satan, too, can bring suffering on us (Job 2:7; Luke 13:16), but the suffering he brings is destructive rather than restorative.

Christ Revealed This book shows how weak people are under the Law, and how unable they are to serve God in their own strength. This drives them to Christ (Rom. 8:3). Even in these poems, however, glimpses of Christ shine through. He is our hope (3:21, 24, 29). He is the manifestation of God's mercy and compassion (3:22, 23, 32). He is our redemption and vindication (3:58, 59).

The Holy Spirit at Work Divine grief over the sins of Israel (2:1–6) reminds us that the Holy Spirit was, and still is, often grieved by our behavior (Is. 63:10). Repentance is also an indication of the work of the Holy Spirit among God's people (3:40–42; John 16:7–11).

Outline of Lamentations

I. The first poem: The misery, sin, and prayer of Jerusalem 1:1–22
- A. The defeat, humiliation, sorrow, and sin of Jerusalem 1:1–11
- B. Telling the uncaring world about her punishment 1:12–19
- C. A prayer for vindication in great suffering 1:20–22

II. The second poem: God's destruction and the prophet's reaction 2:1–22
- A. How God Himself has destroyed Israel 2:1–10
- B. The prophet's sorrow, hopelessness, and exhortation to prayer 2:11–19
- C. Judah's anguished prayer 2:20–22

III. The third poem: God's severity and mercy; man's submissiveness and prayer 3:1–66
- A. The severity of punishment leads to thoughts of mercy 3:1–24
- B. Submissiveness and humility bring mercy 3:25–39
- C. Their repentance comes too late 3:40–47
- D. Prophet and people trust God for eventual vindication 3:48–66

IV. The fourth poem: Devastation, the result of disobedience 4:1–22
- A. The devastation of the people and their leaders 4:1–11
- B. Disobedience and its results 4:12–20
- C. Edom to be punished and Israel to be relieved 4:21, 22

V. The fifth poem: A prayer recording Jerusalem's suffering and final plea 5:1–22
- A. A reminder of their pitiful state 5:1–10
- B. No one exempt from suffering 5:11–14
- C. All joy and pride gone 5:15–18
- D. The final, desperate plea 5:19–22

Jerusalem in Affliction

HOW lonely sits the city
That was full of people!
[a]*How* like a widow is she,
Who *was* great among the
nations!
The [b]princess among the
provinces
Has become a [1]slave!

2 She [a]weeps bitterly in the
[b]night,
Her tears *are* on her cheeks;
Among all her lovers
She has none to comfort *her.*
All her friends have dealt
treacherously with her;
They have become her enemies.

3 [a]Judah has gone into captivity,
Under affliction and hard
servitude;
[b]She dwells among the [1]nations,
She finds no [c]rest;
All her persecutors overtake her
in dire straits.

4 The roads to Zion mourn
Because no one comes to the
[1]set feasts.
All her gates are [a]desolate;
Her priests sigh,
Her virgins are afflicted,
And she *is* in bitterness.

5 Her adversaries [a]have become
[1]the master,
Her enemies prosper;
For the LORD has afflicted her
[b]Because of the multitude of her
transgressions.
Her [c]children have gone into
captivity before the enemy.

6 And from the daughter of Zion
All her splendor has departed.
Her princes have become like
deer
That find no pasture,
That [1]flee without strength
Before the pursuer.

7 In the days of her affliction and
roaming,
Jerusalem [a]remembers all her
pleasant things
That she had in the days of old.
When her people fell into the
hand of the enemy,
With no one to help her,
The adversaries saw her
And mocked at her [1]downfall.

8 [a]Jerusalem has sinned gravely,
Therefore she has become
[1]vile.
All who honored her despise her
Because [b]they have seen her
nakedness;
Yes, she sighs and turns away.

9 Her uncleanness *is* in her skirts;
She [a]did not consider her destiny;
Therefore her collapse was
awesome;
She had no comforter.
"O LORD, behold my affliction,
For *the* enemy is exalted!"

10 The adversary has spread his
hand
Over all her [1]pleasant things;
For she has seen [a]the nations
enter her [2]sanctuary,
Those whom You commanded
[b]Not to enter Your assembly.

11 All her people sigh,
[a]They [1]seek bread;
They have given their [2]valuables
for food to restore life.
"See, O LORD, and consider,
For I am scorned."

12 "*Is it* nothing to you, all you who
[1]pass* by?
Behold and see

CHAPTER 1

1 [a]Is. 47:7–9 [b]1 Kin. 4:21; Ezra 4:20; Jer. 31:7 [1]Lit. *forced laborer*
2 [a]Jer. 13:17 [b]Job 7:3
3 [a]Jer. 52:27 [b]Lam. 2:9 [c]Deut. 28:65 [1]*Gentiles*
4 [a]Is. 27:10 [1]*appointed*
5 [a]Deut. 28:43 [b]Jer. 30:14, 15; Dan. 9:7, 16 [c]Jer. 52:28 [1]Lit. *her head*
6 [1]Lit. *are gone*
7 [a]Ps. 137:1 [1]Vg. *Sabbaths*
8 [a][1 Kin. 8:46] [b]Jer. 13:22; Ezek. 16:37; Hos. 2:10 [1]LXX, Vg. *moved* or *removed*
9 [a]Deut. 32:29; Is. 47:7; Jer. 5:31
10 [a]Ps. 74:4–8; Is. 64:10, 11; Jer. 51:51 [b]Deut. 23:3; Neh. 13:1 [1]*desirable* [2]*holy place,* the temple
11 [a]Jer. 38:9; 52:6 [1]*hunt food* [2]*desirable things*
12 [1]Lit. *pass by this way* *See WW at Josh. 3:4.

1:1 The prophets often depicted Jerusalem as a woman. She was the "daughter of Judah" (2:2), but is now reduced to being a **widow.** She used to be **great** (2:15) and a **princess,** but is now a **slave.**

1:2 The **tears** were understandable (see notes on 2:18, 19) because nations like Egypt, Tyre, and Sidon, whom Judah had thought to be her allies, had forsaken her (4:17). In this verse, they are depicted as **lovers.** When she most *needed someone* **to comfort *her,*** she found that they had deceived her (v. 19).

1:4 People used to arrive for festivals or trading along **the roads** and would perform their transactions at the open spaces just inside the city **gates.**

1:6 The last half of this verse probably refers to the capture of Zedekiah (Jer. 39:4).

1:7 Edom was particularly known to have **mocked at her downfall** (Obad. 12).

1:8 **Nakedness:** Being stripped of clothing was particularly humiliating for someone in the ancient Near East. It was the punishment of a harlot (Ezek. 23:29).

1:9 **Her skirts** were not able to hide **her uncleanness.** It was showing through. At the end of this verse, Jerusalem breaks into the narrative, as she also does in v. 11.

1:10 The Babylonians stripped the temple of all its **pleasant things,** or ornaments. Jerusalem felt like a woman who had been ravished and robbed when the pagans entered the sacred temple. Not even ordinary Jews were allowed into the sanctuary.

1:11 A description of conditions during the siege.

[a]If there is any sorrow like my
sorrow,
Which has been brought on me,
Which the LORD has inflicted
In the day of His fierce anger.

13 "From above He has sent fire into
my bones,
And it overpowered them;
He has [a]spread a net for my feet
And turned me back;
He has made me desolate
And faint all the day.

5 14 "The[a] yoke of my transgressions
was [1]bound;
They were woven together by His
hands,
And thrust upon my neck.
He made my strength fail;
The Lord delivered me into the
hands of *those whom* I am not
able to withstand.

15 "The Lord has trampled underfoot
all my mighty *men* in my midst;
He has called an assembly
against me
To crush my young men;
[a]The Lord trampled *as* in a
winepress
The virgin daughter of Judah.

16 "For these *things* I weep;
My eye, [a]my eye overflows with
water;
Because the comforter, who
should restore my life,
Is far from me.
My children are desolate
Because the enemy prevailed."

17 [a]Zion [1]spreads out her hands,
But no one *comforts her;
The LORD has commanded
concerning Jacob
That those [b]around him *become*
his adversaries;
Jerusalem has become an
unclean thing among them.

1 18 "The LORD is [a]**righteous,**
For I [b]rebelled against His
[1]commandment.

12 [a]Dan. 9:12
13 [a]Ezek. 12:13; 17:20
14 [a]Deut. 28:48 [1]So with MT, Tg.; LXX, Syr., Vg. *watched over*
15 [a]Is. 63:3; [Rev. 14:19]
16 [a]Ps. 69:20; Eccl. 4:1; Jer. 13:17; Lam. 2:18
17 [a][Is. 1:15]; Jer. 4:31 [b]2 Kin. 24:2–4; Jer. 12:9 [1]Prays *See WW at Ps. 23:4.
18 [a]Neh. 9:33; Ps. 119:75; Dan. 9:7, 14 [b]1 Sam. 12:14, 15; Jer. 4:17 [1]Lit. *mouth* *See WW at Ps. 45:14.
20 [a]Job 30:27; Is. 16:11; Jer. 4:19; Lam. 2:11; Hos. 11:8 [b]Deut. 32:25; Ezek. 7:15 [1]Lit. *inward parts*
21 [a]Ps. 35:15; Jer. 48:27; 50:11; Lam. 2:15; Obad. 12 [b]Is. 13; [Jer. 46] [1]*proclaimed*
22 [a]Neh. 4:4, 5; Ps. 109:15; 137:7, 8; Jer. 30:16

Hear now, all peoples,
And behold my sorrow;
My *virgins and my young men
Have gone into captivity.

WORD WEALTH

1:18 righteous, *tsaddiq* (tsahd-*deek*); Strong's #6662: One who is right, just, clear, clean, righteous; a person who is characterized by fairness, integrity, and justice in his dealings. Occurring more than 200 times, *tsaddiq* is derived from the verb *tsadaq,* "to be righteous, justified, clear." *Tsadaq* and its derivatives convey justice and integrity in one's lifestyle. Being righteous brings a person light and gladness (Ps. 97:11). Tsaddiq occurs 66 times in Prov. alone. See especially Prov. 4:18; 18:10; 24:16. It is the *tsaddiq* who shall live by his faith, in Hab. 2:4. In the present verse, Yahweh is *tsaddiq* (just and fair) at all times, even when ordaining punishments.

19 "I called for my lovers,
But they deceived me;
My priests and my elders
Breathed their last in the city,
While they sought food
To restore their life.

20 "See, O LORD, that I *am* in distress;
My [a]soul[1] is troubled;
My heart is overturned within me,
For I have been very rebellious.
[b]Outside the sword bereaves,
At home *it is* like death.

21 "They have heard that I sigh,
But no one comforts me.
All my enemies have heard of my
trouble;
They are [a]glad that You have
done *it.*
Bring on [b]the day You have
[1]announced,
That they may become like me.

22 "Let[a] all their wickedness come
before You,
And do to them as You have done
to me
For all my transgressions;

1:13–15 Fire, net, yoke, and **winepress:** These are all metaphors for suffering. **He has called an assembly against me:** God summoned the enemy forces against Jerusalem (v. 15).
1:14 See section 5 of Truth-In-Action at the end of Lam.
1:16 I weep: See notes on 2:18, 19. The writer takes up the lament again.
1:17 Zion spreads out her hands: A gesture of sorrowful supplication.
1:18 See section 1 of Truth-In-Action at the end of Lam.
1:19 The **priests** and **elders** had been most guilty of disregarding Jeremiah's warnings.
1:20 The **soul,** or inner being, was considered to be the seat of the emotions. The **heart** was considered to be the seat of intelligence and will. **Death** here probably refers to the plague (Jer. 15:2).
1:21 The day You have announced: The great judgment day was coming as God's righteousness would demand the punishment of Babylon. This was Jerusalem's only hope.
1:22 Israel could pray unhesitatingly for a just God to punish the wicked who broke His law.

For my sighs *are* many,
And my heart *is* faint."

God's Anger with Jerusalem

2 How the Lord has covered the daughter of Zion
With a [a]cloud in His anger!
[b]He cast down from heaven to the earth
[c]The beauty of Israel,
And did not remember [d]His footstool
In the day of His anger.

2 The Lord has swallowed up and has [a]not pitied
All the dwelling places of Jacob.
He has thrown down in His wrath
The strongholds of the daughter of Judah;
He has brought *them* down to the ground;
[b]He has profaned the kingdom and its princes.

3 He has cut off in fierce anger
Every [1]horn of Israel;
[a]He has drawn back His right hand
From before the enemy.
[b]He has blazed against Jacob like a flaming fire
Devouring all around.

4 [a]Standing like an enemy, He has bent His bow;
With His right hand, like an adversary,
He has slain [b]all *who were* pleasing to His eye;
On the tent of the daughter of Zion,
He has poured out His fury like fire.

5 [a]The Lord was like an enemy.
He has swallowed up Israel,
He has swallowed up all her palaces;
[b]He has destroyed her strongholds,
And has increased mourning and lamentation
In the daughter of Judah.

6 He has done violence [a]to His [1]tabernacle,
[b]*As if it were* a garden;
He has destroyed His place of assembly;
The LORD has caused
The appointed feasts and Sabbaths to be forgotten in Zion.
In His burning indignation He has [c]spurned the king and the priest.

7 The Lord has spurned His altar,
He has [a]abandoned His sanctuary;
He has [1]given up the walls of her palaces
Into the hand of the enemy.
[b]They have made a noise in the house of the LORD
As on the day of a set feast.

8 The LORD has [1]purposed to destroy
The [a]wall of the daughter of Zion.
[b]He has stretched out a line;
He has not withdrawn His hand from destroying;
Therefore He has caused the rampart and wall to lament;
They languished together.

9 Her gates have sunk into the ground;
He has destroyed and [a]broken her bars.
[b]Her king and her princes *are* among the [1]nations;
[c]The Law *is* no *more*,
And her [d]prophets find no [2]vision from the LORD.

10 The elders of the daughter of Zion
[a]Sit on the ground *and* keep silence;
[1]They [b]throw dust on their heads
And [c]gird themselves with sackcloth.
The virgins of Jerusalem
Bow their heads to the ground.

11 [a]My eyes fail with tears,
My [1]heart is troubled;

CHAPTER 2
1 [a][Lam. 3:44] [b]Matt. 11:23 [c]2 Sam. 1:19 [d]1 Chr. 28:2; Ps. 99:5; Ezek. 43:7
2 [a]Ps. 21:9; Lam. 3:43 [b]Ps. 89:39, 40; Is. 43:28
3 [a]Ps. 74:11; Jer. 21:4, 5 [b]Ps. 89:46 [1]Strength
4 [a]Is. 63:10 [b]Ezek. 24:25
5 [a]Jer. 30:14 [b]2 Kin. 25:9; Jer. 52:13; Lam. 2:2
6 [a]Ps. 80:12; 89:40; Is. 5:5; Jer. 7:14 [b]Is. 1:8; Jer. 52:13 [c]Is. 43:28 [1]Lit. *booth*
7 [a]Ezek. 24:21 [b]Ps. 74:3–8 [1]*delivered*
8 [a]Jer. 52:14 [b][2 Kin. 21:13; Is. 34:11; Amos 7:7–9] [1]*determined*
9 [a]Jer. 51:30 [b]Deut. 28:36; 2 Kin. 24:15; 25:7; Lam. 1:3; 4:20 [c]2 Chr. 15:3 [d]Ps. 74:9; Mic. 3:6 [1]*Gentiles* [2]Prophetic revelation
10 [a]Job 2:13; Is. 3:26 [b]Job 2:12; Ezek. 27:30 [c]Is. 15:3; Jon. 3:6–8 [1]A sign of mourning
11 [a]Ps. 6:7; Lam. 3:48 [1]Lit. *inward parts*

2:1 The beauty of Israel probably refers to the temple (Is. 64:11). The **footstool** was the ark (1 Chr. 28:2), or possibly even the temple itself (Ps. 132:7).
2:2 And has not pitied: See note on 3:40–42. The **dwelling places** were the unwalled villages. The **strongholds** were the fortified towns.
2:3 A **horn** symbolized power. God had **drawn back His right hand** and was no longer protecting them. The **flaming fire** was predicted in Amos 2:5.
2:4 Tent symbolizes a home.
2:6, 7 God had destroyed His own temple, sacrifices, festivals, and priests. Outward forms of worship are not as important as obedience (1 Sam. 15:22). It was the triumphant enemy forces who **made a noise in the house of the LORD.**
2:8 He has stretched out a line: This refers to God's preconceived plan to destroy the nation (2 Kin. 21:13; Amos 7:7–9).
2:10 Dust on their heads: A sign of mourning (Job 2:12).
2:11 Jeremiah was obviously an eyewitness. He did not abandon his disobedient people, but wept with them.

[b]My [2]bile is poured on the ground
Because of the destruction of the daughter of my people,
Because [c]the children and the infants
Faint in the streets of the city.

12 They say to their mothers,
"Where *is* grain and wine?"
As they swoon like the wounded
In the streets of the city,
As their life is poured out
In their mothers' bosom.

13 How shall I [a]console[1] you?
To what shall I liken you,
O daughter of Jerusalem?
What shall I compare with you, that I may comfort you,
O *virgin daughter of Zion?
For your ruin *is* spread wide as the sea;
Who can heal you?

14 Your [a]prophets have seen for you
False and deceptive visions;
They have not [b]uncovered your iniquity,
To bring back your captives,
But have envisioned for you false [c]prophecies and delusions.

15 All who [1]pass by [a]clap *their* hands at you;
They hiss [b]and shake their heads
At the daughter of Jerusalem:
"*Is* this the city that is called
[c]'The perfection of beauty,
The joy of the whole earth'?"

16 [a]All your enemies have opened their mouth against you;
They hiss and gnash *their* teeth.
They say, [b]"We have swallowed *her* up!
Surely this *is* the [c]day we have waited for;
We have found *it*, [d]we have seen *it!*"

11 [b]Job 16:13; Ps. 22:14 [c]Lam. 4:4 [2]Lit. *liver*
13 [a]Lam. 1:12; Dan. 9:12 [1]Or *bear witness to* *See WW at Ps. 45:14.
14 [a]Jer. 2:8; 23:25–29; 29:8, 9; 37:19; Ezek. 13:2 [b]Is. 58:1; Ezek. 23:36; Mic. 3:8 [c]Jer. 23:33–36; Ezek. 22:25, 28
15 [a]1 Kin. 9:8; Job 27:23; Jer. 18:16; Ezek. 25:6; Nah. 3:19 [b]2 Kin. 19:21; Ps. 44:14 [c][Ps. 48:2; 50:2]; Ezek. 16:14 [1]Lit. *pass by this way*
16 [a]Job 16:9, 10; Ps. 22:13; Lam. 3:46 [b]Ps. 56:2; 124:3; Jer. 51:34 [c]Lam. 1:21; [Obad. 12–15] [d]Ps. 35:21
17 [a]Lev. 26:16 [b]Ps. 38:16 [1]Strength
18 [a]Jer. 14:17; Lam. 1:16 [1]Lit. *the daughter of your eye*
19 [a]Ps. 119:147 [b]1 Sam. 1:15; Ps. 42:4; 62:8 [c]Is. 51:20
20 [a]Lev. 26:29; Deut. 28:53; Jer. 19:9; Lam. 4:10; Ezek. 5:10 [1]Vg. *a span long*
21 [a]2 Chr. 36:17; Jer. 6:11 [b]Jer. 18:21
22 [a]Ps. 31:13; Is. 24:17; Jer. 6:25

17 The LORD has done what He [a]purposed;
He has fulfilled His word
Which He commanded in days of old.
He has thrown down and has not pitied,
And He has caused an enemy to [b]rejoice over you;
He has exalted the [1]horn of your adversaries.

18 Their heart cried out to the Lord,
"O wall of the daughter of Zion,
[a]Let tears run down like a river day and night;
Give yourself no relief;
Give [1]your eyes no rest.

19 "Arise, [a]cry out in the night, **2**
At the beginning of the watches;
[b]Pour out your heart like water before the face of the Lord.
Lift your hands toward Him
For the life of your young children,
Who faint from hunger [c]at the head of every street."

20 "See, O LORD, and consider!
To whom have You done this?
[a]Should the women eat their offspring,
The children [1]they have cuddled?
Should the priest and prophet be slain
In the sanctuary of the Lord?

21 "Young[a] and old lie
On the ground in the streets;
My virgins and my young men
Have fallen by the [b]sword;
You have slain *them* in the day of Your anger,
You have slaughtered *and* not pitied.

22 "You have invited as to a feast day
[a]The terrors that surround me.
In the day of the LORD's anger

2:13 To what shall I liken you: It was impossible to comfort Jerusalem by comparing her with any previous event.
2:14 To bring back your captives: This would happen after hardship and repentance (Jer. 28:1–4; 32:42).
2:15 Clap . . . hiss and shake their heads: These were signs of scorn (1 Kin. 9:8; Ps. 22:7).
2:17 The LORD had **done what He purposed.** He had threatened them with this punishment from the days of Moses (Lev. 26:27–33).
2:18 Their heart cried out: If the Lord was dependable in bringing judgment, He would also surely bring restoration if they repented (Lev. 26:44, 45). **Let tears run down:** They were not to bottle up their emotions. Tears provide emotional catharsis (Luke 19:41).
2:19 See section 2 of Truth-In-Action at the end of Lam.
2:19 They were to lament **at the beginning of the watches** (intermittently throughout the night), and were to **lift** their **hands** in prayer (see Ps. 28:2).
2:20 Cannibalism had been predicted a number of times (Deut. 28:53; Jer. 19:9). But this and the killing of their religious leaders was incomprehensible to them.
2:21 The previous verse brought on theological problems. Did God have no mercy? (see note on 3:40–42).
2:22 The terrors were the nations invited by God to the **feast** of destruction.

There was no refugee or survivor.
[b]Those whom I have borne and brought up
My enemies have [c]destroyed."

The Prophet's Anguish and Hope

3 I *am* the man *who* has seen affliction by the rod of His wrath.
2 He has led me and made *me* walk
In darkness and not *in* light.
3 Surely He has turned His hand against me
Time and time again throughout the day.

4 He has aged [a]my flesh and my skin,
And [b]broken my bones.
5 He has besieged me
And surrounded *me* with bitterness and [1]woe.
6 [a]He has set me in dark places
Like the dead of long ago.

7 [a]He has hedged me in so that I cannot get out;
He has made my chain heavy.
8 Even [a]when I cry and shout,
He shuts out my prayer.
9 He has blocked my ways with hewn stone;
He has made my paths crooked.

10 [a]He *has been* to me a bear lying in wait,
Like a lion in [1]ambush.
11 He has turned aside my ways and [a]torn me in pieces;
He has made me desolate.
12 He has bent His bow
And [a]set me up as a target for the arrow.

13 He has caused [a]the [1]arrows of His quiver
To pierce my [2]loins.

14 I have become the [a]ridicule of all my people—
[b]Their taunting song all the day.
15 [a]He has filled me with bitterness,
He has made me drink wormwood.

16 He has also broken my teeth [a]with gravel,
And [1]covered me with ashes.
17 You have moved my soul far from peace;
I have forgotten [1]prosperity.
18 [a]And I said, "My strength and my hope
Have *perished from the LORD."

19 Remember my affliction and roaming,
[a]The wormwood and the [1]gall.
20 My soul still remembers
And [1]sinks within me.
21 This I recall to my mind,
Therefore I have [a]hope.*

22 [a]*Through* the LORD's mercies we are not consumed, **1**
Because His compassions [b]fail not.
23 *They are* new [a]every morning;
*Great *is* Your *faithfulness.
24 "The LORD *is* my [a]portion,"* says my soul,
"Therefore I [b]hope in Him!"

25 The LORD *is* good to those who [a]**wait** for Him, **2**
To the soul *who* seeks Him.

22 [b]Hos. 9:12 [c]Jer. 16:2–4; 44:7

CHAPTER 3

4 [a]Job 16:8 [b]Ps. 51:8; Is. 38:13
5 [1]*hardship* or *weariness*
6 [a][Ps. 88:5, 6; 143:3]
7 [a]Job 3:23; 19:8; Hos. 2:6
8 [a]Job 30:20; Ps. 22:2
10 [a]Is. 38:13 [1]Lit. *secret places*
11 [a]Job 16:12, 13; Jer. 15:3; Hos. 6:1
12 [a]Job 7:20; 16:12; Ps. 38:2
13 [a]Job 6:4 [1]Lit. *sons of* [2]Lit. *kidneys*
14 [a]Ps. 22:6, 7; 123:4; Jer. 20:7 [b]Job 30:9; Ps. 69:12; Lam. 3:63
15 [a]Jer. 9:15
16 [a][Prov. 20:17] [1]Lit. *bent me down in*
17 [1]Lit. *good*
18 [a]Ps. 31:22 *See WW at Judg. 5:31.
19 [a]Jer. 9:15; Lam. 3:5, 15 [1]*bitterness*
20 [1]Lit. *bowed down*
21 [a]Ps. 130:7 *See WW at Mic. 7:7.
22 [a][Mal. 3:6] [b]Ps. 78:38; [Jer. 3:12; 30:11]
23 [a]Is. 33:2; Zeph. 3:5 *See WW at Ps. 31:19. • See WW at Prov. 28:20.
24 [a]Ps. 16:5; 73:26; 119:57; Jer. 10:16 [b]Jer. 17:17; Mic. 7:7 *See WW at Zech. 2:12.
25 [a]Ps. 130:6; Is. 30:18

WORD WEALTH

3:25 wait, *qavah* (kah-*vah*); Strong's #6960: To wait for, look for, expect, hope. This verb is found some 50 times. *Qavah* is the root of the noun *tiqvah*, "hope" or "expectancy." *Qavah* expresses the idea of "waiting hopefully" (Gen. 49:18; Job 30:26; Ps. 40:1; Is. 5:4;

3:1–66 In this chapter, vv. 1–24 use the first person singular. Vv. 25–39 use regular exhortational prose. Vv. 40–47 use the first person plural, and vv. 48–66 use the first person singular. These are the major divisions of this chapter.
3:1 Rod: A picture of God's punishment (Ps. 89:32).
3:4–16 On behalf of Israel Jeremiah sees himself as sick and injured (v. 4), dead and buried (v. 6; see Ps. 143:3), a prisoner (v. 7), tortured (v. 8), a traveler making slow progress (v. 9), attacked by wild animals (vv. 10, 11), a target of arrows (vv. 12, 13), an object of ridicule (v. 14), having to eat bitter food (v. 15), and having to eat contaminated food (v. 16).
3:7, 8 The Assyrians had a form of torture in which prisoners were walled into a very small place. The prophet felt so walled in that even his prayer would be unable to ascend to God (see v. 44).
3:12, 13 See Job 16:12 for a similar experience.
3:20–22 Jeremiah had almost given up hope (v. 20). Then he remembered something that restored his hope again (v. 21). This was the **mercies** of God (v. 22). Mercies (Hebrew *hesed*) can be translated "*covenant* love" or "*steadfast* love." It is linked with compassion (Ps. 103:4), truth and faithfulness (Ex. 34:6), and goodness (Ps. 23:6). The ability to offer sacrifices was gone and everything seemed hopeless, but God's *hesed* remained.
3:22–32 See section 1 of Truth-In-Action at the end of Lam.
3:24 The tribe of Levi received no land. The Lord was to be their portion. With everything taken away except *hesed* (see note on v. 22), Jerusalem could say, **"The LORD is my portion."**
3:25, 26 See section 2 of Truth-In-Action at the end of Lam.

25:9). In the present reference, even in the overwhelming tragedies Jeremiah experienced, he had hope in God's salvation and was willing to wait for it.

26 *It is* good that *one* should
[a]hope [b]and wait quietly
For the salvation of the LORD.
3 27 [a]*It is* good for a man to bear
The yoke in his youth.

28 [a]Let him sit alone and keep silent,
Because *God* has laid *it* on him;
29 [a]Let him put his mouth in the dust—
There may yet be hope.
30 [a]Let him give *his* cheek to the one who strikes him,
And be full of reproach.

1 31 [a]For the Lord will not cast off forever.
32 Though He causes grief,
Yet He will *show compassion
According to the multitude of His mercies.
33 For [a]He does not afflict [1]willingly,
Nor grieve the children of men.

34 To crush under one's feet
All the prisoners of the earth,
35 To turn aside the justice *due* a man
Before the face of the *Most High,
36 Or subvert a man in his cause—
[a]The Lord does not approve.

37 Who *is* he [a]*who* speaks and it comes to pass,
When the Lord has not commanded *it*?
38 *Is it* not from the mouth of the Most High
That [a]woe and well-being proceed?

26 [a][Rom. 4:16–18] [b]Ex. 14:13; Ps. 37:7; Is. 7:4
27 [a]Ps. 94:12
28 [a]Jer. 15:17
29 [a]Job 42:6
30 [a]Job 16:10; Is. 50:6; [Matt. 5:39; 26:67]; Mark 14:65; Luke 22:63
31 [a]Ps. 77:7; 94:14; [Is. 54:7–10]
32 *See WW at Hos. 2:23.
33 [a][Ps. 119:67, 71, 75; Is. 28:21; Ezek. 33:11; Heb. 12:10] [1]Lit. *from His heart*
35 *See WW at Gen. 14:18.
36 [a][Jer. 22:3; Hab. 1:13]
37 [a][Ps. 33:9–11]
38 [a]Job 2:10; [Is. 45:7]; Jer. 32:42; Amos 3:6; [James 3:10, 11]
39 [a]Prov. 19:3 [b]Jer. 30:15; Mic. 7:9; [Heb. 12:5, 6] [1]Or *murmur*
41 [a]Ps. 86:4
42 [a]Neh. 9:26; Jer. 14:20; Dan. 9:5
45 [a]1 Cor. 4:13
46 [a]Job 30:9, 10; Ps. 22:6–8; Lam. 2:16
47 [a]Is. 24:17, 18; Jer. 48:43, 44 [b]Is. 51:19
48 [a]Jer. 4:19; 14:17; Lam. 2:11
49 [a]Ps. 77:2; Jer. 14:17
50 [a]Ps. 80:14; Is. 63:15; Lam. 5:1

39 [a]Why should a living man [1]complain, 4
[b]A man for the punishment of his sins?

40 Let us search out and examine our ways,
And turn back to the LORD;
41 [a]Let us lift our hearts and hands
To God in heaven.
42 [a]We have transgressed and rebelled;
You have not pardoned.

43 You have covered *Yourself* with anger
And pursued us;
You have slain *and* not pitied.
44 You have covered Yourself with a cloud,
That prayer should not pass through.
45 You have made us an
[a]offscouring and refuse
In the midst of the peoples.

46 [a]All our enemies
Have opened their mouths against us.
47 [a]Fear and a snare have come upon us,
[b]Desolation and destruction.
48 [a]My eyes overflow with rivers of water
For the destruction of the daughter of my people.

49 [a]My eyes flow and do not cease,
Without interruption,
50 Till the LORD from heaven
[a]Looks down and sees.
51 My eyes bring suffering to my soul
Because of all the daughters of my city.

3:26 Punishment has to pass eventually. It is good to wait it out. This should be done patiently (v. 26; see Ps. 37:9), quietly (v. 26; see Is. 30:15), and submissively (v. 27).
3:27 See section 3 of Truth-In-Action at the end of Lam.
3:28–30 In someone who is being truly humbled, suffering will take place in silence (v. 28), with submission (**his mouth in the dust**), and with surrender (giving ***his* cheek to the one who strikes him**).
3:31–33 See section 1 of Truth-In-Action at the end of Lam.
3:31–33 In spite of suffering there is a clear view of the nature of God: 1) **The Lord will not cast off forever;** 2) **He will show compassion;** 3) **He does not afflict willingly.**
3:34–36 If vv. 31–33 speak about God, what does He think about the evil men He sometimes uses? **The Lord does not approve** of the maltreatment of prisoners, the waiving of human rights, or the subversion of justice (Deut. 16:19).
3:37, 38 God is sovereign over human affairs and can use both good and evil (Is. 45:7). He can also bring good out of evil (Rom. 8:28).
3:39–42 See section 4 of Truth-In-Action at the end of Lam.
3:39 A living man: Being alive is an indication that God has shown mercy.
3:40–42 This is true repentance and prayer (v. 41). It is an acknowledgment that they had **transgressed and rebelled.** But God was not going to remove the punishment. This had been made clear in 2:2, 17, 21. Jeremiah had warned that the captivity would have to take place (Jer. 15:2; 29:18). This is the sense in which the words **You have not pardoned** are to be understood. God was going to continue to pursue them (v. 43).
3:44 God would not be swayed by their pleadings to cancel the captivity. Such prayers would **not pass through** (Jer. 14:12). God had repeatedly told Jeremiah not to pray for Israel in this way. See Jer. 7:16; 11:14; 14:11.
3:48, 49 See note on 2:18.

52 My enemies [a]without cause
Hunted me down like a bird.
53 They [1]silenced my life [a]in the pit
And [b]threw [2]stones at me.
54 [a]The waters flowed over my head;
[b]I said, "I am cut off!"

55 [a]I called on Your name, O LORD,
From the lowest [b]pit.
56 [a]You have heard my voice:
"Do not hide Your ear
From my sighing, from my cry for help."
57 You [a]drew near on the day I called on You,
And said, [b]"Do not fear!"

1 58 O Lord, You have [a]pleaded the case for my soul;
[b]You have *redeemed my life.
59 O LORD, You have seen [1]*how* I am wronged;
[a]Judge my case.
60 You have seen all their vengeance,
All their [a]schemes against me.

61 You have heard their reproach, O LORD,
All their schemes against me,
62 The lips of my enemies
And their whispering against me all the day.
63 Look at their [a]sitting down and their rising up;
I *am* their taunting song.

64 [a]Repay them, O LORD,
According to the work of their hands.
65 Give them [1]a veiled heart;
Your curse *be* upon them!
66 In Your anger,
Pursue and destroy them
[a]From under the heavens of the [b]LORD.

52 [a]Ps. 35:7, 19 **53** [a]Jer. 37:16 [b]Dan. 6:17 [1]LXX *put to death* [2]Lit. *a stone on* **54** [a]Ps. 69:2; Jon. 2:3–5 [b]Is. 38:10 **55** [a]Ps. 130:1; Jon. 2:2 [b]Jer. 38:6–13 **56** [a]Ps. 3:4 **57** [a]James 4:8 [b]Is. 41:10, 14; Dan. 10:12 **58** [a]Ps. 35:1; Jer. 51:36 [b]Ps. 71:23 *See WW at Is. 52:9. **59** [a]Ps. 9:4 [1]Lit. *my wrong* **60** [a]Jer. 11:19 **63** [a]Ps. 139:2 **64** [a]Ps. 28:4; Jer. 11:20; 2 Tim. 4:14 **65** [1]A Jewish tradition *sorrow of* **66** [a]Deut. 25:19; Jer. 10:11 [b]Ps. 8:3

CHAPTER 4

1 [1]Lit. *poured out* **2** [a]Is. 30:14; Jer. 19:11; [2 Cor. 4:7] [1]Lit. *Weighed against* [2]*reckoned* **3** [a]Job 39:14–17 **4** [a]Ps. 22:15 **5** [a]Job 24:8 **6** [a]Ezek. 16:48 [b]Gen. 19:25; Jer. 20:16 **7** [1]Or *nobles* [2]Or *purer*

The Degradation of Zion

4 How the gold has become dim!
How changed the fine gold!
The stones of the sanctuary are [1]scattered
At the head of every street.

2 The precious sons of Zion,
[1]Valuable as fine gold,
How they are [2]regarded [a]as clay pots,
The work of the hands of the potter!

3 Even the jackals present their breasts
To nurse their young;
But the daughter of my people *is* cruel,
[a]Like ostriches in the wilderness.

4 The tongue of the infant clings
To the roof of its mouth for thirst;
[a]The young children ask for bread,
But no one breaks *it* for them.

5 Those who ate delicacies
Are desolate in the streets;
Those who were brought up in scarlet
[a]Embrace ash heaps.

6 The punishment of the iniquity of the daughter of my people
Is greater than the punishment of the [a]sin of Sodom,
Which was [b]overthrown in a moment,
With no hand to help her!

7 Her [1]Nazirites were [2]brighter than snow
And whiter than milk;
They were more ruddy in body than rubies,

3:53 It is difficult to tell whether Jeremiah is referring to his own experience (see Jer. 38:6), or using **the pit** to symbolize either death (Ps. 30:3) or trouble (Ps. 40:2). He may have been referring to the story of his own imprisonment to interpret the national experience. He would personify the sufferings of the nation.
3:54 The waters flowed over my head: This symbolized trouble and misfortune (Ps. 69:2, 15).
3:58–66 See section 1 of Truth-In-Action at the end of Lam.
3:58–64 God is often portrayed as a righteous Judge, who vindicates the innocent and at the same time punishes their oppressors. This *is seen in* Paul's expressed desire in 2 Tim. 4:14.
3:64–66 These verses are typical of what are called "taunt songs," which people used against their enemies in wartime. A taunt song was supposed to be rather vindictive (Ps. 137:8, 9; Hab. 2:6–19). This one was based on God's promise ultimately to vindicate them (Jer. 50:9).
4:1–22 The three-line stanzas of ch. 3 are now followed by two-line stanzas. This is followed in turn by one-line stanzas in ch. 5 together with no acrostic form. It is possible that this was done purposely to indicate a denouement to the highlights of ch. 3.
4:1, 2 The Jews esteemed their land in terms of **gold, fine gold,** and **stones of the sanctuary.** They esteemed their men as **precious sons . . . valuable as fine gold.** This made the contrast with the present all the more painful.
4:3 The **ostriches** were known to abandon their eggs to be hatched by the sun (Job 39:13–18). Hardship had changed the care of motherhood into this kind of indifference.
4:6 Israel had enjoyed greater privileges than Sodom. This meant that she also had to bear more responsibility and was more accountable for her sin (see Luke 12:47).
4:7–11 This section has a structure similar to vv. 1–6. Both begin with great worth, of the people on the one hand, (v. 1) and the Nazirites on the other (v. 7). This is followed by

Like sapphire in their
[3]appearance.

8 *Now* their appearance is blacker
than soot;
They go unrecognized in the
streets;
[a]Their skin clings to their bones,
It has become as dry as wood.

9 *Those* slain by the sword are
better off
Than *those* who die of hunger;
For these [a]pine away,
Stricken *for lack* of the fruits of
the [b]field.

10 The hands of the [a]compassionate
women
Have [1]cooked their [b]own
children;
They became [c]food for them
In the destruction of the daughter
of my people.

11 The LORD has fulfilled His fury,
[a]He has poured out His fierce
anger.
[b]He kindled a fire in Zion,
And it has devoured its
foundations.

5 12 The kings of the earth,
And all inhabitants of the world,
Would not have believed
That the adversary and the
enemy
Could [a]enter the gates of
Jerusalem—

13 [a]Because of the sins of her
prophets
And the iniquities of her priests,
[b]Who shed in her midst
The blood of the just.

14 They wandered blind in the
streets;
[a]They have defiled themselves
with blood,
[b]So that no one would touch their
garments.

15 They cried out to them,
"Go away, [a]unclean!
Go away, go away,
Do not touch us!"
When they fled and wandered,
Those among the nations said,
"They shall no longer *dwell *here*."

16 The [1]face of the LORD scattered
them;
He no longer regards them.
[a]*The people* do not respect the
priests
Nor show favor to the elders.

17 Still [a]our eyes failed us,
Watching vainly for our help;
In our watching we *watched
For a nation *that* could not save
us.

18 [a]They [1]tracked our steps
So that we could not walk in our
streets.
[b]Our end was near;
Our days were over,
For our end had come.

19 Our pursuers were [a]swifter
Than the eagles of the heavens.
They pursued us on the
mountains
And lay in wait for us in the
wilderness.

20 The [a]breath of our nostrils, the
*anointed of the LORD,
[b]Was caught in their pits,
Of whom we said, "Under his
shadow
We shall live among the nations."

7 [3]Lit. *polishing*
8 [a]Job 19:20; Ps. 102:5
9 [a]Lev. 26:39; Ezek. 24:23 [b]Jer. 16:4
10 [a]Lev. 26:29; Deut. 28:57; 2 Kin. 6:29; Jer. 19:9; Lam. 2:20; Ezek. 5:10 [b]Is. 49:15 [c]Deut. 28:57 [1]*boiled*
11 [a]Jer. 7:20; Lam. 2:17; Ezek. 22:31 [b]Deut. 32:22; Jer. 21:14
12 [a]Jer. 21:13
13 [a]Jer. 5:31; Ezek. 22:26, 28; Zeph. 3:4 [b]Jer. 2:30; 26:8, 9; Matt. 23:31
14 [a]Jer. 2:34 [b]Num. 19:16
15 [a]Lev. 13:45, 46 *See WW at Jer. 42:17.
16 [a]Lam. 5:12 [1]Tg. *anger*
17 [a]2 Kin. 24:7 *See WW at Hos. 9:8.
18 [a]2 Kin. 25:4 [b]Ezek. 7:2, 3, 6; Amos 8:2 [1]Lit. *hunted*
19 [a]Deut. 28:49
20 [a]Gen. 2:7 [b]Jer. 52:9; Ezek. 12:13 *See WW at Dan. 9:25.

the great tragedy of the devastation of these groups. The sections both end with a verse speaking theologically about the events (vv. 6, 11). The word for **Nazirites** has been translated in different ways. It indicates someone who is conspicuous because of his rank. For the fate of the **children** in v. 10, see the note on 2:20.

4:12–16 See section 5 of Truth-In-Action at the end of Lam.

4:12 The hills and walls of Jerusalem made assault both difficult and costly.

4:13 The prophets and priests had **shed . . . the blood of the just** prophet Urijah (Jer. 26:20–23), and had attempted to assassinate Jeremiah for predicting what had happened. As the ones who suppressed the truth, they were the real culprits (Jer. 26:11). They had preferred to believe the more comforting words of the false prophets (2:14). This condition was similar to that of Jesus' day (John 8:44).

4:15 The deceptions of the leaders described in v. 13 had caught up with them. The people of Judah seem to have been outraged at being deceived. So the people would refuse the company of a leader.

4:17 We watched for a nation: Some scholars feel that the surviving remnant was still expecting help. Vv. 18 and 19 refer to this remnant. But these words probably refer to their attitude before the destruction of Jerusalem. They hoped that some nation would come to their aid. These hopes were dashed in 587 B.C. (see note on 1:2).

4:18, 19 The occupying troops harassed the remnant at every opportunity.

4:20 The breath of our nostrils, the anointed of the LORD: These are probably titles used for King Zedekiah, for whom some of the people had had great hopes.

21 Rejoice and be glad, O daughter
of [a]Edom,
You who dwell in the land of Uz!
[b]The cup shall also pass over to
you
And you shall become drunk and
make yourself naked.

22 [a]*The punishment of* your iniquity
[1]is accomplished,
O daughter of Zion;
He will no longer send you into
captivity.
[b]He will punish your iniquity,
O daughter of Edom;
He will uncover your sins!

A Prayer for Restoration

5 Remember, [a]O LORD, what has
come upon us;
Look, and behold [b]our reproach!
2 [a]Our inheritance has been turned
over to aliens,
And our houses to foreigners.
3 We have become orphans and
waifs,
Our mothers *are* like [a]widows.

4 We pay for the water we drink,
And our wood comes at a price.
5 [a]*They* pursue at our [1]heels;
We labor *and* *have no rest.
6 [a]We have given our hand
[b]*to* the Egyptians
And the [c]Assyrians, to be
*satisfied with bread.

7 [a]Our fathers sinned *and are* no
more,
But we bear their iniquities.
8 Servants rule over us;
There is none to deliver *us* from
their hand.

21 [a]Ps. 83:3–6 [b]Jer. 25:15; Obad. 10
22 [a][Is. 40:2; Jer. 33:7, 8] [b]Ps. 137:7 [1]*has been completed*

CHAPTER 5

1 [a]Ps. 89:50 [b]Ps. 79:4; Lam. 2:15
2 [a]Ps. 79:1
3 [a]Ex. 22:24; Jer. 15:8; 18:21
5 [a]Deut. 28:48; Jer. 28:14 [1]Lit. *necks* *See WW at Ex. 33:14.
6 [a]Gen. 24:2 [b]Hos. 9:3; 12:1 [c]Jer. 2:18; Hos. 5:13 *See WW at Amos 4:8.
7 [a]Jer. 31:29

11 [a]Is. 13:16; Zech. 14:2
13 [a]Judg. 16:21
14 [a]Is. 24:8; Jer. 7:34
15 [a]Jer. 25:10; Amos 8:10
16 [a]Job 19:9; Ps. 89:39; Jer. 13:18
17 [a]Ps. 6:7
18 [a]Is. 27:10
19 [a]Ps. 9:7; Hab. 1:12 [b]Ps. 45:6 *See WW at Esth. 9:28.

9 We get our bread *at the risk* of
our lives,
Because of the sword in the
wilderness.

10 Our skin is hot as an oven,
Because of the fever of famine.
11 They [a]ravished the women in
Zion,
The maidens in the cities of
Judah.
12 Princes were hung up by their
hands,
And elders were not respected.
13 Young men [a]ground at the
millstones;
Boys staggered under *loads of*
wood.
14 The elders have ceased *gathering*
at the gate,
And the young men from their
[a]music.

15 The joy of our heart has ceased;
Our dance has turned into
[a]mourning.
16 [a]The crown has fallen *from* our
head.
Woe to us, for we have sinned!
17 Because of this our heart is faint;
[a]Because of these *things* our eyes
grow dim;
18 Because of Mount Zion which is
[a]desolate,
With foxes walking about on it.

19 You, O LORD, [a]**remain** forever;
[b]Your throne from *generation to
generation.

WORD WEALTH

5:19 remain, *yashab* (yah-*shahv*); Strong's #3427: To sit down, stay, re-

4:21 The opposition of **Edom** caused bitterness at this difficult time. **Rejoice and be glad** probably means "Laugh away, but you too will be judged and made to drink **the cup** of God's wrath" (Jer. 25:15).
4:22 Most of the people were in captivity. ***The punishment*** was **accomplished.** It is possible that God offered a new opportunity to the remnant left behind: **He will no longer send you into captivity.** This seems to be implied in Jer. 42:10–12; 50:20.
5:1–22 This is the final prayer and the only part of the book that is not an acrostic. It is also the shortest poem (see note on 4:1–22).
5:2 Inheritance: This word refers to the land of Judah (Lev. 20:24).
5:3 Widows: *This word describes* their unprotected and disinherited state (see v. 2).
5:4 The occupying forces exercised a strict control over the remnant.
5:6 Given our hand to means "submitted to." Assyria is sometimes used for Babylon (Jer. 2:18).
5:7 This statement is not meant to be an excuse (Jer. 3:25). They were acknowledged to be worse than their fathers (Jer. 16:12).
5:8 Servants: These probably were members of nations subject to Babylon. This was objectionable to the Jews (Prov. 19:10; 30:21, 22).
5:9 The sword in the wilderness probably refers to marauding bands. Deut. 28:48 was fulfilled.
5:10 Hot: This metaphor can also be translated "wrinkled."
5:11–14 This is the only section that does not use the first person plural. It is a short passage in the middle of the prayer covering all classes of people. No one has escaped the tragedy. The **young men** were doing work normally done by women. This was therefore probably forced labor (Judg. 16:21).
5:14 The elders normally gathered at the gate to dispense justice and give advice (Josh. 20:4).
5:16 The crown has fallen: Israel no longer had a place of honor among the nations.
5:19 God had not abdicated His **throne** (Ps. 45:6). He was still in control. This verse is the preparation for the final petition.

main, abide, endure, dwell, continue, settle down; to make one's home in a permanent location; to inhabit a particular place. This verb occurs more than 500 times. *Yashab* may be translated as "dwell" in most of its occurrences (2 Sam. 7:2; Jer. 23:8). The sense of sitting down is apparent in Neh. 1:4. Ps. 132:14 illustrates the idea of settling down permanently. From *yashab* are derived *yeshiba* (a religious school where young rabbinical students sit in study) and *yishub* (the total body of Jewish inhabitants in the land of Israel). In the present reference, God's permanence is contrasted with Zion's temporary desolation.

20 [a]Why do You forget us forever,
And forsake us for so long a time?
21 [a]Turn us back to You, O LORD, and we will be [1]restored;
Renew our days as of old,
22 Unless You have utterly rejected us,
And are very angry with us!

20 [a]Ps. 13:1; 44:24
21 [a]Ps. 80:3, 7, 19; Jer. 31:18
[1]*returned*

5:20–22 Forsake us for so long . . . utterly rejected . . . angry with us was a desperate prayer. Their faith, though sometimes strong, was often very weak. But at the heart of this prayer are the words **Turn us back to You, O LORD.** The Hebrew word for "turn back" is used by Jeremiah. See Jer. 3:1, 12, 14, and the following verses. It means to turn from sin to God.

LAMENTATIONS: THE ROAD TO RENEWAL (5:21)

Sin → Suffering (1:8)
Sorrow → Repentance (1:20)
Prayer → Hope (3:19–24)
Faith → Restoration (5:21)

TRUTH-IN-ACTION through LAMENTATIONS

Letting the LIFE of the Holy Spirit Bring Faith's Works Alive in You!

Truth Lamentations Teaches	Text	**Action** Lamentations Invites
1 Steps to Knowing God and His Ways Lam. calls attention to God's faithfulness and righteousness in judgment. No judgment, chastisement, or reproof ever comes as the result of divine caprice. It is always God's righteous response to sin and rebellion. God loves us and allows calamity only as a last resort to restore us to righteousness.	1:18	**Remember** that the Lord is always righteous in His judgment. **Know** that judgment is the fruit of sin and rebellion.
	3:22–32	**Acknowledge** that the Lord is faithful to His Word. **Wait** on the Lord and **expect** daily expressions of His mercy to you.
	3:31–33	**Be confident** that judgment will often be followed by compassion and restoration because of God's love. **Understand** that God does not relish judgment as a disciplinary means, even though it is sometimes necessary.
	3:58–66	**Entrust** yourself completely to the care of the Lord, who is completely just in all His dealings.
2 Guidelines for Growing in Godliness The godly person responds to judgment with intercession and prayer, recognizing that only the repentance of his people can effect the healing of their land (see 2 Chr. 7:14).	2:19	**Let** impending judgment call you to seasons of intercession for God's people. **Implore** God to pour out a spirit of repentance and to show mercy.
	3:25, 26	**Seek the Lord, expecting** that He will bring good things to pass for you. **Wait** quietly for Him to show you His salvation in any distress.

Truth Lamentations Teaches	Text	**Action** Lamentations Invites
3 A Key Step to Dynamic Devotion All too often God's people wait too long to develop good devotional habits. It is vitally important that we train our youth to seek God earnestly.	3:27	**Realize** that it is never too early to begin spiritual development. **Encourage** young people to become earnest and fruitful in their pursuit of God. **Challenge** and **inspire** those who would otherwise postpone godliness until later in life.
4 Keys to Wise Living The wise person does not complain about adversity knowing that it can contribute to godliness. Response with dependence on God's Word and repentance, when needed, will bring restoration.	3:39–42	**Do not complain** about adversity in your life. **Accept** God's discipline as an expression of His love to turn us from rebellion or disobedience.
5 Lessons for Leaders All of the major prophets put a great deal of responsibility for Israel's and Judah's sins squarely on the shoulders of their leaders: their priests, their prophets, and their kings. This should become a strong admonition for those who lead God's church today. When God's people are judged due to the sins of their leaders, God's people tend to lose all respect even for legitimate leadership and faithful leaders thus often lose righteous influence.	1:14 4:12–16	Leaders, **be reminded** that when God's leaders fail to deal with sin, He holds them responsible for the judgment, which inevitably follows. Leaders, **walk obediently, remembering** that your sins can cause the downfall of God's people, bringing judgment to whole churches or fellowships of churches.

The Book of EZEKIEL

Author: Ezekiel
Date: 593 B.C.–573 B.C.
Theme: Destruction of Jerusalem and Its Restoration
Key Words: Judgment, Blessing, Individual Moral Responsibility

Author The author, whose name means "God Strengthens," is identified as "Ezekiel the priest, the son of Buzi" (1:3). Although this identification has been challenged, there seems to be no valid reason for doubting it. He was probably a member of the Zadokite priestly family that came into prominence during the reforms of Josiah (621 B.C.). He was trained in the priesthood during the reign of Jehoiakim, was deported to Babylon (1:1; 33:21; 40:1) in 597 B.C., and settled in Tel Abib on the Chebar Canal near Nippur (1:1). His ministry briefly overlapped Jeremiah's.

Date Ezekiel's call came to him in 593 B.C., the fifth year of Jehoiachin's reign. The latest date given for an oracle (29:17) is probably 571 B.C., making his ministry about twenty years long. The death of his wife occurred about the time of the destruction of Jerusalem in 587 B.C. (24:1, 15–17). Exiled in the second siege of Jerusalem, he wrote to those yet in Jerusalem about its imminent and total destruction, including the departure of God's presence. Parts were also apparently written after Jerusalem's overthrow.

Content Ezekiel's personality reflects a mystical strain. The immediacy of his contact with the Spirit, his visions, and the frequency with which the word of the Lord came to him provide a connection between the older ecstatic prophets and the classical writing prophets. His spiritual experiences also anticipated the activity of the Holy Spirit in the New Testament. To him rightly belongs the title "charismatic."

Ezekiel's message was addressed to a demoralized remnant of Judah exiled in Babylon. The moral responsibility of the individual is a primary theme in his message. Corporate responsibility no longer shields the individual. Each individual must accept personal responsibility for the national calamity. Each individual is responsible for his or her individual sin (18:2–4). It is the weight of the cumulative sin of each individual that contributed to the breaking of God's covenant with Israel, and each bears a share of the blame for the judgment that resulted in the exile to Babylon.

The book is easily divided into three sections, Judah's judgment (chs. 4—24), the heathen nations' judgment (chs. 25—32), and future blessings for God's covenant people (chs. 33—48).

Two theological themes act as a counterpoise in the prophet's thought. In Ezekiel's doctrine of man, he placed the emphasis on personal responsibility (18:4, "the soul who sins shall die"). On the other hand, he emphasized the divine grace in the rebirth of the nation. The repentance of the faithful remnant among the exiles would result in the re-creation of Israel from the dry bones (37:11–14). The divine Spirit would quicken them to a new life. By this emphasis on the Holy Spirit in regeneration Ezekiel anticipated the New Testament doctrine of the Holy Spirit, especially in the Gospel of John.

Christ Revealed In Ezekiel, Christology and the Person and work of the Holy Spirit are inextricably bound together. Although a messianic figure is not clearly discernible in Ezekiel's final vision, several messianic titles and functions in the book indicate that a Messiah is part of his eschatological vision.

The title "Son of Man" occurs some ninety times in Ezekiel. While the title is applied to Ezekiel himself, it was appropriated by Jesus as His favorite self-designation. Therefore, Ezekiel may be regarded as a type of Christ. As such, Ezekiel was empowered as a prophetic voice of the messianic age when "the Spirit of the LORD fell" upon him (11:5). The descent of the Holy Spirit upon Jesus at Jordan empowered Him to articulate the advent of the messianic kingdom (Luke 4:18, 19).

Another messianic title is reflected in the vision of the Lord God as the divine Shepherd who gathers again His scattered flock (34:11–16). The figure evokes images of Jesus as the Good Shepherd (John 10:11–16).

Ezekiel further develops the fundamental idea of Israel as "a kingdom of priests and a holy nation," which was rooted in the covenant of Sinai (Ex. 19:6). A restored sanctuary in the midst of a regathered people whose head is the King-priest, the Davidic Messiah (37:22–28), foreshadows the restored tabernacle of David, the church (Amos 9:11; Acts 15:16).

A final messianic prophecy of Christ employs the figure of a sprig of cedar planted by the Lord Himself on a lofty mountain, which becomes a lofty cedar providing fruit and nests for birds. This nature metaphor, like "the Root of Jesse" (Is. 11:1, 10; Rom. 15:12), serves to represent the future Messiah. Birds and trees represent Gentile nations to show Christ's universal reign.

The Holy Spirit at Work Whether the prophetic revelation is presented symbolically in visions, signs, parabolic actions, or in human speech, Ezekiel claims for them the power and authority of the Holy Spirit. In addition, there are numerous references to the Spirit of God in the book. One might almost characterize the Book of Ezekiel as the "Acts of the Holy Spirit" in the Old Testament. Several of these references merit special notice.

In 11:5, the prophet asserts autobiographically that "the Spirit of the LORD fell upon me, and said to me." The oracle that follows is thus God's Word in Ezekiel's words, inspired by the Holy Spirit. The same chapter (11:24) presents the Spirit as active in a vision: "Then the Spirit took me up and brought me in a vision by the Spirit of God into Chaldea, to those in captivity."

Perhaps the best-known instance of the Spirit's activity is in chapter 37, the vision of the valley of dry bones: "The hand of the LORD came upon me and brought me out in the Spirit of the LORD, and set me down in the midst of the valley; and it *was* full of bones"

(v. 1). The subsequent vision relates the spiritual rebirth of the remnant then in exile.

A final aspect of the Spirit's action in the life of the prophet is found in 36:26, "I will give you a new heart and put a new spirit within you." It is not solely an external act of the Spirit "falling upon" someone, but the prophesied subjective experience of the Spirit's presence within, such as Ezekiel uniquely experienced when "the Spirit entered" him (2:2). Ezekiel anticipated the new covenant's "new birth" experience, which would be by the Spirit.

Personal Application Three very important personal, relevant lessons can be learned in Ezekiel. First is the importance of individual moral responsibility. Although it is true that God still blesses and corrects entire local churches (Rev. 2; 3), His primary dealings are with individuals. As such, one cannot appeal to the righteousness of others as his righteousness nor need he fear personal correction for the sins of another (18:20).

Second, Ezekiel teaches that though God is reluctant to discipline His people severely, He must. He is a righteous and jealous God as much as He is merciful and forgiving (12:1–16).

Third, Ezekiel assures us that God will ultimately triumph in history. His enemies may be winning battles now, but future judgment will totally destroy them (35:1–15).

Outline of Ezekiel

I. The opening vision and call of Ezekiel 1:1—3:21
- A. Introductory visions 1:1–28
- B. The prophet's commission 2:1—3:21

II. Prophecies and visions of Jerusalem's destruction 3:22—24:27
- A. Oracles of judgment 3:22—7:27
  - 1. Against Jerusalem 3:22—5:17
  - 2. Against the whole nation 6:1—7:27
- B. Visions of idolatry in the temple 8:1—11:25
- C. Judah's exile and captivity 12:1—24:27
  - 1. Messages of judgment against Judah 12:1—19:14
  - 2. Oracles before the fall of Jerusalem 20:1—24:27

III. Oracles of doom against foreign nations 25:1—32:32
- A. Against Ammon 25:1–7
- B. Against Moab 25:8–11
- C. Against Edom 25:12–14
- D. Against Philistia 25:15–17
- E. Against Tyre 26:1—28:19
- F. Against Sidon 28:20–26
- G. Against Egypt 29:1—32:32

IV. Prophecies of restoration 33:1—48:35
- A. Ezekiel as watchman 33:1–33
- B. God as shepherd 34:1–31
- C. Judgment against Edom 35:1–15
- D. Restoration of Israel 36:1—37:28
- E. Judgment against Gog 38:1—39:29
- F. Restoration of the temple 40:1—46:24
- G. Restoration of the land 47:1—48:35

Ezekiel's Vision of God

NOW it came to pass in the thirtieth
year, in the fourth *month,* on the
fifth *day* of the month, as I *was* among
the captives by [a]the River Chebar, *that*
[b]the heavens were opened and I saw
[c]visions[1] of *God.

CHAPTER 1
1 [a]Ezek. 3:15, 23; 10:15 [b]Rev. 4:1; 19:11 [c]Ezek. 8:3

[1]So with MT, LXX, Vg.; Syr., Tg. *a vision*
*See WW at 2 Kin. 19:15.

1:1 The thirtieth year is probably the age of Ezekiel when he began his ministry. **The River Chebar:** A navigable canal on the Euphrates River flowing southeast from above Babylon. **Visions** is a special term used by Ezekiel to introduce his major revelations (see 8:3; 40:2), always with the word "God" to indicate their source. Given while he was awake, they were actual pictures likely accompanied by God's audible voice.

2 On the fifth *day* of the month, which
was in the fifth year of King Jehoiachin's captivity,
3 the word of the LORD came expressly to Ezekiel the priest, the son
of Buzi, in the land of the [1]Chaldeans
by the River Chebar; and [a]the hand of
the LORD was upon him there.
4 Then I looked, and behold, [a]a whirlwind was coming [b]out of the north, a
great cloud with raging fire engulfing
itself; and brightness *was* all around
it and radiating out of its midst like the
color of amber, out of the midst of the
fire.
5 [a]Also from within it *came* the likeness of four living creatures. And
[b]this *was* their appearance: they had
[c]the likeness of a man.
6 Each one had four faces, and each
one had four wings.
7 Their [1]legs *were* straight, and the
soles of their feet *were* like the soles
of calves' feet. They sparkled [a]like the
color of burnished bronze.
8 [a]The hands of a man *were* under
their wings on their four sides; and
each of the four had faces and wings.
9 Their wings touched one another.
The creatures did not turn when they
went, but each one went straight
[a]forward.
10 As for [a]the likeness of their faces,
each [b]had the face of a man; each of
the four had [c]the face of a lion on the
right side, [d]each of the four had the
face of an ox on the left side, [e]and each
of the four had the face of an eagle.
11 Thus *were* their faces. Their wings
stretched upward; two *wings* of each

3 [a]1 Kin. 18:46; 2 Kin. 3:15; Ezek. 3:14, 22 [1]Or *Babylonians*, and so elsewhere in the book
4 [a]Is. 21:1; Jer. 23:19; 25:32; Ezek. 13:11, 13 [b]Jer. 1:14
5 [a]Ezek. 10:15, 17, 20; Rev. 4:6–8 [b]Ezek. 10:8 [c]Ezek. 10:14
7 [a]Dan. 10:6; Rev. 1:15 [1]Lit. *feet*
8 [a]Ezek. 10:8, 21
9 [a]Ezek. 1:12; 10:20–22
10 [a]Ezek. 10:14; Rev. 4:7 [b]Num. 2:10 [c]Num. 2:3 [d]Num. 2:18 [e]Num. 2:25
11 [a]Is. 6:2; Ezek. 1:23
12 [a]Ezek. 10:11, 22
*See WW at 2 Sam. 23:2.
13 [a]Ps. 104:4; Rev. 4:5
14 [a]Zech. 4:10; [Matt. 24:27; Luke 17:24]
15 [a]Ezek. 10:9
16 [a]Ezek. 10:9, 10 [b]Dan. 10:6
18 [a]Ezek. 10:12; [Zech. 4:10]; Rev. 4:6, 8
19 [a]Ezek. 10:16, 17

one touched one another, and [a]two
covered their bodies.
12 And [a]each one went straight forward; they went wherever the *spirit
wanted to go, and they did not turn
when they went.
13 As for the likeness of the living
creatures, their appearance *was* like
burning coals of fire, [a]like the appearance of torches going back and forth
among the living creatures. The fire
was bright, and out of the fire went
lightning.
14 And the living creatures ran back
and forth, [a]in appearance like a flash
of lightning.
15 Now as I looked at the living creatures, behold, [a]a wheel *was* on the
earth beside each living creature with
its four faces.
16 [a]The appearance of the wheels and
their workings *was* [b]like the color of
beryl, and all four had the same likeness. The appearance of their workings *was*, as it were, a wheel in the middle of a wheel.
17 When they moved, they went toward any one of four directions; they
did not turn aside when they went.
18 As for their rims, they were so high
they were awesome; and their rims
were [a]full of eyes, all around the four
of them.
19 [a]When the living creatures went,
the wheels went beside them; and
when the living creatures were lifted
up from the earth, the wheels were
lifted up.
20 Wherever the spirit wanted to go,
they went, *because* there the spirit

1:2 If **Jehoiachin** was taken captive from Jerusalem to Babylon in 597 B.C., the **fifth year** would be 593 B.C.
1:3 **Ezekiel** means "God Strengthens" or "God Is Strong." Ezekiel was a member of the priesthood. **Chaldeans:** Babylonians. **Hand of the LORD:** A phrase used six more times by Ezekiel (3:14, 22; 8:1; 33:22; 37:1; 40:1) to express how God's Spirit came upon him in revelation.
1:4–28 This highly symbolic and apocalyptic vision of God can be divided into three parts: vv. 4–14 (the storm and the creatures); vv. 15–21 (wheels and the glory of God); and vv. 22–28 (the firmament and throne). A similar vision is described in ch. 10 where the presence of God leaves the temple. Though the vision is intricate and difficult to interpret at points, its intent is to reveal that the sovereign Lord God Himself is about to intervene in history to judge Judah; He has chosen Ezekiel, who responds with incredible awe (v. 28), to warn them.
1:4 **A whirlwind** *symbolized* the coming of God Himself (see 2 Kin. 2:1, 11; Job 38:1; 40:6; Zech. 9:14). **Out of the north:** Either God chose to follow the path of the exiles, by which He identifies with their plight, or He has come from the direction where the Babylonians believed their gods were located and must, therefore, have overcome them on the way.
1:5 **Four living creatures:** The number 4, which is used 12 times in this chapter and over 40 times in the book, is a symbol of completeness. See 37:9 (four winds); Gen. 13:14 (four directions); Is. 11:12 (four corners). These creatures are further defined in v. 10 and are called "cherubim" in ch. 10.
1:10 The various **faces** symbolize God's rule over all of creation.
1:11 Each creature is described as having four wings (v. 6), and in reverence for God's presence they each **covered their bodies** with two of them.
1:13 The difficulty Ezekiel has in communicating his vision is apparent when he tells us that in addition to the creatures' appearance in the form of a man, **their appearance *was* like burning coals.**
1:15–21 Beside each creature was a **wheel** (v. 15), which gave the appearance of a **wheel in the middle of a wheel,** perhaps intersecting at right angles (v. 16). The wheels had high **rims** (perhaps reaching from Earth to heaven), were **full of eyes** (symbolizing God's all-seeing nature, v. 18), and their spirits were **in the wheels** (vv. 20, 21). The whole description seems to symbolize the omnipresence of God. He is capable of moving in any direction.

went; and the wheels were lifted together with them, [a]for the spirit of the
[1]living creatures *was* in the wheels.
21 When those went, *these* went; when
those stood, *these* stood; and when
those were lifted up from the earth, the
wheels were lifted up together with
them, for the spirit of the [1]living creatures *was* in the wheels.
22 [a]The likeness of the [1]firmament
above the heads of the [2]living creatures
was like the color of an awesome
[b]crystal, stretched out [c]over their
heads.
23 And under the firmament their
wings *spread out* straight, one toward
another. Each one had two which covered one side, and each one had two
which covered the other side of the
body.
24 [a]When they went, I heard the noise
of their wings, [b]like the noise of many
*waters, like [c]the voice of the *Al-
mighty, a tumult like the noise of an
army; and when they stood still, they
let down their wings.
25 A voice came from above the firmament that *was* over their heads; whenever they stood, they let down their
wings.
26 [a]And above the firmament over
their heads *was* the likeness of a
throne, [b]in appearance like a sapphire
stone; on the likeness of the throne *was*
a likeness with the appearance of a
man high above [c]it.
27 Also from the appearance of His
waist and upward [a]I saw, as it were,
the color of amber with the appearance
of fire all around within it; and from
the appearance of His waist and downward I saw, as it were, the appearance
of fire with brightness all around.
28 [a]Like the appearance of a rainbow
in a cloud on a rainy day, so *was* the
appearance of the brightness all
around it. [b]This *was* the appearance
of the likeness of the glory of the LORD.

Ezekiel Sent to Rebellious Israel

So when I saw *it,* [c]I fell on my face,
and I heard a voice of One speaking.
2 And He said to me, "Son of man,
[a]stand on your feet, and I will
speak to you."
2 Then [a]the Spirit entered me when
He spoke to me, and set me on my feet;
and I heard Him who spoke to me.
3 And He said to me: "Son of man, I 5
am sending you to the children of Israel, to a rebellious nation that has
[a]rebelled against Me; [b]they and their
fathers have transgressed against Me
to this very *day.
4 [a]"For *they are* [1]impudent and stubborn children. I am sending you to
them, and you shall say to them, 'Thus
says the Lord GOD.'
5 [a]"As for them, whether they hear
or whether they refuse—for they *are*
a [b]rebellious house—yet they [c]will
know that a *prophet has been among
them.
6 "And you, son of man, [a]do not be
afraid of them nor be afraid of their
words, though [b]briers and thorns *are*
with you and you dwell among scorpions; [c]do not be afraid of their words
or dismayed by their looks, [d]though
they *are* a rebellious house.
7 [a]"You shall speak My *words to
them, whether they hear or whether
they refuse, for they *are* rebellious.
8 "But you, son of man, hear what I
say to you. Do not be rebellious like
that rebellious house; open your mouth
and [a]eat what I give you."
9 Now when I looked, there was
[a]a hand stretched out to me; and behold, [b]a scroll of a book *was* in it.
10 Then He spread it before me; and

20 [a]Ezek. 10:17 [1]Lit. *living creature;* LXX, Vg. *spirit of life;* Tg. *creatures*
21 [1]See note at v. 20
22 [a]Ezek. 10:1 [b]Rev. 4:6 [c]Ezek. 10:1 [1]Or *expanse* [2]So with LXX, Tg., Vg.; MT *living creature*
24 [a]Ezek. 3:13; 10:5 [b]Rev. 1:15 [c]Job 37:4, 5 *See WW at Is. 43:2. • See WW at Ps. 91:1.
26 [a]Ezek. 10:1 [b]Ex. 24:10, 16 [c]Ezek. 8:2
27 [a]Ezek. 8:2
28 [a]Rev. 4:3; 10:1 [b]Ezek. 3:23; 8:4 [c]Dan. 8:17

CHAPTER 2

1 [a]Dan. 10:11
2 [a]Ezek. 3:24
3 [a]Ezek. 5:6; 20:8, 13, 18 [b]Jer. 3:25 *See WW at Zeph. 1:7.
4 [a]Ezek. 3:7 [1]Lit. *stiff-faced and hard-hearted sons*
5 [a]Ezek. 3:11, 26, 27 [b]Ezek. 3:26 [c]Ezek. 33:33 *See WW at 1 Sam. 3:20.
6 [a]Jer. 1:8, 17 [b]Mic. 7:4 [c][1 Pet. 3:14] [d]Ezek. 3:9, 26, 27
7 [a]Jer. 1:7, 17 *See WW at Deut. 1:1.
8 [a]Rev. 10:9
9 [a][Ezek. 8:3] [b]Ezek. 3:1

1:22 Above the creatures was a **firmament,** the same word used of the expanse God created on the second day and called "Heaven" (Gen. 1:6–8). There it separated the waters above from the waters below; here it separated the creatures from the throne.

1:26–28 The **throne** above the firmament has an occupant described as **a man** obscured by the brilliance of **fire.** The important lesson for Ezekiel was that God was present in Babylonia as well as in Jerusalem.

1:28 The glory of the LORD refers to God in all His fullness, especially as He interacts with man (Ex. 33:17—34:9). It is a favorite theme of Ezekiel, used 16 times in the book (3:12, 23; 8:4; 9:3; 10:4, 18, 19; 11:22, 23; 39:21; 43:2 [occurs twice], 4, 5; 44:4). Ezekiel sees this glory both leave the temple (chs. 10; 11) and later return to another temple (chs. 43; 44). **I fell on my face:** A common response when Ezekiel is in God's presence (3:23; 43:3; 44:4).

2:1 Son of man: A term used around 90 times to refer to Ezekiel. It stresses his humanity in contrast to the transcendent God who spoke to him. See also Introduction to Ezekiel: Christ Revealed.

2:2 The Spirit entered me: The Spirit of God entered Ezekiel and equipped him for his task. See Introduction to Ezekiel: The Holy Spirit at Work.

2:3–8 See section 5 of Truth-In-Action at the end of Ezek.

2:3 Rebellious nation: Like many of the prophets before him (see Is. 6:9–13; Jer. 1:17–19), Ezekiel faced a difficult task because the people were in rebellion against God.

2:4 The Lord GOD: A title used 217 times in Ezekiel (only 103 times in the rest of the OT). "Lord" translates the Hebrew *Adonai,* a term that emphasizes sovereignty; "GOD" translates *Yahweh,* the personal name of the God who made Himself known and entered into covenant with His people.

2:5 A rebellious house: Used frequently in the early chapters of Ezek. to describe the nation (vv. 6, 8; 3:9, 26, 27; 12:2, 3, 9, 25; 17:12; 24:3).

2:10 Most ancient scrolls had writing on one side only. **Writing on the inside and on the outside** indicates the

there was writing on the inside and on
the outside, and written on it *were*
lamentations and mourning and woe.

3 Moreover He said to me, "Son of
man, eat what you find; [a]eat this
scroll, and go, speak to the house of
Israel."
2 So I opened my mouth, and He
caused me to eat that scroll.
3 And He said to me, "Son of man,
feed your belly, and *fill your stomach
with this scroll that I give you." So I
[a]ate, and it was in my mouth [b]like
honey in sweetness.
4 Then He said to me: "Son of man,
go to the house of Israel and speak
with My words to them.
5 "For you *are* not sent to a people
of unfamiliar speech and of hard language, *but* to the house of Israel,
6 "not to many people of unfamiliar
speech and of hard language, whose
words you cannot understand. Surely,
[a]had I sent you to them, they would
have listened to you.
3 7 "But the house of Israel will not listen to you, [a]because they will not listen
to Me; [b]for all the house of Israel *are*
[1]impudent and hard-hearted.
8 "Behold, I have made your face
strong against their faces, and your
forehead strong against their foreheads.
9 [a]"Like adamant stone, harder than
flint, I have made your forehead;
[b]do not be afraid of them, nor be dismayed at their looks, though they *are*
a rebellious house."
10 Moreover He said to me: "Son of
man, receive into your heart all My
words that I speak to you, and *hear
with your ears.
11 "And go, get to the captives, to the
children of your people, and speak to
them and tell them, [a]'Thus says the
Lord GOD,' whether they hear, or
whether they refuse."
12 Then [a]the Spirit lifted me up, and I
heard behind me a great thunderous
voice: "Blessed *is* the [b]glory of the
LORD from His place!"
13 *I* also *heard* the [a]noise of the wings
of the living creatures that touched one
another, and the noise of the wheels
beside them, and a great thunderous
noise.
14 So the Spirit lifted me up and took
me away, and I went in bitterness, in
the [1]heat of my spirit; but [a]the hand
of the LORD was strong upon me.
15 Then I came to the captives at Tel
Abib, who dwelt by the River Chebar;
and [a]I sat where they sat, and remained there astonished among them
seven days.

Ezekiel Is a Watchman

16 Now it [a]came to pass at the end of 5
seven days that the word of the LORD
came to me, saying,
17 [a]"Son of *man, I have made you
[b]a *watchman for the house of Israel;
therefore hear a word from My mouth,
and give them [c]warning from Me:
18 "When I say to the wicked, 'You
shall surely die,' and you give him no
warning, nor speak to warn the wicked
from his wicked way, to save his life,
that same wicked *man* [a]shall die in his
iniquity; but his *blood I will require
at your hand.
19 "Yet, if you warn the wicked, and
he does not turn from his wickedness,

CHAPTER 3
1 [a]Ezek. 2:8, 9
3 [a]Jer. 15:16; Rev. 10:9 [b]Ps. 19:10; 119:103 *See WW at Jer. 23:24.
6 [a]Jon. 3:5–10; Matt. 11:21
7 [a]John 15:20, 21 [b]Ezek. 2:4 [1]Lit. *strong of forehead*
9 [a]Is. 50:7; Jer. 1:18; Mic. 3:8 [b]Jer. 1:8, 17; Ezek. 2:6
10 *See WW at 1 Kin. 20:8.
11 [a]Ezek. 2:5, 7
12 [a]1 Kin. 18:12; Ezek. 8:3; Acts 8:39 [b]Ezek. 1:28; 8:4
13 [a]Ezek. 1:24; 10:5
14 [a]2 Kin. 3:15; Ezek. 1:3; 8:1 [1]Or *anger*
15 [a]Job 2:13; Ps. 137:1
16 [a]Jer. 42:7
17 [a]Ezek. 33:7–9 [b]Is. 52:8; 56:10; Jer. 6:17 [c][Lev. 19:17; Prov. 14:25]; Is. 58:1 *See WW at Gen. 1:26. • See WW at Hos. 9:8.
18 [a]Ezek. 33:6; [John 8:21, 24] *See WW at Lev. 17:11.

---

voluminous extent of the message and the lack of space for additions by the prophet himself. Most of this message consisted of **lamentations and mourning and woe,** the theme of Ezekiel until the destruction of Jerusalem.

3:1 Eat this scroll: Before the prophet can deliver the message he must first assimilate it.

3:3 Like honey: The word of God is sweet when it is received (see Ps. 19:10; 119:103).

3:4 House of Israel: A reference to the whole nation, including the southern tribe of Judah and the northern tribes of Israel.

3:7–9 See section 3 of Truth-In-Action at the end of Ezek.

3:8 Face strong against their faces: His determination to prophesy must be stronger than Israel's refusal to listen.

3:10 Hear with your ears: A marked contrast to the people who are rebellious and will not listen (v. 7).

3:11 Go, get to the captives: *The call of Ezekiel was to the exiles, to prepare them for the destruction of Jerusalem and the temple.*

3:12 The Spirit lifted me up: A favorite expression of Ezekiel to indicate the active involvement of the Spirit in the revelatory process (see v. 14; 8:3; 11:1, 24; 43:5).

3:14 I went in bitterness, in the heat of my spirit: The prophet has fully identified with the Lord and experiences righteous anger against sin. **Hand of the LORD:** See v. 22 and note on 1:3.

3:15 Tel Abib (unrelated to modern Tel Aviv) is a site near Nippur on the Chebar Canal (see 1:1), where some of the exiles were settled. **Astonished among them seven days:** Ezekiel is overwhelmed as a result of his encounter with God and is in a state of spiritual shock (see Ezra 9:4; Job 2:13; Acts 9:9); he needs time to adjust to the new situation. **Seven days** is the time of mourning for the dead (Gen. 50:10), the period during which one is unclean after touching a corpse (Num. 19:11), and the period of consecration for a priest (Lev. 8:33). Ezekiel is a priest commissioned to carry out the work of a prophet.

3:16–27 See section 5 of Truth-In-Action at the end of Ezek.

3:17 Watchman: In ancient Israel watchmen were stationed on the walls to warn people of danger and the approach of messengers (see 2 Sam. 18:24–27; 2 Kin. 9:17–20). Prophets were also called watchmen (see Jer. 6:17; Hos. 9:8; Hab. 2:1). Ezekiel is to warn them that each person is responsible for his or her own behavior. This theme of personal responsibility is repeated in 33:7–9 and is spelled out in detail in ch. 18.

nor from his wicked way, he shall die
in his iniquity; [a]but you have delivered
your soul.
20 "Again, when a [a]righteous *man*
turns from his righteousness and commits iniquity, and I lay a stumbling
block before him, he shall die; because
you did not give him warning, he shall
die in his sin, and his righteousness
which he has done shall not be remembered; but his blood I will require at
your hand.
21 "Nevertheless if you warn the righteous *man* that the righteous should
not sin, and he does not sin, he shall
surely live because he took warning;
also you will have delivered your
soul."
22 [a]Then the hand of the LORD was
upon me there, and He said to me,
"Arise, go out [b]into the plain, and there
I shall talk with you."
23 So I arose and went out into the
plain, and behold, [a]the *glory of the
LORD stood there, like the glory which
I [b]saw by the River Chebar; [c]and I fell
on my face.
24 Then [a]the Spirit entered me and set
me on my feet, and spoke with me and
said to me: "Go, shut yourself inside
your house.
25 "And you, O son of man, surely
[a]they will put ropes on you and bind
you with them, so that you cannot go
out among them.
26 [a]"I will make your tongue cling to
the roof of your mouth, so that you
shall be mute and [b]not be [1]one to rebuke them, [c]for they *are* a rebellious
house.
27 [a]"But when I speak with you, I will
*open your mouth, and you shall say
to them, [b]'Thus says the Lord GOD.' He
who hears, let him hear; and he who
refuses, let him refuse; for they *are* a
rebellious house.

The Siege of Jerusalem Portrayed

4 "You also, son of man, take a
clay tablet and lay it before you,
and portray on it a city, Jerusalem.
2 [a]"Lay siege against it, build a
[b]siege wall against it, and heap up a
mound against it; set camps against it
also, and place battering rams against
it all around.
3 "Moreover take for yourself an iron
plate, and set it *as* an iron wall between
you and the city. Set your face against
it, and it shall be [a]besieged, and you
shall lay siege against it. [b]This *will be*
a *sign to the house of Israel.
4 "Lie also on your left side, and lay
the iniquity of the house of Israel upon
it. *According* to the number of the days
that you lie on it, you shall bear their
iniquity.
5 "For I have laid on you the years
of their iniquity, according to the number of the days, three hundred and
ninety days; [a]so you shall bear the iniquity of the house of Israel.
6 "And when you have completed
them, lie again on your right side; then
you shall bear the iniquity of the house
of Judah forty days. I have laid on you
a day for each year.
7 "Therefore you shall set your face
toward the siege of Jerusalem; your
arm *shall be* uncovered, and you shall
prophesy against it.
8 [a]"And surely I will [1]restrain you so
that you cannot turn from one side to
another till you have ended the days
of your siege.
9 "Also take for yourself wheat, barley, beans, lentils, millet, and spelt; put
them into one vessel, and make bread
of them for yourself. *During* the number of days that you lie on your side,
three hundred and ninety days, you
shall eat it.
10 "And your food which you eat *shall
be* by weight, twenty shekels a day;
from time to time you shall eat it.
11 "You shall also drink water by measure, one-sixth of a hin; from time to
time you shall drink.
12 "And you shall eat it *as* barley
cakes; and bake it using fuel of human
waste in their sight."

19 [a]Is. 49:4, 5; Ezek. 14:14, 20; Acts 18:6; 20:26; 1 Tim. 4:16
20 [a]Ps. 125:5; Ezek. 18:24; 33:18; Zeph. 1:6
22 [a]Ezek. 1:3 [b]Ezek. 8:4
23 [a]Ezek. 1:28; Acts 7:55 [b]Ezek. 1:1 [c]Ezek. 1:28 *See WW at Is. 60:1.
24 [a]Ezek. 2:2
25 [a]Ezek. 4:8
26 [a]Ezek. 24:27; Luke 1:20, 22 [b]Hos. 4:17; Amos 8:11 [c]Ezek. 2:5–7 [1]Lit. *one who rebukes*
27 [a]Ex. 4:11, 12; Ezek. 24:27; 33:22 [b]Ezek. 3:11 *See WW at Jer. 40:4.

CHAPTER 4

2 [a]Jer. 6:6; Ezek. 21:22 [b]2 Kin. 25:1
3 [a]Jer. 39:1, 2; Ezek. 5:2 [b]Ezek. 12:6, 11; 24:24, 27 *See WW at Ps. 86:17.
5 [a]Num. 14:34
8 [a]Ezek. 3:25 [1]Lit. *put ropes on*

3:22 Hand of the LORD: See note on 1:3.
3:23 The glory of the LORD again causes Ezekiel to fall on his face. See note on 1:28.
3:24 Shut yourself inside your house: Limited contact between prophet and people is the result of their refusal to listen to God's Word.
3:26 You shall be mute: If the people will not listen, Ezekiel will not speak.
4:1 On a moist **clay tablet,** the common writing material for the cuneiform language in Mesopotamia, Ezekiel is to draw the city of **Jerusalem.** Around this tablet he sets up the siege works (v. 2) and places an iron plate between himself and the city (v. 3) to symbolize that the siege cannot be broken.
4:4–8 A second element in the siege symbolism is Ezekiel's lying on the **left side** for 390 days (v. 5) for **the iniquity of the house of Israel,** and on the **right side** 40 days for **the iniquity of the house of Judah** (v. 6). Why these particular numbers were used is difficult to determine. Symbolically Ezekiel was bearing the punishment they were actually suffering.
4:9–17 A third element in the siege is the **food** preparation. A scant vegetarian diet is represented by the **wheat, barley, beans, lentils, millet, and spelt** (an inferior kind of wheat).
4:10 Twenty shekels: About eight ounces.
4:11 One-sixth of a hin: Two-thirds of a quart.

13 Then the LORD said, "So [a]shall the
children of Israel eat their defiled
bread among the *Gentiles, where I
will drive them."
14 So I said, [a]"Ah, Lord GOD! Indeed
I have never defiled myself from my
youth till now; I have never eaten
[b]what died of itself or was torn by
beasts, nor has [c]abominable[1] flesh
ever come into my mouth."
15 Then He said to me, "See, I am giving you cow dung instead of human
waste, and you shall prepare your
bread over it."
16 Moreover He said to me, "Son of
man, surely I will cut off the [a]supply
of bread in Jerusalem; they shall
[b]eat bread by weight and with anxiety,
and shall [c]drink water by measure and
with dread,
17 "that they may lack bread and water, and be dismayed with one another,
and [a]waste away because of their iniquity.

A Sword Against Jerusalem

5 "And you, son of man, take a sharp
sword, take it as a barber's razor,
[a]and pass *it* over your head and your
beard; then take scales to weigh and
divide the hair.
2 [a]"You shall burn with fire one-third
in the midst of [b]the city, when [c]the
days of the siege are finished; then you
shall take one-third and strike around
it with the sword, and one-third you
shall scatter in the wind: I will draw
out a sword after [d]them.
3 [a]"You shall also take a small number of them and bind them in the edge
of your *garment*.
4 "Then take some of them again and
[a]throw them into the midst of the fire,
and burn them in the fire. From there
a fire will go out into all the house of
Israel.
5 "Thus says the Lord GOD: 'This *is*
Jerusalem; I have set her in the midst
of the nations and the countries all
around her.
6 'She has rebelled against My judgments by doing wickedness more than
the nations, and against My statutes
more than the countries that *are* all
around her; for they have refused My
judgments, and they have not walked
in My statutes.'
7 "Therefore thus says the Lord GOD:
'Because you have [1]multiplied *disobedience* more than the nations that *are*
all around you, have not walked in My
statutes [a]nor kept My judgments, [2]nor
even done according to the judgments of the nations that *are* all around
you'—
8 "therefore thus says the Lord GOD:
'Indeed I, even I, *am* against you and
will execute judgments in your midst
in the sight of the nations.
9 [a]'And I will do among you what I
have never done, and the like of which
I will never do again, because of all
your abominations.
10 'Therefore fathers [a]shall eat *their*
sons in your midst, and sons shall eat
their fathers; and I will execute judgments among you, and all of you who
remain I will [b]scatter to all the winds.
11 'Therefore, *as* I live,' says the Lord
GOD, 'surely, because you have [a]defiled
My sanctuary with all your [b]detestable
things and with all your abominations,
therefore I will also diminish *you;*
[c]My eye will not spare, nor will I have
any pity.
12 [a]'One-third of you shall die of the
pestilence, and be consumed with famine in your midst; and one-third shall
fall by the sword all around you; and
[b]I will scatter another third to all the
winds, and I will draw out a sword after [c]them.
13 'Thus shall My anger [a]be spent, and

13 [a]Hos. 9:3 *See WW at Ps. 106:47.
14 [a]Acts 10:14 [b]Lev. 17:15; 22:8 [c]Deut. 14:3 [1]Ritually unclean flesh, Lev. 7:18
16 [a]Is. 3:1 [b]Ezek. 4:10, 11; 12:19 [c]Ezek. 4:11
17 [a]Lev. 26:39

CHAPTER 5

1 [a]Is. 7:20
2 [a]Ezek. 5:12 [b]Ezek. 4:1 [c]Ezek. 4:8, 9 [d]Lev. 26:25
3 [a]Jer. 40:6; 52:16
4 [a]Jer. 41:1, 2; 44:14
7 [a]Jer. 2:10, 11 [1]Or *raged* [2]So with MT, LXX, Tg., Vg.; many Heb. mss., Syr. *but have done* (cf. 11:12)
9 [a][Amos 3:2]
10 [a]Jer. 19:9 [b]Zech. 2:6; 7:14
11 [a][Jer. 7:9–11] [b]Ezek. 11:21 [c]Ezek. 7:4, 9; 8:18; 9:10
12 [a]Ezek. 6:12 [b]Jer. 9:16 [c]Jer. 43:10, 11; 44:27
13 [a]Lam. 4:11

4:15 Cow dung is commonly used in the Near East as a fuel for baking. The **human waste** (v. 12) was repulsive and "unclean" to a priest such as Ezekiel, so God allowed the substitution.

5:1–17 Ezekiel is told to **take a sharp sword,** cut off his **hair** and **beard,** and then **divide the hair** into three parts, each of which symbolized inhabitants of Jerusalem (v. 5) killed by different methods: burning, striking with the sword, and scattering to the wind. A few strands were laid aside to represent a remnant, some of whom will also be burned with fire.

5:1 A sharp sword: What Ezekiel does as prophetic symbolism, Isaiah expresses in a metaphor (Is. 7:20).

5:2 Burn with fire: This is defined more specifically as pestilence and famine in v. 12. **When the days of the siege are finished** is after the 390 symbolic days of 4:5.

5:5 Midst of the nations: God had placed Israel in a strategic position, and thus her punishment will be more severe.

5:8 I, even I, *am* against you: A phrase used often by Ezekiel to express God's judgment. See 13:8 (prophets); 21:3 (land of Israel); 26:3 (Tyre); 28:22 (Sidon); 29:3, 10; 30:22 (Pharaoh king of Egypt); 34:10 (shepherds); 35:3 (Mt. Seir); 38:3; 39:1 (Gog).

5:10 Fathers shall eat: Cannibalism is possible during siege. It is predicted in Deut. 28:53 and Jer. 19:9, and attested in 2 Kin. 6:28, 29.

5:11 As I live: A divine oath found several times in Ezek. (14:16, 18, 20; 16:48; 17:16, 19; 18:3; 20:3, 31, 33; 33:11, 27; 34:8; 35:6, 11) and in Is. 49:18; Jer. 22:24; and Zeph. 2:9.

5:12 The threefold judgment of **pestilence, famine,** and **sword** is found several times in Ezek. (6:11, 12; 7:15; 12:16); in 5:17 and 14:21 a fourth judgment of wild beasts is added.

I will [b]cause My fury to rest upon them, [c]and I will be avenged; [d]and they shall know that I, the LORD, have spoken *it* in My zeal, when I have spent My fury upon them.
14 'Moreover [a]I will make you a waste and a reproach among the nations that *are* all around you, in the sight of all who pass by.
15 'So [1]it shall be a [a]reproach, a taunt, a [b]lesson,* and an astonishment to the nations that *are* all around you, when I execute judgments among you in anger and in fury and in [c]furious rebukes. I, the LORD, have spoken.
16 'When I [a]send against them the terrible arrows of famine which shall be for destruction, which I will send to destroy you, I will increase the famine upon you and cut off your [b]supply of bread.
17 'So I will send against you famine and [a]wild beasts, and they will bereave you. [b]Pestilence and blood shall pass through you, and I will bring the sword against you. I, the LORD, have spoken.' "

Judgment on Idolatrous Israel

6 Now the word of the LORD came to me, saying:
2 "Son of man, [a]set your face toward the [b]mountains of Israel, and prophesy against them,
3 "and say, 'O mountains of Israel, hear the word of the Lord GOD! Thus says the Lord GOD to the mountains, to the hills, to the ravines, and to the valleys: "Indeed I, *even* I, will bring a sword against you, and [a]I will destroy your [1]**high places.**

WORD WEALTH

6:3 high places, *bamah* (bah-*mah*); Strong's #1116: A height; high place, mountain, hilltop, crest, ridge, summit; a shrine upon a lofty site. Geographically speaking, *bamah* refers to any hilltop or elevated place. The high places were often those hilltops upon which idolaters offered sacrifices to pagan gods. These places became a snare for the Israelites, who mixed the worship of Yahweh with the worship of idols. In Num. 33:52, the Lord commands: "Demolish all their high places." He is not a God who endorses mixture.

4 "Then your altars shall be desolate, your incense altars shall be broken, and [a]I will cast down your slain *men* before your idols.
5 "And I will lay the corpses of the children of Israel before their idols, and I will scatter your bones all around your altars.
6 "In all your dwelling places the cities shall be laid waste, and the [1]high places shall be desolate, so that your altars may be laid waste and made desolate, your idols may be broken and made to cease, your incense altars may be cut down, and your works may be abolished.
7 "The slain shall fall in your midst, and [a]you shall know that I *am* the LORD.
8 [a]"Yet I will leave a remnant, so that you may have *some* who escape the sword among the nations, when you are [b]scattered through the countries.
9 "Then those of you who escape will [a]remember Me among the nations where they are carried captive, because [b]I was crushed by their adulterous heart which has departed from Me, and [c]by their eyes which play the harlot after their idols; [d]they will loathe themselves for the evils which they committed in all their abominations.
10 "And they shall know that I *am* the LORD; I have not said in vain that I would bring this calamity upon them."
11 'Thus says the Lord GOD: [a]"Pound[1] your fists and stamp your feet, and say,

13 [b]Ezek. 21:17 [c][Deut. 32:36]; Is. 1:24 [d]Is. 59:17; Ezek. 36:6; 38:19
14 [a]Lev. 26:31; Neh. 2:17
15 [a]Deut. 28:37; 1 Kin. 9:7; Ps. 79:4; Jer. 24:9; Lam. 2:15 [b][Is. 26:9]; Jer. 22:8, 9; 1 Cor. 10:11 [c]Is. 66:15, 16; Ezek. 5:8; 25:17 [1]LXX, Syr., Tg., Vg. *you* *See WW at Prov. 4:13.
16 [a]Deut. 32:23 [b]Lev. 26:26; Ezek. 4:16; 14:13
17 [a]Lev. 26:22; Deut. 32:24; Ezek. 14:21; 33:27; 34:25; Rev. 6:8 [b]Ezek. 38:22

CHAPTER 6

2 [a]Ezek. 20:46; 21:2; 25:2 [b]Ezek. 36:1
3 [a]Lev. 26:30 [1]Places for pagan worship
4 [a]Lev. 26:30
6 [1]Places for pagan worship
7 [a]Ezek. 7:4, 9
8 [a]Jer. 44:28; Ezek. 5:2, 12; 12:16; 14:22 [b]Ezek. 5:12
9 [a][Deut. 4:29]; Ps. 137; Jer. 51:50 [b]Ps. 78:40; Is. 7:13; 43:24; Hos. 11:8 [c]Num. 15:39; Ezek. 20:7, 24 [d]Lev. 26:39; Job 42:6; Ezek. 20:43; 36:31
11 [a]Ezek. 21:14 [1]Lit. *Strike your hands*

5:15 A reproach, a taunt, a lesson, and an astonishment: Another use of four items. See note on 1:5.
6:1–14 An oracle against the mountains because here is where the idolatry of the people was manifest. **On every high hill, on all the mountaintops** (v. 13) they had built **altars.** The punishment now to be poured out is on the accumulation of sin over many years and not necessarily for the sin of the present inhabitants only.
6:3 The **high places** were open-air sanctuaries built on hilltops, under green trees, or in other select places (v. 13; Jer. 2:20). Solomon worshiped at the high place of Gibeon (1 Kin. 3:4; 2 Chr. 1:3) because the temple had not yet been built at Jerusalem. Many others also legitimately worshiped at these sites. The problem with the high places was that it was too easy for them to be used for Canaanite practices or the worship of Yahweh simply as a nature god. The high places (v. 3), altars, incense altars, and idols (v. 4) make up another list of four (see note on 1:5).
6:4 Idols: A derogatory term meaning "little dung balls," usually applied to foreign gods (see note on Jer. 50:2). It is a common expression of Ezekiel who uses it about 40 times.
6:8 Remnant: The few hairs saved in 5:3. A remnant is also mentioned in 11:13 and 14:22.
6:9, 10 Will remember Me: The goal of the punishment is corrective and redemptive, that **they shall know that I *am* the LORD** (vv. 7, 10, 13, 14). This latter phrase is one of the most characteristic expressions of Ezekiel. It occurs in this form over 50 times, and with expansion another 18 times.
6:11 Pound your fists and stamp your feet: A sign of deep emotion, a personal involvement and rejoicing in the

'Alas, for all the evil abominations of
the house of Israel! [b]For they shall fall
by the sword, by famine, and by pestilence.
12 'He who is far off shall die by the
pestilence, he who is near shall fall by
the sword, and he who remains and is
besieged shall die by the famine.
[a]Thus will I spend My fury upon them.
13 'Then you shall know that I *am* the
LORD, when their slain are among their
idols all around their altars, [a]on every
high hill, [b]on all the mountaintops,
[c]under every green tree, and under
every thick oak, wherever they offered
sweet incense to all their idols.
14 'So I will [a]stretch out My hand
against them and make the land desolate, yes, more desolate than the wilderness toward [b]Diblah, in all their
dwelling places. Then they shall know
that I *am* the LORD.'"'"

Judgment on Israel Is Near

7 Moreover the word of the LORD came to me, saying,
2 "And you, son of man, thus says the
Lord GOD to the land of Israel:

[a]'An end! The end has come upon
the four corners of the land.
3 Now the end *has come* upon you,
And I will send My anger against
you;
I will judge you [a]according to
your ways,
And I will repay you for all your
abominations.
4 [a]My eye will not spare you,
Nor will I have pity;
But I will repay your ways,
And your abominations will be in
your midst;
[b]Then you shall know that I *am*
the LORD!'

5 "Thus says the Lord GOD:

'A disaster, a singular [a]disaster;
Behold, it has come!
6 An end has come,
The end has come;
It has dawned for you;
Behold, it has come!

11 [b]Ezek. 5:12
12 [a]Lam. 4:11, 22; Ezek. 5:13
13 [a]Jer. 2:20; 3:6 [b]1 Kin. 14:23; 2 Kin. 16:4; Ezek. 20:28; Hos. 4:13 [c]Is. 57:5
14 [a]Is. 5:25; Ezek. 14:13; 20:33, 34 [b]Num. 33:46

CHAPTER 7

2 [a]Ezek. 7:3, 5, 6; 11:13; Amos 8:2, 10; [Matt. 24:6, 13, 14]
3 [a][Rom. 2:6]
4 [a]Ezek. 5:11 [b]Ezek. 12:20
5 [a]2 Kin. 21:12, 13; Nah. 1:9

7 [a]Ezek. 7:10 [b]Zeph. 1:14, 15
8 [a]Ezek. 20:8, 21
9 [1]Lit. *give*
10 [a]Ezek. 7:7
11 [a]Jer. 6:7 [b]Jer. 16:5, 6; Ezek. 24:16, 22 [1]Or *their wealth*
12 [a]Prov. 20:14; 1 Cor. 7:30 [b]Is. 24:2
*See WW at Joel 1:9.
13 *See WW at 2 Chr. 32:32.

7 [a]Doom has come to you, you who
dwell in the land;
[b]The time has come,
A day of trouble *is* near,
And not of rejoicing in the
mountains.
8 Now upon you I will soon
[a]pour out My fury,
And spend My anger upon you;
I will judge you according to your
ways,
And I will repay you for all your
abominations.

9 'My eye will not spare,
Nor will I have pity;
I will [1]repay you according to
your ways,
And your abominations will be in
your midst.
Then you shall know that I *am*
the LORD who strikes.

10 'Behold, the day!
Behold, it has come!
[a]Doom has gone out;
The rod has blossomed,
Pride has budded.
11 [a]Violence has risen up into a rod
of wickedness;
None of them *shall remain*,
None of their multitude,
None of [1]them;
[b]Nor *shall there be* wailing for
them.
12 The time has come,
The day draws near.

'Let not the buyer [a]rejoice,
Nor the seller [b]mourn,*
For wrath *is* on their whole
multitude.
13 For the seller shall not return to
what has been sold,
Though he may still be alive;
For the *vision concerns the
whole multitude,
And it shall not turn back;
No one will strengthen himself
Who lives in iniquity.

14 'They have blown the trumpet and
made everyone ready,
But no one goes to battle;

judgment (see 25:6). Rejoicing is called for because the accumulated *sin of Israel will be* purged away. **Pestilence:** See note on 5:12.

6:14 Stretch out My hand: Another phrase used multiple times by Ezekiel (14:9, 13; 16:27; 25:7; 35:3) to indicate God's judgment. **The wilderness toward Diblah** represents the ideal southern and northern boundaries of Israel envisaged before the Conquest (Num. 34:7–9).

7:2 Four corners: The whole land. See note on 1:5.

7:7 A day of trouble: The Day of the Lord, a day of judgment for Israel. See note on Obad. 15.

7:8 Pour out My fury: Another common expression in Ezek. (9:8; 14:19; 20:8, 13, 21; 22:31; 30:15; 36:18).

7:14, 15 Judgment is severe and extensive. No one escapes since **the sword** is in the field and **famine and pestilence** are inside the city. See note on 5:12.

For My wrath *is* on all their
multitude.
15 [a]The sword *is* outside,
And the pestilence and famine
within.
Whoever *is* in the field
Will die by the sword;
And whoever *is* in the city,
Famine and pestilence will
devour him.

16 'Those who [a]survive will escape
and be on the mountains
Like doves of the valleys,
All of them mourning,
Each for his iniquity.
17 Every [a]hand will be feeble,
And every knee will be *as* weak
as water.
18 They will also [a]be girded with
sackcloth;
Horror will cover them;
Shame *will be* on every face,
Baldness on all their heads.

19 'They will throw their silver into
the streets,
And their gold will be like refuse;
Their [a]silver and their gold will
not be *able to deliver them
In the day of the wrath of the
LORD;
They will not satisfy their souls,
Nor fill their stomachs,
Because it became their
stumbling block of iniquity.

20 'As for the beauty of his
ornaments,
He set it in majesty;
[a]But they made from it
The images of their
abominations—
Their detestable things;
Therefore I have made it
Like refuse to them.
21 I will give it as [a]plunder
Into the hands of strangers,
And to the wicked of the earth as
spoil;
And they shall defile it.
22 I will turn My face from them,
And they will defile My secret
place;
For robbers shall enter it and
defile it.

23 'Make a chain,
For [a]the land is filled with crimes
of blood,
And the city is full of violence.
24 Therefore I will bring the
[a]worst of the Gentiles,
And they will possess their
houses;
I will cause the pomp of the
strong to cease,
And their holy places shall be
[b]defiled.
25 [1]Destruction comes;
They will seek peace, but *there
shall be* none.
26 [a]Disaster will come upon disaster, **1**
And rumor will be upon rumor.
[b]Then they will seek a vision from
a prophet;
But the law will perish from the
priest,
And counsel from the *elders.

27 'The king will mourn,
The prince will be clothed with
desolation,
And the hands of the common
people will tremble.
I will do to them according to
their way,
And according to what they
deserve I will judge them;
Then they shall know that I *am*
the LORD!' "

Abominations in the Temple

8 And it came to pass in the sixth
year, in the sixth *month,* on the
fifth *day* of the month, as I sat in my
house with [a]the elders of Judah sitting
before me, that [b]the hand of the Lord
GOD fell upon me there.
2 [a]Then I looked, and there was a
likeness, like the appearance of fire—
from the appearance of His waist
and downward, fire; and from His
waist and upward, like the appearance of brightness, [b]like the color of
amber.

15 [a]Deut. 32:25; Jer. 14:18; Lam. 1:20; Ezek. 5:12
16 [a]Ezra 9:15; Is. 37:31; Ezek. 6:8; 14:22
17 [a]Is. 13:7; Jer. 6:24; Ezek. 21:7; Heb. 12:12
18 [a]Is. 3:24; 15:2, 3; Jer. 48:37; Ezek. 27:31; Amos 8:10
19 [a]Prov. 11:4; Jer. 15:13; Zeph. 1:18
*See WW at Num. 13:30.
20 [a]Jer. 7:30
21 [a]2 Kin. 24:13; Jer. 20:5
23 [a]2 Kin. 21:16
24 [a]Ezek. 21:31; 28:7 [b]2 Chr. 7:20; Ezek. 24:21
25 [1]Lit. *Shuddering*
26 [a]Deut. 32:23; Is. 47:11; Jer. 4:20 [b]Ps. 74:9; Lam. 2:9; Ezek. 20:1, 3; Mic. 3:6
*See WW at Ps. 119:100.

CHAPTER 8

1 [a]Ezek. 14:1; 20:1; 33:31 [b]Ezek. 1:3; 3:22
2 [a]Ezek. 1:26, 27 [b]Ezek. 1:4, 27

7:19 Silver and **gold** are worthless in time of siege since there is nothing to buy. This is especially true on **the day of the wrath of the LORD,** for wealth will not save. On the contrary, it is wealth that was the **stumbling block of iniquity.**
7:22 My secret place: The temple at Jerusalem will be desecrated by the Babylonians when God withdraws His protection (**turn My face from them**).
7:26, 27 See section 1 of Truth-In-Action at the end of Ezek.
7:26 Disaster after disaster is made even worse by the rumors.
8:1—11:25 Ezekiel is sitting with the elders when he is suddenly transported in spirit to Jerusalem. In a vision he reports the idolatry and abominations taking place at the temple, speaks judgment against Jerusalem and the priests, and describes the throne of God and the departure of the divine glory from the temple.
8:1 The date is Sept. 17, 592 B.C.

3 He [a]stretched out the form of a
hand, and took me by a lock of my
hair; and [b]the Spirit lifted me up between earth and heaven, and [c]brought
me in visions of God to Jerusalem, to
the door of the north gate of the inner
court, [d]where the seat of the image of
jealousy *was,* which [e]provokes[1] to jealousy.
4 And behold, the [a]glory of the God
of Israel *was* there, like the vision that
I [b]saw in the plain.
5 Then He said to me, "Son of man,
lift your eyes now toward the north."
So I lifted my eyes toward the north,
and there, north of the altar gate,
was this image of jealousy in the entrance.
6 Furthermore He said to me, "Son
of man, do you see what they are doing, the great [a]abominations that the
house of Israel commits here, to make
Me go far away from My sanctuary?
Now turn again, you will see greater
abominations."
7 So He brought me to the door of
the court; and when I looked, there was
a hole in the wall.
8 Then He said to me, "Son of man,
dig into the wall"; and when I dug into
the wall, there was a door.
9 And He said to me, "Go in, and see
the wicked abominations which they
are doing there."
10 So I went in and saw, and there—
every [a]sort of [b]creeping thing, abominable beasts, and all the idols of the
house of Israel, [1]portrayed all around
on the walls.
11 And there stood before them [a]sev-
enty men of the *elders of the house
of Israel, and in their midst stood Jaazaniah the son of Shaphan. Each man
had a censer in his hand, and a thick
cloud of incense went up.
12 Then He said to me, "Son of man,
have you seen what the elders of the
house of Israel do in the dark, every
man in the room of his idols? For they
say, [a]'The LORD does not see us, the
LORD has forsaken the land.' "
13 And He said to me, "Turn again,
and you will see greater abominations
that they are doing."
14 So He brought me to the door of
the north gate of the LORD's house; and
to my dismay, women were sitting
there weeping for [1]Tammuz.
15 Then He said to me, "Have you seen
this, O son of man? Turn again, you
will see greater abominations than
these."
16 So He brought me into the inner
court of the LORD's house; and there,
at the door of the temple of the LORD,
[a]between the porch and the altar,
[b]*were* about twenty-five men [c]with
their backs toward the temple of the
LORD and their faces toward the east,
and they were worshiping [d]the sun
toward the east.
17 And He said to me, "Have you seen
this, O son of man? Is it a trivial thing
to the house of Judah to commit the
abominations which they commit
here? For they have [a]filled the land
with violence; then they have returned
to *provoke Me to anger. Indeed they
put the branch to their nose.
18 [a]"Therefore I also will act in fury.
My [b]eye will not spare nor will I have
pity; and though they [c]cry in My
ears with a loud voice, I will not hear
them."

The Wicked Are Slain

9 Then He called out in my hearing
with a loud voice, saying, "Let
those who have charge over the city
draw near, each *with* a [1]deadly
weapon in his hand."
2 And suddenly six men came from
the direction of the upper gate, which
faces north, each with his [1]battle-ax in
his hand. [a]One man among them *was*
clothed with linen and had a writer's

3 [a]Dan. 5:5 [b]Ezek. 3:14; Acts 8:39 [c]Ezek. 11:1, 24; 40:2 [d]Jer. 7:30; 32:34; Ezek. 5:11 [e]Ex. 20:4; Deut. 32:16, 21 [1]Arouses the LORD's jealousy
4 [a]Ezek. 3:12; 9:3 [b]Ezek. 1:28; 3:22, 23
6 [a]2 Kin. 23:4, 5; Ezek. 5:11; 8:9, 17
10 [a]Ex. 20:4; Deut. 4:16–18 [b]Rom. 1:23 [1]Or *carved*
11 [a]Num. 11:16, 25; Luke 10:1 *See WW at Ps. 119:100.
12 [a]Ps. 14:1; Is. 29:15; Ezek. 9:9
14 [1]A Sumerian fertility god similar to the Gr. god Adonis
16 [a]Joel 2:17 [b]Ezek. 11:1 [c]2 Chr. 29:6; Jer. 2:27; 32:33; Ezek. 23:39 [d]Deut. 4:19; 2 Kin. 23:5, 11; Job 31:26; Jer. 44:17
17 [a]Ezek. 9:9; Amos 3:10; Mic. 2:2 *See WW at 1 Kin. 16:2.
18 [a]Ezek. 5:13; 16:42; 24:13 [b]Ezek. 5:11; 7:4, 9; 9:5, 10 [c]Prov. 1:28; Is. 1:15; Jer. 11:11; 14:12; Mic. 3:4; Zech. 7:13

CHAPTER 9

1 [1]Or *destroying*
2 [a]Lev. 16:4; Ezek. 10:2; Rev. 15:6 [1]Lit. *shattering weapon*

8:3 Brought me in visions of God to Jerusalem: Ezekiel had prophesied severe judgment against Jerusalem in chs. 1—7. Now he is given additional reasons for this judgment. "Visions of God": See note on 1:1. **Image of jealousy:** Any image would provoke God's jealousy. This one, however, seems to be the image of Asherah, a fertility goddess who may be identified with Ashtarte (Ashtoreth) and the queen of heaven (see 2 Kin. 21:7; 23:4–6; Jer. 44:17–19).

8:10 ***Portrayed all around on the walls:*** Perhaps the type of relief drawings seen on the walls of Egyptian temples.

8:11 The **seventy men** represented the laity and had been appointed by God to guide Israel against such abominations as idolatry (Ex. 24:9, 10; Num. 11:16).

8:14 Tammuz: In pagan practices he was a Sumerian shepherd who married the goddess Ishtar. When he died, fertility ceased on Earth. Since he was a vegetation deity, the **women** of Judah were **weeping** for him (probably in the spring) in order to restore fertility by bringing him back from the dead.

8:16 The **temple** at Jerusalem was oriented to the **east;** to worship **the sun** one had to turn his back **toward the temple.**

8:17 The branch refers to the worship of Tammuz (v. 14), for the cedar branch was a symbol of immortality associated with the cult of Tammuz. To **put . . . to their nose** was their attempt to inhale the supposed life-giving powers of a revived Tammuz.

9:2 Six men: Angel-warriors who carry out God's judgment. They symbolize the Chaldeans who would ravage Jerusalem five years later.

inkhorn [2]at his side. They went in and
stood beside the bronze altar.
3 Now [a]the glory of the God of Israel
had gone up from the cherub, where
it had been, to the threshold of the
[1]temple. And He called to the man
clothed with linen, who *had* the writer's inkhorn at his side;
4 and the LORD said to him, "Go
through the midst of the city, through
the midst of Jerusalem, and put [a]a
mark on the foreheads of the men
[b]who sigh and cry over all the abominations that are done within it."
5 To the others He said in my [1]hear-
ing, "Go after him through the city
and [a]kill;[2] [b]do not let your eye spare,
nor have any pity.
6 [a]"Utterly[1] slay old *and* young men,
maidens and little children and
women; but [b]do not come near anyone
on whom *is* the mark; and [c]begin at
My sanctuary." [d]So they began with
the elders who *were* before the [2]tem-
ple.
7 Then He said to them, "Defile the
[1]temple, and fill the courts with the
slain. Go out!" And they went out and
killed in the city.
8 So it was, that while they were killing them, I was left *alone;* and I
[a]fell on my face and cried out, and said,
[b]"Ah, Lord GOD! Will You destroy all
the remnant of Israel in pouring out
Your fury on Jerusalem?"
9 Then He said to me, "The iniquity
of the house of Israel and Judah *is* exceedingly great, and [a]the land is full
of bloodshed, and the city full of perversity; for they say, [b]'The LORD has
forsaken the land, and [c]the LORD does
not see!'
10 "And as for Me also, My [a]eye will
neither spare, nor will I have pity, *but*
[b]I will recompense their deeds on their
own head."
11 Just then, the man clothed with
linen, who *had* the inkhorn at his side,
reported back and said, "I have done
as You commanded me."

The Glory Departs from the Temple

10 And I looked, and there in the
[a]firmament[1] that was above the
head of the *cherubim, there appeared
something like a sapphire stone, having the appearance of the likeness of
a throne.
2 [a]Then He spoke to the man clothed
with linen, and said, "Go in among
the wheels, under the cherub, fill
your hands with [b]coals of fire from
among the cherubim, and [c]scatter
them over the city." And he went in as
I watched.
3 Now the cherubim were standing
on the [1]south side of the [2]temple when
the man went in, and the [a]cloud filled
the inner court.
4 [a]Then the glory of the LORD went
up from the cherub, *and paused* over
the threshold of the [1]temple; and
[b]the house was filled with the cloud,
and the court was full of the brightness
of the LORD's [c]glory.
5 And the [a]sound of the wings of the
cherubim was heard *even* in the outer
court, like [b]the voice of *Almighty God
when He speaks.
6 Then it happened, when He commanded the man clothed in linen,
saying, "Take fire from among the
wheels, from among the cherubim,"
that he went in and stood beside the
wheels.
7 And the cherub stretched out his
hand from among the cherubim to the
fire that *was* among the cherubim, and
took *some of it* and put *it* into the
hands of the *man* clothed with linen,
who took *it* and went out.
8 [a]The cherubim appeared to have
the form of a man's hand under their
wings.
9 [a]And when I looked, there were
four wheels by the cherubim, one
wheel by one cherub and another
wheel by each other cherub; the
wheels appeared *to have* the color of
a [b]beryl stone.

2 [b]Lit. *upon his loins*
3 [a]Ezek. 3:23; 8:4; 10:4, 18; 11:22, 23 [1]Lit. *house*
4 [a]Rev. 7:2, 3; 9:4; 14:1 [b]Jer. 13:17
5 [a]Ezek. 7:9 [b]Ezek. 5:11 [1]Lit. *ears* [2]Lit. *strike*
6 [a]2 Chr. 36:17 [b]Rev. 9:4 [c]Jer. 25:29 [d]Ezek. 8:11, 12, 16 [1]Lit. *Slay to destruction* [2]Lit. *house*
7 [1]Lit. *house*
8 [a]Josh. 7:6 [b]Ezek. 11:13
9 [a]2 Kin. 21:16 [b]Ezek. 8:12 [c]Is. 29:15
10 [a]Ezek. 5:11; 7:4; 8:18 [b]Ezek. 11:21

CHAPTER 10

1 [a]Ezek. 1:22, 26 [1]*expanse* *See WW at Ex. 25:18.
2 [a]Dan. 10:5 [b]Ezek. 1:13 [c]Rev. 8:5
3 [a]1 Kin. 8:10, 11 [1]Lit. *right* [2]Lit. *house*
4 [a]Ezek. 1:28 [b]Ezek. 43:5 [c]Ezek. 11:22, 23 [1]Lit. *house*
5 [a]Ezek. 1:24 [b][Ps. 29:3] *See WW at Ps. 91:1.
8 [a]Ezek. 1:8; 10:21
9 [a]Ezek. 1:15 [b]Ezek. 1:16

9:4 Put a mark: The Hebrew word for "mark" is *taw,* the final letter of the Hebrew alphabet, which in the ancient script looked like an "X" or a cross. This mark, placed by a seventh warrior angel "clothed with linen" (v. 3), was for protection (see Rev. 7:3) and symbolized that God would spare the righteous remnant.

9:6 Begin at My sanctuary: Judgment begins at the house of God (see 1 Pet. 4:17).

9:8 Ah, Lord GOD: Ezekiel questions whether God is going too far, but his attempt to intercede is of no avail for the evil is too great. This same theme is found in 11:13; 14:14; Jer. 7:16; 11:14; 14:11; 15:1.

10:1–22 Ezekiel here sees another vision of God's chariot-throne. See notes on ch. 1. An additional figure is "the man clothed with linen" from ch. 9, whose role has changed to that of an agent of judgment (v. 2). The significance of the vision is to verify that God will depart from the temple before Jerusalem is burned.

10:2 Coals of fire: Reflects the description of the cherubim (living creatures) in 1:13. These coals suggest the judgment of God on the city.

10:4 The glory of the LORD departed from the temple by stages: first to the threshold (v. 4), then over the cherubim (v. 18), to the east gate (v. 19), and finally to the Mount of Olives (11:23) to the east of the city.

10 *As for* their appearance, all four
looked alike—as it were, a wheel in the
middle of a wheel.
11 [a]When they went, they went toward
any of their four directions; they did
not turn aside when they went, but followed in the direction the head was
facing. They did not turn aside when
they went.
12 And their whole body, with their
back, their hands, their wings, and the
wheels that the four had, *were* [a]full of
eyes all around.
13 As for the wheels, they were called
in my [1]hearing, "Wheel."
14 [a]Each one had four faces: the first
face *was* the face of a cherub, the second face the face of a man, the third
the face of a lion, and the fourth the
face of an eagle.
15 And the cherubim were lifted up.
This *was* [a]the living creature I saw by
the River Chebar.
16 [a]When the cherubim went, the
wheels went beside them; and when
the cherubim lifted their wings to
mount up from the earth, the same
wheels also did not turn from beside
them.
17 [a]When [1]*the cherubim* stood still,
the wheels stood still, and when [2]*one*
was lifted up, [3]*the other* lifted itself
up, for the spirit of the living creature *was* in them.
18 Then [a]the glory of the LORD [b]de-
parted from the threshold of the
[1]temple and stood over the cherubim.
19 And [a]the cherubim lifted their
wings and mounted up from the earth
in my sight. When they went out, the
wheels *were* beside them; and they
stood at the door of the [b]east gate of
the LORD's house, and the glory of the
God of Israel *was* above them.
20 [a]This *is* the living creature I saw under the God of Israel [b]by the River
Chebar, and I knew they *were* cherubim.
21 [a]Each one had four faces and each
one four wings, and the likeness of the
hands of a man *was* under their wings.
22 And [a]the likeness of their faces *was*
the same *as* the faces which I had seen
by the River Chebar, their appearance
and their persons. [b]They each went
straight forward.

11 [a]Ezek. 1:17
12 [a]Rev. 4:6, 8
13 [1]Lit. *ears*
14 [a]1 Kin. 7:29, 36; Ezek. 1:6, 10, 11; Rev. 4:7
15 [a]Ezek. 1:3, 5
16 [a]Ezek. 1:19
17 [a]Ezek. 1:12, 20, 21 [1]Lit. *they* [2]Lit. *they were* [3]Lit. *they lifted them*
18 [a]Ezek. 10:4 [b]Hos. 9:12 [1]Lit. *house*
19 [a]Ezek. 11:22 [b]Ezek. 11:1
20 [a]Ezek. 1:22 [b]Ezek. 1:1
21 [a]Ezek. 1:6, 8; 10:14; 41:18, 19
22 [a]Ezek. 1:10 [b]Ezek. 1:9, 12

CHAPTER 11

1 [a]Ezek. 3:12, 14 [b]Ezek. 10:19 [c]Ezek. 8:16
2 [1]Advice
3 [a]Ezek. 12:22, 27; 2 Pet. 3:4 [b]Jer. 1:13; Ezek. 11:7, 11; 24:3, 6 [1]Pot
5 [a]Ezek. 2:2; 3:24 [b][Jer. 16:17; 17:10]
6 [a]Is. 1:15; Ezek. 7:23; 22:2–6, 9, 12, 27
7 [a]Ezek. 24:3, 6; Mic. 3:2, 3 [b]2 Kin. 25:18–22; Jer. 52:24–27; Ezek. 11:9
8 [a]Jer. 42:16
9 [a]Ezek. 5:8
10 [a]2 Kin. 25:19–21; Jer. 39:6; 52:10 [b]1 Kin. 8:65; 2 Kin. 14:25 [c]Ps. 9:16; Ezek. 6:7; 13:9, 14, 21, 23
11 [a]Ezek. 11:3, 7 [1]Pot
12 [a]Lev. 18:3, 24; Deut. 12:30, 31; Ezek. 8:10, 14, 16

Judgment on Wicked Counselors

11 Then [a]the Spirit lifted me up
and brought me to [b]the East
Gate of the LORD's house, which faces
eastward; and there [c]at the door of the
gate were twenty-five men, among
whom I saw Jaazaniah the son of Azzur, and Pelatiah the son of Benaiah,
princes of the people.
2 And He said to me: "Son of man,
these *are* the men who devise iniquity
and give wicked [1]counsel in this city,
3 "who say, '*The time is* not [a]near to
build houses; [b]this *city is* the [1]caldron,
and we *are* the meat.'
4 "Therefore prophesy against them,
prophesy, O son of man!"
5 Then [a]the Spirit of the LORD fell
upon me, and said to me, "Speak!
'Thus says the LORD: "Thus you have
said, O house of Israel; for [b]I know the
things that come into your mind.
6 [a]"You have multiplied your slain in
this city, and you have filled its streets
with the slain."
7 'Therefore thus says the Lord GOD:
[a]"Your slain whom you have laid in
its midst, they *are* the meat, and this
city is the caldron; [b]but I shall bring
you out of the midst of it.
8 "You have [a]feared the sword; and
I will bring a sword upon you," says
the Lord GOD.
9 "And I will bring you out of its
midst, and deliver you into the hands
of strangers, and [a]execute judgments
on you.
10 [a]"You shall fall by the sword. I will
judge you at [b]the border of Israel.
[c]Then you shall know that I *am* the
LORD.
11 [a]"This *city* shall not be your [1]cal-
dron, nor shall you be the meat in
its midst. I will judge you at the border
of Israel.
12 "And you shall know that I *am* the
LORD; for you have not walked in My
statutes nor executed My judgments,
but [a]have done according to the customs of the Gentiles which *are* all
around you."'"

10:14 Four faces: See note on 1:10. For reasons that are not clear, *the face of the ox in ch. 1 is replaced here by* ***the face of a cherub.***

11:1 The **twenty-five men** were the city's counselors who set its official policies.

11:3 This *city is* the caldron, and we *are* the meat: Because these 25 men had not gone into exile, they assumed they were in a favored position. Their pride is evident in their boasting that they are the meat; and as a caldron protects its contents from the flame, so Jerusalem will protect them from the Babylonian attack. For a more accurate evaluation see v. 7 and Jer. 24:1–10.

11:7 Your slain: Those whom they have killed are **the meat** (see v. 3), and the sinners now living will be removed from Jerusalem.

13 Now it happened, while I was
prophesying, that [a]Pelatiah the son of
Benaiah died. Then [b]I fell on my face
and cried with a loud voice, and said,
"Ah, Lord GOD! Will You make a complete end of the remnant of Israel?"

God Will Restore Israel

14 Again the word of the LORD came
to me, saying,
15 "Son of man, your brethren, your
relatives, your countrymen, and all the
house of Israel in its entirety, *are* those
about whom the inhabitants of Jerusalem have said, 'Get far away from the
LORD; this land has been given to us
as a possession.'
16 "Therefore say, 'Thus says the Lord
GOD: "Although I have cast them far
off among the Gentiles, and although
I have scattered them among the countries, [a]yet I shall be a little [1]sanctuary
for them in the countries where they
have gone." '
17 "Therefore say, 'Thus says the Lord
GOD: [a]"I will gather you from the peoples, assemble you from the countries
where you have been scattered, and I
will give you the land of Israel." '
18 "And they will go there, and they
will take away all its [a]detestable things
and all its abominations from there.
19 "Then [a]I will give them one heart,
and I will put [b]a new spirit within
[1]them, and take [c]the stony heart out
of their flesh, and give them a heart
of flesh,
20 [a]"that they may walk in My statutes
and keep My judgments and do them;
[b]and they shall be My people, and I
will be their God.
21 "But *as for those* whose hearts follow the desire for their detestable
things and their abominations, [a]I will
recompense their deeds on their own
heads," says the Lord GOD.
22 So the cherubim [a]lifted up their
wings, with the wheels beside them,
and the glory of the God of Israel *was*
high above them.
23 And [a]the glory of the LORD went up
from the midst of the city and stood
[b]on the mountain, [c]which *is* on the east
side of the city.
24 Then [a]the Spirit took me up and
brought me in a vision by the Spirit
of God into [1]Chaldea, to those in captivity. And the vision that I had seen
went up from me.
25 So I spoke to those in captivity of
all the things the LORD had shown me.

Judah's Captivity Portrayed

12 Now the word of the LORD came 3
to me, saying:
2 "Son of man, you dwell in the midst
of [a]a rebellious house, which [b]has eyes
to see but does not see, and ears to hear
but does not hear; [c]for they *are* a rebellious house.
3 "Therefore, son of man, prepare
your belongings for captivity, and go
into captivity by day in their sight. You
shall go from your place into captivity
to another place in their sight. It may
be that they will consider, though they
are a rebellious house.
4 "By day you shall bring out your
belongings in their sight, as though going into captivity; and at evening you
shall go in their sight, like those who
go into captivity.
5 "Dig through the wall in their sight,
and carry your belongings out through
it.
6 "In their sight you shall bear *them*
on *your* shoulders *and* carry *them* out
at twilight; you shall cover your face,
so that you cannot see the ground,
[a]for I have made you a *sign to the
house of Israel."
7 So I did as I was commanded. I
brought out my belongings by day, as
though going into captivity, and at evening I dug through the wall with my
hand. I brought *them* out at twilight,

13 [a]Acts 5:5 [b]Ezek. 9:8
16 [a]Ps. 90:1; 91:9; Is. 8:14; Jer. 29:7, 11 [1]*holy place*
17 [a]Is. 11:11–16; Jer. 3:12, 18; 24:5; Ezek. 20:41, 42; 28:5
18 [a]Ezek. 37:23
19 [a]Jer. 32:39; Ezek. 36:26; Zeph. 3:9 [b]Ps. 51:10; [Jer. 31:33]; Ezek. 18:31 [c]Zech. 7:12; [Rom. 2:4, 5] [1]Lit. *you* (pl.)
20 [a]Ps. 105:45 [b]Jer. 24:7; Ezek. 14:11; 36:28; 37:27
21 [a]Ezek. 9:10
22 [a]Ezek. 1:19
23 [a]Ezek. 8:4; 9:3 [b]Zech. 14:4 [c]Ezek. 43:2
24 [a]Ezek. 8:3; 2 Cor. 12:2–4 [1]Or *Babylon,* and so elsewhere in the book

CHAPTER 12

2 [a]Is. 1:23; Ezek. 2:3, 6–8 [b]Is. 6:9; 42:20; Jer. 5:21; Matt. 13:13, 14; Mark 4:12; 8:18; [Luke 8:10; John 9:39–41; 12:40]; Acts 28:26; Rom. 11:8 [c]Ezek. 2:5
6 [a]Is. 8:18; Ezek. 4:3; 24:24 *See WW at Zech. 3:8.

11:13 Pelatiah means "Yahweh's Remnant." Ezekiel feared that his death meant the death of the righteous remnant as well as the wicked.
11:16, 17 A little sanctuary for them: Or, God will be a sanctuary "briefly" or "a little while," since v. 17 goes on to say that God **will gather** [them] **from the peoples** and return them to Jerusalem.
11:17–20 These prophetic verses have a twofold interpretation. In a limited way they refer to the postexilic period when the Judahites will return. However, the broad intent is messianic, prophesying the inheritance of God's future people (2 Cor. 3:3). See also the notes on Obad. 15 and Zech. 2:1–13; 8:1–17. Dispensational interpretation sees here a restored national end-time Israel as well.
11:19 Give them one heart: A spiritual and moral transformation will take place that will enable the people to follow God wholeheartedly.
11:22–25 See note on 10:4.
12:1, 2 See section 3 of Truth-In-Action at the end of Ezek.
12:3–16 A symbolic act by Ezekiel to demonstrate the fate of King Zedekiah and the other exiles at Jerusalem.
12:3 Prepare your belongings for captivity: Only those items that could be carried on the shoulder (v. 6) were to be taken.
12:5 Dig through the wall: The wall of Ezekiel's house is meant. Evidently it was made of sun-dried bricks, a common practice in Babylonia.

and I bore *them* on *my* shoulder in
their sight.
8 And in the morning the word of the
LORD came to me, saying,
9 "Son of man, has not the house of
Israel, [a]the rebellious house, said to
you, [b]'What are you doing?'
10 "Say to them, 'Thus says the Lord
GOD: "This [a]burden[1] *concerns* the
prince in Jerusalem and all the house
of Israel who are among them." '
11 "Say, [a]'I *am* a sign to you. As I have
done, so shall it be done to them;
[b]they shall be carried away into captivity.'
12 "And [a]the prince who *is* among
them shall bear *his belongings* on *his*
shoulder at twilight and go out. They
shall dig through the wall to carry
them out through it. He shall cover his
face, so that he cannot see the ground
with *his* eyes.
13 "I will also spread My [a]net over
him, and he shall be caught in My
snare. [b]I will bring him to Babylon,
to the land of the Chaldeans; yet he
shall not see it, though he shall die
there.
14 [a]"I will scatter to every wind all
who *are* around him to help him, and
all his troops; and [b]I will draw out the
sword after them.
15 [a]"Then they shall know that I *am*
the LORD, when I scatter them among
the nations and disperse them throughout the countries.
16 [a]"But I will spare a few of their men
from the sword, from famine, and from
pestilence, that they may declare all
their abominations among the Gentiles
wherever they go. Then they shall
know that I *am* the LORD."

Judgment Not Postponed

17 Moreover the word of the LORD
came to me, saying,
18 "Son of man, [a]eat your bread with
[1]quaking, and drink your water with
trembling and anxiety.
19 "And say to the people of the land,
'Thus says the Lord GOD to the inhabitants of Jerusalem *and* to the land of
Israel: "They shall eat their bread with
anxiety, and drink their water with
dread, so that her land may [a]be emptied of all who are in it, [b]because of
the violence of all those who dwell in
it.
20 "Then the cities that are inhabited
shall be laid waste, and the land shall
become desolate; and you shall know
that I *am* the LORD." ' "
21 And the word of the LORD came to
me, saying,
22 "Son of man, what *is* this *proverb
that you *people* have about the land
of Israel, which says, [a]'The days are
prolonged, and every vision fails'?
23 "Tell them therefore, 'Thus says the
Lord GOD: "I will lay this proverb to
rest, and they shall no more use it as
a proverb in Israel." But say to them,
[a]"The days are at hand, and the [1]ful-
fillment of every vision.
24 "For [a]no more shall there be any
[b]false[1] vision or flattering divination
within the house of Israel.
25 "For I *am* the LORD. I speak, and
[a]the word which I speak will come to
pass; it will no more be postponed; for
in your days, O rebellious house, I will
say the word and [b]perform it," says the
Lord GOD.' "
26 Again the word of the LORD came
to me, saying,
27 [a]"Son of man, look, the house of Israel is saying, 'The vision that he sees
is [b]for many days *from now*, and he
prophesies of *times far off.'
28 [a]"Therefore say to them, 'Thus says
the Lord GOD: "None of My words will
be postponed any more, but the word
which I speak [b]will be done," says the
Lord GOD.' "

Woe to Foolish Prophets

13 And the word of the LORD came 3
to me, saying,

9 [a]Ezek. 2:5 [b]Ezek. 17:12; 24:19
10 [a]Mal. 1:1 [1]*oracle, prophecy*
11 [a]Ezek. 12:6 [b]2 Kin. 25:4, 5, 7
12 [a]2 Kin. 25:4; Jer. 39:4; 52:7; Ezek. 12:6
13 [a]Job 19:6; Jer. 52:9; Lam. 1:13; Ezek. 17:20 [b]2 Kin. 25:7; Jer. 52:11; Ezek. 17:16
14 [a]2 Kin. 25:4; Ezek. 5:10 [b]Ezek. 5:2, 12
15 [a][Ps. 9:16]; Ezek. 6:7, 14; 12:16, 20
16 [a]2 Kin. 25:11, 22; Ezek. 6:8–10
18 [a]Lam. 5:9; Ezek. 4:16 [1]*shaking*
19 [a]Jer. 10:22; Ezek. 6:6, 7, 14; Mic. 7:13; Zech. 7:14 [b]Ps. 107:34
22 [a]Jer. 5:12; Ezek. 11:3; 12:27; Amos 6:3; 2 Pet. 3:4 *See WW at Prov. 1:6.
23 [a]Ps. 37:13; Joel 2:1; Zeph. 1:14 [1]Lit. *word*
24 [a]Jer. 14:13–16; Ezek. 13:6; Zech. 13:2–4 [b]Lam. 2:14 [1]Lit. *vain*
25 [a][Is. 55:11]; Dan. 9:12; [Luke 21:33] [b]Num. 23:19; [Is. 14:24]
27 [a]Ezek. 12:22 [b]Dan. 10:14 *See WW at Is. 33:6.
28 [a]Ezek. 12:23, 25 [b]Jer. 4:7

12:8 In the morning: The divine explanation for this symbolic act is given to the prophet after he has faithfully obeyed the command.

12:9 What are you doing? This is the first indication that the people to whom Ezekiel ministered showed any response to his message or action.

12:10 This burden: A play on the two meanings of the Hebrew *massa'*, meaning both "oracle" and "burden" (see Jer. 23:33).

12:12–14 The fate of Zedekiah corresponds to the symbolic action of Ezekiel (vv. 5–7). **The prince** (v. 12) is Zedekiah. Ezekiel never calls Zedekiah "king," for he regarded Jehoiachin (who was already in exile) as the true king. Several details of these three verses are confirmed by 2 Kin. 25.

12:17–20 This section is a dramatization of the fate of the people. The **quaking** and **trembling** indicate the terror of the people at the approach of the Babylonian army.

12:21–28 Many of the prophecies of doom by prophets such as Isaiah, Micah, and Jeremiah had not yet come to pass. It was assumed by the people that these prophecies were not merely delayed or suspended but annulled (**every vision fails,** v. 22). Ezekiel is now informed that **the days are at hand** (v. 23) when the Word of God **will come to pass** (v. 25) and **none of** His **words will be postponed any more** (v. 28). Ezekiel began his ministry in 593 B.C. (see 1:2), and by 586 B.C. judgment had come.

13:1–12 See section 3 of Truth-In-Action at the end of Ezek.

2 "Son of man, prophesy [a]against the
prophets of Israel who prophesy, and
say to [b]those who prophesy out of their
own [c]heart,[1] 'Hear the word of the
LORD!' "
3 Thus says the Lord GOD: "Woe to
the foolish prophets, who follow their
own spirit and have seen [1]nothing!
4 "O Israel, your prophets are [a]like
foxes in the deserts.
5 "You [a]have not gone up into the
[1]gaps* to build a wall for the house of
Israel to stand in battle on the day of
the LORD.
6 [a]"They have envisioned futility and
false divination, saying, 'Thus says the
LORD!' But the LORD has [b]not sent
them; yet they *hope that the word may
[1]be confirmed.
7 "Have you not seen a futile vision,
and have you not spoken false divination? You say, 'The LORD says,' but I
have not spoken."
1 8 Therefore thus says the Lord GOD:
"Because you have spoken nonsense
and envisioned lies, therefore I *am* indeed against you," says the Lord GOD.
9 "My hand will be [a]against the
prophets who envision futility and who
[b]divine lies; they shall not be in the assembly of My people, [c]nor be written
in the record of the house of Israel,
[d]nor shall they enter into the land of
Israel. [e]Then you shall know that I *am*
the Lord GOD.
10 "Because, indeed, because they
have seduced My people, saying,
[a]'Peace!' when *there is* no peace—and
one builds a wall, and they [b]plaster[1]
it with untempered *mortar*—
11 "say to those who plaster *it* with untempered *mortar,* that it will fall.
[a]There will be flooding rain, and you,
O great hailstones, shall fall; and a
stormy wind shall tear *it* down.
12 "Surely, when the wall has fallen,
will it not be said to you, 'Where *is* the
mortar with which you plastered *it?*' "

CHAPTER 13
2 [a]Is. 28:7; Jer. 23:1–40; Lam. 2:14; Ezek. 22:25–28 [b]Ezek. 13:17 [c]Jer. 14:14; 23:16, 26 [1]Inspiration
3 [1]No vision
4 [a]Song 2:15
5 [a]Ps. 106:23; [Jer. 23:22]; Ezek. 22:30 [1]*breaches* *See WW at Ezek. 22:30.
6 [a]Jer. 29:8; Ezek. 22:28 [b]Jer. 27:8–15 [1]Come true *See WW at Mic. 7:7.
9 [a]Jer. 23:30 [b]Jer. 20:3–6 [c]Ezra 2:59, 62; Neh. 7:5; [Ps. 69:28] [d]Jer. 20:3–6 [e]Ezek. 11:10, 12
10 [a]Jer. 6:14; 8:11 [b]Ezek. 22:28 [1]Or *whitewash*
11 [a]Ezek. 38:22
14 [a]Ezek. 13:9, 21, 23; 14:8
16 [a]Jer. 6:14; 8:11; 28:9; Ezek. 13:10
17 [a]Ezek. 20:46; 21:2 [b]Ezek. 13:2; Rev. 2:20 [1]Inspiration
18 [a][2 Pet. 2:14] [1]Lit. *over all the joints of My hands;* Vg. *under every elbow;* LXX, Tg. *on all elbows of the hands*
19 [a]1 Sam. 2:15–17; Prov. 28:21; Mic. 3:5; Rom. 16:18; 1 Pet. 5:2
20 [1]Lit. *flying ones*

13 Therefore thus says the Lord GOD:
"I will cause a stormy wind to break
forth in My fury; and there shall be a
flooding rain in My anger, and great
hailstones in fury to consume *it.*
14 "So I will break down the wall you
have plastered with untempered *mortar,* and bring it down to the ground,
so that its foundation will be uncovered; it will fall, and you shall be consumed in the midst of it. [a]Then you
shall know that I *am* the LORD.
15 "Thus will I accomplish My wrath
on the wall and on those who have
plastered it with untempered *mortar;*
and I will say to you, 'The wall *is* no
more, nor those who plastered it,
16 '*that is,* the prophets of Israel who
prophesy concerning Jerusalem, and
who [a]see visions of peace for her when
there is no peace,' " says the Lord GOD.
17 "Likewise, son of man, [a]set your
face against the daughters of your people, [b]who prophesy out of their own
[1]heart; prophesy against them,
18 "and say, 'Thus says the Lord GOD:
"Woe to the *women* who sew *magic*
charms [1]on their sleeves and make
veils for the heads of people of every
height to hunt souls! Will you [a]hunt the
souls of My people, and keep yourselves alive?
19 "And will you profane Me among 3
My people [a]for handfuls of barley and
for pieces of bread, killing people
who should not die, and keeping people alive who should not live, by
your lying to My people who listen to
lies?"
20 'Therefore thus says the Lord GOD:
"Behold, I *am* against your *magic*
charms by which you hunt souls there
like [1]birds. I will tear them from your
arms, and let the souls go, the souls
you hunt like birds.
21 "I will also tear off your veils and
deliver My people out of your hand,
and they shall no longer be as prey in

13:2, 3 Out of their own heart: They used their own intellect and followed **their own spirit** (v. 3), rather than listening to God.

13:4 Like foxes in the deserts: Foxes and jackals were not clearly distinguished in the OT. Foxes usually were solitary creatures, but jackals traveled in packs, hid during the day in caves, and fed on carrion. Perhaps the jackal is the better illustration of the foolish prophets.

13:5 Have not gone up into the gaps: Workmen were busy repairing the physical wall of Jerusalem, and the prophets should have strengthened the moral and spiritual defenses as well.

13:8–23 See section 1 of Truth-In-Action at the end of Ezek.

13:9 A threefold punishment is predicted for the prophets who prophesy **lies:** 1) they will lose their honored place **in the assembly;** 2) their names will be omitted from the citizenship records of Israel; 3) they will not return from exile to the land of Israel.

13:10–13 Untempered *mortar:* Whitewash will not sustain the wall when the **flooding rain** of God's judgment falls (vv. 11, 13).

13:17–23 Warning to the false prophetesses. These seem to be female sorceresses and diviners.

13:18 Sew *magic* charms: The use of such paraphernalia is attested in the magical practices from Babylonia. This may refer to some function in black magic, but the exact meaning here is unclear. The charms and **veils** are used by the sorceresses themselves; and to put an end to such practice, God will tear them off (vv. 20, 21).

13:19 See section 3 of Truth-In-Action at the end of Ezek.

13:19 You profane Me: The use of the name "Yahweh" in any of these incantations would be a misuse of that name.

your hand. [a]Then you shall know that I *am* the LORD.

22 "Because with [a]lies you have made the heart of the righteous sad, whom I have not made sad; and you have [b]strengthened the hands of the wicked, so that he does not turn from his wicked way to save his life.

23 "Therefore [a]you shall no longer envision futility nor practice divination; for I will deliver My people out of your hand, and you shall know that I *am* the LORD." ' "

Idolatry Will Be Punished

14 Now [a]some of the elders of Israel came to me and sat before me.

2 And the word of the LORD came to me, saying,

3 "Son of man, these men have set up their idols in their hearts, and put before them [a]that which causes them to stumble into iniquity. [b]Should I let Myself be inquired of at all by them?

4 "Therefore speak to them, and say to them, 'Thus says the Lord GOD: "Everyone of the house of Israel who sets up his idols in his heart, and puts before him what causes him to stumble into iniquity, and then comes to the prophet, I the LORD will answer him who comes, according to the multitude of his idols,

5 "that I may seize the house of Israel by their heart, because they are all estranged from Me by their idols." '

6 "Therefore say to the house of Israel, 'Thus says the Lord GOD: "Repent, turn away from your idols, and [a]turn your faces away from all your abominations.

4 7 "For anyone of the house of Israel, or of the strangers who dwell in Israel, who separates himself from Me and sets up his idols in his heart and puts before him what causes him to stumble into iniquity, then comes to a prophet to inquire of him concerning Me, I the LORD will answer him by Myself.

8 [a]"I will set My face against that man and make him a [b]sign and a proverb, and I will cut him off from the midst of My people. [c]Then you shall know that I *am* the LORD.

9 "And if the prophet is induced to speak anything, I the LORD [a]have induced that prophet, and I will stretch out My hand against him and destroy him from among My people Israel.

10 "And they shall bear their iniquity; the punishment of the prophet shall be the same as the punishment of the one who inquired,

11 "that the house of Israel may [a]no longer stray from Me, nor be profaned anymore with all their *transgressions, [b]but that they may be My people and I may be their God," says the Lord GOD.' "

Judgment on Persistent Unfaithfulness

12 The word of the LORD came again to me, saying:

13 "Son of man, when a land sins against Me by persistent unfaithfulness, I will stretch out My hand against it; I will cut off its [a]supply of bread, send famine on it, and cut off man and beast from it.

14 [a]"Even *if* these three men, Noah, Daniel, and Job, were in it, they would deliver *only* themselves [b]by their righteousness," says the Lord GOD.

15 "If I cause [a]wild beasts to pass 2
through the land, and they [1]empty it, and make it so desolate that no man may pass through because of the beasts,

16 "*even* [a]*though* these three men *were* [1]in it, *as* I live," says the Lord GOD, "they would deliver neither sons nor daughters; only they would be delivered, and the land would be [b]desolate.

17 "Or *if* [a]I bring a sword on that land, and say, 'Sword, go through the land,' and I [b]cut off man and beast from it,

18 "even [a]*though* these three men *were* in it, *as* I live," says the Lord GOD, "they would deliver neither sons nor daughters, but only they themselves would be delivered.

19 "Or *if* I send [a]a pestilence into that land and [b]pour out My fury on it in blood, and cut off from it man and beast,

20 "even [a]*though* Noah, Daniel, and Job *were* in it, *as* I live," says the Lord GOD, "they would deliver neither son

21 [a]Ezek. 13:9
22 [a]Jer. 28:15 [b]Jer. 23:14
23 [a]Ezek. 12:24; 13:6; Mic. 3:5, 6; Zech. 13:3

CHAPTER 14

1 [a]2 Kin. 6:32; Ezek. 8:1; 20:1; 33:31
3 [a]Ezek. 7:19; Zeph. 1:3 [b]2 Kin. 3:13; Is. 1:15; Jer. 11:11; Ezek. 20:3, 31
6 [a]1 Sam. 7:3; Neh. 1:9; Is. 2:20; 30:22; 55:6, 7; Ezek. 18:30
8 [a]Lev. 17:10; 20:3, 5, 6; Jer. 44:11; Ezek. 15:7 [b]Num. 26:10; Deut. 28:37; Ezek. 5:15 [c]Ezek. 6:7; 13:14
9 [a]1 Kin. 22:23; Job 12:16; Is. 66:4; Jer. 4:10; 2 Thess. 2:11
11 [a]Ps. 119:67, 71; Jer. 31:18, 19; [Heb. 12:11]; 2 Pet. 2:15 [b]Ezek. 11:20; 37:27 *See WW at Ezek. 18:31.
13 [a]Lev. 26:26; 2 Kin. 25:3; Is. 3:1; Jer. 52:6; Ezek. 4:16; 5:16
14 [a]Jer. 15:1 [b][Prov. 11:4]
15 [a]Lev. 26:22; Num. 21:6; Ezek. 5:17; 14:21 [1]Lit. *bereave it* of children
16 [a]Ezek. 14:14, 18, 20 [b]Ezek. 15:8; 33:28, 29 [1]Lit. *in the midst of it*
17 [a]Lev. 26:25; Ezek. 5:12; 21:3, 4; 29:8; 38:21 [b]Ezek. 25:13; Zeph. 1:3
18 [a]Ezek. 14:14
19 [a]2 Sam. 24:15; Ezek. 38:22 [b]Ezek. 7:8
20 [a]Ezek. 14:14

14:1 Elders of Israel: Probably the same as "elders of Judah" in 8:1.

14:3 In their hearts: They have centered their affections on the idols.

14:6 Repent: Three times Ezekiel calls on the people to repent (see 18:30; 33:11).

14:7 See section 4 of Truth-In-Action at the end of Ezek.

14:14 Noah, Daniel, and Job: Three examples of famous men who showed integrity and faithfulness. The people should not think that individuals such as these could help them out of their dilemma, for the sin of the land is so great that these men could only save themselves.

14:15–20 See section 2 of Truth-In-Action at the end of Ezek.

nor daughter; they would deliver *only*
themselves by their righteousness."
21 For thus says the Lord GOD: "How
much more it shall be when [a]I send My
four [1]severe judgments on Jerusalem—
the sword and famine and wild beasts
and pestilence—to cut off man and
beast from it?
22 [a]"Yet behold, there shall be left in
it a remnant who will be [b]brought out,
both sons and daughters; surely they
will come out to you, and [c]you will
see their ways and their doings. Then
you will be comforted concerning the
disaster that I have brought upon Jerusalem, all that I have brought upon
it.
23 "And they will comfort you, when
you see their ways and their doings;
and you shall know that I have done
nothing [a]without cause that I have
done in it," says the Lord GOD.

The Outcast Vine

15 Then the word of the LORD came
to me, saying:
2 "Son of man, how is the wood of
the vine *better* than any other wood,
the vine branch which is among the
trees of the forest?
3 "Is wood taken from it to make any
object? Or can *men* make a peg from
it to hang any vessel on?
4 "Instead, [a]it is thrown into the fire
for fuel; the fire devours both ends of
it, and its middle is burned. Is it useful
for *any* work?
5 "Indeed, when it was whole, no object could be made from it. How much
less will it be useful for *any* work when
the fire has devoured it, and it is
burned?
6 "Therefore thus says the Lord GOD:
'Like the wood of the vine among the
trees of the forest, which I have given
to the fire for fuel, so I will give up
the inhabitants of Jerusalem;
7 'and [a]I will set My face against
them. [b]They will go out from *one* fire,
but *another* fire shall devour them.
[c]Then you shall know that I *am* the
LORD, when I set My face against them.
8 'Thus I will make the land desolate,
because they have persisted in unfaithfulness,' says the Lord GOD."

God's Love for Jerusalem

16 Again the word of the LORD
came to me, saying,
2 "Son of man, [a]cause Jerusalem to
know her abominations,
3 "and say, 'Thus says the Lord GOD
to Jerusalem: "Your [1]birth [a]and your
nativity *are* from the land of Canaan;
[b]your *father *was* an Amorite and your
mother a Hittite.
4 "*As for* your nativity, [a]on the day
you were born your navel cord was not
cut, nor were you washed in water to
cleanse *you;* you were not rubbed with
salt nor wrapped in swaddling cloths.
5 "No eye pitied you, to do any of
these things for you, to have compassion on you; but you were thrown out
into the open field, when you yourself
were [1]loathed on the day you were
born.
6 "And when I passed by you and saw
you struggling in your own blood, I
said to you in your blood, 'Live!' Yes,
I said to you in your blood, 'Live!'
7 [a]"I made you [1]thrive like a plant in
the field; and you grew, matured, and
became very beautiful. *Your* breasts
were formed, your hair grew, but you
were naked and bare.
8 "When I passed by you again and
looked upon you, indeed your time *was*
the time of love; [a]so I spread [1]My wing
over you and covered your nakedness.

21 [a]Ezek. 5:17; 33:27; Amos 4:6–10; Rev. 6:8 [1]Lit. *evil*
22 [a]2 Kin. 25:11, 12; Ezra 2:1; Ezek. 12:16; 36:20 [b]Ezek. 6:8 [c]Ezek. 20:43
23 [a]Jer. 22:8, 9

CHAPTER 15

4 [a][John 15:6]
7 [a]Lev. 26:17; [Ps. 34:16]; Jer. 21:10; Ezek. 14:8 [b]Is. 24:18 [c]Ezek. 7:4

CHAPTER 16

2 [a]Is. 58:1; Ezek. 20:4; 22:2
3 [a]Ezek. 21:30 [b]Gen. 15:16; Deut. 7:1; Josh. 24:15; Ezek. 16:45 [1]*origin and your birth* *See WW at Ps. 68:5.
4 [a]Hos. 2:3
5 [1]*abhorred*
7 [a]Ex. 1:7; Deut. 1:10 [1]Lit. *a myriad*
8 [a]Ruth 3:9; Jer. 2:2 [1]Or *the corner of My garment*

14:21 Four judgments are mentioned in this verse and discussed in this section: **the sword** (v. 17); **famine** (v. 13); **wild beasts**—rabid animals (v. 15); **pestilence**—massive death by disease (v. 19).

15:1–8 The inhabitants of Jerusalem (v. 6) are likened to the vine that is only good **for fuel** for **the fire** (v. 4). The emphasis is not on fruitfulness (John 15:1–17), but on the lack of value of the wood itself for constructive use. Both Isaiah (Is. 5:1–7) and Jeremiah (Jer. 2:21) speak of Israel's failure to produce proper fruit; Ezekiel speaks of total uselessness (v. 5).

15:3 Make a peg: See Is. 22:23–25. The expected answer here is "No!"

15:7 *One* fire: Fire is a figurative expression for an invading army.

16:1–43 An allegory on **Jerusalem** seen first as a child bride and a queen (vv. 1–14), and then a **harlot** (vv. 15–34).

16:3 Jerusalem is used symbolically to designate the southern kingdom (or all Israel). **Your birth and your nativity** speak of the ancient history of the city before the time of the Israelites (see Gen. 14:18 where Salem is another name for Jerusalem). The **Amorite** was a Semitic element in Canaan (v. 45; Gen. 48:22; Josh. 5:1; 10:5), and the **Hittite** was a non-Semitic element (Gen. 23:10–20; 26:34). This has nothing to do with the origin of the Israelites (see v. 45).

16:4 Rubbed with salt: This practice survived until the early years of this century. The purpose was to prevent the growth of harmful bacteria.

16:5 Thrown out into the open field: A child abandoned in a marketplace or other well-traveled area had a chance to be **pitied** and saved; but this child was **loathed,** thrown out, and abandoned to die.

16:8 Spread My wing over you: Similar to the phrase in Ruth 3:9, "Take your maidservant under your wing," a symbolic expression for marriage.

Yes, I [b]swore an oath to you and entered into a [c]covenant with you, and
[d]you became Mine," says the Lord
GOD.
9 "Then I washed you in water; yes,
I thoroughly washed off your blood,
and I anointed you with oil.
10 "I clothed you in embroidered cloth
and gave you sandals of [1]badger skin;
I clothed you with fine linen and covered you with silk.
11 "I adorned you with ornaments,
[a]put bracelets on your wrists, [b]and a
chain on your neck.
12 "And I put a [1]jewel in your nose,
earrings in your ears, and a beautiful
crown on your head.
13 "Thus you were adorned with gold
and silver, and your clothing *was of*
fine linen, silk, and embroidered cloth.
[a]You ate *pastry of* fine flour, honey,
and oil. You were exceedingly [b]beauti-
ful, and succeeded to royalty.
14 [a]"Your fame went out among the
nations because of your *beauty, for it
was perfect through My splendor
which I had bestowed on you," says
the Lord GOD.

Jerusalem's Harlotry

15 [a]"But you trusted in your own
beauty, [b]played the harlot because of
your fame, and poured out your harlotry on everyone passing by who *would
have* it.
16 [a]"You took some of your garments
and adorned multicolored [1]high places
for yourself, and played the harlot on
them. *Such* things should not happen,
nor be.
17 "You have also taken your beautiful
jewelry from My gold and My silver,
which I had given you, and made for
yourself male images and played the
harlot with them.
18 "You took your embroidered garments and covered them, and you set
My oil and My incense before them.

8 [b]Gen. 22:16–18 [c]Ex. 24:6–8 [d][Ex. 19:5]
10 [1]Or *dolphin* or *dugong*
11 [a]Gen. 24:22, 47 [b]Prov. 1:9
12 [1]Lit. *ring*
13 [a]Deut. 32:13, 14 [b]Ps. 48:2
14 [a]Lam. 2:15 *See WW at Ezek. 28:12.
15 [a]Mic. 3:11 [b]Is. 1:21; 57:8
16 [a]Ezek. 7:20 [1]Places for pagan worship
19 [a]Hos. 2:8 [1]Or *a sweet aroma*
20 [a]Jer. 7:31
21 [a]Jer. 19:5
22 [a]Jer. 2:2 [b]Ezek. 16:4–6
24 [a]Jer. 11:13 [b]Jer. 2:20; 3:2 [1]Place for pagan worship
25 [a]Prov. 9:14
26 [a]Ezek. 16:26; 20:7, 8 [b]Deut. 31:20
27 [a]Ezek. 16:57 [1]Allowance of food
28 [a]Jer. 2:18, 36
29 [a]Ezek. 23:14–17

19 "Also [a]My food which I gave you—
the pastry of fine flour, oil, and honey
which I fed you—you set it before them
as [1]sweet incense; and *so* it was," says
the Lord GOD.
20 [a]"Moreover you took your sons and
your daughters, whom you bore to Me,
and these you sacrificed to them to be
devoured. *Were* your *acts* of harlotry
a small matter,
21 "that you have slain My children
and offered them up to them by causing them to pass through *the* [a]*fire?*
22 "And in all your abominations and
acts of harlotry you did not remember
the days of your [a]youth, [b]when you
were naked and bare, struggling in
your blood.
23 "Then it was so, after all your wickedness—'Woe, woe to you!' says the
Lord GOD—
24 "*that* [a]you also built for yourself a
shrine, and [b]made a [1]high place for
yourself in every street.
25 "You built your high places [a]at the
head of every road, and made your
beauty to be abhorred. You offered
yourself to everyone who passed by,
and multiplied your acts of harlotry.
26 "You also committed harlotry with
[a]the Egyptians, your very fleshly
neighbors, and increased your acts of
harlotry to [b]provoke Me to anger.
27 "Behold, therefore, I stretched out
My hand against you, diminished your
[1]allotment, and gave you up to the will
of those who hate you, [a]the daughters
of the Philistines, who were ashamed
of your lewd behavior.
28 "You also played the harlot with the
[a]Assyrians, because you were insatiable; indeed you played the harlot with
them and still were not satisfied.
29 "Moreover you multiplied your acts
of harlotry as far as the land of the
trader, [a]Chaldea; and even then you
were not satisfied.
30 "How degenerate is your heart!"
says the Lord GOD, "seeing you do all

16:10 Embroidered cloth was variegated material fit for royalty (see 26:16; Judg. 5:30; Ps. 45:14). **Sandals of badger skin:** The same material that covered the tabernacle (Ex. 25:5; 26:14).

16:14 Fame went out: This was especially true during the time of David and Solomon.

16:15 Played the harlot means not just adultery, but unbridled lust. She has given herself to **everyone passing by;** and, *instead of* being paid for her services, she has paid her lovers (vv. 31, 33, 34).

16:20, 21 The logical outcome of Jerusalem's idolatry is the sacrifice of the firstborn (20:26, 31; Jer. 7:31) whom they caused **to pass through *the fire.***

16:24 A shrine: The harlotry moved from the high places outside Jerusalem to the heart of the city itself, **in every street.** The **high place** is a brothel.

16:26 Harlotry with the Egyptians indicates international relations. Israel often appealed to foreign nations rather than to trust in God.

16:27 Gave you up: Sennacherib took some of the land of Judah away from King Hezekiah and gave it to Mitinti king of Ashdod, Padi king of Ekron, and Silbel king of Gaza. **Daughters of the Philistines** refers to the Philistine cities.

16:28 Assyrians: Ahaz entered into an alliance with the Assyrians when he was threatened by Pekah of Israel and Rezin of Syria (see 2 Kin. 16:5–18; Is. 7).

16:29 Chaldea probably refers to Hezekiah's reception of the envoys from the Babylonian king Merodach-Baladan (see 2 Kin. 20:12–19).

these *things*, the deeds of a brazen harlot.

Jerusalem's Adultery

31 [a]"You erected your shrine at the
head of every road, and built your
[1]high place in every street. Yet you
were not like a harlot, because you
scorned [b]payment.
32 "*You are* an adulterous wife, *who*
takes strangers instead of her husband.
33 "Men make payment to all harlots,
but [a]you made your payments to all
your lovers, and [1]hired them to come
to you from all around for your harlotry.
34 "You are the opposite of *other*
women in your harlotry, because no
one solicited you to be a harlot. In that
you gave payment but no payment was
given you, therefore you are the opposite."

Jerusalem's Lovers Will Abuse Her

35 'Now then, O harlot, hear the word
of the LORD!
36 'Thus says the Lord GOD: "Because
your filthiness was poured out and
your nakedness uncovered in your harlotry with your lovers, and with all
your abominable idols, and because of
[a]the blood of your children which you
gave to them,
37 "surely, therefore, [a]I will gather all
your lovers with whom you took pleasure, all those you loved, *and* all those
you hated; I will gather them from all
around against you and will uncover
your nakedness to them, that they may
see all your nakedness.
38 "And I will judge you as [a]women
who break wedlock or [b]shed blood are
judged; I will bring blood upon you in
fury and jealousy.
39 "I will also give you into their hand,
and they shall throw down your
shrines and break down [a]your [1]high
places. [b]They shall also strip you of
your clothes, take your beautiful jewelry, and leave you naked and bare.
40 [a]"They shall also bring up an assembly against you, [b]and they shall
stone you with stones and thrust you
through with their swords.
41 "They shall [a]burn your houses with
fire, and [b]execute judgments on you
in the sight of many women; and I
will make you [c]cease playing the
harlot, and you shall no longer hire
lovers.
42 "So [a]I will lay to rest My fury toward you, and My jealousy shall depart
from you. I will be quiet, and be angry
no more.
43 "Because [a]you did not remember
the days of your youth, but [1]agitated
Me with all these *things*, surely [b]I will
also recompense your [2]deeds on *your
own* head," says the Lord GOD. "And
you shall not commit lewdness in addition to all your abominations.

*More Wicked than Samaria and
Sodom*

44 "Indeed everyone who quotes proverbs will use *this* proverb against you:
'Like mother, like daughter!'
45 "You *are* your mother's daughter,
[1]loathing husband and children; and
you *are* the [a]sister of your sisters, who
loathed their husbands and children;
[b]your mother *was* a Hittite and your
father an Amorite.
46 "Your elder sister *is* Samaria, who
dwells with her daughters to the north
of you; and [a]your younger sister, who
dwells to the south of you, *is* Sodom
and her daughters.
47 "You did not walk in their ways nor
act according to their abominations;
but, as *if that were* too little, [a]you became more corrupt than they in all
your ways.
48 "*As* I live," says the Lord GOD, "neither [a]your sister Sodom nor her daughters have done as you and your daughters have done.
49 "Look, this was the iniquity of your
sister Sodom: She and her daughter
had pride, [a]fullness of food, and abundance of idleness; neither did she
strengthen the hand of the poor and
needy.
50 "And they were haughty and [a]com-
mitted abomination before Me; therefore [b]I took them away as [1]I saw *fit*.
51 "Samaria did not commit [a]half of
your sins; but you have multiplied your

31 [a]Ezek. 16:24, 39 [b]Is. 52:3 [1]Place for pagan worship
33 [a]Hos. 8:9, 10 [1]Or *bribed*
36 [a]Jer. 2:34
37 [a]Lam. 1:8
38 [a]Lev. 20:10 [b]Gen. 9:6
39 [a]Ezek. 16:24, 31 [b]Hos. 2:3 [1]Places for pagan worship
40 [a]Ezek. 23:45–47 [b]John 8:5, 7
41 [a]Deut. 13:16 [b]Ezek. 5:8; 23:10, 48 [c]Ezek. 23:27
42 [a]Ezek. 5:13; 21:17
43 [a]Ps. 78:42 [b]Ezek. 9:10; 11:21; 22:31 [1]So with LXX, Syr., Tg., Vg.; MT *were agitated with Me* [2]Lit. *way*
45 [a]Ezek. 23:2–4 [b]Ezek. 16:3 [1]Or *despising*
46 [a]Is. 1:10
47 [a]Ezek. 5:6, 7
48 [a]Matt. 10:15; 11:24
49 [a]Gen. 13:10
50 [a]Gen. 13:13; 18:20; 19:5 [b]Gen. 19:24 [1]Vg. *you saw;* LXX *he saw;* Tg. *as was revealed to Me*
51 [a]Ezek. 23:11

16:38 I will judge you: The usual punishment for adultery was death (see Lev. 20:10; Deut. 22:22) by stoning (see v. 40; 23:47; Deut. 22:21, 24; John 8:3–7), burning (see Gen. 38:24), or sword (see v. 40; 23:47).
16:41 Burn your houses: Used as a punishment in Judg. 12:1.
16:44 Like mother, like daughter: Jerusalem is personified as a woman, and the most apt proverb of Jerusalem is this one signifying the long and continuous bent toward sinning.
16:45 Mother *was* a Hittite: See v. 3, but here the emphasis is on the mother and the Canaanite origin of the city of Jerusalem.
16:46 Both **Samaria** and **Sodom** are described as sisters to Jerusalem. **Daughters** refers to the suburbs or small hamlets around the major cities.

abominations more than they, and
[b]have justified your sisters by all the
abominations which you have done.
52 "You who judged your sisters, bear
your own shame also, because the sins
which you committed were more
abominable than theirs; they are more
righteous than you. Yes, be disgraced
also, and bear your own shame, because you justified your sisters.
53 [a]"When I bring back their captives,
the captives of Sodom and her daughters, and the captives of Samaria and
her daughters, then *I will also bring
back* [b]the captives of your captivity
among them,
54 "that you may bear your own
shame and be disgraced by all that you
did when [a]you *comforted them.
55 "When your sisters, Sodom and her
daughters, return to their former state,
and Samaria and her daughters return
to their former state, then you and your
daughters will return to your former
state.
56 "For your sister Sodom was not a
byword in your mouth in the days of
your pride,
57 "before your wickedness was uncovered. It was like the time of the
[a]reproach of the daughters of [1]Syria
and all *those* around her, and of
[b]the daughters of the Philistines, who
despise you everywhere.
58 [a]"You have paid for your lewdness
and your abominations," says the
LORD.
59 'For thus says the Lord GOD: "I will
deal with you as you have done, who
[a]despised [b]the oath by breaking the
covenant.

An Everlasting Covenant

60 "Nevertheless I will [a]remember My
covenant with you in the days of your
youth, and I will establish [b]an everlasting covenant with you.
61 "Then [a]you will remember your
ways and be ashamed, when you receive your older and your younger sisters; for I will give them to you for
[b]daughters, [c]but not because of My
covenant with you.
62 [a]"And I will establish My covenant
with you. Then you shall know that I
am the LORD,
63 "that you may [a]remember and be
ashamed, [b]and never open your mouth
anymore because of your shame, when
I provide you an atonement for all you
have done," says the Lord GOD.' "

51 [b]Jer. 3:8–11; Matt. 12:41
53 [a]Is. 1:9; [Ezek. 16:60] [b]Jer. 20:16
54 [a]Ezek. 14:22 *See WW at Ps. 23:4.
57 [a]2 Kin. 16:5; 2 Chr. 28:18; Is. 7:1; Ezek. 5:14, 15; 22:4 [b]Ezek. 16:27 [1]Heb. *Aram;* so with MT, LXX, Tg., Vg.; many Heb. mss., Syr. *Edom*
58 [a]Ezek. 23:49
59 [a]Ezek. 17:13 [b]Deut. 29:12
60 [a]Lev. 26:42–45; Ps. 106:45 [b]Is. 55:3; Jer. 32:40; 50:5; Ezek. 37:26
61 [a]Jer. 50:4, 5; Ezek. 20:43; 36:31 [b]Is. 54:1; 60:4; [Gal. 4:26] [c]Jer. 31:31
62 [a]Hos. 2:19, 20
63 [a]Ezek. 36:31, 32; Dan. 9:7, 8 [b]Ps. 39:9; [Rom. 3:19]

CHAPTER 17

2 [a]Ezek. 20:49; 24:3
3 [a]Jer. 48:40; Ezek. 17:12; Hos. 8:1 [b]2 Kin. 24:12
5 [a]Deut. 8:7–9 [b]Is. 44:4
6 [a]Ezek. 17:14

WORD WEALTH

16:63 ashamed, *bush* (boosh); Strong's #954: To be ashamed, shamed, disappointed, or embarrassed. This verb occurs approximately 100 times. Among its derivatives are *busha* (shame) and *boshet,* which is translated "shame," but refers to an idol. The idol itself was considered a shame or an embarrassment. An idol also guaranteed that its worshipers would eventually be shamed and greatly disappointed in their choice of an object of worship. *Bosh* is used for the sense of disappointment one experiences when one's hope fails in an embarrassing way; but those who trust in the Lord shall never be ashamed (Ps. 25:2, 3; Joel 2:26, 27). In the present reference, being ashamed is the result of remembering the path we walked before coming into God's covenant (v. 62) and realizing that our deeds necessitated the atonement.

The Eagles and the Vine

17 And the word of the LORD came
to me, saying,
2 "Son of man, pose a riddle, and
speak a [a]parable to the house of Israel,
3 "and say, 'Thus says the Lord GOD:

[a]"A great eagle with large wings
and long pinions,
Full of feathers of various colors,
Came to Lebanon
And [b]took from the cedar the
highest branch.
4 He cropped off its topmost young
twig
And carried it to a land of trade;
He set it in a city of merchants.
5 Then he took some of the seed of
the land
And planted it in [a]a fertile field;
He placed *it* by abundant waters
And set it [b]like a willow tree.
6 And it grew and became a
spreading vine [a]of low stature;

16:60 My covenant: The covenant the Lord remembers is the *marriage* covenant, the covenant which Jerusalem has violated. But God will establish **an everlasting covenant,** one based on the new heart and the new spirit (11:19, 20; 36:25–28).

17:1–24 An allegory of an **eagle,** a **cedar,** and a **vine.** The riddle is given in vv. 3–10, the explanation in vv. 11–21, and a concluding allegory of hope in vv. 22–24.

17:3 Great eagle: Nebuchadnezzar of Babylon (v. 12).

17:4 Topmost young twig: King Jehoiachin. The **land of trade** is Babylonia, and the **city of merchants** is Babylon (see 2 Kin. 24:12, 15).

17:5 Seed of the land refers to King Zedekiah, who was **planted** (put on the throne) by Nebuchadnezzar (see 2 Kin. 24:17).

Its branches turned toward him,
But its roots were under it.
So it became a vine,
Brought forth branches,
And put forth shoots.

7 "But there was [1]another great
eagle with large wings and
many feathers;
And behold, [a]this vine bent its
roots toward him,
And stretched its branches
toward him,
From the garden terrace where it
had been planted,
That he might water it.
8 It was planted in [1]good* soil by
many waters,
To bring forth branches, bear
fruit,
And become a majestic vine." '

9 "Say, 'Thus says the Lord GOD:

"Will it thrive?
[a]Will he not pull up its roots,
Cut off its fruit,
And leave it to wither?
All of its spring leaves will wither,
And no great power or many
people
Will be needed to pluck it up by
its roots.
10 Behold, *it is* planted,
Will it thrive?
[a]Will it not utterly wither when the
east wind touches it?
It will wither in the garden terrace
where it grew." ' "

11 Moreover the word of the LORD
came to me, saying,
12 "Say now to [a]the rebellious house:
'Do you not know what these *things*
mean?' Tell *them,* 'Indeed [b]the king of
Babylon went to Jerusalem and took
its king and princes, and led them with
him to Babylon.
13 [a]'And he took the king's offspring,
*made a covenant with him, [b]and put
him under oath. He also took away the
mighty of the land,
14 'that the kingdom might be

7 [a]Ezek. 17:15 [1]So with LXX, Syr., Vg.; MT, Tg. *one*
8 [1]Lit. *a good field* *See WW at Ezek. 34:14.
9 [a]2 Kin. 25:7
10 [a]Ezek. 19:12; Hos. 13:15
12 [a]Ezek. 2:3–5; 12:9 [b]2 Kin. 24:11–16; Ezek. 1:2; 17:3
13 [a]2 Kin. 24:17; Jer. 37:1; Ezek. 17:5 [b]2 Chr. 36:13 *See WW at Ex. 34:27.
14 [a]Ezek. 29:14
15 [a]2 Kin. 24:20; 2 Chr. 36:13; Jer. 52:3; Ezek. 17:7 [b]Deut. 17:16; Is. 31:1, 3; 36:6, 9 [c]Ezek. 17:9
16 [a]Jer. 52:11; Ezek. 12:13
17 [a]Jer. 37:7; Ezek. 29:6 [b]Jer. 52:4; Ezek. 4:2 [1]Or *siege wall*
18 [a]1 Chr. 29:24; Lam. 5:6 [1]Took an oath
20 [a]Ezek. 12:13 [b]Jer. 2:35; Ezek. 20:36 [1]Lit. *unfaithful act*
21 [a]Ezek. 12:14 [b]Ezek. 12:15; 22:15 [1]So with MT, Vg.; many Heb. mss., Syr. *choice men;* Tg. *mighty men;* LXX omits *All his fugitives*
22 [a][Is. 11:1; Jer. 23:5; Zech. 3:8] [b]Is. 53:2 [c][Ps. 2:6]
23 [a][Is. 2:2, 3]; Ezek. 20:40; [Mic. 4:1] [b]Ezek. 31:6; Dan. 4:12

[a]brought low and not lift itself up, *but*
that by keeping his covenant it might
stand.
15 'But [a]he rebelled against him by
sending his ambassadors to Egypt,
[b]that they might give him horses and
many people. [c]Will he prosper? Will
he who does such *things* escape? Can
he break a covenant and still be delivered?
16 '*As* I live,' says the Lord GOD,
'surely [a]in the place *where* the king
dwells who made him king, whose oath
he despised and whose covenant he
broke—with him in the midst of Babylon he shall die.
17 [a]'Nor will Pharaoh with *his* mighty
army and great company do anything
in the war, [b]when they heap up a siege
mound and build a [1]wall to cut off
many persons.
18 'Since he despised the oath by
breaking the covenant, and in fact
[a]gave[1] his hand and still did all these
things, he shall not escape.' "
19 Therefore thus says the Lord GOD:
"*As* I live, surely My oath which he despised, and My covenant which he
broke, I will recompense on his own
head.
20 "I will [a]spread My net over him, and
he shall be taken in My snare. I will
bring him to Babylon and [b]try him
there for the [1]treason which he committed against Me.
21 [a]"All his [1]fugitives with all his
troops shall fall by the sword, and
those who remain shall be [b]scattered
to every wind; and you shall know that
I, the LORD, have spoken."

Israel Exalted at Last

22 Thus says the Lord GOD: "I will take
also *one* of the highest [a]branches of
the high cedar and set *it* out. I will crop
off from the topmost of its young twigs
[b]a tender one, and will [c]plant *it* on a
high and prominent mountain.
23 [a]"On the mountain height of Israel
I will plant it; and it will bring forth
boughs, and bear fruit, and be a majestic cedar. [b]Under it will dwell birds of

---

17:7 Another great eagle is an Egyptian pharaoh, and the vine which had been planted by abundant waters (Babylon, v. 5) now turns toward Egypt (v. 15).

17:10 East wind: Usually refers to the hot, dry wind known as khamsin. Here it is Nebuchadnezzar and his army.

17:15 Break a covenant: The action of Zedekiah in sending **ambassadors to Egypt** broke his oath to Nebuchadnezzar. This verse and vv. 16, 18–20 stress the importance of keeping an international agreement.

17:19 My covenant which he broke: The oath of Zedekiah to Nebuchadnezzar was sworn by invoking the name of God (see 2 Kin. 24:17; 2 Chr. 36:13). By breaking the oath to Nebuchadnezzar, he at the same time broke his covenant with God.

17:20 God would **bring him to Babylon** for judgment. It was already mentioned that he would die there (v. 16).

17:22 I will take signifies the divine intervention of God to establish a descendant of David on the throne. The former planting (v. 4) was of human origin and action.

every sort; in the shadow of its
branches they will dwell.
24 "And all the trees of the field shall
know that I, the LORD, [a]have brought
down the high tree and exalted the low
tree, dried up the green tree and made
the dry tree flourish; [b]I, the LORD, have
spoken and have done *it*."

A False Proverb Refuted

18 The word of the LORD came to
me again, saying,
2 "What do you mean when you use
this proverb concerning the land of Israel, saying:

'The [a]fathers have eaten sour
grapes,
And the children's teeth are set
on edge'?

3 "*As* I live," says the Lord GOD, "you
shall no longer use this *proverb in Israel.

4 "Behold, all souls are [a]Mine;
The soul of the father
As well as the soul of the son is
Mine;
[b]The soul who sins shall die.
5 But if a man is just
And does what is lawful and
right;
6 [a]If he has not eaten [1]on the
mountains,
Nor lifted up his eyes to the idols
of the house of Israel,
Nor [b]defiled his neighbor's wife,
Nor approached [c]a woman
during her impurity;
7 If he has not [a]oppressed anyone,
But has restored to the debtor his
[b]pledge;
Has robbed no one by violence,
But has [c]given his bread to the
hungry
And covered the naked with
[d]clothing;
8 If he has not [1]exacted [a]usury
Nor taken any increase,
But has withdrawn his hand from
iniquity
And [b]executed true [2]judgment
between man and man;
9 *If* he has walked in My statutes
And kept My judgments
faithfully—
He *is* just;
He shall surely [a]live!"
Says the Lord GOD.

10 "If he begets a son *who is* a robber
Or [a]a shedder of blood,
Who does any of these *things*
11 And does none of those *duties,*
But has eaten [1]on the mountains
Or defiled his neighbor's wife;
12 If he has oppressed the poor and
needy,
Robbed by violence,
Not restored the pledge,
Lifted his eyes to the idols,
Or [a]committed abomination;
13 If he has exacted usury
Or taken increase—
Shall he then live?
He shall not live!
If he has done any of these
abominations,
He shall surely die;
[a]His blood shall be upon him.

14 "*If,* however, he begets a son
Who sees all the sins which his
father has done,
And considers but does not do
likewise;
15 [a]*Who* has not eaten [1]on the
mountains,
Nor lifted his eyes to the idols of
the house of Israel,
Nor defiled his neighbor's wife;
16 Has not oppressed anyone,
Nor withheld a pledge,
Nor robbed by violence,
But has given his bread to the
hungry
And covered the naked with
clothing;
17 *Who* has withdrawn his hand
from [1]the poor

24 [a]Ezek. 37:3; Amos 9:11; Luke 1:52; [Rom. 11:23, 24] [b]Ezek. 22:14

CHAPTER 18

2 [a]Jer. 31:29; Lam. 5:7
3 *See WW at Prov. 1:6.
4 [a]Num. 16:22; 27:16; Is. 42:5; 57:16 [b]Ezek. 18:20; [Rom. 6:23]
6 [a]Ezek. 22:9 [b]Lev. 18:20; 20:10 [c]Lev. 18:19; 20:18 [1]At the mountain shrines
7 [a]Ex. 22:21; Lev. 19:15; 25:14 [b]Ex. 22:26; Deut. 24:12 [c]Deut. 15:7, 11; Ezek. 18:16; [Matt. 25:35–40]; Luke 3:11 [d]Is. 58:7
8 [a]Ex. 22:25; Lev. 25:36; Deut. 23:19; Neh. 5:7; Ps. 15:5 [b]Deut. 1:16; Zech. 8:16 [1]Lent money at interest [2]*justice*
9 [a]Ezek. 20:11; Amos 5:4; [Hab. 2:4; Rom. 1:17]
10 [a]Gen. 9:6; Ex. 21:12; Num. 35:31
11 [1]At the mountain shrines
12 [a]2 Kin. 21:11; Ezek. 8:6, 17
13 [a]Lev. 20:9, 11–13, 16, 27; Ezek. 3:18; Acts 18:6
15 [a]Ezek. 18:6 [1]At the mountain shrines
17 [1]So with MT, Tg., Vg.; LXX *iniquity* (cf. v. 8)

17:24 All the trees are foreign nations. The **high tree** is Jehoiachin, the **low tree** is a scion of David (and Jehoiachin).
18:2 This proverb: See Jer. 31:29, 30. A stress on corporate solidarity led to the false view that the individual had no responsibility for his own sin. Ezekiel traces three generations to show that each suffers only for his own sin. Each example contains a random list of righteous or unrighteous behavior. See Introduction to Ezekiel: Content.
18:6 Eaten on the mountains: According to Deut. 12:7, 18, the Israelites were to eat their offerings only where God designated. **Defiled his neighbor's wife:** See 22:11. Adultery is prohibited in Ex. 20:14; Deut. 22:22. **During her impurity:** A woman is ritually unclean during her menstruation (see 22:10; Lev. 15:19; 18:19; 20:18).
18:7 Oppressed: See 22:7, 12, 29. Usually the rich take advantage of the poor.
18:8 Exacted usury: See v. 13; 22:12. The charging of interest is prohibited in Lev. 25:36; Deut. 23:19, 20.
18:10–13 The second generation is evil and will pay for his sin.
18:14–18 The third generation is righteous and will live. The sin of his father will not be charged to him (v. 17), but his wicked father will die (v. 18).

And not received usury or
increase,
But has executed My judgments
And walked in My statutes—
He shall not die for the iniquity
of his father;
He shall surely live!

18 "*As for* his father,
Because he cruelly oppressed,
Robbed his brother by violence,
And did what *is* not good among
his people,
Behold, [a]he shall die for his
iniquity.

Turn and Live

19 "Yet you say, 'Why [a]should the son
not bear the guilt of the *father?' Because the son has done what is lawful
and right, and has kept all My statutes
and observed them, he shall surely live.
20 [a]"The soul who sins shall die.
[b]The son shall not bear the guilt of the
father, nor the father bear the guilt of
the son. [c]The righteousness of the righteous shall be upon himself, [d]and the
wickedness of the wicked shall be
upon himself.
21 "But [a]if a wicked man turns from
all his sins which he has committed,
keeps all My statutes, and does what
is lawful and right, he shall surely live;
he shall not die.
22 [a]"None of the transgressions which
he has committed shall be *remembered against him; because of the righteousness which he has done, he shall
[b]live.
23 [a]"Do I have any pleasure at all that
the wicked should die?" says the Lord
GOD, "*and* not that he should turn from
his ways and live?
24 "But [a]when a righteous man turns
away from his righteousness and commits iniquity, and does according to all
the abominations that the wicked *man*
does, shall he live? [b]All the righteousness which he has done shall not
be remembered; because of the
unfaithfulness of which he is guilty and
the sin which he has committed, because of them he shall die.
25 "Yet you say, [a]'The way of the Lord
is not fair.' Hear now, O house of Israel, is it not My way which is fair, and
your ways which are not fair?
26 [a]"When a righteous *man* turns
away from his righteousness, commits
iniquity, and dies in it, it is because of
the iniquity which he has done that he
dies.
27 "Again, [a]when a wicked *man* turns
away from the wickedness which he
committed, and does what is lawful
and right, he preserves himself alive.
28 "Because he [a]considers and turns
away from all the transgressions which
he committed, he shall surely live; he
shall not die.
29 [a]"Yet the house of Israel says, 'The
way of the Lord is not fair.' O house
of Israel, is it not My ways which are
fair, and your ways which are not fair?
30 [a]"Therefore I will judge you, O 4
house of Israel, every one according to
his ways," says the Lord GOD. [b]"Repent, and turn from all your transgressions, so that iniquity will not be your
ruin.
31 [a]"Cast away from you all the **transgressions** which you have committed,
and get yourselves a [b]new heart and
a new spirit. For why should you die,
O house of Israel?

WORD WEALTH

18:31 transgressions, *pesha'* (*peh*-shah); Strong's #6588: Rebellion, transgression, trespass. *Pesha'* comes from the verb *pasha'*, which means "to revolt, rebel, and trespass." Whether as noun or verb, a trespass had to do with revolting against law, God, or government, and was a transgressing, that is, going beyond established limits. "Rebellion," or "breaking out against," might also describe *pesha'*. Is. 53:5 shows that the Messiah was wounded on account of our transgressions (*pesha'*), and v. 12 shows Him interceding for transgressors (*pasha'*).

32 "For [a]I have no pleasure in the
death of one who dies," says the Lord
GOD. "Therefore turn and [b]live!"

Israel Degraded

CHAPTER 19

19 "Moreover [a]take up a lamentation for the princes of Israel,

18 [a]Ezek. 3:18 **19** [a]Ex. 20:5; Deut. 5:9; 2 Kin. 23:26; 24:3, 4 *See WW at Ps. 68:5. **20** [a]2 Kin. 14:6; 22:18–20; Ezek. 18:4 [b]Deut. 24:16; 2 Kin. 14:6; 2 Chr. 25:4; Jer. 31:29, 30 [c]1 Kin. 8:32; Is. 3:10, 11; [Matt. 16:27] [d]Rom. 2:6–9 **21** [a]Ezek. 18:27; 33:12, 19 **22** [a]Is. 43:25; Jer. 50:20; Ezek. 18:24; 33:16; Mic. 7:19 [b][Ps. 18:20–24] *See WW at Is. 62:6. **23** [a]Lam. 3:33; [Ezek. 18:32; 33:11; 1 Tim. 2:4; 2 Pet. 3:9] **24** [a]1 Sam. 15:11; 2 Chr. 24:2, 17–22; Ezek. 3:20; 18:26; 33:18 [b][2 Pet. 2:20] **25** [a]Ezek. 18:29; 33:17, 20; Mal. 2:17; 3:13–15

26 [a]Ezek. 18:24 **27** [a]Ezek. 18:21 **28** [a]Ezek. 18:14 **29** [a]Ezek. 18:25 **30** [a]Ezek. 7:3; 33:20 [b]Matt. 3:2; Rev. 2:5 **31** [a]Is. 1:16; 55:7; Eph. 4:22, 23 [b]Ps. 51:10; Jer. 32:39; Ezek. 11:19; 36:26 **32** [a]Lam. 3:33; Ezek. 33:11; [2 Pet. 3:9] [b][Prov. 4:2, 5, 6]

CHAPTER 19

1 [a]Ezek. 26:17; 27:2

18:19–32 A sinner who **turns from** his wicked way will **live** (v. 21), and **a righteous man** who **turns away** to iniquity will **die** (v. 24). Each person is judged by what is done. Therefore everyone is urged to **repent** (vv. 30, 32).
18:30–32 See section 4 of Truth-In-Action at the end of Ezek.
18:31 New heart and a new spirit: See note on 11:19.
19:1–14 An allegory in two parts (vv. 1–9; vv. 10–14) in the form of a lament, a measured format of three beats followed by two beats, used for funerals. Here Ezekiel uses it to predict the death of the nation of Israel, and it is placed here to follow the concluding words of ch. 18, "For I have no pleasure in the death of one who dies."

2 "and say:

'What *is* your mother? A lioness:
She lay down among the lions;
Among the young lions she
nourished her cubs.
3 She brought up one of her cubs,
And [a]he became a young lion;
He learned to catch prey,
And he devoured men.
4 The nations also heard of him;
He was trapped in their pit,
And they brought him with
chains to the land of [a]Egypt.

5 'When she saw that she *waited,
that her hope was lost,
She took [a]another of her cubs *and*
made him a young lion.
6 [a]He roved among the lions,
And [b]became a young lion;
He learned to catch prey;
He devoured men.
7 [1]He knew their desolate places,
And laid waste their cities;
The land with its fullness was
desolated
By the noise of his roaring.
8 [a]Then the nations set against him
from the provinces on every
side,
And spread their net over him;
[b]He was trapped in their pit.
9 [a]They put him in a cage with
[1]chains,
And brought him to the king of
Babylon;
They brought him in nets,
That his voice should no longer
be heard on [b]the mountains of
Israel.

10 'Your mother *was* [a]like a vine in
your [1]bloodline,
Planted by the waters,
[b]Fruitful and full of branches
Because of many waters.
11 She had strong branches for
scepters of rulers.
[a]She towered in stature above the
thick branches,
And was seen in her height amid
the [1]dense foliage.
12 But she was [a]plucked up in fury,
She was cast down to the ground,
And the [b]east wind dried her
fruit.
Her strong branches were broken
and withered;
The fire consumed them.
13 And now she *is* planted in the
wilderness,
In a dry and thirsty land.
14 [a]Fire has come out from a rod of
her branches
And devoured her fruit,
So that she has no strong
branch— a scepter for ruling.' "

[b]This *is* a lamentation, and has become a lamentation.

The Rebellions of Israel

20 It came to pass in the seventh
year, in the fifth *month*, on the
tenth *day* of the month, *that* [a]certain
of the elders of Israel came to inquire
of the LORD, and sat before me.
2 Then the word of the LORD came to
me, saying,
3 "Son of man, speak to the elders of
Israel, and say to them, 'Thus says the
Lord GOD: "Have you come to inquire
of Me? *As* I live," says the Lord GOD,
[a]"I will not be inquired of by you." '
4 "Will you judge them, son of man,
will you judge *them?* Then [a]make
known to them the abominations of
their fathers.
5 "Say to them, 'Thus says the Lord
GOD: "On the day when [a]I chose Israel
and raised My hand in an oath to the
descendants of the house of Jacob, and
made Myself [b]known to them in the
land of Egypt, I raised My hand in an
oath to them, saying, [c]'I *am* the LORD
your God.'
6 "On that day I raised My hand in
an oath to them, [a]to bring them out of
the land of Egypt into a land that I had
searched out for them, [b]'flowing with
milk and honey,' [c]the glory of all lands.
7 "Then I said to them, 'Each of you,
[a]throw away [b]the abominations which
are before his eyes, and do not defile

3 [a]Ezek. 19:2; 2 Kin. 23:31, 32
4 [a]2 Kin. 23:33, 34; 2 Chr. 36:4
5 [a]2 Kin. 23:34 *See WW at Mic. 7:7.
6 [a]2 Kin. 24:8, 9 [b]Ezek. 19:3
7 [1]LXX *He stood in insolence;* Tg. *He destroyed its palaces;* Vg. *He learned to make widows*
8 [a]2 Kin. 24:2, 11 [b]Ezek. 19:4
9 [a]2 Chr. 36:6; Jer. 22:18 [b]Ezek. 6:2 [1]Or *hooks*
10 [a]Ezek. 17:6 [b]Deut. 8:7–9 [1]Lit. *blood,* so with MT, Syr., Vg.; LXX *like a flower on a pomegranate tree;* Tg. *in your likeness*
11 [a]Ezek. 31:3; Dan. 4:11 [1]Or *many branches*
12 [a]Jer. 31:27, 28 [b]Ezek. 17:10; Hos. 13:5
14 [a]Judg. 9:15; 2 Kin. 24:20; Ezek. 17:18 [b]Lam. 2:5

CHAPTER 20

1 [a]Ezek. 8:1, 11, 12; 14:1
3 [a]Ezek. 7:26; 14:3
4 [a]Ezek. 16:2; 22:2; Matt. 23:32
5 [a]Ex. 6:6–8; Deut. 7:6 [b]Ex. 3:8; 4:31; Deut. 4:34 [c]Ex. 20:2
6 [a]Ex. 3:8, 17; Deut. 8:7–9; Jer. 32:22 [b]Ex. 3:8 [c]Ex. 3:8, 17; 13:5; 33:3; Ps. 48:2; Jer. 11:5; 32:22; Ezek. 20:15; Dan. 8:9; Zech. 7:14
7 [a]Ezek. 18:31 [b]2 Chr. 15:8

19:2 Lioness: It is not clear if the **mother** of the **cubs** is the nation, the city of Jerusalem, or Hamutal, the mother of both Jehoahaz and Zedekiah (see 2 Kin. 23:31; 24:18). In *vv. 10–14* the mother is the kingdom of Judah and perhaps should be here also.
19:3 One of her cubs: Jehoahaz. See 2 Kin. 23:31–34; Jer. 22:10–12.
19:5 Another of her cubs: Zedekiah. See 2 Kin. 24:17.
19:10 A vine: In v. 2 the mother was a lioness, here a vine. The lament emphasizes the death of the vine, Judah.
19:12 The east wind: See note on 17:10.
20:1–44 An overview of the history of Israel: her sin and rebellion (vv. 5–32); her restoration (vv. 33–44).
20:1 The date is August 14, 591 B.C. Jerusalem fell in 586 B.C.
20:5 Raised My hand: A symbolic gesture used when taking an oath (vv. 15, 23, 42; 36:7). **I *am* the LORD your God:** See vv. 19, 42, 44; Ex. 3:6, 14, 15.
20:6 Flowing with milk and honey: Refers to the lushness of the Promised Land.

yourselves with [c]the idols of Egypt. I
am the LORD your God.'
8 "But they rebelled against Me and
would not [1]obey Me. They did not all
cast away the abominations which
were before their eyes, nor did they
forsake the idols of Egypt. Then I said,
'I will [a]pour out My fury on them and
fulfill My anger against them in the
midst of the land of Egypt.'
9 [a]"But I acted for My name's sake,
that it should not be profaned before
the Gentiles among whom they *were*,
in whose sight I had made Myself
[b]known to them, to bring them out of
the land of Egypt.
10 "Therefore I [a]made them go out of
the land of Egypt and brought them
into the wilderness.
11 [a]"And I gave them My statutes and
[1]showed them My judgments, [b]'which,
if a man does, he shall live by them.'
12 "Moreover I also gave them My
[a]Sabbaths, to be a *sign between them
and Me, that they might know that I
am the LORD who sanctifies them.
13 "Yet the house of Israel [a]rebelled
against Me in the wilderness; they did
not walk in My statutes; they [b]despised
My judgments, [c]'which, *if* a man does,
he shall live by them'; and they greatly
[d]defiled My Sabbaths. Then I said I
would pour out My fury on them in the
[e]wilderness, to consume them.
14 [a]"But I acted for My name's sake,
that it should not be profaned before
the Gentiles, in whose sight I had
brought them out.
15 "So [a]I also raised My hand in an
oath to them in the wilderness, that I
would not bring them into the land
which I had given *them*, [b]'flowing with
milk and honey,' [c]the glory of all lands,
16 [a]"because they despised My judgments and did not walk in My statutes,
but profaned My Sabbaths; for [b]their
heart went after their idols.
17 [a]"Nevertheless My eye spared them
from destruction. I did not make an end
of them in the wilderness.
18 "But I said to their children in the
wilderness, 'Do not walk in the *statutes of your fathers, nor observe their
judgments, nor defile yourselves with
their idols.
19 'I *am* the LORD your God: [a]Walk in
My statutes, keep My judgments, and
do them;
20 [a]'hallow My Sabbaths, and they will

7 [c]Lev. 18:3
8 [a]Ezek. 7:8 [1]Lit. *listen to*
9 [a]Num. 14:13 [b]Josh. 2:10; 9:9, 10
10 [a]Ex. 13:18
11 [a]Neh. 9:13 [b]Lev. 18:5 [1]Lit. *made known to*
12 [a]Deut. 5:12 *See WW at Ps. 86:17.
13 [a]Num. 14:22 [b]Prov. 1:25 [c]Lev. 18:5 [d]Ex. 16:27 [e]Num. 14:29
14 [a]Ezek. 20:9, 20
15 [a]Num. 14:28 [b]Ex. 3:8 [c]Ezek. 20:6
16 [a]Ezek. 20:13, 24 [b]Amos 5:25
17 [a][Ps. 78:38]
18 *See WW at Neh. 9:13.
19 [a]Deut. 5:32
20 [a]Jer. 17:22
21 [a]Num. 25:1 [b]Lev. 18:5
22 [1]Refrained from judgment
23 [a]Lev. 26:33
24 [a]Ezek. 20:13, 16 [b]Ezek. 6:9 *See WW at Amos 2:4.
25 [a]Rom. 1:24
26 [a]Jer. 32:35 [b]Ezek. 6:7; 20:12, 20 [1]Lit. *that open the womb*
27 [a]Rom. 2:24
28 [a]Ezek. 6:13 [b]Ezek. 16:19
29 [1]Place for pagan worship [2]Lit. *High Place*
30 [a]Judg. 2:19 [b]Jer. 7:26; 16:12
31 [a]Ezek. 16:20; 20:26

be a sign between Me and you, that
you may know that I *am* the LORD your
God.'
21 "Notwithstanding, [a]the children rebelled against Me; they did not walk
in My statutes, and were not careful
to observe My judgments, [b]'which, *if*
a man does, he shall live by them'; but
they profaned My Sabbaths. Then I
said I would pour out My fury on them
and fulfill My anger against them in
the wilderness.
22 "Nevertheless I [1]withdrew My hand
and acted for My name's sake, that it
should not be profaned in the sight of
the Gentiles, in whose sight I had
brought them out.
23 "Also I raised My hand in an oath
to those in the wilderness, that [a]I
would scatter them among the Gentiles
and disperse them throughout the
countries,
24 [a]"because they had not executed
My judgments, but had *despised My
statutes, profaned My Sabbaths, and
[b]their eyes were fixed on their fathers'
idols.
25 "Therefore [a]I also gave them up to
statutes *that were* not good, and judgments by which they could not live;
26 "and I pronounced them unclean
because of their ritual gifts, in that they
caused all [1]their firstborn to pass
[a]through *the fire*, that I might make
them desolate and that they [b]might
know that I am the LORD." '
27 "Therefore, son of man, speak to
the house of Israel, and say to them,
'Thus says the Lord GOD: "In this too
your fathers have [a]blasphemed Me, by
being unfaithful to Me.
28 "When I brought them into the land
concerning which I had raised My
hand in an oath to give them, and
[a]they saw all the high hills and all the
thick trees, there they offered their sacrifices and provoked Me with their offerings. There they also sent up their
[b]sweet aroma and poured out their
drink offerings.
29 "Then I said to them, 'What *is* this
[1]high place to which you go?' So its
name is called [2]Bamah to this day." '
30 "Therefore say to the house of Israel, 'Thus says the Lord GOD: "Are
you defiling yourselves in the manner
of your [a]fathers, and committing harlotry according to their [b]abominations?
31 "For when you offer [a]your gifts and

20:8 Rebelled against Me . . . pour out My fury: See vv. 13, 21 and note on 7:8.

20:25, 26 The meaning of these very difficult verses is obscure. They are perhaps saying that due to Israel's continued rebellion, God **gave them up to statutes *that were* not good,** including the abominable practice of child sacrifice to Molech (see Rom. 1:24).

make your sons pass through the fire,
you defile yourselves with all your
idols, even to this day. So shall I be
inquired of by you, O house of Israel?
As I live," says the Lord GOD, "I will
[b]not be inquired of by you.
32 [a]"What you have in your mind shall
never be, when you say, 'We will be
like the Gentiles, like the *families in
other countries, serving wood and
stone.'

God Will Restore Israel

33 "*As* I live," says the Lord GOD,
"surely with a mighty hand, [a]with an
outstretched arm, and with fury poured
out, I will rule over you.
34 "I will bring you out from the peoples and gather you out of the countries where you are scattered, with a
mighty hand, with an outstretched
arm, and with fury poured out.
35 "And I will bring you into the wilderness of the peoples, and there [a]I
will plead My case with you face to
face.
36 [a]"Just as I pleaded My case with
your fathers in the wilderness of the
land of Egypt, so I will plead My case
with you," says the Lord GOD.
37 "I will make you [a]pass under the
rod, and I will bring you into the bond
of the [b]covenant;
38 [a]"I will purge the rebels from
among you, and those who transgress
against Me; I will bring them out of the
country where they dwell, but [b]they
shall not enter the land of Israel. Then
you will know that I *am* the LORD.
39 "As for you, O house of Israel," thus
says the Lord GOD: [a]"Go, serve every
one of you his idols—and hereafter—
if you will not obey Me; [b]but profane
My holy name no more with your gifts
and your idols.
40 "For [a]on My holy mountain, on the
mountain height of Israel," says the
Lord GOD, "there [b]all the house of Israel, all of them in the land, shall serve
Me; there [c]I will accept them, and there
I will require your offerings and the
firstfruits of your [1]sacrifices, together
with all your holy things.

31 [b]Ezek. 20.3
32 [a]Ezek. 11:5
*See WW at Gen. 12:3.
33 [a]Jer. 21:5
35 [a]Jer. 2:9, 35; Ezek. 17:20
36 [a]Num. 14:21–23, 28
37 [a]Lev. 27:32; Jer. 33:13 [b]Ps. 89:30–34; Ezek. 16:60, 62
38 [a]Ezek. 34:17; Amos 9:9, 10; Zech. 13:8, 9; [Mal. 3:3; 4:1–3; Matt. 25:32] [b]Jer. 44:14
39 [a]Judg. 10:14; Ps. 81:12; Amos 4:4 [b]Is. 1:13–15; Ezek. 23:38
40 [a]Is. 2:2, 3; Ezek. 17:23; Mic. 4:1 [b]Ezek. 37:22 [c]Is. 56:7; 60:7; Ezek. 43:27; Zech. 8:20–22; Mal. 3:4; [Rom. 12:1] [1]*offerings*
41 [a]Eph. 5:2; Phil. 4:18
42 [a]Ezek. 36:23; 38:23 [b]Ezek. 11:17; 34:13; 36:24
43 [a]Ezek. 16:61 [b]Lev. 26:39; Ezek. 6:9; Hos. 5:15 [1]Or *despise*
44 [a]Ezek. 24:24 [b]Ezek. 36:22
46 [a]Ezek. 21:2; Amos 7:16 [1]*proclaim*, lit. *drop* [2]Heb. *Negev*
47 [a]Is. 9:18, 19; Jer. 21:14 [b]Luke 23:31 [c]Ezek. 21:4
49 [a]Ezek. 12:9; 17:2; Matt. 13:13; John 16:25

CHAPTER 21

2 [a]Ezek. 20:46 [b]Amos 7:16 [1]*proclaim*, lit. *drop*

41 "I will accept you as a [a]sweet aroma
when I bring you out from the peoples
and gather you out of the countries
where you have been scattered; and I
will be hallowed in you before the Gentiles.
42 [a]"Then you shall know that I *am*
the LORD, [b]when I bring you into the
land of Israel, into the country *for*
which I raised My hand in an oath to
give to your fathers.
43 "And [a]there you shall remember
your ways and all your doings with
which you were defiled; and [b]you shall
[1]loathe yourselves in your own sight
because of all the evils that you have
committed.
44 [a]"Then you shall know that I *am*
the LORD, when I have dealt with you
[b]for My name's sake, not according to
your wicked ways nor according to
your corrupt doings, O house of Israel," says the Lord GOD.'"

Fire in the Forest

45 Furthermore the word of the LORD
came to me, saying,
46 [a]"Son of man, set your face toward
the south; [1]preach against the south
and prophesy against the forest land,
the [2]South,
47 "and say to the forest of the South,
'Hear the word of the LORD! Thus says
the Lord GOD: "Behold, [a]I will kindle
a fire in you, and it shall devour
[b]every green tree and every dry tree
in you; the blazing flame shall not be
quenched, and all faces [c]from the
south to the north shall be scorched by
it.
48 "All flesh shall see that I, the LORD,
have kindled it; it shall not be
quenched." ' "
49 Then I said, "Ah, Lord GOD! They
say of me, 'Does he not speak [a]par-
ables?' "

Babylon, the Sword of God

21 And the word of the LORD came
to me, saying,
2 [a]"Son of man, set your face toward
Jerusalem, [b]**preach**[1] against the holy

20:33–38 See note on 11:17–20.
20:33 A mighty hand, with an outstretched arm is familiar OT language (Ex. 6:6; Deut. 4:34; 5:15; 7:19; 26:8; Ps. 136:12) to describe God's immutable power.
20:37 Pass under the rod: The method used by the shepherd to count or separate his flock (see Jer. 33:13).
20:40–44 See note on 11:17–20.
20:44 This summary verse indicates that it is **for My name's sake** that Israel will be restored in spite of their **wicked ways** and **corrupt doings.** When God is finished they will know that He is **the LORD.**
20:46 The south: Judah and Jerusalem.
20:47 I will kindle a fire in you: Figurative language used for the destruction caused by an invading army. See 15:7; Is. 10:16–19; Jer. 15:14; 17:27; 21:14.
21:1–32 There are five oracles on the **sword** in this passage: vv. 3–7; vv. 8–17; vv. 18–24; vv. 25–27; vv. 28–32.

places, and prophesy against the land
of Israel;

WORD WEALTH

21:2 preach, *nataph* (nah-*tahf*); Strong's #5197: To drop down as water, to fall in drops; to flow, drip, ooze, distill, trickle; to cause words to flow. This verb occurs 18 times and refers to the dripping or flowing of water, rain, honey, myrrh, sweet wine, and words, especially words in a prophetic discourse. *Nataph* is here translated "preach," but actually means "drop your word." In Mic. 2:6, 11, *nataph* is translated "prophesy," or, "let your words flow."

3 "and say to the land of Israel, 'Thus
says the LORD: "Behold, I *am* [a]against
you, and I will draw My sword out of
its sheath and cut off both [b]righteous
and wicked from you.
4 "Because I will cut off both righteous and wicked from you, therefore
My sword shall go out of its sheath
against all flesh [a]from south *to* north,
5 "that all flesh may know that I, the
LORD, have drawn My sword out of its
sheath; it [a]shall not return anymore." '
6 [a]"Sigh therefore, son of man, with
[1]a breaking heart, and sigh with bitterness before their eyes.
7 "And it shall be when they say to
you, 'Why are you sighing?' that you
shall answer, 'Because of the news;
when it comes, every heart will melt,
[a]all hands will be feeble, every spirit
will faint, and all knees will be weak
as water. Behold, it is coming and shall
be brought to pass,' says the Lord
GOD."
8 Again the word of the LORD came
to me, saying,
9 "Son of man, prophesy and say,
'Thus says the LORD!' Say:

[a]'A sword, a sword is sharpened
And also polished!
10 Sharpened to make a dreadful
slaughter,
Polished to flash like lightning!
Should we then make mirth?
It despises the scepter of My son,
As it does all wood.

3 [a]Jer. 21:13; Ezek. 5:8; Nah. 2:13; 3:5 [b]Job 9:22
4 [a]Jer. 12:12; Ezek. 20:47
5 [a][Is. 45:23; 55:11]
6 [a]Is. 22:4; Jer. 4:19; Luke 19:41 [1]Emotional distress, lit. *the breaking of your loins*
7 [a]Ezek. 7:17
9 [a]Deut. 32:41; Ezek. 5:1; 21:15, 28
11 [a]Ezek. 21:19
12 [a]Jer. 31:19
13 [a]Job 9:23; 2 Cor. 8:2 [b]Ezek. 21:27
14 [a]Num. 24:10; Ezek. 6:11 [b]1 Kin. 20:30
15 [a]Ezek. 21:10, 28
16 [a]Ezek. 14:17 [1]Lit. *Sharpen yourself!* or *Unite yourself!* [2]Lit. *face*
17 [a]Ezek. 22:13 [b]Ezek. 5:13; 16:42; 24:13

11 And He has given it to be
polished,
That it may be handled;
This sword is sharpened, and it
is polished
To be given into the hand of
[a]the slayer.'

12 "Cry and wail, son of man;
For it will be against My people,
Against all the princes of Israel.
Terrors including the sword will
be against My people;
Therefore [a]strike *your* thigh.

13 "Because *it is* [a]a testing,
And what if *the sword* despises
even the scepter?
[b]*The scepter* shall be no *more,*"

says the Lord GOD.

14 "You therefore, son of man,
prophesy,
And [a]strike *your* hands together.
The third time let the sword do
double *damage.*
It *is* the sword *that* slays,
The sword that slays the great
men,
That enters their [b]private
chambers.
15 I have set the point of the sword
against all their gates,
That the heart may melt and
many may stumble.
Ah! [a]*It is* made bright;
It is grasped for slaughter:

16 "Swords[a1] at the ready!
Thrust right!
Set your blade!
Thrust left—
Wherever your [2]edge is ordered!

17 "I also will [a]beat My fists together,
And [b]I will cause My fury to rest;
I, the LORD, have spoken."

18 The word of the LORD came to me
again, saying:
19 "And son of man, appoint for yourself two ways for the sword of the king
of Babylon to go; both of them shall
go from the same land. Make a sign;

21:3 Draw My sword: The sword here refers to Nebuchadnezzar and Babylonia (see v. 19). **Both righteous and wicked** will suffer in Jerusalem's destruction; no one will escape.
21:6 Sigh: The pronouncement includes a symbolic act to stress the bitterness of grief that will accompany the judgment (v. 7). See vv. 12, 14 and note on 6:11.
21:8–17 A song of the **sword** that is **sharpened** and **polished** (v. 9) and **given into the hand of the slayer.** The sword is used against the **people** and **the princes of Israel.**
21:12 Cry and wail and **strike *your* thigh** are both signs of mourning and are used as symbolic acts to accompany the prophecy (see v. 6).
21:14 Strike *your* hands together: See v. 17 and note on 6:11.
21:17 Beat my fists together: God does exactly what He commands Ezekiel to do (v. 14).

put *it* at the head of the road to the
city.
20 "Appoint a road for the sword to
go to [a]Rabbah of the Ammonites, and
to Judah, into fortified Jerusalem.
21 "For the king of Babylon stands at
the parting of the road, at the fork of
the two roads, to use divination: he
shakes the arrows, he consults the
[1]images, he looks at the liver.
22 "In his right hand is the divination
for Jerusalem: to set up battering rams,
to call for a slaughter, to [a]lift the voice
with *shouting, [b]to set battering rams
against the gates, to heap up a *siege*
mound, and to build a wall.
23 "And it will be to them like a false
divination in the eyes of those who
[a]have *sworn oaths with them; but he
will bring their iniquity to remembrance, that they may be taken.
24 "Therefore thus says the Lord GOD:
'Because you have made your iniquity
to be remembered, in that your transgressions are uncovered, so that in all
your doings your sins appear—because
you have come to remembrance, you
shall be taken in hand.
25 'Now to you, O [a]profane, wicked
prince of Israel, [b]whose day has come,
whose iniquity *shall* end,
26 'thus says the Lord GOD:

"Remove the turban, and take off
the crown;
Nothing *shall remain* the same.
[a]Exalt the humble, and humble the
exalted.
27 [1]Overthrown, overthrown,
I will make it overthrown!
[a]It shall be no *longer*,
Until He comes whose right it is,
And I will give it *to* [b]*Him*." '

A Sword Against the Ammonites

28 "And you, son of man, prophesy
and say, 'Thus says the Lord GOD
[a]concerning the Ammonites and concerning their reproach,' and say:

'A sword, a sword *is* drawn,
Polished for slaughter,
For consuming, for flashing—
29 While they [a]see false visions for
you,
While they divine a lie to you,
To bring you on the necks of the
wicked, the slain
[b]Whose day has come,
Whose iniquity *shall* end.

30 'Return[a] *it* to its sheath.
[b]I will judge you
In the place where you were
created,
[c]In the land of your [1]nativity.
31 I will [a]pour out My indignation
on you;
I will [b]blow against you with the
fire of My wrath,
And deliver you into the hands of
brutal men *who are* skillful to
[c]destroy.
32 You shall be fuel for the fire;
Your blood shall be in the midst
of the land.
[a]You shall not be remembered,
For I the LORD have spoken.' "

Sins of Jerusalem

22 Moreover the word of the LORD
came to me, saying,
2 "Now, son of man, [a]will you judge,
will you judge [b]the bloody city? Yes,
show her all her abominations!
3 "Then say, 'Thus says the Lord
GOD: "The city sheds [a]blood in her own
midst, that her time may come; and she
makes idols within herself to defile
herself.
4 "You have *become guilty by the
blood which you have [a]shed, and have
defiled yourself with the idols which
you have made. You have caused your

20 [a]Deut. 3:11; Jer. 49:2; Ezek. 25:5; Amos 1:14
21 [1]Heb. *teraphim*
22 [a]Jer. 51:14 [b]Ezek. 4:2 *See WW at Ezra 3:11.
23 [a]Ezek. 17:16, 18 *See WW at Gen. 26:3.
25 [a]2 Chr. 36:13; Jer. 52:2; Ezek. 12:10; 17:19 [b]Ezek. 21:29
26 [a]Luke 1:52
27 [a]Gen. 49:10; [Luke 1:32, 33; John 1:49] [b]Ps. 2:6; 72:7, 10; [Jer. 23:5, 6; Ezek. 34:24; 37:24] [1]Or *Distortion, Ruin*
28 [a]Jer. 25:21; 49:1–6; Ezek. 25:1–7; Amos 1:13; Zeph. 2:8–11
29 [a]Jer. 27:9; Ezek. 12:24; 13:6–9; 22:28 [b]Job 18:20; Ps. 37:17; Is. 10:3; Ezek. 7:2, 3, 7
30 [a]Jer. 47:6, 7 [b]Gen. 15:14 [c]Ezek. 16:3 [1]Or *origin*
31 [a]Ezek. 7:8 [b]Ps. 18:15; Is. 30:33; Ezek. 22:20, 21; Hag. 1:9 [c]Jer. 6:22, 23; 51:20, 21; Hab. 1:6–10
32 [a]Ezek. 25:10

CHAPTER 22

2 [a]Ezek. 20:4 [b]Nah. 3:1
3 [a]Ezek. 24:6, 7
4 [a]2 Kin. 21:16; Ezek. 24:7, 8 *See WW at Lev. 4:13.

21:19, 20 Two ways for the sword: Nebuchadnezzar, the **king of Babylon,** must choose his direction at the fork in the road, and it is Ezekiel's task to put up signs to guide him. One road leads to **Rabbah of the Ammonites** and the other to **Judah** (v. 20).

21:21 Divination: Three methods to determine the will of Nebuchadnezzar's gods are mentioned: shaking **the arrows** (similar to drawing straws, but here the names of the places are written on the arrows and are drawn from the quiver), consulting **images** or teraphim (consulting such "gods" is mentioned in Hos. 3:4 and Zech. 10:2, but the method used is unclear), and looking **at the liver** (hepatoscopy, the examination of the configurations and markings of sheep livers, a common practice in ancient Babylonia).

21:25 Prince of Israel: King Zedekiah.

21:26 Turban: Usually worn by the priest, this is its only mention as royal headgear. This would serve as a base for the **crown.**

21:27 Overthrown: The threefold use is for emphasis. See note on Jer. 7:4. **Until He comes** is perhaps a reference to the messianic allusion in Gen. 49:10.

21:28–32 With similar phraseology (vv. 8–10), Ezekiel declares that the Ammonites will suffer the same fate as Judah (see 25:1–7). This is part of God's judgment on Israel's enemies (see note on Zech. 12:1–9) and may have had an immediate reference to the Ammonites' plundering Judah after Jerusalem's downfall.

22:2 The bloody city: Jerusalem.

22:3 Two types of sins are stressed: social injustice (expressed by the **blood** shed in her midst) and idolatry (the making of **idols**).

days to draw near, and have come to
the end of your years; [b]therefore I have
made you a reproach to the nations,
and a mockery to all countries.
5 "*Those* near and *those* far from you
will mock you as [1]infamous *and* full
of tumult.
6 "Look, [a]the princes of Israel: each
one has used his [1]power to shed blood
in you.
7 "In you they have [a]made light of father and mother; in your midst they
have [b]oppressed the stranger; in you
they have mistreated the [1]fatherless
and the widow.
8 "You have despised My holy things
and [a]profaned My Sabbaths.
9 "In you are [a]men who slander to
cause bloodshed; [b]in you are those
who eat on the mountains; in your
midst they commit lewdness.
10 "In you men [a]uncover their fathers'
nakedness; in you they violate women
who are [b]set apart during their impurity.
11 "One commits abomination [a]with
his neighbor's wife; [b]another lewdly
defiles his daughter-in-law; and another in you violates his sister, his father's [c]daughter.
12 "In you [a]they take bribes to shed
blood; [b]you take usury and increase;
you have made profit from your neighbors by extortion, and [c]have forgotten
Me," says the Lord GOD.
13 "Behold, therefore, I [a]beat My fists
at the dishonest profit which you have
made, and at the bloodshed which has
been in your midst.
14 [a]"Can your heart endure, or can
your hands remain strong, in the days
when I shall deal with you? [b]I, the
LORD, have spoken, and will do *it*.
15 [a]"I will scatter you among the nations, disperse you throughout the
countries, and [b]remove your filthiness
completely from you.
16 "You shall defile yourself in the
sight of the nations; then [a]you shall
know that I *am* the LORD." ' "

Israel in the Furnace

17 The word of the LORD came to me,
saying,
18 "Son of man, [a]the house of Israel
has become dross to Me; they *are* all
bronze, tin, iron, and lead, in the midst
of a [b]furnace; they have become dross
from silver.
19 "Therefore thus says the Lord GOD:
'Because you have all become dross,
therefore behold, I will gather you into
the midst of Jerusalem.
20 '*As men* gather silver, bronze, iron,
lead, and tin into the midst of a furnace, to blow fire on it, to [a]melt *it;* so
I will gather *you* in My anger and in
My fury, and I will leave *you there* and
melt you.
21 'Yes, I will gather you and blow on
you with the fire of My wrath, and you
shall be melted in its midst.
22 'As silver is melted in the midst of
a furnace, so shall you be melted in
its midst; then you shall know that I,
the LORD, have [a]poured out My fury
on you.' "

Israel's Wicked Leaders

23 And the word of the LORD came to
me, saying,
24 "Son of man, say to her: 'You *are*
a land that is [a]not [1]cleansed* or rained
on in the day of indignation.'
25 [a]"The conspiracy of her [1]prophets
in her midst is like a roaring lion tearing the prey; they [b]have devoured [2]peo-
ple; [c]they have taken treasure and precious things; they have made many
widows in her midst.
26 [a]"Her priests have [1]violated My law
and [b]profaned My holy things; they
have not [c]distinguished between the
holy and unholy, nor have they made
known *the difference* between the *unclean and the clean; and they have hidden their eyes from My Sabbaths, so
that I am profaned among them.
27 "Her [a]princes in her midst *are* like
wolves tearing the prey, to shed blood,
to destroy [1]people, and to get dishonest
gain.
28 [a]"Her prophets plastered them with
untempered *mortar,* [b]seeing false visions, and divining [c]lies for them, saying, 'Thus says the Lord GOD,' when
the LORD had not spoken.
29 "The people of the land have used
oppressions, committed robbery, and
mistreated the poor and needy; and

4 [b]Deut. 28:37
5 [1]Lit. *defiled of name*
6 [a]Is. 1:23 [1]Lit. *arm*
7 [a]Lev. 20:9 [b]Ex. 22:22 [1]Lit. *orphan*
8 [a]Lev. 19:30
9 [a]Lev. 19:16 [b]Ezek. 18:6, 11
10 [a]Lev. 18:7, 8 [b]Lev. 18:19; 20:18
11 [a]Ezek. 18:11 [b]Lev. 18:15 [c]Lev. 18:9
12 [a]Ex. 23:8 [b]Ex. 22:25 [c]Ezek. 23:35
13 [a]Ezek. 21:17
14 [a]Ezek. 21:7 [b]Ezek. 17:24
15 [a]Deut. 4:27 [b]Ezek. 23:27, 48
16 [a]Ps. 9:16
18 [a]Is. 1:22 [b]Prov. 17:3
20 [a]Is. 1:25
22 [a]Ezek. 20:8, 33
24 [a]Ezek. 24:13 [1]So with MT, Syr., Vg.; LXX *showered upon* *See WW at Lev. 14:31.
25 [a]Hos. 6:9 [b]Matt. 23:14 [c]Mic. 3:11 [1]So with MT, Vg.; LXX *princes;* Tg. *scribes* [2]Lit. *souls*
26 [a]Mal. 2:8 [b]1 Sam. 2:29 [c]Lev. 10:10 [1]Lit. *done violence to* *See WW at Lev. 10:10.
27 [a]Is. 1:23 [1]Lit. *souls*
28 [a]Ezek. 13:10 [b]Ezek. 13:6, 7 [c]Jer. 23:25–32

22:7 The **stranger,** the **fatherless,** and the **widow** are high on God's social agenda. See Jer. 5:28 and 7:6.

22:8 My Sabbaths: The Sabbath was given as a sign to Israel (20:12), and its observance was considered as important as the keeping of any of the laws (see Jer. 17:19–27).

22:18 Dross from silver: Jerusalem is described as a furnace also in Is. 1:21–26 and Jer. 6:27–30. The people are depicted as the worthless residue left over in the smelting process after the desired metal is extracted; nothing is left to be refined.

22:23–31 All classes of society are singled out for punishment: **her prophets, her priests, her princes,** and **the people of the land.**

they wrongfully [a]oppress the stranger.
30 [a]"So I sought for a man among
them who would [b]make a wall, and
[c]stand in the **gap** before Me on behalf
of the land, that I should not destroy
it; but I found no one.

WORD WEALTH

22:30 gap, *perets* (*peh*-rets); Strong's #6556: A break, gap, or breach; especially a gap in a wall. *Perets* comes from the verb *parats,* "to break forth, break open, or break down." *Perets* occurs about 25 times. Two verses (Is. 58:12; Amos 9:11) show that gaps or breaches need to be repaired; the former verse refers to the physical and spiritual ruins of Zion, and the latter to the tabernacle of David. In the present reference, standing in the gap is a metaphor for committed intercession. There is a gap between God and man that an intercessor tries to repair.

KINGDOM DYNAMICS

22:30 Intercession in Spiritual Warfare, FAITH'S WARFARE. It is a sad day in Israel's history when God commands Ezekiel to prophesy against the sins of Jerusalem, declaring He has no choice but to judge the land. This chapter describes this condition that deteriorates so shamefully that God finally cries, "Enough!" Then God makes a startling declaration: this could have been avoided if only one intercessor had stood before Him on behalf of the land. He says succinctly, "I sought for a man!"

The text says, "I sought for a man . . . who would . . . stand . . . before Me on behalf of." This clearly identifies this passage with intercession. No single phrase in Scripture more accurately describes the work of an intercessor than the phrase "stand before Me on behalf of." The intercessor always comes "before God" on "behalf of" others.

Also significant is the intercessor's twofold responsibility. Not only would he "make a wall," which suggests he would restore a breach caused by an enemy, but he would "stand in the gap," or plug up that breach against that enemy throughout the building process.

(Acts 6:1–4/Ps. 5:1–3) D.E.

KINGDOM DYNAMICS

22:30 Intercessors Link God's Mercy with Human Need, PRAYER. In Ezekiel's day, Judah was all that remained of God's vineyard, His chosen people. The idolatrous kingdom of Israel had been destroyed and its people exiled under the Assyrian ruler Sargon in 722 B.C. Now, almost a century and a half later, sin had made a horrendous gap in Judah's protective wall. A "gap" was a break in the protective thorny hedge or wall of stones that surrounded a vineyard and invited trouble. To bar intruders, someone had to stand guard until the gap could be repaired. Therefore, the Word employs this figure of speech to describe God's search for an intercessor among Judah's priests, prophets, princes, or people—for those who would stand in the gap, linking God's mercy with man's need. In our day, the protective hedge about families, churches, and nations is often in a state of terrible disrepair. God is still searching for intercessors to stand guard "in the gap" and by prayer to help repair the breaches.

(Is. 36:1—37:40/Eph. 3:14–21) L.L.

31 "Therefore I have [a]poured out My
indignation on them; I have consumed
them with the fire of My wrath; and I
have recompensed [b]their deeds on
their own heads," says the Lord GOD.

Two Harlot Sisters

23 The word of the LORD came
again to me, saying:

2 "Son of man, there were [a]two
women,
The daughters of one mother.
3 [a]They committed harlotry in
Egypt,
They committed harlotry in
[b]their youth;
Their breasts were there
embraced,
Their virgin bosom was there
pressed.
4 Their names: [1]Oholah the elder
and [2]Oholibah [a]her sister;
[b]They were Mine,
And they bore sons and
daughters.
As for their names,
Samaria *is* Oholah, and
Jerusalem *is* Oholibah.

The Older Sister, Samaria

5 "Oholah played the harlot even
though she was Mine;

29 [a]Ex. 23:9; Lev. 19:33
30 [a]Is. 59:16; 63:5; Jer. 5:1 [b]Ezek. 13:5 [c]Ps. 106:23; Jer. 15:1
31 [a]Ezek. 22:22 [b]Ezek. 9:10; [Rom. 2:8, 9]

CHAPTER 23

2 [a]Jer. 3:7, 8; Ezek. 16:44–46
3 [a]Lev. 17:7; Josh. 24:14; Jer. 3:9 [b]Ezek. 16:22
4 [a]Jer. 3:6, 7 [b]Ezek. 16:8, 20 [1]Lit. *Her Own Tabernacle* [2]Lit. *My Tabernacle Is in Her*

22:30 I sought for a man: See Is. 59:16; 63:5. Probably not just any man, but rather a king who would lead the people in righteousness.

23:1–49 An allegory of the two sisters, **Oholah** (Samaria) and **Oholibah** (Jerusalem), with an emphasis on the unfaithfulness of Israel in relation to other nations.

23:4 Oholah means "Her Own Tabernacle," and **Oholibah** means "My Tabernacle Is in Her."

23:5–10 Oholah played the harlot (entered into political alliance) when several of her kings paid tribute to Assyria:

And she lusted for her lovers, the
neighboring [a]Assyrians,
6 *Who were* clothed in purple,
Captains and rulers,
All of them desirable young men,
Horsemen riding on horses.
7 Thus she committed her harlotry
with them,
All of them choice men of
Assyria;
And with all for whom she lusted,
With all their idols, she defiled
herself.
8 She has never given up her
harlotry *brought* [a]from Egypt,
For in her youth they had lain
with her,
Pressed her virgin bosom,
And poured out their immorality
upon her.

9 "Therefore I have delivered her
Into the hand of her lovers,
Into the hand of the [a]Assyrians,
For whom she lusted.
10 They uncovered her nakedness,
Took away her sons and
daughters,
And slew her with the sword;
She became a byword among
women,
For they had executed judgment
on her.

The Younger Sister, Jerusalem

11 "Now [a]although her sister Oholibah
saw *this,* [b]she became more corrupt in
her lust than she, and in her harlotry
more corrupt than her sister's harlotry.

12 "She lusted for the neighboring
[a]Assyrians,
[b]Captains and rulers,
Clothed most gorgeously,
Horsemen riding on horses,
All of them desirable young men.
13 Then I saw that she was defiled;
Both *took* the same way.
14 But she increased her harlotry;
She looked at men portrayed on
the wall,
Images of [a]Chaldeans portrayed
in vermilion,

5 [a]2 Kin. 15:19; 16:7; 17:3; Ezek. 16:28; Hos. 5:13; 8:9, 10
8 [a]Ex. 32:4; 1 Kin. 12:28; 2 Kin. 10:29; 17:16; Ezek. 23:3, 19
9 [a]2 Kin. 17:3
11 [a]Jer. 3:8 [b]Jer. 3:8–11; Ezek. 16:51, 52
12 [a]2 Kin. 16:7, 8; Ezek. 16:28 [b]Ezek. 23:6, 23
14 [a]Jer. 50:2; Ezek. 8:10; 16:29
16 [a]2 Kin. 24:1 [b]Is. 57:9
17 [a]Ezek. 23:22, 28 [1]Lit. *sons of Babel*
18 [a]Jer. 6:8 [b]Ps. 78:59; 106:40; Jer. 12:8
19 [a]Lev. 18:3; Ezek. 23:2
20 [1]Illicit lovers
21 [a]Ezek. 16:26
22 [a]Ezek. 16:37–41; 23:28

15 Girded with belts around their
waists,
Flowing turbans on their heads,
All of them looking like captains,
In the manner of the Babylonians
of Chaldea,
The land of their nativity.
16 [a]As soon as her eyes saw them,
She lusted for them
And sent [b]messengers to them in
Chaldea.

17 "Then the [1]Babylonians came to
her, into the bed of love,
And they defiled her with their
immorality;
So she was defiled by them, [a]and alienated herself from
them.
18 She revealed her harlotry and
uncovered her nakedness.
Then [a]I [b]alienated Myself from
her,
As I had alienated Myself from
her sister.

19 "Yet she multiplied her harlotry
In calling to remembrance the
days of her youth,
[a]When she had played the harlot
in the land of Egypt.
20 For she lusted for her
[1]paramours,
Whose flesh *is like* the flesh of
donkeys,
And whose issue *is like* the issue
of horses.
21 Thus you called to remembrance
the lewdness of your youth,
When the [a]Egyptians pressed
your bosom
Because of your youthful breasts.

Judgment on Jerusalem

22 "Therefore, Oholibah, thus says the
Lord GOD:

[a]'Behold, I will stir up your lovers
against you,
From whom you have alienated
yourself,
And I will bring them against you
from every side:

Jehu to Shalmaneser III; Jehoahaz to Adad-Nirari; Menahem to Tiglath-Pileser (2 Kin. 15:19–29); and Hoshea to Shalmaneser V (2 Kin. 17:1–14).

23:6 Clothed in purple: The Assyrian army was dressed in purple (or blue) uniforms.

23:10 Uncovered her nakedness: The Assyrians captured Samaria in 722 B.C. and took the people into exile.

23:11–21 The younger **sister, Oholibah,** was worse than her older sister Oholah. She entered into political alliance with Assyria (v. 12) and **Chaldea** (vv. 14–17), just as she had done earlier with **Egypt** (vv. 19–21). Examples of political alliances with Assyria are: Ahaz and Tiglath-Pileser III (2 Kin. 16:7–9); Hezekiah and Sennacherib (2 Kin. 18:1–36); and Manasseh and Esarhaddon. Examples with Chaldea or Babylon are: Hezekiah and the envoys of Merodach-Baladan of Babylon (2 Kin. 20:12–21); Jehoiakim and Zedekiah both served Nebuchadnezzar (2 Kin. 24:1, 17).

23:14 Portrayed in vermilion: The Babylonian soldiers were dressed in vermilion (or red) uniforms.

23 The Babylonians,
All the Chaldeans,
[a]Pekod, Shoa, Koa,
[b]All the Assyrians with them,
All of them desirable young men,
Governors and rulers,
Captains and men of renown,
All of them riding on horses.
24 And they shall come against you
With chariots, wagons, and war-horses,
With a *horde of people.
They shall array against you
Buckler, shield, and helmet all around.

'I will delegate judgment to them,
And they shall judge you according to their judgments.
25 I will set My [a]jealousy against you,
And they shall deal furiously with you;
They shall remove your nose and your ears,
And your remnant shall fall by the sword;
They shall take your sons and your daughters,
And your remnant shall be devoured by fire.
26 [a]They shall also strip you of your clothes
And take away your beautiful jewelry.

27 'Thus [a]I will make you cease your lewdness and your [b]harlotry
Brought from the land of Egypt,
So that you will not lift your eyes to them,
Nor remember Egypt anymore.'

28 "For thus says the Lord GOD:
'Surely I will deliver you into the hand
of [a]those you hate, into the hand *of*
those [b]from whom you alienated yourself.
29 [a]'They will deal hatefully with you,
take away all you have worked for, and
[b]leave you naked and bare. The nakedness of your harlotry shall be uncovered, both your lewdness and your harlotry.
30 'I will do these *things* to you because you have [a]gone as a harlot after
the Gentiles, because you have become
defiled by their idols.
31 'You have walked in the way of
your sister; therefore I will put her
[a]cup in your hand.'
32 "Thus says the Lord GOD:

'You shall drink of your sister's cup,
The deep and wide one;
[a]You shall be laughed to scorn
And held in derision;
It contains much.
33 You will be filled with drunkenness and sorrow,
The cup of horror and desolation,
The cup of your sister Samaria.
34 You shall [a]drink and drain it,
You shall break its [1]shards,
And tear at your own breasts;
For I have spoken,'
Says the Lord GOD.

35 "Therefore thus says the Lord GOD:

'Because you [a]have forgotten Me
and [b]cast Me behind your back,
Therefore you shall bear the *penalty*
Of your lewdness and your harlotry.' "

Both Sisters Judged

36 The LORD also said to me: "Son of
man, will you [a]judge Oholah and
Oholibah? Then [b]declare to them their
abominations.
37 "For they have committed adultery,
and [a]blood *is* on their hands. They
have committed adultery with their
idols, and even sacrificed their sons
[b]whom they bore to Me, passing them
through *the fire,* to devour *them.*
38 "Moreover they have done this to
Me: They have [a]defiled My sanctuary
on the same day and [b]profaned My
Sabbaths.
39 "For after they had slain their children for their idols, on the same day
they came into My sanctuary to profane it; and indeed [a]thus they have
done in the midst of My house.
40 "Furthermore you sent for men to
come from afar, [a]to whom a messenger
was sent; and there they came. And

23 [a]Jer. 50:21 [b]Ezek. 23:12
24 *See WW at Lev. 16:17.
25 [a]Ex. 34:14; Ezek. 5:13; 8:17, 18; Zeph. 1:18
26 [a]Is. 3:18–23; Ezek. 16:39
27 [a]Ezek. 16:41; 22:15 [b]Ezek. 23:3, 19
28 [a]Jer. 21:7–10; Ezek.16:37–41 [b]Ezek. 23:17
29 [a]Deut. 28:48; Ezek. 23:25, 26, 45–47 [b]Ezek. 16:39
30 [a]Ezek. 6:9
31 [a]2 Kin. 21:13; Jer. 7:14, 15; 25:15; Ezek. 23:33
32 [a]Ezek. 22:4, 5
34 [a]Ps. 75:8; Is. 51:17
[1]Earthenware fragments
35 [a]Is. 17:10; Jer. 3:21; Ezek. 22:12; Hos. 8:14; 13:6 [b]1 Kin. 14:9; Jer. 2:27; 32:33; Neh. 9:26
36 [a]Jer. 1:10; Ezek. 20:4; 22:2 [b]Is. 58:1; Ezek. 16:2; Mic. 3:8
37 [a]Ezek. 16:38 [b]Ezek. 16:20, 21, 36, 45; 20:26, 31
38 [a]2 Kin. 21:4, 7; Ezek. 5:11; 7:20 [b]Ezek. 22:8
39 [a]2 Kin. 21:2–8
40 [a]Is. 57:9

23:23 Pekod, Shoa, Koa *were perhaps* famous Chaldean *leaders.*
23:25 Remove your nose and your ears: Mutilation was a common practice in Mesopotamia especially as punishment to an adulteress.
23:30 The Gentiles: Or, "the nations."
23:31 The **cup** of God's wrath brings judgment and causes men to stagger and go mad. It is a symbol of God's compelling man to experience the harvest of all his deeds. See Ps. 75:8; Is. 51:17, 22; Jer. 25:15–17.
23:39 On the same day . . . profane it: They worshiped in the temple on the same day they sacrificed their children to Molech, thus putting God and Molech on the same level.

you [b]washed yourself for them,
[c]painted your eyes, and adorned yourself with ornaments.
41 "You sat on a stately [a]couch, with
a table prepared before it, [b]on which
you had set My incense and My oil.
42 "The sound of a carefree multitude
was with her, and [1]Sabeans *were*
brought from the wilderness with men
of the common sort, who put bracelets
on their [2]wrists and beautiful crowns
on their heads.
43 "Then I said concerning *her who
had grown* old in adulteries, 'Will they
commit harlotry with her now, and she
with them?'
44 "Yet they went in to her, as men
go in to a woman who plays the harlot;
thus they went in to Oholah and Oholibah, the lewd women.
45 "But righteous men will [a]judge
them after the manner of adulteresses,
and after the manner of women who
shed blood, because they *are* adulteresses, and [b]blood *is* on their hands.
46 "For thus says the Lord GOD:
[a]'Bring up an assembly against them,
give them up to trouble and plunder.
47 [a]'The assembly shall stone them
with stones and [1]execute them with
their swords; [b]they shall slay their
sons and their daughters, and burn
their houses with fire.
48 'Thus [a]I will cause lewdness to
cease from the land, [b]that all women
may be taught not to practice your
lewdness.
49 'They shall repay you for your lewdness, and you shall [a]pay for your
idolatrous sins. [b]Then you shall know
that I *am* the Lord GOD.' "

Symbol of the Cooking Pot

24 Again, in the ninth year, in the
tenth month, on the tenth *day*
of the month, the word of the LORD
came to me, saying,
2 "Son of man, write down the name
of the day, this very day—the king of
Babylon started his siege against Jerusalem [a]this very day.
3 [a]"And utter a parable to the rebellious house, and say to them, 'Thus
says the Lord GOD:

40 [b]Ruth 3:3 [c]2 Kin. 9:30; Jer. 4:30
41 [a]Esth. 1:6; Is. 57:7; Amos 2:8; 6:4 [b]Prov. 7:17; Ezek. 16:18, 19; Hos. 2:8
42 [1]Or *drunkards* [2]Lit. *hands*
45 [a]Ezek. 16:38 [b]Ezek. 23:37
46 [a]Ezek. 16:40
47 [a]Lev. 20:10; Ezek. 16:40 [b]2 Chr. 36:17, 19; Ezek. 24:21 [1]Lit. *cut down*
48 [a]Ezek. 22:15 [b]Deut. 13:11; Ezek. 22:15; 2 Pet. 2:6
49 [a]Is. 59:18; Ezek. 23:35 [b]Ezek. 20:38, 42, 44; 25:5

CHAPTER 24

2 [a]2 Kin. 25:1; Jer. 39:1; 52:4
3 [a]Ezek. 17:12 [b]Jer. 1:13; Ezek. 11:3
4 [1]Lit. *bones*
6 [a]2 Kin. 24:3, 4; Ezek. 22:2, 3, 27; Mic. 7:2; Nah. 3:1 [b]2 Sam. 8:2; Joel 3:3; Obad. 11; Nah. 3:10
7 [a]Lev. 17:13; Deut. 12:16
8 [a][Matt. 7:2]
9 [a]Ezek. 24:6; Nah. 3:1; Hab. 2:12
10 [1]Lit. *bones*
11 [a]Ezek. 22:15
12 [1]Or *wearied Me* [2]Or *toil*
13 [a]Ezek. 23:36–48

[b]"Put on a pot, set *it* on,
And also pour water into it.
4 Gather pieces *of meat* in it,
Every good piece,
The thigh and the shoulder.
Fill *it* with choice [1]cuts;
5 Take the choice of the flock.
Also pile *fuel* bones under it,
Make it boil well,
And let the cuts simmer in it."

6 'Therefore thus says the Lord GOD:

"Woe to [a]the bloody city,
To the pot whose scum *is* in it,
And whose scum is not gone from
it!
Bring it out piece by piece,
On which no [b]lot has fallen.
7 For her blood is in her midst;
She set it on top of a rock;
[a]She did not pour it on the ground,
To cover it with dust.
8 That it may raise up fury and take
vengeance,
[a]I have set her blood on top of a
rock,
That it may not be covered."

9 'Therefore thus says the Lord GOD:

[a]"Woe to the bloody city!
I too will make the pyre great.
10 Heap on the wood,
Kindle the fire;
Cook the meat well,
Mix in the spices,
And let the [1]cuts be burned up.

11 "Then set the pot empty on the
coals,
That it may become hot and its
bronze may burn,
That [a]its filthiness may be melted
in it,
That its scum may be consumed.
12 She has [1]grown weary with
[2]lies,
And her great scum has not gone
from her.
Let her scum *be* in the fire!
13 In your [a]filthiness *is* lewdness.
Because I have cleansed you, and
you were not cleansed,

24:1–14 Ezekiel reaches his climax in justifying Jerusalem's coming judgment. The poetic allegory of a **pot** set on fire symbolizes the siege (vv. 3–5). The prose interpretation (vv. 6–14) specifies Jerusalem's woe.
24:1 The date given is January 15, 588 B.C., the day Nebuchadnezzar began the siege of Jerusalem (v. 2).
24:3–5 The **pot** is Jerusalem, the ***meat*** her inhabitants and the ***fuel*** Nebuchadnezzar's siege. Similar imagery with a different interpretation was used in 11:3, 7, 11.
24:6 The "choice cuts" (v. 4) are here termed **scum,** indicating the inhabitants' actual corrosion as evidenced in their bloodguiltiness. See note on 22:3.
24:9, 10 The activity of vv. 3–5 is now attributed to God. He will **heap on the wood** and **cook the meat well.**
24:11 The empty pot is placed on the fire (exile) to purify the pot of corrosion, **its filthiness,** and **its scum.**

You will [b]not be cleansed of your
filthiness anymore,
[c]Till I have caused My fury to rest
upon you.
14 [a]I, the LORD, have spoken *it;*
[b]It shall come to pass, and I will
do *it;*
I will not hold back,
[c]Nor will I spare,
Nor will I relent;
According to your ways
And according to your deeds
[1]They will judge you,"
Says the Lord GOD.' "

The Prophet's Wife Dies

15 Also the word of the LORD came to
me, saying,
16 "Son of man, behold, I take away
from you the desire of your eyes with
one stroke; yet you shall [a]neither
mourn nor weep, nor shall your tears
run down.
17 "Sigh in silence, [a]make no mourning for the dead; [b]bind your turban on
your head, and [c]put your sandals on
your feet; [d]do not cover *your* [1]lips, and
do not eat man's bread *of sorrow.*"
18 So I spoke to the people in the
morning, and at evening my wife died;
and the next morning I did as I was
commanded.
19 And the people said to me, [a]"Will
you not tell us what these *things signify*
to us, that you behave so?"
20 Then I answered them, "The word
of the LORD came to me, saying,
21 'Speak to the house of Israel, "Thus
says the Lord GOD: 'Behold, [a]I will profane My sanctuary, [1]your arrogant
boast, the desire of your eyes, the
[2]delight of your soul; [b]and your sons
and daughters whom you left behind
shall fall by the sword.
22 'And you shall do as I have done;
[a]you shall not cover *your* [1]lips nor eat
man's bread *of sorrow.*
23 'Your turbans shall be on your
heads and your sandals on your feet;
[a]you shall neither mourn nor weep, but
[b]you shall pine away in your *iniquities and mourn with one another.
24 'Thus [a]Ezekiel is a *sign to you; according to all that he has done you
shall do; [b]and when this comes,
[c]you shall know that I *am* the Lord
GOD.' "
25 'And you, son of man—*will it* not
be in the day when I take from them
[a]their stronghold, their joy and their
glory, the desire of their eyes, and
[1]that on which they set their minds,
their sons and their daughters:
26 '*that* on that day [a]one who escapes
will come to you to let *you* hear *it* with
your ears?
27 [a]'On that day your mouth will be
opened to him who has escaped; you
shall speak and no longer be mute.
Thus you will be a sign to them, and
they shall know that I *am* the LORD.' "

Proclamation Against Ammon

25 The word of the LORD came to
me, saying,
2 "Son of man, [a]set your face
[b]against the Ammonites, and prophesy
against them.
3 "Say to the Ammonites, 'Hear the
word of the Lord GOD! Thus says the
Lord GOD: [a]"Because you said, 'Aha!'
against My sanctuary when it was profaned, and against the land of Israel
when it was desolate, and against the
house of Judah when they went into
captivity,
4 "indeed, therefore, I will deliver you
as a possession to the [1]men of the East,
and they shall set their encampments
among you and make their *dwellings

13 [b]Jer. 6:28–30 [c]Ezek. 5:13; 8:18; 16:42
14 [a][1 Sam. 15:29] [b]Is. 55:11 [c]Ezek. 5:11 [1]LXX, Syr., Tg., Vg. *I*
16 [a]Jer. 16:5
17 [a]Jer. 16:5 [b]Lev. 10:6; 21:10 [c]2 Sam. 15:30 [d]Mic. 3:7 [1]Lit. *moustache*
19 [a]Ezek. 12:9; 37:18
21 [a]Jer. 7:14 [b]Ezek. 23:25, 47 [1]Lit. *the pride of your strength* [2]Lit. *compassion*
22 [a]Jer. 16:6, 7 [1]Lit. *moustache*
23 [a]Job 27:15 [b]Lev. 26:39 *See WW at Ps. 130:3.
24 [a]Is. 20:3 [b]Jer. 17:15 [c]Ezek. 6:7; 25:5 *See WW at Zech. 3:8.
25 [a]Ezek. 24:21 [1]Lit. *the lifting up of their soul*
26 [a]Ezek. 33:21
27 [a]Ezek. 3:26; 33:22

CHAPTER 25

2 [a]Ezek. 35:2 [b]Jer. 49:1
3 [a]Ezek. 26:2
4 [1]Lit. *sons* *See WW at Is. 32:18.

24:15–27 On the death of his wife, Ezekiel is prohibited from showing the usual signs of mourning. Vv. 16, 17 give us one of the fullest accounts of customary mourning rites in all of Scripture. The reason for God's command is in vv. 22, 23: when the temple at Jerusalem is destroyed, the people are not to mourn.

24:24 A sign to you: See note on 12:6. Again the personal experience of Ezekiel is to be a guide to the people in their time of sorrow.

25:1—32:32 Oracles are given against seven nations. Most of these prophecies are never heard by the nations *themselves, but are delivered* to Israel to emphasize the sovereignty of God, which includes His guidance of His own people and His rule over and judgment of the nations with whom Israel had come into contact. The nations fall into two groups: One consists of the Ammonites (25:1–7), Moabites (25:8–11), Edomites (25:12–14), and Philistines (25:15–17), all of whom were probably involved with Judah in rebellion against Nebuchadnezzar. The other group consists of the nations of Tyre (26:1—28:19), Sidon (28:20–24), and Egypt (chs. 29—32). For further information on the import of these oracles, see notes on Zeph. 2:4–15 and Amos 1:3—2:3.

25:3 Ammonites: Ammon was situated just east of Judah across the Jordan (see 21:20, 28–32; Jer. 49:1–6; Amos 1:13–15). The Ammonites and Israelites were long-time enemies. Conflict began in the period of the judges with Jephthah (see Judg. 10:6—11:33) and continued with Saul (see 1 Sam. 11:1–11; 14:47), David (see 2 Sam. 11:1; 1 Chr. 19:1—20:3), and Jehoshaphat (see 2 Chr. 20:1–23). Because Judah was attacked by Nebuchadnezzar instead of Ammon, the Ammonites gloated and said **Aha,** which is a cry of joy for the misfortune of another (see 26:2; 36:2; Ps. 35:21).

25:4 Men of the East: Perhaps nomadic tribes. See v. 10; Gen. 29:1; Judg. 6:33.

among you; they shall eat your fruit,
and they shall drink your milk.
5 "And I will make [a]Rabbah [b]a stable
for camels and Ammon a resting place
for flocks. [c]Then you shall know that
I *am* the LORD."
6 'For thus says the Lord GOD: "Because you [a]clapped *your* hands,
stamped your feet, and [b]rejoiced in
heart with all your disdain for the land
of Israel,
7 "indeed, therefore, I will [a]stretch
out My hand against you, and give you
as plunder to the nations; I will cut you
off from the peoples, and I will cause
you to perish from the countries; I will
destroy you, and you shall know that
I *am* the LORD."

Proclamation Against Moab

8 'Thus says the Lord GOD: "Because
[a]Moab and [b]Seir say, 'Look! The house
of Judah *is* like all the nations,'
9 "therefore, behold, I will clear the
territory of Moab of cities, of the cities
on its frontier, the glory of the country,
Beth Jeshimoth, Baal Meon, and
[a]Kirjathaim.
10 [a]"To the men of the East I will
give it as a possession, together with
the Ammonites, that the Ammonites
[b]may not be remembered among the
nations.
11 "And I will execute judgments upon
Moab, and they shall know that I *am*
the LORD."

Proclamation Against Edom

12 'Thus says the Lord GOD: [a]"Because
of what Edom did against the house
of Judah by taking vengeance, and has
greatly offended by avenging itself on
them,"
13 'therefore thus says the Lord GOD:
"I will also stretch out My hand against
Edom, cut off man and beast from it,
and make it desolate from Teman;
[1]Dedan shall fall by the sword.
14 [a]"I will lay My vengeance on Edom
by the hand of My people Israel, that
they may do in Edom according to My
anger and according to My fury; and
they shall know My vengeance," says
the Lord GOD.

Proclamation Against Philistia

15 'Thus says the Lord GOD: [a]"Because
[b]the Philistines dealt vengefully and
took vengeance with [1]a spiteful heart,
to destroy because of the [2]old hatred,"
16 'therefore thus says the Lord GOD:
[a]"I will stretch out My hand against
the Philistines, and I will cut off the
[b]Cherethites [c]and destroy the remnant
of the seacoast.
17 "I will [a]execute great vengeance on
them with furious rebukes; [b]and they
shall know that I *am* the LORD, when
I lay My vengeance upon them." ' "

Proclamation Against Tyre

26 And it came to pass in the eleventh year, on the first *day* of the
month, *that* the word of the LORD came
to me, saying,
2 "Son of man, [a]because Tyre has
said against Jerusalem, [b]'Aha! She is
broken who *was* the gateway of the
peoples; now she is turned over to me;
I shall be filled; she is laid waste.'

5 [a]Deut. 3:11; 2 Sam. 12:26; Jer. 49:2; Ezek. 21:20 [b]Is. 17:2 [c]Ezek. 24:24
6 [a]Job 27:23; Lam. 2:15; Nah. 3:19; Zeph. 2:15 [b]Ezek. 36:5
7 [a]Ezek. 35:3
8 [a]Is. 15:6; Jer. 48:1; Amos 2:1, 2 [b]Ezek. 35:2, 5
9 [a]Num. 32:3, 38; Josh. 13:17; 1 Chr. 5:8; Jer. 48:23
10 [a]Ezek. 25:4 [b]Ezek. 21:32
12 [a]2 Chr. 28:17; Ps. 137:7; Jer. 49:7, 8; Amos 1:11; Obad. 10–14
13 [1]Or *even to Dedan they shall fall*
14 [a]Is. 11:14
15 [a]Jer. 25:20; Amos 1—6 [b]2 Chr. 28:18 [1]Lit. *spite in soul* [2]Or *perpetual*
16 [a]Zeph. 2:4 [b]1 Sam. 30:14 [c]Jer. 47:4
17 [a]Ezek. 5:15 [b]Ps. 9:16

CHAPTER 26

2 [a]2 Sam. 5:11; Is. 23:1; Jer. 25:22; Amos 1:9; Zech. 9:2 [b]Ezek. 25:3

25:6 Clapped *your* hands, stamped your feet: See note on 6:11.
25:7 Stretch out My hand: See vv. 13, 16 and note on 6:14.
25:8 Moab was situated east of the Dead Sea and south of Ammon. When the northern kingdom of Israel was strong, she controlled the land of Moab. **Seir** is another name for Edom (see v. 12).
25:12 Edom was situated south of Moab and south of the Dead Sea. Edom was an enemy of Israel throughout its history. She refused to allow the Israelites under Moses to cross her territory (Num. 20:14–21). She fought wars with Saul (1 Sam. 14:47), David (2 Sam. 8:13, 14), Solomon (1 Kin. 11:14–22), Jehoram (2 Kin. 8:20–22), and Ahaz (2 Chr. 28:16, 17). Edom joined with Nebuchadnezzar in the invasion that led to Judah's destruction (Jer. 49:7–22). See also note on Obad. 10, 11.
25:13 Teman: An area in central Edom near Petra (see Jer. 49:7, 20; Amos 1:12). **Dedan:** A tribe and territory in southern Edom (see 27:20; 38:13; Jer. 49:8).
25:15 The **Philistines** occupied the southern coast of Canaan along the Mediterranean Sea. They entered Canaan in large numbers in the early part of the thirteenth century B.C. At least three of the judges had conflicts with them: Shamgar (Judg. 3:31), Samson (Judg. 13—16), and Samuel (1 Sam. 7:7–14). They controlled much of the territory of Israel during the reign of Saul (see 1 Sam. 13:3—14:23; 14:46; 17:51–53; 28:1–5; 29:1; 31:1–4), but were subdued by David (see 2 Sam. 5:17–25; 8:1). During the divided monarchy they again were a threat. Tribute was paid by them to Jehoshaphat (see 2 Chr. 17:10, 11), they successfully attacked and plundered Jehoram (see 2 Chr. 21:16, 17), they were defeated by Uzziah (see 2 Chr. 26:6, 7), and they took territory from Ahaz (see 2 Chr. 28:16–18). They were finally deported by Nebuchadnezzar and passed from history.
25:16 The **Cherethites** lived between Gerar and Sharuhen and may be synonymous with **Philistines** (1 Sam. 30:14). They are one of the groups, along with the Pelethites, which formed David's bodyguard (see 2 Sam. 8:18; 15:18; 20:7) and may originally have come from Caphtor, that is, Crete (Jer. 47:4).
26:1—28:19 Oracles directed against **Tyre.**
26:1–21 Tyre will be destroyed by **Nebuchadnezzar.** This pronouncement can be divided into four sections (vv. 3–6; vv. 7–14; vv. 15–18; vv. 19–21) by the phrase **Thus says the Lord GOD.**
26:2 Tyre was an important seaport of the Phoenicians

3 "Therefore thus says the Lord GOD:
'Behold, I *am* against you, O Tyre, and
will cause many nations to come up
against you, as the sea causes its waves
to come up.
4 'And they shall destroy the walls of
Tyre and break down her towers; I will
also scrape her dust from her, and
[a]make her like the top of a rock.
5 'It shall be *a place for* spreading
nets [a]in the midst of the sea, for I have
spoken,' says the Lord GOD; 'it shall
become plunder for the nations.
6 'Also her daughter *villages* which
are in the fields shall be slain by the
sword. [a]Then they shall know that I
am the LORD.'
7 "For thus says the Lord GOD: 'Behold, I will bring against Tyre from the
north [a]Nebuchadnezzar[1] king of Babylon, [b]king of kings, with horses, with
chariots, and with horsemen, and an
army with many people.
8 'He will slay with the sword your
daughter *villages* in the fields; he will
[a]heap up a siege mound against you,
build a wall against you, and raise a
[1]defense against you.
9 'He will direct his battering rams
against your walls, and with his axes
he will break down your towers.
10 'Because of the abundance of his
horses, their dust will cover you; your
walls will shake at the noise of the
horsemen, the wagons, and the chariots, when he enters your gates, as men
enter a city that has been breached.
11 'With the hooves of his [a]horses he
will trample all your streets; he will
slay your people by the sword, and
your strong pillars will fall to the
ground.
12 'They will plunder your riches and
pillage your merchandise; they will
break down your walls and destroy
your pleasant houses; they will lay
your stones, your timber, and your soil
in the [a]midst of the water.
13 [a]'I will put an end to the sound of
[b]your songs, and the sound of your
harps shall be heard no more.
14 [a]'I will make you like the top of a
rock; you shall be *a place for* spreading
nets, and you shall never be rebuilt, for
I the LORD have spoken,' says the Lord
GOD.
15 "Thus says the Lord GOD to Tyre:
'Will the coastlands not [a]shake at the
sound of your fall, when the wounded
cry, when slaughter is made in the
midst of you?
16 'Then all the [a]princes of the sea will
[b]come down from their thrones, lay
aside their robes, and take off their embroidered garments; they will clothe
themselves with trembling; [c]they will
sit on the ground, [d]tremble *every* moment, and [e]be astonished at you.
17 'And they will take up a [a]lamenta-
tion for you, and say to you:

"How you have perished,
O one inhabited by seafaring
men,
O renowned city,
Who was [b]strong at sea,
She and her inhabitants,
Who caused their terror *to be* on
all her inhabitants!
18 Now [a]the coastlands tremble on
the day of your fall;
Yes, the coastlands by the sea are
troubled at your departure." '

19 "For thus says the Lord GOD: 'When
I make you a desolate city, like cities
that are not inhabited, when I bring the
deep upon you, and great waters cover
you,
20 'then I will bring you down [a]with
those who descend into the Pit, to the
people of old, and I will make you
dwell in the lowest part of the earth,
in places desolate from antiquity, with
those who go down to the Pit, so that
you may never be inhabited; and I shall
establish glory [b]in the land of the living.
21 [a]'I will make you a terror, and you
shall be no *more;* [b]though you are
sought for, you will never be found
again,' says the Lord GOD."

Lamentation for Tyre

27 The word of the LORD came
again to me, saying,

4 [a]Ezek. 26:14 **5** [a]Ezek. 27:32 **6** [a]Ezek. 25:5 **7** [a]Jer. 27:3–6; Ezek. 29:18 [b]Ezra 7:12; Is. 10:8; Jer. 52:32; Dan. 2:37, 47 [1]Heb. *Nebuchadrezzar,* and so elsewhere in the book **8** [a]Jer. 52:4; Ezek. 21:22 [1]Lit. *a large shield* **11** [a]Hab. 1:8 **12** [a]Ezek. 27:27, 32 **13** [a]Is. 14:11; 24:8; Jer. 7:34; 25:10; Amos 6:5 [b]Is. 23:16; Ezek. 28:13; Rev. 18:22 **14** [a]Ezek. 26:4, 5
15 [a]Jer. 49:21; Ezek. 27:28 **16** [a]Is. 23:8 [b]Jon. 3:6 [c]Job 2:13 [d]Ezek. 32:10; Hos. 11:10 [e]Ezek. 27:35 **17** [a]Ezek. 27:2–36; Rev. 18:9 [b]Josh. 19:29; Is. 23:4 **18** [a]Ezek. 26:15 **20** [a]Ezek. 32:18 [b]Ezek. 32:23 **21** [a]Ezek. 27:36; 28:19 [b]Ps. 37:10, 36; Ezek. 28:19

along the northern coast of the Mediterranean, in present-day Lebanon. There were two cities, one on the coast and the other on an island a half-mile offshore. Amos condemned Tyre for selling Israelites to the Edomites (Amos 1:9). Jeremiah prophesied that Tyre (along with Moab, Edom, Ammon, and Sidon) would be given into the hands of Nebuchadnezzar (Jer. 27:1–6). Ezekiel here prophesies the destruction of Tyre (vv. 3–21), which came about in two phases. The city on the mainland may have been destroyed by Nebuchadnezzar after a 13-year siege (585–572 B.C.), but the island city was not touched at all. Alexander the Great, during a 7-month siege in 332 B.C., built a causeway from the mainland to the island, captured the city, and destroyed it. He thus fulfilled the words of vv. 4 and 14, "I will also scrape her dust from her, and make her like the top of a rock," and v. 12, "they will lay your stones, your timber, and your soil in the midst of the water." Indeed, all the debris on the mainland was cast into the sea by Alexander to build the causeway.

27:1–36 The destruction of Tyre is sure, so Ezekiel is told

2 "Now, son of man, [a]take up a lamentation for Tyre,
3 "and say to Tyre, [a]'You who [1]are
situated at the entrance of the sea, [b]mer-
chant of the peoples on many coastlands, thus says the Lord GOD:

"O Tyre, you have said,
[c]'I *am* perfect in beauty.'
4 Your borders *are* in the midst of
the seas.
Your builders have perfected
your beauty.
5 They [1]made all *your* planks of fir
trees from [a]Senir;
They took a cedar from Lebanon
to make you a mast.
6 *Of* [a]oaks from Bashan they made
your oars;
The company of Ashurites have
inlaid your planks
With ivory from [b]the coasts of
[1]Cyprus.
7 Fine embroidered linen from
Egypt was what you spread for
your sail;
Blue and purple from the coasts
of Elishah was what covered
you.

8 "Inhabitants of Sidon and Arvad
were your oarsmen;
Your wise men, O Tyre, were in
you;
They became your pilots.
9 *Elders of [a]Gebal and its wise men
Were in you to caulk your seams;
All the ships of the sea
And their oarsmen were in you
To market your merchandise.

10 "Those from Persia, [1]Lydia, and
[2]Libya
Were in your army as men of war;
They hung shield and helmet in
you;
They gave splendor to you.
11 Men of Arvad with your army
were on your walls *all* around,
And the men of Gammad were in
your towers;
They hung their shields on your
walls *all* around;
They made [a]your beauty perfect.

12 [a]"Tarshish *was* your merchant because of your many luxury goods.
They gave you silver, iron, tin, and lead
for your goods.
13 [a]"Javan, Tubal, and Meshech *were*
your traders. They bartered [b]human
lives and vessels of bronze for your
merchandise.
14 "Those from the house of [a]Togar-
mah traded for your wares with horses,
steeds, and mules.
15 "The men of [a]Dedan *were* your
traders; many isles *were* the market of
your hand. They brought you ivory
tusks and ebony as payment.
16 "Syria *was* your merchant because
of the abundance of goods you made.
They gave you for your wares emer-
alds, purple, embroidery, fine linen,
corals, and rubies.
17 "Judah and the land of Israel *were*
your traders. They traded for your
merchandise wheat of [a]Minnith, millet,
honey, oil, and [b]balm.
18 "Damascus *was* your merchant because of the abundance of goods you
made, because of your many luxury
items, with the wine of Helbon and
with white wool.
19 "Dan and Javan paid for your
wares, [1]traversing back and forth.
Wrought iron, cassia, and cane were
among your merchandise.

CHAPTER 27

2 [a]Ezek. 26:17 **3** [a]Ezek. 26:17; 28:2 [b]Is. 23:3 [c]Ezek. 28:12 [1]Lit. *sit* or *dwell* **5** [a]Deut. 3:9; 1 Chr. 5:23; Song 4:8 [1]*built* **6** [a]Is. 2:12, 13; Zech. 11:2 [b]Gen. 10:4; Is. 23:1, 12; Jer. 2:10 [1]Heb. *Kittim,* western lands, especially Cyprus **9** [a]Josh. 13:5; 1 Kin. 5:18; Ps. 83:7 *See WW at Ps. 119:100. **10** [1]Heb. *Lud* [2]Heb. *Put*

11 [a]Ezek. 27:3 **12** [a]Gen. 10:4; 2 Chr. 20:36; Ezek. 38:13 **13** [a]Gen. 10:2; Is. 66:19; Ezek. 27:19 [b]Joel 3:3–6; Rev. 18:13 **14** [a]Gen. 10:3; Ezek. 38:6 **15** [a]Gen. 10:7; Is. 21:13 **17** [a]Judg. 11:33; 1 Kin. 5:9, 11; Ezra 3:7; Acts 12:20 [b]Jer. 8:22 **19** [1]LXX, Syr. *from Uzal*

to **take up a lamentation for Tyre.** The demise of Tyre is portrayed as a sinking ship (vv. 32, 34), probably because of her extensive maritime activity and the fact that the city itself was an island.
27:4–7 The various materials used in the ship's construction are described as to their function and place of origin. This in itself indicates extensive trade.
27:5 Senir: Hermon, the mountain range famous for its cedars.
27:6 Bashan: An excellent pastureland east of the Sea of Galilee, known for its cattle (39:18; Amos 4:1) and oak forests (Is. 2:13).
27:7 Elishah: Probably a city in Cyprus, but the identification is uncertain.
27:8–11 The craftsmen, ship personnel, and soldiers were from various nationalities, indicating the cosmopolitan makeup of Tyre.
27:8, 9 Sidon and **Arvad** were cities in Phoenicia, as was **Gebal,** or Byblos (v. 9).
27:10–24 The image of a ship changes to a literal city with **walls** and **towers.**
27:10 Persia is modern Iran, **Lydia** is an area in Asia Minor, and **Libya,** or Put, is in North Africa to the west of Egypt (see 30:5; 38:5).
27:11 Gammad has not been identified with certainty.
27:12–24 The most complete and extensive list of trading communities found anywhere in Scripture. The list moves geographically from west to east, and shows an amazingly accurate knowledge of the commercial activity of that day.
27:12 Tarshish is generally identified as a city or territory in the western Mediterranean, perhaps Tartessus in Spain.
27:13 Javan may be Greece (Gen. 10:2); **Tubal** and **Meshech** are in Asia Minor (38:1–9).
27:14 House of Togarmah is Beth Togarmah in eastern Asia Minor (38:6).
27:15 Dedan may be an Arab tribe in Edom or it may be Rhodes.
27:18 Helbon is a famous vine-growing area northeast of Damascus.

20 [a]"Dedan *was* your merchant in
saddlecloths for riding.
21 "Arabia and all the princes of
[a]Kedar *were* your regular merchants.
They traded with you in lambs, rams,
and goats.
22 "The merchants of [a]Sheba and
Raamah *were* your merchants. They
traded for your wares the choicest
spices, all kinds of precious stones, and
gold.
23 [a]"Haran, Canneh, Eden, the merchants of [b]Sheba, Assyria, *and* Chilmad *were* your merchants.
24 "These *were* your merchants in
choice items—in purple clothes, in embroidered garments, in chests of multicolored apparel, in sturdy woven
cords, which were in your marketplace.

25 "The [a]ships of Tarshish were
carriers of your merchandise.
You were filled and very glorious
[b]in the midst of the seas.
26 Your oarsmen brought you into
many waters,
But [a]the east wind broke you in
the midst of the seas.

27 "Your [a]riches, wares, and
merchandise,
Your mariners and pilots,
Your caulkers and
merchandisers,
All your men of war who *are* in
you,
And the entire company which *is*
in your midst,
Will fall into the midst of the seas
on the day of your ruin.
28 The [a]common-land[1] will shake at
the sound of the cry of your
pilots.

29 "All [a]who handle the oar,
The mariners,
All the pilots of the sea
Will come down from their ships
and stand on the [1]shore.

20 [a]Gen. 25:3
21 [a]Gen. 25:13; Is. 60:7; Jer. 49:28;
22 [a]Gen. 10:7; 1 Kin. 10:1, 2; Ps. 72:10; Is. 60:6; Ezek. 38:13
23 [a]Gen. 11:31; 2 Kin. 19:12; Is. 37:12 [b]Gen. 25:3
25 [a]Ps. 48:7; Is. 2:16 [b]Ezek. 27:4
26 [a]Ps. 48:7; Jer. 18:17; Acts 27:14
27 [a][Prov. 11:4]
28 [a]Ezek. 26:15 [1]*open lands* or *pasturelands*
29 [a]Rev. 18:17 [1]Lit. *land*
30 [a]1 Sam. 4:12; 2 Sam. 1:2; Job 2:12; Lam. 2:10; Rev. 18:19 [b]Esth. 4:1, 3; Jer. 6:26; Jon. 3:6
31 [a]Is. 15:2; Jer. 16:6; Ezek. 29:18
32 [a]Ezek. 26:17 [b]Ezek. 26:4, 5; Rev. 18:18
33 [a]Rev. 18:19
34 [a]Ezek. 26:19 [b]Ezek. 27:27
35 [a]Is. 23:6; Ezek. 26:15, 16
36 [a]Jer. 18:16; Zeph. 2:15 [b]Ezek. 26:2 [c]Ps. 37:10, 36; Ezek. 28:19

CHAPTER 28

2 [a]Jer. 49:16; Ezek. 31:10 [b]Is. 14:14; 47:8; Ezek. 28:9; 2 Thess. 2:4 [c]Ezek. 27:3, 4 [d]Is. 31:3; Ezek. 28:9 [1]Proud

30 They will make their voice heard
because of you;
They will cry bitterly and
[a]cast dust on their heads;
They [b]will roll about in ashes;
31 They will [a]shave themselves
completely bald because of you,
Gird themselves with sackcloth,
And weep for you
With bitterness of heart *and* bitter
wailing.
32 In their wailing for you
They will [a]take up a lamentation,
And lament for you:
[b]'What *city is* like Tyre,
Destroyed in the midst of the sea?

33 'When[a] your wares went out by
sea,
You satisfied many people;
You enriched the kings of the
earth
With your many luxury goods
and your merchandise.
34 But [a]you are broken by the seas
in the depths of the waters;
[b]Your merchandise and the entire
company will fall in your midst.
35 [a]All the inhabitants of the isles will
be astonished at you;
Their kings will be greatly afraid,
And *their* countenance will be
troubled.
36 The merchants among the
peoples [a]will hiss at you;
[b]You will become a horror, and *be*
no [c]more forever.'"'"

Proclamation Against the King of Tyre

28 The word of the LORD came to
me again, saying,
2 "Son of man, say to the prince of
Tyre, 'Thus says the Lord GOD:

"Because your heart *is* [a]lifted[1] up,
And [b]you say, 'I *am* a god,
I sit *in* the seat of gods,
[c]In the midst of the seas,'
[d]Yet you *are* a man, and not a god,

27:21 Arabia and **Kedar** represent the Bedouin tribes from Aram and the Arabian Desert.
27:22 Sheba (38:13) and **Raamah** are located in southern Arabia.
27:23 Haran is on the Balikh River in Mesopotamia; **Canneh** and **Eden** (Beth Eden, Amos 1:5) are southeast and south of Haran, respectively. **Assyria** is Asshur south of Nineveh, while **Chilmad** is unidentified, but presumably in Mesopotamia.
27:25–36 The image used by Ezekiel now returns to that of a ship.
27:25 Ships of Tarshish refers to a type of ship capable of travel on the open sea.
27:26 The **east wind** is destructive at sea (see Ps. 48:7), as well as on land (see 17:10; 19:12; Jer. 18:17).
27:36 Will hiss: A sign of astonishment (see 1 Kin. 9:8).
28:1–10 An oracle against **the prince of Tyre.**
28:2 Prince of Tyre: Probably Ittobaal II, whom Josephus said was king during the siege of Nebuchadnezzar. **I *am* a god:** Because of the wisdom and wealth of the king, he attributes to himself a position greater than warranted. This same presumptuous claim is seen in Is. 14:12–15, where the king of Babylon exalts himself to a high position. The term "god" may be compared to its use in Ps. 82 (there also these "divine rulers" die as men do). In all these passages the one claiming "divine" status will "die the death of the uncircumcised" (v. 10), will be brought down to Sheol (Is. 14:15), or die like men (Ps. 82:7).

Though you set your heart as the heart of a god
3 (Behold, [a]you *are* wiser than Daniel!
There is no secret that can be hidden from you!
4 With your wisdom and your understanding
You have gained [a]riches for yourself,
And gathered gold and silver into your treasuries;
5 [a]By your great wisdom in trade you have increased your riches,
And your heart is lifted up because of your riches),"

6 'Therefore thus says the Lord GOD:

"Because you have set your heart as the heart of a god,
7 Behold, therefore, I will bring [a]strangers against you,
[b]The most terrible of the nations;
And they shall draw their swords against the beauty of your wisdom,
And defile your splendor.
8 They shall throw you down into the [a]Pit,
And you shall die the death of the slain
In the midst of the seas.

9 "Will you still [a]say before him who slays you,
'I *am* a god'?
But you *shall be* a man, and not a god,
In the hand of him who slays you.
10 You shall die the death of [a]the uncircumcised
By the hand of aliens;
For I have spoken," says the Lord GOD.' "

3 [a]Ezek. 14:14; Dan. 1:20; 2:20–23, 28; 5:11, 12; Zech. 9:3
4 [a]Ezek. 27:33; Zech. 9:1–3
5 [a]Ps. 62:10; Zech. 9:3
7 [a]Ezek. 26:7 [b]Ezek. 7:24; 21:31; 30:11; Hab. 1:6–8
8 [a]Is. 14:15
9 [a]Ezek. 28:2
10 [a]1 Sam. 17:26, 36; Ezek. 31:18; 32:19, 21, 25, 27
12 [a]Ezek. 27:2 [b]Ezek. 27:3; 28:3
13 [a]Gen. 2:8; Is. 51:3; Ezek. 31:8, 9; 36:35 [b]Ezek. 26:13
*See WW at Gen. 1:1.
14 [a]Ex. 25:20; Ezek. 28:16

Lamentation for the King of Tyre

11 Moreover the word of the LORD came to me, saying,
12 "Son of man, [a]take up a lamentation for the king of Tyre, and say to him, 'Thus says the Lord GOD:

[b]"You *were* the seal of perfection,
Full of wisdom and perfect in **beauty.**

WORD WEALTH

28:12 beauty, *yophi* (yoh-*fee*); Strong's #3308: Beauty, splendor, brightness, fairness; perfect in physical form; flawless in symmetry. *Yophi* is derived from the verb *yaphah,* "to be beautiful, lovely, fair, and graceful." *Yophi* occurs 18 times in the OT, and one-half of these occurrences are in Ezek. In the present reference, the king of Tyre is described as being "perfect in beauty" at his origin. In Ezek. 16:14, 15, the beauty that God bestowed upon Israel was so extraordinary that it became famous throughout the world. Zion is called "the perfection of beauty" (Ps. 50:2). The most beautiful sight in Scripture is the messianic King's enjoying His rightful reign without end (Is. 33:17).

13 You were in [a]Eden, the garden of God;
Every precious stone *was* your covering:
The sardius, topaz, and diamond,
Beryl, onyx, and jasper,
Sapphire, turquoise, and emerald with gold.
The workmanship of [b]your timbrels and pipes
Was prepared for you on the day you were *created.

14 "You *were* the anointed [a]cherub who covers;

28:3 Daniel: See note on 14:14.
28:7 The most terrible of the nations is Babylon.
28:8 Death: Here and in v. 10 the plural form is used and would better be translated "violent death."
28:11–19 This lamentation is similar to a taunt song (see note on 19:1–14) addressed to **the king of Tyre** (v. 12). Many see in this passage (and in Is. 14) the fall of Satan, a view held by several of the church fathers in the second half of the fourth century A.D. Such an interpretation is strengthened in light of its extreme descriptions (vv. 16, 17), but does not take full account of the context. The fall of the king of Tyre might equally reflect the fall of Adam, the first king, as well as the fall of any proud man. In this sense one can also see Satan's fall for the fall of any proud person reflects the fall of Satan, who in himself personifies pride. Like Adam or like Satan prior to his fall, the king of Tyre belongs to God in a unique way and is perfect in creation (**the seal of perfection,** see Gen. 1:27, 31). He is destined to carry out God's plans and is placed **in Eden** (v. 13) in the presence of God. Unlike Adam, who was naked (Gen. 2:25), the king of Tyre is covered with **every precious stone** to denote his beauties and glories (see Ex. 28:17–20 for the stones on the breastplate of the high priest).

Vv. 14, 15 are the most conclusive evidence that this text likely refers to Satan's fall. **Anointed cherub who covers** indicates high office with authority and responsibility to protect and defend (cover) **the holy mountain of God,** an allusion to God's throne. The high order and specific placement of Lucifer prior to his fall afforded unique opportunity to bring glory to God. (Some see in v. 13 musical reference that suggests his role included leading heaven's choirs in the worship of the Most High.) His fall was occasioned by his seeking to have this glory for himself (see Is. 14:12–17).

The sin of the king of Tyre is that in **the abundance of** his **trading** he **became filled with violence within,** and God **cast** him **out of the mountain of God** (v. 16).

I established you;
You were on [b]the holy mountain of God;
You walked back and forth in the midst of fiery stones.
15 You *were* perfect in your ways from the day you were created,
Till [a]iniquity was found in you.

16 "By the abundance of your trading
You became filled with violence within,
And you sinned;
Therefore I cast you as a profane thing
Out of the mountain of God;
And I destroyed you, [a]O covering cherub,
From the midst of the fiery stones.

17 "Your [a]heart was [1]lifted up because of your beauty;
You corrupted your wisdom for the sake of your splendor;
I cast you to the ground,
I laid you before kings,
That they might gaze at you.

18 "You defiled your sanctuaries
By the multitude of your iniquities,
By the iniquity of your trading;
Therefore I brought fire from your midst;
It devoured you,
And I turned you to ashes upon the earth
In the sight of all who saw you.
19 All who knew you among the peoples are astonished at you;
[a]You have become a horror,
And *shall be* no [b]more forever." ' "

Proclamation Against Sidon

20 Then the word of the LORD came to
me, saying,
21 "Son of man, [a]set your face [b]toward
Sidon, and prophesy against her,
22 "and say, 'Thus says the Lord GOD:

[a]"Behold, I *am* against you,
O Sidon;
I will be glorified in your midst;
And [b]they shall know that I *am* the LORD,

14 [b]Is. 14:13; Ezek. 20:40
15 [a][Is. 14:12]
16 [a]Ezek. 28:14
17 [a]Ezek. 28:2, 5 [1]Proud
19 [a]Ezek. 26:21 [b]Ezek. 27:36
21 [a]Ezek. 6:2; 25:2; 29:2 [b]Gen. 10:15, 19; Is. 23:2, 4, 12; Ezek. 27:8; 32:30
22 [a]Ex. 14:4, 17; Ezek. 39:13 [b]Ps. 9:16 [c]Ezek. 28:25
23 [a]Ezek. 38:22
24 [a]Num. 33:55; Josh. 23:13; Is. 55:13; Ezek. 2:6 [b]Ezek. 16:57; 25:6, 7
25 [a]Ps. 106:47; Is. 11:12, 13; Jer. 32:37; Ezek. 11:17; 20:41; 34:13; 37:21 [b]Ezek. 28:22
26 [a]Jer. 23:6; Ezek. 36:28 [b]Is. 65:21; Jer. 32:15, 43, 44; Amos 9:13, 14 [c]Jer. 31:5; Amos 9:14 [1]*securely* *See WW at Deut. 33:12.

CHAPTER 29

2 [a]Ezek. 28:21 [b]Is. 19:1; Jer. 25:19; 46:2, 25; Ezek. 30:1—32:32; Joel 3:19
3 [a]Jer. 44:30; Ezek. 28:22; 29:10 [b]Ps. 74:13, 14; Is. 37:1; 51:9; Ezek. 32:2 [c]Ezek. 28:2 [1]The Nile
4 [a]2 Kin. 19:28; Is. 37:29; Ezek. 38:4

When I execute judgments in her
and am [c]hallowed in her.
23 [a]For I will send pestilence upon her,
And blood in her streets;
The wounded shall be judged in her midst
By the sword against her on every side;
Then they shall know that I *am* the LORD.

24 "And there shall no longer be a
pricking brier or [a]a painful thorn for
the house of Israel from among all *who*
are around them, who [b]despise them.
Then they shall know that I *am* the
Lord GOD."

Israel's Future Blessing

25 'Thus says the Lord GOD: "When I
have [a]gathered the house of Israel
from the peoples among whom they
are scattered, and am [b]hallowed in
them in the sight of the Gentiles, then
they will dwell in their own land which
I gave to My servant Jacob.
26 "And they will [a]dwell [1]safely* there,
[b]build houses, and [c]plant vineyards;
yes, they will dwell securely, when I
execute judgments on all those around
them who despise them. Then they
shall know that I *am* the LORD their
God." ' "

Proclamation Against Egypt

29 In the tenth year, in the tenth
month, on the twelfth *day* of the
month, the word of the LORD came to
me, saying,
2 "Son of man, [a]set your face against
Pharaoh king of Egypt, and prophesy
against him, and [b]against all Egypt.
3 "Speak, and say, 'Thus says the
Lord GOD:

[a]"Behold, I *am* against you,
O Pharaoh king of Egypt,
O great [b]monster who lies in the midst of his rivers,
[c]Who has said, 'My [1]River *is* my own;
I have made *it* for myself.'
4 But [a]I will put hooks in your jaws,

28:20–23 An oracle against **Sidon,** a rival seaport to the north of Tyre (see 27:8). After the action of Nebuchadnezzar against Tyre, Sidon became more important. What happened to Tyre will also happen to Sidon.
28:24–26 This note on the restoration of **Israel** closes the first section of the oracles concerning foreign nations.
29:1—32:32 Seven oracles against Egypt and Pharaoh, each of which is dated (29:1; 29:17; 30:20; 31:1; 32:1; 32:17) except one (30:1).
29:1 The date of this oracle is January 7, 587 B.C., seven months before the fall of Jerusalem.
29:3 O great monster: In this allegorical poem Pharaoh is likened to a crocodile in the Nile River.
29:4 Fish of your rivers: The Egyptian people.

And cause the fish of your rivers
to stick to your scales;
I will bring you up out of the
midst of your rivers,
And all the fish in your rivers will
stick to your scales.
5 I will leave you in the wilderness,
You and all the fish of your rivers;
You shall fall on the [1]open
[a]field;
[b]You shall not be picked up or
[2]gathered.
[c]I have given you as food
To the beasts of the field
And to the birds of the heavens.

6 "Then all the inhabitants of Egypt
Shall know that I *am* the LORD,
Because they have been a
[a]staff of reed to the house of
Israel.
7 [a]When they took hold of you with
the hand,
You broke and tore all their
[1]shoulders;
When they leaned on you,
You broke and made all their
backs quiver."

8 'Therefore thus says the Lord GOD:
"Surely I will bring [a]a sword upon
you and cut off from you man and
beast.
9 "And the land of Egypt shall become [a]desolate and waste; then they
will know that I *am* the LORD, because
he said, 'The River *is* mine, and I have
made *it.*'
10 "Indeed, therefore, I *am* against you
and against your rivers, [a]and I will
make the land of Egypt utterly waste
and desolate, [b]from [1]Migdol *to* Syene,
as far as the border of Ethiopia.
11 [a]"Neither foot of man shall pass
through it nor foot of beast pass
through it, and it shall be uninhabited
forty years.
12 [a]"I will make the land of Egypt desolate in the midst of the countries *that
are* desolate; and among the cities *that
are* laid waste, her cities shall be desolate forty years; and I will [b]scatter the
Egyptians among the nations and disperse them throughout the countries."
13 'Yet, thus says the Lord GOD: "At
the [a]end of forty years I will gather the
Egyptians from the peoples among
whom they were scattered.
14 "I will bring back the captives of
Egypt and cause them to return to the
land of Pathros, to the land of their origin, and there they shall be a [a]lowly
kingdom.
15 "It shall be the lowliest of kingdoms; it shall never again exalt itself
above the nations, for I will diminish
them so that they will not rule over the
nations anymore.
16 "No longer shall it be [a]the confidence of the house of Israel, but will
remind them of *their* iniquity when
they turned to follow them. Then they
shall know that I *am* the Lord GOD." ' "

Babylonia Will Plunder Egypt

17 And it came to pass in the twenty-
seventh year, in the first *month,* on the
first *day* of the month, *that* the word
of the LORD came to me, saying,
18 "Son of man, [a]Nebuchadnezzar
king of Babylon caused his army to labor strenuously against Tyre; every
head *was* made [b]bald, and every shoulder rubbed raw; yet neither he nor
his army received wages from Tyre,
for the labor which they expended on
it.
19 "Therefore thus says the Lord GOD:
'Surely I will give the land of Egypt to
[a]Nebuchadnezzar king of Babylon; he
shall take away her wealth, carry off
her spoil, and remove her pillage; and
that will be the wages for his army.
20 'I have given him the land of Egypt
for his labor, because they [a]worked for
Me,' says the Lord GOD.
21 'In that day [a]I will cause the [1]**horn**
of the house of Israel to spring forth,
and I will [b]open your mouth to speak
in their midst. Then they shall know
that I *am* the LORD.' "

5 [a]Ezek. 32:4–6 [b]Jer. 8:2; 16:4; 25:33 [c]Jer. 7:33; 34:20; Ezek. 39:4 [1]Lit. *face of the field* [2]So with MT, LXX, Vg.; some Heb. mss., Tg. *buried*
6 [a]2 Kin. 18:21; Is. 36:6; Ezek. 17:15
7 [a]Jer. 37:5, 7, 11; Ezek. 17:17 [1]So with MT, Vg.; LXX, Syr. *hand*
8 [a]Jer. 46:13; Ezek. 14:17; 32:11–13
9 [a]Ezek. 30:7, 8
10 [a]Ezek. 30:12 [b]Ezek. 30:6 [1]Or *the tower*
11 [a]Jer. 43:11, 12; 46:19; Ezek. 32:13
12 [a]Jer. 25:15–19; 27:6–11; Ezek. 30:7, 26 [b]Jer. 46:19; Ezek. 30:23, 26
13 [a]Is. 19:23; Jer. 46:26
14 [a]Ezek. 17:6, 14
16 [a]Is. 30:2, 3; 36:4, 6; Lam. 4:17; Ezek. 17:15; 29:6
18 [a]Jer. 25:9; 27:6; Ezek. 26:7–12 [b]Jer. 48:37; Ezek. 27:31
19 [a]Jer. 43:10–13; Ezek. 30:10
20 [a]Is. 10:6, 7; 45:1–3; Jer. 25:9
21 [a]1 Sam. 2:10; Ps. 92:10; 132:17 [b]Ezek. 24:27; Amos 3:7, 8; [Luke 21:15] [1]Strength

29:6 Staff of reed: The lesser sin of Egypt is that she has been unreliable, a charge also made by the Rabshakeh (2 Kin. 18:19–21).

29:9 The greater sin of **Egypt** was her pride. She believed she had created **the River** just because she had learned to use it.

29:10 Migdol to Syene: Migdol was probably in northern Egypt; Syene is Aswan at the First Cataract of the Nile. The entire extent of Egypt is meant by these names just as Dan to Beersheba was used for the whole of Israel.

29:11 Forty years: A period of time sufficient to accomplish the task. Often used symbolically (see vv. 12, 13; 4:6).

29:14 Pathros is the Hebrew name for upper Egypt or southern Egypt, between Cairo and Aswan.

29:17–21 The second oracle against **Egypt,** dated April 26, 571 B.C. This is Ezekiel's latest dated oracle, and it came just after the siege of **Tyre.**

29:18 Tyre: The siege of Tyre is described in detail in 26:7–14. The implication is that the 13-year siege was unsuccessful from an economic standpoint because the wealth of the mainland city had been shipped to the offshore island. Deprived of that booty, the spoils of Egypt will be substituted for those of Tyre (v. 19).

WORD WEALTH

29:21 horn, *qeren* (*keh*-ren); Strong's #7161: A horn of an animal; a flask or cornet; a symbol of strength, power, and victory. This noun occurs more than 75 times. Horned animals, such as oxen, goats, and rams, are symbols of strength. Thus Hebrew speakers refer to a person's horn's being exalted (Ps. 89:24; 112:9; 148:14), or contrarily, picture defeat as the breaking of the horn (Lam. 2:3). The "horns of the altar" (Lev. 4:7; 9:9; Ps. 118:27) are symbolic of the powerful presence of God. The root from which *qeren* comes is *qaran,* "to have horns," "to shine." In Ex. 34:29, 30, 35, Moses' face shone, speaking of the projecting rays of glory that streamed from Moses' face.

Egypt and Her Allies Will Fall

30 The word of the LORD came to
me again, saying,
2 "Son of man, prophesy and say,
'Thus says the Lord GOD:

[a]"Wail, 'Woe to the day!'
3 For [a]the day *is* near,
Even the day of the LORD *is* near;
It will be a day of clouds, the time
of the Gentiles.
4 The sword shall come upon
Egypt,
And great anguish shall be in
[1]Ethiopia,
When the slain fall in Egypt,
And they [a]take away her wealth,
And [b]her foundations are broken
down.

5 "Ethiopia, [1]Libya, [2]Lydia, [a]all the
mingled people, Chub, and the men of
the lands who are allied, shall fall with
them by the sword."
6 'Thus says the LORD:

"Those who uphold Egypt shall
fall,
And the pride of her power shall
come down.
[a]From [1]Migdol *to* Syene
Those within her shall fall by the
sword,"
Says the Lord GOD.

CHAPTER 30
2 [a]Is. 13:6; 15:2; Ezek. 21:12; Joel 1:5, 11, 13
3 [a]Ezek. 7:7, 12; Joel 2:1; Obad. 15; Zeph. 1:7
4 [a]Ezek. 29:19 [b]Jer. 50:15 [1]Heb. *Cush*
5 [a]Jer. 25:20, 24 [1]Heb. *Put* [2]Heb. *Lud*
6 [a]Ezek. 29:10 [1]Or *the tower*
7 [a]Jer. 25:18–26; Ezek. 29:12
9 [a]Is. 18:1, 2 [1]Or *secure*
10 [a]Ezek. 29:19
11 [a]Ezek. 28:7; 31:12
12 [a]Is. 19:5, 6 [b]Is. 19:4
13 [a]Is. 19:1; Jer. 43:12; 46:25; Zech. 13:2 [b]Zech. 10:11 [c]Is. 19:16 [1]Ancient Memphis
14 [a]Is. 11:11; Jer. 44:1, 15; Ezek. 29:14 [b]Ps. 78:12, 43; Is. 19:11, 13 [c]Jer. 46:25; Ezek. 30:15, 16; Nah. 3:8–10 [1]Ancient Thebes
15 [1]Ancient Pelusium

7 "They[a] shall be desolate in the
midst of the desolate countries,
And her cities shall be in the
midst of the cities *that are* laid
waste.
8 Then they will know that I *am* the
LORD,
When I have set a fire in Egypt
And all her helpers are destroyed.
9 On that day [a]messengers shall go
forth from Me in ships
To make the [1]careless Ethiopians
afraid,
And great anguish shall come
upon them,
As on the day of Egypt;
For indeed it is coming!"

10 'Thus says the Lord GOD:

[a]"I will also make a multitude of
Egypt to cease
By the hand of Nebuchadnezzar
king of Babylon.
11 He and his people with him,
[a]the most terrible of the
nations,
Shall be brought to destroy the
land;
They shall draw their swords
against Egypt,
And fill the land with the slain.
12 [a]I will make the rivers dry,
And [b]sell the land into the hand
of the wicked;
I will make the land waste, and
all that is in it,
By the hand of aliens.
I, the LORD, have spoken."

13 'Thus says the Lord GOD:

"I will also [a]destroy the idols,
And cause the images to cease
from [1]Noph;
[b]There shall no longer be princes
from the land of Egypt;
[c]I will put fear in the land of Egypt.
14 I will make [a]Pathros desolate,
Set fire to [b]Zoan,
[c]And execute judgments in
[1]No.
15 I will pour My fury on [1]Sin, the
strength of Egypt;

30:1–19 The third oracle against Egypt, probably given between January and April, 587 B.C.
30:3 Since the time of Amos the **day of the LORD** was connected with judgment. See note on Obad. 15.
30:5 Lydia: Perhaps located somewhere in northern Africa, but not the Lydia in Asia Minor (see 27:10). **Chub:** A people allied with Egypt against the Babylonians. Perhaps the name should be read as Hebrew *Lub,* that is, "Libya."
30:6 Migdol to Syene: See note on 29:10.
30:11 Most terrible of the nations: Babylonia (28:7).
30:13 Noph: Memphis, on the western bank of the Nile 15 miles south of Cairo (see v. 16; Is. 19:13).
30:14 Pathros: See note on 29:14. **Zoan** is a city in northeast Egypt (see Is. 19:11, 13; 30:4), also known as Tanis. **No** is Thebes, the ancient capital of Egypt. The great temples of Karnak and Luxor stand there today (see vv. 15, 16).
30:15 Sin is usually identified with Pelusium, a city on the eastern side of the Nile Delta (see v. 16).

[a]I will cut off the multitude of
[2]No,
16 And [a]set a fire in Egypt;
Sin shall have great pain,
No shall be split open,
And Noph *shall be in* distress
daily.
17 The young men of [1]Aven and Pi
Beseth shall fall by the sword,
And these *cities* shall go into
captivity.
18 [a]At [1]Tehaphnehes the day shall
also be [2]darkened,
When I break the yokes of Egypt
there.
And her arrogant strength shall
cease in her;
As for her, a cloud shall cover her,
And her daughters shall go into
captivity.
19 Thus I will [a]execute judgments on
Egypt,
Then they shall know that I *am*
the LORD." ' "

Proclamation Against Pharaoh

20 And it came to pass in the eleventh
year, in the first *month,* on the seventh
day of the month, *that* the word of the
LORD came to me, saying,
21 "Son of man, I have [a]broken the
arm of Pharaoh king of Egypt; and see,
[b]it has not been bandaged for healing,
nor a [1]splint put on to bind it, to make
it strong enough to hold a sword.
22 "Therefore thus says the Lord GOD:
'Surely I *am* [a]against Pharaoh king of
Egypt, and will [b]break his arms, both
the strong one and the one that was
broken; and I will make the sword fall
out of his hand.
23 [a]'I will scatter the Egyptians among
the nations, and disperse them
throughout the countries.
24 'I will strengthen the arms of the
king of Babylon and put My sword in
his hand; but I will break Pharaoh's
arms, and he will groan before him
with the groanings of a mortally
wounded *man.*

15 [a]Jer. 46:25 [2]Ancient Thebes
16 [a]Ezek. 30:8
17 [1]Ancient On, Heliopolis
18 [a]Jer. 2:16 [1]*Tahpanhes,* Jer. 43:7 [2]So with many Heb. mss., Bg., LXX, Syr., Tg., Vg.; MT *refrained*
19 [a][Ps. 9:16]; Ezek. 5:8; 25:11
21 [a]Jer. 48:25 [b]Jer. 46:11 [1]Lit. *bandage*
22 [a]Jer. 46:25; Ezek. 29:3 [b]Ps. 37:17
23 [a]Ezek. 29:12; 30:17, 18, 26
25 [a]Ps. 9:16
26 [a]Ezek. 29:12

CHAPTER 31

1 [a]Jer. 52:5, 6; Ezek. 30:20; 32:1
2 [a]Ezek. 31:18
3 [a]Is. 10:33, 34; Ezek. 17:3, 4, 22; 31:16; Dan. 4:10, 20–23
4 [a]Jer. 51:36; Ezek. 29:3–9 [1]Or *channels*
5 [a]Dan. 4:11
6 [a]Ezek. 17:23; 31:13; Dan. 4:12, 21; Matt. 13:32

25 'Thus I will strengthen the arms of
the king of Babylon, but the arms of
Pharaoh shall fall down; [a]they shall
know that I *am* the LORD, when I put
My sword into the hand of the king of
Babylon and he stretches it out against
the land of Egypt.
26 [a]'I will scatter the Egyptians among
the nations and disperse them throughout the countries. Then they shall
know that I *am* the LORD.' "

Egypt Cut Down Like a Great Tree

31 Now it came to pass in the
[a]eleventh year, in the third
month, on the first *day* of the month,
that the word of the LORD came to me,
saying,
2 "Son of man, say to Pharaoh king
of Egypt and to his multitude:

[a]'Whom are you like in your
greatness?
3 [a]Indeed Assyria *was* a cedar in
Lebanon,
With fine branches that shaded
the forest,
And of high stature;
And its top was among the thick
boughs.
4 [a]The waters made it grow;
Underground waters gave it
height,
With their rivers running around
the place where it was planted,
And sent out [1]rivulets to all the
trees of the field.

5 'Therefore [a]its height was exalted
above all the trees of the field;
Its boughs were multiplied,
And its branches became long
because of the abundance of
water,
As it sent them out.
6 All the [a]birds of the heavens
made their nests in its boughs;
Under its branches all the beasts
of the field brought forth their
young;

30:17 Aven is the ancient Egyptian city of On or Heliopolis, just north of Memphis. **Pi Beseth** is located about 30 miles southwest of Zoan.
30:18 Tehaphnehes is Tahpanhes, a city on the eastern frontier of Lower Egypt in the area of the Nile Delta. Jews fled there after the death of Gedaliah (Jer. 43:8, 9).
30:20–26 The fourth oracle against Egypt, dated April 29, 587 B.C., three months before the fall of Jerusalem. God had **broken the arm of Pharaoh** Hophra by Nebuchadnezzar's victory the year before, and Pharaoh had failed to provide aid to Judah (see 29:6; Jer. 37:7). Now God will break both of Pharaoh's arms (v. 24).
31:1–18 The fifth oracle against Egypt, dated June 21, 587 B.C. Ezekiel uses an allegory of a cedar tree to show the unsurpassed greatness of the Assyrian Empire. This is similar to what he did with Tyre, using the image of a grand ship for the purpose (27:3–9). As with Tyre (28:1–5), the cause of Assyria's fall was pride: **its heart was lifted up in its height** (v. 10), and the tree was cut down by Babylon, **the most terrible of the nations** (v. 12). Pharaoh is warned that he, too, will **be brought down** (v. 18) and **lie in the midst of the uncircumcised** (see 28:10; 32:19).
31:4 The waters: The Tigris and Euphrates rivers.

And in its shadow all great
nations [1]made their home.

7 'Thus it was beautiful in greatness
and in the length of its
branches,
Because its roots reached to
abundant waters.
8 The cedars in the [a]garden of God
could not hide it;
The fir trees were not like its
boughs,
And the [1]chestnut trees were not
like its branches;
No tree in the garden of God was
like it in *beauty.
9 I made it beautiful with a
multitude of branches,
So that all the trees of Eden
envied it,
That *were* in the garden of God.'

10 "Therefore thus says the Lord GOD:
'Because you have increased in height,
and it set its top among the thick
boughs, and [a]its heart was [1]lifted up
in its height,
11 'therefore I will deliver it into the
hand of the [a]mighty one of the nations,
and he shall surely deal with it; I have
driven it out for its wickedness.
12 'And aliens, [a]the most terrible of the
nations, have cut it down and left it;
its branches have fallen [b]on the mountains and in all the valleys; its boughs
lie [c]broken by all the rivers of the land;
and all the peoples of the earth have
gone from under its shadow and left
it.

13 'On [a]its ruin will remain all the
birds of the heavens,
And all the beasts of the field will
come to its branches—

14 'So that no trees by the waters may
ever again exalt themselves for their
height, nor set their tops among the
thick boughs, that no tree which drinks
water may ever be high enough to
reach up to them.

'For [a]they have all been delivered
to death,
[b]To the depths of the earth,
Among the children of men who
go down to the Pit.'

15 "Thus says the Lord GOD: 'In the
day when it [a]went down to [1]hell,* I
caused mourning. I covered the deep
because of it. I restrained its rivers, and
the great waters were held back. I
caused Lebanon to [2]mourn for it, and
all the trees of the field wilted because
of it.
16 'I made the nations [a]shake at the
sound of its fall, when I [b]cast it down
to [1]hell together with those who descend into the Pit; and [c]all the trees
of Eden, the choice and best of Lebanon, all that drink water, [d]were comforted in the depths of the earth.
17 'They also went down to hell with
it, with those *slain* by the sword; and
those who were its *strong* arm [a]dwelt
in its shadows among the nations.
18 [a]'To which of the trees in Eden
will you then be likened in glory and
greatness? Yet you shall be brought
down with the trees of Eden to the
depths of the earth; [b]you shall lie in
the midst of the uncircumcised, with
those slain by the sword. This *is* Pharaoh and all his multitude,' says the
Lord GOD."

Lamentation for Pharaoh and Egypt

32 And it came to pass in the
twelfth year, in the [a]twelfth
month, on the first *day* of the month,
that the word of the LORD came to me,
saying,
2 "Son of man, [a]take up a lamentation for Pharaoh king of Egypt, and say
to him:

[b]'You are like a young lion among
the nations,
And [c]you *are* like a monster in
the seas,
[d]Bursting forth in your rivers,
Troubling the waters with your
feet,
And [e]fouling their rivers.'

3 "Thus says the Lord GOD:

'I will therefore [a]spread My net
over you with a company of
many people,
And they will draw you up in My
net.
4 Then [a]I will leave you on the land;

6 [1]Lit. *dwelled*
8 [a]Gen. 2:8, 9; 13:10; Is. 51:3; Ezek. 28:13; 31:16, 18 [1]Or *plane,* Heb. *armon* *See WW at Ezek. 28:12.
10 [a]2 Chr. 32:25; Is. 10:12; 14:13, 14; Ezek. 28:17; Dan. 5:20 [1]Proud
11 [a]Ezek. 30:10; Dan. 5:18, 19
12 [a]Ezek. 28:7; 30:11; 32:12 [b]Ezek. 32:5; 35:8 [c]Ezek. 30:24, 25
13 [a]Is. 18:6; Ezek. 32:4
14 [a]Ps. 82:7 [b]Ezek. 32:18
15 [a]Ezek. 32:22, 23 [1]Or *Sheol* [2]Lit. *be darkened* *See WW at Hos. 13:14.
16 [a]Ezek. 26:15; Hag. 2:7 [b]Is. 14:15; Ezek. 32:18 [c]Is. 14:8; Hab. 2:17 [d]Ezek. 32:31 [1]Or *Sheol*
17 [a]Lam. 4:20
18 [a]Ezek. 32:19 [b]Jer. 9:25, 26; Ezek. 28:10; 32:19, 21

CHAPTER 32

1 [a]Ezek. 31:1; 33:21
2 [a]Ezek. 27:2 [b]Jer. 4:7; Ezek. 19:2–6; Nah. 2:11–13 [c]Is. 27:1; Ezek. 29:3 [d]Jer. 46:7, 8 [e]Ezek. 34:18
3 [a]Ezek. 12:13; 17:20
4 [a]Ezek. 29:5

32:1–16 The sixth oracle against **Egypt,** dated March 3, 585 B.C. The oracle takes the form of a funeral lament (see note on 19:1–14), for God will draw Pharaoh up in His **net** (v. 3) and expose him as food for the **birds** and **beasts** (v. 4). Darkness will come as in the Day of the Lord (v. 7; Joel 2:2, 10; Amos 5:18–20), and Egypt will become a lifeless wasteland (vv. 13–15).

32:2 Young lion: The lion is often associated with royalty (see 19:1–14). **Monster in the seas:** See note on 29:3.

32:3 Draw you up: See the similar treatment of Egypt (29:4, 5).

I will cast you out on the open
fields,
[b]And cause to [1]settle on you all the
birds of the heavens.
And with you I will fill the beasts
of the whole earth.
5 I will lay your flesh [a]on the
mountains,
And fill the valleys with your
carcass.

6 'I will also water the land with the
flow of your blood,
Even to the mountains;
And the riverbeds will be full of
you.
7 When *I* put out your light,
[a]I will cover the heavens, and
make its stars dark;
I will cover the sun with a cloud,
And the moon shall not give her
light.
8 All the [1]bright lights of the
heavens I will make dark over
you,
And bring darkness upon your
land,'
Says the Lord GOD.

9 'I will also trouble the hearts of
many peoples, when I bring your destruction among the nations, into the
countries which you have not known.
10 'Yes, I will make many peoples astonished at you, and their kings shall
be horribly afraid of you when I bran-
dish My sword before them; and [a]they
shall tremble *every* moment, every
man for his own life, in the day of your
fall.'
11 [a]"For thus says the Lord GOD: 'The
sword of the king of Babylon shall
come upon you.
12 'By the swords of the mighty warriors, all of them [a]the most terrible of
the nations, I will cause your multitude
to fall.

[b]'They shall plunder the pomp of
Egypt,
And all its multitude shall be
destroyed.
13 Also I will destroy all its animals
From beside its great waters;
[a]The foot of man shall muddy
them no more,
Nor shall the hooves of animals
muddy them.
14 Then I will make their waters
[1]clear,
And make their rivers run like
oil,'
Says the Lord GOD.

15 'When I make the land of Egypt
desolate,
And the country is destitute of all
that once filled it,
When I strike all who dwell in it,
[a]Then they shall know that I *am*
the LORD.

16 'This *is* the [a]lamentation
With which they shall lament her;
The daughters of the nations shall
lament her;
They shall lament for her, for
Egypt,
And for all her multitude,'
Says the Lord GOD."

Egypt and Others Consigned to the Pit

17 It came to pass also in the twelfth
year, on the fifteenth *day* of the month,
[a]*that* the word of the LORD came to me,
saying:

18 "Son of man, wail over the
multitude of Egypt,
And [a]cast them down to the
depths of the earth,
Her and the daughters of the
famous nations,
With those who go down to the
Pit:
19 'Whom [a]do you surpass in beauty?
[b]Go down, be placed with the
uncircumcised.'

20 "They shall fall in the midst of
those slain by the sword;
She is delivered to the sword,
[a]Drawing her and all her
multitudes.
21 [a]The strong among the mighty
Shall speak to him out of the
midst of hell
With those who help him:
'They have [b]gone down,
They lie with the uncircumcised,
slain by the sword.'

4 [b]Is. 18:6; Ezek. 31:13 [1]Lit. *sit* or *dwell*
5 [a]Ezek. 31:12
7 [a]Is. 13:10; Joel 2:31; 3:15; Amos 8:9; Matt. 24:29; Mark 13:24; Luke 21:25; Rev. 6:12, 13; 8:12
8 [1]Or *shining*
10 [a]Ezek. 26:16
11 [a]Jer. 46:26; Ezek. 30:4
12 [a]Ezek. 28:7; 30:11; 31:12 [b]Ezek. 29:19
13 [a]Ezek. 29:11
14 [1]Lit. *sink;* settle, grow clear
15 [a]Ex. 7:5; 14:4, 18; Ps. 9:16; Ezek. 6:7
16 [a]2 Sam. 1:17; 2 Chr. 35:25; Jer. 9:17; Ezek. 26:17
17 [a]Ezek. 32:1; 33:21
18 [a]Ezek. 26:20; 31:14
19 [a]Jer. 9:25, 26; Ezek. 31:2, 18 [b]Ezek. 28:10
20 [a]Ps. 28:3
21 [a]Is. 1:31; 14:9, 10; Ezek. 32:27 [b]Ezek. 32:19, 25

32:17–32 The seventh and last oracle against Egypt, dated perhaps April 27, 586 B.C. This oracle is also a lament or funeral dirge directed against Pharaoh and all the Egyptians. Like Tyre (28:10), Egypt will **be placed with the uncircumcised** heathen (v. 19; 31:18). Other former great powers await the Pharaoh in **the Pit** (v. 18) or in **hell** (v. 21): **Assyria** (v. 22); **Elam** (v. 24); **Meshech and Tubal** (v. 26); **Edom** (v. 29); **the princes of the north** and **the Sidonians** (v. 30). In each case the nation is personified by one typical figure (perhaps the last king), and the graves of the warriors are all around. In this oracle the language is poetic and symbolic. We should not try to determine the state of the dead from this passage. The clear message is that Egypt will go the way of all nations who forget God.

22 "Assyria[a] *is* there, and all her company,
With their graves all around her,
All of them slain, fallen by the sword.
23 [a]Her graves are set in the recesses of the Pit,
And her company is all around her grave,
All of them slain, fallen by the sword,
Who [b]caused terror in the land of the living.

24 "There *is* [a]Elam and all her multitude,
All around her grave,
All of them slain, fallen by the sword,
Who have [b]gone down uncircumcised to the lower parts of the earth,
[c]Who caused their terror in the land of the living;
Now they bear their shame with those who go down to the Pit.
25 They have set her [a]bed in the midst of the slain,
With all her multitude,
With her graves all around it,
All of them uncircumcised, slain by the sword;
Though their terror was caused
In the land of the living,
Yet they bear their shame
With those who go down to the Pit;
It was put in the midst of the slain.

26 "There *are* [a]Meshech and Tubal and all their multitudes,
With all their graves around it,
All of them [b]uncircumcised, slain by the sword,
Though they caused their terror in the land of the living.
27 [a]They do not lie with the mighty
Who are fallen of the uncircumcised,
Who have gone down to hell with their weapons of war;
They have laid their swords under their heads,
But their iniquities will be on their bones,
Because of the terror of the mighty in the land of the living.
28 Yes, you shall be broken in the midst of the uncircumcised,
And lie with *those* slain by the sword.

29 "There *is* [a]Edom,
Her kings and all her princes,
Who despite their might
Are laid beside *those* slain by the sword;
They shall lie with the uncircumcised,
And with those who go down to the Pit.
30 [a]There *are* the princes of the north,
All of them, and all the [b]Sidonians,
Who have gone down with the slain
In shame at the terror which they caused by their might;
They lie uncircumcised with *those* slain by the sword,
And bear their shame with those who go down to the Pit.

31 "Pharaoh will see them
And be [a]comforted over all his multitude,
Pharaoh and all his army,
Slain by the sword,"
Says the Lord GOD.

32 "For I have caused My terror in the land of the living;
And he shall be placed in the midst of the uncircumcised
With *those* slain by the sword,
Pharaoh and all his multitude,"
Says the Lord GOD.

The Watchman and His Message

33 Again the word of the LORD came to me, saying, 5
2 "Son of man, speak to [a]the children

22 [a]Ezek. 31:3, 16
23 [a]Is. 14:15 [b]Ezek. 32:24–27, 32
24 [a]Gen. 10:22; 14:1; Is. 11:11; Jer. 25:25; 49:34–39 [b]Ezek. 32:21 [c]Ezek. 32:23
25 [a]Ps. 139:8
26 [a]Gen. 10:2; Ezek. 27:13; 38:2, 3; 39:1 [b]Ezek. 32:19
27 [a]Is. 14:18, 19
29 [a]Is. 9:25, 26; 34:5, 6; Jer. 49:7–22; Ezek. 25:12–14
30 [a]Jer. 1:15; 25:26; Ezek. 38:6, 15; 39:2 [b]Jer. 25:22; Ezek. 28:21–23
31 [a]Ezek. 14:22; 31:16

CHAPTER 33

2 [a]Ezek. 3:11

32:24 Elam is a country to the east of Assyria in present-day Iran (Jer. 49:34–39).
32:26 Meshech and Tubal are either tribes or territories in Asia Minor (see 27:13).
32:30 Princes of the north are perhaps the petty kings in northern Syria. The **Sidonians** are part of the southern Phoenicians. See note on 28:20–23.
33:1—39:29 Oracles of restoration. Now that the fate of Jerusalem was sealed, and while Ezekiel waited for word of the fall of the city, God spoke of building a new community. A restored, united, and cleansed Israel with a new heart would emerge. Evangelical Christianity basically interprets these prophecies in one of two ways. Dispensational hermeneutics interprets them literally, applying them to a physical end-times national Israel. Classical hermeneutics interprets them more symbolically, with Israel here being primarily the church but also end-time national Israel to some degree; the time frame of fulfillment is in three phases: the church age, the Millennium, and the world to come. Both of these perspectives will be interwoven into the comments on these oracles. See also the note on Obad. 15.
33:1–9 See section 5 of Truth-In-Action at the end of Ezek.
33:1–9 Responsibility of the **watchman.** Vv. 2–9 are similar to 3:17–21, but here the parallel between Ezekiel and the watchman is more clearly set forth (vv. 2–6), but the danger to the righteous is not mentioned (see 3:20, 21).

of your people, and say to them:
[b]'When I bring the sword upon a land,
and the people of the land take a man
from their territory and make him their
[c]watchman,*
3 'when he sees the sword coming
upon the land, if he *blows the trumpet
and warns the people,
4 'then whoever hears the sound of
the *trumpet and does [a]not take warning, if the sword comes and takes him
away, [b]his blood shall be on his *own*
head.
5 'He heard the sound of the trumpet,
but did not take warning; his blood
shall be upon himself. But he who
takes warning will [1]save his life.
6 'But if the watchman sees the sword
coming and does not blow the trumpet,
and the people are not warned, and the
sword comes and takes *any* person
from among them, [a]he is taken away
in his iniquity; but his blood I will require at the watchman's hand.'
7 [a]"So you, son of man: I have made
you a watchman for the house of Israel; therefore you shall hear a word
from My mouth and warn them for Me.
8 "When I say to the wicked, 'O
wicked *man,* you shall surely die!' and
you do not speak to warn the wicked
from his way, that wicked *man* shall
die in his iniquity; but his blood I will
require at your hand.
9 "Nevertheless if you warn the
wicked to turn from his way, and he
does not turn from his way, he shall
die in his iniquity; but you have [1]de-
livered your soul.
10 "Therefore you, O son of man, say
to the house of Israel: 'Thus you say,
"If our transgressions and our sins *lie*
upon us, and we [a]pine[1] away in them,
[b]how can we then live?" '
11 "Say to them: '*As* I live,' says the
Lord GOD, [a]'I have no pleasure in the
death of the wicked, but that the
wicked [b]turn from his way and live.
Turn, turn from your evil ways! For
[c]why should you die, O house of
Israel?'

The Fairness of God's Judgment

12 "Therefore you, O son of man, say
to the children of your people: 'The

2 [b]Ezek. 14:17 [c]2 Sam. 18:24, 25 *See WW at Hos. 9:8.
3 *See WW at Ps. 47:1.
4 [a]Zech. 1:4 [b][Acts 18:6] *See WW at Hos. 8:1.
5 [1]Or *deliver his soul*
6 [a]Ezek. 33:8
7 [a]Is. 62:6
9 [1]Or *saved your life*
10 [a]Ezek. 24:23 [b]Is. 49:14 [1]Or *waste away*
11 [a][2 Sam. 14:14] [b][Acts 3:19] [c]Ezek. 18:30, 31
12 [a]Ezek. 3:20; 18:24, 26 [b][2 Chr. 7:14]
13 [a]Ezek. 3:20; 18:24
14 [a]Ezek. 3:18, 19; 18:27 [1]*justice* [2]*righteousness*
15 [a]Ezek. 18:7 [b]Lev. 6:2, 4, 5 [c]Ezek. 20:11, 13, 21
16 [a][Is. 1:18; 43:25] *See WW at Is. 62:6.
17 [a]Ezek. 18:25, 29 [1]Or *equitable*
18 [a]Ezek. 18:26
20 [a]Ezek. 18:25, 29 [1]Or *equitable*
21 [a]Ezek. 1:2 [b]Ezek. 24:26 [c]2 Kin. 25:4 [1]Lit. *struck down*
22 [a]Ezek. 1:3; 8:1; 37:1 [b]Ezek. 24:27

[a]righteousness of the righteous man
shall not deliver him in the day of his
transgression; as for the wickedness of
the wicked, [b]he shall not fall because
of it in the day that he turns from his
wickedness; nor shall the righteous
be able to live because of *his righteousness* in the day that he sins.'
13 "When I say to the righteous *that*
he shall surely live, [a]but he trusts in
his own righteousness and commits iniquity, none of his righteous works
shall be remembered; but because of
the iniquity that he has committed, he
shall die.
14 "Again, [a]when I say to the wicked,
'You shall surely die,' if he turns from
his sin and does [1]what is lawful and
[2]right,
15 "*if* the wicked [a]restores the pledge,
[b]gives back what he has stolen, and
walks in [c]the statutes of life without
committing iniquity, he shall surely
live; he shall not die.
16 [a]"None of his sins which he has
committed shall be *remembered
against him; he has done what is lawful
and right; he shall surely live.
17 [a]"Yet the children of your people
say, 'The way of the LORD is not
[1]fair.' But it is their way which is not
fair!
18 [a]"When the righteous turns from
his righteousness and commits iniquity, he shall die because of it.
19 "But when the wicked turns from
his wickedness and does what is lawful
and right, he shall live because of
it.
20 "Yet you say, [a]'The way of the LORD
is not [1]fair.' O house of Israel, I will
judge every one of you according to
his own ways."

The Fall of Jerusalem

21 And it came to pass in the twelfth
year [a]of our captivity, in the tenth
month, on the fifth *day* of the month,
[b]*that* one who had escaped from Jerusalem came to me and said, [c]"The city
has been [1]captured!"
22 Now [a]the hand of the LORD had
been upon me the evening before the
man came who had escaped. And He
had [b]opened my mouth; so when he

33:6 Although this verse is often used to press Christians to witness lest God **require** of them the **blood** of lost associates, this is not its intent. It reflects a word to Ezekiel and an ancient law (Gen. 9:5), not a NT precept.

33:11 ***As I live:*** See v. 27; 34:8 and note on 5:11. **Turn, turn:** See note on 14:6.

33:12–20 This passage is similar to 18:19–32. Each day a person has the opportunity to choose to live a righteous life. The individual is responsible for his or her actions, and one's destiny may be determined by the choice for that day.

33:21 The fall of **Jerusalem** was reported to Ezekiel on January 8, 585 B.C.

33:22 Hand of the LORD: See note on 1:3. **My mouth . . . was no longer mute:** With the announcement that the city

came to me in the morning, my mouth
was opened, and I was no longer mute.

The Cause of Judah's Ruin

23 Then the word of the LORD came to
me, saying:
24 "Son of man, [a]they who inhabit
those [b]ruins in the land of Israel are
saying, [c]'Abraham was only one, and
he *inherited the land. [d]But we *are*
many; the land has been given to us
as a [e]possession.'
25 "Therefore say to them, 'Thus says
the Lord GOD: [a]"You eat *meat* with
blood, you [b]lift up your eyes toward
your idols, and [c]shed blood. Should
you then possess the [d]land?
26 "You rely on your sword, you commit abominations, and you [a]defile one
another's wives. Should you then possess the land?" '
27 "Say thus to them, 'Thus says the
Lord GOD: "*As* I live, surely [a]those who
are in the ruins shall fall by the sword,
and the one who *is* in the open field
[b]I will give to the beasts to be devoured, and those who *are* in the
strongholds and [c]caves shall die of the
pestilence.
28 [a]"For I will make the land most desolate, [1]her [b]arrogant strength shall
cease, and [c]the mountains of Israel
shall be so desolate that no one will
pass through.
29 "Then they shall know that I *am* the
LORD, when I have made the land most
desolate because of all their abominations which they have committed." '

Hearing and Not Doing

5 30 "As for you, son of man, the children of your people are talking about
you beside the walls and in the doors
of the houses; and they [a]speak to one
another, everyone saying to his
brother, 'Please come and hear what
the word is that comes from the LORD.'
31 "So [a]they come to you as people do,
they [b]sit before you *as* My people, and
they [c]hear your words, but they do not
do them; [d]for with their mouth they
show much love, *but* [e]their hearts pursue their *own* gain.
32 "Indeed you *are* to them as a very
lovely song of one who has a pleasant
voice and can play well on an instrument; for they hear your words, but
they do [a]not do them.
33 [a]"And when this comes to pass—
surely it will come—then [b]they will
know that a prophet has been among
them."

Irresponsible Shepherds

34 And the word of the LORD came 5
to me, saying,
2 "Son of man, prophesy against the
shepherds of Israel, prophesy and say
to them, 'Thus says the Lord GOD to
the shepherds: [a]"Woe to the shepherds
of Israel who feed themselves! Should
not the shepherds feed the flocks?
3 [a]"You eat the fat and clothe yourselves with the wool; you [b]slaughter
the fatlings, *but* you do not *feed the
flock.
4 [a]"The weak you have not strengthened, nor have you *healed those who
were sick, nor bound up the broken,
nor brought back what was driven
away, nor [b]sought what was lost; but
with [c]force and [1]cruelty you have ruled
them.
5 [a]"So they were [b]scattered because
there was no shepherd; [c]and they became food for all the beasts of the field
when they were scattered.

24 [a]Ezek. 34:2 [b]Ezek. 36:4 [c]Is. 51:2 [d][Matt. 3:9] [e]Ezek. 11:15 *See WW at Deut. 8:1. **25** [a]Lev. 3:17; 7:26;17:10–14; 19:26 [b]Ezek. 18:6 [c]Ezek. 22:6, 9 [d]Deut. 29:28 **26** [a]Ezek. 18:6; 22:11 **27** [a]Ezek. 33:24 [b]Ezek. 39:4 [c]1 Sam. 13:6 **28** [a]Jer. 44:2, 6, 22 [b]Ezek. 7:24; 24:21 [c]Ezek. 6:2, 3, 6 [1]Lit. *pride of her strength*

30 [a]Is. 29:13 **31** [a]Ezek. 14:1 [b]Ezek. 8:1 [c]Is. 58:2 [d]Ps. 78:36, 37 [e][Matt. 13:22] **32** [a][Matt. 7:21–28] **33** [a]1 Sam. 3:20 [b]Ezek. 2:5

CHAPTER 34

2 [a]Zech. 11:17 **3** [a]Zech. 11:16 [b]Ezek. 33:25, 26 *See WW at Is. 40:11. **4** [a]Zech. 11:16 [b]Luke 15:4 [c][1 Pet. 5:3] [1]*harshness* or *rigor* *See WW at Ex. 15:26. **5** [a]Ezek. 33:21 [b]Matt. 9:36 [c]Is. 56:9

---

had fallen (v. 21), all of Ezekiel's prophecies had come to pass. As God had promised (24:27), Ezekiel is now able to speak. His new role is to minister comfort.

33:23–29 The Jews in Jerusalem, who were not exiled in 586 B.C., boasted that their potential was greater than **Abraham**'s because he **was only one,** and they ***are* many.** Their sin, however, will not allow them to inherit the land (v. 24); instead they will **fall by the sword,** be **devoured** by **beasts,** or **die of the pestilence** (see 5:17 and note on 5:12).

33:30–33 See section 5 of Truth-In-Action at the end of Ezek.

33:30–33 *Ezekiel* is informed that the people desire to **hear** what he has to say (he is popular because his prophecies have all come to pass); but they will not act upon his words because they desire their own way and the **gain** they think will come from their improved situation.

34:1–31 The king, prophet, and priest as shepherd was an ancient image dating back more than 1,000 years before Ezekiel. The king had the responsibility to supply food and water for his flock, to destroy those who would harm them, and to defend the right of the weak—the widow, the orphan, and the alien. But Israel's kings had failed. Instead of feeding the flock, they **feed themselves** (v. 2) and **clothe** themselves **with the wool** (v. 3). As a result of neglect, the sheep are **scattered** (vv. 5, 6). God will intervene and gather the scattered sheep as the Good Shepherd (see vv. 11–16; Is. 40:11; Jer. 31:10). He will **judge** the sheep who have done wrong (vv. 17–22), and will place His **servant David** over them as a **shepherd** (vv. 23, 24). Finally, He will **make a covenant of peace with them;** they will be His people and He will be their God (vv. 25–31). The prophets and priests had also failed (v. 4).

34:1–10 See section 5 of Truth-In-Action at the end of Ezek.

34:5 They were scattered: Out in the field the sheep could be separated from the flock by a storm or darkness or by wandering away. The lack of a shepherd allowed wild **beasts,** hostile foreign powers, to scatter the sheep by exile.

6 "My sheep [a]wandered through all
the mountains, and on every high hill;
yes, My flock was scattered over the
whole face of the earth, and no one was
seeking or searching *for them.*"
7 'Therefore, you shepherds, hear the
word of the LORD:
8 "*As* I live," says the Lord GOD,
"surely because My flock became a
prey, and My flock [a]became food for
every beast of the field, because *there*
was no shepherd, nor did My shepherds search for My flock, [b]but the
shepherds fed themselves and did not
feed My flock"—
9 'therefore, O shepherds, hear the
word of the LORD!
10 'Thus says the Lord GOD: "Behold,
I *am* [a]against the shepherds, and
[b]I will require My flock at their hand;
I will cause them to cease feeding the
sheep, and the shepherds shall [c]feed
themselves no more; for I will [d]deliver
My flock from their mouths, that they
may no longer be food for them."

KINGDOM DYNAMICS

34:1–10 Restoration and the Corruption of Leadership, RESTORATION. This text displays the corruption of leadership and the need for restoration at that dimension. The entire concept of "The Holy Spirit and Restoration" is developed in the study article that begins on page 2012.

(Jer. 8:8, 9/Amos 5:21–23) J.R.

God, the True Shepherd

11 'For thus says the Lord GOD: "Indeed I Myself will search for My sheep
and seek them out.
12 "As a [a]shepherd seeks out his flock
on the day he is among his scattered
sheep, so will I seek out My sheep and
deliver them from all the places where
they were scattered on [b]a cloudy and
dark day.
13 "And [a]I will bring them out from
the peoples and gather them from the
countries, and will bring them to their
own land; I will feed them on the
mountains of Israel, [1]in the valleys and
in all the inhabited places of the country.
14 [a]"I will feed them in **good** pasture,
and their fold shall be on the high
mountains of Israel. [b]There they shall
lie down in a good fold and feed in rich
pasture on the mountains of Israel.

WORD WEALTH

34:14 good, *tob* (*tohv*); Strong's #2896: Good, goodness; whatever is right, pleasant, or happy; opposite of sorrow or evil. This adjective occurs more than 500 times, with a much wider range of meaning than the word "good" has in English. In its first occurrence (Gen. 1:4), the Creator evaluates His product: "God saw the light, that *it was* good." Shortly thereafter, *tob* is used in contrast with its antonym *ra'* (bad or evil) in the phrase "good and evil" (Gen. 2:17; see also Gen. 31:24; Is. 5:20; 7:15). In the present reference, God assures His flock that He will rescue them from their cruel leaders; He will find good pasture to nourish them and will provide a fold where they can rest in safety.

15 "I will feed My flock, and I will
make them lie down," says the Lord
GOD.
16 [a]"I will seek what was lost and
bring back what was driven away, bind
up the broken and strengthen what
was sick; but I will destroy [b]the fat and
the strong, and feed them [c]in judgment."
17 'And *as for* you, O My flock, thus
says the Lord GOD: [a]"Behold, I shall
judge between sheep and sheep, between rams and goats.
18 "*Is it* too little for you to have eaten
up the good pasture, that you must
tread down with your feet the [1]residue
of your pasture—and to have drunk of
the clear waters, that you must foul the
residue with your feet?
19 "And *as for* My flock, they eat what
you have trampled with your feet, and
they drink what you have fouled with
your feet."
20 'Therefore thus says the Lord GOD
to them: [a]"Behold, I Myself will judge
between the fat and the lean sheep.
21 "Because you have pushed with
side and shoulder, butted all the weak
ones with your horns, and scattered
them abroad,
22 "therefore I will save My flock, and
they shall no longer be a prey; and I

6 [a]Jer. 40:11, 12; 50:6; Ezek. 7:16; 1 Pet. 2:25
8 [a]Ezek. 34:5, 6 [b]Ezek. 34:2, 10
10 [a]Jer. 21:13; 52:24–27; Ezek. 5:8; 13:8; Zech. 10:3 [b]Ezek. 3:18; Heb. 13:17 [c]Ezek. 34:2, 8 [d]Ps. 72:12–14; Ezek. 13:23
12 [a]Jer. 31:10 [b]Jer. 13:16; Ezek. 30:3; Joel 2:2
13 [a]Is. 65:9, 10; Jer. 23:3; Ezek. 11:17; 20:41; 28:25; 36:24; 37:21, 22 [1]Or *by the streams*
14 [a]Ps. 23:2; Jer. 3:15; [John 10:9] [b]Jer. 33:12
16 [a]Is. 40:11; Mic. 4:6; [Matt. 18:11; Mark 2:17; Luke 5:32] [b]Is. 10:16; Amos 4:1 [c]Jer. 10:24
17 [a]Ezek. 20:37; Mal. 4:1; [Matt. 25:32]
18 [1]*remainder*
20 [a]Ezek. 34:17

34:8 *As* I live: See note on 5:11.
34:10 I *am* against the shepherds: See note on 5:8.
34:11–16 This prophecy is best understood eschatologically since the shepherd is clearly messianic, described in v. 23 as a descendant of David. The dispensational view interprets this literally, applying to a restored end-times national Israel. The classical view interprets the passage more symbolically, the gathered people being both the church and national Israel.
34:16 The fat and the strong are those sheep that have sought their own welfare at the expense of others (vv. 17–22).

will judge between sheep and sheep.
23 "I will establish one [a]shepherd over
them, and he shall feed them—[b]My
servant David. He shall feed them and
be their shepherd.
24 "And [a]I, the LORD, will be their God,
and My servant David [b]a prince among
them; I, the LORD, have spoken.
25 [a]"I will make a covenant of peace
with them, and [b]cause wild beasts to
cease from the land; and they [c]will
dwell safely in the wilderness and
sleep in the woods.
26 "I will make them and the places
all around [a]My hill [b]a blessing; and I
will [c]cause showers to come down in
their season; there shall be [d]showers
of blessing.
27 "Then [a]the trees of the field shall
yield their fruit, and the earth shall
yield her increase. They shall be safe
in their land; and they shall know that
I *am* the LORD, when I have [b]broken
the bands of their yoke and delivered
them from the hand of those who
[c]enslaved them.
28 "And they shall no longer be a prey
for the nations, nor shall beasts of the
land devour them; but [a]they shall dwell
safely, and no one shall make *them*
afraid.
29 "I will raise up for them a [a]garden[1]
of renown, and they shall [b]no longer
be consumed with hunger in the land,
[c]nor bear the shame of the Gentiles
anymore.
30 "Thus they shall know that [a]I, the
LORD their God, *am* with them, and
they, the house of Israel, *are* [b]My people," says the Lord GOD.' "
31 "You are My [a]flock, the flock of My
pasture; you *are* men, *and* I *am* your
God," says the Lord GOD.

Judgment on Mount Seir

35 Moreover the word of the LORD
came to me, saying,

23 [a][Is. 40:11] [b]Jer. 30:9
24 [a]Ex. 29:45 [b]Ezek. 37:24, 25
25 [a]Ezek. 37:26 [b]Is. 11:6–9 [c]Jer. 23:6
26 [a]Is. 56:7 [b]Zech. 8:13 [c]Lev. 26:4 [d]Ps. 68:9
27 [a]Is. 4:2 [b]Jer. 2:20 [c]Jer. 25:14
28 [a]Jer. 30:10
29 [a][Is. 11:1] [b]Ezek. 36:29 [c]Ezek. 36:3, 6, 15 [1]Lit. *planting place*
30 [a]Ezek. 34:24 [b]Ezek. 14:11; 36:28
31 [a]Ps. 100:3

CHAPTER 35

2 [a]Ezek. 25:12–14 [b]Amos 1:11
3 [a]Ezek. 6:14 [1]Lit. *a desolation and a waste*
5 [a]Ezek. 25:12 [b]Ps. 137:7 [1]Or *everlasting*
6 [a]Is. 63:1–6 [b]Ps. 109:17 [1]Or *bloodshed*
7 [a]Judg. 5:6 [1]Lit. *a waste and a desolation*
9 [a]Jer. 49:13 [b]Ezek. 36:11 [1]Lit. *desolated forever*
10 [a]Ps. 83:4–12 [b][Ps.48:1–3; 132:13, 14]
11 [a][James 2:13]
12 [a]Ps. 9:16

2 "Son of man, set your face against
[a]Mount Seir and [b]prophesy against it,
3 "and say to it, 'Thus says the Lord
GOD:

"Behold, O Mount Seir, I *am*
against you;
[a]I will stretch out My hand against
you,
And make you [1]most desolate;
4 I shall lay your cities waste,
And you shall be desolate.
Then you shall know that I *am*
the LORD.

5 [a]"Because you have had an [1]ancient
hatred, and have shed *the blood of* the
children of Israel by the power of the
sword at the time of their calamity,
[b]*when* their iniquity *came to an* end,
6 "therefore, *as* I live," says the Lord
GOD, "I will prepare you for [a]blood,
and blood shall pursue you; [b]since you
have not hated [1]blood, therefore blood
shall pursue you.
7 "Thus I will make Mount Seir
[1]most desolate, and cut off from it the
[a]one who leaves and the one who returns.
8 "And I will fill its mountains with
the slain; on your hills and in your valleys and in all your ravines those who
are slain by the sword shall fall.
9 [a]"I will make you [1]perpetually desolate, and your cities shall be uninhabited; [b]then you shall know that
I *am* the LORD.
10 "Because you have said, 'These two
nations and these two countries shall
be mine, and we will [a]possess them,'
although [b]the LORD was there,
11 "therefore, *as* I live," says the Lord
GOD, "I will do [a]according to your anger and according to the envy which
you showed in your hatred against
them; and I will make Myself known
among them when I judge you.
12 [a]"Then you shall know that I *am*

34:23 My servant David is a messianic ruler from the line of David who will truly be a man after God's own heart (see Ps. 89:3, 4, 20; Jer. 23:5). This is clearly fulfilled in Jesus Christ.
34:25–31 Here is another eschatological prophecy, which seems to be using symbolic rather than strictly literal language, a practice common in Ezek. Applied to the church, the fulfillment can be seen in three stages with both literal and spiritual applications. The blessings and prosperity *during the* current church age would be *largely* spiritual (for example, **wild beasts** [v. 25] symbolize spiritual enemies). In the Millennium and the world to come, the fulfillment will be both literal and spiritual as then we shall know the full consummation of **showers of blessing** (v. 26), **a garden of renown** (v. 29), and **no . . . hunger** (v. 29).
34:29 A garden of renown: The prophets often describe the future as a return to Paradise, the Garden of Eden (see Is. 35:1–10; 65:17–25).
35:2 Mount Seir is used for Edom (v. 15), the home of Esau the brother of Jacob (Gen. 32:3). There was enmity between the brothers even before birth (Gen. 25:22–34), and this hostility continued in their descendants (25:12–14; Amos 1:11) especially after Edom's occupation of southern Judah (Jer. 49:7–22). Edom seems to be representative of all Israel's enemies who must be disposed of before God's people are restored (ch. 36). Again, Edom can represent national or spiritual enemies. See note on 25:12.
35:6 Blood shall pursue you: Justice or retribution promised in Gen. 9:6. This same type of judgment is reflected in v. 11, "I will do according to your anger and according to [your] envy."

the LORD. I have [b]heard all your
[c]blasphemies which you have spoken
against the mountains of Israel, saying,
'They are desolate; they are given to
us to consume.'
13 "Thus [a]with your mouth you have
[1]boasted against Me and multiplied
your [b]words against Me; I have heard
them."
14 'Thus says the Lord GOD: [a]"The
whole earth will rejoice when I make
you desolate.
15 [a]"As you rejoiced because the inheritance of the house of Israel was
desolate, [b]so I will do to you; you shall
be desolate, O Mount Seir, as well as
all of Edom—all of it! Then they shall
know that I *am* the LORD." '

Blessing on Israel

36 "And you, son of man, prophesy
to the [a]mountains of Israel, and
say, 'O mountains of Israel, hear the
word of the LORD!
2 'Thus says the Lord GOD: "Because
[a]the enemy has said of you, 'Aha!
[b]The [1]ancient heights [c]have become
our possession,' " '
3 "therefore prophesy, and say, 'Thus
says the Lord GOD: "Because they
made *you* desolate and swallowed you
up on every side, so that you became
the possession of the rest of the nations, [a]and you are taken up by the lips
of [b]talkers and slandered by the people"—
4 'therefore, O mountains of Israel,
hear the word of the Lord GOD! Thus
says the Lord GOD to the mountains,
the hills, the [1]rivers, the valleys, the
desolate wastes, and the cities that
have been forsaken, which [a]became
plunder and [b]mockery to the rest of the
nations all around—
5 'therefore thus says the Lord GOD:
[a]"Surely I have spoken in My burning
jealousy against the rest of the nations
and against all Edom, [b]who gave My
land to themselves as a possession,
with wholehearted joy *and* [1]spiteful

12 [b]Zeph. 2:8 [c]Is. 52:5
13 [a][1 Sam. 2:3] [b]Ezek. 36:3 [1]Lit. *made yourself great*
14 [a]Is. 65:13, 14
15 [a]Obad. 12, 15 [b]Jer. 50:11; Lam. 4:21

CHAPTER 36

1 [a]Ezek. 6:2, 3
2 [a]Jer. 33:24; Ezek. 25:3; 26:2 [b]Deut. 32:13; Ps. 78:69; Is. 58:14; Hab. 3:19 [c]Ezek. 35:10 [1]Or *everlasting*
3 [a]Deut. 28:37; 1 Kin. 9:7; Lam. 2:15; Dan. 9:16 [b]Ps. 44:13, 14; Jer. 18:16; Ezek. 35:13
4 [a]Ezek. 34:8, 28 [b]Ps. 79:4; Jer. 48:27 [1]Or *ravines*
5 [a]Deut. 4:24; Ezek. 38:19 [b]Ezek. 35:10, 12 [1]Lit. *scorning souls*
6 [a]Ps. 74:10; 123:3, 4; Ezek. 34:29
7 [a]Ezek. 20:5 [b]Jer. 25:9, 15, 29
10 [a]Is. 58:12; 61:4; Amos 9:14
11 [a]Jer. 31:27; 33:12 [b]Job 42:12; Is. 51:3 [c]Ezek. 35:9; 37:6, 13 [1]Lit. *be fruitful*
12 [a]Obad. 17 [b]Jer. 15:7; Ezek. 22:12, 27
13 [a]Num. 13:32
15 [a]Is. 60:14; Ezek. 34:29

minds, in order to plunder its open
country." '
6 "Therefore prophesy concerning
the land of Israel, and say to the mountains, the hills, the rivers, and the valleys, 'Thus says the Lord GOD: "Behold, I have spoken in My jealousy and
My fury, because you have [a]borne the
shame of the nations."
7 'Therefore thus says the Lord GOD:
"I have [a]raised My hand in an oath that
surely the nations that *are* around you
shall [b]bear their own shame.
8 "But you, O mountains of Israel,
you shall shoot forth your branches
and yield your fruit to My people Israel, for they are about to come.
9 "For indeed I *am* for you, and I will
turn to you, and you shall be tilled and
sown.
10 "I will multiply men upon you, all
the house of Israel, all of it; and the
cities shall be inhabited and [a]the ruins
rebuilt.
11 [a]"I will multiply upon you man and
beast; and they shall increase and
[1]bear young; I will make you inhabited
as in former times, and do [b]better *for
you* than at your beginnings. [c]Then
you shall know that I *am* the LORD.
12 "Yes, I will cause men to walk on
you, My people Israel; [a]they shall take
possession of you, and you shall be
their inheritance; no more shall you
[b]bereave them *of children*."
13 'Thus says the Lord GOD: "Because
they say to you, [a]'You devour men and
bereave your nation *of children*,'
14 "therefore you shall devour men no
more, nor bereave your nation anymore," says the Lord GOD.
15 [a]"Nor will I let you hear the taunts
of the nations anymore, nor bear the
reproach of the peoples anymore, nor
shall you cause your nation to stumble
anymore," says the Lord GOD.' "

The Renewal of Israel

16 Moreover the word of the LORD
came to me, saying:

36:1–38 Interpreted dispensationally (see note on 33:1—39:29), this is a prophecy concerning the restoration of national Israel to a transformed land, likely during the Millennium of Rev. 20. Though Israel was dispossessed by other nations (2 Kin. 17:24), and especially by Edom (35:1–15), God will restore Israel to her inheritance (v. 12; Mal. 1:2–5). The transformation of Israel as a people is preceded by the transformation of the land. Some see this as having begun in a minor way with the restoration of national Israel in 1948.

36:2 Aha: See note on 25:3.

36:7 Raised My hand: See note on 20:5.

36:10 All the house of Israel, all of it: Emphasis upon the combined kingdom of Israel and Judah (37:15–23).

36:12 You bereave them *of children*: The land is accused of causing a depopulation of its inhabitants. Two reasons may be given. The position of the land is such that it is exposed to all invading armies and to the encroachment of nomad tribes from the east. The life of the people is threatened by inadequate rainfall, locust invasions, pestilence, and other natural catastrophes. A spiritual factor may also be included: The hills were the sites of high places for the Canaanite fertility cult, which was the source of religious practices that led Israel astray.

36:16–38 Summary of the past sinful acts of Israel and the merciful restoration to the land in spite of the people.

17 "Son of man, when the house of Israel dwelt in their own land, [a]they defiled it by their own ways and deeds;
to Me their way was like [b]the uncleanness of a woman in her customary impurity.
18 "Therefore I poured out My fury on
them [a]for the blood they had shed on
the land, and for their idols *with which*
they had defiled it.
19 "So I [a]scattered them among the
nations, and they were dispersed
throughout the countries; I judged
them [b]according to their ways and
their deeds.
20 "When they came to the nations,
wherever they went, they [a]profaned
My holy name—when they said of
them, 'These *are* the people of the
LORD, *and* yet they have gone out of
His land.'
21 "But I had concern [a]for My holy
name, which the house of Israel had
profaned among the nations wherever
they went.
22 "Therefore say to the house of Israel, 'Thus says the Lord GOD: "I do
not do *this* for your sake, O house of
Israel, [a]but for My holy name's sake,
which you have profaned among the
nations wherever you went.
23 "And I will sanctify My great name,
which has been profaned among the
nations, which you have profaned in
their midst; and the nations shall know
that I *am* the LORD," says the Lord GOD,
"when I am [a]hallowed in you before
their eyes.
24 "For [a]I will take you from among
the nations, gather you out of all countries, and bring you into your own
land.
25 [a]"Then I will sprinkle clean water
on you, and you shall be clean; I will
*cleanse you [b]from all your filthiness
and from all your idols.
2 26 "I will give you a [a]new heart and
put a new spirit within you; I will take
the heart of stone out of your flesh and
give you a heart of flesh.
27 "I will put My [a]Spirit within you
and cause you to walk in My statutes,
and you will keep My judgments and
do *them*.
28 [a]"Then you shall dwell in the land
that I gave to your fathers; [b]you shall
be My people, and I will be your God.
29 "I will [a]deliver you from all your
uncleannesses. [b]I will call for the grain
and multiply it, and [c]bring no famine
upon you.
30 [a]"And I will multiply the fruit of
your trees and the increase of your
fields, so that you need never again
bear the reproach of famine among the
nations.
31 "Then [a]you will remember your evil
ways and your deeds that *were* not
good; and you [b]will [1]loathe yourselves
in your own sight, for your iniquities
and your abominations.
32 [a]"Not for your sake do I do *this*,"
says the Lord GOD, "let it be known
to you. Be ashamed and confounded
for your own ways, O house of Israel!"
33 'Thus says the Lord GOD: "On the
day that I cleanse you from all your
iniquities, I will also enable *you* to
dwell in the cities, [a]and the ruins shall
be rebuilt.
34 "The desolate land shall be tilled instead of lying desolate in the sight of
all who pass by.
35 "So they will say, 'This land that
was desolate has become like the garden of [a]Eden; and the wasted, desolate,
and ruined cities *are now* fortified *and*
inhabited.'
36 "Then the nations which are left all
around you shall know that I, the LORD,
have rebuilt the ruined places *and*
planted what was desolate. [a]I, the
LORD, have spoken *it*, and I will do *it*."
37 'Thus says the Lord GOD: [a]"I will

17 [a]Jer. 2:7 [b]Lev. 15:19
18 [a]Ezek. 16:36, 38; 23:37
19 [a]Deut. 28:64 [b][Rom. 2:6]
20 [a]Rom. 2:24
21 [a]Ezek. 20:9, 14
22 [a]Ps. 106:8
23 [a]Ezek. 20:41; 28:22
24 [a]Ezek. 34:13; 37:21
25 [a]Heb. 9:13, 19; 10:22 [b]Jer. 33:8 *See WW at Lev. 14:31.
26 [a]Ezek. 11:19
27 [a]Ezek. 11:19; 37:14
28 [a]Ezek. 28:25; 37:25 [b]Jer. 30:22
29 [a][Rom. 11:26] [b]Ps. 105:16 [c]Ezek. 34:27, 29
30 [a]Ezek. 34:27
31 [a]Ezek. 16:61, 63 [b]Ezek. 6:9; 20:43 [1]*despise*
32 [a]Deut. 9:5
33 [a]Ezek. 36:10
35 [a]Joel 2:3
36 [a]Ezek. 17:24; 22:14; 37:14
37 [a]Ezek. 14:3; 20:3, 31

36:18 Poured out My fury: See note on 7:8.

36:19 I scattered them: For their sins the people were driven from the land, and in exile they continued in those same sins (v. 20).

36:20 They profaned My holy name: When the Israelites were exiled as a judgment by God, their enemies assumed that they were removed from the land because God was helpless to protect or rescue them. It was God's plan that His people would be prosperous and blessed, and through them the heathen would learn of God's mercy and holiness. *Israel had failed, and* as a result God was seen to have failed, and His name was profaned.

36:22 God is bringing restoration, not because of the merits of the exiles, but for His **holy name's sake** (see 20:9). The restoration will vindicate God; He is not powerless, but He is holy and righteous (see Mal. 1:11).

36:25 Sprinkle clean water: The sprinkling with water was a ritual for cleansing the unclean (see Lev. 14:51; Num. 19:18; Heb. 10:22). This is the first step of inward renewal for restoration (Ps. 51:7). The second step will be the new heart and spirit (Ps. 51:10).

36:26, 27 See section 2 of Truth-In-Action at the end of Ezek.

36:26, 27 This **new heart** will be pliable and teachable, the opposite of a stone heart. **New spirit:** Transformation of the will and spirit is necessary as the second step in renewal. The parallel passage in 11:19 and the command in 18:31 suggest that the human will and the whole inner life are involved in the renewal. A new will and a new attitude of spirit enable the individual to walk in God's **statutes** and keep His **judgments** (see v. 27). This passage is similar in concept to Jer. 31:31–34 (see note). Hence, part of Ezekiel's prophecy is messianic.

also let the house of Israel inquire of
Me to do this for them: I will [b]increase
their men like a flock.
38 "Like a [1]flock *offered as* holy *sacri-*
fices, like the flock at Jerusalem on its
[2]feast days, so shall the ruined cities
be filled with flocks of men. Then they
shall know that I *am* the LORD." ' "

The Dry Bones Live

37 The [a]hand of the LORD came
upon me and brought me out
[b]in the Spirit of the LORD, and set me
down in the midst of the valley; and it
was full of bones.
2 Then He caused me to pass by them
all around, and behold, *there were* very
many in the open valley; and indeed
they were very dry.
3 And He said to me, "Son of man,
can these bones live?" So I answered,
"O Lord GOD, [a]You know."
4 Again He said to me, "Prophesy to
these bones, and say to them, 'O dry
bones, *hear the word of the LORD!
5 'Thus says the Lord GOD to these
bones: "Surely I will [a]cause *breath to
enter into you, and you shall live.
6 "I will put sinews on you and bring
*flesh upon you, cover you with skin
and put breath in you; and you shall
live. [a]Then you shall know that I *am*
the LORD." ' "
7 So I prophesied as I was commanded; and as I prophesied, there
was a noise, and suddenly a rattling;
and the bones came together, bone to
bone.
8 Indeed, as I looked, the sinews and
the flesh came upon them, and the skin
covered them over; but *there was* no
breath in them.
9 Also He said to me, "Prophesy to
the breath, prophesy, son of man, and
say to the [1]breath, 'Thus says the Lord
GOD: [a]"Come from the four winds, O
breath, and breathe on these slain, that
they may live." ' "
10 So I prophesied as He commanded
me, [a]and [1]breath* came into them, and
they lived, and stood upon their feet,
an exceedingly great army.
11 Then He said to me, "Son of man,
these bones are the [a]whole house of
Israel. They indeed say, [b]'Our bones
are dry, our *hope is lost, and we ourselves are cut off!'
12 "Therefore prophesy and say to
them, 'Thus says the Lord GOD: "Behold, [a]O My people, I will open your
graves and cause you to come up from
your graves, and [b]bring you into the
land of Israel.
13 "Then you shall *know that I *am*
the LORD, when I have opened your
graves, O My people, and brought you
up from your graves.
14 "I [a]will put My Spirit in you, and
you *shall live, and I will place you in
your own land. Then you shall know
that I, the LORD, have spoken *it* and
performed *it,*" says the LORD.' "

One Kingdom, One King

15 Again the word of the LORD came
to me, saying,

37 [b]Ezek. 36:10
38 [1]Lit. *holy flock* [2]*appointed feasts*

CHAPTER 37

1 [a]Ezek. 1:3 [b]Ezek. 3:14; 8:3; 11:24
3 [a][1 Sam. 2:6]
4 *See WW at 1 Kin. 20:8.
5 [a]Ps. 104:29, 30 *See WW at 2 Sam. 23:2.
6 [a]Joel 2:27; 3:17 *See WW at Job 19:26.
9 [a][Ps. 104:30] [1]Breath of life
10 [a]Rev. 11:11 [1]Breath of life *See WW at 2 Sam. 23:2.
11 [a]Ezek. 36:10 [b]Ps. 141:7 *See WW at Hos. 2:15.
12 [a]Is. 26:19; 66:14 [b]Ezek. 36:24
13 *See WW at Ex. 3:7.
14 [a]Ezek. 36:27 *See WW at Hab. 2:4.

37:1–14 The vision of the **valley** or plain of dry **bones** has been variously interpreted. Some see it as teaching the postexilic return of the exiles; as an OT doctrine of bodily resurrection; or as an analogy for spiritual regeneration and the birth of the church (vv. 11–14). Dispensational interpreters see here the resurrection and restoration of end-times national Israel (v. 12).

Contextually, it is designed to be a message of hope to a despondent people whose Jerusalem was ravaged and whose people were exiled (v. 11). Whatever may be the precise meaning of **the whole house of Israel** (v. 11) or **My people** brought **into the land of Israel** (v. 12), it is clear that God has a future beyond Babylon for those who believe in Him. He will see to it they continue, no matter how great a miracle is required. The miracle required two stages (see notes on vv. 8 and 9, 10).

37:1 Hand of the LORD: See note on 1:3. **The valley:** The same Hebrew word is translated "plain" in 3:22, 23 and 8:4. Where judgment had been pronounced previously, hope is now proclaimed. **Bones:** Contextually, these represent the exiles, who, according to v. 11, have given up all hope of reviving the kingdom of Israel because they have been in Babylon 10 years.

37:2 Very many: The total number of exiles, virtually all that was left of the nation. **Very dry** indicates the condition of Israel's hope and the miracle required to bring the nation back to life.

37:5 Breath: Hebrew *ruah* can be translated "breath," "wind," or "spirit." There is a constant wordplay in vv. 7–10, 14.

37:6 A fourfold list (see note on 1:5) consisting of **sinews, flesh, skin,** and **breath.**

37:8 No breath: Similar to the creation of man described in Gen. 2:7, there was no life until God "breathed into his nostrils the breath of life." The first phase of this vision (vv. 7, 8) seems to correspond to Ezekiel's ministry of calling the spiritually dead Judahites to hear God.

37:9, 10 Four winds represent either the four quarters of the Earth or God's omnipresence. See note on 1:5. This second phase of the vision was synonymous with Ezekiel's praying, asking God to effect a miracle.

37:12 Graves figuratively describes the condition of the people. The imagery has moved from the scattered bones on a battlefield to the cemetery.

37:14 Spirit (Hebrew *ruah*) is used here for the Spirit of God, but the same word is translated "breath" and "wind" in other verses. See note on 37:5. Only the infusion of the Spirit of God can bring about the miracle described in this passage. **I will place you in your own land** indicates national restoration for the exiles.

37:15–28 Oracle of the two sticks. This is the last symbolic act of Ezekiel with a material object. It is clear from v. 19

16 "As for you, son of man, [a]take a
stick for yourself and write on it: 'For
Judah and for [b]the children of Israel,
his *companions.' Then take another
stick and write on it, 'For Joseph, the
stick of Ephraim, and *for* all the house
of Israel, his companions.'
17 "Then [a]join them *one to another
for yourself into one stick, and they
will become one in your hand.
18 "And when the children of your
people speak to you, saying, [a]'Will you
not show us what you *mean* by
these?'—
19 [a]"say to them, 'Thus says the Lord
GOD: "Surely I will take [b]the stick of
Joseph, which *is* in the hand of
Ephraim, and the tribes of Israel, his
companions; and I will join them with
it, with the stick of Judah, and make
them one stick, and they will be one
in My hand." '
20 "And the sticks on which you write
will be in your hand [a]before their eyes.
21 "Then say to them, 'Thus says the
Lord GOD: "Surely [a]I will take the children of Israel from among the nations,
wherever they have gone, and will
gather them from every side and bring
them into their own land;
22 "and [a]I will make them one nation
in the land, on the mountains of Israel;
and [b]one king shall be king over them
all; they shall no longer be two nations,
nor shall they ever be divided into two
kingdoms again.
23 [a]"They shall not defile themselves
anymore with their idols, nor with their
detestable things, nor with any of their
transgressions; but [b]I will deliver them
from all their dwelling places in which

16 [a]Num. 17:2, 3 [b]2 Chr. 11:12, 13, 16; 15:9; 30:11, 18 *See WW at Ps. 119:63.
17 [a]Hos. 1:11 *See WW at Deut. 6:4.
18 [a]Ezek. 12:9; 24:19
19 [a]Zech. 10:6 [b]Ezek. 37:16, 17
20 [a]Ezek. 12:3
21 [a]Ezek. 36:24
22 [a]Jer. 3:18 [b]Ezek. 34:23
23 [a]Ezek. 36:25 [b]Ezek. 36:28, 29
24 [a]Is. 40:11 [b][John 10:16] [c]Ezek. 36:27
25 [a]Ezek. 36:28 [b]Is. 60:21 [c]John 12:34 *See WW at Ps. 136:1.
26 [a]Is. 55:3 [b]Ezek. 36:10 [c][2 Cor. 6:16] [1]Lit. *cut* *See WW at Gen. 17:7.
27 [a][John 1:14] [b]Ezek. 11:20
28 [a]Ezek. 36:23 [b]Ezek. 20:12

CHAPTER 38

2 [a]Ezek. 39:1 [b]Ezek. 35:2, 3 [c]Rev. 20:8 [d]Gen. 10:2 [e]Ezek. 32:26 [1]Tg., Vg., Aquila *the chief prince of Meshech,* also v. 3
4 [a]2 Kin. 19:28

they have sinned, and will cleanse
them. Then they shall be My people,
and I will be their God.
24 [a]"David My servant *shall be* king
over them, and [b]they shall all have one
shepherd; [c]they shall also walk in My
judgments and observe My statutes,
and do them.
25 [a]"Then they shall dwell in the land
that I have given to Jacob My servant,
where your fathers dwelt; and they
shall dwell there, they, their children,
and their children's children, [b]forever;
and [c]My servant David *shall be* their
prince *forever.
26 "Moreover I will [1]make [a]a *covenant of peace with them, and it shall
be an everlasting covenant with them;
I will establish them and [b]multiply
them, and I will set My [c]sanctuary in
their midst forevermore.
27 [a]"My tabernacle also shall be with
them; indeed I will be [b]their God, and
they shall be My people.
28 [a]"The nations also will know that
I, the LORD, [b]sanctify Israel, when My
sanctuary is in their midst forevermore." ' "

Gog and Allies Attack Israel

38 Now the word of the LORD came
to me, saying,
2 [a]"Son of man, [b]set your face
against [c]Gog, of the land of [d]Magog,
[1]the prince of Rosh, [e]Meshech, and
Tubal, and prophesy against him,
3 "and say, 'Thus says the Lord GOD:
"Behold, I *am* against you, O Gog, the
prince of Rosh, Meshech, and Tubal.
4 [a]"I will turn you around, put hooks

---

that both kingdoms, Judah and Ephraim, will be united as one nation and there will be one king (v. 22). This, together with the futuristic explanation of vv. 21–28, makes this oracle messianic. As such, it can have either a dispensational or classical interpretation. See notes on 33:1—39:29; 34:11–16, 25–31.

37:16 Take a stick: Each piece of wood symbolized one kingdom, either Judah or Ephraim. Zechariah uses a similar image with two staffs named "Beauty" and "Bonds" (Zech. 11:7–14).

37:22 One king: Ezekiel normally uses "prince" to refer to the future ruler (v. 25). Here and in v. 24, he uses "king."

37:24 David My servant: See note on 34:23.

37:26 Covenant of peace: See 34:25 and note on 34:1–31.

38:1—39:29 The oracles concerning Gog and Magog have given rise to various interpretations. As to the time they will occur, 38:8, 11, 12, 14 suggest it will be after the restoration and unification described in chs. 36 and 37. The only other mention of Gog in Scripture is Rev. 20:7–10, which seems to be postmillennial. See notes on Rev. 20:1–8 and 20:7–10. The participants, for the most part, are tribes on the fringes of the then-known world. To the north is **Gog . . . of Magog, Meshech, Tubal, Gomer,** and **the house of Togarmah;** to the east is **Persia;** to the south is **Cush** (Ethiopia) and **Put** (Libya). Rev. 20:8 describes them as "the nations which are in the four corners of the earth"; and we do well to see them as generically representing resisting forces, rather than endeavoring to find precise counterparts in modern nations. Though some interpreters stress this battle and its implications for the restored nation of Israel, the most important aspect of these two chapters is the glorification of the name of Yahweh before the nations (38:16, 23; 39:6, 7, 13, 21, 22, 27, 28). See note on Zech. 12:1–9.

38:2 Gog is the leader of the coalition. **Magog** is the land of Gog and may be simply "place of Gog." The **prince of Rosh** is "chief prince." **Meshech** is the Assyrian "Mushku," south of Gomer in central Asia Minor (27:13), and **Tubal** is the Assyrian "Tabab," south of (Beth) Togarmah in eastern Asia Minor (27:13).

38:4 I will turn you around: God is in control of the situation, and those who think they are acting independently are merely fooling themselves (39:2). **Put hooks in your jaws** is imagery drawn from capturing a huge, destructive fish.

into your jaws, and [b]lead you out, with
all your army, horses, and horsemen,
[c]all splendidly clothed, a great company *with* bucklers and shields, all of
them handling swords.
5 "Persia, [1]Ethiopia, and [2]Libya are
with them, all of them *with* shield and
helmet;
6 [a]"Gomer and all its troops; the
house of [b]Togarmah *from* the far north
and all its troops—many people *are*
with you.
7 [a]"Prepare yourself and be ready,
you and all your companies that are
gathered about you; and be a guard for
them.
8 [a]"After many days [b]you will be visited. In the latter years you will come
into the land of those brought back
from the sword [c]*and* gathered from
many people on [d]the mountains of Israel, which had long been desolate;
they were brought out of the nations,
and now all of them [e]dwell safely.
9 "You will ascend, coming [a]like a
storm, covering the [b]land like a cloud,
you and all your troops and many peoples with you."
10 'Thus says the Lord GOD: "On that
day it shall come to pass *that* thoughts
will arise in your mind, and you will
make an evil plan:
11 "You will say, 'I will go up against
a land of [a]unwalled villages; I will
[b]go to a peaceful people, [c]who dwell
[1]safely, all of them dwelling without
walls, and having neither bars nor
gates'—
12 "to take plunder and to take booty,
to stretch out your hand against the
waste places *that are again* inhabited,
[a]and against a people gathered from
the nations, who have acquired livestock and goods, who dwell in the
midst of the land.
13 [a]"Sheba, [b]Dedan, the merchants
[c]of Tarshish, and all [d]their young lions
will say to you, 'Have you come to take
plunder? Have you gathered your army
to take booty, to carry away silver and
gold, to take away livestock and goods,
to take great plunder?' " '
14 "Therefore, son of man, prophesy
and say to Gog, 'Thus says the Lord
GOD: [a]"On that day when My people
Israel [b]dwell safely, will you not know
it?
15 [a]"Then you will come from your
place out of the far north, you and
many peoples with you, all of them riding on horses, a great company and a
mighty army.
16 "You will come up against My people Israel like a cloud, to cover the
land. It will be in the latter days that I
will bring you against My land, so that
the nations may [a]know Me, when I am
[b]hallowed in you, O Gog, before their
eyes."
17 'Thus says the Lord GOD: "Are *you*
he of whom I have spoken in former
days by My servants the prophets of
Israel, who prophesied for years in
those days that I would bring you
against them?

Judgment on Gog

18 "And it will come to pass at the
same time, when Gog comes against
the land of Israel," says the Lord GOD,
"*that* My fury will show in My face.
19 "For [a]in My jealousy [b]*and* in the fire
of My wrath I have spoken: [c]'Surely
in that day there shall be a great
[1]earthquake in the land of Israel,
20 'so that [a]the fish of the sea, the birds
of the heavens, the beasts of the field,
all creeping things that creep on the
earth, and all men who *are* on the face
of the earth shall shake at My presence. [b]The mountains shall be thrown
down, the steep places shall fall, and
every wall shall fall to the ground.'
21 "I will [a]call for [b]a sword against
Gog throughout all My mountains,"
says the Lord GOD. [c]"Every man's
sword will be against his brother.

4 [b]Is. 43:17 [c]Ezek. 23:12
5 [1]Heb. *Cush* [2]Heb. *Put*
6 [a]Gen. 10:2 [b]Gen. 10:3; Ezek. 27:14
7 [a]Is. 8:9, 10; Jer. 46:3, 4
8 [a]Deut. 4:30; Is. 24:22 [b]Is. 29:6 [c]Ezek. 34:13 [d]Ezek. 36:1, 4 [e]Jer. 23:6; Ezek. 34:25; 39:26
9 [a]Is. 28:2 [b]Jer. 4:13
11 [a]Zech. 2:4 [b]Jer. 49:31 [c]Ezek. 38:8 [1]*securely*
12 [a]Ezek. 38:8
13 [a]Ezek. 27:22 [b]Ezek. 27:15, 20 [c]Ezek. 27:12 [d]Ezek. 19:3, 5
14 [a]Is. 4:1 [b]Jer. 23:6; Ezek. 38:8, 11; [Zech. 2:5, 8]
15 [a]Ezek. 39:2
16 [a]Ezek. 35:11 [b]Is. 5:16; 8:13; 29:23; Ezek. 28:22
19 [a]Deut. 32:21, 22; Ps. 18:7, 8; Ezek. 36:5, 6; [Nah. 1:2]; Heb. 12:29 [b]Ps. 89:46 [c]Joel 3:16; Hag. 2:6, 7; Rev. 16:18 [1]Lit. *shaking*
20 [a]Hos. 4:3 [b]Jer. 4:24; Nah. 1:5, 6
21 [a]Ps. 105:16 [b]Ezek. 14:17 [c]Judg. 7:22; 1 Sam. 14:20; 2 Chr. 20:23; Hag. 2:22

38:5 Persia is an area to the east on the Iranian plateau, a nation just coming to prominence at the time of Ezekiel. **Ethiopia** is the modern name for Cush, south of Egypt (see 29:10; 30:4, 5, 9), and **Libya** is the modern name for Put in Africa (see 27:10; 30:5).

38:6 Gomer is the Assyrian "Gimirrai" (Cimmerians), northwest of Meshech in central Asia Minor. **House of Togarmah** or Beth Togarmah is the Assyrian "Til-garimmu" on the upper Euphrates in Cappadocia (eastern Asia Minor) north of Tubal (27:14). **Far north:** See v. 15; 39:2. Almost all invasions were from the north (Jer. 1:13), but these will be from the distant borders.

38:13 Sheba is in the southwest part of the Arabian Peninsula (27:22); **Dedan:** See notes on 25:13 and 27:15; **the merchants of Tarshish:** See note on 27:12; see also Jer. 10:9.

38:16 I will bring you: The sovereignty of God is again evident. Though Gog and his cohorts believe they have planned the invasion, God is responsible for their action. Rev. 20:8 has Satan as the instigator of this attack, but he is merely the instrument by which God carries out His will.

38:18–23 Against Gog and his allies God summons the forces of nature and an **earthquake** devastates the land (v. 19), affecting the fish, birds, beasts, and man (v. 20). No human army is needed, for dissension (v. 21), **pestilence, bloodshed,** and in the form of **rain, great hailstones, fire, and brimstone** (v. 22), will do the work. By His intervention God will magnify Himself. This is describing final events of the Day of the Lord. See note on Obad. 15.

22 "And I will [a]bring him to judgment
with [b]pestilence and bloodshed;
[c]I will rain down on him, on his troops,
and on the many peoples who *are* with
him, flooding rain, [d]great hailstones,
fire, and brimstone.
23 "Thus I will magnify Myself and
[a]sanctify Myself, [b]and I will be known
in the eyes of many nations. Then they
shall know that I *am* the LORD."'

Gog's Armies Destroyed

39 "And [a]you, son of man, prophesy against Gog, and say, 'Thus
says the Lord GOD: "Behold, I *am*
against you, O Gog, [1]the prince of
Rosh, Meshech, and Tubal;
2 "and I will [a]turn you around and
lead you on, [b]bringing you up from the
far north, and bring you against the
mountains of Israel.
3 "Then I will knock the bow out of
your left hand, and cause the arrows
to fall out of your right hand.
4 [a]"You shall [1]fall upon the mountains of Israel, you and all your troops
and the peoples who *are* with you;
[b]I will give you to birds of prey of every
sort and *to* the beasts of the field to
be devoured.
5 "You shall [1]fall on [2]the open field;
for I have spoken," says the Lord GOD.
6 [a]"And I will send fire on Magog and
on those who live [1]in security in
[b]the coastlands. Then they shall know
that I *am* the LORD.
7 [a]"So I will make My holy *name
known in the midst of My people Israel, and I will not *let them* [b]profane
My holy name anymore. [c]Then the nations shall know that *I am* the LORD,
the Holy One in Israel.
8 [a]"Surely it is coming, and it shall
be done," says the Lord GOD. "This *is*
the day [b]of which I have spoken.
9 "Then those who dwell in the cities
of Israel will go out and set on fire and
burn the weapons, both the shields and
bucklers, the bows and arrows, the
[1]javelins and spears; and they will

22 [a]Is. 66:16; Jer. 25:31 [b]Ezek. 5:17 [c]Ps. 11:6; Is. 30:30; Ezek. 13:11 [d]Rev. 16:21
23 [a]Ezek. 36:23 [b]Ps. 9:16; Ezek. 37:28; 38:16

CHAPTER 39

1 [a]Ezek. 38:2, 3 [1]Tg., Vg., Aquila *the chief prince of Meshech*
2 [a]Ezek. 38:8 [b]Ezek. 38:15
4 [a]Ezek. 38:4, 21 [b]Ezek. 33:27 [1]Be slain
5 [1]Be slain [2]Lit. *the face of the field*
6 [a]Ezek. 38:22; Amos 1:4, 7, 10; Nah. 1:6 [b]Ps. 72:10; Is. 66:19; Jer. 25:22 [1]*securely* or *confidently*
7 [a]Ezek. 39:25 [b]Lev. 18:21; Ezek. 36:23 [c]Ezek. 38:16 *See WW at Deut. 18:5.
8 [a]Rev. 16:17; 21:6 [b]Ezek. 38:17
9 [1]Lit. *hand staffs*
10 [a]Is. 14:2; 33:1; Mic. 5:8; Hab. 2:8
11 [1]Lit. *The Multitude of Gog*
12 [a]Deut. 21:23; Ezek. 39:14, 16
13 [a]Jer. 33:9; Zeph. 3:19, 20 [b]Ezek. 28:22
14 [a]Ezek. 39:12 [1]Lit. *those who pass through*
15 [1]*build*
16 [a]Ezek. 39:12 [1]Lit. *Multitude*
17 [a]Is. 56:9; [Jer. 12:9]; Ezek. 39:4; Rev. 19:17, 18 [b]Is. 18:6 [c]Is. 34:6, 7; Jer. 46:10; Zeph. 1:7

make fires with them for seven years.
10 "They will not take wood from the
field nor cut down *any* from the forests,
because they will make fires with the
weapons; [a]and they will plunder those
who plundered them, and pillage those
who pillaged them," says the Lord
GOD.

The Burial of Gog

11 "It will come to pass in that day *that*
I will give Gog a burial place there in
Israel, the valley of those who pass by
east of the sea; and it will obstruct travelers, because there they will bury Gog
and all his multitude. Therefore they
will call *it* the Valley of [1]Hamon Gog.
12 "For seven months the house of Israel will be burying them, [a]in order to
cleanse the land.
13 "Indeed all the people of the land
will be burying, and they will gain
[a]renown for it on the day that [b]I am
glorified," says the Lord GOD.
14 "They will set apart men regularly
employed, with the help of [1]a search
party, to pass through the land and
bury those bodies remaining on the
ground, in order [a]to cleanse it. At the
end of seven months they will make a
search.
15 "The search party will pass through
the land; and *when anyone* sees a
man's bone, he shall [1]set up a marker
by it, till the buriers have buried it in
the Valley of Hamon Gog.
16 "*The* name of *the* city *will* also *be*
[1]Hamonah. Thus they shall [a]cleanse
the land."'

A Triumphant Festival

17 "And as for you, son of man, thus
says the Lord GOD, [a]'Speak to every
sort of bird and to every beast of the
field:

[b]"Assemble yourselves and come;
Gather together from all sides to
My [c]sacrificial meal

39:9 Seven years: The seven years may be a symbol of finality, but they also indicate the magnitude of the invading army and the huge quantity of war materiel left on the battlefield. Although some interpret this as an end-times battle fought with ancient weapons, which are then literally *burned, it is perhaps best to see it as using* ancient imagery *to describe a future* battle, which would use modern weaponry, as well as symbolically portraying the dynamics of spiritual warfare.

39:11 Burial place: The dispensational view sees here the actual burial of the battle's bodies east of the Jordan in Transjordan. This will allow Israel proper to be free of defilement (v. 12). So many will be buried (seven months will be needed) that the valley will no longer be accessible to **travelers,** and the area will be named **Valley of Hamon Gog** (valley of the hordes of Gog). Again, this may be apocalyptic, symbolic language.

39:12 Seven months: Used as in v. 9 to indicate finality and the multitude of soldiers. **Cleanse the land:** As a priest, Ezekiel puts much stress on ritual purity (22:26; 24:13; 36:25, 33; 37:23). All dead bodies need to be buried, since they were especially unclean (see Lev. 5:2; 21:1, 11; 22:4; Num. 5:2; 6:6, 7; 19:16; 31:19).

39:13 I am glorified: The main theme of this unit is the glory of God. See note on 38:1—39:29.

Which I am sacrificing for you,
A great sacrificial meal [d]on the
mountains of Israel,
That you may eat flesh and drink
blood.
18 [a]You shall eat the flesh of the
mighty,
Drink the blood of the princes of
the earth,
Of rams and lambs,
Of goats and bulls,
All of them [b]fatlings of Bashan.
19 You shall eat fat till you are full,
And drink blood till you are
drunk,
At My sacrificial meal
Which I am sacrificing for you.
20 [a]You shall be filled at My table
With horses and riders,
[b]With mighty men
And with all the men of war,"
says the Lord GOD.

Israel Restored to the Land

21 [a]"I will set My glory among the nations; all the nations shall see My judgment which I have executed, and
[b]My hand which I have laid on
them.
22 [a]"So the house of Israel shall know
that I *am* the LORD their God from that
day forward.
23 [a]"The Gentiles shall know that the
house of Israel went into captivity for
their iniquity; because they were
unfaithful to Me, therefore [b]I hid My
face from them. I [c]gave them into the
hand of their enemies, and they all fell
by the sword.
24 [a]"According to their uncleanness
and according to their transgressions
I have dealt with them, and hidden My
face from them."'
25 "Therefore thus says the Lord GOD:
[a]'Now I will bring back the captives
of Jacob, and have mercy on the
[b]whole house of Israel; and I will be
*jealous for My holy name—
26 [a]'after they have borne their shame,
and all their unfaithfulness in which
they were unfaithful to Me, when they
[b]dwelt safely in their *own* land and no
one made *them* afraid.
27 [a]'When I have brought them back
from the peoples and gathered them
out of their enemies' lands, and I
[b]am hallowed in them in the sight of
many nations,
28 [a]'then they shall know that I *am* the
LORD their God, who sent them into
captivity among the nations, but also
brought them back to their land, and
left none of them [1]captive any longer.
29 [a]'And I will not hide My face from
them anymore; for I shall have [b]poured
out My Spirit on the house of Israel,'
says the Lord GOD."

A New City, a New Temple

40 In the twenty-fifth year of our
captivity, at the beginning of the
year, on the tenth *day* of the month,
in the fourteenth year after [a]the city
was [1]captured, on the very same day
[b]the hand of the LORD was upon me;
and He took me there.
2 [a]In the visions of God He took me
into the land of Israel and [b]set me on
a very high mountain; on it toward the
south *was* something like the structure
of a city.
3 He took me there, and behold, *there*
was a man whose appearance *was*
[a]like the appearance of bronze. [b]He
had a line of flax [c]and a measuring rod
in his hand, and he stood in the gateway.
4 And the man said to me, [a]"Son of
man, look with your eyes and hear
with your ears, and [1]fix your mind on
everything I show you; for you *were*
brought here so that I might show

17 [d]Ezek. 39:4
18 [a]Rev. 19:18 [b]Deut. 32:14
20 [a]Ps. 76:5, 6 [b]Rev. 19:18
21 [a]Ezek. 36:23; 38:23 [b]Ex. 7:4
22 [a]Ex. 39:7, 28
23 [a]Ezek. 36:18–20, 23 [b]Is. 1:15; 59:2 [c]Lev. 26:25
24 [a]Ezek. 36:19
25 [a]Ezek. 34:13; 36:24 [b]Hos. 1:11 *See WW at Zech. 8:2.
26 [a]Dan. 9:16 [b]Lev. 26:5, 6
27 [a]Ezek. 28:25, 26 [b]Ezek. 36:23, 24; 38:16
28 [a]Ezek. 34:30 [1]Lit. *there*
29 [a]Is. 54:8, 9 [b][Joel 2:28]

CHAPTER 40

1 [a]Ezek. 33:21 [b]Ezek. 1:3; 3:14, 22; 37:1 [1]Lit. *struck*
2 [a]Ezek. 1:1; 3:14; 8:3; 37:1 [b]Rev. 21:10
3 [a]Dan. 10:6 [b]Ezek. 47:3 [c]Rev. 11:1; 21:15
4 [a]Ezek. 44:5 [1]Lit. *set your heart*

39:29 My Spirit: See note on 36:26.
40:1—48:35 These closing chapters describe the new temple and a new order of worship for Israel. Most importantly they conclude with the name of the city, **THE LORD *IS* THERE.** This is the key for understanding this whole vision of Ezekiel, which is paralleled by Rev. 21:1—22:15. As John has an angel guide to show him around his New Jerusalem, so Ezekiel has an angel to explain to him his temple vision. Though scholars vary in their interpretation, the temple is best interpreted symbolically, representing the worshiping community of the Messiah, during the church age, the Millennium, and climaxing in the world to come.

The description is based largely on the temple of Solomon, which Ezekiel had seen before his exile, but the measurements are not the same. This "perfect" temple therefore contrasts sharply with the past and points out clearly its failure. In the end, this temple gives way to the city (48:30–35) and to the presence of the Lord. This is the central issue. Two other similarities with Rev. are: 1) Ezekiel describes water **flowing from under the threshold of the temple,** which quickly becomes a mighty river too deep to cross (47:1–5). John speaks of the "river of water of life . . . proceeding from the throne of God and of the Lamb" (Rev. 22:1). 2) Both speak of fruit-yielding trees along the banks (47:12; Rev. 22:2).
40:1 Twenty-fifth year: April 28, 573 B.C.
40:2 Very high mountain: Mt. Zion is not very high in physical elevation, but extremely high in spiritual significance (see 17:22; Is. 2:2; Mic. 4:1).
40:3 Appearance of bronze: This description is used of angels or nonhuman beings. **Line of flax** is a measuring tape used for long distances. **A measuring rod** is equal to 6 long cubits (v. 5), or about 10 feet 4 inches, used to measure short distances.

them to you. [b]Declare to the house of Israel everything you see."
5 Now there was [a]a wall all around the outside of the [1]temple. In the man's hand was a measuring rod six [2]cubits *long, each being a* cubit and a handbreadth; and he measured the width of the wall structure, one rod; and the height, one rod.

4 [b]Ezek. 43:10
5 [a][Is. 26:1]; Ezek. 42:20 [1]Lit. *house* [2]A royal cubit of about 21 inches
6 [a]Ezek. 43:1 *See WW at Ex. 19:20. • See WW at Amos 9:6.

The Eastern Gateway of the Temple

6 Then he went to the gateway which faced [a]east; and he *went up its *stairs and measured the threshold of the gateway, *which was* one rod wide, and the other threshold *was* one rod wide.
7 Each gate chamber *was* one rod long and one rod wide; between the

40:6–16 The description of the eastern gateway (similar to those on the north and south) mentions three alcoves on each side for the use of the guards (v. 10). Gates of similar design and dimensions have been found at Gezer, Megiddo, and Hazor, all dating to the time of Solomon (see 1 Kin. 9:15).

EZEKIEL'S TEMPLE (40:5)

Ezekiel's restored temple is not a blueprint, but a vision that stresses the purity and spiritual vitality of the ideal place of worship and those who will worship there. It is not intended for an earthly, physical fulfillment, but expresses the truth found in the name of the new city: "THE LORD *IS* THERE" (Ezek. 48:35). God will dwell in the new temple and among His people.

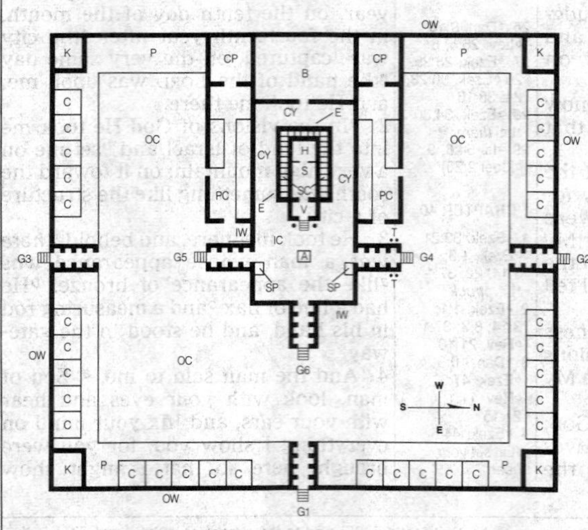

The Temple Complex
OW Wall of outer court (40:5)
G1 Eastern outer gateway (40:6–16)
OC Outer court (40:17)
C Chambers in outer court (40:17)
P Pavement (40:17, 18)
G2 Northern outer gateway (40:20–22)
G4 Northern inner gateway (40:23, 35–37)
G3 Southern outer gateway (40:24–26)
G5 Southern inner gateway (40:27–31)
IC Inner court (40:32)
G6 Eastern inner gateway (40:32–34)
T Tables for killing sacrifices (40:38–43)
SP Chambers for singers and priests (40:44–46)
A Altar (40:47; 43:13–27)
V Vestibule of temple (40:48, 49)
S Sanctuary or holy place (41:1, 2)
H Most Holy Place (41:3, 4)
SC Side chambers (41:5–7)
E Elevation around temple (41:8)
CY Separating courtyard (41:10)
B Building at west end (41:12)
PC Priest's chambers (42:1–14)
IW Wall of inner court (42:10)
CP Priest's cooking places (46:19, 20)
K Kitchens (46:21–24)

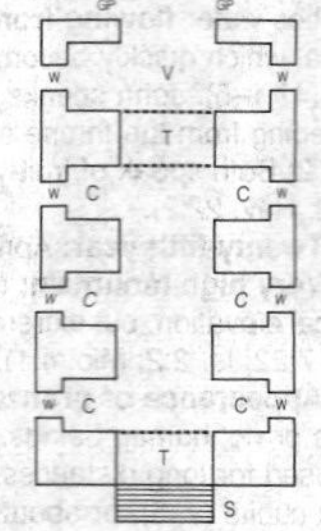

The Gateway
S Steps (40:6)
T Thresholds (40:6, 7)
C Gate chambers (40:7, 10, 12)
W Windows (40:16)
V Vestibule (40:8, 9)
GP Gateposts (40:10, 14)

gate chambers *was a space of* five cubits; and the threshold of the gateway
by the vestibule of the inside gate *was*
one rod.
8 He also measured the vestibule of
the inside gate, one rod.
9 Then he measured the vestibule of
the gateway, eight cubits; and the gateposts, two cubits. The vestibule of the
gate *was* on the inside.
10 In the eastern gateway *were* three
gate chambers on one side and three
on the other; the three *were* all the
same size; also the gateposts were of
the same size on this side and that
side.
11 He measured the width of the entrance to the gateway, ten cubits; *and*
the length of the gate, thirteen cubits.
12 *There was* a [1]space in front of the
gate chambers, one cubit *on this side*
and one cubit on that side; the gate
chambers *were* six cubits on this side
and six cubits on that side.
13 Then he measured the gateway
from the roof of *one* gate chamber to
the roof of the other; the width *was*
twenty-five cubits, as door faces door.
14 He measured the gateposts, sixty
cubits high, and the court all around
the gateway *extended* to the gatepost.
15 *From* the front of the entrance gate
to the front of the vestibule of the inner
gate *was* fifty cubits.
16 *There were* [a]beveled window
frames in the gate chambers and in
their intervening archways on the inside of the gateway all around, and
likewise in the vestibules. *There were*
windows all around on the inside. And
on each gatepost *were* [b]palm trees.

The Outer Court

17 Then he brought me into [a]the outer
court; and *there were* [b]chambers and
a pavement made all around the
court; [c]thirty chambers faced the pavement.
18 The pavement was by the side of
the gateways, corresponding to the
length of the gateways; *this was* the
lower pavement.
19 Then he measured the width from
the front of the lower gateway to the
front of the inner court exterior, one
hundred cubits toward the east and the
north.

The Northern Gateway

20 On the outer court was also a gateway facing north, and he measured its
length and its width.
21 Its gate chambers, three on this side
and three on that side, its gateposts
and its archways, had the same measurements as the first gate; its length
was fifty cubits and its width twenty-
five cubits.
22 Its windows and those of its archways, and also its palm trees, *had* the
same measurements as the gateway
facing east; it was ascended by seven
*steps, and its archway *was* in front
of it.
23 A gate of the inner court was opposite the northern gateway, just as the
eastern *gateway;* and he measured
from gateway to gateway, one hundred
cubits.

The Southern Gateway

24 After that he brought me toward the
south, and there a gateway was facing
south; and he measured its gateposts
and archways according to these same
measurements.
25 *There were* windows in it and in its
archways all around like those windows; its length *was* fifty cubits and
its width twenty-five cubits.
26 Seven steps led up to it, and its archway *was* in front of them; and it had
palm trees on its gateposts, one on this
side and one on that side.
27 *There was* also a gateway on the
inner court, facing south; and he measured from gateway to gateway toward
the south, one hundred cubits.

Gateways of the Inner Court

28 Then he brought me to the inner
court through the southern gateway;
he measured the southern gateway according to these same measurements.
29 Also its gate chambers, its gateposts, and its archways *were* according
to these same measurements; *there
were* windows in it and in its archways
all around; *it was* fifty cubits long and
twenty-five cubits wide.
30 *There were* archways all around,
[a]twenty-five cubits long and five cubits
wide.

12 [1]Lit. *border*
16 [a]1 Kin. 6:4; Ezek. 41:16, 26 [b]1 Kin. 6:29, 32, 35; 2 Chr. 3:5; Ezek. 40:22, 26, 31, 34, 37; 41:18–20, 25, 26
17 [a]Ezek. 10:5; 42:1; 46:21; Rev. 11:2 [b]1 Kin. 6:5; 2 Chr. 31:11; Ezek. 40:38 [c]Ezek. 45:5

22 *See WW at Amos 9:6.
30 [a]Ezek. 40:21, 25, 33, 36

40:16 Palm trees were a common decorative motif in the ancient Near East, and Solomon's temple had palm trees carved on the walls (1 Kin. 6:29).
40:28 The inner court: The temple proper (40:48—41:26) contains an outer court (40:5–27), an inner court (40:28–37) with rooms for the preparation of sacrifices (40:38–43) and for the singers and priests (40:44–47), an altar (43:13–27), and adjacent buildings for the priests (42:1–14).

31 Its archways faced the outer court, palm trees *were* on its gateposts, and going up to it *were* eight steps.

32 And he brought me into the inner court facing east; he measured the gateway according to these same measurements.

33 Also its gate chambers, its gateposts, and its archways *were* according to these same measurements; and *there were* windows in it and in its archways all around; *it was* fifty cubits long and twenty-five cubits wide.

34 Its archways faced the outer court, and palm trees *were* on its gateposts on this side and on that side; and going up to it *were* eight steps.

35 Then he brought me to the north gateway and measured *it* according to these same measurements—

36 also its gate chambers, its gateposts, and its archways. It had windows all around; its length *was* fifty cubits and its width twenty-five cubits.

37 Its gateposts faced the outer court, palm trees *were* on its gateposts on this side and on that side, and going up to it *were* eight steps.

Where Sacrifices Were Prepared

38 *There was* a chamber and its entrance by the gateposts of the gateway, where they [a]washed the burnt offering.

39 In the vestibule of the gateway *were* two tables on this side and two tables on that side, on which to slay the burnt offering, [a]the sin offering, and [b]the trespass offering.

40 At the outer side of the vestibule, as one goes up to the entrance of the northern gateway, *were* two tables; and on the other side of the vestibule of the gateway *were* two tables.

41 Four tables *were* on this side and four tables on that side, by the side of the gateway, eight tables on which they slaughtered *the sacrifices.*

42 *There were* also four tables of hewn stone for the burnt offering, one cubit and a half long, one cubit and a half wide, and one cubit high; on these they laid the instruments with which they slaughtered the burnt offering and the sacrifice.

43 Inside *were* hooks, a handbreadth wide, fastened all around; *and the flesh* of the sacrifices *was* on the tables.

38 [a]2 Chr. 4:6
39 [a]Lev. 4:2, 3 [b]Lev. 5:6; 6:6; 7:1
44 [a]1 Chr. 6:31, 32; 16:41–43; 25:1–7
45 [a]Lev. 8:35; Num. 3:27, 28, 32, 38; 18:5; 1 Chr. 9:23; 2 Chr. 13:11; Ps. 134:1
46 [a]Lev. 6:12, 13; Num. 18:5; Ezek. 44:15 [b]1 Kin. 2:35; Ezek. 43:19; 44:15, 16
48 [a]1 Kin. 6:3; 2 Chr. 3:4
49 [a]1 Kin. 6:3 [b]1 Kin. 7:15–22; 2 Chr. 3:17; Jer. 52:17–23; [Rev. 3:12]

CHAPTER 41

1 [a]Ezek. 40:2, 3, 17 [1]Heb. *heykal;* the main room in the temple, the holy place, Ex. 26:33 *See WW at Hag. 2:15.
4 [a]1 Kin. 6:20; 2 Chr. 3:8

Chambers for Singers and Priests

44 Outside the inner gate *were* the chambers for [a]the singers in the inner court, one facing south at the side of the northern gateway, and the other facing north at the side of the southern gateway.

45 Then he said to me, "This chamber which faces south *is* for [a]the priests who have charge of the temple.

46 "The chamber which faces north *is* for the priests [a]who have charge of the altar; these *are* the sons of [b]Zadok, from the sons of Levi, who come near the LORD to minister to Him."

Dimensions of the Inner Court and Vestibule

47 And he measured the court, one hundred cubits long and one hundred cubits wide, foursquare. The altar *was* in front of the temple.

48 Then he brought me to the [a]vestibule of the temple and measured the doorposts of the vestibule, five cubits on this side and five cubits on that side; and the width of the gateway was three cubits on this side and three cubits on that side.

49 [a]The length of the vestibule *was* twenty cubits, and the width eleven cubits; and by the steps which led up to it *there were* [b]pillars by the doorposts, one on this side and another on that side.

Dimensions of the Sanctuary

41 Then he [a]brought me into the [1]sanctuary and measured the doorposts, six cubits wide on one side and six cubits wide on the other side—the width of the *tabernacle.

2 The width of the entryway *was* ten cubits, and the side walls of the entrance *were* five cubits on this side and five cubits on the other side; and he measured its length, forty cubits, and its width, twenty cubits.

3 Also he went inside and measured the doorposts, two cubits; and the entrance, six cubits *high;* and the width of the entrance, seven cubits.

4 [a]He measured the length, twenty cubits; and the width, twenty cubits, beyond the sanctuary; and he said to me, "This *is* the Most Holy *Place.*"

40:39 The offerings mentioned include **the burnt offering, the sin offering, and the trespass offering.** See notes on Lev. 1:3; 1:4; 4:3; 5:14. Conspicuous by its absence is the peace offering (43:27).

41:1–26 This chapter occupies itself with the temple's measurements. It varies from that of Solomon's in order to draw attention away from a temporary, earthly model. See note on 40:1—48:35.

The Side Chambers on the Wall

5 Next, he measured the wall of the
[1]temple, six cubits. The width of each side chamber all around the temple *was* four cubits on every side.
6 [a]The side chambers *were* in three stories, one above the other, thirty chambers in each story; they rested on [1]ledges which *were* for the side chambers all around, that they might be supported, but [b]not fastened to the wall of the temple.
7 As one went up from story to story, the side chambers [a]became wider all around, because their supporting ledges in the wall of the temple ascended like steps; therefore the width of the structure increased as one went up *from* the lowest *story* to the highest by way of the middle one.
8 I also saw an elevation all around the temple; it was the foundation of the side chambers, [a]a full rod, *that is,* six cubits *high.*
9 The thickness of the outer wall of the side chambers *was* five cubits, and so also the remaining terrace by the place of the side chambers of the [1]temple.
10 And between *it and* the *wall* chambers was a width of twenty cubits all around the temple on every side.
11 The doors of the side chambers opened on the terrace, one door toward the north and another toward the south; and the width of the terrace *was* five cubits all around.

The Building at the Western End

12 The building that faced the separating courtyard at its western end *was* seventy cubits wide; the wall of the building *was* five cubits thick all around, and its length ninety cubits.

Dimensions and Design of the Temple Area

13 So he measured the temple, one [a]hundred cubits long; and the separating courtyard with the building and its walls *was* one hundred cubits long;
14 also the width of the eastern face of the temple, including the separating courtyard, *was* one hundred cubits.
15 He measured the length of the building behind it, facing the separating courtyard, with its [a]galleries on the one side and on the other side, one hundred cubits, as well as the inner [1]temple and the porches of the court,
16 their doorposts and [a]the beveled window frames. And the galleries all around their three stories opposite the threshold were paneled with [b]wood from the ground to the windows—the windows were covered—
17 from the space above the door, even to the inner [1]room, as well as outside, and on every wall all around, inside and outside, by measure.
18 And *it was* made [a]with *cherubim and [b]palm trees, a palm tree between cherub and cherub. *Each* cherub had two faces,
19 [a]so that the face of a man *was* toward a palm tree on one side, and the face of a young lion toward a palm tree on the other side; thus *it was* made throughout the temple all around.
20 From the floor to the space above the door, and on the wall of the sanctuary, cherubim and palm trees *were* carved.
21 The [a]doorposts of the temple *were* square, *as was* the front of the sanctuary; their appearance was similar.
22 [a]The altar *was* of wood, three cubits high, and its length two cubits. Its corners, its length, and its sides *were* of wood; and he said to me, "This *is* [b]the table that *is* [c]before the LORD."
23 [a]The temple and the sanctuary had two doors.
24 The doors had two [a]panels *apiece,* two folding panels: two *panels* for one door and two panels for the other *door.*
25 Cherubim and palm trees *were* carved on the doors of the temple just as they *were* carved on the walls. A wooden canopy *was* on the front of the vestibule outside.
26 *There were* [a]beveled window *frames* and palm trees on one side and on the other, on the sides of the vestibule—also on the side chambers of the temple and on the canopies.

The Chambers for the Priests

42
Then he [a]brought me out into the outer court, by the way toward the [b]north; and he brought me into [c]the chamber which *was* opposite the separating courtyard, and which *was* opposite the building toward the north.
2 Facing the length, *which was* one

5 [1]Lit. *house*
6 [a]1 Kin. 6:5–10 [b]1 Kin. 6:6, 10 [1]Lit. *the wall*
7 [a]1 Kin. 6:8
8 [a]Ezek. 40:5
9 [1]Lit. *house*
13 [a]Ezek. 40:47
15 [a]Ezek. 42:3, 5 [1]Or *sanctuary*
16 [a]1 Kin. 6:4; Ezek. 40:16, 25 [b]1 Kin. 6:15
17 [1]Lit. *house;* the Most Holy Place
18 [a]1 Kin. 6:29; 2 Chr. 3:7 [b]2 Chr. 3:5; Ezek. 40:16 *See WW at Ex. 25:18.
19 [a]Ezek. 1:10; 10:14
21 [a]1 Kin. 6:33; Ezek. 40:9, 14, 16; 41:1
22 [a]Ex. 30:1–3; 1 Kin. 6:20; Rev. 8:3 [b]Ex. 25:23, 30; Lev. 24:6; Ezek. 23:41; 44:16; Mal. 1:7, 12 [c]Ex. 30:8
23 [a]1 Kin. 6:31–35
24 [a]1 Kin. 6:34
26 [a]Ezek. 40:16

CHAPTER 42

1 [a]Ezek. 41:1 [b]Ezek. 40:20 [c]Ezek. 41:12, 15

41:18 Cherubim: Unlike the cherubim described in ch. 10, these have only two faces, the face of a man and the face of a lion (v. 19).

41:22 The **altar** of **wood** is the table of the presence on which the bread was placed.

hundred cubits (the width was fifty cubits), was the north door.
3 Opposite the inner court of twenty
cubits, and opposite the [a]pavement of
the outer court, *was* [b]gallery against
gallery in three *stories.*
4 In front of the chambers, toward the
inside, *was* a walk ten cubits wide, at
a distance of one cubit; and their doors
faced north.
5 Now the upper chambers *were*
shorter, because the galleries took
away *space* from them more than from
the lower and middle stories of the
building.
6 For they *were* in three *stories* and
did not have pillars like the pillars of
the courts; therefore *the upper level*
was [1]shortened more than the lower
and middle levels from the ground
up.
7 And a wall which *was* outside ran
parallel to the chambers, at the front
of the chambers, toward the outer
court; its length *was* fifty cubits.
8 The length of the chambers toward
the outer court *was* fifty cubits,
whereas that facing the temple *was*
one [a]hundred cubits.
9 At the lower chambers *was* the entrance on the east side, as one goes into
them from the outer court.
10 Also *there were* chambers in the
thickness of the wall of the court toward the east, opposite the separating
courtyard and opposite the building.
11 [a]*There was* a walk in front of them
also, and their appearance *was* like the
chambers which *were* toward the
north; they *were* as long and as wide
as the others, and all their exits and
entrances *were* according to plan.
12 And corresponding to the doors of
the chambers that *were* facing south,
as one enters them, *there was* a door
in front of the walk, the way directly
in front of the wall toward the east.
13 Then he said to me, "The north
chambers *and* the south chambers,
which *are* opposite the separating
courtyard, *are* the holy chambers
where the priests who approach the
LORD [a]shall eat the most holy offerings.
There they shall lay the most holy offerings—[b]the grain offering, the sin offering, and the trespass offering—for
the place *is* holy.
14 [a]"When the priests enter them, they
shall not go out of the holy *chamber*
into the outer court; but there they
shall leave their garments in which
they minister, for they *are* holy. They
shall put on other garments; then they
may approach *that* which *is* for the
people."

Outer Dimensions of the Temple

15 Now when he had finished measuring the inner [1]temple, he brought me
out through the gateway that faces toward the [a]east, and measured it all
around.
16 He measured the east side with the
[1]measuring rod, five hundred rods by
the measuring rod all around.
17 He measured the north side, five
hundred rods by the measuring rod all
around.
18 He measured the south side, five
hundred rods by the measuring rod.
19 He came around to the west side
and measured five hundred rods by the
measuring rod.
20 He measured it on the four sides;
[a]it had a wall all around, [b]five hundred
cubits long and five hundred wide, to
separate the holy areas from the
[1]common.

The Temple, the LORD's Dwelling Place

43 Afterward he brought me to the
gate, the gate [a]that faces toward
the east.
2 [a]And behold, the glory of the God
of Israel came from the way of the east.
[b]His voice *was* like the sound of many
waters; [c]and the earth shone with His
glory.
3 *It was* [a]like the appearance of the
vision which I saw—like the vision
which I saw when [1]I came [b]to destroy
the city. The visions *were* like the vision which I saw [c]by the River Chebar;
and I fell on my face.
4 [a]And the glory of the LORD came
into the [1]temple by way of the gate
which faces toward the east.

3 [a]Ezek. 40:17 [b]Ezek. 41:15, 16; 42:5
6 [1]Or *narrowed*
8 [a]Ezek. 41:13, 14
11 [a]Ezek. 42:4
13 [a]Lev. 6:16, 26; 24:9; Ezek. 43:19 [b]Lev. 2:3, 10; 6:14, 17, 25
14 [a]Ezek. 44:19
15 [a]Ezek. 40:6; 43:1 [1]Lit. *house*
16 [1]About 10.5 feet, Ezek. 40:5
20 [a][Is. 60:18]; Ezek. 40:5; Zech. 2:5 [b]Ezek. 45:2; Rev. 21:16 [1]Or *profane*

CHAPTER 43

1 [a]Ezek. 10:19; 46:1
2 [a]Ezek. 11:23 [b]Ezek. 1:24; Rev. 1:15; 14:2 [c]Ezek. 10:4; Rev. 18:1
3 [a]Ezek. 1:4–28 [b]Jer. 1:10; Ezek. 9:1, 5; 32:18 [c]Ezek. 1:28; 3:23 [1]Some Heb. mss., Vg. *He*
4 [a]Ezek. 10:19; 11:23 [1]Lit. *house*

42:13 Priests who approach the LORD are priests from the line of Zadok (see 43:19; 44:15; 1 Kin. 4:2). **Most holy offerings:** The priests were allowed to eat part of the grain offerings, sin offerings, and trespass offerings (44:29, 30).
43:2 Glory of the God of Israel: Ezekiel described God's glory leaving the temple and going to the east (10:18; 11:23); now the glory returns to consecrate the temple by His presence, symbolizing that Judah's exile will not be God's final dealing with those who believe in Him. He has a future for believers beyond Jerusalem's fall. See note on 37:1–14. **Voice was like the sound of many waters:** See 1:24.
43:3 The vision which I saw: Ezekiel refers to the previous vision of God on the plain in Babylon (1:1–28) and to the vision in the temple (8:4; 10:4). Here, however, no cherubim are mentioned. **I fell on my face:** See note on 1:28.

5 [a]The Spirit lifted me up and brought
me into the inner court; and behold,
[b]the glory of the LORD filled the [1]tem-
ple.
6 Then I heard *Him* speaking to me
from the temple, while [a]a man stood
beside me.
7 And He said to me, "Son of man,
this is [a]the place of My throne and
[b]the place of the soles of My feet,
[c]where I will *dwell in the midst of the
children of Israel forever. [d]No more
shall the house of Israel defile My holy
name, they nor their kings, by their
[1]harlotry or with [e]the carcasses of their
kings on their high places.
8 [a]"When they set their threshold by
My threshold, and their doorpost by
My doorpost, with a wall between them
and Me, they defiled My holy name by
the abominations which they committed; therefore I have consumed them
in My anger.
9 "Now let them put their harlotry
and the carcasses of their kings far
away from Me, and I will dwell in their
midst forever.
10 "Son of man, [a]describe the [1]temple
to the house of Israel, that they may
be ashamed of their iniquities; and let
them measure the pattern.
11 "And if they are ashamed of all that
they have done, make known to them
the design of the [1]temple and its arrangement, its exits and its entrances,
its entire design and all its [a]ordinances,
all its forms and all its laws. Write *it*
down in their sight, so that they may
keep its whole design and all its ordinances, and [b]perform them.
12 "This *is* the law of the [1]temple: The
whole area surrounding [a]the mountaintop *is* most holy. Behold, this *is* the
law of the temple.

Dimensions of the Altar

13 "These are the measurements of the
[a]altar in cubits [b](the [1]*cubit is* one cubit
and a handbreadth): the base one cubit
high and one cubit wide, with a rim
all around its edge of one span. This
is the height of the altar:
14 "from the base on the ground to the
lower ledge, two cubits; the width of
the ledge, one cubit; from the smaller
ledge to the larger ledge, four cubits;
and the width of the ledge, *one* cubit.
15 "The altar hearth *is* four cubits
high, with four [a]horns extending upward from the [1]hearth.
16 "The altar hearth *is* twelve cubits
long, twelve wide, [a]square at its four
corners;
17 "the ledge, fourteen *cubits* long and
fourteen wide on its four sides, with a
rim of half a cubit around it; its base,
one cubit all around; and [a]its *steps
face toward the east."

Consecrating the Altar

18 And He said to me, "Son of man,
thus says the Lord GOD: 'These *are* the
ordinances for the altar on the day
when it is made, for sacrificing [a]burnt
offerings on it, and for [b]sprinkling
blood on it.
19 'You shall give [a]a young bull for a
sin offering to [b]the priests, the Levites,
who are of the seed of [c]Zadok, who
approach Me to minister to Me,' says
the Lord GOD.
20 'You shall take some of its blood
and put *it* on the four *horns of the
altar, on the four corners of the ledge,
and on the rim around it; thus you shall
cleanse it and make atonement for it.
21 'Then you shall also take the bull
of the sin offering, and [a]burn it in the
appointed place of the [1]temple, [b]out-
side the sanctuary.
22 'On the second day you shall offer
a kid of the goats *without blemish for
a sin offering; and they shall cleanse
the altar, as they cleansed *it* with the
bull.
23 'When you have finished cleansing
it, you shall offer a young bull without
blemish, and a ram from the flock without blemish.
24 'When you offer them before the
LORD, [a]the priests shall throw salt on
them, and they will offer them up *as* a
burnt offering to the LORD.
25 'Every day for [a]seven days you
shall prepare a goat *for* a sin offering;
they shall also prepare a young bull
and a ram from the flock, both without
blemish.
26 'Seven days they shall make atonement for the altar and purify it, and
so [1]consecrate [2]*it*.
27 [a]'When these days are over it shall
be, on the eighth day and thereafter,
that the priests shall offer your burnt

5 [a]Ezek. 3:12, 14; 8:3; 2 Cor. 12:2–4 [b]Ezek. 40:34; 1 Kin. 8:10, 11 [1]Lit. *house*
6 [a]Ezek. 1:26; 40:3
7 [a]Ps. 99:1; Is. 60:13 [b]1 Chr. 28:2; Ps. 99:5 [c]Ex. 29:45; Ps. 68:16; 132:14; Ezek. 37:26–28; Joel 3:17; [John 1:14; 2 Cor. 6:16] [d]Ezek. 39:7 [e]Lev. 26:30; Jer. 16:18; Ezek. 6:5, 13 [1]Unfaithful idolatry *See WW at Num. 10:12.
8 [a]2 Kin. 16:14; 21:4, 5, 7; Ezek. 8:3; 23:39; 44:7
10 [a]Ezek. 40:4 [1]Lit. *house*
11 [a]Ezek. 44:5 [b]Ezek. 11:20 [1]Lit. *house*
12 [a]Ezek. 40:2 [1]Lit. *house*
13 [a]Ex. 27:1–8; 2 Chr. 4:1 [b]Ezek. 41:8 [1]A royal cubit of about 21 inches
15 [a]Ex. 27:2; Lev. 9:9; 1 Kin. 1:50 [1]Heb. *ariel*
16 [a]Ex. 27:1
17 [a]Ex. 20:26 *See WW at Amos 9:6.
18 [a]Ex. 40:29 [b]Lev. 1:5, 11; [Heb. 9:21, 22]
19 [a]Ex. 29:10; Lev. 8:14; Ezek. 45:18, 19 [b]Ezek. 44:15, 16 [c]1 Kin. 2:35; Ezek. 40:46
20 *See WW at Ezek. 29:21.
21 [a]Ex. 29:14; Lev. 4:12 [b]Heb. 13:11 [1]Lit. *house*
22 *See WW at Lev. 23:12.
24 [a]Lev. 2:13; Num. 18:19; [Mark 9:49, 50; Col. 4:6]
25 [a]Ex. 29:35; Lev. 8:33
26 [1]Lit. *fill its hands* [2]LXX, Syr. *themselves*
27 [a]Lev. 9:1–4

43:5 Spirit lifted me up: See note on 3:12. **Filled the temple:** See also 44:4. The glory of the Lord filled the temple as He filled the tabernacle (Ex. 40:34, 35), the temple of Solomon at its dedication (1 Kin. 8:11), and the temple in the vision of Isaiah (Is. 6:4).

43:7 Place of My throne: See Is. 6:1; Jer. 3:17.

43:13 The altar was mentioned in 40:47, and is here described in detail. Presumably cut stones are used, and there are steps (v. 17), perhaps because of the size of the altar.

offerings and your peace offerings on
the altar; and I will [b]accept you,' says
the Lord GOD."

The East Gate and the Prince

44 Then He brought me back to the
outer gate of the sanctuary
[a]which faces toward the east, but it
was shut.
2 And the LORD said to me, "This gate
shall be shut; it shall not be opened,
and no man shall enter by it, [a]because
the LORD God of Israel has entered by
it; therefore it shall be shut.
3 "*As for* the [a]prince, *because* he *is*
the prince, he may sit in it to [b]eat bread
before the LORD; he shall enter by way
of the vestibule of the gateway, and go
out the same way."

Those Admitted to the Temple

4 Also He brought me by way of the
north gate to the front of the [1]temple;
so I looked, and [a]behold, the glory of
the LORD filled the house of the LORD;
[b]and I fell on my face.
5 And the LORD said to me, [a]"Son of
man, [1]mark well, see with your eyes
and hear with your ears, all that I say
to you concerning all the [b]ordinances
of the house of the LORD and all its
laws. Mark well who may enter the
house and all who go out from the
sanctuary.
6 "Now say to the [a]rebellious, to the
house of Israel, 'Thus says the Lord
GOD: "O house of Israel, [b]let Us have
no more of all your abominations.
7 [a]"When you brought in [b]foreigners,
[c]uncircumcised in heart and uncircumcised in flesh, to be in My sanctuary
to defile it—My house—and when you
offered [d]My food, [e]the fat and the
blood, then they broke My covenant
because of all your abominations.
8 "And you have not [a]kept charge of
My holy things, but you have set *others*
to keep charge of My sanctuary for
you."
9 'Thus says the Lord GOD: [a]"No foreigner, uncircumcised in heart or uncircumcised in flesh, shall enter My
sanctuary, including any foreigner
who *is* among the children of Israel.

Laws Governing Priests

10 [a]"And the Levites who went far
from Me, when Israel went astray, who
strayed away from Me after their idols,
they shall bear their iniquity.
11 "Yet they shall be *ministers in My
sanctuary, [a]*as* gatekeepers of the
house and ministers of the house;
[b]they shall slay the burnt offering and
the sacrifice for the people, and
[c]they shall stand before them to minister to them.
12 "Because they ministered to them
before their idols and [a]caused[1] the
house of Israel to fall into iniquity,
therefore I have [b]raised My hand in
an oath against them," says the Lord
GOD, "that they shall bear their iniquity.
13 [a]"And they shall not come near Me
to minister to Me as priest, nor come
near any of My holy things, nor into
the Most Holy *Place;* but they shall
[b]bear their shame and their abominations which they have committed.
14 "Nevertheless I will make them
[a]keep charge of the temple, for all its
work, and for all that has to be done
in it.
15 [a]"But the priests, the Levites, [b]the
sons of Zadok, who kept charge
of My sanctuary [c]when the children of
Israel went astray from Me, they shall
come near Me to minister to Me; and
they [d]shall stand before Me to offer to
Me the [e]fat and the blood," says the
Lord GOD.
16 "They shall [a]enter My sanctuary,
and they shall come near [b]My table to
minister to Me, and they shall keep My
charge.
17 "And it shall be, whenever they enter the gates of the inner court, that
[a]they shall put on linen garments; no
wool shall come upon them while they
minister within the gates of the inner
court or within the house.
18 [a]"They shall have linen turbans on
their heads and linen trousers on their
bodies; they shall not clothe them-

27 [b]Ezek. 20:40, 41

CHAPTER 44

1 [a]Ezek. 43:1
2 [a]Ezek. 43:2–4
3 [a]Gen. 31:54 [b]Ezek. 46:2, 8
4 [a]Ezek. 3:23; 43:5 [b]Ezek. 1:28; 43:3 [1]Lit. *house*
5 [a]Ezek. 40:4 [b]Ezek. 43:10, 11 [1]Lit. *set your heart*
6 [a]Ezek. 2:5 [b]1 Pet. 4:3
7 [a]Acts 21:28 [b]Lev. 22:25 [c]Lev. 26:41 [d]Lev. 21:17 [e]Lev. 3:16
8 [a]Lev. 22:2
9 [a]Ezek. 44:7
10 [a]2 Kin. 23:8
11 [a]1 Chr. 26:1–19 [b]2 Chr. 29:34; 30:17 [c]Num. 16:9 *See WW at 1 Chr. 15:2.
12 [a]Is. 9:16 [b]Ps. 106:26 [1]Lit. *became a stumbling block of iniquity to the house of Israel*
13 [a]2 Kin. 23:9 [b]Ezek. 32:30
14 [a]Num. 18:4
15 [a]Ezek. 40:46 [b][1 Sam. 2:35] [c]Ezek. 44:10 [d]Deut. 10:8 [e]Ezek. 44:7
16 [a]Num. 18:5, 7, 8 [b]Ezek. 41:22
17 [a]Ex. 28:39–43; 39:27–29
18 [a]Ex. 28:40; 39:28

44:3 The prince: See 34:24, where the prince is synonymous with "My servant David."
44:4 Glory of the LORD filled: See note on 43:5. **I fell on my face:** See note on 1:28.
44:10–14 Cherethite temple guards (2 Kin. 11:4) had contributed to the downfall of Judah's former temple. God's "restored temple" is to be administrated only by covenant priests.
44:15–31 Specific regulations for those serving as **priests** are detailed. The priests from the line of **Zadok** (chief priest under David and a descendant of Aaron, 1 Kin. 1:8) are commended for their faithfulness (v. 15), and they are distinguished from the Levites who went astray (vv. 10–14). Because of their faithfulness they are elevated, and they participate in the offering of **the fat and the blood** (v. 15).
44:17 Linen garments: Linen was ritually clean, but **wool,** coming from an animal, might be unclean. See Ex. 28:42; 39:27–29; Lev. 6:10; 16:4, 23.

selves with *anything that causes*
sweat.
19 "When they go out to the outer
court, to the *outer* court to the people,
[a]they shall take off their garments in
which they have ministered, leave
them in the holy chambers, and put on
other garments; and in their holy garments they shall [b]not sanctify the people.
20 [a]"They shall neither shave their
heads nor let their hair grow [b]long, but
they shall keep their hair well trimmed.
21 [a]"No priest shall drink wine when
he enters the inner court.
22 "They shall not take as wife a
[a]widow or a divorced woman, but take
virgins of the descendants of the house
of Israel, or widows of priests.
23 "And [a]they shall *teach My people
the difference between the holy and the
unholy, and cause them to [b]discern between the unclean and the clean.
24 [a]"In controversy they shall stand as
judges, *and* judge it according to My
judgments. They shall keep My laws
and My statutes in all My appointed
meetings, [b]and they shall hallow My
Sabbaths.
25 "They shall not defile *themselves*
by coming near a dead person. Only
for father or mother, for son or daughter, for brother or unmarried sister
may they defile themselves.
26 [a]"After he is cleansed, they shall
count seven days for him.
27 "And on the day that he goes to the
sanctuary to minister in the sanctuary,
[a]he must offer his sin offering [b]in the
inner court," says the Lord GOD.
28 "It shall be, in regard to their inheritance, *that* I [a]*am* their inheritance. You
shall give them no [b]possession* in Israel, for I *am* their possession.
29 [a]"They shall eat the grain offering,
the sin offering, and the trespass offering; [b]every dedicated thing in Israel
shall be theirs.
30 "The [a]best[1] of all firstfruits of any
kind, and every sacrifice of any kind
from all your sacrifices, shall be the
priest's; also you [b]shall give to the
priest the first of your ground meal,
[c]to cause a blessing to *rest on your
house.
31 "The priests shall not eat anything,
bird or beast, that [a]died naturally or
was torn *by wild beasts.*

The Holy District

45 "Moreover, when you [a]divide
the land by lot into inheritance,
you shall [b]set apart a district for the
LORD, a holy section of the land; its
length *shall be* twenty-five thousand
cubits, and the width ten thousand. It
shall be holy throughout its territory
all around.
2 "Of this there shall be a square plot
for the sanctuary, [a]five hundred by five
hundred *rods,* with fifty cubits around
it for an open space.
3 "So this is the district you shall
measure: twenty-five thousand *cubits*
long and ten thousand wide; [a]in it shall
be the sanctuary, the Most Holy *Place.*
4 "It shall be [a]a holy *section* of the
land, belonging to the priests, the ministers of the sanctuary, who come near
to minister to the LORD; it shall be a
place for their houses and a holy place
for the sanctuary.
5 [a]"*An area* twenty-five thousand *cubits* long and ten thousand wide shall
belong to the Levites, the ministers of
the [1]temple; they shall have [b]twenty[2]
chambers as a possession.

Properties of the City and the Prince

6 [a]"You shall appoint as the property
of the city *an area* five thousand *cubits*
wide and twenty-five thousand long,
adjacent to the district of the holy *section;* it shall belong to the whole house
of Israel.
7 [a]"The prince shall have *a section*
on one side and the other of the holy
district and the city's property; and
bordering on the holy district and the
city's property, extending westward on
the west side and eastward on the east
side, the length *shall be* side by side

19 [a]Ezek. 42:14 [b]Lev. 6:27
20 [a]Lev. 21:5 [b]Num. 6:5
21 [a]Lev. 10:9
22 [a]Lev. 21:7, 13, 14
23 [a]Mal. 2:6–8 [b]Lev. 20:25 *See WW at Ps. 32:8.
24 [a]Deut. 17:8, 9 [b]Ezek. 22:26
26 [a]Num. 6:10; 19:11, 13–19
27 [a]Lev. 5:3, 6 [b]Ezek. 44:17
28 [a]Num. 18:20 [b]Ezek. 45:4 *See WW at Josh. 22:9.
29 [a]Lev. 7:6 [b]Lev. 27:21, 28
30 [a]Num. 3:13; 18:12 [b]Neh. 10:37 [c][Mal. 3:10] [1]Lit. *first* *See WW at Ex. 33:14.
31 [a]Lev. 22:8

CHAPTER 45

1 [a]Ezek. 47:22 [b]Ezek. 48:8, 9
2 [a]Ezek. 42:20
3 [a]Ezek. 48:10
4 [a]Ezek. 48:10, 11
5 [a]Ezek. 48:13 [b]Ezek. 40:17 [1]Lit. *house* [2]So with MT, Tg., Vg.; LXX *a possession,cities of dwelling*
6 [a]Ezek. 48:15
7 [a]Ezek. 48:21

44:20 To **shave their heads** was a sign of mourning, and this made the priest unclean (Lev. 21:5). To **let their hair grow long** seems to refer to a vow that might prevent the priest from carrying out his duties. For the Nazirite vow see Num. 6:5; 1 Sam. 1:11.
44:21 Drink wine: See Lev. 10:9.
44:22 Take as wife: The same prohibition is given by Moses (Lev. 21:7, 13, 14).
44:23 *Difference* between the holy and the unholy: This is a major concern for Ezekiel, since he himself was a priest. The priest was responsible for making the distinction between holy and unholy and for teaching this to the people (Lev. 10:10, 11). According to Mic. 3:11 the priests taught for pay, and by the time of Ezekiel they may have neglected to teach at all (see 22:26; Jer. 2:8).
44:25 Contact with a **dead person** made the priest ritually unclean (see Lev. 21:1–4; Hag. 2:13).
44:28 I *am* their inheritance: Similar to instructions given earlier to Moses and Joshua (see Num. 18:20; Deut. 10:9; Josh. 13:33; 18:7), the priests receive no inheritance in the land. They are to be supported by the gifts and offerings of the people (vv. 29, 30). In the distribution of the land, however, the priests receive an area where the temple is located on which to live (45:4).

with one of the *tribal* portions, from
the west border to the east border.
8 "The land shall be his possession
in Israel; and [a]My princes shall no
more oppress My people, but they shall
give *the rest of* the land to the house
of Israel, according to their tribes."

Laws Governing the Prince

9 'Thus says the Lord GOD: [a]"Enough,
O princes of Israel! [b]Remove violence
and plundering, execute justice and
righteousness, and stop dispossessing
My people," says the Lord GOD.
10 "You shall have [a]honest scales, an
honest ephah, and an honest bath.
11 "The ephah and the bath shall be
of the same measure, so that the bath
contains one-tenth of a homer, and the
ephah one-tenth of a homer; their measure shall be according to the homer.
12 "The [a]shekel *shall be* twenty gerahs; twenty shekels, twenty-five shekels, *and* fifteen shekels shall be your
mina.
13 "This *is* the offering which you shall
offer: you shall give one-sixth of an
ephah from a homer of wheat, and one-
sixth of an ephah from a homer of barley.
14 "The ordinance concerning oil, the
bath of oil, *is* one-tenth of a bath from
a kor. A kor *is* a homer or ten baths,
for ten baths *are* a homer.
15 "And one lamb shall be given from
a flock of two hundred, from the rich
pastures of Israel. These shall be for
grain offerings, burnt offerings, and
peace offerings, [a]to make atonement
for them," says the Lord GOD.
16 "All the people of the land shall give
this offering for the prince in Israel.
17 "Then it shall be the [a]prince's part
to give burnt offerings, grain offerings,
and drink offerings, at the feasts, the
New Moons, the Sabbaths, and at all
the appointed seasons of the house of
Israel. He shall prepare the *sin offering, the grain offering, the burnt offering, and the peace offerings to make
atonement for the house of Israel."

Keeping the Feasts

18 'Thus says the Lord GOD: "In the
first *month,* on the first *day* of the
month, you shall take a young bull
without blemish and [a]cleanse the sanctuary.
19 [a]"The priest shall take some of the
blood of the sin offering and put *it* on
the doorposts of the [1]temple, on the
four corners of the ledge of the altar,
and on the gateposts of the gate of the
inner court.
20 "And so you shall do on the seventh
day of the month [a]for everyone who
has sinned unintentionally or in ignorance. Thus you shall make atonement
for the temple.
21 [a]"In the first *month,* on the fourteenth day of the month, you shall observe the Passover, a feast of seven
days; unleavened bread shall be eaten.
22 "And on that day the prince shall
prepare for himself and for all the people of the land [a]a bull *for* a sin offering.
23 "On the [a]seven days of the feast he
shall prepare a burnt offering to the
LORD, seven bulls and seven rams
*without blemish, daily for seven days,
[b]and a kid of the goats daily *for* a sin
offering.
24 [a]"And he shall prepare a grain offering of one ephah for each bull and
one ephah for each ram, together with
a hin of oil for each ephah.
25 "In the seventh *month,* on the fifteenth day of the month, at the [a]feast,
he shall do likewise for seven days, according to the sin offering, the burnt
offering, the grain offering, and the
oil."

The Manner of Worship

46 'Thus says the Lord GOD: "The
gateway of the inner court that
faces toward the east shall be shut the

8 [a][Is. 11:3–5]; Jer. 22:17; Ezek. 22:27
9 [a]Ezek. 44:6 [b]Jer. 22:3; Zech. 8:16
10 [a]Lev. 19:36; Deut. 25:15; Prov. 16:11; Amos 8:4–6; Mic. 6:10, 11
12 [a]Ex. 30:13; Lev. 27:25; Num. 3:47
15 [a]Lev. 1:4; 6:30
17 [a]Ezek. 46:4–12 *See WW at Lev. 9:2.
18 [a]Lev. 16:16, 33; Ezek. 43:22, 26
19 [a]Lev. 16:18–20; Ezek. 43:20 [1]Lit. *house*
20 [a]Lev. 4:27; Ps. 19:12
21 [a]Ex. 12:18; Lev. 23:5, 6; Num. 9:2, 3; 28:16, 17; Deut. 16:1
22 [a]Lev. 4:14
23 [a]Lev. 23:8 [b]Num. 28:15, 22, 30; 29:5, 11, 16, 19 *See WW at Lev. 23:12.
24 [a]Num. 28:12–15; Ezek. 46:5, 7
25 [a]Lev. 23:34; Num. 29:12; Deut. 16:13; 2 Chr. 5:3; 7:8, 10

45:9–12 Just weights and measures are established to prevent the sins of the past. Similar instruction had been given before. See Lev. 19:35, 36; Deut. 25:13–15; Mic. 6:10, 11.
45:11 The **homer** was a little over 6 bushels (about 220 liters). The **bath** was a liquid measure, the **ephah** was a dry measure. Both were a tenth of a homer.
45:12 *The* ***shekel*** *weighed* about 11.4 grams. The **mina** was usually about 50 shekels in the Canaanite system, but Ezekiel redefines it at 60 shekels, the same as the Babylonian system.
45:13 The offering the prince is to give from his income is a sixtieth of the produce.
45:14 The **kor** and **homer** were the same. The kor was used to measure flour, wheat, and barley.
45:18–25 Only three great feasts are mentioned: New Year's Day (vv. 18–20); Passover, combined with Unleavened Bread (vv. 21–24; Ex. 23:15; Lev. 23:4–8; Deut. 16:1–8); and the Feast of Tabernacles or Ingathering (v. 25; Ex. 23:16; Lev. 23:33–36; Deut. 16:13–15). Surprisingly omitted is a third feast required for all Israelite males, the Feast of Weeks or Pentecost (see Ex. 23:16; Lev. 23:15–21; Deut. 16:9–12) and the Day of Atonement (see Lev. 23:26–32). The ceremony on the first day of the first month (v. 18) and the seventh day of the month (v. 20) seems to replace the Day of Atonement. There is no clear explanation for why certain feasts were chosen for mention by Ezekiel.

six [a]working days; but on the Sabbath
it shall be opened, and on the day of
the New Moon it shall be opened.
2 [a]"The prince shall enter by way of
the vestibule of the gateway from the
outside, and stand by the gatepost. The
priests shall prepare his burnt offering
and his peace offerings. He shall *worship at the threshold of the gate. Then
he shall go out, but the gate shall not
be shut until evening.
3 "Likewise the people of the land
shall worship at the entrance to this
gateway before the LORD on the Sabbaths and the New Moons.
4 "The burnt offering that [a]the prince
offers to the LORD on the [b]Sabbath day
shall be six lambs without blemish, and
a ram without blemish;
5 [a]"and the grain offering *shall be*
one ephah for a ram, and the grain offering for the lambs, [1]as much as he
wants to give, as well as a hin of oil
with every ephah.
6 "On the day of the New Moon *it*
shall be a young bull without blemish,
six lambs, and a ram; they shall be
without blemish.
7 "He shall prepare a grain offering
of an ephah for a bull, an ephah for a
ram, [1]as much as he wants to give for
the lambs, and a hin of oil with every
ephah.
8 [a]"When the prince enters, he shall
go in by way of the vestibule of the
gateway, and go out the same way.
9 "But when the people of the land
[a]come before the LORD on the appointed feast days, whoever enters by
way of the north [b]gate to worship shall
go out by way of the south gate; and
whoever enters by way of the south
gate shall go out by way of the north
gate. He shall not return by way of the
gate through which he came, but shall
go out through the opposite gate.
10 "The prince shall then be in their
midst. When they go in, he shall go
in; and when they go out, he shall go
out.
11 "At the festivals and the appointed
feast days [a]the grain offering shall be
an ephah for a bull, an ephah for a ram,
as much as he wants to give for the
lambs, and a hin of oil with every
ephah.
12 "Now when the prince makes a voluntary burnt offering or voluntary
peace offering to the LORD, the gate

CHAPTER 46

1 [a]Ex. 20:9
2 [a]Ezek. 44:3 *See WW at Ps. 99:5.
4 [a]Ezek. 45:17 [b]Num. 28:9, 10
5 [a]Num. 28:12; Ezek. 45:24; 46:7, 11 [1]Lit. *the gift of his hand*
7 [1]Lit. *as much as his hand can reach*
8 [a]Ezek. 44:3; 46:2
9 [a]Ex. 23:14–17; 34:23; Deut. 16:16, 17; Ps. 84:7; Mic. 6:6 [b]Ezek. 48:31, 33
11 [a]Ezek. 46:5, 7
12 [a]Ezek. 44:3; 46:1, 2, 8
13 [a]Ex. 29:38; Num. 28:3–5 [1]Lit. *morning by morning*
15 [a]Ex. 29:42; Num. 28:6
17 [a]Lev. 25:10 *See WW at Lev. 25:10.
18 [a]Ezek. 45:8
19 [a]Ezek. 42:13
20 [a]2 Chr. 35:13 [b]Lev. 2:4, 5, 7 [c]Ezek. 44:19

that faces toward the east [a]shall then
be opened for him; and he shall prepare his burnt offering and his peace
offerings as he did on the Sabbath day.
Then he shall go out, and after he goes
out the gate shall be shut.
13 [a]"You shall daily make a burnt offering to the LORD *of* a lamb of the first
year without blemish; you shall prepare it [1]every morning.
14 "And you shall prepare a grain offering with it every morning, a sixth
of an ephah, and a third of a hin of
oil to moisten the fine flour. This grain
offering is a perpetual ordinance, to be
made regularly to the LORD.
15 "Thus they shall prepare the lamb,
the grain offering, and the oil, *as* a
[a]regular burnt offering every morning."

The Prince and Inheritance Laws

16 'Thus says the Lord GOD: "If the
prince gives a gift *of some* of his inheritance to any of his sons, it shall belong
to his sons; it is their possession by inheritance.
17 "But if he gives a gift of some of
his inheritance to one of his servants,
it shall be his until [a]the year of *liberty,
after which it shall return to the prince.
But his inheritance shall belong to his
sons; it shall become theirs.
18 "Moreover [a]the prince shall not
take any of the people's inheritance by
evicting them from their property; he
shall provide an inheritance for his
sons from his own property, so that
none of My people may be scattered
from his property." ' "

How the Offerings Were Prepared

19 Now he brought me through the entrance, which *was* at the side of the
gate, into the holy [a]chambers of the
priests which face toward the north;
and there a place *was* situated at their
extreme western end.
20 And he said to me, "This *is* the place
where the priests shall [a]boil the trespass offering and the sin offering, *and*
where they shall [b]bake the grain offering, so that they do not bring *them* out
into the outer court [c]to sanctify the
people."
21 Then he brought me out into the

46:9 Specific directions are given for worshipers entering the temple area. They enter by one gate and exit by the other. This symbolizes the order that is to characterize the community of the new order of worshipers.

46:17 The year of liberty: The Year of Jubilee, which theoretically came every 50 years (Lev. 25:8–17).

outer court and caused me to pass by
the four corners of the court; and in
fact, in every corner of the court *there
was another* court.
22 In the four corners of the court *were*
enclosed courts, forty *cubits* long and
thirty wide; all four corners *were* the
same size.
23 *There was* a row *of building stones*
all around in them, all around the four
of them; and [1]cooking hearths were
made under the rows of stones all
around.
24 And he said to me, "These *are* the
[1]kitchens where the ministers of the
[2]temple shall [a]boil the sacrifices of the
people."

The Healing Waters and Trees

[6] 47 Then he brought me back to the
door of the [1]temple; and there
was [a]water, flowing from under the
threshold of the temple toward the
east, for the front of the temple faced
east; the water was flowing from under
the right side of the temple, south of
the *altar.
2 He brought me out by way of the
north gate, and led me around on the
outside to the outer gateway that faces
[a]east; and there was water, running out
on the right side.
3 And when [a]the man went out to the
east with the line in his hand, he measured one thousand cubits, and he
brought me through the waters; the
water *came up to my* ankles.
4 Again he measured one thousand
and brought me through the waters;
the water *came up to my* knees. Again
he measured one thousand and
brought me through; the water *came
up to my* waist.
5 Again he measured one thousand,
and it was a river that I could not cross;
for the water was too deep, water in

23 [1]Lit. *boiling places*
24 [a]Ezek. 46:20 [1]Lit. *house of those who boil* [2]Lit. *house*

CHAPTER 47

1 [a]Ps. 46:4; Is. 30:25; 55:1; [Jer. 2:13]; Joel 3:18; Zech. 13:1; 14:8; [Rev. 22:1, 17] [1]Lit. *house* *See WW at 2 Kin. 12:9.
2 [a]Ezek. 44:1, 2
3 [a]Ezek. 40:3
7 [a][Is. 60:13, 21; 61:3; Ezek. 47:12; Rev. 22:2]
8 [1]Or *Arabah,* The Jordan Valley
9 [1]Lit. *two rivers*
10 [a]Num. 34:3; Josh. 23:4; Ezek. 48:28
12 [a]Ezek. 47:7; [Rev. 22:2] [b]Job 18:16; [Ps. 1:3; Jer. 17:8] [c][Rev. 22:2] [1]Or *healing*
13 [a]Num. 34:1–29 [b]Gen. 48:5; 1 Chr. 5:1; Ezek. 48:4, 5

which one must swim, a river that
could not be crossed.
6 He said to me, "Son of man, have
you seen *this?*" Then he brought me
and returned me to the bank of the
river.
7 When I returned, there, along the
bank of the river, *were* very many
[a]trees on one side and the other.
8 Then he said to me: "This water
flows toward the eastern region, goes
down into the [1]valley, and enters the
sea. *When it* reaches the sea, *its* waters
are healed.
9 "And it shall be *that* every living
thing that moves, wherever [1]the rivers
go, will live. There will be a very great
multitude of fish, because these waters
go there; for they will be healed, and
everything will live wherever the river
goes.
10 "It shall be *that* fishermen will
stand by it from En Gedi to En Eglaim;
they will be *places* for spreading their
nets. Their fish will be of the same
kinds as the fish [a]of the Great Sea, exceedingly many.
11 "But its swamps and marshes will
not be healed; they will be given over
to salt.
12 [a]"Along the bank of the river, on
this side and that, will grow all *kinds
of* trees used for food; [b]their leaves will
not wither, and their fruit will not fail.
They will bear fruit every month, because their water flows from the sanctuary. Their fruit will be for food, and
their leaves for [c]medicine."[1]

Borders of the Land

13 Thus says the Lord GOD: "These *are*
the [a]borders by which you shall divide
the land as an inheritance among the
twelve tribes of Israel. [b]Joseph *shall
have two* portions.
14 "You shall inherit it equally with

47:1–12 See section 6 of Truth-In-Action at the end of Ezek.
47:1–12 A sacred river **from under the threshold of the temple** flowed to **the east.** Four times the water is measured at increments of 1,000 cubits, and the river rises to ankle-depth (v. 3), to the knees (v. 4), to the waist (v. 4), and finally to a depth too deep to cross. Allusions to this river are found in other scriptures (see Joel 3:18; Zech. 14:8; Rev. 22:1), and there is a strong connection with the river of Paradise (see Gen. 2:10–14; Ps. 46:4). The trees along the bank of the river (vv. 7, 12) provide abundant fruit all year *long as in Amos 9:13.* Such prophecies which relate the flowing waters of blessing may also anticipate the Holy Spirit's work in NT believers (John 7:37, 38).
47:8 Valley: The Arabah, the dry, waterless area between Jerusalem and the Dead Sea.
47:13 Joseph *shall have two portions*: The two sons of Joseph, Ephraim and Manasseh, were adopted by Jacob (Gen. 48:5); since Levi receives no territorial inheritance, they make up two of the Twelve Tribes.
47:15–20 The borders of the land closely resemble those of Num. 34:1–12. The northern border begins on the Phoenician coast of the Mediterranean above Byblos and moves east to Lebo Hamath (modern Lebwe), Zedad, and Hazar Enan on the edge of the desert. The eastern boundary includes the environs of Damascus and the region of Bashan, descending southwestward to the eastern shore of the Sea of Galilee along the Yarmuk Valley. It then follows the Jordan River to the Dead Sea. The southern border begins at the southeastern edge of the Dead Sea, encompasses Zoar and Tamar, and then moves south of Kadesh Barnea and follows the Brook of Egypt to the Mediterranean. The western boundary is the Mediterranean. In dispensational interpretation these boundaries define literal borders in a restored, national Israel.

one another; for I [a]raised My hand in
an oath to give it to your fathers, and
this land shall [b]fall to you as your inheritance.
15 "This *shall be* the border of the land
on the north: from the Great Sea, *by*
[a]the road to Hethlon, as one goes to
[b]Zedad,
16 [a]"Hamath, [b]Berothah, Sibraim
(which *is* between the border of Damascus and the border of Hamath), to
Hazar Hatticon (which *is* on the border
of Hauran).
17 "Thus the boundary shall be from
the Sea to [a]Hazar Enan, the border of
Damascus; and as for the north, northward, it is the border of Hamath. *This*
is the north side.

14 [a]Gen. 12:7; 13:15; 15:7; 17:8; 26:3; 28:13; Deut. 1:8; Ezek. 20:5, 6, 28, 42 [b]Ezek. 48:29
15 [a]Ezek. 48:1 [b]Num. 34:7, 8
16 [a]Num. 34:8 [b]2 Sam. 8:8
17 [a]Num. 34:9; Ezek. 48:1
19 [a]Num. 20:13; Deut. 32:51; Ps. 81:7; Ezek. 48:28 [1]Heb. *Negev* [2]Lit. *Strife*
21 [a]Ezek. 45:1

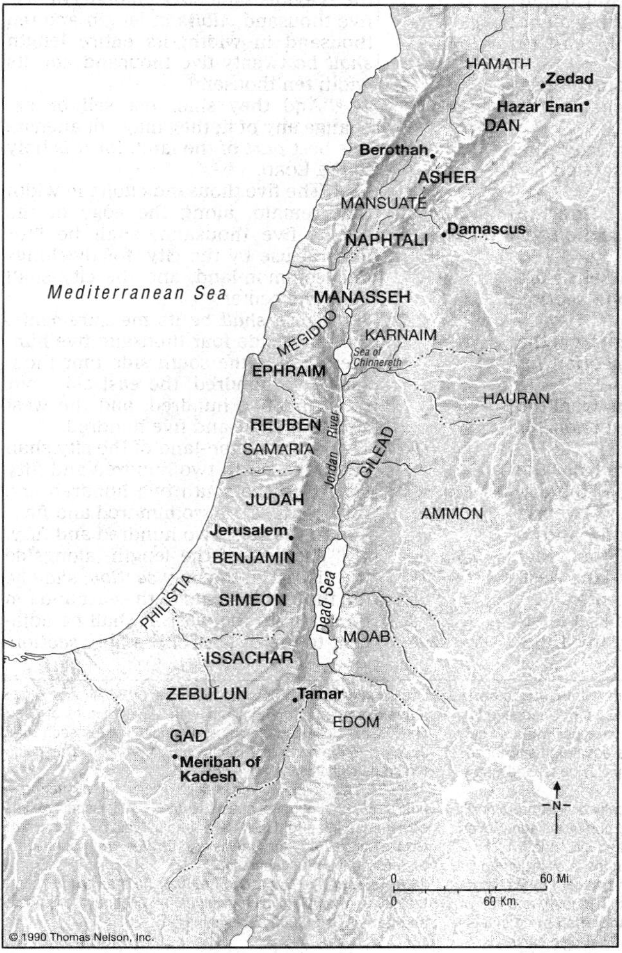

18 "On the east side you shall mark
out the border from between Hauran
and Damascus, and between Gilead
and the land of Israel, along the Jordan, and along the eastern side of the
sea. *This is* the east side.
19 "The south side, toward the [1]South,
shall be from Tamar to [a]the waters of
[2]Meribah by Kadesh, along the brook
to the Great Sea. *This is* the south side,
toward the South.
20 "The west side *shall be* the Great
Sea, from the *southern* boundary until
one comes to a point opposite Hamath.
This *is* the west side.
21 "Thus you shall [a]divide this land
among yourselves according to the
tribes of Israel.

Ezekiel's Vision of the Restoration of the Land. The boundaries of the restored nation of Israel approach the boundaries of the land as it was under David and Solomon. However, the area east of the Jordan—Gilead and Transjordan—will not be a part of this new inheritance. It was not part of the land that had been promised.

The tribes are not arranged as they were historically when the land was divided under Joshua (Josh. 13—19). God will do something new in the restoration.

The central portion of the land around Jerusalem will be set apart for religion and government.

To the north of the central district are seven tribes—Dan, Asher, Naphtali, Manasseh, Ephraim, Reuben, Judah.

To the south are the remaining five tribes—Benjamin, Simeon, Issachar, Zebulun, Gad.

22 "It shall be that you will divide it
by [a]lot as an inheritance for yourselves, [b]and for the strangers who
*dwell among you and who bear chil-
dren among you. [c]They shall be to you
as native-born among the children of
Israel; they shall have an inheritance
with you among the tribes of Israel.
23 "And it shall be *that* in whatever
tribe the stranger dwells, there you
shall give *him* his inheritance," says
the Lord GOD.

Division of the Land

48 "Now these *are* the names of the
tribes: [a]From the northern border along the road to Hethlon at the
entrance of Hamath, to Hazar Enan,
the border of Damascus northward, in
the direction of Hamath, *there shall be*
one *section for* [b]Dan from its east to
its west side;
2 "by the border of Dan, from the east
side to the west, one *section for*
[a]Asher;
3 "by the border of Asher, from the
east side to the west, one *section for*
[a]Naphtali;
4 "by the border of Naphtali, from the
east side to the west, one *section for*
[a]Manasseh;
5 "by the border of Manasseh, from
the east side to the west, one *section*
for [a]Ephraim;
6 "by the border of Ephraim, from the
east side to the west, one *section for*
[a]Reuben;
7 "by the border of Reuben, from the
east side to the west, one *section for*
[a]Judah;
8 "by the border of Judah, from the
east side to the west, shall be [a]the district which you shall set apart, twenty-
five thousand *cubits* in width, and *in*
length the same as one of the *other*
portions, from the east side to the west,
with the [b]sanctuary in the center.
9 "The district that you shall set apart
for the LORD *shall be* twenty-five thousand *cubits* in length and ten thousand
in width.
10 "To these—to the priests—the holy
district shall belong: on the north
twenty-five thousand *cubits in length,*
on the west ten thousand in width, on
the east ten thousand in width, and on
the south twenty-five thousand in
length. The sanctuary of the LORD shall
be in the center.
11 [a]"*It shall be* for the priests of the
sons of Zadok, who are sanctified, who
have kept My charge, who did not go
astray when the children of Israel went
astray, [b]as the Levites went astray.
12 "And *this* district of land that is set
apart shall be to them a thing most
[a]holy by the border of the Levites.
13 "Opposite the border of the priests,
the [a]Levites *shall have an area* twenty-
five thousand *cubits* in length and ten
thousand in width; its entire length
shall be twenty-five thousand and its
width ten thousand.
14 [a]"And they shall not sell or exchange any of it; they may not alienate
this best *part* of the land, for *it is* holy
to the LORD.
15 [a]"The five thousand *cubits* in width
that remain, along the edge of the
twenty-five thousand, shall be [b]for
general use by the city, for dwellings
and common-land; and the city shall
be in the center.
16 "These *shall be* its measurements:
the north side four thousand five hundred *cubits,* the south side four thousand five hundred, the east side four
thousand five hundred, and the west
side four thousand five hundred.
17 "The common-land of the city shall
be: to the north two hundred and fifty
cubits, to the south two hundred and
fifty, to the east two hundred and fifty,
and to the west two hundred and fifty.
18 "The rest of the length, alongside
the district of the holy *section, shall be*
ten thousand *cubits* to the east and ten
thousand to the west. It shall be adjacent to the district of the holy *section,*

22 [a]Num. 26:55, 56 [b][Eph. 3:6; Rev. 7:9, 10] [c][Acts 11:18; 15:9; Gal. 3:28; Eph. 2:12–14; Col. 3:11] *See WW at Jer. 42:17.

CHAPTER 48

1 [a]Ezek. 47:15 [b]Josh. 19:40–48
2 [a]Josh. 19:24–31
3 [a]Josh. 19:32–39
4 [a]Josh. 13:29–31; 17:1–11, 17, 18
5 [a]Josh. 16:5–10; 17:8–10, 14–18
6 [a]Josh. 13:15–23
7 [a]Josh. 15:1–63; 19:9
8 [a]Ezek. 45:1–6 [b][Is. 12:6; 33:20–22]; Ezek. 45:3, 4
11 [a]Ezek. 40:46; 44:15 [b]Ezek. 44:10, 12
12 [a]Ezek. 45:4
13 [a]Ezek. 45:5
14 [a]Ex. 22:29; Lev. 27:10, 28, 33; Ezek. 44:30
15 [a]Ezek. 45:6 [b]Ezek. 42:20

47:22 For the strangers: Aliens were not allowed to own land in Israel, as is attested by the rebuke of Shebna in Is. 22:15–19. Shebna was apparently a foreigner who had cut a tomb for himself. Ezekiel now gives equal rights to these people, a major prophecy of Gentile inclusion is God's new covenant order.

48:1–29 The land is ideally and logically divided from north *to south. Each tribe receives* an equal portion of land. Seven tribes are to the north of the temple and city, and five are south. The former settlement of the tribes is disregarded. Issachar and Zebulun, who had been northern tribes, find themselves in the extreme south. Gad, Reuben, and half of Manasseh must be moved out of Transjordan since that is not included in Ezekiel's boundaries. The logic behind Ezekiel's distribution puts the four sons of Bilhah and Zilpah at the extreme north and south, with the eight sons of Leah and Rachel closest to the city and temple, four on each side. Judah is to the north and Benjamin to the south. This holds the same significance as 47:15–20.

48:8–22 This section gives details for the land allotted to holy use. The amount of space devoted to this aspect makes obvious the intent of Ezekiel—a land in which the temple of God is central, and the priests and Levites are properly performing their functions.

48:8 Twenty-five thousand *cubits*: The area set aside for the city and temple, which includes the allotment for priests and Levites, is 25,000 cubits square (v. 20).

and its produce shall be food for the
workers of the city.
19 [a]"The workers of the city, from all
the tribes of Israel, shall cultivate it.
20 "The entire district *shall be* twenty-
five thousand *cubits* by twenty-five
thousand *cubits,* foursquare. You shall
set apart the holy district with the
property of the city.
21 [a]"The rest *shall belong* to the
prince, on one side and on the other
of the holy district and of the city's
property, next to the twenty-five thousand *cubits* of the *holy* district as far
as the eastern border, and westward
next to the twenty-five thousand as far
as the western border, adjacent to the
tribal portions; *it shall belong* to the
prince. It shall be the holy district,
[b]and the sanctuary of the [1]temple *shall
be* in the center.
22 "Moreover, apart from the possession of the Levites and the possession
of the city *which are* in the midst of
what *belongs* to the prince, *the area*
between the border of Judah and the
border of [a]Benjamin shall belong to the
prince.
23 "As for the rest of the tribes, from
the east side to the west, Benjamin
shall have one *section;*
24 "by the border of Benjamin, from
the east side to the west, [a]Simeon *shall
have* one *section;*
25 "by the border of Simeon, from the
east side to the west, [a]Issachar *shall
have* one *section;*
26 "by the border of Issachar, from the
east side to the west, [a]Zebulun *shall
have* one *section;*
27 "by the border of Zebulun, from the
east side to the west, [a]Gad *shall have*
one *section;*
28 "by the border of Gad, on the south
side, toward the [1]South, the border
shall be from Tamar *to* [a]the waters of
[2]Meribah *by* Kadesh, along the brook
to the [b]Great Sea.
29 [a]"This *is* the land which you shall
divide by lot as an inheritance among
the tribes of Israel, and these *are* their
portions," says the Lord GOD.

The Gates of the City and Its Name

30 "These *are* the exits of the city. On
the north side, measuring four thousand five hundred *cubits*
31 [a]"(the gates of the city *shall be*
named after the tribes of Israel), the
three gates northward: one gate for
Reuben, one gate for Judah, and one
gate for Levi;
32 "on the east side, four thousand five
hundred *cubits,* three gates: one gate
for Joseph, one gate for Benjamin, and
one gate for Dan;
33 "on the south side, measuring four
thousand five hundred *cubits,* three
gates: one gate for Simeon, one gate
for Issachar, and one gate for Zebulun;
34 "on the west side, four thousand
five hundred *cubits* with their three
gates: one gate for Gad, one gate for
Asher, and one gate for Naphtali.
35 "All the way around *shall be* eighteen thousand *cubits;* [a]and the name
of the city from *that* day *shall be:*
[b]THE[1] LORD *IS* THERE."

19 [a]Ezek. 45:6
21 [a]Ezek. 34:24; 45:7; 48:22 [b]Ezek. 48:8, 10 [1]Lit. *house*
22 [a]Josh. 18:21–28
24 [a]Josh. 19:1–9
25 [a]Josh. 19:17–23
26 [a]Josh. 19:10–16
27 [a]Josh. 13:24–28
28 [a]Gen. 14:7; 2 Chr. 20:2; Ezek. 47:19 [b]Ezek. 47:10, 15, 19, 20 [1]Heb. *Negev* [2]Lit. *Strife*
29 [a]Ezek. 47:14, 21, 22
31 [a][Rev. 21:10–14]
35 [a]Jer. 23:6; 33:16 [b]Is. 12:6; 14:32; 24:23; Jer. 3:17; 8:19; 14:9; Ezek. 35:10; Joel 3:21; Zech. 2:10; Rev. 21:3; 22:3 [1]Heb. *YHWH Shammah*

48:30–35 The city has twelve **gates,** three on each side. These are named after the Twelve Tribes, Levi included, and Ephraim and Manasseh united in Joseph.

48:35 THE LORD *IS* THERE (Hebrew *Yahweh Shammah*): The city receives a new name, corresponding to the new state of salvation.

TRUTH-IN-ACTION through EZEKIEL

Letting the LIFE of the Holy Spirit Bring Faith's Works Alive in You!

Truth Ezekiel Teaches	Text	**Action** Ezekiel Invites
1 Steps to Knowing God and His Ways God's Word reveals that He was silent as a judgment against His people, neither answering their prayers nor speaking through prophets.	7:26, 27	**Understand** lack of prophetic leadership and vision comes to any people who refuse to obey God's revealed will.
God rejects false teachers and prophets who speak out of their own imaginations.	13:8–23	**Remember** that God says that teaching or prophesying falsehood is "lying."

Truth Ezekiel Teaches	Text	**Action** Ezekiel Invites
2 Guidelines for Growing in Godliness Godliness is not inherited. Each individual must seek out God and establish a personal relationship with Him. Godliness comes by divine transformation of our hardened or rebellious hearts, not by self-effort.	14:15–20 36:26, 27	**Be assured** that you will not be saved by another's righteousness or be judged for another's sin. **Understand** that God will bring about true transformation among His people by renewing their minds and hearts and filling them with His Spirit. **Welcome** the exchange of heart and spirit God offers to you. **Yield** to God's Spirit and **receive** His law of life in your heart to be truly transformed.
3 Keys to Wise Living The wise person knows that his flesh is at war with his spiritual desires. The carnal nature attempts to reject the Word of God and its renewing work, and to defend the fortress of self-will (see 2 Cor. 10:4–6).	3:7–9 12:1, 2 13:1–12 13:19	**Understand** that the carnal ear is rebellious and stubborn against God's Word. **Remember** that the evidence of rebellion is spiritual blindness and deafness. **Be assured** that God is against those who speak falsely in His name. **Know** that He has set Himself against those who speak things He has not said and who teach His Word falsely. **Understand** that the false teacher, whose motive is gain, causes injustice and iniquity among God's people.
4 Steps to Dealing with Sin The prophet laments that God's people and their leaders "heal their sins lightly." Only paying lip service to sin and its devastation, they fail to confront or deal thoroughly with sin.	14:7 18:30–32	**Be advised** that God will not answer the unrepentant prayers of an idolater or one who continually entertains sin in his heart, although he may be of God's people. **Repent** in sincerity. **Seek God** for a new heart and a renewed spirit. **Understand** that true spiritual transformation involves repentance.
5 Lessons for Leaders Ezek. focuses on the common failure of God's servants. This results from their gauging their success by man's approval rather than by God's standards. Ezek. is rich with insight into the hearts of God's people. Though ostensibly desiring God's will and way, some seek their own benefit and personal gain. God warns the prophets not to presume the outward devotion of people is genuine unless sacrificial and transformed living is manifest.	2:3–8 3:16–27; 33:1–9 33:30–33 34:1–10	Leaders, **do not use** "success" alone to gauge how well people seem to receive you. Leaders, **remember** the principle of your responsibility as God's spokesman or watchman: **Accept** your tasks to teach and correct, whether people listen or not. Leaders, **remember** that popularity is no final measure of righteousness or your true effectiveness. **Beware** of people's tendency to view preaching as a form of entertainment. Leaders, **be warned** that God sets Himself against pastors who take care of themselves and not the welfare of His people.
6 A Key Lesson in Faith God will ultimately supply the final answer to mankind's most perplexing problems through the outflow of the Holy Spirit.	47:1–12	**Rejoice** that the prophesied outflow of God's Spirit will produce healing and restoration. **Welcome** this grace in your life and circumstance.

The Book of DANIEL

Author: Daniel
Date: Late Sixth Century B.C.
Theme: God Controls the Destiny of All Nations
Key Words: Kings, Kingdoms, Visions, Dreams

Author Daniel was deported as a teenager in 605 B.C. to Babylon where he lived over sixty years. He was likely from an upper-class family in Jerusalem. The deportation of the royal descendants into Babylon had been prophesied by Isaiah to Hezekiah (Is. 39:7). Daniel initially served as a trainee in Nebuchadnezzar's court; he was later an advisor to foreign kings.

His importance as a prophet was confirmed by Jesus in Matthew 24:15.

Daniel means "God Is My Judge." His unshakable consecration to Yahweh and his loyalty to God's people strongly affirmed that truth in his life.

Date Although the siege and carrying away of captives into Babylon lasted several years, the mighty men of valor, the skilled, and the educated were taken from Jerusalem early in the war (2 Kin. 24:14). The date usually given for Daniel's captivity is 605 B.C. His prophecy covers the time span of his life.

Background Along with thousands of captives from Judah who were taken into Babylonian exile between 605 B.C. and 582 B.C., the treasures of Solomon's palace and the temple were also transported. The Babylonians had subdued all the provinces ruled by Assyria and had consolidated their empire into an area that covered much of the Middle East.

To govern such a diversified kingdom over such an expanse of space required a skillful administrative bureaucracy. Slaves who were educated or possessed needed skills became the manpower for the government. Because of their wisdom, knowledge, and handsome appearance, four young Hebrews were selected for the training program (1:4). The outstanding character of Daniel, Hananiah, Mishael, and Azariah secured positions for them in the king's palace; and it was Daniel who rose to excel all the wise men of that vast empire (6:1–3).

Purpose The purpose is to show that the God of Israel, the only God, is in control of the destiny of all nations.

Content Daniel has three main sections: Introduction to the person of Daniel (ch. 1), Daniel's key tests of character and the development of his prophetic interpretation skills (chs. 2—7), and his series of visions about future kingdoms and events (chs. 8—12). In this final section, Daniel emerges as a key prophetic book for understanding much of the Bible. Many insights into end-times prophecies are dependent upon an understanding of this book. Jesus' comments in the Olivet Discourse (Matt. 24; 25) and many of the revelations given to the apostle Paul find harmony and cohesion in Daniel (see Rom. 11; 2 Thess. 2). Likewise, it becomes a necessary study companion to the Book of Revelation.

Although the interpretation of Daniel, like Revelation, is subject to great diversity, for many the dispensational approach has become quite popular. It is an interpretive approach that sees in Daniel keys to help unlock the mysteries of such subjects as the Antichrist, the Great Tribulation, the Second Coming of Christ, the Times of the Gentiles, future resurrections, and judgments. This approach also sees most unfulfilled prophecy as revolving around two major focal points: 1) the future destiny of the city of Jerusalem; 2) the future destiny of Daniel's people, national Jews (9:24). See Introduction to Revelation: Methods of Interpretation.

Daniel's writing covers the reign of two kingdoms, Babylon and Medo-Persia, and four kings: Nebuchadnezzar (2:11—4:37); Belshazzar (5:1–31); Darius (6:1–28); and Cyrus (10:1—11:1).

Personal Application One of the beautiful themes of this book is the emphasis on separation to God, with Daniel as the ultimate example. From their decision not to eat the king's food to the refusal to bow to the image of the king, Daniel and his three friends (now named Shadrach, Meshach, and Abed-Nego) displayed such an uncompromising spirit that spectacular opportunities were opened for God to display His power on their behalf. Their courageous commitment presents a timeless challenge to believers not to compromise their testimony of Jesus Christ. Even though it may mean a fiery-furnace testing, the Lord's protection and deliverance will be there.

Another theme of Daniel is the absolute superiority of God over occult attempts to reveal or interpret spiritual mysteries. Try as they did, all the magicians, soothsayers, wise men, and astrologers of the king's court could not arrive at the truth (5:8). This is an enduring encouragement to believers. Spiritual counterfeiters can never stand before the wisdom and power of the Holy Spirit (2 Cor. 10:3–6).

The prophetic section not only gives future understanding to a believer's future, but serves to reassure us that God has history under His sovereign control.

Prophetic Key According to many interpreters, Daniel 9 contains a pivotal prophecy. It has come to be known as "Daniel's Seventy Weeks of Years." An understanding of these weeks is crucial to one school of interpretation of latter-day prophetic events. Unfortunately, but understandably, the interpretation of this section is diverse among equally dedicated, committed Christians. These notes shall reflect the frequently accepted dispensational approach. However, additional entries in certain footnotes and at the end of this section will address the more historic classical/conservative view (indicated by the words ***CLASSICAL INTERPRETATION***). Both are valid considerations for dedicated students to examine, and the exercise occasions the healthy reminder that prophetic Scripture interpretation is not a place for committed Christians to part company, although differences exist.

As Daniel sought the Lord to find out how long the Babylonian captivity would last, God showed him that the original prophecy of Jeremiah, indicating that the captivity would last seventy years, would be extended to "seventy sevens," or 490 years (Jer. 29). This revelation, in fact, covers the history of Jerusalem and the Jews from the time that Artaxerxes decreed they should rebuild the city of Jerusalem (Neh. 2:1–10) to the time of the Great Tribulation (Matt. 24:15–31).

This whole period is called "the Times of the Gentiles" because Gentile political authority will be the major force until the final destruction of all Israel's enemies at the end of the Great Tribulation. This will culminate in the Battle of Armageddon and the Second Advent of the Messiah. He will at that time destroy all the armies that have come against Jerusalem. See note on Revelation 16:12–16.

The "seventy sevens" are divided into three sections: seven weeks, sixty-two weeks, and one week. Each week represents seven years. The decree of Artaxerxes was in 446–445 B.C. (Neh. 2:1). The first two sections of weeks total 69 weeks or 483 years. This period ended in A.D. 32 when the Messiah was "cut off" (9:26), or when Jesus was crucified on Calvary.

The Abomination of Desolation, which Daniel prophesied would be part of the Seventieth Week, was clearly dated by Jesus as being part of the Great Tribulation or end-time period (Matt. 24:15). Nearly two thousand years have passed and the Seventieth Week has not happened. We are still living in the parenthetical time called the Times of the Gentiles, which precedes that culminative prophetic "week."

From this interpretive perspective, the Book of Daniel unveils a march of events in God's relationship, not only with His people, but with the world political system. Basic facts distilled from this book seem to illuminate other difficult passages, presenting these apparent forthcoming events:

1. The Messiah will return before the millennial period (2:31–37, 44, 45; 7:13, 14).
2. God's kingdom will literally be established on the Earth with the Messiah-King as ruler (2:44, 45; 7:26, 27).
3. The four metals of Nebuchadnezzar's dream image symbolizes four empires: Babylonian, Medo-Persian, Macedonian-Greek, and Roman (2:37–40).
4. The fourth kingdom, Rome, will enjoy a last-day revival in the form of a united confederacy in Europe. Out of this system the Antichrist will emerge (7:8, 20, 21; 8:23).
5. The False Prophet and the Antichrist are persons, not merely a system (7:7, 8, 20–26; 9:27; 11:36–45).
6. God will continue to deal with the nation of Israel (9:20–27).
7. National Israel is the prophetic time clock for last-day events (9:24).
8. The False Prophet and the Antichrist will dominate the last portion of the last week of Daniel's Seventy Weeks of Years. At the end of the "week," after the Great Tribulation, Jesus the Messiah will return to establish the kingdom of God, which will resolve all the prophecies of Daniel (9:24, 27).

CLASSICAL INTERPRETATION: As previously indicated in the Introduction, the notations for the Book of Daniel are interpreted using dispensational hermeneutical principles. In contrast to this prophetic approach, many evangelicals interpret Daniel using classical (Covenant) hermeneutical principles. Classical interpreters do so, realizing that biblical prophecy may have multiple levels of fulfillment. See note on the Day of the Lord in Obadiah 15.

The classical view sees the initial fulfillment of Daniel's prophetic sections in past historical events, such as the second-century B.C. invasion of Jerusalem by Antiochus Epiphanes and the events of the fall of Jerusalem in A.D. 70. Classical interpreters do, however, also see ultimate fulfillment of many of the prophecies at the end of this age. For an example, see the note on 9:26, 27.

Furthermore, the classical approach does not always press for strict literalness, especially when the New Testament itself makes nonliteral application. For example, see James's quote of Amos 9:11, 12 in Acts 15:16, 17.

The words ***CLASSICAL INTERPRETATION*** at various places in the notations that follow indicate the classical alternative to the dispensational approach taken by Dr. Phillips.

Christ Revealed Christ is first seen as the "fourth man" standing with Shadrach, Meshach, and Abed-Nego in the fiery furnace (3:25). The three had remained faithful to their God; now God stands faithful with them in the fire of their judgment and delivers them from the very "smell of fire" (3:27).

Another reference to Christ is found in Daniel's night vision (7:13). He describes "*One* like the Son of Man, coming with the clouds of heaven," a reference to the Second Advent of Jesus Christ.

A further vision of Christ is found in 10:5, 6, where the description of Jesus is almost identical to John's in Revelation 1:13–16.

The Holy Spirit at Work The Holy Spirit never announces His presence in Daniel, but He is clearly at work. The ability of Daniel and the other Hebrews to interpret dreams was through the power of the Holy Spirit. The predictive prophecies, both with local and future applications, indicate the supernatural insights given to Daniel by the Holy Spirit.

Outline of Daniel

I. The religious convictions of Daniel **1:1–21**
- A. Judah's exile 1:1, 2
- B. Daniel's decision to maintain his separation 1:3–21

II. Nebuchadnezzar's first dream **2:1–49**
- A. The dream forgotten 2:1–28
- B. Daniel's revelation and interpretation 2:29–45
- C. Daniel honored by promotion 2:46–49

III. Deliverance from the fiery furnace **3:1–30**
- A. *Call* to worship the golden image 3:1–7
- B. Refusal of the three Hebrews to bow to the image 3:8–18
- C. The three Hebrews miraculously protected 3:19–25
- D. The king's confession of the true God 3:26–30

IV. Nebuchadnezzar's second dream **4:1–37**
- A. Nebuchadnezzar's dream 4:1–18
- B. Daniel's interpretation 4:19–27
- C. Fulfillment of the dream 4:28–33
- D. Nebuchadnezzar's prayer and restoration 4:34–37

V. Belshazzar's blasphemous feast **5:1–31**
- A. The handwriting on the wall 5:1–9
- B. Daniel's interpretation of the writing on the wall 5:10–31

VI. Daniel in the lions' den **6:1–28**
- A. Plot against Daniel 6:1–9

B. Daniel cast into the lions' den 6:10–17
C. Daniel delivered 6:18–28
VII. Daniel's first vision 7:1–28
A. Daniel's dream of four beasts 7:1–14
B. Daniel's interpretation 7:15–28
VIII. Daniel's second vision 8:1–27
A. Daniel's dream of a ram, a goat, and the horns 8:1–14
B. Gabriel's interpretation 8:15–27
IX. Prophecy of the Seventy Weeks 9:1–27
A. Daniel's prayer 9:1–19
B. Daniel's vision 9:20–27
X. Daniel's final vision 10:1—12:13
A. Daniel's vision of a glorious being 10:1–9
B. Angelic visitation 10:10–21
C. Wars of kings of north and south 11:1–45
D. The time of trouble 12:1–13

Daniel and His Friends Obey God

IN the third year of the reign of
[a]Jehoiakim king of Judah, Nebuchadnezzar king of Babylon came to
Jerusalem and besieged it.
2 And the Lord gave Jehoiakim king
of Judah into his hand, with [a]some of
the articles of [1]the house of God, which
he carried [b]into the land of Shinar to
the house of his god; [c]and he brought
the articles into the treasure house of
his god.
3 Then the king instructed Ashpenaz,
the master of his eunuchs, to bring
[a]some of the children of Israel and
some of the king's descendants and
some of the nobles,
4 young men [a]in whom *there was* no
blemish, but good-looking, gifted in all
wisdom, possessing knowledge and
quick to understand, who *had* ability
to serve in the king's palace, and
[b]whom they might *teach the language
and [1]literature of the Chaldeans.
5 And the king appointed for them a
daily provision of the king's delicacies
and of the wine which he drank, and
three years of training for them, so that
at the end of *that time* they might
[a]serve before the king.
6 Now from among those of the sons
of Judah were Daniel, Hananiah,
Mishael, and Azariah.
7 [a]To them the chief of the eunuchs
gave names: [b]he gave Daniel *the name*
Belteshazzar; to Hananiah, Shadrach;
to Mishael, Meshach; and to Azariah,
Abed-Nego.
2 8 But Daniel purposed in his heart
that he would not defile himself
[a]with the portion of the king's delicacies, nor with the wine which he drank;
therefore he requested of the chief of
the eunuchs that he might not defile
himself.
9 Now [a]God had brought Daniel into
the favor and [1]goodwill of the chief of
the eunuchs.
10 And the chief of the eunuchs said
to Daniel, "I fear my lord the king, who
has appointed your food and drink. For
why should he see your faces looking
worse than the young men who *are*
your age? Then you would endanger
my head before the king."
11 So Daniel said to [1]the steward
whom the chief of the eunuchs had set
over Daniel, Hananiah, Mishael, and
Azariah,
12 "Please test your servants for ten
days, and let them give us vegetables
to eat and water to drink.
13 "Then let our appearance be examined before you, and the appearance
of the young men who eat the portion
of the king's delicacies; and as you see
fit, *so* deal with your servants."
14 So he consented with them in this
matter, and tested them ten days.
15 And at the end of ten days their features appeared better and fatter in
flesh than all the young men who ate
the portion of the king's delicacies.
16 Thus [1]the steward took away their
portion of delicacies and the wine that
they were to drink, and gave them
vegetables.
17 As for these four young men,
[a]God gave them [b]knowledge and skill
in all literature and wisdom; and Daniel had [c]understanding in all *visions
and dreams.
18 Now at the end of the days, when
the king had said that they should be
brought in, the chief of the eunuchs
brought them in before Nebuchadnezzar.

CHAPTER 1

1 [a]2 Kin. 24:1, 2; 2 Chr. 36:5–7; Jer. 25:1; 52:12–30
2 [a]2 Chr. 36:7; Jer. 27:19, 20; Dan. 5:2 [b]Gen. 10:10; 11:2; Is. 11:11; Zech. 5:11 [c]2 Chr. 36:7 [1]The temple
3 [a]2 Kin. 20:17, 18; Is. 39:7
4 [a]Lev. 24:19, 20 [b]Acts 7:22 [1]Lit. *writing* or *book* *See WW at Is. 48:17.
5 [a]Gen. 41:46; 1 Sam. 16:22; 1 Kin. 10:8; Dan. 1:19
7 [a]Gen. 41:45; 2 Kin. 24:17 [b]Dan. 2:26; 4:8; 5:12
8 [a]Lev. 11:47; Deut. 32:38; Ezek. 4:13; Hos. 9:3
9 [a]Gen. 39:21; 1 Kin. 8:50; [Job 5:15, 16]; Ps. 106:46; [Prov. 16:7]; Acts 7:10; 27:3 [1]*kindness*
11 [1]Or *Melzar*
16 [1]Or *Melzar*
17 [a]1 Kin. 3:12, 28; 2 Chr. 1:10–12; [Luke 21:15; James 1:5–7] [b]Acts 7:22 [c]Num. 12:6; 2 Chr. 26:5; Dan. 5:11, 12, 14; 10:1 *See WW at 2 Chr. 32:32.

1:1 The third year . . . of Jehoiakim was 605 B.C.
1:2 Shinar is another term for Babylon, modern southeastern Iraq.
1:8–16 See section 2 of Truth-In-Action at the end of Dan.
1:8 Daniel **purposed** not to eat the king's food which was forbidden to Jews. Such separation is twofold: it is toward the Lord, and away from things that defile.

19 Then the king [1]interviewed them,
and among them all none was found
like Daniel, Hananiah, Mishael, and
Azariah; therefore [a]they served before
the king.
20 [a]And in all matters of wisdom *and*
understanding about which the king
examined them, he found them ten
times better than all the magicians *and*
astrologers who *were* in all his realm.
21 [a]Thus Daniel continued until the
first year of King Cyrus.

Nebuchadnezzar's Dream

2 Now in the second year of Nebuchadnezzar's reign, Nebuchadnezzar had *dreams; [a]and his spirit was
so troubled that [b]his sleep left him.
2 [a]Then the king gave the command
to call the magicians, the astrologers,
the sorcerers, and the Chaldeans to tell
the king his dreams. So they came and
stood before the king.
3 And the king said to them, "I have
had a *dream, and my spirit is anxious
to [1]know the dream."
4 Then the Chaldeans spoke to the
king in Aramaic, [a]"O[1] king, live forever! Tell your servants the dream, and
we will give the interpretation."
5 The king answered and said to the
Chaldeans, "My [1]decision is firm: if
you do not make known the dream to
me, and its interpretation, you shall be
[a]cut in pieces, and your houses shall
be made an ash heap.
6 [a]"However, if you tell the dream
and its interpretation, you shall receive
from me gifts, rewards, and great
honor. Therefore tell me the dream and
its interpretation."
7 They answered again and said, "Let
the king tell his servants the dream,
and we will give its interpretation."
8 The king answered and said, "I
know for certain that you would gain
time, because you see that my decision
is firm:
9 "if you do not make known the
dream to me, *there is only* one decree
for you! For you have agreed to speak
lying and corrupt words before me till
the [1]time has changed. Therefore tell
me the dream, and I shall know that

19 [a]Gen. 41:46; [Prov. 22:29]; Dan. 1:5 [1]Lit. *talked with them*
20 [a]1 Kin. 10:1
21 [a]Dan. 6:28; 10:1

CHAPTER 2

1 [a]Gen. 40:5–8; 41:1, 8; Job 33:15–17; Dan. 2:3; 4:5 [b]Esth. 6:1; Dan. 6:18 *See WW at Joel 2:28.
2 [a]Gen. 41:8; Ex. 7:11; Is. 47:12, 13; Dan. 1:20; 2:10, 27; 4:6; 5:7
3 [1]Or *understand* *See WW at Joel 2:28.
4 [a]1 Kin. 1:31; Dan. 3:9; 5:10; 6:6, 21 [1]The original language of Daniel 2:4b through 7:28 is Aramaic.
5 [a]2 Kin. 10:27; Ezra 6:11; Dan. 3:29 [1]The command
6 [a]Dan. 5:16
9 [1]Situation [2]Or *declare to me*
11 [a]Gen. 41:39; Dan. 5:11 [1]Or *rare*
13 [a]Dan. 1:19, 20
15 [1]Or *harsh*
18 [a][Dan. 9:9; Matt. 18:19]
19 [a]Num. 12:6; Job 33:15; [Prov. 3:32]; Amos 3:7
20 [a]Ps. 113:2 [b][1 Chr. 29:11, 12; Job 12:13; Ps. 147:5; Jer. 32:19; Matt. 6:13; Rom. 11:33]
21 [a]Ps. 31:15; Esth. 1:13; Dan. 2:9; 7:25 [b]Job 12:18; [Ps. 75:6, 7; Jer. 27:5; Dan. 4:35] [c]1 Kin. 3:9, 10; 4:29; [James 1:5]

you can [2]give me its interpretation."
10 The Chaldeans answered the king,
and said, "There is not a man on earth
who can tell the king's matter; therefore no king, lord, or ruler has *ever*
asked such things of any magician, as-
trologer, or Chaldean.
11 "*It is* a [1]difficult thing that the king
requests, and there is no other who can
tell it to the king [a]except the gods,
whose dwelling is not with flesh."
12 For this reason the king was angry
and very furious, and gave the command to destroy all the wise *men* of
Babylon.
13 So the decree went out, and they
began killing the wise *men;* and they
sought [a]Daniel and his companions, to
kill *them.*

God Reveals Nebuchadnezzar's Dream

14 Then with counsel and wisdom 5
Daniel answered Arioch, the captain of
the king's guard, who had gone out to
kill the wise *men* of Babylon;
15 he answered and said to Arioch the
king's captain, "Why is the decree
from the king so [1]urgent?" Then Arioch made the decision known to
Daniel.
16 So Daniel went in and asked the
king to give him time, that he might
tell the king the interpretation.
17 Then Daniel went to his house, and 5
made the decision known to Hananiah,
Mishael, and Azariah, his companions,
18 [a]that they might seek mercies from
the God of heaven concerning this secret, so that Daniel and his companions might not perish with the rest of
the wise *men* of Babylon.
19 Then the secret was revealed to
Daniel [a]in a night vision. So Daniel
blessed the God of heaven.
20 Daniel answered and said: 3

[a]"Blessed be the name of God
forever and ever,
[b]For wisdom and might are His.
21 And He changes [a]the times and
the seasons;
[b]He removes kings and raises up
kings;
[c]He gives wisdom to the wise

1:20 The occult forces were no match for the Spirit of God. Modern cultic movements are merging many of these spiritual counterfeits into a contemporary revival of occultism. Their influence will continue to rise as a final showdown between Jesus Christ and Satan nears. **In all matters of wisdom *and* understanding** believers who seek to walk in the full life of the Holy Spirit will find, as did the Hebrews, that they are **ten times better** than those who pursue such practices.

1:21 This verse summarizes more than 60 years, **the first year of King Cyrus** being 539 B.C., the year he captured Babylon.

2:14 See section 5 of Truth-In-Action at the end of Dan.

2:17, 18 See section 5 of Truth-In-Action at the end of Dan.

2:20–23 See section 3 of Truth-In-Action at the end of Dan.

And knowledge to those who
have understanding.
22 [a]He reveals deep and secret things;
[b]He knows what *is* in the darkness,
And [c]light dwells with Him.

23 "I thank You and praise You,
O God of my fathers;
You have given me wisdom and
might,
And have now made known to me
what we [a]asked of You,
For You have made known to us
the king's [1]demand."

Daniel Explains the Dream

24 Therefore Daniel went to Arioch,
whom the king had appointed to destroy the wise *men* of Babylon. He
went and said thus to him: "Do not destroy the wise *men* of Babylon; take
me before the king, and I will tell the
king the interpretation."
25 Then Arioch quickly brought Daniel before the king, and said thus to
him, "I have found a man of the
[1]captives of Judah, who will make
known to the king the interpretation."
26 The king answered and said to Daniel, whose name *was* Belteshazzar,
"Are you able to make known to me
the dream which I have seen, and its
interpretation?"
5 27 Daniel answered in the presence of
the king, and said, "The secret which
the king has demanded, the wise *men*,
the astrologers, the magicians, and the
soothsayers cannot declare to the king.
28 [a]"But there is a God in heaven who
reveals secrets, and He has made
known to King Nebuchadnezzar
[b]what will be in the latter days. Your
dream, and the visions of your head
upon your bed, were these:
29 "As for you, O king, thoughts came
to your *mind while* on your bed, *about*
what would come to pass after this;
[a]and He who reveals secrets has made
known to you what will be.
30 [a]"But as for me, this secret has not
been revealed to me because I have
more wisdom than anyone living, but
for *our* sakes who make known the interpretation to the king, [b]and that you
may [1]know the thoughts of your heart.
31 "You, O king, were watching; and
behold, a great image! This great image, whose splendor *was* excellent,
stood before you; and its form *was*
awesome.
32 [a]"This image's head *was* of fine
gold, its chest and arms of silver, its
belly and [1]thighs of bronze,
33 "its legs of iron, its feet partly of
iron and partly of [1]clay.
34 "You watched while a stone was cut
out [a]without hands, which struck the
image on its feet of iron and clay, and
broke them in pieces.
35 [a]"Then the iron, the clay, the
bronze, the silver, and the gold were
crushed together, and became [b]like
chaff from the summer threshing
floors; the wind carried them away so
that [c]no trace of them was found. And
the stone that struck the image [d]be-
came a great mountain [e]and filled the
whole earth.
36 "This *is* the dream. Now we will tell
the interpretation of it before the king.
37 [a]"You, O king, *are* a king of kings.
[b]For the God of heaven has given you
a kingdom, power, strength, and glory;
38 [a]"and wherever the children of men
dwell, or the beasts of the field and the
birds of the heaven, He has given *them*
into your hand, and has made you ruler
over them all—[b]you *are* this head of
gold.
39 "But after you shall arise [a]another
kingdom [b]inferior to yours; then another, a third kingdom of bronze,
which shall rule over all the earth.

22 [a]Job 12:22; Ps. 25:14; [Prov. 3:22] [b]Job 26:6; Ps. 139:12; [Is. 45:7; Jer. 23:24; Heb. 4:13] [c][Ps. 36:9]; Dan. 5:11, 14; [1 Tim. 6:16; James 1:17; 1 John 1:5]
23 [a]Ps. 21:2, 4; Dan. 2:18, 29, 30 [1]Lit. *word*
25 [1]Lit. *sons of the captivity*
28 [a]Gen. 40:8; Amos 4:13 [b]Gen. 49:1; Is. 2:2; Dan. 10:14; Mic. 4:1
29 [a][Dan. 2:22, 28]
30 [a]Acts 3:12 [b]Dan. 2:47 [1]Understand
32 [a]Dan. 2:38, 45 [1]Or *sides*
33 [1]Or *baked clay,* also vv. 34, 35, 42
34 [a]Dan. 8:25; [Zech. 4:6]; 2 Cor. 5:1; Heb. 9:24
35 [a]Dan. 7:23–27; [Rev. 16:14] [b]Ps. 1:4; Is. 17:13; 41:15, 16; Hos. 13:3 [c]Ps. 37:10, 36 [d][Is. 2:2, 3]; Mic. 4:1 [e]Ps. 80:9
37 [a]Ezra 7:12; Is. 47:5; Jer. 27:6, 7; Ezek. 26:7; Hos. 8:10 [b]Ezra 1:2
38 [a]Ps. 50:10, 11; Jer. 27:6; Dan. 4:21, 22 [b]Dan. 2:32
39 [a]Dan. 5:28, 31 [b]Dan. 2:32

2:27, 28 See section 5 of Truth-In-Action at the end of Dan.

2:28 In the latter days refers to the future, from **Nebuchadnezzar** throughout the remainder of human history.

2:31–45 The matter of understanding the various kingdoms of the **great image** has led to many diverse opinions. The two most common understandings are that it represents either four successive kingdoms (the Babylonian, Medo-Persian, Grecian, and Roman) or four successive reigns (kings) over one kingdom (Babylon: the reigns of Nebuchadnezzar through Nabonidus). The differences lie in the fact that the kingdoms are not identified and in the fact that the Hebrew word for "kingdom" can also be translated "reign."

Clearly, however, the image represents governments over whom God has ultimate sovereignty. Whatever their identity, before God's power they are frail; they have "feet of clay." God alone is the ultimate Sovereign of history, both in Daniel's day and throughout this age.

2:34, 35 The **stone . . . cut out without hands** represents God's sovereign power over history, a sovereignty that is implemented through human rulers. To Daniel's immediate readers this "stone" would have been King Cyrus who invaded Babylon, brought it under the dominion of the Medes, and was used by God to release the Hebrews to return to Jerusalem. The fact that it is described as ultimately becoming **a great mountain** that **filled the whole earth** shows the long-range development of the stone imagery. See note on Obad. 15. Hence, the stone ultimately prefigures Jesus Christ, God's consummate Ruler over all governments and all history. Upon His return, He shall "set up a kingdom which shall never be destroyed . . . and consume all these kingdoms" (v. 44).

40 "And [a]the fourth kingdom shall be
as strong as iron, inasmuch as iron
breaks in pieces and shatters everything; and like iron that crushes, *that
kingdom* will break in pieces and crush
all the others.
41 "Whereas you saw the feet and
toes, partly of potter's clay and partly
of iron, the kingdom shall be divided;
yet the strength of the iron shall be in
it, just as you saw the iron mixed with
ceramic clay.
42 "And *as* the toes of the feet *were*
partly of iron and partly of clay,
[a]*so* the kingdom shall be partly strong
and partly [1]fragile.
43 "As you saw iron mixed with ceramic clay, they will mingle with the
seed of men; but they will not adhere
to one another, just as iron does not
mix with clay.
44 "And in the days of these kings
[a]the God of heaven will set up a kingdom [b]which shall never be destroyed;
and the kingdom shall not be left to
other people; [c]it shall [1]break in pieces
and [2]consume all these kingdoms, and
it shall stand forever.
45 [a]"Inasmuch as you saw that the
stone was cut out of the mountain without hands, and that it broke in pieces
the iron, the bronze, the clay, the silver,
and the gold—the great God has made
known to the king what will come to
pass after this. The dream is certain,
and its interpretation is sure."

Daniel and His Friends Promoted

46 [a]Then King Nebuchadnezzar fell on
his face, prostrate before Daniel, and
commanded that they should present
an offering [b]and incense to him.
47 The king answered Daniel, and
said, "Truly [a]your God *is* the God of
[b]gods, the Lord of kings, and a revealer
of secrets, since you could reveal this
secret."
48 [a]Then the king promoted Daniel
[b]and gave him many great gifts; and
he made him ruler over the whole
province of Babylon, and [c]chief administrator over all the wise *men* of Babylon.
49 Also Daniel petitioned the king,
[a]and he set Shadrach, Meshach, and
Abed-Nego over the affairs of the province of Babylon; but Daniel [b]*sat* in
[1]the gate of the king.

The Image of Gold

3 Nebuchadnezzar the king made an
image of gold, whose height *was*
[1]sixty cubits *and* its width six cubits.
He set it up in the plain of Dura, in
the province of Babylon.
2 And King Nebuchadnezzar sent
word to gather together the satraps, the
administrators, the governors, the
counselors, the treasurers, the judges,
the magistrates, and all the officials of
the provinces, to come to the dedication of the image which King Nebuchadnezzar had set up.
3 So the satraps, the administrators,
the governors, the counselors, the treasurers, the judges, the magistrates, and
all the officials of the provinces gathered together for the dedication of the
image that King Nebuchadnezzar had
set up; and they stood before the image
that Nebuchadnezzar had set up.
4 Then a herald cried [1]aloud: "To you
it is commanded, [a]O peoples, nations,
and languages,
5 "*that* at the time you hear the sound
of the horn, flute, harp, lyre, *and* psaltery, in symphony with all kinds of music, you shall fall down and worship
the gold image that King Nebuchadnezzar has set up;
6 "and whoever does not fall down
and worship shall [a]be cast immediately
into the midst of a burning fiery furnace."
7 So at that time, when all the people
heard the sound of the horn, flute,
harp, *and* lyre, in symphony with all
kinds of music, all the people, nations,
and languages fell down *and* worshiped the gold image which King
Nebuchadnezzar had set up.

Daniel's Friends Disobey the King

8 Therefore at that time certain Chaldeans [a]came forward and accused the
Jews.
9 They spoke and said to King Nebu-

40 [a]Dan. 7:7, 23
42 [a]Dan. 7:24 [1]Or *brittle*
44 [a]Dan. 2:28, 37 [b]Is. 9:6, 7; Ezek. 37:25; Dan. 4:3, 34; 6:26; 7:14, 27; Mic. 4:7; [Luke 1:32, 33] [c]Ps. 2:9; Is. 60:12; Dan. 2:34, 35; [1 Cor. 15:24] [1]Or *crush* [2]Lit. *put an end to*
45 [a]Dan. 2:35; Is. 28:16
46 [a]Dan. 3:5, 7; Acts 10:25; 14:13; Rev. 19:10; 22:8 [b]Lev. 26:31; Ezra 6:10
47 [a]Dan. 3:28, 29; 4:34–37 [b][Deut. 10:17]
48 [a][Prov. 14:35; 21:1] [b]Dan. 2:6 [c]Dan. 4:9; 5:11
49 [a]Dan. 1:7; 3:12 [b]Esth. 2:19, 21; 3:2; Amos 5:15 [1]The king's court

CHAPTER 3

1 [1]About 90 feet
4 [a]Dan. 4:1; 6:25 [1]Lit. *with strength*
6 [a]Jer. 29:22; Ezek. 22:18–22; Matt. 13:42, 50; Rev. 9:2; 13:15; 14:11
8 [a]Ezra 4:12–16; Esth. 3:8, 9; Dan. 6:12, 13

3:1–7 Although God's providence had established Nebuchadnezzar as the leading ruler at the time, honoring him with great privileges (2:37, 38), God did not intend for the Hebrews to worship either him or his god. The **image of gold** may have been a statue of Nebuchadnezzar or of Bel, his chief idol or demon-god. At any rate, the four Hebrews were presented with the first major challenge of their allegiance to God alone since their promotion (2:49).

3:8–18 The absolute refusal of the Hebrews to bow to the image offers an inspiring illustration for believers. Satan, as the god of this age (2 Cor. 4:4), forms many images by which he seeks to intimidate and seduce into bowing to the spirit of the world. Jesus Christ stands as the consummate example of uncompromising commitment in resisting this tactic of the Adversary (Matt. 4:1–11).

chadnezzar, [a]"O king, live forever!

10 "You, O king, have made a decree that everyone who hears the sound of the horn, flute, harp, lyre, *and* psaltery, in symphony with all kinds of music, shall fall down and worship the gold image;

11 "and whoever does not fall down and worship shall be cast into the midst of a burning fiery furnace.

2 12 [a]"There are certain Jews whom you have set over the affairs of the province of Babylon: Shadrach, Meshach, and Abed-Nego; these men, O king, have [b]not paid due regard to you. They do not serve your gods or worship the gold image which you have set up."

13 Then Nebuchadnezzar, in [a]rage and fury, gave the command to bring Shadrach, Meshach, and Abed-Nego. So they brought these men before the king.

14 Nebuchadnezzar spoke, saying to them, "*Is it* true, Shadrach, Meshach, and Abed-Nego, *that* you do not serve my gods or worship the gold image which I have set up?

15 "Now if you are ready at the time you hear the sound of the horn, flute, harp, lyre, *and* psaltery, in symphony with all kinds of music, and you fall down and worship the image which I have made, [a]*good!* But if you do not worship, you shall be cast immediately into the midst of a burning fiery furnace. [b]And who *is* the god who will deliver you from my hands?"

5 **16** Shadrach, Meshach, and Abed-Nego answered and said to the king, "O Nebuchadnezzar, [a]we have no need to answer you in this matter.

17 "If that *is the case,* our [a]God whom we serve is able to [b]deliver us from the burning fiery furnace, and He will deliver *us* from your hand, O king.

18 "But if not, let it be known to you, O king, that we do not serve your gods, nor will we [a]worship the gold image which you have set up."

Saved in Fiery Trial

19 Then Nebuchadnezzar was full of fury, and the expression on his face changed toward Shadrach, Meshach, and Abed-Nego. He spoke and commanded that they heat the furnace seven times more than it was usually heated.

20 And he commanded certain mighty men of valor who *were* in his army to bind Shadrach, Meshach, and Abed-Nego, *and* cast *them* into the burning fiery furnace.

21 Then these men were bound in their coats, their trousers, their turbans, and their *other* garments, and were cast into the midst of the burning fiery furnace.

22 Therefore, because the king's command was [1]urgent, and the furnace exceedingly hot, the flame of the fire killed those men who took up Shadrach, Meshach, and Abed-Nego.

23 And these three men, Shadrach, Meshach, and Abed-Nego, fell down bound into the midst of the burning fiery furnace.

24 Then King Nebuchadnezzar was astonished; and he rose in haste *and* spoke, saying to his [1]counselors, "Did we not cast three men bound into the midst of the fire?" They answered and said to the king, "True, O king."

25 "Look!" he answered, "I see four men loose, [a]walking in the midst of the fire; and they are not hurt, and the form of the fourth is like [b]the[1] Son of God."

Nebuchadnezzar Praises God

26 Then Nebuchadnezzar went near the [1]mouth of the burning fiery furnace *and* spoke, saying, "Shadrach, Meshach, and Abed-Nego, servants of the [a]Most High God, come out, and come *here.*" Then Shadrach, Meshach, and Abed-Nego came from the midst of the fire.

27 And the satraps, administrators, governors, and the king's counselors gathered together, and they saw these men [a]on whose bodies the fire had no power; the hair of their head was not singed nor were their garments affected, and the smell of fire was not on them.

28 Nebuchadnezzar spoke, saying, "Blessed be the God of Shadrach, Meshach, and Abed-Nego, who sent His [a]Angel[1] and delivered His servants who trusted in Him, and they have frustrated the king's word, and yielded their bodies, that they should not serve

9 [a]Dan. 2:4; 5:10; 6:6, 21
12 [a]Dan. 2:49 [b]Dan. 1:8; 6:12, 13
13 [a]Dan. 2:12; 3:19
15 [a]Ex. 32:32; Luke 13:9 [b]Ex. 5:2; 2 Kin. 18:35; Is. 36:18–20; Dan. 2:47
16 [a][Matt. 10:19]
17 [a]Job 5:19; [Ps. 27:1, 2; Is. 26:3, 4]; Jer. 1:8; 15:20, 21; Dan. 6:19–22 [b]1 Sam. 17:37; Jer. 1:8; 15:20, 21; 42:11; Dan. 6:16, 19–22; Mic. 7:7; 2 Cor. 1:10
18 [a]Job 13:15
22 [1]Or *harsh*
24 [1]High officials
25 [a][Ps. 91:3–9]; Is. 43:2 [b]Job 1:6; 38:7; [Ps. 34:7]; Dan. 3:28 [1]Or *a son of the gods*
26 [a][Dan. 4:2, 3, 17, 34, 35] [1]Lit. *door*
27 [a][Is. 43:2]; Heb. 11:34
28 [a][Ps. 34:7, 8]; Is. 37:36; [Jer. 17:7]; Dan. 6:22, 23; Acts 5:19; 12:7 [1]Or *angel*

3:12 See section 2 of Truth-In-Action at the end of Dan.
3:16–18 See section 5 of Truth-In-Action at the end of Dan.
3:19–25 This is a dramatic illustration of the personal presence and protection of the Lord with His people who suffer for their testimony. The **fourth** man is a Christophany (preincarnate appearance of the Messiah) whom even **Nebuchadnezzar** recognized to be **like the Son of God.**
3:26–28 **Nebuchadnezzar** acknowledged that the deliverance was of **God.**

nor worship any god except their own God!
29 [a]"Therefore I make a decree that
any people, nation, or language which
speaks anything amiss against the
[b]God of Shadrach, Meshach, and
Abed-Nego shall be [c]cut in pieces, and
their houses shall be made an ash
heap; [d]because there is no other God
who can deliver like this."
30 Then the king [1]promoted Shadrach,
Meshach, and Abed-Nego in the province of Babylon.

Nebuchadnezzar's Second Dream

4 Nebuchadnezzar the king,

[a]To all peoples, nations, and
languages that dwell in all the
earth:

Peace be multiplied to you.

2 I thought it good to declare the
signs and wonders [a]that the Most
High God has worked for me.

3 [a]How great *are* His signs,
And how mighty His wonders!
His kingdom *is* [b]an everlasting
kingdom,
And His dominion *is* from
generation to generation.

4 I, Nebuchadnezzar, was at rest in
my house, and flourishing in my
palace.
5 I saw a dream which made me
afraid, [a]and the thoughts on my
bed and the visions of my head
[b]troubled me.
6 Therefore I issued a decree to
bring in all the wise *men* of
Babylon before me, that they
might make known to me the
interpretation of the dream.
7 [a]Then the magicians, the
astrologers, the Chaldeans, and
the soothsayers came in, and I
told them the dream; but they did
not make known to me its
interpretation.
8 But at last Daniel came before me
[a](his name *is* Belteshazzar,
according to the name of my god;
[b]in him *is* the Spirit of the Holy
God), and I told the dream before
him, *saying:*
9 "Belteshazzar, [a]chief of the
magicians, because I know that
the Spirit of the Holy God *is* in
you, and no secret troubles you,
explain to me the visions of my
dream that I have seen, and its
interpretation.
10 "These *were* the visions of my
head *while* on my bed:

I was looking, and behold,
[a]A tree in the midst of the earth,
And its height was great.
11 The tree grew and became strong;
Its height reached to the heavens,
And it could be seen to the ends
of all the earth.
12 Its leaves *were* lovely,
Its fruit abundant,
And in it *was* food for all.
[a]The beasts of the field found
shade under it,
The birds of the heavens dwelt in
its branches,
And all flesh was fed from it.

13 "I saw in the visions of my head
while on my bed, and there was
[a]a watcher, [b]a holy one, coming
down from heaven.
14 He cried [1]aloud and said thus:

[a]'Chop down the tree and cut off
its branches,
Strip off its leaves and scatter its
fruit.
[b]Let the beasts get out from under
it,
And the birds from its branches.
15 Nevertheless leave the stump and
roots in the earth,
Bound with a band of iron and
bronze,
In the tender grass of the field.
Let it be wet with the dew of
heaven,
And *let* him graze with the beasts
On the grass of the earth.
16 Let his heart be changed from
that of a man,

29 [a]Dan. 6:26 [b]Dan. 2:46, 47; 4:34–37 [c]Ezra 6:11; Dan. 2:5 [d]Dan. 6:27
30 [1]Lit. *caused to prosper*

CHAPTER 4

1 [a]Ezra 4:17; Dan. 3:4; 6:25
2 [a]Dan. 3:26
3 [a]2 Sam. 7:16; Ps. 89:35–37; Dan. 6:27; 7:13, 14; [Luke 1:31–33] [b][Dan. 2:44; 4:34; 6:26]
5 [a]Dan. 2:28, 29 [b]Dan. 2:1
7 [a]Dan. 2:2
8 [a]Dan. 1:7 [b]Is. 63:11; Dan. 2:11; 4:18; 5:11, 14
9 [a]Dan. 2:48; 5:11
10 [a]Ezek. 31:3; Dan. 4:20
12 [a]Jer. 27:6; Ezek. 17:23; 31:6; Lam. 4:20
13 [a][Dan. 4:17, 23] [b]Deut. 33:2; Ps. 89:7; Dan. 8:13; Zech. 14:5; Jude 14
14 [a]Ezek. 31:10–14; Dan. 4:23; [Matt. 3:10; 7:19; Luke 13:7–9] [b]Ezek. 31:12, 13; Dan. 4:12 [1]Lit. *with strength*

3:29 Nebuchadnezzar's favor is bestowed upon the three Hebrew young men. This is a beautiful picture of the blessing of the Lord bringing with it the favor of man (Gen. 39:4; 41:40–44).

4:1–18 Although **Nebuchadnezzar** has seen the miraculous works of Yahweh and believes that it is **the Spirit of the Holy God** (v. 8) who gives Daniel his ability to interpret dreams, his own heart is still filled with pride. He has not submitted the rulership over his own kingdom to the kingdom of God. God deals with him about his pride and exalted opinion of his rulership in the vision of a **great tree,** which symbolizes both him and his dynasty.

4:8 Belteshazzar means "May Bel Protect His Life." Bel was Babylon's chief god.

4:13, 17, 23 Watcher(s): Angels on special appointment of the Lord.

Let him be given the heart of a beast,
And let seven [a]times[1] pass over him.

17 'This decision *is* by the decree of the watchers,
And the sentence by the word of the holy ones,
In order [a]that the living may know
[b]That the Most High rules in the kingdom of men,
[c]Gives it to whomever He will,
And sets over it the [d]lowest of men.'

18 "This dream I, King Nebuchadnezzar, have seen. Now you, Belteshazzar, declare its interpretation, [a]since all the wise *men* of my kingdom are not able to make known to me the interpretation; but you *are* able, [b]for the Spirit of the Holy God *is* in you."

Daniel Explains the Second Dream

19 Then Daniel, [a]whose name was Belteshazzar, was astonished for a time, and his thoughts [b]troubled him. *So* the king spoke, and said, "Belteshazzar, do not let the dream or its interpretation trouble you." Belteshazzar answered and said,
"My lord, *may* [c]the dream [1]concern those who hate you, and its interpretation [2]concern your enemies!
20 [a]The tree that you saw, which grew and became strong, whose height reached to the heavens and which *could be seen* by all the earth,
21 whose leaves *were* lovely and its fruit abundant, in which *was* food for all, under which the beasts of the field dwelt, and in whose branches the birds of the heaven had their home—
22 [a]it *is* you, O king, who have grown and become strong; for your greatness has grown and reaches to the heavens, [b]and your dominion to the end of the earth.
23 [a]And inasmuch as the king saw a watcher, a holy one, coming down from heaven and saying, 'Chop down the tree and destroy it, but leave its stump and roots in the earth, *bound* with a band of iron and bronze in the tender grass of the field; let it be wet with the dew of heaven, [b]and let him graze with the beasts of the field, till seven [1]times pass over him';
24 this is the interpretation, O king, and this is the decree of the Most High, which has come upon my lord the king:
25 They shall [a]drive you from men, your dwelling shall be with the beasts of the field, and they shall make you [b]eat grass like oxen. They shall wet you with the dew of heaven, and seven [1]times shall pass over you, [c]till you know that the Most High rules in the kingdom of men, and [d]gives it to whomever He chooses.
26 And inasmuch as they gave the command to leave the stump *and* roots of the tree, your kingdom shall be assured to you, after you come to know that [a]Heaven[1] rules.
27 Therefore, O king, let my advice be acceptable to you; [a]break off your sins by *being* righteous, and your iniquities by showing mercy to *the* poor. [b]Perhaps there may be [c]a [1]lengthening of your prosperity."

Nebuchadnezzar's Humiliation

28 All *this* came upon King Nebuchadnezzar.
29 At the end of the twelve months he was walking [1]about the royal palace of Babylon.
30 The king [a]spoke, saying, "Is not this great Babylon, that I have built for a royal dwelling by my mighty power and for the honor of my majesty?"
31 [a]While the word *was still* in the king's mouth, [b]a voice fell from heaven: "King Nebuchadnezzar, to you it is spoken: the kingdom has departed from you!
32 And [a]they shall drive you from men, and your dwelling *shall be* with the beasts of the field. They

16 [a]Dan. 11:13; 12:7 [1]Possibly *years*
17 [a]Ps. 9:16; 83:18 [b]Dan. 2:21; 4:25, 32; 5:21 [c]Jer. 27:5–7; Ezek. 29:18–20; Dan. 2:37; 5:18 [d]1 Sam. 2:8; Dan. 11:21
18 [a]Gen. 41:8, 15; Dan. 5:8, 15 [b]Dan. 4:8, 9; 5:11, 14
19 [a]Dan. 4:8 [b]Jer. 4:19; Dan. 7:15, 28; 8:27 [c]2 Sam. 18:32; Jer. 29:7; Dan. 4:24; 10:16 [1]*be for* [2]*for*
20 [a]Dan. 4:10–12
22 [a]Dan. 2:37, 38 [b]Jer. 27:6–8
23 [a]Dan. 4:13–15 [b]Dan. 5:21 [1]Possibly *years*
25 [a]Dan. 4:32; 5:21 [b]Ps. 106:20 [c]Ps. 83:18; Dan. 4:2, 17, 32 [d]Jer. 27:5 [1]Possibly *years*
26 [a]Matt. 21:25; Luke 15:18 [1]God
27 [a][Prov. 28:13]; Is. 55:7; Ezek. 18:21, 22; [Rom. 2:9–11; 1 Pet. 4:8] [b][Ps. 41:1–3]; Is. 58:6, 7, 10 [c]1 Kin. 21:29 [1]*prolonging*
29 [1]Or *upon*
30 [a]Prov. 16:18; Is. 13:19; Dan. 5:20
31 [a]Dan. 5:5; Luke 12:20 [b]Dan. 4:24
32 [a][Dan. 4:25]

4:19–27 Daniel's interpretation shows God's merciful attitude even toward arrogant pagans, as well as His desire that world powers surrender control to His lordship.
4:25 This is an insight into the coming universal kingdom of God. All human government will eventually come under the transcendent authority of the living God.
4:28–33 As the king boasts about his mighty power, the judgment prophesied by Daniel falls upon him. He becomes insane, begins to behave like an animal, and is banished from the very society over which he had exercised rulership.

shall make you eat grass like
oxen; and seven [1]times shall pass
over you, until you know that the
Most High rules in the kingdom
of men, and gives it to whomever
He chooses."
33 That very hour the word was
fulfilled concerning
Nebuchadnezzar; he was driven
from men and ate grass like oxen;
his body was wet with the dew
of heaven till his hair had grown
like eagles' *feathers* and his nails
like birds' *claws.*

Nebuchadnezzar Praises God

34 And [a]at the end of the [1]time I,
Nebuchadnezzar, lifted my eyes
to heaven, and my understanding
returned to me; and I blessed the
Most High and praised and
honored Him [b]who lives forever:

For His dominion *is* [c]an
everlasting dominion,
And His kingdom *is* from
generation to generation.
35 [a]All the inhabitants of the earth
are reputed as nothing;
[b]He does according to His will in
the army of heaven
And *among* the inhabitants of the
earth.
[c]No one can restrain His hand
Or say to Him, [d]"What have You
done?"

36 At the same time my reason
returned to me, [a]and for the glory
of my kingdom, my honor and
splendor returned to me. My
counselors and nobles resorted to
me, I was [b]restored to my
kingdom, and excellent majesty
was [c]added to me.
37 Now I, Nebuchadnezzar, [a]praise
and extol and honor the King of
heaven, [b]all of whose works *are*
truth, and His ways justice.
[c]And those who walk in pride He
is able to put down.

Belshazzar's Feast

5 Belshazzar the king [a]made a great
feast for a thousand of his lords,
and drank wine in the presence of the
thousand.
2 While he tasted the wine, Belshazzar gave the command to bring the
gold and silver vessels [a]which his
[1]father Nebuchadnezzar had taken
from the temple which *had been* in Jerusalem, that the king and his lords,
his wives, and his concubines might
drink from them.
3 Then they brought the gold [a]vessels
that had been taken from the temple
of the house of God which *had been*
in Jerusalem; and the king and his
lords, his wives, and his concubines
drank from them.
4 They drank wine, [a]and praised the
gods of gold and silver, bronze and
iron, wood and stone.
5 [a]In the same hour the fingers of a
man's hand appeared and wrote opposite the lampstand on the plaster of the
wall of the king's palace; and the king
saw the part of the hand that wrote.
6 Then the king's countenance
changed, and his thoughts troubled
him, so that the joints of his hips were
loosened and his [a]knees knocked
against each other.
7 [a]The king cried [1]aloud to bring in
[b]the astrologers, the Chaldeans, and
the soothsayers. The king spoke, saying to the wise *men* of Babylon, "Whoever reads this writing, and tells me its
interpretation, shall be clothed with
purple and *have* a chain of gold around
his neck; [c]and he shall be the third
ruler in the kingdom."
8 Now all the king's wise *men* came,
[a]but they could not read the writing,
or make known to the king its interpretation.
9 Then King Belshazzar was greatly
[a]troubled, his countenance was
changed, and his lords were [1]aston-
ished.
10 The queen, because of the words of
the king and his lords, came to the banquet hall. The queen spoke, saying, "O

32 [1]Possibly *years*
34 [a]Dan. 4:26 [b]Ps. 102:24–27; Dan. 6:26; 12:7; [Rev. 4:10] [c][Ps. 10:16]; Dan. 2:44; 7:14; Mic. 4:7; [Luke 1:33] [1]Lit. *days*
35 [a]Ps. 39:5; Is. 40:15, 17 [b]Ps. 115:3; 135:6; Dan. 6:27 [c]Job 34:29; Is. 43:13 [d]Job 9:12; Is. 45:9; Jer. 18:6; Rom. 9:20; [1 Cor. 2:16]
36 [a]Dan. 4:26 [b]2 Chr. 20:20 [c]Job 42:12; [Prov. 22:4; Matt. 6:33]
37 [a]Dan. 2:46, 47; 3:28, 29 [b]Deut. 32:4; [Ps. 33:4]; Is. 5:16; [Rev. 15:3] [c]Ex. 18:11; Job 40:11, 12; Dan. 5:20

CHAPTER 5

1 [a]Esth. 1:3; Is. 22:12–14
2 [a]2 Kin. 24:13; 25:15; Ezra 1:7–11; Jer. 52:19; Dan. 1:2 [1]Or *ancestor*
3 [a]2 Chr. 36:10
4 [a]Is. 42:8; Dan. 5:23; Rev. 9:20
5 [a]Dan. 4:31
6 [a]Ezek. 7:17; 21:7
7 [a]Dan. 4:6, 7; 5:11, 15 [b]Is. 47:13 [c]Dan. 6:2, 3 [1]Lit. *with strength*
8 [a]Gen. 41:8; Dan. 2:27; 4:7; 5:15
9 [a]Job 18:11; Is. 21:2–4; Jer. 6:24; Dan. 2:1; 5:6 [1]*perplexed*

4:34–37 The degree to which **Nebuchadnezzar** had a personal, ongoing relationship with Yahweh is not clear here. The emphasis is on his recognizing God's kingship rather than his own authority. His restoration is designed to show God's ideal for all rulers—surrendering their kingship to God's ultimate rule.

5:1 Belshazzar, whose name means "Bel Protect the King," was the eldest son of the last Babylonian king, Nabonidus. He assumed his father's kingly functions during Nabonidus's 10-year absence from Babylon.

5:2–16 God's response to Belshazzar's irreverent use of God's holy **vessels** is a warning that whatever God has sanctified is not to be profaned. According to 1 Sam. 24:10, "the LORD's anointed" were not to be touched, that is, human vessels who are set apart to Him. Attributing the work of the Holy Spirit to the Devil is considered blasphemy, because the Spirit's work is holy (Matt. 12:31, 32). Therefore, regarding holy things as common is always dangerous. Those guilty will be "weighed in the balances, and found wanting" (v. 27).

king, live forever! Do not let your
thoughts trouble you, nor let your
countenance change.
11 [a]"There is a man in your kingdom
in whom *is* the Spirit of the Holy God.
And in the days of your [1]father, light
and understanding and wisdom, like
the wisdom of the gods, were found in
him; and King Nebuchadnezzar your
[1]father—your father the king—made
him chief of the magicians, astrologers,
Chaldeans, *and* soothsayers.
12 "Inasmuch as an excellent spirit,
knowledge, understanding, interpreting dreams, solving riddles, and [1]ex-
plaining enigmas were found in this
Daniel, [a]whom the king named Belteshazzar, now let Daniel be called,
and he will give the interpretation."

The Writing on the Wall Explained

13 Then Daniel was brought in before
the king. The king spoke, and said to
Daniel, "*Are* you that Daniel [1]who is
one of the captives from Judah, whom
my [2]father the king brought from Judah?
14 "I have heard of you, that [a]the
[1]Spirit of God *is* in you, and *that* light
and understanding and excellent wisdom are found in you.
15 "Now [a]the wise *men*, the astrologers, have been brought in before me,
that they should read this writing and
make known to me its interpretation,
but they could not give the interpretation of the thing.
16 "And I have heard of you, that you
can give interpretations and [1]explain
enigmas. [a]Now if you can read the
writing and make known to me its interpretation, you shall be clothed with
purple and *have* a chain of gold around
your neck, and shall be the third ruler
in the kingdom."
17 Then Daniel answered, and said before the king, "Let your gifts be for
yourself, and give your rewards to another; yet I will read the writing to the
king, and make known to him the interpretation.
18 "O king, [a]the Most High God gave
Nebuchadnezzar your [1]father a kingdom and majesty, glory and honor.
19 "And because of the majesty that
He gave him, [a]all peoples, nations, and
languages trembled and feared before
him. Whomever he wished, he [b]exe-
cuted; whomever he wished, he kept
alive; whomever he wished, he set
up; and whomever he wished, he put
down.
20 [a]"But when his heart was lifted up,
and his spirit was hardened in pride,
he was deposed from his kingly throne,
and they took his glory from him.
21 "Then he was [a]driven from the sons
of men, his heart was made like the
beasts, and his dwelling *was* with the
wild donkeys. They fed him with grass
like oxen, and his body was wet with
the dew of heaven, [b]till he [1]knew that
the Most High God rules in the kingdom of men, and appoints over it
whomever He chooses.
22 "But you his son, Belshazzar, **1**
[a]have not humbled your heart, although you knew all this.
23 [a]"And you have [1]lifted yourself up
against the Lord of heaven. They have
brought the [b]vessels of [2]His house before you, and you and your lords, your
wives and your concubines, have
drunk wine from them. And you have
praised the gods of silver and gold,
bronze and iron, wood and stone,
[c]which do not see or hear or know; and
the God who *holds* your breath in His
hand [d]and owns all your ways, you
have not glorified.
24 "Then the [1]fingers of the hand were
sent from Him, and this writing was
written.
25 "And this is the inscription that was **1**
written:

[1]MENE, MENE, [2]TEKEL,
[3]UPHARSIN.

26 "This *is* the interpretation of *each*
word. MENE: God has numbered your
kingdom, and finished it;
27 "TEKEL: [a]You have been weighed in
the balances, and found wanting;
28 "PERES: Your kingdom has been divided, and given to the [a]Medes and
[b]Persians."[1]
29 Then Belshazzar gave the command, and they clothed Daniel with
purple and *put* a chain of gold around
his neck, and made a proclamation

11 [a]Dan. 2:48; 4:8, 9, 18 [1]Or *ancestor*
12 [a]Dan. 1:7; 4:8 [1]Lit. *untying knots*
13 [1]Lit. *who is of the sons of the captivity* [2]Or *ancestor*
14 [a]Dan. 4:8, 9, 18; 5:11, 12 [1]Or *spirit of the gods*
15 [a]Dan. 5:7, 8
16 [a]Dan. 5:7, 29 [1]Lit. *untie knots*
18 [a]Jer. 27:5–7; Dan. 2:37, 38; 4:17, 22, 25 [1]Or *ancestor*
19 [a]Jer. 27:7 [b]Dan. 2:12, 13; 3:6
20 [a]Ex. 9:17; Job 15:25; Is. 14:13–15; Dan. 4:30, 37
21 [a]Job 30:3–7; Dan. 4:32, 33 [b]Ex. 9:14–16; Ps. 83:17, 18; Ezek. 17:24; [Dan. 4:17, 34, 35] [1]Recognized
22 [a]Ex. 10:3; 2 Chr. 33:23; 36:12
23 [a]Dan. 5:3, 4 [b]Ex. 40:9; Num. 18:3; Is. 52:11; Heb. 9:21 [c]Ps. 115:5, 6; Is. 37:19; Hab. 2:18, 19; Acts 17:24–26; Rom. 1:21 [d]Ps. 139:3; Prov. 20:24; [Jer. 10:23] [1]Exalted [2]The temple
24 [1]Lit. *palm*
25 [1]Lit. *a mina* (50 shekels) from the verb "to number" [2]Lit. *a shekel* from the verb "to weigh" [3]Lit. *and half-shekels* from the verb "to divide"; pl. of *Peres*, v. 28
27 [a]Job 31:6; Ps. 62:9; Jer. 6:30
28 [a]Is. 21:2; Dan. 5:31; 9:1 [b]Dan. 6:28; Acts 2:9 [1]Aram. *Paras*, consonant with *Peres*

5:22–24 See section 1 of Truth-In-Action at the end of Dan.
5:22 Belshazzar is termed Nebuchadnezzar's son as part of his continued dynasty. Belshazzar should have learned to recognize God's authority from his predecessor's humiliation.
5:25–28 See section 1 of Truth-In-Action at the end of Dan.
5:25–28 Daniel gives the inscription's significance, which puzzles Belshazzar because it was like a merchant's shout, "Reckoned at a mina, a shekel, and two halves!" The reason for Belshazzar's downfall is that God evaluated him and found him deficient. Through presumptuous pride and brazen irreverence, he failed to acknowledge God's ultimate lordship over the Earth and, therefore, over Babylon (v. 27).

concerning him [a]that he should be the
third ruler in the kingdom.

Belshazzar's Fall

30 [a]That very night Belshazzar, king
of the Chaldeans, was slain.
31 [a]And Darius the Mede received the
kingdom, *being* about sixty-two years
old.

The Plot Against Daniel

6 It pleased Darius to set over the
kingdom one hundred and twenty
satraps, to be over the whole kingdom;
2 and over these, three governors, of
whom Daniel *was* one, that the satraps
might give account to them, so that the
king would suffer no loss.
3 Then this Daniel distinguished himself above the governors and satraps,
[a]because an excellent spirit *was* in
him; and the king gave thought to setting him over the whole realm.
2 4 [a]So the governors and satraps
sought to find *some* charge against
Daniel concerning the kingdom; but
they could find no charge or fault, because he *was* faithful; nor was there
any error or fault found in him.
5 Then these men said, "We shall not
find any charge against this Daniel unless we find *it* against him concerning
the law of his God."
6 So these governors and satraps
thronged before the king, and said thus
to him: [a]"King Darius, live forever!
7 "All the governors of the kingdom,
the administrators and satraps, the
counselors and advisors, have [a]con-
sulted together to establish a royal statute and to make a firm decree, that
whoever petitions any god or man for
thirty days, except you, O king, shall
be cast into the den of lions.
8 "Now, O king, establish the decree
and sign the writing, so that it cannot
be changed, according to the [a]law of
the Medes and Persians, which [1]does
not alter."
9 Therefore King Darius signed the
written decree.

29 [a]Dan. 5:7, 16
30 [a]Jer. 51:31, 39, 57
31 [a]Dan. 2:39; 9:1

CHAPTER 6
3 [a]Dan. 5:12
4 [a]Eccl. 4:4
6 [a]Neh. 2:3; Dan. 2:4; 6:21
7 [a]Ps. 59:3; 62:4; 64:2–6
8 [a]Esth. 1:19; 8:8; Dan. 6:12, 15 [1]Lit. *does not pass away*
10 [a]1 Kin. 8:29, 30, 46–48; Ps. 5:7; Jon. 2:4 [b]Ps. 55:17; Acts 2:1, 2, 15; [Phil. 4:6]; 1 Thess. 5:17, 18
12 [a]Dan. 3:8–12; Acts 16:19–21 [b]Esth. 1:19; Dan. 6:8, 15 [1]Lit. *does not pass away*
13 [a]Dan. 1:6; 5:13 [b]Esth. 3:8; Dan. 3:12; Acts 5:29 [1]Lit. *of the sons of the captivity*
14 [a]Mark 6:26 [1]*strove*
15 [a]Esth. 8:8; Ps. 94:20, 21; Dan. 6:8, 12 [1]Lit. *thronged before*
17 [a]Lam. 3:53 [b]Matt. 27:66

Daniel in the Lions' Den

10 Now when Daniel knew that the 2
writing was signed, he went home. And
in his upper room, with his windows
open [a]toward Jerusalem, he knelt
down on his knees [b]three times that
day, and prayed and gave thanks before his God, as was his custom since
early days.
11 Then these men assembled and
found Daniel praying and making supplication before his God.
12 [a]And they went before the king, and
spoke concerning the king's decree:
"Have you not signed a decree that
every man who petitions any god or
man within thirty days, except you, O
king, shall be cast into the den of
lions?" The king answered and said,
"The thing *is* true, [b]according to the
law of the Medes and Persians, which
[1]does not alter."
13 So they answered and said before
the king, "That Daniel, [a]who is [1]one
of the captives from Judah, [b]does not
show due regard for you, O king, or
for the decree that you have signed,
but makes his petition three times a
day."
14 And the king, when he heard *these*
words, [a]was greatly displeased with
himself, and set *his* heart on Daniel to
deliver him; and he [1]labored till the going down of the sun to deliver him.
15 Then these men [1]approached the
king, and said to the king, "Know, O
king, that *it is* [a]the law of the Medes
and Persians that no decree or statute
which the king establishes may be
changed."
16 So the king gave the command, and
they brought Daniel and cast *him* into
the den of lions. *But* the king spoke,
saying to Daniel, "Your God, whom
you serve continually, He will deliver
you."
17 [a]Then a stone was brought and laid
on the mouth of the den, [b]and the king
sealed it with his own signet ring and
with the signets of his lords, that the
purpose concerning Daniel might not
be changed.

5:31 The Persian king Cyrus, who captured the Medes in 549 B.C., took Babylon in 539 B.C. **Darius the Mede** is either his temporary vassal-king or an alternate title for Cyrus. He is not to be confused with Darius I (Ezra 4:5).

6:1 Satraps is a general term for government officials.

6:4–9 See section 2 of Truth-In-Action at the end of Dan.

6:6–9 All the officials knew Daniel's distinctive characteristic could also be his point of vulnerability—steadfast commitment to God. They appeal to Darius's pride and vanity in order to trap Daniel.

6:10–16 See section 2 of Truth-In-Action at the end of Dan.

6:16–24 Contemporary believers rarely confront literal **lions,** but our Adversary "walks about like a roaring lion, seeking whom he may devour" (1 Pet. 5:8). Not only will the mouth of the most ferocious predator be locked shut, but as we "resist the devil . . . he will flee" from us (James 4:7).

Darius's turmoil (vv. 14, 18) shows God's power to convict sinners, bringing them to the point of acknowledging His name (vv. 25–27).

Daniel Saved from the Lions

18 Now the king went to his palace and
spent the night fasting; and no
[1]musicians were brought before him.
[a]Also his sleep [2]went from him.
19 Then the [a]king arose very early in
the morning and went in haste to the
den of lions.
20 And when he came to the den, he
cried out with a [1]lamenting voice to
Daniel. The king spoke, saying to Daniel, "Daniel, servant of the living God,
[a]has your God, whom you serve continually, been able to deliver you from
the lions?"
2 21 Then Daniel said to the king,
[a]"O king, live forever!
22 [a]"My God sent His angel and
[b]shut the lions' mouths, so that they
have not hurt me, because I was found
innocent before Him; and also, O king,
I have done no wrong before you."
23 Now the king was exceedingly glad
for him, and commanded that they
should take Daniel up out of the
den. So Daniel was taken up out of the
den, and no injury whatever was found
on him, [a]because he believed in his
God.

Darius Honors God

24 And the king gave the command,
[a]and they brought those men who had
accused Daniel, and they cast *them*
into the den of lions—them, [b]their children, and their wives; and the lions
overpowered them, and broke all their
bones in pieces before they ever came
to the bottom of the den.
25 [a]Then King Darius wrote:

To all peoples, nations, and
languages that dwell in all the
earth:

Peace be multiplied to you.

26 [a]I make a decree that in every
dominion of my kingdom *men*
must [b]tremble and fear before the
God of Daniel.
[c]For He *is* the living God,
And steadfast forever;
His kingdom *is the one* which
shall not be [d]destroyed,
And His dominion *shall endure* to
the end.
27 He delivers and rescues,
[a]And He works signs and wonders
In heaven and on earth,
Who has delivered Daniel from
the [1]power of the lions.

28 So this Daniel prospered in the
reign of Darius [a]and in the reign of
[b]Cyrus the Persian.

Vision of the Four Beasts

7 In the first year of Belshazzar king
of Babylon, [a]Daniel [1]had a dream
and [b]visions of his head *while* on his
bed. Then he wrote down the dream,
telling [2]the main facts.
2 Daniel spoke, saying, "I saw in my
vision by night, and behold, the four
winds of heaven were stirring up the
Great Sea.
3 "And four great beasts [a]came up
from the sea, each different from the
other.
4 "The first *was* [a]like a lion, and had
eagle's wings. I watched till its wings
were plucked off; and it was lifted up
from the earth and made to stand on
two feet like a man, and a [b]man's heart
was given to it.
5 [a]"And suddenly another beast, a
second, like a bear. It was raised up
on one side, and *had* three ribs in its
mouth between its teeth. And they said
thus to it: 'Arise, devour much flesh!'
6 "After this I looked, and there was
another, like a leopard, which had on
its back four wings of a bird. The beast
also had [a]four heads, and dominion
was given to it.
7 "After this I saw in the night visions, and behold, [a]a fourth beast,
dreadful and terrible, exceedingly
strong. It had huge iron teeth; it was
devouring, breaking in pieces, and
trampling the residue with its feet. It
was different from all the beasts that

18 [a]Esth. 6:1; Ps. 77:4; Dan. 2:1 [1]Exact meaning unknown [2]Or *fled*
19 [a]Dan. 3:24
20 [a]Gen. 18:14; Num. 11:23; Jer. 32:17; Dan. 3:17; [Luke 1:37] [1]Or *grieved*
21 [a]Dan. 2:4; 6:6
22 [a]Num. 20:16; Is. 63:9; Dan. 3:28; Acts 12:11; [Heb. 1:14] [b]Ps. 91:11–13; 2 Tim. 4:17; Heb. 11:33
23 [a]Heb. 11:33
24 [a]Deut. 19:18, 19; Esth. 7:10 [b]Deut. 24:16; 2 Kin. 14:6; Esth. 9:10
25 [a]Ezra 1:1, 2; Esth. 3:12; 8:9; Dan. 4:1
26 [a]Ezra 6:8–12; 7:13; Dan. 3:29 [b]Ps. 99:1 [c]Dan. 4:34; 6:20; Hos. 1:10; Rom. 9:26 [d]Dan. 2:44; 4:3; 7:14, 27; [Luke 1:33]
27 [a]Dan. 4:2, 3 [1]Lit. *hand*
28 [a]Dan. 1:21 [b]Ezra 1:1, 2

CHAPTER 7

1 [a]Num. 12:6; [Amos 3:7] [b][Dan. 2:28] [1]Lit. *saw* [2]Lit. *the head* or *chief of the words*
3 [a]Dan. 7:17; Rev. 13:1; 17:8
4 [a]Deut. 28:49; 2 Sam. 1:23; Jer. 48:40; Ezek. 17:3; Hab. 1:8 [b]Dan. 4:16, 34
5 [a]Dan. 2:39
6 [a]Dan. 8:8, 22
7 [a]Dan. 2:40

6:21, 22 See section 2 of Truth-In-Action at the end of Dan.
6:28 The Hebrew for **and** can be translated "that is." See note on 5:31.
7:1–28 Although details of Daniel's dream are at times difficult to interpret, the main emphasis is clear: history will continue to be filled with turmoil. Yet God, who is the Lord of international politics, will still be involved, until He makes a final intervention. Furthermore, His faithful shall continue to survive during, and at times be delivered from, pressure.
7:1 Daniel's **dream** would have been about 550 B.C. This would have been some 10 years before the events of ch. 5.
7:4–6 As with the kingdoms of the great image of ch. 2, the identity of the kingdoms represented by the various beasts is difficult. It is generally agreed that they represent three successive kingdoms. The main interpretations are that the **lion** represents Babylon, the **bear** represents either Media or the Medo-Persian Empire, and the **leopard** represents either Persia or Greece.

were before it, [b]and it had ten horns.
8 "I was considering the horns, and
[a]there was another horn, a little one,
coming up among them, before whom
three of the first horns were plucked
out by the roots. And there, in this
horn, *were* eyes like the eyes [b]of a
man, [c]and a mouth speaking [1]pomp-
ous words.

Vision of the Ancient of Days

9 "I[a] watched till thrones were
[1]put in place,
And [b]the Ancient of Days was
seated;
[c]His garment *was* white as snow,
And the hair of His head *was* like
pure wool.
His throne *was* a fiery flame,
[d]Its wheels a burning fire;
10 [a]A fiery stream issued
And came forth from before Him.
[b]A thousand thousands ministered
to Him;
Ten thousand times ten thousand
stood before Him.
[c]The [1]court was seated,
And the books were opened.

11 "I watched then because of the
sound of the [1]pompous words which
the horn was speaking; [a]I watched till
the beast was slain, and its body destroyed and given to the burning flame.
12 "As for the rest of the beasts, they
had their dominion taken away, yet
their lives were prolonged for a season
and a time.

13 "I was watching in the night
visions,
And behold, [a]*One* like the Son of
Man,
Coming with the clouds of
heaven!
He came to the Ancient of Days,
And they brought Him near
before Him.
14 [a]Then to Him was given dominion
and glory and a kingdom,
That all [b]peoples, nations, and
languages should serve Him.
His dominion *is* [c]an everlasting
dominion,
Which shall not pass away,
And His kingdom *the one*
Which shall not be destroyed.

Daniel's Visions Interpreted

15 "I, Daniel, was grieved in my spirit
[1]within *my* body, and the visions of my
head troubled me.
16 "I came near to one of those who
stood by, and asked him the truth of
all this. So he told me and made known
to me the interpretation of these
things:
17 'Those great beasts, which are four,
are four [1]kings *which* arise out of the
earth.
18 'But [a]the saints of the Most High
shall receive the kingdom, and possess
the kingdom forever, even forever and
ever.'
19 "Then I wished to know the truth
about the fourth beast, which was different from all the others, exceedingly
dreadful, *with* its teeth of iron and its
nails of bronze, *which* devoured, broke
in pieces, and trampled the residue
with its feet;
20 "and the ten horns that *were* on its
head, and the other *horn* which came
up, before which three fell, namely,
that horn which had eyes and a mouth
which spoke [1]pompous words, whose
appearance *was* greater than his fellows.
21 "I was watching; [a]and the same
horn was making war against the
saints, and prevailing against them,
22 "until the Ancient of Days came,
[a]and a judgment was made *in favor* of
the saints of the Most High, and the
time came for the saints to possess the
kingdom.

7 [b]Dan. 2:41; Rev. 12:3; 13:1
8 [a]Dan. 8:9 [b]Rev. 9:7 [c]Ps. 12:3; Rev. 13:5, 6 [1]Lit. *great things*
9 [a][Rev. 20:4] [b]Ps. 90:2 [c]Ps. 104:2; Rev. 1:14 [d]Ezek. 1:15 [1]Or *set up*
10 [a]Ps. 50:3; Is. 30:33; 66:15 [b]Deut. 33:2; 1 Kin. 22:19; Ps. 68:17; Rev. 5:11 [c]Dan. 12:1; [Rev. 20:11–15] [1]Or *judgment*
11 [a][Rev. 19:20; 20:10] [1]Lit. *great*
13 [a]Ezek. 1:26; [Matt. 24:30; 26:64; Mark 13:26; 14:62; Luke 21:27; Rev. 1:7, 13; 14:14]
14 [a]Ps. 2:6–8; Dan. 7:27; [Matt. 28:18; John 3:35, 36; 1 Cor. 15:27; Eph. 1:22; Phil. 2:9–11; Rev. 1:6; 11:15] [b]Dan. 3:4 [c]Ps. 145:13; Mic. 4:7; [Luke 1:33]; John 12:34; Heb. 12:28
15 [1]Lit. *in the midst of its sheath*
17 [1]Representing their kingdoms, v. 23
18 [a]Ps. 149:5–9; Is. 60:12–14; Dan. 7:14; [2 Tim. 2:11; Rev. 2:26, 27; 20:4; 22:5]
20 [1]Lit. *great things*
21 [a]Rev. 11:7; 13:7; 17:14
22 [a][Rev. 1:6]

KINGDOM DYNAMICS

7:21, 22 Old Testament: Possessing the Kingdom, PROPHECY AND THE KING-DOM. Daniel's prophecy in ch. 7 not only spans the spiritual struggle covering the

7:7 The interpretation of the **fourth beast** depends on one's interpretation of the previous three. If the third beast represents Persia, this is Greece; if it represents Greece, *this is Rome.* ***Ten horns*** *symbolize* an unspecified and yet complete number of kings within the fourth kingdom.

7:8 God's sovereignty over kings is seen in His plucking out **three of the first horns.** Dispensational interpretation sees the fourth kingdom as Rome with **another horn** generally being regarded as its Caesars.

CLASSICAL INTERPRETATION: Classical interpretation sees the fourth kingdom and **another horn** as representing Greece and Antiochus Epiphanes.

In either case, this **little one** clearly embodies the antichrist spirit and becomes an archetype of the Antichrist of the Book of Revelation (see vv. 21–27).

7:13 Son of Man was Jesus' favorite self-designation. Hence, Daniel's dream is in part messianic, announcing that the Messiah's coming will inaugurate a new phase of God's rule on Earth. Christ did this by bringing the kingdom of God into human experience (v. 18).

ages through Messiah's First and Second Coming, but it uses two terms important to perceiving the biblical truth of the kingdom of God: "dominion" and "possess." "Dominion" (from Chaldee, *shelet,* "to govern, prevail, dominate") is in the hands of world powers (vv. 6, 12) until the Coming of the Son of Man, at which time it is taken by Him forever (vv. 13, 14). But an interim struggle is seen between the First and Second Coming of Messiah. During this season, the saints "possess" (Chaldee, *chacan,* "to hold on or occupy") the kingdom. This communicates a process of long struggle as the redeemed ("saints") "possess" what they have "received" (v. 18). The scenario reads: 1) After the "judgment was made in favor of the saints" (a forecast of the pivotal impact of Christ's Cross upon which hinged both man's redemption as well as his reinstatement to the potential of his rule under God), an extended struggle ensues. 2) This struggle is described as the "time [which] came for the saints to possess the kingdom." They do battle against sinister adversaries and experience a mix of victories and apparent defeats (v. 25). The prophecy unveils the present age of the kingdom, which is one of ongoing struggle—with victory upon victory for the church. Yet it withholds its conclusive triumph until Christ comes again.

This prophecy also balances the question of divine sovereignty and human responsibility. 1) God's sovereignty accomplishes the foundational victory (v. 22) and in the Cross achieves the decisive victory allowing the saints new dimensions for advance and conquest. 2) He entrusts the responsibility for that advance to His own to "possess the kingdom," entering into conflict with the adversary, at times at the expense of their apparent defeat (v. 26). 3) However, movement toward victory is theirs as they press the "judgment" of the "court" (vv. 22, 26) and seize realms controlled by evil. They wrestle the dominion from hellish powers, continuing in warfare until the ultimate seating of the Son of Man (vv. 14, 27).

Prophetic systems vary as to how and when these words unfold on the calendar of church history, for the passage is subject to different schemes of interpretation, each with different projected chronologies. But the foundational fact remains that an agelong struggle between "the saints" and the power of evil in the world calls each believer to a commitment to steadfast battle, a mixture of victories with setbacks, and a consummate triumph anticipated at Christ's Coming. In the meantime, we "receive" the kingdom and pursue victories for our King, by His power, making intermittent gains—all of which are based on "the judgment" achieved through the Cross. See Rev. 12:10, 11.

(1 Pet. 2:9/Rev. 12:10, 11) J.W.H.

23 "Thus he said:

'The fourth beast shall be
[a]A fourth kingdom on earth,
Which shall be different from all
other kingdoms,
And shall devour the whole earth,
Trample it and break it in pieces.
24 [a]The ten horns *are* ten kings
Who shall arise from this
kingdom.
And another shall rise after them;
He shall be different from the first
ones,
And shall subdue three kings.
25 [a]He shall speak *pompous* words
against the Most High,
Shall [b]persecute[1] the saints of the
Most High,
And shall [c]intend to change times
and law.
Then [d]*the saints* shall be given
into his hand
[e]For a time and times and half a
time.

26 'But[a] the court shall be seated,
And they shall [b]take away his
dominion,
To consume and destroy *it*
forever.
27 Then the [a]kingdom and
dominion,
And the greatness of the
kingdoms under the whole
heaven,
Shall be given to the people, the
saints of the *Most High.
[b]His kingdom *is* an everlasting
kingdom,
[c]And all dominions shall serve and
obey Him.'

23 [a]Dan. 2:40 **24** [a]Dan. 7:7; Rev. 13:1; 17:12 **25** [a]Is. 37:23; Dan. 11:36; Rev. 13:1–6 [b]Rev. 17:6 [c]Dan. 2:21 [d]Rev. 13:7; 18:24 [e]Dan. 12:7; Rev. 12:14 [1]Lit. *wear out* **26** [a][Dan. 2:35; 7:10, 22] [b]Rev. 19:20 **27** [a]Is. 54:3; Dan. 7:14, 18, 22; Rev. 20:4 [b]2 Sam. 7:16; Ps. 89:35–37; Is. 9:7; Dan. 2:44; 4:34; 7:14; [Luke 1:33, 34]; John 12:34; [Rev. 11:15; 22:5] [c]Ps. 2:6–12; 22:27; 72:11; 86:9; Is. 60:12; Rev. 11:1 *See WW at Gen. 14:18.

7:25 A time and times and half a time is another way of saying three and one-half years. It refers to the last half of the Seventieth Week (see note on 9:24, 26), the time for the most intense manifestation of Satan's power in his persecution of the Jews and believers in Christ who still remain on Earth. This reference gives strong evidence that the last half of Daniel's Seventieth Week (week of years) refers to the Great Tribulation (9:27; Rev. 11:2; 13:5).

CLASSICAL INTERPRETATION: Classical interpretation does not associate the "time and times and half a time" with a literal three-and-one-half-year period. Rather, it views it as representing an indefinite, divinely controlled time period. In referring to Antiochus Epiphanes, it indicates his destructive time will end when God so deems. The same is true with reference to the final ploys of the Antichrist.

4 28 "This *is* the end of the [1]account. As
for me, Daniel, [a]my thoughts greatly
troubled me, and my countenance
changed; but I [b]kept the matter in my
heart."

Vision of a Ram and a Goat

8 In[1] the third year of the reign of
King Belshazzar a *vision appeared *to* me—to me, Daniel—after the
one that appeared to me [a]the first time.
2 I saw in the vision, and it so happened while I was looking, that I *was*
in [a]Shushan,[1] the [2]citadel, which *is* in
the province of Elam; and I saw in the
vision that I was by the River Ulai.
3 Then I lifted my eyes and saw, and
there, standing beside the river, was a
ram which had two horns, and the two
horns *were* high; but one *was* [a]higher
than the other, and the higher *one*
came up last.
4 I saw the ram pushing westward,
northward, and southward, so that no
animal could [1]withstand him; nor *was
there any* that could deliver from his
hand, [a]but he did according to his will
and became great.
5 And as I was considering, suddenly
a male goat came from the west, across
the surface of the whole earth, without
touching the ground; and the goat *had*
a notable [a]horn between his eyes.
6 Then he came to the ram that had
two horns, which I had seen standing
beside the river, and ran at him with
furious power.
7 And I saw him confronting the ram;
he was moved with rage against him,
[1]attacked the ram, and broke his two
horns. There was no power in the ram
to withstand him, but he cast him down
to the ground and trampled him; and
there was no one that could deliver the
ram from his hand.
8 Therefore the male goat grew very
great; but when he became strong, the
large horn was broken, and in place
of it [a]four notable ones came up toward
the four winds of heaven.
9 [a]And out of one of them came a little *horn which grew exceedingly great
toward the south, [b]toward the east, and
toward the [c]Glorious *Land.*
10 [a]And it grew up to [b]the *host of
heaven; and [c]it cast down *some* of the
host and *some* of the stars to the
ground, and trampled them.
11 [a]He even exalted *himself* as high as
[b]the Prince of the host; [c]and by him
[d]the daily *sacrifices* were taken away,
and the place of [1]His sanctuary was
cast down.
12 Because of transgression, [a]an army
was given over *to the horn* to oppose
the daily *sacrifices;* and he cast [b]truth
down to the ground. He [c]did *all this*
and prospered.
13 Then I heard [a]a holy one speaking;
and *another* holy one said to that certain *one* who was speaking, "How long
will the vision *be, concerning* the daily
sacrifices and the transgression [1]of
desolation, the giving of both the sanctuary and the host to be trampled underfoot?"
14 And he said to me, "For two thousand three hundred [1]days; then the
sanctuary shall be cleansed."

Gabriel Interprets the Vision

15 Then it happened, when I, Daniel,
had seen the vision and [a]was seeking
the meaning, that suddenly there stood
before me [b]one having the appearance
of a man.
16 And I heard a man's voice [a]between
the banks of the Ulai, who called, and
said, [b]"Gabriel, make this *man* *understand the vision."
17 So he came near where I stood, and
when he came I was afraid and [a]fell
on my face; but he said to me, "Understand, son of man, that the vision *refers*
to the time of the end."
18 [a]Now, as he was speaking with me,
I was in a deep sleep with my face to
the ground; [b]but he touched me, and
stood me upright.
19 And he said, "Look, I am making
known to you what shall happen in the
latter time of the indignation; [a]for at
the appointed time the end *shall be.*
20 "The ram which you saw, having

28 [a]Dan. 8:27 [b]Luke 2:19, 51 [1]Lit. *word*

CHAPTER 8

1 [a]Dan. 7:1 [1]The Hebrew language resumes in Dan. 8:1. *See WW at 2 Chr. 32:32.
2 [a]Esth. 1:2; 2:8 [1]Or *Susa* [2]Or *fortified palace*
3 [a]Dan. 7:5
4 [a]Dan. 5:19 [1]Lit. *stand before him*
5 [a]Dan. 8:8, 21; 11:3
7 [1]Lit. *struck*
8 [a]Dan. 7:6; 8:22; 11:4
9 [a]Dan. 11:21 [b]Dan. 11:25 [c]Ps. 48:2 *See WW at Ezek. 29:21.
10 [a]Dan. 11:28 [b]Is. 14:13 [c]Rev. 12:4 *See WW at Ps. 68:11.
11 [a]Dan. 8:25; 11:36, 37 [b]Josh. 5:14 [c]Dan. 11:31; 12:11 [d]Ex. 29:38 [1]The temple
12 [a]Dan. 11:31 [b]Is. 59:14 [c]Dan. 8:4; 11:36
13 [a]Dan. 4:13, 23 [1]Or *making desolate*
14 [1]Lit. *evening-mornings*
15 [a]1 Pet. 1:10 [b]Ezek. 1:26
16 [a]Dan. 12:6, 7 [b]Luke 1:19, 26 *See WW at Neh. 8:8.
17 [a]Rev. 1:17
18 [a]Luke 9:32 [b]Ezek. 2:2
19 [a]Hab. 2:3

7:28 See section 4 of Truth-In-Action at the end of Dan.

8:1–22 The precise fulfillment of Daniel's prophecies concerning the defeat of the Medo-Persians (**the ram,** v. 4) by the Greeks (***a male goat,*** v. 5) and the events that led up to Antiochus Epiphanes has caused secular historians to declare that the Book of Daniel could not have been written earlier than 200 B.C., for they deny the supernatural source of the Scriptures. But for all who embrace the validity of this part of the Word's having been written in the sixth century B.C., it is a confirming testimony to the remarkable prophetic anointing that rested upon Daniel for the detailed foretelling of forthcoming events.

8:9–14 The **little horn** is Antiochus Epiphanes, who came out of Syria to persecute the Jews and profane the temple between 171 and 164 B.C. He is a type of the Antichrist of the last days, as well as of all godless world rulers who actively oppose God's people.

CLASSICAL INTERPRETATION: Classical interpretation identifies this "little horn" with the one mentioned in 7:8, while dispensational interpretation does not. See note on 7:8.

the two horns—*they are* the kings of
Media and Persia.
21 "And the [1]male goat *is* the [2]king-
dom of Greece. The large horn that
is between its eyes [a]*is* the first king.
22 [a]"As for the broken *horn* and the
four that stood up in its place, four
kingdoms shall arise out of that nation,
but not with its power.

23 "And in the latter time of their
kingdom,
When the transgressors have
reached their fullness,
A king shall arise,
[a]Having fierce [1]features,
Who understands sinister
schemes.
24 His power shall be mighty,
[a]but not by his own power;
He shall destroy [1]fearfully,
[b]And shall prosper and thrive;
[c]He shall destroy the mighty, and
also the holy people.

25 "Through[a] his cunning
He shall cause deceit to prosper
under his [1]rule;
[b]And he shall exalt *himself* in his
heart.
He shall destroy many in *their*
prosperity.
[c]He shall even rise against the
Prince of princes;
But he shall be [d]broken without
human [1]means.

26 "And the vision of the evenings
and mornings
Which was told is true;
[a]Therefore seal up the vision,
For *it refers* to many days *in the
future.*"

4 **27** [a]And I, Daniel, fainted and was sick
for days; afterward I arose and went
about the king's business. I was
[1]astonished by the vision, but no one
understood it.

Daniel's Prayer for the People

9 In the first year [a]of Darius the *son
of Ahasuerus, of the lineage of the

21 [a]Dan. 11:3 [1]*shaggy male* [2]Lit. *king,* representing his kingdom, Dan. 7:17, 23
22 [a]Dan. 11:4
23 [a]Deut. 28:50 [1]Lit. *countenance*
24 [a]Rev. 17:13 [b]Dan. 11:36 [c]Dan. 7:25 [1]Or *extraordinarily*
25 [a]Dan. 11:21 [b]Dan. 8:11–13; 11:36; 12:7 [c]Dan. 11:36; Rev. 19:19, 20 [d]Job 34:20; Lam. 4:6 [1]Lit. *hand*
26 [a]Ezek. 12:27; Dan. 12:4, 9; Rev. 22:10
27 [a]Dan. 7:28; 8:17; Hab. 3:16 [1]*amazed*

CHAPTER 9

1 [a]Dan. 1:21 *See WW at Gen. 29:32.
2 [a]2 Chr. 36:21; Ezra 1:1; Jer. 25:11, 12; 29:10; Zech. 7:5 *See WW at 2 Sam. 8:15. • See WW at Neh. 8:8.
3 [a]Neh. 1:4; Dan. 6:10; 10:15 *See WW at 2 Chr. 6:20. • See WW at Jon. 3:5.
4 [a]Ex. 20:6 *See WW at Mic. 6:8.
5 [a]1 Kin. 8:47, 48; Neh. 9:33; Ps. 106:6; Is. 64:5–7; Jer. 14:7
6 [a]2 Chr. 36:15; Jer. 44:4, 5
7 [a]Neh. 9:33
9 [a][Neh. 9:17; Ps. 130:4, 7]
11 [a]Is. 1:3–6; Jer. 8:5–10 [b]Lev. 26:14; Neh. 1:6; Ps. 106:6
12 [a]Is. 44:26; Jer. 44:2–6; Lam. 2:17; Zech. 1:6

Medes, who was made king over the
realm of the Chaldeans—
2 in the first year of his *reign I, Daniel, *understood by the books the number of the years *specified* by the word
of the LORD through [a]Jeremiah the
prophet, that He would accomplish
seventy years in the desolations of Jerusalem.
3 [a]Then I set my face toward the Lord
God to make request by *prayer and
supplications, with *fasting, sackcloth,
and ashes.
4 And I prayed to the LORD my God, 3
and made confession, and said, "O
[a]Lord, great and awesome God, who
keeps His covenant and *mercy with
those who love Him, and with those
who keep His commandments,
5 [a]"we have sinned and committed
iniquity, we have done wickedly and
rebelled, even by departing from Your
precepts and Your judgments.
6 [a]"Neither have we heeded Your servants the prophets, who spoke in Your
name to our kings and our princes, to
our fathers and all the people of the
land.
7 "O Lord, [a]righteousness *belongs* to
You, but to us shame of face, as *it is*
this day—to the men of Judah, to the
inhabitants of Jerusalem and all Israel,
those near and those far off in all the
countries to which You have driven
them, because of the unfaithfulness
which they have committed against
You.
8 "O Lord, to us *belongs* shame of
face, to our kings, our princes, and our
fathers, because we have sinned
against You.
9 [a]"To the Lord our God *belong*
mercy and forgiveness, though we
have rebelled against Him.
10 "We have not obeyed the voice of
the LORD our God, to walk in His laws,
which He set before us by His servants
the prophets.
11 "Yes, [a]all Israel has transgressed
Your law, and has departed so as not
to obey Your voice; therefore the curse
and the oath written in the [b]Law of
Moses the servant of God have been
poured out on us, because we have
sinned against Him.
12 "And He has [a]confirmed His words,

8:21, 22 The large horn is Alexander the Great who ruled Greece from 336 to 323 B.C. At his death, his empire was divided into **four kingdoms.**
8:23–27 See note on 8:9–14.
8:27 See section 4 of Truth-In-Action at the end of Dan.
9:1–19 Daniel teaches us that an appropriate response to prophecy is often penitent prayer. His joining of fasting with prayer (9:3; 10:2, 3) is clearly an instrument of spiritual preparation and supplication and is not to be dismissed as a superstitious or ascetic action. (See Matt. 9:14, 15 for Jesus' words on fasting as a disciple's discipline.)
9:1 See note on 5:31.
9:2 See note on Ezra 1:1.
9:4–19 See section 3 of Truth-In-Action at the end of Dan.

which He spoke against us and against
our judges who judged us, by bringing
upon us a great disaster; [b]for under the
whole heaven such has never been
done as what has been done to Jerusalem.
13 [a]"As *it is* written in the Law of Moses, all this disaster has come upon us;
[b]yet we have not made our prayer before the LORD our God, that we might
turn from our iniquities and understand Your *truth.
14 "Therefore the LORD has [a]kept
the disaster in mind, and brought
it upon us; for [b]the LORD our God *is*
righteous in all the works which He
does, though we have not obeyed His
voice.
15 "And now, O Lord our God, [a]who
brought Your people out of the land
of Egypt with a mighty hand, and made
Yourself [b]a name, as *it is* this day—
we have sinned, we have done wickedly!
16 "O Lord, [a]according to all Your
righteousness, I pray, let Your anger
and Your fury be turned away from
Your city Jerusalem, [b]Your holy
mountain; because for our sins, [c]and
for the iniquities of our fathers, [d]Jeru-
salem and Your people [e]*are* a reproach
to all *those* around us.
17 "Now therefore, our God, hear the
prayer of Your servant, and his supplications, [a]and [b]for the Lord's sake
[1]cause Your face to shine on [2]Your
sanctuary, [c]which is desolate.
18 [a]"O my God, incline Your ear and
hear; open Your eyes [b]and see our desolations, and the city [c]which is called
by Your name; for we do not present
our supplications before You because
of our righteous deeds, but because of
Your great mercies.
19 "O Lord, hear! O Lord, *forgive! O
Lord, listen and act! Do not delay for
Your own sake, my God, for Your city

12 [b]Lam. 1:12; 2:13
13 [a]Deut. 28:15–68 [b]Is. 9:13 *See WW at Ps. 25:5.
14 [a]Jer. 31:28; 44:27 [b]Neh. 9:33
15 [a]Neh. 1:10 [b]Neh. 9:10
16 [a]1 Sam. 12:7 [b]Zech. 8:3 [c]Ex. 20:5 [d]Lam. 2:16 [e]Ps. 79:4
17 [a]Num. 6:24–26 [b]Lam. 5:18 [c][John 16:24] [1]Be gracious [2]The temple
18 [a]Is. 37:17 [b]Ex. 3:7 [c]Jer. 25:29
19 *See WW at Ps. 103:3.
21 [a]Dan. 8:16 [1]Or *being weary with weariness*
23 [a]Dan. 10:11, 19 [b]Matt. 24:15 [1]Lit. *word*
24 [a][Is. 53:10] [b]Rev. 14:6 [c]Ps. 45:7 [1]Lit. *sevens,* and so throughout the chapter [2]So with Qr., LXX, Syr., Vg.; Kt., Theodotion *To seal up* [3]The Most Holy Place *See WW at Num. 15:25. • See WW at Is. 61:1.
25 [a]John 1:41; 4:25 [b]Is. 55:4 [1]Or *open square* [2]Or *moat*

and Your people are called by Your
name."

The Seventy-Weeks Prophecy

20 Now while I *was* speaking, praying,
and confessing my sin and the sin of
my people Israel, and presenting my
supplication before the LORD my God
for the holy mountain of my God,
21 yes, while I *was* speaking in prayer,
the man [a]Gabriel, whom I had seen in
the vision at the beginning, [1]being
caused to fly swiftly, reached me about
the time of the evening offering.
22 And he informed *me,* and talked
with me, and said, "O Daniel, I have
now come forth to give you skill to understand.
23 "At the beginning of your supplications the [1]command went out, and I
have come to tell *you,* for you *are*
greatly [a]beloved; therefore [b]consider
the matter, and understand the vision:

24 "Seventy [1]weeks are determined
For your people and for your holy city,
To finish the transgression,
[2]To make an end of sins,
[a]To *make reconciliation for iniquity,
[b]To bring in everlasting righteousness,
To seal up vision and prophecy,
[c]And to *anoint [3]the Most Holy.

25 "Know therefore and understand,
That from the going forth of the command
To restore and build Jerusalem
Until [a]**Messiah** [b]the Prince,
There shall be seven weeks and sixty-two weeks;
The [1]street shall be built again, and the [2]wall,
Even in troublesome times.

9:16–19 In spite of Daniel's impeccable life and testimony, Daniel's intercession and supplication were not based on his own righteousness but on the **great mercies** of the Lord. Titus 3:5 declares it is "not by works of righteousness which we have done, but according to His mercy He saved us."

9:24–27 The revelation to Daniel of **seventy weeks** came as an answer to his prayer. God showed him that the refining judgments of Israel would come to an end, and their acceptance of the Messiah would bring in everlasting righteousness. This prophecy provides a time frame for messianic prediction from the time of Daniel to the establishing of the millennial kingdom. See note on vv. 24, 26. Along with Rom. 11, it also establishes the fact that God is not finished with Israel as a nation. To a great extent, Israel becomes God's prophetic clock.

9:24, 26 The time frame of the **seventy weeks** or "Seventy Sevens of Years" is associated with Daniel's people, the Jews, and the holy city, Jerusalem. The fact that the weeks of years (490 years) are 360-day years is established by a comparison of 7:25 with Rev. 11:2, 3; 12:6, 14; and 13:5. The weeks of years began with the commandment by Artaxerxes in 445 B.C. to restore Jerusalem. Chronologically, they are divided as:

Seven sevens	49 years—445 to 396 B.C. (From Artaxerxes' decree to the arrival of Nehemiah and the covenant renewal celebration at Jerusalem)
Sixty-two sevens	434 years—396 B.C. to A.D. 32 (From the dedication of the second temple to the crucifixion of the Lord Jesus Christ)
One seven	7 years—Unfulfilled. See note on vv. 26, 27.

WORD WEALTH

9:25 Messiah, *mashiach* (mah-*shee*-ahch); Strong's #4899: Anointed one, messiah. Found 39 times in the OT, *mashiach* is derived from the verb *mashach,* "to anoint," "to consecrate by applying the holy anointing oil to an individual." *Mashiach* describes the high priest (Lev. 4:3, 16) and anointed kings, such as Saul (2 Sam. 1:14) and David (2 Sam. 19:21; Ps. 18:50). In Ps. and in Dan., *mashiach* is particularly used for David's anointed heir, the king of Israel and ruler of all nations (see Ps. 2:2; 28:8; Dan. 9:25, 26). When the earliest followers of Jesus spoke of Him, they called Him Jesus the Messiah, or in Hebrew, *Yeshua ha-Mashiach.* "Messiah" or "Anointed One" is *Christos* in Greek and is the origin of the English form "Christ." Whenever the Lord is called "Jesus Christ," He is being called "Jesus the Messiah."

26 "And after the sixty-two weeks
[a]Messiah shall [1]be cut off,
[b]but not for Himself;
And [c]the people of the prince who
is to come
[d]Shall destroy the city and the
sanctuary.
The end of it *shall be* with a
flood,
And till the end of the war
desolations are determined.
27 Then he shall confirm [a]a
[1]covenant with [b]many for one
week;
But in the middle of the
week
He shall bring an end to sacrifice
and offering.
And on the wing of abominations
shall be one who makes
desolate,
[c]Even until the consummation,
which is determined,
Is poured out on the [2]desolate."

Vision of the Glorious Man

10 In the third year of Cyrus king
of Persia a message was *revealed to Daniel, whose [a]name was
called Belteshazzar. The message *was*
true, [1]but the appointed time *was* long;
and he understood the message, and
had understanding of the vision.
2 In those days I, Daniel, was mourning three full weeks.
3 I ate no [1]pleasant food, no meat or
wine came into my mouth, nor did I
anoint myself at all, till three whole
weeks were fulfilled.
4 Now on the twenty-fourth day of
the first month, as I was by the side
of the great river, that *is,* the [1]Tigris,
5 I lifted my eyes and looked, and behold, a certain man clothed in [a]linen,
whose waist *was* [b]girded with gold of
Uphaz!
6 His body *was* like beryl, his face
like the appearance of lightning, his
eyes like torches of fire, his arms and
feet like burnished bronze in color,
[a]and the sound of his words like the
voice of a multitude.
7 And I, Daniel, alone saw the vision,
for the men who were with me did not
see the vision; but a great terror fell
upon them, so that they fled to hide
themselves.
8 Therefore I was left alone when I 4
saw this great vision, and no strength
remained in me; for my [1]vigor was
turned to [2]frailty in me, and I retained
no strength.
9 Yet I heard the sound of his words;
and while I heard the sound of his

26 [a][Is. 53:8]; Matt. 27:50; Mark 9:12; 15:37; [Luke 23:46; 24:26]; John 19:30; Acts 8:32 [b][1 Pet. 2:21] [c]Matt. 22:7 [d]Matt. 24:2; Mark 13:2; Luke 19:43, 44 [1]Suffer the death penalty
27 [a]Is. 42:6 [b][Matt. 26:28] [c]Dan. 11:36 [1]Or *treaty* [2]Or *desolator*

CHAPTER 10

1 [a]Dan. 1:7 [1]Or *and of great conflict;* *See WW at Amos 3:7.
3 [1]*desirable*
4 [1]Heb. *Hiddekel*
5 [a]Ezek. 9:2; 10:2 [b]Rev. 1:13; 15:6
6 [a][Rev. 1:15]
8 [1]Lit. *splendor* [2]Lit. *ruin*

9:26, 27 One who makes desolate: National Israel will enter into a covenant with the future little horn, the Roman prince (7:8; 11:36) or Antichrist for seven years (Daniel's final or Seventieth Week). In the middle of the week, the Antichrist will break the covenant and demand that the blood sacrifices, restored by Israel in the last days, must cease. He will then set up his image in the Jewish temple and require worship (Matt. 24:15; 2 Thess. 2:3, 4).

CLASSICAL INTERPRETATION: The classical approach to 9:24–27 differs, seeing such numerical computation as arbitrary. It views the 490 as representing not a literal period but a lifetime punishment seven times over (Jer. 25:11; Lev. 26:28). In other words, to this viewpoint, in some form or other Israel's desolation will last for centuries, the postexilic return not marking that end; but an end will come.

This view also confines this prophecy to the second century B.C., that time when Jerusalem would suffer greatly at the hands of Antiochus Epiphanes (**one who makes desolate**). His "abominations" included setting up a heathen altar in the temple, the time of the "cutting off" of Onias III, God's anointed high priest of that time. ("Messiah" [vv. 25, 26], which can be translated "anointed one," is thus seen by the classical school as not necessarily referring to Christ but to the high priest.) The prophesied **consummation** is interpreted as Antiochus's overthrow at the time of the Maccabean revolt.

The classical approach does not, however, rule out antitype fulfillment of the broader principles in Jesus Christ, in the destruction of Jerusalem in A.D. 70, nor in the last days' rampages of the Antichrist. Daniel's language is clearly eschatological at points, denoting a multilevel prophetic fulfillment. See note on Obad. 15.

10:1 This verse summarizes chs. 10—12. It is 536 B.C., some two years after Zerubbabel's return (Ezra 3:8).

10:2–8 Daniel is likely **mourning** because of continued reports on the state of Jerusalem. The heavenly messenger is awesome and full of splendor, resembling the beings of Ezek. 1.

10:8, 9 See section 4 of Truth-In-Action at the end of Dan.

words I was in a deep sleep on my face,
with my face to the ground.

Prophecies Concerning Persia and Greece

10 [a]Suddenly, a hand touched me,
which made me tremble on my knees
and *on* the palms of my hands.
11 And he said to me, "O Daniel,
[a]man greatly beloved, understand the
words that I speak to you, and stand
upright, for I have now been sent to
you." While he was speaking this word
to me, I stood trembling.
12 Then he said to me, [a]"Do not fear,
Daniel, for from the first day that you
set your heart to understand, and to
humble yourself before your God,
[b]your words were heard; and I have
come because of your words.
13 [a]"But the prince of the kingdom of
Persia withstood me twenty-one days;
and behold, [b]Michael, one of the chief
princes, came to help me, for I had
been left alone there with the kings of
Persia.

KINGDOM DYNAMICS

10:13 Angels' Influence over Nations, ANGELS. Some angels have influence over nations. The ruling prince of Persia, an evil angel whose abode is in the heavenlies (the invisible realm), attempted to keep the captive Israelites from returning to their homeland. This gives us insight into the powerful control such principalities and rulers of darkness may exercise over nations and national issues. In this same chapter we see two other angelic "princes" who rule nations: Michael, "one of the chief princes," who rules and guards the activities of Israel (v. 13); and the "prince of Greece" (v. 20), who, as it was prophesied, would eventually come and take predominance over the "prince of Persia" then in control.

(Col. 1:16/Acts 8:26) M.H.

14 "Now I have come to make you understand what will happen to your people [a]in the latter days, [b]for the vision
refers to *many* days yet *to come*."
15 When he had spoken such words to 4
me, [a]I [1]turned my face toward the
ground and became speechless.
16 And suddenly, [a]*one* having the likeness of the [1]sons of men [b]touched my
lips; then I opened my mouth and
spoke, saying to him who stood before
me, "My lord, because of the vision
[c]my sorrows have [2]overwhelmed me,
and I have retained no strength.
17 "For how *can this servant of my
lord talk with you, my lord? As for me,
no strength remains in me now, nor is
any *breath left in me."
18 Then again, *the one* having the
likeness of a man touched me and
strengthened me.
19 [a]And he said, "O man greatly beloved, [b]fear not! Peace *be* to you; be
strong, yes, be strong!" So when he
spoke to me I was strengthened, and
said, "Let my lord speak, for you have
strengthened me."
20 Then he said, "Do you know why I
have come to you? And now I must return to fight [a]with the prince of Persia;
and when I have gone forth, indeed the
prince of Greece will come.
21 "But I will tell you what is noted
in the Scripture of Truth. (No one upholds me against these, [a]except Michael your prince.

11 "Also [a]in the first year of
[b]Darius the Mede, I, *even* I,
stood up to confirm and strengthen
him.)
2 "And now I will tell you the truth:
Behold, three more kings will arise in
Persia, and the fourth shall be far
richer than *them* all; by his strength,
through his riches, he shall stir up all
against the realm of Greece.
3 "Then [a]a mighty king shall arise,
who shall rule with great dominion,
and [b]do according to his will.
4 "And when he has arisen, [a]his kingdom shall be broken up and divided
toward the four winds of heaven, but

10 [a]Dan. 9:21
11 [a]Dan. 9:23
12 [a]Rev. 1:17 [b]Dan. 9:3, 4, 22, 23; Acts 10:4
13 [a]Dan. 10:20 [b]Dan. 10:21; 12:1; Jude 9; [Rev. 12:7]
14 [a]Gen. 49:1; Deut. 31:29; Dan. 2:28 [b]Dan. 8:26; 10:1
15 [a]Dan. 8:18; 10:9 [1]Lit. *set*
16 [a]Dan. 8:15 [b]Jer. 1:9; Dan. 10:10 [c]Dan. 10:8, 9 [1]Theodotion, Vg. *the son;* LXX *a hand* [2]Or *turned upon*
17 *See WW at Num. 13:30. • See WW at Ps. 150:6.
19 [a]Dan. 10:11 [b]Judg. 6:23; Is. 43:1; Dan. 10:12
20 [a]Dan. 10:13
21 [a]Dan. 10:13; Jude 9; [Rev. 12:7]

CHAPTER 11

1 [a]Dan. 9:1 [b]Dan. 5:31
3 [a]Dan. 7:6; 8:5 [b]Dan. 8:4; 11:16, 36
4 [a]Jer. 49:36; Ezek. 37:9; Dan. 7:2; 8:8; Zech. 2:6; Rev. 7:1

10:10—11:1 The visitation of the heavenly beings is to reinforce that Daniel's message (11:2—12:3) is indeed from heaven.
10:13 This is one of the clearest OT examples that demonic armies oppose God's purposes and that earthly struggles often reflect what is happening in the heavenlies, and that prayer with fasting may affect the outcome. **The prince . . . Persia** *would* be the head of the spiritual forces marshaled on behalf of sinful Persia, especially in relation to its destructive interaction with God's people. **Michael** is a senior angel. The exact nature of the conflict and why the messenger could not defeat the prince are not stated.
10:15–17 See section 4 of Truth-In-Action at the end of Dan.
10:20 Here the messenger anticipates victory for himself. In spiritual conflict, he will fight to make sure that **Persia** and **Greece** are kept from blocking God's purposes.
11:2–39 This section requires familiarity with the history of the Persian and Greek periods. Its focus is the career of Antiochus Epiphanes who ruled Persia from 175 to 163 B.C. It also shows the conflicts of governments, as kings seek power and wealth through war, invasion, and marriage. While these events are past now, they occurred centuries after Daniel's prophesying, which again emphasizes the supernatural insight the prophet was given.
11:2 The reference to four Persian kings may include all Persian kings, down to the last one, Darius III (331 B.C.).
11:3 **A mighty king** is Alexander the Great who conquered Persia in 331 B.C. See note on 8:21, 22.

not among his posterity [b]nor according
to his *dominion with which he ruled;
for his kingdom shall be uprooted,
even for others besides these.

Warring Kings of North and South

5 "Also the king of the South shall
become strong, as well as *one* of his
princes; and he shall gain power over
him and have dominion. His dominion
shall be a great dominion.
6 "And at the end of *some* years they
shall join forces, for the daughter of
the king of the South shall go to the
king of the North to make an agreement; but she shall not retain the
power of her [1]authority, and neither he
nor his [1]authority shall stand; but she
shall be given up, with those who
brought her, and with him who begot
her, and with him who strengthened
her in *those* times.
7 "But from a branch of her roots *one*
shall arise in his place, who shall come
with an army, enter the fortress of the
king of the North, and deal with them
and prevail.
8 "And he shall also carry their gods
captive to Egypt, with their [1]princes
and their precious articles of silver and
gold; and he shall continue *more* years
than the king of the North.
9 "Also *the king of the North* shall
come to the kingdom of the king of the
South, but shall return to his own land.
10 "However his sons shall stir up
strife, and assemble a multitude of
great forces; and *one* shall certainly
come [a]and overwhelm and pass
through; then he shall return [b]to his
fortress and stir up strife.
11 "And the king of the South shall be
[a]moved with rage, and go out and fight
with him, with the king of the North,
who shall muster a great multitude; but
the [b]multitude shall be given into the
hand of his *enemy*.
12 "When he has taken away the multitude, his heart will be [1]lifted up; and
he will cast down tens of thousands,
but he will not prevail.
13 "For the king of the North will return and muster a multitude greater
than the former, and shall certainly

4 [b]Dan. 8:22 *See WW at Zech. 9:10. **6** [1]Lit. *arm* **8** [1]Or *molded images* **10** [a]Is. 8:8; Jer. 46:7, 8; 51:42; Dan. 9:26; 11:26, 40 [b]Dan. 11:7 **11** [a]Prov. 16:14 [b][Ps. 33:10, 16] **12** [1]Proud

14 [a]Job 9:13 [1]Or *robbers*, lit. *sons of breakage* [2]Lit. *to establish* **15** [a]Jer. 6:6; Ezek. 4:2; 17:17 [1]Lit. *arms* **16** [a]Dan. 8:4, 7 [b]Josh. 1:5 [1]Lit. *hand* **17** [a]2 Kin. 12:17; 2 Chr. 20:3; Ezek. 4:3, 7 [b]Dan. 9:26 [1]Or *bring equitable terms* **19** [a]Ps. 27:2; Jer. 46:6 [b]Job 20:8; Ps. 37:36; Ezek. 26:21 **21** [a]Dan. 7:8 *See WW at 1 Chr. 29:11. **22** [a]Dan. 9:26 [b]Dan. 8:10, 11 [1]Lit. *arms* **23** [a]Dan. 8:25

come at the end of some years with a
great army and much equipment.
14 "Now in those times many shall rise
up against the king of the South. Also,
[1]violent men of your people shall exalt
themselves [2]in fulfillment of the vision,
but they shall [a]fall.
15 "So the king of the North shall
come and [a]build a siege mound, and
take a fortified city; and the [1]forces of
the South shall not withstand *him*.
Even his choice troops *shall have* no
strength to resist.
16 "But he who comes against him
[a]shall do according to his own will, and
[b]no one shall stand against him. He
shall stand in the Glorious Land with
destruction in his [1]power.
17 "He shall also [a]set his face to enter
with the strength of his whole kingdom, and [1]upright ones with him; thus
shall he do. And he shall give him the
daughter of women to destroy it; but
she shall not stand *with him*, [b]or be
for him.
18 "After this he shall turn his face to
the coastlands, and shall take many.
But a ruler shall bring the reproach
against them to an end; and with the
reproach removed, he shall turn back
on him.
19 "Then he shall turn his face toward
the fortress of his own land; but he
shall [a]stumble and fall, [b]and not be
found.
20 "There shall arise in his place one
who imposes taxes *on* the glorious
kingdom; but within a few days he
shall be destroyed, but not in anger or
in battle.
21 "And in his place [a]shall arise a vile
person, to whom they will not give the
*honor of royalty; but he shall come
in peaceably, and seize the kingdom
by intrigue.
22 "With the [1]force of a [a]flood they
shall be swept away from before him
and be broken, [b]and also the prince of
the covenant.
23 "And after the league *is made* with
him [a]he shall act deceitfully, for he
shall come up and become strong with
a small *number of* people.
24 "He shall enter peaceably, even into
the richest places of the province; and

11:5 The South refers to Egypt. Six of her kings are mentioned (vv. 5, 6, 7–9, 10–12, 14–17, 25–28).
11:6 The North is Syria. Seven of her kings are mentioned (vv. 5, 6, 7–9, 10–19, 20, 21–45).
11:7 A branch is the Egyptian Pharaoh, Ptolemy III, who ruled from 246 to 221 B.C.
11:16 The Glorious Land is Israel, which Antiochus the Great conquered in 199 B.C.
11:21 A vile person is Antiochus IV, the Syrian king who ruled from 175 to 163 B.C. He gave himself the name Epiphanes, "God Is Manifest," but was called Epimanes ("Madman") by his enemies. The exact nature of his gaining control **by intrigue** is uncertain.
11:22 The prince of the covenant was the Jewish high priest, Onias III. See Editorial Note on 9:26, 27.

he shall do *what* his fathers have not
done, nor his forefathers: he shall disperse among them the plunder, [1]spoil,
and riches; and he shall devise his
plans against the strongholds, but *only*
for a time.
25 "He shall stir up his power and his
courage against the king of the South
with a great army. And the king of the
South shall be stirred up to battle with
a very great and mighty army; but he
shall not stand, for they shall devise
plans against him.
26 "Yes, those who eat of the portion
of his delicacies shall destroy him; his
army shall [1]be swept away, and many
shall fall down slain.
27 "Both these kings' hearts *shall be*
bent on evil, and they shall speak lies
at the same table; but it shall not prosper, for the end *will* still *be* at the
[a]appointed time.
28 "While returning to his land with
great riches, his heart shall be *moved*
against the holy covenant; so he shall
do *damage* and return to his own land.

The Northern King's Blasphemies

29 "At the appointed time he shall return and go toward the south; but it
shall not be like the former or the latter.
30 [a]"For ships from [1]Cyprus shall
come against him; therefore he shall
be grieved, and return in rage against
the holy covenant, and do *damage*. So
he shall return and show regard for
those who forsake the holy covenant.
31 "And [1]forces shall be mustered by
him, [a]and they shall defile the sanctuary fortress; then they shall take away
the daily *sacrifices*, and place *there* the
abomination of desolation.
32 "Those who do wickedly against
the covenant he shall [1]corrupt with
flattery; but the people who know their
God shall be strong, and carry out
great exploits.
33 "And those of the people who understand shall instruct many; yet *for
many* days they shall fall by sword and
flame, by captivity and plundering.
34 "Now when they fall, they shall be
aided with a little help; but many shall
join with them by [1]intrigue.
35 "And *some* of those of *understanding shall fall, [a]to refine them, purify
them, and make *them* white, *until* the
time of the end; because *it is* still for
the appointed time.
36 "Then the king shall do according
to his own will: he shall [a]exalt and
magnify himself above every god, shall
speak blasphemies against the God of
gods, and shall prosper till the wrath
has been accomplished; for what has
been determined shall be done.
37 "He shall regard neither the [1]God
of his fathers nor the desire of women,
[a]nor regard any god; for he shall exalt
himself above *them* all.
38 "But in their place he shall honor
a god of fortresses; and a god which
his fathers did not know he shall honor
with gold and silver, with precious
stones and pleasant things.
39 "Thus he shall act against the
strongest fortresses with a foreign god,
which he shall acknowledge, *and* advance *its* glory; and he shall cause
them to rule over many, and divide the
land for [1]gain.

The Northern King's Conquests

40 "At the [a]time of the end the king
of the South shall attack him; and the
king of the North shall come against
him [b]like a whirlwind, with chariots,
[c]horsemen, and with many ships; and
he shall enter the countries, overwhelm *them*, and pass through.
41 "He shall also enter the Glorious
Land, and many *countries* shall be
overthrown; but these shall escape
from his hand: [a]Edom, Moab, and the
[1]prominent people of Ammon.
42 "He shall stretch out his hand
against the countries, and the land of
[a]Egypt shall not escape.
43 "He shall have power over the treasures of gold and silver, and over all
the precious things of Egypt; also the
Libyans and Ethiopians *shall follow*
[a]at his heels.
44 "But news from the east and the
north shall trouble him; therefore he

24 [1]*booty*
26 [1]Or *overflow*
27 [a]Dan. 8:19; Hab. 2:3
30 [a]Gen. 10:4; Num. 24:24; Is. 23:1, 12; Jer. 2:10 [1]Heb. *Kittim*, western lands, especially Cyprus
31 [a]Dan. 8:11–13; 12:11 [1]Lit. *arms*
32 [1]*pollute*
34 [1]Or *slipperiness, flattery*
35 [a][Deut. 8:16; Prov. 17:3]; Dan. 12:10; Zech. 13:9; Mal. 3:2, 3 *See WW at Jer. 3:15.
36 [a]Dan. 7:8, 25
37 [a]Is. 14:13; 2 Thess. 2:4 [1]Or *gods*
39 [1]*profit*
40 [a]Dan. 11:27, 35; 12:4, 9 [b]Is. 21:1 [c]Ezek. 38:4; Rev. 9:16
41 [a]Is. 11:14 [1]Lit. *chief of the sons of Ammon*
42 [a]Joel 3:19
43 [a]Ex. 11:8

11:29–39 Antiochus's invasion against Jerusalem included regulations against circumcision, Sabbath observance, and dietary practices. See Editorial Note on 7:25.

11:30 Ships from Cyprus were a delegation from Rome.

11:31 The abomination of desolation was the erection of the altar of Zeus over the altar of burnt offerings in the temple. See Editorial Note on 9:26, 27.

11:36–45 The king shall do according to his own will: In dispensational interpretation, the king is the head of the revised Roman Empire, the "little horn" of ch. 7, the Antichrist. This passage predicts his end, when no one will help him, and he will be destroyed by Christ. Thus the end of the governments and rulers of this world is depicted.

CLASSICAL INTERPRETATION: In this context classical interpreters see this in reference to Antiochus Epiphanes, archetype of the Antichrist, who is seen as being particularly described in vv. 40–45.

shall go out with great fury to destroy
and annihilate many.
45 "And he shall plant the tents of his
palace between the seas and [a]the glorious holy mountain; [b]yet he shall come
to his end, and no one will help him.

Prophecy of the End Time

12 "At that time Michael shall
stand up,
The great prince who stands
watch over the sons of your
people;
[a]And there shall be a time of
trouble,
Such as never was since there
was a nation,
Even to that time.
And at that time your people
[b]shall be delivered,
Every one who is found [c]written
in the book.
2 And many of those who sleep in
the dust of the earth shall
awake,
[a]Some to everlasting life,
Some to shame [b]*and* everlasting
[1]contempt.
3 Those who are wise shall
[a]shine
Like the brightness of the
firmament,
[b]And those who turn many to
righteousness
[c]Like the stars *forever and *ever.

4 "But you, Daniel, [a]shut up the
words, and seal the book until the time
of the end; many shall [b]run to and

45 [a]Ps. 48:2 [b]Rev. 19:20

CHAPTER 12

1 [a]Jer. 30:7 [b]Rom. 11:26 [c]Ex. 32:32
2 [a][John 5:28, 29] [b][Is. 66:24] [1]Lit. *abhorrence*
3 [a]Matt. 13:43 [b][James 5:19, 20] [c]1 Cor. 15:41 *See WW at Ps. 136:1. • See WW at Mic. 4:5.
4 [a]Rev. 22:10 [b]Amos 8:12
5 [a]Dan. 10:4
6 [a]Ezek. 9:2 [b]Dan. 8:13; 12:8
7 [a]Deut. 32:40 [b]Dan. 4:34 [c]Dan. 7:25 [d]Luke 21:24 [e]Dan. 8:24 *See WW at Num. 9:2.
10 [a]Zech. 13:9 [b]Is. 32:6, 7 [c]John 7:17; 8:47 *See WW at Zech. 13:9. • See WW at Prov. 10:16.
13 [a]Rev. 14:13 [b]Ps. 1:5

fro, and knowledge shall increase."
5 Then I, Daniel, looked; and there
stood two others, one on this riverbank
and the other on that [a]riverbank.
6 And *one* said to the man clothed in
[a]linen, who *was* above the waters of
the river, [b]"How long shall the fulfillment of these wonders *be?*"
7 Then I heard the man clothed in
linen, who *was* above the waters of the
river, when he [a]held up his right hand
and his left hand to heaven, and swore
by Him [b]who lives forever, [c]that *it
shall be* for a *time, times, and half *a
time;* [d]and when the power of [e]the holy
people has been completely shattered,
all these *things* shall be finished.
8 Although I heard, I did not understand. Then I said, "My lord, what *shall
be* the end of these *things?*"
9 And he said, "Go *your way,* Daniel,
for the words *are* closed up and sealed
till the time of the end.
10 [a]"Many shall be purified, made
white, and *refined, [b]but the *wicked
shall do wickedly; and none of the
wicked shall understand, but [c]the wise
shall understand.
11 "And from the time *that* the daily
sacrifice is taken away, and the abomination of desolation is set up, *there
shall be* one thousand two hundred and
ninety days.
12 "Blessed *is* he who waits, and
comes to the one thousand three hundred and thirty-five days.
13 "But you, go *your way* till the end;
[a]for you shall rest, [b]and will arise to
your inheritance at the end of the
days."

12:1 A time of trouble: The last three and one-half years of Daniel's Seventieth Week (Matt. 24:21–28).

CLASSICAL INTERPRETATION: The classical view sees this **time of trouble** as a resumption of the events of Antiochus IV described in 11:36–45. But again, this school of thought suggests that an ultimate antitype may also be found in the events of the Book of Revelation, affirming the principle of multilevel prophetic fulfillment.

12:2 These two resurrections are further explained in Rev. 20:4–15. The first resurrection takes place before the Millennium and the second after the Millennium, just prior to the Great White Throne Judgment. Regarding the Millennium, see Kingdom Dynamics: Prophecy and the Scriptures.

12:4–9 Shut up the words, and seal the book: Many dispensational writers believe this time of the end refers to the fact that Daniel's vision of the Seventy Weeks was not understood until the nineteenth century A.D. Others feel this seems highly unlikely. The most obvious meaning seems to be that the latter events of the Book of Daniel will not have great relevance until later in history.

CLASSICAL INTERPRETATION: The classical prophetic writers view this time as being from the period of Antiochus IV onward.

12:10–13 Through all the various afflictions of history (vv. 11, 12), God's faithful are to keep themselves **purified, made white, and refined.** This is the closing message to the Book of Daniel.

TRUTH-IN-ACTION through DANIEL

Letting the LIFE of the Holy Spirit Bring Faith's Works Alive in You!

Truth Daniel Teaches	Text	**Action** Daniel Invites
1 Steps to Knowing God We must know that God will judge and that everyone will give an account to God for his/her conduct.	5:22–24	**Understand** that God judges as idolatry and blasphemy the arrogance of all who refuse to honor Him.
	5:25–28	**Recognize** that God measures, judges, or rewards us according to our conduct.
2 Guidelines for Growing in Godliness Godly living requires that we exhibit faith during times of adversity and want, as well as during times of prosperity and peace. Compromising our faith when threatened with persecution forfeits the most powerful opportunities for God to manifest His glory.	1:8–16	**Stand fast** for your righteous standards, despite pressure to sin. **Believe** that God will give you a means of escape. **Trust** that He will show you favor and give you wisdom through "creative alternatives."
	3:12	**Reject compromise** of your godly convictions, and **refuse** to "run with the multitude" to do evil and worship false gods.
	6:4–9	**Live in such a way** that no charge (except your commitment to your faith) can be found against you.
	6:10–16	**Continue to practice righteousness** even when it may be socially frowned upon or politically prohibited.
	6:21, 22	**Maintain** a clear conscience by living a blameless life.
3 Steps to Dynamic Devotion The individual devoted to God affirms that the Lord is sovereign and seeks to glorify His name.	2:20–23	**Recognize** and **speak open praise** to God for His sovereignty over all circumstances, even those strongly adverse to you. **Believe** that He will equip you to prevail in adversity.
	9:4–19	**Intercede** before God, identifying with the sins of those for whom you pray. **Base** all petitions on the desire to **glorify** God's name.
4 Keys to Wise Living Wisdom is necessary to achieving one's full spiritual potential. The spiritually wise man knows when and when not to speak of things he has seen and heard and knows when and when not to pursue certain spiritual experiences.	7:28	**Be wise** and **understand** that certain of God's secrets and visions are not to be shared but to be kept in your heart. **Be assured** that if you share God's secrets unwisely, He may not entrust them to you again.
	8:27; 10:8, 9, 15–17	**Understand** that experiencing the spiritual reality of visions and other divine encounters may have physiological consequences. Pursue them neither frivolously nor lightly.

Truth Daniel Teaches	Text	**Action** Daniel Invites
5 Key Lessons in Faith Daniel and his friends provide the model for a faithful testimony under the threat of torture and death. Although relatively few believers are required to face this ultimate test, those who do are consistently given the highest honor in the heavenly rolls (see Heb. 11:33, 34).	2:14	**Trust** God to give you wise and tactful words. When speaking to antagonists, **seek to speak** words that are entreating and not full of threats.
	2:17, 18	When facing threatening circumstances, **turn quickly** to the Lord for help.
	2:27, 28	**Bear testimony** that God enables you to overcome otherwise impossible circumstances. **Believe** that God is still in the miracle-working business.
	3:16–18	**Believe** that God is able to deliver you from the most difficult circumstances. **Be willing to endure** death rather than deny your faith in God's power to deliver you.

The Book of HOSEA

Author: Hosea
Date: About 750 B.C.
Theme: Return to God
Key Words: Sin, Judgment, Love

Author Hosea, whose name means "Salvation" or "Deliverance," was chosen by God to live out his message to his people by marrying a woman who would be unfaithful to him. His sensitivity toward the sinful condition of his countrymen and his sensitivity toward the loving heart of God fitted him for this difficult ministry.

Background and Date Hosea gives the historical setting for his ministry by naming the kings of the southern kingdom of Judah (Uzziah, Jotham, Ahaz, and Hezekiah) and the king of the northern kingdom of Israel (Jeroboam II) who ruled during the period of his prophecy (1:1). This sets the dates from 755 B.C. to 715 B.C. Though all the gauges of outward success seemed positive for Israel, underneath disaster was lurking. The people of this period enjoyed peace, plenty, and prosperity; but anarchy was brewing, and it would bring the political collapse of the nation in a few short years. Hosea describes the characteristic social conditions of his day: corrupt leaders, unstable family life, widespread immorality, class hatred, and poverty. Though people continued a form of worship, idolatry was more and more accepted and the priests were failing to guide the people into ways of righteousness. In spite of the darkness of these days, Hosea holds out hope to inspire his people to turn back to God.

Content The Book of Hosea is about a people who needed to hear the love of God, a God who wanted to tell them, and the unique way God chose to demonstrate His love to His people. The people thought that love could be bought ("Ephraim has hired lovers," 8:9), that love was the pursuit of self-gratification ("I will go after my lovers who give *me*," 2:5), and that loving unworthy objects could bring positive benefits ("They became an abomination like the thing they loved," 9:10). God wanted Israel to know His love, which reached out for unlikely and unworthy objects ("When Israel *was* a child, I loved him," 11:1), which guided with gentle discipline ("bands of love," 11:4), and which persisted in spite of the peoples' running and resisting ("How can I give you up?" 11:8).

The problem was how to get this message of God's love to a people not inclined to listen, and not likely to understand if they did listen. God's solution was to let the prophet be his own sermon. Hosea would marry an impure woman ("wife of harlotry," 1:2), love her fully and have children by her (1:3), and go after her and bring her back when she strays ("Go again, love," 3:1). In sum, Hosea was to show by his own love for Gomer the kind of love God had for Israel.

Personal Application These lessons stand out clearly from the Book of Hosea:

1. If the people around us do not see the love of God in us, they will not find it anywhere. Like Hosea, all believers are called to

demonstrate to their neighbors by their attitudes and by their actions God's love in Christ to a world blindly groping for indications of authentic love.

2. We cannot separate our witness and our ministries from our lives. Hosea's strongest sermon was his relationship with his wife. The source of his power for preaching was his home and his family.
3. The only perfect example of love is found in God Himself. When God enters into marriage with His people, He recites vows that promise permanence, a right relationship, fair treatment, love unfailing, tenderness, security, and continuing self-revelation (2:19, 20). Our love must drink from this spring; then draw for others, offering to them, not the best form of human love we can give, but the pure, undiluted love of God in Christ.

Christ Revealed The New Testament writers draw upon Hosea for teaching about the life and ministry of Christ. Matthew sees in 11:1 a prophecy that was fulfilled when Jesus as a baby was literally taken into and brought out of Egypt, parallel to Israel's long stay in Egypt and the Exodus (Matt. 2:15). The writer of Hebrews finds in Jesus the One who enables believers to offer acceptable sacrifices of praise by which we become recipients of God's merciful forgiveness (14:2; Heb. 13:15). For Peter, Jesus provides the basis by which those who were outside the family of God are now admitted to a relationship with Him (1:6, 9; 1 Pet. 2:10). To Paul, Jesus fulfills Hosea's promise that One would break the power of death and the grave, and bring resurrection victory (13:14; 1 Cor. 15:55). Paul's teaching on Christ as the Groom and the church as the bride corresponds to the marriage ceremony and vows whereby God enters into a permanent relationship with Israel (2:19, 20; Eph. 5:25–32).

Jesus also, in at least two of His sermons to the Pharisees, takes His text from Hosea. When questioned about His spending time in the homes of tax collectors and sinners, Jesus quotes Hosea to show that God desires not just empty words or heartless rituals, but genuine care and concern for people (6:6; Matt. 9:13). And, when the Pharisees accuse Jesus' disciples of Sabbath breaking, Jesus defends them with the same reminder that the heart of God places concern for human need above religious form (Matt. 12:7).

The Holy Spirit at Work The Book of Hosea teaches two outstanding lessons concerning the Holy Spirit: 1) It is important to depend on the presence of the Spirit, and 2) negative things happen when the Holy Spirit is missing from a life. Twice Hosea uses the phrase "the spirit of harlotry" (4:12; 5:4), and tells the consequences of being filled with an unholy spirit. Like Paul in Ephesians, Hosea connects such a spirit with wine, which enslaves the heart. This spirit of harlotry also causes people to stray into false ways and false worship in contrast to the Holy Spirit who guides us in true ways and true worship (4:11–13; Eph. 5:17–21). John records the words of Jesus concerning the ministry of the Holy Spirit who will witness to Christ; on the other hand, the spirit of harlotry keeps people from knowing God (5:4; John 15:26).

The love of Hosea for his wayward wife reminds us that the preeminent fruit of the Spirit is love (Gal. 5:22). "The love of God has been poured out in our hearts by the Holy Spirit who was given to us" (Rom. 5:5).

Outline of Hosea

I. Hosea and Gomer 1:1—3:5
- A. Hosea's marriage to Gomer 1:1–9
  - 1. The setting 1:1
  - 2. The marriage 1:2, 3
  - 3. The children 1:3–9
- B. Yahweh's marriage to Israel 1:10—2:23
  - 1. Israel as God's people 1:10—2:1
  - 2. Israel's unfaithfulness 2:2–8
  - 3. Israel's punishment for unfaithfulness 2:9–13
  - 4. God's love for Israel 2:14–23
- C. Hosea's taking back of Gomer 3:1–5
  - 1. Gomer bought out of slavery 3:1–3
  - 2. Israel's return to God 3:4, 5

II. Yahweh and Israel 4:1—14:9
- A. Sin and judgment 4:1—10:15
  - 1. Israel's sinful state 4:1–19
  - 2. Announcement of judgment 5:1—6:11
  - 3. Israel's sins listed 7:1—8:14
  - 4. Forms of judgment specified 9:1—10:15
- B. Love and restoration 11:1—14:9
  - 1. God's father love for Israel 11:1–12
  - 2. God in Israel's history 12:1—13:6
  - 3. God in Israel's future 13:7–16
  - 4. God's promise of restoration 14:1–9

THE word of the LORD that came to
Hosea the son of Beeri, in the days
of [a]Uzziah, [b]Jotham, [c]Ahaz, *and* [d]Hez-
ekiah, kings of Judah, and in the days
of [e]Jeroboam the son of Joash, king
of Israel.

The Family of Hosea

[2] 2 When the LORD began to speak by
Hosea, the LORD said to Hosea:

[a]"Go, take yourself a wife of
harlotry
And children of harlotry,
For [b]the land has committed great
[1]harlotry
By departing from the LORD."

3 So he went and took Gomer the
daughter of Diblaim, and she conceived and bore him a son.
4 Then the LORD said to him:

"Call his name Jezreel,
For in a little *while*
[a]I will avenge the *bloodshed of
Jezreel on the house of Jehu,
[b]And bring an end to the kingdom
of the house of Israel.
5 [a]It shall come to pass in that day
That I will break the bow of Israel
in the Valley of Jezreel."

6 And she conceived again and bore
a daughter. Then *God* said to him:

"Call her name [1]Lo-Ruhamah,
[a]For I will no longer have mercy
on the house of Israel,
[2]But I will utterly take them away.
7 [a]Yet I will have mercy on the
house of Judah,
Will save them by the LORD their
God,
And [b]will not save them by bow,
Nor by sword or battle,
By horses or horsemen."

CHAPTER 1

1 [a]Amos 1:1 [b]2 Chr. 27 [c]2 Chr. 28 [d]2 Chr. 29:1—32:33 [e]2 Kin. 13:13; 14:23–29
2 [a]Hos. 3:1 [b]Jer. 2:13 [1]Spiritual adultery
4 [a]2 Kin. 10:11 [b]2 Kin. 15:8–10; 17:6, 23; 18:11 *See WW at Lev. 17:11.
5 [a]2 Kin. 15:29
6 [a]2 Kin. 17:6 [1]Lit. *No-Mercy* [2]Or *That I may forgive them at all*
7 [a]2 Kin. 19:29–35 [b][Zech. 4:6]

1:1 Uzziah, Jotham, Ahaz, and Hezekiah reigned in the southern kingdom and Jeroboam II in the northern kingdom (which was Hosea's homeland), indicating that Hosea's ministry covered about 40 years (755–715 B.C.).
1:2, 3 See section 2 of Truth-In-Action at the end of Hos.
1:2 Wife of harlotry has been interpreted three ways: 1) as an allegory showing God's relationship with Israel; 2) Gomer fell into an immoral life after Hosea married her; 3) Hosea knew that Gomer was a prostitute when he married *her. The simple direct reading of* the text commends the third view as correct.

The reason for God's call to His prophet is quickly given: **for the land has committed great harlotry.** From the very beginning the connection between Hosea's experience and that of the Lord is seen, so setting the major theme of the book.
1:4 Jezreel means "God Scatters" or "God Sows." Jezreel was the name of the place where Jehu had killed the 70 sons of Ahab (2 Kin. 10:11). As Jehu brought an end to the line of Ahab, so now God will **bring an end to** the whole dynasty of Israel. By 722 B.C. the northern kingdom and its capital, Samaria, will fall.
1:5 Break the bow: Symbolic of Israel's military power. Hosea emphasizes his point here by playing on the similar sounds of the words **Israel** (Hebrew *yisra'el*) and **Jezreel** (Hebrew *yizre'el*).
1:6 Lo-Ruhamah, meaning "No Mercy," indicates a lifting of the Lord's compassion from the rebellious nation.
1:7 Judah, the southern kingdom, still maintains the true worship of the Lord. **Save them by the LORD:** In the reign of Hezekiah (v. 1), the angel of the Lord killed 185,000 Assyrians, thus postponing the fall of Jerusalem for almost 150 years (2 Kin. 19).

8 Now when she had weaned Lo-Ruhamah, she conceived and bore a son.
9 Then *God* said:

"Call his name [1]Lo-Ammi,
For you *are* not My people,
And I will not be your *God.*

The Restoration of Israel

10 "Yet [a]the number of the children of Israel
Shall be as the sand of the sea,
Which cannot be measured or numbered.
[b]And it shall come to pass
In the place where it was said to them,
'You *are* [1]not My [c]people,'*
There it shall be said to them,
'*You are* [d]sons of the living God.'
11 [a]Then the children of Judah and the children of Israel
Shall be gathered together,
And appoint for themselves one head;
And they shall come up out of the land,
For great *will be* the day of Jezreel!

2 Say to your brethren, [1]'My people,'
And to your sisters, [2]'Mercy *is* shown.'

God's Unfaithful People

2 "Bring[1] charges against your mother, [2]bring charges;
For [a]she *is* not My wife, nor *am* I her Husband!
Let her put away her [b]harlotries from her sight,
And her adulteries from between her breasts;
3 Lest [a]I strip her naked
And expose her, as in the day she was [b]born,
And make her like a wilderness,
And set her like a dry land,
And slay her with [c]thirst.

9 [1]Lit. *Not-My-People*
10 [a]Gen. 22:17; 32:12; Jer. 33:22 [b]1 Pet. 2:10 [c]Rom. 9:26 [d]Is. 63:16; 64:8; [John 1:12] [1]Heb. *lo-ammi,* v. 9 *See WW at Ruth 1:16.
11 [a]Is. 11:11–13; Jer. 3:18; 50:4; [Ezek. 34:23; 37:15–28]

CHAPTER 2

1 [1]Heb. *Ammi,* Hos. 1:9, 10 [2]Heb. *Ru-hamah,* Hos. 1:6
2 [a]Is. 50:1 [b]Ezek. 16:25 [1]Or *Contend with* [2]Or *contend*
3 [a]Jer. 13:22, 26; Ezek. 16:37–39 [b]Ezek. 16:4–7, 22 [c]Jer. 14:3; Amos 8:11–13
4 [a]John 8:41
5 [a]Ezek. 23:5; Hos. 2:8, 12
6 [a]Job 19:8; Lam. 3:7, 9 [1]Lit. *wall up her wall*
7 [a]Luke 15:17, 18 [b]Is. 54:5–8; Jer. 2:2; 3:1; Ezek. 16:8; 23:4 [1]Or *pursue*
8 [a]Is. 1:3; Ezek. 16:19

4 "I will not have mercy on her children,
For they *are* the [a]children of harlotry.
5 For their mother has played the harlot;
She who conceived them has behaved shamefully.
For she said, 'I will go after my lovers,
[a]Who give *me* my bread and my water,
My wool and my linen,
My oil and my drink.'

6 "Therefore, behold,
[a]I will hedge up your way with thorns,
And [1]wall her in,
So that she cannot find her paths.
7 She will [1]chase her lovers,
But not overtake them;
Yes, she will seek them, but not find *them.*
Then she will say,
[a]'I will go and return to my [b]first husband,
For then *it was* better for me than now.'
8 For she did not [a]know
That I gave her grain, new wine, and oil,
And multiplied her silver and gold—
Which they prepared for **Baal.**

WORD WEALTH

2:8 Baal, *ba'al* (*bah*-ahl); Strong's #1167: *Ba'al,* literally lord or master; also, possessor, owner, obtainer, and husband. The Israelites sometimes became contaminated with the worship of a false deity of the Canaanites named Baal. *Ba'al* was also the regular word for "husband" or "master," and was used throughout the OT for human husbands or property-owning men (see Ex. 21:22, 28; 22:8; Deut. 22:22; Judg. 9:6, 7, 18; Prov. 31:11; Is. 1:3). Because of its use for Canaanite deities and because it implied ownership rather than relationship, God disassociated Himself from use of the term *ba'al,* asking rather to be called *'ishi,* "My Husband" (Hos. 2:16, 17).

1:9 Lo-Ammi, meaning "Not My People," indicates the end of the relationship. Note the progression in the three names: "Jezreel," active judgment; "Lo-Ruhamah," passive tolerance; "Lo-Ammi," no connection.
1:11 Though some reunification of the two kingdoms will occur after the Exile, their coming under **one head** will not be completely fulfilled until Messiah brings them together. **Jezreel,** used in 1:4, 5 to mean "God Scatters," now takes its positive meaning, "God Plants."
2:2 God calls on the individuals in the nation to seek justice, as children of a home broken by adultery. **She *is* not My wife** because her adulterous actions have broken the relationship.
2:4 Her children continue in the sins of their mother.
2:6 God's mercy is displayed as He uses all means to keep Israel from running from Him.
2:7 Sin will not bring the satisfaction Israel is seeking.

9 "Therefore I will return and take
away
My grain in its time
And My new wine in its season,
And will take back My wool and
My linen,
Given to cover her nakedness.
10 Now [a]I will uncover her lewdness
in the sight of her lovers,
And no one shall deliver her from
My hand.
11 [a]I will also cause all her mirth to
cease,
Her feast days,
Her New Moons,
Her Sabbaths—
All her appointed feasts.

12 "And I will destroy her vines and
her fig trees,
Of which she has said,
'These *are* my wages that my
lovers have given me.'
So I will make them a forest,
And the beasts of the field shall
eat them.
13 I will punish her
For the days of the Baals to which
she burned incense.
She decked herself with her
earrings and jewelry,
And went after her lovers;
But Me she forgot," says the
LORD.

God's Mercy on His People

14 "Therefore, behold, I will allure
her,
Will bring her into the wilderness,
And speak [1]comfort to her.
15 I will give her her vineyards from
there,
And [a]the Valley of Achor as a
door of **hope;**
She shall sing there,
As in [b]the days of her youth,
[c]As in the day when she came up
from the land of Egypt.

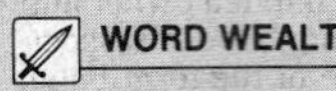

WORD WEALTH

2:15 hope, *tiqvah* (teek-*vah*); Strong's #8615: Hope; expectation; something yearned for and anticipated eagerly; something for which one waits. *Tiqvah* comes from the verb *qavah,* meaning "to wait for" or "to look hopefully" in a particular direction. Its original meaning was "to stretch like a rope." *Tiqvah* occurs 33 times. In Josh. 2:18, 21, it is translated "line" or "cord"; Rahab was instructed to tie a scarlet *tiqvah* (cord or rope) in her window as her hope for rescue. Yahweh Himself is the hope of the godly (Ps. 71:5). Here God's blessing on His land will transform the Valley of Achor ("trouble") into the "door of hope."

10 [a]Ezek. 16:37
11 [a]Jer. 7:34; 16:9; Hos. 3:4; Amos 5:21; 8:10
14 [1]Lit. *to her heart*
15 [a]Josh. 7:26 [b]Jer. 2:1–3; Ezek. 16:8–14 [c]Ex. 15:1

16 "And it shall be, in that day,"
Says the LORD,
"*That* you will call Me [1]'My
Husband,'
And no longer call Me [2]'My
Master,'
17 For [a]I will take from her mouth
the names of the Baals,
And they shall be remembered by
their name no more.

KINGDOM DYNAMICS

2:16, 17, 19, 20 Forgiveness Can Save and Transform a Marriage, FAMILY ORDER. Through the tragic story of Hosea and Gomer, God reveals both the depth and power 1) of His love for Israel and 2) of the marriage bond. God describes His suffering the pain and humiliation of Israel's unfaithfulness; and in obedience to God, Hosea suffers the same pain and humiliation of his own wife's unfaithfulness. But God shows him how the marriage can be saved: through suffering and forgiveness.

This is one of the most profound revelations about marriage found anywhere in Scripture. Successful marriage is not a business of perfect people living perfectly by perfect principles. Rather, marriage is a state in which very imperfect people often hurt and humiliate one another, yet find the grace to extend forgiveness to one another, and so allow the redemptive power of God to transform their marriage.

(Col. 3:18, 19, 23, 24/1 Cor. 7:3, 4) L.C.

18 In that day I will make a
[a]covenant for them

16 [1]Heb. *Ishi* [2]Heb. *Baali*
17 [a]Ex. 23:13; Josh. 23:7; Ps. 16:4
18 [a]Job 5:23; Is. 11:6–9; Ezek. 34:25

2:10 Lewdness: Immodesty or shamelessness.
2:11 God has established the **feast days** so the people *could remember His* blessings to them. Without this element, they had lost their true meaning and so will be brought to an end.
2:14 The wilderness is not here a place of punishment, but a place of privacy.
2:15 Achor means "Trouble," and was the scene of Achan's sin (Josh. 7:26). God redeems situations, bringing present **hope** in the place of previous trouble.
2:16 My Master interprets the Hebrew word *Baali,* implying "owner" or "possessor," while **my husband** expresses the affection of a family relationship.
2:17 The names of the Baals were used in place names that tied the worship of the Baals with the land. Because it was materialistic, sensual, magical, and lacked ethical content, all traces of Baal worship must be removed.

With the beasts of the field,
With the birds of the air,
And *with* the creeping things of
the ground.
Bow and sword of battle
[b]I will shatter from the earth,
To make them [c]lie down safely.

19 "I will betroth you to Me forever;
Yes, I will betroth you to Me
In righteousness and justice,
In lovingkindness and mercy;
20 I will betroth you to Me in
*faithfulness,
And [a]you shall know the LORD.

21 "It shall come to pass in that day
That [a]I will answer," says the
LORD;
"I will answer the heavens,
And they shall answer the earth.
22 The earth shall answer
With grain,
With new wine,
And with oil;
They shall answer [1]Jezreel.
23 Then [a]I will sow her for Myself
in the earth,
[b]And I will **have mercy** on *her who*
had [1]not obtained mercy;
Then [c]I will say to *those who*
were [2]not My people,
'You *are* [3]My people!'
And they shall say, '*You are* my
God!' "

18 [b]Is. 2:4; Ezek. 39:1–10 [c]Lev. 26:5; Is. 32:18; Jer. 23:6; Ezek. 34:25
20 [a][Jer. 31:33, 34]; Hos. 6:6; 13:4; [John 17:3] *See WW at Prov. 28:20.
21 [a]Is. 55:10; Zech. 8:12; [Mal. 3:10, 11]
22 [1]Lit. *God Will Sow*
23 [a]Jer. 31:27; Amos 9:15 [b]Hos. 1:6 [c]Hos. 1:10; Zech. 13:9; Rom. 9:25, 26; [Eph. 2:11–22]; 1 Pet. 2:10 [1]Heb. *lo-ruhamah* [2]Heb. *lo-ammi* [3]Heb. *ammi*

CHAPTER 3

1 [a]Jer. 3:20 [1]Lit. *friend* or *husband* *See WW at Prov. 17:17.
3 [a]Deut. 21:13

WORD WEALTH

2:23 have mercy, *racham* (rah-*chahm*): Strong's #7355: To feel or show compassion, to love deeply, to show pity or mercy; to tenderly regard someone; to tenderly love (especially as parents love their infant child). *Racham* is the origin of the Hebrew word for "womb" (*rechem*). In Is. 49:15, God asks, "Can a woman forget her nursing child, and not have compassion on [*racham*] the son of her womb [*rechem*]?" Fathers, too, can show this feeling for their offspring (Ps. 103:13). God wants parents to tenderly love their offspring and to show compassion toward all who are weak and defenseless. God sets the example by His constant compassion for the helpless and undeserving (Is. 54:8, 10).

Israel Will Return to God

3 Then the LORD said to me, "Go 2
again, love a woman *who is* loved
by a [a]lover[1]* and is committing adultery, just like the love of the LORD for
the children of Israel, who look to other
gods and love *the* raisin cakes *of the*
pagans."
2 So I bought her for myself for fifteen *shekels* of silver, and one and one-
half homers of barley.
3 And I said to her, "You shall
[a]stay with me many days; you shall not
play the harlot, nor shall you have a
man—so, too, *will* I *be* toward you."

2:19, 20 God renews His covenant with Israel in the form of wedding vows. He promises a relationship characterized by permanence, right standards, fair treatment, love unfailing, tenderness, security, and continuing self-revelation.
2:21–23 Heaven and earth conspire under God to bring fruitfulness to the people.
3:1–5 See section 2 of Truth-In-Action at the end of Hos.
3:1 The Lord renews the call of Hosea to love his wife who has returned to her immoral life-style.
3:2 Ex. 21:32 gives the price of a slave as 30 shekels, so Hosea pays part of the price in silver and part in goods. **Fifteen *shekels* of silver** was about 4/10 of an ounce. **One and one-half homers** is about 5 bushels.
3:3 The return to the home involves a period of discipline.

ISRAEL'S APOSTASY AND HOSEA'S MARRIAGE (3:1)

The stages of Israel's relationship with God are depicted in the prophecies of Jeremiah and Ezekiel, as well as in Hosea's relationship with Gomer.

Stage	Israel's Prophets	Hosea's Marriage
Betrothal	Jeremiah 2:2	Hosea 1:2
Marriage	Ezekiel 16:8–14	Hosea 1:3
Adultery	Jeremiah 5:7; Ezekiel 16:15–34	Hosea 3:1
Estrangement	Jeremiah 3:8–10; Ezekiel 16:35–52	Hosea 3:3, 4
Restoration	Ezekiel 16:53–63	Hosea 3:5

4 For the children of Israel shall abide
many days [a]without king or prince,
without sacrifice or *sacred* pillar, without [b]ephod* or [c]teraphim.
5 Afterward the children of Israel
shall return and [a]seek the LORD their
God and [b]David their king. They shall
fear the LORD and His goodness in the
[c]latter days.

> **WORD WEALTH**
>
> **3:5 fear,** *pachad* (pah-*chad*); Strong's #6342: To be startled, to tremble; to stand in awe; to revere, or fear; be amazed. *Pachad* concerns a person's reaction to something sudden and startling to the point of trembling. The verb appears 24 times. The noun *pachad,* which refers to something dreadful and awe-producing, occurs more than 40 times. Here Israel will tremble because of God's startling, sudden, amazing goodness showered upon them in the latter days! This verse shows how positive the Hebrew concept of fear, trembling, and reverence can be, as does Prov. 28:14, "Happy is the man who is always reverent [*pachad*]."

God's Charge Against Israel

4 Hear the *word of the LORD,
You children of Israel,
For the LORD *brings* a [a]charge[1]
against the inhabitants of the
land:

"There is no truth or *mercy
Or [b]knowledge of God in the
land.
2 *By* swearing and lying,
Killing and stealing and
committing adultery,
They break all restraint,
With bloodshed [1]upon blood-
shed.
3 Therefore [a]the land will *mourn;
And [b]everyone who dwells there
will waste away
With the beasts of the field
And the birds of the air;
Even the fish of the sea will be
taken away.

4 "Now let no man contend, or
rebuke another;
For your people *are* like those
[a]who contend with the priest.
5 Therefore you shall stumble
[a]in the day;
The prophet also shall stumble
with you in the night;
And I will destroy your mother.
6 [a]My people are destroyed for lack 4
of *knowledge.
Because you have rejected
knowledge,
I also will reject you from being
priest for Me;
[b]Because you have forgotten the
law of your God,
I also will forget your children.

7 "The more they increased,
The more they sinned against
Me;
[a]I[1] will change [2]their glory into
shame.
8 They eat up the sin of My people;
They set their [1]heart on their
iniquity.
9 And it shall be: [a]like people, like
*priest.
So I will punish them for their
ways,
And [1]reward them for their
deeds.
10 For [a]they shall eat, but not have
enough;
They shall commit harlotry, but
not increase;
Because they have ceased
obeying the LORD.

4 [a]Hos. 10:3 [b]Ex. 28:4–12; 1 Sam. 23:9–12 [c]Gen. 31:19, 34; Judg. 17:5; 18:14, 17; [1 Sam. 15:23] *See WW at Ex. 35:27.
5 [a]Jer. 50:4 [b]Jer. 30:9; Ezek. 34:24 [c][Is. 2:2, 3]; Jer. 31:9

CHAPTER 4

1 [a]Is. 1:18; Hos. 12:2; Mic. 6:2 [b]Jer. 4:22 [1]A legal complaint *See WW at Deut. 1:1. • See WW at Mic. 6:8.
2 [1]Lit. *touching*
3 [a]Is. 24:4; 33:9; Jer. 4:28; 12:4; Amos 5:16; 8:8 [b]Zeph. 1:3 *See WW at Joel 1:9.
4 [a]Deut. 17:12
5 [a]Jer. 15:8; Hos. 2:2, 5
6 [a]Is. 5:13 [b]Ezek. 22:26 *See WW at Mal. 2:7.
7 [a]1 Sam. 2:30; Mal. 2:9 [1]So with MT, LXX, Vg.; scribal tradition, Syr., Tg. *They will change* [2]So with MT, LXX, Syr., Tg., Vg.; scribal tradition *My glory*
8 [1]Desires
9 [a]Is. 24:2; Jer. 5:30, 31; 2 Tim. 4:3, 4 [1]*repay* *See WW at Lev. 5:6.
10 [a]Lev. 26:26; Is. 65:13; Mic. 6:14; Hag. 1:6

3:4 During the Exile, Israel would be **without** all the structures and resources they had depended on for help and guidance. The list of things Israel would be without for guidance was a mixture of essentials ordained of God for Israel's worship and practices forbidden by God, indicating how far the people had moved toward a syncretistic form of religion.

For example, the **ephod** was the part of the high priest's clothing to which the Urim and Thummim were attached, but the **teraphim** were household gods, probably images of ancestors.

3:5 David is here the messianic king. To **fear . . . His goodness** is to marvel at the gracious dealings of God with a people who had rebelled against Him.

4:1, 2 Two kinds of sins characterized the people: 1) they lacked the basic ethical elements necessary for society; 2) they broke the basic commandments.

4:1 Knowledge of God refers to intimate fellowship with Him rather than to an understanding of who He is. They have rejected relationship with God, and this will eventually destroy them (v. 6).

4:2 The commandments that govern relationships with one's fellowman are constantly being broken.

4:3 Man's sin has a detrimental effect on his environment.

4:4 To **contend with the priest** is to reject God-ordained authority.

4:5 Prophet here represents the false prophets. **Mother** is the nation.

4:6–10 This section addresses the particular sins of the priests.

4:6, 7 See section 4 of Truth-In-Action at the end of Hos.

4:7 Glory into shame: Their office, which was intended as one of high honor, has been used in disgraceful ways.

4:8 Sin: Sin-offering.

The Idolatry of Israel

11 "Harlotry, wine, and new wine
[a]enslave the heart.
12 My people ask counsel from their
[a]wooden *idols,*
And their [1]staff informs them.
For [b]the spirit of harlotry has
caused *them* to stray,
And they have played the harlot
against their God.
13 [a]They offer sacrifices on the
mountaintops,
And burn incense on the hills,
Under oaks, poplars, and
terebinths,
Because their shade *is* good.
[b]Therefore your daughters commit
harlotry,
And your brides commit adultery.

4 14 "I will not punish your daughters
when they commit harlotry,
Nor your brides when they
commit adultery;
For *the men* themselves go apart
with harlots,
And offer sacrifices with a
[a]ritual harlot.
Therefore people *who* do not
understand will be trampled.

15 "Though you, Israel, play the
harlot,
Let not Judah offend.
[a]Do not come up to Gilgal,
Nor go up to [b]Beth[1] Aven,
[c]Nor swear an oath, *saying,* 'As the
LORD lives'—

16 "For Israel [a]is stubborn
Like a stubborn calf;
Now the LORD will let them
*forage
Like a lamb in [1]open country.

11 [a]Prov. 20:1; Is. 5:12; 28:7
12 [a]Jer. 2:27 [b]Is. 44:19, 20 [1]Diviner's rod
13 [a]Is. 1:29; 57:5, 7; Jer. 2:20; Ezek. 6:13; 20:28 [b]Amos 7:17; [Rom. 1:28–32]
14 [a]Deut. 23:18
15 [a]Hos. 9:15; 12:11 [b]1 Kin. 12:29; Josh. 7:2; Hos. 10:8 [c]Jer. 5:2; 44:26; Amos 8:14 [1]Lit. *House of Idolatry* or *Wickedness*
16 [a]Jer. 3:6; 7:24; 8:5; Zech. 7:11 [1]Lit. *a large place* *See WW at Is. 40:11.
17 [a]Matt. 15:14
18 [a]Mic. 3:11 [1]Or *has turned aside* [2]Lit. *shields* [3]Heb. difficult; a Jewish tradition *shamefully love, 'Give!'*
19 [a]Jer. 51:1 [b]Is. 1:29

CHAPTER 5

1 [a]Hos. 6:9 [1]Or *to you*
2 [a]Is. 29:15; Hos. 4:2; 6:9
3 [a]Amos 3:2; 5:12 [b]Hos. 4:17
4 [a]Hos. 4:12 [1]Or *Their deeds will not allow them to turn*
5 [a]Hos. 7:10
6 [a]Prov. 1:28; Is. 1:15; Jer. 11:11; Ezek. 8:18; Mic. 3:4; John 7:34

17 "Ephraim *is* joined to idols,
[a]Let him alone.
18 Their drink [1]is rebellion,
They commit harlotry
continually.
[a]Her [2]rulers [3]dearly love dishonor.
19 [a]The wind has wrapped her up in
its wings,
And [b]they shall be ashamed
because of their sacrifices.

Impending Judgment on Israel and Judah

5 "Hear this, O priests!
Take heed, O house of Israel!
Give ear, O house of the king!
For [1]yours *is* the judgment,
Because [a]you have been a snare
to Mizpah
And a net spread on Tabor.
2 The revolters are [a]deeply
involved in slaughter,
Though I rebuke them all.
3 [a]I know Ephraim,
And Israel is not hidden from Me;
For now, O Ephraim, [b]you
commit harlotry;
Israel is defiled.

4 "They[1] do not direct their deeds
Toward turning to their God,
For [a]the spirit of harlotry is in
their midst,
And they do not know the LORD.
5 The [a]pride of Israel testifies to his
face;
Therefore Israel and Ephraim
stumble in their iniquity;
Judah also stumbles with them.

6 "With their flocks and herds
[a]They shall go to seek the LORD,
But they will not find *Him;*
He has withdrawn Himself from
them.

4:11 What God wanted most from the people, **the heart,** has been stolen away by immorality and drunkenness.
4:12–14 Their idolatry led them into foolish practices, infected their spirit, and caused their families to follow them into sin.
4:12 Staff: Sticks were used in their attempt to find direction. See marginal note.
4:14 See section 4 of Truth-In-Action at the end of Hos.
4:14 People *who* do not understand will be trampled: Ruin is the sure end of those who reject relationship with God.
4:15 Judah can avoid Israel's fate if she will stay close to God. **Beth Aven** ("House of Iniquity") is used for Bethel ("House of God"). **Gilgal** and Bethel were places of idol worship.
4:16 A lamb in open country will get lost or fall prey to predators.
4:17 Ephraim is used throughout the rest of Hosea as a synonym for the northern kingdom of Israel.
4:18 An unusual word for **rulers** is used here. Normally it means "shield," the implication here being that those who should have protected their people have left them uncovered.
4:19 The enemy will come with strength and suddenness like a storm.
5:1 Mizpah was a site in Gilead on the east side of the Jordan River. **Tabor** is a dome-shaped mountain in the Valley of Jezreel on the west side of the Jordan. Both had become places of idolatrous worship.
5:2 The leaders of the land were guilty of **slaughter,** either many murders or abundance of idolatrous sacrifices.
5:5 Their **pride** witnessed against them and condemned them.
5:6 They take **flocks and herds** for sacrifices.

7 They have [a]dealt treacherously
with the LORD,
For they have begotten [1]pagan
children.
Now a New Moon shall devour
them and their heritage.

8 "Blow[a] the ram's horn in Gibeah,
The trumpet in Ramah!
[b]Cry aloud *at* [c]Beth Aven,
'*Look* behind you, O Benjamin!'
9 Ephraim shall be desolate in the
day of rebuke;
Among the tribes of Israel I make
known what is sure.

10 "The princes of Judah are like
those who [a]remove a landmark;
I will pour out My wrath on them
like water.
11 Ephraim is [a]oppressed *and*
broken in judgment,
Because he willingly walked by
[b]*human* precept.
12 Therefore I *will be* to Ephraim
like a moth,
And to the house of Judah
[a]like rottenness.

13 "When Ephraim saw his sickness,
And Judah *saw* his [a]wound,
Then Ephraim went [b]to Assyria
And sent to King Jareb;
Yet he cannot cure you,
Nor heal you of your wound.
14 For [a]I *will be* like a lion to
Ephraim,
And like a young lion to the house
of Judah.
[b]I, *even* I, will tear *them* and go
away;
I will take *them* away, and no one
shall rescue.
5 15 I will return again to My place
Till they [1]acknowledge their
offense.
Then they will **seek** My face;
In their affliction they will
earnestly seek Me."

7 [a]Is. 48:8; Jer. 3:20; Hos. 6:7 [1]Lit. *strange*
8 [a]Hos. 8:1; Joel 2:1 [b]Is. 10:30 [c]Josh. 7:2
10 [a]Deut. 19:14; 27:17
11 [a]Deut. 28:33 [b]Mic. 6:16
12 [a]Prov. 12:4
13 [a]Jer. 30:12–15 [b]2 Kin. 15:19; Hos. 7:11; 10:6
14 [a]Ps. 7:2; Lam. 3:10; Hos. 13:7, 8 [b]Ps. 50:22
15 [1]Lit. *become guilty* or *bear punishment*

WORD WEALTH

5:15 seek, *baqash* (bah-*kahsh*); Strong's #1245: To seek, to diligently look for, to search earnestly until the object of the search is located. *Baqash* can apply to seeking a person, a particular item, or a goal (such as seeking to destroy a city, 2 Sam. 20:19). *Baqash* occurs more than 210 times in the Bible. Peace is to be searched for earnestly (Ps. 34:14). The Lord's face, that is, His presence, must especially be sought (Ps. 27:8).

A Call to Repentance

6 Come,[a] and let us return to the 1
LORD;
For [b]He has torn, but [c]He will
heal us;
He has stricken, but He will
[1]bind us up.
2 [a]After two days He will revive us;
On the third day He will raise us
up,
That we may live in His sight.
3 [a]Let us know,
Let us pursue the knowledge of
the LORD.
His going forth is established
[b]as the morning;
[c]He will come to us [d]like the rain,
Like the latter *and* former rain to
the earth.

Impenitence of Israel and Judah

4 "O Ephraim, what shall I do to
you?
O Judah, what shall I do to you?
For your faithfulness is like a
morning cloud,
And like the early dew it goes
away.
5 Therefore I have hewn *them* by
the prophets,

CHAPTER 6

1 [a]Is. 1:18; Acts 10:43 [b]Deut. 32:39; Hos. 5:14 [c]Jer. 30:17; Hos. 14:4 [1]Bandage
2 [a]Luke 24:46; Acts 10:40; [1 Cor. 15:4]
3 [a]Is. 54:13 [b]2 Sam. 23:4 [c]Ps. 72:6; Joel 2:23 [d]Job 29:23

5:7 Dealt treacherously means literally that they have "clothed themselves," or acted under cover, so deceitfully. The monthly sacrifices, **new moon,** will be offered in vain.
5:8 Gibeah was 3 miles north of Jerusalem; **Ramah,** 5 miles north of Jerusalem. **Beth Aven:** See note on 4:15.
5:10 The leaders of **Judah** conspire to commit the most serious offenses, **like those who remove a landmark,** a practice strongly condemned in Deut. 19:14; 27:17.
5:11 The people suffer because they follow the way of other men in worshiping idols.
5:12 ***Moth** and **rottenness*** both work silently, surely, and from the inside to bring devastation.
5:13 Jareb means "Quarrelsome, Contentious," indicating that in their desperation, Israel sought help from one opposed to them.
5:15 See section 5 of Truth-In-Action at the end of Hos.
5:15 Having acted as a lion coming out to take his prey, now God will withdraw to His **place,** to heaven, and leave Israel to consider the consequences of their evil actions.
6:1–3 See section 1 of Truth-In-Action at the end of Hos.
6:1–3 An apparently repentant Israel returns to God, but their language betrays them. They still blame God for their trouble (**He has torn**); and they presume on His grace, implying that since He, not they, is the guilty one, He is obliged to restore them.
6:4 The spirit of this response of God toward His sinful people is reflected in Jesus' words in Matt. 23:37: "O Jerusalem, . . . How often I wanted to gather your children together, . . . but you were not willing." Israel's show of repentance was merely transitory, like a **cloud** or **dew.**
6:5 God had sent **the prophets** to shape the nation, but by rejecting them the people have called upon themselves the penalty that now must follow.

I have slain them by [a]the words
of My mouth;
And [1]your judgments *are like*
light *that* goes forth.
1 6 For I desire [a]mercy[1] and
[b]not sacrifice,
And the [c]knowledge* of God
more than burnt offerings.

7 "But like [1]men they transgressed
the covenant;
There they dealt treacherously
with Me.
8 [a]Gilead *is* a city of evildoers
And [1]defiled with blood.
9 As bands of robbers lie in wait
for a man,
So the company of [a]priests
[b]murder on the way to
Shechem;
Surely they commit [c]lewdness.
10 I have seen a horrible thing in the
house of Israel:
There *is* the [1]harlotry of Ephraim;
Israel is defiled.
11 Also, O Judah, a harvest is
appointed for you,
When I return the captives of My
people.

7

"When I would have healed Israel,
Then the iniquity of Ephraim was
uncovered,
And the wickedness of Sa-
maria.
For [a]they have committed fraud;
A thief comes in;
A band of robbers [1]takes spoil
outside.
2 They [1]do not consider in their
hearts
That [a]I remember all their
wickedness;
Now their own deeds have
surrounded them;
They are before My face.

5 [a][Jer. 23:29] [1]Or *the judgments on you*
6 [a]Matt. 9:13; 12:7 [b]Is. 1:12, 13; [Mic. 6:6–8] [c][John 17:3] [1]Or *faithfulness* or *loyalty* *See WW at Mal. 2:7.
7 [1]Or *Adam*
8 [a]Hos. 12:11 [1]Lit. *foot-tracked*
9 [a]Hos. 5:1 [b]Jer. 7:9, 10; Hos. 4:2 [c]Ezek. 22:9; 23:27; Hos. 2:10
10 [1]Spiritual adultery

CHAPTER 7

1 [a]Ezek. 23:4–8; Hos. 5:1 [1]*plunders*
2 [a]Ps. 25:7; Jer. 14:10; 17:1; Hos. 8:13; 9:9; Amos 8:7 [1]Lit. *do not say to*
3 [a]Hos. 1:1 [b]Mic. 7:3; [Rom. 1:32]
4 [a]Jer. 9:2; 23:10
5 [a]Is. 28:1, 7 [1]Lit. *with the heat of*
6 [1]So with MT, Vg.; Syr., Tg. *Their anger;* LXX *Ephraim*
7 [a]Is. 64:7
8 [a]Ps. 106:35
9 [a]Is. 1:7; 42:25; Hos. 8:7
10 [a]Hos. 5:5 [b]Is. 9:13
11 [a]Hos. 11:11 [b]Is. 30:3 [c]Hos. 5:13; 8:9 [1]Lit. *heart*

3 They make a [a]king glad with their
wickedness,
And princes [b]with their lies.

4 "They[a] *are* all adulterers.
Like an oven heated by a baker—
He ceases stirring *the fire* after
kneading the dough,
Until it is leavened.
5 In the day of our king
Princes have made *him* sick,
[1]inflamed with [a]wine;
He stretched out his hand with
scoffers.
6 They prepare their heart like an
oven,
While they lie in wait;
[1]Their baker sleeps all night;
In the morning it burns like a
flaming fire.
7 They are all hot, like an oven,
And have devoured their judges;
All their kings have fallen.
[a]None among them calls upon Me.

8 "Ephraim [a]has mixed himself
among the peoples;
Ephraim is a cake unturned.
9 [a]Aliens have devoured his
strength,
But he does not know *it;*
Yes, gray hairs are here and there
on him,
Yet he does not know *it.*
10 And the [a]pride of Israel testifies
to his face,
But [b]they do not return to the
LORD their God,
Nor seek Him for all this.

Futile Reliance on the Nations

11 "Ephraim[a] also is like a silly dove,
without [1]sense—
[b]They call to Egypt,
They go to [c]Assyria.

6:6 See section 1 of Truth-In-Action at the end of Hos.
6:6 Mercy (Hebrew *hesed*) is a loyal covenant love, extended to others because it has been experienced in one's own relationship with God.
6:7 Like men can also mean "like Adam," who violated his relationship with God.
6:9 The **priests,** intended to bring blessing and a way of life to those they served, have instead taken advantage of the people and led them into deadly paths. **Shechem,** designated a city of refuge, became the scene of **murder.**
6:10 The Hebrew root for **horrible thing** is the same as the word for "hair," thus bristling, something that makes the hair stand on end.
6:11 When . . . people parallels the phrase at the beginning of 7:1, and means "When I would turn around the captivity of My people."
7:1 Surgical attempts to heal sometimes only reveal the depth of the problem.
7:3 Evil rulers delighted in the sins of their subjects.
7:4–7 Their passions burn in them, find gratification, then quickly return in an endless cycle, like the **baker** at his **oven.**
7:5 The day of our king, the coronation day, was celebrated with drunkenness and mockery.
7:8 Because Israel had entered into foreign alliances and assimilated other cultures, it had lost the distinctions that gave it worth.
7:9 Their alliances, rather than empowering them, have sapped their strength.
7:10 Pride: See note on 5:5.
7:11 A silly dove is one open to deception, easily misled. Israel's foolishness was shown in their thinking that they could find help in any human resource, even powerful **Egypt** and **Assyria.**

12 Wherever they go, I will [a]spread
My net on them;
I will bring them down like birds
of the air;
I will *chastise them
[b]According to what their
*congregation has heard.

13 "Woe to them, for they have fled
from Me!
Destruction to them,
Because they have transgressed
against Me!
Though [a]I redeemed them,
Yet they have spoken lies against
Me.
14 [a]They did not cry out to Me with
their heart
When they wailed upon their
beds.

"They [1]assemble together for grain
and new [b]wine,
[2]They rebel against Me;
15 Though I disciplined *and*
strengthened their arms,
Yet they devise evil against Me;
16 They return, *but* not [1]to the Most
High;
[a]They are like a treacherous bow.
Their princes shall fall by the
sword
For the [b]cursings of their tongue.
This *shall be* their derision
[c]in the land of Egypt.

The Apostasy of Israel

8 "*Set* the [1]**trumpet** to your mouth!
He shall come [a]like an eagle
against the house of the LORD,
Because they have transgressed
My covenant
And rebelled against My law.

WORD WEALTH

8:1 trumpet, *shophar* (shoh-*fahr*); Strong's #7782: A trumpet made from a curved animal horn; a cornet. The *shofar* is mentioned 72 times, first in Ex. 19:16, 19 and 20:18, where a trumpet sounded at Mt. Sinai, heralding the Lord's descent (19:20) and the giving of the Law. In the account of the fall of Jericho in Josh. 6:1–20, *shofar* appears 14 times. In Ezek. 33:2–9, the sound of a trumpet (which warns a city of danger) is compared to the prophet's voice. The *shofar* was sounded not only as a call to arms but also to herald the Day of Atonement, the Year of Jubilee, and events such as the return of the ark. See Lev. 25:9; 2 Sam. 6:15.

2 [a]Israel will cry to Me,
'My God, [b]we know You!'
3 Israel has rejected the good;
The enemy will pursue him.

4 "They[a] set up kings, but not by Me; 2
They made princes, but I did not
acknowledge *them.*
From their silver and gold
They made idols for themselves—
That they might be cut off.
5 Your [1]calf [2]is rejected,
O Samaria!
My anger is aroused against
them—
[a]How long until they attain to
innocence?
6 For from Israel *is* even this:
A [a]workman made it, and it *is* not
God;
But the calf of Samaria shall be
broken to pieces.

7 "They[a] sow the wind,
And reap the whirlwind.
The stalk has no bud;
It shall never produce meal.
If it should produce,
[b]Aliens would swallow it up.
8 [a]Israel is swallowed up;
Now they are among the
*Gentiles
[b]Like a vessel in which *is* no
pleasure.
9 For they have gone up to Assyria,
Like [a]a wild donkey alone by
itself;
Ephraim [b]has hired lovers.

12 [a]Ezek. 12:13 [b]Lev. 26:14; Deut. 28:15; 2 Kin. 17:13 *See WW at Jer. 10:24. • See WW at Josh. 22:17.
13 [a]Ex. 18:8; Mic. 6:4
14 [a]Job 35:9, 10; Ps. 78:36; Jer. 3:10; Zech. 7:5 [b]Judg. 9:27; Amos 2:8 [1]So with MT, Tg.; Vg. *thought upon;* LXX *slashed themselves for* (cf. 1 Kin. 18:28) [2]So with MT, Syr., Tg.; LXX omits *They rebel against Me;* Vg. *They departed from Me*
16 [a]Ps. 78:57 [b]Ps. 73:9; Dan. 7:25; Mal. 3:13, 14 [c]Deut. 28:68; Ezek. 23:32; Hos. 8:13; 9:3 [1]Or *upward*

CHAPTER 8

1 [a]Deut. 28:49; Jer. 4:13 [1]*ram's horn,* Heb. *shophar*
2 [a]Ps. 78:34; Hos. 5:15; 7:14 [b]Titus 1:16
4 [a]1 Kin. 12:20; 2 Kin. 15:23, 25; Hos. 13:10, 11
5 [a]Ps. 19:13; Jer. 13:27 [1]Golden calf image [2]Or *has rejected you*
6 [a]Is. 40:19
7 [a]Prov. 22:8 [b]Hos. 7:9
8 [a]2 Kin. 17:6; Jer. 51:34 [b]Jer. 22:28; 25:34 *See WW at Ps. 106:47.
9 [a]Hos. 7:11; 12:1; Jer. 2:24 [b]Ezek. 16:33, 34

7:12 The punishment for their wickedness was what had already been told them by the prophets (see 6:5).
7:13 God wanted to and would have **redeemed them,** but they rejected His offer.
7:14 They pray for provision, although they have removed themselves from a relationship with the Provider.
7:16 A treacherous bow is literally a "slack, loose," one that does not shoot straight.
8:1 The Assyrian army will come on them, as swiftly as **an eagle** descending on its prey.
8:4 See section 2 of Truth-In-Action at the end of Hos.
8:4 They tried to establish their own government, and even their own religion, apart from God.
8:5 Your calf was the idolatrous golden image. **How long?** Will Israel ever be able to return to the pure worship of the Lord?
8:7 The seed of their wickedness will produce an abundant harvest of punishment.
8:9 Even **a wild donkey** can survive independently, but Israel has become dependent on its foreign alliances. **Hired lovers:** Israel sought to obtain by purchase what God had freely promised: His protection and provision.

10 Yes, though they have hired
among the nations,
Now [a]I will gather them;
And they shall [1]sorrow a little,
Because of the [2]burden of
[b]the king of princes.

11 "Because Ephraim has made many
altars for sin,
They have become for him altars
for sinning.
12 I have *written for him [a]the great
things of My law,
But they were considered a
strange thing.
13 *For* the sacrifices of My offerings
[a]they *sacrifice flesh and eat *it*,
[b]*But* the LORD does not accept
them.
[c]Now He will *remember their
iniquity and punish their sins.
They shall return to Egypt.

14 "For[a] Israel has forgotten
[b]his Maker,
And has built [1]temples;
Judah also has multiplied
[c]fortified cities;
But [d]I will send fire upon his
cities,
And it shall devour his [2]palaces."

Judgment of Israel's Sin

9 Do[a] not rejoice, O Israel, with joy
like *other* peoples,
For you have played the harlot
against your God.
You have made love *for* [b]hire on
every threshing floor.
2 The threshing floor and the
winepress
Shall not feed them,
And the new wine shall fail in her.

3 They shall not dwell in [a]the
LORD's land,
[b]But Ephraim shall return to
Egypt,
And [c]shall eat *unclean *things* in
Assyria.
4 They shall not offer wine
offerings to the LORD,
Nor [a]shall their [b]sacrifices be
pleasing to Him.
It shall be like bread of mourners
to them;
All who eat it shall be defiled.
For their bread *shall be* for their
own life;
It shall not come into the house
of the LORD.

5 What will you do in the appointed
day,
And in the day of the feast of the
LORD?
6 For indeed they are gone because
of destruction.
Egypt shall gather them up;
Memphis shall bury them.
[a]Nettles shall possess their
valuables of silver;
Thorns *shall be* in their tents.

7 The [a]days of punishment have
come;
The days of recompense have
come.
Israel knows!
The prophet *is* a [b]fool,
[c]The spiritual man *is* insane,
Because of the greatness of your
iniquity and great enmity.
8 The [a]**watchman** of Ephraim *is*
with my God;
But the prophet *is* a [1]fowler's
snare in all his ways—
Enmity in the house of his God.

WORD WEALTH

9:8 watchman, *tsaphah* (tsah-*fah*); Strong's #6822: To look out, peer into the distance, spy, keep watch; to scope something out, especially in order to see approaching danger, and to warn those who are endangered. This verb occurs 80 times. Often it is translated "watchmen," referring to the king's guards (1 Sam. 14:16) or to those who look out from a tower in the city wall (2 Kin. 9:17, 18). In other instances, it is spiritual watchmen, or prophets, who look out, see danger, and report to the people. See Is. 52:8; Jer. 6:17; Ezek. 33:2–7. In Prov. 31:27, the ideal woman "watches over" the ways of her household.

10 [a]Ezek. 16:37; 22:20 [b]Is. 10:8; Ezek. 26:7; Dan. 2:37 [1]Or *begin to diminish* [2]Or *oracle* or *proclamation*
12 [a][Deut. 4:6–8]; Ps. 119:18; 147:19, 20
*See WW at Deut. 31:9.
13 [a]Zech. 7:6 [b]Jer. 14:10; Hos. 6:6; 9:4; 1 Cor. 4:5 [c]Hos. 9:9; Amos 8:7; Luke 12:2
*See WW at Deut. 16:2. • See WW at Is. 62:6.
14 [a]Deut. 32:18; [Hos. 2:13; 4:6; 13:6] [b]Is. 29:23 [c]Num. 32:17; 2 Kin. 18:13 [d]Jer. 17:27 [1]Or *palaces* [2]Or *citadels*

CHAPTER 9

1 [a]Is. 22:12, 13; Hos. 10:5 [b]Jer. 44:17
3 [a][Lev. 25:23]; Jer. 2:7 [b]Hos. 7:16; 8:13 [c]Ezek. 4:13
*See WW at Lev. 10:10.
4 [a]Jer. 6:20 [b]Hos. 8:13; Amos 5:22
6 [a]Is. 5:6; 7:23; Hos. 10:8
7 [a]Is. 10:3; Jer. 10:15; Mic. 7:4; Luke 21:22 [b]Lam. 2:14; [Ezek. 13:3, 10] [c]Mic. 2:11
8 [a]Jer. 6:17; 31:6; Ezek. 3:17; 33:7 [1]One who catches birds in a trap or snare

8:10 Sorrow a little: Seeking help from Assyria will not mean gain, but loss to them.
8:11 Adding idolatrous altars increased their transgression, rather than remitting it.
8:13 Egypt is symbolic of a place of exile and bondage.
9:1 Love *for* hire: Israel considered their crops to be the payoff of their worship of idols rather than a gift from God.
9:3 Egypt: See note on 8:13.
9:4 Bread of mourners: Num. 19:14, 15 declares that things in the home of one who has died become unclean and, therefore, unacceptable offerings.
9:6 Memphis was south of Cairo alongside the Nile, noted for its large burial grounds.
9:7 As **punishment** comes, Israel will realize that the false prophets who predicted victory and prosperity were mistaken.
9:8 In contrast to the false prophets of v. 7, a true prophet like Hosea is considered by the people and the priests to be a hostile element in their midst.

9 [a]They are deeply corrupted,
As in the days of [b]Gibeah.
He will remember their iniquity;
He will punish their sins.

10 "I found Israel
Like grapes in the [a]wilderness;
I saw your fathers
As the [b]firstfruits on the fig tree
in its first season.
But they went to [c]Baal Peor,
And [1]separated themselves *to*
that shame;
[d]They became an abomination like
the thing they loved.
11 *As for* Ephraim, their glory shall
fly away like a bird—
No birth, no pregnancy, and no
conception!
12 Though they bring up their
children,
Yet I will bereave them to the last
man.
Yes, [a]woe to them when I depart
from them!
13 Just [a]as I saw Ephraim like Tyre,
planted in a pleasant place,
So Ephraim will bring out his
children to the murderer."

14 Give them, O LORD—
What will You give?
Give them [a]a miscarrying womb
And dry breasts!

15 "All their wickedness *is* in
[a]Gilgal,
For there I hated them.
Because of the evil of their deeds
I will drive them from My house;
I will love them no more.
[b]All their princes *are* rebellious.
16 Ephraim is [a]stricken,
Their root is dried up;
They shall bear no fruit.
Yes, were they to bear children,
I would kill the darlings of their
womb."

5 17 My God will [a]cast them away,
Because they did not obey Him;
And they shall be [b]wanderers
among the nations.

Israel's Sin and Captivity

10 Israel [a]empties *his* vine;
He brings forth fruit for
himself.
According to the multitude of his
fruit
[b]He has increased the altars;
According to the bounty of his
land
They have embellished *his sacred*
pillars.
2 Their heart is [a]divided;[1]
Now they are held guilty.
He will break down their altars;
He will ruin their *sacred* pillars.

3 For now they say,
"We have no king,
Because we did not fear the LORD.
And as for a king, what would he
do for us?"
4 They have spoken words,
Swearing falsely in *making a
covenant.
Thus judgment springs up
[a]like hemlock in the furrows of
the field.

5 The inhabitants of Samaria fear
Because of the [a]calf[1] of Beth
Aven.
For its people mourn for it,
And [2]its priests *shriek for it—
Because its [b]glory has departed
from it.
6 *The idol* also shall be carried to
Assyria
As a present for King [a]Jareb.
Ephraim shall receive shame,
And Israel shall be ashamed of
his own counsel.

7 *As for* Samaria, her king is cut off
Like a twig on the water.
8 Also the [a]high places of [1]Aven,
[b]the sin of Israel,
Shall be destroyed.

9 [a]Hos. 10:9 [b]Judg. 19:22 **10** [a]Jer. 2:2 [b]Is. 28:4; Mic. 7:1 [c]Num. 25:3; Ps. 106:28 [d]Ps. 81:12 [1]Or *dedicated* **12** [a]Deut. 31:17; Hos. 7:13 **13** [a]Ezek. 26—28 **14** [a]Luke 23:29 **15** [a]Hos. 4:15; 12:11 [b]Is. 1:23; Hos. 5:2 **16** [a]Hos. 5:11 **17** [a]2 Kin. 17:20; [Zech. 10:6] [b]Lev. 26:33

CHAPTER 10

1 [a]Nah. 2:2 [b]Jer. 2:28; Hos. 8:11; 12:11 **2** [a]1 Kin. 18:21; Zeph. 1:5; [Matt. 6:24] [1]Divided in loyalty **4** [a]Deut. 31:16, 17; 2 Kin. 17:3, 4; Amos 5:7 *See WW at Ex. 34:27. **5** [a]1 Kin. 12:28, 29; Hos. 8:5, 6; 13:2 [b]Hos. 9:11 [1]Lit. *calves,* images [2]*idolatrous priests* *See WW at Hab. 3:18. **6** [a]Hos. 5:13 **8** [a]Hos. 4:15 [b]Deut. 9:21; 1 Kin. 13:34 [1]Lit. *Idolatry* or *Wickedness*

9:9 Judg. 19 tells how men of **Gibeah** raped and murdered the concubine of a Levite.

9:10 Though the Lord bestowed His special favor on Israel, she abandoned Him to worship such idols as **Baal Peor** (Num. 25).

9:13 Tyre, a major seaport of considerable wealth and influence, would be destroyed (Is. 23). The same fate awaited Ephraim.

9:15 Gilgal, the place where Israel camped upon crossing the Jordan into the Promised Land, had become a center of idolatrous worship.

9:16 The **darlings of their womb** are their desirable, precious children.

9:17 See section 5 of Truth-In-Action at the end of Hos.

10:1 Israel is like a fruitful **vine,** but their prosperity only leads them into more and more sin.

10:3 Having abandoned God, their true King, an earthly **king** cannot help them.

10:4 Because their system of justice is wrong, it is like **hemlock,** a deadly poison, which destroys the possibility of life and fruitfulness in the land.

10:5 Beth Aven: See note on 4:15. The Hebrew word for **priests** here is not the usual *cohen,* but *comer,* priests who served pagan gods.

10:6 King Jareb: See note on 5:13.

The thorn and thistle shall grow
on their altars;
[c]They shall say to the mountains,
"Cover us!"
And to the hills, "Fall on us!"

9 "O Israel, you have sinned from
the days of [a]Gibeah;
There they stood.
The [b]battle in Gibeah against the
children of [1]iniquity
Did not [2]overtake them.
10 When *it is* My desire, I will
*chasten them.
[a]Peoples shall be gathered against
them
When I bind them [1]for their two
transgressions.
11 Ephraim *is* [a]a trained heifer
That loves to thresh *grain;*
But I harnessed her fair neck,
I will make Ephraim [1]pull *a plow.*
Judah shall plow;
Jacob shall break his clods."

5 12 **Sow** for yourselves
righteousness;
Reap in mercy;
[a]Break up your fallow ground,
For *it is* time to seek the LORD,
Till He [b]comes and rains
righteousness on you.

WORD WEALTH

10:12 sow, *zara'* (zah-*rah*); Strong's #2232: To sow; to scatter seed; to plant seed in order to increase the returns; to disseminate. The verb *zara'* appears 55 times in the OT for the sowing of grain, as well as the planting and increasing of humans and animals (Ps. 107:37; Jer. 31:27, 28). In Ps. 97:11, such unusual seed as "light" and "gladness" is sown for the Lord's saints. From the verb *zara'* is derived the noun *zera'*, "seed," whether it is fruit, grain, a male's fluid, or the line of descendants that proceeds from an individual ("seed of Abraham" in Ps. 105:6). The present reference indicates that those who plant righteousness shall harvest tender kindness. Compare planting tears and harvesting joy (Ps. 126:5).

3 13 [a]You have plowed wickedness;
You have reaped iniquity.

8 [c]Is. 2:19; Luke 23:30; Rev. 6:16
9 [a]Hos. 9:9 [b]Judg. 20 [1]So with many Heb. mss., LXX, Vg.; MT *unruliness* [2]Or *overcome*
10 [a]Jer. 16:16 [1]Or *in their two habitations* *See WW at Jer. 10:24.
11 [a][Jer. 50:11; Hos. 4:16; Mic. 4:13] [1]Lit. *to ride*
12 [a]Jer. 4:3 [b]Hos. 6:3
13 [a][Job 4:8; Prov. 22:8; Gal. 6:7, 8]

CHAPTER 11

1 [a]Matt. 2:15 [b]Ex. 4:22, 23 [1]Or *youth* *See WW at Ps. 97:10. • See WW at Jer. 33:3.
2 [a]2 Kin. 17:13–15 [1]So with MT, Vg.; LXX *Just as I called them;* Tg. interprets as *I sent prophets to a thousand of them.* [2]So with MT, Tg., Vg.; LXX *from My face*
3 [a]Deut. 1:31; 32:10, 11 [b]Ex. 15:26 [1]Some Heb. mss., LXX, Syr., Vg. *My arms*
4 [a]Lev. 26:13 [b]Ex. 16:32; Ps. 78:25 [1]Lit. *cords of a man* [2]Lit. *jaws*

You have eaten the fruit of lies,
Because you trusted in your own
way,
In the multitude of your mighty
men.
14 Therefore tumult shall arise
among your people,
And all your fortresses shall be
plundered
As Shalman plundered Beth
Arbel in the day of battle—
A mother dashed in pieces upon
her children.
15 Thus it shall be done to you,
O Bethel,
Because of your great
wickedness.
At dawn the king of Israel
Shall be cut off utterly.

God's Continuing Love for Israel

11 "When Israel *was* a [1]child, I
*loved him,
And out of Egypt [a]I *called My
[b]son.
2 [1]*As* they called them,
So they [a]went [2]from them;
They sacrificed to the Baals,
And burned incense to carved
images.

3 "I[a] taught Ephraim to walk,
Taking them by [1]their arms;
But they did not know that
[b]I healed them.
4 I drew them with [1]gentle cords,
With bands of love,
And [a]I was to them as those who
take the yoke from their [2]neck.
[b]I stooped *and* fed them.

KINGDOM DYNAMICS

11:1, 3, 4 God's Nurturing Heart in Parents Flows to Children, FAMILY ORDER. God reveals Himself as a Father who is tender, close to His children, and sensitive to their needs—teaching, encouraging, helping, and healing them. Growing up is not something that He leaves to chance. He is a God who conscientiously nurtures His children. God's

(*cont. on next page*)

10:9 Gibeah: See note on 9:9.
10:10 God will punish them for **their two transgressions,** which refer either to the two calf images at Dan and Bethel (6:5, 8), or to their rebellions against God and the king (6:3).
10:11 In their own land Israel had worked hard and enjoyed the fruit of their work, but in the Exile they will be subjected to servile labor.
10:12 See section 5 of Truth-In-Action at the end of Hos.
10:12 Fallow ground is land left uncultivated.
10:13 See section 3 of Truth-In-Action at the end of Hos.
10:14 Shalman refers to the Assyrian king Shalmaneser, who defeated the 10 northern tribes of Israel (see 2 Kin. 17:3). **Beth Arbel** is a town in Galilee.
11:1 That this section on the fatherly love of God for His people follows so closely on a prophecy of the total destruction of Israel (ch. 10) demonstrates Hosea's incapacity to point to punishment without balancing it with God's special care and concern for Israel.
11:2 They called: The prophets called.

(cont. from preceding page)
heart toward His children is tenderly portrayed in the meaning behind Hosea's name. *Hoshea* means "Deliverer" or "Helper." The Hebrew root *yasha* indicates that deliverance or help is freely and openly offered, providing a haven of safety for every child of God.

This is the biblical model for parents: God entrusts children to parents, allowing His own nurturing heart to flow through them to the children.
(Ps. 68:5, 6/Ps. 127:3–5) L.C.

5 "He shall not return to the land of
Egypt;
But the Assyrian shall be his king,
Because they refused to repent.
6 And the sword shall slash in his
cities,
Devour his districts,
And consume *them,*
Because of their own counsels.
7 My people are bent on
[a]backsliding* from Me.
Though [1]they call [2]to the Most
High,
None at all exalt *Him.*

8 "How[a] can I give you up, Ephraim?
How can I hand you over, Israel?
How can I make you like
[b]Admah?
How can I set you like Zeboiim?
My *heart [1]churns within Me;
My sympathy is stirred.
9 I will not execute the fierceness
of My anger;
I will not again destroy Ephraim.
[a]For I *am* God, and not man,
The Holy One in your midst;
And I will not [1]come with terror.

10 "They shall walk after the LORD.
[a]He will *roar like a lion.
When He roars,
Then *His* sons shall come
trembling from the west;
11 They shall come trembling like a
bird from Egypt,
[a]Like a dove from the land of
Assyria.
[b]And I will let them dwell in their
houses,"
Says the LORD.

God's Anger with Judah

12 "Ephraim has encircled Me with
lies,
And the house of Israel with
deceit;
But Judah still walks with God,
Even with the [1]Holy One *who is*
faithful.

12 "Ephraim [a]feeds on the wind,
And pursues the east wind;
He daily increases lies and
[1]desolation.
[b]Also they make a [2]covenant with
the Assyrians,
And [c]oil is carried to Egypt.

2 "The[a] LORD also *brings* a [1]charge
against Judah,
And will punish Jacob according
to his ways;
According to his deeds He will
recompense him.
3 He took his brother [a]by the heel
in the womb,
And in his strength he [b]struggled
with God.
4 Yes, he struggled with the *Angel
and prevailed;
He wept, and sought favor from
Him.
He found Him *in* [a]Bethel,
And there He spoke to us—
5 That is, the LORD God of hosts.
The LORD *is* His [a]memorable
name.
6 [a]So you, by *the help of* your God,
return;
Observe mercy and justice,
And *wait on your God
continually.

7 "A cunning [1]Canaanite!
[a]Deceitful scales *are* in his hand;
He loves to oppress.
8 And Ephraim said,
[a]'Surely I have become rich,

7 [a]Jer. 3:6, 7; 8:5 [1]The prophets [2]Or *upward* *See WW at Jer. 5:6.
8 [a]Jer. 9:7 [b]Gen. 14:8; 19:24, 25; Deut. 29:23 [1]Lit. *turns over* *See WW at Ps. 37:4.
9 [a]Num. 23:19 [1]Or *enter a city*
10 [a]Is. 31:4; [Joel 3:16]; Amos 1:2 *See WW at Joel 3:16.
11 [a]Is. 11:11; 60:8; Hos. 7:11 [b]Ezek. 28:25, 26; 34:27, 28
12 [1]Or *holy ones*

CHAPTER 12

1 [a]Job 15:2, 3; Hos. 8:7 [b]2 Kin. 17:4; Hos. 8:9 [c]Is. 30:6 [1]*ruin* [2]Or *treaty*
2 [a]Hos. 4:1; Mic. 6:2 [1]A legal complaint
3 [a]Gen. 25:26 [b]Gen. 32:24–28
4 [a][Gen. 28:12–19; 35:9–15] *See WW at 2 Chr. 32:21.
5 [a]Ex. 3:15
6 [a]Hos. 14:1; Mic. 6:8 *See WW at Lam. 3:25.
7 [a]Prov. 11:1; Amos 8:5; Mic. 6:11 [1]Or *merchant*
8 [a]Ps. 62:10; Hos. 13:6; Rev. 3:17

11:5–7 Hosea returns to the inevitable result of Israel's sin if they persist in turning from God.

11:8 Admah and **Zeboiim** are mentioned in connection with the destruction of Sodom and Gomorrah in Gen. 14:8 and Deut. 29:23.

11:9 *This verse furnishes* one of the keys to understanding the message of the Book of Hosea. A man like Hosea can reflect some aspects of God's nature and love, but he is limited in this capacity. But God has no limits to His patience and love.

11:10, 11 When God calls His people back from captivity, they will respond as certainly as young lions called back to the lair and as swiftly as birds returning to their roost.

11:12 Beginning with this verse and continuing through ch. 12, Hosea reviews Israel's history, especially as epitomized in Jacob, to show a continuing propensity to turn away from God's way of truth to follow their own deceitful paths.

12:1 Feeds on the wind means that they sought futile, empty ways to satisfy desires that only God could fill.

12:3, 4 Hosea makes a wordplay on the Hebrew names of Jacob: **Heel** is the root of the name "Jacob"; **struggled** is the root of the name "Israel."

12:7 Canaanite also means "trader," implying one whose business practices are dishonest.

I have found wealth for myself;
In all my labors
They shall find in me no iniquity
that *is* sin.'

9 "But I *am* the LORD your God,
Ever since the land of Egypt;
[a]I will again make you dwell in
tents,
As in the days of the appointed
feast.
10 [a]I have also spoken by the
prophets,
And have multiplied *visions;
I have given [1]symbols [2]through
the witness of the prophets."

11 Though [a]Gilead *has* idols—
Surely they are [1]vanity—
Though they sacrifice bulls in
[b]Gilgal,
Indeed their altars *shall be* heaps
in the furrows of the field.

12 Jacob [a]fled to the country of
Syria;
[b]Israel served for a spouse,
And for a wife he tended *sheep.*
13 [a]By a prophet the LORD brought
Israel out of Egypt,
And by a prophet he was
*preserved.
14 Ephraim [a]provoked* *Him* to
anger most bitterly;
Therefore his *Lord will leave the
guilt of his bloodshed upon
him,
[b]And return his reproach upon
him.

Relentless Judgment on Israel

13 When Ephraim spoke,
trembling,
He exalted *himself* in Israel;
But when he offended through
Baal *worship,* he died.
2 Now they sin more and more,
And have made for themselves
molded images,
Idols of their silver, according to
their skill;
All of it *is* the work of craftsmen.
They say of them,
"Let [1]the men who sacrifice
[2]kiss the calves!"
3 Therefore they shall be like the
morning cloud
And like the early dew that passes
away,
[a]Like chaff blown off from a
threshing floor
And like smoke from a chimney.

4 "Yet [a]I *am* the LORD your God
Ever since the land of Egypt,
And you shall know no God but
Me;
For [b]*there is* no savior besides
Me.
5 [a]I [1]knew you in the wilderness,
[b]In the land of [2]great drought.
6 [a]When they had pasture, they
were filled;
They were filled and their heart
was *exalted;
Therefore they forgot Me.

7 "So [a]I will be to them like a lion;
Like [b]a leopard by the road I will
lurk;
8 I will meet them [a]like a bear
deprived *of her cubs;*
I will tear open their rib cage,
And there I will devour them like
a lion.
The [1]wild beast shall tear them.

9 "O Israel, [1]you are destroyed,
But [2]your help *is* from Me.
10 [1]I will be your King;
[a]Where *is any other,*
That he may save you in all your
cities?
And your judges to whom
[b]you said,
'Give me a king and princes'?
11 [a]I gave you a king in My anger,
And took *him* away in My wrath.

12 "The[a] iniquity of Ephraim *is* bound
up;
His sin *is* stored up.
13 [a]The sorrows of a woman in
childbirth shall come upon him.
He *is* an unwise son,
For he should not stay long where
children are born.

9 [a]Lev. 23:42
10 [a]2 Kin. 17:13; Jer. 7:25 [1]Or *parables* [2]Lit. *by the hand* *See WW at 2 Chr. 32:32.
11 [a]Hos. 6:8 [b]Hos. 9:15 [1]*worthless*
12 [a]Gen. 28:5; Deut. 26:5 [b]Gen. 29:20, 28
13 [a]Ex. 12:50, 51; 13:3; Ps. 77:20; Is. 63:11, 12; Mic. 6:4 *See WW at Job 10:12.
14 [a]Ezek. 18:10–13 [b]Dan. 11:18; Mic. 6:16 *See WW at 1 Kin. 16:2. • See WW at Mic. 4:13.

CHAPTER 13

2 [1]Or *those who offer human sacrifice* [2]Worship with kisses
3 [a]Ps. 1:4; Is. 17:13; Dan. 2:35
4 [a]Is. 43:11 [b]Is. 43:11; 45:21, 22; [1 Tim. 2:5]
5 [a]Deut. 2:7; 32:10 [b]Deut. 8:15 [1]Cared for you [2]Lit. *droughts*
6 [a]Deut. 8:12, 14; 32:13–15; Jer. 5:7 *See WW at Ps. 18:46.
7 [a]Lam. 3:10; Hos. 5:14 [b]Jer. 5:6
8 [a]2 Sam. 17:8; Prov. 17:12 [1]Lit. *beast of the field*
9 [1]Lit. *it or he destroyed you* [2]Lit. *in your help*
10 [a]Deut. 32:38 [b]1 Sam. 8:5, 6 [1]LXX, Syr., Tg., Vg. *Where is your king?*
11 [a]1 Sam. 8:7; 10:17–24
12 [a]Deut. 32:34, 35; Job 14:17; [Rom. 2:5]
13 [a]Is. 13:8; Mic. 4:9, 10

12:10 Among the **symbols** by which the prophets represented God's message was the life of Hosea himself and his relationship with his wife Gomer, intended to depict God's love for Israel.
12:11 Gilead (6:8) and **Gilgal** (see note on 9:15) were places thoroughly devoted to the worship of idols.
13:2 How far Israel has departed from the true worship of the Lord is seen in the call of the idolatrous priests to worship the calf images of Baal by kissing them. See 1 Kin. 19:18.
13:3 Cloud, dew: See note on 6:4.
13:4 Shall know no God: See note on 4:1.
13:5 God **knew** Israel, that is, He entered into a relationship with them characterized by love and concern.
13:10, 11 The succession of human kings from Saul onward proved a failure in representing God, their true King.
13:13 Like an **unwise** child in the birth process, Israel refuses to come to birth, to newness of life.

14 "I will *ransom them from the
[1]power of [2]the **grave;**
I will redeem them from death.
[a]O Death, [3]I will be your plagues!
O [4]Grave, [5]I will be your
destruction!
[b]Pity is hidden from My eyes."

WORD WEALTH

13:14 grave, *she'ol* (sheh-*oal*); Strong's #7585: The grave; the abode of the dead; the netherworld; hell. This noun occurs 65 times, its use broad enough to include the visible grave that houses a dead body and the abyss, that unseen world to which the soul departs in death. The meaning of "grave" is seen in Gen. 37:35; 42:38; and 1 Kin. 2:6. *She'ol* speaks of the realm of departed souls in such verses as Ps. 9:17; 16:10; 55:15; 139:8; Is. 14:9–11; Ezek. 31:15–17; 32:21. The assumed root of *she'ol* is *sha'al,* "to ask, demand, require." Thus "hell" is a hungry, greedy devourer of humanity, is never full or satisfied, but is always asking for more (see Prov. 27:20). God's promise in the present verse is that He will save His people from the power of *she'ol* and that He will actually destroy *she'ol* in the end!

15 Though he is fruitful among *his*
*brethren,
[a]An east wind shall come;
The wind of the LORD shall come
up from the wilderness.
Then his spring shall become dry,
And his fountain shall be dried
up.
He shall plunder the treasury of
every desirable prize.
16 Samaria [1]is held guilty,
For she has [a]rebelled against her
God.
They shall fall by the sword,
Their infants shall be dashed in
pieces,
And their women with child
[b]ripped open.

Israel Restored at Last

14

O Israel, [a]return to the LORD
your God,
For you have stumbled because of
your iniquity;
2 Take words with you,
And return to the LORD.
Say to Him,
"Take away all iniquity;
Receive *us* graciously,
For we will offer the [a]sacrifices[1]
of our lips.
3 Assyria shall [a]not save us,
[b]We will not ride on horses,
Nor will we say anymore to the
work of our hands,
'*You are* our gods.'
[c]For in You the fatherless finds
mercy."

4 "I will *heal their [a]backsliding,*
I will [b]love them freely,
For My anger has turned away
from him.
5 I will be like the [a]dew to Israel;
He shall [1]grow like the lily,
And [2]lengthen his roots like
Lebanon.
6 His branches shall [1]spread;
[a]His beauty shall be like an olive
tree,
And [b]his fragrance like Lebanon.
7 [a]Those who dwell under his
shadow shall *return;
They shall be revived *like* grain,
And [1]grow like a vine.
Their [2]scent *shall be* like the wine
of Lebanon.

8 "Ephraim *shall say,*
'What have I to do anymore with
idols?'
I have heard and observed him.
I *am* like a green cypress tree;
[a]Your fruit is found in Me."

9 Who *is* wise?
Let him *understand these
things.
Who is prudent?
Let him know them.
For [a]the ways of the LORD *are*
right;
The righteous walk in them,
But transgressors stumble in
them.

2

14 [a][1 Cor. 15:54, 55] [b]Jer. 15:6 [1]Lit. *hand* [2]Or *Sheol* [3]LXX *where is your punishment?* [4]Or *Sheol* [5]LXX *where is your sting?* *See WW at Neh. 1:10.
15 [a]Gen. 41:6; Jer. 4:11, 12; Ezek. 17:10; 19:12 *See WW at Ps. 133:1.
16 [a]2 Kin. 18:12 [b]2 Kin. 15:16 [1]LXX *shall be disfigured*

CHAPTER 14

1 [a]Hos. 12:6; [Joel 2:13]
2 [a][Ps. 51:16, 17; Hos. 6:6; Heb. 13:15] [1]Lit. *bull calves;* LXX *fruit*
3 [a]Hos. 7:11; 10:13; 12:1 [b][Ps. 33:17]; Is. 31:1 [c]Ps. 10:14; 68:5
4 [a]Jer. 14:7 [b][Eph. 1:6] *See WW at Ex. 15:26. • See WW at Jer. 5:6.
5 [a]Job 29:19; Prov. 19:12; Is. 26:19 [1]Lit. *bud or sprout* [2]Lit. *strike*
6 [a]Ps. 52:8; 128:3 [b]Gen. 27:27 [1]Lit. *go*
7 [a]Dan. 4:12 [1]Lit. *bud* or *sprout* [2]Lit. *remembrance* *See WW at Ruth 4:15.
8 [a][John 15:4]
9 [a][Ps. 111:7, 8; Prov. 10:29]; Zeph. 3:5 *See WW at Neh. 8:8.

13:14 God will not only release people **from the power of the grave** and **death,** but He will also take away the threat of death. God can bring back His people from certain extinction in a land of exile in Hosea's time; and, as Paul indicates in 1 Cor. 15:15, God can once and for all remove the abiding menace of death on the basis of the victory won through the resurrection of Christ.
14:2 The **sacrifices** God desires are words of true repentance (see Heb. 13:15).
14:5–8 Hosea uses a series of examples from nature to show how God will restore His people with fruitfulness (**the lily**), stability (**roots like** the cedars of **Lebanon**), beauty (**olive tree**), and fragrance (**wine**). Then God Himself promises to be an evergreen place of shelter (**cypress tree**).
14:9 See section 2 of Truth-In-Action at the end of Hos.
14:9 Hosea here summarizes the message of his book: the main thing is to know God and His ways, to follow Him and so find righteousness, and to avoid paths that lead to destruction.

TRUTH-IN-ACTION through HOSEA

Letting the LIFE of the Holy Spirit Bring Faith's Works Alive in You!

Truth Hosea Teaches	Text	**Action** Hosea Invites
1 Steps to Knowing God Hosea, perhaps more than any other prophet, reveals the loving heart of God. God desires to bless, not to chastise His people. The Lord puts a premium value on His relationship with us.	6:1–3	**Recognize** that God's heart is for the full restoration of His people. **Understand** that He calls us to press on to know Him so that He can bring rich blessings to us.
	6:6	**Be assured** God values our relationship with Him more than He desires our service.
2 Guidelines for Growing in Godliness Paul caught the essence of godliness when he wrote, "Therefore be imitators of God as dear children" (Eph. 5:1). Just as God called Hosea to live out His undying, eternal love for His people by instructing him to marry an unfaithful woman, He calls us to illustrate His Word and His very character in the way we live.	1:2, 3	**Recognize** that a person's life is the most powerful sermon he or she can preach. **Understand** that God calls us to act out His Word in our lives.
	3:1–5	**Know** that Hosea acted out God's loving forgiveness for His people. **Emulate** God's forgiveness for His people in the way you continually forgive others.
	8:4	**Inquire** of the Lord and **invoke** His hand in any selection of leadership in the church.
	14:9	**Be prudent, wise,** and **righteous. Choose** to walk in the way of the Lord.
3 Steps to Holiness Holiness demands rather than requests our total dependence on God and His provision.	10:13	**Depend** wholly on the Lord. **Reject** the deceptive fruit of wickedness, the lie of self-sufficient strength and wisdom.
4 Keys to Wise Living The pursuit of spiritual knowledge and understanding should be high on our list of priorities.	4:6, 7	**Recognize** that what you do not know **can** hurt you. **Pursue** and value true spiritual knowledge. **Do not neglect** God's Word.
	4:14	**Pursue** and value spiritual understanding. **Seek** to lay hold of it. **Recognize** that understanding keeps you from ruin.
5 Steps to Dealing with Sin Give sin no place to develop in your life. A fallow heart is excellent soil in which to cultivate sin. Deal with sin quickly and ruthlessly whenever it is found. Do not be lulled to sleep by those who claim God does not care about obedience. He looks for those who obey His Word and honor it by their behavior.	5:15	**Recognize** that God often allows misery into the lives of His people to cause them to seek him earnestly. **Be quick** to admit your guilt of sin. **Do not deny** that you are a sinner. **Confess, repent,** and **be restored** to God.
	9:17	**Settle it** in your heart: God **does reject** those who continue to disobey him.
	10:12	**Beware** of any hardness of heart. **Seek** radical remedy for a fallow spiritual life. **Believe** that the Lord will honor and visit those who seek Him with their whole heart.

The Book of JOEL

Author: Joel
Date: Probably 835–805 B.C.
Theme: The Judgment and Grace of God
Key Words: Great and Awesome Day of the Lord

Author The name "Joel" means literally, "Yahweh Is God." This is a very common name in Israel, and Joel the prophet is specified as the son of Pethuel. Nothing is known about him or his life circumstances. It is likely that he lived in Judah and prophesied in Jerusalem.

Date There is no way to date the book with absolute certainty, and scholars vary in their opinions. There are references in both Amos and Isaiah, which are also in Joel. (Compare Amos 1:2 with Joel 3:16 and Is. 13:6 with Joel 1:15.) It is the opinion of most conservatives that Amos and Isaiah borrowed from Joel, making him one of the very earliest of the minor prophets.

Furthermore, the worship of God, which the high priest Jehoiada restored during the reign of Joash (2 Kin. 11; 2 Chr. 23:16), is assumed by Joel. Therefore, many hold that Joel prophesied during the first thirty years of the reign of Joash (835–796 B.C.) when Jehoiada was the king's adviser. This would place Joel's ministry around 835–805 B.C.

Background Joel prophesied at a time of great devastation to the entire land of Judah. An enormous plague of locusts had denuded the countryside of all vegetation, destroyed the pastures of both the sheep and the cattle, even stripped the bark off the fig trees. In only a few hours what was once a beautiful, verdant land had become a place of desolation and destruction. Contemporary descriptions of the destructive power of swarms of locusts corroborate Joel's picture of the plague in his time.

The plague of locusts Joel wrote about was greater than anyone had ever seen. All crops were lost and the seed crops for the next planting were destroyed. A famine and drought had seized the entire land. Both people and animals were dying. It was so profound and disastrous that Joel saw only one explanation; it was the judgment of God.

Content The Book of Joel is naturally divided into two sections. The first (1:1—2:27) deals with the present judgment of God, a call to repentance, and a promise of restoration.

In Moses' sermon to Israel (Deut. 28:38–46) he warned that, if the nation was disobedient, "Locusts shall consume all your trees and the produce of your land." The prophet sees that just such a day has come. He graphically describes the horrible armies of locusts in prophetic and poetic language. Four waves of these army-like creatures have consumed everything. Drinkers have no wine.

The priests have nothing to offer in sacrifice to God. Farmers and vinedressers have nothing to care for. There is no part of Judah's life that has not been dramatically and tragically affected.

The second section (2:28—3:21) explains that this plague, horrible as it may be, is nothing compared to the judgment of God that is coming. This will be a time when not only Judah, but all the nations of the world, will be called before God. It will be a time when the sounds of locusts will be muted as "the LORD also will roar from Zion, and utter His voice from Jerusalem; the heavens and earth will shake" (3:16).

Terrifying heavenly portents will take place. "The sun shall be turned into darkness and the moon into blood" (2:31). This will be none other than "the great and awesome day of the LORD" (2:31).

However, we must not overlook the most remarkable section of this short prophecy. Through the anointing of the Holy Spirit, Joel looks hundreds of years ahead to a time when God will pour out His Spirit "on all flesh" (2:28). This will be a prelude to the devastation and judgment of the Day of the Lord. It will be a time when all believers will experience the indwelling of the Spirit of God and will form a prophetic community on Earth. It will be a time when prophecy will come from young and old alike; when both men and women will prophesy. Salvation will not just be the unique blessing on Judah. It will be a time when "whoever calls on the name of the LORD shall be saved" (2:32).

Personal Application

Joel prophesies the inauguration of the age of the church—a time when all people everywhere can call on the name of the Lord, be saved from their sins, and become participants in the kingdom of God. Through the indwelling of the Holy Spirit, the church becomes the body of Christ in the world. The redemptive purposes of God are therefore extended and made available through every Spirit-filled believer.

This is the time in which we now live. Ours is the wonderful privilege of not only experiencing salvation ourselves, but also of being those who bring the Good News to all who will listen. What Joel was to ravaged Judah, the church is to a ravaged world; namely, a prophetic voice, bringing God's viewpoint into clear focus, calling for repentance, and extending the hope of salvation from the final and terrible Day of the Lord.

The message of Joel is concise and clear: "If you think the plague of locusts is bad, wait until you see the final judgment of the Lord." But, as every true prophet of God, Joel does not stop with the prediction of doomsday. He clearly announces the day of God's grace.

Christ Revealed

Joel looked forward to a time when the Lord would bring judgment to the enemies of God and of Israel, when the nations would be called to give account for their actions. He also saw a day of great plenty flowing from the righteous reign of the Lord in Zion. The instrument through which these great events would come was the Messiah. Jesus is the One who will bring this age to a close, defeating His enemies, rewarding His church, and setting up His final kingdom of righteousness.

Furthermore, it is Jesus who promises the coming of the Spirit in response to His finished work of redemption and return to the Father (John 14:15–18; 16:5–24). In the coming of the Spirit at Pentecost we have the spiritual return of Christ to indwell His people and direct His body, the church. His literal and physical return is foretold here in Joel.

The Holy Spirit at Work Joel is remarkable in his references to the Holy Spirit. It is obviously the Holy Spirit who has inspired the prophet to see God's hand in all that is taking place and to be able to leap forward to the terrible Day of the Lord.

But the most astounding passage in Joel is 2:28–32. Here the prophet sees a time in the future, "afterward," when the Spirit of God will be poured out "on all flesh." Young and old alike, both women and men, will experience this outpouring. This section of Scripture hangs suspended for nearly eight hundred years. Though the Spirit had come upon prophets and priests, never had there been such a general outpouring of the Spirit. Then, on the Day of Pentecost, the Spirit came with such power and force that it captured the attention of the masses gathered in Jerusalem for the festival. Peter takes hold of this prophetic section and declares, "But this is what was spoken by the prophet Joel" (Acts 2:16). A new age is born, the church is empowered, and now "whoever calls on the name of the LORD shall be saved."

Outline of Joel

I. The Lord's hand in the present **1:1—2:27**
- A. The destruction by the locusts 1:2—2:11
- B. The repentance of Judah 2:12–17
- C. The restoration of the Lord 2:18–27

II. The Lord's day in the future 2:28—3:21
- A. The grace of the Lord 2:28–32
- B. The judgment of the Lord 3:1–17
- C. The blessing of the Lord 3:18–21

THE word of the LORD that came to [a]Joel the son of Pethuel.

The Land Laid Waste

2 Hear this, you elders,
And give ear, all you inhabitants
of the land!
[a]Has *anything like* this happened
in your days,
Or even in the days of your
fathers?
1 3 [a]Tell your children about it,
Let your children *tell* their
children,
And their children another
generation.
4 [a]What the chewing [1]locust left, the
[b]swarming locust has eaten;
What the swarming locust left,
the crawling locust has eaten;
And what the crawling locust left,
the consuming locust has eaten.
5 Awake, you [a]drunkards, and
weep;
And wail, all you drinkers of
wine,
Because of the new wine,
[b]For it has been cut off from your
mouth.
6 For [a]a nation has come up against
My land,
Strong, and without number;

CHAPTER 1

1 [a]Acts 2:16
2 [a]Jer. 30:7; Joel 2:2
3 [a]Ex. 10:2; Ps. 78:4; Is. 38:19
4 [a]Deut. 28:38; Joel 2:25; Amos 4:9 [b]Is. 33:4 [1]Exact identity of these locusts unknown
5 [a]Is. 5:11; 28:1; Hos. 7:5 [b]Is. 32:10
6 [a]Prov. 30:25; Joel 2:2, 11, 25

1:2–20 Ch. 1 is a lengthy call to Judah to lament because of God's unleashed judgment. The destruction comes through a locust invasion (vv. 4–7), a drought and famine *(vv. 9–12, 16–18), and fire (vv. 19, 20).*

1:2 This question, addressed to the leaders, is designed to show that this is no mere natural calamity, but is, in fact, a judgment of the Lord.

1:3 See section 1 of Truth-In-Action at the end of Joel.

1:4 Chewing locust . . . swarming locust . . . crawling locust . . . consuming locust: The locust is a jumping, flying insect, similar to a grasshopper. These four designations may be four stages of a locust's development, or a poetic form used to indicate the total devastation of the land. The best explanation, however, is that this is a description of four separate waves of locusts, each one eating what the other had left until the land is totally denuded of foliage.

1:6 Here the locusts are described as a warlike nation too large to number. Its teeth are its weapons that crush and devour everything.

[b]His teeth *are* the teeth of a
lion,
And he has the fangs of a
[1]fierce lion.
7 He has [a]laid waste My vine,
And [1]ruined My fig tree;
He has stripped it bare and
thrown *it* away;
Its branches are made white.
8 [a]Lament like a virgin girded with
sackcloth
For [b]the *husband of her youth.
9 [a]The grain offering and the drink
offering
Have been cut off from the house
of the LORD;
The priests [b]**mourn,** who minister
to the LORD.

6 [b]Rev. 9:8 [1]Or *lioness*
7 [a]Is. 5:6 [1]Or *splintered*
8 [a]Is. 22:12 [b]Jer. 3:4 *See WW at Hos. 2:8.
9 [a]Joel 1:13; 2:14 [b]Joel 2:17

1:8 Sackcloth is a rough, coarse cloth made into a baglike garment. It was worn to symbolize deep grief or contrition and repentance before God. It was often used by prophets to symbolize their brokenness in the face of messages of calamity and judgment. **Husband of her youth:** The bridegroom was often referred to as the husband of his engaged bride. The loss of a husband brought the deepest and most painful grief.

1:9, 10 The lack of offerings reflected greatest calamity for Israel, for when there was no longer **grain** or **wine** for the sacrifices, the covenant relationship with God was suspended. This was a sign that God had rejected His people.

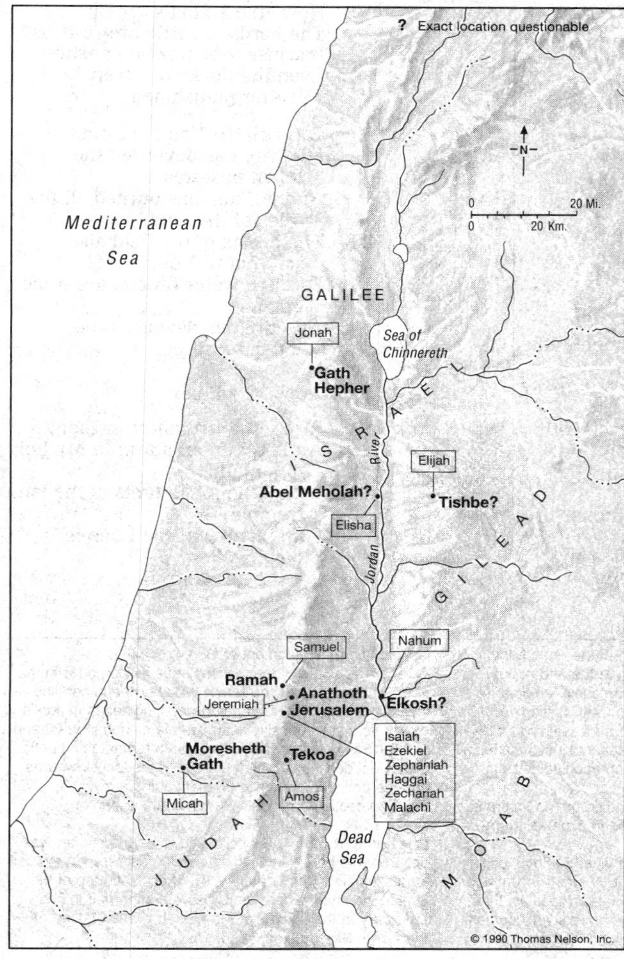

The Prophets of Israel and Judah. From the Scriptures we learn where some of the prophets were born or where they prophesied.

Samuel, who served as prophet and judge, used his hometown of Ramah as a base from which he made his yearly circuit to other places. Two other prophets of the early monarchy, Elijah and Elisha, had their homes in the northern kingdom.

Among the "writing prophets," only Hosea and Jonah were from the North. The exact location of Hosea's home and ministry are unknown. Jonah was from Gath Hepher, but his ministry extended beyond his homeland to the foreign city of Nineveh.

Some prophets had homes in the South, but prophesied to the North. Amos came from Tekoa but preached against the northern kingdom's worship at Bethel. Micah's message addressed Israel as well as Judah.

The ministry of several prophets centers on Judah and the capital city of Jerusalem. The messages of Isaiah, Jeremiah, Zephaniah, Ezekiel, Haggai, Zechariah, and Malachi span a long time period, but all concern either Jerusalem's approaching destruction, fall, or later rebuilding.

For some prophets, such as Joel, Obadiah, and Habakkuk, geographical information is lacking. The home of Nahum is indicated only by his designation as "the Elkoshite."

WORD WEALTH

1:9 mourn, *'abal* (ah-*vahl*); Strong's #56: To weep, lament, mourn, droop, sink down, languish. This verb occurs nearly 40 times and describes mourning over a death, over sin, or over the tragedies of Jerusalem (Is. 66:10). In the present reference, *'abal* describes the reaction of godly priests to the plight of the Lord's people.

10 The field is wasted,
[a]The land mourns;
For the grain is ruined,
[b]The new wine is dried up,
The oil fails.

11 [a]Be ashamed, you farmers,
Wail, you vinedressers,
For the wheat and the barley;
Because the harvest of the field
has perished.
12 [a]The vine has dried up,
And the fig tree has withered;
The pomegranate tree,
The palm tree also,
And the apple tree—
All the trees of the field are
withered;
Surely [b]joy has withered away
from the sons of men.

Mourning for the Land

3 13 [a]Gird yourselves and lament, you
priests;
Wail, you who minister before the
altar;
Come, lie all night in sackcloth,
You who minister to my God;
For the grain offering and the
drink offering
Are withheld from the house of
your God.
3 14 [a]Consecrate a *fast,
Call [b]a sacred assembly;
Gather the elders
And [c]call the inhabitants of the
land
Into the house of the LORD your
God,
And cry out to the LORD.

15 [a]Alas for the *day!
For [b]the day of the LORD *is* at
hand;
It shall come as destruction from
the *Almighty.
16 Is not the food [a]cut off before our
eyes,
[b]Joy and gladness from the house
of our God?
17 The seed shrivels under the clods,
Storehouses are in shambles;
Barns are broken down,
For the grain has withered.
18 How [a]the animals groan!
The herds of cattle are restless,
Because they have no pasture;
Even the flocks of sheep
[1]suffer punishment.

19 O LORD, [a]to You I cry out;
For [b]fire has devoured the
[1]open pastures,
And a flame has burned all the
trees of the field.
20 The beasts of the field also
[a]cry out to You,
For [b]the water brooks are dried
up,
And fire has devoured the
[1]open pastures.

The Day of the LORD

2 Blow [a]the [1]trumpet* in Zion, 3
And [b]sound an alarm in My holy
mountain!
Let all the inhabitants of the land
tremble;
For [c]the day of the LORD is
coming,
For it is at hand:

10 [a]Jer. 12:11; Hos. 3:4 [b]Is. 24:7
11 [a]Jer. 14:3, 4; Amos 5:16
12 [a]Joel 1:10; Hab. 3:17 [b]Is. 16:10; 24:11; Jer. 48:33
13 [a]Jer. 4:8; Ezek. 7:18
14 [a]2 Chr. 20:3; Joel 2:15, 16 [b]Lev. 23:36 [c]2 Chr. 20:13 *See WW at Jon. 3:5.
15 [a][Is. 13:9; Jer. 30:7]; Amos 5:16 [b]Is. 13:6; Ezek. 7:2–12 *See WW at Zeph. 1:7. • See WW at Ps. 91:1.
16 [a]Is. 3:1; Amos 4:6 [b]Deut. 12:7; Ps. 43:4
18 [a]1 Kin. 8:5; Jer. 12:4; 14:5, 6; Hos. 4:3 [1]LXX, Vg. *are made desolate*
19 [a][Ps. 50:15]; Mic. 7:7 [b]Jer. 9:10; Amos 7:4 [1]Lit. *pastures of the wilderness*
20 [a]Job 38:41; Ps. 104:21; 147:9; Joel 1:18 [b]1 Kin. 17:7; 18:5 [1]Lit. *pastures of the wilderness*

CHAPTER 2

1 [a]Jer. 4:5; Joel 2:15; Zeph. 1:16 [b]Num. 10:5 [c]Joel 1:15; 2:11, 31; 3:14; [Obad. 15]; Zeph. 1:14 [1]*ram's horn* *See WW at Hos. 8:1.

1:13 See section 3 of Truth-In-Action at the end of Joel.
1:14 See section 3 of Truth-In-Action at the end of Joel.
1:14 To **consecrate a fast** is to set an assigned time for a national service of prayer in connection with fasting. For this purpose, the priests are to **call a sacred assembly,** a meeting of the full congregation of Judah, not just the priests.
1:15 The day in this instance is the approaching devastating judgment of God.
1:16 Because of the destruction of the crops, no firstfruits or thank offerings are available for use in expressing **joy and gladness** to the Lord.
1:19 Fire is here a graphic picture of what the land looks like after the locusts have destroyed it. It is not uncommon for fires to break out on land left desolate by locusts. Fire is a well-understood figure used of God and also of judgment. It is, therefore, an apt figure tying together the natural calamity and the judgment of God.
2:1–11 The figure of the locust plague is merged with that of the coming **day of the LORD.** Whether the impending invasion is from a literal army threatening Judah in Joel's day or from the apocalyptic armies mentioned in v. 20 and in 3:9–15 is not clear. Nevertheless, in remarkable poetic style, Joel describes both the terror of the locust swarms and the ominous presence of an invading army.
2:1 See section 3 of Truth-In-Action at the end of Joel.
2:1 Trumpet: The ram's horn, known as the shofar, was used both to herald impending danger, as here, and to call the assembly together as in v. 15. **Zion** is the top of the temple mountain where the Lord was enthroned in His sanctuary at the summit of Mt. Moriah (Ps. 2:6). **Day of the LORD:** See note on Obad. 15.

2 [a]A day of darkness and
gloominess,
A day of clouds and thick
darkness,
Like the morning *clouds* spread
over the mountains.
[b]A people *come,* great and strong,
[c]The like of whom has never been;
Nor will there ever be any *such*
after them,
Even for many successive
generations.

3 A fire devours before them,
And behind them a flame burns;
The land *is* like [a]the Garden of
Eden before them,
[b]And behind them a desolate
wilderness;
Surely nothing shall escape them.
4 [a]Their appearance is like the
appearance of horses;
And like [1]swift steeds, so they
run.
5 [a]With a noise like chariots
Over mountaintops they leap,
Like the noise of a flaming fire
that devours the stubble,
Like a strong people set in battle
array.

6 Before them the people writhe in
pain;
[a]All faces [1]are drained of color.
7 They run like mighty men,
They climb the wall like men of
war;
Every one marches in formation,
And they do not break [a]ranks.
8 They do not push one another;
Every one marches in his own
[1]column.
Though they lunge between the
weapons,
They are not [2]cut down.
9 They run to and fro in the city,
They run on the wall;
They climb into the houses,
They [a]enter at the windows
[b]like a thief.

10 [a]The earth quakes before them,
The heavens tremble;
[b]The sun and moon grow dark,
And the stars diminish their
brightness.
11 [a]The LORD gives voice before His
army,
For His camp is very great;
[b]For strong *is the One* who
executes His word.
For the [c]day of the LORD *is* great
and very terrible;
[d]Who can endure it?

A Call to Repentance

12 "Now, therefore," says the LORD, 3
[a]"Turn to Me with all your heart,
With fasting, with weeping, and
with mourning."
13 So [a]rend your heart, and not
[b]your garments;
Return to the LORD your God,
For He *is* [c]gracious and merciful,
Slow to anger, and of great
kindness;
And He relents from doing
harm.
14 [a]Who knows *if* He will turn and
relent,
And leave [b]a blessing behind
Him—

2 [a]Amos 5:18 [b]Joel 1:6; 2:11, 25 [c]Dan. 9:12; 12:1
3 [a]Is. 51:3 [b]Zech. 7:14
4 [a]Rev. 9:7 [1]Or *horsemen*
5 [a]Rev. 9:9
6 [a]Nah. 2:10 [1]LXX, Tg., Vg. *gather blackness*
7 [a]Prov. 30:27
8 [1]Lit. *highway* [2]Halted by losses
9 [a]Jer. 9:21 [b]John 10:1
10 [a]Ps. 18:7 [b]Is. 13:10; 34:4
11 [a]Jer. 25:30 [b]Rev. 18:8 [c]Amos 5:18 [d][Mal. 3:2]
12 [a]Jer. 4:1
13 [a][Ps. 34:18; 51:17] [b]Gen. 37:34 [c][Ex. 34:6]
14 [a]Jer. 26:3 [b]Hag. 2:19

2:2 Like the morning *clouds* . . . mountains can be read, "like morning dawn, it is spread over the mountains." This refers to the bright reflection of the sun on the wings of the swarming locusts. Bright glimmers of light dancing off the wings of the myriads of locusts literally turn the sky to a yellow, foglike texture. This phenomenon is observed a day or more before the creatures actually arrive. For several days the swarms are so thick and continuous that they turn the sky black as night.

2:3 A fire devours: This reference to the judgment of God may also describe a literal fire, which often accompanies terrible locust swarms. **Garden of Eden** is a reference to the garden paradise of unfallen man (Gen. 2:8).

2:4 Like the appearance of horses: The head of the locust looks very much like that of a horse. The German word for locust means literally "hay-horses."

2:5 Noise like chariots . . . noise of a flaming fire: Eyewitnesses declare that the locusts, when running and flying, have a clicking, rattling sound. When they eat, they can sound like a stubble field on fire.

2:7–9 There are many accounts of the unalterable and unstoppable columns of locusts. "There is no road impassable to locusts; they penetrate into fields, and crops, and trees, and cities, and houses, and even the recesses of the bedchambers" (Jerome).

2:11 His army: Here the figures again merge to that future day when the Lord Himself shall lead His armies against the nations and accomplish His judgment, a day when even the natural universe recoils (v. 10). **Who can endure it?** is a rhetorical question, underlining the fact that no one will be able to stand before the Lord's day.

2:12–17 This call to repentance and mourning is similar to that in ch. 1.

2:12–14 See section 3 of Truth-In-Action at the end of Joel.

2:13, 14 When we are dealing with God, we are never without hope. Even in the midst of extreme circumstances, which, as in this case, are His judgments, we can turn our hearts to Him and find help and salvation. He is never vindictive or cruel. Rather, He is **gracious and merciful, slow to anger, and of great kindness.**

2:13 Rend your heart, and not your garments: The tearing of one's garment was a common practice in times of grief or contrition. It symbolized a broken and torn spirit. Here Joel is calling for Judah to actually experience what this symbolism portrays: hearts that are torn with grief and the confession of their sins.

[c]A grain offering and a drink
offering
For the LORD your God?

15 [a]Blow the [1]trumpet in Zion,
[b]Consecrate a fast,
Call a sacred assembly;
16 Gather the people,
[a]Sanctify the congregation,
Assemble the elders,
Gather the children and nursing
babes;
[b]Let the bridegroom go out from
his chamber,
And the bride from her dressing
room.
17 Let the priests, who *minister to
the LORD,
Weep [a]between the porch and the
altar;
Let them say, [b]"Spare Your
people, O LORD,
And do not give Your heritage to
reproach,
That the nations should [1]rule over
them.
[c]Why should they say among the
peoples,
'Where *is* their God?' "

The Land Refreshed

18 Then the LORD will [a]be* zealous
for His land,
And pity His people.
19 The LORD will answer and say to
His people,
"Behold, I will send you [a]grain and
new wine and oil,
And you will be *satisfied by
them;
I will no longer make you a
reproach among the nations.

20 "But [a]I will remove far from you
[b]the northern *army*,
And will drive him away into a
barren and desolate land,
With his face toward the eastern
sea
And his back [c]toward the western
sea;
His stench will come up,
And his foul odor will rise,
Because he has done [1]monstrous
things."

21 *Fear not, O land;
*Be glad and rejoice,
For the LORD has done
[1]marvelous things!
22 Do not be afraid, you beasts of
the field;
For [a]the open pastures are
springing up,
And the tree bears its fruit;
The fig tree and the vine yield
their strength.
23 Be glad then, you children of
Zion,
And [a]rejoice in the LORD your
God;
For He has given you the
[1]former rain faithfully,
And He [b]will cause the rain to
come down for you—
The former rain,
And the latter rain in the first
month.
24 The threshing floors shall be full
of wheat,
And the vats shall overflow with
new wine and oil.

25 "So I will restore to you the years
[a]that the swarming [1]locust has
eaten,
The crawling locust,

14 [c]Joel 1:9, 13 **15** [a]Num. 10:3; 2 Kin. 10:20 [b]Joel 1:14 [1]*ram's horn* **16** [a]Ex. 19:10 [b]Ps. 19:5 **17** [a]Matt. 23:35 [b]Ex. 32:11, 12; [Is. 37:20]; Amos 7:2, 5 [c]Ps. 42:10 [1]Or *speak a proverb against them* *See WW at 1 Chr. 15:2. **18** [a][Is. 60:10; 63:9, 15] *See WW at Zech. 8:2. **19** [a]Jer. 31:12; Hos. 2:21, 22; Joel 1:10; [Mal. 3:10] *See WW at Amos 4:8.

20 [a]Ex. 10:19 [b]Jer. 1:14, 15 [c]Deut. 11:24 [1]Lit. *great* **21** [1]Lit. *great* *See WW at Ex. 1:17. • See WW at Hab. 3:18. **22** [a]Joel 1:19 **23** [a]Deut. 11:14; Is. 41:16; Jer. 5:24; Hab. 3:18; Zech. 10:7 [b]Lev. 26:4; Hos. 6:3; Zech. 10:1; James 5:7 [1]Or *teacher of righteousness* **25** [a]Joel 1:4–7; 2:2–11 [1]Exact identity of these locusts unknown

2:15–17 See section 3 of Truth-In-Action at the end of Joel.
2:15 Blow the trumpet in Zion: The first trumpet was to sound an alarm of impending danger. See note on v. 1. Here the second trumpet is to call the nation to repentance and contrition before God.
2:16 As the sin and judgment had touched every person from **the elders** to the **nursing babes,** so, too, repentance was to include every person. It was even to interrupt **the bride** and **bridegroom.**
2:17 Between the porch and the altar: Between the porch of the temple and the altar of burnt offering. This would place them directly in front of the door of the holy place, where the presence of God is enthroned. Here **the priests,** as mediators for the nation, would intercede with tears. **Your heritage:** The nation of Judah was considered to be God's own possession. For Him to reject them would mean to reject His own heritage. If Judah were destroyed, it would bring **reproach** on **God** Himself.
2:18–27 This promise of relief and blessing (without a specific time reference) prophesies an era in which both physical and spiritual needs will be met.
2:18 Will be zealous: In the Hebrew language, this can also be understood to be a present, rather than a future, reality. Typical to poetic prophecy is the merging of time. The prayer offered in v. 17 is seen as answered and the restoration of the land as begun.
2:20 The northern *army*: This should be taken to mean the army of locusts. The **eastern sea** is the Dead Sea. The **western sea** is the Mediterranean Sea. One way these swarms are stopped is by a wind that drives the locusts into large bodies of water. **Stench . . . foul odor:** The dead locusts are washed ashore by the waves. Their putrefying remains fill the air with a terrible stench.
2:23 Children of Zion represents all the people of Judah, not just those living in **Zion. Former rain** refers to the autumn rain, which came at planting time. **Latter rain** is the spring rain that occurs just before harvest. This outpouring of refreshing rain which renews the fertility of the parched ground prefigures the outpouring of the Spirit, which will bring spiritual renewal (vv. 28–32).

The consuming locust,
And the chewing locust,
My great army which I sent
among you.
26 You shall [a]eat in plenty and be
satisfied,
And *praise the *name of the
LORD your God,
Who has dealt *wondrously with
you;
And My people shall never be put
to [b]shame.
27 Then you shall know that I *am*
[a]in the midst of Israel:
[b]I *am* the LORD your God
And there is no other.
My people shall never be put to
shame.

God's Spirit Poured Out

 28 "And[a] it shall come to pass
afterward
That [b]I will pour out My Spirit on
all *flesh;
[c]Your sons and your [d]daughters
shall prophesy,
Your old men shall dream
dreams,
Your young men shall see visions.

WORD WEALTH

2:28 dreams, *chalom* (kah-*lohm*); Strong's #2472: A dream; a vision in the night. The root of this noun is the verb *chalam,* "to dream." Dreams of various types are mentioned in Scripture, ranging from the product of one's imagination to the vehicle of God's communication with a person (compare Eccl. 5:3 and Gen. 20:6; see also "false dreams," Jer. 23:32). Many biblical figures, such as Jacob, Laban, Pharaoh, Solomon, Nebuchadnezzar, are known for having dreams (see 1 Kin. 3:5; Dan. 2:1). Joseph and Daniel are the biblical champions of dream-revelation; each not only received his own dreams but also interpreted the dreams of others as well.

26 [a]Lev. 26:5; Deut. 11:15; Is. 62:9 [b]Is. 45:17 *See WW at 1 Chr. 23:30. • See WW at Deut. 18:5. • See WW at Judg. 13:19.
27 [a]Lev. 26:11, 12; [Joel 3:17, 21] [b][Is. 45:5, 6]
28 [a]Ezek. 39:29; Acts 2:17–21 [b]Zech. 12:10 [c]Is. 54:13 [d]Acts 21:9 *See WW at Job 19:26.
29 [a][1 Cor. 12:13; Gal. 3:28]
30 [a]Matt. 24:29; Mark 13:24, 25; Luke 21:11, 25, 26; Acts 2:19
31 [a]Is. 13:9, 10; 34:4; Joel 2:10; 3:15; Matt. 24:29; Mark 13:24; Luke 21:25; Acts 2:20; Rev. 6:12, 13 [b]Is. 13:9; Zeph. 1:14–16; [Mal. 4:1, 5, 6]

29 And also on *My* [a]menservants
and on *My* maidservants
I will pour out My Spirit in those
days.

 **KINGDOM DYNAMICS**

2:28, 29 The Holy Spirit: The Agent of Restoration, RESTORATION. This text designates the Holy Spirit as the Promised One who brings full restoration as a possibility to any human situation. The entire concept of "The Holy Spirit and Restoration" is developed in the study article that begins on page 2012.
(Rev. 19:7–9/John 10:10) J.R.

30 "And [a]I will show wonders in the 1
heavens and in the earth:
Blood and fire and pillars of
smoke.
31 [a]The sun shall be turned into
darkness,
And the moon into blood,
[b]Before the coming of the great
and awesome day of the LORD.
32 And it shall come to pass 2

2:26, 27 Never be put to shame: Repeated in v. 27, this is in direct answer to the priest's prayer in v. 17, "Do not give Your heritage to reproach." For three reasons they will not be ashamed: 1) God **has dealt wondrously with you;** 2) **I *am* in the midst of Israel;** 3) **I *am* the LORD your God.**
2:28, 29 See section 1 of Truth-In-Action at the end of Joel.
2:28, 29 Come to pass afterward: This is the bridge to the final section (2:28—3:21), the application of the plague of locusts to the final judgment of God on the nations at the end of this age.

Pour out signifies great abundance. As the physical rains came in sufficient volume to restore the denuded and parched land, as well as to replenish the dried streams and rivers, so this coming of the Spirit will be an outpouring.

All flesh refers to every class of person, not every individual. As the repentance in v. 16 reached to the youngest and the oldest, so this outpouring of the Spirit also reaches to every age and status, to both men and women.

Prophesy means to bring God's viewpoint to earthly matters. A prophet is one who sees and speaks for God. **Dreams** and **visions** were the common ways in which prophecy came in OT times. The point here is that prophetic ministry would be no longer relegated to a few, but would be the characteristic of even the **young men.**

Manservants . . . maidservants are the slaves. This was absolutely unprecedented. In the OT there is not even one instance of a slave functioning as a prophet.

In Acts 2, Peter sees the outpouring of the Spirit at Pentecost as the fulfillment of this prophecy. See Introduction to Joel: Background; The Holy Spirit at Work.

That this coming of the Spirit was not relegated to the apostles and their contemporaries is made clear by Peter's statement in Acts 2:39, "The promise is to you and to your children, and to all who are afar off, as many as the Lord our God will call."

2:30, 31 See section 1 of Truth-In-Action at the end of Joel.
2:30 Wonders are forerunners of God's judgment. They are patterned after the plagues God brought upon Egypt at the time of Israel's deliverance (see Ex. 7—11). They are also the phenomena that accompany war.
2:31 Moon into blood: The moon appears red as when it is viewed through heavy smoke. The days previous to the **awesome day of the LORD** will be days of great violence and war.
2:32 See section 2 of Truth-In-Action at the end of Joel.
2:32 When the world order is falling apart, **whoever calls on the name of the LORD shall be saved.** These signs of God's judgment are disastrous for those who will continue in their sin. They are, however, signs of redemption and deliverance for those who turn to the Lord.

Mount Zion . . . Jerusalem are to be understood as figures for the dwelling place or presence of God.

That [a]whoever calls on the name
of the LORD
Shall be [1]saved.
For [b]in Mount Zion and in
Jerusalem there shall be
[2]deliverance,
As the LORD has said,
Among [c]the remnant whom the
LORD calls.

God Judges the Nations

3 "For behold, [a]in those days and at
that time,
When I bring back the captives
of Judah and Jerusalem,
2 [a]I will also gather all nations,
And bring them down to the
Valley of Jehoshaphat;
And I [b]will enter into judgment
with them there
On account of My people, My
heritage Israel,
Whom they have scattered
among the nations;
They have also divided up My
land.
3 They have [a]cast lots for My
people,
Have given a boy *as payment* for
a harlot,
And sold a girl for wine, that they
may drink.

4 "Indeed, what have you to do with
Me,
[a]O Tyre and Sidon, and all the
coasts of Philistia?
Will you [1]retaliate against Me?
But if you [2]retaliate against Me,
Swiftly and speedily I will return
your [3]retaliation upon your
own head;
5 Because you have taken My silver
and My gold,
And have carried into your
temples My [1]prized
possessions.
6 Also the people of Judah and the
people of Jerusalem
You have sold to the Greeks,
That you may remove them far
from their borders.

7 "Behold, [a]I will raise them
Out of the place to which you
have sold them,
And will return your [1]retaliation
upon your own head.
8 I will sell your sons and your
daughters
Into the hand of the people of
Judah,
And they will sell them to the
[a]Sabeans,[1]
To a people [b]far off;
For the LORD has spoken."

9 [a]Proclaim this among the *nations:
"Prepare for war!
Wake up the mighty men,
Let all the men of war draw
near,
Let them come up.

32 [a]Jer. 33:3; Acts 2:21; Rom. 10:13 [b]Is. 46:13; [Rom. 11:26] [c]Is. 11:11; Jer. 31:7; [Mic. 4:7]; Rom. 9:27 [1]Or *delivered* [2]Or *salvation*

CHAPTER 3

1 [a]Jer. 30:3; Ezek. 38:14
2 [a]Is. 66:18; Mic. 4:12; Zech. 14:2 [b]Is. 66:16; Jer. 25:31; Ezek. 38:22
3 [a]Obad. 11; Nah. 3:10
4 [a]Is. 14:29–31; Jer. 47:1–7; Ezek. 25:15–17; Amos 1:6–8; Zech. 9:5–7 [1]Or *render Me repayment* [2]Or *repay Me* [3]Or *repayment*
5 [1]Lit. *precious good things*
7 [a]Is. 43:5, 6; Jer. 23:8; Zech. 9:13 [1]Or *repayment*
8 [a]Ezek. 23:42 [b]Jer. 6:20 [1]Lit. *Shebaites,* Is. 60:6; Ezek. 27:22
9 [a]Jer. 6:4; Ezek. 38:7; Mic. 3:5 *See WW at Ps. 106:47.

Remnant: Those who are saved, those who have called on **the name of the LORD.** See note on Zeph. 2:7.

Whom the LORD calls: Here we see that salvation is twofold. It is both the calling on God by men and the calling of God to men. God is calling to men through the miraculous wonders. Men can respond by calling on God and will then **be saved** or delivered.

No event in Joel's time answers this prophetic section (vv. 28–32). It has its initial fulfillment on the Day of Pentecost when the outpouring of the Spirit began "the last days." Joel's prophecy will culminate with the coming again of the Messiah, Jesus Christ, and the subsequent end of this world. We are now living in these prolonged last days. The rising crescendo of violence and war that characterizes contemporary history should be understood as the beckoning of God for men to call upon Him and be saved. See note on Obad. 15.

3:1 In those days points back to 2:28–32. It begins a more complete explanation of exactly how the judgment of the Lord on the nations will be carried out. **Captives** contextually are those of Judah and Israel who had been disbursed throughout the nations of the Earth. It answers to v. 2, "whom they have scattered among the nations." In a broader sense, some scholars interpret it as applying to dispersed Jews returning to a restored end-times Israel. Others see it as symbolically referring to the church.

3:2 Valley of Jehoshaphat: In Jewish tradition this is thought to be part of the Kidron Valley between the temple and the Mount of Olives. "Jehoshaphat" means "Yahweh Is Judge." This, therefore, may be a symbolic place of judgment and decision rather than an actual place in Joel's mind.

3:3 Cast lots for My people: When a nation was conquered, it was a common practice to distribute the slaves by drawing lots. **Boy *as payment* for a harlot . . . girl for wine:** The terrible condition of actually using boys and girls as currency to pay for a night with a prostitute or to get a glass of wine.

3:4–8 This section deals with the contemporary nations in Joel's day. They also represent God's enemies throughout history.

3:4 Tyre and Sidon: These were the main cities of the Phoenicians and here stand for all the Phoenicians. **Coasts of Philistia:** A coalition of five major city-kingdoms that were the age-old enemies of Israel. These include the modern area of the Gaza Strip.

3:5 This may refer to the plundering of Judah and Jerusalem during the time of Jehoram. See 2 Chr. 21:16, 17.

3:8 Sabeans were well-known traders in Arabia.

3:9–17 This passage returns to the judgment referred to in v. 2.

3:9 Prepare for war: This is not a call to Judah, but to the heathen nations.

10 [a]Beat your plowshares into swords
And your [1]pruning hooks into
spears;
[b]Let the weak say, 'I *am* strong.' "
11 Assemble and come, all you
nations,
And gather together all around.
Cause [a]Your mighty ones to go
down there, O LORD.

12 "Let the nations be wakened, and
come up to the Valley of
Jehoshaphat;
For there I will sit to [a]judge all
the surrounding nations.
13 [a]Put in the sickle, for [b]the harvest
is ripe.
Come, go down;
For the [c]winepress is full,
The vats overflow—
For their wickedness *is* great."

14 Multitudes, multitudes in the
valley of decision!
For [a]the day of the LORD *is* near
in the valley of decision.
15 The sun and moon will grow
dark,
And the stars will diminish their
brightness.
16 The LORD also will **roar** from
Zion,
And utter His voice from
Jerusalem;
The heavens and *earth will
shake;
[a]But the LORD will be a shelter for
His people,
And the strength of the children
of Israel.

WORD WEALTH

3:16 roar, *sha'ag* (shah-*ahg*); Strong's #7580: To roar, especially to roar as a lion; to rumble or thunder. This verb occurs 22 times, about half of these referring to roaring lions. A few references describe angry, growling men (see Ps. 22:13; 74:4; Zeph. 3:3). Most of the remaining occurrences pertain to the roaring that God will do as He goes to battle. The present reference, as well as Amos 1:2, states that Yahweh will "roar from Zion." Here it refers to His roaring against Israel's enemies, and in Amos it concerns His response to Israel's transgressions.

10 [a][Is. 2:4; Mic. 4:3] [b]Zech. 12:8 [1]*pruning knives*
11 [a]Ps. 103:20; Is. 13:3
12 [a][Ps. 96:13]; Is. 2:4
13 [a][Matt. 13:39]; Rev. 14:15 [b]Jer. 51:33; Hos. 6:11 [c][Is. 63:3]; Lam. 1:5; Rev. 14:19
14 [a]Joel 2:1
16 [a][Is. 51:5, 6] *See WW at Ex. 32:13.
17 [a]Obad. 16; Zech. 8:3
18 [a]Ps. 46:4; Ezek. 47:1; Zech. 14:8; [Rev. 22:1] [1]Heb. *Shittim*
20 *See WW at Esth. 9:28.
21 [a]Is. 4:4 *See WW at Num. 14:18.

17 "So you shall know that I *am* the
LORD your God,
Dwelling in Zion My [a]holy
mountain.
Then Jerusalem shall be holy,
And no aliens shall ever pass
through her again."

God Blesses His People

18 And it will come to pass in that
day
That the mountains shall drip
with new wine,
The hills shall flow with milk,
And all the brooks of Judah shall
be flooded with water;
A [a]fountain shall flow from the
house of the LORD
And water the Valley of [1]Acacias.

19 "Egypt shall be a desolation,
And Edom a desolate wilderness,
Because of violence *against* the
people of Judah,
For they have shed innocent
blood in their land.
20 But Judah shall abide forever,
And Jerusalem from *generation
to generation.
21 For I will [a]acquit* them of the 3
guilt of bloodshed, whom I had
not acquitted;
For the LORD dwells in Zion."

3:10 Beat your plowshares . . . pruning hooks: This is an inversion of Is. 2:4. There the weapons of war are to be made into instruments of peace. Here the implements of peaceful agriculture are to be made into weapons of war. The language is symbolic.
3:11 Your mighty ones are the heroes of God or the heavenly armies, which carry out His bidding.
3:13 The harvest is ripe . . . the winepress is full refers to the fact that the nations are ripe for God's judgment. These figures are also used for the last judgment of God in Rev. 4.
3:14 Multitudes: The word can also be translated "tumult" and refers to the noisy multitudes flowing into the **valley of decision,** the place of God's final verdict.
3:16 It is only to His enemies that the Lord is terrible and fearful. To His remnant, those people who have responded to His call by calling on Him (2:32), He is a **shelter** and a **strength.**
3:17 Jerusalem stands not for the capital of earthly Israel, but for the purified city where God dwells with His people. **No aliens:** That is, no unrighteous will be permitted to enter after the judgment and cleansing by the Lord (Rev. 21:27).
3:18 The Valley of Acacias is the barren valley of the Jordan, just above the Dead Sea. The acacia plant is able to survive in very barren and dry surroundings.
3:21 See section 3 of Truth-In-Action at the end of Joel.
3:21 I will acquit . . . whom I had not acquitted: Some make this the pardoning of the nations who have now been judged by God and therefore can be pardoned. Others see this as a statement indicating that all guilt can now be forgiven since **the LORD dwells in Zion.** Joel now uses this dwelling in Zion to mean that the Lord has established His kingdom and all the enemies of His people have been eliminated. This is the beginning of the world to come.

TRUTH-IN-ACTION through JOEL

Letting the LIFE of the Holy Spirit Bring Faith's Works Alive in You!

Truth Joel Teaches	Text	**Action** Joel Invites
1 Steps to Knowing God and His Ways The knowledge of God is to be passed from generation to generation by instructing our children in the nature, character, and ways of God. Thus trained, a deeper understanding of God's current move, whether in judgment or revival, is possible. This understanding avoids reliance on fleshly or demonic sources of guidance, and allows the alignment of our priorities with God's purpose.	1:3	**Train up** your children in the nurture and admonition of the Lord. **Be an example** your children can follow to know the ways of the Lord and walk in them.
	2:28, 29	**Gratefully receive** the Holy Spirit, by whom God accomplishes His purposes on the Earth. **Be renewed** by the outpouring of the Holy Spirit.
	2:30, 31	**Believe** that signs, wonders, and miracles are part of God's unchanging nature and working.
2 Steps to Receiving God's Grace Receiving the grace of God is neither complex nor difficult. It requires only the decision that God is both able and willing to save, and the act of humbly calling on His name. He is ready to be our Deliverer. The choice is ours.	2:32	**Choose to call** on the name of Jesus for salvation and deliverance. **Recognize** that "calling on His name" relates to inviting His saving and delivering action in all facets of your life, not only your initial experience of New Birth.
3 Steps to Dealing with Corporate Sin Joel's prophecies explain how a people must deal with corporate sin. His prophetic warnings and exhortations are addressed primarily to the spiritual leaders. He calls them first to lead in wholehearted repentance and then to confront the people's sin. Corporate fasts and solemn assemblies to cry out to the Lord are some of the practices Joel recommends to deal with corporate sin.	1:13	**Understand** that the sin of God's people is serious and calls for serious repentance and mourning on the part of spiritual leaders.
	2:1	**Warn God's people** of the consequences of sin.
	1:14	**Teach the church** to repent corporately for corporate sin. **Declare** a time for corporate fasting and solemn assemblies to identify sin and pray for restoration in the body.
	2:12–14	**Repent quickly** with mourning when sin is discovered in you. **Confess** your sin and **let God work** in your heart. **Continually turn** to God and set your affections on His will and His ways.
	2:15–17	**Call for revival. Enjoin** the elders to lead in fasting and prayer.
	3:21	**Be assured** that there is no sin for which Jesus' blood cannot atone.

The Book of AMOS

Author: Amos
Date: 760–750 B.C.
Theme: The Judgment of God Is About to Fall on Israel
Key Words: Judgment, Righteousness, Justice

Author Amos, whose name means "Burden-Bearer," was a native of the small town of Tekoa in the Judean hills, about 16 kilometers (10 miles) south of Jerusalem. He is the first of the so-called "writing prophets" of the eighth century B.C. The others include Hosea to Israel, and Micah and Isaiah to Judah. Amos disclaimed training as a professional prophet, admitting he was a shepherd and one who tended sycamore-fig trees. In spite of his nonprofessional background, Amos was called to deliver God's message to the northern kingdom of Israel.

Date Amos prophesied during the reigns of Uzziah of Judah (792–740 B.C.) and Jeroboam II of Israel (793–753 B.C.). His ministry was between 760 and 750 B.C. and seems to have occupied less than two years.

Background The middle of the eighth century B.C. was a time of great prosperity for both Israel and Judah. Under Jeroboam, Israel had again gained control of the international trade routes—the King's Highway through Transjordan, and the Way of the Sea through the Jezreel Valley and along the coastal plain. According to 2 Kings 14:25, he restored the borders of Israel from Lebo Hamath (in the north) to the Sea of the Arabah (the Dead Sea in the south). Judah, under Uzziah, regained Elath (the seaport on the Gulf of Aqaba), and expanded to the southwest at the expense of the Philistines. Israel and Judah had reached new political and military heights, but the religious situation was at an all-time low. Idolatry was rampant; the rich were living in luxury while the poor were oppressed; there was widespread immorality; and the judicial system was corrupt. The people interpreted their prosperity as a sign of God's blessing on them. Amos's task was to deliver the message that God was displeased with the nation. His patience was exhausted. Punishment was inevitable. The nation would be destroyed unless there was a change of heart—a change that would "let justice run down like water, and righteousness like a mighty stream" (5:24).

Content The Book of Amos is basically a message of judgment: judgment on the nations, oracles and visions of divine judgment on Israel. The central theme of the book is that the people of Israel have broken their covenant with God. As a result, God's punishment of their sin will be severe. Amos begins with a series of indictments against the seven neighbors of Israel, including Judah, and then he indicts Israel, too (1:3—2:16). Each foreign nation is to be punished for specific offenses either against Israel or some other nation.

This judgment on the nations teaches us that God is a universal Monarch. All nations are under His control. They must answer to Him for their mistreatment of other nations and peoples. Israel and Judah, however, will be punished because they have broken their covenant with God. The next section (3:1—6:14) is a series of three oracles or sermons directed against Israel. These include the threat of exile. A third section (7:1—9:10) is a series of five visions of judgment, in two of which God withdraws. Finally, Amos promises restoration for Israel (9:11–15).

Literary Features Even though Amos downplays his professional training, his style suggests a well-educated person. He skillfully uses puns or wordplays. In 8:1, 2, for example, the Hebrew word for "summer fruit" sounds similar to the word for "end." Like summer fruit, Israel is ripe for harvest. The geographical-psychological approach in the judgment of the nations (1:3—2:16) is another indication of literary craftsmanship. Beginning with the nations on the four corners (Damascus, Gaza, Tyre and Edom), Amos crosses the land twice and draws the circle ever tighter with Ammon, Moab, and Judah. He uses a literary method known as graduated numbers or numerical parallelism: "For three transgressions . . . and for four" (see, for example, 1:3, 6, 9). This numerical system suggests the meaning, "For enough transgressions . . . for more than enough." Similar uses of graduated numerals are found in Proverbs 6:16; 30:15, 18, 21, 29; Micah 5:5.

Amos uses the messenger style of speech, indicating he is speaking in the name of another: "Thus says the LORD" (1:3, 6) or "Hear this word" (3:1; 4:1; 5:1). Amos sings a funeral dirge for Israel in anticipation of her demise (5:1, 2). He uses many metaphors from the country life he knew as a shepherd and farmer (1:3; 2:13; 3:12; 4:1; 9:9). Amos has the ability to develop a series of sayings into a powerful climax: the oracles against the nations (1:3—2:10), the recitation of calamities leading to God's visitation (4:6–12), and the visions that move from God's forbearance to His judgment (7:1–19; 8:1–3).

Personal Application Amos stresses that righteousness and justice are essential to a healthy society. Religion is more than observing feast days and holding sacred assemblies; true religion demands righteous living. The way a man treats his neighbor reveals his relationship with God. Jesus said the greatest commandment is to love God. The second is to love our neighbor as ourselves. This is the message of Amos. This is the message needed today. We also are living in a prosperous, materialistic society. Because we are prosperous, we may also deceive ourselves into believing that we have God's blessing on us. The tendency to give God material goods and believe we have satisfied Him is ever with us. Material prosperity often leads to religious and moral corruption. Observation of external rites is not enough. God demands our obedience—a heartfelt attitude that issues in action to meet the needs of our fellow human beings.

Christ Revealed There are no direct references to Christ in Amos. No typology is present either. There does seem to be an allusion, however, to Amos 1:9, 10 in Jesus' statement in Matthew 11:21, 22. Amos speaks of the judgment to come upon Tyre. Jesus says that if the mighty works performed in Chorazin and Bethsaida "had been done in Tyre and Sidon, they would have repented long ago in sackcloth and ashes." One other concept from Amos is picked up by John in Revelation. Amos speaks of God's prophets as servants and says that God does nothing without revealing His plan to His servants the prophets (Amos 3:7). John speaks about the sounding of the seventh trumpet when the "mystery of God would be finished, as He declared to His servants the prophets" (Rev. 10:7).

The Holy Spirit at Work The work of the Holy Spirit is not mentioned specifically in Amos. The process of inspiring the prophet and revealing God's message is usually attributed by other prophets to the Spirit (see Is. 48:16; Ezek. 3:24; Mic. 3:8). As is the case in most of the prophets, it is almost impossible to draw a distinction between the Lord and His Spirit. Amos does not happen to mention the Spirit in his work, but those activities ascribed to the Spirit by other prophets are present in Amos.

Outline of Amos

I. Introduction **1:1, 2**

II. Judgment on the nations **1:3—2:16**
- A. Damascus 1:3–5
- B. Gaza 1:6–8
- C. Tyre 1:9, 10
- D. Edom 1:11, 12
- E. Ammon 1:13–15
- F. Moab 2:1–3
- G. Judah 2:4, 5
- H. Israel 2:6–16

III. Oracles against Israel **3:1—6:14**
- A. Judgment on God's chosen people 3:1–15
  1. Punishment announced 3:1, 2
  2. Punishment deserved 3:3–10
  3. Punishment described 3:11–15
- B. Judgment on God's unresponsive people 4:1–13
  1. The oppressive women of Samaria 4:1–3
  2. Sacrificial transgression 4:4, 5
  3. Failure of Israel to respond to calamities 4:6–11
  4. Punishment on hardened people 4:12, 13
- C. Judgment on God's unrepentant people 5:1—6:14
  1. A funeral dirge for Israel 5:1–3
  2. A call to repentance 5:4–9
  3. Enumeration of evil acts 5:10–13
  4. A second call to repentance 5:14, 15
  5. Judgment will bring wailing and mourning 5:16, 17
  6. The Day of the Lord 5:18–20
  7. Need for justice instead of festivals 5:21–27
  8. Woe to those who are complacent 6:1–7
  9. Judgment on unrepentant people 6:8–14

IV. Visions of judgment **7:1—9:10**
- A. Relented visions 7:1–6
  1. Locust swarms 7:1–3
  2. Consuming fire 7:4–6
- B. Unrelented visions 7:7—9:10
  1. The plumb line 7:7–17
     - a. The vision 7:7–9
     - b. Opposition of Amaziah 7:10–17
  2. The basket of summer fruit 8:1–14
     - a. The vision 8:1–3
     - b. The exposition 8:4–14
  3. The Lord beside the altar 9:1–10
     - a. The vision 9:1–4
     - b. The exposition 9:5–10

V. Restoration of Israel **9:11–15**
- A. Tabernacle of David raised up 9:11, 12
- B. The land and people restored and blessed 9:13–15

THE words of Amos, who was among the [a]sheepbreeders of [b]Tekoa, which he saw concerning Israel in the days of [c]Uzziah king of Judah, and in the days of [d]Jeroboam the son of Joash, king of Israel, two years before the [e]earthquake.
2 And he said:

"The LORD [a]roars* from Zion,
And utters His voice from Jerusalem;
The pastures of the shepherds *mourn,
And the top of [b]Carmel withers."

Judgment on the Nations

3 Thus says the LORD:

"For three *transgressions of [a]Damascus, and for four,
I will not turn away its *punishment*,
Because they have [b]threshed Gilead with implements of iron.
4 [a]But I will send a fire into the house of Hazael,
Which shall devour the palaces of [b]Ben-Hadad.
5 I will also break the *gate* [a]bar of Damascus,
And cut off the inhabitant from the Valley of Aven,
And the one who [1]holds the scepter from [2]Beth Eden.
The people of Syria shall go captive to Kir,"
Says the LORD.

6 Thus says the LORD:

"For three transgressions of [a]Gaza, and for four,
I will not turn away its *punishment*,
Because they took captive the whole captivity
To deliver *them* up to Edom.
7 [a]But I will send a fire upon the wall of Gaza,
Which shall devour its palaces.
8 I will cut off the inhabitant [a]from Ashdod,
And the one who holds the scepter from Ashkelon;
I will [b]turn My hand against Ekron,
And [c]the remnant of the Philistines shall *perish,"
Says the Lord GOD.

9 Thus says the LORD:

"For three transgressions of [a]Tyre, and for four,
I will not turn away its *punishment*,
Because they delivered up the whole captivity to Edom,
And did not remember the covenant of brotherhood.

CHAPTER 1

1 [a]2 Kin. 3:4; Amos 7:14 [b]2 Sam. 14:2 [c]2 Chr. 26:1–23 [d]Amos 7:10 [e]Zech. 14:5
2 [a]Joel 3:16 [b]1 Sam. 25:2 *See WW at Joel 3:16. • See WW at Joel 1:9.
3 [a]Is. 8:4; 17:1–3 [b]2 Kin. 10:32, 33 *See WW at Ezek. 18:31.
4 [a]Jer. 49:27; 51:30 [b]2 Kin. 6:24
5 [a]Jer. 51:30 [1]Rules [2]Lit. *House of Eden*
6 [a]Jer. 47:1, 5
7 [a]Jer. 47:1
8 [a]Zeph. 2:4 [b]Ps. 81:14 [c]Ezek. 25:16 *See WW at Judg. 5:31.
9 [a]Is. 23:1–18

1:1 Amos: The name, used only in this book, means "Burden-Bearer." **Sheepbreeders:** This term appears in the OT with reference to one other man (Mesha, king of Moab) and probably means a "breeder" of small cattle (sheep and goats). **Tekoa:** See Introduction to Amos: Author. **Saw:** Received by revelation. Amos reports five visions. **Earthquake:** Mentioned also in Zech. 14:5. The excavators at Hazor found evidence of an earthquake, which they date to about 760 B.C.

1:2 Roars: The voice of the Lord thunders from Jerusalem, south of Israel, to Mt. Carmel in the north. Amos will tell us in 3:8 that "a lion [the Lord] has roared," and this is why he is prophesying. The Lord's voice is described as producing drought, which affects the verdant area of Carmel (see Ps. 29).

1:3—2:3 This section consists of various oracles against the nations. The specific atrocities mentioned apparently occurred in connection with various border wars during the previous 200 years. The list of specific nations given here is the most comprehensive of all the prophetic oracles against the nations. Although specific judgments against specific nations are apparently in view, precise historical fulfillment of all the judgments is difficult to determine. In this sense, it is best to see Amos's larger purpose in keeping with the futuristic judgment oracles of the Day of the Lord. See notes on Obad. 15 and Zech. 9—14.

1:3 Three transgressions: See Introduction to Amos: Literary Features, for the use of graduated numerals. **Damascus:** Capital of Aram, a city-state to the northeast of Israel. Also translated "Syria" (v. 5), Aram was constantly at war with Israel. **Threshed Gilead** is a description of the cruel military campaigns waged against the Israelite inhabitants of Gilead, the territory east of the Jordan. This may be the campaign recorded in 2 Kin. 13:3–7.

1:4 Hazael murdered the ruling Ben-Hadad (2 Kin. 8:7–15) and ruled from about 842 to 806 B.C. The son of Hazael was also named Ben-Hadad (2 Kin. 13:3).

1:5 Valley of Aven may be a pun on the name "On," the ancient city of Baalbek. "Aven" and "On" look similar in Hebrew. **Beth Eden:** If this is the Bit-adini mentioned in Akkadian texts, it is another Aramean city-state far to the north of Damascus. **Kir:** According to 9:7, God brought the Arameans from Kir, an area in Mesopotamia near Elam. God will now send them back to where they came from.

1:6 Gaza was one of the five main cities of the Philistines. The others were Ashdod, Ashkelon, Ekron (v. 8), and Gath. **Took captive:** This charge of selling an entire population to Edom is also brought against Tyre (v. 9). **Edom** was the country southeast of the Dead Sea. It was the home of Esau, the brother of Jacob. See notes on Obad. 10, 11.

1:8 The **Philistines** were part of the Sea Peoples who invaded Canaan in the thirteenth century B.C. The name "Palestine" comes from this word.

1:9 Tyre is situated on the Mediterranean coast, north of Israel. Tyre represents the nation of Phoenicia. **Covenant of brotherhood** refers to an international treaty between Tyre and another state.

10 But I will send a fire upon the wall
of Tyre,
Which shall devour its palaces."

11 Thus says the LORD:

"For three transgressions of
[a]Edom, and for four,
I will not turn away its
punishment,
Because he pursued his [b]brother
with the sword,
And cast off all pity;
His anger tore perpetually,
And he kept his wrath forever.
12 But [a]I will send a fire upon
Teman,
Which shall devour the palaces of
Bozrah."

13 Thus says the LORD:

"For three transgressions of
[a]the people of Ammon, and for
four,
I will not turn away its
punishment,
Because they ripped open the
women with child in Gilead,
That they might enlarge their
territory.
14 But I will kindle a fire in the wall
of [a]Rabbah,
And it shall devour its palaces,
[b]Amid *shouting in the day of
battle,
And a tempest in the day of the
whirlwind.
15 [a]Their king shall go into captivity,
He and his princes together,"
Says the LORD.

2

Thus says the LORD:

[a]"For three transgressions of Moab,
and for four,
I will not turn away its
punishment,
Because he [b]burned the bones of
the king of Edom to lime.
2 But I will send a fire upon Moab,
And it shall devour the palaces of
[a]Kerioth;
Moab shall die with tumult,
With shouting *and* trumpet
sound.
3 And I will cut off [a]the judge from
its midst,
And slay all its princes with him,"
Says the LORD.

Judgment on Judah

4 Thus says the LORD:

"For three transgressions of
[a]Judah, and for four,
I will not turn away its
punishment,
[b]Because they have **despised** the
law of the LORD,
And have not kept His
commandments.
[c]Their lies lead them astray,
Lies [d]which their fathers
followed.

11 [a]Is. 21:11; Jer. 49:8; Ezek. 25:12–14; Mal. 1:2–5 [b]Num. 20:14–21; 2 Chr. 28:17; Obad. 10–12
12 [a]Jer. 49:7, 20; Obad. 9, 10
13 [a]Jer. 49:1; Ezek. 25:2; Zeph. 2:8, 9
14 [a]Deut. 3:11; 1 Chr. 20:1; Jer. 49:2 [b]Ezek. 21:22; Amos 2:2 *See WW at Ezra 3:11.
15 [a]Jer. 49:3

CHAPTER 2

1 [a]Is. 15:1–16; Jer. 25:21; Ezek. 25:8–11; Zeph. 2:8–11 [b]2 Kin. 3:26, 27
2 [a]Jer. 48:24, 41
3 [a]Num. 24:17; Jer. 48:7
4 [a]2 Kin. 17:19; Hos. 12:2; Amos 3:2 [b]Lev. 26:14 [c]Is. 9:15, 16; 28:15; Jer. 16:19; Hab. 2:18 [d]Jer. 9:14; 16:11, 12; Ezek. 20:13, 16, 18

WORD WEALTH

2:4 despised, *ma'as* (mah-*ahs*); Strong's #3988: To reject, refuse, abhor, despise, disregard; spurn, disdain; to regard as unimportant or worthless. This verb occurs 75 times. It represents the opposite of choosing something, thus rejecting, casting away, or having aversion to something. *Ma'as* is translated "rejected" in Ps. 118:22, speaking of the stone that the builders threw away as unfit. *Ma'as* also appears in 1 Sam. 8:7, where the people rejected God. Compare the use of *ma'as* in 1 Sam. 16:1, 7; Is. (*cont. on next page*)

1:11 Edom: See note on v. 6. **Pursued his brother** is probably a reference to Judah.
1:12 Teman was the most important city in southern Edom, and **Bozrah** held the same position in the north. Thus Teman and Bozrah designate the whole nation.
1:13 Ammon was a state on the east side of Jordan between Moab to the south and Gilead to the north. The atrocity charged, **they ripped open the women with child,** is a reference to a border war when Ammon tried to expand her territory north into Gilead. Ammon attempted to expand on every possible occasion (see Judg. 10:7–9; 11:4–33; 1 Sam. 11:1–11; 14:47).
1:14 Rabbah: Also known as Rabbath Ammon, this city was the Ammonite capital. It is the present city of Amman in Jordan.
1:15 Captivity: Previously Amos had spoken of people and rulers "cut off" (v. 5) from their land. Here he alludes to captivity, which introduces the motif of exile. This is the fate facing Israel.
2:1 Moab was situated east of the Dead Sea, with the northern border along the Arnon River. **Burned the bones:** This act was considered an outrage in the culture of that time.
2:2 Kerioth may be simply the plural form of "cities," but Jer. 48:24 lists it as a city. The site is unknown. Its identification with Ar is a possibility.
2:3 Again the country and rulers are destroyed. The term **judge** is a synonym for "king."
2:4–16 The final two oracles are against God's people. They suggest a long history of rebellion and a lack of gratitude.
2:4 See section 2 of Truth-In-Action at the end of Amos.
2:4 The judgment on **Judah** is not for an atrocity against another state or people, but for the breach of contract with Yahweh.

(*cont. from preceding page*)
5:24; Ezek. 20:16; Hos. 4:6. In the present reference, Jerusalem's citizens disregarded God's written instructions.

5 [a]But I will send a fire upon Judah,
And it shall devour the palaces of
Jerusalem."

Judgment on Israel

6 Thus says the LORD:

"For three transgressions of
[a]Israel, and for four,
I will not turn away its
punishment,
Because [b]they sell the *righteous
for silver,
And the [c]poor for a pair of
sandals.
7 They [1]pant after the dust of the
earth *which is* on the head of
the poor,
And [a]pervert the way of the
humble.
[b]A man and his father go in to the
same girl,
[c]To defile My holy name.
8 They lie down [a]by every altar on
clothes [b]taken in pledge,
And drink the wine of [1]the
condemned *in* the house of their
god.

5 [a]Hos. 8:14
6 [a]2 Kin. 17:7–18; 18:12 [b]Is. 29:21 [c]Amos 4:1; 5:11; 8:6 *See WW at Lam. 1:18.
7 [a]Amos 5:12 [b]Ezek. 22:11 [c]Lev. 20:3 [1]Or *trample on*
8 [a]1 Cor. 8:10 [b]Ex. 22:26 [1]Or *those punished by fines*
9 [a]Num. 21:25 [b]Ezek. 31:3 [c][Mal. 4:1]
10 [a]Ex. 12:51 [b]Deut. 2:7
11 [a]Num. 12:6 [b]Num. 6:2, 3
12 [a]Is. 30:10
13 [a]Is. 1:14 [1]Or *tottering under* [2]Or *totters*
14 [a]Jer. 46:6 [b]Ps. 33:16 [1]Or *the place of refuge* [2]Lit. *save his soul or life*

9 "Yet *it was* I *who* destroyed the
[a]Amorite before them,
Whose height *was* like the
[b]height of the cedars,
And he *was as* strong as the oaks;
Yet I [c]destroyed his fruit above
And his roots beneath.
10 Also *it was* [a]I *who* brought you
up from the land of Egypt,
And [b]led you forty years through
the wilderness,
To possess the land of the
Amorite.
11 I raised up some of your sons as 2
[a]prophets,
And some of your young men as
[b]Nazirites.
Is it not so, O you children of
Israel?"
Says the LORD.
12 "But you gave the Nazirites wine
to drink,
And commanded the prophets
[a]saying,
'Do not prophesy!'

13 "Behold,[a] I am [1]weighed down by
you,
As a cart full of sheaves [2]is
weighed down.
14 [a]Therefore [1]flight shall perish
from the swift,
The strong shall not strengthen
his power,
[b]Nor shall the mighty [2]deliver
himself;

2:5 Although a prophet primarily to northern Israel, Amos prophesied **fire upon Judah** as well. Judah fell to Babylon in 587 B.C.

2:6 After crisscrossing the land from northeast to southwest and northwest to southeast, Amos tightened the circle with Ammon, Moab, and Judah. Now he reaches the climax, the goal for which he has been striving from the first. **Israel,** too, is guilty before God. Specific sins that spell out the alienation of the people from God are enumerated. In a society where justice and righteousness prevail, the sins mentioned here would never occur. **Sell the righteous** refers to selling persons into slavery. People captured in war or people with debts were candidates for slavery (see 2 Kin. 4:1–7). The **righteous** one is the innocent party in the lawsuit (see 5:12). **Pair of sandals** may mean "a cheap price." On the other hand, since a sandal played a part in transactions for land (see Ruth 4:7, 8), perhaps the person is sold for land.

2:7 An alternate reading for **pant after the dust** is "trample on the head of the poor" (see 8:4). This statement parallels v. 6. The legal process has been perverted. The courts are used to oppress the poor rather than to defend their rights. ***The same girl*** *could* refer to a cultic prostitute, but it may also refer to a woman who is a bondservant and is forced to be a concubine for both a **man and his father.** Both are forbidden (see Deut. 23:17; 22:28–30). **Defile My holy name:** See Lev. 18:21; 19:12; Jer. 34:16.

2:8 Social practices are placed within a ceremonial setting. **Clothes** were regularly given as pledge for a debt. **Wine** is payment in kind from a debtor. The practice in itself may be legal, but Amos sees something here that borders on the oppression of the poor by the rich. The rich are engaged in worship at the **altar** or in the **house of their God** and see no incongruity between their social action and their worship.

2:9 Amorite is used for the pre-Israelite inhabitants of Canaan (Gen. 15:16). Since they were tall and strong, only Yahweh could have defeated them. **Fruit above and his roots beneath:** Totally.

2:10 The historical relationship upon which the covenant is based is here recited by Amos. God delivered the people and brought them to the land (see 3:1; 9:7).

2:11, 12 See section 2 of Truth-In-Action at the end of Amos.

2:11 Amos considered himself one of the **prophets** God had raised up. **Nazirites** were dedicated wholly to God. The vow of the Nazirites prohibited them from drinking wine. **Children of Israel:** Israel was used to designate the 10 tribes who made up the northern kingdom as distinct from Judah, the southern kingdom. Here, however, he may merely be calling attention to their descent from Jacob, and thus all the people—both north and south—are included.

2:13 I am weighed down can be read "I will press you" or "I let [the ground] totter under you." **Cart full of sheaves:** A metaphor drawn from the pastoral experience of Amos.

2:14–16 Amos presents successive scenes of the powerlessness of men too frightened to function properly. The appearance of Yahweh will render them helpless.

15 He shall not stand who handles
the bow,
The swift of foot shall not
[1]escape,
Nor shall he who rides a horse
deliver himself.
16 The most [1]courageous men of
might
Shall flee naked in that day,"
Says the LORD.

Authority of the Prophet's Message

3 Hear this word that the LORD has
spoken against you, O children of
Israel, against the whole family which
I brought up from the land of Egypt,
saying:

2 "You[a] only have I known of all the
*families of the earth;
[b]Therefore I will punish you for all
your iniquities."

3 Can two walk together, unless
they are agreed?
4 Will a lion roar in the forest, when
he has no prey?
Will a young lion [1]cry out of
his den, if he has caught
nothing?
5 Will a bird fall into a snare on the
earth, where there is no [1]trap
for it?
Will a snare spring up from the
earth, if it has caught nothing
at all?
1 6 If a [1]trumpet is blown in a city,
will not the people be afraid?
[a]If there is calamity in a city,
will not the LORD have done
it?

1 7 Surely the Lord GOD does
nothing,
Unless [a]He **reveals** His secret to
His servants the prophets.

15 [1]Or *save*
16 [1]Lit. *strong of his heart among the mighty*

CHAPTER 3

2 [a][Gen. 18:19; Ex. 19:5, 6; Deut. 7:6; Ps. 147:19] [b]Jer. 14:10; Ezek. 20:36; Dan. 9:12; Matt. 11:22; [Rom. 2:9]
*See WW at Gen. 12:3.
4 [1]Lit. *give his voice*
5 [1]Or *bait* or *lure*
6 [a]Is. 45:7 [1]*ram's horn*
7 [a]Gen. 6:13; 18:17; [Jer. 23:22]; Dan. 9:22; [John 15:15]
8 [a]Jer. 20:9; [Mic. 3:8]; Acts 4:20; 1 Cor. 9:16
*See WW at Joel 3:16. • See WW at Ex. 1:17.
9 [1]So with MT; LXX *Assyria* [2]Or *oppression*
10 [a]Ps. 14:4; Jer. 4:22; Amos 5:7; 6:12 [1]Or *devastation*
11 *See WW at Jer. 16:19.

WORD WEALTH

3:7 reveals, *galah* (gah-*lah*); Strong's #1540: To uncover, reveal, open, lay bare, strip away, denude, expose, disclose, unveil; to depart, or to go into exile. In the present reference, *galah* has to do with the Lord's laying bare, exposing, revealing, uncovering, and disclosing His secret plans to the prophets, who are His servants. Other usages of *galah* include "uncovering" a near relative's nakedness (Lev. 20); "going away" or "departing" into captivity, as though such an exile was a stripping bare of the blessed life (2 Kin. 25:21); the "departing" (literally the "stripping away") of God's glory from Israel (1 Sam. 4:21, 22).

8 A lion has *roared!
Who will not *fear?
The Lord GOD has spoken!
[a]Who can but prophesy?

Punishment of Israel's Sins

9 "Proclaim in the palaces at
[1]Ashdod,
And in the palaces in the land of
Egypt, and say:
'Assemble on the mountains of
Samaria;
See great tumults in her midst,
And the [2]oppressed within
her.
10 For they [a]do not know to do
right,'
Says the LORD,
'Who store up violence and
[1]robbery in their palaces.' "

11 Therefore thus says the Lord GOD:

"An adversary *shall be* all around
the land;
He shall sap your *strength from
you,
And your palaces shall be
plundered."

2:16 That day: The day God visits His people to carry out His plan of punishment. See note on 5:18–20.
3:1—6:14 Further oracles directed specifically against Israel to demonstrate Israel's sin and God's judgment.
3:1 Hear this word: A proclamation formula used by Amos (see 4:1; 5:1), directed specifically to the **children of Israel** (see note on 2:11).
3:2 You only have I known: God has a special relationship with Israel. This is expressed in the Hebrew word "to know." It is more than cognitive, for God is aware of all the nations, as Amos so forcefully demonstrates in 1:3—2:3. Here it involves concern, pity, sympathy, and care. Because of this relationship Israel has special responsibility.
3:3–8 Amos uses a series of rhetorical questions involving well-known cause and effect relationships (vv. 3–6) designed to elicit a positive agreement from the audience. He lays a foundation for the explanation (vv. 7, 8) of his radical prophesying.
3:6 See section 1 of Truth-In-Action at the end of Amos.
3:7 See section 1 of Truth-In-Action at the end of Amos.
3:8 Lion has roared: God has spoken (see 1:2).
3:9 Prominent people from **Ashdod** (see 1:8) and **Egypt** (the empire to the south) are summoned to come and see what **Samaria** (Israel) is like. Instead of order there are **great tumults,** and instead of justice there is oppression.
3:10 To do right: A phrase signifying what was the acceptable norm, the standard by which actions were judged. **Who store up:** What is stored up is the result of **violence and robbery,** the proceeds from their wrongful acts.

12 Thus says the LORD:

"As a shepherd [1]takes from the
mouth of a lion
Two legs or a piece of an ear,
So shall the children of Israel be
taken out
Who dwell in Samaria—
In the corner of a bed and
[2]on the edge of a couch!
13 Hear and testify against the house
of Jacob,"
Says the Lord GOD, the God of
hosts,
14 "That in the day I punish Israel for
their transgressions,
I will also visit *destruction* on the
altars of [a]Bethel;
And the horns of the altar shall
be cut off
And fall to the ground.
15 I will [1]destroy [a]the winter house
along with [b]the summer house;
The [c]houses of ivory shall perish,
And the great houses shall have
an end,"
Says the LORD.

4 Hear this word, you [a]cows of
Bashan, who *are* on the
mountain of Samaria,
Who oppress the [b]poor,
Who crush the needy,
Who say to [1]your husbands,
"Bring *wine,* let us [c]drink!"
2 [a]The Lord GOD has sworn by His
holiness:
"Behold, the days shall come upon
you
When He will take you away
[b]with fishhooks,
And your posterity with
fishhooks.
3 [a]You will go out *through* broken
walls,
Each one straight ahead of her,
And you will [1]be cast into
Harmon,"
Says the LORD.

4 "Come[a] to Bethel and transgress,
At [b]Gilgal multiply transgression;
[c]Bring your sacrifices every
morning,
[d]Your tithes every three [1]days.
5 [a]Offer a sacrifice of *thanksgiving
with leaven,
Proclaim *and* announce [b]the
freewill offerings;
For this you love,
You children of Israel!"
Says the Lord GOD.

Israel Did Not Accept Correction

6 "Also I gave you [1]cleanness of
teeth in all your cities.
And lack of bread in all your
places;
[a]Yet you have not returned to Me,"
Says the LORD.

7 "I also withheld rain from you,
When *there were* still three
months to the harvest.
I made it rain on one city,
I withheld rain from another city.
One part was rained upon,

12 [1]Or *snatches* [2]Heb. uncertain, possibly *on the cover*
14 [a]2 Kin. 23:15; Hos. 10:5–8, 14, 15; Amos 4:4
15 [a]Jer. 36:22 [b]Judg. 3:20 [c]1 Kin. 22:39; Ps. 45:8 [1]Lit. *strike*

CHAPTER 4

1 [a]Ps. 22:12; Ezek. 39:18 [b]Amos 2:6 [c]Prov. 23:20 [1]Lit. *their masters* or *lords*
2 [a]Ps. 89:35 [b]Jer. 16:16; Ezek. 29:4; Hab. 1:15
3 [a]Ezek. 12:5 [1]Or *cast them*
4 [a]Ezek. 20:39; Amos 3:14 [b]Hos. 4:15 [c]Num. 28:3; Amos 5:21, 22 [d]Deut. 14:28 [1]Or *years,* Deut. 14:28
5 [a]Lev. 7:13 [b]Lev. 22:18; Deut. 12:6 *See WW at Ps. 95:2.
6 [a]2 Chr. 28:22; Is. 26:11; Jer. 5:3; Hag. 2:17 [1]Hunger

3:12 The **shepherd** saved what he could to prove to the owner that the animal was killed by a wild beast, not stolen and sold by him. In the same way, only a chewed-up remnant of the rich of **Samaria** will be found.
3:13 Hear and testify: The prominent people (v. 9) are called upon to testify against Israel. **House** is a catchword in these verses. House of Jacob—the Israelites; Bethel—the house of God (v. 14); the winter house, the summer house, and the houses of ivory (v. 15). Both temple and mansion will be destroyed.
3:14 Altars of Bethel: Bethel marked the southern boundary of Israel, just 10 miles north of Jerusalem. Here Jeroboam I had set up one of the golden calves, and the city became a center of religious life.
3:15 Houses of ivory: Mansions decorated with ivory inlay (see 6:4).
4:1 Hear this word: See note on 3:1. **Cows of Bashan:** The wives of the principal men of Samaria are likened to the cows raised in the verdant pastures of Bashan in Transjordan. **Mountain of Samaria:** The capital city of the *northern kingdom* was built by Omri on a hill he purchased from Shemer (1 Kin. 16:24). **Oppress the poor:** The same charge of ruthless exploitation of the poor is brought against the women. Their desire for more wealth and luxury spurs their husbands to do more wicked deeds.
4:2 GOD has sworn emphasizes the solemnity and certainty of God's action. **His holiness** is in contrast to the people's wickedness. **The days shall come** are the days of Yahweh (5:18). **Fishhooks:** Assyrian reliefs depict prisoners led away with hooks through the nose or lip.
4:3 The meaning of **Harmon** is unclear. It may be the name of a place.
4:4 The customary priestly invitation is turned to sarcasm and irony by Amos as he calls the people to come and **transgress.** Similar irony is used by Jeremiah (Jer. 7:21). For **Bethel** see note on 3:14. **Gilgal** was an ancient shrine connected with Joshua (Josh. 4:19) and Saul (1 Sam. 11:14, 15). **Sacrifices every morning:** According to Ex. 29:38, 39, a lamb was to be offered every morning and evening. If this is a peace offering, the worshiper would do it only once a year or, at most, three times a year; thus, Amos is continuing his irony. **Tithes:** Usually considered to be a tenth of the yield of the land. Deut. (14:28; 26:12) speaks of paying tithes every three years. Amos may be using hyperbole by making it every three days, but sometimes the Hebrew word for "days" stands for years (see Lev. 25:29; 1 Sam. 27:7).
4:5 This you love: The people loved the form and ritual, but this is not what God wanted.
4:6–11 A series of "natural disasters" (famine, drought, crop-failure, plague, war, natural calamity) were used by God to awaken the people to their sin, but these have not been successful. They **have not returned.**
4:6 Cleanness of teeth: Their teeth were clean because they had nothing to eat.

And where it did not rain the part
withered.
8 So two *or* three cities wandered
to another city to drink water,
But they were not **satisfied;**
Yet you have not returned to Me,"
Says the LORD.

WORD WEALTH

4:8 satisfied, *sabe'a* (sah-vay-ah); Strong's #7646: To be filled to satisfaction; to sate, satiate, fill, supply abundantly. This verb occurs about 100 times. Related words appear in Gen. 41:29, seven years of "plenty"; in Job 42:17, Job died when satisfied with his long life ("full of days"); in Ps. 16:11, "fullness" of joy is found in God's presence; and in Is. 23:18, God's people may eat "sufficiently." The most common usage of *sabe'a* concerns being filled with food or drink until one is satisfied. According to Prov. 27:20, two things that are never satisfied are hell and man's eyes.

9 "I[a] blasted you with blight and
mildew.
When your gardens increased,
Your vineyards,
Your fig trees,
And your olive trees,
[b]The locust devoured *them;*
Yet you have not returned to Me,"
Says the LORD.

10 "I sent among you a plague
[a]after the manner of Egypt;
Your young men I killed with a
sword,
Along with your captive horses;
I made the stench of your camps
come up into your nostrils;
Yet you have not returned to Me,"
Says the LORD.

11 "I overthrew *some* of you,
As God overthrew [a]Sodom and
Gomorrah,
And you were like a firebrand
plucked from the burning;
Yet you have not returned to Me,"
Says the LORD.

9 [a]Deut. 28:22; Hag. 2:17 [b]Joel 1:4, 7; Amos 7:1, 2
10 [a]Ex. 9:3, 6; Lev. 26:25; Deut. 28:27, 60; Ps. 78:50
11 [a]Gen. 19:24, 25; Deut. 29:23; Is. 13:19; Jer. 49:18; Lam. 4:6
12 [a]Jer. 5:22
13 [a]Ps. 139:2; Dan. 2:28 [b]Mic. 1:3 [c]Is. 47:4; Jer. 10:16 [1]Or *spirit* [2]Or *His* *See WW at Deut. 18:5.

CHAPTER 5

1 [a]Jer. 7:29; 9:10, 17; Ezek. 19:1
2 *See WW at Ps. 45:14.
4 [a][Deut. 4:29; 2 Chr. 15:2; Jer. 29:13] [b][Is. 55:3]
5 [a]1 Kin. 12:28, 29; Amos 4:4 [b]Gen. 21:31–33; Amos 8:14 [c]Hos. 4:15

12 "Therefore thus will I do to you,
O Israel;
Because I will do this to you,
[a]Prepare to meet your God,
O Israel!"

13 For behold,
He who forms mountains,
And creates the [1]wind,
[a]Who declares to man what
[2]his thought *is,*
And makes the morning
darkness,
[b]Who treads the high places of the
earth—
[c]The LORD God of hosts *is* His
*name.

A Lament for Israel

5 Hear this word which I [a]take up
against you, a lamentation, O
house of Israel:

2 The *virgin of Israel has fallen;
She will rise no more.
She lies forsaken on her land;
There is no one to raise her up.

3 For thus says the Lord GOD:

"The city that goes out by a
thousand
Shall have a hundred left,
And that which goes out by a
hundred
Shall have ten left to the house
of Israel."

A Call to Repentance

4 For thus says the LORD to the house
of Israel:

[a]"Seek Me [b]and live;
5 But do not seek [a]Bethel,
Nor enter Gilgal,
Nor pass over to [b]Beersheba;
For Gilgal shall surely go into
captivity,
And [c]Bethel shall come to
nothing.

4:11 Sodom and Gomorrah were totally destroyed by brimstone and fire from heaven (Gen. 19:24, 25).
4:12 Prepare to meet your God: Because Israel has not returned to God, God will now come to them in punishment. This is a solemn warning.
4:13 Amos inserts a part of a hymn here and at 5:8, 9 and 9:5, 6. All three share the same concluding line, **The LORD . . . *is* His name.** All portray God as Creator and Sustainer.
5:1 Hear this word: See note on 3:1. **Lamentation:** A dirge in the form of a funeral song. Amos considers Israel already dead.
5:2 Virgin of Israel: Or "Virgin Israel." The phrase occurs for the first time in Scripture. Jeremiah uses the identical expression (Jer. 18:13; 31:4, 21) as a personification of the nation.
5:4 Seek Me: God, not the sanctuaries, is to be sought. If they turn to Him, there is a chance to live. This alternative to judgment is offered also in vv. 6, 14, and 24. Ps. 27:8 uses the expression, "Seek My face." It was expected that God could be found at the sanctuaries, but the priests seem to have offered "life" through the cult offerings without stressing the kind of living required by those who "seek God."
5:5 Bethel: See note on 3:14. **Gilgal:** See note on 4:4. **Beersheba** was in the south. Abraham (Gen. 21:31–33),

6 [a]Seek the LORD and live,
Lest He break out like fire *in* the house of Joseph,
And devour *it*,
With no one to quench *it* in Bethel—
7 You who [a]turn justice to wormwood,
And lay righteousness to rest in the earth!"

8 He made the [a]Pleiades and Orion;
He turns the shadow of death into morning
[b]And makes the day dark as night;
He [c]calls for the waters of the sea
And pours them out on the face of the earth;
[d]The LORD *is* His name.
9 He [1]rains ruin upon the strong,
So that fury comes upon the fortress.

10 [a]They hate the one who rebukes in the gate,
And they [b]abhor the one who speaks uprightly.
11 [a]Therefore, because you [1]tread down the poor
And take grain [2]taxes from him,
Though [b]you have built houses of hewn stone,
Yet you shall not dwell in them;
You have planted [3]pleasant vineyards,
But you shall not drink wine from them.
12 For I [a]know your *manifold transgressions
And your mighty sins:
[b]Afflicting the just *and* taking bribes;
[c]Diverting the poor *from justice* at the gate.
13 Therefore [a]the prudent keep silent at that time,
For it *is* an evil time.

14 Seek *good and not evil,
That you may live;
So the LORD God of hosts will be with you,
[a]As you have spoken.
15 [a]Hate evil, love good;
Establish justice in the gate.
[b]It may be that the LORD God of hosts
Will be gracious to the remnant of Joseph.

The Day of the LORD

16 Therefore the LORD God of hosts, the Lord, says this:

"*There shall be* wailing in all streets,
And they shall say in all the highways,
'Alas! Alas!'
They shall call the farmer to mourning,
[a]And skillful lamenters to wailing.
17 In all vineyards *there shall be* wailing,
For [a]I will pass through you,"
Says the LORD.

18 [a]Woe to you who desire the day of the LORD!
For what good *is* [b]the day of the LORD to you?
It *will be* darkness, and not light.

6 [a][Is. 55:3, 6, 7; Amos 5:14] **7** [a]Amos 6:12 **8** [a]Job 9:9; 38:31 [b]Ps. 104:20 [c]Job 38:34 [d][Amos 4:13] **9** [1]Or *flashes forth destruction* **10** [a]Is. 29:21; 66:5; Amos 5:15 [b]1 Kin. 22:8; Is. 59:15; Jer. 17:16–18 **11** [a]Amos 2:6 [b]Deut. 28:30, 38, 39; Mic. 6:15; Zeph. 1:13; Hag. 1:6 [1]*trample* [2]Or *tribute* [3]*desirable* **12** [a]Hos. 5:3 [b]Is. 1:23; 5:23; Amos 2:6 [c]Is. 29:21 *See WW at Ps. 31:19. **13** [a]Amos 6:10 **14** [a]Mic. 3:11 *See WW at Ezek. 34:14. **15** [a]Ps. 97:10; Rom. 12:9 [b]Joel 2:14 **16** [a]2 Chr. 35:25; Jer. 9:17 **17** [a]Ex. 12:12 **18** [a]Is. 5:19; Jer. 17:15; Joel 1:15; 2:1, 11, 31 [b]Is. 5:30; Joel 2:2

Isaac (Gen. 26:23–25), and Jacob (Gen. 46:1) all worshiped God at Beersheba. It was a place of pilgrimage for some from Israel even after the kingdom divided. **Bethel shall come to nothing:** "Nothing" is the Hebrew word "aven." Hosea speaks of Bethel with a similar pun, as Beth Aven, "House of Nothing" (Hos. 4:15; 5:8; 10:5).

5:6 House of Joseph: The northern kingdom of Israel. Ephraim and Manasseh were sons of Joseph.

5:7 Justice and **righteousness** are two of the most important concepts in the prophets. They are used in a similar way in v. 24 and 6:12. Righteousness is the quality of life demonstrated by those who live up to the established norms in a relationship. They "do right by" another person. Justice is the judicial process of determining who is right in a case of law. The just party was helped by the court. Amos's contention is that the poor are not being defended in the court. *Therefore, justice is not done.* **Wormwood:** A plant of the genus *Artemisia.* The juice of the leaves has a bitter taste. In 6:12 it is used in parallel with "gall."

5:8, 9 Part of a hymn. See note on 4:13.

5:8 Pleiades is the star cluster in the constellation Taurus, near the constellation **Orion** (see Job 9:9; 38:31). God is Creator and Sustainer. He regulates nature so that **morning** follows **night** and night follows day; **waters** are drawn up from the **sea** and return as rain to the sea (see Eccl. 1:7).

5:10 Who rebukes: This is the one who judges, reproves, or decides the case **in the gate.** Court was held in the gate of the city (see vv. 12, 15; Ruth 4:1).

5:11 Hewn stone: Most houses were made of mud brick or, at most, of uncut field stones. Only large public buildings, such as the temple and palace, used cut stones.

5:16, 17 The punishment of evildoers is portrayed as a funeral scene with wailing in the streets.

5:18–20 Israel looked on the **day of the LORD** as a time of joy and vindication. Israel would be exalted, her enemies brought low (see note on Obad. 15). Amos questions the validity of their assumptions. **Darkness** can be expected because it is God's judgment upon Israel for sin. Two metaphors speak of persons who think they have escaped, only to find disaster: from the **lion** to the **bear** and from the supposed safety of the **house** to the **serpent** bite. Israel fell captive to Sargon II of Assyria within four decades in 722 B.C.

5:18 Woe is the cry of grief over the dead (1 Kin. 13:30; Jer. 22:18; 34:5). Here Amos uses it to call attention to impending doom (see 6:3).

19 It *will be* [a]as though a man fled
from a lion,
And a bear met him!
Or *as though* he went into the
house,
Leaned his hand on the wall,
And a serpent bit him!
20 *Is* not the day of the LORD
darkness, and not light?
Is it not very dark, with no
brightness in it?

21 "I[a] hate, I *despise your feast days,
And [b]I do not savor your sacred
assemblies.
22 [a]Though you offer Me burnt
offerings and your grain
offerings,
I will not accept *them,*
Nor will I regard your fattened
peace offerings.
23 Take away from Me the noise of
your songs,
For I will not hear the melody of
your stringed instruments.

KINGDOM DYNAMICS

5:21–23 Restoration and the Futility of Religious Ritual, RESTORATION. This text reminds of the futility of religious ritual and the need for restoration at that dimension. The entire concept of "The Holy Spirit and Restoration" is developed in the study article that begins on page 2012.

(Ezek. 34:1–10/Heb. 12:26, 27) J.R.

24 [a]But let justice run down like
water,
And righteousness like a mighty
stream.

19 [a]Job 20:24; Is. 24:17, 18; Jer. 48:44
21 [a]Is. 1:11–16; Amos 4:4, 5; 8:10 [b]Lev. 26:31; Jer. 14:12; Hos. 5:6 *See WW at Amos 2:4.
22 [a]Is. 66:3; Mic. 6:6, 7
24 [a]Jer. 22:3; Ezek. 45:9; Hos. 6:6; Mic. 6:8
25 [a]Deut. 32:17; Josh. 24:14; Neh. 9:18–21; Acts 7:42, 43 *See WW at Num. 29:6.
26 [a]1 Kin. 11:33 [1]LXX, Vg. *tabernacle of Moloch* [2]A pagan deity
27 [a]2 Kin. 17:6; Amos 7:11, 17; Mic. 4:10 [b]Amos 4:13

CHAPTER 6

1 [a]Luke 6:24 [b]Ps. 123:4; Is. 32:9–11; Zeph. 1:12 [c]Is. 31:1; Jer. 49:4 [d]Ex. 19:5; Amos 3:2
2 [a]Jer. 2:10 [b]Gen. 10:10; Is. 10:9 [c]1 Kin. 8:65; 2 Kin. 18:34 [d]Nah. 3:8
3 [a]Is. 56:12; Ezek. 12:27; Amos 9:10; Matt. 24:37–39 [b]Amos 5:18 [c]Amos 5:12 [d]Ps. 94:20

25 "Did[a] you offer Me sacrifices and
*offerings
In the wilderness forty years,
O house of Israel?
26 You also carried [1]Sikkuth[2]
[a]your king
And [2]Chiun, your idols,
The star of your gods,
Which you made for yourselves.
27 Therefore I will send you into
captivity [a]beyond Damascus,"
Says the LORD, [b]whose name *is*
the God of hosts.

Warnings to Zion and Samaria

6 Woe [a]to you *who are* at [b]ease in
Zion, 3
And [c]trust in Mount Samaria,
Notable persons in the [d]chief
nation,
To whom the house of Israel
comes!
2 [a]Go over to [b]Calneh and see;
And from there go to [c]Hamath the
great;
Then go down to Gath of the
Philistines.
[d]*Are you* better than these
kingdoms?
Or is their territory greater than
your territory?

3 *Woe to* you who [a]put far off the 3
day of [b]doom,
[c]Who cause [d]the seat of violence
to come near;
4 Who lie on beds of ivory,
Stretch out on your couches,
Eat lambs from the flock

5:21–24 The Lord does not delight in sacrifices at the shrines (vv. 21–23) as much as He delights in **justice** and **righteousness** in the courts and markets (v. 24). Unless the proper relationships are maintained between the worshiper and God and the worshiper and his neighbor, sacrifices are meaningless (see Is. 1:10–17). The list of **feast days, sacred assemblies, burnt offerings, peace offerings,** and **songs** makes it clear that all of Israel's worship is rejected. The people were zealous in their public worship, but they neglected the weightier matters—justice and righteousness.

5:21 Hate is a very strong verb (see v. 15; Is. 1:14).

5:24 For **justice** and **righteousness** see note on v. 7; Is. 1:10–17; Hos. 6:6; Mic. 6:6–8.

5:25–27 Amos contends that sacrifice had no real place in the relationship of God with His people in the wilderness experience. Instead, Israel responded to God with obedience, justice, and righteousness (see Jer. 2:2, 3; Hos. 2:14–20).

5:26 Sikkuth and **Chiun** are difficult to identify. Their present forms are the result of reading the Hebrew consonants with the vowel letters for "abomination." This process of disparaging the names of false gods is found also in 2 Sam. 2:8 (Ishbosheth for Ish-Baal) and 2 Kin. 1:2 (Baal-Zebub for Baal-Zebul). The gods were probably Sakkut and Kaiwan, both known as names for Saturn in Assyrian sources. Some prefer to translate "tabernacle" and "pedestal," but names seem to have support from the LXX (the Greek translation of the OT) and Acts 7:43.

5:27 Ultimate punishment will be exile **beyond Damascus,** being removed from land God had promised to Abraham, Isaac, and Jacob.

6:1 See section 3 of Truth-In-Action at the end of Amos.

6:1 The middle of the eighth century B.C. was a time of great economic prosperity for both Israel and Judah. Those **at ease in Zion** and those who **trust in Mount Samaria** are one of a kind. They are complacent because of their wealth and exalted position. They consider themselves the **chief nation** because of their newly acquired power and wealth. Their optimism is unwise.

6:2 Israel compares herself to **Calneh** and **Hamath** (two cities in the north taken by Jeroboam II) and **Gath** (a Philistine city conquered by Uzziah). They gloat over their exalted position.

6:3–8 See section 3 of Truth-In-Action at the end of Amos.

6:3 Day of doom is another term for the Day of the Lord. See note on 5:18–20.

6:4 Beds of ivory: See note on 3:15.

And calves from the midst of the stall;
5 [a]Who sing idly to the sound of stringed instruments,
And invent for yourselves [b]musical instruments [c]like David;
6 Who [a]drink wine from bowls,
And anoint yourselves with the best ointments,
[b]But are not grieved for the affliction of Joseph.
7 Therefore they shall now go [a]captive as the first of the captives,
And those who recline at banquets shall be removed.

8 [a]The Lord GOD has sworn by Himself,
The LORD God of hosts says:
"I abhor [b]the pride of Jacob,
And hate his palaces;
Therefore I will deliver up *the* city
And all that is in it."

9 Then it shall come to pass, that if
ten men remain in one house, they
shall die.
10 And when [1]a relative *of the dead,*
with one who will burn *the bodies,*
picks up the [2]bodies to take them out
of the house, he will say to one inside
the house, "*Are there* any more with
you?" Then someone will say, "None."
And he will say, [a]"Hold your tongue!
[b]For we dare not mention the name of
the LORD."

11 For behold, [a]the LORD gives a command:
[b]He will break the great house into bits,
And the little house into pieces.

5 [a]Is. 5:12; Amos 5:23 [b]1 Chr. 15:16; 16:42 [c]1 Chr. 23:5
6 [a]Amos 2:8; 4:1 [b]Gen. 37:25
7 [a]Amos 5:27
8 [a]Gen. 22:16; Jer. 51:14; Amos 4:2; 8:7; Heb. 6:13–17 [b]Ps. 47:4; Ezek. 24:21; Amos 8:7
10 [a]Amos 5:13 [b]Amos 8:3 [1]Lit. *his loved one* or *uncle* [2]Lit. *bones*
11 [a]Is. 55:11 [b]2 Kin. 25:9; Amos 3:15
12 [a]1 Kin. 21:7–13; Is. 59:13, 14; Hos. 10:4; Amos 5:7, 11, 12
13 [1]Lit. *Nothing* [2]Lit. *Horns,* a symbol of strength
14 [a]Jer. 5:15 [b]Num. 34:7, 8; 1 Kin. 8:65; 2 Kin. 14:25

CHAPTER 7

1 [1]Lit. *beginning of the sprouting of*
2 [a]Is. 51:19 [1]Or *How shall Jacob stand* *See WW at Ps. 103:3.
3 [a]Deut. 32:36; Jer. 26:19; Hos. 11:8; Amos 5:15; Jon. 3:10; [James 5:16]
4 [1]*to contend* [2]Lit. *portion*

12 Do horses run on rocks?
Does *one* plow *there* with oxen?
Yet [a]you have turned justice into gall,
And the fruit of righteousness into wormwood,
13 You who rejoice over [1]Lo Debar,
Who say, "Have we not taken [2]Karnaim for ourselves
By our own strength?"

14 "But, behold, [a]I will raise up a nation against you,
O house of Israel,"
Says the LORD God of hosts;
"And they will afflict you from the [b]entrance of Hamath
To the Valley of the Arabah."

Vision of the Locusts

7 Thus the Lord GOD showed me: Behold, He formed locust swarms at
the [1]beginning of the late crop; indeed
it was the late crop after the king's
mowings.
2 And so it was, when they had finished eating the grass of the land, that
I said:

"O Lord GOD, *forgive, I pray!
[a]Oh,[1] that Jacob may stand,
For he *is* small!"
3 *So* [a]the LORD relented concerning this.
"It shall not be," said the LORD.

Vision of the Fire

4 Thus the Lord GOD showed me: Behold, the Lord GOD called [1]for conflict
by fire, and it consumed the great deep
and devoured the [2]territory.

6:5 Like David: See 1 Chr. 23:5; Neh. 12:36.
6:7 First of the captives: The upper class, usually better educated and trained, will be the first to go into exile, and they will "lead" the columns of refugees.
6:8 The Lord GOD has sworn: See note on 4:2.
6:10 Burn *the bodies:* Cremation was not a usual practice in Israel. The burning of the bodies of Saul and his sons (1 Sam. 31:12) is exceptional and seems to follow a Greek custom. If a pestilence was the cause of death, perhaps burning the body was practiced (as did also the Greeks), but there is no evidence for this. **Hold your tongue** continues the sense of dread. The speaker is interrupted so that he will not continue and inadvertently **mention the name of the LORD.** The Lord's appearance was responsible for the disaster that has come upon the people, and the mention of His name may touch off another round of punishment.
6:12 Plow *there* with oxen: The Hebrew text may also be translated "plow the sea with an ox." Either meaning would require an answer of "no." For **justice** and **righteousness** see note on 5:7. **Wormwood:** See note on 5:7.
6:13 Lo Debar and **Karnaim** are used as puns by Amos. Lo Debar, as Amos pronounced it, means "Nothing," and Karnaim means "Horns," which is a symbol for strength. Both were cities recovered by Jeroboam. Lo Debar is located in Gilead, and Karnaim was on the Yarmuk River farther to the northeast.
6:14 Hamath to the Valley of the Arabah indicates the full extent of the territory of Jeroboam (the Orontes River to the Dead Sea), just as Dan to Beersheba designates all the land of Israel and Judah.
7:1–9 Three of the five visions of Amos. The first two—locusts and fire—are relented because Amos intercedes with God and asks for a change in His intention. The third vision—the plumb line—is not relented.
7:1–3 Vision of locusts. See notes on Joel 1:4; 2:3.
7:1 Late crop: The late planting. It is uncertain whether this is a food crop, such as grain, or a grass that would provide pasture for the flocks and herds. The loss of either would be devastating for the people. **King's mowings:** The tax or tribute due the king had already been collected.
7:3 Relented: Man's way of describing God's decision not to send the locusts. See v. 6.
7:4 Great deep: Either the underground water that is the source of springs and rivers, or the Mediterranean Sea.

5 Then I said:

"O Lord GOD, cease, I pray!
[a]Oh, that Jacob may stand,
For he *is* small!"
6 *So* the LORD relented concerning
this.
"This also shall not be," said the
Lord GOD.

Vision of the Plumb Line

1 7 Thus He showed me: Behold, the
Lord stood on a wall *made* with a
plumb line, with a plumb line in His
*hand.
8 And the LORD said to me, "Amos,
what do you see?" And I said, "A
plumb line." Then the Lord said:

"Behold, [a]I am setting a plumb line
In the midst of My people Israel;
[b]I will not pass by them anymore.
9 [a]The [1]high places of Isaac shall be
desolate,
And the [2]sanctuaries of Israel
shall be laid waste.
[b]I will rise with the sword against
the house of Jeroboam."

Amaziah's Complaint

10 Then Amaziah the [a]priest of
[b]Bethel sent to [c]Jeroboam king of Israel, saying, "Amos has conspired
against you in the midst of the house
of Israel. The land is not able to
[1]bear* all his words.
11 "For thus Amos has said:

5 [a]Amos 7:2, 3
7 *See WW at Josh. 4:24.
8 [a]2 Kin. 21:13; Is. 28:17; 34:11; Lam. 2:8 [b]Mic. 7:18
9 [a]Gen. 46:1; Hos. 10:8; Mic. 1:5 [b]2 Kin. 15:8–10; Amos 7:11 [1]Places of pagan worship [2]Or *holy places*
10 [a]1 Kin. 12:31, 32; 13:33 [b]1 Kin. 13:32; Amos 4:4 [c]2 Kin. 14:23 [1]Or *endure* *See WW at Ps. 55:22.
11 [a]Amos 5:27; 6:7
13 [a]Amos 2:12; Acts 4:18 [b]1 Kin. 12:29, 32; Amos 7:9 [1]Or *holy place* [2]Lit. *house*
14 [a]1 Kin. 20:35; 2 Kin. 2:5; 2 Chr. 19:2 [b]2 Kin. 3:4; Amos 1:1; Zech. 13:5 *See WW at 1 Sam. 3:20.
15 [a]Amos 3:8 [1]Lit. *from behind*
16 [a]Deut. 32:2; Ezek. 21:2; Mic. 2:6 [1]Lit. *drip*
17 [a]Jer. 28:12; 29:21, 32 [b]Is. 13:16; Lam. 5:11; Hos. 4:13; Zech. 14:2

'Jeroboam shall die by the sword,
And Israel shall surely be led
away [a]captive
From their own land.' "

12 Then Amaziah said to Amos:

"Go, you seer!
Flee to the land of Judah.
There eat bread,
And there prophesy.
13 But [a]never again prophesy at
Bethel,
[b]For it *is* the king's [1]sanctuary,
And it *is* the royal [2]residence."

14 Then Amos answered, and said to
Amaziah:

"I *was* no *prophet,
Nor *was* I [a]a son of a prophet,
But I *was* a [b]sheepbreeder
And a tender of sycamore fruit.
15 Then the LORD took me [1]as I
followed the flock,
And the LORD said to me,
'Go, [a]prophesy to My people
Israel.'
16 Now therefore, hear the word of 2
the LORD:
You say, 'Do not prophesy
against Israel,
And [a]do not [1]spout against the
house of Isaac.'

17 "Therefore[a] thus says the LORD:

[b]'Your wife shall be a harlot in the
city;

Territory: The area portioned out or assigned to Israel. See Mic. 2:4.
7:7–9 See section 1 of Truth-In-Action at the end of Amos.
7:7 A vision of a wall built with the use of a **plumb line.** The plumb line is symbolic. Israel had been built "true" to God's standard; now she will be measured or tested by that same standard.
7:8 My people Israel: Israel will be judged as a covenant people. She has been tested and found defective. The principal structures, the shrines and the dynasty, will be torn down. **I will not pass by:** The time of forgiveness has passed, and judgment is approaching. Amos has no opportunity to intercede for the people. Their fate is sealed.
7:10–17 The opposition of Amaziah, the priest of Bethel. This confrontation points up the tension between a functionary at the shrine and a prophet called by God. See a similar situation with Jeremiah and Pashhur in Jer. 20:1–6.
7:10 Amos has conspired: The prophets often interfered in the life of the monarchy. Ahijah informed Jeroboam I that God would tear the kingdom from Solomon, and Jeroboam would rule 10 tribes (1 Kin. 11:29–32). A man of God anointed Jehu king of Israel and instructed him to destroy the house of Ahab (2 Kin. 9:6–10).
7:12 Seer: An alternate term for prophet. **There prophesy:** Amaziah insinuates that Amos makes his living as a prophet. Therefore he should return to Judah and ply his trade there. This forms the basis for the reply in v. 14.
7:13 Amaziah was in command at Bethel and had authority to order Amos not to prophesy anymore at the sanctuary.
7:14 No prophet: Amos denies that he is a professional prophet. **Sheepbreeder:** See note on 1:1. **Tender of sycamore fruit:** The sycamore-fig tree is from the mulberry family. The fruit must be punctured or scraped while it is ripening so that it will sweeten and be edible.
7:15 Go, prophesy: Amos is in Bethel because God commanded him to go. Here is where he needs to be, not in Judah. And he is to prophesy to the people of **Israel,** not at his home in Judah. The authority is not Amaziah's, but the Lord's, and Amos must obey the Lord.
7:16, 17 See section 2 of Truth-In-Action at the end of Amos.
7:17 Amos does not stop prophesying, but he repeats his message of exile. This time the judgment is directed not to the house of Jeroboam, but to the family of Amaziah. **Harlot:** Deprived of family and support, the wife of Amaziah will have to support herself as a prostitute, or at the very least would be violated by the conquerors. **Defiled land:** A land where Amaziah will have difficulty observing the ritual laws of a priest. **And Israel:** These last two lines are a repetition of the summary of Amos's message given by Amaziah in v. 11.

Your sons and daughters shall
fall by the sword;
Your land shall be divided by
survey line;
You shall die in a [c]defiled land;
And Israel shall surely be led
away captive
From his own land.' "

Vision of the Summer Fruit

8 Thus the Lord GOD showed me: Behold, a basket of summer fruit.
2 And He said, "Amos, what do you
see?" So I said, "A basket of summer
fruit." Then the LORD said to me:

[a]"The end has come upon My
people Israel;
[b]I will not pass by them anymore.
3 And [a]the songs of the temple
Shall be wailing in that day,"
Says the Lord GOD—
"Many dead bodies everywhere,
[b]They shall be thrown out in
silence."

4 Hear this, you who [1]swallow up
the *needy,
And make the poor of the land
fail,

5 Saying:

"When will the New Moon be past,
That we may sell grain?
And [a]the Sabbath,
That we may [1]trade wheat?
[b]Making the ephah small and the
shekel large,
Falsifying the scales by [c]deceit,

6 That we may buy the poor for
[a]silver,
And the needy for a pair of
sandals—
Even sell the bad wheat?"

7 The LORD has sworn by [a]the pride
of Jacob:
"Surely [b]I will never forget any of
their works.
8 [a]Shall the land not tremble for this,
And everyone mourn who dwells
in it?
All of it shall swell like [1]the River,
Heave and subside
[b]Like the River of Egypt.

9 "And it shall come to pass in that
day," says the Lord GOD,
[a]"That I will make the sun go down
at noon,
And I will darken the earth in
[1]broad daylight;
10 I will turn your feasts into
[a]mourning,
[b]And all your songs into
lamentation;
[c]I will bring sackcloth on every
waist,
And baldness on every head;
I will make it like mourning for
an *only *son,*
And its end like a bitter day.

11 "Behold, the days are coming," 2
says the Lord GOD,
"That I will send a famine on the
land,
Not a famine of bread,
Nor a thirst for water,

17 [c]2 Kin. 17:6; Ezek. 4:13; Hos. 9:3

CHAPTER 8

2 [a]Ezek. 7:2 [b]Amos 7:8
3 [a]Amos 5:23 [b]Amos 6:9, 10
4 [1]Or *trample on,* Amos 2:7 *See WW at Ps. 70:5.
5 [a]Ex. 31:13–17; Neh. 13:15 [b]Mic. 6:10, 11 [c]Lev. 19:35, 36; Deut. 25:13–15 [1]Lit. *open*
6 [a]Amos 2:6
7 [a]Deut. 33:26, 29; Ps. 68:34; Amos 6:8 [b]Ps. 10:11; Hos. 7:2; 8:13
8 [a]Hos. 4:3 [b]Jer. 46:7, 8; Amos 9:5 [1]The Nile; some Heb. mss., LXX, Tg., Syr., Vg. *River* (cf. 9:5); MT *the light*
9 [a]Job 5:14; Is. 13:10; 59:9, 10; Jer. 15:9; [Mic. 3:6]; Matt. 27:45; Mark 15:32; Luke 23:44 [1]Lit. *a day of light*
10 [a]Lam. 5:15; Ezek. 7:18 [b]Is. 15:2, 3; Jer. 48:37; Ezek. 27:31 [c]Jer. 6:26; [Zech. 12:10] *See WW at Gen. 22:2.

8:1–3 Amos's fourth vision, a basket of summer fruit. The message is the same as the third vision (see 7:7–9).
8:2 A pun or sound-play is used with the Hebrew words for **summer fruit** (*qayiṣ*) and **end** (*qēṣ*). The "end" has come for attempts to correct and for passing by. All that is left now is death and destruction. A similar wordplay is found in Jeremiah's vision of the almond rod (Jer. 1:11, 12 and note). **I will not pass by:** See note on 7:8.
8:3 In that day: See note on Obad. 15. The sound of **wailing** and the sight of **dead bodies** will signal that the Day of the Lord has come. The **songs of the temple** will be silenced on that Day.
8:4–14 Indictments against religious hypocrisy. The wealthy are continuing in their religious duty, but are exploiting the poor. God **will never forget** their social injustices in spite of their being strict Sabbath-keepers.
8:5 The **New Moon** and **Sabbath** were days when all customary work was forbidden (Lev. 23:3; Num. 28:18; 29:6; Hos. 2:11). **The ephah small and the shekel large** are both means of cheating the customer through dishonest scales. The ephah was a dry measurement for grain, and the shekel was a basic weight for payment. Therefore, a small ephah and a large shekel meant the customer received less and paid more (see Deut. 25:13–16).
8:6 See note on 2:6. **Bad wheat:** A mixture of chaff and other impurities with the wheat.
8:7 In 4:2 and 6:8 God swore by Himself. In 6:8 the **pride of Jacob** is the people's pride that God abhors. Here, however, it seems to be positive and may be a synonym for God Himself.
8:8 Using the analogy of the Nile River, which rose and fell annually, Amos speaks of an earthquake that will cause the land to **heave** and **subside.**
8:9 Sun go down: Amos earlier described that Day as one of darkness (5:18).
8:10 Sackcloth and **baldness** were signs of mourning (Gen. 37:34; Lev. 21:5; Jer. 16:6). **An only *son*:** This cut off all hope for the future.
8:11, 12 See section 2 of Truth-In-Action at the end of Amos.
8:11 Famine and drought were two of the punishments God had used against Israel (4:6–8). Now Amos speaks of a new kind of famine—a lack of the word of God. This refers specifically to the message delivered by a prophet. No assurance will be available that God has heard their cry for help. No direction from God will guide them in their time of need. All will be silent.

But [a]of hearing the words of the
LORD.
12 They shall wander from sea to
sea,
And from north to east;
They shall run to and fro, seeking
the word of the LORD,
But shall [a]not find *it*.

13 "In that day the fair virgins
And strong young men
Shall faint from thirst.
14 Those who [a]swear by [b]the
[1]sin of Samaria,
Who say,
'As your god lives, O Dan!'
And, 'As the way of [c]Beersheba
lives!'
They shall fall and never rise
again."

The Destruction of Israel

9 I saw the Lord standing by the altar, and He said:

"Strike the [1]doorposts, that the
thresholds may shake,
And [a]break them on the heads of
them all.
I will slay the last of them with
the sword.
[b]He who flees from them shall not
get away,
And he who escapes from them
shall not be delivered.

2 "Though[a] they dig into [1]hell,
From there My hand shall take
them;
[b]Though they climb up to heaven,
From there I will bring them
down;
3 And though they [a]hide
themselves on top of Carmel,
From there I will search and take
them;
Though they hide from My sight
at the bottom of the sea,
From there I will command the
serpent, and it shall bite them;
4 Though they go into captivity
before their enemies,
From there [a]I will command the
sword,
And it shall slay them.
[b]I will set My eyes on them for
harm and not for good."

5 The Lord GOD of hosts,
He who touches the earth and it
[a]melts,
[b]And all who dwell there mourn;
All of it shall swell like [1]the River,
And subside like the River of
Egypt.
6 He who builds His [a]**layers**[1] in the
sky,
And has founded His strata in the
earth;
Who [b]calls for the waters of the
sea,
And pours them out on the face
of the earth—
[c]The LORD *is* His name.

WORD WEALTH

9:6 layers, *ma'alah* (mah-ah-*lah*); Strong's #4609: Steps, stairs, upper chambers; ascents, lofts. This noun occurs 45 times and is derived from the verb *'alah*, "to ascend," "to go up." Often it is translated "steps" as in 1 Kin. 10:19. In 2 Kin. 20:9–11, *ma'alah* is translated "degrees," referring to the ten steps the shadow regressed on the king's sundial. Fifteen psalms are labeled songs of "ascents" (Ps. 120—134). These were probably sung by the Levites as they proceeded up the steps to the temple. In the present reference, the Lord has built His staircase in the sky, a picture of His vast palace through which He walks.

7 "*Are* you not like the [1]people of
Ethiopia to Me,
O children of Israel?" says the
LORD.

11 [a]1 Sam. 3:1; 2 Chr. 15:3; Ps. 74:9; Ezek. 7:26; Mic. 3:6
12 [a]Hos. 5:6
14 [a]Hos. 4:15 [b]Deut. 9:21 [c]Amos 5:5 [1]Or *Ashima*, a Syrian goddess

CHAPTER 9

1 [a]Ps. 68:21; Hab. 3:13 [b]Amos 2:14 [1]Capitals of the pillars
2 [a]Ps. 139:8; Jer. 23:24 [b]Job 20:6; Jer. 51:53; Obad. 4; Matt. 11:23 [1]Or *Sheol*
3 [a]Jer. 23:24
4 [a]Lev. 26:33 [b]Lev. 17:10; Jer. 21:10; 39:16; 44:11
5 [a]Ps. 104:32; 144:5; Is. 64:1; Mic. 1:4 [b]Amos 8:8 [1]The Nile
6 [a]Ps. 104:3, 13 [b]Amos 5:8 [c]Amos 4:13; 5:27 [1]Or *stairs*
7 [1]Lit. *sons of the Ethiopians*

8:12 Sea to sea: From the Mediterranean to the Dead Sea. The whole extent of the land is meant. **Seeking the word:** Trying to find or obtain a divine oracle.
8:14 Sin of Samaria: Perhaps the goddess Ashimah, the patron deity of the men of Hamath. Prominent shrines were located at **Dan** and **Beersheba.** The use of these two names encompasses the whole of the land.
9:1–4 Amos's fifth vision: **the Lord standing by the altar.** Destruction of the people is ordered; none will escape.
9:1 I saw the Lord: As Isaiah saw the Lord in the temple (Is. 6:1), so Amos sees the Lord. He is present, not to bring blessing and assurance but judgment and destruction. **Doorposts:** See Is. 6:4 where the doorposts were shaken. **On the heads:** The fall of the temple will kill most of the people (see Judg. 16:30). **Flees:** A scene similar to 5:19. No one will be able to escape.
9:2–4 No matter where mankind tries to flee, they will not escape. Every place belongs to God, and He is present. **Hell** and **heaven** are the extremes of the universe; Mt. **Carmel** and **the bottom of the sea** are the extremes of the Earth.
9:5, 6 Part of a hymn. See note on 4:13.
9:5 Swell like the River: See note on 8:8.
9:6 His strata: The Hebrew word is used of "something bound together." Perhaps the idea is that the heavens are gathered and bound together as a vault, and the ends of this vault are on Earth.
9:7–10 Statements verifying how Israel can be Yahweh's object of wrath rather than protection.
9:7 A series of rhetorical questions to emphasize the

"Did I not bring up Israel from the land of Egypt,
The [a]Philistines from [b]Caphtor,[2]
And the Syrians from [c]Kir?

8 "Behold, [a]the eyes of the Lord GOD *are* on the sinful kingdom,
And I [b]will destroy it from the face of the earth;
Yet I will not utterly destroy the house of Jacob,"
Says the LORD.

9 "For surely I will command,
And will [1]sift the house of Israel among all nations,
As *grain* is sifted in a sieve;
[a]Yet not the smallest [2]grain shall fall to the ground.
10 All the sinners of My people shall die by the sword,
[a]Who say, 'The calamity shall not overtake nor confront us.'

Israel Will Be Restored

11 "On[a] that day I will raise up
The [1]tabernacle of David, which has fallen down,
And [2]repair its damages;
I will raise up its ruins,
And rebuild it as in the days of old;
12 [a]That they may possess the remnant of [b]Edom,[1]
And all the Gentiles who are called by My name,"
Says the LORD who does this thing.

13 "Behold, [a]the days are coming," says the LORD,
"When the plowman shall overtake the reaper,
And the *treader of grapes him who sows seed;
[b]The mountains shall *drip with sweet wine,
And all the hills shall flow *with it*.
14 [a]I will bring back the captives of My people Israel;
[b]They shall build the waste cities and inhabit *them;*
They shall plant vineyards and drink wine from them;
They shall also make gardens and eat fruit from them.
15 I will plant them in their land,
[a]And no longer shall they be pulled up
From the land I have given them,"
Says the LORD your God.

7 [a]Jer. 47:4 [b]Deut. 2:23 [c]Amos 1:5 [2]Crete
8 [a]Jer. 44:27; Amos 9:4 [b]Jer. 5:10; 30:11; [Joel 2:32]; Amos 3:12; [Obad. 16, 17]
9 [a][Is. 65:8–16] [1]*shake* [2]Lit. *pebble*
10 [a][Is. 28:15]; Jer. 5:12; Amos 6:3
11 [a]Acts 15:16–18 [1]Lit. *booth;* a figure of a deposed dynasty [2]Lit. *wall up its breaches*
12 [a]Obad. 19 [b]Num. 24:18; Is. 11:14 [1]LXX *mankind*
13 [a]Lev. 26:5 [b]Joel 3:18 *See WW at Deut. 11:25. • See WW at Ezek. 21:2.
14 [a]Ps. 53:6; Is. 60:4; Jer. 30:3, 18 [b]Is. 61:4
15 [a]Is. 60:21; Ezek. 34:28; 37:25

sovereignty and control of God over the nations. **People of Ethiopia:** The Ethiopians or Cushites lived in the Nile Valley, south of Syene, modern Aswan (Ezek. 29:10). The color of their skin is mentioned by Jeremiah (Jer. 13:23). They serve as slaves and officials (2 Sam. 18:21; Jer. 38:7), and they are from a distant country. Any of these factors may be the reason God mentions them here, for they are compared to the **children of Israel.** As they view the Ethiopians, so God views them. The Israelites can claim no more favored position than any other nation. **Bring up Israel** is a reference to the Exodus (see Ex. 20:2). **Philistines from Caphtor:** The migration of the Philistines (a part of the Sea Peoples) from Caphtor (Crete and parts of Asia) and the **Syrians from Kir** (see 1:5), occurred in the twelfth century B.C. The Philistines and Syrians had been enemies of Israel for centuries, but God claims His guiding hand was responsible for their presence.

9:8 The sinful nation is any nation that is morally guilty (see 1:3—2:8).

9:9 Sift: Shake. God will shake Israel as a sieve is shaken. In a large mesh screen the impurities, such as chaff and pebbles, are separated from the grain which falls through to the ground. This sifting by God will not allow **the smallest grain** (pebble) to fall through. Anything undesirable will be removed.

9:11–15 The restoration of Israel. In light of James's quote of vv. 11, 12 in Acts 15:16, 17, the fulfillment of vv. 11–15 can be seen in the church. The returned remnant in the time of Ezra and Nehemiah will also fulfill Amos's words.

9:11 On that day: See note on Obad. 15. Here, its blessings and not its punishments are emphasized. **Tabernacle of David** is literally a "booth" or "hut," usually made of branches. Here it stands for the dynasty of David and its descendants, which is most often termed a "house" (2 Sam. 7:5, 11).

9:12 Remnant of Edom: Whatever is left of this enemy of Israel (1:11, 12). Edom was particularly hostile to Judah when the final assault was made on Jerusalem by the Babylonians (Obad. 11–15). Ultimately, God's people shall **possess** all their enemies. **All the Gentiles:** All the nations that had ever been possessed by Yahweh (or by Israel) are referred to as those **called by My name.** They will be included in the future kingdom.

9:13–15 A poetic picture of the fertility of the land and the security and stability of life for God's people, especially in His future kingdom. This blessing is seen as reversing the fortunes of the Israelites in Amos's day (**I will bring back the captives**); conditions will be the opposite of those portrayed in 4:6–11.

9:13 The plowman . . . sows seed: The blessings will be so great that Amos compares them to land producing so quickly and so richly that it is difficult to finish one cycle before the next cycle begins.

9:15 I will plant: In v. 14 God says that the Israelites will plant vineyards and make gardens and enjoy the fruit of their labor. But God will also plant the people **in their land,** and they will never **be pulled up.** This promise reverses much of what has been proclaimed by Amos in the earlier part of the book. The restoration and blessing is usually associated with repentance on the part of God's people. No mention of that is made here as Amos stresses God's mercy and grace. The possession of the land is part of the promise to Abraham and his descendants, and its fulfillment is based on the unconditional blessing of God.

TRUTH-IN-ACTION through AMOS

Letting the LIFE of the Holy Spirit Bring Faith's Works Alive in You!

Truth Amos Teaches	Text	**Action** Amos Invites
1 Steps to Knowing God and His Ways God's judgments should never be a complete surprise because we already know what His standards are. His Word (both the Scriptures and also as incarnate in the Lord Jesus Christ) will announce beforehand any judgment to give His people ample opportunity to repent and turn from their sin (see 2 Chr. 7:14).	3:6	**Understand** that God sent calamity to turn the people back to Him.
	3:7	**Understand** that God never does anything He has not announced beforehand through His prophets. **Develop** an ear to hear what the Spirit is saying (through the prophets) to the churches.
	7:7–9	**Know** that God judges everyone equally by the standards of His Word and by the life of Jesus Christ.
2 Guidelines for Growing in Godliness The rebellious and disobedient among God's people tend to actively discourage godly and righteous behavior on the part of others. God says He will bring severe judgment against these. God wants us to do all we can to encourage His people to seek Him and obey His Word.	2:4	**Understand** that ignorance of God's Word leads to believing lies. **Know** that empty traditions tend to transmit deception.
	2:11, 12	**Do not discourage** godliness, **nor put** roadblocks in the way of those who pursue godliness and truth.
	7:16, 17	**Allow** the full expression of the prophetic ministry so that God's people can be warned. **Encourage** the straightforward preaching of God's Word.
	8:11, 12	**Hunger** and **thirst** for the Word of God while it is available.
3 Keys to Wise Living The wise person does not depend on past achievement of spiritual experience to guarantee success in the future. Nor is he idle and self-indulgent today. God rejects both complacency and self-indulgence.	6:1	**Be zealous** for the things of God. **Reject** any attitude of spiritual elitism.
	6:3–8	**Exercise control** in your appetites. **Practice temperance** in all things. **Be unselfish. Let** Christ's zeal and selfless love characterize your life.

The Book of OBADIAH

Author: Obadiah
Date: Shortly After 586 B.C.
Theme: God's Judgment on Edom
Key Words: Day, Day of the Lord

Background Relations between Israel and Edom were marked by animosity throughout the Old Testament period. The bitterness began when the twin brothers Esau and Jacob parted company in dispute (see Gen. 27; 32; 33). Esau's descendants eventually settled in the area called Edom, south of the Dead Sea, while Jacob's descendants continued the promised line, inhabited Canaan, and grew into the people of Israel. Over the years, numerous conflicts between the Edomites and Israelites developed. The events recorded in Numbers 20:14–21 are an example of this hostility.

This bitter rivalry forms the background to Obadiah's prophecy. Over a period of some twenty years (605–586 B.C.), the Babylonians invaded the land of Israel and made repeated attacks on the sacred city of Jerusalem, which was finally devastated in 586 B.C. The Edomites saw these incursions as an opportunity to quench their bitter thirst against Israel. So the Edomites joined with the Babylonians against their distant relatives and helped to desecrate the land of Israel. Psalm 137:7, Lamentations 4:21, 22, and Ezekiel 25:12–14 decry the participation of the Edomites in the destruction of Jerusalem.

Date The background of Jerusalem's destruction places the date of Obadiah's prophecy shortly after 586 B.C., the year in which the sacred city fell to the Babylonians. The message likely was given during the period of Judah's exile, as Obadiah warns Edom of God's impending vengeance and assures Judah of the Lord's continued concern.

Author The prophet through whom the denunciation comes is known only as Obadiah, "Servant/Worshiper of Yahweh." No additional information is available about him. More than ten men bear the name *Obadiah* in the Old Testament. See 1 Kings 18:3–16; 1 Chronicles 3:21; 7:3; 8:38; 9:16; 12:9. One tradition connects the author of the prophecy with the Obadiah identified as King Ahab's steward. See 1 Kings 18:3–16. But Ahab reigned in the northern kingdom from 874 through 853 B.C., a period that likely does not coincide with the dating of the prophecy of Obadiah.

Purpose Obadiah's prophecy speaks to people mourning over the ruin of their beloved city of Jerusalem and the deaths of family, friends, and relatives. The inhabitants of Judah who had not been carried off into captivity were few in number and confined to a fragment of the territory they once had claimed as their country. They subsisted on a virtual rubbish heap that once had been their sacred city. The Book of Lamentations rehearses the grief experienced by the people of Judah.

Into this setting, Obadiah brings his message of assurance that God has neither forgotten His people nor overlooked the wickedness of the Edomites. He will intervene to redress the situation, to punish Edom, and to restore His people. His message confronts Edom as a severe word of condemnation, but comforts the people of Judah with the promise of God's continued care, His victory, and their eventual restoration.

Content Obadiah is the shortest book in the Old Testament. It begins with a heading identifying the prophecy as "the vision of Obadiah" and attributing the pronouncement to the Lord God (v. 1).

The body of the book divides into two major sections. The first (vv. 1–14) is addressed to Edom and announces her inevitable fall. From her position of pride and false security, God will bring her down (vv. 2–4). The land and the people will be pillaged and plundered, the destruction complete and final (vv. 5–9). Why? Because of the violence Edom undertook against his brother Jacob (v. 10), because Edom rejoiced over the suffering of Israel and joined with her attackers to rob and rape Jerusalem in the day of her calamity (vv. 11–13), and because the Edomites prevented the escape of the people of Judah and handed them over to the invaders (v. 14).

The second major section of the prophecy contemplates the Day of the Lord (vv. 15–21). This Day will be a time of retribution, of reaping what has been sown. For Edom, this is a pronouncement of doom (vv. 15, 16), but for Judah, a proclamation of deliverance (vv. 17–20). Edom will be judged severely, but the people of God will experience blessing and glorious restoration to their land. Mount Zion will rule the mountains of Esau, and the kingdom will belong to the Lord (v. 21). See also the footnote on v. 15.

Personal Application Obadiah forcefully addresses the matter of relationships. How easy it is for those we know best to become the objects of our most bitter resentment. Logically, Edom should have sided with Judah against Babylonia, but years of hatred caused emotions to override good sense. Such fractured relationships almost inevitably result from personal pride, pride that prevents our seeing the error of our own ways, pride that builds barriers to block the way to reconciliation. The Book of Obadiah calls us to confront the incredible cost of pride, and to realize that the importance of preserving our pride fades into oblivion when we must stand face-to-face with an angry God and try to justify our arrogance. The book calls us to repent of our pride, to seek reconciliation in broken relationships, and to model a life-style of forgiveness and acceptance. See Matthew 5:21–26.

The prevailing theme of Obadiah is well stated by Paul in Galatians 6:7: "Do not be deceived, God is not mocked; for whatever a man sows, that he will also reap." Or, in the words of Obadiah himself, "As you have done, it shall be done to you" (v. 15). Retribution is a reality. God is just, and He will punish injustices perpetrated against other people, both individuals and nations. The Lord takes very seriously the covenant promises He makes. In Genesis 12:1–3 He had promised to bless those who bless His people and curse those who curse them. The Lord so closely identifies Himself with His people, that to curse His people is to curse Him, to reject them is to reject Him. Edom's end then foreshadows the fate of all who abuse the people of God. The Lord is determined to keep faith with His people, even when His people are faithless and disobedient.

And He will keep faith—in spite of appearances. The desecration of Jerusalem and the people of Judah sent a message to the world of Obadiah's day: The God of Israel had been defeated by the gods of Babylon, Edom, and the other oppressing nations. But that was a false message, because appearances can be deceiving. In His sovereignty God uses circumstances to accomplish His purposes, to purify and protect His people. As Lord of all the Earth He was already masterminding Edom's doom, announcing victory in the face of smoldering defeat, and controlling the course of the future in order to accomplish His plan. The Lord who did all that for Israel is the Lord who still works for His people today.

Christ Revealed The final verse of Obadiah makes reference to "saviors" through whom God would exercise His dominion over the mountains of Esau. They would function as "judges" or "deliverers" from their center at Mount Zion or Jerusalem. Hebrew judges were "saviors" for the people. They liberated them from the oppression of foreigners, provided help for the widows and orphans, and executed justice in disputes among men. These saviors foreshadow God's ultimate Deliverer, Jesus Christ Himself, the Messiah who comes as the final Judge, both to be and to bring God's most glorious Word concerning the kingdom. Through Jesus, God offers His lordship and His dominion to all mankind. Especially to the downtrodden and oppressed does He carry the message of deliverance (see Luke 4:16–21).

The "day of the LORD" (v. 15) and the kingdom of God (v. 21) proclaimed by Obadiah anticipate the entry of Jesus Christ into the world. The prophet's announcement that "the kingdom shall be the LORD's" (v. 21) is a theme that occupied much of the teaching of Jesus Christ. Time and again He spoke of the "kingdom of God" (see Luke 6:20; 9:27; 13:18–21) or the "kingdom of heaven" (see Matt. 5:3; 13:1–52). The nature of that kingdom and the manner of its coming are different from the image of Obadiah. Jesus ushers in a quiet kingdom of peace, a spiritual kingdom entered by faith in the Person of Christ. But truly, the "day of the LORD" and the coming of His kingdom are inseparable from Jesus Christ. The Second Coming of Jesus will conform more closely to the picture painted in the prophecy of Obadiah than did His first coming. See the note on verse 15.

The Holy Spirit at Work Nowhere in Obadiah is there specific reference to the Holy Spirit or the Spirit of God. His working, however, must be assumed. He serves as Obadiah's source of inspiration, as the One who imparts the "vision" (v. 1) that constitutes Obadiah's message. In addition, although not specifically identified as such, He functions as the One who instigates the judgment of Edom, calling forth the nations to rise up against the enemy of God's people. Though God uses human agents to carry out His justice, behind it all is the working of His Spirit, pushing, prompting, and punishing according to the plan of God.

Outline of Obadiah

The Coming Judgment on Edom

CHAPTER 1

THE *vision of Obadiah.
Thus says the Lord GOD
[a]concerning Edom
[b](We have heard a report from the LORD,
And a messenger has been sent among the nations, *saying*,
"Arise, and let us rise up against her for battle"):

2 "Behold, I will make you small among the nations;
You shall be greatly despised.
3 The [a]pride of your heart has deceived you,
You who dwell in the clefts of the rock,
Whose habitation is high;
[b]*You* who say in your heart,
'Who will bring me down to the ground?'
4 [a]Though you ascend *as* high as the eagle,
And though you [b]set your nest among the stars,
From there I will bring you down," says the LORD.

5 "If [a]thieves had come to you,
If robbers by night—
Oh, how you will be cut off!—
Would they not have stolen till they had *enough?
If grape gatherers had come to you,
[b]Would they not have left *some* gleanings?

6 "Oh, how Esau shall be searched out!
How his hidden treasures shall be sought after!
7 All the men in your confederacy
Shall force you to the border;
[a]The men at peace with you
Shall deceive you *and* prevail against you.
Those who eat your bread shall lay a [1]trap for you.
[b]No[2] one is aware of it.

8 "Will[a] I not in that day," says the LORD,
"Even destroy the wise *men* from Edom,
And understanding from the mountains of Esau?
9 Then your [a]mighty men,
O [b]Teman, shall be dismayed,
To the end that everyone from the mountains of Esau
May be cut off by slaughter.

1 [a]Is. 21:11; Ezek. 25:12; Joel 3:19; Mal. 1:3 [b]Jer. 49:14–16; Obad. 1–4 *See WW at 2 Chr. 32:32. **3** [a]Is. 16:6; Jer. 49:16 [b]Is. 14:13–15; Rev. 18:7 **4** [a]Job 20:6 [b]Hab. 2:9; Mal. 1:4 **5** [a]Jer. 49:9 [b]Deut. 24:21 *See WW at Mal. 3:10. **7** [a]Jer. 38:22 [b]Is. 19:11; Jer. 49:7 [1]Or *wound* or *plot* [2]Or *There is no understanding in him* **8** [a][Job 5:12–14]; Is. 29:14 **9** [a]Ps. 76:5 [b]Gen. 36:11; 1 Chr. 1:45; Job 2:11; Jer. 49:7

1 Vision: A term signifying a divine revelation, especially as delivered to a prophet. Obadiah affirms the divine authority of his message with the assertion **thus says the Lord GOD.** The prophet speaks neither his own words nor under his own authority. "**GOD**" translates the name *Yahweh*, the special covenant name for God. **Edom** can signify both the geographical area lying to the south of the Dead Sea and the people who occupied that territory, descendants of Esau, the twin brother of Jacob. Edom is also known as Esau, Seir, and Hor. The **messenger** carries a summons to arms **among the nations.** A coalition of Edom's enemies, rising to attack her, confirms God's word of impending judgment. The Lord works His judgment through unsuspecting human instruments. **Arise** is a typical summons to battle.
2 I will make you small: The manner in which this is stated in Hebrew indicates that God's judgment is as good as done. Compare the modern expression to "cut someone down to size." The bubble of Edom's inflated pride is about to burst.
3 See section 2 of Truth-In-Action at the end of Obad.
3 Pride is the sin God judges, and it will result in Edom's fatal miscalculation. She boasts in her high and haughty position, taunting her enemies: **Who will bring me down?** She reckons herself secure **in the clefts of the rock,** but her trust in earthly fortifications will prove deadly. **Rock** translates Hebrew *Sela*, the name of the capital city of Edom, an almost impregnable fortress hidden in the rocky hills about 50 miles south of the Dead Sea (see 2 Kin. 14:7). It is likely the site of the later city called Petra, which also means "Rock."
4 See section 1 of Truth-In-Action at the end of Obad.
4 The **eagle** was noted for its strength and powerful flight. But a **nest** set even **among the stars** was never out of reach of God's sovereign power.
5 Robbers and thieves would never have inflicted such massive devastation in Edom as that which God has ordered.
6 Edom will be "cleaned out" totally. Even her **hidden treasures,** valuables the Edomites had stored in vaults in the rocks, will be plundered. The nation will be ruthlessly vandalized.
7 Edom's allies likely lured her out of her fortress, then pounced on her troops in the open frontiers. Close friends, those who shared **bread** with Edom, betrayed her, even as Edom had done to Judah.
8, 9 That day is the Day of the Lord's judgment and

Edom Mistreated His Brother

10 "For [a]violence against your brother Jacob,
Shame shall cover you,
And [b]you shall be cut off forever.
11 In the day that you [a]stood on the other side—
In the day that strangers carried captive his forces,
When foreigners entered his gates
And [b]cast lots for Jerusalem—
Even you *were* as one of them.

2 12 "But you should not have [a]gazed[1] on the day of your brother
[2]In the day of his captivity;
Nor should you have [b]rejoiced over the children of Judah
In the day of their destruction;
Nor should you have spoken proudly
In the day of distress.
13 You should not have entered the gate of My people
In the day of their calamity.
Indeed, you should not have [1]gazed on their affliction
In the day of their calamity,
Nor laid *hands* on their substance
In the day of their calamity.
14 You should not have stood at the crossroads
To cut off those among them who escaped;
Nor should you have [1]delivered up those among them who remained
In the day of distress.

15 "For[a] the day of the LORD upon all the nations *is* near; 1
[b]As you have done, it shall be done to you;
Your [1]reprisal shall return upon your own head.

10 [a]Gen. 27:41; Ezek. 25:12; Amos 1:11 [b]Ezek. 35:9; Joel 3:19
11 [a]Ps. 83:5–8; Amos 1:6, 9 [b]Joel 3:3; Nah. 3:10
12 [a]Mic. 4:11; 7:10 [b][Prov. 17:5]; Ezek. 35:15; 36:5 [1]Gloated over [2]Lit. *On the day he became a foreigner*
13 [1]Gloated over
14 [1]Handed over to the enemy
15 [a]Ezek. 30:3; [Joel 1:15; 2:1, 11, 31; Amos 5:18, 20] [b]Jer. 50:29; 51:56; Hab. 2:8 [1]Or *reward*

KINGDOM DYNAMICS

15 The "Day of the Lord" in Prophecy, PROPHECY. The "day of the LORD" is a term used by the OT prophets to signify a time in the history of mankind when God directly intervenes to bring salvation to His people and punishment to the rebellious. By it God restores His righteous order in the Earth. The terms "that

devastation, a Day that foreshadows the destruction of all God's enemies (see note on v. 15). Edom's reputation for wisdom was widely known, but, in a twist of irony, her **wise *men*** fail her. They are no match for the wisdom and the work of God. **Esau** and **Teman** are synonyms for "Edom." One of Job's counselors was a Temanite (Job 2:11).

10, 11 Edom is charged with **violence** against **Jacob,** a total disregard for human life. Murder is bad enough, but the killing of one's brother is disgraceful. Because of her mistreatment of her **brother,** Edom will be covered with **shame.** So complete is God's retribution that Edom will become extinct, **cut off forever.** Edom was brought under Israelite subjection from 400 to 100 B.C., after which time its history is not accurately known. In this regard, Obadiah is likely speaking not only of the downfall of this particular nation, but is using Edom as a type of the enemies of God's people. As such they will be destroyed throughout history by the intervention of the Day of the Lord (see note on v. 15).

12–14 See the marginal note on v. 12 for the more appropriate sense of **gazed.** The haughty, hostile actions of Edom are cataloged as a list of criminal charges committed against God's people. The general charge of v. 12 is described in greater detail in vv. 13, 14. Edom gloated and **rejoiced** over Judah's misfortune. Edom trespassed by entering the **gate** of the sacred city of Jerusalem and stole from the **substance** of God's people by taking part in the looting process. But worst of all, Edom set ambushes and roadblocks at the **crossroads** to prevent the escape of Jerusalem's refugees. In 586 B.C., when the wall of *Jerusalem fell* before the Babylonians, King Zedekiah and his army fled toward the east at night. But they were captured in the plains of Jericho, their escape apparently halted by Edomite roadblocks. These tactics caused God's people to suffer even greater pain and **distress.** See Ps. 137 and Ezek. 35:12–15.

12 See section 2 of Truth-In-Action at the end of Obad.

15 See section 1 of Truth-In-Action at the end of Obad.

15 The word *day* occurs 11 times in vv. 8–14. Now it becomes **the day of the LORD,** a season of judgment and divine justice **upon all the nations** around Israel. The OT looked ever forward to this time.

"The Day of the Lord" is used by the OT prophets to signify a time in the history of mankind when God directly intervenes to bring salvation to His people and punishment to the rebellious. By it God restores His righteous order in the Earth. As noted, the terms "that Day," or simply "the Day," are sometimes used as synonyms for the fuller expression "The Day of the Lord."

The fulfillment of the Day must be seen, however, in four different stages: 1) In the times of the prophets, it was revealed by such events as the invasion of Israel by foreign powers (Amos), the awesome plagues of locusts (Joel), and the return of Israelite exiles from captivity (Ezra-Nehemiah). 2) In that prophetic insight has the quality of merging periods of eschatology so that even the prophets themselves could not always distinguish the various times of the fulfillment of their prophecies, that Day developed into a broad biblical concept. Prophetic fulfillments closest to the prophets' own day were mingled with those reaching as far as the culmination of all things. Hence, the First Coming of Christ and the church age began another phase of the Day of the Lord. As participants in this aspect of the Day of the Lord, the church can call on the risen Christ to cast down spiritual forces that hinder God's work in this present world and to bring about innumerable blessings. This is made clear by comparing Is. 61:1, 2 with Luke 4:18, 19, and Joel 2:25–32 with Acts 2:16–21. 3) The Second Coming of Christ will inaugurate the third aspect of the Day of the Lord, during which Christ's personal, righteous, and universal rule will restore God's order to the Earth (Is. 11:6–9; Amos 9:13). 4) The ultimate fulfillment of the Day of the Lord awaits the full arrival of the world to come, with its new heaven and new earth. Compare Ezek. 47:1–12 with Rev. 22:1–5.

Day" and simply "the Day" are sometimes used as synonyms for the fuller expression "the day of the LORD."

The fulfillment of the Day may be seen in four different ways: 1) In the times of the prophets it was revealed by such events as the invasion of Israel by foreign powers (Amos), the awesome plagues of locusts (Joel), and the return of Israelite exiles from captivity (Ezra-Neh.). 2) In that prophetic insight had the quality of merging periods of eschatology so that even the prophets themselves could not always distinguish the various times of the fulfillment of their prophecies, that Day developed into a broad biblical concept. Prophetic fulfillments closest to the prophets' own day were mingled with those reaching as far as the final culmination of all things. Hence, the First Coming of Christ and the church age began another phase of the Day of the Lord. As participants in this aspect of the Day, the church can call on the risen Christ to cast down forces that hinder God's work in this present world and to bring about innumerable blessings. This is clear in comparing Is. 61:1, 2 with Luke 4:18, 19 and Joel 2:28–32 with Acts 2:16–21. 3) The Second Coming of Christ will inaugurate the third aspect of the Day of the Lord, during which Christ's righteous and universal rule will restore God's order to the Earth (Amos 9:13; Is. 11:6–9). 4) The ultimate fulfillment of the Day of the Lord awaits the full arrival of the world to come, with its new heaven and new earth. Compare Ezek. 47:1–12 with Rev. 22:1–5.

(Rev. 4:1/Ps. 122:6) J.W.H.

16 [a]For as you drank on My holy
mountain,
So shall all the nations drink
*continually;
Yes, they shall drink, and
swallow,
And they shall be as though they
had never been.

Israel's Final Triumph

17 "But on Mount Zion there
[a]shall be [1]deliverance,
And there shall be holiness;
The house of Jacob shall possess
their possessions.
18 The house of Jacob shall be a fire,
And the house of Joseph
[a]a flame;
But the house of Esau *shall be*
stubble;
They shall kindle them and
devour them,
And no survivor shall *remain* of
the house of Esau,"
For the LORD has spoken.

19 The [1]South [a]shall possess the
mountains of Esau,
[b]And the Lowland shall possess
Philistia.
They shall possess the fields of
Ephraim
And the fields of Samaria.
Benjamin *shall possess* Gilead.
20 And the captives of this host of
the children of Israel

16 [a]Joel 3:17 *See WW at Ex. 28:30.
17 [a]Is. 14:1, 2; Joel 2:32; Amos 9:8 [1]Or *salvation*
18 [a]Is. 5:24; 9:18, 19; Zech. 12:6
19 [a]Is. 11:14; Amos 9:12 [b]Zeph. 2:7 [1]Heb. *Negev*

16 The Edomites who invaded Jerusalem **drank** and caroused on God's **holy mountain** after the city had been plundered, desecrating holy territory. Now **all the nations** will be forced to drink a bitter cup of divine judgment (see Jer. 25:15, 16). The authority of the Lord cannot be flaunted without dire consequences. They will drink themselves into oblivion, **as though they had never been.**
17, 18 The counterpart to judgment on God's enemies is blessing on God's elect. The desecrated site, **Mount Zion,** would be sanctified again. Those who escaped the earlier destruction, a remnant, would gather again in the sacred city to **possess their possessions,** to claim what was rightfully theirs by God's decree. **Holiness** is essential for this remnant to be God's people and to procure His covenant promises. Their holiness qualifies them to become the instrument of God against Edom. **Fire, flame,** and **stubble** refer to divine judgment on the wicked. See Ex. 15:7; Is. 10:17; Matt. 3:12. **The house of Jacob** refers to the southern kingdom and **the house of Joseph** refers to the northern kingdom. The restoration of both kingdoms is in view. In v. 1 Obadiah predicted a confederacy of nations rising up to destroy Edom. Here he attributes the destruction to God's people. The final blow, no doubt, would be delivered by God's people to an Edom already crippled by other foreign forces.
19, 20 The territory of God's people will expand to the extent of Israel's glory days, confirming that God is maintaining His covenant with His people. **South** translates the Hebrew *Negev,* the area southwest of the Dead Sea and directly west of Edom. The Israelites living there will move eastward to **possess the mountains of Esau.** The **Lowland** is a foothill region between the northern Dead Sea and the Mediterranean. **Philistia,** the area occupied by the Philistines, was the coastal plain. **Ephraim** is mountainous terrain between the Jordan River and Mediterranean Sea north of Jerusalem. **Samaria** was its chief city. **Benjamin,** named for the tribe who settled there, was a small strip of land north of Jerusalem. **Gilead** was a rich pasture and wooded area east of the Jordan River. The **captives** are Israelites returning from exile. **Zarephath** was a city near the Mediterranean coast, between Tyre and Sidon. See 1 Kin. 17:9–24. **Sepharad** is of uncertain location, perhaps Sardis (in present-day Turkey) or the Greek city of Sparta. The intent is to affirm that no matter how far away the exiles might be, God would restore them to Jerusalem.

In keeping with the multifaceted aspects of the blessings of the Day of the Lord (see note on v. 15), the restoration prophecies of vv. 17–21 find their fulfillment in part in the return of the exiles and subsequent Israelite history, but more completely in the church age and the world to come. As such, the lands possessed here should not be limited to national Israel, either ancient or restored; rather, they are to be seen as fulfilled in possessing the fullness of our heritage in Christ.

Shall possess the land of the
Canaanites
As [a]far as Zarephath.
The captives of Jerusalem who
are in Sepharad
[b]Shall possess the cities of the
[1]South.

20 [a]1 Kin. 17:9 [b]Jer. 32:44 [1]Heb. *Negev*

21 Then [a]saviors[1] shall come to
Mount Zion
To judge the mountains of
Esau,
And the [b]kingdom shall be the
LORD'S.

21 [a][James 5:20] [b][Rev. 11:15] [1]*deliverers*

21 Some translate **saviors** as "those who have been saved." These are God's people, reestablished upon the holy mountain, exalted over Edom, and executing judgment as the representatives of God. The apex of the prophecy is reached in the final line: **the kingdom shall be the LORD'S.** The objective is not merely the exaltation of Israel, nor is it the destruction of Edom. Rather, the objective is that all the world and all mankind come under the dominion of the one true God.

TRUTH-IN-ACTION through OBADIAH

Letting the LIFE of the Holy Spirit Bring Faith's Works Alive in You!

Truth Obadiah Teaches	Text	**Action** Obadiah Invites
1 Steps to Knowing God and His Ways God hates pride. It is pride to believe we are invulnerable and to place our trust in any other than God. He will humble those who exalt themselves in this way.	v. 4 v. 15	**Exalt** God. **Glorify** Him for the security and success you experience. **Refuse to judge** others, knowing that any judgment or criticism you pass may return to you. **Do not rejoice** in judgment on others.
2 Guidelines for Growing in Godliness The godly person does not rejoice in the destruction of God's people, but, like God, he seeks their reconciliation to God and their restoration to holiness and blessing. He avoids pride and the deception it produces within human hearts.	v. 3 v. 12	**Ask God to reveal** any areas in which your heart is deceived because of pride. **Receive** the reconciliation and restoration that come through repentance.

The Book of JONAH

Author: Jonah or Narrator
Date: About 760 B.C. or After 612 B.C.
Theme: God's Compassion for All Men
Key Words: Arise, Prepared, Relent

Background The pagan Assyrians, long-standing enemies of Israel, were a dominant force among the ancients from about 885 to 665 B.C. Old Testament accounts describe their forays against Israel and Judah in which they ravaged the countryside and carried away captives. Assyrian power was weaker during Jonah's time, and Jeroboam II was able to reclaim areas of Palestine from Hamath southward to the Dead Sea, as had been prophesied by Jonah (2 Kin. 14:25).

Author and Date The matters of author and date of Jonah are closely related. If Jonah wrote the book, then it would obviously date during the reign of Jeroboam II in the early eighth century, approximately 793–753 B.C. If a narrator wrote the book, it could have been written any time after the incident described therein.

Of those who hold to an author other than Jonah (usually referred to as a narrator), some date the book in the late eighth century or early seventh, based on the dates for the preexilic reign of Jeroboam II. Others prefer a postexilic date after the destruction of Nineveh in 612 B.C., some as late as the third century B.C. This contention is based upon 3:3, which says that Nineveh *was* a great city. Those who support the preexilic dating explain that this could be merely a literary form used in telling the story, or that Nineveh was in existence, but not a great city.

Jonah As indicated in 2 Kings 14:25, Jonah was the son of Amittai and a native of Gath Hepher, a village 3 miles northeast of Nazareth, within the tribal borders of Zebulun. Prophesying during the reign of Jeroboam II and immediately preceding Amos, he was a strong nationalist who was fully aware of the havoc the Assyrians had wrought in Israel over the years. Jonah found it difficult to accept the fact that God would offer mercy to Nineveh of Assyria when its inhabitants deserved severe judgment.

He was the only prophet sent to preach to the Gentiles. Elijah was sent to Sarepta to live for a season (1 Kin. 17:8–10) and Elisha journeyed to Damascus (2 Kin. 8:7), but only Jonah was given a message of repentance and mercy to preach directly to a Gentile city. His reluctance to preach at Nineveh was based upon a desire to see their decline culminate in a complete loss of power. Also he feared that God would show mercy, thus extending the Assyrians' opportunity to harass Israel.

Jonah's name means "Dove" or "Pigeon." Dispositionally, he is represented as strong-willed, fretful, pouting, hasty, and clannish.

Politically, it is obvious that he was a loyal lover of Israel and a committed patriot. Religiously, he professed a fear of the Lord as God of heaven, the Creator of the sea and land. But his initial willful disobedience, his later reluctant obedience, and his anger over the extension of mercy to the Ninevites reveal obvious inconsistencies in the application of his faith. The story ends without indicating how Jonah responded to God's object lesson and exhortation.

Purpose The book was written to emphasize that God loves all people and desires to show them mercy based upon repentance. It has been called the outstanding missionary book of the Old Testament. God declared that all nations of the Earth would be blessed through the Abrahamic covenant (Gen. 12:3). The Scriptures reveal that Israel became very nationalistic and exclusivistic and refused to fulfill that mission. Jonah had a strong commitment to this same viewpoint. The love of God for all men was dramatically revealed to Jonah when He answered the prayers of the Gentile sailors and responded to the repentance of the pagan Ninevites. The message was further amplified by the lesson of the plant, the worm, and the east wind.

Content The Book of Jonah, though placed among the prophets in the canon, is different from other prophetical books in that it has no prophecy that contains a message; the story is the message. That story recalls one of the most profound theological concepts found in the Old Testament. God loves all people and desires to share His forgiveness and mercy with them. Israel had been charged with revealing that message but somehow did not grasp the importance of it. This failure eventually led to extreme religious pride. In Jonah can be found the seedbed of New Testament Pharisaism.

Jonah the prophet is asked by God to arise and go eight hundred miles east to Nineveh, a city of the dreaded and hated Assyrians. His message is to be a call to repentance and a promise of mercy if they respond affirmatively. Jonah knows that if God spares Nineveh, then that city will be free to plunder and pillage Israel again. This nationalistic patriotism and his disdain that mercy will be offered to noncovenant people, prompt Jonah to decide to leave Israel and the "presence of the LORD." No doubt he hopes that the Spirit of prophecy will not follow. Jonah is displeased and somehow convinces himself that a trip to Tarshish will relieve him of the responsibility God has placed upon him.

The trip to Tarshish soon provides evidence that Yahweh's presence and influence are not confined to Palestine. God sends a storm to buffet the ship and causes circumstances that bring Jonah face-to-face with his missionary call. After determining that Jonah and his God are responsible for the storm, and after exhausting all alternatives, the sailors throw Jonah overboard. No doubt the sailors and Jonah assume this will end Jonah's earthly existence; but God has prepared a great fish to swallow Jonah and, after three days and nights, the fish deposits him upon land.

Again God instructs Jonah to arise and go to Nineveh to deliver the message of deliverance. This time the prophet reluctantly agrees to make the journey and declare God's message. To his dismay the Ninevites, from the common people to the king, respond and indicate their repentance by ceremonial fasting, sackcloth, and ashes. Even the animals are forced to participate in this humbling behavior.

Jonah's heart is still unchanged and he reacts with anger and confusion. Why would God have mercy on people who had abused the nation of Israel? Perhaps hoping that the repentance is not genuine, or that God will choose another strategy, Jonah builds a shelter on a hill overlooking the city from the east. There he waits for the appointed day of judgment.

God uses this waiting time to teach a valuable lesson to Jonah. He prepares a plant to grow overnight in a location that shaded Jonah's head. The prophet rejoices in his good fortune. Then God prepares a worm to cut the stem of the plant and cause it to wither. He further intensifies Jonah's uncomfortable situation by preparing a hot east wind to dry Jonah's parched body. Jonah laments the death of the vine and expresses his displeasure to God. God responds by showing the inconsistency of being concerned for a gourd, but being totally unconcerned about the fate of the inhabitants of Nineveh whom God loved.

Personal Application Jonah's story has much to say about the heart of God and the mission of God's people. God desires to show His mercy and offer forgiveness to all peoples of the Earth. He has committed this ministry of reconciliation and the message of reconciliation (2 Cor. 5:18, 19) to the church. Just as Israel was commissioned to reveal God to the world (Gen. 12:3), so the church has been commissioned to go into all the world and preach the gospel (Matt. 28:18–20). When the church has the attitude of exclusiveness exhibited by Jonah and Israel, it fails to accomplish its task. But, when the church takes seriously the command of God to arise and go to the nations of the world, those people who hear the Word and respond in faith experience the mercy and forgiveness of God in life-changing, culture-impacting measure.

Christ Revealed God's words to Jonah in 4:10, 11 are paralleled by Jesus' words in John 3:16. God is concerned for all the inhabitants of the Earth. It is true that Christ has a special relationship with members of His body, the church, but Christ's love for the world was dramatically demonstrated when He died on the Cross for the sins of all mankind. John the Baptist acknowledged the universality of this love when he cried, "Behold! The Lamb of God who takes away the sin of the world!" (John 1:29). God's love for all men as taught to Jonah was demonstrated ultimately in Jesus Christ who declared a coming Day when the elect will be gathered from the north, east, south, and west (Matt. 24:31).

The Holy Spirit at Work God's Spirit inspired Jonah to prophesy that land and position would be recovered by Israel. This happened under the leadership of Jeroboam II (2 Kin. 14:25). When the Spirit directed Jonah to go to Nineveh and prophesy against the people there, the prophet refused to follow the Lord's guidance. The Spirit of God did not cease His work, but continued to intervene in Jonah's life and induce him to do God's will. When Jonah relented, the Spirit worked godly sorrow in the hearts of the people and they responded to the message of judgment. When Jonah refused to accept this divine work, the Holy Spirit showed him the contrast between his concern for a gourd and God's concern for the inhabitants of Nineveh.

Outline of Jonah

I. Determined retreat 1:1–3
- A. "Arise, go to Nineveh" 1:1, 2
- B. Jonah flees to Tarshish 1:3

II. Providential return 1:4—2:10
- A. The Lord sends a storm 1:4–9
- B. The sailors throw him overboard 1:10–16
- C. The Lord prepares a great fish 1:17
- D. Jonah prays 2:1–9
- E. He is deposited on land 2:10

III. Successful revival 3:1–10
- A. A second chance is given to "arise and go" 3:1–3
- B. Jonah preaches 3:4
- C. The population repents 3:5–9
- D. God relents 3:10

IV. Negative reaction 4:1–11
- A. Jonah is angry 4:1–5
- B. God teaches a lesson 4:6–11

Jonah's Disobedience

2 NOW the word of the LORD came to
[a]Jonah the son of Amittai, saying,
2 "Arise, go to [a]Nineveh, that [b]great
city, and cry out against it; for [c]their
wickedness has come up before Me."
3 But Jonah arose to flee to Tarshish
from the presence of the LORD. He went
down to [a]Joppa, and found a ship going to Tarshish; so he paid the fare,
and went down into it, to go with them
to [b]Tarshish [c]from the presence of the
LORD.

The Storm at Sea

4 4 But [a]the LORD [1]sent out a great wind
on the sea, and there was a mighty
tempest on the sea, so that the ship was
about to be broken up.
5 Then the mariners were afraid; and
every man cried out to his god, and
threw the cargo that *was* in the ship
into the sea, to lighten [1]the load. But
Jonah had gone down [a]into the lowest
parts of the ship, had lain down, and
was fast asleep.
6 So the captain came to him, and
said to him, "What do you mean,
sleeper? Arise, [a]call on your God;
[b]perhaps your God will consider us, so
that we may not perish."

CHAPTER 1
1 [a]2 Kin. 14:25; Matt. 12:39–41; 16:4; Luke 11:29, 30, 32
2 [a]Is. 37:37 [b]Gen. 10:11, 12; 2 Kin. 19:36; Jon. 4:11; Nah. 1:1; Zeph. 2:13 [c]Gen. 18:20; Hos. 7:2
3 [a]Josh. 19:46; 2 Chr. 2:16; Ezra 3:7; Acts 9:36, 43 [b]Is. 23:1 [c]Gen. 4:16; Job 1:12; 2:7
4 [a]Ps. 107:25 [1]Lit. *hurled*
5 [a]1 Sam. 24:3 [1]Lit. *from upon them*
6 [a]Ps. 107:28 [b]Joel 2:14
7 [a]Josh. 7:14; 1 Sam. 14:41, 42; Prov. 16:33
8 [a]Josh. 7:19; 1 Sam. 14:43
9 [a][Neh. 9:6]; Ps. 146:6; Acts 17:24 [1]Heb. *YHWH*
12 [a]John 11:50 [1]Lit. *hurl*

7 And they said to one another,
"Come, let us [a]cast lots, that we may
know for whose cause this trouble *has
come* upon us." So they cast lots, and
the lot fell on Jonah.
8 Then they said to him, [a]"Please tell
us! For whose cause *is* this trouble
upon us? What is your occupation?
And where do you come from? What
is your country? And of what people
are you?"
9 So he said to them, "I *am* a Hebrew;
and I fear [1]the LORD, the God of
heaven, [a]who made the sea and the dry
land."

Jonah Thrown into the Sea

10 Then the men were exceedingly
afraid, and said to him, "Why have you
done this?" For the men knew that he
fled from the presence of the LORD, because he had told them.
11 Then they said to him, "What shall
we do to you that the sea may be calm
for us?"—for the sea was growing
more tempestuous.
12 And he said to them, [a]"Pick me up
and [1]throw me into the sea; then the
sea will become calm for you. For I
know that this great tempest *is* because
of me."
13 Nevertheless the men rowed hard

1:1–3 See section 2 of Truth-In-Action at the end of Jon.
1:2 Wickedness: The Hebrew word is also translated "trouble," "misery," "difficulty," and "harm." God is concerned about Nineveh's distresses and its evil ways. Its situation is extreme enough to get the attention of God.
1:3 Tarshish is considered by most to be Tartessus on the coast of southwestern Spain. As such it represents a distant place where God had not revealed Himself. Jonah is trying to escape the **presence of the LORD.** This indicates that he had a very localized view of God's presence or perhaps a belief that the Spirit of prophecy would not follow him there. He begins his voyage at the port city of **Joppa,** about 35 miles northwest of Jerusalem, a seaport for Israel.
1:4–15 See section 4 of Truth-In-Action at the end of Jon.
1:5 Probably each of the **mariners** (perhaps Phoenicians) has a personal god, a family god, and a national god. Jonah is **fast asleep,** maybe because of stress, exhaustion, and depression.
1:7 The **lots** cast may have been a kind of dice, alternately dark and light in color. Casting lots was an ancient form of divination and indicates the sailors' assumption that the **trouble** was a divine punishment.
1:9, 10 Note the inconsistency. Jonah is trying to escape the presence of **the God of heaven.**
1:12 Jonah volunteers to be sacrificed for the pagan sailors, an obvious change of attitude toward non-Israelites.
1:13 The hesitation of the sailors indicates a relationship with Jonah and a fear of his God.

to return to land, [a]but they could not,
for the sea continued to grow more
tempestuous against them.
14 Therefore they cried out to the LORD
and said, "We pray, O LORD, please do
not let us perish for this man's life, and
[a]do not charge us with innocent blood;
for You, O LORD, [b]have done as it
pleased You."
15 So they picked up Jonah and threw
him into the sea, [a]and the sea ceased
from its raging.
16 Then the men [a]feared the LORD exceedingly, and offered a sacrifice to the
LORD and took vows.

Jonah's Prayer and Deliverance

3 **17** Now the LORD had prepared a great
fish to swallow Jonah. And [a]Jonah was
in the belly of the fish three days and
three nights.

2

Then Jonah prayed to the LORD his
God from the fish's belly.
2 And he said:

"I [a]cried out to the LORD because
of my affliction,
[b]And He answered me.

"Out of the belly of Sheol I cried,
And You heard my voice.
3 [a]For You cast me into the deep,
Into the heart of the seas,
And the floods surrounded me;
[b]All Your billows and Your waves
*passed over me.
4 [a]Then I said, 'I have been cast out
of Your sight;
Yet I will look again [b]toward
Your holy temple.'
5 The [a]waters surrounded me, *even*
to my soul;
The deep closed around me;
Weeds were wrapped around my
head.
6 I went down to the [1]moorings of
the mountains;
The earth with its bars *closed*
behind me forever;
Yet You have brought up my
[a]life from the pit,
O LORD, my God.

7 "When my soul fainted within me, 3
I remembered the LORD;
[a]And my *prayer went *up* to You,
Into Your holy temple.

8 "Those who regard [a]worthless
idols
Forsake their own [1]Mercy.
9 But I will [a]sacrifice to You
With the voice of *thanksgiving;
I will pay what I have [b]vowed.
[c]Salvation *is* of the [d]LORD."

10 So the LORD spoke to the fish, and
it vomited Jonah onto dry *land*.

Jonah Preaches at Nineveh

3

Now the word of the LORD came
to Jonah the second time, saying,
2 "Arise, go to Nineveh, that great
city, and preach to it the message that
I tell you."
3 So Jonah arose and went to Nin- 3

13 [a][Prov. 21:30] **14** [a]Deut. 21:8 [b]Ps. 115:3; [Dan. 4:35] **15** [a][Ps. 89:9; 107:29]; Luke 8:24 **16** [a]Mark 4:41; Acts 5:11 **17** [a][Matt. 12:40; Luke 11:30]

CHAPTER 2

2 [a]1 Sam. 30:6; Ps. 120:1; Lam. 3:55 [b]Ps. 65:2 **3** [a]Ps. 88:6 [b]Ps. 42:7 *See WW at Josh. 3:4. **4** [a]Ps. 31:22; Jer. 7:15 [b]1 Kin. 8:38; 2 Chr. 6:38; Ps. 5:7 **5** [a]Ps. 69:1; Lam. 3:54 **6** [a]Job 33:28; [Ps. 16:10; Is. 38:17] [1]*foundations* or *bases* **7** [a]2 Chr. 30:27; Ps. 18:6 *See WW at 2 Chr. 6:20. **8** [a]2 Kin. 17:15; Ps. 31:6; Jer. 10:8 [1]Or *Lovingkindness* **9** [a]Ps. 50:14, 23; Jer. 33:11; Hos. 14:2 [b]Job 22:27; [Eccl. 5:4, 5] [c]Ps. 3:8; [Is. 45:17] [d][Jer. 3:23] *See WW at Ps. 95:2.

1:14, 15 The sailors pray to Jonah's God for forgiveness of their act of throwing **him into the sea,** fearing they will further antagonize Him.
1:16 The **sacrifice** was offered on board if animals were present; if not, when they returned to land. The significance of their sacrifice and the content of their **vows** are not revealed. They may merely have added Yahweh to their list of gods.
1:17 See section 3 of Truth-In-Action at the end of Jon.
1:17 The LORD had prepared indicates God's control of the situation. The **great fish** simply did what it was told. This is an obvious miracle, the precise details of which are not stated. We do not know if the fish was a specially created one or a modified whale; nor do we know how Jonah breathed for 72 hours. God likely chose that Jonah stay inside the fish for **three days and three nights** because that was the time ancients thought someone needed to come back from Sheol. Hence, Jonah's return from the fish would represent a miraculous rescue from death and destruction.
Jesus confirms the veracity of this OT event and uses this incident to describe the time He would be "in the heart of the earth," preceding His resurrection (Matt. 12:40).
2:2 The **belly of Sheol:** This is the inner part of the Earth, the grave, away from God's presence. Jonah is aware of his serious, life-threatening situation.
2:6 Moorings: See the marginal note on this word. The **bars** of Sheol were also in the land of the dead beneath the great deep. **From the pit** refers to Sheol.
2:7 See section 3 of Truth-In-Action at the end of Jon.
2:8 The person who has **regard** for **idols** cannot appropriate the mercy God desires to bestow.
2:9 As with the sailors, Jonah's vow is not revealed. The mercy of God is revealed in **salvation** (deliverance) for Jonah.
2:10 The **dry *land*** is not identified, but it was probably on the coast of Israel. Arab tradition says it was north of Israel on the coast of Syria.
3:3 See section 3 of Truth-In-Action at the end of Jon.
3:3 The city of **Nineveh** was approximately 800 miles east of Israel on the eastern bank of the Tigris River, opposite the city of Mosul in modern Iraq. Its walls were over 100 feet high and wide enough for three chariots to ride abreast. **Nineveh was:** The theory that the book was not actually written until after the destruction of Nineveh in 612 B.C. rests upon the tense of this verb. **An exceedingly great city** can also be translated "a city important to God," a designation reinforcing the theological import of Jonah's charge. Various theories have been advanced concerning Nineveh as a city requiring three days to traverse: it was approximately 60 miles across, thus requiring three 20-mile travel days. Another view suggests it was approximately 60 miles in circumference. It could have required one day for the

eveh, according to the word of the
LORD. Now Nineveh was an exceedingly great city, [1]a three-day journey
in extent.
4 And Jonah began to enter the city
on the first day's walk. Then [a]he cried
out and said, "Yet forty days, and
Nineveh shall be overthrown!"

The People of Nineveh Believe

5 So the [a]people of Nineveh *believed
God, proclaimed a **fast,** and put on
sackcloth, from the greatest to the least
of them.

WORD WEALTH

3:5 fast, *tsom* (*tsohm*); Strong's #6685: A fast; a day of fasting; a time set aside to mourn or pray with no provision for one's normal food needs. This noun comes from the verb *tsum,* "to fast." The verb occurs 22 times and the noun 26 times. Fasting is a voluntary denial of food. In the OT, the verb "fast" is sometimes coupled with the words "weep," "mourn," or "lay in sackcloth," all expressing intensity. Fasting is an action contrary to that first act of sin in the human race, which was eating what was forbidden. Fasting is refusing to eat what is allowed. Compare Dan. 1:8–16; 9:3–23; Joel 2:12–19.

6 Then word came to the king of
Nineveh; and he arose from his throne
and laid aside his robe, covered *himself*
with sackcloth [a]and sat in ashes.
7 [a]And he caused *it* to be proclaimed
and published throughout Nineveh by
the decree of the king and his [1]nobles,
saying,

> Let neither man nor beast, herd
> nor flock, *taste anything; do not
> let them *eat, or drink water.

8 But let man and beast be covered
with sackcloth, and cry mightily
to God; yes, [a]let every one turn
from his evil way and from
[b]the violence that is in his hands.
9 [a]Who can tell *if* God will turn and
relent, and turn away from His
fierce anger, so that we may not
perish?

10 [a]Then God saw their works, that
they turned from their evil way; and
God relented from the disaster that He
had said He would bring upon them,
and He did not do it.

Jonah's Anger and God's Kindness

4 But it displeased Jonah exceed- 1
ingly, and he became angry.
2 So he *prayed to the LORD, and said,
"Ah, LORD, was not this what I said
when I was still in my country? Therefore I [a]fled previously to Tarshish; for
I know that You *are* a [b]gracious and
merciful God, slow to anger and *abundant in lovingkindness, One who relents from doing harm.
3 [a]"Therefore now, O LORD, please
take my life from me, for [b]*it is* better
for me to die than to live!"
4 Then the LORD said, "*Is it* right for
you to be angry?"
5 So Jonah went out of the city and
sat on the east side of the city. There
he made himself a shelter and sat under it in the shade, till he might see
what would become of the city.
6 And the LORD God prepared a
[1]plant and made it come up over Jonah, that it might be shade for his head
to deliver him from his misery. So Jonah [2]was very grateful for the plant.
7 But as morning dawned the next
day God prepared a worm, and it *so*
damaged the plant that it withered.

CHAPTER 3
3 [1]Exact meaning unknown
4 [a][Deut. 18:22]
5 [a][Matt. 12:41; Luke 11:32] *See WW at 2 Chr. 20:20.
6 [a]Job 2:8
7 [a]2 Chr. 20:3; Dan. 3:29; Joel 2:15 [1]Lit. *great ones* *See WW at Ps. 34:8. • See WW at Is. 40:11.
8 [a]Is. 58:6 [b]Is. 59:6
9 [a]2 Sam. 12:22; Joel 2:14; Amos 5:15
10 [a]Ex. 32:14; Jer. 18:8; Amos 7:3, 6

CHAPTER 4
2 [a]Jon. 1:3 [b]Ex. 34:6; Num. 14:18; Ps. 86:5, 15; Joel 2:13 *See WW at Job 42:10. • See WW at Ps. 31:19.
3 [a]1 Kin. 19:4; Job 6:8, 9 [b]Jon. 4:8
6 [1]Heb. *kikayon,* exact identity unknown [2]Lit. *rejoiced with great joy*

---

immigration process, one day for visiting and business, and one day for legal exiting: three days to accomplish everything were a person to visit Nineveh.

3:4 How did Jonah preach this terse, yet powerful, message? Some scholars believe the Aramaic language was included in his education. Perhaps he spoke this short declaration phonetically, as have some modern short-term missionaries.

3:5, 6 Sackcloth: A baglike garment made of coarse cloth and worn as a symbol of mourning or repentance. **Ashes** were also a sign of mourning and repentance. A fast can be: abstinence from both food and water (absolute fast); abstinence from food only (normal fast); abstinence from certain kinds of food (partial fast). This biblical practice is employed frequently and ought not to be denigrated as a superstitious or outdated practice for believers today (see Luke 5:35; Acts 13:2, 3; 2 Cor. 6:5; 11:27).

3:9, 10 God's message of judgment always has the intent of repentance and reconciliation. Nineveh's repentance releases God's mercy (**God relented**).

4:1–11 See section 1 of Truth-In-Action at the end of Jon.

4:1–3 These verses clearly define Jonah's reason for fleeing: he is angry that God should even conceive of sparing Nineveh, a noncovenant enemy of Israel.

4:2 Jonah finds it difficult to separate his patriotism and misguided theology from his knowledge of the character of God.

4:4 The didactic aspect of this book comes clearly into view in this and following verses. God desires to teach His prophet a lesson concerning the value of all men, the wideness of divine mercy and the wrongness of Jonah's theology.

4:5 Jonah's isolated vantage point on the east side of the city provides an ideal situation for God's instruction.

4:6 God prepared a plant: This was probably a bottle-gourd plant, which grows very quickly and has large palmlike leaves.

8 And it happened, when the sun
arose, that God prepared a vehement
east wind; and the sun beat on Jonah's
head, so that he grew faint. Then he
*wished death for himself, and said,
[a]"*It is* better for me to die than to
live."
9 Then God said to Jonah, "*Is it* right
for you to be angry about the plant?"
And he said, "*It is* right for me to be
angry, even to death!"
10 But the LORD said, "You have had
pity on the plant for which you have
not labored, nor made it grow, which
[1]came up in a night and *perished in
a night.
11 "And should I not pity Nineveh,
[a]that great city, in which are more than
one hundred and twenty thousand persons [b]who cannot discern between
their right hand and their left—and
much livestock?"

8 [a]Jon. 4:3 *See WW at Ps. 122:6.
10 [1]Lit. *was a son of a night* *See WW at Judg. 5:31.
11 [a]Jon. 1:2; 3:2, 3 [b]Deut. 1:39; Is. 7:16

4:10 Jonah **had pity** on an insignificant portion of God's creation.
4:11 Jonah's misplaced values become painfully obvious. God challenges him to consider the value of the Ninevites. **Who cannot discern between their right hand and their left** is an idiom indicating that the Ninevites, though not morally innocent, were helpless to know how to escape their plight before God. Without a prophet, they would remain trapped in their wickedness.

TRUTH-IN-ACTION through JONAH

Letting the LIFE of the Holy Spirit Bring Faith's Works Alive in You!

Truth Jonah Teaches	Text	**Action** Jonah Invites
1 Knowing God and His Ways God's prevailing self-revelation is His love, graciousness, forgiveness, and mercy. We must allow this knowledge of God's nature to shape our character accordingly.	4:1–11	**Never underestimate** the Lord's mercy and His willingness to forgive. **Never discourage** repentance, **nor be grieved** when an enemy decides to repent and escape the judgment you may feel he deserves.
2 A Guideline for Godliness A godly person displays instant, willing obedience to God's bidding. Godly people are not stubborn people.	1:1–3	**Promptly do** what the Lord directs you to do. **Remember** that your stubbornness causes trouble—for you!
3 A Key to Wise Living The wise person understands that God responds to disobedience by making circumstances oppose us. He knows what is required to cause a change in our hearts and behavior. The path by which we flee from God will become the highway to repentance because of His intervention.	1:17; 2:7; 3:3	**Recognize** God's opposition to your disobedience. **Repent** and **obey.** **Change your heart** as well as your behavior.
4 Understanding Sin God cannot allow known sin to remain unconfronted in the lives of any who love and serve Him. Because sin cannot stand in the presence of God's holiness, prayer is vain and useless until confession of sin removes the spiritual barrier we have constructed between ourselves and Him.	1:4–15	**Confront sin** in your life. **Readily confess** any wrongdoing. **Remember** that you cannot hide from God.

The Book of MICAH

Author: Micah
Date: Between 704 B.C. and 696 B.C.
Theme: Incomparability of the Compassionate Lord
Key Words: Sin, Daughter of Zion, Remnant, Compassion

Author Micah was contemporary with Isaiah in the eighth century before Christ. Both concentrated their ministry in the southern kingdom, Judah, yet included Samaria (Israel) and "the nations" within the scope of their prophecies. For a few years in his early career Micah also was contemporary with Hosea, a prophet located in the northern kingdom. Micah lived in a town about 20 miles southwest of Jerusalem and prophesied mostly in that region.

Micah's name predicates a likeness to the Lord: "He Who Is Like Yahweh." See note at 7:18–20. Micah was so completely and sincerely committed that he was even willing to go stripped naked on occasion to get his message across (1:8). Micah's prophecy had an impact that extended far beyond his local ministry. A century later his prophecy was remembered and quoted (Jer. 26:17–19), and events seven centuries later attest to the authenticity of Micah's prophecy (Matt. 2:1–6; John 7:41–43).

Date Micah prophesied according to his own statement (1:1) during the reigns of the southern kings Jotham (740–731 B.C.), Ahaz (731–716 B.C.), and Hezekiah (716–686 B.C.). Since he died during the administration of Hezekiah and before Manasseh's partly overlapping era (696–642 B.C.), a date between 704 and 696 B.C. seems likely.

Background In the period between the beginning of the divided Solomonic kingdom (Israel to the north, and Judah to the south) and the destruction of the temple, many "high places" had been introduced in Judah through the influence of Samaria. This placed Canaanite idolatry in competition with the true temple worship of the Lord (1:5). Micah shows how this spiritual declension will inevitably lead to judgment on the whole land. And, although King Hezekiah had won a notable victory over Sennacherib and the Assyrian army, Judah was bound to fall unless the nation turned back to God in wholehearted repentance.

Style Micah's introductory statement (1:1) is in prose form, but the entire compilation of prophecies after that is poetry. The advantage of poetry to his contemporaries was that the rhythmic message would be easier to remember. The disadvantage to us is that poetry is more difficult to translate into another language without loss. Micah depends on shortened units of thought (with the nonessential words implied), plentiful parallelisms and nameplays (since name meanings were important to Hebrews), and poetic prepositions. He also uses an abundance of word pictures. For instance, instead of abstractly saying the Lord will conceal or otherwise make invisible our sins, he declares: "You will cast all our sins into the depths of the sea" (7:19). He cannot avoid the abstract word "sins," but he concretely depicts for us their burial like weights into the ocean depths, never to be recoverable again.

Content Micah is a prophecy about the Lord, who has no rivals in pardoning sins and having compassion on sinners. His compassionate faithfulness keeps covenant with Abraham and his descendants. "The majesty of the name of the LORD" (5:4; see also 4:5; 6:9) is featured, as well as the Lord's face (3:4), His glory (2:9), His ways (4:2), His thoughts (4:12), His strength (5:4), His righteousness (6:5; 7:9), and His consequent indignation (7:9) and anger (5:15; 7:18) against all forms of moral rebellion.

In the opening vision, the Lord comes from His holy sanctuary in heaven to witness against the people (1:2). The most remarkable factor in the Lord's handling of His case is how far down He has come to make His complaint (6:2), even being willing to sit at the defendant's table and let His people bring any grievances with the way God has treated them (6:3). Moreover, one who truly repents will have the Lord as his defense lawyer (7:9)!

While Babylon was not yet a world power that could stand independently of Assyria, the Babylonian captivity (over a century later) was clearly predicted as the judgment of God for rebellion against Him (1:16; 2:3, 10; 4:10; 7:13). But as with Isaiah, Micah's colleague, hope was held out for a remnant to be restored, whether from this captivity or from a spiritually restored people (the church) in the days of the Messiah (2:12, 13; 4:6, 7; 5:3, 7, 8; 7:18). The Lord would deliver the remnant (2:12, 13; 4:3–8, 10; 5:9; 7:7).

Micah had to censure the leadership of the nation for consuming the flock with which they were entrusted. Nevertheless, God's great compassion colors His every attitude and action toward His people, portrayed as an errant daughter (1:13; 4:8, 10, 13), for His compassion that once redeemed Israel from Egypt (6:4) will also redeem Judah from Babylon (4:10). His compassionate faithfulness to Abraham and the patriarchs (7:20) is updated with each new generation. This message is focused on the one central question for the entire prophecy: "Who *is* a God like You, pardoning iniquity and passing over the transgression of the remnant of His heritage?" (7:18). Yahweh's compassion (7:18, 19) is the precious attribute no false deity can match. Compassion and covenant faithfulness are unique with God. The people's hope to live under God's full blessing was bound up with the coming of the Messiah. God in His love, foreseeing the glories of His grace to be manifested in Jesus, kept declaring that future Day and kingdom as the event in which the faithful should place their hopes.

Christ Revealed Prophecies of Christ make Micah's book glow with hope and encouragement. The book opens with a magnificent display of Yahweh's coming (1:3–5). It will be for later prophecies to assert the personal aspect of His arrival in historical time. But the disposition of God to come down and interact is established at the outset.

The first messianic prophecy occurs in a shepherding scene. After their homeland had been defiled and destroyed, a remnant of the captives would be rounded up like sheep enclosed in a fold. Then one would break open the enclosure and lead them out the gate into freedom (2:12, 13). This one is their "king" and "LORD." The whole episode accords beautifully with Jesus' announcement of liberty to captives (Luke 4:18), while actually setting the physical and spiritual captives free.

Micah 5:2 is one of the most famous of all Old Testament prophecies. It authenticates biblical prophecy as "the word of the LORD" (1:1; 2:7; 4:2). The term Yahweh's "word" (4:2) is a title applicable to Christ (John 1:1; Rev. 19:13). The Micah 5:2 prophecy is explicitly messianic ("Ruler in Israel") and specifies His birthplace as Bethlehem at a time when Bethlehem was hardly known. His words were given many centuries before the event; he had no local cues to draw on. Another feature of this prophecy is that it cannot refer to just any leader who might originate from Bethlehem. Christ is the only one to whom it could refer, because it equates the Ruler with the eternal One: "Whose goings forth *are* from of old, from everlasting." This prophecy asserts both the humanity and deity of the Messiah in a sublime manner.

The prophecy of Micah 5:4, 5 asserts the Messiah's shepherdhood ("feed His *flock*"), His anointing ("in the strength of the LORD"), His deity ("in the majesty of the name of the LORD") and humanity ("His God"), His universal dominion ("He shall be great to the ends of the earth"), and His being the leader of a peaceful kingdom ("this *One* shall be peace").

The climax of the prophecy (7:18, 19) plus the final verse (7:20), while not including the name of the Messiah, definitely refer to Him. In the expression of divine mercy and compassion, He is the One who "will subdue our iniquities," dropping them into the ocean depths that God might pardon sins and replace sin with truth.

The Holy Spirit at Work One outstanding reference to the Spirit of God occurs in Micah's contrast of the authority behind his ministry with that of the counterfeit prophets of his day. While other men were made bold by intoxicants to fabricate tales in the format of prophecies, the true power, might, and justice behind Micah's message came from his anointing "by the Spirit of the LORD" (3:8).

Personal Application Micah has much to contribute to the knowledge of one's ongoing relationship with the Lord Jesus Christ. Relief from the foremost moral and religious sins of greed and idolatry in that ancient day can be had today by following Jesus into the kingdom of God. Micah's prophecy should make everyone stand in awe of the incomparable Yahweh who revealed Himself in the humanity of Jesus as the compassion and truth of God personified.

Micah's generation was overrun by mercenary activities of faithless rulers, priests, and prophets (3:11). Contrast these with that greatest of all "Shepherd of the sheep" (Heb. 13:20), whose compassion caused Him to give Himself for the sheep, even to pouring out His blood. Likewise, Micah, a true prophet of God, was willing to pay any personal price to perform his ministry, even to being stripped naked for the sake of his message.

Outline of Micah

Theme: Who is like the Lord?

I. The Lord's dramatic coming in judgment 1:1—2:13
1. On the capital cities of Samaria and Jerusalem 1:1–9
2. On the towns southwest of Jerusalem 1:10–16
3. On the crimes that bring foreign occupation 2:1–11
4. On all but a remnant delivered by Yahweh 2:12, 13

II. The Lord's condemnation of the leadership 3:1–12
1. On leaders who consume the people 3:1–4
2. On the prophets, excepting Micah 3:5–8
3. On officials: rulers, priests, prophets 3:9–12

III. The Lord's coming universal kingdom 4:1—5:15
1. Attraction of all nations to Yahweh's name 4:1–5
2. Compassion on His outcast, dependent people 4:6–13
3. Messiah's birthplace and administration 5:1–6
4. Restoration of a remnant in an idol-free zone 5:7–15

IV. The Lord's presentation of His case 6:1—7:6
1. His redemptive care in their history 6:1–5
2. His expectations for a proper response 6:6–8
3. His basis for judgment of the wicked 6:9—7:6

V. The Lord's salvation as the nation's hope 7:7–20
1. In spite of the temporary judgment 7:7–9
2. In spite of the nation's enemies 7:10–17
3. Because of His incomparable compassion 7:18–20

THE word of the LORD that came to [a]Micah of Moresheth in the days
of [b]Jotham, Ahaz, *and* Hezekiah, kings
of Judah, which he saw concerning Samaria and Jerusalem.

The Coming Judgment on Israel

2 Hear, all you peoples!
Listen, O earth, and all that is in it!
Let the Lord GOD be a witness against you,
The Lord from [a]His holy temple.

3 For behold, the LORD is coming out of His place;
He will come down
And tread on the high places of the earth.

4 [a]The mountains will melt under Him,
And the valleys will split
Like wax before the fire,
Like waters poured down a steep place.

5 All this is for the transgression of Jacob
And for the sins of the house of Israel.
What *is* the transgression of Jacob?
Is it not Samaria?
And what *are* the [a]high places of Judah?
Are they not Jerusalem?

6 "Therefore I will make Samaria [a]a heap of ruins in the field,
Places for planting a vineyard;

CHAPTER 1

1 [a][2 Pet. 1:21]; Jer. 26:18 [b]2 Kin. 15:5, 7, 32–38; 2 Chr. 27:1–9; Is. 1:1; Hos. 1:1
2 [a][Ps. 11:4]
4 [a]Amos 9:5
5 [a]Deut. 32:13; 33:29; Amos 4:13
6 [a]2 Kin. 19:25; Mic. 3:12

1:1 The word of the LORD: The signal that what follows is holy prophecy, not a chronicle, personal journal, or political commentary. **Moresheth** is an alternative spelling for Micah's hometown, spelled "Mareshah" in v. 15. The three kings named reigned in the southern kingdom of Judah from 740 to 686 B.C. **Samaria,** the capital of the northern kingdom of Israel, fell to the Assyrians (722 B.C.).

1:2 The **Lord GOD** needs no one's approval to do what He does. Any permission implied by **let** is granted only by Himself. He has come forward as a witness in a lawsuit to testify against His people.

1:3 His place: Micah pictures the coming of God to the people symbolically as one who lives in another location and now arrives on the scene.

1:4 The Lord's descent (v. 3) is portrayed as having the effects of intense heat (melting the mountains) and pressure (caving in the valleys), making the formations of Earth like hot wax and cascading water. The scene depicts everything under God, helplessly giving way before Him.

1:5 What is the transgression of Jacob? Question: "Who is responsible for the transgression of Jacob?" Answer: The strong influence of **Samaria** was to be credited with the increase of idolatry and sin in the southern kingdom. Question: "Who is responsible for the **the high places** (a designation for the elevated idol altars) **of Judah**?" Answer: **Jerusalem** (the southern capital).

I will pour down her stones into
the valley,
And I will [b]uncover her
foundations.
7 All her carved images shall be
beaten to pieces,
And all her [a]pay as a harlot shall
be burned with the fire;
All her idols I will lay desolate,
For she gathered *it* from the pay
of a harlot,
And they shall return to the
[b]pay of a harlot."

Mourning for Israel and Judah

8 Therefore I will wail and howl,
I will go stripped and naked;
[a]I will make a wailing like the
jackals
And a mourning like the
ostriches,
9 For her wounds *are* incurable.
For [a]it has come to Judah;
It has come to the gate of My
people—
To Jerusalem.

10 [a]Tell *it* not in Gath,
Weep not at all;
In [1]Beth Aphrah
Roll yourself in the dust.
11 Pass by in naked shame, you
inhabitant of [1]Shaphir;
The inhabitant of [2]Zaanan does
not go out.
Beth Ezel mourns;
Its place to stand is taken away
from you.

12 For the inhabitant of [1]Maroth
[2]pined for good,
But [a]disaster came down from the
LORD
To the gate of Jerusalem.
13 O inhabitant of [a]Lachish,
Harness the chariot to the swift
steeds
(She *was* the beginning of sin to
the daughter of Zion),
For the *transgressions of Israel
were [b]found in you.

14 Therefore you shall [a]give
presents to [1]Moresheth Gath;
The houses of [b]Achzib[2] *shall be*
a lie to the kings of Israel.
15 I will yet bring an heir to you,
O inhabitant of [a]Mareshah;[1]
The glory of Israel shall come to
[b]Adullam.[2]
16 Make yourself [a]bald and cut off
your hair,
Because of your [b]precious
children;
Enlarge your baldness like an
eagle,
For they shall go from you into
[c]captivity.

Woe to Evildoers

2 Woe to those who devise iniquity,
And [1]work out evil on their
beds!
At [a]morning light they practice it,
Because it is in the power of their
hand.
2 They [a]covet fields and take *them*
by violence,
Also houses, and seize *them*.
So they oppress a man and his
house,
A man and his inheritance.

6 [b]Ezek. 13:14
7 [a]Hos. 2:5 [b]Deut. 23:18; Is. 23:17
8 [a]Ps. 102:6
9 [a]2 Kin. 18:13; Is. 8:7, 8
10 [a]2 Sam. 1:20 [1]Lit. *House of Dust*
11 [1]Lit. *Beautiful* [2]Lit. *Going Out*
12 [a]Is. 59:9–11; Jer. 14:19; Amos 3:6 [1]Lit. *Bitterness* [2]Lit. *was sick*
13 [a]Josh. 10:3; 2 Kin. 14:19; 18:14; Is. 36:2 [b]Ezek. 23:11 *See WW at Ezek. 18:31.
14 [a]2 Sam. 8:2 [b]Josh. 15:44 [1]Lit. *Possession of Gath* [2]Lit. *Lie*
15 [a]Josh. 15:44 [b]2 Chr. 11:7 [1]Lit. *Inheritance* [2]Lit. *Refuge*
16 [a]Job 1:20 [b]Lam. 4:5 [c]2 Kin. 17:6; Amos 7:11, 17; [Mic. 4:10]

CHAPTER 2

1 [a]Hos. 7:6, 7 [1]Plan
2 [a]Is. 5:8

1:7 They shall return to the pay of a harlot: Money contributed in the practice of idolatry is comparable to funds squandered on for-hire fornication, since all idolatry constitutes spiritual adultery.

1:8 To insure a hearing and to guarantee that his message would be passed on to others, Micah adopts a radical behavior. He moves through the town stripped of his clothes like a naked captive being expatriated, and raises the pitch and intensity of his voice like those publicly mourning for the dead. Thus he warns the nation of an impending invasion of foreign armies. Micah's contemporary Isaiah on occasion followed the same tactic (Is. 20:3, 4).

1:9 Her wounds: Samaria's exporting of idolatry into Judah. The spiritual vitality of the southern kingdom was damaged more by this than by physical harassments.

1:10–15 Micah, through numerous Hebrew wordplays, attached a prophecy to names of the towns he served in the corridor between Gath and Jerusalem. Then whenever the people pronounced the name of their hometown or a neighboring town, they would be reminded of Micah's prophecy; the pun either affirmed, contradicted, or expounded the meaning of the town's name. These English translations approximate the sense of the Hebrew text:

1:10 Beth Aphrah="House of Dust"
1:11 Shaphir="Town of Beauty"
Zaan="Town of Going Out"
Beth Ezel="Retreat House"
1:12 Maroth="Bitter Places"
1:13 Lachish="Town of Horses"
1:14 Moresheth Gath="Possession of Gath"
Achzib="Town of a Lie"
1:15 Mareshah="Town of Inheritance"
Adullam="Town of Refuge"

1:10 Tell *it* not in Gath: This prohibition was by now a classical quote from David's lament for the slain Saul and his son Jonathan. Since Gath was a Philistine city, the residents would be pleased to hear any kind of bad news about Judah.

1:16 Shaving one's head bald, inclusive of the beard, was an act of humiliation associated with mourning. **Eagle:** This species is actually a vulture having a bare head and neck. **Captivity:** This ultimately would be fulfilled in the exiles of 597 and 586 B.C., when their sons were carried into Babylon.

3 Therefore thus says the LORD:

"Behold, against this [a]family I am devising [b]disaster,
From which you cannot remove your necks;
Nor shall you walk haughtily,
For this *is* an evil time.
4 In that day *one* shall take up a proverb against you,
And [a]lament with a bitter lamentation, saying:
'We are utterly destroyed!
He has changed the [1]heritage of my people;
How He has removed *it* from me!
To [2]a turncoat He has divided our fields.' "
5 Therefore you will have no [1]one to determine boundaries by lot
In the assembly of the LORD.

Lying Prophets

5 6 "Do not *prattle," *you say to those* who [1]prophesy.
So they shall not prophesy [2]to you;
[3]They shall not return insult for insult.
3 7 *You who are* named the house of Jacob:
"Is the Spirit of the LORD restricted?
Are these His doings?
Do not My words do good
To him who walks uprightly?
8 "Lately My people have risen up as an enemy—
You pull off the robe with the garment
From those who trust *you*, as they pass by,
Like men returned from war.
9 The women of My people you cast out
From their pleasant houses;
From their children
You have taken away My glory forever.
10 "Arise and depart,
For this *is* not *your* [a]rest;*
Because it is [b]defiled, it shall destroy,
Yes, with utter destruction.
11 If a man should walk in a false spirit 4
And speak a lie, *saying,*
'I will [1]prophesy* to you [2]of wine and drink,'
Even he would be the [a]prattler of this people.

Israel Restored

12 "I[a] will surely assemble all of you, O Jacob,
I will surely gather the remnant of Israel;
I will put them together [b]like sheep of [1]the fold,
Like a flock in the midst of their pasture;
[c]They shall make a loud noise because of *so many* people.
13 The one who breaks open will come up before them;
They will break out,
Pass through the gate,
And go out by it;
[a]Their king will pass before them,
[b]With the LORD at their head."

Wicked Rulers and Prophets

3 And I said:

"Hear now, O heads of Jacob,
And you [a]rulers of the house of Israel:
[b]*Is it* not for you to know justice?
2 You who hate good and love *evil;
Who strip the skin from [1]My people,
And the flesh from their bones;
3 Who also [a]eat the flesh of My people,
Flay their skin from them,

3 [a]Ex. 20:5; Jer. 8:3; Amos 3:1, 2 [b]Amos 5:13
4 [a]2 Sam. 1:17 [1]Lit. *portion* [2]Lit. *one turning back,* an apostate
5 [1]Lit. *one casting a surveyor's line*
6 [1]Or *preach,* lit. *drip* words [2]Lit. *to these* [3]Vg. *He shall not take shame*
*See WW at Ezek. 21:2.
10 [a]Deut. 12:9 [b]Lev. 18:25 *See WW at Is. 28:12.
11 [a]Is. 30:10; Jer. 5:30, 31; 2 Tim. 4:3, 4 [1]Or *preach,* lit. *drip* [2]*concerning* *See WW at Ezek. 21:2.
12 [a][Mic. 4:6, 7] [b]Jer. 31:10 [c]Ezek. 33:22; 36:37 [1]Heb. *Bozrah*
13 [a][Hos. 3:5] [b]Is. 52:12

CHAPTER 3

1 [a]Ezek. 22:27 [b]Ps. 82:1–5; Jer. 5:4, 5
2 [1]Lit. *them* *See WW at Ps. 5:4.
3 [a]Ps. 14:4; 27:2; Zeph. 3:3

2:3 Disaster will bear down like a yoke on their necks.
2:5 The meaning of the Hebrew imagery is this: When conquerors hold a land lottery and the surveyor's lines are stretched, the subdivision of the land will not be for the benefit of those who are local residents.
2:6, 7 See section 5 of Truth-In-Action at the end of Mic.
2:6 Since the normal words for "to prophesy" and "prophets" are not used here, the speakers are the wealthy land-grabbers of v. 5, asking Micah not to continue speaking words of judgment against them (vv. 1–4).
2:7 See section 3 of Truth-In-Action at the end of Mic.
2:11 See section 4 of Truth-In-Action at the end of Mic.
2:12, 13 This prophecy of the shepherd-king, the divine deliverer, would have brought joy to Micah's hearers and thus would have moderated the difficult words of judgment spoken earlier. The prophecy of exile is now paralleled by a promise of return by divine agency. **The one who breaks open** is also a messianic title, meaning "deliverer," and adding to the comforting assurance of return from exile the hope of one who will be a shepherd-king to all who recognize His caring authority. See note on Obad. 15 concerning the Day of the Lord.
3:3 The analogy of cannibalism is not meant to say those who loved evil were actually butchering people and cooking

Break their bones,
And chop *them* in pieces
Like *meat* for the pot,
[b]Like flesh in the caldron."

4 Then [a]they will cry to the LORD,
But He will not hear them;
He will even hide His face from
them at that time,
Because they have been evil in
their deeds.

5 5 Thus says the LORD [a]concerning
the prophets
Who make my people stray;
Who chant [1]"Peace"
[2]While they [b]chew with their
teeth,
But who prepare war against him
[c]Who puts nothing into their
mouths:
6 "Therefore[a] you shall have night
without [1]vision,
And you shall have darkness
without divination;
The sun shall go down on the
prophets,
And the day shall be dark for
[b]them.
7 So the seers shall be ashamed,
And the diviners abashed;
Indeed they shall all cover their
lips;
[a]For *there is* no answer from God."

8 But truly I am full of *power by
the Spirit of the LORD,
And of justice and might,
[a]To declare to Jacob his
transgression
And to Israel his sin.
9 Now hear this,
You heads of the house of Jacob

3 [b]Ezek. 11:3, 6, 7
4 [a]Ps. 18:41; Prov. 1:28; Is. 1:15; Jer. 11:11
5 [a]Is. 56:10, 11; Jer. 6:13; Ezek. 13:10, 19 [b]Matt. 7:15 [c]Ezek. 13:18 [1]All is well [2]For those who feed them
6 [a]Is. 8:20–22; 29:10–12 [b]Is. 29:10; [Jer. 23:33–40]; Ezek. 13:23 [1]Prophetic revelation
7 [a]Amos 8:11
8 [a]Is. 58:1 *See WW at Deut. 8:18.
9 [1]Lit. *twist*
10 [a]Jer. 22:13, 17 [b]Ezek. 22:27; Hab. 2:12
11 [a]Is. 1:23; Mic. 7:3 [b]Jer. 6:13 [c]Is. 48:2; Jer. 7:4 [1]Lit. *silver* *See WW at Lev. 5:6.
12 [a]Jer. 26:18 [b]Ps. 79:1; Jer. 9:11 [c]Mic. 4:1, 2 [1]Lit. *house*

CHAPTER 4

1 [a]Is. 2:2–4; Ezek. 17:22; Dan. 2:28; 10:14; Hos. 3:5
2 *See WW at Ps. 32:8.

And rulers of the house of Israel,
Who abhor justice
And [1]pervert all equity,
10 [a]Who build up Zion with
[b]bloodshed
And Jerusalem with iniquity:
11 [a]Her heads judge for a bribe, 5
[b]Her *priests teach for pay,
And her prophets divine for
[1]money.
[c]Yet they lean on the LORD, and
say,
"Is not the LORD among us?
No harm can come upon us."
12 Therefore because of you
Zion shall be [a]plowed *like* a field,
[b]Jerusalem shall become heaps of
ruins,
And [c]the mountain of the
[1]temple
Like the bare hills of the forest.

The LORD's Reign in Zion

4 Now [a]it shall come to pass in the
latter days
That the mountain of the LORD's
house
Shall be established on the top of
the mountains,
And shall be exalted above the
hills;
And peoples shall flow to it.
2 Many nations shall come and say,
"Come, and let us go up to the
mountain of the LORD,
To the house of the God of Jacob;
He will *teach us His ways,
And we shall walk in His paths."
For out of Zion the law shall go
forth,
And the word of the LORD from
Jerusalem.

---

them in caldrons, but immoral leaders were "consuming" the defenseless, taking all they had and divesting them of their means of making a living.

3:4 Cry to the LORD: "Call out a prayer to the Lord," not "Weep before the Lord," for a prayer of true repentance would bring the relief and restoration they seek.

3:5–7 See section 5 of Truth-In-Action at the end of Mic.

3:5 Chew: The cannibalistic biting of people in order to consume them (see v. 3) is extended to the prophets as well.

3:8 Micah had to set himself apart from the prophets he had condemned in vv. 5–7. It is the Lord's Spirit that empowers him to stand up to his generation and boldly point out their sins.

3:10 Build up Zion with bloodshed: This is irony, thus the wrong way to improve a city. Jews were treating one another as enemies rather than as brothers. God always puts the highest value on people, not on cities, real estate, or displays of power.

3:11 See section 5 of Truth-In-Action at the end of Mic.

4:1–5 Although this is a familiar OT passage, its interpretation varies among Christians. It is obviously prophesying end-time realities, but the degree to which it is to be taken literally (an end-times war involving a return to the use of actual **swords,** which are afterward literally beaten into **plowshares**) or symbolically (**shall beat their swords into plowshares,** symbolizing the eventual cessation of war and evil) is not totally clear. We can, however, grasp its essence—a world under God's authority and craving instruction in His ways.

As for the fulfillment of its essence, we know from the NT concept of the kingdom of God that many of these dynamics have already begun through the kingdom's current reign exercised by the church; the Millennium will see more realization of Micah's prophecy; and the world to come will see its consummation. See note on Obad. 15.

4:1, 2 The mountain of the LORD's house can be seen as referring to the spiritual kingdom of God (Luke 17:20, 21) that Micah says would come **in the latter days,** a term signifying the coming epoch of the Messiah some seven centuries after Micah. **The law** here means "instruction," or "teaching," and is not a technical term for the Mosaic code.

3 He shall judge between many peoples,
And rebuke strong nations afar off;
They shall beat their swords into [a]plowshares,
And their spears into [1]pruning hooks;
Nation shall not lift up sword against nation,
[b]Neither shall they learn war anymore.

4 [a]But everyone shall sit under his vine and under his fig tree,
And no one shall make *them* afraid;
For the mouth of the LORD of hosts has spoken.
5 For all people walk each in the name of his god,
But [a]we will walk in the name of the LORD our God
Forever and **ever.**

WORD WEALTH

4:5 ever, *'ad (ahd)*; Strong's #5703: Everlastingness, perpetuity; eternity, evermore, forever; time passing on and on; world without end; for all time forward; continually. This noun appears nearly 50 times in the OT. Its first occurrence is in Ex. 15:18: "The LORD shall reign forever and ever" (compare Ps. 10:16; Is. 45:17). God dwells eternally in Zion (Ps. 132:14). God inhabits "eternity" (Is. 57:15). In Mic. 4:5, Israel vows that they will own Him as their God *Le'Olam Ve'Ad,* forever and ever. In Ps. 132:11, 12, *'ad* describes the length of time that the throne of David shall be occupied by his royal seed: "forevermore." In Is. 9:6, Messiah is called "Everlasting Father," which is in Hebrew, *'Abi-'Ad,* literally "Father of Eternity," that is, the architect, builder, begetter, producer, and creator of the ages to come.

3 [a]Is. 2:4; Joel 3:10 [b]Ps. 72:7 [1]*pruning knives*
4 [a]1 Kin. 4:25; Zech. 3:10
5 [a]Zech. 10:12
6 [a]Ezek. 34:16 [b]Ps. 147:2
7 [a]Mic. 2:12 [b][Is. 9:6; 24:23; Luke 1:33; Rev. 11:15]
9 [a]Jer. 8:19 [b]Is. 13:8; Jer. 30:6 [1]*childbirth*
10 [a]2 Chr. 36:20; Amos 5:27 [b][Is. 45:13; Mic. 7:8–12] [c]Ezra 1:1–3; 2:1; Ps. 18:17
11 [a]Lam. 2:16 [b]Obad. 12

Zion's Future Triumph

6 "In that day," says the LORD,
[a]"I will assemble the lame,
[b]I will gather the outcast
And those whom I have afflicted;
7 I will make the lame [a]a remnant,
And the outcast a strong nation;
So the LORD [b]will reign over them in Mount Zion
From now on, even forever.
8 And you, O tower of the flock,
The stronghold of the daughter of Zion,
To you shall it come,
Even the former dominion shall come,
The kingdom of the daughter of Jerusalem."

9 Now why do you cry aloud?
[a]*Is there* no king in your midst?
Has your counselor perished?
For [b]pangs have seized you like a woman in [1]labor.
10 Be in pain, and labor to bring forth,
O daughter of Zion,
Like a woman in birth pangs.
For now you shall go forth from the city,
You shall dwell in the field,
And to [a]Babylon you shall go.
There you shall be delivered;
There the [b]LORD will [c]redeem you
From the hand of your enemies.

11 [a]Now also many nations have gathered against you,
Who say, "Let her be defiled,
And let our eye [b]look upon Zion."

4:4 The authentic look of this peaceful kingdom (1 Kin. 4:25) is portrayed in the rural imagery of a farmer resting outdoors under his grape arbor, or in the shade of his fig tree. The guarantee of peace is secured by the fact the Lord has His angelic armies (**hosts**) to back up His promise of security.
4:5 Walking **in the name of** one's god indicates identification with that deity. Because human beings are dependent, they take on their deity's manners and are unashamed to have their name associated with him or her as followers. The faithful boldly assert that the only true God is their God, **the LORD** (Yahweh). This verse is a stark reminder that vv. 1–4 are yet future, for men are still worshiping other gods.
4:8 The daughter of Zion is not a third party as if there were God, Zion, and a mysterious daughter who descended from Zion. Zion itself is portrayed as God's daughter. Zion is the high elevation in Jerusalem that was David's favorite terrain and site of his royal castle. By substituting the most glorious part for the whole, Zion came to stand for the entire city of Jerusalem.
4:10 Babylon, which in Micah's time was still under the dominion of Assyria, was about 600 miles east of Judah, across the desert to the modern country of Iraq. Micah's prophecy of deportation to Babylon was fulfilled in 586 B.C. The prophecy of their deliverance or redemption mentioned here was fulfilled in three stages of return for a remnant: 1) 538 B.C., in the time of the Persian monarch Cyrus, under the leadership of Sheshbazzar, Zerubbabel, and Jeshua (Ezra 1—6); 2) 485 B.C., under Ezra (Ezra 7—10); and 3) 444 B.C., under Nehemiah (Neh. 1—13).
4:13 See section 3 of Truth-In-Action at the end of Mic.
4:13 Zion is pictured as a threshing animal with metal reinforcing its hoofs and horns. The nations (vv. 11, 12) will be "threshed" by Zion so their valuables fall out like kernels of grain. Fulfillment occurred, in part, in the second century B.C. under the Maccabees (meaning "Hammers") who purified the temple and gained independence from the encircling nations. Beyond this, the fulfillment is left indefinite. See note on 4:1–5.

12 But they do not know [a]the thoughts of the LORD,
Nor do they *understand His counsel;
For He will gather them [b]like sheaves to the threshing floor.

3 13 "Arise[a] and [b]thresh, O daughter of Zion;
For I will make your *horn iron,
And I will make your hooves bronze;
You shall [c]beat in pieces many peoples;
[d]I will consecrate their gain to the LORD,
And their substance to [e]the **Lord** of the whole earth."

WORD WEALTH

4:13 Lord, *'adon* (ah-*don*); Strong's #113: Owner, master, lord, sir. The primary meaning is "master." It may refer both to a human master and the divine Lord. A citizen may address his king or any other noble person as *'adon.* It was the title applied to Joseph repeatedly by his brothers in Egypt. *'Adon* is used in modern Hebrew to convey the meaning of "mister" or "sir." The intensive form is *'Adonai,* a kind of plural form that is used only in reference to the glorious Lord in all His powers and attributes.

5 Now gather yourself in troops,
O daughter of troops;
He has laid siege against us;
They will [a]strike the judge of Israel with a rod on the cheek.

The Coming Messiah

2 "But you, [a]Bethlehem [b]Ephrathah,
Though you are little [c]among the [d]thousands of Judah,
Yet out of you shall come forth to Me
The One to be [e]Ruler in Israel,
[f]Whose goings forth *are* from of old,
From [1]everlasting."

3 Therefore He shall give them up,
Until the time *that* [a]she who is in labor has given birth;
Then [b]the remnant of His *brethren
Shall return to the children of Israel.

4 And He shall stand and [a]feed[1] *His flock*
In the *strength of the LORD,
In the majesty of the name of the LORD His God;
And they shall abide,
For now He [b]shall be great
To the ends of the earth;

5 And this *One* [a]shall be peace.

KINGDOM DYNAMICS

5:2, 4, 5 Messiah Born at Bethlehem, MESSIAH'S COMING. Bethlehem—the name means "House of Bread," and at the "House of Bread" the Bread of Life was born into the world.

The scribes knew that Messiah was to be born there. When the wise men inquired about the birth of the new King, the scribes referred to Micah's prophecy (Matt. 2:1–12). Yet none of the theologians bothered to accompany the wise men to see if, indeed, the Messiah had come. The "little town of Bethlehem" is now a point of pilgrimage for thousands yearly. But let us learn from those who did not make that first pilgrimage: Neither our orthodoxy, biblical knowledge, nor religious status guarantees that we will see what God is doing in our midst today. We must be willing to follow the

12 [a][Is. 55:8, 9] [b]Is. 21:10 *See WW at Neh. 8:8. **13** [a]Jer. 51:33; [Zech. 12:1–8; 14:14] [b]Is. 41:15 [c]Dan. 2:44 [d]Is. 18:7 [e]Zech. 4:14 *See WW at Ezek. 29:21.

CHAPTER 5

1 [a]1 Kin. 22:24; Job 16:10; Lam. 3:30; Matt. 27:30; Mark 15:19
2 [a]Is. 11:1; Matt. 2:6; Luke 2:4, 11; John 7:42 [b]Gen. 35:19; 48:7; Ruth 4:11 [c]1 Sam. 23:23 [d]Ex. 18:25 [e][Gen. 49:10; Is. 9:6] [f]Ps. 90:2; [John 1:1] [1]Lit. *the days of eternity*
3 [a]Hos. 11:8; Mic. 4:10 [b]Mic. 4:7; 7:18 *See WW at Ps. 133:1.
4 [a][Is. 40:11; 49:9; Ezek. 34:13–15, 23, 24]; Mic. 7:14 [b]Ps. 72:8; Is. 52:13; Zech. 9:10; [Luke 1:32] [1]*shepherd* *See WW at Jer. 16:19.
5 [a][Is. 9:6]; Luke 2:14; [Eph. 2:14; Col. 1:20]

5:1 The triumph of the people of God over the nations is yet a long time away. This verse indicates trouble both now (Sennacherib's invasion) and in the future. The future **siege** occurred under the Roman general Titus; it was terminated when Jerusalem fell to him in A.D. 70. **Daughter of troops** suggests a "huddling [crowded together] daughter." **The judge of Israel** refers historically to Hezekiah, but this prophecy could also be understood messianically, for we read of Jesus that the soldiers "struck Him on the head with a reed" (Mark 15:19).

5:2 Bethlehem means "House of Bread" and is the birthplace of the Davidic dynasty. Many Jews contemporary with Jesus saw this as messianic and believed that the Messiah would be born in Bethlehem (Matt. 2:5, 6; John 7:41, 42). **Ephrathah:** A place-name comparable in our culture to the name of the county inclusive of the town. **The One to be Ruler in Israel:** Here is one of the greatest prophecies about Jesus proclaimed seven centuries in advance of its fulfillment explicitly and only in Him. **Of old, from everlasting:** Though the Messiah's lineage could be traced back to His royal ancestor David, His roots go all the way back to eternity.

5:3 She who is in labor is an allusion to the Messiah's birth (see Is. 7:14). The people of Judah will be in enemy hands until the Messiah is born; then the **remnant** will respond to Him. See notes on Is. 10:20–23; 11:10–16.

5:4 Note how His deity and humanity are combined: He shares **the majesty of the name of the LORD** (the Deity), and yet He is fully human, having **His God** (see John 20:17). **They shall abide:** This clause is incomplete; "with Him" is implied.

5:5, 6 These verses rally Israel to the hope of triumph over Assyria. The victory will be led by God Himself (**He shall deliver us**) and an indefinite, yet adequate, number of unnamed others (**seven shepherds and eight princely men**). Knowledge of the fulfillment of this prophecy is uncertain. But it is known that the Assyrians were never able to overcome the southern kingdom, Judah. **The land of Assyria . . . the land of Nimrod** refer to the same place (Gen. 10:8, 9).

leading of God and His Word if we wish to see the promise fulfilled.
(Is. 7:14/Zech. 9:9) J.H.

Judgment on Israel's Enemies

When the Assyrian comes into
our land,
And when he treads in our
palaces,
Then we will raise against him
Seven shepherds and eight
princely men.
6 They shall [1]waste with the sword
the land of Assyria,
And the land of [a]Nimrod at its
entrances;
Thus He shall [b]deliver *us* from the
Assyrian,
When he comes into our land
And when he treads within our
borders.

7 Then [a]the remnant of Jacob
Shall be in the midst of many
peoples,
[b]Like dew from the LORD,
Like showers on the grass,
That [1]tarry* for no man
Nor [2]wait* for the sons of men.
8 And the remnant of Jacob
Shall be among the *Gentiles,
In the midst of many peoples,
Like a [a]lion among the beasts of
the forest,
Like a young lion among flocks
of sheep,
Who, if he passes through,
Both treads down and tears in
pieces,
And none can deliver.
9 Your hand shall be lifted against
your adversaries,
And all your enemies shall be
[1]cut off.

2 10 "And it shall be in that day," says
the LORD,
"That I will [a]cut[1] off your
[b]horses from your midst
And destroy your [c]chariots.
11 I will cut off the cities of your land
And throw down all your
strongholds.
12 I will cut off sorceries from your
hand,
And you shall have no
[a]soothsayers.
13 [a]Your carved images I will also cut
off,
And your *sacred* pillars from your
midst;
You shall [b]no more worship the
work of your hands;
14 I will pluck your [1]wooden images
from your midst;
Thus I will destroy your cities.
15 And I will [a]execute vengeance in
anger and fury
On the nations that have not
[1]heard."

God Pleads with Israel

6 Hear now what the LORD says:

"Arise, plead your case before the
mountains,
And let the hills hear your voice.
2 [a]Hear, O you mountains, [b]the
LORD's complaint,
And you strong foundations of
the earth;
For [c]the LORD has a complaint
against His people,
And He will [1]contend with Israel.

3 "O My people, what [a]have I done
to you?
And how have I [b]wearied you?
Testify against Me.
4 [a]For I brought you up from the
land of Egypt,
I *redeemed you from the house
of bondage;
And I sent before you Moses,
Aaron, and Miriam.
5 O My people, remember now
What [a]Balak king of Moab
counseled,
And what Balaam the son of Beor
answered him,
From [1]Acacia Grove to Gilgal,
That you may know [b]the
righteousness of the LORD."

6 With what shall I come before the
LORD,
And bow myself before the High
God?
Shall I come before Him with
burnt offerings,
With calves a year old?

6 [a]Gen. 10:8–11 [b]Is. 14:25; Luke 1:71 [1]*devastate*
7 [a]Mic. 5:3 [b]Gen. 27:28; Deut. 32:2; Ps. 72:6; Hos. 14:5 [1]*wait* [2]*delay* *See WW at Lam. 3:25. • See WW at Mic. 7:7.
8 [a]Gen. 49:9; Num. 24:9 *See WW at Ps. 106:47.
9 [1]*destroyed*
10 [a]Zech. 9:10 [b]Deut. 17:16 [c]Is. 2:7; 22:18; Hos. 14:3 [1]*destroy*
12 [a]Deut. 18:10–12; Is. 2:6
13 [a]Zech. 13:2 [b]Is. 2:8
14 [1]Heb. *Asherim,* Canaanite deities
15 [a][2 Thess. 1:8] [1]*obeyed*

CHAPTER 6

2 [a]Ps. 50:1, 4 [b][Is. 1:18]; Hos. 12:2 [c][Is. 1:18] [1]*bring charges against*
3 [a]Is. 5:4; Jer. 2:5, 31 [b]Is. 43:22, 23; Mal. 1:13
4 [a][Deut. 4:20] *See WW at Neh. 1:10.
5 [a]Num. 22:5, 6; Josh. 24:9 [b]Judg. 5:11 [1]Heb. *Shittim,* Num. 25:1; Josh. 2:1; 3:1

5:7, 8 Then shifts the scene to another distant time—after the Babylonian assault and subsequent captivity in 586 B.C.
5:10–15 See section 2 of Truth-In-Action at the end of Mic.
6:1–3 God presses charges in a lawsuit against His people, with **the mountains, the hills,** and the **strong foundations of the earth** as the judicial authority before whom **the LORD** as plaintiff argues His case.
6:6–8 These verses are Israel's reply to God's lawsuit in which she claims ignorance, posing questions to **the LORD** about what is acceptable to Him. The implied answer is that nothing is acceptable unless one is in a proper relationship with God and his neighbor (v. 8). The passage also shows the inadequacy of the entire sacrificial system without accompanying obedient faith (Heb. 9:11–14; 10:1–14).

7 [a]Will the LORD be pleased with
thousands of rams,
Ten thousand [b]rivers of oil?
[c]Shall I give my firstborn *for* my
transgression,
[1]The fruit of my body *for* the sin
of my soul?

 8 He has [a]shown you, O man, what
is good;
And what does the LORD require
of you
But [b]to do justly,
To love [1]**mercy,**
And to walk humbly with your
God?

WORD WEALTH

6:8 mercy, *chesed* (*cheh*-sed); Strong's #2617: Kindness, mercy, lovingkindness; unfailing love; tenderness, faithfulness. *Chesed* occurs 250 times in the Bible. It may best be translated "kindness"; however, faithfulness is sometimes the main idea. Most often in Scripture, *chesed* is used for God's mercy. In Ps. 136, the phrase "His mercy endures forever" occurs 26 times. Jesus quotes Hos. 6:6 ("I desire mercy and not sacrifice") in Matt. 9:13 and calls mercy one of "the weightier matters of the law" (Matt. 23:23). A derivative is *chasid,* generally translated "merciful," "saint," "godly," "holy," or "good" man (Ps. 4:3; 16:10; 18:25; 97:10; Prov. 2:8; Jer. 3:12). Kindness is thus a trait that God expects man to possess.

Punishment of Israel's Injustice

9 The LORD's voice cries to the
city—
Wisdom shall see Your name:

"Hear the rod!
Who has appointed it?
10 Are there yet the treasures of
wickedness
In the house of the *wicked,
And the short measure *that is* an
abomination?
11 Shall I count pure *those* with
[a]the wicked scales,
And with the bag of deceitful
weights?

7 [a]Ps. 50:9; Is. 1:11 [b]Job 29:6 [c]Lev. 18:21; 20:1–5; 2 Kin. 16:3; Jer. 7:31; Ezek. 23:37 [1]My own child
8 [a][Deut. 10:12; 1 Sam. 15:22]; Hos. 6:6; 12:6 [b]Gen. 18:19; Is. 1:17 [1]Or *lovingkindness*
10 *See WW at Prov. 10:16.
11 [a]Lev. 19:36; Hos. 12:7
12 [a]Is. 1:23; 5:7; Amos 6:3, 4; Mic. 2:1, 2 [b]Jer. 9:2–6, 8; Hos. 7:13; Amos 2:4
13 [a]Lev. 26:16; Ps. 107:17
14 [a]Lev. 26:26 [1]Or *Emptiness* or *Humiliation* [2]Tg., Vg. *You shall take hold*
15 [a]Deut. 28:38–40; Amos 5:11; Zeph. 1:13; Hag. 1:6
16 [a]1 Kin. 16:25, 26 [b]1 Kin. 16:30; 21:25, 26; 2 Kin. 21:3; Hos. 5:11 [c]Is. 25:8 [1]Or *object of horror* [2]So with MT, Tg., Vg.; LXX *nations*

CHAPTER 7

1 [a]Is. 17:6 [b]Is. 28:4; Hos. 9:10
2 [a]Ps. 12:1; Is. 57:1 [b]Hab. 1:15 [1]Or *loyal*

12 For her rich men are full of
[a]violence,
Her inhabitants have spoken lies,
And [b]their tongue is deceitful in
their mouth.

13 "Therefore I will also [a]make *you*
sick by striking you,
By making *you* desolate because
of your sins.
14 [a]You shall eat, but not be satisfied;
[1]Hunger *shall be* in your midst.
[2]You may carry *some* away, but
shall not save *them;*
And what you do rescue I will
give over to the sword.

15 "You shall [a]sow, but not reap;
You shall tread the olives, but not
anoint yourselves with oil;
And *make* sweet wine, but not
drink wine.
16 For the statutes of [a]Omri are
[b]kept;
All the works of Ahab's house *are*
done;
And you walk in their counsels,
That I may make you a
[1]desolation,
And your inhabitants a hissing.
Therefore you shall bear the
[c]reproach of [2]My people."

Sorrow for Israel's Sins

7 Woe is me!
For I am like those who gather
summer fruits,
Like those who [a]glean vintage
grapes;
There is no cluster to eat
Of the first-ripe fruit *which*
[b]my soul desires.
2 The [a]faithful[1] *man* has perished
from the earth,
And *there is* no one upright
among men.
They all lie in wait for blood;
[b]Every man hunts his brother with
a net.
3 That they may successfully do
evil with both hands—

6:8 See section 1 of Truth-In-Action at the end of Mic.
6:8 God was really looking for an ethical response from His Old Covenant people. The rabbis analyzed the law and found 613 precepts. Those are reduced to 11 principles in Ps. 15 *and down to 6 commands* in Is. 33:15. But here they have been condensed into 3: 1) Remain honest in all you do; 2) cherish compassionate faithfulness; 3) commit yourself to live in submission to your God.
6:9 Wisdom shall see Your name: It is wise to have regard for the Lord. Instead, Judah is committing the same abominations as Israel. **Hear the rod!** Pay attention to the possibility of punishment.
6:10 The short measure refers to an undersized container used by dishonest vendors where grains were sold in the city.
6:16 The renegade father-and-son kings of the northern kingdom, **Omri** and **Ahab,** in the preceding century had championed idolatry. **Hissing** was a common expression of contempt in the ancient world.
7:1 The prophet comes looking for evidences of loyal, godly character, but finds none.

The prince asks *for gifts,*
The judge *seeks* a [a]bribe,
And the great *man* utters his evil
desire;
So they scheme together.
4 The best of them *is* [a]like a brier;
The most upright *is sharper* than
a thorn hedge;
The day of your watchman and
your punishment comes;
Now shall be their perplexity.

5 [a]Do not trust in a *friend;
Do not put your confidence in a
companion;
Guard the doors of your mouth
From her who lies in your
[b]bosom.
6 For [a]son dishonors father,
Daughter rises against her
mother,
Daughter-in-law against her
mother-in-law;
A man's enemies *are* the men of
his own household.
7 Therefore I will look to the LORD;
I will [a]**wait** for the God of my
salvation;
My God will hear me.

WORD WEALTH

7:7 wait, *yachal* (yah-*chal*); Strong's #3176: To wait, tarry, hope, trust, expect; be patient; remain in anticipation. *Yachal* appears 38 times in the OT. Its first occurrence is in Gen. 8:10, in the account of Noah's waiting seven days, from the time he first sent out the dove until he sent her out again. *Yachal* is often translated "hope" (Ps. 31:24; 33:18; 130:5, 7; 147:11). The correct way to hope and wait for the Lord is to steadfastly expect His mercy, His salvation, and His rescue, and while waiting, not take matters into one's own hand (compare Gen. 15:1—17:22).

Israel's Confession and Comfort

3 8 [a]Do not rejoice over me, my
enemy;
[b]When I fall, I will arise;
When I sit in darkness,
The LORD *will be* a light to me.
9 [a]I will bear the indignation of the
LORD,
Because I have sinned against
Him,
Until He pleads my [b]case
And executes justice for me.
He will bring me forth to the light;
I will see His righteousness.
10 Then *she who is* my enemy will
see,
And [a]shame will cover her who
said to me,
[b]"Where is the LORD your God?"
My eyes will see her;
Now she will be trampled down
Like mud in the streets.

11 *In* the day when your [a]walls are
to be *built,
In that day [1]the decree shall go
far and wide.
12 *In* that day [a]they[1] shall come to
you
From Assyria and the [2]fortified
cities,
From the [3]fortress to [4]the River,
From sea to sea,
And mountain *to* mountain.
13 Yet the land shall be desolate
Because of those who dwell in it,
And [a]for the fruit of their deeds.

God Will Forgive Israel

14 Shepherd Your people with Your
staff,
The flock of Your heritage,
Who dwell [1]solitarily *in* a
[a]woodland,
In the midst of Carmel;
Let them feed *in* Bashan and
Gilead,
As in days of old.

15 "As[a] in the days when you came
out of the land of Egypt,
I will show [1]them [b]wonders."

3 [a]Amos 5:12; Mic. 3:11
4 [a]Is. 55:13; Ezek. 2:6
5 [a]Jer. 9:4 [b]Deut. 28:56 *See WW at Prov. 17:17.
6 [a]Matt. 10:36; Mark 3:21; Luke 8:19; John 7:5
7 [a]Ps. 130:5; Is. 25:9; Lam. 3:24, 25
8 [a]Prov. 24:17; Obad. 12; [Acts 10:43] [b]Ps. 37:24; [Prov. 24:16]; 2 Cor. 4:9
9 [a]Lam. 3:39, 40; [2 Cor. 5:21] [b]Jer. 50:34
10 [a]Ps. 35:26 [b]Ps. 42:3
11 [a]Is. 54:11; [Amos 9:11] [1]Or *the boundary shall be extended* *See WW at Zech. 1:16.
12 [a][Is. 11:16; 19:23–25] [1]Lit. *he,* collective of the captives [2]Heb. *arey mazor,* possibly *cities of Egypt* [3]Heb. *mazor,* possibly *Egypt* [4]The Euphrates
13 [a]Jer. 21:14
14 [a]Is. 37:24 [1]Alone
15 [a]Ps. 68:22; 78:12 [b]Ex. 34:10 [1]Lit. *him,* collective for the captives

7:4 Day of your watchman: This is the Day of the Lord predicted by the prophets. "Watchman" means "examination."
7:5 Do not trust in a friend is not a universal principle, but is counsel strictly for that time of apostasy in which no one is assumed to be trustworthy.
7:6 Jesus indicated that coming persecution against His people could be explained by these words of Micah (Matt. 10:35, 36). His emphasis was on the division of families according to how they responded to Him.
7:7 These statements are Micah's creed for crisis times. They make specific what the vision, attitude, and faith of a believer should be.
7:8, 9 See section 3 of Truth-In-Action at the end of Mic.
7:8, 9 This is the proper attitude for one who would repent and participate in personal revival. The speaker, Zion (God's people), expresses her trust in Yahweh and her understanding that the suffering is due to her sin.
7:11 In this context **the day** must refer to the time of Jerusalem's victory and rebuilding after a long period of desolation.
7:12 Sea to sea . . . mountain *to* mountain suggests the entire region from the Mediterranean to the Persian Gulf, from Mt. Sinai to Mt. Hermon.
7:15–17 This prophecy of mighty miracles as at the time of Israel's exodus is probably best interpreted messianically. The nations will be chagrined when they compare the divine deeds of the Messiah with their own power. The comparison

16 The nations [a]shall see and be
ashamed of all their might;
[b]They shall put *their* hand over
their mouth;
Their ears shall be deaf.
17 They shall lick the [a]dust like a
serpent;
[b]They shall crawl from their holes
like [1]snakes of the earth.
[c]They shall be afraid of the LORD
our God,
And shall fear because of You.
18 [a]Who *is* a God like You,
[b]Pardoning iniquity
And passing over the
transgression of [c]the remnant
of His heritage?
[d]He does not retain His anger
forever,
Because He *delights *in* [e]mercy.[1]
19 He will again *have compassion
on us,
And will subdue our iniquities.

You will cast all [1]our sins
Into the depths of the sea.
20 [a]You will give truth to Jacob
And [1]mercy to Abraham,
[b]Which You have sworn to our
fathers
From days of old.

16 [a]Is. 26:11 [b]Job 21:5 **17** [a][Is. 49:23] [b]Ps. 18:45 [c]Jer. 33:9 [1]Lit. *crawlers* **18** [a]Ex. 15:11 [b]Ex. 34:6, 7, 9 [c]Mic. 4:7 [d]Ps. 103:8, 9, 13 [e][Ezek. 33:11] [1]Or *loving-kindness* *See WW at Ps. 112:1. **19** [1]Lit. *their* *See WW at Hos. 2:23. **20** [a]Luke 1:72, 73 [b]Ps. 105:9 [1]Or *lovingkindness*

will be psychologically devastating to them. Examples of the nations (Gentiles) taking a lowly place in the presence of the manifested power of God are: the Roman centurion (Luke 7:6, 7); Simon the Samaritan (Acts 8:24); Cornelius (Acts 10:25); the people of Lystra (Acts 14:11–15); the city officials at Philippi (Acts 16:39, 40); Governor Festus (Acts 25:25); and the 275 men on board ship with Paul (Acts 27:34–37).

7:18–20 Micah makes a play on his own name: **Mi** ["who"] **c** ["like"] **ah** ["*Yah*"weh] means "Who Is Like the LORD?" or "He Who Is Like Yahweh." The generic name for God ("El," v. 18) is equivalent to the personal name ("Yahweh"). It is not the greatness of God's power that these texts emphasize, but His immense compassion and His will to forgive and forget sin in covenant faithfulness to all generations.

TRUTH-IN-ACTION through MICAH

Letting the LIFE of the Holy Spirit Bring Faith's Works Alive in You!

Truth Micah Teaches	Text	**Action** Micah Invites
1 Understanding Godliness In its simplest definition, godliness means for us to be overflowing with the fruit of the Spirit.	6:8	**Adopt** the four consummate virtues of Christian living: justice, mercy, humility, and faithfulness.
2 A Step to Holiness Holiness is relying totally upon God's ways and resources and turning from your own.	5:10–15	**Understand** that God will eventually root out any dependence we show upon things that He has not established or ways He has not directed.
3 Key Lessons in Faith Faith is simpler than it seems. It is a choice rather than an ability.	2:7	**Remember** that God's Word always accomplishes the good for which it is intended.
Many of God's promises are so astounding that we are not able to comprehend them, let alone fully "believe" them. But we can always	4:13	**Believe** that God will eventually funnel the world's wealth to those who will serve His kingdom's concerns and interests.
choose to believe, or to *commit* to His Word, regardless of the magnitude of the challenge.	7:8, 9	**Understand** that only God can judge His people. **Trust** that He will also restore them.
4 Keys to Wise Living Wisdom teaches us to accept God's assessment of man, as difficult as it may be due to our humanistic milieu.	2:11	**Be warned** that only listening to what we want to hear will breed disobedience and ungodliness.

Truth Micah Teaches	Text	**Action** Micah Invites
5 Lessons for Leaders Spiritual leadership is a sacred trust. Though often coveted by the spiritual neophyte, it is a costly role for anyone who serves in it. Leaders are asked to speak forth boldly and must not use their positions to secure financial position or undue power for themselves.	2:6, 7	**Never discourage** leaders from speaking the whole counsel of God. **Do not reprove** teachers and preachers for speaking correction or warning. **Refuse** to listen to God's Word selectively. **Receive** the corrective as well as the affirmative.
	3:5–7	Leaders, **believe** that God will stop speaking in revelation to leaders who become mercenary in their ministries.
	3:11	Leaders, **be warned: never, never set a price** on your ministry. **Never deceitfully seduce** people to become your financial support by using psychological or spiritual manipulation.

The Book of NAHUM

Author: Nahum
Date: Shortly Before 612 B.C.
Theme: God's Judgment on the City of Nineveh
Key Words: Evil, Cut Off, "I am against you"

Author Nahum, whose name means "Comforter" or "Full of Comfort," is unknown except for the brief caption that opens his prophecy. His identification as an "Elkoshite" does not help greatly, since the location of Elkosh is uncertain. Capernaum, the city in Galilee so prominent in the ministry of Jesus, means "Village of Nahum," and some have speculated, but without solid proof, that its name derives from the prophet. He prophesied to Judah during the reigns of Manasseh, Amon, and Josiah. His contemporaries were Zephaniah, Habakkuk, and Jeremiah.

Date In Nahum 3:8–10, the prophet recounts the fate of the Egyptian city of Thebes, which was destroyed in 663 B.C. Nineveh's fall, around which the entire book revolves, occurred in 612 B.C. Nahum's prophecy must date between these two events, since he looks backward to one and forward to the other. Most likely, his message was delivered shortly before the destruction of Nineveh, perhaps as Assyria's enemies were marshalling their forces for the final attack.

Background The kingdom of the Assyrians, with their capital at Nineveh, had been a thriving nation for centuries by the time the prophet Nahum appeared on the scene. Their territory, which changed over the years with the conquests and defeats of various rulers, lay north of Babylonia, between and beyond the Tigris and Euphrates rivers. Ancient documents attest the cruelty of the Assyrians against other nations. Assyrian kings boast of their savagery, celebrating the abuse and torture they inflicted on conquered peoples.

In 722–721 B.C., the Assyrians conquered the northern kingdom of Israel. At that time they also severely threatened Judah, the southern kingdom. Only divine intervention prevented the desecration of Jerusalem a few years later in 701 B.C. (see 1 Kin. 17—19). Now, over a century later, the empire whose atrocities made the world tremble and who acted as God's instrument against a sinful Israel, teetered on the verge of divine destruction.

The fall of the Assyrian Empire, climaxed by the destruction of the capital city of Nineveh in 612 B.C., is the subject of the prophecy of Nahum. The doom about to descend upon the world's great oppressor is the single occasion for Nahum's pronouncement. Consequently, the prophecy is judicial in style, incorporating ancient "judgment oracles." The language is poetic, forceful, and figurative, underscoring the intensity of the topic with which Nahum wrestles.

While the judgment of Assyria is the overwhelming theme of Nahum, the book is primarily a message of comfort to the people of Judah. News of the destruction of the world's great tyrant would come as welcome relief to people shuddering with apprehension and anxiety. Political bondage was always a theological problem for the people of Israel, because this was one of the curses God had promised for disobedience (Deut. 28:33, 36, 37, 49–52). Release from the terror of Assyrian domination would bring with it a renewed sense of God's good favor. Nahum's two-pronged proclamation of condemnation and comfort is well summarized in 1:7–9. Unfortunately, Judah failed to heed the warning seen in Assyria's fall and the subsequent rise to power of Babylon. She continued in moral rebellion, which would result in her fall to Babylon in 586 B.C.

Content The Book of Nahum focuses on a single concern: the fall of the city of Nineveh. Three major sections, corresponding to the three chapters, comprise the prophecy. The first describes God's great power and how that power works itself out in the form of protection for the righteous but judgment for the wicked. Though God is never quick to judge, His patience cannot forever be taken for granted. All the Earth is under His control; and when He appears in power, even nature shrinks before Him (1:1–8). In her state of distress and affliction (1:12), Judah could easily doubt God's goodness and even question His power. But the Lord promises to restore peace (1:15), to defeat the enemies of His people (1:13–15), and to remove the threat of renewed affliction (1:9). The prediction of Nineveh's doom forms a message of consolation to Judah (1:15).

The second major section of the prophecy describes the coming destruction of Nineveh (2:1–13). Attempts to defend the city against her attackers will be in vain because the Lord has decreed the fall of Nineveh and the rise of Judah (2:1–7). Floods will inundate the city, sweeping away all the mighty, man-made structures (2:6). Nineveh's citizens will be carried away captive (2:7); others will flee in terror (2:8). Precious treasures will be plundered (2:9); all strength and self-confidence will melt away (2:10). The mighty lion's den will be reduced to desolation, because "'I *am* against you,' says the LORD of hosts" (2:11–13).

The third chapter forms the final section of the book. God's judgment may seem overly harsh, but He is justified in His condemnation. Nineveh was a "bloody city" (3:1), a city guilty of shedding the innocent blood of other people. She was a city known for deceit, falsehood, theft, and debauchery (3:1, 4). Such vice was an offense to God, so His verdict of judgment was inevitable (3:2, 3, 5–7). Like No Amon, an Egyptian city that fell despite numerous allies and strong defenses, Nineveh cannot escape divine judgment (3:8–13). All efforts to survive prove futile (3:14, 15). Troops scatter, leaders perish, and the people run for the hills (3:16–18). God's judgment has fallen, and the peoples Assyria once victimized so mercilessly rejoice and celebrate in response to the news (3:19).

Personal Application Nahum graphically portrays the seriousness of sin in the sight of God. Though His mercy and patience may cause Him to withhold judgment for a season, God will ultimately announce a day of reckoning. When His righteous judgment is unleashed, no human or superhuman power can withstand its force. His dominion extends over all that exists, and He sits on the bench as Judge over both individuals and nations.

Nahum calls us to serious self-examination and warns against the subtle sin of believing that life can be lived apart from the will and the ways of God. He chides us for becoming overly smug and secure in our faith, for Assyria, once used as God's instrument (Is. 10:5, 6), now becomes the object of His wrath. The most frightening words anyone could ever experience are those directed toward Nineveh by the Lord: "Behold, I *am* against you" (2:13). With such prospects in view, serious self-examination should lead us into wholehearted repentance.

Misuse and abuse of other people is sin in God's sight. Assyria built an empire by raping and plundering others, but national or personal kingdoms founded on deceit and tyranny also are displeasing to the Lord and will be judged by Him. A life of wickedness eventually will lead to isolation, not only from other people, but also from God. Others will withdraw from you, and God will finally be forced to judge (3:19).

Graciously, His judgment against the sinful is offset by His mercy toward the faithful. To the proud, the arrogant, and the rebellious He comes with condemnation. To the humble, the devoted, and the faithful He comes with comfort.

Assyria's long-awaited doom teaches that God's goodness and justice will prevail, though circumstances may seem contradictory. His concern for His people is unceasing, though He may sometimes seem slow to act or far removed. The antidote for discouragement among believers is a revitalized vision of the person and power of God. It is a renewed understanding that vengeance is the work of God, not of ourselves. True faith leaves judgment in the hands of God.

The truth of God's judgment upon sin and the sinner should prompt believers to a renewed evangelistic mission. Those we fail to reach with the saving message of the gospel will indeed suffer the wrath of God.

Christ Revealed The Book of Nahum pronounces God's judgment on sin and evil, personified in the wickedness of the Assyrians. Nineveh was indeed destroyed, but that partial and temporary defeat of evil awaited the complete and permanent conquest that would come only through Jesus Christ. Nahum's prophecy proclaims that God cannot countenance evil, that sin must be cut off from the Earth. At the crucifixion of Christ, God drove the final nail into sin's coffin by cutting off His own Son. See Matt. 27:46; 2 Cor. 5:21. God's final judgment on wickedness and evil took place at the Cross. That is surely reason for even greater celebration than that prompted by the fall of Nineveh (Nah. 3:19).

But the counterpart, God's greatest demonstration of His goodness, is also revealed in Jesus Christ. Nahum proclaims that God is good, but His goodness was brought to its climax only in Christ (Rom. 5:6–11). God's goodness was enfleshed in Jesus, a living declaration of the good tidings of peace. Now humanity has a way to return to its God-appointed tasks and calling (Nah. 1:15). The wicked lioness (Nah. 2:11, 12) has been defeated and replaced by the righteous Lion of the tribe of Judah (Rev. 5:5). God's vengeance against sin has been satisfied through the sacrifice of His Son.

The Holy Spirit at Work No specific references to the Holy Spirit occur in the Book of Nahum. However, the Spirit's work in the production of the prophecy and in the direction of the events depicted in the book must be assumed.

The heading of the book describes it as "the vision of Nahum" (1:1). The Holy Spirit functions here as the Revealer, the One who opens to Nahum the drama that unfolds before him and imparts the message from the Lord he is commissioned to deliver.

The Holy Spirit must also function as the Great Instigator in the downfall of Nineveh. Enemies, among them the Babylonians, Medes, and Scythians, gather forces against the Assyrians and sack the city. God uses human agents to carry out His judgment, but behind it all is the working of His Spirit, prompting, pushing, and punishing according to the will of God. By the work of the Spirit, the Lord mustered His troops and led them into victorious battle.

Outline of Nahum

I. Title	**1:1**
II. The verdict of God	**1:2–15**
A. The jealousy of God	1:2–6
B. The gentleness of God	1:7
C. The judgment of Nineveh	1:8–14
D. The joy of Judah	1:15
III. The vengeance of God	**2:1–13**
A. The destruction of Nineveh	2:1–12
B. The declaration of the Lord	2:13
IV. The victory of God	**3:1–19**
A. The sins of Nineveh	3:1–4
B. The siege of Nineveh	3:5–18
C. The celebration over Nineveh	3:19

THE [1]burden [a]against Nineveh. The book of the vision of Nahum the Elkoshite.

God's Wrath on His Enemies

2 God *is* [a]jealous, and the LORD avenges;
The LORD avenges and *is* furious.
The LORD will take vengeance on His adversaries,
And He reserves *wrath* for His enemies;
3 The LORD *is* [a]slow to *anger and [b]great in power,
And will not at all acquit *the wicked.*

[c]The LORD has His way
In the whirlwind and in the storm,
And the clouds *are* the dust of His feet.
4 [a]He rebukes the sea and makes it dry,
And dries up all the rivers.
[b]Bashan and Carmel wither,
And the flower of Lebanon wilts.
5 The mountains quake before Him,
The hills melt,
And the earth [1]heaves at His presence,
Yes, the *world and all who dwell in it.

6 Who can stand before His indignation?
And [a]who can endure the fierceness of His anger?
His fury is poured out like fire,

CHAPTER 1

1 [a]2 Kin. 19:36; Jon. 1:2; Nah. 2:8; Zeph. 2:13 [1]*oracle, prophecy*
2 [a]Ex. 20:5; Josh. 24:19
3 [a]Ex. 34:6, 7; Neh. 9:17; Ps. 103:8 [b][Job 9:4] [c]Ps. 18:17 *See WW at Judg. 10:7.
4 [a]Josh. 3:15, 16; Ps. 106:9; Is. 50:2; Matt. 8:26 [b]Is. 33:9
5 [1]Tg. *burns* *See WW at Jer. 51:15.
6 [a]Jer. 10:10; [Mal. 3:2]

1:1 Burden: A threatening word. Nahum's message is the only prophecy in the OT identified as a **book. Nineveh,** representing the entire Assyrian Empire, was a magnificent city located on the eastern bank of the Tigris River in modern Iraq. It was founded by Nimrod (Gen. 10:8–11) and was surrounded by a wall almost 8 miles in circumference. The city could accommodate an estimated 300,000 people. See note on Jon. 3:3.

1:2, 3 The LORD translates the Hebrew *Yahweh,* the covenant name for God. He is **jealous,** demanding undivided devotion, and is intent on protecting and vindicating His people. His mercy and patience make Him **slow to anger.**

1:4 Nahum refers to the Lord's parting **the sea** and leading Israel out of Egypt (Ex. 14) and to His cutting off the river when Israel crossed the Jordan to enter Canaan (Josh. 3). **Bashan, Carmel,** and **Lebanon** were areas renowned for their fertility.

1:5 Even the greatest emblems of strength and stability, **mountains, hills,** and **the earth,** shudder in the presence of God.

And the rocks are thrown down
by Him.

7 [a]The LORD *is* *good,
A stronghold in the day of
trouble;
And [b]He knows those who *trust
in Him.
8 But with an overflowing flood
He will make an utter end of its
place,
And darkness will pursue His
enemies.

9 [a]What do you [1]conspire against
the LORD?
[b]He will make an utter end *of it.*
Affliction will not rise up a second
time.
10 For while tangled [a]*like* thorns,
[b]And while drunken *like*
drunkards,
[c]They shall be devoured like
stubble fully dried.
11 From you comes forth *one*
Who plots evil against the LORD,
A [1]wicked counselor.

12 Thus says the LORD:

"Though *they are* [1]safe, and
likewise many,
Yet in this manner they will be
[a]cut down
When he passes through.
Though I have afflicted you,
I will afflict you no more;
13 For now I will break off his yoke
from you,
And burst your bonds apart."

14 The LORD has given a command
concerning you:
[1]"Your name shall be perpetuated
no longer.
Out of the house of your gods
I will cut off the carved image and
the molded image.
I will dig your [a]grave,
For you are [b]vile."[2]

15 Behold, on the mountains
The [a]feet of him who brings good
tidings,
Who proclaims **peace!**
O Judah, keep your appointed
feasts,
Perform your vows.
For the [1]wicked one shall no more
pass through you;
He is [b]utterly cut off.

WORD WEALTH

1:15 peace, *shalom* (shah-*loam*); Strong's #7965: Completeness, wholeness, peace, health, welfare, safety, soundness, tranquility, prosperity, perfectness, fullness, rest, harmony; the absence of agitation or discord. *Shalom* comes from the root verb *shalam,* meaning "to be complete, perfect, and full." Thus *shalom* is much more than the absence of war and conflict; it is the wholeness that the entire human race seeks. The word *shalom* occurs about 250 times in the OT (see Ps. 4:8; Is. 48:18; Jer. 29:11). In Ps. 35:27, God takes delight in the *shalom* (the wholeness, the total well-being) of His servant. In Is. 53:5, the chastisement necessary to bring us *shalom* was upon the suffering Messiah. The angels understood at His birth that Jesus was to be the great peace-bringer, as they called out, "Glory to God in the highest: and on earth peace, goodwill toward men!" (Luke 2:14–17; compare Is. 9:7).

The Destruction of Nineveh

2 He[1] who scatters has come up
before your face.

---

7 [a]Ps. 25:8; 37:39, 40; 100:5; [Jer. 33:11]; Lam. 3:25 [b]Ps. 1:6; John 10:14; 2 Tim. 2:19 *See WW at Ezek. 34:14. • See WW at Zeph. 3:12.
9 [a]Ps. 2:1; Nah. 1:11 [b]1 Sam. 3:12 [1]Or *devise*
10 [a]2 Sam. 23:6; Mic. 7:4 [b]Is. 56:12; Nah. 3:11 [c]Is. 5:24; 10:17; Mal. 4:1
11 [1]Lit. *counselor of Belial*
12 [a][Is. 10:16–19, 33, 34] [1]Or *at peace* or *complete*
14 [a]Ezek. 32:22, 23 [b]Nah. 3:6 [1]Lit. *No more of your name shall be fruitful* [2]Or *contemptible*
15 [a]Is. 40:9; 52:7; Rom. 10:15 [b]Is. 29:7, 8 [1]Lit. *one of Belial*

CHAPTER 2

1 [1]Vg. *He who destroys*

1:7 See section 1 of Truth-In-Action at the end of Nah.
1:7 The Assyrians regarded Nineveh as an invincible fortress. Beyond its massive walls, a system of canals, moats, outworks, and armed guards provided strong defenses. But as strong as Nineveh was, the Lord is the real **stronghold** for **those who trust in Him.**
1:8 The **flood** probably refers to natural disaster combined with enemy invasion. The **end** came for Nineveh in 612 B.C. at the hands of a coalition headed by the Medes and Babylonians.
1:9 The Lord would not allow Assyria to defeat His people **a second time.** They had been used previously against Israel in 722 B.C.
1:11 The ***one* who plots evil** is probably a general reference to the habitually wicked character of the Assyrian rulers. It could refer either to Sennacherib, whose planned attack on Jerusalem in 701 B.C. was thwarted (2 Kin. 18), or to Ashurbanipal, the last great Assyrian ruler (669–627 B.C.), who conquered Egypt and forced King Manasseh of Judah to submit as his puppet (2 Chr. 33:11–13).
1:12, 13 See section 1 of Truth-In-Action at the end of Nah.
1:12, 13 The Assyrians could not rely on numbers, allies, and past victories to anticipate continued dominion over their kingdom. They failed to reckon with the God of Israel, who had previously used them as His instrument to **afflict** His own people (Is. 10:5). Now He would break their dominion and remove the **yoke** of slavery from Judah.
1:14 As God had previously used the Assyrians, He uses the Medes, the Babylonians, and the Scythians to **dig** the **grave** for Nineveh. Ezek. 32:22, 23 confirms this prophecy.
1:15 See section 1 of Truth-In-Action at the end of Nah.
1:15 The mountains are those surrounding Jerusalem. The message is one of deliverance from the oppression of the enemy, which allows the people of Judah to resume their appointed **feasts** and fulfill their **vows** without the threat of the **wicked one.** See Is. 52:7 and Rom. 10:15.
2:1 He who scatters is the coalition of Medes, Babylonians, and Scythians about to attack Nineveh. The Assyrians practiced a policy of deporting conquered peoples from their homelands and scattering them throughout their empire,

Man the fort!
Watch the road!
Strengthen *your* flanks!
Fortify *your* power mightily.

2 For the LORD will restore the
excellence of Jacob
Like the excellence of Israel,
For the emptiers have emptied
them out
And ruined their vine branches.

3 The shields of his mighty men *are*
made red,
The valiant men *are* in scarlet.
The chariots *come* with flaming
torches
In the day of his preparation,
And [1]the spears are brandished.
4 The chariots rage in the streets,
They jostle one another in the
broad roads;
They seem like torches,
They run like lightning.

5 He remembers his nobles;
They stumble in their walk;
They make haste to her walls,
And the defense is prepared.
6 The gates of the rivers are
opened,
And the palace is dissolved.
7 [1]It is decreed:
She shall be led away captive,
She shall be brought up;
And her maidservants shall lead
her as with the voice of doves,
Beating their breasts.

3 [1]Lit. *the cypresses are shaken;* LXX, Syr. *the horses rush about;* Vg. *the drivers are stupefied*
7 [1]Heb. *Huzzab*
8 [1]Lit. *Stand*
9 [a]Ezek. 7:19; Zeph. 1:18 [1]*Plunder*
10 [1]LXX, Tg., Vg. *gather blackness;* Joel 2:6
11 [a]Job 4:10, 11; Ezek. 19:2–7
12 [a]Is. 10:6; Jer. 51:34 [1]Lit. *Strangled* [2]Torn flesh *See WW at Mal. 3:10.
13 [a]Jer. 21:13; Ezek. 5:8; Nah. 3:5 [b]2 Kin. 18:17–25; 19:9–13, 23 [1]Lit. *her*

8 Though Nineveh of old *was* like
a pool of water,
Now they flee away.
[1]"Halt! Halt!" *they cry;*
But no one turns back.
9 [1]Take spoil of silver!
Take spoil of [a]gold!
There is no end of treasure,
Or wealth of every desirable
prize.
10 She is empty, desolate, and
waste!
The heart melts, and the knees
shake;
Much pain *is* in every side,
And all their faces [1]are drained
of color.

11 Where *is* the dwelling of the
[a]lions,
And the feeding place of the
young lions,
Where the lion walked, the
lioness *and* lion's cub,
And no one made *them* afraid?
12 The lion tore in pieces *enough
for his cubs,
[1]Killed for his lionesses,
[a]Filled his caves with prey,
And his dens with [2]flesh.

13 "Behold, [a]I *am* against you," says
the LORD of hosts, "I will burn [1]your
chariots in smoke, and the sword shall
devour your young lions; I will cut off
your prey from the earth, and the voice
of your [b]messengers shall be heard no
more."

---

thereby stripping them of identity and continuity. The tribes of the northern kingdom suffered this fate. But Assyria the great scatterer will be scattered by others. The short, staccato lines **Man the fort! Watch the road!** depict the urgency of preparing for impending attack; but a sense of irony pervades, because all the efforts of the Assyrians are futile in the face of the judgment of God.

2:2 The ruin of Assyria is offset by the restoration of God's people. **The LORD will restore** their **excellence. Jacob** and **Israel** refer to the southern and northern kingdoms respectively. In that the northern kingdom never returned, Nahum's reference is likely to include the future blessings of God's covenant people in the church age, Millennium, and world to come; all these are part of the OT Day of the Lord. See note on Obad. 15.

2:3, 4 The conflict between the **mighty men** of the invaders and Nineveh's troops is engaged. Military weaponry is graphically described: **shields** are **made red** in preparation for the battle. The **valiant men** are clad in **scarlet,** the battle colors of the invaders. The **chariots,** the zenith of military weaponry in the seventh century B.C., surge forward like flaming steel.

2:5 He, the king of Assyria, musters his best troops, but their efforts are bumbling in the face of the skill of the attackers. By this point, the invaders have likely crossed the 150-foot moat outside Nineveh and have moved battering rams into position against one or more of the 15 gates in the wall around the city.

2:6 Besides the Tigris River on the west, the Khoser, a spring-fed stream, traversed Nineveh. A canal also ran through the city. Sennacherib (705–681 B.C.) had built a series of dams to control water flow. The invaders likely closed **the gates of the rivers** to stop the flow of water and make their approach to Nineveh easier, then suddenly opened the gates to release torrents of water and unleash a destructive flood on the city. The **palace,** likely constructed of dried mud bricks, would literally dissolve.

2:7 Nineveh is disgraced and humiliated.

2:8–10 Nineveh was once like a beautiful **pool of water,** with all her waterways neatly designed, but now God has pulled the plug, and everything is draining away. Ancient records attest to the great amounts of plunder taken from Nineveh.

2:11, 12 In a twist of irony, Nahum employs the figure of a **lion** to mock the fall of Nineveh. The lion was the symbol of the nation (Hos. 5:13, 14), and Assyrian rulers often depicted themselves as the "king of the beasts."

2:13 Nineveh's fall is an act of divine retribution. Ancient records and modern excavations confirm that portions of the city were burned. The fall of Nineveh silenced the **voice** of Assyria forever.

The Woe of Nineveh

3 Woe to the [a]bloody city!
It *is* all full of lies *and* robbery.
Its [1]victim never departs.
2 The noise of a whip
And the noise of rattling wheels,
Of galloping horses,
Of [1]clattering chariots!
3 Horsemen charge with bright sword and glittering spear.
There is a multitude of slain,
A great number of bodies,
Countless corpses—
They stumble over the corpses—
4 Because of the multitude of [1]harlotries of the [2]seductive harlot,
[a]The mistress of sorceries,
Who sells nations through her harlotries,
And families through her sorceries.

5 "Behold, I *am* [a]against you," says the LORD of hosts;
[b]"I will lift your skirts over your face,
I will show the nations your nakedness,
And the kingdoms your shame.
6 I will cast abominable filth upon you,
Make you [a]vile,[1]
And make you [b]a spectacle.
7 It shall come to pass *that* all who look upon you
[a]Will flee from you, and say,
[b]'Nineveh is laid waste!
[c]Who will bemoan her?'
Where shall I seek *comforters for you?"

8 [a]Are you better than [b]No[1] Amon
That was situated by the [2]River,
That had the waters around her,
Whose rampart *was* the sea,
Whose wall *was* the sea?
9 Ethiopia and Egypt *were* her strength,
And *it was* boundless;
[a]Put and Lubim were [1]your helpers.
10 Yet she *was* carried away,
She went into captivity;
[a]Her young children also were dashed to pieces
[b]At the head of every street;
They [c]cast lots for her honorable men,
And all her great men were bound in chains.
11 You also will be [a]drunk;
You will be hidden;
You also will seek refuge from the enemy.

12 All your strongholds *are* [a]fig trees with ripened figs:
If they are shaken,
They fall into the mouth of the eater.
13 Surely, [a]your people in your midst *are* women!
The gates of your land are wide open for your enemies;
Fire shall devour the [b]bars of your *gates.*

14 Draw your water for the siege!
[a]Fortify your strongholds!
Go into the clay and tread the mortar!
Make strong the brick kiln!
15 There the fire will devour you,
The sword will cut you off;
It will eat you up like a [a]locust.

Make yourself many—like the locust!
Make yourself many— like the *swarming* locusts!
16 You have multiplied your

CHAPTER 3

1 [a]Ezek. 22:2, 3; 24:6–9; Hab. 2:12 [1]Lit. *prey*
2 [1]*bounding* or *jolting*
4 [a]Is. 47:9–12; Rev. 18:2, 3 [1]Spiritual unfaithfulness [2]Lit. *goodly charm,* in a bad sense
5 [a]Jer. 50:31; Ezek. 26:3; Nah. 2:13 [b]Is. 47:2, 3; Jer. 13:26
6 [a]Nah. 1:14 [b]Heb. 10:33 [1]*despicable*
7 [a]Rev. 18:10 [b]Jon. 3:3; 4:11 [c]Is. 51:19; Jer. 15:5 *See WW at Ps. 23:4.
8 [a]Amos 6:2 [b]Jer. 46:25; Ezek. 30:14–16 [1]Ancient Thebes; Tg., Vg. *populous Alexandria* [2]Lit. *rivers,* the Nile and the surrounding canals
9 [a]Gen. 10:6; Jer. 46:9; Ezek. 27:10 [1]LXX *her*
10 [a]Ps. 137:9; Is. 13:16; Hos. 13:16 [b]Lam. 2:19 [c]Joel 3:3; Obad. 11
11 [a]Is. 49:26; Jer. 25:27; Nah. 1:10
12 [a]Rev. 6:12, 13
13 [a]Is. 19:16; Jer. 50:37; 51:30 [b]Ps. 147:13; Jer. 51:30
14 [a]Nah. 2:1
15 [a]Joel 1:4

3:1–4 The wickedness of Assyria is cataloged in graphic fashion. Nineveh was indeed a **bloody city,** guilty of shedding the innocent blood of multitudes of victims. Her wealth and power made Nineveh a **seductive** ally, but she was really a **harlot,** demanding heavy payment for her services.
3:5–7 Nineveh receives the judgment of the prostitute and the adulteress—public exposure and disgrace. Ezek. 16:35–39 describes similar judgment on Jerusalem.
3:8, 9 Amon was the supreme sun-god of Egypt. **No Amon,** meaning "City of Amon," was also known as Thebes. Thebes, located on the upper Nile River about 350 miles south of modern Cairo, was the center of the Egyptian Empire for nearly 1,400 years, until Assyria conquered it in 663 B.C. It was surrounded by waterways and sacred temples, much like Nineveh, and boasted allies like **Put** (Somaliland) **and Lubim** (Libya). The greatness of Thebes was legendary. Nahum mentioned her as a reminder that even the greatest fall.
3:10 The punishment inflicted on Thebes by Assyria will now fall on Nineveh.
3:12 Nineveh is ripe for judgment, and her enemies are eager to partake of the fruit. The conquest is as easy as shaking ripe figs from a tree.
3:13 **Women** were not trained for war, and they could not withstand men in hand-to-hand combat.
3:14 These were the normal preparations for a siege. **Water** was always the target of enemy efforts; shortage of water would wilt any attempted defense. More **brick** would be necessary to repair damage to the fortifications.
3:15–17 All the frantic effort is in vain. Ancient sources indicate that the Assyrian king died in the **fire** that consumed his palace.

[a]merchants more than the stars
of heaven.
The locust plunders and flies
away.
17 [a]Your commanders *are* like
swarming locusts,
And your generals like great
grasshoppers,
Which camp in the hedges on a
cold day;
When the sun rises they flee
away,
And the place where they *are* is
not known.

18 [a]Your shepherds slumber,
O [b]king of Assyria;
Your nobles rest *in the dust.*
Your people are [c]scattered on the
mountains,
And no one gathers them.
19 Your injury *has* no healing,
[a]Your wound is severe.
[b]All who hear news of you
Will *clap *their* hands over
you,
For upon whom has not your
wickedness passed
continually?

16 [a]Rev. 18:3, 11–19 **17** [a]Rev. 9:7

18 [a]Ex. 15:16; Ps. 76:5, 6; Is. 56:10; Jer. 51:57 [b]Jer. 50:18; Ezek. 31:3 [c]1 Kin. 22:17; Is. 13:14 **19** [a]Jer. 46:11; Mic. 1:9 [b]Job 27:23; Lam. 2:15; Zeph. 2:15 *See WW at Ps. 47:1.

3:18 The **shepherds** are leaders, ones upon whom the **king** would depend. But instead of rallying to defend Nineveh, they **slumber** in death. Without leadership, the **people** are **scattered:** the "Queen City" of the ancient East has lost all her subjects.
3:19 The ruin of Nineveh evokes the rejoicing of the nations.

TRUTH-IN-ACTION through NAHUM

Letting the LIFE of the Holy Spirit Bring Faith's Works Alive in You!

Truth Nahum Teaches	Text	**Action** Nahum Invites
1 Key Lessons in Faith A key test of faith for God's people comes when God judges the nations around them. For Christians, this can mean that God may judge the nation in which they live. He is able to protect and spare His people from judgments that fall even on their neighbors.	1:7	**Trust** that: (a) God is good! (b) He is a place of safety for us when we are in trouble. (c) He is faithful to care for those who trust Him to do so.
	1:12, 13	**Believe** that God is willing and able to deliver us from any bondage. **Know** that He will eventually stop any attack upon us.
	1:15	**Hear** and **believe** the good news of deliverance from our soul's enemy through Jesus Christ. See Rom. 16:20.

The Book of HABAKKUK

Author: Habakkuk
Date: About 600 B.C.
Theme: The Just Shall Live by Faith
Key Words: Faith, Why?, Woe

Author The name "Habakkuk" means "Embrace," either signifying that he was "embraced by God" and thus strengthened by Him for his difficult task, or "embracing others" and so encouraging them in time of national crisis. The musical notation in 3:19 may indicate that Habakkuk was qualified to lead in temple worship as a member of the Levitical family. The prophet is imbued with a sense of justice, which will not let him ignore the rampant unrighteousness around him. He has also learned the necessity of bringing the major questions of life to the One who created and redeems life.

Background and Date Habakkuk lived during one of Judah's most critical periods. His country had fallen from the heights of Josiah's reforms to the depths of violent treatment of its citizens, oppressive measures against the poor, and collapse of the legal system. The world around Judah was at war, with Babylonia rising to ascendancy over Assyria and Egypt. The threat of invasion from the north added to Judah's internal turmoil. Habakkuk probably wrote during the interval between the fall of Nineveh in 612 B.C. and the fall of Jerusalem in 586 B.C.

Content The Book of Habakkuk gives the account of a spiritual journey, telling of one man's pilgrimage from doubt to worship. The difference between the beginning of the book (1:1–4) and the end of the book (3:17–19) is striking.

In the first four verses Habakkuk is overwhelmed by the circumstances all about him. He can think of nothing except the iniquity and violence he sees among his people. Although Habakkuk addresses God (1:2), he believes God has removed Himself from the earthly scene: His words are forgotten; His hand is not manifest; God is nowhere to be found. Men are in control, and evil men at that. And they act just as one would expect men to act without God's restraint. These words and phrases describe the scene: "iniquity . . . trouble . . . plundering . . . violence . . . strife . . . contention . . . law is powerless . . . justice never goes forth . . . wicked surround the righteous . . . perverse judgment proceeds."

How different is the scene in the last three verses of the book (3:17–19)! All has changed. The prophet is no longer controlled by or even anxious over his circumstances, for his sights have been raised. Temporal affairs no longer fill his thoughts, but his thoughts are on things above. Instead of being ruled by worldly considerations, Habakkuk has fixed his hopes on God, for he realizes that God does take an interest in His creatures. He is the Source of the prophet's strength and joy. Habakkuk has discovered that he is made for higher ground: "He will make me walk on my high hills" (3:19). The words in the last paragraph contrast sharply with those in the first: "rejoice in the LORD . . . joy in the God of my salvation . . . God is my strength . . . feet like deer's *feet* . . . walk on my high hills" (3:18, 19). So Habakkuk has gone from complaining to confidence, from doubt to trust, from man to God, from the valley to the high hills.

If the heart of the gospel is change and transformation, the Book of Habakkuk demonstrates evangelical renewal. At the center of the change and at the center of the book stands this clear credo of faith: "The just shall live by his faith" (2:4). For the prophet, the promise is for physical protection in time of great upheaval and war. When the predicted invasion by foreign armies becomes a reality, that righteous remnant whose God is the Lord, whose trust and dependence is in Him, will be delivered and they will live. For New Testament writers, such as Paul and the author of Hebrews, this statement of confident faith becomes demonstration of the power of the gospel to give assurance of eternal salvation. For Martin Luther, Habakkuk's theme becomes the watchword of the Reformation.

Personal Application Habakkuk reminds us that the question "Why?" can, should, and must be asked. His circumstances demanded that he ask God about the apparent reign of unrighteousness around him. Because he believed in God, he believed that God had an answer to his problem. His questions demonstrated the presence of faith, not the lack of it. For an atheist the question "Why?" has no meaning; for a believer the question "Why?" finds its ultimate answer in God.

Paul the apostle takes the statement of Habakkuk 2:4 and makes it the heart of the gospel. The righteousness of God is attained only through faith, so that the right way to live is to trust. Habakkuk calls all believers in all times to trust God, to be faithful to Him, and so to find life as God means it to be lived.

The final verses of this prophecy teach that it is possible to rise above circumstances, and even to rejoice in them, by focusing on God who stands above all. Habakkuk does not deny his problems, nor does he treat them lightly; instead, he finds God sufficient in the midst of his troubles.

Christ Revealed The terms used by Habakkuk in 3:13 join the idea of salvation with the Lord's Anointed. The Hebrew roots of these words reflect the two names of our Lord: Jesus, meaning "Salvation," and Christ, meaning "the Anointed One." The context here is God's great power manifested in behalf of His people through a Davidic King to bring them deliverance from their enemies. The Messiah came in the fullness of time (2:3; Gal. 4:4), was given the name "Jesus" as a prenatal prophecy of His ministry (Matt. 1:21), and was born "in the city of David a Savior, who is Christ the Lord" (Luke 2:11).

As Habakkuk waits for the answer to his questions, God grants him the gift of a truth that satisfies his unspoken longings as well as provides the solution to his present situation: "The just shall live by his faith" (2:4). The apostle Paul sees this statement of Habakkuk as the foundation stone of the gospel of Christ (Rom. 1:16, 17). Christ is the answer to human needs, including cleansing from sin, relationship with God, and hope for the future.

The Holy Spirit at Work Though no direct references to the Holy Spirit are found in Habakkuk, there are intimations of His life working in the prophet. As Habakkuk surveys the ruin brought about by the invading armies, he nevertheless expresses an abiding joy that even disaster on so large a scale cannot steal from him, reminding us that "the fruit of the Spirit is . . . joy" (Gal. 5:22).

Also, in Galatians, Paul links the most famous verse from Habakkuk with the reception of the promised Holy Spirit through faith (2:4; Gal. 3:11–14). The righteous person lives by his faith in all aspects of his life, including entering into the life of the Spirit.

Outline of Habakkuk

I. Habakkuk's questions 1:1–17
- A. A question about God's concern 1:1–11
  1. The question stated: "Why doesn't God do something?" 1:1–5
  2. The answer given: "I will use the Chaldeans." 1:6–11
- B. A question about God's methods: "Why does God use wicked men?" 1:12–17

II. God's answer 2:1–20
- A. The prophet waiting 2:1
- B. The Lord responding 2:2–20
  1. The significance of the reply 2:2, 3
  2. The central truth for believers 2:4
  3. The consequences of the truth for unbelievers 2:5–20
     - a. Woe to the greedy 2:5–8
     - b. Woe to the complacent 2:9–11
     - c. Woe to the violent 2:12–14
     - d. Woe to the shameless 2:15–17
     - e. Woe to the idolaters 2:18–20

III. Habakkuk's prayer 3:1–19
- A. The Lord's power 3:1–16
  1. A call for mercy 3:1, 2
  2. Power in nature 3:3–11
  3. Power over nations 3:12–16
- B. The prophet's faith 3:17–19
  1. Confidence in spite of circumstances 3:17, 18
  2. Confidence because of God 3:19

THE [1]burden which the prophet Habakkuk saw.

The Prophet's Question

2 O LORD, how long shall I cry,
[a]And You will not hear?
Even cry out to You, [b]"Violence!"
And You will [c]not save.
3 Why do You show me iniquity,
And cause *me* to see [1]trouble?
For plundering and violence *are* before me;
There is strife, and contention arises.
4 Therefore the law is powerless,
And justice never goes forth.
For the [a]wicked surround the righteous;
Therefore perverse judgment proceeds.

The LORD's Reply

5 "Look[a] among the nations and watch—
Be utterly astounded!
For *I will* work a work in your days
Which you would not believe,
though it were told *you*.
6 For indeed I am [a]raising up the Chaldeans,
A bitter and hasty [b]nation
Which marches through the breadth of the earth,
To possess *dwelling places *that are* not theirs.

CHAPTER 1

1 [1]*oracle, prophecy*
2 [a]Lam. 3:8 [b]Mic. 2:1, 2; 3:1–3 [c][Job 21:5–16]
3 [1]Or *toil*
4 [a]Jer. 12:1
5 [a]Is. 29:14; Ezek. 12:22–28
6 [a]Deut. 28:49, 50; 2 Kin. 24:2; 2 Chr. 36:17; Jer. 4:11–13; Mic. 4:10 [b]Ezek. 7:24; 21:31
*See WW at Is. 32:18.

1:1 The seriousness and weight of Habakkuk's concern was a **burden** to him. Other prophets, such as Nahum and Zechariah, also refer to their prophecy as a "burden," heavy for them to carry and hard on the nation on which it falls.
1:2 By a *series of questions* Habakkuk calls on God to set in order those in his nation who are mistreating the weak and helpless among them.
1:3 God is charged with passivity for allowing these evil actions to continue.
1:4 Perverse judgment results when evil men control the justice system and overturn righteous decisions.
1:5, 6 The Lord responds to the prophet's questions by offering to bring in foreign invaders who will seize power from wicked Israelites.
1:6 The Chaldeans, with their soldiers from Babylonia, are a **bitter . . . nation,** acting impetuously as they move violently across the land.

7 They are terrible and dreadful;
Their judgment and their dignity proceed from themselves.
8 Their horses also are [a]swifter than leopards,
And more fierce than evening wolves.
Their [1]chargers [2]charge ahead;
Their cavalry comes from afar;
They fly as the [b]eagle *that* hastens to eat.

9 "They all come for violence;
Their faces are set *like* the east wind.
They gather captives like sand.
10 They scoff at kings,
And princes are scorned by them.
They deride every stronghold,
For they heap up earthen *mounds* and seize it.
11 Then *his* [1]mind changes, and he transgresses;
He commits offense,
[a]*Ascribing* this power to his god."

The Prophet's Second Question

12 Are You not [a]from everlasting,
O LORD my God, my Holy One?
We shall not die.
O LORD, [b]You have appointed them for judgment;
O Rock, You have marked them for [c]correction.
13 *You are* of purer eyes than to behold evil,
And cannot look on wickedness.
Why do You look on those who deal treacherously,
And hold Your tongue when the wicked devours
A *person* more righteous than he?
14 *Why* do You make men like fish of the sea,
Like creeping things *that have* no ruler over them?
15 They take up all of them with a hook,
They catch them in their net,
And gather them in their dragnet.
Therefore they rejoice and are glad.
16 Therefore [a]they *sacrifice to their net,
And burn incense to their dragnet;
Because by them their share *is* [1]sumptuous
And their food plentiful.
17 Shall they therefore empty their net,
And continue to slay nations without pity?

2 I will [a]stand my watch 1
And set myself on the rampart,
And watch to see what He will say to me,
And what I will answer when I am corrected.

The Just Live by Faith

2 Then the LORD answered me and said: 1

[a]"Write* the *vision
And make *it* plain on tablets,
That he may run who reads it.
3 For [a]the vision *is* yet for an appointed time;
But at the end it will speak, and it will [b]not lie.
Though it tarries, [c]wait for it;
Because it will [d]surely come,
It will not tarry.

4 "Behold the proud, 2
His soul is not upright in him;

8 [a]Jer. 4:13 [b]Job 9:26; 39:29, 30; Lam. 4:19; Ezek. 17:3; Hos. 8:1; Matt. 24:28; Luke 17:37 [1]Lit. *horsemen* [2]Lit. *spring about*
11 [a]Dan. 5:4 [1]Lit. *spirit* or *wind*
12 [a]Deut. 33:27; Ps. 90:2; 93:2; Mal. 3:6 [b]Is. 10:5–7; Mal. 3:5 [c]Jer. 25:9
16 [a]Deut. 8:17 [1]Lit. *fat* *See WW at Deut. 16:2.

CHAPTER 2

1 [a]Is. 21:8, 11
2 [a]Is. 8:1 *See WW at Deut. 31:9. • See WW at 2 Chr. 32:32.
3 [a]Dan. 8:17, 19; 10:14 [b]Ezek. 12:24, 25 [c][Heb. 10:37, 38] [d]Ps. 27:13, 14; [James 5:7, 8; 2 Pet. 3:9]

1:7 From themselves: They are accountable only to themselves for their actions, for they owe their power to no one else.
1:9 *Like* the east wind, the army moves relentlessly forward, driving all that stands before it from its path.
1:11 Mind is literally "wind," suggesting that the army blasts across the land allowing nothing to keep it in bounds. **His** only **god** is his **power**.
1:12 God's solution to the prophet's original problem (v. 2) only raises more questions. How can God use a cruel invading army to solve an internal problem among His people?
1:13 God's very nature cannot allow Him **to behold evil** without punishing the guilty ones.
1:15–17 The imagery of fishing is used to describe the way the Babylonians gather up booty and peoples from the nations they conquer.
1:16 Again (see v. 11) they worship their own might as their only god.
2:1 See section 1 of Truth-In-Action at the end of Hab.
2:1 Having completed his questioning, Habakkuk stands like a sentinel to await his answer from God.
2:2, 3 See section 1 of Truth-In-Action at the end of Hab.
2:2 He may run who reads it: The message is clear and can be read quickly and easily.
2:4 See section 2 of Truth-In-Action at the end of Hab.
2:4 The evil and the arrogant Babylonians are contrasted with the righteous and the trusting among God's people. The transient and unstable nature of one who attempts to find life in himself is compared to the dependability and reliability of one who trusts God for his life. (See Introduction to Habakkuk: Content; Personal Application.) The Jewish Talmud states: "Moses gave Israel 613 commandments. David reduced them to 10, Isaiah to 2, but Habakkuk to one: 'The just shall live by his faith.' "

But the [a]just* **shall live** by his
faith.

WORD WEALTH

2:4 shall live, *chayah* (chah-*yah*); Strong's #2421: To live, to stay alive, be preserved; to flourish, to enjoy life; to live in happiness; to breathe, be alive, be animated, recover health, live continuously. The fundamental idea is "to live and breathe," breathing being the evidence of life in the Hebrew concept. Hence the Hebrew words for "living being" or "animal" (*chay*) and "life" (*chayyim*) derive from *chayah.* This verb occurs about 250 times in the OT. Many references contain the suggestion that "living" is the result of doing the right thing (Deut. 4:1; 30:19, 20; Prov. 4:4; 9:6; Amos 5:4). The present reference is one of the giant pillars of the faith; not only does it appear several times in the NT; it also sparked the Reformation. It literally reads, "The righteous person in (or by) his faithfulness (firmness, consistency, belief, faith, steadfastness) shall live!"

Woe to the Wicked

5 "Indeed, because he transgresses
by wine,
He is a proud man,
And he does not stay at home.
Because he [a]enlarges his desire
as [1]hell,
And he *is* like death, and cannot
be satisfied,
He gathers to himself all nations
And heaps up for himself all
peoples.

6 "Will not all these [a]take up a
proverb against him,
And a taunting riddle against
him, and say,
'Woe to him who increases
What is not his—how long?
And to him who loads himself
with [1]many pledges'?
7 Will not [1]your creditors rise up
suddenly?
Will they not awaken who
oppress you?
And you will become their booty.
8 [a]Because you have plundered
many nations,
All the remnant of the people
shall plunder you,
Because of men's [1]blood
And the violence of the land *and*
the city,
And of all who dwell in it.

9 "Woe to him who covets evil gain **4**
for his house,
That he may [a]set his nest on high,
That he may be delivered from
the [1]power of disaster!
10 You give shameful counsel to
your house,
Cutting off many peoples,
And sin *against* your soul.
11 For the stone will cry out from the
wall,
And the beam from the timbers
will answer it.

12 "Woe to him who builds a town **4**
with *bloodshed,
Who establishes a city by
iniquity!
13 Behold, *is it* not of the LORD of
hosts
That the peoples labor [1]to feed
the fire,
And nations weary themselves in
vain?
14 For the *earth will be *filled
With the knowledge of the glory
of the LORD,
As the waters cover the sea.

15 "Woe to him who gives drink to
his neighbor,
[1]Pressing *him to* your [a]bottle,
Even to make *him* drunk,
That you may look on [2]his
nakedness!
16 You are filled with shame instead
of glory.
You also—drink!

4 [a][John 3:36]; Rom. 1:17; Heb. 10:38 *See WW at Lam. 1:18.
5 [a]Prov. 27:20; 30:16; Is. 5:11–15 [1]Or *Sheol*
6 [a]Mic. 2:4 [1]Syr., Vg. *thick clay*
7 [1]Lit. *those who bite you*
8 [a]Is. 33:1; Jer. 27:7; Ezek. 39:10; Zech. 2:8 [1]Or *bloodshed*
9 [a]Jer. 49:16; Obad. 4 [1]Lit. *hand of evil*
12 *See WW at Lev. 17:11.
13 [1]Lit. *for what satisfies fire,* for what is of no lasting value
14 *See WW at Ex. 32:13. • See WW at Jer. 23:24.
15 [a]Hos. 7:5 [1]Lit. *Attaching* or *Joining* [2]Lit. *their*

2:5 The prophet now begins to list the qualities of the Babylonians that will eventually lead to their downfall. Their **desire** for more, like **hell** (Sheol) and **death,** will not be satisfied until it has taken in all.

2:6 Habakkuk pronounces a series of woes (vv. 6, 9, 12, 15, 19) on the Babylonians, indicating the underlying moral weaknesses that will result in their defeat. **Loads himself with many pledges:** Babylon is like a moneylender, exacting exorbitant interest, but the oppressed will gain the upper hand and take back all that was wrongly seized from them.

2:9 See section 4 of Truth-In-Action at the end of Hab.

2:9 Nest on high: They thought themselves safely above retaliation for their wicked deeds.

2:11 Stone will cry out: As often occurs in Scripture, inanimate objects take the role of witness against cruelty.

2:12–14 See section 4 of Truth-In-Action at the end of Hab.

2:13 It is **of the LORD** that gain through unrighteous means will prove unprofitable.

2:14 God's actions in bringing down the wicked (v. 13) demonstrate His sovereignty in all the Earth.

2:15 The Babylonians' subjugation and humiliation of other nations is compared to a person who makes his neighbor drunk and then takes advantage of his weakness.

2:16 What they have done to others (v. 15) will happen to them; they will **drink** and **be exposed.**

And [1]be exposed as
uncircumcised!
The cup of the LORD's right hand
will be turned against you,
And utter shame will be on your
glory.
17 For the violence *done to* Lebanon
will cover you,
And the plunder of beasts *which*
made them afraid,
Because of men's blood
And the violence of the land *and*
the city,
And of all who dwell in it.

3 18 "What profit is the image, that its
maker should carve it,
The molded image, a teacher of
lies,
That the maker of its mold should
trust in it,
To make mute idols?
19 Woe to him who says to wood,
'Awake!'
To silent stone, 'Arise! It shall
*teach!'
Behold, it is overlaid with gold
and silver,
Yet in it there is no breath at all.

20 "But[a] the LORD is in His holy
temple.
Let all the earth keep silence
before Him."

The Prophet's Prayer

3 A prayer of Habakkuk the prophet,
on [1]Shigionoth.

2 O LORD, I have heard Your speech
and was afraid;
O LORD, revive Your work in the
midst of the years!
In the midst of the years make *it*
known;
In wrath remember *mercy.

3 God came from Teman,
The Holy One from Mount Paran.
Selah
His *glory covered the heavens,
And the earth was full of His
*praise.
4 *His* brightness was like the light;
He had rays *flashing* from His
hand,
And there His power *was* hidden.
5 Before Him went pestilence,
And fever followed at His feet.

6 He stood and measured the earth;
He looked and startled the
nations.
[a]And the everlasting mountains
were scattered,
The perpetual hills bowed.
His ways *are* everlasting.
7 I saw the tents of Cushan in
*affliction;
The curtains of the land of Midian
trembled.

8 O LORD, were *You* displeased
with the rivers,
Was Your anger against the
rivers,
Was Your wrath against the sea,
That You rode on Your horses,
Your chariots of salvation?
9 Your bow was made quite ready;
Oaths were sworn over *Your*
[1]arrows.* Selah

You divided the earth with rivers.
10 The mountains saw You *and*
trembled;
The overflowing of the water
passed by.
The deep uttered its voice,
And [a]lifted its hands on high.
11 The [a]sun and moon stood still in
their habitation;
At the light of Your arrows they
went,
At the shining of Your glittering
spear.

12 You marched through the land in
indignation;
You [1]trampled the nations in
anger.

16 [1]DSS, LXX *reel!;* Syr., Vg. *fall fast asleep!*
19 *See WW at Ps. 32:8.
20 [a]Zeph. 1:7; Zech. 2:13

CHAPTER 3

1 [1]Exact meaning unknown
2 *See WW at Hos. 2:23.
3 *See WW at 1 Chr. 29:11. • See WW at Ps. 100:4.
6 [a]Nah. 1:5
7 *See WW at Prov. 22:8.
9 [1]Lit. *tribes* or *rods,* cf. v. 14 *See WW at Ex. 38:22.
10 [a]Ex. 14:22
11 [a]Josh. 10:12–14
12 [1]Or *threshed*

2:18–20 See section 3 of Truth-In-Action at the end of Hab.
2:20 In contrast to lifeless, powerless idols (vv. 18, 19), **the LORD** is present and about to act in strength.
3:1 Shigionoth: A musical notation probably indicating that the song is to be sung with emotion and a sense of victory. (See marginal note on Ps. 7:title.) This stands in contrast with the note of doom that characterizes the woes of ch. 2.
3:2 The prophet appeals to God to work in behalf of His people **in the midst of the years,** during the period of waiting for the final resolution of the intolerable situation (2:3).
3:3 This verse reflects Moses' rehearsal of God's coming to Israel in the wilderness (Deut. 33:2). **Teman** is another name for Edom, southeast of the Dead Sea. **Paran** represents the mountainous region west of Edom.
3:5 God brings **pestilence** and **fever** as vengeance against the Chaldeans.
3:7 Cushan is probably an alternate form of Cush, Ethiopia. **Midian** is the country on the Arabian side of the Red Sea. Both are in the direction from which the Lord will make His appearance (v. 3).
3:9 Oaths were sworn over *Your* arrows: God guarantees by an oath that He brings judgment against His enemies. See Deut. 32:40–42.

13 You went forth for the salvation
of Your *people,
For salvation with Your
*Anointed.
You struck the *head from the
house of the wicked,
By laying bare from foundation
to neck. Selah

14 You thrust through with his own
*arrows
The head of his villages.
They came out like a whirlwind
to scatter me;
Their rejoicing was like feasting
on the poor in secret.
15 [a]You walked through the sea with
Your horses,
Through the heap of great waters.

2 16 When I heard, [a]my body
trembled;
My lips quivered at *the* voice;
Rottenness entered my bones;
And I trembled in myself,
That I might rest in the day of
trouble.
When he comes up to the people,
He will invade them with his
troops.

A Hymn of Faith

17 Though the fig tree may not
blossom,
Nor fruit be on the vines;
Though the labor of the olive may
fail,
And the fields yield no food;
Though the flock may be cut off
from the fold,
And there be no herd in the
stalls—
18 Yet I will [a]rejoice in the LORD,
I will **joy** in the God of my
salvation.

WORD WEALTH

3:18 joy, *gil* (*geel*); Strong's #1523: To joy, rejoice, be glad, be joyful. *Gil* contains the suggestion of "dancing for joy," or "leaping for joy," since the verb originally meant "to spin around with intense motion." This lays to rest the notion that the biblical concept of joy is only "a quiet, inner sense of well-being." God dances for joy over Jerusalem and because of His people (Is. 65:19; Zeph. 3:17). The righteous Messiah shall rejoice in God's salvation with an intensity that the psalmist cannot find words to describe (Ps. 21:1). In turn, His redeemed citizens are joyful in their King; they praise Him with dances, with instruments, and with singing (Ps. 149:2, 3). Although everything is wrong in Habakkuk's external world, he is leaping for joy over his fellowship with Yahweh.

19 [1]The LORD God is my *strength;
He will make my feet like
[a]deer's *feet*,
And He will make me [b]walk* on
my high hills.

To the Chief Musician. With my stringed instruments.

13 *See WW at Ruth 1:16. • See WW at Dan. 9:25. • See WW at Gen. 3:15.
14 *See WW at Ex. 38:22.
15 [a]Ps. 77:19; Hab. 3:8
16 [a]Ps. 119:120
18 [a]Is. 41:16; 61:10
19 [a]2 Sam. 22:34; Ps. 18:33 [b]Deut. 32:13; 33:29 [1]Heb. *YHWH* *See WW at Jer. 16:19. • See WW at Deut. 11:25

3:13 Your Anointed in Hebrew is a form of the word "Messiah," here representing God's anointed King from the line of David. (See Introduction to Habakkuk: Christ Revealed.) Striking down the **head** and the **neck** of the house means the complete devastation of the Babylonian dynasty.
3:14 The enemies are like bandits lying in wait to destroy their victims.
3:16–19 See section 2 of Truth-In-Action at the end of Hab.
3:16 Though the judgments of God are right and necessary, they bring a sense of awe to all who witness them.
3:17, 18 The destructive results of the Babylonian invasion will be felt throughout the land, but the prophet finds the source of his joy in God and not in his circumstances. See Introduction to Habakkuk: Content.
3:19 By the strength of God, he can move swiftly as the deer. **To the Chief Musician** and **With my stringed instruments** are musical notations, giving directions for the use of this chapter in worship. Both terms are used at the beginning of some of the psalms (Ps. 4; 6; 54; 55; 67; 76).

TRUTH-IN-ACTION through HABAKKUK

Letting the LIFE of the Holy Spirit Bring Faith's Works Alive in You!

Truth Habakkuk Teaches	Text	**Action** Habakkuk Invites
1 Steps to Dynamic Devotion God requires that we make our relationship with Him our highest priority, that we bring our deepest questions and turmoils before Him, expecting His answers and guidance.	2:1 2:2, 3	**Set aside** a regular time and place that is holy to the Lord. **Spend time listening** for His word as you read, study, and meditate on Scripture. **Be faithful** in daily prayer. **Document** those things the Lord speaks to you or quickens to your heart. **Record** biblical promises He makes alive to you, and **hold fast to them,** knowing they will come to pass.
2 The Life of Faith When all the circumstances of our life present a negative picture—in failure and loss or when the natural reaction would be grief or complaint—this is the time to put faith in God and in His Word. Thus we can see through God's eyes to the final glorious outcome. This brings worship and praise even before our circumstances have changed.	2:4; 3:16–19	**Determine to praise** and worship and thank God for His faithfulness, no matter how devastating the circumstances. **Look with the eye of faith** at God's plan for the future.
3 A Step to Holiness Though some only think of idols as material images, what truly defines an idol is the place it occupies in a person's life. Any person, thing, or desire that stands in the way of an immediate, wholehearted "Yes, Lord!" to anything He asks of us is an idol and must be eliminated.	2:18–20	**Examine yourself! Ask the question,** "Is there anything in my life that hinders my obedience to God?" **Take down** any idol in your life by humbling yourself before God and by refusing other interests to rule your heart.
4 Keys to Wise Living The worldly theory of success that centers on personal power and the amassing of financial riches is a highly deceptive trap. The wise person defines success in the light of God's plan for his life. Living in a manner that honors God and relies on His promises, brings success.	2:9 2:12–14	**Know** that success by the world's measure is a vain pursuit. **Build** your house—your life and vocation—on the rock of God's Word. **Plan your life** by the wisdom of God. **Be a success in Him.**

The Book of ZEPHANIAH

Author: Zephaniah
Date: About 630 B.C.
Theme: The Wrath of a Loving God
Key Words: The Day of the Lord, The Lord Is in Your Midst

Author Zephaniah ("The LORD Has Hidden") was a prophet to Judah. He identified himself better than any other of the minor prophets, tracing his ancestry back four generations to Hezekiah, a good king who had led the people back to God during the prophet Isaiah's time. King Josiah, whose reform brought about a period of renewal in Jerusalem, was not only a contemporary of Zephaniah, but a distant relative. Thus the men could have been friends and equally zealous for a return to the pure worship of God.

The intimacy of emotion as well as the familiarity of place when Zephaniah writes about Jerusalem (1:10, 11) indicate that he had grown up there and was deeply troubled by prophesying the city's destruction. According to the arrangement of Hebrew Scriptures, Zephaniah was the last of the prophets to write before the captivity. His prophecy was the swan song of the southern kingdom of Judah.

Date Zephaniah gives the general time of his writing as being "in the days of Josiah, the son of Amon, king of Judah" (1:1), about 640 to 609 B.C. The height of Josiah's reform was in the 620s. Since the fall of Nineveh in 612 B.C. had not yet taken place (2:13–15), most scholars set the date of writing between 630 and 627 B.C. His contemporaries included Jeremiah and Nahum.

Background About 100 years before this prophecy, the northern kingdom (the ten tribes of Israel) had fallen to Assyria. The people had been carried away by their captors, and the land had been resettled by foreigners. Under King Manasseh and King Amon, King Josiah's father, tribute had been paid to keep Assyria from invading the southern kingdom.

The alliance with Assyria not only affected Judah politically, but also Assyria's religious, social, and fashion practices set the trend in Judah. Official protection was given in Judah to the magical arts of diviners and enchanters. Astral religion became so popular that Judah's King Manasseh erected altars for the worship of the sun, moon, stars, zodiac signs, and all the host of heaven, on the roof of the temple (2 Kin. 23:11). The worship of the mother-goddess of Assyria became a practice that involved all members of Judean families (Jer. 7:18). However, as the young Josiah took over the reins of government, the Assyrian threat was diminishing. The final blow to their power came with a Babylonian uprising that eventually resulted in the destruction of Nineveh.

After a long silence, true prophetic voices were once again heard in Judah. Along with Zephaniah, Jeremiah was encouraging the revival led by King Josiah. The Book of the Law had been found in the temple. As a consequence, the land was purged of idolatrous practices and priests, the temple was cleansed, and thousands of sacrifices were offered when Passover was once again observed (2 Chr. 34; 35).

In retrospect the reform was one of externals, since the hearts of the people had not been changed. Even so, there was a sense that everything was right with God and the world, for they were living in momentary peace and prosperity. Into this complacent atmosphere the devastating message of Zephaniah comes like a searing blast.

Content Zephaniah viewed the political development of Israel (the northern kingdom), Judah (the southern kingdom), and all the surrounding nations from the perspective that the people should learn that God was involved in all the affairs of history. Speaking as an oracle of God, he understands that God uses foreign governments to bring about judgment upon His rebellious chosen people. Zephaniah is appalled that, after the catastrophe of the northern tribes, the people of Judah still maintain the preposterous notion that God is helpless to do good or evil (1:12).

As is true in most of the prophets, Zephaniah's writings has three components: 1) the pronouncement of specific and often universal judgment for sin; 2) an appeal for repentance because God is righteous and willing to forgive; 3) a promise that the remnant who have made God their refuge will be saved.

Few biblical writers describe the wrath of God or the joy of God as vividly as does Zephaniah. God is seen searching the streets of Jerusalem with lamps to find the wicked He will punish (1:12); the prophecy describing the Day of the Lord in 1:14–18 is a terrible chant of doom. A call to repentance appropriately follows these passages. The first two and a half chapters prophesy judgment so complete that even nature will be consumed (1:2, 3) and "all the earth shall be devoured with the fire of My jealousy" (3:8).

Because of the repeated use of the term "the day of the LORD," the Book of Zephaniah has meaning for end times. The Day of the Lord is either the period of time or the actual day when God will bring His purposes to culmination for mankind and for the Earth. The righteous will be rewarded with eternal blessing, and the wicked will be consigned to eternal damnation.

Amos was probably the first to use the term "the day of the LORD" (Amos 5:18–20). Isaiah, Jeremiah, Obadiah, and Joel all speak of it as a time of final judgment. In the New Testament "the day of Jesus Christ" (Phil. 1:6) carries the same meaning. For elaboration of this concept see the note on Obadiah 15.

While the message of Zephaniah has future significance, Judah and the surrounding nations expected an immediate and local fulfillment of the prophecies. Beginning with Assyria, the judgments were fulfilled in a few years when the temple was utterly destroyed and the Jews were carried into Babylonian captivity.

Though the prophets were called by God to convey a dreadful message, they were also aware that wrath and judgment expressed only one side of God's nature. Habakkuk eloquently reminded the Holy One "in wrath [to] remember mercy" (Hab. 3:2). In the Book of Zephaniah, God does remember, for He promises that He will purify and restore the faithful remnant (3:9). He assures this humbled people that no one will make them afraid again, for He has cast out their enemy (3:13, 15).

Then He bids them to sing, to shout, to rejoice with all their hearts. And God joins in the celebration like a victorious general returning with the comrades he has rescued. In jubilation God sings and dances and shouts for joy as He tells them of His love (3:14–17).

Zephaniah ends with God's tender promise that He will gather all those who have been driven out and will give them fame and praise among all the people of the Earth (3:20).

Personal Application Four timeless lessons for both believers and unbelievers are found in Zephaniah:

1. God is perfect justice as well as perfect love (3:5). If the call to repentance is continually ignored, God's judgment must consequently fall.
2. Punishment is not God's choice, for "God so loved the world that He gave His only begotten Son that whoever believes in Him should not perish but have everlasting life" (John 3:16).
3. To settle into the complacency of financial prosperity (1:10–13) and to participate in the ritual of a well-structured religious life without obeying God's voice, receiving correction, or drawing near to Him (3:2) is an ever-present possibility. Even more tragic is to have no awareness of such spiritual emptiness.
4. Even to the rebellious, God offers last-minute reprieve (2:1–3). The remnant who humble themselves and seek righteousness will be hidden in the Day of the Lord's anger (2:3). They will be gathered to Him and healed (3:18), for God dwells in their midst (3:17). This abiding promise to God's people is the essence of the gospel.

Christ Revealed The meaning of Zephaniah's name ("The LORD Has Hidden") conveys the ministry of Jesus Christ. The truth of the Passover in Egypt, where those hidden behind blood-marked doors were protected from the angel of death, is repeated in the promise of 2:3, where those meek of the Earth who have upheld God's justice will be hidden in the Day of the Lord's anger. Colossians 3:2, 3 spells out this aspect of Christ's ministry: "Set your mind on things above, not on things on the earth. For you died, and your life is hidden with Christ in God."

The rejoicing over a saved remnant (3:16, 17) is connected with the work of Jesus, the Savior. Jesus spoke, "I say to you that likewise there will be more joy in heaven over one sinner who repents than over ninety-nine just persons who need no repentance" (Luke 15:7). The picture of a joyful Redeemer who waits to receive His own is again depicted in Hebrews 12:2, "Looking unto Jesus, the author and finisher of *our* faith, who for the joy that was set before Him endured the cross, despising the shame, and has sat down at the right hand of the throne of God."

The Holy Spirit at Work Jesus said that one of the works of the Holy Spirit would be to convict the world of judgment because the ruler of the world is judged (John 16:8–11). Since His coming, the Holy Spirit has been crying out to the world as Zephaniah did: "Gather yourselves ... before the decree is issued, *or* the day passes like chaff, before the

LORD's fierce anger comes upon you, before the day of the LORD's anger comes upon you" (2:1, 2).

Now as then, a refusal of the warning is a rejection of the Holy Spirit. In the address that sealed his martyrdom, Stephen declared to the council, "*You* stiffnecked and uncircumcised in heart and ears! You always resist the Holy Spirit; as your fathers *did,* so *do* you" (Acts 7:51).

A more joyous work of the Holy Spirit is found in the promise that God will restore to the peoples a pure language that they may serve Him with one accord (3:9). The curse of Babel was the confusion of languages, which prevented people from working in unity to achieve their evil goals (Gen. 11:1–9). The outpouring of the Spirit promised in Joel 2:28–32 came to pass on the Day of Pentecost (Acts 2:1–11) to begin God's process of messianic restoration. In light of Zephaniah's prophecy, it is interesting to note that Pentecost included the dimension of languages.

Furthermore, the gift of tongues was used to bring believing Gentiles and astonished Jews together in unity of faith and purpose during Peter's reluctant visit to the home of Cornelius (Acts 10:44–48). It is this pure language, this gift of tongues, that has also served to merge believers of widely divergent theological persuasions into the modern charismatic movement. They have been enabled to transcend boundaries of tradition and nationality and serve the Lord together in the unity of the Spirit. These may be partial fulfillments of 3:9.

Outline of Zephaniah

Introduction **1:1**
- A. Identification of author 1:1
- B. Time of writing 1:1

I. The day of judgment against Judah **1:2–13**
- A. Judgment on all creation 1:2, 3
- B. Judgment against religious leaders 1:4–7
- C. Judgment against political leaders 1:8, 9
- D. Judgment against business leaders 1:10, 11
- E. Judgment against unbelievers 1:12, 13

II. The Day of the Lord **1:14–18**
- A. Near and coming quickly 1:14
- B. A day of wrath 1:15, 16
- C. The whole land to be devoured 1:18

III. A call to repentance **2:1–3**
- A. A call to gather 2:1, 2
- B. A call to seek the Lord 2:3

IV. The day of judgment against surrounding nations **2:4–15**
- A. To the west—Philistines 2:4–7
- B. To the east—Moab and Ammon 2:8–11
- C. To the south—Ethiopia 2:12
- D. To the north—Assyria 2:13–15

V. The day of judgment against Jerusalem **3:1–7**
- A. Against the leaders 3:1–4
- B. The Lord an unfailing witness in her midst 3:5
- C. Jerusalem has not changed 3:6, 7

VI. A faithful remnant **3:8–20**
- A. To speak with purity and honesty 3:8–13
- B. Judgments to be taken away and their enemy cast out 3:14, 15
- C. God Himself celebrating 3:16, 17
- D. The people restored 3:18–20

THE word of the LORD which came to Zephaniah the son of Cushi, the son of Gedaliah, the son of Amariah, the son of Hezekiah, in the days of [a]Josiah the son of Amon, king of Judah.

The Great Day of the LORD

2 "I will [1]utterly consume everything
From the face of the land,"
Says the LORD;
3 "I[a] will consume man and beast;
I will consume the birds of the heavens,
The fish of the sea,
And the [1]stumbling blocks along with the wicked.
I will cut off man from the face of the [2]land,"
Says the LORD.

4 "I will stretch out My hand against Judah,
And against all the inhabitants of Jerusalem.
[1]I will cut off every trace of Baal from this place,
The names of the [a]idolatrous[2] priests with the *pagan* priests—
5 Those [a]who worship the host of heaven on the housetops;
Those who worship and swear *oaths* by the LORD,
But who *also* swear [b]by [1]Milcom;
2 6 [a]Those who have turned back from *following* the LORD,
And [b]have not sought the LORD, nor inquired of Him."

7 [a]Be silent in the presence of the Lord GOD;
[b]For the **day** of the LORD *is* at hand,
For [c]the LORD has prepared a sacrifice;
He has [1]invited His guests.

WORD WEALTH

1:7 day, *yom (yoam)*; Strong's #3117: Day; daylight; a day consisting of nighttime and daytime; also, a certain period of time. *Yom* occurs more than 2,200 times with a variety of meanings. *Yom* occurs first in Gen. 1:5, where God called the light "Day"; the remainder of the verse shows that day is not only the period of light, but also a period consisting of evening and morning. (Because God placed evening before morning throughout the week of creation, the Jewish day begins at sundown.) *Yom* may represent a time period or the occasion of a major event. "Day of trouble" (Zeph. 1:15) is thus a troubled time. In Gen. 3:5 and Is. 12:4, *yom* expresses an indefinite future time. *Yom Yahweh* ("day of the LORD") may refer to a time when God reveals Himself through judgment and supernatural events. "The day of the LORD" may also refer to the return of the Lord Jesus to judge and rule the world.

8 "And it shall be, 3
In the day of the LORD's sacrifice,
That I will punish [a]the princes and the king's children,
And all such as are clothed with foreign apparel.
9 In the same day I will punish

CHAPTER 1

1 [a]2 Kin. 22:1, 2; 2 Chr. 34:1–33; Jer. 1:2; 22:11
2 [1]Lit. *make a complete end of,* Jer. 8:13
3 [a]Hos. 4:3 [1]Idols [2]*ground*
4 [a]2 Kin. 23:5; Hos. 10:5 [1]Fulfilled in 2 Kin. 23:4, 5 [2]Heb. *chemarim*
5 [a]2 Kin. 23:12; Jer. 19:13 [b]Josh. 23:7 [1]Or *Malcam,* An Ammonite god, 1 Kin. 11:5; Jer. 49:1; *Molech,* Lev. 18:21
6 [a]Is. 1:4; Jer. 2:13 [b]Hos. 7:7
7 [a]Hab. 2:20; Zech. 2:13 [b]Is. 13:6 [c]Deut. 28:26; Is. 34:6; Jer. 46:10; Ezek. 39:17–19 [1]Lit. *set apart, consecrated*
8 [a]Jer. 39:6

1:1 The days of Josiah: Indicators that the book was written early in Josiah's reign (640–609 B.C.) are: 1) No mention is made of Josiah's reformation in 621 B.C.; 2) Nineveh (2:13–15) was destroyed in 612 B.C., just three years before the end of his reign; 3) Huldah the prophetess was called (instead of Jeremiah whose ministry began in Josiah's thirteenth year) when the Book of the Law was found (2 Kin. 22:14).

1:2–6 Using poetic language, Zephaniah prophesies a worldwide judgment, which includes an erring Judah (vv. 4, 6). His prophecy is partially fulfilled in the fall of Jerusalem in 587 B.C. Its broader intent, however, refers to God's dealing with both His spiritual and physical enemies throughout history. This would be especially true during the time of the Messiah, ultimately finding its consummation in the world to come. Because of its poetry and eschatological intent, Zephaniah often speaks with fluid language whose meaning should not be pressed with strict literalness. Also, precise historical fulfillment of prophesied events is not always easy to determine.

1:2 From the face of the land is the same expression used regarding the Noachic flood (Gen. 6:7).

1:3 Nature, with its inhabitants in land, sea, and air, suffers for man's sin (see Gen. 3:17). Creation itself waits for deliverance (Rom. 8:18–22).

1:4 God begins judgment with **Jerusalem,** His own house (1 Pet. 4:17). **Baal:** A Canaanite deity who took various forms—god of nature, the heavens, the underworld, fertility. **Idolatrous priests:** Hebrew *chemarin* ("black"), so called from the black garments they wore.

1:5 Milcom, or Molech, was the idol of fire to which children were offered (Lev. 18:21).

1:6 See section 2 of Truth-In-Action at the end of Zeph.

1:6 God's judgment will fall not only on the wicked and idolatrous, but also on those who have turned back from following the Lord.

1:7—2:3 This section is a single sermon comprised of several unrelated subunits. Its concern is the judgments of **the day of the LORD** (see note on Obad. 15). Again, it had immediate and future application.

1:7 The **sacrifice** is the guilty nation of Judah being offered to divine justice. His **guests** are the nations summoned to execute His judgment.

1:8 See section 3 of Truth-In-Action at the end of Zeph.

1:8 Rather than examples of righteousness, the **princes** are leaders in evil. Costly **foreign apparel** was worn not only for luxury, but also to imitate pagan peoples.

1:9 Leap over the threshold: Possibly an imitation of the Philistine custom of avoiding stepping on the threshold because the head and hands of Dagon were broken off on the threshold before the ark (1 Sam. 5:5).

All those who [a]leap over the
threshold,
Who fill their *masters' houses
with violence and deceit.

10 "And there shall be on that day,"
says the LORD,
"The sound of a mournful cry from
[a]the Fish Gate,
A wailing from the Second
Quarter,
And a loud crashing from the
hills.
11 [a]Wail, you inhabitants of
[1]Maktesh!
For all the merchant people are
cut down;
All those who handle money are
cut off.

2 12 "And it shall come to pass at that
time
That I will search Jerusalem with
lamps,
And punish the men
Who are [a]settled[1] in
complacency,
[b]Who say in their heart,
'The LORD will not do good,
Nor will He do evil.'
13 Therefore their goods shall
become booty,
And their houses a desolation;
They shall build houses, but not
inhabit *them;*
They shall plant vineyards, but
[a]not drink their wine."

14 [a]The great day of the LORD *is* near;
It is near and hastens quickly.
The noise of the day of the LORD
is bitter;
There the mighty men shall cry
out.
15 [a]That day *is* a day of wrath,
A day of trouble and distress,
A day of devastation and
desolation,
A day of darkness and
gloominess,
A day of clouds and thick
darkness,
16 A day of [a]trumpet and alarm
Against the fortified cities
And against the high towers.

17 "I will bring distress upon men,
And they shall [a]walk like blind
men,
Because they have sinned against
the LORD;
Their blood shall be poured out
like dust,
And their flesh like refuse."

18 [a]Neither their silver nor their gold
Shall be able to deliver them
In the day of the LORD's wrath;
But the whole land shall be
devoured
By the fire of His jealousy,
For He will make speedy riddance
Of all those who dwell in the land.

A Call to Repentance

2 Gather[a] yourselves together, yes,
gather together,
O [1]undesirable nation,
2 Before the decree is issued,
Or the day passes like chaff,
Before the LORD's fierce anger
comes upon you,

9 [a]1 Sam. 5:5 *See WW at Mic. 4:13. 10 [a]2 Chr. 33:14; Neh. 3:3; 12:39 11 [a]James 5:1 [1]A market district of Jerusalem, lit. *Mortar* 12 [a]Jer. 48:11; Amos 6:1 [b]Ps. 94:7 [1]Lit. *on their lees;* like the dregs of wine 13 [a]Deut. 28:39 14 [a]Jer. 30:7; Joel 2:1, 11

15 [a]Is. 22:5 16 [a]Is. 27:13; Jer. 4:19 17 [a]Deut. 28:29 18 [a]Ezek. 7:19

CHAPTER 2

1 [a]2 Chr. 20:4; Joel 1:14; 2:16 [1]Or *shameless*

1:10 The **Fish Gate** was in the northeast wall of the city, so called because fish from Jordan and Galilee passed through it. The **Second Quarter** (Hebrew *Mishneh*) was the upper city, populated by the upper class, overlooking the temple near the main commercial center.
1:11 Maktesh: Probably the lower area that separated the upper city from the temple mountain.
1:12 See section 2 of Truth-In-Action at the end of Zeph.
1:12 Settled: *Literally, "settled on their lees," meaning* confirmed or hardened in their evil habits. The figure comes from old wine that has not been poured off and so becomes thick. They do not openly scoff, but **say in their heart, "The LORD will not do good, nor will He do evil,"** thus placing Yahweh in the same category as idols.
1:13 Their goods have become their strength, but will become the **booty** of the enemy.
1:14–18 Greater detail of the Day of the Lord.
1:14 Mighty men shall cry out: Complacent men (v. 12) who would not listen to the prophets will now listen to the bitter **noise of the day of the LORD.**
1:15 The Hebrew words, *shoah* and *meshoah,* because of the similarity of their sounds, are used here to emphasize in poetic terms the terror of coming **devastation and desolation.**
1:16 The **trumpet** was used to signal the approach of an enemy. **Alarm** is a war shout. **High towers** were built at the corners of the walls. Thus besiegers could be assailed from all sides and caught in a crossfire of arrows and stones.
1:17 Jer. 9:22 uses similar language to imply that the bodies were left unburied to rot on the ground.
1:18 Neither their silver nor their gold: Though kings Manasseh and Amon paid tribute to Assyria to gain Judah's freedom, Judah will not be able to bribe the Lord.
2:1–3 Zephaniah calls sinful Judah to repent.
2:1 Gather yourselves together in an assembly for prayer to avert judgment. See 2 Chr. 20:4; Joel 2:16. **Undesirable nation** (literally "shameless nation") has two possible meanings: 1) They have no desire for God; 2) they have nothing to recommend themselves to God.
2:2 Before the decree is issued: As the fetus in the womb will emerge in due season if not interrupted, so will God's judgment. ***Or the day passes like chaff:*** Once judgment emerges, the people will be devastated in a breath, in a moment of time.

Before the day of the LORD's
anger comes upon you!
3 [a]Seek the LORD, [b]all you meek of
the earth,
Who have upheld His justice.
Seek righteousness, seek
humility.
[c]It may be that you will be hidden
In the day of the LORD's anger.

Judgment on Nations

4 For [a]Gaza shall be forsaken,
And Ashkelon desolate;
They shall drive out Ashdod
[b]at noonday,
And Ekron shall be uprooted.
5 Woe to the inhabitants of
[a]the seacoast,
The nation of the Cherethites!
The word of the LORD *is* against
you,
O [b]Canaan, land of the
Philistines:
"I will destroy you;
So there shall be no inhabitant."

6 The seacoast shall be pastures,
With [1]shelters for shepherds
[a]and folds for flocks.
7 The coast shall be for [a]the
remnant of the house of Judah;
They shall feed *their* flocks
there;
In the houses of Ashkelon they
shall lie down at evening.
For the LORD their God will
[b]intervene[1] for them,
And [c]return their captives.

8 "I[a] have heard the reproach of
Moab,
And [b]the insults of the people of
Ammon,
With which they have reproached
My people,
And [c]made arrogant threats
against their borders.
9 Therefore, as I live,"
Says the LORD of hosts, the God
of Israel,
"Surely [a]Moab shall be like
Sodom,
And [b]the people of Ammon like
Gomorrah—
[c]Overrun[1] with weeds and saltpits,
And a [2]perpetual desolation.
The residue of My people shall
plunder them,
And the remnant of My people
shall possess them."

10 This they shall have [a]for their
pride,
Because they have reproached
and made arrogant threats
Against the people of the LORD of
hosts.
11 The LORD *will be* awesome to
them,
For He will reduce to nothing all
the gods of the earth;
[a]*People* shall *worship Him,
Each one from his place,
Indeed all [b]the shores of the
nations.

12 "You[a] Ethiopians also,
You shall be slain by [b]My sword."

3 [a]Ps. 105:4; Amos 5:6 [b]Ps. 76:9 [c]Joel 2:14; Amos 5:14, 15
4 [a]Jer. 47:1, 5; Amos 1:7, 8; Zech. 9:5 [b]Jer. 6:4
5 [a]Ezek. 25:15–17 [b]Josh. 13:3
6 [a]Is. 17:2 [1]Underground huts or cisterns, lit. *excavations*
7 [a][Mic. 5:7, 8] [b]Luke 1:68 [c]Jer. 29:14 [1]Lit. *visit them*
8 [a]Jer. 48:27; Amos 2:1–3 [b]Ezek. 25:3; Amos 1:13 [c]Jer. 49:1
9 [a]Is. 15:1–9; Jer. 48:1–47 [b]Amos 1:13 [c]Deut. 29:23 [1]Lit. *Possessed by nettles* [2]Or *permanent ruin*
10 [a]Is. 16:6
11 [a]Mal. 1:11 [b]Gen. 10:5 *See WW at Ps. 99:5.
12 [a]Is. 18:1–7; Ezek. 30:4, 5 [b]Ps. 17:13

2:3 To seek the LORD is to seek righteousness and humility. Zephaniah hopes (**it may be**) this will avert judgment, but he will not presume upon God to avert His "fierce anger" (v. 2).

2:4–15 This is a series of sermons against various foreign nations. The main purpose is to establish God's sovereignty over nations. See note on 1:2–6 regarding the fulfillment of these prophecies.

2:4–7 Normally, five cities of Philistia are mentioned. Gath is omitted here, having been conquered by David (1 Chr. 18:1).

2:4 Again, the writer uses similar sounds in Hebrew to add drama to the calamity. **Gaza, Ashkelon, Ashdod,** and **Ekron,** thriving city-states, were to be left desolate. The most unlikely time for attack was **noonday,** when the heat is worst.

2:5 The seacoast was all of the country lying on the Mediterranean Sea from Egypt to Joppa. The name **Cherethites** came from Crete.

2:6 Instead of populous cities, the region became pasture for nomadic shepherds' flocks.

2:7 The remnant refers in part to the returnees from the Babylonian captivity. In a broader sense, it refers to God's yet future church. To some biblical scholars, this also refers to a Jewish remnant who will physically occupy an end-times national Israel.

2:8–11 Moabites and Ammonites, both descendants of Lot, were neighboring countries located near the sites of Sodom and Gomorrah on the east side of the Dead Sea. **Reproach, insults,** and **arrogant threats** against the people of the Lord of hosts were made by these two bitter enemies. They had shown their arrogance periodically by violating Israel's borders; now the weakness of Judah has given them occasion for contempt.

2:8 I have heard: Even though God does not immediately punish, He keeps records.

2:9 As I live: God pledges the certainty of His existence as the guarantee of His judgment. They had only to remember **Sodom** and **Gomorrah** to convince themselves that God's warnings were to be taken seriously. The promise of the land to **the remnant** has meaning for returning exiles from Babylonia; as in v. 7, for some scholars it also holds significance for an end-time remnant occupying certain lands as a restored national Israel.

2:11 Reduce to nothing literally reads: "The Lord will famish the gods of this world." He will starve them out of their strongholds. **Each one from his place:** Interpreted messianically, people will no longer need to go to Jerusalem to worship God, but wherever they are they will have access to Him through Jesus.

2:12 The **Ethiopians** were closely allied with Egypt. Nebuchadnezzar's sword became God's instrument of judgment when he conquered Egypt during the reign of King Josiah's son, Jehoiakim (Jer. 46:2).

13 And He will stretch out His hand
against the north,
[a]Destroy Assyria,
And make Nineveh a desolation,
As dry as the wilderness.
14 The herds shall lie down in her
midst,
[a]Every beast of the nation.
Both the [b]pelican and the
bittern
Shall lodge on the capitals *of* her
pillars;
Their voice shall sing in the
windows;
Desolation *shall be* at the
threshold;
For He will lay bare the [c]cedar
work.
15 This is the rejoicing city
[a]That dwelt securely,
[b]That said in her heart,
"I *am it,* and *there is* none besides
me."
How has she become a
desolation,
A place for beasts to lie down!
Everyone who passes by her
[c]Shall hiss and [d]shake his fist.

The Wickedness of Jerusalem

3 Woe to her who is rebellious and
polluted,
To the oppressing city!
[4] 2 She has not obeyed *His* voice,
She has not received correction;
She has not trusted in the LORD,
She has not drawn near to her
God.

[4] 3 [a]Her princes in her midst *are*
*roaring lions;
Her *judges *are* [b]evening wolves
That leave not a bone till
morning.

4 Her [a]prophets are insolent, [4]
treacherous people;
Her priests have [1]polluted the
sanctuary,
They have done [b]violence to the
law.
5 The LORD *is* righteous in her [2]
midst,
He will do no unrighteousness.
[1]Every morning He brings His
justice to light;
He never fails,
But [a]the unjust knows no shame.
6 "I have cut off nations,
Their fortresses are devastated;
I have made their streets desolate,
With none passing by.
Their cities are destroyed;
There is no one, no inhabitant.
7 [a]I said, 'Surely you will fear Me,
You will receive *instruction'—
So that her dwelling would not be
cut off,
Despite everything for which I
punished her.
But [1]they rose early and
[b]corrupted all their deeds.

A Faithful Remnant

8 "Therefore [a]wait for Me," says the
LORD,
"Until the day I rise up [1]for
plunder;
My determination *is* to [b]gather
the nations
To My assembly of kingdoms,
To pour on them My indignation,
All My fierce anger;
All the earth [c]shall be devoured
With the fire of My jealousy.

9 "For then I will restore to the [1]
peoples [a]a pure [1]language,

13 [a]Is. 10:5–27; 14:24–27; Mic. 5:5, 6
14 [a]Is. 13:21 [b]Is. 14:23; 34:11 [c]Jer. 22:14
15 [a]Is. 47:8 [b]Rev. 18:7 [c]Lam. 2:15 [d]Nah. 3:19

CHAPTER 3

3 [a]Ezek. 22:27 [b]Jer. 5:6; Hab. 1:8 *See WW at Joel 3:16. • See WW at Judg. 2:18.
4 [a]Hos. 9:7 [b]Ezek. 22:26; Mal. 2:7, 8 [1]Or *profaned*
5 [a]Jer. 3:3 [1]Lit. *Morning by morning*
7 [a]Jer. 8:6 [b]Gen. 6:12 [1]They were eager *See WW at Prov. 4:13.
8 [a]Prov. 20:22; Mic. 7:7; Hab. 2:3 [b]Is. 66:18; Ezek. 38:14–23; Joel 3:2; Mic. 4:12; Matt. 25:32 [c]Zeph. 1:18 [1]LXX, Syr. *for witness;* Tg. *for the day of My revelation for judgment;* Vg. *for the day of My resurrection that is to come*
9 [a]Is. 19:18; 57:19 [1]Lit. *lip*

2:13–15 Nothing seemed more improbable than that **Assyria,** which had literally carried off the 10 northern tribes, would itself become a **desolation.** Walls 100 feet high encompassed **Nineveh** for 60 miles. The walls were so wide that three chariots abreast could ride on them. With its 1,500 watchtowers, Nineveh felt justified to boast, ***there is* none besides me.**

3:1–5 Specifics regarding the pending judgment against Jerusalem: Her sins are more abominable than Nineveh's because God had revealed to her His covenant righteousness.

3:2 See section 4 of Truth-In-Action at the end of Zeph.

3:2 Signs of Judah's spiritual demise: 1) They do not obey; 2) they do not receive correction; 3) they do not trust in God; 4) they do not draw near to God.

3:3, 4 Princes are like **roaring lions,** predators seeking prey; **judges** are like **evening wolves,** predators hunting under cover of darkness. **Prophets** betray the souls of the people for profit. **Priests** profane the Law by corrupting the sense of it.

3:3 See section 4 of Truth-In-Action at the end of Zeph.

3:4 See section 4 of Truth-In-Action at the end of Zeph.

3:5 See section 2 of Truth-In-Action at the end of Zeph.

3:5 In contrast to the sinning Jews (v. 2), God remains constant: 1) He is in their midst; 2) He is righteous; 3) He does no wrong; 4) He daily shows justice; 5) He never fails.

3:6–8 God's intent for judging **the nations** is that His people might **fear** Him.

3:7 Rose early: Because of the intense heat of the area, early morning was the time for transacting business. Not only did Judah remain unrepentant, but they pursued sin with diligent design.

3:9–13 See section 1 of Truth-In-Action at the end of Zeph.

3:9–13 This section is a promise of salvation for all **the peoples** and for **the remnant of Israel.** In its broadest application it anticipates the salvation of both Jews and Gentiles through Christ Jesus (Eph. 2:14–16). Characteristics of these people will be: serving **Him with one accord** (v. 9), humility (v. 12), righteousness, no lying, no deceit, and no fear (v. 13).

That they all may call on the
name of the LORD,
To *serve Him with one accord.
10 [a]From beyond the rivers of
Ethiopia
My worshipers,
The daughter of My dispersed
ones,
Shall bring My offering.
11 In that day you shall not be
shamed for any of your deeds
In which you transgress against
Me;
For then I will take away from
your midst
Those who [a]rejoice in your
pride,
And you shall no longer be
haughty
In My holy mountain.
12 I will leave in your midst
[a]A meek and humble people,
And they shall **trust** in the name
of the LORD.

WORD WEALTH

3:12 trust, *chasah* (chah-*sah*); Strong's #2620: To trust; to hope; to make someone a refuge. This verb occurs 36 times in the OT. Ps. 57:1 beautifully illustrates the verb, for it pictures David as nestling under God's wings for refuge, in the same manner that a defenseless but trusting baby bird hides itself under its parent's feathers (Ruth 2:12; 2 Sam. 22:3; Ps. 91:4). The middle verse of the Bible is Ps. 118:8, which states, *"It is* better to trust [*chasah*] in the LORD than to put confidence in man," a fitting centerpiece of the Bible.

13 [a]The remnant of Israel [b]shall do
no unrighteousness
[c]And speak no lies,
Nor shall a deceitful tongue be
found in their mouth;
For [d]they shall feed *their* flocks
and lie down,
And no one shall make *them*
afraid."

Joy in God's Faithfulness

14 [a]Sing, O daughter of Zion!
Shout, O Israel!
Be glad and rejoice with all *your*
heart,
O daughter of Jerusalem!
15 The LORD has taken away your
judgments,
He has cast out your enemy.
[a]The King of Israel, the LORD,
[b]*is* in your midst;
You shall [1]see disaster no more.

16 In that day [a]it shall be said to
Jerusalem:
"Do not fear;
Zion, [b]let not your hands be
weak.
17 The LORD your God [a]in your
midst,
The Mighty One, will save;
[b]He will *rejoice over you with
gladness,
He will quiet *you* with His love,
He will *rejoice over you with
singing."

18 "I will gather those who [a]sorrow
over the appointed assembly,
Who are among you,
To whom its reproach *is* a burden.
19 Behold, at that time
I will deal with all who afflict you;
I will save the [a]lame,
And gather those who were
driven out;
I will appoint them for praise and
fame
In every land where they were put
to shame.
20 At that time [a]I will bring you
back,
Even at the time I gather you;
For I will give you [1]fame and
praise
Among all the peoples of the
earth,
When I return your captives
before your eyes,"
Says the LORD.

9 *See WW at Ps. 100:2.
10 [a]Ps. 68:31; Is. 18:1; Acts 8:27
11 [a]Is. 2:12; 5:15; Matt. 3:9
12 [a]Is. 14:32; Zech. 13:8, 9
13 [a]Is. 10:20–22; [Mic. 4:7] [b]Is. 60:21 [c]Zech. 8:3, 16; Rev. 14:5 [d]Ezek. 34:13–15, 28
14 [a]Is. 12:6
15 [a][John 1:49] [b]Ezek. 48:35; [Rev. 7:15] [1]So with Heb. mss., LXX, Bg.; MT, Vg. *fear*
16 [a]Is. 35:3, 4 [b]Job 4:3; Heb. 12:12
17 [a]Zeph. 3:5, 15 [b]Deut. 30:9; Is. 62:5; 65:19; Jer. 32:41 *See WW at Is. 64:5. • See WW at Hab. 3:18.
18 [a]Lam. 2:6
19 [a][Ezek. 34:16; Mic. 4:6, 7]
20 [a]Is. 11:12; Ezek. 28:25; Amos 9:14 [1]Lit. *a name*

3:9 A pure language: See Introduction to Zephaniah: The Holy Spirit at Work.
3:14–20 Similar in style to Ps. 47, 95, and 97, this closing section is one of hope. It gives further positive aspects of **that** future **day** of the Lord. There shall be singing, shouting, and rejoicing (v. 14), deliverance from enemies (v. 15), and the exaltation of God's people (v. 20). Again, this is partially *fulfilled* through Jesus' reign in the church and consummated in the world to come. See note on Obad. 15.
3:17 Zephaniah describes God's victory and admiration of His redeemed people. As Victor, He will be a Hero who helps (**The Mighty One will save**). His love will be seen as deeply felt thoughtfulness and admiration (**He will quiet *you* with His love**). His satisfaction with His people will be expressed through loud, demonstrative singing (**He will rejoice over you with singing**).

TRUTH-IN-ACTION through ZEPHANIAH

Letting the LIFE of the Holy Spirit Bring Faith's Works Alive in You!

Truth Zephaniah Teaches	Text	**Action** Zephaniah Invites
1 Growing in Godliness The sin of pride is most often revealed by the words that we speak. Language becomes unclean with repeated expressions of self-will, or the profane use of God's name.	3:9–13	**Purify your heart** and your speech will be pure also. **Allow** God to purify your lips and language.
2 Steps to Dynamic Devotion The key to knowing God is to continually seek Him. The chief danger in this quest is the temptation to be satisfied with past encounters so that no fresh pursuits are made. Complacency is the enemy of spiritual growth.	1:6 1:12 3:5	**Persevere** in following the Lord. **Do not turn back. Find your answer** in God. **Remain zealous. Refuse** complacency. **Seek God faithfully** every day. Trust that the Lord behaves justly. **Keep your appointments** with the Father.
3 A Step to Holiness Avoid letting attitudes and character be shaped by the worldliness that surrounds. We are citizens of another kingdom.	1:8	**Reject** anything foreign to God's kingdom rule in your life.
4 Lessons for Leaders The wise leader accepts the Scripture's testimony about man and rejects the prevailing, humanistic doctrine that teaches man's intrinsic goodness. An unteachable attitude is the tip of the iceberg of ungodliness. This wisdom should influence one's self-view, causing all of us to guard ourselves from insincerity and pride in any of its manifestations.	3:2 3:3 3:4	Leaders, **understand** that the clearest evidence that someone does not trust the Lord or seek Him diligently is a rebellious, disobedient, and unteachable nature. Leaders, **avoid** being among those who speak loudly, who promise great things, but produce nothing that lasts or bears fruit in the long run. Leaders, **avoid diligently** any form of arrogance or pride in your ministry. **Do not profane** the ministry by mishandling God's Word in any way. **Never teach** your own opinions as God's Word.

The Book of HAGGAI

Author: Haggai
Date: 520 B.C.
Theme: Rebuilding the Temple
Key Words: The Lord's House, Consider, Glory

Author Haggai, whose name means "Festive," was one of the postexilic prophets, a contemporary of Zechariah. Haggai had the qualities of a good pastor. An encourager whose word was in tune with the hearts of the people and the mind of God, he was the Lord's messenger with the Lord's message, bringing to his discouraged band the assurance of God's presence.

Date Haggai's ministry covered a period of slightly less than four months during the second year of the reign of King Darius, who ruled Persia from 522 to 486 B.C. This fixes Haggai in history at 520 B.C.

Background As Haggai came to his task in 520 B.C., he joined the exiles who had returned to their homeland in 536 B.C. to rebuild the temple of the Lord. They had started well, building an altar and offering sacrifices, then laying the foundation for the Lord's house the following year. Construction had ceased, however, as enemies mocked the builders' efforts. But the ministry of Haggai and Zechariah caused the people to rally and complete the task within five years. The rebuilt temple was dedicated in 515 B.C.

Content The Book of Haggai addresses three problems common to all people of all times, and gives three inspired solutions to those problems. The first problem is *disinterest* (1:1–15). The people had returned from exile for the stated purpose of rebuilding the temple in Jerusalem (Ezra 1:2–4) and had made a start on their assigned task; but opposition had appeared and the work had stopped. The people had become more concerned with building beautiful houses for themselves, perhaps in an attempt to blot out the memory of their exile in a strange land (1:4). To wake them from their apathetic attitude, God speaks twice to the people. They first need to realize that they are fruitless (1:5, 6) because they have turned from God's house to their own houses (1:7–9). All their efforts at building their own kingdom can never produce lasting results. After seeing their problem, the people then need to understand that God will accept what they do, that He will be glorified if they will only yield to Him what they have (1:8).

The second problem is *discouragement* (2:1–9). Some of the older people in the band of returned exiles had seen Solomon's temple when they were children, so that no building, however beautiful, could compare with the glory of that former temple (2:3). The discouragement of the older people had quickly influenced the younger ones until, less than a month after the rebuilding began, work on the temple had ceased. But again Haggai brings a message designed to deal decisively with discouragement. The solution has two parts:

one to deal with the immediate problem, the other to bring a long-range resolution. For the present it is enough for the people to "be strong . . . be strong . . . be strong . . . and work" (2:4). The other key to overcoming discouragement is for the builders to know that they are building for the day when God will so fill this house with glory that it will surpass the glory of Solomon's temple (2:9).

The final issue that Haggai has to face is the problem of *dissatisfaction* (2:10–23). Now that the people are working, they expect an immediate reversal of all their years of inactivity. So the prophet comes with a question for the priests (2:12, 13) about clean and unclean things and their influence on one another. The response of the priests is that uncleanness is infectious while holiness is not. The application is obvious: Do not expect the work of three months to undo the neglect of sixteen years. The Lord's next word to the people is a surprise: "*But* from this day I will bless *you*" (2:19). The people needed to understand that God's blessings cannot be earned, but come as gracious gifts from a giving God. God has chosen Zerubbabel to be a sign (2:23), that is, to represent the servant nature to be fulfilled ultimately in Zerubbabel's greatest Son, Jesus. Note Zerubbabel's name in both the genealogical lists in the Gospels (Matt. 1; Luke 3), indicating that God's final, highest blessing is a Person, His Son Jesus Christ.

Personal Application Haggai issues a clear call to his own people and to us that we should set ourselves to the task assigned to us by God. We should not allow difficulties, enemies, or selfish pursuits to turn us aside from our divinely given responsibilities. The noble nature of our calling and the promised presence of God and His Holy Spirit encourage us to fulfill our commission.

By emphasizing the cooperative roles of prophet, priest, prince, and people, Haggai also demonstrates the necessity for teamwork in carrying out God's purposes on Earth.

Christ Revealed Two references to Christ in the Book of Haggai are highlighted. The first is 2:6–9, which begins by explaining that what God will do in the new temple will one day gain international attention. After an upheaval among the peoples of the Earth, the nations will be drawn to the temple to discover what they had been looking for: the One whom all the nations have desired will be displayed in splendor in the temple. The presence of this One will cause the memory of Solomon's glorious temple to fade so that only Christ's glory remains. Along with the glory of Christ's presence will come great peace, since the resplendent Prince of Peace Himself will be there.

The second reference to the coming Messiah is 2:23. The book closes with a mention of Zerubbabel, which ties this book, near the end of the Old Testament, with the first book in the New Testament: Zerubbabel is one of the people listed in the genealogies of Jesus. Two things make Zerubbabel significant and link him to Christ:

1. Zerubbabel is a *sign* of a man chosen by God, from whose yielded nature God causes to flow life, leadership, and ministry. What Zerubbabel did in part, Jesus did in full as the Servant of the Lord.
2. Zerubbabel is also in the *line* of the Messiah. The lists of Jesus'

ancestors in Matthew and Luke include the name of Zerubbabel the son of Shealtiel, whose own personal significance was surpassed by his role as one who pointed ahead to the coming Savior of the world.

The Holy Spirit at Work A brief but beautiful reference to the Holy Spirit is found in 2:5. The previous verses show the people of God discouraged as they compare the temple they are now building with the glorious temple of Solomon, which the new temple is meant to replace. The word of the Lord to them is: "Be strong . . . and work." The motivation to do this is also stated: "For I *am* with you."

Haggai 2:5 then explains how the Spirit of God is meant to interact with the spirit of the people in order to get the work accomplished. Verse 5 includes these significant points:

1. The Holy Spirit is a vital part of God's covenant with His people, "*according to* the word that I covenanted with you."
2. The Holy Spirit is an abiding gift to the people of God: "My Spirit remains among you."
3. The presence of the Holy Spirit removes fear from the hearts of God's people. Therefore, "Do not fear!"

These principles remain the same for the people of God today. At the heart of God's covenant with His people is the constant operation of the Holy Spirit, working to release them from fear, so that they may move boldly in fulfilling the divine commission.

Outline of Haggai

I. The Lord's first message: Consider your ways 1:1–15
- A. Consider what you have done: neglected God's house 1:1–6
- B. Consider what you should do: build God's house 1:7–11
- C. Results of considering your ways 1:12–15

II. The Lord's second message: Be strong and work 2:1–9
- A. Comparison of the new temple with Solomon's temple 2:1–3
- B. Call to be strong 2:4, 5
- C. Coming glory of the new temple 2:6–9

III. The Lord's third message: I will bless you 2:10–23
- A. A question for the priests 2:10–19
- B. A promise for Zerubbabel 2:20–23

The Command to Build God's House

1 IN [a]the second year of King Darius,
in the sixth month, on the first day
of the month, the word of the LORD
came by [b]Haggai the prophet to
[c]Zerubbabel the son of Shealtiel, governor of Judah, and to [d]Joshua the son
of [e]Jehozadak, the high priest, saying,
2 "Thus speaks the LORD of hosts,
saying: 'This people says, "The time
has not come, the time that the LORD's
*house should be built." ' "
3 Then the word of the LORD [a]came
by Haggai the prophet, saying,

CHAPTER 1

1 [a]Ezra 4:24 [b]Ezra 5:1; 6:14 [c]Ezra 2:2 [d]Ezra 5:2, 3 [e]1 Chr. 6:15
2 *See WW at 2 Sam. 7:11.
3 [a]Ezra 5:1

1:1–4 See section 1 of Truth-In-Action at the end of Hag.
1:1 The precise dating given for the messages of God to **Haggai** sets Haggai's ministry among the returned exiles during a four-month period in 520 B.C. The message is from **the LORD** through Haggai **to Zerubbabel** and **Joshua** for all the people, thus calling for a unique collaboration of the prophetic, priestly, and political leadership in seeing that God's will is accomplished in His people.
1:2 Haggai's favorite designation for God is **the LORD of hosts,** which occurs 14 times in this short book. "Hosts" means either "angels," "stars," or "the armies of Israel" and is used by the prophet to emphasize God's greatness and might. **This people says** sets the scene for God's dispute against the people of Jerusalem.

4 "*Is it* [a]time for you yourselves to dwell in your paneled houses, and this [1]temple *to lie* in ruins?"
5 Now therefore, thus says the LORD of hosts: [a]"Consider your ways!

6 "You have [a]sown much, and bring
in little;
You eat, but do not have enough;
You drink, but you are not filled
with drink;
You clothe yourselves, but no one
is warm;
And [b]he who earns wages,
Earns wages *to put* into a bag
with holes."

7 Thus says the LORD of hosts: "Consider your ways!
8 "Go up to the [a]mountains and bring wood and build the [1]temple, that I may take pleasure in it and be glorified," says the LORD.
9 [a]"*You* looked for much, but indeed *it came to* little; and when you brought it home, [b]I blew it away. Why?" says the LORD of hosts. "Because of My house that *is in* ruins, while every one of you runs to his own house.
10 "Therefore [a]the heavens above you withhold the dew, and the earth withholds its fruit.
11 "For I [a]called for a drought on the land and the mountains, on the grain and the new wine and the oil, on whatever the ground brings forth, on men and livestock, and on [b]all the labor of *your* hands."

The People's Obedience

12 [a]Then Zerubbabel the son of Shealtiel, and Joshua the son of Jehozadak, the high priest, with all the remnant of the people, obeyed the voice of the LORD their God, and the words of Haggai the *prophet, as the LORD their God had sent him; and the people feared the presence of the LORD.

4 [a]2 Sam. 7:2 [1]Lit. *house*
5 [a]Lam. 3:40
6 [a]Deut. 28:38–40; Hos. 8:7; Hag. 1:9, 10; 2:16, 17 [b]Zech. 8:10
8 [a]Ezra 3:7 [1]Lit. *house*
9 [a]Hag. 2:16 [b]Hag. 2:17
10 [a]Lev. 26:19; Deut. 28:23; 1 Kin. 8:35; Joel 1:18–20
11 [a]1 Kin. 17:1; 2 Kin. 8:1 [b]Hag. 2:17
12 [a]Ezra 5:2 *See WW at 1 Sam. 3:20.
13 [a][Matt. 28:20; Rom. 8:31]
14 [a]2 Chr. 36:22; Ezra 1:1 [b]Hag. 2:21 [c]Ezra 5:2, 8; Neh. 4:6

CHAPTER 2

1 [1]Lit. *by the hand of*
3 [a]Ezra 3:12, 13 [1]Lit. *house*

13 Then Haggai, the LORD's messenger, spoke the LORD's message to the people, saying, [a]"I *am* with you, says the LORD."
14 So [a]the LORD **stirred up** the spirit of Zerubbabel the son of Shealtiel, [b]governor of Judah, and the spirit of Joshua the son of Jehozadak, the high priest, and the spirit of all the remnant of the people; [c]and they came and worked on the house of the LORD of hosts, their God,

WORD WEALTH

1:14 stirred up, *'ur* (*oor*); Strong's #5782: To rouse, awaken, stir up, excite, raise up; to incite; to arouse to action; to open one's eyes. Occurring about 75 times in the OT, *'ur* is used of an eagle stirring up its nest (Deut. 32:11) and of a musical instrument being awakened or warmed up for playing (Ps. 108:2). In Is. 50:4, the Lord awakens the prophet each morning and "awakens" his ear to hear God's message. See also Is. 51:9, which speaks of the arm of the Lord being awakened or roused into action. The present reference is similar: God wakes up the spirit of Zerubbabel, inciting him to repair God's temple.

15 on the twenty-fourth day of the sixth month, in the second year of King Darius.

The Coming Glory of God's House

2 In the seventh *month,* on the twenty-first of the month, the word of the LORD came [1]by Haggai the prophet, saying:
2 "Speak now to Zerubbabel the son of Shealtiel, governor of Judah, and to Joshua the son of Jehozadak, the high priest, and to the remnant of the people, saying:
3 [a]'Who is left among you who saw this [1]temple in its former glory? And how do you see it now? In comparison

1:4 Paneled houses: The people, though neglecting the temple, beautified their own homes by covering the walls with expensive paneling, as in Solomon's temple where "all *was* cedar; there was no stone *to be* seen" (1 Kin. 6:18).
1:5, 7 Consider your ways! in Hebrew is literally, "Set your heart on your ways!" (see 2:15, 18).
1:6 The people were apparently using their poverty, food shortages, and inflation as excuses not to finish the temple. In actuality, they are judgments for failing to build (vv. 9–11).
1:8 Lacking the resources of Solomon, who built with cedar from Lebanon and gold from Ophir, they can still glorify God by the use of common materials at hand.
1:10, 11 Nature itself reflects divine judgment when the will of God is ignored.
1:13 Haggai, the LORD's messenger, spoke the LORD's message defines Haggai's character and his mission.
1:14 The message of the prophet (v. 13) is complemented by the direct activity of God who **stirred up** in cold hearts a renewed desire for doing His will. The result is that the builders begin working again with renewed energy.
1:15 The twenty-fourth day of the sixth month: Twenty-three days passed between Haggai's proclamation of his first message and the people's beginning work on the temple.
2:1 Haggai's second message ("Be strong . . . and work," v. 4) comes approximately two months after the first and about one month after work on the temple had begun.
2:3 Temple in its former glory refers to Solomon's temple. Some of the elderly had been children at the time of Jerusalem's fall.

with it, [b]*is this* not in your eyes as nothing?
4 'Yet now [a]be* strong, Zerubbabel,'
says the LORD; 'and be strong, Joshua,
son of Jehozadak, the high priest; and
be strong, all you people of the land,'
says the LORD, 'and work; for I *am* with
you,' says the LORD of hosts.
5 [a]'*According to* the word that I covenanted with you when you came out
of Egypt, so [b]My Spirit remains among
you; do not fear!'
1 6 "For thus says the LORD of hosts:
[a]'Once more (it *is* a little while) [b]I will
shake heaven and earth, the sea and
dry land;
7 'and I will shake all nations, and
they shall come to [a]the [1]Desire of All
Nations, and I will fill this [2]temple with
[b]glory,' says the LORD of hosts.
8 'The silver *is* Mine, and the gold *is*
Mine,' says the LORD of hosts.
9 [a]'The glory of this latter [1]temple
shall be greater than the former,' says
the LORD of hosts. 'And in this place I
will give [b]peace,' says the LORD of
hosts."

The People Are Defiled

10 On the twenty-fourth *day* of the
ninth *month,* in the second year of Darius, the word of the LORD came by
Haggai the prophet, saying,
11 "Thus says the LORD of hosts: 'Now,
[a]ask the priests *concerning the* law,
saying,
12 "If one carries holy meat in the
fold of his garment, and with the edge
he touches bread or stew, wine or oil,
or any food, will it become holy?" ' "
Then the priests answered and said,
"No."
13 And Haggai said, "If *one who is*
[a]unclean *because* of a dead body
touches any of these, will it be unclean?" So the priests answered and
said, "It shall be unclean."
14 Then Haggai answered and said,
[a]" 'So is this people, and so is this nation before Me,' says the LORD, 'and so
is every work of their hands; and what
they offer there is unclean.

Promised Blessing

15 'And now, carefully [a]consider from 1
this day forward: from before stone
was laid upon stone in the **temple** of
the LORD—

> **WORD WEALTH**
>
> **2:15 temple,** *heychal* (hay-*chahl*); Strong's #1964: Temple, palace; any splendid building; edifice, citadel, tabernacle, or sanctuary; a spacious, royal building, such as a king would possess. This noun occurs about 80 times, sometimes translated "palace," as in Ps. 45:8, 15; Is. 39:7. However, in the great majority of occurrences, it refers to the Lord's temple in Jerusalem. In several references *heychal* refers to the "inside" aspect of the temple (2 Chr. 29:16; Ps. 11:4; 27:4; Is. 6:1; Jon. 2:7).

16 'since those *days,* [a]when *one* came
to a heap of twenty ephahs, there were
but ten; when *one* came to the wine
vat to draw out fifty baths from the
press, there were *but* twenty.
17 [a]'I struck you with blight and mildew and hail [b]in all the labors of your
hands; [c]yet you did not *turn* to Me,'
says the LORD.
18 'Consider now from this day forward, from the twenty-fourth day of
the ninth month, from [a]the day that the
foundation of the LORD's temple was
laid—consider it:
19 [a]'Is the seed still in the barn? As yet
the vine, the fig tree, the pomegranate,

3 [b]Zech. 4:10 **4** [a]Deut. 31:23; 1 Chr. 22:13; 28:20; Zech. 8:9; Eph. 6:10 *See WW at Josh. 1:9. **5** [a]Ex. 29:45, 46 [b][Neh. 9:20]; Is. 63:11, 14 **6** [a]Heb. 12:26 [b][Joel 3:16] **7** [a]Gen. 49:10; Mal. 3:1 [b]1 Kin. 8:11; Is. 60:7; Zech. 2:5 [1]Or *desire of all nations* [2]Lit. *house* **9** [a][John 1:14] [b]Ps. 85:8, 9; Luke 2:14; [Eph. 2:14] [1]Lit. *house* **11** [a]Lev. 10:10, 11; Deut. 33:10; Mal. 2:7 **13** [a]Lev. 22:4–6; Num. 19:11, 22 **14** [a][Titus 1:15] **15** [a]Hag. 1:5, 7; 2:18 **16** [a]Hag. 1:6, 9; Zech. 8:10 **17** [a]Deut. 28:22; 1 Kin. 8:37; Amos 4:9 [b]Hag. 1:11 [c]Jer. 5:3; Amos 4:6–11 **18** [a]Ezra 5:1, 2, 16; Zech. 8:9 **19** [a]Zech. 8:12

2:5 The promise of the Holy **Spirit** was affirmed by a covenant at the beginning of Israel's history. The promise continues to be fulfilled as God's Spirit remains among the Israelites to take away their **fear.** See Introduction to Haggai: The Holy Spirit at Work.
2:6–9 See section 1 of Truth-In-Action at the end of Hag.
2:6–9 This passage is best seen as referring to God's final inbreaking into history, the culmination of "the day of the LORD" (see note on Obad. 15).
2:6 **It *is* a little while** denotes its assurance.
2:7 **I will shake all nations** is God's final dealing with evil *just before the world to come.* ***I will fill this temple with* glory** refers in part to the dedication of Zerubbabel's actual temple, but also prophesies God's indwelling of human temples through Christ Jesus (1 Cor. 6:19, 20).
2:9 In Jewish tradition **this latter temple** is called "The Second Temple," Solomon's temple being **the former** temple. This is the temple that would be standing in the time of Jesus, though enlarged and beautified under Herod. See note on v. 7 for the importance of "latter temple." See Introduction to Haggai: Christ Revealed.
2:10 Haggai's third message ("I will bless you," v. 18) comes approximately two months after the second message (v. 1).
2:11–14 Before Haggai's message of blessing, he reminds them that holiness is not transferable. Its intent is to teach that three month's work, even on the temple, will not undo the effects of the years of neglect. The temple is not magical. The people still lack reformed lives.
2:12 **Holy meat** refers to a sacrifice.
2:15–19 See section 1 of Truth-In-Action at the end of Hag.
2:15–19 By asking the people to look backward God reinforces the blessings of putting His purposes first (**from this day . . .**).
2:19 ***But* from this day I will bless *you*** are words of God's sure, and yet unmerited, provision.

and the olive tree have not yielded
fruit. But from this day I will [b]bless*
you.' "

Zerubbabel Chosen as a Signet

20 And again the word of the LORD
came to Haggai on the twenty-fourth
day of the month, saying,
21 "Speak to Zerubbabel, [a]governor of
Judah, saying:

[b]'I will shake heaven and earth.
22 [a]I will overthrow the throne of
kingdoms;
I will destroy the strength of the
Gentile kingdoms.
[b]I will overthrow the chariots
And those who ride in them;
The horses and their riders shall
come down,
Every one by the sword of his
brother.

23 'In that day,' says the LORD of hosts,
'I will take you, Zerubbabel My ser-
vant, the son of Shealtiel,' says the
LORD, [a]'and will make you like a signet
ring; for [b]I have *chosen you,' says the
LORD of hosts."

19 [b][Mal. 3:10] *See WW at Ps. 145:2. **21** [a]Zech. 4:6–10 [b]Hag. 2:6, 7 **22** [a][Dan. 2:44] [b]Mic. 5:10

23 [a]Song 8:6 [b]Is. 42:1; 43:10 *See WW at 1 Kin. 11:34.

2:20–23 See note on v. 7. See also note on Zech. 4:7.
2:22 Sword of his brother: God will turn the powers opposing His people against each other so that they end up destroying themselves.
2:23 A signet *ring* represented an article of special value to its owner. Zerubbabel's name remains recorded for all to see as a sign of the special place granted him by God, for he is listed in the genealogies of our Lord Jesus (see Matt. 1:12, 13; Luke 3:27). See also Introduction to Haggai: Christ Revealed.

TRUTH-IN-ACTION through HAGGAI

Letting the LIFE of the Holy Spirit Bring Faith's Works Alive in You!

Truth Haggai Teaches	Text	**Action** Haggai Invites
1 Key Lessons in Faith The challenge to faith is the same in every generation; seek first the things of God and trust Him to provide the daily necessities of life. The glorification of any work we pursue comes by the presence of God in it. God calls us to commit what we are, what we have, and all that we do to Him.	1:1–4 2:6–9 2:15–19	**Make the work of God a priority,** both with your time and with your money. **Understand** that it is the presence of Jesus that produces glory. See 2 Cor. 3:18. **Choose to believe** and **reckon as true** that when we turn from selfish ambition and personal agenda to focus on advancing God's kingdom, He will bless us toward that end.

The Book of ZECHARIAH

Author: Zechariah
Date: 520–475 B.C.
Theme: The Lord Remembers Zion
Key Words: Jerusalem, the Day of the Lord, That Day

Author Zechariah, whose name means "Yahweh Remembers," was one of the postexilic prophets, a contemporary of Haggai. With Haggai, he was called to arouse the returned Jews to complete the task of reconstructing the temple (see Ezra 6:14). As the son of Berechiah and grandson of Iddo, he came from one of the priestly families of the tribe of Levi. He is one of the most messianic of all the Old Testament prophets, giving distinct, verifiable references to the coming Messiah.

Date Zechariah's prophetic ministry began in 520 B.C., two months after Haggai had completed his prophecy. The vision of the early chapters was apparently given while the prophet was still a young man (see 2:4). Chapters 7 and 8 occur two years later in 518 B.C. The reference to Greece in 9:13 may indicate that chapters 9—14 were written after 480 B.C., when Greece replaced Persia as the great world power. The prophecies comprising the Book of Zechariah were reduced to writing between 520 and 475 B.C.

Background The exiles who returned to their homeland in 536 B.C. under the edict of Cyrus were among the poorer of the Jewish captives. Some fifty thousand people returned to Jerusalem under the leadership of Zerubbabel and Joshua. Quickly they rebuilt the altar and began construction on the temple. Soon, however, apathy set in as they were beset with opposition from the neighboring Samaritans who eventually were able to get an order from the Persian government to halt construction. For about twelve years construction had been choked by discouragement and preoccupation with other pursuits. Zechariah and Haggai urged the people to return to the Lord and His purpose to restore the ruined temple. Zechariah encouraged God's people by pointing them to a day when the Messiah would rule from a restored temple in a restored city.

Content The Book of Zechariah begins with the impassioned word of the Lord for the people to repent and turn again to their God. The book is replete with Zechariah's references to the word of the Lord. The prophet does not deliver his own message, but he faithfully transmits the message given to him by God. The people are called on to repent of their lethargy and complete the unfinished task.

God then assures His people of His love and care for them through a series of eight visions. The vision of the man and the horses reminds the people of God's watchful care. The vision of the four horns and four craftsmen recalls God's judgment, first on Judah and then on her enemies. In the vision of the man with the measuring line there is an apocalyptic glimpse of God's beautiful, peaceful city. Joshua, the high priest, portrays cleansing from sin. The magnificent vision of the lampstand among the olive trees assures Zerubbabel that God's purposes will be accomplished only by His Spirit. The flying scroll emits God's pronouncement against stealing and lying. The vision of the woman in a basket signifies the holiness of God and the removal of sin. The vision of the four chariots depicts God's sovereign control over the Earth.

The visions are followed by a coronation scene in which Joshua is crowned as both king and priest. This is powerfully symbolic of the coming Messiah.

In chapters 7 and 8 God takes the occasion of a question concerning fasting to reinforce His mandate for justice and righteousness to supersede religious formalities.

Chapters 9—14 contain much eschatology (the study of the last things). Zion is restored and radiates the glory of her ruling King. Two prophetic messages emerge. The first prophecy, or "burden," is in chapters 9—11. God will deliver His people (ch. 9), there will be a restoration of prosperity for the people of God (ch. 10), and, the Shepherd of Israel will initially be rejected, bringing great desolation (ch. 11). The second prophecy is in chapters 12—14. Again God delivers His people, and they mourn for the One they have pierced (ch. 12). A fountain is then opened to cleanse from sin and uncleanness (ch. 13). Then the Lord will reign from a restored Zion as King over all nations (ch. 14).

Personal Application Zechariah challenges his contemporaries and he challenges us to complete the task God has given us. This entails repentance for neglecting the building up of the house of God. Under the New Covenant, we are to give ourselves to the restoration and cleansing of the temple of God individually and corporately in the church. The glory of God emanating from a restored Zion is not the result of human ingenuity but rather the renewing ministry of the Holy Spirit.

Many Bible students believe the promises of a restored Zion are to apply primarily to a cleansed, invigorated church. A fountain of cleansing is opened to all who repent and look to the One who was pierced for them. William Cowper received the inspiration for the hymn "There Is a Fountain" from this beautiful truth in 13:1.

As we live in harmony with God's purpose to restore what has lain desolate, we rest in the assurance that God sovereignly governs the affairs of Earth. The smitten Shepherd will be worshiped as King, and Israel will receive her Messiah. The task of world evangelization will be accomplished. Jesus shall reign.

Christ Revealed Zechariah is sometimes referred to as the most messianic of all the Old Testament books. Chapters 9—14 are the most quoted section of the Prophets in the passion narratives of the Gospels. In the Revelation Zechariah is quoted more than any prophet except Ezekiel.

Zechariah prophesies that the Messiah will come as the Lord's Servant the Branch (3:8), as the Man the Branch (6:12); as both King and Priest (6:13), and as the True Shepherd (11:4–11). He bears eloquent testimony to Christ's betrayal for thirty pieces of silver (11:12, 13), His crucifixion (12:10), His sufferings (13:7), and His Second Advent (14:4).

Two references to Christ are of profound significance. Jesus' triumphal entry into Jerusalem is described in detail in 9:9, four hundred years before the event (see Matt. 21:5; Mark 11:7–10). One of the most dramatic verses of prophetic Scriptures is found in 12:10 when in the majority of manuscripts the first person is used: "Then they will look on Me whom they pierced." Jesus Christ personally prophesied His eventual reception by the house of David.

The Holy Spirit at Work The most often quoted Old Testament verse in reference to the work of the Holy Spirit is 4:6. Zerubbabel is comforted in the assurances 1) that the rebuilding of the temple will not be by military might or human prowess but by the ministry of the Spirit of God; 2) that the Holy Spirit will remove every obstacle that stands against the completion of God's temple.

A sad commentary in 7:12 reminds the people of their rebellion against the words of the Lord delivered by the prophets. These words were transmitted by His Spirit.

Although the reference to *ruach* (spirit/Spirit) in 12:10 is translated by some as God's disposition rather than as the Holy Spirit, others translate it as the Holy Spirit. As such it is one of the most beautiful titles for the Holy Spirit found in Scripture. God's promise is to pour on the house of David and Jerusalem's population "the Spirit of grace and supplication." This immediately precedes their reception and mourning over the One they had pierced. The preparation of the heart by the Holy Spirit is always antecedent to conversion.

Outline of Zechariah

I. The call to repentance 1:1–6
II. The eight visions 1:7—6:15
- A. The man and horses: God's mercy 1:7–17
- B. The four horns and four craftsmen: God's judgment 1:18–21
- C. The man with the measuring line: God's city 2:1–13
- D. The high priest: God's cleansing 3:1–10
- E. The lampstand and olive trees: God's Spirit 4:1–14
- F. The flying scroll: God's pronouncement 5:1–4
- G. The woman in a basket: God's holiness 5:5–11
- H. The four chariots: God's sovereignty 6:1–8

III. The crowning of the high priest 6:9–15
IV. Religious ritual or real repentance? 7:1–14
V. The restoration of Zion 8:1–23
VI. The triumph of the kingdom of God 9:1—14:21
- A. The first prophecy: The Messiah rejected 9:1—11:17
- B. The second prophecy: The Messiah reigns 12:1—14:21

A Call to Repentance

IN the eighth month [a]of the second
year of Darius, the word of the LORD
came [b]to Zechariah the son of Berechiah, the son of [c]Iddo the prophet,
saying,
2 "The LORD has been very angry 1
with your fathers.
3 "Therefore say to them, 'Thus says
the LORD of hosts: "Return [a]to Me,"
says the LORD of hosts, "and I will return to you," says the LORD of hosts.
4 "Do not be like your fathers, [a]to

CHAPTER 1
1 [a]Zech. 7:1 [b]Matt. 23:35 [c]Neh. 12:4, 16
3 [a][Mal. 3:7–10]
4 [a]2 Chr. 36:15, 16

1:2–6 See section 1 of Truth-In-Action at the end of Zech.

1:2 God reminds His people of the judgment that came on their fathers in 586 B.C., when Nebuchadnezzar defeated King Zedekiah, resulting in the destruction of the city and temple and the deportation of many Jews to Babylon.

1:3 The term, **the LORD of hosts,** is used 53 times in this book and refers to the truth that God is the Lord of all the armies of the universe, both spiritual and material.

whom the former prophets preached,
saying, 'Thus says the LORD of hosts:
[b]"Turn now from your evil ways and
your evil deeds." ' But they did not
hear nor heed Me," says the LORD.

5 "Your fathers, where *are* they?
And the prophets, do they live
forever?
6 Yet surely [a]My words and My
statutes,
Which I commanded My servants
the prophets,
Did they not overtake your
fathers?

"So they returned and said:

[b]'Just as the LORD of hosts
determined to do to us,
According to our ways and
according to our deeds,
So He has dealt with us.' " ' "

Vision of the Horses

7 On the twenty-fourth day of the
eleventh month, which is the month
Shebat, in the second year of Darius,
the word of the LORD came to Zechariah the son of Berechiah, the son of Iddo the prophet:
8 I saw by night, and behold, [a]a man
riding on a red horse, and it stood
among the myrtle trees in the hollow;
and behind him *were* [b]horses: red, sorrel, and white.
9 Then I said, [a]"My lord, what *are*
these?" So the *angel who talked with
me said to me, "I will show you what
they *are*."
10 And the man who stood among the
myrtle trees answered and said,
[a]"These *are the ones* whom the LORD
has sent to walk to and fro throughout
the earth."
11 [a]So they answered the Angel of the
LORD, who stood among the myrtle
trees, and said, "We have walked to
and fro throughout the earth, and behold, all the earth is [1]resting quietly."

The LORD Will Comfort Zion

12 Then the Angel of the LORD answered and said, "O LORD of hosts,
[a]how long will You not *have mercy
on Jerusalem and on the cities of

4 [b]Is. 31:6; Jer. 3:12; 18:11; Ezek. 18:30; [Hos. 14:1] 6 [a][Is. 55:11] [b]Lam. 1:18; 2:17
8 [a]Is. 55:13; Zech. 6:2; [Rev. 6:4] [b][Zech. 6:2–7; Rev. 6:2] 9 [a]Zech. 4:4, 5, 13; 6:4 *See WW at 2 Chr. 32:21. 10 [a][Heb. 1:14] 11 [a][Ps. 103:20, 21] [1]Lit. *sitting and quiet* 12 [a]Ps. 74:10; Jer. 12:4; Hab. 1:2 *See WW at Hos. 2:23.

1:7 The following eight visions were received on **the twenty-fourth day of . . . the month Shebat, in the second year of Darius,** king of Persia. Accordingly, most modern scholarship dates the visions on February 15, 520 B.C.
1:7–17 The major message of this first vision is that God is about to act to aid the postexilic Israelites in restoring the temple and the cities. It is a message of comfort, assurance, and watchful care to a people who have been waiting a long time (**these seventy years**) for God to lift His judgment and again bring prosperity to His people.
1:9 My lord is a title of respect used here to address the unidentified angel who plays a major interpretative role in the visions.

ZECHARIAH'S VISIONS (1:7)

The visions of Zechariah had historical meaning for his day, but they also have meaning for all time. God will save His people and bring judgment on the wicked.

Vision	Significance
Man and horses among the myrtle trees (1:8)	The Lord will again be merciful to Jerusalem (1:14, 16, 17).
Four horns, four craftsmen (1:18–20)	Those who scattered Judah are cast out (1:21).
Man with measuring line (2:1)	God will be a protective wall of fire around Jerusalem (2:3–5).
Cleansing of Joshua (3:4)	The Servant, the Branch, comes to save (3:8, 9).
Golden lampstand and olive trees (4:2, 3)	The Lord empowers Israel by His Spirit (4:6).
Flying scroll (5:1)	Dishonesty is cursed (5:3).
Woman in the basket (5:6, 7)	Wickedness will be removed (5:9).
Four chariots (6:1)	The spirits of heaven execute judgment on the whole Earth (6:5, 7).

Judah, against which You were angry [b]these seventy years?"
13 And the LORD answered the angel who talked to me, *with* [a]good *and* comforting words.
14 So the angel who spoke with me said to me, [1]"Proclaim, saying, 'Thus says the LORD of hosts:

"I am [a]zealous[2] for Jerusalem
And for Zion with great [3]zeal.
15 I am exceedingly angry with the nations at ease;
For [a]I was a little angry,
And they helped—*but* with evil *intent*."

 16 'Therefore thus says the LORD:

[a]"I am returning to Jerusalem with mercy;
My [b]house [c]shall be **built** in it,"
says the LORD of hosts,
"And [d]a *surveyor's* line shall be stretched out over Jerusalem." '

WORD WEALTH

1:16 built, *banah* (bah-*nah*); Strong's #1129: To build, construct, found, set up; obtain children ("build" a family). *Banah* is generally translated "build" in the English versions; its object is usually a city, house, temple, room, gate, or an altar. Occasionally it means "to build up" something, as in Ps. 102:16, "The LORD shall build up Zion; He shall appear in His glory." It is thought that *banah* is the root of *ben* (son) and *banim* (children), as if the linguistic suggestion is that sons are the builders or building blocks of future generations.

17 "Again proclaim, saying, 'Thus says the LORD of hosts:

"My cities shall again [1]spread out through prosperity;
[a]The LORD will again *comfort Zion,
And [b]will again choose Jerusalem." ' "

12 [b]2 Chr. 36:21; Jer. 25:11, 12; 29:10; Dan. 9:2; Zech. 7:5
13 [a]Jer. 29:10
14 [a]Joel 2:18; Zech. 8:2 [1]Lit. *Cry out* [2]Or *jealous* [3]Or *jealousy*
15 [a]Is. 47:6
16 [a][Is. 12:1; 54:8; Zech. 2:10; 8:3] [b]Ezra 6:14, 15; Hag. 1:4; Zech. 4:9 [c]2 Chr. 36:23; Ezra 1:2, 3; Is. 44:28 [d]Zech. 2:1–3
17 [a][Is. 40:1, 2; 51:3] [b]Is. 14:1; Zech. 2:12 [1]Or *overflow with good*
*See WW at Ps. 23:4.
18 [a][Lam. 2:17] *See WW at Ezek. 29:21.
19 [a]Ezra 4:1, 4, 7 [1]Kingdoms or powers
21 [a][Ps. 75:10] [b]Ps. 75:4, 5 [1]Lit. *these*
*See WW at Ps. 106:47.

CHAPTER 2

1 [a]Jer. 31:39; Ezek. 40:3; 47:3; Zech. 1:16
2 [a]Rev. 11:1
4 [a]Jer. 31:27
5 [a][Is. 26:1] [b][Is. 60:19]
6 [a]Is. 48:20 [b]Deut. 28:64
7 [a]Is. 48:20; Jer. 51:6; [Rev. 18:4]

Vision of the Horns

18 Then I raised my eyes and looked, and there *were* four [a]horns.*
19 And I said to the angel who talked with me, "What *are* these?" So he answered me, [a]"These *are* the [1]horns that have scattered Judah, Israel, and Jerusalem."
20 Then the LORD showed me four craftsmen.
21 And I said, "What are these coming to do?" So he said, "These *are* the [a]horns that scattered Judah, so that no one could lift up his head; but [1]the craftsmen are coming to terrify them, to cast out the horns of the *nations that [b]lifted up *their* horn against the land of Judah to scatter it."

Vision of the Measuring Line

2 Then I raised my eyes and looked, and behold, [a]a man with a measuring line in his hand.
2 So I said, "Where are you going?" And he said to me, [a]"To measure Jerusalem, to see what *is* its width and what *is* its length."
3 And there *was* the angel who talked with me, going out; and another angel was coming out to meet him,
4 who said to him, "Run, speak to this young man, saying: [a]'Jerusalem shall be inhabited *as* towns without walls, because of the multitude of men and livestock in it.
5 'For I,' says the LORD, 'will be [a]a wall of fire all around her, [b]and I will be the glory in her midst.' "

Future Joy of Zion and Many Nations

6 "Up, up! Flee [a]from the land of the north," says the LORD; "for I have [b]spread you abroad like the four winds of heaven," says the LORD.
7 "Up, Zion! [a]Escape, you who dwell with the daughter of Babylon."
8 For thus says the LORD of hosts: "He sent Me after glory, to the nations

1:14 God is passionately protective of His covenant people. Whoever would harm the people of God "touches the apple of His eye" (see 2:8).

1:16, 17 See section 1 of Truth-In-Action at the end of Zech.

1:18–21 Some commentators believe the **four horns** of this second vision are the four kingdoms described in Dan. 2 and 7. Probably they should be viewed in the larger sense as any nation from the four quarters of the Earth that has scattered Israel and Judah, acting beyond their divine intention to punish Judah. This, too, then is a message of comfort.

2:1–13 The third vision is a further elaboration of 1:16. Although many of the details are ambiguous, its intent is clear: **Jerusalem** will be rebuilt. Zechariah's immediate reference is obviously to the postexilic Jerusalem. However, the scope of the language here may indicate the yet future and magnificent New Jerusalem of the world to come (Rev. 21:9–27).

2:8 He sent Me after glory is evidently a reference to the Messiah's being sent from God as the Lord of glory. To **[touch] the apple of His eye** means to stick a finger in the pupil of His eye. Whenever anyone accosts the people of God, it is actually a blasphemous assault against God Himself.

which plunder you; for he who
[a]touches you touches the [1]apple of His
eye.
9 "For surely I will [a]shake My hand
against them, and they shall become
[1]spoil for their servants. Then [b]you will
know that the LORD of hosts has sent
Me.
10 [a]"Sing and rejoice, O daughter of
Zion! For behold, I am coming and I
[b]will dwell in your midst," says the
LORD.
11 [a]"Many nations shall be joined to
the LORD [b]in that day, and they shall
become [c]My people. And I will dwell
in your midst. Then [d]you will know
that the LORD of hosts has sent Me to
you.
12 "And the LORD will [a]take possession of Judah as His **inheritance** in the
Holy Land, and will again choose Jerusalem.

WORD WEALTH

2:12 inheritance, *cheleq* (*chay*-lek); Strong's #2506: A portion, part, inheritance, allotment. This noun occurs more than 60 times. It comes from the verb *chalaq,* "to be smooth." From this root are derived such words as "smooth stones" and "flattery," which is smooth words. Perhaps because smooth stones were used for casting "lots," *chalaq* came to mean "to apportion, deal out, divide up, allot." Thus a *cheleq* is an apportionment, allotment, a parcel of land that a person receives as an inheritance. David calls the Lord "my portion" (Ps. 73:26; 142:5). The present reference indicates that Yahweh's portion (allotment, share, inheritance) is the people of Judah in the Holy Land.

13 [a]"Be silent, all flesh, before the
LORD, for He is aroused [b]from His holy
habitation!"

Vision of the High Priest

3 Then he showed me [a]Joshua the
high priest standing before the Angel of the LORD, and [b]Satan[1]* standing
at his right hand to oppose him.
2 And the LORD said to Satan, [a]"The
LORD rebuke you, Satan! The LORD
who [b]has chosen Jerusalem rebuke
you! [c]*Is* this not a brand plucked from
the fire?"
3 Now Joshua was clothed with **1**
[a]filthy garments, and was standing before the Angel.
4 Then He answered and spoke to
those who stood before Him, saying,
"Take away the filthy garments from
him." And to him He said, "See, I have
removed your iniquity from you,
[a]and I will clothe you with rich robes."
5 And I said, "Let them put a clean
[a]turban on his head." So they put a
clean turban on his head, and they put
the clothes on him. And the Angel of
the LORD stood by.

The Coming Branch

6 Then the Angel of the LORD admonished Joshua, saying,
7 "Thus says the LORD of hosts:

'If you will walk in My ways,
And if you will [a]keep My
command,
Then you shall also [b]judge* My
house,
And likewise have charge of My
courts;
I will give you places to walk
Among these who [c]stand here.

8 'Hear, O Joshua, the high priest,
You and your companions who
sit before you,
For they are [a]a[1] **wondrous sign;**
For behold, I am bringing forth
[b]My Servant the [c]BRANCH.

WORD WEALTH

3:8 wondrous sign, *mophet* (moh-*fayt*); Strong's #4159: A miracle, sign, token, wonder. Used 36 times in the OT, its first occurrence is in Ex. 4:21, where God mentions the "wonders" that Moses will perform before Pharaoh. *Mophet* is (*cont. on next page*)

8 [a]Deut. 32:10; Ps. 17:8 [1]Lit. *pupil*
9 [a]Is. 19:16 [b]Zech. 4:9 [1]*booty* or *plunder*
10 [a]Is. 12:6 [b][Lev. 26:12]
11 [a][Is. 2:2, 3] [b]Zech. 3:10 [c]Ex. 12:49 [d]Ezek. 33:33
12 [a][Deut. 32:9]; Ps. 33:12; Jer. 10:16
13 [a]Hab. 2:20; Zeph. 1:7 [b]Ps. 68:5

CHAPTER 3

1 [a]Ezra 5:2; Hag. 1:1; Zech. 6:11 [b]1 Chr. 21:1; Job 1:6; Ps. 109:6; [Rev. 12:9, 10] [1]Lit. *the Adversary* *See WW at Job 1:6.
2 [a]Mark 9:25; [Jude 9] [b][Rom. 8:33] [c]Amos 4:11; Jude 23
3 [a]Ezra 9:15; Is. 64:6
4 [a]Gen. 3:21; Is. 61:10
5 [a]Ex. 29:6
7 [a]Lev. 8:35; Ezek. 44:16 [b]Deut. 17:9, 12 [c]Zech. 3:4 *See WW at Deut. 32:36.
8 [a]Ps. 71:7 [b]Is. 42:1 [c]Is. 11:1; 53:2; Jer. 23:5; 33:15; Zech. 6:12 [1]Lit. *men of a sign* or *wonder*

2:11 This verse encourages us in the task of world evangelization. Far from being "the tribal God of the Hebrews," as some suggest, God is the Lord over all nations. See Matt. 28:19, 20; John 10:16. **That day:** See note on Obad. 15.

3:1–10 The Lord Himself, not the interpreting angel, shows Zechariah this vision. This marks the fourth vision as unique among the eight. The essence of this vision is the cleansing of the priests and the land. There was religious and moral impurity among the recently returned exiles. Ezra addressed this same impurity (Ezra 9; 10).

3:1 Satan is part of the heavenly council, speaking directly to God as an accuser. Compare his role in Job 1.

3:3–5 See section 1 of Truth-In-Action at the end of Zech.

3:8 The cleansing of Joshua is symbolic of God's cleansing of the people; the cleansing takes place through God's **Servant the BRANCH,** a definite type of Christ. When Christ first came to cleanse national Israel, Israel was blinded to His true identity. At His Second Advent they will receive Him as their Messiah. In the interim, Jesus Christ is cleansing His spiritual Israel, the church (see 6:12–15).

(*cont. from preceding page*)
translated "miracle" in Ex. 7:9. Generally it is translated "sign" (2 Chr. 32:24) or "wonder" (Ps. 105:27). While *mophet* contains the idea of something miraculous, in some references it seems to connote an illustration or an example. For instance, the psalmist appears to make a complaint when he states, "I have become as a wonder to many" (Ps. 71:7). Ezekiel is described as a "sign" to the house of Israel (Ezek. 12:6, 11; 24:24, 27).

9 For behold, the stone
That I have laid before Joshua:
[a]Upon the stone *are* [b]seven eyes.
Behold, I will engrave its
inscription,'
Says the LORD of hosts,
'And [c]I will remove the iniquity of
that land in one day.
10 [a]In that day,' says the LORD of
hosts,
'Everyone will invite his neighbor
[b]Under his vine and under his fig
tree.' "

Vision of the Lampstand and Olive Trees

3 4 Now [a]the angel who talked with
me came back and wakened me,
[b]as a man who is wakened out of his
sleep.
2 And he said to me, "What do you
see?" So I said, "I am looking, and
there *is* [a]a lampstand of solid gold with
a bowl on top of it, [b]and on the *stand*
seven lamps with seven pipes to the
seven lamps.
3 [a]"Two olive trees *are* by it, one at
the right of the bowl and the other at
its left."
4 So I answered and spoke to the angel who talked with me, saying, "What
are these, my lord?"
5 Then the angel who talked with me
answered and said to me, "Do you not
know what these are?" And I said, "No,
my lord."
6 So he answered and said to me:

"This *is* the word of the LORD to
[a]Zerubbabel:
[b]'Not by **might** nor by *power, but
by My Spirit,'
Says the LORD of hosts.

9 [a][Zech. 4:10; Rev. 5:6] [b]Ps. 118:22 [c]Jer. 31:34; 50:20; Zech. 3:4
10 [a]Zech. 2:11 [b]1 Kin. 4:25; Is. 36:16; Mic. 4:4

CHAPTER 4

1 [a]Zech. 1:9; 2:3 [b]Dan. 8:18
2 [a]Rev. 1:12 [b]Ex. 25:37; [Rev. 4:5]
3 [a]Rev. 11:3, 4
6 [a]Hag. 1:1 [b]Is. 30:1; Hos. 1:7; Hag. 2:4, 5 *See WW at Deut. 8:18.
7 [a]Ps. 114:4, 6; Is. 40:4; Jer. 51:25; Nah. 1:5; Zech. 14:4, 5; [Matt. 21:21] [b]Ps. 118:22 [c]Ezra 3:10, 11, 13; Ps. 84:11 *See WW at Zech. 12:10.
9 [a]Ezra 3:8–10; 5:16; Hag. 2:18 [b]Ezra 6:14, 15; Zech. 6:12, 13 [c]Zech. 2:9, 11; 6:15 [1]Lit. *house*

WORD WEALTH

4:6 might, *chayil* (*cha*-yeel); Strong's #2428: Strength, power, force, might (especially an army); valor, substance, wealth. *Chayil* occurs more than 230 times. Its basic meaning is force, especially military strength. It may refer to the power of accumulated goods, that is, "wealth," as in Deut. 8:17. Occasionally *chayil* is translated "valor," especially when describing a military man (Judg. 3:29). It is translated "army" in such references as Deut. 11:4 and 2 Chr. 14:8. In the present reference, God informs the rebuilder of the temple that the task would not be accomplished through the force of an army (*chayil*) nor through the muscular power or physical stamina of the workmen; rather, it would be accomplished by the empowering of the Spirit of God.

7 'Who *are* you, [a]O great mountain? 4
Before Zerubbabel *you shall*
become a plain!
And he shall bring forth [b]the
capstone
[c]With shouts of *"Grace, grace to
it!" ' "
8 Moreover the word of the LORD
came to me, saying:
9 "The hands of Zerubbabel
[a]Have laid the foundation of this
[1]temple;
His hands [b]shall also finish *it*.
Then [c]you will know

3:9 There is no unanimity among scholars regarding what **the stone** with **seven eyes** (or facets) represents. It may be another designation of the Messiah. See Is. 8:14; Matt. 21:42.
4:1–14 The fifth vision consists of the vision (vv. 1–5, 11–14) and two speeches (vv. 6–10) to **Zerubbabel,** the governor. The essence is that Zerubbabel will complete the temple project **by My Spirit.**
4:1–6 See section 3 of Truth-In-Action at the end of Zech.
4:2 The intended representation of the **lampstand** is unclear; it may symbolize the people of Israel, or it may symbolize the presence of God. If the latter, the **seven lamps** correspond to "these seven . . . eyes of the LORD" (v. 10).
4:6 As governor of Judah, Zerubbabel is ultimately responsible for rebuilding the temple, but he is forbidden to trust the resources of man to accomplish the task. So today God's holy temple, the church, must be built and sustained, not by wealth, by members, by virtue, nor by sheer strength, but **by My Spirit.**
4:7–10 See section 4 of Truth-In-Action at the end of Zech.
4:7 When the temple is completed, all will acknowledge its beauty and realize it is not the result of human achievements, but rather, of God's **grace** and more **grace. O great mountain** could be the opposition of the adversaries of the temple project, the discouraged group of builders, or some type of turmoil among the people. At any rate, God will see to it that it **shall become a plain.** The NT use of "mountain" and Zechariah's obvious allusion to Is. 40:4 make this a future promise as well. The Messiah's future NT reign will see the removal of many "mountains" by God's grace.
4:9 After years of discouragement, **Zerubbabel** is assured that he will see the fulfillment of God's purpose for him (see Rom. 11:29).

That the [d]LORD of hosts has sent
Me to you.
10 For who has despised the day of
[a]small things?
For these seven rejoice to see
The [1]plumb line in the hand of
Zerubbabel.
[b]They are the eyes of the LORD,
Which scan to and fro throughout
the whole earth."

11 Then I answered and said to him,
"What *are* these [a]two olive trees—at
the right of the lampstand and at its
left?"
12 And I further answered and said to
him, "What *are these* two olive
branches that *drip* [1]into the receptacles
of the two gold pipes from which the
golden *oil* drains?"
13 Then he answered me and said, "Do
you not know what these *are*?" And I
said, "No, my lord."
14 So he said, [a]"These *are* the two
[1]anointed ones, [b]who stand beside the
Lord of the whole earth."

Vision of the Flying Scroll

5 Then I turned and raised my eyes,
and saw there a flying [a]scroll.
2 And he said to me, "What do you
see?" So I answered, "I see a flying
scroll. Its length *is* twenty cubits and
its width ten cubits."
3 Then he said to me, "This *is* the
[a]curse that goes out over the face of
the whole earth: 'Every thief shall be
expelled,' according *to* this side of *the
scroll;* and, 'Every perjurer shall be expelled,' according *to* that side of it."

4 "I will send out *the curse,*" says
the LORD of hosts;
"It shall enter the house of the
[a]thief
And the house of [b]the one who
swears falsely by My name.
It shall remain in the midst of his
house
And consume [c]it, with its timber
and stones."

Vision of the Woman in a Basket

5 Then the angel who talked with me
came out and said to me, "Lift your
eyes now, and see what this *is* that goes
forth."
6 So I asked, "What *is* it?" And he
said, "It *is* a [1]basket that is going
forth." He also said, "This *is* their resemblance throughout the earth:
7 "Here *is* a lead disc lifted up, and
this *is* a woman sitting inside the basket";
8 then he said, "This *is* Wickedness!"
And he thrust her down into the basket, and threw the lead [1]cover over its
mouth.
9 Then I raised my eyes and looked,
and there *were* two women, coming
with the wind in their wings; for they
had wings like the wings of a [a]stork,
and they lifted up the basket between
earth and heaven.
10 So I said to the [a]angel who talked
with me, "Where are they carrying the
basket?"
11 And he said to me, "To [a]build a
house for it in [b]the land of [1]Shinar;
when it is ready, *the basket* will be set
there on its base."

Vision of the Four Chariots

6 Then I turned and raised my eyes
and looked, and behold, four chariots *were* coming from between two
mountains, and the mountains *were*
mountains of bronze.
2 With the first chariot *were* [a]red

9 [d][Is. 43:16]; Zech. 2:8
10 [a]Neh. 4:2–4; Amos 7:2, 5; Hag. 2:3 [b]2 Chr. 16:9; Prov. 15:3; Zech. 3:9 [1]Lit. *plummet stone*
11 [a]Zech. 4:3; Rev. 11:4
12 [1]Lit. *into the hands of*
14 [a]Rev. 11:4 [b]Zech. 3:1–7 [1]Lit. *sons of fresh oil*

CHAPTER 5

1 [a]Jer. 36:2; Ezek. 2:9; Rev. 5:1
3 [a]Mal. 4:6
4 [a]Ex. 20:15; Lev. 19:11 [b]Ex. 20:7; Lev. 19:12; Is. 48:1; Jer. 5:2; Zech. 8:17; Mal. 3:5 [c]Lev. 14:34, 35; Job 18:15
6 [1]Heb. *ephah,* a measuring container, and so elsewhere
8 [1]Lit. *stone*
9 [a]Lev. 11:13, 19; Ps. 104:17; Jer. 8:7
10 [a]Zech. 5:5
11 [a]Jer. 29:5, 28 [b]Gen. 10:10; Is. 11:11; Dan. 1:2 [1]Babylon

CHAPTER 6

2 [a]Zech. 1:8; Rev. 6:4

4:14 The two anointed ones ("two olive trees," v. 3) are Joshua, representing the religious authority, and Zerubbabel, representing the civil authority. They are archetypes of the two witnesses mentioned in Rev. 11:3, 4.

5:1–4 The sixth vision of the **flying scroll,** said to be **twenty cubits** (30 feet) by **ten cubits** (15 feet), denounces the sins of breaking oaths sworn in God's name and of thievery. The size of the scroll denotes the seriousness of the matter; the fact that it is flying shows that the judgment is from God.

5:5–11 The seventh vision promises the removal of **Wickedness** from the land, symbolized by a **woman** trying to escape in **a basket** but forced back into it. The basket is finally removed altogether from the land.

5:11 Wickedness is consigned to the land of **Shinar** (Babylon). By the time of this prophecy, Babylon had become the world focus of idolatry and wickedness. Symbolically, then, wickedness is taken from Judah to Babylon. The exiled Jews return from Babylon to Judah, and wickedness is to be banished from Judah to Babylon.

6:1–8 The final vision of the **four chariots** depicts God's sovereign control over the Earth. Some commentators see a parallel between the four horses in this passage and the four horses of Rev. 6. However, apart from having similar colors, their connection is not clear. Furthermore, there is no apparent significance to the various colors. Similarly, the identity of the **south country** and **north country** are symbolic of governments **of all the earth,** rather than types of particular modern nations. God's Spirit is seen as resting in the north country because at that time Babylon was Judah's greatest potential enemy.

6:1 The number **four** represents God's control of the four quarters of the Earth. **Chariots** were not used for transportation but for war. This vision, therefore, deals with God's sovereign judgment over the Earth.

horses, with the second chariot [b]black
horses,
3 with the third chariot white horses,
and with the fourth chariot dappled
horses—strong *steeds.*
4 Then I answered [a]and said to the
angel who talked with me, "What *are*
these, my lord?"
5 And the angel answered and said
to me, [a]"These *are* four spirits of
heaven, who go out from *their* [b]station
before the Lord of all the earth.
6 [1]"The one with the black horses is
going to [a]the north country, the white
are going after them, and the dappled
are going toward the south country."
7 Then the strong *steeds* went out, eager to go, that they might [a]walk to and
fro throughout the earth. And He said,
"Go, walk to and fro throughout the
earth." So they walked to and fro
throughout the earth.
8 And He called to me, and spoke to
me, saying, "See, those who go toward
the north country have given rest to
My [a]Spirit in the north country."

The Command to Crown Joshua

9 Then the word of the LORD came to
me, saying:
5 10 "Receive *the gift* from the captives—from Heldai, Tobijah, and Jedaiah, who have come from Babylon—
and go the same day and enter the
house of Josiah the son of Zephaniah.
11 "Take the silver and gold, make
[a]an[1] elaborate crown, and set *it* on the
head of [b]Joshua the son of Jehozadak,
the high priest.
12 "Then speak to him, saying, 'Thus
says the LORD of hosts, saying:

"Behold, [a]the Man whose name *is*
the [b]BRANCH!
From His place He shall [1]branch
out,
[c]And He shall build the temple of
the LORD;
13 Yes, He shall build the temple of
the LORD.
He [a]shall bear the *glory,
And shall sit and rule on His
throne;
So [b]He shall be a priest on His
throne,
And the **counsel** of peace shall be
between [1]them both."'

WORD WEALTH

6:13 counsel, *'etsah* (ayst-*ah*); Strong's #6098: Advice; plan; counsel; purpose. This noun comes from the verb *ya'ats,* "to counsel, to advise." *'Etsah* occurs about 85 times, referring both to the Lord's counsel (Ps. 73:24; Jer. 32:19) and the counsel of a true friend, or a group of wise persons (2 Chr. 10:8; Prov. 27:9). The superiority of divine counsel is shown in Ps. 33:11, "The counsel of the LORD stands forever." The present reference refers ultimately to the Lord Jesus, who shall sit as King and Priest on His throne. The counsel of peace (an agreement, plan, and purpose that results in wholeness) shall exist between His kingly and priestly roles. Someday, by God's plan or advice, all powers will be laid on the Messiah's shoulder.

14 "Now the [1]elaborate crown shall be
[a]for a *memorial in the temple of the
LORD [2]for Helem, Tobijah, Jedaiah, and
Hen the son of Zephaniah.
15 "Even [a]those from afar shall come
and build the temple of the LORD. Then
you shall know that the LORD of hosts
has sent Me to you. And *this* shall
come to pass if you diligently obey the
voice of the LORD your God."

Obedience Better than Fasting

7 Now in the fourth year of King Darius it came to pass *that* the word
of the LORD came to Zechariah, on the
fourth day of the ninth month, Chislev,
2 when [1]*the people* sent [2]Sherezer,
with Regem-Melech and his men, *to*
[3]the house of God, [4]to pray before the
LORD,
3 *and* to [a]ask the priests who *were* in

2 [b]Rev. 6:5
4 [a]Zech. 5:10
5 [a][Ps. 104:4; Heb. 1:7, 14] [b]1 Kin. 22:19; Dan. 7:10; Zech. 4:14; Luke 1:19
6 [a]Jer. 1:14; Ezek. 1:4 [1]The chariot
7 [a]Gen. 13:17; Zech. 1:10
8 [a]Eccl. 10:4
11 [a]Ex. 29:6 [b]Ezra 3:2; Hag. 1:1; Zech. 3:1 [1]Lit. *crowns*
12 [a]John 1:45 [b]Is. 4:2; 11:1; Jer. 23:5; 33:15; Zech. 3:8 [c][Matt. 16:18; Eph. 2:20; Heb. 3:3] [1]Lit. *sprout up*
13 [a]Is. 22:24 [b]Ps. 110:4; [Heb. 3:1] [1]Both offices *See WW at 1 Chr. 29:11.
14 [a]Ex. 12:14; Mark 14:9 [1]Lit. *crowns* [2]So with MT, Tg., Vg.; Syr. *for Heldai* (cf. v. 10); LXX *for the patient ones* *See WW at Ex. 39:7.
15 [a]Is. 57:19; [Eph. 2:13]

CHAPTER 7

2 [1]Lit. *they,* cf. v. 5 [2]Or *Sar-Ezer* [3]Heb. *Bethel* [4]Or *to entreat the favor of*
3 [a]Deut. 17:9; Mal. 2:7

6:5 The imagery is changed from chariots to **spirits,** or winds. Having already referred to the four winds of heaven in 1:10, these winds may again refer to the four points of the Earth. The Holy Spirit scans the entire Earth to fulfill God's purposes.

6:10–15 See section 5 of Truth-In-Action at the end of Zech.

6:11 The **elaborate crown** is plural in Hebrew. No high priest in the OT was ever crowned king. While he was allowed to wear a turban, he was forbidden to wear a crown. Thus Joshua clearly prefigures the One who will wear the crown, filling both offices of king and priest. The many crowns are probably reflected in Rev. 19:12 where "on His head *were* many crowns."

6:13 The **counsel of peace** is the wisdom that results in reconciliation and inner tranquility. The Messiah will wisely and harmoniously execute **them both,** the offices of king and priest.

6:15 Those from afar who come and **build the** [spiritual] **temple** are believing Gentiles who submit to the Messiah.

7:1 The date for this two-chapter collection of sermons is almost two years after the date given in 1:7. The sermons stress certain themes from the visions—the rebuilding of Jerusalem and the temple, obedience, and participation of the nations in God's future reign.

7:3–7 The **fast in the fifth month** likely commemorated the destruction of the temple in 587 B.C. Zechariah used their

the house of the LORD of hosts, and the
prophets, saying, "Should I weep in
[b]the fifth month and [1]fast as I have
done for so many years?"
2 4 Then the word of the LORD of hosts
came to me, saying,
5 "Say to all the people of the land,
and to the priests: 'When you [a]fasted
and mourned in the fifth [b]and seventh
months [c]during those seventy years,
did you really fast [d]for Me—for Me?
6 [a]'When you eat and when you
drink, do you not eat and drink *for
yourselves?*
7 *'Should you* not *have obeyed* the
words which the LORD proclaimed
through the [a]former prophets when Jerusalem and the cities around it were
inhabited and prosperous, and [b]the
[1]South and the Lowland were inhabited?' "

Disobedience Resulted in Captivity

8 Then the word of the LORD came to
Zechariah, saying,
9 "Thus says the LORD of hosts:

[a]'Execute true justice,
Show [1]mercy and compassion
Everyone to his brother.
10 [a]Do not oppress the widow or the
fatherless,
The alien or the *poor.
[b]Let none of you plan evil in his
heart
Against his brother.'

2 11 "But they refused to heed,
[a]shrugged[1] their shoulders, and
[b]stopped[2] their ears so that they could
not hear.
12 "Yes, they made their [a]hearts like
flint, [b]refusing to hear the law and the
words which the LORD of hosts had
sent by His Spirit through the former
prophets. [c]Thus great wrath came
from the LORD of hosts.
13 "Therefore it happened, *that* just as
He proclaimed and they would not
hear, so [a]they called out and I would
not listen," says the LORD of hosts.
14 "But [a]I scattered them with a whirlwind among all the nations which they

3 [b]Zech. 8:19 [1]Lit. *consecrate myself*
5 [a][Is. 58:1–9] [b]Jer. 41:1 [c]Zech. 1:12 [d][Rom. 14:6]
6 [a]Deut. 12:7; 14:26; 1 Chr. 29:22
7 [a]Is. 1:16–20; Jer. 7:5, 23; Zech. 1:4 [b]Jer. 17:26 [1]Heb. *Negev*
9 [a]Is. 58:6, 7; Jer. 7:28 [1]Or *lovingkindness*
10 [a]Ex. 22:22; Ps. 72:4; Is. 1:17; Jer. 5:28 [b]Ps. 36:4; Ezek. 38:10; 45:9; Mic. 2:1; Zech. 8:16, 17 *See WW at Ps. 40:17.
11 [a]Neh. 9:29 [b]Jer. 17:23; Acts 7:57 [1]Lit. *gave a stubborn* or *rebellious shoulder* [2]Lit. *made their ears heavy*
12 [a]Ezek. 11:19 [b]Neh. 9:29, 30 [c]2 Chr. 36:16; Dan. 9:11, 12
13 [a]Prov. 1:24–28; Is. 1:15; Jer. 11:11; Mic. 3:4
14 [a]Lev. 26:33; Deut. 4:27; 28:64; Neh. 1:8

CHAPTER 8

2 [a]Joel 2:18; Nah. 1:2; Zech. 1:14 [1]Or *jealous* [2]Or *jealousy* [3]Lit. *heat* or *rage*
3 [a]Zech. 1:16 [b]Zech. 2:10, 11 [c]Is. 1:21 [d][Is. 2:2, 3] [e]Jer. 31:23
4 [a]1 Sam. 2:31; Is. 65:20 [1]Lit. *many days*

had not known. Thus the land became
desolate after them, so that no one
passed through or returned; for they
made the pleasant land desolate."

Jerusalem, Holy City of the Future

8 Again the word of the LORD of
hosts came, saying,
2 "Thus says the LORD of hosts:

[a]'I am [1]**zealous** for Zion with great
[2]zeal;
With great [3]fervor I am zealous
for her.'

WORD WEALTH

8:2 zealous, *qanah* (kah-*nah*); Strong's #7065: To be zealous, filled with zeal, full of emotion; to be passionate; also to be jealous or envious; to be highly possessive of something. *Qanah* and its derivatives appear approximately 90 times in the OT, often in the context of the Lord's becoming provoked to jealousy by the flirtations of His people with false gods. This is not a negative word, though, as it is the zeal of the Lord that will bring about the Messiah's eternal reign (Is. 9:7). In the present reference, God is either zealous with burning zeal for Zion, or jealous with burning jealousy, or perhaps, fanatic over His Jerusalem. Every nation has its plans for Jerusalem; God, too, has His plans (vv. 3–15), which must overrule all human schemes.

3 "Thus says the LORD:

[a]'I will return to Zion,
And [b]dwell in the midst of
Jerusalem.
Jerusalem [c]shall be called the
City of Truth,
[d]The Mountain of the LORD of
hosts,
[e]The Holy Mountain.'

4 "Thus says the LORD of hosts:

[a]'Old men and old women shall
again sit
In the streets of Jerusalem,
Each one with his staff in his hand
Because of [1]great age.

---

theological question to remind Judah that the real matter behind fasting is motive and attitude.

7:4–7 See section 2 of Truth-In-Action at the end of Zech.

7:9, 10 Clear, specific instructions are given to ensure the favor of God.

7:11, 12 See section 2 of Truth-In-Action at the end of Zech.

7:11, 14 Refusing to hear the Word of the Lord, judgment was swift as God **scattered them . . . among all the nations.**

8:1–17 The God who is jealous for Zion promises to **return to Zion, and dwell in the midst of Jerusalem.** The broad scope with which Zechariah speaks, together with the similarities to Ezek. 43, categorize these words as eschatological. Some see this passage as partially fulfilled in God's building of a new people in the church age, their focus being God's perfected people enjoying perfected worship in the New Jerusalem of Rev. 21. See notes on 2:1–13 and Obad. 15.

5 The streets of the city
Shall be [a]full of boys and girls
Playing in its streets.'

6 "Thus says the LORD of hosts:

'If it is [1]marvelous in the eyes of the remnant of this people in these days,
[a]Will it also be marvelous in My eyes?'
Says the LORD of hosts.

7 "Thus says the LORD of hosts:

'Behold, [a]I will save My people from the land of the [1]east
And from the land of the [2]west;
8 I will [a]bring them *back*,
And they shall dwell in the midst of Jerusalem.
[b]They shall be My people
And I will be their God,
[c]In truth and righteousness.'

9 "Thus says the LORD of hosts:

[a]'Let your hands be strong,
You who have been hearing in these days
These words by the mouth of [b]the prophets,
Who *spoke* in [c]the day the foundation was laid
For the house of the LORD of hosts,
That the temple might be *built.
10 For before these days
There were no [a]wages for man nor any hire for beast;
There was no peace from the enemy for whoever went out or came in;
For I set all men, everyone, against his neighbor.

11 [a]'But now I *will* not *treat* the remnant of this people as in the former
days,' says the LORD of hosts.

12 'For[a] the [1]seed *shall be* prosperous,
The vine shall give its fruit,
[b]The ground shall give her increase,
And [c]the heavens shall give their dew—
I will cause the remnant of this people
To possess all these.
13 And it shall come to pass
That just as you were [a]a curse among the nations,
O house of Judah and house of Israel,
So I will save you, and [b]you shall be a blessing.
Do not fear,
Let your hands be strong.'

14 "For thus says the LORD of hosts:

[a]'Just as I determined to [1]punish you
When your fathers provoked Me to wrath,'
Says the LORD of hosts,
[b]'And I would not relent,
15 So again in these days
I am determined to do good
To Jerusalem and to the house of Judah.
Do not fear.
16 These *are* the things you shall [a]do: 3
[b]Speak each man the truth to his neighbor;
Give judgment in your gates for truth, justice, and peace;
17 [a]Let none of you think evil in [1]your heart against your neighbor;
And do not love a false oath.
For all these *are things* that I hate,'
Says the LORD."

18 Then the word of the LORD of hosts
came to me, saying,
19 "Thus says the LORD of hosts:

[a]'The *fast of the fourth *month*,
[b]The fast of the fifth,
[c]The fast of the seventh,
[d]And the fast of the tenth,
Shall be [e]joy and gladness and cheerful *feasts
For the house of Judah.
[f]Therefore love *truth and peace.'

20 "Thus says the LORD of hosts:

5 [a]Jer. 30:19, 20
6 [a][Gen. 18:14; Luke 1:37] [1]Or *wonderful*
7 [a]Ps. 107:3; Is. 11:11; Ezek. 37:21 [1]Lit. *rising sun* [2]Lit. *setting sun*
8 [a]Zeph. 3:20; Zech. 10:10 [b][Jer. 30:22; 31:1, 33; Zech. 13:9] [c]Jer. 4:2
9 [a]1 Chr. 22:13; Is. 35:4; Hag. 2:4 [b]Ezra 5:1, 2; 6:14; Zech. 4:9 [c]Hag. 2:18 *See WW at Zech. 1:16.
10 [a]Hag. 1:6, 9
11 [a][Ps. 103:9]; Is. 12:1; Hag. 2:15–19
12 [a]Joel 2:22 [b]Ps. 67:6 [c]Hag. 1:10 [1]Lit. *seed of peace*
13 [a]Jer. 42:18 [b]Gen. 12:2; Ruth 4:11, 12; Is. 19:24, 25; Ezek. 34:26; [Zeph. 3:20]
14 [a]Jer. 31:28 [b][2 Chr. 36:16] [1]Lit. *bring calamity to you*
16 [a]Zech. 7:9, 10 [b]Ps. 15:2; [Prov. 12:17–19]; Zech. 8:3; [Eph. 4:25]
17 [a]Prov. 3:29; Jer. 4:14; Zech. 7:10 [1]Lit. *his*
19 [a]Jer. 52:6 [b]Jer. 52:12 [c]2 Kin. 25:25; Jer. 41:1, 2 [d]Jer. 52:4 [e]Esth. 8:17 [f]Zech. 8:16; Luke 1:74, 75 *See WW at Jon. 3:5. • See WW at Num. 9:2. • See WW at Ps. 25:5.

8:14, 15 The days of judgment now past, God is **determined to do good to Jerusalem.** Consequently, His people are admonished not to be afraid to approach Him with intimate devotion.
8:16, 17 See section 3 of Truth-In-Action at the end of Zech.
8:16 A restoration of fellowship with God begins by repentant attitudes producing godly actions toward our neighbors.
8:19 These fasts commemorate various events in Israel's history. **The fast of the fourth *month*** commemorates Jerusalem's capture in 587 B.C.; **the seventh** is either the Day of Atonement or an honoring of the assassination of Gedaliah, Judah's governor after Jerusalem's fall; **the tenth** is in memory of Jerusalem's siege in 588 B.C.

'Peoples shall yet come,
Inhabitants of many cities;
21 The inhabitants of one *city* shall go to another, saying,
[a]"Let us continue to go and pray before the LORD,
And *seek the LORD of hosts.
I myself will go also."
22 Yes, [a]many peoples and strong nations
Shall come to seek the LORD of hosts in Jerusalem,
And to pray before the LORD.'

23 "Thus says the LORD of hosts: 'In
those days ten men [a]from every language of the nations shall [b]grasp the
[1]sleeve of a Jewish man, saying, "Let
us go with you, for we have heard
[c]*that* God *is* with you." ' "

21 [a][Is. 2:2, 3; Mic. 4:1, 2] *See WW at Hos. 5:15.
22 [a]Is. 60:3; 66:23; [Zech. 14:16–21]
23 [a]Is. 3:6 [b][Is. 45:14] [c]1 Cor. 14:25 [1]Lit. *wing,* corner of a garment

CHAPTER 9

1 [a]Is. 17:1; Jer. 23:33 [b]Amos 1:3–5 [1]*oracle, prophecy*
2 [a]Jer. 49:23 [b]Is. 23; Jer. 25:22; 47:4; Ezek. 26; Amos 1:9, 10 [c]1 Kin. 17:9 [d]Ezek. 28:3
4 [a]Is. 23:1 [b]Ezek. 26:17
5 [a]Zeph. 2:4, 5

Israel Defended Against Enemies

9 The [1]burden of the word of the LORD
Against the land of Hadrach,
And [a]Damascus its resting place
(For [b]the eyes of men
And all the tribes of Israel
Are on the LORD);
2 Also *against* [a]Hamath, *which* borders on it,
And *against* [b]Tyre and [c]Sidon, though they are very [d]wise.

3 For Tyre built herself a tower,
Heaped up silver like the dust,
And gold like the mire of the streets.
4 Behold, [a]the LORD will cast her out;
He will destroy [b]her power in the sea,
And she will be devoured by fire.

5 Ashkelon shall see *it* and fear;
Gaza also shall be very sorrowful;
And [a]Ekron, for He dried up her expectation.
The king shall perish from Gaza,
And Ashkelon shall not be inhabited.

6 "A[1] mixed race shall settle [a]in Ashdod,
And I will cut off the pride of the [b]Philistines.
7 I will take away the blood from his mouth,
And the abominations from between his teeth.
But he who remains, even he *shall be* for our God,
And shall be like a leader in Judah,
And Ekron like a Jebusite.
8 [a]I will camp around My house
Because of the army,
Because of him who passes by and him who returns.
No more shall an oppressor pass through them,
For now I have seen with My eyes.

The Coming King

9 "Rejoice [a]greatly, O daughter of Zion!
Shout, O daughter of Jerusalem!
Behold, [b]your King is coming to you;
He *is* just and having salvation,
Lowly and riding on a donkey,
A colt, the foal of a donkey.

6 [a]Amos 1:8; Zeph. 2:4 [b]Ezek. 25:15–17 [1]Lit. *An illegitimate one*
8 [a][Ps. 34:7]
9 [a]Zeph. 3:14, 15; Zech. 2:10 [b][Ps. 110:1; Is. 9:6, 7; Jer. 23:5, 6]; Matt. 21:5; Mark 11:7, 9; Luke 19:38; John 12:15

KINGDOM DYNAMICS

9:9 The Lord of Lords or a Rabbi on a Colt?, MESSIAH'S COMING. This is the prophecy of the Lord's Triumphal Entry. We find accounts of its fulfillment in Matt. 21:1–11; Mark 11:1–11; Luke 19:28–44; and John 12:12–19. In this verse we see again how much God's ways differ from man's. Men looked for a conquering king, high and exalted, to come and deliver Jerusalem with an army of mighty men. What they saw was a meek and lowly Rabbi, riding upon a donkey's colt, and attended by a crowd of rejoicing peasants. He did not look like a conqueror. Yet one week later He had risen from the dead, having conquered death and hell.

(Mic. 5:2, 4, 5/Ps. 41:9) J.H.

8:22, 23 God's predisposition of grace toward Zion elicits a global attraction to the God of Israel as **many peoples and strong nations shall come to seek the LORD.**

9:1 The message of judgment is difficult to bear and is therefore described as a **burden.** Zechariah now changes his emphasis. The historical setting of chs. 9—14 is very difficult to identify. It is clearly apocalyptic and messianic, referring in symbolic language to events associated with the promised Messiah. Although the NT sheds great light on much of its fulfillment, this section is difficult. Bible students would do well to be cautious in drawing interpretive conclusions. Dogmatism in prophetic passages is generally unwise where the obvious interpretation is not evident.

9:9, 10 We do not know what, if any, specific historical reference Zechariah would have associated with this prophecy. What is clear is that Matthew refers it to Christ's Triumphal Entry (Matt. 21:5). This clear prediction of Christ's entry into Jerusalem was delivered some 400 years before its fulfillment.

10 I [a]will cut off the chariot from
Ephraim
And the horse from Jerusalem;
The [b]battle bow shall be cut off.
He shall speak peace to the
nations;
His **dominion** *shall be* [c]'from sea
to sea,
And from the River to the ends
of the earth.'

> **WORD WEALTH**
>
> **9:10 dominion,** *moshel* (moh-*shel*); Strong's #4915: Dominion, sovereignty, jurisdiction, rulership. This noun comes from the verb *mashal,* meaning "to rule, to govern, to reign, have dominion, exercise authority." This verb conveys the thought of a strong and sovereign ruling over one's subjects. Note its use in Gen. 37:8; Deut. 15:6; 1 Chr. 29:12; Ps. 8:6; 103:19. The noun *moshel* thus refers to the realm of rulership (both geographical and governmental) that belongs to a sovereign authority. In the present reference, the Messiah's dominion is described as universal, extending to the ends of the Earth.

God Will Save His People

11 "As for you also,
Because of the *blood of your
covenant,
I will set your [a]prisoners free
from the waterless pit.
12 Return to the stronghold,
[a]You prisoners of *hope.
Even today I declare
That I will restore [b]double to you.
13 For I have bent Judah, My *bow,*
Fitted the bow with Ephraim,
And raised up your sons, O Zion,
Against your sons, O Greece,
And made you like the sword of
a mighty man."

14 Then the LORD will be seen over
them,
And [a]His arrow will go forth like
lightning.
The Lord GOD will blow the
trumpet,
And go [b]with whirlwinds from
the south.
15 The LORD of hosts will [a]defend
them;
They shall devour and subdue
with slingstones.
They shall drink *and* roar as if
with wine;
They shall be filled *with blood*
like [1]basins,
Like the corners of the altar.
16 The LORD their God will [a]save
them in that day,
As the flock of His people.
For [b]they *shall be like* the
[1]jewels of a crown,
[c]Lifted like a banner over His
land—
17 For [a]how great is [1]its goodness
And how great [1]its [b]beauty!*
[c]Grain shall make the young men
thrive,
And new wine the young women.

Restoration of Judah and Israel

10 Ask [a]the LORD for [b]rain
In [c]the time of the [1]latter rain.
The LORD will make [2]flashing
clouds;
He will give them showers of rain,
Grass in the field for everyone.

2 For the [a]idols[1] speak delusion; **6**
The diviners envision [b]lies,
And tell false *dreams;
They [c]comfort in vain.
Therefore *the people* wend their
way like [d]sheep;
They are [2]in trouble [e]because
there is no shepherd.

3 "My anger is kindled against the
[a]shepherds,
[b]And I will punish the [1]goatherds.
For the LORD of hosts [c]will visit
His flock,
The house of Judah,

---

10 [a]Hos. 1:7; Mic. 5:10 [b]Ps. 46:9; Is. 2:4; Hos. 2:18; Mic. 4:3 [c]Ps. 72:8
11 [a]Is. 42:7 *See WW at Lev. 17:11.
12 [a]Is. 49:9; Jer. 17:13; Heb. 6:18–20 [b]Is. 61:7 *See WW at Hos. 2:15.
14 [a]Ps. 18:14; Hab. 3:11 [b]Is. 21:1
15 [a]Is. 37:35; Zech. 12:8 [1]Sacrificial basins
16 [a]Jer. 31:10, 11 [b]Is. 62:3; Mal. 3:17 [c]Is. 11:12 [1]Lit. *stones*
17 [a][Ps. 31:19] [b][Ps. 45:1–16] [c]Joel 3:18 [1]Lit. *His* *See WW at Ezek. 28:12.

CHAPTER 10

1 [a][Jer. 14:22] [b][Deut. 11:13, 14] [c][Joel 2:23] [1]Spring rain [2]Or *lightning flashes*
2 [a]Jer. 10:8 [b]Jer. 27:9; [Ezek. 13] [c]Job 13:4 [d]Jer. 50:6, 17 [e]Ezek. 34:5–8; Matt. 9:36; Mark 6:34 [1]Heb. *teraphim* [2]*afflicted* *See WW at Joel 2:28.
3 [a]Jer. 25:34–36; Ezek. 34:2; Zech. 11:17 [b]Ezek. 34:17 [c]Luke 1:68 [1]Leaders

---

9:10 The **dominion** of the Lord will eventually reach **to the ends of the earth** as many people experience God's covenant. The Great Commission, given by Jesus in Matt. 28:19, 20, contributes to the fulfillment of this prophecy.

9:15–17 These verses describe a warring, victorious people whom their Lord prizes as being ***like* the jewels of a crown.** The lesson for the people of God under the New Covenant is that God delights in a people who will engage in spiritual warfare, and He will exhibit them as a banner of victory (see Matt. 11:12).

9:16 That day: See note on Obad. 15.

10:1 Zechariah reminds Judah that God controls the **rain,** even **in the time of the latter rain** (spring), when one assumes there will be sufficient rain. Spiritually applied, only God can send sufficient blessings and power to enable one to mature in Christ. We are to ask for His blessing and not merely to assume it.

10:2 See section 6 of Truth-In-Action at the end of Zech.

10:3–12 This deals with God's indictment against past and present leaders of Judah and the future role of the Messiah as a Good Shepherd, including the restorative effect this will have. Again, this is best seen as messianic and apocalyptic.

10:3 The leadership, who should be **shepherds** to the people, more accurately resemble **goatherds,** an uncomplimentary term that can mean "male goats."

And [d]will make them as His royal
horse in the battle.
4 From him comes [a]the
cornerstone,
From him [b]the tent peg,
From him the battle bow,
From him every [1]ruler together.
5 They shall be like mighty men,
Who [a]tread down *their enemies*
In the mire of the streets in the
battle.
They shall fight because the LORD
is with them,
And the riders on horses shall be
put to shame.

6 "I will strengthen the house of
Judah,
And I will save the house of
Joseph.
[a]I will bring them back,
Because I [b]have* mercy on
them.
They shall be as though I had not
cast them aside;
For I *am* the LORD their God,
And I [c]will hear them.
7 *Those of* Ephraim shall be like a
mighty man,
And their [a]heart shall rejoice as
if with wine.
Yes, their children shall see *it* and
be glad;
Their heart shall *rejoice in the
LORD.
8 I will [a]whistle for them and
gather them,
For I will *redeem them;
[b]And they shall increase as they
once increased.
9 "I[a] will [1]sow* them among the
peoples,
And they shall [b]remember Me in
far countries;
They shall live, together with
their children,
And they shall return.
10 [a]I will also bring them back from
the land of Egypt,
And gather them from Assyria.
I will bring them into the land of
Gilead and Lebanon,
[b]Until no *more room* is found for
them.

3 [d]Song 1:9
4 [a]Is. 28:16 [b]Is. 22:23 [1]Or *despot*
5 [a]Ps. 18:42
6 [a]Jer. 3:18; Ezek. 37:21 [b]Hos. 1:7; Zech. 1:16 [c]Zech. 13:9 *See WW at Hos. 2:23.
7 [a]Ps. 104:15 *See WW at Hab. 3:18.
8 [a]Is. 5:26 [b]Is. 49:19; Ezek. 36:37; Zech. 2:4 *See WW at Neh. 1:10.
9 [a]Hos. 2:23 [b]Deut. 30:1 [1]Or *scatter* *See WW at Hos. 10:12.
10 [a]Is. 11:11; Hos. 11:11 [b]Is. 49:19, 20
11 [a]Is. 11:15 [b]Is. 14:25; Zeph. 2:13 [c]Ezek. 30:13 [1]The Nile
12 [a]Mic. 4:5

CHAPTER 11

1 [a]Zech. 10:10
2 [a]Ezek. 31:3 [b]Is. 32:19
3 [a]Jer. 25:34–36 [1]Or *floodplain, thicket*
5 [a][Jer. 2:3]; 50:7 [b]Deut. 29:19; Hos. 12:8; 1 Tim. 6:9 [c]Ezek. 34:2, 3 *See WW at Lev. 4:13.
6 [1]Lit. *strike*
7 [a]Jer. 39:10; Zeph. 3:12; Matt. 11:5 [1]So with MT, Tg., Vg.; LXX *for the Canaanites*

11 [a]He shall pass through the sea
with affliction,
And strike the waves of the sea:
All the depths of [1]the River shall
dry up.
Then [b]the pride of Assyria shall
be brought down,
And [c]the scepter of Egypt shall
depart.

12 "So I will strengthen them in the
LORD,
And [a]they shall walk up and
down in His name,"
Says the LORD.

Desolation of Israel

11 Open [a]your doors, O Lebanon,
That fire may devour your
cedars.
2 Wail, O cypress, for the [a]cedar
has fallen,
Because the mighty *trees* are
ruined.
Wail, O oaks of Bashan,
[b]For the thick forest has come
down.
3 *There is* the sound of wailing
[a]shepherds!
For their glory is in ruins.
There is the sound of roaring
lions!
For the [1]pride of the Jordan is in
ruins.

Prophecy of the Shepherds

4 Thus says the LORD my God, "Feed
the flock for slaughter,
5 "whose owners slaughter them and
[a]feel no *guilt; those who sell them
[b]say, 'Blessed be the LORD, for I am
rich'; and their shepherds do [c]not pity
them.
6 "For I will no longer pity the inhabitants of the land," says the LORD. "But
indeed I will give everyone into his
neighbor's hand and into the hand of
his king. They shall [1]attack the land,
and I will not deliver *them* from their
hand."
7 So I fed the flock for slaughter,
[1]in particular [a]the poor of the flock. I
took for myself two staffs: the one I

10:4 The Messiah is **the cornerstone, the tent peg** on which humankind's destiny hinges, **the battle bow** that conquers, and the **ruler** over all.
10:9 Though the covenant people be sown among the nations, God promises that **they shall return.** This prophecy was partially fulfilled in Zechariah's day in the return of the exiled Jews from Babylon. The prophecy will have a final fulfillment in the New Jerusalem, where not only Jews but all nations come to worship God.
11:1–3 The protracted strife in **Lebanon** in the latter decades of the twentieth century may be a partial fulfillment of this prophecy of judgment.
11:4–17 The main lesson is that if people will not listen to a good leader, they will surely suffer under numerous evil ones (**the three shepherds**). Interpretation of the details of this passage vary widely.

*called [2]Beauty, and the other I called
[3]Bonds; and I fed the flock.
8 I [1]dismissed the three shepherds
[a]in one month. My soul loathed them,
and their soul also abhorred me.
9 Then I said, "I will not feed you.
[a]Let what is dying die, and what is perishing perish. Let those that are left eat
each other's flesh."
10 And I took my staff, [1]Beauty, and
cut it in two, that I might break the covenant which I had *made with all the
peoples.
11 So it was broken on that day. Thus
[a]the[1] poor of the flock, who were
watching me, knew that it *was* the
word of the LORD.
12 Then I said to them, "If it is
[1]agreeable to you, give *me* my wages;
and if not, refrain." So they [a]weighed
out for my wages thirty *pieces* of silver.
13 And the LORD said to me, "Throw
it to the [a]potter"—that princely price
they set on me. So I took the thirty
pieces of silver and threw them into
the house of the LORD for the potter.
14 Then I cut in two my other staff,
[1]Bonds, that I might break the brotherhood between Judah and Israel.
15 And the LORD said to me, [a]"Next,
take for yourself the implements of a
foolish shepherd.
16 "For indeed I will raise up a shepherd in the land *who* will not care for
those who are cut off, nor seek the
young, nor *heal those that are broken,
nor *feed those that still stand. But he
will eat the flesh of the fat and tear
their hooves in [a]pieces.

17 "Woe[a] to the worthless shepherd,
Who leaves the flock!
A sword *shall be* against his arm
And against his right eye;
His arm shall completely wither,
And his right eye shall be totally
blinded."

The Coming Deliverance of Judah

12 The [1]burden of the word of the
LORD against Israel. Thus says
the LORD, [a]who stretches out the heavens, lays the foundation of the earth,
and [b]forms the spirit of man within
him:
2 "Behold, I will make Jerusalem
[a]a cup of [1]drunkenness to all the surrounding peoples, when they lay siege
against Judah and Jerusalem.
3 [a]"And it shall happen in that day
that I will make Jerusalem [b]a very
heavy stone for all peoples; all who
would heave it away will surely be cut
in pieces, though all nations of the
earth are gathered against it.
4 "In that day," says the LORD,
[a]"I will strike every horse with confusion, and its rider with madness; I will
open My eyes on the house of Judah,
and will strike every horse of the peoples with blindness.
5 "And the governors of Judah shall
say in their heart, 'The inhabitants of
Jerusalem *are* my strength in the LORD
of hosts, their God.'
6 "In that day I will make the governors of Judah [a]like a firepan in the
woodpile, and like a fiery torch in the
sheaves; they shall devour all the surrounding peoples on the right hand
and on the left, but Jerusalem shall be
inhabited again in her own place—Jerusalem.
7 "The LORD will save the tents of Judah first, so that the glory of the house
of David and the glory of the inhabitants of Jerusalem shall not become
greater than that of Judah.
8 "In that day the LORD will defend
the inhabitants of Jerusalem; the one
who is feeble among them in that day
shall be like David, and the house of
David *shall be* like God, like the Angel
of the LORD before them.
9 "It shall be in that day *that* I will
seek to [a]destroy all the nations that
come against Jerusalem.

Mourning for the Pierced One

10 [a]"And I will pour on the house of
David and on the inhabitants of Jerusalem the Spirit of **grace** and supplica-

7 [2]Or *Grace* [3]Or *Unity* *See WW at Jer. 33:3.
8 [a]Hos. 5:7 [1]Or *destroyed,* lit. *cut off*
9 [a]Jer. 15:2
10 [1]Or *Grace* *See WW at Ex. 34:27.
11 [a]Zeph. 3:12; Matt. 27:50; Mark 15:37; Luke 23:46; Acts 8:32 [1]So with MT, Tg., Vg.; LXX *the Canaanites*
12 [a]Gen. 37:28; Ex. 21:32; Matt. 26:15; 27:9, 10 [1]*good in your sight*
13 [a]Matt. 27:3–10; Acts 1:18, 19
14 [1]Or *Unity*
15 [a]Is. 56:11; Ezek. 34:2
16 [a]Ezek. 34:1–10; Mic. 3:1–3 *See WW at Ex. 15:26. • See WW at Ps. 55:22.
17 [a]Jer. 23:1; Ezek. 34:2; Zech. 10:2; 11:15; John 10:12, 13

CHAPTER 12

1 [a]Is. 42:5; 44:24 [b]Num. 16:22; [Eccl. 12:7; Is. 57:16]; Heb. 12:9 [1]*oracle, prophecy*
2 [a]Is. 51:17 [1]Lit. *reeling*
3 [a]Zech. 12:4, 6, 8; 13:1 [b]Matt. 21:44
4 [a]Ps. 76:6; Ezek. 38:4
6 [a]Is. 10:17, 18; Obad. 18; Zech. 11:1
9 [a]Hag. 2:22
10 [a]Jer. 31:9; 50:4; Ezek. 39:29; [Joel 2:28, 29

11:12, 13 Thirty *pieces* of silver was the price of a slave. See Ex. 21:32 and Matt. 27:3–9.

11:7, 10, 14 The shepherd uses two staffs to do his work (see Ps. 23:4): **Beauty,** representing God's gracious actions to protect His flock, and **Bonds,** indicating His desire to bring unity among them.

12:1–9 This passage describes God's judgment against the nations that attack **Jerusalem.** Both Jerusalem and **Israel** represent all God's people; **all the surrounding peoples** are the physical and spiritual enemies of His people. God's manner of judgment (**I will strike**) will take many forms, as exemplified in the totality of biblical history. Armageddon (Rev. 16:16) may be its large-scale climax.

12:9 That day: See note on Obad. 15.

12:10 The outpouring of **the Spirit of grace and supplication** results in conviction and repentance. See John 16:8–11. Both "grace " and "supplication" have the same Hebrew root, meaning "to become amenable to someone." The Holy Spirit breaks through any hostility to the Messiah, making the **inhabitants of Jerusalem** receptive to Him.

12:10–14 These verses depict great future mourning among God's people for piercing God Himself (**Me whom they pierced**). The allusion is obviously to Is. 53, referring to a future event during the time of the Messiah and coinciding

tion; then they will [b]look on Me whom
they pierced. Yes, they will mourn for
Him [c]as one mourns for *his* *only *son*,
and grieve for Him as one grieves for
a firstborn.

WORD WEALTH

12:10 grace, *chen* (*chayn*); Strong's #2580: Favor, grace, graciousness, kindness, beauty, pleasantness, charm, attractiveness, loveliness, affectionate regard. The root *chanan* means "to act graciously or mercifully toward someone; to be compassionate, to be favorably inclined." God's grace poured out upon Jerusalem enables them to look longingly and beseechingly toward their pierced King. God's grace will result in Israel's seeing Jesus as someone of infinite beauty. His goodness enables them to repent. The Holy Spirit is called "the Spirit of grace" in Heb. 10:29, a title no doubt inspired by this reference in Zech.

11 "In that day there shall be a great
[a]mourning in Jerusalem, [b]like the
mourning at Hadad Rimmon in the
plain of [1]Megiddo.
12 [a]"And the land shall mourn, every
family by itself: the family of the house
of David by itself, and their wives by
themselves; the family of the house of
[b]Nathan by itself, and their wives by
themselves;
13 "the family of the house of Levi by
itself, and their wives by themselves;
the family of Shimei by itself, and their
wives by themselves;
14 "all the *families that remain, every
family by itself, and their wives by
themselves.

Idolatry Cut Off

13 "In that [a]day [b]a fountain shall
be opened for the house of Da-
vid and for the inhabitants of Jerusalem, for sin and for [c]uncleanness.
2 "It shall be in that day," says the
LORD of hosts, "*that* I will [a]cut off the
names of the idols from the land, and

10 [b]John 19:34, 37; 20:27; [Rev. 1:7] [c]Jer. 6:26; Amos 8:10 *See WW at Gen. 22:2. **11** [a][Matt. 24:30]; Acts 2:37; [Rev. 1:7] [b]2 Kin. 23:29 [1]Heb. *Megiddon* **12** [a][Matt. 24:30; Rev. 1:7] [b]Luke 3:31 **14** *See WW at Gen. 12:3.

CHAPTER 13

1 [a]Acts 10:43; [Rev. 21:6, 7] [b]Ps. 36:9; [Heb. 9:14; 1 John 1:7] [c]Num. 19:17; Is. 4:4; Ezek. 36:25 **2** [a]Ex. 23:13; Hos. 2:17 [b]Jer. 23:14, 15; 2 Pet. 2:1

3 [a]Deut. 18:20; [Ezek. 14:9] [b]Deut. 13:6–11; [Matt. 10:37] **4** [a]Jer. 6:15; 8:9; [Mic. 3:6, 7] [b]2 Kin. 1:8; Is. 20:2; Matt. 3:4 **5** [a]Amos 7:14 **6** [1]Or *hands* **7** [a]Is. 40:11; Ezek. 34:23, 24; 37:24; Mic. 5:2, 4 [b][John 10:30] [c]Matt. 26:31, 56, 67; Mark 14:27; 1 Pet. 5:4; Rev. 7:16, 17 [d]Luke 12:32 **8** [a]Is. 6:13; Ezek. 5:2, 4, 12 [b][Rom. 11:5] **9** [a]Is. 48:10; Ezek. 20:38; Mal. 3:3 [b]1 Pet. 1:6, 7 [c]Ps. 50:15; Zeph. 3:9; [Zech. 12:10] [d]Jer. 30:22; Hos. 2:23

they shall no longer be remembered. I
will also cause [b]the prophets and the
unclean spirit to depart from the land.
3 "It shall come to pass *that* if anyone
still prophesies, then his father and
mother who begot him will say to him,
'You shall [a]not live, because you have
spoken lies in the name of the LORD.'
And his father and mother who begot
him [b]shall thrust him through when he
prophesies.
4 "And it shall be in that day *that*
[a]every prophet will be ashamed of his
vision when he prophesies; they will
not wear [b]a robe of coarse hair to deceive.
5 [a]"But he will say, 'I *am* no prophet,
I *am* a farmer; for a man taught me to
keep cattle from my youth.'
6 "And *one* will say to him, 'What are
these wounds between your [1]arms?'
Then he will answer, '*Those* with
which I was wounded in the house of
my friends.'

The Shepherd Savior

7 "Awake, O sword, against
[a]My Shepherd,
Against the Man [b]who is My
Companion,"
Says the LORD of hosts.
[c]"Strike the Shepherd,
And the sheep will be scattered;
Then I will turn My hand against
[d]the little ones.
8 And it shall come to pass in all
the land,"
Says the LORD,
"*That* [a]two-thirds in it shall be cut
off *and* die,
[b]But *one*-third shall be left in it:
9 I will bring the *one*-third 4
[a]through the fire,
Will [b]**refine** them as silver is
refined,
And test them as gold is tested.
[c]They will call on My name,
And I will answer them.
[d]I will say, 'This *is* My people';
And each one will say, 'The LORD
is my God.' "

with many truths of Ezek. 36. John applies it directly to Jesus Christ at the time of His crucifixion (John 19:37).

13:1 The gushing **fountain** is a beautiful type of cleansing through union with Christ. No longer forsaking the fountain of living waters (see Jer. 2:13), the recipients are washed from **sin** (missing the mark) and **uncleanness** (ritual and sexual impurity).

13:2 God's cleansing during the age of the Messiah will be radical. **The unclean spirit** is a rare OT reference to God's decisive dealing with demons. **The prophets** are false prophets who continue to speak during the days of the Messiah.

13:7 Strike the Shepherd, and the sheep will be scattered is a tragic principle that is illustrated time and again throughout church history. Jesus applied this verse to Himself in Matt. 26:31.

13:8, 9 The idea here is one of a purified remnant, **as silver is refined** and **as gold is tested.**

13:9 See section 4 of Truth-In-Action at the end of Zech.

WORD WEALTH

13:9 refine, *tsaraph* (tsah-*rahf*); Strong's #6884: To melt; to refine, test, or purify metal; any refining, whether literal or figurative; to prove, smelt, examine; to try by fire. This verb, which occurs more than 30 times, refers to that melting process whereby impurities are removed from precious metals, such as gold or silver. In Ps. 26:2, David beseeches God, "Try [refine] my mind and my heart." In Ps. 12:6, God's pure words are compared to silver purified seven times in a furnace. Compare Ps. 17:3; 66:10; Is. 1:25.

The Day of the LORD

14 Behold, [a]the day of the LORD
is coming,
And your [1]spoil will be divided in
your midst.
2 For [a]I will gather all the nations
to battle against Jerusalem;
The city shall be taken,
The houses [1]rifled,
And the women ravished.
Half of the city shall go into
captivity,
But the remnant of the people
shall not be cut off from the
city.

3 Then the LORD will go forth
And fight against those nations,
As He fights in the day of battle.
4 And in that day His feet will stand
[a]on the Mount of Olives,
Which faces Jerusalem on the
east.
And the Mount of Olives shall be
split in two,
From east to west,
[b]*Making* a very large valley;
Half of the mountain shall move
toward the north
And half of it toward the south.

5 Then you shall flee *through* My
mountain valley,
For the mountain valley shall
reach to Azal.
Yes, you shall flee
As you fled from the [a]earthquake
In the days of Uzziah king of
Judah.

[b]Thus the LORD my God will come,
And [c]all the saints with [1]You.

6 It shall come to pass in that day
That there will be no light;
The [1]lights will diminish.
7 It shall be one day
[a]Which is known to the LORD—
Neither day nor night.
But at [b]evening *time it shall
happen
That it will be light.

8 And in that day it shall be
That living [a]waters shall flow
from Jerusalem,
Half of them toward [1]the eastern
sea
And half of them toward
[2]the western sea;
In both summer and winter it
shall occur.
9 And the LORD shall be [a]King over
all the earth.
In that *day it shall be—
[b]"The LORD *is* one,"
And His *name one.

10 All the land shall be turned into a
plain from Geba to Rimmon south of
Jerusalem. [1]*Jerusalem* shall be raised
up and [a]inhabited in her place from
Benjamin's Gate to the place of the
First Gate and the Corner Gate, [b]and
from the Tower of Hananel to the
king's winepresses.

11 *The people* shall dwell in it;
And [a]no longer shall there be
utter destruction,
[b]But Jerusalem shall be safely
inhabited.

12 And this shall be the plague with
which the LORD will strike all the people who fought against Jerusalem:

CHAPTER 14

1 [a][Is. 13:6, 9; Joel 2:1; Mal. 4:1] [1]*plunder* or *booty*
2 [a]Joel 3:2; Zech. 12:2, 3 [1]Or *plundered*
4 [a]Ezek. 11:23; Acts 1:9–12 [b]Joel 3:12
5 [a]Is. 29:6; Amos 1:1 [b][Ps. 96:13]; Is. 66:15, 16; Matt. 24:30, 31; 25:31; Jude 14 [c]Joel 3:11 [1]Or *you;* LXX, Tg., Vg. *Him*
6 [1]Lit. *glorious ones*
7 [a]Matt. 24:36 [b]Is. 30:26 *See WW at Is. 33:6.
8 [a]Ezek. 47:1–12; Joel 3:18; [John 7:38; Rev. 22:1, 2] [1]The Dead Sea [2]The Mediterranean Sea
9 [a][Jer. 23:5, 6; Rev. 11:15] [b][Eph. 4:5, 6]; Deut. 6:4 *See WW at Zeph. 1:7. • See WW at Deut. 18:5.
10 [a]Jer. 30:18; Zech. 12:6 [b]Neh. 3:1; Jer. 31:38 [1]Lit. *She*
11 [a]Jer. 31:40 [b]Jer. 23:6; Ezek. 34:25–28; Hos. 2:18

14:1–5 The day of the LORD (see note on Obad. 15) refers to end times. It coincides with many of the events in Rev. The nature of the language, like that in Rev., is apocalyptic (highly symbolic, prophetic language). This makes it very difficult to determine what is to take place literally and what *is symbolic, happening only in type or in the spiritual realm.* What the NT (Acts 1:11) does make clear is the literal return of the Messiah, depicted here in v. 4.

14:4 When the Lord returns, **His feet will stand on the Mount of Olives,** from which He ascended into heaven (see Acts 1:9–12).

14:9–21 Final references to end-time events and God's reign in the world to come are again stated in apocalyptic language.

14:9 The LORD shall be King over all the earth: The task of world evangelization will be accomplished and all things will be consummated in Christ. This is the fulfillment of the covenant God made with David that he would have a descendant to sit on his throne forever. See 2 Sam. 7:12–16; Luke 1:32, 33.

14:12 The rapidity with which **the plague** strikes **the people who fought against Jerusalem** is graphically described. Some feel this may be an ancient prophetic description of the ghastly effects of modern warfare.

Their flesh shall [1]dissolve while
they stand on their feet,
Their eyes shall dissolve in their
sockets,
And their tongues shall dissolve
in their mouths.

13 It shall come to pass in that day
That [a]a great panic from the LORD
will be among them.
Everyone will seize the hand of
his neighbor,
And raise [b]his hand against his
neighbor's hand;
14 Judah also will fight at Jerusalem.
[a]And the wealth of all the
surrounding nations
Shall be gathered together:
Gold, silver, and apparel in great
abundance.

15 [a]Such also shall be the plague
On the horse *and* the mule,
On the camel and the donkey,
And on all the cattle that will be
in those camps.
So *shall* this plague *be*.

The Nations Worship the King

16 And it shall come to pass *that*
everyone who is left of all the nations
which came against Jerusalem shall
[a]go up from year to year to [b]worship
the King, the LORD of hosts, and to
*keep [c]the Feast of Tabernacles.
17 [a]And it shall be *that* whichever of
the families of the earth do not come
up to Jerusalem to worship the King,
the LORD of hosts, on them there will
be no rain.
18 If the family of [a]Egypt will not come
up and enter in, [b]they *shall have* no
rain; they shall receive the plague with
which the LORD strikes the nations who
do not come up to keep the Feast of
Tabernacles.
19 This shall be the [1]punishment of
Egypt and the punishment of all the
nations that do not come up to keep
the Feast of Tabernacles.
20 In that day [a]"HOLINESS TO THE
LORD" shall be *engraved* on the bells
of the horses. The [b]pots in the LORD's
house shall be like the bowls before the
altar.
21 Yes, [1]every pot in Jerusalem and
Judah shall be holiness to the LORD of
hosts. Everyone who sacrifices shall
come and take them and cook in them.
In that day there shall no longer be a
[a]Canaanite [b]in the house of the LORD
of hosts.

12 [1]Lit. *decay*
13 [a]1 Sam. 14:15, 20 [b]Judg. 7:22; 2 Chr. 20:23; Ezek. 38:21
14 [a]Ezek. 39:10, 17
15 [a]Zech. 14:12
16 [a][Is. 2:2, 3; 60:6–9; 66:18–21; Mic. 4:1, 2] [b]Is. 27:13 [c]Lev. 23:34–44; Neh. 8:14; Hos. 12:9; John 7:2 *See WW at Ex. 23:14.
17 [a]Is. 60:12
18 [a]Is. 19:21 [b]Deut. 11:10
19 [1]Lit. *sin*
20 [a]Ex. 28:36; 39:30; Is. 23:18; Jer. 2:3 [b]Ezek. 46:20
21 [a]Is. 35:8; Ezek. 44:9; Joel 3:17; Rev. 21:27; 22:15 [b][Eph. 2:19–22] [1]Or *on every pot . . . shall be engraved "HOLINESS TO THE LORD OF HOSTS"*

14:20, 21 When the Lord reigns, **HOLINESS TO THE LORD** will be inscribed, not only on outer artifacts, but on the hearts of His people. **No longer** will any **Canaanite** (a negative term for a greedy, unclean merchant) pollute **the house of the LORD of hosts.**

TRUTH-IN-ACTION through ZECHARIAH

Letting the LIFE of the Holy Spirit Bring Faith's Works Alive in You!

Truth Zechariah Teaches	Text	**Action** Zechariah Invites
1 Steps to Knowing God and His Ways Anything that God has said He will do, He will do. He does not make empty promises or vain threats. We must not interpret His patience and longsuffering toward disobedience as a failure to execute judgment. Rather, He desires our repentance and return. If we will return to Him, He will complete the work of perfecting He has promised.	1:2–6 1:16, 17 3:3–5	**Understand** that God does not issue threats of judgment in vain, and He always keeps His word. **Believe** and **understand** that God fully intends to bring His people to the maturity and prosperity He has always promised. **Believe** and **accept** that God forgives the sins of all who repent and turn to Him. **Be clothed** with His righteousness.

Truth Zechariah Teaches	Text	**Action** Zechariah Invites
2 Guidelines for Growing in Godliness Godliness involves godly practices from a godly heart. God rebukes those who fast or practice other religious acts to serve their own ends. The godly person keeps an open ear for God's Word, even when it is not pleasant or calls for change.	7:4–7	**Make sure** that when you fast your motives are unselfish. **Accompany** your fastings with attitudes and actions of righteousness and obedience.
	7:11, 12	**Open your ears** to prophetic or solemn warnings. **Know** that not to do so can result in calamity.
3 Steps to Holiness Holiness is a commitment to live exclusively for God in the way He has instructed.	4:1–6	**Depend on** the Holy Spirit to accomplish the things God has called you to do.
	8:16, 17	**Practice** honesty, truth, integrity, and justice in all interpersonal dealings. **Examine** your heart, and **avoid** any form of insincerity or hypocrisy.
4 Keys to Wise Living We must learn how to interpret circumstances from God's standpoint.	4:7–10	**Do not** allow yourself to be discouraged by "small things." **Understand** that God does not give the importance we do to the size of things. **Be assured** that what God has begun, He will complete in triumph.
	13:9	**Understand** that God's refining works are to purify His people and to train them in righteousness.
5 A Lesson in Faith The work of establishing and completing the ultimate temple (His body) is assigned to Jesus, but He wants our participation through obedience to His voice. Our gift becomes a memorial, but the glory is all His.	6:10–15	**Understand** that Jesus Christ has committed Himself to building His church and to completing it as a manifestation of His glory. **Remember** that your gift (v. 10) is important to the task and that your privilege is to **render all glory** to Him (v. 11).
6 A Lesson for Leaders Remember that God's Word is always true! Teach God's Word faithfully so that the long-term result will be fruitfulness and well being.	10:2	Leaders, **understand** that false prophecies, teaching that is erroneous or diluted, and personal opinion taught as truth all result in a church that lacks power, stability, and security.

The Book of MALACHI

Author: Malachi
Date: About 450 B.C.
Theme: Reassurance of God's Love and Justice
Key Words: Messenger, Priests, Sun of Righteousness, Day of Judgment

Author Though some attribute Malachi to an anonymous writer, thought by some to have been Ezra, using the pseudonym *Mal'aki* ("My Messenger"), it is best to see the book as written by the named prophet himself. Malachi is not mentioned anywhere else in the Bible, but from his writing we learn he had a great love for the people of Judah and the temple ceremonies. He was likely a contemporary of Nehemiah.

Date The lack of the mention of any kings or identifiable historical incidents makes dating the book somewhat difficult. The use of various Persian words in the text and the reference to a rebuilt temple (1:10) make a postexilic date concurrent with Nehemiah the most likely (about 450 B.C.). Malachi wrote as the last of the twelve Minor Prophets, the final inspired writer of Scripture until the New Testament.

Background As noted, Malachi is the last of a number of divinely inspired men who, over a period of a thousand years, foretold the coming of the Just One. Not only did they prophesy about the coming Messiah, but they clearly spelled out to the people their sins and warned them of God's righteous judgment.

Following their return from exile, the people of Israel lived as a restored community in the land of Palestine. Instead of learning from their past negative experiences and returning to the worship and service of the God of their ancestors, Abraham, Isaac, and Jacob, they became immoral and careless. The ritual and political reforms initiated by the postcaptivity leaders Nehemiah and Ezra had not prevented a serious spiritual decline among the Israelite population. This grave situation caused Malachi to be burdened heavily with the spiritual problems of his people. With divine fervency he addressed their common disregard for their loving Lord.

Content In his opening statement Malachi points out God's unchanging love for His people, due to His mercy that endures forever. This is the background for the following rebukes and exhortations. First, the prophet addresses the arrogant, open contempt of the priests for the Law and their negative influence upon the people. He points out to them that they cause many to stumble in sin. Therefore he warns them that the Lord will not be an idle spectator but, unless they repent, will severely punish them.

Next he addresses, in no uncertain terms, the treachery of priests and laymen in divorcing faithful wives and marrying heathen women who practice idol worship. This is followed by an earnest plea to guard their passions and be faithful to the wives of their youth, given to them by the Lord.

The prophet furthermore rebukes the irreligious practices of the people, their denial of God's justice, and their defrauding the Lord by withholding the required tithes and offerings.

In glowing and fervent language Malachi continues to describe the original type of priesthood. He prophesies of the Sun of Righteousness, the Messenger of the covenant, and the great and terrible day of divine judgment in which the righteous will be rewarded and the wicked punished.

Finally, Malachi exhorts the people to observe the laws given to Israel through Moses and promises a coming Messiah and His forerunner Elijah (John the Baptist). This statement concludes the Old Testament and ties it to the good news of God's provision in the Sun of Righteousness described in the New Testament.

Personal Application Malachi's criticism of abuses and religious indifference is still valid today. God's people always need to confess their inadequate response to divine love. Initial devotion to God and enthusiasm may diminish. Genuine worship frequently turns into mechanical observance of religious practices. Delinquent tithing, divorce of faithful spouses, and intermarriage between God's covenant people and nonbelievers often create havoc in families. Selfish desires, combined with proud and arrogant attitudes, lead to serious problems for which God is blamed. Instead of acknowledging our neglect and changing our lives by the power of the Holy Spirit, we ask the question, "Where *is* the God of justice?" (2:17). However, true repentance still prepares the way for necessary reforms and Holy Spirit-inspired revivals.

Christ Revealed In this last book of the Old Testament we find clear prophetic utterances regarding the sudden appearance of Christ—the Messenger of the (new) covenant (3:1). That day is a time of judgment. "Who can stand when He appears?" (3:2). No one can in his own strength, but for those who fear the Lord, "the Sun of Righteousness ['the Messenger of the covenant,' Jesus (3:1)] shall arise with healing in His wings," that is, in victorious triumph (4:2).

The Holy Spirit at Work The working of the Holy Spirit in Malachi is evident in his own personal life and prophetic ministry. His writings show him to have been a dedicated prophet—a person clearly in tune with the Holy Spirit. As such, he could be used effectively to warn people of their sinful behavior and to urge them to conform their lives to the law of the Lord. The Holy Spirit furthermore granted to him the privilege of bringing the line of faithful, dedicated writing prophets to a close by allowing him to proclaim with clarity and fervency his telescopic vision of Christ's coming.

Outline of Malachi

THE [1]burden of the word of the LORD
to Israel [2]by Malachi.

Israel Beloved of God

2 "I[a] have loved you," says the LORD.
"Yet you say, 'In what way have
You loved us?'
Was not Esau Jacob's brother?"
Says the LORD.
"Yet [b]Jacob I have loved;
3 But Esau I have hated,
And [a]laid waste his mountains
and his heritage
For the jackals of the wilderness."

4 Even though Edom has said,
"We have been impoverished,
But we will return and build the
desolate places,"

Thus says the LORD of hosts:

"They may build, but I will
[a]throw down;
They shall be called the Territory
of Wickedness,
And the people against whom the
LORD will have indignation
forever.
5 Your eyes shall see,
And you shall say,
[a]'The LORD is magnified beyond the
border of Israel.'

Polluted Offerings

6 "A son [a]honors *his* father,
And a servant *his* master.
[b]If then I am the Father,
Where *is* My honor?
And if I *am* a Master,
Where *is* My *reverence?
Says the LORD of hosts
To you priests who despise My
name.
[c]Yet you say, 'In what way have
we despised Your name?'

7 "You offer [a]defiled food on My
altar,
But say,
'In what way have we defiled
You?'
By saying,
[b]'The table of the LORD is
[1]contemptible.'
8 And [a]when you offer the blind as
a sacrifice,
Is it not evil?
And when you offer the lame and
sick,
Is it not evil?
Offer it then to your governor!
Would he be pleased with you?
Would he [b]accept[1] you
favorably?"
Says the LORD of hosts.

9 "But now entreat God's favor,
That He may **be gracious** to us.
[a]*While* this is being *done* by your
hands,
Will He accept you favorably?"
Says the LORD of hosts.

WORD WEALTH

1:9 be gracious, *chanan* (chah-*nahn*); Strong's #2603: To be graciously in-
(*cont. on next page*)

CHAPTER 1

1 [1]*oracle, prophecy* [2]*Lit. by the hand of*
2 [a]Deut. 4:37; 7:8; 23:5; Is. 41:8, 9; [Jer. 31:3]; John 15:12 [b]Rom. 9:13
3 [a]Jer. 49:18; Ezek. 35:9, 15
4 [a]Jer. 49:16–18
5 [a]Ps. 35:27; Mic. 5:4
6 [a][Ex. 20:12]; Prov. 30:11, 17; [Matt. 15:4–8; Eph. 6:2, 3] [b][Is. 63:16; 64:8]; Jer. 31:9; Luke 6:46 [c]Mal. 2:14 *See WW at Is. 8:13.
7 [a]Deut. 15:21 [b]Ezek. 41:22 [1]Or *to be despised*
8 [a]Lev. 22:22; Deut. 15:19–23 [b][Job 42:8] [1]Lit. *lift up your face*
9 [a]Hos. 13:9

1:1 The burden of the word of the LORD to Israel by Malachi: This threatening word from the Lord to His "messenger" (*Mal'aki*) created a considerable burden, causing him a significant amount of anxiety. With 23 probing questions the prophet delivers a self-examination, full of sharp reproaches against the priests and the people of Israel. This small colony, the remnant of the kingdoms of Israel and Judah, returned to their land after the Babylonian captivity and became the central focus of the divine promises and threats.

1:2–4 The whole prophecy, framed in a question-and-answer format, clearly represents the covenant relationship of the Lord to His people. He is their Father and Lord, their only God, and their final Judge. God's chosen people had made a poor return for His unfailing divine love, even though the Lord's covenant love called them to love Him in return and to keep His commandments. Still, because of His divine love, the Lord shows His care in admonishing His chosen people. In reply to the people's request for proofs of His love for them, He refers to the historical fact of His free choice of their ancestor **Jacob** over his brother **Esau** (vv. 2, 3). God **loved,** or "preferred," Jacob and his descendants and **hated,** or "rejected," his brother Esau and **Edom** his offspring for reasons only He knows. Paul refers to this passage as an example of divine electing love (Rom. 9:13).

If they reflect upon the Lord's love for them and contrast their condition with that of Edom, the people of Israel will be convinced of His gracious care and guidance. They will confess that **the LORD is magnified beyond the border of Israel,** that is, "the fame of His great power goes far beyond our borders!" (v. 5).

1:3 Laid waste . . . his heritage: See notes on Obad. 10, 11.

1:6—2:9 The second topic, the condemnation of the priests, is introduced in Hebrew parallel form by the questions in 1:6: "As Father and Master, where are My honor and reverence?" The open contempt of the sacrificial requirements (Lev. 1:10; 22:17–25; Deut. 17:1) is a disgrace to the loving and caring Lord God of Israel. Imperfect sacrifices, offered without sincerity, are unbecoming to governors and displeasing to the Lord. Pure offerings and incense from the peoples around the world, **from the rising of the sun, even to its going down,** are preferred by the Lord of hosts (1:11). The Lord pronounces a **curse** (retributive judgment) upon the priests for their open contempt of His instructions (2:2). It includes some type of severe humiliation: **spread refuse on your faces** (2:3).

My covenant with Levi (2:4) likely refers to Moses' blessing of Levi (Deut. 33:8–11) since no specific covenant with Levi is mentioned in the Pentateuch.

(*cont. from preceding page*)
clined toward someone; to have compassion on someone; to bestow favor on a person in need. This verb, which occurs 81 times, speaks of an attitude marked by compassion, generosity, and kindness. Note the use of *chanan* in Gen. 33:5, 11; Ps. 119:132; 123:3. "Have pity on me," Job repeatedly and pathetically cries out to his friends (Job 19:21). *Chanan*, as it appears in that context (vv. 14–22), denotes the kind of compassion, kindness, and consideration that will cause one to refrain from further wounding any individual who is bruised and suffering. God is very merciful, by His own choice (Ex. 33:19) and by His very nature (Is. 30:18, 19).

10 "Who *is there* even among you
who would shut the doors,
[a]So that you would not kindle fire
on My altar in vain?
I have no pleasure in you,"
Says the LORD of hosts,
[b]"Nor will I accept an offering from
your hands.
11 For [a]from the rising of the sun,
even to its going down,
My name *shall be* great [b]among
the *Gentiles;
[c]In every place [d]incense *shall be*
offered to My name,
And a pure offering;
[e]For My name shall be great
among the nations,"
Says the LORD of hosts.

3 12 "But you profane it,
In that you say,
[a]'The table of the [1]LORD is defiled;
And its fruit, its food, *is*
contemptible.'
13 You also say,
'Oh, what a [a]weariness!'
And you sneer at it,"
Says the LORD of hosts.
"And you bring the stolen, the
lame, and the sick;
Thus you bring an offering!
[b]Should I accept this from your
hand?"
Says the LORD.
14 "But cursed *be* [a]the deceiver
Who has in his flock a male,
And takes a vow,
But sacrifices to the Lord
[b]what is blemished—
For [c]I *am* a great King,"
Says the LORD of hosts,
"And My name *is to be* feared
among the nations.

10 [a]1 Cor. 9:13 [b]Is. 1:11
11 [a]Is. 59:19 [b]Is. 60:3, 5 [c]1 Tim. 2:8 [d]Rev. 8:3 [e]Is. 66:18, 19 *See WW at Ps. 106:47.
12 [a]Mal. 1:7 [1]So with Bg.; MT *Lord*
13 [a]Is. 43:22 [b]Lev. 22:20
14 [a]Mal. 1:8 [b]Lev. 22:18–20 [c]Ps. 47:2

CHAPTER 2

1 [a]Mal. 1:6
2 [a][Lev. 26:14, 15; Deut. 28:15] [b]Mal. 3:9 *See WW at Is. 60:1.
3 [a]Ex. 29:14 [b]1 Kin. 14:10 [1]Lit. *to it*
5 [a]Num. 25:12; Ezek. 34:25 [b]Deut. 33:9 *See WW at Is. 8:13.
6 [a]Deut. 33:10 [b]Jer. 23:22; [James 5:20] [1]Or *True instruction* [2]Or *unrighteousness*
7 [a]Num. 27:21; Deut. 17:8–11; Jer. 18:18 [b][Gal. 4:14] *See WW at Lev. 5:6.

Corrupt Priests

2 "And now, O [a]priests, this
commandment is for you. 4
2 [a]If you will not hear,
And if you will not take *it* to
heart,
To give *glory to My name,"
Says the LORD of hosts,
"I will send a curse upon you,
And I will curse your blessings.
Yes, I have cursed them [b]already,
Because you do not take *it* to
heart.

3 "Behold, I will rebuke your
descendants
And spread [a]refuse on your faces,
The refuse of your solemn feasts;
And *one* will [b]take you away
[1]with it.
4 Then you shall know that I have
sent this commandment to you,
That My covenant with Levi may
continue,"
Says the LORD of hosts.
5 "My[a] covenant was with him, *one*
of life and peace,
And I gave them to him [b]*that he
might* *fear *Me;*
So he feared Me
And was reverent before My
name.
6 [a]The[1] law of truth was in his
mouth,
And [2]injustice was not found on
his lips.
He walked with Me in peace and
equity,
And [b]turned many away from
iniquity.

7 "For[a] the lips of a *priest should
keep **knowledge,**
And *people* should seek the law
from his mouth;
[b]For he is the messenger of the
LORD of hosts.

WORD WEALTH

2:7 knowledge, *da'at* (*dah*-aht); Strong's #1847: Knowledge; knowing, understanding, intelligence, wisdom, discernment, skill. *Da'at* comes from the verb *yada'*, "to know." Occurring more than 90 times, its first mention is in Gen. 2:9, describing the tree of knowledge of good and evil. Hos. 4:6 states that the lack of knowledge destroys God's people. In Ex. 31:3, *da'at* refers to craftsmanship and

1:12, 13 See section 3 of Truth-In-Action at the end of Mal. **2:1–9** See section 4 of Truth-In-Action at the end of Mal.

artistic abilities; God gave Bezalel knowledge to design artistic works. Is. 53:11 ("By His knowledge My righteous Servant shall justify many") can be taken to mean that knowledge of Him (that is, knowing Him) justifies them, or that He uses His knowledge and skills to obtain their justification: that is, He, by His priestly intercession, knows how to justify believers.

8 But you have departed from the
way;
You [a]have caused many to
stumble at the law.
[b]You have corrupted the covenant
of Levi,"
Says the LORD of hosts.
9 "Therefore [a]I also have made you
contemptible and base
Before all the people,
Because you have not kept My
ways
But have shown [b]partiality in the
law."

Treachery of Infidelity

10 [a]Have we not all one Father?
[b]Has not one God created us?
Why do we deal treacherously
with one another
By profaning the covenant of the
fathers?
2 11 Judah has dealt treacherously,
And an abomination has been
committed in Israel and in
Jerusalem,
For Judah has [a]profaned
The LORD's holy *institution* which
He loves:
He has married the daughter of
a foreign god.
12 May the LORD cut off from the
tents of Jacob
The man who does this, being
[1]awake and aware,
Yet [a]who brings an offering to the
LORD of hosts!

13 And this is the second thing you
do:
You cover the altar of the LORD
with tears,
With weeping and crying;
So He does not regard the
offering anymore,
Nor receive *it* with goodwill from
your hands.
14 Yet you say, "For what reason?"
Because the LORD has been
witness
Between you and [a]the wife of
your youth,
With whom you have dealt
treacherously;
[b]Yet she is your companion
And your wife by covenant.
15 But [a]did He not make *them* one,
Having a remnant of the Spirit?
And why one?
He seeks [b]godly offspring.
Therefore take heed to your
spirit,
And let none deal treacherously
with the wife of his youth.

16 "For [a]the LORD God of Israel says
That He hates divorce,
For it covers one's garment with
violence,"
Says the LORD of hosts.
"Therefore take heed to your
spirit,
That you do not deal
treacherously."

8 [a]Jer. 18:15 [b]Num. 25:12, 13; Neh. 13:29; Ezek. 44:10
9 [a]1 Sam. 2:30 [b]Deut. 1:17; Mic. 3:11; 1 Tim. 5:21
10 [a]Jer. 31:9; 1 Cor. 8:6; [Eph. 4:6] [b]Job 31:15
11 [a]Ezra 9:1, 2; Neh. 13:23
12 [a]Neh. 13:29 [1]Talmud, Vg. *teacher and student*
14 [a]Prov. 5:18; Jer. 9:2; Mal. 3:5 [b]Prov. 2:17
15 [a]Gen. 2:24; Matt. 19:4, 5 [b]Ezra 9:2; [1 Cor. 7:14]
16 [a]Deut. 24:1; [Matt. 5:31; 19:6–8]

KINGDOM DYNAMICS

2:13, 14, 16 God Backs Up the Covenant of Marriage, FAMILY ORDER. When two people marry, God stands as a witness to the marriage, sealing it with the strongest possible word: covenant. "Covenant" speaks of faithfulness and enduring commitment. It stands like a divine sentinel over marriage, for blessing or for judgment.

Divorce is here described as violence. To initiate divorce does violence to God's intention for marriage and to the mate to whom one has been joined.

Yet, where husband and wife live according to their marriage vows, all the power of a covenant-keeping God stands behind them and their marriage. What a confidence, to know that God backs up our marriage. His power and authority stand against every enemy that would violently threaten it from without or within. (Is. 54:5/Matt. 19:1–9) L.C.

2:10–16 The reprehensible practice of divorce of Israelite wives (vv. 14–16) and intermarriage with women serving pagan deities was a violation of **the covenant of the fathers** (Deut. 7:1–4). The early postexilic enforcement of this law (Ezra 9; 10) was followed by a gradual return to this abominable practice, producing offspring with diluted religious beliefs (v. 15). **He hates divorce** answers their question as to why God **does not regard** their worship, in spite of their **weeping and crying** (v. 13). The husbands' sending away their wives is a violation of the covenant that God witnessed between them, and He is displeased. This truth goes back to Gen. 1 and 2, and is a basis for Jesus' teaching in Matt. 5:31, 32; 19:4–9.

2:11–16 See section 2 of Truth-In-Action at the end of Mal.

[1] 17 [a]You have wearied the LORD with
your words;
Yet you say,
"In what way have we wearied
Him?"
In that you say,
[b]"Everyone who does evil
Is good in the sight of the LORD,
And He *delights in them,"
Or, "Where *is* the God of justice?"

The Coming Messenger

3 "Behold, [a]I send My messenger,
And he will [b]prepare the way
before Me.
And the Lord, whom you seek,
Will suddenly come to His temple,
[c]Even the Messenger of the
covenant,
In whom you delight.
Behold, [d]He is coming,"
Says the LORD of hosts.

[3] 2 "But who can endure [a]the day of
His coming?
And [b]who can stand when He
appears?
For [c]He *is* like a *refiner's fire
And like launderers' soap.
3 [a]He will sit as a refiner and a
purifier of silver;
He will purify the sons of Levi,
And [1]purge them as gold and
silver,
That they may [b]offer to the LORD
An offering in righteousness.

4 "Then [a]the offering of Judah and
Jerusalem
Will be [1]pleasant to the LORD,
As in the days of old,
As in former years.
5 And I will come near you for
judgment;

17 [a]Is. 43:22, 24 [b]Is. 5:20; Zeph. 1:12 *See WW at Ps. 112:1.

CHAPTER 3

1 [a]Matt. 11:10; Mark 1:2; Luke 1:76; 7:27; John 1:23; 2:14, 15 [b][Is. 40:3] [c]Is. 63:9 [d]Hab. 2:7
2 [a]Jer. 10:10; Joel 2:11; Nah. 1:6; [Mal. 4:1] [b]Is. 33:14; Ezek. 22:14; Rev. 6:17 [c]Is. 4:4; Zech. 13:9; [Matt. 3:10–12; 1 Cor. 3:13–15] *See WW at Zech. 13:9.
3 [a]Is. 1:25; Dan. 12:10; Zech. 13:9 [b][1 Pet. 2:5] [1]Or *refine*
4 [a]Mal. 1:11 [1]*pleasing*
5 [a]Lev. 19:12; Zech. 5:4; [James 5:12] [b]Lev. 19:13; James 5:4 [c]Ex. 22:22
6 [a][Num. 23:19; Rom. 11:29; James 1:17] [b][Lam. 3:22]
7 [a]Acts 7:51 [b]Zech. 1:3 [c]Mal. 1:6 *See WW at Ruth 4:15.
8 [a]Neh. 13:10–12
10 [a]Prov. 3:9, 10 [b]1 Chr. 26:20 [c]Gen. 7:11 *See WW at 1 Kin. 8:23.

I will be a swift witness
Against sorcerers,
Against adulterers,
[a]Against perjurers,
Against those who [b]exploit wage
earners and [c]widows and
orphans,
And against those who turn away
an alien—
Because they do not fear Me,"
Says the LORD of hosts.

6 "For I *am* the LORD, [a]I do not
change;
[b]Therefore you are not consumed,
O sons of Jacob.
7 Yet from the days of [a]your fathers
You have gone away from My
ordinances
And have not kept *them.*
[b]Return* to Me, and I will return
to you,"
Says the LORD of hosts.
[c]"But you said,
'In what way shall we return?'

Do Not Rob God

8 "Will a man rob God? [5]
Yet you have robbed Me!
But you say,
'In what way have we robbed
You?'
[a]In tithes and offerings.
9 You are cursed with a curse,
For you have robbed Me,
Even this whole nation.
10 [a]Bring all the tithes into the
[b]storehouse,
That there may be food in My
house,
And try Me now in this,"
Says the LORD of hosts,
"If I will not open for you the
[c]windows of *heaven

2:17—3:5 The priests and Levites held an arrogant and distorted view of worship, stating that evildoers who question God's justice please Him (2:17). The Lord will vindicate Himself. He **will suddenly come to His temple** (3:1) and judge sorcerers, adulterers, those who swear falsely, those who cheat their hired hands, those who take advantage of widows and orphans or do not welcome aliens, that is, all those who **do not fear Me** (3:5). **My messenger . . . before Me** is linked in the NT with John the Baptist, indicating that Malachi's prophecy had both a historical and a messianic application. Malachi's own name is reflected in the Hebrew word meaning "My Messenger."

2:17 *See section 1 of Truth-*In-Action at the end of Mal.

3:2–5 See section 3 of Truth-In-Action at the end of Mal.

3:6, 7 Although the Lord abhors and condemns the hypocritical, corrupt, and immoral acts of His people, there is hope because the Lord never changes (v. 6). He is faithful to His covenant promises and will not abandon His people. Therefore, He exhorts them, **return to Me, and I will return to you** (v. 7).

3:8–12 These verses teach the following principles: 1) Israel was neglecting her covenant relationship with God by robbing Him of the **tithes and offerings.** 2) Her neglect brought retributive judgment. 3) God challenged her to counter her neglect by proving His faithfulness in this matter of giving. If she would give **all the tithes,** He would **open . . . the windows of heaven** (send the needed rains) and **rebuke the devourer** (destroy the locusts that devour crops). Although there is no consensus in the contemporary church as to the NT applicability of the principle of tithing, of testing God financially, of God's promised rebuking of those things that devour finances, or of God's providing financially for those who faithfully give, there is general agreement that the NT teaches us to give substantially to the Lord. It is also agreed that He is a God who delights to respond with gracious provision, especially to meet essential needs (Matt. 6:25–34).

3:8–10 See section 5 of Truth-In-Action at the end of Mal.

And [d]pour out for you *such*
blessing
That *there will* not *be* **room**
enough *to receive it.*

11 "And I will rebuke [a]the devourer
for your sakes,
So that he will not destroy the
fruit of your ground,
Nor shall the vine fail to bear fruit
for you in the field,"
Says the LORD of hosts;

WORD WEALTH

3:10 ***room* enough,** *day (dye)*; Strong's #1767: Sufficient, enough; a large enough quantity; plenty; measurelessness. *Day* occurs about 40 times in the OT. Its first reference is in Ex. 36:5, which concerns a freewill offering of gold and other materials; the people gave so lavishly that the Scripture describes their gifts as "much more than enough." *Day* appears in the title of the famous Passover song of thanks entitled *dayenu*, meaning "it would be enough for us." Each verse lists a favor that God did for Israel at the Exodus and concludes that, had He only done that much and no more, "it would have been enough."

KINGDOM DYNAMICS

3:8–10 God's Prosperity Plan Includes Tithing, GOD'S PROSPERITY. Many people are handicapped by their own poverty, and too often their poverty is caused by their own disobedience to the Word. There are many ways in which people are disobedient; one way is in robbing God! This passage clearly tells us that those who withhold their tithes and offerings are robbing God. As a consequence, they are also robbing themselves of the blessings that God wants to bestow upon them. You see, when you do not tithe you are breaking the law; and if you are breaking the law, then the benevolent law of God cannot work on your behalf.

Nothing will keep a wise believer from tithing and giving, but he or she will never be found to tithe or give offerings just to get something in return. Rather, the act arises from obedience, and God always rewards obedience!

(*/Luke 6:38) F.P.

10 [d]2 Chr. 31:10
11 [a]Amos 4:9

KINGDOM DYNAMICS

3:10, 11 Your Giving Proves God, Opens the Windows of Heaven to You, and Causes the Devourer to Be Rebuked, SEED FAITH. In this passage of Scripture, God actually invites people to try (prove) Him—to verify His trustworthiness with their giving. He says that by withheld giving we rob Him of the privilege of pouring out great and overflowing blessings. He calls for renewed giving with this promise. First, there will be "food" or resources for God's work ("in My house"). Second, He says those who give will be placed in position to receive great, overflowing blessings. You can experience the windows of heaven actually opening with blessings you will not be able to "receive" or contain! Third, God says that He will "rebuke the devourer" for your sakes. He will cause every blessing that has your name written on it to be directed to you, and Satan himself cannot stop it. Do not be afraid to prove God with your giving; He is God and He will stand the test every time.

(Gal. 6:7–9/Mark 11:22–24) O.R.

12 "And all nations will call you
*blessed,
For you will be [a]a delightful
land,"
Says the LORD of hosts.

The People Complain Harshly

13 "Your[a] words have been [1]harsh
against Me,"
Says the LORD,
"Yet you say,
'What have we spoken against
You?'
14 [a]You have said,
'It is useless to *serve God;
What profit *is it* that we have kept
His ordinance,
And that we have walked as
mourners
Before the LORD of hosts?
15 So now [a]we call the proud
blessed,
For those who do wickedness are
[1]raised up;
They even [b]tempt God and go
free.'"

12 [a]Dan. 8:9 *See WW at Prov. 31:28.
13 [a]Mal. 2:17 [1]Lit. *strong*
14 [a]Job 21:14 *See WW at Ps. 100:2.
15 [a]Ps. 73:12 [b]Ps. 95:9 [1]Lit. *built*

3:13—4:3 The names of those who fear the Lord are written in a **book of remembrance.** In contrast with the end of the wicked, the righteous **shall be mine . . . jewels** (or special possession) on **the day** (see note on Obad. 15) when I act (see 3:16, 17; Ex. 32:32; Ps. 56:8). At that Day of Judgment, **the righteous and the wicked** will be clearly distinguishable (3:18). That **day is coming** and **shall burn them up** who do not serve the Lord (4:1). But the same heat that burns up the wicked will bring healing warmth to the righteous (4:2). **The Sun of Righteousness** occurs as a symbolic designation of Yahweh only here in the OT. It pictures God rising in victorious triumph (**with healing in His wings**), likely through the Messiah.

A Book of Remembrance

16 Then those [a]who feared the LORD
[b]spoke to one another,
And the LORD listened and heard
them;
So [c]a book of remembrance was
written before Him
For those who fear the LORD
And who [1]meditate on His name.

1 17 "They[a] shall be Mine," says the
LORD of hosts,
"On the day that I make them My
[b]jewels.[1]*
And [c]I will spare them
As a man spares his own son who
serves him."
18 [a]Then you shall again discern
Between the righteous and the
wicked,
Between one who serves God
And one who does not serve Him.

The Great Day of God

4 "For behold, [a]the day is coming,
Burning like an oven,
And all [b]the proud, yes, all who
do wickedly will be [c]stubble.
And the day which is coming
shall burn them up,"
Says the LORD of hosts,
"That will [d]leave them neither root
nor branch.
2 But to you who [a]fear My name
The [b]Sun of Righteousness shall
arise
With **healing** in His wings;
And you shall go out
And grow fat like stall-fed
calves.
3 [a]You shall trample the wicked,
For they shall be ashes under the
soles of your feet
On the day that I do *this,*"
Says the LORD of hosts.

4 "Remember the [a]Law of Moses,
My servant,
Which I commanded him in
Horeb for all Israel,
With [b]*the* statutes and
judgments.
5 Behold, I will send you [a]Elijah the
*prophet
[b]Before the coming of the great
and dreadful day of the LORD.
6 And he will turn
The hearts of the fathers to the
children,
And the hearts of the children to
their fathers,
Lest I come and [a]strike the earth
with [b]a curse."

16 [a]Ps. 66:16 [b]Heb. 3:13 [c]Ps. 56:8 [1]Or *esteem* **17** [a]Ex. 19:5; Deut. 7:6; Is. 43:21; [1 Pet. 2:9] [b]Is. 62:3 [c]Ps. 103:13 [1]Lit. *special treasure* *See WW at Deut. 26:18. **18** [a][Ps. 58:11]

CHAPTER 4

1 [a]Ps. 21:9; [Nah. 1:5, 6; Mal. 3:2, 3; 2 Pet. 3:7] [b]Mal. 3:18 [c]Is. 5:24; Obad. 18 [d]Amos 2:9 **2** [a]Mal. 3:16 [b]Matt. 4:16; Luke 1:78; Acts 10:43; 2 Cor. 4:6; Eph. 5:14

3 [a]Mic. 7:10 **4** [a]Ex. 20:3 [b]Deut. 4:10 **5** [a][Matt. 11:14; 17:10–13; Mark 9:11–13; Luke 1:17]; John 1:21 [b]Joel 2:31 *See WW at 1 Sam. 3:20. **6** [a]Zech. 14:12 [b]Zech. 5:3

WORD WEALTH

4:2 healing, *marpe'* (mar-*peh*); Strong's #4832: Restoration of health, remedy, cure, medicine; tranquility, deliverance, refreshing. Occurring 13 times, *marpe'* comes from the verb *rapha'*, "to heal, cure, repair." Salvation is God's rescue of the entire person, and healing is His complete repair of that person, as *marpe'* illustrates. Compare the application of *rapha'* in Ps. 41:4 and 147:3, referring to the healing of a soul that has sinned and the healing of a broken heart. In the present reference, the Messiah is compared to a rising sun, which has visible, radiant beams of sunlight streaming outward in all directions. From each of these beams of glorious light, healing flows.

3:17, 18 See section 1 of Truth-In-Action at the end of Mal.
4:4–6 In conclusion, the prophet admonishes the people to **remember the Law of Moses** (v. 4). Then follows the promise of the coming of **Elijah the prophet,** earlier referred to as "My messenger" (see note on 2:17—3:5).

This prophetic utterance closes the OT with the hope of unity and healing. Malachi, like Obadiah and other predecessors, looks with telescopic vision toward Christ's First Advent and salvation for all who believe in Him. But he also views Christ's Second Advent, with the final judgment of the wicked and ultimate salvation of those who fear His name (v. 6).

TRUTH-IN-ACTION through MALACHI

Letting the LIFE of the Holy Spirit Bring Faith's Works Alive in You!

Truth Malachi Teaches	Text	**Action** Malachi Invites
1 Steps to Knowing God and His Ways God sees and rewards, not according to our timetable, but by His. We must not think that either good or evil conduct goes unrecognized or unjudged. God will honor the faithful.	2:17 3:17, 18	**Be assured** that God never honors evil conduct. **Do not speak against** the justice of God. **Believe** that God differentiates between good and evil behavior.
2 Steps to Covenant Life The covenant relationship of marriage is highly esteemed by the Spirit of God. He instructs believers to seek a believing partner to insure holiness in the marriage. He also requires just and faithful behavior within the marriage bonds. God hates the hard-hearted attitudes that destroy this sacred covenant and produce divorce.	2:11–16	**Obey God; marry only in the Lord. Be loving** and **faithful** to your marriage partner. **Reject divorce** as an answer to marital problems. **Honor** your covenant with God. **Trust** Him to recover the hope in a seemingly "hopeless" marriage. **Be willing** to relearn love, understanding, and forgiveness.
3 Keys to Personal Purity Christ comes as the purifier and refiner of His people, that they, being clean, may offer service and worship acceptable to God. To offer the Lord less than our best is unworthy of His holy name.	1:12, 13 3:2–5	**Give** the best that you have to the Lord. **Submit** to the work of the Lord as refiner and purifier. **Worship** God from a purified heart, and **serve** Him from clean motives. **Commit** to true worship, and **avoid** mere formalism.
4 Lessons for Leaders The personal conduct of God's chosen leaders and the example of their ministry causes God to be received or rejected by the world. If leadership rejects the law of God, the people will not be taught justice, and so cannot live in peace.	2:1–9	Leaders, **make sure** that your conduct and your ministry cause people to **give the Lord honor and glory.**
5 Keys to Generous Living Tithing, though included in the Law, was part of the Abrahamic life of faith and is part of faithful living. Tithing obediently expresses faith that God is our true source. To fail to tithe is to dishonor and rob God.	3:8–10	**Practice tithing! Understand** that the tenth already belongs to God (Lev. 27:30). **Expect** financial well-being to follow when you tithe. **Realize** that tithing is not only a part of the Mosaic Law. It is a timeless covenant of privilege to exercise in joyous faith—not as a grudging legal requirement (2 Cor. 9:7).

BRIDGING THE TESTAMENTS:

Ezra
500 B.C.

HISTORY OF ISRAEL

THE KINGDOM | THE REMNANT

Cyrus the Great
Roman Republic Begins
Socrates
Plato
Aristotle

750 612 550 539 529 509 469 428 384

ASSYRIA
BABYLON
PERSIA
Esther becomes Queen

722 605 586 539 538 478 457 444 Under Nehemiah

ISRAEL
Nebu-chad-nezzar destroys Jerusalem
Fall of Babylon
Under Zerub-babel
Under Ezra
425

JUDAH
Southern Kingdom
EXILE
Temple RETURN

Jeremiah
Habakkuk
Ezekiel
Daniel
Haggai • Ezra • Malachi
Zechariah • Nehemiah

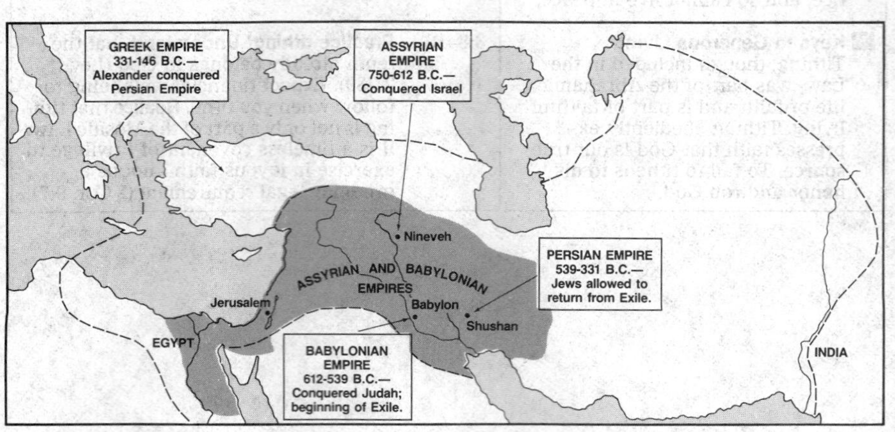

Seeing the picture of how the Old Testament concludes in history and how the period between the Testaments unfolded

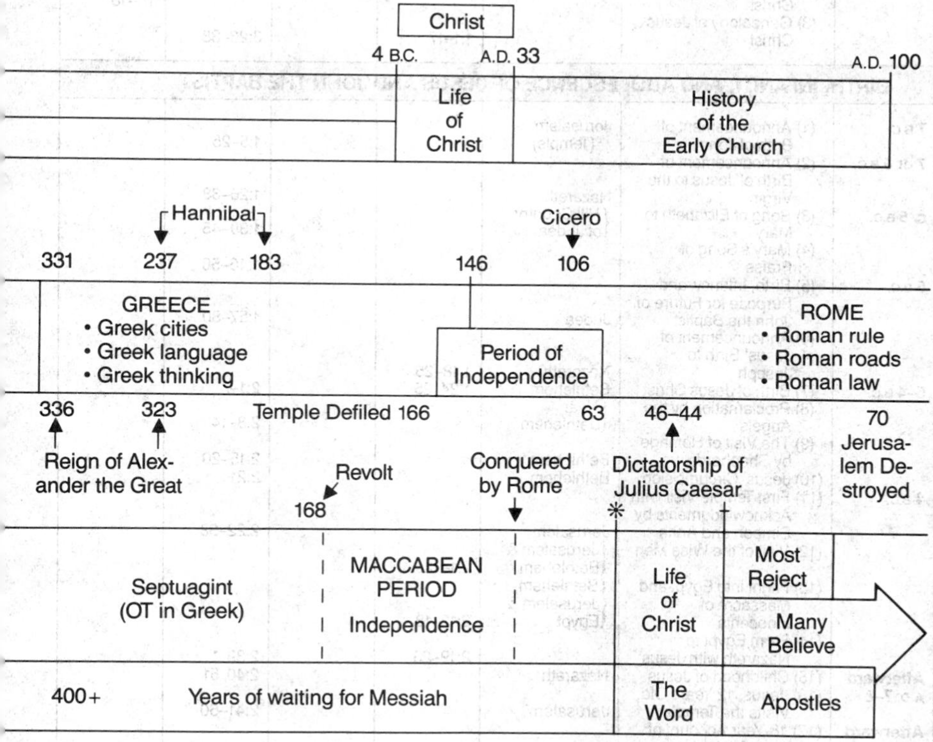

Christ
4 B.C. — A.D. 33 — A.D. 100
Life of Christ | History of the Early Church

Hannibal 237–183 · Cicero 106
331 · 146

GREECE
- Greek cities
- Greek language
- Greek thinking

Period of Independence

ROME
- Roman rule
- Roman roads
- Roman law

336 · 323 · Temple Defiled 166 · 63 · 46–44 · 70

336 Reign of Alexander the Great
168 Revolt
63 Conquered by Rome
46–44 Dictatorship of Julius Caesar
70 Jerusalem Destroyed

Septuagint (OT in Greek)

MACCABEAN PERIOD
Independence

Life of Christ | Most Reject | Many Believe

400+ Years of waiting for Messiah

The Word | Apostles

The chart above outlines the events that led to the fall of both the northern and southern kingdoms (Israel's 10 tribes and Judah's 2 tribes). Sometime after the return of Judah's exiles from captivity to Babylon/Persia, the Old Testament concludes. The voice of the prophets is silent, and the inspired Word of the Old Covenant is closed. Still, history moves forward, and God's purposes sovereignly move toward the manifestation of the world's Redeemer.

Lessons from the postexilic period: True restoration results from being molded by the Word within rather than the world without (Ezra 7:10; 9:10–15; Is. 46:3, 4; Acts 7:51–53). Even after the chastening of the Exile, most of God's returning people became enmeshed once again in the affairs of the world and neglected their relationship with Him. For some, the problem was external religiosity without internal reality; for others, the problem was being more influenced by culture than by God's Word. God has always found a remnant—a faithful minority who love Him enough to stand against the tide of the world system and the ways of the flesh. The church was forthcoming—to be that people in this our era.

Harmony of the Gospels

Date	Event	Location	Matthew	Mark	Luke	John
INTRODUCTIONS TO JESUS CHRIST						
	(1) Luke's Introduction				1:1–4	
	(2) Pre-fleshly state of Christ					1:1–18
	(3) Genealogy of Jesus Christ		1:1–17		3:23–38	
BIRTH, INFANCY, AND ADOLESCENCE OF JESUS AND JOHN THE BAPTIST						
7 B.C.	(1) Announcement of Birth of John	Jerusalem (Temple)			1:5–25	
7 or 6 B.C.	(2) Announcement of Birth of Jesus to the Virgin	Nazareth			1:26–38	
c. 5 B.C.	(3) Song of Elizabeth to Mary	Hill Country of Judea			1:39–45	
	(4) Mary's Song of Praise				1:46–56	
5 B.C.	(5) Birth, Infancy, and Purpose for Future of John the Baptist	Judea			1:57–80	
	(6) Announcement of Jesus' Birth to Joseph	Nazareth	1:18–25			
5–4 B.C.	(7) Birth of Jesus Christ	Bethlehem	1:24, 25		2:1–7	
	(8) Proclamation by the Angels	Near Bethlehem			2:8–14	
	(9) The Visit of Homage by Shepherds	Bethlehem			2:15–20	
	(10) Jesus' Circumcision	Bethlehem			2:21	
4 B.C.	(11) First Temple Visit with Acknowledgments by Simeon and Anna	Jerusalem			2:22–38	
	(12) Visit of the Wise Men	Jerusalem & Bethlehem	2:1–12			
	(13) Flight into Egypt and Massacre of Innocents	Bethlehem, Jerusalem & Egypt	2:13–18			
	(14) From Egypt to Nazareth with Jesus		2:19–23		2:39	
Afterward	(15) Childhood of Jesus	Nazareth			2:40, 51	
A.D. 7–8	(16) Jesus, 12 Years Old, Visits the Temple	Jerusalem			2:41–50	
Afterward	(17) 18-Year Account of Jesus' Adolescence and Adulthood	Nazareth			2:51, 52	
TRUTHS ABOUT JOHN THE BAPTIST						
c. A.D. 25–27	(1) John's Ministry Begins	Judean Wilderness	3:1	1:1–4	3:1, 2	1:19–28
	(2) Man and Message		3:2–12	1:2–8	3:3–14	
	(3) His Picture of Jesus		3:11, 12	1:7, 8	3:15–18	1:26, 27
	(4) His Courage		14:4–12		3:19, 20	
BEGINNING OF JESUS' MINISTRY						
c. A.D. 27	(1) Jesus Baptized	Jordan River	3:13–17	1:9–11	3:21–23	1:29–34
	(2) Jesus Tempted	Wilderness	4:1–11	1:12, 13	4:1–13	
	(3) Calls First Disciples	Beyond Jordan				1:35–51
	(4) The First Miracle	Cana in Galilee				2:1–11
	(5) First Stay in Capernaum	(Capernaum is "His" city)				2:12
A.D. 27	(6) First Cleansing of the Temple	Jerusalem				2:13–22
	(7) Received at Jerusalem	Judea				2:23–25

Date	Event	Location	Matthew	Mark	Luke	John
A.D. 27	(8) Teaches Nicodemus about Second Birth	Judea				3:1–21
	(9) Co-Ministry with John	Judea				3:22–30
	(10) Leaves for Galilee	Judea	4:12	1:14	4:14	4:1–4
	(11) Samaritan Woman at Jacob's Well	Samaria				4:5–42
	(12) Returns to Galilee			1:15	4:15	4:43–45
THE GALILEAN MINISTRY OF JESUS						
A.D. 27–29						
A.D. 27	(1) Healing of the Nobleman's Son	Cana				4:46–54
	(2) Rejected at Nazareth	Nazareth			4:16–30	
	(3) Moved to Capernaum	Capernaum	4:13–17			
	(4) Four Become Fishers of Men	Sea of Galilee	4:18–22	1:16–20	5:1–11	
	(5) Demoniac Healed on the Sabbath Day	Capernaum		1:21–28	4:31–37	
	(6) Peter's Mother-in-Law Cured, Plus Others	Capernaum	8:14–17	1:29–34	4:38–41	
C. A.D. 27	(7) First Preaching Tour of Galilee	Galilee	4:23–25	1:35–39	4:42–44	
	(8) Leper Healed and Response Recorded	Galilee	8:1–4	1:40–45	5:12–16	
	(9) Paralytic Healed	Capernaum	9:1–8	2:1–12	5:17–26	
	(10) Matthew's Call and Reception Held	Capernaum	9:9–13	2:13–17	5:27–32	
	(11) Disciples Defended via a Parable	Capernaum	9:14–17	2:18–22	5:33–39	
A.D. 28	(12) Goes to Jerusalem for Second Passover; Heals Lame Man	Jerusalem				5:1–47
	(13) Plucked Grain Precipitates Sabbath Controversy	En Route to Galilee	12:1–8	2:23–28	6:1–5	
	(14) Withered Hand Healed Causes Another Sabbath Controversy	Galilee	12:9–14	3:1–6	6:6–11	
	(15) Multitudes Healed	Sea of Galilee	12:15–21	3:7–12	6:17–19	
	(16) Twelve Apostles Selected After a Night of Prayer	Near Capernaum		3:13–19	6:12–16	
	(17) Sermon on the Mt.	Near Capernaum	5:1—7:29		6:20–49	
	(18) Centurion's Servant Healed	Capernaum	8:5–13		7:1–10	
	(19) Raises Widow's Son from Dead	Nain			7:11–17	
	(20) Jesus Allays John's Doubts	Galilee	11:2–19		7:18–35	
	(21) Woes Upon the Privileged		11:20–30			
	(22) A Sinful Woman Anoints Jesus	Simon's House, Capernaum			7:36–50	
	(23) Another Tour of Galilee	Galilee			8:1–3	
	(24) Jesus Accused of Blasphemy	Capernaum	12:22–37	3:20–30	11:14–23	
	(25) Jesus' Answer to a Demand for a Sign	Capernaum	12:38–45		11:24–26, 29–36	
	(26) Mother, Brothers Seek Audience	Capernaum	12:46–50	3:31–35	8:19–21	

Date	Event	Location	Matthew	Mark	Luke	John
A.D. 28	(27) Famous Parables of Sower, Seed, Tares, Mustard Seed, Leaven, Treasure, Pearl, Dragnet, Lamp Told	By Sea of Galilee	13:1–52	4:1–34	8:4–18	
	(28) Sea Made Serene	Sea of Galilee	8:23–27	4:35–41	8:22–25	
	(29) Gadarene Demoniac Healed	E. Shore of Galilee	8:28–34	5:1–20	8:26–39	
	(30) Jairus' Daughter Raised and Woman with Hemorrhage Healed		9:18–26	5:21–43	8:40–56	
	(31) Two Blind Men's Sight Restored		9:27–31			
	(32) Mute Demoniac Healed		9:32–34			
	(33) Nazareth's Second Rejection of Christ	Nazareth	13:53–58	6:1–6		
	(34) Twelve Sent Out		9:35—11:1	6:7–13	9:1–6	
	(35) Fearful Herod Beheads John	Galilee	14:1–12	6:14–29	9:7–9	
Spring A.D. 29	(36) Return of 12, Jesus Withdraws, 5000 Fed	Near Bethsaida	14:13–21	6:30–44	9:10–17	6:1–14
	(37) Walks on the Water	Sea of Galilee	14:22–33	6:45–52		6:15–21
	(38) Sick of Gennesaret Healed	Gennesaret	14:34–36	6:53–56		
	(39) Peak of Popularity Passes in Galilee	Capernaum				6:22–71 7:1
A.D. 29	(40) Traditions Attacked		15:1–20	7:1–23		
	(41) Aborted Retirement in Phoenicia: Syro-Phoenician Healed	Phoenicia	15:21–28	7:24–30		
	(42) Afflicted Healed	Decapolis	15:29–31	7:31–37		
	(43) 4000 Fed	Decapolis	15:32–39	8:1–9		
	(44) Pharisees Increase Attack	Magdala	16:1–4	8:10–13		
	(45) Disciples' Carelessness Condemned; Blind Man Healed		16:5–12	8:14–26		
	(46) Peter Confesses Jesus Is the Christ	Near Caesarea Philippi	16:13–20	8:27–30	9:18–21	
	(47) Jesus Foretells His Death	Caesarea Philippi	16:21–26	8:31–38	9:22–25	
	(48) Kingdom Promised		16:27, 28	9:1	9:26, 27	
	(49) The Transfiguration	Mountain Unnamed	17:1–13	9:2–13	9:28–36	
	(50) Epileptic Healed	Mt. of Transfiguration	17:14–21	9:14–29	9:37–42	
	(51) Again Tells of Death, Resurrection	Galilee	17:22, 23	9:30–32	9:43–45	
	(52) Taxes Paid	Capernaum	17:24–27			
	(53) Disciples Contend About Greatness; Jesus Defines; also Patience, Loyalty, Forgiveness	Capernaum	18:1–35	9:33–50	9:46–62	
	(54) Jesus Rejects Brothers' Advice	Galilee				7:2–9
c. Sept. A.D. 29	(55) Galilee Departure and Samaritan Rejection		19:1		9:51–56	7:10
	(56) Cost of Discipleship		8:18–22		9:57–62	
LAST JUDEAN AND PEREAN MINISTRY OF JESUS						
A.D. 29–30						
Oct. A.D.29	(1) Feast of Tabernacles	Jerusalem				7:2, 10–52
	(2) Forgiveness of Adulteress	Jerusalem				7:53—8:11

Date	Event	Location	Matthew	Mark	Luke	John
A.D. 29	(3) Christ—the Light of the World	Jerusalem				8:12–20
	(4) Pharisees Can't Meet the Prophecy Thus Try to Destroy the Prophet	Jerusalem—Temple				8:21–59
	(5) Man Born Blind Healed; Following Consequences	Jerusalem				9:1–41
	(6) Parable of the Good Shepherd	Jerusalem				10:1–21
	(7) The Service of the Seventy	Probably Judea			10:1–24	
	(8) Lawyer Hears the Story of the Good Samaritan	Judea (?)			10:25–37	
	(9) The Hospitality of Martha and Mary	Bethany			10:38–42	
	(10) Another Lesson on Prayer	Judea (?)			11:1–13	
	(11) Accused of Connection with Beelzebub				11:14–36	
	(12) Judgment Against Lawyers and Pharisees				11:37–54	
	(13) Jesus Deals with Hypocrisy, Covetousness, Worry, and Alertness				12:1–59	
	(14) Repent or Perish				13:1–5	
	(15) Barren Fig Tree				13:6–9	
	(16) Crippled Woman Healed on Sabbath				13:10–17	
	(17) Parables of Mustard Seed and Leaven	Probably Perea			13:18–21	
Winter A.D. 29	(18) Feast of Dedication	Jerusalem				10:22–39
	(19) Withdrawal Beyond Jordan					10:40–42
	(20) Begins Teaching Return to Jerusalem with Special Words About Herod	Perea			13:22–35	
	(21) Meal with a Pharisee Ruler Occasions Healing Man with Dropsy; Parables of Ox, Best Places, and Great Supper				14:1–24	
	(22) Demands of Discipleship	Perea			14:25–35	
	(23) Parables of Lost Sheep, Coin, Son				15:1–32	
	(24) Parables of Unjust Steward, Rich Man and Lazarus				16:1–31	
	(25) Lessons on Service, Faith, Influence				17:1–10	
	(26) Resurrection of Lazarus	Perea to Bethany				11:1–44
	(27) Reaction to It: Withdrawal of Jesus					11:45–54
A.D. 30	(28) Begins Last Journey to Jerusalem via Samaria & Galilee	Samaria, Galilee			17:11	
	(29) Heals Ten Lepers				17:12–19	
	(30) Lessons on the Coming Kingdom				17:20–37	
	(31) Parables: Persistent Widow, Pharisee and Tax Collector				18:1–14	
	(32) Doctrine on Divorce		19:1–12	10:1–12		

Date	Event	Location	Matthew	Mark	Luke	John
A.D. 30	(33) Jesus Blesses Children: Objections	Perea	19:13–15	10:13–16	18:15–17	
	(34) Rich Young Ruler	Perea	19:16–30	10:17–31	18:18–30	
	(35) Laborers of the 11th Hour		20:1–16			
	(36) Foretells Death and Resurrection	Near Jordan	20:17–19	10:32–34	18:31–34	
	(37) Ambition of James and John		20:20–28	10:35–45		
	(38) Blind Bartimaeus Healed	Jericho		10:46–52	18:35–43	
	(39) Interview with Zacchaeus	Jericho			19:1–10	
	(40) Parable: the Minas	Jericho			19:11–27	
	(41) Returns to Home of Mary and Martha	Bethany				11:55—12:1
	(42) Plot to Kill Lazarus	Bethany				12:9–11
JESUS' FINAL WEEK OF WORK AT JERUSALEM						
Spring A.D. 30						
Sunday	(1) Triumphal Entry	Bethany, Jerusalem, Bethany	21:1–9	11:1–11	19:28–44	12:12–19
Monday	(2) Fig Tree Cursed and Temple Cleansed	Bethany to Jerusalem	21:10–19	11:12–18	19:45–48	
	(3) The Attraction of Sacrifice	Jerusalem				12:20–50
Tuesday	(4) Withered Fig Tree Testifies	Bethany to Jerusalem	21:20–22	11:19–26		
	(5) Sanhedrin Challenges Jesus. Answered by Parables: Two Sons, Wicked Vinedressers and Marriage Feast	Jerusalem	21:23—22:14	11:27—12:12	20:1–19	
	(6) Tribute to Caesar	Jerusalem	22:15–22	12:13–17	20:20–26	
	(7) Sadducees Question the Resurrection	Jerusalem	22:23–33	12:18–27	20:27–40	
	(8) Pharisees Question Commandments	Jerusalem	22:34–40	12:28–34		
	(9) Jesus and David	Jerusalem	22:41–46	12:35–37	20:41–44	
	(10) Jesus' Last Sermon	Jerusalem	23:1–39	12:38–40	20:45–47	
	(11) Widow's Mite	Jerusalem		12:41–44	21:1–4	
	(12) Jesus Tells of the Future	Mt. Olives	24:1–51	13:1–37	21:5–36	
	(13) Parables: Ten Virgins, Talents, The Day of Judgment	Mt. Olives	25:1–46			
	(14) Jesus Tells Date of Crucifixion		26:1–5	14:1, 2	22:1, 2	
	(15) Anointing by Mary at Simon's Feast	Bethany	26:6–13	14:3–9		12:2–8
	(16) Judas Contracts the Betrayal		26:14–16	14:10, 11	22:3–6	
Thursday	(17) Preparation for the Passover	Jerusalem	26:17–19	14:12–16	22:7–13	
Thursday P.M.	(18) Passover Eaten, Jealousy Rebuked	Jerusalem	26:20	14:17	22:14–16, 24–30	
	(19) Feet Washed	Upper Room				13:1–20
	(20) Judas Revealed, Defects	Upper Room	26:21–25	14:18–21	22:21–23	13:21–30
	(21) Jesus Warns About Further Desertion; Cries of Loyalty	Upper Room	26:31–35	14:27–31	22:31–38	13:31–38
	(22) Institution of the Lord's Supper	Upper Room	26:26–29	14:22–25	22:17–20	

Date	Event	Location	Matthew	Mark	Luke	John
Thursday P.M.	(23) Last Speech to the Apostles and Intercessory Prayer	Jerusalem				14:1—17:26
Thursday-Friday	(24) The Grief of Gethsemane	Mt. of Olives	26:30, 36–46	14:26, 32–42	22:39–46	18:1
Friday	(25) Betrayal, Arrest, Desertion	Gethsemane	26:47–56	14:43–52	22:47–53	18:2–12
	(26) First Examined by Annas	Jerusalem				18:12–14, 19–23
	(27) Trial by Caiaphas and Council; Following Indignities	Jerusalem	26:57, 59–68	14:53, 55–65	22:54, 63–65	18:24
	(28) Peter's Triple Denial	Jerusalem	26:58, 69–75	14:54, 66–72	22:54–62	18:15–18, 25–27
	(29) Condemnation by the Council	Jerusalem	27:1	15:1	22:66–71	
	(30) Suicide of Judas	Jerusalem	27:3–10			
	(31) First Appearance Before Pilate	Jerusalem	27:2, 11–14	15:1–5	23:1–7	18:28–38
	(32) Jesus Before Herod	Jerusalem			23:6–12	
	(33) Second Appearance Before Pilate	Jerusalem	27:15–26	15:6–15	23:13–25	18:39—19:16
	(34) Mockery by Roman Soldiers	Jerusalem	27:27–30	15:16–19		
	(35) Led to Golgotha	Jerusalem	27:31–34	15:20–23	23:26–33	19:16, 17
	(36) 6 Events of First 3 Hours on Cross	Calvary	27:35–44	15:24–32	23:33–43	19:18–27
	(37) Last 3 Hours on Cross	Calvary	27:45–50	15:33–37	23:44–46	19:28–30
	(38) Events Attending Jesus' Death		27:51–56	15:38–41	23:45, 47–49	
	(39) Burial of Jesus	Jerusalem	27:57–60	15:42–46	23:50–54	19:31–42
Friday-Saturday	(40) Tomb Sealed	Jerusalem	27:61–66		23:55, 56	
	(41) Women Watch	Jerusalem		15:47		
THE RESURRECTION THROUGH THE ASCENSION						
A.D. 30						
Dawn of First Day (Sunday, "Lord's Day")	(1) Women Visit the Tomb	Near Jerusalem	28:1–10	16:1–8	24:1–11	
	(2) Peter and John See the Empty Tomb				24:12	20:1–10
	(3) Jesus' Appearance to Mary Magdalene	Jerusalem		16:9–11		20:11–18
	(4) Jesus' Appearance to the Other Women	Jerusalem	28:9, 10			
	(5) Guards' Report of the Resurrection		28:11–15			
Sunday Afternoon	(6) Jesus' Appearance to Two Disciples on Way to Emmaus			16:12, 13	24:13–35	
Late Sunday	(7) Jesus' Appearance to Ten Disciples Without Thomas	Jerusalem			24:36–43	20:19–25
One Week Later	(8) Appearance to Disciples with Thomas	Jerusalem				20:26–31
During 40 Days until Ascension	(9) Jesus' Appearance to Seven Disciples by Sea of Galilee	Galilee				21:1–25
	(10) Great Commission		28:16–20	16:14–18	24:44–49	
	(11) The Ascension	Mt. Olivet		16:19, 20	24:50–53	

THE

NEW TESTAMENT

Words of Christ in Red

The Gospel According to MATTHEW

Author: Anonymous, But Early Tradition Unanimously Ascribes It to Matthew

Date: A.D. 50–75

Theme: Jesus Is the Fulfillment of Old Testament Prophecies Concerning the Messiah; His Disciples Are Called to a New Covenant, to Live at a Higher Dimension than the Old Ever Realized

Key Words: Fulfill, the Kingdom of Heaven, Son of Man, Son of God, Church

Author Although this Gospel does not identify its author, early church tradition attributes it to Matthew, the apostle and former tax collector. Other than his name and occupation, little is known about him. Tradition says that for fifteen years following the resurrection of Jesus he preached in Palestine and then conducted missionary campaigns in other nations.

Date The external evidence, such as quotations in Christian literature of the first century, testifies to the early existence and use of Matthew. Church leaders of the second and third centuries generally agreed that Matthew was the first Gospel to be written, and various statements in their writings indicate a date between A.D. 50 and 65. However, many modern scholars feel that both Matthew and Luke relied heavily on Mark in writing their Gospels, and accordingly date Matthew later. The ongoing tension between Jew and Gentile that is reflected in the Gospel suggests a period when Judaism and Christianity still overlapped.

Purpose Matthew's aim is to present Jesus, not only as the Messiah, but as the Son of David, and to elaborate this truth in such a way that it would aid the Christians in their controversies with the Jews. He shows how Jesus fulfilled Old Testament prophecy, and how the Law is filled with new meaning and supplemented in the Person, words, and work of Christ. Matthew also points out how Israel's rejection of Christ is in accordance with prophecy, and how that rejection caused the transference of the divine privileges of the chosen people from the Jewish to the Christian community. "The kingdom of God will be taken from you [Israel] and given to a nation bearing the fruits of it" (21:43).

Content The purpose of Matthew is evident in the structure of his book, which groups the teachings and deeds of Jesus into five divisions. The fivefold structure, common in Judaism, may reveal Matthew's purpose of showing Jesus as the fulfillment of the Law. Each division concludes with the formula, "And when Jesus had ended these sayings" (7:28; 11:1; 13:53; 19:1; 26:1).

In the prologue (1:1—2:23), Matthew shows that Jesus is the Messiah by linking Him with promises made to Abraham and David. The birth of Jesus highlights the fulfillment theme, portrays Jesus' royalty, and underscores the significance of Jesus for the Gentiles. The first division (chs. 3—7) contains the Sermon on the Mount, in which Jesus describes how people should live under God's reign.

The second division (chs. 8:1—11:1) features the instructions of Jesus to His disciples when He sent them out on their missionary journey.

The third division (11:2—13:52) records several controversies in which Jesus was involved and seven parables describing some aspect of the kingdom of heaven, coupled with the necessary human response.

The major discourse in the fourth division (13:53—18:35) concerns the conduct of believers within the Christian fellowship (ch. 18).

Matthew's fifth division (19:1—25:46) narrates the final journey of Jesus to Jerusalem and reveals His climactic conflict with Judaism. Chapters 24 and 25 contain the teaching of Jesus relating to the last things. The remainder of the book (26:1—28:20) details events and teachings pertaining to the Crucifixion, the Resurrection, and the Lord's commission to the church. Except at the beginning and at the end of the Gospel, Matthew's arrangement is not chronological and not strictly biographical, but is designed to show that in Jesus Judaism finds the fulfillment of its hopes.

Personal Application Matthew's emphasis on Jesus as the fulfillment of prophecy (41 OT quotes) shows that Jesus' life and ministry were part of the single plan of God throughout the history of Israel, and not an act of desperation. The entire Gospel stresses that Jesus is Immanuel—God-With-Us.

Jesus' teachings in Matthew's Gospel call for obedience and continue to expose sham and hypocrisy in personal and corporate life.

The book also gives to the church a clarion call to mission, the proclamation of the good news to all peoples. Christian disciples must learn to live within the tension of two ages, the present age of fulfillment in the Person of Jesus (in His words and works through His church by the Spirit's power) and the Age to Come, that is, the consummation of all things. In the interim, Christians are called to be humble, patient, genuine, faithful, watchful, and responsible—assured of the risen Jesus' presence as they are expectant of His return when faith will give way to sight.

Christ Revealed This Gospel presents Jesus as the fulfillment of all messianic hopes and expectations. Matthew carefully structures his narratives to reveal Jesus as fulfilling specific prophecies. Therefore, he saturates his Gospel with both quotations from and allusions to the Old Testament, introducing many of them with the formula "that it might be fulfilled."

In the Gospel, Jesus often refers to Himself as the Son of Man, a veiled reference to His messiahship (see Dan. 7:13, 14). Not only did the term allow Jesus to avoid common misunderstandings stemming from more popular messianic titles, but it enabled Him to interpret both His redemptive mission (as in 17:12, 22; 20:28; 26:24) and His return in glory (as in 13:41; 16:27; 19:28; 24:30, 44; 26:64).

Matthew's use of the title "Son of God" clearly underscores Jesus' deity (see 1:23; 2:15; 3:17; 16:16). As the Son, Jesus has a direct and unmediated relationship with the Father (11:27).

Matthew presents Jesus as Lord and Teacher of the church, the new community, which is called to live out the new ethic of the kingdom of heaven. Jesus declares "the church" as His select instrument for fulfilling the purposes of God on Earth (16:18; 18:15–20). Matthew's Gospel may have served as a teaching manual for the early church, including the amazing world-oriented Great Commission (28:12–20), with its guarantee of Jesus' living presence.

The Holy Spirit at Work

The activity of the Holy Spirit is evident at every phase of the life and ministry of Jesus. It was by the power of the Spirit that Jesus was conceived in Mary's womb (1:18, 20).

Before Jesus began His public ministry, He was filled with the Spirit of God (3:16), and followed the Spirit's leading into the wilderness to be tempted by the Devil as further preparation for His messianic role (4:1). The power of the Spirit enabled Jesus to heal (12:15–21) and to cast out demons (12:28).

Just as John immersed his followers in water, Jesus will immerse His followers in the Holy Spirit (3:11). In 7:21–23 we find a warning directed against false charismatics, those in the church who prophesy, cast out demons, and do wonders, but do not do the will of the Father. Presumably, the same Holy Spirit who inspires charismatic activities, must also empower the people of the church to do the will of God (7:21).

Jesus declared that His works were done in the power of the Holy Spirit, giving evidence that the kingdom of God had come and that the power of Satan was being overthrown. Therefore, to ascribe the power of the Spirit to the Devil was to commit an unpardonable sin (12:28–32).

In 12:28 the Holy Spirit is connected to Jesus' exorcisms and the present reality of the kingdom of God, not solely by the fact of exorcism per se, for the Pharisees' sons (disciples) also practice exorcism (12:27). Rather, the Holy Spirit is with the Messiah effecting a new event—"the kingdom of God has come upon you" (v. 28).

Finally, the Holy Spirit is found in the Great Commission (28:16–20). The disciples are commanded to go and make disciples of all nations, "baptizing them in the name of the Father and of the Son and of the Holy Spirit" (v. 19). That is, they are to baptize them "unto/with reference to" the name, or authority, of the triune God. In their obedience to this commission, Jesus' disciples are assured of His ongoing presence with them.

Outline of Matthew

Prologue: Genealogy and infancy narratives **1:1—2:23**
- A. The genealogy of Jesus 1:1–17
- B. Jesus' birth 1:18–25
- C. Worship of the wise men 2:1–12
- D. Flight into Egypt, the slaughter of the infants, and the return to Israel 2:13–23

I. Part One: Proclamation of the kingdom of heaven **3:1—7:29**
- A. Narrative: Beginning of Jesus' ministry 3:1—4:25
- B. Discourse: Sermon on the Mount 5:1—7:29

II. Part Two: Jesus' ministry in Galilee **8:1—11:1**
- A. Narrative: Ten miracle stories 8:1—9:34
- B. Discourse: Mission and martyrdom 9:35—11:1

III. Part Three: Controversy stories and parables **11:2—13:52**
- A. Narrative: Controversy which escalates 11:2—12:50
- B. Discourse: Parables of the kingdom 13:1–52

IV. Part Four: Narrative, controversy, and discourse **13:53—18:35**
- A. Narrative: Various episodes preceding Jesus' final journey to Jerusalem 13:53—17:27
- B. Discourse: Teaching on the church 18:1–35

V. Part Five: Jesus in Judea and Jerusalem **19:1—25:46**
- A. Narrative: Jesus' final journey and the mounting conflict 19:1—23:39
- B. Discourse: Jesus' eschatological teaching 24:1—25:46

The Passion narrative **26:1—27:66**

The Resurrection narrative **28:1–20**

The Genealogy of Jesus Christ

THE book of the [a]genealogy[1] of *Jesus *Christ, [b]the Son of David, [c]the Son of Abraham:

2 [a]Abraham begot Isaac, [b]Isaac begot Jacob, and Jacob begot [c]Judah and his brothers.

3 [a]Judah begot Perez and Zerah by Tamar, [b]Perez begot Hezron, and Hezron begot Ram.

4 Ram begot Amminadab, Amminadab begot Nahshon, and Nahshon begot Salmon.

5 Salmon begot [a]Boaz by Rahab, Boaz begot Obed by Ruth, Obed begot Jesse,

6 and [a]Jesse begot David the king. [b]David the king begot Solomon by her [1]*who had been the wife* of Uriah.

7 [a]Solomon begot Rehoboam, Rehoboam begot [b]Abijah, and Abijah begot [1]Asa.

8 Asa begot [a]Jehoshaphat, Jehoshaphat begot Joram, and Joram begot [b]Uzziah.

9 Uzziah begot Jotham, Jotham begot [a]Ahaz, and Ahaz begot Hezekiah.

10 [a]Hezekiah begot Manasseh, Manasseh begot [1]Amon, and Amon begot [b]Josiah.

11 [a]Josiah begot [1]Jeconiah and his brothers about the time they were [b]carried away to Babylon.

12 And after they were brought to Babylon, [a]Jeconiah begot Shealtiel, and Shealtiel begot [b]Zerubbabel.

13 Zerubbabel begot Abiud, Abiud begot Eliakim, and Eliakim begot Azor.

14 Azor begot Zadok, Zadok begot Achim, and Achim begot Eliud.

15 Eliud begot Eleazar, Eleazar begot Matthan, and Matthan begot Jacob.

16 And Jacob begot Joseph the husband of [a]Mary, of whom was born Jesus who is called Christ.

17 So all the generations from Abraham to David *are* fourteen generations, from David until the captivity in Babylon *are* fourteen generations, and from the captivity in Babylon until the Christ *are* fourteen generations.

CHAPTER 1

1 [a]Luke 3:23 [b]John 7:42 [c]Gen. 12:3; 22:18 [1]Lit. *generation* *See WW at Phil. 4:23. • See WW at 2 Tim. 4:22. **2** [a]Gen. 21:2, 12 [b]Gen. 25:26; 28:14 [c]Gen. 29:35 **3** [a]Gen. 38:27; 49:10 [b]Ruth 4:18–22 **5** [a]Ruth 2:1; 4:1–13 **6** [a]1 Sam. 16:1 [b]2 Sam. 7:12; 12:24 [1]Words in italic type have been added for clarity. They are not found in the original Greek. **7** [a]1 Chr. 3:10 [b]2 Chr. 11:20 [1]NU *Asaph* **8** [a]1 Chr. 3:10 [b]2 Kin. 15:13 **9** [a]2 Kin. 15:38 **10** [a]2 Kin. 20:21 [b]1 Kin. 13:2

[1]NU *Amos* **11** [a]1 Chr. 3:15, 16 [b]2 Kin. 24:14–16 [1]Or *Coniah* or *Jehoiachin* **12** [a]1 Chr. 3:17 [b]Ezra 3:2 **16** [a]Matt. 13:55

1:1–17 Matthew follows the legal Jewish system in giving the **genealogy** of the father even though Joseph was father only by adoption. Matthew's purpose in recording the genealogy was twofold: 1) to demonstrate continuity between the Israel of the OT and Jesus; 2) to demonstrate Jesus' royal lineage (**Son of David**) and His link with the founder of the Jewish race (**Son of Abraham**).

Christ Born of Mary

18 Now the [a]birth of Jesus Christ was
as follows: After His mother Mary was
betrothed to Joseph, before they came
together, she was found with child
[b]of the Holy Spirit.
19 Then Joseph her husband, being
[1]a **just** *man,* and not *wanting [a]to make
her a public example, was minded to
put her away secretly.

WORD WEALTH

1:19 just, *dikaios* (*dik*-ah-yoss); Strong's *#1342:* Upright, blameless, righteous, conforming to God's laws and man's. The word was originally used to describe people who lived in accordance with *dike,* "rule," "custom." In the NT it is used primarily of persons who correspond to the divine standard of right made possible through justification and sanctification.

20 But while he thought about these
things, behold, an angel of the Lord appeared to him in a dream, saying, "Joseph, son of David, do not be afraid
to take to you Mary your wife, [a]for that
which is [1]conceived in her is of the
Holy Spirit.
21 [a]"And she will bring forth a Son,
and you shall *call His *name [1]JESUS,
[b]for He will *save His people from their
sins."
22 So all this was done that it might
be fulfilled which was spoken by the
Lord through the prophet, saying:
23 [a]*"Behold,*[1] *the virgin shall be with
child, and bear a Son, and they shall
call His name Immanuel,"* which is
translated, "God with us."
24 Then Joseph, being aroused from
sleep, did as the angel of the Lord commanded him and took to him his wife,
25 and [1]did not know her till she had
brought forth [a]her[2] firstborn Son. And
he called His name JESUS.

18 [a]Matt. 12:46; Luke 1:27 [b]Is. 7:14; 49:5; Luke 1:35
19 [a]Deut. 24:1; John 8:4, 5 [1]*an upright* *See WW at Matt. 8:2.
20 [a]Luke 1:35 [1]Lit. *begotten*
21 [a][Is. 7:14; 9:6, 7]; Luke 1:31; 2:21 [b]Luke 2:11; John 1:29; [Acts 4:12; 5:31; 13:23, 38; Rom. 5:18, 19; Col. 1:20–23] [1]Lit. *Savior* *See WW at Gal. 1:6. • See WW at John 12:13. • See WW at Luke 7:50.
23 [a]Is. 7:14 [1]Words in oblique type in the New Testament are quoted from the Old Testament.
25 [a]Ex. 13:2; Luke 2:7, 21 [1]Kept her a virgin [2]NU *a Son*

CHAPTER 2

1 [a]Mic. 5:2; Luke 2:4–7 [b]Gen. 25:6; 1 Kin. 4:30 [1]Gr. *magoi*
2 [a]Luke 2:11 [b][Num. 24:17; Is. 60:3]
3 *See WW at Luke 24:38.
4 [a]2 Chr. 36:14 [b]2 Chr. 34:13 [c]Mal. 2:7
6 [a]Mic. 5:2; John 7:42 [b]Gen. 49:10; [Rev. 2:27]

Wise Men from the East

2 Now after [a]Jesus was born in Bethlehem of Judea in the days of
Herod the king, behold, [1]wise men
[b]from the East came to Jerusalem,
2 saying, [a]"Where is He who has
been born King of the Jews? For we
have seen [b]His star in the East and
have come to worship Him."
3 When Herod the king heard *this,* he
was *troubled, and all Jerusalem with
him.
4 And when he had gathered all
[a]the chief priests and [b]scribes of the
people together, [c]he inquired of them
where the Christ was to be born.
5 So they said to him, "In Bethlehem
of Judea, for thus it is written by the
prophet:

6 *'But*[a] *you, Bethlehem, in the land*
of Judah,
Are not the least among the rulers
of Judah;
For out of you shall come a Ruler
[b] *Who will shepherd My people*
Israel.' "

WORD WEALTH

2:5 prophet, *prophetes* (prof-*ay*-tace); Strong's *#4396:* From *pro,* "forth," and *phemi,* "to speak." A prophet, therefore, is primarily a forth-teller, one who speaks forth a divine message that can at times include foretelling future events. Among the Greeks, the prophet was the interpreter of the divine will, and this idea is dominant in biblical usage. Prophets are therefore specially endowed with insights into the counsels of the Lord and serve as His spokesmen. Prophecy is a gift of the Holy Spirit (1 Cor. 12:12), which the NT encourages believers to exercise, although at a level different from those with the prophetic office (Eph. 4:11).

1:18, 19 Betrothal was as binding as the actual marriage and could be broken only by divorce. Joseph's character is evidenced in his unwillingness to expose his betrothed wife by repudiating her before witnesses.

1:21 The name **JESUS** means "Yahweh Is Salvation."

1:23 The Hebrew text of Is. 7:14 uses a word which indicates a young girl of marriageable age, while the Greek translation clearly uses the word **virgin.** Whatever its immediate historical meaning was, Matthew views the prophecy of Isaiah as fulfilled in the birth of Jesus by the Virgin Mary. The name **Immanuel** here declares the presence of God with His people in a way altogether new.

1:25 The language indicates that Mary and Joseph entered into normal marital relations following the birth of Jesus.

2:1 The **wise men** were Eastern astrologers, but not to be construed as of the same spirit as modern astrology. Their visit serves to emphasize Jesus' kingly identity (v. 11), affirm the Bethlehem origin of the Messiah (v. 6), and emphasize the Gentile faith and worship (v. 8) in contrast to Jewish hostility (v. 3).

2:2 Star in the East: As trained students of the stars, the wise men observed an unexplained phenomenon in the heavens, which was somehow interpreted by them as a sign of the birth of the King of the Jews. The reference in v. 1 to "Herod the king" ("Herod the Great") would make their visit prior to 4 B.C. when he died and was succeeded by his son Archelaus (v. 22). Matthew consistently uses the verb **worship** to describe the attitude and posture of people before Jesus (vv. 8, 11; 8:2; 9:18; 14:33).

2:5, 6 The birth of Jesus fulfilled Mic. 5:2 and 2 Sam. 5:2, which link the Ruler with David's family (1:6).

7 Then Herod, when he had secretly
called the [1]wise men, determined from
them what *time the [a]star appeared.
8 And he sent them to Bethlehem and
said, "Go and search carefully for the
young Child, and when you have found
Him, bring back word to me, that I may
come and worship Him also."
9 When they heard the king, they departed; and behold, the star which they
had seen in the East went before them,
till it came and stood over where the
young Child was.
10 When they saw the star, they rejoiced with exceedingly great joy.
11 And when they had come into the
house, they saw the young Child with
Mary His mother, and fell down and
worshiped Him. And when they had
opened their treasures, [a]they presented gifts to Him: gold, frankincense,
and myrrh.
12 Then, being divinely warned [a]in
a dream that they should not return to
Herod, they departed for their own
country another way.

The Flight into Egypt

13 Now when they had departed, behold, an angel of the Lord appeared
to Joseph in a dream, saying, "Arise,
take the young Child and His mother,
flee to Egypt, and stay there until I
bring you word; for Herod will seek
the young Child to *destroy Him."
14 When he arose, he took the young
Child and His mother by night and departed for Egypt,
15 and was there until the death of
Herod, that it might be fulfilled which
was spoken by the Lord through the
prophet, saying, [a]*"Out of Egypt I called
My Son."*

Massacre of the Innocents

16 Then Herod, when he saw that he
was deceived by the wise men, was exceedingly angry; and he sent forth and
put to death all the male children who
were in Bethlehem and in all its districts, from two years old and under,
according to the time which he had determined from the wise men.
17 Then was fulfilled what was spoken
by Jeremiah the *prophet, saying:

18 *"A [a]voice was heard in Ramah,*
Lamentation, weeping, and great
mourning,
Rachel weeping for her children,
Refusing to be comforted,
Because they are no more."

The Home in Nazareth

19 Now when Herod was dead, behold,
an angel of the Lord appeared in a
dream to Joseph in Egypt,
20 [a]saying, "Arise, take the young
Child and His mother, and go to the

7 [a]Num. 24:17 [1]Gr. *magoi* *See WW at Acts 1:7.
11 [a]Ps. 72:10; Is. 60:6
12 [a][Job 33:15, 16]; Matt. 1:20
13 *See WW at Luke 9:56.
15 [a]Num. 24:8; Hos. 11:1
17 *See WW at Matt. 2:5.
18 [a]Jer. 31:15
20 [a]Luke 2:39

2:13–23 The accounts of the flight into Egypt (vv. 13–15), the massacre of the innocents (vv.16–18), and the settlement in Nazareth (vv. 19–23) underscore the theme of fulfillment. See Hos. 11:1; Jer. 31:15; Is. 11:1; 49:6.
2:15, 16 Out of Egypt: Matthew intends that his readers see an implicit link with a new **Son** who emerges from Egypt (Hos. 11:1). Matthew reinterprets Son (Israel in Hos.) to mean Jesus, who comes out of Egypt with Joseph and Mary and settles in Nazareth. Herod's attempt to destroy Jesus is analogous to Pharaoh's attempt to kill Moses (Ex. 1:15—2:10).
2:18 The distress of the Hebrew mothers at the time of the Babylonian captivity (Jer. 31:15) received a deeper significance by the weeping mothers of Bethlehem.

The Journeys of Jesus' Birth. Fulfillment of prophecy was involved both when Joseph and Mary went to Bethlehem (Mic. 5:2), obeying the imperial decree (Luke 2:1–5), and when they went to Egypt (Hos. 11:1), following the angel's command (Matt. 2:13).

Mediterranean Sea
GALILEE
Sea of Galilee
Nazareth
Samaria
SAMARIA
Jerusalem
Ashkelon
Gaza
Bethlehem
JUDEA
Dead Sea
IDUMEA
To Egypt
NABATEA
N
0 100 Mi.
0 100 Km.

land of Israel, for those who [b]sought
the young Child's life are dead."
21 Then he arose, took the young Child
and His mother, and came into the land
of Israel.
22 But when he heard that Archelaus
was reigning over Judea instead of his
father Herod, he was afraid to go there.
And being warned by God in a [a]dream,
he turned aside [b]into the region of Galilee.
23 And he came and dwelt in a city
called [a]Nazareth, that it might be fulfilled [b]which was spoken by the prophets, "He shall be called a Nazarene."

John the Baptist Prepares the Way

3 In those days [a]John the Baptist
came preaching [b]in the wilderness
of Judea,
2 and saying, "**Repent,** for [a]the kingdom of heaven is at hand!"

WORD WEALTH

3:2 repent, *metanoeo* (met-an-ah-*eh*-oh); Strong's *#3340:* From *meta,* "after," and *noeo,* "to think." Repentance is a decision that results in a change of mind, which in turn leads to a change of purpose and action.

KINGDOM DYNAMICS

3:1, 2 Defining the Hope, TERMINOLOGY OF THE KINGDOM. The NT records 137 references to "the kingdom," and over 100 of these are during Jesus' ministry, as His entire teaching and approach as Messiah—the Savior-King—center on this theme. To what does "the kingdom" refer? It refers to God's sovereign rule in the universe—He is the King of the heavens. (See Gen. 1:1.) But more specifically, here it refers to the entry of God's long-anticipated Anointed One—the prophesied Messiah, the promised Son of David who would not only be the Savior, Deliverer, and King of Israel, but of all mankind. "The Gentiles" (or all nations)—all flesh—were promised recipients of this hope (Is. 9:6, 7; 11:10; 40:5). Declaring the kingdom "at hand," that is, "drawing near," John was announcing that the rule of God's King was about to overthrow the power and rule of all evil—both human and hellish. The "kingdom" was near because the King was here. And His presence, introducing the power of "the kingdom of God," meant a new world of potential hope to mankind. Man would no more need be held hostage to either the rule of death over mankind, resultant from human sin and sinning, or to the deadening rule of oppressive human systems, political or otherwise. Further, the kingdom of darkness would be confronted and the death, deprivation, disease, and destruction levied by satanic power would begin to be overthrown. As God's King, Jesus offers the blessing of God's rule, now available to bring life to every human experience, as well as deliverance from the dominance of either flesh or the Devil.

(1 Chr. 29:10–16/Matt. 19:23, 24) J.W.H.

KINGDOM DYNAMICS

3:1, 2; 4:17 Repentance, THE MESSAGE OF THE KINGDOM. The first call of the kingdom is to repentance. The implications of biblical repentance are threefold: 1) renunciation and reversal, 2) submission and teachability, and 3) continual shapeability. There is no birth into the kingdom without hearing the call to salvation, renouncing one's sin, and turning from sin toward Christ the Savior (Acts 3:19).

There is no growth in the kingdom without obedience to Jesus' commandments and a childlike responsiveness as a disciple of Jesus, yielding to the teaching of God's Word (James 1:21–25).

There is no lifelong increase of fruit as a citizen of the kingdom without a willingness to accept the Holy Spirit's correction and guidance (Eph. 4:30).

(Mark 1:14, 15/John 3:1–5) J.W.H.

3 For this is he who was spoken of
by the prophet Isaiah, saying:

[a]*"The voice of one crying in the*
wilderness:
[b]*'Prepare the way of the* LORD*;*
Make His paths straight.' "

4 Now [a]John himself was clothed in
camel's hair, with a leather belt around
his waist; and his food was [b]locusts
and [c]wild honey.
5 [a]Then Jerusalem, all Judea, and all
the region around the Jordan went out
to him

20 [b]Matt. 2:16
22 [a]Matt. 2:12, 13, 19 [b]Matt. 3:13; Luke 2:39
23 [a]Luke 1:26; 2:39; John 1:45, 46 [b]Judg. 13:5

CHAPTER 3

1 [a]Matt. 3:1–12; Mark 1:3–8; Luke 3:2–17; John 1:6–8, 19–28 [b]Josh. 14:10
2 [a]Dan. 2:44; Mal. 4:6; Matt. 4:17; Mark 1:15; Luke 1:17; 10:9; 11:20; 21:31
3 [a]Is. 40:3; Luke 3:4; John 1:23 [b]Luke 1:76
4 [a]2 Kin. 1:8; Zech. 13:4; Matt. 11:8; Mark 1:6 [b]Lev. 11:22 [c]1 Sam. 14:25, 26
5 [a]Mark 1:5

2:23 The term **Nazarene** may be a reference to the Hebrew term for "branch," "sprout," or "shoot" in Is. 11:1.
3:1 The expression **in those days** is not chronological but theological, that is, "in that critical period of OT fulfillment."
3:2 The nearness of God's reign, confronting people with an inescapable decision, explains the urgency of John's message of repentance. Jesus announced the same message (4:17).
3:3 Isaiah's prophecy likens John to a royal herald ordering the repair of the roads in preparation for the coming of the King.
3:4 The description of John's clothing connects him with Elijah (see 2 Kin. 1:8; Zech. 13:4).

6 [a]and were baptized by him in the Jordan, confessing their sins.
7 But when he saw many of the Pharisees and Sadducees coming to his *baptism, he said to them, [a]"Brood of vipers! Who warned you to flee from [b]the wrath to come?
8 "Therefore bear fruits worthy of repentance,
9 "and do not think to say to yourselves, [a]'We have Abraham as *our* father.' For I say to you that God is able to raise up children to Abraham from these stones.
10 "And even now the ax is laid to the root of the trees. [a]Therefore every tree which does not bear good fruit is cut down and thrown into the fire.
11 11 [a]"I indeed baptize you with water unto repentance, but He who is coming after me is mightier than I, whose sandals I am not worthy to carry. [b]He will baptize you with the Holy Spirit [1]and fire.
12 [a]"His winnowing fan *is* in His hand, and He will thoroughly clean out His threshing floor, and gather His wheat into the barn; but He will [b]burn up the chaff with unquenchable fire."

John Baptizes Jesus

13 [a]Then Jesus came [b]from Galilee to John at the Jordan to be baptized by him.
14 And John *tried to* prevent Him, saying, "I need to be baptized by You, and are You coming to me?"
15 But Jesus answered and said to him, "Permit *it to be so* now, for thus it is fitting for us to fulfill all *righteousness." Then he allowed Him.
16 [a]When He had been baptized, Jesus came up immediately from the water; and behold, the heavens were opened to Him, and [1]He saw [b]the Spirit of God descending like a dove and alighting upon Him.
17 [a]And suddenly a voice *came* from heaven, saying, [b]"This is My beloved Son, in whom I am well pleased."

Satan Tempts Jesus

4 Then [a]Jesus was led up by [b]the Spirit into the wilderness to be tempted by the devil.
2 And when He had fasted forty days and forty nights, afterward He was hungry.
3 Now when the tempter came to Him, he said, "If You are the Son of God, command that these stones become bread."
4 But He answered and said, "It is written, [a]*'Man shall not live by bread alone, but by every* **word** *that proceeds from the mouth of God.'*"

> **WORD WEALTH**
>
> **4:4 word,** *rhema* (*hray*-mah); Strong's *#4487:* That which is said or spoken, an utterance, in contrast to *logos,* which is the expression of a thought, a message, a discourse. *Logos* is the message; *rhema* is the communication of the message. In reference to the Bible, *logos* is the Bible in its entirety; *rhema* is a verse from the Bible. The meaning of *rhema* in distinction to *logos* is illustrated in Eph. 6:17, where the reference is not to the Scriptures as a whole, but to that portion which the believer wields as a sword in the time of need.

5 Then the devil took Him up [a]into the holy city, set Him on the pinnacle of the temple,

6 [a]Acts 19:4, 18 **7** [a]Matt. 12:34; Luke 3:7–9 [b][Rom. 5:9; 1 Thess. 1:10] *See WW at Matt. 21:25. **9** [a]John 8:33; Acts 13:26; [Rom. 4:1, 11, 16; Gal. 3:29] **10** [a][Ps. 92:12–14]; Matt. 7:19; Luke 13:7, 9; [John 15:6] **11** [a]Mark 1:4, 8; Luke 3:16; John 1:26; Acts 1:5 [b][Is. 4:4; John 20:22; Acts 2:3, 4; 1 Cor. 12:13] [1]M omits *and fire* **12** [a]Mal. 3:3 [b]Mal. 4:1; Matt. 13:30 **13** [a]Matt. 3:13–17; Mark 1:9–11; Luke 3:21, 22; John 1:31–34 [b]Matt. 2:22 **15** *See WW at 2 Tim. 4:8. **16** [a]Mark 1:10 [b][Is. 11:2]; Luke 3:22; John 1:32; Acts 7:56 [1]Or *he*
17 [a]John 12:28 [b]Ps. 2:7; Is. 42:1; Mark 1:11; Luke 1:35; 9:35; Col. 1:13

CHAPTER 4

1 [a]Matt. 4:1–11; Mark 1:12; Luke 4:1 [b]Ezek. 3:14; Acts 8:39 **4** [a]Deut. 8:3 **5** [a]Neh. 11:1, 18; Dan. 9:24; Matt. 27:53

3:7 John uses the metaphor of snakes fleeing from a desert brushfire to depict the religious leaders' posture before **the wrath to come.**
3:9 Physical descent from Abraham does not automatically place one in the kingdom of God.
3:11, 12 See section 11 of Truth-In-Action through the Synoptics at the end of Luke.
3:11 John's baptism is a type of the salvation experience of being baptized in the Spirit. As John's baptism placed the individual in the medium of **water,** so the baptism of Jesus places the Christian in the Spirit, identifying him as bound over totally to the Lord. **Fire** either purifies or destroys. Hence, salvation in Jesus Christ will be purifying for the true Jews who accept Him as Messiah and destructive for those who reject Him.
3:14, 15 *John's* question arises from the apparent incongruity of an inferior one baptizing his superior (v. 11). **All righteousness:** Jesus affirms both God's standard of righteousness and His own will to accomplish that standard in His life. He also gives approval to John's message of repentance and confession of sin as a necessity for entering the kingdom of heaven.
3:16 The Spirit anointed Jesus for His ministry. The **dove** symbolizes gentleness, innocence, and meekness, and it was offered in sacrifice (Lev. 12:6; 14:22; see Luke 2:24). The gentle, innocent, and meek Jesus would be a sacrifice for sin.
3:17 The words of the heavenly voice, taken from Ps. 2:7, a royal psalm, and Is. 42:1, a Servant song, affirm that Jesus is King Messiah who is to carry out the mission of the Servant.
4:1 To be **tempted,** from the divine standpoint, means a positive test; from the Devil's standpoint it implies enticement to sin; from Jesus' standpoint it is a challenge from Satan to test God's sovereignty and plan (v. 6).
4:3 If does not imply doubt, but expresses an assumed fact, and may be translated "since."
4:4 Jesus' appeal to Scripture provides the clue for interpreting the Temptation narrative. Using the Word of God, He is victorious over the same temptations to which Israel had succumbed in the wilderness, when they forced a test upon God in time of need.

6 and said to Him, "If You are the Son of God, throw Yourself down. For it is written:

[a]*'He shall give His angels charge over you,'*

and,

[b]*'In their hands they shall bear you up,*
Lest you dash your foot against a stone.'"

7 Jesus said to him, "It is written again, [a]*'You shall not* [1]*tempt the* LORD *your God.'"*
8 Again, the devil took Him up on an exceedingly high mountain, and [a]showed Him all the kingdoms of the world and their glory.
9 And he said to Him, "All these things I will give You if You will fall down and worship me."
10 Then Jesus said to him, [1]"Away with you, Satan! For it is written, [a]*'You shall worship the* LORD *your God, and Him only you shall serve.'"*
11 Then the devil [a]left Him, and behold, [b]**angels** came and ministered to Him.

WORD WEALTH

4:11 angels, *angelos* (*ang*-el-oss); Strong's *#32:* From *angello*, "to deliver a message"; hence, a messenger. In the NT the word has the special sense of a spiritual, heavenly personage attendant upon God and functioning as a messenger from the Lord sent to Earth to execute His purposes and to make them known to men. Angels are invisibly present in the assemblies of Christians and are appointed by God to minister to believers (Heb. 1:14).

Jesus Begins His Galilean Ministry

12 [a]Now when Jesus heard that John had been put in prison, He departed to Galilee.
13 And leaving Nazareth, He came and dwelt in Capernaum, which is by the sea, in the regions of Zebulun and Naphtali,
14 that it might be fulfilled which was spoken by Isaiah the prophet, saying:

15 *"The* [a] *land of Zebulun and the land of Naphtali,*
By the way of the sea, beyond the Jordan,
Galilee of the Gentiles:
16 [a]*The people who sat in darkness have seen a great light,*
And upon those who sat in the region and shadow of death
Light has dawned."

17 [a]From that time Jesus began to preach and to say, [b]"Repent,* for the kingdom of heaven [1]is at hand."

Four Fishermen Called as Disciples

18 [a]And Jesus, walking by the Sea of Galilee, saw two brothers, Simon [b]called Peter, and Andrew his brother, casting a net into the sea; for they were fishermen.
19 Then He said to them, "Follow Me, and [a]I will make you fishers of men."
20 [a]They *immediately left *their* nets and followed Him.
21 [a]Going on from there, He saw two other brothers, James *the son* of Zebedee, and John his brother, in the boat with Zebedee their father, *mending their nets. He called them,
22 and immediately they left the boat and their father, and followed Him.

Jesus Heals a Great Multitude

23 And Jesus went about all Galilee, [a]teaching in their synagogues, preaching [b]the *gospel of the kingdom, [c]and healing all kinds of sickness and all kinds of disease among the people.
24 Then [1]His fame went throughout all Syria; and they [a]brought* to Him all sick people who were *afflicted with various diseases and torments, and those who were demon-possessed, epileptics, and paralytics; and He *healed them.
25 [a]Great multitudes followed Him—

6 [a]Ps. 91:11 [b]Ps. 91:12
7 [a]Deut. 6:16 [1]*test*
8 [a][Matt. 16:26; 1 John 2:15–17]
10 [a]Deut. 6:13; 10:20; Josh. 24:14 [1]M *Get behind Me*
11 [a][James 4:7] [b]Matt. 26:53; Luke 22:43; [Heb. 1:14]
12 [a]Matt. 14:3; Mark 1:14; Luke 3:20; John 4:43
15 [a]Is. 9:1, 2
16 [a]Is. 42:7; Luke 2:32
17 [a]Mark 1:14, 15 [b]Matt. 3:2; 10:7 [1]*has drawn near* *See WW at Matt. 3:2.
18 [a]Matt. 4:18–22; Mark 1:16–20; Luke 5:2–11; John 1:40–42 [b]Matt. 10:2; 16:18; John 1:40–42
19 [a]Luke 5:10
20 [a]Matt. 19:27; Mark 10:28 *See WW at John 6:21.
21 [a]Mark 1:19 *See WW at Heb. 11:3.
23 [a]Ps. 22:22; Matt. 9:35; Mark 1:21; 6:2; 10:1; Luke 4:15; 6:6; 13:10; John 6:59; 18:20 [b][Matt. 24:14]; Mark 1:14; Luke 4:43; 8:1; 16:16 [c]Mark 1:34; Luke 4:40; 7:21; Acts 10:38 *See WW at Mark 1:1.
24 [a]Mark 1:32, 33; Luke 4:40 [1]Lit. *the report of Him* *See WW at Heb. 9:28. • See WW at 2 Cor. 5:14. • See WW at Matt. 12:22.
25 [a]Matt. 5:1; 8:1, 18; Mark 3:7, 8

4:6 The temptation solicits a compelling messianic proof.
4:10 Rather than earthly power, Jesus affirms exclusive worship of God and His vocation of humble obedience and suffering.
4:11 Jesus emerges as Victor in His repudiation of a false messiahship based upon compromise and power.
4:13–16 Capernaum was located on the western shore of the Sea of Galilee, on the border of the two ancient tribes of **Zebulun and Naphtali.** Jesus' arrival there fulfilled the prophecy of Isaiah (Is. 8:21—9:2) that these northern tribes, which had suffered severely, would be delivered from their enemies.
4:17 The verb **is at hand** means "has come," "has arrived," or "is here," and suggests the inauguration of the reign of God, which still awaits its consummation.
4:18, 19 These men had already met Jesus (see John 1:40–42), but now they left their secular occupations to follow Him.
4:23–25 Jesus' powerful Galilean ministry resulted in increasing popularity.

from Galilee, and *from* [1]Decapolis, Jerusalem, Judea, and beyond the Jordan.

KINGDOM DYNAMICS

4:23–25 The Extent of Jesus' Healing Ministry and Commission, DIVINE HEALING. These verses show the large extent of Jesus' healing ministry. Jesus' ministry consisted of teaching, preaching, making disciples, healing the sick, and casting out demons. This passage is the first NT record of Jesus healing physical afflictions and bringing deliverance to the demonically tormented. Some argue that Jesus healed during His ministry only in order to demonstrate His deity. Look, however, at such passages as 9:36, 37 and 14:14, where it is clear that He healed out of compassion for the suffering multitudes. Therefore, it seems obvious that Jesus intended healing to be a part of the Christian mission of deliverance. His Great Commission includes the promise: "They will lay hands on the sick, and they will recover" (Mark 16:18). He extends this commission on the basis of His atonement, His compassion, and His promise of power to fulfill His word.

(Is. 53:4, 5/Matt. 8:16, 17) N.V.

The Beatitudes

5 And seeing the multitudes, [a]He went up on a mountain, and when He was seated His disciples came to Him.

KINGDOM DYNAMICS

5:1—7:27 Basic Traits, CHARACTER AND THE KINGDOM. In the Sermon on the Mount, Jesus outlines the primary attributes of people who receive the rule of the kingdom He brings. Nine direct references to "the kingdom" are in this sermon, calling for: humility (5:3), willingness to suffer persecution (5:10), earnest attention to God's commandments (5:19), refusal to substitute false piety for genuinely right behavior (5:20), a life of prayer (6:10, 13), prioritizing spiritual over material values (6:33), and above all, acknowledging Christ's lordship by obeying the revealed will of God (7:21). Clearly, the authority Christ hopes to delegate to His own is intended to be exercised by disciples willing to accept renewal in soul and behavior, as well as rebirth through forgiveness of sin. To these, obviously, the call to "kingdom" living and ministry includes the expectation that Holy Spirit-begotten fruit and gifts will develop in the believer. The same Spirit that distributes gifts of power for kingdom service also works in us to beget kingly qualities of life, love, and a holy character (John 15:1–17; Gal. 5:22, 23).

(Luke 17:20, 21/Matt. 18:1–4) J.W.H.

2 Then He opened His mouth and [a]taught them, saying:

3 "**Blessed**[a] *are* the poor in spirit,
For theirs is the kingdom of heaven.
4 [a]Blessed *are* those who *mourn,
For they shall be comforted.
5 [a]Blessed *are* the *meek,
For [b]they shall inherit the [1]earth.
6 Blessed *are* those who [a]hunger and thirst for righteousness,
[b]For they shall be *filled.
7 Blessed *are* the **merciful,**
[a]For they shall obtain *mercy.
8 [a]Blessed *are* the **pure** in heart,
For [b]they shall see God.
9 Blessed *are* the peacemakers,
For they shall be called sons of God.
10 [a]Blessed *are* those who are persecuted for righteousness' sake,
For theirs is the kingdom of heaven.

WORD WEALTH

5:3 blessed, *makarios* (mak-*ar*-ee-oss); Strong's *#3107:* From the root *mak,* indicating large or of long duration. The word is an adjective suggesting happy, supremely blessed, a condition in which congratulations are in order. It is a grace word that expresses the special joys and satisfaction granted the person who experiences salvation.

25 [1]Lit. *Ten Cities*

CHAPTER 5

1 [a]Matt. 14:23; 15:29; 17:1; Mark 3:13; Luke 6:17; 9:28; John 6:3, 15
2 [a][Matt. 7:29]; Mark 10:1; 12:35; John 8:2
3 [a]Prov. 16:19; Is. 66:2; Luke 6:20–23
4 [a]Is. 61:2, 3; Luke 6:21; [John 16:20]; Acts 16:34; [2 Cor. 1:7]; Rev. 21:4 *See WW at Rev. 18:11.
5 [a]Ps. 37:11; Is. 29:19 [b][Rom. 4:13] [1]Or *land* *See WW at Matt. 21:5.
6 [a]Luke 1:53; Acts 2:4 [b][Is. 55:1; 65:13; John 4:14; 6:48; 7:37] *See WW at Matt. 15:33.
7 [a]Ps. 41:1; Mark 11:25 *See WW at Rom. 9:15.
8 [a]Ps. 15:2; 24:4; Heb. 12:14 [b]Acts 7:55, 56; 1 Cor. 13:12
10 [a][2 Cor. 4:17]; 1 Pet. 3:14

5:1 The location of the **mountain** is uncertain, but it was likely in the vicinity of Capernaum. Following the custom of the rabbis, Jesus sat while teaching. The **disciples** included a wider audience *than the 12 disciples* (see 7:28, 29).
5:3 Each Beatitude includes a pronouncement of blessing, a description of the ones considered as blessed, and an explanation (**for**) of the blessing. **The poor in spirit** are those who recognize their spiritual poverty and, casting aside all self-dependence, seek God's grace.
5:4 Those who mourn are not necessarily people in bereavement, but those who experience the sorrow of repentance.
5:5 Meek does not connote weakness, but rather controlled strength. The word carries the ideas of humility and self-discipline.
5:9 God is the supreme Peacemaker, and His **sons** follow His example.
5:10 The cause of persecution is loyalty to righteousness which Jesus makes specific in v. 11.

WORD WEALTH

5:7 merciful, *eleemon* (el-eh-*ay*-mone); Strong's *#1655:* Related to the words *eleeo* (to have mercy), *eleos* (active compassion), and *eleemosune* (compassion for the poor). *Eleemon* is a kind, compassionate, sympathetic, merciful, and sensitive word, combining tendencies with action. A person with this quality finds outlets for his merciful nature. The English word "eleemosynary" or charitable philanthropic relief, finds its origin in this word.

WORD WEALTH

5:8 pure, *katharos* (kath-ar-*oss*); Strong's *#2513:* Without blemish, clean, undefiled, pure. The word describes physical cleanliness (Matt. 23:26; 27:59); ceremonial purity (Luke 11:41; Rom. 14:20); and ethical purity (John 13:10; Acts 18:6). Sin pollutes and defiles, but the blood of Jesus washes the stains away.

KINGDOM DYNAMICS

5:8 6. Can I Live a Holy Life?, SPIRITUAL ANSWERS. For the answer to this and other probing questions about God and the power life in His kingdom, see the study article "Spiritual Answers to Hard Questions," which begins on page 1996. P.R.

11 [a]"Blessed are you when they *revile
and persecute you, and say all kinds of
[b]evil against you falsely for My sake.
12 [a]"Rejoice and be exceedingly glad,
for great *is* your reward in heaven, for
[b]so they persecuted the prophets who
were before you.

Believers Are Salt and Light

2 13 "You are the salt of the earth;
[a]but if the salt loses its flavor, how
shall it be seasoned? It is then good
for nothing but to be thrown out and
trampled underfoot by men.
14 [a]"You are the light of the *world.
A city that is set on a hill cannot be
hidden.
15 "Nor do they [a]light a lamp and put
it under a basket, but on a lampstand,
and it gives light to all *who are* in the
house.
16 "Let your light so shine before men,
[a]that they may see your good works
and [b]glorify your Father in heaven.

Christ Fulfills the Law

17 [a]"Do not think that I came to de- 1
stroy the Law or the Prophets. I did
not come to destroy but to fulfill.
18 "For assuredly, I say to you, [a]till
heaven and earth pass away, one
[1]jot or one [2]tittle will by no means pass
from the law till all is fulfilled.
19 [a]"Whoever therefore breaks one of
the least of these commandments, and
teaches men so, shall be called least
in the kingdom of heaven; but whoever
does and teaches *them,* he shall be
called great in the kingdom of heaven.
20 "For I say to you, that unless your
righteousness exceeds [a]*the righteousness* of the scribes and Pharisees, you
will by no means enter the kingdom
of heaven.

Murder Begins in the Heart

21 "You have heard that it was said 6
to those [1]of old, [a]'*You shall not murder,* and whoever murders will be in
danger of the judgment.'
22 "But I say to you that [a]whoever is
*angry with his brother [1]without a
cause shall be in danger of the **judgment.** And whoever says to his brother,

11 [a]Luke 6:22 [b]1 Pet. 4:14 *See WW at James 1:5. **12** [a]Luke 6:23; Acts 5:41; 1 Pet. 4:13, 14 [b]2 Chr. 36:16; Neh. 9:26; Matt. 23:37; Acts 7:52; 1 Thess. 2:15; Heb. 11:35–37; James 5:10 **13** [a]Mark 9:50; Luke 14:34 **14** [a][Prov. 4:18; John 8:12]; Phil. 2:15 *See WW at John 18:36. **15** [a]Mark 4:21; Luke 8:16; Phil. 2:15 **16** [a]1 Pet. 2:12 [b][John 15:8]; 1 Cor. 14:25 **17** [a]Rom. 10:4 **18** [a]Matt. 24:35; Luke 16:17 [1]Gr. *iota,* Heb. *yod,* the smallest letter [2]The smallest stroke in a Heb. letter **19** [a][James 2:10] **20** [a][Rom. 10:3] **21** [a]Ex. 20:13; Deut. 5:17 [1]*in ancient times* **22** [a][1 John 3:15] [1]NU omits *without a cause* *See WW at Rev. 12:17.

5:13–16 See section 2 of Truth-In-Action through the Synoptics at the end of Luke.

5:13–16 The Beatitudes describe the essential character of kingdom citizens, and the metaphors of **salt** and **light** indicate the citizens' influence for good as they penetrate secular society.

5:17–20 See section 1 of Truth-In-Action through the Synoptics at the end of Luke.

5:17 The negative imperative indicates that some people, disturbed by the teachings of Jesus, charged that He was abrogating **the Law** and **the Prophets.** However, He came to **fulfill** the OT in the sense of bringing to completion its partial revelation, in bringing to pass its messianic predictions, and in giving the true interpretation to its moral precepts.

5:18 Jot refers either to the Greek *iota* or the Hebrew *yod,* the smallest letters in their respective alphabets. A **tittle** is a tiny mark used to distinguish certain Hebrew letters.

5:20 Entrance into **the kingdom** is by a **righteousness** of heart, not by a hypocritical or external legalism. Such righteousness is possible only through the Messiah's personal reign, which the Beatitudes presuppose to be active in those who accept Him.

5:21–48 Jesus gives six specific examples of how His teaching fulfills the Law and the Prophets (v. 17). In each example, He contrasts Pharisaic distortions of the Law with His own interpretation, thereby demonstrating the higher righteousness (v. 20).

5:21, 22 See section 6 of Truth-In-Action through the Synoptics at the end of Luke.

5:22 The sixth Commandment not only prohibits the actual deed of murder, but extends to thought and word, to unrighteous anger and destructive insults. **Raca** is a colloquial expression of contempt for someone's mind, similar to "blockhead," or "stupid," while **fool** expresses contempt for someone's character. They both insinuate the person should be doomed to hell. **The council** initially designated the synagogue, but at the writing of this Gospel

[b]'Raca!'[2] shall be in danger of the council. But whoever says, [3]'You fool!' shall be in danger of [4]hell fire.

WORD WEALTH

5:22 judgment, *krisis* (*kree*-sis); Strong's *#2920:* Compare "crisis." Carries the idea of a separating, the process of distinguishing and selecting, making a decision. The NT uses the word primarily in a forensic sense, especially of the divine judgment. Time is heading for the event when all sin will be confronted, dealt with, and judged accordingly. Because of the atoning work of Christ, believers will stand uncondemned.

23 "Therefore [a]if you bring your gift to the altar, and there remember that your brother has something against you,
6 24 [a]"leave your gift there before the altar, and go your way. First be reconciled to your brother, and then come and offer your gift.
25 [a]"Agree with your adversary *quickly, [b]while you are on the way with him, lest your adversary deliver you to the judge, the judge hand you over to the officer, and you be thrown into prison.
26 "Assuredly, I say to you, you will by no means get out of there till you *have paid the last penny.

Adultery in the Heart

11 27 "You have heard that it was said [1]to those of old, [a]*'You shall not commit adultery.'*

KINGDOM DYNAMICS

5:27 18. What Is the Difference Between Adultery and Fornication?, SPIRITUAL ANSWERS. For the answer to this and other probing questions about God and the power life in His kingdom, see the study article "Spiritual Answers to Hard Questions," which begins on page 1996. P.R.

28 "But I say to you that whoever [a]looks at a woman to *lust for her has already committed adultery with her in his heart.
29 [a]"If your right eye causes you to [1]sin, [b]pluck it out and cast *it* from you; for it is more profitable for you that one of your members perish, than for your whole body to be cast into hell.
30 "And if your right hand causes you to [1]sin, cut it off and cast *it* from you; for it is more profitable for you that one of your members perish, than for your whole body to be cast into hell.

Marriage Is Sacred and Binding

31 "Furthermore it has been said, 1
[a]'Whoever divorces his wife, let him give her a certificate of divorce.'
32 "But I say to you that [a]whoever divorces his wife for any reason except [1]sexual immorality causes her to commit adultery; and whoever marries a woman who is divorced commits adultery.

Jesus Forbids Oaths

33 "Again you have heard that [a]it was said to those of [1]old, [b]'You shall not swear falsely, but [c]shall perform your oaths to the Lord.'
34 "But I say to you, [a]do not swear at all: neither by heaven, for it is [b]God's throne;
35 "nor by the earth, for it is His footstool; nor by Jerusalem, for it is the city of [a]the great King.
36 "Nor shall you swear by your head, because you cannot make one hair white or black.
37 [a]"But let [1]your 'Yes' be 'Yes,' and

22 [b][James 2:20; 3:6] [2]Lit., in Aram., *Empty head* [3]Gr. *More* [4]Gr. *Gehenna*
23 [a]Matt. 8:4
24 [a][Job 42:8; 1 Tim. 2:8; 1 Pet. 3:7]
25 [a][Prov. 25:8]; Luke 12:58, 59 [b][Ps. 32:6; Is. 55:6] *See WW at Rev. 22:20.
26 *See WW at Matt. 22:21.
27 [a]Ex. 20:14; Deut. 5:18 [1]NU, M omit *to those of old*
28 [a]2 Sam. 11:2–5; Job 31:1; Prov. 6:25; [Matt. 15:19; James 1:14, 15] *See WW at Matt. 13:17.
29 [a]Mark 9:43 [b][Col. 3:5] [1]Lit. *stumble* or *offend*
30 [1]Lit. *stumble* or *offend*
31 [a]Deut. 24:1; [Jer. 3:1]; Mark 10:2
32 [a][Matt. 19:9; Mark 10:11; Luke 16:18; Rom. 7:3]; 1 Cor. 7:11 [1]Or *fornication*
33 [a]Matt. 23:16 [b][Ex. 20:7]; Lev. 19:12; Num. 30:2 [c]Deut. 23:23 [1]*ancient times*
34 [a]Matt. 23:16; James 5:12 [b]Is. 66:1
35 [a]Ps. 48:2; [Matt. 5:2, 19; 6:10]
37 [a][Col. 4:6]; James 5:12 [1]Lit. *your word be yes yes*

it may have referred to an investigative body of the church. **Hell fire** is literally "Gehenna," the Greek translation of the Hebrew "Valley of Hinnom." The valley was a ravine south of Jerusalem where refuse was burned. It was most likely symbolic of the fires and judgments of Hades itself.

5:24, 25 See section 6 of Truth-In-Action through the Synoptics at the end of Luke.

5:28–30 Jesus does not stop short at overt adultery, but points to *adulterous desire.* He demands complete self-control over the members of the body. He does not prescribe literal self-mutilation, but a rigid, moral self-denial.

5:27–30 See section 11 of Truth-In-Action through the Synoptics at the end of Luke.

5:31, 32 See section 1 of Truth-In-Action through the Synoptics at the end of Luke.

5:31, 32 The Pharisees interpreted Moses' teaching on divorce (Deut. 24:1) to mean that a man could divorce his wife at virtually any whim. Jesus here counters their abuse, restricting divorce to the grounds of **sexual immorality,** a term which means any deviation from the clearly defined biblical standards for sexual activity (for example, homosexuality, adultery, fornication, and prostitution). See also the text and note on 1 Cor. 7:10, 11.

5:33–37 The Pharisees developed elaborate rules governing vows, and only those employing the divine name were binding. Jesus teaches that a vow is binding regardless of what formula is used. The use of oaths is superfluous when one's word ought to suffice. Oath-taking is an implicit confession that we do not always tell the truth.

your 'No,' 'No.' For whatever is *more than these is from the evil one.

Go the Second Mile

38 "You have heard that it was said, [a]'*An eye for an eye and a tooth for a tooth.*'
39 [a]"But I tell you not to *resist an evil person. [b]But whoever slaps you on your right cheek, turn the *other to him also.
40 "If anyone wants to sue you and take away your tunic, let him have *your* cloak also.
41 "And whoever [a]**compels** you to go one mile, go with him two.

WORD WEALTH

5:41 compels, *angareuo* (ang-ar-*you*-oh); Strong's *#29:* A verb derived from the Persian, where it described a courier with the authority to impress people into public service. The word carried the same idea in NT times, referring to the privilege of Roman officials and soldiers to press into service a person, his horses, his equipment, and his family members, usually without advance notice.

42 *"Give to him who asks you, and [a]from him who *wants to borrow from you do not turn away.

Love Your Enemies

5 43 "You have heard that it was said, [a]'*You shall love your neighbor* [b]and hate your enemy.'
44 [1]"But I say to you, [a]love your enemies, bless those who curse you, [b]do good to those who hate you, and pray [c]for those who spitefully use you and persecute you,
45 "that you may be sons of your Father in heaven; for [a]He makes His sun rise on the evil and on the good, and sends rain on the *just and on the unjust.

37 *See WW at John 10:10
38 [a]Ex. 21:24; Lev. 24:20; Deut. 19:21
39 [a][Prov. 20:22]; Luke 6:29; [Rom. 12:17; 1 Cor. 6:7; 1 Pet. 3:9] [b]Is. 50:6; Lam. 3:30 *See WW at Eph. 6:13. • See WW at John 14:16.
41 [a]Matt. 27:32
42 [a]Deut. 15:7–11; Luke 6:30–34; 1 Tim. 6:18 *See WW at Acts 20:35. • See WW at Matt. 8:2.
43 [a]Lev. 19:18 [b]Deut. 23:3–6; Ps. 41:10
44 [a]Luke 6:27; Rom. 12:14 [b][Rom. 12:20] [c]Luke 23:34; Acts 7:60; 1 Cor. 4:12; 1 Pet. 2:23 [1]NU *But I say to you, love your enemies and pray for those who persecute you*
45 [a]Job 25:3; Ps. 65:9–13; Luke 12:16, 17; Acts 14:17 *See WW at Matt. 1:19.
46 [a]Luke 6:32
47 [1]M *friends* [2]NU *Gentiles*
48 [a]Gen. 17:1; Lev. 11:44; 19:2; Luke 6:36; [Col. 1:28; 4:12]; James 1:4; 1 Pet. 1:15 [b]Eph. 5:1 *See WW at James 3:2.

KINGDOM DYNAMICS

5:43, 44 22. How Do I Forgive My Enemies?, SPIRITUAL ANSWERS. For the answer to this and other probing questions about God and the power life in His kingdom, see the study article "Spiritual Answers to Hard Questions," which begins on page 1996. P.R.

KINGDOM DYNAMICS

5:44 Love Those Who Have Animosity Toward You, BROTHERLY LOVE. The word "enemy" does not suit any limited, convenient meaning, as though merely referring to those whom we may not particularly like. The command to love our enemies means much more than simply changing our feelings about people with whom we do not get along. Rather, "enemy" (Greek *echthros*) means "adversary or foe" and refers to those whose actions and words manifest hatred for you: the in-law who will not speak to you, the associate who tried to get you fired. We are called to love those filled with animosity toward us. Jesus leaves no room for speculation in this passage, commanding love for those who hate, despise, and persecute us. Such love is only possible through the power of Jesus Christ, who Himself loved in that way and now seeks vessels through whom to love again the hate-filled who assail Him as they oppose you.

(Ps. 86:5/Luke 6:31–35) D.S.

46 [a]"For if you love those who love you, what reward have you? Do not even the tax collectors do the same?
47 "And if you greet your [1]brethren only, what do you do more *than others?* Do not even the [2]tax collectors do so?
48 [a]"Therefore you shall be *perfect, just [b]as your Father in heaven is perfect.

Do Good to Please God

6 "Take heed that you do not do your charitable deeds before men, to be

5:38–42 See section 5 of Truth-In-Action through the Synoptics at the end of Luke.
5:38–42 The law of retaliation (see Ex. 21:24; Lev. 24:20; Deut. 19:21) was not intended to encourage personal revenge, but to protect the offender from punishment harsher than his offense warranted. Jesus forbids revenge by insisting upon positive good in the face of evil in terms of personal insult (v. 39), legal contention (v. 40), forced labor (v. 41), and requests for gifts or loans (v. 42).
5:43–48 See section 5 of Truth-In-Action through the Synoptics at the end of Luke.
5:43 The OT precept of love is found in Lev. 19:18, but hatred of one's enemies was a Pharisaic addition.
5:44 Love is not a matter of sentiment alone, but practical concern, blessing, prayer, and positive wishes for well-being, extended to friend and enemy alike.
5:45 Just as God indiscriminately sends rain and sunshine upon the just and unjust alike, so Jesus' disciples must be indiscriminate in their extension of love to friend and enemy.
5:48 The emphasis in the command to **be perfect** is not on a flawless moral nature, but on an all-inclusive love that seeks the good of all. Instead of following the example of sinners who love only those who love them, we are to be like the **Father** in also loving those who do not love us.
6:1–8 Jesus gives three specific examples of how our practice of piety should be different from the hypocritical or

seen by them. Otherwise you have no
reward from your Father in heaven.
2 "Therefore, [a]when you do a charitable deed, do not sound a trumpet before you as the **hypocrites** do in the
synagogues and in the streets, that
they may have glory from men. Assuredly, I say to you, they *have their
reward.

WORD WEALTH

6:2 hypocrites, *hupokrites* (hoop-ok-ree-*tace*); Strong's *#5273:* In Bible days actors wore masks, which included mechanisms for amplifying the voice. Since the dramas were questions and answers, the word describing the dialogue was *hupokrinomai,* to reply or to answer. *Hupokrites* is one who is playacting, reading a script, or one who puts on an act. The *hypocrite* conceals his true motives under a cloak of make-believe.

3 "But when you do a charitable deed,
do not let your left hand know what
your right hand is doing,
4 "that your charitable deed may be
in secret; and your Father who sees in
secret [a]will Himself *reward you
[1]openly.*

The Model Prayer

3 5 "And when you pray, you shall not
be like the [1]hypocrites. For they love
to pray standing in the synagogues and
on the corners of the streets, that they
may be seen by men. Assuredly, I say
to you, they have their reward.
6 "But you, when you **pray,** [a]go into
your room, and when you have shut
your door, pray to your Father who *is*
in the secret *place;* and your Father
who sees in secret will reward you
[1]openly.

CHAPTER 6
2 [a]Rom. 12:8 *See WW at Philem. 15.
4 [a]Luke 14:12–14 [1]NU omits *openly* *See WW at Matt. 22:21. • See WW at 1 Cor. 11:19.
5 [1]*pretenders*
6 [a]2 Kin. 4:33 [1]NU omits *openly*

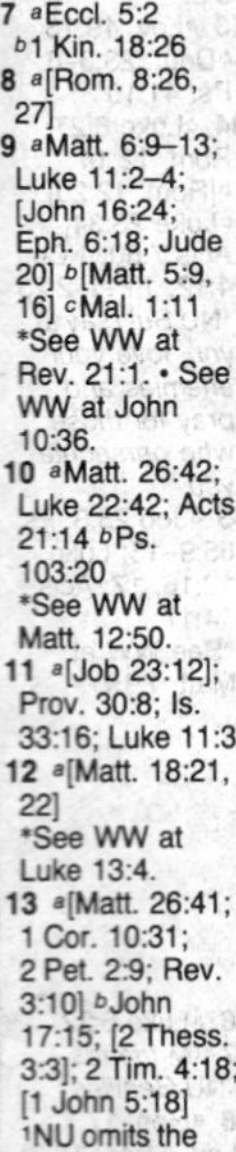

7 [a]Eccl. 5:2 [b]1 Kin. 18:26
8 [a][Rom. 8:26, 27]
9 [a]Matt. 6:9–13; Luke 11:2–4; [John 16:24; Eph. 6:18; Jude 20] [b][Matt. 5:9, 16] [c]Mal. 1:11 *See WW at Rev. 21:1. • See WW at John 10:36.
10 [a]Matt. 26:42; Luke 22:42; Acts 21:14 [b]Ps. 103:20 *See WW at Matt. 12:50.
11 [a][Job 23:12]; Prov. 30:8; Is. 33:16; Luke 11:3
12 [a][Matt. 18:21, 22] *See WW at Luke 13:4.
13 [a][Matt. 26:41; 1 Cor. 10:31; 2 Pet. 2:9; Rev. 3:10] [b]John 17:15; [2 Thess. 3:3]; 2 Tim. 4:18; [1 John 5:18] [1]NU omits the rest of v. 13. *See WW at Matt. 28:20.

WORD WEALTH

6:6 pray, *proseuchomai* (pros-yoo-khom-ahee); Strong's *#4336:* The word is progressive. Starting with the noun, *euche,* which is a prayer to God that also includes making a vow, the word expands to the verb *euchomai,* a special term describing an invocation, request, or entreaty. Adding *pros,* "in the direction of" (God), *proseuchomai* becomes the most frequent word for prayer.

7 "And when you pray, [a]do not use
vain repetitions as the heathen *do.*
[b]For they think that they will be heard
for their many words.
8 "Therefore do not be like them. For
your Father [a]knows the things you
have need of before you ask Him.
9 "In this [a]manner, therefore, pray: 3

[b]Our Father in *heaven,
*Hallowed be Your [c]name.
10 Your kingdom come.
[a]Your *will be done
On earth [b]as *it is* in heaven.
11 Give us this day our [a]daily bread.
12 And [a]forgive us our debts,
As we forgive our *debtors.
13 [a]And do not lead us into
temptation,
But [b]deliver us from the evil one.
[1]For Yours is the kingdom and the
power and the glory *forever.
Amen.

KINGDOM DYNAMICS

6:9–13 The Lord's Prayer, PRAYER. The Lord's Prayer is a prayer outline with seven major topics, each representing a basic human need: 1) The Paternal Need: "Our Father" (v. 9). When you pray, all needs are met by the benevolence of a loving Father. 2) God's Presence: "Hallowed be Your name" (v. 9). Enter His

---

external practices of the Pharisees. The general principle for Christians is that the motive in religious observances is to please God and not to gain praise from others.

6:2 In contrast to **hypocrites** Christians are not to call attention to their almsgiving. The reward of such playactors (hypocrites) is present and human, contrasted with the divine reward for unostentatious giving.

6:5–8 See section 3 of Truth-In-Action through the Synoptics at the end of Luke.

6:5, 6 Jesus does not criticize public prayer, but He does condemn *pretentious, ostentatious* prayer that attracts attention.

6:7 Vain repetitions refers not to repeating a request, but to an empty babbling and long prayers that confuse meaningless verbosity with piety. By way of contrast, Jesus teaches focused prayer, which acknowledges God's needed reign in every facet of life and society (vv. 9–13).

6:9–13 See section 3 of Truth-In-Action through the Synoptics at the end of Luke.

6:9 Father: A new note of personal intimacy with Yahweh originates with Jesus (see Rom. 8:15; Gal. 4:6). **Hallowed be** establishes the principle of prayer on the precept of worship.

6:10 Your kingdom come: The petitioner asks for the establishment of God's rule, not only in its consummation in the Age to Come, but in lives and situations now. This is further defined as God's **will** being done **on earth.**

6:11 Jesus encourages prayer for physical needs, which are vitally linked with kingdom concerns.

6:12 Prayer for forgiveness is qualified by a readiness to forgive personal injury (see vv. 14, 15).

6:13 The final petition requests God's strength to withstand moral peril lest the petitioner fail or be overwhelmed by the temptation of the **evil one.**

presence through praise (Ps. 100:4), and call Him "Father" because of Christ's atoning blood (Heb. 10:19–22; Gal. 4:4–6). 3) God's Priorities: "Your kingdom come" (v. 10). Declare that His kingdom priorities (Rom. 14:17) shall be established in yourself, your loved ones, your church, and your nation. 4) God's Provision: "Give us" (v. 11). Jesus, the need-meeter, told us to pray daily, asking Him to supply all our needs. 5) God's Forgiveness: "And forgive us" (v. 12). You need God's forgiveness, and you need to forgive others. Daily set your will to walk in love and forgiveness. 6) Power Over Satan: "And do not lead us . . . deliver us from the evil one" (v. 13). Pray a hedge of protection about yourself and your loved ones (Job 1:9, 10; Ps. 91), and verbally put on the armor of God (Eph. 6:14–18). 7) Divine Partnership: "For Yours is the kingdom" (v. 13). Praise God for sharing His kingdom, power, and glory with you (2 Tim. 4:18; Luke 10:19; John 17:22). This is the prayer that teaches you how to pray.

(Acts 12:1–17/1 John 5:14, 15) L.L.

6 14 [a]"For if you forgive men their trespasses, your heavenly Father will also forgive you.
15 "But [a]if you do not forgive men their trespasses, neither will your Father forgive your trespasses.

Fasting to Be Seen Only by God

16 "Moreover, [a]when you fast, do not be like the [1]hypocrites,* with a sad countenance. For they disfigure their faces that they may appear to men to be fasting. Assuredly, I say to you, they have their reward.
17 "But you, when you fast, [a]anoint your head and wash your face,
18 "so that you do not appear to men to be fasting, but to your Father who *is* in the secret *place;* and your Father who sees in secret will reward you [1]openly.

14 [a][Matt. 7:2]; Mark 11:25; [Eph. 4:32; Col. 3:13]
15 [a]Matt. 18:35; James 2:13
16 [a]Is. 58:3–7; Luke 18:12 [1]*pretenders* *See WW at Matt. 6:2.
17 [a]Ruth 3:3; 2 Sam. 12:20; Dan. 10:3
18 [1]NU, M omit *openly*
19 [a]Prov. 23:4; [1 Tim. 6:17; Heb. 13:5]; James 5:1
20 [a]Matt. 19:21; Luke 12:33; 18:22; 1 Tim. 6:19; 1 Pet. 1:4
22 [a]Luke 11:34, 35 [1]Clear, or healthy
23 [1]Evil, or unhealthy
24 [a]Luke 16:9, 11, 13 [b][Gal. 1:10; 1 Tim. 6:17; James 4:4; 1 John 2:15] [1]Lit., in Aram., *riches* *See WW at Acts 4:12.
25 [a][Ps. 55:22]; Luke 12:22; [Phil. 4:6; 1 Pet. 5:7] *See WW at Luke 21:19.

Lay Up Treasures in Heaven

19 [a]"Do not lay up for yourselves trea- **10**
sures on earth, where moth and rust destroy and where thieves break in and steal;
20 [a]"but lay up for yourselves treasures in heaven, where neither moth nor rust destroys and where thieves do not break in and steal.
21 "For where your treasure is, there your heart will be also.

The Lamp of the Body

22 [a]"The lamp of the body is the eye. **4**
If therefore your eye is [1]good, your whole body will be full of light.
23 "But if your eye is [1]bad, your whole body will be full of darkness. If therefore the light that is in you is darkness, how great *is* that darkness!

You Cannot Serve God and Riches

24 [a]"No one can serve two masters; for **2**
either he will hate the one and love the *other, or else he will be loyal to the one and despise the other. [b]You cannot serve God and [1]mammon.

Do Not Worry

25 "Therefore I say to you, [a]do not **11**
worry about your *life, what you will eat or what you will drink; nor about your body, what you will put on. Is not life more than food and the body more than clothing?

WORD WEALTH

6:25 worry, *merimnao* (mer-im-*nah*-oh); Strong's *#3309:* From *merizo,* "to divide into parts." The word suggests a distraction, a preoccupation with things causing anxiety, stress, and pressure. Jesus speaks against worry and anxiety (*cont. on next page*)

6:14 See section 6 of Truth-In-Action through the Synoptics at the end of Luke.
6:16 Advertized fasting is another example of a merely external and degenerate piety. All forms of self-denial are to be secret, without parade.
6:19–34 Jesus warns against avarice and its corresponding anxiety, contrasting the uncertain temporal nature of earthly treasure with heavenly treasure, which is enduring.
6:19–24 See section 10 of Truth-In-Action through the Synoptics at the end of Luke.
6:21 Jesus does not prohibit material possessions, nor the enjoyment of material things (see 1 Tim. 6:17), but He does forbid a selfish and extravagant materialism that ties a person to this Earth.
6:22–24 The person with the **good** ("healthy") eye is one whose intent is to serve God and not **mammon** (the money-god, used here to indicate the whole system of materialism). The person with the **bad** eye is selfish, covetous, and miserly. The one's life is full of light, meaning, and purpose; the other's life is plunged into darkness, deprived of meaning.
6:22, 23 See section 4 of Truth-In-Action through the Synoptics at the end of Luke.
6:24 See section 2 of Truth-In-Action through the Synoptics at the end of Luke.
6:25–34 See section 11 of Truth-In-Action through the Synoptics at the end of Luke.
6:25–34 Jesus resumes the theme of single-hearted devotion to God and deals with the related attitude of freedom from anxiety over daily needs. He illustrates the worthlessness of worry by showing that it is unnecessary (vv. 26, 28–30), unfruitful (v. 27), and unbecoming to a Christian (vv. 31, 32).

(*cont. from preceding page*)
because of the watchful care of a heavenly Father who is ever mindful of our daily needs.

26 [a]"Look at the birds of the air, for
they neither sow nor reap nor gather
into barns; yet your heavenly Father
feeds them. Are you not of more value
than they?
27 "Which of you by worrying can add
one [1]cubit to his [2]stature?
28 "So why do you worry about clothing? Consider the lilies of the field, how
they grow: they neither toil nor spin;
29 "and yet I say to you that even Solomon in all his glory was not [1]arrayed
like one of these.
30 "Now if God so clothes the grass
of the field, which today is, and tomorrow is thrown into the oven, *will He*
not much more *clothe* you, O you of
*little faith?
31 "Therefore do not worry, saying,
'What shall we eat?' or 'What shall we
drink?' or 'What shall we wear?'
32 "For after all these things the Gentiles seek. For your heavenly Father
knows that you need all these things.
33 "But [a]seek first the kingdom of God
and His righteousness, and all these
things shall be added to you.
34 "Therefore do not *worry about tomorrow, for tomorrow will worry
about its own things. Sufficient for the
day *is* its own trouble.

Do Not Judge

6 7 [1]"Judge* [a]not, that you be not
judged.
2 "For with what [1]judgment* you
judge, you will be judged; [a]and with
the measure you use, it will be measured back to you.
3 [a]"And why do you look at the speck
in your brother's eye, but do not consider the plank in your own eye?
4 "Or how can you say to your
brother, 'Let me remove the speck
from your eye'; and look, a plank *is*
in your own eye?
5 "Hypocrite! First remove the plank
from your own eye, and then you will
see clearly to remove the speck from
your brother's eye.
6 [a]"Do not give what is holy to the
dogs; nor cast your pearls before
swine, lest they trample them under
their feet, and turn and tear you in
pieces.

Keep Asking, Seeking, Knocking

7 [a]"**Ask,** and it will be given to you;
seek, and you will find; knock, and it
will be opened to you.
8 "For [a]everyone who asks receives,
and he who seeks finds, and to him
who knocks it will be opened.

WORD WEALTH

7:7 ask, *aiteo* (ahee-*teh*-oh); Strong's *#154:* To request, petition. The word usually describes a suppliant making request of someone in higher position, such as an individual asking something from God (21:22), a subject from a king (Mark 6:25), a child from a parent (Luke 11:11), or a beggar from a person of substance (Acts 3:2). The word denotes insistent asking without qualms, not "commanding" God, but solidly presenting a requisition whose items He longs to distribute.

KINGDOM DYNAMICS

7:7, 8 34. What Kingdom Law Is Necessary for the Laws of Reciprocity and Use to Work?, SPIRITUAL ANSWERS. For the answer to this and other probing questions about God and the power life in His kingdom, see the study article "Spiritual Answers to Hard Questions," which begins on page 1996. P.R.

9 [a]"Or what man is there among you
who, if his son asks for bread, will give
him a stone?
10 "Or if he asks for a fish, will he give
him a serpent?
11 "If you then, [a]being evil, know how

26 [a]Job 38:41; Ps. 147:9; Matt. 10:29; Luke 12:24
27 [1]About 18 inches [2]*height*
29 [1]*dressed*
30 *See WW at Matt. 8:26.
33 [a]1 Kin. 3:13; Luke 12:31; [1 Tim. 4:8]
34 *See WW at Matt. 6:25.

CHAPTER 7

1 [a]Matt. 7:1–5; Luke 6:37; Rom. 14:3; [1 Cor. 4:3, 4] [1]Condemn *See WW at John 18:31.
2 [a]Mark 4:24; Luke 6:38 [1]Condemnation *See WW at Rev. 20:4.
3 [a]Luke 6:41
6 [a]Prov. 9:7, 8; Acts 13:45
7 [a][Matt. 21:22; Mark 11:24]; Luke 11:9–13; 18:1–8; [John 15:7; James 1:5, 6; 1 John 3:22]
8 [a]Prov. 8:17; Jer. 29:12
9 [a]Luke 11:11
11 [a]Gen. 6:5; 8:21; Ps. 84:11; Is. 63:7; [Rom. 8:32; James 1:17]; 1 John 3:1

6:33 Rather than being preoccupied with material things, our ambition should be to **seek first** God's **kingdom** and **righteousness,** knowing that as we do so, He has pledged Himself with covenant faithfulness to respond—**all these things shall be added to you.**

7:1–5 *See section 6 of Truth-In-Action through the* Synoptics at the end of Luke.

7:1–5 Jesus does not forbid criticism, opinions, or the condemnation of wrongdoing. What He forbids is censoriousness, the spirit of faultfinding that overlooks one's own shortcomings while assuming the role of supreme judge in regard to the sins of others.

7:6 Some discrimination in preaching the gospel is necessary. To preach the gospel to those who manifest a contemptuous blasphemy toward it is not only to cheapen it, but also to endanger ourselves. The two metaphors here (**dogs, swine**) are Jewish and refer to inviting totally uninterested pagans to join in Yahwistic practices.

7:7–11 The Greek imperatives, **ask, seek,** and **knock** (v. 7) are in the present tense, suggesting continued petition. The human father-son relationship portrays the human-divine relationship and gives further grounds for continued petition in an attitude of filial trust.

to give *good gifts to your children,
how much more will your Father who
is in heaven give good things to those
who ask Him!
12 "Therefore, [a]whatever you want
men to do to you, do also to them, for
[b]this is the Law and the Prophets.

KINGDOM DYNAMICS

7:12 33. What Kingdom Law Is at the Heart of All Relationships?, SPIRITUAL ANSWERS. For the answer to this and other probing questions about God and the power life in His kingdom, see the study article "Spiritual Answers to Hard Questions," which begins on page 1996.
P.R.

The Narrow Way

9 13 [a]"Enter by the narrow gate; for
wide *is* the gate and broad *is* the way
that leads to destruction, and there are
many who go in by it.
14 [1]"Because narrow *is* the gate and
[2]difficult *is* the way which leads to life,
and there are few who find it.

You Will Know Them by Their Fruits

9 15 [a]"Beware of false prophets, [b]who
come to you in sheep's clothing, but
inwardly they are ravenous wolves.
16 [a]"You will *know them by their
fruits. [b]Do men gather grapes from
thornbushes or figs from thistles?
17 "Even so, [a]every good tree bears
good fruit, but a bad tree bears bad
fruit.
18 "A good tree cannot bear bad fruit,
nor *can* a bad tree bear good fruit.
19 [a]"Every tree that does not bear
good fruit is cut down and thrown into
the fire.
20 "Therefore by their fruits you will
know them.

I Never Knew You

9 21 "Not everyone who says to Me,
[a]'Lord, Lord,' shall enter the kingdom
of heaven, but he who [b]does the will
of My Father in heaven.
22 "Many will say to Me in that day,
'Lord, Lord, have we [a]not prophesied
in Your name, cast out demons in Your
name, and done many wonders in Your
name?'
23 "And [a]then I will declare to them,
'I never knew you; [b]depart from Me,
you who practice lawlessness!'

Build on the Rock

24 "Therefore [a]whoever hears these
sayings of Mine, and does them, I will
liken him to a wise man who built his
house on the rock:
25 "and the rain descended, the floods
came, and the winds blew and beat on
that house; and it did not fall, for it
was founded on the rock.
26 "But everyone who hears these sayings of Mine, and does not do them,
will be like a foolish man who built his
house on the sand:
27 "and the rain descended, the floods
came, and the winds blew and beat on
that house; and it fell. And great was
its fall."
28 And so it was, when Jesus had
ended these sayings, that [a]the people
were astonished at His teaching,
29 [a]for He taught them as one having
*authority, and not as the scribes.

Jesus Cleanses a Leper

8 When He had come down from the
mountain, great multitudes followed Him.
2 [a]And behold, a leper came and
[b]worshiped Him, saying, "Lord, if You
are **willing,** You can make me clean."

WORD WEALTH

8:2 willing, *thelo* (*thel*-oh); Strong's *#2309:* To wish, desire, will, take delight in. It carries the idea of being ready, preferring, and having in mind. A related NT word is *boulomai,* a stronger expression of the will, signifying the determinant will deliberately exercised.

11 *See WW at Phil. 1:6. **12** [a]Luke 6:31 [b]Matt. 22:40; Rom. 13:8; Gal. 5:14; [1 Tim. 1:5] **13** [a]Luke 13:24 **14** [1]NU, M *How narrow . . . !* [2]*confined* **15** [a]Deut. 13:3; Jer. 23:16; Ezek. 22:28; Mark 13:22; [Luke 6:26]; Rom. 16:17; Eph. 5:6; [Col. 2:8; 2 Pet. 2:1; 1 John 4:1–3] [b]Mic. 3:5 **16** [a]Matt. 7:20; 12:33; Luke 6:44; James 3:12 [b]Luke 6:43 *See WW at Luke 5:22. **17** [a]Jer. 11:19; Matt. 12:33 **19** [a]Matt. 3:10; Luke 3:9; [John 15:2, 6] **21** [a]Hos. 8:2; Matt. 25:11; Luke 6:46; Acts 19:13 [b]Rom. 2:13; James 1:22 **22** [a]Num. 24:4 **23** [a]Matt. 25:12; Luke 13:25; [2 Tim. 2:19] [b]Ps. 5:5; 6:8; [Matt. 25:41]; Luke 13:27 **24** [a]Matt. 7:24–27; Luke 6:47–49 **28** [a]Matt. 13:54; Mark 1:22; 6:2; Luke 4:32; John 7:46 **29** [a][John 7:46] *See WW at Mark 3:15.

CHAPTER 8

2 [a]Matt. 8:2–4; Mark 1:40–45; Luke 5:12–14 [b]Matt. 2:11; 9:18; 15:25; John 9:38; Acts 10:25

7:12 As an expression of the law of love, Jesus' new version of the Jewish "Golden Rule" summarizes all that Christ requires of us in relation to others as taught in 5:1—7:11.

7:13, 14 See section 9 of Truth-In-Action through the Synoptics at the end of Luke.

7:15–20 See section 9 of Truth-In-Action through the Synoptics at the end of Luke.

7:15, 16 There are many **false prophets** who pretend to be Christian guides, but whose real purpose is selfish and destructive. We must test those claiming to prophesy by their fruit, that is, by their life-style, character, teaching, and influence.

7:21–23 See section 9 of Truth-In-Action through the Synoptics at the end of Luke.

7:21–23 Jesus warns against self-deception, a mere verbal profession of lordship without obedience to the will of God. It is even possible for a self-deluded person to exercise a spectacular ministry, using the authority of the Scriptures and of the name of Jesus, without walking in genuine, obedient discipleship.

7:24–27 Therefore: The parable of the **wise** and the **foolish** builders both serves as a conclusion to the Sermon on the Mount and illustrates the absolute necessity of doing the will of God (that is, what God has told us to do).

7:28, 29 Jesus spoke in His own name and on His own authority, quite unlike the usual teachers.

8:1—9:34 Matthew introduces a series of miracles that portray the authority of Jesus.

3 Then Jesus put out *His* hand and
touched him, saying, "I am willing; be
cleansed." Immediately his leprosy
[a]was cleansed.
4 And Jesus said to him, [a]"See that
you tell no one; but go your way, show
yourself to the priest, and offer the gift
that [b]Moses [c]commanded, as a testimony to them."

Jesus Heals a Centurion's Servant

5 [a]Now when Jesus had entered Capernaum, a [b]centurion came to Him,
pleading with Him,
6 saying, "Lord, my servant is lying
at home paralyzed, dreadfully tormented."
7 And Jesus said to him, "I will come
and *heal him."
8 The centurion answered and said,
"Lord, [a]I am not worthy that You
should come under my roof. But only
[b]speak a word, and my servant will be
healed.
9 "For I also am a man under authority, having soldiers under me. And I
say to this *one,* 'Go,' and he goes; and
to another, 'Come,' and he comes; and
to my servant, 'Do this,' and he does
it."
10 When Jesus heard *it,* He marveled,
and said to those who followed, "Assuredly, I say to you, I have not found
such great faith, not even in Israel!
11 "And I say to you that [a]many will
come from east and west, and sit down
with Abraham, Isaac, and Jacob in the
kingdom of heaven.
12 "But [a]the sons of the kingdom
[b]will be cast out into outer darkness.
There will be weeping and gnashing
of teeth."
13 Then Jesus said to the centurion,
"Go your way; and as you have *believed, *so* let it be done for you." And
his servant was healed that same
hour.

Peter's Mother-in-Law Healed

14 [a]Now when Jesus had come into Peter's house, He saw [b]his wife's mother
lying sick with a fever.

3 [a]Matt. 11:5; Luke 4:27
4 [a]Matt. 9:30; Mark 5:43; Luke 4:41; 8:56; 9:21 [b]Lev. 14:3, 4, 10; Mark 1:44; Luke 5:14 [c]Lev. 14:4–32; Deut. 24:8
5 [a]Luke 7:1–3 [b]Matt. 27:54; Acts 10:1
7 *See WW at Matt. 12:22.
8 [a]Luke 15:19, 21 [b]Ps. 107:20
11 [a][Gen. 12:3; Is. 2:2, 3; 11:10]; Mal. 1:11; Luke 13:29; [Acts 10:45; 11:18; 14:27; Rom. 15:9–13; Eph. 3:6]
12 [a][Matt. 21:43] [b]Matt. 13:42, 50; 22:13; 24:51; 25:30; Luke 13:28; 2 Pet. 2:17; Jude 13
13 *See WW at Rom. 10:9.
14 [a]Matt. 8:14–16; Mark 1:29–31; Luke 4:38, 39 [b]1 Cor. 9:5
15 [1]NU, M *Him* *See WW at Mark 1:20.
16 [a]Mark 1:32–34; Luke 4:40, 41
17 [a]Is. 53:4; 1 Pet. 2:24

15 So He touched her hand, and the
fever *left her. And she arose and
served [1]them.

Many Healed After Sabbath Sunset

16 [a]When evening had come, they
brought to Him many who were demon-possessed. And He cast out the
spirits with a word, and healed all who
were sick,
17 that it might be fulfilled which
was spoken by Isaiah the prophet,
saying:

[a]*"He Himself took our infirmities*
And bore our sicknesses."

KINGDOM DYNAMICS

8:16, 17 The Biblical Grounds for Divine Healing, DIVINE HEALING. The provision of divine healing must rest on clear grounds. Obviously it is biblically based, but from what source is this great mercy of God derived? Some link it to just that—God's mercy. While that is certainly a truth—for His compassion is great—the question at issue is this: What are the redemptive grounds of divine healing? Is healing included in God's saving provision in Christ, or is it simply a loving gesture of His benevolent character? This text, together with our discussion of Is. 53:4, 5, gives clear evidence for divine healing as being provided in the atonement of Christ's redeeming work on the Cross. To avoid this truth, some suggest that Isaiah's prophecy was fulfilled completely by the healings of that one day. Such would be impossible, for the prophecy of Isaiah states that the Servant of Yahweh would bear sickness in the same way that He would bear sins—that is, vicariously (see Kingdom Dynamics at Is. 53:4, 5). Furthermore, He was to suffer for our sins and sicknesses. If "our" means all of us in regard to our sin and our being given a Savior, then it also means all of us in regard to sickness and our having been given a Divine Healer. (See Mark 1:40–45.)

(Matt. 4:23–25/Mark 1:40–45) N.V.

8:3, 4 Jesus **touched** the leper, exhibiting an authority over both disease *and the Law, which prohibited such* physical contact with a leper (see Lev. 13:45–59). He then instructed the leper to **show** himself **to the priest,** balancing His authority over the Law with His commitment to it (see Lev. 14:2–32).

8:5–13 The **great faith** of the centurion (v. 10) is the key to this paragraph. Many other Gentiles would follow his example and enter **the kingdom of heaven** (v. 11), while many Jews would be excluded (v. 12).

8:15 The cure was immediate and complete as evidenced by the detail, **she . . . served them.**

8:17 Matthew interprets Jesus' healings and exorcisms as a fulfillment of the prophesied messianic Servant's role (Is. 53:4). See also the text and note on 1 Pet. 2:24.

The Cost of Discipleship

7 18 And when Jesus saw great multitudes about Him, He gave a command to depart to the other side.
19 [a]Then a certain scribe came and said to Him, "Teacher, I will follow You wherever You go."
20 And Jesus said to him, "Foxes have holes and birds of the air *have* nests, but the Son of Man has nowhere to lay *His* head."
21 [a]Then another of His disciples said to Him, "Lord, [b]let me first go and bury my father."
22 But Jesus said to him, "Follow Me, and let the dead bury their own dead."

Wind and Wave Obey Jesus

23 Now when He got into a boat, His disciples followed Him.
24 [a]And suddenly a great tempest arose on the sea, so that the boat was covered with the waves. But He was asleep.
25 Then His disciples came to *Him* and awoke Him, saying, "Lord, save us! We are perishing!"
26 But He said to them, "Why are you fearful, O you of **little faith?**" Then [a]He arose and rebuked the winds and the sea, and there was a great calm.

WORD WEALTH

8:26 little faith, *oligopistos* (ol-ig-op-is-tus); Strong's *#3640:* From *oligos,* "small," and *pistis,* "faith," describing a faith that lacks confidence or trusts too little. Jesus used the word in various situations as a tender rebuke or corrective chiding (6:30; 8:26; 14:31; 16:8; Luke 12:28). Another way to term it is "underdeveloped faith" as opposed to outright unbelief or distrust (*apistis*).

19 [a]Matt. 8:19–22; Luke 9:57, 58
21 [a]Luke 9:59, 60 [b]1 Kin. 19:20
24 [a]Mark 4:37; Luke 8:23–25
26 [a]Ps. 65:7; 89:9; 107:29
27 [1]Lit. *What sort of Man is this* *See WW at Rom. 6:17.
28 [a]Mark 5:1–4; Luke 8:26–33 [1]NU *Gadarenes* *See WW at 2 Tim. 3:1.
31 [1]NU *send us into*
34 [a]Deut. 5:25; 1 Kin. 17:18; Amos 7:12; Luke 5:8; Acts 16:39

CHAPTER 9

1 [a]Matt. 4:13; 11:23; Mark 5:21
2 [a]Mark 2:3–12; Luke 5:18–26 [b]Matt. 8:10

27 So the men marveled, saying, [1]"Who can this be, that even the winds and the sea *obey Him?"

Two Demon-Possessed Men Healed

28 [a]When He had come to the other side, to the country of the [1]Gergesenes, there met Him two demon-possessed *men,* coming out of the tombs, exceedingly *fierce, so that no one could pass that way.
29 And suddenly they cried out, saying, "What have we to do with You, Jesus, You Son of God? Have You come here to torment us before the time?"
30 Now a good way off from them there was a herd of many swine feeding.
31 So the demons begged Him, saying, "If You cast us out, [1]permit us to go away into the herd of swine."
32 And He said to them, "Go." So when they had come out, they went into the herd of swine. And suddenly the whole herd of swine ran violently down the steep place into the sea, and perished in the water.
33 Then those who kept *them* fled; and they went away into the city and told everything, including what *had happened* to the demon-possessed *men.*
34 And behold, the whole city came out to meet Jesus. And when they saw Him, [a]they begged *Him* to depart from their region.

Jesus Forgives and Heals a Paralytic

9 So He got into a boat, crossed over, [a]and came to His own city.
2 [a]Then behold, they brought to Him a paralytic lying on a bed. [b]When Jesus saw their faith, He said to the paralytic,

8:18–22 See section 7 of Truth-In-Action through the Synoptics at the end of Luke.
8:18–22 Matthew relates two stringent sayings that illustrate the demands of genuine discipleship.
8:19, 20 Jesus warns against a rash fervor that has not counted the cost.
8:21, 22 The man used filial responsibilities as an excuse for delay. The response of Jesus stresses the urgency of following Him.
8:24, 25 Matthew contrasts Jesus' physical state of peaceful sleep with the great tempest of nature and the disciples' fearful cry.
8:26 Rebuked . . . sea demonstrates Jesus' authoritative reign over the entire Earth, including inclement elements that might find their source in the destructive power of the Evil One.
8:28–32 Gergesenes is an alternate reading for Gadarenes (Mark 5:1). Matthew's mention of **two demon-possessed men** as opposed to Mark's (5:2) and Luke's (8:26) "one" is difficult; it is likely that one was more prominent, the details of whom Mark and Luke chose to emphasize. See the text and notes of Mark 5:1–20 for a more complete explanation of this miracle.
8:29 The time: Jesus' overthrow of satanic forces anticipates their final destruction on the Day of Judgment.
9:1 His own city refers to Capernaum.
9:2 The miracles of the previous chapter demonstrate the authority of Jesus over disease, nature, and demons. Now He reveals His power over sin. The response of Jesus to the **faith** (here a confidence in God's providential power) of the paralytic's friends shows the effectiveness of faith on behalf of others.

"Son, be of good cheer; your sins are *forgiven you."

3 And at once some of the scribes said within themselves, "This Man blasphemes!"

4 But Jesus, [a]knowing their thoughts, said, "Why do you think evil in your hearts?

5 "For which is easier, to say, '*Your* sins are forgiven you,' or to say, 'Arise and walk'?

6 "But that you may know that the Son of Man has power on earth to forgive sins"—then He said to the paralytic, "Arise, take up your bed, and go to your house."

7 And he arose and departed to his house.

8 Now when the multitudes saw *it,* they [a]marveled[1] and glorified God, who had given such power to men.

Matthew the Tax Collector

9 [a]As Jesus passed on from there, He saw a man named Matthew sitting at the tax office. And He said to him, "Follow Me." So he arose and followed Him.

10 [a]Now it happened, as Jesus sat at the table in the house, *that* behold, many tax collectors and sinners came and sat down with Him and His disciples.

11 And when the Pharisees saw *it,* they said to His disciples, "Why does your Teacher eat with [a]tax collectors and [b]sinners?"

12 When Jesus heard *that,* He said to them, "Those who are well have no need of a physician, but those who are sick.

13 "But go and learn what *this* means: [a]*'I desire *mercy and not sacrifice.'* For I did not come to call the righteous, [b]but *sinners, [1]to repentance."

Jesus Is Questioned About Fasting

14 Then the disciples of John came to Him, saying, [a]"Why do we and the Pharisees fast [1]often, but Your disciples do not fast?"

15 And Jesus said to them, "Can [a]the [1]friends of the bridegroom *mourn as long as the bridegroom is with them? But the days will come when the bridegroom will be taken away from them, and [b]then they will fast.

16 "No one puts a piece of unshrunk 11
cloth on an old garment; for [1]the patch pulls away from the garment, and the tear is made worse.

17 "Nor do they put *new wine into old wineskins, or else the wineskins [1]break, the wine is spilled, and the wineskins are ruined. But they put new wine into new wineskins, and both are preserved."

A Girl Restored to Life and a Woman Healed

18 [a]While He spoke these things to them, behold, a ruler came and worshiped Him, saying, "My daughter has just died, but come and lay Your hand on her and she will live."

19 So Jesus arose and followed him, and so *did* His [a]disciples.

20 [a]And suddenly, a woman who had a flow of blood for twelve years came from behind and [b]touched the hem of His garment.

21 For she said to herself, "If only I may touch His garment, I shall be made well."

22 But Jesus turned around, and when He saw her He said, "Be of good cheer,

2 *See WW at Mark 1:20.
4 [a]Matt. 12:25
8 [a]John 7:15 [1]NU *were afraid*
9 [a]Luke 5:27
10 [a]Mark 2:15
11 [a]Matt. 11:19 [b][Gal. 2:15]
13 [a]Hos. 6:6 [b]1 Tim. 1:15 [1]NU omits *to repentance* *See WW at 2 Tim. 1:16. • See WW at James 5:20.
14 [a]Luke 5:33–35; 18:12 [1]NU brackets *often* as disputed.
15 [a]John 3:29 [b]Acts 13:2, 3; 14:23 [1]Lit. *sons of the bridechamber* *See WW at Rev. 18:11.
16 [1]Lit. *that which is put on*
17 [1]*burst* *See WW at 2 Cor. 5:17.
18 [a]Luke 8:41–56
19 [a]Matt. 10:2–4
20 [a]Luke 8:43 [b]Matt. 14:36; 23:5

9:3 The charge of blasphemy would have been correct if Jesus had not been the Son of God. **Blasphemes:** A blasphemy is a verbal affront to God's majesty and the penalty for such was death by stoning (Lev. 24:15, 16).

9:5–8 Among the many principles of this incident is the interconnection of this man's paralysis with his undisclosed sin. Having dealt with his sin, Jesus healed him and established His delegated authority (**power**) **to forgive sins** (v. 6).

9:9–13 In having fellowship with publicly acknowledged sinners, Jesus defied accepted social custom, thus demonstrating His authority over man-made customs that disregarded the laws of God.

9:12, 13 *See note on Mark 2:17.*

9:14–17 The response of Jesus to the question of fasting shows His authority over religious observances and, at the same time, reveals the relationship of Christianity to Judaism.

9:15 Fasting suggests mourning, but the presence of Jesus with His disciples, which inaugurated the kingdom of heaven, is an occasion for joyful celebration, such as is seen at a wedding banquet. Jesus' rhetorical response further demonstrates the error of mechanical fasts, which fail to discern God's specific directive.

9:16, 17 See section 11 of Truth-In-Action through the Synoptics at the end of Luke.

9:16, 17 The old forms of Judaism could not contain the spiritual freshness of the gospel. Grace cannot be sewed onto nor poured into the system of legalism. Rather than patching up a brittle, worn-out, and obsolete system, Jesus came to offer a new life imparted by faith in Him.

9:18–34 Another series of miracles demonstrates the authority of Jesus over despair and death.

9:20 The woman **touched the hem** of Jesus' garment, the tassels hanging from the edge of a Jewish cloak to remind the Jews of the Torah (see Num. 15:38).

9:22 The woman's **faith,** which included not only her confidence in Christ's restorative power but her importunate initiative as an unclean woman (Lev. 15:19), occasions her healing.

daughter; [a]your faith has made you
well." And the woman was made well
from that hour.
23 [a]When Jesus came into the ruler's
house, and saw [b]the flute players and
the noisy crowd wailing,
24 He said to them, [a]"Make room, for
the girl is not dead, but sleeping." And
they ridiculed Him.
25 But when the crowd was put outside, He went in and [a]took her by the
hand, and the girl arose.
26 And the [a]report of this went out into
all that land.

Two Blind Men Healed

27 When Jesus departed from there,
[a]two blind men followed Him, crying
out and saying, [b]"Son of David, have
mercy on us!"
28 And when He had come into the
house, the blind men came to Him. And
Jesus said to them, "Do you believe
that I am able to do this?" They said
to Him, "Yes, Lord."
29 Then He touched their eyes, saying,
"According to your faith let it be to
you."
30 And their eyes were opened. And
Jesus *sternly warned them, saying,
[a]"See *that* no one knows *it*."
31 [a]But when they had departed, they
[1]spread the news about Him in all that
[2]country.

A Mute Man Speaks

32 [a]As they went out, behold, they
brought to Him a man, mute and
demon-possessed.
33 And when the demon was cast out,
the mute spoke. And the multitudes
marveled, saying, "It was never seen
like this in Israel!"
34 But the Pharisees said, [a]"He casts
out demons by the ruler of the demons."

The Compassion of Jesus

35 Then Jesus went about all the cities
and villages, [a]teaching in their synagogues, preaching the gospel of the
kingdom, and healing every sickness
and every disease [1]among the people.
36 [a]But when He saw the multitudes,
He was *moved with compassion for
them, because they were [1]weary and
scattered, [b]like sheep having no *shepherd.
37 Then He said to His disciples,
[a]"The harvest truly *is* plentiful, but the
laborers *are* few.
38 [a]"Therefore pray the Lord of the
harvest to send out laborers into His
harvest."

The Twelve Apostles

10 And [a]when He had called His
twelve **disciples** to *Him*, He gave
them power *over* unclean spirits, to
cast them out, and to heal all kinds of
sickness and all kinds of disease.

WORD WEALTH

10:1 disciples, *mathetes* (math-ay-*tace*); Strong's *#3101:* From the verb *manthano,* "to learn," whose root *math* suggests thought with effort put forth. A disciple is a learner, one who follows both the teaching and the teacher. The word is used first of the Twelve and later of Christians generally.

2 Now the names of the twelve *apostles are these: first, Simon, [a]who is
called Peter, and Andrew his brother;
James the *son* of Zebedee, and John
his brother;
3 Philip and Bartholomew; Thomas
and Matthew the tax collector; James
the *son* of Alphaeus, and [1]Lebbaeus,
whose surname was Thaddaeus;
4 [a]Simon the [1]Cananite, and Judas
[b]Iscariot, who also betrayed Him.

Sending Out the Twelve

5 These twelve Jesus sent out and
commanded them, saying: [a]"Do not go
into the way of the Gentiles, and do
not enter a city of [b]the Samaritans.

22 [a]Luke 7:50; 8:48; 17:19; 18:42
23 [a]Mark 5:38 [b]2 Chr. 35:25
24 [a]Acts 20:10
25 [a]Mark 1:31
26 [a]Matt. 4:24
27 [a]Matt. 20:29–34 [b]Luke 18:38, 39
30 [a]Matt. 8:4 *See WW at John 11:38.
31 [a]Mark 7:36 [1]Lit. *made Him known* [2]Lit. *land*
32 [a]Matt. 12:22, 24
34 [a]Luke 11:15
35 [a]Matt. 4:23 [1]NU omits *among the people*
36 [a]Mark 6:34 [b]Num. 27:17 [1]NU, M *harassed* *See WW at Matt. 14:14. • See WW at John 10:2.
37 [a]Luke 10:2
38 [a]2 Thess. 3:1

CHAPTER 10

1 [a]Luke 6:13
2 [a]John 1:42 *See WW at 1 Cor. 12:28.
3 [1]NU omits *Lebbaeus, whose surname was*
4 [a]Acts 1:13 [b]John 13:2, 26 [1]NU *Cananaean*
5 [a]Matt. 4:15 [b]John 4:9

9:23, 24 Matthew describes the professional mourners, whose superficial grief is evidenced by their ridicule (v. 24).

9:27–31 The title **Son of David** was a popular messianic term, which most often carried an intense nationalistic meaning. (Jesus thus avoided the title in referring to Himself.) This may account for His test of their sincerity, which then elicits the response **Lord.**

9:32–34 This incident serves to demonstrate Jesus' reign over diseases directly attributable to a **demon** (v. 33). The accusation of the Pharisees is repeated and answered in 12:22–30.

9:35–38 Matthew summarizes the Galilean ministry of Jesus and introduces the commission He gave to His disciples.

10:1, 2 Jesus bestows upon **His twelve disciples** the delegated **power** that He Himself possessed that is, "authority" to advance the messianic ministry through exorcism healing.

10:5–15 Jesus instructs His disciples concerning the scope of their mission, the substance of their message, the works they are to perform, the equipment they are to take, and their procedure. As a microcosm of the church (Luke 12:32), the mission of the **twelve** foreshadowed the ongoing mission of the church, which would extend beyond **the house of Israel** (v. 6) to include a global scope (Acts 1:8).

6 [a]"But go rather to the [b]lost sheep
of the house of Israel.
7 [a]"And as you go, preach, saying,
[b]'The kingdom of heaven [1]is at hand.'
8 "Heal the sick, [1]cleanse the lepers,
[2]raise the dead, cast out demons.
[a]Freely you have received, freely give.

KINGDOM DYNAMICS

10:8 26. What Power Do Christians Have over Demons?, SPIRITUAL ANSWERS. For the answer to this and other probing questions about God and the power life in His kingdom, see the study article "Spiritual Answers to Hard Questions," which begins on page 1996. P.R.

9 [a]"Provide neither gold nor silver
nor [b]copper in your money belts,
10 "nor bag for *your* journey, nor two
tunics, nor sandals, nor staffs; [a]for a
worker is worthy of his food.
11 [a]"Now whatever city or town you
enter, inquire who in it is worthy, and
stay there till you go out.
12 "And when you go into a household,
greet it.
13 [a]"If the household is worthy, let
your *peace come upon it. [b]But if it is
not worthy, let your peace return to
you.
14 [a]"And whoever will not receive you
nor hear your words, when you depart
from that house or city, [b]shake off the
dust from your feet.
15 "Assuredly, I say to you, [a]it will be
more tolerable for the land of Sodom
and Gomorrah in the day of *judgment
than for that city!

Persecutions Are Coming

16 [a]"Behold, I send you out as sheep
in the midst of wolves. [b]Therefore be
wise as serpents and [c]harmless[1] as
doves.
7 17 "But beware of men, for [a]they will
deliver you up to councils and [b]scourge
you in their synagogues.
18 [a]"You will be brought before governors
and kings for My sake, as a testimony
to them and to the Gentiles.
19 [a]"But when they deliver you up, do
not *worry about how or what you
should speak. For [b]it will be given to
you in that hour what you should
speak;
20 [a]"for it is not you who speak, but
the Spirit of your Father who speaks
in you.
21 [a]"Now brother will deliver up
brother to death, and a father *his* child;
and children will rise up against parents
and cause them to be put to death.
22 "And [a]you will be hated by all for
My name's sake. [b]But he who *endures
to the end will be saved.
23 [a]"When they persecute you in this
city, flee to another. For assuredly, I
say to you, you will not have [b]gone
through the cities of Israel [c]before the
Son of Man comes.
24 [a]"A disciple is not above *his*
teacher, nor a servant above his master.
25 "It is enough for a disciple that he
be like his teacher, and a servant like
his master. If [a]they have called the
master of the house [1]Beelzebub, how
much more *will they call* those of his
household!
26 "Therefore do not **fear** them.
[a]For there is nothing covered that will
not be revealed, and hidden that will
not be known.

6 [a]Matt. 15:24 [b]Jer. 50:6
7 [a]Luke 9:2 [b]Matt. 3:2 [1]*has drawn near*
8 [a][Acts 8:18] [1]NU *raise the dead, cleanse the lepers* [2]M omits *raise the dead*
9 [a]1 Sam. 9:7 [b]Mark 6:8
10 [a]1 Tim. 5:18
11 [a]Luke 10:8
13 [a]Luke 10:5 [b]Ps. 35:13 *See WW at Luke 1:79.
14 [a]Mark 6:11 [b]Acts 13:51
15 [a]Matt. 11:22, 24 *See WW at Matt. 5:22.
16 [a]Luke 10:3 [b]Eph. 5:15 [c][Phil. 2:14–16] [1]*innocent*
17 [a]Mark 13:9 [b]Acts 5:40; 22:19; 26:11
18 [a]2 Tim. 4:16
19 [a]Luke 12:11, 12; 21:14, 15 [b]Ex. 4:12 *See WW at Matt. 6:25.
20 [a]2 Sam. 23:2
21 [a]Mic. 7:6
22 [a]Luke 21:17 [b]Mark 13:13 *See WW at Matt. 24:13.
23 [a]Acts 8:1 [b][Mark 13:10] [c]Matt. 16:28
24 [a]John 15:20
25 [a]John 8:48, 52 [1]NU, M *Beelzebul;* a Philistine deity, 2 Kin. 1:2, 3
26 [a]Mark 4:22

WORD WEALTH

10:26 fear, *phobeo* (fob-*eh*-oh); Strong's *#5399: Phobeo* is defined as a panic that grips a person causing him to run away, be alarmed, scared, frightened, dismayed, filled with dread, intimidated, anxious, and apprehensive. (Compare "phobia.") Jesus is urging His followers

10:6 Lost sheep: The OT background (Ezek. 34) indicates that all Israel is scattered like sheep. Jesus' ministry was primarily directed to the Jews.

10:7 Both John the Baptist (3:2) and Jesus (4:17) proclaimed the same message.

10:8 The disciples have received without pay the authority to exorcise and heal (v. 1) and must do Jesus' work without pay.

10:10 The disciples, unencumbered by possessions, must trust in God's provision through the hospitality of others.

10:16–23 In carrying out their mission, the disciples must be prepared to face persecution and martyrdom.

10:17–20 See section 7 of Truth-In-Action through the Synoptics at the end of Luke.

10:22 The one who perseveres in faith will receive eternal salvation.

10:23 Jesus will come to His followers before they **have gone through the cities of Israel.** This difficult verse has been variously interpreted as referring to His coming in the Transfiguration, Pentecost, in the destruction of Jerusalem in A.D. 70 (a coming in judgment), or in the Second Coming. Perhaps the simplest meaning answers these questions: Jesus was simply saying, "I'll join you later."

10:24 The disciples are encouraged in the fact that their Master has experienced the same rejection and persecution.

10:25 Beelzebub was the Philistine god of flies, used by the Jews to denote the Devil.

10:26, 27 Though persecuted, nothing will stop the disciples from publicly proclaiming the gospel truths (**speak in the light**) they have learned privately (**in the dark**), if they will stand against **fear.** Public announcements were made from **housetops.**

not to have a *phobeo* of men, which is destructive, but a reverential awe or fear of God, which is constructive. Prov. 29:25 addresses the fear syndrome: "The fear of man brings a snare, but whoever trusts in the LORD shall be secure." The NT upgrades this thought with 1 John 4:18, "Perfect love casts out fear." Being filled with God's Spirit will cause you to become fearless (2 Tim. 1:7).

Jesus Teaches the Fear of God

27 "Whatever I tell you in the *dark,
[a]speak in the light; and what you hear
in the ear, preach on the housetops.
2 28 [a]"And do not fear those who kill the
body but cannot kill the soul. But
rather [b]fear Him who is able to *destroy both soul and body in [1]hell.
29 "Are not two [a]sparrows sold for a
[1]copper coin? And not one of them falls
to the ground apart from your Father's
will.
30 [a]"But the very hairs of your head
are all numbered.
31 "Do not fear therefore; you are of
more value than many sparrows.

Confess Christ Before Men

1 **32** [a]"Therefore whoever confesses
Me before men, [b]him I will also confess before My Father who is in
heaven.
33 [a]"But whoever denies Me before
men, him I will also deny before My
Father who is in heaven.

Christ Brings Division

7 **34** [a]"Do not think that I came to bring
peace on earth. I did not come to bring
peace but a sword.
35 "For I have come to [a]*'set[1] a man
against his father, a daughter against
her mother, and a daughter-in-law
against her mother-in-law'*;
36 "and [a]*'a man's enemies will be
those of his own household.'*
37 [a]"He who *loves father or mother 7
more than Me is not worthy of Me. And
he who loves son or daughter more
than Me is not worthy of Me.
38 [a]"And he who does not take his
cross and follow after Me is not worthy
of Me.
39 [a]"He who finds his life will lose it,
and he who loses his life for My sake
will find it.

A Cup of Cold Water

40 [a]"He who receives you receives Me,
and he who receives Me receives Him
who sent Me.
41 [a]"He who receives a prophet in the
name of a prophet shall receive a
prophet's reward. And he who receives
a righteous man in the name of a righteous man shall receive a righteous
man's reward.
42 [a]"And whoever gives one of these
little ones only a cup of cold *water* in
the name of a disciple, assuredly, I say
to you, he shall by no means lose his
reward."

John the Baptist Sends Messengers to Jesus

11 Now it came to pass, when Jesus finished commanding His
twelve disciples, that He departed from
there to [a]teach and to preach in their
cities.
2 [a]And when John had heard [b]in
prison about the *works of Christ, he
[1]sent two of his disciples
3 and said to Him, "Are You [a]the
Coming One, or do we look for another?"
4 Jesus answered and said to them,
"Go and tell John the things which you
hear and see:

27 [a]Acts 5:20 *See WW at John 12:46. **28** [a]Luke 12:4 [b]Luke 12:5 [1]Gr. *Gehenna* *See WW at Luke 9:56. **29** [a]Luke 12:6, 7 [1]Gr. *assarion*, a coin worth about 1/16 of a denarius **30** [a]Luke 21:18 **32** [a]Luke 12:8 [b][Rev. 3:5] **33** [a]2 Tim. 2:12 **34** [a][Luke 12:49] **35** [a]Mic. 7:6 [1]*alienate a man from*

36 [a]John 13:18 **37** [a]Luke 14:26 *See WW at John 21:15. **38** [a][Mark 8:34] **39** [a]John 12:25 **40** [a]Luke 9:48 **41** [a]1 Kin. 17:10 **42** [a]Mark 9:41

CHAPTER 11

1 [a]Luke 23:5 **2** [a]Luke 7:18–35 [b]Matt. 4:12; 14:3 [1]NU *sent by his* *See WW at John 9:4. **3** [a]John 6:14

10:28 See section 2 of Truth-In-Action through the Synoptics at the end of Luke.
10:32, 33 See section 1 of Truth-In-Action through the Synoptics at the end of Luke.
10:32, 33 Jesus leaves no room for secret discipleship.
10:34–39 Jesus does not attack family relationships, but indicates that no earthly tie, however intimate, should detract from aggressive loyalty to Him. This loyalty may even result in certain family members being shunned by others (vv. 35, 36).
10:34–36 See section 7 of Truth-In-Action through the Synoptics at the end of Luke.
10:37–39 See section 7 of Truth-In-Action through the Synoptics at the end of Luke.
10:38 The **cross** is an instrument of death, symbolizing here not the bearing of any particular burden or distress, but a willingness to give one's life sacrificially for the Master.
10:40–42 Those who give support to the messengers of the Lord will receive blessing; because in receiving the Lord's representatives, they are receiving Him.
10:40 Basic to the argument is the Jewish principle that a person's representative is regarded as the person himself/herself. To receive a person, a prophet, a righteous one, or a little one is tantamount to receiving Jesus and the One (Father) who sent Jesus.
11:2, 3 While he was languishing in prison (see 14:1–12), John the Baptist needed reassurance from Jesus. While he had been positive about the identity of the Messiah (see 3:14; John 1:29), he was evidently expecting an eschatological judgment, which had not yet taken place.
11:4, 5 Jesus' present activities are the fulfillment of Is. 35:5, 6. In the present age Jesus accomplishes His messianic task by granting salvation through a response to preaching, healings, exorcisms, and miracles. The judgment expected

5 [a]"*The* blind see and *the* lame walk;
the lepers are cleansed and *the* deaf
hear; *the* dead are raised up and
[b]*the* poor have the gospel preached to
them.
6 "And blessed is he who is not
[a]**offended** because of Me."

WORD WEALTH

11:6 offended, *skandalizo* (skan-dal-*id*-zoe); Strong's *#4624:* Originally, to put a snare or stumbling block in the way. The noun to which it is related referred to the bait-stick of a trap. In the NT *skandalizo* is always used metaphorically of that which hinders right conduct or thought, hence, "to cause to stumble."

7 [a]As they departed, Jesus began to
say to the multitudes concerning John:
"What did you go out into the wilderness to see? [b]A reed shaken by the
wind?
8 "But what did you go out to see? A
man clothed in soft garments? Indeed,
those who wear soft *clothing* are in
kings' houses.
9 "But what did you go out to see? A
prophet? Yes, I say to you, [a]and more
than a prophet.
10 "For this is *he* of whom it is written:

> [a]'*Behold, I send My messenger*
> *before Your face,*
> *Who will prepare Your way*
> *before You.'*

11 "Assuredly, I say to you, among
those born of women there has not
risen one greater than John the Baptist; but he who is least in the kingdom
of heaven is greater than he.
8 12 [a]"And from the days of John the
Baptist until now the kingdom of
heaven suffers violence, and the violent *take it by force.

KINGDOM DYNAMICS

11:12 Taking It by Force, CONFLICT AND THE KINGDOM. Jesus asserts the "violence" of the kingdom. The unique grammatical construction of the text does not make clear if the kingdom of God is the victim of violence or if, as the kingdom advances in victory, it does so through violent spiritual conflict and warfare. But the context does. Jesus' references to the nonreligious style of John and the confrontive, miraculous ministry of Elijah teach that the kingdom of God makes its penetration by a kind of violent entry opposing the human status quo. It transcends the "softness" (v. 8) of staid religious formalism and exceeds the pretension of child's play (vv. 16, 17). It refuses to "dance to the music" of society's expectation that the religious community provide either entertainment ("we played the flute") or dead traditionalism ("we mourned").

Jesus defines the "violence" of His kingdom's expansion by defining the "sword" and "fire" He has brought as different from the battle techniques of political or military warfare (compare Matt. 10:34–39 and Luke 12:49–53 with John 18:36). The upheaval caused by the kingdom of God is not caused by political provocation or armed advance. It is the result of God's order shaking relationships, households, cities, and nations by the entry of the Holy Spirit's power working in people. (See also Luke 16:16.)

(Luke 4:1–12/Col. 2:13–15) J.W.H.

13 [a]"For all the prophets and the law
prophesied until John.
14 "And if you are willing to receive
it, he is [a]Elijah who is to come.
15 [a]"He who has ears to hear, let him
hear!
16 [a]"But to what shall I liken this generation? It is like children sitting in the
marketplaces and calling to their companions,
17 "and saying:

> 'We played the flute for you,
> And you did not dance;
> We mourned to you,
> And you did not [1]lament.'

18 "For John came neither eating nor
drinking, and they say, 'He has a demon.'

5 [a]Is. 29:18; 35:4–6; John 2:23 [b]Ps. 22:26; Is. 61:1; Luke 4:18; James 2:5
6 [a]Is. 8:14, 15; [Rom. 9:32]; 1 Pet. 2:8
7 [a]Luke 7:24 [b][Eph. 4:14]
9 [a]Matt. 14:5; 21:26; Luke 1:76; 20:6
10 [a]Mal. 3:1; Mark 1:2; Luke 1:76
12 [a]Luke 16:16 *See WW at 1 Thess. 4:17.
13 [a]Mal. 4:4–6
14 [a]Mal. 4:5; Matt. 17:10–13; Mark 9:11–13; Luke 1:17; John 1:21
15 [a]Matt. 13:9; Luke 8:8; Rev. 2:7, 11, 17, 29; 3:6, 13
16 [a]Luke 7:31
17 [1]Lit. *beat your breast*

---

by John will take place at the consummation in the Age to Come.

11:7–11 Jesus commends John as a man of courage (v. 7), consecration (v. 8), and greatness (vv. 9–11). Yet, the **least in the kingdom of heaven is greater** in privilege than John.

11:12–14 See section 8 of Truth-In-Action through the Synoptics at the end of Luke.

11:12 Though the Greek here is somewhat difficult to translate, the idea in this verse is that **the kingdom of heaven,** which Jesus set up as a powerful movement or reign among men (**suffers violence**), requires of them an equally strong and radical reaction. **The violent** then who **take it by force** are people of keen enthusiasm and commitment who are willing to respond to and propagate with radical abandonment the message and dynamic of God's reign (see Luke 16:16).

11:14 A proof for the threshold of the Christian era is found in the identification of John the Baptist with Elijah (Mal. 4:5).

11:16–19 Jesus illustrates the fickle and even caustic response of the people to John's ministry and to His own. Unbelief will not respond to truth, however well it is presented and demonstrated.

19 "The Son of Man came eating and
drinking, and they say, 'Look, a glutton
and a [1]winebibber, [a]a *friend of tax
collectors and sinners!' [b]But wisdom
is *justified by her [2]children."

Woe to the Impenitent Cities

20 [a]Then He began to *rebuke the cit-
ies in which most of His mighty works
had been done, because they did not
repent:
21 "Woe to you, Chorazin! Woe to you,
Bethsaida! For if the mighty works
which were done in you had been done
in Tyre and Sidon, they would have repented long ago [a]in sackcloth and
ashes.
22 "But I say to you, [a]it will be more
tolerable for Tyre and Sidon in the day
of judgment than for you.
23 "And you, Capernaum, [a]who[1] are
*exalted to heaven, will be brought
down to Hades; for if the mighty works
which were done in you had been done
in Sodom, it would have remained until
this day.
24 "But I say to you [a]that it shall be
more tolerable for the land of Sodom
in the day of judgment than for you."

Jesus Gives True Rest

25 [a]At that time Jesus answered and
said, "I thank You, Father, Lord of
heaven and earth, that [b]You have hidden these things from *the* wise and
prudent [c]and have revealed them to
babes.
26 "Even so, Father, for so it seemed
good in Your sight.
27 [a]"All things have been delivered to
Me by My Father, and no one *knows
the Son except the Father. [b]Nor does
anyone know the Father except the
Son, and *the one* to whom the Son wills
to reveal *Him*.
28 "Come to [a]Me, all *you* who labor
and are heavy laden, and I will give
you *rest.

19 [a]Matt. 9:10 [b]Luke 7:35 [1]*wine drinker* [2]NU *works* *See WW at John 11:11. • See WW at Matt. 12:37.
20 [a]Luke 10:13–15, 18 *See WW at James 1:5.
21 [a]Jon. 3:6–8
22 [a]Matt. 10:15; 11:24
23 [a]Is. 14:13 [1]NU *will you be exalted to heaven? No, you will be* *See WW at James 4:10.
24 [a]Matt. 10:15
25 [a]Luke 10:21, 22 [b]Ps. 8:2 [c]Matt. 16:17
27 [a]Matt. 28:18 [b]John 1:18; 6:46; 10:15 *See WW at Luke 5:22.
28 [a][John 6:35–37] *See WW at Rev. 14:13.
29 [a][Phil. 2:5] [b]Zech. 9:9 [c]Jer. 6:16 [1]*meek* *See WW at 2 Cor. 7:6.
30 [a][1 John 5:3]

CHAPTER 12

1 [a]Luke 6:1–5 [b]Deut. 23:25 *See WW at Col. 4:5.
3 [a]1 Sam. 21:6 *See WW at Mark 13:14.
4 [a]Lev. 24:5 [b]Ex. 29:32
5 [a]Num. 28:9 [1]*desecrate*
6 [a][Is. 66:1, 2]
7 [a][Hos. 6:6]

29 "Take My yoke upon you [a]and
learn from Me, for I am [1]gentle and
[b]lowly* in heart, [c]and you will find rest
for your souls.
30 [a]"For My yoke *is* **easy** and My burden is light."

WORD WEALTH

11:30 easy, *chrestos* (khrase-*toss*); Strong's *#5543:* From the verb *chraomai,* "to use." The word denotes that which is useful, pleasant, good, comfortable, suitable, and serviceable. The legalistic religious system was a severe burden, but service to Jesus does not chafe, because it is well-fitting and built on personal relationship with God by the indwelling Spirit.

Jesus Is Lord of the Sabbath

12 At that *time [a]Jesus went
through the grainfields on the
Sabbath. And His disciples were hungry, and began to [b]pluck heads of grain
and to eat.
2 And when the Pharisees saw *it,*
they said to Him, "Look, Your disciples
are doing what is not lawful to do on
the Sabbath!"
3 But He said to them, "Have you not
*read [a]what David did when he was
hungry, he and those who were with
him:
4 "how he entered the house of God
and ate [a]the showbread which was not
lawful for him to eat, nor for those who
were with him, [b]but only for the
priests?
5 "Or have you not read in the
[a]law that on the Sabbath the priests
in the temple [1]profane the Sabbath,
and are blameless?
6 "Yet I say to you that in this place
there is [a]*One* greater than the temple.
7 "But if you had known what *this*
means, [a]*'I desire mercy and not sacri-*
fice,' you would not have condemned
the guiltless.

11:20 The woes pronounced upon the cities serve as *warning to the unresponsive generation.* Not only does Jesus condemn the wicked, but also the indifferent, insisting that greater opportunity for belief calls for greater condemnation for rejecting Him.
11:25–30 Jesus concludes this discourse with thanksgiving for revelation (vv. 25–27) and an invitation to come to Him as the source of revelation (vv. 28–30).
11:27 Jesus has a unique and incomparable relationship with **the Father.** Because His relationship is immediate and unmediated, He alone can reveal God.
11:28–30 In contrast to the heavy burden of Jewish legalism, Jesus calls for an open, free, and loyal relationship (**My yoke**), which enables obedience to the Law's righteousness (**My burden**).
12:1–21 The growing opposition to the ministry of Jesus by the religious leaders finds its fullest expression in the observance of the Sabbath, the most sacred institution among the Jews.
12:3 Jesus supports His disciples' action by His appeal to David's example (1 Sam. 21:1–6), verifying that normal Sabbath regulations may need to yield to human need.
12:4, 5 Human need takes precedence over a strict interpretation of the Law, which misses its broadest intent.
12:6–8 In claiming to be **greater than the temple** and **Lord even of the Sabbath,** Jesus was actually claiming deity. Since He gave the Sabbath, He can do with it what He wills.

8 "For the Son of Man is Lord [1]even
of the Sabbath."

Healing on the Sabbath

9 [a]Now when He had departed from
there, He went into their synagogue.
10 And behold, there was a man who
had a withered hand. And they asked
Him, saying, [a]"Is it lawful to heal on
the Sabbath?"—that they might accuse
Him.
11 Then He said to them, "What man
is there among you who has one sheep,
and if it falls into a pit on the Sabbath,
will not lay hold of it and lift *it* out?
12 "Of how much more value then is
a man than a sheep? Therefore it is
lawful to do good on the Sabbath."
13 Then He said to the man, "Stretch
out your hand." And he stretched *it*
out, and it was restored as whole as
the other.
14 Then [a]the Pharisees went out and
plotted against Him, how they might
destroy Him.

Behold, My Servant

15 But when Jesus knew *it,* [a]He withdrew from there. [b]And great [1]multi-
tudes followed Him, and He healed
them all.
16 Yet He [a]warned them not to *make
Him known,
17 that it might be fulfilled which was
spoken by Isaiah the prophet, saying:

18 *"Behold![a] My Servant whom I*
have chosen,
My Beloved [b]in whom My soul is
well pleased!
I will put My Spirit upon Him,
And He will declare justice to the
Gentiles.
19 *He will not quarrel nor cry out,*
Nor will anyone hear His voice in
the streets.
20 *A *bruised reed He will not break,*
And smoking flax He will not
quench,
Till He sends forth justice to
victory;
21 *And in His name Gentiles will*
trust."

A House Divided Cannot Stand

22 [a]Then one was brought to Him who
was demon-possessed, blind and mute;
and He **healed** him, so that the [1]blind
and mute man both spoke and saw.

> **WORD WEALTH**
>
> **12:22 healed,** *therapeuo* (ther-ap-yoo-oh); Strong's *#2323:* Compare "therapy" and "therapeutic." Originally, to serve in a menial way, such as household domestics attending to the members of a family. Since their duties included the care of sick family members, the word took on a medical connotation in the sense of taking care of, tending, and providing for the sick. From there it came to mean to heal, restore to health, cure.

23 And all the multitudes were amazed
and said, "Could this be the [a]Son of
David?"
24 [a]Now when the Pharisees heard *it*
they said, "This *fellow* does not cast
out demons except by [1]Beelzebub, the
ruler of the demons."
25 But Jesus [a]knew their thoughts, and
said to them: "Every kingdom divided
against itself is brought to desolation,
and every city or house divided against
itself will not stand.
26 "If Satan casts out Satan, he is divided against himself. How then will
his kingdom stand?
27 "And if I cast out demons by Beelzebub, by whom do your sons cast *them*
out? Therefore they shall be your
judges.

8 [1]NU, M omit *even*
9 [a]Mark 3:1–6; Luke 6:6–11
10 [a]Luke 13:14; 14:3; John 9:16
14 [a]Ps. 2:2; Matt. 27:1; Mark 3:6; [Luke 6:11]; John 5:18; 10:39; 11:53
15 [a]Matt. 10:23; Mark 3:7 [b]Matt. 19:2 [1]NU brackets *multitudes* as disputed.
16 [a]Matt. 8:4; 9:30; 17:9 *See WW at 1 Cor. 11:19.
18 [a]Is. 42:1–4; 49:3 [b]Matt. 3:17; 17:5
20 *See WW at Rom. 16:20.
22 [a]Matt. 9:32; [Mark 3:11]; Luke 11:14, 15 [1]NU omits *blind and*
23 [a]Matt. 9:27; 21:9
24 [a]Matt. 9:34; Mark 3:22; Luke 11:15 [1]NU, M *Beelzebul,* a Philistine deity
25 [a]Matt. 9:4; John 2:25; Rev. 2:23

12:9–14 Healing was not allowed on the Sabbath except when there was danger to life. Even then, measures could be taken only to prevent the condition from getting worse; nothing could be done to improve it. Jesus countered this obvious fallacy, saying it is indeed **lawful to do good on the Sabbath.**

12:14 Ironically, those who were outraged by a supposed violation of the Sabbath had no qualms about plotting **how they might destroy Him.**

12:15–21 Matthew interprets the withdrawal of Jesus and the injunction to silence about His healing power as a fulfillment of Isaiah's prophecy (Is. 42:1–4) concerning the gentle and unpretentious manner of the Messiah's ministry.

12:24 Beelzebub: See note on 10:25. Since an obvious miracle had taken place, the Pharisees' only alternative was to discredit the source of Jesus' authority.

12:25–29 In this very climactic encounter with the Pharisees over Jesus' reshaped definition of the **kingdom of God,** He shows the absurdity of the charge of casting out demons by Satan's power. On the contrary, the exorcisms demonstrate the penetration of Satan's **kingdom** by the kingdom of God in Jesus. Jesus' binding and plundering of the **strong** man was further inaugurated by His crucifixion and resurrection, is propagated by the church, and will be consummated through the events of the Age to Come.

12:25 The repetition of the term **divided** in vv. 25, 26 reveals the absurdity of the charge. Jesus does not say that the break-up of Satan's kingdom will occur by internal dissension ("divided"), but rather by the external aggression of the Stronger One over the strong one (v. 29; see Is. 49:24–26; 53:12).

28 "But if I cast out demons by the
Spirit of God, [a]surely the kingdom of
God has come upon you.
29 [a]"Or how can one enter a strong
man's house and plunder his goods,
unless he first binds the strong man?
And then he will plunder his house.
30 "He who is not with Me is against
Me, and he who does not gather with
Me scatters abroad.

The Unpardonable Sin

31 "Therefore I say to you, [a]every sin
and blasphemy will be forgiven men,
[b]but the blasphemy *against* the Spirit
will not be forgiven men.

KINGDOM DYNAMICS

12:31 9. What Is the Unpardonable Sin?, SPIRITUAL ANSWERS. For the answer to this and other probing questions about God and the power life in His kingdom, see the study article "Spiritual Answers to Hard Questions," which begins on page 1996. P.R.

32 "Anyone who [a]speaks a word
against the Son of Man, [b]it will be forgiven him; but whoever speaks against
the Holy Spirit, it will not be forgiven
him, either in this age or in the *age* to
come.

A Tree Known by Its Fruit

33 "Either make the tree good and
[a]its fruit good, or else make the tree
bad and its fruit bad; for a tree is
known by *its* fruit.
34 [a]"Brood[1] of vipers! How can you,
being evil, speak good things? [b]For out
of the abundance of the heart the
mouth speaks.
35 "A good man out of the good treasure [1]of his heart brings forth good
things, and an evil man out of the evil
treasure brings forth evil things.
36 "But I say to you that for every idle

28 [a][Dan. 2:44; 7:14; Luke 1:33]; 11:20; [17:20, 21; 1 John 3:8]
29 [a]Is. 49:24; [Luke 11:21–23]
31 [a]Mark 3:28–30; Luke 12:10; [Heb. 6:4–6; 10:26, 29; 1 John 5:16] [b]Acts 7:51
32 [a]Matt. 11:19; 13:55; John 7:12, 52 [b]1 Tim. 1:13
33 [a]Matt. 7:16–18; Luke 6:43, 44; [John 15:4–7]
34 [a]Matt. 3:7; 23:33; Luke 3:7 [b]1 Sam. 24:13; Is. 32:6; [Matt. 15:18]; Luke 6:45; Eph. 4:29; [James 3:2–12] [1]*Offspring*
35 [1]NU, M omit *of his heart*
36 *See WW at Matt. 4:4.
38 [a]Matt. 16:1; Mark 8:11; Luke 11:16; John 2:18; 1 Cor. 1:22
39 [a]Is. 57:3; Matt. 16:4; Mark 8:38; [Luke 11:29–32]; John 4:48
40 [a]Jon. 1:17; Luke 24:46; Acts 10:40; 1 Cor. 15:4
41 [a]Jon. 3:5; Luke 11:32 [b]Jer. 3:11; Ezek. 16:51; [Rom. 2:27] [c]Jon. 3:5
42 [a]1 Kin. 10:1–13; 2 Chr. 9:1; Luke 11:31 *See WW at Acts 6:10.
43 [a]Luke 11:24–26 [b][Job 1:7; 1 Pet. 5:8]

*word men may speak, they will give
account of it in the day of judgment.
37 "For by your words you will be **justified,** and by your words you will be
condemned."

WORD WEALTH

12:37 justified, *dikaioo* (dik-ah-*yah*-oh); Strong's *#1344:* A legal term signifying to acquit, declare righteous, show to be righteous. In this passage Jesus refers to the day of judgment as the day of His determining condemnation or justification, based on our hearts' response to the Spirit.

The Scribes and Pharisees Ask for a Sign

38 [a]Then some of the scribes and Pharisees answered, saying, "Teacher, we
want to see a sign from You."
39 But He answered and said to them,
"An evil and [a]adulterous generation
seeks after a sign, and no sign will be
given to it except the sign of the
prophet Jonah.
40 [a]"For as Jonah was three days and
three nights in the belly of the great
fish, so will the Son of Man be three
days and three nights in the heart of
the earth.
41 [a]"The men of Nineveh will rise up
in the judgment with this generation
and [b]condemn it, [c]because they repented at the preaching of Jonah; and
indeed a greater than Jonah *is* here.
42 [a]"The queen of the South will rise
up in the judgment with this generation
and condemn it, for she came from the
ends of the earth to hear the *wisdom
of Solomon; and indeed a greater than
Solomon *is* here.

An Unclean Spirit Returns

43 [a]"When an unclean spirit goes out 11
of a man, [b]he goes through dry places,
seeking rest, and finds none.

12:28 The miracle was performed **by the Spirit of God** as an indication of the presence of **the kingdom of God.**
12:31, 32 The Pharisees slandered the Holy Spirit by knowledgeably attributing His work to the Devil, thus committing the "unpardonable sin." Their sin was not an act of impulse or ignorance, but the result of a continued and willful rejection of the truth concerning Jesus. It was a sin against spiritual knowledge, for they had ample evidence of the truth from the words and deeds of Jesus. In deliberately choosing to insult the Spirit, they forfeited His ministry in their lives and **will not be forgiven.**
12:33–37 This analogy demonstrates that the blasphemy was not merely an utterance of the lips, but an expression of character.
12:38, 39 Further evidence of the blindness and opposition of the religious leaders is their demand for a display of supernatural power that will authenticate Jesus as the Messiah. They had already witnessed many such signs. The problem was not the lack of signs, but their own unfaithfulness to God. Later, they will refuse even the greatest sign of all—that of the Resurrection (see 28:11–15).
12:42 Queen of the South: The expression means the queen of Sheba (1 Kin. 10:1–13).
12:43–45 See section 11 of Truth-In-Action through the Synoptics at the end of Luke.
12:43–45 Jesus' teaching specifically applies to the emptiness of Judaism in substituting reformation for

44 "Then he says, 'I will return to my
house from which I came.' And when
he comes, he finds *it* empty, swept, and
*put in order.
45 "Then he goes and takes with him
seven other spirits more wicked than
himself, and they enter and dwell
there; [a]and the last *state* of that man
is worse than the first. So shall it also
be with this wicked generation."

Jesus' Mother and Brothers Send for Him

46 While He was still talking to the
multitudes, [a]behold, His mother and
[b]brothers stood outside, seeking to
speak with Him.
47 Then one said to Him, "Look,
[a]Your mother and Your brothers are
standing outside, seeking to speak with
You."
48 But He answered and said to the
one who told Him, "Who is My mother
and who are My brothers?"
49 And He stretched out His hand toward His disciples and said, "Here are
My mother and My [a]brothers!
50 "For [a]whoever does the **will** of My
Father in heaven is My brother and sister and mother."

WORD WEALTH

12:50 will, *thelema* (*thel*-ay-mah); Strong's *#2307:* Used objectively of that which is willed, designed, or desired (18:14; Luke 12:47; John 5:30), and subjectively of the emotion of being desirous (Luke 23:25; John 1:13; 1 Pet. 3:17). The word is used both of the human will and the divine will.

The Parable of the Sower

4 **13** On the same day Jesus went out
of the house [a]and sat by the sea.

KINGDOM DYNAMICS

13:1–52 A Present and Future Kingdom, THE MESSAGE OF THE KINGDOM. In this chapter, Jesus introduces parables as a means of teaching "kingdom" truths (vv. 10, 11). Of the 40 parables Jesus gave, He made direct references to the kingdom in 19. These stories clearly relate to different time frames. Some impact the present, teaching 1) the need for kingdom people to have hearing ears (vv. 3–23); 2) the breadth of the kingdom's spread (vv. 31–35); and 3) the cost of the kingdom's acquisition (vv. 44–46). Others relate to the future, teaching 1) the final disposing of the fruit of the Adversary's hindrance (vv. 36–43) and 2) the final disposition of the mixed ingathering from kingdom outreach (vv. 47–51). In mixing these two aspects of the "kingdom," Jesus helps us appreciate the kingdoms as both present and prospective. The message of the kingdom is two-edged and relates to two frames of time: First, God, in Christ, is now recovering man from his double loss—relationship with God and of rulership under God. He promised this at man's Fall, illustrated it in the patriarchs and Israel's history, and now the King has come to begin fully bringing it about. The kingdom is being realized presently, in partial and personal ways, as it is spread through all the Earth by the Holy Spirit's power in the church. Second, the kingdom will be realized finally in consummate and conclusive ways only at the return of Jesus Christ and by His reign over all the Earth. What we experience of His triumph now, in part, will then be fully manifest (1 Cor. 15:24; Rev. 11:15; 1 Cor. 13:9, 10). This complete view allows for our understanding and applying the principles of "kingdom come" without falling into the confusion of expecting now what the Bible says will only be then.

(John 3:1–5/Col. 1:13) J.W.H.

2 [a]And great multitudes were gathered together to Him, so that [b]He got
into a boat and sat; and the whole multitude stood on the shore.
3 Then He spoke many things to them
in parables, saying: [a]"Behold, a sower
went out to sow.
4 "And as he sowed, some *seed* fell
by the wayside; and the birds came and
devoured them.
5 "Some fell on stony places, where
they did not have much earth; and they

44 *See WW at Matt. 25:7. **45** [a]Mark 5:9; Luke 11:26; [Heb. 6:4–8; 10:26; 2 Pet. 2:20–22] **46** [a]Mark 3:31–35; Luke 8:19–21 [b]Matt. 13:55; Mark 6:3; John 2:12; 7:3, 5; Acts 1:14; 1 Cor. 9:5; Gal. 1:19 **47** [a]Matt. 13:55, 56; John 2:12; Acts 1:14 **49** [a]John 20:17; [Rom. 8:29] **50** [a]John 15:14; [Gal. 5:6; 6:15; Col. 3:11; Heb. 2:11]

CHAPTER 13

1 [a]Matt. 13:1–15; Mark 4:1–12; Luke 8:4–10 **2** [a]Luke 8:4 [b]Luke 5:3 **3** [a]Luke 8:5

regeneration. Israel will be in a worse state than before. Once the nation rejects Jesus, nothing is left to replace the vacuum except satanic deception.

12:46–50 Jesus does not disclaim His family, but enlarges the circle to include spiritual relationships.

13:1–23 See section 4 of Truth-In-Action through the Synoptics at the end of Luke.

13:3–9 This parable constitutes one of eight major **parables** of the kingdom of God. Its central message is that the gospel of the kingdom will meet with varying levels of success in the human heart. The Jews were awaiting a dynamic apocalyptic kingdom, which could not be resisted and which would entirely destroy evil. They could not conceive of a servanthood-type kingdom coming quietly to invade evil and solicit human responses. From Jesus' interpretation (vv. 18–23), we also learn that the kingdom is currently present (though not consummated), that self-sufficiency opposes the gospel, and that measurably great response can be expected from many ("some a hundredfold," v. 23).

13:3 About one-third of Jesus' teaching was **in parables,** brief stories from everyday life told by way of analogy to illustrate spiritual truths. Whereas in interpreting parables,

immediately sprang up because they
had no depth of earth.
6 "But when the sun was up they
were scorched, and because they had
no root they withered away.
7 "And some fell among thorns, and
the thorns sprang up and choked them.
8 "But others fell on good ground and
yielded a crop: some [a]a hundredfold,
some sixty, some thirty.
9 [a]"He who has ears to hear, let him
hear!"

The Purpose of Parables

10 And the disciples came and said to
Him, "Why do You speak to them in
parables?"
11 He answered and said to them, "Because [a]it has been given to you to know
the [1]mysteries* of the kingdom of
heaven, but to them it has not been
given.
12 [a]"For whoever has, to him more
will be given, and he will have abundance; but whoever does not have,
even what he has will be taken away
from him.
13 "Therefore I speak to them in parables, because seeing they do not see,
and hearing they do not hear, nor do
they understand.
14 "And in them the *prophecy of Isaiah is fulfilled, which says:

[a]'*Hearing you will hear and shall*
not understand,
And seeing you will see and not
[b]*perceive;*
15 *For the hearts of this people have*
grown dull.
Their ears [a]*are hard of hearing,*
And their eyes they have
[b]*closed,*
Lest they should see with their
eyes and hear with their ears,
Lest they should understand with
their hearts and turn,
So that I [1]*should* [c]*heal them.'*

16 "But [a]blessed *are* your eyes for they
see, and your ears for they hear;

8 [a]Gen. 26:12
9 [a]Matt. 11:15
11 [a]Mark 4:10, 11 [1]*secret* or *hidden truths* *See WW at Mark 4:11.
12 [a]Matt. 25:29
14 [a]Is. 6:9, 10 [b][John 3:36] *See WW at 1 Thess. 5:20.
15 [a]Heb. 5:11 [b]Luke 19:42 [c]Acts 28:26, 27 [1]NU, M *would*
16 [a]Luke 10:23, 24
17 [a]Heb. 11:13
18 [a]Mark 4:13–20
19 [a]Matt. 4:23 *See WW at 1 Thess. 4:17.
20 [a]Is. 58:2
21 [a][Acts 14:22] [b]Matt. 11:6 *See WW at John 16:33. • See WW at Matt. 11:6.
22 [a]1 Tim. 6:9 [b]Jer. 4:3 *See WW at 1 Pet. 5:7.
23 [a]Col. 1:6

17 "for assuredly, I say to you [a]that
many prophets and righteous *men* **de-**
sired to see what you see, and did not
see *it,* and to hear what you hear, and
did not hear *it.*

WORD WEALTH

13:17 desired, *epithumeo* (ep-ee-thoo-*meh*-oh); Strong's *#1937:* To set one's heart upon, eagerly long for, covet, greatly desire, lust after. The word emphasizes the intensity of the desire rather than the object desired. It describes both good and evil desires.

The Parable of the Sower Explained

18 [a]"Therefore hear the parable of the
sower:
19 "When anyone hears the word
[a]of the kingdom, and does not understand *it,* then the wicked *one* comes
and *snatches away what was sown in
his heart. This is he who received seed
by the wayside.
20 "But he who received the seed on
stony places, this is he who hears the
word and immediately [a]receives it with
joy;
21 "yet he has no root in himself, but
endures only for a while. For when
[a]tribulation* or persecution arises because of the word, immediately [b]he
*stumbles.
22 "Now [a]he who received seed
[b]among the thorns is he who hears
the word, and the *cares of this world
and the deceitfulness of riches
choke the word, and he becomes
unfruitful.
23 "But he who received seed on the
good ground is he who hears the word
and understands *it,* who indeed bears
[a]fruit and produces: some a hundredfold, some sixty, some thirty."

The Parable of the Wheat and the Tares

24 Another parable He put forth to
them, saying: "The kingdom of heaven

one must guard against fanciful allegorization of details, staying primarily with the major point of the story, Jesus' own interpretation (vv. 18–23) demonstrates that the details of a parable can indeed hold symbolic significance and application. Determining such significance can at times be difficult and easily abused; yet, we should not rule out such a revelatory search by the leading of the same indwelling Spirit who first inspired the teaching. A general approach would be to find the primary point (using grammatical-historical principles and staying consistent with the original purpose and message of the parable). Then move on to secondary points of application, using the whole of Scripture's revelation to guide interpretation.

13:9 Ears to hear notes the essential need for a teachable, hearing heart to be present if the "seed" of the kingdom truth is to be received and become fruitful.

13:10–17 The purpose of parables was to make spiritual truths clearer to hearers; to put truth in a form easily remembered; to avoid offense with hostile people who would not receive the truth; and to declare judgment upon those who were willfully blind. See note on Mark 4:12.

13:11 See note on Mark 4:11.

13:16, 17 The disciples were privileged to see and hear things not given to God's servants in the OT.

13:24–30 The central message of this parable is that the consummated kingdom of God will be different from the

is like a man who sowed good seed in
his field;
25 "but while men slept, his enemy
came and sowed tares among the
wheat and went his way.
26 "But when the grain had sprouted
and produced a crop, then the tares
also appeared.
27 "So the servants of the owner came
and said to him, 'Sir, did you not sow
good seed in your field? How then does
it have tares?'
28 "He said to them, 'An enemy has
done this.' The servants said to him,
'Do you want us then to go and gather
them up?'
29 "But he said, 'No, lest while you
gather up the tares you also uproot the
wheat with them.
30 'Let both grow together until the
harvest, and at the time of harvest I
will say to the reapers, "First gather
together the tares and bind them in
bundles to burn them, but [a]gather the
wheat into my barn." ' "

The Parable of the Mustard Seed

11 31 Another parable He put forth to
them, saying: [a]"The kingdom of
heaven is like a mustard seed, which
a man took and sowed in his field,
32 "which indeed is the least of all the
seeds; but when it is grown it is greater
than the herbs and becomes a [a]tree,
so that the birds of the air come and
nest in its branches."

The Parable of the Leaven

33 [a]Another parable He spoke to them:
"The kingdom of heaven is like leaven,
which a woman took and hid in three
[1]measures of meal till [b]it was all leavened."

Prophecy and the Parables

34 [a]All these things Jesus spoke to the
multitude in parables; and without a
parable He did not speak to them,
35 that it might be fulfilled which was
spoken by the prophet, saying:

> [a]"I will open My mouth in parables;
> [b]I will utter things kept secret from
> the foundation of the world."

The Parable of the Tares Explained

36 Then Jesus sent the multitude away
and went into the house. And His disciples came to Him, saying, "Explain to
us the parable of the tares of the field."
37 He answered and said to them: "He
who sows the good seed is the Son of
Man.
38 [a]"The field is the world, the good
seeds are the sons of the kingdom, but
the tares are [b]the sons of the wicked
one.

KINGDOM DYNAMICS

13:37, 38 His Field—A Promise of Harvest, WORLD EVANGELISM. To the farmer, the field is a promise of harvest. This area of land prompts his vision of a yielding crop. Having given the parables of the Sower (vv. 3–9) and the Wheat and the Tares (vv. 24–30), Jesus interprets the parabolic picture: "The field is the world." Christ's own imagery points to the process of world evangelism: Go and sow. The field may or may not appear fertile; the field may be ravished by drought (spiritual need) or insect (spiritual opponents), but in either case the field is itself the summons. Lift up your eyes (Prov. 29:18; John 4:35–37).

(Is. 40:8–11/Matt. 24:14) G.C.

39 "The enemy who sowed them is the
devil, [a]the harvest is the end of the age,
and the reapers are the angels.
40 "Therefore as the tares are gathered
and burned in the fire, so it will be at
the end of this age.
41 "The Son of Man will send out His
*angels, [a]and they will gather out of
His kingdom all things that *offend,
and those who practice lawlessness,
42 [a]"and will cast them into the fur-

30 [a]Matt. 3:12
31 [a][Is. 2:2, 3; Mic. 4:1]; Mark 4:30; Luke 13:18, 19
32 [a]Ps. 104:12; Ezek. 17:22–24; 31:3–9; Dan. 4:12
33 [a]Luke 13:20, 21 [b][1 Cor. 5:6; Gal. 5:9] [1]Gr. *sata,* same as a Heb. *seah;* approximately 2 pecks in all
34 [a]Mark 4:33, 34; John 10:6; 16:25
35 [a]Ps. 78:2 [b]Rom. 16:25, 26; 1 Cor. 2:7; Eph. 3:9; Col. 1:26
38 [a]Matt. 24:14; 28:19; Mark 16:15; Luke 24:47; Rom. 10:18; Col. 1:6 [b]Gen. 3:15; John 8:44; Acts 13:10
39 [a]Joel 3:13; Rev. 14:15
41 [a]Matt. 18:7; 2 Pet. 2:1, 2 *See WW at Matt. 4:11. • See WW at Matt. 16:23.
42 [a]Matt. 3:12; Rev. 19:20; 20:10

present kingdom (reign) in that the consummated kingdom will be in a perfected environment of only sons of the kingdom. Currently, sons of the kingdom and sons of the Evil One live together in human society.

13:25 Tares were very common in Palestine and closely resemble wheat; they are *not really* distinguishable from wheat until the grain appears at harvesttime.

13:30 The question of separation or relative purity in conduct or doctrine among the disciples and the church is answered by Jesus' directive. This is not to be done by the disciples nor by the church—but will ultimately be done by God's angels (vv. 39, 41). Premature separation in the present age is out of the question and becomes more destructive than it is purifying.

13:31, 32 See section 11 of Truth-In-Action through the Synoptics at the end of Luke.

13:31, 32 The parable of the **mustard seed** teaches the destined greatness of the kingdom. The kingdom fulfilled by Jesus now looks insignificant, but its greatness will be apparent in its consummation at the end of the Age.

13:33 At present the kingdom is not fully manifest, but at the consummation in the Age to Come, it will be known to all. Meanwhile, it does its work of permeating human society, penetrating evil and transforming lives.

nace of fire. [b]There will be wailing and
gnashing of teeth.
43 [a]"Then the righteous will shine
forth as the sun in the kingdom of their
Father. [b]He who has ears to hear, let
him hear!

The Parable of the Hidden Treasure

8 44 "Again, the kingdom of heaven is
like treasure hidden in a field, which
a man found and hid; and for joy over
it he goes and [a]sells all that he has and
[b]buys that field.

The Parable of the Pearl of Great Price

45 "Again, the kingdom of heaven is
like a merchant seeking beautiful
pearls,
46 "who, when he had found [a]one
pearl of great price, went and sold all
that he had and bought it.

The Parable of the Dragnet

47 "Again, the kingdom of heaven is
like a dragnet that was cast into the
sea and [a]gathered some of every kind,
48 "which, when it was full, they drew
to shore; and they sat down and gathered the **good** into vessels, but threw
the bad away.

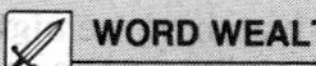

WORD WEALTH

13:48 good, ***kalos*** **(kal-*oss*);** Strong's *#2570:* A descriptive word signifying that which is beautiful, pleasing, acceptable, excellent, serviceable, attractive, honest. Its synonym is *agathos,* good in a physical and moral sense.

49 "So it will be at the end of the age.
The angels will come forth, [a]separate
the wicked from among the just,
50 "and cast them into the furnace of
fire. There will be wailing and gnashing of teeth."

51 [1]Jesus said to them, "Have you understood all these things?" They said
to Him, "Yes, [2]Lord."*
52 Then He said to them, "Therefore
every [1]scribe instructed [2]concerning
the kingdom of heaven is like a householder who brings out of his treasure
[a]*things* new and old."

Jesus Rejected at Nazareth

53 Now it came to pass, when Jesus
had finished these parables, that He
departed from there.
54 [a]When He had come to His own
country, He taught them in their synagogue, so that they were astonished
and said, "Where did this *Man* get this
wisdom and *these* mighty works?
55 [a]"Is this not the carpenter's son? Is
not His mother called Mary? And
[b]His brothers [c]James, [1]Joses, Simon,
and Judas?
56 "And His sisters, are they not all
with us? Where then did this *Man* get
all these things?"
57 So they [a]were offended at Him. But
Jesus said to them, [b]"A prophet is not
without honor except in his own country and in his own house."
58 Now [a]He did not do many mighty
works there because of their unbelief.

John the Baptist Beheaded

14 At that time [a]Herod the tetrarch
heard the report about Jesus
2 and said to his servants, "This is
John the Baptist; he is risen from the
dead, and therefore these powers are
at work in him."
3 [a]For Herod had laid hold of John
and bound him, and put *him* in prison
for the sake of Herodias, his brother
Philip's wife.
4 Because John had said to him,
[a]"It is not lawful for you to have her."
5 And although he wanted to put him
to death, he feared the multitude,

42 [b]Matt. 8:12; 13:50
43 [a][Dan. 12:3; 1 Cor. 15:42, 43, 58] [b]Matt. 13:9
44 [a]Phil. 3:7, 8 [b][Is. 55:1; Rev. 3:18]
46 [a]Prov. 2:4; 3:14, 15; 8:10, 19
47 [a]Matt. 22:9, 10
49 [a]Matt. 25:32

51 [1]NU omits *Jesus said to them* [2]NU omits *Lord*
*See WW at John 6:68.
52 [a]Song 7:13 [1]A scholar of the Old Testament [2]Or *for*
54 [a]Ps. 22:22; Matt. 2:23; Mark 6:1; Luke 4:16; John 7:15
55 [a]Is. 49:7; Mark 6:3; [Luke 3:23]; John 6:42 [b]Matt. 12:46 [c]Mark 15:40 [1]NU *Joseph*
57 [a]Matt. 11:6; Mark 6:3, 4 [b]Luke 4:24; John 4:44
58 [a]Mark 6:5, 6; John 5:44, 46, 47

CHAPTER 14

1 [a]Mark 6:14–29; Luke 9:7–9
3 [a]Matt. 4:12; Mark 6:17; Luke 3:19, 20
4 [a]Lev. 18:16; 20:21

13:44–52 See section 8 of Truth-In-Action through the Synoptics at the end of Luke.

13:44–46 The parables of the hidden treasure and the pearl of great price both stress the superlative value of the kingdom. A common interpretation is that a person should be willing to part with everything in order to possess the kingdom. However, the meaning could be that Jesus is the purchaser who gave His all to secure the kingdom (see Acts 20:28).

13:47–50 The parable of the **dragnet,** like the parable of the tares (vv. 24–30), deals with saints (**the good**) and sinners (**the bad**) in a mixed society. Its uniqueness is that it alludes to the church's responsibility to cast the gospel message before all of society, realizing it will attract all types of people, some of whom will be found unredeemed by **the angels at the end of the age.**

13:52 In response to the disciples' affirmation concerning their understanding, Jesus likens them to a householder able to integrate the new with the old. The disciple who has been properly instructed has at his command both Judaism (old) and Christianity (new).

13:53–58 Those who had the best opportunity to know Jesus rejected Him. Familiarity had bred contempt of Him among those **in his own country.**

14:3 Herod had seduced **Herodias,** who was his niece and wife of his brother Philip. Then he persuaded her to divorce her husband and marry him. The grisly account of John's death, including Herod's cowardly role, explains Herod's paranoid response to the report about Jesus (v. 1).

[a]because they counted him as a prophet.

6 But when Herod's birthday was celebrated, the daughter of Herodias danced before them and pleased Herod.

7 Therefore he promised with an oath to give her whatever she might *ask.

8 So she, having been prompted by her mother, said, "Give me John the Baptist's head here on a platter."

9 And the king was sorry; nevertheless, because of the oaths and because of those who sat with him, he commanded *it* to be given to *her*.

10 So he sent and had John beheaded in prison.

11 And his head was brought on a platter and given to the girl, and she brought *it* to her mother.

12 Then his disciples came and took away the body and buried it, and went and told Jesus.

Feeding the Five Thousand

13 [a]When Jesus heard *it*, He departed from there by boat to a deserted place by Himself. But when the multitudes heard it, they followed Him on foot from the cities.

14 And when Jesus went out He saw a great multitude; and He [a]was **moved with compassion** for them, and healed their sick.

WORD WEALTH

14:14 moved with compassion, *splanchnizomai* (splangkh-*nid*-zom-ahee); Strong's *#4697:* To be moved with deep compassion or pity. The Greeks regarded the bowels (*splanchna*) as the place where strong and powerful emotions originated. The Hebrews regarded *splanchna* as the place where tender mercies and feelings of affection, compassion, sympathy, and pity originated. It is the direct motive for at least five of Jesus' miracles.

15 [a]When it was evening, His disciples came to Him, saying, "This is a deserted place, and the hour is already late. Send the multitudes away, that they may go into the villages and buy themselves food."

5 [a]Matt. 21:26; Luke 20:6
7 *See WW at Matt. 7:7.
13 [a]Matt. 10:23; 12:15; Mark 6:32–44; Luke 9:10–17; John 6:1, 2
14 [a]Matt. 9:36; Mark 6:34
15 [a]Mark 6:35; Luke 9:12
19 [a]1 Sam. 9:13; Matt. 15:36; 26:26; Mark 6:41; 8:7; 14:22; Luke 24:30; Acts 27:35; [Rom. 14:6] *See WW at Luke 6:28.
20 *See WW at Matt. 15:33.
22 [1]*invited, strongly urged*
23 [a]Mark 6:46; Luke 9:28; John 6:15 [b]John 6:16 *See WW at Matt. 6:6.
24 [1]NU *many furlongs away from the land*
26 [a]Job 9:8 *See WW at 1 John 4:18.
27 [a]Acts 23:11; 27:22, 25, 36 [1]*Take courage* [2]Lit. *I am*
30 [1]NU brackets *that* and *boisterous* as disputed.
31 [a]Matt. 6:30; 8:26 *See WW at Matt. 8:26.

16 But Jesus said to them, "They do not need to go away. You give them something to eat."

17 And they said to Him, "We have here only five loaves and two fish."

18 He said, "Bring them here to Me."

19 Then He commanded the multitudes to sit down on the grass. And He took the five loaves and the two fish, and looking up to heaven, [a]He *blessed and broke and gave the loaves to the disciples; and the disciples gave to the multitudes.

20 So they all ate and were *filled, and they took up twelve baskets full of the fragments that remained.

21 Now those who had eaten were about five thousand men, besides women and children.

Jesus Walks on the Sea

22 Immediately Jesus [1]made His disciples get into the boat and go before Him to the other side, while He sent the multitudes away.

23 [a]And when He had sent the multitudes away, He went up on the mountain by Himself to *pray. [b]Now when evening came, He was alone there.

24 But the boat was now [1]in the middle of the sea, tossed by the waves, for the wind was contrary.

25 Now in the fourth watch of the night Jesus went to them, walking on the sea.

26 And when the disciples saw Him [a]walking on the sea, they were troubled, saying, "It is a ghost!" And they cried out for *fear.

27 But immediately Jesus spoke to them, saying, [1]"Be of good [a]cheer! [2]It is I; do not be afraid."

28 And Peter answered Him and said, "Lord, if it is You, command me to come to You on the water."

29 So He said, "Come." And when Peter had come down out of the boat, he walked on the water to go to Jesus.

30 But when he saw [1]that the wind *was* boisterous, he was afraid; and beginning to sink he cried out, saying, "Lord, save me!"

31 And immediately Jesus stretched out *His* hand and caught him, and said to him, "O you of [a]little* faith, why did you doubt?"

14:13 Jesus withdrew from Galilee to avoid a premature conflict with Herod. His death would be according to God's will, not Herod's.

14:15–21 The feeding of the 5,000 is the only miracle recorded by all four Gospel writers. Its significance may be seen in the sermon delivered by the Lord after the miracle, in which He declared Himself to be "the bread of life" (see John 6:22–71).

14:25 The **fourth watch** was between 3:00 A.M. and 6:00 A.M.

14:31 Jesus underscores the greatness of faith in the life of discipleship. He gives His followers the power to follow

32 And when they got into the boat, the wind ceased.

33 Then those who were in the boat [1]came and worshiped Him, saying, "Truly [a]You are the Son of God."

Many Touch Him and Are Made Well

34 [a]When they had crossed over, they came [1]to the land of Gennesaret.

35 And when the men of that place recognized Him, they sent out into all that surrounding region, brought to Him all who were sick,

36 and begged Him that they might only [a]touch the hem of His garment. And [b]as many as touched *it* were made perfectly well.

Defilement Comes from Within

1 **15** Then [a]the scribes and Pharisees who were from Jerusalem came to Jesus, saying,

2 [a]"Why do Your disciples *transgress the tradition of the elders? For they do not wash their hands when they eat bread."

3 He answered and said to them, "Why do you also *transgress the commandment of God because of your tradition?

4 "For God commanded, saying, [a]*'Honor your father and your mother'*; and, [b]*'He who curses father or mother, let him be put to death.'*

5 "But you say, 'Whoever says to his father or mother, [a]"Whatever profit you might have received from me *is* a gift *to God*"—

6 'then he need not honor his father [1]or mother.' Thus you have made the [2]commandment of God of no effect by your tradition.

7 [a]"Hypocrites!* Well did Isaiah prophesy about you, saying:

8 *'These[a] people [1]draw near to Me with their mouth,*
And honor Me with their lips,
But their heart is far from Me.

9 *And in vain they worship Me,*
[a]*Teaching as doctrines the commandments of men.'"*

33 [a]Ps. 2:7 [1]NU omits *came and*
34 [a]Mark 6:53 [1]NU *to land at*
36 [a][Mark 5:24–34] [b][Luke 6:19]

CHAPTER 15
1 [a]Mark 7:1
2 [a]Mark 7:5 *See WW at Acts 1:25.
3 *See WW at Acts 1:25.
4 [a][Deut. 5:16] [b]Ex. 21:17
5 [a]Mark 7:11, 12
6 [1]NU omits *or mother* [2]NU *word*
7 [a]Mark 7:6 *See WW at Matt. 6:2.
8 [a]Is. 29:13 [1]NU omits *draw near to Me with their mouth, And*
9 [a][Col. 2:18–22]
10 [a]Mark 7:14
11 [a][Acts 10:15]
12 *See WW at Matt. 11:6.
13 [a][John 15:2]
14 [a]Luke 6:39

KINGDOM DYNAMICS

15:7–9 Keeping Your Confession Without Hypocrisy, FAITH'S CONFESSION. Jesus quotes from Is. 29:13 in charging the Pharisees with setting aside God's Word by their traditions. Jesus dismisses their worship because their hearts were not aligned with their lips. Living faith—true worship—requires that the mouth and the heart be together to avoid Jesus' charge of hypocrisy.

Praises and true faith emanate from lips that draw from the depths of the heart. As a living principle, faith's confession is not a ritual recitation of slogans; otherwise, it is only acting out a human tradition and, as Jesus notes, is potentially hypocritical.

Just as we are called to genuine praise and worship, not as pretenders or ritual performers, so let our confessing of God's promises be without hypocrisy. Let us speak what God's Holy Spirit has truly birthed in our hearts, thereby bringing us to faithfully speak with our lips.

(Prov. 16:23, 24/Mark 11:22–24) R.H.

10 [a]When He had called the multitude to *Himself*, He said to them, "Hear and understand: 9

11 [a]"Not what goes into the mouth defiles a man; but what comes out of the mouth, this defiles a man."

12 Then His disciples came and said to Him, "Do You know that the Pharisees were *offended when they heard this saying?"

13 But He answered and said, [a]"Every plant which My heavenly Father has not planted will be uprooted.

14 "Let them alone. [a]They are blind leaders of the blind. And if the blind leads the blind, both will fall into a ditch."

Him, even in adversity, and encourages adventurous discipleship (vv. 28, 29). **Little faith:** See Word Wealth on 8:26.

15:1–20 See notes on Mark 7:1–23.

15:1–9 See section 1 of Truth-In-Action through the Synoptics at the end of Luke.

15:2 Tradition of the elders: The term refers to Jewish oral tradition, regarded as a "fence" for preserving the integrity of the Law. These traditions were believed by the Pharisees to be equally binding as the written Law. **Wash their hands** refers not to hygiene but to ritual purifying.

15:3 Jesus charges His opponents with actual disobedience of God's commandment through their slavish adherence to the oral law.

15:4 Jesus substantiates His charge (v. 3) contrasting Moses' commandment (Ex. 20:12; 21:17) with their current practice.

15:5 Gift: The term ("Corban" in Mark 7:11) denotes an offering made to God, withdrawn from its originally intended use, and no longer available for persons, not even for those in need.

15:6 Jesus pictures the "needy ones" as parents who are deprived of financial assistance from a son whose "Corban" offering is regarded as sacrosanct, though it could meet their need. Thereby, the son violates the fifth Commandment, "Honor your father and your mother."

15:8 Jesus views their hypocrisy as a fulfillment of Is. 29:13.

15:10–20 See section 9 of Truth-In-Action through the Synoptics at the end of Luke.

15:12 The Pharisees are offended at the saying (v. 11) while the disciples are given a fuller explanation (v. 15).

15 [a]Then Peter answered and said to
Him, "Explain this parable to us."
16 So Jesus said, [a]"Are you also still
without understanding?
17 "Do you not yet understand that
[a]whatever enters the mouth goes into
the stomach and is eliminated?
18 "But [a]those things which proceed
out of the mouth come from the heart,
and they defile a man.
19 [a]"For out of the heart proceed evil
*thoughts, murders, *adulteries, **fornications,** thefts, false witness, blasphemies.

WORD WEALTH

15:19 fornications, *porneia* (por-*ni*-ah); Strong's *#4202:* Compare "pornography," "pornographic." Illicit sexual intercourse, including prostitution, whoredom, incest, licentiousness, adultery, and habitual immorality. The word describes both physical immorality and spiritual, signifying idolatry (Rev. 2:21; 14:8; 17:2).

20 "These are *the things* which defile
a man, but to eat with unwashed hands
does not defile a man."

15 [a]Mark 7:17 **16** [a]Matt. 16:9; Mark 7:18 **17** [a][1 Cor. 6:13] **18** [a][Matt. 12:34]; Mark 7:20; [James 3:6] **19** [a]Gen. 6:5; 8:21; Prov. 6:14; Jer. 17:9; Mark 7:21; [Rom. 1:29–32; Gal. 5:19–21] *See WW at Luke 2:35. • See WW at John 8:3.

21 [a]Mark 7:24–30 **22** [a]Matt. 1:1; 22:41, 42 **24** [a]Matt. 10:5, 6; [Rom. 15:8] **26** [a]Matt. 7:6; Phil. 3:2 **28** [a]Luke 7:9

A Gentile Shows Her Faith

21 [a]Then Jesus went out from there
and departed to the region of Tyre and
Sidon.
22 And behold, a woman of Canaan
came from that region and cried out
to Him, saying, "Have mercy on me,
O Lord, [a]Son of David! My daughter
is severely demon-possessed."
23 But He answered her not a word.
And His disciples came and urged Him,
saying, "Send her away, for she cries
out after us."
24 But He answered and said, [a]"I was
not sent except to the lost sheep of the
house of Israel."
25 Then she came and worshiped Him,
saying, "Lord, help me!"
26 But He answered and said, "It is not
good to take the children's bread and
throw *it* to the little [a]dogs."
27 And she said, "Yes, Lord, yet even
the little dogs eat the crumbs which fall
from their masters' table."
28 Then Jesus answered and said to
her, "O woman, [a]great *is* your faith!
Let it be to you as you desire." And
her daughter was healed from that
very hour.

15:16–20 Jesus explains v. 11 privately to His disciples by means of a contrast between the literal use of **stomach** (v. 17) and the figurative use of **heart** (v. 18).
15:19 The **heart** is the source of all **evil** action.
15:20 The summary statement not only confirms the explanation in v. 11, but frees the disciples from adherence to the tradition of the elders (v. 2).
15:21–28 See notes on Mark 7:24–30.
15:21 Tyre and Sidon: Jesus is in Gentile territory.
15:24 Lost sheep: For the limitation of Jesus' ministry to Israel see 10:5, 6.
15:24 Jesus spoke a similar word in His instructions to the disciples concerning their own ministry (10:5, 6). The restriction on His mission did not involve racial exclusivism, but was strictly a matter of His limitations as a person and distinct priorities set by the Father. In God's plan the gospel must first be offered to the Old Covenant people, because of their calling and the responsibilities it entailed. The gathering of Israel must precede and prepare for the gathering of the Gentiles (Rom. 1:16).
15:27 The woman acknowledges Israel's privilege and priority, yet appeals to Jesus' unconditional kindness for her demon-possessed daughter.

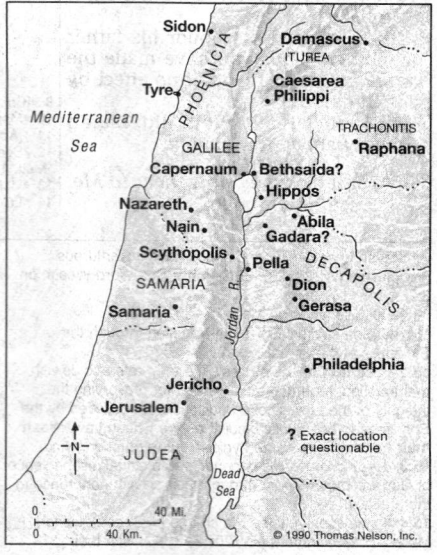

Jesus' Ministry Beyond Galilee. Near Tyre, Jesus cast out a demon from the daughter of a Syro-Phoenician woman (Mark 7:24–30). Peter made his great confession at Caesarea Philippi (Matt. 16:13–19). Jesus returned to Galilee via the Decapolis region, crossing the Jordan River south of the Sea of Galilee. Knowing Jesus toured Galilee and *"all the region," and that customarily He went into the synagogues in each community on the Sabbath (Luke 4:14, 15), we gain a sense of the time required for His itinerary. In noting these cities, this does not begin to number the many villages in the area, explaining why Jesus commissioned the Twelve and the Seventy to assist in the spread of the gospel (Matt. 10:5–8; Luke 10:1).

Jesus Heals Great Multitudes

29 [a]Jesus departed from there, [b]skirted the Sea of Galilee, and went up on the mountain and sat down there.

30 [a]Then great multitudes came to Him, having with them *the* lame, blind, mute, [1]maimed, and many others; and they laid them down at Jesus' [b]feet, and He healed them.

31 So the multitude marveled when they saw *the* mute speaking, *the* [1]maimed made whole, *the* lame walking, and *the* blind seeing; and they [a]glorified the God of Israel.

Feeding the Four Thousand

32 [a]Now Jesus called His disciples to *Himself* and said, "I *have compassion on the multitude, because they have now continued with Me three days and have nothing to eat. And I do not want to send them away hungry, lest they faint on the way."

33 [a]Then His disciples said to Him, "Where could we get enough bread in the wilderness to **fill** such a great multitude?"

> **WORD WEALTH**
>
> **15:33 fill,** *chortazo* (khor-*tad*-zoe); Strong's *#5526:* Originally, to feed or fatten animals. Stoic philosophers began to hold the common people in contempt and transferred *chortazo* from the agriculture field to the dinner table. The word came to signify being satisfied with food in abundance.

34 Jesus said to them, "How many loaves do you have?" And they said, "Seven, and a few little fish."

35 So He commanded the multitude to sit down on the ground.

36 And [a]He took the seven loaves and the fish and [b]gave* thanks, broke *them* and gave *them* to His disciples; and the disciples *gave* to the multitude.

37 So they all ate and were filled, and they *took up seven large baskets full of the fragments that were left.

38 Now those who ate were four thousand men, besides women and children.

39 [a]And He sent away the multitude, got into the boat, and came to the region of [1]Magdala.

The Pharisees and Sadducees Seek a Sign

16 Then the [a]Pharisees and Sadducees came, and testing Him asked that He would show them a sign from heaven.

2 He answered and said to them, "When it is evening you say, *'It will be* fair weather, for the sky is red';

3 "and in the morning, *'It will be* foul weather today, for the sky is red and threatening.' [1]Hypocrites!* You know how to discern the face of the sky, but you cannot *discern* the signs of the times.

4 [a]"A wicked and adulterous generation seeks after a sign, and no sign shall be given to it except the sign of [1]the prophet Jonah." And He left them and departed.

The Leaven of the Pharisees and Sadducees

5 Now [a]when His disciples had come to the other side, they had forgotten to take bread.

6 Then Jesus said to them, [a]"Take heed and beware of the [1]leaven of the Pharisees and the Sadducees."

7 And they reasoned among themselves, saying, *"It is* because we have taken no bread."

8 But Jesus, being aware of *it,* said to them, "O you of *little faith, why do you reason among yourselves because you [1]have brought no bread?

9 [a]"Do you not yet understand, or remember the five loaves of the five thousand and how many baskets you took up?

10 [a]"Nor the seven loaves of the four thousand and how many large baskets you took up?

11 "How is it you do not understand that I did not speak to you concerning

29 [a]Matt. 15:29–31; Mark 7:31–37 [b]Matt. 4:18
30 [a]Is. 35:5, 6; Matt. 11:5; Luke 7:22 [b]Mark 7:25; Luke 7:38; 8:41; 10:39 [1]*crippled*
31 [a]Luke 5:25, 26; 19:37, 38 [1]*crippled*
32 [a]Mark 8:1–10 *See WW at Matt. 14:14.
33 [a]2 Kin. 4:43
36 [a]Matt. 14:19; 26:27; Luke 22:17, 19; John 6:11, 23; Acts 27:35; [Rom. 14:6] [b]1 Sam. 9:13; Luke 22:19 *See WW at John 6:11.
37 *See WW at John 16:22.
39 [a]Mark 8:10 [1]NU *Magadan*

CHAPTER 16

1 [a]Matt. 12:38; Mark 8:11; Luke 11:16; 12:54–56; 1 Cor. 1:22
3 [1]NU omits *Hypocrites* *See WW at Matt. 6:2.
4 [a]Prov. 30:12; Matt. 12:39; Luke 11:29; 24:46 [1]NU omits *the prophet*
5 [a]Mark 8:14
6 [a]Mark 8:15; Luke 12:1 [1]*yeast*
8 [1]NU *have no bread* *See WW at Matt. 8:26.
9 [a]Matt. 14:15–21; Mark 6:30–44; Luke 9:10–17; John 6:1–14
10 [a]Matt. 15:32–38; Mark 8:1–9

15:29–31 Jesus was in Decapolis (Mark 7:31), a Gentile area. This "exception" to His general focus (v. 24) shows not only God's flexibility but His intense compassion for hurting people (v. 32).

15:32–39 See notes on Mark 8:2–9 and John 6:22–71.

16:1 Sign: See note on 12:38, 39.

16:2, 3 They knew how to interpret weather signs but were ignorant of **the signs of the times,** that is, the fulfillment of the kingdom in the Person of Jesus.

16:4 The Resurrection, of which the experience of **Jonah** with the fish is a type, would be the greatest evidence of His authenticity.

16:6 Leaven symbolized the false doctrine of the religious leaders (see v. 12). The **Pharisees** were legalists who reduced religion to form and ceremony. The **Sadducees** were rationalists and materialists, denying the supernatural elements in religion.

bread?—*but* to beware of the [1]leaven of the Pharisees and Sadducees."

12 Then they understood that He did not tell *them* to beware of the leaven of bread, but of the [1]doctrine of the Pharisees and Sadducees.

Peter Confesses Jesus as the Christ

13 When Jesus came into the region of Caesarea Philippi, He asked His *disciples, saying, [a]"Who do men say that I, the Son of Man, am?"

14 So they said, [a]"Some *say* John the Baptist, some Elijah, and others Jeremiah or [b]one of the prophets."

15 He said to them, "But who do [a]you say that I am?"

16 Simon Peter answered and said, [a]"You are the Christ, the Son of the living God."

17 Jesus answered and said to him, *"Blessed are you, Simon Bar-Jonah, [a]for flesh and blood has not revealed *this* to you, but [b]My Father who is in heaven.

18 "And I also say to you that [a]you are Peter, and [b]on this rock I will build My *church, and [c]the gates of Hades shall not [1]prevail against it.

19 [a]"And I will give you the keys of the kingdom of heaven, and whatever you bind on earth [1]will be bound in heaven, and whatever you loose on earth will be loosed in heaven."

20 [a]Then He commanded His disciples that they should tell no one that He was Jesus the Christ.

11 [1]*Yeast*
12 [1]*teaching*
13 [a]Luke 9:18 *See WW at Matt. 10:1.
14 [a]Matt. 14:2 [b]Matt. 21:11
15 [a]John 6:67
16 [a]Acts 8:37; 9:20
17 [a][Eph. 2:8] [b]Gal. 1:16 *See WW at Matt. 5:3.
18 [a]John 1:42 [b][Eph. 2:20] [c]Is. 38:10 [1]*be victorious* *See WW at Acts 8:1.
19 [a]Matt. 18:18 [1]*Or will have been bound . . . will have been loosed*
20 [a]Luke 9:21
21 [a]Luke 9:22; 18:31; 24:46 *See WW at Acts 17:3.
22 [1]*Lit. Merciful to You* (May God be merciful)

KINGDOM DYNAMICS

16:13–20 Hearing God, LEADER TRAITS. The godly leader "hears" God; that is, his or her spirit is tuned to the promptings and lessons of the Holy Spirit. At Caesarea Philippi, a stronghold of the ancient demon-gods of Syria, Greece, and Rome, Jesus deliberately set Himself against the background of the world's religions' error and confusion; and here He inquired of His disciples about His identity. Peter's answer (v. 16) is set apart from and beyond human reason, as Jesus commended his having heard from God (v. 17). Then Jesus emphasized that leadership in His church would always lead and be based not on man's ability to reason things out as much as on his readiness and receptivity to hear God through "revelation knowledge," the things that God unfolds by the work of the Holy Spirit (Eph. 1:17, 18; 3:14–19).

(Is. 6:8, 9/Gen. 12; 17; 22) J.B.

Jesus Predicts His Death and Resurrection

21 From that time Jesus began [a]to show to His disciples that He must go to Jerusalem, and *suffer many things from the elders and chief priests and scribes, and be killed, and be raised the third day.

22 Then Peter took Him aside and began to rebuke Him, saying, [1]"Far be it from You, Lord; this shall not happen to You!"

16:13–20 This incident, which took place six months before the Crucifixion, was pivotal in Jesus' ministry, marking the climax of His teaching concerning His own Person. Here, as well, He began preparing His disciples for His approaching death.

16:13 Caesarea Philippi was in the extreme north of Galilee, near Mt. Hermon.

16:16 Peter confessed Jesus as both the promised Messiah and as divine.

16:17 The deity of Christ is a truth known only by divine revelation.

16:18 The **rock** is not Peter as an individual, since Jesus substituted *petra,* a foundation rock or boulder, for *petros,* a fragment of the *petra.* Jesus may have meant that He Himself is the Rock (*petra*) upon which the church is built (see 1 Cor. 3:10, 11; 10:4), and that the church is built out of those stones (*petroi*) that partake of the nature of the *petra* by their confession of faith in Him (see 1 Pet. 2:5). Peter, therefore, is the first of many building stones in the church. The expression **gates of Hades** means "the power of death" cannot prevent the advance of the kingdom, nor claim victory over those who belong to God.

16:19 The implications of this significant verse are diverse and need to be understood. Jesus' terminology has elements of symbolism and entails a complex Greek construction; therefore, different interpretations are viable.

Keys denote authority. Through Peter, a representative of the church throughout the ages, Jesus is passing on to His church His authority or control to **bind** and to **loose on earth.** The Greek construction behind **will be bound** and **will be loosed** indicates that Jesus is the One who has activated the provisions through His Cross; the church is then charged with implementation of what He has released through His life, death, and resurrection.

Clearly rabbinic in imagery, binding and loosing have to do with forbidding or permitting. In other words, Jesus is stating that the church will be empowered to continue in the privileged responsibility of leavening the earth with His kingdom power and provision. For example, if someone is bound by sin, the church can "loose" him by preaching the provision of freedom from sin in Jesus Christ (Rom. 6:14). If someone is indwelt by a demon, the church can "bind" the demon by commanding its departure (Acts 16:18), realizing that Jesus alone made this provision possible (Matt. 12:29). How the church binds and looses is diverse and would most certainly extend far beyond the mere use of these terms in prayerful petitions.

16:20 Public confession of Jesus' messiahship would have created an unwanted national fervor.

16:21 Peter's confession marks a turning point in Jesus' ministry, for at **that time** he begins to teach explicitly about His atoning death. **Must** indicates a divine necessity.

23 But He turned and said to Peter, "Get behind Me, [a]Satan! [b]You are [1]an **offense** to Me, for you are not mindful of the things of God, but the things of men."

WORD WEALTH

16:23 offense, *skandalon* (*skan*-da-lahn); Strong's *#4625:* Originally, a trapstick, a bent sapling, or a movable stick with bait used to catch animals. The word then came to denote a snare or stumbling block. Metaphorically, it signifies that which causes error or sin.

Take Up the Cross and Follow Him

7 24 [a]Then Jesus said to His disciples, "If anyone desires to come after Me, let him deny himself, and take up his cross, and [b]follow Me.
25 "For [a]whoever desires to save his life will lose it, but whoever loses his life for My sake will find it.
26 "For what [a]profit is it to a man if he gains the whole world, and loses his own soul? Or [b]what will a man give in exchange for his soul?
27 "For [a]the Son of Man will come in the glory of His Father [b]with His angels, [c]and then He will reward each according to his works.

Jesus Transfigured on the Mount

28 "Assuredly, I say to you, [a]there are some standing here who shall not *taste death till they see the Son of Man coming in His kingdom."

17 Now [a]after six days Jesus took Peter, James, and John his brother, led them up on a high mountain by themselves;
2 and He was transfigured before them. His face shone like the sun, and His clothes became as white as the light.
3 And behold, Moses and Elijah appeared to them, talking with Him.
4 Then Peter answered and said to Jesus, "Lord, it is good for us to be here; if You wish, [1]let us make here three tabernacles: one for You, one for Moses, and one for Elijah."
5 [a]While he was still speaking, behold, a bright cloud overshadowed them; and suddenly a voice came out of the cloud, saying, [b]"This is My beloved Son, [c]in whom I am well pleased. [d]Hear Him!"
6 [a]And when the disciples heard *it,* they fell on their faces and were greatly afraid.
7 But Jesus came and [a]touched them and said, "Arise, and do not be afraid."
8 When they had lifted up their eyes, they saw no one but Jesus only.
9 Now as they came down from the mountain, Jesus commanded them, saying, "Tell the vision to no one until the Son of Man is risen from the dead."
10 And His disciples asked Him, saying, [a]"Why then do the scribes say that Elijah must come first?"
11 Jesus answered and said to them, "Indeed, Elijah is coming [1]first and will [a]restore all things.
12 [a]"But I say to you that Elijah has come already, and they [b]did not know him but did to him whatever they wished. Likewise [c]the Son of Man is also about to suffer at their hands."
13 [a]Then the disciples understood that He spoke to them of John the Baptist.

A Boy Is Healed

14 [a]And when they had come to the multitude, a man came to Him, kneeling down to Him and saying,

23 [a]Matt. 4:10 [b][Rom. 8:7] [1]a *stumbling block*
24 [a][2 Tim. 3:12] [b][1 Pet. 2:21]
25 [a]John 12:25
26 [a]Luke 12:20, 21 [b]Ps. 49:7, 8
27 [a]Mark 8:38 [b][Dan. 7:10] [c]Rom. 2:6
28 [a]Luke 9:27 *See WW at John 8:52.

CHAPTER 17

1 [a]Mark 9:2–8
4 [1]NU *I will make*
5 [a]2 Pet. 1:17 [b]Mark 1:11 [c]Matt. 3:17; 12:18 [d][Deut. 18:15, 19]
6 [a]2 Pet. 1:18
7 [a]Dan. 8:18
10 [a]Mal. 4:5
11 [a][Mal. 4:6] [1]NU omits *first*
12 [a]Mark 9:12, 13 [b]Matt. 14:3, 10 [c]Matt. 16:21
13 [a]Matt. 11:14
14 [a]Mark 9:14–28

16:23 Get behind Me, Satan: The words are identical with those of 4:10. Jesus recognized in Peter's words the same diabolically inspired temptation to avoid suffering as part of His messianic vocation as He had heard in the wilderness.
16:24–27 Jesus explains the paradox of discipleship. To lose life is to find it; to die is to live. To **deny** oneself is not to assume some false, external asceticism, but to put the interests of the kingdom first and foremost in one's life. To **take up** the **cross** does not mean to endure some irritating burden, but to renounce self-centered ambitions. Such sacrifice results in eternal life and the fullest experience of kingdom life now (see Mark 10:30).
16:24–26 See section 7 of Truth-In-Action through the Synoptics at the end of Luke.
16:28 Jesus is pointing toward the encounter that **some standing here** will **see** at His transfiguration (17:1–8).
17:1 Peter, James, and John made up the inner circle of those closest to Jesus (20:20; 26:37).
17:2 While the verb **transfigured** may denote spiritual transformation (Rom. 12:2; 2 Cor. 3:18), here it indicates a visible transformation, affirming the essential glory of Jesus the Messiah.
17:3 The appearance of **Moses** and **Elijah** signifies that the Law and the Prophets support Jesus in His redemptive mission.
17:4 Peter may have been suggesting a desire to prolong the visit. Luke says Peter spoke "not knowing what he said" (Luke 9:33).
17:5 The affirmation by the heavenly Father of Jesus' redemptive mission commands the disciples to accept Jesus' instructions about His suffering.
17:9 The secrecy charge is to be suspended after the Resurrection when the others will more fully understand Jesus and His mission.
17:10 The question was prompted by Elijah's appearance on the mountain.
17:12 The prophecy of Mal. 4:5, 6 was fulfilled in the ministry of John the Baptist.

15 "Lord, have mercy on my son, for
he is [1]an epileptic and suffers severely;
for he often falls into the fire and often
into the water.
16 "So I *brought him to Your disciples, but they could not cure him."
17 Then Jesus answered and said, "O
[1]faithless and [a]perverse generation,
how long shall I be with you? How long
shall I *bear with you? Bring him here
to Me."
18 And Jesus [a]rebuked the demon, and
it came out of him; and the child was
cured from that very hour.
19 Then the disciples came to Jesus
privately and said, "Why could we not
cast it out?"
20 So Jesus said to them, "Because of
your [1]unbelief; for assuredly, I say to
you, [a]if you have *faith as a mustard
seed, you will say to this mountain,
'Move from here to there,' and it will
move; and nothing will be impossible
for you.

KINGDOM DYNAMICS

17:19, 20 God Has a Way for Getting Your Need Met, Your Problem Solved. That Way Is Rooted in Your Faith's Becoming a Seed, SEED FAITH. When you plant a seed, God changes the nature of that seed so that it becomes a plant; and the power of life surges in that tender young plant to such a great extent that even a mountain of earth cannot stop it from pushing upward!

Jesus says our faith in God is like a seed. When we put our faith into action, that is, when we release it to God, it takes on a totally new nature. It takes on the nature of a miracle in the making.

What is the mountain in your life? Loneliness, loss of a job, disease, a wounded relationship, trouble in your home? Something else? Be encouraged! Jesus shows the way to see that mountain removed!

First, God says that you have a measure of faith (Rom. 12:3). It is resident within you. Second, God says that this faith comes alive by "hearing . . . the word of God" (Rom. 10:17). Third, God says that you can apply your faith to see your daily needs met. How? You do something as an act of your faith. You sow the mustard-seed smallness of your faith into an action of love (Matt. 17:20).

15 [1]Lit. *moonstruck*
16 *See WW at Heb. 9:28.
17 [a]Deut. 32:5; Phil. 2:15 [1]*unbelieving* *See WW at 2 Thess. 1:4.
18 [a]Luke 4:41
20 [a]Matt. 21:21; Mark 11:23; Luke 17:6; [1 Cor. 12:9] [1]NU *little faith* *See WW at Mark 11:22.
21 [1]NU omits v. 21.
22 [a]Matt. 16:21; 26:57; Mark 8:31; Luke 9:22, 44; John 18:12 [1]NU *gathering together*
23 [a]Matt. 26:22; 27:50; Luke 23:46; 24:46; John 16:6; 19:30; Acts 10:40
24 [a]Mark 9:33 [1]NU *Capharnaum,* here and elsewhere [2]Lit. *double drachma*
25 [a][Is. 60:10–17]
27 [1]Gr. *stater,* the exact temple tax for two

CHAPTER 18

1 [a]Mark 9:33–37; Luke 9:46–48; 22:24–27

Then, when your faith has been planted and is growing, speak to your mountain and watch God set about its removal.

(2 Chr. 25:9/John 10:10) O.R.

KINGDOM DYNAMICS

17:20 8. How Do I Pray for a Miracle?, SPIRITUAL ANSWERS. For the answer to this and other probing questions about God and the power life in His kingdom, see the study article "Spiritual Answers to Hard Questions," which begins on page 1996. P.R.

21 [1]"However, this kind does not go
out except by prayer and fasting."

Jesus Again Predicts His Death and Resurrection

22 [a]Now while they were [1]staying in
Galilee, Jesus said to them, "The Son
of Man is about to be betrayed into the
hands of men,
23 "and they will kill Him, and the
third day He will be raised up." And
they were exceedingly [a]sorrowful.

Peter and His Master Pay Their Taxes

24 [a]When they had come to [1]Caper-
naum, those who received the [2]*temple*
tax came to Peter and said, "Does your
Teacher not pay the *temple* tax?"
25 He said, "Yes." And when he had
come into the house, Jesus anticipated
him, saying, "What do you think, Simon? From whom do the kings of the
earth take customs or taxes, from their
sons or from [a]strangers?"
26 Peter said to Him, "From strangers." Jesus said to him, "Then the
sons are free.
27 "Nevertheless, lest we offend them,
go to the sea, cast in a hook, and take
the fish that comes up first. And when
you have opened its mouth, you will
find a [1]piece of money; take that and
give it to them for Me and you."

Who Is the Greatest?

18 At [a]that time the disciples came 8
to Jesus, saying, "Who then is
greatest in the kingdom of heaven?"

17:20 Faith that appears small or weak to us still can accomplish the humanly impossible. **This mountain** was a figure for an obstacle, hindrance, or humanly insurmountable problem—none of which is **impossible** for God to deal with through committed people who accurately understand their authority and know His power, will, purposes, and provision.
17:23 The disciples lacked an understanding of the victorious Resurrection.
17:24 The ***temple* tax** was an annual tax for the maintenance of the temple (Ex. 30:13–15).
17:27 While Jesus claims exemption from the tax as the Son of God, His concern is that of possible offense. Had He refused to pay, He would have been branded as profane and irreligious.
18:1–5 See section 8 of Truth-In-Action through the Synoptics at the end of Luke.

2 Then Jesus called a little [a]child to
Him, set him in the midst of them,
3 and said, "Assuredly, I say to you,
[a]unless you are converted and become
as little children, you will by no means
enter the kingdom of heaven.
4 [a]"Therefore whoever **humbles** himself as this little child is the greatest
in the kingdom of heaven.

WORD WEALTH

18:4 humbles, *tapeinoo* (tap-eye-*nah*-oh); Strong's *#5013:* Literally, "to make low," used of a mountain in Luke 3:5. Metaphorically, the word means to debase, humble, lower oneself. It describes a person who is devoid of all arrogance and self-exaltation—a person who is willingly submitted to God and His will.

KINGDOM DYNAMICS

18:1–4 Childlikeness, CHARACTER AND THE KINGDOM. Jesus confronts the tendency of humankind to associate authority with an exercise of dominance over others. The dominion or authority in kingdom life God wants to reinstate in us, is for victorious, fruitful living and for the overthrow of hellish powers, not for gaining control of others or for serving our own interests. His call to childlike humility and a servantlike heart (John 13:1–17) establishes the spirit and style by which the authority of the believer is to be exercised as an agent of God's kingdom power. (See Matt. 19:14; Mark 10:14, 15; Luke 18:16, 17.)

(Matt. 5—7/Matt. 18:18–25) J.W.H.

KINGDOM DYNAMICS

18:1–4 30. What Is the Greatest Virtue in the Kingdom?, SPIRITUAL ANSWERS. For the answer to this and other probing questions about God and the power life in His kingdom, see the study article "Spiritual Answers to Hard Questions," which begins on page 1996. P.R.

5 [a]"Whoever receives one little child
like this in My name receives Me.

Jesus Warns of Offenses

6 [a]"But whoever causes one of these
little ones who believe in Me to sin, it
would be better for him if a millstone
were hung around his neck, and he
were drowned in the depth of the
sea.
7 "Woe to the world because of
[1]offenses!* For [a]offenses must come,
but [b]woe to that man by whom the offense comes!
8 [a]"If your hand or foot causes you
to sin, cut it off and cast *it* from you.
It is better for you to enter into life
lame or maimed, rather than having
two hands or two feet, to be cast into
the everlasting fire.
9 "And if your eye causes you to sin,
pluck it out and cast *it* from you. It is
better for you to enter into life with one
eye, rather than having two eyes, to
be cast into [1]hell fire.

The Parable of the Lost Sheep

10 "Take heed that you do not despise
one of these little ones, for I say to you
that in heaven [a]their angels always
[b]see the face of My Father who is in
heaven.
11 [a]"For[1] the Son of Man has come to
save that which was lost.
12 [a]"What do you think? If a man has
a hundred sheep, and one of them goes
astray, does he not leave the ninety-
nine and go to the mountains to seek
the one that is straying?
13 "And if he should find it, assuredly,
I say to you, he rejoices more over that
sheep than over the ninety-nine that
did not go astray.
14 "Even so it is not the [a]will of your
Father who is in heaven that one of
these little ones should perish.

Dealing with a Sinning Brother

15 "Moreover [a]if your brother sins
against you, go and tell him his fault
between you and him alone. If he hears
you, [b]you have gained your brother.
16 "But if he will not hear, take with

2 [a]Matt. 19:14; Mark 10:14; Luke 18:14–17 **3** [a]Ps. 131:2; Matt. 19:14; Mark 10:15; Luke 18:16; [1 Cor. 14:20; 1 Pet. 2:2] **4** [a][Matt. 20:27; 23:11] **5** [a][Matt. 10:42]; Luke 9:48
6 [a]Mark 9:42; Luke 17:2; [1 Cor. 8:12] **7** [a]Luke 17:1; [1 Cor. 11:19]; 1 Tim. 4:1 [b]Matt. 26:24; 27:4, 5 [1]*enticements to sin* *See WW at Matt. 16:23. **8** [a]Matt. 5:29, 30; Mark 9:43, 45 **9** [1]Gr. *Gehenna* **10** [a][Ps. 34:7]; Zech. 13:7; [Heb. 1:14] [b]Esth. 1:14; Luke 1:19; Acts 12:15; [Rev. 8:2] **11** [a]Luke 9:56; John 3:17 [1]NU omits v. 11. **12** [a]Matt. 18:12–14; Luke 15:4–7 **14** [a][1 Tim. 2:4] **15** [a]Lev. 19:17; [Luke 17:3, 4; Gal. 6:1]; 2 Thess. 3:15; [James 5:19] [b][James 5:20]; 1 Pet. 3:1

18:1–5 The way into **the kingdom of heaven** is by the simple trust and dependence of a child; and the way to greatness in the kingdom is by the humility of a child, expressed in humble service.
18:6–9 Jesus proclaims the severe consequences of causing another (vv. 6, 7) or oneself (vv. 8, 9) **to sin** (become apostate). See note on 5:28–30.
18:10 We are not to **despise** childlike believers for they are honored **in heaven. Their angels** are likely guardian angels of the highest rank: they **always see the face of My Father.** Note: The term **little ones** is also linked with "lost" (v. 11) and the "astray" (v. 12) by the connective "for," which begins v. 11, calling for concern toward members of the community who have fallen away.
18:12–14 The care and concern of a shepherd not only illustrate God's love, but serve as examples of the mutual care and nurture that we should practice.
18:15–20 Jesus shows the proper procedure for disciplining an erring brother (see 1 Cor. 5:1–5; Gal. 6:1). Three steps are specified: 1) in private; 2) with witnesses; 3) before the church.

you one or two more, that [a]*'by the
mouth of two or three witnesses every
word may be established.'*
17 "And if he refuses to hear them, tell
it to the church. But if he refuses even
to hear the church, let him be to you
like a [a]heathen and a tax collector.
18 "Assuredly, I say to you, [a]whatever
you bind on earth will be bound in
heaven, and whatever you loose on
earth will be loosed in heaven.
19 [a]"Again[1] I say to you that if two of
you **agree** on earth concerning anything that they ask, [b]it will be done for
them by My Father in heaven.

WORD WEALTH

18:19 agree, *sumphoneo* (soom-foe-*neh*-oh); Strong's *#4856:* From *sum,* "together," and *phoneo,* "to sound." *Sumphoneo* is to sound together, be in accord, be in harmony. The word "symphony" comes from *sumphoneo.* Metaphorically, the word means to agree together in prayer that is concordant.

20 "For where two or three are gathered [a]together in My name, I am there
in the midst of them."

The Parable of the Unforgiving Servant

5 21 Then Peter came to Him and said,
"Lord, how often shall my brother sin
against me, and I forgive him? [a]Up to
seven times?"
22 Jesus said to him, "I do not say to
you, [a]up to seven times, but up to seventy times seven.
23 "Therefore the kingdom of heaven
is like a certain king who wanted to
settle accounts with his servants.
24 "And when he had begun to settle
accounts, one was brought to him who
*owed him ten thousand talents.
25 "But as he was not able to pay, his
master commanded [a]that he be sold,
with his wife and children and all that
he had, and that payment be made.
26 "The servant therefore fell down
before him, saying, 'Master, have patience with me, and I will pay you all.'
27 "Then the master of that servant
was *moved with compassion, released
him, and forgave him the debt.
28 "But that servant went out and
found one of his fellow servants who
owed him a hundred denarii; and he
laid hands on him and took *him* by the
throat, saying, 'Pay me what you owe!'
29 "So his fellow servant fell down
[1]at his feet and begged him, saying,
'Have patience with me, and I will pay
you [2]all.'
30 "And he would not, but went and
threw him into prison till he should pay
the debt.
31 "So when his fellow servants saw
what had been done, they were very
grieved, and came and told their master all that had been done.
32 "Then his master, after he had
called him, said to him, 'You wicked
servant! I forgave you [a]all that debt because you begged me.
33 'Should you not also have had compassion on your fellow servant, just as
I had pity on you?'
34 "And his master was *angry, and
delivered him to the torturers until he
should pay all that was due to him.
35 [a]"So My heavenly Father also will
do to you if each of you, from his heart,
does not forgive his brother [1]his trespasses."

KINGDOM DYNAMICS

18:18–35 Forgiveness, CHARACTER AND THE KINGDOM. Jesus' prefacing words make this "kingdom" parable of the unforgiving servant especially crucial. The human capacity to forget God's gracious gift of forgiveness and allow smallness of soul to breed unforgiveness

16 [a]Deut. 17:6; 19:15; John 8:17; 2 Cor. 13:1; 1 Tim. 5:19; Heb. 10:28
17 [a]Rom. 16:17; 1 Cor. 5:9; [2 Thess. 3:6, 14; 2 John 10]
18 [a]Matt. 16:19; [John 20:22, 23; 1 Cor. 5:4]
19 [a][1 Cor. 1:10] [b][1 John 3:22; 5:14] [1]NU, M *Again, assuredly, I say*
20 [a]Acts 20:7; 1 Cor. 14:26
21 [a]Luke 17:4
22 [a][Matt. 6:14; Mark 11:25]; Col. 3:13
24 *See WW at Luke 13:4.
25 [a]Ex. 21:2; Lev. 25:39; 2 Kin. 4:1; Neh. 5:5, 8
27 *See WW at Matt. 14:14.
29 [1]NU omits *at his feet* [2]NU, M omit *all*
32 [a]Luke 7:41–43
34 *See WW at Rev. 12:17.
35 [a]Prov. 21:13; Matt. 6:12; Mark 11:26; James 2:13 [1]NU omits *his trespasses*

18:18 When a church is acting under the lordship of Jesus in administering discipline, heaven sanctions the action. This is one specific example of the principle more fully explained in 16:19.
18:19 The promise that Jesus gives may apply to prayer in general, but more specifically it concerns the divine guidance that is sought and received in matters of discipline. In such cases, prayer guards against a vindictive spirit.
18:20 The promise of Jesus' presence also has a larger application, but it immediately applies to decisions in matters of church discipline (see 1 Cor. 5:4).
18:21–35 See section 5 of Truth-In-Action through the Synoptics at the end of Luke.
18:21 Peter's question must be considered in the light of the preceding subject of church discipline.
18:22 Jesus does not give a legalistic or mathematical formula. He means limitless forgiveness (see 1 Cor. 13:4, 5).
18:23–35 The parable illustrates the principle of forgiveness, a vital element in the process of church discipline, already made explicit in the disciples' prayer (6:12). God has freely forgiven our debt; therefore, we also should practice forgiveness.
18:24 Ten thousand talents represents the largest sum imaginable, while a hundred denarii (v. 28) represents a highly insignificant amount by way of contrast.
18:35 This is not legalism nor is it a scare tactic. Rather, it states the seriousness of responsible forgiving and demonstrates how unforgiveness clogs the channel of communication and sanctification between God and His people.

is soberingly warned against. 1) Jesus showed how unforgiveness can restrict what God would do in others. (Note: the jailed fellow-servant is still in prison at the story's end, revealing the power of unforgiveness to "bind" circumstances to an undesirable level of perpetual problem.) 2) Jesus teaches how the spirit of unforgiveness (the torturers, literally "bill collectors") exacts its toll on our bodies, minds, and emotions. Finally, every "kingdom" person is advised to sustain a forgiving heart toward all other persons. Kingdom privileges and power must not be mishandled. The "binding" power of unforgiveness is potentially dangerous to any of us.

Matt. 18:18, 19 is frequently quoted to assert the believer's authority in prayer. But the power to "bind and loose" is quickly shown to be as much of a liability as an asset if unforgiveness remains in the people of God's kingdom.

(Matt. 18:1–4/1 Cor. 6:9, 10) J.W.H.

KINGDOM DYNAMICS

18:21–35 38. What Sin Particularly Blocks the Flow of Kingdom Power?, SPIRITUAL ANSWERS. For the answer to this and other probing questions about God and the power life in His kingdom, see the study article "Spiritual Answers to Hard Questions," which begins on page 1996. P.R.

Marriage and Divorce

19 Now it came to pass, [a]when Jesus had finished these sayings,
that He departed from Galilee and
came to the region of Judea beyond the
Jordan.
2 [a]And great multitudes followed
Him, and He healed them there.
3 The Pharisees also came to Him,
testing Him, and saying to Him, "Is it
lawful for a man to divorce his wife
for *just* any reason?"
1 4 And He answered and said to them,
"Have you not read that He who
[1]made *them* at the beginning [a]*'made
them male and female,'*
5 "and said, [a]*'For this reason a man
shall leave his father and mother and
be *joined to his wife, and [b]the two
shall become one flesh'*?
6 "So then, they are no longer two but
one flesh. Therefore what God has
joined together, let not man separate."
7 They said to Him, [a]"Why then did
Moses command to give a certificate
of divorce, and to put her away?"
8 He said to them, "Moses, because
of the [a]hardness of your hearts, permitted you to divorce your [b]wives, but
from the beginning it was not so.
9 [a]"And I say to you, whoever divorces his wife, except for [1]sexual* immorality, and marries another, commits adultery; and whoever marries
her who is divorced commits adultery."

KINGDOM DYNAMICS

19:1–9 Divorce Is a Case of a Heart Hardened Toward God, FAMILY ORDER. In this text Jesus frankly addresses a pivotal issue: the cause of divorce is hardness of heart. Behind every broken marriage is a heart hardened against God, then hardened against one's mate. From the very beginning, God's intention for marriage was that it be for life. Realizing this, believers should exercise care in choosing a life mate (see 2 Cor. 6:14). Yet no marriage will be so free of differences and difficulties that it could not end up in divorce if husband and wife were deceived into following their natural inclinations.

The Devil will exaggerate your mate's failures and inadequacies, sow suspicion and jealousy, indulge your self-pity, insist that you deserve something better, and hold out the hollow promise that things would be better with someone else. But hear Jesus' words, and remember: God can change hearts and remove all hardness if we will allow Him.

(Mal. 2:13, 14, 16/Ps. 68:5, 6) L.C.

10 His disciples said to Him, [a]"If such
is the case of the man with *his* wife, it
is better not to marry."

Jesus Teaches on Celibacy

11 But He said to them, [a]"All cannot
accept this saying, but only *those* to
whom it has been given:
12 "For there are [1]eunuchs who were

CHAPTER 19

1 [a]Matt. 19:1–9; Mark 10:1–12; John 10:40
2 [a]Matt. 12:15
4 [a]Gen. 1:27; 5:2; [Mal. 2:15] [1]NU *created*
5 [a]Gen. 2:24; Mark 10:5–9; Eph. 5:31 [b][1 Cor. 6:16; 7:2] *See WW at Mark 10:7.
7 [a]Deut. 24:1–4; Matt. 5:31
8 [a]Heb. 3:15 [b]Mal. 2:16
9 [a][Matt. 5:32]; Mark 10:11; Luke 16:18; 1 Cor. 7:10 [1]Or *fornication* *See WW at Matt. 15:19.
10 [a][Prov. 21:19]
11 [a][1 Cor. 7:2, 7, 9, 17]
12 [1]Emasculated men

19:3 The rabbis were divided in the interpretation of the law concerning divorce (Deut. 24:1). The conservatives of the school of Shammai held that adultery was the only ground for divorce; while the liberals of the school of Hillel advocated divorce **for just any reason,** even personal dislike.
19:4–6 See section 1 of Truth-In-Action through the Synoptics at the end of Luke.
19:4–6 God's design is that marriage be an abiding state.
19:8 Moses' law was a concession to human weakness, and was not given to make divorce easier; rather, it was a restriction of easy divorce, giving the wife some protection.
19:9 See notes on 5:32 and 1 Cor. 7:10, 11.
19:10 According to the disciples, **it is better not to marry** if there is no escape from a bad marriage.
19:11, 12 Jesus, while recognizing that marriage is the norm, commends the single state in the case of one born impotent, one castrated, or one who voluntarily refrains from marriage in order to give undivided attention to the Lord's service.

born thus from *their* mother's womb,
and [a]there are eunuchs who were
made eunuchs by men, and there are
eunuchs who have made themselves
eunuchs for the kingdom of heaven's
sake. He who is able to accept *it,* let
him accept *it.*"

Jesus Blesses Little Children

13 [a]Then little children were brought
to Him that He might put *His* hands
on them and pray, but the disciples rebuked them.
14 But Jesus said, *"Let the little children come to Me, and do not forbid
them; for [a]of such is the kingdom of
heaven."
15 And He laid *His* hands on them and
departed from there.

Jesus Counsels the Rich Young Ruler

16 [a]Now behold, one came and said to
Him, [b]"Good[1] Teacher, what good
thing shall I do that I may have eternal
life?"
17 So He said to him, [1]"Why do you
call Me good? [2]No one *is* [a]good but
One, *that is,* God. But if you want to
enter into life, [b]keep the commandments."
18 He said to Him, "Which ones?" Jesus said, [a]"*'You shall not murder,'*
'You shall not commit adultery,' 'You
shall not steal,' 'You shall not bear
false witness,'
19 [a]*'Honor your father and your*
mother,' and, [b]*'You shall love your*
neighbor as yourself.'"
20 The young man said to Him, "All
these things I have [a]kept [1]from my
youth. What do I still *lack?"
10 21 Jesus said to him, "If you want to
be perfect, [a]go, sell what you have and
give to the poor, and you will have
treasure in heaven; and come, follow
Me."
22 But when the young man heard that
saying, he went away sorrowful, for he
had great possessions.

12 [a][1 Cor. 7:32]
13 [a]Matt. 20:31; Mark 10:13; Luke 18:15
14 [a]Matt. 18:3, 4; Mark 10:15; Luke 18:17; [1 Cor. 14:20; 1 Pet. 2:2] *See WW at Mark 1:20.
16 [a]Matt. 19:16–29; Mark 10:17–30; Luke 18:18–30 [b]Luke 10:25 [1]NU omits *Good*
17 [a]Ps. 25:8; 34:8; Nah. 1:7; [Rom. 2:4] [b]Lev. 18:5; Deut. 4:40; 6:17; 7:11; 11:22; 28:9; Neh. 9:29; Ezek. 20:21; [Gal. 3:10] [1]NU *Why do you ask Me about what is good?* [2]NU *There is One who is good. But*
18 [a]Ex. 20:13–16; Deut. 5:17–20
19 [a]Ex. 20:12–16; Deut. 5:16–20; Matt. 15:4 [b]Lev. 19:18; Matt. 22:39; [Rom. 13:9; Gal. 5:14; James 2:8]
20 [a][Phil. 3:6, 7] [1]NU omits *from my youth* *See WW at Luke 22:35.
21 [a]Matt. 6:20; Luke 12:33; Acts 2:45; 4:34, 35; 1 Tim. 6:18, 19
23 [a][Matt. 13:22]; Mark 10:24; 1 Cor. 1:26; [1 Tim. 6:9]
26 [a]Gen. 18:14; Num. 11:23; Job 42:2; Is. 59:1; Jer. 32:17; Zech. 8:6; Luke 1:37
27 [a]Deut. 33:9; Matt. 4:20; Luke 5:11

With God All Things Are Possible

23 Then Jesus said to His disciples,
"Assuredly, I say to you that [a]it is hard
for a rich man to enter the kingdom
of heaven.
24 "And again I say to you, it is easier
for a camel to go through the eye of a
needle than for a rich man to enter the
kingdom of God."

KINGDOM DYNAMICS

19:23, 24 Synonymous Expressions, TERMINOLOGY OF THE KINGDOM. This text uses the phrases "kingdom of heaven" and "kingdom of God" interchangeably. In doing so, it sufficiently demonstrates that the two terms are meant to refer to one and the same thing: the kingdom. Although some make a labored distinction between them, this text and 10 others in the Gospels clearly show that the "kingdom of heaven" and "kingdom of God" are verifiably synonyms. Matthew is the only NT writer who used the term "kingdom of heaven." Doing so, he showed a sensitivity toward his originally intended audience of Jewish readers, for whom too frequent a use of the name of "God" would have seemed irreverent. By a variety of terms Matthew refers to "the kingdom" 50 times in his Gospel: 32 times as "kingdom of heaven"; 5 times as "kingdom of God"; 4 times as the "Father's" kingdom; and twice as the kingdom of "the Son of Man." The remaining 7 references are simply to "the kingdom" without other designation. This variety in the usage, made by the only one using the phrase "kingdom of heaven," surely shows these terms to be synonyms for the kingdom.

(Matt. 3:1, 2/John 18:36) J.W.H.

25 When His disciples heard *it,* they
were greatly astonished, saying, "Who
then can be saved?"
26 But Jesus looked at *them* and
said to them, "With men this is impossible, but [a]with God all things are **pos-**
sible."
27 Then Peter answered and said to
Him, "See, [a]we have left all and fol-

19:16 The question reveals that this man felt that **eternal life** could be earned.
19:17 Jesus directs attention to God, the final norm of goodness. Because of man's sinful nature, it is impossible for anyone to **keep the commandments** perfectly, which is why salvation is by grace. This is what Jesus is trying to lead the man to understand.
19:21 Jesus issues a stern challenge designed to show the man that he has not observed the spirit of the commandments, in spite of his claim (v. 20). In fact, his selfish attitude in making an idol of wealth reveals that he had broken the very first Commandment (Ex. 20:3).
19:21–26 See section 10 of Truth-In-Action through the Synoptics at the end of Luke.
19:23, 24 Jesus uses an exaggeration to teach that it is impossible for one who trusts in riches over God to enter heaven. His parallel use of **the kingdom of heaven** (v. 23) and **the kingdom of God** (v. 24) show these designations to be synonymous.
19:25 Supposedly, wealth was an evidence of God's favor. Jesus shows the fallacy of such a view by stating that it may be a hindrance to receiving God's favor.
19:27 Peter, missing the point of Jesus' teaching, rather proudly claims to have fulfilled the condition of forsaking wealth in order to follow Him.

lowed You. Therefore what shall we
have?"

WORD WEALTH

19:26 possible, *dunatos* (doo-nat-*oss*); Strong's *#1415:* Compare "dynasty," "dynamite," "dynamo," and "dynamic." Strong, mighty, powerful. In the neuter form, the word means "possible." The inherent idea is that of having the ability to act and the power to accomplish. Christ gives assurance that however powerless our efforts to make things happen, He can demonstrate the dynamic power that translates people from Satan's realm to God's kingdom.

28 So Jesus said to them, "Assuredly
I say to you, that in the regeneration,
when the Son of Man sits on the throne
of His *glory, [a]you who have followed
Me will also sit on twelve thrones,
judging the twelve tribes of Israel.
29 [a]"And everyone who has left
houses or brothers or sisters or father
or mother [1]or wife or children or
[2]lands, for My name's sake, shall receive a hundredfold, and inherit eternal life.
30 [a]"But many *who are* first will be
last, and the last first.

The Parable of the Workers in the Vineyard

20 "For the kingdom of heaven is
like a landowner who went out
early in the morning to hire laborers
for his vineyard.
2 "Now when he had *agreed with the
laborers for a denarius a day, he sent
them into his vineyard.
3 "And he went out about the third
hour and saw others standing idle in
the marketplace,
4 "and said to them, 'You also go into
the vineyard, and whatever is right I
will give you.' So they went.
5 "Again he went out about the sixth
and the ninth hour, and did likewise.
6 "And about the eleventh hour he
went out and found others standing
[1]idle, and said to them, 'Why have you
been standing here idle all day?'
7 "They said to him, 'Because no one
hired us.' He said to them, 'You also
go into the vineyard, [1]and whatever is
right you will receive.'
8 "So when evening had come, the
owner of the vineyard said to his steward, 'Call the laborers and give them
their wages, beginning with the last to
the first.'
9 "And when those came who *were
hired* about the eleventh hour, they
each received a denarius.
10 "But when the first came, they supposed that they would receive more;
and they likewise received each a denarius.
11 "And when they had received *it,*
they [1]complained against the landowner,
12 "saying, 'These last *men* have
worked *only* one hour, and you made
them equal to us who have borne the
burden and the heat of the day.'
13 "But he answered one of them and
said, 'Friend, I am *doing you no
wrong. Did you not *agree with me for
a denarius?
14 'Take *what is* yours and go your
way. I wish to give to this last man *the
same* as to you.
15 [a]'Is it not lawful for me to do what
I wish with my own things? Or [b]is your
eye evil because I am good?'
16 [a]"So the last will be first, and the
first last. [b]For[1] many are called, but
few *chosen."

Jesus a Third Time Predicts His Death and Resurrection

**17 [a]Now Jesus, going up to Jerusalem,
took the twelve disciples aside on the
road and said to them,**

28 [a]Matt. 20:21; Luke 22:28–30; [1 Cor. 6:2; Rev. 2:26] *See WW at John 2:11. **29** [a][Matt. 6:33]; Mark 10:29, 30; Luke 18:29, 30 [1]NU omits *or wife* [2]Lit. *fields* **30** [a][Matt. 20:16; 21:31, 32]; Mark 10:31; Luke 13:30

CHAPTER 20

2 *See WW at Matt. 18:19.

6 [1]NU omits *idle* **7** [1]NU omits the rest of v. 7. **11** [1]*grumbled* **13** *See WW at Acts 25:10. • See WW at Matt. 18:19. **15** [a][Rom. 9:20, 21] [b]Deut. 15:9; Prov. 23:6; [Matt. 6:23]; Mark 7:22 **16** [a]Matt. 19:30; Mark 10:31; Luke 13:30 [b]Matt. 22:14 [1]NU omits the rest of v. 16. *See WW at 1 Pet. 2:9. **17** [a]Matt. 20:17–19; Mark 10:32–34; Luke 18:31–33; John 12:12

19:28 The former warnings about riches give way to the promise of reward for those who have left riches for Jesus' sake. Blessing **in the regeneration** (the Age to Come) will far outweigh material loss in this age. **Twelve tribes:** The church, patterned after the old, is the new Israel. Jesus assures the disciples of unspecified special exaltation in the Age to Come.
19:29 The promise to the disciples is generalized to include all followers of Christ.
19:30 Rewards will be given by heaven's standards, not earth's. This saying introduces the parable of 20:1–15 and concludes it (20:16).
20:1–16 The parable grows out of the attitude that the disciples had shown toward service and rewards. Although rewards are forthcoming, Jesus rebukes the spirit of serving for the reward itself rather than out of love.
20:2 A **denarius** was the standard wage for a full day's work.
20:3 The first laborers began at 6:00 A.M. (v. 1). Now it is 9:00 A.M.
20:8 Beginning with the last: Within the parable, the problem is produced by the reverse order of payment. The earliest workers' expectations are raised (v. 10).
20:11, 12 Their complaint was that those who rendered less service received the same wage.
20:15 The parable affirms that God is absolutely sovereign and gracious in granting rewards. Those who serve Him can trust His grace.
20:17–19 In the third announcement of His sufferings, Jesus is more explicit than in the first two (16:21; 17:22, 23), referring to Gentile torment and crucifixion.

18 [a]"Behold, we are going up to Jerusalem, and the Son of Man will be betrayed to the chief priests and to the
scribes; and they will condemn Him to
death,
19 [a]"and deliver Him to the Gentiles
to [b]mock and to [c]scourge and to
[d]crucify. And the third day He will
[e]rise again."

Greatness Is Serving

9 20 [a]Then the mother of [b]Zebedee's
sons came to Him with her sons, kneeling down and asking something from
Him.
21 And He said to her, "What do you
wish?" She said to Him, "Grant that
these two sons of mine [a]may sit, one
on Your right hand and the other on
the left, in Your kingdom."
22 But Jesus answered and said, "You
do not know what you *ask. Are you
*able to drink [a]the cup that I am about
to drink, [1]and be baptized with [b]the
*baptism that I am baptized with?"
They said to Him, "We are able."
23 So He said to them, [a]"You will indeed drink My cup, [1]and be baptized
with the baptism that I am baptized
with; but to sit on My right hand and
on My left is not Mine to give, but *it
is for those* for whom it is prepared by
My Father."
24 [a]And when the ten heard *it*, they
were greatly displeased with the two
brothers.
25 But Jesus called them to *Himself*
and said, "You know that the rulers
of the Gentiles lord it over them, and
those who are great exercise authority
over them.
26 "Yet [a]it shall not be so among you;
but [b]whoever desires to become great
among you, let him be your servant.
27 [a]"And whoever desires to be first
among you, let him be your slave—
28 [a]"just as the [b]Son of Man did not
come to be served, [c]but to serve, and
[d]to give His *life a **ransom** [e]for many."

WORD WEALTH

20:28 ransom, *lutron* (loo-trahn); Strong's *#3083:* From the verb *luo,* "to loose." The word signifies a release from slavery or captivity brought about by the payment of a price. Sin demands an expiation, an atonement, a price paid because of the penalty of death that was upon us. Jesus' gift to us was Himself, a universal ransom (for many) that was of a vicarious nature. *Lutron* defines the price paid canceling our debt.

Two Blind Men Receive Their Sight

29 [a]Now as they went out of Jericho,
a great multitude followed Him.
30 And behold, [a]two blind men sitting
by the road, when they heard that Jesus was passing by, cried out, saying,
"Have mercy on us, O Lord, [b]Son of
David!"
31 Then the multitude [a]warned them
that they should be quiet; but they
cried out all the more, saying, "Have
mercy on us, O Lord, Son of David!"
32 So Jesus stood still and called them,
and said, "What do you want Me to
do for you?"
33 They said to Him, "Lord, that our
eyes may be opened."
34 So Jesus *had [a]compassion and
touched their eyes. And immediately
their eyes received sight, and they followed Him.

The Triumphal Entry

21 Now [a]when they drew near Jerusalem, and came to [1]Beth-
phage, at [b]the Mount of Olives, then
Jesus *sent two disciples,
2 saying to them, "Go into the village
opposite you, and immediately you will

18 [a]Matt. 16:21; 26:47–57
19 [a]Matt. 27:2 [b]Matt. 26:67, 68; 27:29, 41 [c]Matt. 27:26 [d]Acts 3:13–15 [e]Matt. 28:5, 6
20 [a]Mark 10:35–45 [b]Matt. 4:21; 10:2
21 [a][Matt. 19:28]
22 [a]Luke 22:42 [b]Luke 12:50 [1]NU omits *and be baptized with the baptism that I am baptized with* *See WW at Matt. 7:7. • See WW at Jude 24. • See WW at Matt. 21:25.
23 [a][Acts 12:2] [1]NU omits *and be baptized with the baptism that I am baptized with*
24 [a]Mark 10:41
26 [a][1 Pet. 5:3] [b]Matt. 23:11
27 [a][Matt. 18:4]
28 [a]John 13:4 [b][Phil. 2:6, 7] [c]Luke 22:27 [d][Is. 53:10, 11] [e][Rom. 5:15, 19] *See WW at Luke 21:19.
29 [a]Mark 10:46–52
30 [a]Matt. 9:27 [b][Ezek. 37:21–25]
31 [a]Matt. 19:13
34 [a]Matt. 9:36; 14:14; 15:32; 18:27 *See WW at Matt. 14:14.

CHAPTER 21

1 [a]Luke 19:29–38 [b][Zech. 14:4] [1]M *Bethsphage* *See WW at John 20:21.

20:20–28 See section 9 of Truth-In-Action through the Synoptics at the end of Luke.

20:21 This request contrasts the self-sacrifice that Jesus has just described with the self-seeking of His followers. The **right** and the **left** are positions of honor in the consummated kingdom.

20:22 The **cup** was used to signify either great joy or great sorrow. See Ps. 23:5; Jer. 25:15. Here it refers to Jesus' death and, more specifically, to God's judgment against sin (see 26:39, 42). **Baptism** speaks of being immersed in the divinely appointed suffering.

20:23 James and John did indeed suffer. James was the first of the apostles to be martyred (Acts 12:2); and, in his later years, John suffered persecution and exile (Rev. 1:9). According to tradition, he also was martyred.

20:26–28 True greatness is measured in terms of service, and Jesus Himself provided the highest standard of service in His atoning death.

20:26 Yet: Gentile practice (v. 25) forms a sharp contrast to the practice Jesus expects from His disciples.

20:28 Jesus models the service that He expects from the disciples. **Ransom:** The idea of payment for resultant freedom is expressed and can only be understood through the Passion of Jesus.

20:31 Son of David occurs twice (v. 30), indicating the men were rendering to Jesus this messianic title.

21:1–11 During the last week of His ministry, Jesus deliberately fulfilled messianic prophecies. The Triumphal Entry into Jerusalem, which took place on Sunday before the Crucifixion, was an enacted parable, a dramatic way in which Jesus proclaimed His messiahship. This fulfilled in minute detail the prophecy of Zech. 9:9.

find a donkey tied, and a colt with her.
Loose *them* and bring *them* to Me.
3 "And if anyone says anything to
you, you shall say, 'The Lord has need
of them,' and immediately he will send
them."
4 [1]All this was done that it might be
fulfilled which was spoken by the
prophet, saying:

5 *"Tell*[a] *the daughter of Zion,*
'Behold, your King is coming to
you,
Lowly, *and sitting on a donkey,*
A colt, the foal of a donkey.'"

WORD WEALTH

21:5 lowly, *praus* (prah-*ooce*); Strong's *#4235* and *#4239:* A humility that is considerate, unassuming, gentle, mild, meek. The Zealots were looking for a warlike Messiah who would use force. Jesus showed a greater power than armed might, the power of humble wisdom and penetrating love. Meekness is not weakness, but power under perfect control.

6 [a]So the disciples went and did as
Jesus commanded them.
7 They brought the donkey and the
colt, [a]laid their clothes on them,
[1]and set *Him* on them.
8 And a very great multitude spread
their clothes on the road; [a]others cut
down branches from the trees and
spread *them* on the road.
9 Then the multitudes who went before and those who followed cried out,
saying:

"Hosanna to the Son of David!
[a]*'Blessed is He who comes in the*
name of the L*ORD*!'
Hosanna in the highest!"

10 [a]And when He had come into Jerusalem, all the city was moved, saying,
"Who is this?"
11 So the multitudes said, "This is Jesus, [a]the prophet from Nazareth of
Galilee."

Jesus Cleanses the Temple

12 [a]Then Jesus went into the temple
[1]of God and drove out all those who
bought and sold in the temple, and
overturned the tables of the [b]money
changers and the seats of those who
sold doves.
13 And He said to them, "It is written,
[a]*'My house shall be called a house of*
prayer,' but you have made it a [b]*'den*
of thieves.' "
14 Then *the* blind and *the* lame came
to Him in the temple, and He healed
them.
15 But when the chief priests and
scribes saw the wonderful things that
He did, and the children crying out in
the temple and saying, "Hosanna to the
[a]Son of David!" they were [1]indignant
16 and said to Him, "Do You hear what
these are saying?" And Jesus said to
them, "Yes. Have you never read,

[a]*'Out of the mouth of babes and*
nursing infants
You have perfected praise'?"

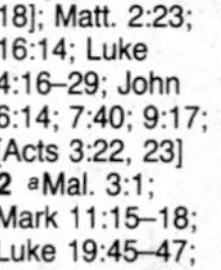

KINGDOM DYNAMICS

21:16 Perfected Praise Produces Power, PRAISE PATHWAY. In response to the criticism levelled against this verbal praise, which was powerful, vocal, and strong, Jesus quotes Ps. 8:2 and reminds us of a great secret. Perfected praise will produce strength! It is powerful! At the very moment Jesus is being rejected by the leaders, these young people are captivated by the full meaning of who Jesus is. Capturing this revelation about Him causes loud and powerful praise to come forth. How heartening this must have been to Jesus as He marched toward the Cross! (Is. 61:3/Acts 16:25, 26) C.G.

17 Then He left them and [a]went out
of the city to Bethany, and He lodged
there.

4 [1]NU omits *All*
5 [a]Is. 62:11; Zech. 9:9; John 12:15
6 [a]Mark 11:4
7 [a]2 Kin. 9:13 [1]NU *and He sat*
8 [a]Lev. 23:40; John 12:13
9 [a]Ps. 118:26; Matt. 23:39
10 [a]John 2:13, 15
11 [a][Deut. 18:15, 18]; Matt. 2:23; 16:14; Luke 4:16–29; John 6:14; 7:40; 9:17; [Acts 3:22, 23]
12 [a]Mal. 3:1; Mark 11:15–18; Luke 19:45–47; John 2:13–16 [b]Deut. 14:25 [1]NU omits *of God*
13 [a]Is. 56:7 [b]Jer. 7:11
15 [a]Matt. 1:1; John 7:42 [1]*angry*
16 [a]Ps. 8:2; Matt. 11:25
17 [a]Matt. 26:6; Mark 11:1, 11, 12; 14:3; Luke 19:29; 24:50; John 11:1, 18; 12:1

21:8 A king's subjects paid homage to him by providing a carpet for him to walk or ride on.
21:9 Hosanna means "Save now." It was more than a cry of acclamation. Essentially, it was a plea from an oppressed people to their Savior for deliverance. Later it came to be a standard shout of praise. Ps. 118:25, 26, from which the quote comes, is messianic; therefore, the people were publicly acknowledging Jesus as the Messiah.
21:10 The verb **moved** is often used of an earthquake showing that the dramatic arrival of Jesus caused a great commotion.
21:12 The **money changers** and other merchants were fraudulent in their transactions. Jesus fulfills the prophecy of Mal. 3:1–3 by another enacted parable, this one demonstrating His messianic authority with respect to the fraudulence and the commercialization of the sacrificial system. This was most likely His second temple cleansing (see John 2:13–22).
21:13 The OT quotation is from Is. 56:7 and Jer. 7:11.
21:14 Jesus' miracles were additional assertions of His kingly authority.
21:17 Jesus likely **lodged** in the home of Martha, Mary, and Lazarus.

The Fig Tree Withered

18 [a]Now in the morning, as He returned to the city, He was hungry.
19 [a]And seeing a fig tree by the road,
He came to it and found nothing on it
but leaves, and said to it, "Let no fruit
grow on you ever again." Immediately
the fig tree withered away.

The Lesson of the Withered Fig Tree

20 [a]And when the disciples saw *it,*
they marveled, saying, "How did the
fig tree wither away so soon?"
21 So Jesus answered and said to
them, "Assuredly, I say to you, [a]if you
have faith and [b]do* not doubt, you will
not only do what was done to the fig
tree, [c]but also if you say to this mountain, 'Be removed and be cast into the
sea,' it will be done.
22 "And [a]whatever things you ask in
prayer, believing, you will receive."

Jesus' Authority Questioned

23 [a]Now when He came into the temple, the chief priests and the elders of
the people confronted Him as He was
teaching, and [b]said, "By what authority are You doing these things? And
who gave You this authority?"
24 But Jesus answered and said to
them, "I also will ask you one thing,
which if you tell Me, I likewise will tell
you by what authority I do these
things:
25 "The [a]**baptism** of [b]John—where
was it from? From heaven or from
men?" And they reasoned among
themselves, saying, "If we say, 'From
heaven,' He will say to us, 'Why then
did you not believe him?'

WORD WEALTH

21:25 baptism, *baptisma* (*bap*-tis-mah); Strong's *#908:* From the verb *baptizo,* to dip, immerse. *Baptisma* emphasizes the result of the act rather than the act itself. In Christian baptism the stress is on the baptized person's identification with Christ in death, burial, and resurrection. The word describes the experience of a convert from initial acceptance of Christ to initiation into the Christian community.

18 [a]Mark 11:12–14, 20–24 **19** [a]Mark 11:13 **20** [a]Mark 11:20 **21** [a]Matt. 17:20 [b]James 1:6 [c]1 Cor. 13:2 *See WW at Acts 11:12. **22** [a]Matt. 7:7–11; Mark 11:24; Luke 11:9; [John 15:7; James 5:16; 1 John 3:22; 5:14] **23** [a]Mark 11:27–33; Luke 20:1–8 [b]Ex. 2:14; Acts 4:7; 7:27 **25** [a][John 1:29–34] [b]John 1:15–28

26 [a]Matt. 14:5; 21:46; Luke 20:6 [b]Matt. 14:5; Mark 6:20 **28** [a]Matt. 20:1; 21:33 **31** [a]Luke 7:29, 37–50 **32** [a]Luke 3:1–12; 7:29 [b]Luke 3:12, 13 [1]*regret it* **33** [a]Ps. 80:9; Mark 12:1–12; Luke 20:9–19 [b]Matt. 25:14

26 "But if we say, 'From men,' we
[a]fear the multitude, [b]for all count John
as a prophet."
27 So they answered Jesus and said,
"We do not know." And He said to
them, "Neither will I tell you by what
authority I do these things.

The Parable of the Two Sons

28 "But what do you think? A man had
two sons, and he came to the first and
said, 'Son, go, work today in my
[a]vineyard.'
29 "He answered and said, 'I will not,'
but afterward he regretted it and went.
30 "Then he came to the second and
said likewise. And he answered and
said, 'I *go,* sir,' but he did not go.
31 "Which of the two did the will of
his father?" They said to Him, "The
first." Jesus said to them, [a]"Assuredly,
I say to you that tax collectors and harlots enter the kingdom of God before
you.
32 "For [a]John came to you in the way
of righteousness, and you did not believe him; [b]but tax collectors and harlots believed him; and when you saw
it, you did not afterward [1]relent and
believe him.

The Parable of the Wicked Vinedressers

33 "Hear another parable: There was
a certain landowner [a]who planted a
vineyard and set a hedge around it, dug
a winepress in it and built a tower. And
he leased it to vinedressers and [b]went
into a far country.

21:19 On **a fig tree** the fruit is first formed, and then the **leaves** appear; so one would expect to find satisfying fruit on a tree in full leaf. The fig tree is used here to designate Israel of Jesus' time, whose religious system and heritage appeared to hold promise of satisfaction. So the curse extended not only to the tree but also to the nation of Israel, an enacted parable, showing the judgment that was to come upon Israel's false profession. The nation had professed righteousness and had maintained all the external forms of godliness, but while professing faith in God, they rejected the Son of God.

21:20–22 The positive lesson to be learned from the withered fig tree is the incredible power of believing prayer authoritatively spoken in accordance with God's will and purposes.

21:23 By asking Jesus the **authority** for His actions, the religious authorities hoped to trap Him in a statement of blasphemy.

21:25 Countering with His own question, Jesus impales His opponents upon the horns of a dilemma.

21:28–32 Jesus speaks a parable of judgment. Repentant sinners of the vilest kind will enter heaven, but not religious pretenders.

21:33–44 The second parable pronounces even more severe judgment on Israel, which had not only maltreated God's prophets through the ages, but was now conspiring to kill His Son.

21:33 The parable begins with the language of the Song of

34 "Now when vintage-time drew
near, he sent his servants to the vinedressers, that they might receive its
fruit.
35 [a]"And the vinedressers took his servants, beat one, killed one, and stoned
another.
36 "Again he sent other servants, more
than the first, and they did likewise to
them.
37 "Then last of all he sent his [a]son
to them, saying, 'They will respect my
son.'
38 "But when the vinedressers saw the
son, they said among themselves,
[a]'This is the heir. [b]Come, let us kill him
and seize his inheritance.'
39 [a]"So they took him and cast *him* out
of the vineyard and killed *him*.
40 "Therefore, when the owner of the
vineyard comes, what will he do to
those vinedressers?"
41 [a]They said to Him, [b]"He will destroy those wicked men miserably,
[c]and lease *his* vineyard to other vinedressers who will [1]render to him the
fruits in their seasons."
42 Jesus said to them, "Have you never
read in the Scriptures:

[a]*'The stone which the builders*
rejected
Has become the chief
cornerstone.
This was the LORD's doing,
And it is marvelous in our eyes'?

43 "Therefore I say to you, [a]the kingdom of God will be taken from you and
given to a nation bearing the fruits of
it.
44 "And [a]whoever falls on this stone
will be broken; but on whomever it
falls, [b]it will grind him to powder."
45 Now when the chief priests and
Pharisees heard His parables, they
[1]perceived* that He was speaking of
them.
46 But when they sought to lay hands
on Him, they [a]feared the multitudes,
because [b]they took Him for a prophet.

The Parable of the Wedding Feast

22 And Jesus answered [a]and spoke
to them again by parables and
said:
2 "The kingdom of heaven is like a
certain king who arranged a marriage
for his son,
3 "and sent out his servants to call
those who were invited to the wedding;
and they were not willing to come.
4 "Again, he sent out other servants,
saying, 'Tell those who are invited,
"See, I have prepared my dinner;
[a]my oxen and fatted cattle *are* killed,
and all things *are* ready. Come to the
wedding." '
5 "But they made light of it and went
their ways, one to his own farm, another to his business.
6 "And the rest seized his servants,
*treated *them* [1]spitefully, and killed
them.
7 "But when the king heard *about it*,
he was *furious. And he sent out
[a]his armies, destroyed those murderers, and burned up their city.
8 "Then he said to his servants, 'The
wedding is ready, but those who were
invited were not [a]worthy.
9 'Therefore go into the highways,
and as many as you find, invite to the
wedding.'
10 "So those servants went out into the
highways and [a]gathered together all
whom they found, both bad and good.
And the wedding *hall* was filled with
guests.
11 "But when the king came in to see
the guests, he saw a man there [a]who
did not have on a wedding garment.
12 "So he said to him, 'Friend, how did
you come in here without a wedding
garment?' And he was [a]speechless.
13 "Then the king said to the servants,
'Bind him hand and foot, [1]take him

35 [a][1 Thess. 2:15]
37 [a][John 3:16]
38 [a][Heb. 1:2] [b]John 11:53
39 [a][Acts 2:23]
41 [a]Luke 20:16 [b][Luke 21:24] [c][Acts 13:46] [1]*give*
42 [a]Ps. 118:22, 23
43 [a][Matt. 8:12]
44 [a]Is. 8:14, 15 [b][Dan. 2:44]
45 [1]*knew* *See WW at John 8:32.
46 [a]Matt. 21:26 [b]Matt. 21:11

CHAPTER 22

1 [a][Rev. 19:7–9]
4 [a]Prov. 9:2
6 [1]*insolently* *See WW at Luke 18:32.
7 [a][Dan. 9:26] *See WW at Rev. 12:17.
8 [a]Matt. 10:11
10 [a]Matt. 13:38, 47, 48
11 [a][Col. 3:10, 12]
12 [a][Rom. 3:19]
13 [1]NU omits *take him away, and*

the Vineyard (Is. 5:1–7), and will underscore the same message, "Your judgment is well deserved!" The vine/vineyard, like the fig tree, is a biblical metaphor that designates the people of God.

21:37 Son: Jesus veils Himself and His fate with this designation.

21:42 The rejection and death of Jesus were divinely ordained and will issue in triumph and exaltation as prophesied in Ps. 118:22, 23.

21:43 In rejecting Jesus they rejected **the kingdom of God,** which will be given to a **nation,** a term signifying a new people (Jew and Gentile) who will render to God the appropriate fruit.

21:44 Those who stumble in unbelief on the **stone** will be shattered, and those who try to pull it down will be utterly destroyed.

22:1–14 This chapter continues the controversy of the previous chapter. Jesus reveals the guilt of Israel in rejecting the invitation to enter the kingdom. As a result, the nation forfeited its privileges and would witness the destruction of Jerusalem.

22:7–9 The destruction of Jerusalem historically marked the end of Israel. God's redemptive purpose would be carried out among the Gentiles until the Gentile era is completed (see Luke 21:24; Rom. 11:11–27).

22:11–13 The **wedding garment** introduces imagery to show that faithfulness and obedience to the will of God are important for members of the new community who have responded to the wedding invitation.

away, and cast *him* [a]into outer darkness; there will be weeping and gnashing of teeth.'
14 [a]"For many are called, but few *are*
chosen."

The Pharisees: Is It Lawful to Pay Taxes to Caesar?

2 15 [a]Then the Pharisees went and
plotted how they might entangle Him
in *His* talk.
16 And they sent to Him their disciples
with the [a]Herodians, saying, "Teacher,
we know that You are *true, and teach
the way of God in *truth; nor do You
care about anyone, for You do not
[1]regard the person of men.
17 "Tell us, therefore, what do You
think? Is it lawful to pay taxes to Caesar, or not?"
18 But Jesus [1]perceived their wickedness, and said, "Why do you test Me,
you *hypocrites?
19 "Show Me the tax money." So they
brought Him a denarius.
20 And He said to them, "Whose image
and inscription *is* this?"
21 They said to Him, "Caesar's." And
He said to them, [a]"**Render**[1] therefore
to Caesar the things that are [b]Caesar's,
and to God the things that are [c]God's."

WORD WEALTH

22:21 render, *apodidomi* (ap-od-*eed*-oh-mee); Strong's *#591:* To fulfill one's duty to someone, give what is due, give back, recompense, restore.

22 When they had heard *these words,*
they marveled, and left Him and went
their way.

13 [a]Matt. 8:12; 25:30; Luke 13:28
14 [a]Matt. 20:16
15 [a]Mark 12:13–17; Luke 20:20–26
16 [a]Mark 3:6; 8:15; 12:13 [1]Lit. *look at the face of*
*See WW at Rom. 3:4. • See WW at John 4:24.
18 [1]*knew*
*See WW at Matt. 6:2.
21 [a]Matt. 17:25 [b][Rom. 13:1–7; 1 Pet. 2:13–15] [c][1 Cor. 3:23; 6:19, 20; 12:27] [1]*Pay*
23 [a]Mark 12:18–27; Luke 20:27–40 [b]Acts 23:8
24 [a]Deut. 25:5
29 [a]John 20:9 [1]*deceived*
30 [a][1 John 3:2] [1]NU omits *of God*
32 [a]Gen. 17:7; 26:24; 28:21; Ex. 3:6, 15; Mark 12:26; Luke 20:37; Acts 7:32; [Heb. 11:16]
33 [a]Matt. 7:28
34 [a]Mark 12:28–31; Luke 10:25–37

The Sadducees: What About the Resurrection?

23 [a]The same day the Sadducees,
[b]who say there is no resurrection,
came to Him and asked Him,
24 saying: "Teacher, [a]Moses said that
if a man dies, having no children, his
brother shall marry his wife and raise
up offspring for his brother.
25 "Now there were with us seven
brothers. The first died after he had
married, and having no offspring, left
his wife to his brother.
26 "Likewise the second also, and the
third, even to the seventh.
27 "Last of all the woman died also.
28 "Therefore, in the resurrection,
whose wife of the seven will she be?
For they all had her."
29 Jesus answered and said to them,
"You are [1]mistaken, [a]not knowing the
Scriptures nor the power of God.
30 "For in the resurrection they neither
marry nor are given in marriage, but
[a]are like angels [1]of God in heaven.
31 "But concerning the resurrection of
the dead, have you not read what was
spoken to you by God, saying,
32 [a]*'I am the God of Abraham, the God
of Isaac, and the God of Jacob'*? God
is not the God of the dead, but of the
living."
33 And when the multitudes heard
this, [a]they were astonished at His
teaching.

The Scribes: Which Is the First Commandment of All?

34 [a]But when the Pharisees heard that 3
He had silenced the Sadducees, they
gathered together.

22:14 The **chosen** ones have met all the requirements.
22:15–40 Because of Jesus' popularity, the religious authorities must first entrap and discredit Him among the people in order to justify His death.
22:15–22 See section 2 of Truth-In-Action through the Synoptics at the end of Luke.
22:16 The **Herodians** were a Jewish political party favoring a continuation of the dynasty of Herod. Although they and the Pharisees were natural enemies, the two parties united in common opposition to Jesus.
22:17 If Jesus answered "Yes," He would lose favor with the people, who hated Roman domination. If He answered "No," His enemies would report Him to the Roman authorities as a traitor.
22:20 Their very possession of a Roman coin evidenced their subservience to Roman rule.
22:21 An earthly state provides for the welfare of its citizens, who are thus obligated to support the government. But citizens of God's kingdom also owe allegiance to Him. Ideally, there should be no conflict between the two kingdoms (see Rom. 13:1–7), but where there is disharmony allegiance to God takes precedence (see Acts 4:18–20).
22:23–28 The hypothetical case stated by **the Sadducees** is based on Deut. 25:5–10, but is ludicrous in light of their denial of the resurrection (v. 23).
22:29, 30 It is erroneous to think of heaven in terms of Earth. Life in heaven will not be an extension of this present temporal existence. **The power of God** will provide for new and greater relationships that transcend the physical relationships of the present order.
22:31, 32 The Sadducees accepted only the first five books of the OT as Scripture, and rejected a resurrection because they saw nothing in their Scriptures to support the doctrine. Jesus pointed out that when God spoke the words of Ex. 3:6, Abraham, Isaac, and Jacob had been physically dead for many years. So evidently there is life after death.
22:34–40 See section 3 of Truth-In-Action through the Synoptics at the end of Luke.
22:34–40 The Pharisees' code of morality consisted of countless minute rules and regulations. Jesus summed up all moral obligations in the word **love,** expressed in the twofold direction of **God** and **neighbor.** The quotation in v. 37 is from the Jewish Shema (Deut. 6:4, 5), which all Jews repeated twice daily.

35 Then one of them, [a]a lawyer, asked *Him a question,* testing Him, and saying,

36 "Teacher, which *is* the great commandment in the law?"

37 Jesus said to him, [a]" '*You shall *love the* LORD *your God with all your heart, with all your soul, and with all your *mind.*'

38 "This is *the* first and great commandment.

39 "And *the* second *is* like it: [a]'*You shall love your neighbor as yourself.*'

40 [a]"On these two commandments hang all the Law and the Prophets."

Jesus: How Can David Call His Descendant Lord?

41 [a]While the Pharisees were gathered together, Jesus asked them,

42 saying, "What do you think about the Christ? Whose Son is He?" They said to Him, "*The* [a]*Son* of David."

43 He said to them, "How then does David in the Spirit call Him *'Lord,'* saying:

44 *'The[a]* LORD *said to my Lord,*
"Sit at My right hand,
Till I make Your enemies Your footstool" '?

45 "If David then calls Him *'Lord,'* how is He his Son?"

46 [a]And no one was able to answer Him a word, [b]nor from that day on did anyone dare question Him anymore.

Woe to the Scribes and Pharisees

23 Then Jesus spoke to the multitudes and to His disciples,

35 [a]Luke 7:30; 10:25; 11:45, 46, 52; 14:3
37 [a]Deut. 6:5; 10:12; 30:6 *See WW at John 3:16. • See WW at Mark 12:30.
39 [a]Lev. 19:18
40 [a][Matt. 7:12]
41 [a]Luke 20:41–44
42 [a]Matt. 1:1; 21:9
44 [a]Ps. 110:1
46 [a]Luke 14:6 [b]Mark 12:34

CHAPTER 23

2 [a]Neh. 8:4, 8
3 [a][Rom. 2:19] [1]NU omits *to observe*
4 [a]Luke 11:46
5 [a][Matt. 6:1–6, 16–18] *See WW at Acts 5:13.
6 [a]Luke 11:43; 20:46 [1]Or *place of honor*
8 [a][James 3:1] [1]*Leader* [2]NU omits *the Christ*
9 [a][Mal. 1:6]
11 [a]Matt. 20:26, 27
12 [a]Luke 14:11; 18:14 [1]*put down* [2]*lifted up* *See WW at James 4:10. • See WW at Matt. 18:4.
13 [a]Luke 11:52

2 saying: [a]"The scribes and the Pharisees sit in Moses' seat.

KINGDOM DYNAMICS

23:2–12 31. What Is the Greatest Sin in the Kingdom?, SPIRITUAL ANSWERS. For the answer to this and other probing questions about God and the power life in His kingdom, see the study article "Spiritual Answers to Hard Questions," which begins on page 1996. P.R.

3 "Therefore whatever they tell you
[1]to observe, *that* observe and do, but do not do according to their works; for [a]they say, and do not do.

4 [a]"For they bind heavy burdens, hard to bear, and lay *them* on men's shoulders; but they *themselves* will not move them with one of their fingers.

5 "But all their works they do to [a]be seen by men. They make their phylacteries broad and *enlarge the borders of their garments.

6 [a]"They love the [1]best places at feasts, the best seats in the synagogues,

7 "greetings in the marketplaces, and to be called by men, 'Rabbi, Rabbi.'

8 [a]"But you, do not be called 'Rabbi'; for One is your [1]Teacher, [2]the Christ, and you are all brethren.

9 "Do not call anyone on earth your father; [a]for One is your Father, He who is in heaven.

10 "And do not be called teachers; for One is your Teacher, the Christ.

11 "But [a]he who is greatest among you shall be your servant.

12 [a]"And whoever *exalts himself will be [1]humbled,* and he who humbles himself will be [2]exalted.

13 "But [a]woe to you, scribes and

22:41–46 Jesus seized the offensive with a countering question concerning the Person of Christ. The favorite messianic title among the Jews was ***Son of David,*** which they interpreted in highly nationalistic and revolutionary terms. Jesus quotes Ps. 110:1, recognized by all Jews as one of the greatest messianic psalms, to assert not only His humanity, but His deity. His scriptural logic completely confounded His enemies.

22:42–45 A father does not call his son, "lord," but rather the reverse; a son calls his father, "lord." Therefore, if the Lord (God) said to my Lord (Messiah), how can the Messiah be the **Son** of David? Thus, the title "Son of David" is inadequate. To be sure, Jesus Christ is the "Son of David" (1:1), but no less is He the "Son of God."

23:1–36 Jesus delivers a blistering rebuke to the Pharisees after first warning His followers against them. The Lord directs His condemnation at hypocritical self-righteousness, full of outward form but devoid of inner spiritual reality.

23:2, 3 The Pharisees were the authoritative teachers of the Mosaic Law even though they failed to follow their own precepts. Much of their teaching was sound, but Jesus confronts those points in which their hypocrisy neutralized the validity of their instruction.

23:4 Jesus refers to their countless rules and regulations, which reduced religion to a burdensome and confusing system of ritual observance that kept people in perpetual bondage.

23:5 The Pharisees paraded their piety in public to win praise. **Phylacteries** were small leather cases, which contained certain Scripture texts, and which the Jews wore around their arms and on their foreheads. **Borders** refers to the tassels the Jews wore on the corners of their outer garments. See 9:20; 14:36; Num. 15:38; Deut. 22:12.

23:6–12 Jesus warns against a prideful seeking of public praise, exemplified by the desire for places of prominence, and titles signifying superiority. The titles themselves may be used as terms of respect or to indicate certain duties and places of responsibility. It is the attitude behind the seeking of such recognition that Jesus condemns. As believers, we are equal and owe our reverence to Christ alone.

23:13–33 Jesus issues a series of eight scathing

Pharisees, *hypocrites! For you shut up
the kingdom of heaven against men;
for you neither go in *yourselves,* nor
do you allow those who are entering
to go in.
14 [1]"Woe to you, scribes and Pharisees, hypocrites! [a]For you devour widows' houses, and for a pretense make
long prayers. Therefore you will receive greater condemnation.
15 "Woe to you, scribes and Pharisees,
hypocrites! For you travel land and sea
to win one proselyte, and when he is
won, you make him twice as much a
son of [1]hell as yourselves.
16 "Woe to you, [a]blind guides, who
say, [b]'Whoever swears by the temple,
it is nothing; but whoever swears by
the gold of the temple, he is obliged
to perform it.'
17 "Fools and blind! For which is
greater, the gold [a]or the temple that
[1]sanctifies the gold?
18 "And, 'Whoever swears by the altar, it is nothing; but whoever swears
by the gift that is on it, he is obliged
to perform it.'
19 "Fools and blind! For which is
greater, the gift [a]or the altar that sanctifies the gift?
20 "Therefore he who [1]swears by the
altar, swears by it and by all things on
it.
21 "He who swears by the temple,
swears by it and by [a]Him who [1]dwells
in it.
22 "And he who swears by heaven,
swears by [a]the throne of God and by
Him who sits on it.
23 "Woe to you, scribes and Pharisees,
hypocrites! [a]For you pay tithe of mint
and anise and cummin, and [b]have neglected the weightier *matters* of the

13 *See WW at Matt. 6:2.
14 [a]Mark 12:40 [1]NU omits v. 14.
15 [1]Gr. *Gehenna*
16 [a]Matt. 15:14; 23:24 [b][Matt. 5:33, 34]
17 [a]Ex. 30:29 [1]NU *sanctified*
19 [a]Ex. 29:37
20 [1]Swears an oath
21 [a]1 Kin. 8:13 [1]M *dwelt*
22 [a]Matt. 5:34
23 [a]Luke 11:42; 18:12 [b][Hos. 6:6]
25 [a]Luke 11:39 [1]M *unrighteousness*
27 [a]Acts 23:3
28 *See WW at Gal. 2:13.
29 [a]Luke 11:47, 48 [1]*decorate* *See WW at Matt. 25:7.
31 [a][Acts 7:51, 52]
32 [a][1 Thess. 2:16]
33 [a]Matt. 3:7; 12:34 [1]*offspring*
34 [a]Luke 11:49 [b]Acts 7:54–60; 22:19 [c]2 Cor. 11:24, 25

law: justice and mercy and faith. These
you ought to have done, without leaving the others undone.
24 "Blind guides, who strain out a gnat
and swallow a camel!
25 "Woe to you, scribes and Pharisees,
hypocrites! [a]For you cleanse the outside of the cup and dish, but inside
they are full of extortion and [1]self-
indulgence.
26 "Blind Pharisee, first cleanse the inside of the cup and dish, that the outside of them may be clean also.
27 "Woe to you, scribes and Pharisees,
hypocrites! [a]For you are like whitewashed tombs which indeed appear
beautiful outwardly, but inside are full
of dead *men's* bones and all uncleanness.
28 "Even so you also outwardly appear
righteous to men, but inside you are
full of *hypocrisy and lawlessness.
29 [a]"Woe to you, scribes and Pharisees, hypocrites! Because you build the
tombs of the prophets and [1]adorn* the
monuments of the righteous,
30 "and say, 'If we had lived in the
days of our fathers, we would not have
been partakers with them in the blood
of the prophets.'
31 "Therefore you are witnesses
against yourselves that [a]you are
sons of those who murdered the prophets.
32 [a]"Fill up, then, the measure of your
fathers' *guilt.*
33 "Serpents, [a]brood[1] of vipers! How
can you escape the condemnation of
hell?
34 [a]"Therefore, indeed, I send you
prophets, wise men, and scribes:
[b]*some* of them you will kill and crucify,
and [c]*some* of them you will scourge

---

denunciations in charging the Pharisees with specific examples of hypocrisy.

23:13 Not only did they themselves refuse the truth, but by their legalism they erected barriers before those who were seeking the truth.

23:14 While professing righteousness, they were unjust in conduct.

23:15 They were zealous missionaries of evil.

23:16–22 They were habitual liars, betraying their moral stupidity by having developed an elaborately absurd system of taking oaths that were binding and nonbinding.

23:23 They were flagrantly inconsistent, having lost all sense of proportion in the importance of spiritual matters. Scrupulously attentive to external things of the most trivial kind, such as tithing small seeds and plants, they forgot the major principles of morality. **Ought to have done** is significant in that Jesus affirms the moral rectitude that His disciples practice tithing, not as a law but as an accepted discipline.

23:24 Jesus uses a ludicrous hyperbole to illustrate the spiritual blindness, which allowed them to see trivial matters while overlooking gigantic items. **Strain:** Strainers were used in the mouths of decanters to remove foreign matter and to avoid ritual impurity that one might inadvertently consume.

23:25, 26 They paid detailed attention to matters pertaining to ceremonial cleansing, while ignoring God's demand for inner holiness. See notes on Mark 7:1–5.

23:27, 28 Outwardly, they appeared to be righteous, but inwardly they were morally defiled.

23:27 Whitewashed tombs: The language is strong. Whitewashing of tombs is still done in Palestine today. It served to identify tombs so that one might not accidentally touch the tomb and incur ritual defilement.

23:29–33 They were self-deceived, falsely claiming to surpass their forefathers in righteousness. Even though they built monuments to prophets whom their fathers murdered, they themselves were plotting to kill the Son of God. Therefore, they will suffer the same condemnation.

23:34–36 Jesus gives a stern warning of judgment upon the nation. The prophecy of Jesus came to pass with the destruction of Jerusalem in A.D. 70. All of the righteous blood shed, from the first victim (**Abel,** Gen. 4:8) to the last (**Zechariah,** 2 Chr. 24:20–22), will be required of Israel.

in your synagogues and persecute
from city to city,
35 [a]"that on you may come all the righteous blood shed on the earth, [b]from
the blood of righteous Abel to [c]the
blood of Zechariah, son of Berechiah,
whom you murdered between the temple and the altar.
36 "Assuredly, I say to you, all these
things will come upon this generation.

Jesus Laments over Jerusalem

37 [a]"O Jerusalem, Jerusalem, the one
who kills the prophets [b]and stones
those who are sent to her! How often
[c]I wanted to gather your children together, as a hen gathers her chicks
[d]under *her* wings, but you were not
willing!
38 "See! Your house is left to you desolate;
39 "for I say to you, you shall see Me
no more till you say, [a]*'Blessed* is*
He who comes in the name of the
LORD!' "

Jesus Predicts the Destruction of the Temple

24 Then [a]Jesus went out and departed from the temple, and His
disciples came up to show Him the
buildings of the temple.
2 And Jesus said to them, "Do you
not see all these things? Assuredly, I
say to you, [a]not *one* stone shall be left
here upon another, that shall not be
thrown down."

The Signs of the Times and the End of the Age

3 Now as He sat on the Mount of Olives, [a]the disciples came to Him privately, saying, [b]"Tell us, when will
these things be? And what *will be* the
sign of Your *coming, and of the end
of the age?"
4 And Jesus answered and said to
them: [a]"Take heed that no one deceives you.
5 "For [a]many will come in My name,
saying, 'I am the Christ,' [b]and will deceive many.
6 "And you will hear of [a]wars and rumors of wars. See that you are not troubled; for [1]all *these things* must come
to pass, but the end is not yet.
7 "For [a]nation will rise against nation, and kingdom against kingdom.
And there will be [b]famines, [1]pesti-
lences, and earthquakes in various
places.
8 "All these *are* the beginning of sorrows.
9 [a]"Then they will deliver you up to
tribulation and kill you, and you will
be hated by all nations for My name's
sake.
10 "And then many will be offended,
will betray one another, and will hate
one another.
11 "Then [a]many false prophets will
rise up and [b]deceive many.
12 "And because lawlessness will
abound, the *love of many will grow
[a]cold.
13 [a]"But he who **endures** to the end
shall be saved.
14 "And this [a]gospel of the kingdom
[b]will be preached in all the world as a
*witness to all the nations, and then the
end will come.

35 [a]Rev. 18:24 [b]Gen. 4:8 [c]2 Chr. 24:20, 21
37 [a]Luke 13:34, 35 [b]2 Chr. 24:20, 21; 36:15, 16 [c]Deut. 32:11, 12 [d]Ps. 17:8; 91:4
39 [a]Ps. 118:26 *See WW at Luke 6:28.

CHAPTER 24

1 [a]Mark 13:1
2 [a]Luke 19:44
3 [a]Mark 13:3 [b][1 Thess. 5:1–3] *See WW at 1 Cor. 15:23.
4 [a][Col. 2:8, 18]
5 [a]John 5:43 [b]Matt. 24:11
6 [a][Rev. 6:2–4] [1]NU omits *all*
7 [a]Hag. 2:22 [b]Rev. 6:5, 6 [1]NU omits *pestilences*
9 [a]Matt. 10:17
11 [a]2 Pet. 2:1 [b][1 Tim. 4:1]
12 [a][2 Thess. 2:3] *See WW at Rom. 5:5.
13 [a]Matt. 10:22
14 [a]Matt. 4:23 [b]Rom. 10:18 *See WW at Rev. 15:5.

WORD WEALTH

24:13 endures, *hupomeno* (hoop-ahm-*en*-oh); Strong's *#5278:* To hold one's ground in conflict, bear up against adversity, hold out under stress, stand firm, persevere under pressure, wait calmly and courageously. It is not passive resignation to fate and mere patience, but the active, energetic resistance to defeat that allows calm and brave endurance.

23:38 They have rejected the King, and so He leaves them to their own desires. (See Jer. 12:7; 22:5; Ezek. 10:18, 19; 11:22, 23.) All that will remain to them will be an empty system of religion, without even its temple and sacrifices.
23:39 Jesus voices a note of hope as He looks toward His glorious return, when He will be recognized as King (see Phil. 2:10, 11).
24:1–51 In His private teaching to the disciples on the Mount of Olives, Jesus responded to three questions, concerning 1) the destruction of the temple, 2) His Second Coming, and 3) the End. These topics are interwoven and sometimes it is difficult to determine which event is being described. This difficulty is partially resolved with the realization that most prophecy is capable of both a near and a remote fulfillment. Jesus uses the tragic events surrounding the destruction of Jerusalem as a picture of conditions preceding His own return. One should bear this in mind throughout the chapter.
24:4–14 In warning the disciples against false signs, Jesus sketches the prevailing conditions of their present age down to the very end and states their continuing task. There will be religious deception, social and political upheavals, natural calamities, disloyalty, and persecution—all of which are precursors of the end times. In the midst of the difficulties, the Lord's followers are to persevere in spreading the gospel.
24:8 Beginning of sorrows: The term means "labor pains," which were expected to precede the end, marking the transition from this age to the Age to Come. The severe labor pains, followed by delivery and fulfillment, are also a pledge of the end and of the joy at the time of "delivery."

KINGDOM DYNAMICS

24:14 The Gospel and "The End," WORLD EVANGELISM. In these words, Jesus linked the worldwide witness of the gospel to His Second Coming. The text contains: 1) an anticipation of ministry—"This gospel . . . will be preached," involving the declaration of the kingdom message of grace for forgiveness and power for deliverance; 2) an arena of effort—"to all the nations," including every group of people; 3) a certainty of "signs" for a witness (see Mark 16:15–20), insuring "proof" of Christ's resurrection life and present power to save and heal. How pointedly Jesus' words speak of the Father's desire toward the nations of the world: God cares for all people; Jesus died for every person; and the Word of God is for every nation—before "the end."

(Matt. 13:37, 38/Matt. 28:18–20) G.C.

The Great Tribulation

15 [a]"Therefore when you see the
[b]*'abomination of desolation,'* spoken
of by Daniel the prophet, standing in
the holy place" [c](whoever reads, let
him understand),
16 "then let those who are in Judea flee
to the mountains.
17 "Let him who is on the housetop not
go down to take anything out of his
house.
18 "And let him who is in the field not
go back to get his clothes.
19 "But [a]woe to those who are pregnant
and to those who are nursing babies
in those days!
20 "And pray that your flight may not
be in winter or on the Sabbath.
21 "For [a]then there will be great tribulation,
such as has not been since the
beginning of the world until this time,
no, nor ever shall be.
22 "And unless those days were shortened,
no flesh would be saved; [a]but for
the [1]elect's sake those days will be
shortened.
23 [a]"Then if anyone says to you,
'Look, here *is* the Christ!' or 'There!'
do not believe *it.*
24 "For [a]false christs and false prophets
will rise and show great signs and
*wonders to deceive, [b]if possible, even
the elect.
25 "See, I have told you beforehand.
26 "Therefore if they say to you, 'Look,
He is in the desert!' do not go out; *or*
'Look, *He is* in the inner rooms!' do not
believe *it.*
27 [a]"For as the lightning comes from
the east and flashes to the west, so also
will the coming of the Son of Man be.
28 [a]"For wherever the carcass is, there
the eagles will be gathered together.

The Coming of the Son of Man

29 [a]"Immediately after the tribulation
of those days [b]the sun will be darkened,
and the moon will not give its
light; the stars will fall from heaven,
and the powers of the heavens will be
shaken.
30 [a]"Then the sign of the Son of Man
will appear in heaven, [b]and then all the
tribes of the earth will mourn, and they
will see the Son of Man coming on the
clouds of heaven with power and great
glory.
31 [a]"And He will send His angels with
a great sound of a trumpet, and they
will gather together His [1]elect from the
four winds, from one end of heaven to
the other.

The Parable of the Fig Tree

32 "Now learn [a]this parable from the
fig tree: When its branch has already
become tender and puts forth leaves,
you know that summer *is* near.

15 [a]Mark 13:14; Luke 21:20; [John 11:48]; Acts 6:13; 21:28 [b]Dan. 9:27; 11:31; 12:11 [c]Dan. 9:23 **19** [a]Luke 23:29 **21** [a]Dan. 9:26 **22** [a]Is. 65:8, 9; [Zech. 14:2] [1]*chosen ones* **23** [a]Mark 13:21; Luke 17:23 **24** [a]Deut. 13:1; John 4:48; [2 Thess. 2:9]; Rev. 13:13 [b][John 6:37; Rom. 8:28; 2 Tim. 2:19] *See WW at Acts 15:12. **27** [a]Luke 17:24 **28** [a]Job 39:30; Ezek. 39:17; Hab. 1:8; Luke 17:37 **29** [a][Dan. 7:11] [b]Is. 13:10; 24:23; Ezek. 32:7; Joel 2:10, 31; 3:15; Amos 5:20; 8:9; Zeph. 1:15; Matt. 24:29–35; Acts 2:20; Rev. 6:12–17; 8:12 **30** [a][Dan. 7:13, 14; Matt. 16:27; 24:3, 37, 39] [b]Zech. 12:12 **31** [a]Ex. 19:16; Deut. 30:4; Is. 27:13; Zech. 9:14; [1 Cor. 15:52; 1 Thess. 4:16]; Heb. 12:19; Rev. 8:2; 11:15 [1]*chosen ones* **32** [a]Luke 21:29

24:15–28 Jesus foretells the destruction of Jerusalem, a catastrophe that pictures the tribulation preceding His return.

24:15 The **abomination of desolation,** prophesied in Dan. (9:27; 11:31; 12:11), was applied by the author of the apocryphal book 1 Maccabees (I:54, 59; 6:7) to the desecration of the temple in 168 B.C. by the Syrian ruler Antiochus Epiphanes. However, Jesus views the prophecy as referring to another profanation—the arrival of the Roman army, which besieged Jerusalem and destroyed the temple in A.D. 70. That event foreshadows the conditions connected with Christ's return, so the prophecy awaits ultimate fulfillment in a manner not clearly specified in Scripture. See note on Dan. 9:27 for an alternate view of this text.

24:16–20 Jesus gives sound practical advice to flee the city before escape is impossible. Christians heeded the warning and fled to the small town of Pella, near the Sea of Galilee.

24:21, 22 The Jewish historian Josephus, who witnessed the destruction of Jerusalem, gives a vivid account of the city's fall, reporting that more than 1,000,000 Jews perished in one day.

24:23–27 True followers of Christ will not be deceived by bogus deliverers, but will await the coming of the Lord from heaven.

24:28 Jesus here uses birds of prey (**eagles** or vultures) gathering over **the carcass** to describe the destruction that will surround Jerusalem's fall and events of the final judgment. This is most likely a proverbial statement.

24:29–31 Jesus uses vivid, prophetic, and symbolic language to describe His glorious return.

24:32–51 The teachings of Jesus should create a spirit of watchfulness among His followers.

24:32–35 As the budding of trees signifies the coming of summer, the signs described by Jesus will give warning of His coming. Even the present generation would witness the destruction of Jerusalem (v. 34), which was a type of events connected with Christ's return.

33 "So you also, when you see all these
things, know [a]that [1]it is near—at the
doors!
34 "Assuredly, I say to you, [a]this generation will by no means pass away till
all these things take place.
35 [a]"Heaven and earth will pass away,
but My *words will by no means pass
away.

No One Knows the Day or Hour

36 [a]"But of that day and hour no one
knows, not even the angels of [1]heaven,
[b]but My Father only.
37 "But as the days of Noah *were*, so
also will the coming of the Son of Man
be.
38 [a]"For as in the days before the
flood, they were eating and drinking,
marrying and giving in marriage, until
the day that Noah entered the ark,
39 "and did not know until the flood
came and took them all away, so also
will the coming of the Son of Man
be.
40 [a]"Then two *men* will be in the field:
one will be taken and the other left.
41 "Two *women will be* grinding at the
mill: one will be taken and the other
left.
42 [a]"Watch therefore, for you do not
know what [1]hour your Lord is coming.

KINGDOM DYNAMICS

24:42 10. When Is Jesus Christ Coming Again?, SPIRITUAL ANSWERS. For the answer to this and other probing questions about God and the power life in His kingdom, see the study article "Spiritual Answers to Hard Questions," which begins on page 1996. P.R.

43 [a]"But know this, that if the master
of the house had known what [1]hour
the thief would come, he would have
watched and not allowed his house to
be broken into.
44 [a]"Therefore you also be ready, for
the Son of Man is coming at an hour
you do not expect.

33 [a][James 5:9; Rev. 3:20] [1]Or *He*
34 [a][Matt. 10:23; 16:28; 23:36]
35 [a]Ps. 102:25, 26; Is. 51:6; Mark 13:31; Luke 21:33; [1 Pet. 1:23–25; 2 Pet. 3:10] *See WW at Acts 19:20.
36 [a]Mark 13:32; Acts 1:7; 1 Thess. 5:2; 2 Pet. 3:10 [b]Zech. 14:7 [1]NU adds *nor the Son*
38 [a][Gen. 6:3–5]; Luke 17:26; [1 Pet. 3:20]
40 [a]Luke 17:34
42 [a]Matt. 25:13; Luke 21:36; 1 Thess. 5:6 [1]NU *day*
43 [a]Luke 12:39; 1 Thess. 5:2; Rev. 3:3 [1]Lit. *watch of the night*
44 [a]Luke 12:35–40; [1 Thess. 5:6]
45 [a]Luke 12:42–46; [Acts 20:28] [1]*at the right time*
46 [a]Rev. 16:15 *See WW at Matt. 5:3.
47 [a]Matt. 25:21, 23; Luke 22:29
48 [a][2 Pet. 3:4–9] [1]NU omits *his coming*
50 [a]Mark 13:32
51 [a]Matt. 8:12; 25:30 *See WW at Matt. 6:2.

CHAPTER 25

1 [a][Eph. 5:29, 30; Rev. 19:7; 21:2, 9]
2 [a]Matt. 13:47; 22:10
5 [a]1 Thess. 5:6
6 [a][Matt. 24:31; 1 Thess. 4:16] [1]NU omits *is coming*
7 [a]Luke 12:35

The Faithful Servant and the Evil Servant

45 [a]"Who then is a faithful and wise
servant, whom his master made ruler
over his household, to give them food
[1]in due season?
46 [a]"Blessed* *is* that servant whom his
master, when he comes, will find so doing.
47 "Assuredly, I say to you that
[a]he will make him ruler over all his
goods.
48 "But if that evil servant says in his
heart, 'My master [a]is delaying [1]his
coming,'
49 "and begins to beat *his* fellow servants, and to eat and drink with the
drunkards,
50 "the master of that servant will
come on a day when he is not looking
for *him* and at an hour that he is
[a]not aware of,
51 "and will cut him in two and appoint *him* his portion with the *hypocrites. [a]There shall be weeping and
gnashing of teeth.

The Parable of the Wise and Foolish Virgins

25 "Then the kingdom of heaven
shall be likened to ten virgins
who took their lamps and went out to
meet [a]the bridegroom.
2 [a]"Now five of them were wise, and
five *were* foolish.
3 "Those who *were* foolish took their
lamps and took no oil with them,
4 "but the wise took oil in their vessels with their lamps.
5 "But while the bridegroom was delayed, [a]they all slumbered and slept.
6 "And at midnight [a]a cry was *heard*:
'Behold, the bridegroom [1]is coming; go
out to meet him!'
7 "Then all those virgins arose and
[a]**trimmed** their lamps.

WORD WEALTH

25:7 trimmed, *kosmeo* (kos-*meh*-oh); Strong's *#2885:* Compare "cosmetic." To (*cont. on next page*)

24:36 If Jesus in His incarnate state is ignorant of the time of the Second Coming, it is futile for others to speculate.
24:37–44 In a time of indifference and carelessness the Lord will appear with startling suddenness. Some will be taken to meet Him, while others will be left. The thought of that event urges watchfulness and preparedness upon us.
24:45–51 While they await the Lord's return, His followers are to be faithful and responsible in their service.
25:1–13 Jesus teaches the necessity of preparedness for His return. He compares the Second Coming to a joyful wedding procession in which the unprepared cannot participate.
25:4 The wisdom of the five virgins consists in their taking a supply of oil in vessels, in addition to the oil already in their lamps. Thereby they are prepared for the unexpected delay of the bridegroom (v. 5).
25:5 There is an implicit association of the bridegroom with Christ as well as the bridegroom's delay, that is, the delay of the Parousia (arrival and presence) of Jesus.

(*cont. from preceding page*)
beautify, arrange, decorate, furnish, embellish, adorn, put in order. Here is a picture of revival before the Second Coming of Christ.

8 "And the foolish said to the wise,
'Give us *some* of your oil, for our lamps
are going out.'
9 "But the wise answered, saying,
'*No,* lest there should not be enough
for us and you; but go rather to those
who sell, and buy for yourselves.'
10 "And while they went to buy, the
bridegroom came, and those who were
ready went in with him to the wedding;
and [a]the door was shut.
11 "Afterward the other virgins came
also, saying, [a]'Lord, Lord, open to us!'
12 "But he answered and said, 'Assuredly, I say to you, [a]I do not know
you.'
13 [a]"Watch therefore, for you [b]know
neither the day nor the hour [1]in which
the Son of Man is coming.

KINGDOM DYNAMICS

25:13 Only the Father Knows When Christ Will Return, MESSIAH'S COMING. This is a critical verse to remember whenever one considers the Second Coming. Throughout history believers have mistakenly tried to determine when the Lord will return, and an ignorance of the history of this folly has led some in every decade to presume to pinpoint the time of Jesus' coming. But here, as well as in 24:36 and Mark 13:32, Jesus tells us directly that no one but the Father knows the time of His return. People have interpreted the expression "hour or day" to mean that we may discover the month or year, but this is incorrect. We cannot be sure that it will be in any particular year, decade, or even in our lifetime.

However, Jesus began His sentence with the command, "Watch." The challenge the Lord gives us is to be constantly and eagerly waiting for His return. Therefore, our duty is twofold: to prepare ourselves for His coming, so that the Lord will receive a bride without "spot or wrinkle" (Eph. 5:27), and to "do business" until He returns, so that the kingdom of God is preserved and extended on the Earth (Luke 19:11–27). Let us be about the Father's business, live in expectation of the Master's return, and be done with all idle speculation or superstitious date-setting regarding the time of His coming.

(1 Thess. 4:15–18/Rev. 22:20) J.H.

10 [a][Matt. 7:21]; Luke 13:25
11 [a][Matt. 7:21–23; Luke 13:25–30]
12 [a][Ps. 5:5; Hab. 1:13; John 9:31]
13 [a]Mark 13:35; [Luke 21:36]; 1 Thess. 5:6 [b]Matt. 24:36, 42 [1]NU omits the rest of v. 13.

The Parable of the Talents

14 [a]"For *the kingdom of heaven is*
[b]like a man traveling to a far country,
who called his own servants and delivered his goods to them.

KINGDOM DYNAMICS

25:14–30 32. What Kingdom Law Underlies All Personal and Corporate Development?, SPIRITUAL ANSWERS. For the answer to this and other probing questions about God and the power life in His kingdom, see the study article "Spiritual Answers to Hard Questions," which begins on page 1996. P.R.

15 "And to one he gave five talents, to
another two, and to another one, [a]to
each according to his own ability; and
immediately he went on a journey.
16 "Then he who had received the five
talents went and traded with them, and
made another five talents.
17 "And likewise he who *had received*
two gained two more also.
18 "But he who had received one went
and dug in the ground, and hid his
lord's money.
19 "After a long time the lord of those
servants came and settled accounts
with them.
20 "So he who had received five talents came and brought five other talents, saying, 'Lord, you delivered to me
five talents; look, I have gained five
more talents besides them.'
21 "His lord said to him, 'Well *done,*
good and faithful servant; you were
[a]faithful over a few things, [b]I will make
you ruler over many things. Enter into
[c]the joy of your lord.'
22 "He also who had received two talents came and said, 'Lord, you delivered to me two talents; look, I have
gained two more talents besides them.'
23 "His lord said to him, [a]'Well *done,*
good and faithful servant; you have

14 [a]Luke 19:12–27 [b]Matt. 21:33
15 [a][Rom. 12:6; 1 Cor. 12:7, 11, 29; Eph. 4:11]
21 [a][Luke 16:10; 1 Cor. 4:2; 2 Tim. 4:7, 8] [b][Matt. 24:47; 25:34, 46; Luke 12:44; 22:29, 30; Rev. 3:21; 21:7] [c][2 Tim. 2:12; Heb. 12:2; 1 Pet. 1:8]
23 [a]Matt. 24:45, 47; 25:21

25:9 The lack of benevolence on the part of the five wise virgins is part of the parable proper, and need not be pressed into allegorical significance.
25:12 The message is, "Too late!"
25:13 The point of the parable is found here. In view of the Parousia's delay (24:48; 25:5), be prepared and watch since **you know neither the day nor the hour.**
25:14–30 Watchfulness does not mean idleness, but a faithful discharge of one's responsibilities. The wise use of gifts and abilities entrusted to us results in greater opportunities, while their neglect results not only in the loss of more opportunities, but of that which was entrusted to us.
25:15 A talent was worth about $1,000.

been faithful over a few things, I will
make you ruler over many things. Enter into [b]the joy of your lord.'
24 "Then he who had received the one
talent came and said, 'Lord, I knew you
to be a hard man, reaping where you
have not sown, and gathering where
you have not scattered seed.
25 'And I was afraid, and went and hid
your talent in the ground. Look, *there*
you have *what is* yours.'
26 "But his lord answered and said to
him, 'You [a]wicked and lazy servant,
you knew that I reap where I have not
sown, and gather where I have not
scattered seed.
27 'So you ought to have deposited my
money with the bankers, and at my
coming I would have received back
my own with interest.
28 'Therefore take the talent from him,
and give *it* to him who has ten talents.
29 [a]'For to everyone who has, more
will be given, and he will **have abundance;** but from him who does not
have, even what he has will be taken
away.

WORD WEALTH

25:29 have abundance, *perisseuo* (per-is-*syoo*-oh); Strong's *#4052:* To superabound, have in excess, greatly surpass, excel. The word shows the generosity of God's grace, giving assurance that faithful use of one's talents and gifts sets the stage for one's own advancement.

30 'And cast the unprofitable servant
[a]into the outer darkness. [b]There will
be weeping and [c]gnashing of teeth.'

The Son of Man Will Judge the Nations

31 [a]"When the Son of Man comes in
His glory, and all the [1]holy angels with
Him, then He will sit on the throne of
His glory.
32 [a]"All the nations will be gathered
before Him, and [b]He will separate
them one from another, as a *shepherd
divides *his* sheep from the goats.
33 "And He will set the [a]sheep on His
right hand, but the goats on the left.
34 "Then the King will say to those on
His right hand, 'Come, you blessed of
My Father, [a]inherit the kingdom
[b]prepared for you from the foundation
of the world:
35 [a]'for I was hungry and you gave Me
food; I was thirsty and you gave Me
drink; [b]I was a stranger and you took
Me in;
36 'I *was* [a]naked and you clothed Me;
I was sick and you visited Me; [b]I was
in prison and you came to Me.'
37 "Then the righteous will answer
Him, saying, 'Lord, when did we see
You hungry and feed *You,* or thirsty
and give *You* drink?
38 'When did we see You a stranger
and take *You* in, or naked and clothe
You?
39 'Or when did we see You sick, or
in prison, and come to You?'
40 "And the King will answer and say
to them, 'Assuredly, I say to you,
[a]inasmuch as you did *it* to one of the
least of these My brethren, you did *it*
to Me.'

23 [b][Ps. 16:11; John 15:10, 11] **26** [a]Matt. 18:32; Luke 19:22 **29** [a]Matt. 13:12; Mark 4:25; Luke 8:18; [John 15:2] **30** [a]Matt. 8:12; 22:13; [Luke 13:28] [b]Matt. 7:23; 8:12; 24:51 [c]Ps. 112:10 **31** [a][Zech. 14:5]; Matt. 16:27; Mark 8:38; Acts 1:11; [1 Thess. 4:16]; 2 Thess. 1:7; [Jude 14]; Rev. 1:7 [1]NU omits *holy* **32** [a][Rom. 14:10; 2 Cor. 5:10; Rev. 20:12] [b]Ezek. 20:38 *See WW at John 10:2. **33** [a]Ps. 79:13; 100:3; [John 10:11, 27, 28] **34** [a][Rom. 8:17; 1 Pet. 1:4, 9; Rev. 21:7] [b]Matt. 20:23; Mark 10:40; 1 Cor. 2:9; Heb. 11:16 **35** [a]Is. 58:7; Ezek. 18:7, 16; [James 1:27; 2:15, 16] [b]Job 31:32; [Heb. 13:2]; 3 John 5 **36** [a]Is. 58:7; Ezek. 18:7, 16; [James 2:15, 16] [b]2 Tim. 1:16 **40** [a]Prov. 14:31; Matt. 10:42; Mark 9:41; Heb. 6:10

KINGDOM DYNAMICS

25:34–40 All of Our Giving Is to Be as to God Our Source, SEED FAITH. Whenever you and I give, or plant our seeds of faith, we are doing it for Jesus. The person we feed becomes as Jesus to us. The person we visit in prison or in the sickbed becomes as Jesus to us. How may we know our Lord? We know Him in doing His works and in doing them as much to Him as for Him. We know Him in putting our arms around those who are desperate or alone. He said that when we do this we are putting our arms around Him—Jesus Christ, our blessed Savior.

Although our giving is to take on very real and tangible forms as we reach out to people, as we give through individuals and churches and ministries to meet great needs around the world, the focus of our faith is to be on Jesus and Jesus alone. He is God—and He is our Source. He is the object of our worship and our love. He alone is worthy of our lives, and He alone can supply our needs.

We give to others, but let us keep our vision clear. We look past them, with our faith directed to God and offered as a service of love for Him.

(Mark 11:22–24/Mark 4:1–20) O.R.

25:26 The reward of further responsibility (first two servants) is contrasted by judgment upon the inactive and lazy servant. In view of the day of reckoning, faithful discharge of one's responsibilities is required.

25:30 This need not be concluded as referring to the loss of one's justification, but may instead portray the forfeiting of one's reward for committed service in the kingdom, a loss of joy, with **weeping and gnashing** one's **teeth,** reflecting the remorse for lost opportunity.

25:31–46 The return of the Lord will usher in a judgment, which will divide people. The judgment will be based on moral character, and the character is revealed by charitable deeds or the lack of them. Outward evidence demonstrates inner righteousness or unrighteousness. Good works do not produce good character; good character produces good works.

KINGDOM DYNAMICS

25:37–40 Christ Mandates Social Concern, HUMAN WORTH. Christ mandates social consciousness and concern (vv. 31–46). Here are the principles by which men will be judged: their treatment of those who are hungry, homeless, poor, diseased, and imprisoned. Social concern cannot biblically be divorced from the Christian walk. "He who has pity on the poor lends to the LORD, and He will pay back what he has given" (Prov. 19:17). Jesus equates our treatment of those who are destitute or distressed with our treatment of Himself. What we do for them, we do for Him. We must not allow the Christian walk to be only a spiritual enterprise, unrelated to the service of humanity. When we fail to care for social need, we fail to place proper value on others, decreasing our own merit in the eyes of the Lord and inviting His condemnation (see James 2:14–17).

(John 13:34, 35/Rom. 12:3–5) C.B.

41 "Then He will also say to those
on the left hand, [a]'Depart from Me,
you cursed, [b]into the everlasting
fire prepared for [c]the devil and his
angels:
42 'for I was hungry and you gave Me
no food; I was thirsty and you gave Me
no drink;
43 'I was a stranger and you did not
take Me in, naked and you did not
clothe Me, sick and in prison and you
did not visit Me.'
44 "Then they also will answer [1]Him,
saying, 'Lord, when did we see You
hungry or thirsty or a stranger or
naked or sick or in prison, and did not
minister to You?'
45 "Then He will answer them, saying,
'Assuredly, I say to you, [a]inasmuch
as you did not do *it* to one of
the least of these, you did not do *it* to
Me.'
46 "And [a]these will go away into everlasting
punishment, but the righteous
into eternal life."

41 [a]Ps. 6:8; Matt. 7:23; Luke 13:27 [b]Matt. 13:40, 42 [c][2 Pet. 2:4]; Jude 6
44 [1]NU, M omit *Him*
45 [a]Prov. 14:31; Zech. 2:8; Acts 9:5
46 [a][Dan. 12:2; John 5:29; Acts 24:15; Rom. 2:7]

CHAPTER 26

2 [a]Matt. 27:35; Mark 14:1, 2; Luke 22:1, 2; John 13:1; 19:18
3 [a]Ps. 2:2; John 11:47; Acts 4:25 [1]NU omits *the scribes*
4 [a]John 11:47; Acts 4:25–28 [1]*deception*
5 [a]Matt. 21:26
6 [a]Matt. 8:2; Mark 14:3–9; Luke 7:37–39; John 11:1, 2; 12:1–8
8 [a]John 12:4
11 [a][Deut. 15:11; Mark 14:7]; John 12:8 [b][Matt. 18:20; 28:20; John 13:33; 14:19; 16:5, 28; 17:11]
12 [a]Matt. 27:60; Luke 23:53; John 19:38–42
14 [a]Mark 14:10, 11; Luke 22:3–6; John 13:2, 30 [b]Matt. 10:4

The Plot to Kill Jesus

26 Now it came to pass, when Jesus had finished all these sayings, *that* He said to His disciples,
2 [a]"You know that after two days is
the Passover, and the Son of Man will
be delivered up to be crucified."
3 [a]Then the chief priests, [1]the scribes,
and the elders of the people assembled
at the palace of the high priest, who
was called Caiaphas,
4 and [a]plotted to take Jesus by
[1]trickery and kill *Him.*
5 But they said, "Not during the feast,
lest there be an uproar among the
[a]people."

The Anointing at Bethany

6 And when Jesus was in [a]Bethany
at the house of Simon the leper,
7 a woman came to Him having an
alabaster flask of very costly fragrant
oil, and she poured *it* on His head as
He sat *at the table.*
8 [a]But when His disciples saw *it,* they
were indignant, saying, "Why this
waste?
9 "For this fragrant oil might have
been sold for much and given to *the*
poor."
10 But when Jesus was aware of *it,* He
said to them, "Why do you trouble the
woman? For she has done a good work
for Me.
11 [a]"For you have the poor with you
always, but [b]Me you do not have always.
12 "For in pouring this fragrant oil on
My body, she did *it* for My [a]burial.
13 "Assuredly, I say to you, wherever
this gospel is preached in the whole
world, what this woman has done will
also be told as a memorial to her."

Judas Agrees to Betray Jesus

14 [a]Then one of the twelve, called
[b]Judas Iscariot, went to the chief
priests

26:1, 2 For six months Jesus had been announcing to His disciples His impending death. Now He names the precise date. While those who were involved in the Crucifixion are not guiltless, He was in control of events throughout. He would be slain as the sacrificial **Passover** lamb, voluntarily fulfilling all of the OT types and prophecies.
26:3–5 Hundreds of thousands of pilgrims thronged Jerusalem during Passover, and the religious leaders did not want to risk **an uproar** that might bring about intervention by the Romans.
26:7 John identifies the **woman** as Mary of Bethany (John 12:3).
26:10 Expense is no consideration in performing an act of devotion for a loved one soon to die.
26:11 The inference is, "It is appropriate to give to Me while I am still with you." Service that will have no other opportunity takes preference over perpetual duties.
26:12 Jesus was anointed by the Spirit for ministry (3:16); now He is anointed with costly oil for His burial.
26:13 Sacrifice for the sake of Jesus will have perpetual influence.
26:14–16 Matthew clearly reveals the motive of **Judas** to be greed; therefore, all attempts to soften the crime are useless.

15 and said, [a]"What are you willing to
give me if I deliver Him to you?" And
they counted out to him thirty pieces
of silver.
16 So from that time he sought opportunity to betray Him.

Jesus Celebrates Passover with His Disciples

17 [a]Now on the first *day of the Feast*
of Unleavened Bread the disciples
came to Jesus, saying to Him, "Where
do You want us to prepare for You to
eat the Passover?"
18 And He said, "Go into the city to a
certain man, and say to him, 'The
Teacher says, [a]"My time is at hand; I
will keep the Passover at your house
with My disciples." ' "
19 So the disciples did as Jesus had directed them; and they *prepared the
Passover.
20 [a]When evening had come, He sat
down with the twelve.
21 Now as they were eating, He said,
"Assuredly, I say to you, one of you
will [a]betray Me."
22 And they were exceedingly sorrowful, and each of them began to say to
Him, "Lord, is it I?"
23 He answered and said, [a]"He who
dipped *his* hand with Me in the dish
will betray Me.
24 "The Son of Man indeed goes just
[a]as it is written of Him, but [b]woe to
that man by whom the Son of Man is
betrayed! [c]It would have been good for
that man if he had not been born."
25 Then Judas, who was betraying
Him, answered and said, "Rabbi, is it
I?" He said to him, "You have said it."

Jesus Institutes the Lord's Supper

3 **26** [a]And as they were eating, [b]Jesus
took bread, [1]blessed and broke *it,* and
gave *it* to the disciples and said, "Take,
eat; [c]this is My body."

15 [a]Zech. 11:12
17 [a]Ex. 12:6, 18–20
18 [a]Luke 9:51
19 *See WW at Rev. 21:2.
20 [a]Mark 14:17–21
21 [a]John 6:70, 71; 13:21
23 [a]Ps. 41:9
24 [a]1 Cor. 15:3 [b]Luke 17:1 [c]John 17:12
26 [a]Mark 14:22–25 [b]1 Cor. 11:23–25 [c][1 Pet. 2:24] [1]M *gave thanks for*

27 Then He took the cup, and gave
thanks, and gave *it* to them, saying,
[a]"Drink from it, all of you.
28 "For [a]this is My *blood [b]of the
[1]new *covenant, which is shed [c]for
many for the [2]remission* of *sins.

KINGDOM DYNAMICS

26:28 God Sovereignly Inaugurates the New Covenant, THE BLOOD. Jesus used the occasion of the Passover meal to inaugurate the New Covenant. The symbolism of the Passover meal under the Old Covenant was about to be fully satisfied through Christ's crucifixion. In this historic moment, Jesus transformed the meaning of the elements of the Passover meal into New Covenant thought. The bread now represented His body, which would be given, and the cup His blood, which would be shed for the forgiveness of sins. The holy requirements of God and the Old Covenant were about to be forever satisfied. A new and living way into the presence and provision of God was being prepared through Christ, the Lamb of God. A new and eternal bond was being established by the blood of Jesus Christ. God was sovereignly inaugurating the new and ultimate covenant.
(Gen. 3:21/Rom. 3:25) C.S.

29 "But [a]I say to you, I will not drink
of this fruit of the vine from now on
[b]until that day when I drink it new with
you in My Father's kingdom."
30 [a]And when they had sung a hymn,
they went out to the Mount of Olives.

Jesus Predicts Peter's Denial

31 Then Jesus said to them, [a]"All of
you will [b]be [1]made to stumble because
of Me this night, for it is written:

[c]'I will strike the Shepherd,
And the sheep of the flock will be scattered.'

32 "But after I have been raised,
[a]I will go before you to Galilee."

27 [a]Mark 14:23
28 [a][Ex. 24:8] [b]Jer. 31:31 [c]Matt. 20:28 [1]NU omits *new* [2]*forgiveness* *See WW at 1 John 1:7. • See WW at Mark 14:24. • See WW at Heb. 9:22. • See WW at John 1:29.
29 [a]Mark 14:25 [b]Acts 10:41
30 [a]Mark 14:26–31
31 [a]John 16:32 [b][Matt. 11:6] [c]Zech. 13:7 [1]*caused to take offense at Me*
32 [a]Matt. 28:7, 10, 16

26:17–35 On Thursday evening Jesus observes the **Passover** meal with His disciples. The next day He would accomplish the redemption, which Passover foreshadowed; henceforth, the Lord's Supper would replace the Passover feast as a commemoration of an even greater deliverance.
26:17 **Prepare:** This is the key word for the paragraph. The Passover preparations are made as the disciples and Jesus are being prepared for the Passion.
26:21 Note that Jesus is not taken by surprise.
26:23 The custom of dipping bread into the same sauce bowl indicated trust and intimacy, which made the deed of Judas even more traitorous (see Ps. 41:9).
26:24 Betrayal was necessary for accomplishing God's purpose, but in no way did it lessen the guilt of the betrayer.
26:26–29 See section 3 of Truth-In-Action through the Synoptics at the end of Luke.
26:26–28 Judas was not present when Jesus instituted the Lord's Supper (see John 13:30). The bread and the wine are symbols to remind Christ's followers through the ages of His redemptive sacrifice. For the **new covenant,** see Jer. 31:31–33.
26:29 The Lord's Supper not only reminds participants of the redemptive death of Jesus; it anticipates His return, when the memorial supper will give way to the festivities of the marriage feast of the Bridegroom.
26:30 It was customary to conclude the Passover meal by singing the *Hallel,* a part of Ps. 115—118.
26:31 The stumbling would fulfill prophecy (see Zech. 13:7).
26:32 Matthew records the fulfillment of this prophecy in 28:9–20.

33 Peter answered and said to Him, "Even if all are [1]made to *stumble because of You, I will never be made to stumble."
34 Jesus said to him, [a]"Assuredly, I say to you that this night, before the rooster crows, you will deny Me three times."
35 Peter said to Him, "Even if I have to die with You, I will not deny You!" And so said all the disciples.

The Prayer in the Garden

36 [a]Then Jesus came with them to a place called Gethsemane, and said to the disciples, "Sit here while I go and pray over there."
37 And He took with Him Peter and [a]the two sons of Zebedee, and He began to be sorrowful and deeply distressed.
38 Then He said to them, [a]"My soul is exceedingly sorrowful, even to death. Stay here and watch with Me."

39 He went a little farther and fell on His face, and [a]prayed, saying, [b]"O My Father, if it is possible, [c]let this cup pass from Me; nevertheless, [d]not as I will, but as You *will*."
40 Then He came to the disciples and found them sleeping, and said to Peter, "What? Could you not watch with Me one hour?
41 [a]"Watch and pray, lest you enter into temptation. [b]The spirit indeed *is* willing, but the **flesh** *is* weak."

WORD WEALTH

26:41 flesh, *sarx (sarks);* Strong's *#4561:* In its literal sense, *sarx* refers to the substance of the body, whether of animals or persons (1 Cor. 15:39; 2 Cor. 12:7). In its idiomatic use, the word indicates the human race or personhood (Matt. 24:22; 1 Pet. 1:24). In an ethical and spiritual sense, *sarx* is the lower nature of a person, the seat and vehicle of sinful desires (Rom. 7:25; 8:4–9, Gal. 5:16, 17).

42 Again, a second time, He went away and prayed, saying, "O My Father, [1]if this cup *cannot pass away from Me unless I drink it, Your *will be done."
43 And He came and found them asleep again, for their eyes were heavy.
44 So He left them, went away again, and prayed the third time, saying the same words.
45 Then He came to His disciples and said to them, "Are *you* still sleeping and *resting? Behold, the hour [1]is at hand, and the Son of Man is being [a]betrayed into the hands of *sinners.
46 "Rise, let us be going. See, My betrayer is at hand."

Betrayal and Arrest in Gethsemane

47 And [a]while He was still speaking, behold, Judas, one of the twelve, with a great multitude with swords and clubs, came from the chief priests and elders of the people.
48 Now His betrayer had given them a sign, saying, "Whomever I kiss, He is the One; seize Him."
49 *Immediately he went up to Jesus and said, "Greetings, Rabbi!" [a]and kissed Him.
50 But Jesus said to him, [a]"Friend, why have you come?" Then they came and laid hands on Jesus and took Him.
51 And suddenly, [a]one of those *who were* with Jesus stretched out *his* hand and drew his sword, struck the servant of the high priest, and cut off his ear.
52 But Jesus said to him, "Put your sword in its place, [a]for all who take the sword will [1]perish by the sword.
53 "Or do you think that I cannot now pray to My Father, and He will provide Me with [a]more than twelve legions of angels?
54 "How then could the *Scriptures be fulfilled, [a]that it must happen thus?"

KINGDOM DYNAMICS

26:47–54; Luke 22:47–51; John 18:10, 11 Vulnerability, LEADER TRAITS. Being vulnerable as a leader means to stand totally open as a human being, hiding nothing and refusing to defend oneself. Few things elicit more of a response from peo-

33 [1]*caused to take offense at You* *See WW at Matt. 11:6.
34 [a]John 13:38
36 [a]Mark 14:32–35
37 [a]Matt. 4:21; 17:1
38 [a]John 12:27
39 [a][Heb. 5:7–9] [b]John 12:27 [c]Matt. 20:22 [d]John 5:30; 6:38
41 [a]Luke 22:40, 46 [b][Gal. 5:17]
42 [1]NU *if this may not pass away unless* *See WW at Jude 24. • See WW at Matt. 12:50.
45 [a]Matt. 17:22, 23; 20:18, 19 [1]*has drawn near* *See WW at Rev. 14:13. • See WW at James 5:20.
47 [a]Acts 1:16
49 [a]2 Sam. 20:9 *See WW at John 6:21.
50 [a]Ps. 41:9; 55:13
51 [a]John 18:10
52 [a]Rev. 13:10 [1]*M die*
53 [a]Dan. 7:10
54 [a]Is. 50:6; 53:2–11 *See WW at John 5:39.

26:35 All the others join Peter in affirming loyalty.
26:36 Gethsemane means "Oil Press." It was probably an enclosed olive orchard, which included a press for crushing oil from the olives.
26:37–46 The agony Jesus experienced was not occasioned by fear of physical death, but by the association of His death with sin (see 2 Cor. 5:21). His holy nature shrank from the thought. (For **cup**, see note on 20:22.)
26:39 See section 4 of Truth-In-Action through the Synoptics at the end of Luke.
26:44 Prayer sustained Him through all the events surrounding the Crucifixion.
26:49 The Greek word for **kissed** indicates more than a casual greeting. Judas gave to Jesus the affectionate and fervent greeting of intimate friends.
26:51 Peter was the disciple who attempted to defend Jesus (John 18:10).
26:52 The statement of Jesus should be interpreted in its context, and not as a general endorsement of pacifism. He was laying down His life in fulfillment of the Scriptures.
26:53 A legion was 6,000 soldiers.

ple than to sense they are dealing with someone who feels their pain and understands their need, which they only discover if the leader is vulnerable enough to disclose as much. When Jesus refused to defend Himself the night of His arrest, Peter's protective action severed the ear of the high priest's bodyguard. Immediately, Jesus reached out to heal His enemy, making Himself vulnerable to a return sword thrust, since His reaching for the man's head easily could have been interpreted as another hostile move. Vulnerability may expose to misunderstanding, but it will also bring healing.
(Acts 13:22/John 13:1–17) J.B.

55 In that hour Jesus said to the multitudes, "Have you come out, as against
a robber, with swords and clubs to take
Me? I sat daily with you, teaching in
the temple, and you did not seize Me.
56 "But all this was done that the
[a]Scriptures of the prophets might be
fulfilled." Then [b]all the *disciples forsook Him and fled.

Jesus Faces the Sanhedrin

57 [a]And those who had laid hold of Jesus led *Him* away to Caiaphas the high
priest, where the scribes and the elders
were assembled.
58 But [a]Peter *followed Him at a distance to the high priest's courtyard.
And he went in and sat with the servants to see the end.
59 Now the chief priests, [1]the elders,
and all the council sought [a]false testimony against Jesus to put Him to
death,
60 [1]but found none. Even though
[a]many false witnesses came forward,
they found none. But at last [b]two
[2]false witnesses came forward
61 and said, "This *fellow* said, [a]'I am
able to destroy the temple of God and
to build it in three days.'"
62 [a]And the high priest arose and said
to Him, "Do You answer nothing?
What *is it* these men testify against
You?"
63 But [a]Jesus kept silent. And the high
priest answered and said to Him,
[b]"I put You under oath by the living
God: Tell us if You are the Christ, the
Son of God!"
64 Jesus said to him, "*It is as* you said.
Nevertheless, I say to you, [a]hereafter
you will see the Son of Man [b]sitting
at the right hand of the *Power, and
coming on the clouds of heaven."
65 [a]Then the high priest tore his
clothes, saying, "He has spoken blasphemy! What further need do we have
of witnesses? Look, now you have
heard His [b]blasphemy!
66 "What do you think?" They answered and said, [a]"He is deserving of
death."
67 [a]Then they spat in His face and beat
Him; and [b]others struck *Him* with
[1]the palms of their hands,
68 saying, [a]"Prophesy to us, Christ!
Who is the one who struck You?"

Peter Denies Jesus, and Weeps Bitterly

69 [a]Now Peter sat outside in the courtyard. And a servant girl came to him,
saying, "You also were with Jesus of
Galilee."
70 But he denied it before *them* all,
saying, "I do not know what you are
saying."
71 And when he had gone out to the
gateway, another *girl* saw him and said
to those *who were* there, "This *fellow*
also was with Jesus of Nazareth."
72 But again he denied with an oath,
"I do not know the Man!"
73 And a little later those who stood
by came up and said to Peter, "Surely
you also are *one* of them, for your
[a]speech betrays you."
74 Then [a]he began to [1]curse and
[2]swear, *saying*, "I do not know the
Man!" Immediately a rooster crowed.
75 And Peter remembered the word of
Jesus who had said to him, [a]"Before
the rooster crows, you will deny Me
three times." So he went out and wept
bitterly.

Jesus Handed Over to Pontius Pilate

27 When morning came, [a]all the
chief priests and elders of the
people plotted against Jesus to put Him
to death.

56 [a]Lam. 4:20 [b]John 18:15 *See WW at Matt. 10:1. **57** [a]John 18:12, 19–24 **58** [a]John 18:15, 16 *See WW at John 13:36. **59** [a]Ps. 35:11 [1]NU omits *the elders* **60** [a]Mark 14:55 [b]Deut. 19:15 [1]NU *but found none, even though many false witnesses came forward.* [2]NU omits *false witnesses* **61** [a]John 2:19 **62** [a]Mark 14:60 **63** [a]Is. 53:7 [b]Lev. 5:1

64 [a]Dan. 7:13 [b][Acts 7:55] *See WW at Acts 4:33. **65** [a]2 Kin. 18:37 [b]John 10:30–36 **66** [a]Lev. 24:16 **67** [a]Is. 50:6; 53:3 [b]Luke 22:63–65 [1]Or *rods,* **68** [a]Mark 14:65 **69** [a]John 18:16–18, 25–27 **73** [a]Luke 22:59 **74** [a]Mark 14:71 [1]*call down curses* [2]*Swear oaths* **75** [a]Matt. 26:34

CHAPTER 27

1 [a]John 18:28

26:57–68 The Jews violated their own laws by holding a trial at night.
26:59 To give a semblance of legality to the verdict on which they had already decided, the authorities needed two or three witnesses to agree in testimony. See Num. 35:30; Deut. 17:6; 19:15.
26:61 They distorted Jesus' teaching about His resurrection.
26:64 Jesus acknowledges His deity, and He adds that despite the present circumstances a time will come when they will see Him in fulfillment of the messianic prophecy of Dan. 7:13.
26:67, 68 Once again they disregard their own laws by striking Jesus in the hopes of revealing the falsities of His claims.
26:73 Peter's Galilean accent was easily detectable in Jerusalem.
26:74 Each denial is more emphatic.

2 And when they had bound Him,
they led Him away and [a]delivered*
Him to [1]Pontius Pilate the governor.

Judas Hangs Himself

3 [a]Then Judas, His betrayer, seeing
that He had been condemned, was re-
morseful and brought back the thirty
[b]pieces of silver to the chief priests and
elders,
4 saying, "I have sinned by betraying
innocent blood." And they said, "What
is that to us? You see *to it!*"
5 Then he threw down the pieces of
silver in the temple and [a]departed, and
went and hanged himself.
6 But the chief priests took the silver
pieces and said, "It is not lawful to put
them into the treasury, because they
are the price of blood."
7 And they consulted together and
bought with them the potter's field, to
bury strangers in.
8 Therefore that field has been called
[a]the Field of Blood to this day.
9 Then was fulfilled what was spoken
by Jeremiah the prophet, saying,
[a]*"And they took the thirty pieces of sil-*
ver, the value of Him who was priced,
whom they of the children of Israel
priced,
10 *"and* [a]*gave them for the potter's*
field, as the LORD *directed me."*

Jesus Faces Pilate

11 Now Jesus stood before the governor. [a]And the governor asked Him,
saying, "Are You the King of the
Jews?" Jesus said to him, [b]*"It is as* you
say."
12 And while He was being accused by
the chief priests and elders, [a]He answered nothing.
13 Then Pilate said to Him, [a]"Do You
not hear how many things they testify
against You?"
14 But He answered him not one word,
so that the governor marveled greatly.

Taking the Place of Barabbas

15 [a]Now at the feast the governor was
accustomed to releasing to the multitude one prisoner whom they wished.
16 And at that time they had a notorious prisoner called [1]Barabbas.
17 Therefore, when they had gathered
together, Pilate said to them, "Whom
do you want me to release to you? Barabbas, or Jesus who is called Christ?"
18 For he knew that they had handed
Him over because of [a]envy.
19 While he was sitting on the **judg-**
ment seat, his wife sent to him, saying,
"Have nothing to do with that just
Man, for I have suffered many things
today in a dream because of Him."

WORD WEALTH

27:19 judgment seat, *bema* (*bay*-mah); Strong's *#968:* From *baino,* "to go," the word described a step or a stride (Acts 7:5). Then it was used for a raised platform reached by steps, especially from which orations were made. Later it denoted the tribune or tribunal of a ruler where litigants stood trial. In the NT it mostly refers to earthly magistrates (Acts 18:12, 16, 17), but twice is used of the divine tribunal before which believers will stand (Rom. 14:10; 2 Cor. 5:10).

20 [a]But the chief priests and elders
persuaded the multitudes that they
should ask for Barabbas and destroy
Jesus.
21 The governor answered and said to
them, "Which of the two do you want
me to release to you?" They said,
[a]"Barabbas!"
22 Pilate said to them, "What then
shall I do with Jesus who is called
Christ?" *They* all said to him, "Let Him
be crucified!"
23 Then the governor said, [a]"Why,
what evil has He done?" But they cried
out all the more, saying, "Let Him be
crucified!"
24 When Pilate saw that he could not
prevail at all, but rather *that* a [1]tumult
was rising, he [a]took water and washed
his hands before the multitude, saying,
"I am innocent of the blood of this
[2]just Person. You see *to it.*"
25 And all the people answered and
said, [a]"His blood *be* on us and on our
children."
26 Then he released Barabbas to them;

2 [a]Matt. 20:19; Luke 18:32; Acts 3:13 [1]NU omits *Pontius* *See WW at Luke 23:25. **3** [a]Matt. 26:14 [b]Matt. 26:15 **5** [a]2 Sam. 17:23; Matt. 18:7; 26:24; John 17:12; Acts 1:18 **8** [a]Acts 1:19 **9** [a]Zech. 11:12 **10** [a]Jer. 32:6–9; Zech. 11:12, 13 **11** [a]Mark 15:2–5; Luke 23:2, 3; John 18:29–38 [b]John 18:37; 1 Tim. 6:13 **12** [a]Ps. 38:13, 14; Matt. 26:63; John 19:9 **13** [a]Matt. 26:62; John 19:10 **15** [a]Mark 15:6–15; Luke 23:17–25; John 18:39—19:16

16 [1]NU *Jesus Barabbas* **18** [a]Matt. 21:38; [John 15:22–25] **20** [a]Mark 15:11; Luke 23:18; John 18:40; Acts 3:14 **21** [a]Acts 3:14 **23** [a]Acts 3:13 **24** [a]Deut. 21:6–8 [1]*an uproar* [2]NU omits *just* **25** [a]Deut. 19:10; Josh. 2:19; 2 Sam. 1:16; 1 Kin. 2:32; Acts 5:28

27:2 The Romans had taken from the Jews the right to inflict capital punishment. Thus Pilate would have to execute the death sentence.
27:3–8 See note on Acts 1:18.
27:6 The Law prohibited money obtained by base means to be given to the temple (Deut. 23:18).
27:11 The Sanhedrin's charge of blasphemy would be meaningless to Pilate, so they accused Jesus of sedition in claiming to be a king.
27:18 Pilate knows Jesus to be innocent, but he will disregard his own conscience.
27:19 The dream stresses the fact that Jesus was not regarded as a criminal by the Roman authorities. In chs. 1 and 2 dreams are used as vehicles of divine revelation.
27:26 A victim to be scourged was stripped and tied to a whipping post. Then he was beaten mercilessly with a whip

and when [a]he had [1]scourged Jesus, he delivered *Him* to be crucified.

The Soldiers Mock Jesus

27 [a]Then the soldiers of the governor took Jesus into the [1]Praetorium and gathered the whole [2]garrison around Him.
28 And they [a]stripped Him and [b]put a scarlet robe on Him.
29 [a]When they had [1]twisted a crown of thorns, they put *it* on His head, and a reed in His right hand. And they bowed the knee before Him and mocked Him, saying, "Hail, King of the Jews!"
30 Then [a]they spat on Him, and took the reed and struck Him on the head.
31 And when they had mocked Him, they took the robe off Him, put His *own* clothes on Him, [a]and led Him away to be crucified.

The King on a Cross

32 [a]Now as they came out, [b]they found a man of Cyrene, Simon by name. Him they *compelled to bear His cross.

KINGDOM DYNAMICS

27:32 The Cross-Cultural Nature of God's Word and Work, HUMAN WORTH. This text reminds us that different cultures were represented at Calvary and in the church. 1) Simon: Wise men of all ages would be honored to be allowed to perform the task that was conferred upon Simon of Cyrene, a black man from northwestern Africa. Whether it was voluntary or by force, in any case, black hands were extended to help the Savior bear His cross. 2) The Ethiopian eunuch from Africa (Acts 8:26) was the first Gentile convert mentioned by name in the Book of Acts. History reports that he returned to Ethiopia to found the Abyssinian Christian Church, which exists until this day.

(Luke 10:33/1 Pet. 1:18, 19) C.B.

33 [a]And when they had come to a place called Golgotha, that is to say, Place of a Skull,
34 [a]they gave Him [1]sour wine mingled with gall to drink. But when He had *tasted *it*, He would not drink.
35 [a]Then they crucified Him, and divided His garments, casting lots, [1]that it might be fulfilled which was spoken by the *prophet:

[b]*"They divided My garments*
among them,
And for My clothing they cast
lots."

36 [a]Sitting down, they kept watch over Him there.
37 And they [a]put up over His head the accusation written against Him:

THIS IS JESUS THE KING
OF THE JEWS.

38 [a]Then two robbers were crucified with Him, one on the right and another on the left.
39 And [a]those who passed by blasphemed Him, wagging their heads
40 and saying, [a]"You who destroy the temple and build *it* in three days, save Yourself! [b]If You are the Son of God, come down from the cross."
41 Likewise the chief priests also, mocking with the [1]scribes and elders, said,
42 "He [a]saved others; Himself He cannot save. [1]If He is the King of Israel, let Him now come down from the cross, and we will believe [2]Him.
43 [a]"He trusted in God; let Him deliver Him now if He will have Him; for He said, 'I am the Son of God.' "
44 [a]Even the robbers who were crucified with Him *reviled Him with the same thing.

Jesus Dies on the Cross

45 [a]Now from the sixth hour until the ninth hour there was darkness over all the land.
46 And about the ninth hour [a]Jesus cried out with a loud voice, saying, "Eli, Eli, lama sabachthani?" that is, [b]*"My God, My God, why have You forsaken Me?"*

26 [a][Is. 50:6; 53:5] [1]*flogged* with a Roman scourge
27 [a]Mark 15:16–20 [1]The governor's headquarters [2]*cohort*
28 [a]John 19:2 [b]Luke 23:11
29 [a]Is. 53:3 [1]Lit. *woven*
30 [a]Matt. 26:67
31 [a]Is. 53:7
32 [a]Heb. 13:12 [b]Mark 15:21 *See WW at Matt. 5:41.
33 [a]John 19:17
34 [a]Ps. 69:21 [1]NU omits *sour* *See WW at John 8:52.
35 [a]Luke 23:34 [b]Ps. 22:18 [1]NU, M omit the rest of v. 35. *See WW at Matt. 2:5.
36 [a]Matt. 27:54
37 [a]John 19:19
38 [a]Is. 53:9, 12
39 [a]Mark 15:29
40 [a]John 2:19 [b]Matt. 26:63
41 [1]M *scribes, the Pharisees, and the elders*
42 [a][John 3:14, 15] [1]NU omits *If* [2]NU, M *in Him*
43 [a]Ps. 22:8
44 [a]Luke 23:39–43 *See WW at James 1:5.
45 [a]Mark 15:33–41
46 [a][Heb. 5:7] [b]Ps. 22:1

consisting of several leather thongs, each loaded with jagged pieces of metal or bone and weighted at the end with lead. Fragments of flesh would be torn from the victims, some of whom did not survive the ordeal.
27:27 The **Praetorium** was the official residence of the governor.
27:34 Victims to be executed customarily received wine drugged with myrrh to dull the senses (see Prov. 31:6). Jesus' refusal not only reflects His prayer (26:39, 41, 42), but His will to avoid nothing of the cup given to Him by the Father (see 20:22).
27:35 The Roman custom was to strip victims naked and to allow the soldiers in the crucifixion detail to keep their clothing, in Jesus' case a fulfillment of Ps. 22:18.
27:37 See note on John 19:19–22.
27:42 He could not save Himself and be the Savior of others.
27:45 From noon to 3:00 P.M.
27:46 The cry of dereliction from Jesus, quoting Ps. 22:1, reflects the burden of humanity's sin, complete identification with sinners, and a real abandonment by His Father. See 2 Cor. 5:21; Gal. 3:13.

47 Some of those who stood there,
when they heard *that,* said, "This Man
is calling for Elijah!"
48 Immediately one of them ran and
took a sponge, [a]filled *it* with sour wine
and put *it* on a reed, and offered it to
Him to drink.
49 The rest said, "Let Him alone; let
us see if Elijah will come to save Him."
50 And Jesus [a]cried out again with a
loud voice, and [b]yielded up His spirit.
51 Then, behold, [a]the veil of the temple
was torn in two from top to bottom;
and the earth quaked, and the rocks
were split,
52 and the graves were opened; and
many bodies of the saints who had
fallen asleep were raised;
53 and coming out of the graves after
His resurrection, they went into the
holy city and *appeared to many.
54 [a]So when the centurion and those
with him, who were guarding Jesus,
saw the earthquake and the things that
had happened, they feared greatly,
saying, [b]"Truly this was the Son of
God!"
55 And many women [a]who followed
Jesus from Galilee, ministering to Him,
were there looking on from afar,
56 [a]among whom were Mary Magdalene, Mary the mother of James and
[1]Joses, and the mother of Zebedee's
sons.

Jesus Buried in Joseph's Tomb

57 Now [a]when evening had come,
there came a rich man from Arimathea, named Joseph, who himself had
also become a disciple of Jesus.
58 This man went to Pilate and asked
for the body of Jesus. Then Pilate commanded the body to be given to him.
59 When Joseph had taken the body,
he wrapped it in a clean linen cloth,
60 and [a]laid it in his new tomb which
he had hewn out of the rock; and he
rolled a large stone against the door
of the tomb, and departed.
61 And Mary Magdalene was there,
and the other Mary, sitting [1]opposite
the tomb.

Pilate Sets a Guard

62 On the next day, which followed the
Day of Preparation, the chief priests
and Pharisees gathered together to Pilate,
63 saying, "Sir, we remember, while
He was still alive, how that deceiver
said, [a]'After three days I will rise.'
64 "Therefore command that the tomb
be made secure until the third day, lest
His disciples come [1]by night and steal
Him *away,* and say to the people, 'He
has risen from the dead.' So the last
*deception will be worse than the
first."
65 Pilate said to them, "You have a
guard; go your way, make *it* as secure
as you know how."
66 So they went and made the tomb
secure, [a]sealing the stone and setting
the guard.

He Is Risen

28 Now [a]after the Sabbath, as the
first *day* of the week began to
dawn, Mary Magdalene [b]and the other
Mary came to *see the tomb.
2 And behold, there was a great
earthquake; for [a]an angel of the Lord
descended from heaven, and came and
rolled back the stone [1]from the door,
and sat on it.
3 [a]His countenance was like lightning, and his clothing as white as
snow.
4 And the guards shook for fear of
him, and became like [a]dead *men.*
5 But the angel answered and said to
the women, "Do not be *afraid, for I
know that you seek Jesus who was crucified.
6 "He is not here; for He is risen,
[a]as He said. Come, see the place where
the Lord lay.
7 "And go *quickly and tell His disciples that He is risen from the dead, and

48 [a]Ps. 69:21
50 [a]Luke 23:46 [b][John 10:18]
51 [a]Ex. 26:31
53 *See WW at John 14:21.
54 [a]Mark 15:39 [b]Matt. 14:33
55 [a]Luke 8:2, 3
56 [a]Mark 15:40, 47; 16:9 [1]NU *Joseph*
57 [a]John 19:38–42
60 [a]Is. 53:9
61 [1]*in front of*
63 [a]Mark 8:31; 10:34
64 [1]NU omits *by night* *See WW at Jude 11.
66 [a]Dan. 6:17

CHAPTER 28

1 [a]Luke 24:1–10 [b]Matt. 27:56, 61 *See WW at John 20:14.
2 [a]Mark 16:5 [1]NU omits *from the door*
3 [a]Dan. 7:9; 10:6
4 [a]Rev. 1:17
5 *See WW at Matt. 10:26.
6 [a]Matt. 12:40; 16:21; 17:23; 20:19
7 *See WW at Rev. 22:20.

27:51 The **veil** was the thick curtain between the Holy Place and the Holy of Holies (see Heb. 6:19; 9:3; 10:20). The fact that it **was torn in two from top to bottom** indicates that this was not an act of man. Jesus' death opens the way to the presence of God.

27:52, 53 Evidently the earthquake opened the tombs, and the bodies were raised after the resurrection of Jesus (see Is. 26:19).

27:54 Son of God: This confession of Jesus' divinity by Gentile soldiers is a fitting climax to the Crucifixion narrative, in that preparation is made for the charge to evangelize "all the nations" (28:19).

27:57 See note on John 19:38, 39.

27:60 Rock tombs, common in that area, were normally closed by means of a large stone rolled into the mouth of the hollow.

27:62 The Day of Preparation was Friday. In visiting **Pilate the next day** the Jewish leaders violated their own rules concerning the Sabbath.

27:64 The presence of a Roman guard refutes the later assertion that Jesus' disciples stole His body (28:11–15).

28:2 The **stone** was rolled away, not that Jesus might escape, but that witnesses might see the evidence of an empty tomb.

indeed [a]He is going before you into
Galilee; there you will see Him. Behold,
I have told you."
8 So they went out quickly from the
tomb with fear and great joy, and ran
to bring His disciples word.

The Women Worship the Risen Lord

9 And [1]as they went to tell His disciples, behold, [a]Jesus met them, saying,
"Rejoice!" So they came and held Him
by the feet and worshiped Him.
10 Then Jesus said to them, "Do not
be afraid. Go *and* tell [a]My brethren to
go to Galilee, and there they will see
Me."

The Soldiers Are Bribed

11 Now while they were going, behold,
some of the guard came into the city
and reported to the chief priests all the
things that had happened.
12 When they had assembled with the
elders and consulted together, they
gave a large sum of money to the soldiers,
13 saying, "Tell them, 'His disciples
came at night and stole Him *away*
while we slept.'
14 "And if this comes to the governor's
ears, we will appease him and make
you secure."
15 So they took the money and did as
they were instructed; and this saying
is commonly reported among the Jews
until this day.

The Great Commission

16 Then the eleven disciples went
away into Galilee, to the mountain

7 [a]Matt. 26:32; 28:10, 16; Mark 16:7
9 [a]Mark 16:9; John 20:14 [1]NU omits *as they went to tell His disciples*
10 [a]Ps. 22:22; John 20:17; Rom. 8:29; [Heb. 2:11]

28:10 Note the fulfillment of 26:32.
28:13 The deception was absurd. If the guards were asleep, how did they know what had happened? It is manifest that the opponents are not at all concerned with the truth of the event, but with the effect of a rumor upon the people (27:64).

THE APPEARANCES OF THE RISEN CHRIST (28:7)

Central to Christian faith is the bodily resurrection of Jesus. By recording the resurrection appearances, the New Testament leaves no doubt about this event.

- In or around Jerusalem
  - To Mary Magdalene (Mark 16:9; John 20:11–18)
  - To the other women (Matt. 28:8–10)
  - To Peter (Luke 24:34)
  - To ten disciples (Luke 24:36–43; John 20:19–25)
  - To the Eleven, including Thomas (Mark 16:14; John 20:26–29)
  - At His ascension (Mark 16:19, 20; Luke 24:50–53; Acts 1:4–12)
- To the disciples on the Emmaus road (Mark 16:12, 13; Luke 24:13–35)
- In Galilee (Matt. 28:16–20; John 21:1–24)
- To five hundred people (1 Cor. 15:6)
- To James and the apostles (1 Cor. 15:7)
- To Paul on the road to Damascus (Acts 9:1–6; 18:9, 10; 22:1–8; 23:11; 26:12–18; 1 Cor. 15:8)

[a]which Jesus had appointed for them.
17 When they saw Him, they worshiped Him; but some [a]doubted.
7 18 And Jesus came and spoke to them, saying, [a]"All authority has been given to Me in heaven and on earth.
19 [a]"Go [1]therefore and [b]make disciples of all the nations, baptizing them in the *name of the Father and of the Son and of the Holy Spirit,
20 [a]"teaching them to observe all things that I have commanded you; and lo, I am [b]with you always, *even* to the end of the **age.**" [1]Amen.

WORD WEALTH

28:20 age, *aion* (ahee-*ohn*); Strong's *#165:* Denotes an indefinitely long period, with emphasis on the characteristics of the period rather than on its duration. In idiomatic usage it designates "forever" or "forever and ever" (21:19; Rom. 16:27; Eph. 3:21). The word is also used as a designation for the present age (Matt. 12:32; 13:22; 1 Tim. 6:17) and for the time after Christ's Second Coming (Mark 10:30; Luke 20:35).

16 [a]Matt. 26:32; 28:7, 10; Mark 14:28; 15:41; 16:7
17 [a]John 20:24–29
18 [a][Dan. 7:13, 14]; Matt. 11:27; Luke 1:32; 10:22; John 3:35; Acts 2:36; Rom. 14:9; 1 Cor. 15:27; [Eph. 1:10, 21]; Phil. 2:9, 10; [Heb. 1:2]; 1 Pet. 3:22
19 [a]Mark 16:15 [b]Is. 52:10; Luke 24:47; [Acts 2:38, 39]; Rom. 10:18; Col. 1:23 [1]M omits *therefore* *See WW at John 12:13.
20 [a][Acts 2:42] [b][Acts 4:31; 18:10; 23:11] [1]NU omits *Amen*

KINGDOM DYNAMICS

28:18–20 Commissioned Under the King's Call, WORLD EVANGELISM. Since Matthew's theme is Christ as King, it is unsurprising Jesus' final commission to His disciples reflects His global perspective. In teaching kingdom life and principles ("kingdom" appears over 50 times in Matt.), Jesus leads His followers to think, live, and pray that His kingdom come to our entire planet (6:10). In ch. 13, His parables illustrated the kingdom's global expansion (v. 33). As His disciples began to minister, He told them to preach everywhere: "The kingdom of God is at hand." Then, before His ascension, the King gave the Great Commission. This climaxing command to go to all nations directed that their teaching and preaching seek to bring all nations into His kingdom (28:18–20). Prophetically, He forecast that the end would come only as "this gospel of the kingdom" was preached "in all the world as a witness to all nations" (24:14). "Nations" (Greek *ethne*) means "people groupings"—today, about 22,000 on this globe.

(Matt. 24:14/Mark 16:15–18) G.C.

28:17 Though **some doubted,** it is important to note that the church's "Great Commission" is born in a context of worship.
28:18–20 See section 7 of Truth-In-Action through the Synoptics at the end of Luke.
28:18 The humiliated Servant is now the exalted Lord, having received the authority promised in Dan. 7:14.
28:19 While Jesus' ministry had been to Israel (see 10:5, 6), proclamation of and adherence to His lordship is extended to **all the nations. Disciples** are to acknowledge openly their allegiance to Christ by the seal of water baptism, which is ministered under the authority of the entire godhead.
28:20 The content of the apostles' future teaching will stem from what Jesus had **commanded** them. Jesus assures them of His constant presence as they go on their divinely commanded mission.

The Gospel According to MARK

Author: Mark
Date: A.D. 65–70
Theme: The Suffering Son of Man Who Is in Fact the Son of God
Key Words: Authority, Son of Man, Son of God, Suffering, Faith, Discipline, Gospel

Author Even though the Gospel of Mark is anonymous, early tradition is unanimous that the author of this Gospel was John Mark, a close associate of Peter (see 1 Pet. 5:13) and a companion of Paul and Barnabas on their first missionary journey. The earliest witness to Markan authorship stems from Papias, bishop of the church at Hierapolis (about A.D. 135–140), a witness that is preserved in Eusebius's *Ecclesiastical History*. Papias describes Mark as "the interpreter of Peter." Although the early church was careful to maintain direct apostolic authorship for the Gospels, the church fathers consistently attributed this Gospel to Mark, who was not an apostle. This fact furnishes indirect confirmation of Mark's authorship.

Date The church fathers state that the Gospel of Mark was written after Peter's death, which occurred during the persecutions by the Emperor Nero in about A.D. 67. The Gospel itself, particularly chapter 13, indicates that it was written before the destruction of the temple in A.D. 70. The bulk of the evidence supports a date between A.D. 65 and 70.

Background In A.D. 64 Nero accused the Christian community of setting the city of Rome on fire, and thereupon instigated a fearful persecution in which Paul and Peter perished. In the milieu of a persecuted church, living constantly under the threat of death, the evangelist Mark writes his "good news." Clearly he wants his readers to draw encouragement and strength from the life and example of Jesus. What was true for Jesus was to be true for the apostles and disciples of all ages. At the heart of the Gospel is the explicit pronouncement "that the Son of Man must suffer many things, and be rejected by the elders and chief priests and scribes, and be killed, and after three days rise again" (8:31). This pronouncement of suffering and death not only is repeated (9:31; 10:32–34), but becomes the norm for committed discipleship: "Whoever desires to come after Me, let him deny himself, and take up his cross and follow Me" (8:34). Mark leads his readers to the Cross of Jesus, where they can discover meaning and hope in their suffering.

Content Mark structures his Gospel around various geographical movements of Jesus, which are climaxed by His death and subsequent resurrection. After the introduction (1:1–13), Mark narrates the public ministry of Jesus in Galilee (1:14—9:50) and Judea (chs. 10—13), culminating in the Passion and Resurrection (chs. 14—16). The Gospel may be viewed as two halves joined together by the hinge of Peter's confession of Jesus as the Messiah (8:27–30) and Jesus' first announcement of His crucifixion (8:31).

Mark is the shortest of the Gospels, containing no genealogy and no account of the birth and early Judean ministry of Jesus. It is the Gospel of action, moving rapidly from one scene to another. John's Gospel is a studied portrait of the Lord, Matthew and Luke present what might be described as a series of colored slides, while Mark's Gospel is like a motion picture of the life of Jesus. Mark accents the activity he records by the use of the Greek word *eutheos,* usually translated "immediately." The word occurs forty-two times in Mark, more than in all the rest of the New Testament. Mark's frequent use of the Greek imperfect tense, denoting continuous action, also moves the narrative at a rapid pace.

Mark is also the Gospel of vividness. Graphic, striking phrases occur frequently to allow the reader to form a mental picture of the scene described. The looks and gestures of Jesus receive unusual attention. There are many Latinisms in the Gospel (see 4:21; 12:14; 6:27; 15:39). Mark places little emphasis on Jewish law and customs, always interpreting them for the reader when he does mention them. This feature tends to support the tradition that Mark wrote for a Gentile, Roman audience.

In many ways, Mark emphasizes the Passion of Jesus so that it becomes the gauge by which the whole of Jesus' ministry and the ministry of His disciples may be measured: "For even the Son of Man did not come to be served, but to serve, and to give His life a ransom for many" (10:45). Jesus' entire ministry (miracles, table-fellowship with sinners, choice of disciples, teaching on the kingdom of God, etc.) is set within the context of the self-giving love of the Son of God, climaxed in the Cross and Resurrection.

Personal Application Mark's Gospel teaches that the life of discipleship means following Jesus along the same path of misunderstanding and rejection that He encountered. For followers of Jesus in all ages the warning and promise are sure: "Whoever desires to come after Me, let him deny himself, and take up his cross, and follow Me. For whoever desires to save his life will lose it, but whoever loses his life for My sake and the gospel's will save it" (8:34, 35).

Mark underscores the need for faith in the person, message, and power of Jesus to help those in need (see 1:15; 2:5; 4:40; 5:34, 36; 6:6; 9:19; 11:22–24). The opposite of such faith can be seen in the motif of hard hearts (see 3:5; 7:14–23; 8:17). The incarnate Christ that Mark describes is One who is willing and able to help those in extreme need.

Finally, Mark's Gospel assures Christian workers of all generations that the same attesting miracles that accredited the ministries of the apostles will continue as characteristic features of God's people under the New Covenant (16:17, 18).

Christ Revealed This book is not a biography, but a concise history of redemption accomplished through the atoning work of Christ. Mark substantiates the messianic claims of Jesus by emphasizing His authority as a Teacher (1:22) and His authority over Satan and unclean spirits (1:27; 3:19–30), sin (2:1–12), the Sabbath (2:27, 28; 3:1–6), nature (4:35–41; 6:45–52), disease (5:21–34), death (5:35–43), legalistic traditions (7:1–13, 14–20), and the temple (11:15–18).

The opening title of Mark's work, "The beginning of the gospel of Jesus Christ, Son of God" (1:1), provides his central thesis concerning the identity of Jesus as the Son of God. Both the Baptism and the Transfiguration testify to His sonship (1:11; 9:7). On two occasions evil spirits confess Him to be the Son of God (3:11; 5:7; see also 1:24, 34). The Parable of the Wicked Vinedressers alludes to Jesus' divine sonship (12:6). Finally, the narrative of the Crucifixion concludes with the centurion's confession, "Truly this Man was the Son of God" (15:39).

The title that Jesus uses most frequently for Himself, a total of fourteen times in Mark, is "Son of Man." As a designation for the Messiah, this term (see Dan. 7:13) was not as popular among the Jews as the highly nationalistic title "Son of David." Jesus chose the title "Son of Man" both to reveal and to conceal His messiahship and to relate Himself to both God and man.

Mark, with his eye upon discipleship, suggests that Jesus' disciples must possess a penetrating insight into the mystery of His identity. Even though many people misunderstand His person and mission, while demons confess His divine sonship, Jesus' disciples must see through to His mission, take up their crosses, and follow Him. The Second Coming of the vindicated Son of Man will fully unveil His power and glory.

The Holy Spirit at Work

Along with the other Gospel writers, Mark records the prophecy of John the Baptist that Jesus "will baptize you with the Holy Spirit" (1:8). Believers would be just as thoroughly immersed in the Spirit as John's candidates were in the waters of the Jordan River.

The Holy Spirit descended upon Jesus at His baptism (1:10), empowering Him for His messianic work in fulfillment of Isaiah's prophecy (Is. 42:1; 48:16; 61:1, 2). The account of the subsequent ministry of Christ bears witness to the fact that His miracles and teaching resulted from the anointing of the Holy Spirit.

Mark graphically states that "the Spirit drove Him into the wilderness" (1:12) to be tempted, suggesting the urgency of meeting and defeating Satan's attempts to defile Him before He embarked on a mission of breaking the enemy's power in others.

The sin against the Holy Spirit is set in contrast to "all sins" (3:28) for these sins and blasphemies can be forgiven. The context defines the meaning of this frightening truth. The scribes blasphemed against the Holy Spirit in that they attributed Jesus' Holy Spirit-effected exorcisms to Satan (3:22). Their prejudiced vision made them incapable of true discernment. Mark's explanation confirms this as why Jesus makes this severe pronouncement (3:30).

Jesus also refers to the Holy Spirit's inspiration of the Old Testament (12:36). Of particular encouragement to Christians facing the hostility of unjust authorities is the Lord's assurance that the Holy Spirit will speak through them when they testify of Christ (13:11).

In addition to explicit references to the Holy Spirit, Mark employs words associated with the gift of the Spirit, such as power, authority, prophet, healing, laying on of hands, Messiah, and kingdom.

Outline of Mark

Introduction	**1:1–13**
A. Summary statement	1:1
B. Fulfillment of Old Testament Prophecy	1:2, 3
C. John the Baptist's ministry	1:4–8
D. Jesus' baptism	1:9–11
E. Jesus' temptation	1:12, 13
I. Jesus' Galilean ministry	**1:14—9:50**
A. Beginnings: initial success and conflict	1:14—3:6
B. Later stages: heightened popularity and opposition	3:7—6:13
C. Ministry outside of Galilee	6:14—8:26
D. Ministry on the way to Judea	8:26—9:50
II. Jesus' Judean ministry	**10:1—16:20**
A. Ministry in the Transjordan	10:1–52
B. Ministry in Jerusalem	11:1—13:37
C. The Passion	14:1—15:47
D. The Resurrection	16:1–20

John the Baptist Prepares the Way

THE [a]beginning of the **gospel** of Jesus Christ, [b]the Son of God.

WORD WEALTH

1:1 gospel, *euangelion* (yoo-ang-*ghel*-ee-on); Strong's *#2098:* Compare "evangel," "evangelize," "evangelistic." In ancient Greece *euangelion* designated the reward given for bringing good news. Later it came to mean the good news itself. In the NT the word includes both the promise of salvation and its fulfillment by the life, death, resurrection, and ascension of Jesus Christ. *Euangelion* also designates the written narratives of Matthew, Mark, Luke, and John.

2 As it is written in [1]the Prophets:

[a]*"Behold, I send My messenger*
before Your face,
Who will prepare Your way
before You."
3 *"The[a] voice of one crying in the*
wilderness:
'Prepare the way of the LORD;
Make His paths straight.' "

CHAPTER 1
1 [a]Luke 3:22 [b]Matt. 14:33
2 [a]Mal. 3:1 [1]NU *Isaiah the prophet*
3 [a]Is. 40:3 *See WW at Rev. 21:2.
4 [a]Matt. 3:1 [1]Or *because of forgiveness* *See WW at Matt. 21:25. • See WW at Heb. 9:22.
5 [a]Matt. 3:5
6 [a]Matt. 3:4
7 [a]John 1:27
8 [a]Acts 1:5; 11:16 [b]Is. 44:3
9 [a]Matt. 3:13–17
10 [a]Matt. 3:16 [b]Acts 10:38 [1]NU *out of* [2]*torn open*

4 [a]John came baptizing in the wilderness and preaching a *baptism of repentance [1]for the *remission of sins.
5 [a]Then all the land of Judea, and
those from Jerusalem, went out to him
and were all baptized by him in the
Jordan River, confessing their sins.
6 Now John was [a]clothed with camel's hair and with a leather belt around
his waist, and he ate locusts and wild
honey.
7 And he preached, saying, [a]"There
comes One after me who is mightier
than I, whose sandal strap I am not
worthy to stoop down and loose.
8 [a]"I indeed baptized you with water, 11
but He will baptize you [b]with the Holy
Spirit."

John Baptizes Jesus

9 [a]It came to pass in those days *that*
Jesus came from Nazareth of Galilee,
and was baptized by John in the Jordan.
10 [a]And immediately, coming up
[1]from the water, He saw the heavens
[2]parting and the Spirit [b]descending
upon Him like a dove.

1:1 The gospel literally means "good news" and is concerned with Jesus, who is identified by name and title.
1:2 The comparative **as** links "the beginning" (v. 1) of the gospel with the announcement of **the Prophets** (see Is. 40:3; Mal. 3:1). Isaiah is the primary prophet who foretold the Day of the Lord. Malachi builds upon Isaiah's prophecy, which had not yet been fulfilled. See note on Matt. 3:3.
1:4 The prophetic promise (vv. 2, 3) is interpreted by Mark to be fulfilled in the ministry of John the Baptist, the messenger who paves the way *for the Lord.* Repentance is a prerequisite to baptism.
1:5 The Greek tense, translated **went out,** suggests a continual exodus of the people of Judea, extending over a period of time.
1:6 John's clothing and diet link him with Elijah (2 Kin. 1:8; Zech. 13:4).
1:8 See section 11 of Truth-In-Action through the Synoptics at the end of Luke.
1:8 John's baptism **with water** was symbolic; only Jesus can **baptize . . . with the Holy Spirit,** and only after His exaltation following the Ascension. Jesus connected John's prophecy with Pentecost (Acts 1:5, 8).
1:9 Jesus was not baptized for His own sins, because He was guiltless. His baptism gave approval to the ministry of John and was an act of dedication to His own ministry. In effect, He was identifying Himself with the people He came to save (see Luke 12:50).
1:10 The Holy Spirit empowers Jesus for His ministry. The **dove** not only suggests gentleness and purity, but was also used as a sacrificial offering. The scene presents a picture of the character and manner of Jesus' redemptive ministry.

11 Then a voice came from heaven,
[a]"You are My beloved Son, in whom
I am well pleased."

Satan Tempts Jesus

12 [a]Immediately the Spirit [1]drove Him
into the wilderness.
13 And He was there in the wilderness
forty days, tempted by Satan, and was
with the wild beasts; [a]and the angels
ministered to Him.

Jesus Begins His Galilean Ministry

14 [a]Now after John *was put in prison,
Jesus came to Galilee, [b]preaching the
gospel [1]of the kingdom of God,
15 and saying, [a]"The *time is fulfilled,
and [b]the kingdom of God [1]is at hand.
Repent, and believe in the gospel."

11 [a][Ps. 2:7]; Is. 42:1; Matt. 3:17; 12:18; Mark 9:7; Luke 3:22
12 [a]Matt. 4:1–11; Luke 4:1–13 [1]*sent Him out*
13 [a]Matt. 4:10, 11
14 [a]Matt. 4:12 [b]Matt. 4:23 [1]NU omits *of the kingdom* *See WW at Luke 23:25.
15 [a]Dan. 9:25; [Gal. 4:4; Eph. 1:10; 1 Tim. 2:6]; Titus 1:3 [b]Matt. 3:2; 4:17; [Acts 20:21] [1]*has drawn near* *See WW at Col. 4:5.
16 [a]Matt. 4:18–22; Luke 5:2–11; John 1:40–42

KINGDOM DYNAMICS

1:14, 15 The Gospel of the Kingdom, THE MESSAGE OF THE KINGDOM. The synoptic Gospels and Acts make at least 20 direct references to the preaching of "the gospel of the kingdom" from John the Baptist (Matt. 3:1, 2), throughout Jesus' ministry (Mark 1:14,15), in the disciples' ministry during Jesus' ministry (Luke 9:1, 2), and throughout Acts. Jesus prophesied this same message shall be taken to the ends of the world (Matt. 24:14), commissioning His disciples to do this and promising the Holy Spirit's power for the task (Mark 16:15–18; Acts 1:3–8).

It is clear that the early church proclaimed the same message Jesus preached, that is, "the gospel of the kingdom of God" (Acts 8:12; 19:8; 20:25; 28:23, 30, 31). Also, they experienced the same confirming evidences present in His ministry.

There is only one gospel: Jesus preached it, transmitted it to His disciples, and has committed it to His church. Paul warned against ever receiving any other gospel. "Any other" may be either a message of outright error or an argument for a diluted message, devoid of power though nominally Christian. Jude 3 urges us always to contend for the original, "the faith which was once for all delivered to the saints." Hold to the full "gospel of the kingdom," and expect the Lord to confirm that "word" with the signs He promised (Mark 16:15–18).

(Col. 1:27, 28/Matt. 3:1, 2; 4:17) J.W.H.

KINGDOM DYNAMICS

1:15 The Holy Spirit, MINISTRY OF THE KINGDOM. Jesus' ministry did not begin until He received His "anointing" as Messiah—the empowering that came through the descent of the Holy Spirit upon Him (v. 10). Though conceived and born by the Spirit's power (Luke 1:35) and sinless His whole lifetime (John 8:46), He did not attempt ministry without the Spirit's power. He insisted John baptize Him, not for repentance, but because He knew the Holy Spirit would come upon Him at that time (Matt. 3:13–17). From that time, He is led of the Spirit (v. 12) and moves into ministry—declaring the presence of God's kingdom and manifesting its miracles, signs, and wonders (Luke 4:14, 15; Matt. 4:23–25).

This pathway points each believer to the need for power, if kingdom ministry is to be advanced through us—His church. Like Him, we, too, are "born of the Spirit" (John 3:5, 6). Though obviously, our spiritual birth is not as His biological Virgin Birth, the point remains. Spiritual rebirth saves, but spiritual enduement is needed for ministering in kingdom power. Similarly, our justification in Christ—being declared sinless (2 Cor. 5:21)—does not qualify for kingdom power in ministry. In His incarnation Jesus' Person and perfection exceeded ours in every way, yet Jesus still acknowledged the need for His own receiving of the power of the Holy Spirit to pursue His ministry. What more needs to be said? Let each of us personally hear His command: "Receive the Holy Spirit!" (John 20:22).

(1 Cor. 6:9, 10/Luke 9:1, 2) J.W.H.

Four Fishermen Called as Disciples

16 [a]And as He walked by the Sea of
Galilee, He saw Simon and Andrew his

1:11 Note the inner bond between "the Son of God" (v. 1) and the Father. The heavenly voice speaks the combined words of Ps. 2:7 in which God addresses the anointed King as His Son, and Is. 42:1, in which God addresses His Servant in whom He delights and upon whom He has put His Spirit. Thus, the Son of God will perform the ministry of the Servant of God by the power of the Spirit.

1:12 The word **drove** does not imply reluctance on the part of Jesus, but rather emphasizes the conviction the Spirit gave Him of the necessity of the experience.

1:13 **Wild beasts** may refer to literal animals, but some interpreters see an allusion to demons, since literature written between the Old and New Testament periods contains many such references in a similar wilderness setting. If this is the case here, we see two rival kingdoms locked in a violent conflict: Satan with his demons against Jesus with the angels.

1:14 The Galilean ministry actually began about a year after Jesus' baptism and temptation, with most of the time spent in a Judean ministry. See John 2:1—4:43. The **gospel** concerns the rule of God evidenced in the person and proclamation of Jesus (see 1:1).

1:15 Jesus announced the inauguration of a new era of salvation, of which repentance and belief in the gospel were prerequisites.

1:16–20 To repent and believe the gospel is simply to follow

brother casting a net into the sea; for they were fishermen.
17 Then Jesus said to them, "Follow Me, and I will make you become [a]fishers of men."
18 [a]They immediately left their nets and *followed Him.
19 When He had gone a little farther from there, He saw James the *son* of Zebedee, and John his brother, who also *were* in the boat mending their nets.
20 And immediately He called them, and they **left** their father Zebedee in the boat with the hired servants, and went after Him.

17 [a]Matt. 13:47, 48
18 [a]Matt. 19:27; [Luke 14:26] *See WW at John 13:36.
21 [a]Matt. 4:13; Luke 4:31–37 [b]Ps. 22:22; Matt. 4:23; Luke 4:16; 13:10
22 [a]Matt. 7:28, 29; 13:54
23 [a][Matt. 12:43]; Mark 5:2; 7:25; Luke 4:33
24 [a]Matt. 8:28, 29; Mark 5:7, 8; Luke 8:28 [b]Mark 3:11; Luke 4:41; James 2:19 [c]Ps. 16:10

WORD WEALTH

1:20 left, *aphiemi* (af-*ee*-ay-mee): Strong's *#863:* A compound of *apo,* "away from," and *hiemi,* "to send." *Aphiemi* has three main categories of meanings: 1) To let go, send away, remit, forgive. In this sense the word is used in connection with divorce (1 Cor. 7:11–13), debts (Matt. 18:27), and especially sins (Matt. 9:2; 1 John 1:9); 2) To permit, let (Matt. 3:15; 5:40; 19:14); 3) To neglect, forsake, leave alone (Matt. 4:11; Mark 7:8; Luke 13:35; John 4:3).

Jesus Casts Out an Unclean Spirit

21 [a]Then they went into Capernaum, and immediately on the Sabbath He entered the [b]synagogue and taught.
22 [a]And they were astonished at His teaching, for He taught them as one having authority, and not as the scribes.
23 Now there was a man in their synagogue with an [a]unclean spirit. And he cried out,
24 saying, "Let *us* alone! [a]What have we to do with You, Jesus of Nazareth? Did You come to destroy us? I [b]know who You are—the [c]Holy One of God!"
25 But Jesus [a]rebuked him, saying, [1]"Be quiet, and come out of him!"
26 And when the unclean spirit [a]had convulsed him and cried out with a loud voice, he came out of him.
27 Then they were all amazed, so that they questioned among themselves, saying, [1]"What is this? What new [2]doctrine *is* this? For with authority He commands even the unclean spirits, and they obey Him."
28 And immediately His [a]fame spread throughout all the region around Galilee.

25 [a][Luke 4:39] [1]Lit. *Be muzzled*
26 [a]Mark 9:20
27 [1]NU *What is this? A new doctrine with authority. He* [2]*teaching*
28 [a]Matt. 4:24; 9:31
29 [a]Matt. 8:14, 15; Luke 4:38, 39
30 *See WW at John 6:21.
32 [a]Matt. 8:16, 17; Luke 4:40, 41
34 [a]Matt. 9:33; Luke 13:32 [b]Mark 3:12; Luke 4:41; Acts 16:17, 18 *See WW at Matt. 12:22.

Peter's Mother-in-Law Healed

29 [a]Now as soon as they had come out of the synagogue, they entered the house of Simon and Andrew, with James and John.
30 But Simon's wife's mother lay sick with a fever, and they told Him about her *at once.
31 So He came and took her by the hand and lifted her up, and immediately the fever left her. And she served them.

Many Healed After Sabbath Sunset

32 [a]At evening, when the sun had set, they brought to Him all who were sick and those who were demon-possessed.
33 And the whole city was gathered together at the door.
34 Then He *healed many who were sick with various diseases, and [a]cast out many demons; and He [b]did not allow the demons to speak, because they knew Him.

Jesus, but note as well two distinct "call-narratives" (vv. 16–18 and vv. 19, 20). Some of these men had already met Him (John 1), but now He calls them to leave their occupations in order to follow Him continuously. They will form a new society who would be formally appointed (3:14) and sent out in mission (6:7).

1:21 Capernaum served as the headquarters of Jesus' Galilean ministry. The leaders of a **synagogue** could invite anyone that they felt was competent to teach.

1:22 Jesus taught independently without appealing to previous authorities, whereas **the scribes** only repeated what others had said. Both *the substance* and *the manner* of the Lord's teaching differed from that of the official interpreters of the Law.

1:23 Many people dismiss the idea of demons (**unclean spirit**) as a superstition of the ancient world, and suggest that Jesus was merely accommodating their beliefs without bothering to change them, knowing it would be a fruitless endeavor. However, the biblical record will not allow this view, making it clear that both the writers of Scripture and Jesus accepted the reality of demons. In fact, Jesus used His authority over them as a sign that He had brought the kingdom of God near (see Matt. 12:28; Luke 11:20). Furthermore, He gave to His followers authority over evil spirits. See Luke 10:19; 2 Cor. 10:3; Eph 6:12.

1:24 Knowledge about Jesus is not necessarily faith in Him (see James 2:19).

1:25 Be quiet is literally "Be muzzled!" Jesus does not seek testimony from demons (see Acts 16:17, 18).

1:31 And she served them: This detail emphasizes the reality of her healing. The cure was instantaneous and complete.

1:34 Many does not imply that there were some that Jesus could not heal, but simply that those He did heal were numerous (see Matt. 8:16).

Preaching in Galilee

35 Now [a]in the morning, having risen
a long while before daylight, He went
out and departed to a [1]solitary place;
and there He [b]prayed.
36 And Simon and those *who were*
with Him searched for Him.
37 When they found Him, they said to
Him, [a]"Everyone [b]is looking for You."
38 But He said to them, [a]"Let us go
into the next towns, that I may preach
there also, because [b]for this purpose I
have come forth."
39 [a]And He was preaching in their
synagogues throughout all Galilee, and
[b]casting out demons.

Jesus Cleanses a Leper

40 [a]Now a leper came to Him, imploring Him, kneeling down to Him and
saying to Him, "If You are willing, You
can make me clean."
41 Then Jesus, moved with [a]compas-
sion,* stretched out *His* hand and
touched him, and said to him, "I am
willing; be cleansed."
42 As soon as He had spoken, [a]imme-
diately the leprosy left him, and he was
cleansed.
43 And He *strictly warned him and
sent him away at once,
44 and said to him, "See that you say
nothing to anyone; but go your way,
show yourself to the priest, and offer
for your cleansing those things [a]which
Moses commanded, as a testimony to
them."
45 [a]However, he went out and began
to proclaim *it* freely, and to spread the
matter, so that Jesus could no longer
openly enter the city, but was outside
in deserted places; [b]and they came to
Him from every direction.

KINGDOM DYNAMICS

1:40–45 The Lord's Willingness to Heal, DIVINE HEALING. Here Jesus declares His willingness to heal the sick. Some insist that we must always preface our prayer for healing with, "If it is Your will." How can one have positive faith who begins a request with an "if"? We do not pray for salvation with an "if."

The leper was certain that Jesus was able to heal him; he was not sure that it was His will. But Jesus' response settled that question: "I am willing; be cleansed." May we not be certain that it is the Lord's will to do that for which He has made redemptive provision? At the same time, one cannot intentionally be living in violation of God's will and expect His promises will be fulfilled. Where biblical conditions for participating in God's processes are present, they must be met; but let us not avoid either God's readiness or God's remedies by reason of the question of His willingness. "If it is Your will" is more often an expression of fear, a proviso to "excuse God of blame" if our faith or His sovereign purposes do not bring healing. If His will is questioned, leave the issue to His sovereignty and remove it from your prayer. Our faith may be weak or incomplete in some regards. We, in fact, may not be healed at times, which should never be viewed as reason for condemnation (Rom. 8:1). Nevertheless, in all things, let us praise Him for His faithfulness and compassion. This is a great environment for healing to be realized and is consistent with the Scriptures, which reveal Jesus as willing to heal.

(Matt. 8:16, 17/Mark 5:24–34) N.V.

35 [a]Luke 4:42, 43 [b]Matt. 26:39, 44; Mark 6:46; Luke 5:16; 6:12; 9:28, 29; Heb. 5:7 [1]*deserted*
37 [a]Matt. 4:25; John 3:26; 12:19 [b][Heb. 11:6]
38 [a]Luke 4:43 [b][Is. 61:1, 2; Mark 10:45; John 16:28; 17:4, 8]
39 [a]Ps. 22:22; Matt. 4:23; 9:35; Mark 1:21; 3:1; Luke 4:44 [b]Mark 5:8, 13; 7:29, 30
40 [a]Matt. 8:2–4; Luke 5:12–14
41 [a]Luke 7:13 *See WW at Matt. 14:14.
42 [a]Matt. 15:28; Mark 5:29
43 *See WW at John 11:38.
44 [a]Lev.14:1–32
45 [a]Matt. 28:15; Luke 5:15 [b]Mark 2:2, 13; 3:7; Luke 5:17; John 6:2

Jesus Forgives and Heals a Paralytic

2 And again [a]He entered Capernaum
after *some* days, and it was heard
that He was in the house.
2 [1]Immediately many gathered together, so that there was no longer
room to receive *them,* not even near
the door. And He preached the word
to them.
3 Then they came to Him, bringing a
[a]paralytic who was carried by four
men.
4 And when they could not come near

CHAPTER 2

1 [a]Matt. 9:1
2 [1]NU omits *Immediately*
3 [a]Matt. 4:24; 8:6; Acts 8:7; 9:33

1:35 Even though Jesus had demonstrated power over demons and disease, He shows the need of prayer for sustained spiritual effectiveness. The time connects this event with the activity of the previous day and evening.
1:38 Jesus refuses to have His agenda dictated by the demands of the people, but clearly states His avowed purpose—to preach in the neighboring towns.
1:41 Touched him: Jesus exhibits an authoritative freedom over the Law which prohibited such physical contact with a leper (see Lev. 13:45, 46).
1:44 Had the man broadcast his healing, the resulting publicity would have aroused an excitement that would have interfered with the preaching of Jesus. In instructing the leper to **show** himself **to the priest,** Jesus shows that His freedom over the Law is balanced by His commitment to that very Law (see Lev. 14:2–32).
1:45 Jesus' purpose of preaching in the next towns (1:38) is frustrated by the leper's disobedience. His fame as a healer is becoming a hindrance to His preaching mission.
2:1 Mark begins to relate a series of events that illustrate the conflict between Jesus and the religious leaders. **The house** probably refers to Simon Peter's residence, where Jesus likely stayed in Capernaum.
2:4 Houses had a flat **roof,** reached by an outside stair and used for additional living space. The persistence and determination of the paralytic's friends demonstrate their faith.

Him because of the crowd, they uncovered the roof where He was. So when they had broken through, they let down the bed on which the paralytic was lying.

5 When Jesus saw their faith, He said to the paralytic, "Son, your sins are forgiven you."

6 And some of the scribes were sitting there and reasoning in their hearts,

7 "Why does this *Man* speak blasphemies like this? [a]Who can *forgive sins but God alone?"

8 But immediately, when Jesus *perceived in His spirit that they reasoned thus within themselves, He said to them, "Why do you reason about these things in your hearts?

9 [a]"Which is easier, to say to the paralytic, '*Your* sins are forgiven you,' or to say, 'Arise, take up your bed and walk'?

10 "But that you may know that the Son of Man has [1]power on earth to forgive sins"—He said to the paralytic,

11 "I say to you, arise, take up your bed, and go to your house."

12 Immediately he arose, took up the bed, and went out in the presence of them all, so that all were amazed and [a]glorified God, saying, "We never saw *anything* like this!"

Matthew the Tax Collector

13 [a]Then He went out again by the sea; and all the multitude came to Him, and He taught them.

14 [a]As He passed by, He saw Levi the *son* of Alphaeus sitting at the tax office. And He said to him, [b]"Follow Me." So he arose and [c]followed Him.

15 [a]Now it happened, as He was dining in *Levi's* house, that many tax collectors and sinners also sat together with Jesus and His *disciples; for there were many, and they followed Him.

16 And when the scribes [1]and Pharisees saw Him eating with the tax collectors and *sinners, they said to His disciples, "How *is it* that He eats and drinks with tax collectors and sinners?"

17 When Jesus heard *it,* He said to them, [a]"Those who are well have no need of a physician, but those who are sick. I did not come to call *the* righteous, but sinners, [1]to repentance."

Jesus Is Questioned About Fasting

18 [a]The disciples of John and of the Pharisees were fasting. Then they came and said to Him, "Why do the disciples of John and of the Pharisees fast, but Your disciples do not fast?"

19 And Jesus said to them, "Can the [1]friends of the bridegroom fast while the bridegroom is with them? *As long as they have the bridegroom with them they cannot fast.

20 "But the days will come when the bridegroom will be [a]taken away from them, and then they will fast in those days.

21 "No one sews a piece of unshrunk cloth on an old garment; or else the 11
new piece pulls away from the old, and the tear is made worse.

7 [a]Job 14:4; Is. 43:25; Dan. 9:9 *See WW at Mark 1:20.
8 *See WW at Luke 5:22.
9 [a]Matt. 9:5
10 [1]*authority*
12 [a]Matt. 15:31; [Phil. 2:11]
13 [a]Matt. 9:9
14 [a]Matt. 9:9–13; Luke 5:27–32 [b]Matt. 4:19; 8:22; 19:21; John 1:43; 12:26; 21:22 [c]Luke 18:28
15 [a]Matt. 9:10 *See WW at Matt. 10:1.
16 [1]NU *of the* *See WW at James 5:20.
17 [a]Matt. 9:12, 13; 18:11; Luke 5:31, 32; 19:10 [1]NU omits *to repentance*
18 [a]Matt. 9:14–17; Luke 5:33–38
19 [1]Lit. *sons of the bridechamber* *See WW at Acts 1:7.
20 [a]Acts 1:9; 13:2, 3; 14:23

2:5 The response of Jesus reflects the Jewish view that forgiveness of sins must precede physical healing. Whether or not this particular disease was the consequence of sin, Jesus went to the heart of the matter. Sin and disease are effects of evil, and Jesus reveals God's opposition to evil in any way it may manifest. His goal is to bring complete wholeness to people.

2:6 In their hearts: The secret reasoning of the scribes "in their hearts" contrasts to Jesus' openness (see v. 8).

2:7 The scribes were correct in their proclamation that only God can forgive sins. They were also correct in their charge of blasphemy against Jesus unless He could provide visible evidence of His authority and ability to grant forgiveness.

2:9–12 The obvious healing of the paralytic effectively establishes the divine prerogative of Jesus to forgive sins. **Son of Man** was a messianic title stemming from Dan. 7:13. Jesus chose it as a self-designation rather than the more popular title "Son of David," which carried nationalistic and materialistic overtones.

2:14 Jesus continues to form His following by summoning a tax collector, a man held in public contempt because of his vocation. **Levi** was his given name, and Matthew ("Gift of God") became his apostolic name (see Matt. 9:9; 10:3).

2:15 Tax collectors and **sinners** are often grouped together, and signify those people who by vocation or morality place themselves outside the society of God's covenant people. For Jesus to have fellowship with such people would bring Him into conflict with the Pharisees.

2:16 By consorting with persons labeled as sinners, Jesus had crossed over the Jewish boundary lines. Tax collectors and sinners were not even to be taught the statutes of God, since their vocation and life-style made them ritually unclean.

2:17 Jesus likens Himself to a **physician** who goes where there is genuine need. It is just as absurd for Jesus to refuse to deal with publicly acknowledged sinners as it is for a doctor to refuse to treat the sick.

2:18 The OT prescribed fasting only on the Day of Atonement (Lev. 16:29), but the Pharisees prescribed fasting on Mondays and Thursdays (see Luke 18:12).

2:19 The present is a time of joy and celebration while **the bridegroom** is with them.

2:20 Jesus alludes to His coming death.

2:21, 22 See section 11 of Truth-In-Action through the Synoptics at the end of Luke.

2:21 To try to tack the new gospel of Jesus to the old legalistic system of Judaism would be like patching **an old garment** with a new, **unshrunk cloth,** which will be ruined by the first wash.

22 "And no one puts new wine into old wineskins; or else the new wine bursts the wineskins, the wine is spilled, and the wineskins are ruined. But new wine must be put into new wineskins."

Jesus Is Lord of the Sabbath

23 [a]Now it happened that He went through the grainfields on the Sabbath; and as they went His disciples began [b]to pluck the heads of grain.
24 And the Pharisees said to Him, "Look, why do they do what is [a]not lawful on the Sabbath?"
25 But He said to them, "Have you never *read [a]what David did when he was in need and hungry, he and those with him:
26 "how he went into the house of God *in the days* of Abiathar the high priest, and ate the *showbread, [a]which is not lawful to eat except for the priests, and also gave some to those who were with him?"
27 And He said to them, "The Sabbath was made for man, and not man for the [a]Sabbath.
28 "Therefore [a]the Son of Man is also Lord of the Sabbath."

Healing on the Sabbath

3 And [a]He entered the synagogue again, and a man was there who had a withered hand.
2 So they [a]watched Him closely, whether He would [b]heal him on the Sabbath, so that they might [1]accuse Him.
3 And He said to the man who had the withered hand, [1]"Step forward."
4 Then He said to them, "Is it lawful on the Sabbath to do good or to do evil, to save life or to kill?" But they kept silent.
5 And when He had looked around at them with anger, being grieved by the [a]hardness* of their hearts, He said to the man, "Stretch out your hand." And he stretched *it* out, and his hand was restored [1]as whole as the *other.
6 [a]Then the Pharisees went out and immediately plotted with [b]the Herodians against Him, how they might destroy Him.

A Great Multitude Follows Jesus

7 But Jesus withdrew with His disciples to the sea. And a great multitude from Galilee *followed Him, [a]and from Judea
8 and Jerusalem and Idumea and beyond the Jordan; and those from Tyre and Sidon, a great multitude, when they heard how [a]many things He was doing, came to Him.
9 So He told His disciples that a small boat should be kept ready for Him because of the multitude, lest they should crush Him.
10 For He healed [a]many, so that as many as had afflictions pressed about Him to [b]touch Him.
11 [a]And the unclean spirits, whenever they saw Him, fell down before Him and cried out, saying, [b]"You are the Son of God."
12 But [a]He sternly warned them that they should not make Him known.

The Twelve Apostles

13 [a]And He went up on the mountain and called to *Him* those He Himself wanted. And they came to Him.
14 Then He appointed twelve, [1]that

23 [a]Luke 6:1–5 [b]Deut. 23:25
24 [a]Ex. 20:10; 31:15
25 [a]1 Sam. 21:1–6 *See WW at Mark 13:14.
26 [a]Lev. 24:5–9 *See WW at Rom. 8:28.
27 [a]Deut. 5:14
28 [a]Matt. 12:8

CHAPTER 3

1 [a]Luke 6:6–11
2 [a]Luke 14:1; 20:20 [b]Luke 13:14 [1]*bring charges against*
3 [1]Lit. *Arise into the midst*
5 [a]Zech. 7:12 [1]NU omits *as whole as the other* *See WW at Rom. 11:25. • See WW at John 14:16.
6 [a]Mark 12:13 [b]Matt. 22:16
7 [a]Luke 6:17 *See WW at John 13:36.
8 [a]Mark 5:19
10 [a]Luke 7:21 [b]Matt. 9:21; 14:36
11 [a]Luke 4:41 [b]Matt. 8:29; 14:33
12 [a]Mark 1:25, 34
13 [a]Luke 9:1
14 [1]NU adds *whom He also named apostles*

2:22 The joy of the new message cannot be contained within Jewish legalism any more than fermenting **wine** can be held by brittle old **wineskins.**

2:23—3:6 See note on Matt. 12:1–14. In these two incidents, Jesus and His disciples were not guilty of violating any scriptural law governing the Sabbath, but only the Pharisaic interpretation of it. Jesus establishes two new positive principles in 2:27, 28. First, God intended the Sabbath to be for the spiritual and physical benefit of His people, not an impossible burden in striving to observe narrow man-made rules. This attitude is in direct contrast to that of the religious authorities, many of whom taught that the only reason God created man was so He would have somebody to observe the Sabbath. The second principle amounts to a claim of deity. If the Sabbath is made for man then **the Son of Man,** as man's Lord and representative, has authority over it. By this claim Jesus is actually stating equality with God, since the Sabbath is the Lord's day.

3:5 Jesus is aware of their inner thoughts before the physical healing (see 2:8). They are silent (v. 4), but He proceeds, though **grieved by the hardness of their hearts.** Note the two imperatives: "Step forward" (v. 3), and **Stretch out your hand.** The miracle was deliberate and aggressive.

3:6 The Herodians were a minor political party favoring the continuation of the dynasty of Herod. Normally, they and the Pharisees were archenemies, but here they are united in their common purpose to destroy Jesus. Evil, as well as righteousness, can unite people.

3:8 The geographical references emphasize both the immense popularity of Jesus and the extreme need of the people. This reference is general and probably embraces an extended period of time.

3:11, 12 Only those who have experienced God's grace can sincerely testify concerning the person and work of Christ.

3:14 Appointed: The Greek verb means "to make someone into something." Jesus selects the **twelve** from the larger group, to form His closest following. The purpose of the appointment is that they **might be with Him** in order to learn from Him and then go out in divine power to extend His work.

they might be with Him and that He might send them out to preach,
15 and to have [1]**power** [2]to *heal sicknesses and to cast out demons:

WORD WEALTH

3:15 power, *exousia* (ex-oo-*see*-ah); Strong's *#1849:* One of four power words (*dunamis, exousia, ischus,* and *kratos*), *exousia* means the authority or right to act, ability, privilege, capacity, delegated authority. Jesus had the *exousia* to forgive sin, heal sicknesses, and cast out devils. *Exousia* is the right to use *dunamis,* "might." Jesus gave His followers *exousia* to preach, teach, heal, and deliver (v. 15), and that authority has never been rescinded (John 14:12). Powerless ministries become powerful upon discovering the *exousia* power resident in the name of Jesus and the blood of Jesus.

16 [1]Simon, [a]to whom He gave the *name Peter;
17 James the *son* of Zebedee and John the brother of James, to whom He gave the name Boanerges, that is, "Sons of Thunder";
18 Andrew, Philip, Bartholomew, Matthew, Thomas, James the *son* of Alphaeus, Thaddaeus, Simon the Cananite;
19 and Judas Iscariot, who also betrayed Him. And they went into a house.

A House Divided Cannot Stand

20 Then the multitude came together again, [a]so that they could not so much as eat bread.
21 But when His [a]own people heard *about this,* they went out to lay hold of Him, [b]for they said, "He is out of His mind."
22 And the scribes who came down from Jerusalem said, [a]"He has Beelzebub," and, "By the [b]ruler of the demons He casts out demons."
23 [a]So He called them to *Himself* and said to them in parables: "How can Satan cast out Satan?
24 "If a kingdom is divided against itself, that kingdom cannot stand.
25 "And if a house is divided against itself, that house cannot stand.
26 "And if Satan has risen up against himself, and is divided, he cannot stand, but has an end.
27 [a]"No one can enter a strong man's house and plunder his goods, unless he first binds the strong man. And then he will plunder his house.

The Unpardonable Sin

28 [a]"Assuredly, I say to you, all sins will be forgiven the sons of men, and whatever blasphemies they may utter;
29 "but he who blasphemes against the Holy Spirit *never has *forgiveness, but is subject to eternal condemnation"—
30 because they [a]said, "He has an unclean spirit."

Jesus' Mother and Brothers Send for Him

31 [a]Then His brothers and His mother came, and standing outside they sent to Him, calling Him.
32 And a multitude was sitting around Him; and they said to Him, "Look, Your mother and Your brothers [1]are outside seeking You."
33 But He answered them, saying, "Who is My mother, or My brothers?"
34 And He looked around in a circle at those who sat about Him, and said, "Here are My mother and My brothers!
35 "For whoever does the [a]will* of God is My brother and My sister and mother."

The Parable of the Sower

4 And [a]again He began to teach by the sea. And a great multitude was

---

15 [1]*authority* [2]NU omits *to heal sicknesses and* *See WW at Matt. 12:22.
16 [a]Matt. 16:18; John 1:42 [1]NU *and He appointed the twelve: Simon . . .* *See WW at John 12:13.
20 [a]Mark 6:31
21 [a]Ps. 69:8; Matt. 13:55; Mark 6:3; John 2:12 [b]John 7:5; 10:20; Acts 26:24; [2 Cor. 5:13]
22 [a]Matt. 9:34; 10:25; Luke 11:15; John 7:20; 8:48, 52; 10:20 [b][John 12:31; 14:30; 16:11; Eph. 2:2]
23 [a]Matt. 12:25–29; Luke 11:17–22
27 [a][Is. 49:24, 25]; Matt. 12:29
28 [a]Matt. 12:31, 32; Luke 12:10; [1 John 5:16]
29 *See WW at Matt. 28:20. • See WW at Heb. 9:22.
30 [a]Matt. 9:34; John 7:20; 8:48, 52; 10:20
31 [a]Matt. 12:46–50; Luke 8:19–21
32 [1]NU, M add *and Your sisters*
35 [a]Eph. 6:6; Heb. 10:36; 1 Pet. 4:2; [1 John 2:17] *See WW at Matt. 12:50.

CHAPTER 4

1 [a]Matt. 13:1–15; Luke 8:4–10

3:21 His own people: The Greek expression may well denote Jesus' immediate family (see 3:31), who misinterpreted His zeal as mental or emotional imbalance.
3:22–30 See note on Matt. 12:24–37.
3:22 Beelzebub was a Canaanite deity, which the Jews used to denote Satan. The **scribes** charge that Jesus *Himself is possessed by Beelzebub* and that He casts out demons by demonic power.
3:23–27 Speaking in **parables,** Jesus shows the absolute absurdity of the charge.
3:24 See Matt. 12:25–29.
3:27 Rather than being allied with Satan, Jesus is in opposition to him and has overpowered him.
3:28–30 The unpardonable sin is not so much an act as a state of sin, a settled attitude that regards good as evil and evil as good. The scribes had repeatedly witnessed the deeds and heard the teachings of Jesus, but their willful blindness to the truth had resulted in such spiritual insensibility that they could no longer recognize the truth and were immune to its convicting power. See note on Matt. 12:31, 32 and Introduction to Mark: The Holy Spirit at Work.
3:31–35 Jesus does not disown His family. He simply states the truth that spiritual kinship with Him goes beyond physical relationships.
4:1–20 See section 4 of Truth-In-Action through the Synoptics at the end of Luke.

gathered to Him, so that He got into a
boat and sat *in it* on the sea; and the
whole multitude was on the land facing
the sea.
2 Then He taught them many things
by parables, [a]and said to them in His
teaching:
3 "Listen! Behold, a sower went out
to sow.
4 "And it happened, as he sowed,
that some *seed* fell by the wayside; and
the birds [1]of the air came and devoured
it.
5 "Some fell on stony ground, where
it did not have much earth; and immediately it sprang up because it had no
depth of earth.
6 "But when the sun was up it was
scorched, and because it had no root
it withered away.
7 "And some *seed* fell among thorns;
and the thorns grew up and choked it,
and it yielded no [1]crop.
8 "But other *seed* fell on good ground
and yielded a crop that sprang up,
increased and produced: some
thirtyfold, some sixty, and some a hundred."
9 And He said [1]to them, "He who has
ears to hear, let him hear!"

The Purpose of Parables

10 [a]But when He was alone, those
around Him with the twelve asked Him
about the parable.
11 And He said to them, "To you it has
been given to [a]know the [1]**mystery** of
the kingdom of God; but to [b]those who
are outside, all things come in parables,
12 "so that

[a]'*Seeing they may see and not*
perceive,
And hearing they may hear and
not understand;
Lest they should turn,
And their sins be forgiven
them.'"

2 [a]Mark 12:38
4 [1]NU, M omit *of the air*
7 [1]Lit. *fruit*
9 [1]NU, M omit *to them*
10 [a]Matt. 13:10; Luke 8:9
11 [a][Matt. 11:25; 1 Cor. 2:10–16; 2 Cor. 4:6] [b][1 Cor. 5:12, 13; Col. 4:5; 1 Thess. 4:12; 1 Tim. 3:7] [1]*secret or hidden truths*
12 [a]Is. 6:9, 10; 43:8; Jer. 5:21; Ezek. 12:2; Matt. 13:14; Luke 8:10; John 12:40; Rom. 11:8
14 [a]Matt. 13:18–23; Luke 8:11–15
17 *See WW at Matt. 11:6.
19 [a]Luke 21:34 [b]Prov. 23:5; Eccl. 5:13; Luke 18:24; 1 Tim. 6:9, 10, 17 *See WW at 1 Pet. 5:7.
20 [a][John 15:2, 5; Rom. 7:4] [1]*receive*

WORD WEALTH

4:11 mystery, *musterion* (moos-*tay*-ree-on); Strong's *#3466:* From *mueo,* "to initiate into the mysteries," hence a secret known only to the initiated, something hidden requiring special revelation. In the NT the word denotes something that people could never know by their own understanding and that demands a revelation from God. The secret thoughts, plans, and dispensations of God remain hidden from unregenerate mankind, but are revealed to all believers. In nonbiblical Greek *musterion* is knowledge withheld, concealed, or silenced. In biblical Greek it is truth revealed (see Col. 1:26). NT *musterion* focuses on Christ's sinless life, atoning death, powerful resurrection, and dynamic ascension.

The Parable of the Sower Explained

13 And He said to them, "Do you not
understand this parable? How then will
you understand all the parables?
14 [a]"The sower sows the word.
15 "And these are the ones by the wayside where the word is sown. When
they hear, Satan comes immediately
and takes away the word that was
sown in their hearts.
16 "These likewise are the ones sown
on stony ground who, when they hear
the word, immediately receive it with
gladness;
17 "and they have no root in themselves, and so endure only for a time.
Afterward, when tribulation or persecution arises for the word's sake, immediately they *stumble.
18 "Now these are the ones sown
among thorns; *they are* the ones who
hear the word,
19 "and the [a]cares* of this world,
[b]the deceitfulness of riches, and the desires for other things entering in choke
the word, and it becomes unfruitful.
20 "But these are the ones sown on
good ground, those who hear the word,
[1]accept *it,* and bear [a]fruit: some thirtyfold, some sixty, and some a hundred."

4:2 About a third of Jesus' teaching was **by parables**. A parable ("a casting alongside") is a brief story told by way of analogy to illustrate a spiritual truth. See note on Matt. 13:3 for interpreting parables.
4:1–9 See note on Matt. 13:3–9.
4:11 Mystery: In biblical thought the term "mystery" means something formerly hidden, but now revealed, which people cannot understand except by divine revelation. The "mystery of the kingdom of God" means that the kingdom of God has come in the person of Jesus of Nazareth, in His words and works, a kingdom which began to penetrate the human situation in a new way in and through His ministry, which continues to do so through the church, and which awaits ultimate consummation at the end of the age. Only by faith can one recognize in the lowly figure of Jesus of Nazareth, the manifestation of God's rule. Gaining a grasp of this "mystery" is the theme for the parables of ch. 4.
4:12 Jesus' followers will understand the lessons taught by parables, or will be stimulated to probe for deeper understanding. Those who have already shut their eyes and ears to the truth will not realize the significance of what they are seeing and hearing, and consequently will not repent and receive forgiveness.
4:13–20 See note on Matt. 13:3–9.

KINGDOM DYNAMICS

4:1–20 Be Wise As to Where You Plant Your Seeds of Faith. God Multiplies Seed Sown in Good Soil, SEED FAITH. We are not only responsible to plant seeds of our faith through actual acts of giving as to the Lord; we are also responsible for selecting the soil in which we plant. It is the quality of the soil that determines the quantity of our harvest. Jesus clearly outlines how we should direct our giving.

First, we must take charge of our giving. We plant our seeds of faith. We do so with patience and diligence (see Luke 8:15).

Second, we must look for places where the Holy Spirit is at work. Look for places alive with the Word of God—where spiritual results are found; where miracles, signs, and wonders confirm the preaching of the Word. Plant your seeds of faith there!

Third, look for people whose ministries already bear fruit for the kingdom of God. Are souls being saved? Are the sick being healed? Are people being delivered? Plant there!

Our Savior Himself tells you what you can expect when you follow His principles for planting: a multiplied harvest! You can look for 30-, 60-, and 100-fold returns when seed is sown wisely.

(Matt. 25:34–40/Luke 5:1–11) O.R.

Light Under a Basket

21 [a]Also He said to them, "Is a lamp
brought to be put under a basket or
under a bed? Is it not to be set on a
lampstand?
22 [a]"For there is nothing hidden which
will not be *revealed, nor has anything
been kept secret but that it should
come to light.
23 [a]"If anyone has ears to hear, let him
hear."
24 Then He said to them, "Take heed
what you hear. [a]With the same measure
you use, it will be measured to
you; and to you who hear, more will
be given.
25 [a]"For whoever has, to him more
will be given; but whoever does not
have, even what he has will be taken
away from him."

The Parable of the Growing Seed

26 And He said, [a]"The kingdom of God
is as if a man should [1]scatter seed on
the ground,
27 "and should sleep by night and rise
by day, and the seed should sprout and
[a]grow, he himself does not know
how.
28 "For the earth [a]yields crops by itself:
first the blade, then the head, after
that the full grain in the head.
29 "But when the grain ripens, immediately
[a]he puts in the sickle, because
the harvest has come."

The Parable of the Mustard Seed

30 Then He said, [a]"To what shall 11
we liken the kingdom of God? Or
with what parable shall we picture
it?
31 "*It is* like a mustard seed which,
when it is sown on the ground, is
smaller than all the seeds on earth;
32 "but when it is sown, it grows up
and becomes greater than all herbs,
and shoots out large branches, so that
the birds of the air may nest under its
shade."

Jesus' Use of Parables

33 [a]And with many such parables He
spoke the word to them as they were
able to hear *it*.
34 But without a parable He did not
speak to them. And when they were
alone, [a]He explained all things to His
disciples.

21 [a]Matt. 5:15; Luke 8:16; 11:33
22 [a]Eccl. 12:14; Matt. 10:26, 27; Luke 12:3; [1 Cor. 4:5] *See WW at Col. 3:4.
23 [a]Matt. 11:15; 13:9, 43; Mark 4:9; Luke 8:8; 14:35; Rev. 3:6, 13, 22; 13:9
24 [a]Matt. 7:2; Luke 6:38; 2 Cor. 9:6
25 [a]Matt. 13:12; 25:29; Luke 8:18; 19:26
26 [a][Matt. 13:24–30, 36–43]; Luke 8:1 [1]*sow*
27 [a][2 Cor. 3:18; 2 Pet. 3:18]
28 [a][John 12:24]
29 [a][Mark 13:30, 39]; Rev. 14:15
30 [a]Matt. 13:31, 32; Luke 13:18, 19; [Acts 2:41; 4:4; 5:14; 19:20]
33 [a]Matt. 13:34, 35; [John 16:12]
34 [a]Luke 24:27, 45

4:21 This parable stresses the need for proper hearing in terms of receiving blessing (v. 24) or judgment (v. 25).

4:22 Precious items, such as jewelry and silverware, are kept concealed until the proper time for their use. In the same way, certain aspects of divine truth may be reserved for full manifestation later, after the ascension of Christ. Jesus taught in parables, not for the ultimate purpose of concealing the truth, but to hide the truth temporarily from His enemies. He then charged His disciples with the ultimate responsibility of bringing it into the open.

4:23 Jesus exhorts them to hear and to heed His admonition.

4:24, 25 Jesus appeals for spiritual perception. Those who receive and assimilate truth will have their capacity for understanding enlarged and their knowledge increased. Those who disbelieve or are indifferent will lose whatever ability for understanding they had, and therefore will continue in ignorance.

4:26–29 This parable is unique to Mark and teaches the supernatural character of God's kingdom. Man is responsible for sowing the kingdom message, but only God can produce effects. In the final analysis, it is totally His deed.

4:30–32 See section 11 of Truth-In-Action through the Synoptics at the end of Luke.

4:30–32 This parable speaks of the destined greatness of the kingdom, contrasting its limited present significance in a small band of original followers with worldwide domination at Jesus' Return.

4:33, 34 Jesus adapted His teaching to the ability of His hearers to understand.

Wind and Wave Obey Jesus

35 [a]On the same day, when evening
had come, He said to them, "Let us
cross over to the other side."
36 Now when they had left the multitude, they took Him along in the boat
as He was. And other little boats were
also with Him.
37 And a great windstorm arose, and
the waves beat into the boat, so that it
was already filling.
38 But He was in the stern, asleep on
a pillow. And they awoke Him and said
to Him, [a]"Teacher, [b]do You not care
that we are perishing?"
39 Then He arose and [a]rebuked the
wind, and said to the sea, [b]"Peace,[1] be
still!" And the wind ceased and there
was a great calm.
40 But He said to them, "Why are you
so fearful? [a]How[1] *is it* that you have
no faith?"
41 And they feared exceedingly, and
said to one another, "Who can this be,
that even the wind and the sea *obey
Him!"

A Demon-Possessed Man Healed

5 Then [a]they came to the other side
of the sea, to the country of the
[1]Gadarenes.
2 And when He had come out of the
boat, immediately there met Him out
of the tombs a man with an [a]unclean
spirit,

KINGDOM DYNAMICS

5:2–5 25. What Is a Demon?, SPIRITUAL ANSWERS. For the answer to this and other probing questions about God and the power life in His kingdom, see the study article "Spiritual Answers to Hard Questions," which begins on page 1996. P.R.

3 who had *his* dwelling among the
tombs; and no one could bind [1]him, not
even with chains,
4 because he had often been bound
with shackles and chains. And the
chains had been pulled apart by him,
and the shackles *broken in pieces;
neither could anyone tame him.
5 And always, night and day, he was
in the mountains and in the tombs, crying out and cutting himself with stones.
6 When he saw Jesus from afar, he
ran and worshiped Him.
7 And he cried out with a loud voice
and said, "What have I to do with You,
Jesus, Son of the Most High God? I
[a]implore[1] You by God that You do not
torment me."
8 For He said to him, [a]"Come out of
the man, unclean spirit!"
9 Then He asked him, "What *is* your
name?" And he answered, saying, "My
name *is* Legion; for we are many."
10 Also he begged Him earnestly that
He would not *send them out of the
country.
11 Now a large herd of [a]swine was
feeding there near the mountains.
12 So all the demons begged Him, saying, "Send us to the swine, that we may
enter them."
13 And [1]at* once Jesus gave them permission. Then the unclean spirits went
out and entered the swine (there were
about two thousand); and the herd ran
violently down the steep place into the
sea, and drowned in the sea.
14 So those who fed the swine fled, and
they told *it* in the city and in the country. And they went out to see what it
was that had happened.
15 Then they came to Jesus, and saw
the one *who had been* [a]demon-
possessed and had the legion, [b]sitting
and [c]clothed and in his **right mind.**
And they were afraid.

WORD WEALTH

5:15 right mind, *sophroneo* (so-fron-*eh*-oh); Strong's *#4993:* To be of sound mind, sane, self-controlled, serious, moderate, sober-minded, restrained, disciplined, able to reason. From *sozo,* "to save," and *phren,* "the mind." The word describes our behavior and attitude as we approach the ending of the age (1 Pet. 4:7).

35 [a]Matt. 8:18, 23–27; Luke 8:22, 25
38 [a][Matt. 23:8–10] [b]Ps. 44:23
39 [a]Mark 9:25; Luke 4:39 [b]Ps. 65:7; 89:9; 93:4; 104:6, 7; Matt. 8:26; Luke 8:24 [1]Lit. *Be quiet*
40 [a]Matt. 14:31, 32; Luke 8:25 [1]NU *Have you still no faith?*
41 *See WW at Rom. 6:17.

CHAPTER 5

1 [a]Matt. 8:28–34; Luke 8:26–37 [1]NU *Gerasenes*
2 [a]Mark 1:23; 7:25; [Rev. 16:13, 14]
3 [1]NU adds *anymore*
4 *See WW at Rom. 16:20.
7 [a]Matt. 26:63; Mark 1:24; Acts 19:13 [1]*adjure*
8 [a]Mark 1:25; 9:25; [Acts 16:18]
10 *See WW at John 20:21.
11 [a]Lev. 11:7, 8; Deut. 14:8; Luke 15:15, 16
13 [1]NU *He gave* *See WW at John 6:21.
15 [a]Matt. 4:24; 8:16; Mark 1:32 [b]Luke 10:39 [c][Is. 61:10]

4:40 Jesus contrasts fear with faith and equates fear with **no faith**. Faith here means trust in God's helping power in crisis, a help that is both present and active in Jesus.
5:2 Matthew (8:28) mentions two demonized men, while Mark and Luke (8:27) mention one, probably the more violent and more prominent of the two.
5:7 The demon fears being thrown into the abyss before the Day of Judgment (see Matt. 8:29; Luke 8:31).
5:8 The Greek tense behind **He said** indicates that Jesus had been repeatedly ordering the **unclean spirit** to leave. Demons do not want to be disembodied and often wage severe contest.
5:9 Legion: At full strength a Roman legion numbered 6,000 men. The name had come to signify a well-organized group possessing great power.
5:13–17 Why Jesus allowed the demons to enter the **swine** is uncertain. Perhaps He was teaching an object lesson to the people of the region, who obviously were more concerned with the loss of property than rejoicing over the deliverance of their countryman (vv. 14–17). Clearly, Jesus valued people more than property.

16 And those who saw it told them how it happened to him *who had been* demon-possessed, and about the swine.
17 Then [a]they began to plead with Him to depart from their region.
18 And when He got into the boat, [a]he who had been demon-possessed begged Him that he might be with Him.
19 However, Jesus did not permit him, but said to him, "Go home to your friends, and tell them what great things the Lord has done for you, and how He has had compassion on you."
20 And he departed and began to [a]proclaim in [1]Decapolis all that Jesus had done for him; and all [b]marveled.

A Girl Restored to Life and a Woman Healed

21 [a]Now when Jesus had crossed over again by boat to the other side, a great multitude gathered to Him; and He was by the sea.
22 [a]And behold, one of the rulers of the synagogue came, Jairus by name. And when he saw Him, he fell at His feet
23 and begged Him earnestly, saying, "My little daughter lies at the point of death. Come and [a]lay Your hands on her, that she may be healed, and she will live."
24 So *Jesus* went with him, and a great multitude followed Him and thronged Him.
25 Now a certain woman [a]had a flow of blood for twelve years,
26 and had suffered many things from many physicians. She had spent all that she had and was no better, but rather grew worse.
27 When she heard about Jesus, she came behind *Him* in the crowd and [a]touched His garment.
28 For she said, "If only I may touch His clothes, I shall be *made well."
29 Immediately the fountain of her blood was dried up, and she felt in *her* body that she was healed of the [1]affliction.
30 And Jesus, immediately knowing in Himself that [a]power had gone out of Him, turned around in the crowd and said, "Who touched My clothes?"
31 But His disciples said to Him, "You see the multitude thronging You, and You say, 'Who touched Me?' "
32 And He looked around to see her who had done this thing.
33 But the woman, [a]fearing and trembling, knowing what had happened to her, came and fell down before Him and told Him the whole truth.
34 And He said to her, "Daughter, [a]your *faith has made you well. [b]Go in *peace, and be healed of your affliction."

KINGDOM DYNAMICS

5:24–34 The Place of Persistent Faith, DIVINE HEALING. This passage relates the account of a desperate woman whose healing was the result of great and persistent faith. Her illness made her ceremonially unclean and disqualified her for mixing with crowds of people, yet she was certain that "if only I may touch His clothes, I shall be made well" (v. 28). Jesus did not rebuke her, but delayed His mission to the home of Jairus, whose daughter was dying, in order to assure her of healing and salvation.

Jesus later raised Jairus's daughter from the dead, but here He took time to minister to one with positive faith. That such persistence is rewarded is not to suggest healing or any other work of God is earned by human effort. It rather illustrates the need to be bold in what we believe—to not be deterred by circumstance or discouraged by others. "All things *are* possible to him [or her] who believes" (9:23); and they all are by God's grace (Eph. 2:8, 9).

(Mark 1:40–45/Mark 9:22, 23) N.V.

35 [a]While He was still speaking, *some* came from the ruler of the synagogue's *house* who said, "Your daughter is dead. Why trouble the Teacher any further?"
36 As soon as Jesus heard the word that was spoken, He said to the ruler of the synagogue, "Do not be afraid; only [a]believe."
37 And He permitted no one to follow

17 [a]Matt. 8:34; Acts 16:39
18 [a]Luke 8:38, 39
20 [a]Ex. 15:2; Ps. 66:16 [b]Matt. 9:8, 33; John 5:20; 7:21; Acts 3:12; 4:13 [1]Lit. *Ten Cities*
21 [a]Matt. 9:1; Luke 8:40
22 [a]Matt. 9:18–26; Luke 8:41–56; Acts 13:15
23 [a]Matt. 8:15; Mark 6:5; 7:32; 8:23, 25; 16:18; Luke 4:40; Acts 9:17; 28:8
25 [a]Lev. 15:19, 25; Matt. 9:20
27 [a]Matt. 14:35, 36; Mark 3:10; 6:56
28 *See WW at Luke 7:50.
29 [1]*suffering*
30 [a]Luke 6:19; 8:46
33 [a][Ps. 89:7]
34 [a]Matt. 9:22; Mark 10:52; Acts 14:9 [b]1 Sam. 1:17; 20:42; 2 Kin. 5:19; Luke 7:50; 8:48; Acts 16:36; [James 2:16] *See WW at Mark 11:22. • See WW at Luke 1:79.
35 [a]Luke 8:49
36 [a][Mark 9:23; John 11:40]

5:19 Instead of commanding the man to be quiet, as in the cases of Galilean healings, Jesus commissioned him to bear witness to his deliverance, possibly because in that Gentile region the fires of Jewish messianism would not be fueled.
5:22–43 These two miracles demonstrate the power of Jesus over disease and death, and His response to simple faith.
5:30–34 Jesus desires to perfect the woman's faith and to lead her to a public confession of faith. He rewards her testimony with the assurance that she can **go in peace**.
5:35 The implication of the person's statement is that Jesus can heal one who is sick, but cannot raise one from the dead.
5:36 The importance of faith in the midst of crisis is underscored (4:40; 5:34).
5:37 Jesus provides special instruction to this inner circle (see 9:2; 14:33).

Him except Peter, James, and John the
brother of James.
38 Then He came to the house of the
ruler of the synagogue, and saw
[1]a tumult and those who [a]wept and
wailed loudly.
39 When He came in, He said to them,
"Why make this commotion and weep?
The child is not dead, but [a]sleeping."
40 And they ridiculed Him. [a]But when
He had put them all outside, He took
the father and the mother of the child,
and those *who were* with Him, and entered where the child was lying.
41 Then He took the child by the hand,
and said to her, "Talitha, cumi," which
is translated, "Little girl, I say to you,
arise."
42 Immediately the girl arose and
walked, for she was twelve years *of
age.* And they were [a]overcome with
great amazement.
43 But [a]He commanded them strictly
that no one should know it, and said
that *something* should be given her to
eat.

Jesus Rejected at Nazareth

6 Then [a]He went out from there and
came to His own country, and His
disciples followed Him.
2 And when the Sabbath had come,
He began to teach in the synagogue.
And many hearing *Him* were [a]aston-
ished, saying, [b]"Where *did* this Man
get these things? And what *wisdom
is this which is given to Him, that such
mighty works are performed by His
hands!
3 "Is this not the carpenter, the Son
of Mary, and [a]brother of James, Joses,
Judas, and Simon? And are not His sisters here with us?" So they [b]were *offended at Him.
4 But Jesus said to them, [a]"A
*prophet is not without honor except

38 [a]Acts 9:39 [1]*an uproar*
39 [a]John 11:4, 11
40 [a]Acts 9:40
42 [a]Mark 1:27; 7:37
43 [a][Matt. 8:4; 12:16–19; 17:9]

CHAPTER 6

1 [a]Matt. 13:54
2 [a]Matt. 7:28 [b]John 6:42 *See WW at Acts 6:10.
3 [a]Matt. 12:46 [b][Matt. 11:6] *See WW at Matt. 11:6.
4 [a]John 4:44 *See WW at Matt. 2:5.
5 [a]Gen. 19:22; 32:25
6 [a]Is. 59:16 [b]Matt. 9:35
7 [a]Mark 3:13, 14 [b][Eccl. 4:9, 10]
9 [a][Eph. 6:15]
10 [a]Matt. 10:11
11 [a]Matt. 10:14 [b]Acts 13:51; 18:6 [1]NU *whatever place* [2]NU omits the rest of v. 11.
12 *See WW at Matt. 3:2.
13 [a][James 5:14]
14 [a]Luke 9:7–9 [b]Luke 19:37 *See WW at 1 Cor. 11:19. See WW at 1 Thess. 2:13.
15 [a]Mark 8:28 [b]Matt. 21:11 [1]NU, M *a prophet, like one*

in his own country, among his own relatives, and in his own house."
5 [a]Now He could do no mighty work
there, except that He laid His hands
on a few sick people and healed *them.*
6 And [a]He marveled because of their
unbelief. [b]Then He went about the villages in a circuit, teaching.

Sending Out the Twelve

7 [a]And He called the twelve to *Himself,* and began to send them out
[b]two *by* two, and gave them power
over unclean spirits.
8 He commanded them to take nothing for the journey except a staff—no
bag, no bread, no copper in *their*
money belts—
9 but [a]to wear sandals, and not to put
on two tunics.
10 [a]Also He said to them, "In whatever
place you enter a house, stay there till
you depart from that place.
11 [a]"And [1]whoever will not receive
you nor hear you, when you depart
from there, [b]shake off the dust under
your feet as a testimony against them.
[2]Assuredly, I say to you, it will be more
tolerable for Sodom and Gomorrah in
the day of judgment than for that city!"
12 So they went out and preached that
people should *repent.
13 And they cast out many demons,
[a]and anointed with oil many who were
sick, and healed *them.*

John the Baptist Beheaded

14 [a]Now King Herod heard *of Him,* for
His name had become *well known.
And he said, "John the Baptist is risen
from the dead, and therefore [b]these
powers are at *work in him."
15 [a]Others said, "It is Elijah." And others said, "It is [1]the Prophet, [b]or like
one of the prophets."

5:38 It was customary to employ professional mourners to display grief at funerals.
5:39 Jesus speaks figuratively of death, indicating a temporary condition. His words are both a rebuke to unbelief and an encouragement to bereaved people then and now.
5:41 Mark translates Jesus' Aramaic for his Roman readers.
5:43 A great outburst of excitement might interfere with His teaching ministry and perhaps precipitate a crisis before His ministry was completed.
6:1–6 This was Jesus' second rejection at Nazareth, the first one occurring at the beginning of His Galilean ministry (Luke 4:16–30).
6:2, 3 The people were perplexed because they knew about the background of Jesus, whereas the coming of the Messiah was supposed to be shrouded in mystery. The reference to Jesus' brothers and sisters clearly shows that following Jesus' birth as Mary's "firstborn Son" (Luke 2:7), she and Joseph entered into normal marriage relations (see Matt. 1:25). The failure to mention Joseph probably indicates that he had already died.
6:7–13 Jesus delegated His own power to **the twelve,** gave them instructions concerning their provisions and concerning their public acceptance or rejection, then sent them on a mission tour.
6:11 To **shake off the dust,** was an act of extreme contempt. When a Jew reentered Jewish territory from a pagan land, he shook the defiled heathen dust from his feet. The apostles were to treat those who rejected them as though they were pagans.
6:12 A preliminary fulfillment of the appointment of the Twelve (3:14, 15), showing as well a similarity to the preaching of repentance by John the Baptist (1:4) and by Jesus (1:14, 15).
6:14 Herod Antipas was the son of Herod the Great.

16 [a]But when Herod heard, he said, "This is John, whom I beheaded; he has been raised from the dead!"
17 For Herod himself had sent and laid hold of John, and bound him in prison for the sake of Herodias, his brother Philip's wife; for he had married her.
18 Because John had said to Herod, [a]"It is not lawful for you to have your brother's wife."
19 Therefore Herodias [1]held it against him and wanted to kill him, but she could not;
20 for Herod [a]feared John, knowing that he *was* a just and holy man, and he protected him. And when he heard him, he [1]did many things, and heard him gladly.
21 [a]Then an opportune day came when Herod [b]on his birthday gave a feast for his nobles, the high officers, and the chief *men* of Galilee.
22 And when Herodias' daughter herself came in and danced, and pleased Herod and those who sat with him, the king said to the girl, "Ask me whatever you want, and I will give *it* to you."
23 He also swore to her, [a]"Whatever you ask me, I will give you, up to half my kingdom."
24 So she went out and said to her mother, "What shall I ask?" And she said, "The head of John the Baptist!"
25 Immediately she came in with haste to the king and asked, saying, "I want you to give me at once the head of John the Baptist on a platter."
26 [a]And the king was exceedingly sorry; *yet,* because of the oaths and because of those who sat with him, he did not want to refuse her.
27 Immediately the king sent an executioner and commanded his head to be brought. And he went and beheaded him in prison,
28 brought his head on a platter, and gave it to the girl; and the girl gave it to her mother.
29 When his disciples heard *of it,* they came and [a]took away his corpse and laid it in a tomb.

16 [a]Matt. 14:2; Luke 3:19
18 [a]Lev. 18:16; 20:21
19 [1]*held a grudge*
20 [a]Matt. 14:5; 21:26 [1]NU *was very perplexed, yet*
21 [a]Matt. 14:6 [b]Gen. 40:20
23 [a]Esth. 5:3, 6; 7:2
26 [a]Matt. 14:9
29 [a]1 Kin. 13:29, 30; Matt. 27:58–61; Acts 8:2
30 [a]Luke 9:10
31 [a]Matt. 14:13 [b]Mark 3:20 *See WW at Rev. 14:13.
32 [a]Matt. 14:13–21; Luke 9:10–17; John 6:5–13
33 [a][Col. 1:6] [1]NU, M *they*
34 [a]Matt. 9:36; 14:14; [Heb. 5:2] [b]Num. 27:17; 1 Kin. 22:17; 2 Chr. 18:16; Zech. 10:2 [c][Is. 48:17; 61:1–3]; Luke 9:11 *See WW at Matt. 14:14. • See WW at John 10:2.
35 [a]Matt. 14:15; Luke 9:12
36 [1]NU *something to eat* and omits the rest of v. 36.
37 [a]Num. 11:13, 22; 2 Kin. 4:43
38 [a]Matt. 14:17; Luke 9:13; John 6:9
39 [a]Matt. 15:35; Mark 8:6
41 [a]John 11:41, 42 [b]1 Sam. 9:13; Matt. 15:36; 26:26; Mark 8:7; Luke 24:30

Feeding the Five Thousand

30 [a]Then the apostles gathered to Jesus and told Him all things, both what they had done and what they had taught.
31 [a]And He said to them, "Come aside by yourselves to a deserted place and *rest a while." For [b]there were many coming and going, and they did not even have time to eat.
32 [a]So they departed to a deserted place in the boat by themselves.
33 But [1]the multitudes saw them departing, and many [a]knew Him and ran there on foot from all the cities. They arrived before them and came together to Him.
34 [a]And Jesus, when He came out, saw a great multitude and was *moved with compassion for them, because they were like [b]sheep not having a *shepherd. So [c]He began to teach them many things.
35 [a]When the day was now far spent, His disciples came to Him and said, "This is a deserted place, and already the hour *is* late.
36 "Send them away, that they may go into the surrounding country and villages and buy themselves [1]bread; for they have nothing to eat."
37 But He answered and said to them, "You give them something to eat." And they said to Him, [a]"Shall we go and buy two hundred denarii worth of bread and give them *something* to eat?"
38 But He said to them, "How many loaves do you have? Go and see." And when they found out they said, [a]"Five, and two fish."
39 Then He [a]commanded them to make them all sit down in groups on the green grass.
40 So they sat down in ranks, in hundreds and in fifties.
41 And when He had taken the five loaves and the two fish, He [a]looked up to heaven, [b]blessed and broke the loaves, and gave *them* to His disciples

6:16 Herod's response to the ministry of the Twelve is mentioned twice (vv. 14, 16). He is convinced that John the Baptist has been raised from the dead.

6:17 Herod had seduced his niece **Herodias,** who was married to his brother Philip, and persuaded her to divorce her husband and marry him. In turn, he divorced his own wife.

6:31 Jesus withdrew with His disciples from the crowds in order to rest, to avoid the hostility of the Jewish religious leaders and the jealousy of Herod, and to teach them in solitude.

6:34 Because: Explanation is given for Jesus' compassion upon the multitude. **Sheep not having a shepherd:** The characteristic of such a leaderless crowd is helplessness and bewilderment.

6:35–44 See notes on John 6:22–71.

6:41 Blessed: According to Jewish custom, at the beginning of the meal, the host or head of a family takes bread and blesses God for the meal. Beyond the actual blessing, Jesus relies upon the Father for the miracle that will meet the needs of the people.

to set before them; and the two fish He
divided among *them* all.
42 So they all ate and were filled.
43 And they took up twelve baskets
full of fragments and of the fish.
44 Now those who had eaten the
loaves were [1]about five thousand men.

Jesus Walks on the Sea

45 [a]Immediately He [1]made His disciples get into the boat and go before
Him to the other side, to Bethsaida,
while He sent the multitude away.
46 And when He had sent them away,
He [a]departed to the mountain to pray.
47 Now when evening came, the boat
was in the middle of the sea; and He
was alone on the land.
48 Then He saw them straining at row-
ing, for the wind was against them.
Now about the fourth watch of the
night He came to them, walking on the
sea, and [a]would have passed them by.
49 And when they saw Him walking
on the sea, they supposed it was a
[a]ghost, and cried out;
50 for they all saw Him and were *troubled. But immediately He talked with
them and said to them, [a]"Be[1] of good
cheer! It is I; do not be [b]afraid."
51 Then He went up into the boat to
them, and the wind [a]ceased. And they
were greatly [b]amazed in themselves
beyond measure, and marveled.
52 For [a]they had not understood about
the loaves, because their [b]heart was
*hardened.

Many Touch Him and Are Made Well

53 [a]When they had crossed over, they
came to the land of Gennesaret and an-
chored there.
54 And when they came out of the
boat, immediately [1]the people recognized Him,
55 ran through that whole surrounding
region, and began to carry about on

44 [1]NU, M omit *about*
45 [a]Matt. 14:22–32; John 6:15–21 [1]*invited, strongly urged*
46 [a]Mark 1:35; Luke 5:16
48 [a]Luke 24:28
49 [a]Matt. 14:26; Luke 24:37
50 [a]Matt. 9:2; John 16:33 [b]Is. 41:10 [1]*Take courage* *See WW at Luke 24:38.
51 [a]Ps. 107:29 [b]Mark 1:27; 2:12; 5:42; 7:37
52 [a]Matt. 16:9–11; Mark 8:17, 18 [b]Is. 63:17; Mark 3:5; 16:14 *See WW at Mark 8:17.
53 [a]Matt. 14:34–36; John 6:24, 25
54 [1]Lit. *they*
56 [a]Matt. 9:20; Mark 5:27, 28; [Acts 19:12] [b]Num. 15:38, 39

CHAPTER 7

1 [a]Matt.15:1–20
2 [a]Matt. 15:20 [1]NU omits *when* [2]NU omits *they found fault*
3 [a]Mark 7:5, 8, 9, 13; Gal. 1:14; 1 Pet. 1:18 [1]Lit. *with the fist*
5 [a]Matt. 15:2
6 [a]Matt. 23:13–29 [b]Is. 29:13 *See WW at Matt. 6:2. • See WW at Philem. 15.
8 [1]NU omits the rest of v. 8.

beds those who were sick to wherever
they heard He was.
56 Wherever He entered, into villages,
cities, or the country, they laid the sick
in the marketplaces, and begged Him
that [a]they might just touch the [b]hem
of His garment. And as many as
touched Him were made well.

Defilement Comes from Within

7 Then [a]the Pharisees and some of 1
the scribes came together to Him,
having come from Jerusalem.
2 Now [1]when they saw some of His
disciples eat bread with defiled, that is,
with [a]unwashed hands, [2]they found
fault.
3 For the Pharisees and all the Jews
do not eat unless they wash *their* hands
[1]in a special way, holding the [a]tra-
dition of the elders.
4 *When they come* from the marketplace, they do not eat unless they wash.
And there are many other things which
they have received and hold, *like* the
washing of cups, pitchers, copper vessels, and couches.
5 [a]Then the Pharisees and scribes
asked Him, "Why do Your disciples
not walk according to the tradition of
the elders, but eat bread with unwashed hands?"
6 He answered and said to them,
"Well did Isaiah prophesy of you
[a]hypocrites,* as it is written:

[b]*'This people honors Me with their*
lips,
*But their heart *is far from Me.*
7 *And in vain they worship Me,*
Teaching as doctrines the
commandments of men.'

8 "For laying aside the commandment of God, you hold the tradition of
men—[1]the washing of pitchers and
cups, and many other such things you
do."

6:48 The fourth watch was between 3:00 and 6:00 A.M.
6:52 For: Mark explains the disciples' fear. They had just seen Jesus multiply **loaves** for the masses in need, but now they are unable to apply His all-sufficiency to their own need.
6:54–56 Even with this tremendous popularity, the people turned away from Jesus that very day (see John 6:66).
6:55 Whenever Jesus makes a geographical move, He is besieged by the masses (1:45; 3:7, 19, 20; 4:1; 5:24; 6:32, 33).
6:56 Touch: The touch of Jesus' garment by the woman with the hemorrhage was public (5:27), which may account for a similar action by the masses.
7:1–13 See section 1 of Truth-In-Action through the Synoptics at the end of Luke.
7:1–5 The charge was not that the disciples were guilty of poor hygiene, but that they did not observe rituals of cleansing. The Pharisees taught that religious defilement could be spread by touch, so they prescribed elaborate ceremonies of cleansing. These were part of **the tradition,** or oral law, which they regarded as having equal authority with the written Law.
7:6, 7 Worship is **vain** when it is scrupulous in external regulations devised by men, but subtly evasive of the things required by God.
7:8, 9 Jesus charges His opponents with actual disobedience of God's commandment through their preference for the oral law.

9 He said to them, *"All too well*
[a]you [1]reject the commandment of
God, that you may keep your tradition.
10 "For Moses said, [a]*'Honor your fa-*
ther and your mother'; and, [b]*'He who*
curses father or mother, let him be put
to death.'
11 "But you say, 'If a man says to his
father or mother, [a]"Whatever profit
you might have received from me *is*
Corban"—' (that is, a gift *to God*),
12 "then you no longer let him do anything for his father or his mother,
13 "making the word of God of no effect through your tradition which you
have handed down. And many such
things you do."

9 [a]Prov. 1:25; Jer. 7:23, 24; Is. 24:5 [1]*set aside* 10 [a]Ex. 20:12; Deut. 5:16; Matt. 15:4 [b]Ex. 21:17; Lev. 20:9; Prov. 20:20
11 [a]Matt. 15:5; 23:18

7:9 That you may keep: The purpose clause indicates that their tradition is more important than God's commandments. They reject what is primary "in order to keep" that which is secondary.
7:10–13 Jesus substantiates the charge by contrasting Moses' commandment (Ex. 20:12; 21:17) with their current tradition of **Corban,** a word denoting withdrawing something from its intended use as though it were an offering made to God. Therefore, if a man wanted to be relieved of the responsibility of caring for his aged and infirm parents, he could declare his property Corban. No one else could then share his possession, although he himself could continue to enjoy its benefits throughout his lifetime. Such a practice was deceitful and in direct violation of God's Commandment (Ex. 20:12).

Cities of the Galilean Ministry.
"And Jesus went about all Galilee, teaching in their synagogues, preaching the gospel of the kingdom, and healing all kinds of sickness and all kinds of disease among the people. Then His fame went throughout all Syria . . . Great multitudes followed Him—from Galilee, and from Decapolis, Jerusalem, Judea, and beyond the Jordan" (Matt. 4:23–25)

Jesus began His public ministry at Cana, where He graced a wedding party with His presence and turned water into wine (John 2:1–11). In the synagogue of Nazareth, Jesus announced that He was the fulfillment of prophecy from the Book of Isaiah (Luke 4:16–22). But His hometown rejected Him, so He went to Capernaum, a prosperous fishing town situated along an international trade route. There He established a base of ministry.

In Capernaum He called Matthew to be His disciple (Mark 2:14) and healed the paralyzed servant of a centurion (Matt. 8:5–13), as well as Peter's mother-in-law (Matt. 8:14, 15). The Sea of Galilee, with its fishing industry, was the setting for many miracles. At Nain, Jesus mercifully raised to life the only son of a widow (Luke 7:11–17). Chorazin and Bethsaida were cities Jesus chastised for their unbelief (Matt. 11:21). The area of Gergesa was possibly where Jesus healed the demoniacs (Matt. 8:28–34).

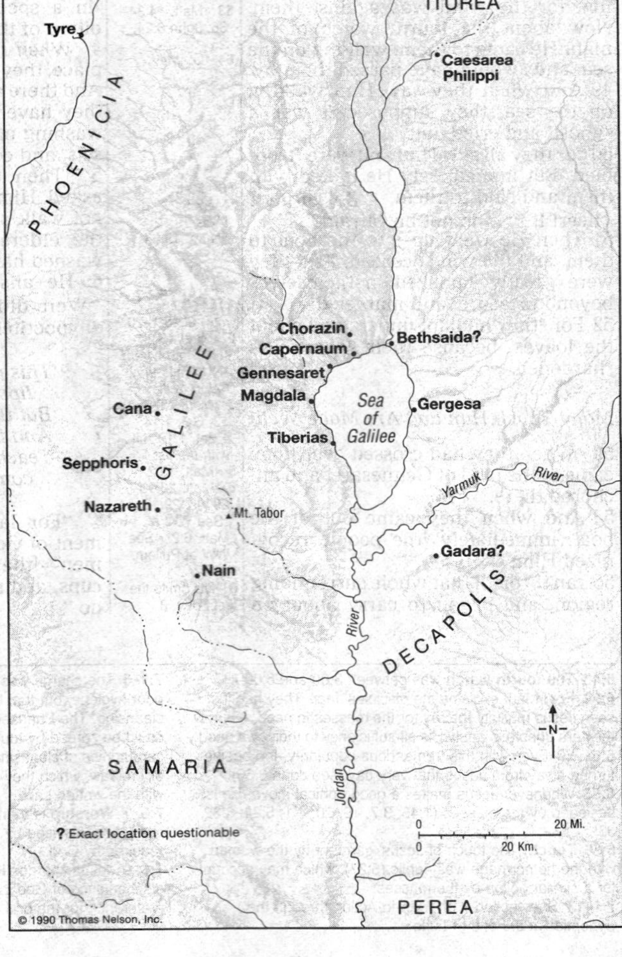

9 14 [a]When He had called all the multitude to *Himself,* He said to them, "Hear
Me, everyone, and [b]understand:
15 "There is nothing that enters a man
from outside which can defile him; but
the things which come out of him,
those are the things that [a]defile a man.
16 [a]"If[1] anyone has ears to hear, let
him hear!"
17 [a]When He had entered a house
away from the crowd, His disciples
asked Him concerning the parable.
18 So He said to them, [a]"Are you thus
without understanding also? Do you
not perceive that whatever enters a
man from outside cannot defile him,
19 "because it does not enter his heart
but his stomach, and is eliminated,
[1]*thus* purifying all foods?"
20 And He said, [a]"What comes out of
a man, that defiles a man.
21 [a]"For from within, out of the heart
of men, [b]proceed evil *thoughts,
[c]adulteries,* [d]fornications, murders,
22 "thefts, [a]covetousness, wickedness,
[b]deceit, [c]lewdness,* an evil eye, [d]blas-
phemy, [e]**pride,** foolishness.

WORD WEALTH

7:22 pride, *huperephania* (hoop-er-ay-fan-*ee*-ah); Strong's *#5243:* Twelfth on the list of thirteen inner vices, the word means haughtiness, arrogance, ostentatious pride bordering on insolence, and a disdainful attitude toward others. It is a pharisaical sin characterized by superiority of attitude. The word is a combination of *huper,* "over," and *phainomai,* "to appear." It is a state of pride that is the very opposite of Jesus' claim for Himself, meek (*praotes*) and lowly (*tapeinos*).

23 "All these evil things come from
within and defile a man."

A Gentile Shows Her Faith

24 [a]From there He arose and went to
the region of Tyre [1]and Sidon. And He
entered a house and wanted no one to
*know *it,* but He could not be [b]hidden.
25 For a woman whose young daughter had an unclean spirit heard about
Him, and she came and [a]fell at His feet.
26 The woman was a [1]Greek, a [2]Syro-
Phoenician by birth, and she kept
[3]asking Him to cast the demon out of
her daughter.
27 But Jesus said to her, "Let the children be *filled first, for it is not good
to take the children's bread and throw
it to the little dogs."
28 And she answered and said to Him,
"Yes, Lord, yet even the little dogs under the table eat from the children's
crumbs."
29 Then He said to her, "For this saying go your way; the demon has gone
out of your daughter."
30 And when she had come to her
house, she found the demon gone out,
and her daughter lying on the bed.

Jesus Heals a Deaf-Mute

31 [a]Again, departing from the region
of Tyre and Sidon, He came through
the midst of the region of Decapolis to
the Sea of Galilee.
32 Then [a]they brought to Him one who
was deaf and had an impediment in his
speech, and they begged Him to put
His hand on him.
33 And He took him aside from the
multitude, and put His fingers in his
ears, and [a]He spat and touched his
tongue.
34 Then, [a]looking up to heaven,
[b]He sighed, and said to him, "Ephpha-
tha," that is, "Be opened."
35 [a]Immediately his ears were opened,
and the [1]impediment of his tongue was
loosed, and he spoke plainly.
36 Then [a]He commanded them that
they should tell no one; but the more
He commanded them, the more widely
they proclaimed *it.*
37 And they were [a]astonished beyond
measure, saying, "He has done all

14 [a]Matt. 15:10 [b]Matt. 16:9, 11, 12
15 [a]Is. 59:3
16 [a]Matt. 11:15 [1]NU omits v. 16.
17 [a]Matt. 15:15
18 [a][Heb. 5:11–14]
19 [1]NU sets off the final phrase as Mark's comment that Jesus has declared all foods clean.
20 [a]Ps. 39:1
21 [a]Gen. 6:5; 8:21 [b][Gal. 5:19–21] [c]2 Pet. 2:14 [d]1 Thess. 4:3
*See WW at Luke 2:35. • See WW at John 8:3.
22 [a]Luke 12:15 [b]Rom. 1:28, 29 [c]1 Pet. 4:3 [d]Rev. 2:9 [e]1 John 2:16
*See WW at 1 Pet. 4:3.
24 [a]Matt. 15:21 [b]Mark 2:1, 2 [1]NU omits *and Sidon*
*See WW at John 8:32.
25 [a]John 11:32
26 [1]*Gentile* [2]A Syrian of Phoenicia [3]*begging*
27 *See WW at Matt. 15:33.
31 [a]Matt. 15:29
32 [a]Luke 11:14
33 [a]Mark 8:23
34 [a]Mark 6:41 [b]John 11:33, 38
35 [a]Is. 35:5, 6 [1]Lit. *bond*
36 [a]Mark 5:43
37 [a]Mark 6:51; 10:26

7:14–23 See section 9 of Truth-In-Action through the Synoptics at the end of Luke.
7:15–23 Jesus teaches that the true source of defilement is not a disregard for external rituals or dietary laws, but a polluted heart that plots evil.
7:24 This was the only time Jesus left Jewish territory.
7:27 The Jews insultingly referred to Gentiles as **dogs**. Even though Jesus softens the barb by using the word for house pets instead of wild and unclean scavengers, His response to the woman still sounds harsh. Actually, in assuming the appearance of traditional Jewish prejudice, Jesus was drawing from her a confession of triumphant faith.
7:28 The woman exhibits an understanding of the implication of Jesus that the gospel must first be offered to the covenant people.
7:31 Decapolis was a Gentile area east of Galilee.
7:33 Jesus personally indicates to the man the ministry He is going to perform. The touch and spittle (representing Jesus' own life, which was to be the source of the healing) gain the man's confidence and encourage him to expect healing.
7:37 The words of the people may have been a simple expression of wonder and praise, although some commentators see a deliberate reference to Is. 35:5, 6, which prophesies the coming of the era of salvation. If that is the case, then the people were acknowledging the miracle as a sign that the age of which Isaiah spoke had arrived in Jesus.

things well. He [b]makes both the deaf
to hear and the mute to speak."

Feeding the Four Thousand

8 In those days, [a]the multitude being
very great and having nothing to
eat, Jesus called His disciples *to Him*
and said to them,
2 "I have [a]compassion* on the multitude, because they have now continued
with Me three days and have nothing
to eat.
3 "And if I send them away hungry
to their own houses, they will faint on
the way; for some of them have come
from afar."
4 Then His disciples answered Him,
"How can one *satisfy these people
with bread here in the wilderness?"
5 [a]He asked them, "How many loaves
do you have?" And they said, "Seven."
6 So He commanded the multitude to
sit down on the ground. And He took
the seven loaves and gave thanks,
broke *them* and gave *them* to His disciples to set before *them;* and they set
them before the multitude.
7 They also had a few small fish; and
[a]having blessed them, He said to set
them also before *them.*
8 So they ate and were filled, and they
took up seven large baskets of leftover
fragments.
9 Now those who had eaten were
about four thousand. And He sent them
away,
10 [a]immediately got into the boat with
His disciples, and came to the region
of Dalmanutha.

The Pharisees Seek a Sign

11 [a]Then the Pharisees came out and
began to dispute with Him, seeking
from Him a sign from heaven, testing
Him.
12 But He [a]sighed deeply in His spirit,
and said, "Why does this generation
seek a sign? Assuredly, I say to you,
[b]no sign shall be given to this generation."

37 [b]Matt. 12:22

CHAPTER 8

1 [a]Matt. 15:32–39; Mark 6:34–44; Luke 9:12
2 [a]Matt. 9:36; 14:14; Mark 1:41; 6:34 *See WW at Matt. 14:14.
4 *See WW at Matt. 15:33.
5 [a]Matt. 15:34; Mark 6:38; John 6:9
7 [a]Matt. 14:19; Mark 6:41
10 [a]Matt. 15:39
11 [a]Matt. 12:38; 16:1; Luke 11:16; John 2:18; 6:30; 1 Cor. 1:22
12 [a]Mark 7:34 [b]Matt. 12:39
14 [a]Matt. 16:5 [1]NU, M *they*
15 [a]Matt. 16:6; Luke 12:1 [1]*yeast*
17 [a]Mark 6:52; 16:14 [1]NU omits *still*
19 [a]Matt. 14:20; Mark 6:43; Luke 9:17; John 6:13
20 [a]Matt. 15:37 *See WW at Eph. 3:19.
21 [a][Mark 6:52]
22 [a]Matt. 9:27; John 9:1 [b]Luke 18:15

Beware of the Leaven of the Pharisees and Herod

13 And He left them, and getting into
the boat again, departed to the other
side.
14 [a]Now [1]the disciples had forgotten
to take bread, and they did not have
more than one loaf with them in the
boat.
15 [a]Then He charged them, saying,
"Take heed, beware of the [1]leaven of
the Pharisees and the leaven of
Herod."
16 And they reasoned among themselves, saying, "*It is* because we have
no bread."
17 But Jesus, being aware of *it,* said
to them, "Why do you reason because
you have no bread? [a]Do you not yet
perceive nor understand? Is your heart
[1]still **hardened?**

WORD WEALTH

8:17 hardened, *poroo* (po-*rah*-oh); Strong's *#4456:* To petrify, form a callous, make hard. The word is used metaphorically of spiritual deafness and blindness. Hearers of the gospel who repeatedly resist its convicting truth become insensitive and dull and lose the power of understanding.

18 "Having eyes, do you not see? And
having ears, do you not hear? And do
you not remember?
19 [a]"When I broke the five loaves for
the five thousand, how many baskets
full of fragments did you take up?"
They said to Him, "Twelve."
20 "Also, [a]when I broke the seven for
the four thousand, how many large
baskets *full of fragments did you take
up?" And they said, "Seven."
21 So He said to them, "How *is it*
[a]you do not understand?"

A Blind Man Healed at Bethsaida

22 Then He came to Bethsaida; and
they brought a [a]blind man to Him, and
begged Him to [b]touch him.
23 So He took the blind man by the

8:2–9 The feeding of the 4,000 follows closely the pattern of 6:30–44. Apparently, the disciples' spiritual dullness clouded their memory of the former miracle.

8:10 The exact location of **Dalmanutha** is unknown, but since Jesus and the others journeyed there from Decapolis in a boat, and since Pharisees were present there (v. 11), it must have been in Galilee, on the western side of the lake.

8:11, 12 See notes on Matt. 12:38, 39 and 16:1–4.

8:15 Leaven: Often the term has an evil connotation, that is, what is small may corrupt the whole. The context suggests a link with the Pharisees' demand for a sign (v. 11). Herod's "leaven" embraces the evil portrayed in 6:14–29, that is, godlessness of the worldly man. See note on Matt. 16:6. For **Herod,** see note on Mark 3:6.

8:22 This healing is unique in that it is accomplished in stages.

hand and led him out of the town. And when [a]He had spit on his eyes and put His hands on him, He asked him if he saw anything.
24 And he looked up and said, "I see men like trees, walking."
25 Then He put *His* hands on his eyes again and made him look up. And he was restored and saw everyone clearly.
26 Then He sent him away to his house, saying, [1]"Neither go into the town, [a]nor tell anyone in the town."

Peter Confesses Jesus as the Christ

27 [a]Now Jesus and His disciples went out to the towns of Caesarea Philippi; and on the road He asked His disciples, saying to them, "Who do men say that I am?"
28 So they answered, [a]"John the Baptist; but some *say,* [b]Elijah; and others, one of the prophets."
29 He said to them, "But who do you say that I am?" Peter answered and said to Him, [a]"You are the *Christ."
30 [a]Then He strictly warned them that they should tell no one about Him.

Jesus Predicts His Death and Resurrection

31 And [a]He began to teach them that the Son of Man must *suffer many things, and be [b]rejected by the elders and chief priests and scribes, and be [c]killed, and after three days rise again.
32 He spoke this word *openly. Then Peter took Him aside and began to rebuke Him.
33 But when He had turned around and looked at His disciples, He [a]rebuked Peter, saying, "Get behind Me, Satan! For you are not [1]mindful of the things of God, but the things of men."

Take Up the Cross and Follow Him

7 **34** When He had called the people to *Himself,* with His disciples also, He said to them, [a]"Whoever desires to come after Me, let him deny himself, and take up his cross, and follow Me.
35 "For [a]whoever desires to save his life will lose it, but whoever loses his life for My sake and the gospel's will save it.
36 "For what will it profit a man if he gains the whole *world, and loses his own soul?
37 "Or what will a man give in exchange for his *soul?
38 [a]"For whoever [b]is ashamed of Me and My words in this adulterous and sinful generation, of him the Son of Man also will be ashamed when He comes in the glory of His Father with the holy angels."

Jesus Transfigured on the Mount

9 And He said to them, [a]"Assuredly, I say to you that there are some standing here who will not *taste death till they see [b]the kingdom of God [1]present with power."
2 [a]Now after six days Jesus took Peter, James, and John, and led them up on a high mountain apart by themselves; and He was transfigured before them.
3 His clothes became shining, exceedingly [a]white, like snow, such as no launderer on earth can whiten them.
4 And Elijah appeared to them with Moses, and they were talking with Jesus.
5 Then Peter answered and said to Jesus, "Rabbi, it is *good for us to be here; and let us make three tabernacles: one for You, one for Moses, and one for Elijah"—
6 because he did not know what to say, for they were greatly afraid.
7 And a [a]cloud came and overshadowed them; and a voice came out of the cloud, saying, "This is [b]My beloved Son. [c]Hear Him!"
8 Suddenly, when they had looked around, they saw no one anymore, but only Jesus with themselves.
9 [a]Now as they came down from the mountain, He commanded them that they should tell no one the things they had seen, till the Son of Man had risen from the dead.
10 So they kept this word to themselves, questioning [a]what the rising from the dead meant.

23 [a]Mark 7:33
26 [a]Mark 5:43; 7:36 [1]NU *"Do not even go into the town."*
27 [a]Luke 9:18–20
28 [a]Matt. 14:2 [b]Luke 9:7, 8
29 [a]John 1:41; 4:42; 6:69; 11:27 *See WW at 2 Tim. 4:22.
30 [a]Matt. 8:4; 16:20
31 [a]Matt. 16:21; 20:19 [b]Mark 10:33 [c]Mark 9:31; 10:34 *See WW at Acts 17:3.
32 *See WW at Acts 4:31.
33 [a][Rev. 3:19] [1]*setting your mind on*
34 [a]Luke 14:27
35 [a]John 12:25
36 *See WW at John 18:36.
37 *See WW at Luke 21:19.
38 [a]Matt. 10:33 [b]2 Tim. 1:8, 9; 2:12

CHAPTER 9

1 [a]Luke 9:27 [b][Matt. 24:30] [1]*having come* *See WW at John 8:52.
2 [a]Matt. 17:1–8
3 [a]Dan. 7:9
5 *See WW at Matt. 13:48.
7 [a]Ex. 40:34 [b]Mark 1:11 [c]Acts 3:22
9 [a]Matt. 17:9–13
10 [a]John 2:19–22

8:27–38 See notes on Matt. 16:13–27.
8:31 Must indicates a divine necessity stemming from God's will. This is the first of three explicit pronouncements concerning Jesus' death (9:31; 10:33, 34), and serves as a hinge for the second half of Mark's Gospel (see Introduction to Mark: Content).
8:32 Rebuke: Note the contrasting subjects and objects of the two rebukes (v. 33).
8:34–36 See section 7 of Truth-In-Action through the Synoptics at the end of Luke.
9:1 Present with power: The Transfiguration, a visible experience of kingdom power, observed six days later by three disciples, was a foretaste of both the Resurrection and Second Coming of Jesus.
9:2–13 See notes on Matt. 17:1–13.

11 And they asked Him, saying, "Why
do the scribes say [a]that Elijah must
come first?"
12 Then He answered and told them,
"Indeed, Elijah is coming first and restores all things. And [a]how is it written
concerning the Son of Man, that He
must suffer many things and [b]be
treated with contempt?
13 "But I say to you that [a]Elijah has
also come, and they did to him whatever they wished, as it is written of
him."

A Boy Is Healed

14 [a]And when He came to the disciples, He saw a great multitude around
them, and scribes disputing with them.
15 Immediately, when they saw Him,
all the people were greatly amazed,
and running to *Him*, greeted Him.
16 And He asked the scribes, "What
are you discussing with them?"
17 Then [a]one of the crowd answered
and said, "Teacher, I brought You my
son, who has a mute spirit.
18 "And wherever it *seizes him, it
throws him down; he foams at the
mouth, gnashes his teeth, and becomes
rigid. So I spoke to Your disciples, that
they should cast it out, but they could
not."
19 He answered him and said, "O
[a]faithless[1] generation, how long shall
I be with you? How long shall I [2]bear*
with you? Bring him to Me."
20 Then they brought him to Him. And
[a]when he saw Him, immediately the
spirit convulsed him, and he fell on the
ground and wallowed, foaming at the
mouth.
21 So He asked his father, *"How long
has this been happening to him?" And
he said, "From childhood.
22 "And often he has thrown him both
into the fire and into the water to
destroy him. But if You can do anything, have compassion on us and help
us."
23 Jesus said to him, [a]"If[1] you can *believe, all things *are* *possible to him
who believes."

11 [a]Mal. 4:5; Matt. 17:10
12 [a]Ps. 22:6; Is. 53:3; Dan. 9:26 [b]Luke 23:11; Phil. 2:7
13 [a]Mal. 4:5; Matt. 11:14; 17:12; Luke 1:17
14 [a]Matt. 17:14–19; Luke 9:37–42
17 [a]Matt. 17:14; Luke 9:38
18 *See WW at John 1:5.
19 [a]John 4:48 [1]*unbelieving* [2]*put up with* *See WW at 2 Thess. 1:4.
20 [a]Mark 1:26; Luke 9:42
21 *See WW at Acts 1:7.
23 [a]Matt. 17:20; Mark 11:23; Luke 17:6; John 11:40 [1]NU *" 'If You can!' All things* *See WW at Rom. 10:9. • See WW at Matt. 19:26.

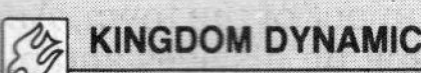

9:22, 23 Cultivating a Climate of Faith for Healing, DIVINE HEALING. In this passage Jesus tells us that "believing" is the condition for answered prayer for a healing. The father of the demon-possessed boy answered in tears, "I believe," then added, "Help my unbelief!" Since faith is a gift, we may pray for it as this father did. Note how quickly God's grace answered; but there is another lesson. Where an atmosphere of unbelief makes it difficult to believe, we should seek a different setting. Even Jesus' ability to work miracles was reduced where unbelief prevailed (Matt. 13:58).

Prayer and praise provide an atmosphere of faith in God. In this text Jesus explained yet another obstacle to faith's victory—why their prayers had been fruitless: "This kind can come out by nothing but prayer and fasting" (Mark 9:29). His explanation teaches: 1) some (not all) affliction is demonically imposed; and 2) some kinds of demonic bondage do not respond to exorcism, but only to fervent prayer. Continuance in prayer, accompanied by praise and sometimes fasting, provides a climate for faith that brings deliverance.

(Mark 5:24–34/Luke 5:16–26) N.V.

24 Immediately the father of the child
cried out and said with tears, "Lord, I
believe; [a]help my unbelief!"
25 When Jesus saw that the people
came running together, He [a]rebuked
the unclean spirit, saying to it: "Deaf
and dumb spirit, I command you,
come out of him and enter him no
more!"
26 Then *the spirit* cried out, convulsed
him greatly, and came out of him. And
he became as one dead, so that many
said, "He is dead."
27 But Jesus took him by the hand and
lifted him up, and he arose.
28 [a]And when He had come into the
house, His *disciples asked Him
privately, "Why could we not cast it
out?"
29 So He said to them, "This kind can
come out by nothing but [a]prayer
[1]and fasting."

24 [a]Luke 17:5
25 [a]Mark 1:25
28 [a]Matt. 17:19 *See WW at Matt. 10:1.
29 [a][James 5:16] [1]NU omits *and fasting*

9:14 The **scribes** were apparently taking advantage of the disciples' failure to deliver the demonized boy (vv. 16, 17).

9:22 The inability of the disciples had weakened the father's faith.

9:23 If you can: The question can be understood, "Is that what you said?" Jesus' exclamation picks up the doubting words of the father. The question deciding the issue is not Jesus' power, but the man's faith. The Lord's statement concerning faith does not grant us the liberty to presume upon God's goodness by irresponsibly asking for selfish things. Our desires must be in accord with God's will. See 1 John 5:14, 15.

9:24 His faith has been shaken, and he is conscious of its imperfection. Therefore, he asks Jesus to remove all doubt and to grant him unquestioning faith.

9:26 The evil spirit had to obey Jesus, but performed a last act of violence.

9:29 Some demons are stronger than others, and we must be adequately prepared to engage in spiritual battle.

Jesus Again Predicts His Death and Resurrection

30 Then they departed from there and
passed through Galilee, and He did not
want anyone to know *it*.
31 [a]For He taught His disciples and
said to them, "The Son of Man is being betrayed into the hands of men,
and they will [b]kill Him. And after
He is killed, He will [c]rise the third
day."
32 But they [a]did not understand this
saying, and were afraid to ask Him.

Who Is the Greatest?

8 **33** [a]Then He came to Capernaum. And
when He was in the house He asked
them, "What was it you [1]disputed
among yourselves on the road?"
34 But they kept silent, for on the road
they had [a]disputed among themselves
who *would be the* [b]greatest.
35 And He sat down, called the twelve,
and said to them, [a]"If anyone desires
to be first, he shall be last of all and
servant of all."
36 Then [a]He took a little child and set
him in the midst of them. And when
He had taken him in His arms, He said
to them,
37 "Whoever receives one of these little children in My name receives Me;
and [a]whoever receives Me, receives
not Me but Him who sent Me."

Jesus Forbids Sectarianism

38 [a]Now John answered Him, saying,
"Teacher, we saw someone who does
not follow us casting out demons in
Your name, and we forbade him because he does not follow us."
39 But Jesus said, "Do not forbid him,
[a]for no one who works a miracle in
My name can soon afterward speak
evil of Me.
40 "For [a]he who is not against [1]us is
on [2]our side.
41 [a]"For whoever gives you a cup of
water to drink in My name, because
you belong to Christ, assuredly, I say
to you, he will by no means lose his
reward.

Jesus Warns of Offenses

42 [a]"But whoever causes one of these
little ones who believe in Me [1]to stumble, it would be better for him if a millstone were hung around his neck, and
he were thrown into the sea.
43 [a]"If your hand causes you to sin,
cut it off. It is better for you to enter
into life [1]maimed, rather than having
two hands, to go to [2]hell, into the fire
that shall never be quenched—
44 [1]"where

> [a]'*Their worm does not die,*
> *And the fire is not quenched.*'

45 "And if your foot causes you to sin,
cut it off. It is better for you to enter
life lame, rather than having two feet,
to be cast into [1]hell, [2]into the fire that
shall never be quenched—
46 "where

> [a]'*Their worm does not die,*
> *And the fire is not quenched.*'

47 "And if your eye causes you to sin,
pluck it out. It is better for you to enter
the kingdom of God with one eye,
rather than having two eyes, to be cast
into [1]hell fire—
48 "where

> [a]'*Their worm does not die,*
> *And the* [b]*fire is not quenched.*'

31 [a]Matt. 17:22; Luke 9:44 [b]Matt. 16:21; 27:50; Luke 18:33; 23:46; Acts 2:23 [c]Matt. 20:19; Luke 24:46; Acts 10:40; 1 Cor. 15:4
32 [a]Luke 2:50; 18:34; John 12:16
33 [a]Matt. 18:1–5; Mark 14:53, 64; Luke 9:46–48; 22:24; John 18:12; 19:7 [1]*discussed*
34 [a][Prov. 13:10]; Mark 15:20, 31 [b]Matt. 18:4; [Mark 9:50]; 14:65; 15:15, 37; Luke 22:24; 23:46; 24:46
35 [a]Matt. 20:26, 27; 23:11; Mark 10:43, 44; Luke 22:26, 27
36 [a]Mark 10:13–16
37 [a]Matt. 10:40; Luke 10:16; John 13:20
38 [a]Num. 11:27–29; Luke 9:49
39 [a]1 Cor. 12:3
40 [a][Matt. 12:30]; Luke 11:23 [1]M *you* [2]M *your*
41 [a]Matt. 10:42
42 [a]Matt. 18:6; Luke 17:1, 2; [1 Cor. 8:12] [1]To fall into sin
43 [a][Deut. 13:6]; Matt. 5:29, 30; 18:8, 9 [1]*crippled* [2]Gr. *Gehenna*
44 [a]Is. 66:24 [1]NU omits v. 44.
45 [1]Gr. *Gehenna* [2]NU omits the rest of v. 45 and all of v. 46.
46 [a]Is. 66:24
47 [1]Gr. *Gehenna*
48 [a]Is. 66:24 [b]Jer. 7:20; [Rev. 21:8]

9:31, 32 In the second announcement of His death, Jesus refers to the betrayal that will take place. The present tense, **is being betrayed,** suggests that the deed was already in the heart of Judas.
9:33–37 See section 8 of Truth-In-Action through the Synoptics at the end of Luke.
9:33 Jesus wants His disciples to confess to their petty discussion, even though He already knows the answer to His question.
9:36, 37 Jesus effectively illustrates the lesson He has just taught. To render service, even to those whom the world regards as insignificant, in the name of Christ and for His sake, is actually to render the service to Him.
9:37 Substantiation for the above example is found in the Jewish legal principle that a man's representative is as himself. Thus, receiving a little child equals receiving Jesus equals receiving God.
9:38 The teaching of Jesus concerning service prompted John to relate an incident that reveals a sectarian attitude among the disciples. The man they rebuke is a true follower of Jesus, although he is not one of the Twelve.
9:39 There is no place for narrow exclusivism in the church. All genuine Christians are to be tolerant toward their fellow believers, regardless of their denomination. A crucial test in determining true service is motive. Is the work done for the sake of Christ and for His glory? The disciples prove to be sectarian (v. 38). Jesus' words **"Do not forbid him"** are followed by a threefold explanation as to why the prohibition of the disciples was wrong (vv. 39–41). Each explanation is introduced by "for."
9:42 Jesus warns of the severe consequences of endangering the immortal soul of another.
9:43–48 See note on Matt. 5:28–30.

Tasteless Salt Is Worthless

49 "For everyone will be [a]seasoned
with fire, [b]and[1] every sacrifice will be
seasoned with salt.
2 50 [a]"Salt *is* good, but if the salt loses
its flavor, how will you season it?
[b]Have salt in yourselves, and [c]have
peace with one another."

49 [a][Matt. 3:11] [b]Lev. 2:13 [1]NU omits the rest of v. 49.
50 [a]Matt. 5:13 [b]Col. 4:6 [c]Rom. 12:18; 14:19

CHAPTER 10

1 [a]Matt 19:1–9
2 [a]Matt. 19:3

Marriage and Divorce

10 Then [a]He arose from there and
came to the region of Judea by
the other side of the Jordan. And multitudes gathered to Him again, and as
He was accustomed, He taught them
again.
2 [a]The Pharisees came and asked

9:49 Jesus is referring to the rigid self-discipline of vv. 43–48. **Fire** purifies and **salt** preserves from corruption. It is better to experience the present pain of self-denial than future and eternal torment.
9:50 See section 2 of Truth-In-Action through the Synoptics at the end of Luke.
9:50 If the disciples lose the flavor of true discipleship in striving after selfish ambition, they become useless as Christians (see Matt. 5:13). Instead of bickering for a position of preference (v. 33), they are to allow the salt of the gospel to preserve them from selfish ambitions, so they will be at **peace with one another**.
10:2–12 See notes on Matt. 5:32 and 19:3–12.

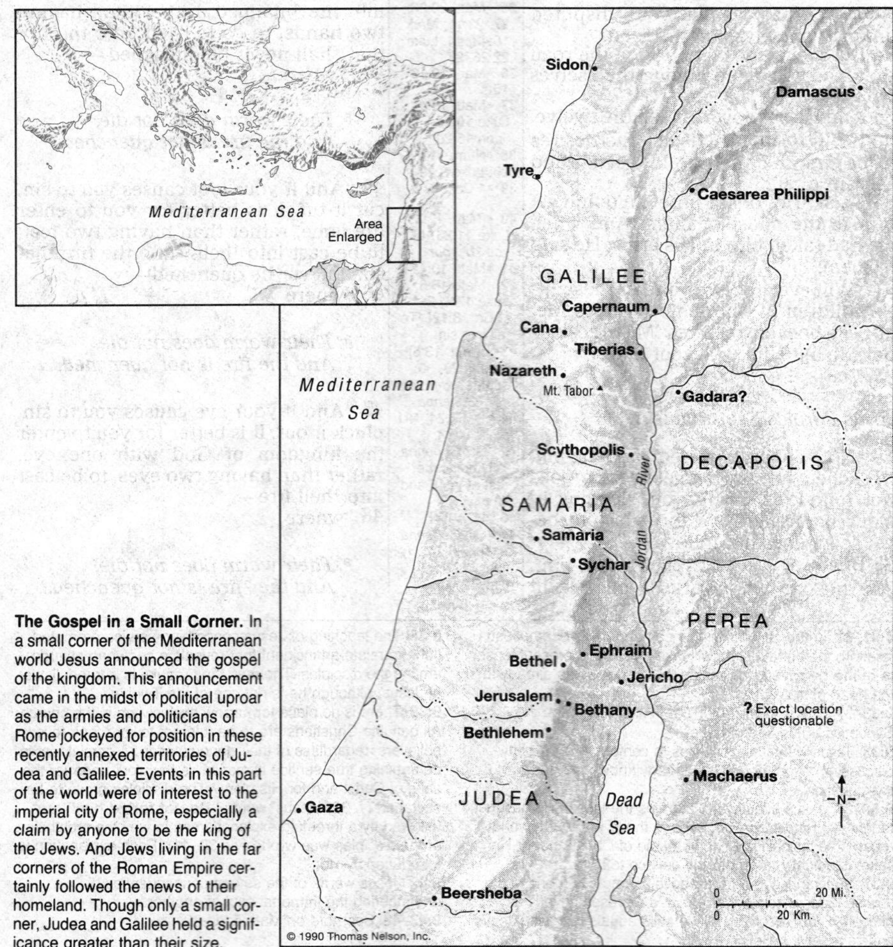

The Gospel in a Small Corner. In a small corner of the Mediterranean world Jesus announced the gospel of the kingdom. This announcement came in the midst of political uproar as the armies and politicians of Rome jockeyed for position in these recently annexed territories of Judea and Galilee. Events in this part of the world were of interest to the imperial city of Rome, especially a claim by anyone to be the king of the Jews. And Jews living in the far corners of the Roman Empire certainly followed the news of their homeland. Though only a small corner, Judea and Galilee held a significance greater than their size.

Him, "Is it lawful for a man to divorce
his wife?" testing Him.
3 And He answered and said to
them, "What did Moses command
you?"
4 They said, [a]"Moses permitted *a*
man to write a certificate of divorce,
and to dismiss *her*."
5 And Jesus answered and said to
them, "Because of the hardness of your
heart he wrote you this [1]precept.
 6 "But from the beginning of the *cre-
ation, God [a]*'made them male and fe-*
male.'
7 [a]*'For this reason a man shall leave*
his father and mother and be ***joined***
to his wife,

WORD WEALTH

10:7 joined, *proskollao* (pros-*kol*-lah-oh): Strong's *#4347:* To glue or cement together, stick to, adhere to, join firmly. The word in the NT primarily describes the union of husband and wife. The addition of *pros* to *kollao* intensifies the relationship of husband and wife. *Proskollao* includes faithfulness, loyalty, and permanency in relationships.

8 *'and the two shall become one*
flesh'; so then they are no longer two,
but one flesh.
9 "Therefore what God has joined together, let not man separate."
10 In the house His disciples also
asked Him again about the same *mat-*
ter.
11 So He said to them, [a]"Whoever divorces his wife and marries another
commits adultery against her.
12 "And if a woman divorces her husband and marries another, she commits adultery."

4 [a]Deut. 24:1–4; Matt. 5:31; 19:7
5 [1]*command*
6 [a]Gen. 1:27; 5:2 *See WW at Col. 1:15.
7 [a]Gen. 2:24; [1 Cor. 6:16]; Eph. 5:31
11 [a]Ex. 20:14; [Matt. 5:32; 19:9]; Luke 16:18; [Rom. 7:3]; 1 Cor. 7:10, 11
13 [a]Matt. 19:13–15; Luke 18:15–17 *See WW at Heb. 9:28.
14 [a][1 Cor. 14:20; 1 Pet. 2:2]
15 [a]Matt. 18:3, 4; 19:14; Luke 18:17 [b]Luke 13:28
16 *See WW at Luke 6:28.
17 [a]Matt. 19:16–30; Luke 18:18–30 [b]John 6:28; Acts 2:37 *See WW at Phil. 1:6. • See WW at 1 John 5:20.
18 [a]1 Sam. 2:2
19 [a]Ex. 20:12–16; Deut. 5:16–20; [Rom. 13:9; James 2:10, 11]
20 [a]Phil. 3:6
21 [a][Luke 12:33; 16:9] [b]Matt. 6:19, 20; 19:21 [c][Mark 8:34] *See WW at Luke 22:35. • See WW at John 16:22.

Jesus Blesses Little Children

13 [a]Then they *brought little children
to Him, that He might touch them; but
the disciples rebuked those who
brought *them*.
14 But when Jesus saw *it*, He was
greatly displeased and said to them,
"Let the little children come to Me, and
do not forbid them; for [a]of such is the
kingdom of God.
15 "Assuredly, I say to you, [a]whoever
does not receive the kingdom of God
as a little child will [b]by no means enter
it."
16 And He took them up in His arms,
laid *His* hands on them, and *blessed
them.

Jesus Counsels the Rich Young Ruler

17 [a]Now as He was going out on the
road, one came running, knelt before
Him, and asked Him, *"Good Teacher,
what shall I [b]do that I may inherit eternal *life?"
18 So Jesus said to him, "Why do you
call Me good? No one *is* good but One,
that is, [a]God.
19 "You know the commandments:
[a]*'Do not commit adultery,' 'Do not*
murder,' 'Do not steal,' 'Do not bear
false witness,' 'Do not defraud,' *'Honor*
your father and your mother.' "
20 And he answered and said to Him,
"Teacher, all these things I have
[a]kept from my youth."
21 Then Jesus, looking at him, loved 10
him, and said to him, "One thing you
*lack: Go your way, [a]sell whatever you
have and give to the poor, and you
will have [b]treasure in heaven; and
come, [c]take* up the cross, and follow
Me."
22 But he was sad at this word, and

10:6–12 See section 1 of Truth-In-Action through the Synoptics at the end of Luke.
10:13 The disciples evidently felt that children were too insignificant to be allowed to interrupt the work of Jesus.
10:14 The indignant response of Jesus shows that no one is too insignificant for the loving attention of Jesus. See note on Matt. 18:1–5.
10:15 The kingdom of God is only for those who come to Jesus in the humble dependence and trust of little children. The kingdom of God belongs to them, not because of merit, but because God wills to give it to the humble, and the apparently insignificant or unimportant. **Whoever:** Jesus moves beyond the specific incident to the general principle.
10:17 The question reveals the man's belief that eternal life is the reward for doing the right things.
10:18 True goodness is the prerogative of God, yet the man had called Jesus "Good Teacher." If Jesus was only a teacher, then He did not deserve to be called "good." On the other hand, if He was indeed good, then He was God. Whether or not this is a veiled claim to deity, Jesus directs the man's attention to God, the ultimate standard of goodness.
10:19 The commandments (except for "Do not defraud") are taken from the Decalogue (Ex. 20:12–16). Some suggest that the prohibition of fraud is an application of the eighth and ninth Commandments.
10:21–27 See section 10 of Truth-In-Action through the Synoptics at the end of Luke.
10:21 Loved: Jesus' love for the man is expressed in a challenge, both stern and gracious. The **one thing** the man lacked was a wholehearted allegiance to God. So Jesus gave him a stern test to reveal the fact that he had made an idol of wealth, thus breaking the first Commandment (Ex. 20:3). **Treasure in heaven:** This is a common Jewish expression, but, for Jesus, it contains no idea of merit. Jesus looks beyond specific requirements to single-hearted devotion to God, that is, in taking up the cross of discipleship.

went away sorrowful, for he had great possessions.

With God All Things Are Possible

23 [a]Then Jesus looked around and said to His disciples, "How hard it is for those who have riches to enter the kingdom of God!"

24 And the disciples were astonished at His words. But Jesus answered again and said to them, "Children, how hard it is [1]for those [a]who trust in riches to enter the kingdom of God!

25 "It is easier for a camel to go through the eye of a needle than for a [a]rich man to enter the kingdom of God."

26 And they were greatly astonished, saying among themselves, "Who then can be saved?"

27 But Jesus looked at them and said, "With men *it is* impossible, but not [a]with God; for with God all things are possible."

KINGDOM DYNAMICS

10:17–27 Using Things, Not Loving Them, GOD'S PROSPERITY. God is not opposed to Christians having material things. He is opposed to material things "having," or controlling, Christians. The rich young ruler in this passage had kept the Law all his life, but his riches controlled him rather than his controlling the riches. He could not let go of those material things—not even for eternal life. There is no reason to doubt that if he had let those material things go, Jesus would have told him to keep them. This episode is a sad example of what can happen when people begin to trust in their material goods instead of trusting in God who has provided them.

(Ps. 35:27/1 Tim. 6:17) F.P.

28 [a]Then Peter began to say to Him, "See, we have left all and followed You."

29 So Jesus answered and said, "Assuredly, I say to you, there is no one who has left house or brothers or sisters or father or mother [1]or wife or children or [2]lands, for My sake and the gospel's,

30 [a]"who shall not receive a hundredfold now in this time—houses and brothers and sisters and mothers and children and lands, with [b]persecutions—and in the age to come, eternal life.

31 [a]"But many *who are* first will be last, and the last first."

Jesus a Third Time Predicts His Death and Resurrection

32 [a]Now they were on the road, going up to Jerusalem, and Jesus was going before them; and they were amazed. And as they followed they were afraid. [b]Then He took the twelve aside again and began to tell them the things that would happen to Him:

33 "Behold, we are going up to Jerusalem, and the Son of Man will be betrayed to the chief priests and to the scribes; and they will condemn Him to death and deliver Him to the Gentiles;

34 "and they will mock Him, and [1]scourge Him, and spit on Him, and kill Him. And the third day He will rise again."

Greatness Is Serving

35 [a]Then James and John, the sons of 9
Zebedee, came to Him, saying, "Teacher, we want You to do for us whatever we ask."

36 And He said to them, "What do you want Me to do for you?"

37 They said to Him, "Grant us that we may sit, one on Your right hand and the other on Your left, in Your glory."

38 But Jesus said to them, "You do not know what you *ask. Are you able to drink the [a]cup that I drink, and be baptized with the [b]baptism that I am baptized with?"

39 They said to Him, "We are able." So Jesus said to them, [a]"You will indeed drink the cup that I drink, and with the baptism I am baptized with you will be baptized;

23 [a]Matt. 19:23; [Mark 4:19]; Luke 18:24 **24** [a]Job 31:24; Ps. 52:7; 62:10; [Prov. 11:28; 1 Tim. 6:17] [1]NU omits *for those who trust in riches* **25** [a][Matt. 13:22; 19:24] **27** [a]Job 42:2; Jer. 32:17; Matt. 19:26; Luke 1:37 **28** [a]Matt. 19:27; Luke 18:28 **29** [1]NU omits *or wife* [2]Lit. *fields*

30 [a]2 Chr. 25:9; Luke 18:29, 30 [b]1 Thess. 3:3; 2 Tim. 3:12; [1 Pet. 4:12, 13] **31** [a]Matt. 19:30; 20:16; Luke 13:30 **32** [a]Matt. 20:17–19; Luke 18:31–33 [b]Mark 8:31; 9:31; Luke 9:22; 18:31 **34** [1]*flog Him* with a Roman scourge **35** [a][James 4:3] **38** [a]Matt. 26:39, 42; Mark 14:36; Luke 22:42; John 18:11 [b]Luke 12:50 *See WW at Matt. 7:7. **39** [a]Matt. 10:17, 18, 21, 22; 24:9; John 16:33; Acts 12:2; Rev. 1:9

10:24, 25 The Jews saw wealth as a mark of God's favor and thought it inconceivable that riches would be a hindrance to kingdom life. Jesus shows the fallacy of such a view and uses it to teach through exaggeration that it is impossible for one who trusts *in riches* to enter heaven.

10:26, 27 Human achievement cannot attain salvation; only God has the power to bestow it.

10:28 Peter, missing the point altogether, wants Jesus to appreciate the fact that the disciples have forsaken everything and therefore have met the requirements of discipleship He gave to the rich man.

10:29–31 Jesus will be a debtor to no one. The blessings He gives will far outweigh material loss and persecution incurred in service to Him. See Phil. 3:7, 8.

10:32 The disciples feared the danger they would meet in Jerusalem.

10:33, 34 For the third time Jesus announces His death, this time with added details.

10:35–45 See section 9 of Truth-In-Action through the Synoptics at the end of Luke.

10:35–45 See note on Matt. 20:20–28. Matthew includes the mother of James and John in the request.

40 "but to sit on My right hand and
on My left is not Mine to give, but *it
is for those* [a]for whom it is prepared."
41 [a]And when the ten heard *it,* they
began to be greatly displeased with
James and John.
42 But Jesus called them to *Himself*
and said to them, [a]"You know that
those who are considered rulers over
the Gentiles lord it over them, and their
great ones exercise authority over
them.
43 [a]"Yet it shall not be so among you;
but whoever desires to become great
among you shall be your servant.
44 "And whoever of you desires to be
first shall be slave of all.
45 "For even [a]the Son of Man did not
come to be served, but to serve, and
[b]to give His life a *ransom for many."

Jesus Heals Blind Bartimaeus

46 [a]Now they came to Jericho. As He
went out of Jericho with His disciples
and a great multitude, blind Bartimaeus, the son of Timaeus, sat by the
road begging.
47 And when he heard that it was Jesus of Nazareth, he began to cry out
and say, "Jesus, [a]Son of David, [b]have*
mercy on me!"
48 Then many warned him to be quiet;
but he cried out all the more, "Son of
David, have mercy on me!"
49 So Jesus stood still and commanded
him to be called. Then they called the
blind man, saying to him, "Be of good
cheer. Rise, He is calling you."
50 And throwing aside his garment, he
rose and came to Jesus.
51 So Jesus answered and said to him,
"What do you want Me to do for you?"
The blind man said to Him, [1]"Rabboni,
that I may receive my sight."
52 Then Jesus said to him, "Go your
way; [a]your faith has [1]made you well."
And immediately he received his sight
and followed Jesus on the road.

The Triumphal Entry

11 Now [a]when they drew near Jerusalem, to [1]Bethphage and
Bethany, at the Mount of Olives, He
sent two of His *disciples;
2 and He said to them, "Go into the
village opposite you; and as soon as
you have entered it you will find a colt
tied, on which no one has sat. Loose
it and bring *it.*
3 "And if anyone says to you, 'Why
are you doing this?' say, 'The Lord has
need of it,' and *immediately he will
send it here."
4 So they went their way, and found
[1]the colt tied by the door outside on
the street, and they loosed it.
5 But some of those who stood there
said to them, "What are you doing,
loosing the colt?"
6 And they spoke to them just as Jesus had commanded. So they let them
go.
7 Then they brought the colt to Jesus
and threw their clothes on it, and He
sat on it.
8 [a]And many spread their clothes on
the road, and others cut down leafy
branches from the trees and spread
them on the road.
9 Then those who went before and
those who followed cried out, saying:

"Hosanna!
[a]*'Blessed is He who comes in the
name of the* LORD!'
10 Blessed *is* the kingdom of our
father David
That comes [1]in the name of the
Lord!
[a]Hosanna in the highest!"

11 [a]And Jesus went into Jerusalem
and into the temple. So when He had

40 [a][Matt. 25:34; John 17:2, 6, 24; Rom. 8:30; Heb. 11:16]
41 [a]Matt. 20:24
42 [a]Luke 22:25
43 [a]Matt. 20:26, 28; Mark 9:35; Luke 9:48
45 [a]Luke 22:27; John 13:14; [Phil. 2:7, 8] [b]Matt. 20:28; [2 Cor. 5:21; 1 Tim. 2:5, 6; Titus 2:14] *See WW at Matt. 20:28.
46 [a]Matt. 20:29–34; Luke 18:35–43
47 [a]Jer. 23:5; Matt. 22:42; Rom. 1:3, 4; Rev. 22:16 [b]Matt. 15:22; Luke 17:13 *See WW at Rom. 9:15.
51 [1]Lit. *My Great One*
52 [a]Matt. 9:22; Mark 5:34 [1]Lit. *saved you*

CHAPTER 11

1 [a]Matt. 21:1–9; Luke 19:29; John 2:13 [1]M *Bethsphage* *See WW at Matt. 10:1.
3 *See WW at John 6:21.
4 [1]NU, M *a*
8 [a]Matt. 21:8
9 [a]Ps. 118:25, 26; Matt. 21:9
10 [a]Ps. 148:1 [1]NU omits *in the name of the Lord*
11 [a]Matt. 21:12

10:45 The **Son of Man** saying substantiates the expected service from the disciples. **Ransom:** The idea of payment for resultant freedom is expressed and can only be understood through the Passion (14:36; 15:34). In vv. 33, 34, the sufferings of Jesus stem from the religious leaders, but in v. 45 Jesus takes the initiative—**to serve, and to give His life a ransom for many.**

10:47 Bartimaeus acknowledges the messiahship of Jesus in his use of the title **Son of David**. The confession is all the more significant since Jesus is headed toward the Cross.

10:48 The blind man would let nothing stand in his way of getting to Jesus.

10:52 Bartimaeus's faith leads to sight. He, like the woman of 5:34, is undeterred by the crowd. He "sat by the road" (v. 46), but later followed Jesus **on the road.**

11:1 In the final days of His ministry, Jesus openly declares His messiahship, deliberately fulfilling prophecies pertaining to the Messiah and performing deeds that show His kingly authority.

11:2–10 Jesus presents Himself to the nation in dramatic fulfillment of Zech. 9:9. This event took place on Sunday before the Crucifixion on Friday.

11:2 The fact that the **colt** had never been ridden is of special significance, since objects used for sacred purposes must never have been used for any other reason. See Num. 19:2; Deut. 21:3; 1 Sam. 6:7.

11:8 This was the customary way for a king's subjects to pay homage to him (see 2 Kin. 9:13).

11:9, 10 In acclaiming Jesus with the words of Ps. 118:25, 26, the people were publicly acknowledging Him as their Messiah. **Hosanna,** meaning "Save now" came to be a customary shout of praise like "Hallelujah."

11:11 Jesus' preliminary observation of the temple was in preparation for the events of the next day.

looked around at all things, as the hour was already late, He went out to Bethany with the twelve.

The Fig Tree Withered

12 [a]Now the next day, when they had come out from Bethany, He was hungry.
13 [a]And seeing from afar a fig tree having leaves, He went to see if perhaps He would find something on it. When He came to it, He found nothing but leaves, for it was not the season for figs.
14 In response Jesus said to it, "Let no one eat fruit from you ever again." And His disciples heard *it.*

Jesus Cleanses the Temple

15 [a]So they came to Jerusalem. Then Jesus went into the temple and began to drive out those who bought and sold in the temple, and overturned the tables of the money changers and the seats of those who sold [b]doves.
16 And He would not allow anyone to carry wares through the temple.
17 Then He taught, saying to them, "Is it not written, [a]*'My house shall be called a house of prayer for all nations'*? But you have made it a [b]*'den of thieves.'* "
18 And [a]the scribes and chief priests heard it and sought how they might *destroy Him; for they feared Him, because [b]all the people were astonished at His teaching.
19 When evening had come, He went out of the city.

The Lesson of the Withered Fig Tree

20 [a]Now in the morning, as they passed by, they saw the fig tree dried up from the roots.
21 And Peter, remembering, said to Him, "Rabbi, look! The fig tree which You cursed has withered away."
22 So Jesus answered and said to them, "Have **faith** in God.
23 "For [a]assuredly, I say to you, whoever says to this mountain, 'Be removed and be cast into the sea,' and *does not doubt in his heart, but believes that those things he says will be done, he will have whatever he says.
24 "Therefore I say to you, [a]whatever things you ask when you pray, believe that you receive *them,* and you will have *them.*

12 [a]Matt. 21:18–22
13 [a]Matt. 21:19
15 [a]Mal. 3:1; Matt. 21:12–16; Luke 19:45–47; John 2:13–16 [b]Lev. 14:22
17 [a]Is. 56:7 [b]Jer. 7:11
18 [a]Ps. 2:2; Matt. 21:45, 46; Luke 19:47 [b]Matt. 7:28; Mark 1:22; 6:2; Luke 4:32 *See WW at Luke 9:56.
20 [a]Matt. 21:19–22
23 [a]Matt. 17:20; 21:21; Luke 17:6 *See WW at Acts 11:12.
24 [a]Matt. 7:7; Luke 11:9; [John 14:13; 15:7; 16:24; James 1:5, 6]

WORD WEALTH

11:22 faith, *pistis* (*pis*-tis); Strong's *#4102:* Conviction, confidence, trust, belief, reliance, trustworthiness, and persuasion. In the NT setting, *pistis* is the divinely implanted principle of inward confidence, assurance, trust, and reliance in God and all that He says. The word sometimes denotes the object or content of belief (Acts 6:7; 14:22; Gal. 1:23).

KINGDOM DYNAMICS

11:20–24 Taking Authority and Victorious Warfare, FAITH'S WARFARE. Our Savior's action in cursing the fig tree indicates a passion in prayer and faith that we need to learn. When the disciples later noticed with surprise that the tree had withered completely (v. 20), Jesus responded with a sharp command, "Have faith in God." Then, calling His followers to "speak to mountains," He led them to prepare for situations in which they would find it necessary to take direct authority in the spiritual realm to impact things in the natural realm.

(Rev. 12:7–11/Num. 10:1–10) D.E.

KINGDOM DYNAMICS

11:22–24 Jesus on "Faith's Confession," FAITH'S CONFESSION. From Jesus' own lips we receive the most direct and practical instruction concerning our exercise of faith. Consider three points: 1) It is to be "in God." Faith that speaks is first faith that seeks. The Almighty One is the Source and Grounds of our faith and being. Faith only flows to Him because of the faithfulness that flows from Him. 2) Faith is not a trick performed with our lips, but a spoken expression that springs from the conviction of our hearts. The idea that faith's confession is a "formula" for getting things from God is unbiblical. But the fact that the faith in our hearts is to be spoken, and thereby becomes active and effective toward specific results, is taught here by the Lord Jesus. 3) Jesus' words "whatever things" apply this principle to every aspect of our lives. The only restrictions

11:12–14 See note on Matt. 21:19.
11:15–17 The temple authorities had established a kind of religious mafia, which siphoned off enormous profits from fraudulent transactions. By purging the temple in fulfillment of Mal. 3:1–3, Jesus dramatized His messianic authority.
11:16 The people had shown disrespect for the temple by using the area as a shortcut from the city to the Mount of Olives.
11:20–24 The positive lesson to be learned from the cursing of the fig tree is the power of believing prayer. **A mountain** is symbolic of an obstacle, hindrance, or insurmountable problem. Faith is the key that releases the resources of heaven into our situation (v. 24).

are (a) that our faith be "in God" our living Father and in alignment with His will and word; and (b) that we "believe"—not doubting in our hearts. Thus, "speaking to the mountain" is not a vain or superstitious exercise or indulgence in humanistic mind-science, but instead becomes an applied release of God's creative word of promise.

(Matt. 15:7–9/Acts 3:6) R.H.

 **KINGDOM DYNAMICS**

11:22–24 Your Faith in God Is the Key to Your Receiving, SEED FAITH. Believing can take opposite forms. It can be faith or it can be doubt. When you believe that God exists and that He loves you and wants to meet your needs, then your believing creates faith in your heart.

On the other hand, doubt is just as real. The reverse of faith, doubt tells you that God does not exist or that He is unloving and uncaring about your needs. Doubt gives rise to fear, which brings torment, not peace. Fear actually keeps you from receiving the good things God desires to send your way. Capture this truth: Doubt, and do without; with faith believe, and receive. I have said for years, "Expect a miracle!"

Expectancy opens your life to God and puts you in a position to receive salvation, joy, health, financial supply, or peace of mind—everything good your heart longs for, and more!

(Mal. 3:10, 11/Matt. 25:34–40) O.R.

 **KINGDOM DYNAMICS**

11:22, 23 35. What Law Guarantees the Possibility of Accomplishing Impossible Things?, SPIRITUAL ANSWERS. For the answer to this and other probing questions about God and the power life in His kingdom, see the study article "Spiritual Answers to Hard Questions," which begins on page 1996. P.R.

Forgiveness and Prayer

6 25 "And whenever you stand praying,
[a]if you have anything against anyone,
forgive him, that your Father in heaven
may also forgive you your trespasses.
26 [1]"But [a]if you do not forgive, neither
will your Father in heaven forgive your
trespasses."

Jesus' Authority Questioned

27 Then they came again to Jerusalem.
[a]And as He was walking in the temple,
the chief priests, the scribes, and the
elders came to Him.
28 And they said to Him, "By what
[a]authority are You doing these things?
And who gave You this authority to
do these things?"
29 But Jesus answered and said to
them, "I also will ask you one question;
then answer Me, and I will tell you by
what authority I do these things:
30 "The [a]baptism* of John—was it
from heaven or from men? Answer
Me."
31 And they reasoned among themselves, saying, "If we say, 'From
heaven,' He will say, 'Why then did
you not believe him?'
32 "But if we say, 'From men' "—they
feared the people, for [a]all counted John
to have been a prophet indeed.
33 So they answered and said to Jesus,
"We do not know." And Jesus answered and said to them, "Neither will
I tell you by what authority I do these
things."

The Parable of the Wicked Vinedressers

12 Then [a]He began to speak to
them in parables: "A man
planted a vineyard and set a hedge
around *it,* dug *a place for* the wine vat
and built a tower. And he leased it to
[1]vinedressers and went into a far country.
2 "Now at vintage-time he sent a servant to the vinedressers, that he might
receive some of the fruit of the vineyard from the vinedressers.
3 "And they took *him* and beat him
and sent *him* away empty-handed.
4 "Again he sent them another servant, [1]and at him they threw stones,
wounded *him* in the head, and sent *him*
away shamefully treated.
5 "And again he sent another, and
him they killed; and many others,
[a]beating some and killing some.
6 "Therefore still having one son,
his beloved, he also sent him to them
last, saying, 'They will respect my
son.'
7 "But those [1]vinedressers said
among themselves, 'This is the heir.
Come, let us kill him, and the inheritance will be ours.'
8 "So they took him and [a]killed *him*
and cast *him* out of the vineyard.
9 "Therefore what will the owner of
the vineyard do? He will come and destroy the vinedressers, and give the
vineyard to others.

25 [a]Matt. 6:14; 18:23–35; Eph. 4:32; [Col. 3:13]
26 [a]Matt. 6:15; 18:35 [1]NU omits v. 26.
27 [a]Matt. 21:23–27; Luke 20:1–8
28 [a]John 5:27
30 [a][Mark 1:4, 5, 8]; Luke 7:29, 30 *See WW at Matt. 21:25.
32 [a]Matt. 3:5; 14:5; Mark 6:20

CHAPTER 12

1 [a]Matt. 21:33–46; Luke 20:9–19 [1]*tenant farmers*
4 [1]NU omits *and at him they threw stones*
5 [a]2 Chr. 36:16
7 [1]*tenant farmers*
8 [a][Acts 2:23]

11:25, 26 A condition of prevailing prayer is a forgiving spirit (see Matt. 6:14, 15).
11:25 See section 6 of Truth-In-Action through the Synoptics at the end of Luke.
11:27–33 See notes on Matt. 21:23–27.
12:1–12 See notes on Matt. 21:33–46.

10 "Have you not even read this Scripture:

[a]*'The stone which the builders rejected*
Has become the chief cornerstone.
11 *This was the LORD's doing,*
And it is marvelous in our eyes'?"

12 [a]And they sought to lay hands on Him, but feared the multitude, for they knew He had spoken the parable against them. So they left Him and went away.

The Pharisees: Is It Lawful to Pay Taxes to Caesar?

2 13 [a]Then they sent to Him some of the Pharisees and the Herodians, to catch Him in *His* words.
14 When they had come, they said to Him, "Teacher, we know that You are *true, and [1]care about no one; for You do not [2]regard the person of men, but teach the [a]way of God in truth. Is it lawful to pay taxes to Caesar, or not?
15 "Shall we pay, or shall we not pay?" But He, knowing their [a]hypocrisy,* said to them, "Why do you test Me? Bring Me a denarius that I may see *it.*"
16 So they brought *it.* And He said to them, "Whose image and inscription *is* this?" They said to Him, "Caesar's."
17 And Jesus answered and said to them, [1]"Render* to Caesar the things that are Caesar's, and to [a]God the things that are God's." And they marveled at Him.

The Sadducees: What About the Resurrection?

18 [a]Then *some* Sadducees, [b]who say there is no resurrection, came to Him; and they asked Him, saying:
19 "Teacher, [a]Moses wrote to us that if a man's brother dies, and leaves *his* wife behind, and leaves no children, his brother should take his wife and raise up offspring for his brother.
20 "Now there were seven brothers. The first took a wife; and dying, he left no offspring.
21 "And the second took her, and he died; nor did he leave any offspring. And the third likewise.

10 [a]Ps. 118:22, 23
12 [a]Matt. 21:45, 46; Mark 11:18; John 7:25, 30, 44
13 [a]Matt. 22:15–22; Luke 20:20–26
14 [a]Acts 18:26 [1]Court no man's favor [2]Lit. *look at the face of men* *See WW at Rom. 3:4.
15 [a]Matt. 23:28; Luke 12:1 *See WW at Gal. 2:13.
17 [a][Eccl. 5:4, 5] [1]*Pay* *See WW at Matt. 22:21.
18 [a]Matt. 22:23–33; Luke 20:27–38 [b]Acts 23:8
19 [a]Deut. 25:5

22 "So the seven had her and left no offspring. Last of all the woman died also.
23 "Therefore, in the resurrection, when they rise, whose wife will she be? For all seven had her as wife."
24 Jesus answered and said to them, "Are you not therefore [1]mistaken, because you do not know the Scriptures nor the power of God?
25 "For when they rise from the dead, they neither marry nor are given in marriage, but [a]are like angels in heaven.
26 "But concerning the dead, that they [a]rise, have you not read in the book of Moses, in the *burning* bush *passage,* how God spoke to him, saying, [b]*'I am the God of Abraham, the God of Isaac, and the God of Jacob'*?
27 "He is not the God of the dead, but the God of the living. You are therefore greatly [1]mistaken."

The Scribes: Which Is the First Commandment of All?

28 [a]Then one of the scribes came, and having heard them reasoning together, [1]perceiving that He had answered them well, asked Him, "Which is the [2]first commandment of all?" 3
29 Jesus answered him, "The [1]first of all the commandments *is:* [a]*'Hear, O Israel, the LORD our God, the LORD is one.*
30 *'And you shall* [a]*love the LORD your God with all your heart, with all your soul, with all your* ***mind,*** *and with all your strength.'* [1]This *is* the first commandment.

WORD WEALTH

12:30 mind, *dianoia* (dee-*an*-oy-ah); Strong's *#1271:* Literally, "a thinking through." *Dianoia* combines *nous,* "mind," and *dia,* "through." The word suggests understanding, insight, meditation, reflection, perception, the gift of apprehension, the faculty of thought. When this faculty is renewed by the Holy Spirit, the whole mind-set changes from the fearful negativism of the carnal mind to the vibrant, positive thinking of the quickened spiritual mind.

31 "And the second, like *it, is* this: [a]*'You shall *love your neighbor as*

24 [1]Or *deceived*
25 [a][1 Cor. 15:42, 49, 52]
26 [a][John 5:25, 28, 29]; Acts 26:8; Rom. 4:17; [Rev. 20:12, 13] [b]Ex. 3:6, 15
27 [1]Or *deceived*
28 [a]Matt. 22:34–40; Luke 10:25–28; 20:39 [1]NU *seeing* [2]*foremost*
29 [a]Deut. 6:4, 5; Is. 44:8; 45:22; 46:9; 1 Cor. 8:6 [1]*foremost*
30 [a][Deut. 10:12; 30:6]; Luke 10:27 [1]NU omits the rest of v. 30.
31 [a]Lev. 19:18; Matt. 22:39; Gal. 5:14; James 2:8 *See WW at John 3:16.

12:13–17 See section 2 of Truth-In-Action through the Synoptics at the end of Luke.
12:13–17 See note on Matt. 22:15–22.
12:18–27 See note on Matt. 22:23–33.
12:28–34 See section 3 of Truth-In-Action through the Synoptics at the end of Luke.
12:28–31 See note on Matt. 22:34–40.

yourself.' There is no other commandment greater than [b]these."

32 So the scribe said to Him, "Well *said,* Teacher. You have spoken the *truth, for there is one God, [a]and there is no other but He.

33 "And to love Him with all the heart, with all the *understanding, [1]with all the soul, and with all the strength, and to love one's neighbor as oneself, [a]is more than all the whole burnt offerings and sacrifices."

34 Now when Jesus saw that he answered wisely, He said to him, "You are not far from the kingdom of God." [a]But after that no one dared question Him.

Jesus: How Can David Call His Descendant Lord?

35 [a]Then Jesus answered and said, while He taught in the temple, "How *is it* that the scribes say that the Christ is the Son of David?

36 "For David himself said [a]by the Holy Spirit:

> [b]*'The LORD said to my Lord,*
> *"Sit at My right hand,*
> *Till I make Your enemies Your*
> *footstool."'*

37 "Therefore David himself calls Him *'Lord';* how is He *then* his [a]Son?" And the common people heard Him gladly.

Beware of the Scribes

38 Then [a]He said to them in His teaching, [b]"Beware of the scribes, who desire to go around in long robes, [c]*love* greetings in the marketplaces,

39 "the [a]best seats in the synagogues, and the best places at feasts,

40 [a]"who devour widows' houses, and [1]for a pretense make long prayers. These will receive *greater *condemnation."

The Widow's Two Mites

41 [a]Now Jesus sat opposite the treasury and saw how the people put money [b]into the treasury. And many *who were* rich put in much.

42 Then one poor widow came and threw in two [1]mites, which make a [2]quadrans.

43 So He called His disciples to *Himself* and said to them, "Assuredly, I say to you that [a]this poor widow has put in more than all those who have given to the treasury;

44 "for they all put in out of their *abundance, but she out of her poverty put in all that she had, [a]her whole livelihood."

Jesus Predicts the Destruction of the Temple

13 Then [a]as He went out of the temple, one of His disciples said to Him, "Teacher, see what manner of stones and what buildings *are here!"*

2 And Jesus answered and said to him, "Do you see these great buildings? [a]Not *one* stone shall be left upon another, that shall not be thrown down."

The Signs of the Times and the End of the Age

3 Now as He sat on the Mount of Olives opposite the temple, [a]Peter, [b]James, [c]John, and [d]Andrew asked Him privately,

4 [a]"Tell us, when will these things be? And what *will be* the sign when all these things will be fulfilled?"

5 And Jesus, answering them, began to say: [a]"Take heed that no one deceives you.

6 "For many will come in My name, saying, 'I am *He,*' and will deceive many.

7 "But when you hear of wars and rumors of wars, do not be troubled; for *such things* must happen, but the end *is* not yet.

8 "For nation will rise against nation, and [a]kingdom against kingdom. And there will be earthquakes in various places, and there will be famines [1]and troubles. [b]These *are* the beginnings of [2]sorrows.

31 [b][Rom. 13:9]
32 [a]Deut. 4:39; Is. 45:6, 14; 46:9; [John 1:14, 17; 14:6] *See WW at John 4:24.
33 [a][1 Sam. 15:22; Hos. 6:6; Mic. 6:6–8; Matt. 9:13; 12:7] [1]NU omits *with all the soul* *See WW at Luke 2:47.
34 [a]Matt. 22:46
35 [a]Matt. 22:41–46; Luke 20:41–44
36 [a]2 Sam. 23:2 [b]Ps. 110:1
37 [a][Acts 2:29–31]
38 [a]Mark 4:2 [b]Matt. 23:1–7; Luke 20:45–47 [c]Matt. 23:7; Luke 11:43
39 [a]Luke 14:7
40 [a]Matt. 23:14 [1]*for appearance' sake* *See WW at John 10:10. • See WW at Rev. 20:4.
41 [a]Luke 21:1–4 [b]2 Kin. 12:9
42 [1]Gr. *lepta,* very small copper coins [2]A Roman coin
43 [a][2 Cor. 8:12]
44 [a]Deut. 24:6; [1 John 3:17] *See WW at Matt. 25:29.

CHAPTER 13

1 [a]Matt. 24:1; Luke 21:5–36
2 [a]Luke 19:44
3 [a]Matt. 16:18; Mark 1:16 [b]Mark 1:19 [c]Mark 1:19 [d]John 1:40
4 [a]Matt. 24:3; Luke 21:7
5 [a]Jer. 29:8; Eph. 5:6; [Col. 2:8]; 1 Thess. 2:3; 2 Thess. 2:3
8 [a]Hag. 2:22 [b]Matt. 24:8 [1]NU omits *and troubles* [2]Lit. *birth pangs*

12:33 The scribe not only agrees with Jesus but places this twofold love commandment above the whole Jewish religion.
12:34 Not far: The scribe is in the presence of the One who embodied the kingdom of God (1:14, 15).
12:35–37 See notes on Matt. 22:41–46.
12:38–40 Jesus strongly condemns the **scribes** for their prideful desire for prominence, their display of false piety, and their cruel avarice.
12:41–44 The sincere devotion of the **poor widow** stands in sharp contrast to the sham righteousness of the scribes.
12:41 The treasury was located in the Court of Women. Offerings were placed in 13 chests shaped like trumpets. Rich people called attention to their gifts by making a great show of putting in their money.
12:42 A mite was the smallest coin in circulation in Palestine, and was worth about 1/8 of a cent. For the benefit of his Roman readers, Mark explains their value in Roman coinage. **A quadrans** was 1/64 of a denarius, a laborer's daily wage.
12:44 The important thing to Jesus is not the amount of the gift but the commitment and sacrifice it represents. He judges our gift not by how much we give, but by how much we have left after we give.
13:1–37 See notes on Matt. 24:1–51.

9 "But [a]watch out for yourselves, for
they will deliver you up to councils,
and you will be beaten in the synagogues. You will [1]be brought before
rulers and kings for My sake, for a *testimony to them.
10 "And [a]the gospel must first be
preached to all the nations.
11 [a]"But when they arrest *you* and deliver you up, do not worry beforehand,
[1]or premeditate what you will speak.
But whatever is given you in that hour,
speak that; for it is not you who speak,
[b]but the Holy Spirit.
12 "Now [a]brother will betray brother
to death, and a father *his* child; and
children will rise up against parents
and cause them to be put to death.
13 [a]"And you will be hated by all for
My name's sake. But [b]he who [1]en-
dures* to the end shall be saved.

The Great Tribulation

14 [a]"So when you see the [b]*'abomina-*
tion of desolation,' [1]spoken of by Daniel the prophet, standing where it ought
not" (let the **reader** understand), "then
[c]let those who are in Judea flee to the
mountains.

WORD WEALTH

13:14 reader, *anaginosko* (an-ag-in-oce-koe); Strong's *#314:* Originally, "to know exactly"; to know over and over again, to recognize. The word came to mean reading aloud to oneself or to the congregation (Acts 8:28, 30; Col. 4:16).

15 "Let him who is on the housetop not
go down into the house, nor enter to
take anything out of his house.
16 "And let him who is in the field not
go back to get his clothes.
17 [a]"But woe to those who are pregnant and to those who are nursing babies in those days!
18 "And pray that your flight may not
be in winter.
19 [a]"For *in* those days there will be
tribulation, such as has not been since
the beginning of the creation which
God created until this time, nor ever
shall be.
20 "And unless the Lord had shortened those days, no flesh would be
saved; but for the elect's sake, whom
He *chose, He shortened the days.

9 [a]Matt. 10:17, 18; 24:9 [1]NU, M *stand* *See WW at Rev. 15:5.
10 [a]Matt. 24:14
11 [a]Luke 12:11; 21:12–17 [b]Acts 2:4; 4:8, 31 [1]NU omits *or premeditate*
12 [a]Mic. 7:6
13 [a]Luke 21:17 [b]Matt. 10:22; 24:13 [1]*bears patiently* *See WW at Matt. 24:13.
14 [a]Matt. 24:15 [b]Dan. 9:27; 11:31; 12:11 [c]Luke 21:21 [1]NU omits *spoken of by Daniel the prophet*
17 [a]Luke 21:23
19 [a]Dan. 9:26; 12:1
20 *See WW at 1 Pet. 2:9.
21 [a]Luke 17:23; 21:8
22 [a]Rev. 13:13, 14 [1]*chosen ones* *See WW at Acts 15:12.
23 [a][2 Pet. 3:17]
24 [a]Zeph. 1:15 *See WW at John 16:33.
25 [a]Is. 13:10; 34:4
26 [a][Dan. 7:13, 14] *See WW at Acts 4:33. • See WW at John 2:11.
27 [1]*chosen ones*
28 [a]Luke 21:29
29 [1]Or *He*
31 [a]Is. 40:8
32 [a]Matt. 25:13 [b]Acts 1:7 *See WW at Matt. 4:11.
33 [a]1 Thess. 5:6
34 [a]Matt. 24:45; 25:14 [b][Matt. 16:19]
35 [a]Matt. 24:42, 44

21 [a]"Then if anyone says to you,
'Look, here *is* the Christ!' or, 'Look, *He*
is there!' do not believe it.
22 "For false christs and false prophets
will rise and show signs and [a]wonders*
to deceive, if possible, even the
[1]elect.
23 "But [a]take heed; see, I have told you
all things beforehand.

The Coming of the Son of Man

24 [a]"But in those days, after that *tribulation, the sun will be darkened, and
the moon will not give its light;
25 "the stars of heaven will fall, and
the powers in the heavens will be
[a]shaken.
26 [a]"Then they will see the Son of Man
coming in the clouds with great *power
and *glory.
27 "And then He will send His angels,
and gather together His [1]elect from the
four winds, from the farthest part of
earth to the farthest part of heaven.

The Parable of the Fig Tree

28 [a]"Now learn this parable from the
fig tree: When its branch has already
become tender, and puts forth leaves,
you know that summer is near.
29 "So you also, when you see these
things happening, know that [1]it is
near—at the doors!
30 "Assuredly, I say to you, this generation will by no means pass away till
all these things take place.
31 "Heaven and earth will pass away,
but [a]My words will by no means pass
away.

No One Knows the Day or Hour

32 "But of that day and hour [a]no one
knows, not even the *angels in heaven,
nor the Son, but only the [b]Father.
33 [a]"Take heed, watch and pray; for
you do not know when the time is.
34 [a]"*It is* like a man going to a far
country, who left his house and gave
[b]authority to his servants, and to each
his work, and commanded the doorkeeper to watch.
35 [a]"Watch therefore, for you do not
know when the master of the house is
coming—in the evening, at midnight,
at the crowing of the rooster, or in the
morning—

13:32–37 Watching for the Lord's return does not mean idly speculating about the time of His Coming or setting dates that the Father has not revealed. Neither does it give license to neglect earthly responsibilities and the penetration of kingdom authority in daily situations.

36 "lest, coming suddenly, he find you
sleeping.
37 "And what I say to you, I say to all:
Watch!"

The Plot to Kill Jesus

14 After [a]two days it was the Passover and [b]*the Feast* of Unleavened Bread. And the chief priests and
the scribes sought how they might
take Him by [1]trickery and put *Him* to
death.
2 But they said, "Not during the feast,
lest there be an uproar of the people."

The Anointing at Bethany

3 [a]And being in Bethany at the house
of Simon the leper, as He sat at the
table, a woman came having an alabaster flask of very costly [1]oil of spikenard. Then she *broke the flask and
poured *it* on His head.
4 But there were some who were indignant among themselves, and said,
"Why was this fragrant oil wasted?
5 "For it might have been sold for
more than three hundred [a]denarii and
given to the poor." And they [b]criti-
cized[1]* her sharply.
6 But Jesus said, "Let her alone. Why
do you trouble her? She *has done a
good *work for Me.
7 [a]"For you have the poor with you
always, and whenever you wish you
may do them good; [b]but Me you do not
have always.
8 "She has done what she could. She
has come beforehand to anoint My
body for burial.
9 "Assuredly, I say to you, wherever
this gospel is [a]preached in the whole
world, what this woman has done
will also be told as a memorial to
her."

CHAPTER 14
1 [a]Matt. 26:2–5; Luke 22:1, 2; John 11:55; 13:1 [b]Ex. 12:1–27; Mark 14:12 [1]*deception*
3 [a]Matt. 26:6; Luke 7:37; John 12:1, 3 [1]Perfume of pure nard *See WW at Rom. 16:20.
5 [a]Matt. 18:28; Mark 12:15 [b]Matt. 20:11; John 6:61 [1]*scolded* *See WW at John 11:38.
6 *See WW at John 3:21. • See WW at John 9:4.
7 [a]Deut. 15:11; Matt. 26:11; John 12:8 [b][John 7:33; 8:21; 14:2, 12; 16:10, 17, 28]
9 [a]Matt. 28:19, 20; Mark 16:15; Luke 24:47
10 [a]Ps. 41:9; 55:12–14; Matt. 10:2–4
11 *See WW at Acts 7:5.
12 [a]Ex. 12:8; Matt. 26:17–19; Luke 22:7–13 [1]*sacrificed*
17 [a]Matt. 26:20–24; Luke 22:14, 21–23
18 [a]Ps. 41:9; Matt. 26:46; Mark 14:42; John 6:70, 71; 13:18
19 [1]NU omits the rest of v. 19.

Judas Agrees to Betray Jesus

10 [a]Then Judas Iscariot, one of the
twelve, went to the chief priests to betray Him to them.
11 And when they heard *it*, they were
glad, and *promised to give him
money. So he sought how he might
conveniently betray Him.

Jesus Celebrates the Passover with His Disciples

12 [a]Now on the first day of Unleavened Bread, when they [1]killed the
Passover *lamb*, His disciples said to
Him, "Where do You want us to go and
prepare, that You may eat the Passover?"
13 And He sent out two of His disciples
and said to them, "Go into the city, and
a man will meet you carrying a pitcher
of water; follow him.
14 "Wherever he goes in, say to the
master of the house, 'The Teacher says,
"Where is the guest room in which I
may eat the Passover with My disciples?" '
15 "Then he will show you a large upper room, furnished *and* prepared;
there make ready for us."
16 So His disciples went out, and came
into the city, and found it just as He
had said to them; and they prepared
the Passover.
17 [a]In the evening He came with the
twelve.
18 Now as they sat and ate, Jesus said,
"Assuredly, I say to you, [a]one of you
who eats with Me will betray Me."
19 And they began to be sorrowful,
and to say to Him one by one, "*Is* it
I?" [1]And another *said*, "*Is* it I?"
20 He answered and said to them, "*It
is* one of the twelve, who dips with Me
in the dish.

14:1 Both the terms **Passover** and **Unleavened Bread** were used of the feast commemorating the deliverance of the Jews from Egyptian bondage (see Luke 22:1). The point of the discussion was not whether to kill Jesus, but **how**. The decision had already been made (see 11:18; John 11:50–53).
14:2 Hundreds of thousands of pilgrims crowded into Jerusalem during the Passover, many of them perhaps supporters of Jesus from Galilee. The Jewish authorities did not want to risk **an uproar** that might bring Roman intervention.
14:3 John 12:3 names the **woman** as Mary of Bethany. **Spikenard** was a perfumed ointment, which came from India.
14:5 Since a denarius was a day's wages, the ointment represented almost a year's wages.
14:6, 7 See note on Matt. 26:7–10.
14:8 Just as Jesus was anointed with the Spirit for ministry, He is anointed with oil **for burial**.
14:9 The influence of an act of service for Christ, if not its memory, will not end.
14:10, 11 Matt. 26:15 makes it clear that the motive of Judas was greed, a trait that had **possessed** him all along, since he had been embezzling funds entrusted to him (John 12:6). Therefore, it is futile to offer explanations lessening his guilt.
14:12 The day **when they killed the Passover *lamb*** was Thursday.
14:13 **A man . . . carrying a pitcher of water** was an unusual sight in a society where women always did this kind of work.
14:15 Tradition suggests that the **upper room** was in the home of Mark, based primarily on the supposition that the young man of 14:51, 52 was Mark himself.
14:17–21 See note on Matt. 26:17–24.

21 [a]"The Son of Man indeed goes just as it is written of Him, but woe to that man by whom the Son of Man is betrayed! It would have been good for that man if he had never been born."

Jesus Institutes the Lord's Supper

3 **22** [a]And as they were eating, Jesus took bread, blessed and broke *it*, and *gave *it* to them and said, "Take, [1]eat; this is My [b]body."
23 Then He took the cup, and when He had *given thanks He gave *it* to them, and they all drank from it.
24 And He said to them, "This is My blood of the [1]new **covenant,** which is shed for many.

WORD WEALTH

14:24 covenant, *diatheke* (dee-ath-*ay*-kay); Strong's *#1242:* A will, testament, pact, contract, an agreed upon plan to which both parties subscribe. While the word may signify an agreement between two parties, with each accepting mutual obligations, most often it is a declaration of one person's will. In the Bible, God initiated the whole action, set the conditions, and defined as a decree a declaration of purposes. God covenanted with Noah, Abraham, Moses, and Israel. In the NT Jesus ratified by His death on the cross a new covenant, termed in Heb. 7:22 "a better covenant."

25 "Assuredly, I say to you, I will no longer drink of the fruit of the vine until that day when I drink it new in the kingdom of God."
26 [a]And when they had sung [1]a hymn, they went out to the Mount of Olives.

Jesus Predicts Peter's Denial

27 [a]Then Jesus said to them, "All of you will be made to *stumble [1]because of Me this night, for it is written:

> [b]*'I will strike the *Shepherd,*
> *And the sheep will be scattered.'*

28 "But [a]after I have been raised, I will go before you to Galilee."
29 [a]Peter said to Him, "Even if all are made to [1]stumble, yet I *will* not *be*."
30 Jesus said to him, "Assuredly, I say to you that today, *even* this night, before the rooster crows twice, you will deny Me three times."
31 But he spoke more vehemently, "If I have to die with You, I will not deny You!" And they all said likewise.

The Prayer in the Garden

32 [a]Then they came to a place which was named Gethsemane; and He said to His disciples, "Sit here while I *pray."
33 And He [a]took Peter, James, and John with Him, and He began to be troubled and deeply distressed.
34 Then He said to them, [a]"My soul is exceedingly sorrowful, *even* to death. Stay here and watch."
35 He went a little farther, and fell on the ground, and prayed that if it were *possible, the hour might pass from Him.
36 And He said, [a]"Abba, Father, 4
[b]all things *are* possible for You. Take this cup away from Me; [c]nevertheless, not what I will, but what You *will*."
37 Then He came and found them sleeping, and said to Peter, "Simon, are you sleeping? Could you not watch one hour?
38 [a]"Watch and pray, lest you enter into temptation. [b]The spirit indeed *is* willing, but the flesh *is* weak."
39 Again He went away and prayed, and spoke the same words.
40 And when He returned, He found them asleep again, for their eyes were heavy; and they did not know what to answer Him.
41 Then He came the third time and said to them, "Are you still sleeping and *resting? It is enough! [a]The hour has come; behold, the Son of Man is being betrayed into the hands of sinners.
42 [a]"Rise, let us be going. See, My betrayer is at hand."

Betrayal and Arrest in Gethsemane

43 [a]And immediately, while He was still speaking, Judas, one of the twelve, with a great multitude with swords and

21 [a]Matt. 26:24; Luke 22:22; Acts 1:16–20
22 [a]Matt. 26:26–29; Luke 22:17–20; 1 Cor. 11:23–25 [b][1 Pet. 2:24] [1]NU omits *eat* *See WW at Acts 20:35.
23 *See WW at John 6:11.
24 [1]NU omits *new*
26 [a]Matt. 26:30 [1]Or *hymns*
27 [a]Matt. 26:31–35; Mark 14:50; John 16:32 [b][Is. 53:5, 10]; Zech. 13:7 [1]NU omits *because of Me this night* *See WW at Matt. 11:6. • See WW at John 10:2.
28 [a]Matt. 28:16; Mark 16:7; John 21:1
29 [a]Matt. 26:33, 34; Luke 22:33, 34; John 13:37, 38 [1]*fall away*
32 [a]Matt. 26:36–46; Luke 22:40–46; John 18:1 *See WW at Matt. 6:6.
33 [a]Mark 5:37; 9:2; 13:3
34 [a]Is. 53:3, 4; Matt. 26:38; John 12:27
35 *See WW at Matt. 19:26.
36 [a]Rom. 8:15; Gal. 4:6 [b][Heb. 5:7] [c]Is. 50:5; John 5:30; 6:38
38 [a]Luke 21:36 [b][Rom. 7:18, 21–24; Gal. 5:17]
41 [a]John 13:1; 17:1 *See WW at Rev. 14:13.
42 [a]Matt. 26:46; Mark 14:18; Luke 9:44; John 13:21; 18:1, 2
43 [a]Ps. 3:1; Matt. 26:47–56; Luke 22:47–53; John 18:3–11

14:22–26 See note on Matt. 26:26–30.
14:22–25 *See section 3 of Truth-In-Action* through the Synoptics at the end of Luke.
14:26 The **hymn** was the Hallel, composed of sections of Ps. 115 and 118, which were sung at the close of a Passover meal.
14:27 The stumbling of the disciples fulfills the prophecy of Zech. 13:7.
14:28 The angel at the empty tomb made the same announcement. The resurrected Shepherd will lead His sheep to Galilee (see 16:7).
14:31 All the others join Peter in affirming loyalty.
14:32–50 See note on Matt. 26:36–56.
14:36 See section 4 of Truth-In-Action through the Synoptics at the end of Luke.

clubs, came from the chief priests and *the* scribes and the elders.

44 Now His betrayer had given them a signal, saying, "Whomever I [a]kiss,* He is the One; seize Him and lead *Him* away safely."

45 As soon as he had come, immediately he went up to Him and said to Him, "Rabbi, Rabbi!" and kissed Him.

46 Then they laid their hands on Him and took Him.

47 And one of those who stood by drew his sword and struck the servant of the high priest, and cut off his ear.

48 [a]Then Jesus answered and said to them, "Have you come out, as against a robber, with swords and clubs to take Me?

49 "I was daily with you in the temple [a]teaching, and you did not seize Me. But [b]the Scriptures must be fulfilled."

50 [a]Then they all forsook Him and fled.

A Young Man Flees Naked

51 Now a certain young man *followed Him, having a linen cloth thrown around *his* naked *body*. And the young men laid hold of him,

52 and he left the linen cloth and fled from them naked.

Jesus Faces the Sanhedrin

53 [a]And they led Jesus away to the high priest; and with him were [b]assembled all the [c]chief priests, the elders, and the scribes.

54 But [a]Peter followed Him at a distance, right into the courtyard of the high priest. And he sat with the servants and warmed himself at the fire.

55 [a]Now the chief priests and all the council sought *testimony against Jesus to put Him to death, but found none.

56 For many bore [a]false witness against Him, but their testimonies [1]did not agree.

57 Then some rose up and bore false witness against Him, saying,

58 "We heard Him say, [a]'I will destroy this temple made with hands, and within three days I will build another made without hands.' "

59 But not even then did their testimony agree.

60 [a]And the high priest stood up in the midst and asked Jesus, saying, "Do

44 [a][Prov. 27:6] *See WW at John 21:15.
48 [a]Matt. 26:55
49 [a]Matt. 21:23 [b]Is. 53:7
50 [a]Ps. 88:8
51 *See WW at John 13:36.
53 [a]Matt. 26:57–68 [b]Mark 15:1 [c]John 7:32; 18:3; 19:6
54 [a]John 18:15
55 [a]Matt. 26:59 *See WW at John 19:35.
56 [a]Ex. 20:16 [1]*were not consistent*
58 [a]John 2:19
60 [a]Matt. 26:62
61 [a]Is. 53:7 [b]Luke 22:67–71
62 [a]Luke 22:69
64 [a]John 10:33, 36 [b]John 19:7
65 [a]Is. 50:6; 52:14 [1]NU *received Him with slaps*
66 [a]John 18:16–18, 25–27
67 [a]John 1:45
69 [a]Matt. 26:71
70 [a]Luke 22:59 [b]Acts 2:7 [1]NU omits the rest of v. 70. [2]*accent*
72 [a]Matt. 26:75 *See WW at Matt. 4:4.

CHAPTER 15
1 [a]Ps. 2:2

You answer nothing? What *is it* these men testify against You?"

61 But [a]He kept silent and answered nothing. [b]Again the high priest asked Him, saying to Him, "Are You the Christ, the Son of the Blessed?"

62 Jesus said, "I am. [a]And you will see the Son of Man sitting at the right hand of the Power, and coming with the clouds of heaven."

63 Then the high priest tore his clothes and said, "What further need do we have of witnesses?

64 "You have heard the [a]blasphemy! What do you think?" And they all condemned Him to be deserving of [b]death.

65 Then some began to [a]spit on Him, and to blindfold Him, and to beat Him, and to say to Him, "Prophesy!" And the officers [1]struck Him with the palms of their hands.

Peter Denies Jesus, and Weeps

66 [a]Now as Peter was below in the courtyard, one of the servant girls of the high priest came.

67 And when she saw Peter warming himself, she looked at him and said, "You also were with [a]Jesus of Nazareth."

68 But he denied it, saying, "I neither know nor understand what you are saying." And he went out on the porch, and a rooster crowed.

69 [a]And the servant girl saw him again, and began to say to those who stood by, "This is one of them."

70 But he denied it again. [a]And a little
later those who stood by said to Peter
again, "Surely you are *one* of them;
[b]for you are a Galilean, [1]and your
[2]speech shows *it*."

71 Then he began to curse and swear, "I do not know this Man of whom you speak!"

72 [a]A second time *the* rooster crowed. Then Peter called to mind the *word that Jesus had said to him, "Before the rooster crows twice, you will deny Me three times." And when he thought about it, he wept.

Jesus Faces Pilate

15

Immediately, [a]in the morning, the chief priests held a consultation with the elders and scribes and the whole council; and they bound

14:51, 52 The addition of this curious detail has suggested to many that this may have been Mark himself. See note on v. 15.

14:53–72 See note on Matt. 26:57–75.

15:1 The Sanhedrin took **Jesus** to **Pilate** because the Romans had denied them the authority to inflict capital punishment. Pilate would have to pronounce the legal sentence.

Jesus, led *Him* away, and [b]delivered*
Him to Pilate.
2 [a]Then Pilate asked Him, "Are You
the King of the Jews?" He answered
and said to him, "*It is as* you say."
3 And the chief priests accused Him
of many things, but He [a]answered
nothing.
4 [a]Then Pilate asked Him again, saying, "Do You answer nothing? See
how many things [1]they testify against
You!"
5 [a]But Jesus still answered nothing,
so that Pilate marveled.

Taking the Place of Barabbas

6 Now [a]at the feast he was accustomed to releasing one prisoner to
them, whomever they requested.
7 And there was one named Barabbas, *who was* chained with his fellow
rebels; they had committed murder in
the rebellion.
8 Then the multitude, [1]crying aloud,
began to ask *him to do* just as he had
always done for them.
9 But Pilate answered them, saying,
"Do you want me to release to you the
King of the Jews?"
10 For he knew that the chief priests
had handed Him over because of envy.
11 But [a]the chief priests stirred up the
crowd, so that he should rather release
Barabbas to them.
12 Pilate answered and said to them
again, "What then do you want me to
do *with Him* whom you call the
[a]King of the Jews?"
13 So they cried out again, "Crucify
Him!"
14 Then Pilate said to them, "Why,
[a]what evil has He done?" But they
cried out all the *more, "Crucify Him!"
15 [a]So Pilate, wanting to gratify the
crowd, released Barabbas to them; and
he delivered Jesus, after he had
scourged *Him*, to be [b]crucified.

The Soldiers Mock Jesus

16 [a]Then the soldiers led Him away
into the hall called [1]Praetorium, and
they called together the whole garrison.
17 And they clothed Him with purple;
and they twisted a crown of thorns, put
it on His *head*,
18 and began to salute Him, "Hail,
King of the Jews!"
19 Then they [a]struck Him on the head
with a reed and spat on Him; and bowing the knee, they *worshiped Him.
20 And when they had [a]mocked Him,
they took the purple off Him, put His
own clothes on Him, and led Him out
to crucify Him.

The King on a Cross

21 [a]Then they *compelled a certain
man, Simon a Cyrenian, the father of
Alexander and Rufus, as he was coming out of the country and passing by,
to bear His cross.
22 [a]And they brought Him to the place
Golgotha, which is translated, Place of
a Skull.
23 [a]Then they gave Him wine mingled
with myrrh to drink, but He did not
take *it*.
24 And when they crucified Him,
[a]they divided His garments, casting
lots for them to determine what every
man should take.
25 Now [a]it was the third hour, and they
crucified Him.
26 And [a]the inscription of His [1]accusa-
tion was written above:

THE KING OF THE JEWS.

27 [a]With Him they also crucified two
robbers, one on His right and the other
on His left.
28 [1]So the *Scripture was fulfilled
which says, [a]*"And He was *numbered
with the transgressors."*
29 And [a]those who passed by blasphemed Him, [b]wagging their heads
and saying, "Aha! [c]*You* who destroy
the temple and build *it* in three days,
30 "save Yourself, and come down
from the cross!"
31 Likewise the chief priests also,
[a]mocking among themselves with the
scribes, said, "He saved [b]others; Himself He cannot save.

1 [b]Acts 3:13 *See WW at Luke 23:25.
2 [a]Matt. 27:11–14
3 [a]John 19:9
4 [a]Matt. 27:13 [1]NU *of which they accuse You*
5 [a]Is. 53:7
6 [a]Matt. 27:15–26
8 [1]NU *going up*
11 [a]Acts 3:14
12 [a]Mic. 5:2
14 [a]1 Pet. 2:21–23 *See WW at 2 Cor. 2:4.
15 [a]Matt. 27:26 [b][Is. 53:8]
16 [a]Matt. 27:27–31 [1]The governor's headquarters
19 [a][Is. 50:6; 52:14; 53:5] *See WW at Rev. 4:10.
20 [a]Luke 22:63; 23:11
21 [a]Matt. 27:32 *See WW at Matt. 5:41.
22 [a]John 19:17–24
23 [a]Matt. 27:34
24 [a]Ps. 22:18
25 [a]John 19:14
26 [a]Matt. 27:37 [1]*crime*
27 [a]Luke 22:37
28 [a]Is. 53:12 [1]NU omits v. 28. *See WW at John 5:39. • See WW at Rom. 4:3.
29 [a]Ps. 22:6, 7; 69:7 [b]Ps. 109:25 [c]John 2:19–21
31 [a]Luke 18:32 [b]John 11:43, 44

15:2 Jewish religious matters were of little concern to Pilate, so he would not be impressed with the charge of blasphemy. Therefore, the Sanhedrin twisted the claims of Jesus to mean that He was plotting rebellion against the Romans.
15:10 *Pilate knows Jesus to be innocent, but he disregards* his conscience in order to please the Jewish religious leaders (see v. 15).
15:15 **Scourged:** See note on Matt. 27:26.
15:16 The **Praetorium** was the official residence of the governor.
15:21 The victim was required to carry his own cross to the place of execution, but Jesus, in His weakened condition, could not bear its weight. **Alexander and Rufus** were apparently known by Mark's readers (see Rom. 16:13).
15:22 The English word Calvary comes from the Latin *calvaria*, "a skull."
15:24 The Roman custom was to strip the condemned man and allot his clothes to members of the crucifixion detail.
15:25 **The third hour** was 9:00 A.M.
15:26 See note on John 19:19–22.
15:31 He could not save Himself and be the Savior of others.

32 "Let the Christ, the King of Israel,
descend now from the cross, that we
may see and [1]believe." Even [a]those
who were crucified with Him *reviled
Him.

Jesus Dies on the Cross

33 Now [a]when the sixth hour had
come, there was *darkness over the
whole land until the ninth hour.
34 And at the ninth hour Jesus cried
out with a loud voice, saying, "Eloi,
Eloi, lama sabachthani?" which is
translated, [a]*"My God, My God, why
have You forsaken Me?"*
35 Some of those who stood by, when
they heard *that,* said, "Look, He is calling for Elijah!"
36 Then [a]someone ran and filled a
sponge full of sour wine, put *it* on a
reed, and [b]offered *it* to Him to drink,
saying, "Let Him alone; let us see if
Elijah will come to take Him down."
37 [a]And Jesus cried out with a loud
voice, and breathed His last.
38 Then [a]the veil of the temple was
torn in two from top to bottom.
39 So [a]when the centurion, who stood
opposite Him, saw that [1]He cried out
like this and breathed His last, he said,
"Truly this Man was the Son of God!"
40 [a]There were also women looking on
[b]from afar, among whom were Mary
Magdalene, Mary the mother of James
the Less and of Joses, and Salome,
41 who also [a]followed Him and ministered to Him when He was in Galilee,
and many other women who came up
with Him to Jerusalem.

Jesus Buried in Joseph's Tomb

42 [a]Now when evening had come, because it was the Preparation Day, that
is, the day before the Sabbath,
43 Joseph of Arimathea, a prominent
council member, who [a]was himself
waiting for the kingdom of God, coming and taking courage, went in to Pilate and asked for the body of Jesus.
44 Pilate marveled that He was already
dead; and summoning the centurion,

32 [a]Matt. 27:44 [1]M *believe Him* *See WW at James 1:5.
33 [a]Luke 23:44–49 *See WW at Luke 11:35.
34 [a]Ps. 22:1
36 [a]John 19:29 [b]Ps. 69:21
37 [a]Matt. 27:50
38 [a]Ex. 26:31–33
39 [a]Luke 23:47 [1]NU *He thus breathed His last*
40 [a]Matt. 27:55 [b]Ps. 38:11
41 [a]Luke 8:2, 3
42 [a]John 19:38–42
43 [a]Luke 2:25, 38; 23:51
46 [a]Matt. 27:59, 60

CHAPTER 16

1 [a]John 20:1–8 [b]Luke 23:56
2 [a]Luke 24:1
5 [a]John 20:11, 12
6 [a]Matt. 28:6
7 [a]Matt. 26:32; 28:16, 17 [1]*ahead of*
8 [a]Matt. 28:8 [1]NU, M omit *quickly* *See WW at Rev. 22:20.
9 [1]Vv. 9–20 are bracketed in NU as not in the original text. They are lacking in Codex Sinaiticus and Codex Vaticanus, although nearly all other mss. of Mark contain them.

he asked him if He had been dead for
some time.
45 So when he found out from the centurion, he granted the body to Joseph.
46 [a]Then he bought fine linen, took
Him down, and wrapped Him in the
linen. And he laid Him in a tomb which
had been hewn out of the rock, and
rolled a stone against the door of the
tomb.
47 And Mary Magdalene and Mary *the
mother* of Joses observed where He
was laid.

He Is Risen

16 Now [a]when the Sabbath was
past, Mary Magdalene, Mary
the mother of James, and Salome
[b]bought spices, that they might come
and anoint Him.
2 [a]Very early in the morning, on the
first *day* of the week, they came to the
tomb when the sun had risen.
3 And they said among themselves,
"Who will roll away the stone from the
door of the tomb for us?"
4 But when they looked up, they saw
that the stone had been rolled away—
for it was very large.
5 [a]And entering the tomb, they saw
a young man clothed in a long white
robe sitting on the right side; and they
were alarmed.
6 [a]But he said to them, "Do not be
alarmed. You seek Jesus of Nazareth,
who was crucified. He is risen! He is
not here. See the place where they laid
Him.
7 "But go, tell His disciples—and Peter—that He is going [1]before you into
Galilee; there you will see Him, [a]as He
said to you."
8 So they went out [1]quickly* and fled
from the tomb, for they trembled and
were amazed. [a]And they said nothing
to anyone, for they were afraid.

Mary Magdalene Sees the Risen Lord

9 [1]Now when *He* rose early on the
first *day* of the week, He appeared first

15:34 The cry of dereliction from Jesus (Ps. 22:1) reflects the burden of humanity's sin, complete identification with sinners, and a real abandonment by God (see 14:36; 2 Cor. 5:21; Gal. 3:13). See note on Matt. 27:46.
15:38 See note on Matt. 27:51.
15:43 See note on John 19:38, 39.
15:46 Rock tombs were normally closed by means of a large stone rolled into the mouth of the hollow.
16:1 **The Sabbath** ended at sunset on Saturday, about 6:00 P.M. There is unanimity in the Gospels regarding the prominence of women in this event as the first ones who received news of the Resurrection.
16:2 Even though Jesus had promised to rise from the dead on the third day His followers either disbelieved the promise or in their grief had forgotten it.
16:5 The **young man** was an angel (see Matt. 28:2–7).
16:6 The angel emphasizes the evidence of the Resurrection.
16:7 The special reference to Peter is an assurance of forgiveness and restoration after his denials.
16:9–20 Many scholars question the authenticity of vv. 9–20, primarily because of omission of these verses in some of the earliest manuscripts, and because their style is somewhat different from the rest of Mark. However, Christian

to Mary Magdalene, [a]out of whom He
had cast seven demons.
10 [a]She went and told those who had
been with Him, as they *mourned and
wept.
11 [a]And when they heard that He was
alive and had been seen by her, they
did not believe.

Jesus Appears to Two Disciples

12 After that, He *appeared in *another form [a]to two of them as they
walked and went into the country.
13 And they went and told *it* to the
rest, *but* they did not believe them either.

The Great Commission

14 [a]Later He appeared to the eleven as
they sat at the table; and He *rebuked
their unbelief and hardness of heart,
because they did not believe those who
had seen Him after He had risen.
15 [a]And He said to them, "Go into all
the world [b]and preach the gospel to every creature.
16 [a]"He who believes and is baptized
will be saved; [b]but he who does not
believe will be condemned.
17 "And these [a]signs will follow those
who [1]believe: [b]In My name they will
cast out demons; [c]they will speak with
new tongues;
18 [a]"they[1] will take up serpents; and
if they drink anything deadly, it will
by no means hurt them; [b]they will lay
hands on the sick, and they will recover."

KINGDOM DYNAMICS

16:15–18 Commissioned in Christ's Servant Spirit, WORLD EVANGELISM. To understand the Great Commission in Mark, we must capture the spirit of Mark's focus on Jesus as the Servant. Messianic prophecies, such as Is. 42:1–21, 49:1–7, 50:4–11, and 53:12, forecast Jesus' servant-character would do a specific work and act with unqualified and unsullied obedience.

Mark shows Christ's servant-character by omitting His genealogy (by which other Gospels establish His identity), showing that, as servants of Christ, we, too, might learn the servant-spirit essential to fulfilling the Great Commission. Christ seeks those who will serve without seeking recognition, selflessly and obediently seeking to exalt Christ and make Him known. Such servants establish their personhood and ministries by their devotion and obedience to Jesus, their disposition to serve unselfishly—their only exercise of power being to extend the love of God—ministering His life to the lost, the sick, and those in bondage. They do so wherever and however God sovereignly directs, whether it be through their giving, their going, or their prayerful intercession. The Servant Jesus' love and obedience compel His servants to loyal and unreserved service.

(Matt. 28:18–20/Luke 24:45–48) G.C.

Christ Ascends to God's Right Hand

19 So then, [a]after the *Lord had spoken to them, He was [b]received up into
heaven, and [c]sat down at the right
hand of God.
20 And they went out and preached
everywhere, the Lord *working with
them [a]and **confirming** the *word
through the accompanying signs.
Amen.

WORD WEALTH

16:20 confirming, *bebaioo* (beb-ah-*yah*-oh); Strong's *#950:* To make firm, establish, secure, corroborate, guarantee. The miracles that accompanied the disciples' preaching confirmed to the people that the messengers were telling the truth, that God was backing up their message with supernatural phenomena, and that a new dispensation, the age of grace, had entered the world.

9 [a]Luke 8:2
10 [a]Luke 24:10 *See WW at Rev. 18:11.
11 [a]Matt. 28:17; Luke 24:11, 41; John 20:25
12 [a]Luke 24:13–35 *See WW at Col. 3:4. • See WW at Acts 4:12.
14 [a]Luke 24:36; John 20:19, 26; 1 Cor. 15:5 *See WW at James 1:5.
15 [a]Matt. 28:19; [John 15:16; Acts 1:8]; Col. 1:6 [b][Col. 1:23]
16 [a][John 3:18, 36; Acts 2:38; 16:30, 31; Rom. 10:8–10] [b][John 12:48]
17 [a]Acts 5:12 [b]Mark 9:38; Luke 10:17; Acts 5:16; 8:7; 16:18; 19:12 [c][Acts 2:4; 1 Cor. 12:10] [1]*have believed*
18 [a][Luke 10:19]; Acts 28:3–6 [b][Acts 5:15]; James 5:14 [1]NU *and in their hands they will*
19 [a]Acts 1:2, 3 [b]Ps. 68:18; Luke 9:51; 24:51; John 6:62; 20:17; Acts 1:2, 9–11; [1 Tim. 3:16; Rev. 4:2] [c][Ps. 110:1]; Luke 22:69; [Acts 7:55]; 1 Pet. 3:22 *See WW at John 6:68.
20 [a]Acts 5:12; [1 Cor. 2:4, 5; Heb. 2:4] *See WW at James 2:22. • See WW at Acts 19:20.

writers of the second century, such as Justin Martyr, Irenaeus, and Tatian, testify to the inclusion of these verses, and the earliest translations, such as the Latin, Syriac, and Coptic, all include them. In any case, the passage does reflect the experience and expectation of the early church concerning the practice of charismatic gifts, and the question of its authenticity should remain open.

16:12 See notes on Luke 24:13–35.

16:15 See notes on Matt. 28:18–20.

16:16 See note on *Rom. 6:3. Belief* is the inward reception of Christ, and baptism is the outward testimony of that belief.

16:17, 18 The **signs** accredit the gospel message, and cannot be limited to the apostolic age, any more than the Lord's commission to carry the gospel throughout the world. The signs, therefore, confirm the ministries of Christ's ambassadors in every generation. Casting out demons, speaking in tongues, and healing all appear in other passages in the NT, and there is no scriptural warrant for their cessation before the Lord returns. Taking up **serpents** does not refer to handling snakes in religious ceremonies, but casting them away without being harmed (see Acts 28:3–6). The Greek verb *airō*, "take up," can also mean "remove," "take away," "cast away." See Matt. 14:12; Luke 11:52; 1 Cor. 5:2; Eph. 4:31. Similarly, a servant of the Lord may look for divine protection in matters pertaining to food and drink. Many missionaries have testified to God's miraculous protection in heathen territories, where they experienced no ill effects from impure food and drink. All of the signs listed here have occurred repeatedly in Christian history.

16:19 These words are an echo of Ps. 110:1, a verse quoted more frequently in the NT than any other OT passage.

The Gospel of LUKE

Author: Luke
Date: A.D. 59–75
Theme: Jesus the Savior of the World
Key Words: Prayer, Thanksgiving, Joy, Save, Kingdom, Holy Spirit, Repentance

Author Both style and language offer convincing evidence that the same person wrote Luke and Acts. "The former account" of Acts 1:1 then is likely a reference to the third Gospel as the first of a two-volume series, and the fact that the writer dedicates both books to Theophilus also strongly argues for common authorship. Since church tradition unanimously attributes these two works to Luke the physician, a close associate of Paul (Col. 4:14; Philem. 24; 2 Tim. 4:11), and since the internal evidence supports this view, there is no reason to dispute the Lukan authorship.

Date Scholars who assume that Luke used Mark's Gospel as a source in writing his own account date the third Gospel in the A.D. seventies. Others, however, point out that Luke wrote his Gospel prior to Acts, which he wrote during Paul's first Roman imprisonment, about A.D. 63. Since Luke was in Caesarea during Paul's two-year incarceration there (Acts 27:1), he would have had ample opportunity during that time to conduct the investigation he mentions in 1:1–4. If this is the case, then Luke's Gospel may be dated around A.D. 59–60, but as late as A.D. 75.

Purpose Luke clearly states that his purpose in writing this Gospel is to present "an orderly account" (1:3) "of all that Jesus began both to do and teach" (Acts 1:1), so that Theophilus may have historical evidence of the teachings he had received (1:4). While the Gospel is specifically addressed to one individual, apparently a high official, its intent is to give all believers the assurance that Christianity is not one of many speculative systems searching for theological or ethical values, but that this movement is bound up with an event in history. Luke substantiates the certainty/accuracy of his work with four reasons: 1) his concern with early origins, with priority given to eyewitnesses (v. 2); 2) his aim to be comprehensive, "all things"; 3) chronological, "an orderly account"; 4) accurate, "the certainty" (v. 4).

In achieving his purpose, Luke traces in his two volumes the Christian movement from its beginnings with Jesus of Nazareth to its development into a worldwide fellowship transcending the limits of Jewish nationality and embracing Jews and Gentiles impartially. Luke presents Jesus not as a mere Jewish Messiah, but as a world Savior.

Content A distinguishing feature of Luke's Gospel is its emphasis on the universality of the Christian message. From Simeon's song praising Jesus as "a light . . . to the Gentiles" (2:32) to the risen Lord's commission to preach "to all nations" (24:47), Luke stresses the fact that Jesus is not merely the Jewish Deliverer, but the Savior of the entire world.

In order to support this theme, Luke omits much material that is strictly Jewish in character. For example, he does not include Jesus' pronouncement of condemnation upon the scribes and Pharisees (Matt. 23), nor the discussion about Jewish tradition (Matt. 15:1–20; Mark 7:1–23). Luke also excludes the teachings of Jesus in the Sermon on the Mount that deal directly with His relation to the Jewish Law (see Matt. 5:21–48; 6:1–8, 16–18). Luke also omits the instructions of Jesus to the Twelve to refrain from ministering to the Gentiles and Samaritans (Matt. 10:5).

On the other hand, Luke includes many features that demonstrate universality. He sets the birth of Jesus in a Roman context (2:1, 2; 3:1), showing that what he records has meaning for all people. While Matthew traces Jesus' ancestry from Abraham, Luke follows it back to Adam, connecting the Lord to the entire human race.

However, Luke also emphasizes the Jewish roots of Jesus. Of all the Gospel writers, he alone records the circumcision and dedication of Jesus (2:21–24), as well as His temple visit as a Boy of twelve (2:41–52). Luke alone relates the birth and infancy of Jesus in the context of pious Jews such as Simeon, Anna, Zacharias, and Elizabeth, who were among the faithful remnant "waiting for the Consolation of Israel" (2:25). Throughout his Gospel, Luke makes it clear that Jesus is the fulfillment of Old Testament expectations concerning salvation.

A key verse in Luke's Gospel is 19:10, which states that Jesus "has come to seek and to save that which was lost." In presenting Jesus as the Savior of all sorts of people, Luke includes material not found in the other Gospels, such as the account of the Pharisee and the sinful woman (7:36–50); the parables of the lost sheep, coin, and son (15:1–32); the parable of the Pharisee and the tax collector (18:9–14); the story of Zacchaeus (19:1–10); and the pardon of the thief on the cross (23:39–43).

Luke highlights Jesus' warnings about the danger of riches and His sympathy for the poor (see 1:53; 4:18; 6:20, 21, 24, 25; 12:13–21; 14:13; 16:19–31; 19:1–10).

This Gospel has more references to prayer than do the other Gospels. Luke especially emphasizes the prayer life of Jesus, recording seven occasions on which Jesus prayed that are not found elsewhere (see 3:21; 5:16; 6:12; 9:18, 29; 11:1; 23:34, 46). Luke alone has the Lord's lessons on prayer taught in the parables of the persistent friend (11:5–10), the persistent widow (18:1–8), and the Pharisee and the tax collector (18:9–14). In addition, the Gospel abounds in notes of praise and thanksgiving (see 1:28, 46–56, 68–79; 2:14, 20, 29–32; 5:25, 26; 7:16; 13:13; 17:15; 18:43).

Christ Revealed In addition to presenting Jesus as the Savior of the world, Luke gives the following witness to Him:

1. Jesus is the Prophet whose role becomes equated with Servant and Messiah (see 4:24; 7:16, 39; 9:19; 24:19).

2. Jesus is the ideal Man, the perfect Savior of imperfect humankind. The title "Son of Man" is found twenty-six times in the Gospel. The term not only emphasizes the humanity of Christ in contrast to the expression "Son of God," which stresses His deity, but it describes Jesus as the perfect, ideal Man, the true representative of the entire human race.

3. Jesus is Messiah. Not only does Luke affirm Jesus' messianic identity, but he is careful to define the nature of His messiahship. Jesus is preeminently the Servant who steadfastly sets His face to go to Jerusalem to fulfill His role (9:31, 51). Jesus is the Son of David (20:41–44), the Son of Man (5:24), and the Suffering Servant (4:17–19) who was numbered with transgressors (22:37).

4. Jesus is the exalted Lord. Luke refers to Jesus as "Lord" eighteen times in his Gospel (fifty times in Acts). Even though the title takes on new significance after the Resurrection (see Acts 2:36), it denotes the divine Person of Jesus even during His earthly ministry.

5. Jesus is the friend of lowly outcasts. He is consistently gracious to society's rejected ones—publicly acknowledged sinners, Samaritans, Gentiles, and the poor. His attitude toward women in a patriarchal age is likewise affirming and sensitive. Luke includes much material that underscores Jesus' positive ministry of kindness and sympathy toward these groups.

The Holy Spirit at Work

There are seventeen explicit references to the Holy Spirit in Luke, stressing His activity both in the life of Jesus and in the continuing ministry of the church.

First, the Holy Spirit's action is seen in the lives of various faithful people connected with the births of John the Baptist and Jesus (1:35, 41, 67; 2:25–27), as well as in the fact that John fulfilled his ministry under the anointing of the Holy Spirit (1:15). The same Spirit enabled Jesus to carry out His messianic role.

Second, the Holy Spirit enables Jesus to fulfill His ministry—the Spirit-anointed Messiah. In chapters 3 and 4, there are five explicit references to the Spirit, used with progressive force. 1) The Spirit comes upon Jesus in bodily form like a dove (3:22); 2) He leads Jesus into the wilderness to be tempted (4:1); 3) following His victory over temptation, Jesus returns to Galilee in the power of the same Spirit (4:14); 4) In the Nazareth synagogue Jesus reads the messianic passage, "The Spirit of the LORD *is* upon Me . . ." (4:18; Is. 61:1, 2) claiming their fulfillment in Him (4:21). Then, 5) evidence for His charismatic ministry abounds (4:31–44), and continues into the whole of His ministry of power and compassion.

Third, the Holy Spirit, through petitionary prayer, effects the messianic ministry. At critical junctures in that ministry, Jesus prays, before, during, or after the crucial event (3:21; 6:12; 9:18, 28; 10:21). The same Holy Spirit that was effective through Jesus' prayers will empower the disciples' prayers (18:1–8), and link the messianic ministry of Jesus to their mighty ministry through the church (see 24:48, 49).

Fourth, the Holy Spirit spreads joy, both to Jesus and the new community. Five Greek words denoting joy or exultation are used twice as often in Luke as they are in Matthew or Mark. At the time when the disciples return with joy from their mission (10:17), "In that hour Jesus rejoiced in the Spirit and said . . . " (10:21). As the disciples are waiting for the promised Spirit (24:49), "they worshiped Him, and returned to Jerusalem with great joy, and were continually in the temple, praising and blessing God" (24:52, 53).

Personal Application No one who reads this book should feel that he is beyond the reach of the gospel of salvation. Throughout the book, Luke presents Jesus as the Savior of the whole world. This is true from Simeon's song about Jesus being "a light . . . to the Gentiles" (2:32) to the final instructions of the risen Lord to His disciples, in which He told them that "repentance and remission of sins should be preached in His name to all nations" (24:47). Luke emphasizes the fact that the gospel is not only for Jews, but for all peoples—Greeks, Romans, Samaritans, and all others without regard to race or condition. It is not only for males, but also for females, including widows and prostitutes as well as the socially prominent. It is not only for freemen, but also for slaves and all others rejected by society—the lowly poor, the helplessly weak, the crucified thief, the outcast sinner, the despised tax collector.

Outline of Luke

I. Prologue 1:1–4

II. The infancy narrative 1:5—2:52

- A. Announcement of John the Baptist's birth 1:5–25
- B. Announcement of Jesus' birth 1:26–38
- C. Visit of the two mothers 1:39–56
- D. John the Baptist's birth 1:57–80
- E. Jesus' birth 2:1–40
- F. The Boy Jesus in the temple 2:41–52

III. Preparation for public ministry 3:1—4:13

- A. John the Baptist's ministry 3:1–20
- B. Jesus' baptism 3:21, 22
- C. Jesus' genealogy 3:23–38
- D. The Temptation 4:1–13

IV. The Galilean ministry 4:14—9:50

- A. At Nazareth and Capernaum 4:14–44
- B. From the call of Peter to the call of the Twelve 5:1—6:16
- C. Sermon on the Plain 6:17–49
- D. Narrative and dialogue 7:1—9:50

V. The travel narrative (on the way to Jerusalem) 9:51—19:28

VI. The Jerusalem ministry 19:29—21:38

- A. Events at Jesus' entry 19:29–48
- B. Controversy stories 20:1—21:4
- C. Eschatological discourse 21:5–38

VII. The passion and glorification of Jesus 22:1—24:53

- A. The Passover meal 22:1–38
- B. The passion, death, and burial of Jesus 22:39—23:56
- C. The Resurrection and the Ascension 24:1–53

Dedication to Theophilus

INASMUCH as many have taken in hand to set in order a narrative of those [a]things which [1]have been fulfilled among us,
2 just as those who [a]from the beginning were [b]eyewitnesses and ministers of the word [c]delivered them to us,
3 it seemed good to me also, having [1]had perfect understanding of all things from the very first, to write to

CHAPTER 1
1 [a]John 20:31 [1]Or *are most surely believed*
2 [a]Acts 1:21, 22 [b]Acts 1:2 [c]Heb. 2:3
3 [1]Lit. *accurately followed*

1:1, 2 The inspiration of the Holy Spirit in the writing of Scripture does not preclude careful research on the part of the human author. Luke's sources, which he does not regard as inaccurate but as inadequate, were twofold: written and oral. **Many** people had attempted to arrange in orderly fashion fragmentary collections of Jesus' teachings and works, and **eyewitnesses** had been faithful in preserving and narrating what they had witnessed. Luke is not concerned to write religious theory; he tells the good news **of those things which have been fulfilled**.

1:3 The expression **having had perfect understanding** is more accurately translated "having followed up all things carefully," stressing Luke's diligent care as a historian. The **orderly account** he writes does not necessarily refer to

you an orderly account, [a]most excellent Theophilus,
4 [a]that you may *know the certainty of
those things in which you were instructed.

John's Birth Announced to Zacharias

5 There was [a]in the days of Herod,
the king of Judea, a certain priest
named Zacharias, [b]of the division of
[c]Abijah. His [d]wife *was* of the daughters of Aaron, and her name *was* Elizabeth.
6 And they were both *righteous before God, walking in all the commandments and ordinances of the Lord
blameless.
7 But they had no child, because Elizabeth was barren, and they were both
well advanced in years.
8 So it was, that while he was serving
as priest before God in the order of his
division,
9 according to the custom of the
priesthood, [1]his lot fell [a]to burn incense when he went into the temple of
the Lord.
10 [a]And the whole multitude of the
people was praying outside at the hour
of incense.
11 Then an angel of the Lord appeared
to him, standing on the right side of
[a]the altar of incense.

3 [a]Acts 1:1
4 [a][John 20:31] *See WW at Luke 5:22.
5 [a]Matt. 2:1 [b]1 Chr. 24:1, 10 [c]Neh. 12:4 [d]Lev. 21:13, 14
6 *See WW at Matt. 1:19.
9 [a]Ex. 30:7, 8; 1 Chr. 23:13; 2 Chr. 29:11 [1]*he was chosen by lot*
10 [a]Lev. 16:17
11 [a]Ex. 30:1
12 [a]Judg. 6:22; Dan. 10:8; Luke 2:9; Acts 10:4; Rev. 1:17
13 [a]Luke 1:57, 60, 63
14 [a]Luke 1:58
15 [a][Luke 7:24–28] [b]Num. 6:3; Judg. 13:4; Matt. 11:18 [c]Jer. 1:5; Gal. 1:15 *See WW at Rom. 7:6.
17 [a]Mal. 4:5, 6; Matt. 3:2; 11:14; Mark 1:4; 9:12
18 [a]Gen. 17:17
19 [a]Dan. 8:16; [Matt. 18:10]; Heb. 1:4 [b]Luke 2:10 [1]*this good news*

12 And when Zacharias saw *him*,
[a]he was troubled, and fear fell upon
him.
13 But the angel said to him, "Do not
be afraid, Zacharias, for your prayer
is heard; and your wife Elizabeth will
bear you a son, and [a]you shall call his
name John.
14 "And you will have joy and gladness, and [a]many will rejoice at his
birth.
15 "For he will be [a]great in the sight
of the Lord, and [b]shall drink neither
wine nor strong drink. He will also be
filled with the Holy *Spirit, [c]even from
his mother's womb.
16 "And he will turn many of the
children of Israel to the Lord their
God.
17 [a]"He will also go before Him in the
spirit and power of Elijah, *'to turn the
hearts of the fathers to the children,'*
and the disobedient to the wisdom of
the just, to make ready a people prepared for the Lord."
18 And Zacharias said to the angel,
[a]"How shall I know this? For I am an
old man, and my wife is well advanced
in years."
19 And the angel answered and said
to him, "I am [a]Gabriel, who stands in
the presence of God, and was sent to
speak to you and bring you [1]these glad
[b]tidings.

Herod's Kingdom at Jesus' Birth

chronological arrangement, but rather to a logical arrangement of the material that will best carry out his theme. The identity of **Theophilus** ("Friend of God") is unknown, although the address indicates that he was a person of rank.
1:4 Luke wants to establish the authenticity and trustworthiness of the Christian message.
1:5 **Herod** reigned during 37–4 B.C. John the Baptist and Jesus were therefore born a few years before A.D. 1. The discrepancy happened through an erroneous calculation in devising the Christian calendar in the sixth century. Priests were divided into 24 sections, of which **Abijah** was one (see 1 Chr. 24:6–19).
1:7 The Jews considered children to be a sign of God's favor, and childlessness was considered a sign of His displeasure. This was not the case with Zacharias and Elizabeth, since they were righteous in God's sight (v. 6).
1:8 Each section of priests served at the temple for one week twice a year.
1:9 Priestly duties were assigned by **lot**. A priest could have the privilege of burning incense in the Holy Place only once during his lifetime, and sometimes never.
1:13 **John** means "The Lord (Yahweh) Has Shown Favor (Grace)." It signifies the purpose of John's birth, for he was to herald the arrival of the Messiah, the gift of God's grace.
1:15 The boy will be dedicated as a Nazirite (see Num. 6; Judg. 13:5; 1 Sam. 1:11). The source of his prophetic inspiration is not physical but **the Holy Spirit**.
1:17 John will fulfill the prophecy of Mal. 4:5, 6.
1:19 **Gabriel** ("Mighty Man of God") foretold the Messiah's coming (Dan. 9:25), and according to the traditional interpretation of 1 Thess. 4:16, will sound the trumpet for His Return.

20 "But behold, [a]you will be mute and
not able to speak until the day these
things take place, because you did not
believe my words which will be fulfilled in their own time."
21 And the people waited for Zacharias, and marveled that he lingered so
long in the temple.
22 But when he came out, he could not
speak to them; and they perceived that
he had seen a vision in the temple, for
he beckoned to them and remained
speechless.
23 So it was, as soon as [a]the days of
his **service** were completed, that he departed to his own house.

WORD WEALTH

1:23 service, *leitourgia* (lie-toorg-*ee*-ah); Strong's *#3009:* Compare "liturgy," "liturgical." From *laos,* "people," and *ergon,* "work." The word was used originally of citizens serving in public office at their own expense. Later it included military service or community participation. In the NT *leitourgia* is used both for priestly service and unselfish giving. Here it refers to priestly service in the temple. In 2 Cor. 9:12, it denotes charitable gifts as a service to the needy. Paul names his service to the Christian church *leitourgia* in Phil. 2:17.

24 Now after those days his wife Elizabeth conceived; and she hid herself five
months, saying,
25 "Thus the Lord has dealt with me,
in the days when He looked on *me,* to
[a]take away my reproach among people."

Christ's Birth Announced to Mary

26 Now in the sixth month the angel
Gabriel was sent by God to a city of
Galilee named Nazareth,

KINGDOM DYNAMICS

1:26–56 Faithful Mother: Obedient Disciple (Mary), WOMEN. There is a wonder surrounding Mary, the mother of Jesus, that transcends traditional religious thought. That she was a privileged vessel, chosen to bear God's Son, is wonder enough, for she is a participant in the miracle of the Incarnation at a level no other human being can comprehend. It is clear that she did not claim to understand it herself, but simply worshiped God in humble acknowledgment of the phenomenon engulfing her existence: "My soul magnifies the Lord," she exclaims (v. 46). We can hardly fathom the bewildering moments she experienced 1) when Simeon prophesied future mental/emotional suffering (2:35); 2) when she and Joseph spoke with Jesus after they thought He was lost in Jerusalem (2:49, 50); 3) when Jesus gently rebuffed her at the wedding in Cana (John 2:4); 4) when Jesus seemed to reject her and His brothers' efforts at helping Him, though they clearly misunderstood Him at that time (Matt. 12:46–50). These instances prompt our learning the wisdom of persistence and obedience in following God's basic directive on our lives, even when the details of the outworking of His will are unclear or mystifying.

Mary is also a study in the pathway forward in God's will. She might have sought elevation in position among those who saw Jesus for who He was—Messiah—but instead 1) she remained steadfast with Him all the way to the Cross, rather than protect herself (John 19:25); and 2) she obediently joined other of Jesus' disciples in the Upper Room, waiting as He commanded for the coming of the Holy Spirit (Acts 1:14).

Mary is a model of responsive obedience, one who lived out her own directive to the servants at Cana—timeless advice for all ages: "Whatever He [Jesus] says to you, do it" (John 2:5).

(Esth. 4:1/Luke 2:36–38) F.L.

27 to a virgin [a]betrothed to a man
whose name was Joseph, of the house
of David. The virgin's name *was* Mary.
28 And having come in, the angel said
to her, [a]"Rejoice, highly favored *one,*
[b]the Lord *is* with you; [1]blessed* *are*
you among women!"
29 But [1]when she saw *him,* [a]she was
troubled at his saying, and considered
what manner of greeting this was.
30 Then the angel said to her, "Do not
be afraid, Mary, for you have found
[a]favor with God.
31 [a]"And behold, you will conceive in
your womb and bring forth a Son, and
[b]shall call His name *JESUS.
32 "He will be great, [a]and will be
called the Son of the Highest; and
[b]the Lord God will give Him the
[c]throne of His [d]father David.
33 [a]"And He will reign over the house
of Jacob forever, and of His kingdom
there will be no end."

20 [a]Ezek. 3:26; 24:27
23 [a]2 Kin. 11:5; 1 Chr. 9:25
25 [a]Gen. 30:23; Is. 4:1; 54:1, 4
27 [a]Matt. 1:18; Luke 2:4, 5
28 [a]Dan. 9:23 [b]Judg. 6:12 [1]NU omits *blessed are you among women* *See WW at Luke 6:28.
29 [a]Luke 1:12 [1]NU omits *when she saw him*
30 [a]Luke 2:52
31 [a]Is. 7:14; Matt. 1:21, 25; Gal. 4:4 [b]Luke 2:21; [Phil. 2:9–11] *See WW at Phil. 4:23.
32 [a]Matt. 3:17; 17:5; Mark 5:7; Luke 1:35, 76; 6:35; Acts 7:48 [b]2 Sam. 7:12, 13, 16; Ps. 132:11; [Is. 9:6, 7; 16:5; Jer. 23:5] [c]2 Sam. 7:14–17; Acts 2:33; 7:55 [d]Matt. 1:1
33 [a][Dan. 2:44; Obad. 21; Mic. 4:7]; John 12:34; [Heb. 1:8]; 2 Pet. 1:11

1:20 Mute: From v. 62 we can infer that Zacharias is also deaf.
1:31 Jesus is the Greek equivalent of the Hebrew Joshua, "The Lord Is Salvation."
1:32, 33 The position of Jesus as heir of **the throne of His father David** and the eternity of His reign identify Him as the Messiah (see 2 Sam. 7:12–16; Is. 9:6, 7; Ps. 132:11, 12; Dan.7:14; Hos. 3:5).

34 Then Mary said to the angel, "How
can this be, since I [1]do not know a
man?"
35 And the angel answered and said
to her, [a]"*The* Holy Spirit will come
upon you, and the power of the Highest
will overshadow you; therefore, also,
that Holy One who is to be born will
be called [b]the Son of God.
36 "Now indeed, Elizabeth your relative has also conceived a son in her
old age; and this is now the sixth
month for her who was called barren.
37 "For [a]with God nothing will be impossible."
4 38 Then Mary said, "Behold the maidservant of the Lord! Let it be to me according to your *word." And the angel
departed from her.

Mary Visits Elizabeth

39 Now Mary arose in those days and
went into the hill country with haste,
[a]to a city of Judah,
40 and entered the house of Zacharias
and greeted Elizabeth.
41 And it happened, when Elizabeth
heard the greeting of Mary, that the
babe leaped in her womb; and Elizabeth was [a]filled with the Holy Spirit.
42 Then she spoke out with a loud
voice and said, [a]"Blessed *are* you
among women, and blessed *is* the fruit
of your womb!
43 "But why *is* this *granted* to me, that
the mother of my Lord should come
to me?
44 "For indeed, as soon as the voice
of your greeting sounded in my ears,
the babe leaped in my womb for joy.
45 [a]"Blessed *is* she who [1]believed, for
there will be a fulfillment of those
things which were told her from the
Lord."

The Song of Mary

46 And Mary said:

[a]"My soul [1]magnifies* the Lord,

34 [1]Am a virgin
35 [a]Matt. 1:20 [b][Heb. 1:2, 8]
37 [a]Jer. 32:17
38 *See WW at Matt. 4:4.
39 [a]Josh. 21:9
41 [a]Acts 6:3
42 [a]Judg. 5:24
45 [a]John 20:29 [1]Or *believed that there*
46 [a]1 Sam. 2:1–10 [1]Declares the greatness of *See WW at Acts 5:13.
47 [a]Hab. 3:18 [b]1 Tim. 1:1; 2:3
48 [a]Ps. 138:6 [b]Luke 11:27
49 [a]Ps. 71:19; 126:2, 3 [b]Ps. 111:9 *See WW at Matt. 19:26. • See WW at Acts 2:11.
50 [a]Ps. 103:17
51 [a]Ps. 98:1; 118:15 [b][1 Pet. 5:5] *See WW at 1 Tim. 6:16. • See WW at Mark 12:30.
52 [a]1 Sam. 2:7, 8 *See WW at Acts 8:27. • See WW at James 4:10. • See WW at 2 Cor. 7:6.
53 [a][Matt. 5:6]
54 [a]Is. 41:8 [b][Jer. 31:3]
55 [a]Gen. 17:19 [b][Rom. 11:28] [c]Gen. 17:7
58 [a][Rom. 12:15] *See WW at Acts 5:13.
59 [a]Gen. 17:12

47 And my spirit has [a]rejoiced in
[b]God my Savior.
48 For [a]He has regarded the lowly
state of His maidservant;
For behold, henceforth [b]all
generations will call me
blessed.
49 For He who is *mighty [a]has done
*great things for me,
And [b]holy *is* His name.
50 And [a]His mercy *is* on those who
fear Him
From generation to generation.
51 [a]He has shown *strength with His
arm;
[b]He has scattered *the* proud in the
*imagination of their hearts.
52 [a]He has put down the *mighty
from *their* thrones,
And *exalted *the* *lowly.
53 He has [a]filled *the* hungry with
good things,
And *the* rich He has sent away
empty.
54 He has helped His [a]servant Israel,
[b]In remembrance of *His* mercy,
55 [a]As He spoke to our [b]fathers,
To Abraham and to his [c]seed
forever."

56 And Mary remained with her about
three months, and returned to her
house.

Birth of John the Baptist

57 Now Elizabeth's full time came for
her to be delivered, and she brought
forth a son.
58 When her neighbors and relatives
heard how the Lord had *shown great
mercy to her, they [a]rejoiced with her.

Circumcision of John the Baptist

59 So it was, [a]on the eighth day, that
they came to circumcise the child; and
they would have called him by the
name of his father, Zacharias.

1:35 The conception of Jesus took place through the direct action of ***the Holy Spirit.* Overshadowed** is the same word used for the cloud from which the voice spoke at the Transfiguration. Both uses refer to the cloud that manifested the glory of God (Ex. 40:34–38).

1:36, 37 The angel encourages Mary's faith.

1:38 See section 4 of Truth-In-Action through the Synoptics at the end of Luke.

1:38 Mary's acquiescence would risk the loss of her reputation.

1:45 Note the clear contrast between Mary's faith response and Zacharias's unbelief (v. 20). We should also note in chs. 1 and 2 how the new era is signaled by the renewal of the gift of prophecy, which has been dormant. The various prophecies and songs of these two chapters reflect the best of OT piety and prophecy. The songs and prophecies of Mary (the Magnificat, vv. 46–55), Zacharias (Benedictus, vv. 68–79), Simeon (Nunc Dimittis, 2:29–32), and Anna (2:36–38) reflect a naturalness with and sensitivity to God's former revelation in the OT (see, for example, the song of Hannah, 1 Sam. 2:1–10).

1:46–55 Mary's song (the Magnificat) is taken from the song of Hannah (1 Sam. 2:1–10) in a similar condition of miraculous birth. In Jewish prophecy, new messages are often elaborations of former revelations, with new meaning and application.

1:59 Male babies were named **on the eighth day,** at which

60 His mother answered and said,
[a]"No; he shall be called John."
61 But they said to her, "There is no
one among your relatives who is called
by this name."
62 So they made signs to his father—
what he would have him called.
63 And he asked for a writing tablet,
and wrote, saying, "His *name is
John." So they all marveled.
64 Immediately his mouth was opened
and his tongue *loosed,* and he spoke,
praising God.
65 Then fear came on all who dwelt
around them; and all these sayings
were discussed throughout all the hill
country of Judea.
66 And all those who heard *them*
[a]kept *them* in their hearts, saying,
"What kind of child will this be?" And
[b]the hand of the Lord was with him.

Zacharias' Prophecy

67 Now his father Zacharias [a]was
filled with the Holy Spirit, and prophesied, saying:

68 "Blessed[a] *is* the Lord God of Israel,
For [b]He has visited and redeemed
His people,
69 [a]And has raised up a horn of
*salvation for us
In the house of His servant David,
70 [a]As He spoke by the mouth of His
holy prophets,
Who *have been* [b]since the world
began,
71 That we should be saved from our
enemies
And from the hand of all who hate
us,
72 [a]To perform the mercy *promised*
to our fathers
And to remember His holy
*covenant,
73 [a]The oath which He swore to our
father Abraham:
74 To grant us that we,
Being delivered from the hand of
our enemies,
Might [a]serve Him without fear,
75 [a]In holiness and righteousness
before Him all the days of our
life.

76 "And you, child, will be called the
[a]prophet of the Highest;
For [b]you will go before the face
of the Lord to prepare His
ways,
77 To give [a]knowledge of salvation
to His people
By the *remission of their sins,
78 Through the tender mercy of our
God,
With which the [1]Dayspring from
on high [2]has visited us;
79 [a]To give light to those who sit in
*darkness and the shadow of
death,
To [b]guide our feet into the way
of **peace.**"

WORD WEALTH

1:79 peace, *eirene* (eye-*ray*-nay); Strong's *#1515:* Compare "irenic" and "Irene." A state of rest, quietness, and calmness; an absence of strife; tranquility. It generally denotes a perfect well-being. *Eirene* includes harmonious relationships between God and men, men and men, nations, and families. Jesus as Prince of Peace gives peace to those who call upon Him for personal salvation.

80 So [a]the child grew and became
strong in spirit, and [b]was in the deserts
till the day of his manifestation to Israel.

Christ Born of Mary

2 And it came to pass in those days
that a decree went out from Caesar
Augustus that all the world should be
registered.
2 [a]This census first took place while
Quirinius was governing Syria.
3 So all went to be registered, everyone to his own city.
4 Joseph also went up from Galilee,
out of the city of Nazareth, into Judea,

60 [a]Luke 1:13, 63
63 *See WW at John 12:13.
66 [a]Luke 2:19 [b]Gen. 39:2; Acts 11:21
67 [a]Joel 2:28
68 [a]1 Kin. 1:48; Ps. 106:48 [b]Ex. 3:16
69 [a]2 Sam. 22:3; Ps. 132:17; Ezek. 29:21 *See WW at Luke 19:9.
70 [a]Jer. 23:5; Rom. 1:2 [b]Acts 3:21
72 [a]Lev. 26:42 *See WW at Mark 14:24.
73 [a]Gen. 12:3; 22:16–18; [Heb. 6:13]
74 [a][Rom. 6:18; Heb. 9:14]
75 [a]Jer. 32:39; [Eph. 4:24; 2 Thess. 2:13]
76 [a]Matt. 3:3; 11:9; Mark 3:2, 3; Luke 3:4; John 1:23 [b]Is. 40:3; Mal. 3:1; Matt. 11:10
77 [a][Jer. 31:34; Mark 1:4]; Luke 3:3 *See WW at Heb. 9:22.
78 [1]Lit. *Dawn;* the Messiah [2]NU *shall visit*
79 [a]Is. 9:2; Matt. 4:16; [Acts 26:18; 2 Cor. 4:6; Eph. 5:14] [b][John 10:4; 14:27; 16:33] *See WW at Luke 11:35.
80 [a]Luke 2:40 [b]Matt. 3:1

CHAPTER 2

2 [a]Dan. 9:25; Acts 5:37

time they were circumcised. Ordinarily the child would have been named after his father.
1:62 Apparently Zacharias has been temporarily deaf as well as mute (v. 20).
1:68–79 This song is commonly known as the Benedictus, from the first word in the Latin text. The first part (vv. 68–75) deals with the salvation which is about to appear in the Person of the Messiah, Mary's child. The redemption He accomplishes is a visit of God, a direct intervention. It is also the raising up of **a horn of salvation,** symbolic of strength (see Ezek. 29:21). The second part of the song (vv. 76–79) relates to the prophetic ministry of John as the forerunner of the Messiah.
2:1, 2 Luke meticulously establishes the historical circumstances surrounding the birth of Jesus, relating it to events in the Roman Empire. **Caesar Augustus** was emperor from 30 B.C. until A.D. 14. **Quirinius** was governor of Syria during 10–7 B.C. and later served a second term during A.D. 6–9. The **census** was for the purpose of taxation.
2:3, 4 The head of each family journeyed to the town where the ancestral records were kept.

to [a]the city of David, which is called Bethlehem, [b]because he was of the house and lineage of David,

5 to be registered with Mary, [a]his betrothed [1]wife, who was with child.

6 So it was, that while they were there, the days were completed for her to be delivered.

7 And [a]she brought forth her firstborn Son, and wrapped Him in swaddling cloths, and laid Him in a [1]manger, because there was no room for them in the inn.

Glory in the Highest

8 Now there were in the same country shepherds living out in the fields, keeping watch over their flock by night.

9 And [1]behold, an angel of the Lord stood before them, and the *glory of the Lord shone around them, [a]and they were greatly afraid.

10 Then the angel said to them, [a]"Do not be afraid, for behold, I bring you good tidings of great joy [b]which will be to all people.

11 [a]"For there is born to you this day in the city of David [b]a *Savior, [c]who is Christ the Lord.

12 "And this *will be* the sign to you: You will find a Babe wrapped in swaddling cloths, lying in a [1]manger."

13 [a]And suddenly there was with the angel a multitude of the heavenly host praising God and saying:

14 "Glory[a] to God in the highest,
And on earth [b]peace, [c]goodwill[1] toward men!"

15 So it was, when the *angels had gone away from them into heaven, that the *shepherds said to one another, "Let us now go to Bethlehem and see this thing that has come to pass, which the Lord has made known to us."

16 And they came with haste and found Mary and Joseph, and the Babe lying in a manger.

17 Now when they had seen *Him*, they made [1]widely known the saying which was told them concerning this Child.

4 [a]1 Sam. 16:1 [b]Matt. 1:16
5 [a][Matt. 1:18] [1]NU omits *wife*
7 [a]Matt. 1:25 [1]*feed trough*
9 [a]Luke 1:12 [1]NU omits *behold* *See WW at John 2:11.
10 [a]Luke 1:13, 30 [b]Gen. 12:3
11 [a]Is. 9:6 [b]Matt. 1:21 [c]Acts 2:36 *See WW at John 4:42.
12 [1]*feed trough*
13 [a]Dan. 7:10
14 [a]Luke 19:38 [b]Is. 57:19 [c][Eph. 2:4, 7] [1]NU *toward men of goodwill*
15 *See WW at Matt. 4:11. • See WW at John 10:2.
17 [1]NU omits *widely*
19 [a]Gen. 37:11 *See WW at Rev. 2:23.
20 [a]Luke 19:37 *See WW at John 10:2.
21 [a]Lev. 12:3 [b][Matt. 1:21] [c]Luke 1:31 [1]NU *for His circumcision*
22 [a]Lev. 12:2–8
23 [a]Deut. 18:4 [b]Ex. 13:2, 12, 15
24 [a]Lev. 12:2, 8
25 [a]Mark 15:43
26 [a][Heb. 11:5]
27 [a]Matt. 4:1
29 [a]Gen. 46:30 *See WW at Jude 4. • See WW at Rev. 19:5.

18 And all those who heard *it* marveled at those things which were told them by the shepherds.

19 [a]But Mary kept all these things and pondered *them* in her *heart.

20 Then the *shepherds returned, glorifying and [a]praising God for all the things that they had heard and seen, as it was told them.

Circumcision of Jesus

21 [a]And when eight days were completed [1]for the circumcision of the Child, His name was called [b]JESUS, the name given by the angel [c]before He was conceived in the womb.

Jesus Presented in the Temple

22 Now when [a]the days of her purification according to the law of Moses were completed, they brought Him to Jerusalem to present *Him* to the Lord

23 [a](as it is written in the law of the Lord, [b]*"Every male who opens the womb shall be called holy to the LORD"*),

24 and to offer a sacrifice according to what is said in the law of the Lord, [a]*"A pair of turtledoves or two young pigeons."*

Simeon Sees God's Salvation

25 And behold, there was a man in Jerusalem whose name was Simeon, and this man was just and devout, [a]waiting for the Consolation of Israel, and the Holy Spirit was upon him.

26 And it had been revealed to him by the Holy Spirit that he would not [a]see death before he had seen the Lord's Christ.

27 So he came [a]by the Spirit into the temple. And when the parents brought in the Child Jesus, to do for Him according to the custom of the law,

28 he took Him up in his arms and blessed God and said:

29 *"Lord, [a]now You are letting Your
*servant depart in peace,

2:7 The term **firstborn** suggests other sons born at a later time (contrast "only son" in 7:12). **Swaddling cloths** were long strips of cloth used to wrap infants.
2:8 Sheep were kept out in the open between March and December. No certain date can be established for the birth of Jesus. We do not know exactly when or why the church chose December 25. The first recorded celebration of Christmas was in Rome in A.D. 354.
2:14 In the highest refers not to the highest degree, but to the highest realm, heaven. **Goodwill:** See marginal note. People cannot be at peace with each other until they are at peace with God.
2:22 The ceremony of purification, described in Lev. 12:2–8, took place 40 days after the birth of a male child.
2:24 The sacrifice is of the kind prescribed for the poor (Lev. 12:8).
2:25–27 Luke emphasizes the activity of **the Holy Spirit. The Consolation of Israel** refers to the comfort the Messiah would bring to His people (see Is. 40:1, 2).
2:29–32 Simeon's prophetic utterance is known as the Nunc

According to Your word;
30 For my eyes [a]have seen Your
*salvation
31 Which You have prepared before
the face of all peoples,
32 [a]A light to *bring* revelation to the
Gentiles,
And the glory of Your people
Israel."

33 [1]And Joseph and His mother marveled at those things which were spoken of Him.
34 Then Simeon blessed them, and
said to Mary His mother, "Behold, this
Child is destined for the [a]fall and rising
of many in Israel, and for [b]a sign which
will be spoken against
35 "(yes, [a]a sword will pierce through
your own soul also), that the **thoughts**
of many hearts may be revealed."

WORD WEALTH

2:35 thoughts, *dialogismos* (dee-al-og-is-*moss*); Strong's *#1261:* Compare "dialogue." Inward reasoning, questioning, consideration, and deliberation; turning thoughts over in the mind; reckoning by mental questions, opinions, designs, and disputes. *Dialogismos* is the thinking of a man who is 1) deliberating with himself, 2) settling accounts, and 3) suspicious because of his state of indecision. Through one's acceptance or rejection of Christ, the real thoughts of one's heart toward himself and toward God become clear.

Anna Bears Witness to the Redeemer

36 Now there was one, Anna, a prophetess, the daughter of Phanuel, of the
tribe of [a]Asher. She was of a great age,
and had lived with a husband seven
years from her virginity;
37 and this woman *was* a widow
[1]of about eighty-four years, who did
not depart from the temple, but served
God with fastings and prayers [a]night
and day.
38 And coming in that instant she gave
thanks to [1]the Lord, and spoke of Him
to all those who [a]looked for redemption in Jerusalem.

30 [a]Ps. 119:166, 174; [Is. 52:10; Luke 3:6] *See WW at Acts 28:28.
32 [a]Is. 9:2; 42:6; 49:6; 60:1–3; Matt. 4:16; Acts 10:45; 13:47; 28:28; [Rom. 9:24; Gal. 3:14]
33 [1]NU *And His father and mother*
34 [a]Is. 8:14; Hos. 14:9; Matt. 21:44; [Rom. 9:32]; 1 Cor. 1:23; [2 Cor. 2:16; 1 Pet. 2:7, 8] [b]Matt.28:12–15; Acts 4:2; 17:32; 28:22; [1 Pet. 2:12; 4:14]
35 [a]Ps. 42:10; John 19:25
36 [a]Josh. 19:24
37 [a]Acts 26:7; 1 Tim. 5:5 [1]NU *until she was eighty-four*
38 [a]Lam. 3:25, 26; Mark 15:43; Luke 24:21 [1]NU *God*
40 [a]Luke 1:80; 2:52; [1 Cor. 1:24, 30] [1]NU omits *in spirit*
41 [a]John 4:20 [b]Ex. 23:15, 17; 34:23; Deut. 16:1, 16; Luke 22:15
42 [a]Ex. 23:14, 15
43 *See WW at 1 John 2:5.

KINGDOM DYNAMICS

2:36–38 An Effective Older Woman and Widow (Anna), WOMEN. Anna the prophetess came from Asher, the tribe that was to be blessed and that was to "dip his foot in oil" (Deut. 33:24)—a sign of joy and happiness. But also, Asher's descendants were to have shoes of "iron and bronze," denoting strength (Deut. 33:25). Anna exemplified these qualities of anointing and steadfastness. After being married only seven years, her husband died, and this widow chose a life of fasting and prayer in the temple. She "did not depart from the temple, but served God" (Luke 2:36, 37), clearly walking in moral purity and dedicated service.

Her prophetic anointing was untainted by the spirit of the age. Her historic prophecy regarding Jesus called the attention of all present to the uniqueness of the Child just then being brought into the temple for dedication (v. 22)..

The name "Anna" means "Favor" or "Grace," and originates from the Hebrew *chanan,* meaning "to bend or stoop in kindness" and "to find favor and show favor." She did find favor in God's eyes, for He revealed the Messiah, the Hope of Israel, to her aged eyes. Her anointed ministry during later years of life holds forth a promise for older women. There is always ministry awaiting the sensitive, obedient, and pure—ministry that can influence and shape the rising generation (Titus 2:2–5).

(Luke 1:26–56/Luke 8:2) F.L.

The Family Returns to Nazareth

39 So when they had performed all
things according to the law of the Lord,
they returned to Galilee, to their *own*
city, Nazareth.
40 [a]And the Child grew and became
strong [1]in spirit, filled with wisdom;
and the grace of God was upon Him.

The Boy Jesus Amazes the Scholars

41 His parents went to [a]Jerusalem
[b]every year at the Feast of the Passover.
42 And when He was twelve years old,
they went up to Jerusalem according
to the [a]custom of the feast.
43 When they had *finished the

Dimittis, from the first words of the Latin text. The song stresses that Jesus is the universal Savior.

2:34 Not everyone will accept the salvation that Jesus offers; some will stumble over Him.

2:35 The opposition to Jesus will reach its climax at the Cross, where Mary will experience piercing anguish.

2:40 Luke emphasizes the complete humanity of Jesus.

2:41 Jewish law required that males attend the feasts of Passover, Pentecost, and Tabernacles (Ex. 23:14–17; Deut. 16:16).

2:42 At the age of 12 a Jewish boy became "a son of the Law" and began to observe the requirements of the Law.

[a]days, as they returned, the Boy Jesus
*lingered behind in Jerusalem. And
[1]Joseph and His mother did not know
it;
44 but supposing Him to have been in
the company, they went a day's journey, and sought Him among *their* relatives and acquaintances.
45 So when they did not find Him, they
returned to Jerusalem, seeking Him.
46 Now so it was *that* after three days
they found Him in the temple, sitting
in the midst of the teachers, both listening to them and asking them questions.
47 And [a]all who heard Him were astonished at His **understanding** and
answers.

WORD WEALTH

2:47 understanding, *sunesis* (*soon*-es-is); Strong's *#4907:* Literally, "a putting together," hence, quickness of apprehension, the critical faculty for clear apprehension, intelligently assessing a situation. Comparable to the modern idiom, "putting two and two together." The NT uses two words for understanding, *phronesis* and *sunesis. Phronesis* acts while *sunesis* judges. *Phronesis* is the practical side of the mind while *sunesis* is the analyzing and discerning side.

48 So when they saw Him, they were
amazed; and His mother said to Him,
"Son, why have You done this to us?
Look, Your father and I have sought
You anxiously."
49 And He said to them, "Why did you
seek Me? Did you not know that I must
be [a]about [b]My Father's business?"
50 But [a]they did not understand the
statement which He spoke to them.

Jesus Advances in Wisdom and Favor

51 Then He went down with them and
came to Nazareth, and was [1]subject*
to them, but His mother [a]kept all these
things in her heart.
52 And Jesus [a]increased in *wisdom
and stature, [b]and in favor with God
and men.

43 [a]Ex. 12:15 [1]NU *His parents* *See WW at Matt. 24:13.
47 [a]Matt. 7:28; 13:54; 22:33; Mark 1:22; 6:2; 11:18; Luke 4:32; John 7:15
49 [a]John 9:4 [b][Mark 1:22; Luke 4:22, 32; John 4:34; 5:17, 36]
50 [a]Mark 9:32; Luke 9:45; 18:34; John 7:15, 46
51 [a]Dan. 7:28 [1]*obedient* *See WW at 1 Cor. 14:32.
52 [a][Is. 11:2, 3; Col. 2:2, 3] [b]1 Sam. 2:26; [Prov. 3:1–4] *See WW at Acts 6:10.

CHAPTER 3

1 [a]Matt. 27:2
2 [a]John 11:49; 18:13; Acts 4:6 [b]Luke 1:13 [1]NU, M *in the high priesthood of Annas and Caiaphas* *See WW at Matt. 4:4.
3 [a]Matt. 3:1; Mark 1:4 [b]Luke 1:77 *See WW at Acts 9:20. • See WW at Matt. 21:25.
4 [a]Is. 40:3–5; Matt. 3:3; Mark 1:3
5 *See WW at Matt. 18:4.

John the Baptist Prepares the Way

3 Now in the fifteenth year of the
reign of Tiberius Caesar, [a]Pontius
Pilate being governor of Judea, Herod
being tetrarch of Galilee, his brother
Philip tetrarch of Iturea and the region
of Trachonitis, and Lysanias tetrarch
of Abilene,

KINGDOM DYNAMICS

3:1–20 Boldness, LEADER TRAITS. John the Baptist began his prophetic ministry not only with the positive message announcing the coming Messiah, but in confrontively calling the people to repentance. It would have been much safer to simply proclaim good news, but John was obedient to the prophetic ministry that challenged human carelessness and sinning. His ministry was marked by boldness, daring to preach what was unpopular. He rebuked the religious (v. 8), called to unselfishness (vv. 10, 11), denounced dishonesty (vv. 12, 13) and required equitable administration of authority (v. 14). Later, he confronted immorality tolerated in leadership (Mark 6:18), and for this he eventually was arrested and beheaded. Jesus' tribute to John's ministry (Matt. 11:11) abides as a testimony to faithfulness and boldness as worthy traits for leaders.

(Judg. 4; 5/1 Cor. 12:28) J.B.

2 [1]while [a]Annas and Caiaphas were
high priests, the *word of God came
to [b]John the son of Zacharias in the
wilderness.
3 [a]And he went into all the region
around the Jordan, *preaching a *baptism of repentance [b]for the remission
of sins,
4 as it is written in the book of the
words of Isaiah the prophet, saying:

[a]*"The voice of one crying in the*
wilderness:
'Prepare the way of the LORD;
Make His paths straight.
5 *Every valley shall be filled*
And every mountain and hill
**brought low;*
The crooked places shall be made
straight
And the rough ways smooth;

2:44 Company: Villagers who made pilgrimages to Jerusalem usually traveled in caravans, with women and children in the front. Each parent thought that Jesus was with the other.
2:49 Jesus shows an awareness of His unique relationship to the Father, as well as a consciousness of His mission.
2:51 Even as the Son of God, Jesus remained under the care and guidance of His earthly parents.

3:1 Tiberius Caesar began ruling the provinces of Rome as coemperor with Augustus in A.D. 12, and ruled alone as emperor during A.D. 14–37. **The fifteenth year** was about A.D. 26. **Pontius Pilate** was **governor** during A.D. 26–36.
3:2 Although **Caiaphas** was the high priest, his father-in-law **Annas,** who was the ex–high priest, was the real power behind the office.
3:3–9 See notes on Matt. 3:1–10.

6 *And [a]all *flesh shall see the*
**salvation of God.' "*

John Preaches to the People

7 Then he said to the multitudes that
came out to be baptized by him,
[a]"Brood[1] of vipers! Who warned you
to flee from the wrath to come?
8 "Therefore bear fruits [a]worthy of
repentance, and do not begin to say to
yourselves, 'We have Abraham as *our*
father.' For I say to you that God is
able to raise up children to Abraham
from these stones.
9 "And even now the ax is laid to the
root of the trees. Therefore [a]every tree
which does not bear good fruit is cut
down and thrown into the fire."
10 So the people asked him, saying,
[a]"What shall we do then?"
11 He answered and said to them,
[a]"He who has two tunics, let him *give
to him who has none; and he who has
food, [b]let him do likewise."
12 Then [a]tax collectors also came to
be baptized, and said to him, "Teacher,
what shall we do?"
13 And he said to them, [a]"Collect no
more than what is appointed for you."
14 Likewise the soldiers asked him,
saying, "And what shall we do?" So
he said to them, "Do not [1]intimidate
anyone [a]or accuse falsely, and be content with your wages."
15 Now as the people were in expectation, and all reasoned in their hearts
about John, whether he was the Christ
or not,
11 16 John answered, saying to all,
[a]"I indeed baptize you with water; but
One mightier than I is coming, whose
sandal strap I am not worthy to loose.
He will [b]baptize you with the Holy
Spirit and fire.
17 "His winnowing fan *is* in His hand,
and He will thoroughly clean out His
threshing floor, and [a]gather the wheat
into His barn; but the chaff He will
burn with unquenchable fire."
18 And with many other exhortations
he preached to the people.
19 [a]But Herod the tetrarch, being rebuked by him concerning Herodias, his
[1]brother Philip's wife, and for all the
evils which Herod had done,
20 also added this, above all, that he
shut John up in prison.

John Baptizes Jesus

21 When all the people were baptized,
[a]it came to pass that Jesus also was
baptized; and while He prayed, the
heaven was opened.
22 And the Holy Spirit descended in
bodily form like a dove upon Him, and
a voice came from heaven which said,
"You are My beloved Son; in You I am
[a]well pleased."

The Genealogy of Jesus Christ

23 Now Jesus Himself began *His ministry at* [a]about thirty years of age, being (as was supposed) [b]*the* son of Joseph, *the son* of Heli,
24 *the son* of Matthat, *the son* of Levi,
the son of Melchi, *the son* of Janna,
the son of Joseph,
25 *the son* of Mattathiah, *the son* of
Amos, *the son* of Nahum, *the son* of
Esli, *the son* of Naggai,
26 *the son* of Maath, *the son* of Mattathiah, *the son* of Semei, *the son* of Joseph, *the son* of Judah,

6 [a]Ps. 98:2; Is. 52:10; Luke 2:10; [Rom. 10:8–18] *See WW at Matt. 26:41. • See WW at Acts 28:28.
7 [a]Matt. 3:7; 12:34; 23:33 [1]*Offspring*
8 [a][2 Cor.7:9–11]
9 [a]Matt. 7:19; Luke 13:6–9
10 [a]Luke 3:12, 14; [Acts 2:37, 38; 16:30, 31]
11 [a]Luke 11:41; 2 Cor. 8:14; James 2:15, 16; [1 John 3:17; 4:20] [b]Is. 58:7; [1 Tim. 6:17, 18] *See WW at Rom. 1:11.
12 [a]Matt. 21:32; Luke 7:29
13 [a]Luke 19:8
14 [a]Ex. 20:16; 23:1; Lev. 19:11 [1]Lit. *shake down* for money
16 [a]Matt. 3:11, 12; Mark 1:7, 8 [b]John 7:39; 20:22; Acts 2:1–4
17 [a]Mic. 4:12; Matt.13:24–30
19 [a]Matt. 14:3; Mark 6:17 [1]NU *brother's wife*
21 [a]Matt. 3:13–17; John 1:32
22 [a]Ps. 2:7; [Is. 42:1]; Matt. 3:17; 17:5; Mark 1:11; Luke 1:35; 9:35; 2 Pet. 1:17
23 [a][Num. 4:3, 35, 39, 43, 47] [b]Matt. 13:55; John 6:42

3:7 To be baptized: Jews baptized Gentiles who wished to become Jews (proselytes). Gentile candidates not only were baptized, but their males were circumcised, and they offered sacrifice. The fact that John baptizes Jews is radical; that is, they are viewed as no less needy than Gentiles. Physical descent from Abraham is not sufficient (v. 8).
3:8 Repentance: The term here means an internal sorrow that results in "turning." The expression of such "turning" from the people (v. 11), the tax collectors (v. 13), and the soldiers (v. 14) is concrete and practical. Each of the three groups is commanded to change a type of behavior, within their given sphere of life. **Children:** There is a conscious wordplay between "children" and "stones," which in Aramaic (and Hebrew) sound almost identical.
3:10–14 In response to the people's questions, John insisted that repentance was not an abstract theological term or a matter of form and ceremony. Rather, it was a radical change from a self-centered existence of greed, dishonesty, and discontent to a practical expression of moral and ethical relationships with others.
3:15 John's prophetic ministry stirred the messianic hopes of the people.
3:16–18 See note on Matt. 3:11.
3:16, 17 See section 11 of Truth-In-Action through the Synoptics at the end of Luke.
3:19, 20 See note on Matt. 14:3.
3:21, 22 See notes on Matt. 3:14–17.
3:23–38 Concerning the two Gospel genealogies of Jesus, Matthew traces the lineage of Jesus from Abraham through Joseph (Matt. 1:1–16), although he is careful to point out that Joseph was not Jesus' actual father (Matt. 1:18). His purpose, since he was writing for a Jewish audience, was to prove that Jesus was the promised Messiah. Specifically stating that Jesus was the **supposed** son of Joseph, Luke ascends the family line all the way to Adam, thus identifying Jesus universally with the human race. Some commentators account for the differences in the two genealogies by assuming that Matthew gives the legal line of royal descent, while Luke gives the lineage of Mary, the only human parent of Jesus. If this is the case, Joseph may be reckoned as the son of her father **Heli** through marriage (v. 23).

27 *the son* of Joannas, *the son* of
Rhesa, *the son* of [a]Zerubbabel, *the son*
of Shealtiel, *the son* of Neri,
28 *the son* of Melchi, *the son* of Addi,
the son of Cosam, *the son* of Elmodam,
the son of Er,
29 *the son* of Jose, *the son* of Eliezer,
the son of Jorim, *the son* of Matthat,
the son of Levi,
30 *the son* of Simeon, *the son* of Judah,
the son of Joseph, *the son* of Jonan,
the son of Eliakim,
31 *the son* of Melea, *the son* of Menan,
the son of Mattathah, *the son* of
[a]Nathan, [b]*the son* of David,
32 [a]*the son* of Jesse, *the son* of Obed,
the son of Boaz, *the son* of Salmon,
the son of Nahshon,
33 *the son* of Amminadab, *the son* of
Ram, *the son* of Hezron, *the son* of
Perez, *the son* of Judah,
34 *the son* of Jacob, *the son* of Isaac,
the son of Abraham, [a]*the son* of Terah,
the son of Nahor,
35 *the son* of Serug, *the son* of Reu,
the son of Peleg, *the son* of Eber, *the*
son of Shelah,
36 [a]*the son* of Cainan, *the son* of
[b]Arphaxad, [c]*the son* of Shem, *the son*
of Noah, *the son* of Lamech,
37 *the son* of Methuselah, *the son* of
Enoch, *the son* of Jared, *the son* of Mahalalel, *the son* of Cainan,
38 *the son* of Enosh, *the son* of Seth,
the son of Adam, [a]*the son* of God.

Satan Tempts Jesus

4 Then [a]Jesus, being filled with the
*Holy Spirit, returned from the Jor-
dan and [b]was led by the Spirit [1]into
the wilderness,

27 [a]Ezra 2:2; 3:8
31 [a]Zech. 12:12 [b]2 Sam. 5:14; 7:12
32 [a]Ruth 4:18–22
34 [a]Gen. 11:24, 26–30; 12:3
36 [a]Gen. 11:12 [b]Gen. 10:22, 24; 11:10–13 [c]Gen. 5:6–32; 9:27; 11:10
38 [a]Gen. 5:1, 2

CHAPTER 4

1 [a]Matt. 4:1–11 [b]Luke 2:27 [1]NU *in* *See WW at Acts 7:33.
2 [a]Ex. 34:28 [1]*tested* *See WW at Rev. 2:10.
3 [a]John 20:31
4 [a]Deut. 8:3 [1]NU omits *but by every word of God*
5 [1]NU *And taking Him up, he showed Him*
6 [a][Rev. 13:2, 7]
8 [a]Deut. 6:13; 10:20 [1]NU omits *Get behind Me, Satan* [2]NU, M omit *For* *See WW at Rev. 4:10.
9 [a]Matt. 4:5–7
10 [a]Ps. 91:11
11 [a]Ps. 91:12

2 being [1]tempted* for forty days by
the devil. And [a]in those days He ate
nothing, and afterward, when they had
ended, He was hungry.
3 And the devil said to Him, "If You
are [a]the Son of God, command this
stone to become bread."
4 But Jesus answered him, saying, "It
is written, [a]*'Man shall not live by bread*
alone, [1]*but by every word of God.'* "
5 [1]Then the devil, taking Him up on
a high mountain, showed Him all the
kingdoms of the world in a moment of
time.
6 And the devil said to Him, "All this
authority I will give You, and their
glory; for [a]*this* has been delivered to
me, and I give it to whomever I wish.
7 "Therefore, if You will worship before me, all will be Yours."
8 And Jesus answered and said to
him, [1]"Get behind Me, Satan! [2]For it
is written, [a]*'You shall *worship the*
LORD your God, and Him only you shall
serve.' "
9 [a]Then he brought Him to Jerusalem, set Him on the pinnacle of the
temple, and said to Him, "If You are
the Son of God, throw Yourself down
from here.
10 "For it is written:

[a]*'He shall give His angels charge*
over you,
To keep you,'

11 "and,

[a]*'In their hands they shall bear you*
up,
Lest you dash your foot against
a stone.' "

4:1–12 See notes on Matt. 4:1–10.

TEMPTATION: THE TWO ADAMS CONTRASTED (4:1, 2)

Both Adam and Christ faced three aspects of temptation. Adam yielded, bringing upon humankind sin and death. Christ resisted, resulting in justification and life.

1 John 2:16	Genesis 3:6 First Adam	Luke 4:1–13 Second Adam—Christ
"the lust of the flesh"	"the tree was good for food"	"command this stone to become bread"
"the lust of the eyes"	"it was pleasant to the eyes"	"the devil...showed Him all the kingdoms"
"the pride of life"	"a tree desirable to make one wise"	"throw Yourself down from here"

12 And Jesus answered and said to him, "It has been said, [a]*'You shall not* [1]*tempt the* LORD *your God.'"*

KINGDOM DYNAMICS

4:1–12 Earth's Evil "Ruler," CONFLICT AND THE KINGDOM. As Jesus confronts Satan, He dramatically exposes the Adversary's relationship to this present world. Note the significance in Satan's offer to Jesus of "all the kingdoms of the world." Here we see the Adversary as administrator of the curse on this planet, a role he has held since man's dominion was lost and forfeited at the Fall. Because of this, Jesus does not contest the Devil's right to make that offer of this world's kingdoms and glory, but He pointedly denies the terms for their being gained. Jesus knows He is here to regain and ultimately win them, but He will do so on the Father's terms, not the Adversary's. Still, the present world systems are largely grounded by the limited but powerful and destructive rule of the one Jesus calls "the ruler of this world" (John 12:31; 16:30). Understanding these facts, we are wise not to attribute to God anything of the disorder of our confused, sin-riddled, diseased, tragedy-ridden, and tormented planet. "This present evil age" (Gal. 1:4) "lies *under the sway of* the wicked one" (1 John 5:19). But Jesus also said that Satan's rule "will be cast down," and that he "has nothing in Me," that is, no control over Christ or Christ's own. "He who is in you is greater than he who is in the world" (1 John 4:4).

(Acts 1:3–8/Matt. 11:12) J.W.H.

KINGDOM DYNAMICS

4:12 24. Is There Anything Wrong with Gambling?, SPIRITUAL ANSWERS. For the answer to this and other probing questions about God and the power life in His kingdom, see the study article "Spiritual Answers to Hard Questions," which begins on page 1996. P.R.

13 Now when the devil had ended every [1]temptation, he departed from Him [a]until an opportune time.

12 [a]Deut. 6:16 [1]*test*
13 [a][John 14:30; Heb. 4:15; James 4:7] [1]*testing*
14 [a]Matt. 4:12 [b]John 4:43 [c]Acts 10:37 [d]Matt. 4:24
15 [a]Ps. 22:22; Matt. 4:23 [b]Is. 52:13
16 [a]Matt. 2:23; 13:54; Mark 6:1 [b]Mark 1:21; John 18:20; Acts 13:14–16; 17:2 *See WW at Mark 13:14.
18 [a]Is. 49:8, 9; 61:1, 2; Matt. 11:5; 12:18; John 3:34 [b][Dan. 9:24] [1]NU omits *to heal the brokenhearted* [2]*downtrodden* *See WW at Rom. 16:20.
21 [a]Matt. 1:22, 23; Acts 13:29
22 [a][Ps. 45:2]; Matt. 13:54; Mark 6:2; Luke 2:47; [John 1:14, 17] [b]John 6:42

Jesus Begins His Galilean Ministry

14 [a]Then Jesus returned [b]in the power of the Spirit to [c]Galilee, and [d]news of Him went out through all the surrounding region.
15 And He [a]taught in their synagogues, [b]being glorified by all.

Jesus Rejected at Nazareth

16 So He came to [a]Nazareth, where He had been brought up. And as His custom was, [b]He went into the synagogue on the Sabbath day, and stood up to *read.
17 And He was handed the book of the prophet Isaiah. And when He had opened the book, He found the place where it was written:

18 *"The*[a] *Spirit of the* LORD *is upon*
Me,
Because He has anointed Me
To preach the gospel to the poor;
He has sent Me [1]*to heal the*
**brokenhearted,*
To proclaim liberty to the
captives
And recovery of sight to the
blind,
To [b]*set at liberty those who are*
[2]*oppressed;*
19 *To proclaim the acceptable year*
of the LORD*."*

20 Then He closed the book, and gave *it* back to the attendant and sat down. And the eyes of all who were in the synagogue were fixed on Him.
21 And He began to say to them, "Today this Scripture is [a]fulfilled in your hearing."
22 So all bore witness to Him, and [a]marveled at the gracious words which proceeded out of His mouth. And they said, [b]"Is this not Joseph's son?"

4:13 The three temptations just described were only typical of a much wider struggle in which Jesus engaged with **the devil**. The attacks of Satan continued throughout Jesus' ministry (see Heb. 2:18; 4:15).
4:14 The Galilean ministry began about a year after Jesus' baptism and temptation, with most of the time spent in a Judean ministry (see John 2:1—4:43). Luke emphasizes **the power of the Spirit** in Jesus' ministry, resulting in His subsequent fame.
4:16 The synagogue originated during the Exile, when the Jews were separated from the temple services in Jerusalem. It was both a religious and educational institution. A member or a visitor who was judged worthy was frequently asked to read the Scripture and make appropriate comments.
4:17–21 The prophecy of Is. 61:1, 2 describes the deliverance of Israel from exile in Babylon in terms of the Year of Jubilee, but its ultimate fulfillment awaited the coming of the messianic age. Jesus boldly claims to be the promised Messiah, and His defined ministry here becomes the ongoing essence of the good news of the gospel of the kingdom of God. Luke later makes it clear He passed this same ministry on to the disciples (9:1, 2) and ultimately to the entire church (Acts 1:1, 2).
4:21, 22 The response of marvel at the words of Jesus is qualified by skepticism since His hearers know His earthly origin.

23 He said to them, "You will surely
say this proverb to Me, 'Physician, heal
yourself! Whatever we have heard
done in [a]Capernaum,[1] do also here in
[b]Your country.'"
24 Then He said, "Assuredly, I say to
you, no [a]prophet is accepted in his own
country.
25 "But I tell you *truly, [a]many widows
were in Israel in the days of Elijah,
when the heaven was shut up three
years and six months, and there was
a great famine throughout all the
land;
26 "but to none of them was Elijah
sent except to [1]Zarephath, *in the region* of Sidon, to a woman *who was* a
widow.
27 [a]"And many lepers were in Israel
in the time of Elisha the *prophet, and
none of them was cleansed except Naaman the Syrian."
28 So all those in the synagogue, when
they heard these things, were [a]filled
with [1]**wrath,**

WORD WEALTH

4:28 wrath, ***thumos*** (thoo-*moss*); Strong's *#2372:* Compare "thyme." Inflammatory rage, exploding anger, turbulent commotion, boiling agitation, impulsive outbursts of hot anger. Another word, *orge,* presents anger as a settled habit.

29 [a]and rose up and thrust Him out of
the city; and they led Him to the brow
of the hill on which their city was built,
that they might throw Him down over
the cliff.
30 Then [a]passing through the midst of
them, He went His way.

Jesus Casts Out an Unclean Spirit

31 Then [a]He went down to Capernaum, a city of Galilee, and was teaching them on the Sabbaths.

23 [a]Matt. 4:13; 11:23 [b]Matt. 13:54; Mark 6:1 [1]NU *Capharnaum,* here and elsewhere
24 [a]Matt. 13:57; Mark 6:4; John 4:44
25 [a]1 Kin. 17:9; James 5:17 *See WW at John 4:24.
26 [1]Gr. *Sarepta*
27 [a]2 Kin. 5:1–14 *See WW at Matt. 2:5.
28 [a]Luke 6:11 [1]*rage*
29 [a]Luke 17:25; John 8:37; 10:31
30 [a]John 8:59; 10:39
31 [a]Is. 9:1; Matt. 4:13; Mark 1:21
32 [a]Matt. 7:28, 29 [b]Luke 4:36; [John 6:63; 7:46; 8:26, 28, 38, 47; 12:49, 50]
33 [a]Mark 1:23
34 [a]Luke 4:41 [b]Ps. 16:10; Is. 49:7; Dan. 9:24; Luke 1:35 *See WW at Luke 9:56.
35 [1]Lit. *Be muzzled*
38 [a]Matt. 8:14, 15; Mark 1:29–31 [b]Mark 5:23 [1]*afflicted with* *See WW at 2 Cor. 5:14.
39 [a]Luke 8:24 *See WW at Mark 1:20.
40 [a]Matt. 8:16, 17; Mark 1:32–34 *See WW at Matt. 12:22.
41 [a]Mark 1:34; 3:11; Acts 8:7 [b]Mark 8:29 [c]Mark 1:25, 34; 3:11; Luke 4:34, 35 [1]NU omits *the Christ* [2]Or *say that they knew*

32 And they were [a]astonished at His
teaching, [b]for His word was with authority.
33 [a]Now in the synagogue there was
a man who had a spirit of an unclean
demon. And he cried out with a loud
voice,
34 saying, "Let *us* alone! What have
we to do with You, Jesus of Nazareth?
Did You come to *destroy us? [a]I know
who You are—[b]the Holy One of
God!"
35 But Jesus rebuked him, saying,
[1]"Be quiet, and come out of him!" And
when the demon had thrown him in
their midst, it came out of him and did
not hurt him.
36 Then they were all amazed and
spoke among themselves, saying,
"What a word this *is!* For with authority and power He commands
the unclean spirits, and they come
out."
37 And the report about Him went out
into every place in the surrounding region.

Peter's Mother-in-Law Healed

38 [a]Now He arose from the synagogue
and entered Simon's house. But Simon's wife's mother was [1]sick* with a
high fever, and they [b]made request of
Him concerning her.
39 So He stood over her and [a]rebuked
the fever, and it *left her. And immediately she arose and served them.

Many Healed After Sabbath Sunset

40 [a]When the sun was setting, all those
who had any that were sick with various diseases brought them to Him; and
He laid His hands on every one of them
and *healed them.
41 [a]And demons also came out of
many, crying out and saying, [b]"You
are [1]the Christ, the Son of God!" And
He, [c]rebuking *them,* did not allow
them to [2]speak, for they knew that He
was the Christ.

4:23 Jesus anticipates the demands of the people that He perform in Nazareth the miracles He had done in Capernaum. However, His signs are not for the skeptic but for the believer, and He consistently refuses to produce compelling signs of His messiahship.
4:24 Those most familiar with great people sometimes are the least appreciative of their greatness.
4:25 Elijah: The introduction of Elijah and Elisha (v. 27), not only explains why Jesus the Prophet was rejected, but also emphasizes the transfer of the kingdom from rebellious Israel to the Gentiles. The two regions, Zarephath (Sidon—1 Kin. 17:9) and Syria (2 Kin. 5:1–14), are notably Gentile.
4:29 Out of the city emphasizes His excommunication by His hometown people, but the expression also seems to anticipate Jesus' fate outside the city of Jerusalem. He who opens the kingdom to the Gentiles (vv. 24–28) is Himself rejected as a Gentile and cast out.
4:32 Unlike other teachers, who monotonously quoted former rabbis, Jesus taught **with authority**—a consciousness of His calling, backed by divine display and approval.
4:33–35 See notes on Mark 1:23–25.
4:40 The Jews reckoned a day to be the period from one sunset to the next.
4:41 Jesus does not seek testimony from demons (see Acts 16:17, 18).

Jesus Preaches in Galilee

42 [a]Now when it was day, He departed and went into a deserted place. And the crowd sought Him and came to Him, and tried to keep Him from leaving them;
43 but He said to them, "I must [a]preach the kingdom of God to the other cities also, because for this purpose I have been sent."
44 [a]And He was preaching in the synagogues of [1]Galilee.

Four Fishermen Called as Disciples

5 So [a]it was, as the multitude pressed about Him to [b]hear the word of God, that He stood by the Lake of Gennesaret,
2 and saw two boats standing by the lake; but the fishermen had gone from them and were washing *their* nets.
3 Then He got into one of the boats, which was Simon's, and asked him to put out a little from the land. And He [a]sat down and taught the multitudes from the boat.
4 When He had stopped speaking, He said to Simon, [a]"Launch out into the deep and let down your nets for a catch."
5 But Simon answered and said to Him, "Master, we have toiled all night and caught [a]nothing; nevertheless [b]at Your word I will let down the net."
6 And when they had done this, they caught a great number of fish, and their net was breaking.
7 So they signaled to *their* *partners in the other boat to come and help them. And they came and filled both the boats, so that they began to sink.
8 When Simon Peter saw *it,* he fell down at Jesus' knees, saying, [a]"Depart from me, for I am a sinful man, O Lord!"
9 For he and all who were with him were [a]astonished at the catch of fish which they had taken;
10 and so also *were* James and John, the sons of Zebedee, who were partners with Simon. And Jesus said to Simon, "Do not be afraid. [a]From now on you will catch men."

42 [a]Mark 1:35–38; Luke 9:10
43 [a]Mark 1:14; [John 9:4]
44 [a]Matt. 4:23; 9:35; Mark 1:39 [1]NU *Judea*

CHAPTER 5

1 [a]Matt. 4:18–22; Mark 1:16–20; John 1:40–42 [b]Acts 13:44
3 [a]John 8:2
4 [a]John 21:6
5 [a]John 21:3 [b]Ps. 33:9
7 *See WW at Heb. 3:14.
8 [a]2 Sam. 6:9; 1 Kin. 17:18
9 [a]Mark 5:42; 10:24, 26
10 [a]Matt. 4:19; Mark 1:17
11 [a]Matt. 4:20; 19:27; [Mark 1:18; 8:34, 35; Luke 9:59–62]; John 12:26 [1]*left behind*
12 [a]Matt. 8:2–4; Mark 1:40–44 [b]Lev. 13:14 [1]*begged*
13 [a]Matt. 20:34; Luke 8:44; John 5:9
14 [a]Matt. 8:4; Luke 17:14 [b]Lev. 13:1–3; 14:2–32
15 [a]Mark 1:45 [b]Matt. 4:25; Mark 3:7; John 6:2

11 So when they had brought their boats to land, [a]they [1]forsook all and followed Him.

KINGDOM DYNAMICS

5:1–11 God Multiplies Your Seed to More Than Meet Your Greatest Need, SEED FAITH. Jesus taught a great lesson about seed-sowing and the importance of sowing in good soil (see Mark 4:1–20). Then, as if to illustrate His point, He told this group of discouraged and tired fishermen to launch out with their faith for a miracle catch.

These men had just planted their boat as a seed into the ministry of Jesus. They had given Him their greatest possession as a platform from which to preach the gospel. They had served the greatest need Jesus had at that moment, and here Jesus multiplied that gift into the means that met the greatest need they had at that moment in their lives. As commercial fishermen, they had a need for fish in order to make a living. They also had a need to see God working in their lives—to see both that Jesus was who He claimed to be and that their faith was operating effectively. Jesus met both of those needs!

When you give something to God, He will give it back in a way that is even better—plus He will be in it with all His grace and power!

(Mark 4:1–20/2 Cor. 9:8–10) O.R.

Jesus Cleanses a Leper

12 [a]And it happened when He was in a certain city, that behold, a man who was full of [b]leprosy saw Jesus; and he fell on *his* face and [1]implored Him, saying, "Lord, if You are willing, You can make me clean."
13 Then He put out *His* hand and touched him, saying, "I am willing; be cleansed." [a]Immediately the leprosy left him.
14 [a]And He charged him to tell no one, "But go and show yourself to the priest, and make an offering for your cleansing, as a testimony to them, [b]just as Moses commanded."
15 However, [a]the report went around concerning Him all the more; and [b]great multitudes came together to

4:42–44 Jesus refused to capitalize on the popularity He gained through His miracles. His agenda is not dictated by the crowd's demand that He stay.
5:1 The Lake of Gennesaret is another name for the Sea of Galilee. Since it measures only about 8 by 13 miles, it technically is not a sea and Luke never refers to it as such.
5:5 The best time for fishing was at night.
5:8 Peter's doubts about Jesus' fishing abilities progress to doubts about himself. The first doubt is overcome by a miracle; the second doubt is overcome by a promise (v. 10).
5:10 The Greek word for **catch** means "to capture alive," and its tense suggests continuous action. From now on Peter and the others are continuously to capture people for the kingdom of God.
5:12–15 See notes on Mark 1:40–45.

hear, and to be healed by Him of their
infirmities.
16 [a]So He Himself *often* withdrew into
the wilderness and [b]prayed.

Jesus Forgives and Heals a Paralytic

17 Now it happened on a certain day,
as He was teaching, that there were
Pharisees and teachers of the law sitting by, who had come out of every
town of Galilee, Judea, and Jerusalem.
And the power of the Lord was *present*
[1]to heal them.
18 [a]Then behold, men brought on a
bed a man who was paralyzed, whom
they sought to bring in and lay before
Him.
19 And when they could not find how
they might bring him in, because of the
crowd, they went up on the housetop
and let him down with *his* bed through
the tiling into the midst [a]before Jesus.
20 When He saw their faith, He said
to him, "Man, your sins are forgiven
you."
21 [a]And the scribes and the Pharisees
began to reason, saying, "Who is this
who speaks blasphemies? [b]Who can
forgive sins but God alone?"
22 But when Jesus [a]**perceived** their
*thoughts, He answered and said to
them, "Why are you reasoning in your
hearts?

WORD WEALTH

5:22 perceived, *epiginosko* (ep-ig-in-*oce*-koe); Strong's *#1921: Gnosis* is the noun, "knowledge," and *ginosko* is the verb, "to know." *Epiginosko* is to know fully; to know with a degree of thoroughness and competence; to be fully acquainted in a discerning, recognizing manner.

23 "Which is easier, to say, 'Your sins
are forgiven you,' or to say, 'Rise up
and walk'?
24 "But that you may know that the
Son of Man has *power on earth to forgive sins"—He said to the man who
was paralyzed, [a]"I say to you, arise,
take up your bed, and go to your
house."
25 Immediately he rose up before
them, took up what he had been lying
on, and departed to his own house,
[a]glorifying God.
26 And they were all amazed, and they
[a]glorified God and were filled with
fear, saying, "We have seen strange
things today!"

KINGDOM DYNAMICS

5:16–26 Which Is Easier, Pardon or Healing?, DIVINE HEALING. While not all affliction is the result of a specific sin, in this case sin was the cause, for the man was healed when Jesus said, "Your sins are forgiven you." From Jesus' words it is clear that Jesus could have said either, "Rise up and walk," or "Your sins are forgiven you." In many cases prayer for healing should begin with confession of sin and repentance (James 5:16; 1 John 1:8, 9).

Jesus' linking of healing with forgiveness is also evidence that human wholeness at every point of need is His concern. Obviously, forgiveness of sins is our greater need, but Jesus does not assert that need for divine forgiveness without affirming His partnering concern for human suffering.

Of further note, this episode teaches how healing often comes when a united group prays together in one accord (v. 16; also Matt. 18:19). The paralytic's healing came by means of men who cared, their faith overcoming all obstacles.

(Mark 9:22, 23/Luke 8:36) N.V.

Matthew the Tax Collector

27 [a]After these things He went out and
saw a tax collector named Levi, sitting
at the tax office. And He said to him,
[b]"Follow Me."
28 So he left all, rose up, and [a]followed
Him.
29 [a]Then Levi gave Him a great feast
in his own house. And [b]there were a
great number of tax collectors and
*others who sat down with them.
30 [1]And their scribes and the Pharisees [2]complained against His disciples,
saying, [a]"Why do You eat and drink
with tax collectors and sinners?"
31 Jesus answered and said to them,
"Those who are *well have no need of
a physician, but those who are sick.
32 [a]"I have not come to call *the* righteous, but sinners, to repentance."

Jesus Is Questioned About Fasting

33 Then they said to Him, [a]"Why[1] do
the disciples of John fast often and

16 [a]Luke 9:10 [b]Matt. 14:23; Mark 1:35; Luke 6:12; 9:18; 11:1
17 [1]NU *with Him to heal*
18 [a]Matt. 9:2–8; Mark 2:3–12
19 [a]Matt. 15:30
21 [a]Matt. 9:3; 26:65; Mark 2:6, 7; John 10:33 [b]Ps. 32:5; 130:4; Is. 43:25
22 [a]Luke 9:47; John 2:25 *See WW at Luke 2:35.
24 [a]Mark 2:11; 5:41; Luke 7:14 *See WW at Mark 3:15.
25 [a]Luke 17:15, 18; Acts 3:8
26 [a]Luke 1:65; 7:16
27 [a]Matt. 9:9–17; Mark 2:13–22 [b][Mark 8:34]; Luke 9:59; John 12:26; 21:19, 22
28 [a]Matt. 4:22; 19:27; Mark 10:28
29 [a]Matt. 9:9, 10; Mark 2:15 [b]Luke 15:1 *See WW at John 14:16.
30 [a]Matt. 11:19; Luke 15:2; Acts 23:9 [1]NU *But the Pharisees and their scribes* [2]*grumbled*
31 *See WW at 3 John 2.
32 [a]Matt. 9:13; 1 Tim. 1:15
33 [a]Matt. 9:14; Mark 2:18; Luke 7:33 [1]NU omits *Why do,* making the verse a statement

5:16 The Greek verb tense indicates that Jesus habitually **withdrew** for prayer.
5:17 The power of the Lord is equivalent to "the Spirit of the Lord" (4:18).
5:18–26 See notes on Mark 2:1–12.
5:27–32 See notes on Mark 2:14–17.
5:33–38 See notes on Matt. 9:14–17; Mark 2:18–22.

make prayers, and likewise those of
the Pharisees, but Yours eat and
drink?"
34 And He said to them, "Can you
make the friends of the bridegroom
fast while the [a]bridegroom is with
them?
35 "But the days will come when the
bridegroom will be taken away from
them; then they will fast in those
days."
11 36 [a]Then He spoke a parable to them:
"No one [1]puts a piece from a new garment on an old one; otherwise the new
makes a tear, and also the piece that
was *taken* out of the new does not
*match the old.
37 "And no one puts new wine into old
wineskins; or else the new wine will
burst the wineskins and be spilled, and
the wineskins will be ruined.
38 "But new wine must be put into new
wineskins, [1]and both are preserved.
39 "And no one, having drunk old
wine, [1]immediately desires new; for he
says, 'The old is [2]better.' "*

Jesus Is Lord of the Sabbath

6 Now [a]it happened [1]on the second
Sabbath after the first that He went
through the grainfields. And His disciples plucked the heads of grain and ate
them, rubbing *them* in *their* hands.
2 And some of the Pharisees said to
them, "Why are you doing [a]what is not
lawful to do on the Sabbath?"
3 But Jesus answering them said,
"Have you not even read this, [a]what
David did when he was hungry, he and
those who were with him:
4 "how he went into the house of God,
took and ate the *showbread, and also
gave some to those with him, [a]which
is not lawful for any but the priests to
eat?"
5 And He said to them, "The Son of
Man is also Lord of the Sabbath."

Healing on the Sabbath

6 [a]Now it happened on another Sabbath, also, that He entered the synagogue and taught. And a man was
there whose right hand was withered.

34 [a]John 3:29
36 [a]Matt. 9:16, 17; Mark 2:21, 22 [1]NU *tears a piece from a new garment and puts it on an old one* *See WW at Matt. 18:19.
38 [1]NU omits *and both are preserved*
39 [1]NU omits *immediately* [2]NU *good* *See WW at Matt. 11:30.

CHAPTER 6

1 [a]Matt. 12:1–8; Mark 2:23–28 [1]NU *on a Sabbath that He went*
2 [a]Ex. 20:10
3 [a]1 Sam. 21:6
4 [a]Lev. 24:9 *See WW at Rom. 8:28.
6 [a]Matt. 12:9–14; Mark 3:1–6; Luke 13:14; 14:3; John 9:16
7 [a]Luke 13:14; 14:1–6 [b]Luke 20:20
8 [a]Matt. 9:4; John 2:24, 25
9 [a]John 7:23 [1]M *to kill*
10 [1]NU, M *him* [2]NU omits *as whole as the other*
12 [a]Matt. 14:23; Mark 1:35; Luke 5:16; 9:18; 11:1
13 [a]John 6:70 [b]Matt. 10:1
14 [a]John 1:42
16 [a]Jude 1 [b]Luke 22:3–6
17 [a]Matt. 4:25; Mark 3:7, 8
19 [a]Matt. 9:21; 14:36; Mark 3:10

7 So the scribes and Pharisees
watched Him closely, whether He
would [a]heal on the Sabbath, that they
might find an [b]accusation against
Him.
8 But He [a]knew their thoughts, and
said to the man who had the withered
hand, "Arise and stand here." And he
arose and stood.
9 Then Jesus said to them, "I will ask
you one thing: [a]Is it lawful on the Sabbath to do good or to do evil, to save
life or [1]to destroy?"
10 And when He had looked around
at them all, He said to [1]the man,
"Stretch out your hand." And he did
so, and his hand was restored [2]as
whole as the other.
11 But they were filled with rage, and
discussed with one another what they
might do to Jesus.

The Twelve Apostles

12 Now it came to pass in those days
that He went out to the mountain to
pray, and continued all night in
[a]prayer to God.
13 And when it was day, He called His
disciples to *Himself;* [a]and from them
He chose [b]twelve whom He also
named apostles:
14 Simon, [a]whom He also named Peter, and Andrew his brother; James
and John; Philip and Bartholomew;
15 Matthew and Thomas; James the
son of Alphaeus, and Simon called the
Zealot;
16 Judas [a]*the son* of James, and
[b]Judas Iscariot who also became a traitor.

Jesus Heals a Great Multitude

17 And He came down with them and
stood on a level place with a crowd of
His disciples [a]and a great multitude of
people from all Judea and Jerusalem,
and from the seacoast of Tyre and Sidon, who came to hear Him and be
healed of their diseases,
18 as well as those who were tormented with unclean spirits. And they
were healed.
19 And the whole multitude [a]sought to

5:36–39 See section 11 of Truth-In-Action through the Synoptics at the end of Luke.
5:39 Jesus sadly describes people who are satisfied with the old legalistic system and who are reluctant to accept the gospel.
6:1–11 See notes on Matt. 12:1–14; Mark 2:23—3:6.
6:12 Once again Luke emphasizes the fact that Jesus prayed before critical events.
6:17 The geographical references emphasize both the immense popularity of Jesus and the extreme need of the people.

[b]touch Him, for [c]power went out from Him and healed *them* all.

The Beatitudes

20 Then He lifted up His eyes toward His disciples, and said:

[a]"Blessed* *are you* poor,
For yours is the kingdom of God.
21 [a]Blessed *are you* who hunger now,
For you shall be [b]filled.[1]*
[c]Blessed *are you* who weep now,
For you shall [d]laugh.
22 [a]Blessed are you when men hate you,
And when they [b]exclude you,
And *revile *you,* and cast out your name as evil,
For the Son of Man's sake.
23 [a]Rejoice in that day and leap for joy!
For indeed your *reward *is* great in heaven,
For [b]in like manner their fathers did to the prophets.

Jesus Pronounces Woes

24 "But[a] woe to you [b]who are rich,
For [c]you have *received your consolation.
25 [a]Woe to you who are full,
For you shall hunger.
[b]Woe to you who laugh now,
For you shall *mourn and [c]weep.
26 [a]Woe [1]to you when [2]all men speak well of you,
For so did their fathers to the false prophets.

19 [b]Mark 5:27, 28 [c]Luke 8:46
20 [a]Matt. 5:3–12; [11:5] *See WW at Matt. 5:3.
21 [a]Is. 55:1; 65:13 [b][Rev. 7:16] [c][Is. 61:3] [d]Ps. 126:5 [1]*satisfied* *See WW at Matt. 15:33.
22 [a]1 Pet. 2:19; 3:14; 4:14 [b][John 16:2] *See WW at James 1:5.
23 [a]James 1:2 [b]Acts 7:51 *See WW at Rev. 22:12.
24 [a]James 5:1–6 [b]Luke 12:21 [c]Luke 16:25 *See WW at Philem. 15.
25 [a][Is. 65:13] [b][Prov. 14:13] [c]James 4:9 *See WW at Rev. 18:11.
26 [a][John 15:19] [1]NU, M omit *to you* [2]M omits *all*
27 [a]Rom. 12:20 *See WW at John 3:16.
28 [a]Rom. 12:14 [b]Acts 7:60
29 [a]Matt. 5:39–42 [b][1 Cor. 6:7]
30 [a]Deut. 15:7, 8
31 [a]Matt. 7:12
32 [a]Matt. 5:46
34 [a]Matt. 5:42

Love Your Enemies

27 [a]"But I say to you who hear: *Love 5
your enemies, do good to those who hate you,
28 [a]"**bless** those who curse you, and [b]pray for those who spitefully use you.

WORD WEALTH

6:28 bless, *eulogeo* (yoo-log-*eh*-oh); Strong's *#2127:* Compare "eulogy" and "eulogize." From *eu,* "well" or "good," and *logos,* "speech" or "word." *Eulogeo* is to speak well of, praise, extol, bless abundantly, invoke a benediction, give thanks. *Eulogeo* can be from men to God, from men to men, and from God to men. When God blesses men, He grants them favor and confers happiness upon them.

29 [a]"To him who strikes you on the 5
one cheek, offer the other also. [b]And from him who takes away your cloak, do not withhold *your* tunic either.
30 [a]"Give to everyone who asks of you. And from him who takes away your goods do not ask *them* back.
31 [a]"And just as you want men to do to you, you also do to them likewise.
32 [a]"But if you love those who love 5
you, what credit is that to you? For even sinners love those who love them.
33 "And if you do good to those who do good to you, what credit is that to you? For even sinners do the same.
34 [a]"And if you lend *to those* from whom you hope to receive back, what credit is that to you? For even sinners lend to sinners to receive as much back.

6:20–49 The Sermon on the Plain parallels Matthew's Sermon on the Mount (Matt. 5—7) in general structure, sequence, and thought. In line with his purpose, Luke omits much material of particular interest to Jews.
6:20–23 There are spiritual implications in the terms **poor, hunger, weep,** and **hate**. Jesus does not commend poverty, hunger, sorrow, and reproach in themselves. These sufferings bring blessings only when they are endured through discipleship **for the Son of Man's sake** (v. 22). Therefore, poverty of spirit, hungering after righteousness, weeping over one's sins, and social ostracism for the sake of Christ are sources of blessing. "Poor": The term denotes the humble poor whose trust is in God's help in the midst of their poverty (compare with "poor in spirit," Matt. 5:3).
6:21 There is a clear contrast in several of these Beatitudes between present lot and future reward. Each of the four blessings corresponds by way of contrast to each of the woes.
6:22–24 There is continuity of suffering and persecution between Jesus' disciples' ("you") suffering for following the Son of Man, and the prophets' suffering for proclaiming God's message (v. 23). In contrast, consolation is promised in this present age and the coming age when situations will be reversed.
6:24–26 Jesus does not condemn riches, abundance, laughter, and social acceptance in themselves. Preference for earthly things over things of the kingdom of God is what leads to ultimate **woe.**
6:26 The rejection of God's true prophets (v. 23) is contrasted with the easy-going and shallow reception of the false prophets.
6:27–38 The essence of the Christian life is love, with the general principle stated in v. 31. This love is manifested by responding to personal insult and injustice, not with retaliation or even passive endurance, but with positive and aggressive acts of goodness designed to redeem the offenders. See notes on Matt. 5:38–45.
6:27, 28 See section 5 of Truth-In-Action through the Synoptics at the end of Luke.
6:29, 30 See section 5 of Truth-In-Action through the Synoptics at the end of Luke.
6:32–36 See section 5 of Truth-In-Action through the Synoptics at the end of Luke.
6:32–34 Doing good merely for the sake of recompense betrays a self-interest that has no place in the Christian life.

35 "But [a]love your enemies, [b]do good, and [c]lend, [1]hoping for nothing in return; and your reward will be great, and [d]you will be sons of the Most High. For He is *kind to the unthankful and evil.

KINGDOM DYNAMICS

6:31–35 God's Love Loves the Unlovable, BROTHERLY LOVE. To love the unlovable is to separate ourselves from the world's self-serving kind of love—to share Christ's love with people who have no apparent ability to return anything at all. Jesus calls us to love as He did—to love those who finish last, those who are ugly, those who are poor, or who are powerless to help us. This response is only possible by a supernatural transformation that begets in us a different order of response than is usual to mankind. Just as the human mind separates man from animals, so Christian love is to be so dramatically different that it separates the believer from the world. It is to remove us from animal responses that snarl, attack, or retaliate. It is to transcend human responses that expect an earthly reward for service or kindness. Such love will become a beacon light, drawing the worldling to us, to question what causes us to radiate love in the midst of unlovable, unloving people. Stephen exemplifies this love (Acts 7:59, 60), and Saul (Paul) reflects the impact of such love (Acts 9:5). Note "the goads" of conviction that had begun piercing him, doubtless through Stephen's love. The perfection of God's love in us can gain a curious and attentive audience.

(Matt. 5:44/John 12:26) D.S.

36 [a]"Therefore be merciful, just as your Father also is merciful.

Do Not Judge

6 37 [a]"Judge not, and you shall not be judged. Condemn not, and you shall not be condemned. [b]Forgive, and you will be forgiven.
38 [a]"Give, and it will be given to you: *good measure, pressed down, shaken together, and running over will be put into your [b]bosom. For [c]with the same measure that you use, it will be measured back to you."

KINGDOM DYNAMICS

6:38 God Expects You to Receive a Harvest from Your Giving. He Wants Us to Expect a Miracle Return!, SEED FAITH. Jesus opened up a whole new way of giving. He gave Himself totally to and for the needs of the people. We can no longer pay or sacrifice our way into God's mercy. Jesus Christ has paid our debt before God, and His Cross is a completed work in our eternal interest. Our giving, then, is no longer a debt that we owe, but a seed that we sow! The life and power source is from Him. Ours is simply to act on the power potential in that seed-life He has placed in us by His power and grace!

Notice that when Jesus said, "Give," He also said, "and it will be given to you." Giving and receiving belong together. Only when we give are we in a position to expect to reach out and receive a harvest. And Jesus said the harvest will be "good measure, pressed down, shaken together, and running over."

We give as to God, and we receive as from God; but we should remain sensitive at all times to the different ways in which God may deliver our harvest. I often say, "A miracle is either coming toward you or going past you all the time. Reach out and take it! Do not let it pass by!" (see Matt. 9:20–22). God's miracle for you may be coming as an idea, an opportunity, an invitation, or a previously unknown or unidentified association. Watch expectantly for the ways in which God may choose to deliver your miracle to you in His "due season" (which, for you, may be today).

(John 10:10/Gal. 6:7–9) O.R.

KINGDOM DYNAMICS

6:38 The Law of Divine Reciprocity, GOD'S PROSPERITY. There is a universal law of divine reciprocity. You give; God gives in return. When you plant a seed, the ground yields a harvest. That is a reciprocal relationship. The ground can only give to you as you give to the ground. You put money in the bank, and the bank returns interest. That is reciprocity.

But many people want something for

35 [a][Rom. 13:10] [b]Heb. 13:16 [c]Lev. 25:35–37; Ps. 37:26 [d]Matt. 5:46 [1]*expecting* *See WW at Matt. 11:30.
36 [a]Matt. 5:48; Eph. 4:32
37 [a]Matt. 7:1–5; Rom. 14:4; [1 Cor. 4:5] [b]Matt. 18:21–35
38 [a][Prov. 19:17; 28:27] [b]Ps. 79:12; Is. 65:6, 7; Jer. 32:18 [c]Matt. 7:2; Mark 4:24; James 2:13 *See WW at Matt. 13:48.

6:35, 36 Christian love finds its motivation in God's love for us. His mercy to us is the basis of the mercy we extend to others.
6:35 Substantiation for the love-commandment is found in the divine example. Because God does not give or withhold His kindness dependent upon the character of the recipient, so Jesus' disciples must be indifferent in their extension of kindness to friend and enemy alike (see Lev. 19:18).
6:37, 38 See section 6 of Truth-In-Action through the Synoptics at the end of Luke.
6:37 The practice of Christian love and forgiveness is a deterrent to a censorious attitude, while at the same time allowing us to exercise moral judgment of issues. Jesus describes judging, condemning and withholding forgiveness as prerogatives that belong to God alone.
6:38 God rewards unselfish giving to those in need with boundless liberality.

nothing when it comes to the things of God. They know that it does not work that way in the world system. Yet they always expect God to send them something when they have not invested in the kingdom of God.

If you are not investing your time, talent, commitment, and your money, why do you want something? How can you get something when you have not planted any seed? How can you expect God to honor your desire when you have not honored His command to give? Prosperity begins with investment.

(Mal. 3:8–10/3 John 2) F.P.

39 And He spoke a parable to them:
[a]"Can the blind lead the blind? Will
they not both fall into the ditch?
40 [a]"A disciple is not above his
teacher, but everyone who is *perfectly
trained will be like his teacher.
[6] 41 [a]"And why do you look at the speck
in your brother's eye, but do not perceive the plank in your own eye?
42 "Or how can you say to your
brother, 'Brother, let me remove the
speck that *is* in your eye,' when you
yourself do not see the plank that *is*
in your own eye? Hypocrite! First remove the plank from your own eye,
and then you will see clearly to remove
the speck that is in your brother's eye.

A Tree Is Known by Its Fruit

[9] 43 [a]"For a good tree does not bear bad
fruit, nor does a bad tree bear good
fruit.
44 "For [a]every tree is known by its
own fruit. For *men* do not gather figs
from thorns, nor do they gather grapes
from a bramble bush.
45 [a]"A *good man out of the good treasure of his heart brings forth good; and
an evil man out of the evil [1]treasure
of his heart brings forth evil. For out
[b]of the abundance of the heart his
mouth speaks.

Build on the Rock

[9] 46 [a]"But why do you call Me 'Lord,
Lord,' and not do the things which I
say?

39 [a]Matt. 15:14; 23:16; Rom. 2:19
40 [a]Matt. 10:24; [John 13:16; 15:20] *See WW at Heb. 11:3.
41 [a]Matt. 7:3
43 [a]Matt. 7:16–18, 20
44 [a]Matt. 12:33
45 [a]Matt. 12:35 [b]Prov. 15:2, 28; 16:23; 18:21; Matt. 12:34 [1]NU omits *treasure of his heart* *See WW at Phil. 1:6.
46 [a]Mal. 1:6; Matt. 7:21; 25:11; Luke 13:25
47 [a]Matt. 7:24–27; [John 14:21]; James 1:22–25
48 [1]NU *well built*
49 [1]NU *collapsed*

CHAPTER 7

1 [a]Matt. 8:5–13
6 *See WW at Philem. 15. • See WW at John 11:11.
7 [a]Ps. 33:9; 107:20
8 [a][Mark 13:34]

47 [a]"Whoever comes to Me, and hears
My sayings and does them, I will show
you whom he is like:
48 "He is like a man building a house,
who dug deep and laid the foundation
on the rock. And when the flood arose,
the stream beat vehemently against
that house, and could not shake it, for
it was [1]founded on the rock.
49 "But he who heard and did nothing
is like a man who built a house on the
earth without a foundation, against
which the stream beat vehemently; and
immediately it [1]fell. And the ruin of
that house was great."

Jesus Heals a Centurion's Servant

7 Now when He concluded all His
sayings in the hearing of the people, He [a]entered Capernaum.
2 And a certain centurion's servant,
who was dear to him, was sick and
ready to die.
3 So when he heard about Jesus, he
sent elders of the Jews to Him, pleading with Him to come and heal his servant.
4 And when they came to Jesus, they
begged Him earnestly, saying that the
one for whom He should do this was
deserving,
5 "for he loves our nation, and has
built us a synagogue."
6 Then Jesus went with them. And
*when He was already not far from the
house, the centurion sent *friends to
Him, saying to Him, "Lord, do not trouble Yourself, for I am not worthy that
You should enter under my roof.
7 "Therefore I did not even think myself worthy to come to You. But
[a]say the word, and my servant will be
healed.
8 "For I also am a man placed under
[a]authority, having soldiers under me.
And I say to one, 'Go,' and he goes;
and to another, 'Come,' and he comes;
and to my servant, 'Do this,' and he
does *it.*"
9 When Jesus heard these things, He
marveled at him, and turned around
and said to the crowd that followed
Him, "I say to you, I have not found

6:39–45 Jesus is still dealing with the matter of hypocritical judgment, which violates the law of love. A person who is quick to condemn the faults of others, while ignoring his own shortcomings, will be of little help to others. He particularly has in mind the Pharisees and their disciples (see Matt. 15:14). See notes on Matt. 7:15, 16; 12:33–37.

6:41, 42 See section 6 of Truth-In-Action through the Synoptics at the end of Luke.

6:43–45 See section 9 of Truth-In-Action through the Synoptics at the end of Luke.

6:46–49 See note on Matt. 7:24–27.

6:46 See section 9 of Truth-In-Action through the Synoptics at the end of Luke.

7:1–10 See note on Matt. 8:5–13.

7:9 Such great faith: The great faith of the Gentile centurion is the key to the passage, "great faith" being explained as

such great faith, not even in Israel!”
10 And those who were sent, returning
to the house, found the servant *well
[1]who had been sick.

Jesus Raises the Son of the Widow of Nain

11 Now it happened, the day after, *that*
He went into a city called Nain; and
many of His disciples went with Him,
and a large crowd.
12 And when He came near the gate
of the city, behold, a dead man was being carried out, the only son of his
mother; and she was a widow. And a
large crowd from the city was with her.
13 When the Lord saw her, He had
[a]compassion* on her and said to her,
[b]“Do not weep.”
14 Then He came and touched the
open coffin, and those who carried *him*
stood still. And He said, “Young man,
I say to you, [a]arise.”
15 So he who was dead [a]sat up and
began to speak. And He [b]presented
him to his mother.
16 [a]Then fear [1]came upon all, and they
[b]glorified God, saying, [c]“A great
prophet has risen up among us”; and,
[d]“God has visited His people.”
17 And this report about Him went
throughout all Judea and all the surrounding region.

John the Baptist Sends Messengers to Jesus

18 [a]Then the disciples of John reported
to him concerning all these things.
19 And John, calling two of his disciples to *him,* sent *them* to [1]Jesus, saying, “Are You [a]the Coming One, or
[2]do we look for another?”
20 When the men had come to Him,
they said, “John the Baptist has sent
us to You, saying, ‘Are You the Coming
One, or do we look for another?’ ”
21 And that very hour He cured many
of [1]infirmities, afflictions, and evil spirits; and to many blind He *gave sight.
22 [a]Jesus answered and said to them,
“Go and tell John the things you have
seen and heard: [b]that *the* blind [c]see,
the lame [d]walk, *the* lepers are
[e]cleansed, *the* deaf [f]hear, *the* dead are
raised, [g]*the* poor have the gospel
preached to them.
23 “And blessed is *he* who is not
[1]offended* because of Me.”
24 [a]When the messengers of John had
departed, He began to speak to the
multitudes concerning John: “What
did you go out into the wilderness to
see? A reed shaken by the wind?
25 “But what did you go out to see? A
man clothed in soft garments? Indeed
those who are gorgeously appareled
and live in luxury are in kings’ courts.
26 “But what did you go out to see? A
prophet? Yes, I say to you, and *more
than a prophet.
27 “This is *he* of whom it is written:

[a]‘Behold, I send My messenger
before Your face,
Who will prepare Your way
before You.’

28 “For I say to you, among those born
of women there is [1]not a [a]greater
prophet than John the Baptist; but he
who is least in the kingdom of God is
greater than he.”
29 And when all the people heard *Him,*
even the tax collectors [1]justified* God,
[a]having been baptized with the baptism of John.
30 But the Pharisees and [1]lawyers rejected [a]the will of God for themselves,
not having been baptized by him.
31 [1]And the Lord said, [a]“To what then
shall I liken the men of this generation,
and what are they like?
32 “They are like children sitting in the
marketplace and calling to one another, saying:

‘We played the flute for you,
And you did not dance;
We mourned to you,
And you did not weep.’

33 “For [a]John the Baptist came [b]nei-
ther eating bread nor drinking wine,
and you say, ‘He has a demon.’
34 “The Son of Man has come [a]eating
and drinking, and you say, ‘Look, a
glutton and a [1]winebibber, a friend of
tax collectors and sinners!’
35 [a]“But wisdom is justified by all her
children.”

10 [1]NU omits *who had been sick* *See WW at 3 John 2.
13 [a]John 11:35 [b]Luke 8:52 *See WW at Matt. 14:14.
14 [a]Acts 9:40
15 [a]John 11:44 [b]2 Kin. 4:36
16 [a]Luke 1:65 [b]Luke 5:26 [c]Luke 24:19 [d]Luke 1:68 [1]*seized them all*
18 [a]Matt. 11:2–19
19 [a][Zech. 9:9] [1]NU *the Lord* [2]*should we expect*
21 [1]*illnesses* *See WW at Col. 3:13.
22 [a]Matt. 11:4 [b]Is. 35:5 [c]John 9:7 [d]Matt. 15:31 [e]Luke 17:12–14 [f]Mark 7:37 [g][Is. 61:1–3]
23 [1]*caused to stumble* *See WW at Matt. 11:6.
24 [a]Matt. 11:7
26 *See WW at John 10:10.
27 [a]Mal. 3:1
28 [a][Luke 1:15] [1]NU *none greater than John;*
29 [a]Luke 3:12 [1]*declared the righteousness of* *See WW at Matt. 12:37.
30 [a]Acts 20:27 [1]*the experts in the law*
31 [a]Matt. 11:16 [1]NU, M omit *And the Lord said*
33 [a]Matt. 3:1 [b]Luke 1:15
34 [a]Luke 15:2 [1]An excessive drinker
35 [a]Matt. 11:19

the centurion’s understanding and response to an authoritative word (vv. 7, 8) from Jesus. His faith stands in stark contrast to the curious doubt in Israel.
7:11–17 Luke emphasizes the compassion of Jesus as His motivation to minister this miracle. **Nain** was about a day’s journey south of Capernaum.
7:16 Perhaps the people recall how two OT prophets had restored dead sons to their mothers (1 Kin. 17:17–24; 2 Kin. 4:32–37).
7:18–35 See notes on Matt. 11:2–19.

A Sinful Woman Forgiven

36 [a]Then one of the Pharisees asked Him to eat with him. And He went to the Pharisee's house, and sat down to eat.

37 And behold, a woman in the city who was a sinner, when she knew that *Jesus* sat at the table in the Pharisee's house, brought an alabaster flask of fragrant oil,

38 and stood at His feet behind *Him* weeping; and she began to wash His feet with her tears, and wiped *them* with the hair of her head; and she kissed His feet and anointed *them* with the fragrant oil.

39 Now when the Pharisee who had invited Him saw *this,* he spoke to himself, saying, [a]"This Man, if He were a prophet, would know who and what manner of woman *this is* who is touching Him, for she is a sinner."

40 And Jesus answered and said to him, "Simon, I have something to say to you." So he said, "Teacher, say it."

41 "There was a certain creditor who had two debtors. One owed five hundred [a]denarii, and the other fifty.

42 "And when they had nothing with which to repay, he freely forgave them both. Tell Me, therefore, which of them will love him more?"

43 Simon answered and said, "I suppose the *one* whom he forgave more." And He said to him, "You have rightly judged."

44 Then He turned to the woman and said to Simon, "Do you see this woman? I entered your house; you gave Me no [a]water for My feet, but she has washed My feet with her tears and wiped *them* with the hair of her head.

45 "You gave Me no [a]kiss, but this woman has not ceased to kiss My feet since the time I came in.

46 [a]"You did not anoint My head with oil, but this woman has anointed My feet with fragrant oil.

47 [a]"Therefore I say to you, her *sins, *which are* many, are *forgiven, for she loved much. But to whom little is forgiven, *the same* loves little."

48 Then He said to her, [a]"Your sins are forgiven."

49 And those who sat at the table with Him began to say to themselves, [a]"Who is this who even forgives sins?"

50 Then He said to the woman, [a]"Your faith has **saved** you. Go in peace."

36 [a]Matt. 26:6; Mark 14:3; John 11:2
39 [a]Luke 15:2
41 [a]Matt. 18:28; Mark 6:37
44 [a]Gen. 18:4; 19:2; 43:24; Judg. 19:21; 1 Tim. 5:10
45 [a]Rom. 16:16
46 [a]2 Sam. 12:20; Ps. 23:5; Eccl. 9:8; Dan. 10:3
47 [a][1 Tim. 1:14] *See WW at John 1:29. • See WW at Mark 1:20.
48 [a]Matt. 9:2; Mark 2:5
49 [a]Matt. 9:3; [Mark 2:7]; Luke 5:21
50 [a]Matt. 9:22; Mark 5:34; 10:52; Luke 8:48; 18:42

CHAPTER 8
1 [1]*proclaiming the good news*
2 [a]Matt. 27:55; Mark 15:40, 41; Luke 23:49, 55 [b]Matt. 27:56; Mark 16:9 [1]*sicknesses*

WORD WEALTH

7:50 saved, *sozo* (*sode*-zoe); Strong's *#4982:* To save, heal, cure, preserve, keep safe and sound, rescue from danger or destruction, deliver. *Sozo* saves from physical death by healing, and from spiritual death by forgiving sin and its effects. *Sozo* in primitive cultures is translated simply, "to give new life" and "to cause to have a new heart."

Many Women Minister to Jesus

8 Now it came to pass, afterward, that He went through every city and village, preaching and [1]bringing the glad tidings of the kingdom of God. And the twelve *were* with Him,

2 and [a]certain women who had been healed of evil spirits and [1]infirmities—Mary called Magdalene, [b]out of whom had come seven demons,

KINGDOM DYNAMICS

8:2 Freed to Become Fruitful (Mary Magdalene), WOMEN. Mary Magdalene first appears in the Gospels among a number of other women who constitute a part of the support-team assisting Jesus in His ministry. She had been delivered from demonic bondage, the nature of which is not related.

There is an almost indestructible body of myth that has come to surround her, primarily by reason of speakers, writers, novelists, and screenplays, which have created a fantasy that generally suggests *(cont. on next page)*

7:36 The fact that the Pharisee did not extend common courtesies to Jesus (v. 38) indicates that his motive in inviting Jesus was curiosity.

7:37 The description of the **woman** suggests that she was a prostitute. She is not to be confused with Mary of Bethany (John 12:3).

7:39 Simon reasons that a genuine prophet could discern the character of the woman. In His reply Jesus shows that He knows what sort of man Simon is and what he is thinking (vv. 40–47).

7:41–43 Jesus teaches the principle that the greater the forgiveness, the greater is the love.

7:41 The parable is a parable of contrast, between two debtors, the amount of debt, the forgiveness of the debts, and the contrasting gratitude of both. The woman and Simon are represented by the two debtors. Simon's minimal hospitality (vv. 44–46) is contrasted with the woman's lavish devotion. The love that she displayed is the fruit of a penitent heart.

7:44–47 In applying the principle to Simon and the woman, Jesus shows that one who realizes the depth of his own sin, and the greatness of God's mercy, must love as this woman does. Her love resulted from her forgiveness.

7:50 **Faith** secured her pardon, and the realization of God's forgiveness brought forth her expression of gratitude.

8:1–3 Luke emphasizes the place of devout women in the ministry of Jesus, here calling special attention to their financial support.

(*cont. from preceding page*)
three things, none of which are in the Bible: 1) that she had been a prostitute, 2) that she was young and attractive, and 3) that she had a romantic affection for Jesus. She has also been frequently confused with the sinful woman forgiven by Jesus (7:36–50) and/or the woman who broke the alabaster box of perfumed ointment (Mark 14:3–9). In fact, all these proposals are speculation, yet through frequent allusion or direct reference have taken on the appearance of fact for multitudes. What is true of Mary Magdalene?

First, she was a grateful soul, because she had been freed from terrible torment. This text suggests her service for Christ was motivated by that gratitude. Second, she was a witness of the Crucifixion, though apparently not beside the Cross as were Mary, Jesus' mother, and John the Beloved (Matt. 27:55, 56). (The fact that the other women with whom she kept company were all older women supports the reasoning that she was likely their peer in age.) Third, she was present at Jesus' burial (Mark 15:47), among those who came early Easter morning to complete the embalming of Jesus' body (Mark 16:1), among the first to hear the angelic announcement of Jesus' resurrection (Mark 16:6), and the first person actually to talk with Jesus after He was risen (John 20:11–18). It is foolish to conclude that her movement toward greeting Jesus with an embrace following His resurrection suggests anything other than the most logical response of joy at the discovery of His being alive. Jesus' directive that she not do so was not because there was anything unworthy in her approach. His words apparently indicate some yet uncompleted aspect of His post-crucifixion mission.

Mary Magdalene was a steadfast disciple of Jesus and is best seen as a case study of how no dimension of satanic bondage can prohibit any individual's being released to fruitful service for Jesus Christ.

(Luke 2:36–38/Luke 10:38–42) F.L.

3 and Joanna the wife of Chuza, Herod's steward, and Susanna, and many others who provided for [1]Him from their [2]substance.

The Parable of the Sower

4 4 [a]And when a great multitude had gathered, and they had come to Him from every city, He spoke by a parable:

5 "A sower went out to sow his seed. And as he sowed, some fell by the wayside; and it was trampled down, and the birds of the air devoured it.

6 "Some fell on rock; and as soon as it sprang up, it withered away because it lacked moisture.

7 "And some fell among thorns, and the thorns sprang up with it and choked it.

8 "But others fell on good ground, sprang up, and yielded [1]a crop a hundredfold." When He had said these things He cried, [a]"He who has ears to hear, let him hear!"

The Purpose of Parables

9 [a]Then His disciples asked Him, saying, "What does this parable mean?"

10 And He said, "To you it has been given to know the [1]mysteries* of the kingdom of God, but to the rest *it is given* in parables, that

[a]*'Seeing they may not see,*
And hearing they may not
understand.'

The Parable of the Sower Explained

11 [a]"Now the parable is this: The seed is the [b]word of God.

12 "Those by the wayside are the ones who hear; then the devil comes and takes away the word out of their hearts, lest they should believe and be saved.

13 "But the ones on the rock *are those* who, when they hear, receive the word with joy; and these have no root, who believe for a while and in time of [1]temptation fall away.

14 "Now the ones *that* fell among thorns are those who, when they have heard, go out and are choked with *cares, [a]riches, and pleasures of life, and bring no fruit to maturity.

15 "But the ones *that* fell on the good ground are those who, having heard the word with a noble and good heart, keep *it* and bear fruit with [a]patience.[1]*

The Parable of the Revealed Light

16 [a]"No one, when he has lit a lamp, covers it with a vessel or puts *it* under a bed, but sets *it* on a lampstand, that those who enter may see the [b]light.

3 [1]NU, M *them* [2]*possessions*
4 [a]Matt. 13:2–9; Mark 4:1–9
8 [a]Matt. 11:15; Mark 7:16; Luke 14:35; Rev. 2:7, 11, 17, 29; 3:6, 13, 22; 13:9 [1]Lit. *fruit*
9 [a]Matt. 13:10–23; Mark 4:10–20
10 [a]Is. 6:9; Matt. 13:14; Acts 28:26 [1]*secret* or *hidden truths* *See WW at Mark 4:11.
11 [a]Matt. 13:18; Mark 4:14; [1 Pet. 1:23] [b]Luke 5:1; 11:28
13 [1]*testing*
14 [a]Matt. 19:23; 1 Tim. 6:9, 10 *See WW at 1 Pet. 5:7.
15 [a][Rom. 2:7; Heb. 10:36–39; James 5:7, 8] [1]*endurance* *See WW at Heb. 10:36.
16 [a]Matt. 5:15; Mark 4:21; Luke 11:33 [b]Matt. 5:14

8:4–15 See section 4 of Truth-In-Action through the Synoptics at the end of Luke.
8:4 For Jesus' use of parables, see note on Mark 4:2.
8:5–15 See notes on Matt. 13:3–23; Mark 4:3–20.
8:16–18 See notes on Mark 4:21–25.

17 [a]"For nothing is secret that will not
be [b]revealed, nor *anything* hidden that
will not be known and come to light.
18 "Therefore take heed how you hear.
[a]For whoever has, to him *more* will be
given; and whoever does not have,
even what he [1]seems to [b]have will be
taken from him."

Jesus' Mother and Brothers Come to Him

19 [a]Then His mother and brothers
came to Him, and could not approach
Him because of the crowd.
20 And it was told Him *by some,* who
said, "Your mother and Your brothers
are standing outside, desiring to see
You."
21 But He answered and said to them,
"My mother and My brothers are these
who hear the word of God and do it."

Wind and Wave Obey Jesus

22 [a]Now it happened, on a certain day,
that He got into a boat with His disciples. And He said to them, "Let us
cross over to the other side of the
lake." And they launched out.
23 But as they sailed He fell asleep.
And a windstorm came down on the
lake, and they were filling *with water,*
and were in [1]jeopardy.
24 And they came to Him and awoke
Him, saying, "Master, Master, we are
perishing!" Then He arose and rebuked the wind and the raging of the
water. And they ceased, and there was
a calm.
25 But He said to them, [a]"Where is
your *faith?" And they were afraid,
and marveled, saying to one another,
[b]"Who can this be? For He commands
even the winds and water, and they
obey Him!"

A Demon-Possessed Man Healed

26 [a]Then they sailed to the country of
the [1]Gadarenes, which is opposite Galilee.
27 And when He stepped out on the
land, there met Him a certain man
from the city who had demons [1]for a
long time. And he wore no clothes, nor
did he live in a house but in the tombs.
28 When he saw Jesus, he [a]cried out,
fell down before Him, and with a loud
voice said, [b]"What have I to do with
[c]You, Jesus, Son of the Most High
God? I beg You, do not torment me!"
29 For He had commanded the unclean
spirit to come out of the man. For it
had often seized him, and he was kept
under guard, bound with chains and
shackles; and he broke the bonds and
was driven by the demon into the wilderness.
30 Jesus asked him, saying, "What is
your name?" And he said, "Legion,"
because many demons had entered
him.
31 And they begged Him that He
would not command them to go out
[a]into the abyss.
32 Now a herd of many [a]swine was
feeding there on the mountain. So they
begged Him that He would permit
them to enter them. And He permitted
them.
33 Then the demons went out of the
man and entered the swine, and the
herd ran violently down the steep place
into the lake and drowned.
34 When those who fed *them* saw what
had happened, they fled and told *it* in
the city and in the country.
35 Then they went out to see what had
happened, and came to Jesus, and
found the man from whom the demons
had departed, [a]sitting at the [b]feet of
Jesus, clothed and in his [c]right* mind.
And they were afraid.
36 They also who had seen *it* told them
by what means he who had been
demon-possessed was [1]healed.

17 [a]Matt. 10:26; Luke 12:2; [1 Cor. 4:5] [b][Eccl. 12:14; 2 Cor. 5:10]
18 [a]Matt. 25:29 [b]Matt. 13:12 [1]*thinks that he has*
19 [a]Ps. 69:8; Matt. 12:46–50; Mark 3:31–35
22 [a]Matt. 8:23–27; Mark 4:36–41
23 [1]*danger*
25 [a]Luke 9:41 [b]Luke 4:36; 5:26 *See WW at Mark 11:22.
26 [a]Matt. 8:28–34; Mark 5:1–17 [1]NU *Gerasenes*
27 [1]NU *and for a long time wore no clothes*
28 [a]Mark 1:26; 9:26 [b]Mark 1:23, 24 [c]Luke 4:41
31 [a]Rom. 10:7; [Rev. 20:1, 3]
32 [a]Lev. 11:7; Deut. 14:8
35 [a][Matt. 11:28] [b]Matt. 28:9; Mark 7:25; Luke 10:39; 17:16; John 11:32 [c][2 Tim. 1:7] *See WW at Mark 5:15.
36 [1]*delivered*

KINGDOM DYNAMICS

8:36 The Healing of Spirit, Soul, and Body, DIVINE HEALING. The Greek word *sozo* ("heal, save, make well or whole") appears in this chapter, offering Luke's unique perspective as a physician. A full range of encounters appears, manifesting Jesus' healing power: 1) The Gadarene, delivered from the demonic powers dominating him, is "healed," freed of evil powers that countermanded his own rational mind and physical actions. 2) The woman with the issue of blood (vv. 43–48) touches the hem of Jesus' garment, and Jesus says, "Your faith has made you well." 3) In v. 50, after being told the little girl is dead, Jesus declares: "Only believe, and she will be made well." 4) In v. 12, as Jesus explains the parable of the Sower, the word "saved" is used of one's restored

(*cont. on next page*)

8:19–21 See notes on Matt. 12:46–50; Mark 3:31–35.
8:22–25 See notes on Matt. 8:24–27; Mark 4:40.
8:26–39 See notes on Matt. 8:28–32; Mark 5:1–20.

(cont. from preceding page)
relationship with God through faith. Luke's precise account offers a complete picture of the Savior's concern to restore every part of man's life: (a) our relationship with God the Father; (b) our broken personalities and bondages; (c) our physical health; and (d) ultimately our rescue from death itself at the Resurrection. Jesus Christ is the Savior of the whole man.

(Luke 5:16–26/Luke 10:8, 9) N.V.

37 [a]Then the whole multitude of the
surrounding region of the [1]Gadarenes
[b]asked Him to [c]depart from them, for
they were *seized with great [d]fear. And
He got into the boat and returned.
38 Now [a]the man from whom the demons had departed begged Him that
he might be with Him. But Jesus sent
him away, saying,
39 "Return to your own house, and tell
what great things God has done for
you." And he went his way and proclaimed throughout the whole city
what great things Jesus had done for
him.

A Girl Restored to Life and a Woman Healed

40 So it was, when Jesus returned, that
the multitude welcomed Him, for they
were all waiting for Him.
41 [a]And behold, there came a man
named Jairus, and he was a ruler of
the synagogue. And he fell down at
Jesus' feet and begged Him to come
to his house,
42 for he had an only daughter about
twelve years of age, and she [a]was dying. But as He went, the multitudes
thronged Him.
43 [a]Now a woman, having a [b]flow of
blood for twelve years, who had spent
all her livelihood on physicians and
could not be *healed by any,
44 came from behind and [a]touched the
border of His garment. And immediately her flow of blood stopped.
45 And Jesus said, "Who touched
Me?" When all denied it, Peter [1]and
those with him said, "Master, the multitudes throng and press You, [2]and You
say, 'Who touched Me?'"
46 But Jesus said, "Somebody touched
Me, for I perceived [a]power going out
from Me."
47 Now when the woman saw that she
was not hidden, she came trembling;
and falling down before Him, she declared to Him in the presence of all the
people the reason she had touched Him
and how she was healed immediately.
48 And He said to her, "Daughter,
[1]be of good cheer; [a]your faith has made
you well. [b]Go in peace."
49 [a]While He was still speaking, someone came from the ruler of the synagogue's *house,* saying to him, "Your
daughter is dead. Do not trouble the
[1]Teacher."
50 But when Jesus heard *it,* He answered him, saying, "Do not be afraid;
[a]only believe, and she will be made
well."
51 When He came into the house, He
permitted no one to go [1]in except
[2]Peter, James, and John, and the father
and mother of the girl.
52 Now all wept and mourned for her;
but He said, [a]"Do not weep; she is not
dead, [b]but sleeping."
53 And they ridiculed Him, knowing
that she was dead.
54 But He [1]put them all outside, took
her by the hand and called, saying,
"Little girl, [a]arise."
55 Then her spirit returned, and she
arose immediately. And He commanded that she be given *something*
to eat.
56 And her parents were astonished,
but [a]He charged them to tell no one
what had happened.

Sending Out the Twelve

9 Then [a]He called His twelve disciples together and [b]gave them
power and authority over all demons,
and to cure diseases.
2 [a]He sent them to preach the kingdom of God and to heal the sick.

KINGDOM DYNAMICS

9:1, 2 Authority for Ministry, MINISTRY OF THE KINGDOM. Luke shows the flow of power of Jesus the King, who extends the delivering and benevolent rule of the kingdom of God over hell's works (demon power) and human hurt (disease). The order of ministry that began with Jesus (8:1) continues to be exercised by His disciples as He trained them for ministry (9:1, 2), and later will issue in the same type of ministry in the church as it spreads the gospel message (Acts

37 [a]Matt. 8:34 [b]Mark 1:24; Luke 4:34 [c]Job 21:14; Acts 16:39 [d]Luke 5:26 [1]NU *Gerasenes* *See WW at 2 Cor. 5:14.
38 [a]Mark 5:18–20
41 [a]Matt. 9:18–26; Mark 5:22–43
42 [a]Luke 7:2
43 [a]Matt. 9:20 [b]Luke 15:19–22 *See WW at Matt. 12:22.
44 [a]Mark 6:56; Luke 5:13
45 [1]NU omits *and those with him* [2]NU omits the rest of v. 45.
46 [a]Mark 5:30; Luke 6:19
48 [a]Mark 5:34; Luke 7:50 [b]John 8:11 [1]NU omits *be of good cheer*
49 [a]Mark 5:35 [1]NU adds *anymore*
50 [a][Mark 11:22–24]
51 [1]NU adds *with Him* [2]NU, M *Peter, John, and James*
52 [a]Luke 7:13 [b][John 11:11, 13]
54 [a]Luke 7:14; John 11:43 [1]NU omits *put them all outside*
56 [a]Matt. 8:4; 9:30; Mark 5:43

CHAPTER 9

1 [a]Matt. 10:1, 2; Mark 3:13; 6:7 [b]Mark 16:17, 18; [John 14:12]
2 [a]Matt. 10:7, 8; Mark 6:12; Luke 10:1, 9

8:41–56 See notes on Matt. 9:18–34; Mark 5:22–43.
9:1–6 Jesus gives the **disciples** the **authority** to use the **power** He transfers to them. See notes on Matt. 10:1–15; Mark 6:7–13.

8:4–12). This gospel throbs with confidence in the full transparency of power and authority for ministry by Jesus to His disciples, then and now:

- We may expect victory over the powers of darkness and their operations (10:19).
- We are assigned to "do business" as authorized representatives of our Lord until He returns (19:13).
- We are promised the Father's pleasure "to give" us the kingdom, that is, to supply us with His peace and power (12:32).

Dominion over evil has been given, but we can expect to see spiritual breakthrough to the degree we receive and apply that authority in prayer, preaching, teaching, and personal ministry.
(Mark 1:15/Luke 11:2–4) J.W.H.

3 [a]And He said to them, "Take nothing for the journey, neither staffs nor bag nor bread nor money; and do not have two tunics apiece.
4 [a]"Whatever house you enter, stay there, and from there depart.
5 [a]"And whoever will not receive you, when you go out of that city, [b]shake off the very dust from your feet as a testimony against them."
6 [a]So they departed and went through the towns, preaching the gospel and healing everywhere.

Herod Seeks to See Jesus

7 [a]Now Herod the tetrarch heard of all that was done by Him; and he was perplexed, because it was said by some that John had risen from the dead,
8 and by some that Elijah had appeared, and by others that one of the old prophets had risen again.
9 Herod said, "John I have beheaded, but who is this of whom I hear such things?" [a]So he sought to see Him.

Feeding the Five Thousand

10 [a]And the apostles, when they had returned, told Him all that they had done. [b]Then He took them and went aside privately into a deserted place belonging to the city called Bethsaida.
11 But when the multitudes knew *it,* they followed Him; and He received them and spoke to them about the kingdom of God, and healed those who had need of healing.
12 [a]When the day began to wear away, the twelve came and said to Him, "Send the multitude away, that they may go into the surrounding towns and country, and lodge and get provisions; for we are in a deserted place here."
13 But He said to them, "You give them something to eat." And they said, "We have no more than five loaves and two fish, unless we go and buy food for all these people."
14 For there were about five thousand men. Then He said to His *disciples, "Make them sit down in groups of fifty."
15 And they did so, and made them all sit down.
16 Then He took the five loaves and the two fish, and looking up to heaven, He [a]blessed and broke *them,* and gave *them* to the disciples to set before the multitude.
17 So they all ate and were [1]filled, and twelve baskets of the leftover fragments were taken up by them.

Peter Confesses Jesus as the Christ

18 [a]And it happened, as He was alone praying, *that* His disciples joined Him, and He asked them, saying, "Who do the crowds say that I am?"
19 So they answered and said, [a]"John the Baptist, but some *say* Elijah; and others *say* that one of the old prophets has risen again."
20 He said to them, "But who do you say that I am?" [a]Peter answered and said, "The Christ of God."

Jesus Predicts His Death and Resurrection

21 [a]And He strictly warned and commanded them to tell this to no one,
22 saying, [a]"The Son of Man must suffer many things, and be rejected by the elders and chief priests and scribes, and be killed, and be raised the third day."

Take Up the Cross and Follow Him

23 [a]Then He said to *them* all, "If any- 7
one desires to come after Me, let him

3 [a]Matt. 10:9–15; Mark 6:8–11; Luke 10:4–12; 22:35
4 [a]Matt. 10:11; Mark 6:10
5 [a]Matt. 10:14 [b]Luke 10:11; Acts 13:51
6 [a]Mark 6:12; Luke 8:1
7 [a]Matt. 14:1, 2; Mark 6:14
9 [a]Luke 23:8
10 [a]Mark 6:30 [b]Matt. 14:13
12 [a]Matt. 14:15; Mark 6:35; John 6:1, 5
14 *See WW at Matt. 10:1.
16 [a]Luke 22:19; 24:30
17 [1]*satisfied*
18 [a]Matt. 16:13–16; Mark 8:27–29
19 [a]Matt. 14:2
20 [a]Matt. 16:16; John 6:68, 69
21 [a]Matt. 8:4; 16:20; Mark 8:30
22 [a]Matt. 16:21; 17:22; Luke 18:31–33; 23:46; 24:46
23 [a]Matt. 10:38; 16:24; Mark 8:34; Luke 14:27

9:9 Herod's intent was evil (see 13:31). He finally got to see Jesus on the day of the Lord's death (23:6–12).
9:10 Jesus withdrew to rest, to instruct His disciples, and to avoid confrontation with Herod. **Bethsaida** was on the northeastern shore of the lake.
9:12–17 See notes on John 6:22–40.
9:18–21 See notes on Matt. 16:13–20.
9:22 See notes on Matt. 16:21–23.
9:23–25 See section 7 of Truth-In-Action through the Synoptics at the end of Luke.
9:23–26 See notes on Matt. 16:24–27. Luke adds the word **daily** to the Lord's requirement of cross-bearing, indicating

deny himself, and take up his cross
[1]daily, and follow Me.
24 [a]"For whoever desires to save his
life will lose it, but whoever loses his
life for My sake will save it.
25 [a]"For what profit is it to a man if
he gains the whole world, and is himself destroyed or lost?
26 [a]"For whoever is ashamed of Me
and My words, of him the Son of Man
will be [b]ashamed when He comes in
His *own* glory, and *in His* Father's, and
of the holy angels.

Jesus Transfigured on the Mount

27 [a]"But I tell you truly, there are some
standing here who shall not taste death
till they see the kingdom of God."
28 [a]Now it came to pass, about eight
days after these sayings, that He took
Peter, John, and James and went up
on the mountain to pray.
29 As He prayed, the appearance of
His face was altered, and His robe *became* white *and* glistening.
30 And behold, two men talked with
Him, who were [a]Moses and [b]Elijah,
31 who appeared in glory and spoke
of His [1]decease which He was about
to accomplish at Jerusalem.
32 But Peter and those with him
[a]were heavy with sleep; and when they
were fully awake, they saw His glory
and the two men who stood with
Him.
33 Then it happened, as they were
parting from Him, *that* Peter said to
Jesus, "Master, it is good for us to be
here; and let us make three [1]taberna-
cles: one for You, one for Moses, and
one for Elijah"—not knowing what he
said.
34 While he was saying this, a cloud
came and overshadowed them; and
they were fearful as they entered the
[a]cloud.
35 And a voice came out of the cloud,
saying, [a]"This is [1]My beloved Son.
[b]Hear Him!"
36 When the voice had ceased, Jesus
was found alone. [a]But they kept quiet,
and told no one in those days any of
the things they had seen.

23 [1]M omits *daily*
24 [a]Matt. 10:39; Luke 17:33; [John 12:25]
25 [a]Matt. 16:26; Mark 8:36; [Luke 16:19–31]; Acts 1:18, 25
26 [a][Rom. 1:16] [b]Matt. 10:33; Mark 8:38; Luke 12:9; 2 Tim. 2:12
27 [a]Matt. 16:28; Mark 9:1; Acts 7:55, 56; Rev. 20:4
28 [a]Matt. 17:1–8; Mark 9:2–8
30 [a]Heb. 11:23–29 [b]2 Kin. 2:1–11
31 [1]Death, lit. *departure*
32 [a]Dan. 8:18; 10:9; Matt. 26:40, 43; Mark 14:40
33 [1]*tents*
34 [a]Ex. 13:21; Acts 1:9
35 [a]Ps. 2:7; [Is. 42:1; Matt. 3:17; 12:18]; Mark 1:11; Luke 3:22 [b]Acts 3:22 [1]NU *My Son, the Chosen One*
36 [a]Matt. 17:9; Mark 9:9
37 [a]Matt. 17:14–18; Mark 9:14–27
39 *See WW at Rom. 16:20.
41 [1]*unbelieving* [2]*put up with* *See WW at 2 Thess. 1:4.
44 [a]Matt. 17:22; Mark 10:33; 14:53; Luke 22:54; John 18:12
45 [a]Mark 9:32; Luke 2:50; 18:34

A Boy Is Healed

37 [a]Now it happened on the next day,
when they had come down from the
mountain, that a great multitude met
Him.
38 Suddenly a man from the multitude
cried out, saying, "Teacher, I implore
You, look on my son, for he is my only
child.
39 "And behold, a spirit seizes him,
and he suddenly cries out; it convulses
him so that he foams *at the mouth;*
and it departs from him with great difficulty, *bruising him.
40 "So I implored Your disciples to
cast it out, but they could not."
41 Then Jesus answered and said, "O
[1]faithless and perverse generation,
how long shall I be with you and
[2]bear* with you? Bring your son here."
42 And as he was still coming, the demon threw him down and convulsed
him. Then Jesus rebuked the unclean
spirit, healed the child, and gave him
back to his father.

Jesus Again Predicts His Death

43 And they were all amazed at the
majesty of God. But while everyone
marveled at all the things which Jesus
did, He said to His disciples,

WORD WEALTH

9:43 majesty, *megaleiotes* (meg-al-eye-*ot*-ace); Strong's *#3168:* Compare "megalomania." Sublimity, grandeur, glory, magnificence, splendor, superbness, greatness. In Acts 19:27, the silversmith Demetrius expressed a fear that the preaching of Paul would destroy the *magnificence* of the goddess Diana. Here and in 2 Pet. 1:16 the word magnifies the Lord and His far-surpassing greatness.

44 [a]"Let these words sink down into
your ears, for the Son of Man is about
to be betrayed into the hands of men."
45 [a]But they did not understand this
saying, and it was hidden from them
so that they did not perceive it; and
they were afraid to ask Him about this
saying.

a progressive and continuous renouncing of one's natural self-centeredness (v. 23).

9:27–36 See notes on Matt. 16:28—17:9. Luke reports that the topic of conversation with Moses and Elijah was Jesus' **decease** (v. 31). The experience confirmed Jesus in His decision to go to Jerusalem to suffer. The fulfillment of God's plan comes through the Cross. Since the word for "decease" is literally "exodus," suggesting Jesus' departure from the world, the conversation probably included a discussion of the Resurrection and the Ascension as well as the Crucifixion. The appearance of Moses and Elijah with Jesus signifies that the Law and the Prophets support Jesus in His messianic mission.

9:37–42 See notes on Mark 9:14–29.

9:43–45 Suffering and messiahship seemed so incompatible that the disciples could not connect them.

Who Is the Greatest?

8 46 [a]Then a *dispute arose among them
as to which of them would be greatest.
47 And Jesus, [a]perceiving the thought
of their heart, took a [b]little child and
set him by Him,
48 and said to them, [a]"Whoever receives this little child in My name receives Me; and [b]whoever receives Me
[c]receives Him who sent Me. [d]For he
who is least among you all will be
great."

Jesus Forbids Sectarianism

49 [a]Now John answered and said,
"Master, we saw someone casting out
demons in Your name, and we forbade
him because he does not follow with
us."
50 But Jesus said to him, "Do not forbid *him,* for [a]he who is not against
[1]us is on [2]our side."

A Samaritan Village Rejects the Savior

51 Now it came to pass, when the time
had come for [a]Him to be received up,
that He steadfastly set His face to go
to Jerusalem,
52 and sent messengers before His
face. And as they went, they entered
a village of the Samaritans, to prepare
for Him.
53 But [a]they did not receive Him, because His face was *set* for the journey
to Jerusalem.
54 And when His disciples [a]James and
John saw *this,* they said, "Lord, do You
want us to command fire to come down
from heaven and consume them,
[1]just as [b]Elijah did?"
55 But He turned and rebuked them,
[1]and said, "You do not know what
manner of [a]spirit you are of.
56 [1]"For [a]the Son of Man did not come
to **destroy** men's lives but to save
them." And they went to another village.

WORD WEALTH

9:56 destroy, *apollumi* (ap-*ol*-loo-mee); Strong's *#622:* To lay waste, destroy utterly, disintegrate. The NT often uses the word to describe spiritual destitution. Destruction for the sinner does not result in annihilation or extinction. It is not the loss of being, but of well-being.

The Cost of Discipleship

57 [a]Now it happened as they jour- 7
neyed on the road, *that* someone said

46 [a]Matt. 18:1–5 *See WW at Luke 2:35.
47 [a]Matt. 9:4 [b]Luke 18:17
48 [a]Matt. 18:5 [b]John 12:44 [c]John 13:20 [d]Eph. 3:8
49 [a]Mark 9:38–40
50 [a]Luke 11:23 [1]NU *you* [2]NU *your*
51 [a]Mark 16:19
53 [a]John 4:4, 9
54 [a]Mark 3:17 [b]2 Kin. 1:10, 12 [1]NU omits *just as Elijah did*
55 [a][2 Tim. 1:7] [1]NU omits the rest of v. 55.
56 [a]John 3:17; 12:47 [1]NU omits *For the Son of Man did not come to destroy men's lives but to save them.*
57 [a]Matt. 8:19–22

Jewish Pilgrimage from Galilee to Jerusalem. The popular route passed directly through Samaria. However, some pious Jews took an alternate route through Jericho to avoid Samaria.

9:46–48 See section 8 of Truth-In-Action through the Synoptics at the end of Luke.
9:46–48 See notes on Matt. 18:1–5; Mark 9:33–37.
9:49, 50 See notes on Mark 9:38–40.
9:51 Received up: The term refers to the entire sequence of events: suffering, death, resurrection, and finally ascension. This verse begins a new section in Luke's gospel, Jesus' resolute journey to Jerusalem.
9:52 The Jews and **the Samaritans** had been enemies for centuries. Pilgrims to Jerusalem ordinarily avoided Samaria.
9:53 They were inhospitable, not only because Jesus was a Jew, but because He did not recognize the Samaritan temple on Mt. Gerizim.
9:54 The disciples wish to use the authority and power, given to them for their mission (v. 1), for destruction. They demonstrate real faith but it is insensitive and is utterly out of character with Jesus' objective of saving people (v. 56).
9:57–62 See section 7 of Truth-In-Action through the Synoptics at the end of Luke.
9:57, 58 The three candidates for discipleship illustrate the demands involved in following Jesus. The first incident teaches that an emotional enthusiasm that has not considered the cost of abandoning material security is insufficient.

to Him, "Lord, I will follow You wherever You go."
58 And Jesus said to him, "Foxes have
holes and birds of the air *have* nests,
but the Son of Man [a]has nowhere to
lay *His* head."
59 [a]Then He said to another, "Follow
Me." But he said, "Lord, let me first
go and bury my father."
60 Jesus said to him, "Let the dead
bury their own dead, but you go and
preach the kingdom of God."
61 And another also said, "Lord,
[a]I will follow You, but let me first go
and bid them farewell who are at my
house."
62 But Jesus said to him, "No one, having put his hand to the plow, and looking back, is [a]fit for the kingdom of
God."

The Seventy Sent Out

10 After these things the Lord appointed [1]seventy others also,
and [a]sent* them two by two before His
face into every city and place where
He Himself was about to go.
2 Then He said to them, [a]"The harvest truly *is* great, but the laborers *are*
few; therefore [b]pray the Lord of the
harvest to send out laborers into His
harvest.
3 "Go your way; [a]behold, I send you
out as lambs among wolves.
4 [a]"Carry neither money bag, knapsack, nor sandals; and [b]greet no one
along the road.
5 [a]"But whatever house you enter,
first say, 'Peace to this house.'
6 "And if a son of peace is there, your
peace will rest on it; if not, it will return
to you.
7 [a]"And remain in the same house,
[b]eating and drinking such things as
they give, for [c]the laborer is worthy

58 [a]Luke 2:7; 8:23
59 [a]Matt. 8:21, 22
61 [a]1 Kin. 19:20
62 [a]2 Tim. 4:10

CHAPTER 10

1 [a]Matt. 10:1; Mark 6:7 [1]NU *seventy-two others* *See WW at John 20:21.
2 [a]Matt. 9:37, 38; John 4:35 [b]2 Thess. 3:1; [1 Cor. 3:9]
3 [a]Matt. 10:16
4 [a]Matt. 10:9–14; Mark 6:8–11; Luke 9:3–5 [b]2 Kin. 4:29
5 [a]1 Sam. 25:6; Matt. 10:12
7 [a]Matt. 10:11 [b]1 Cor. 10:27 [c][Matt. 10:10]; 1 Cor. 9:4–8; 1 Tim. 5:18

of his wages. Do not go from house to
house.
8 "Whatever city you enter, and they
receive you, eat such things as are set
before you.
9 [a]"And heal the sick there, and say
to them, [b]'The kingdom of God has
come near to you.'

KINGDOM DYNAMICS

10:8, 9 The Disciples Instructed to Heal, DIVINE HEALING. Jesus' instructions to the 70 sent out in the surrounding countryside are direct and clear: "Heal the sick there, and say to them, 'The kingdom of God has come near to you.' " The coming of God's kingdom and the ministry of healing are not separated. The same point is made with the 12 disciples in 9:1, 2. The authority to heal has been given to Jesus' disciples as they are willing to exercise the privileges of being messengers and participants in the kingdom of God. This ministry should not be divided from the complete declaration of the coming of the kingdom. The Holy Spirit delights to confirm the presence of the kingdom by glorifying the King's power, verifying Jesus Christ's working through the ministry of healing. This ministry of healing is experienced throughout the whole of the Book of Acts, and in James 5:13–16 is declared as one of the responsibilities of eldership in a local congregation.

(Luke 8:36/Luke 17:12–19) N.V.

10 "But whatever city you enter, and
they do not receive you, go out into its
streets and say,
11 [a]'The very dust of your city which
clings to [1]us we wipe off against you.
Nevertheless know this, that the kingdom of God has come near you.'
12 [1]"But I say to you that [a]it will be
more tolerable in that Day for Sodom
than for that city.

9 [a]Mark 3:15 [b]Matt. 3:2; 10:7; Luke 10:11
11 [a]Matt. 10:14; Mark 6:11; Luke 9:5; Acts 13:51 [1]NU *our feet*
12 [a]Gen. 19:24–28; Lam. 4:6; Matt. 10:15; 11:24; Mark 6:11 [1]NU, M omit *But*

9:59, 60 Loyalty to Christ takes precedence over all lesser loyalties. The man was offering the excuse that he must care for his father until he died. The spiritually **dead** are to **bury their own** physically **dead,** but followers of Christ have the urgent task of proclaiming the good news of life in Him. This does not argue for insensitivity or disrespect with reference to the propriety of funerals. It is a lesson against procrastination.

9:61, 62 This should not be construed as a teaching on backsliding or losing one's salvation. Jesus focuses on the truth that service for His enterprise demands undivided attention. **Is** [not] **fit for the kingdom of God** means that halfhearted discipleship eliminates one from God's maximum use. This may be what Paul warns against in 1 Cor. 3:12–15.

10:1–11 This may have been a deliberate and dramatic way of emphasizing the universality of Jesus' mission, since the Jews considered 70 to be the number of the Gentile nations (see Gen. 10). The instructions given are similar to those given to the 12 disciples (see Matt. 10:5–14).

10:2 Harvest: Since the messianic harvest is already in process, time is of the utmost importance (v. 4), and the consequences of rejection are final (vv. 11, 13–16).

10:4 Greet no one: The instructions underscore the urgency of the mission, in that ordinary Near Eastern greetings, which tend to be drawn out, are not to deter them from their task.

10:11 The very dust: Before reentering Jewish territory, the dust of heathen lands was carefully removed, as something defiling. The action declares that the place that rejects them is heathen, that is, unclean.

10:12 Even though **Sodom** represented the most wicked of Gentile cities, its judgment will be less severe than for those cities that reject the messengers of Jesus.

Woe to the Impenitent Cities

13 [a]"Woe to you, Chorazin! Woe to
you, Bethsaida! [b]For if the mighty
works which were done in you had
been done in Tyre and Sidon, they
would have *repented long ago, sitting
in sackcloth and ashes.
14 "But it will be more tolerable for
Tyre and Sidon at the judgment than
for you.
15 [a]"And you, Capernaum, [1]who are
[b]exalted* to heaven, [c]will be brought
down to Hades.
16 [a]"He who hears you hears Me,
[b]he who rejects you rejects Me, and
[c]he who rejects Me rejects Him who
sent Me."

The Seventy Return with Joy

17 Then [a]the [1]seventy returned with
joy, saying, "Lord, even the demons
are subject to us in Your name."
18 And He said to them, [a]"I saw Satan
fall like lightning from heaven.
19 "Behold, [a]I give you the authority
to trample on serpents and scorpions,
and over all the power of the enemy,
and nothing shall by any means *hurt
you.
20 "Nevertheless do not rejoice in this,
that the spirits are subject to you, but
[1]rather rejoice because [a]your names
are written in heaven."

Jesus Rejoices in the Spirit

21 [a]In that hour Jesus rejoiced in the
Spirit and said, "I thank You, Father,
Lord of heaven and earth, that You
have hidden these things from *the* wise
and prudent and revealed them to
babes. Even so, Father, for so it seemed
good in Your sight.
22 [a]"All[1] things have been delivered to
Me by My Father, and [b]no one knows
who the Son is except the Father, and
who the Father is except the Son, and
the one to whom the Son wills to reveal
Him."
23 Then He turned to *His* disciples and
said privately, [a]"Blessed *are* the eyes
which see the things you see;
24 "for I tell you [a]that many prophets
and kings have desired to see what you
see, and have not seen *it*, and to hear
what you hear, and have not heard *it*."

The Parable of the Good Samaritan

25 And behold, a certain [1]lawyer stood 3
up and tested Him, saying, [a]"Teacher,
what shall I do to inherit eternal life?"
26 He said to him, "What is written in
the law? What is your reading *of it*?"
27 So he answered and said, [a]"'*You
shall love the* LORD *your God with all
your heart, with all your *soul, with all
your strength, and with all your mind,*'
and [b]'*your neighbor as yourself.*'"
28 And He said to him, "You have answered rightly; do this and [a]you will
live."
29 But he, *wanting to [a]justify himself,
said to Jesus, "And who is my neighbor?"
30 Then Jesus answered and said: "A
certain *man* went down from Jerusalem to Jericho, and fell among [1]thieves,

13 [a]Matt. 11:21–23 [b]Ezek. 3:6 *See WW at Matt. 3:2. **15** [a]Matt. 11:23 [b]Is. 14:13–15 [c]Ezek. 26:20 [1]NU *will you be exalted to heaven? You will be thrust down to Hades!* *See WW at James 4:10. **16** [a]John 13:20 [b]1 Thess. 4:8 [c]John 5:23 **17** [a]Luke 10:1 [1]NU *seventy-two* **18** [a]John 12:31 **19** [a]Mark 16:18 *See WW at Acts 25:10. **20** [a]Is. 4:3 [1]NU, M omit *rather* **21** [a]Matt. 11:25–27 **22** [a]John 3:35; 5:27; 17:2 [b][John 1:18; 6:44, 46] [1]M *And turning to the disciples He said, "All* **23** [a]Matt. 13:16, 17 **24** [a]1 Pet. 1:10, 11 **25** [a]Matt. 19:16–19; 22:35 [1]*expert in the law* **27** [a]Deut. 6:5 [b]Lev. 19:18 *See WW at Luke 21:19. **28** [a]Ezek. 20:11, 13, 21 **29** [a]Luke 16:15 *See WW at Matt. 8:2.

30 [1]*robbers*

10:13, 14 Greater privilege means greater responsibility. Heavier condemnation comes upon those who have light but reject it.
10:15 **Capernaum** was the headquarters for Jesus' Galilean ministry, but rejected Him. **Hades,** the realm of the dead, suggests the total desolation Jesus prophesied would come upon the area. Today Capernaum is deserted.
10:17 The **name** of Jesus signifies His authority.
10:18 This was not a vision in which Jesus **saw Satan** cast out of **heaven;** rather, He saw in their ministry the present and ultimate defeat of Satan.
10:19 **Serpents and scorpions** are symbols of spiritual enemies and demonic power, over which Jesus has given His followers power.
10:20 Even though Christians may rejoice in charismatic operations realized through the name of Jesus, a greater occasion for rejoicing is the registration of their names in **heaven,** both the grounds of their authority over demons and the certainty of their eternal destiny in a heavenly home.
10:21 The successful mission of the 70 caused Jesus to burst forth in a spontaneous demonstration of worship **in the Spirit** (the Greek word suggests "shouting and leaping with joy"). He also expressed gratitude that God's revelation is given to the simple and not to those, particularly the scribes, who consider themselves **wise** in religious matters.
10:22 Jesus has an immediate and exclusive relationship with the Father, and therefore He is able to reveal God to whom He chooses.
10:23, 24 Jesus contrasts the disciples' privileged position with those of former prophets and kings.
10:25–28 See section 3 of Truth-In-Action through the Synoptics at the end of Luke.
10:27 The lawyer gives the rabbinic summary of OT law (Deut. 6:5; Lev. 19:18).
10:29 The lawyer's question suggests that there must be some to whom the obligation to love does not apply, thus seeking to set a limit on his duty to love. It also emphasizes the worthiness of the object of love rather than the attitude of the one who is to do the loving.
10:30–35 While the lawyer quibbles over a definition, Jesus teaches that love is not a matter of theoretical discussion, but of practical demonstration. Professional religionists, exemplified by the **priest** and the **Levite,** could argue the question with great skill. However, the **Samaritan,** though despised as a man of a mongrel race and of a polluted religion, is commended because he did not theorize but acted.

who stripped him of his clothing,
wounded *him,* and departed, leaving
him half dead.
31 "Now by chance a certain priest
came down that road. And when he
saw him, [a]he passed by on the other
side.
32 "Likewise a Levite, when he arrived
at the place, came and looked, and
passed by on the other side.
33 "But a certain [a]Samaritan, as he
journeyed, came where he was. And
when he saw him, he had [b]com-
passion.*

KINGDOM DYNAMICS

10:33 Help from a Despised Source, HUMAN WORTH. There was distinct racial strain between Jews and Samaritans (John 4:9). They did not frequently interact with one another; and in some cases, outright hostility and hatred existed. But Jesus, early in His ministry, taught the Samaritans the truth of God. He ministered to the "woman of Samaria" and to the people of Samaria (John 4:4–42). Here in this parable the source of assistance was not a kinsman or fellow citizen of Israel but a despised Samaritan. We are reminded that one of the great tragedies of prejudice is that it may separate one from a potential source of assistance. The compassion of the Samaritan was all the more commendable in that the person he assisted, under normal circumstances, probably would not have even spoken to him. Christ has come to break down such division.

(James 2:1–9/Matt. 27:32) C.B.

34 "So he went to *him* and bandaged
his wounds, pouring on oil and wine;
and he set him on his own animal,
brought him to an inn, and took care
of him.
35 "On the next day, [1]when he departed, he took out two [a]denarii, gave
them to the innkeeper, and said to him,
'Take care of him; and whatever more
you spend, when I come again, I will
repay you.'
36 "So which of these three do you
think was neighbor to him who fell
among the thieves?"
37 And he said, "He who showed
*mercy on him." Then Jesus said to
him, [a]"Go and do likewise."

31 [a]Ps. 38:11
33 [a]John 4:9 [b]Luke 15:20 *See WW at Matt. 14:14.
35 [a]Matt. 20:2 [1]NU omits *when he departed*
37 [a]Prov. 14:21; [Matt. 9:13; 12:7] *See WW at 2 Tim. 1:16.
38 [a]John 11:1; 12:2, 3
39 [a][1 Cor. 7:32–40] [b]Luke 8:35; Acts 22:3 [1]NU *the Lord's*
41 [1]NU *the Lord* *See WW at Matt. 6:25.
42 [a][Ps. 27:4; John 6:27]

Mary and Martha Worship and Serve

38 Now it happened as they went that 3
He entered a certain village; and a certain woman named [a]Martha welcomed
Him into her house.
39 And she had a sister called Mary,
[a]who also [b]sat at [1]Jesus' feet and heard
His word.
40 But Martha was distracted with
much serving, and she approached
Him and said, "Lord, do You not care
that my sister has left me to serve
alone? Therefore tell her to help
me."
41 And [1]Jesus answered and said to
her, "Martha, Martha, you are *worried and troubled about many things.
42 "But [a]one thing is needed, and
Mary has chosen that good part,
which will not be taken away from
her."

KINGDOM DYNAMICS

10:38–42 Balancing Devotion and Duty (Martha and Mary), WOMEN. Martha and Mary were sisters who lived in the village of Bethany, a suburb of Jerusalem. It appears Martha was the elder, for v. 38 speaks of Martha's receiving Jesus "into her house." Thus, Martha felt more keenly the domestic responsibilities of keeping house and the demands of providing hospitality. On the occasion Martha complained to Jesus that Mary was not helping her in the kitchen, Jesus gently reminded her that "Mary has chosen that good part"—sitting at His feet (vv. 39–42). Many have tended to distinguish Martha as "the practical one" and Mary as "the spiritual one." However, the Scriptures indicate that Martha also sat at Jesus' feet (v. 39) and that Mary also served (v. 40). Both of these women reveal unique spiritual gifts with which they lovingly served God. They remind us of the importance of balancing personal devotion with practical duties. These are not irreconcilable facts of believing life and should never be allowed to be pitted against one another.

(Luke 8:2/Rom. 16:1) F.L.

10:36 Jesus throws the question back to the lawyer, but changes its emphasis. It is not, "Who *was* the **neighbor?**" but "Who *proved* to be the neighbor?" Love does not consider the worth of its object, but simply responds to human need.

10:38–42 See section 3 of Truth-In-Action through the Synoptics at the end of Luke.

10:40 Distracted: Martha's legitimate concern was to be a proper hostess. Mary's concern was to be a proper disciple (v. 39, "heard His word"). Jesus does not negate Martha's hospitable activities, but is concerned with her distraction, worry, and trouble about many things (v. 41), which cause her to underemphasize the one thing that is needed (v. 42), that is, to hear the word of Jesus.

The Model Prayer

11 Now it came to pass, as He was praying in a certain place, when He ceased, *that* one of His disciples said to Him, "Lord, teach us to pray, as John also taught his disciples."

3 2 So He said to them, "When you pray, say:

[a]Our[1] Father [2]in heaven,
Hallowed be Your name.
Your kingdom come.
[3]Your will be done
On earth as *it is* in heaven.
3 Give us day by day our daily bread.
4 And [a]forgive us our sins,
For we also forgive everyone who is indebted to us.
And do not lead us into temptation,
[1]But deliver us from the evil one."

KINGDOM DYNAMICS

11:2–4 Prayer and Intercession, THE MINISTRY OF THE KINGDOM. Jesus' words "Your kingdom come" are more than a suggestion to pray for a distant millennial day, for everything in this prayer is current. This prayer is not a formula for repetition so much as it is an outline for expansion. Worship is to be longer than a sentence. Petitions are not confined to bread. Forgiveness is to be requested in specifics, not generalities, and prayer for the entry of God's kingdom into present earthborn situations is not accomplished in a momentary utterance. The verb mood and tense of "Your kingdom come" essentially says, "Father, let Your kingdom come here and now!"

Such prayerful intervention is called intercession. Motivation toward such prayer occurs when we recognize the importance Jesus placed on prayer in helping us serve in our roles as "kingdom administrators." Without the intervention of God's kingdom rule through prayer, Earth's circumstances will succumb to inevitable consequences. Earthly scenes of need must be penetrated by God's "will here as in heaven." Either the weakness of man's rule (the flesh) or the viciousness of hell's works (the Devil) will prevail. God's power alone can change things and bring heaven's rule (kingdom) instead, and the honor and the glory for prayer's answers are His. However, the praying is ours to do: unless we ask for the intervention of His kingdom and obey His prayer-lessons, nothing will change. All kingdom ministry begins with, is sustained by, and will triumph through prayer.

(Luke 9:1, 2/Luke 11:20) J.W.H.

CHAPTER 11

2 [a]Matt. 6:9–13 [1]NU omits *Our* [2]NU omits *in heaven* [3]NU omits the rest of v. 2.
4 [a][Eph. 4:32] [1]NU omits *But deliver us from the evil one*

A Friend Comes at Midnight

5 And He said to them, "Which of you shall have a friend, and go to him at midnight and say to him, 'Friend, lend me three loaves;
6 'for a friend of mine has come to me on his journey, and I have nothing to set before him';
7 "and he will answer from within and say, 'Do not trouble me; the door is now shut, and my children are with me in bed; I cannot rise and give to you'?
8 "I say to you, [a]though he will not rise and give to him because he is his friend, yet because of his persistence he will rise and give him as many as he needs.

Keep Asking, Seeking, Knocking

9 [a]"So I say to you, ask, and it will be given to you; [b]seek, and you will find; knock, and it will be opened to you.
10 "For everyone who asks receives, and he who seeks finds, and to him who knocks it will be opened.
11 [a]"If a son asks for [1]bread from any father among you, will he give him a stone? Or if *he asks* for a fish, will he give him a serpent instead of a fish?
12 "Or if he asks for an egg, will he offer him a scorpion?

8 [a][Luke 18:1–5]
9 [a]Ps. 50:14, 15; Jer. 33:3; [Matt. 7:7; 21:22; Mark 11:24; John 15:7; James 1:5, 6; 1 John 3:22; 5:14, 15] [b]Is. 55:6
11 [a]Matt. 7:9 [1]NU omits *bread from any father among you, will he give him a stone? Or if he asks for*

11:1–4 Although Jesus says we are actually to **say** this prayer (v. 2), He does not intend that His prayer be used as a mere rigid ritual, but that it be a guide to prayer as well. This is clear from Matthew's teaching on it. See notes on Matt. 6:9–13.

11:2–4 See section 3 of Truth-In-Action through the Synoptics at the end of Luke.

11:5–10 Jesus teaches **persistence** in prayer, along with a sense of urgency and boldness. He does not suggest that we must overcome God's reluctance to respond to our requests, but that we must be earnest and wholehearted in prayer. The persistence is necessary for our benefit, not for God's.

11:8 Persistence can also be translated importunity, overboldness, or shamelessness.

11:9 The three imperatives are in the Greek present tense, denoting a continuous asking, seeking, and knocking.

11:11–13 Jesus encourages prayer by reminding us of the nature of the One to whom we are praying. He argues from the lesser to the greater. If faulty human parents will meet the real needs of their children, instead of deceiving them with harmful gifts, **how much more** can we expect our **heavenly Father** to bless us with the best gift, **the Holy Spirit,** as well as lesser gifts. Our primary needs are spiritual, and a proper relationship with God through the Holy Spirit is the ground of assurance that He will provide both spiritual and material needs.

13 "If you then, being evil, know how
to give [a]good gifts to your children,
how much more will *your* heavenly Father give the Holy Spirit to those who
*ask Him!"

A House Divided Cannot Stand

14 [a]And He was casting out a demon,
and it was mute. So it was, when the
demon had gone out, that the mute
spoke; and the multitudes marveled.
15 But some of them said, [a]"He casts
out demons by [1]Beelzebub, the ruler
of the demons."
16 Others, testing *Him*, [a]sought from
Him a sign from heaven.
17 [a]But [b]He, knowing their thoughts,
said to them: "Every kingdom divided
against itself is brought to desolation,
and a house *divided* against a house
falls.
18 "If Satan also is divided against
himself, how will his kingdom stand?
Because you say I cast out demons by
Beelzebub.

KINGDOM DYNAMICS

11:17, 18 36. How Is It Possible That a Kingdom Can Be Destroyed?, SPIRITUAL ANSWERS. For the answer to this and other probing questions about God and the power life in His kingdom, see the study article "Spiritual Answers to Hard Questions," which begins on page 1996. P.R.

19 "And if I cast out demons by Beelzebub, by whom do your sons cast *them*
out? Therefore they will be your
judges.
20 "But if I cast out demons [a]with the
finger of God, surely the kingdom of
God has come upon you.

KINGDOM DYNAMICS

11:20 Casting Out Demons, MINISTRY OF THE KINGDOM. Jesus indicates that one signal of a true ministry of the kingdom includes the casting out of demons. He models this in His ministry and promises it as a timeless sign confirming the preaching of the gospel of the kingdom (Mark 16:17). He also balances this aspect of ministry for His disciples, who at first were amazed to experience such power, exclaiming, "Lord, even the demons are subject to us in Your name" (Luke 10:17). While affirming the place and value of this ministry (vv. 18, 19), Jesus still reminds them of a foundational truth. Power over demons is not the central reason for rejoicing; rather, their salvation has registered them as heaven's representatives. That is the real grounds for authority in the spiritual realm.

(Luke 11:2–4/Acts 1:3–8) J.W.H.

13 [a]James 1:17 *See WW at Matt. 7:7. **14** [a]Matt. 9:32–34; 12:22, 24 **15** [a]Matt. 9:34; 12:24 [1]NU, M *Beelzebul* **16** [a]Matt. 12:38; 16:1; Mark 8:11 **17** [a]Matt. 12:25–29; Mark 3:23–27 [b]Matt. 9:4; John 2:25 **20** [a]Ex. 8:19

21 [a]Matt. 12:29; Mark 3:27 **22** [a][Is. 53:12; Col. 2:15] [1]*plunder* **23** [a]Matt. 12:30; Mark 9:40 **24** [a]Matt. 12:43–45; Mark 1:27; 3:11; 5:13; Acts 5:16; 8:7 **25** *See WW at Matt. 25:7. **26** [a]John 5:14; [Heb. 6:4–6; 10:26; 2 Pet. 2:20]

21 [a]"When a strong man, fully armed,
guards his own palace, his goods are
in peace.
22 "But [a]when a stronger than he
comes upon him and overcomes him,
he takes from him all his armor in
which he trusted, and divides his
[1]spoils.
23 [a]"He who is not with Me is against
Me, and he who does not gather with
Me scatters.

An Unclean Spirit Returns

24 [a]"When an unclean spirit goes out **11**
of a man, he goes through dry places,
seeking rest; and finding none, he says,
'I will return to my house from which
I came.'
25 "And when he comes, he finds *it*
swept and *put in order.
26 "Then he goes and takes with *him*
seven other spirits more wicked than
himself, and they enter and dwell
there; and [a]the last *state* of that man
is worse than the first."

Keeping the Word

27 And it happened, as He spoke these
things, that a certain woman from the
crowd raised her voice and said to

11:14–23 See notes on Matt. 12:24–37.
11:19 The Pharisees condemn Jesus, while they praise their own disciples for engaging in the same activity.
11:20 The finger of God is a figure of speech for the power of God (see Ex. 8:19; 31:18; Ps. 8:3).
11:21, 22 Satan is **strong,** but Jesus is **stronger**.
11:23 In a spiritual conflict neutrality is impossible.
11:24–26 See section 11 of Truth-In-Action through the Synoptics at the end of Luke.
11:24–26 The application of this parable is explicit in Matt. 12:43, wherein Jesus likens the present "generation" (that is, circumstance He addresses) to the man who has been exorcised. He is warning that a situation confronted by His exorcising presence is liable to a worse state than before if there is no fundamental reform. Jesus teaches the peril of an empty life. The vacuum left by the departure of an evil spirit must be filled with the Holy Spirit, or else the individual is open to worse demonic activity. The immediate application of the teaching is to those who lack the spiritual discernment to recognize Jesus as the Savior. In rejecting Him they have nothing left but empty rites and ceremonies, making them even more susceptible to Satan's deception (see note on Matt. 12:43–45).
11:27, 28 It may indeed be a privilege to have a close human

Him, [a]"Blessed *is* the womb that bore
You, and *the* breasts which nursed
You!"
28 But He said, [a]"More than that,
blessed *are* those who hear the word
of God and keep it!"

Seeking a Sign

29 [a]And while the crowds were thickly
gathered together, He began to say,
"This is an evil generation. It seeks a
[b]sign, and no sign will be given to it
except the sign of Jonah [1]the *prophet.
30 "For as [a]Jonah became a sign to the
Ninevites, so also the Son of Man will
be to this generation.
31 [a]"The queen of the South will rise
up in the judgment with the men of this
generation and condemn them, for she
came from the ends of the earth to hear
the wisdom of Solomon; and indeed a
[b]greater than Solomon *is* here.
32 "The men of Nineveh will rise up
in the judgment with this generation
and condemn it, for [a]they repented at
the preaching of Jonah; and indeed a
greater than Jonah *is* here.

The Lamp of the Body

2 **33** [a]"No one, when he has lit a lamp,
puts *it* in a secret place or under a
[b]basket, but on a lampstand, that those
who come in may see the light.
4 34 [a]"The lamp of the body is the eye.
Therefore, when your eye is [1]good,
your whole body also is full of light.
But when *your eye* is [2]bad, your body
also *is* full of darkness.
35 "Therefore take heed that the light
which is in you is not **darkness.**

WORD WEALTH

11:35 darkness, *skotos* (*skot*-oss); Strong's *#4655:* From the root *ska,* "to cover." The word is used literally for physical darkness and metaphorically for spiritual, moral, and intellectual darkness. The darkness arises from error, ignorance, disobedience, willful blindness, and rebellion. Darkness is an evil system absolutely opposed to the light.

36 "If then your whole body *is* full of
light, having no part dark, *the* whole
body will be full of light, as when the
bright shining of a lamp gives you
light."

Woe to the Pharisees and Lawyers

37 And as He spoke, a certain Pharisee
asked Him to dine with him. So He
went in and sat down to eat.
38 [a]When the Pharisee saw *it,* he marveled that He had not first washed before dinner.
39 [a]Then the Lord said to him, "Now
you Pharisees make the outside of the
cup and dish clean, but [b]your inward
part is full of [1]greed and wickedness.
40 "Foolish ones! Did not [a]He who
made the outside make the inside
also?
41 [a]"But rather give alms of [1]such
things as you have; then indeed all
things are clean to you.
42 [a]"But woe to you Pharisees! For you
tithe mint and rue and all manner of
herbs, and [b]pass by *justice and the
[c]love of God. These you ought to have
done, without leaving the others undone.
43 [a]"Woe to you Pharisees! For you
love the [1]best seats in the synagogues
and greetings in the marketplaces.
44 [a]"Woe to you, [1]scribes and Pharisees, *hypocrites! [b]For you are like
graves which are not seen, and the men
who walk over *them* are not aware *of
them.*"

27 [a]Luke 1:28, 48 **28** [a][Luke 8:21] **29** [a]Matt. 12:38–42 [b]1 Cor. 1:22 [1]NU omits *the prophet* *See WW at Matt. 2:5. **30** [a]Jon. 1:17; 2:10; 3:3–10 **31** [a]1 Kin. 10:1–9 [b][Rom. 9:5] **32** [a]Jon. 3:5 **33** [a]Mark 4:21 [b]Matt. 5:15 **34** [a]Matt. 6:22, 23 [1]Clear, or healthy [2]Evil, or unhealthy

38 [a]Mark 7:2, 3 **39** [a]Matt. 23:25 [b]Titus 1:15 [1]Lit. *eager grasping* or *robbery* **40** [a]Gen. 1:26, 27 **41** [a][Luke 12:33; 16:9] [1]Or *what is inside* **42** [a]Matt. 23:23 [b][Mic. 6:7, 8] [c]John 5:42 *See WW at Matt. 5:22. **43** [a]Mark 12:38, 39 [1]Or *places of honor* **44** [a]Matt. 23:27 [b]Ps. 5:9 [1]NU omits *scribes and Pharisees, hypocrites* *See WW at Matt. 6:2.

relationship with Jesus, but it is much better to have a spiritual kinship manifested by obedience to the **word of God** (see 8:21).

11:29–32 See notes on Matt. 12:38, 39.

11:33 See section 2 of Truth-In-Action through the Synoptics at the end of Luke.

11:33–36 The unbelief of the Jews was not due to lack of "signs," or evidence, but to their own blindness. Light does little good for one with diseased eyes. Jesus is God's light, but their spiritual blindness kept them from seeing Him.

11:34–36 See section 4 of Truth-In-Action through the Synoptics at the end of Luke.

11:34 Eye: The eye is regarded as the lens of the soul and reflects the total orientation of one's life. The image of the "good eye" is coupled with that of a useful lamp (v. 33). Both images speak of the positive effect of true enlightenment.

11:38 The washing of hands was not a matter of hygiene, but of ritual cleansing to remove any moral pollution acquired by contact with sinners or unholy things. See note on Mark 7:1–5.

11:39–44 They were meticulously scrupulous in matters pertaining to ceremonial cleansing, but ignored God's demand for inner holiness and for charity toward the poor. Hypocrisy is always more concerned with the form than the reality.

11:42 See note on Matt. 23:23.

11:43 Their parade of piety was only a means to enhance their own vanity rather than to bring glory to God.

11:44 Since stepping on a grave was defiling to a Jew (Num. 19:16), unmarked graves were a menace. Usually tombs were whitewashed in order to identify them (see Matt. 23:27). The attractive outward display of religion concealed the deadness within the hearts of the hypocrites.

45 Then one of the lawyers answered
and said to Him, "Teacher, by saying
these things You *reproach us also."
46 And He said, "Woe to you also, lawyers! [a]For you load men with burdens
hard to bear, and you yourselves do
not touch the burdens with one of your
fingers.
47 [a]"Woe to you! For you build the
tombs of the prophets, and your fathers killed them.
48 "In fact, you bear witness that you
approve the deeds of your fathers; for
they indeed killed them, and you build
their tombs.
49 "Therefore the wisdom of God also
said, [a]'I will send them prophets and
apostles, and *some* of them they will
kill and persecute,'
50 "that the blood of all the prophets
which was shed from the foundation
of the world may be required of this
generation,
51 [a]"from the blood of Abel to [b]the
blood of Zechariah who perished between the altar and the temple. Yes, I
say to you, it shall be required of this
generation.
52 [a]"Woe to you lawyers! For you have
taken away the key of knowledge. You
did not enter in yourselves, and those
who were entering in you hindered."
53 [1]And as He said these things to
them, the scribes and the Pharisees began to assail *Him* vehemently, and to
cross-examine Him about many things,
54 lying in wait for Him, [1]and [a]seeking
to catch Him in something He might
say, [2]that they might accuse Him.

Beware of Hypocrisy

12 In [a]the meantime, when an innumerable multitude of people
had gathered together, so that they
trampled one another, He began to say
to His disciples first *of all,* [b]"Beware
of the [1]leaven of the Pharisees, which
is *hypocrisy.
2 [a]"For there is nothing covered that
will not be revealed, nor hidden that
will not be *known.
3 "Therefore whatever you have spoken in the *dark will be heard in the
light, and what you have spoken in the
ear in inner rooms will be proclaimed
on the housetops.

Jesus Teaches the Fear of God

4 [a]"And I say to you, [b]My friends, do 2
not be afraid of those who kill the
body, and after that have no more that
they can do.
5 "But I will show you whom you
should fear: Fear Him who, after He
has killed, has power to cast into hell;
yes, I say to you, [a]fear Him!
6 "Are not five sparrows sold for two
[1]copper coins? And [a]not one of them
is forgotten before God.
7 "But the very hairs of your head are
all numbered. Do not fear therefore;
you are of more value than many sparrows.

Confess Christ Before Men

8 [a]"Also I say to you, whoever con- 1
fesses Me [b]before men, him the Son
of Man also will confess before the angels of God.
9 "But he who [a]denies Me before men
will be denied before the angels of God.
10 "And [a]anyone who speaks a word
against the Son of Man, it will be forgiven him; but to him who blasphemes
against the Holy Spirit, it will not be
forgiven.
11 [a]"Now when they bring you to the
synagogues and magistrates and authorities, do not *worry about how or
what you should answer, or what you
should say.

45 *See WW at Luke 18:32.
46 [a]Matt. 23:4
47 [a]Matt. 23:29
49 [a]Matt. 23:34
51 [a]Gen. 4:8 [b]2 Chr. 24:20, 21
52 [a]Matt. 23:13
53 [1]NU *And when He left there*
54 [a]Mark 12:13 [1]NU omits *and seeking* [2]NU omits *that they might accuse Him*

CHAPTER 12

1 [a]Mark 8:15 [b]Matt. 16:12 [1]*yeast* *See WW at Gal. 2:13.
2 [a]Matt. 10:26 [1 Cor. 4:5] *See WW at John 8:32.
3 *See WW at John 12:46.
4 [a]Is. 51:7, 8, 12, 13 [b][John 15:13–15]
5 [a]Ps. 119:120
6 [a]Matt. 6:26 [1]Gr. *assarion,* a coin worth about 1/16 of a denarius
8 [a]Matt. 10:32 [b]Ps. 119:46
9 [a]Matt. 10:33
10 [a][Matt. 12:31, 32]
11 [a]Mark 13:11 *See WW at Matt. 6:25.

11:45 The lawyers, or scribes, were especially blameworthy, since they were the official interpreters of the Law.
11:46 They place intolerable legalistic requirements on the people, but contrive ways of avoiding the regulations themselves.
11:47–51 See notes on Matt. 23:29–36.
11:52 See note on Matt. 23:13.
12:1 Leaven signifies the evil doctrine of the Pharisees (see Matt. 16:6, 12).
12:2, 3 God will unmask all hypocrisy, while, on the other hand, He will provide opportunity for greater proclamation of the gospel. See notes on Matt. 10:26, 27.
12:4, 5 See section 2 of Truth-In-Action through the Synoptics at the end of Luke.
12:4, 5 Disciples are not to fear their enemies, whose judgment is merely physical and temporal. They are to reverence God, whose judgment is final and of eternal consequence.
12:6, 7 Fearing God involves trust, not terror. Nothing that happens to His witnesses, not even death, takes place apart from the providential care of the One who is concerned with the smallest details of life.
12:8, 9 See section 1 of Truth-In-Action through the Synoptics at the end of Luke.
12:8, 9 Acknowledgment of Christ on Earth results in acknowledgment by Him in heaven. The reverse is also true.
12:10 See notes on Matt. 12:31, 32.
12:11, 12 Witnesses for Christ are to testify openly and fearlessly in a hostile environment, knowing that **the Holy Spirit** is at work in and through them (see Acts 4:13; 7:1–53; 2 Tim. 4:16, 17).

12 "For the Holy Spirit will [a]teach you in that very hour what you ought to say."

The Parable of the Rich Fool

 **13** Then one from the crowd said to Him, "Teacher, tell my brother to divide the inheritance with me."

14 But He said to him, [a]"Man, who made Me a judge or an arbitrator over you?"

15 And He said to them, [a]"Take heed and beware of [1]covetousness, for one's life does not consist in the *abundance of the things he possesses."

> **KINGDOM DYNAMICS**
>
> **12:15 Sharpening Our Priorities,** GOD'S PROSPERITY. Life consists of far more than just obtaining and possessing things. Rather, God wants us to enjoy a full, complete, and balanced life; and He has made provisions through His Word for us to be fulfilled in that way. He has promised to supply our every need (Phil. 4:19), and He has promised to fulfill the desires of our hearts (Ps. 37:4). But He also wants us to keep our priorities clear: "Seek first the kingdom of God." In that way—with all His promises and priorities in balanced application to your life—"all these things shall be added to you" (Matt. 6:33).
>
> (Ps. 1:1–3/Phil. 4:19) F.P.

16 Then He spoke a parable to them, saying: "The ground of a certain rich man yielded plentifully.

17 "And he thought within himself, saying, 'What shall I do, since I have no room to store my crops?'

18 "So he said, 'I will do this: I will pull down my barns and build greater, and there I will store all my crops and my goods.

19 'And I will say to my soul, [a]"Soul, you have many goods laid up for many years; take your *ease; [b]eat, drink, *and* be merry." '

20 "But God said to him, 'Fool! This night [a]your soul will be required of you; [b]then whose will those things be which you have provided?'

21 "So *is* he who lays up treasure for himself, [a]and is not rich toward God."

Do Not Worry

22 Then He said to His disciples, 11
"Therefore I say to you, [a]do not worry about your life, what you will eat; nor about the body, what you will put on.

23 "Life is more than food, and the body *is more* than clothing.

24 "Consider the ravens, for they neither sow nor reap, which have neither storehouse nor barn; and [a]God feeds them. Of how much more value are you than the birds?

25 "And which of you by worrying can add one cubit to his stature?

26 "If you then are not able to do *the* least, why [1]are you anxious for the rest?

27 "Consider the lilies, how they grow: they neither toil nor spin; and yet I say to you, even [a]Solomon in all his glory was not [1]arrayed like one of these.

28 "If then God so clothes the grass, which today is in the field and tomorrow is thrown into the oven, how much more *will He clothe* you, O *you* of [a]little* faith?

29 "And do not seek what you should eat or what you should drink, nor have an anxious mind.

30 "For all these things the nations of the *world seek after, and your Father [a]knows that you need these things.

31 [a]"But seek [1]the kingdom of God,

12 [a][John 14:26]
14 [a][John 18:36]
15 [a][1 Tim. 6:6–10] [1]NU *all covetousness* *See WW at Matt. 25:29.
19 [a]Eccl. 11:9; 1 Cor. 15:32; James 5:5 [b][Eccl. 2:24; 3:13; 5:18: 8:15] *See WW at Rev. 14:13.
20 [a]Job 27:8; Ps. 52:7; [James 4:14] [b]Ps. 39:6; Jer. 17:11
21 [a][Matt. 6:20; Luke 12:33; 1 Tim. 6:18, 19; James 2:5; 5:1–5]
22 [a]Matt. 6:25–33
24 [a]Job 38:41; Ps. 147:9
26 [1]*do you worry*
27 [a]1 Kin. 10:4–7; 2 Chr. 9:3–6 [1]*clothed*
28 [a]Matt. 6:30; 8:26; 14:31; 16:8 *See WW at Matt. 8:26.
30 [a]Matt. 6:31, 32 *See WW at John 18:36.
31 [a]Matt. 6:33 [1]NU *His kingdom, and these things*

12:13–15 See section 10 of Truth-In-Action through the Synoptics at the end of Luke.

12:13, 14 Jesus refuses to enter into a civil dispute, but uses the occasion to teach a lesson on covetousness.

12:15 Jesus' parable underscores the ultimacy of "life." True life has nothing to do with possessions. The sin of covetousness is directed toward the acquisition of more possessions and, thus, is self-defeating and futile. It does not know the meaning of "life."

12:16–20 Jesus enforces His message with a parable underscoring the dangers of materialism. Possessions neither give life nor provide security, because death separates from things. The **fool** in the parable mistakenly looked upon his possessions as his own, not as gifts dependent upon the will of God and to be used unselfishly.

12:21 So: The fate of the rich fool is generalized to all those who are concerned with possessions. He **lays up treasure for himself** and is not **rich toward God,** and thus fails to understand life's true objective. Further explanation of this statement follows in vv. 22–34.

12:22–34 See section 11 of Truth-In-Action through the Synoptics at the end of Luke.

12:22–34 Therefore connects these verses with the teaching concerning covetousness. A proper attitude toward material things, based on a simple trust in a caring Father, frees one from a nagging anxiety about the physical necessities of life. Worry is useless because life is in God's hands (vv. 24–26); because God's concern for transitory things indicates His greater care for His highest creation (vv. 27, 28); and because God knows our needs better than we do (v. 30). Therefore, we should not allow material concerns to distract us from our primary aim of seeking the total lordship of God (v. 31). See notes on Matt. 6:25–34. Provision in life follows those whose priorities are concerned with God's ways, work, and will—His rule (kingdom).

and all these things shall be added to
you.
32 "Do not *fear, little flock, for
[a]it is your Father's good pleasure to
give you the kingdom.
10 33 [a]"Sell what you have and give
[b]alms; [c]provide yourselves money
bags which do not grow old, a treasure
in the heavens that does not fail, where
no thief approaches nor moth destroys.
34 "For where your treasure is, there
your heart will be also.

The Faithful Servant and the Evil Servant

35 [a]"Let your waist be girded and
[b]*your* lamps burning;
36 "and you yourselves be like men
who wait for their master, when he will
return from the wedding, that when he
comes and knocks they may open to
him immediately.
37 [a]"Blessed *are* those *servants
whom the master, when he comes, will
find watching. Assuredly, I say to you
that he will gird himself and have them
sit down *to eat*, and will come and
serve them.
38 "And if he should come in the second watch, or come in the third watch,
and find *them* so, blessed are those servants.
39 [a]"But know this, that if the master
of the house had known what hour the
thief would come, he would [1]have
watched and not allowed his house to
be broken into.
40 [a]"Therefore you also be ready, for
the Son of Man is coming at an hour
you do not expect."
41 Then Peter said to Him, "Lord, do
You speak this parable *only* to us, or
to all *people?*"

32 [a][Matt. 11:25, 26] *See WW at Matt. 10:26.
33 [a]Matt. 19:21 [b]Luke 11:41 [c]Matt. 6:20
35 [a][1 Pet. 1:13] [b][Matt. 25:1–13]
37 [a]Matt. 24:46 *See WW at Rev. 19:5.
39 [a]Rev. 3:3; 16:15 [1]NU *not have allowed*
40 [a]Mark 13:33
42 [a]Matt. 24:45, 46; 25:21 [1]*at the right time* *See WW at 1 Pet. 4:10.
44 [a]Matt. 24:47; 25:21
45 [a]2 Pet. 3:3, 4
46 [a]1 Thess. 5:3
47 [a]Deut. 25:2 [b][James 4:17]
48 [a][Lev. 5:17]
49 [a]Luke 12:51
50 [a]Mark 10:38 [b]John 12:27; 19:30 *See WW at Matt. 21:25. • See WW at 2 Cor. 5:14.
51 [a]Matt. 10:34–36 [b]John 7:43; 9:16; 10:19

42 And the Lord said, [a]"Who then is
that faithful and wise *steward, whom
his master will make ruler over his
household, to give *them their* portion
of food [1]in due season?
43 "Blessed *is* that servant whom his
master will find so doing when he
comes.
44 [a]"Truly, I say to you that he will
make him ruler over all that he has.
45 [a]"But if that servant says in his
heart, 'My master is delaying his coming,' and begins to beat the male and
female servants, and to eat and drink
and be drunk,
46 "the master of that servant will
come on a [a]day when he is not looking
for *him*, and at an hour when he is not
aware, and will cut him in two and appoint *him* his portion with the unbelievers.
47 "And [a]that servant who [b]knew his 1
master's will, and did not prepare *himself* or do according to his will, shall
be beaten with many *stripes*.
48 [a]"But he who did not know, yet
committed things deserving of stripes,
shall be beaten with few. For everyone
to whom much is given, from him
much will be required; and to whom
much has been committed, of him they
will ask the more.

Christ Brings Division

49 [a]"I came to send fire on the earth,
and how I wish it were already kindled!
50 "But [a]I have a *baptism to be baptized with, and how *distressed I am
till it is [b]accomplished!
51 [a]"Do *you* suppose that I came to 7
give peace on earth? I tell you, not at
all, [b]but rather division.

12:32 Little flock is a reference to the OT idea of Israel as God's sheep (Is. 40:11). Jesus' use of it here for His disciples clearly designates them, and the church birthed through them, the new, true Israel—the propagators and inheritors of His present and consummated **kingdom**.
12:33, 34 See section 10 of Truth-In-Action through the Synoptics at the end of Luke.
12:33 Sacrificial giving for the needs of others assures us of treasures that can never be lost.
12:34 A life totally occupied with things of the kingdom will be free from covetousness.
12:35 In order to have freedom of activity, men tucked the skirts of their long robes into their belts. **Girded** signifies a readiness for action.
12:36, 40 The parable calls for alertness and preparedness for the Lord's return, which will be as unexpected as the coming of a thief at night (vv. 39, 40; see 1 Thess. 5:2; 2 Pet. 3:10; Rev. 16:15). Those who are watchful and ready will have the reward of fellowship with Christ.
12:41–48 In response to Peter's question, Jesus teaches that watchfulness is especially required of those in leadership positions. Greater privileges bring greater temptations and greater responsibilities (see James 3:1). Those who use their authority selfishly or unkindly will suffer severe punishment. The Lord indicates that at the judgment there will be degrees both of punishments and rewards.
12:47, 48 See section 1 of Truth-In-Action through the Synoptics at the end of Luke.
12:49, 50 Some commentators feel that **fire** symbolizes the divisive nature of Christ's ministry, consuming the destructible and purifying the indestructible. However, in light of His **wish** that the fire **were already kindled,** and the obvious reference to His death as a prerequisite to the fire's appearing, it is better to understand the statement to be a reference to the burning zeal of believers, which is connected with the outpouring of the Holy Spirit (see Acts 2). The fervor of Spirit-filled witnesses would arouse the antagonism of unbelievers.
12:51–53 See section 7 of Truth-In-Action through the Synoptics at the end of Luke.

52 [a]"For from now on five in one house
will be divided: three against two, and
two against three.
53 [a]"Father will be divided against son
and son against father, mother against
daughter and daughter against mother,
mother-in-law against her daughter-in-
law and daughter-in-law against her
mother-in-law."

Discern the Time

54 Then He also said to the multitudes,
[a]"Whenever you see a cloud rising out
of the west, immediately you say, 'A
shower is coming'; and so it is.
55 "And when you see the [a]south wind
blow, you say, 'There will be hot
weather'; and there is.
56 *"Hypocrites! You can discern the
face of the sky and of the earth, but
how *is it* you do not discern [a]this time?

Make Peace with Your Adversary

6 **57** "Yes, and why, even of yourselves,
do you not judge what is right?
58 [a]"When you go with your adversary
to the magistrate, make every effort
[b]along the way to settle with him, lest
he drag you to the judge, the judge deliver you to the officer, and the officer
throw you into prison.
59 "I tell you, you shall not depart from
there till you have paid the very last
mite."

Repent or Perish

13 There were present at that season some who told Him about
the Galileans whose blood Pilate had
[1]mingled with their sacrifices.
2 And Jesus answered and said to
them, "Do you suppose that these Galileans were worse sinners than all *other*
Galileans, because they suffered such
things?
3 "I tell you, no; but unless you *repent you will all likewise *perish.
4 "Or those eighteen on whom the
tower in Siloam fell and killed them,
do you think that they were worse
sinners than all *other* men who dwelt
in Jerusalem?

WORD WEALTH

13:4 sinners, *opheiletes* (of-eye-*let*-ace); Strong's *#3781:* A debtor, one who owes a moral obligation, an offender, a delinquent, a moral transgressor. The debt concept comes from this sequence: we are morally bound to live a life free from violation of God's commandments; failing in performance, we become delinquent transgressors and debtors to divine justice.

5 "I tell you, no; but unless you repent
you will all likewise perish."

The Parable of the Barren Fig Tree

6 He also spoke this parable: [a]"A certain *man* had a fig tree planted in his
vineyard, and he came seeking fruit on
it and found none.
7 "Then he said to the keeper of his
vineyard, 'Look, for three years I have
come seeking fruit on this fig tree and
find none. Cut it down; why does it
[1]use up the ground?'
8 "But he answered and said to him,
'Sir, let it alone this year also, until I
dig around it and fertilize *it*.
9 [1]'And if it bears fruit, *well*. But if
not, after that you can [a]cut it down.'"

A Spirit of Infirmity

10 Now He was teaching in one of the
synagogues on the Sabbath.
11 And behold, there was a woman
who had a spirit of infirmity eighteen
years, and was bent over and could in
no way [1]raise *herself* up.

52 [a]Matt. 10:35; Mark 13:12
53 [a]Matt. 10:21, 36
54 [a]Matt. 16:2, 3
55 [a]Job 37:17
56 [a]Luke 19:41–44 *See WW at Matt. 6:2.
58 [a]Prov. 25:8; Matt. 5:25, 26 [b][Ps. 32:6; Is. 55:6]

CHAPTER 13

1 [1]*mixed*
3 *See WW at Matt. 3:2. • See WW at Luke 9:56.
6 [a]Is. 5:2; Matt. 21:19
7 [1]*waste*
9 [a][John 15:2] [1]NU *And if it bears fruit after that, well. But if not, you can*
11 [1]*straighten up*

12:51–53 The gospel creates division even among members of the same family.

12:54–56 See note on Matt. 16:2, 3.

12:57, 58 See section 6 of Truth-In-Action through the Synoptics at the end of Luke.

12:57–59 God's judgment is coming, and people would be wise to make a settlement with Him beforehand.

13:1 Pilate had apparently put to death some **Galileans** as they were offering worship sacrifices in Jerusalem. No explanation of the reason is given. They had perhaps transgressed a Roman law, prompting the response from the notoriously hard-hearted Pilate.

13:2 Since their theology attributed individual suffering to individual sin, the Jews interpreted the fate of the Galileans as God's punishment of their guilt.

13:3 Jesus transfers the meaning of these incidents to the spiritual sphere. He does not deal with a retribution theory, but points to the urgent demand of the present, **unless you repent you will all likewise perish** (see v. 5).

13:4, 5 Jesus refers to a recent calamity in which 18 workers perished in an accident. Rather than speculating on their guilt, others should regard their fate as a warning calling themselves to repentance.

13:6–9 The parable's immediate application is to Israel. The nation had failed to produce spiritual fruit, but God gives the people one more opportunity in their attitude toward Jesus.

13:10–17 For views concerning the Sabbath, see notes on Matt. 12:1–14.

12 But when Jesus saw her, He called *her* to *Him* and said to her, "Woman, you are loosed from your [a]infirmity."

13 [a]And He laid *His* hands on her, and immediately she was made straight, and glorified God.

14 But the ruler of the synagogue answered with indignation, because Jesus had [a]healed on the Sabbath; and he said to the crowd, [b]"There are six days on which men ought *to work; therefore come and be healed on them, and [c]not on the Sabbath day."

15 The Lord then answered him and said, [1]"Hypocrite! [a]Does not each one of you on the Sabbath loose his ox or donkey from the stall, and lead *it* away to water it?

16 "So ought not this woman, [a]being a daughter of Abraham, whom Satan has bound—think of it—for eighteen years, be loosed from this bond on the Sabbath?"

17 And when He said these things, all His adversaries were put to shame; and all the multitude rejoiced for all the glorious things that were [a]done by Him.

The Parable of the Mustard Seed

11 18 [a]Then He said, "What is the kingdom of God like? And to what shall I
compare it?

19 "It is like a mustard seed, which a man took and put in his garden; and it grew and became a [1]large tree, and the birds of the air nested in its branches."

The Parable of the Leaven

20 And again He said, "To what shall I liken the kingdom of God?

21 "It is like [1]leaven, which a woman took and hid in three [a]measures[2] of meal till it was all leavened."

The Narrow Way

22 [a]And He went through the cities and villages, teaching, and journeying toward Jerusalem.

23 Then one said to Him, "Lord, are 9
there [a]few who are saved?" And He
said to them,

24 [a]"Strive to enter through the nar- 9
row gate, for [b]many, I say to you, will
seek to enter and will not be able.

25 [a]"When once the Master of the house has risen up and [b]shut the door, and you begin to stand outside and knock at the door, saying, [c]'Lord, Lord, open for us,' and He will answer and say to you, [d]'I do not know you, where you are from,'

26 "then you will begin to say, 'We ate and drank in Your presence, and You taught in our streets.'

27 [a]"But He will say, 'I tell you I do not know you, where you are from. [b]Depart from Me, all you workers of iniquity.'

28 [a]"There will be weeping and gnashing of teeth, [b]when you see Abraham and Isaac and Jacob and all the prophets in the kingdom of God, and yourselves thrust out.

29 "They will come from the east and the west, from the north and the south, and sit down in the kingdom of God.

30 [a]"And indeed there are last who will be first, and there are first who will be last."

31 [1]On that very day some Pharisees came, saying to Him, "Get out and depart from here, for Herod wants to kill You."

32 And He said to them, "Go, tell that fox, 'Behold, I cast out demons and

12 [a]Luke 7:21; 8:2
13 [a]Mark 16:18; Acts 9:17
14 [a][Luke 6:6–11; 14:1–6]; John 5:16 [b]Ex. 20:9; 23:12 [c]Matt. 12:10; Mark 3:2; Luke 6:7; 14:3 *See WW at John 3:21.
15 [a][Matt. 7:5; 23:13]; Luke 14:5 [1]NU, M *Hypocrites*
16 [a]Luke 19:9
17 [a]Mark 5:19, 20
18 [a]Matt. 13:31, 32; Mark 4:30–32
19 [1]NU omits *large*
21 [a]Matt. 13:33 [1]*yeast* [2]Gr. *sata,* same as Heb. *seah;* approximately 2 pecks in all
22 [a]Matt. 9:35; Mark 6:6
23 [a][Matt. 7:14; 20:16]
24 [a][Matt. 7:13] [b][John 7:34; 8:21; 13:33; Rom. 9:31]
25 [a][Ps. 32:6]; Is. 55:6 [b]Matt. 25:10; Rev. 22:11 [c]Luke 6:46 [d]Matt. 7:23; 25:12
27 [a][Matt. 7:23; 25:41] [b]Ps. 6:8; [Matt. 25:41]; Titus 1:16
28 [a]Matt. 8:12; 13:42; 24:51 [b]Matt. 8:11
30 [a][Matt. 19:30; 20:16]; Mark 10:31
31 [1]NU *In that very hour*

13:15, 16 Animals routinely receive care on the Sabbath. Are not people of far greater value? **Whom Satan has bound** clearly attributes the woman's disease of what was apparently a rigidly fused spine to a demon, called a "spirit of infirmity" (v. 11).

13:18, 19 See section 11 of Truth-In-Action through the Synoptics at the end of Luke.

13:18, 19 See note on Matt. 13:31, 32.

13:20, 21 See note on Matt. 13:33.

13:23, 24 See section 9 of Truth-In-Action through the Synoptics at the end of Luke.

13:23 The rabbis often discussed this theoretical question. Jesus answers the questioner instead of the question, stressing the seriousness of the need for repentance.

13:24–30 See section 9 of Truth-In-Action through the Synoptics at the end of Luke.

13:24 The **gate** is **narrow** because Christ is the only Door (John 10:7–9), and repentance and faith are the only means of admission.

13:25–27 At the Last Judgment the door will be closed, and those who are now indifferent to Christ will claim acquaintance with Him. However, superficial knowledge about Christ and His teaching will not substitute for personal repentance and faith, which bring a true relationship with Him.

13:28 The Jews claimed to be automatically in **the kingdom of God** by virtue of their physical relationship to **Abraham**.

13:29, 30 Believing Gentiles, who were called **last,** will enter the kingdom, while unbelieving Jews, who were called **first,** will be excluded.

13:31 The **Pharisees** may have been trying to force Jesus into Jerusalem or some other area where they might more easily seize Him.

13:32 Jesus is not threatened by a conniving politician's scheme but continues on His predetermined course, fully cognizant of what His "course" involves. He must have His rendezvous in Jerusalem (see 9:51) as a part of the divine program. **Today and tomorrow:** The expression is Hebrew

perform **cures** today and tomorrow, and the third *day* [a]I shall be [1]perfected.'

WORD WEALTH

13:32 cures, *iasis* (*ee*-as-is); Strong's *#2392:* The act of healing, curing the sick. *Iasis* is akin to *iaomai,* "to heal," and *iatros,* "a physician." By the second century A.D., *iasis* included bodily healing, forgiveness of sins, and deliverance from demonic possession. The gospel frees the entire person.

33 "Nevertheless I must journey today, tomorrow, and the *day* following; for it cannot be that a prophet should perish outside of Jerusalem.

Jesus Laments over Jerusalem

34 [a]"O Jerusalem, Jerusalem, the one who kills the prophets and stones those who are sent to her! How often I wanted to gather your children together, as a hen *gathers* her brood under *her* wings, but you were not willing!
35 "See! [a]Your house is left to you desolate; and [1]assuredly, I say to you, you shall not see Me until *the time* comes when you say, [b]*'Blessed is He who comes in the name of the* LORD!'"

A Man with Dropsy Healed on the Sabbath

14 Now it happened, as He went into the house of one of the rulers of the Pharisees to eat bread on the Sabbath, that they watched Him closely.
2 And behold, there was a certain man before Him who had dropsy.
3 And Jesus, answering, spoke to the lawyers and Pharisees, saying, [a]"Is it lawful to heal on the [1]Sabbath?"
4 But they kept silent. And He took *him* and healed him, and let him go.
5 Then He answered them, saying, [a]"Which of you, having a [1]donkey or an ox that has fallen into a pit, will not immediately pull him out on the Sabbath day?"
6 And they could not answer Him regarding these things.

Take the Lowly Place

7 So He told a parable to those who were invited, when He noted how they chose the best places, saying to them: 5
8 "When you are invited by anyone to a wedding feast, do not sit down in the best place, lest one more honorable than you be invited by him;
9 "and he who invited you and him come and say to you, 'Give place to this man,' and then you begin with shame to take the lowest place.
10 [a]"But when you are invited, go and sit down in the lowest place, so that when he who invited you comes he may say to you, 'Friend, go up higher.' Then you will have glory in the presence of those who sit at the table with you.
11 [a]"For whoever *exalts himself will be [1]humbled, and he who *humbles himself will be exalted."
12 Then He also said to him who invited Him, "When you give a dinner or a supper, do not ask your friends, your brothers, your relatives, nor rich neighbors, lest they also invite you back, and you be repaid.
13 "But when you give a feast, invite [a]*the* poor, *the* [1]maimed, *the* lame, *the* blind.
14 "And you will be [a]blessed, because they cannot repay you; for you shall be repaid at the resurrection of the just."

32 [a]Luke 24:46; Acts 10:40; 1 Cor. 15:4; [Heb. 2:10; 5:9; 7:28] [1]Resurrected
34 [a]Matt. 23:37–39; 2 Chr. 24:20, 21; 36:15, 16
35 [a]Lev. 26:31, 32; Ps. 69:25; Is. 1:7; Jer. 22:5; Dan. 9:27; Mic. 3:12 [b]Ps. 118:26; Matt. 21:9; Mark 11:10; Luke 19:38; John 12:13 [1]NU, M omit *assuredly*

CHAPTER 14

3 [a]Matt. 12:10 [1]NU adds *or not*
5 [a][Ex. 23:5; Deut. 22:4]; Luke 13:15 [1]NU, M *son*
10 [a]Prov. 25:6, 7
11 [a]Job 22:29; Ps. 18:27; Prov. 29:23; Matt. 23:12; Luke 18:14; James 4:6; [1 Pet. 5:5] [1]*put down* *See WW at James 4:10. • See WW at Matt. 18:4.
13 [a]Neh. 8:10, 12 [1]*crippled*
14 [a][Matt. 25:34–40]

and suggests a short, indeterminate period of time followed by an impending, sure climax.
13:33 The real danger of death was not from Herod, but from the religious leaders in Jerusalem.
13:34, 35 See notes on Matt. 23:38, 39.
14:1 The outward courtesy shown to Jesus was a sham, for the Pharisees were seeking opportunities to criticize Him. **Eat:** Vv. 1–24 are loosely joined together by the theme of dining situations. A healing takes place at dinner (vv. 1–6), providing the setting for two sayings (vv. 7–14), and the Parable of the Great Supper (vv. 15–24). This is Luke's sixth dinner episode (5:29; 7:36; 9:16; 10:39; 11:37; see also 19:8; 22:14; 24:30).
14:2 Dropsy is a swelling of the body caused by excess fluid in the tissues.
14:5 Jesus exposes their distorted sense of values.
14:7–11 See section 5 of Truth-In-Action through the Synoptics at the end of Luke.
14:7–11 Jesus not only rebukes social pride, but enforces a lesson on character. God honors those who recognize their own lowliness and unworthiness and who rely solely on His mercy.
14:12–14 The Lord's concern is more than the guest list at a social occasion; He teaches the principle of unselfish motives in performing deeds of kindness.
14:13 The **lame** and **blind** were excluded from the temple.
14:14 God's invitation includes the lowly and the poor—those who have no means to repay. Reward that will not be returned in the present age will be given **at the resurrection of the just,** that is, in the consummation. In the future age, God will reward those who have been merciful in this age.

The Parable of the Great Supper

15 Now when one of those who sat at
the table with Him heard these things,
he said to Him, [a]"Blessed *is* he who
shall eat [1]bread in the kingdom of
God!"
16 [a]Then He said to him, "A certain
man gave a great supper and invited
many,
17 "and [a]sent his servant at supper
time to say to those who were invited, 'Come, for all things are now
ready.'
18 "But they all with one *accord* began
to make excuses. The first said to him,
'I have bought a piece of ground, and
I must go and see it. I ask you to have
me excused.'
19 "And another said, 'I have bought
five yoke of oxen, and I am going to
test them. I ask you to have me excused.'
20 "Still another said, 'I have married a wife, and therefore I cannot
come.'
21 "So that servant came and reported
these things to his master. Then the
master of the house, being *angry, said
to his servant, 'Go out quickly into the
streets and lanes of the city, and bring
in here *the* poor and *the* [1]maimed and
the lame and *the* blind.'
22 "And the servant said, 'Master, it is
done as you commanded, and still
there is room.'
23 "Then the master said to the servant, 'Go out into the highways and
hedges, and compel *them* to come in,
that my house may be filled.
24 'For I say to you [a]that none of those
men who were invited shall *taste my
supper.' "

15 [a]Rev. 19:9 [1]M *dinner*
16 [a]Matt. 22:2–14
17 [a]Prov. 9:2, 5
21 [1]*crippled* *See WW at Rev. 12:17.
24 [a][Matt. 21:43; 22:8; Acts 13:46] *See WW at John 8:52.

Leaving All to Follow Christ

25 Now great multitudes went with
Him. And He turned and said to
them,
26 [a]"If anyone comes to Me [b]and does 7
not hate his father and mother, wife
and children, brothers and sisters,
[c]yes, and his own life also, he cannot
be My disciple.
27 "And [a]whoever does not bear his
cross and come after Me cannot be My
disciple.
28 "For [a]which of you, intending to
build a tower, does not sit down first
and count the cost, whether he has
enough to finish *it*—
29 "lest, after he has laid the foundation, and is not able to finish, all who
see *it* begin to mock him,
30 "saying, 'This man began to build
and was not able to finish.'
31 "Or what king, going to make war
against another king, does not sit down
first and consider whether he is able
with ten thousand to meet him who
comes against him with twenty thousand?
32 "Or else, while the other is still a
great way off, he sends a delegation
and asks conditions of peace.
33 "So likewise, whoever of you
[a]does not forsake all that he has cannot
be My disciple.

Tasteless Salt Is Worthless

34 [a]"Salt *is* *good; but if the salt 2
has lost its flavor, how shall it be seasoned?
35 "It is neither fit for the land nor for
the [1]dunghill, *but* men throw it out. He
who has ears to hear, let him hear!"

26 [a]Deut. 13:6; 33:9; Matt. 10:37 [b]Rom. 9:13 [c]Rev. 12:11
27 [a]Matt. 16:24; Mark 8:34; Luke 9:23; [2 Tim. 3:12]
28 [a]Prov. 24:27
33 [a]Matt. 19:27
34 [a]Matt. 5:13; [Mark 9:50] *See WW at Matt. 13:48.
35 [1]*rubbish heap*

14:15 Shall eat bread: The mention of the "resurrection" (v. 14) suggests the future. The person who pronounces the blessing is thinking of the *future* messianic banquet at the time of the consummation. But, in the parable, Jesus announces that the messianic banquet is not simply future, but present. Jesus counters the false assumption. The messianic banquet is already in process, seen, for example, in the extension of the gospel to all the poor, sick, and socially dispossessed. See notes on Matt. 22:1–14.

14:16, 17 A host would issue an invitation in advance, and then would send notice when the meal was ready. Evidently the guests in this parable had accepted the advance invitation.

14:18–24 Israel had accepted God's invitation to the kingdom, given through the prophets. The arrival of Jesus signals the arrival of the kingdom, but in its rejection of Him the nation is declining God's offer of grace. However, God's purpose will not be thwarted, so He will send His gracious invitation to the Gentiles.

14:25 The **multitudes** were attracted by Jesus' miracles and expected Him to establish an earthly kingdom. Interested in quality more than quantity, He defined the cost of true discipleship.

14:26, 27 See section 7 of Truth-In-Action through the Synoptics at the end of Luke.

14:26 A **disciple** must subordinate all earthly relationships to loyalty to Christ. **Hate** does not mean to bear ill will, but to choose Christ over all others.

14:27 A disciple must die to self-centeredness and be willing to endure suffering and even martyrdom.

14:28–32 Erecting a stately building is costly and waging war is dangerous, illustrating the costliness and danger that disciples of Jesus must be willing to face.

14:33 Discipleship means the total renunciation of all selfish interest for the sake of Jesus. **Cannot be My disciple** is dealing with issues of total commitment and maximum realization of Christ's purpose for our lives in this age.

14:34, 35 See section 2 of Truth-In-Action through the Synoptics at the end of Luke.

14:34, 35 In order to flavor society, disciples must retain a spirit of self-sacrifice (see Matt. 5:13).

The Parable of the Lost Sheep

15 Then [a]all the tax collectors and
the *sinners drew near to Him
to hear Him.
2 And the Pharisees and scribes complained, saying, "This Man [1]receives
sinners [a]and eats with them."
3 So He spoke this parable to them,
saying:
4 [a]"What man of you, having a hundred sheep, if he loses one of them,
does not leave the ninety-nine in the
wilderness, and go after the one which
is lost until he finds it?
5 "And when he has found *it,* he lays
it on his shoulders, rejoicing.
6 "And when he comes home, he calls
together *his* *friends and neighbors,
saying to them, [a]'Rejoice with me, for
I have found my sheep [b]which was
lost!'
7 "I say to you that likewise there will
be more joy in heaven over one sinner
who repents [a]than over ninety-nine
[1]just persons who [b]need no repentance.

The Parable of the Lost Coin

8 "Or what woman, having ten silver
[1]coins, if she loses one coin, does
not light a lamp, sweep the house,
and search carefully until she finds
it?
9 "And when she has found *it,* she
calls *her* friends and neighbors together, saying, 'Rejoice with me,
for I have found the piece which I
lost!'
10 "Likewise, I say to you, there is joy
in the presence of the angels of God
over one sinner who repents."

CHAPTER 15
1 [a][Matt. 9:10–13] *See WW at James 5:20.
2 [a]Acts 11:3; Gal. 2:12 [1]*welcomes*
4 [a]Matt. 18:12–14; 1 Pet. 2:25
6 [a][Rom. 12:15] [b][Luke 19:10; 1 Pet. 2:10, 25] *See WW at John 11:11.
7 [a][Luke 5:32] [b][Mark 2:17] [1]*upright*
8 [1]Gr. *drachma,* a valuable coin often worn in a ten-piece garland by married women
12 [a]Mark 12:44
13 [1]*wasteful*
14 *See WW at Luke 22:35.
16 [1]*carob pods* *See WW at Matt. 13:17.
18 [a]Ex. 9:27; 10:16; Num. 22:34; Josh. 7:20; 1 Sam. 15:24, 30; 26:21; 2 Sam. 12:13; 24:10, 17; Ps. 51:4; Matt. 27:4
19 *See WW at Gal. 1:6.
20 [a][Jer. 3:12]; Matt. 9:36; [Acts 2:39; Eph. 2:13, 17] *See WW at Philem. 15. • See WW at Matt. 14:14.
21 [a]Ps. 51:4

The Parable of the Lost Son

11 Then He said: "A certain man had
two sons.
12 "And the younger of them said to
his father, 'Father, give me the portion
of goods that falls *to me.'* So he divided
to them [a]*his* livelihood.
13 "And not many days after, the
younger son gathered all together,
journeyed to a far country, and there
wasted his possessions with [1]prodigal
living.
14 "But when he had spent all, there
arose a severe famine in that land, and
he began to be in *want.
15 "Then he went and joined himself
to a citizen of that country, and he sent
him into his fields to feed swine.
16 "And he would *gladly have filled
his stomach with the [1]pods that the
swine ate, and no one gave him *anything.*
17 "But when he came to himself, he
said, 'How many of my father's hired
servants have bread enough and to
spare, and I perish with hunger!
18 'I will arise and go to my father, and
will say to him, "Father, [a]I have sinned
against heaven and before you,
19 "and I am no longer worthy to be
*called your son. Make me like one of
your hired servants." '
20 "And he arose and came to his father. But [a]when* he was still a great
way off, his father saw him and had
*compassion, and ran and fell on his
neck and kissed him.
21 "And the son said to him, 'Father,
I have sinned against heaven [a]and in
your sight, and am no longer worthy
to be called your son.'
22 "But the father said to his servants,

15:1–3 The Pharisees' criticism of Jesus' open association with known **sinners** and social outcasts occasioned three parables, which illustrate God's love and concern for sinners. His attitude is sharply opposed to that of the self-righteous. **The Pharisees** correspond to the 99 sheep, the 9 coins, and the elder brother. **The tax collectors and sinners** correspond to the lost sheep, the lost coin, and the prodigal son.

15:4–10 The **or** of v. 8 indicates that the two parables illustrate the same point. God is concerned with one lost person and rejoices in his recovery. Those who are legalistically self-righteous are not even aware of their need.

15:5 Sheep that are lost lie down helplessly and refuse to budge.

15:7 Jesus' table-fellowship with sinners (v. 2) is a celebration of joy, analogous to the joy a shepherd must share with his friends and neighbors on finding a lost sheep (v. 6).

15:10 Likewise: The same word is used in v. 7, indicative of a joy that must be shared.

15:11–32 The fact that a penitent sinner pleases God more than a ceremonially correct Pharisee is quite evident in this parable.

15:12 At a father's death Jewish Law allotted one-third of the estate to the younger son and two-thirds to the elder (Deut. 21:17). The younger son's request betrayed his rebellious nature in wanting to live independently of his father's will. A Jewish father could abdicate his wealth prior to his death (1 Kin. 1; 2).

15:15 To his immorality (v. 13), the son adds apostasy. He joins himself to a Gentile farmer who raises pigs, which were regarded by Jesus' audience as especially "unclean."

15:17 Note how the father is present in the son's memory in the far country.

15:18, 19 Repentance is sorrow for sin, confession that the offense has been committed against a holy God, and change of heart that manifests itself in change of action.

15:21 Compare what the son actually says to his father with his prepared confession (vv. 18, 19). He does not even have a chance to finish his confession before his father calls for a celebration of joy.

15:22–24 The father's reception shows that genuine repentance brings not only pardon but complete restoration.

[1]'Bring out the best robe and put *it* on
him, and put a ring on his hand and
sandals on *his* feet.
23 'And bring the fatted calf here and
kill *it*, and let us eat and be merry;
24 [a]'for this my son was dead and is
alive again; he was lost and is found.'
And they began to be merry.
25 "Now his older son was in the field.
And as he came and drew near to the
house, he heard music and dancing.
26 "So he called one of the servants
and asked what these things meant.
27 "And he said to him, 'Your brother
has come, and because he has received
him *safe and sound, your father has
killed the fatted calf.'
28 "But he was *angry and would not
go in. Therefore his father came out
and pleaded with him.
29 "So he answered and said to *his* father, 'Lo, these many years I have been
serving you; I never transgressed your
commandment at any time; and yet
you never gave me a young goat, that
I might make merry with my friends.
30 'But as soon as this son of yours
came, who has devoured your livelihood with harlots, you killed the fatted
calf for him.'
31 "And he said to him, 'Son, you are
always with me, and all that I have is
yours.
32 'It was right that we should make
merry and be glad, [a]for your brother
was dead and is alive again, and was
lost and is found.' "

The Parable of the Unjust Steward

10 **16** He also said to His disciples:
"There was a certain rich man
who had a *steward, and an accusation
was brought to him that this man was
[1]wasting his goods.
2 "So he called him and said to him,
'What is this I hear about you? Give
an [a]account of your stewardship, for
you can no longer be steward.'
3 "Then the steward said within himself, 'What shall I do? For my master
is taking the stewardship away from
me. I cannot dig; I am ashamed to beg.
4 'I have resolved what to do, that
when I am **put out** of the stewardship,
they may receive me into their houses.'

WORD WEALTH

16:4 put out, *methistemi* (meth-*is*-tay-mee); Strong's *#3179:* Literally, "to set aside." The word indicates a change from one place to another, a removal, a transfer, a relocation. The action involved may be either positive (Col. 1:13) or negative (Luke 16:4).

5 "So he called every one of his master's debtors to *him*, and said to the
first, 'How much do you owe my master?'
6 "And he said, 'A hundred [1]mea-
sures of oil.' So he said to him, 'Take
your bill, and sit down quickly and
write fifty.'
7 "Then he said to another, 'And how
much do you owe?' So he said, 'A hundred [1]measures of wheat.' And he said
to him, 'Take your bill, and write
eighty.'
8 "So the master commended the unjust *steward because he had dealt
shrewdly. For the sons of this world
are more shrewd in their generation
than [a]the sons of light.
9 "And I say to you, [a]make friends
for yourselves by *unrighteous [1]mam-
mon, that when [2]you fail, they may receive you into an everlasting home.
10 [a]"He who *is* faithful in *what is* least
is faithful also in much; and he who
is unjust in *what is* least is unjust also
in much.
11 "Therefore if you have not been
faithful in the unrighteous mammon,
who will commit to your trust the true
riches?
12 "And if you have not been faithful
in what is another man's, who will give
you what is your [a]own?

22 [1]NU *Quickly bring*
24 [a]Matt. 8:22; Luke 9:60; 15:32; Rom. 11:15; [Eph. 2:1, 5; 5:14; Col. 2:13; 1 Tim. 5:6]
27 *See WW at 3 John 2.
28 *See WW at Rev. 12:17.
32 [a]Luke 15:24

CHAPTER 16

1 [1]*squandering* *See WW at 1 Pet. 4:10.
2 [a][Rom. 14:12; 2 Cor. 5:10; 1 Pet. 4:5, 6]
6 [1]Gr. *batos*, same as Heb. *bath;* 8 or 9 gallons each
7 [1]Gr. *koros*, same as Heb. *kor;* 10 or 12 bushels each
8 [a][John 12:36; Eph. 5:8]; 1 Thess. 5:5 *See WW at 1 Pet. 4:10.
9 [a]Dan. 4:27; [Matt. 6:19; 19:21]; Luke 11:41; [1 Tim. 6:17–19] [1]Lit., in Aram., *wealth* [2]NU *it fails* *See WW at John 7:18.
10 [a]Matt. 25:21; Luke 19:17
12 [a][1 Pet. 1:3, 4]

15:25–30 The loveless attitude of the elder brother portrays the Pharisees' claim to self-righteousness, their doctrine of salvation by achievement, and their uncharitable attitude toward repenting sinners. Just as the elder brother had no true relationship with his father, so the Pharisees have no real relationship with God.
15:28 Pleaded: The search of the father extends not only to the younger son, but to the elder son as well.
15:30 This son of yours: The joyless attitude of the older brother (who typifies Jesus' critics) is portrayed by this pejorative jibe. He cannot bring himself to say, "my brother."
15:31, 32 God will extend His mercy to whomever He will, despite the objections of those who view salvation in another way.
16:1–13 See section 10 of Truth-In-Action through the Synoptics at the end of Luke.
16:1–3 The parable of the dishonest steward illustrates the stewardship of wealth. Jesus does not approve the steward's fraud (v. 10), but commends his prudence in using present opportunities for his future welfare (v. 8). For the Christian, prudent use of possessions is for the benefit of others.
16:9 Jesus does not suggest that a person may buy entrance into heaven. He indicates that one's stewardship is a valid test of one's relationship to God.
16:10–12 God tests our fitness to receive the **true riches** of heaven by our use of material possessions.

2 13 [a]"No servant can serve two masters; for either he will hate the one and
love the other, or else he will be loyal
to the one and despise the other. You
cannot serve God and mammon."

The Law, the Prophets, and the Kingdom

9 14 Now the Pharisees, [a]who were lovers of money, also heard all these
things, and they [1]derided Him.
15 And He said to them, "You are
those who [a]justify yourselves [b]before
men, but [c]God knows your hearts. For
[d]what is highly esteemed among men
is an abomination in the sight of God.
8 16 [a]"The law and the prophets *were*
until John. Since that time the kingdom
of God has been preached, and everyone is pressing into it.

KINGDOM DYNAMICS

16:16 Pressing In, CONFLICT AND THE KINGDOM. Jesus declares the advance of the kingdom of God is the result of two things: preaching and pressing in. He shows the gospel of the kingdom must be proclaimed with spiritual passion. In every generation believers have to determine whether they will respond to this truth with sensible minds and sensitive hearts. To overlook it will bring a passivity that limits the ministry of God's kingdom to extending the terms of truth and love—that is, teaching or educating and engaging in acts of kindness. Without question, we must do these things. However, apart from 1) an impassioned pursuit of prayer, 2) confrontation with the demonic, 3) expectation of the miraculous, and 4) a burning heart for evangelism, the kingdom of God makes little penetration in the world.

At the same time, overstatement of "pressing" is likely to produce rabid fanatics who justify any behavior in Jesus' name as applying the boldness spoken of here. Such travesties in church history as the Crusades and various efforts at politicizing in a quest to produce righteousness in society through Earth-level rule are extremes we must learn to reject. "Pressing in" is accomplished first in prayer warfare, coupled with a will to surrender one's life and self-interests, in order to gain God's kingdom goals.

(Col. 2:13–15/Acts 14:21, 22) J.W.H.

13 [a]Matt. 6:24; Gal. 1:10
14 [a]Matt. 23:14 [1]Lit. *turned up their nose at*
15 [a]Luke 10:29 [b][Matt. 6:2, 5, 16] [c]1 Chr. 28:9; 2 Chr. 6:30; Ps. 7:9; Prov. 15:11; Jer. 17:10 [d]1 Sam. 16:7; Ps. 10:3; Prov. 6:16–19; 16:5
16 [a]Matt. 3:1–12; 4:17; 11:12, 13; Luke 7:29
17 [a]Ps. 102:26, 27; Is. 40:8; 51:6; Matt. 5:18; 1 Pet. 1:25 [1]The smallest stroke in a Heb. letter

17 [a]"And it is easier for heaven and
earth to pass away than for one
[1]tittle of the law to fail.

KINGDOM DYNAMICS

16:17 Jesus and the Holy Scriptures, THE WORD OF GOD. As the Resurrected King, God's Messiah and our Savior, our Lord Jesus Christ has given us some of the most important statements concerning the authority and nature of the Word of God. 1) Jesus confirms the truth that every word of the Scriptures is given by God. He goes so far as to make direct reference to the smallest letter ("jot," literally *yod,* the Hebrew counterpart to our letter "i" or "j"), and the smallest punctuation point, "tittle." There is no room for debate: Jesus believed and taught the plenary verbal inspiration of the Bible—that every word is God-breathed (see 2 Tim. 3:16). 2) Jesus also contends that every truth the Bible teaches is to be held inviolable. In Matt. 5:17–19 He insists that anyone who teaches anything running at cross-purposes with the Scriptures is not in harmony with His kingdom order. 3) Jesus attests to the indissolubility of the Scriptures (John 10:35). When He says "the Scripture cannot be broken," He literally describes the utter inviolability of God's Word from man's side (do not try to diminish its truth or meaning) and the utter dependability of it from God's side (He will uphold it—His Word will not dissolve or be shaken). Matt. 24:35 is the verse most quoted in this regard. All creation may dissolve: God's Word will stand forever! 4) Jesus affirms the credibility of the OT in general (John 5:39), but also of the miracles of the OT. He did not see them as superstitiously held beliefs, which He tolerated among those He addressed. Rather, He was the

(*cont. on next page*)

16:13 See section 2 of Truth-In-Action through the Synoptics at the end of Luke.
16:13 One's attitude toward money is indicative of one's submission to or rebellion against God's lordship.
16:14, 15 See section 9 of Truth-In-Action through the Synoptics at the end of Luke.
16:14 The Pharisees regarded wealth as the reward for righteousness.
16:15 An outward attitude of righteousness coming out of evil hearts might win the praise of others, but it is detestable to God.
16:16 See section 8 of Truth-In-Action through the Synoptics at the end of Luke.
16:16 The Pharisees supposed that a rigid observance of the Law was the way of righteousness, failing to realize that the Law and the Prophets pointed to the Messiah. Their way of justification was no longer valid since John the Baptist announced that repentance and belief were the means of entrance into the kingdom. Now everyone who desired the kingdom could press into it. See note on Matt. 11:12.
16:17, 18 Tittle: The term means a tiny mark, used to distinguish Hebrew alphabet letters. The saying affirms the enduring quality of the Law, as expressive of the will of God. The gospel did not set aside the Law, but rather fulfilled it at a higher level (see note on Matt. 5:17). As an example of the Law's permanence, Jesus refers to **adultery,** which was still sinful, even if it was justified by civil law (see note on Matt. 5:32).

(cont. from preceding page)
Incarnate Truth; and as the embodiment of truthfulness, His testimony is decisive. Thus, note that Jesus believed the biblical record of: (a) Adam and Eve as the first pair (Matt. 19:4, 5); (b) the literal destruction of Sodom and Gomorrah (Mark 6:11; Luke 17:29, 30); (c) the actuality of Noah and the Flood (Matt. 24:37, 38); (d) the trustworthiness of Daniel's prophecy (Matt. 24:15); (e) the truth of Jonah's being swallowed by the great fish (Matt. 12:39, 40); and (f) the miracle of the manna as well as other miracles during the wilderness journey of Moses' time (John 3:14; 6:31, 32). Finally, 5) Jesus forecast and authorized the writing of the NT Scriptures. In both John 14:26 and 16:12, 13, He indicated that the coming ministry of the Holy Spirit would include His bringing to the apostles' minds the things that should afterward be recorded. His anticipation of that ministry not only places His endorsement upon that facet of their apostolic mission, it also indirectly effects His closure of the canon of Scripture following the completion of this task. (See article at Prov. 30:5, 6.)

(Prov. 30:5, 6/2 Cor. 3:5–8) J.W.H.

1 18 [a]"Whoever divorces his wife and
marries another commits adultery; and
whoever marries her who is divorced
from *her* husband commits adultery.

The Rich Man and Lazarus

19 "There was a certain rich man who
was clothed in purple and fine linen
and [1]fared sumptuously every day.
20 "But there was a certain beggar
named Lazarus, full of sores, who was
laid at his gate,
21 "desiring to be *fed with [1]the
crumbs which fell from the rich man's
table. Moreover the dogs came and
licked his sores.
22 "So it was that the beggar died, and
was carried by the angels to [a]Abra-
ham's bosom. The rich man also died
and was buried.

18 [a]Matt. 5:32; 19:9; Mark 10:11; 1 Cor. 7:10, 11
19 [1]*lived in luxury*
21 [1]NU *what fell* *See WW at Matt. 15:33.
22 [a]Matt. 8:11

KINGDOM DYNAMICS

16:22 Believers Accompanied by Angels, ANGELS. The Bible indicates angels in the future of all believers, at death or at Jesus' Second Coming. Should death occur, at our transition between this life and the next, it will not be a lonely, dreadful experience. Rather, angels will accompany us into everlasting joy just as they carried the beggar to the resting place appointed for him by God. For us, that will be Jesus' presence (2 Cor. 5:1–8). However, if Christ returns before our death, at the Second Coming the angels will gather us to Christ "from the farthest part of earth to the farthest part of heaven" (Mark 13:26, 27).

(Is. 14:12–14/Ps. 103:20, 21*) M.H.

23 "And being in torments in Hades,
he lifted up his eyes and saw Abraham
afar off, and Lazarus in his bosom.

KINGDOM DYNAMICS

16:23 15. What Is Hell Like?, SPIRITUAL ANSWERS. For the answer to this and other probing questions about God and the power life in His kingdom, see the study article "Spiritual Answers to Hard Questions," which begins on page 1996.

P.R.

24 "Then he cried and said, 'Father
Abraham, have mercy on me, and send
Lazarus that he may dip the tip of his
finger in water and [a]cool my tongue;
for I [b]am tormented in this flame.'
25 "But Abraham said, 'Son, [a]remem-
ber that in your lifetime you received
your good things, and likewise Lazarus
evil things; but now he is comforted
and you are tormented.
26 'And besides all this, between us
and you there is a great gulf fixed, so
that those who want to pass from here

24 [a]Zech. 14:12 [b][Is. 66:24; Mark 9:42–48]
25 [a]Job 21:13; Luke 6:24; James 5:5

16:18 See section 1 of Truth-In-Action through the Synoptics at the end of Luke.

16:19–31 As "lovers of money" (v. 14), the Pharisees looked upon wealth as a sign of God's blessings, and looked upon poverty as a sign of His judgment. Jesus teaches that material possessions are a trust from God, to be used responsibly for good. One's attitude toward possessions is a clear indication of whether one is living self-centeredly or under the total Lordship of Christ.

The main intent of this parable is to call those with a godless view of wealth and righteousness to repent and help others with their money. It is an example of "what is highly esteemed among men [being] an abomination in the sight of God" (v. 15).

16:19 The **rich man** is sometimes called Dives, Latin for "a man of wealth."

16:22 To a Jew **Abraham's bosom** suggests the honored place in Paradise (see John 13:23), that is, the beggar received a special welcome in heaven and was seated beside Abraham. The term also apparently may have been used to describe that segment of Hades reserved for the righteous (until following Jesus' resurrection).

16:23, 24 Hades is the abode of the dead. The description leaves no doubt that the rich man was in a place of eternal punishment.

16:25 Wealth does not automatically condemn one to hell, nor does poverty in this life guarantee eternal joy. One's destiny depends upon one's relationship to God, which is often reflected in the attitude toward material possessions.

to you cannot, nor can those from there
pass to us.'
27 "Then he said, 'I beg you therefore,
father, that you would send him to my
father's house,
28 'for I have five brothers, that he may
testify to them, lest they also come to
this place of torment.'
29 "Abraham said to him, [a]'They have
Moses and the prophets; let them hear
them.'
30 "And he said, 'No, father Abraham;
but if one goes to them from the dead,
they will *repent.'
31 "But he said to him, [a]'If they do not
hear Moses and the prophets, [b]neither
will they be persuaded though one rise
from the dead.'"

Jesus Warns of Offenses

17 Then He said to the disciples,
[a]"It is impossible that no
[1]offenses* should come, but [b]woe *to*
him through whom they do come!
2 "It would be better for him if a millstone were hung around his neck, and
he were thrown into the sea, than that
he should [1]offend one of these little
ones.
5 3 "Take heed to yourselves. [a]If your
brother sins [1]against you, [b]rebuke him;
and if he repents, forgive him.
4 "And if he sins against you seven
times in a day, and seven times in a
day returns [1]to you, saying, 'I repent,'
you shall forgive him."

Faith and Duty

5 And the apostles said to the Lord,
"Increase our faith."
6 [a]So the Lord said, "If you have faith
as a mustard seed, you can say to this
mulberry tree, 'Be pulled up by the
roots and be planted in the sea,' and
it would obey you.
7 "And which of you, having a servant plowing or tending sheep, will say
to him when he has come in from the
field, 'Come at once and sit down to
eat'?
8 "But will he not rather say to him,
'Prepare something for my supper, and
gird yourself [a]and serve me till I have
eaten and drunk, and afterward you
will eat and drink'?
9 "Does he thank that servant because he did the things that were commanded [1]him? I think not.
10 "So likewise you, when you have
done all those things which you are
commanded, say, 'We are [a]unprofit-
able servants. We have done what was
our duty to do.'"

Ten Lepers Cleansed

11 Now it happened [a]as He went to Jerusalem that He passed through the
midst of Samaria and Galilee.
12 Then as He entered a certain village, there met Him ten men who were
lepers, [a]who stood afar off.
13 And they lifted up *their* voices and
said, "Jesus, Master, have mercy on
us!"
14 So when He saw *them,* He said to
them, [a]"Go, show yourselves to the
priests." And so it was that as they
went, they were cleansed.
15 And one of them, when he saw that
he was healed, returned, and with a
loud voice [a]glorified God,
16 and fell down on *his* face at His feet,
giving Him thanks. And he was a
[a]Samaritan.
17 So Jesus answered and said, "Were
there not ten cleansed? But where *are*
the nine?
18 "Were there not any found who returned to give glory to God except this
foreigner?"
19 [a]And He said to him, "Arise, go
your way. Your faith has made you
well."

29 [a]Acts 15:21; 17:11
30 *See WW at Matt. 3:2.
31 [a][John 5:46] [b]John 12:10, 11

CHAPTER 17

1 [a][1 Cor. 11:19] [b][2 Thess. 1:6] [1]*stumbling blocks* *See WW at Matt. 16:23.
2 [1]*cause one of these little ones to stumble*
3 [a][Matt. 18:15, 21] [b][Prov. 17:10] [1]NU omits *against you*
4 [1]M omits *to you*
6 [a][Mark 9:23; 11:23]
8 [a][Luke 12:37]
9 [1]NU omits the rest of v. 9; M omits *him*
10 [a]Rom. 3:12; 11:35
11 [a]Luke 9:51, 52
12 [a]Lev. 13:46
14 [a]Matt. 8:4
15 [a]Luke 5:25; 18:43
16 [a]2 Kin. 17:24
19 [a]Matt. 9:22

16:29–31 The Pharisees were constantly demanding signs from Jesus to prove His messiahship. Not only did they reject the scriptural evidence concerning Him, which was sufficient in itself, but they did not receive the witness of the Resurrection, the greatest miracle of all.
17:1, 2 Offenses: The term means "stumbling blocks," lit. the trigger of a trap or a snare. Here it designates something that will cause another to sin. No person sins in a vacuum; others are affected. Jesus issues a strong warning against being the cause of the apostasy of others, particularly those less mature in years or experience (see Matt. 18:6, 7).
17:3, 4 See section 5 of Truth-In-Action through the Synoptics at the end of Luke.
17:3, 4 See notes on Matt. 18:21–35.
17:5 The disciples felt the need for greater **faith** to meet the standard Jesus demanded.
17:6 The amount of faith is not as important as its quality. See notes on Matt. 17:20; Mark 11:23.
17:7–10 A disciple who obeys the commands of God cannot make special claims upon God for merely fulfilling his duty. God's rewards are of grace, not of merit.
17:16 Perhaps the others, who were Jews, felt that healing was their due since they were of the chosen race.
17:17 Ingratitude did not deny Christ's mercy to **the nine,** but did deprive them of fellowship with Him.
17:18 Foreigner: The ungrateful nine lepers seem to represent that nation of people who had been ungrateful and unresponsive to the cleansing work of Jesus the Messiah. They contrast with the grateful response of their hated Samaritan neighbors (v. 16).
17:19 An alternate translation is, "Your faith has saved you," referring to salvation rather than health. The nine ingrates

KINGDOM DYNAMICS

17:12–19 Healing as They Went, DIVINE HEALING. The nature of some healing as "progressive" is noted in the words "as they went, they were cleansed." The 10 lepers' healing affords several lessons: 1) Not all healing is at the moment of prayer. Instant healings are often expected, whereas this illustrates the healing "in process" over a period of time following prayer. 2) Jesus' directive "Go . . . to the priests" not only indicates His affirmation of the Law (Lev. 13:1–59). Since the priests were the physicians of that culture, it indicates His approval of persons who have received healings seeing their physicians for confirmation of the healings. 3) The lepers' obedience to Jesus' command is important to note. As they went in obedience, they were healed. When healing is not instantaneous, one ought not to doubt, but find a possible path of obedience. 4) Of that group of lepers healed by Jesus, only one returned to express gratitude. When healing comes, express thanks with praise and worship, and do not be as the nine who failed to return with thanksgiving.

(Luke 10:8, 9/John 8:58) N.V.

The Coming of the Kingdom

8 **20** Now when He was asked by the
Pharisees when the kingdom of God
would come, He answered them and
said, "The kingdom of God does not
come with observation;
21 [a]"nor will they say, [1]'See here!' or
'See there!' For indeed, [b]the kingdom
of God is [2]within you."

KINGDOM DYNAMICS

17:20, 21 The Kingdom Within You, THE MESSAGE OF THE KINGDOM. Fundamental to NT truth is that the kingdom of God is the spiritual reality and dynamic available to each person who receives Jesus Christ as Savior and Lord. To receive Him—the King—is to receive His kingly rule, not only in your life and over your affairs, but through your life and by your service and love. "The kingdom of God is within you," Jesus said.

This is never to be construed as possible if we operate independently of God's power and grace. The possibility of reinstatement to rulership is brought about only through the forgiveness of sins and full redemption in Christ through the Cross. The Bible never suggests either 1) that there exists in man a divine spark, which may be fanned to flame by noble human efforts, or 2) that godlikeness is somehow resident in man's potential, as though human beings are or may become "gods." To the contrary, man is lost in darkness and alienated from God (Eph. 4:18; 2:12).

However, full salvation brings restored relationship to God and a full potential for His kingdom's ruling "within us" as we walk with Him. Jesus has sent the Holy Spirit to cause the anointing of His messiahship to be transmitted to us (Is. 61:1–3; Luke 4:18; John 1:16; 1 John 2:20, 27; 4:17). So it is, and on these terms only, that a human being can say, "The kingdom of God is within me."

(Col. 1:13/Matt. 5:1—7:27) J.W.H.

KINGDOM DYNAMICS

17:21 29. What Is the Kingdom of God?, SPIRITUAL ANSWERS. For the answer to this and other probing questions about God and the power life in His kingdom, see the study article "Spiritual Answers to Hard Questions," which begins on page 1996. P.R.

21 [a]Luke 17:23 [b][Rom. 14:17] [1]NU reverses *here* and *there* [2]*in your midst*

22 [a]Matt. 9:15; Mark 2:20; Luke 5:35; [John 17:12]
23 [a]Matt. 24:23; Mark 13:21; [Luke 21:8] [1]NU reverses *here* and *there*
24 [a]Matt. 24:27
25 [a]Matt. 26:67; 27:29–31; Mark 8:31; 9:31; 10:33 [b]Luke 9:22 *See WW at Acts 17:3.
26 [a]Matt. 24:37–39 [b][Gen. 6:5–7] [c][Gen. 6:8–13] [d]1 Pet. 3:20

22 Then He said to the disciples,
[a]"The days will come when you will
desire to see one of the days of the Son
of Man, and you will not see *it*.
23 [a]"And they will say to you, [1]'Look
here!' or 'Look there!' Do not go after
them or follow *them*.
24 [a]"For as the lightning that flashes
out of one *part* under heaven shines
to the other *part* under heaven, so also
the Son of Man will be in His day.
25 [a]"But first He must *suffer many
things and be [b]rejected by this generation.
26 [a]"And as it [b]was in the [c]days of
[d]Noah, so it will be also in the days
of the Son of Man:
27 "They ate, they drank, they married

received only physical healing, but the grateful foreigner received more.
17:20, 21 See section 8 of Truth-In-Action through the Synoptics at the end of Luke.
17:20, 21 In contrast to the expectations of the Pharisees, **the kingdom** is not external and physical, in the sense of being a political domain, but rather internal and spiritual. **Within you** (v. 21) may also be translated "in your midst." If so, Jesus is saying that the kingdom is presently embodied in Him, a fact, which, in their unbelief, they failed to recognize.
17:22 The consummation of the kingdom awaits the return of the Lord. In times of weariness believers will often long for that day of victory.
17:23 Until the Lord returns, Christians are to live by faith and avoid those who tamper with dates and signs.
17:24 The Lord's Coming will be as sudden and as visible as **lightning**.
17:26–30 Believers must live in constant expectancy and readiness for Christ's return, in contrast to the careless indifference of unbelievers who are absorbed in routine pursuits of life as though they were permanent.

wives, they were given in marriage, until the [a]day that Noah entered the ark,
and the flood came and [b]destroyed
them all.
28 [a]"Likewise as it was also in the
days of Lot: They ate, they drank, they
bought, they sold, they planted, they
built;
29 "but on [a]the day that Lot went out
of Sodom it rained fire and brimstone
from heaven and destroyed *them* all.
30 "Even so will it be in the day when
the Son of Man [a]is revealed.
31 "In that day, he [a]who is on the
housetop, and his [1]goods *are* in the
house, let him not come down to take
them away. And likewise the one who
is in the field, let him not turn back.
32 [a]"Remember Lot's wife.
33 [a]"Whoever seeks to *save his life
will lose it, and whoever loses his life
will preserve it.
34 [a]"I tell you, in that night there will
be two [1]*men* in one bed: the one will
be taken and the other will be left.
35 [a]"Two *women* will be grinding together: the one will be taken and the
other left.
36 [1]"Two *men* will be in the field: the
one will be taken and the other left."
37 And they answered and said to
Him, [a]"Where, Lord?" So He said to
them, "Wherever the body is, there the
eagles will be gathered together."

The Parable of the Persistent Widow

3 **18** Then He spoke a parable to
them, that men [a]always ought
to pray and not lose heart,
2 saying: "There was in a certain city
a judge who did not fear God nor
[1]regard man.

27 [a]Gen. 7:1–16 [b]Gen. 7:19–23
28 [a]Gen. 19
29 [a]Gen. 19:16, 24, 29; 2 Pet. 2:6, 7
30 [a][Matt. 16:27]; 1 Cor. 1:7; [Col. 3:4; 2 Thess. 1:7]; 1 Pet. 1:7; 4:13; 1 John 2:28
31 [a]Matt. 24:17, 18; Mark 13:15 [1]*possessions*
32 [a]Gen. 19:26
33 [a]Matt. 10:39; 16:25; Mark 8:35; Luke 9:24; John 12:25 *See WW at Luke 7:50.
34 [a]Matt. 24:40, 41; [1 Thess. 4:17] [1]Or *people*
35 [a]Matt. 24:40, 41
36 [1]NU, M omit v. 36.
37 [a]Job 39:30; Matt. 24:28

CHAPTER 18

1 [a]Luke 11:5–10; Rom. 12:12; [Eph. 6:18]; Col. 4:2; 1 Thess. 5:17
2 [1]*respect*
3 [1]*Avenge me on*
5 [a]Luke 11:8 [1]*vindicate*
7 [a]Rev. 6:10 *See WW at 1 Pet. 2:9.
8 [a]Heb. 10:37; [2 Pet. 3:8, 9]
9 [a]Prov. 30:12; Luke 10:29; 16:15
10 *See WW at Matt. 6:6.
11 [a]Ps. 135:2 [b]Is. 1:15; 58:2; Rev. 3:17

3 "Now there was a widow in that
city; and she came to him, saying,
[1]'Get justice for me from my adversary.'
4 "And he would not for a while; but
afterward he said within himself,
'Though I do not fear God nor regard
man,
5 [a]'yet because this widow troubles
me I will [1]avenge her, lest by her continual coming she weary me.' "
6 Then the Lord said, "Hear what the
unjust judge said.
7 "And [a]shall God not avenge His
own *elect who cry out day and night
to Him, though He bears long with
them?
8 "I tell you [a]that He will avenge them
speedily. Nevertheless, when the Son
of Man comes, will He really find faith
on the earth?"

The Parable of the Pharisee and the Tax Collector

9 Also He spoke this parable to some 5
[a]who trusted in themselves that they
were righteous, and despised others:
10 "Two men went up to the temple
to *pray, one a Pharisee and the other
a tax collector.
11 "The Pharisee [a]stood and prayed
thus with himself, [b]'God, I thank You
that I am not like other men—extortioners, unjust, adulterers, or even
as this tax collector.
12 'I fast twice a week; I give tithes of
all that I possess.'
13 "And the tax collector, standing
afar off, would not so much as raise
his eyes to heaven, but beat his breast,
saying, 'God, be merciful to me a sinner!'

17:31, 32 A loose attachment to things of Earth allows for readiness to leave. The fate of **Lot's wife** is a warning against being tied to worldly possessions.
17:33 See notes on Matt. 16:21–27.
17:34–36 Although some commentators dramatize these verses as indicative of the church's "secret" rapture, Jesus' point is to teach that there will be a decisive separation at the Lord's return. The time and manner of fulfillment is not indicated.
17:37 Different views see the **eagles** (vultures) in these ways: 1) as symbols of judgment; 2) as birds gathering where there is the carrion of spiritual decay; 3) as depicting the church being "snatched heavenward," as a bird snatches its prey.
18:1–8 See section 3 of Truth-In-Action through the Synoptics at the end of Luke.
18:1 Prayer encourages steadfastness and guards against disheartedness during the delay of Christ's return.
18:2–8 The parable is a story using contrast rather than comparison. The readiness of God to effect justice lies in contrast to the reluctance of the judge who only dispenses justice out of exasperation with the nuisance of the widow's persistence. The point of contrast is in the fact of God's willingness and readiness; further, we are not widows but members of Christ's own body—His bride. Therefore, we can expect the Just Judge, the Father, to bring us redress from wrong when we pray.
18:8 Christians are not to grow weary in waiting for the Lord, but they are to persevere in faith.
18:9–14 See section 5 of Truth-In-Action through the Synoptics at the end of Luke.
18:9 Not all prayer is genuine. Attitude is just as important as persistence. Jesus also corrects the mistaken notion that righteousness is a human achievement instead of a gift of God's grace.
18:11 A religion based upon a merit system leads to religious pride.
18:12 Some Pharisees went beyond the requirements of the Law by tithing even what they bought, lest they make use of goods which had not been tithed.
18:13 **A sinner** is literally "the sinner," more than all others. He deeply feels his guilt.

14 "I tell you, this man went down to his house *justified *rather* than the other; [a]for everyone who exalts himself will be [1]humbled, and he who *humbles himself will be exalted."

Jesus Blesses Little Children

15 [a]Then they also brought infants to Him that He might touch them; but when the disciples saw *it*, they rebuked them.
16 But Jesus called them to *Him* and said, "Let the little children come to Me, and do not forbid them; for [a]of such is the kingdom of God.
17 [a]"Assuredly, I say to you, whoever does not receive the kingdom of God as a little child will by no means enter it."

Jesus Counsels the Rich Young Ruler

18 [a]Now a certain ruler asked Him, saying, "Good Teacher, what shall I do to inherit eternal life?"
19 So Jesus said to him, "Why do you call Me good? No one *is* good but [a]One, *that is*, God.
20 "You know the commandments: [a]*'Do not commit adultery,' 'Do not murder,' 'Do not steal,' 'Do not bear false witness,'* [b]*'Honor your father and your mother.'* "
21 And he said, "All [a]these things I have kept from my youth."
10 22 So when Jesus heard these things, He said to him, "You still lack one thing. [a]Sell all that you have and distribute to the poor, and you will have treasure in heaven; and come, *follow Me."

KINGDOM DYNAMICS

18:22 21. Do People Have to Be Poor in Order to Be Holy?, SPIRITUAL ANSWERS. For the answer to this and other probing questions about God and the power life in His kingdom, see the study article "Spiritual Answers to Hard Questions," which begins on page 1996. P.R.

23 But when he heard this, he became very sorrowful, for he was very rich.

14 [a]Job 22:29; Matt. 23:12; Luke 14:11; [James 4:6; 1 Pet. 5:5] [1]*put down* *See WW at Matt. 12:37. • See WW at Matt. 18:4.
15 [a]Matt. 19:13–15; Mark 10:13–16
16 [a]Matt. 18:3; 1 Cor. 14:20; 1 Pet. 2:2
17 [a]Matt. 18:3; 19:14; Mark 10:15
18 [a]Matt. 19:16–29; Mark 10:17–30
19 [a]Ps. 86:5; 119:68
20 [a]Ex. 20:12–16; Deut. 5:16–20; Mark 10:19; Rom. 13:9 [b]Eph. 6:2; Col. 3:20
21 [a]Phil. 3:6
22 [a]Matt. 6:19, 20; 19:21; [1 Tim. 6:19] *See WW at John 13:36.
24 [a]Prov. 11:28; Matt. 19:23; Mark 10:23
27 [a]Job 42:2; Jer. 32:17; Zech. 8:6; Matt. 19:26; Luke 1:37
28 [a]Matt. 19:27 [1]NU *our own*
29 [a]Deut. 33:9
30 [a]Job 42:10
31 [a]Matt. 16:21; 17:22; 20:17; Mark 10:32; Luke 9:51 [b]Ps. 22; [Is. 53] [1]*fulfilled*
32 [a]Matt. 26:67; 27:2, 29, 41; Mark 14:65; 15:1, 19, 20, 31; Luke 23:1; John 18:28; Acts 3:13
34 [a]Mark 9:32; Luke 2:50; 9:45; [John 10:6; 12:16]

With God All Things Are Possible

24 And when Jesus saw that he became very sorrowful, He said, [a]"How hard it is for those who have riches to enter the kingdom of God!
25 "For it is easier for a camel to go through the eye of a needle than for a rich man to enter the kingdom of God."
26 And those who heard it said, "Who then can be saved?"
27 But He said, [a]"The things which are impossible with men are possible with God."
28 [a]Then Peter said, "See, we have left [1]all and followed You."
29 So He said to them, "Assuredly, I say to you, [a]there is no one who has left house or parents or brothers or wife or children, for the sake of the kingdom of God,
30 [a]"who shall not receive many times more in this present time, and in the age to come eternal life."

Jesus a Third Time Predicts His Death and Resurrection

31 [a]Then He took the twelve aside and said to them, "Behold, we are going up to Jerusalem, and all things [b]that are written by the prophets concerning the Son of Man will be [1]accomplished.
32 "For [a]He will be delivered to the Gentiles and will be mocked and **insulted** and spit upon.

WORD WEALTH

18:32 insulted, *hubrizo* (hoo-*brid*-zoe); Strong's *#5195:* Compare "hubristic" and "hybrid." To insult; to treat arrogantly, insolently, sarcastically, and injuriously; to commit an outrage against. It is abuse that runs riot, acts wantonly, shamefully, and with affront. Jesus not only received this treatment from His enemies, but He warned His followers not to be surprised when they received the same treatment (Matt. 22:6).

33 "They will scourge *Him* and kill Him. And the third day He will rise again."
34 [a]But they understood none of these things; this saying was hidden from them, and they did not know the things which were spoken.

18:15–17 See notes on Mark 10:13–16.
18:18–30 See notes on Matt. 19:16–29; Mark 10:17–30.
18:22–27 See section 10 of Truth-In-Action through the Synoptics at the end of Luke.
18:31–33 Jesus' third pronouncement of His death includes details not mentioned in the earlier two (9:22, 43–45).
18:34 Luke describes their dullness of apprehension with a threefold emphasis.

A Blind Man Receives His Sight

35 [a]Then it happened, as He was coming near Jericho, that a certain blind
man sat by the road begging.
36 And hearing a multitude passing
by, he asked what it meant.
37 So they told him that Jesus of Nazareth was passing by.
38 And he cried out, saying, "Jesus,
[a]Son of David, have mercy on me!"
39 Then those who went before
warned him that he should be quiet;
but he cried out all the more, "Son of
David, *have mercy on me!"
40 So Jesus stood still and commanded
him to be brought to Him. And when
he had come near, He asked him,
41 saying, "What do you *want Me to
do for you?" He said, "Lord, that I may
receive my sight."
42 Then Jesus said to him, "Receive
your sight; [a]your faith has made you
well."
43 And immediately he received his
sight, and followed Him, [a]glorifying
God. And all the people, when they
saw *it*, gave praise to God.

Jesus Comes to Zacchaeus' House

19 Then *Jesus* entered and passed
through [a]Jericho.
2 Now behold, *there was* a man
named Zacchaeus who was a chief tax
collector, and he was rich.
3 And he sought to [a]see who Jesus
was, but could not because of the
crowd, for he was of short stature.
4 So he ran ahead and climbed up
into a sycamore tree to see Him, for
He was going to pass that *way*.
5 And when Jesus came to the place,
He looked up [1]and saw him, and said
to him, "Zacchaeus, [2]make haste and
come down, for today I must stay at
your house."
6 So he [1]made haste and came down,
and received Him joyfully.
7 But when they saw *it*, they all
[1]complained, saying, [a]"He has gone to
be a guest with a man who is a *sinner."
8 Then Zacchaeus stood and said to
the Lord, "Look, Lord, I give half of
my goods to the [a]poor; and if I have
taken anything from anyone by
[b]false accusation, [c]I restore fourfold."
9 And Jesus said to him, "Today **salvation** has come to this house, because
[a]he also is [b]a son of Abraham;

35 [a]Matt. 20:29–34; Mark 10:46–52
38 [a]Matt. 9:27
39 *See WW at Rom. 9:15.
41 *See WW at Matt. 8:2.
42 [a]Luke 17:19
43 [a]Luke 5:26; Acts 4:21; 11:18

CHAPTER 19

1 [a]Josh. 6:26; 1 Kin. 16:34
3 [a]John 12:21
5 [1]NU omits *and saw him* [2]*hurry*
6 [1]*hurried*
7 [a]Matt. 9:11; Luke 5:30; 15:2 [1]*grumbled* *See WW at James 5:20.
8 [a][Ps. 41:1] [b]Luke 3:14 [c]Ex. 22:1; Lev. 6:5; Num. 5:7; 1 Sam. 12:3; 2 Sam. 12:6
9 [a]Luke 3:8; 13:16; [Rom. 4:16; Gal. 3:7] [b][Luke 13:16]

WORD WEALTH

19:9 salvation, *soteria* (so-tay-*ree*-ah); Strong's *#4991:* Compare "soteriology." Deliverance, preservation, soundness, prosperity, happiness, rescue, general well-being. The word is used both in a material, temporal sense and in a spiritual, eternal sense. The NT especially uses the word for spiritual well-being. Salvation is a present possession (1:77;
(*cont. on next page*)

18:35–43 See notes on Mark 10:47, 48.
19:1 Jericho served as a major customs site for goods entering Palestine from the East.
19:2 As a **chief tax collector Zacchaeus** was both a social and a religious outcast because he was viewed as cooperating with the Roman occupational government.
19:4 The **sycamore tree** (literally, a fig-mulberry) is a sturdy, wide, open tree with low limbs that allow for ease in climbing.
19:5 Today: The word, repeated in v. 9, is suggestive of the present reality of salvation present in Jesus. The present acceptance of a hated chief tax collector expresses the presence of the kingdom's power just as other acts of healing or exorcism.
19:8 Zacchaeus goes far beyond the laws of just restitution (Lev. 6:1–5; Num. 5:5–7), giving evidence of a changed heart.
19:9 Previously, he may have been a physical **son of Abraham,** but by his repentance he has become a spiritual son, and the entire household shares in the blessing.

Scythopolis
SAMARIA
Aenon?
Salim?
Samaria
Sychar
Jordan R.
PEREA (TRANSJORDAN)
Arimathea
Ephraim
Bethel
Emmaus
Jericho
Jerusalem
Bethany
JUDEA
Bethlehem
Dead Sea
IDUMEA
N
? Exact location questionable
0 30 Mi.
0 30 Km.

Last Journey to Jerusalem. Jesus' last ascent to Jerusalem began on the eastern side of the Jordan. After crossing the river, He entered Jericho, then ascended the mountain to Bethany and Jerusalem. There He was crucified.

(cont. from preceding page)
2 Cor. 1:6; 7:10) with a fuller realization in the future (Rom. 13:11; 1 Thess. 5:8, 9).

10 [a]"for the Son of Man has come to
seek and to save that which was lost."

The Parable of the Minas

11 Now as they heard these things, He
spoke another parable, because He
was near Jerusalem and because
[a]they thought the kingdom of God
would appear immediately.
12 [a]Therefore He said: "A certain nobleman went into a far country to receive for himself a kingdom and to return.
13 "So he called ten of his servants,
delivered to them ten [1]minas, and said
to them, 'Do business till I come.'
14 [a]"But his citizens hated him, and
sent a delegation after him, saying,
'We will not have this *man* to reign
over us.'
15 "And so it was that when he returned, having received the kingdom,
he then commanded these servants, to
whom he had given the money, to be
called to him, that he might know how
much every man had gained by trading.
16 "Then came the first, saying, 'Master, your mina has earned ten minas.'
17 "And he said to him, [a]'Well *done*,
good servant; because you were
[b]faithful in a very little, have authority
over ten cities.'
18 "And the second came, saying,
'Master, your mina has earned five minas.'
19 "Likewise he said to him, 'You also
be over five cities.'
20 "Then another came, saying, 'Master, here is your mina, which I have
kept put away in a handkerchief.
21 [a]'For I feared you, because you are
[1]an austere man. You collect what you
did not deposit, and reap what you did
not sow.'
22 "And he said to him, [a]'Out of your
own mouth I will *judge you, *you*
wicked servant. [b]You knew that I was
an austere man, collecting what I did
not deposit and reaping what I did not
sow.
23 'Why then did you not put my
money in the bank, that at my coming
I might have collected it with interest?'
24 "And he said to those who stood by,
'Take the mina from him, and give *it*
to him who has ten minas.'
25 ("But they said to him, 'Master, he
has ten minas.')
26 'For I say to you, [a]that to everyone
who has will be given; and from him
who does not have, even what he has
will be taken away from him.
27 'But bring here those enemies of
mine, who did not want me to reign
over them, and slay *them* before me.' "

The Triumphal Entry

28 When He had said this, [a]He went
on ahead, going up to Jerusalem.
29 [a]And it came to pass, when He drew
near to [1]Bethphage and [b]Bethany, at
the mountain called [c]Olivet, *that* He
sent two of His disciples,
30 saying, "Go into the village opposite *you*, where as you enter you will
find a colt tied, on which no one has
ever sat. Loose it and bring *it here*.
31 "And if anyone asks you, 'Why are
you loosing *it*?' thus you shall say to
him, 'Because the Lord has need of
it.' "
32 So those who were sent went their
way and found *it* just [a]as He had said
to them.
33 But as they were loosing the colt,
the owners of it said to them, "Why
are you loosing the colt?"

10 [a]Matt. 18:11; [Luke 5:32; Rom. 5:8]
11 [a]Acts 1:6
12 [a]Matt. 25:14–30; Mark 13:34
13 [1]Gr. *mna,* same as Heb. *minah,* each worth about three months' salary
14 [a][John 1:11]
17 [a]Matt. 25:21, 23 [b]Luke 16:10
21 [a]Matt. 25:24 [1]*a severe*
22 [a]2 Sam. 1:16; Job 15:6; [Matt. 12:37] [b]Matt. 25:26 *See WW at John 18:31.
26 [a]Matt. 13:12; 25:29; Mark 4:25; Luke 8:18
28 [a]Mark 10:32
29 [a]Matt. 21:1; Mark 11:1 [b]Matt. 26:6; John 12:1 [c]John 8:1; Acts 1:12 [1]M *Bethsphage*
32 [a]Luke 22:13

19:10 In announcing the purpose of His mission, Jesus goes against the political expectations of the people.
19:11 The parable of the minas (vv. 12–26) corrects the Pharisees' false assumption that the kingdom of God would occur immediately. Jesus shows its fullness will be delayed. In view of this, His parable highlights the responsibility of the people of God during this interim period. The immediate need was to correct their false assumption—an especially needed correction, since the presence of Jesus now **near Jerusalem** was fueling anticipations that were not to be fulfilled.
19:12–27 See notes on Matt. 25:14–30.
19:13 A mina was a weight equal to 50 shekels. Here it refers to approximately a pound of money (see marginal note).
19:14 The parable is based upon a historical event. According to the historian Josephus, after the death of Herod the Great, his son Archelaus went to Rome to be confirmed as king of Judea (v. 12). The Jews, however, sent a delegation to protest the appointment.
19:17 For the first two servants, responsible service is rewarded with greater authority, corresponding to their gain.
19:20 Handkerchief: This refers to a neck scarf worn for protection from the sun.
19:26 The conclusion to the parable makes two points: 1) The rule of God demands fearless venture, even risk-taking; 2) The enemies of the king will be slain. The fierce judgment of v. 27 may reflect the fall of Jerusalem (A.D. 70) as a type of the future judgment when Jesus will come in the glory of the kingdom, after His absence (v. 12).
19:28–38 See notes on Matt. 21:1–11; Mark 11:1–10.

34 And they said, "The Lord has need of him."
35 Then they brought him to Jesus. [a]And they threw their own clothes on the colt, and they set Jesus on him.
36 And as He went, *many* spread their clothes on the road.
37 Then, as He was now drawing near the descent of the Mount of Olives, the whole multitude of the disciples began to [a]rejoice and praise God with a loud voice for all the mighty works they had seen,
38 saying:

> [a]" *'Blessed is the King who comes in the name of the LORD!'*
> [b]Peace in heaven and glory in the highest!"

39 And some of the Pharisees called to Him from the crowd, "Teacher, rebuke Your disciples."
40 But He answered and said to them, "I tell you that if these should keep silent, [a]the stones would immediately cry out."

Jesus Weeps over Jerusalem

41 Now as He drew near, He saw the city and [a]wept over it,
42 saying, "If you had known, even you, especially in this [a]your day, the things *that* [b]*make* for your [c]peace! But now they are hidden from your eyes.
43 "For days will come upon you when your enemies will [a]build an embankment around you, surround you and *close you in on every side,
44 [a]"and level you, and your children within you, to the ground; and [b]they will not leave in you one stone upon another, [c]because you did not know the time of your visitation."

Jesus Cleanses the Temple

45 [a]Then He went into the temple and began to drive out those who [1]bought and sold in it,
46 saying to them, "It is written, [a]*'My house [1]is a house of prayer,'* but you have made it a [b]*'den of thieves.'*"
47 And He [a]was teaching daily in the temple. But [b]the chief priests, the scribes, and the leaders of the people sought to destroy Him,
48 and were unable to do anything; for all the people were very attentive to [a]hear Him.

35 [a]2 Kin. 9:13; Matt. 21:7; Mark 11:7
37 [a]Luke 13:17; 18:43
38 [a]Ps. 118:26; Luke 13:35 [b]Luke 2:14; [Eph. 2:14]
40 [a]Hab. 2:11
41 [a]Is. 53:3; John 11:35
42 [a]Ps. 95:7, 8; Heb. 3:13 [b][Luke 1:77–79; Acts 10:36] [c][Rom. 5:1]
43 [a]Is. 29:3, 4; Jer. 6:3, 6; Luke 21:20 *See WW at 2 Cor. 5:14.
44 [a]1 Kin. 9:7, 8; Mic. 3:12 [b]Matt. 24:2; Mark 13:2; Luke 21:6 [c][Dan. 9:24; Luke 1:68, 78; 1 Pet. 2:12]
45 [a]Mal. 3:1; Matt. 21:12, 13; Mark 11:11, 15–17; John 2:13–16 [1]NU *were selling, saying*
46 [a]Is. 56:7 [b]Jer. 7:11 [1]NU *shall be*
47 [a]Luke 21:37; 22:53 [b]Mark 11:18; Luke 20:19; John 7:19; 8:37
48 [a]Luke 21:38

CHAPTER 20

1 [a]Matt. 21:23–27; Mark 11:27–33
2 [a]Acts 4:7; 7:27
4 [a]John 1:26, 31
5 [1]NU, M omit *then*
6 [a]Matt. 14:5; 21:26; Mark 6:20; Luke 7:24–30
9 [a]Ps. 80:8; Matt. 21:33–46; Mark 12:1–12 [1]*tenant farmers* *See WW at Acts 1:7.
10 [a]2 Kin. 17:13, 14; 2 Chr. 36:15, 16; [Acts 7:52; 1 Thess. 2:15] [1]Lit. *the season*

Jesus' Authority Questioned

20 Now [a]it happened on one of those days, as He taught the people in the temple and preached the gospel, *that* the chief priests and the scribes, together with the elders, confronted *Him*
2 and spoke to Him, saying, "Tell us, [a]by what authority are You doing these things? Or who is he who gave You this authority?"
3 But He answered and said to them, "I also will ask you one thing, and answer Me:
4 "The [a]baptism of John—was it from heaven or from men?"
5 And they reasoned among themselves, saying, "If we say, 'From heaven,' He will say, 'Why [1]then did you not believe him?'
6 "But if we say, 'From men,' all the people will stone us, [a]for they are persuaded that John was a prophet."
7 So they answered that they did not know where *it was* from.
8 And Jesus said to them, "Neither will I tell you by what authority I do these things."

The Parable of the Wicked Vinedressers

9 Then He began to tell the people this parable: [a]"A certain man planted a vineyard, leased it to [1]vinedressers, and went into a far country for a long *time.
10 "Now at [1]vintage-time he [a]sent a servant to the vinedressers, that they might give him some of the fruit of the vineyard. But the vinedressers beat him and sent *him* away empty-handed.
11 "Again he sent another servant; and they beat him also, treated *him* shamefully, and sent *him* away empty-handed.
12 "And again he sent a third; and they wounded him also and cast *him* out.
13 "Then the owner of the vineyard said, 'What shall I do? I will send my

19:40 Jesus not only accepted the homage paid to Him as the Messiah, but He insisted that it was legitimate.
19:41–44 Jesus knew that the acclaim of the populace would be short-lived. They were blind to the true nature of His kingdom and would reject Him. As a result, Jerusalem would be destroyed, a prophecy that came to pass in A.D. 70.
19:45, 46 See notes on Matt. 21:12, 13; Mark 11:15–17.
20:1–8 See notes on Matt. 21:23–27.
20:9–19 See notes on Matt. 21:33–46.

beloved son. Probably they will respect
him when they see him.'
14 "But when the vinedressers saw
him, they reasoned among themselves,
saying, 'This is the [a]heir. Come,
[b]let us kill him, that the inheritance
may be [c]ours.'
15 "So they cast him out of the vineyard and [a]killed *him.* Therefore what
will the owner of the vineyard do to
them?
16 "He will come and destroy those
vinedressers and give the vineyard to
[a]others." And when they heard *it* they
said, "Certainly not!"
17 Then He looked at them and said,
"What then is this that is written:

[a]*'The stone which the builders*
rejected
Has become the chief
cornerstone'?

18 "Whoever falls on that stone will be
[a]broken; but [b]on whomever it falls, it
will grind him to powder."
19 And the chief priests and the scribes
that very hour sought to lay hands on
Him, but they [1]feared* the people—for
they knew He had spoken this parable
against them.

The Pharisees: Is It Lawful to Pay Taxes to Caesar?

2 20 [a]So they watched *Him,* and sent
spies who pretended to be righteous,
that they might seize on His words, in
order to deliver Him to the power and
the authority of the governor.
21 Then they asked Him, saying,
[a]"Teacher, we know that You say and
teach rightly, and You do not show
personal favoritism, but teach the way
of God in truth:
22 "Is it lawful for us to pay taxes to
Caesar or not?"
23 But He perceived their *craftiness,
and said to them, [1]"Why do you test
Me?
24 "Show Me a denarius. Whose image and inscription does it have?" They
answered and said, "Caesar's."
25 And He said to them, [a]"Render[1]
therefore to Caesar the things that are
Caesar's, and to God the things that
are God's."
26 But they could not catch Him in His
words in the presence of the people.

14 [a][Heb. 1:1–3] [b]Matt. 27:21–23 [c]John 11:47, 48
15 [a]Luke 23:33; Acts 2:22, 23; 3:15
16 [a][John 1:11–13]; Rom. 11:1, 11; 1 Cor. 6:15; Gal. 2:17; 3:21; 6:14
17 [a]Ps. 118:22; Matt. 21:42; 1 Pet. 2:7, 8
18 [a]Is. 8:14, 15 [b][Dan. 2:34, 35, 44, 45]; Matt. 21:44
19 [1]M *were afraid—for* *See WW at Matt. 10:26.
20 [a]Matt. 22:15
21 [a]Matt. 22:16; Mark 12:14
23 [1]NU omits *Why do you test Me?* *See WW at 1 Cor. 3:19.
25 [a]Matt. 17:24–27; Rom. 13:7; [1 Pet. 2:13–17] [1]*Pay*
27 [a]Matt. 22:23–33; Mark 12:18–27 [b]Acts 23:6, 8
30 [1]NU omits the rest of v. 30.
31 [1]NU, M *also left no children*
35 [a]Phil. 3:11
36 [a][1 Cor. 15:42, 49, 52; 1 John 3:2] [b]Rom. 8:23
37 [a]Ex. 3:1–6, 15; Acts 7:30–32
38 [a][Rom. 6:10, 11; 14:8, 9; Heb. 11:16]
41 [a]Matt. 22:41–46; Mark 12:35–37
42 [a]Ps. 110:1; Acts 2:34, 35

And they marveled at His answer and
kept silent.

The Sadducees: What About the Resurrection?

27 [a]Then some of the Sadducees,
[b]who deny that there is a resurrection,
came to *Him* and asked Him,
28 saying: "Teacher, Moses wrote to
us *that* if a man's brother dies, having
a wife, and he dies without children,
his brother should take his wife and
raise up offspring for his brother.
29 "Now there were seven brothers.
And the first took a wife, and died
without children.
30 "And the second [1]took her as wife,
and he died childless.
31 "Then the third took her, and in like
manner the seven [1]also; and they left
no children, and died.
32 "Last of all the woman died also.
33 "Therefore, in the resurrection,
whose wife does she become? For all
seven had her as wife."
34 Jesus answered and said to them,
"The sons of this age marry and are
given in marriage.
35 "But those who are [a]counted worthy to attain that age, and the resurrection from the dead, neither marry
nor are given in marriage;
36 "nor can they die anymore, for
[a]they are equal to the angels and are
sons of God, [b]being sons of the resurrection.
37 "But even Moses showed in the
burning bush *passage* that the dead are
raised, when he called the Lord
[a]*'the God of Abraham, the God of*
Isaac, and the God of Jacob.'
38 "For He is not the God of the dead
but of the living, for [a]all live to Him."
39 Then some of the scribes answered
and said, "Teacher, You have spoken
well."
40 But after that they dared not question Him anymore.

Jesus: How Can David Call His Descendant Lord?

41 And He said to them, [a]"How can
they say that the Christ is the Son of
David?
42 "Now David himself said in the
Book of Psalms:

[a]*'The LORD said to my Lord,*
"Sit at My right hand,

20:20–26 See section 2 of Truth-In-Action through the Synoptics at the end of Luke.
20:20–26 See notes on Matt. 22:15–22.
20:27–40 See notes on Matt. 22:23–33.
20:41–44 See notes on Matt. 22:41–46.

43 *Till I make Your enemies Your footstool.*" '

44 "Therefore David calls Him *'Lord'*; [a]how is He then his Son?"

Beware of the Scribes

45 [a]Then, in the hearing of all the people, He said to His disciples,
46 [a]"Beware of the scribes, who desire to go around in long robes, [b]love greetings in the marketplaces, the best seats in the synagogues, and the best places at feasts,
47 [a]"who devour widows' houses, and for a [b]pretense make long prayers. These will receive greater condemnation."

The Widow's Two Mites

21 And He looked up [a]and saw the rich putting their gifts into the treasury,
2 and He saw also a certain [a]poor widow putting in two [b]mites.[1]
3 So He said, "Truly I say to you [a]that this poor widow has put in more than all;
4 "for all these out of their abundance have put in offerings [1]for God, but she out of her poverty put in [a]all the livelihood that she had."

Jesus Predicts the Destruction of the Temple

5 [a]Then, as some spoke of the temple, how it was [1]adorned* with beautiful stones and donations, He said,
6 "These things which you see—the days will come in which [a]not *one* stone shall be left upon another that shall not be thrown down."

The Signs of the Times and the End of the Age

7 So they asked Him, saying, "Teacher, but when will these things be? And what *sign *will there be* when these things are about to take place?"
8 And He said: [a]"Take heed that you not be deceived. For many will come in My name, saying, 'I am *He*,' and, 'The time has drawn near.' [1]Therefore do not [2]go after them.
9 "But when you hear of [a]wars and commotions, do not be terrified; for these things must come to pass first, but the end *will not come* *immediately."
10 [a]Then He said to them, "Nation will rise against nation, and kingdom against kingdom.
11 "And there will be great [a]earthquakes in various places, and famines and pestilences; and there will be fearful sights and great signs from heaven.
12 [a]"But before all these things, they will lay their hands on you and persecute *you*, delivering *you* up to the synagogues and [b]prisons. [c]You will be brought before kings and rulers [d]for My name's sake.
13 "But [a]it will turn out for you as an occasion for *testimony.
14 [a]"Therefore settle *it* in your hearts not to meditate beforehand on what you will [1]answer;
15 "for I will give you a mouth and wisdom [a]which all your adversaries will not be able to contradict or [1]resist.*
16 [a]"You will be betrayed even by parents and brothers, relatives and friends; and they will put [b]*some* of you to death.
17 "And [a]you will be hated by all for My name's sake.
18 [a]"But not a hair of your head shall be lost.
19 "By your patience possess your **souls.**

WORD WEALTH

21:19 souls, *psuche* (psoo-*khay*); Strong's *#5590:* Compare "psychology," "psychosis," "psychiatrist," "psychedelic." *Psuche* is the soul as distinguished from the body. It is the seat of the affections, will, desire, emotions, mind, reason, and understanding. *Psuche* is the inner self or the essence of life. The word often denotes person or self (Acts 2:41, 43; 1 Pet. 3:20). *Psuche* is not dissolved by death. Body and spirit may be separated, but spirit and soul can only be distinguished.

The Destruction of Jerusalem

20 [a]"But when you see Jerusalem surrounded by armies, then know that its desolation is near.
21 "Then let those who are in Judea flee to the mountains, let those who are in the midst of her depart, and let not those who are in the country enter her.
22 "For these are the days of ven-

44 [a]Acts 13:22, 23; Rom. 1:3; 9:4, 5
45 [a]Matt. 23:1–7; Mark 12:38–40
46 [a]Matt. 23:5 [b]Luke 11:43; 14:7
47 [a]Matt. 23:14 [b][Matt. 6:5, 6]

CHAPTER 21

1 [a]Mark 12:41–44
2 [a][2 Cor. 6:10] [b]Mark 12:42 [1]Gr. *lepta*, very small copper coins
3 [a][2 Cor. 8:12]
4 [a][2 Cor. 8:12] [1]NU omits *for God*
5 [a]Matt. 24:1; Mark 13:1 [1]*decorated* *See WW at Matt. 25:7.
6 [a]Is. 64:10, 11; Lam. 2:6–9; Mic. 3:12; Luke 19:41–44
7 *See WW at Rev. 16:14.
8 [a]Matt. 24:4; Mark 13:5; Eph. 5:6; 2 Thess. 2:3; [1 John 4:1] [1]NU omits *Therefore* [2]*follow*
9 [a]Rev. 6:4 *See WW at John 6:21.
10 [a]Matt. 24:7
11 [a]Rev. 6:12
12 [a]Mark 13:9; John 16:2; [Rev. 2:10] [b]Acts 4:3; 5:18; 12:4; 16:24 [c]Acts 25:23 [d]1 Pet. 2:13
13 [a][Phil. 1:12–14, 28; 2 Thess. 1:5] *See WW at Rev. 15:5.
14 [a]Matt. 10:19; Mark 13:11; Luke 12:11 [1]*say in defense*
15 [a]Acts 6:10 [1]*withstand* *See WW at Eph. 6:13.
16 [a]Mic. 7:6; Mark 13:12 [b]Acts 7:59; 12:2
17 [a]Matt. 10:22
18 [a]Matt. 10:30; Luke 12:7
20 [a]Matt. 24:15; Mark 13:14

20:45–47 See notes on Matt. 23:5–7, 14; Mark 12:38–40.
21:1–4 See notes on Mark 12:41–44.
21:5–28 See notes on Matt. 24:1–31.

geance, that [a]all things which are written may be fulfilled.
23 [a]"But woe to those who are pregnant and to those who are nursing
babies in those days! For there will be
great distress in the land and wrath
upon this people.
24 "And they will fall by the edge of
the sword, and be led away captive into
all nations. And Jerusalem will be
trampled by Gentiles [a]until the *times
of the Gentiles are fulfilled.

The Coming of the Son of Man

25 [a]"And there will be signs in the sun,
in the moon, and in the stars; and on
the earth distress of nations, with perplexity, the sea and the waves roaring;
26 "men's hearts failing them from
fear and the expectation of those
things which are coming on the earth,
[a]for the powers of the heavens will be
shaken.
27 "Then they will see the Son of Man
[a]coming in a cloud with power and
great glory.
28 "Now when these things begin to
happen, look up and lift up your heads,
because [a]your *redemption draws
near."

The Parable of the Fig Tree

29 [a]Then He spoke to them a parable:
"Look at the fig tree, and all the
trees.
30 "When they are already budding,
you see and know for yourselves that
summer is now near.
31 "So you also, when you see these
things happening, know that the kingdom of God is near.
32 "Assuredly, I say to you, this generation will by no means pass away till
all things take place.
33 [a]"Heaven and earth will pass away,
but My [b]words will by no means pass
away.

22 [a][Dan. 9:24–27]
23 [a]Matt. 24:19
24 [a][Dan. 9:27; 12:7] *See WW at Col. 4:5.
25 [a][2 Pet. 3:10–12]
26 [a]Matt. 24:29
27 [a]Rev. 1:7; 14:14
28 [a][Rom. 8:19, 23] *See WW at Rom. 3:24.
29 [a]Mark 13:28
33 [a]Matt. 24:35 [b]Is. 40:8

34 [a]1 Thess. 5:6 [b]Luke 8:14 [1]*dissipation* *See WW at 1 Pet. 5:7.
35 [a]Rev. 3:3; 16:15
36 [a]Matt. 24:42; 25:13 [b]Luke 18:1 [c]Luke 20:35 [d][Eph. 6:13] [1]NU *have strength to*
37 [a]John 8:1, 2 [b]Luke 22:39

CHAPTER 22

1 [a]Matt. 26:2–5
2 [a]John 11:47
3 [a]Mark 14:10, 11 [b]Matt. 10:2–4
4 *See WW at Luke 23:25.
5 [a]Zech. 11:12
6 [a]Ps. 41:9
7 [a]Matt. 26:17–19 [1]Sacrificed

The Importance of Watching

34 "But [a]take heed to yourselves, lest
your hearts be weighed down with
[1]carousing, drunkenness, and [b]cares*
of this life, and that Day come on you
unexpectedly.
35 "For [a]it will come as a snare on all
those who dwell on the face of the
whole earth.
36 [a]"Watch therefore, and [b]pray always that you may [1]be counted [c]wor-
thy to escape all these things that will
come to pass, and [d]to stand before the
Son of Man."
37 [a]And in the daytime He was teaching in the temple, but [b]at night He went
out and stayed on the mountain called
Olivet.
38 Then early in the morning all the
people came to Him in the temple to
hear Him.

The Plot to Kill Jesus

22 Now [a]the Feast of Unleavened
Bread drew near, which is
called Passover.
2 And [a]the chief priests and the
scribes sought how they might kill
Him, for they feared the people.
3 [a]Then Satan entered Judas, surnamed Iscariot, who was numbered
among the [b]twelve.
4 So he went his way and conferred
with the chief priests and captains,
how he might *betray Him to them.
5 And they were glad, and [a]agreed to
give him money.
6 So he promised and sought opportunity to [a]betray Him to them in the
absence of the multitude.

Jesus and His Disciples Prepare the Passover

7 [a]Then came the Day of Unleavened
Bread, when the Passover must be
[1]killed.
8 And He sent Peter and John, saying,

21:24 The times of the Gentiles refers to the interval between the destruction of Jerusalem in A.D. 70 and the Second Coming of Christ, during which the gospel is proclaimed to the whole world. Inasmuch as **Jerusalem** often symbolizes the Jewish people as a whole (Rev. 11:2), Jesus here is also prophesying the disbelief of the majority of Jews during the church age. "Until" seems to allude to a repentant Israel's welcoming His return (see Matt. 23:39; Rom. 11:11–27).

21:25 The OT frequently uses similar language to describe "the day of the LORD." Whether literal or figurative, the description is of violent change. See note on Obad. 15.

21:26–28 The disturbing phenomena preceding the Lord's return will strike terror in the hearts of the impenitent, but will be a source of hope and expectation to the redeemed. **Redemption** (v. 28) refers to the completion of Christ's saving work, when the unbelieving world will acknowledge that believers are "the sons of God" and the bodies of God's people will be redeemed (Rom. 8:19–25).

21:29–33 See note on Matt. 24:32–35.

21:34–36 Jesus warns against spiritual lethargy and calls for alertness and readiness for His return. See notes on Matt. 24:37–44; Mark 13:32–37.

22:1–6 See notes on Matt. 26:3–5, 14–16; Mark 14:1, 2, 10, 11.

22:7–13 See notes on Matt. 26:17–19; Mark 14:12–15.

"Go and prepare the Passover for us,
that we may eat."
9 So they said to Him, "Where do You
want us to prepare?"
10 And He said to them, "Behold,
when you have entered the city, a man
will meet you carrying a pitcher of water; follow him into the house which
he enters.
11 "Then you shall say to the master
of the house, 'The Teacher says to you,
"Where is the guest room where I may
eat the Passover with My disciples?"'
12 "Then he will show you a large, furnished upper room; there make
ready."
13 So they went and [a]found it just as
He had said to them, and they prepared
the Passover.

Jesus Institutes the Lord's Supper

14 [a]When the hour had come, He sat
down, and the [1]twelve apostles with
Him.
3 15 Then He said to them, "With *fervent*
desire I have *desired to eat this Passover with you before I suffer;
16 "for I say to you, I will no longer
eat of it [a]until it is fulfilled in the kingdom of God."
17 Then He took the cup, and gave
thanks, and said, "Take this and divide
it among yourselves;
18 "for [a]I say to you, [1]I will not drink
of the fruit of the vine until the kingdom of God comes."
19 [a]And He took bread, gave thanks
and broke *it*, and gave *it* to them, saying, "This is My [b]body which is given
for you; [c]do this in remembrance of
Me."
20 Likewise He also *took* the cup after
supper, saying, [a]"This cup *is* the new
*covenant in My blood, which is shed
for you.
21 [a]"But behold, the hand of My betrayer *is* with Me on the table.
22 [a]"And truly the Son of Man goes
[b]as it has been determined, but woe to
that man by whom He is betrayed!"

13 [a]Luke 19:32
14 [a]Matt. 26:20; Mark 14:17 [1]NU omits *twelve*
15 *See WW at Matt. 13:17.
16 [a]Luke 14:15; [Acts 10:41; Rev. 19:9]
18 [a]Matt. 26:29; Mark 14:25 [1]NU adds *from now on*
19 [a]Matt. 26:26; Mark 14:22 [b][1 Pet. 2:24] [c]1 Cor. 11:23–26
20 [a]1 Cor. 10:16 *See WW at Mark 14:24.
21 [a]Ps. 41:9; Matt. 26:21, 23; Mark 14:18; Luke 22:48; John 13:21, 26, 27
22 [a]Matt. 26:24 [b]John 17:12; Acts 2:23
23 [a]Matt. 26:22; John 13:22, 25
24 [a]Mark 9:34; Luke 9:46–48
25 [a][Matt. 20:25–28]; Mark 10:42–45
26 [a]Matt. 20:26; [1 Pet. 5:3] [b]Luke 9:48
27 [a][Luke 12:37] [b]Matt. 20:28; John 13:13, 14; Phil. 2:7
28 [a][Heb. 2:18; 4:15]
29 [a]Matt. 24:47
30 [a][Matt. 8:11; Rev. 19:9] [b]Ps. 49:14; [Matt. 19:28; 1 Cor. 6:2; Rev. 3:21]
31 [a]1 Pet. 5:8 [b]Amos 9:9 [1]NU omits *And the Lord said*
32 [a][John 17:9, 11, 15] [b]John 21:15–17; Acts 1:15; 2:14; 2 Pet. 1:10–15

23 [a]Then they began to question
among themselves, which of them it
was who would do this thing.

The Disciples Argue About Greatness

24 [a]Now there was also a dispute 9
among them, as to which of them
should be considered the greatest.
25 [a]And He said to them, "The kings
of the Gentiles exercise lordship over
them, and those who exercise authority over them are called 'benefactors.'
26 [a]"But not so *among* you; on the contrary, [b]he who is greatest among you,
let him be as the younger, and he who
governs as he who serves.
27 [a]"For who *is* greater, he who sits
at the table, or he who serves? *Is* it not
he who sits at the table? Yet [b]I am
among you as the One who serves.

KINGDOM DYNAMICS

22:25–27 37. How Does One Become Great in the Kingdom of God?, SPIRITUAL ANSWERS. For the answer to this and other probing questions about God and the power life in His kingdom, see the study article "Spiritual Answers to Hard Questions," which begins on page 1996. P.R.

28 "But you are those who have continued with Me in [a]My trials.
29 "And [a]I bestow upon you a kingdom, just as My Father bestowed *one*
upon Me,
30 "that [a]you may eat and drink at My
table in My kingdom, [b]and sit on
thrones judging the twelve tribes of Israel."

Jesus Predicts Peter's Denial

31 [1]And the Lord said, "Simon, Simon!
Indeed, [a]Satan has asked for you, that
he may [b]sift *you* as wheat.
32 "But [a]I have prayed for you, that
your faith should not fail; and when
you have returned to *Me*, [b]strengthen
your brethren."

22:14–23 See notes on Matt. 26:20–29.
22:15–20 See section 3 of Truth-In-Action through the Synoptics at the end of Luke.
22:24–27 See section 9 of Truth-In-Action through the Synoptics at the end of Luke.
22:25, 26 Jesus redefines the meaning of greatness, reversing the values of the world. True greatness is measured in terms of service without thought of reward.
22:27 Jesus reinforces the principle He has just declared, with the example of Himself as **One who serves**.
22:29, 30 The kingdom is a gift that is present both in the Person of Jesus and in His body, the church. It will be fulfilled completely in the future age (v. 30; see vv. 16, 18). Since all granted authority is a gift, personal rivalry for greatness is ruled out. Although the disciples will not experience earthly position and power, they will enjoy places of honor in the heavenly kingdom.
22:31 By calling him **Simon** instead of Peter ("Rock"), Jesus may be implying that the disciple will soon act in accord with his old nature, which is one of human weakness.
22:32 The **you** is plural, signifying that others would also experience testing. Jesus prayed for all the disciples (see John 17:6–19). He knows beforehand of Peter's denial and subsequent repentance, and therefore urges him to encourage the others in their own testing.

33 But he said to Him, "Lord, I am ready to go with You, both to prison and to death."

34 [a]Then He said, "I tell you, Peter, the rooster shall not crow this day before you will deny three times that you know Me."

Supplies for the Road

35 [a]And He said to them, "When I sent you without money bag, knapsack, and sandals, did you **lack** anything?" So they said, "Nothing."

WORD WEALTH

22:35 lack, *hustereo* (hoos-ter-*eh*-oh); Strong's *#5302:* To come late, be behind. With reference to persons, to fail (Heb. 4:1), be inferior to (2 Cor. 11:5), to be in want, to come short of (Matt. 19:20; Rom. 3:23).

36 Then He said to them, "But now, he who has a money bag, let him take *it,* and likewise a knapsack; and he who has no sword, let him sell his garment and buy one.

37 "For I say to you that this which is written must still be [1]accomplished in Me: [a]*'And He was numbered with the transgressors.'* For the things concerning Me have an end."

38 So they said, "Lord, look, here *are* two swords." And He said to them, "It is enough."

The Prayer in the Garden

39 [a]Coming out, [b]He went to the Mount of Olives, as He was accustomed, and His disciples also followed Him.

40 [a]When He came to the place, He said to them, "Pray that you may not enter into temptation."

41 [a]And He was withdrawn from them about a stone's throw, and He knelt down and prayed,

4 42 saying, "Father, if it is Your will, take this cup away from Me; nevertheless [a]not My will, but Yours, be done."

43 [1]Then [a]an angel appeared to Him from heaven, strengthening Him.

34 [a]Matt. 26:33–35; Mark 14:29–31; Luke 22:61; John 13:37, 38
35 [a]Matt. 10:9; Mark 6:8; Luke 9:3; 10:4
37 [a]Is. 53:12; Matt. 27:38; Mark 15:28; Luke 22:32 [1]*fulfilled*
39 [a]Matt. 26:36; John 18:1 [b]Luke 21:37
40 [a]Matt. 26:36–46; Mark 14:32–42
41 [a]Matt. 26:39; Mark 14:35; [Luke 18:11–14]
42 [a]Is. 50:5; John 4:34; 5:30; 6:38; 8:29
43 [a]Matt. 4:11 [1]NU brackets vv. 43 and 44 as not in the original text.
44 [a]John 12:27; [Heb. 5:7] *See WW at 1 John 1:7.
46 [a]Luke 9:32 [b]1 Chr. 16:11; Luke 22:40; [Eph. 6:18]; 1 Thess. 5:17
47 [a]Matt. 26:47–56; Mark 14:43–50; John 18:3–11 [b]Ps. 41:9; Matt. 20:18; Luke 9:44; 22:21; Acts 1:16, 17
48 [a][Prov. 27:6]
50 [a]Matt. 26:51
52 [a]Matt. 26:55 [b]Luke 23:32
53 [a]Luke 19:47, 48 [b][John 12:27]
54 [a]Is. 53:7, 8; Matt. 26:57; Mark 14:53; Luke 9:44; Acts 8:32 [b]Matt. 26:58; Mark 14:54; John 18:15
55 [a]Matt. 26:69–75; Mark 14:66–72; John 18:15, 17, 18
57 [1]NU *it*

44 [a]And being in agony, He prayed more earnestly. Then His sweat became like great drops of *blood falling down to the ground.

45 When He rose up from prayer, and had come to His disciples, He found them sleeping from sorrow.

46 Then He said to them, "Why [a]do you sleep? Rise and [b]pray, lest you enter into temptation."

Betrayal and Arrest in Gethsemane

47 And while He was still speaking, [a]behold, a multitude; and he who was called [b]Judas, one of the twelve, went before them and drew near to Jesus to kiss Him.

48 But Jesus said to him, "Judas, are you betraying the Son of Man with a [a]kiss?"

49 When those around Him saw what was going to happen, they said to Him, "Lord, shall we strike with the sword?"

50 And [a]one of them struck the servant of the high priest and cut off his right ear.

51 But Jesus answered and said, "Permit even this." And He touched his ear and healed him.

52 [a]Then Jesus said to the chief priests, captains of the temple, and the elders who had come to Him, "Have you come out, as against a [b]robber, with swords and clubs?

53 "When I was with you daily in the [a]temple, you did not try to seize Me. But this is your [b]hour, and the power of darkness."

Peter Denies Jesus, and Weeps Bitterly

54 [a]Having arrested Him, they led *Him* and brought Him into the high priest's house. [b]But Peter followed at a distance.

55 [a]Now when they had kindled a fire in the midst of the courtyard and sat down together, Peter sat among them.

56 And a certain servant girl, seeing him as he sat by the fire, looked intently at him and said, "This man was also with Him."

57 But he denied [1]Him, saying, "Woman, I do not know Him."

22:36 Conditions will change after the Crucifixion, and they should be prepared to meet hatred and persecution. Jesus does not suggest that His followers are to use force in extending the gospel, but that they would need perpetual vigilance, using all the resources at their command.

22:38 The disciples took His words with absurd literalness, as though **two swords** were sufficient for 11 men to defend Him. For Jesus to speak literally would be inconsistent with His action in Gethsemane (vv. 49–51). The words **It is enough** do not mean "they are sufficient." They are a curt dismissal of the subject, in the sense of "Enough of that!"

22:39–46 See notes on Matt. 26:36–46.

22:42 See section 4 of Truth-In-Action through the Synoptics at the end of Luke.

22:47–53 See notes on Matt. 26:47–56.

22:53 God granted temporary authority to the enemy.

58 [a]And after a little while another saw
him and said, "You also are of them."
But Peter said, "Man, I am not!"
59 [a]Then after about an hour had
passed, another confidently affirmed,
saying, "Surely this *fellow* also was
with Him, for he is a [b]Galilean."
60 But Peter said, "Man, I do not know
what you are saying!" Immediately,
while he was still speaking, [1]the
rooster crowed.
61 And the Lord turned and looked at
Peter. Then [a]Peter remembered the
word of the Lord, how He had said to
him, [b]"Before the rooster [1]crows, you
will deny Me three times."
62 So Peter went out and wept bitterly.

Jesus Mocked and Beaten

63 [a]Now the men who *held Jesus
mocked Him and [b]beat Him.
64 [1]And having blindfolded Him, they
[a]struck Him on the face and asked
Him, saying, "Prophesy! Who is the
one who struck You?"
65 And many other things they blasphemously spoke against Him.

Jesus Faces the Sanhedrin

66 [a]As soon as it was day, [b]the *elders
of the people, both chief priests and
scribes, came together and led Him
into their council, saying,
67 [a]"If You are the Christ, tell us." But
He said to them, "If I tell you, you will
[b]by no means believe.
68 "And if I [1]also ask *you*, you will by
no means answer [2]Me or let *Me* go.
69 [a]"Hereafter the Son of Man will sit
on the right hand of the power of God."
70 Then they all said, "Are You then
the Son of God?" So He said to them,
[a]"You *rightly* say that I am."
71 [a]And they said, "What further *testimony do we need? For we have heard
it ourselves from His own mouth."

Jesus Handed Over to Pontius Pilate

23 Then [a]the whole multitude of
them arose and led Him to
[b]Pilate.

58 [a]John 18:25
59 [a]Mark 14:70 [b]Acts 1:11; 2:7
60 [1]NU, M *a rooster*
61 [a]Matt. 26:75 [b]John 13:38 [1]NU adds *today*
63 [a]Ps. 69:1, 4, 7–9 [b]Is. 50:6 *See WW at 2 Cor. 5:14.
64 [a]Zech. 13:7 [1]NU *And having blindfolded Him, they asked Him*
66 [a]Matt. 27:1 [b]Acts 4:26 *See WW at 1 Tim. 4:14.
67 [a]Matt. 26:63–66 [b]Luke 20:5–7
68 [1]NU omits *also* [2]NU omits the rest of v. 68.
69 [a]Heb. 1:3; 8:1
70 [a]Matt. 26:64; 27:11
71 [a]Mark 14:63 *See WW at John 19:35.

CHAPTER 23

1 [a]John 18:28 [b]Luke 3:1; 13:1
2 [a]Acts 24:2 [b]Acts 17:7 [c]Matt. 17:27 [d]John 19:12 [1]NU *our*
3 [a]1 Tim. 6:13
4 [a][1 Pet. 2:22]
5 [a]John 7:41
6 [1]NU omits *of Galilee*
7 [a]Luke 3:1; 9:7; 13:31
8 [a]Luke 9:9 [b]Matt. 14:1
9 [a]John 19:9
11 [a]Is. 53:3 [1]*troops*
12 [a]Acts 4:26, 27
13 [a]Mark 15:14
14 [a]Luke 23:1, 2 [b]Luke 23:4

2 And they began to [a]accuse Him,
saying, "We found this *fellow* [b]pervert-
ing [1]the nation, and [c]forbidding to pay
taxes to Caesar, saying [d]that He Himself is Christ, a King."
3 [a]Then Pilate asked Him, saying,
"Are You the King of the Jews?" He
answered him and said, "*It is as* you
say."
4 So Pilate said to the chief priests
and the crowd, [a]"I find no fault in this
Man."
5 But they were the more fierce, saying, "He stirs up the people, teaching
throughout all Judea, beginning from
[a]Galilee to this place."

Jesus Faces Herod

6 When Pilate heard [1]of Galilee, he
asked if the Man were a Galilean.
7 And as soon as he knew that He belonged to [a]Herod's jurisdiction, he sent
Him to Herod, who was also in Jerusalem at that time.
8 Now when Herod saw Jesus,
[a]he was exceedingly glad; for he had
desired for a long *time* to see Him, because [b]he had heard many things
about Him, and he hoped to see some
miracle done by Him.
9 Then he questioned Him with many
words, but He answered him [a]nothing.
10 And the chief priests and scribes
stood and vehemently accused Him.
11 [a]Then Herod, with his [1]men of war,
treated Him with contempt and
mocked *Him*, arrayed Him in a gor-
geous robe, and sent Him back to Pilate.
12 That very day [a]Pilate and Herod became friends with each other, for previously they had been at enmity with
each other.

Taking the Place of Barabbas

13 [a]Then Pilate, when he had called together the chief priests, the rulers, and
the people,
14 said to them, [a]"You have brought
this Man to me, as one who mis-
leads the people. And indeed, [b]having

22:59 Peter's accent betrayed him (Matt. 26:73). A relative of the servant he had attacked in Gethsemane also identified him (John 18:26).
22:61 Jesus' look of compassion pierced Peter's heart. Later the Lord manifests His mercy by appearing to Peter before the other apostles following the Resurrection (24:34).
22:69 This statement referring to Dan. 7:13 is climactic. Jesus substitutes "Son of Man" for "Christ" (vv. 67, 69), and speaks of His future and victorious Parousia (arrival and presence) in glory. Jesus also categorically affirms that He is the "Son of God," a title that expresses His exclusive and unique oneness with God.
23:1–5 See notes on Matt. 27:2, 11; Mark 15:1, 2; John 18:28–38.
23:7 Pilate had two motives in sending Jesus to **Herod.** First, he would be free from an unpleasant case. Second, his gesture of respect for Herod would mend a rift between them, possibly caused by Pilate's brutal treatment of some of Herod's subjects (13:1).
23:13–25 See notes on Matt. 27:18, 26; John 19:5–14.

examined *Him* in your presence, I have
found no fault in this Man concerning
those things of which you accuse
Him;
15 "no, neither did Herod, for [1]I sent
you back to him; and indeed nothing
deserving of death has been done by
Him.
16 [a]"I will therefore chastise Him and
release *Him*"
17 [a](for[1] it was necessary for him to
release one to them at the feast).
18 And [a]they all cried out at once, saying, *"Away with this *Man,* and release
to us Barabbas"—
19 who had been thrown into prison
for a certain rebellion made in the city,
and for murder.
20 Pilate, therefore, wishing to release
Jesus, again called out to them.
21 But they shouted, saying, "Crucify
Him, crucify Him!"
22 Then he said to them the third time,
"Why, what evil has He done? I have
found no reason for death in Him. I will
therefore chastise Him and let *Him*
go."
23 But they were insistent, demanding
with loud voices that He be crucified.
And the voices of these men [1]and of
the chief priests prevailed.
24 So [a]Pilate gave sentence that it
should be as they requested.
25 [a]And he released [1]to them the one
they requested, who for rebellion
and murder had been thrown into
prison; but he **delivered** Jesus to their
*will.

WORD WEALTH

23:25 delivered, *paradidomi* (par-ad-*id*-oh-mee); Strong's *#3860:* From *para,* "alongside," and *didomi,* "to give." The verb is quite common in the NT and is used in a variety of ways, usually reflecting the root meaning of to give over or deliver. It is used in the sense of to hand over to another (Matt. 25:14; Luke 4:6); to commit or commend (Acts 15:40; 1 Pet. 2:23); to deliver up to prison or judgment (Matt. 4:12; 2 Pet. 2:4); to betray (Matt. 10:4; Mark 13:12); to hand down, such as traditions (Mark 7:13; Acts 6:14); to permit (Mark 4:29).

15 [1]NU *he sent Him back to us*
16 [a]John 19:1
17 [a]John 18:39 [1]NU omits v. 17.
18 [a]Acts 3:13–15 *See WW at John 16:22.
23 [1]NU omits *and of the chief priests*
24 [a]Mark 15:15
25 [a]Is. 53:8 [1]NU, M omit *to them* *See WW at Matt. 12:50.
26 [a]Matt. 27:32
29 [a]Matt. 24:19
30 [a]Hos. 10:8; Rev. 6:16, 17; 9:6
31 [a][Jer. 25:29]
32 [a]Is. 53:9, 12 *See WW at Acts 4:12.
33 [a]John 19:17–24
34 [a]1 Cor. 4:12 [b]Acts 3:17 [c]Matt. 27:35 [1]NU brackets the first sentence as a later addition.
35 [a]Ps. 22:17 [b]Matt. 27:39 *See WW at John 20:14.
36 [a]Ps. 69:21
38 [a]John 19:19 [1]NU omits *written* and *in letters of Greek, Latin, and Hebrew*
39 [a]Mark 15:32 [1]NU *Are You not the Christ? Save*

The King on a Cross

26 [a]Now as they led Him away, they
laid hold of a certain man, Simon a
Cyrenian, who was coming from the
country, and on him they laid the cross
that he might bear *it* after Jesus.
27 And a great multitude of the people
followed Him, and women who also
mourned and lamented Him.
28 But Jesus, turning to them, said,
"Daughters of Jerusalem, do not weep
for Me, but weep for yourselves and
for your children.
29 [a]"For indeed the days are coming
in which they will say, 'Blessed *are* the
barren, wombs that never bore, and
breasts which never nursed!'
30 "Then they will begin [a]*'to say to the
mountains, "Fall on us!" and to the
hills, "Cover us!"'*
31 [a]"For if they do these things in the
green wood, what will be done in the
dry?"
32 [a]There were also two *others, criminals, led with Him to be put to death.
33 And [a]when they had come to the
place called Calvary, there they crucified Him, and the criminals, one on the
right hand and the other on the left.
34 [1]Then Jesus said, "Father, [a]forgive
them, for [b]they do not know what they
do." And [c]they divided His garments
and cast lots.
35 And [a]the people stood *looking on.
But even the [b]rulers with them
sneered, saying, "He saved others; let
Him save Himself if He is the Christ,
the chosen of God."
36 The soldiers also mocked Him,
coming and offering Him [a]sour wine,
37 and saying, "If You are the King of
the Jews, save Yourself."
38 [a]And an inscription also was
[1]written over Him in letters of Greek,
Latin, and Hebrew:

THIS IS THE KING OF THE JEWS.

39 [a]Then one of the criminals who
were hanged blasphemed Him, saying,
[1]"If You are the Christ, save Yourself
and us."
40 But the other, answering, rebuked
him, saying, "Do you not even fear

23:26 See note on Mark 15:21.
23:28, 29 Jesus does not renounce the sympathy of the mourning women, but suggests that their own sufferings were more worthy of their tears. The reference is to the terrible judgment soon to fall upon Jerusalem.
23:31 Jesus quotes a proverb suggesting that if His own sufferings are so great, then the sufferings of the Jews will be even more intense.
23:33 Calvary is from the Latin *calvaria,* "a skull." The name probably denotes the shape of the place. For crucifixion, see note on John 19:6.
23:34 Victims were stripped naked, and their clothing was given to the crucifixion detail (see Ps. 22:18).
23:35 He could not save Himself and be the Savior of others.
23:38 See note on John 19:19.

God, seeing you are under the same
*condemnation?
41 "And we indeed justly, for we receive the due reward of our deeds; but
this Man has done [a]nothing wrong."
42 Then he said [1]to Jesus, "Lord, remember me when You come into Your
kingdom."
43 And Jesus said to him, "Assuredly,
I say to you, today you will be with
Me in [a]Paradise."

Jesus Dies on the Cross

44 [a]Now it [1]was about the sixth hour,
and there was darkness over all the
earth until the ninth hour.
45 Then the sun was [1]darkened, and
[a]the veil of the temple was torn in
[2]two.
46 And when Jesus had cried out with
a loud voice, He said, "Father, [a]*'into
Your hands I commit My spirit.'"*
[b]Having said this, He breathed His last.
47 [a]So when the centurion saw what
had happened, he glorified God, saying, "Certainly this was a righteous
Man!"
48 And the whole crowd who came together to that sight, seeing what had
been done, beat their breasts and returned.
49 [a]But all His acquaintances, and the
women who followed Him from Galilee, stood at a distance, watching these
things.

Jesus Buried in Joseph's Tomb

50 [a]Now behold, *there was* a man
named Joseph, a council member, a
good and just man.
51 He had not consented to their decision and deed. *He was* from Arimathea, a city of the Jews, [a]who[1] himself
was also waiting for the kingdom of
God.
52 This man went to Pilate and asked
for the body of Jesus.
53 [a]Then he took it down, wrapped it
in linen, and laid it in a tomb *that was*
hewn out of the rock, where no one
had ever lain before.
54 That day was [a]the Preparation, and
the Sabbath drew near.
55 And the women [a]who had come
with Him from Galilee followed after,
and [b]they observed the tomb and how
His body was laid.
56 Then they returned and [a]prepared*
spices and fragrant oils. And they
rested on the Sabbath [b]according to
the commandment.

He Is Risen

24 Now [a]on the first *day* of the
week, very early in the morning,
they, [1]and certain *other women* with
them, came to the tomb [b]bringing the
spices which they had prepared.
2 [a]But they found the stone rolled
away from the tomb.
3 [a]Then they went in and did not find
the body of the Lord Jesus.
4 And it happened, as they were
[1]greatly perplexed about this, that
[a]behold, two men stood by them in
shining garments.
5 Then, as they were afraid and
bowed *their* faces to the earth, they
said to them, "Why do you seek the
living among the dead?
6 "He is not here, but is risen! [a]Re-
member how He spoke to you when He
was still in Galilee,
7 "saying, 'The Son of Man must be
[a]delivered into the hands of sinful men,
and be crucified, and the third day rise
again.' "
8 And [a]they remembered His words.
9 [a]Then they returned from the tomb
and told all these things to the eleven
and to all the rest.
10 It was Mary Magdalene, [a]Joanna,
Mary *the mother* of James, and the
other *women* with them, who told
these things to the apostles.
11 [a]And their words seemed to them
like [1]idle tales, and they did not believe
them.
12 [a]But Peter arose and ran to the
tomb; and stooping down, he saw the
linen cloths [1]lying by themselves; and
he departed, marveling to himself at
what had happened.

The Road to Emmaus

13 [a]Now behold, two of them were
traveling that same day to a village

40 *See WW at Rev. 20:4.
41 [a][Heb. 7:26]
42 [1]NU *"Jesus, remember me*
43 [a][Rev. 2:7]
44 [a]Matt. 27:45–56 [1]NU adds *already*
45 [a]Matt. 27:51 [1]NU *obscured* [2]*the middle*
46 [a]Ps. 31:5 [b]John 19:30
47 [a]Mark 15:39
49 [a]Ps. 38:11
50 [a]Matt. 27:57–61
51 [a]Luke 2:25, 38 [1]NU *who was waiting*
53 [a]Mark 15:46
54 [a]Matt. 27:62
55 [a]Luke 8:2 [b]Mark 15:47
56 [a]Mark 16:1 [b]Ex. 20:10 *See WW at Rev. 21:2.

CHAPTER 24

1 [a]John 20:1–8 [b]Luke 23:56 [1]NU omits *and certain other women with them*
2 [a]Mark 16:4
3 [a]Mark 16:5
4 [a]John 20:12 [1]NU omits *greatly*
6 [a]Luke 9:22
7 [a]Luke 9:44; 11:29, 30; 18:31–33
8 [a]John 2:19–22
9 [a]Mark 16:10
10 [a]Luke 8:3
11 [a]Luke 24:25 [1]*nonsense*
12 [a]John 20:3–6 [1]NU omits *lying*
13 [a]Mark 16:12

23:43 Paradise, "a garden place," refers to the state of blessedness from death to resurrection.
23:44, 45 See notes on Matt. 27:45, 51.
23:46 Some interpreters view the **loud voice** as indicating that Jesus died not as much from physical exhaustion as from spiritual agony. The words of Jesus are from Ps. 31:5, a prayer of confidence taught to Jewish children.
23:47 See note on Matt. 27:54.
23:50–53 See note on John 19:38, 39.
23:54 The Preparation was a technical term describing the day before the Sabbath.
24:1–12 See notes on Matt. 28:2; Mark 16:1–7; John 20:2, 6, 7.
24:13 Luke identifies one of the two as Cleopas (v. 18).

called Emmaus, *which was [1]seven
miles from Jerusalem.
14 And they talked together of all
these things which had happened.
15 So it was, while they conversed and
reasoned, that [a]Jesus Himself drew
near and went with them.
16 But [a]their eyes were restrained, so
that they did not know Him.
17 And He said to them, "What kind
of conversation *is* this that you have
with one another as you [1]walk and are
sad?"
18 Then the one [a]whose name was
Cleopas answered and said to Him,
"Are You the only stranger in Jerusalem, and have You not known the
things which happened there in these
days?"
19 And He said to them, "What
things?" So they said to Him, "The
things concerning Jesus of Nazareth,
[a]who was a Prophet [b]mighty in *deed
and *word before God and all the people,
20 [a]"and how the chief priests and our
rulers delivered Him to be *condemned
to death, and crucified Him.
21 "But we were hoping [a]that it was
He who was going to redeem Israel.
Indeed, besides all this, today is
the third day since these things happened.
22 "Yes, and [a]certain women of our
company, who arrived at the tomb
early, astonished us.
23 "When they did not find His body,
they came saying that they had also
seen a vision of angels who said He
was alive.
24 "And [a]certain of those *who were*
with us went to the tomb and found *it*
just as the women had said; but Him
they did not see."
25 Then He said to them, "O foolish
ones, and slow of heart to *believe in
all that the prophets have spoken!
26 [a]"Ought not the *Christ to have
*suffered these things and to enter into
His [b]glory?"
27 And beginning at [a]Moses and
[b]all the Prophets, He [1]expounded to
them in all the Scriptures the things
concerning Himself.

13 [1]Lit. *60 stadia* *See WW at Philem. 15.
15 [a][Matt. 18:20]
16 [a]John 20:14; 21:4
17 [1]NU *walk? And they stood still, looking sad.*
18 [a]John 19:25
19 [a]Matt. 21:11 [b]Acts 7:22 *See WW at John 9:4. • See WW at Acts 19:20.
20 [a]Acts 13:27, 28 *See WW at Rev. 20:4.
21 [a]Luke 1:68; 2:38
22 [a]Mark 16:10
24 [a]Luke 24:12
25 *See WW at Rom. 10:9.
26 [a]Acts 17:2, 3 [b][1 Pet. 1:10–12] *See WW at 2 Tim. 4:22. • See WW at Acts 17:3.
27 [a][Deut. 18:15] [b][Is. 7:14; 9:6] [1]*explained*
28 [a]Mark 6:48 [1]*acted as if*
29 [a]Gen. 19:2, 3 [b][John 14:23]
30 [a]Matt. 14:19
34 [a]1 Cor. 15:5 *See WW at John 6:68.
35 [1]*recognized*
36 [a]Mark 16:14
37 [a]Mark 6:49 *See WW at John 20:14.
38 *See WW at Luke 2:35.

The Disciples' Eyes Opened

28 Then they drew near to the village
where they were going, and [a]He
[1]indicated that He would have gone
farther.
29 But [a]they constrained Him, saying,
[b]"Abide with us, for it is toward evening, and the day is far spent." And
He went in to stay with them.
30 Now it came to pass, as [a]He sat at
the table with them, that He took
bread, blessed and broke *it*, and gave
it to them.
31 Then their eyes were opened and
they knew Him; and He vanished from
their sight.
32 And they said to one another, "Did
not our heart burn within us while He
talked with us on the road, and while
He opened the Scriptures to us?"
33 So they rose up that very hour and
returned to Jerusalem, and found the
eleven and those *who were* with them
gathered together,
34 saying, "The *Lord is risen indeed,
and [a]has appeared to Simon!"
35 And they told about the things *that
had happened* on the road, and how
He was [1]known to them in the breaking of bread.

Jesus Appears to His Disciples

36 [a]Now as they said these things,
Jesus Himself stood in the midst of
them, and said to them, "Peace to
you."
37 But they were terrified and frightened, and supposed they had *seen
[a]a spirit.
38 And He said to them, "Why are you
troubled? And why do *doubts arise in
your hearts?

WORD WEALTH

24:38 troubled, *tarasso* (tar-*as*-so); Strong's *#5015:* To unsettle, stir up, agitate, disturb, trouble. The word is used in a physical sense (John 5:7), but its primary use in the NT is metaphorical. It denotes mental agitation from fear or perplexity (Matt. 2:3; 14:26); an upheaval

They are followers of Jesus, but are not of the apostolic band.
24:16 The men are blinded either by their despair (v. 21) or by divine intervention.
24:18 An early tradition identifies **Cleopas** as the brother of Joseph, Mary's husband.
24:19–21 While they still perceived Jesus as **a Prophet,** their messianic hopes had been crushed by His death.
24:25–27 Their spiritual dullness came from a failure to recognize that the Scriptures foretold the necessity of the Messiah's sufferings.
24:30, 31 The manner in which Jesus broke bread revealed His identity to them (see v. 35). Their perception of Jesus went beyond mere physical recognition.
24:36–40 See notes on John 20:19, 20.

in the spirit (John 11:33; 13:21); stirring up a crowd (Acts 17:8, 13); confusion resulting from false doctrine (Acts 15:24; Gal. 1:7; 5:10).

39 "Behold My hands and My feet, that
it is I Myself. [a]Handle Me and see, for
a [b]spirit does not have flesh and bones
as you see I have."
40 [1]When He had said this, He showed
them His hands and His feet.
41 But while they still did not believe [a]for joy, and marveled, He
said to them, [b]"Have you any food
here?"
42 So they gave Him a piece of a
broiled fish [1]and some honeycomb.
43 [a]And He took *it* and ate in their
presence.

The Scriptures Opened

44 Then He said to them, [a]"These
are the words which I spoke to you
while I was still with you, that all
things must be fulfilled which were
written in the Law of Moses and *the*
Prophets and *the* Psalms concerning
Me."
45 And [a]He opened their understanding, that they might comprehend the
*Scriptures.
46 Then He said to them, [a]"Thus it is
written, [1]and thus it was necessary for
the Christ to suffer and to rise from
the dead the third day,
47 "and that repentance and [a]remis-
sion* of sins should be *preached in His
name [b]to all nations, beginning at Jerusalem.
48 "And [a]you are *witnesses of these
things.

39 [a]John 20:20, 27 [b][1 Cor. 15:50]
40 [1]Some printed New Testaments omit v. 40. It is found in nearly all Gr. mss.
41 [a]Gen. 45:26 [b]John 21:5
42 [1]NU omits *and some honeycomb*
43 [a]Acts 10:39–41
44 [a]Matt. 16:21; 17:22; 20:18
45 [a]Acts 16:14 *See WW at John 5:39.
46 [a]Acts 17:3 [1]NU *that the Christ should suffer and rise*
47 [a]Acts 5:31; 10:43; 13:38; 26:18 [b][Jer. 31:34] *See WW at Heb. 9:22. • See WW at Acts 9:20.
48 [a][Acts 1:8] *See WW at Rev. 1:5.
49 [a]Joel 2:28 [1]NU omits *of Jerusalem* *See WW at Acts 13:32. • See WW at Acts 4:33.
50 [a]Acts 1:12
51 [a]Mark 16:19 *See WW at Rev. 21:1.
52 [a]Matt. 28:9
53 [a]Acts 2:46 [1]NU omits *praising and* [2]NU omits *Amen.*

KINGDOM DYNAMICS

24:45–48 Commissioned to Go with Christ's Compassion, WORLD EVANGELISM. Luke's emphasis in the Great Commission is consonant with his theme: Christ, the Son of Man—showing Jesus' humanity and divinity in balance. The beauty and uniqueness of His character—both divine and human—is revealed as this Divine One brings sinful man to a holy God. In His perfect holiness of life, Jesus reflects compassion for sin-stained and suffering mankind—brokenhearted, sick, mistreated, and bereaved. Our fulfillment of the Great Commission requires such a worldwide scope in ministering compassion and human concern. Jesus' style—sensitive and touchable—is a summons to His followers to speedily answer His command and to answer with His compassion. No geographic boundary, no sin barrier, no ethnic, political, or economic partisan interest is ever to restrict our reach or penetration with the gospel.

(Mark 16:15–18/John 20:21–23) G.C.

49 [a]"Behold, I send the *Promise of My
Father upon you; but tarry in the city
[1]of Jerusalem until you are endued
with *power from on high."

The Ascension

50 And He led them out [a]as far as Bethany, and He lifted up His hands and
blessed them.
51 [a]Now it came to pass, while He
blessed them, that He was parted from
them and carried up into *heaven.
52 [a]And they worshiped Him, and returned to Jerusalem with great joy,
53 and were continually [a]in the temple
[1]praising and blessing God. [2]Amen.

24:39 Spirit: The thrust of this appearance is the tangible nature of the body of the resurrected Lord. The risen Jesus has flesh and bones, and thus He is no vaporlike spirit/ghost. He can even eat a piece of broiled fish (v. 42).

24:44–46 Previously the disciples had been unable to comprehend the scriptural teachings concerning the crucifixion and resurrection of Jesus. Now He is able to interpret those teachings to them in the light of their fulfillment.

24:47 The Scriptures not only prophesy the death and resurrection of the Messiah, but decree that the redemptive message is to be offered **to all nations**.

24:48, 49 Jesus not only commissions them as **witnesses,** but promises the enabling power of the Holy Spirit to carry out the task (see note on Acts 1:8). They are not to begin their mission until they receive **the Promise**.

24:50, 51 See notes on Acts 1:9–11.

24:52, 53 The assurance of continued fellowship with the ascended Lord in the Person of the Holy Spirit swept away any despair they might have felt at His departure.

TRUTH-IN-ACTION through THE SYNOPTIC GOSPELS

Letting the LIFE of the Holy Spirit Bring Faith's Works Alive in You!

EDITORIAL NOTE: Scholars refer to Matthew, Mark, and Luke as the synoptic Gospels because they are parallel accounts of the life and ministry of Jesus of Nazareth. To offer maximum insight into a faithful application of the teaching of Jesus recounted in the synoptic Gospels and to avoid unnecessary repetition, we are presenting this summary of the first three Gospels. In this chart, each "Action" will reference, as appropriate, from one to three of the Synoptics.

Truth the Synoptics Teach	Text	**Action** the Synoptics Invite
1 Guidelines for Growing in Godliness With the Gospels, as with the whole NT godliness (or godly living) takes on a new dimension. Jesus has come and demonstrated the desirability of personal godliness, and given the Holy Spirit to live this life through us. As a result, we have the hope of experiencing the very life of God. Jesus' life and teaching gave us instruction in how to live a godly life. Though godliness never earns access to heaven from Earth, through godly living we discover the blessing of heaven on Earth.	Matt. 5:17–20	**Understand** that Jesus' ministry fulfilled the Law; it did not abolish it. **Be warned** that those who teach lawlessness will not be great in the kingdom.
	Matt. 5:31, 32; 19:4–6; Mark 10:6–12; Luke 16:18	**Understand** that divorce must never be employed as an expedient. **Recognize** that divorce upsets the intended created order and is, therefore, sin.
	Matt. 10:32, 33; Luke 12:8, 9	**Boldly confess** Jesus before others; **believe** He will acknowledge you before the Father.
	Matt. 15:1–9; Mark 7:1–13	**Beware** the danger of religious tradition. **Recognize** and **guard against** the tendency of men to teach religious tradition as a substitute for God's Word.
	Luke 12:47, 48	**Know** that those who have the greatest knowledge of truth will be held accountable for the greatest fruitfulness.
2 Steps to Holiness Under the Old Covenant, holiness called Israel to live distinctly from the nations, primarily in the external matters of the Law. However, Jesus calls His people to a holiness that proceeds from the heart. Holiness is now the outcome of personal loyalty to God and the realization of the fulfilling fruitfulness originally intended for mankind.	Matt. 5:13–16; Mark 9:50; Luke 11:33; 14:34, 35	**Recognize** that your life has either a positive or negative effect. **Live** responsibly to bring glory to God.
	Matt. 6:24; Luke 16:13	**Be loyal** to God. **Forsake** any ambition that compromises your commitment to God.
	Matt. 10:28; Luke 12:4, 5	**Acknowledge** that only God has power over death and hell. **Have reverence** for Him.
	Matt. 22:15–22; Mark 12:13–17; Luke 20:20–26	**Discern** between "Caesar's" claims and those of God. **Honor** the Lord as the highest authority.
3 Steps to Dynamic Devotion Whereas the Old Covenant focused on the external practices of devotion, Jesus presents devotion as a matter of the heart. He contrasts sincere, heartfelt devotion with the external, hypocritical, pretentious practices of piety among the Pharisees. He warns His disciples against allowing even genuine,	Matt. 6:5–8	**Always pray** in an honest and sincere manner. **Experience** times of private prayer. **Forsake** any display of religion that is done only for man's approval.
	Matt. 6:9–13; Luke 11:2–4	**Employ** "The Lord's Prayer" daily as an outline for personal worship, intercession, petition, warfare, and praise.

Truth the Synoptics Teach	Text	**Action** the Synoptics Invite
3 good works to distract from wholehearted devotion to Him. Devotion is a matter of developing an intimate relationship with the living God, learning the warmth of a life that draws near to His Father-heart.	Luke 10:38–42	**Avoid** setting the Lord's work as a priority over the Lord's Presence. **Prefer** "Mary's place," learning at the feet of Jesus Himself, but **serve** like Martha whom He commended.
	Luke 18:1–8	**Practice** patient, persistent, persevering prayer.
	Matt. 22:34–40; Mark 12:28–34; Luke 10:25–28	**Know** that only total love for God can empower you to **love rightly** yourself and your neighbor.
	Matt. 26:26–29; Mark 14:22–25; Luke 22:15–20	**Celebrate** the Lord's Supper often. **Approach** it with faith, receiving the life and healing it provides.
4 Steps to Faithful Obedience Obeying the Father was supremely important to Jesus. Obedience is the response of faith to any instruction from God. Jesus taught that true faith will always be manifested in obedience to God's revealed will. Successful Christian living results from seeking and knowing God's will and then doing it in faith.	Luke 1:38	**Adopt** Mary's attitude. **Submit** your plans and future to God's will.
	Matt. 6:22, 23; Luke 11:34–36	**Be full** of the light of life so that there is no darkness in you. Have a "good" eye. **Develop** a personal commitment to the Lord and His will.
	Matt. 13:1–23; Mark 4:1–20; Luke 8:4–15	**Be aware** that the fruitfulness of the Word of God in your life is determined by your receptivity and teachability. **Determine** to obey God's Word.
	Matt. 26:39; Mark 14:36; Luke 22:42	**Prefer** God's will to your own.
5 Steps in Developing Humility Jesus has a great deal to say about humility. And no wonder, since it was pride that first caused man's downfall. As the New Adam, Jesus exemplified this aspect of righteous living. Man fell because he presumed his own way above God's, but restored godliness requires that man do the opposite and humble himself before God's will and way. Then true God-given exaltation and recognition will come to those who least expect it and who least seek it.	Matt. 5:38–42; Luke 6:29, 30	**Renounce** any form of retaliation. **Leave** all vengeance to God.
	Matt. 5:43–48; Luke 6:27, 28, 32–36	**Love** by choice, not by circumstance. **Let** mistreatment by others remind you to **overcome their evil** through love.
	Matt. 18:21–35; Luke 17:3, 4	**Forgive** daily those who have sinned against you. **Allow** God's forgiving nature to guide you in forgiving others.
	Luke 14:7–11	**Humble** yourself. **Be wary** of the serious danger of pride and arrogance. **Avoid striving** for public recognition and **promoting** yourself or your ministry.
	Luke 18:9–14	**Recognize** and **confess** before God any sin in your life. **Do not seek to justify yourself** by comparing yourself with other sinners.
6 Keys to Godly Relationships A major emphasis of Jesus' teaching is how to build and maintain right relationships with God and man. He views these relationships	Matt. 5:21, 22	**Know** that Jesus equates anger with murder. **Be very careful** how you speak to others lest hateful words bring you into God's judgment.

Truth the Synoptics Teach	Text	**Action** the Synoptics Invite
6 as neither unimportant nor extraneous, but as the essence of which life is made. Knowing God is our highest priority, but this pursuit should not replace or diminish our interpersonal relationships with others. Rather, our personal interaction with God should produce within us the qualities of character that build and sustain all our relationships.	Matt. 5:24, 25; Luke 12:57, 58	**Practice** instant reconciliation. **Understand** that conflicts cause much greater damage to relationships when left unresolved.
	Matt. 6:14; Mark 11:25	**Understand** that God forgives us our sins as we forgive others who have sinned against us. **Adopt** the forgiveness of others into your prayer life as a daily discipline.
	Matt. 7:1–5; Luke 6:37, 38, 41, 42	**Correct** your faults and solve your own problems before attempting to correct faults or problems in others. **Let** any judgmental attitude in yourself signal the need to **examine yourself** for things that bother you about others.
7 **How to Develop Dynamic Discipleship** With Jesus, righteousness no longer consists in observance of an external legal code. Jesus defines it as an apprenticeship to Himself as Master Teacher through the Holy Spirit. Righteousness is now defined by the Person of Jesus and not by the Law. However, this Person who is righteousness requires our loyalty: true discipleship requires total commitment without distraction or compromise.	Matt. 10:17–20	**Understand** that legalistic religion is a ferocious enemy of the loving "life" quality of the kingdom of God. **Trust** that Jesus will give you the wisdom and words to overcome such opposition.
	Matt. 10:37–39; Luke 14:26, 27	**Know for certain** that Jesus requires a loyalty to Himself greater than loyalty to any other human being. **Understand** that discipleship means submitting your own interests in favor of God's.
	Matt. 10:34–36; Luke 12:51–53	**Recognize** and **anticipate** that personal discipleship and commitment to Jesus can even result in division and rejection.
	Matt. 16:24–26; Mark 8:34–36; Luke 9:23–25	**Understand** and **accept** that discipleship means forsaking all selfish personal ambition. **Know for certain** that every true disciple must take up his cross.
	Matt. 28:18–20	**Recognize** that Jesus calls His disciples to go to people of all nations and **teach** them how to know Him and live for Him. **Teach** others that Christ must be the center of all their life.
	Matt. 8:18–22; Luke 9:57–62	**Remember** that the demands of discipleship are costly. **Know** that God will test all of your relationships to prove that following Jesus is your highest priority.
8 **Keys to Understanding God's Kingdom** The dominant theme of Jesus' teaching is the kingdom of God. Jesus presents numerous word-pictures of what this supernatural	Matt. 11:12–14; Luke 16:16	**Enter** the kingdom of God by "violent" determination. **Be aggressive** about serving Christ.
	Luke 17:20, 21	**Understand** that the kingdom is an internal rulership unobservable by the natural eye.

Truth the Synoptics Teach	Text	**Action** the Synoptics Invite
8 realm "is like." But the kingdom is not merely to be understood with the mind. Rather, it is spiritual and is to be comprehended and entered into by spiritual means and in practical living. Let us meditate daily on Jesus' words in order to receive the keys of the kingdom.	Matt. 13:44–52	**Recognize** that the kingdom of God requires your highest commitment. **Understand** that the kingdom is worth more than any other pursuit. **Be ready** to forsake any personal goal that hinders your entering into it.
	Matt. 18:1–5; Mark 9:33–37; Luke 9:46–48	**Recognize** that kingdom people are childlike (not childish) in their faith, trust, and blamelessness. **Pursue** childlikeness in all your interpersonal dealings.
9 **Keys to Wise Living** Jesus motivates His disciples to live righteously by emphasizing that such living comes from the heart with love and in trust, more than through observance of an external code of ethics. Consequently, NT wisdom reveals the differences between a correct behavior, based only on the Law, and righteous actions that proceed from the heart of a new life reborn in Christ.	Matt. 7:13, 14; Luke 13:23, 24	**Suspect** things that are popular or favored by the world-minded majority.
	Matt. 15:10–20; Mark 7:14-23	**Understand** that evil originates in the heart.
	Matt. 7:15–20; Luke 6:43–45	**Understand** that the results of an individual's life and work are better indications of personal motives than are appearance or claims.
	Matt. 7:21–23; Luke 6:46; 13:24–30	**Be warned** that what you practice demonstrates your relationship with Jesus. **Never undervalue** obedience. **Know** that many who expect divine approval will receive censure or even judgment instead.
	Luke 16:14, 15	**Beware** of judging yourself and your success by human standards. **Remember** that popularity and human approval do not necessarily indicate God's approval of a situation.
	Matt. 20:20–28; Mark 10:35–37; Luke 22:24–27	**Understand** that God's kingdom authority and the world's systems of authority are often opposites.
10 **Learning the Righteous Use of Money** Although in the Bible wealth is shown as an aspect of God's blessing and approval, the NT brings the added emphasis of the possession and use of wealth or money in connection with heart attitude and internal motivation. A righteous	Matt. 6:19–24; Luke 12:33, 34	**Remember** your heart follows your treasures. **Put your treasures** where you want your life to be. **Avoid** misplacing your affections and loyalty because of personal possessions. **Sell** unnecessary or distracting possessions and give the money to the poor or to the Lord's work.

Truth the Synoptics Teach	Text	**Action** the Synoptics Invite
10 heart does not serve money. Mammon is closely associated with money—perhaps even naming the demonic principality dominating the world's economy. Jesus equates love for money with the service of mammon. Money must be handled carefully and used wisely lest desire for it seduce us from true devotion to God.	Luke 12:13–15	**Practice** generosity toward God! **Stop** any form of hoarding (fear-motivated clamoring for "things") or laying up treasures on Earth.
	Luke 16:1–13	**Employ** material wealth for the kingdom, not for personal selfish ambition. **Remember** that such a use of your financial resources has eternal results.
	Matt. 19:21–26; Mark 10:21–27; Luke 18:22–27	**Free** your heart of your possessions. **Do not seek** your security in financial holdings or material possessions.
11 **Miscellaneous Instructions** Here are several important instructions found in the synoptic Gospels, but which are not included in the above categories.	Matt. 3:11, 12; Mark 1:8; Luke 3:16, 17	**Expect** and **welcome** the refining work of the **Holy Spirit** as the result of His indwelling and continual infilling.
	Matt. 5:27–30	**Develop** a godly hatred for all immorality and sexual sin. **Know** that sexual sin begins with a lustful thought, glance, or inappropriate touch.
	Matt. 6:25–34; Luke 12:22–34	**Name worry** as sin. **Discipline** yourself to turn from any anxiety, and **choose to trust** the Lord.
	Matt. 9:16, 17; Mark 2:21, 22; Luke 5:36–39	**Avoid** imposing past traditional structures on present renewals. **Understand** that yesterday's structures and forms are often incapable of handling today's dynamic of spiritual renewal.
	Matt. 12:43–45; Luke 11:24–26	**Be warned** that returning to a past bondage from which you were once delivered results in deeper bondage.
	Matt. 13:31, 32; Mark 4:30–32; Luke 13:18, 19	**Recognize** that faith is decision and obedience rather than ability. **Understand** that obedient faith releases Holy Spirit power to accomplish the task.

The Gospel According to JOHN

Author: The Apostle John
Date: About A.D. 85
Theme: Knowing God by Believing in Jesus Christ
Key Words: Believe, Bear Witness, Life

Author Early church tradition attributes the Fourth Gospel to John "the beloved disciple" (13:23; 19:26; 20:2; 21:7, 20), who belonged to the "inner circle" of Jesus' followers (see Matt. 17:1; Mark 13:3). According to Christian writers of the second century, John moved to Ephesus, probably during the Jewish War of A.D. 66–70, where he continued his ministry. For instance, Irenaeus, the bishop of Lyons in the latter part of the second century, stated that "John, the disciple of the Lord, who also leaned upon His breast, did himself publish a Gospel during his residence in Ephesus in Asia" (*Against Heresies* 3.1.1).

Some scholars suggest that John 19:35 and 21:24 may reflect another author who faithfully collected the apostle's eyewitness account and testimonials. However, the bulk of the evidence, both internal and external, supports John the apostle as the author.

Date The same tradition that locates John in Ephesus suggests that he wrote his Gospel in the latter part of the first century. In the absence of substantial evidence to the contrary, most scholars accept this tradition.

Purpose In a broad sense, John wrote to provide the Christians of the province of Asia (now in Asia Minor) with a fuller understanding of the life and ministry of Jesus Christ. More specifically, he wrote to lead his readers to a settled faith on the basis of the words and works of Jesus, with the result that they "may have life in His name" (20:31).

John and the Synoptic Gospels While John most likely knew of the other three Gospel accounts, he chose not to follow their chronological sequence of events as much as a topical order. In this case they may have used common oral and/or literary traditions. The broad outline is the same, and some particular events in Jesus' ministry are common to all four books. Some of the distinctive differences are: 1) Instead of the familiar parables, John has lengthy discourses; 2) In place of the many miracles and healings in the Synoptics, John uses seven carefully picked miracles, which serve as "signs"; 3) The ministry of Jesus revolves around three Passover Feasts, instead of the one cited in the Synoptics; 4) The "I am" sayings are uniquely Johannine.

Content John divides the ministry of Jesus into two distinct parts: chapters 2—12 give insight into His public ministry, while chapters 13—21 relate His private ministry to His disciples. In 1:1–18, called the "Prologue," John deals with the theological implications of the first coming of Jesus. He shows Jesus' preexistent state with God, His deity and essence, as well as His incarnation.

Christ Revealed The book presents Jesus as the only begotten Son of God who became flesh. For John, Jesus' humanity meant essentially a twofold mission: 1) As the "Lamb of God" (1:29), He procured the redemption of mankind; 2) Through His life and ministry He revealed the Father. Christ consistently pointed beyond Himself to the Father who had sent Him and whom He sought to glorify. In fact, the very miracles Jesus performed, which John characterized as "signs," bore testimony to the divine mission of the Son of God. As the Son glorified the Father in ministry and passion, so the Father glorified the Son. But, as John shows, the Son's glorification came at the Crucifixion (12:32, 33), not only in the postresurrection exaltation. By believing that Jesus is the Christ, the readers of John's Gospel become participants in the life Jesus brought out of death (20:31).

The Holy Spirit at Work Unique to John is the designation of the Holy Spirit as "Comforter" or "Helper" (14:16), literally "one called alongside." He is "another Helper," namely, one of the same kind as Jesus, thereby extending the ministry of Jesus to the end of this age. It would be a grave error, however, to understand the Spirit's purpose merely in terms of one needed in predicaments. On the contrary, John demonstrates that the Spirit's role encompasses every facet of life. In regard to the world outside of Christ, He works as the agent who convicts of sin, righteousness, and judgment (16:8–11). The experience of being "born of the Spirit" is descriptive of New Birth (3:6). Because God in essence is Spirit, those who worship Him must do so spiritually, that is, as directed and motivated by the Holy Spirit (4:24). Further, in anticipation of Pentecost, the Spirit becomes the divine enabler for authoritative ministry (20:21–23).

The Holy Spirit also fulfills a definite function in relation to Christ. While the Father sent the Spirit in the name of Christ, the Spirit never draws attention to Himself, nor does He speak in His own authority. Instead, His mission is to glorify Jesus and to declare Christ's teaching to the disciples (16:14).

John reveals the function of the Holy Spirit in continuing the work of Jesus, leading believers into an understanding of the meanings, implications, and imperatives of the gospel, and enabling them to do "greater works" than those done by Jesus (14:12). Present-day believers in Christ may thus view Him as their contemporary, not merely as a figure from the distant past.

Personal Application In seeking to fulfill his purpose as stated in 20:20, 31, John confronts his readers with claims of Jesus that demand a personal response. A positive response of faith in "Jesus . . . . the Christ, the Son of God" results in "life in His name." John records the assertion of Jesus that He came "that they might have life and that they might have it more abundantly" (10:10), and he makes it clear that life is not an independent quality unrelated to God or to Christ. The knowledge of "the only true God and Jesus Christ" (17:3), which implies fellowship as well as intellectual understanding, is the key to the meaning of eternal life.

Outline of John

Prologue 1:1–18

I. Jesus' public ministry 1:19—12:50
- A. Preparation 1:19–51
- B. Wedding at Cana 2:1–12
- C. Ministry in Jerusalem 2:13—3:36
- D. Jesus and the Samaritan woman 4:1–42
- E. Healing of the nobleman's son 4:43–54
- F. Sabbath healing at the pool of Bethesda 5:1–15
- G. Honoring the Father and the Son 5:16–29
- H. Witnesses to the Son 5:30–47
- I. Ministry in Galilee 6:1–71
- J. Conflict in Jerusalem 7:1—9:41
- K. Jesus the Good Shepherd 10:1–42
- L. Ministry at Bethany 11:1—12:11
- M. Triumphal entry to Jerusalem 12:12–19
- N. Final rejection: unbelief 12:20–50

II. Jesus' ministry to the disciples 13:1—17:26
- A. Modeling servanthood 13:1–20
- B. Pronouncements of betrayal and denial 13:21–38
- C. Preparation for Jesus' departure 14:1–31
- D. Fruitfulness by abiding 15:1–17
- E. Dealing with rejection 15:18—16:4
- F. Understanding Jesus' departure 16:5–33
- G. Jesus' prayer for His disciples 17:1–26

III. Jesus' passion and resurrection 18:1—21:23
- A. Jesus' arrest 18:1–14
- B. Trial before the high priest 18:15–27
- C. Trial before Pilate 18:28—19:16
- D. Crucifixion and burial 19:17–42
- E. Resurrection and appearances 20:1—21:23

Epilogue 21:24, 25

The Eternal Word

IN the beginning [a]was the *Word, and
the [b]Word was [c]with God, and the
Word was [d]God.
2 [a]He was in the beginning with God.
3 [a]All things were made through
Him, and without Him nothing was
made that was made.
4 [a]In Him was *life, and [b]the life was
the light of men.
5 And [a]the light shines in the *darkness, and the darkness did not [1]**comprehend** it.

WORD WEALTH

1:5 comprehend, *katalambano* (kat-al-am-*ban*-oh); Strong's *#2638:* The word is capable of three interpretations: 1) To seize, lay hold of, overcome. As such, v. 5 could read, "The darkness does not gain control of it." 2) To perceive, attain, lay hold of with the mind; to apprehend with mental or moral effort. With this meaning the verse could be translated, "The darkness is unreceptive and does not understand it." 3) To quench, extinguish, snuff out the light by stifling it. "The darkness will never be able to eliminate it." Light and darkness essentially are antagonistic. The Christian's joy is in knowing that light is not only greater than darkness but will also outlast the darkness.

CHAPTER 1

1 [a]1 John 1:1 [b]Rev. 19:13 [c][John 17:5] [d][1 John 5:20] *See WW at Acts 19:20.
2 [a]Gen. 1:1
3 [a][Col. 1:16, 17]
4 [a][1 John 5:11] [b]John 8:12; 9:5; 12:46 *See WW at 1 John 5:20.
5 [a][John 3:19] [1]Or *overcome* *See WW at John 12:46.
6 [a]Matt. 3:1–17 *See WW at John 20:21.
7 [a]John 3:25–36; 5:33–35 [b][John 3:16] *See WW at Acts 26:22.

John's Witness: The True Light

6 There was a [a]man *sent from God,
whose name *was* John.
7 This man came for a [a]witness,* to
bear witness of the Light, that all
through him might [b]believe.

1:1 In the beginning: An allusion to Gen. 1:1, with the intention of linking Jesus the Word with the God of creation. The event of Jesus' incarnation, therefore, had cosmic significance. **The Word** is Jesus Christ, the eternal, ultimate expression of God. In the OT God spoke the world into existence; in the gospel God spoke His final word through the living Word, His Son. The phrase "the Word was God" attributes deity to the Word without defining all of the Godhead as "the Word."

1:3 John declares that Jesus was the divine agent who was responsible for the entire creation.

1:4, 5 Life and **light** belong to John's fundamental vocabulary in describing the essence and mission of the incarnate Word.

1:6–11 John's Gospel records various testimonies concerning Christ, showing that faith in Him is based upon evidence. The **witness** of John the Baptist, as well as the other evidence, makes the world's rejection of Jesus inexcusable. The phrase **coming into the world** (v. 9) refers to Christ, not to **every man.** By His coming He has become **the true Light** to those who believe, but He is also that Light that, in a general sense, enlightens the human conscience and thereby makes all mankind responsible before God (Rom. 1:19, 20).

8 He was not that Light, but *was sent*
to bear witness of that [a]Light.
9 [a]That[1] was the true Light which
gives light to every man coming into
the world.
10 He was in the world, and the world
was made through Him, and [a]the world
did not *know Him.
11 [a]He came to His [1]own, and His
[2]own did not receive Him.
12 But [a]as many as received Him, to
them He gave the [1]right* to become
children of God, to those who believe
in His name:
13 [a]who were born, not of blood, nor
of the will of the flesh, nor of the will
of man, but of God.

The Word Becomes Flesh

14 [a]And the Word [b]became [c]flesh* and
dwelt among us, and [d]we beheld His
*glory, the glory as of the only begotten
of the Father, [e]full of grace and truth.
15 [a]John bore witness of Him and
cried out, saying, "This was He of
whom I said, [b]'He who comes after me
[1]is preferred before me, [c]for He was
before me.' "
16 [1]And of His [a]fullness* we have all
received, and grace for grace.
17 For [a]the law was given through Moses, *but* [b]grace and [c]truth* came
through Jesus Christ.
18 [a]No one has seen God at any time.
[b]The only begotten [1]Son, who is in the
bosom of the Father, He has declared
Him.

A Voice in the Wilderness

19 Now this is [a]the testimony of John,
when the Jews sent priests and Levites
from Jerusalem to ask him, "Who are
you?"
20 [a]He confessed, and did not deny,
but confessed, "I am not the Christ."
21 And they asked him, "What then?
Are you Elijah?" He said, "I am not."
"Are you [a]the Prophet?" And he answered, "No."
22 Then they said to him, "Who are
you, that we may give an answer to
those who sent us? What do you say
about yourself?"
23 He said: [a]"I *am*

> [b]*'The voice of one crying in the*
> *wilderness:*
> *"Make straight the way of the*
> *LORD,"'*

as the prophet Isaiah said."
24 Now those who were sent were
from the Pharisees.
25 And they asked him, saying, "Why
then do you baptize if you are not the
Christ, nor Elijah, nor the Prophet?"
26 John answered them, saying,

8 [a]Is. 9:2; 49:6 **9** [a]Is. 49:6 [1]Or *That was the true Light which, coming into the world, gives light to every man.* **10** [a]Heb. 1:2 *See WW at John 8:32. **11** [a][Luke 19:14] [1]His own things or domain [2]His own people **12** [a]Gal. 3:26 [1]*authority* *See WW at Mark 3:15. **13** [a][1 Pet. 1:23] **14** [a]Rev. 19:13 [b]Gal. 4:4 [c]Heb. 2:11 [d]Is. 40:5 [e][John 8:32; 14:6; 18:37] *See WW at Matt. 26:41. • See WW at John 2:11. **15** [a]John 3:32 [b][Matt. 3:11] [c][Col. 1:17] [1]*ranks higher than I* **16** [a][Col. 1:19; 2:9] [1]NU *For* *See WW at Eph. 3:19. **17** [a][Ex. 20:1] [b][Rom. 5:21; 6:14] [c][John 8:32; 14:6; 18:37] *See WW at John 4:24. **18** [a]Ex. 33:20 [b]1 John 4:9 [1]NU *God*

19 [a]John 5:33 **20** [a]Luke 3:15 **21** [a]Deut. 18:15, 18 **23** [a]Matt. 3:3 [b]Is. 40:3

1:13 The New Birth does not come by physical descent, human effort, or human volition, but by the power of **God.**
1:14 **Dwelt** literally means "tabernacled." The analogy is that of the tabernacle in the wilderness when God pitched His tent among those of the Hebrews and manifested His glory there, so Jesus identified Himself with humanity by becoming **flesh . . . and we beheld His glory.**
1:16 The fact that John states that **grace** comes from **His fullness** teaches that grace is more than God's disposition or impersonal favor. It is God meeting us at our point of need in the Person of Jesus Christ, including all His power and provision.
1:18 **Only begotten** does not denote Christ's earthly birth but describes the unique, loving relationship of the Son with the Father.
1:23 John prepared the way for the Messiah by his call to repentance. The quote from Isaiah depicts preparations made in advance of a king's visit to a province of his realm. The road is smoothed and leveled.
1:25–27 All John could do was administer the sign; only the Messiah can bestow that which is signified—the cleansing, renewing power of the Holy Spirit.

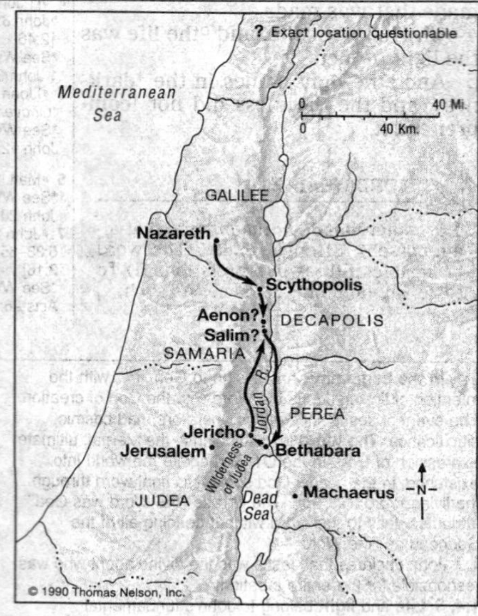

Baptism and Temptation. Jesus came from Nazareth in Galilee to be baptized by John the Baptist in the Jordan River. After His temptation in the wilderness around Jericho, Jesus returned to Galilee.

[a]"I baptize with water, [b]but there
stands One among you whom you do
not know.
27 [a]"It is He who, coming after me,
[1]is preferred before me, whose sandal
strap I am not worthy to loose."
28 These things were done [a]in [1]Beth-
abara beyond the Jordan, where John
was baptizing.

The Lamb of God

29 The next day John saw Jesus coming toward him, and said, "Behold!
[a]The Lamb of God [b]who *takes away
the **sin** of the world!

WORD WEALTH

1:29 sin, *hamartia* (ham-ar-*tee*-ah); Strong's *#266:* Literally, "missing the mark," failure, offense, taking the wrong course, wrongdoing, sin, guilt. The NT uses the word in a generic sense for concrete wrongdoing (8:34, 46; 2 Cor. 11:7; James 1:15); as a principle and quality of action (Rom. 5:12, 13, 20; Heb. 3:13); and as a sinful deed (Matt. 12:31; Acts 7:60; 1 John 5:16).

30 "This is He of whom I said, 'After
me comes a Man who [1]is preferred before me, for He was before me.'
31 "I did not know Him; but that He
should be revealed to Israel, [a]therefore
I came baptizing with water."
32 [a]And John bore witness, saying, "I
saw the *Spirit descending from
heaven like a dove, and He remained
upon Him.
33 "I did not know Him, but He who
sent me to baptize with water said to
me, 'Upon whom you see the Spirit descending, and remaining on Him,
[a]this is He who baptizes with the *Holy
Spirit.'
34 "And I have seen and testified that
this is the [a]Son of God."

The First Disciples

35 Again, the next day, John stood
with two of his disciples.
36 And looking at Jesus as He walked,
he said, [a]"Behold the Lamb of God!"
37 The two disciples heard him speak,
and they [a]followed Jesus.
38 Then Jesus turned, and seeing them
following, said to them, "What do you
seek?" They said to Him, "Rabbi"
(which is to say, when translated,
Teacher), "where are You staying?"
39 He said to them, "Come and see."
They came and saw where He was
staying, and remained with Him that
day (now it was about the tenth hour).
40 One of the two who heard John
speak, and followed Him, was [a]An-
drew, Simon Peter's brother.
41 He first found his own brother Simon, and said to him, "We have found
the [1]Messiah" (which is translated, the
Christ).
42 And he brought him to Jesus. Now
when Jesus looked at him, He said,
"You are Simon the son of [1]Jonah.
[a]You shall be called Cephas" (which
is translated, [2]A Stone).

Philip and Nathanael

43 The following day Jesus wanted to
go to Galilee, and He found [a]Philip and
said to him, "Follow Me."
44 Now [a]Philip was from Bethsaida,
the city of Andrew and Peter.
45 Philip found [a]Nathanael and said to
him, "We have found Him of whom
[b]Moses in the law, and also the
[c]prophets, wrote—Jesus [d]of Nazareth,
the [e]son of Joseph."
46 And Nathanael said to him, [a]"Can
anything good come out of Nazareth?"
Philip said to him, "Come and see."
47 Jesus saw Nathanael coming toward Him, and said of him, "Behold,
[a]an Israelite indeed, in whom is no deceit!"
48 Nathanael said to Him, "How do
You know me?" Jesus answered and
said to him, "Before Philip called you,
when you were under the fig tree, I saw
you."
49 Nathanael answered and said to
Him, "Rabbi, [a]You are the Son of God!
You are [b]the King of Israel!"

26 [a]Matt. 3:11 [b]Mal. 3:1
27 [a]Acts 19:4 [1]*ranks higher than I*
28 [a]Judg. 7:24 [1]NU, M *Bethany*
29 [a]Rev. 5:6–14 [b][1 Pet. 2:24] *See WW at John 16:22.
30 [1]*ranks higher than I*
31 [a]Matt. 3:6
32 [a]Mark 1:10 *See WW at Rom. 7:6.
33 [a]Matt. 3:11 *See WW at Acts 7:33.
34 [a]John 11:27
36 [a]John 1:29
37 [a]Matt. 4:20, 22
40 [a]Matt. 4:18
41 [1]Lit. *Anointed One*
42 [a]Matt. 16:18 [1]NU *John* [2]Gr. *Petros,* usually translated *Peter*
43 [a]John 6:5; 12:21, 22; 14:8, 9
44 [a]John 12:21
45 [a]John 21:2 [b]Luke 24:27 [c][Zech. 6:12] [d][Matt. 2:23] [e]Luke 3:23
46 [a]John 7:41, 42, 52
47 [a]Ps. 32:2; 73:1
49 [a]Matt. 14:33 [b]Matt. 21:5

1:29 The sacrificial language of John's declaration is taken from the OT and points to the universal scope of Christ's mission. Clearly, this was not an awareness that gradually dawned upon Jesus, but one that shaped His entire earthly ministry from the start.

1:33 John's witness was reliable because it came by divine revelation. As **the Lamb of God,** Jesus justifies us and takes away sin (v. 29); as the baptizer **with the Holy Spirit,** He fills us and endues with an enabling power.

1:35–42 Jesus called His first disciples from among those who also followed John the Baptist. Since only Andrew is named as one of the first two disciples (v. 40), the other was probably John, the author of this Gospel.

1:46 Nathanael is not insulting Nazareth. Rather he knows that Nazareth seems too obscure, and further, is not the prophesied birthplace of the Messiah; so he voices his difficulty in accepting Philip's assertion.

1:47–51 Jesus' supernatural insight into Nathanael's character convinces this "true Israelite" that he has been confronted by the Son of God, the King of Israel. Even through the facade of Nathanael's skepticism, Jesus discerned his transparency of spirit.

50 Jesus answered and said to him,
"Because I said to you, 'I saw you under the fig tree,' do you believe? You
will see greater things than these."
51 And He said to him, "Most assuredly, I say to you, [a]hereafter[1] you
shall see heaven open, and the angels
of God ascending and descending upon
the Son of Man."

Water Turned to Wine

2 On the third day there was a
[a]wedding in [b]Cana of Galilee, and
the [c]mother of Jesus was there.
2 Now both Jesus and His disciples
were invited to the wedding.
3 And when they ran out of wine, the
mother of Jesus said to Him, "They
have no wine."
4 Jesus said to her, [a]"Woman, [b]what
does your concern have to do with Me?
[c]My hour has not yet come."
3 5 His mother said to the servants,
"Whatever He says to you, do *it*."
6 Now there were set there six waterpots of stone, [a]according to the manner
of purification of the Jews, containing
twenty or thirty gallons apiece.
7 Jesus said to them, "Fill the waterpots with water." And they filled them
up to the brim.
8 And He said to them, "Draw *some*
out now, and take *it* to the master of
the feast." And they took *it*.
9 When the master of the feast had
*tasted [a]the water that was made wine,
and did not know where it came from
(but the servants who had drawn the
water knew), the master of the feast
called the bridegroom.
10 And he said to him, "Every man at
the beginning sets out the good wine,
and when the *guests* have well drunk,
then the inferior. You have kept the
good wine until now!"
11 This [a]beginning of *signs Jesus did
in Cana of Galilee, [b]and [1]manifested
His **glory;** and His *disciples believed
in Him.

51 [a]Gen. 28:12; [Luke 2:9, 13]; Acts 1:10; 7:55, 56 [1]NU omits *hereafter*

CHAPTER 2

1 [a][Heb. 13:4] [b]John. 4:46 [c]John 19:25
4 [a]John 19:26 [b]2 Sam. 16:10 [c]John 7:6, 8, 30; 8:20
6 [a]Matt. 15:2; [Mark 7:3; Luke 11:39]; John 3:25
9 [a]John 4:46 *See WW at John 8:52.
11 [a]John 4:54 [b][John 1:14] [1]*revealed* *See WW at Rev. 16:14. • See WW at Matt. 10:1.

WORD WEALTH

2:11 glory, *doxa* (*dox*-ah); Strong's *#1391:* Compare "doxology," "paradox," "heterodoxy," and "orthodoxy." Originally, an opinion or estimation in which one is held. Then the word came to denote the reputation, good standing, and esteem given to a person. It progressed to honor or glory given to peoples, nations, and individuals. The NT *doxa* becomes splendor, radiance, and majesty centered in Jesus. Here *doxa* is the majestic, absolute perfection residing in Christ and evidenced by the miracles He performed.

12 After this He went down to [a]Caper-
naum, He, His mother, [b]His brothers,
and His disciples; and they did not stay
there many days.

Jesus Cleanses the Temple

13 [a]Now the Passover of the Jews was
at hand, and Jesus went up to Jerusalem.
14 [a]And He found in the temple those
who sold oxen and sheep and doves,
and the money changers [1]doing business.
15 When He had made a whip of cords,
He drove them all out of the temple,
with the sheep and the oxen, and
poured out the changers' money and
overturned the tables.
16 And He said to those who sold
doves, "Take these things away! Do
not make [a]My Father's house a house
of merchandise!"
17 Then His disciples remembered that
it was written, [a]*"Zeal* for Your house*
[1]*has eaten Me up."*
18 So the Jews answered and said to
Him, [a]"What sign do You show to us,
since You do these things?"
19 Jesus answered and said to them,
[a]"Destroy this temple, and in three
days I will raise it up."
20 Then the Jews said, "It has taken

12 [a]Matt. 4:13; John 4:46 [b]Matt. 12:46; 13:55
13 [a]Ex. 12:14; Deut. 16:1–6; John 5:1; 6:4; 11:55
14 [a]Mal. 3:1; Matt. 21:12; Mark 11:15, 17; Luke 19:45 [1]Lit. *sitting*
16 [a]Luke 2:49
17 [a]Ps. 69:9 [1]NU, M *will eat* *See WW at 2 Cor. 11:2.
18 [a]Matt. 12:38; John 6:30
19 [a]Matt. 26:61; 27:40; [Mark 14:58; 15:29]; Luke 24:46; Acts 6:14; 10:40; 1 Cor. 15:4

2:1 Cana of Galilee was located about 8 miles northeast of Nazareth. According to 21:2, Cana was the home of Nathanael.

2:4 The title **woman** does not convey a lack of respect or affection. It was used in addressing people of rank. Some think Mary wanted Jesus to take this occasion to present Himself openly as the Messiah. However, it is not necessary to suppose she meant anything more than that Jesus assist her in arranging for the supplying of the wine by natural means, since many believe this was probably a relative's wedding.

2:5 See section 3 of Truth-In-Action at the end of John.

2:11 As a sign, the miracle was not meant to draw attention to itself; rather, it was intended to demonstrate the power and glory of Jesus. All the miracles related by John testify to the deity of Christ.

2:13–17 This event took place at the holiest site in Israel and at the most solemn time of the year, when pilgrims thronged Jerusalem. The synoptic Gospels record a second cleansing of the temple near the end of Jesus' ministry. Interpreted in the light of the messianic prophecy of Ps. 69:9 (v. 17), the incident strengthened the conviction of the disciples that Jesus was indeed the Messiah. See note on Matt. 21:12.

2:20 Herod the Great undertook a massive expansion and beautification of the temple in 20 B.C., so it was now about A.D. 26.

forty-six years to build this temple, and
will You raise it up in three days?"
21 But He was speaking [a]of the temple
of His body.
22 Therefore, when He had risen from
the dead, [a]His disciples remembered
that He had said this [1]to them; and they
believed the Scripture and the word
which Jesus had said.

The Discerner of Hearts

23 Now when He was in Jerusalem at
the Passover, during the feast, many
believed in His name when they saw
the [a]signs which He did.
24 But Jesus did not commit Himself
to them, because He [a]knew all *men,*
25 and had no need that anyone should
testify of man, for [a]He knew what was
in man.

The New Birth

3 There was a man of the Pharisees
named Nicodemus, a ruler of the
Jews.
2 [a]This man came to Jesus by night
and said to Him, "Rabbi, we know that
You are a teacher come from God; for
[b]no one can do these signs that You
do unless [c]God is with him."
4 3 Jesus answered and said to him,
"Most assuredly, I say to you, [a]unless
one is born [1]again, he cannot see the
kingdom of God."
4 Nicodemus said to Him, "How can
a man be born when he is old? Can
he enter a second time into his
mother's womb and be born?"
5 Jesus answered, "Most assuredly, I
say to you, [a]unless one is born of water
and the Spirit, he cannot enter the
kingdom of God.

KINGDOM DYNAMICS

3:1–5 New Birth, THE MESSAGE OF THE KINGDOM. Upon repentance, a new order of life opens to the believer in Jesus Christ. Jesus used the figure of "new birth" to dramatically indicate three things: 1) Without New Birth, there is no life and no relationship with God (14:6). 2) In New Birth, new perspective comes as we "see the kingdom of God" (3:3), God's Word becomes clear, and the Holy Spirit's works and wonders are believed and experienced—faith is alive. 3) Through New Birth we are introduced—literally we "enter" (v. 5)—to a new realm, where God's new kingdom order can be realized (2 Cor. 5:17). New Birth is more than simply being "saved." It is a requalifying experience, opening up the possibilities of our whole being to the supernatural dimension of life and fitting us for a beginning in God's kingdom order.

(Matt. 3:1, 2; 4:17/Matt. 13:1–52) J.W.H.

KINGDOM DYNAMICS

3:3 3. What Do I Have to Do to Be Saved?, SPIRITUAL ANSWERS. For the answer to this and other probing questions about God and the power life in His kingdom, see the study article "Spiritual Answers to Hard Questions," which begins on page 1996. P.R.

6 "That which is born of the flesh is
[a]flesh, and that which is born of the
*Spirit is spirit.
7 "Do not marvel that I said to you,
'You must be born again.'
8 [a]"The wind blows where it wishes,
and you hear the sound of it, but cannot tell where it comes from and where
it goes. So is everyone who is born of
the Spirit."
9 Nicodemus answered and said to
Him, [a]"How can these things be?"
10 Jesus answered and said to him,
"Are you the teacher of Israel, and do
not know these things?
11 [a]"Most assuredly, I say to you, We
speak what We know and testify what
We have seen, and [b]you do not receive
Our witness.

21 [a][Col. 2:9; Heb. 8:2; 1 Cor. 3:16; 6:19; 2 Cor. 6:16]
22 [a]Luke 24:8; John 2:17; 12:16; 14:26 [1]NU, M omit *to them*
23 [a][John 5:36; Acts 2:22]
24 [a]Matt. 9:4; John 16:30; Rev. 2:23
25 [a]1 Sam. 16:7; 1 Chr. 28:9; Matt. 9:4; [Mark 2:8]; John 6:64; 16:30; Acts 1:24; Rev. 2:23

CHAPTER 3

2 [a]John 7:50; 19:39 [b]John 9:16, 33; Acts 2:22 [c][Acts 10:38]
3 [a][John 1:13; Gal. 6:15; Titus 3:5; James 1:18; 1 Pet. 1:23; 1 John 3:9] [1]Or *from above*
5 [a]Mark 16:16; [Acts 2:38]
6 [a]John 1:13; 1 Cor. 15:50 *See WW at Rom. 7:6.
8 [a]Ps. 135:7; Eccl. 11:5; Ezek. 37:9; 1 Cor. 2:11
9 [a]John 6:52, 60
11 [a][Matt. 11:27] [b]John 3:32; 8:14

2:23–25 Jesus' knowledge of human nature pierces the superficiality of faith in Him on account of His miracles.
2:23 Many believed in His name: Since the "name" represents the person, no qualitative difference exists between this expression and "believes in Him" (3:16).
3:1 Nicodemus ("Conqueror of the People") was an influential and respected member of the Sanhedrin. As a Pharisee, Nicodemus was thoroughly trained in Jewish law and theology; Jesus therefore called him a "teacher of Israel" (3:10).
3:2 Nicodemus may have come to Jesus at night because he was fearful of losing his reputation and position. More likely he was a particular example of those mentioned in 2:23; if so, his night visit would indicate a lack of certainty that Jesus was the Messiah Himself.
3:3, 4 The Greek word translated **again** can also be rendered "from above." Nicodemus clearly understood it in the former sense, whereas Jesus had both meanings in mind. To enter the kingdom of God, one must be born again, not by experiencing a second biological birth, but by spiritual birth from above.
3:3 See section 4 of Truth-In-Action at the end of John.
3:5 Water may refer to physical birth. The Hebrews used terms such as "water" and "drop" in describing natural birth, and such an explanation fits the context. However, some see a reference to the faith that is expressed in water baptism (not "for" but "because of" salvation). **Spirit** refers to the spiritual birth brought about by the renewing and transforming power of the Holy Spirit.

12 "If I have told you earthly things
and you do not believe, how will you
believe if I tell you heavenly things?
13 [a]"No one has ascended to heaven
but He who came down from heaven,
that is, the Son of Man [1]who is in
heaven.
14 [a]"And as Moses *lifted up the serpent in the wilderness, even so [b]must
the Son of Man be lifted up,
15 "that whoever [a]believes in Him
should [1]not perish but [b]have eternal
life.
16 [a]"For God so **loved** the world that
He gave His only begotten [b]Son, that
whoever *believes in Him should not
*perish but have everlasting life.

WORD WEALTH

3:16 loved, *agapao* (ag-ah-*pah*-oh); Strong's *#25:* Unconditional love, love by choice and by an act of the will. The word denotes unconquerable benevolence and undefeatable goodwill. *Agapao* will never seek anything but the highest good for fellow mankind. *Agapao* (the verb) and *agape* (the noun) are the words for God's unconditional love. It does not need a chemistry, an affinity, or a feeling. *Agapao* is a word that exclusively belongs to the Christian community. It is a love virtually unknown to writers outside the NT.

KINGDOM DYNAMICS

3:16 God Gave to Us First. He Is Our Role Model for Giving and Receiving, SEED FAITH. Do you find it difficult to believe that you should expect to receive back from your giving? Read again this most famous verse in all the Bible and notice these things: 1) God so loved. God's motivation for giving was love. Ours must be, too. 2) God gave. God's love was turned into an act of giving. 3) God gave His only begotten Son. He gave His very best! So must we also give our best. 4) God gave for a specific reason—to get man back from Satan. God's deepest desire is to have man restored to Himself. And to get that need met, He gave. What is your need? Your giving—as an act of your deepest love and strongest faith—is the key to your having that need met. 5) God gave sacrificially. Our salvation cost Jesus His life (see John 12:24). It also costs us—full repentance and the giving of our lives to God. 6) God's plan works! Souls are saved because God gave His best, gave first, and gave expecting to receive! God Himself is our role model for giving . . . and receiving!

(James 5:15, 16/Gen. 8:22*) O.R.

13 [a]Deut. 30:12; Prov. 30:4; Acts 2:34; Rom. 10:6; 1 Cor. 15:47; Eph. 4:9 [1]NU omits *who is in heaven*
14 [a]Num. 21:9 [b]Matt. 27:35; Mark 15:24; Luke 23:33; John 8:28; 12:34; 19:18 *See WW at James 4:10.
15 [a]John 6:47 [b]John 3:36 [1]NU omits *not perish but*
16 [a]Rom. 5:8; Eph. 2:4; 2 Thess. 2:16; [1 John 4:9, 10; Rev. 1:5] [b][Is. 9:6] *See WW at Rom. 10:9. • See WW at Luke 9:56.
17 [a]Matt. 1:21; Luke 9:56; 1 John 4:14 *See WW at John 18:31. • See WW at Luke 7:50.
18 [a]John 5:24; 6:40, 47; 20:31; Rom. 8:1
19 [a][John 1:4, 9–11] *See WW at Luke 11:35.
20 [a]Job 24:13; Eph. 5:11, 13
21 [a][John 15:4, 5]; 1 Cor. 15:10
22 [a]John 4:1, 2
23 [a]1 Sam. 9:4 [b]Matt. 3:5, 6
24 [a]Matt. 4:12; 14:3; Mark 6:17; Luke 3:20
26 [a]John 1:7, 15, 27, 34 [b]Mark 2:2; 3:10; 5:24; Luke 8:19
27 [a][Rom. 12:5–8]; 1 Cor. 3:5, 6; 4:7; Heb. 5:4; [James 1:17; 1 Pet. 4:10, 11]

17 [a]"For God did not send His Son into
the world to *condemn the world, but
that the world through Him might be
*saved.
18 [a]"He who believes in Him is not
condemned; but he who does not believe is condemned already, because he
has not believed in the name of the
only begotten Son of God.
19 "And this is the condemnation,
[a]that the light has come into the world,
and men loved *darkness rather than
light, because their deeds were evil.
20 "For [a]everyone practicing evil hates
the light and does not come to the light,
lest his deeds should be exposed.
21 "But he who does the truth comes
to the light, that his deeds may be
clearly seen, that they have **been**
[a]**done** in God."

WORD WEALTH

3:21 been done, *ergazomai* (er-*gad*-zom-ahee); Strong's *#2038:* Compare "energy." To work, be busy, accomplish something, carry on a trade, produce things, be engaged in, toil, perform, to do business. *Ergazomai* is the opposite of idleness, laziness, or inactivity.

John the Baptist Exalts Christ

22 After these things Jesus and His disciples came into the land of Judea, and
there He remained with them [a]and
baptized.
23 Now John also was baptizing in Aenon near [a]Salim, because there was
much water there. [b]And they came and
were baptized.
24 For [a]John had not yet been thrown
into prison.
25 Then there arose a dispute between
some of John's disciples and the Jews
about purification.
26 And they came to John and said to
him, "Rabbi, He who was with you beyond the Jordan, [a]to whom you have
testified—behold, He is baptizing, and
all [b]are coming to Him!"
27 John answered and said, [a]"A man
can receive nothing unless it has been
given to him from heaven.
28 "You yourselves bear me witness,

3:14 The deliverance from sin described in Num. 21:4–9 is a type of the Crucifixion.

3:16 The theme of this summary of the gospel is God's love made manifest in an infinitely glorious manner.

3:22 Jesus **baptized** in water by means of His disciples (see 4:2).

that I said, [a]'I am not the Christ,' but,
[b]'I have been sent before Him.'
29 [a]"He who has the bride is the bridegroom; but [b]the friend of the bridegroom, who stands and hears him,
rejoices greatly because of the bridegroom's voice. Therefore this joy of
mine is fulfilled.
30 [a]"He must increase, but I *must* de-
crease.
31 [a]"He who comes from above
[b]is above all; [c]he who is of the earth
is earthly and speaks of the earth.
[d]He who comes from heaven is above
all.
32 "And [a]what He has seen and heard,
that He testifies; and no one receives
His testimony.
33 "He who has received His testimony [a]has certified that God is *true.
34 [a]"For He whom God has sent
speaks the words of God, for God does
not give the Spirit [b]by measure.
35 [a]"The Father loves the Son, and has
given all things into His hand.
36 [a]"He who believes in the Son has
everlasting life; and he who does not
believe the Son shall not see life, but
the [b]wrath of God abides on him."

A Samaritan Woman Meets Her Messiah

4 Therefore, when the Lord knew
that the Pharisees had heard that
Jesus made and [a]baptized more disciples than John
2 (though Jesus Himself did not baptize, but His disciples),
3 He left Judea and departed again to
Galilee.
4 But He needed to go through Samaria.
5 So He came to a city of Samaria
which is called Sychar, near the plot
of ground that [a]Jacob [b]gave to his son
Joseph.
6 Now Jacob's well was there. Jesus
therefore, being wearied from *His* journey, sat thus by the well. It was about
the sixth hour.
7 A woman of Samaria came to draw
water. Jesus said to her, "Give Me a
drink."
8 For His disciples had gone away
into the city to buy food.
9 Then the woman of Samaria said
to Him, "How is it that You, being a
Jew, ask a drink from me, a Samaritan
woman?" For [a]Jews have no dealings
with [b]Samaritans.
10 Jesus answered and said to her, "If
you knew the [a]gift of God, and who it
is who says to you, 'Give Me a drink,'
you would have asked Him, and He
would have given you [b]living water."
11 The woman said to Him, "Sir, You
have nothing to draw with, and the
well is deep. Where then do You get
that living water?
12 "Are You greater than our father
Jacob, who gave us the well, and drank
from it himself, as well as his sons and
his livestock?"
13 Jesus answered and said to her,
"Whoever drinks of this water will
thirst again,
14 "but [a]whoever drinks of the water
that I shall give him will *never thirst.
But the water that I shall give him
[b]will become in him a fountain of water springing up into *everlasting life."
15 [a]The woman said to Him, "Sir, give
me this water, that I may not thirst, nor
come here to draw."
16 Jesus said to her, "Go, call your
husband, and come here."
17 The woman answered and said, "I
have no husband." Jesus said to her,
"You have well said, 'I have no husband,'
18 "for you have had five husbands,
and the one whom you now have is not
your husband; in that you spoke truly."
19 The woman said to Him, "Sir,
[a]I perceive that You are a prophet.
20 "Our fathers worshiped on [a]this
mountain, and you *Jews* say that in

28 [a]John 1:19–27 [b]Mal. 3:1
29 [a][2 Cor. 11:2] [b]Song 5:1
30 [a][Is. 9:7]
31 [a]John 3:13; 8:23 [b]Matt. 28:18 [c]1 Cor. 15:47 [d]John 6:33
32 [a]John 3:11; 15:15
33 [a]1 John 5:10 *See WW at Rom. 3:4.
34 [a]John 7:16 [b]John 1:16
35 [a][Heb. 2:8]
36 [a]John 3:16, 17; 6:47 [b]Rom. 1:18

CHAPTER 4

1 [a]John 3:22, 26
5 [a]Gen. 33:19 [b]Gen. 48:22
9 [a]Acts 10:28 [b]2 Kin. 17:24
10 [a][Rom. 5:15] [b]Is. 12:3; 44:3
14 [a][John 6:35, 58] [b]John 7:37, 38 *See WW at Matt. 28:20. • See WW at Rev. 14:6.
15 [a]John 6:34, 35; 17:2, 3
19 [a]Luke 7:16, 39; 24:19
20 [a]Judg. 9:7

3:29 The friend of the bridegroom was John the Baptist himself. His great joy was being privileged, as forerunner, to prepare the people for the heavenly Bridegroom.

3:31 John contrasts his own role with that of Jesus, asserting the supremacy of Jesus.

3:32–36 The **testimony** of Jesus **is true** and should be accepted as such. He Himself is of divine origin; He taught from His own divine experience. He received **the Spirit** in fullness, with nothing held back, and He alone has universal authority. However, since this enduement of the Holy Spirit is given to **He whom God has sent,** 20:21 would suggest a similar unlimited resource of Holy Spirit fullness is available to obedient disciples of His (Jesus).

4:4 The need **to go through Samaria** was not merely a geographical consideration, but a divine compulsion.

4:5 The exact location of **Sychar** is uncertain, but it likely was in the vicinity of Shechem. See Gen. 33:18, 19; Josh. 24:32.

4:6 By Jewish reckoning, **the sixth hour** was 12:00 noon; by Roman reckoning, it was 6:00 A.M. or 6:00 P.M.

4:9 John inserts an explanatory note about the hostility between the Jews and the Samaritans.

4:13, 14 In him a fountain indicates "living water" (v. 10) as a great illustration of regeneration **into everlasting life.** Compare with 7:37–39.

4:20 This mountain refers to Mt. Gerizim, on which the Samaritans built a temple as a rival place of worship, since they were not welcome in the Jerusalem temple (see v. 21).

[b]Jerusalem is the place where one
ought to worship."
2 21 Jesus said to her, "Woman, believe
Me, the hour is coming [a]when you will
neither on this mountain, nor in Jerusalem, worship the Father.
22 "You worship [a]what you do not
know; we know what we worship, for
[b]salvation* is of the Jews.
23 "But the hour is coming, and now
is, when the true worshipers will
[a]worship* the Father in [b]spirit [c]and
truth; for the Father is seeking such to
worship Him.
24 [a]"God *is* Spirit, and those who worship Him must worship in spirit and
truth."

WORD WEALTH

4:24 truth, *aletheia* (al-*ay*-thi-ah); Strong's *#225:* Derived from negative, *a,* and *lanthano,* "to be hidden," "to escape notice." (Compare "latent," "lethargy," "lethal.") *Aletheia* is the opposite of fictitious, feigned, or false. It denotes veracity, reality, sincerity, accuracy, integrity, truthfulness, dependability, and propriety.

25 The woman said to Him, "I know
that Messiah [a]is coming" (who is called
Christ). "When He comes, [b]He will tell
us all things."
26 Jesus said to her, [a]"I who speak to
you am *He.*"

The Whitened Harvest

27 And at this *point* His disciples
came, and they marveled that He
talked with a woman; yet no one said,
"What do You seek?" or, "Why are
You talking with her?"
28 The woman then *left her waterpot,
went her way into the city, and said
to the men,
29 "Come, see a Man [a]who told me all
things that I ever did. Could this be the
Christ?"
30 Then they went out of the city and
came to Him.
31 In the meantime His disciples urged
Him, saying, "Rabbi, eat."
32 But He said to them, "I have food
to eat of which you do not know."
33 Therefore the disciples said to one
another, "Has anyone brought Him
anything to eat?"
34 Jesus said to them, [a]"My food is to
do the will of Him who sent Me, and
to [b]finish* His work.

KINGDOM DYNAMICS

4:34 A Prayerful Quest for God Is the Pathway to Satisfaction, PRAYER. When Jesus refused the food offered by His disciples and declared, "I have food to eat of which you do not know" (v. 32), He was not implying that physical hunger and thirst were sinful (He later made eating and drinking sacramental signs). But His spirit's hunger had priority over physical appetites. He found satisfying food in deep communion with God and in doing His Father's will. Applause and material acquisitions can feed vanity and nourish ambition, but they cannot sustain the spirit. A prayerful quest for God will lead to our finding our food, our spiritual strength and satisfaction in doing God's will. And, like Jesus, we shall discover God's will through daily communion with Him; and we shall receive a fresh, daily anointing to achieve it.

(1 John 5:14, 15/Ps. 51:1–19) L.L.

35 "Do you not say, 'There are still
four months and *then* comes [a]the harvest'? Behold, I say to you, lift up your
eyes and look at the fields, [b]for they
are already white for harvest!
36 [a]"And he who reaps receives
*wages, and gathers fruit for eternal
life, that [b]both he who sows and he
who reaps may rejoice together.
37 "For in this the saying is true:
[a]'One sows and *another reaps.'
38 "I sent you to reap that for which
you have not labored; [a]others have labored, and you have entered into their
labors."

The Savior of the World

39 And many of the Samaritans of that
city believed in Him [a]because of the
word of the woman who testified, "He
told me all that I *ever* did."
40 So when the Samaritans had come
to Him, they urged Him to stay with
them; and He stayed there two days.
41 And many more believed because
of His own [a]word.

20 [b]Deut. 12:5, 11; 1 Kin. 9:3; 2 Chr. 7:12; Ps. 122:1–9
21 [a][Mal. 1:11]; 1 Tim. 2:8
22 [a][2 Kin. 17:28–41] [b][Is. 2:3; Luke 24:47; Rom. 3:1; 9:4, 5] *See WW at Luke 19:9.
23 [a]Matt. 18:20; [Heb. 13:10–14] [b]Phil. 3:3 [c][John 1:17] *See WW at Rev. 4:10.
24 [a]2 Cor. 3:17
25 [a]Deut. 18:15 [b]John 4:29, 39
26 [a]Dan. 9:25; Matt. 26:63, 64; Mark 14:61, 62
28 *See WW at Mark 1:20.
29 [a]John 4:25
34 [a]Ps. 40:7, 8; Heb. 10:9 [b]Job 23:12; [John 6:38; 17:4; 19:30] *See WW at 1 John 2:5.
35 [a]Gen. 8:22 [b]Matt. 9:37; Luke 10:2
36 [a]Dan. 12:3; Rom. 6:22 [b]1 Thess. 2:19 *See WW at Rev. 22:12.
37 [a]1 Cor. 3:5–9 *See WW at John 14:16.
38 [a]Jer. 44:4; [1 Pet. 1:12]
39 [a]John 4:29
41 [a]Luke 4:32; [John 6:63]

4:21–24 See section 2 of Truth-In-Action at the end of John.
4:21–24 What matters is not where one worships, but the attitude of heart and mind. True worship is not mere form and ceremony, but spiritual reality, which is in harmony with the nature of **God,** who ***is* Spirit.** Worship must also be **in truth,** that is, transparent, sincere, and according to biblical mandates.
4:27 The Jews considered it improper for a rabbi to speak to a woman in public.
4:35 The statement concerning **four months** was probably a proverb signifying that there is no need to rush in performing a task.

42 Then they said to the woman, "Now
we believe, not because of what you
said, for [a]we ourselves have heard *Him*
and we know that this is indeed
[1]the Christ, the **Savior** of the world."

WORD WEALTH

4:42 Savior, *soter* (so-*tare*): Strong's *#4990:* Compare "soteriology," the doctrine of salvation. From the same root as *sodzo,* "to save," and *soteria,* "salvation." The word designates a deliverer, preserver, savior, benefactor, rescuer. It is used to describe both God the Father and Jesus the Son.

Welcome at Galilee

43 Now after the two days He departed
from there and went to Galilee.
44 For [a]Jesus Himself testified that a
prophet has no honor in his own country.
45 So when He came to Galilee, the
Galileans received Him, [a]having seen
all the things He did in Jerusalem at
the feast; [b]for they also had gone to
the feast.

A Nobleman's Son Healed

46 So Jesus came again to Cana of Galilee
[a]where He had made the water
wine. And there was a certain [1]nobleman
whose son was sick at Capernaum.
47 When he heard that Jesus had come
out of Judea into Galilee, he went to
Him and implored Him to come down
and heal his son, for he was at the point
of death.
48 Then Jesus said to him, [a]"Unless
you *people* see signs and *wonders,
you will by no means believe."
49 The nobleman said to Him, "Sir,
come down before my child dies!"
50 Jesus said to him, "Go your way;
your son lives." So the man believed
the word that Jesus spoke to him, and
he went his way.
51 And as he was now going down, his
servants met him and told *him,* saying,
"Your son lives!"
52 Then he inquired of them the hour
when he got better. And they said to
him, "Yesterday at the seventh hour
the fever left him."
53 So the father knew that *it was* at
the same hour in which Jesus said to
him, "Your son lives." And he himself
believed, and his whole household.
54 This again *is* the second sign Jesus
did when He had come out of Judea
into Galilee.

A Man Healed at the Pool of Bethesda

5 After [a]this there was a feast of the
Jews, and Jesus [b]went up to Jerusalem.
2 Now there is in Jerusalem [a]by the
Sheep *Gate* a pool, which is called in
Hebrew, [1]Bethesda, having five
porches.
3 In these lay a great multitude of sick
people, blind, lame, [1]paralyzed, [2]waiting
for the moving of the water.
4 For an angel went down at a certain
time into the pool and *stirred up the
water; then whoever stepped in first,
after the stirring of the water, was
made well of whatever disease he had.
5 Now a certain man was there who
had an infirmity thirty-eight years.
6 When Jesus saw him lying there,
and knew that he already had been *in
that condition* a long time, He said to
him, "Do you want to be made well?"
7 The sick man answered Him, "Sir,
I have no man to put me into the pool
when the water is stirred up; but while
I am coming, another steps down before
me."
8 Jesus said to him, [a]"Rise, take up
your bed and walk."
9 And immediately the man was
made well, took up his bed, and
walked. And [a]that day was the Sabbath.

42 [a]John 17:8; 1 John 4:14 [1]NU omits *the Christ*
44 [a]Matt. 13:57; Mark 6:4; Luke 4:24
45 [a]John 2:13, 23; 3:2 [b]Deut. 16:16
46 [a]John 2:1, 11 [1]*royal official*
48 [a]John 6:30; Rom. 15:19; 1 Cor. 1:22; 2 Cor. 12:12; [2 Thess. 2:9]; Heb. 2:4 *See WW at Acts 15:12.

CHAPTER 5

1 [a]Lev. 23:2; Deut. 16:16 [b]John 2:13
2 [a]Neh. 3:1, 32; 12:39 [1]NU *Bethzatha*
3 [1]*withered* [2]NU omits the rest of v. 3 and all of v. 4.
4 *See WW at Luke 24:38.
8 [a]Matt. 9:6; Mark 2:11; Luke 5:24
9 [a]John 9:14

4:46–54 The healing of the nobleman's son not only demonstrates Jesus' power to heal, but it underscores the principle that He did not regard signs and wonders as ends in themselves. Rather, they were at the very least intended to bring the recipients of the miracle to faith in Christ.

5:1 John did not identify this particular **feast,** and it is impossible to determine which one it was. If it was the Passover, it introduces an important chronological device helping provide a clearer calendaring of Jesus' three and one-half years of ministry.

5:2 Sheep *Gate:* Literally, the gate "pertaining to sheep." Based on a later Christian tradition, the KJV incorrectly rendered it "sheep market." **Bethesda:** The Hebrew *beth 'eshda* literally means "Place of Outpouring," or "House of Grace." Today the pool is identified with practical certainty as the double pool at the Church of St. Anne.

5:3–15 Except for the duration of the man's illness, John's emphasis is not as much on the medical details of the case, as on the supernatural cure, its consequences, and its testimony to Christ's life-giving power.

5:4 The last phrase of v. 3 and all of v. 4 are omitted in some ancient Greek manuscripts of John (see marginal note). The statements may reflect a popular tradition associated with the pool that the bubbling of the waters (v. 7), which some scholars feel was caused by an intermittent spring, was supernaturally caused by an angel. Irrespective of the source of the waters being **stirred,** the testimony of God's healing grace was nonetheless present.

10 The Jews therefore said to him who was *cured, "It is the Sabbath; [a]it is not lawful for you to carry your bed."
11 He answered them, "He who made me well said to me, 'Take up your bed and walk.' "
12 Then they asked him, "Who is the Man who said to you, 'Take up your bed and walk'?"
13 But the one who was [a]healed did not know who it was, for Jesus had **withdrawn,** a multitude being in *that* place.

WORD WEALTH

5:13 withdrawn, *ekneuo* (ek-*nyoo*-oh); Strong's *#1593:* Literally "to bend the head aside." To shun, avoid, turn aside, withdraw, retire. Used only here in the NT, *ekneuo* describes Jesus leaving the premises after healing the lame man. Although some believe that Jesus slipped away to escape danger, others believe that He was avoiding audience applause or the crisis precipitated with the religious order by healing a man on the Sabbath.

14 Afterward Jesus found him in the temple, and said to him, "See, you have been made well. [a]Sin no more, lest a worse thing come upon you."
15 The man departed and told the Jews that it was Jesus who had made him well.

Honor the Father and the Son

3 16 For this reason the Jews [a]persecuted Jesus, [1]and sought to kill Him, because He had done these things on the Sabbath.
17 But Jesus answered them, [a]"My Father has been *working until now, and I have been working."
18 Therefore the Jews [a]sought all the more to kill Him, because He not only broke the Sabbath, but also said that God was His Father, [b]making Himself equal with God.
19 Then Jesus answered and said to them, "Most assuredly, I say to you, [a]the Son can do nothing of Himself, but what He sees the Father do; for whatever He does, the Son also does in like manner.
20 "For [a]the Father *loves the Son, and [b]shows Him all things that He Himself does; and He will show Him greater *works than these, that you may marvel.
21 "For as the Father raises the dead and gives life to *them,* [a]even so the Son gives life to whom He will.
22 "For the Father judges no one, but [a]has committed all *judgment to the Son,
23 "that all should honor the Son just as they honor the Father. [a]He who does not honor the Son does not honor the Father who sent Him.

Life and Judgment Are Through the Son

24 "Most assuredly, I say to you, [a]he who hears My word and believes in Him who sent Me has everlasting life, and shall not come into judgment, [b]but has passed from death into life.
25 "Most assuredly, I say to you, the hour is coming, and now is, when [a]the dead will hear the voice of the Son of God; and those who hear will live.
26 "For [a]as the Father has life in Himself, so He has granted the Son to have [b]life in Himself,
27 "and [a]has given Him authority to execute judgment also, [b]because He is the Son of Man.
28 "Do not marvel at this; for the hour is coming in which all who are in the graves will [a]hear His voice
29 [a]"and come forth—[b]those who have done good, to the resurrection of life, and those who have done evil, to the resurrection of condemnation.
30 [a]"I can of Myself do nothing. As I hear, I judge; and My judgment is *righteous, because [b]I do not seek My own will but the will of the Father who sent Me.

10 [a]Jer. 17:21, 22 *See WW at Matt. 12:22. **13** [a]Luke 13:14; 22:51 **14** [a]John 8:11 **16** [a]John 8:37; 10:39 [1]NU omits *and sought to kill Him* **17** [a][John 9:4; 17:4] *See WW at John 3:21. **18** [a]John 7:1, 19 [b]John 10:30 **19** [a]John 5:30; 6:38; 8:28; 12:49; 14:10 **20** [a]Matt. 3:17 [b][Matt. 11:27] *See WW at John 21:15. • See WW at John 9:4. **21** [a][John 11:25] **22** [a][Acts 17:31] *See WW at Matt. 5:22. **23** [a]1 John 2:23 **24** [a]John 3:16, 18; 6:47 [b][1 John 3:14] **25** [a][Col. 2:13] **26** [a]Ps. 36:9 [b]1 Cor. 15:45 **27** [a][Acts 10:42; 17:31] [b]Dan. 7:13 **28** [a][1 Thess. 4:15–17] **29** [a]Is. 26:19 [b]Dan. 12:2 **30** [a]John 5:19 [b]Matt. 26:39 *See WW at Matt. 1:19.

5:16–23 See section 3 of Truth-In-Action at the end of John.
5:16–18 If Jesus' healing on the Sabbath evoked the wrath of the Jewish religious leaders, His claim to equality with God earned Him their charge of blasphemy and its necessary death sentence. From this point on, Jesus was on a collision course with the authorities.
5:19–23 Jesus in no way acted independently of the Father. On the contrary, He understood that, because He and the Father were one, He did only what His Father showed Him. Jesus' authority, then, was not usurped, but derived from the Father's authority. Conversely, one cannot honor the Father apart from honoring the Son.
5:24–47 Jesus addresses the entire discourse of His relationship to the Father to those who accused Him of blasphemy. In the discourse Jesus' love even for His enemies is made crystal clear. While His desire is for them to be saved (v. 34), their problem is not that they cannot believe but that they are unwilling to accept His offer of life (v. 40).

The Fourfold Witness

31 [a]"If I bear witness of Myself, My witness is not [1]true.
32 [a]"There is another who bears witness of Me, and I know that the witness which He witnesses of Me is true.
33 "You have sent to John, [a]and he has borne witness to the truth.
34 "Yet I do not receive testimony from man, but I say these things that you may be saved.
35 "He was the burning and [a]shining lamp, and [b]you were *willing for a time to rejoice in his light.
36 "But [a]I have a greater witness than John's; for [b]the works which the Father has given Me to finish—the very [c]works that I do—bear witness of Me, that the Father has sent Me.
37 "And the Father Himself, who sent Me, [a]has testified of Me. You have neither heard His voice at any time, [b]nor seen His form.
38 "But you do not have His word abiding in you, because whom He sent, Him you do not believe.
39 [a]"You search the **Scriptures,** for in them you think you have eternal life; and [b]these are they which testify of Me.

> **WORD WEALTH**
>
> **5:39 Scriptures,** *graphe* (graf-*ay*); Strong's *#1124:* Compare "graph," "graphic," "biography," "autograph." A document, anything written, holy writ, the Scriptures. *Graphe* points to the divine author with the idea that what is written remains forever identified as the living voice of God. While some scholars restrict *graphe* to the OT writings, 2 Pet. 3:16 includes the NT writings.

40 [a]"But you are not willing to come to Me that you may have life.
41 [a]"I do not receive honor from men.
42 "But I know you, that you do not have the love of God in you.
43 "I have come in My Father's name, and you do not receive Me; if another comes in his own name, him you will receive.
44 [a]"How can you believe, who receive honor from one another, and do not seek [b]the honor that *comes* from the only God?
45 "Do not think that I shall accuse you to the Father; [a]there is *one* who accuses you—Moses, in whom you trust.
46 "For if you believed Moses, you would believe Me; [a]for he wrote about Me.
47 "But if you [a]do not believe his writings, how will you believe My words?"

Feeding the Five Thousand

6 After [a]these things Jesus went over the Sea of Galilee, which is *the Sea* of [b]Tiberias.
2 Then a great multitude followed Him, because they saw His signs which He performed on those who were [a]diseased.[1]
3 And Jesus went up on the mountain, and there He sat with His disciples.
4 [a]Now the Passover, a feast of the Jews, was near.
5 [a]Then Jesus lifted up *His* eyes, and seeing a great multitude coming toward Him, He said to [b]Philip, "Where shall we buy bread, that these may eat?"
6 But this He said to *test him, for He Himself knew what He would do.
7 Philip answered Him, [a]"Two hundred denarii worth of bread is not sufficient for them, that every one of them may have a little."
8 One of His disciples, [a]Andrew, Simon Peter's brother, said to Him,
9 "There is a lad here who has five barley loaves and two small fish, [a]but what are they among so many?"
10 Then Jesus said, "Make the people sit down." Now there was much grass in the place. So the men sat down, in number about five thousand.
11 And Jesus took the loaves, and when He had **given thanks** He distributed *them* [1]to the disciples, and the disciples to those sitting down; and likewise of the fish, as much as they wanted.

> **WORD WEALTH**
>
> **6:11 given thanks,** *eucharisteo* (yoo-khar-is-*teh*-oh); Strong's *#2168:* From
>
> (*cont. on next page*)

31 [a]John 8:14; Rev. 3:14 [1]*valid as testimony*
32 [a][Matt. 3:17; John 8:18; 1 John 5:6]
33 [a][John 1:15, 19, 27, 32]
35 [a]2 Sam. 21:17; 2 Pet. 1:19 [b]Matt. 13:20; Mark 6:20 *See WW at Matt. 8:2.
36 [a]1 John 5:9 [b]John 3:2; 10:25; 17:4 [c]John 9:16; 10:38
37 [a]Matt. 3:17; John 6:27; 8:18 [b]Deut. 4:12; John 1:18; 1 Tim. 1:17; 1 John 4:12
39 [a]Is. 8:20; 34:16; Luke 16:29; Acts 17:11 [b]Deut. 18:15, 18; Luke 24:27
40 [a][John 1:11; 3:19]
41 [a]John 5:44; 7:18; 1 Thess. 2:6
44 [a]John 12:43 [b][Rom. 2:29]
45 [a]Rom. 2:12
46 [a][Gen. 3:15]; Deut. 18:15, 18; John 1:45; Acts 26:22
47 [a]Luke 16:29, 31

CHAPTER 6

1 [a]Matt. 14:13; Mark 6:32; Luke 9:10, 12 [b]John 6:23; 21:1
2 [a]Matt. 4:23; 8:16; 9:35; 14:36; 15:30; 19:2 [1]*sick*
4 [a]Lev. 23:5, 7; Deut. 16:1; John 2:13
5 [a]Matt. 14:14; Mark 6:35; Luke 9:12 [b]John 1:43
6 *See WW at Rev. 2:10.
7 [a]Num. 11:21, 22
8 [a]John 1:40
9 [a]2 Kin. 4:43
11 [1]NU omits *to the disciples, and the disciples*

6:1 John identifies the **Sea of Galilee** with the name by which it was called when he wrote the Gospel. **Tiberias,** a city located on the lake's western shore, was founded about A.D. 20, so the lake probably was not known by its name during the ministry of Jesus.

6:4 John's second reference to the Feast of Passover, likely a year after the one mentioned in 2:13, does not require Jesus to go to Jerusalem. Rather, in this case it serves as backdrop for the discourse on Jesus as the Bread of Life (6:41–58).

6:9–14 Apart from the Resurrection, the feeding of the 5,000 is the only miracle recorded in all four Gospels.

(*cont. from preceding page*)
eu, "well," and *charizomai,* "to give freely." To be grateful, to express gratitude, to be thankful. Eleven of the thirty-nine appearances of the word in the NT refer to partaking of the Lord's Supper, while twenty-eight occurrences describe the praise words given to the Godhead. During the second century, Eucharist became the generic term for the Lord's Supper.

12 So when they were filled, He said
to His disciples, "Gather up the fragments that *remain, so that nothing is
lost."
13 Therefore they gathered *them* up,
and filled twelve baskets with the fragments of the five barley loaves which
were left over by those who had eaten.
14 Then those men, when they had
seen the sign that Jesus did, said, "This
is truly [a]the Prophet who is to come
into the world."

Jesus Walks on the Sea

15 Therefore when Jesus perceived
that they were about to come and take
Him *by force to make Him [a]king, He
departed again to the mountain by
Himself alone.
16 [a]Now when evening came, His disciples went down to the sea,
17 got into the boat, and went over the
sea toward Capernaum. And it was already *dark, and Jesus had not come
to them.
18 Then the sea arose because a great
wind was blowing.
19 So when they had rowed about
[1]three or four miles, they saw Jesus
walking on the sea and drawing near
the boat; and they were [a]afraid.
20 But He said to them, [a]"It is I; do
not be afraid."
21 Then they willingly received Him
into the boat, and **immediately** the boat
was at the land where they were going.

WORD WEALTH

6:21 immediately, *eutheos* (yoo-*theh*-oce); Strong's *#2112:* From the adjective *euthus,* "straight." Speedily, straightway, immediately, directly, presently, suddenly, quickly. The word describes what is happening right now in contrast to what happened before this time.

12 *See WW at Matt. 25:29.
14 [a]Gen. 49:10; Deut. 18:15, 18; John 1:21; 7:40; Acts 3:22; 7:37
15 [a][John 18:36] *See WW at 1 Thess. 4:17.
16 [a]Matt. 14:23; Mark 6:47
17 *See WW at John 12:46.
19 [a]Matt. 17:6 [1]Lit. *25 or 30 stadia*
20 [a]Is. 43:1, 2

22 [1]NU omits *that* [2]NU omits *which His disciples had entered* *See WW at John 14:16.
23 *See WW at John 6:11.
24 [a]Mark 1:37; Luke 4:42
26 *See WW at Matt. 15:33.
27 [a]Matt. 6:19 [b]John 4:14; [Eph. 2:8, 9] [c]Ps. 2:7; Is. 42:1; Matt. 3:17; 17:5; Mark 1:11; 9:7; Luke 3:22; 9:35; John 5:37; Acts 2:22; 2 Pet. 1:17
29 [a]1 Thess. 1:3; James 2:22; [1 John 3:23]; Rev. 2:26
30 [a]Matt. 12:38; 16:1; Mark 8:11; 1 Cor. 1:22
31 [a]Ex. 16:15; Num. 11:7; 1 Cor. 10:3 [b]Ex. 16:4, 15; Neh. 9:15; Ps. 78:24

The Bread from Heaven

22 On the following day, when the people who were standing on the other
side of the sea saw that there was no
*other boat there, except [1]that one
[2]which His disciples had entered, and
that Jesus had not entered the boat
with His disciples, but His disciples
had gone away alone—
23 however, other boats came from
Tiberias, near the place where they
ate bread after the Lord had *given
thanks—
24 when the people therefore saw that
Jesus was not there, nor His disciples,
they also got into boats and came to
Capernaum, [a]seeking Jesus.
25 And when they found Him on the
other side of the sea, they said to Him,
"Rabbi, when did You come here?"
26 Jesus answered them and said,
"Most assuredly, I say to you, you seek
Me, not because you saw the signs, but
because you ate of the loaves and were
*filled.
27 [a]"Do not labor for the food which
perishes, but [b]for the food which endures to everlasting life, which the Son
of Man will give you, [c]because God the
Father has set His seal on Him."
28 Then they said to Him, "What shall
we do, that we may work the works
of God?"
29 Jesus answered and said to them.
[a]"This is the work of God, that you believe in Him whom He sent."
30 Therefore they said to Him, [a]"What
sign will You perform then, that we
may see it and believe You? What
work will You do?
31 [a]"Our fathers ate the manna in the
desert; as it is written, [b]*'He gave them
bread from heaven to eat.'"*
32 Then Jesus said to them, "Most assuredly, I say to you, Moses did not
give you the bread from heaven, but

6:14, 15 The people's response of **This is truly the Prophet** reflects the popular belief that a prophet like Moses, who fed the Israelites with manna, would **come into the world** to establish an earthly paradise. This sparked their messianic fervor, and they wanted to install Jesus as their political "bread-Messiah," making Him king by force. Jesus would have none of it (see Matt. 4:1–4).

6:16–21 In contrast to their concept of Jesus as an earthly ruler with limited power, in walking on the water Jesus reveals Himself as having supreme authority in all the universe.

6:22–71 This lengthy section provides us with the most in-depth NT explanation of the significance of Communion and how it is vastly more than a mere ordinance commemorating Jesus' death.

6:28–30 The people placed primary emphasis on their works for God and on God's works for them (signs), whereas with Jesus, singular focus is on believing (that is, trusting) in the One whom God sent.

[a]My Father gives you the true bread
from heaven.
33 "For the bread of God is He who
comes down from heaven and gives life
to the world."
34 [a]Then they said to Him, "Lord, give
us this bread always."
35 And Jesus said to them, [a]"I am the
bread of life. [b]He who comes to Me
shall never hunger, and he who believes in Me shall never [c]thirst.
36 [a]"But I said to you that you have
seen Me and yet [b]do not believe.
37 [a]"All that the Father gives Me will
come to Me, and [b]the one who comes
to Me I will [1]by no means cast out.
38 "For I have come down from
heaven, [a]not to do My own will,
[b]but the will of Him who sent Me.
39 "This is the will of the Father who
sent Me, [a]that of all He has given Me
I should lose nothing, but should raise
it up at the last day.
40 "And this is the will of Him who
sent Me, [a]that everyone who sees the
Son and believes in Him may have everlasting life; and I will raise him up
at the last day."

Rejected by His Own

41 The Jews then [1]complained about
Him, because He said, "I am the bread
which came down from heaven."
42 And they said, [a]"Is not this Jesus,
the son of Joseph, whose father and
mother we know? How is it then that
He says, 'I have come down from
heaven'?"
43 Jesus therefore answered and said
to them, [1]"Do not murmur among
yourselves.
44 [a]"No one can come to Me unless
the Father who sent Me [b]draws him;
and I will raise him up at the last
day.
45 "It is written in the prophets,
[a]*'And they shall all be taught by God.'*
[b]Therefore everyone who [1]has heard
and learned from the Father comes to
Me.
46 [a]"Not that anyone has seen the Fa-

32 [a]John 3:13, 16
34 [a]John 4:15
35 [a]John 6:48, 58 [b]John 4:14; 7:37; Rev. 7:16 [c]Is. 55:1, 2
36 [a]John 6:26, 64; 15:24 [b]John 10:26
37 [a]John 6:45 [b][Matt. 24:24; John 10:28, 29]; 2 Tim. 2:19; 1 John 2:19 [1]*certainly not*
38 [a]Matt. 26:39; John 5:30 [b]John 4:34
39 [a]John 10:28; 17:12; 18:9
40 [a]John 3:15, 16; 4:14; 6:27, 47, 54
41 [1]*grumbled*
42 [a]Matt. 13:55; Mark 6:3; Luke 4:22
43 [1]*Stop grumbling*
44 [a]Song 1:4 [b][Eph. 2:8, 9; Phil. 1:29; 2:12, 13]
45 [a]Is. 54:13; Jer. 31:34; Mic. 4:2; [Heb. 8:10] [b]John 6:37 [1]*M hears and has learned*
46 [a]John 1:18 [b]Matt. 11:27; [Luke 10:22]; John 7:29
47 [a][John 3:16, 18] [1]NU omits *in Me*
48 [a]John 6:33, 35; [Gal. 2:20; Col. 3:3, 4]
49 [a]John 6:31, 58
50 [a]John 6:51, 58
51 [a]John 3:13 [b]Heb. 10:5
52 [a]John 7:43; 9:16; 10:19
53 [a]Matt. 26:26
54 [a]John 4:14; 6:27, 40
55 [1]NU *true food* [2]NU *true drink*
56 [a][1 John 3:24; 4:15, 16]

ther, [b]except He who is from God; He
has seen the Father.
47 "Most assuredly, I say to you,
[a]he who believes [1]in Me has everlasting life.
48 [a]"I am the bread of life.
49 [a]"Your fathers ate the manna in the
wilderness, and are dead.
50 [a]"This is the bread which comes
down from heaven, that one may eat
of it and not die.
51 "I am the living bread [a]which came
down from heaven. If anyone eats of
this bread, he will live forever; and
[b]the bread that I shall give is My flesh,
which I shall give for the life of the
world."
52 The Jews therefore [a]quarreled
among themselves, saying, "How can
this Man give us *His* flesh to eat?"
53 Then Jesus said to them, "Most as- 2
suredly, I say to you, unless [a]you eat
the flesh of the Son of Man and drink
His blood, you have no life in you.
54 [a]"Whoever eats My flesh and
drinks My blood has eternal life, and
I will raise him up at the last day.

KINGDOM DYNAMICS

6:53, 54 Partaking in the Blood, THE BLOOD. Partaking in the covenant blood of Christ is the means of being joined to God and receiving the benefits of His life. Christ is the covenant sacrifice and is God's provision for our sustenance. When we feed on Him through faith, we become partakers of the divine nature (2 Pet. 1:4), which is life eternal. Through the Holy Spirit's work, we receive His life and partake of His promises (John 6:63). Those who share in this mystery of relationship with Christ are assured of being raised up at the last day into eternal life.

(1 Pet. 1:18, 19/Col. 1:20) C.S.

55 "For My flesh is [1]food indeed, and
My blood is [2]drink indeed.
56 "He who eats My flesh and drinks
My blood [a]abides in Me, and I in him.
57 "As the living Father sent Me, and
I live because of the Father, so he who

6:48 This is the first of the seven **I am** sayings of Jesus, unique to John's Gospel. There is an unmistakable parallel to God's covenant name (Yahweh) by which He revealed Himself to Moses in Ex. 3:14, "I AM WHO I AM." Jesus makes the pronouncement "I am the bread of life" three times (vv. 35, 48, 51). He is the "real" heavenly bread, the true life-sustaining power; anything else, regardless, of its religious significance in past or present, is an inadequate substitute.

6:49–59 Jesus carried the argument a step beyond the essential recognition that He is the Bread of Life. To believe in Him means to partake of Him.

6:53–58 See section 2 of Truth-In-Action at the end of John.

6:53 To eat the flesh of Jesus and to **drink His blood** are to be understood spiritually. The expressions point to the violent sacrificial death He would suffer and the necessity of believers partaking in the benefits of His death by coming to Him and believing in Him (v. 35). Although we need not see in this the necessity of our partaking of the Eucharist in order to obtain salvation, it does teach the very vital importance of Communion in strengthening our souls, bringing healing into our lives, and for testifying to our faith.

feeds on Me will live because of Me.
58 [a]"This is the bread which came
down from heaven—not [b]as your fathers ate the manna, and are dead. He
who eats this bread will live forever."
59 These things He said in the synagogue as He taught in Capernaum.

Many Disciples Turn Away

60 [a]Therefore many of His disciples,
when they heard *this,* said, "This is
a [1]hard saying; who can understand
it?"
61 When Jesus knew in Himself that
His disciples [1]complained about this,
He said to them, "Does this [2]offend
you?
62 [a]"*What* then if you should see the
Son of Man ascend where He was before?
63 [a]"It is the Spirit who gives life; the
[b]flesh profits nothing. The [c]words that
I speak to you are spirit, and *they* are
life.
64 "But [a]there are some of you who
do not believe." For [b]Jesus knew from
the beginning who they were who did
not believe, and who would betray
Him.
65 And He said, "Therefore [a]I have
said to you that no one can come to
Me unless it has been granted to him
by My Father."
66 [a]From that *time* many of His disciples went [1]back and walked with Him
no more.
67 Then Jesus said to the twelve, "Do
you also want to go away?"
68 But Simon Peter answered Him,
"**Lord,** to whom shall we go? You have
[a]the words of eternal life.

WORD WEALTH

6:68 Lord, *kurios* (koo-ree-oss); Strong's *#2962:* Originally, an adjective signifying authority or having power. As a noun the word designates the owner, master, controller, one in authority. In direct address, *kurios* is a title of respect given to masters, teachers, and so on. *Kurios* in the OT was Yahweh, while in the NT the title is transferred to Jesus.

58 [a]John 6:49–51 [b]Ex. 16:14–35
60 [a]John 6:66 [1]*difficult*
61 [1]*grumbled* [2]*make you stumble*
62 [a]Acts 1:9; 2:32, 33
63 [a]2 Cor. 3:6 [b]John 3:6 [c][John 6:68; 14:24]
64 [a]John 6:36 [b]John 2:24, 25; 13:11
65 [a]John 6:37, 44, 45
66 [a]Luke 9:62 [1]Or *away;* lit. *to the back*
68 [a]Acts 5:20
69 [a]Luke 9:20 [1]NU *Holy One of God.*
70 [a]Luke 6:13 [b][John 13:27]
71 [a]John 12:4; 13:2, 26 [b]Matt. 26:14–16

CHAPTER 7

1 [a]John 5:18; 7:19, 25; 8:37, 40 [1]The ruling authorities
2 [a]Lev. 23:34
3 [a]Matt. 12:46 *See WW at John 9:4.
5 [a]Ps. 69:8 [b]Mark 3:21
6 [a]John 2:4; 8:20
7 [a][John 15:19] [b]John 3:19
8 [a]John 8:20 [1]NU omits *yet*
11 [a]John 11:56
12 [a]John 9:16; 10:19 [b]Luke 7:16

69 [a]"Also we have come to believe and
know that You are the [1]Christ, the Son
of the living God."
70 Jesus answered them, [a]"Did I not
choose you, the twelve, [b]and one of
you is a devil?"
71 He spoke of [a]Judas Iscariot, *the
son* of Simon, for it was he who
would [b]betray Him, being one of the
twelve.

Jesus' Brothers Disbelieve

7 After these things Jesus walked in
Galilee; for He did not want to
walk in Judea, [a]because the [1]Jews
sought to kill Him.
2 [a]Now the Jews' Feast of Tabernacles was at hand.
3 [a]His brothers therefore said to Him,
"Depart from here and go into Judea,
that Your disciples also may see the
*works that You are doing.
4 "For no one does anything in secret
while he himself seeks to be known
openly. If You do these things, show
Yourself to the world."
5 For [a]even His [b]brothers did not believe in Him.
6 Then Jesus said to them, [a]"My time
has not yet come, but your time is always ready.
7 [a]"The world cannot hate you, but
it hates Me [b]because I testify of it that
its works are evil.
8 "You go up to this feast. I am not
[1]yet going up to this feast, [a]for My time
has not yet fully come."
9 When He had said these things to
them, He remained in Galilee.

The Heavenly Scholar

10 But when His brothers had gone up,
then He also went up to the feast, not
openly, but as it were in secret.
11 Then [a]the Jews sought Him at the
feast, and said, "Where is He?"
12 And [a]there was much complaining
among the people concerning Him.
[b]Some said, "He is good"; others said,
"No, on the contrary, He deceives the
people."

6:60 The **saying** (vv. 35–58) was **hard** in that it was difficult to accept.

6:71 Iscariot means "Man of Kerioth." Since Kerioth was in southern Judah, Judas Iscariot appears to have been the only non-Galilean disciple.

7:1 John summarizes events that occurred during the six-month period from April to October. The other Gospel writers give a detailed account (see Mark 7—9).

7:2 The Feast of Tabernacles, which is celebrated at the end of September and the beginning of October, is a thanksgiving festival. It also commemorates the divine guidance granted to Israel during the nation's wandering in the wilderness. During the festival the people erect and dwell in temporary shelters made of palm and other tree branches.

7:5 After the resurrection of Jesus, His brothers were among the believers (see Acts 1:14).

13 However, no one spoke openly of
Him [a]for fear of the Jews.
14 Now about the middle of the feast
Jesus went up into the temple and
[a]taught.
15 [a]And the Jews marveled, saying,
"How does this Man know letters, having never studied?"
16 [1]Jesus answered them and said,
[a]"My doctrine is not Mine, but His who
sent Me.
3 17 [a]"If anyone wills to do His will, he
shall know concerning the doctrine,
whether it is from God or *whether* I
speak on My own *authority*.
18 [a]"He who speaks from himself
seeks his own glory; but He who
[b]seeks the glory of the One who sent
Him is true, and [c]no **unrighteousness**
is in Him.

> **WORD WEALTH**
>
> **7:18 unrighteousness,** *adikia* (ad-ee-*kee*-ah); Strong's *#93:* Derived from *a,* negative, and the root *dike,* "right." Misdeeds, injustice, moral wrongdoing, unjust acts, unrighteousness, iniquity. It is the opposite of truthfulness, faithfulness, and rightness.

19 [a]"Did not Moses give you the law,
yet none of you keeps the law? [b]Why
do you seek to kill Me?"
20 The people answered and said,
[a]"You have a demon. Who is seeking
to kill You?"
21 Jesus answered and said to them,
"I did one work, and you all marvel.
22 [a]"Moses therefore gave you circumcision (not that it is from Moses,
[b]but from the fathers), and you circumcise a man on the Sabbath.
23 "If a man receives circumcision on
the Sabbath, so that the law of Moses
should not be broken, are you angry
with Me because [a]I made a man completely well on the Sabbath?
1 24 [a]"Do not judge according to appearance, but judge with righteous
judgment."

13 [a][John 9:22; 12:42; 19:38]
14 [a]Mark 6:34
15 [a]Matt. 13:54
16 [a]John 3:11 [1]NU, M *So Jesus*
17 [a]John 3:21; 8:43
18 [a]John 5:41 [b]John 8:50 [c][2 Cor. 5:21]
19 [a]Deut. 33:4 [b]Matt. 12:14
20 [a]John 8:48, 52
22 [a]Lev. 12:3 [b]Gen. 17:9–14
23 [a]John 5:8, 9, 16
24 [a]Prov. 24:23
25 [a]Matt. 21:38; 26:4
26 [a]John 7:48 [1]NU omits *truly*
27 [a]Luke 4:22
28 [a]John 8:14 [b]John 5:43 [c]Rom. 3:4 [d]John 1:18; 8:55
29 [a]Matt. 11:27 [1]NU, M omit *But*
30 [a]Mark 11:18 [b]John 7:32, 44; 8:20; 10:39
31 [a]Matt. 12:23
33 [a]John 13:33 [b][1 Pet. 3:22] [1]NU, M omit *to them*
34 [a]Hos. 5:6 [b][Matt. 5:20]
35 [a]James 1:1
37 [a]Lev. 23:36

Could This Be the Christ?

25 Now some of them from Jerusalem
said, "Is this not He whom they seek
to [a]kill?
26 "But look! He speaks boldly, and
they say nothing to Him. [a]Do the rulers
know indeed that this is [1]truly the
Christ?
27 [a]"However, we know where this
Man is from; but when the Christ
comes, no one knows where He is
from."
28 Then Jesus cried out, as He taught
in the temple, saying, [a]"You both know
Me, and you know where I am from;
and [b]I have not come of Myself, but
He who sent Me [c]is true, [d]whom you
do not know.
29 [1]"But [a]I know Him, for I am from
Him, and He sent Me."
30 Therefore [a]they sought to take Him;
but [b]no one laid a hand on Him, because His hour had not yet come.
31 And [a]many of the people believed
in Him, and said, "When the Christ
comes, will He do more signs than
these which this *Man* has done?"

Jesus and the Religious Leaders

32 The Pharisees heard the crowd
murmuring these things concerning
Him, and the Pharisees and the chief
priests sent officers to take Him.
33 Then Jesus said [1]to them, [a]"I shall
be with you a little while longer, and
then I [b]go to Him who sent Me.
34 "You [a]will seek Me and not find *Me,*
and where I am you [b]cannot come."
35 Then the Jews said among themselves, "Where does He intend to go
that we shall not find Him? Does He
intend to go to [a]the Dispersion among
the Greeks and teach the Greeks?
36 "What is this thing that He said,
'You will seek Me and not find Me, and
where I am you cannot come'?"

The Promise of the Holy Spirit

37 [a]On the last day, that great *day* of
the feast, Jesus stood and cried out,

7:15 Letters refers not to the basic ability of reading and writing, but to Jesus' knowledge and understanding of the Scriptures. Their puzzlement was over Jesus' extraordinary knowledge without **having . . . studied** at one of the prestigious and official rabbinic schools of Shammai and Hillel.
7:17 See section 3 of Truth-In-Action at the end of John.
7:17 The teachings and claims of Jesus will be accepted by those who are intent on doing God's will.
7:21 The **one work** refers to the healing of the cripple at the pool of Bethesda, the only miracle Jesus had performed in Jerusalem (5:1–15; see v. 23).
7:24 See section 1 of Truth-In-Action at the end of John.
7:27 The people were puzzled because they knew facts about the background of Jesus, whereas they supposed the coming of the Messiah to be shrouded in secrecy.
7:35 The Dispersion refers to Jews scattered throughout the Greek world. Later the term also denoted the Christians scattered abroad (1 Pet. 1:1). The Jews' ignorance was only heightened by their supposition that Jesus was surely not going to preach to the Jews but to the Gentiles instead.
7:37–39 Each day during the Feast of Tabernacles a joyous

saying, [b]"If anyone thirsts, let him
come to Me and drink.
38 [a]"He who believes in Me, as the
Scripture has said, [b]out of his heart
will flow rivers of living water."
39 [a]But this He spoke concerning the
Spirit, whom those [1]believing in Him
would receive; for the [2]Holy Spirit was
not yet *given,* because Jesus was not
yet [b]glorified.

Who Is He?

40 Therefore [1]many from the crowd,
when they heard this saying, said,
"Truly this is [a]the *Prophet."
41 Others said, "This is [a]the Christ."
But some said, "Will the Christ come
out of Galilee?
42 [a]"Has not the Scripture said that
the Christ comes from the seed of David and from the town of Bethlehem,
[b]where David was?"
43 So [a]there was a division among the
people because of Him.
44 Now [a]some of them wanted to take
Him, but no one laid hands on Him.

Rejected by the Authorities

45 Then the officers came to the chief
priests and Pharisees, who said to
them, "Why have you not brought
Him?"
46 The officers answered, [a]"No man
ever spoke like this Man!"
47 Then the Pharisees answered them,
"Are you also deceived?
48 "Have any of the rulers or the Pharisees believed in Him?
49 "But this crowd that does not know
the law is accursed."
50 Nicodemus [a](he who came to
[1]Jesus [2]by night, being one of them)
said to them,
51 [a]"Does our law judge a man before
it hears him and knows what he is doing?"
52 They answered and said to him,
"Are you also from Galilee? Search

37 [b][Is. 55:1]
38 [a]Deut. 18:15
[b]Is. 12:3; 43:20;
44:3; 55:1
39 [a]Is. 44:3
[b]John 12:16;
13:31; 17:5 [1]NU
who believed
[2]NU omits *Holy*
40 [a]Deut. 18:15,
18 [1]NU *some*
*See WW at
Matt. 2:5.
41 [a]John 4:42;
6:69
42 [a]Mic. 5:2
[b]1 Sam. 16:1, 4
43 [a]John 7:12
44 [a]John 7:30
46 [a]Luke 4:22
50 [a]John 3:1, 2;
19:39 [1]Lit. *Him*
[2]NU *before*
51 [a]Deut. 1:16,
17; 19:15
52 [a][Is. 9:1, 2]
[1]NU *is to rise*
53 [1]NU brackets
7:53 through
8:11 as not in the
original text.
They are present
in over 900 mss.
of John.

CHAPTER 8

2 [a]John 8:20;
18:20 [1]M *very
early*
4 [a]Ex. 20:14 [1]M
*we found this
woman*
*See WW at
John 1:5.
5 [a]Lev. 20:10 [1]M
*in our law Moses
commanded*
[2]NU, M *to stone
such* [3]M adds
about her
6 [a]Matt. 22:15
[1]NU, M omit *as
though He did
not hear*
*See WW at
Rev. 2:10.
7 [a]Deut. 17:7 [1]M
He looked up
9 [a]Rom. 2:22
[1]NU, M omit *be-
ing convicted by
their conscience*

and look, for [a]no prophet [1]has arisen
out of Galilee."

An Adulteress Faces the Light of the World

53 [1]And everyone went to his *own*
house.
8 But Jesus went to the Mount of Olives.
2 Now [1]early in the morning He came
again into the temple, and all the people came to Him; and He sat down and
[a]taught them.
3 Then the scribes and Pharisees
brought to Him a woman caught in
adultery. And when they had set her
in the midst,

WORD WEALTH

8:3 adultery, *moicheia* (moy-*khi*-ah); Strong's *#3430:* Unlawful sexual intercourse, illicit connection with a married person, marital infidelity. *Moicheia* is incompatible with the harmonious laws of family life in God's kingdom; and since it violates God's original purpose in marriage, it is under God's judgment.

4 they said to Him, "Teacher, [1]this
woman was *caught in [a]adultery, in the
very act.
5 [a]"Now [1]Moses, in the law, commanded us [2]that such should be
stoned. But what do You [3]say?"
6 This they said, *testing Him, that
they [a]might have *something* of which
to accuse Him. But Jesus stooped down
and wrote on the ground with *His* finger, [1]as though He did not hear.
7 So when they continued asking
Him, He [1]raised Himself up and said
to them, [a]"He who is without sin
among you, let him throw a stone at
her first."
8 And again He stooped down and
wrote on the ground.
9 Then those who heard *it,* [a]being[1]
convicted by *their* conscience, went
out one by one, beginning with the old-

celebration was observed in which the priests brought water (symbolic of the water supplied from the rock in Ex. 17) to the temple from the pool of Siloam in a golden pitcher. During the procession the people recited Is. 12:3. The water was poured out on the altar as an offering to God, while the people shouted and sang. Jesus was the fulfillment of all that the ceremony typified (see 1 Cor. 10:4).

7:38 Those who are satisfied by Jesus will themselves become channels of spiritual refreshment for others. The figure of **rivers** contrasts with "a fountain" (4:14), illustrating the difference between one's new birth and one's experience of the overflowing fullness of the Spirit-filled life.

7:39 John interprets the words of Jesus to refer to the pouring out of the Holy Spirit that was still to come. The Holy Spirit existed from all eternity, but was not yet present in the sense indicated. Soon the fullness of the Spirit would be a blessing that all of God's people could experience (see Acts 2:33).

7:40 The Prophet refers to the promise of Deut. 18:15, 18.

7:53—8:11 That this passage was part of the original text of John's Gospel is disputed. However, there is little doubt that the incident actually occurred. The motive of the Pharisees was not passion for holiness, but a desire to entrap Jesus in a dilemma (v. 6).

est *even* to the last. And Jesus was left
alone, and the woman standing in the
midst.
10 When Jesus had raised Himself up
[1]and saw no one but the woman, He
said to her, "Woman, where are those
accusers [2]of yours? Has no one condemned you?"
11 She said, "No one, Lord." And
Jesus said to her, [a]"Neither do I condemn you; go [1]and [b]sin no more."
12 Then Jesus spoke to them again,
saying, [a]"I am the light of the world.
He who [b]follows Me shall not walk in
*darkness, but have the light of life."

Jesus Defends His Self-Witness

13 The Pharisees therefore said to
Him, [a]"You bear witness of Yourself;
Your witness is not [1]true."
14 Jesus answered and said to them,
"Even if I bear witness of Myself, My
witness is true, for I know where I
came from and where I am going; but
[a]you do not know where I come from
and where I am going.
15 [a]"You judge according to the flesh;
[b]I judge no one.
16 "And yet if I do judge, My judgment
is true; for [a]I am not alone, but I *am*
with the Father who sent Me.
17 [a]"It is also written in your law that
the testimony of two men is true.
18 "I am One who bears witness of Myself, and [a]the Father who sent Me bears
witness of Me."
19 Then they said to Him, "Where is
Your Father?" Jesus answered, [a]"You
know neither Me nor My Father.
[b]If you had known Me, you would have
known My Father also."
20 These words Jesus spoke in [a]the
treasury, as He taught in the temple;
and [b]no one laid hands on Him, for
[c]His hour had not yet come.

Jesus Predicts His Departure

21 Then Jesus said to them again, "I
am going away, and [a]you will seek Me,
and [b]will die in your sin. Where I go
you cannot come."

10 [1]NU omits *and saw no one but the woman;* M *He saw her and said,* [2]NU, M omit *of yours*
11 [a][John 3:17] [b][John 5:14] [1]NU, M add *from now on*
12 [a]John 1:4; 9:5; 12:35 [b]1 Thess. 5:5 *See WW at John 12:46.
13 [a]John 5:31 [1]*valid* as testimony
14 [a]John 7:28; 9:29
15 [a]John 7:24 [b][John 3:17; 12:47; 18:36]
16 [a]John 16:32
17 [a]Deut. 17:6; 19:15
18 [a]John 5:37
19 [a]John 16:3 [b]John 14:7
20 [a]Mark 12:41, 43 [b]John 2:4; 7:30 [c]John 7:8
21 [a]John 7:34; 13:33 [b]John 8:24
23 [a]John 3:31 [b]1 John 4:5
24 [a]John 8:21 [b][Mark 16:16]
25 [a]John 4:26
26 [a]John 7:28 [b]John 3:32; 15:15
28 [a]John 3:14; 12:32; 19:18 [b][Rom. 1:4] [c]John 5:19, 30 [d]John 3:11 [1]Crucify *See WW at John 8:32.
29 [a]John 14:10 [b]John 8:16; 16:32 [c]John 4:34; 5:30; 6:38
30 [a]John 7:31; 10:42; 11:45
31 [a][John 14:15, 23]
32 [a][John 1:14, 17; 14:6] [b][Rom. 6:14, 18, 22] *See WW at Rom. 8:2.

22 So the Jews said, "Will He kill Himself, because He says, 'Where I go you
cannot come'?"
23 And He said to them, [a]"You are
from beneath; I am from above.
[b]You are of this world; I am not of this
world.
24 [a]"Therefore I said to you that you
will die in your sins; [b]for if you do not
believe that I am *He,* you will die in
your sins."
25 Then they said to Him, "Who are
You?" And Jesus said to them, "Just
what I [a]have been saying to you from
the beginning.
26 "I have many things to say and to
judge concerning you, but [a]He who
sent Me is true; and [b]I speak to the
world those things which I heard from
Him."
27 They did not understand that He
spoke to them of the Father.
28 Then Jesus said to them, "When
you [a]lift[1] up the Son of Man, [b]then you
will *know that I am *He,* and [c]*that* I
do nothing of Myself; but [d]as My Father taught Me, I speak these things.
29 "And [a]He who sent Me is with Me.
[b]The Father has not left Me alone,
[c]for I always do those things that
please Him."
30 As He spoke these words, [a]many
believed in Him.

The Truth Shall Make You Free

31 Then Jesus said to those Jews who
believed Him, "If you [a]abide in My
word, you are My disciples indeed.
32 "And you shall **know** the [a]truth,
and [b]the truth shall *make you free."

WORD WEALTH

8:32 know, *ginosko* (ghin-*oce*-koe); Strong's *#1097:* Compare "prognosis," "gnomic," "gnomon," "gnostic." To perceive, understand, recognize, gain knowledge, realize, come to know. *Ginosko* is the knowledge that has an inception, a progress, and an attainment. It is the recognition of truth by personal experience.

8:12 The light of the world: The second of Jesus' self-disclosing declarations in John, presupposing that the world is in darkness apart from Him.

8:13–20 The Pharisees objected that the witness of Jesus was true because He spoke for Himself, whereas two witnesses were necessary. Jesus reported that the Father added His testimony both by the written Word and by the works Jesus did.

8:29 For Jesus, doing the will of the Father was not an occasional choice in times of crucial decisions. Rather, the Father's constant presence in His life signals that there never was a moment when He did not do the Father's will.

8:31–59 The claim of the people to be descendants of Abraham was futile, because their deeds evidenced a lack of any moral relationship to him. If they were truly children of God, they would reverence the Son of God. Instead, their reaction against Jesus only revealed the sobering fact that the Devil was their father. It is not ethnic or family pedigree that makes one acceptable to God, but honoring God by believing in and loving Jesus Christ.

33 They answered Him, [a]"We are Abraham's descendants, and have never been in bondage to anyone. How *can* you say, 'You will be made free'?"
34 Jesus answered them, "Most assuredly, I say to you, [a]whoever commits sin is a slave of sin.
35 "And [a]a slave does not abide in the house forever, *but* a son abides forever.
36 [a]"Therefore if the Son *makes you free, you shall be *free indeed.

Abraham's Seed and Satan's

37 "I know that you are Abraham's descendants, but [a]you seek to kill Me, because My word has no place in you.
38 [a]"I speak what I have seen with My Father, and you do what you have [1]seen with your father."
39 They answered and said to Him, [a]"Abraham is our father." Jesus said to them, [b]"If you were Abraham's children, you would do the works of Abraham.
40 [a]"But now you seek to kill Me, a Man who has told you the truth [b]which I heard from God. Abraham did not do this.
41 "You do the deeds of your father." Then they said to Him, "We were not born of *fornication; [a]we have one Father—God."
42 Jesus said to them, [a]"If God were your Father, you would love Me, for [b]I proceeded forth and came from God; [c]nor have I come of Myself, but He sent Me.
43 [a]"Why do you not understand My speech? Because you are not able to listen to My word.
44 [a]"You are of *your* father the devil, and the [b]desires of your father you want to [c]do. He was a murderer from the beginning, and [d]*does not* stand in the truth, because there is no truth in him. When he speaks a lie, he speaks from his own *resources,* for he is a liar and the father of it.
45 "But because I tell the truth, you do not believe Me.
46 "Which of you convicts Me of sin? And if I tell the truth, why do you not believe Me?
47 [a]"He who is of God hears God's words; therefore you do not hear, because you are not of God."

33 [a]Lev. 25:42; [Matt. 3:9]; Luke 3:8
34 [a]Prov. 5:22; Rom. 6:16; 2 Pet. 2:19
35 [a]Gen. 21:10; Gal. 4:30
36 [a][Rom. 8:2; 2 Cor. 3:17]; Gal. 5:1
*See WW at Rom. 8:2. • See WW at Rev. 6:15.
37 [a]John 7:19
38 [a][John 3:32; 5:19, 30; 14:10, 24] [1]NU *heard from*
39 [a]Matt. 3:9; John 8:37 [b][Rom. 2:28; Gal. 3:7, 29]
40 [a]John 8:37 [b]John 8:26
41 [a]Deut. 32:6; Is. 63:16; Mal. 1:6
*See WW at Matt. 15:19.
42 [a]1 John 5:1 [b]John 16:27; 17:8, 25 [c]John 5:43; Gal. 4:4
43 [a][John 7:17]
44 [a]Matt. 13:38; 1 John 3:8 [b]1 John 2:16, 17 [c][1 John 3:8–10, 15] [d][Jude 6]
47 [a]Luke 8:15; John 10:26; 1 John 4:6
48 [a]John 7:20; 10:20
49 [a]John 5:41
50 [a]John 5:41; 7:18; [Phil. 2:6–8]
51 [a]John 5:24; 11:26
52 [a]John 7:20; 10:20 [b]Zech. 1:5; Heb. 11:13
53 [a]John 10:33; 19:7
54 [a]John 5:31, 32 [b]John 5:41; Acts 3:13 [1]NU, M *our*
55 [a]John 7:28, 29 [b][John 15:10]
56 [a]Luke 10:24 [b]Matt. 13:17; Heb. 11:13
58 [a]Mic. 5:2; John 17:5; Heb. 7:3; Rev. 22:13 [b]Ex. 3:14; Is. 43:13; John 17:5, 24; Col. 1:17; Rev. 1:8

Before Abraham Was, I AM

48 Then the Jews answered and said to Him, "Do we not say rightly that You are a Samaritan and [a]have a demon?"
49 Jesus answered, "I do not have a demon; but I honor My Father, and [a]you dishonor Me.
50 "And [a]I do not seek My *own* glory; there is One who seeks and judges.
51 "Most assuredly, I say to you, [a]if anyone keeps My word he shall never see death."
52 Then the Jews said to Him, "Now we know that You [a]have a demon! [b]Abraham is dead, and the prophets; and You say, 'If anyone keeps My word he shall never taste death.'

WORD WEALTH

8:52 taste, *geuomai* (ghyoo-om-ahee); Strong's *#1089:* Compare "gusto" and "disgust." To eat, partake of, feel, experience. *Geuomai* is used both naturally and metaphorically, especially to describe the personal experience of death, whether Christ's (Heb. 2:9) or the believer's (Matt. 16:28; John 8:52).

53 "Are You greater than our father Abraham, who is dead? And the prophets are dead. [a]Who do You make Yourself out to be?"
54 Jesus answered, [a]"If I honor Myself, My honor is nothing. [b]It is My Father who honors Me, of whom you say that He is [1]your God.
55 "Yet [a]you have not known Him, but I know Him. And if I say, 'I do not know Him,' I shall be a liar like you; but I do know Him and [b]keep His word.
56 "Your father Abraham [a]rejoiced to see My day, [b]and he saw *it* and was glad."
57 Then the Jews said to Him, "You are not yet fifty years old, and have You seen Abraham?"
58 Jesus said to them, "Most assuredly, I say to you, [a]before Abraham was, [b]I AM."

KINGDOM DYNAMICS

8:58 Divine Healing Never Outdated, DIVINE HEALING. Jesus' critics challenged His miracle ministry (5:16–18), His paternity (8:41), His integrity (7:12),

8:58 Before Abraham was: The verb ought to be translated "was born," indicating that Abraham's life had a specific beginning. This stands in sharp contrast to Jesus' self-claim, **"I AM."** In other words, He was without beginning—the ever-present One.

and His spiritual purity (8:48). Their resistance was not unlike that which often is raised today against the present reality of healing/miracle ministry. A foundational answer to such doubt is found in Jesus' assertion to His critics: "Before Abraham was, I AM." Christ's answer ties all facets of His Person and ministry to His own unchanging timelessness. This is a timeless message for us today as well. Jesus is not the great "I was" of yesteryear, but He is the great "I AM," "the same yesterday, and today, and forever" (Heb. 13:8). Some confine miraculous healings to Bible times, but church history annuls that theory. Nothing in Scripture ever indicates that there will be any diminution in the work of Christ or the NT church during the whole church age. Jesus said that His church would do greater works than He had done, because He was going to the Father (John 14:12). Jesus healed through the power of the Holy Spirit, and the same Holy Spirit is still operating in the church (Acts 2:38, 39).

(Luke 17:12–19/Acts 3:16) N.V.

59 Then [a]they took up stones to throw
at Him; but Jesus hid Himself and went
out of the temple, [b]going[1] through the
midst of them, and so passed by.

A Man Born Blind Receives Sight

9 Now as *Jesus* passed by, He saw a
man who was blind from birth.
2 And His disciples asked Him, saying,
"Rabbi, [a]who sinned, this man or
his parents, that he was born blind?"
3 Jesus answered, "Neither this man
nor his parents sinned, [a]but that the
works of God should be *revealed in
him.
4 [a]"I[1] must work the **works** of Him
who sent Me while it is [b]day; *the* night
is coming when no one can work.

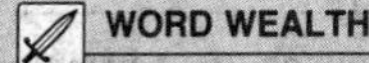
WORD WEALTH

9:4 works, *ergon* (er-gon); Strong's *#2041:* Compare "energy" and "urge." Toil, occupation, enterprise, deed, task, accomplishment, employment, performance, work, labor, course of action. The miraculous accomplishments and deeds of Jesus are works of God implying power and might.

5 "As long as I am in the world,
[a]I am the light of the world."
6 When He had said these things,
[a]He spat on the ground and made clay
with the saliva; and He anointed the
eyes of the blind man with the clay.
7 And He said to him, "Go, wash
[a]in the pool of Siloam" (which is translated,
Sent). So [b]he went and washed,
and came back seeing.
8 Therefore the neighbors and those
who previously had seen that he was
[1]blind said, "Is not this he who sat and
begged?"
9 Some said, "This is he." Others
said, [1]"He is like him." He said, "I am
he."
10 Therefore they said to him, "How
were your eyes opened?"
11 He answered and said, [a]"A Man
called Jesus made clay and anointed
my eyes and said to me, 'Go to [1]the
pool of Siloam and wash.' So I went
and washed, and I received sight."
12 Then they said to him, "Where is
He?" He said, "I do not know."

The Pharisees Excommunicate the Healed Man

13 They brought him who formerly
was blind to the Pharisees.
14 Now it was a Sabbath when Jesus
made the clay and opened his eyes.
15 Then the Pharisees also asked him
again how he had received his sight.
He said to them, "He put clay on my
eyes, and I washed, and I see."
16 Therefore some of the Pharisees
said, "This Man is not from God, because
He does not [1]keep the Sabbath."
Others said, [a]"How can a man who is

59 [a]John 10:31; 11:8 [b]Luke 4:30; John 10:39 [1]NU omits the rest of v. 59.

CHAPTER 9

2 [a]Luke 13:2; John 9:34; Acts 28:4
3 [a]John 11:4 *See WW at Col. 3:4.
4 [a][John 4:34; 5:19, 36; 17:4] [b]John 11:9, 10; 12:35; Gal. 6:10 [1]NU *We*
5 [a][John 1:5, 9; 3:19; 8:12; 12:35, 46]
6 [a]Mark 7:33; 8:23
7 [a]Neh. 3:15; Is. 8:6; Luke 13:4; John 9:11 [b]2 Kin. 5:14
8 [1]NU *a beggar*
9 [1]NU *"No, but he is like him."*
11 [a]John 9:6, 7 [1]NU omits *the pool of*
16 [a]John 3:2; 9:33 [1]*observe*

8:59 The claim of Jesus to be eternal was a claim to be divine. Thus, in the eyes of the Jews He was guilty of blasphemy, a sin punishable by stoning. This and related passages in this Gospel are devastatingly powerful in refuting the presumptuous notions of skeptics who say Jesus never claimed to be very *God* incarnate.

9:1–12 Assuming that an individual case of suffering was due to specific sin, the disciples inquired into the cause of the man's blindness. Jesus, however, notes that beyond the tragedy of human defects, which result in a general way from man's fall and the consequent entry of sin, sickness, affliction, and death into the world, God's merciful and sovereign grace is available.

9:4 Day signifies Jesus' messianic ministry, and **the night** refers to the Crucifixion.

9:13 The perverse reasoning of the Pharisees placed them in a dilemma from which the only escape was to disprove the miracle that had been performed. They argued that no miracle could have occurred because it was the Sabbath, and God would never violate the law of rest by healing a person. However, the fact that a man born blind now had perfect sight refuted their theory. Thus, they must either deny the facts or confess the divine nature of Jesus. The logic of the healed man was simple and irrefutable (vv. 30–33). Unable to deny the man's testimony, the religious authorities took the cowardly way out and excommunicated him.

a *sinner do such signs?" And [b]there was a division among them.
17 They said to the blind man again, "What do you say about Him because He opened your eyes?" He said, [a]"He is a prophet."
18 But the Jews did not believe concerning him, that he had been blind and received his sight, until they called the parents of him who had received his sight.
19 And they asked them, saying, "Is this your son, who you say was born blind? How then does he now see?"
20 His parents answered them and said, "We know that this is our son, and that he was born blind;
21 "but by what means he now sees we do not know, or who opened his eyes we do not know. He is of age; ask him. He will speak for himself."
22 His parents said these *things* because [a]they feared the Jews, for the Jews had agreed already that if anyone confessed *that* He *was* Christ, he [b]would be put out of the synagogue.
23 Therefore his parents said, "He is of age; ask him."
24 So they again called the man who was blind, and said to him, [a]"Give God the glory! [b]We know that this Man is a sinner."
25 He answered and said, "Whether He is a sinner *or not* I do not know. One thing I know: that though I was blind, now I see."
26 Then they said to him again, "What did He do to you? How did He open your eyes?"
27 He answered them, "I told you already, and you did not listen. Why do you want to hear *it* again? Do you also want to become His disciples?"
28 Then they reviled him and said, "You are His disciple, but we are Moses' disciples.
29 "We know that God [a]spoke to [b]Moses; *as for* this *fellow*, [c]we do not know where He is from."
30 The man answered and said to them, [a]"Why, this is a marvelous thing, that you do not know where He is from; yet He has opened my eyes!
31 "Now we know that [a]God does not hear sinners; but if anyone is a worshiper of God and does His will, He hears him.

16 [b]John 7:12, 43; 10:19 *See WW at James 5:20. **17** [a][John 4:19; 6:14] **22** [a]John 7:13; 12:42; 19:38; Acts 5:13 [b]John 16:2 **24** [a]Josh. 7:19; 1 Sam. 6:5; Ezra 10:11; Rev. 11:13 [b]John 9:16 **29** [a]Ex. 19:19, 20; 33:11; 34:29; Num. 12:6–8 [b][John 5:45–47] [c]John 7:27, 28; 8:14 **30** [a]John 3:10 **31** [a]Job 27:9; 35:12; Ps. 18:41; Prov. 1:28; 15:29; 28:9; Is. 1:15; Jer. 11:11; 14:12; Ezek. 8:18; Mic. 3:4; Zech. 7:13; [James 5:16]

33 [a]John 3:2; 9:16 **34** [a]Ps. 51:5; John 9:2 [1]Excommunicated him **35** [a]John 5:14 [b]John 1:7; 16:31 [c]Matt. 14:33; 16:16; Mark 1:1; John 10:36; 1 John 5:13 [1]NU *Man* **37** [a]John 4:26 **38** [a]Matt. 8:2 **39** [a][John 3:17; 5:22, 27; 12:47] [b]Matt. 13:13; 15:14 **40** [a][Rom. 2:19] **41** [a]John 15:22, 24

32 "Since the world began it has been unheard of that anyone opened the eyes of one who was born blind.
33 [a]"If this Man were not from God, He could do nothing."
34 They answered and said to him, [a]"You were completely born in sins, and are you teaching us?" And they [1]cast him out.

True Vision and True Blindness

35 Jesus heard that they had cast him out; and when He had [a]found him, He said to him, "Do you [b]believe in [c]the Son of [1]God?"
36 He answered and said, "Who is He, Lord, that I may believe in Him?"
37 And Jesus said to him, "You have both seen Him and [a]it is He who is talking with you."
38 Then he said, "Lord, I believe!" And he [a]worshiped Him.
39 And Jesus said, [a]"For judgment I have come into this world, [b]that those who do not see may see, and that those who see may be made blind."
40 Then *some* of the Pharisees who were with Him heard these words, [a]and said to Him, "Are we blind also?"
41 Jesus said to them, [a]"If you were blind, you would have no sin; but now you say, 'We see.' Therefore your sin remains.

Jesus the True Shepherd

10 "Most assuredly, I say to you, he who does not enter the sheepfold by the door, but climbs up some other way, the same is a thief and a robber.
2 "But he who enters by the door is the **shepherd** of the sheep.

WORD WEALTH

10:2 shepherd, *poimen* (poy-*mane*); Strong's *#4166:* A herdsman, sheepherder; one who tends, leads, guides, cherishes, feeds, and protects a flock. The NT uses the word for a Christian pastor to whose care and leadership others will commit themselves (Eph. 4:11). The term is applied metaphorically to Christ (John 10:11, 14, 16; Heb. 13:20; 1 Pet. 2:25).

9:35–41 Jesus moved the discussion from physical blindness to spiritual blindness. To believe in Jesus means to see spiritually, whereas those who do not believe in Him remain blind.

10:1–21 The discourse of Jesus as the Good Shepherd must be read in the context of 9:35–41, as 10:21 clearly indicates. Not only were the Pharisees blind, they were also false shepherds, described in vv. 5 and 8 as strangers and thieves.

3 "To him the doorkeeper opens, and
the sheep hear his voice; and he calls
his own sheep by [a]name and leads
them out.
4 "And when he brings out his own
sheep, he goes before them; and the
sheep *follow him, for they know his
voice.
5 "Yet they will by no means follow
a [a]stranger, but will flee from him, for
they do not know the voice of strangers."
6 Jesus used this illustration, but they
did not understand the things which
He spoke to them.

Jesus the Good Shepherd

7 Then Jesus said to them again,
"Most assuredly, I say to you, I am the
door of the sheep.
8 "All who *ever* came [1]before Me are
thieves and robbers, but the sheep did
not hear them.
9 [a]"I am the door. If anyone enters
by Me, he will be saved, and will go
in and out and find pasture.
10 "The thief does not come except to
steal, and to kill, and to destroy. I have
come that they may have life, and that
they may have *it* more **abundantly.**

WORD WEALTH

10:10 abundantly, *perissos* (per-is-*soss*); Strong's *#4053:* Superabundance, excessive, overflowing, surplus, over and above, more than enough, profuse, extraordinary, above the ordinary, more than sufficient.

KINGDOM DYNAMICS

10:10 God Desires Biblical Abundance for You, SEED FAITH. As you give your total self to God, God gives His total self to you. That is the supreme message of the Bible. Inherent in God's "total self" of His own Person is true, Bible-based prosperity—the real possibility of health for your total being (body, mind, emotions, relationships), of your material needs being met. Above all, His prosperity brings eternal life. Stop to think about it. What else is there worth having?

Jesus said that He came to give life—not just ordinary existence, but life in fullness, abundance, and prosperity (3 John 2). On the other hand, the Enemy (Satan) comes only to steal, kill, and destroy. The line is clearly drawn. On one side is God with goodness, life, and "plenty" of all that is necessary for life (see Joel 2:26 and 2 Pet. 1:3), and on the other side is the Enemy of our souls, who comes to rob us of God's blessings, to oppress our bodies through disease and accidents, and to destroy everything that we love and hold dear.

Your first step toward experiencing full biblical prosperity is to believe that it is God's highest desire for you. The next step is to line up your highest desire with His.

(Matt. 17:19, 20/Luke 6:38) O.R.

KINGDOM DYNAMICS

10:10 Abundant Life, GOD'S PROSPERITY. God's covenant to us is a covenant for abundant life. From the very beginning of time, Scripture shows us that God wanted us to be happy and prosperous. In Gen., we are told that God made everything and declared it to be good. Then He gave this beautiful, plentiful Earth to Adam; Adam was given dominion over all of it (Gen. 1:28). God's plan from the beginning was for man to be enriched and to have a prosperous, abundant life. Here Jesus declares His intention to recover and restore to man what was the Father's intent and to break and block the Devil's intent to hinder our receiving it.

(Deut. 8:18/Ps. 1:1–3) F.P.

KINGDOM DYNAMICS

10:10 Abundant Life, HUMAN WORTH. Christ came to Earth in defense of life. By His words and actions He opposed any thing, force, or person that might diminish it. Likewise, He calls us to do everything within our power to preserve and enhance the lives of those around us. In addition to evangelizing, we are to work to reduce poverty, disease, hunger, injustice, and ignorance.

Beyond His defense of life, however, Jesus also came to deliver from death and to introduce abundant living. By His death and resurrection, Christ has opened a new dimension of life for all mankind, that "all things become new" (2 Cor. 5:17).

(1 Pet. 1:18, 19/Gen. 1:26–28*) C.B.

KINGDOM DYNAMICS

10:10 The Meaning of Restoration to an Individual, RESTORATION. This text opens the theme of individual restoration. The entire concept of "The Holy

(*cont. on next page*)

CHAPTER 10

3 [a]John 20:16
4 *See WW at John 13:36.
5 [a][2 Cor. 11:13–15]
8 [1]M omits *before Me*
9 [a][John 14:6; Eph. 2:18]

10:7–9 Jesus' third **I am** pronouncement depicts Him as **the door of the sheep.** The imagery contrasts Jesus' protection of the sheep in the fold with the usurpers, the false prophets of OT times and the false messiahs of more recent times. Entering the sheepfold through Jesus is a saving action and provides the sheep with abundant life and provision. The phrase **go in and out** (v. 9) does not mean that one can vacillate about being in Christ one moment and outside of Him the next. The picture is one of security and safety in Christ as the door to the sheep's daily comings and goings.

(cont. from preceding page)
Spirit and Restoration" is developed in the study article that begins on page 2012.
(Joel 2:28, 29/John 13:34, 35) J.R.

11 [a]"I am the *good shepherd. The
good shepherd gives His *life for the
sheep.
12 "But a [1]hireling, *he who is* not the
shepherd, one who does not own the
sheep, sees the wolf coming and
[a]leaves the sheep and flees; and the
wolf *catches the sheep and scatters
them.
13 "The hireling flees because he is a
hireling and does not care about the
sheep.
14 "I am the good *shepherd; and
[a]I know My *sheep,* and [b]am known by
My own.
15 [a]"As the Father knows Me, even so
I know the Father; [b]and I lay down My
life for the sheep.
16 "And [a]other sheep I have which are
not of this fold; them also I must bring,
and they will hear My voice; [b]and there
will be one flock *and* one shepherd.
17 "Therefore My Father [a]loves Me,
[b]because I lay down My life that I may
take it again.
18 "No one takes it from Me, but I lay
it down of Myself. I [a]have power to lay
it down, and I have power to take it
again. [b]This command I have received
from My Father."
19 Therefore [a]there was a division
again among the Jews because of these
sayings.
20 And many of them said, [a]"He has
a demon and is [1]mad. Why do you listen to Him?"
21 Others said, "These are not the
words of one who has a demon.
[a]Can a demon [b]open the eyes of the
blind?"

The Shepherd Knows His Sheep

22 Now it was the Feast of Dedication
in Jerusalem, and it was winter.

11 [a]Is. 40:11 *See WW at Matt. 13:48. • See WW at Luke 21:19.
12 [a]Zech. 11:16, 17 [1]*hired man* *See WW at 1 Thess. 4:17.
14 [a]2 Tim. 2:19 [b]2 Tim. 1:12 *See WW at John 10:2.
15 [a]Matt. 11:27 [b][John 15:13; 19:30]
16 [a]Is. 42:6; 56:8 [b]Eph. 2:13–18
17 [a]John 5:20 [b][Heb. 2:9]
18 [a][John 2:19; 5:26] [b][John 6:38; 14:31; 17:4; Acts 2:24, 32]
19 [a]John 7:43; 9:16
20 [a]John 7:20 [1]*insane*
21 [a][Ex. 4:11] [b]John 9:6, 7, 32, 33
23 [a]Acts 3:11; 5:12
24 [1]Suspense
25 [a]John 5:36; 10:38 [b]Matt. 11:4
26 [a][John 8:47] [1]NU omits *as I said to you*
27 [a]John 10:4, 14
29 [a]John 14:28 [b][John 17:2, 6, 12, 24] *See WW at 1 Thess. 4:17.
30 [a]John 17:11, 21–24
31 [a]John 8:59
33 [a]Matt 9:3 [b]John 5:18
34 [a]Ps. 82:6
35 [a]Matt. 5:17, 18 [b]1 Pet. 1:25
36 [a]John 6:27 [b]John 3:17 [c]John 5:17, 18 [d]Luke 1:35

23 And Jesus walked in the temple,
[a]in Solomon's porch.
24 Then the Jews surrounded Him and
said to Him, "How long do You keep
us in [1]doubt? If You are the Christ, tell
us plainly."
25 Jesus answered them, "I told you,
and you do not believe. [a]The works
that I do in My Father's name, they
[b]bear witness of Me.
26 "But [a]you do not believe, because
you are not of My sheep, [1]as I said to
you.
27 [a]"My sheep hear My voice, and I
know them, and they follow Me.
28 "And I give them eternal life, and
they shall never perish; neither shall
anyone snatch them out of My hand.
29 [a]"My Father, [b]who has given *them*
to Me, is greater than all; and no one
is able to *snatch *them* out of My Father's hand.
30 [a]"I and *My* Father are one."

Renewed Efforts to Stone Jesus

31 Then [a]the Jews took up stones
again to stone Him.
32 Jesus answered them, "Many good
works I have shown you from My Father. For which of those works do you
stone Me?"
33 The Jews answered Him, saying,
"For a good work we do not stone You,
but for [a]blasphemy, and because You,
being a Man, [b]make Yourself God."
34 Jesus answered them, "Is it not
written in your law, [a]*'I said, "You are
gods"'*?
35 "If He called them gods, [a]to whom
the word of God came (and the Scripture [b]cannot be broken),
36 "do you say of Him [a]whom the Father **sanctified** and [b]sent into the
world, 'You are blaspheming,' [c]be-
cause I said, 'I am [d]the Son of God'?

WORD WEALTH

10:36 sanctified, *hagiadzo* (hag-ee-*ad*-zoe); Strong's *#37:* Compare "hagiography" and "Hagiographa." To hallow, set

10:11–14 Jesus' fourth **I am** pronouncement declares Him to be **the good shepherd,** whose genuine concern for His sheep is in stark contrast to the conduct of a **hireling,** whose only interest is self-preservation.

10:15 The intimate relationship of the Father and the Son provides the *model* for the relationship of the Shepherd and His sheep.

10:16 The reference to **other sheep** anticipates the mission to the Gentiles after Pentecost and their full incorporation into the one church of the Lord Jesus Christ.

10:22 The Feast of Dedication, known today as Hanukkah, had its origin in the liberation and rededication of the temple under the Maccabeans in 165 B.C., after it had been desecrated by the Seleucid king Antiochus Epiphanes.

10:28, 29 The security of the sheep lies in the power of the Shepherd and His relationship to the Father.

10:34, 35 You are gods: The reference, taken from Ps. 82:6, does not attribute deity to the judges to whom it refers, but was a title of commendation, noting the God-given capacities of human life and will—the fruit of being made "in His image." This is clearly seen in the appositional clause, "You are children of the Most High" (Ps. 82:6). Jesus' use here is as an argument from the lesser to the greater, not as a designation of His people. In other words, if God Himself

apart, dedicate, consecrate, separate, sanctify, make holy. *Hagiadzo* as a state of holiness is opposite of *koinon,* common or unclean. In the OT things, places, and ceremonies were named *hagiadzo.* In the NT the word describes a manifestation of life produced by the indwelling Holy Spirit. Because His Father set Him apart, Jesus is appropriately called the Holy One of God (6:69).

5 37 [a]"If I do not do the works of My
Father, do not believe Me;
38 "but if I do, though you do not believe Me, [a]believe the works, that you
may know and [1]believe [b]that the Father *is* in Me, and I in Him."
39 [a]Therefore they sought again to
seize Him, but He escaped out of their
hand.

The Believers Beyond Jordan

40 And He went away again beyond
the Jordan to the place [a]where John
was baptizing at first, and there He
stayed.
41 Then many came to Him and said,
"John performed no sign, [a]but all the
things that John spoke about this Man
were true."
42 And many believed in Him there.

The Death of Lazarus

11 Now a certain *man* was sick,
Lazarus of Bethany, the town of
[a]Mary and her sister Martha.
2 [a]It was *that* Mary who anointed the
Lord with fragrant oil and wiped His
feet with her hair, whose brother Lazarus was sick.
3 Therefore the sisters sent to Him,
saying, "Lord, behold, he whom You
*love is sick."
4 When Jesus heard *that,* He said,
"This sickness is not unto death, but
for the glory of God, that the Son of
God may be glorified through it."
5 Now Jesus loved Martha and her
sister and Lazarus.
6 So, when He heard that he was sick,

37 [a]John 10:25; 15:24
38 [a]John 5:36 [b]John 14:10, 11 [1]NU *understand*
39 [a]John 7:30, 44
40 [a]John 1:28
41 [a][John 1:29, 36; 3:28–36; 5:33]

CHAPTER 11

1 [a]Luke 10:38, 39; John 11:5, 19
2 [a]Matt. 26:7
3 *See WW at John 21:15.

6 [a]John 10:40
8 [a]John 8:59; 10:31
9 [a]Luke 13:33; John 9:4; 12:35 [b]Is. 9:2
10 [a]John 12:35
11 [a]Deut. 31:16; [Dan. 12:2]; Matt. 9:24; Acts 7:60; [1 Cor. 15:18, 51]
16 [a]Matt. 10:3; Mark 3:18; Luke 6:15; John 14:5; 20:26–28; Acts 1:13
18 [1]Lit. *15 stadia*

[a]He stayed two more days in the place
where He was.
7 Then after this He said to *the* disciples, "Let us go to Judea again."
8 *The* disciples said to Him, "Rabbi,
lately the Jews sought to [a]stone You,
and are You going there again?"
9 Jesus answered, "Are there not
twelve hours in the day? [a]If anyone
walks in the day, he does not stumble,
because he sees the [b]light of this world.
10 "But [a]if one walks in the night, he
stumbles, because the light is not in
him."
11 These things He said, and after that
He said to them, "Our **friend** Lazarus
[a]sleeps, but I go that I may wake him
up."

WORD WEALTH

11:11 friend, *philos (fee-*loss); Strong's *#5384:* Compare "philosophy," "philology," "philharmonic." An adjective used as a noun, denoting a loved one, beloved, affectionate friend. The verb is *phileo,* which describes a love of emotion and friendship. *Philos* thus has a congeniality about it.

12 Then His disciples said, "Lord, if he
sleeps he will get well."
13 However, Jesus spoke of his death,
but they thought that He was speaking
about taking rest in sleep.
14 Then Jesus said to them plainly,
"Lazarus is dead.
15 "And I am glad for your sakes that
I was not there, that you may believe.
Nevertheless let us go to him."
16 Then [a]Thomas, who is called the
Twin, said to his fellow disciples, "Let
us also go, that we may die with Him."

I Am the Resurrection and the Life

17 So when Jesus came, He found that
he had already been in the tomb four
days.
18 Now Bethany was near Jerusalem,
about [1]two miles away.
19 And many of the Jews had joined
the women around Martha and Mary,

called the Jews "gods" at that time, as verified by their own Scriptures, how much more was Jesus now justified in calling Himself the Son of God, as verified by His works, which were the Father's?
10:37, 38 See section 5 of Truth-In-Action at the end of John.
11:1 Bethany was located about 2 miles east of Jerusalem. During the final week before the Crucifixion Jesus spent considerable time there with His friends Lazarus, Mary, and Martha.
11:4 Another example of divine sovereignty amid human suffering, and demonstrating God's purposes and grace through Jesus' responses. See notes on 9:1–12; Rom. 9:6–24.
11:6 Jesus' delay of two **days** underscores what He had taught consistently, namely, that His marching orders came exclusively from His Father. Neither the need of His closest friends nor the fury of His enemies determined His actions.

to comfort them concerning their brother.

20 Then Martha, as soon as she heard that Jesus was coming, went and met Him, but Mary was sitting in the house.

21 Now Martha said to Jesus, "Lord, if You had been here, my brother would not have died.

22 "But even now I know that [a]whatever You ask of God, God will give You."

23 Jesus said to her, "Your brother will rise again."

24 Martha said to Him, [a]"I know that he will rise again in the resurrection at the last day."

25 Jesus said to her, "I am [a]the resurrection and the life. [b]He who believes in Me, though he may [c]die, he shall live.

26 "And whoever lives and believes in Me shall never die. Do you believe this?"

27 She said to Him, "Yes, Lord, [a]I believe that You are the Christ, the Son of God, who is to come into the world."

Jesus and Death, the Last Enemy

28 And when she had said these things, she went her way and secretly called Mary her sister, saying, "The Teacher has come and is calling for you."

29 As soon as she heard *that,* she arose *quickly and came to Him.

30 Now Jesus had not yet come into the town, but [1]was in the place where Martha met Him.

31 [a]Then the Jews who were with her in the house, and comforting her, when they saw that Mary rose up quickly and went out, followed her, [1]saying, "She is going to the tomb to weep there."

32 Then, when Mary came where Jesus was, and saw Him, she [a]fell down at His feet, saying to Him, [b]"Lord, if You had been here, my brother would not have died."

33 Therefore, when Jesus saw her weeping, and the Jews who came with her weeping, He *groaned in the spirit and was troubled.

34 And He said, "Where have you laid him?" They said to Him, "Lord, come and see."

35 [a]Jesus wept.

36 Then the Jews said, "See how He loved him!"

37 And some of them said, "Could not this Man, [a]who opened the eyes of the blind, also have kept this man from dying?"

Lazarus Raised from the Dead

38 Then Jesus, again **groaning** in Himself, came to the tomb. It was a cave, and a [a]stone lay against it.

WORD WEALTH

11:38 groaning, *embrimaomai* (em-brim-*ah*-om-ahee); Strong's *#1690:* Derived from *en,* "in," and *brime,* "strength." The word is used to express anger (Mark 14:5), to indicate a speaking or acting with deep feeling (John 11:33, 38), and for stern admonishment (Matt. 9:30; Mark 1:43).

39 Jesus said, "Take away the stone." Martha, the sister of him who was dead, said to Him, "Lord, by this time there is a stench, for he has been *dead* four days."

40 Jesus said to her, "Did I not say to 5
you that if you would believe you would [a]see the glory of God?"

41 Then they took away the stone [1]*from the place* where the dead man was lying. And Jesus lifted up *His* eyes and said, "Father, I thank You that You have heard Me.

42 "And I know that You always hear Me, but [a]because of the people who are standing by I said *this,* that they may believe that You sent Me."

43 Now when He had said these things, He cried with a loud voice, "Lazarus, come forth!"

44 And he who had died came out bound hand and foot with [a]graveclothes, and [b]his face was wrapped with a cloth. Jesus said to them, "Loose him, and let him go."

The Plot to Kill Jesus

45 Then many of the Jews who had come to Mary, [a]and had seen the things Jesus did, believed in Him.

22 [a][John 9:31; 11:41]
24 [a][Luke 14:14; John 5:29]
25 [a]John 5:21; 6:39, 40, 44; [Rev. 1:18] [b]John 3:16, 36; 1 John 5:10 [c]1 Cor. 15:22; [Heb. 9:27]
27 [a]Matt. 16:16; Luke 2:11; John 4:42; 6:14, 69
29 *See WW at Rev. 22:20.
30 [1]NU *was still*
31 [a]John 11:19, 33 [1]NU *supposing that she was going*
32 [a]Mark 5:22; 7:25; Rev. 1:17 [b]John 11:21
33 *See WW at John 11:38.
35 [a]Luke 19:41
37 [a]John 9:6, 7
38 [a]Matt. 27:60, 66; Mark 15:46; Luke 24:2; John 20:1
40 [a][John 11:4, 23]
41 [1]NU omits *from the place where the dead man was lying*
42 [a]John 12:30; 17:21
44 [a]John 19:40 [b]John 20:7
45 [a]John 2:23; 10:42; 12:11, 18

11:25 The fifth **I am** pronouncement declares Jesus to be **the resurrection and the life.**

11:38–44 The raising of Lazarus was not a resurrection from which followed endless physical life. That was reserved for the Father to initiate in His own Son's resurrection, thereby inaugurating a new order of life to which all those in Christ are still looking forward in hope. Jesus restored Lazarus to physical life, which would cease at his subsequent death. As with all others who have died in Christ, Lazarus awaits the bodily resurrection promised to all who are Christ's people.

11:40 See section 5 of Truth-In-Action at the end of John.

46 But some of them went away to the
Pharisees and [a]told them the things
Jesus did.
47 [a]Then the chief priests and the
Pharisees gathered a council and said,
[b]"What shall we do? For this Man
works many signs.
48 "If we let Him alone like this, everyone will believe in Him, and the Romans will come and take away both
our place and nation."
49 And one of them, [a]Caiaphas, being
high priest that year, said to them,
"You know nothing at all,
50 [a]"nor do you consider that it is ex-
pedient for [1]us that one man should die
for the people, and not that the whole
nation should perish."
51 Now this he did not say on his own
authority; but being high priest that
year he prophesied that Jesus would
die for the nation,
52 and [a]not for that nation only, but
[b]also that He would gather together in
one the children of God who were scattered abroad.
53 Then, from that day on, they plotted
to [a]put Him to death.
54 [a]Therefore Jesus no longer walked
openly among the Jews, but went from
there into the country near the wilderness, to a city called [b]Ephraim, and
there remained with His disciples.
55 [a]And the Passover of the Jews was
near, and many went from the country
up to Jerusalem before the Passover,
to [b]purify themselves.
56 [a]Then they sought Jesus, and spoke
among themselves as they stood in the
temple, "What do you think—that He
will not come to the feast?"
57 Now both the chief priests and the
Pharisees had given a command, that
if anyone knew where He was, he
should report *it,* that they might
[a]seize Him.

The Anointing at Bethany

12 Then, six days before the Passover, Jesus came to Bethany,
[a]where Lazarus was [1]who had been
dead, whom He had raised from the
dead.
2 [a]There they made Him a supper; 2
and Martha served, but Lazarus was
one of those who sat at the table with
Him.
3 Then [a]Mary took a pound of very
costly oil of [b]spikenard, anointed the
feet of Jesus, and wiped His feet with
her hair. And the house was filled with
the fragrance of the oil.
4 But one of His disciples, [a]Judas Iscariot, Simon's *son,* who would betray
Him, said,
5 "Why was this fragrant oil not sold
for [1]three hundred denarii and given
to the poor?"
6 This he said, not that he cared for
the poor, but because he was a thief,
and [a]had the money box; and he used
to take what was put in it.
7 But Jesus said, "Let her alone;
[1]she has kept this for the day of My
burial.
8 "For [a]the poor you have with you
always, but Me you do not have always."

The Plot to Kill Lazarus

9 Now a great many of the Jews knew
that He was there; and they came, not
for Jesus' sake only, but that they
might also see Lazarus, [a]whom He had
raised from the dead.
10 [a]But the chief priests plotted to put
Lazarus to death also,
11 [a]because on account of him many
of the Jews went away and believed
in Jesus.

The Triumphal Entry

12 [a]The next day a great multitude
that had come to the feast, when they
heard that Jesus was coming to Jerusalem,
13 took branches of palm trees and
went out to meet Him, and cried out:

46 [a]John 5:15
47 [a]Ps. 2:2; Matt. 26:3; Mark 14:1; Luke 22:2 [b]John 12:19; Acts 4:16
49 [a]Matt. 26:3; Luke 3:2; John 18:14; Acts 4:6
50 [a]John 18:14 [1]NU *you*
52 [a]Is. 49:6; Acts 10:45; 11:18; 13:46; [1 John 2:2] [b]Ps. 22:27; John 10:16; [Eph. 2:14–17]
53 [a]Matt. 26:4; Luke 6:11; 19:47; 22:2; John 5:16
54 [a]John 4:1, 3; 7:1 [b]2 Chr. 13:19
55 [a]Matt. 26:1; Mark 14:1; Luke 22:1; John 2:13; 5:1; 6:4 [b]Num. 9:10, 13; 31:19, 20; 2 Chr. 30:17; Luke 2:22
56 [a]John 7:11
57 [a]Matt. 26:14–16

CHAPTER 12

1 [a]Matt. 21:17; John 11:1, 43 [1]NU omits *who had been dead*
2 [a]Matt. 26:6; Mark 14:3; Luke 10:38–41
3 [a]Luke 10:38, 39; John 11:2 [b]Song 1:12
4 [a]John 13:26
5 [1]About one year's wages for a worker
6 [a]John 13:29
7 [1]NU *that she may keep*
8 [a]Deut. 15:11; Matt. 26:11; Mark 14:7; John 17:11
9 [a]John 11:43, 44
10 [a]Luke 16:31
11 [a]John 11:45; 12:18
12 [a]Matt. 21:4–9; Mark 11:7–10; Luke 19:35–38

11:49 Caiaphas was high priest during A.D. 18–36.
11:55 This is at least the third Passover John mentions and undoubtedly supports the claim that Jesus' ministry covered approximately three years. See note on 5:1.
12:2–8 See section 2 of Truth-In-Action at the end of John.
12:3 Spikenard: A valuable and fragrant ointment derived from the dried roots of the herbal plant called nard. By the first century A.D. it was already being imported from its native India in alabaster boxes. Because of its costliness, spikenard was used only for very special occasions.
12:8 Jesus did not belittle the poor, and His statement must be read against Judas's reprimand of Mary's extravagant devotion. Judas's apparent concern for the poor, however, was only pretense. The disciples were to serve the disadvantaged, but in this case Mary practiced her servanthood on Jesus while He was still with them.
12:12–18 The pilgrims who had come to Jerusalem for Passover had heard about Jesus' raising of Lazarus and were convinced that Jesus was indeed the Messiah (v. 18). So they accompanied Him into the city, shouting praises to God and singing the words of Ps. 118:25, 26. Their euphoria, however, was at fever pitch because they expected their messianic hopes to be fulfilled along nationalistic lines. See notes on Matt. 21:1–11.

"Hosanna!
[a]'*Blessed* is He who comes in the*
name *of the* LORD!'
The King of Israel!"

WORD WEALTH

12:13 name, *onoma* (*on*-om-ah); Strong's *#3686:* Compare "anonymous," "synonym," "onomatology." In general, the word signifies the name or term by which a person or thing is called (Matt. 10:2; Mark 3:16; Luke 1:63). However, it was quite common both in Hebrew and Hellenistic Greek to use *onoma* for all that the name implies, such as rank or authority (Matt. 7:22; John 14:13; Acts 3:6; 4:7), character (Luke 1:49; 11:2; Acts 26:9), reputation (Mark 6:14; Luke 6:22), representative (Matt. 7:22; Mark 9:37). Occasionally, *onoma* is synonymous for an individual, a person (Acts 1:15; Rev. 3:4; 11:13).

14 [a]Then Jesus, when He had found a
young donkey, sat on it; as it is written:

15 *"Fear[a] not, daughter of Zion;*
Behold, your King is coming,
Sitting on a donkey's colt."

16 [a]His disciples did not understand
these things at first; [b]but when Jesus
was glorified, [c]then they remembered
that these things were written about
Him and *that* they had done these
things to Him.
17 Therefore the people, who were
with Him when He called Lazarus out
of his tomb and raised him from the
dead, bore witness.
18 [a]For this reason the people also met
Him, because they heard that He had
done this sign.
19 The Pharisees therefore said among
themselves, [a]"You see that you are accomplishing nothing. Look, the world
has gone after Him!"

The Fruitful Grain of Wheat

20 Now there [a]were certain Greeks
among those [b]who came up to worship
at the feast.
21 Then they came to Philip, [a]who was
from Bethsaida of Galilee, and asked
him, saying, "Sir, we wish to see
Jesus."
22 Philip came and told Andrew, and
in turn Andrew and Philip told Jesus.
23 But Jesus answered them, saying,
[a]"The hour has come that the Son of
Man should be glorified.
24 "Most assuredly, I say to you,
[a]unless a grain of wheat falls into the
ground and dies, it remains alone; but
if it dies, it produces much [1]grain.
25 [a]"He who loves his life will lose it,
and he who hates his life in this world
will keep it for eternal life.
26 "If anyone serves Me, let him
[a]follow Me; and [b]where I am, there My
servant will be also. If anyone serves
Me, him *My* Father will honor.

KINGDOM DYNAMICS

12:26 Love Is Servant-Spirited, BROTHERLY LOVE. Love is servant-spirited. The world-mind will never understand or accept this call. A servant is one who accepts and acknowledges a place beneath those whom he serves, one willing to forsake the systems of social status on our human scale of values. Servants are viewed as performing the unworthy tasks considered beneath those whom they serve. But Jesus says that those who function as His servants—serving the world in His name—will be honored by the heavenly Father. Every true servant will ultimately be honored by the One whom they serve and who has promised them honor for that service!

If we follow and serve our King, in that act of service we are elevated to a place of honor!

(Luke 6:31–35/John 15:12, 13) D.S.

Jesus Predicts His Death on the Cross

27 [a]"Now My soul is *troubled, and
what shall I say? 'Father, *save Me
from this hour'? [b]But for this purpose
I came to this hour.
28 "Father, glorify Your name."
[a]Then a voice came from heaven, *saying,* "I have both glorified *it* and will
glorify *it* again."
29 Therefore the people who stood by
and heard *it* said that it had thundered.
Others said, "An angel has spoken to
Him."
30 Jesus answered and said, [a]"This
voice did not come because of Me, but
for your sake.

13 [a]Ps. 118:25, 26 *See WW at Luke 6:28. **14** [a]Matt. 21:7 **15** [a]Is. 40:9; Zech. 9:9 **16** [a]Luke 18:34 [b]John 7:39; 12:23 [c][John 14:26] **18** [a]John 12:11 **19** [a]John 11:47, 48 **20** [a]Mark 7:26; Acts 17:4 [b]1 Kin. 8:41, 42; Acts 8:27 **21** [a]John 1:43, 44; 14:8–11 **23** [a]Matt. 26:18, 45; John 13:32; Acts 3:13 **24** [a][Rom. 14:9]; 1 Cor. 15:36 [1]Lit. *fruit* **25** [a]Matt. 10:39; Mark 8:35; Luke 9:24 **26** [a][Matt. 16:24] [b]John 14:3; 17:24; [1 Thess. 4:17] **27** [a][Matt. 26:38, 39]; Mark 14:34; Luke 12:50; John 11:33 [b]Luke 22:53; John 18:37 *See WW at Luke 24:38. • See WW at Luke 7:50. **28** [a]Matt. 3:17; 17:5; Mark 1:11; 9:7; Luke 3:22; 9:35 **30** [a]John 11:42

12:19 The ironic statement that **the world** was going after Jesus, spoken by the frustrated Pharisees, contrasts His success with their failure.
12:20–36 Jesus redefined His impending death. The sufferings of Jesus, and particularly His death, were the Father's profoundest occasion to glorify Him. From the perspective of John, Jesus was not glorified in His resurrection and ascension as much as already in His sacrificial death on the cross. In v. 32 and its commentary in v. 33, we see that the *Cross* is at the heart of the church's mission and message, which draws all peoples to Jesus.

31 "Now is the judgment of this world;
now [a]the ruler of this world will be cast
out.
1 32 "And I, [a]if I am [1]lifted* up from the
earth, will draw [b]all *peoples* to Myself."
33 [a]This He said, signifying by what
death He would die.
34 The people answered Him, [a]"We
have heard from the law that the Christ
remains forever; and how *can* You say,
'The Son of Man must be lifted up'?
Who is this Son of Man?"
35 Then Jesus said to them, "A little
while longer [a]the light is with you.
[b]Walk while you have the light, lest
*darkness *overtake you; [c]he who
walks in darkness does not know
where he is going.
36 "While you have the light, believe
in the light, that you may become
[a]sons of light." These things Jesus
spoke, and departed, and [b]was hidden
from them.

Who Has Believed Our Report?

37 But although He had done so many
[a]signs before them, they did not believe in Him,
38 that the word of Isaiah the prophet
might be fulfilled, which he spoke:

[a]*"Lord, who has believed our*
report?
And to whom has the arm of the
LORD been revealed?"

39 Therefore they could not believe,
because Isaiah said again:

40 *"He[a] has blinded their eyes and*
**hardened their hearts,*
[b]*Lest they should see with their*
eyes,
Lest they should understand with
their hearts and turn,
So that I should heal them."

41 [a]These things Isaiah said [1]when he
saw His glory and spoke of Him.

Walk in the Light

42 Nevertheless even among the rulers
many believed in Him, but [a]because of
the Pharisees they did not confess *Him,*
lest they should be put out of the synagogue;
43 [a]for they loved the praise of men
more than the praise of God.
44 Then Jesus cried out and said,
[a]"He who believes in Me, [b]believes not
in Me [c]but in Him who sent Me.
45 "And [a]he who sees Me sees Him
who sent Me.
46 [a]"I have come *as* a light into the
world, that whoever believes in Me
should not abide in **darkness.**

> **WORD WEALTH**
>
> **12:46 darkness,** *scotia* (skot-*ee*-ah); Strong's *#4653:* Darkness, gloom, evil, sin, obscurity, night, ignorance, moral depravity. The NT especially uses the word in a metaphorical sense of ignorance of divine truth, man's sinful nature, total absence of light, and a lack of spiritual perception. Light equals happiness. *Scotia* equals unhappiness. *Scotia* as spiritual darkness basically describes everything earthly or demonic that is at enmity with God.

47 "And if anyone hears My words and 3
does not [1]believe, [a]I do not judge him;
for [b]I did not come to judge the world
but to save the world.
48 [a]"He who rejects Me, and does not
receive My words, has that which
judges him—[b]the word that I have spoken will judge him in the last day.
49 "For [a]I have not spoken on My own
authority; but the Father who sent Me
gave Me a command, [b]what I should
say and what I should speak.
50 "And I know that His command is
everlasting life. Therefore, whatever I
speak, just as the Father has told Me,
so I [a]speak."

Jesus Washes the Disciples' Feet

13 Now [a]before the Feast of the
Passover, when Jesus knew that
[b]His hour had come that He should
depart from this world to the Father,
having loved His own who were
in the world, He [c]loved them to the
end.
2 And [1]supper being ended, [a]the devil

31 [a]Matt. 12:29; Luke 10:18; [Acts 26:18; 2 Cor. 4:4]
32 [a]John 3:14; 8:28 [b][Rom. 5:18; Heb. 2:9] [1]Crucified *See WW at James 4:10.
33 [a]John 18:32; 21:19
34 [a]Ps. 89:36, 37; Is. 9:6, 7; Mic. 4:7
35 [a][John 1:9; 7:33; 8:12] [b]Jer. 13:16; [Gal. 6:10]; Eph. 5:8 [c]John 11:10; [1 John 2:9–11] *See WW at John 12:46. • See WW at John 1:5.
36 [a]Luke 16:8; John 8:12 [b]John 8:59
37 [a]John 11:47
38 [a]Is. 53:1; Rom. 10:16
40 [a]Is. 6:9, 10 [b]Matt. 13:14 *See WW at Mark 8:17.
41 [a]Is. 6:1 [1]NU *because*
42 [a]John 7:13; 9:22
43 [a]John 5:41, 44
44 [a]Mark 9:37 [b][John 3:16, 18, 36; 11:25, 26] [c][John 5:24]
45 [a][John 14:9]
46 [a]John 1:4, 5; 8:12; 12:35, 36
47 [a]John 5:45 [b]John 3:17 [1]NU *keep them*
48 [a][Luke 10:16] [b]Deut. 18:18, 19; [John 5:45; 8:47]
49 [a]John 8:38 [b]Deut. 18:18
50 [a]John 5:19; 8:28

CHAPTER 13

1 [a]Matt. 26:2 [b]John 12:23; 17:1 [c]John 15:9
2 [a]Luke 22:3 [1]NU *during supper*

12:32 See section 1 of Truth-In-Action at the end of John.
12:37–50 Apart from the trial of Jesus, these were the Master's last words addressed to a public broader than the circle of His disciples. There is a sense of finality ringing from these words—a last appeal, as it were.
12:38–40 See note on Mark 4:12.
12:47–50 See section 3 of Truth-In-Action at the end of John.
13:2 Whether or not the **supper** was the Last Supper or the Passover meal described by the other Gospels is immaterial to John's emphasis on the lesson Jesus taught in the washing of the disciples' feet.

having already put it into the heart of
Judas Iscariot, Simon's *son,* to betray
Him,
3 Jesus, knowing [a]that the Father had
given all things into His hands, and
that He [b]had come from God and
[c]was going to God,
4 [a]rose from supper and laid aside
His garments, took a towel and girded
Himself.
5 After that, He poured water into a
basin and began to wash the disciples'
feet, and to wipe *them* with the towel
with which He was girded.
6 Then He came to Simon Peter. And
Peter said to Him, [a]"Lord, are You
washing my feet?"
7 Jesus answered and said to him,
"What I am doing you [a]do not understand now, [b]but you will know after
this."
8 Peter said to Him, "You shall never
wash my feet!" Jesus answered him,
[a]"If I do not wash you, you have no
part with Me."
9 Simon Peter said to Him, "Lord, not
my feet only, but also *my* hands and
my head!"
10 Jesus said to him, "He who is
bathed needs only to wash *his* feet, but
is completely clean; and [a]you are
clean, but not all of you."
11 For [a]He knew who would betray
Him; therefore He said, "You are not
all clean."
12 So when He had washed their feet,
taken His garments, and sat down
again, He said to them, "Do you
[1]know what I have done to you?
13 [a]"You call Me Teacher and Lord,
and you say well, for so I am.
14 [a]"If I then, *your* Lord and Teacher,
have washed your feet, [b]you also ought
to wash one another's feet.
15 "For [a]I have given you an example,
that you should do as I have done to
you.
16 [a]"Most assuredly, I say to you, a
servant is not greater than his master;
nor is he who is *sent greater than he
who sent him.
5 17 [a]"If you know these things, blessed
are you if you do them.

3 [a]Acts 2:36 [b]John 8:42; 16:28 [c]John 17:11; 20:17
4 [a][Luke 22:27]
6 [a]Matt. 3:14
7 [a]John 12:16; 16:12 [b]John 13:19
8 [a][1 Cor. 6:11]
10 [a][John 15:3]
11 [a]John 6:64; 18:4
12 [1]*understand*
13 [a]Matt. 23:8, 10
14 [a]Luke 22:27 [b][Rom. 12:10]
15 [a][1 Pet. 2:21–24]
16 [a]Matt. 10:24 *See WW at 1 Cor. 12:28.
17 [a][James 1:25]

KINGDOM DYNAMICS

13:1–17 Secure, LEADER TRAITS. As Jesus took the towel and basin to wash His disciples' feet, His assuming a servant's role exhibits more than humility, but also evidences the psychological security essential to a leader. Jesus' lifestyle and lessons establish the mode for a new kind of leader—the servant leader (Matt. 20:26–28). The servant leader leads from a position of personal security, that is, knowing who God has made him or her to be, and resting in the peaceful awareness and confidence that God's hand is ordering his or her personal destiny (see this in v. 3, of Jesus). The godly leader is one who stoops to help another, who counts others better than himself (Phil. 2:3, 4), who lays down his life for others (John 10:11), who seeks to serve rather than to be served (Luke 22:27). Until a person is ready to wash feet he is not qualified to be a kingdom leader.

(Matt. 26:47–54/Judg. 8:22, 23; 9:1–57) J.B.

Jesus Identifies His Betrayer

18 "I do not speak concerning all of
you. I know whom I have chosen; but
that the [a]Scripture may be fulfilled,
[b]*'He who eats* [1]*bread with Me has
lifted up his heel against Me.'*
19 [a]"Now I tell you before it comes,
that when it does come to pass, you
may believe that I am *He.*
20 [a]"Most assuredly, I say to you, he
who receives whomever I send receives Me; and he who receives Me receives Him who sent Me."
21 [a]When Jesus had said these things,
[b]He was troubled in spirit, and testified
and said, "Most assuredly, I say to you,
[c]one of you will betray Me."
22 Then the disciples looked at one another, perplexed about whom He
spoke.
23 Now [a]there was [1]leaning on Jesus'
bosom one of His disciples, whom
Jesus loved.
24 Simon Peter therefore motioned to
him to ask who it was of whom He
spoke.

18 [a]John 15:25; 17:12 [b]Ps. 41:9 [1]NU *My bread has*
19 [a]John 14:29; 16:4
20 [a]Matt. 10:40
21 [a]Luke 22:21 [b]John 12:27 [c]1 John 2:19
23 [a]John 19:26; 20:2; 21:7, 20 [1]*reclining*

13:5 Usually a servant performed the menial task of washing the guests' feet, but since no servant was present and no one else assumed the role, Jesus used the occasion to teach a lesson in humility and selfless service.

13:10 The disciples of Christ already enjoyed a special relationship to Him. Therefore, what is needed is not another "bath," but cleansing from defilement contracted along the way. **Not all** refers to Judas.

13:13–17 Jesus was probably not seeking to institute a literal practice to be observed continually in the church, although some feel this to be the case. But He shows great concern that the meaning of true servanthood be well understood, that no one deem it beneath his dignity to perform the most menial of tasks for others. Ultimately, servanthood is a disposition of the heart and spirit, which expresses itself in concrete actions.

13:17 See section 5 of Truth-In-Action at the end of John.

13:23 Although this disciple is not named, there is no reason to doubt that it was John.

25 Then, leaning [1]back on Jesus'
breast, he said to Him, "Lord, who is
it?"
26 Jesus answered, "It is he to whom
I shall give a piece of bread when I
have dipped *it.*" And having dipped the
bread, He gave *it* to [a]Judas Iscariot,
the son of Simon.
27 [a]Now after the piece of bread, Satan
entered him. Then Jesus said to him,
"What you do, do quickly."
28 But no one at the table knew for
what reason He said this to him.
29 For some thought, because [a]Judas
had the money box, that Jesus had said
to him, "Buy *those things* we need for
the feast," or that he should give something to the poor.
30 Having received the piece of bread,
he then went out immediately. And it
was night.

The New Commandment

31 So, when he had gone out, Jesus
said, [a]"Now the Son of Man is glorified, and [b]God is glorified in Him.
32 "If God is glorified in Him, God will
also glorify Him in Himself, and
[a]glorify Him immediately.
33 "Little children, I shall be with you
a [a]little while longer. You will seek Me;
[b]and as I said to the Jews, 'Where I
am going, you cannot come,' so now I
say to you.
34 [a]"A *new commandment I give to
you, that you love one another; as I
have loved you, that you also love one
another.
35 [a]"By this all will know that you are
My disciples, if you have *love for one
another."

KINGDOM DYNAMICS

13:34, 35 Love—The Testing of Discipleship, HUMAN WORTH. That Christ would command us to love indicates that love is not just a feeling or a preference; it is what one does and how he relates to others—a decision, a commitment, or a way of behaving. Jesus states that the world will know that we are His disciples if we behave lovingly toward one another. Schisms, disputes, unkind criticisms, and defamation of character are contrary to the spirit of Christ. His love was a sacrificial love. It was unconditional love. His love is constant and self-sustaining. His love provides for the best interests of the beloved, and He commands that we should love one another as He has loved us.

(1 Cor. 12:12/Matt. 25:37–40) C.B.

25 [1]NU, M add *thus*
26 [a]Matt. 10:4; John 6:70, 71; 12:4; Acts 1:16
27 [a]Luke 22:3
29 [a]John 12:6
31 [a]John 12:23; Acts 3:13 [b][John 14:13; 17:4; 1 Pet. 4:11]
32 [a]John 12:23
33 [a]John 12:35; 14:19; 16:16–19 [b]Mark 16:19; [John 7:34; 8:21]; Acts 1:9
34 [a]Lev. 19:18; Eph. 5:2; 1 Thess. 4:9; James 2:8; 1 Pet. 1:22; 1 John 2:7 *See WW at 2 Cor. 5:17.
35 [a]1 John 2:5 *See WW at Rom. 5:5.
36 [a]John 13:33; 14:2; 16:5 [b]John 21:17; 2 Pet. 1:14
37 [a]Matt. 26:33–35; Mark 14:29–31; Luke 22:33, 34
38 [a]Matt. 26:74; Mark 14:30; Luke 22:61; John 18:25–27

KINGDOM DYNAMICS

13:34, 35 The Meaning of Restoration to the Church, RESTORATION. This text opens the door on the meaning of restoration in the church, the body of Christ. The entire concept of "The Holy Spirit and Restoration" is developed in the study article that begins on page 2012.

(John 10:10/Acts 3:19–21*) J.R.

Jesus Predicts Peter's Denial

36 Simon Peter said to Him, "Lord,
where are You going?" Jesus answered
him, "Where I [a]am going you cannot
follow Me now, but [b]you shall follow
Me afterward."

WORD WEALTH

13:36 follow, *akoloutheo* (ak-ol-oo-*theh*-oh); Strong's *#190:* To accompany, go along with, go the same way with, follow one who precedes. *A* is in union with, and *keluethos* is a road. *Akoloutheo* is being on the same roadway with someone. Since the word was used for soldiers, servants, and pupils, it can easily be transferred to the life of the Christian. In 78 Gospel occurrences it is used 77 times of following Christ. Metaphorically, it is used for discipleship (Matt. 9:9; Mark 9:38).

37 Peter said to Him, "Lord, why can
I not follow You now? I will [a]lay down
my life for Your sake."
38 Jesus answered him, "Will you lay
down your life for My sake? Most assuredly, I say to you, the rooster shall
not [a]crow till you have denied Me three
times.

13:25, 26 The context implies a private dialogue between John and Jesus, unheard by the others.

13:27 The direct mention of Satan's entering Judas puts three parties behind the Crucifixion event—**Satan** and sinful man (meaning it for evil) and God (divinely ordaining it for reconciliation; see 2 Cor. 5:18, 19).

13:30 The statement that **it was night** has not only a literal meaning but a symbolic/theological meaning as well. To leave the fellowship of Jesus is to exchange the light for inevitable darkness.

13:34, 35 Jesus picked up the theme of vv. 13–17, but now speaks of it as the **new commandment** to **love one another.** It is new because it presents a new standard—the love of Jesus. The servantlike, selfless love that Christians display toward one another witnesses to the world that they are true disciples.

13:36–38 Peter completely missed the main point of Jesus' statement and was preoccupied instead with His departure and where He was going. But behind the overt question were likely the feelings of loss and abandonment. Life without the physical presence of Jesus was unthinkable for Peter.

The Way, the Truth, and the Life

14 "Let [a]not your *heart be *troubled; you believe in God, believe also in Me.
2 "In My Father's house are many [1]mansions; if *it were* not *so,* [2]I would have told you. [a]I go to prepare a place for you.
3 "And if I go and *prepare a place for you, [a]I will come again and receive you to Myself; that [b]where I am, *there* you may be also.

> **KINGDOM DYNAMICS**
>
> **14:1–3 Messiah's Peace, Place, and Promise for His People,** MESSIAH'S COMING. These are among the most comforting words in all of Scripture; from Jesus' own lips, we receive the promise of His return. He spoke these words during His most intimate time with His disciples, and they echo down to us as a precious promise to the bride of Christ.
>
> In this text Jesus tells us of a peace, a place, and a promise. He begins with a comforting exhortation: do not be troubled; be at peace. Our peace is based on our belief in God and Christ. We know that He is trustworthy and that gives us a foundation of peace upon which to build our lives. Second, Jesus spoke of a place. He has promised to prepare for us a place where we will have eternal fellowship with Him. Finally, we have His personal promise that He is returning for us. Think of it! His personal signature is on our salvation; as we have received Him, He is coming to receive us. We look forward to that day in expectation, preparing ourselves for it, for "everyone who has this hope . . . purifies himself" (1 John 3:3).
>
> (Ps. 16:10/Acts 1:10, 11) J.H.

4 "And where I go you know, and the way you know."
5 [a]Thomas said to Him, "Lord, we do not know where You are going, and how can we know the way?"
6 Jesus said to him, "I am [a]the way, 5
[b]the truth, and [c]the life. [d]No one comes to the Father [e]except through Me.

The Father Revealed

7 [a]"If you had known Me, you would have known My Father also; and from now on you know Him and have seen Him."
8 Philip said to Him, "Lord, show us the Father, and it is sufficient for us."
9 Jesus said to him, "Have I been with you *so long, and yet you have not known Me, Philip? [a]He who has seen Me has seen the Father; so how can you say, 'Show us the Father'?
10 "Do you not believe that [a]I am in the Father, and the Father in Me? The words that I speak to you [b]I do not speak on My own *authority;* but the Father who dwells in Me does the works.
11 "Believe Me that I *am* in the Father and the Father in Me, [a]or else believe Me for the sake of the works themselves.

The Answered Prayer

12 [a]"Most assuredly, I say to you, he 5
who believes in Me, the works that I do he will do also; and greater *works* than these he will do, because I go to My Father.
13 [a]"And whatever you *ask in My name, that I will do, that the Father may be [b]glorified in the Son.
14 "If you [1]ask anything in My name, I will do *it.*

Jesus Promises Another Helper

15 [a]"If you love Me, [1]keep My com- 3
mandments.

CHAPTER 14

1 [a][John 14:27; 16:22, 24] *See WW at Rev. 2:23. • See WW at Luke 24:38.
2 [a]John 13:33, 36 [1]Lit. *dwellings* [2]NU *would I have told you that I go or I would have told you; for I go*
3 [a][Acts 1:11] [b][John 12:26] *See WW at Rev. 21:2.
5 [a]Matt. 10:3
6 [a][Heb. 9:8; 10:19, 20] [b][John 1:14, 17; 8:32; 18:37] [c][John 11:25] [d]1 Tim. 2:5 [e][John 10:7–9]
7 [a]John 8:19
9 [a]Col. 1:15 *See WW at Acts 1:7.
10 [a]John 10:38; 14:11, 20 [b]John 5:19; 14:24
11 [a]John 5:36; 10:38
12 [a]Luke 10:17
13 [a]Matt. 7:7 [b]John 13:31 *See WW at Matt. 7:7.
14 [1]NU *ask Me*
15 [a]1 John 5:3 [1]NU *you will keep*

14:1–4 In 13:36 Jesus responded to Peter's question individually; now He answers the same question for all the disciples.
14:2 Mansions literally means "dwelling places." A better translation is "rooms," conveying the idea that there is ample space in heaven for all who come to Jesus as Savior.
14:6, 7 See section 5 of Truth-In-Action at the end of John.
14:6 The sixth **I am** pronouncement is threefold, with the last two expressions explaining the sense in which Jesus is **the way . . . to the Father.** He is **the truth** about God and the very **life** of God. As such, He reveals truth to us and gives life to us.
14:12–14 See section 5 of Truth-In-Action at the end of John.
14:12 The promise is not that disciples of Jesus will perform works that are **greater** in value or significance than His. Rather they are greater in scope and number, in these respects: 1) Because He was crucified, Jesus' earthly ministry was limited to only a few years, but after the Resurrection and Pentecost, His ministry was and continues to be multiplied through Spirit-empowered believers. 2) Our works include the preaching of the gospel, resulting in the blessings of justification, reconciliation, and the gift of the Holy Spirit coming to humankind—all post-Resurrection manifestations of Christ's reign (see 5:20).
14:13 Prayer offered in the **name** of Jesus is in accord with His revealed nature and purpose and has the full weight of His authority behind it.
14:15–24 See section 3 of Truth-In-Action at the end of John.
14:15 The verb **keep** is not imperative, but future (see marginal note). Those who love Christ will prove their devotion by their obedience.

16 "And I will pray the Father, and
[a]He will *give you **another** [1]Helper,*
that He may abide with you forever—
17 [a]"the Spirit of truth, [b]whom the
world cannot receive, because it neither sees Him nor knows Him; but you
know Him, for He dwells with you
[c]and will be in you.

WORD WEALTH

14:16 another, *allos* (*al*-loss); Strong's *#243:* One besides, another of the same kind. The word shows similarities but diversities of operation and ministries. Jesus' use of *allos* for sending another Comforter equals "one besides Me and in addition to Me but one just like Me. He will do in My absence what I would do if I were physically present with you." The Spirit's coming assures continuity with what Jesus did and taught.

KINGDOM DYNAMICS

14:16, 17 The Person of the Holy Spirit, SPIRITUAL GIFTS. The Holy Spirit, who operates as a Helper for the church, is not impersonal. He has all the characteristics of a personality. An elaboration of this and related themes appears in the study article on page 2018, "Holy Spirit Gifts and Power."

(Is. 28:11, 12/Acts 2:4) P.W.

18 [a]"I will not leave you orphans;
[b]I will come to you.

Indwelling of the Father and the Son

19 "A little while longer and the world
will see Me no more, but [a]you will see
Me. [b]Because I live, you will live also.
20 "At that day you will know that
[a]I *am* in My Father, and you in Me,
and I in you.
21 [a]"He who has My commandments
and keeps them, it is he who loves Me.
And he who loves Me will be loved by
My Father, and I will love him and
[1]**manifest** Myself to him."

WORD WEALTH

14:21 manifest, *emphanidzo* (em-fan-*id*-zoe); Strong's *#1718:* A combination of *en,* "in," and *phaino,* "to cause to shine," thus, to appear, come to view, reveal, exhibit, make visible, present oneself to the sight of another, be conspicuous. In v. 21, *emphanidzo* is the self-revelation of Jesus to believers. A secondary meaning of the word is to declare, make known (Acts 23:15, 22; 24:1; 25:2, 15).

KINGDOM DYNAMICS

14:21 Loving God's Word As Jesus' Follower, THE WORD OF GOD. Jesus completely aligned His life and will with the Father's (8:29), which indicates His total allegiance to the Father's Word and commandments. He also said He disapproved of any attitude that would reduce respect for or teach less than full obedience to the entirety of God's revealed Word (Matt. 5:17–19). Thus, in this text, when He explicitly links His disciples' love for Him as Savior with their will to keep His commandments, we conclude Jesus' clear intent: If we love Him, we will love His Father's Word, also.

In John 5:39 our Lord declares that the knowledge of the Scriptures is the pathway to knowing Him well. Further, upon His resurrection, He unveiled the fullness of His own Person as revealed in the OT (Luke 24:27). These texts cluster to teach us: To follow Christ, to know Him, and to grow in insight as people walking with the Resurrected Lord, a basic and continuing requirement is a steadfast commitment to hearing, heeding, and studying the Bible.

(1 Cor. 3:1–5/James 1:23–25) J.W.H.

22 [a]Judas (not Iscariot) said to Him,
"Lord, how is it that You will *manifest
Yourself to us, and not to the world?"
23 Jesus answered and said to him, "If
anyone loves Me, he will keep My
word; and My Father will love him,
[a]and We will come to him and make
Our home with him.
24 "He who does not love Me does not
keep My words; and [a]the word which
you hear is not Mine but the Father's
who sent Me.

The Gift of His Peace

25 "These things I have spoken to you 4
while being present with you.
26 "But [a]the [1]Helper,* the Holy Spirit,
whom the Father will [b]send in My
name, [c]He will teach you all things,
and bring to your [d]remembrance all
things that I said to you.

16 [a][John 15:26; 20:22]; Acts 2:4, 33; Rom. 8:15 [1]*Comforter,* Gr. *Parakletos* *See WW at Acts 20:35. • See WW at John 15:26.
17 [a][John 15:26; 16:13; 1 John 4:6; 5:7] [b][1 Cor. 2:14] [c][1 John 2:27]
18 [a][Matt. 28:20] [b][John 14:3, 28]
19 [a]John 16:16, 22 [b][Rom. 5:10; 1 Cor. 15:20; 2 Cor. 4:10]
20 [a]John 10:38; 14:11
21 [a]1 John 2:5 [1]*reveal*
22 [a]Luke 6:16; Acts 1:13 *See WW at John 14:21.
23 [a]2 Cor. 6:16; Eph. 3:17; [1 John 2:24]; Rev. 3:20; 21:3
24 [a]John 5:19
26 [a]Luke 15:26 [b]John 15:26 [c]1 Cor. 2:13 [d]John 2:22; 12:16; 1 John 2:20 [1]*Comforter,* Gr. *Parakletos* *See WW at John 15:26.

14:18 Jesus refers to His coming in the Person of the Holy Spirit (see 16:16).
14:21 Loving Jesus Christ finds its most comprehensive expression in obeying Jesus' commandments, which are also the Father's commandments. A Christianity satisfied with less may be convenient, but is too cheap to be biblical.
14:25, 26 See section 4 of Truth-In-Action at the end of John.
14:26 The ministry of the Holy Spirit is predominantly Christ-oriented, a part of which is to teach and remind the disciples of what Jesus taught in person. The Spirit, then, is never self-serving.

27 [a]"Peace* I leave with you, My peace
I give to you; not as the world gives
do I give to you. Let not your heart be
troubled, neither let it be afraid.
28 "You have heard Me [a]say to you,
'I am going away and coming *back* to
you.' If you loved Me, you would rejoice because [1]I said, [b]'I am going
to the Father,' for [c]My Father is greater
than I.
29 "And [a]now I have told you before
it comes, that when it does come to
pass, you may believe.
30 "I will no longer talk much with
you, [a]for the ruler of this world is coming, and he has [b]nothing in Me.
31 "But that the world may know that
I love the Father, and [a]as the Father
gave Me commandment, so I do. Arise,
let us go from here.

The True Vine

2 **15** "I am the true vine, and My Father is the vinedresser.
2 [a]"Every branch in Me that does not
bear fruit He [1]takes away; and every
branch that bears fruit He prunes, that
it may bear [b]more fruit.
3 [a]"You are already clean because of
the word which I have spoken to you.
4 [a]"Abide in Me, and I in you. As the
branch cannot bear fruit of itself, unless it abides in the vine, neither can
you, unless you abide in Me.
5 "I am the vine, you *are* the
branches. He who abides in Me, and I
in him, bears much [a]fruit; for without
Me you can do [b]nothing.
6 "If anyone does not abide in Me,
[a]he is cast out as a branch and is withered; and they gather them and throw
them into the fire, and they are burned.
7 "If you abide in Me, and My words
[a]abide in you, [b]you[1] will ask what you
desire, and it shall be done for you.
8 [a]"By this My Father is glorified, that
you bear much fruit; [b]so you will be
My disciples.

27 [a]Luke 1:79; [John 16:33; 20:19; Phil. 4:7]; Col. 3:15 *See WW at Luke 1:79.
28 [a]John 14:3, 18 [b]John 16:16 [c][John 5:18; Phil. 2:6] [1]NU omits *I said*
29 [a]John 13:19
30 [a][John 12:31] [b][John 8:46; 2 Cor. 5:21; Heb. 4:15; 1 Pet. 1:19; 2:22]
31 [a]Is. 50:5; John 10:18; Phil. 2:8

CHAPTER 15

2 [a]Matt. 15:13 [b][Matt. 13:12] [1]Or *lifts up*
3 [a][John 13:10; 17:17]; Eph. 5:26
4 [a]John 17:23; Eph. 3:17; [Col. 1:23]
5 [a]Hos. 14:8; [Gal. 5:22, 23] [b]2 Cor. 3:5
6 [a]Matt. 3:10
7 [a]1 John 2:14 [b]John 14:13; 16:23 [1]NU omits *you will*
8 [a]Ps. 22:23; [Matt. 5:16]; John 13:31; 17:4; [Phil. 1:11]; 1 Pet. 4:11 [b]John 8:31
9 [a]John 5:20; 17:26
10 [a]John 14:15
11 [a][John 16:24]; 1 John 1:4
12 [a]John 13:34; 1 John 3:11 [b]Rom. 12:9
13 [a]Eph. 5:2; 1 John 3:16 *See WW at John 11:11.
14 [a][Matt. 12:50; 28:20]; John 14:15, 21; Acts 10:42; 1 John 3:23, 24

Love and Joy Perfected

9 "As the Father [a]loved Me, I also 1
have loved you; abide in My love.
10 [a]"If you keep My commandments,
you will abide in My love, just as I have
kept My Father's commandments and
abide in His love.
11 "These things I have spoken to you,
that My joy may remain in you, and
[a]*that* your joy may be full.
12 [a]"This is My [b]commandment, that
you love one another as I have loved
you.
13 [a]"Greater love has no one than this,
than to lay down one's life for his
*friends.

KINGDOM DYNAMICS

15:12, 13 The Priority and Pathway of Brotherly Love, BROTHERLY LOVE. Here is summarized the entire duty and direction of the disciple of Jesus. The direct simplicity of this statement establishes the priority and the pathway we are to pursue. 1) Our priority is to love one another. 2) Our pathway is to love as Christ loved us, "laying down His life." Who can measure this love? Christ gave up the comforts, joys, and adoration of heaven to be sullied by the soil of Earth and to carry the sins of sinners. His bearing of agonizing pain through beatings, nails in His hands, the spear in His side, the thorns on His head, all exemplify the measure of His love. We find His love, but we also see His manner of loving and are called to bear with others' sins, with inflicted pain, with stabbing, cruel remarks and treatment. Impossible? Yes, to human nature; but as new temples of the Holy Spirit, who has poured out the love of God into our hearts, we can ask for and receive the grace and guidance to love as Jesus loved.

(John 12:26/2 Pet. 1:7, 8) D.S.

14 [a]"You are My friends if you do
whatever I command you.

14:28, 29 Losing the physical presence of Jesus through His death was a necessary condition of His spiritual return.
14:30 Satan, **the ruler of this world,** had no foothold in the life of Jesus and no authority over Him.
15:1–8 See section 2 of Truth-In-Action at the end of John.
15:1–8 The fruit that the heavenly **vinedresser** looks for in His people is Christlikeness (see Gal. 5:22, 23). In order to be productive, a branch must submit to pruning, that is, to the beneficent discipline of the Father (v. 2; see Heb. 12:10) and must maintain an abiding union with the vine (vv. 4, 5).
15:1 This seventh **I am** and the last self-designation in this Gospel, is repeated in v. 5, describing the relationship between Jesus and His disciples. Its background is Is. 5:1–7, where Israel is compared to a vineyard under God's loving care. But unlike Israel, Jesus is the **true** [real or genuine] **vine.**
15:2 The fruitless branch, which does not abide in the vine (v. 6), is destroyed. The immediate reference was probably to Judas, but the idea applies to all pseudo-believers (see Matt. 15:13).
15:7–11 When we abide in Christ, our prayers are effective (v. 7), we glorify God in our fruitbearing (v. 8), we demonstrate our discipleship (vv. 8–10), and our joy becomes full through experiencing Christ's own joy within us (v. 11).
15:9–14 See section 1 of Truth-In-Action at the end of John.

15 "No longer do I call you servants,
for a servant does not know what his
master is doing; but I have called you
friends, [a]for all things that I heard from
My Father I have made known to you.
16 [a]"You did not choose Me, but I
chose you and [b]appointed you that you
should go and bear fruit, and *that* your
fruit should remain, that whatever you
ask the Father [c]in My name He may
give you.
17 "These things I command you, that
you love one another.

The World's Hatred

18 [a]"If the world hates you, you know
that it hated Me before *it hated* you.
19 [a]"If you were of the world, the
world would *love its own. Yet [b]be-
cause you are not of the world, but I
chose you out of the world, therefore
the world hates you.
20 "Remember the word that I said to
you, [a]'A *servant is not greater than
his master.' If they persecuted Me, they
will also persecute you. [b]If they kept
My word, they will keep yours also.
21 "But [a]all these things they will do
to you for My name's sake, because
they do not know Him who sent Me.
22 [a]"If I had not come and spoken to
them, they would have no sin, [b]but
now they have no excuse for their sin.
23 [a]"He who hates Me hates My Father
also.
24 "If I had not done among them
[a]the works which no one else did, they
would have no sin; but now they have
[b]seen and also hated both Me and My
Father.
25 "But *this happened* that the word
might be fulfilled which is written in
their law, [a]*'They hated Me without a
cause.'*

The Coming Rejection

26 [a]"But when the [1]**Helper** comes,
whom I shall send to you from the Father, the Spirit of truth who proceeds
from the Father, [b]He will testify of Me.

15 [a]Gen. 18:17
16 [a]John 6:70; 13:18; 15:19 [b][Col. 1:6] [c]John 14:13; 16:23, 24
18 [a]1 John 3:13
19 [a]1 John 4:5 [b]John 17:14 *See WW at John 21:15.
20 [a]John 13:16 [b]Ezek. 3:7 *See WW at Rev. 19:5.
21 [a]Matt. 10:22; 24:9
22 [a]John 9:41; 15:24 [b][James 4:17]
23 [a]1 John 2:23
24 [a]John 3:2 [b]John 14:9
25 [a]Ps. 35:19; 69:4; 109:3–5
26 [a]Luke 24:49 [b]1 John 5:6 [1]*Comforter,* Gr. *Parakletos*
27 [a]Luke 24:48 [b]Luke 1:2

CHAPTER 16

1 [a]Matt. 11:6 *See WW at Matt. 11:6.
2 [a]John 9:22 [b]Acts 8:1
3 [a]John 8:19; 15:21 [1]NU, M omit *to you*
4 [1]NU *their*
5 [a]John 7:33; 13:33; 14:28; 17:11
6 [a][John 16:20, 22]
7 [a]Acts 2:33 *See WW at John 15:26.
8 [a]Acts 1:8; 2:1–4, 37 *See WW at John 1:29. • See WW at Matt. 5:22.
9 [a]Acts 2:22

WORD WEALTH

15:26 Helper, *parakletos* (par-*ak*-lay-toss); Strong's *#3875:* From *para,* "beside," and *kaleo,* "to call," hence, called to one's side. The word signifies an intercessor, comforter, helper, advocate, counselor. In nonbiblical literature *parakletos* had the technical meaning of an attorney who appears in court in another's behalf. The Holy Spirit leads believers to a greater apprehension of gospel truths. In addition to general help and guidance, He gives the strength to endure the hostility of the world system.

27 "And [a]you also will bear witness,
because [b]you have been with Me from
the beginning.
16 "These things I have spoken to
you, that you [a]should not be
made to *stumble.
2 [a]"They will put you out of the synagogues; yes, the time is coming [b]that
whoever kills you will think that he offers God service.
3 "And [a]these things they will do
[1]to you because they have not known
the Father nor Me.
4 "But these things I have told you,
that when [1]the time comes, you may
remember that I told you of them. And
these things I did not say to you at the
beginning, because I was with you.

The Work of the Holy Spirit

5 "But now I [a]go away to Him who
sent Me, and none of you asks Me,
'Where are You going?'
6 "But because I have said these
things to you, [a]sorrow has filled your
heart.
7 "Nevertheless I tell you the truth.
It is to your advantage that I go away;
for if I do not go away, the *Helper will
not come to you; but [a]if I depart, I will
send Him to you.
8 "And when He has [a]come, He will 4
convict the world of *sin, and of righteousness, and of *judgment:
9 [a]"of sin, because they do not believe
in Me;

15:15 The servant-master and son-father terminology describes the believer's relationship to Christ and to the Father quite vividly. But none is quite as profound as when Jesus called His disciples **friends,** because it speaks of mutuality and love.
15:18–25 Godless secular society is hostile toward Christ and His followers, simply because Christian standards are in opposition to the world's system.
15:26 Another of the Christ-oriented functions of the Spirit is to witness about Him. That witness will be authentic because God's Spirit is the **Spirit of truth.**
15:27 In response to the antagonism of the world, believers **bear witness** concerning Christ through the power of the Spirit.
16:7 The loss of the bodily presence of Jesus will be more than compensated by the coming of the Holy Spirit.
16:8–11 See section 4 of Truth-In-Action at the end of John.
16:8–11 The ministry of the Spirit to unbelievers is that of conviction. Specifically, He uses their unbelief to prove the gravity **of sin** (v. 9), the triumphant work of Christ to prove the availability **of righteousness** (v. 10), and the defeat of Satan to prove the solemn certainty **of judgment** (v. 11).

10 [a]"of righteousness, [b]because I go to
My Father and you see Me no more;
11 [a]"of judgment, because [b]the ruler
of this world is judged.
4 12 "I still have many things to say to
you, [a]but you cannot bear *them* now.
13 "However, when He, [a]the Spirit of
truth, has come, [b]He will guide you
into all truth; for He will not speak on
His own *authority,* but whatever He
hears He will speak; and He will tell
you things to come.
14 [a]"He will glorify Me, for He will
take of what is Mine and declare *it* to
you.
15 [a]"All things that the Father has are
Mine. Therefore I said that He [1]will
take of Mine and declare *it* to you.

Sorrow Will Turn to Joy

16 "A [a]little while, and you will not see
Me; and again a little while, and you
will see Me, [b]because I go to the Father."
17 Then *some* of His disciples said
among themselves, "What is this that
He says to us, 'A little while, and you
will not see Me; and again a little while,
and you will see Me'; and, 'because I
go to the Father'?"
18 They said therefore, "What is this
that He says, 'A little while'? We do
not [1]know what He is saying."
19 Now Jesus knew that they desired
to ask Him, and He said to them, "Are
you inquiring among yourselves about
what I said, 'A little while, and you will
not see Me; and again a little while,
and you will see Me'?
20 "Most assuredly, I say to you that
you will weep and [a]lament, but the
world will rejoice; and you will be sorrowful, but your sorrow will be turned
into [b]joy.
21 [a]"A woman, when she is in labor,
has sorrow because her hour has
come; but as soon as she has given
birth to the child, she no longer remembers the anguish, for joy that a human

10 [a]Acts 2:32 [b]John 5:32
11 [a]Acts 26:18 [b][Luke 10:18]
12 [a]Mark 4:33
13 [a][John 14:17] [b]John 14:26; Acts 11:28; Rev. 1:19
14 [a]John 15:26
15 [a]Matt. 11:27; John 3:35 [1]NU, M *takes of Mine and will declare*
16 [a]John 7:33; 12:35; 13:33; 14:19;19:40–42; 20:19 [b]John 13:3
18 [1]*understand*
20 [a]Mark 16:10; Luke 23:48; 24:17 [b]Luke 24:32, 41
21 [a]Gen. 3:16; Is. 13:8; 26:17; 42:14; 1 Thess. 5:3

22 [a]Luke 24:41; John 14:1, 27; 20:20; Acts 2:46; 13:52; 1 Pet. 1:8 *See WW at Rev. 2:23.
23 [a]Matt. 7:7; [John 14:13; 15:16] *See WW at Matt. 7:7.
24 [a]John 17:13 [b]John 15:11
25 [a]John 7:13
27 [a][John 14:21, 23] [b]John 3:13
28 [a]John 13:1, 3; 16:5, 10, 17
30 [a]John 21:17

being has been born into the world.
22 "Therefore you now have sorrow;
but I will see you again and [a]your
*heart will rejoice, and your joy no one
will **take** from you.

WORD WEALTH

16:22 take, *airo* (*ahee*-roe); Strong's *#142:* To bear away, take away, carry off, lift from the ground, remove, and take up. The verb is quite common in the NT and in addition to a literal use, it is used of Christ's taking away sin (1:29; 1 John 3:5), of believers' putting aside negative attitudes (Eph. 4:31) and taking up a cross (Matt. 16:24), and of the Devil's snatching away the word of God from hearers.

23 "And in that day you will *ask Me
nothing. [a]Most assuredly, I say to you,
whatever you ask the Father in My
name He will give you.
24 "Until now you have asked nothing 5
in My name. Ask, and you will receive,
[a]that your joy may be [b]full.

Jesus Christ Has Overcome the World

25 "These things I have spoken to you
in figurative language; but the time is
coming when I will no longer speak to
you in figurative language, but I will
tell you [a]plainly about the Father.
26 "In that day you will ask in My
name, and I do not say to you that I
shall pray the Father for you;
27 [a]"for the Father Himself loves you,
because you have loved Me, and
[b]have believed that I came forth from
God.
28 [a]"I came forth from the Father and
have come into the world. Again, I
leave the world and go to the Father."
29 His disciples said to Him, "See, now
You are speaking plainly, and using no
figure of speech!
30 "Now we are sure that [a]You know
all things, and have no need that anyone should question You. By this

16:12–15 See section 4 of Truth-In-Action at the end of John.
16:12, 13 Earlier, Jesus promised the apostles that the Spirit would remind them of His teachings (14:26). Now He promises them that the Spirit **will guide** them into further truth, which they could not bear at that time. Both promises were fulfilled in the writing of the NT. The Holy Spirit also fulfills that work in granting believers today an understanding of that truth (see 1 Cor. 2:14, 15; Eph. 1:17, 18).
16:14 The Spirit's ministry is not only directed to believers and to the world, but also to Christ. What the Spirit teaches He draws from and conveys in the authority of Christ, and glorifies Christ in all that He does. True ministry in the Holy Spirit never serves a private agenda. Rather, working in us and through us, He never exalts Himself, but He continually glorifies Christ who glorifies the Father.
16:16 The first **little while** speaks of the remaining hours before the Crucifixion, while the second reference is to the coming of the Holy Spirit, which afforded a more intimate fellowship with Christ than an earthly acquaintance (see 14:18; 16:7).
16:20–22 Their temporary grief at the separation caused by His death will be lost in the joy of a spiritual reunion.
16:23–28 The Holy Spirit will increase their knowledge of spiritual things and will enhance their prayer life.
16:24 See section 5 of Truth-In-Action at the end of John.

[b]we believe that You came forth from
God."
31 Jesus answered them, "Do you now
believe?
32 [a]"Indeed the hour is coming, yes,
has now come, that you will be scattered, [b]each to his [1]own, and will leave
Me alone. And [c]yet I am not alone, because the Father is with Me.
33 "These things I have spoken to you,
that [a]in Me you may have peace.
[b]In the world you [1]will have **tribulation;** but be of good cheer, [c]I have overcome the world."

WORD WEALTH

16:33 tribulation, *thlipsis* (*thlip*-sis); Strong's *#2347:* Pressure, oppression, stress, anguish, tribulation, adversity, affliction, crushing, squashing, squeezing, distress. Imagine placing your hand on a stack of loose items and manually compressing them. That is *thlipsis,* putting a lot of pressure on that which is free and unfettered. *Thlipsis* is like spiritual bench-pressing. The word is used of crushing grapes or olives in a press.

Jesus Prays for Himself

17 Jesus spoke these words, lifted
up His eyes to heaven, and said:
"Father, [a]the hour has come. Glorify
Your Son, that Your Son also may glorify You,
2 [a]"as You have given Him authority
over all flesh, that He [1]should give eternal life to as many [b]as You have given
Him.
3 "And [a]this is eternal life, that they
may know You, [b]the only true God,
and Jesus Christ [c]whom You have
sent.
4 [a]"I have glorified You on the earth.
[b]I have *finished the work [c]which You
have given Me to do.
5 "And now, O Father, glorify Me together [1]with Yourself, with the glory
[a]which I had with You before the world
was.

Jesus Prays for His Disciples

6 [a]"I have [1]manifested Your name to
the men [b]whom You have given Me
out of the world. [c]They were Yours,
You gave them to Me, and they have
kept Your word.
7 "Now they have known that all
things which You have given Me are
from You.
8 "For I have given to them the words
[a]which You have given Me; and they
have received *them,* [b]and have known
surely that I came forth from You; and
they have believed that [c]You sent
Me.
9 "I pray for them. [a]I do not pray for
the world but for those whom You
have given Me, for they are Yours.
10 "And all Mine are Yours, and
[a]Yours are Mine, and I am glorified in
them.
11 [a]"Now I am no longer in the world,
but these are in the world, and I come
to You. Holy Father, [b]keep[1] through
Your name those whom You have
given Me, that they may be one [c]as
We *are.*
12 "While I was with them [1]in the
world, [a]I kept them in [2]Your name.
Those whom You gave Me I have kept;
and [b]none of them is [3]lost* [c]except the
son of [4]perdition, [d]that the Scripture
might be fulfilled.
13 "But now I come to You, and these
things I speak in the world, that they
may have My joy fulfilled in themselves.
14 "I have given them Your word;
[a]and the world has hated them because
they are not of the world, [b]just as I am
not of the world.
15 "I do not pray that You should take
them out of the world, but [a]that You
should keep them from the evil one.
16 "They are not of the world, just as
I am not of the world.
17 [a]"Sanctify[1]* them by Your truth.
[b]Your word is truth.
18 [a]"As You sent Me into the world, I
also have sent them into the world.
19 "And [a]for their sakes I sanctify Myself, that they also may be sanctified
by the truth.

30 [b]John 17:8 **32** [a]Matt. 26:31, 56 [b]John 20:10 [c]John 8:29 [1]*own things* or *place* **33** [a][Eph. 2:14] [b]2 Tim. 3:12 [c]Rom. 8:37 [1]NU, M omit *will*

CHAPTER 17

1 [a]John 12:23 **2** [a]John 3:35 [b]John 6:37, 39; 17:6, 9, 24 [1]M *shall* **3** [a]Jer. 9:23, 24 [b]1 Cor. 8:4 [c]John 3:34 **4** [a]John 13:31 [b]John 4:34; 19:30 [c]John 14:31 *See WW at 1 John 2:5. **5** [a]Phil. 2:6 [1]Lit. *alongside* **6** [a]Ps. 22:22 [b]John 6:37 [c]Ezek. 18:4 [1]*revealed*

8 [a]John 8:28 [b]John 8:42; 16:27, 30 [c]Deut. 18:15, 18 **9** [a][1 John 5:19] **10** [a]John 16:15 **11** [a]John 13:1 [b][1 Pet. 1:5] [c]John 10:30 [1]NU, M *keep them through Your name which You have given Me* **12** [a]Heb. 2:13 [b]1 John 2:19 [c]John 6:70 [d]Ps. 41:9; 109:8 [1]NU omits *in the world* [2]NU *Your name which You gave Me. And I guarded them;* (or *it;*) [3]*destroyed* [4]*destruction*

*See WW at Luke 9:56. **14** [a]John 15:19 [b]John 8:23 **15** [a]1 John 5:18 **17** [a][Eph. 5:26] [b]Ps. 119:9, 142, 151 [1]*Set them apart* *See WW at John 10:36. **18** [a]John 4:38; 20:21 **19** [a][Heb. 10:10]

16:33 Even in the midst of persecution there is joyful peace in the certainty of Christ's victory.

17:1–26 This chapter, rather than Matt. 6:9–13, might more properly be called "the Lord's Prayer." The prayer contains a threefold petition—that He may be glorified (vv. 1–5), that the apostles may be sanctified (vv. 6–19), and that the church may be unified (vv. 20–26).

17:1–5 The petition of Jesus for Himself is not selfish, since His desire is to **glorify** the Father. To glorify Him is to make Him known. Jesus would soon be manifested as the Savior of the world through His atoning death. Believers in Him will know God and thus possess **eternal life.**

17:6–19 Although He does not pray that His immediate disciples may be removed from the world, He does pray that they will be kept from the world's evil through the Father's name (vv. 6–16). He also prays that they might be sanctified, that is, set apart for the ministry of truth (vv. 17–19).

Jesus Prays for All Believers

1 20 "I do not pray for these alone, but also for those who [1]will believe in Me through their word;

21 [a]"that they all may be one, as [b]You, Father, *are* in Me, and I in You; that they also may be one in Us, that the world may believe that You sent Me.

22 "And the [a]glory which You gave Me I have given them, [b]that they may be one just as We are one:

23 "I in them, and You in Me; [a]that they may be made perfect in one, and that the world may know that You have sent Me, and have loved them as You have loved Me.

24 [a]"Father, I desire that they also whom You gave Me may be with Me where I am, that they may behold My glory which You have given Me; [b]for You loved Me before the foundation of the world.

25 "O righteous Father! [a]The world has not known You, but [b]I have known You; and [c]these have known that You sent Me.

26 [a]"And I have declared to them Your *name, and will declare *it,* that the love [b]with which You loved Me may be in them, and I in them."

Betrayal and Arrest in Gethsemane

18 When Jesus had spoken these words, [a]He went out with His disciples over [b]the Brook Kidron, where there was a garden, which He and His disciples entered.

2 And Judas, who betrayed Him, also knew the place; [a]for Jesus often met there with His disciples.

3 [a]Then Judas, having received a detachment *of troops,* and officers from the chief priests and Pharisees, came there with lanterns, torches, and weapons.

4 Jesus therefore, [a]knowing all things that would come upon Him, went forward and said to them, "Whom are you seeking?"

5 They answered Him, [a]"Jesus [1]of Nazareth." Jesus said to them, "I am *He.*" And Judas, who [b]betrayed Him, also stood with them.

6 Now when He said to them, "I am *He,*" they drew back and fell to the ground.

7 Then He asked them again, "Whom are you seeking?" And they said, "Jesus of Nazareth."

8 Jesus answered, "I have told you that I am *He.* Therefore, if you seek Me, let these go their way,"

9 that the saying might be fulfilled which He spoke, [a]"Of those whom You gave Me I have lost none."

10 [a]Then Simon Peter, having a sword, drew it and struck the high priest's servant, and cut off his right ear. The servant's name was Malchus.

11 So Jesus said to Peter, "Put your sword into the sheath. Shall I not drink [a]the cup which My Father has given Me?"

Before the High Priest

12 Then the detachment *of troops* and the captain and the officers of the Jews arrested Jesus and bound Him.

13 And [a]they led Him away to [b]Annas first, for he was the father-in-law of [c]Caiaphas who was high priest that year.

14 [a]Now it was Caiaphas who advised the Jews that it was [1]expedient that one man should die for the people.

Peter Denies Jesus

15 [a]And Simon Peter followed Jesus, and so *did* [b]another[1] disciple. Now that disciple was known to the high priest, and went with Jesus into the courtyard of the high priest.

16 [a]But Peter stood at the door outside. Then the other disciple, who was known to the high priest, went out and

20 [1]NU, M omit *will*
21 [a][Gal. 3:28] [b]John 10:38; 17:11, 23
22 [a]1 John 1:3 [b][2 Cor. 3:18]
23 [a][Col. 3:14]
24 [a][1 Thess. 4:17] [b]John 17:5
25 [a]John 15:21 [b]John 7:29; 8:55; 10:15 [c]John 3:17; 17:3, 8, 18, 21, 23
26 [a]John 17:6 [b]John 15:9 *See WW at John 12:13.

CHAPTER 18

1 [a]Mark 14:26, 32 [b]2 Sam. 15:23
2 [a]Luke 21:37; 22:39
3 [a]Luke 22:47–53
4 [a]John 6:64; 13:1, 3; 19:28
5 [a]Matt. 21:11 [b]Ps. 41:9 [1]Lit. *the Nazarene*
9 [a][John 6:39; 17:12]
10 [a]Matt. 26:51
11 [a]Matt. 20:22; 26:39
13 [a]Matt. 26:57 [b]Luke 3:2 [c]Matt. 26:3
14 [a]John 11:50 [1]*advantageous*
15 [a]Mark 14:54 [b]John 20:2–5 [1]M *the other*
16 [a]Matt. 26:69

17:20–26 In His final petition Jesus prays for the unity of all believers of subsequent generations. The oneness He requests is not an organizational but a spiritual unity, which, will be visibly manifested in the life of the church and will bear witness to the divine mission of Christ. The church's unity will reach its consummation in heaven (vv. 24–26).

17:20–23 See section 1 of Truth-In-Action at the end of John.

18:1 The Brook Kidron, often dry in summer but rain-swollen in winter, runs along the eastern side of Jerusalem, past the Garden of Gethsemane and the Mt. of Olives. One coming from Jerusalem had to cross the Kidron to reach Gethsemane.

18:5, 6 I am *He:* On the surface these words simply identified Jesus in terms of His Galilean hometown. Just as the other "I am" sayings in John, however, this one also revealed Jesus as God. This explains the impact of His words on the troops, who are involuntarily smitten by this momentary unleashing of His inherent power as God.

18:13 Although **Caiaphas was high priest** at the time of the arrest of Jesus, **Annas,** the ex-high priest, exercised greater influence and authority.

18:15 The other **disciple** has traditionally been identified as John, the writer of this Gospel, who preferred not to divulge his name (see 13:23; 19:25–27).

spoke to her who kept the door, and brought Peter in.
17 Then the servant girl who kept the door said to Peter, "You are not also *one* of this Man's disciples, are you?" He said, "I am [a]not."
18 Now the servants and officers who had made a fire of coals stood there, for it was cold, and they warmed themselves. And Peter stood with them and warmed himself.

Jesus Questioned by the High Priest

19 The high priest then asked Jesus about His disciples and His doctrine.
20 Jesus answered him, [a]"I spoke *openly to the world. I always taught [b]in synagogues and [c]in the temple, where [1]the Jews always meet, and in secret I have said nothing.
21 "Why do you ask Me? Ask [a]those who have heard Me what I said to them. Indeed they know what I said."
22 And when He had said these things, one of the officers who stood by [a]struck[1] Jesus with the palm of his hand, saying, "Do You answer the high priest like that?"
23 Jesus answered him, "If I have spoken evil, bear witness of the evil; but if well, why do you strike Me?"
24 [a]Then Annas sent Him bound to [b]Caiaphas the high priest.

Peter Denies Twice More

25 Now Simon Peter stood and warmed himself. [a]Therefore they said to him, "You are not also *one* of His disciples, are you?" He denied *it* and said, "I am not!"
26 One of the servants of the high priest, a relative *of him* whose ear Peter cut off, said, "Did I not see you in the garden with Him?"
27 Peter then denied again; and [a]immediately a rooster crowed.

In Pilate's Court

28 [a]Then they led Jesus from Caiaphas to the Praetorium, and it was early morning. [b]But they themselves did not go into the [1]Praetorium, lest they should be defiled, but that they might eat the Passover.
29 [a]Pilate then went out to them and said, "What accusation do you bring against this Man?"
30 They answered and said to him, "If He were not [1]an evildoer, we would not have *delivered Him up to you."
31 Then Pilate said to them, "You take Him and **judge** Him according to your law." Therefore the Jews said to him, "It is not lawful for us to put anyone to death,"

WORD WEALTH

18:31 judge, *krino* (*kree*-no); Strong's *#2919:* Compare "criterion" and "critic." To separate, decide, examine, question, select, choose, resolve, make an opinion, determine, decide favorably or unfavorably, pronounce judgment.

32 [a]that the saying of Jesus might be fulfilled which He spoke, [b]signifying by what death He would die.
33 [a]Then Pilate entered the [1]Praetorium again, called Jesus, and said to Him, "Are You the King of the Jews?"
34 Jesus answered him, "Are you speaking for yourself about this, or did others tell you this concerning Me?"
35 Pilate answered, "Am I a Jew? Your own nation and the chief priests have delivered You to me. What have You done?"
36 [a]Jesus answered, [b]"My kingdom is not of this **world.** If My kingdom were of this world, My servants would fight, so that I should not be delivered to the Jews; but now My kingdom is not from here." 1

WORD WEALTH

18:36 world, *kosmos* (*kos*-moss); Strong's *#2889:* Compare "cosmic," "cosmogony," "cosmopolitan." Originally, *kosmos* was orderly arrangement, decor, adorning, beauty, symmetry, and the regularity of the world order. *Kosmos*

(*cont. on next page*)

17 [a]Matt. 26:34
20 [a]Matt. 26:55; Luke 4:15; John 8:26 [b]John 6:59 [c]Mark 14:49; John 7:14, 28 [1]NU *all the Jews meet* *See WW at Acts 4:31.
21 [a]Mark 12:37
22 [a]Job 16:10; Is. 50:6; Jer. 20:2; Lam. 3:30; Acts 23:2 [1]Lit. *gave Jesus a slap,*
24 [a]Matt. 26:57; Luke 3:2; Acts 4:6 [b]John 11:49
25 [a]Matt. 26:71–75; Mark 14:69–72; Luke 22:58–62
27 [a]Matt. 26:74; Mark 14:72; Luke 22:60; John 13:38
28 [a]Matt. 27:2; Mark 15:1; Luke 23:1; Acts 3:13 [b]John 11:55; Acts 10:28; 11:3 [1]The governor's headquarters
29 [a]Matt. 27:11–14; Mark 15:2–5; Luke 23:2, 3
30 [1]*a criminal* *See WW at Luke 23:25.
32 [a]Matt. 20:17–19; 26:2; Mark 10:33; Luke 18:32 [b]John 3:14; 8:28; 12:32, 33
33 [a]Matt. 27:11 [1]The governor's headquarters
36 [a]1 Tim. 6:13 [b][Dan. 2:44; 7:14]; Luke 12:14; John 6:15; 8:15

18:19 In a trial it was illegal for the accused to be interrogated, lest he incriminate himself. Guilt must be established by witnesses.
18:22 The Jews again violated their own law in striking Jesus.
18:28 The Praetorium was the residence of the Roman procurator, in this case, Pilate. During the main Jewish festivals, the Roman governor would reside in Jerusalem in order to forestall any possible uprising. While plotting murder, the religious authorities were careful not to defile themselves ceremonially.
18:32 If the Jews had been allowed to carry out the death penalty, Jesus would have been stoned.
18:33–38 The dialogue between Pilate and Jesus clarifies the true nature of the Lord's kingship and emphasizes its abiding relevance.
18:36 See section 1 of Truth-In-Action at the end of John.

(*cont. from preceding page*)
later focused on "the Earth" (contrasted with heaven) and the secular world. Often in the NT the word describes a world system alienated from and opposed to God, lying in the power of the Evil One.

KINGDOM DYNAMICS

18:36 John's Writings, TERMINOLOGY OF THE KINGDOM. John is the only gospel writer who records these words of Jesus: "My kingdom is not of this world." Near the end of the first century, when John was writing his Gospel, Christians were often assailed with the accusation that their goals were not spiritual, but political. The Roman Empire was being filled with reborn citizens of a heavenly kingdom, but their "kingdom of God" terminology could be misunderstood. Thus, John adopts the phrase "eternal life," as much to show the new quality of life Jesus Christ has brought as to describe its quantity. The idea of "eternal life" describes a divine dimension of life available to mankind, as well as a destined duration of "everlasting" endlessness. The words "eternal life" occur 15 times in John's writings, "the kingdom of God" only 6. Some have thought John's relatively infrequent use of "kingdom of God" suggested this message application was confined only to the time of Jesus' ministry and the birth of "the church age." Notwithstanding the fact that the birth of the church did introduce a new era in human history, the message of "the gospel of the kingdom" was not changed. For example, see the thrust of its being taught/preached throughout Acts (20:25; 28:23, 30, 31).
(Matt. 19:23, 24/Col. 1:27, 28) J.W.H.

37 Pilate therefore said to Him, "Are
You a king then?" Jesus answered,
"You say *rightly* that I am a king. For
this cause I was born, and for this
cause I have come into the world,
[a]that I should bear [b]witness to the
truth. Everyone who [c]is of the truth
[d]hears My voice."
38 Pilate said to Him, "What is truth?"
And when he had said this, he went
out again to the Jews, and said to them,
[a]"I find no fault in Him at all.

Taking the Place of Barabbas

39 [a]"But you have a custom that I
should release someone to you at the
Passover. Do you therefore want me
to release to you the King of the Jews?"
40 [a]Then they all cried again, saying,
"Not this Man, but Barabbas!" [b]Now
Barabbas was a robber.

The Soldiers Mock Jesus

19 So then [a]Pilate took Jesus and
scourged *Him.*
2 And the soldiers twisted a crown of
thorns and put *it* on His head, and they
put on Him a purple robe.
3 [1]Then they said, "Hail, King of the
Jews!" And they [a]struck Him with
their hands.
4 Pilate then went out again, and said
to them, "Behold, I am bringing Him
out to you, [a]that you may know that I
find no fault in Him."

Pilate's Decision

5 Then Jesus came out, wearing the
crown of thorns and the purple robe.
And *Pilate* said to them, "Behold the
Man!"
6 [a]Therefore, when the chief priests
and officers saw Him, they cried out,
saying, "Crucify *Him,* crucify *Him!*" Pilate
said to them, "You take Him and
crucify *Him,* for I find no fault in Him."
7 The Jews answered him, [a]"We have
a law, and according to [1]our law He
ought to die, because [b]He made Himself
the Son of God."
8 Therefore, when Pilate heard that
saying, he was the more afraid,
9 and went again into the Praetorium,
and said to Jesus, "Where are You
from?" [a]But Jesus gave him no answer.
10 Then Pilate said to Him, "Are You
not speaking to me? Do You not know
that I have [1]power to crucify You, and
[1]power to release You?"
11 Jesus answered, [a]"You could have
no power at all against Me unless it
had been given you from above. Therefore
[b]the one who delivered Me to you
has the greater sin."
12 From then on Pilate sought to release
Him, but the Jews cried out, saying,
"If you let this Man go, you are
not Caesar's *friend. [a]Whoever makes
himself a king speaks against Caesar."
13 [a]When Pilate therefore heard that
saying, he brought Jesus out and sat

37 [a][Matt. 5:17; 20:28; Luke 4:43; 12:49; 19:10; John 3:17; 9:39; 10:10; 12:47] [b]Is. 55:4; Rev. 1:5 [c][John 14:6] [d]John 8:47; 10:27; [1 John 3:19; 4:6]
38 [a]Is. 53:9; Matt. 27:24; Luke 23:4; John 19:4, 6; 1 Pet. 2:22–24
39 [a]Matt. 27:15–26; Mark 15:6–15; Luke 23:17–25
40 [a]Is. 53:3; Acts 3:14 [b]Luke 23:19

CHAPTER 19

1 [a]Matt. 20:19; 27:26; Mark 15:15; Luke 18:33
3 [a]Is. 50:6 [1]NU *And they came up to Him and said*
4 [a]Is. 53:9; John 18:33, 38; 1 Pet. 2:22–24
6 [a]Acts 3:13
7 [a]Lev. 24:16 [b]Matt. 26:63–66; John 5:18; 10:33 [1]NU *the law*
9 [a]Is. 53:7; Matt. 27:12, 14; Luke 23:9
10 [1]*authority*
11 [a][Luke 22:53]; John 7:30 [b]John 3:27; Rom. 13:1
12 [a]Luke 23:2; John 18:33; Acts 17:7
*See WW at John 11:11.
13 [a]Deut. 1:17; 1 Sam. 15:24; Prov. 29:25; Is. 51:12; Acts 4:19

19:5 Behold the Man was not meant as a title of honor but was a mingling of pity and scorn. Pilate regarded the claims of Jesus as more fit for ridicule than for serious legal action.

19:6 Crucifixion was the most hideous Roman method of execution, reserved only for slaves and criminals. The victim generally was nailed or tied to a crossbeam which was then mounted to an upright wooden pole. Crucifixion was despised and therefore not practiced by the Jews. Their disgust with this form of punishment is evident in Deut. 21:23: "He who is hanged is accursed of God."

19:13 ***The Pavement,*** also called **Gabbatha** ("an elevated

down in the *judgment seat in a place
that is called *The* Pavement, but in Hebrew, Gabbatha.
14 Now [a]it was the Preparation Day
of the Passover, and about the sixth
hour. And he said to the Jews, "Behold
your King!"
15 But they cried out, "Away with
Him, away with *Him!* Crucify Him!" Pilate said to them, "Shall I crucify your
King?" The chief priests answered,
[a]"We have no king but Caesar!"
16 [a]Then he delivered Him to them to
be crucified. So they took Jesus
[1]and led *Him* away.

The King on a Cross

17 [a]And He, bearing His cross, [b]went
out to a place called *the Place* of a
Skull, which is called in Hebrew, Golgotha,
18 where they crucified Him, and
[a]two others with Him, one on either
side, and Jesus in the center.
19 [a]Now Pilate wrote a title and put *it*
on the cross. And the writing was:

JESUS OF NAZARETH, THE KING
OF THE JEWS.

20 Then many of the Jews *read this
title, for the place where Jesus was
crucified was near the city; and it
was written in Hebrew, Greek, *and*
Latin.
21 Therefore the chief priests of the
Jews said to Pilate, "Do not write, 'The
King of the Jews,' but, 'He said, "I am
the King of the Jews." ' "
22 Pilate answered, "What I have written, I have written."
23 [a]Then the soldiers, when they had
crucified Jesus, took His garments and
made four parts, to each soldier a part,
and also the tunic. Now the tunic was
without seam, woven from the top in
one piece.
24 They said therefore among themselves, "Let us not tear it, but cast lots
for it, whose it shall be," that the Scripture might be fulfilled which says:

13 *See WW at Matt. 27:19.
14 [a]Matt. 27:62; John 19:31, 42
15 [a][Gen. 49:10]
16 [a]Matt. 27:26, 31; Mark 15:15; Luke 23:24 [1]NU omits *and led Him away*
17 [a]Matt. 27:31, 33; Mark 15:21, 22; Luke 23:26, 33 [b]Num. 15:36; Heb. 13:12
18 [a]Ps.22:16–18; Is. 53:12; Matt. 20:19; 26:2
19 [a]Matt. 27:37; Mark 15:26; Luke 23:38
20 *See WW at Mark 13:14.
23 [a]Matt. 27:35; Mark 15:24; Luke 23:34
24 [a]Ps. 22:18
25 [a]Matt. 27:55; Mark 15:40; Luke 2:35; 23:49 [b]Luke 24:18
26 [a]John 13:23; 20:2; 21:7, 20, 24 [b]John 2:4
27 [a]Luke 18:28; John 1:11; 16:32; Acts 21:6
28 [a]Ps. 22:15 [1]M *seeing*
29 [a]Ps. 69:21; Matt. 27:48, 50; Mark 15:36; Luke 23:36
30 [a]Dan. 9:26; Zech. 11:10, 11; John 17:4
31 [a]Matt. 27:62; Mark 15:42; Luke 23:54 [b]Deut. 21:23; Josh. 8:29; 10:26 [c]Ex. 12:16; Lev. 23:6, 7

[a]*"They divided My garments*
among them,
And for My clothing they cast
lots."

Therefore the soldiers did these things.

Behold Your Mother

25 [a]Now there stood by the cross of
Jesus His mother, and His mother's sister, Mary the *wife* of [b]Clopas, and
Mary Magdalene.
26 When Jesus therefore saw His
mother, and [a]the disciple whom He
loved standing by, He said to His
mother, [b]"Woman, behold your son!"
27 Then He said to the disciple, "Behold your mother!" And from that hour
that disciple took her [a]to his own
home.

It Is Finished

28 After this, Jesus, [1]knowing that all
things were now accomplished, [a]that
the Scripture might be fulfilled, said,
"I thirst!"
29 Now a vessel full of sour wine was
sitting there; and [a]they filled a sponge
with sour wine, put *it* on hyssop, and
put *it* to His mouth.
30 So when Jesus had received the
sour wine, He said, [a]"It is finished!"
And bowing His head, He gave up His
spirit.

Jesus' Side Is Pierced

31 [a]Therefore, because it was the Preparation *Day,* [b]that the bodies should
not remain on the cross on the Sabbath
(for that Sabbath was a [c]high day), the
Jews asked Pilate that their legs might
be broken, and *that* they might be
taken away.
32 Then the soldiers came and broke
the legs of the first and of the other
who was crucified with Him.
33 But when they came to Jesus and

place"), was a raised platform upon which Pilate sat in judgment. Archaeologists identify it with an excavated Roman pavement that formed the courtyard of the Tower of Antonia.

19:14 Preparation Day was the day immediately prior to a particular festival, the Passover in this case. Since all religious festivals began on the Sabbath, Preparation Day was Friday.

19:17 The victim was forced to carry only the crossbeam to the place of execution.

19:19 Pilate's bitter irony achieved a measure of revenge against those who had entrapped him into a condemnation of Jesus.

19:25–27 To the very last, Jesus' earthly life demonstrated the priority He placed on love and concern in relationships.

19:30 It is finished: The Greek tense indicates that the work of redemption has been completed once for all and its results are abiding continuously.

19:31–33 Jewish law dictated that the bodies of executed criminals be removed from sight before sunset (Deut. 21:23). When the legs were broken, the victims could no longer ease the strain on their arms and chests, causing a greater constriction in their chests, which hastened death.

saw that He was already dead, they did
not break His legs.
34 But one of the soldiers pierced His
side with a spear, and immediately
[a]blood and water came out.
35 And he who has seen has testified,
and his **testimony** is [a]true; and he
knows that he is telling the truth, so
that you may [b]believe.

WORD WEALTH

19:35 testimony, *marturia* (mar-too-*ree*-ah); Strong's *#3141:* Compare "martyr." Witness, historical attestation, evidence, judicial or general certification. The word describes a testimony based on what one has seen, heard, or knows. The English word "martyr" comes from the Greek root, with the implication that a witness is willing to die for his belief.

36 For these things were done that the
Scripture should be fulfilled, [a]*"Not one*
*of His bones shall be *broken."*
37 And again *another Scripture says,
[a]*"They shall look on Him whom they*
pierced."

Jesus Buried in Joseph's Tomb

38 [a]After this, Joseph of Arimathea,
being a disciple of Jesus, but secretly,
[b]for fear of the Jews, asked Pilate that
he might take away the body of Jesus;
and Pilate gave *him* permission. So
he came and took the body of Jesus.
39 And [a]Nicodemus, who at first came
to Jesus by night, also came, bringing
a mixture of [b]myrrh and aloes, about
a hundred pounds.
40 Then they took the body of Jesus,
and [a]bound it in strips of linen with
the spices, as the custom of the Jews
is to bury.
41 Now in the place where He was crucified there was a garden, and in the
garden a *new tomb in which no one
had yet been laid.
42 So [a]there they laid Jesus, [b]because
of the Jews' Preparation *Day*, for the
tomb was nearby.

The Empty Tomb

20 Now on the [a]first *day* of the
week Mary Magdalene went to
the tomb early, while it was still *dark,
and saw *that* the [b]stone had been
taken away from the tomb.
2 Then she ran and came to Simon
Peter, and to the [a]other disciple,
[b]whom Jesus *loved, and said to them,
"They have taken away the Lord out
of the tomb, and we do not know where
they have laid Him."
3 [a]Peter therefore went out, and the
other disciple, and were going to the
tomb.
4 So they both ran together, and the
other disciple outran Peter and came
to the tomb first.

34 [a][1 John 5:6, 8]
35 [a]John 21:24 [b][John 20:31]
36 [a][Ex. 12:46; Num. 9:12]; Ps. 34:20 *See WW at Rom. 16:20.
37 [a]Zech. 12:10; 13:6 *See WW at Acts 4:12.
38 [a]Luke 23:50–56 [b][John 7:13; 9:22; 12:42]
39 [a]John 3:1, 2; 7:50 [b]Matt. 2:11
40 [a]John 20:5, 7
41 *See WW at 2 Cor. 5:17.
42 [a]Is. 53:9 [b]John 19:14, 31

CHAPTER 20

1 [a]Matt. 28:1–8 [b]Matt. 27:60, 66; 28:2 *See WW at John 12:46.
2 [a]John 21:23, 24 [b]John 13:23; 19:26; 21:7, 20, 24 *See WW at John 21:15.
3 [a]Luke 24:12

19:34–37 Whether or not the **blood and water** may be joint symbols of redemption and evidences of the humanity of Jesus (see 1 John 5:6–8), John sees the piercing of Jesus' side as a fulfillment of prophecy.
19:38, 39 Both **Joseph of Arimathea** and **Nicodemus** were members of the Sanhedrin and had apparently become covert disciples of Jesus.
20:1–10 The first ***day*** **of the week:** The Resurrection distinguishes Christianity from all other religions. In commemoration and celebration of this event, Christians gather on Sunday to worship the resurrected Lord. The graveclothes were not unwound or disarranged, but still retained the shape they had when they covered the body, the upper layer having fallen on the lower from the weight of the spices, and the head wrapping separated from the rest by the length of the neck. Apparently the body had simply passed through the burial shroud.
20:2 The other disciple was John, the writer of this Gospel.

THE DEATH OF JESUS (19:42)

The world viewed Jesus' death as a scandal and as foolishness (1 Cor. 1:18–25). The early believers understood His death as fulfillment of Old Testament prophecy.

Aspect of Jesus' Death	Old Testament Reference
In obedience to His Father (18:11)	Psalm 40:8
Announced by Himself (18:32; see 3:14)	Numbers 21:8, 9
In the place of His people (18:14)	Isaiah 53:4–6
With evildoers (19:18)	Isaiah 53:12
In innocence (19:6)	Isaiah 53:9
Crucified (19:18)	Psalm 22:16
Buried in a rich man's tomb (19:38–42)	Isaiah 53:9

5 And he, stooping down and looking
in, saw [a]the linen cloths lying *there;*
yet he did not go in.
6 Then Simon Peter came, following
him, and went into the tomb; and he
*saw the linen cloths lying *there,*
7 and [a]the [1]handkerchief that had
been around His head, not lying with
the linen cloths, but folded together in
a place by itself.
8 Then the [a]other disciple, who came
to the tomb first, went in also; and he
saw and believed.
9 For as yet they did not [1]know the
[a]Scripture,* that He must rise again
from the dead.
10 Then the disciples went away again
to their own homes.

Mary Magdalene Sees the Risen Lord

11 [a]But Mary stood outside by the
tomb weeping, and as she wept she
stooped down *and looked* into the
tomb.
12 And she saw two *angels in white
sitting, one at the head and the other
at the feet, where the body of Jesus had
lain.
13 Then they said to her, "Woman,
why are you weeping?" She said to
them, "Because they have taken away
my Lord, and I do not know where they
have laid Him."
14 [a]Now when she had said this, she
turned around and **saw** Jesus standing
there, and [b]did not know that it was
Jesus.

WORD WEALTH

20:14 saw, *theoreo* (theh-oh-*reh*-oh); Strong's *#2334:* Compare "theater," "theory," "theoretical." To behold, view attentively, perceive, look with a prolonged and continuous gaze. *Theoreo* conveys looking with a purpose, with interest, and with close scrutiny.

15 Jesus said to her, "Woman, why are
you weeping? Whom are you seeking?" She, supposing Him to be the
gardener, said to Him, "Sir, if You have
carried Him away, tell me where You
have laid Him, and I will take Him
away."
16 Jesus said to her, [a]"Mary!" She
turned and said to [1]Him, "Rabboni!"
(which is to say, Teacher).
17 Jesus said to her, "Do not cling to
Me, for I have not yet [a]ascended to My
Father; but go to [b]My brethren and say
to them, [c]'I am ascending to My Father
and your Father, and *to* [d]My God and
your God.' "
18 [a]Mary Magdalene came and told
the [1]disciples that she had seen the
Lord, and *that* He had spoken these
things to her.

The Apostles Commissioned

19 [a]Then, the same day at evening, being the first *day* of the week, when the
doors were shut where the disciples
were [1]assembled, for [b]fear* of the
Jews, Jesus came and stood in the
midst, and said to them, [c]"Peace *be*
with you."
20 When He had said this, He [a]showed
them *His* hands and His side. [b]Then
the *disciples were glad when they saw
the Lord.
21 So Jesus said to them again, "Peace
to you! [a]As the Father has **sent** Me, I
also send you."
22 And when He had said this, He
breathed on *them,* and said to them,
"Receive the *Holy Spirit.
23 [a]"If you forgive the sins of any, they

5 [a]John 19:40 **6** *See WW at John 20:14. **7** [a]John 11:44 [1]*face cloth* **8** [a]John 21:23, 24 **9** [a]Ps. 16:10 [1]*understand* *See WW at John 5:39. **11** [a]Mark 16:5 **12** *See WW at Matt. 4:11. **14** [a]Matt. 28:9 [b]John 21:4

16 [a]John 10:3 [1]NU adds *in Hebrew* **17** [a]Heb. 4:14 [b]Heb. 2:11 [c]John 16:28; 17:11 [d]Eph. 1:17 **18** [a]Luke 24:10, 23 [1]NU *disciples, "I have seen the Lord,"* **19** [a]Luke 24:36 [b]John 9:22; 19:38 [c]John 14:27; 16:33 [1]NU omits *assembled* *See WW at 1 John 4:18. **20** [a]Acts 1:3 [b]John 16:20, 22 *See WW at Matt. 10:1. **21** [a]John 17:18, 19 **22** *See WW at Acts 7:33. **23** [a]Matt. 16:19; 18:18

20:17, 18 Do not cling to Me reinforces the now changed condition that is to exist between Master and disciple, a condition which Jesus tells Mary will be fully inaugurated with the Ascension. There is no justification for the carnal presumption asserted by sinful minds that some amorous feelings existed between Mary Magdalene and Jesus. There is neither any evidence that she had been a prostitute (only that she had experienced a great deliverance, Luke 8:2), nor that her age was even approximate to Jesus' age. Her companying with a group of older women argues otherwise, John 19:25.

20:19 Closed doors were not a barrier to the risen Lord (see v. 26).

20:20 The appearance of the risen Christ dispelled the fears of the disciples. They were convinced that He was the same Jesus who had been crucified a few days earlier, as the scars in His hands and side showed.

20:21–23 The commissioning of the disciples to the mission of Christ is what made them "apostles," or "sent-forth ones." The empowerment for such mission comes through the Holy Spirit, poured out upon all believers at Pentecost. See note on 3:32–36.

20:22 Breathed: The allusion to Gen. 2:7 is unmistakable. Now Jesus breathed life into His own. Some interpret the statement **Receive the Holy Spirit** as symbolic and as anticipating Pentecost. Others understand the Greek to denote immediacy in the sense of "receive right now," and view the day of the Lord's resurrection as marking the transition from the terms of the Old Covenant to those of the New Covenant. The old creation began with the breath of God; now the new creation begins with the breath of God the Son.

20:23 The disciples are to preach both the way of salvation and the way of damnation explaining how sinners can be forgiven and the danger of rejecting the gospel. Whether or not the hearers' sins are forgiven depends on their acceptance or rejection of Christ.

are forgiven them; if you retain the *sins* of any, they are retained."

WORD WEALTH

20:21 sent, *apostello* (ap-os-*tel*-low); Strong's *#649:* Compare "apostolic." To commission, set apart for a special service, send a message by someone, send out with a mission to fulfill, equip and dispatch one with the full backing and authority of the sender.

KINGDOM DYNAMICS

20:21–23 Commissioned with a Mandate and a Message, WORLD EVANGELISM. John's Gospel presents the deity of Jesus—the Son of God. As God He has created all things (1:1–3), and as God He has come to redeem all—to bring the fullness of forgiveness. This aspect of His mission is conveyed to His disciples as their commission as well: Go with forgiveness. It is stated here as both a mandate and a mission: 1) "I also send you." Precisely as the Father sent the Son to bring salvation as an availability to every human being (3:16), so we are sent to insure that availability is understood by everyone. 2) "If you forgive" indicates the conditional nature of His provision. It cannot be responded to unless it is delivered. There is no escape from the awesome nature of His terminology here. We are not only sent with the substance of the message—salvation; we are sent to bring the spirit of its truth—forgiveness. Only the breath of His Spirit, which He breathed upon those who first heard these words, can enable us to go obediently and to reach lovingly. The message (salvation) and its meaning (forgiveness) are ours to deliver, and we need to receive the Holy Spirit to do both.

(Luke 24:45–58/Acts 1:8) G.C.

Seeing and Believing

24 Now Thomas, [a]called the Twin, one of the twelve, was not with them when Jesus came.
25 The other disciples therefore said to him, "We have seen the Lord." So he said to them, "Unless I see in His hands the print of the nails, and put my finger into the print of the nails, and put my hand into His side, I will not believe."
26 And after eight days His disciples were again inside, and Thomas with them. Jesus came, the doors being shut, and stood in the midst, and said, "Peace to you!"
27 Then He said to Thomas, "Reach your finger here, and look at My hands; and [a]reach your hand *here,* and put *it* into My side. Do not be [b]unbelieving, but believing."
28 And Thomas answered and said to Him, "My Lord and my God!"
29 Jesus said to him, [1]"Thomas, because you have seen Me, you have believed. [a]Blessed* *are* those who have not seen and *yet* have believed."

That You May Believe

30 And [a]truly Jesus did many other *signs in the presence of His disciples, which are not written in this book;
31 [a]but these are written that [b]you may believe that Jesus [c]is the *Christ, the Son of God, [d]and that believing you may have life in His name.

Breakfast by the Sea

21 After these things Jesus showed Himself again to the disciples at the [a]Sea of Tiberias, and in this way He showed *Himself:*
2 Simon Peter, [a]Thomas called the Twin, [b]Nathanael of [c]Cana in Galilee, [d]the *sons* of Zebedee, and two others of His disciples were together.
3 Simon Peter said to them, "I am going fishing." They said to him, "We are going with you also." They went out and [1]immediately got into the boat, and that night they caught nothing.
4 But when the morning had now come, Jesus stood on the shore; yet the disciples [a]did not know that it was Jesus.
5 Then [a]Jesus said to them, "Children, have you any food?" They answered Him, "No."
6 And He said to them, [a]"Cast the net on the right side of the boat, and you will find *some.*" So they cast, and now they were not able to draw it in because of the multitude of fish.
7 Therefore [a]that disciple whom Jesus loved said to Peter, "It is the Lord!" Now when Simon Peter heard that it was the Lord, he put on *his* outer garment (for he had removed it), and plunged into the sea.

24 [a]John 11:16
27 [a]Ps. 22:16; Zech. 12:10; 13:6; 1 John 1:1 [b]Mark 16:14
29 [a]2 Cor. 5:7; 1 Pet. 1:8 [1]NU, M omit *Thomas* *See WW at Matt. 5:3.
30 [a]John 21:25 *See WW at Rev. 16:14.
31 [a]Luke 1:4 [b]John 19:35; 1 John 5:13 [c]Luke 2:11; 1 John 5:1 [d]John 3:15, 16; 5:24; [1 Pet. 1:8, 9] *See WW at 2 Tim. 4:22.

CHAPTER 21

1 [a]Matt. 26:32; Mark 14:28; John 6:1
2 [a]John 20:24 [b]John 1:45–51 [c]John 2:1 [d]Matt. 4:21; Mark 1:19; Luke 5:10
3 [1]NU omits *immediately*
4 [a]Luke 24:16; John 20:14
5 [a]Luke 24:41
6 [a]Luke 5:4,6, 7
7 [a]John 13:23; 20:2

20:30, 31 John states both his method and his purpose in writing.
21:1–14 The appearances of the risen Christ in ch. 20 took place in the vicinity of Jerusalem. But this one was in Galilee, where the disciples had returned to their secular occupation as fishermen. The miraculous catch of fish and breakfast with their Master convinced them of who He was, and yet left them too awed to spoil with words the wonder of His presence and actions.

8 But the other disciples came in the
little boat (for they were not far from
land, but about two hundred cubits),
dragging the net with fish.
9 Then, as soon as they had come to
land, they saw a fire of coals there, and
fish laid on it, and bread.
10 Jesus said to them, "Bring some of
the fish which you have just caught."
11 Simon Peter went up and dragged
the net to land, full of large fish, one
hundred and fifty-three; and although
there were so many, the net was not
broken.
12 Jesus said to them, [a]"Come *and* eat
breakfast." Yet none of the disciples
dared ask Him, "Who are You?"—
knowing that it was the Lord.
13 Jesus then came and took the bread
and gave it to them, and likewise the
fish.
14 This *is* now [a]the third time Jesus
showed Himself to His disciples after
He was raised from the dead.

Jesus Restores Peter

15 So when they had eaten breakfast,
Jesus said to Simon Peter, "Simon, *son*
of [1]Jonah, do you love Me more than
these?" He said to Him, "Yes, Lord;
You know that I [2]**love** You." He said
to him, [a]"Feed My *lambs."

> **WORD WEALTH**
>
> **21:15 love,** *phileo* (fill-*eh*-oh); Strong's *#5368:* Compare "philharmonic," "philosophy," "philology." To be fond of, care for affectionately, cherish, take pleasure in, have personal attachment for. Jesus asked Peter twice if he had *agape* love. Peter answered with *phileo,* which at that moment was all he had to give. Later, when the Holy Spirit imparted to him the fuller understanding of *agape* love, Peter used the *agape/agapao* words nine times in his writings.

16 He said to him again a second time,
"Simon, *son* of [1]Jonah, do you love
Me?" He said to Him, "Yes, Lord; You
know that I [2]love You." [a]He said to
him, "Tend My [b]sheep."
17 He said to him the third time, "Simon,
son of [1]Jonah, do you [2]love Me?"
Peter was grieved because He said to
him the third time, "Do you [2]love Me?"
And he said to Him, *"Lord, [a]You
know all things; You know that I [2]love
You." Jesus said to him, "Feed My
sheep.
18 [a]"Most assuredly, I say to you,
when you were younger, you girded
yourself and walked where you
wished; but when you are old, you will
stretch out your hands, and another
will gird you and carry *you* where you
do not wish."
19 This He spoke, signifying [a]by what
death he would glorify God. And when
He had spoken this, He said to him,
[b]"Follow Me."

The Beloved Disciple and His Book

20 Then Peter, turning around, saw the
disciple [a]whom Jesus loved following,
[b]who also had leaned on His breast at
the supper, and said, "Lord, who is the
one who betrays You?"
21 Peter, seeing him, said to Jesus,
"But Lord, what *about* this man?"
22 Jesus said to him, "If I [1]will that he
remain [a]till I come, what *is that* to you?
You follow Me."
23 Then this saying went out among
the brethren that this disciple would
not die. Yet Jesus did not say to him
that he would not die, but, "If I will
that he remain till I come, what *is that*
to you?"
24 This is the disciple who [a]testifies*
of these things, and wrote these things;
and we know that his *testimony is
true.
25 [a]And there are also many other
things that Jesus did, which if they
were written one by one, [b]I suppose
that even the *world itself could not
contain the books that would be written.
Amen.

12 [a]Acts 10:41
14 [a]John 20:19, 26
15 [a]Acts 20:28; 1 Tim. 4:6; 1 Pet. 5:2 [1]NU *John* [2]*have affection for*
*See WW at Rev. 6:1.
16 [a]Matt. 2:6; Acts 20:28; Heb. 13:20; 1 Pet. 2:25; 5:2, 4 [b]Ps. 79:13; Matt. 10:16; 15:24; 25:33; 26:31 [1]NU *John* [2]*have affection for*
17 [a]John 2:24, 25; 16:30 [1]NU *John* [2]*have affection for*
*See WW at John 6:68.
18 [a]John 13:36; Acts 12:3, 4
19 [a]2 Pet. 1:13, 14 [b][Matt. 4:19; 16:24]; John 21:22
20 [a]John 13:23; 20:2 [b]John 13:25
22 [a][Matt. 16:27, 28; 25:31; 1 Cor. 4:5; 11:26; Rev. 2:25; 3:11; 22:7, 20] [1]*desire*
24 [a]John 19:35; 3 John 12
*See WW at Acts 26:22. • See WW at John 19:35.
25 [a]John 20:30 [b]Amos 7:10
*See WW at John 18:36.

21:15–19 After his threefold denial of Jesus, Peter needed special attention. In his reply to Jesus' threefold question **Do you love Me?** Peter uses a less emphatic word, not daring to claim a complete devotion. In the third form of the question, Jesus uses the same word for love that Peter had used, inquiring if Peter even had the affection that he claimed. Peter can only appeal to the Lord's divine knowledge as proof of his sincerity. The ultimate call for Peter to follow his Master epitomizes the Lord's threefold commission for him to be a shepherd to the sheep.

21:20–23 The emphasis does not rest on the rather mysterious reference to the fate of the beloved disciple, but on the individualization of the call to discipleship. The specifics may vary from one individual to another, but the demand for obedience is the same.

TRUTH-IN-ACTION through JOHN

Letting the LIFE of the Holy Spirit Bring Faith's Works Alive in You!

Truth John Teaches	Text	**Action** John Invites
1 Guidelines for Growing in Godliness To the NT disciple, godly living is living in, through, and for Jesus. Godliness can be summarized in three words: love, obedience, and unity. By living godly lives, we learn to see things as God does and adopt His Word as our only standard.	7:24	**Judge** spiritual things by spiritual standards, not by appearance.
	12:32	**Exalt** Jesus in your life and service to draw men to Him.
	15:9–14	**Recognize** that love obeys Jesus and lays down its life for others.
	17:20–23	**Commit yourself** to bringing about the unity of the church.
	18:36	**Practice** Christian citizenship, but **do not depend on** political means to bring about spiritual ends.
2 Steps to Dynamic Devotion John's Gospel introduces the Holy Spirit as the key to a truly dynamic devotion to God. It anticipates the outpouring of the Holy Spirit who will become the very energy of the believer's devotional life. The Holy Spirit will maximize prayer and worship, minister through the Lord's Supper, and enable the believer to continually draw his life from Jesus Christ Himself.	4:21–24	**Worship** God frequently, employing your spiritual language as well as your understanding.
	6:53–58	**Draw on** Jesus' life and healing while partaking of His body and blood in the Lord's Supper.
	12:2–8	**Do not allow** your ministry for Jesus to distract you from your more important ministry to Him.
	15:1–8	**Reject** independence from God. **Nurture** an increasingly deepened relationship with Jesus Christ.
3 Steps to Faithful Obedience Obeying Jesus is the primary evidence that we love Him and are His disciples. Our decision to obey is the key to understanding the spiritual reality of the Scriptures and frees the Holy Spirit to teach us.	2:5	Follow this advice: **Practice** instant obedience to whatever Jesus tells you to do.
	5:16–23	**Do only** what you see Jesus doing just as He did only what He saw the Father doing.
	7:17	**Determine** to obey the Lord. **Align your will** with His will and **receive** understanding of His Word.
	12:47–50	**Speak** as the Lord commands. **Know** you will be judged by the words of Jesus.
	14:15–24	**Know** that you show your love for Jesus by obeying Him. Diligently **keep** God's Word so that His presence will steadfastly abide with you.
4 Guidelines for Growth in the Spirit John's Gospel introduces the Holy Spirit's role in spiritual growth. The New Birth and the baptism with the Holy Spirit endow the believer with the life and gifts of the Holy Spirit, including the ability to pray in Spirit power. The Holy Spirit is our Teacher, Helper, Advocate, and Guide. He is our source of true spiritual understanding. He lifts up Jesus and builds up believers, enabling them to live the Christian life.	3:3	**Understand** that perceiving the kingdom of God and entering it are impossible without spiritual rebirth.
	14:25, 26	**Understand** that the Holy Spirit enables God's people to understand and live by the truth.
	16:8–11	**Ask** the Holy Spirit to bring conviction to men's hearts. **Understand** that is one of His primary ministries.
	16:12–15	**Understand** that knowing the truth of God's Word is made possible by the Holy Spirit.

Truth John Teaches	Text	**Action** John Invites
5 Key Lessons in Faith The key word in John's Gospel is "believe." Faith unlocks our understanding of Scripture and releases the Spirit's activity in our lives. Faith, like love, evidences itself in obedience. Finally, faith approaches God boldly to receive from Him the things it needs.	10:37, 38	**Believe** in the miracles of Jesus.
	11:40	**Understand** that the glory of God is revealed to those who believe.
	13:17	**Recognize** that it is what you practice of God's Word that brings blessing to yourself and others.
	14:6, 7	**Recognize** that Jesus is the only way to God. **Know** Jesus to know God.
	14:12–14	**Pray for** and **expect** the "greater things" ministry of the church.
	16:24	**Do not neglect** to ask the Father for those things you need to live and do His work.

THE ACTS
of the Apostles

Author: Historically, Luke
Date: About A.D. 62
Theme: The Work of the Holy Spirit in the Early History of Christianity
Key Words: Jesus, Spirit, Resurrection, Apostle, Church

Author The Book of Acts does not specifically mention its author, but many indicators point to Luke, "the beloved physician" (Col. 4:14). The author was the same person as the one who wrote the Third Gospel (1:1, 2). He was a close associate of Paul, as indicated in the "we" sections of the book. The writer was a man of culture, as indicated by his literary style; he had a universal outlook; and he revealed an interest in medical matters. In addition, church tradition uniformly declares that Luke was the author of Acts. Therefore, the bulk of the evidence, both external and internal, supports Luke as the author.

Date Luke tells the story of the early church within the framework of geographical, political, and historical details that could only fit in the first century. For example, Luke's use of regional Roman governmental titles, which only someone living at the time could know precisely, suggests that the book was probably written within its actual time frame. Furthermore, there is no mention of the fall of Jerusalem in A.D. 70, and Nero's persecution of the Christians, which began about A.D. 64. Therefore, because of these facts, and because the book does not record the death of Paul but leaves him a prisoner in Rome, it is logical to date the writing of Acts near the end of the apostle's imprisonment there in about A.D. 62.

Content Acts is a sequel to the life of Christ in the Gospels, and it records the spread of Christianity from Jerusalem to Rome. It is the initiation of Jesus' Great Commission to make disciples of all nations (Matt. 28:18–20; Luke 24:46–49).

Acts 1:8 is the key to the book. Not only does this verse predict the outpouring of the Spirit and its powerful witness, but the geographical references present a simple outline of the narrative. In general, Acts relates the step-by-step expansion of Christianity westward from Palestine to Italy. The book thus begins in Jerusalem (chs. 1—7), with Peter assuming the major role and Jews as the recipients of the gospel.

Following the death of Stephen (7:60—8:1), widespread persecution broke out against the church, and believers scattered, sowing the seed of the gospel in Samaria and among the Gentiles (chs. 8—12). During this period of history the conversion of Saul occurred (ch. 9), an event of such importance that Luke includes three long descriptions of the incident (chs. 9; 22; 26).

The longest section of Acts focuses on the development and expansion of the Gentile ministry directed by Paul and his associates (chs. 13—28). It concludes with Paul's arrival in Rome, capital of the empire and representative of "the end of the earth." The book ends rather abruptly, because in all likelihood, Luke had brought the matter up-to-date, and there was no more to write.

Purpose The key to the purpose of Acts is in the first verse, where Luke implies that the book is a continuation of the Gospel of Luke. The Gospel told what "Jesus began both to do and teach," and Acts tells what the risen Lord continues to do and teach through the Holy Spirit.

Personal Application Acts is a record of *practicing* Christianity under the power of the Holy Spirit. It teaches believers how to live together in meaningful Christian fellowship, sharing freely with one another (2:42; 4:32–35).

Conversely, Acts also shows that Christians inevitably will have disagreements (6:1; 11:1–3; 15:2, 7; 15:36–39), but that God gives wisdom and grace to settle differences (15:12–22). Even though the early church had its share of strong personalities, there was still a willingness to listen and to submit to one another (15:6–14).

Probably the most prominent characteristic of the early Christians was their spiritual power. They fasted and prayed fervently (2:42; 6:4; 13:3), and their faith released the miracle-working power of God (3:16). Acts is about ordinary people doing extraordinary things. Signs followed those who believed! See Mark 16:17, 18.

Christ Revealed The Book of Acts records several examples of the early apostolic proclamation of the gospel of Jesus Christ, and the pattern is consistent. First, Jesus is presented as a historical figure, a man empowered to perform signs and wonders (2:22; 10:38). Next, the death of Jesus is attributed equally to the wickedness of men and to the purpose of God. On the one hand, the Jews had "crucified" Him "by lawless hands" (2:23; see 3:13–15; 4:10; 5:30; 7:52; 10:39; 13:28). On the other hand, Jesus had been "delivered by the determined purpose and foreknowledge of God" (2:23; see 17:3). Then the resurrection of Jesus is emphasized, particularly as the fulfillment of Old Testament prophecy and as God's reversal of men's verdict on Jesus (1:3; 2:24–32; 4:10; 5:30; 10:40, 41; 13:30–37; 17:31). The apostles declare that Jesus has been exalted to a position of unique and universal dominion (2:33–36; 3:21; 5:31). From that place of supreme honor and executive power Jesus had poured out the promised Holy Spirit (2:33), who bears witness to Him (5:32) and empowers believers (1:8). Jesus has been "ordained by God *to be* Judge of the living and the dead" (10:42) and will return in triumph at the end of the age (1:11). Meanwhile, those who believe in Him will receive forgiveness of sins (2:21; 3:19; 4:12; 5:31; 10:43; 13:38, 39) and "the gift of the Holy Spirit" (2:38). Those who do not believe in Him are destined for terrible things (3:23).

The Holy Spirit at Work The power of the Holy Spirit through the church is the most striking feature in Acts. The book has even been called *The Acts of the Holy Spirit.* The work of the Spirit in Acts, however, cannot be understood without seeing the relationship between Acts and the Gospels, which demonstrates an essential continuity. Both the public ministry of Jesus in the Gospels and the public ministry of the church in Acts begin with a life-changing encounter with the Spirit; both are essential accounts of the results of that event.

The power of the Spirit in Jesus' life authorized Him to preach the kingdom of God and to demonstrate kingdom power by healing the sick, casting out demons, and setting the captives free (Luke 4:14–19; Matt. 4:23). The same Spirit power in Acts 2 gave the same authority to the disciples. Jesus is the prototype of the Spirit-filled, Spirit-empowered life (10:38). *The Book of Acts is the story of the disciples receiving what Jesus received in order to do what Jesus did.*

Luke's terminology in describing people's experience with the Holy Spirit in Acts is fluid. He is more interested in conveying a relational dynamic than in delineating a precisely worded theology. He notes that people were "filled with the Holy Spirit" (2:4; 9:17), that "they received the Holy Spirit" (8:17), that "the Holy Spirit fell upon [them]" (10:44), that "the Holy Spirit had been poured out on [them]" (10:45), and that "the Holy Spirit came upon them" (Acts 19:6). These are all then essential equivalents of Jesus' promise that the church would "be baptized with the Holy Spirit" (1:5; see especially its immediate fulfillment in 2:4, which Luke describes as a filling).

Three of these five instances record specific special manifestations of the Spirit in which the people themselves participated. Those on the Day of Pentecost and the Gentiles of Cornelius's house spoke with other tongues (2:4; 10:46); the Ephesians "spoke with tongues and prophesied" (19:6). Although it is not specified, it is generally agreed that there was also some type of manifestation in which the Samaritans participated because Luke says that "when Simon *saw* that . . . the Holy Spirit was given" (8:18).

Outline of Acts

1. Supernatural release from prison 5:17–21
2. The boldness of the apostles 5:22–32
3. The counsel of Gamaliel to release the apostles 5:33–42

V. The ministry of Stephen 6:1—7:60
A. His selection as one of the seven deacons 6:1–7
B. His power, ministry, and arrest 6:8–15
C. His defense before the Sanhedrin 7:1–53
D. His martyrdom 7:54–60

VI. The first ministry to non-Jews 8:1–40
A. To the Samaritans (Philip and Peter) 8:1–25
B. To the Ethiopian (Philip) 8:26–40

VII. The conversion of Saul 9:1–31

VIII. Aeneas and Dorcas healed through Peter's ministry 9:32–43

IX. The story of Cornelius 10:1—11:18
A. Cornelius and his house come to Christ 10:1–48
B. Peter defends his witness to the Gentiles 11:1–18

X. The witness of the early church 11:19—12:24
A. Paul and Barnabas at Antioch 11:19–30
B. Peter's miraculous escape from Herod's prison 12:1–24

Part Two: Paul and the international outreach of the church at Antioch 12:25—28:31

I. Paul's first missionary journey 12:25—14:28
A. Paul's apostolic commission 12:25—13:3
B. Exorcism on Cyprus 13:4–12
C. Preaching and revival at Antioch in Pisidia 13:13–50
D. Signs and wonders at Iconium 13:51—14:5
E. Healing and stoning at Lystra 14:6–20
F. Follow-up ministry and return to Antioch 14:21–28

II. The Council at Jerusalem to discuss law and grace 15:1–35

III. Paul's second missionary journey 15:36—18:22
A. Paul and Barnabas divide over Mark 15:36–41
B. Follow-up ministry with Timothy 16:1–5
C. The vision to evangelize Greece 16:6–10
D. Baptism of Lydia at Philippi 16:11–15
E. Imprisonment at Philippi 16:16–40
F. Riot at Thessalonica 17:1–9
G. Openness to the Word in Berea 17:10–15
H. Philosophizing in Athens 17:16–34
I. One and a half years in Corinth 18:1–17
J. Return to Antioch 18:18–22

IV. Paul's third missionary journey 18:23—21:14
A. Ministry, miracles, and rioting in Ephesus 18:23—19:41
B. Journeys in Greece 20:1–6
C. Paul's all-night sermon in Troas 20:7–12
D. From Troas to Miletus and Paul's farewell address to the Ephesian elders 20:13–38
E. Paul is warned about Jerusalem in Tyre and by Agabus in Caesarea 21:1–14

V. Paul's journey to Rome through Jerusalem 21:15—28:31
A. Paul returns to Jerusalem 21:15—23:35
1. Paul's return and arrest 21:15–36
2. Paul's defense before the Jerusalem mob 21:37—22:29
3. Paul's defense before the Sanhedrin 22:30—23:10
4. The plot to kill Paul 23:11–35
B. Paul's defense before Felix 24:1–27
C. Paul's defense before Festus and Agrippa 25:1—26:32
D. The voyage to Rome 27:1—28:31

Prologue

THE former account I made, O [a]Theophilus, of all that Jesus began both to do and teach,

2 [a]until the day in which [1]He was taken up, after He through the Holy Spirit [b]had given commandments to the apostles whom He had chosen,

3 [a]to whom He also presented Himself alive after His suffering by many [1]infallible proofs, being seen by them during forty days and speaking of the things pertaining to the kingdom of God.

The Holy Spirit Promised

4 [a]And being assembled together with *them,* He commanded them not to depart from Jerusalem, but to wait for the *Promise of the Father, "which," *He said,* "you have [b]heard from Me;

5 [a]"for John truly baptized with water, [b]but you shall be baptized with the Holy Spirit not many days from now."

6 Therefore, when they had come together, they asked Him, saying, "Lord, will You at this time restore the kingdom to Israel?"

7 And He said to them, [a]"It is not for you to [b]know **times** or *seasons which the Father has put in His own *authority.

2 8 [a]"But you shall receive power [b]when the Holy Spirit has come upon you; and [c]you shall be [1]witnesses to Me in Jerusalem, and in all Judea and [d]Samaria, and to the [e]end of the earth."

CHAPTER 1

1 [a]Luke 1:3
2 [a]Mark 16:19; Acts 1:9, 11, 22 [b]Matt. 28:19; Mark 16:15; John 20:21; Acts 10:42 [1]He ascended into heaven.
3 [a]Matt. 28:17; Mark 16:12, 14; Luke 24:34, 36; John 20:19, 26; 21:1, 14; 1 Cor. 15:5–7 [1]*unmistakable*
4 [a]Luke 24:49 [b][John 14:16, 17, 26; 15:26]; Acts 2:33 *See WW at Acts 13:32.
5 [a]Matt. 3:11; Mark 1:8; Luke 3:16; John 1:33; Acts 11:16 [b][Joel 2:28]
7 [a]1 Thess. 5:1 [b]Matt. 24:36; Mark 13:32 *See WW at Col. 4:5. • See WW at Mark 3:15.
8 [a][Acts 2:1, 4] [b]Luke 24:49 [c]Luke 24:48; John 15:27 [d]Acts 8:1, 5, 14 [e]Matt. 28:19; Mark 16:15; Rom. 10:18; Col. 1:23; [Rev. 14:6] [1]NU *My witnesses*

WORD WEALTH

1:7 times, *chronos* (*khron*-oss); Strong's *#5550:* Compare "chronology," "chronic," "chronicles." Duration of time, which may be a point, a lapse, a span, a period, a stretch, a quantity, a measure, a duration, or a length. *Kairos* ("seasons") suggests kind of time. *Chronos* tells what day it is. *Kairos* tells of special happenings occurring during the time frame of *chronos.*

KINGDOM DYNAMICS

1:3–8 Receiving Kingdom Power, MINISTRY OF THE KINGDOM. As Jesus presented post-Resurrection teaching "pertaining to the kingdom of God" (v. 3), His disciples asked if now—with the Cross behind—the ultimate messianic kingdom would come. "It is not yours to know the future," He says, "but it is yours to receive the Spirit's power!" With those words, He makes three points: 1) The Holy Spirit is the Person and the Power by which assistance and ability are given for serving, for sharing the life and power of God's kingdom with others. 2) The Holy Spirit's power must be "received"; it is not an automatic experience. As surely as the Holy Spirit indwells each believer (Rom. 8:9), so surely will He fill and overflow (John 7:37–39) each who receives the Holy Spirit in childlike faith. 3) When the Holy Spirit fills you, you will know it. Jesus said it and the disciples found it true (Acts 1:5; 2:1–4). Have you received the Holy Spirit? (19:1–6). You may, for the promise is as fully yours today as at any time in the past (2:38, 39).

(Luke 11:20/Luke 4:1–12) J.W.H.

1:1 The former account refers to the Gospel of Luke. **Theophilus** is the unknown recipient. His name means "Loved by God," and in Luke 1:3 he is called "most excellent," a formal title of respect. Physicians like Luke (Col. 4:14) were often slaves. Theophilus may have been Luke's former master.

1:2 Acts reveals the transfer of Christ's authority and mission to His disciples. The word **apostles** became a designation for those with the gift to work miracles and start and oversee churches (see note on 1:22).

1:3 Alive . . . by many infallible proofs: The resurrection of Christ is the bedrock of Christianity and the initiating event of Acts (2:32, 33). **The kingdom of God,** the divine rule in human hearts, lives, and situations, was a prominent theme in Jesus' teaching. Jesus began to do and teach the kingdom through the Spirit's power (Luke 4:18, 19), and He is about to transfer that power and responsibility to His disciples by baptizing them in the same Spirit that had authorized His ministry.

1:5 You shall be baptized with the Holy Spirit is the source of the phrase "the baptism 'in' or 'with' the Holy Spirit." Acts has many synonyms for this dynamic. See Introduction to Acts: The Holy Spirit at Work. Many understand this as a work distinct from conversion, which is seen as being referred to in 1 Cor. 12:3, where the Holy Spirit is the Agent performing the baptizing work. See note on 2:4 and Holy Spirit Gifts and Power: How Can Spiritual Integrity Be Maintained?

1:6 The disciples are still thinking of the messianic kingdom in terms of *political* power.

1:7, 8 In His reply Jesus corrects their misconception and adjusts their perspective concerning the kingdom of God. He declares that the kingdom is currently spiritual in its character, international in its membership, and gradual in its expansion. **The Holy Spirit . . . upon** one is an important concept in Luke and Acts, and Jesus is a primary example of the work of the Holy Spirit *within* and *upon* us. Jesus' life was conceived by the Spirit, and the Spirit working *within* Him brought forth the fruit of good character (Luke 2:52). Later the Spirit came *upon* Jesus to bring forth a ministry of power (Luke 3:22; 4:18). The distinctive purpose of the outpouring of the Spirit in Acts is to empower the church for ministry. See Introduction to Acts: The Holy Spirit at Work.

1:8 See section 2 of Truth-In-Action at the end of Acts.

KINGDOM DYNAMICS

1:8 Christ's Final Charter and Promise, WORLD EVANGELISM. In five NT references, Jesus directly charges His disciples to go and preach the gospel to all the world (Matt. 28:18–20; Mark 16:15–18; Luke 24:45–48; John 20:21–23; Acts 1:8). Here His Great Commission is preceded by His promise of the outpouring of the Holy Spirit. Empowerment for world evangelism is tied inseparably to this promise. There is obvious need for power if people are to fully perceive the gospel. But prior to that, another issue awaits resolution. The Spirit has come to convince us to go. We need power to serve effectively, to heal the sick, and to deliver those possessed of unclean spirits. But let us first receive the Holy Spirit's first anointing—power to *act*—to go. Then, He will give 1) power to find the lost; 2) authority to boldly declare Jesus as the Son of God; and 3) power to establish His church—locally and worldwide. The intended borders of expansion are clear: Jerusalem (local), Judea (national), Samaria (cross-cultural) and "the end of the earth" (international). Jesus' last earthly command points to His power and His pathways for global evangelism.
(John 20:21–23/Acts 4:12) G.C.

Jesus Ascends to Heaven

9 [a]Now when He had spoken these
things, while they watched, [b]He was
taken up, and a cloud received Him out
of their sight.
10 And while they looked steadfastly
toward heaven as He went up, behold,
two men stood by them [a]in white apparel,
11 who also said, "Men of Galilee, why
do you stand gazing up into *heaven?
This *same* Jesus, who was taken up
from you into heaven, [a]will so come
in like manner as you saw Him go into
heaven."

KINGDOM DYNAMICS

1:10, 11 Confirmed: Jesus Will Return, MESSIAH'S COMING. Before Jesus left His disciples He promised them that He would return (John 14:1–3). Here, at the ascension of Jesus, the promise is reiterated. In essence, the angels say to the disciples, "Do not stand here looking at the sky! Jesus will return, but now you go and do what He told you to do." We frequently need to be reminded of these words. Often we get so caught up in the precious promise of the Lord's return that we forget that His promise should also affect how we behave toward the world. Jesus has given each of us an assignment, and "blessed *is* that servant whom his master, when he comes, will find so doing" (Matt. 24:46).
(John 14:1–3/1 Thess. 4:15–18) J.H.

9 [a]Luke 24:50, 51 [b]Ps. 68:18; 110:1; Mark 16:19; Luke 23:43; John 20:17; Acts 1:2; [Heb. 4:14; 9:24; 1 Pet. 3:22]
10 [a]Matt. 28:3; Mark 16:5; Luke 24:4; John 20:12; Acts 10:3, 30
11 [a]Dan. 7:13; Mark 13:26; Luke 21:27; [John 14:3]; 2 Thess. 1:10; Rev. 1:7 *See WW at Rev. 21:1.

The Upper Room Prayer Meeting

12 [a]Then they returned to Jerusalem
from the mount called Olivet, which is
near Jerusalem, a Sabbath day's journey.
13 And when they had entered, they
went up [a]into the upper room where
they were staying: [b]Peter, James, John,
and Andrew; Philip and Thomas; Bartholomew and Matthew; James *the son*
of Alphaeus and [c]Simon the Zealot;
and [d]Judas *the son* of James.
14 [a]These all continued *with one
[1]accord in prayer [2]and supplication,
with [b]the women and Mary the mother
of Jesus, and with [c]His brothers.

KINGDOM DYNAMICS

1:14 Unity and Harmony, LEADER TRAITS. Being "of one accord" is a dominant trait of NT leadership. Whenever the early church leaders gathered in Jerusalem, it is said they were in unity and harmony, with each other and with God (2:46; 4:24; 5:12; 15:25). Their agreement was spiritual and practical, not only theological, for they shared their lives and possessions. Acts 2:42–47 gives a description of NT leadership: meeting together, studying together, sharing their material possessions (2:45; 4:32–37; 6:1). They met often to pray, revealing not only relationship with each other but their total reliance on God (2:42; 4:31; 12:5; 13:3).
(Acts 2:22/Ex. 27:1—28:43) J.B.

Matthias Chosen

15 And in those days Peter stood up
in the midst of the [1]disciples (altogether the number [a]of names was

12 [a]Luke 24:52
13 [a]Mark 14:15; Luke 22:12; Acts 9:37, 39; 20:8 [b]Matt. 10:2–4 [c]Luke 6:15 [d]Jude 1
14 [a]Acts 2:1, 46 [b]Luke 23:49, 55 [c]Matt. 13:55 [1]*purpose* or *mind* [2]NU omits *and supplication* *See WW at Acts 2:1.
15 [a]Luke 22:32; Rev. 3:4 [1]NU *brethren*

1:9 The **cloud** is likely a reference to the radiant cloud of God's special glory, the *Shekinah* (see Matt. 17:5).

1:11 Will so come in like manner: Jesus will return bodily, literally.

1:12 The mount called Olivet was just outside Jerusalem, overlooking the city from the east. **A Sabbath day's journey** was about ¾ mile.

1:14 Fervent and persistent **prayer** is prominent in Acts. Here the prayer is an obedient response to Jesus' command to wait in Jerusalem (v. 4).

1:15 The phrase **Peter stood up** points to the beginning of Peter's formal leadership and the first major section of the book.

about a hundred and twenty), and said,
16 "Men *and* brethren, this *Scripture
had to be fulfilled, [a]which the Holy
Spirit spoke before by the mouth of
David concerning Judas, [b]who became
a guide to those who arrested Jesus;
17 "for [a]he was numbered with us and
obtained a part in [b]this ministry."
18 [a](Now this man purchased a field
with [b]the [1]wages* of iniquity; and falling headlong, he burst open in the middle and all his [2]entrails gushed out.
19 And it became known to all those
dwelling in Jerusalem; so that field is
called in their own language, Akel
Dama, that is, Field of Blood.)
20 "For it is written in the Book of
Psalms:

> [a]*'Let his dwelling place be*
> *[1]desolate,*
> *And let no one live in it';*

and,

> [b]*'Let another take his [2]office.'*

21 "Therefore, of these men who have
accompanied us all the time that the
Lord Jesus went in and out among us,
22 "beginning from the *baptism of
John to that day when [a]He was taken
up from us, one of these must [b]become
a *witness with us of His *resurrection."
23 And they proposed two: Joseph
called [a]Barsabas, who was surnamed
Justus, and Matthias.
24 And they prayed and said, "You, O
Lord, [a]who know the hearts of all,
show which of these two You have
chosen
25 [a]"to take part in this ministry and
apostleship from which Judas by **transgression** fell, that he might go to his
own place."

WORD WEALTH

1:25 transgression, *parabaino* (par-ab-*ahee*-no); Strong's *#3845:* Abandoning a trust, departing, stepping aside, overstep, violation, rebellion, aberration, apostasy, disobedience, deviation from an original and true direction. In order to go his own way, Judas abandoned his position of service as one of the Twelve.

26 And they cast their lots, and the lot
fell on Matthias. And he was numbered
with the eleven *apostles.

Coming of the Holy Spirit

2 When [a]the Day of Pentecost had
fully come, [b]they were all [1]**with
one accord** in one place.

WORD WEALTH

2:1 with one accord, *homothumadon* (hom-oth-oo-mad-*on*); Strong's *#3661:* Being unanimous, having mutual consent, being in agreement, having group unity, having one mind and purpose. The disciples had an intellectual unanimity, an emotional rapport, and volitional agreement in the newly founded church. In each of its occurrences, *homothumadon* shows a harmony leading to action.

2 And suddenly there came a sound
from *heaven, as of a rushing mighty
wind, and [a]it filled the whole house
where they were sitting.
3 Then there appeared to them
[1]divided tongues, as of fire, and *one* sat
upon each of them.
4 And [a]they were all filled with the 2

16 [a]Ps. 41:9 [b]Luke 22:47 *See WW at John 5:39.
17 [a]Matt. 10:4 [b]Acts 1:25
18 [a]Matt. 27:3–10 [b]Mark 14:21 [1]*reward of unrighteousness* [2]*intestines* *See WW at Rev. 22:12.
20 [a]Ps. 69:25 [b]Ps. 109:8 [1]*deserted* [2]Gr. *episkopen,* position of overseer
22 [a]Acts 1:9 [b]Acts 1:8; 2:32 *See WW at Matt. 21:25. • See WW at Rev. 1:5. • See WW at Acts 23:6.
23 [a]Acts 15:22
24 [a]1 Sam. 16:7
25 [a]Acts 1:17
26 *See WW at 1 Cor. 12:28.

CHAPTER 2

1 [a]Lev. 23:15 [b]Acts 1:14 [1]NU *together*
2 [a]Acts 4:31 *See WW at Rev. 21:1.
3 [1]Or *tongues as of fire, distributed and resting on each*
4 [a]Acts 1:5

1:18 There is no discrepancy with Matt. 27:5–10. The priests, considering the bribe money paid to Judas to be his legal property, **purchased** the **field** in his name. After Judas hanged himself, his body fell when the rope broke or was cut by someone. Luke describes the gruesome results of the suicide.

1:22 A witness . . . of His resurrection was the essential requirement for serving as one of the original 12 apostles. These, of course, have died, but the general ministry of apostleship remains (Eph. 4:11).

1:26 Casting **lots** was a provision of the Law (Lev. 16:8). It may be significant that following the outpouring of the Holy Spirit at Pentecost there is no more mention of the practice. Notice also that on this occasion the disciples first selected the two men they judged most worthy to fill the vacancy. The final decision was left to the Lord as they prayed (v. 24). To be certain of His will they cast lots. Afterward the Holy Spirit provided the needed guidance.

2:1 Pentecost was an annual Jewish festival, also known as the "Feast of Weeks," or the "Day of Firstfruits," a celebration of the first buds of the harvest. Jewish men were required by law to go to Jerusalem three times each year to celebrate the major feasts (Deut. 16:16): Passover in the spring; Pentecost (Greek *pentekostos,* "fifty") seven weeks and a day later (Lev. 23:15, 16); and Tabernacles at the end of the harvest in the fall. Lev. 23 details the dates and rituals of the Jewish festival calendar. Those who became Christians on Pentecost were the firstfruits of a vast harvest of millions of souls.

2:2 As of a rushing mighty wind: Not a wind, but *like* the sound of a wind (see John 3:8), suggesting the mighty but unseen power of the Spirit.

2:3 Tongues, as of fire: Not fire, but *like* fire. John the Baptist foretold how Spirit baptism would be accompanied by wind and fire (Matt. 3:11, 12). This may also be an allusion to the burning bush (Ex. 3:2–5), which was a symbol of the divine presence. This outward manifestation of the Spirit's coming was another sign of His power.

2:4 See section 2 of Truth-In-Action at the end of Acts.

2:4 This is the initial fulfillment of Jesus' promise in 1:5, 8.

Holy Spirit and began [b]to speak with other tongues, as the Spirit gave them utterance.

4 [b]Mark 16:17; Acts 10:46; 19:6; [1 Cor. 12:10, 28, 30; 13:1]

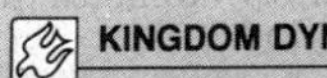

KINGDOM DYNAMICS

2:4 Holy Spirit Baptism: Case Histories, SPIRITUAL GIFTS. The Book of Acts provides the case history accounts of receiving the infilling of or baptism in the Holy Spirit (2:4; 8:14–25; 9:17–20; 10:44–48; 19:1–7). An elaboration of this and related themes appears in the study article on page 2018, "Holy Spirit Gifts and Power."

(John 14:16, 17/Acts 10:46) P.W.

The interchangeable terms in each of the three references is common to Acts. See Introduction to Acts: The Holy Spirit at Work. The OT expectation about the coming of the Spirit and the beginning of a new era is at last fulfilled.

Other tongues here refers to spoken human languages, unknown to the speakers but known by others (v. 6); a distinct practice of the Spirit's fullness that evolved at some later point in the development of the church is that of speaking "with the [unknown] tongues . . . of angels" (1 Cor. 13:1). **Began to speak** indicates that they continued in the process (see 11:15). Luke could be indicating that they continued speaking for an extended time; more likely, however, he is indicating that this practice continued in their lives, just as he records the church's continuation of what Jesus "began both to do and to teach" (1:1).

Many contemporary Christians from all denominational backgrounds, believe that the phenomenon of "speaking with tongues" (languages not formerly learned or known by the speaker) may accompany the occasion of a person's initial surrender to the fullness of the Holy Spirit. In classical Pentecostal tradition, this experience is expected, and is doctrinally expressed in the words, "The initial physical evidence of the baptism with the Holy Spirit is speaking with other tongues." Other Christians and many Charismatics who do not accept this doctrinal terminology still apply its fundamental implications in their practice.

This modified view, which is also accepted by some Pentecostals, places less emphasis on the importance of tongues as the evidence of the baptism with the Holy Spirit, either in terms of one's initial experience or one's ongoing life of Spirit fullness. These focus more on all the gifts, with speaking in tongues seen as but one of them, since all the gifts are deemed contemporarily operational and any one of them may serve as a sign of one's baptism in the Spirit. Further, one's deepened participation in worship is also seen as a fundamental indication of being baptized in the Spirit, with the continual exercise of tongue-speaking as a part of the believer's private devotional expression (see 1 Cor. 14:1, 2, 4, 15, 39, 40).

Some other Christians who disagree with any of the above views usually explain the baptism with the Holy Spirit in one of the following ways:

(a) As an experience subsequent to salvation, bringing needed divine power for Christian witness and service, but without any expectation of the Holy Spirit's gifts attending this experience.

(b) As synonymous with one's conversion experience, when the Holy Spirit merges the individual into the body of Christ at the time the believer places his faith in Jesus as Lord (1 Cor. 12:3, 13).

(c) As unique to the Book of Acts; claiming the baptism with the Holy Spirit, including its miraculous manifestations, was solely a single event of a single divine outpouring, first at Pentecost (though repeated at later junctures, when the ethnic barriers of the Samaritans [ch. 8] and Gentiles [ch. 10] were breached).

The Nations of Pentecost. In the first Christian century, Jewish communities were located primarily in the eastern part of the Roman Empire, where Greek was the common language, but also existed as far west as Italy and as far east as Babylonia. In addition to people from the nations shown here, those present on the Day of Pentecost (Acts 2:9–11) included visitors from Mesopotamia and even farther east, from Parthia, Media, and Elam (present-day Iran).

The Crowd's Response

5 And there were dwelling in Jerusalem Jews, [a]devout men, from every nation under heaven.
6 And when this sound occurred, the [a]multitude came together, and were confused, because everyone heard them speak in his own language.
7 Then they were all amazed and marveled, saying to one another, "Look, are not all these who speak [a]Galileans?
8 "And how *is it that* we hear, each in our own [1]language in which we were born?
9 "Parthians and Medes and Elamites, those dwelling in Mesopotamia, Judea and [a]Cappadocia, Pontus and Asia,
10 "Phrygia and Pamphylia, Egypt and the parts of Libya adjoining Cyrene, visitors from Rome, both Jews and proselytes,
11 "Cretans and [1]Arabs—we hear them speaking in our own tongues the **wonderful works** of God."

5 [a]Luke 2:25; Acts 8:2
6 [a]Acts 4:32
7 [a]Matt. 26:73; Acts 1:11
8 [1]*dialect*
9 [a]1 Pet. 1:1
11 [1]*Arabians*

WORD WEALTH

2:11 wonderful works, *megaleios* (meg-al-*eye*-oss); Strong's *#3167:* Conspicuous, magnificent, splendid, majestic, sublime, grand, beautiful, excellent, favorable. Used here and in Luke 1:49. The amazed visitors at Pentecost heard the disciples in their own languages reciting the sublime greatness of God and His mighty deeds.

12 So they were all amazed and perplexed, saying to one another, "Whatever could this mean?"

2:5 These international Jews had made the pilgrimage to Jerusalem to celebrate the festival of Pentecost (see note on v. 1).

THE WORK OF THE HOLY SPIRIT (2:4)

In the beginning
- Active and present at creation, hovering over the unordered conditions (Gen. 1:2)

In the Old Testament
- The origin of supernatural abilities (Gen. 41:38)
- The giver of artistic skill (Ex. 31:2–5)
- The source of power and strength (Judg. 3:9, 10)
- The inspiration of prophecy (1 Sam. 19:20, 23)
- The mediation of God's message (Mic. 3:8)

In Old Testament prophecy
- The cleansing of the heart for holy living (Ezek. 36:25–29)

In salvation
- Brings conviction (John 16:8–11)
- Regenerates the believer (Titus 3:5)
- Sanctifies the believer (2 Thess. 2:13)
- Completely indwells the believer (John 14:17; Rom. 8:9–11)

In the New Testament
- Imparts spiritual truth (John 14:26; 16:13; 1 Cor. 2:13–15)
- Glorifies Christ (John 16:14)
- Endows with power for gospel proclamation (Acts 1:8)
- Fills believers (Acts 2:4)
- Pours out God's love in the heart (Rom. 5:5)
- Enables believers to walk in holiness (Rom. 8:1–8; Gal. 5:16–25)
- Makes intercession (Rom. 8:26)
- Imparts gifts for ministry (1 Cor. 12:4–11)
- Strengthens the inner being (Eph. 3:16)

In the written Word
- Inspired the writing of Scripture (2 Tim. 3:16; 2 Pet. 1:21)

The New Testament understands the Holy Spirit to be the assurance of the risen Lord Jesus indwelling believers.

13 Others mocking said, "They are full
of new wine."

Peter's Sermon

14 But Peter, standing up with the
eleven, raised his voice and said to
them, "Men of Judea and all who dwell
in Jerusalem, let this be known to you,
and heed my words.
15 "For these are not drunk, as you
suppose, [a]since it is *only* [1]the third
hour of the day.
16 "But this is what was spoken by the
prophet Joel:

17 *'And[a] it shall come to pass in the*
last days, says God,
[b]That I will pour out of My Spirit
*on all *flesh;*
Your sons and [c]your daughters
shall prophesy,
Your young men shall see visions,
Your old men shall dream
dreams.
18 *And on My menservants and on*
My maidservants
I will pour out My Spirit in those
days;
[a]And they shall prophesy.
19 *[a]I will show *wonders in heaven*
above
And signs in the earth beneath:
Blood and fire and vapor of
smoke.
20 *[a]The sun shall be turned into*
darkness,
And the moon into blood,
Before the coming of the great
and awesome day of the LORD.
21 *And it shall come to pass*
That [a]whoever calls on the name
of the LORD
*Shall be *saved.'*

22 "Men of Israel, hear these words:
*Jesus of Nazareth, a Man attested by
God to you [a]by miracles, wonders, and
*signs which God did through Him in
your midst, as you yourselves also
know—

15 [a]1 Thess. 5:7 [1]9 A.M.
17 [a]Is. 44:3; Ezek. 11:19; Joel 2:28–32; [Zech. 12:10; John 7:38] [b]Acts 10:45 [c]Acts 21:9 *See WW at Matt. 26:41.
18 [a]Acts 21:4, 9; 1 Cor. 12:10
19 [a]Joel 2:30 *See WW at Acts 15:12.
20 [a]Is. 13:10; Ezek. 32:7; Matt. 24:29; Mark 13:24, 25; Luke 21:25; Rev. 6:12
21 [a]Rom. 10:13 *See WW at Luke 7:50.
22 [a]Is. 50:5; John 3:2; 5:6; Acts 10:38 *See WW at Phil. 4:23. • See WW at Rev. 16:14.
23 [a]Matt. 26:4; Luke 22:22; Acts 3:18; 4:28; [1 Pet. 1:20] [b]Acts 5:30 [1]NU omits *have taken*
24 [a][Rom. 8:11; 1 Cor. 6:14; 2 Cor. 4:14; Eph. 1:20; Col. 2:12]; 1 Thess. 1:10; Heb. 13:20 [1]*destroyed* or *abolished* [2]Lit. *birth pangs*
25 [a]Ps.16:8–11
27 [a]Acts 13:30–37

KINGDOM DYNAMICS

2:22 Miracles, Signs, and Wonders, LEADER TRAITS. Without exception, miracles, signs, and wonders accompanied the ministry and preaching of early church leaders. Here Peter reminded the people that Jesus' credibility was based on His miracle ministry. This same credibility accompanied those set apart in leadership, such as Stephen, Philip, Barnabas, Silas, and Paul, as well as the original apostles (6:8; 8:6; 15:12; 19:11, 12).

Miracles, signs, and wonders were commonly accepted in the early church; and leaders led the way in giving place to such ministry. Also, the early church leaders prayed for miracles (Acts 4:30), seeing them not as random, occasional events, but as worthy evidences of God's anointing continually glorifying Christ through the church, and therefore to be sought and welcomed.

(Acts 16:6–10/Acts 1:14) J.B.

23 "Him, [a]being delivered by the determined purpose and foreknowledge of
God, [b]you [1]have taken by lawless
hands, have crucified, and put to death;
24 [a]"whom God raised up, having
[1]loosed the [2]pains of death, because it
was not possible that He should be held
by it.
25 "For David says concerning Him:

[a]'I foresaw the LORD always before
my face,
For He is at my right hand, that
I may not be shaken.
26 *Therefore my heart rejoiced, and*
my tongue was glad;
Moreover my flesh also will rest
in hope.
27 *For You will not leave my soul in*
Hades,
Nor will You allow Your Holy
One to see [a]corruption.
28 *You have made known to me the*
ways of life;
You will make me full of joy in
Your presence.'

2:13 The mockers apparently formed this conclusion from the fact that they did not recognize some of the sounds.
2:14 Peter is the spokesman for the disciples and takes the lead role in Acts at this point.
2:15 The third hour of the day was about 9:00 A.M.
2:17, 18 The last days refer to the era of the church from Pentecost to the return of Christ (see Heb. 1:1, 2). They are an overlap of this age and the Age to Come. **I will pour out of My Spirit on all flesh:** Peter explains the unusual events of Pentecost in terms of the outpouring of the Spirit predicted in Joel's messianic word. The outpouring of the Spirit in the OT had been largely reserved for the spiritual and national leaders of Israel. Under the New Covenant, however, the authority of the Spirit is for "all flesh," all who come under the New Covenant. Every believer is anointed to be a priest and king to God. Important evidences of participation in the Spirit's outpouring are **dreams** and prophecies.
2:19–21 Joel prophesied that this present age would end amidst mighty portents and in divine judgment, but that **whoever calls on the name of the LORD shall be saved.** Peter will proceed to establish that Jesus is the Lord who will return in judgment and upon whom people must now call in repentance and faith.

29 "Men *and* brethren, let *me* speak
freely to you [a]of the patriarch David,
that he is both dead and buried, and
his tomb is with us to this day.
30 "Therefore, being a prophet,
[a]and knowing that God had sworn
with an oath to him that of the fruit
of his body, [1]according to the flesh, He
would raise up the Christ to sit on his
throne,
31 "he, foreseeing this, spoke concerning the resurrection of the *Christ,
[a]that His soul was not left in Hades,
nor did His flesh see corruption.
32 [a]"This Jesus God has raised up,
[b]of which we are all witnesses.
33 "Therefore [a]being exalted [1]to
[b]the right hand of God, and [c]having
received from the Father the *promise
of the Holy Spirit, He [d]poured out this
which you now see and hear.
34 "For David did not ascend into the
heavens, but he says himself:

> [a]*'The LORD said to my Lord,*
> *"Sit at My right hand,*
> 35 *Till I make Your enemies Your*
> *footstool."'*

36 "Therefore let all the house of Israel
know assuredly that God has made this
Jesus, whom you crucified, both Lord
and Christ."
37 Now when they heard *this,* [a]they
were cut to the heart, and said to Peter
and the rest of the apostles, "Men *and*
brethren, what shall we do?"
1 38 Then Peter said to them, [a]"Repent,*
and let every one of you be baptized
in the name of Jesus Christ for the
[1]remission of sins; and you shall receive the gift of the Holy Spirit.
39 "For the promise is to you and
[a]to your children, and [b]to all who are
afar off, as many as the Lord our God
will call."

29 [a]Acts 13:36
30 [a]Ps. 132:11
[1]NU *He would seat one on his throne,*
31 [a]Ps. 16:10
*See WW at 2 Tim. 4:22.
32 [a]Acts 2:24
[b]Acts 1:8; 3:15
33 [a][Acts 5:31]
[b][Heb. 10:12]
[c][John 14:26]
[d]Acts 2:1–11, 17; 10:45
[1]Possibly *by*
*See WW at Acts 13:32.
34 [a]Ps. 68:18; 110:1
37 [a]Luke 3:10, 12, 14
38 [a]Luke 24:47
[1]*forgiveness*
*See WW at Matt. 3:2.
39 [a]Joel 2:28, 32
[b]Eph. 2:13

KINGDOM DYNAMICS

2:38, 39 5. How Do I Receive the Baptism in the Holy Spirit?, SPIRITUAL ANSWERS. For the answer to this and other probing questions about God and the power life in His kingdom, see the study article "Spiritual Answers to Hard Questions," which begins on page 1996.

P.R.

A Vital Church Grows

40 And with many *other words he testified and exhorted them, saying, "Be
saved from this [1]perverse generation."
41 Then those who [1]gladly received his
word were baptized; and that day
about three thousand *souls were
added *to them.*
42 [a]And they continued steadfastly in 3
the apostles' [1]doctrine and **fellowship,**
in the breaking of bread, and in prayers.

WORD WEALTH

2:42 fellowship, *koinonia* (koy-nohn-*ee*-ah); Strong's *#2842:* Sharing, unity, close association, partnership, participation, a society, a communion, a fellowship, contributory help, the brotherhood. (Compare "coin," "cenobite," "epicene.") *Koinonia* is a unity brought about by the Holy Spirit. In *koinonia* the individual shares in common an intimate bond of fellowship with the rest of the Christian society. *Koinonia* cements the believers to the Lord Jesus and to each other.

43 Then *fear came upon every soul,
and [a]many wonders and signs were
done through the apostles.
44 Now all who believed were to-

40 [1]*crooked*
*See WW at Acts 4:12.
41 [1]NU omits *gladly*
*See WW at Luke 21:19.
42 [a]Acts 1:14
[1]*teaching*
43 [a]Acts 2:22
*See WW at 1 John 4:18.

2:29–32 Peter proves that the resurrection of Christ is foretold in the OT. Thus, his Jewish audience should readily accept Jesus as their Messiah.
2:33 See note on John 7:39.
2:34–36 The outpouring of the Spirit is a sign that Jesus has been exalted to the right hand of the Father. Pentecost is a sign that Jesus is Lord.
2:38–41 See section 1 of Truth-In-Action at the end of Acts.
2:38 Peter calls upon his audience to change their opinion of and attitude toward Christ and to **be baptized in the name of Jesus Christ** as a public acknowledgment that they had accepted Jesus as Messiah and Lord. "Name" suggested nature or character; therefore, to be baptized "in the name of Jesus" is to confess Him to be all that His name denotes. Baptism in and of itself is not a means of forgiveness and salvation (see 3:19). For the early church, however, there was no separation between ritual and reality. Coming to Christ and being baptized were mutually inclusive. See 22:16; Mark 16:16; 1 Pet. 3:21. **The gift of the Holy Spirit** must be distinguished from the gifts of the Spirit. The former is the Holy Spirit Himself, while the latter are special abilities granted by the Spirit to equip believers for service (see 1 Cor. 12:1–31).
2:39 The promise of the Holy Spirit (see v. 33; 1:4, 5; Luke 24:49) is a gift for every believer in every generation. **All who are afar off** includes Gentiles (see Is. 57:19; Eph. 2:13, 17). Peter's words clearly extend to every believer in every era and everywhere, full reason to expect the same resource and experience that was afforded the first believers who received the Holy Spirit at the birth of the church.
2:42–47 See section 3 of Truth-In-Action at the end of Acts.
2:42 These are four fundamental devotions of the church throughout this age. **The breaking of bread** is probably a reference to the Lord's Supper in conjunction with a full meal.
2:43 Fear is not terror, but awe.
2:44, 45 This was spontaneous and voluntary benevolence as a result of truly understanding God's love. Forced community is communism.

gether, and [a]had all things in common,
45 and [1]sold their possessions and
goods, and [a]divided[2] them among all,
as anyone had need.
46 [a]So continuing daily *with one accord [b]in the temple, and [c]breaking
bread from house to house, they ate
their food with gladness and simplicity
of heart,
47 praising God and having favor with
all the people. And [a]the Lord added
[1]to the *church daily those who were
being saved.

A Lame Man Healed

3 Now Peter and John went up together [a]to the temple at the hour
of prayer, [b]the ninth *hour.*
2 And [a]a certain man lame from his
mother's womb was carried, whom
they laid daily at the gate of the temple
which is called Beautiful, [b]to [1]ask*
alms from those who entered the temple;
3 who, seeing Peter and John about
to go into the temple, asked for alms.
4 And fixing his eyes on him, with
John, Peter said, "Look at us."
5 So he gave them his attention, expecting to receive something from
them.
6 Then Peter said, "Silver and gold I
do not have, but what I do have I give
you: [a]In the *name of Jesus Christ of
Nazareth, rise up and walk."

KINGDOM DYNAMICS

3:6 Jesus' Name: Faith's Complete Authority, FAITH'S CONFESSION. In this first recorded miracle performed by the disciples, we are given the key for use by all believers in exercising faith's authority. When commanding healing for the lame man, Peter employs the full name/title of our Lord: "Jesus Christ [Messiah] of Nazareth." "Jesus" ("Joshua" or "Yeshua") was a common name among the Jews and continues to be in many cultures today. But the declaration of His full name and title, a noteworthy practice in Acts, seems a good and practical lesson for us (see 2:22; 4:10). Let us be complete when claiming our authority over sickness, disease, or demons. In our confession of faith or proclamation of power, confess His deity and His lordship as the Christ (Messiah); use His precious name, as Jesus (Savior). Call upon Him as Lord Jesus, or Jesus Christ, or Jesus of Nazareth, there being no legal or ritual demand intended in this point. But it is wise to remember, just as we pray "in Jesus' name" (John 16:24), so we exercise all authority in Him—by the privilege of power He has given us in His name (Matt. 28:18; Mark 16:12; John 14:13, 14).

Many other compound names for Him are found in the Word of God. Let us declare them in faith, with prayer and full confidence.

(Mark 11:22–24/Acts 4:33) R.H.

7 And he took him by the right hand
and lifted *him* up, and immediately his
feet and ankle bones received strength.
8 So he, [a]leaping up, stood and
walked and entered the temple with
them—walking, leaping, and praising
God.
9 [a]And all the people saw him walking and praising God.
10 Then they knew that it was he who
[a]sat begging alms at the Beautiful Gate
of the temple; and they were filled with
wonder and amazement at what had
happened to him.

Preaching in Solomon's Portico

11 Now as the lame man who was
healed held on to Peter and John, all
the people ran together to them in the
porch [a]which is called Solomon's,
greatly amazed.
12 So when Peter saw *it,* he responded
to the people: "Men of Israel, why do
you marvel at this? Or why look so intently at us, as though by our own
power or godliness we had made this
man walk?
13 [a]"The God of Abraham, Isaac, and
Jacob, the God of our fathers,
[b]glorified His Servant Jesus, whom
you [c]delivered* up and [d]denied in the
presence of Pilate, when he was determined to let *Him* go.
14 "But you denied [a]the Holy One
[b]and the *Just, and [c]asked for a murderer to be granted to you,
15 "and killed the [1]Prince of life,
[a]whom God raised from the dead,
[b]of which we are witnesses.
16 [a]"And His name, through faith in

44 [a]Acts 4:32, 34, 37; 5:2
45 [a]Is. 58:7 [1]*would sell* [2]*distributed*
46 [a]Acts 1:14 [b]Luke 24:53 [c]Luke 24:30; Acts 2:42; 20:7; [1 Cor. 10:16] *See WW at Acts 2:1.
47 [a]Acts 5:14 [1]NU omits *to the church* *See WW at Acts 8:1.

CHAPTER 3

1 [a]Acts 2:46 [b]Ps. 55:17; Matt. 27:45; Acts 10:30
2 [a]Acts 14:8 [b]John 9:8; Acts 3:10 [1]Beg *See WW at Matt. 7:7.
6 [a]Acts 4:10 *See WW at John 12:13.
8 [a]Is. 35:6
9 [a]Acts 4:16, 21
10 [a]John 9:8; Acts 3:2
11 [a]John 10:23; Acts 5:12
13 [a]John 5:30 [b]Is. 49:3; John 7:39; 12:23; 13:31 [c]Matt. 27:2 [d]Matt. 27:20; Mark 15:11; Luke 23:18; John 18:40; Acts 13:28 *See WW at Luke 23:25.
14 [a]Ps. 16:10; Mark 1:24; Luke 1:35 [b]Acts 7:52; 2 Cor. 5:21 [c]John 18:40 *See WW at Matt. 1:19.
15 [a]Acts 2:24 [b]Acts 2:32 [1]Or *Originator*
16 [a]Matt. 9:22; Acts 4:10; 14:9

3:1 At this early point in the history of the church, the Jewish Christians were still praying in **the temple. The ninth *hour*** was about 3:00 P.M.
3:12–26 Most of the sermons in Acts contain four elements: 1) a proclamation that the age of the Messiah has finally come; 2) quotations from the OT to prove that Jesus is the Messiah; 3) a review of the life and ministry of Jesus, especially His resurrection; 4) a call to repentance.
3:16 Healing is by **faith in** the **name** of Jesus. In the cultural setting of the Bible, a name could not be separated from

His name, has made this man strong,
whom you see and know. Yes, the faith
which *comes* through Him has given
him this perfect soundness in the presence of you all.

KINGDOM DYNAMICS

3:16 Healing in Jesus' Incomparable Name, DIVINE HEALING. Immediately after the Spirit's outpouring at Pentecost, it is stated, "many wonders and signs were done through the apostles." Ch. 3 gives the account of the healing of a man who was lame from birth, a fact well known by everyone in Jerusalem. Peter attributed the healing to no unique human powers, but to faith in the name of Jesus (v. 16).

Note how the invoking of the name of "Jesus Christ of Nazareth" (v. 6; 4:10) rings from the apostles' lips. The appeals to Jesus' name as the unmistakable Messiah (Christ), who walked as a Man among men (of Nazareth), is an establishing of His Person, His character, and His kingly office as the authoritative grounds for extending healing grace. The use of another person's name to declare legal rights is called "the power of attorney." This is a privileged power that Jesus has delegated to us in confronting the retreating rule that sickness and Satan seek to sustain over mankind.

(John 8:58/Acts 28:8, 9) N.V.

17 "Yet now, brethren, I know that
[a]you did *it* in ignorance, as *did* also
your rulers.
18 "But [a]those things which God foretold [b]by the mouth of all His prophets,
that the Christ would suffer, He has
thus fulfilled.
1 19 [a]"Repent therefore and be converted, that your sins may be *blotted
out, so that times of refreshing may
come from the presence of the Lord,
20 "and that He may send [1]Jesus
Christ, who was [2]preached to you before,
4 21 [a]"whom heaven must receive until
the times of [b]restoration of all things,
[c]which God has spoken by the mouth
of all His holy prophets since [1]the
world began.

17 [a]Luke 23:34; John 16:3; [Acts 13:27; 17:30]; 1 Cor. 2:8; 1 Tim. 1:13
18 [a]Luke 24:44; Acts 26:22 [b]Ps. 22; Is. 50:6; 53:5; Dan. 9:26; Hos. 6:1; Zech. 13:6; 1 Pet. 1:10
19 [a][Acts 2:38; 26:20] *See WW at Col. 2:14.
20 [1]NU, M *Christ Jesus* [2]NU, M *ordained for you before*
21 [a]Acts 1:11 [b]Matt. 17:11; [Rom. 8:21] [c]Luke 1:70 [1]Or *time*
22 [a]Deut. 18:15, 18, 19; Acts 7:37
24 [a]2 Sam. 7:12; Luke 24:25 [1]NU, M *proclaimed*
25 [a]Acts 2:39; [Rom. 9:4, 8; Gal. 3:26] [b]Gen. 12:3; 18:18; 22:18; 26:4; 28:14 *See WW at Mark 14:24.
26 [a]Matt. 15:24; John 4:22; Acts 13:46; [Rom. 1:16; 2:9] [b]Is. 42:1; Matt. 1:21 *See WW at Luke 6:28.

CHAPTER 4

1 [a]Matt. 22:23

KINGDOM DYNAMICS

3:19–21 New Testament Prophecy, RESTORATION. This text unfolds the NT prophecy of restoration. The entire concept of "The Holy Spirit and Restoration" is developed in the study article, which begins on page 2012.

(*/Job 42:10–12) J.R.

22 "For Moses truly said to the fathers,
[a]*'The* LORD *your God will raise up for*
you a Prophet like me from your breth-
ren. Him you shall hear in all things,
whatever He says to you.
23 *'And it shall be that every soul who*
will not hear that Prophet shall be ut-
terly destroyed from among the peo-
ple.'
24 "Yes, and [a]all the prophets, from
Samuel and those who follow, as many
as have spoken, have also [1]foretold
these days.
25 [a]"You are sons of the prophets, and
of the *covenant which God made with
our fathers, saying to Abraham,
[b]*'And in your seed all the families of*
the earth shall be blessed.'
26 "To you [a]first, God, having raised
up His Servant Jesus, sent Him to
*bless you, [b]in turning away every one
of you from your iniquities."

Peter and John Arrested

4 Now as they spoke to the people,
the priests, the captain of the temple, and the [a]Sadducees came upon
them,

KINGDOM DYNAMICS

4:1–37 Prayer, the Proving Grounds of Our Faith, PRAYER. See the early church's response when persecutors tried to shut down the Christian movement? They went to prayer! Often the things that threaten to suffocate or destroy the church turn out to be the means of its preservation and advance. This persecution was sparked by controversy over a miracle, just as skeptics still debate the relationship of miracles to

---

the person bearing that name, and the very name "Jesus Christ" means "Anointed Savior." Therefore, Peter is saying that it was the Messiah in all His fullness who healed the man. Furthermore, the miracle power was not in Peter's faith, but by **the faith which *comes* through Him** (see Heb. 12:2).
3:19, 20 See section 1 of Truth-In-Action at the end of Acts.
3:21 See section 4 of Truth-In-Action at the end of Acts.
3:21, 24 OT prophecy has a present, *spiritual* fulfillment in the church (v. 24) *and* a future fulfillment in the Second Coming of Christ. Bible prophecy is both realized and unfulfilled. The kingdom of God is both "now" and "later."
Whom heaven must receive: See Ps. 110:1.
3:25 Peter reminds the Jewish leaders that the Abrahamic covenant promise of Gen. 12:1–3 shows that God never intended to limit His covenant blessing to the Jewish bloodline of Abraham's family.
4:1 The captain was the commander of the temple police who were responsible to maintain public order in the temple precincts.

Christianity. These early believers knew that if it could be established that the lame man's healing had been accomplished in the name and power of Jesus, Christ's power and authority would be clearly confirmed. Therefore, they went to prayer. The results? Great grace and boldness. Great power and unity (vv. 32–34). They teach us the pathway to proving the reality of our faith: not debate or argument, but prayer.

(Acts 13:1—14:28/2 Chr. 6:12–42; 7:1) L.L.

2 being greatly disturbed that they
taught the people and preached in
Jesus the resurrection from the dead.
3 And they laid hands on them, and
put *them* in custody until the next day,
for it was already evening.
4 However, many of those who heard
the *word believed; and the number of
the men came to be about five thousand.

Addressing the Sanhedrin

5 And it came to pass, on the next
day, that their rulers, elders, and
scribes,
6 as well as [a]Annas the high priest,
Caiaphas, John, and Alexander, and as
many as were of the family of the high
priest, were gathered together at Jerusalem.
7 And when they had set them in the
midst, they asked, [a]"By what power or
by what name have you done this?"
2 8 [a]Then Peter, filled with the Holy
Spirit, said to them, "Rulers of the people and elders of Israel:
9 "If we this day are judged for a good
deed *done* to a helpless man, by what
means he has been made well,
10 "let it be known to you all, and to
all the people of Israel, [a]that by the
name of Jesus Christ of Nazareth,
whom you crucified, [b]whom God
raised from the dead, by Him this man
stands here before you whole.
11 "This is the [a]*'stone which was rejected by you builders, which has become the chief cornerstone.'*
1 12 [a]"Nor is there *salvation in any
other, for there is no **other** name under
heaven given among men by which we
must be saved."

WORD WEALTH

4:12 other, *heteros* (*het*-er-oss); Strong's *#2087:* Different, generic distinction, another kind, not of the same nature, form, or class. Here *heteros* denotes a distinction and an exclusivity, with no second choices, opinions, or options. "Jesus, You are the One. You are the only One. There is no *heteros*, no other!"

KINGDOM DYNAMICS

4:12 The Sole Avenue of Salvation, WORLD EVANGELISM. The call to take the gospel to the nations is founded in these basic assumptions: 1) that humankind without Christ is lost, whether the entire race or the individual is concerned; 2) that there is "no other name under heaven given among men by which we must be saved"; that is, that no other authority, no other personality, no other system or philosophy can effect the rescue of the human soul. While some propose possibilities for human hope other than personal trust in Jesus Christ, God's Word preempts such propositions. In 2 Cor. 5:17 to be "in Christ" is the only way to enter the "new creation" of God's present promise and His eternal salvation.

(Acts 1:8/Rom. 3:23) G.C.

The Name of Jesus Forbidden

13 Now when they saw the boldness 2
of Peter and John, [a]and *perceived that
they were uneducated and untrained
men, they marveled. And they realized
that they had been with Jesus.
14 And seeing the man who had been
*healed [a]standing with them, they
could say nothing against it.
15 But when they had commanded
them to go aside out of the council,
they conferred among themselves,
16 saying, [a]"What shall we do to these
men? For, indeed, that a [1]notable miracle has been done through them *is*
[b]evident[2] to all who dwell in Jerusalem, and we cannot deny *it*.
17 "But so that it spreads no further

4 *See WW at Acts 19:20. **6** [a]Luke 3:2; John 11:49; 18:13 **7** [a]Ex. 2:14; Matt. 21:23; Acts 7:27 **8** [a]Luke 12:11, 12 **10** [a]Acts 2:22; 3:6, 16 [b]Acts 2:24 **11** [a]Ps. 118:22; Is. 28:16; Matt. 21:42 **12** [a]Is. 42:1, 6, 7; 53:11; Dan. 9:24; [Matt. 1:21; John 14:6; Acts 10:43; 1 Tim. 2:5, 6] *See WW at Luke 19:9.

13 [a]Matt. 11:25; [1 Cor. 1:27] *See WW at John 1:5. **14** [a]Acts 3:11 *See WW at Matt. 12:22. **16** [a]John 11:47 [b]Acts 3:7–10 [1]*remarkable sign* [2]*well known*

4:4 Men suggests that there may have been many women and children who were not counted in this early census (see 5:14).

4:5, 6 This gathering of officials was called the Sanhedrin, a kind of Jewish religious senate and supreme court.

4:8 See section 2 of Truth-In-Action at the end of Acts.

4:8 A believer's interaction with the Spirit is never static; therefore, Luke describes Peter's dynamic, ongoing relationship of the Spirit's power and anointing with the same words he used to describe his initial experience, being **filled with the Holy Spirit.** See notes on 2:4 and Eph. 5:18.

4:12 See section 1 of Truth-In-Action at the end of Acts.

4:13 See section 2 of Truth-In-Action at the end of Acts.

4:13 Uneducated means that the disciples had not received formal instruction in the rabbinical schools. **Untrained** describes them as common laymen, not professional experts.

4:16 The early debate over the Resurrection and other miracles did not concern whether or not such things occurred, but concerned the *meaning* of these events.

among the people, let us severely
threaten them, that from now on they
speak to no man in this name."
18 [a]So they called them and commanded them not to speak at all nor
teach in the name of Jesus.
19 But Peter and John answered and
said to them, [a]"Whether it is right in
the sight of God to listen to you more
than to God, you judge.
20 [a]"For we *cannot but speak the
things which [b]we have seen and
heard."
21 So when they had further threatened them, they let them go, finding
no way of punishing them, [a]because
of the people, since they all [b]glorified
God for [c]what had been done.
22 For the man was over forty years
old on whom this miracle of *healing
had been performed.

Prayer for Boldness

23 And being let go, [a]they went to their
own *companions* and reported all that
the chief priests and elders had said
to them.
3 24 So when they heard that, they
raised their voice to God *with one accord and said: *"Lord, [a]You *are* God,
who made heaven and earth and the
sea, and all that is in them,
25 "who [1]by the mouth of Your servant
David have said:

[a]'Why did the nations rage,
And the people plot vain things?
26 *The kings of the earth took their*
stand,
And the rulers were gathered
together
Against the LORD *and against His*
Christ.'

27 "For [a]truly against [b]Your holy Servant Jesus, [c]whom You anointed, both
Herod and Pontius Pilate, with the
Gentiles and the people of Israel, were
gathered together
28 [a]"to do whatever Your hand and
Your purpose determined before to be
done.
29 "Now, Lord, look on their threats,
and grant to Your servants [a]that with
all boldness they may speak Your
word,
30 "by stretching out Your hand to

18 [a]Acts 5:28, 40
19 [a]Acts 5:29
20 [a]Acts 1:8; 2:32 [b]Acts 22:15; [1 John 1:1, 3] *See WW at Jude 24.
21 [a]Matt. 21:26; Luke 20:6, 19; 22:2; Acts 5:26 [b]Matt. 15:31 [c]Acts 3:7, 8
22 *See WW at Luke 13:32.
23 [a]Acts 2:44–46; 12:12
24 [a]Ex. 20:11; 2 Kin. 19:15; Neh. 9:6; Ps. 146:6 *See WW at Acts 2:1. • See WW at Jude 4.
25 [a]Ps. 2:1, 2 [1]NU *through the Holy Spirit, by the mouth of our father, Your servant David,*
27 [a]Matt. 26:3; Luke 22:2; 23:1, 8 [b][Luke 1:35] [c]Luke 4:18; John 10:36
28 [a]Acts 2:23; 3:18
29 [a]Acts 4:13, 31; 9:27; 13:46; 14:3; 19:8; 26:26; Eph. 6:19
30 [a]Acts 2:43; 5:12 [b]Acts 3:6, 16 [c]Acts 4:27 *See WW at Luke 13:32.
31 [a]Matt. 5:6; Acts 2:2, 4; 16:26 [b]Acts 4:29
32 [a]Acts 5:12; Rom. 15:5, 6; 2 Cor. 13:11; Phil. 1:27; 2:2; 1 Pet. 3:8 [b]Acts 2:44 *See WW at Rev. 2:23.
33 [a][Acts 1:8] [b]Acts 1:22 [c]Rom. 6:15 *See WW at Rev. 15:5. • See WW at Acts 23:6.
34 [a][Matt. 19:21]; Acts 2:45

*heal, [a]and that signs and wonders
may be done [b]through the name of
[c]Your holy Servant Jesus."
31 And when they had prayed, [a]the
place where they were assembled together was shaken; and they were all
filled with the Holy Spirit, [b]and they
spoke the word of God with **boldness.**

WORD WEALTH

4:31 boldness, *parrhesia* (par-rhay-*see*-ah); Strong's *#3954:* Outspokenness, unreserved utterance, freedom of speech, with frankness, candor, cheerful courage, and the opposite of cowardice, timidity, or fear. Here it denotes a divine enablement that comes to ordinary and unprofessional people exhibiting spiritual power and authority. It also refers to a clear presentation of the gospel without being ambiguous or unintelligible. *Parrhesia* is not a human quality but a result of being filled with the Holy Spirit.

Sharing in All Things

32 Now the multitude of those who believed [a]were of one *heart and one
soul; [b]neither did anyone say that any
of the things he possessed was his own,
but they had all things in common.
33 And with [a]great **power** the apostles
gave [b]witness* to the *resurrection of
the Lord Jesus. And [c]great grace was
upon them all.
34 Nor was there anyone among them
who lacked; [a]for all who were pos-
sessors of lands or houses sold them,
and brought the proceeds of the things
that were sold,

WORD WEALTH

4:33 power, *dunamis* (*doo*-nam-is); Strong's *#1411:* One of four great power words. The others are *exousia,* delegated authority; *ischuros,* great strength (especially physical); and *kratos,* dominion authority. *Dunamis* means energy, power, might, great force, great ability, strength. It is sometimes used to describe the powers of the world to come at work upon the Earth and divine power overcoming all resistance. (Compare "dynamic," "dynamite," and "dynamometer.") The *dunamis* in Jesus resulted in dramatic transformations. This is the norm for the Spirit-filled and Spirit-led church.

4:19, 20 The superceding of obedience to God, in instances where human authority resists His will, is modeled in this passage. While it is apparently justifiable in some instances (see 5:40–42; 1 Pet. 2:18–23), there are no grounds in this text for the toleration of a rebellious spirit. Peter and John's demeanor, while asserting a higher moral claim, does not manifest either arrogance or presumption.

4:24–31 See section 3 of Truth-In-Action at the end of Acts.

4:31 See note on 4:8.

KINGDOM DYNAMICS

4:31–34 Faith's Victory Through Prayer, FAITH'S WARFARE. Following the healing of the lame man (3:1–6), Peter and John were commanded to cease their preaching in Jesus' name (4:18). Recognizing the severity of the situation, they returned to the believers (vv. 23, 24) and called for a season of prayer that would release their faith so as to increase the scope of their witness.

Note the progression of events following this prayer (vv. 31–35), resulting in a supernatural shaking. From that moment, further mightiness was manifest: 1) a supernatural fullness—all present experienced the fullness of the Holy Spirit; 2) a supernatural boldness—this prayer led to a baptism of forthright fearlessness to proclaim the Word of God (v. 31); 3) a supernatural unity—the prayer participants were of "one heart and one soul" (v. 32); 4) a supernatural submission; 5) a supernatural fruitfulness—with a new power they went boldly, and fruit was produced for God's glory (v. 33); 6) a supernatural generosity—they were baptized into a spirit of sacrifice and generosity (vv. 34, 35).

(Ps. 5:1–3/2 Kin. 19:8–19) D.E.

KINGDOM DYNAMICS

4:33 Calling for "Great Grace," FAITH'S CONFESSION. Most believers know the common definition of the beautiful word "grace" as "the unmerited favor of God." This is wonderfully true and clearly relates to our salvation apart from the works or energy of our flesh (Eph. 2:7–9).

But "grace," as used in this text ("great grace") and texts such as Luke 2:40 and Acts 11:23, also refers to "operations of the power of God." Just as God in mercy saves us by His grace, so that grace is manifested in great dynamic where the Holy Spirit is at work in power. Zech. 4:7 provides an OT illustration of this truth. The prophet instructed Zerubbabel to speak "grace" to the "mountain"—the hindrance he faced in the trying task of rebuilding God's temple. Speaking "grace" to obstacles we face is an action of faith, drawing on the operations of God's great power. We only speak: the work is entirely His—by His gracious power and for His great glory.

When we accept salvation, we receive it only through the power of His grace. Likewise, we can trust that His same grace will operate in us and through us, as it has been shown to us. As with the early disciples, great authority and power in other issues flowed through them and in their midst. As we call upon the name of the Lord, speaking His grace into the face of our mountainous impossibilities, we have every reason to expect "great power" and "great grace" today, too. (Acts 3:6/Rom. 10:9, 10) R.H.

35 [a]and laid *them* at the apostles' feet;
[b]and they distributed to each as anyone had need.
36 And [1]Joses, who was also named Barnabas by the apostles (which is translated Son of [2]Encouragement),* a Levite of the country of Cyprus,
37 [a]having land, sold *it,* and brought the money and laid *it* at the apostles' feet.

Lying to the Holy Spirit

5 But a certain man named Ananias, with Sapphira his wife, sold a possession.
2 And he kept back *part* of the proceeds, his wife also being aware *of it,* and brought a certain part and laid *it* at the apostles' feet.
3 [a]But Peter said, "Ananias, why has
[b]Satan filled your heart to lie to the Holy Spirit and keep back *part* of the price of the land for yourself?
4 "While it remained, was it not your own? And after it was sold, was it not in your own control? Why have you conceived this thing in your heart? You have not lied to men but to God."
5 Then Ananias, hearing these words,
[a]fell down and breathed his last. So great fear came upon all those who heard these things.
6 And the young men arose and
[a]wrapped him up, carried *him* out, and buried *him.*
7 Now it was about three hours later when his wife came in, not knowing what had happened.
8 And Peter answered her, "Tell me whether you sold the land for so much?" She said, "Yes, for so much."

35 [a]Acts 4:37; 5:2 [b]Acts 2:45; 6:1
36 [1]NU *Joseph* [2]Or *Consolation* *See WW at Acts 9:31.
37 [a]Acts 4:34, 35; 5:1, 2

CHAPTER 5

3 [a]Num. 30:2; Deut. 23:21; Eccl. 5:4 [b]Matt. 4:10; Luke 22:3; John 13:2, 27
5 [a]Ezek. 11:13; Acts 5:10, 11
6 [a]John 19:40

5:1–11 Ananias and **Sapphira** were judged for their hypocrisy and lying to God, not for their decision to retain some of their personal property for themselves (v. 4). The severity of the punishment for such a small offense may seem intolerant and graceless (see Luke 9:54, 55), but it was necessary both to establish apostolic authority in the early church and to safeguard the church's purity. A sobering lesson is that Satan has the power to distort the thinking of Christians (v. 3), thus affirming our need to allow him no place (Eph. 4:27). The believer's best defense against self-deception is through mutual accountability to one another (especially to a local congregation, Eph. 5:21). Constant renewing of the mind through the Word and a sustained "fullness" of the Holy Spirit are also safeguards. See Rom. 12:1, 2; 2 Cor. 10:4, 5; Eph. 5:17–20.

9 Then Peter said to her, "How is it
that you have *agreed together [a]to *test
the Spirit of the Lord? Look, the feet
of those who have buried your husband *are* at the door, and they will
carry you out."
10 [a]Then immediately she fell down at
his feet and breathed her last. And the
young men came in and found her
dead, and carrying *her* out, buried *her*
by her husband.
11 [a]So great fear came upon all the
church and upon all who heard these
things.

Continuing Power in the Church

12 And [a]through the hands of the
apostles many signs and wonders were
done among the people. [b]And they
were all *with one accord in Solomon's
Porch.
13 Yet [a]none of the rest dared join
them, [b]but the people **esteemed** them
highly.

WORD WEALTH

5:13 esteemed, *megaluno* (meg-al-oo-no); Strong's *#3170:* To make great, to enlarge, to magnify, to increase, to make conspicuous, to extol, to show respect, to hold in high esteem. When Ananias and Sapphira were judged, many shrank from associating with the apostles and their services. Despite all this, the public looked at the new Christian worshipers favorably (*megaluno*).

14 And believers were increasingly
added to the Lord, multitudes of both
men and women,
15 so that they brought the sick out
into the streets and laid *them* on beds
and couches, [a]that at least the shadow
of Peter passing by might fall on some
of them.
16 Also a multitude gathered from the
surrounding cities to Jerusalem, bringing [a]sick people and those who were
tormented by unclean spirits, and they
were all healed.

Imprisoned Apostles Freed

17 [a]Then the high priest rose up, and
all those who *were* with him (which is
the *sect of the Sadducees), and they
were filled with [1]indignation,*
18 [a]and laid their hands on the apostles and put them in the common
prison.
19 But at night [a]an angel of the Lord
opened the prison doors and brought
them out, and said,
20 "Go, stand in the temple and speak
to the people [a]all the words of this life."
21 And when they heard *that,* they entered the temple early in the morning
and taught. [a]But the high priest and
those with him came and called the
[1]council together, with all the [2]elders
of the children of Israel, and sent to
the prison to have them brought.

Apostles on Trial Again

22 But when the officers came and did
not find them in the prison, they returned and reported,
23 saying, "Indeed we found the prison
shut securely, and the guards standing
[1]outside before the doors; but when we
opened them, we found no one inside!"
24 Now when [1]the high priest, [a]the
captain of the temple, and the chief
priests heard these things, they wondered what the outcome would be.
25 So one came and told them, [1]saying,
"Look, the men whom you put in
prison are standing in the temple and
teaching the people!"
26 Then the captain went with the officers and brought them without violence, [a]for they feared the people, lest
they should be stoned.
27 And when they had brought them,
they set *them* before the council. And
the high priest asked them,
28 saying, [a]"Did we not strictly *command you not to teach in this name?
And look, you have filled Jerusalem
with your doctrine, [b]and intend to
bring this Man's [c]blood on us!"
29 But Peter and the *other* apostles answered and said: [a]"We ought to obey
God rather than men.
30 [a]"The God of our fathers raised up
Jesus whom you murdered by [b]hang-
ing on a tree.
31 [a]"Him God has *exalted to His right
hand *to be* [b]Prince and [c]Savior, [d]to
give repentance to Israel and *forgiveness of sins.

9 [a]Acts 5:3, 4 *See WW at Matt. 18:19. • See WW at Rev. 2:10.
10 [a]Acts 5:5
11 [a]Acts 2:43; 5:5; 19:17
12 [a]Acts 2:43; 4:30; 6:8; 14:3; 15:12 [b]Acts 3:11; 4:32 *See WW at Acts 2:1.
13 [a]John 9:22 [b]Acts 2:47; 4:21
15 [a]Acts 19:12
16 [a]Mark 16:17, 18
17 [a]Acts 4:1, 2, 6 [1]*jealousy* *See WW at 2 Pet. 2:1. • See WW at 2 Cor. 11:2.
18 [a]Luke 21:12
19 [a]Acts 12:7; 16:26
20 [a][John 6:63, 68; 17:3]
21 [a]Acts 4:5, 6 [1]Sanhedrin [2]*council of elders* or *senate*
23 [1]NU, M omit *outside*
24 [a]Acts 4:1; 5:26 [1]NU omits *the high priest*
25 [1]NU, M omit *saying*
26 [a]Matt. 21:26
28 [a]Acts 4:17, 18 [b]Acts 2:23, 36 [c]Matt. 23:35 *See WW at Acts 16:24.
29 [a]Acts 4:19
30 [a]Acts 3:13, 15 [b][1 Pet. 2:24]
31 [a][Acts 2:33, 36] [b]Acts 3:15 [c]Matt. 1:21 [d]Luke 24:47 *See WW at James 4:10. • See WW at Heb. 9:22.

5:12 Signs and wonders characterized the ministry of the early church and are equally intended to be expected in and through the church today.
5:15 The shadow of Peter was not magic nor was it intended to provide a formula. Sometimes God uses physical objects as a point at which our faith may make a kind of link between the seen and the unseen (see 19:12). The bread and cup of Communion, the water of baptism, and the anointing oil (James 5:14) are some examples.
5:31, 32 The gift of **the Holy Spirit** bears witness to the reality of the exaltation of Jesus (see 2:33; John 7:39).

32 "And [a]we are His witnesses to these things, and *so* also *is* the Holy Spirit [b]whom God has given to those who obey Him."

Gamaliel's Advice

33 When they heard *this,* they were [a]furious[1] and plotted to kill them.

34 Then one in the council stood up, a Pharisee named [a]Gamaliel, a teacher of the law held in respect by all the people, and commanded them to put the apostles outside for a little while.

35 And he said to them: "Men of Israel, [1]take heed to yourselves what you intend to do regarding these men.

36 "For some time ago Theudas rose up, claiming to be somebody. A number of men, about four hundred, [1]joined* him. He was slain, and all who obeyed him were scattered and came to nothing.

37 "After this man, Judas of Galilee rose up in the days of the census, and drew away many people after him. He also perished, and all who obeyed him were dispersed.

38 "And now I say to you, keep away from these men and let them alone; for if this plan or this work is of men, it will come to nothing;

39 [a]"but if it is of God, you cannot overthrow it—lest you even be found [b]to fight against God."

40 And they agreed with him, and when they had [a]called for the apostles [b]and beaten *them,* they commanded that they should not speak in the name of Jesus, and let them go.

41 So they departed from the presence of the council, [a]rejoicing that they were counted worthy to suffer shame for [1]His name.

42 And daily [a]in the temple, and in every house, [b]they did not cease teaching and preaching Jesus *as* the Christ.

32 [a]John 15:26, 27; Acts 15:28; Rom. 8:16; Heb. 2:4 [b]Acts 2:4; 10:44
33 [a]Acts 2:37; 7:54 [1]*cut to the quick*
34 [a]Acts 22:3
35 [1]*be careful*
36 [1]*followed* *See WW at Mark 10:7.
39 [a]Luke 21:15; 1 Cor. 1:25 [b]Acts 7:51; 9:5
40 [a]Acts 4:18 [b]Matt. 10:17; Mark 13:9; Acts 16:22, 23; 21:32; 2 Cor. 11:25
41 [a]Matt. 5:10–12; Rom. 5:3; 2 Cor. 12:10; Heb. 10:34; [James 1:2; 1 Pet. 4:13–16] [1]NU *the name;* M *the name of Jesus*
42 [a]Acts 2:46 [b]Acts 4:20, 29

CHAPTER 6

1 [a]Acts 2:41; 4:4 [b]Acts 9:29; 11:20 [c]Acts 4:35; 11:29 [1]Greek-speaking Jews *See WW at Matt. 10:1.
2 [a]Ex. 18:17
3 [a]Deut. 1:13; 1 Tim. 3:7 [b]Phil. 1:1; 1 Tim. 3:8–13
4 [a]Acts 2:42

Seven Chosen to Serve

6 Now in those days, [a]when *the number of* the *disciples was multiplying, there arose a complaint against the Hebrews by the [b]Hellenists,[1] because their widows were neglected [c]in the daily distribution.

2 Then the twelve summoned the multitude of the disciples and said, [a]"It is not desirable that we should leave the word of God and serve tables.

3 "Therefore, brethren, [a]seek out from among you seven men of *good* reputation, full of the Holy Spirit and wisdom, whom we may appoint over this [b]business;

4 "but we [a]will give ourselves continually to prayer and to the ministry of the word."

KINGDOM DYNAMICS

6:1–4 Faithfulness in Prayer and Spiritual Warfare, FAITH'S WARFARE. The early church learned quickly that their prayer had to be continuous because spiritual warfare is continuous. It became their first priority because Satan sought their defeat as his first priority. Thus, their earliest recorded administrative decision after Pentecost places the ministry of prayer (with the Word) as highest in importance.

As the church grew, circumstances required more of the apostles' time. But realizing they needed more prayer, rather than increased activity, the apostles chose seven men to serve as deacons to care for the church. This freed them to focus on prayer and the ministry of the Word. Of the two, prayer, rightfully, is listed first. Faithfulness to prayer recurs throughout Scripture. Paul would later tell the church at Rome to "*be* kindly affectionate to one another . . . continuing steadfastly in prayer" (Rom. 12:10, 12).

(Prov. 3:5, 6/Ezek. 22:30) D.E.

5:33–40 Gamaliel, Paul's former **teacher** (22:3), did not see Jesus as the Messiah, but his counsel to the Sanhedrin was certainly influenced by divine providence. Luke's more subtle message is that even the highest levels of Jewish leadership had to admit that they had no valid reason for resisting the early church.

5:41 Rejoicing that they were counted worthy to suffer shame for His name is a response that would be unusual for some Christians today. Jesus does not guarantee perpetual happiness if we agree to serve Him, but He does promise us a joy that is "inexpressible and full of glory" (1 Pet. 1:8).

5:42 Both public services in the temple and small group meetings in private homes were employed for the nurturing of believers.

6:1–6 See section 3 of Truth-In-Action at the end of Acts.

6:1 The Hebrews were natives of Palestine and spoke Hebrew (or Aramaic) rather than Greek. **The Hellenists** were Jews who were natives of the Greco-Roman world and spoke Greek. The presence and power of the Spirit does not automatically guarantee that life's difficulties will go away. Often it is necessary for Christians to discuss their differences and ask God for wise solutions.

6:3 Church growth demands organization and delegation. Leadership in the church must be full of *both* **the Holy Spirit and wisdom.** The Holy Spirit gives us God's perspective. Wisdom is the practical side of problem solving. Many interpreters regard the **seven** as the first deacons, although the term does not appear in this passage.

6:4 Prayer and **the ministry of the word** must be the perpetual priority of the leadership of the church. This does not suggest that the ministry of benevolence is on a lower level. It is a matter of the roles that God assigns (see Rom. 12:4–8).

5 And the saying pleased the whole
multitude. And they chose Stephen,
[a]a man full of faith and the Holy Spirit,
and [b]Philip, Prochorus, Nicanor, Ti-
mon, Parmenas, and [c]Nicolas, a proselyte from Antioch,
6 whom they set before the apostles;
and [a]when they had prayed, [b]they laid
hands on them.
7 Then [a]the word of God spread, and
the number of the disciples multiplied
greatly in Jerusalem, and a great many
[b]of the priests were *obedient to the
faith.

Stephen Accused of Blasphemy

8 And Stephen, full of [1]faith and
power, did great [a]wonders and signs
among the people.
9 Then there arose some from what
is called the Synagogue of the Freedmen (Cyrenians, Alexandrians, and
those from Cilicia and Asia), disputing
with Stephen.
10 And [a]they were not able to *resist
the **wisdom** and the Spirit by which he
spoke.

WORD WEALTH

6:10 wisdom, *sophia* (sof-*ee*-ah); Strong's *#4678:* Practical wisdom, prudence, skill, comprehensive insight, Christian enlightenment, a right application of knowledge, insight into the true nature of things. Wisdom in the Bible is often coupled with knowledge (Rom. 11:33; 1 Cor. 12:8; Col. 2:3). In anticipation of our needing guidance, direction, and knowing, God tells us to ask for wisdom, assuring us of a liberal reception (James 1:5).

11 [a]Then they secretly induced men to
say, "We have heard him speak **blasphemous** words against Moses and
God."

5 [a]Acts 6:3; 11:24 [b]Acts 8:5, 26; 21:8 [c]Rev. 2:6, 15
6 [a]Acts 1:24 [b]Num. 8:10; 27:18; Deut. 34:9; [Mark 5:23; Acts 8:17; 9:17; 13:3; 19:6; 1 Tim. 4:14; 2 Tim. 1:6]; Heb. 6:2
7 [a]Acts 12:24; Col. 1:6 [b]John 12:42 *See WW at Rom. 6:17.
8 [a]Acts 2:43; 5:12; 8:15; 14:3 [1]NU *grace*
10 [a]Ex. 4:12; Is. 54:17; Luke 21:15 *See WW at Eph. 6:13.
11 [a]1 Kin. 21:10, 13; Matt. 26:59, 60
13 [1]NU omits *blasphemous* *See WW at Acts 6:11.
14 [a]Acts 10:38; 25:8

CHAPTER 7

2 [a]Acts 22:1 [b]Ps. 29:3; 1 Cor. 2:8 [c]Gen. 11:31, 32 *See WW at John 2:11.
3 [a]Gen. 12:1
4 [a]Gen. 11:31; 15:7; Heb. 11:8–10 [b]Gen. 11:32
5 [a]Gen. 12:7; 13:15; 15:3, 18; 17:8; 26:3 *See WW at Matt. 27:19.

WORD WEALTH

6:11 blasphemous, *blasphemos* (*blas*-fay-moss); Strong's *#989:* Compare "blasphemy." From *blapto,* "to injure," and *pheme,* "speech"; hence, slanderous, abusive speech.

12 And they stirred up the people, the
elders, and the scribes; and they came
upon *him,* seized him, and brought *him*
to the council.
13 They also set up false witnesses
who said, "This man does not cease to
speak [1]blasphemous* words against
this holy place and the law;
14 [a]"for we have heard him say that
this Jesus of Nazareth will destroy this
place and change the customs which
Moses delivered to us."
15 And all who sat in the council, looking steadfastly at him, saw his face as
the face of an angel.

Stephen's Address: The Call of Abraham

7 Then the high priest said, "Are
these things so?"
2 And he said, [a]"Brethren and fathers, listen: The [b]God of *glory appeared to our father Abraham when he
was in Mesopotamia, before he dwelt
in [c]Haran,
3 "and said to him, [a]*'Get out of your
country and from your relatives, and
come to a land that I will show
you.'*
4 "Then [a]he came out of the land of
the Chaldeans and dwelt in Haran.
And from there, when his father was
[b]dead, He moved him to this land in
which you now dwell.
5 "And *God* gave him no inheritance
in it, not even *enough* to *set his foot
on. But even when *Abraham* had no
child, [a]He **promised** to give it to him
for a possession, and to his descendants after him.

6:6 Laid hands on them is an act of ordination, a transferral of authority and responsibility, also indicating an acknowledgment of mutual identification and partnership with those commissioned to service.
6:7 This is the first of six progress reports that appear throughout Acts (v. 7; 9:31; 12:24; 16:5; 19:20; 28:31). Each covers an approximate span of five years.
6:8 Wonders and signs are not an exclusive characteristic of apostolic ministry. **Stephen** was not an apostle, but he was **full of faith and power.**
6:9 Freedmen were former Roman slaves.
6:10 Testifying of your faith is not just a matter of saying the right things. Witnessing is a spiritual battle that requires **the wisdom and** the power of the **Spirit** working in the witness.
6:13, 14 The same argument had been leveled at Jesus (Matt. 26:60, 61). Actually, the coming of Christ meant the end of the temple order, which was the foundation and centerpiece of Judaism.
7:1–53 Stephen's lengthy address is more than a rebuttal of the charges against him. Rather than defending himself, he brought an indictment against his accusers. Instead of manifesting a true zeal for the temple and the Law in their opposition to the gospel, the Jews were displaying the same rebellious spirit of unbelief that characterized their forebears who resisted the purposes of God. In a skillful review of Israel's history he also concludes that God's presence is not limited to a geographical place nor to a particular people.

WORD WEALTH

7:5 promised, *epangello* (ep-ang-*el*-low); Strong's *#1861:* To engage, to profess, to assert something concerning oneself, to announce what one is about to do (an intention), to render a service, to make a commitment, to pledge to do something. Here *epangello* is God's assurance to Abraham that the land He showed him was for him and his descendants.

6 "But God spoke in this way: [a]that
his descendants would *dwell in a foreign land, and that they would bring
them into [b]bondage and oppress *them*
four hundred years.
7 [a]*'And the nation to whom they will
be in bondage I will* [b]*judge,'* said God,
[c]*'and after that they shall come out and
serve Me in this place.'*
8 [a]"Then He gave him the covenant
of circumcision; [b]and so *Abraham* begot Isaac and circumcised him on the
eighth day; [c]and Isaac *begot* Jacob,
and [d]Jacob *begot* the twelve patriarchs.

The Patriarchs in Egypt

9 [a]"And the patriarchs, becoming
*envious, [b]sold Joseph into Egypt.
[c]But God was with him
10 "and delivered him out of all his
troubles, [a]and gave him favor and
*wisdom in the presence of Pharaoh,
king of Egypt; and he made him governor over Egypt and all his house.
11 [a]"Now a famine and great [1]trouble
came over all the land of Egypt and
Canaan, and our fathers found no
sustenance.
12 [a]"But when Jacob heard that there
was grain in Egypt, he sent out our fathers first.
13 "And the [a]second *time* Joseph was
made known to his brothers, and Joseph's family became known to the
Pharaoh.
14 [a]"Then Joseph sent and called his
father Jacob and [b]all his relatives to
him, [1]seventy-five people.
15 [a]"So Jacob went down to Egypt;
[b]and he died, he and our fathers.
16 "And [a]they were carried back to
Shechem and laid in [b]the tomb that
Abraham bought for a sum of money
from the sons of Hamor, *the father* of
Shechem.

6 [a]Gen. 15:13, 14, 16; 47:11, 12 [b]Ex. 1:8–14; 12:40, 41 *See WW at Eph. 2:19. **7** [a]Gen. 15:14 [b]Ex. 14:13–31 [c]Ex. 3:12 **8** [a]Gen. 17:9–14 [b]Gen. 21:1–5 [c]Gen. 25:21–26 [d]Gen. 29:31—30:24; 35:18, 22–26 **9** [a]Gen. 37:4, 11, 28 [b]Gen. 37:28 [c]Gen. 39:2, 21, 23 *See WW at 1 Cor. 14:1. **10** [a]Gen. 41:38–44 *See WW at Acts 6:10. **11** [a]Gen. 41:54; 42:5 [1]*affliction* **12** [a]Gen. 42:1, 2 **13** [a]Gen. 45:4, 16 **14** [a]Gen. 45:9, 27 [b]Deut. 10:22 [1]Or *seventy,* Ex. 1:5 **15** [a]Gen. 46:1–7 [b]Gen. 49:33 **16** [a]Josh. 24:32 [b]Gen. 23:16

17 [a]Gen. 15:13 [b]Ex. 1:7–9 **18** [a]Ex. 1:8 **19** [a]Ex. 1:22 **20** [a]Ex. 2:1, 2 [b]Heb. 11:23 **21** [a]Ex. 2:3, 4 [b]Ex. 2:5–10 **22** [a]Luke 24:19 *See WW at John 9:4. **23** [a]Ex. 2:11, 12 **26** *See WW at Acts 25:10. **27** [a]Ex. 2:14 **29** [a]Heb. 11:27 [b]Ex. 2:15, 21, 22; 4:20; 18:3 *See WW at Eph. 2:19. **30** [a]Ex. 3:1–10 [1]NU omits *of the Lord* **32** [a]Ex. 3:6, 15 **33** [a]Ex. 3:5, 7, 8, 10

God Delivers Israel by Moses

17 "But when [a]the time of the promise
drew near which God had sworn to
Abraham, [b]the people grew and multiplied in Egypt
18 "till another king [a]arose who did
not know Joseph.
19 "This man dealt treacherously with
our people, and oppressed our forefathers, [a]making them expose their babies, so that they might not live.
20 [a]"At this time Moses was born, and
[b]was well pleasing to God; and he was
brought up in his father's house for
three months.
21 "But [a]when he was set out, [b]Pha-
raoh's daughter took him away and
brought him up as her own son.
22 "And Moses was learned in all the
wisdom of the Egyptians, and was
[a]mighty in words and *deeds.
23 [a]"Now when he was forty years old,
it came into his heart to visit his brethren, the children of Israel.
24 "And seeing one of *them* suffer
wrong, he defended and avenged him
who was oppressed, and struck down
the Egyptian.
25 "For he supposed that his brethren
would have understood that God
would deliver them by his hand, but
they did not understand.
26 "And the next day he appeared to
two of them as they were fighting, and
tried to reconcile them, saying, 'Men,
you are brethren; why *do you wrong
one another?'
27 "But he who did his neighbor wrong
pushed him away, saying, [a]*'Who made
you a ruler and a judge over us?*
28 *'Do you want to kill me as you did
the Egyptian yesterday?'*
29 [a]"Then, at this saying, Moses fled
and became a *dweller in the land of
Midian, where he [b]had two sons.
30 [a]"And when forty years had passed,
an Angel [1]of the Lord appeared to him
in a flame of fire in a bush, in the wilderness of Mount Sinai.
31 "When Moses saw *it,* he marveled
at the sight; and as he drew near to
observe, the voice of the Lord came to
him,
32 *"saying,* [a]*'I am the God of your fathers—the God of Abraham, the God
of Isaac, and the God of Jacob.'* And
Moses trembled and dared not look.
33 [a]*'Then the* LORD *said to him, "Take*

7:8 The covenant of circumcision was intended to reflect personal commitment to one's obedience to God's covenant, but the Jews made little distinction between the ritual and the reality. **The twelve patriarchs** are the sons of Jacob, who became the fathers of the 12 tribes of Israel.

your sandals off your feet, for the place where you stand is ***holy*** *ground.*

WORD WEALTH

7:33 holy, *hagios* (*hag*-ee-oss); Strong's #*40:* Compare "Hagiographa" and "hagiography." Sacred, pure, blameless, consecrated, separated, properly revered, worthy of veneration, Godlikeness, God's innermost nature, set apart for God, reserved for God and His service. Since nothing that is polluted could be *hagios,* purity becomes a big part of *hagios.* A holy God calls for a holy people.

34 "*I have surely* [a]*seen the oppression*
of My people who are in Egypt; I have
heard their groaning and have come
down to deliver them. And now come,
I will [b]*send you to Egypt.*" '
35 "This Moses whom they rejected,
saying, [a]*'Who made you a ruler and a*
judge?' is the one God sent *to be* a ruler
and a deliverer [b]by the hand of the Angel who appeared to him in the bush.
36 [a]"He brought them out, after he had
[b]shown *wonders and signs in the land
of Egypt, [c]and in the Red Sea, [d]and
in the wilderness forty years.

Israel Rebels Against God

37 "This is that Moses who said to the
children of Israel, [a]*'The* L*ORD your God*
will raise up for you a Prophet like me
from your brethren. [b]*Him*[1] *you shall*
hear.'
38 [a]"This is he who was in the [1]con-
gregation in the wilderness with
[b]the Angel who spoke to him on Mount
Sinai, and *with* our fathers, [c]the one
who received the living [d]oracles[2] to
give to us,
39 "whom our fathers [a]would not
obey, but rejected. And in their hearts
they turned back to Egypt,
40 [a]"saying to Aaron, *'Make us gods*
to go before us; as for this Moses who
brought us out of the land of Egypt,
we do not know what has become of
him.'
41 [a]"And they made a calf in those
days, offered sacrifices to the idol, and
[b]rejoiced in the works of their own
hands.

34 [a]Ex. 2:24, 25 [b]Ps. 105:26
35 [a]Ex. 2:14 [b]Ex. 14:21
36 [a]Ex. 12:41; 33:1 [b]Ps. 105:27 [c]Ex. 14:21 [d]Ex. 16:1, 35 *See WW at Acts 15:12.
37 [a]Deut. 18:15, 18, 19 [b]Matt. 17:5 [1]NU, M omit *Him you shall hear*
38 [a]Ex. 19:3 [b]Gal. 3:19 [c]Deut. 5:27 [d]Heb. 5:12 [1]Gr. *ekklesia, assembly or church* [2]*sayings*
39 [a]Ps. 95:8–11
40 [a]Ex. 32:1, 23
41 [a]Deut. 9:16 [b]Ex. 32:6, 18, 19

42 "Then [a]God turned and gave them
up to worship [b]the host of heaven, as
it is written in the book of the Prophets:

[c]*'Did you offer Me slaughtered*
animals and sacrifices during
forty years in the wilderness,
O house of Israel?
43 *You also took up the tabernacle*
of Moloch,
And the star of your god
Remphan,
Images which you made to
worship;
And [a]*I will carry you away*
beyond Babylon.'

God's True Tabernacle

44 "Our fathers had the tabernacle of
*witness in the wilderness, as He ap-
pointed, instructing Moses [a]to make it
according to the pattern that he had
seen,
45 [a]"which our fathers, having received it in turn, also brought with
Joshua into the land possessed by the
Gentiles, [b]whom God drove out before
the face of our fathers until the [c]days
of David,
46 [a]"who found favor before God and
[b]asked to find a dwelling for the God
of Jacob.
47 [a]"But Solomon built Him a house.
48 "However, [a]the Most High does not
dwell in temples made with hands, as
the prophet says:

49 *'Heaven*[a] *is My throne,*
And earth is My footstool.
What house will you build for
Me? says the L*ORD,*
Or what is the place of My rest?
50 *Has My hand not* [a]*made all these*
things?'

Israel Resists the Holy Spirit

51 "*You* [a]stiff-necked[1] and [b]uncircum-
cised in heart and ears! You always resist the Holy Spirit; as your fathers *did,*
so *do* you.
52 [a]"Which of the prophets did your
fathers not persecute? And they killed
those who foretold the coming of
[b]the Just One, of whom you now have

42 [a][2 Thess. 2:11] [b]2 Kin. 21:3 [c]Amos 5:25–27
43 [a]Jer. 25:9–12
44 [a][Heb. 8:5] *See WW at Rev. 15:5.
45 [a]Josh. 3:14; 18:1; 23:9 [b]Ps. 44:2 [c]2 Sam. 6:2–15
46 [a]2 Sam. 7:1–13 [b]1 Chr. 22:7
47 [a]1 Kin. 6:1–38; 8:20, 21
48 [a]1 Kin. 8:27
49 [a]Is. 66:1, 2
50 [a]Ps. 102:25
51 [a]Ex. 32:9 [b]Lev. 26:41 [1]*stubborn*
52 [a]2 Chr. 36:16 [b]Acts 3:14; 22:14

7:44 Tabernacle of witness: The stone tables of the Ten Commandments were referred to as "the witness," or "the Testimony," being contained within the ark of the covenant in the tabernacle of Moses.

7:47, 48 Stephen was not opposed to the temple itself, but to the lifeless institutionalism it came to represent.

7:51–53 Stephen's passionate conclusion led to his violent death. **Uncircumcised in heart and ears** describes those who felt self-assured because they had been outwardly circumcised. Ritualism does not bring one into a right standing before God. A change of heart through rebirth and an obedient walk of faith are the real signs of a true relationship with God.

become the betrayers and murderers,
53 [a]"who have received the law by the
direction of *angels and have not kept
it."

Stephen the Martyr

54 [a]When they heard these things they
were [1]cut to the heart, and they
gnashed at him with *their* teeth.
55 But he, [a]being full of the Holy
Spirit, gazed into heaven and saw the
[b]glory of God, and Jesus standing at
the right hand of God,
56 and said, "Look! [a]I *see the heavens
opened and the [b]Son of Man standing
at the right hand of God!"
57 Then they cried out with a loud
voice, *stopped their ears, and ran at
him *with one accord;
58 and they cast *him* out of the city and
stoned *him.* And [a]the *witnesses laid
down their clothes at the feet of a
young man named Saul.
59 And they stoned Stephen as he was
calling on *God* and saying, "Lord
Jesus, [a]receive my spirit."
60 Then he knelt down and cried out
with a loud voice, [a]"Lord, do not
charge them with this *sin." And when
he had said this, he fell asleep.

Saul Persecutes the Church

8 Now Saul was consenting to his
death. At that time a great persecution arose against the **church** which
was at Jerusalem; and [a]they were all
scattered throughout the regions of Judea and Samaria, except the apostles.

WORD WEALTH

8:1 church, *ecclesia* (ek-klay-*see*-ah); Strong's *#1577:* Used in secular Greek for an assembly of citizens and in the Septuagint for the congregation of Israel. The NT uses the word in the former sense in 19:32, 39, 41, and in the latter sense in 7:38 and Heb. 2:12. The dominant use in the NT is to describe an assembly or company of Christians in the following ways: 1) the whole body of Christians; 2) a local church constituting a company of Christians gathering for worship, sharing, and teaching; 3) churches in a district. Other related terms are: "spiritual house," "chosen race," and "God's people." (Compare "ecclesiastic" and "ecclesiastical.") The survival of the Christian church against all its opponents is assured in Jesus' words from Matt. 16:18, "On this rock I will build My church, and the gates of Hades shall not prevail against it."

2 And devout men carried Stephen *to
his burial,* and [a]made great lamentation over him.
3 As for Saul, [a]he made havoc of the
church, entering every house, and
dragging off men and women, committing *them* to prison.

Christ Is Preached in Samaria

4 Therefore [a]those who were scattered went everywhere preaching the
word.
5 Then [a]Philip went down to [1]the city
of Samaria and *preached Christ to
them.
6 And the multitudes *with one accord heeded the things spoken by
Philip, hearing and seeing the miracles
which he did.
7 For [a]unclean spirits, crying with a
loud voice, came out of many who were
possessed; and many who were paralyzed and lame were healed.
8 And there was great joy in that city.

The Sorcerer's Profession of Faith

9 But there was a certain man called
Simon, who previously [a]practiced
[1]sorcery in the city and [b]astonished the
[2]people of Samaria, claiming that he
was someone great,
10 to whom they all gave heed, from
the least to the greatest, saying, "This
man is the great power of God."
11 And they heeded him because he
had astonished them with his [1]sorcer-
ies for a long time.

53 [a]Ex. 20:1; Deut. 33:2; Acts 7:38; Gal. 3:19; Heb. 2:2 *See WW at Matt. 4:11. **54** [a]Acts 5:33 [1]*furious* **55** [a]Matt. 5:8; 16:28; Mark 9:1; Luke 9:27; Acts 6:5 [b][Ex. 24:17] **56** [a]Matt. 3:16 [b]Dan. 7:13 *See WW at John 20:14. **57** *See WW at 2 Cor. 5:14. • See WW at Acts 2:1. **58** [a]Acts 22:20 *See WW at Rev. 1:5. **59** [a]Ps. 31:5 **60** [a]Matt. 5:44; Luke 23:34 *See WW at John 1:29.

CHAPTER 8

1 [a]John 16:2; Acts 8:4; 11:19
2 [a]Gen. 23:2 **3** [a]Acts 7:58; 1 Cor. 15:9; Gal. 1:13; Phil. 3:6; 1 Tim. 1:13 **4** [a]Matt. 10:23 **5** [a]Acts 6:5; 8:26, 30 [1]Or *a* *See WW at Acts 9:20. **6** *See WW at Acts 2:1. **7** [a]Mark 16:17 **9** [a]Acts 8:11; 13:6 [b]Acts 5:36 [1]*magic* [2]Or *nation* **11** [1]*magic arts*

7:55, 56 Son of Man: See Introduction to Matthew: Christ Revealed. Jesus, who sits at the right hand of the Father (Col. 3:1; Heb. 1:3, 13; 10:12), is **standing** here to witness against Stephen's accusers and to receive him into the heavenly kingdom.
7:58 Saul, the one who will become the apostle Paul, was from Tarsus, located in Cilicia. He may have even attended the synagogue where Stephen preached (6:9).
7:60 Stephen's prayer is reminiscent of that of Jesus at His crucifixion (Luke 23:34).
8:4 God turns evil into good (Rom. 8:28). The first official persecution of the church drove the Christians out of Jerusalem, and they preached the gospel everywhere they went.
8:5, 6 Philip was another nonapostle like Stephen (6:8), but that was no hindrance to his miracle ministry. Miracles themselves do not bring salvation, but they often attract people to the message. The miracles of the Bible are "signs," in that each one has an important spiritual message to convey, as well as serving to confirm the veracity of the word of the gospel (Mark 16:20).

12 But when they believed Philip as he
preached the things [a]concerning the
kingdom of God and the name of Jesus
Christ, both men and women were baptized.
13 Then Simon himself also believed;
and when he was baptized he continued with Philip, and was amazed,
seeing the miracles and signs which
were done.

The Sorcerer's Sin

14 Now when the [a]apostles who were
at Jerusalem heard that Samaria had
received the word of God, they sent Peter and John to them,
15 who, when they had come down,
prayed for them [a]that they might receive the Holy Spirit.
16 For [a]as yet He had fallen upon none
of them. [b]They had only been baptized
in [c]the name of the Lord Jesus.
17 Then [a]they laid hands on them, and
they received the Holy Spirit.
18 And when Simon saw that through
the laying on of the apostles' hands the
Holy Spirit was given, he offered them
money,
19 saying, "Give me this power also,
that anyone on whom I lay hands may
receive the Holy Spirit."
20 But Peter said to him, "Your money
perish with you, because [a]you thought
that [b]the gift of God could be purchased with money!
21 "You have neither part nor portion
in this matter, for your [a]heart is not
right in the sight of God.
22 "Repent therefore of this your wickedness, and pray God [a]if perhaps the
thought of your heart may be forgiven
you.
23 "For I see that you are [a]poisoned
by bitterness and bound by *iniquity."
24 Then Simon answered and said,
[a]"Pray to the Lord for me, that none
of the things which you have spoken
may come upon me."
25 So when they had testified and
preached the word of the Lord, they
returned to Jerusalem, preaching the
gospel in many villages of the Samaritans.

Christ Is Preached to an Ethiopian

26 Now an angel of the Lord spoke to
[a]Philip, saying, "Arise and go toward
the south along the road which goes

12 [a]Acts 1:3; 8:4 **14** [a]Acts 5:12, 29, 40 **15** [a]Acts 2:38; 19:2 **16** [a]Acts 19:2 [b]Matt. 28:19; Acts 2:38 [c]Acts 10:48; 19:5 **17** [a]Acts 6:6; 19:6; Heb. 6:2 **20** [a]2 Kin. 5:16; Is. 55:1; Dan. 5:17; [Matt. 10:8] [b][Acts 2:38; 10:45; 11:17] **21** [a]Jer. 17:9 **22** [a]Dan. 4:27; 2 Tim. 2:25 **23** [a]Heb. 12:15 *See WW at John 7:18. **24** [a]Gen. 20:7, 17; Ex. 8:8; Num. 21:7; 1 Kin. 13:6; Job 42:8; James 5:16 **26** [a]Acts 6:5

8:14 Since the Samaritans were the first non-Jews to receive the gospel, the Jerusalem church sent Peter and John to Samaria as an official, apostolic delegation to investigate (see John 4:9 for Jewish-Samaritan relationships). This was a direct fulfillment of 1:8.

8:15–17 This passage has been subject to unnecessary debate. The sequence of events described in v. 12 leaves little doubt that the Samaritans had become Christians. They had already had a conversion experience with the Holy Spirit, evidenced by their water baptism (vv. 12, 16). Now, through the ministry of the apostles, they are being led into another significant experience with the Holy Spirit, which Luke describes both as "receiving the Holy Spirit," including their allowing Him to "fall upon" them. (See Introduction to Acts: The Holy Spirit at Work for the fluidity of Luke's terms.) This, therefore, may best be seen in the sense of their initial baptism with the Holy Spirit. See also note on 1:5.

8:18–25 Simon evidently **saw** some outward phenomenon that convinced him that the Samaritan converts had received **the Holy Spirit . . . through the laying on of the apostles' hands.** Although Luke does not identify the external manifestation, many commentators agree that it may likely have been speaking in tongues. **Your money perish . . . iniquity:** Simon's quest to buy the ability to impart the power of the Spirit was his obvious sin, including a more subtle evil is his desire to use the power of God for his own gain. The word "simony," which is the buying and selling of church offices and influence, originates here. Some ask, Was Simon really saved? "Simon himself also believed" and "was baptized" (v. 13), but Peter's scathing rebuke (v. 21) leaves us uncertain about where Simon really stood with God. Furthermore, the early writings of church history continue to depict Simon as a father of heresies.

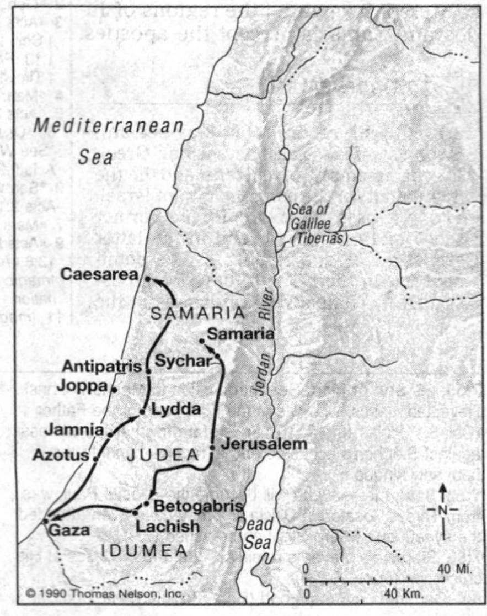

Philip's Missionary Journeys. Two journeys are recorded in Acts 8:5–13 and 8:26–40.

down from Jerusalem to Gaza." This
is [1]desert.

KINGDOM DYNAMICS

8:26 Angels as Messengers, ANGELS. With God's Word as our source of information, we see that angels may be actively involved in assisting the advance of the church on Earth through messages. Philip had evangelized in Jerusalem and Samaria, but it was a messenger angel who told him to go into the desert where he met the Ethiopian eunuch. Acts 10 also reveals angelic intervention on behalf of Cornelius, and the church was enlarged to include Gentiles. As with the supernatural gifts of the Spirit, angelic activity did not cease after the time of the apostles. Angels are still actively involved with building God's kingdom on Earth. Nevertheless, wisdom teaches we would do well to heed Paul's warning: "But even if we, or an angel from heaven, preach any other gospel to you than what we have preached to you, let him be accursed" (Gal. 1:8). Any angelic message must be judged by God's eternal word of truth.

(Dan. 10:13/Ps. 91:11, 12) M.H.

27 So he arose and went. And behold,
[a]a man of Ethiopia, a eunuch of great
authority under Candace the queen of
the Ethiopians, who had charge of all
her treasury, and [b]had come to Jerusalem to worship,

WORD WEALTH

8:27 authority, *dunastes* (doo-*nahs*-tace); Strong's *#1413:* A high official, an important personage, a court official, one invested with power, a ruler, a sovereign, a prince, a royal minister, a potentate. (Compare "dynasty.") Luke 1:52 suggests that the *dunastes* of the world systems will be replaced by the Prince of Peace. In Acts 8:27, the *dunastes* only exists during the reign of Candace, queen of Ethiopia. Jesus' kingdom is a perpetual *dunastes* without end.

28 was returning. And sitting in his
chariot, he was *reading Isaiah the
prophet.
29 Then the Spirit said to Philip, "Go
near and overtake this chariot."

26 [1]Or *a deserted place*
27 [a]Ps. 68:31; 87:4; Is. 56:3; Zeph. 3:10 [b]1 Kin. 8:41, 42; John 12:20
28 *See WW at Mark 13:14.
30 *See WW at Matt. 2:5. • See WW at John 8:32.
31 *See WW at Jude 24.
32 [a]Is. 53:7, 8 [b]Matt. 26:62, 63; 27:12, 14; John 19:9
33 [a]Luke 23:1–25 [b]Luke 23:33–46 *See WW at Matt. 5:22.
35 [a]Luke 24:27; Acts 17:2; 18:28; 28:23
36 [a]Acts 10:47; 16:33
37 [a]Matt. 28:19; [Mark 16:16; Rom. 10:9, 10] [b]Matt. 16:16; John 6:69; 9:35, 38; 11:27 [1]NU, M omit v. 37. It is found in Western texts, including the Latin tradition. *See WW at Rev. 2:23.
39 [a]1 Kin. 18:12; 2 Kin. 2:16; Ezek. 3:12, 14; 2 Cor. 12:2 *See WW at 1 Thess. 4:17.
40 [a]Acts 21:8 [1]Same as Heb. *Ashdod*

CHAPTER 9

1 [a]Acts 7:57; 8:1, 3; 26:10, 11; Gal. 1:13; 1 Tim. 1:13

30 So Philip ran to him, and heard him
reading the *prophet Isaiah, and said,
"Do you *understand what you are
reading?"
31 And he said, "How *can I, unless
someone guides me?" And he asked
Philip to come up and sit with him.
32 The place in the Scripture which he
read was this:

[a]"He was led as a sheep to the
slaughter;
And as a lamb before its shearer
is silent,
[b]So He opened not His mouth.
33 *In His humiliation His [a]justice**
was taken away,
And who will declare His
generation?
For His life is [b]taken from the
earth."

34 So the eunuch answered Philip and
said, "I ask you, of whom does the
prophet say this, of himself or of some
other man?"
35 Then Philip opened his mouth,
[a]and beginning at this Scripture,
preached Jesus to him.
36 Now as they went down the road,
they came to some water. And the eunuch said, "See, *here is* water. [a]What
hinders me from being baptized?"
37 [1]Then Philip said, [a]"If you believe
with all your *heart, you may." And
he answered and said, [b]"I believe that
Jesus Christ is the Son of God."
38 So he commanded the chariot to
stand still. And both Philip and the eunuch went down into the water, and
he baptized him.
39 Now when they came up out of the
water, [a]the Spirit of the Lord *caught
Philip away, so that the eunuch saw
him no more; and he went on his way
rejoicing.
40 But Philip was found at [1]Azotus.
And passing through, he preached in
all the cities till he came to [a]Caesarea.

The Damascus Road: Saul Converted

9 Then [a]Saul, still breathing threats
and murder against the disciples of
the Lord, went to the high priest

8:27 The **man of Ethiopia** was a high-ranking court official of the queen mother who was a God-fearer, a Gentile who worshiped the Jewish God.

8:28 Reading in the ancient world was almost always done aloud. During his stay in Jerusalem, this man had probably heard about the resurrection of Christ and the unusual events of Pentecost, and now he was reading from an **Isaiah** scroll, specifically about the sacrificial death of the Messiah (vv. 32, 33).

8:39, 40 Philip was miraculously transported away by the **Spirit of the Lord.** He next appears in Acts 20 years later, still in Caesarea (21:8).

9:1–19 This is the first of three accounts in Acts of Paul's conversion to Christ (see 22:6–21; 26:12–18).

9:1 Paul earnestly believed he was doing the right thing. A number of OT zealots, like Elijah (see 1 Kin. 18:40), used violence to purge Israel from false religion.

2 and asked [a]letters from him to the synagogues of Damascus, so that if he found any who were of the Way, whether men or women, he might bring them bound to Jerusalem.

3 [a]As he journeyed he came near Damascus, and suddenly a light shone around him from heaven.

4 Then he fell to the ground, and heard a voice saying to him, "Saul, Saul, [a]why are you persecuting Me?"

5 And he said, "Who are You, Lord?" Then the Lord said, "I am Jesus, whom you are persecuting. [1]It *is* hard for you to kick against the goads."

6 So he, trembling and astonished, said, "Lord, what do You want me to do?" Then the Lord *said* to him, "Arise and go into the city, and you will be told what you must do."

7 And [a]the men who journeyed with him stood speechless, hearing a voice but *seeing no one.

8 Then Saul arose from the ground, and when his eyes were opened he saw no one. But they led him by the hand and brought *him* into Damascus.

9 And he was three days without sight, and neither ate nor drank.

Ananias Baptizes Saul

10 Now there was a certain disciple at Damascus [a]named Ananias; and to him the Lord said in a vision, "Ananias." And he said, "Here I am, Lord."

11 So the Lord *said* to him, "Arise and go to the street called Straight, and inquire at the house of Judas for *one* called Saul [a]of Tarsus, for behold, he is praying.

12 "And in a vision he has seen a man named Ananias coming in and putting *his* hand on him, so that he might receive his sight."

13 Then Ananias answered, "Lord, I have heard from many about this man, [a]how much [1]harm he has done to Your saints in Jerusalem.

14 "And here he has authority from the chief priests to bind all [a]who call on Your name."

15 But the Lord said to him, "Go, for [a]he is a chosen vessel of Mine to bear My name before [b]Gentiles, [c]kings, and the [d]children[1] of Israel.

16 "For [a]I will show him how many things he must suffer for My [b]name's sake."

17 [a]And Ananias went his way and entered the house; and [b]laying his hands on him he said, "Brother Saul, the Lord [1]Jesus, who appeared to you on the road as you came, has *sent me that you may receive your sight and [c]be filled with the Holy Spirit."

18 Immediately there fell from his eyes *something* like scales, and he received his sight at once; and he arose and was baptized.

19 So when he had received food, he was strengthened. [a]Then Saul spent some days with the disciples at Damascus.

Saul Preaches Christ

20 Immediately he **preached** [1]the Christ in the synagogues, that He is the Son of God.

WORD WEALTH

9:20 preached, *kerusso* (kay-*roos*-oh); Strong's *#2784:* To herald, tell abroad, publish, propagate, publicly proclaim, exhort, call out with a clear voice, communicate, preach. The herald is to give a public announcement of an official message and to issue whatever demands the message entails. The Christian herald is to proclaim the message of salvation through Jesus Christ and issue a summons to repent and receive forgiveness of sins.

21 Then all who heard were amazed, and said, [a]"Is this not he who destroyed those who called on this name in Jerusalem, and has come here for that purpose, so that he might bring them bound to the chief priests?"

2 [a]Acts 22:5 **3** [a]Acts 22:6; 26:12, 13; 1 Cor. 15:8 **4** [a][Matt. 25:40] **5** [1]NU, M omit the rest of v. 5 and begin v. 6 with *But arise and go* **7** [a]Dan. 10:7; John 12:29; [Acts 22:9; 26:13] *See WW at John 20:14. **10** [a]Acts 22:12 **11** [a]Acts 21:39; 22:3 **13** [a]Acts 9:1 [1]*bad things* **14** [a]Acts 7:59; 9:2, 21; 1 Cor. 1:2; 2 Tim. 2:22

15 [a]Acts 13:2; 22:21; Rom. 1:1; 1 Cor. 15:10; Gal. 1:15; Eph. 3:7, 8; 1 Tim. 2:7; 2 Tim. 1:11 [b]Rom. 1:5; 11:13; Gal. 2:7, 8 [c]Acts 25:22, 23; 26:1 [d]Acts 21:40; Rom. 1:16; 9:1–5 [1]Lit. *sons* **16** [a]Acts 20:23; 2 Cor. 11:23–28; 12:7–10; Gal. 6:17; Phil. 1:29, 30 [b]2 Cor. 4:11 **17** [a]Acts 22:12, 13 [b]Acts 8:17 [c]Acts 2:4; 4:31; 8:17; 13:52 [1]M omits *Jesus* *See WW at John 20:21. **19** [a]Acts 26:20 **20** [1]NU *Jesus* **21** [a]Acts 8:3; 9:13; Gal. 1:13, 23

9:4 Saul was not just persecuting people; he was opposing Christ (see Matt. 25:40, 45).

9:5 A goad is a pointed stick for urging on a team of oxen. This may mean that Paul was already having his conscience pricked about the terrible things he was doing.

9:6 Paul's dramatic conversion is considered by many to be one of the two great proofs of the validity of the Christian religion, the other being the resurrection of Christ. These two key events are the footings of the Book of Acts.

9:7 See note on 22:9.

9:13 Ananias was understandably reluctant about God's command, but the message was clear that he must go (v. 15).

9:16 How many things he must suffer: The call to ministry is bittersweet. See how Paul later describes the ministry in 2 Cor. 4:7–12.

9:17 Be filled with the Holy Spirit: It is generally agreed that Paul was converted three days earlier when he encountered the Lord (vv. 1–9). This experience then, which also included his apostolic commissioning, was likely Paul's initial "baptism with the Holy Spirit." See note on 1:5.

22 But Saul increased all the more in
strength, [a]and confounded the Jews
who dwelt in Damascus, proving that
this *Jesus* is the Christ.

Saul Escapes Death

23 Now after many days were past,
[a]the Jews plotted to kill him.
24 [a]But their plot became known to
Saul. And they watched the gates day
and night, to kill him.
25 Then the disciples took him by
night and [a]let *him* down through the
wall in a large basket.

Saul at Jerusalem

26 And [a]when Saul had come to Jerusalem, he tried to join the disciples; but
they were all afraid of him, and did not
believe that he was a disciple.
27 [a]But Barnabas took him and
brought *him* to the apostles. And he declared to them how he had seen the
Lord on the road, and that He had spoken to him, [b]and how he had preached
boldly at Damascus in the name of
Jesus.
28 So [a]he was with them at Jerusalem,
coming in and going out.
29 And he spoke boldly in the name
of the Lord Jesus and disputed against
the [a]Hellenists,[1] [b]but they attempted to
kill him.
30 When the brethren found out, they
brought him down to Caesarea and
sent him out to Tarsus.

The Church Prospers

31 [a]Then the [1]churches throughout all
Judea, Galilee, and Samaria had peace
and were [b]edified.[2] And walking in the
[c]fear of the Lord and in the [d]**comfort**
of the Holy Spirit, they were [e]multi-
plied.

WORD WEALTH

9:31 comfort, *paraklesis* (par-*ak*-lay-sis); Strong's *#3874:* A calling alongside to help, to comfort, to give consolation or encouragement. The *paraklete* is a strengthening presence, one who upholds those appealing for assistance. *Paraklesis* (comfort) can come to us both by the Holy Spirit (v. 31) and by the Scriptures (Rom. 15:4).

Aeneas Healed

32 Now it came to pass, as Peter went
[a]through all *parts of the country*, that
he also came down to the saints who
dwelt in Lydda.
33 There he found a certain man
named Aeneas, who had been bed-
ridden eight years and was paralyzed.
34 And Peter said to him, "Aeneas,
[a]Jesus the Christ heals you. Arise and
make your bed." Then he arose immediately.

22 [a]Acts 18:28 **23** [a]Acts 23:12; 2 Cor. 11:26 **24** [a]2 Cor. 11:32 **25** [a]Josh. 2:15; 1 Sam. 19:12 **26** [a]Acts 22:17–20; 26:20; Gal. 1:17, 18 **27** [a]Acts 4:36; 13:2 [b]Acts 9:20, 22 **28** [a]Gal. 1:18 **29** [a]Acts 6:1; 11:20 [b]Acts 9:23; 2 Cor. 11:26 [1]Greek-speaking Jews

31 [a]Acts 5:11; 8:1; 16:5 [b][Eph. 4:16, 29] [c]Ps. 34:9 [d]John 14:16 [e]Acts 16:5 [1]NU *church . . . was* [2]*built up* **32** [a]Acts 8:14 **34** [a][Acts 3:6, 16; 4:10]

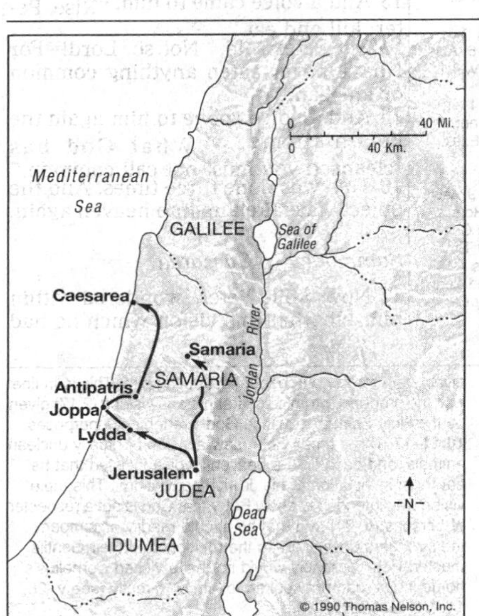

Peter's Missionary Journeys. Two journeys are recorded in Acts 8:14–25 and 9:32—10:48.

9:22 The church's greatest opponent became her greatest advocate.
9:23 After many days: Paul was in Arabia for three years after his conversion (see Gal. 1:18), some of that time having been spent in Damascus.
9:27 Barnabas means "Son of Consolation," which aptly describes his ministry here, bringing Paul and his former victims together.
9:29 Paul evidently spoke in the same synagogue where Stephen had spoken (see 6:9). The tables are now turned as Paul becomes the target of vicious persecution. The prediction of v. 16 has already begun.
9:32 Lydda, known as Lod today, was a small village west of Jerusalem on the way to Joppa (see v. 38).
9:34, 35 Aeneas was the recipient of a great blessing, but v. 35 indicates that the healing was really designed to bring many to Christ. The miracle was not just a marvel; it was a sign.

35 So all who dwelt at Lydda and
[a]Sharon saw him and [b]turned to the
Lord.

Dorcas Restored to Life

36 At Joppa there was a certain disciple named [1]Tabitha, which is translated [2]Dorcas. This woman was full
[a]of good works and charitable deeds
which she did.
37 But it happened in those days that
she became sick and died. When they
had washed her, they laid *her* in
[a]an upper room.
38 And since Lydda was near Joppa,
and the disciples had heard that Peter
was there, they sent two men to him,
imploring *him* not to delay in coming
to them.
39 Then Peter arose and went with
them. When he had come, they brought
him to the upper room. And all the widows stood by him weeping, showing
the tunics and garments which Dorcas
had made while she was with them.
40 But Peter [a]put them all out, and
[b]knelt down and prayed. And turning
to the body he [c]said, "Tabitha, arise."
And she opened her eyes, and when
she saw Peter she sat up.
41 Then he gave her *his* hand and lifted
her up; and when he had called the
saints and widows, he presented her
alive.
42 And it became known throughout
all Joppa, [a]and many believed on the
Lord.
43 So it was that he stayed many days
in Joppa with [a]Simon, a tanner.

Cornelius Sends a Delegation

10 There was a certain man in
[a]Caesarea called Cornelius, a
centurion of what was called the Ital-
ian [1]Regiment,
2 [a]a devout *man* and one who
[b]feared* God with all his household,
who gave [1]alms generously to the people, and prayed to God always.
3 About [1]the ninth hour of the day
[a]he saw clearly in a vision an angel
of God coming in and saying to him,
"Cornelius!"
4 And when he observed him, he was
afraid, and said, "What is it, lord?" So
he said to him, "Your prayers and your
alms have come up for a memorial before God.
5 "Now [a]send men to Joppa, and send
for Simon whose surname is Peter.
6 "He is lodging with [a]Simon, a tanner, whose house is by the sea. [b]He[1]
will tell you what you must do."
7 And when the angel who spoke to
him had departed, Cornelius called two
of his household servants and a devout
soldier from among those who waited
on him continually.
8 So when he had explained all *these*
things to them, he sent them to Joppa.

Peter's Vision

9 The next day, as they went on their
journey and drew near the city, [a]Peter
went up on the housetop to *pray,
about [1]the sixth hour.
10 Then he became very hungry and
wanted to eat; but while they made
ready, he fell into a trance
11 and [a]saw heaven opened and an object like a great sheet bound at the four
corners, descending to him and let
down to the earth.
12 In it were all kinds of four-footed
animals of the earth, wild beasts,
creeping things, and birds of the air.
13 And a voice came to him, "Rise, Peter; kill and eat."
14 But Peter said, "Not so, Lord! [a]For
I have never eaten anything common
or unclean."
15 And a voice *spoke* to him again the
second time, [a]"What God has
[1]cleansed you must not call common."
16 This was done three times. And the
object was taken up into heaven again.

Summoned to Caesarea

17 Now while Peter [1]wondered within
himself what this vision which he had

35 [a]1 Chr. 5:16; 27:29; Is. 33:9; 35:2; 65:10 [b]Acts 11:21; 15:19
36 [a]1 Tim. 2:10; Titus 3:8 [1]Lit., in Aram., *Gazelle* [2]Lit., in Gr., *Gazelle*
37 [a]Acts 1:13; 9:39
40 [a]Matt. 9:25 [b]Luke 22:41; Acts 7:60 [c]Mark 5:41, 42; John 11:43
42 [a]John 11:45
43 [a]Acts 10:6

CHAPTER 10

1 [a]Acts 8:40; 23:23 [1]*Cohort*
2 [a]Acts 8:2; 9:22; 22:12 [b][Acts 10:22, 35; 13:16, 26] [1]*charitable gifts* *See WW at Matt. 10:26.
3 [a]Acts 10:30; 11:13 [1]3 P.M.
5 [a]Acts 11:13, 14
6 [a]Acts 9:43 [b]Acts 11:14 [1]NU, M omit the rest of v. 6.
9 [a]Acts 10:9–32; 11:5–14 [1]Noon *See WW at Matt. 6:6.
11 [a]Ezek. 1:1; Matt. 3:16; Acts 7:56; Rev. 4:1; 19:11
14 [a]Lev. 11:4; 20:25; Deut. 14:3, 7; Ezek. 4:14
15 [a][Matt. 15:11; Mark 7:19]; Acts 10:28; [Rom. 14:14]; 1 Cor. 10:25; [1 Tim. 4:4; Titus 1:15] [1]Declared clean
17 [1]*was perplexed*

9:36 Joppa was just south of modern Tel Aviv.
10:1 A centurion was a noncommissioned Roman military officer responsible for a hundred men.
10:2 Although he was not a Jewish proselyte, Cornelius believed in Jewish monotheism and ethical teachings. In spite of the fact that he was **devout,** he still needed to hear the way of salvation.
10:9, 10 The sixth hour, noon. The flat roof was the customary place for relaxation and privacy. The Greek word for **trance,** of which the English word "ecstasy" is a transliteration of the Greek verb *existemi,* displacing the individual's ordinary state of mind with an elevated, God-given state for the purpose of instructing him. This is in line with the prophetic promise of dreams and visions (2:17) given by the Holy Spirit to advance God's redemptive purposes.
10:11–17 Three times Peter saw a vision of ritually unclean animals, and each time a heavenly voice insisted that he eat them in violation of his Jewish convictions. This triple vision was intended to show Peter that God is not a respecter of persons (v. 34) and that he should readily accompany the strangers downstairs to the residence of their Gentile master. Peter probably would not have visited Cornelius's home if God had not spoken to him so directly (see v. 28; 11:2, 3; Gal. 2:11, 12).

seen meant, behold, the men who had
been sent from Cornelius had made inquiry for Simon's house, and stood before the gate.
18 And they called and asked whether
Simon, whose surname was Peter, was
lodging there.
19 While Peter thought about the vision, [a]the *Spirit said to him, "Behold,
three men are seeking you.
20 [a]"Arise therefore, go down and go
with them, *doubting nothing; for I
have sent them."
21 Then Peter went down to the men
[1]who had been sent to him from Cornelius, and said, "Yes, I am he whom
you seek. For what reason have you
come?"
22 And they said, "Cornelius *the* centurion, a just man, one who fears God
and [a]has a good reputation among all
the nation of the Jews, was divinely instructed by a holy angel to summon
you to his house, and to hear words
from you."
23 Then he invited them in and lodged
them. On the next day Peter went away
with them, [a]and some brethren from
Joppa accompanied him.

Peter Meets Cornelius

24 And the following day they entered
Caesarea. Now Cornelius was waiting
for them, and had called together his
relatives and close *friends.
25 As Peter was coming in, Cornelius
met him and fell down at his feet and
worshiped *him.*
26 But Peter lifted him up, saying,
[a]"Stand up; I myself am also a man."
27 And as he talked with him, he went
in and found many who had come together.
28 Then he said to them, "You know
how [a]unlawful it is for a Jewish man
to keep company with or go to one of
another nation. But [b]God has shown
me that I should not call any man common or unclean.
29 "Therefore I came without objection as soon as I was sent for. I ask,
then, for what reason have you sent
for me?"
30 So Cornelius said, [1]"Four days ago
I was fasting until this hour; and at the
ninth hour I prayed in my house, and
behold, [a]a man stood before me
[b]in bright clothing,
31 "and said, 'Cornelius, [a]your prayer
has been heard, and [b]your [1]alms are
remembered in the sight of God.
32 'Send therefore to Joppa and call Simon here, whose surname is Peter. He
is lodging in the house of Simon, a tanner, by the sea. [1]When he comes, he
will speak to you.'
33 "So I sent to you immediately, and
you have done well to come. Now
therefore, we are all present before
God, to hear all the things commanded
you by God."

Preaching to Cornelius' Household

34 Then Peter opened *his* mouth and
said: [a]"In truth I *perceive that God
shows no **partiality.**

> **WORD WEALTH**
>
> **10:34 partiality,** *prosopoleptes* (pros-oh-pol-*ape*-tace); Strong's *#4381:* A receiver of a face, one who takes sides, showing favoritism, exhibiting bias, showing discrimination, showing partiality, treating one person better than another. While society makes distinctions among people, God's love and grace are available for all, and can be received by anyone.

35 "But [a]in every nation whoever fears
Him and *works righteousness is
[b]accepted by Him.
36 "The word which *God* sent to the
[1]children of Israel, [a]preaching *peace
through Jesus Christ—[b]He is Lord of
all—
37 "that *word you know, which was
proclaimed throughout all Judea, and
[a]began from Galilee after the baptism
which John preached:
38 "how [a]God anointed Jesus of Nazareth with the Holy Spirit and with
*power, who [b]went about doing good
and healing all who were oppressed by
the devil, [c]for God was with Him.
39 "And we are [a]witnesses of all things
which He did both in the land of the
Jews and in Jerusalem, whom [1]they
[b]killed by hanging on a tree.
40 "Him [a]God raised up on the third
day, and showed Him openly,
41 [a]"not to all the people, but to witnesses chosen before by God, *even* to

19 [a]Acts 11:12 *See WW at Rom. 7:6. **20** [a]Acts 15:7–9 *See WW at Acts 11:12. **21** [1]NU, M omit *who had been sent to him from Cornelius* **22** [a]Acts 22:12 **23** [a]Acts 10:45; 11:12 **24** *See WW at John 11:11. **26** [a]Acts 14:14, 15; Rev. 19:10; 22:8 **28** [a]John 4:9; 18:28; Acts 11:3; Gal. 2:12 [b][Acts 10:14, 35; 15:8, 9] **30** [a]Acts 1:10 [b]Matt. 28:3; Mark 16:5 [1]NU *Four days ago to this hour, at the ninth hour* **31** [a]Dan. 10:12 [b]Heb. 6:10 [1]*charitable gifts* **32** [1]NU omits the rest of v. 32. **34** [a]Deut. 10:17; 2 Chr. 19:7; Rom. 2:11; Gal. 2:6; Eph. 6:9 *See WW at John 1:5. **35** [a]Acts 15:9; [1 Cor. 12; 13; Eph. 2:13] [b]Ps. 15:1, 2 *See WW at John 3:21. **36** [a]Is. 57:19; Eph. 2:14; [Col. 1:20] [b]Matt. 28:18; Acts 2:36; Rom. 10:12; 1 Cor. 15:27 [1]Lit. *sons* *See WW at Luke 1:79. **37** [a]Luke 4:14 *See WW at Matt. 4:4. **38** [a]Is. 61:1–3; Luke 4:18 [b]Matt. 4:23 [c]John 3:2; 8:29 *See WW at Acts 4:33. **39** [a]Acts 1:8 [b]Acts 2:23 [1]NU, M *they also* **40** [a]Hos. 6:2; Matt. 12:39, 40; 16:4; 20:19; John 2:19–21; Acts 2:24 **41** [a][John 14:17, 19, 22; 15:27]

10:34–43 See note on 3:12–26
10:34 The fact that **God shows no partiality** means that He wants *everyone,* regardless of their nationality or ethnic orientation, to hear the gospel and believe. In Christ there are no barriers (Gal. 3:26–29).

10:35 Peter is not suggesting that salvation is possible apart from the redemptive work of Christ; rather, he emphasizes that through Christ people of all nations can be saved even if they are not Jews.

us [b]who ate and drank with Him after
He arose from the dead.
42 "And [a]He commanded us to preach
to the people, and to testify [b]that it is
He who was ordained by God *to be*
Judge [c]of the living and the dead.
43 [a]"To Him all the prophets *witness
that, through His name, [b]whoever believes in Him will receive [c]remission[1]*
of sins."

The Holy Spirit Falls on the Gentiles

2 44 While Peter was still speaking these
words, [a]the Holy Spirit fell upon all
those who heard the word.
45 [a]And [1]those of the circumcision
who believed were astonished, as
many as came with Peter, [b]because the
gift of the Holy Spirit had been poured
out on the Gentiles also.
46 For they heard them speak with
tongues and *magnify God. Then Peter
answered,

KINGDOM DYNAMICS

10:46 Tongues as a Sign, SPIRITUAL GIFTS. The experience of "glossolalia" functions as a sign of the indwelling presence of the Holy Spirit, affirming His abiding presence and assuring the believer of an invigorated living witness. An elaboration of this and related themes appears in the study article on page 2018, "Holy Spirit Gifts and Power."

(Acts 2:4/Acts 19:2) P.W.

1 47 "Can anyone forbid water, that
these should not be baptized who have
received the Holy Spirit [a]just as we
have?"
48 [a]And he commanded them to be
baptized [b]in the name of the Lord.
Then they asked him to stay a few
days.

Peter Defends God's Grace

11 Now the apostles and brethren
who were in Judea heard that
the Gentiles had also received the word
of God.
2 And when Peter came up to Jerusalem, [a]those of the circumcision contended with him,

41 [b]Luke 24:30, 41–43
42 [a]Matt. 28:19 [b]John 5:22, 27; Acts 17:31 [c]Rom. 14:9; 2 Tim. 4:1; 1 Pet. 4:5
43 [a][Is. 42:1; 53:11; 61:1]; Jer. 31:34; Dan. 9:24; Hos. 6:1–3; Mic. 7:18; Zech. 13:1; Mal. 4:2 [b][John 3:16, 18; Acts 26:18]; Rom. 10:11; Gal. 3:22 [c]Acts 13:38, 39 [1]*forgiveness* *See WW at Acts 26:22. • See WW at Heb. 9:22.
44 [a]Acts 4:31
45 [a]Acts 10:23 [b]Is. 42:1, 6; 49:6; Luke 2:32; John 11:52; Acts 11:18 [1]The Jews
46 *See WW at Acts 5:13.
47 [a]Acts 2:4; 10:44; 11:17; 15:8
48 [a]1 Cor. 1:14–17 [b]Acts 2:38; 8:16; 19:5

CHAPTER 11

2 [a]Acts 10:45
3 [a]Matt. 9:11; Acts 10:28 [b]Gal. 2:12
4 [a]Luke 1:3
5 [a]Acts 10:9
12 [a][John 16:13]; Acts 10:19; 15:7 [b]Acts 10:23
13 [a]Acts 10:30
15 [a]Acts 2:1–4; 15:7–9 *See WW at Acts 7:33.

3 saying, [a]"You went in to uncircumcised men [b]and ate with them!"
4 But Peter explained *it* to them
[a]in order from the beginning, saying:
5 [a]"I was in the city of Joppa praying;
and in a trance I saw a vision, an object
descending like a great sheet, let down
from heaven by four corners; and it
came to me.
6 "When I observed it intently and
considered, I saw four-footed animals
of the earth, wild beasts, creeping
things, and birds of the air.
7 "And I heard a voice saying to me,
'Rise, Peter; kill and eat.'
8 "But I said, 'Not so, Lord! For nothing common or unclean has at any time
entered my mouth.'
9 "But the voice answered me again
from heaven, 'What God has cleansed
you must not call common.'
10 "Now this was done three times,
and all were drawn up again into
heaven.
11 "At that very moment, three men
stood before the house where I was,
having been sent to me from Caesarea.
12 "Then [a]the Spirit told me to go with
them, **doubting** nothing. Moreover
[b]these six brethren accompanied me,
and we entered the man's house.

WORD WEALTH

11:12 doubting, *diakrino* (dee-ak-*ree*-no); Strong's *#1252:* Has two definitions. 1) To judge thoroughly; to decide between two or more choices; to make a distinction; to separate two components, elements, or factors; to render a decision; to evaluate carefully. 2) The word also connotes a conflict with oneself, in the sense of hesitating, having misgivings, doubting, being divided in decision making, or wavering between hope and fear. This is its use here.

13 [a]"And he told us how he had seen
an angel standing in his house, who
said to him, 'Send men to Joppa, and
call for Simon whose surname is Peter,
14 'who will tell you words by which
you and all your household will be
saved.'
15 "And as I began to speak, the *Holy
Spirit fell upon them, [a]as upon us at
the beginning.

10:44–48 Just as the Jewish believers received the Spirit and praised God in tongues at Pentecost, these Gentile believers now received the identical gift (v. 45; 11:15). The Jewish Christians who were present knew that the Gentiles had received **the gift of the Holy Spirit** (v. 45), **for they heard them speak with tongues** (v. 46). That tongues are at least one means of giving evidence to the baptism in the Holy Spirit is unmistakably clear here. See note on 2:4.

10:44, 45 See section 2 of Truth-In-Action at the end of Acts.

10:47, 48 See section 1 of Truth-In-Action at the end of Acts.

11:4–14 See note on 10:11–17.

16 "Then I remembered the *word of
the Lord, how He said, [a]'John indeed
baptized with water, but [b]you shall be
baptized with the Holy Spirit.'
17 [a]"If therefore God gave them the
same gift as *He gave* us when we believed on the Lord Jesus Christ,
[b]who was I that I could withstand
God?"
18 When they heard these things they
became silent; and they glorified
God, saying, [a]"Then God has also
*granted to the Gentiles repentance to
*life."

Barnabas and Saul at Antioch

19 [a]Now those who were scattered after the persecution that arose over Stephen traveled as far as Phoenicia, Cyprus, and Antioch, preaching the word
to no one but the Jews only.
20 But some of them were men from
Cyprus and Cyrene, who, when they
had come to Antioch, spoke to [a]the
Hellenists, preaching the Lord Jesus.
21 And [a]the hand of the Lord was with
them, and a great number believed and
[b]turned to the Lord.
22 Then news of these things came to
the ears of the church in Jerusalem,
and they sent out [a]Barnabas to go as
far as Antioch.
23 When he came and had seen the
grace of God, he was glad, and [a]en-
couraged them all that with *purpose
of heart they should continue with the
Lord.
24 For he was a *good man, [a]full of
the Holy Spirit and of *faith. [b]And a
great many people were added to the
Lord.
25 Then Barnabas departed for [a]Tar-
sus to seek Saul.
26 And when he had found him, he
brought him to Antioch. So it was that
for a whole year they assembled with
the church and taught a great many
people. And the disciples were first
called Christians in Antioch.

Relief to Judea

27 And in these days [a]prophets came
from Jerusalem to Antioch.
28 Then one of them, named [a]Agabus,
stood up and showed by the Spirit that
there was going to be a great famine
throughout all the world, which also
happened in the days of [b]Claudius
Caesar.
29 Then the disciples, each according
to his ability, determined to send
[a]relief to the brethren dwelling in Judea.
30 [a]This they also did, and sent it to
the elders by the hands of Barnabas
and Saul.

16 [a]Matt. 3:11; Mark 1:8; John 1:26, 33; Acts 1:5; 19:4 [b]Is. 44:3 *See WW at Matt. 4:4.
17 [a][Acts 15:8, 9] [b]Acts 10:47
18 [a]Is. 42:1, 6; 49:6; Luke 2:32; John 11:52; Rom. 10:12, 13; 15:9, 16 *See WW at Acts 20:35. • See WW at 1 John 5:20.
19 [a]Acts 8:1, 4
20 [a]Acts 6:1; 9:29
21 [a]Luke 1:66; Acts 2:47 [b]Acts 9:35; 14:1
22 [a]Acts 4:36; 9:27
23 [a]Acts 13:43; 14:22 *See WW at Rom. 8:28.
24 [a]Acts 6:5 [b]Acts 5:14; 11:21 *See WW at Phil. 1:6. • See WW at Mark 11:22.
25 [a]Acts 9:11, 30
27 [a]Acts 2:17; 13:1; 15:32; 21:9; 1 Cor. 12:28; Eph. 4:11
28 [a]John 16:13; Acts 21:10 [b]Acts 18:2
29 [a]Rom. 15:26; 1 Cor. 16:1; 2 Cor. 9:1
30 [a]Acts 12:25

KINGDOM DYNAMICS

11:27–30 The Office of the Prophet, PROPHECY. Agabus is an example of the "office" of the "prophet" in the NT. This role differs from the operation of the gift of prophecy in the life of the believer, for it entails a Christ-appointed ministry of a person rather than the Holy Spirit-distributed gift through a person. In the NT, this office was not sensationalized as it tends to be today. Such an attitude is unworthy, both in the prophet and in those to whom he ministers, and is certain to result in an unfruitful end. (Apparently Paul was addressing such assumption of the prophetic office when he issued the challenge of 1 Cor. 14:37, calling for submission to spiritual authority rather than self-serving independence.) The office of prophet cannot be taken lightly. There is nothing in the NT that reduces the stringent requirements for serving this role, and Deut. 18:20–22 ought to be regarded seriously. Prophecy is nothing to be "experimented" with, for souls are in the balance in the exercise of every ministry.

Further wisdom may be gained by noting that on biblical terms there is more than one type of ministry by a prophet. While a few exercised remarkable predictive gifts (Daniel, Zechariah, John), other traits of the prophetic office are seen: 1) preaching—especially at a

(cont. on next page)

11:18 This is a pivotal verse. What happened to Cornelius under the ministry of Peter, and the very positive response of the Jerusalem church, set the stage for Paul's extensive ministry to the Gentiles in the remaining chapters.
11:19 Periodically, the Jews had been forcibly relocated during the previous centuries, and they had established worship and teaching centers in order to maintain their religious and cultural identity. Missionary work out of the Jerusalem church was at first limited exclusively to these synagogues of the dispersion.
11:26 Christians is a transliteration of the Greek *christianos,* which was a simple, and most likely a derisive name given to the early followers of Christ (Greek *christos*), not unlike a believer's today being called a "Jesus-person" in an uncomplimentary way.
11:28 Apparently, predictive prophecy about specific future events was the exclusive ministry of "the prophet," while in 1 Cor. 14:1 Paul encouraged everyone to prophesy for the general edification or encouragement of the church (1 Cor. 14:3). The Scriptures, then, seem to distinguish between the gift of prophecy and the office of the prophet. **Claudius Caesar** was the Roman emperor in A.D. 41–54. The Jewish historian Josephus records a famine that occurred in Judea in A.D. 46.

(*cont. from preceding page*)
national or international level (John the Baptist); 2) teaching—especially when unusual insight is present and broad impact made in serving God's people (Ezra); 3) miracles—as remarkable signs to accompany a prophet's preaching (Elijah); 4) renewal—as with Samuel (1 Sam. 3:21; 4:1), or that called for by the psalmist and by Amos (Ps. 74:9; Amos 8:11, 12). The incident of Agabus resulted in effective action by the church's rising to meet a challenging situation. This is a valid test of the prophetic office. It is for edification and not for entertainment—to enlarge and refresh the body, whether locally or beyond.
(Acts 21:11/Deut. 28:1) J.W.H.

Herod's Violence to the Church

12 Now about that time Herod the
king stretched out *his* hand to
harass some from the church.
2 Then he killed James [a]the brother
of John with the sword.
3 And because he saw that it pleased
the Jews, he proceeded further to seize
Peter also. Now it was *during* [a]the
Days of Unleavened Bread.
4 So [a]when he had arrested him, he
put *him* in prison, and delivered *him*
to four [1]squads of soldiers to keep him,
intending to bring him before the people after Passover.

Peter Freed from Prison

3 5 Peter was therefore kept in prison,
but [1]constant prayer was offered to
God for him by the church.
6 And when Herod was about to bring
him out, that night Peter was sleeping,
bound with two chains between two
soldiers; and the guards before the
door were [1]keeping the prison.
7 Now behold, [a]an angel of the Lord
stood by *him*, and a light shone in the
prison; and he struck Peter on the side
and raised him up, saying, "Arise
quickly!" And his chains fell off *his*
hands.
8 Then the angel said to him, "Gird
yourself and tie on your sandals"; and
so he did. And he said to him, "Put on
your garment and follow me."

CHAPTER 12
2 [a]Matt. 4:21; 20:23
3 [a]Ex. 12:15; 23:15; Acts 20:6
4 [a]John 21:18 [1]Gr. *tetrads,* squads of four
5 [1]NU *constantly* or *earnestly*
6 [1]*guarding*
7 [a]Acts 5:19
9 [a]Ps. 126:1 [b]Acts 10:3, 17; 11:5 *See WW at John 13:36. • See WW at Rom. 3:4.
10 [a]Acts 5:19; 16:26
11 [a][Ps. 34:7]; Dan. 3:28; 6:22; [Heb. 1:14] [b]Job 5:19; [Ps. 33:18, 19; 34:22; 41:2]; 2 Cor. 1:10; [2 Pet. 2:9]
12 [a]Acts 4:23 [b]Acts 13:5, 13; 15:37; 2 Tim. 4:11; Philem. 24; 1 Pet. 5:13 [c]Acts 12:5
14 *See WW at Luke 5:22.
15 [a]Gen. 48:16; [Matt. 18:10]
17 [a]Acts 13:16; 19:33; 21:40

9 So he went out and *followed him,
and [a]did not know that what was done
by the angel was *real, but thought
[b]he was seeing a vision.
10 When they were past the first and
the second guard posts, they came to
the iron gate that leads to the city,
[a]which opened to them of its own accord; and they went out and went
down one street, and immediately the
angel departed from him.
11 And when Peter had come to himself, he said, "Now I know for certain
that [a]the Lord has sent His angel, and
[b]has delivered me from the hand of
Herod and *from* all the expectation of
the Jewish people."
12 So, when he had considered *this*,
[a]he came to the house of Mary, the
mother of [b]John whose surname was
Mark, where many were gathered together [c]praying.
13 And as Peter knocked at the door
of the gate, a girl named Rhoda came
to answer.
14 When she *recognized Peter's
voice, because of *her* gladness she did
not open the gate, but ran in and announced that Peter stood before the
gate.
15 But they said to her, "You are beside yourself!" Yet she kept insisting
that it was so. So they said, [a]"It is his
angel."
16 Now Peter continued knocking; and
when they opened *the door* and saw
him, they were astonished.
17 But [a]motioning to them with his
hand to keep silent, he declared to
them how the Lord had brought him
out of the prison. And he said, "Go,
tell these things to James and to the
brethren." And he departed and went
to another place.

KINGDOM DYNAMICS

12:1–17 Unceasing Prayer Is a Key to Deliverance, PRAYER. This conflict is a study in ongoing confrontation with evil. The Herods symbolize Satan's relentless attack on the church. Herod the Great had sought to kill Jesus; his son slew John the Baptist; his grandson beheaded

12:1 Herod is Herod Agrippa I (A.D. 37–44), grandson of Herod the Great. Little is recorded about this man in Scripture, but it is known that he had helped Claudius become emperor of Rome after the notorious Emperor Caligula was murdered. Herod Agrippa I suffered an untimely and humiliating death (vv. 20–24). By including this account here Luke may be showing a connection between the death of Herod and his persecution of Christians.
12:2 James was the first of the 12 apostles to be martyred.
12:3 Days of Unleavened Bread was a part of the Passover festival in the spring (see v. 4 and Lev. 23:4–8).
12:4 Four squads was sixteen soldiers.
12:5 See section 3 of Truth-In-Action at the end of Acts.
12:17 James was the Lord's brother (see Mark 6:3) who became the leader of the Jerusalem church (15:13; 21:18) and who wrote the Epistle of James. Paul refers to him as one of the "pillars" of the church (Gal. 2:9) and as an apostle (Gal. 1:19).

James and now was hiding Peter in prison for execution after Passover. While Peter suffered in chains, the church suffered with him on their knees. Hour after hour they wrestled in prayer; and when they had done all they could do, God began. Suddenly an angel "anesthetized" the 16 guards and removed Peter's chains. (But neither God nor His angel did what Peter could do for himself. He had to put on his garments and sandals and follow.) Nothing hindered their escape. An iron gate opened by itself; and earnest, unceasing prayers brought deliverance. Curiously, the only place Peter found impassable was his friends' front door! Even those who pray sometimes fail to see or believe the speed with which God works when they pray.

(2 Chr. 6:12–42; 7:1/Matt. 6:9–13) L.L.

18 Then, as soon as it was day, there
was no small [1]stir among the soldiers
about what had become of Peter.
19 But when Herod had searched for
him and not found him, he examined
the guards and commanded that *they*
should be put to death. And he went
down from Judea to Caesarea, and
stayed *there.*

Herod's Violent Death

20 Now Herod had been very angry
with the people of [a]Tyre and Sidon; but
they came to him *with one accord, and
having made Blastus [1]the king's personal aide their friend, they asked for
peace, because [b]their country was
[2]supplied with food by the king's *country.*
21 So on a set day Herod, arrayed in
royal apparel, sat on his *throne and
gave an oration to them.
22 And the people kept shouting, "The
voice of a god and not of a man!"
23 Then immediately an angel of the
Lord [a]struck him, because [b]he did not
give glory to God. And he was eaten
by worms and [1]died.
24 But [a]the word of God grew and multiplied.

18 [1]*disturbance* **20** [a]Matt. 11:21 [b]1 Kin. 5:11; Ezra 3:7; Ezek. 27:17 [1]*who was in charge of the king's bedchamber* [2]Lit. *nourished* *See WW at Acts 2:1. **21** *See WW at Matt. 27:19. **23** [a]1 Sam. 25:38; 2 Sam. 24:16, 17; 2 Kin. 19:35; Acts 5:19 [b]Ps. 115:1 [1]*breathed his last* **24** [a]Is. 55:11; Acts 6:7; 19:20

25 [a]Acts 11:30 [b]Acts 11:30 [c]Acts 13:5, 13 [d]Acts 12:12; 15:37 [1]NU, M *to*

CHAPTER 13

1 [a]Acts 14:26 [b]Acts 11:22 [c]Rom. 16:21 **2** [a]Num. 8:14; Acts 9:15; 22:21; Rom. 1:1; Gal. 1:15; 2:9 [b]Matt. 9:38; Acts 14:26; Rom. 10:15; Eph. 3:7, 8; 1 Tim. 2:7; 2 Tim. 1:11; Heb. 5:4 **3** [a]Matt. 9:15; Mark 2:20; Luke 5:35; Acts 6:6

Barnabas and Saul Appointed

25 And [a]Barnabas and Saul returned
[1]from Jerusalem when they had
[b]fulfilled *their* ministry, and they also
[c]took with them [d]John whose surname
was Mark.

13 Now [a]in the church that was at 3
Antioch there were certain
prophets and teachers: [b]Barnabas,
Simeon who was called Niger, [c]Lucius
of Cyrene, Manaen who had been
brought up with Herod the tetrarch,
and Saul.
2 As they **ministered** to the Lord and
fasted, the Holy Spirit said, [a]"Now separate to Me Barnabas and Saul for the
work [b]to which I have called them."
3 Then, [a]having fasted and prayed,
and laid hands on them, they sent *them*
away.

WORD WEALTH

13:2 ministered, *leitourgeo* (lie-toorg-*eh*-oh); Strong's *#3008:* Performing religious or charitable acts, fulfilling an office, discharging a function, officiating as a priest, serving God with prayers and fastings. (Compare "liturgy" and "liturgical.") The word describes the Aaronic priesthood ministering Levitical services (Heb. 10:11). In Rom. 15:27, it is used of meeting financial needs of the Christians, performing a service to the Lord by doing so. Here the Christians at Antioch were fulfilling an office and discharging a normal function by ministering to the Lord in fastings and prayer.

KINGDOM DYNAMICS

13:1—14:28 Prayer and Fasting Birth Signs and Wonders, PRAYER. The signs-and-wonders ministry of Paul and Barnabas was birthed as church leaders prayed, fasted, and sought the Lord. After the Holy Spirit Himself had called the two men, the leaders laid hands upon them and sent them forth (13:1–4). Later, Paul and Barnabas followed that same pattern, traveling from city to city, strengthening disciples and ordaining elders in the churches (14:22, 23). What is that pattern? Every ministry sent forth

(*cont. on next page*)

12:20–23 See note on v. 1. Luke's account of Herod's unusual death is corroborated by the first-century Jewish historian Josephus.

13:1–3 See section 3 of Truth-In-Action at the end of Acts.

13:1 Simeon is not mentioned anywhere else in the Bible. Some commentators speculate he may have been the same person as Simon of Cyrene, the man who bore Jesus' cross (Luke 23:26). **Manaen who had been brought up with Herod:** perhaps they were childhood friends. This suggests that he was probably a man of distinction.

13:2, 3 This is the commissioning of Paul's great apostolic ministry. **Ministered** translates a verb used of the official service of priests. Here it speaks of their ministry of public worship. They **fasted:** Fasting is a spiritual exercise, a voluntary restraint from food for the purpose of seeking God. This practice was encouraged by Jesus' own teaching (Matt. 9:15; Luke 5:35). **The Holy Spirit** probably spoke in a prophecy uttered by one of the "prophets" (v. 1). **Laid hands on them** is an act of spiritual impartation and commissioning.

(*cont. from preceding page*)
is God's intercessor, standing between the overflowing abundance of God and the overwhelming need of humanity. Therefore, those who send them must be moved by the Holy Spirit through prayer, not by their own spirits, to send men and women whom God has anointed and appointed. When today's church discovers direction for and advances all ministry in and through prayer, we will see opposition and unbelief bow before us as, once again, God confirms His Word with signs and wonders (14:3).

(Eph. 3:14–21/Acts 4:1–37) L.L.

 **KINGDOM DYNAMICS**

13:1–3 Fasting and Prayer, LEADER TRAITS. Leaders of the early church arrived at decisions only after fasting and prayer. In Antioch the prophets and teachers fasted and prayed, seeking God's direction for the church. While they waited on God, the Holy Spirit gave direction (v. 2), thus beginning the missionary ministry, which eventually took the gospel to the whole world. Godly leaders rely on God for the direction and the empowering of their lives and ministry. Disciplined fasting and constant prayer are proven means for this, and as such, are mandatory in the lives of leaders (Matt. 9:15).

(Num. 13:1—14:45/Acts 16:6–10) J.B.

Preaching in Cyprus

4 So, being sent out by the Holy
Spirit, they went down to Seleucia, and
from there they sailed to [a]Cyprus.
5 And when they arrived in Salamis,
[a]they preached the word of God in the
synagogues of the Jews. They also had
[b]John as *their* assistant.
6 Now when they had gone through
[1]the island to Paphos, they found
[a]a certain sorcerer, a false prophet, a
Jew whose name *was* Bar-Jesus,
7 who was with the proconsul, Sergius Paulus, an intelligent man. This
man called for Barnabas and Saul and
sought to hear the word of God.
8 But [a]Elymas the sorcerer (for so his
name is translated) [1]withstood* them,
seeking to turn the proconsul away
from the faith.
9 Then Saul, who also *is called* Paul, 2
[a]filled with the Holy Spirit, looked intently at him
10 and said, "O full of all deceit and

4 [a]Acts 4:36
5 [a][Acts 13:46] [b]Acts 12:25; 15:37
6 [a]Acts 8:9 [1]NU *the whole island*
8 [a]Ex. 7:11; 2 Tim. 3:8 [1]*opposed* *See WW at Eph. 6:13.
9 [a]Acts 2:4; 4:8

13:4 This is the beginning of Paul's first missionary journey, which ends in 14:26–28. See map of Paul's first journey.
13:6 Bar-Jesus means "Son of Jesus," but suggests no relationship to our Lord. Jesus, or Joshua, was a common name at the time.
13:7 The Roman Empire was divided into *imperial* provinces, which were administrated by appointed representatives of the emperor called procurators (as Pilate in Judea), and *senatorial* provinces, which were presided over by proconsuls appointed by the Roman senate. **Sergius Paulus** was the **proconsul** of the island of Cyprus.
13:9 See section 2 of Truth-In-Action at the end of Acts.
13:9 See note on 4:8.

Paul Goes to Galatia (The First Missionary Journey, Acts 13; 14). Sent out from the church at Antioch (Acts 13:1–3), Paul and Barnabas went to the cities of Galatia in Asia Minor. The Jewish synagogues in these cities provided Paul a platform for preaching the gospel. At times, however, he even encountered opposition from the synagogues.

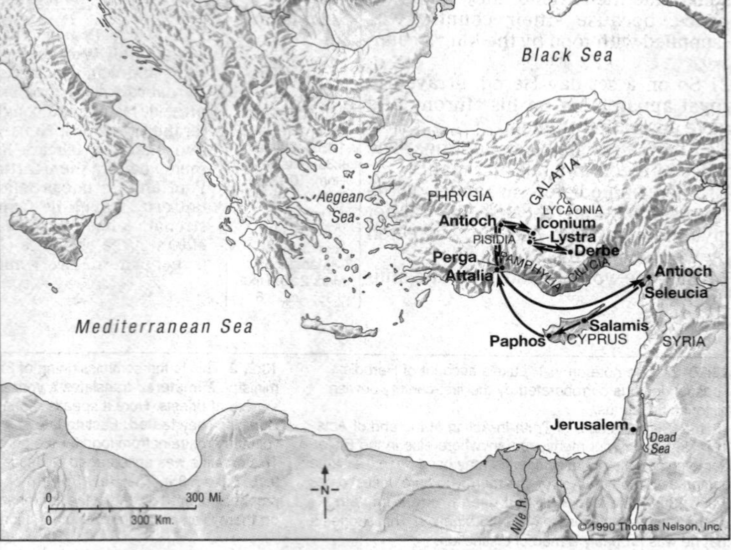

all fraud, [a]*you* son of the devil, *you* enemy of all righteousness, will you not
cease perverting the straight ways of
the Lord?
11 "And now, indeed, [a]the hand of the
Lord *is* upon you, and you shall be
blind, not seeing the sun for a time."
And immediately a *dark mist fell on
him, and he went around seeking
someone to lead him by the hand.
12 Then the proconsul believed, when
he saw what had been done, being astonished at the teaching of the Lord.

At Antioch in Pisidia

13 Now when Paul and his party set
sail from Paphos, they came to Perga
in Pamphylia; and [a]John, departing
from them, returned to Jerusalem.
14 But when they departed from
Perga, they came to Antioch in Pisidia,
and [a]went into the synagogue on the
Sabbath day and sat down.
15 And [a]after the reading of the Law
and the Prophets, the rulers of the
synagogue sent to them, saying, "Men
and brethren, if you have [b]any word
of [1]exhortation for the people, say
on."
16 Then Paul stood up, and motioning
with *his* hand said, "Men of Israel, and
[a]you who fear God, listen:
17 "The God of this people [1]Israel
[a]chose our fathers, and exalted the
people [b]when they dwelt as **strangers**
in the land of Egypt, and with [2]an
uplifted arm He [c]brought them out of
it.

WORD WEALTH

13:17 strangers, *paroikia* (par-oy-*kee*-ah); Strong's *#3940:* Aliens, foreigners, strangers, sojourners, noncitizens dwelling as resident exiles. (Compare "parochial" and "parish.") Israel sojourned in Egypt on a *paroikia* basis. Their permanent home was the land of Canaan. 1 Pet. 1:17 uses *paroikia* in the spiritual sense. Christians live temporarily as aliens in an unfriendly world. The Lord has prepared for them a final home based on permanency, duration, and endless time.

10 [a]Matt. 13:38; John 8:44; [1 John 3:8]
11 [a]Ex. 9:3; 1 Sam. 5:6; Job 19:21; Ps. 32:4; Heb. 10:31 *See WW at Luke 11:35.
13 [a]Acts 15:38
14 [a]Acts 16:13
15 [a]Luke 4:16 [b]Heb. 13:22 [1]*encouragement*
16 [a]Acts 10:35
17 [a]Ex. 6:1, 6; 13:14, 16; Deut. 7:6–8 [b]Acts 7:17 [c]Ex. 14:8 [1]M omits *Israel* [2]Mighty power
18 [a]Ex. 16:35; Num. 14:34; Acts 7:36
19 [a]Deut. 7:1 [b]Josh. 14:1, 2; 19:51; Ps. 78:55
20 [a]Judg. 2:16; 1 Sam. 4:18; 7:15 [b]1 Sam. 3:20; Acts 3:24
21 [a]1 Sam. 8:5 [b]1 Sam. 10:20–24
22 [a]1 Sam. 15:23, 26, 28 [b]1 Sam. 16:1, 12, 13 [c]Ps. 89:20 [d]1 Sam. 13:14 *See WW at Luke 16:4. • See WW at Matt. 12:50.
23 [a]Is. 11:1 [b]Ps. 132:11 [c][Matt. 1:21] [1]M *salvation, after* *See WW at John 4:42.
24 [a]Matt. 3:1; [Luke 3:3]

18 "Now [a]for a time of about forty
years He put up with their ways in the
wilderness.
19 "And when He had destroyed
[a]seven nations in the land of Canaan,
[b]He distributed their land to them by
allotment.
20 "After that [a]He gave *them* judges
for about four hundred and fifty years,
[b]until Samuel the prophet.
21 [a]"And afterward they asked for a
king; so God gave them [b]Saul the son
of Kish, a man of the tribe of Benjamin,
for forty years.
22 "And [a]when He had *removed him,
[b]He raised up for them David as king,
to whom also He gave testimony and
said, [c]*'I have found David* the *son* of
Jesse, [d]*a man after My own heart,* who
will do all My *will.'

KINGDOM DYNAMICS

13:22 A Teachable Spirit, LEADER TRAITS. Only one man in the Bible enjoys the designation of being a man after God's own heart—David. To outward appearance, David is more readily remembered as a gross sinner. He committed adultery, murdered, lied, betrayed his nation, made severe mistakes in judgment, was a poor manager, and finally was unable to manage his home. Yet God said, "I have found David the *son* of Jesse, a man after My *own* heart, who will do all My will" (v. 22). Almost every time we read about David, he was doing something wrong, yet God commended the heart of his leadership. How do we explain it? The answer is in the fact that with every mistake, David repented; and of equal importance, he learned from his mistakes. Not only was he humble and teachable, but he listened to his critics and his enemies as well; and, foremost of all, he heeded the prophets of God. This teachable spirit is the trait that caused God to classify him as Israel's finest leader.

(Judg. 6:1—8:35/Matt. 26:47–54) J.B.

23 [a]"From this man's seed, according
[b]to *the* promise, God raised up for Israel [c]a[1] *Savior—Jesus—
24 [a]"after John had first preached,

13:12 Astonished at the teaching of the Lord: This does not refer to the mere presentation of religious truths. The proconsul was astonished at the *power* of the teaching (see Mark 1:22).
13:14 Antioch was located in present-day Turkey, and is not the same as Antioch in Syria from which Paul was sent in v. 1.
13:15 Jewish synagogues were open forums, and it was quite proper for guests to speak and teach.
13:17–41 A typical Acts sermon (see note on 3:12–26), including 1) a review of Jewish history (vv. 17–22); 2) a sketch of the life of Christ (vv. 23–31) with an emphasis on His resurrection (vv. 30, 33, 34); 3) OT texts to prove that Jesus is the Messiah (vv. 32–37); 4) a call to hear the message, repent, and believe (vv. 38–41). **Justified** (v. 39) here has the idea of being set free.

before His coming, the baptism of repentance to all the people of Israel.
25 "And as John was finishing his
course, he said, [a]'Who do you think I
am? I am not *He.* But behold, [b]there
comes One after me, the sandals of
whose feet I am not worthy to loose.'
26 "Men *and* brethren, sons of the
[1]family of Abraham, and [a]those among
you who fear God, [b]to you the [2]word
of this salvation has been sent.
27 "For those who dwell in Jerusalem,
and their rulers, [a]because they did not
know Him, nor even the voices of the
Prophets which are read every Sabbath, have fulfilled *them* in condemning *Him.*
28 [a]"And though they found no cause
for death *in Him,* they asked Pilate that
He should be put to death.
29 [a]"Now when they had fulfilled all
that was written concerning Him,
[b]they took *Him* down from the tree and
laid *Him* in a tomb.
30 [a]"But God raised Him from the
dead.
31 [a]"He was seen for many days by
those who came up with Him from Galilee to Jerusalem, who are His witnesses to the people.
32 "And we declare to you glad tidings—[a]that **promise** which was made
to the fathers.

WORD WEALTH

13:32 promise, *epangelia* (ep-ang-el-*ee*-ah); Strong's *#1860:* Both a promise and the thing promised, an announcement with the special sense of promise, pledge, and offer. *Epangelia* tells what the promise from God is and then gives the assurance that the thing promised will be done. 2 Cor. 1:20 asserts, "For all the promises [*epangelia*] of God in Him *are* Yes, and in Him Amen, to the glory of God through us."

33 "God has fulfilled this for us their
children, in that He has raised up
Jesus. As it is also written in the second
Psalm:

[a]'You are My Son,
Today I have begotten You.'

34 "And that He raised Him from the
dead, no more to return to [1]corruption,
He has spoken thus:

[a]'I will give you the sure [2]mercies
of David.'

35 "Therefore He also says in another
Psalm:

[a]'You will not allow Your Holy One
to see corruption.'

36 "For David, after he had served
[1]his own generation by the will of God,
[a]fell asleep, was buried with his fathers, and [2]saw corruption;
37 "but He whom God raised up
[1]saw no corruption.
38 "Therefore let it be known to you,
brethren, that [a]through this Man is
preached to you the forgiveness of
sins;
39 "and [a]by Him everyone who believes is *justified from all things from
which you could not be justified by the
law of Moses.
40 "Beware therefore, lest what has
been spoken in the prophets come
upon you:

41 *'Behold,[a] you despisers,*
Marvel and perish!
For I work a work in your days,
A work which you will by no
means believe,
Though one were to declare it to
you.'"

Blessing and Conflict at Antioch

42 [1]So when the Jews went out of the
synagogue, the Gentiles begged that
these words might be preached to them
the next Sabbath.
43 Now when the congregation had
broken up, many of the Jews and devout proselytes *followed Paul and
Barnabas, who, speaking to them,
[a]persuaded them to continue in [b]the
grace of God.
44 On the next Sabbath almost the
whole city came together to hear the
word of God.
45 But when the Jews saw the multitudes, they were filled with envy; and
contradicting and blaspheming, they
[a]opposed the things spoken by Paul.
46 Then Paul and Barnabas grew bold
and said, [a]"It was necessary that the
word of God should be spoken to you
first; but [b]since you reject it, and judge

25 [a]Matt. 3:11; Mark 1:7; Luke 3:16 [b]John 1:20, 27
26 [a]Ps. 66:16 [b]Matt. 10:6 [1]*stock* [2]*message*
27 [a]Luke 23:34
28 [a]Matt. 27:22, 23; Mark 15:13, 14; Luke 23:21–23; John 19:15; Acts 3:14; [2 Cor. 5:21; Heb. 4:15]; 1 Pet. 2:22
29 [a]Luke 18:31 [b]Matt. 27:57–61; Mark 15:42–47; Luke 23:50–56; John 19:38–42
30 [a]Ps. 16:10, 11; Hos. 6:2; Matt. 12:39, 40; 28:6
31 [a]Matt. 28:16; Acts 1:3, 11; 1 Cor. 15:5–8
32 [a][Gen. 3:15]
33 [a]Ps. 2:7; Heb. 1:5
34 [a]Is. 55:3 [1]*the state of decay* [2]*blessings*
35 [a]Ps. 16:10; Acts 2:27
36 [a]Acts 2:29 [1]*in his* [2]*underwent decay*
37 [1]*underwent no decay*
38 [a]Jer. 31:34
39 [a][Is. 53:11; John 3:16] *See WW at Matt. 12:37.
41 [a]Hab. 1:5
42 [1]Or *And when they went out of the synagogue of the Jews;* NU *And when they went out, they begged*
43 [a]Acts 11:23 [b]Titus 2:11; Heb. 12:15; 1 Pet. 5:12 *See WW at John 13:36.
45 [a]Acts 18:6; 1 Pet. 4:4; Jude 10
46 [a]Matt. 10:6; Acts 3:26; Rom. 1:16 [b]Ex. 32:10; Deut. 32:21; Is. 55:5; Matt. 21:43; Rom. 10:19

13:42 The Gentiles here were converts to the Jewish religion.
13:46, 47 These are important transitional verses in the narrative. The preaching of the gospel is beginning to turn away from the Jewish community. Paul began his ministry in each new city by entering the synagogue, but rejection by the Jews forced him to preach to Gentile audiences.

yourselves unworthy of *everlasting
life, behold, [c]we turn to the Gentiles.
47 "For so the Lord has commanded
us:

[a]'I have set you as a light to the
Gentiles,
That you should be for salvation
to the ends of the earth.'"

48 Now when the Gentiles heard this,
they were glad and glorified the word
of the Lord. [a]And as many as had been
appointed to eternal life believed.
49 And the word of the Lord was being
spread throughout all the region.
50 But the Jews stirred up the devout
and prominent women and the chief
men of the city, [a]raised up persecution
against Paul and Barnabas, and expelled them from their region.
51 [a]But they shook off the dust from
their feet against them, and came to
Iconium.
52 And the disciples [a]were filled with
joy and [b]with the Holy Spirit.

At Iconium

14 Now it happened in Iconium
that they went together to the
synagogue of the Jews, and so spoke
that a great multitude both of the Jews
and of the [a]Greeks believed.
2 But the unbelieving Jews stirred
up the Gentiles and [1]poisoned their
[2]minds against the brethren.
4 3 Therefore they stayed there a long
time, speaking boldly in the Lord,
[a]who was bearing witness to the word
of His grace, granting signs and
[b]wonders* to be done by their hands.
4 But the multitude of the city was
[a]divided: part sided with the Jews, and
part with the [b]apostles.
5 And when a violent attempt was
made by both the Gentiles and Jews,
with their rulers, [a]to *abuse and stone
them,
6 they became aware of it and [a]fled
to Lystra and Derbe, cities of Lycaonia,
and to the surrounding region.

46 [c]Acts 18:6 *See WW at Rev. 14:6.
47 [a]Is. 42:6; 49:6; Luke 2:32
48 [a][Acts 2:47]
50 [a]Acts 7:52; 2 Tim. 3:11
51 [a]Matt. 10:14; Mark 6:11; [Luke 9:5]
52 [a]Matt. 5:12; John 16:22 [b]Acts 2:4; 4:8, 31; 13:9

CHAPTER 14

1 [a]John 7:35; Acts 18:4; Rom. 1:14, 16; 1 Cor. 1:22
2 [1]*embittered* [2]Lit. *souls*
3 [a]Mark 16:20; Acts 4:29; 20:32; Heb. 2:4 [b]Acts 5:12 *See WW at Acts 15:12.
4 [a]Luke 12:51 [b]Acts 13:2, 3
5 [a]2 Tim. 3:11 *See WW at Luke 18:32.
6 [a]Matt. 10:23
8 [a]Acts 3:2
9 [1]Lit. *Who*
10 [a][Is. 35:6]
11 [a]Acts 8:10; 28:6
12 [1]*Jupiter* [2]*Mercury*
13 [a]Dan. 2:46
14 [a]Num. 14:6; Matt. 26:65; Mark 14:63
15 [a]Acts 10:26 [b]James 5:17 [c]1 Sam. 12:21; Jer. 8:19; 14:22; Amos 2:4; 1 Cor. 8:4 [d]1 Thess. 1:9 [e]Gen. 1:1; Ex. 20:11; Ps. 146:6; Acts 4:24; 17:24; Rev. 14:7

7 And they were preaching the gospel
there.

Idolatry at Lystra

8 [a]And in Lystra a certain man without strength in his feet was sitting, a
cripple from his mother's womb, who
had never walked.
9 *This* man heard Paul speaking.
[1]Paul, observing him intently and seeing that he had faith to be healed,
10 said with a loud voice, [a]"Stand up
straight on your feet!" And he leaped
and walked.
11 Now when the people saw what
Paul had done, they raised their voices,
saying in the Lycaonian *language,*
[a]"The gods have come down to us in
the likeness of men!"
12 And Barnabas they called [1]Zeus,
and Paul, [2]Hermes, because he was the
chief speaker.
13 Then the priest of Zeus, whose temple was in front of their city, brought
oxen and garlands to the gates, [a]in-
tending to sacrifice with the multitudes.
14 But when the apostles Barnabas 3
and Paul heard this, [a]they tore their
clothes and ran in among the multitude, crying out
15 and saying, "Men, [a]why are you doing these things? [b]We also are men
with the same nature as you, and
preach to you that you should turn
from [c]these **useless** things [d]to the living God, [e]who made the heaven, the
earth, the sea, and all things that are
in them,

WORD WEALTH

14:15 useless, *mataios* (*mat*-ah-yoss); Strong's *#3152:* Fruitless, empty, futile, frivolous, hollow, unreal, unproductive, lacking substance, trifling, ineffectual, void of results, devoid of force, success, or utility, and worthless. The word here describes Greek and Roman mythological ritual. The unregenerate philosophy

(*cont. on next page*)

13:48 The primary significance of the phrase **appointed to eternal life** is not theological but historical, as Luke traces the spread of the gospel from its Jewish origins to the Gentile world. This reference underscores God's initiative in individual salvation. Throughout the Bible there are references to God's hand of providence influencing people and altering the course of human history. Every Christian, in retrospect, can see how God carefully orchestrated particular events that changed his or her life forever. See Prov. 16:9; Dan. 4:34, 35; Acts 2:22–24; Eph. 1:3–5.

13:51 Shook off the dust is a dramatic symbol of divine abandonment. See Matt. 10:14.

13:52 The tense of the verb **were filled** signifies a continuous filling.

14:3 See section 4 of Truth-In-Action at the end of Acts.

14:9 In both the Gospels and Acts faith is often emphasized as the condition of healing (see Matt. 8:10; 9:2, 22, 29; 15:28; Mark 10:52; Luke 17:19; Acts 3:16).

14:12 The worship of **Zeus** and **Hermes** (the father and the messenger of the gods and known to the Romans as Jupiter and Mercury) in ancient Lystra has been established by archaeological research.

14:14–18 See section 3 of Truth-In-Action at the end of Acts.

(*cont. from preceding page*)
of that day made Paul and Barnabas urge the people to turn from these useless (*mataios*) things. Their message was "turn from Zeus, who has never lived, to God who has always been alive. As Creator He is worthy to be served, worshiped, and trusted."

16 [a]"who in bygone generations allowed all nations to walk in their own
ways.
17 [a]"Nevertheless He did not leave
Himself without witness, in that He did
good, [b]gave us rain from heaven and
fruitful seasons, filling our hearts with
[c]food and gladness."
18 And with these sayings they could
scarcely restrain the multitudes from
sacrificing to them.

Stoning, Escape to Derbe

19 [a]Then Jews from Antioch and Iconium came there; and having persuaded the multitudes, [b]they stoned
Paul *and* dragged *him* out of the city,
supposing him to be [c]dead.
20 However, when the disciples gathered around him, he rose up and went
into the city. And the next day he departed with Barnabas to Derbe.

Strengthening the Converts

21 And when they had preached the
gospel to that city [a]and made many disciples, they returned to Lystra, Iconium, and Antioch,
22 strengthening the souls of the disciples, [a]exhorting *them* to continue in
the faith, and *saying*, [b]"We must
through many *tribulations enter the
kingdom of God."

KINGDOM DYNAMICS

14:21, 22 Suffering, Tribulation, CONFLICT AND THE KINGDOM. Paul not only taught the joy and peace of the kingdom of God (Rom. 14:17), its power (1 Cor. 4:20), and its present authority to cause the believer to triumph over evil (2 Tim. 4:18; Rom. 16:20). He also taught that "kingdom people" experience trial, suffering, and not always an "instant victory" (2 Thess. 1:5). Triumph and victory may characterize the attitude of each citizen of the kingdom of God, and Holy Spirit-empowered authority is given to be applied to realize results. Yet, God did not promise life without struggle. The "dominion" being recovered through the presence of the King within us and ministered by the Holy Spirit's power through us is never taught by the apostles as preempting all suffering.

This text reminds us that victory only comes through battle, and triumph only follows trial. Only a weak view of the truth of the kingdom of God pretends otherwise. Another weak view surrenders to negative circumstances on the proposition that we are predestined to problems and therefore should merely tolerate them. The Bible teaches that suffering, trial, and all order of human difficulty are unavoidable; but God's Word also teaches they may all be overcome. The presence of the King and the power of His kingdom in our lives make us neither invulnerable nor immune to life's struggles. But they do bring the promise of victory: provision in need, strength for the day, and healing, comfort, and saving help.

(Luke 16:16/Ex. 19:5–7) J.W.H.

16 [a]Ps. 81:12; Mic. 4:5; 1 Pet. 4:3
17 [a]Acts 17:24–27; Rom. 1:19, 20 [b]Lev. 26:4; Deut. 11:14; [Matt. 5:45] [c]Ps. 145:16
19 [a]Acts 13:45, 50; 14:2–5; 1 Thess. 2:14 [b]Acts 14:5; 2 Cor. 11:25; 2 Tim. 3:11 [c][2 Cor. 12:1–4]
21 [a]Matt. 28:19
22 [a]Acts 11:23 [b]Matt. 10:38; Luke 22:28; [Rom. 8:17; 2 Tim. 2:12; 3:12] *See WW at John 16:33.

23 So when they had [a]appointed elders
in every church, and prayed with fasting, they commended them to the Lord
in whom they had believed.
24 And after they had passed through
Pisidia, they came to Pamphylia.
25 Now when they had preached the
word in Perga, they went down to Atta-
lia.
26 From there they sailed to Antioch,
where they had been commended to
the grace of God for the work which
they had completed.
27 Now when they had come and gathered the church together, [a]they reported all that God had done with
them, and that He had [b]opened the
door of faith to the Gentiles.
28 So they stayed there a long time
with the disciples.

Conflict over Circumcision

15 And [a]certain *men* came down
from Judea and taught the

23 [a]Matt. 9:15; Mark 2:20; Luke 5:35; 2 Cor. 8:19; Titus 1:5
27 [a]Acts 15:4, 12 [b]1 Cor. 16:9; 2 Cor. 2:12; Col. 4:3; Rev. 3:8

CHAPTER 15

1 [a]Gal. 2:12

14:19, 20 Many scholars believe that Paul was describing this near-death experience in 2 Cor. 12:2–5. It is possible that when Paul **rose up and went into the city,** he was actually raised from the dead. At the very least, he was miraculously healed, because **the next day he departed with Barnabas to Derbe.**

14:22 Enduring sufferings does not earn entrance into the kingdom. The meaning is that persecution accompanies entrance into the kingdom.

15:1–35 This section represents a theological milestone in the history of Christianity. All the principal leaders of the early church agreed to meet in Jerusalem to resolve the emerging conflict between legalistic Jewish Christians and Gentile converts to Christianity (vv. 1, 2). The legalists, called Judaizers, believed that in addition to exercising faith in Jesus, one must observe the ceremonial **custom** (v. 1) of

brethren, [b]"Unless you are circumcised according to the custom of Moses, you cannot be saved."
2 Therefore, when Paul and Barnabas
had no small dissension and dispute
with them, they determined that
[a]Paul and Barnabas and certain *others of them should go up to Jerusalem,
to the apostles and elders, about this
question.
3 So, [a]being sent on their way by the
church, they passed through Phoenicia
and Samaria, [b]describing the conversion of the Gentiles; and they caused
great joy to all the brethren.
4 And when they had come to Jerusalem, they were received by the church
and the apostles and the elders; and
they reported all things that God had
done with them.
5 But some of the *sect of the Pharisees who believed rose up, saying, "It
is necessary to circumcise them, and
to command *them* to keep the law of
Moses."

The Jerusalem Council

6 Now the apostles and elders came
together to consider this matter.
7 And when there had been much dispute, Peter rose up and said to them:
[a]"Men and brethren, you know that a
good while ago God chose among us,
that by my mouth the Gentiles should
hear the word of the *gospel and believe.
8 "So God, [a]who knows the heart,
[1]acknowledged them by [b]giving them
the Holy Spirit, just as *He did* to us,
9 [a]"and made no *distinction between
us and them, [b]purifying their hearts by
faith.

1 [b]John 7:22; Acts 15:5; Gal. 5:2; Phil. 3:2; [Col. 2:8, 11, 16]
2 [a]Gal. 2:1 *See WW at John 14:16.
3 [a]Acts 20:38; 21:5; Rom. 15:24; 1 Cor. 16:6, 11; 2 Cor. 1:16; Titus 3:13; 3 John 6 [b]Acts 14:27; 15:4, 12
5 *See WW at 2 Pet. 2:1.
7 [a]Acts 10:20 *See WW at Mark 1:1.
8 [a]1 Chr. 28:9; Acts 1:24 [b]Acts 2:4; 10:44, 47 [1]*bore witness to*
9 [a]Rom. 10:12 [b]Acts 10:15, 28 *See WW at Acts 11:12.
10 [a]Matt. 23:4; Gal. 5:1
11 [a]Rom. 3:4; 5:15; 2 Cor. 13:14; [Eph. 2:5–8; Titus 2:11] [1]NU, M omit *Christ*
12 [a]Acts 14:27; 15:3, 4
13 [a]Acts 12:17 [1]*stopped speaking*
14 [a]Acts 15:7; 2 Pet. 1:1
15 *See WW at Matt. 18:19.
16 [a]Amos 9:11, 12

10 "Now therefore, why do you test
God [a]by putting a yoke on the neck
of the disciples which neither our fathers nor we were able to bear?
11 "But [a]we believe that through the
grace of the Lord Jesus [1]Christ we
shall be saved in the same manner as
they."
12 Then all the multitude kept silent
and listened to Barnabas and Paul declaring how many miracles and **wonders** God had [a]worked through them
among the Gentiles.

WORD WEALTH

15:12 wonders, *teras* (*ter*-as); Strong's *#5059:* Compare "teratology," the science that deals with unexplainable phenomena. *Teras* denotes extraordinary occurrences, supernatural prodigies, omens, portents, unusual manifestations, miraculous incidents portending the future rather than the past, and acts that are so unusual they cause the observer to marvel or be in awe. *Teras* is always in the plural, associated with *semeion* (signs). Signs and wonders are a perfect balance for touching man's intellect, emotions, and will.

13 And after they had [1]become silent,
[a]James answered, saying, "Men *and*
brethren, listen to me:
14 [a]"Simon has declared how God at
the first visited the Gentiles to take out
of them a people for His name.
15 "And with this the words of the
prophets *agree, just as it is written:

16 *'After[a] this I will return*
And will rebuild the tabernacle of
David, which has fallen down;

the OT, especially the rite of circumcision. Judaizers, then, expected Gentile believers to be circumcised and observe the Law of Moses, just as converts to Judaism had been circumcised for generations previously (v. 21). After **much dispute** (v. 7), the Jerusalem Council agreed on what has become the doctrinal foundation of the Christian faith: *salvation is by grace through faith alone* (v. 11). Paul's letter to the Galatians is an extended explanation of this doctrine. See also Rom. 3:28; 2 Cor. 3:7–18; Eph. 2:8, 9; Col. 2:11–17. The clarification of salvation by grace through faith in Jesus Christ alone also led to a final and formal separation of Christianity from Judaism.

15:1 Paul's report of what had happened among the Gentiles on his first missionary journey (14:26–28) had reached Jerusalem and Judea, so **certain *men* came down from Judea** to teach the importance of circumcision. They sincerely believed that converts from paganism would weaken the *moral* standards of the church.

15:2 It is not unusual for Christian leaders to disagree strongly. Acts 15 shows how through the Spirit and open dialogue they are able to resolve their differences.

15:7 Peter refers to his ministry in the house of Cornelius (10:1—11:18).

15:10 To add the Law of Moses to faith is to **test God,** because in effect it means that the sacrificial death of Christ was not quite enough to effect salvation (see Gal. 2:21).

15:12 The irrefutable evidence provided by the demonstrations of the power of the Holy Spirit played a significant role in bringing the Jerusalem Council to its historic decision. See Rom. 15:18, 19; 1 Cor. 2:4; 1 Thess. 1:5.

15:14 There is a subtle play on words here. The root of this statement is Deut. 14:2, which declares that God will call a people (Israel) out of "all the peoples who *are* on the face of the earth [the Gentiles]." But James gives new meaning to the long-understood use of these terms. For James, the "people" that God is calling out are Gentiles *in contrast* to Israel.

15:16, 17 James quotes this OT reference because of its clear prophecy about the salvation of the Gentiles. The rebuilding and restoration of **the tabernacle of David** refers to the building of the church, which in the beginning was

I will rebuild its ruins,
And I will set it up;
17 So that the rest of mankind may seek the LORD,
Even all the Gentiles who are called by My name,
Says the [1]LORD who does all these things.'

18 [1]"Known to God from eternity are all His works.

KINGDOM DYNAMICS

15:16–18 Restoration of David's Tabernacle, RESTORATION. This text prophesies the restoration of the tabernacle of David, a forecast of the global body of Christ united in serving God. The entire concept of "The Holy Spirit and Restoration" is developed in the study article, which begins on page 2012.
(Is. 58:1–14/Is. 4:2, 3) J.R.

19 "Therefore [a]I judge that we should
not trouble those from among the Gentiles who [b]are turning to God,
20 "but that we [a]write to them to abstain [b]from things polluted by idols,
[c]*from* [1]sexual* immorality, [d]*from*
things strangled, and *from* *blood.
21 "For Moses has had throughout
many generations those who preach
him in every city, [a]being read in the
synagogues every Sabbath."

The Jerusalem Decree

22 Then it pleased the apostles and elders, with the whole church, to send
chosen men of their own company to
Antioch with Paul and Barnabas,
namely, Judas who was also named
[a]Barsabas,[1] and Silas, leading men
among the brethren.
23 They wrote this *letter* by them:

The apostles, the elders, and the brethren,

To the brethren who are of the Gentiles in Antioch, Syria, and Cilicia:

Greetings.

24 Since we have heard that [a]some who went out from us have *troubled you with words, [b]unsettling your souls, [1]saying, "*You must* be circumcised and keep the law"—to whom we gave no *such* commandment—
25 it seemed good to us, being assembled *with one [1]accord, to send chosen men to you with our beloved Barnabas and Paul,
26 [a]men who have risked their lives for the name of our Lord Jesus Christ.
27 We have therefore sent Judas and Silas, who will also report the same things by word of mouth.
28 For it seemed good to the Holy Spirit, and to us, to lay upon you no greater burden than these necessary things:
29 [a]that you abstain from things offered to idols, [b]from blood, from things strangled, and from [c]sexual[1] immorality. If you keep yourselves from these, you will do well.

Farewell.

Continuing Ministry in Syria

30 So when they were sent off, they
came to Antioch; and when they had
gathered the multitude together, they
delivered the letter.
31 When they had read it, they rejoiced
over its *encouragement.
32 Now Judas and Silas, themselves
being [a]prophets also, [b]exhorted and
strengthened the brethren with many
words.
33 And after they had stayed *there* for
a time, they were [a]sent back with

17 [1]NU *LORD, who makes these things*
18 [1]NU (continuing v. 17) *known from eternity (of old).'*
19 [a]Acts 15:28; 21:25 [b]1 Thess. 1:9
20 [a]Acts 21:25 [b][1 Cor. 8:1; 10:20, 28] [c][1 Cor. 6:9] [d]Lev. 3:17 [1]Or *fornication* *See WW at Matt. 15:19. • See WW at 1 John 1:7.
21 [a]Acts 13:15, 27
22 [a]Acts 1:23 [1]NU, M *Barsabbas*
24 [a]Titus 1:10, 11 [b]Gal. 1:7; 5:10 [1]NU omits *saying, "You must be circumcised and keep the law"* *See WW at Luke 24:38.
25 [1]*purpose* or *mind* *See WW at Acts 2:1.
26 [a]Acts 13:50; 14:19
29 [a]Acts 15:20; 21:25 [b]Lev. 17:14 [c]Col. 3:5 [1]Or *fornication*
31 *See WW at Acts 9:31.
32 [a]Eph. 4:11 [b]Acts 14:22; 18:23
33 [a]Heb. 11:31

composed of Jews, but now included many Gentiles. The church, therefore, is the instrument by which Gentiles may know God. See note on Amos 9:11–15.
15:20 See note on v. 29.
15:22 The Spirit of God brought harmonious agreement among strong-willed leaders in the face of "no small dissension" (v. 2) and "much dispute" (v. 7).
15:23 The salutation of the letter affirms the unity of the leadership of the church.
15:28 It seemed good to the Holy Spirit, and to us: An earnest and common desire to know the mind of God leads to unanimity. A church possessing an awareness of the guidance of the Holy Spirit (see 10:19, 20; 13:2, 3) need not be unassisted in pursuing its decisions.
15:29 Things offered to idols was meat that had been offered as a sacrifice and was later sold in the market as "used" meat (see 1 Cor. 8). It appears that the early church is substituting three "new" laws for the "old" laws of Judaism. In view of the clear teaching on grace in this chapter (v. 11), these cannot be seen as requirements for salvation. Instead, they represent a basic separation from glaring paganism and its practices, particularly offensive to Jewish scruples.
15:31 Legalism is always accompanied by fear and bondage; the message of grace is "good news," and brings liberty and joy.

greetings from the brethren to [1]the apostles.
34 [1]However, it seemed good to Silas to remain there.
35 [a]Paul and Barnabas also remained in Antioch, teaching and preaching the word of the Lord, with many others also.

Division over John Mark

36 Then after some days Paul said to Barnabas, "Let us now go back and visit our brethren in every city where we have preached the word of the Lord, *and see* how they are doing."
37 Now Barnabas [1]was determined to take with them [a]John called Mark.
38 But Paul insisted that they should not take with them [a]the one who had departed from them in Pamphylia, and had not gone with them to the work.
39 Then the contention became so sharp that they parted from one another. And so Barnabas took Mark and sailed to [a]Cyprus;

33 [1]NU *those who had sent them*
34 [1]NU, M omit v. 34.
35 [a]Acts 13:1
37 [a]Acts 12:12, 25 [1]*resolved*
38 [a]Acts 13:13
39 [a]Acts 4:36; 13:4
40 [a]Acts 11:23; 14:26 [1]*committed*
41 [a]Acts 16:5

CHAPTER 16

1 [a]Acts 14:6 [b]Rom. 16:21 [c]2 Tim. 1:5; 3:15
3 [a][Gal. 2:3; 5:2]
4 [a]Acts 15:19–21 [b]Acts 15:28, 29
5 [a]Acts 2:47; 15:41

40 but Paul chose Silas and departed, [a]being [1]commended by the brethren to the grace of God.
41 And he went through Syria and Cilicia, [a]strengthening the churches.

Timothy Joins Paul and Silas

16 Then he came to [a]Derbe and Lystra. And behold, a certain disciple was there, [b]named Timothy, [c]*the* son of a certain Jewish woman who believed, but his father *was* Greek.
2 He was well spoken of by the brethren who were at Lystra and Iconium.
3 Paul wanted to have him go on with him. And he [a]took *him* and circumcised him because of the Jews who were in that region, for they all knew that his father was Greek.
4 And as they went through the cities, they delivered to them the [a]decrees to keep, [b]which were determined by the apostles and elders at Jerusalem.
5 [a]So the churches were strengthened

15:36–41 The contention (v. 39) between **Paul** and **Barnabas** arose over a difference of opinion concerning the inclusion of **Mark** on the mission team. Paul considered Mark's departure on the previous journey a desertion (see 13:13). Paul later changed his mind about John Mark (see Col. 4:10). Unfortunately, painful divisions in the body of Christ do occur, but God can turn such things to good. In the case of Paul and Barnabas, there are now *two* missionary teams instead of one (vv. 39, 40). This is the beginning of Paul's next trip abroad. See map of Paul's second journey.
16:1–5 See section 3 of Truth-In-Action at the end of Acts.

16:1 Timothy becomes one of Paul's disciples and later is the recipient of 1 and 2 Tim.
16:3 Paul, the chief spokesman of salvation by grace alone, had the half-Jewish Timothy **circumcised** so that he could take him into the Jewish synagogues. This was not compromise; it was simple Christian courtesy. It was a mature recognition that social, cultural, and even religious differences should never become more important issues than the simple message of salvation in Christ. See 1 Cor. 9:19–23.

Paul Goes to Greece (The Second Missionary Journey, Acts 15:39—18:22). Starting from Jerusalem, Paul took Silas to visit again the churches of Galatia. Young Timothy joined them in Lystra. Then they went to Macedonia and Achaia, present-day Greece. On this journey the Philippian jailer was saved, the Bereans "searched the Scriptures daily" (Acts 17:11), and Paul preached at the Areopagus in Athens and then settled in Corinth for a year and a half.

in the faith, and *increased in number
daily.

The Macedonian Call

6 Now when they had gone through
Phrygia and the region of [a]Galatia,
they were forbidden by the Holy Spirit
to preach the *word in [1]Asia.
7 After they had come to Mysia, they
*tried to go into Bithynia, but the
[1]Spirit did not permit them.
8 So passing by Mysia, they [a]came
down to Troas.
9 And a vision appeared to Paul in
the night. A [a]man of Macedonia stood
and pleaded with him, saying, "Come
over to Macedonia and help us."
10 Now after he had seen the vision,
immediately we sought to go [a]to Macedonia, concluding that the Lord had
called us to preach the gospel to
them.

KINGDOM DYNAMICS

16:6–10 Dreams and Visions, LEADER TRAITS. On his missionary journey Paul planned a northward turn into Bithynia. But that night he dreamed of a man begging him, "Come over to Macedonia and help us" (v. 9). On the basis of the dream, Paul altered his direction, and thus exemplifies a trait of Holy Spirit-guided leaders. While ungodly leaders consult horoscopes and diviners for direction in their lives, godly leaders hear from God 1) through the written Word, the Bible, and 2) through dreams and visions (2:17). Their thought channels are cleansed of impurity (2 Cor. 10:5). They are not conformed to the pattern of this world but are transformed by the renewing of their minds (Rom. 12:2). Their affections are on things above, not on earthly things (Col. 3:2). Therefore, when the Holy Spirit chooses to speak to them through visions (daytime mind pictures) and dreams (sleeping revelations), they hear clearly (see also Ps. 16:7; Acts 9:10; 10:3, 17; 18:9).

(Acts 13:1–3/Acts 2:22) J.B.

5 *See WW at Matt. 25:29.
6 [a]Acts 18:23; Gal. 1:1, 2 [1]The Roman province of Asia *See WW at Acts 19:20.
7 [1]NU adds *of Jesus* *See WW at Rev. 2:10.
8 [a]Acts 16:11; 20:5; 2 Cor. 2:12; 2 Tim. 4:13
9 [a]Acts 10:30
10 [a]2 Cor. 2:13
12 [a]Acts 20:6; Phil. 1:1; 1 Thess. 2:2 [1]Lit. *first*
14 [a]Rev. 1:11; 2:18, 24 [b]Luke 24:45
15 [a]Gen. 19:3; 33:11; Judg. 19:21; Luke 24:29; [Heb. 13:2]
16 [a]Lev. 19:31; 20:6, 27; Deut. 18:11; 1 Sam. 28:3, 7; 2 Kin. 21:6; 1 Chr. 10:13; Is. 8:19 [b]Acts 19:24
17 *See WW at Rev. 19:5.
18 [a]Mark 1:25, 34 [b]Mark 16:17 [1]*distressed*
19 [a]Acts 16:16; 19:25, 26 [b]Matt. 10:18
20 [a]1 Kin. 18:17; Acts 17:8

Lydia Baptized at Philippi

11 Therefore, sailing from Troas, we
ran a straight course to Samothrace,
and the next *day* came to Neapolis,
12 and from there to [a]Philippi, which
is the [1]foremost city of that part of
Macedonia, a colony. And we were
staying in that city for some days.
13 And on the Sabbath day we went
out of the city to the riverside, where
prayer was customarily made; and we
sat down and spoke to the women who
met *there.*
14 Now a certain woman named Lydia
heard *us.* She was a seller of purple
from the city of [a]Thyatira, who worshiped God. [b]The Lord opened her
heart to heed the things spoken by
Paul.
15 And when she and her household
were baptized, she begged *us,* saying,
"If you have judged me to be faithful
to the Lord, come to my house and
stay." So [a]she persuaded us.

Paul and Silas Imprisoned

16 Now it happened, as we went to
prayer, that a certain slave girl [a]pos-
sessed with a spirit of divination met
us, who brought her masters [b]much
profit by fortune-telling.
17 This girl followed Paul and us, and
cried out, saying, "These men are the
*servants of the Most High God, who
proclaim to us the way of salvation."
18 And this she did for many days. But
Paul, [a]greatly [1]annoyed, turned and
said to the spirit, "I command you in
the name of Jesus Christ to come out
of her." [b]And he came out that very
hour.
19 But [a]when her masters saw that
their hope of profit was gone, they
seized Paul and Silas and [b]dragged
them into the marketplace to the authorities.
20 And they brought them to the magistrates, and said, "These men, being
Jews, [a]exceedingly trouble our city;

16:7 Luke does not indicate how **the Spirit** communicated His will to the missionaries. It may have been through inner prompting, prophetic utterance, or external circumstances.
16:9 Macedonia is northern Greece, including the cities of Philippi and Thessalonica, to which Paul later addressed three of his epistles.
16:11 This verse begins the "we" sections of Acts, indicating that Luke has joined the mission team and is now giving a firsthand report.
16:13 Since Jewish law required the establishment of a synagogue when there was a population of at least 10 men in a community, the absence of a synagogue in Philippi indicates a small Jewish population.
16:16 The slave girl had **a spirit of divination,** or literally, "a spirit, a python," characterizing her as one inspired by Apollo, the god worshiped at Pytho (Delphi).
16:17 The demon in the slave girl spoke the truth, but mockingly. See Mark 1:24, 25.
16:18 Why Paul delayed to cast out the demon is uncertain. Perhaps he was aware of the peril to which the exorcism would expose the mission team.
16:19–21 This was Paul's first clash with Roman officials. The new Christian sect was not a threat to the peace of Rome. The charges here were false, and Paul and Silas were completely exonerated by Roman justice (vv. 34–39).

21 "and they teach customs which are
not lawful for us, being Romans, to receive or observe."
22 Then the multitude rose up together
against them; and the magistrates tore
off their clothes [a]and commanded
them to be beaten with rods.
23 And when they had laid many
stripes on them, they threw *them* into
prison, commanding the jailer to keep
them securely.
24 Having received such a **charge,** he
put them into the inner prison and fastened their feet in the stocks.

WORD WEALTH

16:24 charge, *parangelia* (par-ang-gel-*ee*-ah); Strong's *#3852:* A chain-of-command word, denoting a general order, instruction, command, precept, or direction. It is used in a way that makes the word self-explanatory. The prison authorities charge the jailer to imprison Paul and Silas (v. 24). The apostles were given a charge not to preach by the authorities at Jerusalem (5:28). Paul gives a charge to the Thessalonians (1 Thess. 4:2). *Parangelia* is the charge Paul gave to Timothy (1 Tim. 1:5, 18).

The Philippian Jailer Saved

25 But at midnight Paul and Silas were
praying and singing hymns to God,
and the prisoners were listening to
them.
26 [a]Suddenly there was a great earthquake, so that the foundations of the
prison were shaken; and immediately
[b]all the doors were opened and everyone's chains were loosed.

KINGDOM DYNAMICS

16:25, 26 Praise Springs Open Prison Doors, PRAISE PATHWAY. Study this example of the power of praise, even in difficult circumstances. Beaten and imprisoned, Paul and Silas respond by singing a hymn of praise—a song sung directly from the heart to God. The relationship between their song of praise and their supernatural deliverance through the earthquake cannot be overlooked. Praise directed toward God can shake open prison doors! A man was converted, his household saved, and satanic captivity overthrown in Philippi. Today, as well, praise will cause every chain of bondage to drop away. When you are serving God and things do not go the way you planned, learn from this text. Praise triumphs gloriously!

(Matt. 21:16/Eph. 5:18, 19) C.G.

27 And the keeper of the prison, awak-
ing from sleep and seeing the prison
doors open, supposing the prisoners
had fled, drew his sword and was
about to kill himself.
28 But Paul called with a loud voice,
saying, "Do yourself no harm, for we
are all here."
29 Then he called for a light, ran in,
and fell down trembling before Paul
and Silas.
30 And he brought them out and said,
[a]"Sirs, what must I do to be *saved?"
31 So they said, [a]"Believe* on the Lord
Jesus Christ, and you will be saved,
you and your household."
32 Then they spoke the word of the
Lord to him and to all who were in his
house.
33 And he took them the same hour
of the night and washed *their* stripes.
And immediately he and all his family
were baptized.
34 Now when he had brought them
into his house, [a]he set food before
them; and he rejoiced, having believed
in God with all his household.

Paul Refuses to Depart Secretly

35 And when it was day, the magistrates sent the [1]officers, saying, "Let
those men go."
36 So the keeper of the prison reported
these words to Paul, saying, "The magistrates have sent to let you go. Now
therefore depart, and go in peace."
37 But Paul said to them, "They have
beaten us openly, uncondemned
[a]Romans, *and* have thrown *us* into
prison. And now do they put us out secretly? No indeed! Let them come
themselves and get us out."

22 [a]2 Cor. 6:5; 11:23, 25; 1 Thess. 2:2
26 [a]Acts 4:31 [b]Acts 5:19; 12:7, 10
30 [a]Luke 3:10; Acts 2:37; 9:6; 22:10 *See WW at Luke 7:50.
31 [a][John 3:16, 36; 6:47; Acts 13:38, 39; Rom. 10:9–11; 1 John 5:10] *See WW at Rom. 10:9.
34 [a]Matt. 5:4; Luke 5:29; 19:6
35 [1]*lictors,* lit. *rod bearers*
37 [a]Acts 22:25–29

16:25 Paul and Silas rejoiced in the face of their terrible circumstances. As he later wrote back to the church he had planted in this very city of Philippi, Paul commanded from another prison cell, "Rejoice in the Lord always" (Phil. 4:4).
16:26 This is the power of praise in action, although it must be remembered that Paul was in prison at other times and this kind of spectacular event did *not* occur.
16:30, 31 Luke was not only recording an important moment in early church history; he was recording a universal question and the precise answer to that question. **You and your household** suggests that God works in family units (see Ex. 12:3).
16:37 This is the first of several instances where Paul appeals to his Roman citizenship. A relatively small proportion of the population of the Roman Empire held citizenship, a rare and valuable status (22:27, 28); and Roman law guaranteed the legal rights of its official citizens, including the right to a fair trial (22:25, 26; 25:16). Paul's insistence on fair treatment is to turn the tables on the lies of his accusers (v. 21).

38 And the officers told these words to the magistrates, and they were *afraid when they heard that they were Romans.
39 Then they came and pleaded with them and brought *them* out, and [a]asked *them* to depart from the city.
40 So they went out of the prison [a]and entered *the house of* Lydia; and when they had seen the brethren, they encouraged them and departed.

Preaching Christ at Thessalonica

17 Now when they had passed through Amphipolis and Apollonia, they came to [a]Thessalonica, where there was a synagogue of the Jews.
2 Then Paul, as his custom was, [a]went in to them, and for three Sabbaths [b]reasoned with them from the Scriptures,
3 explaining and demonstrating [a]that the Christ had to **suffer** and rise again from the dead, and *saying,* "This Jesus whom I preach to you is the Christ."

WORD WEALTH

17:3 suffer, *pascho* (*pas*-kho); Strong's *#3958:* Compare "passion," "passive," "pathos." Being acted upon in a certain way, to experience ill-treatment, roughness, violence, or outrage, to endure suffering, and to undergo evils from without. *Pascho* asks the painful question, "What is happening to me?" Of the 42 times it appears, it is mostly used of Christ's suffering for us.

4 [a]And some of them were persuaded; and a great multitude of the devout Greeks, and not a few of the leading women, joined Paul and [b]Silas.

Assault on Jason's House

5 But the Jews [1]who were not persuaded, [2]becoming [a]envious,* took some of the evil men from the marketplace, and gathering a mob, set all the city in an uproar and attacked the house of [b]Jason, and sought to bring *them out to the people.*

38 *See WW at Matt. 10:26.
39 [a]Matt. 8:34
40 [a]Acts 16:14

CHAPTER 17

1 [a]Acts 17:11, 13; 20:4; 27:2; Phil. 4:16; 1 Thess. 1:1; 2 Thess. 1:1; 2 Tim. 4:10
2 [a]Luke 4:16; Acts 9:20; 13:5, 14; 14:1; 16:13; 19:8 [b]1 Thess. 2:1–16
3 [a]Luke 24:26, 46; Acts 18:5, 28; Gal. 3:1
4 [a]Acts 28:24 [b]Acts 15:22, 27, 32, 40
5 [a]Acts 13:45 [b]Acts 17:6, 7, 9; Rom. 16:21 [1]NU omits *who were not persuaded* [2]M omits *becoming envious* *See WW at 1 Cor. 14:1.
6 [a][Acts 16:20]
7 [a]Luke 23:2; John 19:12; 1 Pet. 2:13 [1]*welcomed*
8 *See WW at Luke 24:38.
10 [a]Acts 9:25; 17:14
11 [a]Is. 34:16; Luke 16:29; John 5:39 [1]Lit. *noble*
14 [a]Matt. 10:23 *See WW at Matt. 24:13.
15 [a]Acts 18:5
16 [a]2 Pet. 2:8 [1]*full of idols*
18 [1]NU, M add *also*

6 But when they did not find them, they dragged Jason and some brethren to the rulers of the city, crying out, [a]"These who have turned the world upside down have come here too.
7 "Jason has [1]harbored them, and these are all acting contrary to the decrees of Caesar, [a]saying there is another king—Jesus."
8 And they *troubled the crowd and the rulers of the city when they heard these things.
9 So when they had taken security from Jason and the rest, they let them go.

Ministering at Berea

10 Then [a]the brethren immediately sent Paul and Silas away by night to Berea. When they arrived, they went into the synagogue of the Jews.
11 These were more [1]fair-minded than those in Thessalonica, in that they received the word with all readiness, and [a]searched the Scriptures daily *to find out* whether these things were so.
12 Therefore many of them believed, and also not a few of the Greeks, prominent women as well as men.
13 But when the Jews from Thessalonica learned that the word of God was preached by Paul at Berea, they came there also and stirred up the crowds.
14 [a]Then immediately the brethren sent Paul away, to go to the sea; but both Silas and Timothy *remained there.
15 So those who conducted Paul brought him to Athens; and [a]receiving a command for Silas and Timothy to come to him with all speed, they departed.

The Philosophers at Athens

16 Now while Paul waited for them at Athens, [a]his spirit was provoked within him when he saw that the city was [1]given over to idols.
17 Therefore he reasoned in the synagogue with the Jews and with the *Gentile* worshipers, and in the marketplace daily with those who happened to be there.
18 [1]Then certain Epicurean and Stoic philosophers encountered him. And

17:2 Paul usually began his ministry in a new city by going into the Jewish synagogue, which offered a relatively open forum for Jews to teach and address current issues. Even though Paul was persecuted by his brethren, the Jews, he never lost his burden for their souls (see Rom. 9:1–5).

17:11 These Jews did not have closed minds; **they received the word with all readiness.** Nor were they gullible; they **searched the Scriptures daily.**

some said, "What does this [2]**babbler** want to say?" Others said, "He seems to be a proclaimer of foreign gods," because he preached to them [a]Jesus and the resurrection.

WORD WEALTH

17:18 babbler, *spermologos* (sper-mol-og-oss); Strong's *#4691:* Athenian slang for: 1) a bird that picks up seeds; 2) men lounging around the marketplace, making a living by picking up whatever falls from the loads of merchandise; 3) a babbler, chatterer, or gossip retailing bits and pieces of misinformation; 4) a pseudo-intellectual who insists on spouting off. Tragically, the super-intellectuals on Mars' Hill failed to see in Paul all the necessary ingredients for being a truth bringer.

19 And they took him and brought him
to the [1]Areopagus, saying, "May we know what this *new doctrine *is* of which you speak?
20 "For you are bringing some strange things to our ears. Therefore we want to know what these things mean."
21 For all the Athenians and the foreigners who were there spent their time in nothing else but either to tell or to hear some new thing.

Addressing the Areopagus

22 Then Paul stood in the midst of the [1]Areopagus and said, "Men of Athens, I perceive that in all things you are very religious;
23 "for as I was passing through and considering the objects of your worship, I even found an altar with this inscription:

TO THE UNKNOWN GOD.

Therefore, the One whom you worship without knowing, Him I proclaim to you:

18 [a]1 Cor. 15:12 [2]Lit. *seed picker,* an idler who makes a living picking up scraps
19 [1]Lit. *Hill of Ares,* or *Mars' Hill*
*See WW at 2 Cor. 5:17.
22 [1]Lit. *Hill of Ares,* or *Mars' Hill*

24 [a]Is. 42:5; Acts 14:15 [b]Deut. 10:14; Ps. 115:16; Matt. 11:25 [c]1 Kin. 8:27; Acts 7:48–50
25 [a]Gen. 2:7; Is. 42:5; Dan. 5:23
26 [a]Deut. 32:8; Job 12:23; Dan. 4:35 [1]NU omits *blood*

KINGDOM DYNAMICS

17:23 1. What Is God Like?, SPIRITUAL ANSWERS. For the answer to this and other probing questions about God and the power life in His kingdom, see the study article "Spiritual Answers to Hard Questions," which begins on page 1996. P.R.

24 [a]"God, who made the world and everything in it, since He is [b]Lord of heaven and earth, [c]does not dwell in temples made with hands.
25 "Nor is He worshiped with men's hands, as though He needed anything, since He [a]gives to all life, breath, and all things.
26 "And He has made from one [1]blood every nation of men to dwell on all the face of the earth, and has determined their preappointed times and [a]the boundaries of their dwellings,

KINGDOM DYNAMICS

17:26 The Unity of the Human Race, HUMAN WORTH. Here the unity of the human race is clearly stated, for through Adam and Eve (Gen. 3:20), and then the sons of Noah (Gen. 9:19), all races and nationalities of men came forth. We all proceed from one blood, both figuratively and literally, for the same blood types are found in all races. Humankind is a universal family. "Have we not all one Father? Has not one God created us?" (Mal. 2:10). We live in a single world community. No race or nation has the right to look down on or disassociate itself from another. The apostle Peter said, "God has shown me that I should not call any man common or unclean . . . In truth I perceive that God shows no partiality. But in every nation, whoever fears Him and works righteousness is accepted by Him" (Acts 10:28, 34, 35). There are only two divisions of humankind: the saved and the unsaved. Other differences are merely skin deep or culturally flavored, but all people are relatives.

(Gen. 9:5, 6/1 Cor. 12:12) C.B.

17:18 The people of the Roman Empire were characterized by a great diversity of religious belief. Epicureanism (seeking tranquility as the highest good) and Stoicism (being free from passion and passively accepting everything in life as inevitable, impersonal fate) were popular philosophies. Polytheism (the belief in multiple gods) was rampant: "The city was given over to idols" (v. 16). These philosophers actually thought that Paul was propagating a religion of two new gods: **Jesus and the resurrection.** Others, however, accused Paul of being a **babbler.** The word originally described one who picked up scraps in the marketplace. Later, it designated one who picked up scraps of learning here and there and peddled them.
17:19 The **Areopagus,** or "Hill of Ares" (Roman, "of Mars"), was an open forum for philosophical debate, and was located southwest of the Parthenon on the Acropolis.
17:22 Athens was the religious center of the Greco-Roman world. There were more statues of gods in Athens than in all the rest of Greece put together. The phrase **very religious** is not a compliment, but a statement of fact. It could be understood as "somewhat superstitious."
17:23 In spite of their religiosity, the Athenians were ignorant of the true God.
17:24–31 Paul did not quote from the Hebrew Scriptures, which were unfamiliar to his Greek audience. For reasons Luke does not explain, results here were meager (v. 34)—no baptisms, no new church, and no letter to the Athenians in the NT—in contrast to other places where the power of God was the front line of his ministry.

27 [a]"so that they should seek the Lord, in the hope that they might grope for Him and find Him, [b]though He is not far from each one of us;

28 "for [a]in Him we live and move and have our being, [b]as also some of your own poets have said, 'For we are also His offspring.'

29 "Therefore, since we are the offspring of God, [a]we ought not to think that the Divine Nature is like gold or silver or stone, something shaped by art and man's devising.

30 "Truly, [a]these times of ignorance God overlooked, but [b]now commands all men everywhere to *repent,

31 "because He has appointed a day on which [a]He will judge the world in righteousness by the Man whom He has ordained. He has given assurance of this to all by [b]raising Him from the dead."

32 And when they heard of the resurrection of the dead, some mocked, while others said, "We will hear you again on this *matter.*"

33 So Paul departed from among them.

34 However, some men joined him and believed, among them Dionysius the Areopagite, a woman named Damaris, and others with them.

Ministering at Corinth

18 After these things Paul departed from Athens and went to Corinth.

2 And he found a certain Jew named [a]Aquila, born in Pontus, who had recently come from Italy with his wife Priscilla (because Claudius had commanded all the Jews to depart from Rome); and he came to them.

3 So, because he was of the same trade, he stayed with them [a]and worked; for by occupation they were tentmakers.

4 [a]And he reasoned in the synagogue every Sabbath, and persuaded both Jews and Greeks.

5 [a]When Silas and Timothy had come from Macedonia, Paul was [b]compelled* [1]by the Spirit, and testified to the Jews *that* Jesus *is* the Christ.

6 But [a]when they opposed him and blasphemed, [b]he shook *his* garments and said to them, [c]"Your blood *be* upon your *own* heads; [d]I *am* clean. [e]From now on I will go to the Gentiles."

7 And he departed from there and entered the house of a certain *man* named [1]Justus, *one* who worshiped God, whose house was next door to the synagogue.

8 [a]Then Crispus, the ruler of the synagogue, believed on the Lord with all his household. And many of the Corinthians, hearing, believed and were baptized.

9 Now [a]the Lord spoke to Paul in the night by a vision, "Do not be afraid, but speak, and do not keep silent;

10 [a]"for I am with you, and no one will attack you to hurt you; for I have many people in this city."

11 And he continued *there* a year and six months, teaching the word of God among them.

12 When Gallio was proconsul of Achaia, the Jews *with one accord rose up against Paul and brought him to the [1]judgment* seat,

13 saying, "This *fellow* persuades men to worship God contrary to the law."

14 And when Paul was about to open *his* mouth, Gallio said to the Jews, "If it were a matter of wrongdoing or wicked crimes, O Jews, there would be reason why I should *bear with you.

15 "But if it is a [a]question of words and names and your own law, look *to it* yourselves; for I do not want to be a judge of such *matters.*"

16 And he drove them from the *judgment seat.

17 Then [1]all the Greeks took [a]Sosthenes, the ruler of the synagogue, and beat *him* before the judgment seat. But Gallio took no notice of these things.

Paul Returns to Antioch

18 So Paul still remained [1]a good while. Then he took leave of the breth-

27 [a][Rom. 1:20] [b]Jer. 23:23, 24
28 [a][Heb. 1:3] [b]Titus 1:12
29 [a]Is. 40:18, 19
30 [a][Rom. 3:25] [b][Titus 2:11, 12] *See WW at Matt. 3:2.
31 [a]Acts 10:42 [b]Acts 2:24

CHAPTER 18

2 [a]1 Cor. 16:19
3 [a]Acts 20:34
4 [a]Acts 17:2
5 [a]Acts 17:14, 15 [b]Acts 18:28 [1]Or *in his spirit* or *in the Spirit* *See WW at 2 Cor. 5:14.
6 [a]Acts 13:45 [b]Neh. 5:13 [c]2 Sam. 1:16 [d][Ezek. 3:18, 19] [e]Acts 13:46–48; 28:28
7 [1]NU *Titius Justus*
8 [a]1 Cor. 1:14
9 [a]Acts 23:11
10 [a]Jer. 1:18, 19
12 [1]Gr. *bema* *See WW at Acts 2:1. • See WW at Matt. 27:19.
14 *See WW at 2 Thess. 1:4.
15 [a]Acts 23:29; 25:19
16 *See WW at Matt. 27:19.
17 [a]1 Cor. 1:1 [1]NU *they all*
18 [1]Lit. *many days*

17:32 To the Greeks the idea of the resurrection of the dead was ridiculous, because they believed that death was a release of the soul from the prison of the body.

18:2 Claudius banished Jews from Rome in A.D. 49.

18:3 Paul, the brilliant and gifted apostle of Christ, was not afraid of manual labor. His vocation was tentmaking, or possibly leatherwork. In ancient Judaism it was improper for a rabbi to receive money for his teaching.

18:4 Greeks in the synagogue were proselytes, converts to Judaism.

18:6 See note on 13:51. **From now on I will go to the Gentiles** must refer only to Corinth, because later Paul goes back to the synagogue in other cities (see 18:19; 19:8).

18:12 Gallio was the brother of the famous Roman orator, Seneca. He became governor of Achaia in A.D. 52.

18:18 This **vow** is difficult to identify. A Nazirite vow could not be undertaken outside of Judea, so this was probably some private vow of thanksgiving for the fulfillment of God's promise to him in vv. 9, 10 and his protection in Corinth.

ren and sailed for Syria, and Priscilla
and Aquila *were* with him. [a]He had *his*
hair cut off at [b]Cenchrea, for he had
taken a vow.
19 And he came to Ephesus, and left
them there; but he himself entered the
synagogue and reasoned with the
Jews.
20 When they asked *him* to stay a
longer time with them, he did not consent,
21 but took leave of them, saying,
[a]"I[1] must by all means keep this coming feast in Jerusalem; but I will return
again to you, [b]God willing." And he
sailed from Ephesus.
22 And when he had landed at [a]Caesa-
rea, and [1]gone up and greeted the
church, he went down to Antioch.
23 After he had spent some time *there,*
he departed and went over the region
of [a]Galatia and Phrygia [1]in order,
[b]strengthening all the disciples.

Ministry of Apollos

24 [a]Now a certain Jew named Apollos,
born at Alexandria, an eloquent man
and *mighty in the *Scriptures, came
to Ephesus.

18 [a]Num. 6:2, 5, 9, 18; Acts 21:24 [b]Rom. 16:1
21 [a]Acts 19:21; 20:16 [b]1 Cor. 4:19; Heb. 6:3; James 4:15 [1]NU omits *I must by all means keep this coming feast in Jerusalem*
22 [a]Acts 8:40 [1]To Jerusalem
23 [a]Gal. 1:2 [b]Acts 14:22; 15:32, 41 [1]*successively*
24 [a]Acts 19:1; 1 Cor. 1:12; 3:4; 16:12; Titus 3:13 *See WW at Matt. 19:26. • See WW at John 5:39.
25 [a]Rom. 12:11 [b][Matt. 3:1–11; Mark 1:7, 8; Luke 3:16, 17; 7:29; John 1:26, 33]; Acts 19:3
27 [a]1 Cor. 3:6

25 This man had been instructed in the
way of the Lord; and being [a]**fervent**
in spirit, he spoke and taught accurately the things of the Lord, [b]though
he knew only the baptism of John.

WORD WEALTH

18:25 fervent, *zeo* (*dzeh*-oh); Strong's *#2204:* Compare "zeal," "zeolite,"or "seethe." Living fervor, fiery hot, full of burning zeal. It is the opposite of dignified, cold, and unemotional. In a Christian context it signifies a high spiritual temperature, inflamed by the Holy Spirit. Apollos was a complete man, articulate in Scripture, and full of spiritual fervency.

26 So he began to speak boldly in the
synagogue. When Aquila and Priscilla
heard him, they took him aside and explained to him the way of God more
accurately.
27 And when he desired to cross to
Achaia, the brethren wrote, exhorting
the disciples to receive him; and when
he arrived, [a]he greatly helped those
who had believed through grace;
28 for he vigorously refuted the Jews

18:22 Greeted the church in Jerusalem.
18:23 This verse is the quiet beginning of Paul's third international trip. See map of Paul's third journey.
18:24 The references Paul makes to Apollos in 1 Cor. 1:12; 3:4 indicate that later he became well known to the Corinthian church.
18:26 Explained . . . more accurately may refer to Apollos's unexpanded view of the Holy Spirit's ministry, which will be discovered by Paul among the Ephesians to whom Apollos had ministered (v. 24; 19:1, 2).

Asia and Greece Revisited (Paul's Third Missionary Journey, Acts 18:23—21:16). Paul visited the churches of Galatia for a third time, and then settled in Ephesus for more than two years. Upon leaving Ephesus, Paul traveled again to Macedonia and Achaia (Greece) for a three-month stay. He returned to Asia by way of Macedonia.

On this third journey Paul wrote 1 Corinthians from Ephesus, 2 Corinthians from Macedonia, and the letter to the Romans from Corinth.

publicly, [a]showing from the Scriptures
that Jesus is the Christ.

Paul at Ephesus

19 And it happened, while [a]Apol-
los was at Corinth, that Paul,
having passed through [b]the upper regions, came to Ephesus. And finding
some disciples
2 he said to them, "Did you receive
the Holy Spirit when you believed?" So
they said to him, [a]"We have not so
much as heard whether there is a Holy
Spirit."

KINGDOM DYNAMICS

19:2 Receiving the Holy Spirit Baptism, SPIRITUAL GIFTS. Although it is recognized that the Holy Spirit is operative in every believer and the varied ministries of the church, still the presence of this question prompts us all to be certain: "Have you received?" An elaboration of this and related themes appears in the study article on page 2018, "Holy Spirit Gifts and Power."
(Acts 10:46/Rom. 8:2) P.W.

3 And he said to them, "Into what
then were you baptized?" So they said,
[a]"Into John's baptism."
4 Then Paul said, [a]"John indeed baptized with a baptism of repentance,
saying to the people that they should
believe on Him who would come after
him, that is, on Christ Jesus."
5 When they heard *this,* they were
baptized [a]in the name of the Lord
Jesus.
6 And when Paul had [a]laid hands on
them, the Holy Spirit came upon them,
and [b]they spoke with tongues and
prophesied.
7 Now the men were about twelve in
all.

28 [a]Acts 9:22; 17:3; 18:5

CHAPTER 19

1 [a]1 Cor. 1:12; 3:5, 6; Titus 3:13 [b]Acts 18:23
2 [a]1 Sam. 3:7; Acts 8:16
3 [a]Luke 7:29; Acts 18:25
4 [a]Matt. 3:11; Mark 1:4, 7, 8; Luke 3:16; [John 1:15, 26, 27]; Acts 13:24
5 [a]Matt. 28:19; Acts 8:12, 16; 10:48
6 [a]Acts 6:6; 8:17 [b]Mark 16:17; Acts 2:4; 10:46
8 [a]Acts 17:2; 18:4 [b]Acts 1:3; 28:23 *See WW at 2 Thess. 3:4.
9 [a]2 Tim. 1:15; 2 Pet. 2:2; Jude 10 [b]Acts 9:2; 19:23; 22:4; 24:14
10 [a]Acts 19:8; 20:31
11 [a]Mark 16:20; Acts 14:3
12 [a]2 Kin. 4:29; Acts 5:15
13 [a]Matt. 12:27; Luke 11:19 [b]Mark 9:38; Luke 9:49 [c]1 Cor. 1:23; 2:2 [1]NU / [2]*adjure,* solemnly command *See WW at Acts 9:20.

8 [a]And he went into the synagogue
and spoke boldly for three months, reasoning and *persuading [b]concerning
the things of the kingdom of God.
9 But [a]when some were hardened and
did not believe, but spoke evil [b]of the
Way before the multitude, he departed
from them and withdrew the disciples,
reasoning daily in the school of Tyran-
nus.
10 And [a]this continued for two years,
so that all who dwelt in Asia heard the
word of the Lord Jesus, both Jews and
Greeks.

Miracles Glorify Christ

11 Now [a]God worked unusual miracles by the hands of Paul,
12 [a]so that even handkerchiefs or
aprons were brought from his body to
the sick, and the diseases left them and
the evil spirits went out of them.
13 [a]Then some of the itinerant Jewish
exorcists [b]took it upon themselves to
call the name of the Lord Jesus over
those who had evil spirits, saying,
[1]"We [2]exorcise you by the Jesus whom
Paul [c]preaches."*

KINGDOM DYNAMICS

19:13 27. What Is Exorcism?, SPIRITUAL ANSWERS. For the answer to this and other probing questions about God and the power life in His kingdom, see the study article "Spiritual Answers to Hard Questions," which begins on page 1996. P.R.

14 Also there were seven sons of
Sceva, a Jewish chief priest, who did
so.
15 And the evil spirit answered and
said, "Jesus I know, and Paul I know;
but who are you?"
16 Then the man in whom the evil

19:1–7 Upon arriving in Ephesus, Paul finds a group of **disciples** (a clear indication that they are true, baptized Christians) whose knowledge about **the Holy Spirit** is defective. Their teachers knew some basics of Christianity from contact with John the Baptist, but they were apparently unaware of the developments of Pentecost. Therefore, these disciples had only been baptized **into John's baptism.** This indicates that their conversion experience was accompanied by the knowledge that a fuller experience with the Holy Spirit would come (Matt. 3:11), but without the realization that it had come (Acts 2:1–4). Paul remedies this by rebaptizing them in water (the only such account in the NT) and by leading them into a fuller experience with the Holy Spirit (v. 6). An obvious parallel to the Day of Pentecost, the Spirit's fullness is displayed by their speaking in tongues and prophesying. See note on 2:4.

19:8 The kingdom of God: See note on 1:3.

19:12 Handkerchiefs were sweat-rags tied around Paul's head while he was working. See Matt. 9:20, 21 and note on Acts 5:15. Although some find a basis here for using anointed prayer cloths today, the passage does not necessarily provide a warrant for the practice as a formula for ministering divine healing.

19:13–17 The authority of **the name of the Lord Jesus** has been granted only to believers (Mark 16:17; see Luke 10:17–20). The name of Jesus is not given as a magical phrase calculated to guarantee good or bad results. There is no guarantee of power when it is capriciously uttered, particularly when the situation involves an ecclesiastical or stylized exercise. However, when employed in faith by the power of the Holy Spirit, His might and glory may be expected to be manifested. Inherent in the name of Jesus is not only the resource of His authority, but also the fullness of His nature and character. Thus, any prayer offered or ministry attempted in the name of Jesus must be in accord with His nature and purpose. See note on John 14:13.

spirit was leaped on them, [1]overpowered them, and prevailed against [2]them, so that they fled out of that house naked and wounded.
17 This became known both to all Jews and Greeks dwelling in Ephesus; and [a]fear fell on them all, and the name of the Lord Jesus was *magnified.
18 And many who had believed came [a]confessing and telling their deeds.
19 Also, many of those who had practiced magic brought their books together and burned *them* in the sight of all. And they counted up the value of them, and *it* totaled fifty thousand *pieces* of silver.
20 [a]So the **word** of the Lord grew *mightily and prevailed.

WORD WEALTH

19:20 word, *logos* (*log*-oss); Strong's *#3056:* A transmission of thought, communication, a word of explanation, an utterance, discourse, divine revelation, talk, statement, instruction, an oracle, divine promise, divine doctrine, divine declaration. Jesus is the living *logos* (John 1:1); the Bible is the written *logos* (Heb. 4:12); and the Holy Spirit utters the spoken *logos* (1 Cor. 2:13).

The Riot at Ephesus

21 [a]When these things were accomplished, Paul [b]purposed in the Spirit, when he had passed through [c]Macedonia and Achaia, to go to Jerusalem, saying, "After I have been there, [d]I must also see Rome."
22 So he sent into Macedonia two of those who ministered to him, [a]Timothy and [b]Erastus, but he himself stayed in Asia for a time.
23 And [a]about that time there arose a great commotion about [b]the Way.
24 For a certain man named Demetrius, a silversmith, who made silver shrines of [1]Diana, brought [a]no small profit to the craftsmen.
25 He called them together with the workers of similar occupation, and said: "Men, you know that we have our prosperity by this trade.
26 "Moreover you see and hear that not only at Ephesus, but throughout almost all Asia, this Paul has persuaded and *turned away many people, saying that [a]they are not gods which are made with hands.
27 "So not only is this trade of ours in danger of falling into disrepute, but also the temple of the great goddess Diana may be despised and [1]her *magnificence destroyed, whom all Asia and the world worship."
28 Now when they heard *this,* they were full of *wrath and cried out, saying, "Great *is* Diana of the Ephesians!"
29 So the whole city was filled with confusion, and rushed into the theater with one accord, having seized [a]Gaius and [b]Aristarchus, Macedonians, Paul's travel companions.
30 And when Paul wanted to go in to the people, the disciples would not allow him.
31 Then some of the [1]officials of Asia, who were his *friends, sent to him pleading that he would not venture into the theater.
32 Some therefore cried one thing and some another, for the assembly was confused, and most of them did not know why they had come together.
33 And they drew Alexander out of the multitude, the Jews putting him forward. And [a]Alexander [b]motioned with his hand, and wanted to make his defense to the people.
34 But when they found out that he was a Jew, all with one voice cried out for about two hours, "Great *is* Diana of the Ephesians!"
35 And when the city clerk had quieted the crowd, he said: "Men of Ephesus, what man is there who does not know that the city of the Ephesians is temple guardian of the great goddess [1]Diana, and of the *image* which fell down from [2]Zeus?
36 "Therefore, since these things cannot be denied, you ought to be quiet and do nothing rashly.
37 "For you have brought these men here who are neither robbers of temples nor blasphemers of [1]your goddess.
38 "Therefore, if Demetrius and his fellow craftsmen have a [1]case against anyone, the courts are open and there are proconsuls. Let them bring charges against one another.
39 "But if you have any other inquiry

16 [1]M *and they overpowered them* [2]NU *both of them*
17 [a]Luke 1:65; 7:16; Acts 2:43; 5:5, 11 *See WW at Acts 5:13.
18 [a]Matt. 3:6
20 [a]Acts 6:7; 12:24 *See WW at 1 Tim. 6:16.
21 [a]Rom. 15:25; Gal. 2:1 [b]Acts 20:22; 2 Cor. 1:16 [c]Acts 20:1; 1 Cor. 16:5 [d]Acts 18:21; 23:11; Rom. 1:13; 15:22–29
22 [a]1 Tim. 1:2 [b]Rom. 16:23; 2 Tim. 4:20
23 [a]2 Cor. 1:8 [b]Acts 9:2
24 [a]Acts 16:16, 19 [1]Gr. *Artemis*
26 [a]Deut. 4:28; Ps. 115:4; Is. 44:10–20; Jer. 10:3; Acts 17:29; 1 Cor. 8:4; 10:19; Rev. 9:20 *See WW at Luke 16:4.
27 [1]NU *she be deposed from her magnificence* *See WW at Luke 9:43.
28 *See WW at Luke 4:28.
29 [a]Acts 20:4; Rom. 16:23; 1 Cor. 1:14; 3 John 1 [b]Acts 20:4; 27:2; Col. 4:10; Philem. 24
31 [1]*Asiarchs, rulers of Asia,* the province *See WW at John 11:11.
33 [a]1 Tim. 1:20; 2 Tim. 4:14 [b]Acts 12:17
35 [1]Gr. *Artemis* [2]*heaven*
37 [1]NU *our*
38 [1]Lit. *matter*

19:19 Even in nonbiblical records of the time, Ephesus had the reputation of being a center of magical practices. **Fifty thousand *pieces* of silver:** This is probably a reference to 50,000 Greek drachmae, a coin which was roughly equivalent to one day's wage, so the cumulative value of these magic books was enormous.

19:24 Diana was the Roman name of Artemis, the Greek goddess of love and fertility; and Ephesus was the home of her great temple (vv. 34, 35), acclaimed as one of the seven wonders of the ancient world.

19:32 Another of many references to show that early opposition to Christianity was at times irrational. Anyone who knew the facts would not be threatened by the Christian message (see vv. 36, 37, 40).

to make, it shall be determined in the lawful assembly.
40 "For we are in danger of being [1]called in question for today's uproar, there being no reason which we may *give to account for this disorderly gathering."
41 And when he had said these things, he dismissed the assembly.

Journeys in Greece

20 After the uproar had ceased, Paul called the disciples to *himself*, embraced *them*, and [a]departed to go to Macedonia.
2 Now when he had gone over that region and encouraged them with many words, he came to [a]Greece
3 and stayed three months. And [a]when the Jews plotted against him as he was about to sail to Syria, he decided to return through Macedonia.
4 And Sopater of Berea accompanied him to Asia—also [a]Aristarchus and Secundus of the Thessalonians, and [b]Gaius of Derbe, and [c]Timothy, and [d]Tychicus and [e]Trophimus of Asia.
5 These men, going ahead, waited for us at [a]Troas.
6 But we sailed away from Philippi after [a]the Days of Unleavened Bread, and in five days joined them [b]at Troas, where we stayed seven days.

Ministering at Troas

7 Now on [a]the first *day* of the week, when the disciples came together [b]to break bread, Paul, ready to depart the next day, spoke to them and continued his message until midnight.
8 There were many lamps [a]in the upper room where [1]they were gathered together.
9 And in a window sat a certain young man named Eutychus, who was sinking into a deep sleep. He was overcome by sleep; and as Paul continued speaking, he fell down from the third story and was *taken up dead.
10 But Paul went down, [a]fell on him, and embracing *him* said, [b]"Do not trouble yourselves, for his life is in him."
11 Now when he had come up, had broken bread and *eaten, and talked *a long while, even* till daybreak, he departed.

40 [1]Or *charged with rebellion concerning today* *See WW at Matt. 22:21.

CHAPTER 20

1 [a]1 Cor. 16:5; 1 Tim. 1:3
2 [a]Acts 17:15; 18:1
3 [a]Acts 9:23; 23:12; 25:3; 2 Cor. 11:26
4 [a]Acts 19:29; Col. 4:10 [b]Acts 19:29 [c]Acts 16:1 [d]Eph. 6:21; Col. 4:7; 2 Tim. 4:12; Titus 3:12 [e]Acts 21:29; 2 Tim. 4:20
5 [a]2 Cor. 2:12; 2 Tim. 4:13
6 [a]Ex. 12:14, 15 [b]Acts 16:8; 2 Cor. 2:12; 2 Tim. 4:13
7 [a]1 Cor. 16:2; Rev. 1:10 [b]Acts 2:42, 46; 20:11; 1 Cor. 10:16
8 [a]Acts 1:13 [1]NU, M *we*
9 *See WW at John 16:22.
10 [a]1 Kin. 17:21; 2 Kin. 4:34 [b]Matt. 9:23, 24; Mark 5:39
11 *See WW at John 8:52.
13 [1]*arranged it*
16 [a]Acts 18:21; 19:21; 21:4 [b]Acts 24:17 [c]Acts 2:1; 1 Cor. 16:8 *See WW at Matt. 19:26.
17 *See WW at Acts 8:1.
18 [a]Acts 18:19; 19:1, 10; 20:4, 16
19 [a]Acts 20:3
20 [a]Acts 20:27
21 [a]Acts 18:5; 19:10

12 And they brought the young man in alive, and they were not a little comforted.

From Troas to Miletus

13 Then we went ahead to the ship and sailed to Assos, there intending to take Paul on board; for so he had [1]given orders, intending himself to go on foot.
14 And when he met us at Assos, we took him on board and came to Mitylene.
15 We sailed from there, and the next *day* came opposite Chios. The following *day* we arrived at Samos and stayed at Trogyllium. The next *day* we came to Miletus.
16 For Paul had decided to sail past Ephesus, so that he would not have to spend time in Asia; for [a]he was hurrying [b]to be at Jerusalem, if *possible, on [c]the Day of Pentecost.

The Ephesian Elders Exhorted

17 From Miletus he sent to Ephesus and called for the elders of the *church.
18 And when they had come to him, he said to them: "You know, [a]from the first day that I came to Asia, in what manner I always lived among you,
19 "serving the Lord with all **humility,** with many tears and trials which happened to me [a]by the plotting of the Jews;

WORD WEALTH

20:19 humility, *tapeinophrosune* (tap-eye-nof-ros-oo-nay); Strong's *#5012:* Modesty, lowliness, humble-mindedness, a sense of moral insignificance, and a humble attitude of unselfish concern for the welfare of others. It is a total absence of arrogance, conceit, and haughtiness. The word is a combination of *tapeinos,* "humble," and *phren,* "mind." The word was unknown in classical nonbiblical Greek. Only by abstaining from self-aggrandizement can members of the Christian community maintain unity and harmony.

20 "how [a]I kept back nothing that was helpful, but proclaimed it to you, and taught you publicly and from house to house,
21 [a]"testifying to Jews, and also to

20:6 Days of Unleavened Bread was another way to refer to the Passover.
20:17–35 This was Paul's emotional farewell address to the Ephesian **elders.** In its written form, this passage also became a permanent word of warning and instruction to all the Gentile churches that Paul had established. **Miletus** was a port city that serviced **Ephesus,** about 30 miles away.

Greeks, [b]repentance toward God and
faith toward our Lord Jesus Christ.
22 "And see, now [a]I go bound in the
spirit to Jerusalem, not knowing the
things that will happen to me there,
23 "except that [a]the Holy Spirit testifies in every city, saying that chains
and tribulations await me.
24 [1]"But [a]none of these things move
me; nor do I count my life dear to myself, [b]so that I may *finish my [2]race
with joy, [c]and the ministry [d]which I
received from the Lord Jesus, to testify
to the gospel of the grace of God.
25 "And indeed, now I know that you
all, among whom I have gone preaching the kingdom of God, will see my
face no more.
26 "Therefore I testify to you this day
that I *am* [a]innocent[1]* of the blood of
all *men.*
3 27 "For I have not [1]shunned to declare
to you [a]the whole counsel of God.
3 28 [a]"Therefore take heed to yourselves
and to all the flock, among which the
Holy Spirit [b]has made you overseers,
to shepherd the church [1]of God [c]which
He purchased [d]with His own blood.
29 "For I know this, that after my departure [a]savage wolves will come in
among you, not sparing the flock.
30 "Also [a]from among yourselves men
will rise up, speaking [1]perverse things,
to draw away the disciples after themselves.
31 "Therefore watch, and remember
that [a]for three years I did not cease to
warn everyone night and day with
tears.
32 "So now, brethren, I commend you
to God and [a]to the word of His grace,
which is able [b]to build you up and give
you [c]an inheritance among all those
who are *sanctified.

21 [b]Mark 1:15
22 [a]Acts 19:21
23 [a]Acts 21:4, 11
24 [a]Acts 21:13
[b]2 Tim. 4:7
[c]Acts 1:17
[d]Gal. 1:1 [1]NU *But I do not count my life of any value or dear to myself* [2]*course*
*See WW at 1 John 2:5.
26 [a]Acts 18:6
[1]Lit. *clean*
*See WW at Matt. 5:8.
27 [a]Luke 7:30
[1]*avoided declaring*
28 [a]1 Pet. 5:2
[b]1 Cor. 12:28
[c]Eph. 1:7, 14
[d]Heb. 9:14 [1]M *of the Lord and God*
29 [a]Matt. 7:15
30 [a]1 Tim. 1:20
[1]*misleading*
31 [a]Acts 19:8, 10; 24:17
32 [a]Heb. 13:9
[b]Acts 9:31
[c][Heb. 9:15]
*See WW at John 10:36.
33 *See WW at Matt. 13:17.
34 [a]Acts 18:3
[1]NU, M omit *Yes*
35 [a]Rom. 15:1
*See WW at Matt. 5:3.
37 [a]Acts 21:13
[b]Gen. 45:14
[1]Lit. *much*
38 *See WW at John 20:14.

33 "I have *coveted no one's silver or
gold or apparel.
34 [1]"Yes, you yourselves know [a]that
these hands have provided for my necessities, and for those who were with
me.
35 "I have shown you in every way,
[a]by laboring like this, that you must
support the weak. And remember the
words of the Lord Jesus, that He said,
'It is more *blessed to **give** than to receive.'"

WORD WEALTH

20:35 give, *didomi* (*did*-oh-mee); Strong's *#1325:* Granting, allowing, bestowing, imparting, permitting, placing, offering, presenting, yielding, and paying. *Didomi* implies giving an object of value. It gives freely and is unforced. Acts 20:35 indicates that the giver takes on the character of Christ, whose nature is to give. Jesus did not say it would be more natural or easier to give than to receive, but that it would be more blessed.

36 And when he had said these things,
he knelt down and prayed with them
all.
37 Then they all [a]wept [1]freely, and
[b]fell on Paul's neck and kissed him,
38 sorrowing most of all for the words
which he spoke, that they would *see
his face no more. And they accompanied him to the ship.

Warnings on the Journey to Jerusalem

21 Now it came to pass, that when
we had departed from them and
set sail, running a straight course we
came to Cos, the following *day* to
Rhodes, and from there to Patara.
2 And finding a ship sailing over to

20:25 Kingdom of God: Paul does not use this precise phraseology often in his epistles. However, an understanding of its significance (see note on 1:3) shows that it is conceptually synonymous with Paul's more familiar "preaching the gospel, the Cross, or life in the Spirit." See Kingdom Dynamics articles on this subject.

20:27 See section 3 of Truth-In-Action at the end of Acts.

20:27 The whole counsel of God refers to the larger picture of God's plan. Deception or diminishing of fullness of experience and ministry by the body of Christ often begins when men and women preach only part of the counsel of God.

20:28–32 See section 3 of Truth-In-Action at the end of Acts.

20:28 This verse is rich with lessons about leadership in the church: 1) **Take heed to yourselves** means "pay close attention." Leaders must first guard themselves before they can oversee the church adequately. 2) Church leaders are not self-made. They are appointed by the Spirit. 3) **Overseers** is from the same Greek root translated "overshadow" in Luke 1:35. An overseer is one who covers and protects the flock. 4) The church belongs to God. He owns it because He bought it. What God does through the leaders of the church does not belong to them. In contrast, Paul warns of false leaders in vv. 29–31.

20:29–31 Characteristics of the wrong kind of leadership in the church: 1) They are more interested in themselves than the care of the flock (v. 29). 2) They will draw people after themselves (v. 30). 3) They will look for quick results that require little sacrifice (v. 31).

20:32 The word of His grace always builds up and releases our spiritual inheritance. **Are sanctified** is best translated "are *being* sanctified," with an emphasis on the unfinished process.

20:33–35 This is Paul's view of money and the ministry. Money was not his motivation (v. 33). He supplemented his ministry by making tents (see 18:3), thereby putting less of a financial burden on the churches where he ministered (v. 34). **It is more blessed to give than to receive** refers to our *time* as well as our money, for **by laboring like this** we **support the weak,** the primary recipients of our giving being those who are less fortunate. This saying of Jesus is not recorded in the Gospels.

Phoenicia, we went aboard and set sail.
3 When we had sighted Cyprus, we
passed it on the left, sailed to Syria,
and landed at Tyre; for there the ship
was to unload her cargo.
4 And finding [1]disciples,* we stayed
there seven days. [a]They told Paul
through the Spirit not to go up to Jerusalem.
5 When we had come to the end of
those days, we departed and went on
our way; and they all accompanied us,
with wives and children, till *we were*
out of the city. And [a]we knelt down
on the shore and prayed.
6 When we had taken our leave of
one another, we boarded the ship, and
they returned [a]home.
7 And when we had finished *our* voyage from Tyre, we came to Ptolemais,
greeted the brethren, and stayed with
them one day.
8 On the next *day* we [1]who were
Paul's companions departed and came
to [a]Caesarea, and entered the house of
Philip [b]the evangelist, [c]who was *one*
of the seven, and stayed with him.
9 Now this man had four virgin
daughters [a]who prophesied.

KINGDOM DYNAMICS

21:9 Women and New Testament Ministry (Philip's Daughters), WOMEN. This reference to Philip's daughters' each exercising the gifts of prophecy makes clear that women did bring God's word by the power of the Holy Spirit and that such ministry was fully accepted in the early church. This is reinforced by Paul in 1 Cor. 11:5, where he directs 1) that a woman may "prophesy," but 2) that she must be properly "covered," that is, rightly related to her husband or other spiritual authority, a regulation incumbent upon all spiritual leaders—male or female (see 1 Tim. 3:1–13).

It is puzzling why the place of women in ministry is contested by some in the church. Women had an equal place in the Upper Room, awaiting the Holy Spirit's coming and the birth of the church (Acts 1:14). Then Peter's prophetic sermon at Pentecost affirmed the OT promise was now to be realized: "your daughters" and "maidservants" would now share fully and equally with men in realizing the anointing, fullness, and ministry of the Holy Spirit, making them effective in witness and service for the spread of the gospel.

Though the place of men seems more pronounced in the number who filled leadership offices, there does not appear to be any direct restriction of privilege. Note: 1) the direct mention of Phoebe as a deacon ("servant," Greek, *diakonia,* Rom. 16:1); 2) John's letter to an "elect [chosen] lady" with instructions concerning whom she allows to minister in her "house" (a designation for early church fellowships, 2 John); and 3) 1 Cor. 1:11 and Phil. 4:2, where Chloe and Euodia seem to be women in whose homes believers gather. The method of designation suggests they were the appointed leaders in their respective fellowships.

The acceptance of women in a public place of ministry in the church is not a concession to the spirit of the feminist movement. But the refusal of such a place might be a concession to an order of male chauvinism, unwarranted by and unsupported in the Scriptures. Clearly, women did speak—preach and prophesy—in the early church (see 1 Tim. 2:8–15).

(Rom. 16:1/1 Pet. 3:1) F.L./J.W.H.

10 And as we stayed many days, a certain prophet named [a]Agabus came
down from Judea.
11 When he had come to us, he took
Paul's belt, bound his *own* hands and
feet, and said, "Thus says the Holy
Spirit, [a]'So shall the Jews at Jerusalem
bind the man who owns this belt, and
deliver *him* into the hands of the Gentiles.' "

KINGDOM DYNAMICS

21:11 The Issue of Personal Prophecy, PROPHECY. The Bible clearly allows for personal prophecy. Nathan brought David a confrontive "word" from God (2 Sam. 12:13); Isaiah predicted Hezekiah's death (Is. 38:1); and in this text Agabus told Paul he faced trouble in Jerusalem. "Personal prophecy" refers to a prophecy ("word") the Holy Spirit may prompt one person to give another, relating to personal matters. Many feel deep reservations about this operation of the gift of prophecy because sometimes it is abused. True "words" may be used to manipulate others, or they may be unwisely or hastily applied. This passage reveals safeguards against abusive uses

CHAPTER 21

4 [a][Acts 20:23; 21:12] [1]NU *the disciples* *See WW at Matt. 10:1.
5 [a]Luke 22:41; Acts 9:40; 20:36
6 [a]John 1:11
8 [a]Acts 8:40; 21:16 [b]Acts 8:5, 26, 40; Eph. 4:11; 2 Tim. 4:5 [c]Acts 6:5 [1]NU omits *who were Paul's companions*
9 [a]Joel 2:28; Acts 2:17
10 [a]Acts 11:28
11 [a]Acts 20:23; 21:33; 22:25

21:4–12 This passage contains several warnings given by the Spirit that Paul would encounter trouble during his visit to Jerusalem (vv. 4, 10–12). But the apostle persisted (v. 14), later being arrested and sent to Rome under guard. Arguments to whether or not Paul was in the perfect will of God are pointless. What is useful is to note 1) prophecies do not have to dictate the decisions or manipulate the will of a godly person; 2) even though they may be true, God's purpose may yet be realized, as was the case in God's will ultimately bringing Paul to Rome.

21:10, 11 See note on 11:28.

of personal prophecy, allowing us to implement this biblical practice. First, the "word" will usually not be new to the mind of the person addressed, but it will confirm something God is already dealing with him about. From Acts 20:22–24 we know Paul was already sensitive to the issue Agabus raised. Second, the character of the person bringing the "word" ought to be weighed. Agabus's credibility is related not to his claim of having a "word," but to his record as a trustworthy man of God used in the exercise of this gift (11:28; 21:10). Third, remember that the prophecy, or "word," is not to be considered "controlling." In other words, such prophecies should never be perceived as dominating anyone's free will. Christian living is never cultish—governed by omens or the counsel of gurus. Paul did not change his plans because of Agabus's prophecy or because of the urging of others (vv. 12–14); he received the "word" graciously but continued his plans nonetheless. Fourth, all prophecy is "in part" (1 Cor. 13:9), which means that as true as that "part" may be, it does not give the whole picture. Agabus's "word" was true, and Paul was bound in Jerusalem. But this also occasioned an opportunity to eventually minister in Rome (Acts 23:11). Finally, in the light of a "word," we should prayerfully consider the word as Mary did the shepherds' report (Luke 2:19). A hasty response is never required: simply wait on God. We should then move ahead with trust in God, as Hezekiah did. He had been told that he would shortly die; but he prayed instead of merely surrendering to the prophecy, and his life realized its intended length—unshortened by his diseased condition. Occasional personal prophecy is not risky if kept on biblical footings, but neither is it to become the way we plan or direct our lives.

(2 Pet. 1:16–19/Acts 11:27–30) J.W.H.

12 Now when we heard these things,
both we and those from that place
pleaded with him not to go up to Jerusalem.
13 Then Paul answered, [a]"What do
you mean by weeping and breaking my
heart? For I am ready not only to be
bound, but also to die at Jerusalem for
the name of the Lord Jesus."
14 So when he would not be persuaded, we ceased, saying, [a]"The *will
of the Lord be done."

Paul Urged to Make Peace

15 And after those days we [1]packed
and went up to Jerusalem.
16 Also some of the disciples from
Caesarea went with us and brought
with them a certain Mnason of Cyprus,
an early disciple, with whom we were
to lodge.
17 [a]And when we had come to Jerusalem, the brethren received us gladly.
18 On the following *day* Paul went in
with us to [a]James, and all the elders
were present.
19 When he had greeted them, [a]he told
in detail those things which God had
done among the Gentiles [b]through his
ministry.
20 And when they heard *it*, they glorified the Lord. And they said to him,
"You see, brother, how many myriads
of Jews there are who have believed,
and they are all [a]zealous* for the law;
21 "but they have been informed about
you that you teach all the Jews who
are among the Gentiles to forsake Moses, saying that they ought not to circumcise *their* children nor to walk according to the customs.
22 [1]"What then? The assembly must
certainly meet, for they will hear that
you have come.
23 "Therefore do what we tell you: We
have four men who have taken a vow.
24 "Take them and be purified with
them, and pay their expenses so that
they may [a]shave *their* heads, and that
all may know that those things of
which they were informed concerning
you are nothing, but *that* you yourself
also walk orderly and keep the law.
25 "But concerning the Gentiles who
believe, [a]we have written *and* decided
[1]that they should observe no such
thing, except that they should keep
themselves from *things* offered to
idols, from blood, from things strangled, and from [2]sexual* immorality."

Arrested in the Temple

26 Then Paul took the men, and the
next day, having been purified with

13 [a]Acts 20:24, 37
14 [a]Matt. 6:10; 26:42; Luke 11:2; 22:42 *See WW at Matt. 12:50.
15 [1]*made preparations*
17 [a]Acts 15:4
18 [a]Acts 15:13; Gal. 1:19; 2:9
19 [a]Acts 15:4, 12; Rom. 15:18, 19 [b]Acts 1:17; 20:24; 1 Tim. 2:7
20 [a]Acts 15:1; 22:3; [Rom. 10:2]; Gal. 1:14 *See WW at Acts 22:3.
22 [1]NU *What then is to be done? They will certainly hear*
24 [a]Num. 6:2, 13, 18; Acts 18:18
25 [a]Acts 15:19, 20, 29 [1]NU omits *that they should observe no such thing, except* [2]*fornication* *See WW at Matt. 15:19.

21:20–25 There was still wide debate about Paul's teaching and Gentile Christianity (v. 21). So the apostolic leadership in Jerusalem asked Paul, out of courtesy to those who were suspicious of him, to purify himself ceremonially. The apostles themselves, however, knew that the accusations were baseless (v. 24). Furthermore, the decree of the Jerusalem Council (ch. 15) was **written *and* decided** (v. 25).

21:24 Pay their expenses was a pious and charitable way for an Israelite to associate himself with those who had taken a Nazirite vow. This involved 30 days of ritual purification, including shaving the head.

21:25 This is a reaffirmation of the apostolic decree in 15:19, 20.

them, [a]entered the temple [b]to announce the [1]expiration of the days of
purification, at which time an **offering**
should be *made for each one of them.

WORD WEALTH

21:26 offering, *prosphora* (pros-for-*ah*); Strong's *#4376:* A bringing to, setting before, presenting, sacrificing, a gift, the act of offering, or the thing offered. The word includes giving kindness and bestowing benefit. Paul engaged in the purification ceremony. It was not necessary for his salvation, but was an act of devotion to God. Paul's principle was being all things to all men in order to win them.

27 Now when the seven days were almost ended, [a]the Jews from Asia, seeing him in the temple, stirred up the
whole crowd and [b]laid hands on him,
28 crying out, "Men of Israel, help!
This is the man [a]who teaches all *men*
everywhere against the people, the
law, and this place; and furthermore
he also brought Greeks into the temple
and has defiled this holy place."
29 (For they had [1]previously seen
[a]Trophimus the Ephesian with him in
the city, whom they supposed that Paul
had brought into the temple.)
30 And [a]all the city was disturbed; and
the people ran together, seized Paul,
and dragged him out of the temple; and
*immediately the doors were shut.
31 Now as they were [a]seeking to kill
him, news came to the commander of
the [1]garrison that all Jerusalem was in
an uproar.
32 [a]He immediately took soldiers and
centurions, and ran down to them. And
when they saw the commander and the
soldiers, they stopped beating Paul.
33 Then the [a]commander came near
and took him, and [b]commanded *him*
to be bound with two chains; and he
asked who he was and what he had
done.
34 And some among the multitude
cried one thing and some another. So
when he could not ascertain the truth
because of the tumult, he commanded
him to be taken into the barracks.
35 When he reached the stairs, he had
to be carried by the soldiers because
of the violence of the mob.

26 [a]John 11:55; Acts 21:24; 24:18 [b]Num. 6:13; Acts 24:18 [1]*completion* *See WW at Heb. 9:28.
27 [a]Acts 20:19; 24:18 [b]Acts 26:21
28 [a][Matt. 24:15]; Acts 6:13; 24:6
29 [a]Acts 20:4 [1]M omits *previously*
30 [a]2 Kin. 11:15; Acts 16:19; 26:21 *See WW at John 6:21.
31 [a]2 Cor. 11:23 [1]*cohort*
32 [a]Acts 23:27; 24:7
33 [a]Acts 24:7 [b]Acts 20:23; 21:11; Eph. 6:20; 2 Tim. 1:16; 2:9
36 [a]Luke 23:18; John 19:15; Acts 22:22
38 [a]Acts 5:36
39 [a]Acts 9:11; 22:3; 2 Cor. 11:22; Phil. 3:4–6 [1]*insignificant*
40 [a]Acts 12:17 [b]John 5:2; Acts 22:2

CHAPTER 22

1 [a]Acts 7:2
2 [a]Acts 21:40
3 [a]Acts 21:39; 2 Cor. 11:22 [b]Deut. 33:3 [c]Acts 5:34 [d]Acts 23:6; 26:5; Phil. 3:6 [e]Acts 21:20; Gal. 1:14 [f][Rom. 10:2]
4 [a]Acts 8:3; 26:9–11; Phil. 3:6; 1 Tim. 1:13
5 [a]Acts 23:14; 24:1; 25:15 [b]Luke 22:66; Acts 4:5; 1 Tim. 4:14 *See WW at 1 Tim. 4:14.

36 For the multitude of the people followed after, crying out, [a]"Away with
him!"

Addressing the Jerusalem Mob

37 Then as Paul was about to be led
into the barracks, he said to the commander, "May I speak to you?" He replied, "Can you speak Greek?
38 [a]"Are you not the Egyptian who
some time ago stirred up a rebellion
and led the four thousand assassins out
into the wilderness?"
39 But Paul said, [a]"I am a Jew from
Tarsus, in Cilicia, a citizen of no
[1]mean city; and I implore you, permit
me to speak to the people."
40 So when he had given him permission, Paul stood on the stairs and
[a]motioned with his hand to the people.
And when there was a great silence,
he spoke to *them* in the [b]Hebrew language, saying,

22 "Brethren[a] and fathers, hear my
defense before you now."
2 And when they heard that he spoke
to them in the [a]Hebrew language, they
kept all the more silent. Then he said:
3 [a]"I am indeed a Jew, born in Tarsus
of Cilicia, but brought up in this city
[b]at the feet of [c]Gamaliel, taught
[d]according to the strictness of our fathers' law, and [e]was **zealous** toward
God [f]as you all are today.

WORD WEALTH

22:3 zealous, *zelotes* (dzay-low-*tace*); Strong's *#2207:* Burning with zeal, having warmth and feeling for or against, deep commitment and eager devotion to something or someone, an enthusiast, uncompromising partisan, admirer, emulator, imitator, follower of anyone. Paul rejected his previous zeal that caused him to become a persecutor of the church, but rejoiced in his *zelotes* for the Lord Jesus Christ.

4 [a]"I persecuted this Way to the
death, binding and delivering into prisons both men and women,
5 "as also the high priest bears me
witness, and [a]all the council of the *elders, [b]from whom I also received letters to the brethren, and went to Da-

21:27–29 The ploy of vv. 23, 24 does not work. These Asian Jews, who made the pilgrimage to Jerusalem for the feast, had opposed Paul in their regions. When some of them recognized Paul himself in the temple, they were enraged, especially when they mistakenly thought he had brought Trophimus, a Gentile, with him into the inner temple precincts. This was an offense so grave that even Roman citizens were not exempt from its death penalty.

21:30–32 The prophecy of Agabus and the warnings of the church are fulfilled (see 21:4, 11, 12).

22:2 The Hebrew language is probably a reference to Aramaic, a dialect related to Hebrew.

22:3 Gamaliel: See note on 5:33–40.

mascus [c]to bring in chains even those
who were there to Jerusalem to be punished.
6 "Now [a]it happened, as I journeyed
and came near Damascus at about
noon, suddenly a great light from
heaven shone around me.
7 "And I fell to the ground and heard
a voice saying to me, 'Saul, Saul, why
are you persecuting Me?'
8 "So I answered, 'Who are You,
Lord?' And He said to me, 'I am Jesus
of Nazareth, whom you are persecuting.'
9 "And [a]those who were with me indeed saw the light [1]and were afraid,
but they did not hear the voice of Him
who spoke to me.
10 "So I said, 'What shall I do, Lord?'
And the Lord said to me, 'Arise and
go into Damascus, and there you will
be told all things which are appointed
for you to do.'
11 "And since I could not see for the
glory of that light, being led by the
hand of those who were with me, I
came into Damascus.
12 "Then [a]a certain Ananias, a devout
man according to the law, [b]having a
good testimony with all the [c]Jews who
dwelt *there,*
13 "came to me; and he stood and said
to me, 'Brother Saul, receive your
sight.' And at that same hour I looked
up at him.
14 "Then he said, [a]'The God of our fathers [b]has chosen you that you should
[c]know His will, and [d]see the Just One,
[e]and hear the voice of His mouth.
15 [a]'For you will be His witness to all
men of [b]what you have seen and heard.
1 16 'And now why are you waiting?
Arise and be baptized, [a]and wash away
your sins, [b]calling on the name of the
Lord.'
17 "Now [a]it happened, when I returned to Jerusalem and was praying
in the temple, that I was in a trance

5 [c]Acts 9:2
6 [a]Acts 9:3; 26:12, 13
9 [a]Dan. 10:7; Acts 9:7 [1]NU omits *and were afraid*
12 [a]Acts 9:17 [b]Acts 10:22 [c]1 Tim. 3:7
14 [a]Acts 3:13; 5:30 [b]Acts 9:15; 26:16; Gal. 1:15 [c]Acts 3:14; 7:52 [d]Acts 9:17; 26:16; 1 Cor. 9:1; 15:8 [e]1 Cor. 11:23; Gal. 1:12
15 [a]Acts 23:11 [b]Acts 4:20; 26:16
16 [a]Acts 2:38; 1 Cor. 6:11; [Eph. 5:26]; Heb. 10:22 [b]Acts 9:14; Rom. 10:13
17 [a]Acts 9:26; 26:20; 2 Cor. 12:2
18 [a]Acts 22:14 [b]Matt. 10:14 *See WW at John 19:35.
19 [a]Acts 8:3; 22:4 [b]Matt. 10:17; Acts 26:11
20 [a]Acts 7:54—8:1 [b]Luke 11:48 [1]NU omits *to his death*
21 [a]Acts 9:15; Rom. 1:5; 11:13; Gal. 2:7, 8; Eph. 3:7, 8; 1 Tim. 2:7; 2 Tim. 1:11
22 [a]Acts 21:36; 1 Thess. 2:16 [b]Acts 25:24
23 [1]Lit. *threw*
25 [a]Acts 16:37

18 "and [a]saw Him saying to me,
[b]'Make haste and get out of Jerusalem
quickly, for they will not receive your
*testimony concerning Me.'
19 "So I said, 'Lord, [a]they know that
in every synagogue I imprisoned and
[b]beat those who believe on You.
20 [a]'And when the blood of Your martyr Stephen was shed, I also was standing by [b]consenting [1]to his death, and
guarding the clothes of those who were
killing him.'
21 "Then He said to me, 'Depart,
[a]for I will send you far from here to
the Gentiles.' "

Paul's Roman Citizenship

22 And they listened to him until this
word, and *then* they raised their voices
and said, [a]"Away with such a *fellow*
from the earth, for [b]he is not fit to live!"
23 Then, as they cried out and [1]tore off
their clothes and threw dust into the
air,
24 the commander ordered him to be
brought into the barracks, and said
that he should be examined under
scourging, so that he might know why
they shouted so against him.
25 And as they bound him with thongs,
Paul said to the centurion who stood
by, [a]"Is it lawful for you to scourge a
man who is a Roman, and uncondemned?"
26 When the centurion heard *that,* he
went and told the commander, saying,
"Take care what you do, for this man
is a Roman."
27 Then the commander came and said
to him, "Tell me, are you a Roman?"
He said, "Yes."
28 The commander answered, "With a
large sum I obtained this citizenship."
And Paul said, "But I was born *a citizen.*"
29 Then immediately those who were
about to examine him withdrew from

22:6 This begins the second of three Pauline conversion narratives in Acts. The first (9:1–19) was Luke's account of the event. The second (vv. 6–21) and the third (26:12–18) were told by Paul himself in his public testimony to the Jews and later to the authorities.
22:7, 8 See note on 9:4.
22:9 **Did not hear the voice** seems to contradict 9:7, where Luke records that they did hear the voice. Actually, the verses contain different grammatical constructions, which say the same thing. The companions of Paul heard the sound of the voice, but did not discern words with understanding.
22:12 The description of **Ananias** here is to show how Paul's conversion and subsequent ministry were compatible with Jewish traditions.
22:16 See section 1 of Truth-In-Action at the end of Acts.
22:16 See note on **be baptized,** 2:38.
22:18 **They will not receive your testimony** refers to the general Jewish leadership and community in Jerusalem, not to the church (see 9:26–28).
22:22 Mention of the "Gentiles" (v. 21) infuriated the Jews.
22:23 Luke is reporting the utter madness of the opposition to Paul and the Christian message he represented (see 23:10). Throughout Acts, believers are shown to be rational; their detractors, irrational (26:24–26). The message of Jesus and the Cross is foolishness to the world, but to those who are saved, it is utterly reasonable. The gospel is the wisdom and power of God (1 Cor. 1:18–25).
22:24 The response of the crowd was so outrageous that the Roman authorities suspected Paul of some greater crime, for which they would force a confession by scourging.
22:25 For his own protection, Paul appeals to his Roman citizenship (see note on 16:37).

him; and the commander was also
afraid after he found out that he was
a Roman, and because he had bound
him.

The Sanhedrin Divided

30 The next day, because he wanted
to know for certain why he was accused by the Jews, he released him
from *his* bonds, and commanded the
chief priests and all their council to appear, and brought Paul down and set
him before them.

23 Then Paul, looking earnestly at
the council, said, "Men *and*
brethren, [a]I have lived in all good conscience before God until this day."
2 And the high priest Ananias commanded those who stood by him
[a]to strike him on the mouth.
3 Then Paul said to him, "God will
strike you, *you* whitewashed wall! For
you sit to judge me according to the
law, and [a]do you command me to be
struck contrary to the law?"
4 And those who stood by said, "Do
you revile God's high priest?"
5 Then Paul said, [a]"I did not know,
brethren, that he was the high priest;
for it is written, [b]*'You shall not speak
evil of a ruler of your people.'*"
6 But when Paul perceived that one
part were Sadducees and the other
Pharisees, he cried out in the council,
"Men *and* brethren, [a]I am a Pharisee,
the son of a Pharisee; [b]concerning the
hope and **resurrection** of the dead I am
being judged!"

WORD WEALTH

23:6 resurrection, *anastasis* (an-*as*-tas-is); Strong's *#386:* A standing up again, restoration to life, rising from the dead. A compound of *ana,* "again," and *histemi,* "to stand." The resurrection of Jesus is the firstfruits or prototype of the future resurrection of all that are in the grave. In v. 6, *anastasis* is the coming resurrection that occurs at the Judgment Day. Another usage of *anastasis* is "a moral recovery of spiritual truth."

7 And when he had said this, a dissension arose between the Pharisees
and the Sadducees; and the assembly
was divided.
8 [a]For Sadducees say that there is no
resurrection—and no angel or spirit;
but the Pharisees confess both.
9 Then there arose a loud outcry. And
the scribes of the Pharisees' party
arose and protested, saying, [a]"We find
no evil in this man; [1]but [b]if a spirit or
an angel has spoken to him, [c]let us not
fight against God."
10 Now when there arose a great dissension, the commander, fearing lest
Paul might be pulled to pieces by them,
commanded the soldiers to go down
and *take him by force from among
them, and bring *him* into the barracks.

The Plot Against Paul

11 But [a]the following night the Lord
stood by him and said, [1]"Be of good
cheer, Paul; for as you have testified
for Me in [b]Jerusalem, so you must also
bear witness at [c]Rome."
12 And when it was day, [a]some of the
Jews banded together and bound
themselves under an oath, saying that
they would neither eat nor drink till
they had [b]killed Paul.
13 Now there were more than forty
who had formed this conspiracy.
14 They came to the chief priests and
[a]elders, and said, "We have bound ourselves under a great *oath that we will
eat nothing until we have killed Paul.
15 "Now you, therefore, together with
the council, *suggest to the commander
that he be brought down to you
[1]tomorrow, as though you were going
to make further inquiries concerning
him; but we are ready to kill him before
he comes near."
16 So when Paul's sister's son heard
of their ambush, he went and entered
the barracks and told Paul.
17 Then Paul called one of the centurions to *him* and said, "Take this young
man to the commander, for he has
something to tell him."
18 So he took him and brought *him* to
the commander and said, "Paul the
prisoner called me to *him* and asked
me to bring this young man to you. He
has something to say to you."

CHAPTER 23

1 [a]Acts 24:16; 1 Cor. 4:4; 2 Cor. 1:12; 4:2; 2 Tim. 1:3; Heb. 13:18
2 [a]1 Kin. 22:24; Jer. 20:2; John 18:22
3 [a]Lev. 19:35; Deut. 25:1, 2; John 7:51
5 [a]Lev. 5:17, 18 [b]Ex. 22:28; Eccl. 10:20; 2 Pet. 2:10
6 [a]Acts 26:5; Phil. 3:5 [b]Acts 24:15, 21; 26:6; 28:20
8 [a]Matt. 22:23; Mark 12:18; Luke 20:27
9 [a]Acts 25:25; 26:31 [b]John 12:29; Acts 22:6, 7, 17, 18 [c]Acts 5:39 [1]NU *what if a spirit or an angel has spoken to him?* omitting the last clause
10 *See WW at 1 Thess. 4:17.
11 [a]Acts 18:9; 27:23, 24 [b]Acts 21:18, 19; 22:1–21 [c]Acts 28:16, 17, 23 [1]*Take courage*
12 [a]Acts 23:21, 30; 25:3 [b]Acts 9:23, 24; 25:3; 26:21; 27:42; 1 Thess. 2:15
14 [a]Acts 4:5, 23; 6:12; 22:5; 24:1; 25:15 *See WW at 1 Cor. 12:3.
15 [1]NU omits *tomorrow* *See WW at John 14:21.

23:2 Ananias, the high priest, is different from the Ananias of 5:1 and 9:10.
23:3–5 Whitewashed wall means new and clean appearance, but rotten on the inside. Perhaps Paul's reaction was improper (see v. 5; 1 Pet. 2:21–23), but even Jesus defended His legal rights (John 18:21–23). **I did not know . . . he was the high priest** may have been spoken in bitter irony, indicating he did not expect to receive justice from the Jewish court.
23:6 See note on Matt. 22:31, 32.
23:11 See note on 21:4–12.
23:16 God speaks through angels, dreams, and visions. At other times He uses people and very ordinary situations. What at first may appear to be everyday circumstances are actually God's providences.

19 Then the commander took him by
the hand, went aside, and asked privately, "What is it that you have to tell
me?"
20 And he said, [a]"The Jews have
agreed to ask that you bring Paul down
to the council tomorrow, as though
they were going to inquire more fully
about him.
21 "But do not yield to them, for more
than forty of them lie in wait for him,
men who have bound themselves by
an oath that they will neither eat nor
drink till they have killed him; and now
they are ready, waiting for the promise
from you."
22 So the commander let the young
man depart, and commanded *him*,
"Tell no one that you have *revealed
these things to me."

Sent to Felix

23 And he called for two centurions,
saying, *"Prepare two hundred soldiers, seventy horsemen, and two hundred spearmen to go to [a]Caesarea at
the third hour of the night;
24 "and provide mounts to set Paul on,
and bring *him* safely to Felix the governor."
25 He wrote a letter in the following
manner:

26 Claudius Lysias,

To the most excellent governor
Felix:

Greetings.

27 [a]This man was seized by the Jews
and was about to be killed by
them. Coming with the troops I
rescued him, having learned that
he was a Roman.
28 [a]And when I wanted to know the
reason they accused him, I
brought him before their council.
29 I found out that he was accused
[a]concerning questions of their
law, [b]but had nothing charged
against him deserving of death or
chains.
30 And [a]when it was told me that
[1]the Jews lay in wait for the man,
I sent him immediately to you,
and [b]also commanded his

20 [a]Acts 23:12
22 *See WW at John 14:21.
23 [a]Acts 8:40; 23:33 *See WW at Rev. 21:2.
27 [a]Acts 21:30, 33; 24:7
28 [a]Acts 22:30
29 [a]Acts 18:15; 25:19 [b]Acts 25:25; 26:31
30 [a]Acts 23:20 [b]Acts 24:8; 25:6 [1]NU *there would be a plot against the man*

accusers to state before you the
charges against him.

Farewell.

31 Then the soldiers, as they were
commanded, took Paul and brought
him by night to Antipatris.
32 The next day they left the horsemen
to go on with him, and returned to the
barracks.
33 When they came to [a]Caesarea and
had delivered the [b]letter to the governor, they also presented Paul to him.
34 And when the governor had read
it, he asked what province he was
from. And when he understood that *he
was* from [a]Cilicia,
35 he said, [a]"I will hear you when your
accusers also have come." And he
commanded him to be kept in [b]Herod's
[1]Praetorium.

Accused of Sedition

24 Now after [a]five days [b]Ananias
the high priest came down with
the elders and a certain orator *named*
Tertullus. These *gave evidence to the
governor against Paul.
2 And when he was called upon, Tertullus began his accusation, saying:
"Seeing that through you we enjoy
great peace, and [1]prosperity is being
brought to this nation by your *foresight,
3 "we accept *it* always and in all
places, most noble Felix, with all
thankfulness.
4 "Nevertheless, not to be tedious to
you any further, I beg you to hear, by
your [1]**courtesy**, a few words from us.

WORD WEALTH

24:4 courtesy, *epieikeia* (ep-ee-*eye*-ki-ah); Strong's *#1932:* Graciousness, gentleness, clemency, moderation, sweet reasonableness, mildness, fairness, kindness, forbearance, what is right or fitting. In 2 Cor. 10:1, *epieikeia* is an attribute of God. Here it is an appeal to Felix to show the customary graciousness befitting his high office. Christians can display *epieikeia* in virtue of their divine calling.

5 [a]"For we have found this man a
plague, a creator of dissension among

33 [a]Acts 8:40 [b]Acts 23:26–30
34 [a]Acts 6:9; 21:39
35 [a]Acts 24:1, 10; 25:16 [b]Matt. 27:27 [1]Headquarters

CHAPTER 24

1 [a]Acts 21:27 [b]Acts 23:2, 30, 35; 25:2 *See WW at John 14:21.
2 [1]Or *reforms are* *See WW at Rom. 13:14.
4 [1]*graciousness*
5 [a]Luke 23:2; Acts 6:13; 16:20; 17:6; 21:28; 1 Pet. 2:12, 15

23:24 Felix served as **governor** of Judea from A.D. 52 to 59 (see note on 25:13).
24:2, 3 A proper but manipulative introduction. In contrast, Paul's introduction is polite, but direct.
24:5 The sect of the Nazarenes, a moderately derisive name given to the Christians (see v. 14, "which they call a sect").

all the Jews throughout the world, and
a ringleader of the *sect of the Nazarenes.
6 [a]"He even tried to profane the temple, and we seized him, [1]and wanted
[b]to judge him according to our law.
7 [a]"But the commander Lysias came
by and with great violence took *him*
out of our hands,
8 [a]"commanding his accusers to
come to you. By examining him yourself you may ascertain all these things
of which we accuse him."
9 And the Jews also [1]assented, maintaining that these things were so.

The Defense Before Felix

10 Then Paul, after the governor had
nodded to him to speak, answered: "Inasmuch as I know that you have been
for many years a judge of this nation,
I do the more cheerfully answer for
myself,
11 "because you may ascertain that it
is no more than twelve days since I
went up to Jerusalem [a]to *worship.
12 [a]"And they neither found me in the
temple disputing with anyone nor inciting the crowd, either in the synagogues or in the city.
13 "Nor can they prove the things of
which they now accuse me.
14 "But this I confess to you, that according to [a]the Way which they call a
*sect, so I worship the [b]God of my fa-
thers, believing all things which are
written in [c]the Law and in the Prophets.
15 [a]"I have hope in God, which they
themselves also accept, [b]that there will
be a *resurrection [1]of *the* dead, both
of *the* just and *the* unjust.
16 [a]"This *being* so, I myself always
strive to have a conscience without offense toward God and men.
17 "Now after many years [a]I came to
bring alms and *offerings to my nation,
18 [a]"in the midst of which some Jews
from Asia found me [b]purified in the
temple, neither with a mob nor with
tumult.
19 [a]"They ought to have been here before you to object if they had anything
against me.
20 "Or else let those who are *here*
themselves say [1]if they found any
wrongdoing in me while I stood before
the council,
21 "unless *it is* for this one statement
which I cried out, standing among
them, [a]'Concerning the resurrection of
the dead I am being judged by you this
day.'"

Felix Procrastinates

22 But when Felix heard these things,
having more accurate knowledge of
the [a]Way, he adjourned the proceedings and said, "When [b]Lysias the
commander comes down, I will make
a decision on your case."
23 So he commanded the centurion to
keep Paul and to let *him* have liberty,
and [a]told him not to forbid any of his
friends to provide for or visit him.
24 And after some days, when Felix
came with his wife Drusilla, who was
Jewish, he sent for Paul and heard him
concerning the [a]faith in Christ.
25 Now as he reasoned about *righteousness, self-control, and the *judgment to come, Felix was afraid and answered, "Go away for now; when I
have a convenient time I will call for
you."
26 Meanwhile he also hoped that
[a]money would be given him by Paul,
[1]that he might release him. Therefore
he sent for him more often and conversed with him.
27 But after two years Porcius Festus
succeeded Felix; and Felix, [a]wanting*
to do the Jews a favor, left Paul bound.

Paul Appeals to Caesar

25 Now when Festus had come to
the province, after three days he
went up from [a]Caesarea to Jerusalem.
2 [a]Then the [1]high priest and the chief
men of the Jews *informed him against
Paul; and they petitioned him,
3 asking a favor against him, that he
would summon him to Jerusalem—
[a]while *they* lay in ambush along the
road to kill him.
4 But Festus answered that Paul

5 *See WW at 2 Pet. 2:1. **6** [a]Acts 21:28 [b]John 18:31 [1]NU ends the sentence here and omits the rest of v. 6, all of v. 7, and the first clause of v. 8. **7** [a]Acts 21:33; 23:10 **8** [a]Acts 23:30 **9** [1]NU, M *joined the attack* **11** [a]Acts 21:15, 18, 26, 27; 24:17 *See WW at Rev. 4:10. **12** [a]Acts 25:8; 28:17 **14** [a]Acts 9:2; 24:22 [b]2 Tim. 1:3 [c]Acts 26:22; 28:23 *See WW at 2 Pet. 2:1. **15** [a]Acts 23:6; 26:6, 7; 28:20 [b][Dan. 12:2] [1]NU omits *of the dead* *See WW at Acts 23:6. **16** [a]Acts 23:1 **17** [a]Rom. 15:25–28 *See WW at Acts 21:26. **18** [a]Acts 21:27; 26:21 [b]Acts 21:26 **19** [a][Acts 23:30; 25:16] **20** [1]NU, M *what wrongdoing they found* **21** [a][Acts 23:6; 24:15; 28:20] **22** [a]Acts 9:2; 18:26; 19:9, 23; 22:4 [b]Acts 23:26; 24:7 **23** [a]Acts 23:16; 27:3; 28:16 **24** [a][Rom. 10:9] **25** *See WW at 2 Tim. 4:8. • See WW at Rev. 20:4. **26** [a]Ex. 23:8 [1]NU omits *that he might release him* **27** [a]Acts 12:3; 23:35; 25:9, 14 *See WW at Matt. 8:2.

CHAPTER 25

1 [a]Acts 8:40; 25:4, 6, 13

2 [a]Acts 24:1; 25:15 [1]NU *chief priests* *See WW at John 14:21. **3** [a]Acts 23:12, 15

24:10 See note on vv. 2, 3.
24:14 Believing all things which are written in the Law and in the Prophets: The followers of Jesus did not reject the Jewish Scriptures (see Matt. 5:17, 18). They simply understood them in a new light: Jesus of Nazareth was the Messiah (18:5); His coming was not merely to fulfill Jewish national interests (1:6, 7); and His kingdom included all nations—the Gentiles (15:15–17). See 26:6, 7, 22, 23; note on 28:23.
24:18 See note on 21:23, 24.
24:27 Festus served as governor from A.D. 59 to 61.

should be kept at Caesarea, and that
he himself was going *there* shortly.
5 "Therefore," he said, "let those who
have authority among you go down
with *me* and accuse this man, to see
[a]if there is any fault in him."
6 And when he had remained among
them more than ten days, he went
down to Caesarea. And the next day,
sitting on the *judgment seat, he commanded Paul to be brought.
7 When he had come, the Jews who
had come down from Jerusalem stood
about [a]and laid many serious complaints against Paul, which they could
not prove,
8 while he answered for himself,
[a]"Neither against the law of the Jews,
nor against the temple, nor against
Caesar have I offended in anything at
all."
9 But Festus, [a]wanting to do the Jews
a favor, answered Paul and said,
[b]"Are you *willing to go up to Jerusalem and there be judged before me concerning these things?"
10 So Paul said, "I stand at Caesar's
judgment seat, where I ought to be
judged. To the Jews **I have done no
wrong,** as you very well know.

WORD WEALTH

25:10 I have done no wrong, *adikeo* (ad-ee-*keh*-oh); Strong's *#91:* To do an injustice, to act criminally or unrighteously, to violate any human or divine law, to do wrong, to mistreat others. The word is a compound of *a,* "without," and *dike,* "right"; hence, an illegal action. *Adikeo* consists of offending legally, general wrongdoing, social injustice, and inflicting hurt or damage on individuals. In his appeal to Caesar, Paul declares his innocence.

11 [a]"For if I am an offender, or have
committed anything deserving of
death, I do not object to dying; but if
there is nothing in these things of
which these men accuse me, no one
can deliver me to them. [b]I appeal to
Caesar."
12 Then Festus, when he had conferred with the council, answered,
"You have appealed to Caesar? To
Caesar you shall go!"

5 [a]Acts 18:14; 25:18
6 *See WW at Matt. 27:19.
7 [a]Mark 15:3; Luke 23:2, 10; Acts 24:5, 13
8 [a]Acts 6:13; 24:12; 28:17
9 [a]Acts 12:2; 24:27 [b]Acts 25:20 *See WW at Matt. 8:2.
11 [a]Acts 18:14; 23:29; 25:25; 26:31 [b]Acts 26:32; 28:19

14 [a]Acts 24:27
15 [a]Acts 24:1; 25:2, 3 *See WW at John 14:21.
16 [a]Acts 25:4, 5 [1]NU omits *to destruction*, although it is implied
17 [a]Matt. 27:19; Acts 25:6, 10
18 [1]*suspected*
19 [a]Acts 18:14, 15; 23:29
21 [a]Acts 25:11, 12
22 [a]Acts 9:15
23 [a]Acts 9:15 [1]*pageantry*
24 [a]Acts 25:2, 3, 7 [b]Acts 21:36; 22:22 *See WW at Heb. 7:25.
25 [a]Acts 23:9, 29; 26:31 *See WW at John 1:5.

Paul Before Agrippa

13 And after some days King Agrippa
and Bernice came to Caesarea to greet
Festus.
14 When they had been there many
days, Festus laid Paul's case before the
king, saying: [a]"There is a certain man
left a prisoner by Felix,
15 [a]"about whom the chief priests and
the elders of the Jews *informed *me,*
when I was in Jerusalem, asking for a
judgment against him.
16 [a]"To them I answered, 'It is not the
custom of the Romans to deliver any
man [1]to destruction before the accused
meets the accusers face to face, and
has opportunity to answer for himself
concerning the charge against him.'
17 "Therefore when they had come together, [a]without any delay, the next
day I sat on the judgment seat and
commanded the man to be brought in.
18 "When the accusers stood up, they
brought no accusation against him of
such things as I [1]supposed,
19 [a]"but had some questions against
him about their own religion and about
a certain Jesus, who had died, whom
Paul affirmed to be alive.
20 "And because I was uncertain of
such questions, I asked whether he was
willing to go to Jerusalem and there
be judged concerning these matters.
21 "But when Paul [a]appealed to be reserved for the decision of Augustus, I
commanded him to be kept till I could
send him to Caesar."
22 Then [a]Agrippa said to Festus, "I
also would like to hear the man myself." "Tomorrow," he said, "you shall
hear him."
23 So the next day, when Agrippa and
Bernice had come with great [1]pomp,
and had entered the auditorium with
the commanders and the prominent
men of the city, at Festus' command
[a]Paul was brought in.
24 And Festus said: "King Agrippa and
all the men who are here present with
us, you see this man about whom
[a]the whole assembly of the Jews *petitioned me, both at Jerusalem and here,
crying out that he was [b]not fit to live
any longer.
25 "But when I *found that [a]he had
committed nothing deserving of death,

25:8 Luke shows repeatedly how the Christian "sect" was no threat to anyone—Jews or Romans.

25:9–11 Paul's destiny takes an unexpected turn. Standing on his rights as a Roman citizen, Paul appeals to the Roman supreme court, **Caesar's judgment seat.** Having been in custody now for two years, Paul's appeal may have been a desperate one, but it enabled him to reach his ultimate destination, Rome, and fulfill 1:8.

25:13 King Agrippa was the son of Herod Agrippa I (12:1) and great-grandson of Herod the Great. He ruled over northern Palestine. **Bernice** was his sister, as well as the sister of Drusilla (24:24).

[b]and that he himself had appealed to
Augustus, I decided to send him.
26 "I have nothing certain to write to
my lord concerning him. Therefore I
have brought him out before you, and
especially before you, King Agrippa, so
that after the examination has taken
place I may have something to write.
27 "For it seems to me unreasonable
to send a prisoner and not to specify
the charges against him."

Paul's Early Life

26 Then Agrippa said to Paul,
"You are permitted to speak for
yourself." So Paul stretched out his
hand and answered for himself:
2 "I think myself [a]happy, King
Agrippa, because today I shall answer
[b]for myself before you concerning all
the things of which I am [c]accused by
the Jews,
3 "especially because you are expert
in all customs and questions which
have to do with the Jews. Therefore I
beg you to hear me patiently.
4 "My manner of life from my youth,
which was spent from the beginning
among my own nation at Jerusalem,
all the Jews know.
5 "They knew me from the first, if
they were willing to testify, that according to [a]the strictest *sect of our religion I lived a Pharisee.
6 [a]"And now I stand and am *judged
for the hope of [b]the promise made by
God to our fathers.
7 "To this *promise* [a]our twelve tribes,
earnestly serving *God* [b]night and day,
[c]hope to attain. For this hope's sake,
King Agrippa, I am accused by the
Jews.
8 "Why should it be thought incredible by you that God raises the dead?
9 [a]"Indeed, I myself thought I must
do many things [1]contrary to the name
of [b]Jesus of Nazareth.
10 [a]"This I also did in Jerusalem, and
many of the saints I shut up in prison,
having received authority [b]from the
chief priests; and when they were
put to death, I cast my vote against
them.
11 [a]"And I punished them often in
every synagogue and compelled *them*
to blaspheme; and being exceedingly

25 [b]Acts 25:11, 12

CHAPTER 26

2 [a][1 Pet. 3:14; 4:14] [b][1 Pet. 3:15, 16] [c]Acts 21:28; 24:5, 6
5 [a][Acts 22:3; 23:6; 24:15, 21]; Phil. 3:5 *See WW at 2 Pet. 2:1.
6 [a]Acts 23:6 [b][Gen. 3:15; 22:18; 26:4; 49:10; Deut. 18:15; 2 Sam. 7:12; Ps. 132:11; Is. 4:2; 7:14; 9:6; 40:10; Jer. 23:5; 33:14–16; Ezek. 34:23; 37:24; Dan. 9:24]; Acts 13:32; Rom. 15:8; [Titus 2:13] *See WW at John 18:31.
7 [a]James 1:1 [b]Luke 2:37; 1 Thess. 3:10; 1 Tim. 5:5 [c]Phil. 3:11
9 [a]John 16:2; 1 Cor. 15:9; 1 Tim. 1:12, 13 [b]Acts 2:22; 10:38 [1]*against*
10 [a]Acts 8:1–3; 9:13; Gal. 1:13 [b]Acts 9:14
11 [a]Matt. 10:17; Acts 22:19
12 [a]Acts 9:3–8; 22:6–11; 26:12–18
16 [a]Acts 22:15; Eph. 3:6–8 *See WW at Rev. 1:5.
17 [a]Acts 22:21 [1]*rescue* [2]NU, M omit *now*
18 [a]Is. 35:5; 42:7, 16; Luke 1:79; [John 8:12; 2 Cor. 4:4]; Eph. 1:18; 1 Thess. 5:5 [b]2 Cor. 6:14; Eph. 4:18; 5:8; [Col. 1:13]; 1 Pet. 2:9 [c]Luke 1:77 [d]Eph. 1:11; Col. 1:12 [e]Acts 20:32 [1]*set apart*

enraged against them, I persecuted
them even to foreign cities.

Paul Recounts His Conversion

12 [a]"While thus occupied, as I journeyed to Damascus with authority and
commission from the chief priests,
13 "at midday, O king, along the road
I saw a light from heaven, brighter
than the sun, shining around me and
those who journeyed with me.
14 "And when we all had fallen to the
ground, I heard a voice speaking to me
and saying in the Hebrew language,
'Saul, Saul, why are you persecuting
Me? *It is* hard for you to kick against
the goads.'
15 "So I said, 'Who are You, Lord?'
And He said, 'I am Jesus, whom you
are persecuting.
16 'But rise and stand on your feet; for
I have appeared to you for this purpose, [a]to make you a minister and a
*witness both of the things which you
have seen and of the things which I
will yet reveal to you.
17 'I will [1]deliver you from the *Jewish*
people, as well as *from* the Gentiles,
[a]to whom I [2]now send you,
18 [a]'to open their eyes, *in order*
[b]to turn *them* from darkness to light,
and *from* the power of Satan to God,
[c]that they may receive forgiveness of
sins and [d]an inheritance among those
who are [e]sanctified[1] by faith in Me.'

Paul's Post-Conversion Life

19 "Therefore, King Agrippa, I was not
disobedient to the heavenly vision,

KINGDOM DYNAMICS

26:19 Total Commitment, LEADER TRAITS. Paul was totally committed to his call to spread the gospel and establish churches throughout the known world. He lived what he wrote, that "the gifts and the calling of God *are* irrevocable" (Rom. 11:29). His life demonstrated three basic concepts of leadership: 1) He was committed to the goals and spirit of his call (Phil. 3:7, 8). 2) He translated his objectives into the lives of his followers (2 Tim. 2:1, 2) and bore with all necessary hardship in pursuing that end (2 Cor. 4:8–11; 11:23–33). 3) He was alert to

26:6, 7 See note on 24:14.
26:12–18 This is the third account in Acts of Paul's conversion (see 9:1–19; 22:6–21). **Kick against the goads:** See note on 9:5.
26:16, 17 These promises are not included in the other conversion accounts. In v. 17 Jesus promises His personal protection to Paul, and His promise is fulfilled. Acts ends with Paul unharmed by the Jews and preaching the gospel freely in Rome.
26:19 God guides through supernatural means (**the heavenly vision**), but all such special guidance must be grounded in the unchanging revelation of the Bible.

change. He adapted to cultural, social, and political changes and thus never lost his relevancy (1 Cor. 9:19–22).
(1 Tim. 3:1–13/Judg. 6:1—8:35) J.B.

20 "but [a]declared first to those in Damascus and in Jerusalem, and throughout all the region of Judea, and *then*
to the Gentiles, that they should repent,
turn to God, and do [b]works befitting
*repentance.
21 "For these reasons the Jews seized
me in the temple and tried to kill *me*.
22 "Therefore, having obtained help
from God, to this day I stand, **witnessing** both to small and great, saying
no other things than those [a]which the
prophets and [b]Moses said would
come—

WORD WEALTH

26:22 witnessing, *martureo* (mar-too-*reh*-oh); Strong's *#3140:* Giving evidence, attesting, confirming, confessing, bearing record, speaking well of, giving a good report, testifying, affirming that one has seen, heard, or experienced something. In the NT it is used particularly for presenting the gospel with evidence. The English word "martyr" comes from this word, suggesting that a witness is one willing to die for his testimony.

23 [a]"that the Christ would suffer,
[b]that He would be the first to rise from
the dead, and [c]would proclaim light to
the *Jewish* people and to the Gentiles."

Agrippa Parries Paul's Challenge

24 Now as he thus made his defense,
Festus said with a loud voice, "Paul,
[a]you are beside yourself! Much learning is driving you mad!"
25 But he said, "I am not [1]mad, most
noble Festus, but speak the words of
truth and reason.

20 [a]Acts 9:19, 20, 22; 11:26 [b]Matt. 3:8; Luke 3:8 *See WW at Matt. 3:2.
22 [a]Luke 24:27; Acts 24:14; 28:23; Rom. 3:21 [b]John 5:46
23 [a]Luke 24:26 [b]1 Cor. 15:20, 23; Col. 1:18; Rev. 1:5 [c]Is. 42:6; 49:6; Luke 2:32; 2 Cor. 4:4
24 [a]2 Kin. 9:11; John 10:20; [1 Cor. 1:23; 2:13, 14; 4:10]
25 [1]*out of my mind*
26 [a]Acts 26:3
29 [a]1 Cor. 7:7
31 [a]Acts 23:9, 29; 25:25
32 [a]Acts 28:18 [b]Acts 25:11

CHAPTER 27

1 [a]Acts 25:12, 25
2 [a]Acts 19:29
3 [a]Acts 24:23; 28:16
6 [a]Acts 28:11

26 "For the king, before whom I also
speak freely, [a]knows these things; for
I am convinced that none of these
things escapes his attention, since this
thing was not done in a corner.
27 "King Agrippa, do you believe the
prophets? I know that you do believe."
28 Then Agrippa said to Paul, "You almost persuade me to become a Christian."
29 And Paul said, [a]"I would to God
that not only you, but also all who hear
me today, might become both almost
and altogether such as I am, except for
these chains."
30 When he had said these things, the
king stood up, as well as the governor
and Bernice and those who sat with
them;
31 and when they had gone aside, they
talked among themselves, saying,
[a]"This man is doing nothing deserving
of death or chains."
32 Then Agrippa said to Festus, "This
man might have been set [a]free [b]if he
had not appealed to Caesar."

The Voyage to Rome Begins

27 And when [a]it was decided that
we should sail to Italy, they delivered Paul and some other prisoners
to *one* named Julius, a centurion of the
Augustan Regiment.
2 So, entering a ship of Adramyttium,
we put to sea, meaning to sail along
the coasts of Asia. [a]Aristarchus, a Macedonian of Thessalonica, was with us.
3 And the next *day* we landed at Sidon. And Julius [a]treated Paul kindly
and gave *him* liberty to go to his
friends and receive care.
4 When we had put to sea from there,
we sailed under *the shelter of* Cyprus,
because the winds were contrary.
5 And when we had sailed over the
sea which is off Cilicia and Pamphylia,
we came to Myra, *a city* of Lycia.
6 There the centurion found [a]an

26:20 Works befitting repentance indicates that a true relationship with God will result in a godly life-style. We are not saved by our own good works, but salvation by grace will certainly change us.
26:22, 23 See note on 24:14.
26:24–26 See note on 22:23.
26:27, 28 Paul's challenge to **Agrippa,** who had a Jewish heritage, put the king in an embarrassing position. If he agreed with Paul he would lose credibility with Festus, who had just declared Paul to be mad (v. 24). Yet if he renounced **the prophets** he would lose favor with the Jews. Therefore, he attempted to escape his dilemma by responding to Paul with what most interpreters feel to be an insincere and cynical comment: "In a short time you think to make me a Christian!"
27:1 This is the beginning of Paul's fourth trip, which takes him to Rome (see map of Paul's fourth journey). Luke shows a remarkably detailed understanding of ancient seamanship. **Augustan Regiment** was one of five Roman regiments stationed near the seaport city of Caesarea.
27:2 Adramyttium was a seaport of the Roman province of Asia (modern Turkey). The ship Paul boarded was based there. **We put to sea** indicates that Luke was accompanying Paul on his final journey.
27:4 Paul's ship sailed to the north of **Cyprus** to protect itself from strong southerly winds.
27:5 Myra is a city in southern Asia Minor (modern Turkey).
27:6 The **Alexandrian ship,** probably a grain ship (v. 38), had its registry in Alexandria, the Roman capital of Egypt. Egypt was the principal source of grain for Rome, and the grain fleet was the lifeblood of the empire.

Alexandrian ship sailing to Italy, and
he put us on board.
7 When we had sailed slowly many
days, and arrived with difficulty off
Cnidus, the wind not permitting us to
proceed, we sailed under *the shelter*
of [a]Crete off Salmone.
8 Passing it with difficulty, we came
to a place called Fair Havens, near the
city *of* Lasea.

Paul's Warning Ignored

9 Now when much time had been
spent, and sailing was now dangerous
[a]because [1]the Fast was already over,
Paul advised them,
10 saying, "Men, I perceive that this
voyage will end with **disaster** and
much loss, not only of the cargo and
ship, but also our lives."

WORD WEALTH

27:10 disaster, *hubris* (*hoo*-bris); Strong's *#5196:* Hurt, loss, injury arising from violence, damage caused by the elements, hardship, detriment, trouble, and danger. In 2 Cor. 12:10, where Paul described the reproaches he endured for the Lord's sake, *hubris* denotes insolence, impudence, a haughty attitude, insult, injury, outrage, persecution, and affront. The word is definitely adversarial. (Compare "hubristic" and "hybrid.")

11 Nevertheless the centurion was
more persuaded by the helmsman and
the owner of the ship than by the
things spoken by Paul.
12 And because the harbor was not
suitable to winter in, the majority advised to set sail from there also, if by
any means they could reach Phoenix,
a harbor of Crete opening toward the
southwest and northwest, *and* winter
there.

In the Tempest

13 When the south wind blew softly,
supposing that they had obtained *their*
*desire, putting out to sea, they sailed
close by Crete.
14 But not long after, a tempestuous
head wind arose, called [1]Euroclydon.
15 So when the ship was caught, and
could not head into the wind, we let
her [1]drive.
16 And running under *the shelter of*
an island called [1]Clauda, we secured
the skiff with difficulty.

7 [a]Acts 2:11; 27:12, 21; Titus 1:5, 12
9 [a]Lev.16:29–31; 23:27–29; Num. 29:7 [1]The Day of Atonement, late September or early October
13 *See WW at Rom. 8:28.
14 [1]A southeast wind that stirs up broad waves; NU *Euraquilon,* a northeaster
15 [1]*be driven*
16 [1]NU *Cauda*

27:9 The Fast is a reference to the Day of Atonement in late September or early October. It was already past, which was a way of saying winter's dangerous sailing weather was about to begin. The dangerous period for sailing began in mid-September and lasted until early November. After that, all navigation on the open sea halted until winter was over.
27:16 The skiff was a smaller rowboat, or dinghy, used to transport people from a larger craft to the shore (see v. 30).

On to Rome (Paul's Fourth Journey, Acts 27:1—28:16). In Jerusalem following his third missionary journey, Paul struggled with Jews who accused him of profaning the temple (Acts 21:26–34). He was placed in Roman custody in Caesarea for two years, but after appealing to Caesar, was sent by ship to Rome. After departing the island of Crete, Paul's party was shipwrecked on Malta by a great storm. Three months later he finally arrived at the imperial city.

17 When they had taken it on board,
they used cables to undergird the ship;
and fearing lest they should run
aground on the [1]Syrtis *Sands,* they
struck sail and so were driven.
18 And because we were exceedingly
tempest-tossed, the next *day* they lightened the ship.
19 On the third *day* [a]we threw the
ship's tackle overboard with our own
hands.
20 Now when neither sun nor stars appeared for many days, and no small
tempest beat on *us,* all hope that we
would be saved was finally given
up.
21 But after long abstinence from food,
then Paul stood in the midst of them
and said, "Men, you should have listened to me, and not have sailed from
Crete and incurred this *disaster and
loss.
22 "And now I urge you to take
[1]heart, for there will be no loss of life
among you, but only of the ship.
23 [a]"For there stood by me this night
an angel of the God to whom I belong
and [b]whom I serve,
24 "saying, 'Do not be afraid, Paul; you
must be brought before Caesar; and indeed God has *granted you all those
who sail with you.'
25 "Therefore take heart, men, [a]for I
believe God that it will be just as it was
told me.
26 "However, [a]we must run aground
on a certain island."
27 Now when the fourteenth night had
come, as we were driven up and down
in the Adriatic *Sea,* about midnight the
sailors sensed that they were drawing
near some land.
28 And they took soundings and found
it to be twenty fathoms; and when they
had gone a little farther, they took
soundings again and found *it* to be fifteen fathoms.
29 Then, fearing lest we should run
aground on the rocks, they dropped
four anchors from the stern, and
[1]prayed for day to come.
30 And as the sailors were seeking to
escape from the ship, when they had
let down the skiff into the sea, under
pretense of putting out anchors from
the prow,
31 Paul said to the centurion and the
soldiers, "Unless these men stay in the
ship, you cannot be saved."
32 Then the soldiers cut away the
ropes of the skiff and let it fall off.
33 And as day was about to dawn, Paul
implored *them* all to take food, saying,
"Today is the fourteenth day you have
waited and continued without food,
and eaten nothing.
34 "Therefore I urge you to take nourishment, for this is for your survival,
[a]since not a hair will fall from the head
of any of you."
35 And when he had said these things,
he took bread and [a]gave thanks to
God in the presence of them all; and
when he had broken *it* he began to
eat.
36 Then they were all encouraged, and
also took food themselves.
37 And in all we were two hundred and
seventy-six [a]persons on the ship.
38 So when they had eaten enough,
they lightened the ship and threw out
the wheat into the sea.

Shipwrecked on Malta

39 When it was day, they did not recognize the land; but they observed a
bay with a beach, onto which they
planned to run the ship if possible.
40 And they [1]let go the anchors and
left *them* in the sea, meanwhile loosing
the rudder ropes; and they hoisted the
mainsail to the wind and made for
shore.
41 But striking [1]a place where two seas
met, [a]they ran the ship aground; and
the prow stuck fast and remained immovable, but the stern was being
broken up by the violence of the
waves.
42 And the soldiers' plan was to kill
the prisoners, lest any of them should
swim away and escape.
43 But the centurion, wanting to save
Paul, kept them from *their* purpose,
and commanded that those who could
swim should jump *overboard* first and
get to land,
44 and the rest, some on boards and
some on *parts* of the ship. And so it
was [a]that they all escaped safely to
land.

17 [1]M *Syrtes*
19 [a]Jon. 1:5
21 *See WW at Acts 27:10.
22 [1]*courage*
23 [a]Acts 18:9; 23:11; 2 Tim. 4:17 [b]Dan. 6:16; Rom. 1:9; 2 Tim. 1:3
24 *See WW at Col. 3:13.
25 [a]Luke 1:45; Rom. 4:20, 21; 2 Tim. 1:12
26 [a]Acts 28:1
29 [1]Or *wished*
34 [a]1 Kin. 1:52; [Matt. 10:30; Luke 12:7; 21:18]
35 [a]1 Sam. 9:13; Matt. 15:36; Mark 8:6; John 6:11; [1 Tim. 4:3, 4]
37 [a]Acts 2:41; 7:14; Rom. 13:1; 1 Pet. 3:20
40 [1]*cast off*
41 [a]2 Cor. 11:25 [1]A reef
44 [a]Acts 27:22, 31

27:17 Cables were used **to undergird the ship** to prevent its breaking apart. **Syrtis:** Quicksands off the coast of north Africa.

27:18, 19 It was common for a ship's crew in a storm, in order to make the craft more buoyant, to throw virtually everything but the passengers overboard. They later disposed of their cargo and remaining food (v. 38).

27:31, 32 Now everyone believed Paul (see vv. 10, 11, 21). The Roman **centurion** and his **soldiers** assumed command of this nonmilitary vessel.

27:38 See note on vv. 18, 19.

Paul's Ministry on Malta

28 Now when they had escaped, they then found out that [a]the island was called Malta.
2 And the [a]natives[1] showed us unusual **kindness;** for they kindled a fire and made us all welcome, because of the rain that was falling and because of the cold.

> **WORD WEALTH**
>
> **28:2 kindness,** *philanthropia* (fil-an-thro-*pee*-ah); Strong's *#5363:* Compare "philanthropist" and "philanthropy." Love for mankind, hospitality, acts of kindness, readiness to help, human friendship, benevolence, and taking thought of others. The word is a compound of *philos,* "love," and *anthropos,* "man." In Titus 3:4, *philanthropia* is used to describe God's lovingkindness toward men.

3 But when Paul had gathered a bundle of sticks and laid *them* on the fire, a viper came out because of the heat, and fastened on his hand.
4 So when the natives saw the creature hanging from his hand, they said to one another, "No doubt this man is a murderer, whom, though he has escaped the sea, yet justice does not allow to live."
5 But he shook off the creature into the fire and [a]suffered no harm.
6 However, they were expecting that he would swell up or suddenly fall down dead. But after they had looked for a long time and saw no harm come to him, they changed their minds and [a]said that he was a god.
7 In that region there was an estate of the [1]leading citizen of the island, whose name was Publius, who received us and entertained us courteously for three days.
8 And it happened that the father of Publius lay *sick of a fever and dysentery. Paul went in to him and [a]prayed, and [b]he laid his hands on him and healed him.

CHAPTER 28

1 [a]Acts 27:26 **2** [a]Acts 28:4; Rom. 1:14; 1 Cor. 14:11; Col. 3:11 [1]Lit. *barbarians*

5 [a]Mark 16:18; Luke 10:19 **6** [a]Acts 12:22; 14:11 **7** [1]Magistrate **8** [a]Acts 9:40; [James 5:14, 15] [b]Matt. 9:18; Mark 5:23; 6:5; 7:32; 16:18; Luke 4:40; Acts 19:11, 12; [1 Cor. 12:9, 28] *See WW at 2 Cor. 5:14.

28:1 Malta is a small **island** just south of Sicily and Italy.
28:4 One of the pagan deities was a goddess called **justice.** The natives assumed she was behind this.
28:5 See note on Mark 16:17, 18.
28:7 Publius was the highest ranking Roman official on the island.

The Influence of Paul. The witness of the apostle Paul began early in Damascus and in Tarsus, the city of his birth. Missionary travels then took him throughout the provinces of Galatia, Asia, Macedonia, and Achaia. Even while under custody in Caesarea and imprisoned in Rome, Paul testified of his salvation in Christ.

9 So when this was done, the rest of
those on the island who had diseases
also came and were *healed.

KINGDOM DYNAMICS

28:8, 9 Paul's Healing Ministry in Malta, DIVINE HEALING. Here is a reference to divine healings in spite of the fact that Luke, a physician, accompanied Paul. This fact is so troublesome to critics of modern healing that some have come forth with the theory that the healings mentioned in v. 9 were the work of Luke who used medical remedies, although Luke is not mentioned by name. The theory is based on the use of *therapeuo*, the Greek word for "healing" (v. 8), which some insist refers to medical therapy.

In fact, however, this word occurs 34 times in the NT. In 32 instances it clearly refers to divine healing; in the other cases the use is general. Both words (*iaomai* and *therapeuo*) are used in reference to the same healing in Matt. 8:7, 8, indicating the terms are used interchangeably in the Bible.

This observation is certainly not to oppose medical treatment or to say medicine or medical aid is wrong. It is not. However, it does clarify that this text is not grounds for the substitution of medical therapy for prayer. God heals by many means: the prayer of faith, natural recuperative powers, medical aid or medicine, miracles.

(Acts 3:16/1 Cor. 12:9, 28) N.V.

10 They also honored us in many
[a]ways; and when we departed, they
provided such things as were [b]neces-
sary.

Arrival at Rome

11 After three months we sailed in
[a]an Alexandrian ship whose figure-
head was the [1]Twin Brothers, which
had wintered at the island.
12 And landing at Syracuse, we stayed
three days.
13 From there we circled round and
reached Rhegium. And after one day
the south wind blew; and the next day
we came to Puteoli,
14 where we found [a]brethren, and
were invited to stay with them seven
days. And so we went toward Rome.
15 And from there, when the brethren
heard about us, they came to meet us
as far as Appii Forum and Three Inns.
When Paul saw them, he *thanked God
and took courage.
16 Now when we came to Rome, the
centurion delivered the prisoners to the
captain of the guard; but [a]Paul was
permitted to dwell by himself with the
soldier who guarded him.

Paul's Ministry at Rome

17 And it came to pass after three days
that Paul called the leaders of the Jews
together. So when they had come together, he said to them: "Men *and*
brethren, [a]though I have done nothing
against our people or the customs of
our fathers, yet [b]I was delivered as a
prisoner from Jerusalem into the
hands of the Romans,
18 "who, [a]when they had examined
me, wanted to let *me* go, because there
was no cause for putting me to death.
19 "But when the [1]Jews spoke against
it, [a]I was compelled to appeal to Caesar, not that I had anything of which
to accuse my nation.
20 "For this reason therefore I have
called for you, to see *you* and speak
with *you*, because [a]for the *hope of Israel I am bound with [b]this chain."
21 Then they said to him, "We neither
received letters from Judea concerning
you, nor have any of the brethren who
came reported or spoken any evil of
you.
22 "But we desire to hear from you
what you think; for concerning this
*sect, we know that [a]it is spoken
against everywhere."
23 So when they had appointed him a
day, many came to him at *his* lodging,
[a]to whom he explained and solemnly
testified of the kingdom of God, persuading them concerning Jesus [b]from
both the Law of Moses and the Prophets, from morning till evening.

9 *See WW at Matt. 12:22.
10 [a]Matt. 15:6; 1 Tim. 5:17 [b][Phil. 4:19]
11 [a]Acts 27:6 [1]Gr. *Dioskouroi*, Zeus's sons Castor and Pollux
14 [a]Rom. 1:8
15 *See WW at John 6:11.
16 [a]Acts 23:11; 24:25; 27:3
17 [a]Acts 23:29; 24:12, 13; 26:31 [b]Acts 21:33
18 [a]Acts 22:24; 24:10; 25:8; 26:32
19 [a]Acts 25:11, 21, 25 [1]The ruling authorities
20 [a]Acts 26:6, 7 [b]Acts 26:29; Eph. 3:1; 4:1; 6:20; 2 Tim. 1:8, 16; Philem. 10, 13 *See WW at 1 Thess. 1:3.
22 [a]Luke 2:34; Acts 24:5, 14; [1 Pet. 2:12; 3:16; 4:14, 16] *See WW at 2 Pet. 2:1.
23 [a]Luke 24:27; [Acts 17:3; 19:8] [b]Acts 26:6, 22

28:11 They had to wait **three months** until the sailing season began, probably in February. **The Twin Brothers** (see margin) were the patron deities of navigation.
28:12 **Syracuse** was the chief city on the island of Sicily.
28:13 **Puteoli,** modern Pozzuoli, was the principal port of southern Italy.
28:15 The party traveled overland to Rome on the Appian Way. **Appii Forum** was a town 43 miles from Rome, and **Three Inns** was located 33 miles from the capital city.
28:16 As a Roman citizen who had committed no flagrant offense and who had no political aspirations, Paul was allowed to live in private quarters.
28:20 **The hope of Israel** is the messianic kingdom in Jesus of Nazareth (see note on 24:14).
28:21 Paul had suffered intense persecution, and the Roman Jews express a sense of surprise that his notoriety had not reached them.
28:22 These Roman Jews have not heard about Paul of Tarsus, but they have heard many negative reports about the Christian **sect.**
28:23 Basing his argument on the OT teachings concerning the Messiah and His **kingdom,** Paul presented the evidence pertaining to **Jesus.**

24 And [a]some were persuaded by the
things which were spoken, and some
disbelieved.
25 So when they did not agree among
themselves, they departed after Paul
had said one *word: "The Holy Spirit
spoke rightly through Isaiah the
prophet to [1]our fathers,
26 "saying,

[a]*'Go to this people and say:*
"Hearing you will hear, and shall
not understand;
And seeing you will see, and not
perceive;
27 *For the hearts of this people have*
grown dull.
Their ears are hard of hearing,
And their eyes they have closed,
Lest they should see with their
eyes and hear with their ears,
Lest they should understand with
their hearts and turn,
So that I should heal them."'

28 "Therefore let it be known to you
that the **salvation** of God has been sent
[a]to the Gentiles, and they will hear
it!"

24 [a]Acts 14:4; 19:9
25 [1]NU *your* *See WW at Matt. 4:4.
26 [a]Is. 6:9, 10; Jer. 5:21; Ezek. 12:2; Matt. 13:14, 15; Mark 4:12; Luke 8:10; John 12:40, 41; Rom. 11:8
28 [a]Is. 42:1, 6; 49:6; Matt. 21:41; Luke 2:32; Rom. 11:11
29 [1]NU omits v. 29.
31 [a]Acts 4:31; Eph. 6:19 *See WW at Acts 9:20. • See WW at John 6:68. • See WW at Acts 4:31.

WORD WEALTH

28:28 salvation, *soterion* (so-*tay*-ree-on); Strong's *#4992:* Rescue, deliverance, safety, liberation, release, preservation, and the general word for Christian salvation. (Compare "soteriology.") *Soterion* only occurs five times. *Soteria,* the generic word, occurs forty-five times. It is an all-inclusive word signifying forgiveness, healing, prosperity, deliverance, safety, rescue, liberation, and restoration. Christ's salvation is total in scope for the total man: spirit, soul, and body.

29 [1]And when he had said these words,
the Jews departed and had a great dispute among themselves.
30 Then Paul dwelt two whole years
in his own rented house, and received
all who came to him,
31 [a]preaching* the kingdom of God
and teaching the things which concern
the *Lord Jesus Christ with all *confidence, no one forbidding him.

28:25–28 The closing message of Acts is that the Jews of Paul's day, from Jerusalem to Rome, rejected Jesus as their Messiah. Individual Jews believed, of course, but the torch of the gospel was passed from the Jewish nation to the Gentiles. Not only has Christianity spread from Jerusalem to Rome, it has also made the transition from an exclusively Jewish religion to a hope for all nations (v. 28). Paul himself thoroughly explains this transition in Rom. 9—11.

28:31 The term **kingdom of God** is not as prominent in Acts as it is in Luke's Gospel. Kingdom teachings, however, are the bookends of Acts. Jesus preached and demonstrated the kingdom; the apostles preached and demonstrated the kingdom in Acts, and Acts portrays Paul as *continuing* to preach *the kingdom.* For an account of Paul's probable activities following the completion of Acts, see Introduction to 1 Timothy: Author; also see Kingdom Dynamics articles on the kingdom of God.

TRUTH-IN-ACTION through ACTS

Letting the LIFE of the Holy Spirit Bring Faith's Works Alive in You!

Truth Acts Teaches	Text	**Action** Acts Invites
1 How to Insure Complete Conversion In Acts we find the historical record of the first conversions to faith in Jesus Christ. Here in detail is the message of the apostles and the response of the people. Here, also, is found the promise of the gift of the Holy Spirit to all who believe, an experience of empowering that was normative in the early church. Our message today should be the same as this, regarding the gift of the *Holy Spirit* and the life He produces.	2:38–41	**Repent, be baptized,** and **receive** the gift of the Holy Spirit. **Be saved.**
	3:19, 20	**Receive** your sins forgiven and forgotten by **being converted. Enjoy** the refreshing that comes from God's presence.
	4:12	**Know** that only the name of Jesus Christ provides salvation.
	10:47, 48	**Insure** that everyone you lead to Jesus is water baptized. **Remember** that water baptism was an integral part of the preaching of the apostles.
	22:16	**Recognize** that the act of water baptism pictures the exchange of guilt and "sin consciousness" for the knowledge of cleansing from sin by the death of Christ and a new consciousness of God's presence.

Truth Acts Teaches	Text	**Action** Acts Invites
2 In the OT only those uniquely called or anointed of God received the Holy Spirit. But under the New Covenant every believer is offered the Promise of the Father (Luke 24:49), the active presence of the Holy Spirit. It is by this activity of the Spirit's fullness in the life of every believer that the ministry of Christ in His church continues.	1:8	**Believe** that the power of God comes only by the Holy Spirit. **Do not attempt** ministry without the Holy Spirit.
	2:4; 4:8; 13:9	**Seek** and **receive** the baptism in the Holy Spirit. Continually be refilled with the Spirit to regularly renew your life and ministry. **Exercise** your prayer language as a part of the Spirit's flow in your life.
	4:13	**Expect** your Spirit-filled relationship with Jesus to help you speak boldly, with courage and spiritual understanding.
	10:44, 45	**Share** Jesus boldly. **Ask** the Holy Spirit to confirm your testimony.
3 **Lessons for Leaders** Acts is indispensable material for those who wish to learn the power principles of Christian leadership. The leadership in Acts is some of the most spiritually powerful the church has ever known. Whenever Christian leadership has forgotten the models shown in Acts, they have lost most of their power. Applying the lessons for leaders given in Acts will help give today's Christian leader a ministry of increased power and effectiveness.	2:42–47	Leaders, **incorporate** these four elements into your congregation's life. **Believe** evangelism will result from a church living in obedience to Jesus' invitations.
	4:24–31	Leaders, **frequently pray** this fervent prayer in your congregational worship.
	6:1–6	Leaders, **share** your ministry. **Do not** weaken your life and ministry by doing work others should do.
	12:5	Leaders, **give** prayer a central place in your church life.
	13:1–3	Leaders, **submit** to the Spirit's guidance when confronting decisions. **Call** leadership to prayer and fasting in such times. **Release** ministry freely when asked to do so by the Holy Spirit.
	14:14–18	Leaders, **do not receive** inordinate praise from people. **Dispel** unrighteous adultation by admirers.
	16:1–5	Leaders, **personally train** young men who are called to ministry.
	20:28–32	Leaders, **guard against** disloyalty. **Insure** that no one makes disciples for himself. **Assume** the responsibility of guarding the flock of God from "savage wolves."
	20:27	Leaders, **make certain** that you teach "the whole counsel of God." **Live** in obedience to the gospel, and see the results in evangelism and spiritual growth.
4 **Key Lessons in Faith** Acts summons us to a bold faith, which may be unfamiliar to many of us. It is refreshing to read about men and women who believed in our great God to do great things in a great way. Let us have the courage to do the same. These accounts invite us to the kinds of risks associated with this bold faith.	3:21	**Believe steadfastly** that God will fulfill everything he has promised in His Word.
	14:3	**Humbly call** to the Lord to perform signs, wonders, and miracles to confirm with power the gospel message of His Son.

The Epistle of Paul the Apostle to the

ROMANS

Author: Paul
Date: A.D. 56
Theme: The Righteousness of God in the Gospel of Christ
Key Words: Righteousness, Faith, Justification, Law, Grace

Background When Paul wrote Romans about A.D. 56, he had not yet been to Rome, but he had been preaching the gospel since his conversion in A.D. 35. During the previous ten years he had founded churches throughout the Mediterranean world. Now he was nearing the end of his third missionary journey. This epistle is therefore a mature statement of his understanding of the gospel. The church at Rome had been founded by other Christians (unknown to us, but see "visitors from Rome" in Acts 2:10); and Paul, through his travels, knew many of the believers there (16:3–15).

Occasion and Date Paul most likely wrote Romans while he was in Corinth in A.D. 56, taking a collection to help the needy Christians in Jerusalem (15:25–28, 31; 2 Cor. 8, 9). He planned to go to Jerusalem with this collection, then visit the church in Rome (1:10, 11; 15:22–24). After being refreshed and supported by the Christians in Rome, he planned to travel to Spain to preach the gospel (15:24). He wrote to tell the Romans of his impending visit. The letter was likely delivered by Phoebe (16:1, 2).

Purpose In view of his personal plans, Paul wrote to introduce himself to a church he had never visited. At the same time he set forth a full and orderly statement of the great principles of the gospel that he preached.

Characteristics Romans is commonly considered the greatest exposition of Christian doctrine anywhere in Scripture. It contains an orderly, logical development of profound theological truths. It is filled with the great themes of redemption: the guilt of all mankind, our inability to earn favor with God, the redeeming death of Christ, and the free gift of salvation to be received by faith alone. Since Paul had not visited Rome, the epistle does not address specific local problems, but contains general teaching applicable to all Christians for all time. Throughout the history of the church, expositions of Romans have sparked many revivals as people have become aware of the magnificence of God and His grace toward us.

Content The overall doctrinal theme that Paul seeks to demonstrate is that God is righteous. In spite of all that happens in this world—even though all men are sinful (1:18—3:20); even though God does not punish but forgives guilty sinners (3:21—5:21); even though believers may not fully live in a way consistent with God's righteousness

(6:1—8:17); even though believers suffer and final redemption is delayed (8:18–39); even though many Jews do not believe (9:1—11:36)—still God is perfectly righteous, and by His grace has forgiven us. Because of this great mercy from an all-righteous God, we should live a pattern of life consistent with God's own righteousness (12:1—16:27).

Personal Application Romans teaches us that we should not trust in ourselves for salvation, but in Christ (chs. 1—5); that we should imitate the faith of Abraham (ch. 4); be patient in times of trouble (5:1–11); rejoice in our representation by Christ (5:12–21); grow in daily death to sin (6:1—7:25); walk according to the Spirit each moment (8:1–17); hope in future glory and trust that God will bring good out of present sufferings (8:18–39); pray for and proclaim the gospel to the lost, especially the Jews (9:1—11:32); and praise God for His great wisdom in the plan of salvation (11:33–36). Especially in chapters 12—15 the letter gives many specific applications to life, showing how the gospel works out in practice both in the church and in the world. Finally, we can even learn to imitate Paul's deeply personal care for many individual believers (ch. 16).

Christ Revealed The whole epistle is the story of God's plan of redemption in Christ: the need for it (1:18—3:20), the detailed description of Christ's work and its implications for Christians (3:21—11:36), and the application of the gospel of Christ to everyday life (12:1—16:27).

More specifically, Jesus Christ is our Savior, who obeyed God perfectly as our representative (5:18, 19), and who died as our substitute sacrifice (3:25; 5:6, 8). He is the One in whom we must have faith for salvation (1:16, 17; 3:22; 10:9, 10). Through Christ we have many blessings: reconciliation to God (5:11); righteousness and eternal life (5:18–21); identification with Him in His death, burial, and resurrection (6:3–5); being alive to God (6:11); freedom from condemnation (8:1); eternal inheritance (8:17); suffering with Him (8:17); being glorified with Him (8:17); being made like Him (8:29); and the fact that He even now prays for us (8:34). Indeed, all of the Christian life seems to be lived through Him: prayer (1:8), rejoicing (5:11), exhortation (15:30), glorifying God (16:27), and, in general, living to God and obeying Him (6:11; 13:14).

The Holy Spirit at Work The Holy Spirit gives power in preaching the gospel and in working miracles (15:19), dwells in all who belong to Christ (8:9–11), and gives us life (8:11). He also makes us progressively more holy in daily life, empowering us to obey God and overcome sin (2:29; 7:6; 8:2, 13; 15:13, 16), giving us a pattern of holiness to follow (8:4), guiding us in it (8:14), and purifying our consciences to bear true witness (9:1). The Holy Spirit pours God's love into our hearts (5:5; 15:30), along with joy, peace, and hope by His power (14:17; 15:13). He enables us to pray rightly (8:26) and to call God our Father, thereby giving inward spiritual assurance that we are God's children (8:16). We are to set our minds on the things of the Spirit if we wish to be pleasing to God (8:5, 6). Though Paul discusses spiritual gifts briefly in Romans (12:3–8), he makes no explicit mention of the Holy Spirit in connection with these gifts, except to refer to them as "spiritual" (or "of the Spirit") in 1:11. The present work of the Holy Spirit in us is only a foretaste of His future heavenly work in us (8:23).

Outline of Romans

Introduction **1:1–17**
- A. Paul's identification 1:1–7
- B. Paul's desire to visit Rome 1:8–15
- C. Summary of the gospel 1:16, 17

I. All have sinned **1:18—3:20**
- A. Gentiles know of God but reject Him 1:18–32
- B. Jews have God's laws but are not righteous 2:1–29
- C. God is just to judge all men 3:1–20

II. Justification is by faith alone **3:21—5:21**
- A. God's righteousness preserved through Christ's death for us 3:21–26
- B. Justification is by faith alone 3:27–31
- C. Abraham justified by faith, not works 4:1–25
- D. Once justified by faith, we triumph even in sufferings 5:1–11
- E. We gained death through Adam's sin, but eternal life through Christ's obedience 5:12–21

III. Practicing righteousness in the Christian life **6:1—8:39**
- A. Overcoming sin in the Christian life 6:1–23
- B. We are dead to the powerless system called "law" 7:1–6
- C. The law cannot empower us to obey 7:7–25
- D. We fulfill God's righteousness by living in the power of the Spirit and according to the Spirit 8:1–17
- E. Longing for complete redemption 8:18–25
- F. Help and assurance in hardship 8:26–39

IV. God and Israel **9:1—11:36**
- A. Though Israel is unfaithful, God is righteous 9:1–33
- B. Israel has willingly rejected the gospel 10:1–21
- C. A remnant now remains, and someday full salvation will come to Israel 11:1–32
- D. Praise for God's infinite wisdom 11:33–36

V. Practical applications **12:1—15:13**
- A. Present yourselves as sacrifices to God 12:1, 2
- B. Use of spiritual gifts 12:3–8
- C. Relating to Christians 12:9–13
- D. Relating to unbelievers 12:14–21
- E. Relating to government 13:1–7
- F. The law of love 13:8–14
- G. Toleration and love in minor things 14:1–23
- H. Caring for each other 15:1–13

VI. Paul's own situation **15:14–33**
- A. His ministry 15:14–22
- B. His plans 15:23–33

VII. Personal greetings **16:1–24**

VIII. Benediction **16:25–27**

Greeting

PAUL, a bondservant of Jesus
Christ, [a]called *to be* an *apostle,
[b]separated to the gospel of God
2 [a]which He promised before
[b]through His prophets in the Holy
Scriptures,
3 concerning His Son Jesus Christ

CHAPTER 1

1 [a]1 Cor. 1:1; 9:1; 15:9; 2 Cor. 1:1; 1 Tim. 1:11 [b]Acts 9:15; 13:2; [Gal. 1:15]

*See WW at 1 Cor. 12:28. **2** [a]Acts 26:6 [b]Gal. 3:8

1:1 Bondservant: Also translated "servant" or "slave," the word refers to an employee who was paid wages, often had considerable skills and responsibilities, and was usually treated well and protected by law. But a *bondservant* could not resign and work for another employer. Highly educated and skilled people, as well as ordinary laborers, were *bondservants.*

Apostle: The use here refers to the unique officers in the early church who had the power to govern the churches with absolute authority (Gal. 1:8, 9; 1 Thess. 4:8; 2 Thess. 3:6, 14), and to speak and write the very words of God without error (2 Cor. 13:3; 1 Thess. 2:13; 4:15), words which would become part of Scripture itself (2:16; 1 Cor. 14:37; 2 Pet. 3:15, 16). The qualifications for being an apostle were: 1) having seen the risen Christ with one's own eyes (Acts 1:22; 1 Cor. 9:1); 2) having been commissioned by Christ as an apostle (Matt. 10:1–7; Acts 1:24–26; 26:16, 17; Gal. 1:1).

In this founding sense, there are no more apostles today, for no one today can write more Scripture. Paul considers himself the "last of all" the apostles to have seen the risen Christ with his own eyes (1 Cor. 15:8). However, some people use the word "apostle" in a broader sense applicable today, denoting an especially anointed church planter or a church leader, commanding widespread respect and authoritative oversight.

1:3 Jesus had both a human nature and a divine nature combined in one person. The words **according to the flesh**

our Lord, who [1]was [a]born of the seed
of David according to the flesh,
4 *and* [a]declared *to be* the Son of God
with power according [b]to the Spirit of
*holiness, by the *resurrection from the
dead.
5 Through Him [a]we have received
grace and apostleship for [b]obedience
to the faith among all nations [c]for His
name,
6 among whom you also are the
called of Jesus Christ;

7 To all who are in Rome, beloved of
God, [a]called *to be* saints:

[b]Grace to you and peace from God
our Father and the Lord Jesus Christ.

3 [a]Gal. 4:4 [1]*came*
4 [a]Acts 9:20; 13:33 [b][Heb. 9:14] *See WW at 1 Thess. 3:13. • See WW at Acts 23:6.
5 [a]Eph. 3:8 [b]Acts 6:7 [c]Acts 9:15 *See WW at 2 Cor. 12:9. • See WW at 2 Cor. 10:5.
7 [a]1 Cor. 1:2, 24 [b]1 Cor. 1:3

Desire to Visit Rome

8 First, [a]I thank my God through
Jesus Christ for you all, that [b]your
faith is spoken of throughout the whole
world.
9 For [a]God is my *witness, [b]whom I
serve [1]with my spirit in the gospel of
His Son, that [c]without ceasing I make
mention of you always in my prayers,
10 making request if, by some means,
now at last I may find a way in the
*will of God to come to you.
11 For I long to see you, that [a]I may

8 [a]1 Cor. 1:4 [b]Rom. 16:19
9 [a]Rom. 9:1 [b]Acts 27:23 [c]1 Thess. 3:10 [1]Or *in* *See WW at Rev. 1:5.
10 *See WW at Matt. 12:50.
11 [a]Rom. 15:29

refer to His human nature, which did not exist before He was conceived in Mary's womb. This was not a human body only, but included a truly human mind and spirit as well.

1:4 Though Jesus has eternally been the Son of God (John 1:1–3; 17:5, 24), in His new role as God-Man He was clearly **declared *to be* the Son of God** by His **resurrection.**

1:7 Saints is a common NT word for all Christians. It could literally be translated "holy people."

1:9 Without ceasing: Paul must have had a continual fellowship of prayer with God through the day. He did not hesitate to speak of his own prayer life in order to encourage others (see 1 Cor. 11:1; 1 Thess. 5:17).

1:11 Paul longed to visit the Roman church not simply for social reasons, but to impart **some spiritual gift** to them in order to strengthen them. "Gift" (Greek *charisma*) is the same word used in 12:6 and in 1 Cor. 12. Paul here adds

THE CAREER OF THE APOSTLE PAUL (1:5)

Origin:	Tarsus in Cilicia (Acts 22:3) Tribe of Benjamin (Phil. 3:5)
Training:	Learned tentmaking (Acts 18:3) Studied under Gamaliel (Acts 22:3)
Early Religion:	Hebrew and Pharisee (Phil. 3:5) Persecuted Christians (Acts 8:1–3; Phil. 3:6)
Salvation:	Met the risen Christ on the road to Damascus (Acts 9:1–8) Received the infilling of the Holy Spirit on the street called Straight (Acts 9:17)
Called to Missions:	Church at Antioch was instructed by the Holy Spirit to send out Paul to the work (Acts 13:1–3) Carried the gospel to the Gentiles (Gal. 2:7–10)
Roles:	Spoke up for the church at Antioch at the council of Jerusalem (Acts 15:1–35) Opposed Peter (Gal. 2:11–21) Disputed with Barnabas about John Mark (Acts 15:36–41)
Achievements:	Three extended missionary journeys (Acts 13—20) Founded numerous churches in Asia Minor, Greece, and possibly Spain (Rom. 15:24, 28) Wrote letters to numerous churches and various individuals which now make up one-fourth of our New Testament
End of Life:	Following arrest in Jerusalem, was sent to Rome (Acts 21:27; 28:16–31) According to Christian tradition, released from prison allowing further missionary work; rearrested, imprisoned again in Rome, and beheaded outside of the city.

impart to you some spiritual *gift, so
that you may be established—

WORD WEALTH

1:11 impart, *metadidomi* (met-ad-*id*-oh-mee); Strong's *#3330:* To give, share, impart, distribute, grant. The word implies liberality or generosity. It is used to exhort those with two outer tunics to give one to someone who has none (Luke 3:11); to encourage people to give with cheerful outflow (Rom. 12:8); and to urge workers to labor with industry in order to give to him who has a need (Eph. 4:28).

12 that is, that I may be encouraged
together with you by [a]the mutual faith
both of you and me.
13 Now I do not *want you to be unaware, brethren, that I often planned
to come to you (but [a]was hindered until
now), that I might have some [b]fruit
among you also, just as among the
other Gentiles.
14 I am a *debtor both to Greeks and
to barbarians, both to wise and to unwise.
15 So, as much as is in me, *I am* ready
to preach the gospel to you who are
in Rome also.

The Just Live by Faith

1 16 For [a]I am not ashamed of the *gospel [1]of Christ, for [b]it is the *power of
God to *salvation for everyone who believes, [c]for the Jew first and also for
the Greek.
17 For [a]in it the *righteousness of God

11 *See WW at 1 Cor. 1:7.
12 [a]Titus 1:4
13 [a][1 Thess. 2:18] [b]Phil. 4:17 *See WW at Matt. 8:2.
14 *See WW at Luke 13:4.
16 [a]Ps. 40:9, 10 [b]1 Cor. 1:18, 24 [c]Acts 3:26 [1]NU omits *of Christ* *See WW at Mark 1:1. • See WW at Acts 4:33. • See WW at Luke 19:9.
17 [a]Rom. 3:21; 9:30 [b]Hab. 2:4 *See WW at 2 Tim. 4:8. • See WW at Matt. 1:19.
18 [a][Acts 17:30] [b]2 Thess. 2:10 [1]*hold down*
19 [a][Acts 14:17; 17:24] [b][John 1:9] [1]*evident* [2]*among* *See WW at Col. 3:4.
20 [a]Ps. 19:1–6 [1]*divine nature, deity* *See WW at Col. 1:15. • See WW at Eph. 2:10.
21 [a]Jer. 2:5 *See WW at Rev. 2:23.
22 [a]Jer. 10:14
23 [a]1 Tim. 1:17; 6:15, 16 [b]Deut. 4:16–18 [1]*perishable*

is revealed from faith to faith; as it is
written, [b]*"The *just shall live by faith."*

God's Wrath on Unrighteousness

18 [a]For the wrath of God is revealed 3
from heaven against all ungodliness
and [b]unrighteousness of men, who
[1]suppress the truth in unrighteousness,
19 because [a]what may be known of
God is [1]manifest [2]in them, for [b]God has
*shown *it* to them.
20 For since the *creation of the world
[a]His invisible *attributes* are clearly
seen, being understood by the *things
that are made, *even* His eternal power
and [1]Godhead, so that they are without
excuse,
21 because, although they knew God,
they did not glorify *Him* as God, nor
were thankful, but [a]became **futile** in
their thoughts, and their foolish
*hearts were darkened.

WORD WEALTH

1:21 futile, *mataioo* (mat-ah-*yah*-oh); Strong's *#3154:* To make empty, vain, foolish, useless, confused. The word describes the perverted logic and idolatrous presumption of those who do not honor God or show Him any gratitude for His blessings on humanity.

22 [a]Professing to be wise, they became
fools,
23 and changed the glory of the
[a]incorruptible [b]God into an image
made like [1]corruptible man—and birds

the adjective "spiritual" (Greek *pneumatikos*), emphasizing that it is from the Holy Spirit, even though Paul's ministry may be the means the Holy Spirit uses to **impart** a gift to them.
1:14 Paul felt an obligation to preach the gospel to every kind of person.
1:16, 17 The theme of this epistle is that Paul was **not ashamed** to speak about **the gospel** because he knew it had **power** to bring people to **salvation.** This happened when people trusted, or put their faith, in Christ to save them.
1:16 See section 1 of Truth-In-Action at the end of Rom.
1:16 For the Jew first: Paul's missionary practice in every city was to begin preaching **the gospel** in the Jewish synagogue, and then, once the Jews had heard or refused to hear, to preach to the Gentiles (see, for example, Acts 13:42–47; 14:1). This follows the pattern of God throughout most of the OT, the pattern of Jesus during His earthly ministry, and the pattern of evangelism in the early church *(Acts 1:8)*.
1:17 The righteousness of God is God's way of justifying sinners, that is, putting them right with Himself without compromising His absolutely pure moral character. **As it is written:** Hab. 2:4 indicates that salvation by faith alone was clearly taught in the OT, also. (Note the examples of Abraham and David in 4:1–8, and see Heb. 11.) People were not saved by works or obedience to the Law in the OT any more than in the NT. In the OT, people put faith in a Messiah who was yet to come (see John 8:56; Heb. 11:13).
1:18–31 God's existence, His moral demands, and His **wrath** against sin are clearly evident in the world around us. See note on v. 21.
1:18–23 See section 3 of Truth-In-Action at the end of Rom.
1:18 Paul's explanation of the gospel always included the fact of the **wrath of God**—His righteous, personal anger against all sin in the universe, which He exercises because, rather than bringing Him glory, sin dishonors Him and contradicts His holy, moral character. People's **unrighteousness** often leads them to **suppress the truth** and hold false views of God or the teachings of the Bible, because they know that the truth would require that they repent.
1:20 Clearly seen: In looking at the created **world,** every person should see abundant evidence of God's existence and power.
1:21 They knew God: All people know in their hearts that God exists, as well as something of His moral requirements (v. 32; 2:14, 15). This statement does not say that people can come to saving faith by observing the created world, for saving faith comes only through hearing and believing the Bible's message about Christ (v. 16; 10:14–17).

and four-footed animals and creeping
things.
24 [a]Therefore God also gave them up
to uncleanness, in the *lusts of their
hearts, [b]to dishonor their bodies
[c]among themselves,
25 who exchanged [a]the truth of God
[b]for the lie, and worshiped and served
the creature rather than the Creator,
who is blessed *forever. Amen.
26 For this reason God gave them up
to [a]vile passions. For even their
[1]women exchanged the natural use for
what is against nature.
27 Likewise also the [1]men, leaving the
natural use of the [2]woman, burned in
their lust for one another, [1]men with
[1]men committing what is shameful,
and receiving in themselves the penalty of their *error which was due.

KINGDOM DYNAMICS

1:27 16. What Does the Bible Say About Homosexuality?, SPIRITUAL ANSWERS. For the answer to this and other probing questions about God and the power life in His kingdom, see the study article "Spiritual Answers to Hard Questions," which begins on page 1996. P.R.

28 And even as they did not like to retain God in *their* knowledge, God gave
them over to a debased mind, to do
those things [a]which are not fitting;
29 being filled with all unrighteousness, [1]sexual* immorality, wickedness, [2]covetousness, [3]maliciousness;
full of envy, murder, strife, deceit, evil-
mindedness; *they are* whisperers,
30 backbiters, haters of God, violent,
proud, boasters, inventors of evil
things, disobedient to parents,
31 [1]undiscerning, untrustworthy, unloving, [2]unforgiving, unmerciful;
32 who, [a]knowing* the righteous judgment of God, that those who practice
such things [b]are deserving of death,
not only do the same but also [c]approve
of those who practice them.

God's Righteous Judgment

2 Therefore you are [a]inexcusable, O
man, whoever you are who judge,
[b]for in whatever you judge another you
condemn yourself; for you who judge
practice the same things.
2 But we know that the *judgment of
God is according to truth against those
who practice such things.
3 And do you think this, O man, you
who judge those practicing such
things, and doing the same, that you
will escape the judgment of God?
4 Or do you despise [a]the riches of His
*goodness, [b]forbearance, and [c]long-
suffering,* [d]not knowing that the
*goodness of God leads you to repen-
tance?
5 But in accordance with your hardness and your [1]impenitent heart
[a]you are [2]treasuring up for yourself
wrath in the day of wrath and revelation of the righteous judgment of God,
6 who [a]*"will *render to each one according to his deeds"*:
7 eternal life to those who by *patient
continuance in doing good seek for
glory, honor, and immortality;
8 but to those who are *self-seeking
and [a]do not obey the truth, but obey
*unrighteousness—indignation and
*wrath,
9 tribulation and anguish, on every
*soul of man who does evil, of the Jew
[a]first and also of the [1]Greek;

24 [a]Eph. 4:18, 19 [b]1 Cor. 6:18 [c]Lev. 18:22 *See WW at 2 Tim. 2:22. **25** [a]1 Thess. 1:9 [b]Is. 44:20 *See WW at Matt. 28:20. **26** [a]Lev. 18:22 [1]Lit. *females* **27** [1]Lit. *males* [2]Lit. *female* *See WW at Jude 11. **28** [a]Eph. 5:4 **29** [1]NU omits *sexual immorality* [2]*greed* [3]*malice* *See WW at Matt. 15:19. **31** [1]*without understanding* [2]NU omits *unforgiving* **32** [a][Rom. 2:2] [b][Rom. 6:21] [c]Hos. 7:3 *See WW at Luke 5:22.

CHAPTER 2

1 [a][Rom. 1:20] [b][Matt. 7:1–5] **2** *See WW at Rev. 20:4. **4** [a][Eph. 1:7, 18; 2:7] [b][Rom. 3:25] [c]Ex. 34:6 [d]Is. 30:18 *See WW at Gal. 5:22. • See WW at Heb. 6:12. • See WW at Matt. 11:30. **5** [a][Deut. 32:34] [1]*unrepentant* [2]*storing* **6** [a]Ps. 62:12; Prov. 24:12 *See WW at Matt. 22:21. **7** *See WW at Heb. 10:36. **8** [a][2 Thess. 1:8] *See WW at Phil. 1:16. • See WW at John 7:18. • See WW at Luke 4:28. **9** [a]1 Pet. 4:17 [1]Gentile *See WW at Luke 21:19.

1:24 Therefore: False religion (v. 23) leads to personal immorality (vv. 24, 26). **God . . . gave them up:** The same Greek phrase is repeated in vv. 26 and 28, indicating the terrible truth that as people continue to reject God, He gives them up to increasingly immoral and self-destructive activities.
1:26 Against nature: Homosexual activity.
1:27 Lust for one another: Even homosexual *desire* is here seen as sinful in God's sight. **Penalty:** Any destructive consequences resulting from homosexuality, whether physical, emotional, or spiritual.
1:29–31 A description of a society totally rebelling against God.
1:32 The deeply irrational nature of sin is seen in the fact that even hardened sinners still know in their hearts that their actions are **deserving of death.** Nevertheless, they go on sinning and even drag others down with them when they **approve of those** who do the same things.
2:4 Sinners who are not yet experiencing God's judgment should not presume that God's mercy will last even another hour. Judgment is withheld only to give time to repent.
2:6 The phrase **according to his deeds** does not contradict the gospel of salvation as a free gift that cannot be earned (1:16, 17; 3:20, 23, 24, 28, 30; 4:5; 6:23). The verse summarizes what will actually happen: unbelievers will be judged for their sins; and believers, who have been freely forgiven of sins because of Christ's work (3:21–26), will be given degrees of reward in heaven according to their actions in this life (see Matt. 16:27; 25:31–46; John 5:29; Rom. 14:10–12; 1 Cor. 3:10–15; 2 Cor. 5:9, 10).
2:7 Although the phrase **doing good** describes Christians, their salvation was not granted because they did good works (3:20, 23, and see note on v. 6), but because they trusted in Christ who earned eternal life for them (1:16, 17; 3:24).
2:9 Racial or religious background will not keep anyone from judgment (see v. 11).

10 [a]but glory, honor, and peace to
everyone who works what is good, to
the Jew first and also to the Greek.
11 For [a]there is no *partiality with
God.
12 For as many as have sinned without
law will also perish without law, and
as many as have sinned in the law will
be *judged by the law
13 (for [a]not the hearers of the law *are*
just in the sight of God, but the doers
of the law will be *justified;
14 for when Gentiles, who do not have
the law, by nature do the things in the
law, these, although not having the
law, are a law to themselves,
15 who show the [a]work of the law written in their hearts, their [b]conscience
also bearing witness, and between
themselves *their* thoughts accusing or
else excusing *them*)
16 [a]in the day when God will judge the
secrets of men [b]by Jesus Christ,
[c]according to my gospel.

The Jews Guilty as the Gentiles

17 [1]Indeed [a]you are called a Jew, and
[b]rest[2] on the law, [c]and make your
boast in God,
18 and [a]know *His* will, and [b]approve
the things that are excellent, being instructed out of the law,
19 and [a]are confident that you yourself
are a guide to the blind, a light to those
who are in *darkness,
20 an instructor of the foolish, a
teacher of babes, [a]having the form of
knowledge and truth in the law.
21 [a]You, therefore, who teach another,
do you not teach yourself? You who
preach that a man should not steal, do
you steal?
22 You who say, "Do not commit adultery," do you commit adultery? You
who abhor idols, [a]do you rob temples?
23 You who [a]make your boast in the
law, do you dishonor God through
breaking the law?
3 24 For [a]*"the name of God is* [b]*blasphemed among the Gentiles because of
you,"* as it is written.

10 [a][1 Pet. 1:7] **11** [a]Deut. 10:17 *See WW at Col. 3:25. **12** *See WW at John 18:31. **13** [a][James 1:22, 25] *See WW at Matt. 12:37. **15** [a]1 Cor. 5:1 [b]Acts 24:25 **16** [a][Matt. 25:31] [b]Acts 10:42; 17:31 [c]1 Tim. 1:11 **17** [a]John 8:33 [b]Mic. 3:11 [c]Is. 48:1, 2 [1]NU *But if* [2]*rely* **18** [a]Deut. 4:8 [b]Phil. 1:10 **19** [a]Matt. 15:14 *See WW at Luke 11:35. **20** [a][2 Tim. 3:5] **21** [a]Matt. 23:3 **22** [a]Mal. 3:8 **23** [a]Rom. 2:17; 9:4 **24** [a]Ezek. 16:27 [b]Is. 52:5; Ezek. 36:22

25 [a][Gal. 5:3] **26** [a][Acts 10:34] **27** [a]Matt. 12:41 [1]Lit. *letter* **28** [a][Gal. 6:15] *See WW at 1 Cor. 11:19 **29** [a][1 Pet. 3:4] [b]Phil. 3:3 [c]Deut. 30:6 [d][1 Cor. 4:5] [1]A play on words—*Jew* is literally *praise.* *See WW at Eph. 1:6.

CHAPTER 3

1 *See WW at John 10:10. **2** [a]Deut. 4:5–8 [1]*sayings,* Scriptures **3** [a]Heb. 4:2 [b][2 Tim. 2:13] **4** [a]Job 40:8 [b][John 3:33] [c]Ps. 62:9 [d]Ps. 51:4 [1]Found true

Circumcision of No Avail

25 [a]For circumcision is indeed profitable if you keep the law; but if you are
a breaker of the law, your circumcision
has become uncircumcision.
26 Therefore, [a]if an uncircumcised
man keeps the righteous requirements
of the law, will not his uncircumcision
be counted as circumcision?
27 And will not the physically uncircumcised, if he fulfills the law, [a]judge
you who, *even* with *your* [1]written *code*
and circumcision, *are* a transgressor of
the law?
28 For [a]he is not a Jew who *is one* *outwardly, nor *is* circumcision that which
is outward in the flesh;
29 but *he is* a Jew [a]who *is one* inwardly; and [b]circumcision *is that* of
the heart, [c]in the Spirit, not in the letter; [d]whose [1]praise* *is* not from men
but from God.

God's Judgment Defended

3 What *advantage then has the Jew,
or what *is* the profit of circumcision?
2 Much in every way! Chiefly because
[a]to them were committed the [1]oracles
of God.
3 For what if [a]some did not believe?
[b]Will their unbelief make the faithfulness of God without effect?
4 [a]Certainly not! Indeed, let [b]God be
[1]**true** but [c]every man a liar. As it is
written:

[d]*"That You may be justified in Your
words,
And may overcome when You are
judged."*

WORD WEALTH

3:4 true, *alethes* (al-ay-*thace*); Strong's *#227:* Compare "latent" and "lethargy." Genuine, real, true, ideal, manifest, unconcealed, actual. *Alethes* is the opposite of falsehood, concealment, and human inconsistency. God is faithful to His promises; He is incapable of falsehood. *Alethes* assures us that His utterances

2:10 Works what is good: See notes on vv. 6, 7.

2:12–16 Paul stresses that both Jews and Gentiles are accountable to God for judgment. They differ from each other in that Jews possess the **law,** while Gentiles do not, even though **by nature** they do some of the things that are stipulated in the Law (v. 14). God has given all people a moral instinct by creation (v. 15), though repeated sin or cultural acceptance may distort their understanding. The point is that people will be judged according to the revelation they have. The standard of judgment for Jews will be the written Law; the standard for pagans will be the unwritten law of **conscience** and nature.

2:24 See section 3 of Truth-In-Action at the end of Rom.

2:24 Often the worst enemy of the gospel and of God's honor is sin in the lives of those who profess to be believers.

2:28, 29 "True Judaism" is found in those who are righteous before God, whether or not they have Jewish parents or the physical sign of **circumcision.**

agree with reality, are authentic, and harmonize with historical fact.

5 But if our unrighteousness demonstrates the righteousness of God, what shall we say? *Is* God unjust who inflicts wrath? [a](I speak as a man.)
6 Certainly not! For then [a]how will God judge the world?
7 For if the truth of God has increased through my lie to His glory, why am I also still judged as a sinner?
8 And *why* not *say,* [a]"Let us do evil that good may come"?—as we are slanderously reported and as some affirm that we say. Their [1]condemnation is just.

All Have Sinned

9 What then? Are we better *than they?* Not at all. For we have previously charged both Jews and Greeks that [a]they are all under *sin.
10 As it is written:

[a]"There is none righteous, no, not one;
11 *There is none who understands;*
There is none who seeks after God.
12 *They have all turned aside;*
They have together become unprofitable;
*There is none who does *good, no, not one."*
13 *"Their[a] throat is an open [1]tomb;*
With their tongues they have practiced deceit";
[b]"The poison of asps is under their lips";
14 *"Whose[a] mouth is full of cursing and bitterness."*
15 *"Their[a] feet are swift to shed blood;*
16 *Destruction and misery are in their ways;*
17 *And the way of peace they have not known."*
18 *"There[a] is no *fear of God before their eyes."*

19 Now we know that whatever
[a]the law says, it says to those who are under the law, that [b]every mouth may be stopped, and all the world may become [1]guilty before God.
20 Therefore [a]by the *deeds of the law no *flesh will be justified in His sight, for by the law *is* the knowledge of sin.

God's Righteousness Through Faith

21 But now [a]the righteousness of God apart from the law is revealed, [b]being *witnessed by the Law [c]and the Prophets,
22 even the righteousness of God, through faith in Jesus Christ, to all [1]and on all who believe. For [a]there is no difference;
23 for [a]all have sinned and *fall short of the glory of God,
24 being *justified [1]freely [a]by His *grace [b]through the **redemption** that is in *Christ Jesus,
25 whom God set forth [a]*as* a [1]propitia-

5 [a]Gal. 3:15
6 [a][Gen. 18:25]
8 [a]Rom. 5:20 [1]Lit. *judgment*
9 [a]Gal. 3:22 *See WW at John 1:29.
10 [a]Ps. 14:1–3; 53:1–3; Eccl. 7:20
12 *See WW at Gal. 5:22.
13 [a]Ps. 5:9 [b]Ps. 140:3 [1]*grave*
14 [a]Ps. 10:7
15 [a]Prov. 1:16; Is. 59:7, 8
18 [a]Ps. 36:1 *See WW at 1 John 4:18.
19 [a]John 10:34 [b]Job 5:16 [1]*accountable*
20 [a][Gal. 2:16] *See WW at John 9:4. • See WW at Matt. 26:41.
21 [a]Acts 15:11 [b]John 5:46 [c]1 Pet. 1:10 *See WW at Acts 26:22.
22 [a][Col. 3:11] [1]NU omits *and on all*
23 [a]Gal. 3:22 *See WW at Luke 22:35.
24 [a][Eph. 2:8] [b][Heb. 9:12, 15] [1]*without any cost* *See WW at Matt. 12:37. • See WW at 2 Cor. 12:9. • See WW at 2 Tim. 4:22.
25 [a]Lev. 16:15 [1]*mercy seat*

3:5 It is true that God's judgment of sin shows His **righteousness** and brings Him glory, but this does not mean that God is unfair. His holy character requires that He judge sin.
3:8 Some had distorted Paul's gospel by claiming that he was preaching that we should **do evil that good may come.** Though God is so great that He can even use evil ultimately to bring glory to Himself, He Himself never does evil; and He never allows us to do evil in order to try to bring about good results.
3:9–20 Paul's conclusion from the argument in 1:18—3:8 is that all people in the **world** are **guilty before God.**
3:9 We includes Jews in contrast to **they,** the Gentiles.
3:18 The underlying reason for the increasing corruption of societies is that they have **no fear of God,** that is, thinking they will not have to answer to God for their immorality.
3:19 That every mouth may be stopped: At the Day of Judgment, no one will be able to say that God has been unfair in His judgment. The Jews had God's written laws in Scripture, and the Gentiles had God's moral standards in their hearts and consciences, enough at least to cause them to seek Him further.
3:21 But underscores the contrast between the revelation of God's wrath (1:18) and the revealing of God's **righteousness.** See note on 1:17. **The Law and the Prophets** refers here to the whole OT.
3:22 Faith in Jesus Christ is a genuine reliance on Christ, a heartfelt trust in Him, rather than in oneself, for salvation.
3:23 No one will ever reach God's standard of absolute moral perfection and be worthy of His **glory** on his own. Therefore, if there is to be any salvation, it must come in another way (see v. 24).
3:24 Justified means to be declared righteous in God's sight.
3:25 Propitiation means the appeasement of divine wrath by a sacrificial offering. Some deny that the Bible contains this idea because they do not think a loving God would ever personally exercise wrath against His creatures. But the idea is clearly implied by the Greek word for "propitiation," and is the only saving solution to the fact of God's wrath against sin that Paul developed in 1:18—3:20. At the heart of the gospel is the fact that if Christ did not bear the wrath of God that we deserved, then that wrath is still stored up for us (2:5, 8; 3:5; 5:9; 9:22; Eph. 5:6; Rev. 6:16, 17). The idea of propitiation is also vividly described in Is. 53:4, 5, 10, 11. **Blood** is a reference to Christ's death as a substitute sacrifice for us. Christ's blood poured out is clear evidence that His life was given for us. **To demonstrate His righteousness:** God had not punished all sins **previously committed** (in the time of the OT). Therefore, He *appeared* to be unjust: for sin had been committed but no penalty had been paid. But when Christ died, He paid even for those

tion* [b]by His *blood, through faith, to
demonstrate His righteousness, because in His forbearance God had
passed over [c]the sins that were previously committed,

WORD WEALTH

3:24 redemption, *apolutrosis* (ap-ol-oo-tro-sis); Strong's *#629:* A release secured by the payment of a ransom, deliverance, setting free. The word in secular Greek described a conqueror releasing prisoners, a master ransoming a slave, and redemption from an alien yoke. In the NT it designates deliverance through Christ from evil and the penalty of sin. The price paid to purchase that liberation was His shed blood.

KINGDOM DYNAMICS

3:23 Christ—The Absolute Need of Every Man, WORLD EVANGELISM. World evangelism requires that we see all people as God sees them—as sinners: 1) by nature (3:10); 2) by choice (3:23); 3) by practice (6:23). Casual attitudes and blinded minds have lured some believers in Christ to overlook the desperate state of the lost: "The wages of sin *is* death" (6:23). Universalism or ultimate reconciliation are terms describing the erroneous belief of some that eventually even the eternally lost will be granted a reprieve from eternal judgment. But Paul said, "We judge that if One died for all, all died" (2 Cor. 5:14). Because he saw the lost as God sees them, he said God's love "constrained" him to world evangelism. The nations—all people—need the gospel desperately and are lost without it. A clear-eyed look into the Word of God will help us capture and retain the conviction that humankind needs the gospel.

(Acts 4:12/Rom. 10:13–15) G.C.

KINGDOM DYNAMICS

3:25 Right Relationship with God Through Blood, THE BLOOD. God presented Jesus as the sacrifice for atonement or reconciliation with separated mankind. Fellowship with a holy God could only be realized through atoning for the sins that separated mankind from God and His covenant promises. It is the shed blood of Christ that ultimately satisfied the requirements of God's justice. God's judgment was fully put upon Christ, the blameless sacrifice, for all sins both past and present. It is through faith in the blood of Christ that mankind is justified in God's eyes. The blood of Christ then also becomes the bond that joins people to God and entitles them to God's covenant provisions. The blood of Christ is forever the only means of right relationship with the holy God.

(Matt. 26:28/Eph. 2:13) C.S.

26 to demonstrate at the present time
His righteousness, that He might be
just and the justifier of the one who
has faith in Jesus.

Boasting Excluded

27 [a]Where *is* boasting then? It is excluded. By what law? Of works? No,
but by the law of faith.
28 Therefore we conclude [a]that a man
is [1]justified by faith apart from the
deeds of the law.
29 Or *is He* the God of the Jews only?
Is He not also the God of the Gentiles?
Yes, of the Gentiles also,
30 since [a]*there is* one God who will
justify the circumcised by faith and the
uncircumcised through faith.
31 Do we then make void the law
through faith? Certainly not! On the
contrary, we establish the law.

Abraham Justified by Faith

4 What then shall we say that
[a]Abraham our [b]father[1] has found
according to the flesh?
2 For if Abraham was [a]justified by
works, he has *something* to boast
about, but not before God.
3 For what does the *Scripture
say? [a]*"Abraham believed God, and it
was [1]**accounted** to him for righteousness."*

25 [b]Col. 1:20 [c]Acts 14:16; 17:30; [Rom. 2:4] *See WW at Heb. 9:5 • See WW at 1 John 1:7.
27 [a]Rom. 2:17, 23; [1 Cor. 1:29]; Eph. 2:9
28 [a]Gal. 2:16 [1]*declared righteous*
30 [a]Rom. 10:12; [Gal. 3:8, 20]

CHAPTER 4

1 [a]Gen. 11:27—25:9; Is. 51:2; [Matt. 3:9]; John 8:33 [b][Luke 3:8]; John 8:53; James 2:21 [1]*Or (fore)father according to the flesh has found?*
2 [a]Rom. 3:20, 27
3 [a]Gen. 15:6; Rom. 4:9, 22; Gal. 3:6; James 2:23 [1]*imputed, credited, reckoned, counted* *See WW at John 5:39.

previous sins that God had forgiven, thereby showing that God is truly just and that He never forgives any sin without full payment of the penalty for that sin.

3:26 Sending Christ to die for our sins was God's amazing solution to the problem of how He could remain just (punish all sin) and still justify us (declare us perfectly righteous in *His sight).*

3:31 God's moral laws are not abolished by the gospel of Christ. Rather, the whole plan of salvation, including Christ's obeying the Law for us and dying to pay the penalty for our breaking the Law, shows that God's moral standards are eternally valid.

4:1–25 The example of **Abraham,** whom faithful Jews thought of as the **father** of their faith, shows that salvation by faith, not works, is clearly taught in the OT as well as in the NT.

4:2 Paul's argument is that Abraham was not **justified by works** or obedience to the Law. The statement of James 2:21 that Abraham was "justified by works" uses the word "justified" in a different sense, not meaning "declared to be righteous" by God (as here), but rather "shown outwardly to be righteous." (The word can take both meanings.) Paul and James agree that Abraham's initial salvation and eternal forgiveness came through faith alone (Gen. 15:6; Rom. 4:3), but that later in his life evidence of that salvation came by his works (Gen. 22:9; James 2:21). So it is with us today.

WORD WEALTH

4:3 accounted, *logidzomai* (log-id-zom-ahee); Strong's *#3049:* Compare "logistic" and "logarithm." Numerically, to count, compute, calculate, sum up. Metaphorically, to consider, reckon, reason, deem, evaluate, value. *Logidzomai* finalizes thought, judges matters, draws logical conclusions, decides outcomes, and puts every action into a debit or credit position.

4 Now [a]to him who works, the
*wages are not counted [1]as grace but
[1]as debt.

David Celebrates the Same Truth

5 But to him who [a]does not work but
believes on Him who justifies [b]the ungodly, his *faith is accounted for righteousness,
6 just as David also [a]describes the
blessedness of the man to whom God
imputes righteousness apart from
works:

7 *"Blessed[a] are those whose lawless*
deeds are forgiven,
And whose sins are covered;
8 **Blessed is the man to whom the*
**Lord shall not impute sin."*

Abraham Justified Before Circumcision

9 *Does* this blessedness then *come*
upon the circumcised *only,* or upon the
uncircumcised also? For we say that
faith was accounted to Abraham for
righteousness.
10 How then was it accounted? While
he was circumcised, or uncircumcised?
Not while circumcised, but while uncircumcised.
11 And [a]he received the sign of circumcision, a seal of the righteousness
of the faith which *he had while still* uncircumcised, that [b]he might be the father of all those who believe, though
they are uncircumcised, that righteousness might be imputed to them
also,
12 and the father of circumcision to
those who not only *are* of the circumcision, but who also walk in the steps
of the faith which our father [a]Abraham
had while still uncircumcised.

The Promise Granted Through Faith

13 For the promise that he would be
the [a]heir of the world *was* not to Abraham or to his seed through the
law, but through the righteousness of
faith.
14 For [a]if those who are of the law *are*
heirs, faith is *made void and the promise made of no effect,
15 because [a]the law brings about
wrath; for where there is no law *there*
is no transgression.
16 Therefore *it is* of faith that *it might*
be [a]according to grace, [b]so that the
promise might be [1]sure to all the seed,
not only to those who are of the law,
but also to those who are of the faith
of Abraham, [c]who is the father of us
all
17 (as it is written, [a]*"I have made you* 1
a father of many nations") in the presence of Him whom he believed—God,
[b]who gives life to the dead and calls
those [c]things which do not exist as
though they did;
18 who, contrary to hope, in hope believed, so that he became the father of
many nations, according to what was
spoken, [a]*"So shall your descendants*
be."
19 And not being weak in faith,
[a]he did not consider his own body, already dead (since he was about a

4 [a]Rom. 11:6 [1]*according to* *See WW at Rev. 22:12. **5** [a][Gal. 2:16; Eph. 2:8, 9] [b]Josh. 24:2 *See WW at Mark 11:22. **6** [a]Ps. 32:1, 2 **7** [a]Ps. 32:1, 2 **8** *See WW at Matt. 5:3. • See WW at John 6:68. **11** [a]Gen. 17:10 [b]Luke 19:9; Rom. 4:16

12 [a]Rom. 4:18–22 **13** [a]Gen.17:4–6; 22:17 **14** [a]Gal. 3:18 *See WW at 1 Cor. 9:15. **15** [a]Rom. 3:20 **16** [a][Rom. 3:24] [b][Gal. 3:22] [c]Is. 51:2 [1]*certain* **17** [a]Gen. 17:5 [b][Rom. 8:11] [c]Rom. 9:26 **18** [a]Gen. 15:5 **19** [a]Gen. 17:17

4:6 Imputes: God imparts **righteousness** to those who believe. The same Greek word occurs in vv. 3, 4, 5, 8, 9, 10, 11, 22, 23, and 24, and is sometimes translated by different English words, such as "accounted" or "reckoned."
4:9 Circumcised refers to Jews. **Uncircumcised** refers to Gentiles. Paul uses Abraham's own life in vv. 9–12 to demonstrate that the free gift of salvation is not restricted to those who have received the physical sign of being included among God's people under the Old Covenant, that is, circumcision. The same argument could be used to show that a person can be forgiven before receiving baptism, because baptism, in the New Covenant, is the outward physical sign of becoming a Christian.
4:11 Much to the surprise of first-century Jews, Paul argues that Abraham is also **the father** of the **uncircumcised** Gentiles **who believe.**
4:16 Many human attitudes, such as love, joy, patience, courage, and mercy, can be somewhat worked up by our own effort. But **faith** occurs when we cease trying to do something by our own efforts, and trust someone else to do it for us. Faith is the one attitude that is exactly the opposite of trusting ourselves. Apparently this is why God decided that faith would be the attitude of heart by which we could obtain salvation, **that *it might be* according to grace,** that is, that it might be an entirely free gift of God, not dependent on any merit of our own.
4:17–18 See section 1 of Truth-In-Action at the end of Rom.
4:17 Abraham's faith that God would fulfill His promise was based on God's power as demonstrated in resurrection and in creation (see v. 21).
4:18 Contrary to hope: Contrary to ordinary human expectation. **In hope:** In expectation that God would fulfill His promises.

hundred years old), [b]and the deadness
of Sarah's womb.
■1 20 He *did not waver at the promise
of God through unbelief, but was
strengthened in faith, giving glory to
God,
21 and being fully convinced that what
He had *promised [a]He was also able
to perform.
22 And therefore [a]*"it was accounted to
him for righteousness."*
23 Now [a]it was not written for his sake
alone that it was imputed to him,
24 but also for us. It shall be imputed
to us who believe [a]in Him who raised
up Jesus our Lord from the dead,
25 [a]who was *delivered up because of
our offenses, and [b]was raised because
of our justification.

Faith Triumphs in Trouble

5 Therefore, [a]having been *justified
by faith, [1]we have [b]peace with God
through our Lord Jesus Christ,
2 [a]through whom also we have access
by faith into this grace [b]in which we
stand, and [c]rejoice in *hope of the
glory of God.
3 And not only *that,* but [a]we also
glory in *tribulations, [b]knowing that
tribulation produces [1]perseverance;
4 [a]and perseverance, [1]character; and
character, hope.
5 [a]Now hope does not disappoint,
[b]because the **love** of God has been
poured out in our hearts by the Holy
Spirit who was given to us.

WORD WEALTH

5:5 love, *agape* (ag-*ah*-pay): Strong's *#26:* A word to which Christianity gave new meaning. Outside of the NT, it rarely occurs in existing Greek manuscripts of the period. *Agape* denotes an undefeatable benevolence and unconquerable goodwill that always seeks the highest good of the other person, no matter what he does. It is the self-giving love that gives freely without asking anything in return, and does not consider the worth of its object. *Agape* is more a love by choice than *philos,* which is love by chance; and it refers to the will rather than the emotion. *Agape* describes the unconditional love God has for the world.

Christ in Our Place

6 For when we were still without
strength, [1]in *due time [a]Christ died for
the ungodly.
7 For scarcely for a righteous man
will one die; yet perhaps for a good
man someone would even dare to die.
8 But [a]God demonstrates His own
*love toward us, in that while we were
still *sinners, Christ died for us.
9 Much more then, having now been
justified [a]by His *blood, we shall be
*saved [b]from wrath through Him.

KINGDOM DYNAMICS

5:9 The Blood, Reconciliation, and Victorious Living, THE BLOOD. Rom. 3:10 establishes that all people are unrighteous and therefore deserving of judgment. The covenant love of God reaches beyond the satisfaction of justice to establish a bond of fellowship in the blood of Jesus Christ. Faith in His blood not only brings our deliverance from the wrath of God, but also is the means of victorious living through participation in His life: 1) the blood of Christ deals with the legal issue of separation from God, reconciling us to Him; and 2) faith in His blood infuses divine life and provision for our continuing triumph over sin.

(Col. 1:20/Rev. 12:11) C.S.

10 For [a]if when we were enemies
[b]we were *reconciled to God through
the death of His Son, much more, having been reconciled, we shall be saved
[c]by His life.
11 And not only *that,* but we also

19 [b]Heb. 11:11
20 *See WW at Acts 11:12
21 [a][Heb. 11:19] *See WW at Acts 7:5.
22 [a]Gen. 15:6
23 [a]Rom. 15:4
24 [a]Acts 2:24
25 [a]Is. 53:4, 5 [b][1 Cor. 15:17] *See WW at Luke 23:25.

CHAPTER 5

1 [a]Is. 32:17 [b][Eph. 2:14] [1]Some ancient mss. *let us have* *See WW at Matt. 12:37.
2 [a][Eph. 2:18; 3:12] [b]1 Cor. 15:1 [c]Heb. 3:6 *See WW at 1 Thess. 1:3.
3 [a]Matt. 5:11, 12 [b]James 1:3 [1]*endurance* *See WW at John 16:33.
4 [a][James 1:12] [1]*approved character*
5 [a]Phil. 1:20 [b]2 Cor. 1:22
6 [a][Rom. 4:25; 5:8; 8:32] [1]*at the right time* *See WW at Col. 4:5.
8 [a][John 3:16; 15:13] *See WW at Rom. 5:5. • See WW at James 5:20.
9 [a]Eph. 2:13 [b]1 Thess. 1:10 *See WW at 1 John 1:7. • See WW at Luke 7:50.
10 [a][Rom. 8:32] [b]2 Cor. 5:18 [c]John 14:19 *See WW at 1 Cor. 7:11.

4:20–25 See section 1 of Truth-In-Action at the end of Rom.
4:20 Was strengthened in faith: Through nearly 10 years of waiting for fulfillment of a seemingly impossible promise, Abraham's faith, rather than growing weak, grew stronger, while he continued to give **glory to God.**
4:25 Though the NT elsewhere describes further benefits that Christ's resurrection brings to us, here His resurrection *specifically obtains* **our justification,** that is, our being declared righteous in God's sight. By raising Christ from the dead God declared both His approval of Christ's completed work of redemption and His approval of all who believe and are thereby united with Christ in His resurrection.
5:2 The whole Christian life is the result of God's **grace in which we stand**—His favor and provision in Christ that we do not deserve. **The glory of God** is the manifestation of God, the outward shining of His inward being. At the Lord's return that glory will be fully revealed (see Titus 2:13), and believers exult in the prospect of seeing Him as He is and of sharing in His glory.
5:4 And character, hope: When our Christian character goes through hardship, hope of receiving what God has promised grows stronger.
5:5 We know that hope of great future blessings will not turn out to be false, because **the Holy Spirit** gives lavish evidence in our hearts of God's **love** for us.
5:8 We did not have to make ourselves righteous before **God** decided to send **Christ** to earn our salvation.
5:11 Even in hardship, we not only hope in God for future

[a]rejoice in God through our Lord Jesus
Christ, through whom we have now received the reconciliation.

Death in Adam, Life in Christ

12 Therefore, just as [a]through one man
sin entered the *world, and [b]death
through sin, and thus death spread to
all men, because all sinned—
13 (For until the law sin was in the
world, but [a]sin is not imputed when
there is no law.
14 Nevertheless death reigned from
Adam to Moses, even over those who
had not sinned according to the likeness of the transgression of Adam,
[a]who is a type of Him who was to
come.
15 But the free *gift *is* not like the
[1]offense. For if by the one man's offense many died, much more the grace
of God and the gift by the grace of the
one Man, Jesus Christ, abounded
[a]to many.
16 And the gift *is* not like *that which
came* through the one who sinned. For
the judgment *which came* from one *offense resulted* in condemnation, but
the free gift *which came* from many
[1]offenses *resulted* in justification.
17 For if by the one man's [1]offense
death reigned through the one, much
more those who receive abundance of
grace and of the gift of righteousness
will reign in life through the One, Jesus
Christ.)
18 Therefore, as through [1]one man's
offense *judgment* came to all men, resulting in condemnation, even so
through [a]one[2] Man's righteous act *the
free gift came* [b]to all men, resulting in
justification of life.
19 For as by one man's disobedience
many were made sinners, so also by
[a]one Man's obedience many will be
made righteous.
20 Moreover [a]the law entered that the
offense might abound. But where *sin
abounded, grace [b]abounded much
more,
21 so that as sin reigned in death, even
so grace might reign through righteousness to *eternal *life through
Jesus Christ our Lord.

Dead to Sin, Alive to God

6 What shall we say then? [a]Shall we 1
continue in sin that grace may
abound?

11 [a][Gal. 4:9]
12 [a][1 Cor. 15:21] [b]Gen. 2:17 *See WW at John 18:36.
13 [a]1 John 3:4
14 [a][1 Cor. 15:21, 22]
15 [a][Is. 53:11] [1]*trespass* or *false step* *See WW at 1 Cor. 1:7.
16 [1]*trespasses*
17 [1]*trespass*
18 [a][1 Cor. 15:21, 45] [b][John 12:32] [1]Or *one trespass* [2]Or *one righteous act*
19 [a][Phil. 2:8]
20 [a]John 15:22 [b]1 Tim. 1:14 *See WW at John 1:29.
21 *See WW at Rev. 14:6. • See WW at 1 John 5:20.

CHAPTER 6

1 [a]Rom. 3:8; 6:15

blessings, we also **rejoice in God** because of present fellowship with Him through Christ.

5:12–21 This passage must be understood within the context of 3:21—5:11, which sets forth the gospel of the grace of God revealed through Jesus Christ. This passage continues to magnify God's grace by presenting the universal scope of Christ's redemptive work. V. 18 summarizes Paul's teaching. One act of **one man** brought **sin** and its penalty of **death** upon the human race. On the other hand, the obedience of **one Man** counteracted this deed and made righteousness and eternal life available for humankind. **Adam** headed the old humanity characterized by sin and death. **Jesus Christ** heads a new humanity characterized by righteousness and life. We come under the consequences of Adam's deed by natural descent. We come under Christ's obedience by faith (see 1 Cor. 15:22; 2 Cor. 5:14).

5:12 The expression **just as** is a key to understanding vv. 12–21. Paul is going to show several parallels between the way Adam affected us and the way Christ affected us. The phrase **because all sinned** probably means that "all sinned" in Adam—that is, when **one man** sinned, God thought of all who would descend from Adam as having sinned, also, since Adam was our representative (see v. 19; 1 Cor. 15:22). However, others understand this phrase to mean merely that all others *later* sinned and therefore they died. But vv. 13, 14 seem to suggest the first view.

5:13, 14 Paul enforces and proves his assertion of v. 12 by pointing out the fact that people died even during the time preceding the giving of the **law** (the written law of the Ten Commandments, Ex. 20). His argument is that they died because all of humanity was counted guilty because of Adam's sin and thus suffered its penalty, not because they deliberately transgressed the Law (which was not yet in existence). Paul states that they **sinned according to the likeness of the transgression of Adam,** that is, they had not sinned by disobeying a specific verbal command of God. A **type** is a living prediction or pattern or model of one who was to come later.

5:15–19 Paul refers to Adam as "a type" (v. 14) of Christ and draws an analogy between Adam and Christ. They are similar in the fact that their deeds have affected many people. However, their differences are more pronounced, and Paul gives a threefold contrast. First, Adam's act was an **offense,** a deliberate going astray; Christ's deed was one of **grace** (v. 15). Second, Adam's sin resulted in **condemnation** and **death,** whereas Christ's deed of grace brought **justification** and **life** (vv. 16, 17). Third, Adam is characterized by **disobedience,** while Christ is characterized by **obedience** (vv. 18, 19). We are in Adam by birth, but we are in Christ by faith. In Adam by birth we are condemned and die, but because of Christ's redemptive work we can be justified and live if we are in Him by faith.

5:18 All men . . . all men: The groups of people are not the same, or the verse would mean that every person ever born would be saved, something Scripture does not teach (see 2:8, 9; Matt. 7:13, 14, 23; 25:46). Rather, the first "all men" refers to all who were represented by Adam, namely, the whole human race. The second "all men" refers to all who were represented by Christ, namely, all who would believe in Him.

5:19 A summary of God's plan of representative heads for the human race. Adam sinned (once), and all whom Adam represented were found guilty. Christ obeyed (through His whole life) and all whom Christ represented will be **made righteous.** Some object to this idea of representative heads for the human race. But if we do not think it fair that we were counted guilty for Adam's sin, then we also should not think it fair that we are counted righteous for Christ's **obedience.**

5:20, 21 One purpose of **the law** was to make sin obvious and thus to make more evident the need for redemption.

6:1–10 See section 1 of Truth-In-Action at the end of Rom.

2 Certainly not! How shall we who
[a]died to sin live any longer in it?
3 Or do you not know that [a]as many
of us as were baptized into Christ Jesus
[b]were baptized into His death?
4 Therefore we were [a]buried with
Him through *baptism into death, that
[b]just as Christ was raised from the
dead by [c]the glory of the Father,
[d]even so we also should walk in newness of *life.
5 [a]For if we have been united together in the likeness of His death, certainly we also shall be *in the likeness*
of *His* *resurrection,
6 knowing this, that [a]our old man was
crucified with *Him,* that [b]the body of
sin might be [1]done away with, that we
should no longer be slaves of sin.
7 For [a]he who has died has been
[1]freed from sin.
8 Now [a]if we died with Christ, we believe that we shall also live with Him,
9 knowing that [a]Christ, having been
raised from the dead, dies no more.
Death no longer has dominion over
Him.
10 For *the death* that He died, [a]He died
to sin once for all; but *the life* that He
lives, [b]He lives to God.
4 11 Likewise you also, [1]reckon yourselves to be [a]dead indeed to sin, but
[b]alive to God in Christ Jesus our Lord.
12 [a]Therefore do not let sin reign in
your mortal body, that you should obey
it in its lusts.
13 And do not present your [a]members
as [1]instruments of unrighteousness to
sin, but [b]present yourselves to God as
being alive from the dead, and your
members *as* [1]instruments of righteousness to God.
14 For [a]sin shall not have dominion
over you, for you are not under law
but under grace.

From Slaves of Sin to Slaves of God

15 What then? Shall we sin [a]because
we are not under law but under grace?
Certainly not!
16 Do you not know that [a]to whom you 4
present yourselves *slaves to obey, you
are that one's slaves whom you obey,
whether of sin *leading* to death, or of
*obedience *leading* to righteousness?
17 But God be thanked that *though*
you were slaves of sin, yet you **obeyed**
from the heart [a]that form of doctrine
to which you were [1]delivered.

2 [a][Gal. 2:19]
3 [a][Gal. 3:27] [b][1 Cor. 15:29]
4 [a]Col. 2:12 [b]1 Cor. 6:14 [c]John 2:11 [d][Gal. 6:15] *See WW at Matt. 21:25. • See WW at 1 John 5:20.
5 [a]Phil. 3:10 *See WW at Acts 23:6.
6 [a]Gal. 2:20; 5:24; 6:14 [b]Col. 2:11 [1]*rendered inoperative*
7 [a]1 Pet. 4:1 [1]*cleared*
8 [a]2 Tim. 2:11
9 [a]Rev. 1:18
10 [a]Heb. 9:27 [b]Luke 20:38
11 [a][Rom. 6:2; 7:4, 6] [b][Gal. 2:19] [1]*consider*
12 [a]Ps. 19:13
13 [a]Col. 3:5 [b]1 Pet. 2:24; 4:2 [1]Or *weapons*
14 [a][Gal. 5:18]
15 [a]1 Cor. 9:21
16 [a]2 Pet. 2:19 *See WW at Rev. 19:5. • See WW at 2 Cor. 10:5.
17 [a]2 Tim. 1:13 [1]*entrusted*

WORD WEALTH

6:17 obeyed, *hupakouo* (hoop-ak-*oo*-oh); Strong's *#5219:* To hear as a subordinate, listen attentively, obey as a subject, answer and respond, submit without reservation. *Hupakouo* was used particu-

6:1 Paul's teaching in 5:20, 21 that increased sin brings increased **grace** was liable to distortion. Some might claim that if by sinning they were providing God an opportunity to display the greatness of His grace then they should sin more and more.

6:2 The idea of a Christian continuing in **sin** is entirely contrary to the gospel. Sin is hateful and destructive, and those who have **died to** the love of **sin** and the ruling power of sin should never want to live in it any longer.

6:3 Water baptism is a symbol of the believer's union with Christ in His death, burial (v. 4), and resurrection (vv. 4, 5; Eph. 2:6; Col. 3:1).

6:6 Our old man is our preconversion life, what we were before becoming Christians under the unrestrained dominion of the flesh (sin nature). **The body of sin** refers to the sinful nature within us, not to the human body. The Greek verb translated **done away with** does not mean to become extinct, but to be defeated or deprived of power (see marginal note).

6:11–14 See section 4 of Truth-In-Action at the end of Rom.

6:11 Dead . . . to sin: Not controlled by the love of sin or its ruling power in our lives, dead to its enslaving power (but not dead to all of its influence: see vv. 12, 13, 15, 16).

6:12 Therefore: A natural conclusion from vv. 2–11 is that if we are dead to the ruling power of **sin,** and if sin has destructive effects in our lives, then, of course, we should **not let** it **reign** in our bodies.

6:13 We have a continual choice day after day whether to yield ourselves to sin or to God. **Members:** The various parts of our bodies, probably as representative of all aspects of our lives.

6:14 Though we can never say in this life that we are free from all sin (James 3:2; 1 John 1:8, 10), we also should never say, "This one sin has defeated me—I give up." The power of Christ's resurrection at work within us (vv. 4, 5, 11) is greater than the power of any **sin,** no matter how long established in our lives. To be **under law** is to be under a system of trying to earn salvation in our own strength by obeying the law, but to be **under grace** is to be justified and to live by the indwelling resurrection power of Christ. We can die to sin, not because of the law forbidding it, but through all the resources that grace provides. Some erroneously interpret this verse to mean that it does not matter if Christians disobey God's moral commands, because they are no longer "under law." Such an interpretation (antinomianism) is contrary to Paul's whole discussion of sin and to Jesus' own words about the law (Matt. 5:17–20).

6:15–23 Once again Paul responds to the supposition that grace encourages or permits sin (see v. 1). He uses the analogy of slavery to combat a casual attitude toward sin and issues a stern warning on the serious consequences of yielding to sin.

6:16–23 See section 4 of Truth-In-Action at the end of Rom.

6:16 A person is a slave of that to which he gives obedience or that which he recognizes as his master. If he obeys the commands of **sin,** then sin is his master and he is moving in the direction of **death.** If he obeys the commands of **righteousness,** then righteousness is his master, and he experiences true life.

6:17, 18 Paul's readers, once **slaves of sin,** have renounced sin as master and have committed themselves as **slaves of righteousness.**

larly of servants who were attentive to the requests made of them and who complied. The word thus contains the ideas of hearing, responding, and obeying.

18 And [a]having been set *free from sin,
you became slaves of righteousness.
19 I speak in human *terms* because of
the weakness of your flesh. For just as
you presented your members *as* slaves
of uncleanness, and of lawlessness
leading to *more* lawlessness, so now
present your members *as* slaves of
righteousness [1]for holiness.
20 For when you were [a]slaves of sin,
you were free in regard to righteousness.
21 [a]What fruit did you have then in
the things of which you are now
ashamed? For [b]the end of those things
is death.
22 But now [a]having been set *free from
sin, and having become slaves of God,
you have your fruit [1]to holiness, and
the end, everlasting life.
23 For [a]the wages of sin *is* death, but
[b]the [1]gift* of God *is* eternal life in
Christ Jesus our Lord.

Freed from the Law

7 Or do you not know, brethren (for
I speak to those who know the
law), that the law [1]has dominion over
a man as long as he lives?
2 For [a]the woman who has a husband
is bound by the law to *her* husband as
long as he lives. But if the husband
dies, she is released from the law of
her husband.

18 [a]John 8:32; Rom. 6:22; 8:2; 1 Cor. 7:22; Gal. 5:1; 1 Pet. 2:16 *See WW at Rom. 8:2.
19 [1]*unto sanctification*
20 [a]John 8:34
21 [a]Jer. 12:13; Ezek. 16:63; Rom. 7:5 [b]Rom. 1:32; Gal. 6:8
22 [a][John 8:32]; Rom. 6:18; 8:2 [1]*unto sanctification* *See WW at Rom. 8:2.
23 [a]Gen. 2:17 [b]Rom. 2:7; 1 Pet. 1:4 [1]*free gift* *See WW at 1 Cor. 1:7.

CHAPTER 7

1 [1]*rules*
2 [a]1 Cor. 7:39
3 [a][Matt. 5:32] *See WW at Rev. 6:15.
4 [a]Rom. 8:2; Gal. 2:19; 5:18; [Col. 2:14] [b]Gal. 5:22
5 [a]Rom. 6:13 [b]Rom. 6:21; Gal. 5:19; James 1:15 *See WW at 1 Thess. 2:13.
6 [a]Rom. 2:29; 2 Cor. 3:6

3 So then [a]if, while *her* husband lives,
she marries another man, she will be
called an adulteress; but if her husband
dies, she is *free from that law, so that
she is no adulteress, though she has
married another man.
4 Therefore, my brethren, you also
have become [a]dead to the law through
the body of Christ, that you may be
married to another—to Him who was
raised from the dead, that we should
[b]bear fruit to God.
5 For when we were in the flesh, the
sinful passions which were aroused by
the law [a]were at *work in our members
[b]to bear fruit to death.
6 But now we have been delivered
from the law, having died to what we
were held by, so that we should serve
[a]in the newness of the **Spirit** and not
in the oldness of the letter.

WORD WEALTH

7:6 Spirit, *pneuma* (*pnyoo*-mah); Strong's *#4151:* Compare "pneumonia," "pneumatology," "pneumatic." Breath, breeze, a current of air, wind, spirit. *Pneuma* is that part of a person capable of responding to God. The Holy Spirit is the third person of the Trinity, who draws us to Christ, convicts us of sin, enables us to accept Christ as our personal Savior, assures us of salvation, enables us to live the victorious life, understand the Bible, pray according to God's will, and share Christ with others.

Sin's Advantage in the Law

7 What shall we say then? *Is* the law
sin? Certainly not! On the contrary,

6:19–23 Paul uses the **human** analogy of slavery in appealing for holiness. In doing so he reminds his readers of the contrast between the old unregenerate life and the new regenerate life. **Slaves of sin** do not recognize the obligation to righteousness, but rather abandon themselves to a process of moral deterioration, which has **death** as its end (v. 21). **Slaves of God,** on the other hand, devote themselves to **holiness,** a road that leads to **everlasting life** (vv. 19, 22). V. 23 summarizes the consequences of the two types of slavery.
7:1 While **the law** still fulfills its function of guiding us to know God's moral standards, we are free from enslavement to it as a way of righteousness (see 6:14).
7:2, 3 Paul illustrates our freedom from **the law** with the analogy of marriage, showing how the death of one partner frees the other from lifelong obligations. The subject under discussion here is not divorce and remarriage but the Christian's relationship to the system called "law." Paul is speaking here in general terms without making detailed qualifications, and his statements should not be pressed to exclude the grounds for divorce and remarriage mentioned in Matt. 19:9 and 1 Cor. 7:15, where divorce and remarriage are specifically under discussion.
7:4 You also have become dead to the law: The analogy is not perfect, for here we died, not the law. But the point is clear. Because a death has occurred, old obligations and powers are broken, and we are no longer under a system of trying to obey in our own strength. We are dead to that system of "law" (3:20; 6:14).
7:5 In our preconversion state our **sinful passions,** originating **in the flesh,** were **aroused by the law,** leading **to death.** As believers, similar struggles with sin in the flesh occur, but need not prevail. The difference is the presence of the Spirit to bring them under Christ's kingdom dominion within us.
7:6 Freedom from the Law does not mean license to sin, but servitude to God. In the **newness** of the New Covenant, the Holy Spirit gives power to obey God, a power the Law by itself could never give.
7:7–25 The law is **good,** but it cannot empower us to obey. In this section, Paul guards against the misunderstanding that he is saying that the Law in itself is evil. He emphasizes several times that it is good, yet vividly describes the impossibility of obeying it in one's own strength.

The frequent uses of the personal pronouns "I" and "me" in vv. 7–25 raise a question: Is Paul a) referring to himself, either as a Christian experiencing present struggles or b) as a former Pharisee, or is he c) referring to people in general

[a]I would not have known sin except
through the law. For I would not have
known covetousness unless the law
had said, [b]*"You shall not *covet."*
8 But [a]sin, taking opportunity by the
commandment, produced in me all
manner of evil desire. For [b]apart from
the law sin *was* dead.
9 I was alive once without the law,
but when the commandment came, sin
revived and I died.
10 And the commandment, [a]which
was to *bring* life, I found to *bring* death.
11 For sin, taking occasion by the commandment, deceived me, and by it
killed *me.*
12 Therefore [a]the law *is* holy, and the
commandment holy and just and good.

Law Cannot Save from Sin

13 Has then what is good become
death to me? Certainly not! But sin,
that it might appear sin, was producing
death in me through what is good, so
that sin through the commandment
might become *exceedingly sinful.
14 For we know that the law is spiritual, but I am carnal, [a]sold under sin.
15 For what I am doing, I do not understand. [a]For what I will to do, that I do
not practice; but what I hate, that I do.
16 If, then, I do what I will not to do,
I agree with the law that *it is* good.

7 [a]Rom. 3:20 [b]Ex. 20:17; Deut. 5:21; Acts 20:33 *See WW at Matt. 13:17. **8** [a]Rom. 4:15 [b]1 Cor. 15:56 **10** [a]Lev. 18:5 **12** [a]Ps. 19:8 **13** *See WW at 2 Cor. 4:7. **14** [a]2 Kin. 17:17 **15** [a][Gal. 5:17]

18 [a][Gen. 6:5; 8:21] **22** [a]Ps. 1:2 [b][2 Cor. 4:16] **23** [a][Gal. 5:17] [b]Rom. 6:13, 19 **24** [a][1 Cor. 15:51, 52] **25** [a]1 Cor. 15:57 *See WW at John 6:11.

CHAPTER 8

1 [a]Gal. 5:16 [1]NU omits the rest of v. 1.

17 But now, *it is* no longer I who do 4
it, but sin that dwells in me.
18 For I know that [a]in me (that is, in
my flesh) nothing good dwells; for to
will is present with me, but *how* to perform what is good I do not find.
19 For the good that I will *to do,* I do
not do; but the evil I will not *to do,*
that I practice.
20 Now if I do what I will not *to do,* it 4
is no longer I who do it, but sin that
dwells in me.
21 I find then a law, that evil is present
with me, the one who wills to do good.
22 For I [a]delight in the law of God according to [b]the inward man.
23 But [a]I see another law in [b]my members, warring against the law of my
mind, and bringing me into captivity
to the law of sin which is in my members.
24 O wretched man that I am! Who will
deliver me [a]from this body of death?
25 [a]I *thank God—through Jesus
Christ our Lord! So then, with the mind
I myself serve the law of God, but with
the flesh the law of sin.

Free from Indwelling Sin

8 *There is* therefore now no condem- 5
nation to those who are in Christ
Jesus, [a]who[1] do not walk according to
the flesh, but according to the Spirit.

who are attempting apart from the work of the Holy Spirit to attain righteousness in their own strength? The first position regards the passage as autobiographical, with Paul sharing his experiences both as a Pharisee (vv. 7–13) and as a Christian (vv. 14–25). Supporting this common view is the fact that the tenses change from the past to the present in vv. 14–25 and the fact that Paul ordinarily uses the pronoun "I" to refer to himself. But it is also true that Paul's experiences are representative of others, first of those seeking righteousness by legalistic practices and then of Christians engaged in warfare between the new nature in Christ and the old nature still resident in the flesh. Since Paul uses "I" in a generic or hypothetical sense in 3:7 and 1 Cor. 13:1–3, some have proposed this passage is not autobiographical, since Paul is such a bold proponent of the victorious life elsewhere (8:2; Phil. 4:8; 2 Tim. 1:13). However, interpreters all agree there remains a struggle with sin in the Christian life (6:12–16; 2 Cor. 7:1; Gal. 5:16, 17; 1 Pet. 2:11).

7:7 Paul's declaration that "we have been delivered from the law" (v. 6) gives rise to the question ***is the law sin?*** His reaction is one of horror. Then he proceeds to show that the Law of God is good, provided we understand its function, which is to reveal sin and to teach what is right. Powerless in itself to produce righteousness, it exposes sin for what it really is.

7:8 Apart from the law, sin was dormant, but the Law aroused a desire to do that which it forbade. The same is true of every Christian.

7:9, 10 Realization of sin through the instrumentality of the Law makes one conscious of his spiritual **death.**

7:11–13 Sin, not **the law,** was to blame. God's law, reflecting His righteous moral principles, **is holy.** It simply does not have the power to make us righteous.

7:14–23 According to position a) mentioned above (see note on 7:7–25), here Paul relates his own experience as a Christian to teach the lesson that the Law cannot deliver one who is struggling against sin. While the Law can enlighten one's conscience, it is powerless to produce holiness of life. The fault, however, is not with the Law of God, which **is spiritual** (v. 14). The fault is with **the law of sin** (v. 23, see vv. 14, 17, 18, 20, 21), the indwelling depravity of human nature, which rebels against God's laws. According to this view, Paul declares that he is **carnal,** a creature of the flesh, **sold under sin,** in captivity to sin (v. 14). Throughout this life a conflict goes on between the new nature and the old, but there is a way to victory: Christ frees us to live in the power of the Holy Spirit (v. 25—8:11).

7:17, 20 See section 4 of Truth-In-Action at the end of Rom.

7:24, 25 This body of death: The figure is of a person chained to a corpse from which he cannot be freed, despairing of deliverance. But despair gives way to a declaration of victory, not because the struggle ceases, but because human strength is exceeded by the power of the Holy Spirit.

8:1–11 See section 5 of Truth-In-Action at the end of Rom.

8:1–11 Paul begins a description of life in the **Spirit.** He first declares that the Spirit assures victory and makes holiness possible.

8:1 Therefore: Because of the fact of salvation by faith alone, explained in 3:21—7:25, but especially picking up the major outline of Christ's redemptive work in 3:21–26 and 5:6–21, Christians are free from God's banishing judgment.

2 For [a]the law of [b]the Spirit of life in
Christ Jesus has **made** me **free** from
[c]the law of sin and death.

WORD WEALTH

8:2 made free, *eleutheroo* (el-yoo-ther-*ah*-oh); Strong's *#1659:* To liberate, acquit, set free, deliver. In the NT the word is used exclusively for Jesus' setting believers at liberty from the dominion of sin.

KINGDOM DYNAMICS

8:2 Names/Symbols of the Holy Spirit, SPIRITUAL GIFTS. The Holy Spirit is given several different names and symbols in Scripture. In this chapter, He is referred to as the Spirit of life (v. 2), the Spirit of God (v. 9), the Spirit of Christ (v. 9), and the Spirit of adoption (v. 15). An elaboration of this and related themes appears in the study article on page 2018, "Holy Spirit Gifts and Power."

(Acts 19:2/Rom. 12:6–8) P.W.

3 For [a]what the law could not do in
that it was weak through the flesh,
[b]God *did* by sending His own Son in
the likeness of sinful *flesh, on account
of sin: He condemned sin in the flesh,
4 that the righteous requirement of
the law might be fulfilled in us who
[a]do not walk according to the flesh but
according to the Spirit.
5 For [a]those who live according to the
flesh set their minds on the things of
the flesh, but those *who live* according
to the Spirit, [b]the things of the Spirit.
6 For [a]to be [1]carnally minded *is*
death, but to be spiritually minded *is*
life and peace.
7 Because [a]the [1]carnal mind *is* enmity 3
against God; for it is not *subject to
the law of God, [b]nor indeed can be.
8 So then, those who are in the flesh
cannot please God.
9 But you are not in the flesh but in
the *Spirit, if indeed the Spirit of God
dwells in you. Now if anyone does not
have the Spirit of Christ, he is not His.
10 And if Christ *is* in you, the body *is*
dead because of sin, but the Spirit *is*
life because of righteousness.
11 But if the Spirit of [a]Him who raised
Jesus from the dead dwells in you,
[b]He who raised Christ from the dead
will also give life to your mortal bodies
[1]through His Spirit who dwells in you.

Sonship Through the Spirit

12 [a]Therefore, brethren, we are *debtors—not to the flesh, to live according
to the flesh.
13 For [a]if you live according to the 5
flesh you will die; but if by the Spirit
you [b]put to death the deeds of the
body, you will live.
14 For [a]as many as are led by the Spirit
of God, these are sons of God.

2 [a]Rom. 6:18, 22 [b][1 Cor. 15:45] [c]Rom. 7:24, 25 **3** [a]Acts 13:39; [Heb. 7:18] [b][2 Cor. 5:21; Gal. 3:13] *See WW at Matt. 26:41. **4** [a][Rom. 6:4; 2 Cor. 5:7]; Gal. 5:16, 25; Eph. 4:1; 5:2, 15; [1 John 1:7; 2:6] **5** [a]John 3:6 [b][Gal. 5:22–25] **6** [a]Gal. 6:8 [1]*fleshly* **7** [a]James 4:4 [b]1 Cor. 2:14 [1]*fleshly* *See WW at 1 Cor. 14:32. **9** *See WW at Rom. 7:6. **11** [a]Acts 2:24; Rom. 6:4 [b]1 Cor. 6:14 [1]Or *because of* **12** [a][Rom. 6:7, 14] *See WW at Luke 13:4. **13** [a]Gal. 6:8 [b]Eph. 4:22; [Col. 3:5–10] **14** [a][Gal. 5:18]

8:2 The law here does not refer to God's written moral commands in the OT (as in 7:12), but to the system of operation that the **Spirit of life,** the Holy Spirit, carries out in our lives, breaking the dominion of the old **law** [principle] **of sin and death.**
8:3 Though given by God, **the law** (the written code in the OT) was powerless to enable people to meet its demands because it had to depend on sinful human nature to carry them out. **In the likeness of sinful flesh:** The human nature of Jesus was real, but sinless (see Phil. 2:7, 8; Heb. 2:17; 4:15; 1 Pet. 2:22).
8:4 Paul presents two ways of life, and they are central to the whole discussion until v. 17. To **walk according to the flesh** is to follow the sinful desires of one's old life. To walk **according to the Spirit** is to follow the desires of the Holy Spirit, to live in a way pleasing to Him.
8:5 Paul expects that Christians ordinarily will live **according to the Spirit.** This involves holiness, not only in actions and words, but also in the thoughts that fill our minds each moment through the day.
8:7, 8 See section 3 of Truth-In-Action at the end of Rom.
8:8 Those who are in the flesh characterizes people's very nature and is a stronger description than the activity of walking according to the flesh. The phrase therefore refers to unbelievers who **cannot please God.** This situation is not true of believers, as the following verse shows.
8:9 He is not His: All Christians have the Holy Spirit within them. Anyone who does not have the Holy Spirit within is not a Christian. Though Paul says that Christians are **in the Spirit,** he also warns that they can from time to time live "according to the flesh" (v. 13).
8:12 To live according to the flesh: See note on v. 4. Although Paul does not state it, the implication is that we are debtors to the Spirit, to live according to the Spirit.
8:13–17 See section 5 of Truth-In-Action at the end of Rom.
8:13 See note on 6:16. Paul lays out two directions of life and shows their ultimate consequences. He implies that Christians have an ability to choose to do what is uncharacteristic of a Christian, namely, to walk "according to the flesh," and he warns them not to do it. **If by the Spirit you put to death the deeds of the body:** A good summary of the process of sanctification (growth in holiness) in the Christian life. We are actively to work at growing in holiness and "putting to death" any sin in our hearts or minds, as well as in our words and deeds. Yet, in spite of the fact that we actively put forth effort, Paul reminds us that it is only "by the Spirit," that is, by the Holy Spirit's power, that we can succeed.
8:14 The phrase **as many as are led by the Spirit of God** is more than a synonym for Christians. It describes the lifestyle of those who are **sons of God.** Paul is giving encouragement *not* to live according to the flesh *but* to put to death the deeds of the body (v. 13). Therefore, being "led by the Spirit of God" involves progressively putting to death the sinful appetites of the lower nature. This implies that, while all Christians are in some general sense being "led by the Spirit of God," there are increasing degrees of being led by the Spirit. The more fully people are led by the Holy Spirit, the more completely will they be obedient to God and be conformed to His holy standards.

Since the Greek word translated **led** is a present participle, it may be translated, "as many as are *continually being led*

15 For [a]you did not receive the spirit of bondage again [b]to *fear, but you received the [c]Spirit of adoption by whom we cry out, [d]"Abba,[1] Father."

16 [a]The Spirit Himself bears witness with our spirit that we are children of God,

17 and if children, then [a]heirs*—heirs of God and joint heirs with Christ, [b]if indeed we suffer with *Him,* that we may also be glorified together.

From Suffering to Glory

18 For I *consider that [a]the sufferings of this present time are not worthy *to be compared* with the *glory which shall be revealed in us.

19 For [a]the earnest expectation of the *creation eagerly waits for the revealing of the sons of God.

20 For [a]the creation was subjected to futility, not willingly, but because of Him who subjected *it* in hope;

21 because the creation itself also will be *delivered from the bondage of [1]corruption into the glorious [a]liberty* of the children of God.

15 [a]Heb. 2:15 [b]2 Tim. 1:7 [c][Is. 56:5] [d]Mark 14:36 [1]Lit., in Aram., *Father* *See WW at 1 John 4:18. **16** [a]Eph. 1:13 **17** [a]Acts 26:18 [b]Phil. 1:29 *See WW at Heb. 11:9. **18** [a]2 Cor. 4:17 *See WW at Rom. 4:3. • See WW at John 2:11. **19** [a][2 Pet. 3:13] *See WW at Col. 1:15. **20** [a]Gen. 3:17–19 **21** [a][2 Cor. 3:17] [1]*decay* *See WW at Rom. 8:2. • See WW at 1 Cor. 10:29. **22** [a]Jer. 12:4, 11 **23** [a]2 Cor. 5:5 [b]2 Cor. 5:2, 4 [c][Luke 20:36] [d]Eph. 1:14; 4:30 *See WW at Rom. 3:24.

22 For we know that the whole creation [a]groans and labors with birth pangs together until now.

23 Not only *that,* but we also who have [a]the firstfruits of the Spirit, [b]even we ourselves groan [c]within ourselves, eagerly waiting for the adoption, the [d]redemption* of our body.

24 For we were saved in this hope, but [a]hope that is seen is not hope; for why does one still hope for what he sees?

25 But if we hope for what we do not see, we eagerly wait for *it* with perseverance.

26 Likewise the Spirit also helps in our weaknesses. For [a]we do not know what we should *pray for as we ought, but [b]the Spirit Himself makes intercession [1]for us with groanings which cannot be uttered.

27 Now [a]He who searches the hearts knows what the mind of the Spirit *is,* because He makes *intercession for the

24 [a]Heb. 11:1 **26** [a]Matt. 20:22 [b]Eph. 6:18 [1]NU omits *for us* *See WW at Matt. 6:6. **27** [a]1 Chr. 28:9 *See WW at Heb. 7:25.

by the Spirit of God." This leading is not to be restricted to objective knowledge of the commands of Scripture and conscious effort to obey them (though it most certainly includes that). Rather, it more fully includes the subjective factor of being sensitive to the promptings of the Holy Spirit throughout the day, promptings that if genuinely from the Holy Spirit will never encourage us to act contrary to Scripture.

What one perceives to be a subjective leading of the Holy Spirit, especially in major decisions or promptings for "unusual" actions, should be subjected to the confirmation of several counselors (Prov. 11:14; 24:6) to help guard against mistakes and to help get a clear picture of Scripture's objective standards.

8:15, 16 The Holy Spirit grants us subjective assurance **that we are children of God. Abba** is the Aramaic word for **Father.**

8:17–30 The Spirit guarantees glory.

8:17 Scripture often indicates that God leads His children through suffering before they reach His glory.

8:18 In us may also be translated "to us."

8:19 Physical **creation** will be redeemed at the consummation of our redemption (see v. 21).

8:20 The whole created universe has suffered the consequences of human sin, being **subjected** to decomposition, futility and corruption. However, that process of deterioration is only temporary, because God has provided **hope** of deliverance.

8:21 At the time of our final redemption (v. 23), **creation itself** will be set free from enslavement to decay and will share our glory.

8:23** Just as* ***the firstfruits *of a harvest are a pledge of* the full crop to come, the Holy Spirit is the pledge of our full adoption as God's children, when our bodies are redeemed. The metaphor also suggests that the Holy Spirit is the foretaste of the life to come (see Eph. 1:14). We **groan** because although our souls are saved, our bodies are still subject to pain and sin. However, we look forward with hope (v. 24) to our resurrection bodies, which will be free from physical frailty and indwelling sin (see 1 Cor. 15:50–54).

8:26 The Greek word translated **helps** is used in Luke 10:40, where Martha wants Mary to come and *help* her. The word does not indicate that the Holy Spirit prays *instead of* us, but that the Holy Spirit takes part *with* us and makes our weak prayers effective. Some interpret the **groanings** as those uttered by the Holy Spirit, since the text says that He uses these groanings to make intercession. Others see Paul referring to our "groanings" in prayer, since: 1) v. 23 says that "we ourselves groan"; 2) such "groanings," which seem to imply a degree of distress or anguish, are appropriate for creatures (vv. 22, 23), but not for the Creator; 3) this sentence explains the first sentence in v. 26, which says that the Spirit "helps" us, not that the Spirit replaces our prayers.

The expression **which cannot be uttered** does not necessarily mean "silent," but can rather mean "not able to be put into words."

If v. 26 refers to "groanings" of the Holy Spirit, which we cannot hear, then the verse simply gives encouragement that the Holy Spirit prays for us and adds effective prayer when we do not pray effectively. But if, as seems more likely, the verse refers to our "groanings" in prayer, then it means that those sighs, groans, loud "cries and tears" (Heb. 5:7), and other expressions of our hearts and spirits in prayer are taken by the Holy Spirit and made into effectual intercession before the throne of God.

Paul is speaking in this verse about the prayer life of Christians generally, and is not specifically discussing the question of speaking in tongues. But there are similarities between speaking in tongues and the activity Paul describes here, for speaking in tongues is often prayer or praise in syllables the speaker does not himself understand (1 Cor. 14:2), and both kinds of speech are made effective by the Holy Spirit (Acts 2:4; 1 Cor. 12:10, 11; 14:15; Eph. 6:18; Jude 20).

saints [b]according to *the will of* God.
28 And we know that all things *work
together for *good to those who love
God, to those [a]who are the called according to *His* **purpose.**

WORD WEALTH

8:28 purpose, *prothesis* (*proth*-es-is); Strong's *#4286:* From *pro,* "before," and *thesis,* "a place," thus "a setting forth." The word suggests a deliberate plan, a proposition, an advance plan, an intention, a design. Of 12 occurrences in the NT, *prothesis* is used 4 times for the Levitical showbread (literally "the bread of setting before"). Most of the other usages point to God's eternal purposes relating to salvation. Our personal salvation was not only well planned but demonstrates God's abiding faithfulness as He awaits the consummation of His great plan for His church.

29 For whom [a]He foreknew, [b]He also
predestined [c]*to be* conformed to the
image of His Son, [d]that He might be
the firstborn among many brethren.
30 Moreover whom He predestined,
these He also [a]called;* whom He
called, these He also [b]justified; and
whom He *justified, these He also
[c]glorified.

God's Everlasting Love

31 What then shall we say to these
things? [a]If God *is* for us, who *can be*
against us?
32 [a]He who did not spare His own Son,
but [b]delivered Him up for us all, how
shall He not with Him also freely *give
us all things?
33 Who shall bring a charge against
God's *elect? [a]*It is* God who justifies.
34 [a]Who *is* he who condemns? *It is*
Christ who died, and furthermore is
also risen, [b]who is even at the right
hand of God, [c]who also makes *intercession for us.
35 Who shall separate us from the love
of Christ? *Shall* tribulation, or distress,
or persecution, or famine, or nakedness, or peril, or sword?
36 As it is written:

> [a]*"For Your sake we are killed all*
> *day long;*
> *We are accounted as sheep for the*
> *slaughter."*

37 [a]Yet in all these things we are **more
than conquerors** through Him who
loved us.

WORD WEALTH

8:37 more than conquerors, *hupernikao* (hoop-er-nik-*ah*-oh); Strong's *#5245:* From *huper,* "over and above," and *nikao,* "to conquer." The word describes one who is super victorious, who wins more than an ordinary victory, but who is overpowering in achieving abundant victory. This is not the language of conceit, but of confidence. Christ's love conquered death, and because of His love, we are *hupernikao.*

38 For I am *persuaded that neither
death nor life, nor *angels nor [a]prin-

27 [b]1 John 5:14
28 [a]2 Tim. 1:9 *See WW at James 2:22. • See WW at Phil. 1:6.
29 [a]2 Tim. 2:19 [b]Eph. 1:5, 11 [c][2 Cor. 3:18] [d]Heb. 1:6
30 [a][1 Pet. 2:9; 3:9] [b][Gal. 2:16] [c]John 17:22 *See WW at Gal. 1:6. • See WW at Matt. 12:37.
31 [a]Num. 14:9
32 [a]Rom. 5:6, 10 [b][Rom. 4:25] *See WW at Col. 3:13.
33 [a]Is. 50:8, 9 *See WW at 1 Pet. 2:9.
34 [a]John 3:18 [b]Mark 16:19 [c]Heb. 7:25; 9:24 *See WW at Heb. 7:25.
36 [a]Ps. 44:22
37 [a]1 Cor. 15:57
38 [a][Eph. 1:21] *See WW at 2 Thess. 3:4. • See WW at Matt. 4:11.

8:28 Even in hardship and suffering, even in bitter disappointments, even when wrongly treated, Christians can know that God will work amidst such situations to fulfill His good **purpose** in His children. The situation may or may not be directly changed by God, but even if situations stay difficult God guarantees ultimate good results, including maturation of character **to those who are the called.** (Note: The certainties of this verse must be kept in union with the responsible participation into which we enter with the Holy Spirit, described in vv. 26, 27.)

8:29, 30 The conjunction **for** introduces the reason for the assurance of v. 28. Paul looks to eternity past and sees that God's purpose for His people has only been good: He **foreknew** and **predestined** believers to be like Christ. Then he looks to the recent past and sees that God **called** and **justified** His people. Finally, Paul looks to the distant future and finds that God's plan is to glorify, that is, to give a resurrection body to all who have been justified. (**Glorified** is used as a "prophetic perfect," speaking of a future event as if it were already done, because it is certain that God will do it.)

But if in eternity past, if in the recent past, and if in the distant future all of God's purposes for His people have only been good, then Paul concludes that His purposes at the present time, even in hardship, must also be only good for His people.

Foreknew: Not just that God knew that we would exist, or knew some fact about us, because it is *persons* whom God foreknew. It may be paraphrased, "those whom God thought of in a personal, saving relationship." **Predestined:** Planned that they would ultimately be like Christ, **conformed to the image of His Son.** These two verses outline a sequence of events and indicate that everyone who has begun the sequence will complete it.

8:31–39 Paul defiantly and triumphantly raises five unanswerable questions designed to give believers a profound assurance of spiritual security.

8:34 It *is* Christ who will be the Judge over all the Earth, but He will not condemn us, and even now He **makes intercession** [brings requests to God the Father] **for us.**

8:35–39 For any Christian who is discouraged this powerful passage gives assurance of Christ's *present* **love,** active at *every moment* in the Christian's life. Are any causes of discouragement greater than those Paul mentions? And if not, then we are never in this life separated from Christ's love. Even in hardships we can be **more than conquerors** (v. 37).

cipalities nor powers, nor things present nor things to come,
39 nor height nor depth, nor any *other
created thing, shall be able to separate
us from the love of God which is in
Christ Jesus our Lord.

Israel's Rejection of Christ

9 I [a]tell the *truth in Christ, I am not
lying, my conscience also bearing
me witness in the Holy Spirit,
2 [a]that I have great sorrow and continual grief in my heart.
3 For [a]I could wish that I myself were
*accursed from Christ for my brethren,
my [1]countrymen according to the flesh,
4 who are Israelites, [a]to whom *pertain* the adoption, [b]the glory, [c]the *covenants, [d]the giving of the law, [e]the service *of God,* and [f]the promises;
5 [a]of whom *are* the fathers and from
[b]whom, according to the flesh, Christ
came, [c]who is over all, *the* eternally
blessed God. Amen.

Israel's Rejection and God's Purpose

6 [a]But it is not that the word of God
has taken no effect. For [b]they *are* not
all Israel who *are* of Israel,
7 [a]nor *are they* all children because
they are the seed of Abraham; but,
[b]*"In Isaac your seed shall be called."*
8 That is, those who *are* the children
of the flesh, these *are* not the children
of God; but [a]the children of the promise are counted as the seed.
9 For this *is* the word of promise:
[a]*"At this time I will come and Sarah
shall have a son."*
10 And not only *this,* but when [a]Re-
becca also had conceived by one man,
even by our father Isaac
11 (for *the children* not yet being born,
nor having done any good or evil, that
the *purpose of God according to election might stand, not of works but of
[a]Him who calls),
12 it was said to her, [a]*"The older shall
serve the younger."*
13 As it is written, [a]*"Jacob I have
loved, but Esau I have hated."*

Israel's Rejection and God's Justice

14 What shall we say then? [a]*Is there*
unrighteousness with God? Certainly
not!
15 For He says to Moses, [a]*"I will **have
mercy** on whomever I will have mercy,
and I will have compassion on whomever I will have compassion."*

WORD WEALTH

9:15 have mercy, *eleeo* (el-eh-*eh*-oh); Strong's *#1653:* Compare "eleemosynary," those supported by charities. To show kindness and concern for someone in serious need, feel compassion for, have pity. Those who take care of the sick are called *eleeo,* or showers of mercy. In the NT the word is often used of Christ's gracious faithfulness and proof of His benevolence. Mercy is not merely a passive emotion, but an active desire to remove the cause of distress in others.

16 So then *it is* not of him who wills,
nor of him who runs, but of God who
shows mercy.
17 For [a]the Scripture says to the Pharaoh, [b]*"For this very purpose I have
raised you up, that I may show My
power in you, and that My name may
be declared in all the earth."*
18 Therefore He has mercy on whom
He wills, and whom He wills He
[a]hardens.
19 You will say to me then, "Why does
He still find fault? For [a]who has *resisted His will?"
20 But indeed, O man, who are you to

39 *See WW at Acts 4:12

CHAPTER 9

1 [a]2 Cor. 1:23 *See WW at John 4:24.
2 [a]Rom. 10:1
3 [a]Ex. 32:32 [1]Or *relatives* *See WW at 1 Cor. 12:3.
4 [a]Ex. 4:22; [Rom. 8:15] [b]1 Sam. 4:21 [c]Gen. 17:2; Deut. 29:14; Luke 1:72; Acts 3:25 [d]Deut. 4:13; Ps. 147:19 [e]Heb. 9:1, 6 [f][Acts 2:39; 13:32; Eph. 2:12] *See WW at Mark 14:24.
5 [a]Deut. 10:15 [b][Luke 1:34, 35; 3:23] [c]Jer. 23:6
6 [a]Num. 23:19 [b][John 8:39; Gal. 6:16]
7 [a][John 8:33, 39; Gal. 4:23] [b]Gen. 21:12; Heb. 11:18
8 [a]Gal. 4:28
9 [a]Gen. 18:10, 14; Heb. 11:11
10 [a]Gen. 25:21
11 [a][Rom. 4:17; 8:28] *See WW at Rom. 8:28.
12 [a]Gen. 25:23
13 [a]Mal. 1:2, 3
14 [a]Deut. 32:4
15 [a]Ex. 33:19
17 [a]Gal. 3:8 [b]Ex. 9:16
18 [a]Ex. 4:21; Deut. 2:30; Josh. 11:20; John 12:40; Rom. 11:7, 25
19 [a]2 Chr. 20:6; Job 9:12; Dan. 4:35 *See WW at Eph. 6:13.

9:1—11:36 Can God be just, even if so many of God's Old Covenant nation, the Jews, are lost? After this long demonstration of the way God's righteousness is preserved in the gospel, and yet sinners can still be saved, another question arises: How can we say that God is righteous or just if, according to the gospel, one must trust in Christ in order to be saved? This would mean that many Jews who have not trusted Christ are lost. But then how could God be true to His promises to the Jews as His people? Paul answers this question in chs. 9—11.
9:2 Paul expresses genuine sorrow over the unbelief of the Jews. See Ezek. 33:11; Matt. 23:37–39.
9:3 Paul does not actually wish that he was cut off from Christ so that other Jews would be saved, but his grief for them is so deep that it brings him virtually to that very point.
9:11 God's choice of Jacob instead of Esau was not based on anything either had done or would do in the future. This is the mystery of divine election.
9:14–18 God is never unjust in dealing with people. As sovereign Creator, He has the right to deal with people according to His will, whether it is in the exercise of His **compassion** (vv. 14–16) or in the exercise of His wrath (vv. 17, 18).
9:19 Paul anticipates this common objection to his teaching in the previous verse. If God chooses to have mercy on "whom He wills" and to harden the heart of "whom He wills" (v. 18), and if His choice is ultimately only based on the "purpose of God" (v. 11), then how can it be fair for God to judge those who refuse to believe?
9:20, 21 To question the morality of God's actions is incongruous. Creatures have no right to object to what their Creator does. However, such teaching should never lead

reply against God? [a]Will the thing
formed say to him who formed *it*,
"Why have you made me like this?"
21 Does not the [a]potter have power
over the clay, from the same lump to
make [b]one vessel for honor and another for dishonor?
22 *What* if God, wanting to show *His*
wrath and to make His power known,
endured with much *longsuffering
[a]the vessels of wrath [b]prepared* for
destruction,
23 and that He might make known
[a]the riches of His glory on the vessels
of mercy, which He had [b]prepared beforehand for glory,
24 *even* us whom He [a]called, [b]not of
the Jews only, but also of the Gentiles?
25 As He says also in Hosea:

[a]"I will call them My people, who
were not My people,
And her beloved, who was not
beloved."
26 *"And[a] it shall come to pass in the*
place where it was said to them,
'You are not My people,'
There they shall be called sons of
the living God."

27 Isaiah also cries out concerning
Israel:

[a]"Though the number of the
children of Israel be as the sand
of the sea,
[b]The remnant will be saved.
28 *For [1]He will finish the work and*
cut it short in righteousness,
[a]Because the LORD *will make a*
short work upon the earth."

29 And as Isaiah said before:

[a]"Unless the LORD *of [1]Sabaoth had*
left us a seed,

20 [a]Is. 29:16
21 [a]Prov. 16:4 [b]2 Tim. 2:20
22 [a][1 Thess. 5:9] [b][1 Pet. 2:8] *See WW at Heb. 6:12. • See WW at Heb. 11:3.
23 [a][Col. 1:27] [b][Rom. 8:28–30]
24 [a][Rom. 8:28] [b]Rom. 3:29
25 [a]Hos. 2:23
26 [a]Hos. 1:10
27 [a]Is. 10:22, 23 [b]Rom. 11:5
28 [a]Is. 10:23; 28:22 [1]NU *the* LORD *will finish the work and cut it short upon the earth*
29 [a]Is. 1:9 [b]Is. 13:19 [1]Lit., in Heb., *Hosts*
30 [a]Rom. 4:11 [b]Rom. 1:17; 3:21; 10:6 *See WW at John 1:5.
31 [a][Rom. 10:2–4] [b][Gal. 5:4] [1]NU omits *of righteousness*
32 [a][1 Cor. 1:23] [1]NU *by works,* omitting *of the law*
33 [a]Is. 8:14; 28:16 [b]Rom. 5:5; 10:11

CHAPTER 10

1 [1]NU *them*
2 [a]Acts 21:20
3 [a][Rom. 1:17] [b][Phil. 3:9] *See WW at 1 Cor. 14:32.
4 [a][Gal. 3:24; 4:5]
5 [a]Lev. 18:5

[b]We would have become like
Sodom,
And we would have been made
like Gomorrah."

Present Condition of Israel

30 What shall we say then? [a]That Gentiles, who did not pursue righteousness, have *attained to righteousness, [b]even the righteousness of
faith;
31 but Israel, [a]pursuing the law of righteousness, [b]has not attained to the law
[1]of righteousness.
32 Why? Because *they did* not *seek it*
by faith, but as it were, [1]by the works
of the law. For [a]they stumbled at that
stumbling stone.
33 As it is written:

[a]"Behold, I lay in Zion a stumbling
stone and rock of offense,
And [b]whoever believes on Him
will not be put to shame."

Israel Needs the Gospel

10 Brethren, my heart's desire and
prayer to God for [1]Israel is that
they may be saved.
2 For I bear them witness [a]that they
have a zeal for God, but not according
to knowledge.
3 For they being ignorant of [a]God's
righteousness, and seeking to establish
their own [b]righteousness, have not
*submitted to the righteousness of
God.
4 For [a]Christ *is* the end of the law for
righteousness to everyone who believes.
5 For Moses writes about the righteousness which is of the law, *[a]"The*
man who does those things shall live
by them."

---

us to think that sinners *could not* believe if they wanted to, for Scripture does not teach that. It repeatedly affirms that "whoever calls on the name of the LORD shall be saved" (10:13). This appeal of Scripture to unbelievers is consistent throughout both the OT and NT (see Ezek. 33:11; John 6:37).

9:22, 23 God exercises His sovereignty in abundant **mercy,** not in strict justice. His longsuffering patience with Israel proves His willingness to save and confirms the fact that the nation's failure was not His fault.

9:24–26 God's mercy is also evident in His dealings with **the Gentiles.** To support his teaching that not all who are called to become "vessels of mercy" (v. 23) belong to physical Israel, Paul quotes from Hos. 2:23 and 1:10. In their original setting the verses refer to the restoration of sinful Israel to God. Paul sees in them the inclusion of the Gentiles (see 1 Pet. 2:10), indicating that there is a spiritual Israel (the church) beyond a national Israel (see Gal. 6:16).

9:27–29 Paul quotes from Is. 10:22, 23 and 1:9 to confirm that God in His mercy has preserved a **remnant** of physical Israel. Had He not done so the entire apostate nation would have been wiped out.

9:32 The **stumbling stone** is Jesus Christ, the Messiah (see 1 Pet. 2:6–8), who offers salvation by faith, not works, and thus requires that human pride be humbled.

10:3 God's righteousness, that is, right standing with Him, comes through faith in Christ alone.

10:4 Some interpret **Christ** to be **the end of the law** in the sense that He is the goal or fulfillment of the law. However, "law" here refers to the system of earning righteousness in one's own strength. Christ indeed is the perfect fulfillment of everything the law requires, but He also put an end to the law as a way of achieving righteousness for **everyone who believes.** Thus, Paul emphasizes the sufficiency of faith in receiving the righteousness of God because in fulfilling the law's demands, Christ terminated its claim. The verse does not mean that a Christian may ignore God's moral standards or commandments (see note on 6:14).

6 But the righteousness of faith
speaks in this way, [a]*"Do not say in
your heart, 'Who will ascend into
heaven?'" (that is, to bring Christ
down *from above*)
7 or, [a]*"'Who will descend into the
abyss?'"* (that is, to bring Christ up
from the dead).
8 But what does it say? [a]*"The word
is near you, in your mouth and in your
heart"* (that is, the word of faith which
we *preach):
9 that [a]if you confess with your
mouth the Lord Jesus and **believe** in
your heart that God has raised Him
from the dead, you will be saved.
10 For with the *heart one believes
unto righteousness, and with the
mouth confession is made unto
salvation.

WORD WEALTH

10:9 believe, *pisteuo* (pist-*yoo*-oh); Strong's *#4100:* The verb form of *pistis,* "faith." It means to trust in, have faith in, be fully convinced of, acknowledge, rely on. *Pisteuo* is more than credence in church doctrines or articles of faith. It expresses reliance upon and a personal trust that produces obedience. It includes submission and a positive confession of the lordship of Jesus.

KINGDOM DYNAMICS

10:9, 10 Continuing in Faith As We Have Begun, FAITH'S CONFESSION. Here is the most foundational lesson in the importance and power of faith's confession found anywhere in the Bible. The principle is established at the very beginning of our life in Christ. Just as salvation (God's righteous working in our behalf) is appropriated by heart belief and spoken confession, so His continuing working in our lives is advanced by the same means.

The word "confess" (Greek *homologeo*) has the connotation of "a binding public declaration by which a legal relation is contractually established" (Kittel). Thus, as our words "contract" from our side the salvation God has fully provided from His by Christ's saving work and power, so we have a principle for all of life. Beginning in this spirit of saving faith, let us grow in active faith—believing in God's mighty power for all our needs, speaking with our lips what our hearts receive and believe of the many promises in His Word. Let us accept God's "contracts" for all our need by endowing them with our confessed belief—just as when we were saved.

(Acts 4:33/1 Cor. 11:23–26) R.H.

6 [a]Deut. 30:12–14 *See WW at Rev. 21:1. **7** [a]Deut. 30:13 **8** [a]Deut. 30:14 *See WW at Acts 9:20. **9** [a]Matt. 10:32; Luke 12:8; Acts 8:37; Rom. 14:9; [1 Cor. 12:3]; Phil. 2:11 **10** *See WW at Rev. 2:23.

11 [a]Is. 28:16; Jer. 17:7; Rom. 9:33 **12** [a]Acts 15:9; Rom. 3:22, 29; Gal. 3:28 [b]Acts 10:36; 1 Tim. 2:5 [c]Eph. 1:7 **13** [a]Joel 2:32; Acts 2:21 [b]Acts 9:14 *See WW at John 12:13. **14** [a]Acts 8:31; Titus 1:3 **15** [a]Is. 52:7; Nah. 1:15 [1]NU omits *preach the gospel of peace, Who* *See WW at John 20:21.

11 For the Scripture says, [a]*"Whoever
believes on Him will not be put to
shame."*
12 For [a]there is no distinction between
Jew and Greek, for [b]the same Lord
over all [c]is rich to all who call upon
Him.
13 For [a]*"whoever calls* [b]*on the *name
of the* LORD *shall be saved."*

Israel Rejects the Gospel

14 How then shall they call on Him in
whom they have not believed? And
how shall they believe in Him of whom
they have not heard? And how shall
they hear [a]without a preacher?
15 And how shall they preach unless
they are *sent? As it is written:

> [a]*"How beautiful are the feet of*
> *those who* [1]*preach the gospel of*
> *peace,*
> *Who bring glad tidings of good*
> *things!"*

KINGDOM DYNAMICS

10:13–15 The Absolute Need for a Messenger, WORLD EVANGELISM. Paul asks, "How shall they hear without a preacher?" (v. 14). This does not mean we must enter public ministry to "preach" the gospel. The Greek word used here for "preacher" means "one who heralds, proclaims, or publishes." Clearly, every believer is assigned a personal "pulpit"—in the home, the community, at the office, or in school—from which to show and tell others the Good News.

In 1:14 Paul declares, "I am a debtor," pointedly noting his sense of obligation. Why? He answers in Eph. 2: Man is dead, needing life (v. 1); man is walking a course of destruction, needing deliverance (v. 12); man is hopeless, needing God (v. 13); man is separated from God, needing Christ (v. 14). Jesus concludes the evidence of man's need: he is lost, needing to be found (Luke 19:10). The answer is here: someone must be sent

10:6–8 Paul asserts that **the righteousness of faith** does not demand human merit or effort. Christ has already achieved all that is necessary for our salvation.
10:9, 10 Oral confession declares, confirms, and seals the belief in the **heart.**
10:11–15 The gospel is universal in its application and demands a universal proclamation.

to preach so that people hear and believe.
There is no other way.
(Rom. 3:23/2 Cor. 10:15, 16) G.C.

16 But they have not all *obeyed the
gospel. For Isaiah says, [a]*"LORD, who
has believed our report?"*
2 17 So then faith *comes* by hearing, and
hearing by the word of God.
18 But I say, have they not heard? Yes
indeed:

> [a]*"Their sound has gone out to all*
> *the earth,*
> [b]*And their words to the ends of the*
> *world."*

19 But I say, did Israel not know? First
Moses says:

> [a]*"I will provoke you to jealousy by*
> *those who are not a nation,*
> *I will move you to anger by a*
> [b]*foolish nation."*

20 But Isaiah is very bold and says:

> [a]*"I was found by those who did not*
> *seek Me;*
> *I was made manifest to those who*
> *did not ask for Me."*

21 But to Israel he says:

> [a]*"All day long I have stretched out*
> *My hands*
> *To a disobedient and contrary*
> *people."*

Israel's Rejection Not Total

11 I say then, [a]has God cast away
His people? [b]Certainly not! For
[c]I also am an Israelite, of the seed of
Abraham, *of* the tribe of Benjamin.
2 God has not cast away His people
whom [a]He foreknew. Or do you not
know what the Scripture says of Elijah,

16 [a]Is. 53:1; John 12:38 *See WW at Rom. 6:17. **18** [a]Ps. 19:4; Matt. 24:14; Mark 16:15; Rom. 1:8; Col. 1:6, 23; 1 Thess. 1:8 [b]1 Kin. 18:10; Matt. 4:8 **19** [a]Deut. 32:21; Rom. 11:11 [b]Titus 3:3 **20** [a]Is. 65:1; Rom. 9:30 **21** [a]Is. 65:2

CHAPTER 11

1 [a]Ps. 94:14; Jer. 46:28 [b]1 Sam. 12:22; Jer. 31:37 [c]2 Cor. 11:22; Phil. 3:5 **2** [a][Rom. 8:29] *See WW at Heb. 7:25. **3** [a]1 Kin. 19:10, 14 **4** [a]1 Kin. 19:18 **5** [a]2 Kin. 19:4; Rom. 9:27 **6** [a]Rom. 4:4 [1]NU omits the rest of v. 6. *See WW at John 9:4. **7** [a]Rom. 9:31 [b]Mark 6:52; Rom. 9:18; 11:25; 2 Cor. 3:14 *See WW at Mark 8:17. **8** [a]Is. 29:10, 13 [b]Deut. 29:3, 4; Is. 6:9; Matt. 13:13, 14; John 12:40; Acts 28:26, 27 **9** [a]Ps. 69:22, 23 *See WW at Matt. 16:23. **11** [a]Is. 42:6, 7; Acts 28:28 [b]Deut. 32:21; Acts 13:46; Rom. 10:19 [1]*trespass* **12** [1]*trespass*

how he *pleads with God against Israel, saying,
3 [a]*"LORD, they have killed Your
prophets and torn down Your altars,
and I alone am left, and they seek my
life"*?
4 But what does the divine response
say to him? [a]*"I have reserved for Myself seven thousand men who have not
bowed the knee to Baal."*
5 [a]Even so then, at this present time
there is a remnant according to the
election of grace.
6 And [a]if by grace, then *it is* no longer
of *works; otherwise grace is no longer
grace. [1]But if *it is* of works, it is no
longer grace; otherwise work is no
longer work.
7 What then? [a]Israel has not obtained
what it seeks; but the elect have obtained it, and the rest were [b]blinded.*
8 Just as it is written:

> [a]*"God has given them a spirit of*
> *stupor,*
> [b]*Eyes that they should not see*
> *And ears that they should not*
> *hear,*
> *To this very day."*

9 And David says:

> [a]*"Let their table become a snare*
> *and a trap,*
> *A *stumbling block and a*
> *recompense to them.*
> 10 *Let their eyes be darkened, so*
> *that they do not see,*
> *And bow down their back*
> *always."*

Israel's Rejection Not Final

11 I say then, have they stumbled that
they should fall? Certainly not! But
[a]through their [1]fall, to provoke them
to [b]jealousy, salvation *has come* to the
Gentiles.
12 Now if their [1]fall *is* riches for the

10:16–21 Israel can plead neither ignorance of the gospel (vv. 16–18) nor that God has been unjust with them (vv. 19–21).
10:17 See section 2 of Truth-In-Action at the end of Rom.
10:17 In God's ordinary means of operating, people do not come to saving faith unless they either read the Bible or have someone tell them the gospel message that is in it. It is the **word of God** that the Holy Spirit uses to awaken a response of faith within us, and it is the reliability of the Word of God on which we rest our faith for salvation. The words of Scripture are the words of eternal life (see James 1:18; 1 Pet. 1:23). This is why preaching the gospel is absolutely necessary (see v. 14).
11:1–6 Paul points to himself as an example of the fact that there is a saved remnant in Israel.
11:7–10 **Israel** refers to the majority of those who are Jews by physical descent, including their recognized leadership. Having failed to obtain the right standing with God they had sought by their own efforts, they have been hardened. Persistent and obstinate unbelief brought God's judgment upon them.
11:11 The unbelief of Israel has opened the door of opportunity for the **Gentiles.** God's purpose is that when unbelieving Jews see many Gentiles turn to Christ they will become jealous and will repent and come to faith.
11:12 Paul begins a theme that will return in vv. 15, 23, 24, 25, and 26: God has planned that in the future there will be a massive ingathering of the Jewish people as they come to belief in Christ and are reconciled to God. This future revival of faith among the Jewish people is here called **their fullness,** "their acceptance" (v. 15), and their being "grafted into their own olive tree" (vv. 23, 24). Many scholars believe the NT does not specify the exact time of this ingathering. See note on v. 26.

world, and their failure riches for the
Gentiles, how much more their *fullness!
13 For I speak to you Gentiles; inasmuch as [a]I am an apostle to the Gentiles, I magnify my ministry,
14 if by any means I may provoke to
jealousy *those who are* my flesh and
[a]save some of them.
15 For if their being cast away *is* the
reconciling of the world, what *will* their
acceptance *be* [a]but life from the dead?
16 For if [a]the firstfruit *is* holy, the lump
is also *holy;* and if the root *is* holy, so
are the branches.
17 And if [a]some of the branches were
broken off, [b]and you, being a wild olive
tree, were grafted in among them, and
with them became a partaker of the
root and [1]fatness of the olive tree,
18 [a]do not boast against the branches.
But if you do boast, *remember that* you
do not support the root, but the root
supports you.
19 You will say then, "Branches were
broken off that I might be grafted in."
20 Well *said.* Because of [a]unbelief they
were broken off, and you stand by
faith. Do not be haughty, but *fear.
21 For if God did not spare the natural
branches, He may not spare you either.
22 Therefore consider the goodness
and severity of God: on those who fell,
severity; but toward you, [1]goodness,*
[a]if you continue in *His* goodness. Otherwise [b]you also will be cut off.
23 And they also, [a]if they do not continue in unbelief, will be grafted in, for
God is *able to graft them in again.
24 For if you were cut out of the olive
tree which is wild by nature, and were
grafted contrary to nature into a cultivated olive tree, how much more will
these, who *are* natural *branches,* be
grafted into their own olive tree?

KINGDOM DYNAMICS

11:19–24 The Church and Present-Day Israel, PROPHECY. While two basically different prophetic positions exist concerning Israel's future, there is only one biblical view concerning the Christian's attitude toward the Jewish people. First, the Bible calls us to honor the fact that since they were the national avenue by which messianic blessing has come to mankind (9:4, 5), there should be a sense of duty to "bless" all Jewry (Gen. 12:3), to "pray" with sincere passion for them (Rom. 10:1), and to be as ready to "bear witness" to any Jew as graciously and sensitively as we would to any other human being (1:16, 17).

Second, the biblical directive to "pray for the peace of Jerusalem" (Ps. 122:6) cannot be said to have been rescinded. Even though the text of this psalm centers on the presence of the temple in ancient Jerusalem, this prayer assignment ought not to be withdrawn. Those taking this text seriously see their prayer responsibility for "Jerusalem" to be an assignment of continuing concern for God's providential hand of protection and grace upon the nation of Israel in particular (as distinguished from paragraph 1, which relates to Jews everywhere). It is wise for believers to avoid the presumption of passivity toward Israel, since the evidence of all history is that God has not forgotten this people (Rom. 11:23, 24). (See Prophecy and the Future of Israel, Ps. 122:6.)

(Ps. 122:6/Rev. 19:10*) J.W.H.

25 For I do not desire, brethren, that
you should be ignorant of this mystery,
lest you should be [a]wise in your own
[1]opinion, that [b]**blindness** in part has
happened to Israel [c]until the fullness
of the Gentiles has come in.

WORD WEALTH

11:25 blindness, *porosis* (po-row-sis); Strong's *#4457:* Hardening, callousness. The word is a medical term describing the process by which extremities of fractured bones are set by an ossifying, or calloused petrifying. Sometimes it describes a hard substance in the eye that blinds. Used metaphorically, *porosis* denotes a dulled spiritual perceptivity, spiritual blindness, and hardness.

26 And so all Israel will be [1]saved, as
it is written:

12 *See WW at Eph. 3:19. **13** [a]Acts 9:15; 22:21; Gal. 1:16; 2:7–9; Eph. 3:8 **14** [a]1 Cor. 9:22; 1 Tim. 4:16; James 5:20 **15** [a][Is. 26:16–19] **16** [a]Lev. 23:10; [James 1:18] **17** [a]Jer. 11:16; [John 15:2] [b]Acts 2:39; [Eph. 2:12] [1]*richness* **18** [a][1 Cor. 10:12] **20** [a]Heb. 3:19 *See WW at Matt. 10:26. **22** [a]1 Cor. 15:2; Heb. 3:6, 14 [b][John 15:2] [1]NU adds *of God* *See WW at Gal. 5:22. **23** [a][2 Cor. 3:16] *See WW at Matt. 19:26.

25 [a]Rom. 12:16 [b]2 Cor. 3:14 [c]Luke 21:24; John 10:16; Rom. 11:12 [1]*estimation* **26** [1]Or *delivered*

11:17–24 Paul warns Gentiles against boastfulness (vv. 17, 18), pride (vv. 19–21), and presumption (vv. 22–24), since they are but **a wild olive tree, grafted in** because of Israel's unbelief.

11:25 Israel's rejection is temporary, until all those who are going to be saved from among **the Gentiles** come to trust in Christ. Then salvation will come to a large number of Jews in the same way it has come to people for centuries—a faith response to the preached gospel of Christ.

11:26 And so: That is, "in this way, in the process just described." **All Israel** does not mean that every Jewish person who has ever lived **will be saved,** for Paul does not teach that (see 10:2, 3). The term must be understood in the same sense as "the fullness of the Gentiles" (v. 25). Paul is therefore speaking in a collective sense. There will be a mighty turning on the part of the Jews to Christ.

Although many scholars believe the NT does not specify the time of Israel's ingathering (see note on v. 12), others see here a possible reference in Paul's statement, **the Deliverer will come.** Those taking this latter view see this

[a]*"The Deliverer will come out of*
Zion,
And He will turn away
ungodliness from Jacob;
27 *For [a]this is My covenant with*
them,
When I take away their sins."

28 Concerning the gospel *they are* enemies for your sake, but concerning the
election *they are* [a]beloved for the sake
of the fathers.
29 For the gifts and the calling of God
are [a]irrevocable.
30 For as you [a]were once disobedient
to God, yet have now obtained *mercy
through their disobedience,
31 even so these also have now been
disobedient, that through the *mercy
shown you they also may obtain
mercy.
32 For God has [1]committed them [a]all
to disobedience, that He might have
mercy on all.
33 Oh, the depth of the riches both
of the *wisdom and knowledge of
God! How unsearchable *are* His
judgments and His ways past finding
out!

34 *"For who has known the [a]mind*
of the LORD?
Or [b]who has become His
counselor?"
35 *"Or[a] who has first given to*
Him
And it shall be repaid to him?"

26 [a]Ps. 14:7; Is. 59:20, 21
27 [a]Is. 27:9; Heb. 8:12
28 [a]Deut. 7:8; 10:15; Rom. 9:5
29 [a]Num. 23:19
30 [a][Eph. 2:2] *See WW at Rom. 9:15.
31 *See WW at 2 Tim. 1:16.
32 [a]Rom. 3:9; [Gal. 3:22] [1]*shut them all up in*
33 *See WW at Acts 6:10.
34 [a]Is. 40:13; Jer. 23:18; 1 Cor. 2:16 [b]Job 36:22
35 [a]Job 41:11
36 [a][1 Cor. 8:6; 11:12]; Col. 1:16; Heb. 2:10 [b]Heb. 13:21

CHAPTER 12

1 [a]1 Cor. 1:10; 2 Cor. 10:1–4 [b]Phil. 4:18; Heb. 10:18, 20 [1]*urge* [2]*rational* *See WW at Acts 7:33.
2 [a]Matt. 13:22; Gal. 1:4; 1 John 2:15 [b]Eph. 4:23; [Titus 3:5] [c][1 Thess. 4:3] *See WW at Titus 3:5. • See WW at James 3:2. • See WW at Matt. 12:50.

36 For [a]of Him and through Him and
to Him *are* all things, [b]to whom *be*
glory forever. Amen.

Living Sacrifices to God

12 I [a]beseech[1] you therefore, 2
brethren, by the mercies of God,
that you present your bodies [b]a living
sacrifice, *holy, acceptable to God,
which is your [2]reasonable service.
2 And [a]do not be **conformed** to this
world, but [b]be transformed by the *renewing of your mind, that you may
[c]prove what *is* that good and acceptable and *perfect *will of God.

WORD WEALTH

12:2 conformed, *suschematizo* (soos-khay-mat-*id*-zoe); Strong's *#4964:* Compare "scheme" and "schematic." Refers to conforming oneself to the outer fashion or outward appearance, accommodating oneself to a model or pattern. *Suschematizo* occurs elsewhere in the NT only in 1 Pet. 1:14, where it describes those conforming themselves to worldly lusts. Even apparent or superficial conformity to the present world system or any accommodation to its ways would be fatal to the Christian life.

KINGDOM DYNAMICS

12:2 7. How Can I Know God's Will?, SPIRITUAL ANSWERS. For the answer to this and other probing questions about (*cont. on next page*)

---

quote of Is. 59:20 as a reference to Christ's return. Hence, many Jews, having seen and heard the truth of the gospel during the Great Tribulation, will accept the Messiah upon His return.

11:28, 29 God is mindful of the covenant promise He gave to **the fathers,** and He will fulfill it. The word **for** shows that v. 29 is a reason given to demonstrate the truthfulness of v. 28. While the immediate reference of **the gifts and the calling of God** is to the privileges of Israel, some interpreters apply the principle stated in v. 29 to spiritual gifts. Others, however, cite passages such as Judg. 16:20 and 1 Sam. 16:14 as indications that one may forfeit his special anointing.

11:33–36 After the longest extended theological argument in the NT (1:16—11:33), Paul reflects on the amazing **wisdom and knowledge of God** in His plan of salvation, and breaks forth into spontaneous praise. **Unsearchable:** Unable to be fully discovered or understood by us.

11:36 All things: The universe, ourselves, our salvation, and everything else, all are from God and work through His sustaining power, and ultimately further His glory. The proper response of every creature is to give God **glory forever.**

12:1—16:27 Paul now adds practical application and personal greetings to his theological discussion of chs. 1—11. In fact, the book may be divided into two large sections—doctrine (chs. 1—11) and application (chs. 12—16).

12:1, 2 See section 2 of Truth-In-Action at the end of Rom.

12:1 Therefore: In light of the great plan of salvation outlined in chs. 1—11, particularly all the **mercies** (benefits) it brings to us as Christians, let us respond appropriately.

A living sacrifice: Since Christians (both Jews and Gentiles) are the new people of God, the "New Israel," then should we not offer sacrifices to God, just as the OT Jews did? Yes, but not animal sacrifices at the temple in Jerusalem; rather, we should offer our **bodies** (all that we are) as "living sacrifices" each day to God.

The Greek word translated **service** is used to refer to ceremonies of Jewish temple worship in 9:4 and Heb. 9:1, 6. The word translated **reasonable** can mean "pertaining to reason." As such it suggests that a rational response to God's "mercies" is to commit ourselves in an act of worship. The word may also be understood as "spiritual" (see 1 Pet. 2:2, where it is translated "pure"). As such, our act of consecration is a supreme form of religious service: physical, in that our "bodies" are presented in worship; rational, in that our reasoning is responsive to His truth; emotional, in that His "mercies" are perceived and awaken our sensitivities to His lovingkindness; and spiritual, in that this is all the fruit of His Spirit's reviving and renewing ours.

12:2 World is literally "age," referring to a godless system. We are not to accept the pattern of an age whose god is the Devil (2 Cor. 4:4). On the contrary, we are to **be transformed** by a renewed **mind** committed to the ideals of the kingdom of God. **Prove** means to test and to prove by practice in everyday life that God's **will** for us is **good and acceptable and perfect.**

(cont. from preceding page)
God and the power life in His kingdom, see the study article "Spiritual Answers to Hard Questions," which begins on page 1996. P.R.

Serve God with Spiritual Gifts

3 For I say, [a]through the *grace
*given to me, to everyone who is
among you, [b]not to think *of himself*
more highly than he ought to think, but
to think *soberly, as God has dealt
[c]to each one a measure of faith.
4 For [a]as we have many members in
one body, but all the members do not
have the same function,
5 so [a]we, *being* many, are one body
in Christ, and individually members of
one another.

KINGDOM DYNAMICS

12:3–5 One Should Not Think Too Highly of Himself, HUMAN WORTH. Because the Bible teaches that human beings are made in God's image, we are to respect the position of each individual under God. This text does not teach that believers should think of themselves as worthless or insignificant beings, but rather that none should consider himself to be more worthy, more important, more deserving of salvation, or more essential than anyone else. Possession of different talents or gifts does not denote differences in worth, for all belong to the one body, to one another, and all are interdependent (vv. 4, 5). To think otherwise is to distort reality. Each individual has intrinsic value and worth, as we are all equal before God and in Christ.
(Matt. 25:37–40/James 2:1–9) C.B.

6 Having then *gifts differing according to the grace that is [a]given to us,
let us use them: if *prophecy, *let
us* [b]*prophesy* in proportion to our
faith;
7 or ministry, *let us use it* in *our* ministering; [a]he who teaches, in teaching;
8 [a]he who exhorts, in *exhortation;
[b]he who *gives, with liberality; [c]he
who leads, with diligence; he who
shows mercy, [d]with **cheerfulness.**

WORD WEALTH

12:8 cheerfulness, *hilarotes* (hil-ar-*ot*-ace); Strong's *#2432:* Compare "hilarious" and "hilarity." Graciousness, joyfulness, gladness, benevolence, amiability, cheerfulness, gaiety, affability. In primitive lands Bible translators define *hilarotes* as, "The heart is laughing and the eyes are dancing." The word was often used for the cheerful demeanor of those visiting the sick and infirm and of those giving alms. The person who exhibits *hilarotes* is a sunbeam lighting up a sickroom with warmth and love.

3 [a]Rom. 1:5; 15:15; 1 Cor. 3:10; 15:10; Gal. 2:9; Eph. 3:7 [b]Prov. 25:27 [c][Eph. 4:7] *See WW at 2 Cor. 12:9. • See WW at Acts 20:35. • See WW at Mark 5:15.
4 [a]1 Cor. 12:12–14; [Eph. 4:4, 16]
5 [a][1 Cor. 10:17]; Gal. 3:28
6 [a][John 3:27] [b]Acts 11:27 *See WW at 1 Cor. 1:7. • See WW at 1 Thess. 5:20.
7 [a]Eph. 4:11
8 [a]Acts 15:32 [b][Matt. 6:1–3] [c][Acts 20:28] [d]2 Cor. 9:7 *See WW at Acts 9:31. • See WW at Rom. 1:11.

12:3–8 Paul calls for lives marked by humility and faithfulness in Christian relationships. Just as the physical body is made up of many members, each with a different function, the church is a body of many members, but all closely related and constituting a unity in Christ, with each one having individual functions and responsibilities. We are not to inflate our own position nor to begrudge others their office.

12:3 Paul refers to his own function in the body as an authoritative apostle **through the grace given to him.** The **measure of faith** is not saving faith but the faith to receive and to exercise the gifts God apportions to us. The "measure of faith" He gives corresponds to the role He assigns as Creator and Redeemer.

12:4, 5 Our different gifts and abilities should make us love and depend more on one another, and therefore should make us more united as **one body in Christ.**

12:6–8 There are basically two interpretative approaches to this passage on **gifts:** 1) To see them as a category distinct from that of other NT passages, often referred to as the Father's creational gifts. See note on Eph. 4:8, 11; or 2) to see them as a repeat or overlap of many of those mentioned in either 1 Cor. 12:12–29 or Eph. 4:11.

12:6 Prophecy refers either to those whose creation gift from the Father enables them to view all of life with special ongoing prophetic insight, independent of public office or special use by the Spirit in giving public prophecy; or to the manifestation of public prophecy, speaking something that God has spontaneously brought to mind (1 Cor. 12:10). **In proportion to our faith** likely means that prophecy of any sort is to be exercised in accordance with the biblical maturity God has granted the speaker, recognizing that God is the originator of the gift.

12:7, 8 Ministry suggests either those whose special creation gift enables them to most effectively serve the body in physical ways; or the rendering of any type of service by anyone in the church (1 Cor. 12:5). **Teaching** refers either to those who are specially gifted to keep an eye on and instruct the revealed truth of God's Word, regardless of public office; or to those in the public office of teacher (Eph. 4:11). **He who exhorts** describes either those whose creation gift enables them to best apply God's truths through encouragement; or to those (such as pastors) who are called to publicly bring encouragement to the church.

He who gives, which does not occur in the 1 Cor. or Eph. listings, refers either to those gifted to contribute to the emotional and/or physical support of others; or to those gifted with abundant financial means so as to support the work of the gospel. **He who leads** refers either to those who are gifted to effectively facilitate all areas of life; or to those with the public function of administration (1 Cor. 12:28) or possibly even to a deacon (Phil. 1:1). **He who shows mercy** defines either those with the special gift of strong, perceptive emotions; or those called to special functions of Christian relief or acts of charity. **With cheerfulness** warns those with this gift not to allow depression or moroseness to overtake them.

KINGDOM DYNAMICS

12:6–8 The Father's Gifts to You, SPIRITUAL GIFTS. The gifts are placed in the church as resources to be utilized at the point of need for ministry in the body. This passage unfolds the Father's gifts, given to each person as a means of affording fulfilling purpose in life. What is the "mix" that constitutes your personal motivation? An elaboration of this and related themes appears in the study article on page 2018, "Holy Spirit Gifts and Power."

(Rom. 8:2/1 Cor. 12:8–10, 28) P.W.

Behave Like a Christian

9 [a]*Let* love *be* *without hypocrisy.
[b]Abhor what is evil. Cling to what is good.
10 [a]*Be* kindly affectionate to one another with *brotherly love, [b]in honor giving preference to one another;
11 not lagging in diligence, *fervent in spirit, serving the Lord;
12 [a]rejoicing in hope, [b]patient[1]* in tribulation, [c]continuing steadfastly in prayer;
13 [a]distributing to the needs of the saints, [b]given[1] to hospitality.
14 [a]Bless* those who persecute you; bless and do not curse.
15 [a]Rejoice with those who rejoice, and weep with those who weep.
16 [a]Be of the same mind toward one another. [b]Do not set your mind on high things, but associate with the *humble. Do not be wise in your own opinion.
17 [a]Repay* no one evil for evil. [b]Have[1] regard for good things in the sight of all men.
18 If it is *possible, as much as depends on you, [a]live peaceably with all men.
19 Beloved, [a]do not avenge yourselves, but *rather* give place to wrath; for it is written, [b]*"Vengeance is Mine, I will repay,"* says the Lord.
20 Therefore

[a]*"If your enemy is hungry, feed him;*
If he is thirsty, give him a drink;
For in so doing you will heap coals of fire on his head."

21 Do not be overcome by evil, but [a]overcome evil with good.

Submit to Government

13 Let every soul be [a]subject to the governing authorities. For there is no *authority except from God, and the authorities that exist are appointed by God.
2 Therefore whoever *resists [a]the authority resists the ordinance of God, and those who resist will [1]bring judgment on themselves.
3 For rulers are not a terror to good works, but to evil. Do you want to be unafraid of the authority? [a]Do what is good, and you will have *praise from the same.
4 For he is God's minister to you for good. But if you do evil, be afraid; for

9 [a]1 Tim. 1:5 [b]Ps. 34:14 *See WW at 1 Pet. 1:22.
10 [a]Heb. 13:1 [b]Phil. 2:3 *See WW at Heb. 13:1.
11 *See WW at Acts 18:25.
12 [a]Luke 10:20 [b]Luke 21:19 [c]Luke 18:1 [1]persevering *See WW at Matt. 24:13.
13 [a]1 Cor. 16:1 [b]1 Tim. 3:2 [1]Lit. *pursuing*
14 [a][Matt. 5:44] *See WW at Luke 6:28.
15 [a][1 Cor. 12:26]
16 [a][Phil. 2:2; 4:2] [b]Jer. 45:5 *See WW at 2 Cor. 7:6.
17 [a][Matt. 5:39] [b]2 Cor. 8:21 [1]Or *Provide good* *See WW at Matt. 22:21.
18 [a]Heb. 12:14 *See WW at Matt. 19:26.
19 [a]Lev. 19:18 [b]Deut. 32:35
20 [a]Prov. 25:21, 22
21 [a][Rom. 12:1, 2]

CHAPTER 13

1 [a]1 Pet. 2:13 *See WW at Mark 3:15.
2 [a][Titus 3:1] [1]Lit. *receive*
*See WW at Eph. 6:13. 3 [a]1 Pet. 2:14 *See WW at Eph. 1:6.

12:9–21 Love is to be the guiding principle in Christian relationships not only with fellow believers (vv. 9–13), but with enemies as well (vv. 14–21). Paul mentions many specific Christian duties, but love is the dominant note in all the exhortations.

12:18 Because some people may remain violently opposed to us, there are times when all efforts toward peace fail. However, the Christian is to make certain that he is not at fault when peace breaks down.

12:19 Instead of taking vengeance ourselves, we should give it over into God's hands and thereby **give place to wrath.** God will exact **vengeance** at the final judgment or even in this life, sometimes through the instrumentality of civil government (13:4).

13:1–7 Paul exhorts his readers to fulfill their duties to the state.

13:1 The authorities that exist are appointed by God: See also Dan. 4:32; Ps. 75:6, 7. Paul does not suggest that God approves a corrupt government, ungodly officials, or unjust legislation. Sometimes, however, in punishment for the sins of a people, or for other reasons known to Him, God allows evil rulers to have authority for a time, as the OT prophets frequently testify. Ideally, God grants authority to serve good ends (vv. 3, 4). How that authority is exercised will be the accounting of each to whom it has been given.

13:2 Although obedience to earthly authority is the general rule, a clear biblical principle is that we may need to disobey government if commanded to sin, for loyalty to God always takes priority over all human authority (see Esth. 4:16; Dan. 3:12–18; 6:10; Matt. 2:12; Acts 5:29; Heb. 11:23).

13:4 When government officials use force to restrain and punish evil, they are not doing wrong. Rather, they are **God's minister** (servant) and are doing **good.** Therefore, Christians may serve as police officers and soldiers in good conscience.

Bear the sword is to carry and use weapons. This implies the right to carry out capital punishment on wrongdoers, for swords were used to take people's lives. The fact that God authorizes governments as His servants to use force even to the point of taking human life does not contradict the command "You shall not murder" in Ex. 20:13. The word used in that commandment refers to criminal murder and does not include judicial taking of life or killing in war, for which the OT uses other words. The same is true of the Greek word translated "kill" or "murder" in such NT passages as Matt. 5:21.

To execute wrath: See note on 12:19. Sometimes God's wrath is carried out through civil government when it punishes wrongdoers. This means that civil punishments should not only be imposed for the purpose of restraining evil, but also for the purpose of retribution.

he does not bear the sword in vain; for
he is God's minister, an avenger to *execute* wrath on him who practices evil.

KINGDOM DYNAMICS

13:3, 4 19. Should a Christian Be Involved in Police or Military Service?, SPIRITUAL ANSWERS. For the answer to this and other probing questions about God and the power life in His kingdom, see the study article "Spiritual Answers to Hard Questions," which begins on page 1996. P.R.

5 Therefore [a]*you* must be *subject,
not only because of wrath [b]but also for
conscience' sake.
6 For because of this you also pay
taxes, for they are God's *ministers attending continually to this very thing.
7 [a]Render therefore to all their due:
taxes to whom taxes *are due,* customs
to whom customs, fear to whom fear,
honor to whom honor.

KINGDOM DYNAMICS

13:7 20. When Should a Christian Disobey Civil Government?, SPIRITUAL ANSWERS. For the answer to this and other probing questions about God and the power life in His kingdom, see the study article "Spiritual Answers to Hard Questions," which begins on page 1996. P.R.

Love Your Neighbor

3 8 Owe no one anything except to love
one another, for [a]he who loves another
has fulfilled the law.
9 For the commandments, [a]"*You
shall not commit adultery," "You shall
not murder," "You shall not steal,"*
[1]*"You shall not bear false witness," "You shall not covet,"* and if *there is*
any other commandment, are *all*
summed up in this saying, namely,
[b]*"You shall love your neighbor as
yourself."*
10 Love *does no harm to a neighbor;
therefore [a]love *is* the *fulfillment of the
law.

Put on Christ

11 And *do* this, knowing the time, that
now *it is* high time [a]to awake out of
sleep; for now our salvation *is* nearer
than when we *first* believed.
12 The night is far spent, the day is at
hand. [a]Therefore let us cast off the
works of darkness, and [b]let us put on
the armor of light.
13 [a]Let us walk [1]properly, as in the
day, [b]not in revelry and drunkenness,
[c]not in *lewdness and lust, [d]not in
strife and *envy.
14 But [a]put on the Lord Jesus Christ,
and [b]make no **provision** for the flesh,
to *fulfill its* lusts.

WORD WEALTH

13:14 provision, *pronoia* (*pron*-oy-ah); Strong's *#4307:* Foreplanning, foresight, forethought, premeditated plan, making preparation for, providing for. Derived from words *pro,* "before," and *noeo,* "to think," "contemplate." Paul prohibited his readers from planning ahead and making any preparations for gratifying their carnal nature.

5 [a]Eccl. 8:2 [b][1 Pet. 2:13, 19] *See WW at 1 Cor. 14:32.
6 *See WW at Heb. 1:7.
7 [a]Matt. 22:21
8 [a][Gal. 5:13, 14]
9 [a]Ex. 20:13–17; Deut. 5:17–21 [b]Lev. 19:18 [1]NU omits *"You shall not bear false witness,"*
10 [a][Matt. 7:12; 22:39, 40] *See WW at John 3:21. • See WW at Eph. 3:19.
11 [a][1 Cor. 15:34]
12 [a]Eph. 5:11 [b][Eph. 6:11, 13]
13 [a]Phil. 4:8 [b]Prov. 23:20 [c][1 Cor. 6:9] [d]James 3:14 [1]*decently* *See WW at 1 Pet. 4:3. • See WW at 2 Cor. 11:2.
14 [a]Gal. 3:27 [b][Gal. 5:16]

13:5 Paul gives two reasons why Christians must obey government: 1) **Because of wrath,** that is, to avoid the punishment that government executes on those who do wrong (v. 4); 2) **For conscience' sake,** that is, because we want to keep a clear conscience before God, who has established government and commands us to obey it. This second reason means that even where there is no likelihood of arrest or punishment, Christians should be fully obedient to government.

13:7 Both Paul and Jesus direct Christians to pay **taxes** to the Roman government, which was certainly not pure or righteous in all its actions. As with all commands of God, we should try to obey this one joyfully, not grudgingly. Whenever we tend to become discouraged with the imperfections of our government, or the burden of taxation *that it imposes upon* us, we would do well to remember that the alternative, anarchy, is far worse (see Judg. 17—21).

13:8–10 See section 3 of Truth-In-Action at the end of Rom.

13:8 Owe no one anything: The Greek present tense of the prohibition may be translated, "Don't continue owing anything to anybody." The verse probably does not forbid all debt, but it certainly forbids an attitude of contentment with indebtedness, or thinking that indebtedness is a normal situation (see Ps. 37:21). **He who loves another has fulfilled the law:** If we truly understood and completely followed the command to love one another, we would fulfill every social duty and would especially observe those commandments that are most fundamental in human relations (v. 9).

13:9 Summed up: Love is a summary of God's moral laws—yet a summary should not be used to contradict one of the items it is summarizing. Therefore, to say that love for another requires one to break some of God's laws from time to time (as in "situation ethics") is a misunderstanding of Scripture.

13:11–14 Paul emphasizes a high standard of moral conduct, particularly in view of the nearness of the Lord's return, when our **salvation** will be consummated (vv. 11, 12). The way to moral excellence is twofold (v. 14). Positively, we must **put on the Lord Jesus Christ,** submitting to His lordship, accepting His moral standards, living in constant fellowship with Him, and depending upon His strength. Negatively, we are to **make no provision for the flesh,** doing nothing to foster its sensual desires and appetites (see Gal. 5:16–25).

KINGDOM DYNAMICS

13:13, 14 23. How Can I Quit Drinking or Depending on Drugs?, SPIRITUAL ANSWERS. For the answer to this and other probing questions about God and the power life in His kingdom, see the study article "Spiritual Answers to Hard Questions," which begins on page 1996.

P.R.

The Law of Liberty

14 Receive[a] one who is weak in the faith, *but* not to disputes over *doubtful things.
2 For one believes he [a]may eat all things, but he who is weak eats *only* vegetables.
3 Let not him who eats despise him who does not eat, and [a]let not him who does not eat judge him who eats; for God has received him.
4 [a]Who are you to judge another's servant? To his own master he stands or falls. Indeed, he will be made to stand, for God is able to make him stand.
5 [a]One person esteems *one* day above another; another esteems every day *alike.* Let each be fully convinced in his own mind.
6 He who [a]observes the day, observes *it* to the Lord; [1]and he who does not observe the day, to the Lord he does not observe *it.* He who eats, eats to the Lord, for [b]he gives God thanks; and he who does not eat, to the Lord he does not eat, and gives God thanks.
7 For [a]none of us lives to himself, and no one dies to himself.
8 For if we [a]live, we live to the Lord; and if we die, we die to the Lord. Therefore, whether we live or die, we are the Lord's.
9 For [a]to this end Christ died [1]and rose and lived again, that He might be [b]Lord of both the dead and the living.
10 But why do you judge your brother? Or why do you show contempt for your brother? For [a]we shall all stand before the *judgment seat of [1]Christ.
11 For it is written:

[a]*"As I live, says the LORD,*
Every knee shall bow to Me,
And every tongue shall confess to God."

12 So then [a]each of us shall *give account of himself to God.
13 Therefore let us not judge one another [1]anymore, but rather resolve this, [a]not to put a *stumbling block or a cause to fall in *our* brother's way.

The Law of Love

14 I know and am convinced by the Lord Jesus [a]that *there is* nothing unclean of itself; but to him who considers anything to be unclean, to him *it is* unclean.
15 Yet if your brother is grieved because of *your* food, you are no longer walking in love. [a]Do not *destroy with your food the one for whom Christ died.
16 [a]Therefore do not let your good be spoken of as evil;
17 [a]for the kingdom of God is not eating and drinking, but righteousness and [b]peace and joy in the Holy Spirit.
18 For he who serves Christ in [1]these things [a]*is* acceptable to God and approved by men.
19 [a]Therefore let us pursue the things *which make* for peace and the things by which [b]one may [1]edify another.
20 [a]Do not destroy the work of God for the sake of food. [b]All things indeed *are* *pure, [c]but *it is* evil for the man who eats with [1]offense.
21 *It is* *good neither to eat [a]meat nor drink wine nor *do anything* by which your brother stumbles [1]or is *offended or is made weak.

CHAPTER 14

1 [a][1 Cor. 8:9; 9:22] *See WW at Luke 2:35.
2 [a][Titus 1:15]
3 [a][Col. 2:16]
4 [a]James 4:11, 12
5 [a]Gal. 4:10
6 [a]Gal. 4:10 [b][1 Tim. 4:3] [1]NU omits the rest of this sentence.
7 [a][Gal. 2:20]
8 [a]2 Cor. 5:14, 15
9 [a]2 Cor. 5:15 [b]Acts 10:36 [1]NU omits *and rose*
10 [a]2 Cor. 5:10 [1]NU *God* *See WW at Matt. 27:19.
11 [a]Is. 45:23
12 [a]1 Pet. 4:5 *See WW at Acts 20:35.
13 [a]1 Cor. 8:9 [1]*any longer* *See WW at Matt. 16:23.
14 [a]1 Cor. 10:25
15 [a]1 Cor. 8:11 *See WW at Luke 9:56.
16 [a][Rom. 12:17]
17 [a]1 Cor. 8:8 [b][Rom. 8:6]
18 [a]2 Cor. 8:21 [1]NU *this thing*
19 [a]Rom. 12:18 [b]1 Cor. 14:12 [1]*build up*
20 [a]Rom. 14:15 [b]Acts 10:15 [c]1 Cor. 8:9–12 [1]A feeling of giving offense *See WW at Matt. 5:8.
21 [a]1 Cor. 8:13 [1]NU omits the rest of v. 21. *See WW at Matt. 13:48. • See WW at Matt. 11:6.

14:1–23 These are guidelines with respect to things that *are neither commanded nor forbidden in Scripture.*

14:2, 3 Among Christians there is room for toleration and differences of strictness regarding such issues as eating habits (vv. 2–4) and observing special days in the Christian life (vv. 5, 6). Since both parties do it to honor the Lord (v. 6), neither should look down on the other. Yet Paul does say that the Christian who refuses to eat certain things is **weak** (immature) in the faith since eating is really morally relative. (v. 1; see 1 Tim. 4:3–5).

14:6 See note on vv. 2, 3.

14:10 Christians are not to **judge** each other with reference to the practice of morally neutral issues (see vv. 3, 4), since each individual is responsible to God (see v. 12). As Lord (v. 9), the right of such judgment belongs to Christ. Weak and strong Christians alike **shall all stand,** not at each other's judgment seats, but **before the judgment seat of Christ.** That judgment will be based on what we have done in this life (2 Cor. 5:10). It will not determine whether or not we enter heaven, but will determine degrees of reward in heaven (see note on 2:6).

14:13 Paul directs this counsel primarily to the mature, urging them to practice self-limitation in exercising their liberty lest they offend others (see vv. 20, 21).

14:14 Christians can eat all foods and need not follow the dietary laws of the OT. See marginal note on Mark 7:19; Acts 10:9–16; Col. 2:16, 17; 1 Tim. 4:3–5.

14:17 Dietary laws are relatively trivial, and their fulfillment is not essential to God's reign. Of far more importance is the fruit of **the Holy Spirit** (see Gal. 5:22, 23).

22 [1]Do you have faith? Have *it* to yourself before God. [a]Happy *is* he who does not condemn himself in what he approves.
23 But he who doubts is condemned if he eats, because *he does* not *eat* from faith; for [a]whatever *is* not from faith is [1]sin.

Bearing Others' Burdens

1 **15** We [a]then who are strong ought to bear with the [1]scruples of the weak, and not to please ourselves.
2 [a]Let each of us please *his* neighbor for *his* good, leading to [1]edification.
3 [a]For even Christ did not please Himself; but as it is written, [b]*"The reproaches of those who *reproached You fell on Me."*
2 4 For [a]whatever things were written before were written for our learning, that we through the [1]patience* and comfort of the Scriptures might have hope.
5 [a]Now may the God of patience and comfort grant you to be like-minded toward one another, according to Christ Jesus,
6 that you may [a]with* one mind *and* one mouth glorify the God and Father of our Lord Jesus Christ.

Glorify God Together

7 Therefore [a]receive one another, just [b]as Christ also received [1]us, to the glory of God.

KINGDOM DYNAMICS

15:5–7 Receiving One Another Is the Way to Oneness, FAMILY ORDER. It has been said that most teaching on family life is simply an application of what it means to live as a Christian. These verses in Rom. are directed to the Christian community at large, yet they are a frequently used wedding text, for they present a beautiful and fitting description of Christian marriage.

The key word is "receive" (Greek *proslambano*), which means "to take to oneself." Its root indicates strong action toward us—that in Christ, God literally came to us and took hold of us "while we were still sinners" (5:8). By that act of acceptance He released the grace of God and set in motion the powers of redemption.

When that power is allowed to work in a family, it will transform the lives of two imperfect people into one life, lived to the praise of God's glory. Therefore, the Lord sets this word like a banner over marriage from the first day until the last, "Receive one another, just as Christ also received us, to the glory of God."

(Prov. 13:24/Gen. 1:26–28*) L.C.

8 Now I say that [a]Jesus Christ has become a [1]servant to the circumcision for the truth of God, [b]to *confirm the *promises *made* to the fathers,
9 and [a]that the Gentiles might glorify God for *His* mercy, as it is written:

[b]*"For this reason I will confess to*
You among the Gentiles,
And sing to Your name."

10 And again he says:

[a]*"Rejoice, O Gentiles, with His*
people!"

11 And again:

[a]*"Praise the* L*ORD, all you Gentiles!*
Laud Him, all you peoples!"

12 And again, Isaiah says:

[a]*"There shall be a root of Jesse;*
And He who shall rise to reign
over the Gentiles,
In Him the Gentiles shall hope."

13 Now may the God of hope fill you with all [a]joy and peace in believing, that you may *abound in hope by the *power of the Holy Spirit.

---

22 [a][1 John 3:21] [1]NU *The faith which you have—have* **23** [a]Titus 1:15 [1]M puts Rom. 16:25–27 here.

CHAPTER 15

1 [a]Rom. 14:1; [Gal. 6:1, 2]; 1 Thess. 5:14 [1]*weaknesses* **2** [a]1 Cor. 9:22; 10:24, 33; 2 Cor. 13:9 [1]*building up* **3** [a]Matt. 26:39; [Phil. 2:5–8] [b]Ps. 69:9 *See WW at James 1:5. **4** [a]Rom. 4:23, 24; 1 Cor. 10:11; 2 Tim. 3:16, 17 [1]*perseverance* *See WW at Heb. 10:36. **5** [a]1 Cor. 1:10; Phil. 1:27 **6** [a]Acts 4:24 *See WW at Acts 2:1. **7** [a]Rom. 14:1, 3 [b]Rom. 5:2 [1]NU, M *you*

8 [a]Matt. 15:24; Acts 3:26 [b][Rom. 4:16]; 2 Cor. 1:20 [1]*minister* *See WW at Mark 16:20. • See WW at Acts 13:32. **9** [a]John 10:16 [b]2 Sam. 22:50; Ps. 18:49 **10** [a]Deut. 32:43 **11** [a]Ps. 117:1 **12** [a]Is. 11:1, 10 **13** [a]Rom. 12:12; 14:17 *See WW at Matt. 25:29. • See WW at Acts 4:33.

14:22 Faith here is one's conviction that he is free from all unnecessary scruples. He must not, however, flaunt his liberty recklessly over the weak in faith.
14:23 A person who has scruples about matters not wrong in and of themselves should not act contrary to his conscience, because to violate the conscience is not acting in **faith** but is **sin.**
15:1–6 Christ is the model of conduct in relationships between weak and strong Christians. His example demands mutual forbearance and love, and if followed will result in a unity of harmonious praise to God (v. 6).
15:1–3 See section 1 of Truth-In-Action at the end of Rom.
15:4 See section 2 of Truth-In-Action at the end of Rom.
15:7–13 Not only are the "strong" to adjust to the "weak" (see note on 14:13), but the matter of acceptance is to be two-way (v. 7). This was modeled by **Christ,** the *Jewish* Messiah who accepted **Gentiles.** This mutual acceptance of Jew and Gentile by Christ is then supported by a catena of OT scriptures.
15:13 The Holy Spirit imparts not only spiritual gifts to the believer, but also **joy** and **peace** and **hope** (see 14:17).

From Jerusalem to Illyricum

14 Now [a]I myself am confident concerning you, my brethren, that you also
are full of **goodness,** [b]filled with all
knowledge, able also to admonish
[1]one another.

WORD WEALTH

15:14 goodness, *agathosune* (ag-ath-*oh*-soo-nay); Strong's *#19:* Compare "Agatha" and possibly "agate." Beneficence, kindness in actual manifestation, virtue equipped for action, a bountiful propensity both to will and to do what is good, intrinsic goodness producing a generosity and a Godlike state or being. *Agathosune* is a rare word that combines being good and doing good.

15 Nevertheless, brethren, I have written more boldly to you on *some* points,
as reminding you, [a]because of the
grace given to me by God,
16 that [a]I might be a *minister of Jesus
Christ to the Gentiles, ministering the
gospel of God, that the [b]offering*
[1]of the Gentiles might be acceptable,
*sanctified by the Holy Spirit.
17 Therefore I have reason to glory in
Christ Jesus [a]in the things *which pertain* to God.
18 For I will not dare to speak of any
of those things [a]which Christ has not
accomplished through me, in word and
deed, [b]to make the Gentiles *obedient—
19 [a]in mighty *signs and *wonders, by
the power of the Spirit of God, so that
from Jerusalem and round about to Illyricum I have fully preached the gospel of Christ.
20 And so I have made it my aim to
preach the gospel, not where Christ
was named, [a]lest I should build on another man's foundation,
21 but as it is written:

[a]*"To whom He was not announced,*
they shall see;
And those who have not heard
shall understand."

Plan to Visit Rome

22 For this reason [a]I also have been
much hindered from coming to you.
23 But now no longer having a place
in these parts, and [a]having a great desire these many years to come to you,
24 whenever I journey to Spain, [1]I
shall come to you. For I hope to see
you on my journey, [a]and to be helped
on my way there by you, if first I may
[b]enjoy your *company* for a while.
25 But now [a]I am going to Jerusalem
to [1]minister to the saints.
26 For [a]it pleased those from Macedonia and Achaia to make a certain *contribution for the poor among the saints
who are in Jerusalem.
27 It pleased them indeed, and they are
their *debtors. For [a]if the Gentiles have
been partakers of their spiritual things,
[b]their duty is also to *minister to them
in material things.
28 Therefore, when I have performed
this and have sealed to them [a]this fruit,
I shall go by way of you to Spain.
29 [a]But I know that when I come to
you, I shall come in the *fullness of the
blessing [1]of the gospel of Christ.
30 Now I beg you, brethren, through
the Lord Jesus Christ, and [a]through the
love of the Spirit, [b]that you strive together with me in prayers to God for
me,

14 [a]2 Pet. 1:12 [b]1 Cor. 1:5; 8:1, 7, 10 [1]M *others*
15 [a]Rom. 1:5; 12:3
16 [a]Rom. 11:13 [b][Is. 66:20] [1]Consisting of *See WW at Heb. 1:7. • See WW at Acts 21:26. • See WW at John 10:36.
17 [a]Heb. 2:17; 5:1
18 [a]Acts 15:12; 21:19 [b]Rom. 1:5 *See WW at 2 Cor. 10:5.
19 [a]Acts 19:11 *See WW at Rev. 16:14. • See WW at Acts 15:12.
20 [a][2 Cor. 10:13, 15, 16]
21 [a]Is. 52:15
22 [a]Rom. 1:13
23 [a]Acts 19:21; 23:11
24 [a]Acts 15:3 [b]Rom. 1:12 [1]NU omits *I shall come to you* and joins *Spain* with the next sentence.
25 [a]Acts 19:21 [1]*serve*
26 [a]1 Cor. 16:1 *See WW at Acts 2:42.
27 [a]Rom. 11:17 [b]1 Cor. 9:11 *See WW at Luke 13:4. • See WW at Acts 13:2.
28 [a]Phil. 4:17
29 [a][Rom. 1:11] [1]NU omits *of the gospel* *See WW at Eph. 3:19.
30 [a]Phil. 2:1 [b]2 Cor. 1:11

15:14 Admonish: Exhort, counsel. Christians are often the best counselors for one another, especially when they understand the will of God as taught in Scripture, and are able to apply Scripture rightly to life.

15:18 Not accomplished: This apparently means that Paul will speak of things that Christ *has* accomplished through him, **in word and deed,** that is, by the proclamation of the truth, by its demonstration in miracles and powerful answers to prayer, and in his own example of a Christlike life.

15:19 Signs and wonders accompanied Paul's preaching to authenticate it in the eyes of those who heard. This was the NT pattern (see Acts 2:43; 4:30; 5:12; 6:8; 14:3; 15:12; 2 Cor. 12:12; Heb. 2:4). Based on that pattern and the gifts described in 1 Cor. 12:9, 10, 28, it seems appropriate to expect miracles today as well. **Illyricum:** A Roman province located in modern day Yugoslavia and Albania, on the east coast of the Adriatic Sea.

15:23 Place: Probably "place to preach the gospel" (see v. 20). **These parts:** Paul was writing from Corinth, but perhaps his meaning was that he had preached in all God's commissioned places for him in Asia Minor and Greece and he was therefore ready to move further west.

15:24 To Spain: Paul was hoping to visit Rome, minister there (1:11), be encouraged and supported by the church in Rome, and then continue westward to preach in Spain. He probably did this after his imprisonment at the end of Acts.

15:25 Paul was **going to Jerusalem** with an offering to help poor Christians there (see Acts 19:21; 20:1—21:16; 2 Cor. 8; 9).

15:26 Macedonia: Northern Greece, including Philippi, Thessalonica, and Berea. **Achaia:** Southern Greece, including Corinth.

15:27 Though Christians in Greece were separated from the poor Christians in Jerusalem by many days in terms of communication and transportation, Paul nonetheless said that they had a **duty** to send aid to meet the needs of those distant believers—a principle the church would do well to heed today, also (see 1 John 3:17).

15:30 Paul knew that even the **prayers** of those whom he had never met could be very effective before God, so he asked that they pray for him.

31 [a]that I may be delivered from those
in Judea who [1]do not believe, and that
[b]my service for Jerusalem may be acceptable to the saints,
32 [a]that I may come to you with joy
[b]by the will of God, and may [c]be refreshed together with you.
33 Now [a]the God of *peace *be* with you
all. Amen.

Sister Phoebe Commended

16 I commend to you Phoebe our
sister, who is a servant of the
church in [a]Cenchrea,

KINGDOM DYNAMICS

16:1 A Radiant Woman Minister (Phoebe), WOMEN. The name "Phoebe" means "Pure or Radiant as the Moon." It is clear that through Phoebe the light of Jesus Christ shone brightly, for Paul calls her not only a servant of the church, but a helper of many (vv. 1, 2). Other versions translate the word "servant" as "deaconess." Still others have called her "minister"—inasmuch as in other scriptures where the Greek word *diakoneo* is used, it is translated "minister." According to many scholars it was Phoebe who carried the written book of Romans to the congregation. This is consonant to Ps. 68:11, which declares the place of women in the spread of God's Word: "The Lord gave the word; great *was* the company [or host of women] . . . who proclaimed it." The inserted words are justified by the Hebrew, and most translators acknowledge this fact. Today multitudes of laywomen and Christian women leaders—licensed or ordained—and prophetesses are helping carry the gospel to the world.

(Luke 10:38–42/Acts 21:9) F.L.

2 [a]that you may receive her in the
Lord [b]in a manner worthy of the saints,
and assist her in whatever business she
has need of you; for indeed she has
been a helper of many and of myself
also.

Greeting Roman Saints

3 Greet [a]Priscilla and Aquila, my fellow workers in Christ Jesus,
4 who risked their own necks for my
life, to whom not only I give thanks,
but also all the churches of the Gentiles.
5 Likewise *greet* [a]the *church that is
in their house. Greet my beloved Epae-
netus, who is [b]the firstfruits of [1]Achaia
to Christ.
6 Greet Mary, who labored much for
us.
7 Greet Andronicus and Junia, my
countrymen and my fellow prisoners,
who are of note among the [a]apostles,
who also [b]were in Christ before me.
8 Greet Amplias, my beloved in the
Lord.
9 Greet Urbanus, our fellow worker
in Christ, and Stachys, my beloved.
10 Greet Apelles, approved in Christ.
Greet those who are of the *household*
of Aristobulus.
11 Greet Herodion, my [1]countryman.
Greet those who are of the *household*
of Narcissus who are in the Lord.
12 Greet Tryphena and Tryphosa, who
have labored in the Lord. Greet the beloved Persis, who labored much in the
Lord.
13 Greet Rufus, [a]chosen* in the Lord,
and his mother and mine.
14 Greet Asyncritus, Phlegon, Hermas,
Patrobas, Hermes, and the brethren
who are with them.
15 Greet Philologus and Julia, Nereus
and his sister, and Olympas, and all the
saints who are with them.
16 [a]Greet one another with a holy

31 [a]2 Tim. 3:11; 4:17 [b]2 Cor. 8:4 [1]*are disobedient*
32 [a]Rom. 1:10 [b]Acts 18:21 [c]1 Cor. 16:18
33 [a]Rom. 16:20; 1 Cor. 14:33; 2 Cor. 13:11; Phil. 4:9; [1 Thess. 5:23]; 2 Thess. 3:16; Heb. 13:20 *See WW at Luke 1:79.

CHAPTER 16

1 [a]Acts 18:18
2 [a]Phil. 2:29 [b]Phil. 1:27
3 [a]Acts 18:2, 18, 26; 1 Cor. 16:19; 2 Tim. 4:19
5 [a]1 Cor. 16:19; Col. 4:15; Philem. 2 [b]1 Cor. 16:15 [1]NU *Asia* *See WW at Acts 8:1.
7 [a]Acts 1:13, 26 [b]Rom. 8:11; 16:3, 9, 10; 2 Cor. 5:17; 12:2; Gal. 1:22
11 [1]Or *relative*
13 [a]2 John 1 *See WW at 1Pet. 2:9.
16 [a]1 Cor. 16:20; 2 Cor. 13:12; 1 Thess. 5:26; 1 Pet. 5:14

16:1 Phoebe probably carried Paul's letter from Corinth to the church in Rome. **Servant:** This word may be translated "servant" or "minister" (as in Mark 9:35; John 2:5, 9; Rom. 13:4; 15:8), or "deacon" (as in Phil. 1:1; 1 Tim. 3:8, 12), depending on whether one thinks that Phoebe held a formally recognized office in the church at **Cenchrea,** a port city very near Corinth. Those who translate servant think that the requirements in 1 Tim. 3:12 make it unlikely that Phoebe would be in the office of deacon. There does not appear to be a consistent NT disposition against women in leading ministry roles.

16:2 *The Greek word for* **helper** is found nowhere else in the NT. Outside the NT, it is sometimes used of a "patroness," a woman who supplied support and funding for worthy causes.

16:3–16 Greetings to Christians whom Paul knows in Rome. The purposes are: 1) to give Phoebe a list of people on whom to call when she arrives; 2) to ensure she knows who is to receive the letter; 3) to show God's awareness of each individual's import in the work of the gospel. The list interestingly contains a number of significant women and numerous names common to slaves and freedmen.

16:3 See note on 1 Cor. 16:19.

16:7 Junia: Sometimes also translated "Junias," indicating a man. It is impossible to tell whether this name refers to a man or a woman. The name could be a feminine name "Junia," or it could be a regularly shortened form of a common man's name, "Junianus," like Silvanus (Silas) and many other names that took long and short forms. **Apostles** may be understood either in the narrow sense of those who could rule the church and write scripture or in the broader sense of the word (see note on 1:1). See also John 13:16; 2 Cor. 8:23; Phil. 2:25.

16:16 Holy kiss: A kiss was a common greeting in the first century (see 1 Thess. 5:26; 1 Pet. 5:14). See note on 1 Cor. 16:20. In western culture, the embrace seems to be the equivalent expression.

kiss. [1]The churches of Christ greet
you.

Avoid Divisive Persons

17 Now I urge you, brethren, note
those [a]who cause divisions and *offenses, contrary to the doctrine which
you learned, and [b]avoid them.
18 For those who are such do not serve
our Lord [1]Jesus Christ, but [a]their own
belly, and [b]by smooth words and flattering speech deceive the hearts of the
simple.
19 For [a]your *obedience has become
known to all. Therefore I am glad on
your behalf; but I want you to be
[b]wise in what is good, and [1]simple concerning evil.
20 And [a]the God of peace [b]will **crush**
Satan under your feet shortly. [c]The
grace of our Lord Jesus Christ *be* with
you. Amen.

WORD WEALTH

16:20 crush, *suntribo* (soon-*tree*-bow); Strong's *#4937:* To trample upon, break in pieces, shatter, bruise, grind down, smash. This statement in v. 20 alludes to Gen. 3:15. Our victory is a continuation of Christ's victory when He bruised the head of the serpent at Calvary. *Suntribo* points to present victories over the powers of darkness as well as to the ultimate destruction of Satan's kingdom at the Second Coming of Christ.

Greetings from Paul's Friends

21 [a]Timothy, my fellow worker, and
[b]Lucius, [c]Jason, and [d]Sosipater, my
countrymen, greet you.
22 I, Tertius, who wrote *this* epistle,
greet you in the Lord.
23 [a]Gaius, my host and *the host* of the
whole church, greets you. [b]Erastus, the
*treasurer of the city, greets you, and
Quartus, a brother.
24 [a]The[1] grace of our Lord Jesus
Christ *be* with you all. Amen.

Benediction

25 [1]Now [a]to Him who is able to establish you [b]according to my gospel and
the preaching of Jesus Christ, [c]accord-
ing to the revelation of the *mystery
[d]kept secret since the *world began
26 but [a]now made manifest, and by the
prophetic Scriptures made known to
all nations, according to the commandment of the everlasting God, for
[b]obedience to the faith—
27 to [a]God, alone wise, *be* glory
through Jesus Christ forever. Amen.

16 [1]NU *All the churches*
17 [a][Acts 15:1] [b][1 Cor. 5:9] *See WW at Matt. 16:23.
18 [a]Phil. 3:19 [b]Col. 2:4 [1]NU, M omit *Jesus*
19 [a]Rom. 1:8 [b]Matt. 10:16 [1]*innocent* *See WW at 2 Cor. 10:5.
20 [a]Rom. 15:33 [b]Gen. 3:15 [c]1 Cor. 16:23
21 [a]Acts 16:1 [b]Acts 13:1 [c]Acts 17:5 [d]Acts 20:4
23 [a]1 Cor. 1:14 [b]Acts 19:22 *See WW at 1 Pet. 4:10.
24 [a]1 Thess. 5:28 [1]NU omits v. 24.
25 [a][Eph. 3:20] [b]Rom. 2:16 [c]Eph. 1:9 [d]Col. 1:26; 2:2; 4:3 [1]M puts Rom. 16:25–27 after Rom. 14:23. *See WW at Mark 4:11. • See WW at Acts 1:7.
26 [a]Eph. 1:9 [b]Rom. 1:5
27 [a]Jude 25

16:19 Simple concerning evil: Christians should not try to become experts about all the details of evil deeds.
16:20 Paul proclaims the ultimate triumph of Christ and His church over all evil in fulfillment of Gen. 3:15. **Shortly** does not mean "soon," but "swiftly." In circumstances of life, as at the end of this age, we may expect God's conquest of **Satan**'s workings to be short and sharp.
16:22 Tertius was the secretary (or amanuensis) who wrote while Paul dictated (see Gal. 6:11).
16:26 Prophetic scriptures refers to the OT (see 1:2).

TRUTH-IN-ACTION through ROMANS

Letting the LIFE of the Holy Spirit Bring Faith's Works Alive in You!

Truth Romans Teaches	Text	**Action** Romans Invites
1 Key Lessons in Faith Faith is choosing boldly and unswervingly to believe what God has said. Twentieth-century faith must learn again to believe totally the testimony of Scripture! Among the keys to faithful living is the truth of our conversion. Faith frees us to live as never before for the good of others.	1:16	**Proclaim** the gospel boldly.
	4:17, 18	**Release** the creative power of God's Word by believing it in the face of challenging circumstances.
	4:20–25	**Stand** when tempted by unbelief, knowing that God can do what He promises.
	6:1–10	**Understand** that through baptism, you have been crucified with Christ. **Choose to believe** that you were also united with Jesus in His death, burial, and resurrection.
	15:1–3	**Live** in a manner that strengthens the weak in faith. **Commit** to the upbuilding of your neighbor.

Truth Romans Teaches	Text	**Action** Romans Invites
2 Steps to Dynamic Devotion The Word of God illuminated by the Holy Spirit is the only true means for transforming the human heart. Salvation by faith is a specific occasion, while the renewing of the mind by the Word is a continuing process. The disciple devotes himself to God's Word to be transformed into a holy person, radiantly Christ-like and radically different from the world. Spiritual disciples devour God's Word because in it is the key to a more dynamic relationship with their living Lord and a greater availability to the Holy Spirit.	10:17	**Be constant** in your reading and study of God's Word. **Recognize** that your faith will grow only as much as you feed on God's Word.
	12:1, 2	**Let** God's Word and His Holy Spirit radically transform your way of thinking. **Renew your mind** to know and do the will of God, giving your body a living sacrifice.
	15:4	**Recognize** that the OT was written through the Spirit for the church. **Incorporate** the OT into your daily Bible study.
3 Keys to Wise Living The believer's two natures often baffle and confuse him or her. The wisdom found in Rom. will help in managing this conflict by identifying which aspects of behavior result from the Holy Spirit's life and which result from the fleshly nature's activity. Thus, we can navigate our new life with Spirit-engendered wisdom and understanding.	1:18–23	**Understand** that judgment is self-induced. **Know** that men choose to reject God.
	2:24	**Be sensitive** to the fact that how you live can bring honor and glory to God, or it can bring reproach and blasphemy against His name.
	8:7, 8	**Be clear** that any hostile or disobedient tendency toward God's Word comes out of your fleshly nature.
	13:8–10	**Recognize** that love is binding and obligatory on believers. **Understand** that any lack of love is lawlessness and rebellion.
4 Steps to Dealing with Sin Rom. reveals a new, victorious method for our dealing with sin. Living free of sin's rule is now possible because we are no longer slaves of sin, but have become slaves of God, able to choose righteousness rather than being bound to the old nature. Obedience to the Word of God gains a new nature of holiness.	6:11–14	**Say "No!" to sin** whenever it confronts you. **Recognize** that you are really free from its demands.
	6:16–23	**Obey Christ,** your new Master, not sin, your old master.
	7:17, 20	**Believe with conviction** that it is your old, sinful nature, not your new nature in Christ that manifests itself in acts of sin.
5 Guidelines for Growth in the Spirit Through the indwelling presence of the Holy Spirit, the very life of Jesus Christ is brought into effect in our mortal bodies. As we yield ourselves to Him, Jesus becomes in and through us the very fulfillment of the Law and Word of God.	8:1–11	**Recognize** that the Law is fulfilled by the Holy Spirit in us. **Know** that His presence in you is the very life of Jesus Christ.
	8:13–17	**Choose** to live by the Spirit. **Put to death** fleshly attitudes and actions. **Acknowledge** your adoption as a child of God, calling Him "Father."

The First Epistle of Paul the Apostle to the CORINTHIANS

Author: Paul
Date: A.D. 56
Theme: Resolving Doctrinal and Practical Church Problems and Growth of a Church in Christ
Key Words: The Cross, Sexual Sins, Spiritual Gifts, Love, the Resurrection

Author The authenticity of 1 Corinthians has never seriously been challenged. In style, language, and theology, the letter belongs to Paul.

Occasion and Date Paul established the church at Corinth about A.D. 50–51, when he spent eighteen months there on his second missionary journey (Acts 18:1–17). He continued to carry on correspondence and exercise care for the church after his departure (see 1 Cor. 5:9; 2 Cor. 12:14). During his three-year ministry in Ephesus, on his third missionary journey (Acts 19), he had received disturbing reports concerning moral laxity among believers in Corinth. To remedy the situation, he sent the church a letter (1 Cor. 5:9–11), which has since been lost. Shortly afterward, a delegation sent by Chloe, a member of the church in Corinth, reported to Paul concerning the existence of divisive factions in the church. Before he could write a corrective letter, another delegation from Corinth arrived with a letter asking him certain questions (1 Cor. 7:1; 16:17). Paul immediately sent Timothy to Corinth to help correct conditions there (1 Cor. 4:17). He then wrote the letter that we know as 1 Corinthians, expecting it to reach Corinth before Timothy (16:10). Since Paul apparently wrote the letter near the end of his Ephesian ministry (16:8), it may be dated about A.D. 56.

Purpose 1 Corinthians is a pastoral letter, written to resolve doctrinal and practical problems within the local church. Paul's authorship gives the letter apostolic application to all "the churches of God" (11:16).

Background The letter reveals some of the typical Greek cultural problems of Paul's day, including the gross sexual immorality of the city of Corinth. The Greeks were known for their idolatry, divisive philosophies, spirit of litigation, and rejection of a bodily resurrection. Corinth was one of the most important commercial cities of the day and controlled much of the shipping between the East and the West. It was located on the narrow neck of land which served as a land-bridge between the mainland of Greece and the Peloponnesian peninsula. The city was infamous for its sensuality and sacred prostitution. Even its name became a notorious proverb: "to Corinthianize" meant to practice prostitution. The city's chief deity was

Aphrodite (Venus), the goddess of licentious love, and a thousand professional prostitutes served in the temple dedicated to her worship. The spirit of the city showed up in the church and explains the kind of problems the people faced.

It also reveals some of the problems the former pagans had in not transferring previous religious experiences to the ministry experience of the Holy Spirit. They may have associated some of the frenzied antics of paganism with the exercise of spiritual gifts (see 12:2).

Content The letter consists of Paul's response to ten separate problems: a sectarian spirit, incest, lawsuits, fornication, marriage and divorce, eating food offered to idols, wearing of the veil, the Lord's Supper, spiritual gifts, and the resurrection of the body.

Personal Application No epistle in the New Testament gives a clearer insight into the life of the first-century church than 1 Corinthians. In it Paul provides straightforward instructions for such moral and theological problems as sectarianism, spiritual immaturity, church discipline, ethical differences, the role of the sexes and the proper use of spiritual gifts. Where these same problems exist in the modern church, the remedies are the same. Those from non-Pentecostal or non-charismatic churches may receive a fresh challenge from the vitality and spiritual gifts evident in the Corinthian church, and may lay aside traditional prejudices against such things. Those from charismatic and Pentecostal churches, where worship is less structured and spiritual gifts are prominent, may reexamine their own practices in the light of Paul's guidelines for congregational services.

Christ Revealed The letter contains an unmatched revelation of the Cross of Christ as a counter to all human boasting (chs. 1—4). Paul cites Christ as our example in all behavior (11:1) and describes the church as His body (ch. 12). Especially important are the powerful consequences of Christ's resurrection for the whole of creation (ch. 15).

The Holy Spirit at Work The manifestations or the gifts of the Spirit make up the best known passages about the Holy Spirit (chs. 12—14). But we should not overlook the role of the Holy Spirit in revealing the things of God to the human spirit in a way that prevents all grounds for pride (2:1–13). Perhaps most illuminating amid current debate in the church at large is the way the apostle leads the Corinthians into a balanced employment of speaking with tongues, affirming this practice and refusing any the right to prohibit it (ch. 14).

Outline of 1 Corinthians

Introduction with greetings and thanksgiving **1:1–9**

I. The problem of a sectarian spirit which arose from a preference for religious leaders because of their supposed superior wisdom **1:10—4:21**

A. The contrast between human and divine wisdom over the Cross shows the fallacy of a sectarian spirit which stems from human wisdom 1:10—3:4

B. The role of religious leaders show they are important but never the cause for boasting 3:5—4:5

C. An open rebuke by ironic comparison of the Corinthians' pride with Paul's foolishness 4:6–21

Greeting

PAUL, [a]called *to be* an apostle of
Jesus Christ [b]through the *will of
God, and [c]Sosthenes *our* brother,

2 To the church of God which is at
Corinth, to those who [a]are [1]sanctified*
in Christ Jesus, [b]called *to be* *saints,
with all who in every place call on the
name of Jesus Christ [c]our Lord,
[d]both theirs and ours:

3 [a]Grace to you and peace from God
our Father and the Lord Jesus Christ.

Spiritual Gifts at Corinth

4 [a]I thank my God always concerning
you for the grace of God which was
given to you by Christ Jesus,
5 that you were enriched in every
thing by Him [a]in all [1]utterance and all
knowledge,
6 even as [a]the *testimony of Christ
was *confirmed [1]in you,
7 so that you *come short in no **gift,**
eagerly [a]waiting for the revelation of
our Lord Jesus Christ,

WORD WEALTH

1:7 gift, *charisma* (*khar*-is-mah); Strong's *#5486:* Related to other words derived from the root *char. Chara* is joy, cheerfulness, delight. *Charis* is grace, goodwill, undeserved favor. *Charisma* is a gift of grace, a free gift, divine gratuity, spiritual endowment, miraculous faculty. It is especially used to designate the gifts of the Spirit (12:4–10). In modern usage, a "charismatic" signifies one who either has one or more of these gifts functioning in his life, or who believes these gifts are for today's church.

8 [a]who will also confirm you to the
end, [b]*that you may be* blameless in the
day of our Lord Jesus Christ.
9 [a]God *is* faithful, by whom you were
*called into [b]the *fellowship of His
Son, Jesus Christ our Lord.

CHAPTER 1

1 [a]Rom. 1:1 [b]2 Cor. 1:1 [c]Acts 18:17 *See WW at Matt. 12:50.
2 [a][Acts 15:9] [b]Rom. 1:7 [c][1 Cor. 8:6] [d][Rom. 3:22] [1]*set apart* *See WW at John 10:36. • See WW at Acts 7:33.
3 [a]Rom. 1:7
4 [a]Rom. 1:8
5 [a][1 Cor. 12:8] [1]*speech*
6 [a]2 Tim. 1:8 [1]Or *among* *See WW at Rev. 15:5. • See WW at Mark 16:20.
7 [a]Phil. 3:20 *See WW at Luke 22:35.
8 [a]1 Thess. 3:13; 5:23 [b]Col. 1:22; 2:7
9 [a]Is. 49:7 [b][John 15:4]

*See WW at Gal. 1:6. • See WW at Acts 2:42.

1:1 Sosthenes was probably the former ruler of the synagogue at Corinth (Acts 18:17).
1:2 All believers in Christ are **saints** by virtue of their call, having been set apart to belong to Him. Having been placed in Christ, they are to grow progressively in holiness.
1:4–9 Paul rejoices in the grace of God at work in their past (vv. 5, 6), present (v. 7), and future (vv. 8, 9). Jesus Christ is validating the eternal purposes of God for His people.
1:5 Enriched: No one is impoverished by becoming a Christian. The particular wealth Paul has in mind is in the realm of spiritual gifts. Noteworthy is his introductory mention of **utterance,** affirmed as enriching, even though he will later bring severe correction regarding their manner of employing vocal gifts.
1:6 The changed lives of the Corinthians gave divine confirmation to Paul's **testimony** to Christ (see 2 Cor. 3:1–3).
1:8, 9 Blameless: Paul's confidence of final approval is based on God's faithfulness.

Sectarianism Is Sin

4 **10** Now I plead with you, brethren, by
the name of our Lord Jesus Christ,
[a]that you all [1]speak the same thing,
and *that* there be no [2]divisions among
you, but *that* you be *perfectly joined
together in the same mind and in the
same judgment.
11 For it has been declared to me concerning you, my brethren, by those of
Chloe's *household,* that there are
[1]contentions among you.
12 Now I say this, that [a]each of you
says, "I am of Paul," or "I am of
[b]Apollos," or "I am of [c]Cephas," or "I
am of Christ."
13 [a]Is Christ divided? Was Paul crucified for you? Or were you baptized in
the name of Paul?
14 I *thank God that I baptized [a]none
of you except [b]Crispus and [c]Gaius,
15 lest anyone should say that I had
baptized in my own name.
16 Yes, I also baptized the household
of [a]Stephanas. Besides, I do not know
whether I baptized any other.
17 For Christ did not *send me to baptize, but to preach the gospel, [a]not with
wisdom of words, lest the cross of
Christ should be *made of no effect.

Christ the Power and Wisdom of God

18 For the [1]message of the cross is
[a]foolishness to [b]those who are *perishing, but to us [c]who are being saved it
is the [d]power of God.
19 For it is written:

> [a]*"I will destroy the wisdom of the wise,*
> *And bring to nothing the *understanding of the prudent."*

20 [a]Where *is* the wise? Where *is* the
scribe? Where *is* the [1]disputer of this
*age? [b]Has not God made foolish the
wisdom of this *world?
21 For since, in the [a]wisdom of God,
the world through wisdom did not
know God, it pleased God through the
foolishness of the message preached to
save those who believe.
22 For [a]Jews request a *sign, and
Greeks seek after wisdom;
23 but we *preach Christ crucified,
[a]to the Jews a [1]stumbling* block and
to the [2]Greeks [b]foolishness,
24 but to those who are called, both
Jews and Greeks, Christ [a]the power of
God and [b]the wisdom of God.
25 Because the foolishness of God is 2
wiser than men, and the weakness of
God is stronger than men.

Glory Only in the Lord

26 For [1]you see your calling, brethren,
[a]that not many wise according to the
*flesh, not many *mighty, not many
[2]noble, *are called.*
27 But [a]God has chosen the foolish
things of the world to put to shame the
wise, and God has chosen the weak
things of the world to put to shame the
things which are mighty;
28 and the [1]base things of the world
and the things which are despised God
has chosen, and the things which are
not, to bring to nothing the things that
are,

10 [a]2 Cor. 13:11 [1]Have a uniform testimony [2]*schisms* or *dissensions* *See WW at Heb. 11:3. **11** [1]*quarrels* **12** [a]1 Cor. 3:4 [b]Acts 18:24 [c]John 1:42 **13** [a]2 Cor. 11:4 **14** [a]John 4:2 [b]Acts 18:8 [c]Rom. 16:23 *See WW at John 6:11. **16** [a]1 Cor. 16:15, 17 **17** [a][1 Cor. 2:1, 4, 13] *See WW at John 20:21. • See WW at 1 Cor. 9:15. **18** [a]1 Cor. 2:14 [b]2 Cor. 2:15 [c][1 Cor. 15:2] [d]Rom. 1:16 [1]Lit. *word* *See WW at Luke 9:56. **19** [a]Is. 29:14 *See WW at Luke 2:47. **20** [a]Is. 19:12; 33:18 [b]Job 12:17 [1]*debater* *See WW at Matt. 28:20. • See WW at John 18:36. **21** [a]Dan. 2:20 **22** [a]Matt. 12:38 *See WW at Rev. 16:14. **23** [a]Luke 2:34 [b][1 Cor. 2:14] [1]Gr. *skandalon, offense* [2]NU *Gentiles* *See WW at Acts 9:20. • See WW at Matt. 16:23.

24 [a][Rom. 1:4] [b]Col. 2:3 **26** [a]John 7:48 [1]*consider* [2]*well-born* *See WW at Matt. 26:41. • See WW at Matt. 19:26. **27** [a]Matt. 11:25 **28** [1]*insignificant* or *lowly*

1:10–17 The first problem addressed is the rivalry and strife that resulted over preference for religious leaders based on their assumed superior wisdom. Probably most were claiming to be of the "Paul-party" (v. 12). As a recipient of revelation, no one stood as close to the fountainhead of Christianity as Paul. He expressed gratitude that he had **baptized** only a few, lest anyone could claim baptism **in the name of Paul** and assume undue allegiance to him or privileged position before others. The gospel has to do with Jesus Christ, and one's allegiance belongs *to* Him and all position is *in* Him.

1:10 See section 4 of Truth-In-Action at the end of 1 Cor.

1:18–25 Message of the cross: A mutual antagonism exists between the wisdom of this world and the wisdom of God, and the conflict shows up supremely in the Cross of Christ. God works most wisely and most powerfully in ways directly opposite human expectations. Even as Jesus hung on the Cross, the Jews asked for a power-sign (Matt. 27:40–43). The Greeks made the pursuit of wisdom a meaningless end in itself, as Paul learned at Athens (Acts 17:21).

1:20 Where *is* the wise?: The deep gap between human and divine ways is evidenced throughout human history, as the quotation from Isaiah in v. 19 and the four questions in v. 20 show. The pro-Egyptian policies of Israel in Isaiah's day seemed to be the only reasonable recourse, but it was completely contrary to the divine plan of salvation (Is. 29:14).

1:24 The power of God: The gospel is the revelation of truth, but in the final analysis it is the operation of God's power with victory over sin and death. Biblical salvation is nothing short of a complete restoration of the universe, with a new heaven and a new earth.

1:25–29 See section 2 of Truth-In-Action at the end of 1 Cor.

1:26 A survey of the converts at Corinth proves the mutual rejection between human and divine wisdom. Only a few came from the world of culture and social sophistication. The heart of true wisdom is knowing the ways and the will of God, and living in harmony with ultimate, created reality. The human wisdom Paul opposes is not intellect or education, but a false independence of God and a bent toward self-sufficiency. God rejects human wisdom because of its pride and self-glory.

29 that no flesh should glory in His
presence.
30 But of Him you are in Christ Jesus,
who became for us wisdom from God—
and [a]righteousness* and sanctification
and *redemption—
31 that, as it is written, [a]*"He who
glories, let him glory in the LORD."*

Christ Crucified

2 And I, brethren, when I came to
you, did not come with excellence
of speech or of *wisdom declaring to
you the [1]testimony of God.
2 For I *determined not to know anything among you [a]except *Jesus
*Christ and Him crucified.
3 [a]I was with you [b]in weakness, in
*fear, and in much trembling.
4 And my speech and my preaching
[a]*were* not with persuasive words of
[1]human wisdom, [b]but in demonstration of the Spirit and of power,
5 that your faith should not be in the
wisdom of men but in the [a]power of
God.

Spiritual Wisdom

6 However, we speak wisdom among
those who are *mature, yet not the wisdom of this age, nor of the rulers of
this age, who are coming to nothing.
7 But we speak the wisdom of God
in a *mystery, the hidden *wisdom*
which God [1]ordained before the ages
for our glory,
8 which none of the rulers of this age
knew; for [a]had they known, they
would not have [b]crucified the *Lord of
glory.
9 But as it is written:

[a]*"Eye has not seen, nor ear heard,*
*Nor have entered into the *heart*
of man
The things which God has
**prepared for those who *love*
Him."

10 But [a]God has revealed *them* to us
through His Spirit. For the Spirit
searches all things, yes, the deep things
of God.
11 For what man knows the things of
a man except the [a]spirit of the man
which is in him? [b]Even so no one
knows the things of God except the
Spirit of God.
12 Now we have received, not the
spirit of the world, but [a]the Spirit who
is from God, that we might know the
things that have been freely *given to
us by God.

30 [a][2 Cor. 5:21] *See WW at 2 Tim. 4:8. • See WW at Rom. 3:24.
31 [a]Jer. 9:23, 24

CHAPTER 2

1 [1]NU *mystery* *See WW at Acts 6:10.
2 [a]Gal. 6:14 *See WW at John 18:31. • See WW at Phil. 4:23. • See WW at 2 Tim. 4:22.
3 [a]Acts 18:1 [b][2 Cor. 4:7] *See WW at 1 John 4:18.
4 [a]2 Pet. 1:16 [b]Rom. 15:19 [1]NU omits *human*
5 [a]1 Thess. 1:5
6 *See WW at James 3:2.
7 [1]*predetermined* *See WW at Mark 4:11.
8 [a]Luke 23:34 [b]Matt. 27:33–50 *See WW at John 6:68.
9 [a][Is. 64:4; 65:17] *See WW at Rev. 2:23. • See WW at Rev. 21:2. • See WW at John 3:16.
10 [a]Matt. 11:25; 13:11; 16:17 **11** [a][James 2:26] [b]Rom. 11:33 **12** [a][Rom. 8:15] *See WW at Col. 3:13.

1:30 Righteousness, a term taken from the courts, is God's judicial determination to right every wrong, His gift to the guilty which removes all condemnation and puts them in a state of justification, including full acquittal from all charges against them. **Sanctification** is a symbol taken from the temple, showing the need for cleansing from pollution. It includes a renewal by the power of the Holy Spirit, which allows acceptable living before God and points to our ultimate perfection in His presence. **Redemption,** taken from a background of slavery and debt, speaks of freedom and final deliverance from all aspects of sin, including the resurrection of the body.

2:1–5 Both the content and the style of Paul's preaching conformed to the ways of God as revealed in the Cross. Paul did not preach to show off his oratorical skills and draw attention to himself; rather, he spoke with **fear, and . . . trembling,** a figure of speech denoting the opposite of self-confidence. **Demonstration of the Spirit and of power** not only refer to the fact that the miraculous accompanied Paul's preaching (2 Cor. 12:12), but also to the Holy Spirit's transforming power in the individual lives of the Corinthians at the time of their conversion. Far from a mere intellectual conversion through human wisdom, they encountered the Spirit Himself who demonstrated His presence in them through various spiritual gifts, including speaking with tongues.

2:7 The very nature of God's **wisdom** renders the wisdom of this world inadequate, for it is not of this age. **Mystery** in the NT does not mean mysterious or difficult to understand, but denotes a truth hidden in God's mind until He chooses to disclose it. God had the plan of redemption in mind before the creation of the world, and it would have remained unknown had He not revealed it in Christ. Believers live by a secret, the essence of which is Christ and His glorious purposes for the world.

2:8 None of the rulers: This passage asserts that Satan ("the god of this age," 2 Cor. 4:4) and the demons of hell ("principalities and powers," Col. 2:15) were completely confounded by the Cross. This is a profound disclosure of Satan's limited ability to anticipate the tactics of Almighty God, the reminder that God's sovereign power and omniscience are always the insurance of the believer's ultimate victory in Christ.

2:9 Eye has not seen: The quotation from Is. 64:4 (v. 9) implies three ways of knowing: perceptual knowledge (**eye, ear**) through observation and sense experience; conceptual knowledge (**heart,** mind) by reason and intellectual inquiry; and spiritual knowledge (**love**) by moral and personal affinity. Since knowledge of the things of God is more of a spiritual than an intellectual nature, there is no basis for glorying in any religious leader for his supposed superior grasp of reality.

2:10 God has revealed: Two elements are necessary to know the things of God: a revelation from God by the Spirit, and an appropriate spiritual response by man (2:14—3:4).

2:11 As one's own inner thoughts are known only to himself, so the mind of God is known only by God's Spirit. God has chosen to make Himself known in Jesus Christ, and the Holy Spirit has brought this revelation of Christ to the church through the apostles.

2 13 These things we also speak, not in
words which man's wisdom teaches
but which the [1]Holy Spirit teaches,
comparing spiritual things with spiritual.
14 [a]But the *natural man does not receive the things of the Spirit of God,
for they are foolishness to him; nor can
he know *them,* because they are *spiritually discerned.
15 But he who is spiritual judges all
things, yet he himself is *rightly* judged
by no one.
16 For [a]*"who has known the mind of
the* LORD *that he may instruct Him?"*
[b]But we have the mind of Christ.

Sectarianism Is Carnal

4 3 And I, brethren, could not speak
to you as to spiritual *people* but as
to carnal, as to [a]babes in Christ.
2 I fed you with [a]milk and not with
solid food; [b]for until now you were not
able *to receive it,* and even now you
are still not able;
3 for you are still carnal. For where
there are *envy, strife, and divisions
among you, are you not carnal and
[1]behaving like *mere* men?
4 For when one says, "I am of Paul,"
and another, "I *am* of Apollos," are you
not carnal?

Watering, Working, Warning

5 Who then is Paul, and who *is* Apollos, but [a]ministers through whom you
believed, as the Lord gave to each one?

KINGDOM DYNAMICS

3:1–5 True Spiritual Growth Requires God's Word, THE WORD OF GOD. Beginning in 1 Cor. 2:10, Paul elaborates our need of Holy Spirit-given wisdom and revelation, and he ties this very firmly to our receiving the "words . . . which the Holy Spirit teaches" (2:13). He immediately turns from these observations to an outright confrontation with the carnality of the Corinthians, attributing it to the shallowness of their intake of God's Word ("not able to receive [solid food]," 3:2; see also Heb. 5:12–14).

The demanding truth of this passage is that no amount of supposed spiritual insight or experience reflects genuine spiritual growth, if it is separated from our basic growth in the knowledge of God's word in the Bible. Without this rootedness in the word, we may be deluded about our growth. Such "rootedness" is in truth and love, not merely in learning knowledge or accomplished study. In order to experience true spiritual growth, we must spend time in the Word and separate ourselves from the hindrances of lovelessness, competitiveness, and strife.

(Ps. 119:105/John 14:21) J.W.H.

6 [a]I planted, [b]Apollos watered,
[c]but God gave the increase.
7 So then [a]neither he who plants is
anything, nor he who waters, but God
who gives the increase.
8 Now he who plants and he who waters are one, [a]and each one will receive
his own *reward according to his own
labor.
9 For [a]we are God's fellow workers;
you are God's field, *you are* [b]God's
building.
10 [a]According to the grace of God
which was given to me, as a wise master builder I have laid [b]the foundation,
and *another builds on it. But let each
one take heed how he builds on it.
11 For no other foundation *can anyone lay than [a]that which is laid,
[b]which is Jesus Christ.
12 Now if anyone builds on this foun-

13 [1]NU omits *Holy*
14 [a]Matt. 16:23 *See WW at James 3:15. • See WW at Rev. 11:8.
16 [a]Is. 40:13 [b][John 15:15]

CHAPTER 3

1 [a]Heb. 5:13
2 [a]1 Pet. 2:2 [b]John 16:12
3 [1]Lit. *walking according to man* *See WW at 2 Cor. 11:2.
5 [a]2 Cor. 3:3, 6; 4:1; 5:18; 6:4
6 [a]Acts 18:4 [b]Acts 18:24–27 [c][2 Cor. 3:5]
7 [a][Gal. 6:3]
8 [a]Ps. 62:12 *See WW at Rev. 22:12.
9 [a]2 Cor. 6:1 [b][Eph. 2:20–22]
10 [a]Rom. 1:5 [b]1 Cor. 4:15 *See WW at John 14:16.
11 [a]Is. 28:16 [b]Eph. 2:20 *See WW at Jude 24.

2:13 Spiritual things with spiritual: Spirit answers to spirit, not spirit to mind. The Holy Spirit interprets spiritual things to spiritual people. This text also may describe the means by which the Word of God has been given to us in the Bible as the Holy Spirit puts spiritual "ideas" into specific spiritual "words" of His selection.
2:13–16 See section 2 of Truth-In-Action at the end of 1 Cor.
2:14—3:4 People fall into three spiritual categories that clarify how the revelation of the Cross by the Spirit is received from the human side. **The natural man,** unregenerate and devoid of the Spirit, has no appreciation for the gospel. The **spiritual** man, regenerate and possessing spiritual maturity, as seen in freedom from sectarian strife (3:3, 4), has a nature that responds to the truth, and unbelievers find him difficult to understand. The **carnal** man, regenerate but living much like an unregenerate, is a believer with childish ways, as seen in a jealous and sectarian spirit. An immature Christian lives more for human opinion than for Christ.
3:1–4 See section 4 of Truth-In-Action at the end of 1 Cor.
3:5–9 Three illustrations put the religious leaders in whom the Corinthians were glorying into proper perspective (3:5—4:5). **You are God's field:** The first example, from agriculture, shows their essential equality, but stresses that they have nothing to boast about since God gives the increase. They have individual rewards, but in terms of goals and servanthood they are one.
3:9–17 ***You are* God's building:** The second metaphor also shows the relative insignificance of religious leaders, but stresses their responsibility. Ministers are like building contractors with restricted permits to build only on the prescribed foundation (vv. 10, 11). In architecture, originality goes into the floor plan; so in the gospel, no man has authored original revelation, but only God in the Father's wise plan, through the Son's willing obedience, and by the Holy Spirit's powerful working.
3:12 To build on the foundation a building of durable material (**gold, silver, precious stones**) is to teach sound doctrine

dation *with* gold, silver, precious
stones, wood, hay, straw,
13 each one's *work will become clear;
for the Day [a]will declare it, because
[b]it will be *revealed by fire; and the
fire will test each one's work, of what
sort it is.
14 If anyone's work which he has built
on *it* endures, he will receive a reward.
15 If anyone's work is burned, he will
suffer loss; but he himself will be
saved, yet so as through fire.
16 [a]Do you not know that you are the
temple of God and *that* the Spirit of
God dwells in you?
1 17 If anyone [1]defiles the temple of
God, God will destroy him. For the
temple of God is holy, which *temple*
you are.

Avoid Worldly Wisdom

18 [a]Let no one deceive himself. If anyone among you seems to be wise in this
age, let him become a fool that he may
become wise.
19 For the wisdom of this world is foolishness with God. For it is written,
[a]*"He catches the wise in their own*
craftiness";

> **WORD WEALTH**
>
> **3:19 craftiness,** *panourgia* (pan-oorg-*ee*-ah); Strong's *#3834:* Versatile cleverness, astute knavery, sophisticated cunning, unscrupulous conduct, evil treachery, deceptive scheming, arrogant shrewdness, and sly arrogance. Used only five times in the NT, it refers to Satan's deceiving Eve (2 Cor. 11:3); the Pharisees' trying to trick Jesus (Luke 20:23); the deception of false teachers (Eph. 4:14); the self-entrapment of the worldly wise (1 Cor. 3:19); and the improper method of presenting the gospel (2 Cor. 4:2).

20 and again, [a]*"The* LORD *knows the*
**thoughts of the wise, that they are*
**futile."*
21 Therefore let no one boast in men.
For [a]all things are yours:
22 whether Paul or Apollos or Cephas,
or the world or *life or death, or things
present or things to come—all are
yours.
23 And [a]you *are* Christ's, and Christ
is God's.

Stewards of the Mysteries of God

4 Let a man so consider us, as
[a]servants of Christ [b]and *stewards
of the mysteries of God.
2 Moreover it is required in *stewards
that one be found faithful.
3 But with me it is a very small thing
that I should be judged by you or by
a human [1]court. In fact, I do not even
judge myself.
4 For I know of nothing against myself, yet I am not justified by this; but
He who judges me is the Lord.
5 [a]Therefore judge nothing before the
time, until the Lord comes, who will
both bring to [b]light the hidden things
of darkness and [c]reveal* the [1]counsels

13 [a]1 Pet. 1:7 [b]Mal. 3:1–3; Luke 2:35 *See WW at John 9:4. • See WW at 1 Cor. 11:19.
16 [a]Rom. 8:9; 1 Cor. 6:19; 2 Cor. 6:16; Eph. 2:21
17 [1]*destroys*
18 [a]Prov. 3:7
19 [a]Job 5:13
20 [a]Ps. 94:11 *See WW at Luke 2:35. • See WW at Acts 14:15.
21 [a][2 Cor. 4:5]
22 *See WW at 1 John 5:20.
23 [a][Rom. 14:8]; 1 Cor. 15:23; 2 Cor. 10:7; [Gal. 3:29]

CHAPTER 4

1 [a]Matt. 24:45; Rom. 13:6; 2 Cor. 3:6; Col. 1:25 [b]Luke 12:42; 1 Cor. 9:17; Titus 1:7; 1 Pet. 4:10 *See WW at 1 Pet. 4:10.
2 *See WW at 1 Pet. 4:10.
3 [1]Lit. *day*
5 [a]Matt. 7:1; Rom. 2:1; [Rev. 20:12] [b]Matt. 10:26 [c]1 Cor. 3:13 [1]*motives* *See WW at Col. 3:4.

---

and live a life of fidelity to the truth, thus leading converts to spiritual maturity. To build with perishable material (**wood, hay, straw**) is to provide inadequate or unsound teaching or to compromise the truth by demonstrating a life-style that contradicts or fails to model it.

3:13 The quality of each builder's work will be tested on **the Day** of the Lord's return. Every leader will stand accountable before the Lord Christ—Builder of His church (Matt. 16:18; 2 Cor. 5:10; Heb. 13:17).

3:14 The **reward** is not salvation, which Scripture teaches is a free gift, but a reward for faithful service.

3:15 The **loss** is the reward this builder might have received, not his salvation. **As through fire:** This person will have a narrow escape, like someone fleeing from a burning building, who loses all his possessions and saves only his life.

3:16 The building is identified as God's **temple,** made holy by the indwelling presence of the Holy Spirit. Here the temple of God is the local church. In 6:19 it is the individual Christian's body, and in Eph. 2:20, 21 it is the church universal.

3:17 See section 1 of Truth-In-Action at the end of 1 Cor.

3:17 Paul does not specify how one may destroy **the temple of God,** that is, the church. The word means "to ruin through corrupting or seducing," thus any number of unworthy, immature or crude means may apply. It may be by false teaching, by pride and spite, or by immorality. Paul does make it clear, however, that one defiling will himself be brought to ruin.

3:18–20 Quotations from Job 5:13 and Ps. 94:11 shame the Corinthians for glorying in the wisdom of their religious leaders.

3:21–23 Here is a conclusive word against exclusive sectarian thinking. **All are yours:** The apostles have been gifted, not in order that the Corinthians might serve them, but in order that the apostles might serve the Corinthians. The appeal is for all believers to see that the leaders they have been given are from Christ (Eph. 4:7–11) and thus are not to be pitted against one another by those who have received them.

4:1–5 The third illustration pictures ministers as **stewards** in God's household, standing between the householder and the household, and charged particularly with the task of feeding the household. A steward was in full charge of a household and was accountable only to the owner, who alone could render final decisions. The steward was expected to be **faithful** in dispensing to the household exactly what had been entrusted to him. In the same way, ministers are to expound nothing more and nothing less than the whole counsel of God.

of the hearts. [d]Then each one's *praise
will come from God.

Fools for Christ's Sake

6 Now these things, brethren, I have
figuratively transferred to myself and
Apollos for your sakes, that you may
learn in us not to think beyond what
is written, that none of you may be
[1]puffed up on behalf of one against the
other.
7 For who [1]makes* you differ *from
another?* And [a]what do you have that
you did not receive? Now if you did
indeed receive *it,* why do you boast as
if you had not received *it?*
8 You are already full! [a]You are already rich! You have reigned as kings
without us—and indeed I could wish
you did reign, that we also might reign
with you!
9 For I think that God has displayed
us, the apostles, last, as men condemned to death; for we have been
made [1]a [a]spectacle to the world, both
to angels and to men.
10 We *are* [a]fools for Christ's sake, but
you *are* wise in Christ! [b]We *are* weak,
but you *are* strong! You *are* distinguished, but we *are* dishonored!
11 To the present hour we both hunger
and thirst, and we are poorly clothed,
and beaten, and homeless.
12 [a]And we labor, working with our
own hands. [b]Being reviled, we bless;
being persecuted, we *endure;
13 being defamed, we [1]entreat. [a]We
have been made as the filth of the
world, the offscouring of all things until now.

5 [d]Rom. 2:29 *See WW at Eph. 1:6
6 [1]*arrogant*
7 [a]John 3:27 [1]*distinguishes you* *See WW at Acts 11:12.
8 [a]Rev. 3:17
9 [a]Heb. 10:33 [1]Lit. *theater*
10 [a]Acts 17:18; 26:24 [b]2 Cor. 13:9
12 [a]Acts 18:3; 20:34 [b]Matt. 5:44 *See WW at 2 Thess. 1:4.
13 [a]Lam. 3:45 [1]*exhort, encourage*
14 [a]1 Thess. 2:11
15 [a]Gal. 4:19 *See WW at Mark 1:1.
16 [a][1 Cor. 11:1]
17 [a]Acts 19:22 [b]1 Tim. 1:2, 18 [c]1 Cor. 11:2 [d]1 Cor. 7:17 [e]1 Cor. 14:33
18 [a]1 Cor. 5:2 [1]*arrogant*
19 [a]Acts 19:21; 20:2 [b]Acts 18:21 *See WW at Matt. 8:2.
20 [a]1 Thess. 1:5 [b]1 Cor. 2:4
21 [a]2 Cor. 10:2 *See WW at 1 Tim. 6:11.

CHAPTER 5

1 [a]Lev. 18:6–8 [1]NU omits *named* *See WW at Matt. 15:19.

Paul's Paternal Care

14 I do not write these things to shame
you, but [a]as my beloved children I
warn *you.*
15 For though you might have ten
thousand instructors in Christ, yet *you
do* not *have* many fathers; for [a]in
Christ Jesus I have begotten you
through the *gospel.
16 Therefore I urge you, [a]imitate me.
17 For this reason I have sent [a]Timo-
thy to you, [b]who is my beloved and
faithful son in the Lord, who will
[c]remind you of my ways in Christ, as
I [d]teach everywhere [e]in every church.
18 [a]Now some are [1]puffed up, as
though I were not coming to you.
19 [a]But I will come to you shortly,
[b]if the Lord *wills, and I will know, not
the word of those who are puffed up,
but the power.
20 For [a]the kingdom of God *is* not in 6
word but in [b]power.
21 What do you want? [a]Shall I come
to you with a rod, or in love and a spirit
of *gentleness?

Immorality Defiles the Church

5 It is actually reported *that there is* 4
*sexual immorality among you,
and such sexual immorality as is not
even [1]named among the Gentiles—that
a man has his father's [a]wife!
2 [a]And you are [1]puffed up, and have
not rather [b]mourned,* that he who has
done this deed might be taken away
from among you.

2 [a]1 Cor. 4:18 [b]2 Cor. 7:7–10 [1]*arrogant* *See WW at Rev. 18:11.

4:6–19 The Corinthians were **puffed up,** bloated with pride (vv. 6, 18, 19). In humbling them without rejecting them (v. 14), Paul appeals to reason (vv. 6, 7); resorts to satire (vv. 8–13); tries tenderness (vv. 14–16); and uses toughness (vv. 17–21). In their pride the Corinthians were arrogantly presuming the full right *in this life* to things promised in part at the present, but only fully realized in the coming of Christ's kingdom (v. 8). They were drawing their values from the false standards or fallacious teaching born of the spirit of this age, forgetting that this era's values stand judged under the Cross of Christ. The apostles, on the other hand, lived like **fools** from any other perspective than faith in Christ. Paul's life-style was ridiculous by the world's opinion (vv. 9–13).

4:9 In contrast to the smug self-satisfaction of the Corinthian Christians, Paul uses a vivid metaphor to paint the actual *condition of the apostles.* **Displayed us, the apostles, last,** is a pitiful analogy drawn from the cruelty of the Roman arena. The apostles were like gladiators fighting to the death, or like criminals thrown to the lions, made a spectacle as the grand finale to a day's sport in a colosseum.

4:15 I have begotten you: Because Paul founded the church, he had a special fatherly role in the life of the people.

4:17 Timothy will prepare them for Paul's future coming (see 16:10, 11).

4:20 See section 6 of Truth-In-Action at the end of 1 Cor.

4:20 Kingdom of God: God's present reign in Christ through the lives of believers is backed up by the dynamic power of the Holy Spirit, which carries a moral authority that Paul can use if necessary.

5:1–13 The Corinthians displayed an apathetic attitude toward an outrageous case of incest, passively ignoring the disgrace. Paul must deal with the problem and instruct the church in godly discipline. However, as evil as this tolerance was, it is the one case of immoral behavior reported in the text. The Corinthians clearly needed correction and needed warning against concession to their immoral environment (6:12–20). This episode, however wrong, often invokes exaggerative comments that this church was "riddled with immoral behavior."

5:1–8 See section 4 of Truth-In-Action at the end of 1 Cor.

5:1 Father's wife: This expression parallels Lev. 18:8 and almost certainly means a stepmother. The offense violated even the social decency of the pagan world, a clear indicator that the Corinthians had either a false notion about God's grace or a too casual attitude about sexual morality.

3 [a]For I indeed, as absent in body but
present in spirit, have already judged
(as though I were present) him who has
so done this deed.
4 In the [a]name of our Lord Jesus
Christ, when you are gathered together, along with my spirit, [b]with the
power of our Lord Jesus Christ,
5 [a]deliver such a one to [b]Satan for the
destruction of the flesh, that his spirit
may be saved in the day of the Lord
[1]Jesus.
6 [a]Your glorying *is* not good. Do you
not know that [b]a little leaven leavens
the whole lump?
7 Therefore [1]purge out the old leaven,
that you may be a new lump, since you
truly are unleavened. For indeed
[a]Christ, our [b]Passover, was sacrificed
[2]for us.
8 Therefore [a]let us keep the feast,
[b]not with old leaven, nor [c]with the
leaven of malice and wickedness, but
with the unleavened *bread* of **sincerity**
and truth.

WORD WEALTH

5:8 sincerity, *eilikrineia* (eye-lik-*ree*-ni-ah); Strong's *#1505:* Literally "judged by sunlight." The word alludes to Oriental bazaars where pottery was displayed in dimly lit rooms. Unscrupulous merchants would patch cracked pottery or cover defects with wax. Intelligent buyers would hold up the pottery to the sun and judge its quality by the sunlight. *Eilikrineia* is transparent honesty, genuine purity, manifested clarity, and unsullied innocence. It describes one who does not fear thorough examination of his motives and intents, because he has nothing to hide.

3 [a]Col. 2:5; 1 Thess. 2:17
4 [a][Matt. 18:20] [b][Matt. 16:19; John 20:23]; 2 Cor. 12:9
5 [a]Ps. 109:6; Prov. 23:14; Luke 22:31; 1 Tim. 1:20 [b][Acts 26:18] [1]NU omits *Jesus*
6 [a]1 Cor. 3:21 [b]Hos. 7:4; Matt. 16:6, 12; Gal. 5:9; 2 Tim. 2:17
7 [a]Is. 53:7 [b]John 19:14 [1]*clean out* [2]NU omits *for us*
8 [a]Ex. 12:15 [b]Deut. 16:3 [c]Matt. 16:6
9 [a]2 Cor. 6:14; Eph. 5:11; 2 Thess. 3:6 [1]*associate*
10 [a]John 17:15 *See WW at 1 Cor. 6:10.
11 [a]Matt. 18:17 [b]Gal. 2:12 *See WW at 1 Cor. 6:10.
13 [a]Deut. 13:5; 17:7, 12; 19:19; 21:21; 22:21, 24; 24:7; 1 Cor. 5:2

CHAPTER 6

1 [a]Dan. 7:22; Matt. 19:28
2 [a]Ps. 49:14

Immorality Must Be Judged

9 I wrote to you in my epistle [a]not to
[1]keep company with sexually immoral
people.
10 Yet *I* certainly *did* not *mean* with
the sexually immoral people of this
world, or with the *covetous, or extortioners, or idolaters, since then you
would need to go [a]out of the world.
11 But now I have written to you not
to keep company [a]with anyone named
a brother, who is sexually immoral, or
*covetous, or an idolater, or a reviler,
or a drunkard, or an extortioner—[b]not
even to eat with such a person.
12 For what *have* I *to do* with judging
those also who are outside? Do you not
judge those who are inside?
13 But those who are outside God
judges. Therefore [a]*"put away from
yourselves the evil person."*

Do Not Sue the Brethren

6 Dare any of you, having a matter
against another, go to law before
the unrighteous, and not before the
[a]saints? 1
2 Do you not know that [a]the saints
will judge the world? And if the world

5:5 Deliver . . . to Satan: More than church ostracism, it implies a removal of God's protective power, which allows Satan to work (Acts 26:18; 1 Tim. 1:20). **Destruction of the flesh:** The discipline administered to the offender and the resultant sufferings would bring about a spirit of humility and repentance. The text does not inform us exactly how "to deliver" in this process. While leaving certain questions unanswered, the final intent is clear: **that his spirit may be saved.** It would seem, however, that certain elements would have included abandoning fellowship (v. 9) and "loosing" the party (Matt. 18:17–20) to the consequences of their persistent disobedience.

5:6–8 On the night of the first Passover in Egypt, the Hebrews removed all the **leaven** from their houses, a practice still carried on among Jewish people (Ex. 12:15). Leaven has a fermenting action that illustrates the corrupting power of evil. Since Christ our Passover Lamb has been sacrificed, the church ought to have an unleavened house; otherwise, the yeast of sin can spread if unchecked. Ignored discipline denies the purpose of Christ's death.

5:9–13 The converts in Corinth had misunderstood Paul's instructions in an earlier letter concerning association with **immoral people,** concluding that he meant withdrawal from all contact with non-Christian sinners. He was actually referring to immoral people who claimed to be Christians.

5:10 Not to mix with the world's sinners would necessitate total withdrawal, as though one entered a monastery to get **out of the world** altogether. Paul implies this is not God's will for us, and the evidence of monastic philosophy in church history verifies its relative fruitlessness for advancing either godliness or the gospel.

5:11 Elsewhere Paul instructs to seek the restoration of erring saints, not to withdraw from them (see Gal. 6:1). Here he instructs that at times we are to withdraw fellowship. This case means to administer strict discipline when church members openly persist in sin and do not heed corrective counsel.

5:12, 13 The church judges (administers corrective discipline to) those inside its fellowship; God judges the world. Christian morality can never successfully be imposed on the world, and such imposition is not to be our attempted mission. **Put away from yourselves the evil person** is a quotation repeated nine times in Deut. as an abiding principle for God's people, applying directly to the case of incest and indirectly to all leavening evil in our lives. This process is redemptive and not punitive (2 Cor 2:5–11).

6:1–11 See section 1 of Truth-In-Action at the end of 1 Cor.

6:1–11 The Corinthian Christians were suing each other in pagan courts, with the underlying motive of greed (v. 8). Paul denounces their shame of taking cases to heathen judges instead of settling disputes themselves (vv. 1–6), and exposes their lovelessness and unrighteousness in harboring grievances (vv. 7–11).

6:2, 3 If Christians are destined to be future coadministrators of justice in the coming **world** (see Matt. 19:28; Rev. 20:4), they should be able to **judge** more petty matters now.

will be judged by you, are you unworthy to judge the smallest matters?
3 Do you not know that we shall
[a]judge *angels? How much more,
things that pertain to this life?
4 If then you have [1]judgments concerning things pertaining to this life,
do you appoint those who are least esteemed by the church to judge?
5 I say this to your shame. Is it so,
that there is not a wise man among
you, not even one, who will be able to
*judge between his brethren?
6 But brother goes to law against
brother, and that before unbelievers!
7 Now therefore, it is already an utter
failure for you that you go to law
against one another. [a]Why do you not
rather *accept wrong? Why do you not
rather *let yourselves* be cheated?
8 No, you yourselves do wrong and
cheat, and *you do* these things *to your*
brethren!
9 Do you not know that the unrighteous will not inherit the kingdom of
God? Do not be deceived. [a]Neither fornicators, nor idolaters, nor adulterers,
nor [1]homosexuals, nor [2]sodomites,
10 nor thieves, nor **covetous,** nor
drunkards, nor revilers, nor extortioners will inherit the kingdom of
God.

WORD WEALTH

6:10 covetous, *pleonektes* (pleh-on-*ek*-tace); Strong's *#4123:* Literally "to have more." This word regresses from good to bad. *Pleon* is the basic word for more in quantity, quality, and number. *Pleonazo* means to do more, make more, or increase. *Pleonekteo* means to overreach. *Pleonexia* is avarice. *Pleonektes* means a greedy covetousness so eager for gain that it will defraud others. A person consumed with *pleonektes* will violate laws for unlawful gain. He will cunningly forge ahead at others' expense. Eph. 5:3 tells us covetousness is idolatry. Idolatry is an aggravated form of self-love motivated by ego-drive. (Compare "pleonasm" or "pleonastic.")

KINGDOM DYNAMICS

6:9, 10 Integrity and Morality, CHARACTER AND THE KINGDOM. The privilege of becoming an authorized and empowered representative of God's kingdom and of ministering Christ's life and the Holy Spirit's gifts to others is not the heritage of the unholy. Twice the text says certain people will not "inherit the kingdom of God," and then designates broad categories of people who are excluded from enjoying the resources and rewards of righteousness. (See also Gal. 5:19–21; Eph. 5:5.)

Although our righteousness before God is through Christ's work alone, and while it remains timelessly true that we cannot earn any spiritual gift or right to function in the power of the Holy Spirit, integrity and morality of character are nonetheless essential to the "kingdom person."

Holiness of heart and life keeps the lines of communication with God unjumbled, by keeping any private or carnal agenda out of the way. They also insure the Holy Spirit free access for distributing His gifts and fulfilling the Father's will in any situation.

(Matt. 18:18–25/Mark 1:15) J.W.H.

11 And such were [a]some of you.
[b]But you were washed, but you were
[1]sanctified, but you were *justified in
the *name of the Lord Jesus and by
the Spirit of our God.

Glorify God in Body and Spirit

12 [a]All things are lawful for me, but
all things are not [1]helpful. All things

3 [a]2 Pet. 2:4 *See WW at Matt. 4:11. **4** [1]*courts* **5** *See WW at Acts 11:12. **7** [a][Prov. 20:22] *See WW at Acts 25:10. **9** [a]Acts 20:32; [1 Cor. 15:50]; Gal. 5:21; Eph. 5:5; 1 Tim. 1:9 [1]*catamites, those submitting to homosexuals* [2]*male homosexuals*

11 [a][1 Cor. 12:2; Col. 3:5–7; Titus 3:3–7] [b]Heb. 10:22 [1]*set apart* *See WW at Matt. 12:37. *See WW at John 12:13. **12** [a]1 Cor. 10:23 [1]*profitable*

6:5 Paul uses irony. The Corinthians prided themselves on their wisdom, yet not a single person among them was wise enough to settle their disputes.

6:6 They were acting improperly in seeking justice at the hands of the unjust and putting their trust in those who have no faith.

6:7, 8 Every believer should be free of a covetous adversary attitude even to the point of being personally cheated. A moral loss is greater than any material gain.

6:9, 10 The OT taught again and again that **the kingdom of God** is a righteous kingdom (see Ps. 45:6, 7), and Jesus affirmed it (see Matt. 6:33). Paul declares, therefore, that **the unrighteous,** of whom he proceeds to give examples, **will not inherit the kingdom of God,** thinking of its future consummation. Paul's point is to warn the Corinthian believers (who were apparently deceived into thinking that life-style is relative for believers) that if they willfully and unrepentantly persist in the evils of the wicked, they face the same final danger as the wicked. As his point is to arrest their attention and stop their deception, he does not address the question as to when such practiced behavior causes saints to cross the line to being "disinherited" in God's sight, nor does he draw conclusions regarding the issue of Christians yet caught in the struggle of these sinful habits but who sincerely desire freedom (see Rom. 7:7–25).

6:11 Evildoers such as those mentioned by Paul can be fully cleansed from sin (**washed**), set apart for God (**sanctified**), and totally accepted in His holy sight (**justified**), because **some** of the Corinthian Christians had known such life-styles in their past. **But** their conversion was **in the name of the Lord Jesus and by the Spirit of our God.** The saving work of Christ is the ground on which and the Holy Spirit is the agent through whom salvation is accomplished. He ends on a positive note, calling them to live according to who they are.

6:12–20 For first-century Greeks the body was of secondary

are lawful for me, but I will not be
brought under the power of [2]any.
13 [a]Foods for the stomach and the
stomach for foods, but God will destroy
both it and them. Now the body *is* not
for [b]sexual immorality but [c]for the
Lord, [d]and the Lord for the body.
14 And [a]God both raised up the Lord
and will also raise us up [b]by His power.
15 Do you not know that [a]your bodies
are members of Christ? Shall I then
*take the members of Christ and make
them members of a harlot? Certainly
not!
16 Or do you not know that he who is
joined to a harlot is one body *with her*?
For [a]*"the two,"* He says, *"shall become
one flesh."*
17 [a]But he who is joined to the Lord
is one spirit *with Him*.
18 [a]Flee sexual immorality. Every sin
that a man does is outside the body,
but he who *commits sexual immorality sins [b]against his own body.
19 Or [a]do you not know that your body
is the temple of the Holy Spirit *who is*
in you, whom you have from God,
[b]and you are not your own?
20 For [a]you were bought at a price;
therefore glorify God in your body
[1]and in your spirit, which are God's.

Principles of Marriage

7 Now concerning the things of
which you wrote to me: [a]*It is* good
for a man not to touch a woman.
2 Nevertheless, because of sexual immorality, let each man have his own
wife, and let each woman have her
own husband.
3 [a]Let the husband *render to his wife
the affection due her, and likewise also
the wife to her husband.
4 The wife does not have authority
over her own body, but the husband
does. And likewise the husband does
not have authority over his own body,
but the wife *does*.

12 [2]Or *anything*
13 [a]Matt. 15:17 [b]Gal. 5:19 [c]1 Thess. 4:3 [d][Eph. 5:23]
14 [a]2 Cor. 4:14 [b]Eph. 1:19
15 [a]Rom. 12:5 *See WW at John 16:22.
16 [a]Gen. 2:24
17 [a][John 17:21–23]
18 [a]Heb. 13:4 [b]Rom. 1:24 *See WW at Rev. 17:2.
19 [a]2 Cor. 6:16 [b]Rom. 14:7
20 [a]2 Pet. 2:1 [1]NU omits the rest of v. 20.

CHAPTER 7

1 [a]1 Cor. 7:8, 26
3 [a]Ex. 21:10 *See WW at Matt. 22:21.

KINGDOM DYNAMICS

7:3, 4 Three Sides of Sex: Unity, Symbol of Love, Reserved for Marriage, FAMILY ORDER. Sexual intercourse is an intimate expression of affection between a husband and wife. The apostle underscores its importance in marriage by declaring that it is in fact a duty: a husband is to be available for his wife at her request, and a wife for her husband at his request.

It is more than an act of biological mating. The Bible calls it a privileged "mystery" by which two people, a man and a woman, become one (Eph. 5:32; see Gen. 2:24). The privilege is abused when people not married to each other have intercourse (see 1 Cor. 5:1; 6:16); then that which God meant for blessing becomes a cause of judgment (see Eph. 5:5).

Marriage is the one and the only place that God has provided for sexual union to take place. In that setting it becomes a powerful symbol of the love between Christ and the church, a pure sharing of joy and delight in one another that is a

(cont. on next page)

importance; what really mattered was the soul. With a libertine philosophy of sex, and surrounded by temple prostitutes, the subject of fornication was bound to arise. Paul had taught the truth of Christian liberty, particularly concerning the observance of certain days and the eating of certain foods. However, lest the Corinthians falsely misapply this fundamental freedom to include illicit sex (as the case in ch. 5 indicated), Paul presses this point. That society argued, as the stomach is designed for food, the genitals are created for sexual experience; and as when one is hungry one eats, so when one is sexually aroused, one gratifies sexual passion. Thus this emphasis was greatly needed. If any were inclined to satisfy sexual desire just as readily as they might satisfy the appetite for food, Paul corrects such a dangerous misconception. He shows how the analogy is false, because **your body is the temple of the Holy Spirit,** and therefore belongs to Christ. Immoral conduct demeans the price paid to redeem sinners, and diminishes the glory believers are to bring to Him who loved so purely and powerfully.

6:12 Things that are morally indifferent and not specifically forbidden by God's law may not be advantageous to the one practicing them or to others. On the contrary, they may lead to evil habit.

6:13 Because of the God-ordained purposes of the body, the digestive and the sexual functions of the body are not in the same category. Eating food is a secondary and temporal arrangement, but sexuality reaches into the eternal and metaphysical depths of one's being.

6:14 Because of God's resurrection designs for the body, an essential identity exists between the present physical body and the future glorified body.

6:15–17 Sexual intercourse is more than a biological experience; it involves a communion of life. Since Jesus is one with the believer's spirit, it is unthinkable to involve Him in immorality.

6:18 Sexuality is a uniquely profound aspect of the personality, involving one's whole being. Sexual immorality has far-reaching effects, with great spiritual significance and social complications.

6:19 Such immorality is not only a sin against the body; it is a sin against **the Holy Spirit,** who dwells in the body.

6:20 Because believers have been purchased by the blood of Christ, they should honor Him to whom they belong.

7:1–40 Paul had received a letter from the Corinthians inquiring about various problems. Among them were questions pertaining to marriage, to which he responds in this section.

7:1 Not to touch a woman is a euphemism for sexual intercourse and represents the spiritual challenge of this chapter. Regardless of how important sex may be, it is still a temporal arrangement and not a part of our eternal existence. Marriage itself is an earthly institution (Matt. 22:30).

(*cont. from preceding page*)
gift from the hand of God. Outside those boundaries, it eventually becomes destructive.
(Hos. 2:16, 17, 19, 20/Is. 54:5) L.C.

5 [a]Do not deprive one another except
with consent for a time, that you may
give yourselves to fasting and prayer;
and come together again so that
[b]Satan does not *tempt you because of
your lack of self-control.
6 But I say this as a concession,
[a]not as a commandment.
7 For [a]I wish that all men were even
as I myself. But each one has his own
*gift from God, one in this manner and
another in that.
8 But I say to the unmarried and to
the widows: [a]It is good for them if they
remain even as I am;
9 but [a]if they cannot exercise self-
control, let them marry. For it is better
to marry than to burn *with passion.*

Keep Your Marriage Vows

1 **10** Now to the married I command, *yet*
not I but the [a]Lord: [b]A wife is not to
depart from *her* husband.
11 But even if she does depart, let her
remain unmarried or be **reconciled** to
her husband. And a husband is not to
*divorce *his* wife.

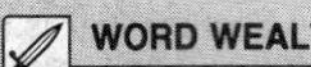
WORD WEALTH

7:11 reconciled, *katallasso* (kat-al-*las*-so); Strong's *#2644:* To change, exchange, reestablish, restore relationships, make things right, remove an enmity. Five times the word refers to God's reconciling us to Himself through the life, death, and resurrection of His Son Jesus (Rom. 5:10; 2 Cor. 5:18). Whether speaking of God and man or husband and wife, *katallasso* describes the reestablishing of a proper, loving, interpersonal relationship, which has been broken or disrupted.

12 But to the rest I, not the Lord, say:
If any brother has a wife who does not
believe, and she is willing to live with
him, let him not divorce her.
13 And a woman who has a husband
who does not believe, if he is willing
to live with her, let her not divorce him.
14 For the unbelieving husband is
sanctified by the wife, and the unbelieving wife is sanctified by the husband; otherwise [a]your children would
be unclean, but now they are holy.
15 But if the unbeliever departs, let
him depart; a brother or a sister is not
under bondage in such *cases.* But God
has called us [a]to *peace.
16 For how do you know, O wife,
whether you will [a]save *your* husband?
Or how do you know, O husband,
whether you will save *your* wife?

Live as You Are Called

17 But as God has distributed to each
one, as the Lord has called each one,
so let him walk. And [a]so I [1]ordain in
all the churches.
18 Was anyone called while circum-

5 [a]Joel 2:16 [b]1 Thess. 3:5 *See WW at Rev. 2:10.
6 [a]2 Cor. 8:8
7 [a]Acts 26:29 *See WW at 1 Cor. 1:7.
8 [a]1 Cor. 7:1, 26
9 [a]1 Tim. 5:14
10 [a]Mark 10:6–10 [b]Mal. 2:14; [Matt. 5:32]
11 *See WW at Mark 1:20.
14 [a]Ezra 9:2; Mal. 2:15
15 [a]Rom. 12:18 *See WW at Luke 1:79.
16 [a]Rom. 11:14; 1 Pet. 3:1
17 [a]1 Cor. 4:17 [1]*direct*

7:5 Christian couples should overcome sexual selfishness and should **not deprive one another.** If sexual activity is interrupted in marriage, three conditions are necessary: mutual consent; a limited time; spiritual, not selfish, reasons.
7:6–9 Paul clearly states that he is speaking from personal preference when he challenges the unmarried to remain celibate (v. 35). Matrimony or celibacy is an individual and a relative matter depending, in part, on one's ability to control sexual passion. The sexual drive is not sinful, and remaining unmarried instead of marrying embodies no superior moral virtue.
7:10–16 See section 1 of Truth-In-Action at the end of 1 Cor.
7:10, 11 Not I but the Lord: Jesus did not address every possible marriage detail. He did, however, ask His disciples to follow God's original creation design and never to sever the oneness of their marriage bond (Matt. 19:3–9). A Christian couple is to bear witness to the world by keeping marriage indissoluble. They represent the truth of covenant love and should live and grow in a spirit of forgiveness and reconciliation. Having dealt with the ideal of marriage, Paul, realizing the reality of stresses and human failure, mentions the permissibility of divorce (**but even if she does depart** [v. 11]). This permitted divorce has a strict regulation—no adultery, meaning there can most likely be no remarriage in this case except to the one from whom she was previously divorced (**let her remain unmarried or be reconciled to *her* husband** [v. 11]). It is not clear why Paul addresses this from the woman's perspective, but the principle applies to both genders.

Whereas this section forms the major Pauline statement on the issues of divorce and remarriage among Christians, it does not exhaust all the Bible has to say about the issues. See the text and notes on Matt. 5:31, 32.
7:12–16 To the rest: This section deals with the marriage between a believer and a nonbeliever. Jesus did not rule on this, so Paul must respond in his apostolic authority. Marriages in which one partner later becomes a Christian are valid and must remain intact. Any separation must be initiated by the unbelieving partner.
7:14 The ultimate reason for keeping a mixed marriage together is the holy influence of the believer's life on the unbelieving partner, resulting in the possible salvation of the entire household.
7:15 When an unbeliever initiates divorce beyond a believer's control, the believer is free from the relationship, and **is not under bondage** to keep it intact. Paul is silent concerning remarriage in such a situation.
7:17–24 The connection between the secular and the spiritual sphere is evident in this passage. In light of our

cised? Let him not become uncircumcised. Was anyone called while
uncircumcised? [a]Let him not be circumcised.
19 [a]Circumcision is nothing and uncircumcision is nothing, but [b]keeping the
commandments of God *is what matters.*
20 Let each one remain in the same
calling in which he was called.
21 Were you called *while* a slave? Do
not be concerned about it; but if you
can be made *free, rather use *it.*
22 For he who is called in the Lord
while a *slave is [a]the Lord's freedman.
Likewise he who is called *while* free
is [b]Christ's slave.
23 [a]You were bought at a price; do not
become slaves of men.
24 Brethren, let each one remain with
[a]God in that *state* in which he was
called.

To the Unmarried and Widows

25 Now concerning virgins: [a]I have no
commandment from the Lord; yet I
give judgment as one [b]whom the Lord
in His *mercy *has made* [c]trustworthy.
26 I suppose therefore that this is good
because of the present distress—[a]that
it is good for a man to remain as he
is:
27 Are you bound to a wife? Do not
seek to be loosed. Are you loosed from
a wife? Do not seek a wife.
28 But even if you do marry, you have
not sinned; and if a virgin marries, she
has not sinned. Nevertheless such will
have *trouble in the flesh, but I would
spare you.
2 29 But [a]this I say, brethren, the time
is short, so that from now on even
those who have wives should be as
though they had none,

18 [a]Acts 15:1
19 [a][Gal. 3:28; 5:6; 6:15] [b][John 15:14]
21 *See WW at Rev. 6:15.
22 [a][John 8:36] [b]1 Pet. 2:16 *See WW at Rev. 19:5.
23 [a]1 Pet. 1:18, 19
24 [a][Col. 3:22–24]
25 [a]2 Cor. 8:8 [b]1 Tim. 1:13, 16 [c]1 Tim. 1:12 *See WW at Rom. 9:15.
26 [a]1 Cor. 7:1, 8
28 *See WW at John 16:33.
29 [a]1 Pet. 4:7
31 [a]1 Cor. 9:18 [b][1 John 2:17]
32 [a]1 Tim. 5:5 [1]*concern* [2]*is concerned about* *See WW at Matt. 6:25.
34 [a]Luke 10:40
36 [1]Or *virgin daughter*
37 [1]Or *virgin daughter*
38 [a]Heb. 13:4 [1]NU *his own virgin*
39 [a]Rom. 7:2 [b]2 Cor. 6:14 *See WW at Acts 1:7.

30 those who weep as though they did
not weep, those who rejoice as though
they did not rejoice, those who buy as
though they did not possess,
31 and those who use this world as not
[a]misusing *it.* For [b]the form of this
world is passing away.
32 But I want you to be without
[1]care. [a]He who is unmarried [2]cares* for
the things of the Lord—how he may
please the Lord.
33 But he who is married cares about
the things of the world—how he may
please *his* wife.
34 There is a difference between a wife
and a virgin. The unmarried woman
[a]cares about the things of the Lord,
that she may be holy both in body and
in spirit. But she who is married cares
about the things of the world—how she
may please *her* husband.
35 And this I say for your own profit,
not that I may put a leash on you, but
for what is proper, and that you may
serve the Lord without distraction.
36 But if any man thinks he is behaving improperly toward his [1]virgin, if
she is past the flower of youth, and
thus it must be, let him do what he
wishes. He does not sin; let them
marry.
37 Nevertheless he who stands steadfast in his heart, having no necessity,
but has power over his own will, and
has so determined in his heart that he
will keep his [1]virgin, does well.
38 [a]So then he who gives [1]*her* in marriage does well, but he who does not
give *her* in marriage does better.
39 [a]A wife is bound by law *as long
as her husband lives; but if her husband dies, she is at liberty to be married to whom she wishes, [b]only in the
Lord.
40 But she is happier if she remains

---

eternal calling and destiny, the political and social distinctions of temporal life are not the most important. What matters is obedience to God. Even such a tragic state as slavery, from a social viewpoint, does not dictate the terms of a life in Christ. The paramount thing is for a believer's spiritual life to remain constant and intact in an unredeemed, changing world.

7:25–40 Paul does not exalt the single state above the marriage state, but he does have a personal preference and urges all groups of the unmarried to consider the wisdom and spiritual benefits of a celibate life. Among these various groups are divorcees (vv. 27, 28); unmarrieds who are free to make their own matrimonial choices (vv. 28–35); unmarrieds whose choices depend on others, most likely fathers (vv. 36–38); and widows (vv. 39, 40).

7:25 Christ Himself gave no teaching on the subject under discussion; but Paul, while not disclaiming inspiration, stresses he is giving sound advice.

7:26 Paul presents his teaching in light of the tension between the temporal, unredeemed secular order and the believer's spiritual life and calling. **The present distress** applies to the whole of this age, and does not refer to some special persecution in the first century. This entire age is stressful (vv. 26–28), temporal (vv. 29, 30), and distracting (vv. 32–35).

7:29–31 See section 2 of Truth-In-Action at the end of 1 Cor.

7:29–31 Because of the nature of this age and the reality of the Coming of Jesus Christ, believers are to adopt the attitude of finding the source of their life in Christ, rather than in earthly institutions, whether marriage, the social sphere, or the economic world. A Christian is to live intently and responsibly and yet see these realities as ultimately temporal.

7:36–38 **Behaving improperly** probably means a father's unfair treatment of a virgin daughter by refusing permission to marry, but other interpretations are possible.

as she is, [a]according to my judgment—
and [b]I think I also have the Spirit of
God.

Be Sensitive to Conscience

8 Now [a]concerning things offered to
idols: We know that we all have
[b]knowledge. [c]Knowledge [1]puffs up,
but love [2]edifies.
2 And [a]if anyone thinks that he
knows anything, he knows nothing yet
as he ought to know.
3 But if anyone loves God, this one
is known by Him.
4 Therefore concerning the eating of
things offered to idols, we know that
[a]an idol *is* nothing in the world,
[b]and that *there is* no other God but
one.
5 For even if there are [a]so-called
gods, whether in heaven or on earth
(as there are many gods and many
lords),
6 yet [a]for us *there is* one God, the Father, [b]of whom *are* all things, and we
for Him; and [c]one Lord Jesus Christ,
[d]through whom *are* all things, and
[e]through whom we *live.*
7 However, *there is* not in everyone
that knowledge; for some, [a]with consciousness of the idol, until now eat *it*
as a thing offered to an idol; and their
conscience, being weak, is [b]defiled.
8 But [a]food does not commend us to
God; for neither if we eat are we the
better, nor if we do not eat are we the
worse.
9 But [a]beware lest somehow this liberty of yours become [b]a [1]stumbling
block to those who are weak.
10 For if anyone sees you who have
knowledge eating in an idol's temple,
will not [a]the conscience of him who is
weak be emboldened to eat those
things offered to idols?
11 And [a]because of your knowledge
shall the weak brother perish, for
whom Christ died?
12 But [a]when you thus sin against the
brethren, and wound their weak conscience, you sin against Christ.
13 Therefore, [a]if food makes my
brother stumble, I will never again eat
meat, lest I make my brother stumble.

A Pattern of Self-Denial

9 Am [a]I not an apostle? Am I not
free? [b]Have I not seen Jesus Christ
our Lord? [c]Are you not my work in
the Lord?
2 If I am not an apostle to others, yet
doubtless I am to you. For you are
[a]the [1]seal of my apostleship in the
Lord.
3 My defense to those who examine
me is this:
4 [a]Do we have no [1]right to eat and
drink?
5 Do we have no right to take along
[1]a believing wife, as *do* also the other
apostles, [a]the brothers of the Lord, and
[b]Cephas?
6 Or *is it* only Barnabas and I [a]*who*
have no right to refrain from working?
7 Who ever [a]goes to war at his own
expense? Who [b]plants a vineyard and

40 [a]1 Cor. 7:6, 25 [b]1 Thess. 4:8

CHAPTER 8

1 [a]Acts 15:20 [b]Rom. 14:14 [c]Rom. 14:3 [1]*makes arrogant* [2]*builds up*
2 [a][1 Cor. 13:8–12]
4 [a]Is. 41:24 [b]Deut. 4:35, 39; 6:4
5 [a][John 10:34]
6 [a]Mal. 2:10 [b]Acts 17:28 [c]John 13:13 [d]John 1:3 [e]Rom. 5:11
7 [a][1 Cor. 10:28] [b]Rom. 14:14, 22
8 [a][Rom. 14:17]
9 [a]Gal. 5:13 [b]Rom. 14:13, 21 [1]*cause of offense*
10 [a]1 Cor. 10:28
11 [a]Rom. 14:15, 20
12 [a]Matt. 25:40
13 [a]Rom. 14:21

CHAPTER 9

1 [a]Acts 9:15 [b]1 Cor. 15:8 [c]1 Cor. 3:6; 4:15
2 [a]2 Cor. 12:12 [1]*certification*
4 [a][1 Thess. 2:6, 9] [1]*authority*
5 [a]Matt. 13:55 [b]Matt. 8:14 [1]*Lit. a sister, a wife*
6 [a]Acts 4:36
7 [a]2 Cor. 10:4 [b]Deut. 20:6

8:1—11:1 Sacrificing food to the gods was a routine pagan ritual in Paul's day, and much confusion and division in the church resulted from the practice. Should they eat food that was connected in some way with a pagan religious service (10:14–22)? How about buying the meat from the local butcher shop (10:25, 26)? What if invitations to dinner come from unbelieving friends (10:27–30)? Paul explains why these matters are resolved by love and not knowledge (8:1–13); he cites himself as one who is willing to live by love for the sake of others (9:1–27); and he applies these principles to the specific problems at Corinth (10:1—11:1).

8:1 Eating food is essentially an ethically neutral act (v. 8), but not all people have the same level of knowledge. Some new converts were uncertain about the power of their former pagan gods; others knew that idols held no power over them. Knowledge has two defects: it tends to center on self, and it is inadequate as the bond in personal relationships. The obligations of love are the determining factor in questions of moral insignificance. The principle of love places limitations on one's liberty of conscience.

8:4–6 Though **an idol *is* nothing** as a random product of human engineering, **there are so-called gods,** demon beings that operate amid idol worship (Deut. 32:17; Ps. 106:37). No place is to be given them in a believer's life (see 10:20; Gal. 4:9; Eph. 4:27).

8:7 The conscience is like a judge in a courtroom. The judge does not make the laws; his role is to interpret them and render decisions. The judgments of the conscience are relative and vary between individuals, depending on what they know. The conscience carries an impulse to obey the right, and it passes judgment on conformity or nonconformity to the right. As a result, the conscience is a very powerful force. Guilt feelings are just as devastating as real guilt; therefore, love and not knowledge must be the basic principle whereby Christians live.

8:9–13 Being a **stumbling block** involves more than upsetting another or ignorantly offending; it is a serious deliberate offense that wounds and weakens another's conscience and ruins a relationship with Christ. Sin against a brother is a sin against Christ (v. 12). Christian liberty must always be exercised in love with a view to strengthening others (see 10:28–30).

9:1–6 Paul enforces the principle of considerate love by using his own action as an example. His apostolic office entitled him to certain privileges, but he renounced them for their sake. Had he insisted on his rights, his motives could be questioned and the work of Christ might be hindered.

9:7–14 Three reasons justify Paul's right to financial support: 1) Society dictates that those who render service, such as soldiers, farmers, and shepherds, receive remuneration (v. 7). 2) The Mosaic Law prescribed just recompense for those

does not eat of its fruit? Or who
[c]tends a flock and does not drink of
the milk of the flock?
8 Do I say these things as a *mere*
man? Or does not the law say the same
also?
9 For it is written in the law of Moses,
[a]*"You shall not muzzle an ox while it
treads out the grain."* Is it oxen God
is concerned about?
10 Or does He say *it* altogether for our
sakes? For our sakes, no doubt, *this* is
written, that [a]he who plows should
plow in hope, and he who threshes
in hope should **be partaker** of his
hope.

WORD WEALTH

9:10 be partaker, *metecho* (met-*ekh*-oh); Strong's *#3348:* Literally "to have with." The word connotes a sharing in, participating of, copartnering, working in association with another, and taking part in a joint venture. Here the sowers and the reapers share the same hopes. Heb. 2:14 describes Jesus, by the incarnation, sharing flesh and blood with humanity for their redemption. 1 Cor. 10:17 states that all the redeemed have a joint-participation in worshiping the Lord Jesus.

1 11 [a]If we have sown spiritual things for
you, *is it* a great thing if we reap your
material things?
12 If others *are partakers of *this* right
over you, *are* we not even more?
[a]Nevertheless we have not used this
right, but endure all things [b]lest we
hinder the gospel of Christ.
13 [a]Do you not know that those who
minister the holy things eat *of the
things* of the [b]temple, and those who
serve at the altar partake of *the offerings of* the altar?
14 Even so [a]the Lord has commanded
[b]that those who preach the gospel
should live from the gospel.
15 But [a]I have used none of these
things, nor have I written these things
that it should be done so to me; for
[b]it *would be* better for me to die than

7 [c]John 21:15
9 [a]Deut. 25:4; 1 Tim. 5:18
10 [a]2 Tim. 2:6
11 [a]Rom. 15:27; 1 Cor. 9:14
12 [a][Acts 18:3; 20:33]; 1 Cor. 9:15, 18 [b]2 Cor. 11:12
*See WW at 1 Cor. 9:10.
13 [a]Lev. 6:16, 26; 7:6, 31 [b]Num. 18:8–31; Deut. 18:1
14 [a]Matt. 10:10; Luke 10:7, 8; 1 Tim. 5:18 [b]Rom. 10:15
15 [a]Acts 18:3; 20:33; 1 Cor. 9:12, 18 [b]2 Cor. 11:10
16 [a]Acts 9:15; [Rom. 1:14]
17 [a]John 4:36; 1 Cor. 3:8, 14; 9:18 [b]1 Cor. 4:1; Gal. 2:7; Eph. 3:2; Col. 1:25
18 [a]1 Cor. 10:33 [b]1 Cor. 7:31; 9:12 [1]NU omits *of Christ*
19 [a]1 Cor. 9:1 [b]2 Cor. 4:5; Gal. 5:13 [c]Matt. 18:15; 1 Pet. 3:1
20 [a]Acts 16:3; 21:23–26; Rom. 11:14 [1]NU adds *though not being myself under the law*
21 [a][Gal. 2:3; 3:2] [b][Rom. 2:12, 14] [c][1 Cor. 7:22; Gal. 6:2] [1]NU *God's law* [2]NU *Christ's law*
22 [a]Rom. 14:1; 15:1; 2 Cor. 11:29 [b]1 Cor. 10:33 [c]Rom. 11:14 [1]NU omits *as*

that anyone should make my boasting
void.

WORD WEALTH

9:15 void, *kenoo* (ken-*ah*-oh); Strong's *#2758:* To abase, neutralize, empty, nullify, render void, divest totally, reduce to nothing. The word is used of the incarnation of Christ in Phil. 2:7, which describes His self-emptying of the glories attendant to His deity, but not of deity itself.

16 For if I preach the gospel, I have
nothing to boast of, for [a]necessity is
laid upon me; yes, woe is me if I do
not preach the gospel!
17 For if I do this willingly, [a]I have a
reward; but if against my will, [b]I have
been entrusted with a stewardship.
18 What is my reward then? That
[a]when I preach the gospel, I may
present the gospel [1]of Christ without
charge, that I [b]may not abuse my authority in the gospel.

Serving All Men

19 For though I am [a]free from all *men,*
[b]I have made myself a servant to all,
[c]that I might win the more;
20 and [a]to the Jews I became as a Jew,
that I might win Jews; to those *who
are* under the law, as under the [1]law,
that I might win those *who are* under
the law;
21 [a]to [b]those *who are* without law, as
without law [c](not being without
[1]law toward God, but under [2]law toward Christ), that I might win those
who are without law;
22 [a]to the weak I became [1]as weak,
that I might win the weak. [b]I have become all things to all *men,* [c]that I might
by all means save some.
23 Now this I do for the gospel's sake,
that I may be partaker of it with *you.*

Striving for a Crown

24 Do you not know that those who
run in a race all run, but one receives

rendering service, a principle which applied even to working animals, like an ox that **treads out the grain** (vv. 8–13).
3) **The Lord** Himself **commanded** the principle of support for **those who preach the gospel** (v. 14).
9:11–14 See section 1 of Truth-In-Action at the end of 1 Cor.
9:15–27 In a way that both justifies his apostleship and illustrates the way of love, Paul states three reasons for giving up his rights: his unique calling as an apostle (vv. 15–18); his evangelistic motivations (vv. 19–23); and his concern for self-discipline (vv. 24–27).

9:16–18 Paul preached by a divine compulsion, and was confident of receiving a **reward.** Even if he really had not wanted to preach, he felt a moral obligation to do so. Because he longed to relate to Christ wholly out of love and by free choice, he chose to forego his rights. His reward was the satisfaction of preaching gratuitously.
9:19–23 While Paul himself was free from rigid scruples, he was constrained by the weakness of others that he might ultimately win them for Christ. Without violating biblical morality, he would go to any length to enter the world of others and lead them to salvation.

the prize? [a]Run in such a way that you
may [1]obtain* *it.*
25 And everyone who competes *for*
the prize [1]is temperate in all things.
Now they *do it* to obtain a perishable
crown, but we *for* [a]an imperishable
crown.
26 Therefore I run thus: [a]not with
uncertainty. Thus I fight: not as *one*
who beats the air.
27 [a]But I discipline my body and
[b]bring *it* into subjection, lest, when I
have preached to others, I myself
should become [c]disqualified.

Old Testament Examples

10 Moreover, brethren, I do not
want you to be unaware that all
our fathers were under [a]the cloud, all
passed through [b]the sea,
2 all were baptized into Moses in the
cloud and in the sea,
3 all ate the same [a]spiritual food,
4 and all drank the same [a]spiritual
drink. For they drank of that spiritual
Rock that *followed them, and that
Rock was Christ.
5 But with most of them God was not
well pleased, for *their bodies* [a]were
scattered in the wilderness.
3 6 Now these things became our examples, to the intent that we should not
*lust after evil things as [a]they also
lusted.
7 [a]And do not become idolaters as
were some of them. As it is written,
[b]*"The people sat down to eat and*
drink, and rose up to play."
8 [a]Nor let us *commit sexual immorality, as [b]some of them did, and
[c]in one day twenty-three thousand fell;
9 nor let us [1]tempt Christ, as [a]some
of them also tempted, and [b]were destroyed by serpents;
10 nor complain, as [a]some of them also
complained, and [b]were destroyed by
[c]the destroyer.
11 Now [1]all these things happened to
them as examples, and [a]they were
written for our [2]admonition, [b]upon
whom the ends of the ages have come.
12 Therefore [a]let him who thinks he
stands take heed lest he fall.
13 No temptation has overtaken you
except such as is common to man; but
[a]God *is* faithful, [b]who will not allow
you to be tempted beyond what you
are able, but with the temptation will
also make the way of escape, that you
may be able to [1]bear *it.*

Flee from Idolatry

14 Therefore, my beloved, [a]flee from
idolatry.
15 I speak as to [a]wise men; judge for
yourselves what I say.
16 [a]The cup of blessing which we
bless, is it not the [1]communion of the
*blood of Christ? [b]The bread which we

24 [a]Gal. 2:2 [1]*win* *See WW at John 1:5.
25 [a]James 1:12 [1]*exercises self-control*
26 [a]2 Tim. 2:5
27 [a][Rom. 8:13] [b][Rom. 6:18] [c]Jer. 6:30

CHAPTER 10

1 [a]Ex. 13:21, 22 [b]Ex. 14:21, 22, 29
3 [a]Ex. 16:4, 15, 35
4 [a]Ex. 17:5–7 *See WW at John 13:36.
5 [a]Num. 14:29, 37; 26:65
6 [a]Num. 11:4, 34 *See WW at Matt. 13:17.
7 [a]1 Cor. 5:11; 10:14 [b]Ex. 32:6
8 [a]Rev. 2:14 [b]Num. 25:1–9 [c]Ps. 106:29 *See WW at Rev. 17:2.
9 [a]Ex. 17:2, 7 [b]Num. 21:6–9 [1]*test*
10 [a]Ex. 16:2 [b]Num. 14:37 [c]Ex. 12:23
11 [a]Rom. 15:4 [b]Phil. 4:5 [1]NU omits *all* [2]*instruction*
12 [a]Rom. 11:20
13 [a]1 Cor. 1:9 [b]Ps. 125:3 [1]*endure*
14 [a]2 Cor. 6:17
15 [a]1 Cor. 8:1
16 [a]Matt. 26:26–28 [b]Acts 2:42 [1]*fellowship* or *sharing* *See WW at Luke 6:28. • See WW at Acts 2:42. • See WW at 1 John 1:7.

9:27 Athletes who break the rules **become disqualified:** Paul's illustration stresses the necessity of self-discipline and the danger of flaunting one's liberties. Believers must practice self-denial and self-control even in matters that are morally indifferent.

10:1–13 Christian liberty has its limits; it does not include flirting with idolatry: although idols are nonentities, the demonic powers behind them are real (vv. 19, 20). History illustrates the danger of self-indulgence. Israel had redemptive experiences that parallel water baptism and eating and drinking the Lord's Supper (vv. 1–4), but many sinned and were destroyed (vv. 5–10). These same lessons apply today (vv. 11–13). This and related texts give full and strong warrant for the NT believer's study of OT passages, to draw lessons from assertions and analogies.

10:4 That Rock was Christ: Christ is central to all of redemptive history. The birth of Jesus was an incarnation, not His beginning. He was behind the miraculous source of manna and water in the wilderness. The rock followed them in the sense that the blessings of Christ, as symbolized in the supply of water, never failed (see Ex. 17:1–7; Num. 21:17, 18).

10:6–12 See section 3 of Truth-In-Action at the end of 1 Cor.

10:11 The First Coming of Christ, not His Second Coming, marks the ends of the ages. The Second Coming concludes what the first unfolds and will bring to accomplishment. We live in an overlap between the former and the new creation.

10:12, 13 Paul gives a solemn warning against independent self-confidence concerning one's moral security (v. 12) and follows with a message of encouragement (v. 13). **Temptation** translates a Greek word which can mean enticement to evil or testing in general, including various kinds of trials. The word should probably be understood in the broad sense, with the further understanding that while God permits testing for the purpose of strengthening faith and character, Satan entices to evil for the purpose of destruction (see James 1:2–4, 12–15). The Corinthians need not despair when they consider two things: 1) Their temptations are not unique, as evidenced by the experiences of Israel in the wilderness (vv. 5–10). 2) God may be trusted not to **allow** them **to be tempted** in excess of their ability to endure and overcome. Not only will He limit trials; He will provide **the way of escape.**

10:14–22 To eat meat that had been sacrificed to idols might be innocent, but to eat such food as part of an idol feast in a pagan temple was quite another matter. Just as believers commune with Christ in the Lord's Supper (vv. 16, 17), and as Hebrew worshipers entered into fellowship with all that the altar represented when they offered sacrifices (v. 18), so sharing food as part of a pagan festival involves **fellowship with demons** (v. 20).

10:16 The cup of blessing refers to the third of the four cups of wine at the Passover meal, and was likely "the cup after supper" of Luke 22:20.

break, is it not the communion of the
body of Christ?

KINGDOM DYNAMICS

10:16 The Significance of Communion's Covenant, THE BLOOD. The Passover celebration was to be the last meal that Christ would share with the disciples before His death (John 16:28). It was also the setting in which He chose to transform the meaning of the cup and the bread into New Covenant thought. Now receiving the cup is a participation in the blood of Christ, and the breaking of bread is a participation in His body. The mystery involved in the covenant meal extends beyond Christ's relationship to the individual. Partakers of the covenant meal are also joined together in the body and blood of Christ. The blessings and responsibilities of the covenant are therefore extended laterally among those who partake of Christ together, as certainly as they are vertically between God and the believer in Christ.

(Rev. 12:11/Gen. 1:3–5*) C.S.

17 For [a]we, *though* many, are one
bread *and* one body; for we all *partake of that one bread.
18 Observe [a]Israel [b]after the flesh:
[c]Are not those who eat of the sacrifices
[1]partakers of the altar?
19 What am I saying then? [a]That an
idol is anything, or what is offered to
idols is anything?
20 Rather, that the things which the
Gentiles [a]sacrifice [b]they sacrifice to
demons and not to God, and I do not
want you to have fellowship with demons.
21 [a]You cannot drink the cup of the
Lord and [b]the cup of demons; you cannot *partake of the [c]Lord's table and
of the table of demons.
22 Or do we [a]provoke the Lord to jealousy? [b]Are we stronger than He?

All to the Glory of God

23 All things are lawful [1]for me, but
not all things are [a]helpful; all things
are lawful [1]for me, but not all things
[2]edify.
24 Let no one seek his own, but each
one [a]the other's *well-being.*

17 [a]Rom. 12:5; 1 Cor. 12:12, 27; Eph. 4:4, 16; Col. 3:15 *See WW at 1 Cor. 9:10.
18 [a]Rom. 4:12 [b]Rom. 4:1 [c]Lev. 3:3; 7:6, 14; Deut. 12:17 [1]*fellowshippers* or *sharers*
19 [a]1 Cor. 8:4
20 [a]Lev. 17:7 [b]Deut. 32:17; Ps. 106:37; Gal. 4:8; Rev. 9:20
21 [a]2 Cor. 6:15, 16 [b]Deut. 32:38 [c][1 Cor. 11:23–29] *See WW at 1 Cor. 9:10.
22 [a]Deut. 32:21 [b]Ezek. 22:14
23 [a]1 Cor. 6:12 [1]NU omits *for me* [2]*build up*
24 [a]Phil. 2:4
25 [a][1 Tim. 4:4]
26 [a]Ex. 19:5; Ps. 24:1; 50:12; 1 Tim. 4:4 *See WW at Eph. 3:19.
27 [a]Luke 10:7, 8
28 [a][1 Cor. 8:7, 10, 12] [b]Deut. 10:14; Ps. 24:1 [1]NU omits the rest of v. 28. *See WW at Eph. 3:19.
29 [a]Rom. 14:16; [1 Cor. 9:19]
30 [a]Rom. 14:6 *See WW at 1 Cor. 9:10.
31 [a]Col. 3:17; 1 Pet. 4:11
32 [a]Rom. 14:13
33 [a]Rom. 15:2; 1 Cor. 9:22; [Gal. 1:10]

CHAPTER 11

1 [a]Eph. 5:1

25 [a]Eat whatever is sold in the meat
market, asking no questions for conscience' sake;
26 for [a]*"the earth is the* LORD*'s, and
all its *fullness."*
27 If any of those who do not believe
invites you *to dinner,* and you desire
to go, [a]eat whatever is set before you,
asking no question for conscience'
sake.
28 But if anyone says to you, "This was
offered to idols," do not eat it [a]for the
sake of the one who told you, and for
conscience' sake; [1]for [b]*"the earth is the
LORD's, and all its *fullness."*
29 "Conscience," I say, not your own,
but that of the other. For [a]why is my
liberty judged by another *man's* conscience?

WORD WEALTH

10:29 liberty, *eleutheria* (el-yoo-ther-*ee*-ah); Strong's *#1657:* Freedom from slavery, independence, absence of external restraint, a negation of control or domination, freedom of access. Paul exulted in the liberty that there is in Christ Jesus. Legalistic believers were critical of his new life-style, but he responded: "I am free from religious bondage. Why does anyone want me to go back to it?" We are free to serve the Lord in all the ways that are consistent with His word, will, nature, and holiness.

30 But if I *partake with thanks, why
am I evil spoken of for *the food*
[a]over which I give thanks?
31 [a]Therefore, whether you eat or
drink, or whatever you do, do all to the
glory of God.
32 [a]Give no offense, either to the Jews
or to the Greeks or to the church of
God,
33 just [a]as I also please all *men* in all
things, not seeking my own profit, but
the *profit* of many, that they may be
saved.
11 Imitate[a] me, just as I also *imitate* Christ.

Head Coverings

2 Now I praise you, brethren, that you
remember me in all things and keep

10:22 Idolatrous activity amounts to a confrontation with God. The quotations "sacrifice to demons and not to God" (v. 20) and **provoke the Lord to jealousy** (v. 22) are from Moses' "Song of Witness," which adds historical solemnity to the warnings (Deut. 32:16, 17).

10:23—11:1 In a nonreligious personal or social situation, food offered to idols can be eaten unless it involves the conscience of another brother. No created thing in itself is sinful, since everything belongs to God, but it is inconsistent to glorify God and hurt others. The final arbiter must be considerate love, not knowledge or liberty.

11:2 Chs. 11—14 cover three problems related to public worship: the wearing of the veil, the Lord's Supper, and spiritual gifts. Paul did not invent these truths, but handed on established Christian **traditions** in his apostolic teaching.

the traditions just as I *delivered *them*
to you.
3 But I want you to know that [a]the
head of every man is Christ, [b]the head
of woman *is* man, and [c]the head of
Christ *is* God.

KINGDOM DYNAMICS

11:3 Jesus and the Father Model Relationship for Marriage, FAMILY ORDER. The relationship between God as "Head" and Christ as Son is given as a model for the relationship between husband and wife. When the Bible reveals how the Father and the Son relate to each other, it also tells us something about the way that husbands and wives should relate to each other.

The following principles for the husband-wife relationship are illustrated in the relationship of Jesus and the Father: 1) Husband and wife are to share a mutual love (John 5:20; 14:31). 2) Husband and wife have different roles and accomplish different functions in the marriage (John 10:17; 14:28; 17:4). 3) Though having different roles, husband and wife are equal; they live in unity (John 10:30; 14:9, 11). 4) Husband and wife esteem one another (John 8:49, 54). 5) Husbands express love for their wives through care, shared life and ministry, attentiveness (John 5:20, 22; 8:29; 11:42; 16:15; 17:2). 6) Wives express love for their husbands by being of one will and purpose with them; by exercising authority entrusted to them with humility and meekness, not striving or competing; in a word, by showing respect both in attitude and action (John 4:34; 5:19, 30; 8:28; 14:31; 15:10; Phil. 2:5, 6, 8; see also Gen. 3:16; 1 Tim. 2:8-15).

(Eph. 3:14, 15/Eph. 5:22–33) L.C.

4 Every man praying or [a]prophesying, having *his* head covered, dishonors his head.

5 But every woman who prays or
prophesies with *her* head uncovered
dishonors her head, for that is one and
the same as if her head were [a]shaved.
6 For if a woman is not covered, let
her also be shorn. But if it is [a]shameful
for a woman to be shorn or shaved,
let her be covered.
7 For a man indeed ought not to cover
his head, since [a]he is the image and
glory of God; but woman is the glory
of man.
8 For man is not from woman, but
woman [a]from man.
9 Nor was man created for the
woman, but woman [a]for the man.
10 For this reason the woman ought to
have *a symbol of* authority on *her* head,
because of the angels.
11 Nevertheless, [a]neither *is* man independent of woman, nor woman independent of man, in the Lord.
12 For as woman *came* from man, even
so man also *comes* through woman;
but all things are from God.
13 Judge among yourselves. Is it
proper for a woman to *pray to God
with her head uncovered?
14 Does not even nature itself teach
you that if a man has long hair, it is a
dishonor to him?
15 But if a woman has long hair, it is
a glory to her; for *her* hair is given
[1]to her for a covering.
16 But [a]if anyone seems to be contentious, we have no such custom,
[b]nor *do* the churches of God.

Conduct at the Lord's Supper

17 Now in giving these instructions I
do not praise *you,* since you come together not for the better but for the
worse.

2 *See WW at Luke 23:25. 3 [a]Eph. 1:22; 4:15; 5:23; Col. 1:18; 2:19 [b]Gen. 3:16; [Eph. 5:23] [c]John 14:28 4 [a]1 Cor. 12:10
5 [a]Deut. 21:12 6 [a]Num. 5:18 7 [a]Gen. 1:26, 27; 5:1; 9:6; James 3:9 8 [a]Gen. 2:21–23; 1 Tim. 2:13 9 [a]Gen. 2:18 11 [a][Gal. 3:28] 13 *See WW at Matt. 6:6. 15 [1]M omits *to her* 16 [a]1 Tim. 6:4 [b]1 Cor. 7:17

11:3–16 A proper understanding of this section is based on understanding Creation principles and Corinthian social customs. Adam and Eve were created mutually interdependent (v. 11). Together they make up humanity in its completed form. The order and design in their creation reveals the glory of God (v. 7) and headship of Christ (v. 3). In addition, **woman is the glory of man** (v. 7) in that she was created as his suitable companion (v. 9) and endowed with a nature to match her role (v. 15).

These creational truths became associated with the social custom of a head covering for women, even in pagan cultures. Both the permanent spiritual truth and the temporal cultural habit then enter into this topic, the essence of which *deals not with a* physical covering but a woman's submissive inner self, especially to her husband.

11:5, 6 A woman who appeared bareheaded in public was considered to be loose and immoral. Uncovered hair or a shaved head could symbolize a loose or unclean condition, (Lev. 14:8, 9; Num. 5:18). Hence, these verses emphasize the disgrace of a woman's unsubmissiveness in public worship.

11:10 The angels represent the spiritual realm and may refer to the efforts of fallen demonic beings to motivate to pride and to invest themselves wherever they can inspire arrogance. The term may also be recalling the original authority that was lost over the Garden of Eden because Eve was "uncovered," that is, she acted independently of Adam. At that time, their privileged authority and access were lost (Gen. 3:24). Behind the symbolism of wearing the veil is the acknowledgment of mankind's need to show submission to divinely appointed authority if he is to regain the dominion lost (Gen. 1:28). True authority comes by submissiveness, and both men and women—husbands and wives—are called to learn it (Eph. 5:21).

11:14 It is not primarily the length of **hair** that is being judged, but hair viewed as an adornment. Man directly reflects the glory of God, and he needs no other adornment or "covering" except Jesus Christ (v. 7). Good grooming is in order, but primping and undue attention to externals betray true manliness and falsely focus on self rather than on Christ, the head of the man.

11:17–34 The desecration of **the Lord's Supper** brought

18 For first of all, when you come together as a church, [a]I hear that there
are divisions among you, and in part I
believe it.
19 For [a]there must also be *factions
among you, [b]that those who are approved may be [1]**recognized** among
you.

WORD WEALTH

11:19 recognized, *phaneros* (fan-er-*oss*); Strong's *#5318:* Compare "phantom," "phenomenon," "phantasm," "fantasy." Conspicuous, apparent, manifest, visible, evident, plain, clear, open to sight. The very nature of the word suggests a visibility that gives the observer an ability to define immediately what is seen. Here Paul stated that the only good that can come out of false brethren is the evident goodness of the true brethren. In Matt. 6:4, 6, and 18, Jesus assures us that the Father observing us in secret, rewards us openly (*phaneros*).

3 20 Therefore when you come together
in one place, it is not to eat the Lord's
Supper.
21 For in eating, each one takes his
own supper ahead of *others;* and one
is hungry and [a]another is drunk.
22 What! Do you not have houses to
eat and drink in? Or do you despise
[a]the church of God and [b]shame
[1]those who have nothing? What shall
I say to you? Shall I praise you in this?
I do not praise *you.*

Institution of the Lord's Supper

23 For [a]I received from the Lord that
which I also delivered to you: [b]that the
Lord Jesus on the *same* night in which
He was betrayed took bread;
24 and when He had given *thanks, He
broke *it* and said, [1]"Take, eat; this is
My body which is [2]broken for you;
do this in remembrance of Me."
25 In the same manner *He* also *took*
the cup after supper, saying, "This cup
is the *new *covenant in My blood.
This do, as often as you drink *it,* in remembrance of Me."
26 For as often as you eat this bread
and drink this cup, you proclaim the
Lord's death [a]till He comes.

18 [a]1 Cor. 1:10–12; 3:3
19 [a]Matt. 18:7; Luke 17:1; 1 Tim. 4:1; 2 Pet. 2:1 [b][Deut. 13:3]; Luke 2:35; 1 John 2:19 [1]Lit. *manifest, evident* *See WW at 2 Pet. 2:1.
21 [a]2 Pet. 2:13; Jude 12
22 [a]1 Cor. 10:32 [b]James 2:6 [1]The poor
23 [a]1 Cor. 15:3; Gal. 1:12; Col. 3:24 [b]Matt. 26:26–28; Mark 14:22–24; Luke 22:17–20; 1 Cor. 10:16
24 [1]NU omits *Take, eat* [2]NU omits *broken* *See WW at John 6:11.
25 *See WW at 2 Cor. 5:17. • See WW at Mark 14:24.
26 [a]John 14:3; [Acts 1:11]
27 [a][John 6:51]

KINGDOM DYNAMICS

11:23–26 Faith At the Lord's Table, FAITH'S CONFESSION. Just as the act of water baptism outwardly declares or confesses an inward experience of salvation through the blood of the Lord Jesus, each observance of the Lord's Table is a powerful occasion for faith's confession. In the ordinance, the Christian confesses before all heaven that he not only has believed, but that he has not forgotten. "In remembrance" involves more than just memory; the word suggests an "active calling to mind" (Wycliffe).

The word "for" introduces the reason the Supper is continually repeated. It is an acted sermon, for it "proclaims" the Lord's death. The outward act of faith, as the bread and cup taken, is explicitly said to be an ongoing, active confession—literally "you are proclaiming" (v. 26). Each occasion of partaking is an opportunity to say, proclaim, or confess again: "I herewith lay hold of all the benefits of Jesus Christ's full redemption for my life—forgiveness, wholeness, strength, health, sufficiency." The Lord's Supper is not to be simply a ritual remembrance, but an active confession, by which you actively will to call to memory and appropriate today all that Jesus has provided and promised through His Cross.

(Rom. 10:9, 10/Phil. 2:9–11) R.H.

Examine Yourself

27 Therefore whoever eats [a]this bread
or drinks *this* cup of the Lord in an

censure from Paul. Its neglect or abuse became a self-induced judgment in the form of physical sickness and even death (v. 30). God's own chastening is also a prospect when such carelessness prevails. This serious problem was caused by their failure to understand the meaning of the Lord's Supper and to observe it in an undivisive, unselfish way. The church was made up largely of the poorer class, including slaves (1:26–28; 7:21); and apparently, the wealthier members, unwilling to share their food, took the supper **ahead of others** and shamed **those who** had **nothing** (vv. 21, 22). After clarifying the problem (vv. 17–22), Paul corrects it (vv. 23–34). He reminds them of the solemn meaning behind the Supper (vv. 23–26); he responds to the divine displeasure among them for their guilty manners (vv. 27–32); and he recommends a proper course of action (vv. 33, 34).

11:18, 19 Paul finds it hard to believe that such grievous **divisions** could exist, but he sees a divine purpose at work in them, revealing who is schismatic and who is true in spirit. See Deut. 13:3; 1 John 2:19.

11:20–29 See section 3 of Truth-In-Action at the end of 1 Cor.

11:24 Broken for you refers to both Jesus' substitutionary role as Savior as well as the One who bore our pain and sicknesses (Is. 53:4–6). **In remembrance of Me** is a summons to keep the purpose and victory of His Cross in focus. It is not a requirement to morbidly reenact Calvary but to celebrate sensitively Christ's triumph there.

11:25 The new covenant, sealed by the **blood** of Jesus, was prophesied in Jer. 31:31–34. That covenant was new in its nature and in its content, securing the forgiveness of sins and writing the law of God in the hearts of believers. The old ritualistic system is replaced by the gospel of Christ, which He established by His death (see Heb. 8:7–13).

11:27 The context describes **an unworthy manner** as a divisive attitude that desecrates the meaning of the Lord's

unworthy manner will be guilty of the
body and [1]blood of the Lord.
28 But [a]let a man examine himself, and
so let him eat of the bread and drink
of the cup.
29 For he who eats and drinks [1]in an
unworthy manner eats and drinks
*judgment to himself, not *discerning
the [2]Lord's body.
30 For this reason many *are* weak and
sick among you, and many [1]sleep.
31 For [a]if we would judge ourselves,
we would not be judged.
32 But when we are judged, [a]we are
chastened by the Lord, that we may
not be condemned with the world.
33 Therefore, my brethren, when you
[a]come together to eat, wait for one another.
34 But if anyone is hungry, let him eat
at home, lest you come together for
judgment. And the rest I will set in order when I come.

Spiritual Gifts: Unity in Diversity

12 Now [a]concerning spiritual *gifts,*
brethren, I do not want you to
be ignorant:
2 You know [a]that[1] you were Gentiles,
carried away to these [b]dumb[2] idols,
however you were led.

27 [1]Nu, M *the blood*
28 [a]2 Cor. 13:5
29 [1]NU omits *in an unworthy manner* [2]NU omits *Lord's* *See WW at Rev. 20:4. • See WW at Acts 11:12.
30 [1]Are dead
31 [a][1 John 1:9]
32 [a]Ps. 94:12
33 [a]1 Cor. 14:26

CHAPTER 12

1 [a]1 Cor. 12:4; 14:1, 37
2 [a]Eph. 2:11 [b]Ps. 115:5 [1]NU, M *that when* [2]*mute, silent*
3 [a]Matt. 16:17 [1]Gr. *anathema*
4 [a]Rom. 12:3–8 [b]Eph. 4:4 [1]*allotments* or *various kinds* *See WW at 1 Cor. 1:7.
5 [a]Rom. 12:6
6 [a]1 Cor. 15:28 [1]*all things in* *See WW at 1 Thess. 2:13.
8 [a]1 Cor. 2:6, 7 [b]Rom. 15:14 *See WW at Rom. 7:6.

3 Therefore I make known to you that
no one speaking by the Spirit of God
calls Jesus [1]**accursed,** and [a]no one can
say that Jesus is Lord except by the
Holy Spirit.

WORD WEALTH

12:3 accursed, ***anathema*** (an-*ath*-em-ah); Strong's *#331:* An animal to be slain as a sacrifice, devoted to destruction. Because of its association with sin, the word had an evil connotation and was synonymous with a curse. In the sacrificial scheme, *anathema* meant alienated from God without hope of being redeemed.

4 [a]There are [1]diversities of *gifts, but 5
[b]the same Spirit.
5 [a]There are differences of ministries,
but the same Lord.
6 And there are diversities of activities, but it is the same God [a]who
*works [1]all in all.
7 But the manifestation of the Spirit
is given to each one for the profit *of
all:*
8 for to one is given [a]the word of wisdom through the *Spirit, to another
[b]the word of knowledge through the
same Spirit,

Supper. It does not refer to a person's examining his or her daily walk with Jesus so as to determine worthiness to partake of Communion. To partake in a "worthy" manner is to attribute the full worth of Christ's redeeming work to this action—to partake with faith in His full forgiveness, full acceptance, and full power to restore, strengthen, and heal.

11:29 The Lord's body refers either to the physical body of Jesus (see v. 27) or to the corporate body of Christ, the church.

11:30 Some Corinthians, in failing to partake of the power potential in judicious celebration of the Lord's Table, or who had abused its meaning, were under affliction, or had suffered a premature death.

11:31, 32 Careful self-examination will help us to avoid God's chastisement, and sensitive participation may prevent illness or premature death (see Ps. 81; 1 John 1:9). Note: This passage warns against meaningless participation in the Eucharist, but it does not present God as vindictively monitoring the participant. The message is, "Remember, Jesus has borne your judgment!" Thus, "Come with humility, confession, and worship, and be strengthened in Him."

12:1 The Corinthians misunderstood the manner in which the Holy Spirit works through individuals, and they abused the use of **spiritual gifts,** apparently regarding them as ends in themselves. In particular, they misunderstood the proper public use of the gift of tongues and it often confused the *order in their meetings.* They also misunderstood the power of the Spirit, viewing gift-operations of the Spirit as a compulsive possession, negating the will (14:32). Paul responds to this problem by showing the need for varied and multiple manifestations of the Spirit (ch. 12); the need for loving and unselfish motives in these manifestations (ch. 13); and the need for self-control and for keeping an orderly, edifying manner in corporate services (ch. 14).

12:2, 3 Paul introduces three guiding principles that distinguish the ways of the **Holy Spirit:** 1) The principle of conscious control. Unlike paganism, the power of the Holy Spirit does not drive people into wild compulsive acts. His gentle dovelike ministry strengthens human personality. He empowers; He does not overpower. 2) The principle that Christ is glorified. All manifestations of the Spirit will harmonize with the truth about Jesus. 3) The principle of creedal faith. The main work of the Holy Spirit is to bring people under the lordship of **Jesus.**

12:4–11 See section 5 of Truth-In-Action at the end of 1 Cor.

12:4–6 The three categories named in these verses coupled with the Trinity show the broad diversity, yet essential unity, in the manifestation of the **Spirit.** Unity does not make the Spirit uniform. The Holy Spirit is not an impersonal power, and His gifts do not spring from a human source; it is the work of **God.** Gifts are from the great gift, the Holy Spirit; ministries are modeled by the main minister, Christ (the **Lord**); and the works of the Spirit come from the chief worker, God the Father.

12:7 Paul identifies a spiritual gift as a supernatural ability bestowed on an individual by the Holy Spirit, not as a heightened natural ability. Thus, each gift is a **manifestation of the Spirit,** that is, visible evidence of His activity. The Holy Spirit bestows the gifts to whom He wills as the occasion recommends from the divine viewpoint.

12:8–11 These nine gifts specify the varied distribution necessary for a full manifestation of the Spirit: **The word of wisdom** is a spiritual utterance at a given moment **through the Spirit,** supernaturally disclosing the mind, purpose, and way of God as applied to a specific situation. **The word of knowledge** is a supernatural revelation of information pertaining to a person or an event, given for a specific

9 [a]to another faith by the same Spirit,
to another [b]gifts of healings by [1]the
same Spirit,
10 [a]to another the working of miracles,
to another [b]prophecy,* to another
[c]discerning of spirits, to another
[d]*different* kinds of tongues, to another the interpretation of tongues.

KINGDOM DYNAMICS

12:8–10, 28 The Holy Spirit's Gifts to You, SPIRITUAL GIFTS. It is important that we not blur the distinction between the gifts given by each member of the Godhead. Discovering the giftedness the Father has begotten in us should not substitute for our earnest availability to operate in any of the nine gifts of the Holy Spirit listed here, as He—of His will—distributes them through the church. An elaboration of this and related themes appears in the study article on page 2018, "Holy Spirit Gifts and Power."

(Rom. 12:6–8/Eph. 4:11) J.W.H.

KINGDOM DYNAMICS

12:9, 28 The Gift of Healing, DIVINE HEALING. In order that the church's mission might not be limited to the abilities of mere human enterprise, the Holy Spirit provides specially designed, distributed, and energized gifts. Among them are "gifts of healings." The clear intent is that the supernatural healing of the sick should be a permanent ministry established in the church alongside and abetting the work of evangelizing the world. This is for today—timeless—for "the gifts and the calling of God *are* irrevocable" (Rom. 11:29).

(Acts 28:8, 9/James 5:13–18) N.V.

9 [a]Matt. 17:19; [1 Cor. 13:2]; 2 Cor. 4:13 [b]Matt. 10:1; Mark 3:15; 16:18; James 5:14 [1]NU *one*
10 [a]Mark 16:17 [b]Rom. 12:6 [c]1 John 4:1 [d]Acts 2:4–11 *See WW at 1 Thess. 5:20.
11 [a]Rom. 12:6; 2 Cor. 10:13 [b][John 3:8]
12 [a]Rom. 12:4, 5; 1 Cor. 10:17; Eph. 4:4 [b][Gal. 3:16]
13 [a][Rom. 6:5] [b]Rom. 3:22; Gal. 3:28; [Eph. 2:13–18]; Col. 3:11

11 But one and the same Spirit works
all these things, [a]distributing to each
one individually [b]as He wills.

Unity and Diversity in One Body

12 For [a]as the body is one and has 4
many members, but all the members
of that one body, being many, are one
body, [b]so also *is* Christ.

KINGDOM DYNAMICS

12:12 All Believers Are Members of the Body of Christ, HUMAN WORTH. The human body is an exquisite organism. Scientists cannot duplicate it or even fully understand it. It is a synthesis of many parts all working together in a comprehensive whole. What affects one part of the body affects the whole. Each member of the body relates to and depends upon other parts of the body. Each contributes to the welfare of the entire body. So are all believers as members of the body of Christ. We should function in Christ's body as the parts of the human body function in it. The amputation of a limb handicaps the entire body. There is no Christian brother whom we do not need. The word "body" (Greek *soma*) is related to *sozo,* meaning "to heal, preserve, be made whole." This clearly shows how our lives are inextricably woven together within the body of Christ, and how well-being depends upon the well-being of others (Rom. 14:7). Let us allow Christ to knit us together in His church.

(Acts 17:26/John 13:34, 35) C.B.

13 For [a]by one Spirit we were all baptized into one body—[b]whether Jews or

purpose, usually having to do with an immediate need. The gift of **faith** is a unique form of faith that goes beyond natural faith and saving faith. It supernaturally trusts and does not doubt with reference to the specific matters involved. **Gifts of healings** are those healings that God performs supernaturally **by the Spirit.** The plural suggests that as there are many sicknesses and diseases, the gift is related to healings of many disorders. **The working of miracles** is a manifestation of power beyond the ordinary course of natural law. It is a divine enablement to do something that could not be done naturally. **Prophecy** is a divine disclosure on behalf of the Spirit, an edifying revelation of the Spirit for the moment (14:3), a sudden insight of the Spirit, prompting exhortation or comfort (14:3, 30). **Discerning of spirits** is the ability to discern the spirit world, and especially to detect the true source of circumstances or motives of people. ***Different* kinds of tongues** is the gift of speaking supernaturally in a language not known to the individual. The plural allows different forms, possibly harmonizing the known spoken languages of Acts 2:4–6 and the unknown transrational utterances in Corinthians, designed particularly for praying and singing in the Spirit, mostly for private worship (14:14–19). **The interpretation of tongues** is the gift of rendering the transrational (but not irrational) message of the Spirit meaningful to others when exercised in public. It is not the translation of a foreign language. Note: None of the gifts require a "public" setting, although each may and should be welcomed in corporate gatherings.

12:12–27 See section 4 of Truth-In-Action at the end of 1 Cor.

12:12–26 In comparing the church to the human body, Paul shows how the wide diversity of gifts assures unity in the church. Each gift contributes something necessary to the common life and growth of the whole. There is no room for pride and no need to feel inferior in the body of Christ, for each individual is essential to the proper function of the body.

12:13 Paul states the basis for the principle of unity within diversity. The gift of the Holy Spirit is the common life of Christians and a greater dynamic than all human distinctives. The Greek grammar in this statement parallels other passages that speak of being "baptized with the Holy Spirit" (see Matt. 3:11; Mark 1:8; Luke 3:16; John 1:33; Acts 1:5; 11:16). While Spirit baptism describes a primary spiritual reality for all believers, Paul still pleads for a Spirit-filled experience (Eph. 5:18) that includes the manifestations listed here.

Greeks, whether slaves or *free—and
[c]have all been made to drink [1]into one
Spirit.
14 For in fact the body is not one member but many.
15 If the foot should say, "Because I
am not a hand, I am not of the body,"
is it therefore not of the body?
16 And if the ear should say, "Because
I am not an eye, I am not of the body,"
is it therefore not of the body?
17 If the whole body *were* an eye,
where *would be* the hearing? If the
whole *were* hearing, where *would be*
the smelling?
18 But now [a]God has set the members,
each one of them, in the body [b]just as
He pleased.
19 And if they *were* all one member,
where *would* the body *be?*
20 But now indeed *there are* many
members, yet one body.
21 And the eye cannot say to the hand,
"I have no need of you"; nor again the
head to the feet, "I have no need of
you."
22 No, much rather, those members of
the body which seem to be weaker are
necessary.
23 And those *members* of the body
which we think to be less honorable,
on these we bestow *greater honor;
and our unpresentable *parts* have
greater modesty,
24 but our presentable *parts* have no
need. But God composed the body,
having given greater honor to that *part*
which lacks it,
25 that there should be no [1]schism
in the body, but *that* the members
should have the same care for one another.
26 And if one member suffers, all the
members suffer with *it;* or if one member is honored, all the members rejoice
with *it.*
27 Now [a]you are the body of Christ,
and [b]members individually.
28 And [a]God has appointed these in
the *church: first [b]**apostles,** second
[c]prophets,* third teachers, after that
[d]miracles, then [e]gifts of healings,
[f]helps, [g]administrations, varieties of
tongues.

13 [c][John 7:37–39] [1]NU omits *into* *See WW at Rev. 6:15.
18 [a]1 Cor. 12:28 [b]Rom. 12:3
23 *See WW at John 10:10.
25 [1]*division*
27 [a]Rom. 12:5; Eph. 1:23; 4:12; 5:23, 30; Col. 1:24 [b]Eph. 5:30
28 [a]Eph. 4:11 [b][Eph. 2:20; 3:5] [c]Acts 13:1; Rom. 12:6 [d]1 Cor. 12:10, 29; Gal. 3:5 [e]Mark 16:18; 1 Cor. 12:9, 30 [f]Num. 11:17 [g]Rom. 12:8; 1 Tim. 5:17; Heb. 13:17, 24 *See WW at Acts 8:1. • See WW at Matt. 2:5.

WORD WEALTH

12:28 apostles, *apostolos* (ap-os-tol-oss); Strong's *#652:* A special messenger, a delegate, one commissioned for a particular task or role, one who is sent forth with a message. In the NT the word denotes both the original twelve disciples and prominent leaders outside the Twelve. Marvin Vincent records three features of an apostle: 1) one who has had a visible encounter with the resurrected Christ; 2) one who plants churches; 3) one who functions in the ministry with signs, wonders, and miracles.

KINGDOM DYNAMICS

12:28 The Administrative Leader, LEADER TRAITS. The NT seems to recognize three basic types of administrative leadership: 1) The Servant Leader or Deacon: Greek *diakonia* means "service or ministry" (2 Cor. 8:19, 20; 9:1, 12). These "deacons" were patterned after the men set apart in Acts 6:1–6 to serve the widows in Jerusalem. 2) The Steward Leader or Manager: Greek *oikonomos* or *oikonomis* means "steward," such as today's pastor. The word literally means "household manager," a slot often held by a slave in the first century. It refers to those who "manage" the church (1 Cor. 4:1, 2; 2 Tim. 1:7). 3) The Steersman Leader or Overseer is found in the office of apostle or bishop. *Kybernesis* is a Greek term borrowed from seafaring, and is used to designate the steersman or pilot who holds the ship on course. The word is rendered "governments" (1 Cor. 12:28) where Paul speaks of the spiritual gift of administration.

(Luke 3:1–20/Is. 6:8, 9*) J.B.

29 *Are* all apostles? *Are* all prophets?
Are all teachers? *Are* all workers of
miracles?
30 Do all have gifts of healings? Do all
speak with tongues? Do all interpret?
31 But [a]earnestly *desire the [1]best
*gifts. And yet I show you a *more ex-
cellent way.

31 [a]1 Cor. 14:1, 39 [1]NU *greater* *See WW at 1 Cor. 14:1. • See WW at 1 Cor. 1:7. • See WW at 2 Cor. 4:7.

12:27–30 Members individually: The lessons from the human body are now practically applied to individuals. No one has all the gifts. Any order of ranking would contradict *the context,* which is a mix of the gifts, ministries, and activities of the Trinity, illustrating how variety and diversity operate in different people (12:4–6). **Helps** describes all forms of loving service and support, a manifestation of the Spirit often overlooked. **Administrations** is another of the less honorable, that is, less noticeable ministries (v. 23), giving guidance and assistance behind the scenes.
12:30 Do all speak with tongues? This question anticipates a negative answer. However, the wish that all did (14:5), and the prevalence of tongues in Paul's own personal prayer life (14:18), indicate that the question likely refers to the fact that all should not expect or strive to speak with tongues in public meetings (14:27). Such breeds chaos.
12:31 Paul's exhortation concerning **the best gifts** seeks to correct the mistaken applications of the public use of tongues. The private use, which is designed mostly for self-edification, was being confused by public exercise. "Best" might be defined as that gift or those gifts most suited to the given situation, and an example is present: for example,

The Greatest Gift

1 **13** Though I speak with the
tongues of men and of *angels,
but have not love, I have become
sounding brass or a clanging cymbal.

KINGDOM DYNAMICS

13:1 Love: The Qualifying Factor, SPIRITUAL GIFTS. Since the basis of all gifts is love, that spirit of love is the qualifying factor for biblical exercise of the gifts of the Holy Spirit. Thus, those in authority must "try the spirits" to assure that those who exercise spiritual gifts actually "follow after love" as well as "desire spiritual gifts." An elaboration of this and related themes appears in the study article on page 2018, "Holy Spirit Gifts and Power."

(Eph. 4:11/1 Cor. 14:27) P.W.

2 And though I have *the gift of*
[a]prophecy,* and understand all mysteries and all knowledge, and though
I have all faith, [b]so that I could *remove mountains, but have not love, I
am nothing.
3 And [a]though I bestow all my goods
to feed *the poor,* and though I give my
body [1]to be burned, but have not love,
it profits me nothing.
4 [a]Love suffers long *and* is [b]kind;
love [c]does not *envy; love does not parade itself, is not [1]puffed up;
5 does not behave rudely, [a]does not
seek its own, is not provoked, [1]thinks*
no evil;
6 [a]does not rejoice in *iniquity, but
[b]rejoices in the *truth;
7 [a]bears all things, believes all things,
hopes all things, *endures all things.
8 *Love never fails. But whether *there
are* *prophecies, they will fail; whether
there are tongues, they will cease;
whether *there is* knowledge, it will
vanish away.
9 [a]For we *know in part and we
prophesy in part.
10 But when that which is [1]perfect* has
come, then that which is in part will
be done away.
11 When I was a child, I spoke as a
child, I understood as a child, I thought
as a child; but when I became a man,
I put away childish things.
12 For [a]now we see in a mirror, dimly,

CHAPTER 13

1 *See WW at Matt. 4:11
2 [a]1 Cor. 12:8–10, 28; 14:1 [b]Matt. 17:20; 21:21 *See WW at 1 Thess. 5:20. • See WW at Luke 16:4.
3 [a]Matt. 6:1, 2 [1]NU *so I may boast*
4 [a]Prov. 10:12; 17:9 [b]Eph. 4:32 [c]Gal. 5:26 [1]*arrogant* *See WW at 1 Cor. 14:1.
5 [a]1 Cor. 10:24 [1]*keeps no accounts of evil* *See WW at Rom. 4:3.
6 [a]Rom. 1:32 [b]2 John 4 *See WW at John 7:18. • See WW at John 4:24.
7 [a]Gal. 6:2 *See WW at Matt. 24:13.
8 *See WW at Rom. 5:5. • See WW at 1 Thess. 5:20.
9 [a]1 Cor. 8:2; 13:12 *See WW at John 8:32.
10 [1]*complete* *See WW at James 3:2.
12 [a]Phil. 3:12

prophecy is functionally "better" than tongues in public because it edifies the church (14:4, 5), unless, of course, the "tongue" is interpreted. However, the example from the human body precludes all value ranking of gifts (12:22–25). No negative conclusion about the worth of tongues may legitimately be drawn from the fact that it appears last in the lists. Is self-control the least important virtue in the fruit of the Spirit because it is listed last (Gal. 5:22, 23)? Using the same logic, love should be of less importance than faith and hope, but Paul calls it the greatest (1 Cor. 13:13). **A more excellent way** is not a negative comparison between gifts and love, since the temporal adverb **yet** indicates the continuation of the subject. All manifestations of the Spirit must at the same time manifest the ways of love, for love is the ultimate issue behind all things.

13:1–13 Paul explains the absolute necessity of **love** (vv. 1–3); defines the essence of love in 14 of its characteristics (vv. 4–7); and contrasts the eternal perfections of love with the temporal imperfections of gifts (vv. 8–13).

13:1–8 See section 1 of Truth-In-Action at the end of 1 Cor.

13:1–3 Without **love** the most magnificent manifestation of gifts and the most heroic self-sacrifice mean nothing. Right things must be done in the right way. Although some view the reference to **tongues of angels** as a poetic hyperbole, it likely denotes the languages of these supernatural beings.

13:4–7 Love suffers long, having patience with imperfect people. Love **is kind,** active in doing good. **Love does not envy;** since it is nonpossessive and noncompetitive, it actually wants other people to get ahead. Hence it **does not parade itself.** Love has a self-effacing quality; it is not ostentatious. Love **is not puffed up,** treating others arrogantly; it **does not behave rudely,** but displays good manners and courtesy. Love **does not seek its own,** insisting on its own rights and demanding precedence; rather, it is unselfish. Love **is not provoked;** it is not irritable or touchy, rough or hostile, but is graceful under pressure. Love **thinks no evil;** it does not keep an account of wrongs done to it; instead, it erases resentments. Love **does not rejoice in iniquity,** finding satisfaction in the shortcomings of others and spreading an evil report; rather, it **rejoices in the truth,** aggressively advertising the good. Love **bears all things,** defending and holding other people up. Love **believes** the best about others, credits them with good intentions, and is not suspicious. Love **hopes all things,** never giving up on people, but affirming their future. Love **endures all things,** persevering and remaining loyal to the end.

13:8–13 Gifts, in contrast to love, are partial, not complete (v. 9); they are temporal, not eternal (vv. 10, 11); they communicate imperfect rather than perfect knowledge (v. 12). Everything in this age compared to the perfection of the new creation is at a child-stage, including all gifts. Rather than suggesting the demise of gifts during this age or at some early point in church history, this passage proves just the opposite.

13:10 That which is perfect refers to the completion of God's purposes after the coming of the Lord Jesus Christ (Rom. 8:18, 19). There is no reason other than human opinion to presume to attribute this reference to the conclusion of the canon of the Scriptures. While the inspired Word of God was completed at the end of the first century, its completion did not signal an end to the continuing operation of the very powers it describes. Rather, that Word instructs us to welcome the Holy Spirit's gifts and ministries in our lives, to round out our sufficiency for ministry to a needy world—through the Word *preached* and the Word *confirmed.*

13:12 Ancient mirrors, which were manufactured at Corinth, were made of metal and gave dim reflections, an illustration of our imperfect knowledge during this age. But knowledge will be full and instantaneous in the future state of glory.

but then [b]face to face. Now I know in
part, but then I shall *know just as I
also am known.
13 And now abide *faith, *hope, love,
these three; but the greatest of these
is love.

12 [b]Gen. 32:30; Num. 12:8; Matt. 18:10; [1 John 3:2] *See WW at Luke 5:22.
13 *See WW at Mark 11:22. • See WW at 1 Thess. 1:3

Prophecy and Tongues

5 **14** Pursue love, and [a]**desire** spiritual *gifts*, [b]but especially that
you may prophesy.

CHAPTER 14

1 [a]1 Cor. 12:31; 14:39 [b]Num. 11:25, 29

WORD WEALTH

14:1 desire, *zeloo* (dzay-*low*-oh), Strong's *#2206:* To be zealous for, to burn with desire, to pursue ardently, to desire eagerly or intensely. Negatively, the word is associated with strong envy and jealousy (Acts 7:9; 17:5; 1 Cor. 13:4; James 4:2).

KINGDOM DYNAMICS

14:1–40 The Pentecostal/Charismatic Context, SPIRITUAL GIFTS. This text bases the gifts of the Spirit on the one sure foundation of love and calls for integrity as the key for the preservation of the sacredness of the sanctuary and the dignity of the worship service. This passage affords the controlling guidelines for governing services in the biblically sensitive Pentecostal/Charismatic context. An elaboration of this and related themes appears in the study article on page 2018, "Holy Spirit Gifts and Power."
(Jude 20/Is. 28:11, 12*) P.W.

KINGDOM DYNAMICS

14:1 The Propriety and Desirability of Prophecy, PROPHECY. The life of the NT church is intended to be blessed by the presence of the gift of prophecy. As Paul states here in noting love as our primary pursuit, prophecy is to be welcomed for the "edification and exhortation and comfort" of the congregation—corporately and individually (v. 3). Such encouragement of each other is "prophecy," not "words" in the sense of the Bible, which uses the very words of God, but in the sense of human words the Holy Spirit uniquely brings to mind.

The practice of the gift of prophecy is one purpose of Holy Spirit fullness (Acts 2:17). It also fulfills Joel's prophecy (Joel 2:28) and Moses' earlier expressed hope (Num. 11:29).

The operation of the gift of prophecy is encouraged by Peter (1 Pet. 4:11), and Paul says that it is within the potential of every believer (1 Cor. 14:31). It is intended as a means of broad participation among the congregation, mutually benefiting each other with anointed, loving words of upbuilding, insight, and affirmation. Such prophecy may provide such insight that hearts are humbled in worship of God, suddenly made aware of His Spirit's knowledge of their need and readiness to answer it (1 Cor. 14:24, 25). Prophecy of this order is also a means by which vision and expectation are prompted and provided, and without which people may become passive or neglectful (1 Sam. 3:1; Prov. 29:18; Acts 2:17). There are specific guidelines for the operation of this gift, as with all gifts of the Holy Spirit, to insure that one gift not supplant the exercise of others or usurp the authority of spiritual leadership. Further, all such prophecy is subordinated to the plumbline of God's Eternal Word, the Bible—the standard by which all prophetic utterance in the church is to be judged (1 Cor. 14:26–33).
(Eph. 1:17–19/2 Pet. 1:16–19) J.W.H.

2 For he who [a]speaks in a tongue
does not speak to men but to God, for
no one understands *him;* however, in
the spirit he speaks mysteries.
3 But he who prophesies speaks
[a]edification and [b]exhortation and comfort to men.
4 He who speaks in a tongue edifies
himself, but he who prophesies edifies
the church.

2 [a]Acts 2:4; 10:46
3 [a]Rom. 14:19; 15:2; 2 Cor. 10:8; 12:19; Eph. 4:12, 29 [b]1 Tim. 4:13; 2 Tim. 4:2; Titus 1:9; 2:15; Heb. 3:13; 10:25

13:13 The virtues of **faith, hope,** and **love** are necessary in this age; but in the age to come, faith will give way to sight (2 Cor. 5:7), and hope will turn into experience (Rom. 8:24). Love alone is eternal, for God is love (1 John 4:8).
14:1–40 Paul provides guidelines for exercising the gifts of prophecy and tongues, comparing their public benefits with private exercise (vv. 2–25), stating their rules of operation (vv. 26–36), and giving a final exhortation (vv. 37–40).
14:1–5 See section 5 of Truth-In-Action at the end of 1 Cor.
14:1 Neither **love** nor ***gifts*** come automatically and should not be a passive matter of indifference. Believers should **desire especially** to **prophesy,** as compared to speaking in tongues in public (vv. 2–5). Tongues are primarily for self-edification and depend on the companion gift of interpretation when exercised in public. Tongues are permitted, but prophecy is preferred (v. 39).
14:2 Paul's assertion clearly establishes the primary purpose for tongues as the gift of the Spirit for private worship. It is a unique Godward and not a manward gift, unless interpreted so the hearers may understand (v. 5). Tongues are intended for personal prayer and praise to God (vv. 14, 17). Therefore, they can take on a strictly spiritual form of expression, since man is not the goal. The seat of their operation is not the mind, but the spirit (vv. 14, 15). They are an enablement of the Spirit for nonconceptual communication directly with God, who is Spirit (John 4:24). This is why they are so vastly important and constantly used by Paul (v. 18) **Mysteries,** as elsewhere in the NT, refers to secrets which have been divinely revealed.
14:3, 4 The use of tongues is a means of private self-edification. This practice does not denote selfishness, but rather, spiritual strengthening. Prophecy, however, builds up, encourages, and comforts others in the church.

5 I wish you all spoke with tongues,
but even more that you prophesied;
[1]for he who prophesies *is* greater than
he who speaks with tongues, unless indeed he interprets, that the church may
receive edification.

Tongues Must Be Interpreted

6 But now, brethren, if I come to you
speaking with tongues, what shall I
profit you unless I speak to you either
by [a]revelation, by knowledge, by
prophesying, or by teaching?
7 Even things without life, whether
flute or harp, when they make a sound,
unless they make a distinction in the
sounds, how will it be known what is
piped or played?
8 For if the trumpet *makes an uncertain sound, who will prepare for battle?
9 So likewise you, unless you utter by
the tongue words easy to understand,
how will it be known what is spoken?
For you will be speaking into the air.
10 There are, it may be, so many kinds
of languages in the world, and none
of them *is* without [1]significance.
11 Therefore, if I do not know the
meaning of the language, I shall be a
[1]foreigner to him who speaks, and he
who speaks *will be* a foreigner to
me.
12 Even so you, since you are
[1]zealous* for spiritual *gifts, let it be* for
the [2]edification of the church *that* you
seek to excel.
13 Therefore let him who speaks in a
tongue pray that he may [a]interpret.
14 For if I pray in a tongue, my spirit
prays, but my understanding is unfruitful.
15 What is *the conclusion* then? I will
pray with the spirit, and I will also pray
with the understanding. [a]I will sing
with the spirit, and I will also sing
[b]with the understanding.
16 Otherwise, if you bless with the
spirit, how will he who occupies the
place of the uninformed say "Amen"
[a]at your giving of thanks, since he does
not understand what you say?
17 For you indeed give thanks well, but
the other is not edified.
18 I thank my God I speak with
tongues more than you all;
19 yet in the church I would rather
speak five words with my understanding, that I may teach others also, than
ten thousand words in a tongue.

Tongues a Sign to Unbelievers

20 Brethren, [a]do not be children in understanding; however, in malice
[b]be babes, but in understanding be mature.
21 [a]In the law it is written:

[b]*"With men of other tongues and*
other lips

5 [1]NU *and*
6 [a]1 Cor. 14:26; Eph. 1:17
8 *See WW at Acts 20:35.
10 [1]*meaning*
11 [1]Lit. *barbarian*
12 [1]*eager* [2]*building up* *See WW at Acts 22:3.
13 [a]1 Cor. 12:10
15 [a]Eph. 5:19; Col. 3:16 [b]Ps. 47:7
16 [a]Deut. 27:15–26; 1 Chr. 16:36; Neh. 5:13; 8:6; Ps. 106:48; Jer. 11:5; 28:6; 1 Cor. 11:24; Rev. 5:14; 7:12
20 [a]Ps. 131:2; [Matt. 11:25; 18:3; 19:14]; Rom. 16:19; 1 Cor. 3:1; Eph. 4:14; Heb. 5:12, 13 [b][Matt. 18:3; 1 Pet. 2:2]
21 [a]John 10:34; 1 Cor. 14:34 [b]Is. 28:11, 12

14:5 Paul's endorsement of prophecy over tongues in corporate gatherings is qualified by his equating the *value* of tongues with prophecy, if the tongue is accompanied by interpretation. Therefore, tongues without interpretation are for personal edification. Prophecy and tongues with interpretation minister to the entire congregation, being understood by all. This understanding serves to affirm the fact of and distinguish the application of the two distinct ways "tongues" may be manifested—in private or public, in personal devotion or in corporate gatherings.

14:6–13 Prophecy is preferred above tongues in public, where clear understanding by the hearers is the goal. Tongues exercised in a church meeting must therefore be interpreted.

14:13–22 See section 3 of Truth-In-Action at the end of 1 Cor.

14:13 The person who speaks in tongues publicly seems to bear the responsibility of interpretation, but 12:10 allows for a diversity in these two gifts. If no interpreter is present, the tongue is to be restrained (v. 28).

14:14–19 Paul reveals the place of tongues in his own personal prayer life. Praying in tongues is praying from the spirit instead of the intellect, and the same is true of singing praises. For Paul, praying and singing, both in tongues and in everyday language, were normal and regular parts of prayer and praise. There is no suggestion of hysteria, emotionalism, or abnormality of any kind.

14:16, 17 Edification of others is always the guideline in the public use of tongues. At the same time v. 17 makes it clear that no censure is intended. It is not clear whether or not corporate singing, praising, or praying in tongues would be permitted or denied by Paul. What is clear is that no individual or group of individuals should so sing or pray in violation of the leadership, the spirit of the group as a whole, or the intent of the meeting. Differences exist in the acceptance of "singing in tongues" in corporate gatherings of believers. Some adhere to a strict disallowance of group exercise of this gift in concert, while others feel that "order" is not violated if the exercise is explained and nonfanatical expression maintained.

14:18 Paul did not depreciate tongues as a lesser gift, but thanked God for the self-edification afforded by the full measure of the gift in his own devotional life. (See also v. 5, "I wish you all spoke with tongues.")

14:21–25 In one respect, Paul's use of Is. 28:11, 12 notes how the harsh, unknown tongues of foreign invaders were a sign of divine judgment upon Israel in Isaiah's day—a warning that they scoffed at and completely rejected. He seems to be noting how tongues in the Corinthian church could have the same effect of hardening **believers** who were present, whose response to the sign of tongues might be **you are out of your mind** (similar to the reaction at Pentecost, Acts 2:13). Prophecy, however, is a sign to believers that God is in their midst, and brings conviction upon unbelievers, leading them to repentance. (In a second respect, Paul might have had double entendre in mind, for the Is. passage also describes a second aspect of possible value in "tongues"—that people would receive a "rest" and "a refreshing." In private exercise, the "edifying" benefit of tongues (v. 4) would doubtless include that.)

I will speak to this people;
And yet, for all that, they will not
hear Me,"
says the Lord.
22 Therefore tongues are for a [a]sign,
not to those who believe but to unbelievers; but prophesying is not for
unbelievers but for those who believe.
23 Therefore if the whole church
comes together in one place, and all
speak with tongues, and there come in
those who are uninformed or unbelievers, [a]will they not say that you are
[1]out of your mind?
24 But if all prophesy, and an unbeliever or an uninformed person comes
in, he is convinced by all, he is convicted by all.
25 [1]And thus the secrets of his heart
are *revealed; and so, falling down on
his face, he will *worship God and report [a]that God is truly among you.

Order in Church Meetings

4 26 How is it then, brethren? Whenever
you come together, each of you has a
psalm, [a]has a teaching, has a tongue,
has a revelation, has an interpretation.
[b]Let all things be done for [1]edification.
27 If anyone speaks in a tongue, *let
there be* two or at the most three, *each*
in turn, and let one interpret.

KINGDOM DYNAMICS

14:27 Limits to Exercising Tongues, SPIRITUAL GIFTS. In a group gathering, the exercise of tongues (with interpretation each time, of course) is to be limited to sequences of two or three at the most. While many hold this to be a rigid number, others understand it to be a flexible guideline to keep a worship service in balance. An elaboration of this and related themes appears in the study article on page 2018, "Holy Spirit Gifts and Power."

(1 Cor. 13:1/Gal. 5:22, 23) P.W.

28 But if there is no interpreter, let him
keep silent in church, and let him
speak to himself and to God.
29 Let two or three prophets speak,
and [a]let the others judge.
30 But if *anything* is revealed to another who sits by, [a]let the first keep
silent.
31 For you can all prophesy one by
one, that all may learn and all may be
encouraged.
32 And [a]the spirits of the prophets are
subject to the prophets.

WORD WEALTH

14:32 subject, *hupotasso* (hoop-ot-*as*-so); Strong's *#5293:* Literally "to stand under." The word suggests subordination, obedience, submission, subservience, subjection. The divine gift of prophetic utterance is put under the control and responsibility of the possessor.

33 For God is not *the author* of [1]confu-
sion but of peace, [a]as in all the
churches of the saints.
34 [a]Let [1]your women keep silent in the
churches, for they are not permitted to
speak; but *they are* to be submissive,
as the [b]law also says.
35 And if they want to learn something, let them ask their own husbands
at home; for it is shameful for women
to speak in church.
36 Or did the word of God come *originally* from you? Or *was it* you only that
it reached?
37 [a]If anyone thinks himself to be a
prophet or spiritual, let him acknowl-

22 [a]Mark 16:17
23 [a]Acts 2:13 [1]*insane*
25 [a]Is. 45:14; Dan. 2:47; Zech. 8:23; Acts 4:13 [1]NU omits *And thus* *See WW at 1 Cor. 11:19. • See WW at Rev. 4:10.
26 [a]1 Cor. 12:8–10; 14:6 [b]1 Cor. 12:7; [2 Cor. 12:19] [1]*building up*
29 [a]1 Cor. 12:10
30 [a][1 Thess. 5:19, 20]
32 [a]1 John 4:1
33 [a]1 Cor. 11:16 [1]*disorder*
34 [a]1 Tim. 2:11; 1 Pet. 3:1 [b]Gen. 3:16 [1]NU omits *your*
37 [a]2 Cor. 10:7; [1 John 4:6]

14:26–40 See section 4 of Truth-In-Action at the end of 1 Cor.

14:26 Each of you: The things of the Spirit are intended for every member of the body of Christ, not an elite few. This verse describes typical Christian worship in the present age.

14:29 In order to preserve balance and prevent confusion in the worship service, Paul regulates prophecy. **Others** present, especially those who function in the gift of prophecy, are to **judge** the authenticity of the prophetic utterances. The judging includes its content, alignment with God's Word, and relevancy to the meeting.

14:34, 35 These verses are very difficult and are subject to great debate. The best interpretation is probably to see Paul as not forbidding women to manifest spiritual gifts in the service (see 11:5; Acts 2:18; 21:9). Rather, he prohibits undisciplined discussion that would disturb the service. Also possible is the forbidden speaking along the lines of 1 Tim. 2:11–15, which precludes women from becoming independent doctrinal (apostolic) authorities over men. One other view sees vv. 34, 35 as Paul's quoting from their letter to him in beginning a new paragraph. Proponents of this view then see v. 36 as his rhetorical answer, essentially saying, "What? Men only? Nonsense!" Perhaps more helpful is noting that the Greek word here for "woman" is also translatable "wife." Thus, the command may confront the impropriety in any age for a wife to domineeringly issue doctrinal commands and enforce authoritative teachings, embarrassing her husband in public. The Bible does not assign rigid social or church roles to men and women, but it does place headship and authority in husbands as an abiding principle for this age.

14:37, 38 The spiritually minded will receive Paul's instructions with apostolic authority. Those who reject them are responsible for the consequences of their ignorance.

edge that the things which I write to
you are the commandments of the
Lord.
38 But [1]if anyone is ignorant, let him
be ignorant.
39 Therefore, brethren, [a]desire* earnestly to prophesy, and do not forbid
to speak with tongues.
40 [a]Let all things be done decently and
in order.

The Risen Christ, Faith's Reality

15 Moreover, brethren, I declare to
you the gospel [a]which I
preached to you, which also you received and [b]in which you stand,
2 [a]by which also you are saved, if you
hold fast that word which I preached
to you—unless [b]you believed in
vain.
3 For [a]I delivered to you first of all
that [b]which I also received: that Christ
died for our sins [c]according to the
*Scriptures,
4 and that He was buried, and that
He rose again the third day [a]according
to the Scriptures,
5 [a]and that He was seen by [1]Cephas,
then [b]by the twelve.
6 After that He was seen by over five
hundred brethren at once, of whom the
greater part remain to the present, but
some have [1]fallen asleep.
7 After that He was seen by James,
then [a]by all the *apostles.
8 [a]Then last of all He was seen by me
also, as by one born out of due time.
9 For I am [a]the least of the apostles,
who am not worthy to be called an
apostle, because [b]I persecuted the
church of God.
10 But [a]by the *grace of God I am what
I am, and His grace toward me was not
in vain; but I labored more abundantly
than they all, [b]yet not I, but the grace
of God *which was* with me.
11 Therefore, whether *it was* I or they,
so we preach and so you *believed.

The Risen Christ, Our Hope

12 Now if Christ is preached that He
has been raised from the dead, how do
some among you say that there is no
resurrection of the dead?
13 But if there is no resurrection of the
dead, [a]then Christ is not risen.
14 And if Christ is not risen, then our
preaching *is* empty and your faith *is*
also empty.
15 Yes, and we are found false *witnesses of God, because [a]we have testified of God that He raised up Christ,
whom He did not raise up—if in fact
the dead do not rise.
16 For if *the* dead do not rise, then
Christ is not risen.
17 And if Christ is not risen, your
faith *is* *futile; [a]you are still in your
sins!
18 Then also those who have [1]fallen
[a]asleep in Christ have perished.
19 [a]If in this life only we have hope
in Christ, we are of all men the most
pitiable.

The Last Enemy Destroyed

20 But now [a]Christ is risen from the
dead, *and* has become [b]the firstfruits
of those who have [1]fallen asleep.

38 [1]NU *if anyone does not recognize this, he is not recognized.*
39 [a]1 Cor. 12:31 *See WW at 1 Cor. 14:1.
40 [a]1 Cor. 14:33

CHAPTER 15

1 [a][Gal. 1:11] [b][Rom. 5:2; 11:20]
2 [a]Rom. 1:16 [b]Gal. 3:4
3 [a]1 Cor. 11:2, 23 [b][Gal. 1:12] [c]Ps. 22:15 *See WW at John 5:39.
4 [a]Ps. 16:9–11; 68:18; 110:1
5 [a]Luke 24:34 [b]Matt. 28:17 [1]Peter
6 [1]Died
7 [a]Acts 1:3, 4 *See WW at 1 Cor. 12:28.
8 [a][Acts 9:3–8; 22:6–11; 26:12–18]
9 [a]Eph. 3:8 [b]Acts 8:3
10 [a]Eph. 3:7, 8 [b]Phil. 2:13 *See WW at 2 Cor. 12:9.
11 *See WW at Rom. 10:9.
13 [a][1 Thess. 4:14]
15 [a]Acts 2:24 *See WW at Acts 26:22.
17 [a][Rom. 4:25] *See WW at Acts 14:15.
18 [a]Job 14:12 [1]Died
19 [a]2 Tim. 3:12
20 [a]1 Pet. 1:3 [b]Acts 26:23 [1]Died

14:39, 40 Discontinuance of spiritual gifts was not Paul's solution to their abuse. The guidelines he has given will provide safeguards assuring **order** in the service.
15:1–58 The Greeks scoffed at the idea of a bodily **resurrection** (see Acts 17:32). They believed the body was a barrier to the immortal soul. Therefore the attainment of the good required an escape from the body. Paul portrays the resurrection as a qualitative life, involving the eternal redemptive plan of God with the destruction of all enemy powers. He shows the importance of the resurrection as it relates to Jesus Christ (vv. 1–11) and to Christians (vv. 12–34); he defines the nature of the resurrection body (vv. 36–49); and he reveals how the resurrection will take place (vv. 50–58).
15:1 The gospel is more than the forgiveness of sins; it includes Christ's resurrection and the subsequent renewal of all creation.
15:2 Only persevering faith is saving faith.
15:4 According to the Scriptures: See Ps. 2:7; 16:10; 61:7; 68:18, 102:25–27; 110:1; Is. 25:8; 26:19; 53:10–12; Dan. 12:2; Hos. 6:2; 13:14.
15:5–8 The gospel is God's historical revelation of Himself in Christ. It is a saving event that literally happened in the crucifixion and resurrection of Jesus as seen by reliable eyewitnesses. The gospel is not speculation or theory; it concerns events that can be reported.
15:8 Paul humbly illustrates his personal unworthiness as a former persecutor. **Out of due time** is a graphic term in which Paul describes himself at the time of the call of the other apostles as an undeveloped, aborted fetus incapable of sustaining life. The conversion of such a devout Jew as Paul is inexplicable apart from an actual appearance of Christ (see Acts 9; 22; 26).
15:12–19 Paul hypothetically assumes the false premise of **no resurrection** to show its far-reaching implication. Christianity completely depends on the real physical resurrection of the dead body of **Christ;** otherwise, it is all a lie.
15:20 The firstfruits are the first ripened part of the harvest, furnishing actual evidence that the entire harvest is on the way. According to Lev. 23:4–14, the firstfruits in connection with the Passover were used to consecrate the coming harvest. Jesus died on the Passover, and His resurrection is a promise of our own resurrection.

21 For [a]since by man *came* death,
[b]by Man also *came* the resurrection of
the dead.
22 For as in Adam all die, even so in
Christ all shall [a]be made alive.
23 But [a]each one in his own order:
Christ the firstfruits, afterward those
who are Christ's at His **coming.**

WORD WEALTH

15:23 coming, *parousia* (par-oo-*see*-ah): Strong's *#3952:* The technical term signifying the second advent of Jesus, was never used to describe His first coming. *Parousia* originally was the official term for a visit by a person of high rank, especially a king. It was an arrival that included a permanent presence from that coming onward. The glorified Messiah's arrival will be followed by a permanent residence with His glorified people.

24 Then *comes* the end, when He delivers [a]the kingdom to God the Father,
when He puts an end to all rule and
all *authority and power.
25 For He must reign [a]till He has put
all enemies under His feet.
26 [a]The last enemy *that* will be destroyed *is* death.
27 For [a]*"He has put all things *under*
His feet." But when He says "all things
are put under *Him," it is* evident that
He who put all things under Him is ex-
cepted.
28 [a]Now when all things are made subject to Him, then [b]the Son Himself will
also be subject to Him who put all
things under Him, that God may be all
in all.

21 [a]Gen. 3:19; Ezek. 18:4; Rom. 5:12; 6:23; Heb. 9:27 [b]John 11:25
22 [a][John 5:28, 29]
23 [a][1 Thess. 4:15–17]
24 [a][Dan. 2:44; 7:14, 27; 2 Pet. 1:11] *See WW at Mark 3:15.
25 [a]Ps. 110:1; Matt. 22:44
26 [a][2 Tim. 1:10; Rev. 20:14; 21:4]
27 [a]Ps. 8:6 *See WW at 1 Cor. 14:32.
28 [a][Phil. 3:21] [b]1 Cor. 3:23; 11:3; 12:6
30 [a]2 Cor. 11:26 [1]*danger*
31 [a]1 Thess. 2:19 [b]Rom. 8:36
32 [a]2 Cor. 1:8 [b]Eccl. 2:24; Is. 22:13; 56:12; Luke 12:19
33 [a][1 Cor. 5:6] *See WW at Matt. 11:30.
34 [a]Rom. 13:11; Eph. 5:14 [b][1 Thess. 4:5] [c]1 Cor. 6:5
35 [a]Ezek. 37:3
36 [a]John 12:24
39 [1]NU, M omit *of flesh*

Effects of Denying the Resurrection

29 Otherwise, what will they do who
are baptized for the dead, if the dead
do not rise at all? Why then are they
baptized for the dead?
30 And [a]why do we stand in [1]jeopardy
every hour?
31 I affirm, by [a]the boasting in you
which I have in Christ Jesus our Lord,
[b]I die daily.
32 If, in the manner of men, [a]I have
fought with beasts at Ephesus, what
advantage *is it* to me? If *the* dead do
not rise, [b]*"Let us eat and drink, for to-*
morrow we die!"
33 Do not be deceived: [a]"Evil company 2
corrupts *good habits."
34 [a]Awake to righteousness, and do
not sin; [b]for some do not have the
knowledge of God. [c]I speak *this* to
your shame.

A Glorious Body

35 But someone will say, [a]"How are
the dead raised up? And with what
body do they come?"
36 Foolish one, [a]what you sow is not
made alive unless it dies.
37 And what you sow, you do not sow
that body that shall be, but mere
grain—perhaps wheat or some other
grain.
38 But God gives it a body as He
pleases, and to each seed its own body.
39 All flesh *is* not the same flesh, but
there is one *kind* [1]of flesh of men, another flesh of animals, another of fish,
and another of birds.

15:21, 22 The resurrection is not a timeless philosophical idea, but an experience in human life. Jesus Christ is an authentic **Man** who acted in behalf of other men (see vv. 45–49; Rom. 5:12–19).

15:23–25 The Second Coming of Christ will complete the resurrection harvest. Having subdued **all enemies,** Christ will turn over the reins of divine government **to God the Father.**

15:28 The goal of history and the consummation of the covenant will occur when the kingdom is delivered up to God, when creation will be completely free of all dissident, antilife forces. Once this redemptive task is completed, the saving mediatorial role that Jesus assumed will be laid aside.

15:29 Baptized for the dead: This difficult verse is subject to many interpretations. Some see a reference to Jesus Himself, that is, "baptized for [or "with reference to"] the dead"—Jesus who died, and with whom one is identifying in baptism (Rom. 6:3–6). This view notes that in Rom. 1:4, the Greek text may be using the same noun form in reference to Jesus as is used here. Others see a reference to vicarious baptism in which someone was baptized on behalf of a Christian friend or relative who died before baptism, a completely meaningless action if we understand personal responsibility properly. Others interpret the phrase to mean that some people were baptized as a result of the witness given to them by someone who later died. Some feel that Paul referred to a literal baptism over the graves of departed loved ones. Whatever the proper interpretation, Paul's point is clear: all is futile if there is no resurrection.

15:30, 31 I die daily: Paul daily faced peril, hardship, and possible martyrdom in order to proclaim the gospel. Why should he take the risk if there is no life after death?

15:32 If there is no resurrection, why not abandon sacrificial living in favor of self-indulgence?

15:33, 34 Paul quotes from a third-century B.C. Athenian writer, Menander, to show that our lives are influenced by what we believe and with whom we associate.

15:33 See section 2 of Truth-In-Action at the end of 1 Cor.

15:36–38 A life-death principle is already at work in creation. A seed must give itself up to a death process so new life can emerge in the form of fruit or grain. Like seed, our present physical bodies potentially contain the resurrection **body that shall be.**

15:39–41 An infinite variety of bodies adapted to live in the different environments of land, sea, air, and the heavens already exists. Is a resurrection body so incredible then?

40 *There are* also [1]celestial bodies and
[2]terrestrial bodies; but the glory of the
celestial *is* one, and the *glory* of the ter-
restrial *is* another.
41 *There is* one glory of the sun, another glory of the moon, and another
glory of the stars; for *one* star differs
from *another* star in glory.
42 [a]So also *is* the resurrection of the
dead. *The body* is sown in corruption,
it is raised in incorruption.
43 [a]It is sown in dishonor, it is raised
in glory. It is sown in weakness, it is
raised in power.
44 It is sown a *natural body, it is
raised a spiritual body. There is a natural body, and there is a spiritual body.
45 And so it is written, [a]*"The first man
Adam became a *living being."* [b]The
last Adam *became* [c]a life-giving spirit.
46 However, the spiritual is not first,
but the *natural, and afterward the
spiritual.
47 [a]The first man *was* of the earth,
[b]*made*[1] of dust; the second Man *is*
[2]the Lord [c]from heaven.
48 As *was* the [1]*man* of dust, so also
are those *who are* [1]*made* of dust;
[a]and as *is* the heavenly *Man*, so also
are those *who are* heavenly.
49 And [a]as we have borne the image
of the *man* of dust, [b]we[1] shall also bear
the image of the heavenly *Man*.

Our Final Victory

50 Now this I say, brethren, that
[a]flesh and *blood cannot inherit the
kingdom of God; nor does corruption
inherit incorruption.
51 Behold, I tell you a [1]mystery:
[a]We shall not all sleep, [b]but we shall
all be changed—
52 in a **moment,** in the twinkling of an
eye, at the last trumpet. [a]For the trumpet will sound, and the dead will be

40 [1]*heavenly* [2]*earthly*
42 [a][Dan. 12:3]
43 [a][Phil. 3:21]
44 *See WW at James 3:15.
45 [a]Gen. 2:7 [b][Rom. 5:14] [c]John 5:21; 6:57 *See WW at Luke 21:19.
46 *See WW at James 3:15.
47 [a]John 3:31 [b]Gen. 2:7; 3:19 [c]John 3:13 [1]*earthy* [2]NU omits *the Lord*
48 [a]Phil. 3:20 [1]*earthy*
49 [a]Gen. 5:3 [b]Rom. 8:29 [1]M *let us also bear*
50 [a][John 3:3, 5] *See WW at 1 John 1:7.
51 [a][1 Thess. 4:15] [b][Phil. 3:21] [1]*hidden truth*
52 [a]Matt. 24:31
53 [a]2 Cor. 5:4
54 [a]Is. 25:8
55 [a]Hos. 13:14 [1]NU *O Death, where is your victory? O Death, where is your sting?*
56 [a][Rom. 3:20; 4:15; 7:8]
57 [a][Rom. 7:25] [b][1 John 5:4]
58 [a]2 Pet. 3:14 [b][1 Cor. 3:8] *See WW at Matt. 25:29.

CHAPTER 16
1 [a]Gal. 2:10

raised incorruptible, and we shall be
changed.

WORD WEALTH

15:52 moment, *atomos* (*at*-om-oss); Strong's *#823:* Compare "atomizer" and "atomic." Uncut, indivisible, undissected, infinitely small. The word is a compound of *a,* "un," and *temnos,* "to cut in two." When used of time, it represents an extremely short unit of time, a flash, an instant, a unit of time that cannot be divided. A second can be calibrated to one-tenth, one one-hundredth, and one one-thousandth of a second. But how do you calibrate an atomic second? Christ's return will be in an atomic second.

53 For this corruptible must put on
incorruption, and [a]this mortal *must*
put on immortality.
54 So when this corruptible has put on
incorruption, and this mortal has put
on immortality, then shall be brought
to pass the saying that is written:
[a]*"Death is swallowed up in victory."*

55 [a]*"O*[1] *Death, where is your sting?*
O Hades, where is your victory?"

56 The sting of death *is* sin, and
[a]the strength of sin *is* the law.
57 [a]But thanks *be* to God, who gives
us [b]the victory through our Lord Jesus
Christ.
58 [a]Therefore, my beloved brethren, 6
be steadfast, immovable, always
*abounding in the work of the Lord,
knowing [b]that your labor is not in vain
in the Lord.

Collection for the Saints

16 Now concerning [a]the collection
for the saints, as I have given

15:42–44 The **resurrection** body will not be subject to death; it will be beautiful and perfect; it will have unlimited capabilities unknown to us in this age; it will be adapted for life in the spiritual realm. **A spiritual body** does not mean an immaterial body but one adapted to the realities of the Age to Come. The resurrection body will be our very own bodies changed, for that which **is sown** is that also which **is raised.**
15:45–49 In other words, our resurrected bodies will be like Christ's. As **a life-giving spirit** the resurrected Christ is the fountainhead of the new creation, as **Adam** was of the old creation. Although we cannot know fully the nature of a spiritual body, Christ's resurrection body reveals something of what kind of bodies resurrected believers will have. During the 40 days of postresurrection appearances, Jesus could pass for an ordinary man. He still had nail prints and He ate food yet He also could materialize at will and pass through locked doors (see John 20; Luke 24). He had complete command over creation, as evidenced by His dominion over the fish (John 21:6–11).
15:50 See note on vv. 42–44.
15:51, 52 God made known to Paul that the dead will be raised up by instantaneous transformation **at the last trumpet.** Trumpets were used to call God's people together (Num. 10:1–10) and at royal coronations in presenting kings to Israel (1 Kin. 1:34). The Rapture of the church not only transforms us but welcomes Christ the coming King on Earth, as we "meet the Lord in the air" at His returning (see 1 Thess. 4:16, 17).
15:56, 57 Strength of sin is the law: See notes on Rom. 7. The Law, good in itself, was given to weak and sinful people. When the Law's moral claim encounters sinful human nature, it activates sin. Rather than bringing salvation, it brings condemnation. However, the resurrection of Christ brings **victory** over sin, the Law, and death.
15:58 See section 6 of Truth-In-Action at the end of 1 Cor.
16:1–24 These rather ordinary remarks sparkle with spiritual vitality. Paul deals with questions about the collection (v. 1)

orders to the churches of Galatia, so
you must do also:
2 [a]On the first *day* of the week let
each one of you lay something aside,
storing up as he may prosper, that
there be no collections when I come.
3 And when I come, [a]whomever you
approve by *your* letters I will send to
bear your gift to Jerusalem.
4 [a]But if it is fitting that I go also, they
will go with me.

Personal Plans

5 Now I will come to you [a]when I pass
through Macedonia (for I am passing
through Macedonia).
6 And it may be that I will remain,
or even spend the winter with you, that
you may [a]send me on my journey,
wherever I go.
7 For I do not wish to see you now
on the way; but I hope to stay a while
with you, [a]if the Lord permits.
8 But I will tarry in Ephesus until
[a]Pentecost.
9 For [a]a great and *effective door has
opened to me, and [b]*there are* many adversaries.
10 And [a]if Timothy comes, see that he
may be with you without fear; for
[b]he does the work of the Lord, as I also
do.
11 [a]Therefore let no one despise him.
But send him on his journey [b]in peace,
that he may come to me; for I am waiting for him with the brethren.
12 Now concerning *our* brother
[a]Apollos, I strongly urged him to come
to you with the brethren, but he was
quite unwilling to come at this time;
however, he will come when he has a
convenient time.

Final Exhortations

13 [a]Watch, [b]stand fast in the faith, be
brave, [c]be strong.
14 [a]Let all *that* you *do* be done with
*love.
15 I urge you, brethren—you know
[a]the household of Stephanas, that it is
[b]the firstfruits of Achaia, and *that* they
have devoted themselves to [c]the ministry of the saints—
16 [a]that you also submit to such, and
to everyone who *works and [b]labors
with *us.*
17 I am glad about the *coming of
Stephanas, Fortunatus, and Achaicus,
[a]for what was lacking on your part
they supplied.
18 [a]For they *refreshed my spirit and
yours. Therefore [b]acknowledge such
men.

Greetings and a Solemn Farewell

19 The churches of Asia greet you. Aquila and Priscilla greet you heartily in
the Lord, [a]with the church that is in
their house.
20 All the brethren greet you. [a]Greet
one another with a holy kiss.
21 [a]The salutation with my own
hand—Paul's.
22 If anyone [a]does not *love the Lord
Jesus Christ, [b]let him be [1]accursed.*
[c]O[2] Lord, come!

2 [a]Acts 20:7
3 [a]2 Cor. 3:1; 8:18
4 [a]2 Cor. 8:4, 19
5 [a]2 Cor. 1:15, 16
6 [a]Acts 15:3
7 [a]James 4:15
8 [a]Lev. 23:15–22
9 [a]Acts 14:27 [b]Acts 19:9 *See WW at Heb. 4:12.
10 [a]Acts 19:22 [b]Phil. 2:20
11 [a]1 Tim. 4:12 [b]Acts 15:33
12 [a]1 Cor. 1:12; 3:5
13 [a]Matt. 24:42 [b]Phil. 1:27; 4:1 [c][Eph. 3:16; 6:10]
14 [a][1 Pet. 4:8] *See WW at Rom. 5:5.
15 [a]1 Cor. 1:16 [b]Rom. 16:5 [c]2 Cor. 8:4
16 [a]Heb. 13:17 [b][Heb. 6:10] *See WW at James 2:22.
17 [a]2 Cor. 11:9 *See WW at 1 Cor. 15:23.
18 [a]Col. 4:8 [b]Phil. 2:29 *See WW at Rev. 14:13.
19 [a]Rom. 16:5
20 [a]Rom. 16:16
21 [a]Col. 4:18
22 [a]Eph. 6:24 [b]Gal. 1:8, 9 [c]Jude 14, 15 [1]Gr. *anathema* [2]Aram. *Marana tha* or *Maranatha;* possibly *Maran atha, Our Lord has come*

*See WW at John 21:15. • See WW at 1 Cor. 12:3.

and about Apollos (v. 12); he touches on events and personalities that affect the Corinthians' future.
16:1–4 According to Rom. 15:26, 27, the Gentile Christians owed the Jews a material debt of love for sharing their spiritual blessings. No doubt Paul hoped to heal the gap between the two (Acts 21:20, 21). The collection was to be systematic, individual, proportionate, and carefully administered.
16:5–9 Paul delays plans to visit Corinth because of the success of the ministry in Ephesus (vv. 8, 9), because he first wants to travel **through Macedonia** (v. 5) to strengthen the work there, and because he desires a prolonged stay in Corinth rather than an immediate visit **on the way** or merely in passing (v. 7). The grave problems at Corinth required unhurried time. His plans, however, depended on God's will (v. 7).
16:10, 11 Paul had already sent Timothy on a mission to Corinth (4:17). Timothy later reported to him in Macedonia prior to the writing of 2 Cor. (2 Cor. 1:1).
16:12 Apollos ministered in Corinth after Paul had established the church there (3:5, 6). He was emphatic in refusing to return there **at this time** perhaps because of the party dissensions that made him appear to be a rival of Paul or perhaps because he was for now too busy.
16:13, 14 The unsettling situation at Corinth could work havoc without vigilance, courage, and love.
16:15, 16 Stephanas and his **household** were among the first converts in southern Greece and were also among the few baptized by Paul himself (1:16). He and his family engaged in a loving ministry to others, and deserved the church's obedient loyalty.
16:17, 18 These visitors from Corinth probably carried the letter written by the church. All three are models of comfort and cheer.
16:19 Aquila and Priscilla were the husband and wife who accompanied Paul to Ephesus from Corinth and who instructed Apollos (Acts 18:18–26). Wherever they went they turned their home into a meeting place for Christians (Rom. 16:3–5).
16:20 Greeting **with a holy kiss** was an affectionate act fostered by the spirit of Christ and not by the culture. Paul sometimes validated his letters by personally signing his own name (see Gal. 6:11; 2 Thess. 3:17).
16:22 O Lord, come translates an Aramaic phrase, *marana tha,* meaning either "Our Lord, come" or "Our Lord has come." The context seems to express a heartfelt desire for Christ's immediate return.

23 [a]The grace of our Lord Jesus Christ *be* with you.

24 My love *be* with you all in Christ Jesus. Amen.

23 [a]Rom. 16:20

16:23, 24 Despite the problems caused by their spiritual immaturity, and even though he had severely rebuked them, Paul assures the Corinthians of his sincere affection.

TRUTH-IN-ACTION through 1 CORINTHIANS

Letting the LIFE of the Holy Spirit Bring Faith's Works Alive in You!

Truth 1 Corinthians Teaches	Text	**Action** 1 Corinthians Invites
1 Guidelines for Growing in Godliness Godliness is transparent, selfless, replete in integrity and excellent character. The godly person views personal relationships as one of life's highest priorities and sees failure in this area as most serious. In order to maintain peace within the church, the godly will refuse to enter legal action against a fellow believer. The godly person seeks reconcilation and healing in the family rather than divorce. He honors and supports those God has set in authority in the church. The godly person accepts any loss in order to secure or maintain right relationships in the family or the church and commits them to God for His restoration and reparation.	3:17	**Recognize** that your body is God's temple. **Refuse to defile** this house of God.
	6:1–11	**Never** go to the law against a fellow believer. **Commit** yourself to keeping your marriage healthy and intact.
	7:10–16	**Do not divorce** an unbelieving spouse if he/she wants to stay with you or restrain him/her if he/she wishes to dissolve marriage bonds. (This does not mean that a believer must accept brutal neglect, abuse, or immoral treatment.)
	9:11–14	**Recognize** and **honor** the devoted minister's right to support from those he serves.
	13:1–8	**Discipline yourself** in the practice of *agape love* in every attitude, thought, word, and deed.
2 Steps to Holiness Holy living calls for us to rely totally on God for spiritual wisdom, rejecting the wisdom of the world. Holiness devotes time and energy to knowing the Lord, choosing to associate with other believers rather than be unduly influenced by the world's values.	1:25–29	**Acknowledge** that there is no spiritual dynamic in mere human abilities. **Understand** that God uses that which without His presence is ineffectual.
	2:13–16	**Recognize** that the natural mind cannot understand or receive from the Holy Spirit. **Know** that only the spiritually alive can discern spiritual wisdom.
	7:29–31	**Remember** that earthly values are transient, and **embrace** the eternal.
	15:33	**Recognize** that evil associations influence your conduct toward evil.
3 Steps to Dynamic Devotion Devotion makes full use of the key resources God has made available for that purpose: the Scriptures and spiritual gifts. Both the OT and NT are important for the believer. Employing spiritual language (tongues) as a private devotional discipline results in a holy self-edification. The devoted disciple knows that the Lord's Table is an important means to nurture spiritual life and growth.	10:6–12	**Recognize** that the OT is an example for the church. **Submit yourself** to the wisdom of the OT. **Read, study,** and **apply** the OT.
	11:20–29	**Celebrate** the Lord's Supper frequently. **Receive** Jesus' life from it through faith. **Approach** Communion humbled and cleansed through confession of sin.
	14:13–22	**Employ** both spiritual and natural language in worship and devotion. **Desire** prophetic utterance. **Differentiate** between prophetic utterances and the prophetic office.

Truth 1 Corinthians Teaches	Text	**Action** 1 Corinthians Invites
4 Vital Keys to Dynamic Church Life The body life of the church, not the independent believer, is the key to understanding God's dealings in the NT. We should not presume that the apostles thought with a predisposition toward rugged individualism. God deals with the church as a body and with individuals as parts or members. Individual members ought to put the body's or congregation's concerns above their own. This will open our understanding to dynamic truth God has intended for the church.	1:10	**Know** that believers are to be unified in their devotion to the gospel of Christ. **Acknowledge** where you fall short, and **repent.**
	3:1–4	**Recognize** that division in the church is sin.
	5:1–8	**Do not neglect** church discipline. **Understand** that such neglect emboldens unrestrained and undisciplined living.
	12:12–27	**Promote** unity within the body of Christ. **Believe** that God places every member in the body as will best serve His purposes.
	14:26–40	**Maintain** order in church gatherings. **Allow** no "tongue" to go uninterpreted. **Allow** no prophetic utterance to go unjudged.
5 Guidelines for Growth in the Spirit Learning how to employ the spiritual gifts is vital, because they are the means God has given us to nurture growth. This occurs in the congregation through edification and beyond it through evangelism.	12:4–11	**Understand** that God works through spiritual gifts to reproduce the ministry of the Lord Jesus Christ in His church. **Recognize** the importance of these gifts for dynamic ministry.
	14:1–5	**Accept** the importance of tongues for holy self-edification.
6 Key Lessons in Faith Faith believes and focuses on proclaiming God's Word without reservation.	4:20	**Recognize** that kingdom ministry involves signs, wonders, and miracles that demonstrate the power of God. **Humbly call** for God to restore the miraculous dimension to the church.
	15:58	**Never give up! Continue steadfastly** in faith and abound in service to God. **Know** that nothing done in Jesus' name is in vain.

The Second Epistle of Paul the Apostle to the CORINTHIANS

Author: Paul
Date: A.D. 55–56
Theme: Powerful Ministry Through Weak Vessels
Key Words: Comfort, Suffering, Ministry, Glory, Power, Weakness

Background and Date In various ways 2 Corinthians reflects Paul's dealings with the church in Corinth during the period from the founding of the church in about A.D. 50 until the writing of this letter in A.D. 55 or 56. The various episodes in the interactions between Paul and the Corinthians can be summarized as follows:

1. The *founding visit* to Corinth lasted about eighteen months (see Acts 18).
2. Paul wrote an *earlier letter* than 1 Corinthians (see 1 Cor. 5:9).
3. Paul wrote *1 Corinthians* from Ephesus, about A.D. 55.
4. A brief but *painful visit* to Corinth caused "sorrow" for Paul and the church (see 2 Cor. 2:1; 13:2).
5. Following the painful visit, Paul wrote a *severe letter,* delivered by Titus (see 2 Cor. 2:4; 7:6–8).
6. Paul wrote *2 Corinthians* from Macedonia, while on his way to Corinth again, in A.D. 55 or 56.
7. Paul's *final visit* to Corinth (Acts 20) was probably when he wrote Romans, just before returning to Jerusalem. The *painful visit,* which Acts does not record, and the *severe letter* provide immediate background for the writing of 2 Corinthians.

We do not possess the *severe letter,* although some scholars have suggested that 2 Corinthians 10—13 may have been part of that epistle. There is no manuscript evidence to support this view, however.

Occasion and Purpose First Corinthians was not as effective as Paul had hoped in settling the crisis at Corinth. The party opposing Paul gained strength, and its leader was particularly obnoxious to him (2:5–11; 10:7–12). Paul hurriedly traveled to Corinth from Ephesus in an attempt to meet the situation. Although this visit is not mentioned in Acts, it is implied in 2 Corinthians 12:14. Paul failed to achieve his desired objective (2:1; 12:14, 21; 13:1, 2), and experienced open hostility from the leader of the opposition (2:5–8; 7:12). Paul then returned to Ephesus, where he wrote a severe letter to the Corinthians, putting into it the full weight of his apostolic authority. He sent the letter by Titus, and then made his way to Macedonia, where Titus met him with an encouraging report (2:12, 13; 7:6–16). The majority had been won back to Paul and had taken disciplinary action against the offender (2:5–11). However, there was still a rebellious minority (chs. 10—13). Paul wrote to express a message of conciliation to the loyal majority and to rebuke the rebellious minority. He also gave instructions concerning the offering he was collecting for the impoverished church in Jerusalem.

Characteristics Second Corinthians is the most autobiographical of Paul's letters, containing numerous references to the hardships he endured in the course of his ministry (see 11:23–33). Paul mentioned these to establish the legitimacy of his ministry and to illustrate the nature of true spirituality.

In defending his ministry, Paul opens his heart, showing his deep emotion. He reveals his strong love for the Corinthians, his ardent zeal for the glory of God, his uncompromising loyalty to the truth of the gospel, and his stern indignation in confronting those who disrupt the fellowship of the church. His life was bound up in the life of his converts, and he was not coldly professional in his ministry (see 1:6; 5:13; 7:3–7; 11:2; 12:14, 15).

Content Second Corinthians consists of three main parts. The first seven chapters contain Paul's defense of his conduct and his ministry. He explains the change in his plans to visit Corinth and responds to a charge of fickleness. In discussing the Christian ministry, he expounds on its nature, its problems, its motivating principles, and its responsibilities.

The second unit, chapters 8 and 9, deals with the offering being raised by Paul for the poor saints in Judea. Paul urged the Corinthians to be liberal and cheerful in giving so that God might bless them in every way.

Chapters 10 through 13 form the third segment of the letter and contain a message of rebuke to the remaining detractors in the church. Paul responds to the jibes and slanders of his critics and fully vindicates his authority as an apostle.

Personal Application Second Corinthians is a valuable guide in examining our own motives for serving the Lord, whether as lay people or as ordained pastors and evangelists. As an instrument of the Holy Spirit, this letter can refine our motives until we reflect the kind of selfless giving best exemplified in Christ, but also found in His servant Paul. The instructions concerning the collection for Jerusalem (chs. 8 and 9) emphasize generosity in the area of financial resources, just as Paul emphasized generosity in self-giving throughout the book.

Christ Revealed Jesus Christ is the focus of our relationship with God. All God's promises to us are Yes in Jesus, and we say "Amen" to God's promises in Jesus (1:19, 20). Jesus is God's Yes to us and our Yes to God. Only in Christ do we see the glory of God, and only in Him are we transformed by that glory (3:14, 18), for Christ is the very image of God (4:4–6). God came to us in Christ, reconciling the world to Himself (5:19). Thus, it is "in Christ" that we have become new creatures (5:17). This change was accomplished through the marvelous act of God's grace in which Christ, "who knew no sin," became "sin for us, that we might become the righteousness of God in Him" (5:21).

Jesus is also the focus of our service to God. We proclaim Jesus as Lord and ourselves as servants for His sake (4:5). We willingly share not only Christ's life and glory but also His dying (4:10–12),

His willingness to be weak so that others might experience the power of God (13:3, 4, 9), and His willingness to be impoverished so that others might be enriched (8:9). We experience His weakness but also His strength as we seek to bring "every thought into captivity to the obedience of Christ" (10:5).

Again, Jesus is the focus of our present life in this world, where we simultaneously experience in our mortal bodies both "the dying of the Lord Jesus" and His life (4:10, 11).

Finally, Jesus is the focus of our future life, for we will be raised up with Jesus (4:14), who is the "betrothed ... husband" of the church (11:2) and the judge of all men (5:10).

The Holy Spirit at Work The Holy Spirit is the power of the New Covenant (3:6), because He makes real to us the present and future provisions of our salvation in Christ. By the gift of "the Spirit in our hearts as a guarantee," we are assured that all God's promises are Yes in Christ, and that we are anointed and "sealed" as belonging to Him (1:20–22). The present experience of the Spirit is specifically "a guarantee" of the glorified bodies we will one day receive (5:1–5).

We do not merely read about the will of God in the "letter" of Scripture, for "the letter [alone] kills." The Spirit who gives life (3:6) changes our way of living by opening our eyes to the living reality of what we read. Thus, we progressively experience and embody the will of God, and we ourselves become epistles of Christ, "known and read by all men" (3:2).

When we submit ourselves to the work of the Spirit, we experience a miracle. We find that "where the Spirit of the Lord *is*, there *is* liberty" (3:17). There is liberty to behold the unveiled glory of the Lord and to be changed more and more into the likeness of what we behold. The Holy Spirit gives us freedom to see and freedom to be what God wants us to be (3:16–18).

The work of the Holy Spirit is evident in daily inward renewal (4:16), spiritual warfare (10:3–5), and the "signs and wonders and mighty deeds" of Paul's ministry in Corinth (12:12). Paul ended his letter with a blessing, which included "the communion [fellowship] of the Holy Spirit" (13:14). This could indicate a sense of the Spirit's presence or, more likely, an enjoyment of the fellowship the Spirit gives us with Christ and with all people who love Christ.

Outline of 2 Corinthians

- **I. Greeting** **1:1, 2**
- **II. Explanation of Paul's ministry** **1:3—7:16**
  - A. Comfort and suffering 1:3–11
  - B. Changes in plans 1:12—2:4
  - C. Forgiving the offender 2:5–11
  - D. Distraction in Troas 2:12, 13
  - E. Nature of Christian ministry 2:14—7:4
    1. Life and death issues 2:14–17
    2. Living letters of commendation 3:1–3
    3. Sufficiency from God 3:4–6
    4. Unveiled in the New Covenant 3:7–18
    5. Integrity and openness 4:1–6
    6. Dying and living with Jesus 4:7–15
    7. Eternal perspective 4:16—5:11
    8. Reconciled and reconciling 5:12—6:2
    9. Paying the price to minister 6:3–10
    10. Heartfelt appeal for holiness 6:11—7:4
  - F. Rejoicing over the report from Corinth 7:5–16

III. Generosity in giving 8:1—9:15
- A. Macedonians and Jesus as examples 8:1–9
- B. Fulfilling good intentions 8:10–12
- C. Sharing resources 8:13–15
- D. A trustworthy delegation 8:16–24
- E. Timely preparation of the gift 9:1–5
- F. Blessings of giving 9:6–15

IV. Defense and use of apostolic authority 10:1—13:10
- A. Rebuke of superficial assessment 10:1–11
- B. Rebuke of foolish comparisons 10:12–18
- C. Godly jealousy for the church 11:1–4
- D. Comparison with false apostles 11:5–15
- E. Corinthians' misguided tolerance 11:16–21
- F. Paul's reluctant boasting 11:22—12:13
- G. Announcement of third visit 12:14—13:10
  1. Integrity of Paul's motives 12:14–19
  2. Warning to remaining rebels 12:20—13:4
  3. Call to self-examination 13:5–10

V. Concluding greetings 13:11–14

Greeting

PAUL, [a]an apostle of Jesus Christ by
the will of God, and [b]Timothy *our*
brother,

To the church of God which is at
Corinth, [c]with all the saints who are
in all Achaia:

2 [a]Grace to you and peace from God
our Father and the Lord Jesus Christ.

Comfort in Suffering

3 [a]Blessed *be* the God and Father of
our Lord Jesus Christ, the Father of
mercies and God of all comfort,
4 who [a]comforts* us in all our tribulation, that we may be able to comfort
those who are in any [1]trouble, with the
comfort with which we ourselves are
comforted by God.
5 For as [a]the sufferings of Christ
abound in us, so our [1]consolation also
abounds through Christ.
6 Now if we are afflicted, [a]*it is* for
your consolation and *salvation, which
is effective for enduring the same sufferings which we also *suffer. Or if we
are comforted, *it is* for your consolation and salvation.
7 And our hope for you *is* steadfast,
because we know that [a]as you are partakers of the sufferings, so also *you will*
partake of the consolation.

Delivered from Suffering

8 For we do not want you to be ignorant, brethren, of [a]our [1]trouble which
came to us in Asia: that we were burdened *beyond measure, above
strength, so that we despaired even of
life.
9 Yes, we had the sentence of death
in ourselves, that we should [a]not trust
in ourselves but in God who raises the
dead,
10 [a]who delivered us from so great a
death, and [1]does deliver us; in whom
we trust that He will still deliver *us,*
11 you also [a]helping together in prayer
for us, that thanks may be given by
many persons on [1]our behalf [b]for the
gift *granted* to us through many.

Paul's Sincerity

12 For our boasting is this: the *testi- 2
mony of our conscience that we conducted ourselves in the world in
[1]simplicity and [a]godly *sincerity,
[b]not with fleshly wisdom but by the
grace of God, and more *abundantly
toward you.

CHAPTER 1

1 [a]2 Tim. 1:1 [b]1 Cor. 16:10 [c]Col. 1:2
2 [a]Rom. 1:7
3 [a]1 Pet. 1:3
4 [a]Is. 51:12; 66:13 [1]*tribulation* *See WW at Acts 9:31.
5 [a]2 Cor. 4:10 [1]*comfort*
6 [a]2 Cor. 4:15; 12:15 *See WW at Luke 19:9. • See WW at Acts 17:3.
7 [a][Rom. 8:17]
8 [a]Acts 19:23 [1]*tribulation* *See WW at 2 Cor. 4:7.
9 [a]Jer. 17:5, 7
10 [a][2 Pet. 2:9] [1]NU *shall*
11 [a]Rom. 15:30 [b]2 Cor. 4:15; 9:11 [1]M *your behalf*
12 [a]2 Cor. 2:17 [b][1 Cor. 2:4] [1]The opposite of duplicity *See WW at Rev. 15:5. • See WW at 1 Cor. 5:8. • See WW at 2 Cor. 2:4.

1:1 Paul's commission as **an apostle** is a key issue of this epistle. **Timothy** was involved in founding the church in Corinth (Acts 18:5). **Achaia:** A region of Greece including Corinth and Cenchrea (Rom. 16:1).
1:4 For some of Paul's troubles, see 11:23–33.
1:8–10 We means Paul himself here and in most contexts of the epistle. **Trouble:** Possibly severe illness or persecution. **Asia:** Not the continent but a province of the Roman Empire, in the western part of modern Turkey. **So great a death:** Such a great danger that, humanly speaking, there was no hope of surviving.
1:12 See section 2 of Truth-In-Action at the end of 2 Cor.
1:12 Simplicity is the opposite of duplicity or deviousness, with which some of Paul's critics had accused him. **More abundantly:** Especially.

13 For we are not writing any other
things to you than what you read or
*understand. Now I trust you will un-
derstand, even to the end
14 (as also you have understood us in
part), [a]that we are your boast as
[b]you also *are* ours, in the day of the
Lord Jesus.

Sparing the Church

15 And in this confidence [a]I intended
to come to you before, that you might
have [b]a second benefit—
16 to pass by way of you to Macedonia,
[a]to come again from Macedonia to you,
and be helped by you on my way to
Judea.
17 Therefore, when I was planning
this, did I do it lightly? Or the things I
plan, do I plan [a]according to the flesh,
that with me there should be Yes, Yes,
and No, No?
18 But *as* God *is* [a]faithful, our [1]word
to you was not Yes and No.
19 For [a]the Son of God, Jesus Christ,
who was preached among you by us—
by me, [b]Silvanus, and [c]Timothy—was
not Yes and No, [d]but in Him was Yes.
20 [a]For all the promises of God in Him
are Yes, and in Him Amen, to the glory
of God through us.
21 Now He who *establishes us with
you in Christ and [a]has anointed us *is*
God,
22 who [a]also has sealed us and [b]given
us the Spirit in our hearts as a **guarantee.**

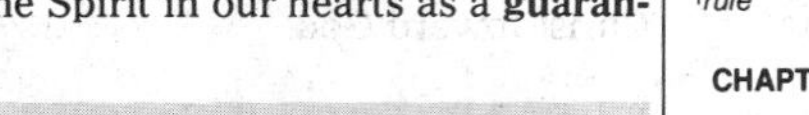

WORD WEALTH

1:22 guarantee, *arrabon* (ar-hrab-*ohn*); Strong's *#728:* A business term that speaks of earnest money, a part of the purchase price paid in advance as a down payment. *Arrabon* is the first installment, which guarantees full possession when the whole is paid later. Sometimes this transaction was called "caution money," "a pledge," "a deposit," "a guarantee." *Arrabon* describes the Holy Spirit as the pledge of our future joys and bliss in heaven. The Holy Spirit gives us a foretaste or guarantee of things to come.

13 *See WW at Luke 5:22.
14 [a]2 Cor. 5:12 [b]Phil. 2:16
15 [a]1 Cor. 4:19 [b]Rom. 1:11; 15:29
16 [a]1 Cor. 16:3–6
17 [a]2 Cor. 10:2; 11:18
18 [a]1 John 5:20 [1]*message*
19 [a]Mark 1:1 [b]1 Pet. 5:12 [c]2 Cor. 1:1 [d][Heb. 13:8]
20 [a][Rom. 15:8, 9]
21 [a][1 John 2:20, 27] *See WW at Mark 16:20.
22 [a][Eph. 4:30] [b][Eph. 1:14]
23 [a]Gal. 1:20 [b]1 Cor. 4:21 *See WW at Rev. 1:5.
24 [a][1 Pet. 5:3] [b]Rom. 11:20 [1]*rule*

CHAPTER 2

1 [a]2 Cor. 1:23
2 [a]2 Cor. 7:8
3 [a]2 Cor. 12:21 [b]Gal. 5:10
4 [a][2 Cor. 2:9; 7:8, 12] [1]*tribulation*

23 Moreover [a]I call God as *witness
against my soul, [b]that to spare you I
came no more to Corinth.
24 Not [a]that we [1]have dominion over
your faith, but are fellow workers for
your joy; for [b]by faith you stand.
2 But I determined this within myself, [a]that I would not come again
to you in sorrow.
2 For if I make you [a]sorrowful, then
who is he who makes me glad but the
one who is made sorrowful by me?

Forgive the Offender

3 And I wrote this very thing to you,
lest, when I came, [a]I should have sorrow over those from whom I ought to
have joy, [b]having confidence in you all
that my joy is *the joy* of you all.
4 For out of much [1]affliction and anguish of heart I wrote to you, with
many tears, [a]not that you should be
grieved, but that you might know the
love which I have so **abundantly** for
you.

WORD WEALTH

2:4 abundantly, *perissoteros* (per-is-sot-*er*-oce); Strong's *#4056:* The adverbial form of a comparative adjective, suggest-
(*cont. on next page*)

1:13, 14 To the end: Fully, in contrast to **in part**.
1:15–17 Paul defends his change in plans. First, he had planned to visit Macedonia, then Corinth (1 Cor. 16:5). Then he decided to visit Corinth before and after the trip to Macedonia (v. 16), with the hope of blessing the Corinthians twice (v. 15). Apparently his recent painful visit to Corinth had prompted him to return to Ephesus rather than proceeding immediately to Macedonia. Now he has gone to Macedonia and is on his way to Corinth again. (See Introduction to 2 Corinthians: Background and Date.)
1:17, 18 The rhetorical form of Paul's questions expects an answer of "No, of course not." He had not been vacillating and frivolously changing his plans, saying **Yes** and **No**. His words and his ministry have reflected the faithfulness and consistency of God.
1:19, 20 Silvanus: Silas (see Acts 18:5). Christ is the positive and completely consistent living Word from God; likewise, Paul's ministry has been consistent. His travel plans may change, but only because of his constant commitment to the unchanging gospel. Christ is the fulfiller and fulfillment of **all the promises of God** because He is their sum and substance. Through Jesus, believers say **Amen** ("Yes, so be it") in response to God.
1:21, 22 Sealed us: God has marked us as belonging to Him. The Holy **Spirit** Himself serves as **guarantee** (Greek *arrabon,* "pledge," "deposit") of God's commitment to complete His work in us (see 5:5; Eph. 1:13, 14; also Rom. 8:23), thus confirming the Yes that is in Jesus (v. 20).
1:23—2:2 Paul delayed his proposed visit to Corinth out of consideration for the church. He cannot be **glad** as long as they remain **sorrowful**.
2:3, 4 Wrote: The previous *severe letter* (or "tearful letter") written as a follow-up to the *painful visit*. Some identify 1 Cor. as the *severe letter*, but it does not seem to fit that description. Others suggest that 2 Cor. 10—13 fits that description, but no manuscript evidence supports the separation of those chapters from the rest of the epistle.

(cont. from preceding page)
ing something done or possessed in a greater degree, excessively, with superfluity.

5 But [a]if anyone has caused grief, he
has not [b]grieved me, but all of you to
some extent—not to be too severe.
6 This punishment which *was inflicted* [a]by the majority *is* sufficient for
such a man,
7 [a]so that, on the contrary, you *ought*
rather to *forgive and comfort *him,* lest
perhaps such a one be swallowed up
with *too much sorrow.
8 Therefore I urge you to reaffirm
your love to him.
2 9 For to this end I also wrote, that I
might put you to the test, whether you
are [a]obedient in all things.
10 Now whom you forgive anything, I
also *forgive.* For [1]if indeed I have forgiven anything, I have forgiven that
one for your sakes in the presence of
Christ,
11 lest Satan should take advantage of
us; for we are not ignorant of his
devices.

Triumph in Christ

12 Furthermore, [a]when I came to
Troas to *preach* Christ's gospel, and
[b]a [1]door was opened to me by the Lord,
13 [a]I had no rest in my spirit, because
I did not find Titus my brother; but taking my leave of them, I departed for
Macedonia.
14 Now thanks *be* to God who always 1
leads us in triumph in Christ, and
through us [1]diffuses the fragrance of
His knowledge in every place.
15 For we are to God the fragrance of
Christ [a]among those who are being
saved and [b]among those who are perishing.
16 [a]To the one *we are* the aroma of
death *leading* to death, and to the other
the aroma of life *leading* to life. And
[b]who *is* sufficient for these things?
17 For we are not, as [1]so many,
[a]peddling[2] the word of God; but as
[b]of *sincerity, but as from God, we
speak in the sight of God in Christ.

Christ's Epistle

3 Do [a]we begin again to commend
ourselves? Or do we need, as some
others, [b]epistles of commendation to
you or *letters* of commendation from
you?
2 [a]You are our epistle written in our 5
hearts, known and *read by all men;
3 clearly *you are* an epistle of Christ,
[a]ministered by us, written not with ink
but by the Spirit of the living God, not
[b]on tablets of stone but [c]on tablets of
flesh, *that is,* of the heart.

The Spirit, Not the Letter

4 And we have such trust through
Christ toward God.

5 [a][1 Cor. 5:1] [b]Gal. 4:12
6 [a]1 Cor. 5:4, 5
7 [a]Gal. 6:1 *See WW at Col. 3:13. • See WW at John 10:10.
9 [a]2 Cor. 7:15; 10:6
10 [1]NU *indeed, what I have forgiven, if I have forgiven anything, I did it for your sakes*
12 [a]Acts 16:8 [b]1 Cor. 16:9 [1]Opportunity
13 [a]2 Cor. 7:6, 13; 8:6
14 [1]*manifests*
15 [a][1 Cor. 1:18] [b][2 Cor. 4:3]
16 [a]Luke 2:34 [b][1 Cor. 15:10]
17 [a]2 Pet. 2:3 [b]2 Cor. 1:12 [1]M *the rest* [2]*adulterating for gain* *See WW at 1 Cor. 5:8.

CHAPTER 3

1 [a]2 Cor. 5:12; 10:12, 18; 12:11 [b]Acts 18:27
2 [a]1 Cor. 9:2 *See WW at Mark 13:14.
3 [a]1 Cor. 3:5 [b]Ex. 24:12; 31:18; 32:15 [c]Ps. 40:8

2:5–11 The conflict that caused the *painful visit* and the *severe letter* involved a challenge to Paul's authority as an apostle. The *severe letter* achieved a degree of correction. The rebel who **caused grief,** not merely for Paul, but for the entire church **to some extent,** had been repudiated **by the majority** (see 7:6–13). With their cooperation, Paul is ready **to forgive and comfort** the offender. To continue to punish him (after he has repented) would damage not only him but the church and Paul's own work, because it would allow **Satan** to **take advantage** of the discord in the church. The traditional identification of the offending person with the incestuous man in 1 Cor. 5:1–5 is possible, but the offense here seems to have been directed particularly at Paul with the charge being grievous, rude conduct, not immorality.
2:9 See section 2 of Truth-In-Action at the end of 2 Cor.
2:12 Troas was a coastal city in Asia Minor (Acts 16:8, 9).
2:14–17 See section 1 of Truth-In-Action at the end of 2 Cor.
2:14–16 Paul begins a long digression on the nature of Christian ministry, *not returning* to the subject of Titus' report until 7:5. Perhaps in response to that good report (7:5–16), Paul abruptly gives praise to God. Although he left Troas in anxiety, he now saw his experience as just one more step in a continuous triumphal procession to the glory of Christ.

The Roman **triumph** was a victory parade for a conquering army and its leader. Both victors and captives were part of the procession, and both groups could smell the fragrance of burning spices which accompanied the parade. The **aroma,** however, meant something different to the two groups. Likewise, the **fragrance of Christ** (the gospel) is to **those who are perishing** an **aroma of death *leading* to death,** for it signifies and leads to their ultimate judgment. **Those who are being saved** find the **knowledge** of Christ to be an **aroma of life *leading* to life,** for it signifies life now and leads to life eternal. For Christians to have such significance for the eternal destinies of others is a serious matter, prompting Paul's question in v. 16 (answered in 3:5). **Sufficient:** Worthy, qualified, or capable.
2:17 Peddling the word of God: Teaching it only as a way of making money, without understanding the seriousness of the responsibility.
3:1–3 You are our epistle: Unlike the intruders trying to discredit Paul and elevate themselves, Paul did not need a letter of introduction and recommendation. His legitimacy as a minister of the gospel was proved by their changed lives.
3:2, 3 See section 5 of Truth-In-Action at the end of 2 Cor.
3:4–6 Paul's **trust** is not self-confidence but confidence in the **sufficiency** (see 2:16) of God's Spirit, who empowers life and ministry in the reality of the **new covenant**. **The letter kills** means that the external code of the Old Covenant produces spiritual death, because the law shows us our need but is powerless to meet the need (Rom. 7:7). Only **the Spirit**

6 5 [a]Not that we are sufficient of ourselves to think of anything as *being* from ourselves, but [b]our sufficiency *is* from God,
6 who also made us sufficient as [a]ministers of [b]the *new covenant, not [c]of the letter but of the [1]Spirit; for [d]the letter kills, [e]but the Spirit gives life.

Glory of the New Covenant

7 But if [a]the ministry of death, [b]written *and* engraved on stones, was glorious, [c]so that the children of Israel could not look steadily at the face of Moses because of the glory of his countenance, which *glory* was passing away,
8 how will [a]the ministry of the Spirit not be more glorious?

KINGDOM DYNAMICS

3:5–8 The Way God's Word Is to Be Ministered, THE WORD OF GOD. Believing in the truthfulness of God's Word does not guarantee that we will minister that truth in the Spirit of God. Eph. 4:15 describes growth and maturity in the body of Christ as being related to our "speaking the truth in love." In the words of 2 Cor. 3:6, the apostle Paul warns of the danger of God's Word being ministered literally but not life-givingly. We need not wonder if this is possible, since the Spirit of Truth (1 John 4:6) and the Spirit of Life (Rom. 8:2) are the same—the Holy Spirit! Blending both will always reveal three things: 1) A faithfulness to "keep straight" (2 Tim. 2:15). "Rightly dividing the word of truth" means putting forward the truth, faithfully and forthrightly. (This verse was never intended to refer to "dividing" the Word by segmenting it, but rather to a straightforward dealing with all the truth and all its implications.) 2) A constant presence of love, even in the most demanding declarations of correction or judgment. In the texts above (2 Cor. 3:6; Eph. 4:15) we have already discussed this, but human tendencies need this reminder. Urgency may attend our message and passion infuse our delivery; but anger, impatience, and irritation are not of the life-giving Spirit, however literally accurate the interpretation of the Bible or preaching thereof may be. 3) An expectation of signs to follow the preaching of God's Word. Jesus promised this, and the early church tasted its beginnings (Mark 16:15–20); Paul described it as normative in his ministry (1 Cor. 2:1–5; 1 Thess. 1:5); and the Book of Hebrews endorsed this as a part of the "so great salvation" we have been provided (Heb. 2:1–4). This last reference shows that the confirmation of God's Word with signs and wonders not only is to verify Christ's living presence where His gospel is preached, but also is to warn us against drifting from the new life to which we have all been called.

(Luke 16:17/1 Pet. 1:23) J.W.H.

9 For if the ministry of condemnation *had* glory, the ministry [a]of righteousness exceeds much more in glory.
10 For even what was made glorious had no glory in this respect, because of the glory that excels.
11 For if what is passing away *was* glorious, what remains *is* much more glorious.
12 Therefore, since we have such *hope, [a]we use great boldness of speech—
13 unlike Moses, [a]*who* put a veil over his face so that the children of Israel could not look steadily at [b]the end of what was passing away.
14 But [a]their minds were *blinded. For until this day the same veil remains unlifted in the reading of the Old Testament, because the *veil* is taken away in Christ.
15 But even to this day, when Moses is read, a veil lies on their heart.
16 Nevertheless [a]when one turns to the Lord, [b]the veil is taken away.
17 Now [a]the Lord is the Spirit; and **5**

5 [a][John 15:5] [b]1 Cor. 15:10
6 [a]1 Cor. 3:5; Eph. 3:7 [b]Jer. 31:31; Matt. 26:28; Luke 22:20 [c]Rom. 2:27 [d][Rom. 3:20]; Gal. 3:10 [e]John 6:63; Rom. 8:2 [1]Or *spirit* *See WW at 2 Cor. 5:17.
7 [a]Rom. 7:10 [b]Ex. 34:1; Deut. 10:1 [c]Ex. 34:29
8 [a][Gal. 3:5]
9 [a][Rom. 1:17; 3:21]
12 [a]Acts 4:13, 29; 2 Cor. 7:4; Eph. 6:19 *See WW at 1 Thess. 1:3.
13 [a]Ex. 34:33–35; 2 Cor. 3:7 [b]Rom. 10:4; [Gal. 3:23]
14 [a]Is. 6:10; 29:10; Acts 28:26; Rom. 11:7, 8; 2 Cor. 4:4 *See WW at Mark 8:17.
16 [a]Ex. 34:34; Rom. 11:23 [b]Is. 25:7
17 [a][1 Cor. 15:45]

gives life. The advantage of the New Covenant is that it is an inward power bearing the Spirit of God Himself, enabling us to keep God's law. See Jer. 31:33; Rom. 8; Heb. 8:6–13.
3:5, 6 See section 6 of Truth-In-Action at the end of 2 Cor.
3:7–10 The ministry of death refers to the dispensation of the OT, which was based on a covenant **engraved on stones** and not on hearts (v. 3) and which brought **condemnation** (v. 9). Nevertheless the giving of that covenant was accompanied by great **glory** because it was God's Word. **Moses,** as minister of that covenant, reflected its glory (see Ex. 34:29–35). Only in comparison to the New Covenant can the Old Covenant be said to have **no glory**.
3:12, 13 Confident **hope** in the lasting glory of the New Covenant makes bold speech appropriate. In contrast, **Moses** wore a **veil** to obscure the temporary nature of the glory on his face.
3:14, 15 Moses' literal veil illustrates the spiritual **veil** which prevents some who read the OT from seeing the true glory of God's Word, which is **Christ** (see 4:6).
3:16, 17 Whenever Moses left the people to go into the presence of the **Lord,** he removed his **veil** (see Ex. 34:34). Likewise, under the New Covenant to turn to the Lord is to be open to the **Spirit,** who gives the **liberty** of unveiled access to God in Christ (see v. 14).
3:17, 18 See section 5 of Truth-In-Action at the end of 2 Cor.

where the Spirit of the Lord *is,* there
is [b]liberty.*
18 But we all, with unveiled face, beholding [a]as in a mirror [b]the glory of
the Lord, [c]are being transformed into
the same image from glory to glory,
just as [1]by the Spirit of the Lord.

The Light of Christ's Gospel

6 **4** Therefore, since we have this ministry, [a]as we have received *mercy,
we [b]do not lose heart.
2 But we have renounced the hidden
things of shame, not walking in *craftiness nor [1]handling the *word of God
deceitfully, but by manifestation of
the *truth [a]commending ourselves to
every man's conscience in the sight of
God.
3 But even if our gospel is veiled,
[a]it is veiled to those who are perishing,
4 whose minds [a]the god of this *age
[b]has blinded, who do not believe, lest
[c]the light of the *gospel of the glory
of *Christ, [d]who is the image of God,
should shine on them.
5 [a]For we do not *preach ourselves,
but Christ Jesus the Lord, and [b]our-
selves your *bondservants for Jesus'
sake.
6 For it is the God [a]who commanded
light to shine out of *darkness, who has
[b]shone in our hearts to *give* the light
of the knowledge of the glory of God
in the face of Jesus Christ.

Cast Down but Unconquered

6 7 But we have this treasure in earthen
vessels, [a]that the **excellence** of
the power may be of God and not of
us.

17 [b]Gal. 5:1, 13 *See WW at 1 Cor. 10:29.
18 [a]1 Cor. 13:12 [b][2 Cor. 4:4, 6] [c][Rom. 8:29, 30] [1]*Or from the Lord, the Spirit*

CHAPTER 4

1 [a]1 Cor. 7:25 [b]2 Cor. 4:16 *See WW at Rom. 9:15.
2 [a]2 Cor. 5:11 [1]*adulterating the word of God* *See WW at 1 Cor. 3:19. • See WW at Acts 19:20. • See WW at John 4:24.
3 [a][1 Cor. 1:18]
4 [a]John 12:31 [b]John 12:40 [c][2 Cor. 3:8, 9] [d][John 1:18] *See WW at Matt. 28:20. • See WW at Mark 1:1. • See WW at 2 Tim. 4:22.
5 [a]1 Cor. 1:13 [b]1 Cor. 9:19 *See WW at Acts 9:20. • See WW at Rev. 19:5.
6 [a]Gen. 1:3 [b]2 Pet. 1:19 *See WW at Luke 11:35.
7 [a]1 Cor. 2:5
8 [a]2 Cor. 1:8; 7:5
9 [a][Heb. 13:5] [b]Ps. 37:24 *See WW at Luke 9:56.
10 [a]Phil. 3:10 [b]Rom. 8:17 *See WW at 1 John 5:20. • See WW at Col. 3:4.

WORD WEALTH

4:7 excellence, *huperbole* (hoop-er-bol-*ay*); Strong's *#5236:* From *huper,* "beyond," and *ballo,* "to throw"; hence, a throwing beyond. The primary idea is that of excellence, superiority, excess, preeminence.

8 *We are* [a]hard-pressed on every side,
yet not crushed; *we are* perplexed, but
not in despair;
9 persecuted, but not [a]forsaken;
[b]struck down, but not *destroyed—
10 [a]always carrying about in the body
the dying of the Lord Jesus, [b]that the
*life of Jesus also may be *manifested
in our body.
11 For we who live [a]are always *delivered to death for Jesus' sake, that the
life of Jesus also may be manifested
in our mortal flesh.
12 So then death is *working in us, but
life in you.
13 And since we have [a]the same spirit
of faith, according to what is written,
[b]*"I believed and therefore I spoke,"* we
also believe and therefore speak,
14 knowing that [a]He who raised up the
Lord Jesus will also raise us up with
Jesus, and will present *us* with you.
15 For [a]all things *are* for your sakes,
that [b]grace,* having spread through
the many, may cause thanksgiving to
abound to the glory of God.

Seeing the Invisible

16 Therefore we [a]do not lose heart. 3
Even though our outward man is per-

11 [a]Rom. 8:36 *See WW at Luke 23:25.
12 *See WW at 1 Thess. 2:13. 13 [a]2 Pet. 1:1 [b]Ps. 116:10 14 [a][Rom. 8:11] 15 [a]Col. 1:24 [b]2 Cor. 1:11 *See WW at 2 Cor. 12:9. 16 [a]2 Cor. 4:1

3:18 Beholding as in a mirror connotes "reflecting" as well as "looking into." As we behold **the glory of the Lord,** we are continually **transformed into the same image** by **the Spirit of the Lord**. We then, with ever-increasing glory, reflect what we behold.

4:1–6 See section 6 of Truth-In-Action at the end of 2 Cor.

4:1 Therefore: An important connecting word. The transcendent glory of the ministry of the New Covenant (ch. 3) provides a basis for courage to be completely honest.

4:2 Commending: Honest behavior is Paul's "letter of recommendation," along with the reality of the Corinthians' faith (see 3:1–3).

4:4 Satan, **the god of this age** (see John 12:31), blinds the **minds** of people, but they choose not to **believe,** resulting in their inability to see **the glory of Christ**.

4:7–15 See section 6 of Truth-In-Action at the end of 2 Cor.

4:7 Treasure: The knowledge of God in the face of Christ. **Earthen vessels** are weak and fragile. This verse is *virtually* thematic for the entire letter, expressing *the paradox* of how weak human beings can be the *instruments* of the **power** of God (see 12:9, 10).

4:8, 9 The providential hand of God was controlling Paul's persecutions, keeping them within manageable proportions.

4:10, 11 Paul enlarges the theme of power through weakness (v. 7) to include life through death. Paul's missionary career was dangerous, and at any time he might suffer martyrdom. As he endured hardships and surrendered himself to the possibility of death, he was following the pattern of Jesus (see 1 Cor. 15:31; Gal. 6:17). However, in the midst of his perils he could experience **the life of Jesus,** strengthening and sustaining him in his present weakness and assuring him of future resurrection.

4:12 Paul was willing to suffer *hardship* or martyrdom so that the Corinthians *could know* the power of God.

4:16–18 See *section 3* of Truth-In-Action at the end of 2 Cor.

***4:16* Not lose heart:** Because of faith in the future *resurrection* (v. 14) and because of the present experience of God's renewing power, Paul continues to preach with courage and determination (see v. 1).

ishing, yet the inward *man* is [b]being
renewed day by day.
17 For [a]our light *affliction, which is
but for a moment, is working for us a
*far more exceeding *and* *eternal
weight of glory,
18 [a]while we do not look at the things
which are seen, but at the things which
are not seen. For the things which are
seen *are* temporary, but the things
which are not seen *are* eternal.

Assurance of the Resurrection

5 For we know that if [a]our earthly
[1]house, *this* tent, is destroyed, we
have a building from God, a house
[b]not made with hands, eternal in the
heavens.
2 For in this [a]we groan, earnestly desiring to be clothed with our [1]habita-
tion which is from *heaven,
3 if indeed, [a]having been clothed, we
shall not be found naked.
4 For we who are in *this* tent groan,
being burdened, not because we want
to be unclothed, [a]but further clothed,
that mortality may be swallowed up by
life.
5 Now He who has prepared us for
this very thing *is* God, who also
[a]has *given us the Spirit as [1]a *guarantee.
6 So *we are* always confident, knowing that while we are at home in the
body we are absent from the Lord.
7 For [a]we walk by faith, not by sight. 3
8 We are confident, yes, [a]well pleased
rather to be absent from the body and
to be present with the Lord.

The Judgment Seat of Christ

9 Therefore we make it our aim,
whether present or absent, to be well
pleasing to Him.
10 [a]For we must all *appear before the 1
*judgment seat of Christ, [b]that each
one may receive the things *done* in the
body, according to what he has done,
whether good or bad.
11 Knowing, therefore, [a]the terror of
the Lord, we *persuade men; but we
are well known to God, and I also trust
are well known in your consciences.

Be Reconciled to God

12 For [a]we do not commend ourselves
again to you, but give you opportunity
[b]to boast on our behalf, that you may
have *an answer* for those who boast
in appearance and not in heart.
13 For [a]if we are beside ourselves, *it
is* for God; or if we are of *sound mind,
it is for you.
14 For the *love of Christ **compels** us,

16 [b][Is. 40:29, 31]
17 [a]Rom. 8:18 *See WW at John 16:33. • See WW at 2 Cor. 4:7. • See WW at Rev. 14:6.
18 [a][Heb. 11:1, 13]

CHAPTER 5

1 [a]Job 4:19 [b]Mark 14:58 [1]Physical body
2 [a]Rom. 8:23 [1]*dwelling* *See WW at Rev. 21:1.
3 [a]Rev. 3:18
4 [a]1 Cor. 15:53
5 [a]Rom. 8:23 [1]*down payment, earnest* *See WW at Acts 20:35. • See WW at 2 Cor. 1:22.
7 [a]Heb. 11:1
8 [a]Phil. 1:23
10 [a]Rom. 2:16; 14:10, 12 [b]Eph. 6:8 *See WW at Col. 3:4. • See WW at Matt. 27:19.
11 [a][Heb. 10:31; 12:29] *See WW at 2 Thess. 3:4.
12 [a]2 Cor. 3:1 [b]2 Cor. 1:14
13 [a]2 Cor. 11:1, 16; 12:11 *See WW at Mark 5:15.
14 *See WW at Rom. 5:5.

4:17 Paul's hardships can be termed **light affliction** (see 11:23–29) only in comparison with the future **eternal weight of glory** (see Rom. 8:18).
4:18 **Do not look** does not mean "ignore," but "do not keep looking at, or gazing at." Paul recognizes that the outward man is perishing (v. 16), but by faith he sees more than the outward and more than the present. We must clearly see **temporary** things in light of the **eternal** (see v. 17; Heb. 11:1).
5:1 The present **earthly** body is like a fragile **tent** in contrast to the future body, which is called **a building**.
5:2 **Groan:** A sigh of frustration with bodily limitations that simultaneously expresses hope. See 4:16; Rom. 8:22, 23. **Clothed:** With the new body. Paul changes imagery from a building (v. 1) to clothing (see 1 Cor. 15:53, 54).
5:3, 4 **Naked:** A spirit or soul without a body. Ancient Greeks often spoke of the body as a *tomb;* Paul said it is a "temple of the Holy Spirit" (1 Cor. 6:19). Thus, he did not desire an escape from the body at death, but rather desired its renewal (1 Cor. 15:35–55).
5:5 **This very thing:** The renewed body for which we long. Our present experience of renewed life by God's **Spirit** is **a guarantee** (Greek *arrabon,* "pledge," "deposit") that He will perfect what He has begun. See note on 1:21, 22; see also Rom. 8:23; Eph. 1:14.
5:6 **Absent from the Lord:** Christ is with us spiritually, but His physical absence means we do not perceive Him as clearly or as fully as we will in the future. See Phil. 1:23; Col. 3:3, 4; 1 John 3:2.
5:7 See section 3 of Truth-In-Action at the end of 2 Cor.
5:8 **To be present with the Lord** is better than our present condition, even if it means to be **absent from the body** between death and the day of our resurrection (see note on v. 6). This text conclusively disproves any notion that the believer experiences any lapse between death and his presence with Christ.
5:9 **Therefore:** Paul's conclusion is that in view of the confident expectation of seeing Christ (v. 8) and our hope for the resurrection (vv. 5, 6) he desires **to be well pleasing to Him.** This holds true whether he is **present or absent,** that is, in the body or out (v. 6).
5:10 See section 1 of Truth-In-Action at the end of 2 Cor.
5:10 **For:** Knowledge of a future accountability for our service is another reason to seek "to be well pleasing to Him" (v. 9).
5:11 **The terror of the Lord** (the appropriate reverential awe or fear of our Creator and Judge) strengthens our resolve to please Christ ourselves (vv. 9, 10) and motivates our attempts to **persuade** others to trust in Christ.
5:12 **Opportunity to boast:** Paul explains his motives to the Corinthians to give them an answer for his detractors, who are preoccupied with superficial judgment.
5:13 If his critics call him irrational (**beside ourselves**), Paul knows he is only trying to serve God. If, on the other hand, Paul is **of sound mind,** that also is for the benefit of others, specifically the Corinthians.
5:14 **The love of Christ:** His love for us, which motivated Him to die for us. **Compels:** Constrains, confines, leaves no option. Christ died as the *substitute* **for all;** therefore, He died as the *representative* of all, and **all died** in Him.

because we *judge thus: that [a]if One
died for all, then all died;

WORD WEALTH

5:14 compels, *sunecho* (soon-*ekh*-oh); Strong's *#4912:* From *sun,* "together," and *echo,* "to hold"; hence, "to hold together," or "to grip tightly." The word describes people who are afflicted with various diseases and pains (Luke 4:38) or paralyzed by fear (Luke 8:37), crowds hemming Christ in (Luke 8:45), an army surrounding Jerusalem (Luke 19:43), soldiers arresting Jesus and holding Him fast (Luke 22:63). In every use of the word, there is a sense of constraint, a tight grip that prevents an escape. The love of Christ leaves us no choice except to live our lives for Him.

[1] 15 and He died for all, [a]that those who
live should live no longer for themselves, but for Him who died for them
and rose again.
16 [a]Therefore, from now on, we regard
no one according to the flesh. Even
though we have known Christ according to the flesh, [b]yet now we know *Him*
thus no longer.
17 Therefore, if anyone [a]*is* in Christ,
he is [b]a new *creation; [c]old things have
passed away; behold, all things have
become [d]**new.**

WORD WEALTH

5:17 new, *kainos* (kahee-*noss*); Strong's *#2537:* New, unused, fresh, novel. The word means new in regard to form or quality, rather than new in reference to time, a thought conveyed by *neos.*

14 [a][Rom. 5:15; 6:6] *See WW at John 18:31.
15 [a][Rom. 6:11]
16 [a]2 Cor. 10:3 [b][Matt. 12:50]
17 [a][John 6:63] [b][Rom. 8:9] [c]Is. 43:18; 65:17 [d][Rom. 6:3–10] *See WW at Col. 1:15.
18 [a]Rom. 5:10 *See WW at 1 Cor. 7:11.
19 [a][Rom. 3:24] [1]*reckoning* *See WW at 1 Cor. 7:11. • See WW at John 18:36. • See WW at Rom. 4:3.
20 [a]Eph. 6:20 *See WW at Eph. 6:20. • See WW at 1 Cor. 7:11.
21 [a]Is. 53:6, 9 [b][Rom. 1:17; 3:21] *See WW at John 8:32. • See WW at John 1:29. • See WW at 2 Tim. 4:8.

CHAPTER 6

1 [a]1 Cor. 3:9 [b]2 Cor. 5:20 *See WW at James 2:22.
2 [a]Is. 49:8
3 [a]Rom. 14:13
4 [a]1 Cor. 4:1 [1]*endurance* *See WW at Heb. 10:36.
5 [a]2 Cor. 11:23

18 Now all things *are* of God, [a]who has
*reconciled us to Himself through
Jesus Christ, and has given us the ministry of reconciliation,
19 that is, that [a]God was in Christ *reconciling the *world to Himself, not
[1]imputing* their trespasses to them,
and has committed to us the word of
reconciliation.
20 Now then, we are [a]ambassadors*
for Christ, as though God were pleading through us: we implore *you* on
Christ's behalf, be *reconciled to God.
21 For [a]He made Him who *knew no
*sin *to be* sin for us, that we might become [b]the *righteousness of God in
Him.

Marks of the Ministry

6 We then, *as* [a]workers* together
with Him also [b]plead with *you* not
to receive the grace of God in vain.
2 For He says:

> [a]*"In an acceptable time I have*
> *heard you,*
> *And in the day of salvation I have*
> *helped you."*

Behold, now *is* the accepted time; behold, now *is* the day of salvation.
3 [a]We give no offense in anything,
that our ministry may not be blamed.
4 But in all *things* we commend ourselves [a]as ministers of God: in much
[1]patience,* in tribulations, in needs, in
distresses,
5 [a]in stripes, in imprisonments, in tumults, in labors, in sleeplessness, in
fastings;

Although the pain of death was Christ's alone, the benefit of His death is given to those who trust Him. See Rom. 6:2–10; Gal. 2:20; Col. 3:3.

5:15–17 See section 1 of Truth-In-Action at the end of 2 Cor.

5:16 According to the flesh suggests external evaluation viewed from an earthly perspective. Since his conversion, Paul no longer estimates a person according to worldly standards of judgment.

5:17 In Christ: Paul's most characteristic expression of what it means to be a Christian. Christ's death and resurrection for us, and our identification with Him by faith, make existence as **a new creation** possible. At present this new creation is only partially experienced, but it is to be our focus as the completion of the re-creation is assured (see 4:16—5:5). Our relationship with Christ affects every aspect of life.

5:18, 19 The ministry of reconciliation is to announce the message of what **God,** who **was in Christ,** has done to provide atonement for sin. Those already reconciled (v. 17) have the commission to bring that message to others. **Imputing:** In His grace, God has refused to reckon our **trespasses** against us.

5:21 This statement is the positive counterpart to the statement in v. 19 that God does not impute our trespasses to us. He imputed them instead to Christ, who was sinless in every respect (see Heb. 4:15; 1 Pet. 2:22; 1 John 3:5). He bore our sins on the Cross and endured the penalty that we deserved, **that we might become the righteousness of God in Him.** See also Rom. 8:3, 4; 1 Cor. 1:30; Gal. 3:13, 14.

6:1 In vain: It is possible to refuse or to miss the benefits of **the grace of God.**

6:2 Time: The Greek word *kairos* denotes an appointed time or "season," rather than a certain length of time. The "right time" to receive God's grace is **now** (see also Heb. 3:7—4:11).

6:3 Offense: Stumbling block. Paul sought diligently to be beyond reproach (see 4:2).

6:4–10 Paul's "letter of recommendation" (see notes on 3:1–3; 4:2) is the price he has paid to be a minister of the gospel, what he has experienced (both good and bad), and the qualities he has demonstrated (regardless of what others have said about him). See also 11:23–33.

6:4, 5 Some hardships are imposed by others; some are the results of disciplines freely chosen for the sake of the ministry.

6 by purity, by knowledge, by *longsuffering, by *kindness, by the Holy
Spirit, by [1]sincere* love,
7 [a]by the word of truth, by [b]the power
of God, by [c]the armor of righteousness
on the right hand and on the left,
8 by honor and dishonor, by evil report and good report; as deceivers, and
yet *true;
9 as unknown, and [a]*yet* well known;
[b]as dying, and behold we live; [c]as
chastened, and *yet* not killed;
10 as sorrowful, yet always rejoicing;
as poor, yet making many [a]rich; as
having nothing, and *yet* possessing all
things.

Be Holy

11 O Corinthians! [1]We have spoken
openly to you, [a]our heart is wide open.
12 You are not restricted by us, but
[a]you are restricted by your *own* affections.
13 Now in return for the same [a](I
speak as to children), you also be open.
2 14 [a]Do not be unequally yoked together with unbelievers. For [b]what
[1]fellowship has righteousness with
lawlessness? And what [2]communion*
has light with *darkness?
15 And what accord has Christ with
Belial? Or what part has a believer with
an unbeliever?
16 And what agreement has the temple
of God with idols? For [a]you[1] are the
temple of the living God. As God has
said:

6 [1]Lit. *unhypocritical* *See WW at Heb. 6:12. • See WW at Gal. 5:22. • See WW at 1 Pet. 1:22.
7 [a]2 Cor. 7:14 [b]1 Cor. 2:4 [c]2 Cor. 10:4
8 *See WW at Rom. 3:4.
9 [a]2 Cor. 4:2; 5:11 [b]1 Cor. 4:9, 11 [c]Ps. 118:18
10 [a][2 Cor. 8:9]
11 [a]2 Cor. 7:3 [1]Lit. *Our mouth is open*
12 [a]2 Cor. 12:15
13 [a]1 Cor. 4:14
14 [a]1 Cor. 5:9 [b]Eph. 5:6, 7, 11 [1]*in common* [2]*fellowship* *See WW at Acts 2:42. • See WW at Luke 11:35.
16 [a][1 Cor. 3:16, 17; 6:19] [b]Ezek. 37:26, 27 [1]NU *we*
17 [a]Is. 52:11
18 [a]2 Sam. 7:14 [b][Rom. 8:14]

CHAPTER 7

1 [a][1 John 3:3] *See WW at Acts 13:32. • See WW at 1 Thess. 3:13. • See WW at 1 John 4:18.
2 [a]Acts 20:33 *See WW at Acts 25:10.

[b]*"I will dwell in them*
And walk among them.
I will be their God,
And they shall be My people."

17 Therefore

[a]*"Come out from among them*
And be separate, says the Lord.
Do not touch what is unclean,
And I will receive you."
18 *"I [a]will be a Father to you,*
And you shall be My [b]sons and
daughters,
Says the LORD *Almighty."*

7 Therefore,[a] having these *promises, beloved, let us cleanse ourselves from all filthiness of the flesh
and spirit, perfecting *holiness in the
*fear of God.

The Corinthians' Repentance

2 Open *your hearts* to us. We have
*wronged no one, we have corrupted
no one, [a]we have cheated no one.
3 I do not say *this* to condemn; for
[a]I have said before that you are in our
hearts, to die together and to live together.
4 [a]Great *is* my *boldness of speech toward you, [b]great *is* my boasting on
your behalf. [c]I am filled with comfort.
I am exceedingly joyful in all our tribulation.
5 For indeed, [a]when we came to

3 [a]2 Cor. 6:11, 12 4 [a]2 Cor. 3:12 [b]1 Cor. 1:4 [c]Phil. 2:17 *See WW at Acts 4:31. 5 [a]2 Cor. 2:13

6:7 Armor can also be translated "weapons" (see 10:4, where the same Greek word is used). See Eph. 6:13–17; 1 Thess. 5:8.

6:8 Not everyone in the church had a positive opinion of Paul. The faithful minister must not let either praise or unfair criticisms affect him too greatly.

6:9 Unknown perhaps refers to the disparagement of those who questioned Paul's apostolic authority. The contrasts between **dying** and living, **chastened** and **not killed,** are based on Ps. 118:17, 18 (see 4:10–12).

6:10 The ministry sometimes gives cause to be **sorrowful** (as in Paul's dealings with the Corinthians). Paul was, at least at times, quite literally **poor** (11:7–9, 27; 1 Cor. 4:11, 12; Phil. 4:11, 12). Yet his ministry enriched his hearers, as he followed the example of the Lord Himself (8:9). See 1 Cor. 3:21–23.

6:11–13 Restricted: The Corinthians have been less than completely forthright with Paul (see note on 6:14—7:1), while he has been very **open** in his words to them (see 2:17; 4:2; 5:11).

6:14—7:1 Paul appears to change subjects abruptly; but, in fact, he is simply repeating and emphasizing previous instructions to avoid all associations with idolatry and any compromising union with unbelievers (1 Cor. 10:1—11:1).

6:14–18 See section 2 of Truth-In-Action at the end of 2 Cor.

6:14 Unequally yoked refers both to Christians joining pagans in idolatrous practices (v. 16) and so closely yoking themselves (in any close relationship) with **unbelievers** that they compromise integrity of faith. His allusion is to Deut. 22:10. A warning against marriage to an unbeliever is obviously an appropriate application.

6:15 Belial, one of the many names for Satan, transliterates a Hebrew word meaning "worthlessness" or perhaps "lawlessness."

6:16 To indulge in idolatrous practices is to defile God's **temple** in a direct way, since Christians, collectively (1 Cor. 3:16, 17) and individually (1 Cor. 6:19), are temples of the Holy Spirit. **The living God:** A frequent OT description of God in comparison with dead idols.

6:17, 18 Paul combines words from Is. 52:11 and 2 Sam. 7:14, which affirm God's desire for an exclusive, loving relationship with His people.

7:1 These promises that God will dwell among us, receive us, and be our Father (6:16–18) should motivate us to **holiness,** as should the proper **fear of God.** See 5:10, 11; 1 John 3:1–3.

7:2 Resuming the appeal begun in 6:13, Paul notes that **no one** in the Corinthian church has a just accusation against him.

7:5 After a long digression (since 2:13), Paul resumes the description of his travels and the acute anxiety he

Macedonia, our bodies had no rest, but
[b]we were troubled on every side.
[c]Outside *were* conflicts, inside *were*
fears.
6 Nevertheless [a]God, who comforts
the **downcast,** comforted us by [b]the
*coming of Titus,

> **WORD WEALTH**
>
> **7:6 downcast,** *tapeinos* (tap-eye-*noss*); Strong's *#5011:* Literally "low to the ground." Metaphorically, the word signifies low estate, lowly in position and power, humble.

7 and not only by his coming, but also
by the [1]consolation with which he was
comforted in you, when he told us of
your earnest desire, your mourning,
your zeal for me, so that I rejoiced even
more.
8 For even if I made you [a]sorry with
my letter, I do not regret it; [b]though I
did regret it. For I perceive that the
same epistle made you sorry, though
only for a while.
9 Now I rejoice, not that you were
made sorry, but that your sorrow led
to repentance. For you were made
sorry in a godly manner, that you
might suffer loss from us in nothing.
10 For [a]godly sorrow produces repentance *leading* to salvation, not to be regretted; [b]but the sorrow of the world
produces death.
11 For observe this very thing, that you
sorrowed in a godly manner: What diligence it produced in you, *what* [a]clear-
ing *of yourselves, what* indignation,
what fear, *what* vehement desire, *what*
zeal, *what* vindication! In all *things*
you proved yourselves to be [b]clear* in
this matter.
12 Therefore, although I wrote to you,
I did not *do it* for the sake of him who
had done the wrong, nor for the sake
of him who suffered wrong, [a]but that
our care for you in the sight of God
might appear to you.

The Joy of Titus

13 Therefore we have been comforted
in your comfort. And we rejoiced exceedingly more for the joy of Titus, because his spirit [a]has been *refreshed
by you all.
14 For if in anything I have boasted to
him about you, I am not ashamed. But
as we spoke all things to you in truth,
even so our boasting to Titus was
found true.
15 And his affections are *greater for
you as he remembers [a]the *obedience
of you all, how with fear and trembling
you received him.
16 Therefore I rejoice that [a]I have confidence in you in everything.

Excel in Giving

8 Moreover, brethren, we make
known to you the grace of God bestowed on the *churches of Macedonia:
2 that in a great trial of affliction the
abundance of their joy and [a]their deep
*poverty abounded in the riches of
their liberality.
3 For I bear *witness that according
to *their* ability, yes, and beyond *their*
ability, *they were* freely willing,
4 imploring us with much urgency
[1]that we would receive the gift and
[a]the fellowship of the ministering to
the saints.
5 And not *only* as we had hoped, but
they first [a]gave themselves to the Lord,

5 [b]2 Cor. 4:8 [c]Deut. 32:25 **6** [a]Is. 49:13; 2 Cor. 1:3, 4 [b]2 Cor. 2:13; 7:13 *See WW at 1 Cor. 15:23. **7** [1]*comfort* **8** [a]2 Cor. 2:2 [b]2 Cor. 2:4 **10** [a]2 Sam. 12:13; Ps. 32:10; Matt. 26:75 [b]Prov. 17:22 **11** [a]Eph. 5:11 [b]2 Cor. 2:5–11 *See WW at 1 John 3:3. **12** [a]2 Cor. 2:4 **13** [a]Rom. 15:32 *See WW at Rev. 14:13. **15** [a]2 Cor. 2:9; Phil. 2:12 *See WW at 2 Cor. 2:4. • See WW at 2 Cor. 10:5. **16** [a]2 Cor. 2:3; 8:22; 2 Thess. 3:4; Philem. 8, 21

CHAPTER 8

1 *See WW at Acts 8:1. **2** [a]Mark 12:44 *See WW at Rev. 2:9. **3** *See WW at Acts 26:22. **4** [a]Acts 11:29; 24:17; Rom. 15:25, 26; 1 Cor. 16:1, 3, 4; 2 Cor. 9:1 [1]NU, M omit *that we would receive,* thus changing text to *urgency for the favor and fellowship* **5** [a][Rom. 12:1, 2]

---

experienced while waiting to hear news from Corinth through Titus.

7:6, 7 Titus brought the good news that the Corinthians had reconciled themselves to Paul and had responded to his *severe letter* with repentance and obedience, which brought him comfort (or encouragement) and joy.

7:8, 9 I did regret it: Paul briefly felt pain in causing them **sorrow,** but the resulting **repentance,** with its lasting benefits, made the pain worthwhile. **Suffer loss from us:** Paul's letter had not hurt them but helped them.

7:10 Godly sorrow: Their response of turning toward God and **repentance** brought **salvation,** which would not be **regretted**.

7:11 The Corinthians' energetic response was gratifying to Paul. Its depth was characterized by **indignation** toward the offender and the *offense, alarm* over the problem (**fear**), *longing or affection* toward Paul (**vehement desire**), and readiness to see justice done (**vindication**). The church also took a stand against the rebel (see 2:9).

7:14 Not ashamed: That is, "You did not let me down."

7:15 Fear and trembling: They demonstrated respect and deference to the apostle's representative. See the same expression in 1 Cor. 2:3; Eph. 6:5; Phil. 2:12.

8:1 Paul turns to a project begun earlier to raise an offering from the churches he had founded to take to the church in Jerusalem (1 Cor. 16:1–4; see also Rom. 15:25–27). **Macedonia** (northern Greece) and Achaia (where Corinth is located; 1:1; 9:2) were natural rivals. Paul mentions the Macedonians a number of times in these two chapters, knowing that the Corinthians would be spurred to action by the comparison. He appeals to this natural motivation but provides other reasons for giving as well (see 8:9, 14; 9:6–12).

8:2 Trial: The Macedonian churches had been persecuted since their founding. See Acts 16; 17; Phil. 1:28–30; 1 Thess. 1:6. They were also financially poor, yet they had great **joy** and **liberality** in giving.

8:3 Beyond *their* ability: Sacrificially.

8:4 Fellowship: They desired to share in financially **ministering** with the other contributing churches to **the saints** in Jerusalem.

8:5 First . . . to the Lord: A model for all Christian giving.

and *then* to us by the [b]will of God.
6 So [a]we urged Titus, that as he had
begun, so he would also complete this
grace in you as well.
7 But as [a]you abound in everything—
in faith, in speech, in knowledge, in all
diligence, and in your love for us—*see*
[b]that you abound in this grace also.

Christ Our Pattern

8 [a]I speak not by commandment, but
I am testing the sincerity of your love
by the diligence of others.
9 For you know the grace of our Lord
Jesus Christ, [a]that though He was rich,
yet for your sakes He **became poor,**
that you through His *poverty might
become [b]rich.

WORD WEALTH

8:9 became poor, *ptocheuo* (pto-*khyoo*-oh); Strong's *#4433:* To be destitute, poor as a beggar, reduced to extreme poverty. The word suggests the bottom rung of poverty, a situation in which one is totally lacking in this world's goods.

10 And in this [a]I give advice: [b]It is to
your advantage not only to be doing
what you began and [c]were desiring to
do a year ago;
11 but now you also must complete the
doing *of it;* that as *there was* a readiness to desire *it,* so *there* also *may be*
a completion out of what *you* have.
12 For [a]if there is first a willing mind,
it is accepted according to what one
has, *and* not according to what he does
not have.
13 For *I do* not *mean* that others should
be eased and you burdened;
14 but by an equality, *that* now at this
time your abundance *may supply* their
lack, that their abundance also may
supply your lack—that there may be
equality.
15 As it is written, [a]*"He who gathered
much had nothing left over, and he
who gathered little had no lack."*

Collection for the Judean Saints

16 But thanks *be* to God who [1]puts the
same earnest care for you into the
heart of Titus.
17 For he not only accepted the exhortation, but being more diligent, he went
to you of his own accord.
18 And we have sent with him [a]the
brother whose *praise *is* in the gospel
throughout all the churches,
19 and not only *that,* but who was also
[a]chosen by the churches to travel with
us with this gift, which is administered
by us [b]to the glory of the Lord Himself
and *to show* your ready mind,
20 avoiding this: that anyone should
blame us in this lavish gift which is
administered by us—
21 [a]providing honorable things, not 1
only in the sight of the Lord, but also
in the sight of men.
22 And we have sent with them our
brother whom we have often proved
diligent in many things, but now much

5 [b][Eph. 6:6]
6 [a]2 Cor. 8:17; 12:18
7 [a][1 Cor. 1:5; 12:13] [b]2 Cor. 9:8
8 [a]1 Cor. 7:6
9 [a]Matt. 8:20; Luke 9:58; Phil. 2:6, 7 [b]Rom. 9:23; [Eph. 1:7; Rev. 3:18] *See WW at Rev. 2:9.
10 [a]1 Cor. 7:25, 40 [b][Prov. 19:17; Matt. 10:42; 1 Tim. 6:18, 19; Heb. 13:16] [c]1 Cor. 16:2; 2 Cor. 9:2
12 [a]Mark 12:43, 44; Luke 21:3, 4; 2 Cor. 9:7
15 [a]Ex. 16:18
16 [1]NU *has put*
18 [a]1 Cor. 16:3; 2 Cor. 12:18 *See WW at Eph. 1:6.
19 [a]Acts 14:23; 1 Cor. 16:3, 4 [b]2 Cor. 4:15
21 [a]Rom. 12:17; Phil. 4:8; 1 Pet. 2:12

8:6 Paul was sending **Titus** back to Corinth, this time to deliver 2 Cor. and to resume supervision of the collection, which was to be completed before Paul's arrival (see 9:5).
8:7 To **abound in this grace** of giving is as important as the other areas in which the Corinthians had shown such zeal (see 1 Cor. 1:4–7).
8:8 Not by commandment: The gift must be voluntary (9:5–7).
8:9 The greatest and most inspiring example of generosity is **the grace** of **Jesus**. **He was rich:** Not a reference to Jesus' material wealth while on Earth, but a recognition of His eternal status as Lord of heaven and Earth. **He became poor** through the total giving of Himself in the Incarnation and the Crucifixion (see Phil. 2:5–8). **Through His poverty** refers to His self-giving.
8:10, 11 Paul gives **advice** (or opinion) rather than a commandment (v. 8), to avoid any appearance of coercion. **A year ago:** The troubles between Paul and the Corinthian church had perhaps delayed this project.
8:12 A willing mind, a desire to give, is the key issue, not the amount given (see Luke 21:1–4).
8:14 Equality: The Corinthians had, at the present time, more resources than the Christians in Jerusalem and, Paul implies, more than the Macedonians who had already given so generously.
8:15 The manna in the wilderness (Ex. 16:18) had provided enough for everyone, a fact illustrating God's will for His people. Equal distribution of the supply, however, depends on giving by those with an abundance (v. 14).
8:16–24 Several unnamed people accompany Titus to Corinth and Paul gives his personal endorsement of them.
8:17 This refers to the present visit of Titus with 2 Cor., not to the previous visit with the *severe letter.*
8:18, 19 Some have suggested that **the brother** was Luke, famous for his great knowledge of the **gospel**. Whoever he was, he was included in the delegation to provide additional assurance that the money collected would be handled properly (v. 20).
8:20, 21 Again Paul shows his concern for **avoiding** unnecessary criticism (**blame**). **Providing honorable things,** that is, "taking into consideration what is right," meant Paul's sharing the administrative responsibilities for the collection with other trusted individuals. What **the Lord** knows is most important, but what **men** think cannot be recklessly ignored without endangering the effectiveness of the ministry (see 4:2; 6:3).
8:21 See section 1 of Truth-In-Action at the end of 2 Cor.
8:22 Paul mentions another unnamed **brother,** who would have been personally present at the first reading of this epistle.

more diligent, because of the great confidence which *we have* in you.
23 If *anyone inquires* about [a]Titus, *he*
is my partner and fellow worker concerning you. Or if our brethren *are in-*
quired about, they are [b]messengers[1] of
the churches, the glory of Christ.
24 Therefore show to them, [1]and before the churches, the proof of your love
and of our [a]boasting on your behalf.

Administering the Gift

9 Now concerning [a]the ministering
to the saints, it is *superfluous for
me to write to you;
2 for I know your willingness, about
which I boast of you to the Macedonians, that Achaia was ready a [a]year
ago; and your *zeal has stirred up the
majority.
3 [a]Yet I have sent the brethren, lest
our boasting of you should be *in vain
in this respect, that, as I said, you may
be ready;
4 lest if *some* Macedonians come with
me and find you unprepared, we (not
to mention you!) should be ashamed
of this [1]confident boasting.
5 Therefore I thought it necessary to
[1]exhort the brethren to go to you ahead
of time, and prepare your generous gift
beforehand, which *you had* previously
promised, that it may be ready as *a*
matter of generosity and not as a
[2]grudging obligation.

The Cheerful Giver

6 [a]But this *I say:* He who sows sparingly will also reap sparingly, and he
who sows [1]bountifully will also reap
[1]bountifully.
7 *So let* each one *give* as he purposes
in his heart, [a]not grudgingly or of
[1]necessity; for [b]God loves a **cheerful**
giver.

WORD WEALTH

9:7 cheerful, *hilaros* (hil-*ar*-oss); Strong's *#2431:* Willing, good-natured, joyfully ready. The word describes a spirit of enjoyment in giving that sweeps away all restraints. The English word "hilarious" is a transliteration.

23 [a]2 Cor. 7:13, 14 [b][John 13:16]; Phil. 2:25 [1]Lit. *apostles,* "sent ones"
24 [a]2 Cor. 7:4, 14; 9:2 [1]NU, M omit *and*

CHAPTER 9

1 [a]Acts 11:29; Rom. 15:26; 1 Cor. 16:1; 2 Cor. 8:4; Gal. 2:10 *See WW at John 10:10.
2 [a]2 Cor. 8:10 *See WW at 2 Cor. 11:2.
3 [a]2 Cor. 8:6, 17 *See WW at 1 Cor. 9:15.
4 [1]NU *confidence.*
5 [1]*encourage* [2]Lit. *covetousness*
6 [a]Prov. 11:24; 22:9; Gal. 6:7, 9 [1]*with blessings*
7 [a]Deut. 15:7 [b]Deut. 15:10; 1 Chr. 29:17; [Prov. 11:25]; Rom. 12:8; [2 Cor. 8:12] [1]*compulsion*
8 [a][Prov. 11:24] *See WW at Matt. 25:29. • See WW at Phil. 1:6.
9 [a]Ps. 112:9
10 [a]Is. 55:10 [b]Hos. 10:12 [1]NU omits *may* [2]NU *will supply* *See WW at Gal. 3:5.
11 [a]2 Cor. 1:11
12 *See WW at Luke 1:23.

8 [a]And God *is* able to make all grace
*abound toward you, that you, always
having all sufficiency in all *things,* may
have an abundance for every *good
work.
9 As it is written:

[a]*"He has dispersed abroad,*
He has given to the poor;
His righteousness endures
forever."

10 Now [1]may He who [a]supplies* seed
to the sower, and bread for food,
[2]supply and multiply the seed you have
sown and increase the fruits of your
[b]righteousness,

KINGDOM DYNAMICS

9:8–10 Give What You Have in Your Hand to Give, SEED FAITH. Note especially these three things as you study this passage: First, God is the One who makes all grace abound toward you and provides you sufficiency in all things. All things beneficial for our lives come from God's hands. Second, we are given sufficiency—even "bounty" so that we might do good works. We are blessed in order to be a blessing to others! (see Gen. 12:2). The word "sufficiency" means "self-satisfaction," "contentedness," or "competence"—earmarks of the believer whose life is truly blessed by these characteristics as God increases him (also see Gen. 12:2). And third, the God who gave you seed in the first place is the One who meets your basic needs, multiplies your seeds sown into an abundance you can share with others, and increases you spiritually with love, joy, peace, and all of the other fruit of the Holy Spirit flowing freely in your life ("the fruits of your righteousness").

How great is our God! We have no lack in Him—only potential!

(Luke 5:1–11/James 5:15, 16) O.R.

11 while *you are* enriched in everything for all liberality, [a]which causes
thanksgiving through us to God.
12 For the administration of this *ser-

9:3 The brethren are the delegation (8:16–24) sent to prepare the offering before Paul arrives.
9:6 *Giving* **bountifully** (literally "with blessings") blesses both the recipients and those who give.
9:7 Of necessity: Under constraint, against one's will.
9:8 All, always, and **every** are the emphases in this verse. God can meet their own needs (financial, spiritual, and so on) and increase their resources to meet the various needs of others.
9:9 Righteousness, an "act of righteousness or piety," refers to the lasting results of generosity. See Ps. 112:9 in its context; also Matt. 6:1, where the same Greek word is translated "charitable deeds."
9:12 Generous giving meets the material needs of others but also produces a spiritual result: **many thanksgivings to God**.

vice not only [a]supplies the needs of the saints, but also is abounding through many thanksgivings to God,
13 while, through the proof of this ministry, they [a]glorify God for the obedience of your confession to the gospel of Christ, and for *your* liberal [b]sharing with them and all *men*,
14 and by their prayer for you, who long for you because of the exceeding [a]grace of God in you.
15 Thanks *be* to God [a]for His indescribable gift!

The Spiritual War

10 Now [a]I, Paul, myself am pleading with you by the *meekness and *gentleness of Christ—[b]who in presence *am* *lowly among you, but being absent am bold toward you.
2 But I beg *you* [a]that when I am present I may not be bold with that confidence by which I intend to be bold against some, who think of us as if we walked according to the flesh.

3 For though we walk in the flesh, we do not war according to the flesh.
4 [a]For the weapons [b]of our warfare *are* not [1]carnal but [c]mighty in God [d]for pulling down strongholds,
5 [a]casting down arguments and every high thing that exalts itself against the knowledge of God, bringing every thought into captivity to the **obedience** of Christ,

WORD WEALTH

10:5 obedience, *hupakoe* (hoop-ak-oh-*ay*); Strong's *#5218:* From *hupo,* "under," and *akouo,* "to hear." The word signifies attentive hearing, to listen with compliant submission, assent, and agreement. It is used for obedience in general, for obedience to God's commands, and for Christ's obedience.

6 [a]and being ready to punish all disobedience when [b]your obedience is fulfilled.

Reality of Paul's Authority

7 [a]Do you look at things according to the outward appearance? [b]If anyone is convinced in himself that he is Christ's, let him again consider this in himself, that just as he *is* Christ's, even [1]so [c]we *are* Christ's.
8 For even if I should boast somewhat more [a]about our authority, which the Lord gave [1]us for [2]edification and not for your destruction, [b]I shall not be ashamed—
9 lest I seem to terrify you by letters.
10 "For *his* letters," they say, "*are* weighty and powerful, but [a]*his* bodily presence *is* weak, and *his* [b]speech contemptible."
11 Let such a person consider this, that what we are in word by letters when we are absent, such *we will* also *be* in deed when we are present.

Limits of Paul's Authority

12 [a]For we dare not class ourselves or compare ourselves with those who commend themselves. But they, measuring themselves by themselves, and comparing themselves among themselves, are not wise.
13 [a]We, however, will not boast beyond measure, but within the limits of the sphere which God appointed us—a sphere which especially includes you.

12 [a]2 Cor. 8:14
13 [a][Matt. 5:16] [b][Heb. 13:16]
14 [a]2 Cor. 8:1
15 [a][John 3:16; 4:10; Rom. 6:23; 8:32; Eph. 2:8; James 1:17]

CHAPTER 10

1 [a]Rom. 12:1 [b]1 Thess. 2:7 *See WW at 1 Tim. 6:11. • See WW at Acts 24:4. • See WW at 2 Cor. 7:6.
2 [a]1 Cor. 4:21; 2 Cor. 13:2, 10
4 [a]Eph. 6:13 [b]1 Cor. 9:7; [2 Cor. 6:7]; 1 Tim. 1:18 [c]Acts 7:22 [d]Jer. 1:10; [2 Cor. 10:8; 13:10] [1]*of the flesh*
5 [a]1 Cor. 1:19
6 [a]2 Cor. 13:2, 10 [b]2 Cor. 7:15
7 [a][John 7:24]; 2 Cor. 5:12 [b]1 Cor. 1:12; 14:37 [c][Rom. 14:8]; 1 Cor. 3:23 [1]NU *as we are.*
8 [a]2 Cor. 13:10 [b]2 Cor. 7:14 [1]NU omits *us* [2]*building up*
10 [a]1 Cor. 2:3, 4; 2 Cor. 12:7; Gal. 4:13 [b][1 Cor. 1:17]; 2 Cor. 11:6
12 [a]2 Cor. 5:12
13 [a]2 Cor. 10:15

9:13 Proof of this ministry: The Corinthians' **obedience** in contributing to the collection will be tangible evidence of the reality behind their **confession to the gospel of Christ**.
10:1—13:10 Paul's tone changes dramatically as he returns to the subject of the challenges to his authority in Corinth. He answers a number of criticisms made against him and rebukes the impure motives of those who seek to undermine his ministry in order to win personal followings. Paul felt joy and encouragement over the response of the majority of the church (7:6–16), but he has stern words of warning to the minority which may still be in rebellion and under the sway of the intruding "false apostles" (11:13).
10:1 Paul's critics accuse him of being too **lowly** (timid) to be a real apostle, although they admit that he writes **bold** letters (v. 10).
10:3–5 See section 5 of Truth-In-Action at the end of 2 Cor.
10:3 Walk in the flesh: Paul admits he is a mortal, living in the realities of the present world, but he does not **war** (fight) with mere human weapons.
10:4, 5 Our warfare is not "against flesh and blood" (Eph. 6:12); therefore, **carnal** (weak, worldly) **weapons** will not do. We need weapons that are God-empowered (**mighty in God**). Their purpose is **for pulling down** [demolishing] **strongholds** (anything opposing God's will). Here Paul refers specifically to warfare in the mind, against arrogant, rebellious ideas and attitudes (which he terms **arguments**), and against **every high thing** (pride) opposed to the true **knowledge of God**. The aim is to bring **every** disobedient **thought into . . . obedience** to Christ.
10:6 Paul is **ready to punish** the rebels who continue to refuse to repent. First he must be assured of the **obedience** of the congregation as a whole.
10:8 Paul reluctantly boasts of his apostolic **authority** because it has been questioned by his detractors.
10:10, 11 Weighty: Severe, burdensome. ***His* bodily presence *is* weak:** His personal presence is unimposing (see v. 2). **Contemptible:** Paul's speaking ability was ridiculed by those who prided themselves on eloquence according to the standards of Greek rhetorical style (see 1 Cor. 2:1–5).

14 For we are not overextending ourselves (as though *our authority* did not extend to you), [a]for it was to you that we came with the gospel of Christ;
15 not boasting of things beyond measure, *that is,* [a]in other men's labors, but having hope, *that* as your faith is increased, we shall be greatly *enlarged by you in our sphere,
16 to preach the gospel in the *regions* beyond you, *and* not to boast in another man's sphere of accomplishment.

KINGDOM DYNAMICS

10:15, 16 The Continuing Call "Beyond," WORLD EVANGELISM. Paul's words of "having hope . . . to preach the gospel in the regions beyond you" reveal he was never content to keep the message within the Christian community. As John Wesley said, "The world is my parish." This text models the church's mandate to reach "beyond you." Christ's orders are clear: "Make disciples of all the nations" (Matt. 28:19); "preach the gospel to every creature" (Mark 16:15); "[preach] repentance and remission of sins" (Luke 24:47); and go "as the Father has sent Me" (John 20:21) "to the end of the earth" (Acts 1:8). When the full command is obeyed, the full promise will be fulfilled.

(Rom. 10:13–15/Gal. 6:7, 8) G.C.

4 17 But [a]*"he who glories, let him glory in the LORD."*
18 For [a]not he who commends himself is approved, but [b]whom the Lord commends.

Concern for Their Faithfulness

11 Oh, that you would *bear with me in a little [a]folly—and indeed you do bear with me.
2 For I am [a]jealous* for you with godly **jealousy.** For [b]I have betrothed you to one husband, [c]that I may present *you* [d]*as* a *chaste virgin to Christ.

WORD WEALTH

11:2 jealousy, *zelos* (*dzay*-loss); Strong's *#2205:* The root of the English word "zeal." It signifies eagerness, enthusiasm, intense desire, passionate commitment. The word carries both the idea of zeal (7:11; 9:2; Phil. 3:6) and jealousy (Acts 5:17; 13:45; Rom. 13:13).

3 But I fear, lest somehow, as [a]the 3
serpent deceived Eve by his *craftiness, so your minds [b]may be corrupted from the [1]simplicity that is in Christ.
4 For if he who comes preaches *another Jesus whom we have not preached, or *if* you receive a *different spirit which you have not received, or a [a]different gospel which you have not accepted—you may well put up with it!

Paul and False Apostles

5 For I consider that [a]I am not at all *inferior to the most eminent apostles.
6 Even though [a]*I am* untrained in speech, yet *I am* not [b]in knowledge. But [c]we have [1]been thoroughly manifested among you in all things.
7 Did I commit sin in [1]humbling* myself that you might be *exalted, because I preached the gospel of God to you [a]free of charge?
8 I robbed other churches, taking wages *from them* to minister to you.
9 And when I was present with you, and in need, [a]I was a burden to no one, for what I lacked [b]the brethren who came from Macedonia supplied. And in everything I kept myself from being burdensome to you, and so I will keep *myself.*
10 [a]As the truth of Christ is in me, [b]no one shall stop me from this boasting in the regions of Achaia.
11 Why? [a]Because I do not love you? God knows!
12 But what I do, I will also continue to do, [a]that I may cut off the opportunity from those who desire an opportu-

14 [a]1 Cor. 3:5, 6
15 [a]Rom. 15:20 *See WW at Acts 5:13.
17 [a]Jer. 9:24
18 [a]Prov. 27:2 [b]Rom. 2:29

CHAPTER 11

1 [a]2 Cor. 11:4, 16, 19 *See WW at 2 Thess. 1:4.
2 [a]Gal. 4:17 [b]Hos. 2:19 [c]Col. 1:28 [d]Lev. 21:13 *See WW at 1 Cor. 14:1. • See WW at 1 John 3:3.
3 [a]Gen. 3:4, 13 [b]Eph. 6:24 [1]NU adds *and purity* *See WW at 1 Cor. 3:19.
4 [a]Gal. 1:6–8 *See WW at John 14:16. • See WW at Acts 4:12.
5 [a]2 Cor. 12:11 *See WW at Luke 22:35.
6 [a][1 Cor. 1:17] [b][Eph. 3:4] [c][2 Cor. 12:12] [1]NU omits *been*
7 [a]1 Cor. 9:18 [1]*putting myself down* *See WW at Matt. 18:4. • See WW at James 4:10.
9 [a]Acts 20:33 [b]Phil. 4:10
10 [a]Rom. 1:9; 9:1 [b]1 Cor. 9:15
11 [a]2 Cor. 6:11; 12:15
12 [a]1 Cor. 9:12

10:17, 18 See section 4 of Truth-In-Action at the end of 2 Cor.
11:1 Folly: Since self-commendation is pointless (10:18), Paul sees boasting about himself as foolish, yet necessary, in the present situation.
11:3, 4 See section 3 of Truth-In-Action at the end of 2 Cor.
11:5 The most eminent apostles could refer to the Twelve, in which case Paul claims to be their equal in apostolic authority (see Gal. 2:6–9). More likely he is sarcastically referring to the intruders, who are in fact "false apostles" (v. 13).
11:7–12 See notes on 1 Cor. 9:1–27.
11:7 Humbling myself: Paul's craft of tentmaking (Acts 18:3) was held in low social esteem by Greeks. His financial independence was not intended to embarrass the Corinthians. Rather, he desired that they be **exalted** (lifted up) by his preaching the **gospel . . . free of charge**.
11:8, 9 Robbed other churches: The Macedonians were poorer than the Corinthians (8:2).
11:12 Cut off the opportunity: Those who falsely **boast** of their superiority to Paul will not want to imitate his financial independence. He is determined to continue his policy in order to distinguish himself from those with selfish motives.

nity to be regarded just as we are in
the things of which they boast.
13 For such [a]*are* false apostles, [b]deceit-
ful workers, transforming themselves
into apostles of Christ.
14 And no wonder! For Satan himself
transforms himself into [a]an angel of
light.
15 Therefore *it is* no great thing if his
ministers also transform themselves
into ministers of righteousness,
[a]whose end will be according to their
works.

Reluctant Boasting

16 I say again, let no one think me a
fool. If otherwise, at least receive
me as a fool, that I also may boast a
little.
17 What I speak, [a]I speak not according to the Lord, but as it were, foolishly, in this confidence of boasting.
18 Seeing that many boast according
to the flesh, I also will boast.
19 For you put up with fools gladly,
[a]since you *yourselves* are wise!
20 For you put up with it [a]if one brings
you into bondage, if one devours *you*,
if one takes *from you*, if one exalts himself, if one strikes you on the face.
21 To *our* shame [a]I say that we were
too weak for that! But [b]in whatever
anyone is bold—I speak foolishly—I
am bold also.

Suffering for Christ

22 Are they [a]Hebrews? So *am* I. Are
they Israelites? So *am* I. Are they the
seed of Abraham? So *am* I.
23 Are they ministers of Christ?—I
speak as a fool—I *am* more: [a]in labors
more *abundant, [b]in stripes above
measure, in prisons more frequently,
[c]in deaths often.
24 From the Jews five times I received
[a]forty [b]*stripes* minus one.
25 Three times I was [a]beaten with
rods; [b]once I was stoned; three times
I [c]was shipwrecked; a night and a day
I have been in the deep;
26 *in* journeys often, *in* perils of waters, *in* perils of robbers, [a]*in* perils of
my own countrymen, [b]*in* perils of the
Gentiles, *in* perils in the city, *in* perils
in the wilderness, *in* perils in the sea,
in perils among false brethren;
27 in weariness and toil, [a]in sleeplessness often, [b]in hunger and thirst, in
[c]fastings often, in cold and nakedness—
28 besides the other things, what
comes upon me daily: [a]my deep *concern for all the churches.
29 [a]Who is weak, and I am not weak?
Who is made to *stumble, and I do not
burn *with indignation?*
30 If I must boast, [a]I will boast in the
things which concern my [1]infirmity.
31 [a]The God and Father of our Lord
Jesus Christ, [b]who is blessed forever,
knows that I am not lying.
32 [a]In Damascus the governor, under
Aretas the king, was *guarding the city
of the Damascenes with a garrison, desiring to arrest me;
33 but I was let down in a basket
through a window in the wall, and escaped from his hands.

The Vision of Paradise

12 It is [1]doubtless not profitable for
me to boast. I will come to
[a]visions and [b]revelations of the Lord:

[1]NU *necessary, though not profitable, to boast*

13 [a]Phil. 1:15 [b]Phil. 3:2
14 [a]Gal. 1:8
15 [a][Phil. 3:19]
17 [a]1 Cor. 7:6
19 [a]1 Cor. 4:10
20 [a][Gal. 2:4; 4:3, 9; 5:1]
21 [a]2 Cor. 10:10 [b]Phil. 3:4
22 [a]Phil. 3:4–6
23 [a]1 Cor. 15:10 [b]Acts 9:16 [c]1 Cor. 15:30 *See WW at 2 Cor. 2:4.
24 [a]Deut. 25:3 [b]2 Cor. 6:5
25 [a]Acts 16:22, 23; 21:32 [b]Acts 14:5, 19 [c]Acts 27:1–44
26 [a]Acts 9:23, 24; 13:45, 50; 17:5, 13 [b]Acts 14:5, 19; 19:23; 27:42
27 [a]Acts 20:31 [b]1 Cor. 4:11 [c]Acts 9:9; 13:2, 3; 14:23
28 [a]Acts 20:18 *See WW at 1 Pet. 5:7.
29 [a][1 Cor. 8:9, 13; 9:22] *See WW at Matt. 11:6.
30 [a][2 Cor. 12:5, 9, 10] [1]*weakness*
31 [a]1 Thess. 2:5 [b]Rom. 9:5
32 [a]Acts 9:19–25 *See WW at 1 Pet. 1:5.

CHAPTER 12

1 [a]Acts 16:9; 18:9; 22:17, 18; 23:11; 26:13–15; 27:23 [b][Gal. 1:12; 2:2]

11:16–18 Christ would not boast in this manner, but Paul feels constrained by the rivals' boasting and its effect on the Corinthians (see note on v. 1).

11:21 In ironic echo of the charge made against him (10:10), Paul admits he was **too weak** to mistreat them.

11:22 Paul matches the claims of the false apostles, who were apparently Jews from Palestine (**Hebrews;** see Acts 6:1; Phil. 3:5).

11:23–33 Very reluctantly, and after several protests concerning the foolishness of it, Paul begins to boast of his experiences as a servant of Christ. Ironically, he focuses attention on experiences that many (then and now) would consider signs of weakness rather than strength. Some of the events here can be found in Acts; many cannot, since Acts is not an exhaustive account. Note also that the hardships endured in Acts 20:3—28:31 all occurred after the writing of 2 Cor. (see 4:17).

11:24 Forty *stripes* minus one: To avoid breaking the Law's limitation (Deut. 25:3), the Jews stopped short of the maximum permitted.

11:25 Beaten with rods: A Roman form of punishment (Acts 16:22). **Stoned:** A Jewish form of execution inflicted on Paul at Jewish instigation (Acts 14:19). **Shipwrecked:** Acts 27:13–44 is later and thus not included here. **In the deep:** Adrift at sea.

11:27 Hunger and thirst: Imposed by the circumstances (see Phil. 4:12), as contrasted with voluntary **fastings. Nakedness:** Without adequate clothing for the weather.

11:28 Besides the other things: The events he has not mentioned. **Deep concern:** His continuing responsibility for **all the churches,** not just Corinth.

11:29 Rather than boasting of his strength and looking with contempt on those who are **weak** or who **stumble,** Paul identifies with them in their hurt (see 1 Cor. 12:26).

11:32, 33 Aretas IV, king of the Nabatean Arabs, and perhaps in control of Damascus at the time of this event, apparently was in collusion with the Jews who were lying in wait (Acts 9:23–25).

2 I know a man [a]in Christ who fourteen years ago—whether in the body I
do not know, or whether out of the
body I do not know, God knows—such
a one [b]was *caught up to the third
heaven.
3 And I know such a man—whether
in the body or out of the body I do not
know, God knows—
4 how he was caught up into [a]Para-
dise and heard inexpressible words,
which it is not lawful for a man to utter.
5 Of such a one I will boast; yet of
myself I will not [a]boast, except in my
infirmities.
6 For though I might desire to boast,
I will not be a fool; for I will speak the
truth. But I refrain, lest anyone should
think of me above what he sees me *to
be* or hears from me.

The Thorn in the Flesh

4 7 And lest I should be exalted above
measure by the *abundance of the revelations, a [a]thorn in the *flesh was
given to me, [b]a messenger of Satan to
[1]buffet me, lest I be exalted above measure.
8 [a]Concerning this thing I pleaded
with the Lord three times that it might
depart from me.
9 And He said to me, "My **grace** is
sufficient for you, for My strength is
made *perfect in weakness." Therefore
most gladly [a]I will rather boast in my
infirmities, [b]that the power of Christ
may rest upon me.

2 [a]Rom. 16:7 [b]Acts 22:17 *See WW at 1 Thess. 4:17.
4 [a]Luke 23:43
5 [a]2 Cor. 11:30
7 [a]Ezek. 28:24 [b]Job 2:7 [1]*beat* *See WW at 2 Cor. 4:7. • See WW at Matt. 26:41.
8 [a]Matt. 26:44
9 [a]2 Cor. 11:30 [b][1 Pet. 4:14] *See WW at 1 John 2:5.
10 [a][Rom. 5:3; 8:35] [b]2 Cor. 13:4 *See WW at Acts 27:10.
11 [a]2 Cor. 5:13; 11:1, 16; 12:6 [b]2 Cor. 11:5 [c]1 Cor. 3:7; 13:2; 15:9 [1]NU omits *in boasting* *See WW at Luke 22:35. • See WW at 1 Cor. 12:28.
12 [a]Rom. 15:18 [b]Acts 15:12 [c]Acts 14:8–10; 16:16–18; 19:11, 12; 20:6–12; 28:1–10 *See WW at Rev. 16:14. • See WW at Acts 15:12.
13 *See WW at John 7:18.
14 [a]2 Cor. 1:15; 13:1, 2 [b][1 Cor. 10:24–33] [c]1 Cor. 4:14

WORD WEALTH

12:9 grace, *charis* (*khar*-ece); Strong's *#5485:* From the same root as *chara,* "joy," and *chairo,* "to rejoice." *Charis* causes rejoicing. It is the word for God's grace as extended to sinful man. It signifies unmerited favor, undeserved blessing, a free gift.

10 Therefore [a]I take pleasure in infirmities, in *reproaches, in needs, in
persecutions, in distresses, for Christ's
sake. [b]For when I am weak, then I am
strong.

Signs of an Apostle

11 I have become [a]a fool [1]in boasting;
you have compelled me. For I ought
to have been commended by you; for
[b]in nothing was I *behind the most eminent *apostles, though [c]I am nothing.
12 [a]Truly the *signs of an apostle were
accomplished among you with all perseverance, in signs and [b]wonders* and
mighty [c]deeds.
13 For what is it in which you were inferior to other churches, except that I
myself was not burdensome to you?
Forgive me this *wrong!

Love for the Church

14 [a]Now *for* the third time I am ready
to come to you. And I will not be burdensome to you; for [b]I do not seek
yours, but you. [c]For the children ought

12:2 I know a man in Christ: Obviously Paul himself, but he speaks with reserve to avoid boasting about himself rather than the Lord who granted such a privilege. **Fourteen years ago:** About A.D. 42, in the period of his Christian life not described in Acts. **Third heaven:** The highest heaven, the presence of God, in contrast to the sky and the starry heavens visible from Earth.

12:4 Paradise: Identified here with "the third heaven" (v. 2); the place of blissful fellowship with God (Luke 23:43; Rev. 2:7). Paul was neither able nor permitted to repeat what he had heard.

12:7–10 See section 4 of Truth-In-Action at the end of 2 Cor.

12:7–10 Because of some ambiguities, it seems very unwise to form dogmatic conclusions about certain particulars of this section. What is clear, however, is a **thorn in the flesh** (an intense, wearying difficulty or affliction) had come by means of a **messenger of Satan** (probably a demonically instigated assault). God's providence clearly allowed this (grammatically, a "divine passive," indicating God as the unseen Agent overseeing the *entire process*) that Paul might *avoid being* **exalted above measure by the abundance of the revelations.**

Though it is futile to try to identify the "thorn," it caused Paul great consternation and ultimately served a good purpose, becoming the occasion for a revelation to him of the overcoming **grace** of God, which proved **sufficient** in the midst of Paul's **weakness** (v. 9).

We must also note that though God does not respond to Paul's repeated pleading **that it might depart from** him by removing it, there is no indication God is upset with Paul for so pleading. In fact, Jesus' answer (v. 9) indicates God's concern to respond, howbeit differently than Paul had prayed.

Finally, it is important to note that Jesus' answer was not seen by Paul as punitive; nor did it cause him to resign himself to buffeting with a defeatist attitude. Rather, it affirmed in Paul that whenever Satan buffets him (either directly as the destructive adversary or indirectly as God's controlled agent to bring about character development) he can **boast in** his **infirmities** because Jesus' **grace** and **strength** will be **sufficient** to enable him to continue in his apostolic ministry. Neither the thorn, any messenger of Satan, nor any character-refining test from God will cause him to cease serving God. He can therefore **take pleasure . . . for when** he is personally **weak, then** he can be **strong** in Jesus.

12:11 The Corinthian Christians **compelled** Paul to boast by being impressed with the boasts of the false apostles.

12:12 What many would list first in an assertion of spiritual authority, Paul mentioned last and did not elaborate, since the Corinthians had witnessed them.

12:14, 15 Third time: See Introduction to 2 Corinthians: Background and Date.

not to lay up for the parents, but the
parents for the children.
15 And I will very gladly spend and be
spent [a]for your souls; though [b]the
more *abundantly I love you, the less
I am loved.
16 But be that *as it may*, [a]I did not burden you. Nevertheless, being crafty, I
caught you by cunning!
17 Did I take advantage of you by any
of those whom I sent to you?
18 I urged Titus, and sent our [a]brother
with *him*. Did Titus take advantage of
you? Did we not walk in the same
spirit? Did *we* not *walk* in the same
steps?
19 [a]Again,[1] do you think that we excuse ourselves to you? [b]We speak before God in Christ. [c]But *we do* all
things, beloved, for your edification.
20 For I *fear lest, when I come, I shall
not find you such as I wish, and *that*
[a]I shall be found by you such as you
do not wish; lest *there be* contentions,
*jealousies, outbursts of *wrath, *self-
ish ambitions, backbitings, whisperings, conceits, tumults;
21 lest, when I come again, my God
[a]will *humble me among you, and I
shall *mourn for many [b]who have
sinned before and have not *repented
of the uncleanness, [c]fornication,* and
*lewdness which they have practiced.

Coming with Authority

13 This *will be* [a]the third *time* I am
coming to you. [b]*"By the mouth
of two or three witnesses every word
shall be established."*
2 [a]I have told you before, and foretell
as if I were present the second time,
and now being absent [1]I write to those
[b]who have sinned before, and to all the
rest, that if I come again [c]I will not
spare—
3 since you seek a proof of Christ
[a]speaking in me, who is not weak toward you, but **mighty** [b]in you.

> **WORD WEALTH**
>
> **13:3 mighty,** *dunateo* (doo-nat-*eh*-oh); Strong's *#1414:* To be able, powerful, mighty. The power at work in believers is that of the same Spirit that raised Jesus from the dead.

4 [a]For though He was crucified in
weakness, yet [b]He lives by the power
of God. For [c]we also are weak in Him,
but we shall live with Him by the
power of God toward you.
5 *Examine yourselves *as to* whether 4
you are in the faith. Test yourselves.
Do you not know yourselves, [a]that
Jesus Christ is in you?—unless indeed
you [1]are [b]disqualified.
6 But I trust that you will know that
we are not disqualified.

Paul Prefers Gentleness

7 Now [1]I pray to God that you do no
evil, not that we should appear approved, but that you should do what
is honorable, though [a]we may seem
disqualified.
8 For we can do nothing against the
truth, but for the truth.
9 For we are glad [a]when we are weak
and you are strong. And this also we
pray, [b]that you may be made **complete.**

> 
> **WORD WEALTH**
>
> **13:9 complete,** *katartisis* (kat-*ar*-tis-is); Strong's *#2676:* An improving, equipping, training, disciplining. It includes making the necessary adjustments and repairs. The related verb, *katartizo,* is used for the disciples' mending their nets (Matt. 4:21).

10 [a]Therefore I write these things being absent, lest being present I should

15 [a][2 Tim. 2:10] [b]2 Cor. 6:12, 13 *See WW at 2 Cor. 2:4. **16** [a]2 Cor. 11:9 **18** [a]2 Cor. 8:18 **19** [a]2 Cor. 5:12 [b][Rom. 9:1, 2] [c]1 Cor. 10:33 [1]NU *You have been thinking for a long time that we* **20** [a]1 Cor. 4:21 *See WW at Matt. 10:26. • See WW at 2 Cor. 11:2. • See WW at Luke 4:28. • See WW at Phil. 1:16. **21** [a]2 Cor. 2:1, 4 [b]2 Cor. 13:2 [c]1 Cor. 5:1 *See WW at Matt. 18:4. • See WW at Rev. 18:11. • See WW at Matt. 3:2. • See WW at Matt. 15:19. • See WW at 1 Pet. 4:3.

CHAPTER 13

1 [a]2 Cor. 12:14 [b]Deut. 17:6; 19:15 **2** [a]2 Cor. 10:2 [b]2 Cor. 12:21 [c]2 Cor. 1:23; 10:11 [1]NU omits *I write* **3** [a]Matt. 10:20 [b][1 Cor. 9:2] **4** [a][1 Pet. 3:18] [b][Rom. 1:4; 6:4] [c][2 Cor. 10:3, 4] **5** [a][Gal. 4:19] [b]1 Cor. 9:27 [1]*do not stand the test* *See WW at Rev. 2:10. **7** [a]2 Cor. 6:9 [1]NU *we* **9** [a]1 Cor. 4:10 [b][1 Thess. 3:10] **10** [a]1 Cor. 4:21

12:16–18 I caught you: Paul echoes an accusation that he had tricked the Corinthians by sending others (**Titus** and the unnamed **brother**) to get their money (supposedly for Jerusalem), which Paul was keeping for himself. He refutes the charge by citing the character of his envoys, whom the Corinthians know to be honest (see 8:6, 16–24).

12:21 Some had resisted Paul's authority because they were unwilling to abandon ungodly behavior, which Paul had already rebuked (see 1 Cor. 5:9–11; 6:18–20).

13:1, 2 Paul wants this **third** visit (12:14) to settle the persistent troubles. Thus he warns that disciplinary action is certain, just as judgment was made sure by the agreement of **two or three witnesses** (see Deut. 19:15).

13:3, 4 Those who think Paul is **weak** (see 10:10) will find that he really does speak with the authority of Christ, who was able to be weak enough to be **crucified** and yet be the ultimate example of **the power of God**. Likewise, Paul can be **weak in Him** and at the same time powerful in acting and speaking as Christ's apostle in dealing with the Corinthians.

13:5–7 Those who seek "proof" from Paul (v. 3) should **examine** and **test** themselves rather than him. If they **know** that they are genuine Christians, they should know that Paul is a genuine apostle (see 3:1–3). If they are not **disqualified** (counterfeit, unapproved, failing the test), neither is Paul. Whether he is **approved** (qualified, genuine, passing the test) or thought to be **disqualified,** Paul's main concern is their right behavior, not their opinion of him.

13:5, 6 See section 4 of Truth-In-Action at the end of 2 Cor.

13:10 Sharpness: Severity or harshness, such as was used in the previous *severe letter* and in chs. 10—13 of this epistle.

use sharpness, according to the [b]authority* which the *Lord has given me for edification and not for destruction.

Greetings and Benediction

11 Finally, brethren, farewell. Become *complete. [a]Be of good comfort, be of one mind, live in peace; and the God of love [b]and peace will be with you.
12 [a]Greet one another with a holy kiss.
13 All the saints greet you.
14 [a]The grace of the Lord Jesus Christ, and the love of God, and [b]the [1]communion* of the Holy Spirit *be* with you all. Amen.

10 [b]2 Cor. 10:8 *See WW at Mark 3:15. • See WW at John 6:68.
11 [a]Rom. 12:16, 18 [b]Rom. 15:33 *See WW at Heb. 11:3.
12 [a]Rom. 16:16
14 [a]Rom. 16:24 [b]Phil. 2:1 [1]*fellowship* *See WW at Acts 2:42.

KINGDOM DYNAMICS

13:14 2. What Does the Bible Say About the Trinity?, SPIRITUAL ANSWERS. For the answer to this and other probing questions about God and the power life in His kingdom, see the study article "Spiritual Answers to Hard Questions," which begins on page 1996. P.R.

13:12 Holy kiss: A sign of unity.
13:14 A Trinitarian benediction. By **the grace** experienced through **Jesus** we know **the love of God** (John 3:16), and our **communion** (fellowship) with God and God's people is given by **the Holy Spirit** (see 1 John 1:3; 4:13).

TRUTH-IN-ACTION through 2 CORINTHIANS

Letting the LIFE of the Holy Spirit Bring Faith's Works Alive in You!

Truth 2 Corinthians Teaches	Text	**Action** 2 Corinthians Invites
1 Guidelines for Growing in Godliness Godly living may result in disfavor with others because it warns of judgment for the ungodly. Godly individuals live by the ethic of love, selflessly asking, "How can I live for the benefit of others?" They are not lawless or sloppy in the way they live; rather, they seek to do right in everything.	2:14–17	**Conduct** yourself with a clear conscience so that you will not be easily shaken by people's reactions. **Realize** that righteousness also sometimes triggers negative reactions.
	5:10	**Know** and **understand** that you will give an account to Jesus as Judge for every thought, word, and deed. **Let this influence** your conduct.
	5:15–17	**Appropriate** the fact that God has called you to live for Him. **Avoid** any selfishness or personal ambition.
	8:21	**Practice** diligence in everything. **Do** what is right. **Make sure** your ethics reflect Jesus Christ in all your conduct
2 Steps to Holiness Holiness requires that we live according to God's standard, not that of the world. Holiness recognizes the serious nature of partnerships and will not enter into them with those who are not believers. Planning a marriage to an unbeliever will produce an unequal alliance that is to be avoided. To experience a happy union, the believer should align with one whose ideals and visions center in Jesus Christ.	1:12	**Conduct** yourself in the sincerity and holiness that come by God's grace. **Turn from** any worldly wisdom toward which you may naturally incline.
	6:14–18	**Refuse to enter** any covenant or partnership with unbelievers. **Live** as a holy person.
	2:9	**Know** and **observe** the necessity of obedience in Christian living.

Truth 2 Corinthians Teaches	Text	**Action** 2 Corinthians Invites
3 Key Lessons in the Faith Faith chooses to believe God's word above the evidence of the senses, knowing natural circumstances are to be kept subject to the Word of God. Faith is not in denying the circumstances; rather, it is in believing God's testimony and living in agreement with it.	4:16–18 5:7 11:3, 4	**Focus** on the *unseen* and eternal. **Consider** and **dwell upon** the glory that follows this life. **Know** the inward man is being renewed. **Live** according to the truth of God's Word and the testimony of His Spirit. **Identify as evil** any who would pervert the Word of God. **Do not accept** distortions of the gospel's truth.
4 Steps in Developing Humility Humility looks to God for what it needs. Humility is not shocked to discover its own weaknesses, having learned to trust God's strength. Nor do the humble take faith for granted, always drawing near to God, distrusting self.	10:17, 18 12:7–10 13:5, 6	**Give God the glory,** and let any commendation be from Him. **Allow** Jesus' strength to be exhibited and exalted through your weakness. **Know** that His grace is large enough to meet you in your problems. **Practice** regular, diligent self-examination.
5 Guidelines for Growth in the Spirit We must be determined to grow spiritually. Such growth is painful because one undergoes stretching, molding, and refining by the Holy Spirit. Spiritual people deal ruthlessly with any carnal thoughts in their own minds.	3:2, 3 3:17, 18 10:3–5	**Be shaped** by the Holy Spirit so that people can come to know Jesus through what they see. **Spend time** in "God's presence." **Expect** the Spirit to transform you into the image of His glorious Son. **Recognize** the spiritual war in your mind. **Take captive** every thought that is hostile to God. **Memorize** Scripture and meditate as a "military discipline."
6 Lessons for Leaders God's leaders depend entirely on Him for their direction and empowering in the ministry. They never exalt or glorify themselves, acknowledging their lack of power and ability to fulfill any mission alone.	3:5, 6 4:1–6 4:7–15	Leaders, **depend** on the Spirit as your only true source of ability. **Beware** building your ministry on mere human training or ability alone. Leaders, **handle** God's Word diligently and with great care. **Be careful** not to read your own ideas into God's Word. **Ask** God to enlighten His Word. Leaders, **never lose sight** of your weakness. **Give room** for the power of Jesus' dying to work in you so that His life-power can result in others.

The Epistle of Paul the Apostle to the GALATIANS

Author: Paul
Date: A.D. 55–56
Theme: Justification by Faith Alone
Key Words: Grace, Gospel, Faith, Justified, Promise, Liberty, Law

Destination Galatians is the only letter Paul specifically addressed to a group of churches. Galatia was not a city, but a region of Asia Minor, which included many towns. Its name originated in the third century B.C. when a tribe of people from Gaul migrated to the area. In the first century A.D. the term "Galatia" was used geographically to denote the north-central region of Asia Minor, where the Gauls had settled, and politically to designate the Roman province in south-central Asia Minor. Paul sent this letter to churches in the province of Galatia, an area that included the towns of Antioch, Iconium, Lystra, and Derbe.

Date The question of the date of Galatians hinges mainly on the correlation of 2:1–10 with Paul's visits to Jerusalem recorded in Acts. Although chapter 2 may be identified with the famine visit of Acts 11:30, fewer difficulties are encountered by identifying it with the events of Acts 15. Paul probably wrote the letter about A.D. 55 or 56, when he was in Macedonia or Corinth on his third missionary journey.

Occasion and Purpose Legalists in the church, called Judaizers, taught that certain Old Testament laws were still binding upon Christians. They reasoned that God's promises extended only to Jews, and that Gentiles must be circumcised before they could fully experience salvation. The Judaizers did not deny that faith in Jesus was necessary, but insisted that it was inadequate. One must add to faith observance of the Law.

This doctrine was in direct contradiction to Paul's insistence that salvation was by grace through faith, so the Judaizers sought to discredit his teachings by challenging his authority. They charged that he was a secondhand apostle, inferior to Peter and James. Furthermore, they argued, he was a compromiser who made the gospel more attractive to Gentiles by removing its valid legal demands.

Paul vehemently reacted to the evil propaganda of the Judaizers by asserting his apostolic authority and explaining the gospel of grace through faith.

Content Galatians contains biographical, doctrinal, and practical divisions of two chapters each. In the first section (chs. 1 and 2), Paul defends his apostolic independence, not in a spirit of personal indignation, but to establish the divine origin of his gospel. In the doctrinal section (chs. 3 and 4), Paul presents a series of masterful arguments and illustrations to prove the inferiority of the Law to the gospel and to establish the true purpose of the Law. In the practical application of his doctrine (chs. 5 and 6), Paul exhorts the Galatians to use properly their Christian liberty and not to abuse it. Rather than giving license to sin, the gospel provides the enabling means to attain the righteousness that the Law demands.

Personal Application The same perversion of the gospel that Paul combats in this letter keeps appearing in various forms. Legalism, which teaches that justification or sanctification depends upon a person's own efforts, thus denying the sufficiency of the Cross, is the most persistent enemy of the gospel of grace. Circumcision and other requirements of the Mosaic Law may no longer be issues pertaining to salvation, but oftentimes the observance of certain rules, regulations, or religious rites is made coordinate with faith in Christ as the condition of Christian maturity. Galatians clearly declares the perils of legalism and establishes the essential truth of salvation by faith alone. This epistle was the battle cry of the Protestant Reformation and is the *Magna Charta* of spiritual liberty for all time.

Christ Revealed Paul teaches that Jesus places those who have faith in Him (2:16; 3:26) in a position of liberty (2:4; 5:1), freeing them from bondage to legalism and to license. The apostle's main emphasis is on the crucifixion of Christ as the basis for the believer's deliverance from the curse of sin (1:4; 6:14), self (2:20; see 5:24), and Law (3:12; 4:5). Paul also describes a dynamic faith-union with Christ (2:20), visibly portrayed in baptism (3:27), which relates all believers to each other as brothers and sisters (3:28). Concerning the Person of Christ, Paul declares both His deity (1:1, 3, 16) and His humanity (3:16; 4:4). Jesus is the substance of the gospel (1:7), which He Himself revealed to Paul (1:12).

The Holy Spirit at Work The Judaizers were as wrong about the means of sanctification as they were about the way of justification. A key passage is 3:2, 3, in which Paul asks the Galatians, who would readily admit that they had begun their Christian life by the Spirit, why they were seeking spiritual maturity by performing works of the Law. The intimation is that the same Spirit who regenerated them causes their new life to grow.

In 3:5 Paul asks a similar question concerning the Holy Spirit. The language he uses indicates an experience of the Spirit that extended beyond the Galatians' initial reception. The verb "supplies" suggests a continual supplying in bountiful measure, while "works" indicates that God was continuing to perform miracles in their midst through Spirit-filled believers who had not slipped into legalism. The word "miracles" refers to the charismatic manifestations of the Spirit evidenced by outward signs, such as those described in 1 Corinthians 12—14. The phrase "the promise of the Spirit" in 3:14 was also used by Peter to explain the outpouring of the Holy Spirit at Pentecost (Acts 2:33).

These verses teach that we receive the Spirit by faith and that the Spirit continues to manifest Himself in power as we walk in faith.

In 5:16–25 Paul graphically describes a fierce and constant

conflict between the flesh, our lower nature prone to sin, and the indwelling Spirit. Only the Holy Spirit, when we passively submit to His control and actively walk in Him, can enable us to die to the flesh (vv. 16, 17), deliver us from the tyranny of the Law (v. 18), and cause the fruit of holiness to grow in our lives (vv. 22, 23).

This section (5:16–25) is a part of Paul's exhortation concerning the proper use of Christian liberty. Apart from the controlling, sanctifying work of the Holy Spirit, liberty is certain to degenerate into license.

Outline of Galatians

I. Introduction **1:1–10**
- A. Salutation 1:1–5
- B. Defection of the Galatians 1:6, 7
- C. Denunciation of the Judaizers 1:8, 9
- D. Statement of Paul's integrity 1:10

II. Biographical: Paul defends his authority **1:11—2:21**
- A. Source of his authority 1:11–24
- B. Recognition of his authority 2:1–10
- C. Manifestation of his authority 2:11–21

III. Doctrinal: Paul defends his gospel **3:1—4:31**
- A. By argument 3:1—4:11
  - 1. Experience of the Galatians 3:1–5
  - 2. Teaching of the Old Testament 3:6–14
  - 3. Character of the covenant with Abraham 3:15–18
  - 4. Purpose of the Law 3:19–24
  - 5. Status of those in Christ 3:25—4:7
  - 6. Folly of reverting to legalism 4:8–11
- B. By appeal 4:12–20
  - 1. Based on their affection for Paul 4:12–18
  - 2. Based on Paul's affection for them 4:19, 20
- C. By allegory 4:21–31

IV. Practical: Paul exhorts the Galatians **5:1—6:10**
- A. To use properly their Christian liberty 5:1–15
- B. To walk by the Spirit 5:16–26
- C. To bear one another's burdens 6:1–10

V. Conclusion **6:11–18**
- A. Warning against the legalists 6:11–13
- B. Centrality of the Cross 6:14–16
- C. Marks of an apostle 6:17
- D. Benediction 6:18

Greeting

PAUL, an apostle (not from men nor
through man, but [a]through Jesus
Christ and God the Father [b]who raised
Him from the dead),
2 and all the brethren who are with
me,

To the churches of Galatia:

3 Grace to you and peace from
God the Father and our Lord Jesus
Christ,
4 [a]who *gave Himself for our sins,
that He might deliver us [b]from this
present evil *age, according to the will
of our God and Father,
5 to whom *be* glory forever and ever.
Amen.

Only One Gospel

6 I marvel that you are turning away 2
so soon [a]from Him who **called** you in
the grace of Christ, to a different gospel,

CHAPTER 1
1 [a]Acts 9:6 [b]Acts 2:24
4 [a][Matt. 20:28] [b]Heb. 2:5 *See WW at Acts 20:35. • See WW at Matt. 28:20.
6 [a][Rom. 8:28]; Gal. 1:15; 5:8

1:1 Paul's apostolic authority was not **from** any human source or **through** any human agency. **God** commissioned him through the risen Lord.

1:4 Paul summarizes the epistle by declaring the fact, the purpose, and the ground of redemption in Christ. Scripture divides history into two ages: **This present evil age,** dominated by Satan (2 Cor. 4:4), and "the age to come" (Matt. 12:32; Mark 10:30; Eph. 1:21), inaugurated by Jesus. Since the present age has not yet passed away, the two ages are currently running on parallel courses. Jesus came to rescue us from the dominion of the old age and to transfer us into life in the Age to Come.

1:6–9 See section 2 of Truth-In-Action at the end of Gal.

1:6, 7 In contrast to his usual practice of expressing thanksgiving for his readers, Paul immediately plunges into his argument. The news of the Galatians is not of progress

WORD WEALTH

1:6 called, *kaleo* (kal-*eh*-oh); Strong's *#2564:* From the root *kal,* the source of the English words "call" and "clamor." The word is used to invite or to summon, and is especially used of God's call to participate in the blessings of the kingdom (Rom. 8:30; 9:24, 25).

7 [a]which is not *another; but there are some [b]who *trouble you and want to [c]pervert[1] the *gospel of Christ.
8 But even if [a]we, or an angel from heaven, preach any other gospel to you than what we have preached to you, let him be [1]accursed.*
9 As we have said before, so now I say again, if anyone preaches any other gospel to you [a]than what you have received, let him be *accursed.
10 For [a]do I now [b]persuade men, or God? Or [c]do I seek to please men? For if I still pleased men, I would not be a bondservant of Christ.

Call to Apostleship

11 [a]But I make known to you, brethren, that the gospel which was preached by me is not according to man.
12 For [a]I neither received it from man, nor was I taught *it,* but *it came* [b]through the revelation of Jesus Christ.
13 For you have heard of my former conduct in Judaism, how [a]I persecuted

7 [a]2 Cor. 11:4 [b]Acts 15:1; Gal. 5:10, 12 [c]2 Cor. 2:17 [1]*distort* *See WW at John 14:16. • See WW at Luke 24:38. • See WW at Mark 1:1.
8 [a]1 Cor. 16:22 [1]Gr. *anathema* *See WW at 1 Cor. 12:3.
9 [a]Deut. 4:2 *See WW at 1 Cor. 12:3.
10 [a][1 Cor. 10:33]; 1 Thess. 2:4 [b]1 Sam. 24:7 [c]1 Thess. 2:4
11 [a][Rom. 2:16]; 1 Cor. 15:1
12 [a]1 Cor. 15:1 [b][Eph. 3:3–5]
13 [a]Acts 9:1

but of retrogression. They are deserting Christ for **a different** [Greek, *heteron,* "another of a different kind"] **gospel, which is not another** [Greek, *allo,* "another of the same kind"]. There is only one gospel, and what the Judaizers preached was a perversion of it.
1:8, 9 The first **if** clause in Greek is a supposition. Paul is not preaching anything contrary to what he previously preached. The second **if** clause describes a present concrete situation—some were actually perverting the gospel. Paul's zeal for the gospel is such that he desires God's judgment (**accursed**) to fall upon himself if he should ever distort it. His pronouncement of judgment is not a harsh, personal reaction toward rival teachers. Rather, he is speaking with apostolic authority, realizing that the glory of the redemptive work of Christ and the destiny of souls are at stake.
1:10 Paul denies the insinuation of the false teachers that he is a compromiser seeking favor by teaching people what they want to hear.
1:11, 12 Paul's gospel came neither from tradition nor instruction, but from God through the agency of Christ.
1:13–24 Paul proves the divine origin of his gospel by relating facts pertaining to his preconversion conduct (vv. 13, 14), his conversion (vv. 15, 16), and his postconversion activities (vv. 17–24).
1:13–16 Only divine intervention could suddenly change

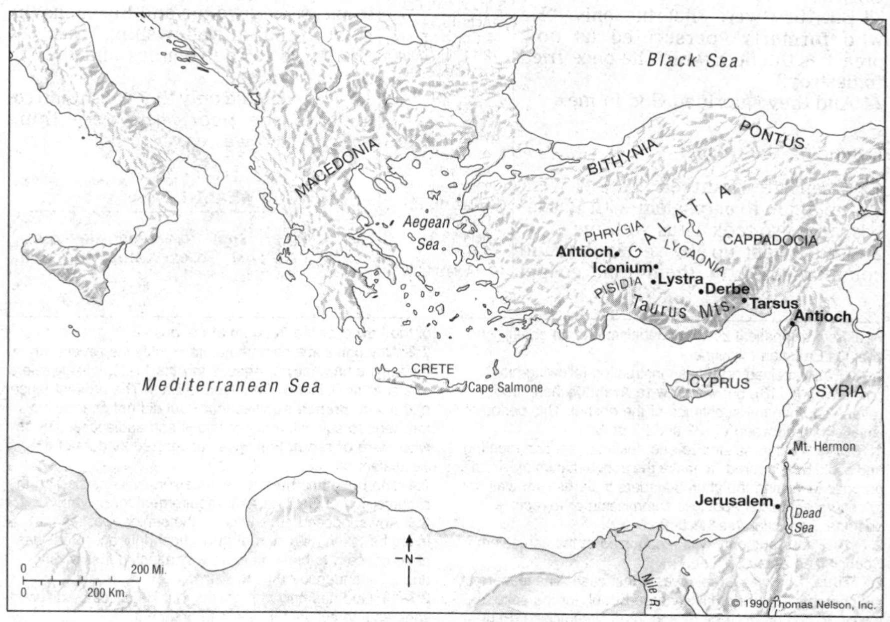

The Churches of Galatia

the *church of God *beyond measure and [b]*tried to* destroy it.
14 And I advanced in Judaism beyond many of my contemporaries in my own nation, [a]being *more exceedingly *zealous [b]for the traditions of my fathers.
15 But when it pleased God, [a]who separated me from my mother's womb and called *me* through His grace,
16 [a]to reveal His Son in me, that [b]I might preach Him among the Gentiles, I did not *immediately confer with [c]flesh and blood,
17 nor did I go up to Jerusalem to those *who were* *apostles before me; but I went to Arabia, and returned again to Damascus.

Contacts at Jerusalem

18 Then after three years [a]I went up to Jerusalem to see [1]Peter, and remained with him fifteen days.
19 But [a]I saw none of the other apostles except [b]James, the Lord's brother.
20 (Now *concerning* the things which I write to you, indeed, before God, I do not lie.)
21 [a]Afterward I went into the regions of Syria and Cilicia.
22 And I was unknown by face to the churches of Judea which [a]*were* in Christ.
23 But they were [a]hearing only, "He who formerly [b]persecuted us now preaches the faith which he once *tried to* destroy."
24 And they [a]glorified God in me.

Defending the Gospel

2 Then after fourteen years [a]I went up again to Jerusalem with Barnabas, and also took Titus with *me.*
2 And I went up [1]by revelation, and communicated to them that gospel which I preach among the Gentiles, but [a]privately to those who were of reputation, lest by any means [b]I might run, or had run, in vain.
3 Yet not even Titus who *was* with me, being a Greek, was compelled to be circumcised.
4 And *this occurred* because of [a]false brethren secretly brought in (who came in by stealth to spy out our [b]liberty* which we have in Christ Jesus, [c]that they might bring us into bondage),
5 to whom we did not yield submission even for an hour, that [a]the truth of the gospel might continue with you.
6 But from those [a]who seemed to be something—whatever they were, it makes no difference to me; [b]God [1]shows personal favoritism to no man—for those who seemed *to be something* [c]added nothing to me.
7 But on the contrary, [a]when they saw that the gospel for the uncircumcised [b]had been committed to me, as *the gospel* for the circumcised *was* to Peter
8 (for He who worked effectively in Peter for the apostleship to the [a]circumcised [b]also [c]worked effectively in me toward the Gentiles),
9 and when James, [1]Cephas, and John, who seemed to be [a]pillars, perceived [b]the grace that had been given to me, they gave me and Barnabas the right hand of fellowship, [c]that we *should go* to the Gentiles and they to the circumcised.
10 *They desired* only that we should remember the poor, [a]the very thing which I also was **eager** to do.

13 [b]Acts 8:3; 22:4, 5 *See WW at Acts 8:1 • See WW at 2 Cor. 4:7.
14 [a]Acts 26:9 [b]Jer. 9:14 *See WW at 2 Cor. 2:4. • See WW at Acts 22:3.
15 [a]Is. 49:1, 5
16 [a][2 Cor. 4:5–7] [b]Acts 9:15 [c]Matt. 16:17 *See WW at John 6:21.
17 *See WW at 1 Cor. 12:28.
18 [a]Acts 9:26 [1]NU *Cephas*
19 [a]1 Cor. 9:5 [b]Matt. 13:55
21 [a]Acts 9:30
22 [a]Rom. 16:7
23 [a]Acts 9:20, 21 [b]Acts 8:3
24 [a]Acts 11:18

CHAPTER 2

1 [a]Acts 15:2
2 [a]Acts 15:1–4 [b]Phil. 2:16 [1]*because of*
4 [a]Acts 15:1, 24 [b]Gal. 3:25; 5:1, 13 [c]Gal. 4:3, 9 *See WW at 1 Cor. 10:29.
5 [a][Gal. 1:6; 2:14; 3:1]
6 [a]Gal. 2:9; 6:3 [b]Acts 10:34 [c]2 Cor. 11:5; 12:11 [1]Lit. *does not receive the face of a man*
7 [a]Acts 9:15; 13:46; 22:21 [b]1 Thess. 2:4
8 [a]1 Pet. 1:1 [b]Acts 9:15 [c][Gal. 3:5]
9 [a]Matt. 16:18 [b]Rom. 1:5 [c]Acts 13:3 [1]Peter
10 [a]Acts 11:30

WORD WEALTH

2:10 eager, *spoudazo* (spoo-*dad*-zoe); Strong's *#4704:* To exert oneself, make

---

Paul from a fanatical zealot of Judaism into an equally zealous Christian missionary.
1:17 Paul received no human instruction following his conversion (v. 16), but withdrew **to Arabia,** where God revealed to him the substance of the gospel. This period of isolation fits between vv. 22 and 23 of Acts 9.
1:18 The word translated **to see** designates a first meeting, and could be rendered "to make the acquaintance of." Paul's purpose in visiting the church leaders in Jerusalem was not to secure an official apostolic commission or to receive doctrinal instruction (see Acts 9:26–30).
2:1–10 Paul's authority was recognized at the Jerusalem Council (see Acts 15:1–29).
2:1 Titus, who was Greek, was a test case. The leaders of the church at Jerusalem likely urged Paul, for the sake of peace, to compromise by having Titus circumcised. Paul refused, for to yield would have been to accept the bondage of the Law over the freedom of the gospel.
2:2 Although some commentators identify the **revelation** as the famine prophecy of Agabus in Acts 11:28, it likely refers to a specific guidance from God to Paul. The present tense of the verb **preach** signifies that Paul did not change his message to suit different occasions and audiences. **Those who were of reputation** were recognized leaders of the Jerusalem church.
2:4 The **false brethren** were Judaizers who insisted on the circumcision of Gentiles as a requirement for salvation.
2:6 Any supposed advantage of the senior apostles that might be taken as a sign of their superiority over Paul was of no concern to him and in no way affected the validity and independence of his ministry.
2:7–10 God has only one gospel, but He allocates different spheres and cultures in which to preach it.

every effort, give diligence, make haste, be zealous, strain every nerve, and further the cause assiduously. *Spoudazo* combines thinking and acting, planning and producing. It sees a need and promptly does something about it. The word covers inception, action, and follow-through.

No Return to the Law

11 [a]Now when [1]Peter had come to Antioch, I [2]withstood* him to his face, because he was to be blamed;
12 for before certain men came from
James, [a]he would eat with the Gentiles;
but when they came, he withdrew and
separated himself, fearing [1]those who
were of the circumcision.
13 And the rest of the Jews also played
the hypocrite with him, so that even
Barnabas was carried away with their
hypocrisy.

WORD WEALTH

2:13 hypocrisy, *hupokrisis* (*hoop*-ok-ree-sis); Strong's *#5272:* Literally "a reply." The word came to denote a theatrical performance by one who spoke in dialogue. Then it was used of playacting, role-playing, pretending; hence, acting insincerely, hypocrisy.

14 But when I saw that they were not
straightforward about [a]the truth of the
gospel, I said to Peter [b]before *them* all,
[c]"If you, being a Jew, live in the manner of Gentiles and not as the Jews,
[1]why do you compel Gentiles to live
as [2]Jews?

11 [a]Acts 15:35 [1]NU *Cephas* [2]*opposed* *See WW at Eph. 6:13.
12 [a][Acts 10:28; 11:2, 3] [1]Jewish Christians
14 [a]Gal. 1:6; 2:5 [b]1 Tim. 5:20 [c][Acts 10:28] [1]NU *how can you* [2]Some interpreters stop the quotation here.
15 [a][Acts 15:10] [b]Matt. 9:11
16 [a]Acts 13:38, 39 [b]Rom. 1:17 [c]Ps. 143:2 [1]*declared righteous* *See WW at Matt. 12:37. • See WW at John 9:4.
17 [a][1 John 3:8]
19 [a]Rom. 8:2 [b][Rom. 6:2, 14; 7:4] [c][Rom. 6:11]
20 [a][Rom. 6:6] [b]2 Cor. 5:15 [c]Eph. 5:2 *See WW at Matt. 26:41. • See WW at John 3:16.
21 [a]Heb. 7:11 [1]*for nothing*

CHAPTER 3

1 [1]NU omits *that you should not obey the truth* [2]NU omits *among you*
2 [a]Rom. 10:16, 17
3 [a][Gal. 4:9]

15 [a]"We *who are* Jews by nature, and
not [b]sinners of the Gentiles,
16 [a]"knowing that a man is not 2
[1]justified* by the *works of the law but
[b]by faith in Jesus Christ, even we have
believed in Christ Jesus, that we might
be justified by faith in Christ and not
[c]by the works of the law; for by the
works of the law no flesh shall be justified.
17 "But if, while we seek to be justified by Christ, we ourselves also are
found [a]sinners, *is* Christ therefore a
minister of sin? Certainly not!
18 "For if I build again those things
which I destroyed, I make myself a
transgressor.
19 "For I [a]through the law [b]died to the 2
law that I might [c]live to God.
20 "I have been [a]crucified with Christ;
it is no longer I who live, but Christ
lives in me; and the *life* which I now
live in the *flesh [b]I live by faith in the
Son of God, [c]who *loved me and gave
Himself for me.
21 "I do not set aside the grace of God;
for [a]if righteousness *comes* through
the law, then Christ died [1]in vain."

Justification by Faith

3 O foolish Galatians! Who has be- 2
witched you [1]that you should not
obey the truth, before whose eyes
Jesus Christ was clearly portrayed
[2]among you as crucified?
2 This only I want to learn from you:
Did you receive the Spirit by the works
of the law, [a]or by the hearing of faith?
3 Are you so foolish? [a]Having begun

2:11–21 Paul's apostolic authority was evident in an ugly clash with Peter. His purpose in relating this incident is to state the very **truth of the gospel** (v. 14).
2:11 Antioch of Syria was the third largest city in the Roman Empire and was the missionary center of the early church (see Acts 11:19–26; 13:1–3).
2:12 Peter's action was not from theological conviction, but from cowardice.
2:13 The rest of the Jews were Jewish Christians, such as **Barnabas,** in the church at Antioch who were not associated with the legalists.
2:14 Paul charges Peter, who no longer observed Jewish food regulations (v. 12), with flagrant inconsistency in separating himself from Gentiles.
2:15 In referring to Gentiles as **sinners,** Paul does not question their moral qualities, but speaks of their nonobservance of the Law.
2:16 See section 2 of Truth-In-Action at the end of Gal.
2:16 Paul and Peter agree that there is no distinction between Jews and Gentiles in the way of salvation.
2:17, 18 Christ does not promote **sin** in releasing us from bondage to a legalistic system. On the contrary, the **transgressor** is one who reverts from Christ to legalism. Paul emphasizes the way of salvation through faith by a threefold statement that is general ("a man"), personal ("we"), and universal ("no flesh").
2:19–21 See section 2 of Truth-In-Action at the end of Gal.
2:19 Through the law Paul received a consciousness of sin, but the Law gave him no power to overcome sin. Therefore, he turned from the Law as a means of acceptance with God.
2:20 The believer, united by faith to Christ in His death, has died to the old life and has risen to a new life. See Rom. 6:1–10; 7:6.
2:21 If we can earn salvation by obedience to the Law, then the Cross is redundant.
3:1–11 See section 2 of Truth-In-Action at the end of Gal.
3:1–5 Paul begins the defense of his gospel by reminding the Galatians that their Christian life, which began with faith in Christ crucified and was certified by the gift of the Holy Spirit, was altogether apart from the Law. They would be foolish to abandon God's way and try to reach perfection by their own efforts.
3:1 The Judaizers are like evil sorcerers diverting their victims' eyes from the Cross to the Law. However, the Galatians are without excuse, because Paul had made clear to them the meaning of the Cross.

in the Spirit, are you now being made
perfect by [b]the flesh?
4 [a]Have you *suffered so [1]many
things in vain—if indeed *it was* in vain?
5 Therefore He who **supplies** the
Spirit to you and works miracles
among you, *does He do it* by the works
of the law, or by the hearing of faith?—

WORD WEALTH

3:5 supplies, *epichoregeo* (ep-ee-khor-ayg-*eh*-oh); Strong's *#2023:* A combination of *epi,* intensive, and *choregeo,* "to defray the expenses of a chorus." The word thus means to supply fully or abundantly, generously provide what is needed, to cover the costs completely. (Compare "chorus.") It is used with the strong connotation of great and free generosity. Paul is chiding the Galatians for regressing to the beggarly elements of legalism, which he contrasts with the abounding surplus of God's provision through grace.

6 just as Abraham [a]*"believed* God,*
*and it was *accounted to him for *righteousness."*
7 Therefore know that *only* [a]those
who are of faith are sons of Abraham.
8 And [a]the Scripture, foreseeing that
God would justify the Gentiles by faith,
preached the gospel to Abraham beforehand,
saying, [b]*"In you all the nations shall be blessed."*
9 So then those who *are* of faith are
blessed with believing Abraham.

The Law Brings a Curse

10 For as many as are of the works of
the law are under the curse; for it is
written, [a]*"Cursed is everyone who*
does not continue in all things which

3 [b]Heb. 7:16
4 [a]Heb. 10:35 [1]Or *great* *See WW at Acts 17:3.
6 [a]Gen. 15:6 *See WW at Rom. 10:9. • See WW at Rom. 4:3. • See WW at 2 Tim. 4:8.
7 [a]John 8:39
8 [a]Rom. 9:17 [b]Gen. 12:3; 18:18; 22:18; 26:4; 28:14
10 [a]Deut. 27:26
11 [a]Hab. 2:4; Rom. 1:17; Heb. 10:38 [1]*declared righteous* *See WW at Matt. 1:19.
12 [a]Rom. 4:4, 5 [b]Lev. 18:5; Rom. 10:5 *See WW at Mark 11:22.
13 [a][Rom. 8:3] [b]Deut. 21:23 *See WW at 2 Tim. 4:22.
14 [a][Rom. 4:1–5, 9, 16; Gal. 3:28] [b]Is. 42:1, 6; 49:6; Luke 2:32; Rom. 3:29, 30 [c]Is. 32:15 *See WW at Acts 13:32.
15 [a]Heb. 9:17
16 [a]Gen. 22:18 [b]Gen. 12:3, 7; 13:15; 24:7 [c][1 Cor. 12:12]
17 [a]Gen. 15:13; Ex. 12:40; Acts 7:6 [b][Rom. 4:13] [1]NU omits *in Christ*
18 [a][Rom. 8:17] [b]Rom. 4:14 *See WW at Col. 3:13.
19 [a]John 15:22

are written in the book of the law, to
do them."
11 But that no one is [1]justified by the
law in the sight of God *is* evident, for
[a]*"the *just shall live by faith."*
12 Yet [a]the law is not of *faith, but
[b]*"the man who does them shall live by*
them."
13 [a]Christ* has redeemed us from the
curse of the law, having become a
curse for us (for it is written, [b]*"Cursed*
is everyone who hangs on a tree"),
14 [a]that the blessing of Abraham 3
might come upon the [b]Gentiles in
Christ Jesus, that we might receive
[c]the *promise of the Spirit through
faith.

The Changeless Promise

15 Brethren, I speak in the manner of
men: [a]Though *it is* only a man's covenant,
yet *if it is* confirmed, no one annuls
or adds to it.
16 Now to Abraham and his Seed were
the promises made. He does not say,
"And to seeds," as of many, but as of
[a]one, [b]*"And to your Seed,"* who is
[c]Christ.
17 And this I say, *that* the law, [a]which
was four hundred and thirty years
later, cannot annul the covenant that
was confirmed before by God [1]in
Christ, [b]that it should make the promise
of no effect.
18 For if [a]the inheritance *is* of the law,
[b]*it is* no longer of promise; but God
*gave *it* to Abraham by promise.

Purpose of the Law

19 What purpose then *does* the law
serve? [a]It was added because of trans-

3:6–9 The Jews regarded **Abraham** as their father and the source of their spiritual blessings. They believed that simple physical descent from Abraham made them righteous. Paul shows that Abraham pleased God by faith and not by doing works of the Law, since the Law did not exist in Abraham's time. He further insists that the true children of Abraham, and thus heirs of the promised blessing, are those who live by the principle of faith.

3:10–14 Paul presents the alternatives of **faith** (v. 11) and **law** (v. 12) as the means of justification. However, rather than justifying, the Law curses (v. 10) because it makes demands that no one can keep. Obedience must not only be absolute in every detail, but it must be continuous (v. 12). Through His death on the Cross, Christ *did for us* what we could not do for *ourselves. His* work, not ours, removed **the curse** upon us because of our disobedience of the Law (v. 13). By faith we receive the benefits provided by His death, including justification (v. 11) and **the promise of the Spirit** (v. 14; see Introduction to Galatians: The Holy Spirit at Work).

3:14 See section 3 of Truth-In-Action at the end of Gal.

3:15–18 In defending his gospel Paul describes the character of the covenant with Abraham, proving that the promise is fulfilled in Christ, not in the Law. **No one annuls** a human agreement (v. 15). How much more is this true of a divine agreement (v. 17). The basis of the covenant with Abraham was faith, and the Law, which came **four hundred and thirty years** after Abraham, cannot possibly set aside this earlier agreement.

3:16 Seed . . . seeds: The promise was not to all descendants of Abraham. It found its fulfillment in Christ, and thus in those who are united with Him.

3:19–24 Paul explains the true purpose of the Law in a fourfold assertion.

3:19, 20 First, the Law was intended to reveal sin, not to secure righteousness (see Rom. 4:15; 5:20). It was a temporary measure, introduced to convince people of their need of justification and of their inability to save themselves, thus leading them to Christ. Second, the Law is inferior to the promise, having come **through angels** and Moses (see

gressions, till the [b]Seed should come
to whom the *promise was made; *and
it was* [c]appointed through angels by
the hand [d]of a **mediator.**

WORD WEALTH

3:19 mediator, *mesites* (mes-ee-tace); Strong's *#3316:* From *mesos,* "middle," and *eimi,* "to go"; hence, a go-between, umpire, reconciler, arbitrator, intermediary. In this passage, the word refers to Moses' bringing the law to the people, along with angelic assistance. In its other occurrences, *mesites* speaks of Jesus' accomplishing salvation by His vicarious death (1 Tim. 2:5) and guaranteeing the terms of the new covenant (Heb. 8:6; 9:15; 12:24).

20 Now a *mediator does not *mediate*
for one *only,* [a]but God is one.
21 *Is* the law then against the promises
of God? Certainly not! For if there had
been a law given which could have
given life, truly righteousness would
have been by the law.
22 But the Scripture has confined
[a]all under sin, [b]that the promise by
faith in Jesus Christ might be given to
those who believe.
2 23 But before faith came, we were
*kept under guard by the law, [1]kept for
the faith which would afterward be revealed.
24 Therefore [a]the law was our [1]tutor
to bring us to Christ, [b]that we might
be justified by faith.
25 But after faith has come, we are no
longer under a tutor.

Sons and Heirs

26 For you [a]are all sons of God 1
through faith in Christ Jesus.
27 For [a]as many of you as were baptized into Christ [b]have put on Christ.
28 [a]There is neither Jew nor Greek,
[b]there is neither slave nor *free, there
is neither male nor female; for you are
all [c]one in Christ Jesus.
29 And [a]if you *are* Christ's, then you
are Abraham's [b]seed, and [c]heirs according to the promise.

4 Now I say *that* the heir, as long
as he is a child, does not differ at
all from a slave, though he is master
of all,
2 but is under guardians and *stewards until the time appointed by the father.
3 Even so we, when we were children,
[a]were in bondage under the elements
of the world.
4 But [a]when the *fullness of the time
had come, God sent forth His Son,
[b]born[1] [c]of a woman, [d]born under the
law,
5 [a]to redeem those who were under
the law, [b]that we might receive the
adoption as sons.
6 And because you are sons, God has

19 [b]Gal. 4:4 [c]Acts 7:53 [d]Ex. 20:19 *See WW at Acts 7:5.
20 [a][Rom. 3:29] *See WW at Gal. 3:19.
22 [a]Rom. 11:32 [b]Rom. 4:11
23 [1]Lit. *confined* *See WW at 1 Pet. 1:5.
24 [a]Rom. 10:4 [b]Acts 13:39 [1]In a household, the guardian responsible for the care and discipline of the children
26 [a]John 1:12
27 [a][Rom. 6:3] [b]Rom. 10:12; 13:14
28 [a]Col. 3:11 [b][1 Cor. 12:13] [c][Eph. 2:15, 16] *See WW at Rev. 6:15.
29 [a]Gen. 21:10 [b]Rom. 4:11 [c]Rom. 8:17

CHAPTER 4

2 *See WW at 1 Pet. 4:10.
3 [a]Col. 2:8, 20
4 [a][Gen. 49:10] [b][John 1:14] [c]Gen. 3:15 [d]Luke 2:21, 27 [1]Or *made* *See WW at Eph. 3:19.
5 [a][Matt. 20:28] [b][John 1:12]

Deut. 33:2; Ps. 68:17; Acts 7:53; Heb. 2:2) in contrast to the promise, which came direct from God to Abraham.
3:21, 22 Third, the Law is not contrary to the promise; rather, the two are complementary. The Law demanded righteousness but was powerless to provide it. Its function was to prepare for the gospel by making people conscious of their sin and their need of a Savior.
3:23–29 See section 2 of Truth-In-Action at the end of Gal.
3:23, 24 Fourth, the Law directed us to Christ. It restricted us as a jailer (v. 22) and as a disciplinarian (vv. 23, 24) until faith in Christ brought us into the freedom of full-grown sons who have received their rightful heritage.
3:25—4:7 Paul shows the new position of those in Christ, contrasting what we are **after faith has come** (v. 25) with what we were **before faith came** (v. 23). Under the Law we were in a state of bondage and immaturity, but under the gospel our status is that of **sons** (v. 26) and **heirs** (v. 29).
3:26–29 See section 1 of Truth-In-Action at the end of Gal.
3:28 In Christ distinctions of race, rank, and sex neither hinder fellowship nor grant special privileges.
3:29 Baptism itself does not secure our union with Christ; it portrays outwardly and visibly the union secured by faith inwardly.
4:1, 2 Under the Law we were like an heir during his minority, subject to **guardians** until he became of age.
4:3 Elements translates a Greek word, which originally referred to the triangle on a sundial for determining time by a shadow-line. From there it came to be applied to a going in order, advancing in steps or rows, elementary beginnings, and learning the letters of the alphabet. In NT usage, the word refers to the elementary principles of the OT (Heb. 5:12), the rudiments of both Jewish and Gentile religion (here and Col. 2:8, 20), and the material elements of the universe (2 Pet. 3:10, 12).

Paul's use of the same word in v. 9 ("the weak and beggarly elements"), along with its usage in Col. 2, lends further insight into "elements." He teaches that spirits of the animistic or demonic dimension (v. 8) find easy allegiance with the rituals and philosophies of human religion and tradition. Hence, **the elements of the world** are actually evil spirits that use the rituals of the Law (v. 10) to enslave and condemn.
4:4–7 In contrast to bondage to the Law, life in Christ is the freedom of sons and daughters.
4:4 The fullness of the time was God's appointed time for the coming of Christ, when world conditions favored His appearing. Paul stresses the deity of Jesus (**His Son**), His humanity (**born of a woman**), and His subjection to **the law.**
4:5 God's purpose in sending Christ was to rescue us from slavery (**redeem**) and to bring slaves into sonship (**adoption**).
4:6 God provides our sonship through Christ and assures us of it through **the Spirit. Abba** is an intimate Aramaic diminutive for **Father,** used by Jesus Himself in addressing God (see Rom. 8:15, 16).

sent forth [a]the *Spirit of His Son into
your hearts, crying out, [1]"Abba, Father!"
7 Therefore you are no longer a slave
but a son, [a]and if a son, then an heir
[1]of God [2]through Christ.

Fears for the Church

8 But then, indeed, [a]when you did not
know God, [b]you served those which by
nature are not gods.
9 But now [a]after you have known
God, or rather are known by God,
[b]how *is it that* you turn again to
[c]the weak and beggarly elements, to
which you desire again to be in bondage?
10 [a]You observe days and months and
seasons and years.
11 I am afraid for you, [a]lest I have labored for you in vain.
12 Brethren, I urge you to become like
me, for I *became* like you. [a]You *have
not injured me at all.
13 You know that [a]because of physical
infirmity I preached the gospel to you
at the first.
14 And my trial which was in my flesh
you did not despise or reject, but you
received me [a]as an [1]angel of God,
[b]*even* as Christ Jesus.
15 [1]What then was the blessing you *enjoyed?* For I *bear you witness that, if
*possible, you would have plucked out
your own eyes and given them to me.
16 Have I therefore become your enemy because I tell you the truth?
17 They [a]zealously* court you, *but* for
no good; yes, they want to exclude you,
that you may be zealous for them.
18 But it is *good to be *zealous in a
good thing always, and not only when
I am present with you.

6 [a][Acts 16:7; Rom. 5:5; 8:9, 15, 16; 2 Cor. 3:17] [1]Lit. in Aram., *Father* *See WW at Rom. 7:6.
7 [a][Rom. 8:16, 17] [1]NU *through God* [2]NU omits *through Christ*
8 [a]1 Cor. 1:21; Eph. 2:12; 1 Thess. 4:5; 2 Thess. 1:8 [b]Rom. 1:25
9 [a][1 Cor. 8:3] [b]Gal. 3:1–3; Col. 2:20 [c]Heb. 7:18
10 [a]Rom. 14:5; Col. 2:16
11 [a]1 Thess. 3:5
12 [a]2 Cor. 2:5 *See WW at Acts 25:10.
13 [a]1 Cor. 2:3
14 [a]Mal. 2:7 [b][Luke 10:16] [1]Or *messenger*
15 [1]NU *Where* *See WW at Acts 26:22. • See WW at Matt. 19:26.
17 [a]Rom. 10:2 *See WW at 1 Cor. 14:1.
18 *See WW at Matt. 13:48. • See WW at 1 Cor. 14:1.
19 [a]1 Cor. 4:15
22 [a]Gen. 16:15 [b]Gen. 21:2
23 [a]Rom. 9:7, 8; Gal. 4:29 [b]Gen. 16:15; 17:15–19; 18:10; 21:1; Gal. 4:28; Heb. 11:11
24 [a]Ex. 24:6–8; Deut. 33:2 [1]NU, M omit *the* *See WW at Mark 14:24.
26 [a][Is. 2:2]

19 [a]My little children, for whom I labor 1
in birth again until Christ is **formed** in
you,

WORD WEALTH

4:19 formed, *morphoo* (mor-*fah*-oh); Strong's *#3445:* To form. *Schema* and *morphoo* are in bold contradistinction. *Schema* (English "scheme") signifies external form or outer appearance. *Morphoo* and *morphe,* its related noun, refer to internal reality. Gal. 4:19 speaks of a change in character, becoming conformed to the character of Christ in actuality, not merely in semblance.

20 I would like to be present with you
now and to change my tone; for I have
doubts about you.

Two Covenants

21 Tell me, you who desire to be under
the law, do you not hear the law?
22 For it is written that Abraham had
two sons: [a]the one by a bondwoman,
[b]the other by a freewoman.
23 But he *who was* of the bondwoman
[a]was born according to the flesh,
[b]and he of the freewoman through
promise,
24 which things are symbolic. For
these are [1]the two *covenants: the one
from Mount [a]Sinai which gives birth
to bondage, which is Hagar—
25 for this Hagar is Mount Sinai in
Arabia, and corresponds to Jerusalem
which now is, and is in bondage with
her children—
26 but the [a]Jerusalem above is free,
which is the mother of us all.
27 For it is written:

4:8–11 Paul declares that going back into legalism would be no better than going back into pagan worship.
4:12–20 Paul appeals to the Galatians on the basis of their affection for him (vv. 12–18) and his love for them (vv. 19, 20).
4:12 Paul claimed no superiority as a Jew, but totally identified himself with Gentiles (see 1 Cor. 9:20–22). Now he wants them to identify with his Christian freedom.
4:13–15 Paul's sojourn in Galatia on his first missionary trip was the result of some unsightly **physical infirmity.** His disfigurement was so repulsive that the Galatians might have rejected his message because of his weakness and *unattractiveness. Instead, they paid* homage to him (see Acts 14:8–18). **Reject** (Greek, *ekptuo*) is literally "to spit out," which some commentators take to be a reference to the custom of spitting in the direction of an epileptic to avert the influence of the evil spirit supposedly residing in him. On that basis they suggest that Paul's ailment was epilepsy. Likely, however, the word carries a metaphorical sense of scorn. Others speculate that Paul suffered from some form of ophthalmia (see v. 15; 6:11), but the evidence is inconclusive.
4:17, 18 Paul exposes the insincere motives of the Judaizers.
4:19, 20 See section 1 of Truth-In-Action at the end of Gal.
4:19 Paul likens his anxiety over the Galatians to the travail of a mother at childbirth.
4:21–31 Paul defends his gospel by an allegorical application of the story of Isaac and Ishmael. Some critics accuse him of spiritualizing Bible history, but, rather than establishing doctrine, he is illustrating a point he has already proved. Paul's premise is that true descent from Abraham is spiritual, not physical. See 3:14; Matt. 3:9; John 8:31–44; Rom. 4:16. Abraham's real heir was the son of the **freewoman,** not the son of the slave girl (vv. 23–27). Isaac represents those who trust in Christ, and Ishmael represents those who are in bondage to the Law. Therefore, Christians are the true sons of God (vv. 28, 31).

[a]"*Rejoice, O barren,*
You who do not bear!
Break forth and shout,
You who are not in labor!
For the desolate has many more
children
Than she who has a husband."

28 Now [a]we, brethren, as Isaac *was,*
are [b]children of promise.
29 But, as [a]he who was born according
to the flesh then persecuted him *who*
was born according to the Spirit,
[b]even so *it is* now.
30 Nevertheless what does [a]the Scripture say? [b]"*Cast out the bondwoman*
and her son, for [c]*the son of the bond-*
woman shall not be heir with the son
of the freewoman."
31 So then, brethren, we are not children of the bondwoman but of the free.

Christian Liberty

1 **5** [a]Stand[1] fast therefore in the *liberty by which Christ has *made us
free, and do not be entangled again
with a [b]yoke of bondage.
2 Indeed I, Paul, say to you that
[a]if you become circumcised, Christ will
profit you nothing.
3 And I testify again to every man
who becomes circumcised [a]that he is
[1]a *debtor to keep the whole law.
1 4 [a]You have become estranged from
Christ, you who *attempt to* be justified
by law; [b]you have fallen from grace.
5 For we through the Spirit eagerly
[a]wait for the hope of righteousness by
faith.
6 For [a]in Christ Jesus neither circumcision nor uncircumcision avails anything, but [b]faith *working through
love.

Love Fulfills the Law

7 You [a]ran well. Who hindered you
from obeying the truth?
8 This persuasion does not *come* from
Him who *calls you.
9 [a]A little leaven leavens the whole
lump.
10 I *have confidence in you, in the
Lord, that you will have no other mind;
but he who *troubles you shall bear his
judgment, whoever he is.
11 And I, brethren, if I still preach circumcision, [a]why do I still suffer persecution? Then [b]the offense of the cross
has ceased.
12 [a]I could wish that those [b]who trouble you would even [1]cut themselves
off!
13 For you, brethren, have been called 4
to *liberty; only [a]do not *use* liberty as
an [b]opportunity for the flesh, but
[c]through *love serve one another.
14 For [a]all the law is fulfilled in one
*word, *even* in this: [b]"*You shall love*
your neighbor as yourself."
15 But if you bite and devour one another, beware lest you be consumed by
one another!

Walking in the Spirit

16 I say then: [a]Walk in the Spirit, and 3
you shall not fulfill the *lust of the
flesh.
17 For [a]the flesh *lusts against the

27 [a]Is. 54:1 28 [a]Gal. 3:29 [b]Acts 3:25 29 [a]Gen. 21:9 [b]Gal. 5:11 30 [a][Gal. 3:8, 22] [b]Gen. 21:10, 12 [c][John 8:35]

CHAPTER 5

1 [a]Phil. 4:1 [b]Acts 15:10 [1]NU *For freedom Christ has made us free; stand fast therefore, and* *See WW at 1 Cor. 10:29. See WW at Rom. 8:2. 2 [a]Acts 15:1 3 [a][Rom. 2:25] [1]*obligated* *See WW at Luke 13:4. 4 [a][Rom. 9:31] [b]Heb. 12:15 5 [a]Rom. 8:24 6 [a][Gal. 6:15] [b]1 Thess. 1:3 *See WW at 1 Thess. 2:13. 7 [a]1 Cor. 9:24 8 *See WW at Gal. 1:6. 9 [a]1 Cor. 5:6 10 *See WW at 2 Thess. 3:4. • See WW at Luke 24:38. 11 [a]1 Cor. 15:30 [b][1 Cor. 1:23] 12 [a]Josh. 7:25 [b]Acts 15:1, 2 [1]*mutilate themselves* 13 [a]1 Cor. 8:9 [b]1 Pet. 2:16 [c]1 Cor. 9:19 *See WW at 1 Cor. 10:29, See WW at Rom. 5:5.

14 [a]Matt. 7:12; 22:40 [b]Lev. 19:18 *See WW at Acts 19:20. 16 [a]Rom. 6:12 *See WW at 2 Tim. 2:22. 17 [a]Rom. 7:18, 22, 23; 8:5 *See WW at Matt. 13:17.

4:29 The historical reference is to Gen. 21:9. True believers must expect persecution.
5:1–15 Paul begins his presentation of the practical issues of the gospel by exhorting the Galatians to use properly their Christian liberty. They are to **stand fast** in it (vv. 1–12) and to guard against lawlessness (vv. 13–15).
5:1–3 See section 1 of Truth-In-Action at the end of Gal.
5:2–4 The Galatians must make a clear choice between law and grace. Those who opt for justification by the works of the Law **have fallen from grace,** because it is impossible to have it both ways. In other words, the effective operating power of God's grace becomes ineffective in the life of anyone who trusts in his own efforts for salvation.
5:4–6 See section 1 of Truth-In-Action at the end of Gal.
5:5, 6 True believers look forward **through the Spirit** to being accepted by God on the ground of faith, not law. The reference is to the end of the age, when God pronounces the final verdict of acquittal upon Christians, and they fully experience the blessings of eternity (see Rom. 8:23).
5:7–12 Paul severely condemns the false teachers who were hindering (v. 7), persuading (v. 8), and troubling (vv. 10, 12) the Galatians.
5:11 The Judaizers not only perverted the gospel, but they also accused Paul of inconsistency in his doctrine by his preaching **circumcision** to Jews and repudiating it among the Gentiles.
5:12 Paul shows his contempt for the Judaizers by mockingly suggesting that, since they prize circumcision so highly, they should emasculate themselves.
5:13–15 Christian freedom is not the removal of moral restraints, but the freedom to **serve one another.** The gospel exchanges the oppressive bondage of legalism for the higher bondage of **love.**
5:13 See section 4 of Truth-In-Action at the end of Gal.
5:16–26 See section 3 of Truth-In-Action at the end of Gal.
5:16 Liberty can degenerate into license, but the Holy Spirit enables us to subdue **the lust of the flesh** when we continuously submit ourselves to His power and control.
5:17 **The Spirit** and **the flesh** are diametrically opposed to one another, as evidenced by their "works" and "fruit" (vv. 19–22). The result is a fierce and unrelenting conflict within Christians in which they cannot be victorious by their own strength. See Rom. 7:15–23.

Spirit, and the Spirit against the flesh;
and these are contrary to one another,
[b]so that you do not do the things that
you wish.
18 But [a]if you are led by the Spirit, you
are not under the law.
19 Now [a]the works of the flesh are *evident, which are: [1]adultery,* [2]fornica-
tion, uncleanness, *lewdness,
20 idolatry, *sorcery, hatred, contentions, *jealousies, outbursts of *wrath,
*selfish ambitions, dissensions, *here-
sies,
21 envy, [1]murders, drunkenness, revelries, and the like; of which I tell you
beforehand, just as I also told *you* in
time past, that [a]those who practice
such things will not inherit the kingdom of God.
22 But [a]the fruit of the Spirit is [b]love,
joy, *peace, *longsuffering, **kindness,**
[c]goodness,* [d]faithfulness,
23 [1]gentleness,* self-control. [a]Against
such there is no law.

WORD WEALTH

5:22 kindness, *chrestotes* (khray-*stot*-ace); Strong's *#5544:* Goodness in action, sweetness of disposition, gentleness in dealing with others, benevolence, kindness, affability. The word describes the ability to act for the welfare of those taxing your patience. The Holy Spirit removes abrasive qualities from the character of one under His control.

KINGDOM DYNAMICS

5:22, 23 A Call to Character, SPIRITUAL GIFTS. Being filled with the Spirit calls us as much to character as it does to charismatic activity. The Holy Spirit's fruit is to be grown in our lives every bit as much as His gifts may be shown through us. An elaboration of this and related themes appears in the study article on page 2018, "Holy Spirit Gifts and Power."

(1 Cor. 14:27/Jude 20) P.W.

24 And those *who are* Christ's [a]have
crucified the flesh with its passions and
desires.
25 [a]If we live in the Spirit, let us also
walk in the Spirit.
26 [a]Let us not become conceited, provoking one another, envying one another.

Bear and Share the Burdens

6 Brethren, if a man is [1]overtaken in 4
any trespass, you who *are* spiritual
*restore such a one in a spirit of
[a]gentleness,* considering yourself lest
you also be *tempted.
2 [a]Bear one another's burdens, and so
fulfill [b]the law of Christ.
3 For [a]if anyone thinks himself to be 5
something, when [b]he is nothing, he deceives himself.
4 But [a]let each one examine his own
work, and then he will have rejoicing
in himself alone, and [b]not in another.
5 For [a]each one shall bear his own
load.

Be Generous and Do Good

6 [a]Let him who is taught the word
share in all good things with him who
teaches.
7 Do not be deceived, God is not 1

17 [b]Rom. 7:15
18 [a][Rom. 6:14; 7:4; 8:14]
19 [a]Eph. 5:3, 11 [1]NU omits *adultery* [2]*sexual immorality* *See WW at 1 Cor. 11:19. • See WW at John 8:3. • See WW at 1 Pet. 4:3.
20 *See WW at Rev. 9:21. • See WW at 2 Cor. 11:2. • See WW at Luke 4:28. • See WW at Phil. 1:16. • See WW at 2 Pet. 2:1.
21 [a]1 Cor. 6:9, 10 [1]NU omits *murders*
22 [a][John 15:2] [b][Col. 3:12–15] [c]Rom. 15:14 [d]1 Cor. 13:7 *See WW at Luke 1:79. • See WW at Heb. 6:12. • See WW at Rom. 15:14.
23 [a]1 Tim. 1:9 [1]*meekness* *See WW at 1 Tim. 6:11.
24 [a]Rom. 6:6
25 [a][Rom. 8:4, 5]
26 [a]Phil. 2:3

CHAPTER 6

1 [a]Eph. 4:2 [1]*caught* *See WW at Heb. 11:3. • See WW at 1 Tim. 6:11. • See WW at Rev. 2:10.
2 [a]Rom. 15:1 [b][James 2:8]
3 [a]Rom. 12:3 [b][2 Cor. 3:5]
4 [a]1 Cor. 11:28 [b]Luke 18:11
5 [a][Rom. 2:6]
6 [a]1 Cor. 9:11, 14

5:18 The person who is **led by the Spirit** will do what is right freely, and not by the compulsion of **the law.** Thus, he is not under the Law's bondage and condemnation.
5:19–21 The works of the flesh may be categorized as sexual sins (v. 19), sins connected with pagan religion (the first two of v. 20), sins of temper (the next nine), and sins of drunkenness (the last two).
5:22, 23 These virtues are characterized as **fruit** in contrast to "works." Only the Holy Spirit can produce them, and not our own efforts. Another contrast is that, whereas the works of the flesh are plural, the fruit of the Spirit is one and indivisible. When the Spirit fully controls the life of a believer, He produces *all* of these graces. The first three concern our attitude toward God, the second triad deals with social relationships, and the third *group* describes principles that *guide* a Christian's conduct.
5:24 Paul describes repentance metaphorically as a crucifixion of the old life of sin, turning from it fully and finally. The tense of the verb indicates a decisive act, which we performed at our conversion.
5:25 The Greek word for **walk** here is literally "walk in line with." It is not the same as "walk" in v. 16, whose Greek form is the word usually used for physical walking. To **walk in the Spirit** is to walk along the path that He lays down.
6:1, 2 See section 4 of Truth-In-Action at the end of Gal.
6:1 The Greek word for **restore** (*katartizo*) was used in secular Greek for setting broken bones, and in Matt. 4:21 for "mending" nets. **Considering yourself:** See 1 Cor. 10:12.
6:2 The law of Christ is to love one another as He loves us. See 5:14; John 13:34; 15:12.
6:3–5 See section 5 of Truth-In-Action at the end of Gal.
6:3–5 Self-conceit leads to pride in one's own accomplishments when compared to those of someone else. Such comparisons are out of order, since each person will be accountable on Judgment Day for his own actions. No one can boast when he measures himself and his work against the standard of God's requirements.
6:6–10 Paul applies the general principle of sowing and reaping to the support of Christian teachers (v. 6), to moral behavior (v. 8), and to Christian service (vv. 9, 10).
6:7–9 See section 1 of Truth-In-Action at the end of Gal.

mocked; for [a]whatever a man sows,
that he will also reap.
8 For he who sows to his flesh will
of the flesh reap corruption, but he who
sows to the Spirit will of the Spirit reap
[a]everlasting* life.
2 9 And [a]let us not grow weary while
doing good, for in due *season we shall
reap [b]if we do not lose heart.

KINGDOM DYNAMICS

6:7–9 God Has a Due Season for All of the Seeds You Plant—Good Seeds As Well As Bad Seeds, SEED FAITH. God has a timetable for every seed we plant. His timetable is not always our timetable. Sometimes the "due season" means a quick return. Sometimes it means a process or a slow return that may take years—even a lifetime. But we can count on three things. First, God will cause a harvest to come from our seeds. Second, God is never early or late—He is always right on time with our best interests at heart. Third, our harvest will have the same nature as our seeds sown: good seeds bring good harvests, bad seeds bring bad harvests.

What are we to do during the growing time of our seeds? 1) Refuse to become discouraged. 2) Determine to keep our faith alive and active. 3) Give and keep on giving; love and keep on loving. Know this—His harvest is guaranteed. Continue in an attitude of expectancy.

(Luke 6:38/Mal. 3:10, 11) O.R.

KINGDOM DYNAMICS

6:7, 8 The Seedtime of Our Lifetime, WORLD EVANGELISM. The law of sowing and reaping is at the heart of world evangelism. In John 4, Jesus declares a divine Now to the time for our laboring for the harvest of souls (see John 4:35–38). Here, we are reminded that our lifetime is our "seedtime," and our life's harvest will yield multiplied times the fruit of the seed sown—if we sow wisely. This truth calls us to cast off reserve and to give God the finest "soil" of our lives in which He may beget a rich harvest. Hos. 8:7 presents the same principle, contrasting the power of "sowing" for evil rather than for God. The truth is amplified by this comparison. If sowing to evil (the flesh) may reap a whirlwind, how much more may righteous sowing (to the Spirit) make room for God's almightiness! He came as a rushing, mighty wind at Pentecost. Might He not work in holy hurricane power if He can find us sowing to the Spirit? A God-possessed life guarantees partnership with God in worldwide increase.

(2 Cor. 10:15, 16/Rev. 5:8–10) G.C.

10 [a]Therefore, as we have opportunity, 1
[b]let* us do good to all, [c]especially to
those who are of the household of faith.

Glory Only in the Cross

11 See with what large letters I have
written to you with my own hand!
12 As many as desire to make a good
showing in the flesh, these *would* compel you to be circumcised, [a]only that
they may not suffer persecution for the
cross of Christ.
13 For not even those who are circumcised keep the law, but they desire to
have you circumcised that they may
boast in your flesh.
14 But God forbid that I should boast
except in the [a]cross of our Lord Jesus
Christ, by [1]whom the world has been
crucified to me, and [b]I to the world.
15 For [a]in Christ Jesus neither circumcision nor uncircumcision avails anything, but a *new *creation.

Blessing and a Plea

16 And as many as walk according to
this rule, peace and *mercy *be* upon
them, and upon the Israel of God.
17 From now on let no one trouble me,
for I bear in my body the marks of the
Lord Jesus.
18 Brethren, the grace of our Lord
Jesus Christ *be* with your spirit. Amen.

7 [a][Rom. 2:6]
8 [a][Rom. 6:8] *See WW at Rev. 14:6.
9 [a]1 Cor. 15:58; 2 Cor. 4:1; 2 Thess. 3:13 [b][Matt. 24:13]; Heb. 12:3, 5; [James 5:7, 8] *See WW at Col. 4:5.
10 [a]Prov. 3:27; [John 9:4; 12:35] [b]Titus 3:8 [c]Rom. 12:13 *See WW at John 3:21.
12 [a]Gal. 5:11; Phil. 3:8
14 [a][1 Cor. 1:18] [b][Gal. 2:20]; Col. 2:20 [1]Or *which,* the cross
15 [a][Rom. 2:26, 28]; 1 Cor. 7:19; [Gal. 5:6] *See WW at 2 Cor. 5:17. • See WW at Col. 1:15.
16 *See WW at 2 Tim. 1:16.

6:9 See section 2 of Truth-In-Action at the end of Gal.
6:10 See section 1 of Truth-In-Action at the end of Gal.
6:11 Paul uses **large letters** to emphasize the importance of what he is about to write.
6:12, 13 The motives of the Judaizers were insincere and selfish.
6:15 What is of primary importance is not the status of a person's ritual observance, but whether or not he has been born again.
6:16 Paul does not mention two groups of Christians. The connective **and** is emphatic, and could be translated "even." All true believers in Christ are **the Israel of God** (see 3:29).
6:17 **The marks** on Paul were the scars of wounds inflicted on him by persecutors. See Acts 14:19; 2 Cor. 11:23–25.

TRUTH-IN-ACTION through GALATIANS *Letting the LIFE of the Holy Spirit Bring Faith's Works Alive in You!*		
Truth Galatians Teaches	Text	**Action** Galatians Invites
1 Guidelines for Growing in Godliness Godliness results from Jesus Christ living through you by the Holy Spirit. It is not achieved by observing some external code. Any attempt to achieve righteousness through a list of external dos and don'ts is fruitless. God calls us to love others and serve others just as Jesus did, by the power of the same Holy Spirit and in the same gracious freedom.	3:26–29 4:19, 20 5:1–3 5:4–6 6:7–9 6:10	**Think** as if you have put on the life of Jesus Christ like clothing. **Let Christ** live freely through you. **Concern yourself** with God's Word becoming incarnate in you. **Consider** yourself as being "under construction" with Christ's likeness the objective. **Walk** in the freedom that Christ purchased. **Do not submit** your soul to legalist rules regardless of how right arguments in their favor may seem. **Cherish** the grace of God. **Do not attempt** to earn what can only be received as a gift. **Love others freely** as an act of obedient faith. **Remember** the "law of sowing and reaping" applies to everyone. **Sow** only those things you desire to reap. God guarantees that harvest will come. **Do "good"** to others when you have opportunity. **Be especially responsive** to your brothers and sisters in Christ.
2 Key Lessons in Faith Faith accepts God's testimony in a trusting, childlike manner, and salvation as a free gift. The Law was given to lead us to Christ; thus any use of the Law as a means of earning our salvation is a distortion. By nature mankind presumes to seek salvation by works. It seems an offense to the flesh to believe we cannot. But God's Word says it is an offense to Him to believe we can.	1:6–9 2:16 2:19–21 3:1–11 3:23–29 6:9	**Do not** change, amend, distort, or add to the gospel. **Know** that severe judgment awaits those who do. **Understand** that justification through observing laws or codes is impossible. **Receive** God's gift of justification through faith. **Understand** that you died with Christ so that Christ can live through you. **Understand** that it is just as impossible to maintain your relationship with God through works as it was to earn it in the first place. **Understand** that God intended the Law to lead His people to Christ. **Continue walking** in faith ceaselessly. **Recognize** and **believe** in the certainty of victory for those who "endure to the end."
3 Guidelines for Growth in the Spirit The Holy Spirit is the key to living under God's grace. Only the indwelling Holy Spirit can fulfill the Law through us as the life of Christ and truly free us from the Law.	3:14 5:16–26	**Understand** that you receive "the promise of the Spirit" (Acts 2:38, 39) the same way you receive salvation through Christ. **Live** under the Holy Spirit's control. **Obey** every leading of the Holy Spirit. **Know** that this will defeat any fleshly or carnal inclination you may have. **Believe** that this will result in Jesus' life being reproduced in you.

Truth Galatians Teaches	Text	**Action** Galatians Invites
4 Steps to Dealing with Sin We must not allow our freedom from the Law to become an occasion for fleshly activity. Also, we are accountable for one another and need to keep watch for one another as well as for ourselves.	5:13 6:1, 2	**Be free** from the controlling influence of sin. **Do not use** the liberty you have in Christ to sin against your brother or sister in Christ. **Recognize** that the outcome of liberty should be loving service to others. **Do not allow** others to remain captive to sin. **Be ready** to do what is needed to restore the brother who is in sin. **Behave gently,** without haughtiness, **being aware** that you, too, can be tempted.
5 One Step in Developing Humility If we believe we are too spiritually mature to fall, we should beware! The Bible portrays the sins of past spiritual leaders as a warning to us to remain humble and open to correction. We each need to reassess our personal walk with God in honesty before Him. Each of us will be held responsible for our actions and attitudes.	6:3–5	**Be sober** in your self-assessment. **Employ only** Jesus' life and teachings as your standard for judgment, not the performance of others.

The Epistle of Paul the Apostle to the
EPHESIANS

Author: Paul
Date: A.D. 60, 61
Theme: The Glorious Church
Key Words: Glory, Body, Heavenly Places

Background Ephesus was a principal port on the west coast of Asia Minor, situated near present-day Izmir. It was one of the seven churches to whom Jesus addressed His letters in Revelation 2 and 3, a relevant fact for studying this epistle since it was originally circulated to approximately the same group of churches.

Although Paul had been to Ephesus earlier (Acts 18:21), he first came there to minister in the winter of A.D. 55. He ministered there for over two full years (Acts 19:8–10), developing so deep a relationship with the Ephesians that his farewell message to them is one of the Bible's most moving passages (Acts 20:17–38).

Occasion and Date While imprisoned in Rome, Paul wrote Ephesians, Philippians, Colossians, and Philemon. Confined and awaiting trial (3:1; 4:1; 6:20), the apostle writes this encyclical letter—one to be read by several congregations. Ephesians is probably the same letter referred to in Colossians 4:16 as being presently at Laodicea while being circulated.

It appears that after writing Colossians, Paul was deeply stirred by an expanding revelation about the church. Now seeing the church as Christ's body and as God's instrument to confound and overthrow evil powers, he writes an elaboration of these themes.

Purpose Ephesians unveils the "mystery" of the church as no other epistle. God's "secret" intention is revealed: 1) to form a body to express Christ's fullness on Earth (1:15–23); 2) to do this by uniting one people—both Jew and Gentile, among whom God Himself dwells (2:11—3:7); and 3) to equip, empower, and mature this people to the end that they extend Christ's victory over evil (3:10–20; 6:12–20).

Content The throbbing message of Ephesians is "to the praise of His [God's] glory" (1:6, 12, 14). The word "glory" occurs eight times and refers to the exceeding excellence of God's love, His wisdom, and His power. The magnificent goal is in Jesus' announced commitment to build a glorious, mature, and ministering church, "not having spot or wrinkle" (5:27).

Ephesians unfolds the process by which God is bringing the church to its destined purpose in Christ. Basic maturing steps are taken toward the church's appointed engagement in battle with dark powers: 1) before the church is called to *war,* she is taught to *walk;* and 2) before being called to *walk,* the church is taught where she *stands.*

The epistle divides into two sections: 1) the Believer's Position, chapters 1—3, and 2) the Believer's Practice, chapters 4—6. In chapter 1, the recurrent term "in Christ" sums up the Christian's position, as having been given "every spiritual blessing." Several of these blessings are enumerated: chosen, blameless (1:4), adopted, accepted (1:5, 6), forgiven, predestined, and sealed (1:7, 11, 13).

With sweeping strokes, this foundational series of statements moves to a bold, new assertion, declared in Paul's first of two prayers in this letter. He prays that each Christian may perceive God's grand purpose in raising Christ to triumph—that now the church may know Christ's victorious fullness as we resist evil and face life's trials (1:15—2:10). Chapter 2 describes how God's grace has formed a united people among whom He can dwell in His fullness and glory. Through this people His high purpose is to be unveiled. Grasping the message of Ephesians requires understanding two words from chapter 3—"dispensation" and "mystery" (vv. 2, 3). The apostle declared that God's "secret" in planning the church is hidden no longer (3:3, 4—*now* the "mystery" is *known*). He has designed the church to administer ("to dispense") Christ's fullness everywhere (3:2, 9), ministering as a living body, spreading over the Earth and penetrating "the heavenlies." God's "manifold wisdom" now demonstrates His glory in the church (3:10, 11), a manifestation that eventually will issue in the believer's strengthening (3:14–20), maturing (4:15), confrontation, and victory (6:10–20). However, the church cannot approach this without a practical understanding of how this present glory of God's grace and presence is to affect everyday living.

The great call to "walk worthy of the calling" introduces this letter's second section (chs. 4—6). Systematically, Paul presents the ethical and moral implications of Spirit-filled living (4:1—6:9). The maturing process of the believer's "equipping" (4:11–16) and the appeal to help each other forward ("speaking the truth in love") will bring growth in the disciplines essential to the triumphant spiritual warrior's life (6:10–20).

Personal Application In short, Ephesians discloses awesome blessings of grace ("accepted in the Beloved," 1:6) and awesome dimensions of spiritual authority over evil ("according to the power that works in us," 3:20). But this awaits the believer's first accepting the disciplines of unity (4:1–16), purity (4:17–31), forgiveness (4:32), and walking in the fullness of the Holy Spirit (5:1–21). With this, relationships at every point must be in order (5:22—6:9), the idea being firmly established that true spiritual power flows from true obedience to the divine order in relationships and personal conduct.

Christ Revealed Ephesians has been called "The Alps of the New Testament," "The Grand Canyon of Scripture," and "The Royal Capstone of the Epistles," not only because of its grand theme, but because of the majesty of Christ revealed here. Chapter 1: He is the Redeemer (1:7), the One in whom and by whom history will ultimately be consummated (1:10); and He is the Resurrected Lord who not only has risen over death and hell, but who reigns as King, pouring His life through His body, the church—the present expression of Himself on Earth (1:15–23). Chapter 2: He is the Peacemaker who has reconciled man to God and who makes possible reconciliation of man to man as well (2:11–18); and He is the Chief Cornerstone of the new temple consisting of His own people to be indwelt by God Himself (2:19–22). Chapter 3: He is the Treasure in whom life's unsearchable riches are found (3:8); and He is the Indweller of human hearts, securing us in the love of God (3:17–19). Chapter 4: Jesus is the Giver of ministry-gifts to His church (4:7–11); and He is the Victor who has broken hell's ability to keep humankind captive (4:8–10). Chapter 5: He is the Model Husband, unselfishly giving Himself to enhance His bride—His church (5:25–27, 32). Chapter 6: He is the Lord, Mighty in Battle, the resource of strength for His own as they arm for spiritual warfare (6:10).

The Holy Spirit at Work As with Christ, the Holy Spirit is revealed in widely varied ministry to and through the believer. In 1:13 He is the Sealer, authorizing the believer to represent Christ; in 1:17 and 3:5 He is the Revealer, enlightening the heart to perceive God's purpose; in 3:16 He is the Empowerer whom Christ gives to strengthen within; in 4:3, 4 He is the Spirit of Unity desiring to sustain the bond of peace in the body of Christ; in 4:30 He is the Spirit of holiness who may be grieved by insistence on carnal pursuits; in 5:18 He is the Fountain, from which all are to be continuously filled; in 6:17, 18 He is the Giver of the Word as a sword for battle and the heavenly Assistant given to aid us in prayer and intercession until victory is won.

Outline of Ephesians

Opening greeting **1:1, 2**

I. The believer's position in Christ **1:3–14**
- A. Blessings of full redemption 1:3–8
- B. Partnership in God's purpose 1:9–14

II. The apostle's prayer for insight **1:15–23**
- A. For hearts that see with hope 1:15–18
- B. For experience that shares Christ's victory 1:19–21
- C. The church: Christ's body 1:22, 23

III. The believer's past, present, and future **2:1–22**
- A. The past order of the living dead 2:1–3
- B. The new order of God's loving life 2:4–10
- C. The past separation and hopelessness 2:11, 12
- D. The new union and present peace 2:13–18
- E. The church: Christ's building 2:19–22

IV. The apostle's ministry and message **3:1–13**
- A. The stewardship Paul has been given 3:1–7
- B. The stewardship each believer is given 3:8–13

V. The apostle's prayer for power **3:14–21**
- A. For strength by the Holy Spirit 3:14–16
- B. For faith and love by Christ's indwelling 3:17–19
- C. The church and God's glory 3:20, 21

VI. The believer's call to responsibility **4:1–16**
- A. To pursue unity with diligence 4:1–6
- B. To accept grace and gifts humbly 4:7–11
- C. To grow in ministry as part of the body 4:12–16

VII. The believer's call to purity **4:17—5:14**
- A. To refuse worldly mindedness 4:17–19
- B. To put off the old and put on the new 4:20–32
- C. To progress in untainted love 5:1–7
- D. To shine as undimmed light bearers 5:8–14

VIII. The believer's call to Spirit-filled living **5:15—6:9**
- A. To pursue God's will and wisdom 5:15–17
- B. To maintain the fullness of the Holy Spirit through worship and humility 5:18–21

C. To conduct all relationships according to God's order 5:22—6:9

IX. The believer's call to spiritual warfare 6:10–20

A. The reality of the invisible conflict 6:10–12

B. Armor for the warrior 6:13–17

C. The action involved in warfare 6:18–20

Concluding remarks 6:21–24

Greeting

PAUL, an apostle of Jesus Christ by
the will of God,

To the saints who are in Ephesus,
and faithful in Christ Jesus:

2 Grace to you and peace from God
our Father and the Lord Jesus Christ.

Redemption in Christ

3 [a]Blessed *be* the God and Father of
our Lord Jesus Christ, who has blessed
us with every spiritual blessing in the
heavenly *places* in Christ,
4 just as [a]He chose us in Him [b]before
the foundation of the world, that we
should [c]be holy and without blame before Him in love,
5 [a]having predestined us to [b]adoption
as sons by Jesus Christ to Himself,
[c]according to the good pleasure of His
*will,
6 to the **praise** of the glory of His
*grace, [a]by which He [1]made us ac-
cepted in [b]the Beloved.

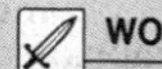

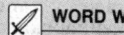

WORD WEALTH

1:6 praise, *epainos* (*ep*-ahee-noss); Strong's *#1868:* Approbation, commendation, approval, praise. *Epainos* expresses not only praise for what God does for us, but also for who He is, recognizing His glory.

7 [a]In Him we have *redemption
through His blood, the *forgiveness of
sins, according to [b]the riches of His
grace
8 which He made to *abound toward
us in all *wisdom and [1]prudence,
9 [a]having made known to us the
*mystery of His will, according to His
good pleasure [b]which He purposed in
Himself,
10 that in the dispensation of [a]the *fullness of the times [b]He might gather together in one [c]all things in Christ,
[1]both which are in heaven and which
are on earth—in Him.
11 [a]In Him also we have obtained an
inheritance, being predestined according to [b]the *purpose of Him who works
all things according to the counsel of
His will,
12 [a]that we [b]who first trusted in Christ
should be to the *praise of His glory.
13 In Him you also *trusted*, after you
heard [a]the word of *truth, the gospel

CHAPTER 1

3 [a]2 Cor. 1:3
4 [a]Rom. 8:28 [b]1 Pet. 1:2 [c]Luke 1:75
5 [a][Rom. 8:29] [b]John 1:12 [c][1 Cor. 1:21] *See WW at Matt. 12:50.
6 [a][Rom. 3:24] [b]Matt. 3:17 [1]Lit. *bestowed grace (favor) upon us* *See WW at 2 Cor. 12:9.
7 [a][Heb. 9:12] [b][Rom. 3:24, 25] *See WW at Rom. 3:24. • See WW at Heb. 9:22.
8 [1]*understanding* *See WW at Matt. 25:29. • See WW at Acts 6:10.
9 [a][Rom. 16:25] [b][2 Tim. 1:9] *See WW at Mark 4:11.
10 [a]Gal. 4:4 [b]1 Cor. 3:22 [c][Col. 1:16, 20] [1]NU, M omit *both* *See WW at Eph. 3:19.
11 [a]Rom. 8:17 [b]Is. 46:10 *See WW at Rom. 8:28.
12 [a]2 Thess. 2:13 [b]James 1:18 *See WW at Eph. 1:6.
13 [a]John 1:17 *See WW at John 4:24.

1:1 Saints is never a merely religious title in the Bible, but a declared state of being. Saints are "holy people," so-called by God because He has made them holy through His salvation.

1:3 Spiritual blessing refers to divine privileges and resources available now, that is, chosen, adopted, forgiven. 1 Cor. 12:1 uses the same Greek word for "spiritual" in referring to the gifts of the Holy Spirit, evidencing that they are among the "blessings" included.

1:5 Predestined does not suggest a fatalism that excludes some while including others, but assures an appointed plan and guaranteed destiny for all the redeemed.

1:6 Accepted is literally "graced with grace." "In Christ" is a recurring term designating the sphere in which all salvation is realized and the realm in which God's kingdom purposes are fulfilled—in the circle of the King's (Christ's) reign.

1:7 This letter repeatedly insists that the ground of all grace is the reconciling death of Jesus Christ on the Cross (2:16), at the expense of **His** redeeming **blood** (2:13). Through this alone God offers forgiveness (4:32). Forgiveness is possible because Christ loved the church and gave Himself to provide it (5:25–27).

1:9 Mystery was formerly a divine secret, but in the NT is now a fully disclosed truth for understanding and application.

1:10 Dispensation is not a restricted period of time. The Greek word refers to the administration or management of a household. Paul is speaking of God's arrangement or "dispensing" of the affairs of history.

1:11 Counsel of His will signifies God's eternal and unchangeable plan. Repeated reference to God's will (vv. 1, 5, 9, 11) establishes the confidence of strong purpose and solid ground for living.

1:13 You were sealed is seen by some as referring to justification, but that term is not used here and the emphasis is different. Justification brings acceptance; sealing brings authority (John 3:33, 34). This verse, therefore, may refer to Acts 19:1–6, where the Ephesians, who had already believed, received the fullness of the Holy Spirit after Paul taught and ministered to them.

of your *salvation; in whom also, having *believed, [b]you were sealed with
the Holy Spirit of promise,
14 [a]who[1] is the [2]guarantee* of our inheritance [b]until the *redemption of
[c]the purchased possession, [d]to the
*praise of His glory.

Prayer for Spiritual Wisdom

15 Therefore I also, [a]after I heard of
your faith in the Lord Jesus and your
love for all the saints,
16 [a]do not cease to give thanks for you,
making mention of you in my prayers:
17 that [a]the God of our Lord Jesus
Christ, the Father of glory, [b]may give
to you the spirit of wisdom and revelation in the knowledge of Him,
18 [a]the eyes of your [1]understanding*
being enlightened; that you may know
what is [b]the hope of His calling, what
are the riches of the glory of His inheritance in the saints,
19 and what *is* the exceeding greatness
of His *power toward us who believe,
[a]according to the *working of His
mighty power
20 which He worked in Christ when
[a]He raised Him from the dead and
[b]seated *Him* at His right hand in the
heavenly *places*,
21 [a]far above all [b]principality[1] and
[2]power and [3]might and dominion, and
every *name that is named, not only
in this *age but also in that which is
to come.
22 And [a]He put all *things* *under His

13 [b][2 Cor. 1:22] *See WW at Luke 19:9 • See WW at Rom. 10:9. **14** [a]2 Cor. 5:5 [b]Rom. 8:23 [c][Acts 20:28] [d]1 Pet. 2:9 [1]NU *which* [2]*down payment, earnest* *See WW at 2 Cor. 1:22. • See WW at Rom. 3:24. • See WW at Eph. 1:6. **15** [a]Col. 1:4; Philem. 5 **16** [a]Rom. 1:9 **17** [a]John 20:17; Rom. 15:6 [b]Is. 11:2; Col. 1:9 **18** [a]Acts 26:18; 2 Cor. 4:6; Heb. 6:4 [b]Eph. 2:12 [1]NU, M *hearts* *See WW at Mark 12:30. **19** [a]Col. 2:12 *See WW at 1 Tim. 6:16. • See WW at Col. 1:29. **20** [a]Acts 2:24 [b]Ps. 110:1 **21** [a]Is. 9:6, 7; Luke 1:32, 33; Phil. 2:9, 10; Rev. 19:12 [b][Rom. 8:38, 39] [1]*rule* [2]*authority* [3]*power* *See WW at John 12:13. • See WW at Matt. 28:20. **22** [a]Ps. 8:6; 110:1; Matt. 28:18; 1 Cor. 15:27 *See WW at 1 Cor. 14:32.

KINGDOM DYNAMICS

1:17–19 The Spirit of Revelation, PROPHECY. In this text, Paul says he prays for people to receive "the spirit of wisdom and revelation," with the dual objective of their knowing Christ and understanding God's purpose and power in their lives. Such "revelation" refers to an unveiling of our hearts that we may receive insight into the way God's word is intended to work in our lives. It may be used of teaching or preaching that is especially anointed in helping people see the glory of Christ and His purpose and power for them. But in making such a biblical use of the term as it appears here in Eph. 1, it is wise to understand its alternate and grander use.

The word "revelation" is used in two ways in the Bible. It is important to distinguish them, not only to avoid confusion in studying the Word of God, but to assure the avoidance of a destructive detour into humanistic ideas and hopeless error. The Holy Scriptures are called "the revealed Word of God." The Bible declares that God's "law" (Deut. 29:29) and the "prophets" (Amos 3:7) are the result of His revealing work, essentially describing the whole of the OT as "revealed." In the NT, this word is used of writings as well (Rom. 16:25; Eph. 3:3; Rev. 1:1)—writings that became part of the closed canon of the Holy Scriptures (see "The Content of God's Word Is Completed," Prov. 30:5, 6).

Wisdom and understanding, as well as sound, practical speech, recommend that today's believer both know and clearly express what is meant when he or she speaks of "revelations." The Holy Spirit does indeed give us revelation, as this text teaches. But such prophetic insight into the Word should never be considered as equal to the actual giving of the Holy Scriptures. As helpful as insight into God's Word may be, the finality of the whole of the revelation of God's Holy Word is the only sure ground for building our lives (Matt. 7:24–29).

(1 John 4:1–6/1 Cor. 14:1) J.W.H.

1:14 Guarantee literally means "deposit," "down payment," or "first installment." The Holy Spirit invested in us is God's title to possessing us entirely and forever.

1:16 For insight into the weight and dimension of prayer life in the early church, study the content of Paul's two prayers recorded in this letter (vv. 16–23; 3:14–21).

1:17 Wisdom and revelation are not to be interpreted as mystical. "Wisdom" concerns practical, workable principles; "revelation" refers to clear perception and applicable understanding. The Holy Spirit is the divine and supernatural source of both.

1:18 Eyes of your understanding being enlightened literally means that your heart may receive the brightness of hope resulting when the wealth of God's investment in you is understood.

1:19 According to occurs repeatedly and means "in the same measure as" or "to the exact degree."

1:20 *Heavenly places* does not refer to heaven in the sense of its being the destined home of the redeemed. Rather, the Greek word here refers to the invisible realm that surrounds our present daily situation, the arena or sphere of spiritual action and activity. Christ's authority, which encompasses every age and exceeds every known power, is here and now (see also v. 3; 2:6; 3:10; 6:12).

1:21 Principality and power and might and dominion are terms consistently used for ruling authorities in both the visible and the invisible realms (see 3:10). The NT reveals an invisible hierarchy of evil powers who deceive and manipulate human behavior, thereby advancing satanic strategies. Christ Himself and all who are in Christ are shown to be placed in authority above these powers, an authority that only spiritual warfare can assert, demonstrate, and sustain (6:12).

1:22, 23 His body: The primary thrust of this letter is to show the church as the present, physical presence of Christ. The church is to be filled with Him by the Holy Spirit, and assigned by the Lord Jesus to represent Him to society to minister His life, love, and power.

feet, and gave Him [b]*to be* head over
all *things* to the church,
23 [a]which is His body, [b]the fullness of
Him [c]who fills all in all.

By Grace Through Faith

2 And [a]you *He made alive,* [b]who
were dead in trespasses and
sins,
2 [a]in which you once walked according to the [1]course of this wo er a the
ing to [b]the prince of th works in
air, the spirit wh ace,
[c]the sons of diso also ve all once
3 [a]among ves in [b]the lusts of
conduct the desires of the
our the *mind and [c]were by
flesh, children of wrath, just as the
fls.
But God, [a]who is rich in *mercy, because of His [b]grea *love with which
He *loved us,
5 [a]even when we were dead in trespasses, [b]made us alive together with
Christ (by *grace you have been
*saved),
6 and raised *us* up together, and made
us sit together [a]in *the* heavenly *places*
in Christ Jesus,
7 that in the ages to come He might
show the exceeding riches of His grace
in [a]*His* *kindness toward us in Christ
Jesus.
8 [a]For by grace you have been saved
[b]through *faith, and that not of yourselves; [c]*it is* the gift of God,
9 not of [a]works, lest anyone should
[b]boast.
10 For we are [a]His **workmanship,** created in Christ Jesus for *good works,
which God prepared beforehand that
we should walk in them.

22 [b]Heb. 2:7
23 [a]Rom. 12:5 [b]Col. 2:9 [c][1 Cor. 12:6]

CHAPTER 2

1 [a]Eph. 2:5; Col. 2:13 [b]Eph. 4:18 Col. 1:21
2 [John 12:31]; Eph. 6:12 [c]Col. 3:6 [1]Gr. *aion,* aeon
3 [a]1 Pet. 4:3 [b]Gal. 5:16 [c][Ps. 51:5] *See WW at Mark 12:30.
4 [a]Ps.103:8–11; Rom. 10:12 [b]John 3:16; 1 John 4:9, 10 *See WW at 2 Tim. 1:16. • See WW at Rom. 5:5. • See WW at John 3:16.
5 [a]Rom. 5:6, 8 [b][Rom. 6:4, 5] *See WW at 2 Cor. 12:9. • See WW at Luke 7:50.
6 [a]Eph. 1:20
7 [a]Titus 3:4 *See WW at Gal. 5:22.
8 [a][2 Tim. 1:9] [b]Rom. 4:16 [c][John 1:12, 13] *See WW at Mark 11:22.
9 [a]Rom. 4:4, 5; 11:6 [b]Rom. 3:27
10 [a]Is. 19:25 *See WW at Phil. 1:6.
11 [a][Rom. 2:28; Col. 2:11]

WORD WEALTH

2:10 workmanship, *poiema* (*poy*-ay-mah); Strong's *#4161:* From the verb *poieo,* "to make." (Compare "poem" and "poetry.") The word signifies that which is manufactured, a product, a design produced by an artisan. *Poiema* emphasizes God as the Master Designer, the universe as His creation (Rom. 1:20), and the redeemed believer as His new creation (Eph. 2:10). Before conversion our lives had no rhyme or reason. Conversion brought us balance, symmetry, and order. We are God's poem, His work of art.

Brought Near by His Blood

11 Therefore remember that you, once
Gentiles in the flesh—who are called
Uncircumcision by what is called
[a]the Circumcision made in the flesh by
hands—
12 that at that time you were without
Christ, being aliens from the commonwealth of Israel and strangers from the
covenants of promise, having no hope
and without God in the world.
13 But now in Christ Jesus you who
once were far off have been brought
near by the blood of Christ.

KINGDOM DYNAMICS

2:13 Gentiles Embraced by Christ's Sacrifice, THE BLOOD. Prior to the New Covenant, Gentiles were excluded from citizenship in the commonwealth of Israel and were foreigners to the covenant promises of God. There was no hope in this life and no ability to know God's presence in the world. The covenant sacrifice of Christ's blood took Gentile (*cont. on next page*)

2:1 Were dead: Man does not merely need a guide or a teacher; he is dead and needs someone able to resurrect his spirit.

2:2 The mood and manner of society is shaped by **the prince of the power of the air,** a title for Satan as he exercises influence globally and within each culture.

2:3 Children of wrath: The inevitable end of "sons of disobedience" (v. 2) is to come under the condemnation of God's righteous anger, a justifiable judgment for having violated known boundaries of spiritual and moral duty (see Rom. 1:18–21).

2:6 Sit together . . . in Christ Jesus: Three "togethers" in vv. 5 and 6 note our union with Christ 1) in His resurrection, 2) in His ascension, and 3) in His present rule at God's right hand. From this place of partnership, He grants that we share in the present works of His kingdom's power (Col. 1:13).

2:7 In the ages to come: Whatever glories of Christ's kingdom dominion and authority may be experienced and enjoyed in the present era, it is clear that there is much that will be unrealized until the consummation of this age and the inauguration of the unimaginable future God reserves for His own.

2:8 Grace describes the undeserved kindness by which salvation is given, but it is also the power-word describing the Holy Spirit's operational means. Grace is a *force* as well as a *favor,* a verb as well as a noun.

2:10 Created . . . that we should walk: The genius of God's new creation work in each believer is that He renovates the nature of His redeemed children to make **good works** a living possibility.

2:11 Uncircumcision is the most direct term to describe the fact that Gentiles were outside any covenant relationship with God.

2:12 Without Christ is the first of five phrases in this verse describing the estrangement of Gentiles before Christ came. Being "without a Messiah" is the fountainhead of futility and hopelessness.

2:13 But now joins with "but God" (v. 4) as gloriously pivotal words upon which everything in life turns from death to life, sin to salvation, and hopelessness to eternal joy.

(cont. from preceding page)
believers who were far from God and joined them together with the Jews in the New Covenant. Gentiles were grafted in to enjoy the covenants of promise through the New Covenant and were included as heirs with the patriarchs of all of God's promises.
(Rom. 3:25/1 Pet. 1:18, 19) C.S.

Christ Our Peace

14 For He Himself is our peace, who
has made both one, and has broken
down the middle wall of separation,
15 having abolished in His flesh the enmity, *that is,* the law of commandments *contained* in ordinances, so as
to create in Himself one [a]new man
from the two, *thus* making peace,
16 and that He might [a]reconcile them
both to God in one body through the
cross, thereby [b]putting to death the enmity.
17 And He came and preached peace
to you who were afar off and to those
who were near.
18 For [a]through Him we both have access [b]by one Spirit to the Father.

Christ Our Cornerstone

19 Now, therefore, you are no longer
strangers and **foreigners,** but fellow
citizens with the saints and members
of the household of God,

WORD WEALTH

2:19 foreigners, *paroikos* (par-oy-koss); Strong's *#3941:* From *para,* "beside," and *oikeo,* "to dwell"; hence, "dwelling near." The word came to denote an alien who dwells as a sojourner in a land without the rights of citizenship. The word describes Abraham and Moses, sojourners in a land not their own (Acts 7:6, 29), and the Christian who is traveling through this world as an alien whose citizenship and ultimate residence are in heaven (1 Pet. 2:11).

15 [a]Gal. 6:15
16 [a]2 Cor. 5:18; [Col. 1:20–22] [b][Rom. 6:6]
18 [a]John 10:9 [b]1 Cor. 12:13; Eph. 4:4
20 [a]1 Pet. 2:4 [b]Matt. 16:18; 1 Cor. 3:10, 11; Rev. 21:14 [c]1 Cor. 12:28; Eph. 3:5 [d]Ps. 118:22; Luke 20:17
21 [a]1 Cor. 3:16, 17
22 [a]1 Pet. 2:5 [b]John 17:23

CHAPTER 3

2 [a]Acts 9:15 [1]*stewardship*
3 [a]Acts 22:17, 21; 26:16 [b][Rom. 11:25; 16:25; Eph. 3:4, 9; 6:19]; Col. 1:26; 4:3
4 *See WW at Mark 13:14. • *See WW at Luke 2:47.
6 [a]Gal. 3:28, 29 *See WW at Heb. 11:9.
7 [a]Rom. 15:16 [b]Rom. 1:5 [c]Rom. 15:18 *See WW at Col. 1:29.
8 [a][1 Cor. 15:9] [b][Col. 1:27; 2:2, 3]
9 [a]John 1:3; Col. 1:16; Heb. 1:2 [1]NU, M *steward-ship* (dispensation) [2]NU omits *through Jesus Christ* *See WW at Acts 2:42.

20 having been [a]built [b]on the foundation of the [c]apostles and prophets,
Jesus Christ Himself being [d]the chief
corner*stone,*
21 in whom the whole building, being
fitted together, grows into [a]a holy temple in the Lord,
22 [a]in whom you also are being built
together for a [b]dwelling place of God
in the Spirit.

The Mystery Revealed

3 For this reas[on I,] Paul, the prisoner of Christ Je[sus for] you Gentiles—
2 if indeed you have he[ard of the]
[1]dispensation of the grace [of God]
[a]which was given to me for you, [...]
3 [a]how that by revelation [b]He made
known to me the mystery (as I have
briefly written already,
4 by which, when you *read, you may
*understand my knowledge in the mys-
tery of Christ),
5 which in other ages was not made
known to the sons of men, as it has
now been revealed by the Spirit to His
holy apostles and prophets:
6 that the Gentiles [a]should be fellow
*heirs, of the same body, and partakers
of His promise in Christ through the
gospel,
7 [a]of which I became a minister
[b]according to the gift of the grace of
God given to me by [c]the effective
*working of His power.

Purpose of the Mystery

8 To me, [a]who am less than the least
of all the saints, this grace was given,
that I should preach among the Gentiles [b]the unsearchable riches of
Christ,
9 and to make all see what *is* the
[1]fellowship* of the mystery, which
from the beginning of the ages has
been hidden in God who [a]created all
things [2]through Jesus Christ;

2:14 The essence of **peace** is dual, to cause a ceasing from separation as well as a ceasing from strife. Peace means "to be united with" as well as "to bring an end to hostility."
2:19 Household literally means "members of the family."
2:20 Apostles and prophets mentioned in this reference should be distinguished from the reference in 4:11. The founding apostles are meant here, as in Rev. 21:14, while the later reference (4:11) is to the ongoing mission of apostles, who serve the church of Christ in a more general way.
2:21, 22 The metaphor of the body (1:22, 23) being filled by Christ is complemented by that of a **building . . . temple** being inhabited by God through the Holy Spirit.
3:1–7 Paul reflects on his mission to help believing Jews and Gentiles accept each other as partners in God's covenant of salvation. This mystery was especially foreign to the OT Jewish mindset, not being understood by either Jew or Gentile until Jesus came. See "revelation" (1:17) and "mystery" (1:9).
3:9 A textual variation suggests "dispensation" here for **fellowship** (see note on 1:10). Paul describes his driving desire to help every believer see the personal role each has in dispensing (*spreading, distributing, administering*) the grand truth of God's purpose in the church.

10 [a]to the intent that now [b]the [1]**manifold** wisdom of God might be made
known by the church [c]to the [2]principal-
ities and powers in the heavenly
places,

WORD WEALTH

3:10 manifold, *polupoikilos* (pol-oo-poy-kil-oss); Strong's *#4182:* From *polus,* "much," and *poikilos,* "varied," "many-colored." The word pictures God's wisdom as much varied, with many shades, tints, hues, and colorful expressions. As a God of variety, He is still entering the human arena displaying many-sided, multicolored, and much variegated wisdom to His people and through His people.

11 [a]according to the eternal *purpose
which He accomplished in Christ Jesus
our Lord,
12 in whom we have boldness and access [a]with confidence through faith in
Him.
13 [a]Therefore I ask that you do not
lose heart at my *tribulations for you,
[b]which is your glory.

Appreciation of the Mystery

14 For this reason I bow my knees to
the [a]Father [1]of our Lord Jesus Christ,
15 from whom the whole family in
heaven and earth is named,

KINGDOM DYNAMICS

3:14, 15 The Identity of Family Is in God, FAMILY ORDER. Humanly speaking, we link the identity of a husband, wife, and children to their particular family-name. This, however, is only a surface identification. Family identity has a deeper root.

"Family" is a word that is rooted in God: God is Father—the Father of our Lord Jesus Christ. In Himself, God is a "divine family." This also expresses itself in the way that God relates to people. The Bible reveals this aspect of God's nature in rich and varied use of family imagery: God is our Father, God is Husband to His people, God is like a nurturing mother, Christ is the Bridegroom of the church.

When a man and a woman come together in marriage, God extends to them this name that in essence belongs to Him—the name of family. Husband, wife, and children live up to the true meaning of this name as they reflect the nature and life of the divine family in their human family.

(Gen. 1:26–28/1 Cor. 11:3) L.C.

KINGDOM DYNAMICS

3:14–21 Spiritual Leaders: Pray As Well As Teach, PRAYER. Spiritual leaders must pray for their people as well as teach them. Paul prayed that his fellow believers might know the strength of the Spirit's reinforcement in the inner person, just as a storm-tossed ship on which he once sailed was strengthened inside by bracings and undergirded outside by cables (Acts 27:17). Knowing that the strength of Christianity is not outward laws but inward character, Paul prayed that Christ might enter through the open door of faith, dwell in their hearts, and imprint His nature upon their minds, wills, and emotions. When Christ enters a life, He brings His life—the very soil in which we take root and blossom, the ground in which our lives are founded. Prayer begets prayer, for the believer in whom Christ's love is bringing the fullness of God will learn to ask and expect great things from Him!

(Ezek. 22:30/Acts 13:1—14:28) L.L.

16 that He would *grant you, [a]accord-
ing to the riches of His glory, [b]to be
strengthened with might through His
Spirit in [c]the inner man,
17 [a]that Christ may dwell in your
hearts through faith; that you, [b]being
rooted and grounded in love,
18 [a]may be able to *comprehend with
all the saints [b]what *is* the width and
length and depth and height—
19 to *know the love of Christ which
passes knowledge; that you may be
filled [a]with all the **fullness** of God.

10 [a]1 Pet. 1:12 [b][1 Tim. 3:16] [c]Eph. 1:21; 6:12; Col. 1:16; 2:10, 15 [1]*variegated* or *many-sided* [2]*rulers*
11 [a][Eph. 1:4, 11] *See WW at Rom. 8:28.
12 [a]2 Cor. 3:4; Heb. 4:16; 10:19, 35; [1 John 2:28; 3:21]
13 [a]Phil. 1:14 [b]2 Cor. 1:6 *See WW at John 16:33.
14 [a]Eph. 1:3 [1]NU omits *of our Lord Jesus Christ*
16 [a][Eph. 1:7; 2:4; Phil. 4:19] [b]1 Cor. 16:13; Phi. 4:13; Col. 1:11 [c]Rom. 7:22 *See WW at Acts 20:35.
17 [a]John 14:23; Rom. 8:9; 2 Cor. 13:5; [Eph. 2:22] [b]Col. 1:23
18 [a]Eph. 1:18 [b]Rom. 8:39 *See WW at John 1:5.
19 [a]Eph. 1:3 *See WW at John 8:

3:10, 11 The eternal purpose is the same here as 1:9, 11. The text soars as Paul cites God's intent to display se church before all evil powers as His instrument to dis d throughout the earth what He has already **accompli** n, **in Christ Jesus our Lord** (that is, through Jesus' resurrection, and ascension).
3:14–21 The second apostolic prayer is for the Spirit's power to fill every believer, which is the logical if the grand objective of vv. 9–12 is to be realized. ne
3:16 Strengthened with might is literally " gs to mighty by His power," which the Holy Spiri work in the believer.
3:17 Rooted like a tree **and grounded** like a building on a strong foundation.
3:18 Comprehend means to receive experientially, not simply to understand intellectually.
3:19 To know the love of Christ is the essence of the greatest fullness. **All the fullness of God** speaks of more than one experience or one aspect of His truth or power. It points to a broad-based spirituality, balanced through participating in all of God's blessings, resources, and wisdom.

WORD WEALTH

***3:19* fullness,** *pleroma* (*play*-row-mah); Strong's *#4138:* Full number, full complement, full measure, copiousness, plenitude, that which has been completed. The word describes a ship with a full cargo and crew, and a town with no empty houses. *Pleroma* strongly emphasizes fullness and completion.

20 Now [a]to Him who is able to do exceedingly *abundantly [b]above all that
we *ask or think, [c]according to the
power that *works in us,
21 [a]to Him *be* glory in the church by
Christ Jesus to all generations, forever
and ever. Amen.

Walk in Unity

1 4 I, therefore, the prisoner [1]of the
Lord, [2]beseech you to [a]walk worthy of the calling with which you were
called,
2 with all *lowliness and *gentleness,
with *longsuffering, *bearing with one
another in love,
3 *endeavoring to keep the unity of
the Spirit [a]in the bond of *peace.
4 [a]*There is* one body and one Spirit,
just as you were called in one *hope
of your calling;
5 [a]one Lord, [b]one faith, [c]one *baptism;
6 [a]one God and Father of all, who *is*
above all, and [b]through all, and in
[1]you all.

20 [a]Rom. 16:25 [b]1 Cor. 2:9 [c]Col. 1:29 *See WW at John 10:10. • See WW at Matt. 7:7. • See WW at 1 Thess. 2:13.
21 [a]Rom. 11:36

CHAPTER 4

1 [a]1 Thess. 2:12 [1]Lit. *in* [2]*exhort, encourage*
2 *See WW at Acts 20:19. • See WW at 1 Tim. 6:11. • See WW at Heb. 6:12. • See WW at 2 Thess. 1:4.
3 [a]Col. 3:14 *See WW at Gal. 2:10. • See WW at Luke 1:79.
4 [a]Rom. 12:5 *See WW at 1 Thess. 1:3.
5 [a]1 Cor. 1:13 [b]Jude 3 [c][Heb. 6:6] *See WW at Matt. 21:25.
6 [a]Mal. 2:10 [b]Rom. 11:36 [1]NU omits *you;* M *us*

7 [a][1 Cor. 12:7, 11]
8 [a]Ps. 68:18
9 [a]John 3:13; 20:17 [1]NU omits *first*
10 [a]Acts 1:9 [b][Eph. 1:23]

Spiritual Gifts

7 But [a]to each one of us grace was
given according to the measure of
Christ's gift.
8 Therefore He says:

[a]*"When He ascended on high,*
He led captivity captive,
And gave gifts to men."

9 [a](Now this, *"He ascended"*—what
does it mean but that He also [1]first descended into the lower parts of the
earth?
10 He who descended is also the One
[a]who ascended far above all the heavens, [b]that He might fill all things.)
11 And He Himself gave some *to be*
*apostles, some prophets, some evan-
gelists, and some *pastors and teachers,

KINGDOM DYNAMICS

4:11 The Gifts Christ Gives, SPIRITUAL GIFTS. Distinguishing among the gifts of Rom. 12:6–8 (from the Father), the gifts of 1 Cor. 12:8–10 (from the Holy Spirit), and those here, which are explicitly given by Christ the Son (v. 8), is pivotal in comprehending the whole scope of spiritual gifts. An elaboration of this and related themes appears in the study article on page 2018, "Holy Spirit Gifts and Power."

(1 Cor. 12:8–10, 28/1 Cor. 13:1) J.W.H.

11 *See WW at 1 Cor. 12:28. • See WW at John 10:2.

4:1 See section 1 of Truth-In-Action at the end of Eph.

4:1 Prisoner of the Lord: See also 3:1 and 6:20, which remind us that although the writer is in jail, he still maintains that his real captor is Christ. **Worthy** means "of sufficient weight," a quality issuing from acknowledging what Christ has poured into us, rather than whatever worth is felt or unfelt in oneself.

4:2–6 Unity is the responsibility of each believer and is to be pursued earnestly.

4:5 One baptism probably refers to water baptism, the common external point of publicly declaring faith in Jesus Christ. The issue is not the form of the ritual as much as the fact of one's obedience. The believer's baptism *by* the Holy Spirit *into* Christ's body (1 Cor. 12:13) and the baptism *in* or *with* the Holy Spirit *for* power-filled service (John 1:33; Acts 1:5, 8) are facts unchallenged by this observation. They clearly stand as spiritual realities linked in a tri-unity with the one baptism in water.

4:8, 11 Gifts . . . gave some: The five ministry offices listed here are gifts that Christ gave for the nurture and equipping of His church, not for hierarchical control or ecclesiastical competition. Beyond the distinct role filled by the original founding apostles (see note on 2:20), the NT mentions enough additional apostles to indicate that this office, with that of prophets, is as continuing a ministry in the church as the more commonly acknowledged offices of evangelists, pasors, and teachers (some make pastor-teacher one office). There is no prescribed formula or "gift-mix" for any particular office, as God uses different people in different waysin each of these five ministries Christ has given. Uniqueness is manifested in individuals according to the varied gifts God the Father has given them (Rom. 12:3–8) and joined with whatever gifts the Holy Spirit distributes to or through them (1 Cor. 12:4–11). The distinct gifts of the Father (Rom. 12), the Son (Eph. 4), and the Spirit (1 Cor. 12) ought not to be confused, nor should any of the five ministry offices in this text be limited to the operation of any particular gift.

4:9, 10 Paul explains that the quote from Ps. 68:18 (v. 8) [illegible]plies to the **ascended** Christ. An ascent implies a prior d[illegible]cent. Christ's descent **into the lower parts of the earth** ha[illegible]een variously interpreted as a descent into hell (ass[illegible]iating it with 1 Pet. 3:19), a descent into Sheol/Hades (the [illegible]m of the dead [see Acts 2:25–35]), or as symbolically referri[illegible] His incarnation (whereby Christ descended to Earth fr[illegible] heaven), a descent carrying Him to the depths of humili[illegible] (see Phil. 2:5–11). With reference to the view that He de[illegible]nded into hell, there is no biblical support for the notion t[illegible]esus suffered in hell, only that He descended to Sheol to [illegible]e the righteous dead into eternal glory, proclaiming th[illegible] [illegible]equacy of the Atonement and validating the testimony o[illegible] prophets.

12 for the **equipping** of the saints for
the work of ministry, [a]for the [1]edifying
of [b]the body of Christ,

WORD WEALTH

4:12 equipping, *katartismos* (kat-ar-tis-*moss*); Strong's *#2677:* A making fit, preparing, training, perfecting, making fully qualified for service. In classical language the word is used for setting a bone during surgery. The Great Physician is now making all the necessary adjustments so the church will not be "out of joint."

13 till we all come to the unity of the
faith [a]and of the knowledge of the Son
of God, to [b]a *perfect man, to the measure
of the stature of the fullness of
Christ;
14 that we should no longer be [a]children,
tossed to and fro and carried
about with every wind of doctrine, by
the trickery of men, in the cunning
craftiness of [b]deceitful plotting,
15 but, speaking the truth in love, may
grow up in all things into Him who is
the [a]head—Christ—
16 [a]from whom the whole body, joined
and knit together by what every joint
supplies, according to the effective
*working by which every part does its
share, causes growth of the body for
the edifying of itself in love.

The New Man

2 17 This I say, therefore, and testify in
the Lord, that you should [a]no longer
walk as [1]the rest of the Gentiles walk,
in the futility of their mind,
18 having their understanding darkened,
being alienated from the life of
God, because of the ignorance that is
in them, because of the [a]blindness* of
their heart;
19 [a]who, being past feeling, [b]have
given themselves over to *lewdness, to
work all uncleanness with greediness.
20 But you have not so learned Christ,
21 if indeed you have heard Him and
have been taught by Him, as the truth
is in Jesus:
22 that you [a]put off, concerning your
former conduct, the old man which
grows corrupt according to the deceitful
*lusts,
23 and [a]be renewed in the spirit of
your mind,
24 and that you [a]put on the *new man
which was created according to God,
in true righteousness and holiness.

Do Not Grieve the Spirit

25 Therefore, putting away lying, 3
[a]*"Let each one of you speak truth with
his neighbor,"* for [b]we are members of
one another.
26 [a]*"Be* angry, and do not sin"*: do not
let the sun go down on your wrath,
27 [a]nor give [1]place to the devil.
28 Let him who stole steal no longer, 7
but rather [a]let him labor, *working
with *his* hands what is *good, that he
may have something [b]to *give him who
has need.
29 [a]Let no corrupt word proceed out 4
of your mouth, but [b]what is good for

12 [a]1 Cor. 14:26 [b]Col. 1:24 [1]*building up*
13 [a]Col. 2:2 [b]1 Cor. 14:20 *See WW at James 3:2.
14 [a]1 Cor. 14:20 [b]Rom. 16:18 *See WW at 1 Cor. 3:19. • See WW at Jude 11.
15 [a]Eph. 1:22
16 [a]Col. 2:19 *See WW at Col. 1:29.
17 [a]Eph. 2:2; 4:22 [1]NU omits *the rest of*
18 [a]Rom. 1:21 *See WW at Rom. 11:25.
19 [a]1 Tim. 4:2 [b]1 Pet. 4:3 *See WW at 1 Pet. 4:3.
22 [a]Col. 3:8 *See WW at 2 Tim. 2:22.
23 [a][Rom. 12:2]
24 [a][Rom. 6:4; 7:6; 12:2] *See WW at 2 Cor. 5:17.
25 [a]Zech. 8:16 [b]Rom. 12:5
26 [a]Ps. 4:4; 37:8 *See WW at Rev. 12:17.
27 [a][Rom. 12:19] [1]*an opportunity*
28 [a]Acts 20:35 [b]Luke 3:11 *See WW at John 3:21. • See WW at Phil. 1:6. • See WW at Rom. 1:11.
29 [a]Col. 3:8 [b]1 Thess. 5:11

4:12 The Greek word for **equipping** implies: 1) a recovered wholeness as when a broken limb is set and mends; 2) a discovered function, as when a physical member is properly operating. The **work of ministry** is the enterprise of each member of the body of Christ and not the exclusive charge of select leaders. Taken together, vv. 11, 12 reveal that the task of the gifted leader is to cultivate the individual and corporate ministries of those he or she leads.

4:13–16 A progress in maturity (v. 13), stability (v. 14), and integrity (v. 15), taking place in every individual member's experience, results in the whole body's **growth** (numerical expansion) and **edifying** (internal strengthening).

4:17–19 Five traits of a worldly walk are summed up in the word **futility** (emptiness, purposelessness): darkened understanding, alienation from God, ignorance of God's way, hardened heart, and an unfeeling state. (The Greek word means "to have ceased to care.")

4:17 See section 2 of Truth-In-Action at the end of Eph.

4:20–32 This section asserts each believer's accountability to live in contrast with the surrounding culture, since the five traits of the worldling are no longer true of him.

4:22, 24 The old man . . . the new man contrasts the old life-style dominated by the spirit of disobedience (2:1–3) with the believer's newly created capacity for a life-style of obedience by the Holy Spirit's power (2:10; 3:16).

4:25–27 See section 3 of Truth-In-Action at the end of Eph.

4:26 Being **angry** may win a moment, but it is not to be allowed to win a day.

4:27 The Greek word for **place** (***topos***) emphasizes that believers can actually give ground in their lives to satanic control. This is a warning against theologized suppositions that argue against the possibility that demonic vexing or oppression may succeed with Christians. But the surrounding commands balance the issue (v. 17—5:14), making clear that responsible believers cannot glibly blame the Devil for sin they yield to in carnal disobedience.

4:28 See section 7 of Truth-In-Action at the end of Eph.

4:28 Note that the first motive for a believer to earn money is **that he may have something to give.** The occupational enterprise of Christians is not simply to make a living, but to make possible their being instruments of God's service to mankind through their work and giving.

4:29 See section 4 of Truth-In-Action at the end of Eph.

4:29 Corrupt is literally "decayed, rotten," as used for spoiled meat, rotted fruit, or crumbled stones.

necessary [1]edification, [c]that it may impart grace to the hearers.
30 And [a]do not grieve the Holy Spirit
of God, by whom you were sealed for
the day of *redemption.
31 [a]Let all bitterness, *wrath, anger,
[1]clamor, and [b]evil speaking be *put
away from you, [c]with all malice.
32 And [a]be *kind to one another,
tenderhearted, [b]forgiving* one another, even as God in Christ forgave
you.

Walk in Love

1 5 Therefore[a] be imitators of God as
dear [b]children.
2 And [a]walk in love, [b]as Christ also
has loved us and *given Himself for us,
an *offering and a sacrifice to God
[c]for a sweet-smelling aroma.
4 3 But *fornication and all [a]unclean-
ness or [b]covetousness, let it not even
be named among you, as is fitting for
saints;
4 [a]neither filthiness, nor [b]foolish talking, nor coarse jesting, [c]which are not
fitting, but rather [d]giving of thanks.
5 For [1]this you know, that no fornicator, unclean person, nor *covetous
man, who is an idolater, has any
[a]inheritance in the kingdom of Christ
and God.
6 Let no one deceive you with empty
words, for because of these things the
wrath of God comes upon the sons of
disobedience.
7 Therefore do not be [a]partakers with
them.

Walk in Light

8 For you were once *darkness, but
now *you are* [a]light in the Lord. Walk
as children of light
9 (for [a]the fruit of the [1]Spirit* *is* in
all *goodness, righteousness, and
truth),
10 [a]finding out what is acceptable to
the Lord.
11 And have [a]no fellowship with the
unfruitful works of darkness, but
rather [1]expose *them.*
12 [a]For it is shameful even to speak
of those things which are done by them
in secret.
13 But [a]all things that are [1]exposed are
*made manifest by the light, for what-
ever makes manifest is light.
14 Therefore He says:

[a]"Awake, you who sleep,
Arise from the dead,
And Christ will give you light."

Walk in Wisdom

15 [a]See then that you walk [1]circum- 6
spectly, not as fools but as wise,
16 [a]redeeming the time, [b]because the
days are evil.
17 [a]Therefore do not be unwise, but
[b]understand [c]what the will of the Lord
is.
18 And [a]do not be drunk with wine, 1
in which is dissipation; but be filled
with the Spirit,
19 speaking to one another [a]in psalms
and hymns and spiritual songs, singing
and making [b]melody in your heart to
the Lord,

KINGDOM DYNAMICS

5:18, 19 Encouraging One Another in Praise, PRAISE PATHWAY. This text in-

29 [c]Col. 3:16 [1]*building up* **30** [a]Is. 7:13 *See WW at Rom. 3:24. **31** [a]Col. 3:8, 19 [b]James 4:11 [c]Titus 3:3 [1]*loud quarreling* *See WW at Luke 4:28. • See WW at John 16:22. **32** [a]2 Cor. 6:10 [b][Mark 11:25] *See WW at Matt. 11:30. • See WW at Col. 3:13.

CHAPTER 5

1 [a]Luke 6:36 [b]1 Pet. 1:14–16 **2** [a]1 Thess. 4:9 [b]Gal. 1:4 [c]2 Cor. 2:14, 15 *See WW at Luke 23:25. • See WW at Acts 21:26. **3** [a]Col. 3:5–7 [b][Luke 12:15] *See WW at Matt. 15:19. **4** [a]Matt. 12:34, 35 [b]Titus 3:9 [c]Rom. 1:28 [d]Phil. 4:6 **5** [a]1 Cor. 6:9, 10 [1]NU *know this* *See WW at 1 Cor. 6:10. **7** [a]1 Tim. 5:22 **8** [a]1 Thess. 5:5 *See WW at Luke 11:35. **9** [a]Gal. 5:22 [1]NU *light* *See WW at Rom. 7:6. • See WW at Rom. 15:14. **10** [a][Rom. 12:1, 2] **11** [a]2 Cor. 6:14 [1]*reprove* **12** [a]Rom. 1:24 **13** [a][John 3:20, 21] [1]*reproved* *See WW at Col. 3:4. **14** [a][Is. 26:19; 60:1] **15** [a]Col. 4:5 [1]*carefully* **16** [a]Col. 4:5 [b]Eccl. 11:2 **17** [a]Col. 4:5 [b][Rom. 12:2] [c]1 Thess. 4:3 **18** [a]Prov. 20:1; 23:31 **19** [a]Acts 16:25 [b]James 5:13

4:30 The Holy Spirit has **sealed** ("authorized as a representative," 1:13) and dwells in the inner man (3:16). If He is grieved, the believer will be the first to know. **Grieve** means to cause injury or distress, the precise feeling the believer senses when sin or disobedience finds its place.
4:32 Jesus taught the duty of **forgiving . . . even as God,** and showed it to be fundamental to having one's own prayers for forgiveness answered (see Matt. 6:14, 15; 18:21–35).
5:1, 2 See section 1 of Truth-In-Action at the end of Eph.
5:2 Sweet-smelling aroma parallels the figure of the OT sacrifices offered in worship. *See also 2 Cor. 2:15, 16, concerning* one's witness, and Heb. 13:15, 16, concerning one's worship.
5:3–7 See section 4 of Truth-In-Action at the end of Eph.
5:3 Fornication encompasses all acts of sexual immorality; **covetousness** identifies the insatiability of human carnality—never able to "get enough."
5:11 Have no fellowship means to have no share in the darkened life-style. See 1 Cor. 5:9–13.
5:15 See section 6 of Truth-In-Action at the end of Eph.
5:15 Circumspectly means to walk cautiously, sensitively, as a person would walk through thorny terrain.
5:16 Redeeming the time is capitalizing on every appropriate opportunity.
5:18–20 See section 1 of Truth-In-Action at the end of Eph.
5:18 The tense of the Greek for **be filled** makes clear that such a Spirit-filled condition does not stop with a single experience, but is maintained by "continually being filled," as commanded here.
5:19 Note the place of songful worship as a means to fulfilling the directive in v. 18—to be filled continually with the Spirit. **Psalms** are scriptural lyrics in song; **hymns** are humanly inspired lyrics in song; **spiritual songs** are impromptu rhythmic lyrics given by the Holy Spirit in one's language or in "tongues" (see 1 Cor. 14:15).

structs interaction in our praise. Paul tells the Ephesians to "[speak] to one another," using psalms and hymns and spiritual songs. Entering a gathering of believers, even with a small offering of praise, our worship begins to be magnified as we join with others. Their voices encourage us, and we inspire them. Separation from the local assembly deprives a person of this relationship and its strength. Let us assemble often and praise much—encouraging one another in praise.

(Acts 16:25, 26/Heb. 2:11, 12) C.G.

20 [a]giving* thanks always for all
things to God the Father [b]in the name
of our Lord *Jesus Christ,
3 21 [a]submitting* to one another in the
*fear of [1]God.

Marriage—Christ and the Church

22 Wives, [a]submit to your own husbands, as to the Lord.
23 For [a]the husband is head of the
wife, as also [b]Christ is head of the
*church; and He is the *Savior of
the body.
24 Therefore, just as the church is subject to Christ, so *let* the wives *be* to
their own husbands [a]in everything.
25 [a]Husbands, love your wives, just as
*Christ also loved the church and
[b]gave Himself for her,
26 that He might [1]sanctify* and
cleanse her [a]with the washing of water
[b]by the word,
27 [a]that He might present her to Himself a glorious church, [b]not having spot
or wrinkle or any such thing, but that
she should be holy and without blemish.
28 So husbands ought to love their
own wives as their own bodies; he who
loves his wife loves himself.
29 For no one ever hated his own flesh,
but nourishes and cherishes it, just as
the Lord *does* the church.
30 For [a]we are members of His body,
[1]of His flesh and of His bones.
31 [a]*"For this reason a man shall leave
his father and mother and be *joined
to his wife, and the [b]two shall become
one flesh."*
32 This is a great mystery, but I speak
concerning Christ and the church.
33 Nevertheless [a]let each one of you
in particular so love his own wife as
himself, and let the wife *see* that she
[b]respects *her* husband.

20 [a]Ps. 34:1 [b][1 Pet. 2:5] *See WW at John 6:11. • See WW at Phil. 4:23.
21 [a][Phil. 2:3]; 1 Pet. 5:5 [1]NU *Christ* *See WW at 1 Cor. 14:32. • See WW at 1 John 4:18.
22 [a]Eph. 5:22—6:9; Col. 3:18—4:1; 1 Pet. 3:1–6
23 [a][1 Cor. 11:3] [b]Col. 1:18 *See WW at Acts 8:1. • See WW at John 4:42.
24 [a]Titus 2:4, 5
25 [a]Eph. 5:28, 33; Col. 3:19; [1 Pet. 3:7] [b]Acts 20:28 *See WW at 2 Tim. 4:22.
26 [a]John 3:5 [b][John 15:3; 17:17; Rom. 10:8; Eph. 6:17] [1]*set it apart* *See WW at John 10:36.
27 [a][2 Cor. 4:14; 11:2]; Col. 1:22 [b]Song 4:7
30 [a]Gen. 2:23 [1]NU omits the rest of v. 30.
31 [a]Gen. 2:24; Matt. 19:5; Mark 10:7 [b][1 Cor. 6:16] *See WW at Mark 10:7.
33 [a]Col. 3:19 [b]1 Pet. 3:1, 6

KINGDOM DYNAMICS

5:22–33 Christ and the Church Model Husband/Wife Relationships, FAMILY ORDER. The specific instructions that the apostle Paul gives to husbands and wives are a glimpse of the Bridegroom and bride—a heavenly model for every marriage on Earth.

As a husband, how should I behave toward my wife? Look to Christ, the divine Bridegroom, in His relationship with the church: love her, sacrifice for her, listen to her concerns, take care of her; be as sensitive to her needs and her hurts as you are to those of your own body.

As a wife, how should I behave toward my husband? Look to the chosen bride, the church, in its relationship with Christ: respect him, acknowledge his calling as "head" of the family, respond to his leadership, listen to him, praise him, be unified in purpose and will with him; be a true helper (see Gen. 2:18).

No husband and wife can do this by mere willpower or resolve, but since you (including your marriage) are "His workmanship" (Eph. 2:8–10), God will help bring this about.

(1 Cor. 11:3/1 Pet. 3:1–7) L.C.

Children and Parents

6 Children, [a]obey* your parents in
the Lord, for this is *right.

CHAPTER 6

1 [a]Prov. 6:20; 23:22; Col. 3:20 *See WW at Rom. 6:17. • See WW at Matt. 1:19.

KINGDOM DYNAMICS

6:1 14. Will I Have My Family in Heaven?, SPIRITUAL ANSWERS. For the answer to this and other probing questions about God and the power life in His kingdom, see the study article "Spiritual Answers to Hard Questions," which begins on page 1996. P.R.

5:21—6:4 See section 3 of Truth-In-Action at the end of Eph.
5:21, 22 Submitting is taking the divinely ordered place in a relationship. Submission can never be required by one human being of another; it can only be given on the basis of trust, that is, to believe God's Word and to be willing to learn to grow in relationships.
5:22 Women are never made second to men in general, but the wife is specifically called to accept her husband's leadership.
5:23 The Bible does not put males over females, but it does call for husbands to accept responsible leadership in the same spirit of self-giving and devotion Christ has shown for His church.
5:24–33 These verses put such demands upon the Christian husband that it is impossible to see how a charge of male chauvinism could justly be made against the Bible, or how a license to exploit women or wives could ever be claimed from such texts.
6:1–4 The guidelines are for the family **in the Lord,** and are not necessarily expected to work outside the believing home.

2 [a]*"Honor your father and mother,"*
which is the first commandment with
promise:
3 *"that it may be well with you and
you may live long on the earth."*
4 And [a]you, fathers, do not provoke
your children to wrath, but [b]bring
them up in the training and admonition
of the Lord.

KINGDOM DYNAMICS

6:4 Parents Responsible to Raise Children, FAMILY ORDER. God holds parents responsible for the upbringing of children—not grandparents, not schools, not the state, not youth groups, not peers and friends. Although each of these groups may influence children, the final duty rests with parents, and particularly with the father, whom God has appointed "head" to lead and serve the family. Two things are necessary for the proper teaching of children: a right attitude and a right foundation. An atmosphere reeking with destructive criticism, condemnation, unrealistic expectations, sarcasm, intimidation, and fear will "provoke a child to wrath." In such an atmosphere, no sound teaching can take place.

The positive alternative would be an atmosphere rich in encouragement, tenderness, patience, listening, affection, and love. In such an atmosphere parents can build into the lives of their children the precious foundation of knowledge of God. (See also Deut. 6:6, 7; Prov. 22:6.)

(Ps. 127:3–5/Prov. 13:24) L.C.

Bondservants and Masters

3 5 [a]Bondservants, be obedient to those
who are your masters according to the
flesh, [b]with fear and trembling, [c]in sincerity of heart, as to Christ;
6 [a]not with eyeservice, as men-
pleasers, but as bondservants of Christ,
doing the will of God from the *heart,
7 with goodwill doing service, as to
the Lord, and not to men,
8 [a]knowing that whatever good anyone does, he will receive the same from
the Lord, whether *he is* a slave or *free.
9 And you, masters, do the same
things to them, giving up threatening,
knowing that [1]your own [a]Master also
is in heaven, and [b]there is no *partiality with Him.

The Whole Armor of God

10 Finally, my brethren, be strong in 5
the Lord and in the *power of His
might.
11 [a]Put on the whole armor of God,
that you may *be able to stand against
the [1]wiles of the devil.
12 For we do not wrestle against flesh
and *blood, but against [a]principalities,
against powers, against [b]the rulers of
[1]the darkness of this age, against spiritual *hosts* of wickedness in the heavenly *places.*
13 [a]Therefore take up the whole armor
of God, that you may be able to **withstand** [b]in the evil day, and having done
all, to stand.

2 [a]Ex. 20:12; Deut. 5:16
4 [a]Col. 3:21 [b]Gen. 18:19; Deut. 6:7; 11:19; Ps. 78:4; Prov. 22:6; 2 Tim. 3:15
5 [a]Col. 3:22; [1 Tim. 6:1]; Titus 2:9; 1 Pet. 2:18 [b]2 Cor. 7:15 [c]1 Chr. 29:17
6 [a]Col. 3:22 *See WW at Luke 21:19.
8 [a]Rom. 2:6 *See WW at Rev. 6:15.
9 [a]Job 31:13; John 13:13; Col. 4:1 [b]Deut. 10:17; Acts 10:34; Rom. 2:11; Col. 3:25 [1]NU *He who is both their Master and yours is* *See WW at Col. 3:25.
10 *See WW at 1 Tim. 6:16.
11 [a][2 Cor. 6:7] [1]*schemings* *See WW at Jude 24.
12 [a]Rom. 8:38 [b]Luke 22:53 [1]NU *this darkness,* *See WW at 1 John 1:7.
13 [a][2 Cor. 10:4] [b]Eph. 5:16

WORD WEALTH

6:13 withstand *anthistemi* (anth-*is*-tay-mee); Strong's *#436:* Compare "antihistamine." From *anti,* "against," and *his-*

6:5–9 In contrast to vv. 1–4, the believer's ethical duty and diligence in the marketplace is to perform as though serving Christ even when the worker's counterpart—employer or employee—is **according to the flesh,** that is, even when the other is not necessarily a Christian.

6:5–8 See section 3 of Truth-In-Action at the end of Eph.

6:10–13 See section 5 of Truth-In-Action at the end of Eph.

6:10 Finally implies not "in conclusion," but rather "insofar as the rest of life and its challenges are concerned."

6:11 The charge is to "brethren" (v. 10), not only each individual, but with corporate implications for the whole church.

6:12 Not . . . **against flesh and blood:** One of the church's greatest demands is to discern between the spiritual struggle and other social, personal, and political difficulties. Otherwise, individual believers and groups become too easily detoured, "wrestling" with human adversaries instead of *prayerfully warring* against the invisible works of hell behind the scenes. **Heavenly *places*** recalls earlier references to: 1) spiritual resources available to the church (1:3); 2) Christ's authority over evil (1:21); 3) the church's being seated together with her ascended Lord (2:6); 4) the Father's will to display His wisdom through the church to the confounding of evil powers (3:10). On these grounds this passage announces the church's corporate assignment to prayer warfare, in order that evil will be driven back and the will of God advanced.

6:13–17 The metaphor here is based on the **armor** and battle dress of the first-century Roman soldier. Clearly the military metaphor is intended to show the reader that we are engaged in an active battle now. Though some suggest that the viewpoint of a continuous aggressive struggle minimizes the accomplished victory of the Cross, it in fact asserts that victory all the more. All spiritual warfare waged today is victorious only on the basis of appropriating the provision of the Cross and Christ's blood (Col. 2:15).
1) Personal faith that positions itself against evil and
2) aggressive prayer warfare that assails demonic strongholds are two distinct and complementary facets of spiritual life.

This entire passage lends further support to this perspective: "To stand against" (v. 11) means to hold at bay aggressively or to stand in front of and oppose; "wrestle" (v. 12) means to engage actively in one-on-one combat; "to stand" (v. 13) means to be found standing after an active battle; and "stand" (v. 14) means take your stand for the next battle.

temi, "to cause to stand." The verb suggests vigorously opposing, bravely resisting, standing face-to-face against an adversary, standing your ground. Just as an antihistamine puts a block on histamine, *anthistemi* tells us that with the authority and spiritual weapons granted to us we can withstand evil forces.

5 14 Stand therefore, [a]having girded
your waist with truth, [b]having put on
the breastplate of *righteousness,
15 [a]and having shod your feet with the
preparation of the gospel of peace;
16 above all, taking [a]the shield of faith
with which you will be able to quench
all the fiery darts of the wicked one.
17 And [a]take the helmet of *salvation,
and [b]the sword of the Spirit, which is
the *word of God;
1 18 [a]praying always with all prayer and
supplication in the Spirit, [b]being
watchful to this end with all perseverance and [c]supplication for all the
saints—

KINGDOM DYNAMICS

6:10–18 Spiritual Warfare, FAITH'S WARFARE. Paul admonishes us to put on the whole armor of God in order to stand against the forces of hell. It is clear that our warfare is not against physical forces, but against invisible powers who have clearly defined levels of authority in a real, though invisible, sphere of activity. Paul, however, not only warns us of a clearly defined structure in the invisible realm, he instructs us to take up the whole armor of God in order to maintain a "battle-stance" against this unseen satanic structure. All of this armor is not just a passive protection in facing the enemy; it is to be used offensively against these satanic forces. Note Paul's final directive: we are to be "praying always with all prayer and supplication in the Spirit" (v. 18). Thus, prayer is not so much a weapon, or even a part of the armor, as it is the means by which we engage in the battle itself and the purpose for which we are armed. To put on the armor of God is to prepare for battle. Prayer is the battle itself, with God's Word being our chief weapon employed against Satan during our struggle.

(*/2 Kin. 6:8–17) D.E.

14 [a]Is. 11:5; Luke 12:35; 1 Pet. 1:13 [b]Is. 59:17; Rom. 13:12; Eph. 6:13; 1 Thess. 5:8 *See WW at 2 Tim. 4:8.
15 [a]Is. 52:7; Rom. 10:15
16 [a]1 John 5:4
17 [a]1 Thess. 5:8 [b]Is. 49:2; Hos. 6:5; [Heb. 4:12] *See WW at Acts 28:28. • See WW at Matt. 4:4.
18 [a]Luke 18:1; Col. 1:3; 4:2; 1 Thess. 5:17 [b][Matt. 26:41] [c]Phil. 1:4
19 [a]Acts 4:29; Col. 4:3 *See WW at Acts 4:31. • See WW at Mark 4:11.
20 [a]2 Cor. 5:20; Philem. 9
21 [a]Acts 20:4; 2 Tim. 4:12; Titus 3:12 [b]1 Cor. 4:1, 2
22 [a]Col. 4:8 [b]2 Cor. 1:6

19 and for me, that utterance may be
given to me, [a]that I may open my
mouth *boldly to make known the
*mystery of the gospel,
20 for which [a]I am an **ambassador** in
chains; that in it I may speak boldly,
as I ought to speak.

WORD WEALTH

6:20 ambassador, *presbeuo* (pres-*byoo*-oh); Strong's *#4243:* Literally "to be the elder," and later "to be an ambassador," a representative of a ruling authority. Ambassadors would be chosen from the ranks of mature, experienced men. To be an ambassador for Christ necessitates spiritual maturity.

A Gracious Greeting

21 But that you also may know my affairs *and* how I am doing, [a]Tychicus,
a beloved brother and [b]faithful minister in the Lord, will make all things
known to you;
22 [a]whom I have sent to you for this
very purpose, that you may know our
affairs, and *that* he may [b]comfort your
hearts.
23 Peace to the brethren, and love with
faith, from God the Father and the
Lord Jesus Christ.
24 Grace *be* with all those who love
our Lord Jesus Christ in sincerity.
Amen.

6:14–17 See section 5 of Truth-In-Action at the end of Eph.
6:15 Preparation refers to that which is already accomplished and ready.
6:16 The wicked one is a direct reference to the personal assault of Satan against believers.
6:18–20 See section 1 of Truth-In-Action at the end of Eph.
6:18 All prayer is literally "every order of praying," the specific method by which spiritual warfare is carried on. Prayer is to include **supplication in the Spirit,** a phrase that elucidates Rom. 8:26, 27 and Jude 20, where Holy Spirit-assisted prayer is taught and directed. In 1 Cor. 14:14, 15 Paul clearly shows that such praying may include prayer "in a tongue" not known to the person praying.
6:19, 20 The focus of all spiritual warfare is ultimately the opening of doors (Col. 4:3; 1 Cor. 16:9) so that the ministry of the gospel may be advanced.

TRUTH-IN-ACTION through EPHESIANS

Letting the LIFE of the Holy Spirit Bring Faith's Works Alive in You!

Truth Ephesians Teaches	Text	**Action** Ephesians Invites
1 Guidelines for Growing in Godliness Simply put, godliness is living the way God wants us to. Few books speak as clearly and succinctly to this subject as does Eph. Here godliness is exhorted in terms of behavior, motivating dynamic, and example. Godly behavior is modeled after God Himself, especially as He has revealed Himself in His fullness in Jesus Christ.	4:1	**Understand** that your conduct is the most effective sermon you will ever preach. **Live** a life that will give consistent, undeniable evidence of the truth of the gospel.
	5:1, 2	**Model** your life after Jesus, imitating Him rather than others. **Understand** that He is the perfect example of the love God requires.
	5:18–20	**Be continually filled** with the Holy Spirit. **Overflow** with a continual song of praise and thanksgiving to maintain a Spirit-filled flow in your life.
	6:18–20	**Give yourself** to constant, faithful prayer. **Let God change** your prayer life to a life of prayer.
2 Steps to Holiness A major facet of holiness is living a life separated from the world. Jesus stressed this by saying that although we live in the world, we are not to be *of the world.*	4:17	**Be careful** to avoid and reject the world's way of thinking. **Realize** that thinking as the world does will unavoidably lead to sensuality and impurity.
3 Keys to Godly Relationships Eph. has much to say about building godly relationships. This is one of the major themes of the NT. Our relationships are to be loving, truthful, selfless, and submissive. Simply put, Eph. exhorts that we relate to others as Jesus relates to the Father and to us.	4:25–27	**Diligently practice** honesty and truthfulness in all your relationships. **Deal with anger** quickly, not allowing it to influence your treatment of others.
	5:21—6:4	**Maintain** a *selflessly submissive attitude* in all your family relationships. **Understand** that this will provide evidence that Christ rules your home.
	6:5–8	**Do not be** merely a people-pleaser at work! **Serve the Lord** in all you do. **Recognize** that it is He who has assigned you to that post of responsibility.
4 How to Tame the Tongue Proper speech is crucial to effective Christian living. Prov. points out that life and death are in the power of the tongue. How important it is for us to realize that our speech can be spiritually motivated.	4:29	**Be careful** how you speak and what you say. **Reject** evil attitudes; and **develop** compassionate, forgiving attitudes toward others.
	5:3–7	**Avoid** and **reject** *any* impure or immoral speech or behavior. **Be certain** that it contradicts your profession of faith in Christ.
5 Guidelines to Gaining Victory Eph. gives us insight into the nature of the spiritual warfare we face daily. Our *combat is against spiritual forces,* not men. Great is the protection and resources God has provided us to meet this enemy.	6:10–13	**Stand in readiness** for spiritual combat. **Recognize** that your demonic enemies are behind much of what comes against you to harm you.
	6:14–17	Each day, consciously **put on** the spiritual armor God supplies. **Learn** and **understand** the nature of this divine protection.

Truth Ephesians Teaches	Text	**Action** Ephesians Invites
6 **Keys to Wise Living** Perhaps wisdom is what is most necessary in governing our use of time.	5:15	**Use** time wisely, and **do not squander** it. **Be certain** that you will give an account of how you use God's gift of time.
7 **Keys to Generous Living** Selflessness is most concretely expressed in generosity.	4:28	**Think** of how you can give rather than how you can get.

The Epistle of Paul the Apostle to the PHILIPPIANS

Author: Paul
Date: A.D. 61
Theme: Joy in Christ
Key Words: Joy, Rejoice

Background Acts 16:12–40 records the founding of the Philippian church. Paul established the church during his second missionary journey, about A.D. 51. From its inception, the church displayed a strong missionary zeal and was consistent in its support of Paul's ministry (4:15, 16; see 2 Cor. 11:8, 9). Paul enjoyed a closer friendship with the Philippians than with any other church.

Occasion and Date Paul most likely wrote his letter to the Philippians during his first Roman imprisonment, about A.D. 61, to thank them for the contribution he had received from them. He also warmly commended Epaphroditus, who had brought the gift from Philippi and whom Paul was sending back.

Purpose While his primary reason for writing the letter was to acknowledge the gift sent by the Philippians, Paul also appealed for a spirit of unity and steadfastness among them. In addition, he warned against dangerous heresies that were threatening them, probably Judaism and Gnosticism.

Characteristics In many respects, this is the most beautiful of Paul's letters, full of tenderness, warmth, and affection. His style is spontaneous, personal, and informal, presenting us with an intimate diary of Paul's own spiritual experiences.

The dominant note throughout the letter is that of triumphant joy. Paul, though a prisoner, was exultantly happy, and called upon his readers to rejoice in Christ always. It is an ethical and practical letter in its emphasis and centers on Jesus Christ. To Paul, Christ was more than an example; He was the apostle's very life.

Content The abiding message of Philippians concerns the nature and grounds of Christian joy. For Paul, true joy is not a surface emotion that depends on favorable circumstances of the moment. Christian joy is independent of outward conditions, and is possible even in the midst of adverse circumstances, such as suffering and persecution.

Joy ultimately arises from fellowship with the risen, glorified Christ. Throughout the letter, Paul speaks of joy in the Lord, emphasizing that through Christ alone is Christian joy realized, as are all other Christian graces. Essential to this joy is the confident conviction of the lordship of Christ, based on experience of the power of His resurrection. Because of this conviction, life for Paul attained meaning. Even death became a friend, because it would bring him *into a fuller* experience of the presence of Christ (1:21–23).

The joy presented in Philippians involves eager expectation of the near return of the Lord. That this expectation was dominant in Paul's thinking is seen in his five references to Christ's return. In the context of each reference is a note of joy (1:6, 10; 2:16; 3:20; 4:5).

Paul further describes a joy that springs from fellowship in the spreading of the gospel. He begins the letter by thanking the Philippians for their partnership in spreading the gospel through their monetary gifts. The gifts, however, are only an expression of their spirit of fellowship, or as he puts it in 4:17, "the fruit that abounds to your account." So Christian joy is an outgrowth of being in the active fellowship of the body of Christ.

Personal Application This letter reveals the timeless message that true joy is to be found only in a dynamic personal relationship with Jesus Christ and in the assurance that God is able to turn adverse circumstances to our good and His glory. Because he was united to Christ by a living faith, Paul could claim contentment in all circumstances. His unadorned testimony was "I rejoice . . . and will rejoice" (1:18), and his unqualified command was, "Rejoice . . . again I will say, rejoice!" (4:4).

Christ Revealed For Paul, Christ is the sum and substance of life. To preach Christ was his consuming passion; to know Him was his highest aspiration; and to suffer for Him was a privilege. His chief desire for his readers was that they might have the mind of Christ. To support his exhortation for self-forgetting humility, the apostle describes the attitude of Christ that moved Him to renounce the glory of heaven and suffer and die for our salvation (2:5–11). In doing so, he presents the most concise statement in the New Testament concerning the preexistence, the incarnation, and the exaltation of Christ. Both the deity and the humanity of Christ are stressed.

The Holy Spirit at Work The Spirit's work in three areas is mentioned in the letter. First, Paul declares that the Spirit of Jesus Christ will direct the accomplishment of God's purpose in his own experience (1:19). The Holy Spirit also promotes unity and fellowship in the body of Christ (2:1). Common participation in Him breeds singleness of purpose and maintains a community of love. Then, in contrast to the lifeless ritual observance of formalists, the Holy Spirit inspires and directs the worship of true believers (3:3).

Outline of Philippians

Introduction **1:1–11**
- A. Salutation 1:1, 2
- B. Thanksgiving 1:3–8
- C. Prayer 1:9–11

I. Circumstances of Paul's imprisonment **1:12–26**
- A. Had advanced the gospel 1:12–18
- B. Had brought assurance of blessing 1:19–21
- C. Had created a dilemma for Paul 1:22–26

II. Exhortations **1:27—2:18**
- A. Live worthy of the gospel 1:27—2:4
- B. Reproduce the mind of Christ 2:5–11
- C. Cultivate the spiritual life 2:12, 13
- D. Leave off murmurings and questionings 2:14–18

III. Commendation of and plans for Paul's companions **2:19–30**
- A. Timothy 2:19–24
- B. Epaphroditus 2:25–30

IV. Warnings against error **3:1–21**
- A. Against the Judaizers 3:1–16
- B. Against sensualism 3:17–21

Conclusion **4:1–23**
- A. Final appeals 4:1–9
- B. Acknowledgment of the Philippians' gift 4:10–20
- C. Greetings 4:21, 22
- D. Benediction 4:23

Greeting

PAUL and Timothy, bondservants of Jesus Christ,

To all the saints in Christ Jesus who are in Philippi, with the [1]bishops and [a]deacons:

2 Grace to you and peace from God our Father and the Lord Jesus Christ.

Thankfulness and Prayer

3 [a]I thank my God upon every remembrance of you,
4 always in [a]every prayer of mine making request for you all with joy,
5 [a]for your *fellowship in the *gospel from the first day until now,
3 6 being confident of this very thing, that He who has begun [a]a **good** work in you will complete *it* until the day of Jesus Christ;

WORD WEALTH

1:6 good, *agathos* (ag-ath-*oss*); Strong's *#18:* Good, in a physical and moral sense, and which produces benefits. The word is used of persons, things, acts, conditions, and so on. A synonym of *agathos* is *kalos,* good in an aesthetic sense, suggesting attractiveness, excellence.

7 just as it is right for me to think this of you all, because I have you in my heart, inasmuch as both in my chains and in the defense and confirmation of the gospel, you all are partakers with me of *grace.
8 For God is my *witness, how greatly I long for you all with the affection of Jesus Christ.
9 And this I *pray, that your *love may *abound still more and more in knowledge and all discernment,
10 that you may approve the things that are excellent, that you may be *sincere and without offense till the day of Christ,
11 being filled with the fruits of *righteousness [a]which *are* by Jesus Christ, [b]to the glory and *praise of God.

CHAPTER 1
1 [a][1 Tim. 3:8–13] [1]Lit. *overseers*
3 [a]1 Cor. 1:4
4 [a]Eph. 1:16; 1 Thess. 1:2
5 [a][Rom. 12:13] *See WW at Acts 2:42. • See WW at Mark 1:1.
6 [a][John 6:29]
7 *See WW at 2 Cor. 12:9.
8 *See WW at Rev. 1:5.
9 *See WW at Matt. 6:6. • See WW at Rom. 5:5. • See WW at Matt. 25:29.
10 *See WW at 2 Pet. 3:1.
11 [a][Eph. 2:10]; Col. 1:6 [b]John 15:8 *See WW at 2 Tim. 4:8. • See WW at Eph. 1:6.
13 [a]Phil. 4:22 [1]Or *Praetorium* *See WW at 1 Cor. 11:19.
14 *See WW at 2 Cor. 2:4.
15 *See WW at Acts 9:20.
16 [1]NU reverses vv. 16 and 17.

Christ Is Preached

12 But I want you to know, brethren, that the things *which happened* to me have actually turned out for the furtherance of the gospel,
13 so that it has become *evident [a]to the whole [1]palace guard, and to all the rest, that my chains are in Christ;
14 and most of the brethren in the Lord, having become confident by my chains, are *much more bold to speak the word without fear.
15 Some indeed *preach Christ even from envy and strife, and some also from goodwill:
16 [1]The former preach Christ from **selfish ambition,** not sincerely, supposing to add affliction to my chains;

WORD WEALTH

1:16 selfish ambition, *eritheia* (er-ith-*eye*-ah); Strong's *#2052:* A word that regressed from denoting honorable work to suggesting dishonorable intrigue. Originally, it meant a field-worker or reaper, and then anyone working for pay, a hireling. *Eritheia* later described a person who was concerned only with his own welfare, a person susceptible to being bribed, an ambitious, self-willed person seeking opportunities for promotion. From there it became electioneering, a partisan factious spirit that would resort to any method for winning followers.

17 but the latter out of love, knowing that I am appointed for the defense of the gospel.

1:1 Because of his close relationship with the Philippian Christians, Paul does not need to insist upon his authority as an apostle as he does in other epistles. **Bishops:** A reference to an official in the local church, stressing the nature of his work as an overseer. In the NT the word refers to the same office as elder, which emphasizes the status of the office, and pastor, which describes the shepherding function of the office. **Deacons:** See note on 1 Tim. 3:8.

1:5 The Philippians had actively supported Paul's ministry from the time that they first became Christians.

1:6 See section 3 of Truth-In-Action at the end of Phil.

1:6 Paul is confident that they will maintain their fruitful activity until Christ returns. He bases his belief, not on their own faithfulness, but on God's purpose and faithfulness until Christ returns.

1:7 The Philippians are united with Paul both in his sufferings and in his witness of the gospel, showing that they share in the grace that he experienced.

1:8 Paul's affection for them is identical with the love of Christ for them.

1:10 Paul intends their love to result in their ability both to discern and choose what is morally best. As a result, their lives will be transparently pure and they will provide others no occasion for stumbling.

1:12–18 Rather than slowing the spread of the gospel, Paul's imprisonment has given him new opportunities for witnessing, particularly among the elite of the Roman army. His experience has also stimulated others to preach more boldly, even though some had the wrong motive. Paul has no scathing remark for these people because their doctrine is correct. His reaction is vastly different to the doctrinal agitators addressed in ch. 3.

18 What then? Only *that* in every way, whether in pretense or in truth, Christ is preached; and in this I rejoice, yes, and will rejoice.

To Live Is Christ

19 For I know that [a]this will turn out for my deliverance through your prayer and the supply of the *Spirit of Jesus Christ,
20 according to my earnest expectation and hope that in nothing I shall be ashamed, but [a]with all *boldness, as always, so now also Christ will be *magnified in my body, whether by life [b]or by death.
[3] 21 For to me, to live *is* Christ, and to die *is* gain.
22 But if *I* live on in the *flesh, this *will mean* fruit from *my* labor; yet what I shall choose I [1]cannot tell.
23 [1]For I am *hard-pressed between the two, having a [a]desire* to depart and be with Christ, *which is* [b]far better.
24 Nevertheless to remain in the flesh *is* more needful for you.
25 And being confident of this, I know that I shall remain and continue with you all for your progress and joy of faith,
26 that [a]your rejoicing for me may be more abundant in Jesus Christ by my *coming to you again.

Striving and Suffering for Christ

[1] **27** Only [a]let your conduct be worthy of the gospel of Christ, so that whether I come and see you or am absent, I may hear of your affairs, that you stand fast in one spirit, [b]with one mind [c]striving together for the faith of the gospel,
28 and not in any way terrified by your adversaries, which is to them a proof of perdition, but [1]to you of salvation, and that from God.
29 For to you [a]it has been *granted on [3]
behalf of Christ, [b]not only to believe in Him, but also to [c]suffer* for His sake,
30 [a]having the same conflict [b]which you saw in me and now hear *is* in me.

19 [a]Job 13:16, LXX *See WW at Rom. 7:6. **20** [a]Eph. 6:19, 20 [b][Rom. 14:8] *See WW at Acts 4:31. • See WW at Acts 5:13. **22** [1]*do not know* *See WW at Matt. 26:41. **23** [a][2 Cor. 5:2, 8] [b][Ps. 16:11] [1]NU, M *But* *See WW at 2 Cor. 5:14. • See WW at 2 Tim. 2:22. **26** [a]2 Cor. 1:14 *See WW at 1 Cor. 15:23. **27** [a]Eph. 4:1 [b]Eph. 4:3 [c]Jude 3 **28** [1]NU *of your salvation* **29** [a][Matt. 5:11, 12] [b]Eph. 2:8 [c][2 Tim. 3:12] *See WW at Col. 3:13. • See WW at Acts 17:3. **30** [a]Col. 1:29; 2:1 [b]Acts 16:19–40

CHAPTER 2

1 [a]Col. 3:12 [1]Or *encouragement* *See WW at Acts 9:31. • See WW at Acts 2:42. **2** [a]John 3:29 [b]Rom. 12:16 [c]Phil. 4:2 **3** [a]Gal. 5:26 [b]Rom. 12:10 *See WW at Phil. 1:16. • See WW at Acts 20:19.

Unity Through Humility

2 Therefore if *there is* any [1]consolation in Christ, if any *comfort of love, if any *fellowship of the Spirit, if any [a]affection and mercy,
2 [a]fulfill my joy [b]by being like- [2]
minded, having the same love, *being* of [c]one accord, of one mind.
3 [a]*Let* nothing *be done* through *self- [1]
ish ambition or conceit, but [b]in *lowliness of mind let each esteem others better than himself.
4 [a]Let each of you look out not only for his own interests, but also for the interests of [b]others.*

The Humbled and Exalted Christ

5 [a]Let this mind be in you which was [2]
also in Christ Jesus,
6 who, [a]being in the form of God, did not consider it [1]robbery to be equal with God,
7 [a]but [1]made* Himself of no reputa-

4 [a]1 Cor. 13:5 [b]Rom. 15:1, 2 *See WW at Acts 4:12. **5** [a][Matt. 11:29] **6** [a]2 Cor. 4:4 [1]Or *something to be held onto to be equal* **7** [a]Ps. 22:6 [1]*emptied Himself* of His privileges *See WW at 1 Cor. 9:15.

1:21–25 Paul does not long for death, but for the closer presence of Christ that death will bring. Meanwhile, he has a strong sense of duty to remain among them for their growth and maturing in the faith.
1:21–24 See section 3 of Truth-In-Action at the end of Phil.
1:23 The word **depart** is also used for pulling up tent pegs or a ship's anchor. For Paul, death is simply breaking camp and moving on, or setting sail to a new port.
1:27 See section 1 of Truth-In-Action at the end of Phil.
1:27 Conduct: This word usually describes one's life as a citizen. The city of Philippi prized its Roman citizenship, but Paul reminds his readers that the most important conduct is to behave in a manner befitting citizens of the kingdom of God.
1:28 The courageous conduct of the Philippian Christians is evidence of the spiritual ruin of their adversaries and proof of their own eternal safety.
1:29 See section 3 of Truth-In-Action at the end of Phil.
2:1 The basis of Christian unity is expressed in conditional clauses (**if . . . if . . . if**). In the Greek these clauses do not convey doubt, but rather are used for emphasis. Each "if" could be translated "since."
2:2 See section 2 of Truth-In-Action at the end of Phil.
2:3, 4 See section 1 of Truth-In-Action at the end of Phil.
2:5–11 See section 2 of Truth-In-Action at the end of Phil.
2:5–11 Paul uses the example of Christ to enforce an appeal for unselfishness. As Christ willingly laid aside His heavenly glory to come to Earth and die, we should be willing to look beyond our own interests for ("not only . . . but also," v. 4) the sake of others. Although his purpose is to strengthen his exhortation rather than to establish doctrine, Paul here presents one of the greatest statements in the NT concerning the Person and work of Jesus Christ.
2:6 Form of God: The reference is not to the physical shape of Christ, but to His divine essence, a quality that is unchangeable. **Equal with God** refers to the mode of Christ's existence. Christ shared in the glories and prerogatives of deity, but did not regard the circumstances of His existence as something to be jealously retained. Rather, He willingly relinquished His glory when He came to Earth, though retaining His deity.
2:7 The reality of the Incarnation is expressed in the complete self-renunciation of Christ as He **made Himself of no reputation** (see marginal note). He veiled the

tion, taking the form [b]of a *bondservant, *and* [c]coming in the likeness
of men.
8 And being found in appearance as
a man, He *humbled Himself and
[a]became [b]obedient to *the point of*
death, even the death of the cross.
9 [a]Therefore God also [b]has **highly exalted** Him and [c]given* Him the *name
which is above every name,
10 [a]that at the name of Jesus every
knee should bow, of those in heaven,
and of those on earth, and of those under the earth,
11 and [a]*that* every tongue should confess that Jesus Christ *is* Lord, to the
glory of God the Father.

WORD WEALTH

2:9 highly exalted, *huperupsoo* (hoop-er-oop-*sah*-oh); Strong's *#5251:* From *huper,* "over," and *hupsoo,* "to lift up." Thus, the word suggests an exaltation to the highest position, an elevation above all others. The context contrasts humiliation and resulting honors. Jesus' obedience to death is followed by a super-exalted position of honor and glory.

KINGDOM DYNAMICS

2:9–11 Faith Exalting Jesus' Lordship, FAITH'S CONFESSION. Scholars note that the word "confess" means "to acknowledge openly and joyfully, to celebrate and give praise" (Thayer/Wycliffe). This eloquently and beautifully stated text is a great point of acknowledgment for all who would learn the power of faith's confession. The exalting and honoring of our Lord Jesus Christ is our fountainhead of power in applying faith. The Father honors Him first, then those who confess His Son as well (John 12:26). All humans, angels, and demon spirits will ultimately bow the knee to Jesus, rendering complete and final homage. That confession of every tongue will one day be heard by every ear as He receives ultimate and complete rule. But until that day, our confession of Jesus Christ as Lord invites and receives His presence and power over all evil whenever we face it now. And as we declare His lordship—in faith—His rule enters those settings and circumstances today.
(1 Cor. 11:23–26/Heb. 4:11–13) R.H.

7 [b]Is. 42:1 [c][John 1:14] *See WW At Rev. 19:5. **8** [a]Matt. 26:39 [b]Heb. 5:8 *See WW at Matt. 18:4. **9** [a]Heb. 2:9 [b]Acts 2:33 [c]Eph. 1:21 *See WW at Col. 3:13. • See WW at John 12:13. **10** [a]Is. 45:23 **11** [a]John 13:13

12 [a]Phil. 1:5, 6; 4:15 [b]John 6:27, 29 [c]Eph. 6:5 *See WW at Rom. 6:17. • See WW at Luke 19:9. • See WW at 1 John 4:18. **13** [a]Heb. 13:20, 21 [b]Eph. 1:5 *See WW at 1 Thess. 2:13. **14** [a]1 Pet. 4:9 [b]Rom. 14:1 [1]*grumbling* [2]*arguing* *See WW at Luke 2:35. **15** [a]Matt. 5:15, 16 [1]*innocent* **16** [a]2 Cor. 1:14 [b]Gal. 2:2 [c]1 Thess. 3:5 *See WW at Acts 19:20. **17** [a]2 Tim. 4:6 [b]Rom. 15:16 [c]2 Cor. 7:4 *See WW at Luke 1:23. **19** [a]Rom. 16:21 [1]*condition* **20** [a]2 Tim. 3:10 **22** [a]1 Cor. 4:17

Light Bearers

12 Therefore, my beloved, [a]as you **2**
have always *obeyed, not as in my
presence only, but now much more in
my absence, [b]work out your own *salvation with [c]fear* and trembling;
13 for [a]it is God who *works in you
both to will and to do [b]for *His* good
pleasure.
14 Do all things [a]without [1]complaining
and [b]disputing,[2]*
15 that you may become blameless and
[1]harmless, children of God without
fault in the midst of a crooked and perverse generation, among whom you
shine as [a]lights in the world,
16 holding fast the *word of life, so that
[a]I may rejoice in the day of Christ that
[b]I have not run in vain or labored in
[c]vain.
17 Yes, and if [a]I am being poured out
as a drink offering on the sacrifice
[b]and *service of your faith, [c]I am glad
and rejoice with you all.
18 For the same reason you also be
glad and rejoice with me.

Timothy Commended

19 But I trust in the Lord Jesus to send
[a]Timothy to you shortly, that I also
may be encouraged when I know your
[1]state.
20 For I have no one [a]like-minded, **2**
who will sincerely care for your state.
21 For all seek their own, not the
things which are of Christ Jesus.
22 But you know his proven character,
[a]that as a son with *his* father he served
with me in the gospel.
23 Therefore I hope to send him at

manifestations of deity and assumed real humanity. **Likeness** suggests that Jesus was really a man, but not merely a man. His humanity was genuine, yet His being was still divine.
2:9 The exaltation of Christ is in consequence of His redemptive work. He now has a higher state of glory than before His Incarnation.
2:10, 11 *Christ's exaltation* is absolute; His lordship is universal.
2:12, 13 See section 2 of Truth-In-Action at the end of Phil.
2:12 In view of the obedience of Christ and His lordship, the Philippians should show a like obedience. Paul does not teach that salvation is dependent on one's continued works, but that salvation must express itself in progressive Christian living and upright character, not only individually, but through obedient participation in God's corporate call to a local church.
2:13 Without denying man's freedom, Paul stresses God's part in man's salvation, both in its initial resolution and in its subsequent progress.
2:15 As the heavenly bodies shine forth in brightness against the blackness of the night, so the lives of true Christians lighten the moral darkness of the world.
2:19–23 Timothy often functioned as Paul's personal envoy (1 Cor. 4:17; 16:10, 11; 1 Thess. 3:6). His purpose in going to Philippi is both to encourage the Christians there and to bring back to Paul news of their welfare.
2:20, 21 See section 2 of Truth-In-Action at the end of Phil.

once, as soon as I see how it goes with
me.
24 But I *trust in the Lord that I myself
shall also come shortly.

Epaphroditus Praised

25 Yet I considered it necessary to
send to you [a]Epaphroditus, my
brother, fellow worker, and [b]fellow
soldier, [c]but your messenger and
[d]the *one who ministered to my need;
26 [a]since he was longing for you all,
and was distressed because you had
heard that he was sick.
27 For indeed he was sick almost unto
death; but God had *mercy on him, and
not only on him but on me also, lest I
should have sorrow upon sorrow.
28 Therefore I sent him the more eagerly, that when you see him again you
may rejoice, and I may be less sorrowful.
29 Receive him therefore in the Lord
with all gladness, and hold such men
in esteem;
30 because for the work of Christ he
came close to death, [1]not regarding his
life, [a]to supply what was lacking in
your *service toward me.

All for Christ

3 Finally, my brethren, [a]rejoice in
the Lord. For me to write the same
things to you *is* not tedious, but for you
it is safe.
2 [a]Beware of dogs, beware of [b]evil
workers, [c]beware of the mutilation!
3 For we are [a]the circumcision,
[b]who worship [1]God in the Spirit, rejoice in Christ Jesus, and have no confidence in the flesh,
4 though [a]I also might have confidence in the flesh. If *anyone else
thinks he may have confidence in the
flesh, I [b]more so:
5 circumcised the eighth day, of the
stock of Israel, [a]*of* the tribe of Benjamin, [b]a Hebrew of the Hebrews; concerning the law, [c]a Pharisee;
6 concerning *zeal, [a]persecuting the
church; concerning the righteousness
which is in the law, blameless.
7 But [a]what things were gain to me, 4
these I have counted loss for Christ.
8 Yet indeed I also count all things
loss [a]for the excellence of the knowledge of Christ Jesus my Lord, for
whom I have suffered the loss of all
things, and count them as rubbish, that
I may gain Christ
9 and be found in Him, not having
[a]my own righteousness, which *is* from
the law, but [b]that which *is* through
faith in Christ, the righteousness which
is from God by faith;
10 that I may know Him and the
[a]power of His *resurrection, and
[b]the fellowship of His sufferings, being
conformed to His death,
11 if, by any means, I may [a]attain[1] to
the resurrection from the dead.

Pressing Toward the Goal

12 Not that I have already [a]attained,[1] 4
or am already [b]perfected;* but I press
on, that I may *lay hold of that for
which Christ Jesus has also laid hold
of me.

• See WW at John 1:5.

24 *See WW at 2 Thess. 3:4. **25** [a]Phil. 4:18 [b]Philem. 2 [c]2 Cor. 8:23 [d]2 Cor. 11:9 *See WW at Heb. 1:7. **26** [a]Phil. 1:8 **27** *See WW at Rom. 9:15. **30** [a]1 Cor. 16:17 [1]*risking* *See WW at Luke 1:23.

CHAPTER 3

1 [a]1 Thess. 5:16 **2** [a]Gal. 5:15 [b]Ps. 119:115 [c]Rom. 2:28 **3** [a]Deut. 30:6 [b]Rom. 7:6 [1]NU, M *in the Spirit of God* **4** [a]2 Cor. 5:16; 11:18 [b]2 Cor. 11:22, 23 *See WW at John 14:16. **5** [a]Rom. 11:1 [b]2 Cor. 11:22 [c]Acts 23:6 **6** [a]Acts 8:3; 22:4, 5; 26:9–11 *See WW at 2 Cor. 11:2. **7** [a]Matt. 13:44 **8** [a]Jer. 9:23 **9** [a]Rom. 10:3 [b]Rom. 1:17 **10** [a]Eph. 1:19, 20 [b][Rom. 6:3–5] *See WW at Acts 23:6. **11** [a]Acts 26:6–8 [1]Lit. *arrive at* **12** [a][1 Tim. 6:12, 19] [b]Heb. 12:23 [1]*obtained it* *See WW at 1 John 2:5.

2:24 Paul is confident of his release from prison. His expectation was fulfilled soon after he wrote this letter.
2:25–30 **Epaphroditus,** as the representative of the Philippian church, has assumed great risk in rendering service to Christ. In effect, he has gambled with his life, displaying reckless courage.
3:1, 2 Paul issues a harsh warning against the Judaizers, who taught that observance of the Law was necessary for salvation and who constantly sought to sabotage his gospel of free grace. The word **mutilation** in v. 2 is a parody. The legalists taught the necessity of circumcision, but in reality a physical ritual without rightness of heart is nothing more than worthless mutilation of the flesh.
3:3 The true sign of a right relation to God is not the observance of an external rite but a manifestation of the three characteristics mentioned. **Worship God in the Spirit** not only refers to one's being alive in the spirit (John 4:24) and thereby qualified for living worship, but also includes the Holy Spirit's enablement in expanded worship expressions: in song (Eph. 5:18, 19), in prayer and singing (1 Cor. 14:15) and in communion with God (1 Cor. 14:1, 2).
3:4–16 Paul gives his personal testimony as an example that one must put no confidence in his own achievements, but must rely entirely on Christ.
3:5 Paul was a genuine Jew by birth, not a proselyte. Furthermore, he was **of the stock of Israel,** directly descended from Abraham, Isaac, and Jacob. His tribe was the elite of Israel, and he was **a Hebrew of the Hebrews** in that his family retained Hebrew customs and spoke the Hebrew language.
3:6 Paul had scrupulously observed the external demands of the Law and fanatically tried to wipe out all opponents of Judaism.
3:7–9 See section 4 of Truth-In-Action at the end of Phil.
3:7 What Paul had considered assets became liabilities. He laid aside all human achievements in order to receive the free grace of God.
3:8 Paul's **knowledge of Christ** involves not merely an intellectual apprehension, but rather an experiential knowledge resulting from his personal communion with Christ. In contrast to the life he now has, his former manner of life is **rubbish,** scraps fit only to be thrown to the dogs.
3:10 Knowing Christ not only means experiencing the power of the risen Lord, but also sharing **His sufferings.**
3:11 **If, by any means:** Not an expression of doubt, but of deep humility and earnest striving.
3:12–14 See section 4 of Truth-In-Action at the end of Phil.

13 Brethren, I do not *count myself to
have [1]apprehended; but one thing *I do,*
[a]forgetting those things which are behind and [b]reaching forward to those
things which are ahead,
14 [a]I press toward the goal for the
prize of [b]the upward call of God in
Christ Jesus.
4 15 Therefore let us, as many as are
[a]mature,* [b]have this mind; and if in
anything you think otherwise, [c]God
will reveal even this to you.
16 Nevertheless, to *the degree* that we
have already [1]attained, [a]let us walk
[b]by the same [2]rule, let us be of the
same mind.

Our Citizenship in Heaven

4 17 Brethren, [a]join in following my example, and note those who so walk, as
[b]you have us for a pattern.
18 For many walk, of whom I have told
you often, and now tell you even weeping, *that they are* [a]the enemies of the
cross of Christ:
19 [a]whose end *is* destruction, [b]whose
god *is their* belly, and [c]*whose* glory *is*
in their shame—[d]who set their mind
on earthly things.
20 For [a]our citizenship is in heaven,
[b]from which we also [c]eagerly wait for
the *Savior, the Lord Jesus Christ,
21 [a]who will transform our lowly body
that it may be [b]conformed to His glorious body, [c]according to the *working
by which He *is able even to [d]subdue*
all things to Himself.

4 Therefore, my beloved and
[a]longed-for brethren, [b]my joy and
crown, so [c]stand fast in the Lord, beloved.

Be United, Joyful, and in Prayer

2 I implore Euodia and I implore Syn-
tyche [a]to be of the same mind in the
Lord.

13 [a]Luke 9:62 [b]Heb. 6:1 [1]*laid hold of it* *See WW at Rom. 4:3.
14 [a]2 Tim. 4:7 [b]Heb. 3:1
15 [a]1 Cor. 2:6 [b]Gal. 5:10 [c]Hos. 6:3 *See WW at James 3:2.
16 [a]Gal. 6:16 [b]Rom. 12:16; 15:5 [1]*arrived* [2]NU omits *rule* and the rest of v. 16.
17 [a][1 Cor. 4:16; 11:1] [b]Titus 2:7, 8
18 [a]Gal. 1:7
19 [a]2 Cor. 11:15 [b]1 Tim. 6:5 [c]Hos. 4:7 [d]Rom. 8:5
20 [a]Eph. 2:6, 19 [b]Acts 1:11 [c]1 Cor. 1:7 *See WW at John 4:42.
21 [a][1 Cor. 15:43–53] [b]1 John 3:2 [c]Eph. 1:19 [d][1 Cor. 15:28] *See WW at Col. 1:29. • See WW at Jude 24. • See WW at 1 Cor. 14:32.

CHAPTER 4

1 [a]Phil. 1:8 [b]2 Cor. 1:14 [c]Phil. 1:27
2 [a]Phil. 2:2; 3:16
3 [a]Rom. 16:3 [b]Luke 10:20 [1]NU, M *Yes*
4 [a]Rom. 12:12
5 [a][James 5:7–9] [1]*graciousness* or *forbearance* *See WW at 1 Tim. 3:3.
6 [a]Matt. 6:25 [b][1 Thess. 5:17, 18]

3 [1]And I urge you also, true companion, help these women who [a]labored
with me in the gospel, with Clement
also, and the rest of my fellow workers,
whose names *are* in [b]the Book of Life.
4 [a]Rejoice in the Lord always. Again 3
I will say, rejoice!
5 Let your [1]gentleness* be known to
all men. [a]The Lord *is* at hand.
6 [a]Be *anxious for nothing, but in
everything by prayer and supplication,
with [b]thanksgiving, let your requests
be made known to God;
7 and [a]the peace of God, which surpasses all understanding, will *guard
your hearts and minds through Christ
Jesus.

Meditate on These Things

8 Finally, brethren, whatever things 2
are [a]true,* whatever things *are* [b]no-
ble,* whatever things *are* [c]just, [d]what-
ever things *are* *pure, whatever things
are [e]lovely, whatever things *are* of
good report, if *there is* any *virtue and
if *there is* anything *praiseworthy—
meditate on these things.

WORD WEALTH

4:8 good report, *euphemos* (yoo-fay-moss); Strong's *#2163:* Compare "euphemism" and "euphemistic." A combination of *eu,* "well," and *pheme,* "a saying." *Euphemos* is speech that is gracious, auspicious, praiseworthy, and fair-sounding. It includes the avoidance of words of ill omen. An OT counterpart is found in Prov. 16:24: "Pleasant words *are like* a honeycomb, sweetness to the soul and health to the bones."

*See WW at Matt. 6:25. 7 [a][John 14:27] *See WW at 1 Pet. 1:5. 8 [a]Eph. 4:25 [b]2 Cor. 8:21 [c]Deut. 16:20 [d]1 Thess. 5:22 [e]1 Cor. 13:4–7 *See WW at Rom. 3:4. • See WW at 1 Tim. 3:11. • See WW at 1 John 3:3. • See WW at 2 Pet. 1:5. • See WW at Eph. 1:6.

3:13 Reaching forward: The imagery is that of a runner on the course straining every muscle as he runs toward the goal, his hand stretched out to grasp it.
3:15 See section 4 of Truth-In-Action at the end of Phil.
3:17–21 In contrast to the Judaizers, other false teachers perverted Christian liberty and took freedom from the Law as license to sin.
3:17–19 See section 4 of Truth-In-Action at the end of Phil.
3:20 Paul again reminds his readers that, although they may be citizens of Rome, they have a higher citizenship and really *are only aliens* on this Earth.
4:3 Paul appeals to a member of the Philippian church to reconcile two women who were in disagreement. Although various suggestions have been made concerning the identity of the **true companion,** including the theory that the Greek word here is a proper name, Syzygus, it remains unknown.
4:4–7 See section 3 of Truth-In-Action at the end of Phil.
4:4 Christians are commanded to rejoice under all circumstances, and obedience is possible because true joy is **in the Lord.** Therefore, Christians can be inwardly joyful when everything around is dreary (see 4:12; Hab. 3:17, 18; 2 Cor. 6:10).
4:6, 7 Supplication is more than petitioning, but suggests an intensity of earnestness in extended prayer—not to gain merit by many words, but to fully transfer the burden of one's soul into God's hands. Prayer and peace are closely connected. One who entrusts cares to Christ instead of fretting over them will experience the peace of God to guard him from nagging anxiety.
4:8, 9 See section 2 of Truth-In-Action at the end of Phil.
4:8 Character and conduct begin in the mind. Our actions are affected by the things we dwell on in our thoughts. Paul cautions his readers to concentrate on things that will result in right living and in God's peace (v. 9).

9 The things which you learned and
received and heard and saw in me,
these do, and [a]the God of peace will
be with you.

Philippian Generosity

10 But I rejoiced in the Lord greatly
that now at last [a]your[1] care for me has
flourished again; though you surely did
care, but you lacked opportunity.
3 11 Not that I speak in regard to need,
for I have learned in whatever state I
am, [a]to be content:
12 [a]I know how to [1]be *abased, and I
know how to [2]abound. Everywhere
and in all things I have learned both
to be *full and to be hungry, both to
abound and to *suffer need.
3 13 I can do all things [a]through [1]Christ
who strengthens me.

KINGDOM DYNAMICS

4:12, 13 Riches Are Not to Be Trusted, GOD'S PROSPERITY. Let this scripture be a guiding light to understanding God's will on the subject of prosperity. It tells us yes (we can have riches), and no (do not trust in them). With the mind of Christ (see Phil. 2:1–5), we will never become high-minded if blessed with wealth. Here is assurance that if our lives are geared to the Word of God, then, through Christ, we can experience either financial wealth or temporary setback, but we will still be steadfast in our living, all because our trust will be only in Him. If the economy should dissolve tomorrow, God's people would not be rendered inoperative, because God is our source. He can keep us through times of scarcity as well as in times of plenty. He fed Elijah by sending ravens to bring him food in the morning and evening (1 Kin. 17:2–6). God can do that now. He is the same today as He was then.

(1 Tim. 6:17/Deut. 8:18) F.P.

14 Nevertheless you have done well
that [a]you shared in my *distress.
15 Now you Philippians know also that
in the beginning of the gospel, when I
departed from Macedonia, [a]no church
shared with me concerning giving and
receiving but you only.
16 For even in Thessalonica you sent
aid once and again for my necessities.
17 Not that I seek the gift, but I seek
[a]the fruit that abounds to your account.
18 Indeed I [1]have* all and abound. I
am full, having received from [a]Epaphroditus
the things *sent* from you,
[b]a sweet-smelling aroma, [c]an acceptable
sacrifice, well pleasing to God.
19 And my God [a]shall supply all your
need according to His riches in glory
by Christ Jesus.

KINGDOM DYNAMICS

4:19 Do Whatever He Says; Then You Will Prosper, GOD'S PROSPERITY. This verse tells us that God will supply our need by a distinct and definite measure, "according to His riches." In declaring this, God makes clear that He is not stingy when it comes to provision. His "riches" encompass all of creation, so there is nothing you need that He cannot provide! Do not misquote or misread this verse. It does not say that God shall supply your needs; it says that He shall supply your need. That includes everything at once, and all of it is adequately covered because He does it according to His riches. This verse cannot be lifted out of the Bible. It underwrites and relates to everything the Scriptures tell us to do in order to prosper. If we do what the Bible tells us to do, then God will provide abundantly.

(Luke 12:15/Gen. 12:1–3*) F.P.

20 [a]Now to our God and Father *be*
glory forever and ever. Amen.

Greeting and Blessing

21 Greet every saint in Christ Jesus.
The brethren [a]who are with me greet
you.
22 All the saints greet you, but especially
those who are of Caesar's household.

9 [a]Rom. 15:33; Heb. 13:20
10 [a]2 Cor. 11:9; Phil. 2:30 [1]*you have revived your care*
11 [a]2 Cor. 9:8; 1 Tim. 6:6, 8; Heb. 13:5
12 [a]1 Cor. 4:11 [1]*live humbly* [2]*live in prosperity* *See WW at Matt. 18:4. • See WW at Matt. 15:33. • See WW at Luke 22:35.
13 [a]John 15:5 [1]NU *Him who*
14 [a]Phil. 1:7 *See WW at John 16:33.
15 [a]2 Cor. 11:8, 9
17 [a]Titus 3:14
18 [a]Phil. 2:25 [b]Heb. 13:16 [c]Rom.12:1; 2 Cor. 9:12 [1]*Or have received all* *See WW at Philem. 15.
19 [a]Ps. 23:1; 2 Cor. 9:8
20 [a]Rom. 16:27
21 [a]Gal. 1:2

4:10 Paul expresses no complaint over the delay in attending to his material needs. Rather, he acknowledges that the Philippians maintained a concern for him all along, but they lacked the opportunity to send help. That **opportunity** had been provided by Epaphroditus.
4:11 See section 3 of Truth-In-Action at the end of Phil.
4:11 The satisfaction of Paul's material needs was neither the reason nor the measure of his joy. **Content:** The Stoics used this word to describe a person who was self-sufficient in all circumstances. In contrast, though he uses the Stoic word, Paul expressly disclaims mere self-sufficiency (see 2 Cor. 3:5; 9:9). His sufficiency is in Christ, whose peace and purpose he enjoys regardless of life's circumstances. (v. 13).
4:13 See section 3 of Truth-In-Action at the end of Phil.
4:13 I can do all things: It is important to note that the emphasis is not so much on achievement as it is on willingness to allow Christ's power to sustain in difficulty and scarcity, and to enhance the enjoyment of abundance and prosperity. Such faith is a stimulant to believe for all Christ's sufficiency in facing all life's circumstances.
4:17 Paul emphasizes the importance of the Philippians' gifts as investments yielding spiritual fruit.
4:22 Caesar's household most likely refers to the slaves and servants in and around the imperial palace.

23 The grace of our Lord **Jesus** Christ be with [1]you all. Amen.

23 [1]NU *your spirit*

WORD WEALTH

4:23 Jesus, *Iesous* (Yay-*soos*); Strong's *#2424:* The Greek transliteration of the Hebrew *Yeshua,* "He Shall Save," which is the shorter form of *Yehoshua* (Joshua), "Yahweh Is Salvation." It was a common male Jewish name. Ten men in the OT were named *Yeshua,* and three men in the NT, in addition to the Lord, were so named.

TRUTH-IN-ACTION through PHILIPPIANS

Letting the LIFE of the Holy Spirit Bring Faith's Works Alive in You!

Truth Philippians Teaches	Text	**Action** Philippians Invites
1 Guidelines for Growing in Godliness Those who observe a godly life see what God is like. This is one of the church's primary functions. Godliness avoids anything that brings disunity or division in the church. It lives unselfishly, making others the primary focus of its concerns.	1:27	**Conduct your life** as a gospel sermon for observers of your life. **Develop** the heart attitude of unity.
	2:3, 4	**Live unselfishly! Turn away from** any selfish ambition or conceited attitudes. **Esteem** others as being more important and more worthy than you are.
2 How to Develop Dynamic Discipleship Discipleship is apprenticeship to the life of Jesus, focusing on Christ as Mentor and Model. Jesus chose to lay aside His divine form and adopt the lowly form of man. Even as a Man He did not choose wealth, power, or worldly position, but came as a servant, and died the death of a criminal. In everything He humbled Himself, trusting God to exalt and establish His name. Discipleship may call the Christian to choose to lay aside rights much valued in our culture, and to accept the life-role assigned by God. This role may not appear to be a place of acknowledgment, but trust God to choose how to establish and promote you.	2:2	**Seek to maintain** unity with other believers in your thoughts, attitudes, love, spirit, and purpose. **Recognize** that a separatist "right to one's own opinion" is not a biblical teaching. **Repent** and **surrender** such arrogance for the sake of unity in the body of Christ.
	2:5–11	**Adopt** Christ's attitude of **unselfishness, servanthood, humility, and obedience.**
	2:12, 13	**Commit yourself** to obedience. **Allow** God's work of salvation to have its full work in you. **Recognize** that your whole Christian life, from *being willing* to *doing it* is all God's work.
	2:20, 21	**Understand** that being concerned for the interests of Jesus Christ means being concerned *selflessly* for the welfare of others.
	4:8, 9	**Determine** your own thought life. **Do not let** others do it for you. **Cause your mind to dwell** on those things that bring peace to you and glory to God. **Follow** holy leadership as a pattern for life and faith.
3 Key Lessons in Faith Our inheritance as believers can only be received fully by taking a stand on what God has said in the face of contradicting circumstances, sometimes *even* suffering and death. The stance of faith eliminates fear and worry and brings	1:6	**Believe** that God always finishes what he starts, including His work in you!
	1:21–24	**Do not fear death. Remember** that dying in God's timing and will is only victory for a believer.
	1:29	**Recognize** and **accept** that true faith in Jesus Christ will involve suffering for His sake.

Truth Philippians Teaches	Text	**Action** Philippians Invites
3 the freedom to "rejoice evermore." True faith never says, "I cannot!" Such an utterance betrays unbelief.	4:4–7	**Rejoice** as a constant discipline! **Refuse** to worry about things. **Understand** that Jesus gives peace to those who trust Him and ask for His help.
	4:11	**Choose** to be contented in all circumstances.
	4:13	**Know** and **believe** that Jesus Christ will enable you to do anything He asks of you. *Nothing is impossible for him who believes!*
4 **Steps to Dynamic Devotion** Devotion focuses on the pursuit of intimacy with God. It is "devoting oneself" to knowing Jesus Christ. One measure of maturity is the degree to which this pursuit becomes our consuming focus and desire. Nowhere is the disciple of Jesus more challenged to become a man or woman "after God's own heart" than here.	3:7–9	**Understand** that no personal achievements earn spiritual position. **Do not be afraid** to lose everything in your quest to know Christ. **Make** "knowing" Christ your main goal in life. **Know** that this quest always involves sacrifice and unselfish living.
	3:12–14	**Aim** to achieve the goal God has set for you. **Spare no cost** in this quest. **Spare no effort** in your pressing toward the mark of knowing Christ.
	3:15	**Recognize** that a single-eyed pursuit of God is the hallmark of true spiritual maturity.
	3:17–19	**Know** that those who offer cheap alternatives to knowing Christ become His enemies.

The Epistle of Paul the Apostle to the COLOSSIANS

Author: Paul
Date: About A.D. 61
Theme: The Supremacy and Sufficiency of Christ
Key Words: Fullness, Wisdom, Knowledge, Mystery

Background Paul had never visited Colosse, a small town in the province of Asia, about 100 miles east of Ephesus. The Colossian church was an outgrowth of his three-year ministry in Ephesus about A.D. 52–55 (see Acts 19:10; 20:31). Epaphras, a native of the town, and probably a convert of the apostle, was likely the church's founder and leader (1:7, 8; 4:12, 13). The church apparently met in Philemon's home (Philem. 2).

Conservative scholars believe Paul wrote this letter during his first Roman imprisonment, around A.D. 61. Tychicus took the letters to the Colossians, to Philemon, and to the Ephesians to their respective destinations.

Occasion and Purpose Sometime during Paul's imprisonment, Epaphras solicited his help in dealing with false teaching which threatened the church at Colosse (2:8, 9). This heresy was apparently a blend of pagan-occultism, Jewish legalism, and Christianity. The error resembles an early form of Gnosticism, which taught that Jesus was not fully God and fully man, but merely one of the semidivine beings that bridged the chasm between God and the world. He, therefore, was said to be lacking in authority and ability to meet the needs of the Colossians. Enlightened believers could, however, achieve spiritual fullness through special knowledge and rigorous self-discipline.

With an urgency heightened by the repatriation of the runaway slave, Onesimus, to his master at Colosse, Paul wrote this epistle with a fourfold purpose: 1) to expose and rebut the heresy; 2) to instruct the Colossians in the truth and alert them to the danger of returning to pagan vices; 3) to express personal interest in the believers; 4) to inspire them to promote mutual love and harmony.

Characteristics No other book of the New Testament sets forth more fully or defends the universal lordship of Christ more thoroughly. Combative in tone and abrupt in style, Colossians bears a close resemblance to Ephesians in language and subject matter. Over seventy of the 155 verses in Ephesians contain expressions echoed in Colossians. On the other *hand,* Colossians has twenty-eight words found nowhere else in Paul's writings and thirty-four found nowhere else in the New Testament.

Content The false teachers at Colosse had undercut the major doctrines of Christianity, not least of which was the deity, absolute lordship, and sufficiency of Christ. Colossians sets forth Christ as supreme Lord in whose sufficiency the believers find completeness (1:15–20). The first two chapters present and defend this truth; the latter two unfold practical implications.

Jesus Christ's supremacy hinges upon His uniqueness as God's eternal, beloved Son and Heir (1:13, 15). In Him dwells the totality of divine attributes, essence, and power (1:19; 2:9). He is the exact revelation and representation of the Father, and has priority in time and primacy in rank over all creation (1:15). His sufficiency depends upon His superiority. The conviction of Christ's absolute sovereignty gave impulse to Paul's missionary activity (1:27–29).

Paul declares Christ's lordship in three primary ways, at the same time proclaiming His adequacy. First, Christ is Lord over all creation. His creative authority encompasses the whole material and spiritual universe (1:16). Since this includes the angels and planets (1:16; 2:10), Christ deserves to be worshiped instead of the angels (2:18). Further, there is no reason to fear demonic spirit-powers or to seek superstitiously for protection from them, because Christ has neutralized their power at the Cross (2:15), and the Colossians shared His triumphant resurrection power (2:20). As sovereign and sufficient Potentate, Christ is not only Creator of the universe but also its Sustainer (1:17), its Uniting Principle, and its Goal (1:16).

Second, Jesus Christ is preeminent in the church as its Creator and Savior (1:18). He is its Life and Leader, and to Him alone may the church submit. The Colossians must remain rooted in Him (2:6, 7) rather than become enchanted with empty speculation and traditions (2:8, 16–18).

Third, Jesus Christ is supreme in salvation (3:11). In Him all man-made distinctions fade and barriers fall. He has made all Christians into one family in which all members are equal in forgiveness and adoption; and He is all that matters, first and last. Therefore, contrary to the heresy, there are no special qualifications or requirements for experiencing God's favor (2:8–20).

Chapters 3 and 4 deal with the practical implications of Christ in the Colossians' daily life. Paul's use of the word "Lord" nine times in 3:1—4:18 indicates that Christ's supremacy impinges upon every aspect of their relationships and activities.

Personal Application Because this is an age of religious pluralism and syncretism (that is, a diluting of truth for the sake of unity), Christ's lordship is deemed irrelevant by many religious groups that believe one religion is as good as the other. His preeminence is denied by others that place the Christian stamp upon a fusion of beliefs from several religions. Usually hailed as an advance beyond apostolic Christianity, this blend promises self-fulfillment and freedom without surrender to Christ.

"Jesus is Lord" is the church's earliest confession. It remains the abiding test of authentic Christianity. Neither the church nor the individual believer can afford to compromise Christ's deity. In His sovereignty lies His sufficiency. He will be Lord of everything or not Lord at all.

Christ Revealed Paul lifts up Christ as the center and circumference of all that exists. The incarnate Son of God, He is the exact revelation and representation of the Father (1:15), as well as the embodiment of full deity (1:19; 2:9). He who is Lord in creation (1:16), in the church (1:18), and in salvation (3:11) indwells believers and is their "hope of glory" (1:27). The supreme Creator and Sustainer of all things (1:16, 17) is also a sufficient Savior for His people (2:10). See also "Content" above.

The Holy Spirit at Work Colossians has a single explicit reference to the Holy Spirit, used in association with love (1:8). Some scholars also understand "wisdom and spiritual understanding" in 1:9 in terms of gifts of the Spirit. For Paul, the lordship of Christ in the believer's life is the most crucial and clearest evidence of the Spirit's presence.

Outline of Colossians

Greeting

PAUL, [a]an apostle of Jesus Christ by the will of God, and Timothy our brother,

2 To the *saints [a]and faithful brethren in Christ *who are* in Colosse:

[b]Grace to you and peace from God our Father [1]and the Lord Jesus Christ.

Their Faith in Christ

3 [a]We give thanks to the God and Father of our Lord Jesus Christ, praying always for you,
4 [a]since we heard of your *faith in Christ Jesus and of [b]your love for all the saints;
5 because of the hope [a]which is laid up for you in *heaven, of which you heard before in the word of the truth of the gospel,
6 which has come to you, [a]as *it has* also in all the world, and [b]is bringing forth [1]fruit, as *it is* also among you since the day you heard and *knew [c]the grace of God in truth;
7 as you also learned from [a]Epaphras, our dear fellow servant, who is [b]a faithful minister of Christ on your behalf,
8 who also declared to us your [a]love in the *Spirit.

CHAPTER 1
1 [a]Eph. 1:1
2 [a]1 Cor. 4:17 [b]Gal. 1:3 [1]NU omits *and the Lord Jesus Christ* *See WW at Acts 7:33.
3 [a]Phil. 1:3
4 [a]Eph. 1:15 [b][Heb. 6:10] *See WW at Mark 11:22.
5 [a][1 Pet. 1:4] *See WW at Rev. 21:1.
6 [a]Matt. 24:14 [b]John 15:16 [c]Eph. 3:2 [1]NU, M add *and growing* *See WW at Luke 5:22.
7 [a]Philem. 23 [b]2 Cor. 11:23 *See WW at Rom. 7:6.
8 [a]Rom. 15:30

1:1 In calling himself Christ's **apostle,** Paul declares his authority to speak to a church he never founded. **Timothy,** who is highly regarded in the churches throughout Asia Minor (modern Turkey), is with Paul at the time of the writing of the epistle.

1:3–8 These verses confirm the genuineness of the Colossians' faith, commend the faithfulness of **Epaphras** in proclaiming a pure apostolic gospel, and reflect Paul's true affection for the believers.

Preeminence of Christ

9 [a]For this reason we also, since the
day we heard it, do not cease to *pray
for you, and to ask [b]that you may be
filled with [c]the knowledge of His will
[d]in all wisdom and spiritual *understanding;
1 10 [a]that you may walk worthy of the
Lord, [b]fully pleasing *Him,* [c]being fruitful in every good work and increasing
in the [d]knowledge of God;
11 [a]**strengthened** with all might, according to His glorious *power, [b]for all
*patience and *longsuffering [c]with joy;

WORD WEALTH

1:11 strengthened, *dunamoo* (doo-nam-*ah*-oh); Strong's *#1412:* To make strong, confirm, enable. There is a family of *duna*-power words: *dunamai* (to be able), *dunamis* (power, usually supernatural), *dunamoo* (to strengthen), *dunastes* (sovereign or ruler), *dunateo* (to be mighty), and *dunatos* (powerful). (Compare "dynasty," "dynamic," "dynamite.")

12 [a]giving thanks to the Father who
has qualified us to be partakers of
[b]the inheritance of the saints in the
light.
13 He has delivered us from [a]the
*power of *darkness [b]and [1]conveyed*
us into the kingdom of the Son of His
love,

KINGDOM DYNAMICS

1:13 People of the Kingdom, THE MESSAGE OF THE KINGDOM. The "transference" of the believer, from under Satan's authority to Christ's, is described as movement into another "kingdom." Ensuing verses describe Christ's redemption as bringing us to a place of "completeness," that is, of spiritual adequacy, authority, or ability to live victoriously over and above the invisible powers of darkness (vv. 14–16; 2:6–10). This becomes functionally true, as opposed to merely theoretically so, when we 1) live and love as citizens of the heavenly kingdom (Phil. 3:20); 2) utilize this kingdom's currency, which is of irresistible value (Acts 3:6); 3) operate as ambassadors authorized to offer kingdom peace and reconciliation to those yet unrenewed in Christ (2 Cor. 5:20); and 4) serve as the kingdom militia, girded for prayerful conflict against the dark powers controlling so much of this present world (Eph. 6:10–20). The terminology of "the kingdom" holds more than poetic pictures. It is practically applicable to all our living.

(Matt. 13/Luke 17:20, 21) J.W.H.

9 [a]Eph. 1:15–17 [b]1 Cor. 1:5 [c][Rom. 12:2] [d]Eph. 1:8 *See WW at Matt. 6:6. • See WW at Luke 2:47.
10 [a]Eph. 4:1 [b]1 Thess. 4:1 [c]Heb. 13:21 [d]2 Pet. 3:18
11 [a][Eph. 3:16; 6:10] [b]Eph. 4:2 [c][Acts 5:41] *See WW at 1 Tim. 6:16. • See WW at Heb. 10:36. • See WW at Heb. 6:12.
12 [a][Eph. 5:20] [b]Eph. 1:11
13 [a]Eph. 6:12 [b]2 Pet. 1:11 [1]*transferred* *See WW at Mark 3:15. • See WW at Luke 11:35. • See WW at Luke 16:4.
14 [a]Eph. 1:7 [1]NU, M omit *through His blood* *See WW at Rom. 3:24. • See WW at 1 John 1:7. • See WW at Heb. 9:22.
15 [a]2 Cor. 4:4 [b]Rev. 3:14
16 [a]Heb. 1:2, 3 [b][Eph. 1:20, 21] [c]Heb. 2:10 [1]*rulers* [2]*authorities*

14 [a]in whom we have *redemption
[1]through His *blood, the *forgiveness
of sins.
15 He is [a]the image of the invisible
God, [b]the firstborn over all **creation.**

WORD WEALTH

1:15 creation, *ktisis* (*ktis*-is); Strong's *#2937:* A founding, establishing, settling, formation. The word is used to denote both the act of creating and the product of the creative act. Salvation gives a person the status of being a new creation (2 Cor. 5:17; Gal. 6:15).

16 For [a]by Him all things were created
that are in heaven and that are on
earth, visible and invisible, whether
thrones or [b]dominions or [1]principali-
ties or [2]powers. All things were created
[c]through Him and for Him.

1:9 Knowledge: The heretics promise their followers new knowledge (Greek *gnosis*) which is self-serving. Paul prays that the Colossians fully attain to and be controlled by the *fullest* and *clearest* knowledge (Greek *epignosis*) of God's will (see also Rom. 12:2).

1:10, 11 See section 1 of Truth-In-Action at the end of Col.

1:10 Walk worthy of the Lord describes a radical commitment of will, affection, and disposition to pleasing Christ. Fruitfulness, growth in godly knowledge, divine empowerment, and thankfulness characterize such a walk (vv. 10–12).

1:12 Qualified means primarily to make competent or sufficient and, secondarily, to entitle, authorize, or enable (see 2 Cor. 3:6). Just as God honored Israel by giving that nation Canaan as an earthly allotment, so He has honored each member of the church with the potential of obtaining the inheritance of spiritual Canaan.

1:13 Delivered us . . . darkness conveys the idea of salvation rescuing us from the tyranny of darkness. Drawing on an important OT theme (see Ex. 6:6; 14:30), it includes rescue from such negatives as danger, death, sickness, and hostile situations in general (see Ps. 33:18, 19). These rescues include both present deliverances and future, consummated deliverances in the world to come. **Conveyed** refers to the deportation or transferrance of captured armies or populations from one country to another.

1:15 Image: The Greek word here means an exact revelation and representation (Heb. 1:3). Jesus is also called the **firstborn,** a title that refers to His exalted position, not the timing of His physical birth (see also Ps. 89:4, 27). Among the Jews, the firstborn son was especially favored by his parents. He inherited the leadership of the family and a double portion of the property upon his father's death.

1:16 In order to give more explicit proof of Jesus' role as "the firstborn over all creation" (v. 15), Paul depicts Him as the Mediator, Agent, and Goal of all things (see John 1:3). This includes declaring His authority above all negative cosmic powers, which are also subjects of His creation who fell from their first estate. Paul's reference point is Gen. 1.

KINGDOM DYNAMICS

1:16 Organized Structure in the Angelic Realm, ANGELS. There is an organized structure in the angelic realm. Profoundly influential in humanity's history, angels are involved according to their designated ranks. Though opinion differs as to the placement of angelic offices, it is clear that the angelic host are part of a highly organized world of angel beings. For example, Dan. 10:13 shows that warring angels have a chief prince, Michael, who is also called an archangel, that is, one who rules over others. Seraphim and cherubim seem to be of a slightly lower rank, just ahead of ministering spirits (Heb. 1:14). However, it may also be that the seraphim and cherubim fill a leadership role in worship while Michael leads the warring angels. As to the dark angels, Eph. 6:12 offers insight into the ranks of the evil angelic realm: principalities, powers, rulers of the darkness of this world, and spiritual wickedness in high places. From the information the Bible gives, we can see that the angelic realm is a distinctly structured society with different levels of authority or power endowed to each according to God's creative order.

(Judg. 13:6/Dan. 10:13) M.H.

17 [a]And He is before all things, and
in Him [b]all things consist.

17 [a][John 17:5] [b]Heb. 1:3
18 [a]1 Cor. 11:3; Eph. 1:22 [b]Rev. 1:5
19 [a]John 1:16
20 [a]Rom. 5:1; Eph. 2:14 [b]2 Cor. 5:18 [c]Eph. 1:10

18 And [a]He is the head of the body,
the church, who is the beginning,
[b]the firstborn from the dead, that in all
things He may have the preeminence.

Reconciled in Christ

19 For it pleased *the Father that*
[a]in Him all the fullness should dwell,
20 and [a]by Him to reconcile [b]all things
to Himself, by Him, whether things on
earth or things in heaven, [c]having
made peace through the blood of His
cross.

KINGDOM DYNAMICS

1:20 Christ's Blood Satisfies Holiness, Thereby Making Peace, THE BLOOD. Mankind was separated from God because of sin and had no acceptable offering to satisfy the demands of God's holy nature. God sent Christ to provide an acceptable sacrifice for sin, establishing a bond with those who received Him, thereby making peace. It was specifically the blood Jesus Christ shed on the cross that satisfied the demand of God's holiness, established a peace bond or covenant with those who received Him, and provided the means for all of creation to be reconciled to God. Lev. 17:11 declares that sin cannot be forgiven without the

1:17 Consist means to hold or stand together, and portrays Christ as the Sustainer and Uniting Principle of the universe.
1:19 Used 8 times in Col. and about 17 times in the NT, the word **fullness** has a variety of meanings. Here it translates a technical term, which the false teachers probably employed to denote the totality of semidivine intermediaries between God and man. Paul sanitizes the word and uses it to describe the sum total of divine attributes resident in Christ and to show His unique and uncontested mediatorship.
1:20–23 Sin's ruinous consequence was universal and pervasive, placing all of creation at odds with God and itself (Rom. 8:20–23). The death of Christ restored the harmony and fellowship that once existed between God and His creation.

THE PREEMINENCE OF CHRIST (1:18)

CHRIST

In universal government	In reconciliation	In wisdom and knowledge	In personal observance	In Christian living
• The visible image of God (1:15) • The agent of creation (1:16) • *The Sustainer* (1:17) • The Head of the church (1:18)	• Pleases the Father (1:19, 20) • Reconciles us through His death (1:21, 22) • Lives in us as our hope of glory (1:27)	• The source of all the treasures (2:2, 3) • Worldly philosophy does not conform to Him (2:8)	• We are alive in Him (2:11–13) • No need for legalism and ritualism (2:16–23)	• He is our life (3:3) • We can avoid immorality and can bless others (3:5–14)

shedding of blood. Because sin takes life, life is required to repay sin's debts. Jesus Christ gave divine life in blood to satisfy all of mankind's sin debts and to restore covenant peace between God and man.

(John 6:53, 54/Rom. 5:9) C.S.

21 And you, [a]who once were alienated
and enemies in your *mind [b]by wicked
works, yet now He has [c]reconciled
22 [a]in the body of His *flesh through
death, [b]to present you holy, and blameless, and above reproach in His sight—
23 if indeed you continue [a]in the faith,
grounded and steadfast, and are
[b]not moved away from the hope of the
*gospel which you heard, [c]which was
preached to every *creature under
heaven, [d]of which I, Paul, became a
minister.

Sacrificial Service for Christ

24 [a]I now rejoice in my sufferings
[b]for you, and fill up in my flesh
[c]what is lacking in the *afflictions of
Christ, for [d]the sake of His body, which
is the *church,
5 25 of which I became a minister according to [a]the [1]stewardship from God
which was given to me for you, to fulfill
the word of God,
26 [a]the [1]mystery* which has been hidden from *ages and from generations,
[b]but now has been revealed to His
saints.
27 [a]To them God willed to make
known what are [b]the riches of the
glory of this mystery among the Gentiles: [1]which is [c]Christ in you, [d]the
hope of glory.
3 28 Him we preach, [a]warning every
man and teaching every man in all
*wisdom, [b]that we may present every
man *perfect in Christ *Jesus.
29 To this *end* I also labor, striving according to His **working** which *works
in me [a]mightily.

21 [a][Eph. 2:1] [b]Titus 1:15 [c]2 Cor. 5:18, 19 *See WW at Mark 12:30.
22 [a]2 Cor. 5:18 [b][Eph. 5:27] *See WW at Matt. 26:41.
23 [a]Eph. 3:17 [b][John 15:6] [c]Col. 1:6 [d]Col. 1:25 *See WW at Mark 1:1. • See WW at Col. 1:15.
24 [a]2 Cor. 7:4 [b]Eph. 3:1, 13 [c][2 Cor. 1:5; 12:15] [d]Eph. 1:23 *See WW at John 16:33. • See WW at Acts 8:1.
25 [a]Gal. 2:7 [1]*dispensation* or *administration*
26 [a][1 Cor. 2:7] [b][2 Tim. 1:10] [1]*secret* or *hidden truth* *See WW at Mark 4:11. • See WW at Matt. 28:20.
27 [a]2 Cor. 2:14 [b]Rom. 9:23 [c][Rom. 8:10, 11] [d]1 Tim. 1:1 [1]M *who*
28 [a]Acts 20:20 [b]Eph. 5:27 *See WW at Acts 6:10. • See WW at James 3:2. • See WW at Phil. 4:23.
29 [a]Eph. 3:7 *See WW at 1 Thess. 2:13.

CHAPTER 2

1 [a]Phil. 1:30 [1]*struggle*

 **WORD WEALTH**

1:29 working, *energeia* (en-*erg*-eye-ah); Strong's *#1753:* Working, action, operative power. The English word "energy" comes from this word. *Energeia* usually describes the working of God, but is used of Satan's empowering "the lawless one" (2 Thess. 2:9).

 **KINGDOM DYNAMICS**

1:27, 28 Paul's Writings, TERMINOLOGY OF THE KINGDOM. "In Christ" is the expression Paul most frequently uses to designate the new life potential through the gospel. The Messiah (Christ) being King, the term clearly places the believer in the circle of all that is represented and contained in the King, His salvation conquest, and His personal rule. The essential truth is that the Savior-King has come, and in Him the rule of God has altered the limits sin has heretofore placed on individuals. People no longer need be ruled by their carnality (flesh) or controlled by evil (the Devil). Being freed, that is, transferred to a new kingdom, they can know the joy of a relationship with God through the power of the Cross and can realize a beginning reinstatement of their rulership under God, through the power of the Holy Spirit. Thereby, living in the King's kingdom brings a dual hope: eternity with Christ and the promise of grace to begin "reigning in life." Now, "in Christ" designates the new life that may be lived in the benefits of, and by the power of, the King Jesus, "who has brought life [reigning in life presently in Christ—Rom. 5:8] and immortality [reigning forever with Christ—Rev. 22:5] to light through the gospel" (2 Tim. 1:10).

(John 18:36/Mark 1:14, 15) J.W.H.

Not Philosophy but Christ

2 For I want you to know what a
great [a]conflict[1] I have for you and
those in Laodicea, and *for* as many as
have not seen my face in the flesh,
2 that their hearts may be encour- 3
aged, being knit together in love, and

1:23 If indeed (Greek *ei ge*) is not an expression of doubt but of confidence. Paul is confident the Colossians will not deny their faith (see 2:5). See the notes on Heb. 6:4–6, 7, 8, and 9–12 for a further understanding of continuing **in the faith.**

1:24–29 Paul neither sees Christ's vicarious suffering as deficient nor his own as having any redemptive value. Rather, to him Christ's sacrificial suffering is past, and his own suffering is a joyous privilege whereby he is identified with his Lord (Acts 9:16; Phil. 3:10). His Lord is identified with His church (Acts 9:4), whose destiny is also suffering (Phil. 1:29). At the risk of personal danger and loss of comfort (2 Cor. 4:8–12), Paul fulfills his responsibility of delivering God's **mystery** to the Gentiles, the open, revealed secret concerning the redemptive work of Christ, through which Jews and Gentiles are united in Him (see Eph. 2:11–22).

1:25–29 See section 5 of Truth-In-Action at the end of Col.

1:28, 29 See section 3 of Truth-In-Action at the end of Col.

2:1–5 Paul expresses the emotions of anguish and joy in these verses. Out of concern for their spiritual welfare, he agonizes in prayer for the believers at Colosse and Laodicea who are threatened by false teachers. Their unity in combating the heresy and a full recognition of their sufficiency in Christ are the burden of his prayer. On the other hand, he expresses joy because the Colossians are standing resolutely in unbroken ranks, their attention still focused on Christ alone (v. 5).

2:2, 3 See section 3 of Truth-In-Action at the end of Col.

attaining to all riches of the full assurance of *understanding, to the knowledge of the mystery of God, [1]both of
the Father and of Christ,
3 [a]in whom are hidden all the treasures of wisdom and knowledge.
4 Now this I say [a]lest anyone should
deceive you with persuasive words.
5 For [a]though I am absent in the flesh,
yet I am with you in spirit, rejoicing
[1]to see [b]your *good* order and the
[c]steadfastness of your faith in Christ.
6 [a]As you therefore have received
Christ Jesus the Lord, so walk in Him,
7 [a]rooted and built up in Him and *established in the faith, as you have been
taught, *abounding [1]in it with thanksgiving.
4 8 Beware lest anyone [1]cheat you
through philosophy and empty deceit,
according to [a]the tradition of men, according to the [b]basic principles of the
world, and not according to Christ.

KINGDOM DYNAMICS

2:8 28. What About Mind Control and Mind-Science Beliefs?, SPIRITUAL ANSWERS. For the answer to this and other probing questions about God and the power life in His kingdom, see the study article "Spiritual Answers to Hard Questions," which begins on page 1996.

P.R.

9 For [a]in Him dwells all the *fullness
of the Godhead [1]bodily;
10 and you are complete in Him, who
is the [a]head of all [1]principality and
power.

Not Legalism but Christ

3 **11** In Him you were also [a]circumcised
with the circumcision made without
hands, by [b]putting off the body [1]of the
sins of the flesh, by the circumcision
of Christ,
12 [a]buried with Him in *baptism, in
which you also were raised with *Him*
through [b]faith in the *working of God,
[c]who raised Him from the dead.
13 And you, being dead in your trespasses and the uncircumcision of your
flesh, He has made alive together with
Him, having forgiven you all trespasses,
14 [a]having **wiped out** the [1]handwriting
of requirements that was against us,
which was contrary to us. And He has
*taken it out of the way, having nailed
it to the cross.
15 [a]Having disarmed [b]principalities
and powers, He made a *public spectacle of them, triumphing over them in
it.

2 [1]NU omits *both of the Father and* *See WW at Luke 2:47.
3 [a]1 Cor. 1:24, 30
4 [a]Rom. 16:18; 2 Cor. 11:13; Eph. 4:14; 5:6
5 [a]1 Thess. 2:17 [b]1 Cor. 14:40 [c]1 Pet. 5:9 [1]Lit. *and seeing*
6 [a]1 Thess. 4:1
7 [a]Eph. 2:21 [1]NU omits *in it* *See WW at Mark 16:20. • See WW at Matt. 25:29.
8 [a]Gal. 1:14 [b]Gal. 4:3, 9, 10; Col. 2:20 [1]Lit. *plunder you* or *take you captive*
9 [a][John 1:14]; Col. 1:19 [1]*in bodily form* *See WW at Eph. 3:19.
10 [a][Eph. 1:20, 21; 1 Pet. 3:22] [1]*rule and authority*
11 [a]Deut. 10:16 [b]Rom. 6:6; 7:24; Gal. 5:24; Col. 3:5 [1]NU omits *of the sins*
12 [a]Rom. 6:4 [b]Eph. 1:19, 20 [c]Acts 2:24 *See WW at Matt. 21:25. • See WW at Col. 1:29.
14 [a][Eph. 2:15, 16]; Col. 2:20 [1]*certificate of debt with its* *See WW at John 16:22.
15 [a][Is. 53:12; Heb. 2:14] [b]Eph. 6:12 *See WW at Acts 4:31.

WORD WEALTH

2:14 wiped out, *exaleipho* (ex-al-*eye*-foe); Strong's *#1813:* From *ek,* "out," and *aleipho,* "to anoint"; hence, to wipe out, wipe off, wash. Used metaphorically, the word signifies a removal or obliteration, whether of sins (Acts 3:19), of writing (Col. 2:14), of a name (Rev. 3:5), or of tears (Rev. 21:4).

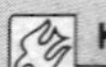

KINGDOM DYNAMICS

2:13–15 Grounds of Authority, CONFLICT AND THE KINGDOM. Jesus Christ's triumph over sin and evil powers was accomplished in "it"—that is, in the Cross. This text, joined to and studied beside others (Eph. 2:13–16; Gal. 3:13, 14; 2 Cor. 5:14–17; Rom. 5:6–15; and Rev. 12:10, 11), firmly establishes Jesus' suffering, shed blood, sacrificial death, and resurrection triumph as the only adequate and available grounds for ransom from sin, reconciliation to God, redemption from slavery, and restoration. The Cross is the sole hope and means for full reinstatement to relationship with God and rulership under Him—to "reign in life" (Rom. 5:17). To avoid presumption or imbalance regarding the message and ministry of the present power of the kingdom of God, we must focus on and regularly review two points; the source

2:6–10 Where the heretics through devious methods promise progressive spirituality in which Christ is demoted and the basics of Christianity denied, Paul summons the Colossians back to **Christ** (v. 6). Progress in faith consists of deepening, not discarding, the basic truths about Christ. What the false teachers call enlightened, liberating Christianity, Paul terms **basic principles of the world** (see *note on Gal. 4:1–3*).
2:8 See section 4 of Truth-In-Action at the end of Col.
2:11–14 See section 3 of Truth-In-Action at the end of Col.
2:11–13 Contrary to the false teaching, salvation is not by ritual observance. Christ is the fulfillment of that which is typified in the rites of the Law, freeing us from the bondage of legalism (see Rom. 2:25–29; 3:27–31; 10:4). In their identification with Jesus, believers share the experiences of their Lord. They need nothing more.
2:14 Handwriting: A word commonly used when a monetary obligation was acknowledged by a debtor. It means a signed confession of indebtedness, bond, or self-confessed indictment. In Eph. 2:15 it is used of the Mosaic Law.
2:15 The conquest of hostile spiritual forces is described in terms of a homecoming victory celebration of a Roman general. The idea here is that God, through the Cross events, divested **principalities and powers** of their uncontested rule and authority over redeemed people who live under Christ's lordship. The fact that **He made a public spectacle of them** affirms that they are not annihilated, but that their authority has been curbed. See notes on 1 Cor. 2:8; Heb. 2:14, 15.

and the grounds for the delegation of such authority and power. 1) God's sovereign authority and almighty power is the source from which mankind derives any ability to share in the exercise of God's kingdom power. 2) But even more important, seeing sinful, fallen man had lost all claim to his early privilege of rulership under God, let us remember the grounds upon which all kingdom privilege or power may be restored and by which such spiritual ministry with authority may be exercised.
(Matt. 11:12/Luke 16:16) J.W.H.

2 16 So let no one [a]judge* you in food
or in drink, or regarding a [1]festival or
a new moon or sabbaths,
17 [a]which are a shadow of things to
come, but the [1]substance is of Christ.
4 18 Let no one cheat you of your reward, taking delight in *false* *humility
and worship of angels, intruding into
those things which he has [1]not seen,
vainly puffed up by his fleshly mind,
19 and not holding fast to [a]the Head,
from whom all the body, *nourished
and knit together by joints and liga-
ments, [b]grows with the increase *that
is* from God.
20 [1]Therefore, if you [a]died with Christ
from the basic principles of the world,
[b]why, as *though* living in the world,
do you subject yourselves to regulations—
21 [a]"Do not touch, do not *taste, do not
handle,"
22 which all concern things which perish with the using—[a]according to the
commandments and doctrines of men?
23 [a]These things indeed have an appearance of wisdom in self-imposed religion, *false* *humility, and [1]neglect of
the body, *but are* of no value against
the indulgence of the flesh.

Not Carnality but Christ

2 3 If then you were [a]raised with
Christ, seek those things which are
above, [b]where Christ is, sitting at the
right hand of God.
2 Set your mind on things above, not
on things on the [a]earth.
3 [a]For you died, [b]and your life is hidden with Christ in God.
4 [a]When Christ *who is* [b]our life **appears,** then you also will appear with
Him in [c]glory.

WORD WEALTH

3:4 appears, *phaneroo* (fan-er-*ah*-oh); Strong's *#5319:* To lay bare, reveal, uncover, make visible, make known what has been hidden or unknown, make clear. *Phaneroo* tells us of Christ's appearing, when we see Him in the full expression of His glorious character.

5 [a]Therefore put to death [b]your mem- 6
bers which are on the earth: [c]fornica-
tion,* uncleanness, passion, evil *desire, and covetousness, [d]which is
idolatry.
6 [a]Because of these things the wrath
of God is coming upon [b]the sons of
disobedience,
7 [a]in which you yourselves once
walked when you lived in them.
8 [a]But now you yourselves are to put
off all these: anger, *wrath, malice,
blasphemy, filthy language out of your
mouth.
9 Do not lie to one another, since you
have put off the old man with his
deeds,
10 and have put on the new *man* who
[a]is renewed in knowledge [b]according
to the image of Him who [c]created
him,
11 where there is neither [a]Greek nor
Jew, circumcised nor uncircumcised,
barbarian, Scythian, slave *nor* *free,
[b]but Christ *is* all and in all.

Character of the New Man

12 Therefore, [a]as *the* *elect of God, 6
holy and beloved, [b]put on tender

16 [a]Rom. 14:3 [1]*feast day* *See WW at John 18:31. **17** [a]Heb. 8:5; 10:1 [1]Lit. *body* **18** [1]NU omits *not* *See WW at Acts 20:19. **19** [a]Eph. 4:15 [b]Eph. 1:23; 4:16 *See WW at Gal. 3:5. **20** [a]Rom. 6:2–5 [b]Gal. 4:3, 9 [1]NU, M omit *Therefore* **21** [a]1 Tim. 4:3 *See WW at John 8:52. **22** [a]Titus 1:14 **23** [a]1 Tim. 4:8 [1]*severe treatment, asceticism* *See WW at Acts 20:19.

CHAPTER 3

1 [a]Col. 2:12 [b]Eph. 1:20 **2** [a][Matt. 6:19–21] **3** [a][Rom. 6:2] [b][2 Cor. 5:7] **4** [a][1 John 3:2] [b]John 14:6 [c]1 Cor. 15:43 **5** [a][Rom. 8:13] [b][Rom. 6:13] [c]Eph. 5:3 [d]Eph. 4:19; 5:3, 5 *See WW at Matt. 15:19. • See WW at 2 Tim. 2:22. **6** [a]Rom. 1:18 [b][Eph. 2:2] **7** [a]1 Cor. 6:11 **8** [a]Eph. 4:22 *See WW at Luke 4:28. **10** [a]Rom. 12:2 [b][Rom. 8:29] [c][Eph. 2:10] **11** [a]Gal. 3:27, 28 [b]Eph. 1:23 *See WW at Rev. 6:15. **12** [a][1 Pet. 1:2] [b]1 John 3:17 *See WW at 1 Pet. 2:9.

2:16–23 See section 2 of Truth-In-Action at the end of Col.
2:16–23 In view of Christ's all-sufficiency, His abolition of the Mosaic Law as a means to justification, and His decisive victory over demonic powers, Paul urges the Colossians to resist legalism, angel-worship, and asceticism that was being forced upon them by the false teachers. Such exercises deny Christ's supremacy and sufficiency, rob Christians of their liberty, and ***are of no value against the indulgence of the flesh.***
2:18–23 See section 4 of Truth-In-Action at the end of Col.
2:20 Basic principles of the world: See note on Gal. 4:3.
3:1–11 See section 2 of Truth-In-Action at the end of Col.
3:1–4 For Paul, demonstrating the life-changing power of the gospel is equally as important as defending it against error. The Colossians are able to fulfill the command daily to display their attention and affection toward spiritual things because of their identification with Christ by death to the past, and their empowerment for the present by the resurrection of Jesus.
3:5–11 See section 6 of Truth-In-Action at the end of Col.
3:5–17 To focus interest and ambition heavenward entails casting away specific vices and cultivating certain virtues. Sins of sensual self-indulgence (v. 5), attitude (v. 8), speech (vv. 8, 9), and prejudice of the mind (v. 11) must be **put to death** once and for all. Christ must govern and be the goal of the relationships and worship of the children of God (vv. 12–17).
3:12–14 See section 6 of Truth-In-Action at the end of Col.

mercies, *kindness, *humility, meekness, *longsuffering;
13 [a]bearing* with one another, and
forgiving one another, if anyone has a
complaint against another; even as
Christ forgave you, so you also *must*
do.

WORD WEALTH

3:13 forgiving, *charizomai* (khar-*id*-zahm-ahee); Strong's *#5483:* To do a favor, show kindness unconditionally, give freely, grant forgiveness, forgive freely. The word is from the same root as *charis,* "grace."

14 [a]But above all these things [b]put on
love, which is the [c]bond of perfection.
6 15 And let [a]the *peace of God rule in
your hearts, [b]to which also you were
called [c]in one body; and [d]be thankful.
5 16 Let the word of Christ dwell in you
richly in all wisdom, teaching and admonishing one another [a]in psalms and
hymns and spiritual songs, singing
with *grace in your hearts to the Lord.
17 And [a]*whatever* you do in word or
deed, *do* all in the name of the Lord
Jesus, *giving thanks to God the Father
through Him.

The Christian Home

4 18 [a]Wives, *submit to your own husbands, [b]as is fitting in the Lord.
19 [a]Husbands, *love your wives and do
not be [b]bitter toward them.
20 [a]Children, *obey your parents [b]in
all things, for this is well pleasing to
the Lord.
21 [a]Fathers, do not provoke your children, lest they become discouraged.
22 [a]Bondservants, obey in all things
your masters according to the flesh,
not with eyeservice, as men-pleasers,
but in sincerity of heart, fearing God.
23 [a]And whatever you do, do it heartily, as to the Lord and not to men,
24 [a]knowing that from the Lord you
will receive the reward of the inheritance; [b]for[1] you serve the Lord Christ.
25 But he who *does wrong will be repaid for what he has done, and [a]there
is no **partiality.**

12 *See WW at Gal. 5:22 • See WW at Acts 20:19 • See WW at Heb. 6:12.
13 [a][Mark 11:25] *See WW at 2 Thess. 1:4.
14 [a]1 Pet. 4:8 [b][1 Cor. 13] [c]Eph. 4:3
15 [a][John 14:27; Phil. 4:7] [b]1 Cor. 7:15 [c]Eph. 4:4 [d][1 Thess. 5:18] *See WW at Luke 1:79.
16 [a]Eph. 5:19 *See WW at 2 Cor. 12:9.
17 [a]1 Cor. 10:31 *See WW at John 6:11.
18 [a]1 Pet. 3:1 [b][Col. 3:18—4:1; Eph. 5:22—6:9] *See WW at 1 Cor. 14:32.
19 [a][Eph. 5:25; 1 Pet. 3:7] [b]Eph. 4:31 *See WW at John 3:16.
20 [a]Eph. 6:1 [b]Eph. 5:24 *See WW at Rom. 6:17.
21 [a]Eph. 6:4
22 [a]Eph. 6:5; [1 Tim. 6:1]; Titus 2:9; 1 Pet. 2:18
23 [a][Eccl. 9:10]
24 [a]Eph. 6:8 [b]1 Cor. 7:22 [1]NU omits *for*
25 [a]Rom. 2:11 *See WW at Acts 25:10.

CHAPTER 4
1 [a]Eph. 6:9

WORD WEALTH

3:25 partiality, *prosopolepsia* (pros-oh-pol-ape-*see*-ah); Strong's *#4382:* Favoritism, partiality, distinction, bias, conditional preference. The word denotes a biased judgment, which gives respect to rank, position, or circumstances instead of considering the intrinsic conditions. God shows no partiality in justice, judgment, or favorable treatment when dealing with people, and He expects us to follow His example.

KINGDOM DYNAMICS

3:18, 19, 23, 24 Husbands and Wives Called to Operate in God's Order, FAMILY ORDER. A Christian renders service to others as a way of serving the Lord Christ. In these verses the relationship to which this truth is specifically applied is the husband-wife relationship. The role and admonition that God assigns to a husband is meant to be a way of serving his wife. Likewise a distinctive role and direction is given to the wife, according to which she serves her husband.

These roles are not self-chosen, nor are they assigned by the culture in which one lives: they are given by God as a means of manifesting the life of Christ on Earth. In this setting the word submission acquires its full biblical significance for family life: husband and wife alike are submissive to God in fulfilling the roles that He has given them. In serving one another, husband and wife serve and honor Christ. The word "submit" (Greek *hupotasso*) is formed from *hupo* ("under") and *tasso* ("to arrange in an orderly manner"). In this context it describes a person who accepts his or her place under God's arranged order. Also, remember that God's directive to submit is not limited to wives. In James 4:7 and Eph. 5:21 we see the directive applied to every believer—in his or her relationships with others—and with God.

(1 Pet. 3:1–7/Hos. 2:16, 17, 19, 20) L.C.

4 Masters,[a] give your bondservants
what is just and fair, knowing that
you also have a Master in heaven.

3:15 See section 6 of Truth-In-Action at the end of Col.
3:16, 17 See section 5 of Truth-In-Action at the end of Col.
3:16 See note on Eph. 5:19.
3:18—4:1 Paul's domestic code contains the duties of household members, not their rights. Domestic regulations such as this were not unheard of in the pagan world. In this section, however, Paul introduces Christ as the new goal and dynamic of the Christian's life and behavior. Before Him each person participates equally in redemption, and through Him all immoral inequalities and all injustices are undermined and destined to crumble.
3:18–22 See section 4 of Truth-In-Action at the end of Col.
3:18 See note on Eph. 5:22.
3:19 See notes on Eph. 5:23 and 5:24–33.
3:20, 21 See note on Eph. 6:1–4. **Provoke** means to irritate or discourage **children** by harsh yelling, nagging, or deriding their efforts. Such provocations wound their spirits (see note on Prov. 18:14) and make them timid (**they become discouraged**).

Christian Graces

5 2 [a]Continue earnestly in prayer, being vigilant in it [b]with thanksgiving;
3 [a]meanwhile praying also for us,
that God would [b]open to us a door
for the word, to speak [c]the [1]mystery
of Christ, [d]for which I am also in
chains,
4 that I may make it manifest, as I
ought to speak.
5 [a]Walk in [b]wisdom toward those
who are outside, [c]redeeming the **time.**

> **WORD WEALTH**
>
> **4:5 time,** *kairos* (kahee-*ross*); Strong's *#2540:* Opportune time, set time, appointed time, due time, definitive time, seasonable time, proper time for action. *Kairos* describes kind, or quality, of time, whereas *chronos* denotes extent, or quantity, of time.

6 *Let* your speech always *be* [a]with
grace, [b]seasoned with salt, [c]that you
may know how you ought to answer
each one.

Final Greetings

7 [a]Tychicus, a beloved brother, faithful minister, and fellow servant in the
Lord, will tell you all the news about
me.
8 [a]I am sending him to you for this
very purpose, that [1]he may know your
circumstances and comfort your
hearts,
9 with [a]Onesimus, a faithful and beloved brother, who is *one* of you. They
will make known to you all things
which *are happening* here.
10 [a]Aristarchus my fellow prisoner
greets you, with [b]Mark the cousin of
Barnabas (about whom you received
instructions: if he comes to you, welcome him),
11 and Jesus who is called Justus.
These *are my* only fellow workers for
the kingdom of God who are of the circumcision; they have proved to be a
comfort to me.
12 [a]Epaphras, who is *one* of you, a
bondservant of Christ, greets you, always [b]laboring fervently for you in
prayers, that you may stand [c]perfect
and [1]complete in all the will of God.
13 For I bear him *witness that he has
a great [1]zeal* for you, and those who
are in Laodicea, and those in Hierapolis.
14 [a]Luke the beloved physician and
[b]Demas greet you.
15 Greet the brethren who are in Laodicea, and [1]Nymphas and [a]the church
that *is* in [2]his house.

Closing Exhortations and Blessing

16 Now when [a]this epistle is *read
among you, see that it is read also in
the church of the Laodiceans, and that
you likewise read the epistle from Laodicea.
17 And say to [a]Archippus, "Take heed
to [b]the ministry which you have received in the Lord, that you may fulfill
it."
18 [a]This salutation by my own hand—
Paul. [b]Remember my chains. Grace *be*
with you. Amen.

2 [a]Luke 18:1 [b]Col. 2:7
3 [a]Eph. 6:19 [b]1 Cor. 16:9 [c]Eph. 3:3, 4; 6:19 [d]Eph. 6:20 [1]*hidden truth*
5 [a]Eph. 5:15 [b][Matt. 10:16] [c]Eph. 5:16
6 [a]Eccl. 10:12 [b]Mark 9:50 [c]1 Pet. 3:15
7 [a]2 Tim. 4:12
8 [a]Eph. 6:22 [1]NU *you may know our circumstances and he may comfort*
9 [a]Philem. 10
10 [a]Acts 19:29; 20:4; 27:2 [b]2 Tim. 4:11
12 [a]Philem. 23 [b]Rom. 15:30 [c]Matt. 5:48 [1]NU *fully assured*
13 [1]NU *concern* *See WW at Acts 26:22. • See WW at 2 Cor. 11:2.
14 [a]2 Tim. 4:11 [b]2 Tim. 4:10
15 [a]Rom. 16:5 [1]NU *Nympha* [2]NU *her*
16 [a]1 Thess. 5:27 *See WW at Mark 13:14.
17 [a]Philem. 2 [b]2 Tim. 4:5
18 [a]1 Cor. 16:21 [b]Heb. 13:3

4:2–6 See section 5 of Truth-In-Action at the end of Col.

4:2–6 Paul singles out three ingredients that should characterize the Colossians' relation and responsibilities to the non-Christian world: persevering prayer (vv. 2–4); a lifestyle of discreet behavior and diligent service (v. 5); winsome and wholesome speech (v. 6).

4:7–18 As in Rom. 16, the long list of greetings is addressed to a church Paul did not establish. It reflects his own need to foster supportive relationships and his genuine concern to strengthen his ties with the Colossians.

4:7 Tychicus is Paul's messenger to the Colossian church. He was a native of the province of Asia (Acts 20:4) and a frequent companion of Paul.

4:9 Onesimus means "Useful." He is likely the same Onesimus in the Book of Philemon. See Introduction to Philemon: Background and notes on Philem. 10, 11, and 13.

4:10 Aristarchus was a Jew, a native of Thessalonica who traveled extensively with Paul (Acts 19:29; 20:4). **Mark,** also a Jew, was a native of Jerusalem (Acts 12:12, 25) and author of the Second Gospel. See Introduction to Mark: Author.

4:11 Jesus whose surname is **Justus** is an otherwise unknown Jewish Christian who was with Paul.

4:12 Epaphras: See Introduction to Colossians: Background.

4:14 Luke: See Introduction to Luke: Author. **Demas** is likely the same person whose temporal interest caused him later to leave Paul for Thessalonica (2 Tim. 4:10).

4:15 Early Christians worshiped in private homes (see Acts 16:15, 40; Philem. 2). Church buildings as we know them emerged in the third century. If **Nymphas** is to be read as "Nympha" (see marginal note), this could designate a woman pastor of a local house church.

4:16 The epistle from Laodicea, a letter similar to Col., did not survive. The apostles obviously wrote letters that were not canonized.

4:17 Archippus was a member of Philemon's household (Philem. 2). He was perhaps a pastor or deacon in Colosse.

TRUTH-IN-ACTION through COLOSSIANS

Letting the LIFE of the Holy Spirit Bring Faith's Works Alive in You!

Truth Colossians Teaches	Text	**Action** Colossians Invites
1 A Definition of Godliness This passage defines NT godliness concisely and completely.	1:10, 11	**Believe** that a "walk worthy of the Lord," 1) pleases the Lord, 2) is fruitful in good works, 3) grows in knowing God, and 4) is strengthened by God's power.
2 Steps to Holiness Under the old covenant the Law's system only allowed limited access to God. The new covenant no longer poses rules for cleansing, but calls to faith and acceptance of the completed work of Jesus. We are not to allow anything other than the Word of God to control or judge us. We are neither judged holy nor unholy by external regulations, but by the condition of our heart.	2:16–23	**Reject** rules that aim to cleanse the spirit by means of humanly contrived regulations. **Realize** that in Christ you are no longer subject to human wisdom or works, but to God.
	3:1–11	**Set** your thinking and affections on Jesus Christ, and **build** your relationship with Him. **Do not allow** worldly pursuits to waste your mental or emotional energy.
3 Lessons for Leaders Wise leaders focus their ministries on Jesus Christ and avoid presumptuous and transient teachings. Let us prioritize believers' maturity, stressing the finished work of Christ.	1:28, 29	Leaders, **concentrate** on the spiritual maturity of your people. **Lessen** your emphasis on any programs that do not foster maturity.
	2:2, 3	Leaders, **focus** on Jesus Christ. **Build** your congregation's unity and understanding on Him.
	2:11–14	Leaders, **teach** your people to base their whole life on the work done in them through Christ's death and resurrection.
4 Keys to Wise Living Many believers are slowed in their spiritual growth for lack of wisdom. Sometimes teaching that stymies spiritual growth is enthusiastically endorsed because believers do not know the Scriptures. We should heed Paul's warning against listening to people who pander to the flesh, rather than edifying in the truth.	2:8	**Be aware** that human philosophy and erroneous religious tradition are contrary to Christ. **Do not be deceived.**
	2:18–23	**Hold fast to Christ** and **honor Him** to please the Father. **Be wise** in evaluating "spiritual experiences," knowing that they are not to produce pride or elitism. **Know** the importance of commitment to a local church and of submission to righteous spiritual authority.
	3:18–22	**Submit** to God's ordained order in the home, church, and workplace.
5 Steps to Dynamic Devotion Always in the NT, the call to wholehearted discipleship is accompanied by the call to a life of devotion. To devote is "to concentrate on a particular *pursuit or purpose.*" A life of devotion to Christ pursues His purpose—His being reproduced in us.	1:25–29	**Understand** that all hope of real "glory" is in discovering Christ's very life in you.
	3:16, 17	**Be diligent** in Bible study and **practice** Scripture memorization and meditation. **Let the Word** in you **produce** praise to God and edification of others. **Serve** Jesus' purposes in every thought, word, and deed.

Truth Colossians Teaches	Text	**Action** Colossians Invites
	4:2–6	**Become** a person of prayer. **Repent** of any prayerlessness in your life. **Recognize** God's gift of time and use it wisely. **Speak with grace and wisdom** in answer to all.
6 **Keys to Godly Relationships** Human relationships were designed to be fueled and filled by righteousness. To the degree we give in to the urging of our flesh nature, we will fail to experience righteous or fulfilling relationships. To the degree we practice those things God commands, our relationships will become a sampling of heaven on Earth.	3:5–11 3:12–14 3:15	**Reject, turn from,** and **refuse to practice** any form of relational unrighteousness or sin: wrong sexual activity, angry exchanges, jealous or envious attitudes, greedy desire for things, gossip, or coarse humor. **Adopt** and **practice diligently** every form of relational righteousness: love, compassion, humble attitudes, self-giving behavior, freely flowing forgiveness, and patience with others. **Choose peace** to govern all of your relationships.

The First Epistle of Paul the Apostle to the THESSALONIANS

Author: Paul
Date: A.D. 50
Theme: The Twin Comforts of Past Ministry and the Future Return of the Lord
Key Words: Thanks, Coming, Faith/Hope/Love

Origin of the Church at Thessalonica The gospel first reached Europe around A.D. 49. That occurred when, on his second mission tour, Paul and his party responded to the night vision of the Macedonian man by sailing from Troas (site of the ancient city of Troy), via the Aegean island of Samothrace, to Neapolis—the port city for Philippi (Acts 16:8–12). Here the apostle met the businesswoman Lydia, cast a spirit of divination out of a young female slave, and was publicly beaten and wrongfully arrested as a result. On learning that Paul and Silas were Roman citizens, the imperial authorities gingerly apologized, freed the apostles, and urged them to leave town. They did (Acts 16:13–40).

Traveling 90 miles southwesterly, Paul and Silas came to Thessalonica. "As his custom was," Luke reports, Paul went to the synagogue there and over several weeks preached by arguing that Jesus, the carpenter's son from Nazareth, was in fact God's Anointed One—the Messiah—long promised in the Jewish scriptures (Acts 17:1–3). Here Paul established the second major church on the European continent.

Among those who accepted the message were not only Jews like Aristarchus (Col. 4:10, 11) but as well "devout Greeks"—Gentiles who attended the synagogue services but never became full converts to Judaism by taking circumcision. In addition, a considerable number of prominent women in the city responded to Paul's message (Acts 17:4). The faith of Christian believers at Thessalonica became widely known (1 Thess. 1:7, 8). Twice, at least, the Philippian church sent financial support to Paul while he was at Thessalonica, where his stay lasted at least several weeks (Phil. 4:16).

While Acts emphasizes the Jewish origins of the church at Thessalonica, Paul's letters to them make it clear that many of them had "turned to God from idols" (1 Thess. 1:9). Since worship of idols in New Testament times was a Gentile and not a Jewish practice, ethnic variety marked the church of the Thessalonians.

Named for his sister by a Macedonian king in the late fourth century B.C., the city of Thessalonica was the capital of its district of the Roman province of Macedonia and possessed of a fine natural harbor. It was located on the famed Via Egnatia, a major Roman military highway that stretched from the western Balkan coast to present-day Istanbul, and was ruled by *politarchs*—a class of officials peculiar to the region. Luke shows his usual historical sensitivity by using this rare term (Acts 17:6, "rulers of the city," NKJV).

As earlier in Philippi and afterward in Berea, Paul's ministry in

Thessalonica caught the attention both of Roman officials and Jewish opponents. Jewish leaders were not pleased with the redirected loyalties of the synagogue adherents. So they brought charges that Paul and his band had "turned the world upside down"—a highly serious charge, much closer to civil rebellion than to tolerable public mischief suggested by long use of familiar words. To call Jesus "Lord" was to employ a title otherwise applied to the emperor: "these are all acting contrary to the decrees of Caesar, saying there is another king—Jesus" (Acts 17:7). Quite possibly, the very Roman authorities who reviewed the case included husbands of the "prominent women" persuaded by Paul. Their ire may have been added to the Jewish hostilities.

When Paul could not be found, his host Jason was arrested and made to pay bail. Under cover of night, Paul and Silas left for Berea—60 miles to the southwest. "But when the Jews from Thessalonica learned that the word of God was preached by Paul at Berea, they came there also, and stirred up the crowds" (Acts 17:13). Thus, from three cities in succession—Philippi, Thessalonica, and Berea—Paul and his team left amid civil unrest and with their work cut short. Such was the initial reception of the gospel on the European continent.

Occasion and Date During his brief ministry in Athens, Paul was deeply concerned with the state of affairs within the infant church at Thessalonica. He had tried to return twice earlier, but Satan hindered (2:18). So when he could no longer endure the uncertainty nor conclusively plan a visit, he sent Timothy back to the church to investigate its progress (3:1, 2).

Timothy brought back a good report. The Thessalonians were thriving in their faith and were equally concerned for Paul. News of their faith amid trouble had spread widely through Macedonia and Achaia, the province to the south. Both Paul and the Thessalonians longed for reunion.

But there was more ministry for Paul in Corinth, about 50 miles west of Athens. From Corinth, it appears, refreshed by the good news from Thessalonica, he wrote the letter today called 1 Thessalonians.

From calculations based on the Gallio inscription—a public copy of a letter from the Roman emperor to the proconsul of Achaia—it can be affirmed that 1 Thessalonians was written in A.D. 50 or 51. The letter (with the possible exception of Galatians) is therefore the earliest preserved letter of Paul and, in fact, the first book of the New Testament to have been written. (The four Gospels, though they describe earlier events, were in their final form published later.)

Character and Content Written primarily in a mood of relief and gratitude, 1 Thessalonians is marked by thankfulness over the growth of the church in Paul's forced absence. The letter contains no elaborate theology like Romans, no rebuke of a threatening heresy like Galatians, no extensive pastoral counsels like 1 Corinthians.

The usual pattern in Paul's letter—theological teaching followed by practical application—is slightly modified in 1 Thessalonians. First Thessalonians 1—3 rehearse Paul's remembrances of his ministry among them, his concern for the state of their faith, his commission of Timothy to return to the church, his conspicuous delight upon learning of their steadfast faith. First Thessalonians 4 and 5 contain the characteristic exhortations toward such matters as sexual purity (4:1–8; 5:23), responsible love (4:9–12), esteem and support for leaders (5:12, 13), patience and helpfulness toward the varieties of human need (5:14, 15).

It is clear that these counsels only repeat what Paul had urged earlier when he was with them and that the Thessalonians already follow his counsel but should do so "more and more" (4:1), "just as you also are doing" (5:11). From the carefully balanced phrases in 1:3 and the repetition of the terms in 5:8, it is likewise clear that Paul and probably other early Christian missionaries repeatedly spoke of faith, hope, and love as a favorite trio of Christian virtues.

One doctrinal and practical concern, probably brought back by Timothy to Paul, led to the major theological emphasis of 1 Thessalonians. They had clearly understood his teaching that Jesus, brought back from the dead by God, would come again in triumph. Since Paul had left Thessalonica, however, several of the Thessalonian believers had died. What would become of them, the Thessalonians wondered, since Christ had not yet returned?

Paul's response fueled hope and therefore comfort to those who grieved the loss of loved ones. The dead in Christ, in fact, would be the first to be resurrected. Then living Christians would join them and all would be caught up to meet the Lord in the air and forever be with Him. Comfort indeed!

Paul's language describing the coming of Jesus lies at a distance from the vocabulary of urban technology two millennia later. First-century Mediterranean people were quite accustomed to the splendorous, joyful, and anticipated arrival ("coming") of a visiting royal figure. On the appointed day, citizens would go outside the city to meet the royal visitor—who came with a vast cortege. Shouts of welcome and acclaim would rise as he passed by, and those who lined the road would then join the monarch as he was borne to an appointed place. Here, special recognitions and awards would be made (2:19). There was joy and awe at the king's splendorous arrival. So shall it be when the living and the dead go up, not out, to meet the King who comes from heaven.

The theme of Christ's return, though concentrated in 4:13–18, spills over into 5:1–11 as well. Indeed, the coming of Christ occurs from one end of the letter (1:10) to the other (5:23; see also 2:19; 3:13). Every chapter in 1 Thessalonians refers to this decisive future event.

Personal Application

Christians of all ages, like Paul ("we who are alive," 4:15), have confidently awaited the return of Christ in their own time. Throughout the history of the church, there have been those who deprived the return of Christ of its intended force by setting dates or specifying limits. Those of any age who do so are claiming to know more than Jesus Himself: "But of that day and hour no one knows, not even the angels in heaven, nor the Son, but only the Father" (Mark 13:32).

Immediately following the prediction of Christ's return (4:13–18), Paul makes the point (5:1–11) that the suddenness of the coming of Jesus will not surprise prepared Christians who have donned the appropriate armor (5:8), which works in all dimensions of time: faith (past), hope (future), and love (present).

Two things are certain: 1) the return of Christ is an assured future event, and 2) that event is closer than it has ever been before. But to specify a date for the Second Coming, or to specify a time by which the Lord must surely return, or to focus solely on detailed prophetic systems that attempt to sequence precisely various final events described in Scripture—such efforts dilute the force of Christ's return as revealed in 1 Thessalonians. Paul's bottom line—twice affirmed (4:18; 5:11: the Greek text uses exactly the same words)—is comfort in the face of death. Such a message encourages as well the contemporary descendants of the Thessalonians who mourn "those who sleep in Jesus." This does not discourage expectancy (5:1–10), but neither does it provide encouragement to presumptuous systems of dating Jesus' return.

Father God Revealed God the Father (1:1, 3; 3:11, 13) is the source of wrath and displeasure (2:15, 16) to those who oppose Him, but for those who serve Him He is the recipient of thanks (1:2; 2:13; 3:9) and the origin of salvation (5:9), courage (2:2), peace (5:23), and approval (2:4). God raised Jesus and will raise the dead who trusted Him (1:10; 4:14). He is the living and genuine God (1:9), the opposite of idols (1:9), the incontestable witness (2:5). God's will relates to moral purity (4:3, 7), but as well to continual thanksgiving (5:18). His word, "the gospel of God" (2:2, 8, 9: compare "gospel of Christ," 3:2), remarkably, comes through human words (2:13; 4:8). In 1 Thessalonians, as elsewhere in the Bible, God is the source and end of all that relates to both natural and spiritual life.

Christ Revealed Jesus is the Son of God (1:10), whose death and resurrection (1:10; 2:14, 15) provide an example to believers who suffer now (1:6; 2:14, 15) but who, as He was, will be raised in the future (1:10; 4:14, 16). Believers then and now have a mystical spiritual position "in the Lord" (1:1, 3; 4:1; 5:18), which, nevertheless, is practical enough to be the ground of respect for ruling elders (5:12). From Christ comes grace (5:28).

But above all in 1 Thessalonians, Christ emerges as the coming King, the conqueror of death, whose awaited return from heaven (1:10) gives comfort to the bereaved (4:17, 18; 5:11) and joy to his expectant subjects (2:19, 20). This will be His day, the "Day of the Lord" (5:2; see 2 Thess. 2:2, "day of Christ").

The Holy Spirit at Work All Christians can affirm that it is God who has "given us His Holy Spirit" (4:8). The Spirit inspires joy even amid affliction (1:6). When the gospel arrived in Thessalonica, it came not only in word "but also in power and in the Holy Spirit and in much assurance" (1:5), suggesting a balanced mix of intellectual argument, the Spirit's power (probably with "signs and wonders"), and deep personal response. First Thessalonians 5:19–21 reveals a lively charismatic character to the worship at Thessalonica—prophetic activity, which some were inclined to subdue but for which Paul asks tested acceptance: his words were to be read "to all the holy brethren" (5:27).

Outline of 1 Thessalonians

I. Typical letter opening **1:1**
- A. Authors
- B. Addressees
- C. Greeting

II. Paul's ministry recalled **1:2—3:13**
- A. Thanks for Thessalonian faith, hope, love 1:2–10

B. How Paul ministered there 2:1–12
 1. Like a nurse: gentle 2:1–8
 2. Like a father: concerned 2:9–12
C. Thanks for Thessalonian endurance 2:13–16
D. Paul's anxiety over the Thessalonians 2:17–20
E. Timothy's mission and Paul's relief 3:1–10
F. Paul's continued hope to see the Thessalonians 3:11–13

III. Christ's return awaited 4:1—5:11

A. For the present: life-style qualities 4:1–12
 1. Marital fidelity 4:1–8
 2. Brotherly love 4:9, 10
 3. Personal responsibility 4:10–12
B. For the future: the return of Christ 4:13—5:11
 1. The coming of the King: comfort for the bereaved 4:13–18
 2. The coming of the King: no surprise for the prepared 5:1–11

IV. Closing counsels 5:12–28

A. Respect for leaders 5:12, 13
B. Peace in the community 5:13
C. Help for the needy 5:14
D. Christian universals 5:15–22
 1. Benevolence toward all 5:15
 2. Joy at all times 5:16
 3. Prayer always 5:17
 4. Thanksgiving everywhere 5:18
 5. Charismatic affirmation 5:19–22

Greeting

PAUL, [a]Silvanus, and Timothy,

To the church of the [b]Thessalonians
in God the Father and the Lord Jesus
Christ:

Grace to you and peace [1]from God
our Father and the Lord Jesus Christ.

Their Good Example

2 [a]We give thanks to God always for
you all, making mention of you in our
prayers,
1 3 remembering without ceasing
[a]your work of faith, [b]labor of love, and
*patience of **hope** in our Lord Jesus
Christ in the sight of our God and
Father,

WORD WEALTH

1:3 hope, *elpis* (el-*peece*); Strong's *#1680:* Hope, not in the sense of an optimistic outlook or wishful thinking without any foundation, but in the sense of confident expectation based on solid certainty. Biblical hope rests on God's promises, particularly those pertaining to Christ's return. So certain is the future of the redeemed that the NT sometimes speaks of future events in the past tense, as though they were already accomplished. Hope is never inferior to faith, but is an extension of faith. Faith is the present possession of grace; hope is confidence in grace's future accomplishment.

4 knowing, beloved brethren, [a]your
election by God.
5 For [a]our gospel did not come to you 2
in word only, but also in power,
[b]and in the *Holy Spirit [c]and in much
assurance, as you know what kind of
men we were among you for your sake.
6 And [a]you became followers of us
and of the Lord, having received the
word in much affliction, [b]with joy of
the Holy Spirit,
7 so that you became examples to all
in Macedonia and Achaia who *believe.

CHAPTER 1

1 [a]1 Pet. 5:12 [b]Acts 17:1–9 [1]NU omits *from God our Father and the Lord Jesus Christ* **2** [a]Rom. 1:8; 2 Thess. 1:3 **3** [a]John 6:29 [b]Rom. 16:6 *See WW at Heb. 10:36. **4** [a]Col. 3:12 **5** [a]Mark 16:20 [b]2 Cor. 6:6 [c]Heb. 2:3 *See WW at Acts 7:33. **6** [a]1 Cor. 4:16; 11:1 [b]Acts 5:41; 13:52; 2 Cor. 6:10; Gal. 5:22 **7** *See WW at Rom. 10:9.

1:1 Paul shared authorship of 1 and 2 Thess. with **Silvanus** and **Timothy**. Timothy, a young Jewish understudy of Paul, also joined with Paul in the writing of 2 Cor., Phil., Col., and Philem. Silvanus, known as Silas in Acts, was a leader in the church in Jerusalem (Acts 15:22) and a prophet (Acts 15:32). Later, Silvanus shared in the writing of 1 Pet. (5:12). He was therefore an associate *both of Peter and Paul.*

1:3 *See section 1* of Truth-In-Action at the end of 1 Thess.

1:3 Faith and **love** and **hope** appear together also at 5:8 in the same sequence. These words occur elsewhere in Paul's writings as well (Rom. 5:1–5; 1 Cor. 13:13; Gal. 5:5, 6; Col. 1:4, 5; see Heb. 10:22–24). This trio of terms was a favorite summary of Christian teaching in the early church.

1:5 See section 2 of Truth-In-Action at the end of 1 Thess.

1:5 The ways in which Christianity reached the Thessalonians model a balanced but full-orbed description of effective preaching. Although there was reasoned argument, the **gospel did not come . . . in word only, but also in power** (Greek *dunamis*), which Jesus had promised with the arrival of the **Holy Spirit** (Acts 1:8). Linkage of the power and the Spirit probably suggests that miraculous manifestations are in view, but these alone are not sufficient to yield the **much assurance,** that is, full and deep personal conviction, which was the outcome of the Pauline mission at Thessalonica.

1:6 Received the word in much affliction: See 2:14 and Acts 17:1–9. Both Jesus (Matt. 12:14) and Paul (2 Cor. 11:26) received similar treatment.

8 For from you the word of the Lord
[a]has sounded forth, not only in Macedonia and Achaia, but also [b]in every
place. Your faith toward God has gone
out, so that we do not need to say anything.
9 For they themselves declare concerning us [a]what manner of entry we
had to you, [b]and how you turned to
God from idols to serve the living and
true God,
10 and [a]to wait for His Son from
heaven, whom He raised from the
dead, *even* Jesus who delivers us
[b]from the wrath to come.

Paul's Conduct

2 For you yourselves know, brethren, that our coming to you was not
in vain.
2 But [1]even after we had suffered before and were *spitefully treated at
[a]Philippi, as you know, we were
[b]bold in our God to speak to you the
gospel of God in much conflict.
3 [a]For our *exhortation *did* not *come*
from *error or uncleanness, nor *was*
it in deceit.
4 But as [a]we have been approved by
God [b]to be entrusted with the gospel,
even so we speak, [c]not as pleasing
men, but God [d]who tests our hearts.
3 5 For [a]neither at any time did we use
flattering words, as you know, nor a
[1]cloak for covetousness—[b]God *is* witness.
6 [a]Nor did we seek glory from men,
either from you or from others, when
[b]we might have [c]made demands
[d]as apostles of Christ.
3 7 But [a]we were gentle among you,

8 [a]Rom. 10:18 [b]Rom. 1:8; 16:19
9 [a]1 Thess. 2:1 [b]1 Cor. 12:2
10 [a][Rom. 2:7] [b]Rom. 5:9

CHAPTER 2

2 [a]Acts 14:5; 16:19–24 [b]Acts 17:1–9 [1]NU, M omit *even* *See WW at Luke 18:32.
3 [a]2 Cor. 7:2 *See WW at Acts 9:31. • See WW at Jude 11.
4 [a]1 Cor. 7:25 [b]Titus 1:3 [c]Gal. 1:10 [d]Prov. 17:3
5 [a]2 Cor. 2:17 [b]Rom. 1:9 [1]*pretext for greed*
6 [a]1 Tim. 5:17 [b]1 Cor. 9:4 [c]2 Cor. 11:9 [d]1 Cor. 9:1
7 [a]1 Cor. 2:3
8 [a]Rom. 1:11 [b]2 Cor. 12:15 *See WW at Rom. 1:11. • See WW at Luke 21:19.
9 [a]Acts 18:3; 20:34, 35 [b]2 Cor. 12:13
10 [a]1 Thess. 1:5 [b]2 Cor. 7:2 *See WW at Rev. 1:5.
11 [1]NU, M *implored*
12 [a]Eph. 4:1 [b]1 Cor. 1:9
13 [a]1 Thess. 1:2, 3 [b]Mark 4:20 [c][Gal. 4:14] [d][1 Pet. 1:23]

just as a nursing *mother* cherishes her
own children.
8 So, affectionately longing for you,
we were well pleased [a]to *impart to
you not only the gospel of God, but also
[b]our own *lives, because you had become dear to us.
9 For you remember, brethren, our **3**
[a]labor and toil; for laboring night and
day, [b]that we might not be a burden
to any of you, we preached to you the
gospel of God.
10 [a]You *are* *witnesses, and God *also*,
[b]how devoutly and justly and blamelessly we behaved ourselves among
you who believe;
11 as you know how we exhorted, and
comforted, and [1]charged every one of
you, as a father *does* his own children,
12 [a]that you would walk worthy of
God [b]who calls you into His own kingdom and glory.

Their Conversion

13 For this reason we also thank God **2**
[a]without ceasing, because when you
[b]received the word of God which you
heard from us, you welcomed *it*
[c]not *as* the word of men, but as it is
in truth, the word of God, which also
effectively [d]works in you who believe.

WORD WEALTH

2:13 effectively, *energeo* (en-erg-*eh*-oh); Strong's *#1754:* One of the four big energy words: *energeo, energes, energeia,* and *energema.* The words all stem from *en,* "in," and *ergon,* "work," and have to do with the active operation or working of power and its effectual results.

1:9 Some of the Thessalonians were Gentiles, who **turned to God from idols**. Others were Jews, as emphasized by Luke's account of Paul's arrival at the synagogue in Thessalonica (Acts 17:1–4).

2:2 Though **spitefully treated at Philippi** by being beaten and jailed in violation of the rights of Roman citizens, Paul and Silas who here write together there sang together (Acts 16:25) and knew the "joy of the Holy Spirit" that flourishes amid adversity (1:6).

2:3–6 Accusations against the apostle, attacks on his integrity, can be detected behind his denial of **error** and **uncleanness** as well as of using **flattering words** or seeking **glory from men.**

2:5, 6 See section 3 of Truth-In-Action at the end of 1 Thess.

2:7 See section 3 of Truth-In-Action at the end of 1 Thess.

2:7 As the italic type in the NKJV shows, no underlying separate word for ***mother*** appears in the Greek text, though the added term seems warranted from the fact that the nurse feeds **her own children.** The loving care expressed in **cherishes** is illumined by the one other place in the NT where this verb is used, likewise in a tender family setting—the husband's owed care for his wife as for himself (Eph. 5:29). The word means literally, "keep warm."

2:9 See section 3 of Truth-In-Action at the end of 1 Thess.

2:9 At least in Thessalonica and Corinth, Paul supported himself—presumably by working as a tentmaker. Yet while in Thessalonica, at least twice he received support from the Philippian church (Phil.4:16), which he had left a few months earlier. To a large extent, the Book of Philippians was written as an extended thank-you letter for much continued support of Paul's ministry. But his general rule was to impose no burden on the churches.

2:12 The charge to **walk worthy of God** is in 1 Thess. one of several clues to the content of Paul's preaching and teaching while at Thessalonica. In general terms, he had taught them how to please God (4:1, 2). He taught marital fidelity (4:6) and explained that believers could expect suffering (3:3, 4). From the second letter, it is clear he taught—though, it seems, they needed a reminder—that apostasy and the emergence of the Man of Sin would precede the Lord's return (2 Thess. 2:3–5). All such teachings Paul called "traditions" and urged their careful recollection and observance.

2:13 See section 2 of Truth-In-Action at the end of 1 Thess.

14 For you, brethren, became imitators
[a]of the churches of God which are in
Judea in Christ Jesus. For [b]you also
suffered the same things from your
own countrymen, just as they *did* from
the Judeans,
15 [a]who killed both the Lord Jesus and
[b]their own prophets, and have persecuted us; and they do not please God
[c]and are [1]contrary to all men,
16 [a]forbidding us to speak to the Gentiles that they may be saved, so as always [b]to fill up *the measure of* their
sins; [c]but wrath has come upon them
to the uttermost.

Longing to See Them

17 But we, brethren, having been
taken away from you for a short time
[a]in presence, not in heart, *endeavored
*more eagerly to see your face with
great *desire.
18 Therefore we wanted to come to
you—even I, Paul, time and again—but
[a]Satan hindered us.
19 For [a]what *is* our hope, or joy, or
[b]crown of rejoicing? *Is it* not even you
in the [c]presence of our Lord Jesus
Christ [d]at His *coming?
20 For you are our glory and joy.

Concern for Their Faith

3 Therefore, when we could no
longer endure it, we thought it
good to be left in Athens alone,
2 and sent [a]Timothy, our brother and
minister of God, and our fellow laborer
in the gospel of Christ, to establish you

14 [a]Gal. 1:22 [b]Acts 17:5
15 [a]Acts 2:23 [b]Matt. 5:12; 23:34, 35 [c]Esth. 3:8 [1]*hostile*
16 [a]Luke 11:52 [b]Gen. 15:16 [c]Matt. 24:6
17 [a]1 Cor. 5:3 *See WW at Gal. 2:10. • See WW at 2 Cor. 2:4. • See WW at 2 Tim. 2:22.
18 [a]Rom. 1:13; 15:22
19 [a]2 Cor. 1:14 [b]Prov. 16:31 [c]Jude 24 [d]1 Cor. 15:23 *See WW at 1 Cor. 15:23.

CHAPTER 3

2 [a]Rom. 16:21
3 [a]Eph. 3:13 [b]Acts 9:16; 14:22
4 [a]Acts 20:24
5 [a]1 Cor. 7:5 [b]Gal. 2:2
6 [a]Acts 18:5 [b]Phil. 1:8
7 [a]2 Cor. 1:4
8 [a]Phil. 4:1
10 [a]2 Cor. 13:9 *See WW at John 10:10. • See WW at Heb. 11:3.
11 [a]Mark 1:3

and encourage you concerning your
faith,
3 [a]that no one should be shaken by
these afflictions; for you yourselves
know that [b]we are appointed to this.
4 [a]For, in fact, we told you before
when we were with you that we would
suffer tribulation, just as it happened,
and you know.
5 For this reason, when I could no
longer endure it, I sent to know your
faith, [a]lest by some means the tempter
had tempted you, and [b]our labor might
be in vain.

Encouraged by Timothy

6 [a]But now that Timothy has come to
us from you, and brought us good news
of your faith and love, and that you always have good remembrance of us,
greatly desiring to see us, [b]as we also
to see you—
7 therefore, brethren, in all our affliction and distress [a]we were comforted concerning you by your faith.
8 For now we live, if you [a]stand fast
in the Lord.
9 For what thanks can we render to
God for you, for all the joy with which
we rejoice for your sake before our
God,
10 night and day praying *exceedingly **1**
that we may see your face [a]and *perfect what is lacking in your faith?

Prayer for the Church

11 Now may our God and Father Himself, and our Lord Jesus Christ, [a]direct
our way to you.

2:16 The arrival of God's **wrath** on the Jews cannot be a reference to the destruction of the temple in Jerusalem, an event two decades future to Paul's writing. The widespread difficulties undergone by Jewish settlements throughout the Mediterranean may have been viewed by the apostle as a foretaste of the "wrath to come" (1:10) from which Jesus rescues believers. Paul may have had in mind the recent (A.D. 49) expulsion of the Jews from Rome by edict of the emperor Claudius, which accounted for the presence in Corinth (from which Paul wrote 1 Thess.) of his friends Priscilla and Aquila who were among those banned (Acts 18:2).

2:18 Satan is called "the tempter" in 3:5.

2:19 The **crown of rejoicing** was actually a wreath woven from plants. These crowns were used as prizes in athletic contests, such as the famed *Isthmian Games held* on the *Corinthian isthmus*: Paul apparently wrote the Thessalonian letters from Corinth. But the notion of crowns **in the presence of our Lord Jesus Christ at His coming** recalls the pomp and splendor of an official imperial visitor that provided the imagery Paul uses to speak of the return of Jesus. At such official visits, awards were made. "Coming" in reference to the return of the Lord occurs six times in the Thessalonian letters and only once (1 Cor. 15:23) elsewhere in Paul's writings—illustrating the central role of the return of Christ in these early letters of Paul. The exact expression "*second* coming" arose after NT times.

3:6 Now that Timothy has come discloses the occasion for writing 1 Thess. Concerned over the state of affairs among the Thessalonians, whom he had to leave abruptly and whom he had, without success, tried repeatedly to see again, Paul sent Timothy back to Thessalonica while Paul first visited at Athens and then went on to Corinth (vv. 1, 2). On his return to Paul, Timothy brought the **good news** about the thriving **faith and love** of the Thessalonians (v. 6). Paul still hopes to see them again (v. 11), and the likelihood is that he did see them on a later mission tour (Acts 20:1–4).

3:10–12 That Paul hoped to see the Thessalonians again to **perfect what is lacking** in their faith need not be taken in any heavy technical sense: no specific spiritual defects are detailed in the letters. The mood is a prayerful wish that they will **increase and abound in love,** along the lines of his later phrases "more and more" (4:1), "just as you also are doing" (5:11).

3:10 See section 1 of Truth-In-Action at the end of 1 Thess.

12 And may the Lord make you increase and [a]abound in love to one another and to all, just as we *do* to you,
13 so that He may establish [a]your hearts blameless in **holiness** before our God and Father at the coming of our Lord Jesus Christ with all His saints.

WORD WEALTH

3:13 holiness, *hagiosune* (hag-ee-ah-*soo*-nay); Strong's *#42:* The process, quality, and condition of a holy disposition and the quality of holiness in personal conduct. It is the principle that separates the believer from the world. *Hagiosune* consecrates us to God's service both in soul and in body, finding fulfillment in moral dedication and a life committed to purity. It causes every component of our character to stand God's inspection and meet His approval.

Plea for Purity

1 **4** Finally then, brethren, we urge and exhort in the Lord Jesus [a]that you should abound more and more, [b]just as you received from us how you ought to walk and to please God;
2 for you know what *commandments we gave you through the Lord Jesus.
4 3 For this is [a]the will of God, [b]your sanctification: [c]that you should abstain from *sexual immorality;
4 [a]that each of you should know how to possess his own vessel in sanctification and honor,
5 [a]not in passion of lust, [b]like the Gentiles [c]who do not know God;
6 that no one should take advantage of and defraud his brother in this matter, because the Lord [a]*is* the avenger of all such, as we also forewarned you and testified.

12 [a]Phil. 1:9
13 [a]2 Thess. 2:17

CHAPTER 4

1 [a]1 Cor. 15:58 [b]Phil. 1:27
2 *See WW at Acts 16:24.
3 [a][Rom. 12:2] [b]Eph. 5:27 [c][1 Cor. 6:15–20] *See WW at Matt. 15:19.
4 [a]Rom. 6:19
5 [a]Col. 3:5 [b]Eph. 4:17, 18 [c]1 Cor. 15:34
6 [a]2 Thess. 1:8
7 [a]Lev. 11:44 *See WW at Gal. 1:6.
8 [a]Luke 10:16 [b]1 Cor. 2:10 [1]NU *who also gives*
9 [a][Jer. 31:33, 34] [b]Matt. 22:39 *See WW at Heb. 13:1. • See WW at John 3:16.
10 [a]1 Thess. 3:12
11 [a]2 Thess. 3:11 [b]Acts 20:35
12 [a]Rom. 13:13
13 [a]Lev. 19:28 [b][Eph. 2:12] [1]Died *See WW at 1 Thess. 1:3.
14 [a]1 Cor. 15:13 [b]1 Cor. 15:20, 23 [1]Or *through Jesus sleep*
15 [a]1 Kin. 13:17; 20:35 [b]1 Cor. 15:51, 52 [1]Dead
16 [a][Matt. 24:30, 31] [b][1 Cor. 15:52] [c][1 Cor. 15:23]
17 [a][1 Cor. 15:51–53] [b]Acts 1:9

7 For God did not *call us to uncleanness, [a]but in holiness. 4
8 [a]Therefore he who rejects *this* does not reject man, but God, [b]who[1] has also given us His Holy Spirit.

A Brotherly and Orderly Life

9 But concerning *brotherly love you have no need that I should write to you, for [a]you yourselves are taught by God [b]to *love one another;
10 and indeed you do so toward all the brethren who are in all Macedonia. But we urge you, brethren, [a]that you increase more and more;
11 that you also aspire to lead a quiet life, [a]to mind your own business, and [b]to work with your own hands, as we commanded you, 1
12 [a]that you may walk properly toward those who are outside, and *that* you may lack nothing.

The Comfort of Christ's Coming

13 But I do not want you to be ignorant, brethren, concerning those who have fallen [1]asleep, lest you sorrow [a]as others [b]who have no *hope.
14 For [a]if we believe that Jesus died and rose again, even so God will bring with Him [b]those who [1]sleep in Jesus.
15 For this we say to you [a]by the word of the Lord, that [b]we who are alive *and* remain until the coming of the Lord will by no means precede those who are [1]asleep.
16 For [a]the Lord Himself will descend from heaven with a shout, with the voice of an archangel, and with [b]the trumpet of God. [c]And the dead in Christ will rise first.
17 [a]Then we who are alive *and* remain shall be **caught up** together with them [b]in the clouds to meet the Lord in the 2

4:1–8 At this point the apostle turns to the exhortations that customarily form the second half of his letters. He urges renewed attention to the **commandments** (v. 2) he had given while with them. Rather a surprise in the context is an appeal to the **will of God** here defined as **your sanctification: that you should abstain from sexual immorality** (v. 3). For a largely Gentile audience, the advice is relevant and specific. An echo of this highly practical definition of sanctification occurs in the closing prayer for entire sanctification, including the body (5:23).
4:1 See section 1 of Truth-In-Action at the end of 1 Thess.
4:3–6 See section 4 of Truth-In-Action at the end of 1 Thess.
4:7, 8 See section 4 of Truth-In-Action at the end of 1 Thess.
4:11, 12 See section 1 of Truth-In-Action at the end of 1 Thess.
4:13 Those who have fallen asleep are Thessalonians who have died, whether or not since Paul left them. Puzzlement arose over how the dead could benefit from Christ's return. Paul's reply is to the point: they shall rise first and the living will follow them (vv. 16, 17).
4:14 God will bring with Him, that is, with Jesus. God will resurrect deceased believers as He has already brought Jesus from the dead.
4:16 Shouts and trumpets heralded the arrival of visiting monarchs in NT times. Heavenly equivalents proclaim the return of Jesus.
4:17 See section 2 of Truth-In-Action at the end of 1 Thess.
4:17 Caught up together with them: The chief biblical source of the doctrine of the Rapture—the catching away to heaven of those, dead or living, who have trusted in Christ and await His return. The exact word "rapture" does not occur in Scripture: it was formed from a word in the Latin translation of the Bible, which, for this phrase, reads *simul rapiemur cum illis.* 2 Thess. 2:3–12 gives the additional information that a great apostasy and the emergence of the Man of Sin will precede the return of the Lord.

air. And thus [c]we shall always be with
the Lord.
18 [a]Therefore comfort one another
with these words.

WORD WEALTH

4:17 caught up, *harpadzo* (har-*pad*-zoe); Strong's *#726:* To seize, snatch away, catch up, take by force. The word describes the Holy Spirit's action in transferring Philip from one location to another (Acts 8:39) and Paul's being caught up to Paradise (2 Cor. 12:2, 4). It suggests the exercise of a sudden force.

KINGDOM DYNAMICS

4:15–18 The Threefold Announcement of the Lord's Coming, MESSIAH'S COMING. This is one of the most beloved passages about the Second Coming, and it is also one of the most detailed. We are told that there will be a threefold announcement of the Lord's coming: a shout, the voice of an archangel, and the trumpet of God (v. 16). In addition, there is a threefold promise to believers: 1) the dead in Christ shall rise; 2) we who are alive will be caught away with them; and 3) we shall always be with the Lord (vv. 16, 17).

It is important to note as well that this is the key text where the idea of a Rapture is taught. The word "Rapture" is not used in the Bible, but the idea of the saints' being "caught up" and gathered together at the Second Coming of the Lord is clearly spoken of here and in Matt. 24:30, 31. The hope of His coming is to be a source of comfort for us who await Him (v. 18).

(Acts 1:10, 11/Matt. 25:13) J.H.

The Day of the Lord

5 But concerning [a]the *times and the
*seasons, brethren, you have no
need that I should write to you.
2 For you yourselves know perfectly
that [a]the day of the *Lord so comes as
a thief in the night.
3 For when they say, "Peace and
safety!" then [a]sudden destruction
comes upon them, [b]as labor pains upon
a pregnant woman. And they shall not
escape.
4 [a]But you, brethren, are not in darkness, so that this Day should overtake
you as a thief.
5 You are all [a]sons of light and sons
of the day. We are not of the night nor
of darkness.
6 [a]Therefore let us not sleep, as oth- 1
ers *do*, but [b]let us watch and be
[1]sober.
7 For [a]those who sleep, sleep at night,
and those who get drunk [b]are drunk
at night.
8 But let us who are of the day be sober, [a]putting on the breastplate of faith
and love, and *as* a helmet the hope of
*salvation.
9 For [a]God did not appoint us to
wrath, [b]but to obtain salvation through
our Lord *Jesus Christ,
10 [a]who died for us, that whether we
wake or sleep, we should live together
with Him.
11 Therefore [1]comfort each other and
[2]edify one another, just as you also are
doing.

Various Exhortations

12 And we urge you, brethren, [a]to rec- 5
ognize those who labor among you,
and are over you in the Lord and
[1]admonish you,
13 and to esteem them *very highly in
love for their work's sake. [a]Be at peace
among yourselves.
14 Now we [1]exhort you, brethren,
[a]warn those who are [2]unruly, [b]comfort
the fainthearted, [c]uphold the weak,
[d]be patient with all.

17 [c]John 14:3; 17:24
18 [a]1 Thess. 5:11

CHAPTER 5

1 [a]Matt. 24:3 *See WW at Acts 1:7. • See WW at Col. 4:5.
2 [a]Luke 21:34; 1 Thess. 5:4; [2 Pet. 3:10]; Rev. 3:3; 16:15 *See WW at John 6:68.
3 [a]Is. 13:6–9 [b]Hos. 13:13
4 [a][Acts 26:18]; Rom. 13:12; Eph. 5:8; 1 John 2:8
5 [a]Eph. 5:8
6 [a]Matt. 25:5 [b]Matt. 25:13; Mark 13:35; [1 Pet. 5:8] [1]*self-controlled*
7 [a][Luke 21:34] [b]Acts 2:15; 2 Pet. 2:13
8 [a]Is. 59:17; Eph. 6:14 *See WW at Luke 19:9.
9 [a]Rom. 9:22 [b][2 Thess. 2:13] *See WW at Phil. 4:23.
10 [a]2 Cor. 5:15
11 [1]Or *encourage* [2]*build one another up*
12 [a]1 Cor. 16:18; 1 Tim. 5:17; Heb. 13:7, 17 [1]*instruct* or *warn*
13 [a]Mark 9:50 *See WW at John 10:10.
14 [a]2 Thess. 3:6, 7, 11 [b]Heb. 12:12 [c]Rom. 14:1; 15:1; 1 Cor. 8:7 [d]Gal. 5:22 [1]*encourage* [2]*insubordinate* or *idle*

4:18—5:2 The Greek words here translated **comfort one another** are precisely repeated at 5:11, "Comfort each other." Biblical teaching about the return of Christ is intended to yield present comfort to the bereaved, not future speculation for the curious. What is important is, as the Thessalonians knew, that **the day of the Lord so comes as a thief in the night.** Sudden unexpectedness is the point of the imagery, and obviously it is not a commendation of thievery.

5:5 Sons of light and sons of the day reflects Paul's Jewish background. The Hebrew *language uses* "son of—" *to identify what is characteristic:* Barnabas, for example, meant "Son of Consolation." The "valiant man" King Saul took for himself in battle is described literally in Hebrew as "a son of might" (1 Sam. 14:52). Christians enjoy the openness of sunlight and avoid the potential destructive surprises of darkness.

5:6–8 Those **who are of the day** (v. 8) are to be awake, sensitive, alert, and prepared.

5:6 See section 1 of Truth-In-Action at the end of 1 Thess.

5:9 Salvation is threefold—past, present and future. We *were* saved (justification) when we first trusted Christ; we *are being* saved (sanctification) as the Holy Spirit continues to work in us; and we will *yet be* saved (glorification) as we share in the Lord's final triumph.

5:10 The true end of the return of Jesus is that Christians, living or dead, **should live together with Him** and "always be with the Lord" (4:17). Such knowledge gives true comfort. On the other hand, the evil will be forever banished "from the presence of the Lord" (2 Thess. 1:9).

5:12, 13 See section 5 of Truth-In-Action at the end of 1 Thess.

5:12 To recognize carries the idea of appreciating a person's true worth. The Thessalonians apparently had not fully realized their leaders' value.

15 [a]See that no one *renders evil for
evil to anyone, but always [b]pursue
what is good both for yourselves and
for all.
 16 [a]Rejoice always,
17 [a]pray* without ceasing,
18 in everything give thanks; for this
is the will of God in Christ Jesus for
you.
19 [a]Do not quench the Spirit.
20 [a]Do not despise **prophecies.**

WORD WEALTH

5:20 prophecies, *propheteia* (prof-ay-*tie*-ah); Strong's *#4394:* From *pro,* "forth," and *phemi,* "to speak." The primary use of the word is not predictive, in the sense of foretelling, but interpretive, declaring, or forth-telling, the will and counsel of God.

15 [a]Lev. 19:18 [b]Gal. 6:10 *See WW at Matt. 22:21. **16** [a][2 Cor. 6:10] **17** [a]Eph. 6:18 *See WW at Matt. 6:6. **19** [a]Eph. 4:30 **20** [a]1 Cor. 14:1, 31 **21** [a]1 John 4:1 [b]Phil. 4:8 *See WW at Matt. 13:48. **23** [a]Phil. 4:9 [b]1 Thess. 3:13 [c]1 Cor. 1:8, 9 [1]*set you apart* *See WW at 1 Cor. 15:23. **24** [a][1 Cor. 10:13] [b]Phil. 1:6 **27** [1]*letter* [2]NU omits *holy* *See WW at Mark 13:14.

21 [a]Test all things; [b]hold fast what is
*good.
22 Abstain from every form of evil.

Blessing and Admonition

23 Now may [a]the God of peace Himself
[b]sanctify[1] you completely; and may
your whole spirit, soul, and body
[c]be preserved blameless at the *coming of our Lord Jesus Christ.
24 He who calls you *is* [a]faithful, who
also will [b]do *it.*
25 Brethren, pray for us.
26 Greet all the brethren with a holy
kiss.
27 I charge you by the Lord that this
[1]epistle be *read to all the [2]holy brethren.
28 The grace of our Lord Jesus Christ
be with you. Amen.

5:16–22 See section 1 of Truth-In-Action at the end of 1 Thess.
5:16–21 These verses may suggest elements of an early Christian service of worship: rejoicing, prayer, thanksgiving, and sifted charismatic prophecy.
5:19, 20 The commands **Do not quench the Spirit** and **Do not despise prophecies,** imply, by their form in Greek, that the Thessalonians were guilty of both. Paul counters these attitudes by endorsing tested, proven, and validated charismatic activities—anticipating the counsels of 1 Cor. 12—14, which later he was to write back to Corinth, where he was when he wrote these words. To quench carries the idea of dampening the flame of Holy Spirit fire, which is poured out to purify, enlighten, warm, melt and consume. Quenching may be either by an inadequate, chilled response or an exaggerated disruptive response.
5:23 Paul's final prayer is that his converts might be wholly sanctified, that is, that their whole being—**spirit, soul, and body**—may be yielded up to the will of God. The power for this accomplishment must come from **the God of peace Himself**. ("Peace" means spiritual prosperity in the broadest sense.)
5:24 God's faithfulness gives assurance that they will "be preserved blameless" until the return of Christ (v. 23).
5:27 This letter, like that to the Colossians (4:16) and the Book of Revelation (1:3) was to be **read** aloud **to all the holy brethren**. The earliest NT was *heard* by many long before it could be *read* by all. "Faith *comes* by hearing" (Rom. 10:17).
5:28 Without exception, every letter of Paul's contains among its closing words a reference to the **grace** of our Lord Jesus Christ.

TRUTH-IN-ACTION through 1 THESSALONIANS

Letting the LIFE of the Holy Spirit Bring Faith's Works Alive in You!

Truth 1 Thessalonians Teaches	Text	**Action** 1 Thessalonians Invites
1 Guidelines For Growing in Godliness Godly believers live unto God and for God. They seek to honor and reflect God in everything they think, say, or do. Godliness lives quietly, is absorbed in doing good for others and works productively. Godliness has a good reputation with unbelievers. Godliness is knowing the commands of Scripture and doing them.	1:3	**Understand** that successful Christian living consists of 1) work that flows from faith, 2) labor that flows from love, and 3) patient endurance that is born of living hope. **Insure** that your life is thus characterized.
	3:10	**Be faithful to intercede** for other believers and other congregations.
	4:1	**Live your life** in order to please God, not yourself.
	4:11, 12	**Live** a quiet, peaceful life. **Never gossip. Be diligent** in whatever work you have chosen to do. **Earn** a good reputation with unbelievers.
	5:6	**Conduct your life,** being alert and self-controlled.
	5:16–22	**Practice** the commands of Scripture.

Truth 1 Thessalonians Teaches	Text	**Action** 1 Thessalonians Invites
2 Key Lessons in Faith The person of faith prays that God will demonstrate His power in the church today. Faith is able to receive God's Word through human beings, believing God's ability to use human vessels. And faith looks forward to the promise that the Lord will appear a second time for salvation's consummation.	1:5 2:13 4:17	**Pray** that your preaching of the gospel will be attended by the power of signs, wonders, and miracles. **Receive** the preaching and teaching as God's Word! **Refuse** to receive the Scripture as merely human opinion, and **avoid** negating its authority or nullifying its effectiveness for growth in your life. **Encourage** brothers and sisters in Christ often, giving hope through expecting Jesus Christ's return.
3 Lessons for Leaders Although righteous spiritual leaders speak the truth of God boldly, they do so gently. They are unmoved by flattery or praise from humankind. They only seek praise from God. They are diligent workers who never take advantage of those they serve.	2:5, 6 2:7 2:9	Leaders, **seek to please** God, rather than cater to humans. **Never employ** flattery; rather, **speak** the truth **forthrightly. Look** only to God for praise. Leaders, **practice gentleness** in your ministry. Leaders, **understand** that ministry means hard work and long hours.
4 Keys to Moral Purity The church must sustain a biblical commitment to sexual purity. The worldly attitude that produces sexually immoral behavior rejects God and His ways.	4:3–6 4:7, 8	**Recognize** that sanctification includes sexual purity and moral self-control. **Never defraud** others; that is, **do not cheat** brothers through wrongful sexual liaisons. **Understand** that living in sexual impurity is a rejection of God as well as His Word.
5 Keys to Relating to Authority Pastoral leadership is a gift from God. We must treat God's appointed leaders and teachers with appropriate respect.	5:12, 13	**Honor** church leadership. **Recognize** that their Bible-based instruction comes with Jesus' own authority.

The Second Epistle of Paul the Apostle to the THESSALONIANS

Author: Paul
Date: A.D. 50
Theme: The Return of the Lord—Advance Indicators and Life-style in the Meanwhile
Key Words: Day of the Lord, Man of Sin, Tradition

Author and Date First and 2 Thessalonians are very similar in language, suggesting that Paul wrote 2 Thessalonians within a few weeks of 1 Thessalonians. The return of the Lord is of central importance in both letters. First Thessalonians reveals that some Thessalonians were perplexed over the death of loved ones and whether they might miss the Lord's return. In 2 Thessalonians, a different problem surfaces—one still related to the coming of the Lord. (On the origins of the church at Thessalonica and Paul's earlier relations with them, see the Introduction to 1 Thessalonians.)

Both in 1 Thessalonians (1:6; 2:14; 3:3–5) and in 2 Thessalonians (1:4–7), it is clear that believers there suffered certain persecutions and hardships—just as Paul and Silas themselves did, leading to their departure by night from the city (Acts 17:5–10; 1 Thess. 2:2). Paul's concern for the spiritual stability of the Thessalonian church had led him to send Timothy and to express, in writing 1 Thessalonians, joyful relief upon learning of their spiritual health (1 Thess. 2:17—3:10). The steadfastness of the Thessalonians, their persistence and patience amid adversity, drew the frequent praise and gratitude of the apostle (1 Thess. 1:3; 2 Thess. 1:4). Still, there were clear concerns over imbalanced attitudes related to Christ's coming.

"We hear," said the apostle (3:11), "that there are some who walk among you in a disorderly manner, not working at all. . . ." Work stoppage, it seems, was prompted by an erroneous teaching that someone, unnamed, had brought to Thessalonica—a doctrine that announced that "the day of Christ had come" (2:2). Such a teaching may have had a falsely claimed charismatic origin ("by spirit," 2:2). Or it may have surfaced in a letter falsely attributed to Paul.

Whatever the source of the erroneous teaching, Paul quickly wrote 2 Thessalonians to round out the proper way to understand the return of the Lord. That day, he clarifies, will not occur until certain events take place. First, there will be a falling away and more importantly, the Man of Sin will be revealed—the "son of perdition" (2:3). This figure, in the letters of John called the Antichrist (1 John 2:18; 4:3; 2 John 7), will blasphemously call himself God (2:4). He will deceive many, for he will possess charismatic powers, including the ability to perform miracles (2:9). The spirit of such a figure, the "mystery of lawlessness" (2:7) was already at work in Paul's day. But a restraining power—not clearly identified by the apostle (see note on 2:6, 7)—controls the Man of Sin in such a way as to keep him from interfering with God's consummation of the course of human events through the return of Christ at the Second Coming.

Twice in 2 Thessalonians (2:15; 3:6), the apostle appeals to the "tradition"—fixed beliefs within the churches—as a check upon charismatic but novel teaching. Frequently in the Thessalonian letters he reminds his readers to continue in the things he earlier taught (1 Thess. 2:11, 12; 3:4; 4:2; 2 Thess. 2:5, 15; 3:4, 6, 10, 14). Already in these letters, probably the earliest of New Testament books to be written, a body of fixed Christian beliefs is developing.

Second Thessalonians, if written only a few weeks after 1 Thessalonians, would therefore also have been written about A.D. 50.

Personal Application Scripture presents both signs and suddenness as descriptions of the Lord's return. That may seem contradictory. But alert Christians observe the signs and know that the "mystery of lawlessness" is perennial. They avoid date-setting, leaving the times and the seasons in the hands of the Lord of history (1 Thess. 5:1). Yet they live expectantly, knowing that whether they live or die they are the Lord's (Rom. 14:8; 1 Thess. 5:10).

Before novel teachings that originated with charismatic prophecy are adopted, they should be tested (1 Thess. 5:19, 20). One such test is surely consistency with the generally accepted beliefs—"traditions"—of the historic church and especially alignment with apostolic beliefs. It is sobering to learn that even the Man of Sin, the Antichrist, will possess miraculous powers. Miracles, surprisingly, are never a sufficient ground for faith (Matt. 7:21–23; John 2:23–25): they can be imitated. But the enduring love of God, which is poured out in the hearts of believers by the Holy Spirit (Rom. 5:5), continues into eternity even after charismatic gifts have passed (1 Cor. 13:8–13). Love, then, is the way believers experience eternity within time.

Father God Revealed As elsewhere in the New Testament, God is seen as the Father (1:1; 2:16), the source of grace (1:12) and love (3:5), and the object of thanks (1:3; 2:13). He has chosen (2:13) those in His kingdom (1:5) and makes them worthy of His saving call (1:11), but as well He repays evildoers (1:6) and allows delusion to those who despise the truth (2:11) and who do not know Him (1:8). The churches are His (1:4), they rest in Him (1:1).

Christ Revealed The coequality of Christ with God receives particular attention in this book. Father and Son together are the source of grace and peace (1:2, 12; 3:16, 18), comfort and stability (2:16, 17), love and patience (3:5). Though the church is located geographically in Thessalonica, its spiritual position lies "in God our Father and the Lord Jesus Christ" (1:1; 3:12). As in 1 Thess., the Lord Jesus will come again (1:7, 10; 2:1); and He will, "with the breath of His mouth" (2:8), discomfit the Man of Sin at the moment of His return (2:8) and take vengeance on those who have no knowledge of God (1:8).

***The Holy* Spirit at Work** *In the single* direct reference to the Holy Spirit in 2 Thessalonians, Paul gives thanks to God for the Thessalonians, whose selection for salvation by God "from the beginning" the apostle describes comprehensively as "through sanctification by the Spirit and belief in the truth" (2:13). The Spirit's sanctifying work can be seen as one way to view the intent of God for His people in saving them.

Prophetic utterance from the Spirit, or alleged to be so (2:2), must always be tested (1 Thess. 5:20, 21; 1 Cor. 14:29).

Outline of 2 Thessalonians

I. Typical letter opening **1:1–4**
- A. Authors 1:1
- B. Addressees 1:1
- C. Greetings 1:2
- D. Thanksgiving 1:3, 4

II. Doctrine **1:5—2:12**
- A. Consequences of the coming 1:5–12
  - 1. To the righteous: established worthiness 1:5, 10–12
  - 2. To the unjust: declared banishment 1:6–9
- B. Indicators of the coming 2:1–12
  - 1. The falling away 2:1–3
  - 2. The Man of Sin 2:3–5
  - 3. The restrainer 2:6
  - 4. The lying wonders 2:7–12

III. Exhortation **2:13—3:16**
- A. To steadfastness 2:13–17
- B. To prayer 3:1–5
- C. Against idleness 3:6–13
- D. To discipline 3:14, 15
- E. To peace 3:16

IV. Concluding comments **3:17, 18**
- A. An accrediting signature 3:17
- B. A wish for grace 3:18

Greeting

PAUL, Silvanus, and Timothy,

To the church of the Thessalonians
in God our Father and the Lord Jesus
Christ:

2 [a]Grace to you and peace from God
our Father and the Lord Jesus Christ.

God's Final Judgment and Glory

3 We are bound to thank God always
for you, brethren, as it is fitting, because your faith grows exceedingly,
and the love of every one of you all
abounds toward each other,

4 so that [a]we ourselves boast of you
among the churches of God [b]for your
*patience and faith [c]in all your perse-
cutions and [1]tribulations that you **endure,**

> **WORD WEALTH**
>
> **1:4 endure,** *anechomai* (an-*ekh*-om-ahee); Strong's *#430:* From *ana,* "up," and *echo,* "to hold." The word carries the idea of persevering, tolerating, bearing with, putting up with, standing firm, and not losing courage under pressure.

5 *which is* [a]manifest[1] evidence of the
righteous *judgment of God, that you
may be counted worthy of the kingdom
of God, [b]for which you also *suffer;
6 [a]since *it is* a righteous thing with
God to repay with [1]tribulation those
who trouble you,
7 and to *give* you who are troubled
[a]rest with us when [b]the Lord Jesus is
revealed from heaven with His *mighty
angels,
8 in flaming fire taking vengeance on
those who do not know God, and on
those who do not *obey the gospel of
our Lord Jesus Christ.
9 [a]These shall be punished with everlasting destruction from the presence
of the Lord and [b]from the glory of His
power,
10 when He comes, in that Day,
[a]to be [b]glorified in His saints and to
be admired among all those who

CHAPTER 1

2 [a]1 Cor. 1:3
4 [a]2 Cor. 7:4; [1 Thess. 2:19] [b]1 Thess. 1:3 [c]1 Thess. 2:14 [1]*afflictions* *See WW at Heb. 10:36.
5 [a]Phil. 1:28 [b]1 Thess. 2:14 [1]*plain* *See WW at Matt. 5:22. • See WW at Acts 17:3.
6 [a]Rev. 6:10 [1]*affliction*
7 [a]Rev. 14:13 [b][1 Thess. 4:16]; Jude 14 *See WW at Acts 4:33.
8 *See WW at Rom. 6:17.
9 [a]Phil. 3:19; 1 Thess. 5:3 [b]Deut. 33:2
10 [a]Matt. 25:31 [b]Is. 49:3; John 17:10; 1 Thess. 2:12

1:1 Paul, Silvanus, and Timothy also wrote 1 Thess. No other letter of Paul links these three, though Timothy's name appears as coauthor elswhere: see note on 1 Thess. 1:1.

1:4 See section 1 of Truth-In-Action at the end of 2 Thess.

1:4 The **patience and faith** of the Thessalonians amid **persecutions and tribulations** are frequently and gratefully described as commendable and exemplary by the apostle in his letters to them (1 Thess. 1:3, 6–8; 2:14; 3:2–4; 2 Thess. 1:6, 7).

1:5–10 The fact that the Thessalonians are increasing in faith and love while bravely enduring persecution is clear **evidence** (v. 5) that God is at work in them preparing them for His **kingdom**. One day the present situation will be reversed, for the persecutors will themselves suffer **tribulation** (v. 6), and the persecuted will find **rest** (v. 7) when Christ returns.

1:7 When the Lord Jesus is revealed from heaven, part of the events surrounding the return of the Lord in the Day of the Lord, the wicked **shall be punished with everlasting destruction from the presence** [literally, "the Face"] **of the Lord.** The evil ones forever will be banished from the Lord's presence, while the saved "shall always be with the Lord" (1 Thess. 4:17). The difference is eternal.

[1]believe, because our *testimony
among you was believed.
1 11 Therefore we also pray always for
you that our God would [a]count you
worthy of *this* calling, and fulfill all the
good pleasure of *His* *goodness and
[b]the work of faith with power,
12 [a]that the name of our Lord Jesus
Christ may be glorified in you, and
you in Him, according to the grace
of our God and the Lord Jesus
Christ.

The Great Apostasy

2 Now, brethren, [a]concerning the
*coming of our Lord Jesus Christ
[b]and our gathering together to Him, we
ask you,
2 [a]not to be soon shaken in mind or
troubled, either by spirit or by word
or by letter, as if from us, as though
the day of [1]Christ had come.
3 Let no one deceive you by any
means; for *that Day will not come*
[a]unless the falling away comes first,
and [b]the man of [1]sin is revealed,
[c]the son of perdition,

KINGDOM DYNAMICS

2:2, 3 11. Who Is the Antichrist?, SPIRITUAL ANSWERS. For the answer to this and other probing questions about God and the power life in His kingdom, see the study article "Spiritual Answers to Hard Questions," which begins on page 1996. P.R.

4 who opposes and [a]exalts himself
[b]above all that is called God or that is
worshiped, so that he sits [1]as God in
the temple of God, showing himself
that he is God.
5 Do you not remember that when I
was still with you I told you these
things?
6 And now you know what is restraining, that he may be revealed in
his own time.
7 For [a]the [1]mystery* of lawlessness
is already at *work; only [2]He who now
restrains *will do so* until [2]He is taken
out of the way.
8 And then the lawless one will be revealed, [a]whom the Lord will consume
[b]with the breath of His mouth and destroy [c]with the brightness of His coming.
9 The coming of the *lawless one* is 3
[a]according to the *working of Satan,
with all power, [b]signs, and lying *wonders,
10 and with all unrighteous deception
among [a]those who perish, because
they did not receive [b]the love of the
truth, that they might be saved.

10 [1]NU, M *have believed* *See WW at Rev. 15:5.
11 [a]Col. 1:12 [b]1 Thess. 1:3 *See WW at Rom. 15:14.
12 [a][Col. 3:17]

CHAPTER 2

1 [a][1 Thess. 4:15–17] [b]Matt. 24:31 *See WW at 1 Cor. 15:23.
2 [a]Matt. 24:4 [1]NU *the Lord*
3 [a]1 Tim. 4:1 [b]Dan. 7:25; 8:25; 11:36 [c]John 17:12 [1]NU *lawlessness*
4 [a]Is. 14:13, 14 [b]1 Cor. 8:5 [1]NU omits *as God*
7 [a]1 John 2:18 [1]*hidden truth* [2]*Or he* *See WW at Mark 4:11. • See WW at 1 Thess. 2:13.
8 [a]Dan. 7:10 [b]Is. 11:4 [c]Heb. 10:27
9 [a]John 8:41 [b]Deut. 13:1 *See WW at Col. 1:29. • See WW at Acts 15:12.
10 [a]2 Cor. 2:15 [b]1 Cor. 16:22

1:11 See section 1 of Truth-In-Action at the end of 2 Thess.
2:2 Upsetting and erroneous teaching can arise **by spirit,** through charismatic prophecy, as well as **by word** through reasoned instruction, and even **by letter, as if from us** (see 3:17). Like a later heresy (2 Tim. 2:18, "the resurrection is already past"), the error at Thessalonica put in the past what belongs to the future **as though the day of Christ had come.** The primary thrust of 2 Thess. is to correct this error by the clarification that certain indicators—especially a great apostasy and the emergence of the Man of Sin—will precede the Day of the Lord.
2:3 The man of sin ("man of lawlessness" in some manuscripts) is called the Antichrist in the letters of John. On **the son of perdition,** see the note on 1 Thess. 5:5.
2:4 Jewish history had already shown in Antiochus Epiphanes (about 167 B.C.) a fiercely ungodly monarch who desecrated the temple at Jerusalem (Dan. 11:31–36; the Book of 1 Maccabees, an intertestamental historical account, tells this story). Roman emperors, such as Gaius Caligula (A.D. 37–41) and Domitian (A.D. 81–96), sought to be regarded as divine. This corrupting potential of political power will mark the final Man of Sin as well.
2:5 From Paul's words **when I was still with you I told you these things,** it is clear that future events formed part of his pastoral instruction during the brief time he was with *the Thessalonians.*
2:6, 7 In grammatical terms, **what is restraining** the Man of Sin is neuter, referring to an impersonal force, while **He who now restrains** is masculine, suggesting a personal figure. Paul apparently expected his readers to understand what or whom he meant (since he had given them instruction when with them), but today's readers should hesitate to clarify by dogmatic opinion what stands unclear in the biblical text itself (it is always helpful to reread 2 Pet. 3:15, 16 and be reminded that even one apostle found difficult passages in the writings of another). The restrainer is mentioned nowhere else in the Bible. Among interpretations proposed for the restraining power that keeps the Antichrist in check have been 1) Paul's incomplete ministry: the son of perdition would emerge once Paul's mission is complete; 2) the Holy Spirit, who keeps things under control until the ripe eschatological moment; 3) God Himself, since it is evil that is held back; 4) the Jewish state at the time; 5) the institution of human government. The last alternative has in its favor Paul's own experience of benefits gained from Roman citizenship (Acts 16:37; 22:26–29). In addition the neuter expression "what is restraining" could refer to the Roman system of government itself and the masculine "he who is now restraining" to the then-reigning Roman emperor, Claudius, whose tenure (A.D. 41-54) was one of the saner eras in Roman imperial history.
2:7, 8, 11, 12 The **mystery of lawlessness,** which was in Paul's day **already at work,** need not be taken as some deep secret. Good and evil alike occur in the world. As the final Day of the Lord approaches, when evil rouses and the limiting forces are withdrawn, **the lawless one will be revealed,** but—as made clear a generation later in the Book of Revelation—the result will be the final destruction of the Antichrist and all the forces of evil, with God and Christ in final triumph. Meanwhile, there are many who **believe the lie, because** they **did not believe the truth.** People will believe *something.*
2:9, 10 See section 3 of Truth-In-Action at the end of 2 Thess.

11 And [a]for this reason God will send
them strong *delusion, [b]that they
should believe the lie,
12 that they all may be condemned
who did not believe the truth but
[a]had pleasure in unrighteousness.

Stand Fast

4 **13** But we are [1]bound to give thanks
to God always for you, brethren beloved by the Lord, because God
[a]from the beginning [b]chose you for
*salvation [c]through [2]sanctification by
the Spirit and belief in the truth,
14 to which He called you by our gospel, for [a]the obtaining of the glory of
our Lord Jesus Christ.
2 15 Therefore, brethren, [a]stand fast and
hold [b]the traditions which you were
taught, whether by word or our
[1]epistle.
16 Now may our Lord Jesus Christ
Himself, and our God and Father,
[a]who has loved us and given *us* *everlasting *consolation and [b]good hope by
grace,
17 comfort your hearts [a]and [1]establish
you in every good word and work.

Pray for Us

2 **3** Finally, brethren, [a]pray for us, that
the word of the Lord may run
swiftly and be glorified, just as *it is*
with you,
2 and [a]that we may be delivered from
unreasonable and wicked men; [b]for
not all have faith.
3 But [a]the Lord is faithful, who will
establish you and [b]guard *you* from the
evil one.

11 [a]Rom. 1:28 [b]1 Tim. 4:1 *See WW at Jude 11.
12 [a]Rom. 1:32; 1 Cor. 13:6
13 [a]Eph. 1:4 [b]1 Thess. 1:4 [c]1 Thess. 4:7; [1 Pet. 1:2] [1]*under obligation* [2]*being set apart by* *See WW at Luke 19:9.
14 [a]1 Pet. 5:10
15 [a]1 Cor. 16:13 [b]Rom. 6:17; 1 Cor. 11:2; 2 Thess. 3:6; Jude 3 [1]*letter*
16 [a][Rev. 1:5] [b]Titus 3:7; 1 Pet. 1:3 *See WW at Rev. 14:6. • See WW at Acts 9:31.
17 [a]1 Cor. 1:8 [1]*strengthen*

CHAPTER 3

1 [a]Eph. 6:19
2 [a]Rom. 15:31 [b]Acts 28:24
3 [a]1 Cor. 1:9; 1 Thess. 5:24 [b]John 17:15
4 [a]2 Cor. 7:16
5 [a]1 Chr. 29:18
6 [a]Rom. 16:17 [b]1 Cor. 5:1 [c]1 Thess. 4:11 [1]NU, M *they*
8 [a]1 Thess. 2:9 [1]Lit. *for nothing*
9 [a]1 Cor. 9:4, 6–14

4 And [a]we have **confidence** in the
Lord concerning you, both that you do
and will do the things we command
you.

WORD WEALTH

3:4 confidence, *peitho* (*pie*-tho); Strong's *#3982:* As an intransitive verb, the word means to be convinced, be confident, have inward certainty, trust (Rom. 2:19; 2 Cor. 2:3). In its transitive use, it means to win over, prevail upon, persuade, induce a change of mind by the use of arguments (Acts 18:4; 19:8, 26; 2 Cor. 5:11).

5 Now may [a]the Lord direct your
hearts into the love of God and into
the patience of Christ.

Warning Against Idleness

6 But we command you, brethren, in 1
the name of our Lord Jesus Christ,
[a]that you withdraw [b]from every
brother who walks [c]disorderly and not
according to the tradition which
[1]he received from us.
7 For you yourselves know how you
ought to follow us, for we were not disorderly among you;
8 nor did we eat anyone's bread
[1]free of charge, but worked with
[a]labor and toil night and day, that we
might not be a burden to any of
you,
9 not because we do not have [a]author-
ity, but to make ourselves an example
of how you should follow us.
10 For even when we were with you,
we commanded you this: If anyone will
not work, neither shall he eat.

2:9 The identical word used six times of the return of the Lord in the two Thessalonian letters refers here to **the coming of the *lawless one*.** Just as God energizes the gifts of the Spirit (1 Cor. 12:6), Satan will empower this figure to produce compelling, but deceptive, **signs and lying wonders.** Not every "miracle" comes from God, nor are such wonders any less miraculous because of their origin.
2:13 See section 4 of Truth-In-Action at the end of 2 Thess.
2:13 Sanctification is but another way to translate the usual word for "holiness"—a term rather characteristic of 1 Thess. and occurring in that book three times (4:3, 4, 7; compare 1 Thess. 5:23), more often than in the Book of Romans. Because the work of the Spirit can be described comprehensively as the cultivation of holiness, the Spirit most frequently is designated the *Holy* Spirit. But a splendid balance is urged between the believer's personal holiness and **belief in the truth,** between subjective piety and objective truth.
2:15 See section 2 of Truth-In-Action at the end of 2 Thess.
2:15 The traditions which you were taught describe emerging fixed beliefs and practices that eventually form a skeletal apostolic orthodoxy. Paul refers to the same idea when, six years later, he conveys tradition to the Corinthian church (1 Cor. 11:2, 17; 15:3) and cites the practice of the churches as a source for his pastoral counsel (1 Cor. 4:17; 7:17; 11:16; 14:33). Such a churchly tradition, this early in the Pauline mission, was violated by the disorderly brothers mentioned in 3:6, and Paul's words in 3:4 illustrate the birth of tradition.
2:16, 17 Here is the first of three benedictions in 2 Thess. The others are at 3:5 and 3:16. Compare 1 Thess. 3:11–13; 5:23.
3:1, 2 See section 2 of Truth-In-Action at the end of 2 Thess.
3:6–15 See section 1 of Truth-In-Action at the end of 2 Thess.
3:6 In vv. 6–15 Paul warns against **every brother who walks disorderly,** urging the severe step of discontinued fellowship with those who persist in such behavior (vv. 6, 14, 15). The term "disorderly" (vv. 6, 7, 11) originally described one conspicuously out of step in a marching military column. The refusal to work may have arisen from the conviction of some of the Thessalonians that the Day of the Lord was just about to occur; therefore, menial labor was thought to be inappropriate and unnecessary.
3:10–12 Paul's counsel and his example, both at Thessalonica (3:7, 8) and at Corinth (1 Cor. 9:3–6, 12, 15),

11 For we hear that there are some
who walk among you in a disorderly
manner, not working at all, but are
[a]busybodies.
12 Now those who are such we command and [1]exhort through our Lord
Jesus Christ [a]that they work in quietness and eat their own bread.
13 But *as for* you, brethren, [a]do not
grow weary *in* doing good.
5 14 And if anyone does not obey our
word in this [1]epistle, note that person
and [a]do not keep company with him,
that he may be ashamed.
15 [a]Yet do not count *him* as an enemy,
[b]but [1]admonish *him* as a brother.

Benediction

16 Now may [a]the Lord of peace Himself give you peace always in every
way. The Lord *be* with you all.
17 [a]The salutation of Paul with my
own hand, which is a *sign in every
[1]epistle; so I write.
18 [a]The grace of our Lord Jesus Christ
be with you all. Amen.

11 [a]1 Pet. 4:15 **12** [a]Eph. 4:28 [1]*encourage* **13** [a]Gal. 6:9 **14** [a]Matt. 18:17 [1]*letter* **15** [a]Lev. 19:17 [b]Titus 3:10 [1]*warn* **16** [a]Rom. 15:33 **17** [a]1 Cor. 16:21 [1]*letter* *See WW at Rev. 16:14. **18** [a]Rom. 16:20, 24

were that **if anyone will not work, neither shall he eat.** Refused employment leads to becoming **busybodies,** who simply should go back to work.

3:14, 15 The disciplinary separation implied in the words **do not keep company with him** are consistent with other instructions about discipline in the NT (Matt. 18:15–17; 1 Cor. 5:11; James 5:19, 20; 1 John 5:16, 17).

3:14 See section 5 of Truth-In-Action at the end of 2 Thess.

3:17 The salutation by Paul in his **own hand** appears also at the end of 1 Cor. (16:21), Gal. (6:11), Col. (4:18), and Philem. (19).

3:18 On **grace,** see the note on 1 Thess. 5:28.

TRUTH-IN-ACTION through 2 THESSALONIANS

Letting the LIFE of the Holy Spirit Bring Faith's Works Alive in You!

Truth 2 Thessalonians Teaches	Text	**Action** 2 Thessalonians Invites
1 Guidelines For Growing in Godliness Three faces of godliness in believers are 1) enduring trials through faith and hope, 2) faithfulness in intercession for other believers, and 3) faithfully confronting those who are out of order, exhorting to repent.	1:4 1:11 3:6–15	**Recognize** the value of perseverance and faith maintained in the face of persecutions and tribulations. **Pray** for other believers and for churches, for the fulfillment of God's purpose for them. **Work diligently,** and **pay** your bills. **Do not encourage** idleness by supporting those who will not work.
2 Key Lessons in Faith Faith is unmoving in the face of tribulation and recognizes that it has a role to play in the effectiveness of other ministries through prayer partnership with them.	2:15 3:1, 2	**Stand fast** and **hold firmly** to the truth of God's Word. **Pray** for church leaders that their evangelistic ministries will be fruitful and that they will be kept safe from those who oppose them.
3 A Key to Wise Living The wise believer correctly discerns between deceptive satanic signs and wonders and the true gifts of the Holy Spirit.	2:9, 10	**Understand** and **beware** of the counterfeit nature of satanic signs and wonders. **Know** that they will deceive those who reject the truth.
4 A Step to Holiness We must realize that practical holiness is not a possession, but it is a process that calls for continual submission to the Spirit's work and *continued* steadfastness in faith.	2:13	**Recognize** and **embrace** the continuing work of God's grace that involves 1) the sanctifying work of God's Holy Spirit and 2) our continuing to advance through believing the truth.
5 A Step to Faithful Obedience We must practice discriminating sensitivity in our fellowshipping.	3:14	**Recognize** the importance of obeying God's Word. **Notice** that restoration is the object of rejecting fellowship with careless disciples.

The First Epistle of Paul the Apostle to
TIMOTHY

Author: Paul
Date: About A.D. 64
Theme: Removal of False Doctrine, Preservation of Public Worship, and Proper Leadership in the Church
Key Words: Carefulness, Watchfulness, Strength, Commitment

Background On their first missionary journey Paul and Barnabas preached in Lystra, a city of Lycaonia, and experienced success amid persecution. It is likely that a Jewess named Lois, and her daughter Eunice, were converted to Christ during that ministry. Eunice was married to a Gentile, by whom she had Timothy, probably an only child. Timothy evidently had been instructed in the Jewish religion, but his father refused to allow his son to be circumcised. From the beginning a close relationship developed between Paul and Timothy.

When Paul returned to Lystra on his second journey, he found Timothy to be a member of the local church and highly recommended by its leaders there and at Iconium. Under the prompting of the Holy Spirit Paul added Timothy to his apostolic party. Since they were going to be ministering among the Jews, Paul admonished Timothy to be circumcised, not for righteousness' sake, but to avoid offending the Jews since his mother was Jewish.

Author All the Pastoral Epistles (1 Tim., 2 Tim., Titus) name the apostle Paul as their author. In addition, early tradition unanimously insists that Paul wrote them. However, many scholars question this claim on the basis of several difficulties. The Pastoral Epistles include words that do not appear in Paul's uncontested letters. Moreover, the Pastorals record certain events that are difficult to harmonize with the account of Paul's journeys in Acts. For example, Paul has conducted a mission in Crete (Titus 1:5), plans to spend the winter in Nicopolis (Titus 3:12), and has made visits to Ephesus (1 Tim. 1:3), to Miletus (2 Tim. 4:20), and to Troas (2 Tim. 4:13). Furthermore, some scholars feel that these letters describe a church organization too far advanced for Paul's time.

So far as vocabulary is concerned, we may conclude that the subject matter of the Pastorals is so different from that of Paul's other letters that he would necessarily use some words he had not previously employed. It would be foolish to restrict an educated man like Paul to a limited vocabulary. The fact that he was writing to close associates is also a consideration.

The obvious answer to the problem of harmonizing the accounts of Paul's journeys in the Pastorals with those in Acts is that Paul was released from the Roman imprisonment described in Acts and continued his ministry for several more years. There is solid evidence from the writings of early Christian leaders that this was the case. During this period of continued activity, Paul wrote 1 Timothy and Titus. Later he was arrested again and wrote 2 Timothy during his second Roman imprisonment.

The mention of elders, bishops, and deacons in the Pastorals does not imply a monarchical episcopacy that demands a date later than Paul's time. Paul appointed elders in the churches on his first missionary journey (Acts 14:23) and greeted bishops and deacons in his Philippian letter. Furthermore, Paul used the terms "bishop" and "elder" interchangeably (see Titus 1:5–7).

The preponderance of evidence supports Paul as the author of the Pastoral Epistles.

Date Paul visited Ephesus in about A.D. 63, following his release from his first Roman imprisonment. Soon thereafter, he left, placing Timothy in charge of the church there. He probably wrote the letter in about A.D. 64.

Purpose The primary purpose of the epistle was to encourage Timothy in his difficult task of dealing with doctrinal errors and practical problems in the church at Ephesus, and to give him instructions concerning pastoral responsibilities and the qualifications and duties of church leadership.

Content The work to which Paul assigned Timothy involved serious difficulties, and he felt it necessary to write a letter of instruction to his young associate as he faced the problems. In the letter he told Timothy how to combat false teachers, how to order the church's worship, how to choose church leaders, and how to deal prudently with different classes in the church. All the while Timothy was to teach the apostolic faith and lead an exemplary life.

Personal Application This letter not only guided Timothy in fulfilling his responsibilities as a church leader, but it has been a handbook for pastors throughout the whole church age. A clear lesson gleaned from Paul's instructions is that the church must have a well-trained, deeply devoted, and highly consecrated ministry. Furthermore, ministers must stay in constant touch with God through prayer and study of the Bible (see 2:1, 8; 4:6, 12–16). The pastor must first nourish his own soul in the words of faith and good doctrine (4:6) and then teach the people the essentials of the faith (4:11). Practicing godliness in his own conduct, he must bring his congregation to do the same (4:16).

Christ Revealed The deity of Jesus is apparent, because Paul equates Him with God the Father (1:1, 2; 3:16) and proclaims His universal sovereignty and eternal nature (6:15, 16). Jesus is the source of grace, mercy, and peace (1:2, 14) who commanded Paul's apostleship (1:1) and enabled him for service (1:12). Christ is both Lord (1:2, 12, 14; 5:21; 6:3, 14, 15) and Savior (1:1, 15) "who gave Himself a ransom for all" (2:6). By virtue of His redemptive work He is the "one Mediator between God and men" (2:5), the way of access to God. He who became incarnate has ascended (3:16). Meanwhile, He is our hope (1:1), and the promise of His return is an incentive to fidelity in service and to purity in life (6:14).

The Holy Spirit at Work Direct references to the Holy Spirit in 1 Timothy are rare, but He was at work from the inception of the church at Ephesus (see Acts 19:1–7). The "intercessions" (2:1) are prayers that involve the Holy Spirit's assistance (Rom. 8:26, 27). The statement that "the Spirit expressly says" (4:1) underscores the continuing activity of the Holy Spirit and Paul's sensitivity to His promptings. In 4:14 Paul reminds Timothy of "the gift" that was given to him "by prophecy," a special ability for ministry given as a *charisma* of the Spirit when hands were laid on him. Further, "a good testimony" (3:7) would also include a leader's being "full of the Holy Spirit" as with the first appointment of leaders (Acts 6:3).

Outline of 1 Timothy

Introduction 1:1–20
- A. Salutation 1:1, 2
- B. Charge to Timothy 1:3–11
- C. Thanksgiving 1:12–17
- D. Restatement of the charge 1:18–20

I. Instructions concerning the church 2:1—3:16
- A. Its worship 2:1–15
- B. Its officers 3:1–13
- C. Its function in relation to the truth 3:14–16

II. Instructions concerning pastoral duties 4:1—6:10
- A. Toward the church as a whole 4:1–16
- B. Toward various classes in the church 5:1—6:10

III. Concluding exhortations 6:11–21
- A. To keep the faith and fight the fight 6:11–16
- B. To present the claims of Christ to the rich 6:17–19
- C. To guard the truth 6:20, 21

Greeting

PAUL, an apostle of Jesus Christ, by
the commandment of God our
*Savior and the Lord Jesus Christ, our
hope,

2 To Timothy, a [a]true son in the faith:

[b]Grace, mercy, *and* peace from God
our Father and Jesus Christ our Lord.

No Other Doctrine

3 3 As I urged you [a]when I went into
Macedonia—remain in Ephesus that
you may [1]charge some [b]that they teach
no other doctrine,
4 [a]nor give heed to fables and endless
genealogies, which cause disputes
rather than godly edification which is
in faith.
5 Now [a]the purpose of the *commandment
is love [b]from a *pure heart,
from a good conscience, and *from*
[1]sincere* faith,
6 from which some, having strayed,
have turned aside to [a]**idle talk,**
7 desiring to be teachers of the law,
understanding neither what they say
nor the things which they affirm.

CHAPTER 1

1 *See WW at John 4:42.
2 [a]Acts 16:1, 2; Rom. 1:7; 2 Tim. 1:2; Titus 1:4 [b]Gal. 1:3
3 [a]Acts 20:1,3 [b]Rom. 16:17; 2 Cor. 11:4; Gal. 1:6, 7; 1 Tim. 6:3 [1]*command*
4 [a]1 Tim. 6:3, 4, 20; Titus 1:14
5 [a]Rom.13:8–10; Gal. 5:14 [b]Eph. 6:24 [1]Lit. *unhypocritical* *See WW at Acts 16:24. • See WW at Matt. 5:8. • See WW at 1 Pet. 1:22.
6 [a]1 Tim. 6:4, 20

WORD WEALTH

1:6 idle talk, *mataiologia* (mat-ah-yol-og-*ee*-ah); Strong's *#3150:* A combination of *mataios,* "vain," and *logos,* "word." The word denotes futile talk, worthless, empty, meaningless babble, and idle prattle. Here it describes would-be teachers who love to hear themselves speak but have nothing of substance to say.

1:1 Paul states his apostleship incidentally. There was no controversy between the teacher and his pupil regarding the chain of authority.
1:2 Timothy was Paul's spiritual **son,** having been converted through his ministry. See Phil. 2:22.
1:3–7 See section 3 of Truth-In-Action at the end of 1 Tim.
1:3 I urged you: False teaching had been sown in the church, and Timothy must prevent its spread. Paul's description of the teachers in the following verses indicates that they were legalists trying to mix law and grace.
1:4 Fables probably refer to the numerous legends which the Jews had added to the OT. See Titus 1:14. The Jews often amplified the OT **genealogies,** inventing names and weaving tales about them.
1:5 God's **commandment** does not lead to strife and debate but rather to love for God and man.
1:7 The false teachers sought to be esteemed as **teachers of the law** who can untie the knotty questions of life, but they did not even understand what they were talking about, let alone comprehend the question at hand.

3 8 But we know that the law *is* [a]good
if one uses it lawfully,
9 knowing this: that the law is not
made for a righteous person, but for
the lawless and insubordinate, for *the*
ungodly and for sinners, for *the* unholy
and profane, for murderers of fathers
and murderers of mothers, for man-
slayers,
10 for fornicators, for sodomites, for
kidnappers, for liars, for perjurers, and
if there is any other thing that is
[1]contrary to *sound doctrine,
11 according to the glorious gospel of
the [a]blessed God which was [b]commit-
ted to my trust.

Glory to God for His Grace

12 And I thank Christ Jesus our Lord
who has [a]enabled me, [b]because He
counted me faithful, [c]putting *me* into
the ministry,
13 although [a]I was formerly a *blasphemer, a persecutor, and an [1]insolent
man; but I obtained mercy because
[b]I did *it* ignorantly in unbelief.
14 [a]And the grace of our Lord was exceedingly abundant, [b]with faith and
love which are in Christ Jesus.
15 [a]This *is* a faithful saying and worthy of all acceptance, that [b]Christ
Jesus came into the world to *save *sinners, of whom I am chief.
16 However, for this reason I obtained
*mercy, that in me first Jesus Christ
might show all *longsuffering, as a pattern to those who are going to believe
on Him for everlasting life.
17 Now to [a]the King *eternal, [b]immor-
tal, [c]invisible, to [1]God [d]who alone is
wise, [e]*be* honor and glory forever and
ever. Amen.

Fight the Good Fight

18 This [1]charge* I commit to you, son 4
Timothy, according to the *prophecies
previously made concerning you, that
by them you may wage the good warfare,
19 having faith and a good conscience,
which some having rejected, concerning the faith have suffered shipwreck,
20 of whom are [a]Hymenaeus and
[b]Alexander, whom I delivered to Satan
that they may learn not to [c]blaspheme.

Pray for All Men

2 Therefore I [1]exhort first of all that 5
supplications, prayers, intercessions, *and* giving of thanks be made
for all men,
2 [a]for kings and [b]all who are in
[1]authority, that we may lead a quiet
and peaceable life in all godliness and
[2]reverence.
3 For this *is* [a]good* and acceptable in
the sight [b]of God our Savior,

8 [a]Rom. 7:12, 16 **10** [1]*opposed* *See WW at 3 John 2. **11** [a]1 Tim. 6:15 [b]1 Cor. 9:17 **12** [a]1 Cor. 15:10 [b]1 Cor. 7:25 [c]Col. 1:25 **13** [a]Acts 8:3 [b]John 4:21 [1]*violently arrogant* *See WW at Acts 6:11. **14** [a]Rom. 5:20 [b]2 Tim. 1:13; 2:22 **15** [a]2 Tim. 2:11 [b]Matt. 1:21; 9:13 *See WW at Luke 7:50. • See WW at James 5:20. **16** *See WW at Rom. 9:15. • See WW at Heb. 6:12.

17 [a]Ps. 10:16 [b]Rom. 1:23 [c]Heb. 11:27 [d]Rom. 16:27 [e]1 Chr. 29:11 [1]NU *the only God,* *See WW at Matt. 28:20. **18** [1]*command* *See WW at Acts 16:24. • See WW at 1 Thess. 5:20. **20** [a]2 Tim. 2:17, 18 [b]2 Tim. 4:14 [c]Acts 13:45

CHAPTER 2

1 [1]*encourage* **2** [a]Ezra 6:10 [b][Rom. 13:1] [1]*a prominent place* [2]*dignity* **3** [a]Rom. 12:2 [b]2 Tim. 1:9 *See WW at Matt. 13:48.

1:8–11 See section 3 of Truth-In-Action at the end of 1 Tim.
1:8 Paul does not disparage **the law** of Moses. In the epistles to the Romans and the Galatians he explains that the Law is necessary to bring conviction of sin (**uses it lawfully**).
1:9 The law is not a needed restrainer for a **righteous person,** the Christian who already shows his regard and allegiance to it. **The lawless** have no respect for the law and have no intention of keeping it. **Insubordinate:** Those who do not acknowledge authority and rule. **Unholy:** Those unclean within and without. **Profane:** Those so unholy they are a shame in any public gathering.
1:10 Fornicators: Those who practice any sexual immorality. **Sodomites:** Perverts, homosexuals, those who defile themselves with other men. **Any other thing that is contrary to sound doctrine:** Paul completes the list with a general statement entailing everything in conflict with the immutable moral law of God, the accepted precepts of Christianity.
1:13 A blasphemer: One who speaks unjustly of Jesus, His doctrines, His ways, and His followers. ***I did it ignorantly:*** Paul acted according to the prejudices he was taught in his nation and by his Pharisaism. God showed him **mercy** because he was misinformed.
1:14 The grace of our Lord was exceedingly abundant: The original Greek is emphatic. The grace of God superabounded toward Paul.
1:15 Of whom I am chief: Paul had not forgotten what he had been. His boasting was never in himself, but rather in the God who redeemed and changed him.
1:17 Now to the King eternal: The King ever living and ever able to redeem; One who will never see decay or corruption; One who cannot be seen but who works everywhere; One who possesses wisdom above any creature, including man; One who is to be respected, honored, and glorified forever.
1:18 See section 4 of Truth-In-Action at the end of 1 Tim.
1:18 Timothy's charge was to stop those who were teaching a doctrine contrary to that delivered by Paul. This responsibility evidently had been prophesied at his ordination (4:14). By meditating upon these prophetic words he would receive the determination to fight a good warfare. This passage would recommend that the ordination of people to ministry today might well be attended by such sensitive and supernatural ministry of the Holy Spirit as godly people pray with and minister to the candidate (see 2 Tim. 1:6).
1:19 Those who abandon the truths and morals of the gospel in favor of false doctrine meet with catastrophe.
1:20 To deliver an offender **to Satan** refers to excommunication, which was remedial as well as punitive (see 1 Cor. 5:5).
2:1–6 See section 5 of Truth-In-Action at the end of 1 Tim.
2:2 We must pray for those **who are in authority** over us if we wish to reap the benefits of good government, which is a prized gift from God for the church's welfare and advancement of the gospel.

4 [a]who desires all men to be saved
[b]and to come to the knowledge of the
truth.
5 [a]For *there is* one God and [b]one *Mediator between God and men, *the* Man
Christ *Jesus,
6 [a]who gave Himself a ransom for all,
to be testified in due time,
7 [a]for which I was appointed a
preacher and an apostle—I am speaking the truth [1]in Christ *and* not lying—
[b]a teacher of the Gentiles in faith and
truth.

Men and Women in the Church

8 I desire therefore that the men pray
[a]everywhere, [b]lifting up holy hands,
without wrath and *doubting;
1 9 in like manner also, that the
[a]women *adorn themselves in modest
apparel, with propriety and [1]modera-
tion, not with braided hair or gold or
pearls or costly clothing,
10 [a]but, which is proper for women
*professing godliness, with good
works.
11 Let a woman learn in silence with
all submission.
12 And [a]I do not permit a woman to
teach or to have authority over a man,
but to be in silence.
13 For Adam was formed first, then
Eve.
14 And Adam was not deceived, but
the woman being deceived, fell into
transgression.
15 Nevertheless she will be saved in
childbearing if they continue in faith,
love, and holiness, with self-control.

Qualifications of Overseers

3 This *is* a faithful saying: If a man 5
*desires the position of a [1]bishop,
he desires a good work.
2 A bishop then must be blameless,
the husband of one wife, temperate,
sober-minded, of good behavior, hospitable, able to teach;
3 not [1]given to wine, not violent,
[2]not greedy for money, but **gentle,** not
quarrelsome, not [3]covetous;

> **WORD WEALTH**
>
> **3:3 gentle,** *epieikes* (ep-ee-eye-*kace*); Strong's *#1933:* From *epi,* "unto," and *eikos,* "likely." The word suggests a character that is equitable, reasonable, forbearing, moderate, fair, and considerate. It is the opposite of harsh, abrasive, sarcastic, cruel, and contentious. The person with *epieikes* does not insist on the letter of the law.

4 one who rules his own house well,
having *his* children in submission with
all reverence
5 (for if a man does not know how

4 [a]Ezek. 18:23, 32; John 3:17; 1 Tim. 4:10; Titus 2:11; 2 Pet. 3:9 [b][John 17:3]
5 [a]1 Cor. 8:6; Gal. 3:20 [b][Heb. 9:15] *See WW at Gal. 3:19. • See WW at Phil. 4:23.
6 [a]Mark 10:45
7 [a]Eph. 3:7, 8; 1 Tim. 1:11; 2 Tim. 1:11 [b][Gal. 1:15, 16] [1]NU omits *in Christ*
8 [a]Luke 23:34 [b]Ps. 134:2 *See WW at Luke 2:35.
9 [a]1 Pet. 3:3 [1]*discretion* *See WW at Matt. 25:7.
10 [a]1 Pet. 3:4 *See WW at Acts 7:5.
12 [a]1 Cor. 14:34; Titus 2:5

CHAPTER 3

1 [1]Lit. *overseer* *See WW at Matt. 13:17.
3 [1]*addicted* [2]NU omits *not greedy for money* [3]*loving money*

2:4 Although God **desires** the salvation of all men, He does not violate their opportunity to choose.
2:5 There is **one God** who is the Maker, Preserver, and Governor of all. **Jesus** is the One who mediates God to us. Jesus does not stand as a third person between God and us, but rather reveals the Father and His goodness.
2:7 Paul received a divine commission as apostle to the **Gentiles**. See Gal. 1:1, 15, 16; 2:7–9.
2:8 Prayer with the **lifting up** of **holy hands** was customary among the Jews and even the heathen. The hands were lifted and spread out toward heaven as a posture of surrender.
2:9, 10 See section 1 of Truth-In-Action at the end of 1 Tim.
2:9, 10 Women should observe a proper sense of modesty, free from vanity and worldly display, at all times, but especially in public worship. A godly woman's attractiveness is her character, not her **costly clothing**. See 1 Pet. 3:3, 4.
2:11, 12 Positively, Paul exhorts women to be disciples and to maintain a conduct that would not discredit the church. The prohibition of v. 12 refers to the authoritative office of apostolic teacher in the church. It does not forbid women to educate, proclaim truth or exhort (prophesy). See Acts 2:17; 18:26; 21:9; 1 Cor. 11:5; Phil. 4:3; 2 Tim. 1:5; 3:14, 15; Titus 2:3–5.
2:13 The fact that **Adam was formed first** by God indicates a priority of responsibility. God appointed the man as the head of the family, and the wife is not to usurp authority over him in this office. Conversely, the man is therewith charged to accept and serve this role, not as a tyrant but as a servant under God's assignment and subject to His holy and loving Spirit.
2:14 Adam acted by deliberate choice, but Eve was **deceived**. Paul does not teach that Adam was morally, intellectually, or spiritually superior to Eve, simply that her trustfulness made her susceptible to deception.
2:15 To be a Christian homemaker, wife, and mother is as lofty a work as can be inspired, especially as we study the abundant historical evidence of a mother's influence in shaping the destiny of children, who have in turn shaped the history of the church and of nations.
3:1–7 See section 5 of Truth-In-Action at the end of 1 Tim.
3:1 The position of a bishop is not the monarchical episcopate, which developed later. The Greek word *episkopos* designates a local pastoral oversight. Hence, a better word than "bishop" to express its meaning may be "supervisor" or "overseer." Paul elsewhere uses the words "presbyter" or "elder" to refer to the same office (see Titus 1:5–9).
3:2 Before the **bishop** takes the oversight of the flock to teach and correct them, he must be **blameless**—not perfect, but one against whom no evil charge can be proved. **The husband of one wife:** Literally, the bishop must be a "one-woman man." Although the phrase obviously prohibits polygamy, that is not the sole point. The dominant thought is monogamous fidelity, that is, the bishop must be a faithful husband. For some, the phrase may refer to prohibiting remarriage after divorce, but Paul's chief concern is the potential bishop's conduct as a husband at the time of his candidacy for office. He should exemplify the principles taught by Paul in Eph. 5:25–33.
3:4, 5 Success or failure in managing the home indicates the ability or inability to handle successfully the administration of the church.

to rule his own house, how will he take
care of the church of God?);
6 not a [1]novice, lest being puffed up
with pride he fall into the *same* condemnation as the devil.
7 Moreover he must have a good testimony among those who are outside,
lest he fall into reproach and the
[a]snare of the devil.

Qualifications of Deacons

5 8 Likewise deacons *must be* *reverent, not double-tongued, [a]not given to
much wine, not greedy for money,
9 holding the [1]mystery* of the faith
with a pure conscience.
10 But let these also first be tested;
then let them serve as deacons, being
found blameless.
11 Likewise, *their* wives *must be* **reverent,** not [1]slanderers, temperate,
faithful in all things.

WORD WEALTH

3:11 reverent, *semnos* (sem-*noss*); Strong's *#4586:* Behavior that is dignified, honorable, decent, august, worthy of respect. Leaders in the church should set a good example, displaying a deportment that commands respect. Since *semnos* is used of both husband and wife, an idealistic attractiveness should characterize all Christian couples.

12 Let deacons be the husbands of one
wife, ruling *their* children and their
own houses well.
13 For those who have served well as
deacons [a]obtain for themselves a good
standing and great *boldness in the
faith which is in Christ Jesus.

KINGDOM DYNAMICS

3:1–13 Character Qualifications, LEADER TRAITS. The dominant idea among NT leaders was that the ministry belonged to the whole believing community. The ordination of leaders was primarily the selecting of individuals of proven maturity and character to lead so the whole church could function effectively in worship, service, outreach, and the fulfillment of individual spiritual gifts. The qualifications for church leaders are carefully outlined in vv. 1–13 and in Titus 1:5–9. They do not emphasize family line or some past rite as the OT priesthood did. Instead the focus is on the leader's certified and sustained ethical character. There are over a dozen significant qualities expected, which include spiritual preparedness, self-control, social graciousness, domestic order, and holy living. The basis for continual ministry is continual commitment to character. If a leader falls from these ethical standards, he or she should accept removal from leadership until an appropriate season of reverifying of character can be fulfilled (Gal. 6:1, 2).

(James 3:1/Acts 26:19) J.B.

The Great Mystery

14 These things I write to you, though 1
I hope to come to you shortly;
15 but if I am delayed, *I write* so that
you may know how you ought to
conduct yourself in the house of
God, which is the church of the living
God, the pillar and [1]ground of the
truth.
16 And without controversy great is
the [1]mystery of godliness:

[a]God[2] was *manifested in the
flesh,
[b]Justified in the Spirit,
[c]Seen by angels,
[d]Preached among the Gentiles,
[e]Believed on in the world,
[f]Received up in glory.

The Great Apostasy

4

Now the Spirit [1]expressly says that 3
in latter times some will depart

6 [1]*new convert* **7** [a]1 Tim. 6:9; 2 Tim. 2:26 **8** [a]Ezek. 44:21 *See WW at 1 Tim. 3:11. **9** [1]*hidden truth* *See WW at Mark 4:11. **11** [1]*malicious gossips* **13** [a]Matt. 25:21 *See WW at Acts 4:31.

15 [1]*foundation, mainstay* **16** [a][John 1:14; 1 Pet. 1:20; 1 John 1:2; 3:5, 8] [b][Matt. 3:16; Rom. 1:4] [c]Matt. 28:2 [d]Acts 10:34; Rom. 10:18 [e]Rom. 16:26; 2 Cor. 1:19; Col. 1:6, 23 [f]Luke 24:51 [1]*hidden truth* [2]NU *Who* *See WW at Col. 3:4.

CHAPTER 4

1 [1]*explicitly*

3:6, 7 Only one who is mature in the faith should be entrusted with the responsibility of leadership.
3:8–13 See section 5 of Truth-In-Action at the end of 1 Tim.
3:8 The NT does not define the exact nature and duties of the office of deacon, but the meaning of the word suggests the function of serving as an attendant (see v. 10). The office probably originated with the choosing of the seven assistants *to the apostles (Acts 6)* but they are not referred to as such officeholders.
3:11 The qualifications laid down for women could well apply to the office of deaconess, an office recognized in the early church (see Rom. 16:1).
3:14–16 See section 1 of Truth-In-Action at the end of 1 Tim.
3:15 The function of **the church** is to support and transmit to the world **the truth God** has revealed.
3:16 Paul delineates the content of "the truth." **The mystery,** or revealed secret, is **great** in its importance, not in its obscurity; and it is **without controversy,** that is, beyond all question. Its purpose and its result are to produce **godliness**. The rhythmic construction of Paul's summary suggests that he may be quoting an early hymn or creedal confession.
4:1, 2 See section 3 of Truth-In-Action at the end of 1 Tim.
4:1 The Holy Spirit speaks openly and prophetically. **Latter times:** This term denotes the period of time between the First Coming and the Second Coming of Christ. See Acts

from the faith, giving heed [a]to deceiving spirits and doctrines of demons,
2 [a]speaking lies in *hypocrisy, having
their own conscience [b]seared with a
hot iron,
2 3 forbidding to marry, *and command-
*ing to abstain from foods which God
created to be received with thanksgiving by those who believe and *know
the *truth.
4 For every *creature of God *is* good,
and nothing is to be refused if it is received with thanksgiving;
5 for it is [1]sanctified by the word of
God and prayer.

A Good Servant of Jesus Christ

6 If you instruct the brethren in these
things, you will be a good minister of
Jesus Christ, [a]nourished in the words
of faith and of the good doctrine which
you have carefully followed.
1 7 But [a]reject profane and old wives'
fables, and [b]exercise yourself toward
godliness.
8 For [a]bodily exercise profits a little,
but godliness is profitable for all
things, [b]having promise of the *life that
now is and of that which is to come.
9 This *is* a faithful saying and worthy
of all acceptance.
10 For to this *end* [1]we both labor and
suffer *reproach, because we trust in
the living God, [a]who is *the* Savior of
all men, especially of those who believe.
5 11 These things command and teach.

Take Heed to Your Ministry

12 Let no one [1]despise your youth, but 1
be an [a]example to the believers in
word, in conduct, in love, [2]in spirit, in
faith, in purity.
13 Till I come, give attention to read- 5
ing, to *exhortation, to [1]doctrine.
14 [a]Do not neglect the *gift that is in
you, which was given to you by
*prophecy [b]with the laying on of the
hands of the **eldership.**

> **WORD WEALTH**
>
> **4:14 eldership,** *presbuterion* (pres-boo-*ter*-ee-on); Strong's *#4244:* A body of elders (literally aged men), composed of men of dignity, wisdom, and maturity. The word is used both of the Sanhedrin (Luke 22:66; Acts 22:5) and of Christian presbyters (1 Tim. 4:14).

15 Meditate on these things; give yourself entirely to them, that your progress may be *evident to all.
16 Take heed to yourself and to the
doctrine. Continue in them, for in doing this you will save both yourself and
those who hear you.

Treatment of Church Members

5 Do not rebuke an older man, but
exhort *him* as a father, younger
men as brothers,

1 [a]2 Tim. 3:13; Rev. 16:14
2 [a]Matt. 7:15 [b]Eph. 4:19 *See WW at Gal. 2:13.
3 *See WW at Luke 5:22. • See WW at John 4:24.
4 *See WW at Rev. 5:13.
5 [1]*set apart*
6 [a]2 Tim. 3:14
7 [a]2 Tim. 2:16; Titus 1:14 [b]Heb. 5:14
8 [a]1 Cor. 8:8 [b]Ps. 37:9 *See WW at 1 John 5:20.
10 [a]Ps. 36:6 [1]NU *we labor and strive,* *See WW at James 1:5.
12 [a]Phil. 3:17; Titus 2:7; 1 Pet. 5:3 [1]*look down on your youthfulness* [2]NU omits *in spirit*
13 [1]*teaching* *See WW at Acts 9:31.
14 [a]2 Tim. 1:6 [b]Acts 6:6; 1 Tim. 5:22 *See WW at 1 Cor. 1:7. • See WW at 1 Thess. 5:20.
15 *See WW at 1 Cor. 11:19.

2:17; Heb. 1:2; 1 John 2:18. **Depart from the faith:** They will apostatize, that is, deny the essential doctrines of Christianity. **Deceiving spirits:** The false teachers are teaching doctrines inspired by Satan; they may even lead astray careless leaders (see John 8:44; 1 John 4:1–6).

4:2 Although they are motivated by evil spirits, the false teachers will pretend divine inspiration. In abandoning God's Word they have become insensitive to spiritual truth.

4:3–5 See section 2 of Truth-In-Action at the end of 1 Tim.

4:3 A person who departs from the true faith falls prey to all sorts of traps that are alleged to make one more spiritual, such as a false asceticism.

4:4, 5 Every creature God made for man's health and nourishment is good for that purpose and is to be received **with thanksgiving**. Our food consumption should be preceded by **the word of God and prayer** as we believe that the Lord will sanctify and bless it.

4:6, 7 The responsibility of the **minister** involves both positive and negative aspects of teaching. He must faithfully teach sound **doctrine,** but resist and shun godless myths.

4:7, 8 See section 1 of Truth-In-Action at the end of 1 Tim.

4:10 The salvation that God has intended for **all men** He gives to **those who believe**. Those who do not believe, who fail to appropriate the riches of God's grace, will have an eternity to express their regrets.

4:11, 12 In his capacity as spiritual leader, Timothy was to meet the false teaching at Ephesus by commanding and teaching sound doctrine. His conduct was to give no cause for criticism, but was to be such as would elicit the respect of his people and serve as an example to them.

4:11 See section 5 of Truth-In-Action at the end of 1 Tim.

4:12 See section 1 of Truth-In-Action at the end of 1 Tim.

4:13 See section 5 of Truth-In-Action at the end of 1 Tim.

4:13 Paul's admonition to Timothy describes the minister's responsibility to study, to expound, and to apply the Scriptures.

4:14 The reference is to the occasion when the elders of Iconium and Lystra laid hands on Timothy and prophesied concerning the gifts and purposes of God. The laying-on of hands, with prophecy, is one of the means the Holy Spirit employs to reveal His will and purposes to His servants. Paul urged Timothy to exercise his gift.

4:15 The purposes of God need to be thoroughly fastened in our heart and mind, and we must give our time and attention to them. Matters of importance do not come automatically. Those around us quickly observe the progress we make or the ground we lose.

4:16 The personal life of God's ministers ought to be as pure as their doctrine. The two were made for each other. If the servant of the Lord does not take heed to himself, his doctrine will be sporadic and fuzzy. God's influence can depart from the human heart through carelessness, and our minds can lose the intensity of His call.

5:1 An older man may refer to an officer of the church. However, the mention of four groups may rather indicate age.

2 older women as mothers, younger
women as sisters, with all purity.

Honor True Widows

5 **3** Honor widows who are really widows.
4 But if any widow has children or
grandchildren, let them first learn to
show piety at home and [a]to repay their
parents; for this is [1]good and acceptable before God.
5 Now she who is really a widow, and
left alone, trusts in God and continues
in supplications and prayers [a]night
and day.
6 But she who lives in [1]pleasure is
dead while she lives.
7 And these things command, that
they may be blameless.
8 But if anyone does not provide for
his own, [a]and especially for those of
his household, [b]he has denied the faith
[c]and is worse than an unbeliever.
9 Do not let a widow under sixty
years old be taken into the number,
and not unless she has been the wife
of one man,
10 well reported for good works: if she
has brought up children, if she has
lodged strangers, if she has washed the
saints' feet, if she has relieved the afflicted, if she has diligently followed
every good work.
11 But [1]refuse *the* younger widows; for
when they have begun to grow wanton
against Christ, they desire to marry,
12 having condemnation because they
have cast off their first [1]faith.
13 And besides they learn *to be* idle,
wandering about from house to house,
and not only idle but also gossips and
busybodies, saying things which they
ought not.
14 Therefore I desire that *the* younger
widows marry, bear children, manage
the house, give no opportunity to the
adversary to speak reproachfully.
15 For some have already turned aside
after Satan.
16 If any believing [1]man or woman has
widows, let them [2]relieve them, and do
not let the church be burdened, that it
may relieve those who are really widows.

Honor the Elders

17 Let the elders who rule well be
counted worthy of double honor, especially those who labor in the word and
doctrine.
18 For the *Scripture says, [a]*"You shall
not muzzle an ox while it treads out
the grain,"* and, [b]"The laborer *is* worthy of his *wages."
19 Do not receive an accusation 5
against an elder except [a]from two or
three witnesses.
20 Those who are sinning rebuke in
the presence of all, that the rest also
may *fear.

CHAPTER 5
4 [a]Gen. 45:10 [1]NU, M omit *good and*
5 [a]Acts 26:7
6 [1]*indulgence*
8 [a]Is. 58:7; 2 Cor. 12:14 [b]2 Tim. 3:5 [c]Matt. 18:17
11 [1]Refuse to enroll
12 [1]Or *solemn promise*
16 [1]NU omits *man or* [2]*give aid to*
18 [a]Deut. 25:4; 1 Cor. 9:7–9 [b]Lev. 19:13; Deut. 24:15; Matt. 10:10; Luke 10:7; 1 Cor. 9:14 *See WW at John 5:39. • See WW at Rev. 22:12.
19 [a]Deut. 17:6; 19:15; Matt. 18:16
20 *See WW at 1 John 4:18.

5:2 Older women must be treated with a great degree of respect, and **younger women** should be treated respectfully as sisters. All social and physical relationships must be clean and wholesome.

5:3–16 See section 5 of Truth-In-Action at the end of 1 Tim.

5:3 Widows who are really widows are those who have no relatives to care for them.

5:4 The responsibility of caring for widows must not fall on the church when the person in question has children and grandchildren. The family must perform their duty to the family patriarchs.

5:5 Widows who are without family should be praying, loving, and God-fearing women. To these the local church has a responsibility.

5:6 A widow who indulges in riotous living, who is physically alive but spiritually dead, is not to receive financial support from the church.

5:8 A person who **does not provide for his own** family not only fails to live up to the principles of the faith that he professes, but fails to live up to the code of unbelievers concerning filial obligations.

5:9, 10 A widow enrolled as a ward of the local church had *to be at least* 60 years old, an age limit probably intended as a safeguard against remarriage. She also must have had a blameless married life, a reputation for good works, and an exemplary Christian life.

5:11, 12 Young widows who are able to work should not be cared for by the church. Furthermore, their youthful impulses will incline them to remarriage or may lead to improper behavior, resulting in a marriage without regard to Christ. Such action would lead to discipline because of unfaithfulness to their vow of service. Paul wants to spare them the **condemnation** that would be incurred by breaking the pledge made when they were placed on the roll to receive support.

5:13 Young widows who do not work or have responsibilities may succumb to the temptation of filling their idle time by meddling in the affairs of other people.

5:14 Young widows will find fulfillment in remarriage and household management, serving as a testimony to the unconverted. Paul sanctioned second marriages if the persons involved stood on scriptural grounds (see notes on 5:11).

5:15 Some widows had already abandoned the true faith, necessitating the restrictions mentioned above.

5:17 Elders who govern and feed the church are to be given the double honor of office and suitable salary. Those who preach and teach should be honored above those who serve in administration.

5:19 See section 5 of Truth-In-Action at the end of 1 Tim.

5:19 An accusation brought against an elder must not be considered unless it can be proved by **two or three witnesses**. We must remember that those who correct others always have enemies, and discipline must be based on fact rather than gossip.

5:20 Public discipline of guilty elders is appropriate as a warning to others.

21 I charge *you* before God and the
Lord Jesus Christ and the [1]elect* angels that you observe these things
without [a]prejudice, doing nothing with
partiality.
5 22 Do not lay hands on anyone hastily,
nor [a]share in other people's sins; keep
yourself *pure.
23 No longer drink only water, but use
a little wine for your stomach's sake
and your frequent [1]infirmities.
24 Some men's sins are [a]clearly evident, preceding *them* to *judgment, but
those of some *men* follow later.
25 Likewise, the good works *of some*
are clearly evident, and those that are
otherwise cannot be hidden.

Honor Masters

6 Let as many [a]bondservants as are
under the yoke count their own
*masters worthy of all honor, so that
the name of God and *His* doctrine may
not be blasphemed.
2 And those who have believing
*masters, let them not despise *them* because they are brethren, but rather
serve *them* because those who are benefited are believers and beloved. Teach
and exhort these things.

Error and Greed

5 3 If anyone teaches otherwise and
does not consent to [a]wholesome*
words, *even* the words of our Lord
Jesus Christ, [b]and to the [1]doctrine
which accords with godliness,
4 he is proud, knowing nothing, but
is obsessed with disputes and arguments over words, from which come
envy, strife, reviling, evil suspicions,
5 [1]useless wranglings of men of corrupt minds and destitute of the truth,
who suppose that godliness is a *means*
of gain. [2]From [a]such withdraw yourself.
6 Now godliness with [a]contentment is
great gain.
7 For we brought nothing into *this*
world, [1]*and it is* [a]certain we can carry
nothing out.
8 And having food and clothing, with
these we shall be [a]content.
9 But those who desire to be rich fall
into temptation and a snare, and *into*
many foolish and harmful *lusts which
drown men in destruction and perdition.
10 For the love of money is a root of
all *kinds of* evil, for which some have
strayed from the faith in their greediness, and pierced themselves through
with many sorrows.

The Good Confession

11 But you, O man of God, flee these
things and pursue righteousness, godliness, faith, love, *patience, **gentleness.**

WORD WEALTH

6:11 gentleness, *praotes* (prah-*ot*-ace); Strong's *#4236:* A disposition that is even-tempered, tranquil, balanced in spirit, unpretentious, and that has the passions under control. The word is best translated "meekness," not as an indication of weakness, but of power and strength under control. The person who possesses this quality pardons injuries, corrects faults, and rules his own spirit well.

12 Fight the good fight of faith, lay 4
hold on *eternal life, to which you were
also called and have confessed the
good confession in the presence of
many witnesses.
13 I urge you in the sight of God who
gives life to all things, and *before*

21 [a]Deut. 1:17 [1]*chosen* *See WW at 1 Pet. 2:9. **22** [a]Eph. 5:6, 7; 2 John 11 *See WW at 1 John 3:3. **23** [1]*illnesses* **24** [a]Gal. 5:19–21 *See WW at Matt. 5:22.

CHAPTER 6

1 [a]Eph. 6:5; Titus 2:9; 1 Pet. 2:18 *See WW at Jude 4. **2** *See WW at Jude 4. **3** [a]2 Tim. 1:13 [b]Titus 1:1 [1]*teaching* *See WW at 3 John 2. **5** [a]2 Tim. 3:5 [1]NU, M *constant friction* [2]NU omits the rest of v. 5. **6** [a]Phil. 4:11; Heb. 13:5 **7** [a]Job 1:21; Ps. 49:17; Eccl. 5:15 [1]NU omits *and it is certain* **8** [a]Prov. 30:8, 9 **9** *See WW at 2 Tim. 2:22. **11** *See WW at Heb. 10:36. **12** *See WW at Rev. 14:6. **13** [a]Matt. 27:2; John 18:36, 37

5:22 See section 5 of Truth-In-Action at the end of 1 Tim.
5:22 Haste must be avoided in the appointment of leaders. Failure to exercise caution implicates those responsible for the ordination of an unwise choice.
5:23 Paul's reference to purity in the previous verse may have led him to insert a personal note to Timothy to the effect that denial of the medicinal use of wine for a stomach disorder had nothing to do with purity. He was to guard against a false asceticism.
5:24, 25 One's character, with attendant sins or good works and their results, will be revealed sooner or later.
6:1 Christian slaves were to serve unbelieving **masters** with respect so that the faith would not be spoken against.
6:2 Equality in Christ does not cancel differences of functions and place in the church or society.
6:3–5 See section 5 of Truth-In-Action at the end of 1 Tim.
6:3 Paul reverts to the necessity of sound doctrine (see 1:3). All teaching is to be judged by its agreement with **the words of our Lord Jesus Christ**.
6:4 Some teachers, inflated by their own importance, had substituted contentious and hair-splitting doctrines for the wholesome teaching of Christ.
6:5 Some arguments are useless and totally unprofitable. There are also those who incite controversy for the sake of gain, knowing that some people love to rally to strange causes. We are to have no religious fellowship with them.
6:6 Godliness is synonymous with true religion, and true religion should be enough to satisfy us.
6:9, 10 A restless desire to be rich subjects one to great spiritual peril.
6:12 See section 4 of Truth-In-Action at the end of 1 Tim.
6:12 Using terms derived from the field of competition, Paul admonishes Timothy to contend for the gospel against all adversaries and to seize the prize of **eternal life**.
6:13 The **good confession** that Christ gave was the truth concerning Himself in His statements to Pilate.

Christ Jesus [a]who witnessed the good
confession before Pontius Pilate,
14 that you keep *this* commandment
without spot, blameless until our Lord
Jesus Christ's appearing,
15 which He will manifest in His own
time, *He who is* the blessed and only
[1]Potentate,* the King of kings and Lord
of lords,
16 who alone has immortality, dwelling in [a]unapproachable light, [b]whom
no man has seen or can see, to whom
be honor and everlasting **power.**
Amen.

WORD WEALTH

6:16 power, *kratos* (*krat*-oss); Strong's *#2904:* Dominion, strength, manifested power. The word especially signifies exerted strength, power shown effectively in a reigning authority. (Compare "theocracy," "aristocracy," "democracy.") Although it is used in Heb. 2:14 of the Devil's power of death, *kratos* primarily refers to God's kingdom authority, dominion, and majesty.

Instructions to the Rich

5 17 Command those who are rich in this
present age not to be haughty, nor to
trust in uncertain [a]riches but in the living God, who gives us richly all things
[b]to enjoy.

KINGDOM DYNAMICS

6:17 Riches Are a Responsibility, GOD'S PROSPERITY. This verse clears up much misunderstanding about the acquisition or possession of material goods. Paul tells us not to trust in uncertain riches. Here, the word "trust" (Greek *elpizo*) means "to expect" or "to hope for." We are not to hope for riches or expect them to bring us security or deliverance. Why does he tell us that? Because riches are so transient. Values change, and earthly riches are only as good as the present value. What is valuable today might not be valuable tomorrow; thus the wisdom of our trusting—putting our hope—in God alone to make provision for us. Further, we must never let the presence of wealth make us think that we are better than others or that we can be irresponsible or indulgent. It is a responsibility, a great responsibility, to have great wealth; and we must always remember that much is required of those to whom much is given (Luke 12:48).

(Mark 10:17–27/Phil. 4:12, 13) F.P.

15 [1]*Sovereign* *See WW at Acts 8:27. **16** [a]Dan. 2:22 [b]John 6:46 **17** [a]Jer. 9:23; 48:7 [b]Eccl. 5:18, 19

19 [a][Matt. 6:20, 21; 19:21] **20** [a][2 Tim. 1:12, 14] [b]Titus 1:14 [1]*empty chatter*

18 *Let them* do good, that they be rich
in good works, ready to give, willing
to share,
19 [a]storing up for themselves a good
foundation for the time to come, that
they may lay hold on eternal life.

Guard the Faith

20 O Timothy! [a]Guard what was com- 3
mitted to your trust, [b]avoiding the profane *and* [1]idle babblings and contradictions of what is falsely called
knowledge—
21 by professing it some have strayed
concerning the faith. Grace *be* with
you. Amen.

6:15 The incentive for faithfulness is the Second Coming of Christ, when the validity of a good confession will be openly demonstrated.
6:17–19 See section 5 of Truth-In-Action at the end of 1 Tim.
6:18, 19 Wealthy people should be good stewards. What they share with others is an investment bringing eternal dividends.
6:20, 21 See section 3 of Truth-In-Action at the end of 1 Tim.
6:20 Paul's final charge to Timothy, which likens the gospel to a treasure committed to his trust, summarizes the entire epistle.

TRUTH-IN-ACTION through 1 TIMOTHY

Letting the LIFE of the Holy Spirit Bring Faith's Works Alive in You!

Truth 1 Timothy Teaches	Text	**Action** 1 Timothy Invites
1 ***Guidelines for Growing in*** **Godliness**	2:9, 10	**Dress** with appropriate modesty. **Stress** internal beauty.
God's Word instructs in godly conduct, which must issue from godly attitudes in life and worship. If the heart is tuned to God, modesty and	3:14–16	Let all those in the church **conform** to the high standards to be observed by leaders. **Acknowledge** the order Christ has set in the church.

Truth 1 Timothy Teaches	Text	**Action** 1 Timothy Invites
1 acceptable worship will be the result. God has defined godliness in the example of the Lord Jesus Christ. Believers are to conform to Christ as an act of faithful obedience.	4:7, 8 4:12	**Recognize** that godliness is necessary to this life and to life eternal. **Be disciplined** in body, soul, and spirit. **Conduct yourself** in an exemplary manner in every detail of your life.
2 **Steps to Holiness** Holiness does not reject that which God has created for man's benefit, nor does it condemn those who rightly use what God has called good. The source of holiness is a personal relationship with Jesus, not a system of works. The stomach does not defile man, but the heart can.	4:3–5	**Reject** teaching that bases holiness on works. **Receive thankfully** the natural blessings from God. **Sanctify** by prayer what you so receive.
3 **Keys to Wise Living** The wise believer sees the trap of theological debate and avoids it. Realizing that truth is more practice than theory, he judges all teaching by what it produces, not by how it sounds. Therefore, he avoids the deception of demonically inspired teachings that sound good, but bring destruction and death in the end.	1:3–7 4:1, 2 1:8–11 6:20, 21	**Teach** only sound, thoroughly biblical doctrine. **Do not attempt to teach** what you do not fully understand. **Operate** from a motive of love, faith, and good conscience in all you do. **Be warned** that some will abandon faith in Jesus Christ for demonically inspired teaching. **Understand** that hypocrisy is an open door to deceiving spirits. Liars will believe "the lie." **Recognize** that the law is to instruct and judge the ungodly, not to induce condemnation in the righteous. **Guard carefully** the truth you have been taught! **Reject** human knowledge that denies the faith.
4 **Key Lessons in Faith** Prophetic "words" can be the basis for much hope and faith for many. We should never despise or reject such ministry. These utterances can encourage us to endure ferocious and demanding battles as we carry out the Lord's will.	1:18 6:12	**Heed** confirmed, prophetic utterances. **Recognize** their value in spiritual warfare and maintaining strong, positive faith. **Know** that faith and a good conscience keep you from spiritual disaster. **Recognize** that excellence in Christian ministry often involves long and arduous struggles. **Do not give up; stand firm. Endure** in your struggle for righteousness regardless of the cost.
5 **Lessons for Leaders** Christian leadership should conform to the scriptural requirements given here, being stable in the basics of life and grounded in the faith. All leadership must be established on the motivation of service, and is to maintain faithful order in	2:1–6 3:1–7	Leaders, **lead** in regular, fervent prayer for civil authority. **Pray** that the gospel will spread and God's people will be protected. Leaders, **open** leadership roles to those who are qualified. **Refuse** leadership responsibility to anyone who is unqualified spiritually.

Truth 1 Timothy Teaches	Text	**Action** 1 Timothy Invites
5 the church. All God's people are to pray constantly for those who have authority and responsibility over the church as well as throughout society.	3:8–13	Leaders, **recognize** and **honor** those who help in practical service to the church. **Insist** on a time of testing before they are recognized.
	4:11	Leaders, **recognize** the imperative nature of biblical truth. **Know** that to teach and not cultivate obedience dilutes scriptural intent and misrepresents divine authority.
	4:13	Leaders, **focus** ministry around the public reading of Scripture.
	5:3–16	Leaders, **establish** a benevolence fund for widows and others who are in genuine need. **Be faithful** to help those who have no other means of legitimate family support.
	5:19	Leaders, **do not welcome** or **consider** unwarranted criticism against fellow leadership.
	5:22	Leaders, **do not involve** others in roles of responsible leadership too quickly.
	6:3–5	Leaders, **avoid** the love of money. **Reprove** any covetousness among God's people. **Reject** teaching motivated by greed. **Rebuke** greedy teachers.
	6:17–19	Leaders, **urge** and **persuade** any wealthy in your congregation to give liberally to God's work. **Teach** against the selfish use of personal wealth.

The Second Epistle of Paul the Apostle to TIMOTHY

Author: Paul
Date: A.D. 66/67
Theme: The Commitment to Ministry
Key Words: Fight, Charge, Instruct

Background As far as we can determine, Paul was released from Roman imprisonment shortly after Acts was written and engaged in additional missionary travels, journeying as far as Spain. During the era of persecutions initiated by Nero in A.D. 64, Paul was again arrested, probably in Troas (4:13), and taken to Rome. The circumstances of his second Roman imprisonment were quite different from those of his first incarceration. Previously, he was in his own hired dwelling and was able to receive visitors freely, but now he was confined in a dungeon and friends could only see him with difficulty. Formerly he had expected to be released, but now he looked forward to death (4:6–8). At the writing of this letter, only Luke was with Paul (4:11), all others having left for various reasons.

Occasion and Date The letter was occasioned by Paul's concern for Timothy's needs as well as for his own. He reminded Timothy of his responsibilities and admonished him to give himself wholeheartedly to his task. As for himself, Paul needed certain personal effects (4:13) and in his loneliness desired to see Timothy and Mark (4:9–11). There is little question that Paul wrote this letter shortly before his death. Therefore, since he was probably executed before Nero's death in A.D. 68, the letter may be dated around 66/67.

Purpose Paul's immediate purpose in the letter was to issue an affectionate appeal to Timothy to come to him (4:9, 11, 13, 21). However, Paul's main concern was the welfare of the church, and he gave Timothy instructions for perfecting its organization and safeguarding the gospel. With the realization that his death was imminent, and that Timothy might not reach him in time for a final visit, Paul injected into this letter solemn words of admonition. His preoccupation was with the gospel, and he expressed to Timothy his concern that his young coworker would faithfully transmit the gospel after the old warrior's death. The letter urges Timothy to be faithful in the face of hardships, desertions, and error.

Characteristics Although Paul is terse and to the point, he is also tender, warm, and affectionate. Second Timothy reveals Paul's emotions more than his intellect, because his heart was speaking. Consequently, the letter is not an orderly, well-planned literary production, but a personal note containing the apostle's last will and testament.

Personal Application This epistle is a handbook for young ministers of the gospel. The church needs more Timothys who are determined to guard the gospel as a sacred deposit committed to them, who are faithful to proclaim it, who are ready to suffer for it, and who will pass it on to faithful followers.

Christ Revealed For Paul, the gospel is more than statements and proposition; it is Christ (see 1:8). Spiritual blessings, such as grace, mercy, peace, and even life itself, reside in Him and are derived from Him (1:1, 2, 9, 10, 13, 16, 18; 2:1). Jesus came to earth as a man (2:8) to be our Savior (1:10; 2:10; 3:15) and was resurrected (2:8) following His death. He is faithful to those who follow Him (1:12; 2:11, 12; 4:17, 18, 22) and consistent in His purpose (2:12, 13). He also grants spiritual understanding (2:7). Christ will appear at His Second Coming as the righteous judge (4:1, 8; see 1:18; 4:14, 16).

The Holy Spirit at Work The Holy Spirit had given Timothy a gift and Paul exhorted him to use it actively (1:6). Furthermore, the Holy Spirit grants power, love, and a sound mind (1:7). The indwelling Holy Spirit enables us to be faithful to the gospel committed to us and to safeguard its purity (1:13, 14).

Outline of 2 Timothy

I. Introduction 1:1–5
- A. Salutation 1:1, 2
- B. Thanksgiving 1:3–5

II. Fidelity in the face of hardships 1:6–14
- A. Because of the nature of Christian experience 1:6–8
- B. Because of the greatness of the gospel 1:9–11
- C. Because of the example of Paul 1:12–14

III. Fidelity in the face of desertions 1:15—2:13
- A. The example of Onesiphorus 1:15–18
- B. The character of Timothy's work 2:1–7
- C. The redemptive work of Christ 2:8–13

IV. Fidelity in the face of error 2:14—4:8
- A. Doctrinal error 2:14–26
- B. Practical error 3:1—4:8

V. Conclusion 4:9–22
- A. Instruction 4:9–13
- B. Warning 4:14, 15
- C. Explanation 4:16–18
- D. Greetings 4:19–21
- E. Benediction 4:22

Greeting

PAUL, an apostle of [1]Jesus Christ by
the will of God, according to the
[a]promise of life which is in Christ
Jesus,

2 To Timothy, a [a]beloved son:

Grace, *mercy, *and* peace from God
the Father and Christ Jesus our Lord.

Timothy's Faith and Heritage

1 3 I thank God, whom I serve with a
*pure conscience, as *my* [a]forefathers
did, as without ceasing I remember you
in my prayers night and day,
4 greatly desiring to see you, being
mindful of your tears, that I may be
filled with joy,
5 when I call to remembrance [a]the
[1]genuine* faith that is in you, which
dwelt first in your grandmother Lois
and [b]your mother Eunice, and I am
persuaded is in you also.
6 Therefore I remind you [a]to stir up 3
the *gift of God which is in you through
the laying on of my hands.
7 For [a]God has not given us a spirit

CHAPTER 1
1 [a]Titus 1:2 [1]NU, M *Christ Jesus*
2 [a]1 Tim. 1:2 *See WW at 2 Tim. 1:16.
3 [a]Acts 24:14 *See WW at Matt. 5:8.
5 [a]1 Tim. 1:5; 4:6 [b]Acts 16:1 [1]Lit. *unhypocritical* *See WW at 1 Pet. 1:22.
6 [a]1 Tim. 4:14 *See WW at 1 Cor. 1:7.
7 [a]Rom. 8:15

1:1 Paul states his office, the authority by which he held it, and the reason it was given to him.
1:3 See section 1 of Truth-In-Action at the end of 2 Tim.
1:3 *As a Jew, Paul* had been taught faith in the true God and the proper way to worship Him. When he became a Christian, he did not abandon those teachings, but discovered the fulfillment of Judaism.
1:5 A Christian upbringing and a spiritual family atmosphere are decided advantages. Timothy's **mother Eunice,** and his **grandmother Lois,** communicated their faith to Timothy.
1:6 See section 3 of Truth-In-Action at the end of 2 Tim.
1:6 Stir up: The initiative for keeping the fires of the soul stirred is upon the recipient. This principle applies to all believers. Thus, Paul urges Timothy to the fullest use of the spiritual equipment given to him for ministry. While he does not specify the **gift,** his use of the Greek word *charisma* suggests a distinct manifestation of the Holy Spirit bestowed upon Timothy through the prayers of the apostle and others. See 1 Tim. 1:18 and the notes on 1 Cor. 12—14.
1:7 Possibly because of his youth or natural temperament,

of fear, [b]but of power and of love and
of a **sound mind.**

WORD WEALTH

1:7 sound mind, *sophronismos* (so-fron-is-*moss*); Strong's *#4995:* A combination of *sos,* "safe," and *phren,* "the mind"; hence, safe-thinking. The word denotes good judgment, disciplined thought patterns, and the ability to understand and make right decisions. It includes the qualities of self-control and self-discipline.

Not Ashamed of the Gospel

5 8 [a]Therefore do not be ashamed of
[b]the testimony of our Lord, nor of me
[c]His prisoner, but share with me in the
sufferings for the gospel according to
the power of God,
9 who has saved us and *called *us*
with a holy calling, [a]not according to
our works, but [b]according to His own
*purpose and grace which was given
to us in Christ Jesus [c]before *time began,
10 but [a]has now been revealed by the
appearing of our *Savior Jesus Christ,
who has abolished death and brought
life and immortality to light through
the gospel,
11 [a]to which I was appointed a
preacher, an apostle, and a teacher
[1]of the Gentiles.
12 For this reason I also suffer these
things; nevertheless I am not ashamed,
[a]for I know whom I have *believed and
am *persuaded that He is *able to keep
what I have committed to Him until
that Day.

Be Loyal to the Faith

5 13 [a]Hold fast [b]the pattern of [c]sound*
words which you have heard from me,

7 [b][Acts 1:8]
8 [a][Mark 8:38; Luke 9:26; Rom. 1:16]; 2 Tim. 1:12, 16 [b]1 Tim. 2:6 [c]Eph. 3:1; 2 Tim. 1:16
9 [a][Rom. 3:20]; Eph. 2:8, 9 [b]Rom. 8:28 [c]Rom. 16:25; Eph. 1:4; Titus 1:2 *See WW at Gal. 1:6. • See WW at Rom. 8:28. • See WW at Acts 1:7.
10 [a]Eph. 1:9 *See WW at John 4:42.
11 [a]Acts 9:15 [1]NU omits *of the Gentiles*
12 [a]1 Pet. 4:19 *See WW at Rom. 10:9. • See WW at 2 Thess. 3:4. • See WW at Matt. 19:26.
13 [a]2 Tim. 3:14; Titus 1:9 [b]Rom. 2:20; 6:17 [c]1 Tim. 6:3 *See WW at 3 John 2.
16 [a]2 Tim. 4:19
18 [a]Matt. 6:4; Mark 9:41 [b]2 Thess. 1:10 [c]Heb. 6:10 [1]*to me* from Vg., a few Gr. mss.

CHAPTER 2

1 [a]1 Tim. 1:2 [b]Eph. 6:10
2 *See WW at Acts 4:12.
3 [a]2 Tim. 4:5 [b]1 Cor. 9:7; 1 Tim. 1:18 [1]NU *You must share* *See WW at Matt. 13:48.

in faith and love which are in Christ
Jesus.
14 That good thing which was committed to you, keep by the Holy Spirit who
dwells in us.
15 This you know, that all those in
Asia have turned away from me,
among whom are Phygellus and Hermogenes.
16 The Lord grant **mercy** to the [a]house-
hold of Onesiphorus, for he often refreshed me, and was not ashamed of
my chain;

WORD WEALTH

1:16 mercy, *eleos* (*el*-eh-oss); Strong's *#1656:* Compassion, tender mercy, kindness, beneficence, an outward manifestation of pity. The word is used of God (Luke 1:50, 54, 58; Rom. 15:9; Eph. 2:4); of Christ (Jude 21); and of men (Matt. 12:7; 23:23; Luke 10:37).

17 but when he arrived in Rome, he
sought me out very zealously and
found *me.*
18 The Lord [a]grant to him that he may
find mercy from the Lord [b]in that
Day—and you know very well how
many ways he [c]ministered [1]*to me* at
Ephesus.

Be Strong in Grace

2 You therefore, [a]my son, [b]be strong 3
in the grace that is in Christ Jesus.
2 And the things that you have heard 5
from me among many witnesses, commit these to faithful men who will be
able to teach *others also.
3 You therefore must [a]endure[1] 5
hardship [b]as a *good soldier of Jesus
Christ.

Timothy was prone to timidity (**fear**) and may have been reluctant to accept heavy responsibilities. In these verses (6, 7) Paul is reminding him that the Holy Spirit's fullness and gifts provide enabling power to exercise one's ministry.
1:8 See section 5 of Truth-In-Action at the end of 2 Tim.
1:8 In those days of persecution, Christian leaders who remained loyal to Christ almost certainly would suffer for the gospel's sake, but they could rely on **the power of God** for endurance.
1:9 Salvation is entirely a matter of God's **purpose and grace,** apart from human **works.**
1:10 What God purposed "before time began" (v. 9) has been historically disclosed **by the appearing of our Savior.** Although physical **death** is still experienced by believers, Christ has **abolished** it by rendering it ineffective. See 1 Cor. 15:54–57.
1:11, 12 Paul encourages Timothy to steadfastness by his own example of fearlessness in the face of death. The basis of his courage is his assurance that Christ will safely guard him **until that Day** of His glorious return. See 1 Thess. 5:23.
1:13, 14 See section 5 of Truth-In-Action at the end of 2 Tim.
1:13, 14 In view of his impending death, and in the face of desertion by false friends, Paul urges Timothy to fidelity by the power of the indwelling **Holy Spirit.**
1:15 Asia refers to the Roman province of which Ephesus was the capital. Nothing is known of **Phygellus and Hermogenes** except this defection.
1:16–18 The devotion and loyalty of **Onesiphorus** served to encourage Timothy. **That Day** refers to the Second Coming (see notes on v. 12 and Obad. 15).
2:1 See section 3 of Truth-In-Action at the end of 2 Tim.
2:2 See section 5 of Truth-In-Action at the end of 2 Tim.
2:2 Paul establishes a pattern for the preservation and transmission of the gospel. Apostolic teaching is to be passed on to succeeding generations without addition or alteration.
2:3–7 See section 5 of Truth-In-Action at the end of 2 Tim.

4 [a]No one engaged in warfare entangles himself with the affairs of *this* life,
that he may please him who enlisted
him as a soldier.
5 And also [a]if anyone competes in
athletics, he is not crowned unless he
competes according to the rules.
6 The hardworking farmer must be
first to partake of the crops.
7 Consider what I say, and [1]may the
Lord [a]give you *understanding in all
things.
8 Remember that Jesus Christ, [a]of
the seed of David, [b]was raised from the
dead [c]according to my gospel,
9 [a]for which I suffer trouble as an
evildoer, [b]*even* to the point of chains;
[c]but the word of God is not chained.
10 Therefore [a]I *endure all things for
the sake of the [1]elect,* [b]that they also
may obtain the salvation which is in
Christ Jesus with *eternal glory.
11 *This is* a faithful saying:

For [a]if we died with *Him*,
We shall also live with *Him*.
12 [a]If we endure,
We shall also reign with *Him*.
[b]If we deny *Him*,
He also will deny us.
13 If we are faithless,
He remains faithful;
He [a]cannot deny Himself.

Approved and Disapproved Workers

4 14 Remind *them* of these things,
[a]charging *them* before the Lord not to
[1]strive about words to no profit, to the
ruin of the hearers.
1 15 [a]Be* diligent to present yourself approved to God, a worker who does not
need to be ashamed, rightly dividing
the word of truth.

KINGDOM DYNAMICS

2:15 God's Word: Read It! Study It! Memorize It! THE WORD OF GOD. The Bible—God's inspired Word—is the only conclusive source of wisdom, knowledge, and understanding concerning ultimate realities. It is a fountainhead of freeing truth (John 8:32) and a gold mine of practical principles (Ps. 19:10), waiting to liberate and/or enrich the person who will pursue its truth and wealth. Thus, Paul's instruction to "be diligent . . . a worker" has been applied by serious Christians through the centuries as a directive to study the Word of God. The only way to healthy, balanced living is through the "rightly dividing" (Greek *orthotomounta*, literally, "cutting straight") of God's Word. Such correct, straight-on application of God's Word is the result of diligent study. The text calls us beyond casual approaches to the Scriptures, telling us to refuse to suit the Bible to our own convenience or ideology.

In his earlier words (1 Tim. 4:13) Paul also told Timothy, "Give attention to reading [God's Word]," but now he emphasizes studying like a "worker" (from Greek *ergon*—"toil, effort"). Ps. 119:11 urges memorizing of the Word of God as a mighty deterrent against sin. Memorizing the Scripture also provides an immediate availability of God's "words" as a sword, ready in witnessing and effective in spiritual warfare (Heb. 4:12; Eph. 6:17).

(Is. 55:10, 11/2 Tim. 3:16*) J.W.H.

16 But shun profane *and* [1]idle babblings, for they will [2]increase to more
ungodliness.

4 [a][2 Pet. 2:20] **5** [a][1 Cor. 9:25] **7** [a]Prov. 2:6 [1]NU *the Lord will give you* *See WW at Luke 2:47. **8** [a]Rom. 1:3, 4 [b]1 Cor. 15:4 [c]Rom. 2:16 **9** [a]Acts 9:16 [b]Eph. 3:1 [c]Acts 28:31; [2 Tim. 4:17] **10** [a]Eph. 3:13 [b]2 Cor. 1:6; 1 Thess. 5:9 [1]*chosen ones* *See WW at Matt. 24:13. • See WW at 1 Pet. 2:9. • See WW at Rev. 14:6. **11** [a]Rom. 6:5, 8; 1 Thess. 5:10 **12** [a][Matt. 19:28]; Luke 22:29; [Rom. 5:17; 8:17] [b]Matt. 10:33; Luke 12:9; 1 Tim. 5:8 **13** [a]Num. 23:19; Titus 1:2 **14** [a]1 Tim. 5:21; 6:4; 2 Tim. 2:23; Titus 3:9 [1]*battle* **15** [a]1 Tim. 4:13; 2 Pet. 1:10 *See WW at Gal. 2:10. **16** [1]*empty chatter* [2]*lead*

2:3–6 Paul illustrates the strenuous duties of a Christian minister with the metaphors of a **soldier,** an athlete, and a **farmer.**
2:4 Rather than entangling himself in civilian matters, the **soldier** must dedicate himself wholeheartedly to the business of soldiery. In like manner, the warfare of the kingdom demands one's full attention.
2:5 An athlete must play by the **rules;** otherwise he will forfeit the prize. Rewards for Christian service depend on faithfulness. See 1 Cor. 3:10–15.
2:6 The hardworking farmer must first plow the ground before he reaps a crop, but if he does he receives the reward of a bountiful harvest. The hardworking laborer in God's field will receive an appropriate reward.
2:8–13 Paul expounds the principle that suffering is the condition of blessing, enforcing it with the experience of ***Jesus Christ*** (v. 8), himself (vv. 9, 10), and every believer (vv. 11–13).
2:8 This principle took **Christ** through lowly birth and even lowlier death to His glorious resurrection and reign.
2:9, 10 The same principle brought Paul's imprisonment, that through his work many **may obtain the salvation**.
2:11–13 Paul reinforces the principle of present suffering followed by future glory with a quotation from an early hymn or confession. His purpose is to call for courage and endurance, even martyrdom, in the service of the Lord.
2:13 Although it is true that Christ **remains faithful** to His promises, here the statement refers to His faithfulness in carrying out the warning that He will disown us in the presence of the Father "if we [willfully and knowledgeably] deny Him" (v. 12) in the midst of peril or scorn. See Matt. 10:33.
2:14 See section 4 of Truth-In-Action at the end of 2 Tim.
2:15–26 Paul uses the metaphors of an unashamed workman, a clean vessel, and a gentle servant to illustrate the Christian minister.
2:15 See section 1 of Truth-In-Action at the end of 2 Tim.
2:15 Rightly dividing: Paul likens **the word of truth** to a road being built or a furrow being plowed, both of which must be straight. The good workman must be accurate and clear in his exposition of God's Word, keeping to the road himself and making it easy for others to follow. The "dividing" of the Word of God does not mean to segment it, but to rightly discern its truth by capturing the spirit of the Word (Heb. 4:12; 1 Cor. 2:13, 14; John 6:63).

17 And their message will spread like
cancer. [a]Hymenaeus and Philetus are
of this sort,
18 who have strayed concerning the
truth, [a]saying that the *resurrection is
already past; and they overthrow the
faith of some.
19 Nevertheless [a]the solid foundation
of God stands, having this seal: "The
Lord [b]knows those who are His," and,
"Let everyone who names the name of
[1]Christ depart from *iniquity."
20 But in a great house there are not
only [a]vessels of gold and silver, but
also of wood and clay, some for honor
and some for dishonor.
21 Therefore if anyone cleanses himself from the latter, he will be a vessel
for honor, [1]sanctified and useful for the
Master, [a]prepared for every good
work.
3 22 [a]Flee also youthful **lusts;** but pursue
righteousness, faith, love, peace with
those who call on the Lord out of a
pure heart.

WORD WEALTH

2:22 lusts, *epithumia* (ep-ee-thoo-*mee*-ah); Strong's *#1939:* A strong desire and intense craving for something. Three times it applies to good desires (Luke 22:15; Phil. 1:23; 1 Thess. 2:17). Its other uses are negative, such as gratifying sensual cravings, desiring the forbidden, longing for the evil, coveting what belongs to someone else, and striving for things, persons, or experiences contrary to the will of God.

23 But avoid foolish and ignorant disputes, knowing that they generate
strife.
4 24 And [a]a servant of the Lord must not
quarrel but be gentle to all, [b]able to
teach, [c]patient,
25 [a]in *humility correcting those who
are in opposition, [b]if God perhaps will
grant them repentance, [c]so that they
may know the truth,
26 and *that* they may come to their
senses *and* [a]*escape* the snare of the
devil, having been taken captive by
him to *do* his will.

17 [a]1 Tim. 1:20
18 [a]1 Cor. 15:12 *See WW at Acts 23:6.
19 [a]Matt. 24:24; [1 Cor. 3:11] [b]Num. 16:5; [Nah. 1:7]; John 10:14, 27 [1]NU, M *the Lord* *See WW at John 7:18.
20 [a]Rom. 9:21
21 [a]2 Cor. 9:8; [Eph. 2:10]; 2 Tim. 3:17 [1]*set apart* *See WW at Jude 4. • See WW at Rev. 21:2.
22 [a]1 Tim. 6:11
24 [a]Titus 3:2 [b]Titus 1:9 [c]1 Tim. 3:3; Titus 1:7
25 [a]Gal. 6:1; Titus 3:2; 1 Pet. 3:15 [b]Acts 8:22 [c]1 Tim. 2:4 *See WW at 1 Tim. 6:11.
26 [a]1 Tim. 3:7

CHAPTER 3

1 [a]1 Tim. 4:1; 2 Pet. 3:3; 1 John 2:18; Jude 17, 18 [1]*times of stress* *See WW at Col. 4:5.
2 *See WW at Acts 6:11.
3 [1]*irreconcilable*
4 [a]2 Pet. 2:10
5 [a]Titus 1:16 [b]1 Tim. 5:8 [c]Matt. 23:3; 2 Thess. 3:6; 1 Tim. 6:5
6 [a]Matt. 23:14; Titus 1:11
7 [a]1 Tim. 2:4
8 [a]Ex. 7:11, 12, 22; 8:7; 9:11 [b]1 Tim. 6:5 [c]Rom. 1:28
9 [a]Ex. 7:11, 12; 8:18; 9:11

Perilous Times and Perilous Men

3 But know this, that [a]in the last days
[1]**perilous** *times will come:

WORD WEALTH

3:1 perilous, *chalepos* (khal-ep-*oss*); Strong's *#5467:* Harsh, savage, difficult, dangerous, painful, fierce, grievous, hard to deal with. The word describes a society that is barren of virtue but abounding with vices.

2 For men will be lovers of themselves, lovers of money, boasters,
proud, *blasphemers, disobedient to
parents, unthankful, unholy,
3 unloving, [1]unforgiving, slanderers,
without self-control, brutal, despisers
of good,
4 [a]traitors, headstrong, haughty, lovers of pleasure rather than lovers of
God,
5 [a]having a form of godliness but 4
[b]denying its power. And [c]from such
people turn away!
6 For [a]of this sort are those who creep
into households and make captives of
gullible women loaded down with sins,
led away by various lusts,
7 always learning and never able
[a]to come to the knowledge of the truth.
8 [a]Now as Jannes and Jambres resisted Moses, so do these also resist the
truth: [b]men of corrupt minds, [c]dis-
approved concerning the faith;
9 but they will progress no further,
for their folly will be manifest to all,
[a]as theirs also was.

2:17, 18 Hymenaeus and Philetus apparently taught that a spiritual rebirth was the only kind of resurrection that would occur.
2:20 Some household utensils are for menial use, and others are for noble use. By use of this metaphor Paul states that in the church there are true and false teachers.
2:21, 22 Christian teachers are to be righteous in character and conduct, because only in their purity will they be fit for the Lord's work.
2:22 See section 3 of Truth-In-Action at the end of 2 Tim.
2:24–26 See section 4 of Truth-In-Action at the end of 2 Tim.
2:24–26 False teachers are in reality ensnared by **the devil,** but the **gentle** correction of the Lord's **servant** may lead false teachers to **repentance.**
3:1–9 Paul exhorts Timothy to continue in the gospel in the face of a great increase of evil. **In the last days,** the time from the first appearing of Christ until His Second Coming (see note on Acts 2:17; see also 1 Tim. 4:1; Heb. 1:1, 2; 1 Pet. 1:20, 1 John 2:18), people will be characterized by all kinds of self-centered and unnatural perversions. Some will maintain an outward pretense, speaking the vocabulary of Christianity, but refusing the reality that Christian faith expresses (v. 5). The **power** they deny is the heart of Christianity—the fact of a risen Redeemer, the truth of the inspired Word and the indwelling and overflowing of the Holy Spirit, working within believers and transforming their lives. The false teachers are compared to **Jannes and Jambres,** Egyptian magicians who opposed Moses because of their base and perverted minds (see Ex. 7).
3:5 See section 4 of Truth-In-Action at the end of 2 Tim.

The Man of God and the Word of God

10 [a]But you have carefully followed
my doctrine, manner of life, *purpose,
faith, longsuffering, love, *perseverance,
11 persecutions, afflictions, which
happened to me [a]at Antioch, [b]at Iconium, [c]at Lystra—what persecutions I
endured. And [d]out of *them* all the Lord
delivered me.
1 12 Yes, and [a]all who desire to live
godly in Christ Jesus will suffer persecution.
13 [a]But evil men and impostors will
grow worse and worse, deceiving and
being deceived.
14 But you must [a]continue in the
things which you have learned and
been assured of, knowing from whom
you have learned *them*,
15 and that from childhood you have
known [a]the Holy Scriptures, which are
able to make you wise for salvation
through faith which is in Christ Jesus.
2 16 [a]All *Scripture *is* given by inspiration of God, [b]and *is* profitable for doctrine, for reproof, for correction, for
[1]instruction in righteousness,

10 [a]Phil. 2:20, 22; 1 Tim. 4:6 *See WW at Rom. 8:28. • See WW at Heb. 10:36.
11 [a]Acts 13:44–52 [b]Acts 14:1–6, 19 [c]Acts 14:8–20 [d]Ps. 34:19
12 [a][Ps. 34:19]
13 [a]2 Thess. 2:11
14 [a]2 Tim. 1:13; Titus 1:9
15 [a]Ps. 119:97–104; John 5:39
16 [a][2 Pet. 1:20] [b]Rom. 4:23; 15:4 [1]*training, discipline* *See WW at John 5:39.
17 [a]1 Tim. 6:11 [b]2 Tim. 2:21; Heb. 13:21

KINGDOM DYNAMICS

3:16 The Divine Inspiration of the Bible, THE WORD OF GOD. The absolute authority of the Bible over our lives is based in our conviction that this Book does not merely contain the Word of God, but that it is the Word of God in its sum and in its parts. This text testifies to this, describing the actual process of this inspiration (inbreathing of life): 1) It is the word of the Holy Spirit. *Theopneustos* (Greek), translated "inspiration of God," literally means "God-breathed." This describes the source of the whole Bible's derivation (that is, "all Scripture") as transcendent of human inspiration. The Bible is not the product of elevated human consciousness or enlightened human intellect, but is directly "breathed" from God Himself. 2) 2 Pet. 1:20, 21 elaborates this truth, and adds that none of what was given was merely the private opinion of the writer (v. 20) and that each writer involved in the production of the Holy Scriptures was "moved by" (literally, "being borne along") the Holy Spirit. This does not mean that the writers were merely robots, seized upon by God's power to write automatically without their conscious participation. God does not override those gifts of intellect and sensitivity that He has given His creatures. (Beware of all instances where individuals claim to "automatically" write anything at any time, for the Holy Spirit never functions that way.) 3) 1 Cor. 2:10–13 expands on this process by which the revelation of the Holy Scriptures was given. V. 13 says that even the words used in the giving of the Bible (not just the ideas, but the precise terminology) were planned by the Holy Spirit, who deployed the respective authors of the Bible books to write, "comparing spiritual things with spiritual" (literally, "matching spiritual words to spiritual ideas"). This biblical view of the Bible's derivation is called the plenary verbal inspiration of the Scriptures, meaning every word is inspired by the Holy Spirit of God. (*/Ps. 19:7) J.W.H.

17 [a]that the man of God may be complete, [b]thoroughly equipped for every
good work.

Preach the Word

4 I [a]charge *you* [1]therefore before
God and the Lord Jesus Christ,
[b]who will *judge the living and the
dead [2]at His appearing and His kingdom:
2 *Preach the word! Be ready in sea- 5
son *and* out of season. [a]Convince,
[b]rebuke, [c]exhort, with all longsuffering and teaching.
3 [a]For the time will come when they
will not *endure [b]sound* doctrine,
[c]but according to their own desires, *because* they have itching ears, they will
heap up for themselves teachers;

CHAPTER 4

1 [a]1 Tim. 5:21; 2 Tim. 4:1 [b]Acts 10:42 [1]NU omits *therefore* [2]NU *and by* *See WW at John 18:31.
2 [a]Titus 2:15 [b]1 Tim. 5:20; Titus 1:13; 2:15 [c]1 Tim. 4:13 *See WW at Acts 9:20.
3 [a]2 Tim. 3:1 [b]1 Tim. 1:10; 2 Tim. 1:13 [c]Is. 30:9–11; Jer. 5:30, 31; 2 Tim. 3:6 *See WW at 2 Thess. 1:4. • See WW at 3 John 2.

3:10–17 The religious **impostors** will steadily degenerate, becoming **worse and worse** (v. 13), and Timothy will **suffer persecution** in opposing them (v. 12). However, Timothy has Paul's own perseverance as an example (vv. 10, 11), and he will also find strength and stability in the Scriptures (vv. 14–17).

3:12 See section 1 of Truth-In-Action at the end of 2 Tim.

3:16 See section 2 of Truth-In-Action at the end of 2 Tim.

3:16 Given by inspiration of God translates the Greek word *theopneustos,* which literally means "God-breathed." This is Scripture's most important statement about itself, meaning that **Scripture** is the product of God's creative breath. Therefore, being God's own utterance, it is properly called "the Word of God." Here Paul only states the fact of inspiration without explaining its process. Elsewhere he elaborates on the Holy Spirit's role in the production of the written Word (1 Cor. 2:9–15; see also 2 Pet. 1:21).

4:1 Paul underscores the urgency of his exhortations to Timothy. The Greek word for **I charge** is used in connection with a solemn and emphatic testimony in a court of law.

4:2 See section 5 of Truth-In-Action at the end of 2 Tim.

4:2 Timothy is to **preach the word** with equal urgency when circumstances are favorable and when they are unfavorable.

4:3–8 Paul bases his urgent appeal on the fact that people will prefer **fables** to **truth** (vv. 3, 4), and on the reality of his imminent death (vv. 6–8). In light of the contemporary situation, Timothy's responsibility was to be faithful in fulfilling his **ministry** (v. 5).

4 and they will turn *their* ears away
from the truth, and [a]be turned aside
to fables.
5 But you be watchful in all things,
[a]endure afflictions, do the work of
[b]an evangelist, fulfill your ministry.

Paul's Valedictory

6 For [a]I am already being poured out
as a drink offering, and the time of
[b]my departure is at hand.
7 [a]I have fought the *good fight, I
have finished the race, I have kept the
faith.
8 Finally, there is laid up for me
[a]the crown of **righteousness,** which the
Lord, the *righteous [b]Judge, will *give
to me [c]on that Day, and not to me only
but also to all who have *loved His appearing.

> **WORD WEALTH**
>
> **4:8 righteousness,** *dikaiosune* (dik-ah-yos-oo-nay); Strong's *#1343:* Just, the quality of being right. Broadly, the word suggests conformity to the revealed will of God in all respects. *Dikaiosune* is both judicial and gracious. God declares the believer righteous, in the sense of acquitting him, and imparts righteousness to him (2 Cor. 5:21).

The Abandoned Apostle

9 *Be diligent to come to me quickly;
10 for [a]Demas has forsaken me,
[b]having loved this present world, and
has departed for Thessalonica—Cres-
cens for Galatia, Titus for Dalmatia.
11 Only Luke is with me. Get [a]Mark
and bring him with you, for he is useful
to me for ministry.
12 And [a]Tychicus I have *sent to Ephesus.
13 Bring the cloak that I left with Car-
pus at Troas when you come—and the
books, especially the parchments.
14 [a]Alexander the coppersmith did me
much harm. May the Lord repay him
according to his works.
15 You also must beware of him, for
he has greatly *resisted our words.
16 At my first defense no one stood
with me, but all forsook me. [a]May it
not be *charged against them.

The Lord Is Faithful

17 [a]But the Lord stood with me and
strengthened me, [b]so that the message
might be preached fully through me,
and *that* all the Gentiles might hear.
Also I was delivered [c]out of the mouth
of the lion.
18 [a]And the Lord will deliver me from
every evil work and preserve *me* for
His heavenly kingdom. [b]To Him *be*
glory forever and ever. Amen!

Come Before Winter

19 Greet [a]Prisca and Aquila, and the
household of [b]Onesiphorus.
20 [a]Erastus stayed in Corinth, but
[b]Trophimus I have left in Miletus sick.
21 *Do your utmost to come before
winter. Eubulus greets you, as well as

4 [a]1 Tim. 1:4
5 [a]2 Tim. 1:8 [b]Acts 21:8
6 [a]Phil. 2:17 [b][Phil. 1:23]
7 [a]1 Cor. 9:24–27 *See WW at Matt. 13:48.
8 [a]James 1:12 [b]John 5:22 [c]2 Tim. 1:12 *See WW at Matt. 1:19. • See WW at Matt. 22:21. • See WW at John 3:16.
9 *See WW at Gal. 2:10.
10 [a]Col. 4:14 [b]1 John 2:15
11 [a]Acts 12:12, 25; 15:37–39
12 [a]Acts 20:4 *See WW at John 20:21.
14 [a]1 Tim. 1:20
15 *See WW at Eph. 6:13.
16 [a]Acts 7:60 *See WW at Rom. 4:3.
17 [a]Acts 23:11 [b]Acts 9:15 [c]1 Sam. 17:37
18 [a]Ps. 121:7 [b]Rom. 11:36
19 [a]Acts 18:2 [b]2 Tim. 1:16
20 [a]Rom. 16:23 [b]Acts 20:4; 21:29
21 *See WW at Gal. 2:10.

4:5 See section 2 of Truth-In-Action at the end of 2 Tim.
4:6 Paul's death was a sacrifice **poured out** before God and, as such, enabled him to share the sufferings of Christ.
4:7, 8 Whether Paul regarded his life as a battle, a race, or a test of the truth of the gospel, he had achieved victory. The past, with its many duties, has been completed; the present is secure in faith; the future promises rewards.
4:11 Because of Mark's early failure in mission work (see Acts 13:13), Paul had spurned him as a deserter and had refused his service (see Acts 15:36–40). However, **Mark** redeemed his reputation and Paul now recognized his sincerity and value as a minister.
4:13 Paul needed his **cloak** in the cold and damp dungeon. The **books,** or papyrus rolls, may have been portions of the OT. The leather **parchments** could have been unused material, which Paul wanted for planned writing endeavors; more probably, however, they were sections of the OT, prized highly by Paul, or perhaps even copies of the Lord's words and early narratives of His life.
4:14 Alexander was possibly the blasphemer mentioned in 1 Tim. 1:20.
4:16, 17 Though men abandoned Paul at his first court hearing, the Lord did not. Evidently Paul was able to use that occasion to preach the gospel. As a Roman citizen, Paul would not be thrown to the lions in the public theater. **Delivered out of the mouth of the lion** was a figurative way of saying that Satan's efforts to bring about a premature death for Paul had been averted for the present.
4:18 Paul does not express an immunity to physical ill. On the contrary, he expects death (vv. 6–8), but no attack upon him could do him abiding harm. His death would bring deliverance from suffering and entrance into heaven.
4:19 Paul first met **Prisca and Aquila** in Corinth (Acts 18:1, 2).
4:20 Erastus was either the treasurer of Corinth (Rom. 16:23) or a messenger whom Paul had sent to Macedonia (Acts 19:22). **Trophimus** was the Ephesian who had traveled with Paul on the third missionary journey (Acts 20:4). That Paul left him **in Miletus sick** expresses an enigma concerning healing. Although divine healing is part of the saints' inheritance (see Matt. 8:14–17), sometimes we are not healed, even when we have prayed in faith and confessed our faith outwardly. The Bible gives no explicit answers to this puzzle, and the fact that a close associate of an apostle was not healed shows that the dilemma has existed from the early days of the church. Such a fact should never discourage or introduce doubt to our prayers. It should, however, serve as a guard against presumption or condemnation.
4:21 Timothy may have reached Rome in response to Paul's appeal, at which time he himself may have been arrested (see Heb. 13:23). Of the others mentioned here nothing

Pudens, Linus, Claudia, and all the brethren.

Farewell

22 The Lord [1]Jesus **Christ** be with your spirit. Grace be with you. Amen.

22 [1]NU omits *Jesus Christ*

WORD WEALTH

4:22 Christ, *Christos* (Khris-*toss*); Strong's *#5547:* The Anointed One. The word comes from the verb *chrio,* "to anoint," referring to the consecration rites of a priest or king. *Christos* translates the Hebrew *Mashiyach,* "Messiah." Unfortunately, the transliteration of *Christos* into English, resulting in the word "Christ," deprives the word of much of its meaning. It would be better to translate *Christos* in every instance as "the Anointed One" or "the Messiah," denoting a *title.* "Jesus Christ" actually means Jesus the Messiah, or Jesus the Anointed One, emphasizing the fact that the man Jesus was God's Anointed One, the promised Messiah.

further is known, except for a tradition that **Linus** was appointed a bishop of Rome.

4:22 The Greek pronoun **you** is plural, indicating that Paul's message was to the entire congregation at Ephesus.

TRUTH-IN-ACTION through 2 TIMOTHY

Letting the LIFE of the Holy Spirit Bring Faith's Works Alive in You!

Truth 2 Timothy Teaches	Text	**Action** 2 Timothy Invites
1 Guidelines for Growing in Godliness Being like God is living like He has told us to live; this involves studying and applying the Scriptures.	1:3	**Strictly maintain** a clear conscience before God and man.
	2:15	**Devote yourself to** responsible Bible study. **Become** a sensible interpreter of Scripture.
Those who do so will become living reproof to those who do not and thus will often encounter persecution.	3:12	**Recognize** that godly living always encounters persecution. **Expect** this because a godly life testifies against godlessness in others.
2 Key Lessons in Faith Faith believes absolutely in the divine inspiration of the Scriptures.	3:16	**Revere** God's Word very highly. **Recognize** its fully divine source of inspiration. **Submit** to it absolutely.
Therefore, the man of faith has a very high view of the Bible, and is able courageously to face opposition unmoved.	4:5	**Do not be frustrated** by opposition. **Continue** to stand strong. **Be tirelessly faithful** in those things God has commissioned you to do.
3 Guidelines for Growth in the Spirit Spiritual growth is learning to depend upon the Holy Spirit's life in you through His indwelling presence and the spiritual gifts He has given you.	1:6	**Faithfully exercise** charismatic gifts that have been imparted to you. **Discipline yourself** continually to employ them in boldness and in love.
	2:1	**Be strong** in grace; **draw deeply** on God's enabling power and energy to accomplish His purpose through you.
	2:22	**Strictly avoid** any fleshly indulgence, and **do not succumb to** fleshly desires. **Devote yourself** to Spirit-filled living, bearing the fruit of the Spirit.

Truth 2 Timothy Teaches	Text	**Action** 2 Timothy Invites
4 Keys to Wise Living One with spiritual wisdom possesses spiritual perception and a wise value system. He realizes that any theological quarreling is unproductive and refuses to be drawn into it. Rather, he learns gently to persuade others to godliness, not being easily deceived by feigned godly behavior. He also recognizes the human tendency to avoid the demands of truth and to listen, rather, to what they want to hear.	2:14 2:24–26 3:5	**Be warned** that theological quarreling is ruinous and almost never helpful. **Avoid** being drawn into arguments or quarrels. **Learn** how to persuade others to believe and practice truth, but **do so** gently and kindly. **Do not be deceived** by jargon or religiosity. **Look for** true spiritual power and godliness in others.
5 Getting Motivated for Ministry Ministry is service, and a "minister" of the gospel is primarily a servant of God's Word, boldly and courageously sharing its message. He treasures the Word of God and defends it tirelessly, being careful to communicate its truth with absolute accuracy. This is no easy task because the Word of God faces violent opposition. Thus the "minister" of God's Word learns that patience, endurance, and hard work are necessary for success in his calling.	1:8 1:13, 14 2:2 2:3–7 4:2	**Preach the gospel** boldly, without fear! **Recognize** that the Word of God is a treasure of inestimable value. **Guard** it diligently. **Hold firmly** to the truth you have received. **Do not let** the Enemy **corrupt** it. **Communicate** truth exactly and accurately. **Train** others to do the same. **Make sure** that none of it is ever distorted, diluted, or deleted. **Learn from** the "ministry" examples of 1) the soldier enduring hardship, 2) the athlete in strict training, and 3) the hardworking, patient farmer, what ministry really means. **Become** a committed servant of God's Word. **Be prepared** at any time, whether convenient or inconvenient, **to proclaim** it and to **patiently instruct** those who do not understand or accept it.

The Epistle of Paul the Apostle to TITUS

Author: Paul
Date: Probably A.D. 64
Theme: Setting the Church at Crete in Order
Key Words: Diligence, Commitment, Responsibility

Background It is strange that a person whose name is listed among the books of the New Testament is so little known. Even though Titus was a companion and valuable coworker of Paul, there is no mention of him in the Acts of the Apostles.

Titus was a Greek and evidently a convert of Paul. The fact that Titus was not circumcised (Gal. 2:3) indicates that he had not been raised in Judaism nor had he become a proselyte. Paul highly esteemed Titus, and the apostle was restless when there was little or no news of the young man's whereabouts and activities.

Occasion and Date Although the New Testament does not record a ministry of Paul in Crete, such passages as 1:5 clearly indicate that he and Titus had conducted a mission there. This campaign probably took place sometime during A.D. 63–64, after Paul's release from his first imprisonment in Rome. Since his time was short, Paul left Titus on Crete to care for the new churches. Then the apostle departed to other fields of labor. Somewhere enroute to Nicopolis of Greece (3:12), he wrote to Titus. The letter gives evidence of having been written during the fall of the year, probably around A.D. 64 (see 3:12).

Purpose Paul gave to Titus, a relatively young preacher of the gospel, the difficult assignment of directing the work in Crete. Later he wrote this letter to give Titus more detailed instructions concerning the performance of his pastoral duties.

Content The letter to Titus has an affinity with 1 Timothy. Both epistles are addressed to young men who had been assigned positions of responsible leadership in their respective churches during Paul's absence. Both epistles are occupied with the qualifications of those who are to lead and teach the churches. The worldly corruptions that face the new churches are the same. Titus has three great themes—church organization, sound doctrine, and holy living. Titus was to ordain elders in every city where the nucleus of a congregation existed. They must be men of high moral character, and must be adamant on questions of principle, maintaining the true apostolic doctrine and able to refute objectors.

Personal Application Difficulties in the church are compounded when there are problems with the leadership. This letter teaches that the supreme aim of church government is the preservation of revealed truth and the safeguarding of ethical standards. Therefore, church leaders must be exemplary in life-style and sound in doctrine. This letter also stresses the close connection between sound doctrine and morals. Truth is always intended to determine life and to promote godliness.

Christ Revealed Underlying the instructions of Paul is the theme that Christ is building His church, carefully choosing the stones that make up this habitation for God. Paul also emphasizes Christ as our Redeemer (2:14; 3:4–7), and presents His Second Coming as an incentive to holy living (2:12, 13).

The Holy Spirit at Work The ministry of the Holy Spirit is understood throughout the entire epistle. The Cretans cannot change themselves (1:12, 13), and regeneration can only be the work of the Holy Spirit (3:5). The one who experiences a new birth receives the Holy Spirit in order to maintain a victorious life-style patterned after that of Christ (3:6–8).

Outline of Titus

Greeting

PAUL, a bondservant of God and an
apostle of Jesus Christ, according
to the faith of God's elect and [a]the acknowledgment of the truth [b]which accords with godliness,
2 in *hope of eternal life which God,
who [a]cannot lie, *promised before time
began,
3 but has in due time manifested His
word through preaching, which was
committed to me according to the commandment of God our Savior;

4 To [a]Titus, a true son in *our* common
faith:
Grace, *mercy, *and* peace from God
the Father and [1]the Lord *Jesus Christ
our Savior.

Qualified Elders

5 For this reason I left you in Crete, **2**
that you should [a]set in order the
things that are lacking, and appoint
elders in every city as I commanded
you—
6 if a man is blameless, the husband
of one wife, [a]having faithful children
not accused of [1]dissipation or insub-
ordination.
7 For a [1]bishop must be blameless, as

CHAPTER 1

1 [a]2 Tim. 2:25 [b][1 Tim. 3:16]
2 [a]Num. 23:19 *See WW at 1 Thess. 1:3. • See WW at Acts 7:5.
4 [a]2 Cor. 2:13; 8:23 [1]NU *Christ Jesus* *See WW at 2 Tim. 1:16. • See WW at Phil. 4:23.
5 [a]1 Cor. 11:34
6 [a]1 Tim. 3:2–4 [1]*debauchery,* lit. *incorrigibility*
7 [1]Lit. *overseer*

1:1 Usually Paul calls himself the bondslave of Jesus Christ. This is the only time he calls himself a **bondservant of God.** The reason for the change is not clear. Though it was once reserved for Israel, the term **God's elect** refers to the Christian church, made up of those who have heard the gospel and have responded to it.

1:2 Eternal life refers both to a new quality of life in this world and the continuation of that Christian life thereafter. Although it is a present possession, many of its aspects are yet unrealized and thus may be described in terms of **hope . . . which God, who cannot lie, promised.** God, whose nature is the absence of falsehood, formulated His purposes before time began.

1:3 In the **time** of His own choosing (see note on Gal. 4:4), God revealed His purposes to Paul, who received a special dispensation of the grace of God.

1:4 Titus was **a true son** of the gospel, as was Timothy, having been converted through Paul's ministry. As father and sons they stood shoulder to shoulder proclaiming their **common faith.**

1:5–9 See section 2 of Truth-In-Action at the end of Titus.

1:5 Luke does not record in the Book of Acts Paul's evangelistic campaign in Crete. Consequently, it must have taken place following Paul's first Roman imprisonment. The word "elder" apparently designates the same office as "bishop" (see v. 7; 1 Tim. 3:1–7).

1:6–9 The spiritual standards of the elders were all the more important because the Cretans had notorious reputations (vv. 12, 13). The list of qualifications parallels the one found in 1 Tim. 3:1–7, with few differences. See notes on 1 Tim. 3:1–7.

a *steward of God, not self-willed, not
quick-tempered, [a]not given to wine,
not violent, not greedy for money,
8 but hospitable, a lover of what is
good, sober-minded, just, holy, self-
controlled,
9 holding fast the faithful word as he
has been taught, that he may be able,
by *sound doctrine, both to exhort and
convict those who contradict.

The Elders' Task

2 10 For there are many insubordinate,
both **idle** [a]**talkers** and deceivers, especially those of the circumcision,

WORD WEALTH

1:10 idle talkers, *mataiologos* (mat-ah-yol-*og*-oss); Strong's *#3151:* From *mataios,* "idle," "useless," and *lego,* "to speak." *Mataiologos* is speaking that lacks reason and worth and that gives evidence of an undisciplined life-style. The counterpart is men speaking as they are moved by the Holy Spirit (2 Pet. 1:21).

11 whose mouths must be stopped,
who subvert whole households, teaching things which they ought not,
[a]for the sake of dishonest gain.
12 [a]One of them, a prophet of their
own, said, "Cretans *are* always liars,
evil beasts, lazy gluttons."
13 This *testimony is *true. [a]Therefore
rebuke them sharply, that they may be
sound in the faith,
14 not giving heed to Jewish fables and

7 [a]Lev. 10:9 *See WW at 1 Pet. 4:10
9 *See WW at 3 John 2.
10 [a]James 1:26
11 [a]1 Tim. 6:5
12 [a]Acts 17:28
13 [a]2 Cor. 13:10; 2 Tim. 4:2 *See WW at John 19:35. • See WW at Rom. 3:4.
14 [a]Is. 29:13
15 [a]Luke 11:41; Rom. 14:14, 20; 1 Cor. 6:12 *See WW at Matt. 5:8.
16 [a]Matt. 7:20–23; 25:12; 1 John 2:4 [b][2 Tim. 3:5, 7] [c]Rom. 1:28 [1]*detestable*

CHAPTER 2

1 *See WW at 3 John 2.
2 *See WW at 1 Tim. 3:11. • See WW at 3 John 2.
5 [a]1 Tim. 5:14 [b]1 Cor. 14:34; 1 Tim. 2:11 [c]Rom. 2:24 *See WW at 1 John 3:3.
6 *See WW at Mark 5:15.
7 [a]Phil. 3:17; 1 Tim. 4:12 [b]Eph. 6:24 [1]NU omits *incorruptibility*
8 [1]NU, M *us*

[a]commandments of men who turn
from the truth.
15 [a]To the pure all things are *pure,
but to those who are defiled and unbelieving nothing is pure; but even their
mind and conscience are defiled.
16 They profess to [a]know God, but
[b]in works they deny Him, being
[1]abominable, disobedient, [c]and disqualified for every good work.

Qualities of a Sound Church

2 But as for you, speak the things 2
which are proper for *sound doctrine:
2 that the older men be sober, *reverent, temperate, *sound in faith, in love,
in patience;
3 the older women likewise, that they
be reverent in behavior, not slanderers,
not given to much wine, teachers of
good things—
4 that they admonish the young
women to love their husbands, to love
their children,
5 to be discreet, *chaste, [a]home-
makers, good, [b]obedient to their own
husbands, [c]that the word of God may
not be blasphemed.
6 Likewise, exhort the young men to
be *sober-minded,
7 in all things showing yourself *to be* 2
[a]a pattern of good works; in doctrine
showing integrity, reverence, [b]incor-
ruptibility,[1]
8 sound speech that cannot be condemned, that one who is an opponent
may be ashamed, having nothing evil
to say of [1]you.

1:9 In addition to good moral character, elders are to maintain true Christian **doctrine** seriously and zealously, both for the purpose of instructing believers and of confuting false teachers.

1:10–16 See section 2 of Truth-In-Action at the end of Titus.

1:10 A spiritual leader must recognize that some people are insubordinate and will not bend their will to the rule of any leader. They love to float from church to church talking about spiritual matters, but in their deception they do not realize they are all talk and no fruit. Paul particularly has in mind **those of the circumcision,** or Jewish legalists.

1:11 The influence of these teachers was widespread.

1:12 Paul quotes Epimenides, a well-known Cretan poet of the sixth century B.C. who was regarded as a prophet by his countrymen, to illustrate the poor reputation of Cretans in the ancient world.

1:14 The erroneous doctrines were **Jewish** in origin (see note on v. 10).

1:15 *While* the Jewish legalists compiled an overwhelming list of "unclean" things that went far beyond the requirements of the OT, Christians no longer need to make distinctions between clean and unclean foods (see Mark 7:15–19; Acts 10:15). However, **those who are defiled** (corrupt) **and unbelieving** soil everything they do and say. This verse does not give Christians license to indulge in evil (see 1 Tim. 4:4, 5).

1:16 Paul agrees with James that works give evidence of faith.

2:1–10 See section 2 of Truth-In-Action at the end of Titus.

2:1 The pronoun **you** is emphatic. No matter what the legalists say and do, Titus is to continue the healthful teaching of the gospel.

2:2–10 In contrast to the disobedient and detestable lives of the false teachers, Paul exhorts Christians of various ages and classes to practice good deeds.

2:2 This exhortation applies to the **older men** in the church and not particularly to the official elders. They are to exhibit special qualities of Christian living consistent with age and experience.

2:3–5 **Older women** are to assume the responsibilities of their new position in the gospel. These include providing a proper example for **the young women** and teaching them Christian character and domestic responsibilities, lest they bring disgrace on the faith by abusing their newfound freedom.

2:6–8 Evidently Titus was young enough to be classified among **the young men.** Therefore, he must present himself in all respects **a pattern of good works.** Church leadership demands exemplary conduct.

2:7, 8 See section 2 of Truth-In-Action at the end of Titus.

2 9 *Exhort* [a]bondservants to be obedient to their own *masters, to be well
pleasing in all *things,* not answering
back,
10 not [1]pilfering, but showing all good
[2]fidelity, that they may *adorn the doctrine of God our Savior in all things.

Trained by Saving Grace

1 11 For [a]the grace of God that brings
*salvation has appeared to all men,
12 teaching us that, denying ungodliness and worldly *lusts, we should live
soberly, righteously, and godly in the
present age,

WORD WEALTH

2:12 soberly, *sophronos* (so-*fron*-oce); Strong's *#4996:* From *sozo,* "to save," and *phren,* "the mind." This word is an adverb signifying acting in a responsible manner, sensibly, prudently, being in self-control and in full possession of intellectual and emotional faculties.

13 [a]looking for the *blessed [b]hope and
glorious appearing of our great God
and Savior Jesus Christ,
14 [a]who gave Himself for us, that He
might redeem us from every lawless
deed [b]and purify for Himself [c]*His* own
special people, *zealous for good
works.
15 Speak these things, [a]exhort, and rebuke with all authority. Let no one despise you.

Graces of the Heirs of Grace

1 3 Remind them [a]to be subject to
rulers and *authorities, to obey,

9 [a]1 Tim. 6:1 *See WW at Jude 4.
10 [1]*thieving* [2]*honesty* *See WW at Matt. 25:7.
11 [a][Rom. 5:15] *See WW at Acts 28:28.
12 *See WW at 2 Tim. 2:22.
13 [a]1 Cor. 1:7 [b][Col. 3:4] *See WW at Matt. 5:3.
14 [a]Gal. 1:4 [b][Heb. 1:3; 9:14] [c]Ex. 15:16 *See WW at Acts 22:3.
15 [a]2 Tim. 4:2

CHAPTER 3

1 [a]1 Pet. 2:13 [b]Col. 1:10 *See WW at Mark 3:15.
2 *See WW at 1 Tim. 3:3. • See WW at 1 Tim. 6:11.
3 [a]1 Cor. 6:11
4 [a]Titus 2:11 [b]1 Tim. 2:3 *See WW at Gal. 5:22. • See WW at Acts 28:2. • See WW at John 4:42.
5 [a][Rom. 3:20] [b]John 3:3
6 [a]Ezek. 36:26
7 [a][Rom. 8:17, 23, 24] *See WW at Rev. 14:6.
8 [a]1 Tim. 1:15

[b]to be ready for every good work,
2 to speak evil of no one, to be peace- 1
able, *gentle, showing all *humility to
all men.
3 For [a]we ourselves were also once
foolish, disobedient, deceived, serving
various lusts and pleasures, living in
malice and envy, hateful and hating
one another.
4 But when [a]the *kindness and the
*love of [b]God our *Savior toward man
appeared,
5 [a]not by works of righteousness
which we have done, but according to
His mercy He saved us, through
[b]the washing of regeneration and **renewing** of the Holy Spirit,

WORD WEALTH

3:5 renewing, *anakainosis* (an-ak-*ahee*-no-sis); Strong's *#342:* A combination of *ana,* "again," and *kainos,* "new." The word suggests a renovation, restoration, transformation, and a change of heart and life. In Rom. 12:2, it indicates a complete change for the better, an adjustment of one's moral and spiritual vision. Here it stresses the work of the Holy Spirit in transforming the life.

6 [a]whom He poured out on us abundantly through Jesus Christ our Savior,
7 that having been justified by His
grace [a]we should become heirs according to the hope of *eternal life.
8 [a]This is a faithful saying, and these 1
things I want you to affirm constantly,
that those who have believed in God
should be careful to maintain good
works. These things are good and
profitable to men.

2:9, 10 See section 2 of Truth-In-Action at the end of Titus.
2:9, 10 See notes on 1 Tim. 6:1, 2.
2:11–15 See section 1 of Truth-In-Action at the end of Titus.
2:11–14 The prerequisite to godly living is **the grace of God.** It teaches Christians discipleship and affords them **the blessed hope** of the Coming of Christ.
2:11 The word **for** introduces the basis of proper conduct. There is a close relationship between ethics and theology, between right living and right believing.
2:13 Paul testifies to the deity of **Jesus Christ** by identifying Him as **our great God and Savior.**
2:14 The purpose of Christ's redemptive work was to create a **special people** cleansed of sin and **zealous for good works.**
3:1 See section 1 of Truth-In-Action at the end of Titus.
3:1 Christians are citizens of heaven (Phil. 3:20), but they also must fulfill their obligations toward civil authorities. See Rom. 13; 1 Pet. 2:13.
3:2 See section 1 of Truth-In-Action at the end of Titus.
3:2 Christians also have obligations toward all their fellow citizens outside the church, and by their gentle dispositions may influence them for good.
3:3–7 Paul states two motives for proper conduct toward the outside world: a remembrance of their own worldly behavior in their preconversion lives and the realization of the love and kindness of God toward them.
3:4 God's special love for humankind is described by a Greek word from which the English word "philanthropy" is derived. God's gift of His Son is the greatest demonstration of His love.
3:5 Salvation comes through a twofold channel. **Through the washing of regeneration** may refer either to baptism (see Acts 2:38, where Peter describes the norm of Christian conversion-initiation), or to the cleansing of the believer from the guilt of sin, accomplished by regeneration. **Renewing of the Holy Spirit** signifies the role of the Holy Spirit in effecting a new birth in the believer and in imparting eternal life to him.
3:8–11 Paul's concluding injunctions to Titus instruct him to teach spiritual truths, to encourage believers **to maintain good works,** to shun strife and factions, and to avoid factious persons. The rejection of works as a basis of salvation (vv. 4–7) does not weaken Paul's insistence that saving faith must be revealed in a transformed life.
3:8 See section 1 of Truth-In-Action at the end of Titus.

Avoid Dissension

1 9 But [a]avoid foolish disputes, genealogies, contentions, and strivings about the law; for they are unprofitable and *useless.
10 [a]Reject a divisive man after the first and second [1]admonition,
11 knowing that such a person is warped and sinning, being self-condemned.

Final Messages

12 When I send Artemas to you, or [a]Tychicus, *be diligent to come to me at Nicopolis, for I have decided to spend the winter there.
13 Send Zenas the lawyer and [a]Apollos on their journey with haste, that they may lack nothing.
14 And let our *people* also learn to maintain good works, to *meet* urgent needs, that they may not be unfruitful.

Farewell

15 All who *are* with me greet you. Greet those who *love us in the faith. Grace *be* with you all. Amen.

9 [a]1 Tim. 1:4; 2 Tim. 2:23 *See WW at Acts 14:15. 10 [a]Matt. 18:17 [1]warning 12 [a]Acts 20:4; Eph. 6:21; Col. 4:7; 2 Tim. 4:12 *See WW at Gal. 2:10. 13 [a]Acts 18:24; 1 Cor. 16:12 15 *See WW at John 21:15.

3:9–11 See section 1 of Truth-In-Action at the end of Titus.
3:10 A divisive man is one who makes a choice pleasing to himself regardless of all other considerations. He is obstinately attached to an opinion that is not sound and threatens the unity of the church. Such a man is to be rebuked; and if he does not heed the rebuke, he is to be avoided.
3:12 Nothing is known of **Artemas** beyond this reference, but **Tychicus** was a trusted messenger (Eph. 6:21; Col. 4:7). Apparently Paul sent one of them to relieve Titus of his duties on Crete. **Nicopolis** was a city in Epirus, a part of Achaia.
3:13 Zenas is not mentioned elsewhere, but the designation **lawyer** identifies him as a secular jurist or, more likely, a converted rabbi. **Apollos** is the well-known teacher who first appears in Ephesus (Acts 18:24) and who exercised a profitable ministry in Corinth (1 Cor. 1:12; 3:4–6). Titus was to equip these two coworkers for the continuation of their journey. They may have been the bearers of this letter.

TRUTH-IN-ACTION through TITUS

Letting the LIFE of the Holy Spirit Bring Faith's Works Alive in You!

Truth Titus Teaches	Text	**Action** Titus Invites
1 **Guidelines for Growing in Godliness** Depending on God's grace (godliness is impossible any other way), the godly person exemplifies self-control. Say "No!" to ungodly and worldly attitudes and behavior and say "Yes!" to righteous and godly living. This involves submissive obedience to governing authorities. A key part of godly living is an eager readiness to do good works! Godly speech is humble, peaceable, and never slanderous or argumentative.	2:11–15	**Stand strongly** in grace. **Say "No!"** to ungodliness and worldliness. **Be self-controlled** in your practice of godly behavior. **Be eager** to do what is good!
	3:1	**Be subject** and **obedient to** authority—civil, family, church, and employers.
	3:2	**Never slander** anyone. **Humbly be at peace** with all men and be considerate of them.
	3:8	**Devote yourself** to doing good works!
	3:9–11	**Warn** those who are divisive and shun them if they do not heed a second warning.
2 **Lessons for Leaders** Christian leaders are not called to lead alone. Rather they are to involve other faithful, qualified persons to help them oversee the people of God. The primary role of the Christian leader is teaching. He is *to instruct* others in godly living, regardless of his station in life. Also, he is to guard God's church from false teachers and deceivers who take advantage of the people of God. The godly leader's teaching	1:5–9	Leaders, **appoint** qualified elders (overseers) to share ministry with you. **Make sure** they practice truth and are able to communicate it effectively.
	1:10–16	Leaders, **silence** the rebellious! **Identify** and **rebuke sharply** those whose lives are only talk and who seek to deceive others. **Aggressively prevent** the ruination of homes and churches by disallowing such to teach false doctrine.
	2:1–10	Leaders, **take an active role** in teaching others how to live self-controlled, exemplary, and fruitful lives.

Truth Titus Teaches	Text	**Action** Titus Invites
2 is to be first through the life that he lives: people should be able to look at the Christian leader and say, "That is how I am supposed to live." Also, he needs to be an able communicator of truth.	2:7, 8	Leaders, **teach** both by precept and example. **Exemplify** excellent character and self-control. **Do not allow** your words to provide an occasion for accusation.
	2:9, 10	Leaders, **teach** your people to be excellent employees, not stealing, not rebelling against their employer's authority—always being loyal and never injuring their employer's reputation.

The Epistle of Paul the Apostle to PHILEMON

Author: Paul
Date: A.D. 60–61
Theme: Brotherly Love
Key Word: Brother

Background This letter is Paul's personal appeal to Philemon, a wealthy Christian slaveowner. It appears that Philemon had been converted under Paul's ministry (v. 19), that he resided in Colosse, and that the Colossian church met in his house (v. 2). Onesimus, one of his slaves, had fled to Rome, apparently after damaging or stealing his master's property (vv. 11, 18). In Rome, Onesimus came in contact with the imprisoned Paul, who led him to Christ (v. 10).

Paul eventually wrote to the church in Colosse and evidently included this letter on Onesimus's behalf. Tychicus and Onesimus apparently delivered both letters. See Colossians 4:7–9; Philemon 12. The close relationship between Paul and Philemon is evidenced by their mutual prayers (vv. 4, 22) and an "open door" hospitality (v. 22). Love, trust, and respect characterized their friendship (vv. 1, 14, 21).

Slavery was an accepted economic and social reality in the Roman world. A slave was his master's property, without rights. Under Roman law, runaway slaves could be severely punished and even condemned to death. Slave uprisings in the first century resulted in fearful and suspicious owners. While the early Christian church did not directly attack the institution of slavery, it reordered the relationship between master and slave. Both were equal before God (Gal. 3:28), and both were accountable for their behavior (Eph. 6:5–9).

Occasion and Date Paul wrote this letter during his first Roman imprisonment about A.D. 61. He desired a genuine Christian reconciliation between a wronged slaveowner and a forgiven slave. Paul tactfully, yet urgently, interceded for Onesimus and expressed complete confidence that Philemon's faith and love would result in restoration (vv. 5, 21).

Purpose Paul's primary goal was to see Philemon freely embrace the fugitive Onesimus as a brother in Christ. He also expressed joy in Philemon's ministry and encouraged him to continue (vv. 4–7). The apostle made clear his desire for Onesimus to stay with him, but insisted on reconciliation first (vv. 13, 14).

Characteristics While the shortest of Paul's epistles, Philemon is a deep revelation of Christ at work in the lives of Paul and those around him. The tone is one of warm, personal friendship rather than apostolic authority. It reveals how Paul politely yet firmly addressed a central issue of the Christian life, namely love through forgiveness, in a very sensitive situation. It presents Paul's persuasion in action.

Content The epistle is a hallmark expression of true Christian relationships. After personally greeting Philemon and his fellow believers, Paul expresses thanksgiving for their love and faith toward Christ and their fellow believers.

Brotherly love often requires practical grace and mercy, and Paul soon comes to this point. He explains the conversion of Onesimus and the slave's new value in the ministry and family of Jesus Christ (vv. 12–16). This transformation, along with Paul's deep friendship with both men, is the basis for a new beginning.

This is no shallow appeal by Paul, for he writes a "blank check" on behalf of Onesimus for any outstanding debts (vv. 17–19). He brings the petition to a close knowing that Philemon's love and character will prevail. As he concludes, one can sense the unity of the Spirit among all the saints involved.

Personal Application This work presents the incredible power of Christ to bring healing to broken lives. It includes the personal reunion between Jesus Christ and the runaway sinner, as well as the wonderful restoration of two believers who were formerly separated. Only with Christ's example of forgiveness through the Cross are we able to overcome our hurts and mistakes and be reconciled to our brothers and sisters in Christ.

Christ Revealed This epistle powerfully applies the message of the gospel. Once an estranged slave, Onesimus is now "a beloved brother" in Christ as well (v. 16). Philemon is challenged to show the same unconditional pardon that he received through the grace and love of Jesus. Paul's offer to pay a debt that was not his own on behalf of a repentant slave is a clear picture of the work of Calvary. Paul's intercession is furthermore analogous to Christ's ongoing intercession with the Father on our behalf.

The Holy Spirit at Work While not specifically mentioned in Philemon, the Holy Spirit was definitely active in Paul's ministry and in the life of the church. It is the Holy Spirit who baptizes all believers, whether slave or free, into the body of Christ (1 Cor. 12:13); and Paul applies this truth to the lives of Philemon and Onesimus. Love, a fruit of the Spirit, is evident throughout the letter.

Outline of Philemon

I. Salutation **1–3**

II. Thanksgiving concerning Philemon **4–7**

A. Personal praise 4

B. Praiseworthy characteristics 5–7

III. Paul's petition for Onesimus **8–21**

A. A plea for acceptance 8–16

B. A pledge to repay 17–19

C. A confidence in obedience 20, 21

IV. Personal concerns **22–25**

A. Hope for release 22

B. Greetings 23, 24

C. Benediction 25

Greeting

PAUL, a [a]prisoner of Christ Jesus,
and Timothy *our* brother,

To Philemon our beloved *friend* and
fellow laborer,
2 to [1]the beloved Apphia, [a]Archippus
our fellow soldier, and to the church
in your house:

3 Grace to you and peace from God
our Father and the Lord Jesus Christ.

Philemon's Love and Faith

4 [a]I thank my God, making mention
of you always in my prayers,
5 [a]hearing of your love and faith
which you have toward the Lord Jesus
and toward all the saints,
1 6 that the *sharing of your faith may
become *effective [a]by the acknowledgment of [b]every good thing which is in
[1]you in Christ Jesus.
7 For we [1]have great [2]joy and [3]con-
solation* in your love, because the
[4]hearts of the saints have been *refreshed by you, brother.

The Plea for Onesimus

1 8 Therefore, though I might be very
bold in Christ to command you what
is fitting,
9 *yet* for love's sake I rather appeal
to you—being such a one as Paul, the
aged, and now also a prisoner of Jesus
Christ—

1 [a]Eph. 3:1
2 [a]Col. 4:17 [1]NU *our sister Apphia*
4 [a]Eph. 1:16; 1 Thess. 1:2; 2 Thess. 1:3
5 [a]Eph. 1:15; Col. 1:4; 1 Thess. 3:6
6 [a]Phil. 1:9; [Col. 1:9; 3:10; James 2:14–17] [b][1 Thess. 5:18] [1]NU, M *us* *See WW at Acts 2:42. • See WW at Heb. 4:12.
7 [1]NU *had* [2]M *thanksgiving* [3]*comfort* [4]Lit. *inward parts,* heart, liver, and lungs *See WW at Acts 9:31. • See WW at Rev. 14:13.
10 [a]Col. 4:9
12 [1]NU *back to you in person, that is, my own heart,* [2]See v. 7.
13 *See WW at Mark 1:1.
14 [a]2 Cor. 9:7; 1 Pet. 5:2
15 *See WW at Rev. 14:6.
16 [a]Eph. 6:5; Col. 3:22 *See WW at Rev. 19:5.

10 I appeal to you for my son [a]Onesi-
mus, whom I have begotten *while* in my
chains,
11 who once was unprofitable to you,
but now is profitable to you and to me.
12 I am sending him [1]back. You therefore receive him, that is, my own
[2]heart,
13 whom I wished to keep with me,
that on your behalf he might minister
to me in my chains for the *gospel.
14 But without your consent I wanted
to do nothing, [a]that your good deed
might not be by compulsion, as it were,
but voluntary.
15 For perhaps he departed for a while
for this *purpose,* that you might **receive**
him *forever,

WORD WEALTH

15 receive, *apecho* (ap-*ekh*-oh); Strong's *#568:* To receive in full, have sufficiency. The prefix *apo,* "from," before *echo,* "to have," stresses the accomplished result of the action. As an intransitive verb, *apecho* signifies to be away, distant (Matt. 15:8; Mark 7:6; Luke 7:6).

16 no longer as a *slave but more than
a slave—a beloved brother, especially
to me but how much more to you, both
in the [a]flesh and in the Lord.

Philemon's Obedience Encouraged

17 If then you count me as a partner,
receive him as *you would* me.

1 Paul sees his situation through the eyes of faith. He is a **prisoner of Christ Jesus,** not of Caesar. He is a captive ambassador.
2 **Apphia** and **Archippus** were, in all probability, a part of Philemon's household. They could have been his wife and son respectively.
6 See section 1 of Truth-In-Action at the end of Philem.
6 Paul prays that Philemon's faith will become productive in loving service and effective witness through a fullness in Christ. The **acknowledgment of every good thing** is both a reminder of our riches in Christ and resources in the Holy Spirit, and a directive to participatively receive and apply those benefits.
7 The position of **brother** in the Greek sentence is emphatic.
8–16 See section 1 of Truth-In-Action at the end of Philem.
8 Paul is confident that he could speak freely and **be very bold in Christ,** demanding as an apostle and friend the exercise of Philemon's proper duty. A "frankness" between two believers is available **in Christ.**
9 ***Yet,*** love is the basis of Paul's appeal, **rather** than an exercise of apostolic authority. Paul, about 60 years old, certainly had the right to call himself **aged.** Yet, the Greek word is very close to the term "ambassador," both having the same root and sometimes interchangeable. Thus, Paul might be affirming himself as "an ambassador in chains" (Eph. 6:20).
10 Paul, the instrument God used to bring **Onesimus** to conversion during his imprisonment, appeals on behalf of his **son.**
11 This is a play on words, since "Onesimus" means "Useful" or "Profitable." In stark contrast to his past, Onesimus is now useful to both Paul and Philemon. He finally lives up to his name.
13 Paul subtly requests that Onesimus serve him by doing what Philemon also would do if he were given the opportunity. A parallel example is that of Epaphroditus in Phil. 2:25–30.
14 As an effective leader and good friend, Paul chooses not to force a **good deed** in violation of Philemon's own free will, but desires that service be rendered with his genuine approval.
15 Paul suggests that God's deeper providence was at work even in Onesimus's initial act of running away. With Onesimus now belonging to Christ, there is a new and eternal relationship between slave and master.
16 The basis of Paul's appeal is the fact that Onesimus is now **a beloved brother.** The new relationship is beyond the temporary master-to-slave in the earthly realm to the eternal brother-to-brother in the spiritual realm. While Paul does not overtly attack the institution of slavery, the principles he espouses lay the foundation for future reformation in abolishing it.

18 But if he has *wronged you or owes
anything, put that on my account.
19 I, Paul, am writing with my own
[a]hand. I will repay—not to mention to
you that you owe me even your own
self besides.
20 Yes, brother, let me have joy from
you in the Lord; refresh my heart in
the Lord.
21 [a]Having *confidence in your *obedience, I write to you, knowing that you
will do even more than I say.
1 22 But, meanwhile, also prepare a
guest room for me, for [a]I trust that
[b]through your prayers I shall be
*granted to you.

Farewell

23 [a]Epaphras, my fellow prisoner in
Christ Jesus, greets you,
24 *as do* [a]Mark, [b]Aristarchus, [c]Demas,
[d]Luke, my fellow laborers.
25 [a]The grace of our Lord Jesus Christ
be with your spirit. Amen.

18 *See WW at Acts 25:10.
19 [a]1 Cor. 16:21
21 [a]2 Cor. 7:16 *See WW at 2 Thess. 3:4. • See WW at 2 Cor. 10:5.
22 [a]Phil. 1:25; 2:24 [b]2 Cor. 1:11 *See WW at Col. 3:13.
23 [a]Col. 1:7; 4:12
24 [a]Acts 12:12, 25; 15:37–39 [b]Acts 19:29; 27:2 [c]Col. 4:14 [d]2 Tim. 4:11
25 [a]2 Tim. 4:22

18 If he has wronged you or owes you anything seems to indicate Onesimus stole money before running away. Repentance often requires restitution, which Onesimus was likely unable to make or guarantee. Paul offers to pay it.
19 Paul intensifies his commitment to repay by personally writing his IOU on behalf of Onesimus. Yet, beyond this, Paul was counting on the appreciation and character of Philemon.
20 There is a suggested wordplay here since the verb **let me have joy** (which can also be translated "profit") is the same verb from which Onesimus's name is derived (see note on v. 11). Paul may be closing with a plea that Onesimus be allowed to join him.
22 See section 1 of Truth-In-Action at the end of Philem.
23, 24 Epaphras was active in ministering in and around Colosse, and he would personally be known by Philemon. The four other **fellow laborers** enjoyed an undefined relationship to Philemon as well.

TRUTH-IN-ACTION through PHILEMON

Letting the LIFE of the Holy Spirit Bring Faith's Works Alive in You!

Truth Philemon Teaches	Text	**Action** Philemon Invites
1 Guidelines for Growing in Godliness Sharing Jesus with others gives us a deeper insight into our inheritance in Christ. The godly person is immediately available for restored relationships. Sharing your home, food, and possessions with strangers is a greater blessing to you who show hospitality than it is to the one who receives it.	v. 6	**Understand** that by sharing your faith in Jesus, you gain a fuller understanding of your inheritance in Christ.
	vv. 8–16	**Practice instant forgiveness** of those who have offended you. **Make room** for the restoration of broken relationships.
	v. 22	**Practice hospitality.** Provide lodging for traveling servants of God.

The Epistle to the HEBREWS

Author: Unknown
Date: Before A.D. 70
Theme: The Superiority of Jesus Christ over the Old Covenant
Key Words: Better, Let Us

Author Hebrews does not name its author, and there is no unanimity of tradition concerning his identity. Some scholars point out certain internal evidences that may indicate a Pauline authorship, while others suggest that one of Paul's associates, such as Barnabas or Apollos, may have written the book. Speculation has proved fruitless, and the best conclusion may be that of Origen in the third century, who stated that only God knows for certain who wrote Hebrews.

Date and Location The content of Hebrews indicates that it was written before the destruction of the temple in A.D. 70 (10:11; 13:11). The only evidence concerning the site of the book's writing is the greeting sent by "those from Italy" (13:24), perhaps indicating that the author was either in Rome or was writing to Christians in Rome.

Background and Purpose The majority of early Christians were Jewish. Apparently they expected Christ to return soon, but the delay in His coming and the persecutions against them (10:32–34) caused them to wonder if they had made the right choice in becoming Christians. Consequently, they were in danger of returning to Judaism.

This epistle was written to wavering Jewish believers, encouraging them to stand fast in their faith. The writer points out the overwhelming superiority of Christ over all that they had experienced under the law. What is offered to them through Christ is so much better than that which is promised under the Mosaic economy they should never consider turning back. The author dwells on the incomparable glory of the Person and work of Christ, showing His supremacy over prophets (1:1–3), angels (1:4—2:18), Moses (3:1–19), Joshua (4:1–13), Aaron (4:14—7:18), and the whole ritual of Judaism (7:19—10:39).

Content A key word of the epistle is "better," used to describe Christ and the benefits of the gospel (1:4; 7:19, 22; 8:6; 9:23; 10:34; 11:16, 35, 40).

Most of the blessings of Judaism had to do with earthly things: an earthly tabernacle or temple, earthly priests, earthly sacrifices, a covenant that promised earthly prosperity. In contrast, Christ is "at the right hand of the Majesty on high" (1:3), where He dispenses heavenly blessings (3:1; 6:4; 8:5; 11:16; 12:22, 23).

The high point of the epistle is the presentation of the high priestly ministry of the Lord. Christ is High Priest, not after the order of Aaron, but after the order of Melchizedek, who had no predecessors and no successors in the priesthood. Thus, Melchizedek was a perfect type of Christ, who received the office of high priest by the direct call of God, not by inheritance (5:5, 6). Whereas the Aaronic priest had to offer sacrifices continually for his own sins, as well as for the sins of the people, Christ once and for all offered His own sinless Person as the perfect sacrifice. In His flesh He experienced the testing that all believers know, and thus He is able to intercede compassionately on their behalf.

Chapter 11 lists some of the great heroes of faith of the Old Testament. Verses 4–35 record marvelous blessings and outstanding victories achieved through faith, while verses 36–38 record those who through faith endured great trial, suffering, and persecution. Significantly, there is no mention of the sins and shortcomings of those listed. The obvious reason is that the blood of Jesus Christ had blotted out the sins and failures, so that their iniquities are remembered against them no more.

Personal Application Although Hebrews is specifically addressed to Jewish Christians, its teachings and practical admonitions are equally applicable to Gentile believers. In Christ there is no distinction between Jew and Gentile (Col. 3:11). The church today needs the teaching provided in the Old Testament laws of worship, which this book so beautifully relates to Christ and the gospel of eternal salvation. Christianity is not something added on to Judaism. It is something new, but a fuller understanding of the Old Covenant gives a richer and more marvelous appreciation of the New Covenant of God's grace through our Lord Jesus Christ.

While the epistle is primarily doctrinal in its content, it is also intensely practical. After each doctrinal passage the writer inserts a section in which he gives some very pointed and powerful admonitions based on the teachings presented. At least fifteen times he uses the expression "let" or "let us" (4:1, 11, 14, 16; 6:1; 10:22, 23, 24; 12:1, 2, 28; 13:1, 5, 13, 15, 17).

Christ Revealed To speak of Christ in Hebrews is to describe the entire book. In striving to keep his readers from apostasy, the writer emphasizes the superiority of Christ to all that has gone before in Old Testament times. Like no other book in the Bible, Hebrews points out the importance and the ministry of the preincarnate Christ. See "Background and Purpose" and "Content" above.

The Holy Spirit at Work The ministry of the Holy Spirit is seen in a variety of ways, applying to both the Old and New Testament periods: gifts of the Holy Spirit for ministry (2:4); witness to the inspiration of the Old Testament (3:7; 10:15); descriptive of the experience of believers (6:4); interpreting spiritual truth (9:8); assisting in the ministry of Jesus (9:14); insulted by apostasy (10:29).

Outline of Hebrews

I. The superiority of Christ Jesus' person **1:1—4:13**
- A. Jesus better than the prophets 1:1–3
- B. Jesus better than the angels 1:4—2:18
  (First warning: against neglect 2:2–4)
- C. Jesus better than Moses 3:1–19
- D. Jesus better than Joshua 4:1–13
  (Second warning: against unbelief 4:1–3, 11–13)

II. The superiority of Christ Jesus' ministry **4:4—10:18**
- A. Jesus better than Aaron 4:14—5:10

1. Understanding and compassionate 4:14—5:4
2. After the order of Melchizedek 5:5–10
   (Third warning: against lack of maturity 5:11—6:20)

B. The Melchizedek priesthood, thus Jesus Christ's, better than Aaron's 7:1—8:5
1. Aaron paid tithes to Melchizedek 7:1–10
2. Aaronic priests made nothing perfect 7:11–22
3. Aaronic priests died 7:23–28
4. Aaronic priests served only shadows 8:1–5

C. Jesus mediates a better Covenant 8:6—10:18
1. The better Covenant 8:6–13
2. The Old Covenant's sanctuary and sacrifices 9:1–10
3. The New Covenant's sanctuary and sacrifices 9:11—10:18

III. The superiority of the walk of faith 10:19—13:25

A. A call to full assurance of faith 10:19—11:40
1. A call to steadfastness of faith 10:19–39
   (Fourth warning: against turning back 10:26–39)
2. A description of faith 11:1–3
3. Heroes of faith 11:4–40

B. The endurance of faith 12:1–29
1. Jesus' endurance 12:1–4
2. The value of chastening 12:5–24
   (Fifth warning: against refusing God 12:25–29)

C. Admonitions to love 13:1–17
1. Love in the social realm 13:1–6
2. Love in the religious realm 13:7–17

D. Conclusion 13:18–25

God's Supreme Revelation

GOD, who [1]at various times and
[a]in various ways spoke in time
past to the fathers by the prophets,
2 has in these last days spoken to us
by *His* Son, whom He has appointed
heir of all things, through whom also
He made the [1]worlds;
3 [a]who being the brightness of *His*
glory and the express [b]image of His
person, and [c]upholding all things by
the word of His power, [d]when He had
[1]by Himself [2]purged [3]our *sins, [e]sat
down at the right hand of the Majesty
on high,
4 having become so much better than
the *angels, as [a]He has by inheritance
obtained a more excellent name than
they.

The Son Exalted Above Angels

5 For to which of the angels did He
ever say:

[a]"*You are My Son,*
Today I have begotten You"?

And again:

[b]"*I will be to Him a Father,*
And He shall be to Me a Son"?

6 But when He again brings [a]the firstborn into the world, He says:

[b]"*Let all the angels of God *worship*
Him."

7 And of the angels He says:

[a]"*Who makes His angels spirits*
And His **ministers** *a flame of*
fire."

CHAPTER 1

1 [a]Num. 12:6, 8 [1]Or *in many portions*
2 [1]Or *ages*, Gr. *aiones*, aeons
3 [a]John 1:14 [b]2 Cor. 4:4 [c]Col. 1:17 [d][Heb. 7:27] [e]Ps. 110:1 [1]NU omits *by Himself* [2]*cleansed* [3]NU omits *our* *See WW at John 1:29.
4 [a][Phil. 2:9, 10] *See WW at Matt. 4:11.
5 [a]Ps. 2:7 [b]2 Sam. 7:14
6 [a][Rom. 8:29] [b]Deut. 32:43, LXX, DSS; Ps. 97:7 *See WW at Rev. 4:10.
7 [a]Ps. 104:4

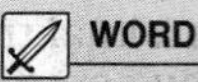

WORD WEALTH

1:7 ministers, *leitourgos* (lie-toorg-oss); Strong's *#3011:* From *laos,* "people," and

---

1:1 God has spoken to and through **the prophets in various ways,** such as dreams (Dan. 2:3), visions (Ezek. 8:4; 11:24), angels (Zech. 1:9), a burning bush (Ex. 3:4), *and direct speech (Gen. 12:1).*

1:2, 3 The writer describes the sevenfold excellencies of God's Son through whom He now speaks. **By** can be translated "in." Christ did not merely speak the **word** of God; He was the Word.

1:4–14 Christ is **better than the angels** because He is the eternal Son of God and the glorified and exalted Man.

1:6 Some view the title **firstborn** as a reference to the Incarnation, and others to the Second Coming. More likely, it refers to Christ's position of preeminence.

1:7–9 The writer contrasts the transitory ministerial and creaturely offices of the angels (see Ps. 104:4) with the eternal reign of **the Son** as divine Sovereign (see Ps. 45:6, 7). **Spirits** (v. 7) may also be translated "winds." Although angels occupy a high place as God's **ministers,** they are as dependent and perishable as the forces of nature.

ergon, "work"; hence, working for the people. The word first denoted someone who rendered public service at his own expense, then generally signified a public servant, a minister. In the NT it is used of earthly rulers (Rom. 13:6); the apostle Paul (Rom. 15:16); Epaphroditus, who attended to Paul's needs (Phil. 2:25); angels (Heb. 1:7); and Christ (Heb. 8:2).

8 But to the Son *He says:*

[a]*"Your throne, O God, is forever*
and ever;
A [1]*scepter of righteousness is the*
scepter of Your kingdom.
9 *You have* **loved righteousness*
and hated lawlessness;
Therefore God, Your God,
[a]*has anointed You*
With the oil of gladness more
than Your **companions."*

10 And:

[a]*"You,* LORD, *in the beginning laid*
the foundation of the earth,
And the heavens are the work of
Your hands.
11 [a]*They will perish, but You remain;*
And [b]*they will all grow old like*
a garment;
12 *Like a cloak You will fold them*
up,
And they will be changed.
But You are the [a]*same,*
And Your years will not fail."

13 But to which of the angels has He ever said:

[a]*"Sit at My right hand,*
Till I make Your enemies Your
footstool"?

14 [a]Are they not all ministering spirits sent forth to minister for those who will [b]inherit salvation?

8 [a]Ps. 45:6, 7 [1]A ruler's staff **9** [a]Is. 61:1, 3 *See WW at John 3:16. • See WW at Heb. 3:14. **10** [a]Ps. 102:25–27 **11** [a][Is. 34:4] [b]Is. 50:9; 51:6; Heb. 8:13 **12** [a]Heb. 13:8 **13** [a]Ps. 110:1; Matt. 22:44; Heb. 1:3 **14** [a]Ps. 103:20; Dan. 7:10 [b]Rom. 8:17

CHAPTER 2

1 [1]*all the more careful attention* *See WW at 2 Cor. 2:4. **2** [a]Deut. 33:2; Acts 7:53; Gal. 3:19 [b]Num. 15:30 [1]*retribution* or *penalty* **3** [a]Heb. 10:28 [b]Matt. 4:17 [c]Mark 16:20; Luke 1:2; 1 John 1:1 *See WW at John 6:68. • See WW at Mark 16:20. **4** [a]Mark 16:20 [b]Acts 2:22, 43; 2 Cor. 12:2 [c]1 Cor. 12:4, 7, 11; Eph. 4:7 [d]Eph. 1:5, 9 [1]*distributions* *See WW at Acts 15:12. **5** [a][2 Pet. 3:13] **6** [a]Job 7:17; Ps. 8:4–6

KINGDOM DYNAMICS

1:14 Ministering Spirits, ANGELS. Surprisingly enough, there are more direct references to angels in the NT than in the OT. A careful study will reveal that the NT activity of angels usually revolves around the ministry of Jesus and the establishment of His church on Earth. They "minister" (Greek *diakonia*), referring to their "serviceable labor, assistance." They are ministering spirits, or heavenly assistants, who are continually active today in building the body of Christ—advancing the ministry of Jesus and the building of His church.

(Rev. 12:7, 9/Is. 6:2) M.H.

Do Not Neglect Salvation

2 Therefore we must give [1]the *more earnest heed to the things we have heard, lest we drift away. **2**
2 For if the word [a]spoken through
angels proved steadfast, and [b]every
transgression and disobedience received a just [1]reward,
3 [a]how shall we escape if we neglect
so great a salvation, [b]which at the first
began to be spoken by the *Lord, and
was [c]confirmed* to us by those who
heard *Him,*
4 [a]God also bearing witness [b]both
with signs and *wonders, with various
miracles, and [c]gifts[1] of the Holy Spirit,
[d]according to His own will?

The Son Made Lower than Angels

5 For He has not put [a]the world to
come, of which we speak, in subjection
to angels.
6 But one testified in a certain place,
saying:

[a]*"What is man that You are mindful*
of him,
Or the son of man that You take
care of him?

1:10–12 Christ is presented as the Creator of **the heavens** and **the earth,** and as the immutable One (see Ps. 102:25–27).
1:13, 14 The superiority of Christ is evident in His enthronement (Ps. 110:1), while **all** the angels are but ministers who serve both Christ and the saints. See, for example, 2 Kin. 6:15–17; Ps. 91:11; 103:20, 21; Matt. 4:11.
2:1–4 See section 2 of Truth-In-Action at the end of Heb.
2:1 Therefore: Because of the greatness of Christ, Christians must be careful lest they **drift away** from what He has spoken. The figure is that of a ship drifting past its safe anchorage. Believers are to take heed lest adverse doctrine sweep them away from their Christian convictions.
2:2 The word spoken through angels refers to the Mosaic Law, which the angels mediated (see Deut. 33:2; Ps. 68:17; Acts 7:53; Gal. 3:19).
2:3, 4 The author argues from the lesser to the greater. If disobedience to a revelation transmitted by angels was severely punished, indifference to the **salvation** brought by Christ receives even greater punishment. The greatness of salvation is confirmed by three facts: it was **spoken by the Lord;** it **was confirmed** by the apostles; it was attested by the ministry **of the Holy Spirit** through **miracles** and spiritual **gifts** (see 1 Cor. 12:8–11). It is an age-long expectation that such manifestations of Christ's glory will be ministered by the Holy Spirit in confirming the spread of the gospel (Mark 16:20; 1 Cor. 2:4).
2:5–9 God has purposed men and not angels to be sovereigns of the created order. **The world to come** is the new eternal order inaugurated by the enthronement of Christ which is to be consummated at His return.

7 *You have made him [1]a little lower*
than the angels;
You have crowned him with glory
and honor,
[2]*And set him over the works of*
Your hands.
8 [a]*You have put all things in*
subjection under his feet."

For in that He put all in subjection under him, He left nothing *that is* not put
under him. But now [b]we do not yet see
all things put under him.
9 But we see *Jesus, [a]who was made
[1]a little lower than the angels, for the
suffering of death [b]crowned with glory
and honor, that He, by the *grace of
God, might *taste death [c]for everyone.

Bringing Many Sons to Glory

10 For it was fitting for Him, [a]for
whom *are* all things and by whom *are*
all things, in bringing many sons to
glory, to make the captain of their salvation [b]perfect* through sufferings.
11 For [a]both He who [1]sanctifies and
those who are being *sanctified [b]*are*
all of one, for which reason [c]He is not
ashamed to call them brethren,
12 saying:

[a]*"I will declare Your name to My*
brethren;
In the midst of the assembly I will
sing praise to You."

KINGDOM DYNAMICS

2:11, 12 Praise Releases the Spirit of Prophecy, PRAISE PATHWAY. This text quotes the messianic prophecy in Ps. 22:22, showing how the Spirit of the Christ fills the NT church, and how Christ identifies Himself so closely with His people when they sing praises. As they do, two important things happen: 1) He joins in the song Himself, and 2) this praise releases the spirit of prophecy. The latter is in the words "I will declare Your name to My brethren." As we joyfully sing praise to our God, Christ comes to flood our minds with the glory of the Father's character ("name"). There is no doubt about it—the praises of the people in the church service release the spirit of prophetic revelation—the magnifying of God through Jesus Christ. Thus, praise introduces edification, exhortation, and comfort to bless the whole body.

(Eph. 5:18, 19/Heb. 13:10–15) C.G.

13 And again:

[a]*"I will put My trust in Him."*

And again:

[b]*"Here am I and the children whom*
God has given Me."

14 Inasmuch then as the children have 1
partaken of flesh and blood, He
[a]Himself likewise *shared in the same,
[b]that through death He might destroy
him who had the *power of [c]death, that
is, the devil,
15 and release those who [a]through
fear of death were all their lifetime subject to bondage.
16 For indeed He does not [1]give aid to
angels, but He does [2]give aid to the
seed of Abraham.
17 Therefore, in all things He had
[a]to be made like *His* brethren, that He
might be [b]a *merciful and faithful High
Priest in things *pertaining* to God, to
make propitiation for the sins of the
people.
18 [a]For in that He Himself has suffered, being [1]tempted, He is able to aid
those who are tempted.

7 [1]Or *for a little while* [2]NU, M omit the rest of v. 7.
8 [a]Matt. 28:18 [b]Ps. 8:6; 1 Cor. 15:25, 27
9 [a]Phil. 2:7–9; Heb. 1:9 [b]Acts 2:33; 3:13; 1 Pet. 1:21 [c]Is. 53:12; [John 3:16] [1]Or *for a little while* *See WW at Phil. 4:23. • See WW at 2 Cor. 12:9. • See WW at John 8:52.
10 [a]Col. 1:16 [b]Heb. 5:8, 9; 7:28 *See WW at 1 John 2:5.
11 [a]Heb. 10:10 [b]Acts 17:26 [c]Matt. 28:10 [1]*sets apart* *See WW at John 10:36.
12 [a]Ps. 22:22
13 [a]2 Sam. 22:3; Is. 8:17 [b]Is. 8:18
14 [a]John 1:14 [b]Col. 2:15 [c][1 Cor. 15:54–57]; 2 Tim. 1:10 *See WW at 1 Cor. 9:10. • See WW at 1 Tim. 6:16.
15 [a]Ps. 68:18; Is. 42:7; 45:13; 49:9; 61:1; [Luke 1:74]
16 [1]Or *take on the nature of* [2]Or *take on*
17 [a]Phil. 2:7; Heb. 2:14 [b][Heb. 4:15; 5:1–10] *See WW at Matt. 5:7.
18 [a][Heb. 4:15, 16] [1]*tested*

2:8, 9 Instead of assuming his intended dominion over creation, man had become a slave, held in bondage by death and Satan. So the eternal Son of God appeared in history on Earth as **Jesus** the Man to provide a way of escape from bondage, access to God's presence, and an entrance into man's intended glory. Jesus the Man, exalted in glory at God's right hand, occupies the position of dominion intended for men, with everything **put,** or to be put, **in subjection under his feet** (v. 8).

2:10 The author emphasizes the genuine humanity of Jesus. The path that He trod as the suffering Redeemer was **fitting,** *for thereby* He was made **perfect.** This does not mean that Jesus had moral shortcomings, but that He became perfect or complete as an all-sufficient Savior. Only by suffering temptation and death did He qualify as our **captain** or leader who has gone ahead of us to open the way of **salvation.** See 2:14, 17.

2:11–13 There is a profound unity between Jesus and those He saves. We are **brethren** because in physical birth Jesus shares our descent from Adam, and in the new birth believers become members of the family of God.

2:14–18 See section 1 of Truth-In-Action at the end of Heb.

2:14, 15 The ultimate purpose of Christ's Incarnation was the destruction of **the devil** and deliverance from the **fear of death** (see 1 Cor. 15:54–57). The destruction of Satan does not mean that he is annihilated, but that his power is curbed in the lives of those committed to Christ.

2:16 Jesus took to Himself the nature of humanity, not that of angels (see marginal note).

2:17 Since a **High Priest** must be one with the people in order to represent them, the Incarnation was indispensable to the atoning work of Jesus.

2:18 Temptation was an exceedingly painful experience for the sinless Son of God. Since He knows all that temptation involves (see 4:15), He empathizes as He enables us to overcome.

The Son Was Faithful

2 3 Therefore, holy brethren, *partakers of the heavenly calling, consider the *Apostle and High Priest of
our confession, Christ Jesus,
2 who was faithful to Him who appointed Him, as [a]Moses also *was faith-
ful in all His house.
3 For this One has been counted worthy of more glory than Moses, inasmuch as [a]He who built the house has
more honor than the house.
4 For every house is built by someone, but [a]He who built all things *is*
God.
5 [a]And Moses indeed *was* faithful in
all His house as [b]a servant, [c]for a *testimony of those things which would be
spoken *afterward,*
1 6 but Christ as [a]a Son over His own
house, [b]whose house we are [c]if we
hold fast the confidence and the rejoicing of the hope [1]firm to the end.

Be Faithful

7 Therefore, as [a]the Holy Spirit
says:

[b]*"Today, if you will hear His voice,*
8 *Do not harden your *hearts as in*
the rebellion,
In the day of trial in the
wilderness,
9 *Where your fathers tested Me,*
tried Me,
And saw My works forty years.
10 *Therefore I was angry with that*
generation,
And said, 'They always go astray
in their heart,
And they have not known My
ways.'
11 *So I swore in My wrath,*
'They shall not enter My rest.'"

CHAPTER 3

1 *See WW at Heb. 3:14. • See WW at 1 Cor. 12:28.
2 [a]Ex. 40:16; Num. 12:7; Heb. 3:5
3 [a]Zech. 6:12, 13
4 [a][Eph. 2:10]
5 [a]Ex. 40:16; Num. 12:7; Heb. 3:2 [b]Ex. 14:31; Num. 12:7 [c]Deut. 18:15, 18, 19 *See WW at Rev. 15:5.
6 [a]Ps. 2:7; 110:4; Heb. 1:2 [b][1 Cor. 3:16]; 1 Tim. 3:15 [c][Matt. 10:22] [1]NU omits *firm to the end*
7 [a]Acts 1:16 [b]Ps. 95:7–11; Heb. 3:15; 4:7
8 *See WW at Rev. 2:23.
13 [1]*encourage*
15 [a]Ps. 95:7, 8
16 [a]Num. 14:2, 11, 30; Deut. 1:35, 36, 38
17 [a]Num. 14:22, 23
18 [a]Num. 14:30
19 [a]Num. 14:1–39; 1 Cor. 10:11, 12

CHAPTER 4

1 [a]2 Cor. 6:1; [Gal. 5:4]; Heb. 12:15 *See WW at Acts 13:32. • See WW at Luke 22:35.

12 Beware, brethren, lest there be in
any of you an evil heart of unbelief in
departing from the living God;
13 but [1]exhort one another daily, while
it is called *"Today,"* lest any of you be
hardened through the deceitfulness of
sin.
14 For we have become **partakers** of
Christ if we hold the beginning of our
confidence steadfast to the end,

WORD WEALTH

3:14 partakers, *metochos* (*met*-okh-oss); Strong's *#3353:* A participant, associate, sharer, partner, companion. The word is a combination of *meta,* "with," and *echo,* "to have."

15 while it is said:

[a]*"Today, if you will hear His voice,*
Do not harden your hearts as in
the rebellion."

Failure of the Wilderness Wanderers

16 [a]For who, having heard, rebelled?
Indeed, *was it* not all who came out
of Egypt, *led* by Moses?
17 Now with whom was He angry forty
years? *Was it* not with those who
sinned, [a]whose corpses fell in the wilderness?
18 And [a]to whom did He swear that
they would not enter His rest, but to
those who did not obey?
19 So we see that they could not enter
in because of [a]unbelief.

The Promise of Rest

4 Therefore, since a *promise re- 3
mains of entering His rest, [a]let us
fear lest any of you seem to have *come
short of it.

3:1 See section 2 of Truth-In-Action at the end of Heb.
3:1 Therefore: Consider all that Christ is and has done, as described in ch. 2. As **apostle,** Christ is God's representative to His people; as **High Priest,** He is their representative to God.
3:2–6 Christ is **worthy of more glory than Moses** because Moses was merely **a servant,** and himself a member of **the house.** In contrast, as God, Christ is both builder and Lord of the house. He is the fulfillment of all that Moses foreshadowed.
3:6 See section 1 of Truth-In-Action at the end of Heb.
3:7–11 The writer testifies to the inspiration of the OT by ascribing the quote from Ps. 95 to the **Holy Spirit.** Using the tragic failure of the Israelites in the wilderness as an example, he solemnly warns his readers of the peril of unbelief (see 1 Cor. 10:11). Their spirit of disobedience resulted in God's **wrath,** excluding them from entrance into the promised **rest** of Canaan (v. 11).
3:12, 13 Unbelief is caused by a **hardened** heart, which is caused by **the deceitfulness of sin.** The result is apostasy, **departing from the living God.** The writer views the abandonment of the Christian faith as turning away from God. Constant encouragement in the midst of a caring fellowship will help believers remain faithful.
3:14, 15 Partaking of Christ requires a continuance in faith, not merely a one-time experience.
4:1–10 See section 3 of Truth-In-Action at the end of Heb.
4:1 Israel's failure to enter Canaan becomes a solemn warning, lest professing Christians fail to enter the **rest** that God has promised. This rest is not entrance to Canaan, as it is in 3:18, but that historical event is a type of the rest to be enjoyed by Christians. Some commentators view rest as a future heavenly rest, while others feel that the term describes the present experience of the believer who has fully surrendered to the lordship of Christ and is totally controlled by the Holy Spirit.

2 For indeed the gospel was preached to us as well as to them; but the word which they heard did not profit them, [1]not being mixed with faith in those who heard *it*.

3 For we who have believed do enter that rest, as He has said:

> [a]*"So I swore in My wrath,*
> *'They shall not enter My rest,' "*

although the works were finished from the foundation of the world.

4 For He has spoken in a certain place of the seventh *day* in this way: [a]*"And God rested on the seventh day from all His works"*;

5 and again in this *place*: [a]*"They shall not enter My rest."*

6 Since therefore it remains that some *must* enter it, and those to whom it was first preached did not enter because of disobedience,

7 again He designates a certain day, saying in David, *"Today,"* after such a long *time, as it has been said:

> [a]*"Today, if you will hear His voice,*
> *Do not harden your hearts."*

3 8 For if [1]Joshua had [a]given them rest, then He would not afterward have spoken of another day.

9 There remains therefore a rest for the people of God.

10 For he who has entered His rest has himself also ceased from his works as God *did* from His.

The Word Discovers Our Condition

11 [a]Let us therefore *be diligent to enter that rest, lest anyone fall according to the same example of disobedience.

1 12 For the word of God *is* [a]living and **powerful,** and [b]sharper than any [c]two-edged sword, piercing even to the division of soul and spirit, and of joints and marrow, and is [d]a discerner of the thoughts and intents of the heart.

13 [a]And there is no *creature hidden from His sight, but all things *are* [b]naked and open to the eyes of Him to whom we *must give* account.

2 [1]NU, M *since they were not united by faith with those who heeded it*
3 [a]Ps. 95:11; Heb. 3:11
4 [a]Gen. 2:2; Ex. 20:11; 31:17
5 [a]Ps. 95:11
7 [a]Ps. 95:7, 8 *See WW at Acts 1:7.
8 [a]Josh. 22:4 [1]Gr. *Jesus,* same as Heb. *Joshua*
11 [a]2 Pet. 1:10 *See WW at Gal. 2:10.
12 [a]Ps. 147:15 [b]Is. 49:2 [c]Eph. 6:17; Rev. 2:12 [d][John 12:48]; 1 Cor. 14:24, 25
13 [a]2 Chr. 16:9; Ps. 33:13–15; 90:8 [b]Job 26:6; Prov. 15:11 *See WW at Col. 1:15.

WORD WEALTH

4:12 powerful, *energes* (en-er-*gace*); Strong's *#1756:* Comparable in meaning to the English word "energetic," which stems from this word. *Energes,* used elsewhere only in 1 Cor. 16:9 and Philem. 6, denotes something at work, active, and effective. It is the opposite of *argos,* "idle," "inactive," "ineffective."

KINGDOM DYNAMICS

4:11–13 Understanding *Rhema* and *Logos,* FAITH'S CONFESSION. This text is among the foremost in understanding faith's call to "confess" the Word of God. The lesson relates to Israel's renunciation of God's promise, which resulted in a whole generation's dying in the wilderness and failing to possess the inheritance God intended for them. In this context, the Bible describes itself: "The word of God is living and powerful." The term for "word" here is the Greek word *logos,* which commonly indicates the expression of a complete idea and is used in referring to the Holy Scriptures. It contrasts with *rhema,* which generally refers to a word spoken or given. This recommends our understanding the difference between all the Bible and the single promise or promises the Holy Spirit may bring to our mind from the Word of God. When facing a situation of need, trial, or difficulty, the promises of God may become a *rhema* to you; that is, a weapon of the Spirit, "the word of God" (Eph. 6:17). Its authority is that this "word" comes from the Bible—God's Word—the completed *logos.* Its immediate significance is that He has "spoken" it to your soul by His Spirit and is calling forth faith just as He did from Israel when He pointed them toward their inheritance. Faith's confession receives God's "words" (*rhema*) and stands firm upon these promises. However, faith's confession is strong not in human willpower, but in the divine will revealed in the whole of the Scriptures—the Holy Bible—the *logos* (completed Word) from which the *rhema* (present "word of promise") has been received.

(Phil. 2:9–11/Heb. 11:13–16) R.H.

4:2 The mere hearing of the gospel is not enough; it must also be believed.

4:3, 4 The believing ones are those who enter His **rest** as *the un*believing Israelites failed to do. The works **finished from the foundation of the world** appear to be God's works of creation.

4:5–9 Through **David,** God promised another rest, which Israel failed to enjoy—the rest that is found in Christ.

4:8–11 See section 3 of Truth-In-Action at the end of Heb.

4:10 Just as God rested from His work of creation, the one who trusts in Christ rests in what God has done for him. He has ceased striving to achieve salvation by his own efforts, and in daily life has begun to learn a dependence upon the Holy Spirit's help.

4:11–14 Two great provisions encourage believers in their faith: 1) **the word of God,** which reveals whether a person is living a soulish or spiritual life; 2) the ministry of Christ our **great High Priest,** who is able to bring us into immediate fellowship with God.

4:12, 13 See section 1 of Truth-In-Action at the end of Heb.

Our Compassionate High Priest

1 **14** Seeing then that we have a great
[a]High Priest who has passed through
the heavens, Jesus the Son of God,
[b]let us hold fast *our* confession.
15 For [a]we do not have a High Priest
who cannot sympathize with our
weaknesses, but [b]was in all *points*
*tempted as *we are,* [c]*yet* without sin.
1 16 [a]Let us therefore come *boldly to
the throne of grace, that we may obtain
*mercy and find grace to help in time
of need.

Qualifications for High Priesthood

5 For every high priest taken from
among men [a]is appointed for men
in things *pertaining* to God, that he
may *offer both gifts and sacrifices for
sins.
2 He can [1]have compassion on those
who are ignorant and going astray,
since he himself is also subject to
[a]weakness.
3 Because of this he is required as for
the people, so also for [a]himself, to offer
sacrifices for sins.
4 And no man takes this honor to
himself, but he who is called by God,
just as [a]Aaron *was.*

A Priest Forever

5 [a]So also Christ did not glorify Himself to become High Priest, *but it* was
He who said to Him:

[b]*"You are My Son,*
Today I have begotten You."

6 As *He* also *says* in another *place:*

[a]*"You are a priest forever*
According to the order of
Melchizedek";

7 who, in the days of His flesh, when
He had [a]offered up prayers and supplications, [b]with vehement cries and tears
to Him [c]who was able to save Him
from death, and was heard [d]because
of His godly fear,
8 though He was a Son, *yet* He 3
learned [a]obedience* by the things
which He suffered.
9 And [a]having been perfected, He became the author of eternal salvation to
all who *obey Him,
10 called by God as High Priest [a]*"according to the order of Melchizedek,"*
11 of whom [a]we have much to say, and
hard to explain, since you have become
[b]dull of hearing.

Spiritual Immaturity

12 For though by this time you ought 4
to be teachers, you need *someone* to
teach you again the first principles of
the [1]oracles of God; and you have
come to need [a]milk and not solid food.
13 For everyone who *partakes *only* of
milk *is* unskilled in the word of righteousness, for he is [a]a babe.
14 But solid food belongs to those who
are [1]of *full age, *that is,* those who by
reason of [2]use have their senses exercised [a]to discern both good and evil.

The Peril of Not Progressing

6 Therefore, [a]leaving* the discussion
of the elementary *principles* of

14 [a]Heb. 2:17; 7:26 [b]Heb. 10:23
15 [a]Is. 53:3–5 [b]Luke 22:28 [c]2 Cor. 5:21 *See WW at Rev. 2:10.
16 [a][Eph. 2:18] *See WW at Acts 4:31. • See WW at 2 Tim. 1:16.

CHAPTER 5

1 [a]Heb. 2:17; 8:3 *See WW at Heb. 9:28.
2 [a]Heb. 7:28 [1]*deal gently with*
3 [a]Lev. 9:7; 16:6
4 [a]Ex. 28:1
5 [a]John 8:54 [b]Ps. 2:7
6 [a]Ps. 110:4
7 [a]Matt. 26:39, 42, 44 [b]Ps. 22:1 [c]Matt. 26:53 [d]Matt. 26:39
8 [a]Phil. 2:8 *See WW at 2 Cor. 10:5.
9 [a]Heb. 2:10 *See WW at Rom. 6:17.
10 [a]Ps. 110:4
11 [a][John 16:12] [b][Matt. 13:15]
12 [a]1 Cor. 3:1–3 [1]*sayings, Scriptures*
13 [a]Eph. 4:14 *See WW at 1 Cor. 9:10.
14 [a]Is. 7:15 [1]*mature* [2]*practice* *See WW at James 3:2.

CHAPTER 6

1 [a]Heb. 5:12

*See WW at Mark 1:20.

4:14 See section 1 of Truth-In-Action at the end of Heb.
4:15 A special encouragement to loyalty is the human sympathy of our great **High Priest.**
4:16 See section 1 of Truth-In-Action at the end of Heb.
4:16 **Come boldly** literally means "without reservation, with frankness, with full and open speech." We approach a **throne of grace,** not of judgment, obtaining **mercy** for the past and **grace** for the present and future.
5:1–4 The writer presents the qualifications and activities of the office of **high priest.** He must be a man with the same nature as those he represents, thus having a capacity for full fellow-feeling with them. His is a public office to which he is appointed as a representative of men to God. He offers both thanksgiving and propitiatory sacrifices. His intercession is full of **compassion, . . . since he himself is also subject to weakness.** Therefore, he must **offer *sacrifices*** for himself as well as for the people. (Christ had no need to purify Himself by sacrifices; see 7:27). He must be divinely chosen and appointed.
5:5–11 Jesus perfectly fulfilled the requirements of high priesthood. He was appointed by God; He experienced genuine humanity; He made a sacrifice for sin "once for all when He offered up Himself" (7:27); and He has an understanding sympathy for us.
5:6 The writer introduces the concept of a priesthood like that of **Melchizedek,** which he develops more fully in ch. 7.
5:7 The prayer of Jesus in Gethsemane was that the Father's will would be done (see Luke 22:42), and His prayer was answered because of **godly fear,** that is, reverent submission to God's will.
5:8–10 See section 3 of Truth-In-Action at the end of Heb.
5:9 Jesus was **perfected,** not in a moral sense since He always possessed moral perfection, but in the sense of being qualified as **the author of eternal salvation.** See note on 2:10.
5:12–14 See section 4 of Truth-In-Action at the end of Heb.
5:12, 13 Their slothful attitude of hearing had resulted in a lack of spiritual growth.
5:14 The more advanced teachings are adapted to mature believers, whose spiritual **senses** are able to discriminate between sound and unsound doctrine and between wholesome and unwholesome conduct.
6:1–3 The six doctrines mentioned are the foundational principles of the spiritual life. Foundations are not to be laid again but built upon. This cannot be done apart from dependence on the help of God.

Christ, let us go on to [1]perfection, not
laying again the foundation of repentance from [b]dead works and of faith
toward God,
2 [a]of the doctrine of baptisms, [b]of laying on of hands, [c]of *resurrection
of the dead, [d]and of eternal *judgment.
3 And this [1]we will do if God permits.
4 For *it is* impossible for those who
were once enlightened, and have
*tasted [a]the heavenly gift, and [b]have
become *partakers of the *Holy Spirit,
5 and have tasted the good *word
of God and the powers of the age to
come,
6 [1]if they fall away, to renew them
again to repentance, [a]since they crucify again for themselves the Son of
God, and put *Him* to an open shame.

KINGDOM DYNAMICS

6:4–6 4. If I Sin, Will I Lose My Salvation?, SPIRITUAL ANSWERS. For the answer to this and other probing questions about God and the power life in His kingdom, see the study article "Spiritual Answers to Hard Questions," which begins on page 1996. P.R.

7 For the earth which drinks in the
rain that often comes upon it, and
bears herbs useful for those by whom
it is cultivated, [a]receives blessing from
God;
8 [a]but if it bears thorns and briers, *it*
is rejected and near to being cursed,
whose end *is* to be burned.

A Better Estimate

9 But, beloved, we are *confident of
better things concerning you, yes,
things that accompany salvation,
though we speak in this manner.
10 For [a]God *is* not unjust to forget
[b]your work and [1]labor of love which
you have shown toward His name, *in*
that you have [c]ministered to the saints,
and do minister.
4 11 And we *desire that each one of you

1 [b][Heb. 9:14] [1]*maturity*
2 [a]Acts 19:3–5 [b][Acts 8:17] [c]Acts 17:31 [d]Acts 24:25 *See WW at Acts 23:6. • See WW at Rev. 20:4.
3 [1]M *let us do*
4 [a][John 4:10] [b][Gal. 3:2, 5] *See WW at John 8:52. • See WW at Heb. 3:14. • See WW at Acts 7:33.
5 *See WW at Matt. 4:4.
6 [a]Heb. 10:29 [1]Or *and have fallen away*
7 [a]Ps. 65:10
8 [a]Is. 5:6
9 *See WW at 2 Thess. 3:4.
10 [a]Rom. 3:4 [b]1 Thess. 1:3 [c]Rom. 15:25 [1]NU omits *labor of*
11 [a]Col. 2:2 *See WW at Matt. 13:17. • See WW at 1 Thess. 1:3.
12 [a]Heb. 10:36 [1]*lazy*
13 [a]Gen. 22:16, 17 *See WW at Acts 7:5.
14 [a]Gen. 22:16, 17 *See WW at Luke 6:28.
15 [a]Gen. 12:4; 21:5
16 [a]Ex. 22:11
17 [a]Heb. 11:9 [b]Rom. 11:29 [1]*unchangeableness of His purpose* [2]*guaranteed*
18 [a]Num. 23:19 [b][Col. 1:5] [1]*unchangeable* [2]M omits *might* *See WW at Acts 9:31.
19 [a]Lev. 16:2, 15
20 [a][Heb. 4:14] [b]Heb. 3:1; 5:10, 11

show the same diligence [a]to the full assurance of *hope until the end,
12 that you do not become [1]sluggish,
but imitate those who through faith
and **patience** [a]inherit the promises.

WORD WEALTH

6:12 patience, *makrothumia* (mak-roth-oo-*mee*-ah); Strong's *#3115:* From *makros,* "long," and *thumos,* "temper." The word denotes lenience, forbearance, fortitude, patient endurance, longsuffering. Also included in *makrothumia* is the ability to endure persecution and ill-treatment. It describes a person who has the power to exercise revenge but instead exercises restraint. This quality is a fruit of the Spirit (Gal. 5:22).

God's Infallible Purpose in Christ

13 For when God made a *promise to
Abraham, because He could swear by
no one greater, [a]He swore by Himself,
14 saying, [a]*"Surely blessing I will*
**bless you, and multiplying I will mul-*
tiply you."
15 And so, after he had patiently endured, he obtained the [a]promise.
16 For men indeed swear by the
greater, and [a]an oath for confirmation
is for them an end of all dispute.
17 Thus God, determining to show
more abundantly to [a]the heirs of promise [b]the [1]immutability of His counsel,
[2]confirmed *it* by an oath,
18 that by two [1]immutable things, in
which it *is* impossible for God to
[a]lie, we [2]might have strong *consolation, who have fled for refuge
to lay hold of the hope [b]set before
us.
19 This *hope* we have as an anchor of
the soul, both sure and steadfast,
[a]and which enters the *Presence* behind
the veil,
20 [a]where the forerunner has entered
for us, *even* Jesus, [b]having become
High Priest forever according to the order of Melchizedek.

6:4–6 The language of vv. 4 and 5 clearly describes those who have experienced the saving grace of God, and the language of v. 6 denotes a complete disowning of Christ, a deliberate and decisive abandonment of the Christian faith. The people described are not backsliders but apostates. They have not merely fallen into sin but have denounced Christ. They have become as those who crucified Jesus.

6:7, 8 The illustration depicts the condemnation of those who turn away from Jesus Christ.

6:9–12 The writer expresses confidence that his readers will remain steadfast, thus tempering his harsh warning with warm encouragement. Faith looks to the One who promises; hope looks to the things promised (vv. 10, 11).

6:11, 12 See section 4 of Truth-In-Action at the end of Heb.

6:13–17 We have in God and in His expressed purpose to bless us in Christ grounds for confident expectation. The fulfillment of His promise to Abraham provides assurance that He is certain to perform what He promises.

6:18 God's confirmation of His promise by His oath and covenant removes all doubt about its certainty.

6:19, 20 An anchor is only as secure as that to which it is fastened.

The King of Righteousness

7 For this [a]Melchizedek, king of Salem, priest of the Most High God, who met Abraham returning from the slaughter of the kings and blessed him,
2 to whom also Abraham gave a tenth part of all, first being translated "king of *righteousness," and then also king of Salem, meaning "king of peace,"
3 without father, without mother, without genealogy, having neither beginning of days nor end of *life, but made like the Son of God, remains a priest continually.
4 Now *consider how great this man *was,* to whom even the patriarch Abraham gave a tenth of the [1]spoils.
5 And indeed [a]those who are of the sons of Levi, who receive the priesthood, have a commandment to receive tithes from the people according to the law, that is, from their brethren, though they have come from the loins of Abraham;
6 but he whose genealogy is not derived from them received tithes from Abraham [a]and blessed [b]him who had the promises.
7 Now beyond all contradiction the lesser is blessed by the better.
8 Here mortal men receive tithes, but there he *receives them,* [a]of whom it is *witnessed that he lives.
9 Even Levi, who receives tithes, paid tithes through Abraham, so to speak,
10 for he was still in the loins of his father when Melchizedek met him.

Need for a New Priesthood

11 [a]Therefore, if perfection were through the Levitical priesthood (for under it the people received the law), what further need *was there* that *another priest should rise according to the order of Melchizedek, and not be called according to the order of Aaron?
12 For the priesthood being changed, of necessity there is also a change of the law.
13 For He of whom these things are spoken *belongs to another tribe, from which no man has [1]officiated at the altar.
14 For *it is* evident that [a]our Lord arose from [b]Judah, of which tribe Moses spoke nothing concerning [1]priesthood.
15 And it is yet far more evident if, in the likeness of Melchizedek, there arises another priest
16 who has come, not according to the law of a fleshly commandment, but according to the power of an endless life.
17 For [1]He testifies:

[a]"You are a priest forever
According to the order of
Melchizedek."

18 For on the one hand there is an annulling of the former commandment because of [a]its weakness and unprofitableness,
19 for [a]the law made nothing [1]perfect; on the other hand, *there is the* bringing in of [b]a better hope, through which [c]we draw near to God.

Greatness of the New Priest

20 And inasmuch as *He was* not *made priest* without an oath
21 (for they have become priests without an oath, but He with an oath by Him who said to Him:

[a]"The LORD has sworn
And will not relent,
'You are a priest [1]forever
According to the order of
Melchizedek'"),

CHAPTER 7

1 [a]Gen.14:18–20; Heb. 7:6 **2** *See WW at 2 Tim. 4:8. **3** *See WW at 1 John 5:20. **4** [1]*plunder* *See WW at John 20:14. **5** [a]Num. 18:21–26; 2 Chr. 31:4 **6** [a]Gen. 14:19, 20 [b][Rom. 4:13] **8** [a]Heb. 5:6; 6:20; [Rev. 1:18] *See WW at Acts 26:22. **11** [a][Rom. 7:7–14]; Gal. 2:21; Heb. 7:18; 8:7 *See WW at Acts 4:12. **13** [1]*served* *See WW at 1 Cor. 9:10. **14** [a]Gen. 49:8–10; Num. 24:17; Is. 1:1; Mic. 5:2; Matt. 1:3; 2:6; Rev. 5:5 [b]Matt. 1:2 [1]NU *priests* **17** [a]Ps. 110:4; Heb. 5:6; 6:20; 7:21 [1]NU *it is testified* **18** [a][Rom. 8:3]; Gal. 3:21; Heb. 7:11 **19** [a][Acts 13:39]; Rom. 3:20; 7:7; Gal. 2:16; 3:21; Heb. 9:9; 10:1 [b]Heb. 6:18, 19 [c]Lam. 3:57; Rom. 5:2; [Eph. 2:18]; Heb. 4:16; James 4:8 [1]*complete* **21** [a]Ps. 110:4; Heb. 5:6; 7:17 [1]NU ends the quotation after *forever.*

7:1, 2 Mentioned only twice in the OT (Gen. 14:18–20; Ps. 110:4), **Melchizedek** is a type of Christ in His high priestly ministry.

7:3 Like Melchizedek, Jesus Christ is a universal **priest,** and He is at once both Priest and King. The silence concerning Melchizedek's ancestry, priestly pedigree, birth, and death illustrates the eternal and changeless priesthood of Christ.

7:4–7 Melchizedek is greater than the Levitical priests, even though they received tithes from the descendants of **Abraham.** The fact that Abraham paid **tithes** to Melchizedek, and was blessed by him, establishes the superiority of Melchizedek.

7:8 The Levitical priests, as **mortal men,** were subject to death, but no mention is made of Mechizedek's death. Thus he is a true typical representative of Christ who is alive forevermore.

7:9, 10 Abraham represented all Israel when he paid tithes to **Melchizedek.**

7:13, 14 The fact that Christ was born of the tribe of Judah, not Levi, emphasizes the inauguration of a new priestly order.

7:15–17 The Greek word here for **another** is not *allos,* which means another of the same kind, but *heteros,* another of a totally different order. The priesthood of Christ supersedes the Levitical priesthood.

7:18, 19 The first covenant proved weak and useless in providing either full access to God's presence or full fitness for His company. Therefore, it had to be annulled and a new and **better hope** introduced to succeed where it had failed.

7:20–22 Jesus' priesthood supersedes Aaron's because His was established by God's solemn **oath.** Men do not give their oath in trivial matters.

22 by so much more Jesus has become
a [1]surety of a [a]better *covenant.
23 Also there were many priests, because they were prevented by death
from continuing.
24 But He, because He continues forever, has an unchangeable priesthood.
25 Therefore He is also [a]able* to save
[1]to the uttermost those who come to
God through Him, since He always
lives [b]to **make intercession** for them.

WORD WEALTH

7:25 make intercession, *entunchano* (en-toong-*khan*-oh); Strong's *#1793:* To fall in with, meet with in order to converse. From this description of a casual encounter, the word progresses to the idea of pleading with a person on behalf of another, although at times the petition may be against another (Acts 25:24; Rom. 11:2).

26 For such a High Priest was fitting
for us, [a]*who is* holy, [1]harmless, undefiled, separate from sinners, [b]and
has become higher than the heavens;
27 who does not need daily, as those
high priests, to offer up sacrifices, first
for His [a]own sins and then for the people's, for this He did once for all when
He offered up Himself.
28 For the law appoints as high priests
men who have weakness, but the word
of the oath, which came after the law,
appoints the Son who has been perfected forever.

The New Priestly Service

8 Now *this is* the main point of the things we are saying: We have
such a High Priest, [a]who is seated at
the right hand of the throne of the Majesty in the heavens,
2 a *Minister of [a]the [1]sanctuary and
of [b]the true tabernacle which the Lord
erected, and not man.
3 For [a]every high priest is appointed
to offer both gifts and sacrifices. Therefore [b]*it is* necessary that this One also
have something to offer.
4 For if He were on earth, He would
not be a priest, since there are priests
who offer the gifts according to the
law;
5 who serve [a]the copy and [b]shadow
of the heavenly things, as Moses was
divinely instructed when he was about
to make the tabernacle. For He said,
[c]*"See that you make all things according to the pattern shown you on the
mountain."*
6 But now [a]He has obtained a more
excellent *ministry, inasmuch as He is
also *Mediator of a [b]better covenant,
which was established on better promises.

A New Covenant

7 For if that [a]first *covenant* had been
faultless, then no place would have
been sought for a second.
8 Because finding fault with them, He
says: [a]*"Behold, the days are coming,
says the LORD, when I will make a *new
covenant with the house of Israel and
with the house of Judah—*
9 *"not according to the covenant that
I made with their fathers in the day
when I took them by the hand to lead
them out of the land of Egypt; because
they did not continue in My covenant,
and I disregarded them, says the LORD.*
10 *"For this is the covenant that I will
make with the house of Israel after
those days, says the [a]LORD: I will put
My laws in their *mind and write them
on their hearts; and [b]I will be their
God, and they shall be My people.*
11 [a]*"None of them shall teach his
neighbor, and none his brother, saying,
'Know the [b]LORD,' for all shall know
Me, from the least of them to the greatest of them.*
12 *"For I will be merciful to their
unrighteousness, [a]and their sins*

7:22 [a]Heb. 8:6 [1]*guarantee* *See WW at Mark 14:24. **25** [a]Jude 24 [b]Rom. 8:34; 1 Tim. 2:5; Heb. 9:24; 1 John 2:1 [1]*completely* or *forever* *See WW at Jude 24. **26** [a][2 Cor. 5:21]; Heb. 4:15 [b]Eph. 1:20 [1]*innocent* **27** [a]Lev. 9:7; 16:6; Heb. 5:3

CHAPTER 8

1 [a]Ps. 68:18; 110:1; Eph. 1:20; Col. 3:1; Heb. 2:17; 3:1; 10:12 **2** [a]Heb. 9:8, 12 [b]Heb. 9:11, 24 [1]Lit. *holies* *See WW at Heb. 1:7. **3** [a][Rom. 4:25; 5:6, 8; Gal. 2:20; Eph. 5:2]; Heb. 5:1; 8:4 [b][Eph. 5:2; Heb. 9:14] **5** [a]Heb. 9:23, 24 [b]Col. 2:17; Heb. 10:1 [c]Ex. 25:40 **6** [a][2 Cor. 3:6–8] [b][Luke 22:20]; Heb. 7:22 *See WW at Luke 1:23. • See WW at Gal. 3:19. **7** [a]Ex. 3:8; 19:5 **8** [a]Jer. 31:31–34 *See WW at 2 Cor. 5:17. **10** [a]Jer. 31:33; Rom. 11:27; Heb. 10:16 [b]Zech. 8:8 *See WW at Mark 12:30. **11** [a]Is. 54:13; John 6:45; [1 John 2:27] [b]Jer. 31:34 **12** [a]Rom. 11:27

7:23–25 Jesus' priestly ministrations are endless and changeless, enabling Him to bring a salvation that lacks nothing.
7:28 Total salvation demands a perfect High Priest and a perfect sacrifice for sins.
8:1–6 The writer turns from the qualifications of Christ a High Priest to His actual atoning work. That work is so superior to the ministry of the Jewish priests that, by it, the old system is done away, replaced by the absolute, eternal, and perfect priesthood of Christ.
8:2 Jesus' ministry is performed in the true **sanctuary,** not of Earth, but of heaven. As Priest and King He occupies the place of supreme power (v. 1).
8:5, 6 The ministry of the **tabernacle** was only a type and symbol of the realities accomplished by Christ. Therefore, His ministry surpasses that of the Levitical priesthood as substance surpasses **shadow.**
8:7 The first covenant was entirely external. It set a standard but provided no power to keep it.
8:8–10 Jesus' ministry is performed under the covenant of God's grace, wrought within the **mind** and **hearts** of believers by the power of the Holy Spirit. Thus, God established a new personal covenant relationship with His people, based not on a compelling force from without, but on an impelling power from within.
8:11 In contrast to Israel's limited and impersonal revelation, under the New Covenant there will be complete, universal and immediate knowledge of God.
8:12, 13 Grace and mercy characterize the ***new covenant*** replacing the inadequate **first** covenant.

[1]*and their lawless deeds I will remem-*
ber no more."
13 [a]In that He says, *"A new covenant,"*
He has made the first obsolete. Now
what is becoming obsolete and growing old is ready to vanish away.

The Earthly Sanctuary

9 Then indeed, even the first *cov-*
enant had ordinances of divine service and [a]the earthly sanctuary.
2 For a tabernacle was prepared: the
first *part*, in which *was* the lampstand,
the table, and the *showbread, which
is called the [1]sanctuary;
3 [a]and behind the second veil, the
part of the tabernacle which is called
the Holiest of All,
4 which had the [a]golden censer and
[b]the ark of the covenant overlaid on
all sides with gold, in which *were*
[c]the golden pot that had the manna,
[d]Aaron's rod that budded, and [e]the
tablets of the covenant;
5 and [a]above it were the cherubim of
glory overshadowing the **mercy seat.**
Of these things we cannot now speak
in detail.

WORD WEALTH

9:5 mercy seat, ***hilasterion*** (hil-as-*tay*-ree-on); Strong's *#2435:* Although used only here and in Rom. 3:25 in the NT, the word is quite common in the Septuagint, where it primarily denotes the mercy seat, the lid of gold above the ark of the covenant. In this verse it has that meaning, indicating the place of atonement. The root meaning of *hilasterion* is that of appeasing and placating an offended god. Applied to the sacrifice of Christ in that regard, the word suggests that Christ's death was propitiatory, averting the wrath of God from the sinner.

Limitations of the Earthly Service

6 Now when these things had been
thus prepared, [a]the priests always
went into the first part of the tabernacle, performing *the services.*
7 But into the second part the high
priest *went* alone [a]once a year, not
without *blood, which he *offered for
[b]himself and *for* the people's sins *com-*
mitted in ignorance;
8 the Holy Spirit indicating this, that
[a]the way into the Holiest of All was
not yet made *manifest while the first
tabernacle was still standing.
9 It *was* symbolic for the present time
in which both gifts and sacrifices are
offered [a]which cannot make him who
performed the service perfect in regard
to the conscience—
10 *concerned* only with [a]foods and
drinks, [b]various [1]washings, [c]and
fleshly ordinances imposed until the
time of reformation.

The Heavenly Sanctuary

11 But Christ came *as* High Priest of 2
[a]the good things [1]to come, with the
greater and more perfect tabernacle
not made with hands, that is, not of
this creation.
12 Not [a]with the blood of goats and
calves, but [b]with His own blood He entered the Most Holy Place [c]once for all,
[d]having obtained eternal redemption.

KINGDOM DYNAMICS

9:12 Christ's Sacrifice, Permanent Relief, THE BLOOD. The Hebrew epistle contrasts the covenants of God through Moses and Christ. The Mosaic covenant provided animal sacrifices that brought temporary relief to man's guilt and demonstrated the lessons of God's justice. The covenant through Moses provided a bond in the blood of animals. These sacrifices, however, had to be repeated annually at the tabernacle, which was only symbolic of God's eternal, heavenly altar. However, Jesus Christ came into history as an eternal priest to offer an eternal sacrifice for sin. The shedding of His blood provided a permanent sacrifice and a permanent covenant bond between God and man. His blood was applied not merely to an earthly altar, but to the very altar of God in heaven, where once and for all it obtained redemption from sin for those who receive Him. The immutable bond that is established through the New Covenant in Christ's blood is the ultimate fulfillment of God's covenant-making nature.

(Is. 1:11/Gen. 3:21) C.S.

---

12 [1]NU omits *and their lawless deeds*
13 [a][2 Cor. 5:17]; Heb. 1:11

CHAPTER 9

1 [a]Ex. 25:8; [Heb. 8:2; 9:11, 24]
2 [1]*holy place,* lit. *holies* *See WW at Rom. 8:28.
3 [a]Ex. 26:31–35; 40:3
4 [a]Lev. 16:12 [b]Ex. 25:10 [c]Ex. 16:33 [d]Num. 17:1–10 [e]Ex. 25:16; 34:29; Deut. 10:2–5
5 [a]Ex. 25:17, 20; Lev. 16:2; 1 Kin. 8:7
6 [a]Num.18:2–6; 28:3
7 [a]Ex. 30:10; Lev. 16:34; Heb. 10:3 [b]Heb. 5:3 *See WW at 1 John 1:7. • See WW at Heb. 9:28.
8 [a][John 14:6; Heb. 10:20] *See WW at Col. 3:4.
9 [a][Gal. 3:21]; Heb. 7:19
10 [a]Lev. 11:2; Col. 2:16 [b]Num. 19:7 [c]Eph. 2:15 [1]Lit. *baptisms*
11 [a][Eph. 1:3–11]; Heb. 10:1 [1]NU *that have come*
12 [a]Heb. 10:4 [b]Is. 53:12; Eph. 1:7 [c]Zech. 3:9 [d][Dan. 9:24]

9:1–10 In order to demonstrate the superiority of the atoning work of Christ, the writer first shows the insufficiency of the Levitical system of worship. Even though the rituals of the ancient tabernacle were observed with dignity and glory, they failed to provide free access to the presence of God.
9:11–15 See section 2 of Truth-In-Action at the end of Heb.
9:11 Jesus introduced the ideal system toward which the old rituals pointed. His ministry took place, not in an earthly sanctuary, but in the sphere of heavenly realities.
9:12–14 Jesus offered as a sacrifice **His own blood.** If the sacrifice of animals could achieve ceremonial cleansing, **how much more** will the spiritual sacrifice of Christ cleanse the soul!

13 For if [a]the blood of bulls and goats
and [b]the ashes of a heifer, sprinkling
the unclean, [1]sanctifies for the [2]purify-
ing of the flesh,
14 how much more shall the blood of
Christ, who through the eternal Spirit
*offered Himself without [1]spot to God,
[a]cleanse your conscience from [b]dead
works [c]to serve the living God?
15 And for this reason [a]He is the *Mediator of the new covenant, by means
of death, for the *redemption of the
transgressions under the first covenant, that [b]those who are called may
receive the promise of the eternal inheritance.

The Mediator's Death Necessary

16 For where there *is* a testament,
there must also of necessity be the
death of the testator.
17 For [a]a testament *is* in force after
men are dead, since it has no power
at all while the testator lives.
18 [a]Therefore not even the first *covenant* was dedicated without blood.
19 For when Moses had spoken every
[1]precept to all the people according to
the law, [a]he took the blood of calves
and goats, [b]with water, scarlet wool,
and hyssop, and sprinkled both the
book itself and all the people,
20 saying, [a]*"This is the* [b]*blood of the
covenant which God has commanded
you."*
21 Then likewise [a]he sprinkled with
blood both the tabernacle and all the
vessels of the *ministry.
22 And according to the law almost all
things are [1]purified with blood, and
[a]without shedding of blood there is no
[2]**remission.**

WORD WEALTH

9:22 remission, *aphesis* (*af*-es-is); Strong's *#859:* From *aphiemi,* "to send away." The word signifies a release from bondage or imprisonment, dismissal, sending away, and forgiveness, with the added quality of canceling out all judgment, punishment, obligation, or debt.

Greatness of Christ's Sacrifice

23 Therefore *it was* necessary that
[a]the copies of the things in the heavens
should be [1]purified with these, but the
heavenly things themselves with better
sacrifices than these.
24 For [a]Christ has not entered the holy
places made with hands, *which are*
[1]copies of [b]the true, but into heaven
itself, now [c]to *appear in the presence
of God for us;
25 not that He should offer Himself often, as [a]the high priest enters the Most
Holy Place every year with blood of
another—
26 He then would have had to suffer
often since the foundation of the world;
but now, once at the end of the ages,
He has appeared to put away sin by
the sacrifice of Himself.
27 [a]And as it is appointed for men to
die once, [b]but after this the *judgment,
28 so [a]Christ was [b]**offered** once to bear
the sins [c]of many. To those who
[d]eagerly wait for Him He will appear
a second time, apart from sin, for salvation.

WORD WEALTH

9:28 offered, *prosphero* (pros-*fer*-oh); Strong's *#4374:* From *pros,* "toward," and *phero,* "to bring." In addition to the more literal sense of bringing or leading to (Matt. 4:24; 8:16; 9:2, 32), the word denotes an offering, whether of gifts, prayers, or sacrifices (Matt. 2:11; 5:24; Mark 1:44; Heb. 8:3).

Animal Sacrifices Insufficient

10 For the law, having a [a]shadow
of the good things to come, *and*
not the very image of the things,

13 [a]Lev. 16:14, 15; Heb. 9:19; 10:4 [b]Num. 19:2 [1]*sets apart* [2]*cleansing*
14 [a]1 John 1:7 [b]Heb. 6:1 [c]Luke 1:74 [1]*blemish* *See WW at Heb. 9:28.
15 [a]Rom. 3:25 [b]Heb. 3:1 *See WW at Gal. 3:19. • See WW at Rom. 3:24.
17 [a]Gal. 3:15
18 [a]Ex. 24:6
19 [a]Ex. 24:5, 6 [b]Lev. 14:4, 7; Num. 19:6, 18 [1]*command*
20 [a][Matt. 26:28] [b]Ex. 24:3–8
21 [a]Ex. 29:12, 36 *See WW at Luke 1:23.
22 [a]Lev. 17:11 [1]*cleansed* [2]*forgiveness*
23 [a]Heb. 8:5 [1]*cleansed*
24 [a]Heb. 6:20 [b]Heb. 8:2 [c]Rom. 8:34 [1]*representations* *See WW at John 14:21.
25 [a]Heb. 9:7
27 [a]Gen. 3:19; Eccl. 3:20 [b][2 Cor. 5:10]; 1 John 4:17 *See WW at Matt. 5:22.
28 [a]Rom. 6:10 [b]Is. 53:12; 1 Pet. 2:24 [c]Matt. 26:28 [d]1 Cor. 1:7; Titus 2:13

CHAPTER 10

1 [a]Heb. 8:5

9:15–23 A testament, or will, has no legal authority until after the **death** of the one who made it, as illustrated by the ratification of the **first covenant** at Sinai (see Ex. 24:5–8). In the same way, the death of Christ was necessary for the establishment of the New Covenant.

9:21, 22 The ancient **tabernacle** needed to be sanctified by the sprinkling of blood. Nothing was considered as ***purified*** *without the* mark of the shed blood. The writer sees here a type of spiritual life. Apart from the **shedding of** Jesus Christ's **blood there is no** forgiveness of sins.

9:23–26 The OT sacrifices were only earthly **copies** of **heavenly** realities, which necessitate **better sacrifices** than the blood of animals. The complete adequacy of the sacrifice Jesus offered is seen by the fact that it needed to be offered only **once.**

9:27 Physical death does not end conscious existence. There is an **after this.**

9:28 Jesus Christ appeared on Earth to accomplish His atoning work (v. 26). Then He entered "into heaven," opening the way of access to God (v. 24); one day He will reappear to consummate our **salvation.**

10:1–4 If the Levitical **sacrifices** had made the worshipers **perfect,** there would have been no need for the yearly repetition. This constant repetition only served to remind the worshipers of their sins instead of removing them from their conscience. Animal sacrifices cannot take away the guilt of sin.

[b]can never with these same sacrifices, which they *offer continually year by year, make those who approach perfect.

2 For then would they not have ceased to be offered? For the worshipers, once [1]purified, would have had no more consciousness of sins.

3 But in those *sacrifices there is* a reminder of sins every year.

4 For [a]*it is* not possible that the blood of bulls and goats could take away sins.

Christ's Death Fulfills God's Will

5 Therefore, when He came into the world, He said:

> [a]*"Sacrifice and *offering You did not desire,*
> *But a body You have *prepared for Me.*
>
> 6 *In burnt offerings and sacrifices for sin*
> *You had no pleasure.*
>
> 7 *Then I said, 'Behold, I have come—*
> *In the volume of the book it is written of Me—*
> *To do Your will, O God.' "*

8 Previously saying, *"Sacrifice and *offering, burnt offerings, and offerings for sin You did not desire, nor had pleasure in them"* (which are offered according to the law),

9 then He said, *"Behold, I have come to do Your will,* [1]*O God."* He takes away the first that He may establish the second.

10 [a]By that will we have been [1]sanctified* [b]through the *offering of the body of Jesus Christ once *for all.*

Christ's Death Perfects the Sanctified

11 And every priest stands [a]ministering* daily and offering repeatedly the same sacrifices, which can never take away sins.

12 [a]But this Man, after He had offered one sacrifice for sins forever, sat down [b]at the right hand of God,

13 from that time waiting [a]till His enemies are made His footstool.

14 For by one *offering He has perfected forever those who are being [1]sanctified.

15 But the Holy Spirit also witnesses to us; for after He had said before,

16 [a]*"This is the *covenant that I will make with them after those days, says the* LORD: *I will put My laws into their hearts, and in their *minds I will write them,"*

17 *then He adds,* [a]*"Their sins and their lawless deeds I will remember no more."*

18 Now where there is [1]remission* of these, *there is* no longer an *offering for sin.

Hold Fast Your Confession

19 Therefore, brethren, having [a]boldness[1] to enter [b]the Holiest by the blood of Jesus,

20 by a new and [a]living way which He consecrated for us, through the veil, that is, His flesh,

21 and *having* a High Priest over the house of God,

22 let us [a]draw near with a true heart 2
[b]in full assurance of faith, having our
hearts sprinkled from an evil conscience and our bodies washed with *pure water.

23 Let us hold fast the confession of 1
our hope without wavering, for [a]He who *promised *is* faithful.

24 And let us consider one another in order to stir up love and good works,

25 [a]not forsaking the assembling of 2
ourselves together, as *is* the manner of some, but exhorting *one another,* and [b]so much the more as you see [c]the Day approaching.

1 [b]Heb. 7:19; 9:9 *See WW at Heb. 9:28.
2 [1]*cleansed*
4 [a]Mic. 6:6, 7
5 [a]Ps. 40:6–8 *See WW at Acts 21:26. • See WW at Heb. 11:3.
8 *See WW at Acts 21:26.
9 [1]NU, M omit *O God*
10 [a]John 17:19 [b][Heb. 9:12] [1]*set apart* *See WW at John 10:36. • See WW at Acts 21:26.
11 [a]Num. 28:3 *See WW at Acts 13:2.
12 [a]Col. 3:1 [b]Ps. 110:1
13 [a]Ps. 110:1
14 [1]*set apart* *See WW at Acts 21:26.
16 [a]Jer. 31:33, 34 *See WW at Mark 14:24. • See WW at Mark 12:30.
17 [a]Jer. 31:34
18 [1]*forgiveness* *See WW at Heb. 9:22. • See WW at Acts 21:26.
19 [a][Eph. 2:18] [b]Heb. 9:8, 12 [1]*confidence*
20 [a]John 14:6
22 [a]Heb. 7:19; 10:1 [b]Eph. 3:12 *See WW at Matt. 5:8.
23 [a]1 Cor. 1:9; 10:13 *See WW at Acts 7:5.
25 [a]Acts 2:42 [b]Rom. 13:11 [c]Phil. 4:5

10:5–10 Though ordained by God, the sacrifices and offerings were unsatisfactory because they were merely shadows and symbols. God willed that they should be fulfilled in **the offering of the body of Jesus Christ.**

10:11–14 The writer contrasts the OT priest, continuously offering ineffective sacrifices, with Christ. Having finished His New Covenant work on Calvary, Christ **sat down** on high to await the manifestation of His triumph over all His enemies.

10:15–17 In addition to the one offering of Christ bringing assurance of salvation, **the Holy Spirit also witnesses to us** through Jeremiah that God will work in us to produce new desires to do His will. Furthermore, whereas the Old Covenant could only bring a reminder of sins (see v. 3), the New Covenant brings real forgiveness.

10:19–21 Confidence to enter God's presence is founded on **the blood of Jesus** and His high priestly ministry.

10:22 See section 2 of Truth-In-Action at the end of Heb.

10:22 Worship from **a true heart,** that is, with complete sincerity of purpose, must be based on an assurance of the justifying power of the blood of Christ (Rom. 5:1) and the sanctifying cleansing of the Word of God (Eph. 5:26).

10:23 See section 1 of Truth-In-Action at the end of Heb.

10:23 The confession of *our* hope of the future consummation of our salvation will never waver as long as it is grounded on the faithfulness of the One **who promised.** See 3:6.

10:24, 25 Love for one another in Christ must manifest itself in works of love and gathering together in His name, especially in the light of His imminent Coming.

10:25 See section 2 of Truth-In-Action at the end of Heb.

The Just Live by Faith

26 For [a]if we sin willfully [b]after we
have received the knowledge of the
truth, there [c]no longer remains a sacrifice for sins,
27 but a certain fearful expectation of
judgment, and [a]fiery *indignation
which will devour the adversaries.
28 Anyone who has rejected Moses'
law dies without mercy on the testimony of two or three [a]witnesses.
29 [a]Of how much worse punishment,
do you suppose, will he be thought
worthy who has trampled the Son of
God underfoot, [b]counted the blood of
the covenant by which he was sanctified a common thing, [c]and insulted the
Spirit of grace?
30 For we know Him who said, [a]*"Vengeance is Mine, I will repay,"* [1]says the
Lord. And again, [b]*"The LORD will
judge His people."
31 [a]It is a fearful thing to fall into the
hands of the living God.
32 But [a]recall the former days in
which, after you were [1]illuminated,
you *endured a great struggle with sufferings:
33 partly while you were made [a]a spectacle both by reproaches and tribulations, and partly while [b]you became
companions of those who were so
treated;
34 for you had compassion on [1]me
[a]in my chains, and [b]joyfully accepted
the plundering of your [2]goods, knowing that [c]you have a better and an
enduring possession for yourselves
[3]in heaven.
35 Therefore do not cast away your
confidence, [a]which has great reward.
36 [a]For you have need of **endurance,**
so that after you have done the will
of God, [b]you may receive the promise:

> **WORD WEALTH**
>
> **10:36 endurance,** *hupomone* (hoop-om-on-*ay*); Strong's *#5281:* Constancy, perseverance, continuance, bearing up, steadfastness, holding out, patient endurance. The word combines *hupo,* "under," and *mone,* "to remain." It describes the capacity to continue to bear up under difficult circumstances, not with a passive complacency, but with a hopeful fortitude that actively resists weariness and defeat.

37 *"For [a]yet a little while,*
And [b]He[1] who is coming will
come and will not [2]tarry.
38 *Now [a]the[1] just shall live by faith;*
But if anyone draws back,
My soul has no pleasure in him."

39 But we are not of those [a]who draw
back to [1]perdition, but of those who
[b]believe to the saving of the soul.

By Faith We Understand

11 Now *faith is the [1]substance of
things hoped for, the [2]evidence
[a]of things not seen.
2 For by it the elders obtained a *good*
testimony.
3 By faith we understand that [a]the
[1]worlds were **framed** by the word of
God, so that the things which are seen
were not made of things which are
visible.

> **WORD WEALTH**
>
> **11:3 framed,** *katartizo* (kat-ar-*tid*-zoe); Strong's *#2675:* To arrange, set in order, equip, adjust, complete what is lacking, make fully ready, repair, prepare. The word is a combination of *kata,* "down," and *artios,* "complete," "fitted." It is used

26 [a]Num. 15:30 [b]2 Pet. 2:20 [c]Heb. 6:6
27 [a]Zeph. 1:18 *See WW at 2 Cor. 11:2.
28 [a]Deut. 17:2–6; 19:15
29 [a][Heb. 2:3] [b]1 Cor. 11:29 [c][Matt. 12:31]
30 [a]Deut. 32:35 [b]Deut. 32:36 [1]NU omits *says the Lord* *See WW at John 18:31.
31 [a][Luke 12:5]
32 [a]Gal. 3:4 [1]*enlightened* *See WW at Matt. 24:13.
33 [a]1 Cor. 4:9 [b]Phil. 1:7
34 [a]2 Tim. 1:16 [b]Matt. 5:12 [c]Matt. 6:20 [1]NU *the prisoners* instead of *me in my chains* [2]*possessions* [3]NU omits *in heaven*
35 [a]Matt. 5:12
36 [a]Luke 21:19 [b][Col. 3:24]
37 [a]Luke 18:8 [b]Hab. 2:3, 4 [1]Or *that which* [2]*delay*
38 [a]Rom. 1:17 [1]NU *My just one*
39 [a]2 Pet. 2:20 [b]Acts 16:31 [1]*destruction*

CHAPTER 11

1 [a]Rom. 8:24 [1]*realization* [2]Or *confidence* *See WW at Mark 11:22.
3 [a]Ps. 33:6 [1]Or *ages,* Gr. *aiones,* aeons

10:26, 27 One of the most solemn warnings against apostasy found in the Scriptures. If one willfully forsakes Christ, there is no other sacrifice for sin.

10:28, 29 There are degrees of punishment. The one who **rejected Moses' law** suffered the judgment prescribed in Deut. 17:2–6. An apostate from Christianity will suffer an even **worse punishment,** for he has treated **the Son of God** with scorn, regarded His **blood** as **common** and unclean, and **insulted** the Holy Spirit.

10:30, 31 The Scriptures testify that God's judgment is *certain and absolute.*

10:32–39 The writer encourages his readers by reminding them of their past endurance in the midst of trials, their compassion toward others, and the imminent return of the Lord.

11:1 The author supports his encouragement to steadfast faith by reviewing the triumphant experiences of Hebrew heroes. First he provides, not a definition, but a description of how faith works. Faith is established conviction concerning things unseen and settled expectation of future reward. The Greek word translated **substance** literally means "a standing under," and was used in the technical sense of "title deed." The root idea is that of standing under the claim to the property to support its validity. Thus, faith is the title deed **of things hoped for.** Throughout the chapter the writer emphasizes that assurance rests on God's promises.

11:2 The elders were the OT saints, many of whom are mentioned in this chapter. They obtained a ***good*** report, not because of achievements, personal holiness, or passive acceptance of divine promises, but by an active certitude expressed in obedience, persistence, and sacrifice.

11:3 Our belief concerning God's creative act exemplifies the "evidence of things not seen" (v. 1).

for the disciples' mending their nets (Matt. 4:21) and for restoring a fallen brother (Heb. 13:21).

Faith at the Dawn of History

4 By faith [a]Abel *offered to God a
more excellent sacrifice than Cain,
through which he obtained witness
that he was righteous, God testifying
of his gifts; and through it he being
dead still [b]speaks.
5 By faith Enoch was taken away so
that he did not see death, [a]*"and was
not found, because God had taken
him"*; for before he was taken he had
this testimony, that he pleased God.
2 6 But without faith *it is* impossible to
please *Him*, for he who comes to God
must believe that He is, and *that* He
is a rewarder of those who diligently
seek Him.
7 By faith [a]Noah, being divinely
warned of things not yet seen, moved
with godly fear, [b]prepared an ark for
the saving of his household, by which
he condemned the world and became
heir of [c]the righteousness which is according to faith.

Faithful Abraham

8 By faith [a]Abraham obeyed when he
was called to go out to the place which
he would receive as an inheritance.
And he went out, not knowing where
he was going.
9 By faith he dwelt in the land of
*promise as *in* a foreign country,
[a]dwelling in tents with Isaac and Jacob, [b]the **heirs** with him of the same
promise;

WORD WEALTH

11:9 heirs, *sunkleronomos* (soong-klay-ron-om-oss); Strong's *#4789:* From *sun*, "with," *klero*, "a lot," and *nemomai*, "to possess." The word denotes a joint participant, coheir, fellow heir, one who receives a lot with another.

4 [a]Gen. 4:3–5; Matt. 23:35; 1 John 3:12 [b]Gen. 4:8–10; Heb. 12:24 *See WW at Heb. 9:28.
5 [a]Gen. 5:21–24
7 [a]Gen. 6:13–22 [b]1 Pet. 3:20 [c]Rom. 3:22
8 [a]Gen. 12:1–4; Acts 7:2–4
9 [a]Gen. 12:8; 13:3, 18; 18:1, 9 [b]Heb. 6:17 *See WW at Acts 13:32.
10 [a][Heb. 12:22; 13:14] [b][Rev. 21:10]
11 [a]Gen. 17:19; 18:11–14; 21:1, 2 [b]Luke 1:36 [c]Heb. 10:23 [1]NU omits *she bore a child*
12 [a]Rom. 4:19 [b]Gen. 15:5; 22:17; 32:12
13 [a]Heb. 11:39 [b]Gen. 12:7 [c]John 8:56; Heb. 11:27 [d]Gen. 23:4; 47:9; 1 Chr. 29:15; Ps. 39:12; Eph. 2:19; 1 Pet. 1:17; 2:11 [1]NU, M omit *were assured of them*
14 [a]Heb. 13:14 *See WW at John 14:21.
15 [a]Gen. 11:31
16 [a]Gen. 26:24; 28:13; Ex. 3:6, 15; 4:5 [b][John 14:2]; Heb. 11:10; [Rev. 21:2] *See WW at Rev. 21:2.

10 for he waited for [a]the city which has
foundations, [b]whose builder and
maker *is* God.
11 By faith [a]Sarah herself also received strength to conceive seed, and
[b]she[1] bore a child when she was past
the age, because she judged Him
[c]faithful who had promised.
12 Therefore from one man, and him
as good as [a]dead, were born *as many*
as the [b]stars of the sky in multitude—
innumerable as the sand which is by
the seashore.

The Heavenly Hope

13 These all died in faith, [a]not having
received the [b]promises, but [c]having
seen them afar off [1]were assured of
them, embraced *them* and [d]confessed
that they were strangers and pilgrims
on the earth.
14 For those who say such things
[a]declare* plainly that they seek a
homeland.
15 And truly if they had called to mind
[a]that *country* from which they had
come out, they would have had opportunity to return.
16 But now they desire a better, that
is, a heavenly *country*. Therefore God
is not ashamed [a]to be called their God,
for He has [b]prepared* a city for them.

KINGDOM DYNAMICS

11:13–16 Faith's Confession Is Steadfast, FAITH'S CONFESSION. This chapter records glorious victories of faith's champions, yet vv. 13–16 speak of those who died, "not having received the promises." Even then, the Bible says "these all died in faith," being content to confess that they were only strangers and pilgrims traveling, as it were, through the land: "For true believers, to (*cont. on next page*)

11:4 Abel's act of worship still testifies to the fact that a true worshiper must come in faith, presenting the sacrifice required by God.
11:5 Enoch's translation to heaven, without physical **death,** took place because he pleased God by taking Him at His word and living his life accordingly.
11:6 See section 2 of Truth-In-Action at the end of Heb.
11:6 Nothing so pleases God as a steadfast **faith** in all that He is and promises to do.
11:7 Noah's obedience in building the ark far inland was physical evidence of his trust in God's word.
11:8–10 Abraham demonstrated his **faith** by obedience in leaving his home in Ur and journeying to unknown lands, in living long years in the Promised Land as a foreigner in temporary quarters (Acts 7:5), and by patiently awaiting his permanent abode.
11:11 Sarah gave birth to Isaac when she was 90 years of age because she looked away from her physical inability and **judged** God **faithful** to keep His word.
11:12 Abraham was 100 years old when Isaac was born.
11:13–16 Although they received only a partial fulfillment of what God had promised, these elders maintained their faith that God would do what He said. Because of their close relationship with God, they could not feel at home in earthly surroundings. They looked for something better; and because of their longings, **God** gladly acknowledged them as His own people.

(cont. from preceding page)
live by faith is to die by faith" (Wycliffe).

The key to the "confession" (v. 13) of this admirable group in Heb. 11 is that when given a promise by God, as were Abraham and his descendants, they became "fully persuaded" that the promise was true. Thus they embraced (literally "greeted") that promise in their hearts. The word "confess" helps us to understand how easily these of the gallery of faith established their ways before God and left the testimony, which His Word records with tribute. While each of these persons did receive many victories through faith, the text says that none of them received everything that was promised. Whether or not we receive what we "confess" (ask, pray, or hope for) does not change the behavior or the attitude of the steadfast believer. Faith's worship and walk do not depend on answered or unanswered prayers. Our confession of His lordship in our lives is to be consistent—a daily celebration, with deep gratitude.
(Heb. 4:11–13/Rev. 12:11) R.H.

The Faith of the Patriarchs

17 By faith Abraham, [a]when he was
tested, offered up Isaac, and he who
had received the promises offered up
his only begotten *son,*
18 [1]of whom it was said, [a]*"In Isaac*
your seed shall be called,"
19 *concluding that God [a]*was* able to
raise *him* up, even from the dead, from
which he also received him in a figurative sense.
20 By faith [a]Isaac blessed Jacob and
Esau concerning things to come.
21 By faith Jacob, when he was dying,
[a]blessed each of the sons of Joseph,
and worshiped, *leaning* on the top of
his staff.
22 By faith [a]Joseph, when he was dying, made mention of the departure of
the children of Israel, and gave instructions concerning his bones.

The Faith of Moses

23 By faith [a]Moses, when he was born,
was hidden three months by his parents, because they saw *he was* a beautiful child; and they were not afraid of
the king's [b]command.
24 By faith [a]Moses, when he became
of age, refused to be called the son of
Pharaoh's daughter,
25 choosing rather to suffer affliction
with the people of God than to enjoy
the [1]passing pleasures of sin,
26 esteeming [a]the [1]reproach of Christ
greater riches than the treasures [2]in
Egypt; for he **looked** to the [b]reward.

> **WORD WEALTH**
>
> **11:26 looked,** *apoblepo* (ap-ob-*lep*-oh); Strong's *#578:* A graphic word combining *apo,* "away from," and *blepo,* "to see." The word literally means "to look away from everything else in order to look intently on one object." Moses looked away from the wealth of world systems toward a messianic future.

27 By faith [a]he forsook Egypt, not fearing the *wrath of the king; for he endured as seeing Him who is invisible.
28 By faith [a]he kept the Passover and
the sprinkling of blood, lest he who destroyed the firstborn should touch
them.
29 By faith [a]they passed through the
Red Sea as by dry *land, whereas* the
Egyptians, attempting *to do* so, were
drowned.

By Faith They Overcame

30 By faith [a]the walls of Jericho fell
down after they were encircled for
seven days.
31 By faith [a]the harlot Rahab did not
perish with those who [1]did not believe,
when [b]she had received the spies with
peace.
32 And what more shall I say? For the
time would fail me to tell of [a]Gideon
and [b]Barak and [c]Samson and [d]Jeph-
thah, also *of* [e]David and [f]Samuel and
the *prophets:
33 who through faith subdued king-

17 [a]Gen. 22:1–14; James 2:21
18 [a]Gen. 21:12; Rom. 9:7 [1]*to*
19 [a]Rom. 4:17 *See WW at Rom. 4:3.
20 [a]Gen. 27:26–40
21 [a]Gen. 48:1, 5, 16, 20
22 [a]Gen. 50:24, 25; Ex. 13:19
23 [a]Ex. 2:1–3 [b]Ex. 1:16, 22
24 [a]Ex. 2:11–15
25 [1]*temporary*
26 [a]Heb. 13:13 [b]Rom. 8:18; 2 Cor. 4:17 [1]*reviling because of* [2]NU, M *of*
27 [a]Ex. 10:28 *See WW at Luke 4:28.
28 [a]Ex. 12:21
29 [a]Ex.14:22–29; Jude 5
30 [a]Josh. 6:20
31 [a]Josh. 2:9; 6:23; James 2:25 [b]Josh. 2:1 [1]*were disobedient*
32 [a]Judg. 6:11; 7:1–25 [b]Judg. 4:6–24 [c]Judg. 13:24—16:31 [d]Judg. 11:1–29; 12:1–7 [e]1 Sam. 16; 17 [f]1 Sam. 7:9–14 *See WW at Matt. 2:5.

11:20 No mention is made of **Jacob**'s deceit, revealing how grace covers all.
11:21 Though his natural sight was gone, Jacob's eye of faith was clear as he crossed his hands and pronounced *the greater blessing* on Ephraim, the younger son (Gen. 48:13–20).
11:22 Joseph expressed complete **faith** in the promises concerning the land of Canaan, and spoke of a **departure** from Egypt centuries in the future.
11:23 The story of Moses' faith begins with the **faith** of **his parents.**
11:24–26 Only **faith** could influence such a great choice, which looked far beyond the present scene.
11:27 Probably refers to the night of the Exodus. Only a godly **faith** can see the invisible.
11:31 Rahab's **faith** was based on the record of God's mighty deeds and promises to Israel (Josh. 2:9–11).
11:32 A detailed study of the lives of these mentioned shows the outstanding place that faith had in the experience and service of each. Personal shortcomings were victoriously overcome as they looked away from themselves to the greatness of God.

doms, worked righteousness, obtained promises, [a]stopped the mouths of lions,
34 [a]quenched the violence of fire, escaped the edge of the sword, out of weakness were made strong, became valiant in battle, turned to flight the armies of the aliens.
35 [a]Women received their dead raised to life again. Others were [b]tortured, not accepting *deliverance, that they might obtain a better resurrection.
36 Still others had trial of mockings and scourgings, yes, and [a]of chains and imprisonment.
37 [a]They were stoned, they were sawn in two, [1]were tempted, were slain with the sword. [b]They wandered about [c]in sheepskins and goatskins, being *destitute, afflicted, tormented—
38 of whom the world was not worthy. They wandered in deserts and mountains, [a]*in* dens and caves of the earth.
39 And all these, [a]having obtained a good testimony through faith, did not receive the promise,
40 God having provided something better for us, that they should not be [a]made *perfect apart from us.

The Race of Faith

4 **12** Therefore we also, since we are surrounded by so great a cloud of witnesses, [a]let us lay aside every weight, and the sin which so easily ensnares *us,* and [b]let us run [c]with endurance the race that is set before us,
2 **looking** unto Jesus, the [1]author and [2]finisher of *our* faith, [a]who for the joy that was set before Him [b]endured* the cross, despising the shame, and [c]has sat down at the right hand of the throne of God.

33 [a]Dan. 6:22
34 [a]Dan. 3:23–28
35 [a]1 Kin. 17:22 [b]Acts 22:25 *See WW at Rom. 3:24.
36 [a]Gen. 39:20
37 [a]1 Kin. 21:13 [b]2 Kin. 1:8 [c]Zech. 13:4 [1]NU omits *were tempted* *See WW at Luke 22:35.
38 [a]1 Kin. 18:4, 13; 19:9
39 [a]Heb. 11:2, 13
40 [a]Heb. 5:9 *See WW at 1 John 2:5.

CHAPTER 12

1 [a]Col. 3:8 [b]1 Cor. 9:24 [c]Rom. 12:12
2 [a]Luke 24:26 [b]Phil. 2:8 [c]Ps. 110:1 [1]*originator* [2]*perfecter* *See WW at Matt. 24:13.
3 [a]Matt. 10:24 [b]Gal. 6:9
4 [a][1 Cor. 10:13]
5 [a]Prov. 3:11, 12 [1]*discipline*
6 [a]Rev. 3:19
7 [a]Deut. 8:5 [b]Prov. 13:24; 19:18; 23:13 [1]NU, M *It is for discipline that you endure; God*
8 [a]1 Pet. 5:9 *See WW at Heb. 3:14.
9 [a][Job 12:10]

WORD WEALTH

12:2 looking, *aphorao* (af-or-*ah*-oh); Strong's *#872:* From *apo,* "away from," and *horao,* "to see." The word signifies undivided attention, looking away from all distractions in order to fix one's gaze on one object. *Aphorao* in Heb. 12:2 is having eyes for no one but Jesus.

The Discipline of God

3 [a]For consider Him who endured such hostility from sinners against Himself, [b]lest you become weary and discouraged in your souls.
4 [a]You have not yet resisted to bloodshed, striving against sin. 4
5 And you have forgotten the exhortation which speaks to you as to sons:

[a]*"My son, do not despise the*
[1]chastening of the L*ORD,*
Nor be discouraged when you are
rebuked by Him;
6 *For [a]whom the* L*ORD loves He*
chastens,
And scourges every son whom He
receives."

7 [a]If[1] you endure chastening, God deals with you as with sons; for what [b]son is there whom a father does not chasten?
8 But if you are without chastening, [a]of which all have become *partakers, then you are illegitimate and not sons.
9 Furthermore, we have had human fathers who corrected *us,* and we paid *them* respect. Shall we not much more readily be in subjection to [a]the Father of spirits and live?
10 For they indeed for a few days chastened *us* as seemed *best* to them, but

11:35–38 The fact that **others were tortured** and suffered in various other ways indicates that faith does not provide an automatic exemption from hardships, trials, or tragedy. Furthermore, the experience of such difficulties does not mean that the people undergoing them possess less faith than those who are not afflicted. The same faith that enables some to escape trouble enables others to endure it. The same faith that delivers some from death enables others to die victoriously. Faith is not a bridge over troubled waters, but is a pathway through them. Discerning the pathway and the source of any hardships encountered requires aggressive prayer and worship. Through these means, God's perspective becomes focused.

11:39, 40 In spite of the **good testimony** resulting from their **faith,** the OT saints **did not receive the promise** of the blessings of the New Covenant brought by Christ. **Made perfect:** The body of Christ will be complete with saints from both OT and NT times.

12:1–3 See section 4 of Truth-In-Action at the end of Heb.

12:1 The heroes of faith are not spectators watching us from heaven; rather their lives are **witnesses** to us, having successfully overcome. The Christian life is often likened to a race (see 1 Cor. 9:24; 2 Tim. 4:7). We are to **lay aside** anything that hinders our progress, particularly every form of **sin.**

12:2 The runner must not look to other contestants, but must ever keep his eyes fixed on **Jesus.**

12:4–10 See section 4 of Truth-In-Action at the end of Heb.

12:5–11 The readers must not assume that the sufferings they are enduring as a result of their Christian profession mean that God is unconcerned about their welfare. Far from neglecting them, He shows Himself to be a true **Father** in the experience of discipline. **Chastens** describes corrective discipline used in training a child. Such treatment is administered not harshly, but in love, with the well-being of the child in mind. Instead of becoming discouraged, the readers should view their persecutions as evidence of God's love for them as His children, bringing them to spiritual maturity. The writer does not suggest that God is responsible for the sufferings that hostile sinners bring upon them, but he does indicate that God uses even adverse circumstances as instruments to accomplish His purpose.

He for *our* profit, [a]that *we* may be partakers of His holiness.
4 11 Now no [1]chastening seems to be
joyful for the present, but painful;
nevertheless, afterward it yields
[a]the peaceable fruit of righteousness
to those who have been trained by it.

Renew Your Spiritual Vitality

12 Therefore [a]strengthen the hands
which hang down, and the feeble
knees,
13 and make straight paths for your
feet, so that what is lame may not be
dislocated, but rather be healed.
14 [a]Pursue peace with all *people*, and
holiness, [b]without which no one will
see the Lord:
15 looking carefully lest anyone
[a]fall short of the grace of God; lest any
[b]root of bitterness springing up cause
trouble, and by this many become defiled;
16 lest there *be* any [a]fornicator or
[1]profane person like Esau, [b]who for
one morsel of food sold his birthright.
17 For you know that afterward, when
he wanted to inherit the blessing, he
was [a]rejected, for he found no place
for repentance, though he sought it diligently with tears.

The Glorious Company

18 For you have not come [1]to [a]the
mountain that may be touched and that
burned with fire, and to blackness and
[2]darkness and tempest,
19 and the sound of a trumpet and the
voice of words, so that those who
heard *it* [a]begged that the word should
not be spoken to them anymore.
20 (For they could not endure what
was commanded: [a]*"And if so much as
a beast touches the mountain, it shall
be stoned* [1]*or shot with an arrow."*

10 [a]Lev. 11:44
11 [a]Is. 32:17; 2 Tim. 4:8; James 3:17, 18 [1]*discipline*
12 [a]Is. 35:3
14 [a]Ps. 34:14 [b]Matt. 5:8; [Heb. 9:28]
15 [a]2 Cor. 6:1; Gal. 5:4; Heb. 4:1 [b]Deut. 29:18
16 [a][1 Cor. 6:13–18] [b]Gen. 25:33 [1]*godless*
17 [a]Gen. 27:30–40
18 [a]Ex. 19:12, 16; 20:18; Deut. 4:11; 5:22 [1]NU *to that which* [2]NU *gloom*
19 [a]Ex. 20:18–26; Deut. 5:25; 18:16
20 [a]Ex. 19:12, 13 [1]NU, M omit the rest of v. 20.
21 [a]Deut. 9:19
23 [a][James 1:18] [b]Luke 10:20 [c]Gen. 18:25; Ps. 50:6; 94:2 [d][Phil. 3:12] [1]*festal gathering* *See WW at Acts 8:1.
24 [a]1 Tim. 2:5; Heb. 8:6; 9:15 [b]Ex. 24:8 [c]Gen. 4:10; Heb. 11:4 *See WW at Gal. 3:19.
25 [a]Heb. 2:2, 3
26 [a]Hag. 2:6 [1]NU *will shake*
27 [a][Is. 34:4; 54:10; 65:17; Rom. 8:19, 21]; 1 Cor. 7:31; Heb. 1:10

21 And so terrifying was the sight *that*
Moses said, [a]*"I am exceedingly afraid*
and trembling.")
22 But you have come to Mount Zion
and to the city of the living God, the
heavenly Jerusalem, to an innumerable company of angels,
23 to the [1]general assembly and
*church of [a]the firstborn [b]*who are* registered in heaven, to God [c]the Judge
of all, to the spirits of just men [d]made
perfect,
24 to Jesus [a]the *Mediator of the new
covenant, and to [b]the blood of sprinkling that speaks better things [c]than
that of Abel.

Hear the Heavenly Voice

25 See that you do not refuse Him who 3
speaks. For [a]if they did not escape who
refused Him who spoke on earth, much
more *shall we not escape* if we turn
away from Him who *speaks* from
heaven,
26 whose voice then shook the earth;
but now He has promised, saying,
[a]*"Yet once more I* [1]*shake not only the
earth, but also heaven."*
27 Now this, *"Yet once more,"* indicates the [a]removal of those things that
are being shaken, as of things that are
made, that the things which cannot be
shaken may remain.

KINGDOM DYNAMICS

12:26, 27 Restoration and the Shaking of Man's Works, RESTORATION. This text warns of God's shaking the works of man's hands so that divine restoration can begin. The entire concept of "The Holy Spirit and Restoration" is developed in the study article, which begins on page 2012.

(Amos 5:21–23/Is. 58:1–14) J.R.

12:11 See section 4 of Truth-In-Action at the end of Heb.
12:12 Therefore, because of the beneficial results of suffering, they are to put aside all fear and faintheartedness.
12:13 They are to set an example that will encourage those who are wavering not to falter.
12:14 In their conflict with the world, they are to seek **peace,** but not at the expense of sacrificing **holiness.**
12:15 They are to watch over one another with jealous care, **lest anyone** leave the faith. The **root of bitterness** is a deliberate turning away from God, as exemplified by the disobedience of Israel in the wilderness (see Deut. 29:18). Such sin contaminates the entire Christian community.
12:16, 17 The fate of **Esau** serves as a solemn warning to anyone who forfeits permanent spiritual blessings for immediate passing fleshly gratification. Once such a choice is made and acted on, its consequences cannot be reversed, and the blessings that might have been realized are lost forever.
12:18–24 The writer presents another dramatic contrast between Judaism, pictured as Mt. Sinai, and Christianity, represented by **Mount Zion . . . the heavenly Jerusalem.** The Old Covenant of the Law brought fear and separation (see Ex. 19:12, 13; 20:18, 19), but the New Covenant brings overwhelming blessings.
12:25–29 The author issues a final warning to those who contemplated turning away from Christ. If severe punishment fell upon those who rejected the revelation of Sinai, **much more** severe will be the penalty upon those who disregard the fuller revelation they have in Christ. The return of the Lord will signal the removal of all that is earthly and temporal, in order that only heavenly and spiritual realities **may remain** (v. 27). **Therefore, . . . let us have grace** to **serve God acceptably.**
12:25 See section 3 of Truth-In-Action at the end of Heb.

28 Therefore, since we are receiving a
kingdom which cannot be shaken, let
us have grace, by which we [1]may
[a]serve God acceptably with reverence
and godly fear.
29 For [a]our God *is* a consuming fire.

Concluding Moral Directions

13 Let [a]**brotherly love** continue.
2 [a]Do not forget to entertain
strangers, for by so *doing* [b]some have
unwittingly entertained angels.

WORD WEALTH

13:1 brotherly love, *philadelphia* (fil-ad-el-*fee*-ah); Strong's *#5360:* From *phileo,* "to love," and *adelphos,* "brother." The word denotes the love of brothers, fraternal affection. In the NT it describes the love Christians have for other Christians.

3 [a]Remember the prisoners as if
chained with them—those who are
mistreated—since you yourselves are
in the body also.
4 [a]Marriage *is* honorable among all,
and the bed undefiled; [b]but fornicators
and adulterers God will judge.
5 *Let your* conduct *be* without covetousness; *be* content with such things
as you have. For He Himself has said,
[a]*"I will never leave you nor forsake
you."*
6 So we may boldly say:

[a]*"The* Lord *is my* **helper;**
*I will not *fear.*
What can man do to me?"

28 [a]Heb. 13:15, 21 [1]M omits *may*
29 [a]Ex. 24:17

CHAPTER 13

1 [a]Rom. 12:10
2 [a]Matt. 25:35; Rom. 12:13 [b]Gen. 18:1–22; 19:1
3 [a]Matt. 25:36; Heb. 10:34
4 [a]Prov. 5:18, 19 [b]1 Cor. 6:9; Gal. 5:19, 21; 1 Thess. 4:6
5 [a]Gen. 28:15; Deut. 31:6, 8; Josh. 1:5
6 [a]Ps. 27:1; 118:6 *See WW at Matt. 10:26.
7 [1]*lead*
8 [a][John 8:58]; 2 Cor. 1:19; Heb. 1:12
9 [1]NU, M *away* *See WW at Mark 16:20.
12 [1]*set apart* *See WW at Acts 17:3.
13 [a]1 Pet. 4:14
15 [a]Eph. 5:20

WORD WEALTH

13:6 helper, *boethos* (bah-ay-*thoss*); Strong's *#998:* From *boe,* "a cry for help," and *theo,* "to run." *Boethos* is one who comes running when we cry for help. The word describes the Lord as poised and ready to rush to the relief of His oppressed children when they shout for His assistance.

Concluding Religious Directions

7 Remember those who [1]rule over 4
you, who have spoken the word of God
to you, whose faith follow, considering
the outcome of *their* conduct.
8 Jesus Christ *is* [a]the same yesterday,
today, and forever.
9 Do not be carried [1]about with various and strange doctrines. For *it is*
good that the heart be *established by
grace, not with foods which have not
profited those who have been occupied
with them.
10 We have an altar from which those
who serve the tabernacle have no right
to eat.
11 For the bodies of those animals, 1
whose blood is brought into the sanctuary by the high priest for sin, are
burned outside the camp.
12 Therefore Jesus also, that He might
[1]sanctify the people with His own
blood, *suffered outside the gate.
13 Therefore let us go forth to Him, outside the camp, bearing [a]His reproach.
14 For here we have no continuing
city, but we seek the one to come.
15 [a]Therefore by Him let us continu- 2

13:1 The writer begins his concluding exhortations. Love is a manifestation of growth in the Lord (see John 13:34, 35).
13:2 Hospitality, which literally refers to opening one's home to traveling strangers who share in the faith, may bring unexpected blessings.
13:3 They must minister to those suffering for their faith, remembering that they are liable to the same hostility.
13:4 In order to guard against sexual immorality, God has ordained the sacred relationship of marriage. **Undefiled** contains more than an approval of conjugal relationship, but also entails the married couples' responsibility to preserve their intimacy from the perverse and debasing practices of a lewd society.
13:5, 6 Covetousness and financial **fear** are overcome by a contentment founded on the assurance of God's constant presence and the promises He extends to us to supply our daily needs. Because of the word of assurance that **He Himself** has spoken, **we may boldly** respond with a declaration of confidence.
13:7 See section 4 of Truth-In-Action at the end of Heb.
13:7 Teachers who have been faithful unto death are worthy examples of persevering faith.
13:8 The same Christ who sustained the leaders mentioned in the previous verse will support them.
13:9 One of the chief causes of instability of faith is false and novel teaching. Note that **doctrines** is in the plural (see Col. 2:22; 1 Tim. 4:1). Truth is always in the singular (see John 7:17; Rom. 16:17; 1 Tim. 4:16; 2 John 9). Faith comes from **the heart** (see Rom. 10:10), which alone can appreciate the fullness of God's **grace.**
13:10 Our **altar** is the Cross of Christ. Those who still trust in the old rituals are excluded from the saving benefits of His death.
13:11–13 See section 1 of Truth-In-Action at the end of Heb.
13:11, 12 On the Day of Atonement the bodies of the animals whose blood was carried into the Holy of Holies were **burned outside the camp** (see Lev. 16:14, 27). Jesus, the antitype of this sacrifice, was crucified outside the city of Jerusalem (see John 19:16, 17).
13:13, 14 Loyalty to Christ means separation. It may involve the loss of friends and **bearing His reproach.** However, departure from earthly ties results in entering the "continuing city . . . to come" (v. 14).
13:15, 16 As priests of God (see Rev. 1:6), believers **offer the sacrifice of praise to God** and loving service to others. **The fruit of *our* lips** notes the fact that, as with the fruit God creatively brings forth from plant life, so the Holy Spirit will beget new and living worship unto God from our lips and our whole being.
13:15 See section 2 of Truth-In-Action at the end of Heb.

ally offer [b]the sacrifice of praise to God, that is, [c]the fruit of *our* lips, [1]giving thanks to His name.

KINGDOM DYNAMICS

13:10–15 The Sacrifice of Praise, PRAISE PATHWAY. Why is praising God a sacrifice? The word "sacrifice" (Greek *thusia*) comes from the root *thuo*, a verb meaning "to kill or slaughter for a purpose." Praise often requires that we "kill" our pride, fear, or sloth—anything that threatens to diminish or interfere with our worship of the Lord. We also discover here the basis of all our praise: the sacrifice of our Lord Jesus Christ. It is by Him, in Him, with Him, to Him, and for Him that we offer our sacrifice of praise to God. Praise will never be successfully hindered when we keep its focus on Him—the Founder and Completer of our salvation. His Cross, His Blood—His love gift of life and forgiveness to us—keep praise as a living sacrifice!

(Heb. 2:11, 12/1 Pet. 2:9) C.G.

16 [a]But do not forget to do good and to share, for [b]with such sacrifices God is well pleased.
3 17 [a]Obey those who [1]rule over you, and be submissive, for [b]they watch out for your souls, as those who must give account. Let them do so with joy and not with grief, for that would be unprofitable for you.

15 [b]Lev. 7:12 [c]Is. 57:19; Hos. 14:2 [1]Lit. *confessing*
16 [a]Rom. 12:13 [b]2 Cor. 9:12; Phil. 4:18
17 [a]Phil. 2:29 [b]Is. 62:6; Ezek. 3:17; Acts 20:28 [1]*lead*
18 [a]Eph. 6:19 [b]Acts 23:1 *See WW at Matt. 8:2.
19 *See WW at 2 Cor. 2:4.
20 [a]Rom. 5:1, 2, 10; 15:33 [b]Ps. 16:10, 11; Hos. 6:2; Rom. 4:24 [c]Ps. 23:1; Is. 40:11; 63:11; John 10:11; 1 Pet. 2:25; 5:4 [d]Zech. 9:11; Heb. 10:29 *See WW at John 10:2. • See WW at Mark 14:24.
21 [a]Phil. 2:13 [1]*perfect* [2]NU, M *us* *See WW at Heb. 11:3. • See WW at Phil. 1:6.
22 *See WW at 2 Thess. 1:4.
24 [1]*lead*

Prayer Requested

18 [a]Pray for us; for we are confident that we have [b]a good conscience, in all things *desiring to live honorably.
19 But I *especially urge *you* to do this, that I may be restored to you the sooner.

Benediction, Final Exhortation, Farewell

20 Now may [a]the God of peace [b]who brought up our Lord Jesus from the dead, [c]that great *Shepherd of the sheep, [d]through the blood of the everlasting *covenant,
21 make you [1]complete* in every *good work to do His will, [a]working in [2]you what is well pleasing in His sight, through Jesus Christ, to whom *be* glory forever and ever. Amen.
22 And I appeal to you, brethren, *bear with the word of exhortation, for I have written to you in few words.
23 Know that *our* brother Timothy has been set free, with whom I shall see you if he comes shortly.
24 Greet all those who [1]rule over you, and all the saints. Those from Italy greet you.
25 Grace *be* with you all. Amen.

13:17, 18 See section 3 of Truth-In-Action at the end of Heb.
13:17 Christians are not only to remember past church leaders (v. 7), but are to heed present leaders who are responsible in discharging their duties in providing spiritual oversight to the congregation. The obedience commanded denotes assenting to someone else's directions, and submission means yielding one's contrary opinions in favor of another's. The writer does not suggest blind, unquestioning obedience to everything a leader says, even in decisions pertaining to changing jobs, making purchases, taking a trip, and the like. The NT teaches the necessity of discernment (1 John 4:1), personal accountability to God (Rom. 14:12; Gal. 6:5), and mutual submission (Rom. 12:10; Gal. 5:13; Eph. 5:21; Phil. 2:3, 4). Furthermore, church leaders are not autocratic chiefs who lord it over the congregation, but are servants who exercise authority with concern and care (see Rom.12:8; 1 Thess. 5:12, 13; 1 Tim. 3:5; 5:17).
13:18, 19 The writer had formerly ministered among them, but some obstacle was hindering his return. Prayer could clear the way.
13:20, 21 Having requested prayer from them, the writer now prays for them. The benediction summarizes all that has been said. God has provided everything necessary for our spiritual well-being through the atoning work of Christ. The **covenant** He inaugurated is eternal.
13:23 The NT does not reveal the time or circumstances of Timothy's confinement.
13:24 The greetings sent by **those from Italy** do not necessarily indicate the place of writing or the destination of the letter.

TRUTH-IN-ACTION through HEBREWS

Letting the LIFE of the Holy Spirit Bring Faith's Works Alive in You!

Truth Hebrews Teaches	Text	**Action** Hebrews Invites
1 Key Lessons in Faith Faith accepts the Bible's record of who Jesus is and what He has accomplished on our behalf. It also draws near to God and clings to Him tenaciously. The believer accepts the benefits of Jesus' sacrifice and enters God's presence with confidence. Faith believes the Bible implicitly, knowing it is God's living self-expression and so submits to its judgment. Finally, faith is willing to suffer with Christ, knowing it will receive a good reward.	2:14–18	**Recognize** that Jesus has destroyed the fear of death for you by overcoming the Devil.
	3:6	**Consciously hold onto** the courage and hope that is implied by your confession of faith.
	4:12, 13	**Allow** the Word of God to judge the intents and thoughts of your heart.
	4:14	**Be tenacious** in holding onto God's promises. **Aggressively pursue** God, **study** His Word, and **build up** your faith.
	4:16	**Draw near to** God with confidence when in need. **Believe** He understands your suffering.
	10:23	**Hold on to** hope! **Develop** a sense of high destiny.
	13:11–13	**Recognize** that following Jesus brings reproach. **Do not fear** human mockery, rejection, and scorn.
2 Steps to Dynamic Devotion Devotion is concentration on a particular pursuit, purpose, or cause. He who is devoted to Jesus recognizes his fleshly tendency to become lackadaisical and studies to avoid it. The Scriptures shape his thinking, and he devotes time to prayer, to waiting upon the Lord, and to praise and thanksgiving.	2:1–4	**Give your full attention** to God's Word and your relationship with Jesus.
	3:1	**Let** Jesus and His Word be the foundation and sustainer of your thinking.
	9:11–15	**Celebrate daily** that you have gained access to God through the shed blood of Jesus Christ.
	10:22	**Continually draw near** to God with a blameless heart and faith.
	10:25	**Gather often** with God's people to encourage and urge them on in righteousness.
	11:6	**Seek God** diligently. **Believe** that He will reward you for it.
	13:15	**Practice** persistent and patient praise.
3 Steps to Faithful Obedience Faith believes what God says and acts in line with His Word. Faith allows the believer to enter the rest into which God has called all His people. It acknowledges the completed work of salvation, while faithfully obeying every instruction from God.	4:1–10	**Enter** the rest promised by God. **Mix** your faith with God's Word. **Do not allow** rebellion to harden your heart.
	4:8–11	**Devote your whole heart** to obeying God and His Word. **Trust** Him to do the things He says He will do.
	5:8–10	**Study** Jesus' life as your model for suffering and obedience.
	12:25	**Never reject** a message because it makes you uncomfortable. **Accept** correction from God's Word.
	13:17, 18	**Obey** church leadership. **Recognize** and **cooperate** with leadership to make their job easier. **Pray** for them continuously and faithfully.

Truth Hebrews Teaches	Text	**Action** Hebrews Invites
4 **How to Develop Dynamic Discipleship** The disciple is an apprentice to Jesus, learning to live as He did. God disciplines His children, correcting and training them to live in His kingdom. Correction, if received with the right attitude of heart, produces the fruit of righteousness. The Father's object is to bring His children to maturity.	5:12–14	**Recognize** that it is only through a sustained daily effort to apply God's Word to your life that you will become mature.
	6:11, 12	**Turn** from laziness and **patiently endure,** sustaining diligence in your pursuit of Christlikeness.
	12:1–3	**Discard** any attitude or practice that hinders your walk with Christ. **Model** your life after Jesus. **Give careful thought and study** to the life of Jesus for encouragement in your struggle with sin.
	12:4–10	**Embrace** God's discipline. **Know** that it is evidence that He is training you as His child.
	12:11	**Accept** God's correction as necessary for spiritual growth.
	13:7	**Honor, consider,** and **imitate** those God has put over you to lead you.

The Epistle of JAMES

Author: James, Brother of Jesus
Date: A.D. 48–62
Theme: Faith That Works
Key Words: Faith, Riches, Tongue, Pride, Prayer

Author The author of this letter identifies himself simply as James. The name was quite common; and the New Testament lists at least five men named James, two of whom were Jesus' disciples and one of whom was His brother. Tradition has ascribed the book to the Lord's brother, and there is no reason to question this view. Evidently the writer was well known, and James the brother of Jesus became the leader of the church in Jerusalem at an early date (Acts 12:17; 15:13–21; 21:18; Gal. 1:19; 2:9, 12). The language of the epistle is similar to James's speech in Acts 15. James apparently was an unbeliever during the ministry of Jesus (John 7:3–5). A post-Resurrection appearance of Christ to him (1 Cor. 15:7) probably led to his conversion, for he is numbered with the believers in Acts 1:14.

Date The Jewish historian Josephus indicates that James was stoned to death in the year A.D. 62, so if he is the author the letter was evidently written before that date. The contents of the book suggest that it may have been written as early as a date shortly before the church council of Acts 15, which convened about A.D. 49. We cannot be dogmatic, and can only conclude that the letter was likely written between A.D. 48 and 62.

Purpose James is primarily practical and ethical, emphasizing duty rather than doctrine. The author wrote to rebuke the shameful neglect of certain Christian duties. In doing so, he analyzed the nature of genuine faith and urged his readers to demonstrate the validity of their experience with Christ. His supreme concern was reality in religion, and he set forth the practical claims of the gospel.

Content Rather than speculating or debating on religious theories, James directs his readers toward godly living. From beginning to end the mood of his letter is imperative. In 108 verses, 54 clear commands are given, and 7 times James calls attention to his statements by using terms that are imperative in nature. This "bondservant of God" (1:1) writes as one supervising other slaves. The result is a statement of Christian ethics, which stands on a par with any such teaching in the New Testament.

Personal Application The book's call for ethical living based on the gospel provides its relevance. James gives a practical exposition of "pure and undefiled religion" (1:27). His two fundamental emphases are personal growth in the spiritual life and sensitivity in social relationships. Any faith that does not deal with both personal and social issues is a dead faith. The message of James speaks especially to those who are inclined to talk their way to heaven instead of walk their way there.

Christ Revealed Beginning in the first verse and continuing throughout the letter, James recognizes the lordship of Jesus, referring to himself as the Lord's "bondservant," or slave. That term is applicable to all Christians, because all true disciples of Christ acknowledge His sovereignty over their lives and willingly commit themselves to His service. Christ is the object of our faith (2:1), the One in whose name and by whose power we perform our ministry (5:14, 15), the Rewarder of those who are steadfast in the midst of trials (1:12), and the Coming One for whom we patiently wait (5:7–9). James identifies Christ as the "glory" (2:1), referring to the Shekinah, the glorious manifestation of the presence of God among His people. Not only glorious Himself, He is the divine Glory, the presence of God on Earth (see Luke 2:30–32; John 1:14; Heb. 1:3).

Of considerable interest is the close parallel between the content of this letter and the teachings of Jesus, particularly the Sermon on the Mount. Although James does not quote any statement of Jesus exactly, there are more verbal reminiscences of the Lord's teachings in this letter than in all the rest of the New Testament epistles combined. These allusions indicate a close association between James and Jesus and give evidence of the strong influence of the Lord in the author's life.

The Holy Spirit at Work The letter specifically mentions the Holy Spirit only in 4:5, which states the indwelling Spirit's strong desire for our undivided loyalty, jealously brooking no rivals.

The activity of the Holy Spirit may be seen in the ministry to the sick described in 5:14–16. In light of other biblical terminology connecting anointing with the Spirit (see Is. 61:1; Luke 4:18; 1 John 2:20–27), anointing with oil is best understood as symbolic of the Holy Spirit. Furthermore, in the Greek the definite article used with the word for "faith" in 5:15 particularizes this faith, suggesting that James is referring to the manifestation of the gift of faith (1 Cor. 12:9).

Outline of James

I.	**Salutation**	**1:1**
II.	**Practical religion and trials**	**1:2–18**
	A. Outward adversities	1:2–12
	B. Inward enticements	1:13–18
III.	**Practical religion and God's Word**	**1:19–27**
	A. Hear the Word	1:19, 20
	B. *Receive the Word*	1:21
	C. Obey the Word	1:22–27
IV.	**Practical religion and human relationships**	**2:1–26**
	A. Negative partiality	2:1–13
	B. Positive compassion	2:14–26
V.	**Practical religion and speech**	**3:1–18**
VI.	**Practical religion and worldliness**	**4:1–12**
VII.	**Practical religion and business affairs**	**4:13—5:6**
VIII.	**Final appeals**	**5:7–20**
	A. For patience	5:7–11
	B. For pure speech	5:12
	C. For prayer	5:13–18
	D. For compassion	5:19, 20

Greeting to the Twelve Tribes

JAMES, [a]a bondservant of God and
of the Lord Jesus Christ,

To the twelve tribes which are scattered abroad:

Greetings.

Profiting from Trials

1 2 My brethren, [a]count it all joy
[b]when you fall into various trials,
1 3 [a]knowing that the testing of your
faith produces [1]patience.
1 4 But let patience have *its* perfect
work, that you may be [1]perfect and
complete, lacking nothing.
1 5 [a]If any of you lacks *wisdom,
[b]let him ask of God, who gives to all
liberally and without **reproach,** and
[c]it will be given to him.

WORD WEALTH

1:5 reproach, *oneidizo* (on-eye-*did*-zoe); Strong's *#3679:* Originally, to behave in a very juvenile and immature way, describing youngsters who make fun of, tease, and taunt each other. Then the word came to denote mocking, ridiculing, scolding, insulting, and using words angrily or sarcastically. James 1:5 assures us that God gives without reminding us of our unworthiness.

6 [a]But let him *ask in faith, with no
*doubting, for he who doubts is like a
wave of the sea driven and tossed by
the wind.
7 For let not that man suppose that
he will receive anything from the Lord;
8 *he is* [a]a double-minded man, unstable in all his ways.

The Perspective of Rich and Poor

9 Let the *lowly brother glory in his
exaltation,
10 but the rich in his humiliation, be- 6
cause [a]as a flower of the field he will
pass away.
11 For no sooner has the sun risen with
a burning heat than it withers the
grass; its flower falls, and its beautiful
appearance perishes. So the rich man
also will fade away in his pursuits.

Loving God Under Trials

12 [a]Blessed* *is* the man who *endures
temptation; for when he has been approved, he will receive [b]the crown of
life [c]which the Lord has *promised to
those who love Him.
13 Let no one say when he is tempted,
"I am tempted by God"; for God cannot

CHAPTER 1

1 [a]Acts 12:17
2 [a]Acts 5:41 [b]1 Pet. 1:6
3 [a]Rom. 5:3–5 [1]*endurance* or *perseverance*
4 [1]*mature*
5 [a]1 Kin. 3:9; James 3:17 [b]Prov. 2:3–6; Matt. 7:7 [c]Jer. 29:12 *See WW at Acts 6:10.
6 [a][Mark 11:23, 24]; Acts 10:20 *See WW at Matt. 7:7. • See WW at Acts 11:12.
8 [a]James 4:8
9 *See WW at 2 Cor. 7:6.
10 [a]Job 14:2
12 [a]Job 5:17; Luke 6:22; Heb. 10:36; James 5:11; [1 Pet. 3:14; 4:14] [b][1 Cor. 9:25] [c]Matt. 10:22 *See WW at Matt. 5:3. • See WW at Matt. 24:13. • See WW at Acts 7:5.

1:1 James made no boast about his personal relationship to Jesus, nor did he identify himself as a church leader. His greatest honor was to be **a bondservant of God**. **The twelve tribes** designates the nation Israel, and **scattered abroad** translates a technical term (Greek *diaspora*) describing Jews scattered throughout Gentile lands. Thus, this letter is addressed to Jewish Christians living outside Palestine.

1:2, 3 Becoming a Christian does not automatically exclude a believer from difficulties (see John 15:20; 2 Tim. 3:12; 1 Pet. 1:6, 7; 4:12–19). The proper attitude in meeting adversity is to **count it all joy,** which is not an emotional reaction but a deliberate intelligent appraisal of the situation from God's perspective, viewing **trials** as a means of moral and spiritual growth. We do not rejoice in the trials themselves, but in their possible results. **Testing** carries the idea of proving genuineness. Trials serve as a discipline to purge faith of dross, stripping away what is false. **Patience** is not a passive resignation to adverse circumstances, but a positive steadfastness that bravely endures.

1:2 See section 1 of Truth-In-Action at the end of James.

1:3 See section 1 of Truth-In-Action at the end of James.

1:4 See section 1 of Truth-In-Action at the end of James.

1:4 Perfect does not denote absolute sinlessness, but carries the idea of being fully developed or mature. **Complete** underscores the thought of fullness and wholeness.

1:5 See section 1 of Truth-In-Action at the end of James.

1:5 The **wisdom** which may be had by asking "in faith" (v. 6) is not intellectual knowledge or philosophical speculation, but spiritual understanding of the purpose of trials. When God grants a gift He does so **liberally and without reproach,** that is, generously, not stintingly, condescendingly, or grudgingly.

1:8 A double-minded man is a person drawn in two opposite directions. His allegiance is divided and because of his lack of sincerity he vacillates between belief and disbelief, sometimes thinking that God will help him and at other times giving up all hope in Him. Such a person is **unstable in all his ways,** not only in his prayer life. The lack of consistency in his exercise of faith betrays his general character.

1:9–11 Both poverty and prosperity are concrete examples of trials that test our faith. Either may result in spiritual disaster. The Christian who is poor materially can rejoice in his high spiritual position as a child of God, while **the rich** person can rejoice in new values, realizing the temporal nature of earthly wealth as opposed to the eternal benefits of spiritual possessions. **Fade away** refers to the certain destruction of people who are rich only in temporal things.

1:10 See section 6 of Truth-In-Action at the end of James.

1:12 Those who remain steadfast under testing **will receive the crown of life,** which refers not to life hereafter, but to life here and now, enjoyed more abundantly and in greater fullness.

1:13 Having discussed temptation in the form of outward trials (vv. 2–12), James now turns to temptation as enticement to evil. Many Scriptures reveal that God sometimes sends trials as a means of testing (see, for example, Gen. 22:1; Deut. 8:2; 2 Chr. 32:31), but James emphatically declares that God's perfect holiness puts Him beyond the reach of temptation and that He does not solicit to sin.

be tempted by evil, nor does He Himself tempt anyone.
14 But each one is tempted when he
is drawn away by his own desires and
enticed.
15 Then, [a]when *desire has conceived,
it gives birth to *sin; and sin, when it
is full-grown, [b]brings forth death.
16 Do not be deceived, my beloved
brethren.
17 [a]Every *good gift and every *perfect
gift is from above, and comes down
from the Father of lights, [b]with whom
there is no variation or shadow of turning.
18 [a]Of His own will He brought us
forth by the [b]word of truth, [c]that we
might be a kind of firstfruits of His
*creatures.

Qualities Needed in Trials

19 [1]So then, my beloved brethren, let
every man be swift to hear, [a]slow to
speak, [b]slow to wrath;
20 for the wrath of man does not produce the righteousness of God.

Doers—Not Hearers Only

21 Therefore [a]lay aside all filthiness
and [1]overflow of wickedness, and receive with meekness the implanted
word, [b]which is able to save your
souls.
2 22 But [a]be doers of the word, and not
hearers only, deceiving yourselves.
23 For [a]if anyone is a hearer of the
word and not a doer, he is like a man
observing his natural face in a mirror;
24 for he observes himself, goes away,

15 [a]Job 15:35; Ps. 7:14; Is. 59:4 [b][Rom. 5:12; 6:23] *See WW at 2 Tim. 2:22. • See WW at John 1:29.
17 [a]John 3:27 [b]Num. 23:19 *See WW at Phil. 1:6. • See WW at James 3:2.
18 [a]John 1:13 [b]2 Cor. 6:7; 1 Thess. 2:13; 2 Tim. 2:15; [1 Pet. 1:3, 23] [c][Eph. 1:12, 13]; Heb. 12:23; Rev. 14:4 *See WW at Rev. 5:13.
19 [a]Prov. 10:19; 17:27 [b]Prov. 14:17; 16:32; Eccl. 7:9 [1]NU *Know this* or *This you know*
21 [a]Col. 3:8 [b]Acts 13:26 [1]*abundance*
22 [a]Matt. 7:21–28; Luke 6:46–49; [Rom. 2:13; James 1:22–25; 2:14–20]
23 [a]Luke 6:47
24 *See WW at John 6:21.
25 [a][John 8:32; Rom. 8:2; 2 Cor. 3:17]; Gal. 2:4; 6:2; James 2:12; 1 Pet. 2:16 [b]John 13:17 *See WW at 1 Cor. 10:29.
26 [a]Ps. 34:13 [1]NU omits *among you*

and *immediately forgets what kind of
man he was.
25 But [a]he who looks into the perfect
law of *liberty and continues *in it*, and
is not a forgetful hearer but a doer of
the work, [b]this one will be blessed in
what he does.

KINGDOM DYNAMICS

1:23–25 God's Word: Purifier unto Holy Living, THE WORD OF GOD. Purity of life is not a quest for perfection as much as it is a quest for liberation from those things that may inhibit effectiveness and reduce power-filled living. This text shows the Word of God as a means of reflection—a mirror into which we are to look and see ourselves. The call is not only to heed what we see and accept the Bible's corrective instruction, but there is an unwritten lesson here. We should avoid the temptation to see (and judge) others in the Word, analyzing what they ought to do, instead of what we need to do. 2 Cor. 3:18 also likens God's Word to a mirror, but describes the image seen as no less than the Lord Jesus Himself. The sum of the two texts: 1) The Bible shows us Christ's likeness in order that 2) we may measure our conduct and character against His and allow God to shape us into Christ's likeness (Rom. 8:29). Other promises for cleansing through God's Word: Jer. 20:9 speaks of the "fire" in the Word, which can purge as well as ignite; and Ps. 119:9 holds special promise to the one who wants a pure life of holy power. God's Word is a powerful, cleansing, delivering agent.

(John 14:21/Is. 55:10, 11) J.W.H.

26 If anyone [1]among you thinks he is
religious, and [a]does not bridle his

1:14, 15 When inner **desires** respond to outward enticement, sin is spawned. James does not mention Satan's role in temptation. His purpose is not to discuss the origin of sin but to explain that enticement to evil is not from God. In stressing the inward nature of temptation, James leaves sinners no excuse. Satan is indeed the external source of temptation, but no one can blame him for the roots of sinful deeds, which lie within the individual. See Mark 7:1–23.

1:17 Not only is God not responsible for human sin, He is the source of all good. In contrast to the wandering heavenly bodies He created, God is unchangeable. He always keeps His promises.

1:18 God's greatest gift to us is regeneration. By the exercise **of His own will He brought us forth** into new life. His instrument was **the word of truth,** which Paul identifies as "the gospel of . . . salvation" (Eph. 1:13). God's purpose was to present believers as ***a kind of firstfruits.*** *(The first part of* the crop was the pledge of a greater harvest to come.) As such, James and the other Christians of his generation were a foretaste of a great host of believers to come. The phrase **of His creatures** may indicate that believers are the first stage of the ultimate redemption of all creation, which is now under the divine curse since the Fall.

1:19, 20 The anger that springs from self-centeredness does not accomplish **the righteousness of God,** but is conducive only to malice and destruction.

1:21 Salvation comes not from the use of worldly methods, but from a meek, gentle acceptance of **the implanted word,** which God has caused to take root in the heart.

1:22–25 See section 2 of Truth-In-Action at the end of James.

1:22 Salvation leads to service. It is self-deception to believe that God's goal for church attendance is merely to hear the word, instead of to experience a transformation of life that results in ministry.

1:23–25 The one who merely hears **the word** quickly forgets it; only the one who acts on the word and **continues *in it*** is **blessed**. God's Word is **the perfect law of liberty**. It does not enslave us to the bondage of legalism, but rather frees us to keep its precepts by an inward compulsion.

1:26, 27 An uncontrolled **tongue** and a deceived **heart** are companions of an empty religion. True religion will issue in practical living, as exemplified in pure speech, pure love, and pure character. While James does not give an exhaustive list of the positive duties of genuine religion, he presents these as typical characteristics.

tongue but deceives his own heart, this
one's religion *is* *useless.
27 [a]Pure* and undefiled religion before
God and the Father is this: [b]to visit orphans and widows in their trouble,
[c]*and* to keep oneself unspotted from
the world.

26 *See WW at Acts 14:15.
27 [a]Matt. 25:34–36 [b]Is. 1:17 [c][Rom. 12:2] *See WW at Matt. 5:8.

CHAPTER 2

1 [a]Acts 7:2; 1 Cor. 2:8 [b]Lev. 19:15 *See WW at Col. 3:25.
2 [1]*bright* [2]*vile*
3 [1]Lit. *look upon*
4 [1]*differentiated* *See WW at Luke 2:35.
5 [a]Job 34:19; John 7:48; 1 Cor. 1:27 [b]Luke 12:21; 1 Tim. 6:18; Rev. 2:9 [c]Ex. 20:6
6 [a]1 Cor. 11:22 [b]Acts 13:50
7 [a]Acts 11:26; 1 Pet. 4:16
8 [a]Lev. 19:18
9 [a]Lev. 19:15; Deut. 1:17 [1]Lit. *receive the face*
10 [a]Gal. 3:10 [b]Deut. 27:26
11 [a]Ex. 20:14; Deut. 5:18 [b]Ex. 20:13; Deut. 5:17
12 [a]James 1:25 *See WW at 1 Cor. 10:29.
13 [a]Job 22:6 [b]Prov. 21:13; Matt. 18:32–35; [Luke 6:37] [c]Mic. 7:18; [Matt. 5:7] [d]Rom. 12:8 *See WW at Matt. 5:22. • See WW at 2 Tim. 1:16.
14 [a]Matt. 7:21–23, 26; 21:28–32

Beware of Personal Favoritism

3 **2** My brethren, do not hold the faith
of our Lord Jesus Christ, [a]*the Lord*
of glory, with [b]partiality.*
2 For if there should come into your
assembly a man with gold rings, in
[1]fine apparel, and there should also
come in a poor man in [2]filthy clothes,
3 and you [1]pay attention to the one
wearing the fine clothes and say to
him, "You sit here in a good place,"
and say to the poor man, "You stand
there," or, "Sit here at my footstool,"
4 have you not [1]shown partiality
among yourselves, and become judges
with evil *thoughts?
5 Listen, my beloved brethren:
[a]Has God not chosen the poor of this
world *to be* [b]rich in faith and heirs of
the kingdom [c]which He promised to
those who love Him?
6 But [a]you have dishonored the poor
man. Do not the rich oppress you
[b]and drag you into the courts?
7 Do they not blaspheme that noble
name by which you are [a]called?
8 If you really fulfill *the* royal law according to the Scripture, [a]*"You shall*
love your neighbor as yourself," you
do well;
3 9 but if you [1]**show partiality,** you
commit sin, and are convicted by the
law as [a]transgressors.

WORD WEALTH

2:9 show partiality, *prosopolepteo* (pros-oh-pol-ape-*teh*-oh); Strong's *#4380:* From *prosopon,* "a face," and *lambano,* "to lay hold of." The word denotes making distinctions among people based on their rank or influence, showing preference for the rich and powerful. The impartial God shows to all people the same love, grace, blessings, and benefits of His salvation.

KINGDOM DYNAMICS

2:1–9 Respect of Persons, HUMAN WORTH. Human value cannot be equated with race, wealth, social standing, or educational level. All are significant and valuable in God's order. To regard a race, group, or individual as less important than another is sin in view of the fact that Christ died for all people and for each one in particular. At the foot of the Cross we are equal, both in our worth to God (He sent His Son to die for each of us) and in our need to accept His gift of salvation. Let us learn to respect and honor every person and each people regardless of their station or color. Christ said, "Inasmuch as you did *it* to one of the least of these My brethren, you did *it* to Me" (Matt. 25:40).

(Rom. 12:3–5/Luke 10:33) C.B.

10 For whoever shall keep the whole
law, and yet [a]stumble in one *point,*
[b]he is guilty of all.
11 For He who said, [a]*"Do not commit*
adultery," also said, [b]*"Do not murder."*
Now if you do not commit adultery, but
you do murder, you have become a
transgressor of the law.
12 So speak and so do as those who
will be judged by [a]the law of *liberty.
13 For [a]judgment* is without *mercy
to the one who has shown [b]no [c]mercy.
[d]Mercy triumphs over judgment.

Faith Without Works Is Dead

14 [a]What *does it* profit, my brethren,
if someone says he has faith but does

2:1–13 An empty religion will betray itself in relationships. To make superficial distinctions among people, preferring those of prestige and position, is incompatible with **the faith of our Lord** (v. 1), which excludes favoritism based on wealth or class.
2:1–8 See section 3 of Truth-In-Action at the end of James.
2:2 **Assembly** is literally "synagogue," possibly suggesting that the letter was written before Jewish Christians adopted a different name for their gatherings. On the other hand, the term may have been used interchangeably with the word "church" (see 5:14).
2:4 Those who fawn upon the rich, while despising the poor, determine the true value of a person by worldly standards and reveal **evil thoughts,** such as covetousness and pride.
2:6, 7 James is not speaking exhaustively, characterizing all rich people. He is obviously describing certain rich unbelievers who were exploiting the poor and blaspheming Jesus.
2:8 ***The* royal law,** commanding us to love, is the king of laws, comprehending all other commandments dealing with human relationships.
2:9 See section 3 of Truth-In-Action at the end of James.
2:9 Believers cannot love their neighbors as themselves and **show partiality,** because the two are mutually exclusive. To show the favoritism described in this passage is to **commit sin.**
2:10–13 James does not teach that to commit one sin, such as **murder** or **adultery,** is to be **guilty** of every other individual sin listed in the **law.** He views the law as an expression of God's will, which is an unfragmented **whole,** so that breaking any part of the law constitutes breaking the law as a whole. To disregard God's will as revealed in the law is not merely to break an isolated rule; it is to rebel against God Himself.
2:14–26 James does not set faith against works, but rather discusses two kinds of faith: a dead faith and a saving faith.

not have works? Can faith save him?
15 [a]If a brother or sister is naked and destitute of daily food,
16 and [a]one of you says to them, "Depart in peace, be warmed and *filled," but you do not give them the things which are needed for the body, what *does it* profit?
17 Thus also faith by itself, if it does not have works, is dead.
18 But someone will say, "You have faith, and I have works." [a]Show me your faith without [1]your works, [b]and I will show you my faith by [2]my works.
19 You believe that there is one God. You do well. Even the demons believe—and tremble!
20 But do you want to know, O foolish man, that faith without works is [1]dead?
21 Was not Abraham our father justified by works [a]when he offered Isaac his son on the altar?
22 Do you see [a]that faith was **working together** with his works, and by [b]works faith was made [1]perfect?*

WORD WEALTH

2:22 working together, *sunergeo* (soon-erg-*eh*-oh); Strong's *#4903:* Compare "synergist" and "synergism." From *sun,* "together," and *ergeo,* "to work"; hence, to cooperate, help, collaborate, colabor. There is a practical harmony or synergism between vertical faith in God and horizontal works to a needy world. Faith is both spiritual and practical.

23 And the Scripture was fulfilled which says, [a]*"Abraham believed God, and it was* [1]*accounted* to him for righteousness."* And he was called [b]the *friend of God.
24 You see then that a man is justified by works, and not by faith only.
25 Likewise, [a]was not Rahab the harlot also justified by works when she received the messengers and sent *them* out another way?
26 For as the body without the spirit is dead, so faith without works is dead also.

15 [a]Matt. 25:35; Luke 3:11
16 [a][1 John 3:17, 18] *See WW at Matt. 15:33.
18 [a]Col. 1:6; 1 Thess. 1:3; Heb. 6:10 [b][Gal. 5:6]; James 3:13 [1]NU omits *your* [2]NU omits *my*
20 [1]NU *useless*
21 [a]Gen. 22:9, 10, 12, 16–18
22 [a][John 6:29]; Heb. 11:17 [b]John 8:39 [1]*complete* *See WW at 1 John 2:5.
23 [a]Gen. 15:6; Rom. 4:3 [b]2 Chr. 20:7; Is. 41:8 [1]*credited* *See WW at Rom. 4:3. • See WW at John 11:11.
25 [a]Heb. 11:31

CHAPTER 3

1 [a][Matt. 23:8]; Rom. 2:21; 1 Tim. 1:7 [b]Luke 6:37 *See WW at Rev. 20:4.
2 [a]1 Kin. 8:46 [b]Ps. 34:13 [c][Matt. 12:34–37; James 3:2–12] [1]*mature*

The Untamable Tongue

3 My brethren, [a]let not many of you 4
become teachers, [b]knowing that
we shall receive a stricter *judgment.

KINGDOM DYNAMICS

3:1 The High Standard for Leadership, LEADER TRAITS. Leaders are judged with a higher standard than those who follow. 1 Tim. 3 and Titus 1 give great attention to details, but here James reminds that those in leadership will be held accountable for exemplifying Jesus Christ in their spirit and behavior, as well as in their words and duties. Government, military, and business leaders are seldom judged on their personal lives. Leaders in the kingdom, however, are judged not so much by what they accomplish as by the character they reveal—who they are before what they do. This high standard applies not so much to the leader's achievements as to the condition of his or her heart and spirit. It is possible to have grand accomplishments and even orthodox behavior but still manifest a loveless, ungodly spirit. But if first the leader's heart is right, godly behavior will always follow and good leadership will be manifested.

(Gen. 12; 17; 22/1 Tim. 3:1–13) J.B.

2 For [a]we all stumble in many things. 4
[b]If anyone does not stumble in word,
[c]he *is* a [1]**perfect** man, able also to bridle the whole body.

WORD WEALTH

3:2 perfect, *teleios* (*tel*-eye-oss); Strong's *#5046:* From *telos,* "end." *Teleios* refers to that which has reached an end, that is, finished, complete, perfect. When ap-

---

Saving faith is not simply a profession or an empty claim (vv. 14–17), nor is it merely the acceptance of a creed (vv. 18–20). Saving faith is that which produces an obedient life (vv. 21–26).

2:14 The question is literally, "**Can** that kind of **faith** (the kind that does not issue in good works) **save him?**" The implied answer is, "No."

2:18 Our **works** show the genuineness of what we profess.

2:19 Intellectual assent to a creed is not saving faith.

2:21–24 God pronounced **Abraham** righteous the moment he **believed** (Gen. 15:4–6), but it was only by his later obedience that he demonstrated the reality of his **righteousness**.

2:22 Faith creates **works,** works perfect faith.

2:24 James and Paul do not contradict each other. Paul emphasizes that faith is not religious deeds without a born-again heart; James stresses that faith is not a born-again heart without deeds. Neither would agree to the validity of an empty creedal faith.

2:25 Abraham was an upright, founding patriarch while **Rahab** represents the average person at the other end of the social and moral scale. Both, however, were justified on the same basis.

3:1 See section 4 of Truth-In-Action at the end of James.

3:1 Teachers are responsible not only for themselves but for all those they influence (see Matt. 23).

3:2–12 The tongue is a little member (v. 5), but its power and influence for good or bad are out of proportion to its size.

3:2 See section 4 of Truth-In-Action at the end of James.

plied to persons, it signifies consummate soundness, and includes the idea of being whole. More particularly, when applied to believers, it denotes maturity.

3 [1]Indeed, [a]we put bits in horses' mouths that they may *obey us, and we turn their whole body.
4 Look also at ships: although they are so large and are driven by fierce winds, they are turned by a very small rudder wherever the pilot desires.
5 Even so [a]the tongue is a little member and [b]boasts great things. See how great a forest a little fire kindles!
6 And [a]the tongue *is* a fire, a world of [1]iniquity.* The tongue is so set among our members that it [b]defiles the whole body, and sets on fire the course of [2]nature; and it is set on fire by [3]hell.
7 For every kind of beast and bird, of reptile and creature of the sea, is tamed and has been tamed by mankind.
8 But no man can tame the tongue. *It is* an unruly evil, [a]full of deadly poison.
4 9 With it we *bless our God and Father, and with it we curse men, who have been made [a]in the [1]similitude of God.
10 Out of the same mouth proceed blessing and cursing. My brethren, these things ought not to be so.
11 Does a spring send forth fresh *water* and bitter from the same opening?
12 Can a [a]fig tree, my brethren, bear olives, or a grapevine bear figs? [1]Thus no spring yields both salt water and fresh.

Heavenly Versus Demonic Wisdom

13 [a]Who *is* wise and understanding among you? Let him show by good conduct *that* his works *are done* in the meekness of wisdom.
14 But if you have [a]bitter envy and [1]self-seeking* in your hearts, [b]do not boast and lie against the truth.

3 [a]Ps. 32:9 [1]NU *Now if* *See WW at 2 Thess. 3:4.
5 [a]Prov. 12:18; 15:2 [b]Ps. 12:3; 73:8
6 [a]Prov. 16:27 [b][Matt. 12:36; 15:11, 18] [1]*unrighteousness* [2]*existence* [3]Gr. *Gehenna* *See WW at John 7:18.
8 [a]Ps. 140:3
9 [a]Gen. 1:26; 5:1; 9:6 [1]*likeness* *See WW at Luke 6:28.
12 [a]Matt. 7:16–20 [1]NU *Neither can a salty spring produce fresh water.*
13 [a]Gal. 6:4
14 [a]Rom. 13:13 [b]Rom. 2:17 [1]*selfish ambition* *See WW at Phil. 1:16.
15 [a]Phil. 3:19
16 [a]1 Cor. 3:3 *See WW at Phil. 1:16.
17 [a]1 Cor. 2:6, 7 [b]James 2:1 [c]Rom. 12:9 *See WW at 1 John 3:3. • See WW at 1 Tim. 3:3. • See WW at 1 Pet. 1:22.
18 [a]Prov. 11:18

CHAPTER 4

1 [a]Rom. 7:23 [1]*battles*
2 [1]*battle* [2]NU, M omit *Yet* *See WW at 1 Cor. 14:1.
3 [a]Job 27:8, 9 [b][Ps. 66:18]
4 [a]1 John 2:15 [b]Gal. 1:4 [1]NU omits *Adulterers and* *See WW at John 11:11.
5 [a]Gen. 6:5

15 [a]This wisdom does not descend from above, but *is* earthly, **sensual,** demonic.

WORD WEALTH

3:15 sensual, *psuchikos* (psoo-khee-*koss*); Strong's *#5591:* Belonging to the natural or physical, unspiritual. It is living in the domain of the five senses, concerned with this life only. Being sensual is being in common with lusts, illicit desires, and unclean practices that open a person to the demonic. Gal. 5:16 admonishes, "Walk in the Spirit, and you shall not fulfill the lust of the flesh."

16 For [a]where envy and *self-seeking *exist,* confusion and every evil thing *are* there.
17 But [a]the wisdom that is from above is first *pure, then peaceable, *gentle, willing to yield, full of mercy and good fruits, [b]without partiality [c]and *without hypocrisy.
18 [a]Now the fruit of righteousness is sown in peace by those who make peace.

Pride Promotes Strife

4 Where do [1]wars and fights *come* 5
from among you? Do *they* not *come* from your *desires for* pleasure [a]that war in your members?
2 You lust and do not have. You murder and *covet and cannot obtain. You fight and [1]war. [2]Yet you do not have because you do not ask.
3 [a]You ask and do not receive, [b]because you ask amiss, that you may spend *it* on your pleasures.
4 [1]Adulterers and adulteresses! Do you not know that [a]friendship with the world is enmity with God? [b]Whoever therefore wants to be a *friend of the world makes himself an enemy of God.
5 Or do you think that the Scripture says in vain, [a]"The Spirit who dwells in us yearns jealously"?
6 But He gives more grace. Therefore He says:

3:6–8 The true source of the **unruly evil** produced by the tongue is **hell**. At one end the tongue spits **deadly poison;** at the other end it is manipulated by wicked spirits. Therefore, **no man can tame** it.
3:9–12 See section 4 of Truth-In-Action at the end of James.
3:9–12 James's previous comment does not mean the tongue does not also speak good. It is notoriously inconsistent, and its propensity is to speak evil.
3:13–18 James continues his discussion of teaching with a contrast of **demonic** and divine **wisdom**.
3:13 A teacher should practice what he teaches.
3:14 A teacher who is motivated by selfish ambition will always **lie against the truth**.
3:17 James describes practical, moral **wisdom,** not theoretical knowledge.
4:1, 2 See section 5 of Truth-In-Action at the end of James.
4:1, 2 In contrast to the heavenly wisdom that produces an atmosphere of peace, in which the seed of righteousness will grow (3:18), earthly wisdom causes chronic interpersonal warfare. The source is a contentious, selfish nature.
4:4 Adulterers and adulteresses are metaphorical terms in the OT for those who break their vows to love and serve God, and instead follow idols. An illicit affair with worldliness results in estrangement and hostility with God.
4:4–10 Nevertheless, God will receive the adulterer who returns in humility, submitting to God and not the **devil.**

[a]*"God resists the proud,*
*But gives grace to the *humble."*

Humility Cures Worldliness

5 7 Therefore *submit to God. [a]Resist*
the devil and he will flee from you.
5 8 [a]Draw near to God and He will
draw near to you. [b]Cleanse *your*
hands, *you* sinners; and [c]purify *your*
hearts, *you* double-minded.
9 [a]Lament and mourn and weep! Let
your laughter be turned to *mourning
and *your* joy to gloom.
10 [a]Humble* yourselves in the sight of
the Lord, and He will **lift** you **up.**

WORD WEALTH

4:10 lift up, *hupsoo* (hoop-*sah*-oh); Strong's *#5312:* Related to the noun *hupsos,* "height," the verb signifies to lift or raise up. It is used literally (John 3:14; 8:28; 12:32, 34); figuratively, of spiritual privileges given to a city (Matt. 11:23; Luke 10:15); and metaphorically, in the sense of exalting or uplifting (Acts 2:33; 5:31; 13:17). The Bible warns us that exalting ourselves will result in a disgraceful fall, but humbling ourselves leads to exaltation in this and the next world.

Do Not Judge a Brother

5 11 [a]Do not speak evil of one another,
brethren. He who speaks evil of a
brother [b]and judges his brother,
speaks evil of the law and judges the
law. But if you judge the law, you are
not a doer of the law but a judge.
12 There is one [1]Lawgiver, [a]who is
able to save and to destroy. [b]Who[2] are
you to judge [3]another?

Do Not Boast About Tomorrow

5 13 Come now, you who say, "Today or
tomorrow [1]we will go to such and such

6 [a]Prov. 3:34 *See WW at 2 Cor. 7:6.
7 [a][Eph. 4:27; 6:11] *See WW at 1 Cor. 14:32. • See WW at Eph. 6:13.
8 [a]2 Chr. 15:2 [b]Is. 1:16 [c]1 Pet. 1:22
9 [a]Matt. 5:4 *See WW at Rev. 18:11.
10 [a]Job 22:29 *See WW at Matt. 18:4.
11 [a]1 Pet. 2:1–3 [b][Matt. 7:1–5]
12 [a][Matt. 10:28] [b]Rom. 14:4 [1]NU adds *and Judge* [2]NU, M *But who* [3]NU *a neighbor*
13 [1]M *let us*
14 [a]Job 7:7
15 [a]Acts 18:21
16 [a]1 Cor. 5:6
17 [a][Luke 12:47]

CHAPTER 5

1 [a][Luke 6:24]
2 [a]Matt. 6:19 [b]Job 13:28 [1]*have rotted*
3 [a]Rom. 2:5 *See WW at Rev. 15:5.
4 [a]Lev. 19:13 [b]Deut. 24:15 [1]Lit., in Heb., *Hosts* *See WW at Rev. 22:12.
5 [1]*indulgence* [2]Lit. *nourished* [3]NU omits *as*
6 *See WW at Matt. 1:19.
7 *See WW at 1 Cor. 15:23.

a city, spend a year there, buy and sell,
and make a profit";
14 whereas you do not know what *will*
happen tomorrow. For what *is* your
life? [a]It is even a vapor that appears
for a little time and then vanishes
away.
15 Instead you *ought* to say, [a]"If the
Lord wills, we shall live and do this
or that."
16 But now you boast in your arrogance. [a]All such boasting is evil.
17 Therefore, [a]to him who knows to do 5
good and does not do *it,* to him it is
sin.

Rich Oppressors Will Be Judged

5 Come now, *you* [a]rich, weep and 6
howl for your miseries that are
coming upon *you!*
2 Your [a]riches [1]are corrupted, and
[b]your garments are moth-eaten.
3 Your gold and silver are corroded,
and their corrosion will be a *witness
against you and will eat your flesh like
fire. [a]You have heaped up treasure in
the last days.
4 Indeed [a]the *wages of the laborers
who mowed your fields, which you
kept back by fraud, cry out; and
[b]the cries of the reapers have reached
the ears of the Lord of [1]Sabaoth.
5 You have lived on the earth in pleasure and [1]luxury; you have [2]fattened
your hearts [3]as in a day of slaughter.
6 You have condemned, you have
murdered the *just; he does not resist
you.

Be Patient and Persevering

7 Therefore be patient, brethren, until 1
the *coming of the Lord. See *how* the
farmer waits for the precious fruit of
the earth, waiting patiently for it until
it receives the early and latter rain.
8 You also be patient. Establish your

4:7 See section 5 of Truth-In-Action at the end of James.
4:8 See section 5 of Truth-In-Action at the end of James.
4:8 A **double-minded** person attempts to hold to God and the world at the same time. See note on 1:8.
4:11 See section 5 of Truth-In-Action at the end of James.
4:11, 12 Those who **judge** others in the sense of condemning them are guilty of assuming the prerogatives of God Himself.
4:13–16 See section 5 of Truth-In-Action at the end of James.
4:13–16 *A clear characteristic of having an affair with worldliness* is making plans without consulting God. Such action is **boasting,** that is, a presumption that oneself, not God, is in control of the circumstances of life.
4:17 See section 5 of Truth-In-Action at the end of James.
4:17 Sin is not only actively committing evil deeds; it is also passively failing to do what you know God wants you to do.
5:1–6 See section 6 of Truth-In-Action at the end of James.
5:1–6 See note on 1:9–11. When a rich person appears at the judgment of God, dishonestly gained wealth will not protect, but will attack.
5:4 The Lord of Sabaoth is literally "the Lord of Hosts." He is commander of the armies of heaven.
5:5 The rich oppressors are like **fattened** pampered animals that are unaware of their approaching **day of slaughter.**
5:6 The unjust rich controlled the courts through bribery or other forms of injustice, and their exploitation of the poor often had legal sanction.
5:7–9 James encourages his readers to **be patient,** with the reminder that **the coming of the Lord** is near, at which time God will fulfill His function as **Judge** to reward the righteous and punish the wicked.
5:7, 8 See section 1 of Truth-In-Action at the end of James.

hearts, for the coming of the Lord
[1]is at hand.
9 Do not [1]grumble against one another, brethren, lest you be [2]con-
demned. Behold, the Judge is standing
at the door!
10 [a]My brethren, take the prophets,
who spoke in the name of the Lord,
as an example of suffering and [b]pa-
tience.*
11 Indeed [a]we count them blessed who
[b]endure. You have heard of [c]the perseverance of Job and seen [d]the end *intended by* the Lord—that [e]the Lord is
very compassionate and merciful.
12 But above all, my brethren, [a]do not
swear, either by heaven or by earth or
with any other oath. But let your "Yes"
be "Yes," and *your* "No," "No," lest
you fall into [1]judgment.*

Meeting Specific Needs

13 Is anyone among you suffering? Let
him [a]pray. Is anyone cheerful? [b]Let
him sing psalms.
14 Is anyone among you sick? Let him
call for the elders of the church, and
let them *pray over him, [a]anointing
him with oil in the name of the Lord.
15 And the prayer of faith will save the
sick, and the Lord will raise him up.
[a]And if he has committed sins, he will
be forgiven.

8 [1]*has drawn near*
9 [1]Lit. *groan* [2]NU, M *judged*
10 [a]Matt. 5:12 [b]Heb. 10:36 *See WW at Heb. 6:12.
11 [a][Ps. 94:12; Matt. 5:10]; James 1:2 [b][James 1:12] [c]Job 1:21, 22; 2:10 [d]Job 42:10 [e]Num. 14:18
12 [a]Matt. 5:34–37 [1]M *hypocrisy* *See WW at Gal. 2:13.
13 [a]Ps. 50:14, 15 [b]Eph. 5:19
14 [a]Mark 6:13; 16:18 *See WW at Matt. 6:6.
15 [a]Is. 33:24
16 [a]Num. 11:2 [1]NU *Therefore confess your sins* [2]*supplication* *See WW at 1 Thess. 2:13.
17 [a]Acts 14:15 [b]1 Kin. 17:1; 18:1
18 [a]1 Kin. 18:1, 42

16 [1]Confess *your* trespasses to one another, and pray for one another, that
you may be healed. [a]The *effective,
[2]fervent prayer of a righteous man
avails much.
17 Elijah was a man [a]with a nature like
ours, and [b]he prayed earnestly that it
would not rain; and it did not rain on
the land for three years and six
months.
18 And he prayed [a]again, and the
heaven gave rain, and the earth produced its fruit.

KINGDOM DYNAMICS

5:13–18 The New Testament Divine Healing Covenant, DIVINE HEALING. Just as Ex. 15:26 is called the OT Divine Healing Covenant, James 5:13–18 is viewed as the NT Divine Healing Covenant. The inspired apostle affirms that those sick persons whom the elders of the church anoint with oil and for whom they pray will be healed.

Some critics of healing for today contend that oil was a medicinal remedy with which the sick were to be massaged, but it is clear the oil is intended as a symbol of the work of the Holy Spirit, who is present to glorify Jesus in healing works (John 16:14, 15). The text plainly states that "the Lord [not the oil] will raise him up" (v. 15). This practice was

(*cont. on next page*)

5:10 See Heb. 11 for the testimonies of **the prophets**.
5:11 Only by Job's suffering could he intimately experience and comprehend the Lord as **compassionate and merciful**.
5:12 Originally, swearing was an attempt to involve the character and authority of God to support a claim or a promise (Lev. 19:12; Deut. 23:23). Then, as often is the case today, the Lord's name was debased by using it to excessively emphasize a trivial point. James cites Jesus (Matt. 5:37), insisting that we should have integrity in what we utter, and that after a divine oath, failure to perform perfectly one's word besmirches God's holiness to observers.
5:14 The initiative lies with the **sick** person in sending **for the elders** who are the officers **of the church** (see 1 Tim. 3:1–7; Titus 1:5–9). Their qualifications characterize them as men of personal uprightness and spiritual maturity, having special ability, particularly in the area of discernment. As overseers they hold positions of authority and presumably are men of faith and prayer. **Anointing . . . with oil** does not refer to a medicinal act (see Mark 6:13) or to a magic potion, but is symbolic of the consecration of the sick person and the joyous presence of the Holy Spirit, in this case to bring healing. James stresses God's healing power through prayer that accompanies the anointing.
5:15 **The prayer of faith** in Greek is literally "the prayer of the faith," referring to the gift of faith the Holy Spirit gives (see note on 1 Cor. 12:9). Here the faith is granted to one or more of the elders to believe for the healing. **Save** in this instance refers to physical restoration rather than to spiritual salvation. The healing of the **sick** person would indicate the forgiveness of any **sins** that may have been responsible for that particular illness. Not all sickness is caused by one's sin, but in some cases there is a connection (see Mark 2:5–11; 1 Cor. 11:30).
5:16 Having spoken of the place of prayer in regard to sickness (vv. 13–15), James offers a summarizing inference (see marginal note, "therefore") which illustrates the power of prayer. The **trespasses** James particularly has in mind may be those of the sick person, which could have been the root of his sickness, or they may be those of believers in general. Regardless, he does not enjoin a general public confession of all sins without any discretion whatever. Certainly, public wrongdoings that have tainted the whole church should be confessed before the church, but James especially refers to confessing sins to the individuals injured by them (see Matt. 5:23, 24). There is also a place for confidential confession to godly intercessors who will offer prevailing prayer for the offender and provide wise counsel to him. James stresses the effectual nature of the **fervent prayer of a righteous man**. Although a literal translation of the Greek phrase is awkward, and different versions vary in their translations, the basic idea is that of a supplication "having energy." Effective prayer is characterized by earnestness, fervency, and energy, and is illustrated in the case study the following verses provide.
5:17 In spite of his greatness, **Elijah** was subject to the same feelings and liable to the same weaknesses we all experience. Effectual, that is, miracle-producing, prayer is not limited to a certain few, such as apostles or prophets. All believers can "pray for one another" (v. 16) with the same results. (Study the specifics for comparing Elijah's prayer, which inaugurated and then ended the drought, 1 Kin. 17:1; 18:41–46).

(cont. from preceding page)
probably intended to be a sacrament, even as baptism and the Lord's Supper are continually observed today. (This should not be confused with "last rites," which some Christians observe when no recovery is possible.)

Here is an abiding healing covenant to be held as such and practiced today. 1) The sick are to exercise faith in calling for the "elders," that is, for pastoral leadership (v. 14). 2) Confession of sin and heart preparation are important, since our physical well-being is never separated from or made primary above our spiritual health (vv. 15, 16). 3) Healing may come as a result of corporate, group, or personal prayer. 4) The anointing with oil is not a superstitious exercise, but a prophetic action—declaring the present dependence upon the Anointed One—Christ Jesus, whose power is ministered by the present work of the Holy Spirit in our midst.

(1 Cor. 12:9, 28/Ex. 15:26*) N.V.

KINGDOM DYNAMICS

5:13–18 Effectivity in Spiritual Warfare, FAITH'S WARFARE. James pictures a level of prayer that is beyond any believer's normal capacity—it is divinely energized by the direct involvement of the Holy Spirit. The Greek word for "fervent" actually does not appear in the original text. It is an amplification of the word for "effectual" which does appear in the Greek text. The Greek word *energeo* means "effectual, or that which is effective." Yet, to simply say prayer is "effective when offered by a righteous person" was deemed by the translators to be shallow in the context, and therefore "fervent" was rightly added to the text. To fully understand the word *energeo* one needs to examine another passage where the word is used. Paul used the word in describing the power of God's Word as it works special energy in those who believe (1 Thess. 2:13). The foundational premise of the Greek word *energeo* is that something "effectively works." Yet it only works in those who "believe." Applied to this text, this suggests that our praying, when energized by the power of the Holy Spirit, causes things to happen. Our prayers work!

(2 Kin. 19:8–19/Jer. 29:11–14) D.E.

19 [a]Matt. 18:15; Gal. 6:1
20 [a]Rom. 11:14; 1 Cor. 1:21; James 1:21 [b]Prov. 10:12; [1 Pet. 4:8] [1]NU *his soul* *See WW at Jude 11.

KINGDOM DYNAMICS

5:15, 16 You Can Always Give a Seed of Prayer . . . A Seed of Forgiveness . . . A Seed of Love and Joy, SEED FAITH. Do you ever feel you have absolutely nothing to give to God? Well, you can always plant a seed of faith-believing, love-motivated prayer in another person's life!

What does this type of prayer do? It saves the sick. Now "save" and "heal" are virtually interchangeable words in the Greek language; and "sickness" may broadly refer to any weakness or inability, disease or sin—anything that is "wrong" in life. In other words, the prayer of faith works to do good in whatever area life has gone bad.

And when people pray this kind of prayer, they are healed as they pray! Jesus also said that we are forgiven as we forgive (see Matt. 6:14, 15). We experience love as we give love away. We are blessed as we bless others. God gives to us as we give to others.

We can always plant a faith-believing prayer in the life of another person. Do it with love . . . with joy . . . with a spirit of forgiveness . . . and expect God to multiply that seed in your own life!

(2 Cor. 9:8–10/John 3:16) O.R.

Bring Back the Erring One

19 Brethren, if anyone among you
wanders from the truth, and someone
[a]turns him back,
20 let him know that he who turns a
sinner from the *error of his way
[a]will save [1]a soul from death and
[b]cover a multitude of sins.

WORD WEALTH

5:20 sinner, *hamartolos* (ham-ar-toe-*loss*); Strong's *#268:* An archer's term for missing the mark or a traveler leaving the familiar road and taking twisted paths that cause him to lose his way. The word denotes one devoted to sin by choice, a transgressor whose thoughts, words, and deeds are contrary to the eternal laws of God.

5:19, 20 James turns from a discussion of physical affliction to spiritual sickness, urging the restoration of backsliders (see Gal. 6:1). The expression **among you** suggests that the erring one is a member of the church. In addition, the phrase **turns . . . back** is not necessarily limited to the original turning from sin to God, but to the subsequent experience of returning to God after a Christian has become involved in sin. A person may wander **from the truth** of the gospel (see 1:18; 3:14) in either belief or conduct or both. Whether doctrinal or moral, the straying is a serious departure from the Christian way of life, not merely a minor difference of theological opinion or trivial ethical inconsistency. Truth and error are mutually exclusive, and a person either walks in God's truth or **his** own **way** (v. 20).

Since the straying individual is a Christian, the **death** is probably physical death as a result of his sins (see Deut. 34:4, 5; 1 Cor. 5:5; 11:29, 30). **Cover** is a Hebrew idiom meaning "forgive" or "overlook" (see Ps. 32:1; 85:2; Prov. 10:12; 1 Pet. 4:8). The **soul** and the **sins** covered are those of the one restored. By bringing the errant one to repentance and confession, forgiveness is procured.

TRUTH-IN-ACTION through JAMES

Letting the LIFE of the Holy Spirit Bring Faith's Works Alive in You!

Truth James Teaches	Text	**Action** James Invites
1 How to Have Patience in Trials The testing of faith produces patience (the ability to endure), which is the hallmark of the mature believer. Only under the pressure of trials can the believer test the true depth of his faith in God. The established heart will not waver, but will rejoice in the knowledge of the goodness of God.	1:2	**Rejoice** when trials come to test your faith.
	1:3	**Know** that patience results when your faith is tested by trials.
	1:4	**Endure** so that God has enough time to bring about the Christlikeness He intends through trial (see Rom. 8:28, 29).
	1:5	**Ask** God for wisdom! When a trial comes, if you do not know what to do, He does. And He wants to help you through your trials.
	5:7, 8	**Develop patience:** To receive the harvest and the crown of life that you desire, you must persevere.
2 Being a Doer of the Word Obedience to the Word of God brings about the work of God. We are to hear the Word and do the work. To hear and to do nothing is one sign of a deceived heart. Faith acts. To believe is to do!	1:22–25	**Evaluate!** In what areas do you claim faith, while your actions declare unbelief? **Acknowledge** those areas. **Decide** to act on the faith you have! **Practice today** what you proclaim.
3 Learning to Avoid Partiality Some may argue that preferring the rich and famous is only human, but the Bible rejects partiality. God is not an exalter of persons; neither should His children be.	2:1–8	**Be uninfluenced** by a person's social station. **Show love** to all without partiality.
	2:9	**Differentiate** between sinful partiality and "due honor" (Rom. 13:7).
4 How to Tame the Tongue Nothing can cause more damage than the tongue. Keeping our speech under closer control is a discipline believers must develop.	3:1	**Avoid presumptuousness!** Do not take the position of being a teacher until God has placed you there. You increase your liability for judgment if you do.
	3:2	**Bridle your tongue!** Monitoring every word we speak may seem cumbersome at first, but it will serve to advance righteousness.
	3:9–12	**Speak well of others.** Criticism, slander, backbiting, and gossip are "bitter waters," which issue out of demonic, worldly wisdom.
5 Steps in Developing Humility True faith is humble. And humility is the opposite of the proud selfishness and self-centered ambition that characterizes this present evil age. Selfcenteredness is the essence of worldliness. Therefore, to be a self-centered person is to be at enmity with God. James calls for believers to humble themselves.	4:1, 2	**Renounce strife!** Refuse unnecessary argument and personal strife. Seek to be at peace with others, preferring them to yourself.
	4:7	**Renounce rebellion!** Submit yourself to God. Renounce the Devil and reject all his suggestions.
	4:8	**Be quick to confess sin!** Nothing more effectively humbles a man than to admit sincerely that he is a sinner.
	4:11	**Renounce slander!** Rather, **speak highly** of others, even to your own discredit.

Truth James Teaches	Text	**Action** James Invites
	4:13–16	**Express** continued dependence upon God! An independent spirit wars against godly humility.
	4:17	**Do the good you know to do,** regardless of the cost. Not to do so is sin!
6 The Dangers of Money The consistent scriptural witness is that money, though necessary and a blessing from God, can be a dangerous commodity. Things we think *we* own may really own *us!* God calls us to put material goods into proper perspective and to use them wisely under His direction.	1:10	**Recognize** the fact that all material possessions will perish and have no eternal value.
	5:1–6	**Avoid** unnecessary acquisition. Acquired wealth can bring unwelcomed problems to your life. **Embrace simplicity!** Simplicity and poverty are not the same. Simplicity is simply acting responsibly with what God gives you!

The First Epistle of PETER

Author: Peter
Date: Early A.D. Sixties
Theme: Suffering as a Christian
Key Words: Suffer, Suffering

Author The letter claims to be from the apostle Peter, and there is no evidence that Petrine authorship was ever challenged in the early church. Silvanus, who accompanied Paul on his second missionary journey, was likely Peter's secretary in composing 1 Peter (5:12), which probably explains the polished Greek style of the letter.

There are linguistic and literary parallels between 1 Peter and Peter's speeches as recorded in Acts. Peter's Pentecost address and 1 Peter have the following in common: Christ's sacrifice was "foreordained" (compare 1 Pet. 1:20 with Acts 2:23); Christ's resurrection and ascension glory are presented together (compare 1 Pet. 1:21 with Acts 2:32–35); the role of baptism is related to forgiveness of sins (compare 1 Pet. 3:21 with Acts 2:38). Peter's speech at the Jerusalem Council and 1 Peter yield the following: God's "choice" in salvation (compare 1 Pet. 1:2; 2:9 with Acts 15:7); purity of heart with response to the gospel (compare 1 Pet. 1:22 with Acts 15:9). Other examples could be noted.

Occasion and Date Peter addresses Christians living in various parts of Asia Minor who are suffering rejection in the world because of their obedience to Christ (4:1–4, 12–16). He therefore reminds them that they have a heavenly inheritance (1:3–5).

Peter has learned of their trials and thus addresses them as "pilgrims of the Dispersion" (1:1), a phrase reminiscent of exiled Israel in the Old Testament, but also appropriate for these Christians (see 1:17; 2:11). They are mostly converted Gentiles. At one time they were "not a people" (2:10, hardly true of Jews). Their former life was one of lewdness, drunkenness, and idolatries (4:3), more descriptive of pagan Gentiles than of first-century Jews. Their compatriots are surprised that they now live differently (4:4). Although suffering is a "fiery trial" (4:12), it apparently does not entail martyrdom as yet. Furthermore, persecution is often the exception (see 3:13, 14; 4:16).

Ancient tradition suggests that Peter was martyred in Rome in conjunction with Nero's severe persecution of Christians after the burning of Rome in A.D. 64. This letter was likely written toward the end of Peter's life, but while he could still say, "Honor the king" (2:17). The early sixties are a good estimate for the composition of 1 Peter.

Content Accompanying the several exhortations for faithful living while in a society that is ungodly, the salvation promised in the gospel is also very much in view. The future salvation that awaits believers at the revelation of Christ is especially prominent at the outset of the letter (1:3–13). This is the "hope" of the Christian referred to in 1:3, 13, 21; 3:15. Even as Christ suffered and then was glorified, so Christians should anticipate the glory ahead, though they may be persecuted for their faith in this life (1:6, 7; 4:12, 13). Patience in the midst of unjust suffering is "commendable before God" (2:20).

Also addressed is the important goal of believers' pointing others to God by their godly life-styles. They thus proclaim the praises of God (2:9), influence pagans to glorify God (2:12), silence foolish people by doing good works (2:15), win spouses to Christ by their examples (3:1), shame their ungodly critics (3:15, 16), and puzzle former companions (4:4). Christians are to be a redeeming force in the world, though they suffer.

Personal Application Since all true Christians experience hostility from an ungodly world, the call to patience and holiness amid suffering is applicable to all. However, the message is most pertinent where the opposition is severe. Persecution of Christians is as great in many areas of the world today as it was in the first century, and 1 Peter offers hope to those suffering for Christ's sake.

Christ Revealed In four separate passages Peter links Christ's sacrificial sufferings with His glory that followed death (1:11; 3:18; 4:13; 5:1). The letter details the fruits of Christ's suffering and victory, including provision for a new life now and hope for the future (see 1:3, 18, 19; 3:18). Anticipation of Christ's return in glory causes believers to rejoice (1:4–7). In other ways also Christ now makes a profound difference in the lives of Christians: they love Him (1:8); they come to Him (2:4); they offer "spiritual sacrifices" through Him (2:5); they are reproached because of Him (4:14); they should expect to be rewarded when He returns (5:4).

The Holy Spirit at Work The Holy Spirit is active in the entire process of salvation: the "Spirit of Christ" in the Old Testament prophets "testified beforehand" concerning the Cross and the subsequent glory (1:11); Christ was raised from the dead "by the Spirit" (3:18); evangelists preached the gospel by the Spirit; believers responded in obedience "through the Spirit" (1:2, 22); a foretaste of the coming glory is had through the Spirit (compare 4:14 with v. 13 and 5:1).

Outline of 1 Peter

Introduction **1:1, 2**
- A. Salutation 1:1
- B. Addressees 1:2

I. Believers' faith and hope in the world **1:3—2:10**
- A. Rejoicing in the hope of Christ's return 1:3–12
- B. Righteous living because of the hope 1:13—2:3
- C. Renewal for God's people 2:4–10

II. Believers' conduct in everyday circumstances **2:11—5:11**
- A. Submission and respect toward others 2:11—3:12
- B. Suffering for Christ's sake 3:13—4:19
- C. Serving humbly while suffering 5:1–11

Conclusion **5:12–14**
- A. Silvanus, coauthor of this letter 5:12
- B. Greetings 5:13
- C. Final exhortation with benediction 5:14

Greeting to the Elect Pilgrims

PETER, an apostle of Jesus Christ,

To the [1]pilgrims [a]of the Dispersion in Pontus, Galatia, Cappadocia, Asia, and Bithynia,

3 2 [a]elect [b]according to the foreknowledge of God the Father, [c]in sanctification of the Spirit, for [d]obedience* and [e]sprinkling of the blood of Jesus Christ:

[f]Grace to you and *peace be multiplied.

A Heavenly Inheritance

3 [a]Blessed *be* the God and Father of our Lord Jesus Christ, who [b]according to His abundant *mercy [c]has begotten us again to a living *hope [d]through the *resurrection of Jesus Christ from the dead,

4 to an inheritance [1]incorruptible and undefiled and that does not fade away, [a]reserved in *heaven for you,

5 [a]who are **kept** by the *power of God through faith for *salvation ready to be revealed in the last *time.

WORD WEALTH

1:5 kept, *phroureo* (froo-*reh*-oh); Strong's *#5432:* A military term picturing a sentry standing guard as protection against the enemy. We are in spiritual combat, but God's power and peace (Phil. 4:7) are our sentinels and protectors.

6 [a]In this you greatly rejoice, though 4
now [b]for a little while, if need be,
[c]you have been [1]grieved by various
trials,

CHAPTER 1

1 [a]James 1:1 [1]*sojourners, temporary residents* **2** [a]Eph. 1:4 [b][Rom. 8:29] [c]2 Thess. 2:13 [d]Rom. 1:5 [e]Heb. 10:22; 12:24 [f]Rom. 1:7 *See WW at 2 Cor. 10:5. • See WW at Luke 1:79. **3** [a]Eph. 1:3 [b]Gal. 6:16 [c][John 3:3, 5] [d]1 Cor. 15:20 *See WW at 2 Tim. 1:16. • See WW at 1 Thess. 1:3. • See WW at Acts 23:6.

4 [a]Col. 1:5 [1]*imperishable* *See WW at Rev. 21:1.

5 [a]John 10:28 *See WW at Acts 4:33. • See WW at Luke 19:9. • See WW at Col. 4:5. **6** [a]Matt. 5:12 [b]2 Cor. 4:17 [c]James 1:2 [1]*distressed*

1:1 Although the phrase **pilgrims of the Dispersion** has as its background the exiles of the OT Jewish dispersion, the recipients of this letter were predominantly Gentile Christians.
1:2 See section 3 of Truth-In-Action at the end of 1 Pet.
1:2 Elect: Even as God chose Israel, in the counsels of eternity He chose the church as His own people.
1:3 Begotten us again refers to the New Birth (see v. 23 where the same Greek verb is rendered "having been born again"). The living Christ makes possible **a living hope**.
1:4 Unlike ancient Israel's **inheritance** of Canaan, the Christian's inheritance is eternal life in the kingdom of God (see Mark 10:17, 29, 30).
1:5 Salvation in the NT is past, present, and future. Here our final glorious salvation at the Second Coming of Christ is in view.
1:6–9 The prospect of salvation at the Second Coming of Christ inspires great joy in the midst of suffering. There is also a present foretaste of this **salvation** through **faith** (v. 9).
1:6, 7 See section 4 of Truth-In-Action at the end of 1 Pet.
1:6 In comparison with the eternal inheritance and salvation to come (see vv. 4, 5), present trials are **for a little while**.

A Letter to Christians Abroad. The First Epistle of Peter is addressed to "the pilgrims of the Dispersion in Pontus, Galatia, Cappadocia, Asia, and Bithynia." Writing from Rome, the author encourages them to be strong in the faith as they encounter persecutions.

7 that [a]the genuineness of your faith,
being much more precious than gold
that perishes, though [b]it is tested by
fire, [c]may be found to *praise, honor,
and glory at the revelation of Jesus
Christ,
8 [a]whom having not [1]seen you love.
[b]Though now you do not see *Him,*
yet believing, you rejoice with joy inexpressible and full of glory,
9 receiving the end of your faith—the
salvation of *your* souls.
4 10 Of this salvation the prophets have
inquired and searched carefully, who
prophesied of the grace *that would
come* to you,
11 searching what, or what manner of
time, [a]the Spirit of Christ who was in
them was indicating when He testified
beforehand the sufferings of Christ
and the glories that would follow.
12 To them it was revealed that, not
to themselves, but to [1]us they were
ministering the things which now have
been reported to you through those
who have preached the gospel to you
by the *Holy Spirit *sent from
heaven—things which [a]angels *desire
to look into.

Living Before God Our Father

13 Therefore gird up the loins of your
*mind, be sober, and rest *your* hope
fully upon the grace that is to be
brought to you at the revelation of
Jesus Christ;
3 14 as *obedient children, not [a]conform-
ing* yourselves to the former lusts, *as*
in your ignorance;
2 15 [a]but as He who called you *is* holy,
you also be holy in all *your* conduct,
16 because it is written, [a]*"Be holy, for
I am holy."*
2 17 And if you call on the Father, who
[a]without partiality judges according to
each one's work, conduct yourselves
throughout the time of your [1]stay* *here*
in fear;
18 knowing that you were not redeemed with [1]corruptible things, *like*

7 [a]James 1:3 [b]Job 23:10 [c][Rom. 2:7] *See WW at Eph. 1:6.
8 [a]1 John 4:20 [b]John 20:29 [1]M *known*
11 [a]2 Pet. 1:21
12 [a]Eph. 3:10 [1]NU, M *you* *See WW at Acts 7:33. • See WW at John 20:21. • See WW at Matt. 13:17.
13 *See WW at Mark 12:30.
14 [a][Rom. 12:2]; 1 Pet. 4:2 *See WW at 2 Cor. 10:5. • See WW at Rom. 12:2.
15 [a][2 Cor. 7:1]
16 [a]Lev. 11:44, 45; 19:2; 20:7
17 [a]Acts 10:34 [1]*sojourning, dwelling* as resident aliens *See WW at Acts 13:17.
18 [1]*perishable* *See WW at Acts 14:15.
19 [a]Acts 20:28; 1 Pet. 1:2 [b]Ex. 12:5; Is. 53:7
20 [a]Rom. 3:25 [b]Gal. 4:4 [1]*revealed* *See WW at John 18:36.

silver or gold, from your *aimless conduct *received* by tradition from your fathers,
19 but [a]with the precious blood of
Christ, [b]as of a lamb without blemish
and without spot.

KINGDOM DYNAMICS

1:18, 19 Bought Back By the Blood, THE BLOOD. "Redeemed" means "bought back." The redeemer pays a worthy price to reclaim something previously owned. Mankind was once God's by creation, but became lost through sin. The blood of Christ is the price of our purchase, or redemption. God offers Christ's blood to us as our substitutionary sacrifice and accepts it when we offer it back to Him. Our transaction with God is therefore not a gold-and-silver economy; it is a life-and-death economy. Christ gave His life's blood to buy us out of sin and death. His blood is a worthy price and provides an imperishable bond between God and man.

(Eph. 2:13/John 6:53, 54) C.S.

KINGDOM DYNAMICS

1:18, 19 Man's Greatest Need Is for Salvation, HUMAN WORTH. The value of the human being can be inferred from the price paid to redeem man (John 3:16; 1 Cor. 6:20). God the Son, the Divine One through whom the worlds were created, became flesh and died for the sins of humanity. That He willingly shed His blood and died for us reveals not only the value of the human personality, but also the importance of salvation. Through Christ, believers are forgiven, reckoned to be righteous, and by New Birth are renewed in the image of God. Fallen men and women can only produce the works of the flesh. Only the Spirit, by the New Birth, can renew and recover that which was destroyed by the Fall (John 3:5, 6). To reach highest human potential, to have abundant life, one must accept Jesus Christ by faith.

(Matt. 27:32/John 10:10) C.B.

20 [a]He indeed was foreordained before
the foundation of the *world, but was
[1]manifest [b]in these last times for you

1:7 Revelation (Greek *apocalypsis*) refers to the return of Christ and suggests disclosure of what was unseen before (see v. 8).
1:10–12 See section 4 of Truth-In-Action at the end of 1 Pet.
1:10–12 *Though the OT prophets* had an incomplete vision of the Christ event, they foretold through the Spirit **this salvation** that Christians now have and will experience (see vv. 5–9).
1:13, 14 Therefore: The assuredness of salvation (vv. 10–12) is basic for holy living. The figure **gird up the loins of your mind** comes from Orientals necessarily gathering up their long robes with a belt to prepare for action.
1:14 See section 3 of Truth-In-Action at the end of 1 Pet.
1:15, 16 The holy nature of God is the motivation for Christian holiness.
1:15 See section 2 of Truth-In-Action at the end of 1 Pet.
1:17 See section 2 of Truth-In-Action at the end of 1 Pet.
1:17 The certainty that God will judge our **work** is another incentive to holiness. **Fear** has the sense of reverence.
1:18, 19 Slaves in the ancient world could be **redeemed** (freed) by payment of the ransom price.
1:20 These last times were inaugurated with the First Coming of Christ (see Acts 2:17; Heb. 1:2).

21 who through Him believe in God,
[a]who raised Him from the dead and
[b]gave Him glory, so that your faith and
hope are in God.

The Enduring Word

3 22 Since you [a]have purified your souls
in *obeying the truth [1]through the
Spirit in [2]**sincere** [b]love* of the brethren, love one another fervently with a
*pure heart,
23 [a]having been born again, not of
[1]corruptible seed but [2]incorruptible,
[b]through the word of God which lives
and abides [3]forever,

WORD WEALTH

1:22 sincere, *anupokritos* (an-oo-*pock*-ree-toss); Strong's *#505:* From *a,* negative, and *hupokrisis,* "hypocrisy"; thus, "without hypocrisy." Since hypocrisy originally denoted the acting in a play, *anupokritos* signifies a sincerity void of pretension and without putting on an act.

KINGDOM DYNAMICS

1:23 The Regenerating Power of God's Word, THE WORD OF GOD. Just as we owe our natural existence to the Creator's spoken word and life-giving breath, so we owe our New Birth to the power of God's Word and the Holy Spirit's activation of its power. God's intent for our created being is only completely fulfilled when our spirits are alive toward Him. As sin has produced spiritual death in people (Eph. 2:1–3), so salvation in Jesus Christ has provided spiritual life. This text tells us that the "seed" that has produced new life in us is the Word of God, which has begotten us again by the Holy Spirit's power (Titus 3:5) and made us members of God's new creation (2 Cor. 5:17). The power of God's Word—the Holy Scriptures—is in no way more manifest than in this: its power to bring spiritual life to all who open to its truth. James 1:18 elaborates the fact that God's "word of truth" is the means by which He brought us new life, emphasizing that He has done this as a direction of His own will. God's will to save us (2 Pet. 3:9) has been effectively expressed in His Word, which accomplishes that work (John 1:13).

(2 Cor. 3:5–8/Ps. 119:89–91) J.W.H.

21 [a]Acts 2:24 [b]Acts 2:33
22 [a]Acts 15:9 [b]John 13:34; Rom. 12:10; Heb. 13:1; 1 Pet. 2:17; 3:8 [1]NU omits *through the Spirit* [2]Lit. *unhypocritical* *See WW at 2 Cor. 10:5. • See WW at Heb. 13:1. • See WW at Matt. 5:8.
23 [a]John 1:13 [b]1 Thess. 2:13; James 1:18 [1]*perishable* [2]*imperishable* [3]NU omits *forever*
24 [a]Is. 40:6–8; James 1:10 [1]NU *its glory as*
25 [a]Is. 40:8 [b][John 1:1] [1]*spoken word* *See WW at Matt. 4:4.

CHAPTER 2

1 [a]Heb. 12:1 *See WW at Gal. 2:13.
2 [a][Matt. 18:3; 19:14; Mark 10:15; Luke 18:17]; 1 Cor. 14:20 [b]1 Cor. 3:2 [1]NU adds *up to salvation*
3 [a]Ps. 34:8; Titus 3:4; Heb. 6:5 *See WW at John 8:52. • See WW at Matt. 11:30.
4 [a]Ps. 118:22
6 [a]Is. 28:16; Rom. 9:32, 33; 10:11; 1 Pet. 2:8
7 [a]Ps. 118:22; Matt. 21:42; Luke 2:34 [1]NU *disbelieve*
8 [a]Is. 8:14 *See WW at Matt. 16:23.

24 because

[a]"All flesh is as grass,
And all [1]the glory of man as the
flower of the grass.
The grass withers,
And its flower falls away,
25 *[a]But the [1]word* of the* L*ORD*
endures forever."

[b]Now this is the word which by the
gospel was preached to you.

2 Therefore, [a]laying aside all malice, 2
all deceit, *hypocrisy, envy, and all
evil speaking,
2 [a]as newborn babes, desire the pure
[b]milk of the word, that you may grow
[1]thereby,
3 if indeed you have [a]tasted* that the
Lord *is* *gracious.

The Chosen Stone and His Chosen People

4 Coming to Him *as to* a living stone,
[a]rejected indeed by men, but chosen
by God *and* precious,
5 you also, as living stones, are being
built up a spiritual house, a holy priesthood, to offer up spiritual sacrifices acceptable to God through Jesus Christ.
6 Therefore it is also contained in the
Scripture,

[a]"Behold, I lay in Zion
A chief cornerstone, elect,
precious,
And he who believes on Him will
by no means be put to shame."

7 Therefore, to you who believe, *He
is* precious; but to those who [1]are
disobedient,

[a]"The stone which the builders
rejected
Has become the chief
cornerstone,"

8 and

[a]"A stone of stumbling
*And a rock of *offense."*

1:22, 23 The New Birth brings inner purity which is manifested in love for fellow believers.
1:22 See section 3 of Truth-In-Action at the end of 1 Pet.
2:1–3 Genuine love for the brethren and eager desire for **the word** (gospel, see 1:25) go together and result in spiritual growth.
2:1 See section 2 of Truth-In-Action at the end of 1 Pet.
2:4, 5 By **coming to Him** (Christ) believers constitute God's **spiritual house** (temple, see 1 Cor. 3:16, 17; Eph. 2:19–22), wherein believers as **a holy priesthood . . . offer up spiritual sacrifices.**
2:7, 8 Peter contrasts what Christ means to believers with what He means to **disobedient** ones who do not receive Him as **precious.** Though Israel nationally rejected Him, Jesus **has become the chief cornerstone** in God's new house.

[b]They stumble, being disobedient to
the word, [c]to which they also were appointed.
9 But you *are* a **chosen** generation, a
royal priesthood, a holy nation, His
own special people, that you may proclaim the *praises of Him who *called
you out of [a]darkness* into His marvelous light;

WORD WEALTH

2:9 chosen, *eklektos* (ek-lek-*toss*); Strong's *#1588:* Compare "eclectic." From *ek,* "out of," and *lego,* "to pick, gather." The word designates one picked out from among the larger group for special service or privileges. It describes Christ as the chosen Messiah of God (Luke 23:35), angels as messengers from heaven (1 Tim. 5:21), and believers as recipients of God's favor (Matt. 24:22; Rom. 8:33; Col. 3:12). The NT traces the source of election to God's grace.

KINGDOM DYNAMICS

2:9 Priority of Worship, WORSHIP AND THE KINGDOM. As a "royal" priesthood, the kingly nature of the redeemed worshiper is noted. This passage is rooted in God's call to ancient Israel (see Ex. 19:5–7). Peter and John (Rev. 1:5, 6) draw this truth to full application and prophetic fulfillment in the NT believer. As with Israel, deliverance through the blood of the Lamb is but the beginning. As promised, dominion and destiny will unfold as their priestly duty is fulfilled. True authority is always related to a walk in purity and a constancy in worship. The spirit of worship is essential to all advance of the kingdom. Just as ancient Israel will only take the Promised Land while doing battle from a foundation of righteous worship before the Lord, so with the contemporary church. We will only experience promised power for evangelism and spiritual victories as we prioritize and grow in our worship of the living God. Kingdom power is kept from pollution this way, as kingdom people keep humbly praiseful before the King—and witness His works of power with joy. See also Rev. 1:5, 6.

(Rev. 1:5, 6/Dan. 7:21, 22) J.W.H.

8 [b]1 Cor. 1:23; Gal. 5:11 [c]Rom. 9:22
9 [a]Is. 9:2; 42:16; [Acts 26:18; 2 Cor. 4:6] *See WW at 2 Pet. 1:5. • See WW at Gal. 1:6. • See WW at Luke 11:35.
10 [a]Hos. 1:9, 10; 2:23; Rom. 9:25; 10:19 *See WW at Rom. 9:15.
11 [a][Rom. 8:13]; Gal. 5:17; James 4:1 *See WW at Eph. 2:19.
12 [a]2 Cor. 8:21; Phil. 2:15; Titus 2:8; 1 Pet. 2:15; 3:16 [b]Matt. 5:16; 9:8; John 13:31; 1 Pet. 4:11, 16
13 [a]Matt. 22:21 [1]*institution* *See WW at Col. 1:15.

KINGDOM DYNAMICS

2:9 Worshipful Walk with God, PRAISE PATHWAY. This text not only appoints praise, but represents a basic revelation of the Bible: God wants a people who will walk with Him in prayer, march with Him in praise, and thank and worship Him. Note the progression in Peter's description of the people of the New Covenant: 1) We are a chosen generation—a people begun with Jesus' choice of the Twelve, who became 120, to whom were added thousands at Pentecost. We are a part of this continually expanding generation, "chosen" when we receive Christ. 2) We are a royal priesthood. Under the Old Covenant the priesthood and royalty were separated. We are now—in the Person of our Lord—all "kings and priests to His God" (Rev. 1:6), a worshiping host and a kingly band, prepared for walking with Him in the light or warring beside Him against the hosts of darkness. 3) We are a holy nation, composed of Jews and Gentiles—of one blood, from every nation under heaven. 4) We are His own special people. God's intention from the time of Abraham has been to call forth a people with a special mission—to proclaim His praise and to propagate His blessing throughout the Earth.

(Heb. 13:10–15/Gen. 29:35*) C.G.

10 [a]who once *were* not a people but
are now the people of God, who had
not *obtained mercy but now have obtained mercy.

Living Before the World

11 Beloved, I beg *you* as *sojourners **2**
and pilgrims, abstain from fleshly lusts
[a]which war against the soul,
12 [a]having your conduct honorable **1**
among the Gentiles, that when they
speak against you as evildoers, [b]they
may, by *your* good works which they
observe, glorify God in the day of visitation.

Submission to Government

13 [a]Therefore submit yourselves to **5**
every [1]ordinance* of man for the

2:9, 10 The church is the new "Israel," now including Gentile believers **who once *were* not a people** and **who had not obtained mercy**. This quote from Hos. 1 is an indication that the apostles could view OT prophecies about national Israel as fulfilled in the church, the new spiritual Israel.
2:11 See section 2 of Truth-In-Action at the end of 1 Pet.
2:12 See section 1 of Truth-In-Action at the end of 1 Pet.
2:12 Gentiles: Here, "pagans" or "heathen." **The day of visitation** is any time God comes in a special act of judgment or mercy. See Deut. 5:9; Luke 1:68; Acts 15:14. In this context *visitation* is either God's time for a special dealing with the unsaved or it is the glorious return of Christ.
2:13—3:6 Particular attention is given to the outworking of 2:11, 12 in specific life situations "among the Gentiles" (v. 12).
2:13–17 See section 5 of Truth-In-Action at the end of 1 Pet.
2:13 The king refers here and in v. 17 to Nero, the Roman emperor, who reigned from A.D. 54 to 68.

Lord's sake, whether to the king as supreme,
14 or to governors, as to those who are sent by him for the punishment of evildoers and *for the* *praise of those who do good.
15 For this is the will of God, that by doing good you may put to silence the ignorance of foolish men—
16 [a]as *free, yet not [b]using *liberty as a cloak for [1]vice, but as bondservants of God.
17 Honor all *people.* Love the brotherhood. Fear [a]God. Honor the king.

Submission to Masters

5 18 [a]Servants, *be* submissive to *your* *masters with all fear, not only to the good and *gentle, but also to the harsh.
19 For this *is* [a]commendable, if because of conscience toward God one endures grief, suffering wrongfully.
20 For [a]what credit *is it* if, when you are beaten for your faults, you take it patiently? But when you do good and suffer, if you take it patiently, this *is* commendable before God.
1 21 For [a]to this you were called, because Christ also *suffered for [1]us, [b]leaving [2]us an **example,** that you should follow His steps:

WORD WEALTH

2:21 example, *hupogrammos* (hoop-og-ram-*moss*); Strong's *#5261:* From *hupo,* "under," and *grapho,* "to write"; hence, an underwriting. The word referred to tracing letters, copying the writings of the teacher. Then it came to denote an example to be followed. The example of Christ enables us to endure when we suffer for our faith.

22 *"Who[a] committed no sin,*
Nor was deceit found in His mouth";

14 *See WW at Eph. 1:6.
16 [a]Rom. 6:14, 20, 22; 1 Cor. 7:22; [Gal. 5:1] [b]Gal. 5:13 [1]*wickedness* *See WW at Rev. 6:15. • See WW at 1 Cor. 10:29.
17 [a]Prov. 24:21
18 [a]Eph. 6:5–8 *See WW at Jude 4. • See WW at 1 Tim. 3:3.
19 [a]Matt. 5:10
20 [a]Luke 6:32–34
21 [a]Matt. 16:24; 1 Thess. 3:3, 4 [b][1 John 2:6] [1]NU *you* [2]NU, M *you* *See WW at Acts 17:3.
22 [a]Is. 53:9; 2 Cor. 5:21
23 [a]Is. 53:7; Heb. 12:3; 1 Pet. 3:9 [b]Luke 23:46
24 [a]Is. 53:4, 11; 1 Cor. 15:3; [Heb. 9:28] [b]Rom. 7:6 [c]Is. 53:5 [1]*wounds*
25 [a]Is. 53:5, 6 [b]Is. 40:11; [Ezek. 34:23]; Zech. 13:7 [1]Gr. *Episkopos* *See WW at John 10:2.

CHAPTER 3

1 [a]Gen. 3:16; 1 Cor. 14:34; Eph. 5:22; Col. 3:18 [b]1 Cor. 7:16 [c]Matt. 18:15

23 [a]who, when He was reviled, did not revile in return; when He suffered, He did not threaten, but [b]committed *Himself* to Him who judges righteously; 1
24 [a]who Himself bore our sins in His own body on the tree, [b]that we, having died to sins, might live for righteousness—[c]by whose [1]stripes you were healed.
25 For [a]you were like sheep going astray, but have now returned [b]to the *Shepherd and [1]Overseer of your souls.

Submission to Husbands

3 Wives, likewise, *be* [a]submissive to your own husbands, that even if some do not obey the word, [b]they, without a word, may [c]be won by the conduct of their wives, 6

KINGDOM DYNAMICS

3:1 A Word of Wisdom to Wives, WOMEN. The spirit of submission, whereby a woman voluntarily acknowledges her husband's leadership responsibility under God, is an act of faith. The Bible nowhere "submits" or subordinates women to men, generically. But this text calls a woman to submit herself to her husband (Eph. 5:22), and the husband is charged to lovingly give himself to caring for his wife—never exploiting the trust of her submission (v. 7; Eph. 5:25–29). This divinely ordered arrangement is never shown, nor was it ever given, to reduce the potential, purpose, or fulfillment of the woman. Only fallen nature or persistent church traditionalism, finding occasion through "proof-texts" separated from their full biblical context, can make a case for the social exploitation of women or the restriction of women from church ministry.

1 Tim. 2:12 and 1 Cor. 14:34, 35, which disallow a woman's teaching (in an unwelcomed manner), usurping authority, or creating a nuisance by public

(*cont. on next page*)

2:18 See section 5 of Truth-In-Action at the end of 1 Pet.
2:18 Household **servants** (Greek *oiketai,* probably "slaves" here) are to be **submissive** out of **fear** (reverence) of God (see vv. 17, 19). Today this is relevant for contractual agreements wherein one is under authority to another.
2:21 See section 1 of Truth-In-Action at the end of 1 Pet.
2:23 See section 1 of Truth-In-Action at the end of 1 Pet.
2:24, 25 In v. 21 Christ is our Example; here He is our Redeemer. Christ's vicarious death makes possible our response of death **to sins** (repentance) and life for God (**righteousness**). This is NT Christian conversion in its broadest application, which Peter describes when he says, **by whose stripes you were healed.** Peter's intent in quoting Is. 53:5 is to show that personal wholeness—mental, psychological, physical, and spiritual—flows from this conversion.
3:1–6 See section 6 of Truth-In-Action at the end of 1 Pet.
3:1 Likewise: A comparison is drawn between wives' obedience to their husbands and servants' obedience to their masters (2:18; see also 2:13). Both situations call for reverent behavior from servants and wives (2:18; 3:2) toward ungodly masters and husbands (2:18, 19; 3:1). As vv. 3–6 indicate, a wife's obedience is not from intimidation, but from a quiet confidence which is the fruit of trust in God. Such a comparison between servants and wives was appropriate in a first-century setting with its slavery and the subordinate role of women in society. However, the principles of respectful godly behavior and a quiet spirit transcend time boundaries.

(cont. from preceding page)
argument, all relate to the woman's relationship with her husband. (The Greek word for "man" in 1 Tim. 2:12 is *aner,* which is as readily translated "husband" as "man." The context clearly recommends "husband," as does the evidence of the rest of the NT related to the viability of a woman's public voice in Christian assemblies.)

The Bible's word of wisdom to women seems to be summarized in Peter's word here: counsel given to a woman whose husband is an unbeliever. She is told that her "words" are not her key to success in winning her husband to Christ; but her Christlike, loving spirit is. Similarly, this wisdom would apply to any woman with the potential for a public ministry of leadership in the church. Her place will most likely be given when she is not argumentatively insistent upon it, so much as given to "winning" it by a gracious, loving, servantlike spirit—the same spirit that ought to be evident in the life of a man who would lead.

(Acts 21:9/Gen. 4:25*) F.L./J.W.H.

2 [a]when they observe your *chaste conduct *accompanied* by fear.
3 [a]Do not let your adornment be *merely* outward—arranging the hair, wearing gold, or putting on *fine* apparel—
4 rather *let it be* [a]the hidden person of the heart, with the [1]incorruptible *beauty* of a *gentle and quiet spirit, which is very precious in the sight of God.
5 For in this manner, in former times, the holy women who trusted in God also *adorned themselves, being submissive to their own husbands,
6 as Sarah *obeyed Abraham, [a]calling him lord, whose daughters you are if you do good and are not afraid with any terror.

A Word to Husbands

6 7 [a]Husbands, likewise, dwell with *them* with understanding, giving honor to the wife, [b]as to the weaker vessel, and as *being* *heirs together of the grace of life, [c]that your prayers may not be hindered.

2 [a]1 Pet. 2:12; 3:6 *See WW at 1 John 3:3.
3 [a]Is. 3:18; 1 Tim. 2:9
4 [a]Rom. 2:29 [1]*imperishable* *See WW at Matt. 21:5.
5 *See WW at Matt. 25:7.
6 [a]Gen. 18:12 *See WW at Rom. 6:17.
7 [a]1 Cor. 7:3; [Eph. 5:25]; Col. 3:19 [b]1 Cor. 12:23 [c]Job 42:8 *See WW at Heb. 11:9.

8 [1]NU *humble*
9 [a][Prov. 17:13] [b]Matt. 5:44 [c]Matt. 25:34
10 [a]Ps. 34:12–16 [b]James 1:26 [1]*restrain*
11 [a]Ps. 37:27 [b]Rom. 12:18
12 [a]John 9:31
13 [a]Prov. 16:7
14 [a]James 1:12

KINGDOM DYNAMICS

3:1–7 Attitudes Toward God Determine Attitudes Toward Mates, FAMILY ORDER. Our attitudes toward our mates are governed by our attitudes toward God. A husband may fall short of a wife's expectations and of God's ideal for a husband. Nevertheless, she seeks in every way to be a good wife, modeling her behavior on Christ, who obeyed and trusted the Father even when His own people rejected Him (John 1:11). Or, a wife may disappoint her husband, disregard his authority, or withhold her respect. Nevertheless, a husband honors his wife, cares for her, and prays for her, modeling his behavior on the Father, who "knows our frame" (Ps. 103:14).

(Eph. 5:22–33/Col. 3:18, 19, 23, 24) L.C.

Called to Blessing

8 Finally, all *of you be* of one mind, having compassion for one another; love as brothers, *be* tenderhearted, *be* [1]courteous;
9 [a]not returning evil for evil or reviling for reviling, but on the contrary [b]blessing, knowing that you were called to this, [c]that you may inherit a blessing. 1
10 For

> [a]*"He who would love life*
> *And see good days,*
> [b]*Let him* [1]*refrain his tongue from evil,*
> *And his lips from speaking deceit.*
> 11 *Let him* [a]*turn away from evil and do good;*
> [b]*Let him seek peace and pursue it.*
> 12 *For the eyes of the* LORD *are on the righteous,*
> [a]*And His ears are open to their prayers;*
> *But the face of the* LORD *is against those who do evil."*

Suffering for Right and Wrong

13 [a]And who *is* he who will harm you if you become followers of what is good?
14 [a]But even if you should suffer for righteousness' sake, *you are* blessed.

3:7 *See section 6 of Truth-In-Action at the end of 1 Pet.*
3:7 Likewise invokes the preceding directives upon the husbands as well, and they are to **dwell with . . . understanding, giving honor** to their spouses, indicating a certain reciprocity between the sexes in marriage. A husband is to consider the lesser physical strength and vulnerability of his wife (**the weaker vessel**). See Kingdom Dynamics.
3:9 See section 1 of Truth-In-Action at the end of 1 Pet.
3:13–15 Suffering **for righteousness' sake** evokes two responses: 1) reverence toward **the Lord God** (or toward Christ as Lord, see marginal note); 2) readiness to answer for one's **hope** (see 1:3, 13, 21) with **meekness and fear,** ("gentleness and reverence").

[b]*"And do not be afraid of their threats,*
*nor be *troubled."*
1 15 But [1]sanctify [2]the Lord God in your
hearts, and always [a]*be* ready to *give* a
defense to everyone who asks you a
reason for the [b]hope that is in you, with
meekness and fear;
16 [a]having a good conscience, that
when they defame you as evildoers,
those who revile your good conduct in
Christ may be ashamed.
17 For *it is* better, if it is the will of
God, to suffer for doing good than for
doing evil.

Christ's Suffering and Ours

18 For Christ also suffered once for
sins, the just for the unjust, that He
might bring [1]us to God, being put to
death in the flesh but made alive by
the Spirit,
19 by whom also He went and
preached to the spirits in prison,
20 who formerly were disobedient,
[1]when once the Divine longsuffering
waited in the days of Noah, while *the*
ark was being prepared, in which a
few, that is, eight souls, were saved
through water.
21 [a]There is also an antitype which
now saves us—baptism [b](not the removal of the filth of the flesh, [c]but the
answer of a good conscience toward
God), through the resurrection of Jesus
Christ,
22 who has gone into heaven and
[a]is at the right hand of God, [b]angels
and authorities and powers having
been made subject to Him.
4 **4** Therefore, since Christ suffered
[1]for us in the flesh, arm yourselves
also with the same mind, for he who
has suffered in the flesh has ceased
from sin,
2 that he no longer should live the 2
rest of *his* time in the flesh for the lusts
of men, [a]but for the will of God.
3 For we *have spent* enough of our
past [1]lifetime in doing the will of the
Gentiles—when we walked in **lewd-**
ness, lusts, drunkenness, revelries,
drinking parties, and abominable
idolatries.

WORD WEALTH

4:3 lewdness, *aselgeia* (as-elg-*eye*-ah); Strong's *#766:* Total debauchery, unashamed indecency, unbridled lust, unrestrained depravity. The person with this characteristic has an insolent defiance of public opinion, sinning in broad daylight with arrogance and contempt.

4 In regard to these, they think it
strange that you do not run with *them*
in the same flood of dissipation, speaking evil of *you.*
5 They will give an account to Him
who is ready [a]to judge the living and
the dead.
6 For this reason [a]the gospel was
preached also to those who are dead,
that they might be judged according to
men in the flesh, but [b]live according
to God in the spirit.

Serving for God's Glory

7 But [a]the end of all things is at hand; 2
therefore be *serious and watchful in
your prayers.
8 And above all things have fervent 6

14 [b]Is. 8:12 *See WW at Luke 24:38. **15** [a]Ps. 119:46 [b][Titus 3:7] [1]*set apart* [2]NU *Christ as Lord* **16** [a]1 Tim. 1:5; Heb. 13:18; 1 Pet. 3:21 **18** [1]NU, M *you* **20** [1]NU, M *when the longsuffering of God waited patiently* **21** [a]Acts 16:33; Eph. 5:26 [b][Titus 3:5] [c][Rom. 10:10] **22** [a]Ps. 110:1 [b]Rom. 8:38; Heb. 1:6

CHAPTER 4

1 [1]NU omits *for us* **2** [a]John 1:13 **3** [1]NU *time* **5** [a]Acts 10:42; Rom. 14:9; 2 Tim. 4:1 **6** [a]1 Pet. 1:12; 3:19 [b][Rom. 8:9, 13]; Gal. 5:25 **7** [a]Rom. 13:11; Heb. 9:26; James 5:8, 9; 1 John 2:18 *See WW at Mark 5:15.

3:15 See section 1 of Truth-In-Action at the end of 1 Pet.
3:18–20 This difficult passage, undoubtedly clearer to its first readers, has been variously interpreted. It probably refers to Christ's proclaiming, through the event of His resurrection, the fruits of His victory to **spirits in prison** (demon spirits). These spirits apparently were also behind the corruption of the world in Noah's day. See Gen. 6:1–8; 2 Pet. 2:4, 5; Jude 6. This proclamation may be part of Christ's subsequent sovereignty over "angels and authorities and powers" (v. 22). Nothing is said of a response from the hearers, and the passage ought not to be interpreted as referring to a second chance for salvation for those who refuse the truth in this life. See note on Eph. 4:9, 10.
3:18 Christ is the model for unjust suffering (see vv. 15–17).
3:21 It is the response of faith on the occasion of **baptism** that saves. In early Christianity water baptism was much more closely linked to the initial confession of faith than is often the case today (see Rom. 6:3, 4).
4:1, 2 See section 4 of Truth-In-Action at the end of 1 Pet.
4:1, 2 Therefore: Because Christ suffered (see 3:18), believers are to be prepared to follow Him in suffering. This frame of mind has a purging effect, disciplining one to live **for the will of God**. The believer is to reckon himself "dead indeed to sin" (Rom. 6:11).
4:2 See section 2 of Truth-In-Action at the end of 1 Pet.
4:5 Ready to judge the living and the dead refers to judgment at Christ's return (see 2 Tim. 4:1), which is drawing near (v. 7; see also 5:4).
4:6 Those who are dead are people who heard the gospel preached when alive and thus were given an opportunity to **live according to God in the spirit.** "In the spirit" here refers to the realm of the Spirit, with eternal life especially in view (see 3:18, where Christ was "made alive, by [or "in"] the Spirit"). This opportunity also meant they were **judged according to men in the flesh,** meaning that the issue of eternal judgment is determined by one's response to the gospel while alive. See Heb. 9:27.
4:7, 8 See section 2 of Truth-In-Action at the end of 1 Pet.
4:7 Since the **end** of the present order with the return of Christ is ever approaching (see James 5:7–9), Christians are to be **watchful**. See Matt. 24:42–44; 1 Thess. 5:1–11.
4:8 See section 6 of Truth-In-Action at the end of 1 Pet.

love for one another, for [a]*"love will cover a multitude of sins."*

1 9 [a]*Be* hospitable to one another [b]without grumbling.

10 [a]As each one has received a *gift, minister it to one another, [b]as good **stewards** of [c]the manifold grace of God.

> **WORD WEALTH**
>
> **4:10 stewards,** *oikonomos* (oy-kon-*om*-oss); Strong's *#3623:* Compare "economy." From *oikos,* "house," and *nemo,* "to arrange." The word originally referred to the manager of a household or estate, and then in a broader sense denoted an administrator or a steward in general. In 1 Cor. 4:1 and Titus 1:7, it refers to Christian ministers; but in 1 Pet. 4:10, it denotes Christians in general, using the gifts entrusted to them by the Lord for the strengthening and encouragement of fellow believers.

11 [a]If anyone speaks, *let him speak* as the [1]oracles of God. If anyone ministers, *let him do it* as with the ability which God supplies, that [b]in all things God may be glorified through Jesus Christ, to whom belong the glory and the [2]dominion* forever and ever. Amen.

Suffering for God's Glory

4 12 Beloved, do not think it strange concerning the fiery trial which is to try you, as though some strange thing happened to you;

13 but rejoice [a]to the extent that you partake of Christ's sufferings, that [b]when His glory is revealed, you may also be glad with exceeding joy.

14 If you are [1]reproached* for the name of Christ, [a]blessed *are you,* for the Spirit of glory and of God *rests upon you. [2]On their part He is blasphemed, [b]but on your part He is glorified.

15 But let none of you suffer as a murderer, a thief, an evildoer, or as a [1]busybody in other people's matters.

16 Yet if *anyone suffers* as a Christian, let him not be ashamed, but let him glorify God in this [1]matter.

17 For the time *has come* [a]for judgment to begin at the house of God; and if *it begins* with us first, [b]what will *be* the end of those who do not obey the gospel of God?

18 Now

[a]"If the righteous one is scarcely saved,
*Where will the ungodly and the *sinner appear?"*

19 Therefore let those who suffer according to the will of God [a]commit their souls *to Him* in doing good, as to a faithful Creator.

Shepherd the Flock

5

The elders who are among you I exhort, I who am a fellow elder and a [a]witness* of the sufferings of Christ, and also a partaker of the [b]glory that will be revealed:

2 [a]Shepherd the flock of God which is among you, serving as overseers, [b]not by compulsion but [1]willingly, [c]not for dishonest gain but eagerly;

3 nor as [a]being [1]lords over [b]those entrusted to you, but [c]being examples to the flock;

4 and when [a]the Chief Shepherd appears, you will receive [b]the crown of *glory that does not fade away.

Submit to God, Resist the Devil

5 Likewise you younger people, submit yourselves to *your* elders. Yes, [a]all of *you* be submissive to one another, and be clothed with *humility, for 5

[b]"God resists the proud,
*But [c]gives grace to the *humble."*

6 Therefore *humble yourselves under the mighty hand of God, that He may *exalt you in due time,

8 [a][Prov. 10:12]
9 [a]Heb. 13:2 [b]2 Cor. 9:7
10 [a]Rom. 12:6–8 [b]1 Cor. 4:1, 2 [c][1 Cor. 12:4] *See WW at 1 Cor. 1:7.
11 [a]Eph. 4:29 [b][1 Cor. 10:31] [1]*utterances* [2]*sovereignty* *See WW at 1 Tim. 6:16.
13 [a]James 1:2 [b]2 Tim. 2:12
14 [a]Matt. 5:11 [b]Matt. 5:16 [1]*insulted* or *reviled* [2]NU omits the rest of v. 14. *See WW at James 1:5. • See WW at Rev. 14:13.
15 [1]*meddler*
16 [1]NU *name*
17 [a]Is. 10:12 [b]Luke 10:12
18 [a]Prov. 11:31 *See WW at James 5:20.
19 [a]2 Tim. 1:12

CHAPTER 5

1 [a]Matt. 26:37 [b]Rom. 8:17, 18 *See WW at Rev. 1:5.
2 [a]Acts 20:28 [b]1 Cor. 9:17 [c]1 Tim. 3:3 [1]NU adds *according to God*
3 [a]Ezek. 34:4 [b]Ps. 33:12 [c]Phil. 3:17 [1]*masters*
4 [a]Heb. 13:20 [b]2 Tim. 4:8 *See WW at John 2:11.
5 [a]Eph. 5:21 [b]Prov. 3:34 [c]Is. 57:15 *See WW at Acts 20:19. • See WW at 2 Cor. 7:6.
6 *See WW at Matt. 18:4. • See WW at James 4:10.

4:9 See section 1 of Truth-In-Action at the end of 1 Pet.
4:10, 11 See Rom. 12:1–8 and 1 Cor. 12.
4:12–16 See section 4 of Truth-In-Action at the end of 1 Pet.
4:16 One of three times that the word **Christian** appears in the NT. See Acts 11:26; 26:28.
4:17 Christian suffering is explained (**for**) in part as the beginning of God's appointed **time . . . for judgment**. Such suffering has a cleansing effect (vv. 1, 2) on **the house of God,** which is the church (compare believers as "a spiritual house" in 2:5). Divine judgment will culminate in the terrible outpouring of wrath upon those choosing to refuse the gospel. A similar sequence of judgment is found in Mal. 3:1–3; 4:1–6.
5:1 The apostle humbly refers to himself as a **fellow elder**. Suffering in this time and the subsequent glory when Christ returns are also linked elsewhere in this letter (1:5–7, 11; 3:13; 5:9, 10).
5:2, 3 Simon Peter himself was told by the risen Lord to feed the **flock of God** out of love for Him (John 21:15–17).
5:5–7 See section 5 of Truth-In-Action at the end of 1 Pet.
5:5 Likewise is a transition word denoting a shift to a different group.
5:6 Humble interpersonal relations (vv. 2, 3, 5) are to be

7 casting all your **care** upon Him, for
He cares for you.

WORD WEALTH

5:7 care, *merimna* (*mer*-im-nah); Strong's *#3308:* From *meiro,* "to divide," and *noos,* "the mind." The word denotes distractions, anxieties, burdens, and worries. *Merimna* means to be anxious beforehand about daily life. Such worry is unnecessary, because the Father's love provides for both our daily needs and our special needs.

8 Be [1]sober, be [2]vigilant; [3]because
your adversary the devil walks about
like a roaring lion, seeking whom he
may devour.
9 *Resist him, steadfast in the faith,
knowing that the same sufferings are
experienced by your brotherhood in
the world.

8 [1]*self-controlled* [2]*watchful* [3]NU, M omit *because*
9 *See WW at Eph. 6:13.
10 [a]1 Cor. 1:9; 1 Thess. 2:12 [1]NU *the God of all grace,* [2]NU, M *you* [3]NU *will perfect* *See WW at Heb. 11:3.
11 [a]Rev. 1:6
12 [a]2 Cor. 1:19; 1 Thess. 1:1; 2 Thess. 1:1 [b]Acts 20:24 *See WW at Rom. 4:3. • See WW at Rom. 3:4.
13 [a]Acts 12:12, 25; 15:37, 39; Col. 4:10; Philem. 24

10 But [1]may the God of all grace,
[a]who called [2]us to His eternal glory
by Christ Jesus, after you have suffered a while, [3]perfect,* establish,
strengthen, and settle *you.*
11 [a]To Him *be* the glory and the dominion forever and ever. Amen.

Farewell and Peace

12 By [a]Silvanus, our faithful brother as
I *consider him, I have written to you
briefly, exhorting and testifying
[b]that this is the *true grace of God in
which you stand.
13 She who is in Babylon, elect together with *you,* greets you; and *so
does* [a]Mark my son.
14 Greet one another with a kiss of
love. Peace to you all who are in Christ
Jesus. Amen.

lived out **under the mighty hand of God** (observe **therefore** at the beginning of the verse). It is He who will **exalt** the humble **in due time,** that is, when the "Chief Shepherd appears" (v. 4). "The mighty hand of God" perhaps alludes especially to the Exodus, when deliverance came to Israel. See Ex. 3:19; 6:1; 7:5; 13:3; Deut. 5:15.

5:8, 9 Resist: The active imperative indicates an assertive stance against the Adversary's operations. Because of the Devil's aggressive hostility, Christians must be spiritually alert, not only to withstand his attacks (employing the armor described in Eph. 6:10–18), but in prayer and spiritual warfare *opposing* him.

5:10 God's **eternal glory** (vv. 1, 4) is contrasted with the comparatively brief period during which these Christians suffer (see 1:6). Trials are temporary in light of eternity.

5:12 Silvanus also appears as a coworker of Paul in 2 Cor. 1:19, 1 Thess. 1:1, and 2 Thess. 1:1. He is probably the Silas (possibly the Greek form of the Latinized Silvanus) who accompanied Paul on his second missionary journey. Silvanus seems to have had a significant part in the writing of this letter. See Introduction to 1 Peter: Author.

5:13 Most scholars suggest that **Babylon** is a symbolic reference to imperial Rome, with which early church tradition associates both Peter and John Mark. It less likely refers to a sister congregation located in Babylon. Mark may have been converted by means of Peter's Jerusalem ministry (see Acts 12:1–16).

TRUTH-IN-ACTION through 1 PETER

Letting the LIFE of the Holy Spirit Bring Faith's Works Alive in You!

Truth 1 Peter Teaches	Text	**Action** 1 Peter Invites
1 Guidelines for Growing in Godliness Godliness invites others to ask why we have so much hope. Godly living involves suffering. We know this because Jesus suffered as our example. The godly person returns good for evil. When insulted, he blesses; and when caused to suffer, he never threatens in return.	2:12	**Live** so unbelievers will give God glory because your life is righteous.
	2:21	**Recognize** that Jesus suffered as our example. **Know** that you must suffer also.
	2:23	**Refuse** to retaliate against any who attack you. **Never threaten** those who cause you suffering.
	3:9	**Always bless** those who insult you.
	3:15	**Always be prepared** to explain the difference that Jesus has made in your life.
	4:9	**Practice** hospitality.
2 Steps to Holiness Being holy is being set apart *unto* God and *from* the world. People	1:15	**Set your life apart** fully to God, and **be holy** as God has commanded.
	1:17	**Live** as strangers in this world.

Truth 1 Peter Teaches	Text	**Action** 1 Peter Invites
2 committed to God's holiness say "No!" to fleshly demands and live for the will of God. The holy person is always alert, keeping his mind clear, fit for his walk with God.	2:1 2:11 4:2 4:7, 8	**Be honest, sincere,** and **pure** in all your relationships. **Refuse** to succumb to any demands of the flesh. **Do not live** solely for your own desires; **do** the will of God. **Pray** with dedication, knowing the time is short. **Love** one another fervently.
3 Steps to Faithful Obedience God calls His people to obedience. As Jesus was absolutely obedient to His Father's will, so His church is to be to His. Obedience is to characterize the lives of the saints. This means that they do God's will and deny the desires that formerly controlled them. Faithful obedience purifies God's people.	1:2 1:14 1:22	**Understand** that we were chosen in God and set apart by the Holy Spirit in order to live obediently to Jesus Christ. **Become** characteristically obedient! **Do not let** former desires continue to shape or direct your life. **Let** obedient living purify your life!
4 Key Lessons in Faith Faith in the Person of Christ and in the completed work of the Cross allows a Christian to endure rejection by the world. This rejection may even lead to death. The faith-filled Christian glorifies God and can count it as a blessing to stand for his Lord. Such a stand for Christ is preceded by the denial of fleshly lust so that the Spirit is in control.	1:6, 7 1:10–12 4:1, 2 4:12–16	**Know** that the steadfastness of your faith brings glory to Jesus. **Value** your faith more than gold. **Understand** that the OT can be fully understood in the light of the NT. **Live** according to the will of God by ceasing from sin. **Count** as a blessing any reproach or suffering for the name of Christ.
5 Keys to Relating to Authority All rightful authority is derived from God; therefore, to submit to authority honors God. Submission is an act of faith, establishing God as the ultimate authority over the relationship, be it connected with government, church, employment, or home. The higher the authority, the greater the accountability to God.	2:13–17 2:18 5:5–7	**Submit** to and **respect** all authority. **Do not use** your freedom in Christ as an excuse for sin. **Obey** and **respect** your employer. **Submit** yourself to the authority of those who govern the church. **Humble** yourself before God; **trust** Him to promote you as He wills.
6 Keys to Godly Relationships God designed marriage to illustrate the relationship He intends to have with His people. The husband is to give his wife honor and understanding, protecting her and acknowledging that she is a fully partnered heir of God. The wife is to accept the care and authority of the husband, living in a manner *that honors him*. The beauty of character and gentleness of spirit of such a woman will be precious to God and to her husband.	3:1–6 3:7 4:8	Wife, **place** yourself in submission to your husband. **Live** in a way that honors your husband and God. **Believe** that this godly conduct will win an unsaved husband to Christ. Husband, **be kind** and **gentle** with your wife. **Honor** her as your very best friend. **Listen** to her and **spend time** with her. **Cherish** her and make her feel extremely important. **Recognize** that not doing so will hinder your prayer life and obstruct answers. **Love** all believers fervently.

The Second Epistle of PETER

Author: Traditionally Peter
Date: A.D. 65–68
Theme: Remaining True to the Biblical Faith
Key Words: Know, Knowledge, Promise

Author and Date This letter gives instruction and exhortation from the apostle Peter as he nears the end of his life (1:1, 12–15). According to early church tradition, Peter was martyred in Rome during the reign of Nero. If the tradition is reliable, then his death occurred before A.D. 68, when Nero died.

Many New Testament scholars question Peter's authorship of this letter, primarily because it differs in style and thought from 1 Peter and because there is little evidence from the early church fathers supporting Peter as the author. Some scholars maintain that an author passed on apostolic teaching after Peter's martyrdom by writing in his name, suggesting that this was an accepted literary practice in the first century. However, conservative scholars usually hold that Peter wrote both epistles attributed to him, explaining the differences by Peter's use of an amanuensis (stenographic reporter) other than Silvanus (1 Pet. 5:12), or by his writing the letter without scribal help. In addition, certain references in 2 Peter indicate Petrine authorship: The author identifies himself as Simon Peter, an apostle (1:1); he claims to have been with Christ on the Mount of Transfiguration (1:16–18); he had written a previous letter to the people to whom 2 Peter is addressed (3:1); and he uses many words and phrases similar to those found in 1 Peter. These factors point to 2 Peter as a genuine work of the apostle Peter.

Background Whereas 1 Peter encourages Christians facing opposition from the world, 2 Peter warns Christians against false teachers within their fellowship who would lead them into apostasy. Fidelity to the apostolic teaching is the main concern (see especially 1:12–16; 3:1, 2, 15, 16). Heretical teachers will appear (2:1, 2) and in fact are already on the scene (2:12–22). They deny the Lord, exhibit a sensuous lifestyle, and are destined for destruction. They ridicule the idea of the Lord's return. These characteristics fit the Gnostic heresy, which developed more fully in the second century, but whose roots were fixed in the first century.

The author evidently has a specific community in mind (3:15), and if that community is the same as that addressed in 1 Peter (see 3:1), then this letter was intended for Christians somewhere in Asia Minor.

Content The answer to encroaching error is steadfastness through growing in the knowledge of the Lord. The letter opens and closes with the theme of cultivating Christian maturity (1:2–11; 3:14–18). "Knowledge" in 2 Peter is more than intellectual perception. It is an experience of God and Christ that results in moral transformation (1:2,

3; 2:20). This is the true *gnosis* (knowledge), which combats heretical Gnostic influence. The basis for that knowledge is the Scriptures, called the "prophetic word" (1:19–21) and the apostolic teaching (3:1, 2, 15, 16).

Chapter 2 gives a lengthy description of and warning against the false teachers. Apparently they at one time had "escaped the pollutions of the world through the knowledge of the Lord and Savior Jesus Christ" (2:20).

The last chapter emphasizes the Second Coming, an object of attack by scoffers, and explains why this hope is yet unfulfilled. It also assures the fulfillment of the promise of the Lord's return and teaches that its expectation should motivate Christians to godly behavior.

Personal Application The concerns of 2 Peter are also concerns of the contemporary church as it counteracts worldliness and humanistic philosophy. There are still false teachers who deal in half-truths regarding the Christian faith, and this letter provides a clear response to them.

Christ Revealed The deity of Christ is evident in the way that God and Christ are closely linked in 1:1, 2. God knows Christ as His "Son" (1:17). The divine purpose and activity are centered in Jesus Christ, as His grace and power are given to believers (1:2, 3, 8; 2:9, 20; 3:18), who are to look for His Coming (1:16) and the arrival of His eternal kingdom (1:11).

It is the Scriptures that assure the believer of a destiny with Jesus Christ (1:16–21; see also 3:1, 2).

The Holy Spirit at Work The only direct reference to the Holy Spirit is in 1:21, which describes the Spirit's work in "moving" the human authors of the prophetic Scriptures, which in turn disqualifies any "private interpretation" (see note on 1:20). However, the Spirit is obviously at work in providing the "divine power" that makes possible growth in the grace and knowledge of Christ (1:2–8; 3:18).

Outline of 2 Peter

I. Greeting **1:1, 2**
II. True versus false teaching **1:3—2:3**
- A. Pursuit of moral graces 1:3–11
- B. Peter's testament 1:12–15
- C. Prophetic Scriptures versus false teachers 1:16—2:3

III. Exposure and doom of false teachers **2:4–22**
- A. Destruction of the false teachers 2:4–10
- B. Description of the false teachers 2:10–22

IV. Warning against end-time deceivers **3:1–18**
- A. Scoffers in the last days 3:1–7
- B. Believers and the day of the Lord 3:8–18

Greeting the Faithful

1 SIMON Peter, a bondservant and [a]apostle of Jesus Christ,

To those who have [1]obtained [b]like[2] precious faith with us by the righteousness of our God and Savior Jesus Christ:

CHAPTER 1
1 [a]Gal. 2:8 [b]Eph. 4:5 [1]*received* [2]*faith of the same value*

1:1 In place of **Simon,** some ancient manuscripts have "Symeon," a Hebraic form of the name.

2 [a]Grace and peace be multiplied to
you in the knowledge of God and of
Jesus our Lord,
3 3 as His [a]divine power has given to
us all things that *pertain* to life and
godliness, through the knowledge of
Him [b]who* called us by *glory and
*virtue,
5 4 [a]by which have been given to us exceedingly great and precious *promises, that through these you may be
[b]partakers of the divine nature, having
escaped the [1]corruption *that is* in the
world through lust.

Fruitful Growth in the Faith

2 5 But also for this very reason,
[a]giving all diligence, *add to your faith
virtue, to virtue [b]knowledge,

WORD WEALTH

1:5 virtue, *arete* (ar-*et*-ay); Strong's *#703:* Used in classical Greek to describe any quality that elicited preeminent estimation for a person. Later the word signified intrinsic value, moral excellency, and goodness. It is used both of God (1 Pet. 2:9) and persons (Phil. 4:8; 2 Pet. 1:3, 5). Many scholars feel that in biblical times *arete* was commonly used to refer to manifestations of God's miracle power.

6 to knowledge self-control, to self-
control [1]perseverance, to perseverance
godliness,
7 to godliness *brotherly kindness,
and [a]to brotherly kindness love.
8 For if these things are yours and
abound, *you will be* neither [1]barren
[a]nor unfruitful in the knowledge of our
Lord Jesus Christ.

2 [a]Dan. 4:1
3 [a]1 Pet. 1:5 [b]1 Thess. 2:12; 2 Thess. 2:14; 1 Pet. 5:10 *See WW at Gal. 1:6. • See WW at John 2:11. • See WW at 2 Pet. 1:5.
4 [a]2 Cor. 1:20; 7:1 [b][2 Cor. 3:18] [1]*depravity* *See WW at 2 Pet. 3:13.
5 [a]2 Pet. 3:18 [b]2 Pet. 1:2 *See WW at Gal. 3:5.
6 [1]*patience*
7 [a]Gal. 6:10 *See WW at Heb. 13:1.
8 [a][John 15:2] [1]*useless*
9 [a]1 John2:9–11
10 [a]2 Cor. 13:5; 1 John 3:19 *See WW at Gal. 2:10.
11 *See WW at Gal. 3:5.
12 [a]Phil. 3:1; 1 John 2:21; Jude 5 [b]1 Pet. 5:12
13 [a][2 Cor. 5:1, 4]; 2 Pet. 1:14 *See WW at Matt. 1:19.

KINGDOM DYNAMICS

1:7, 8 Brotherly Love Flows from the Divine Nature, BROTHERLY LOVE. In 1:4 Peter describes God's "great and precious promises" intended to enable us 1) to be "partakers" in His divine nature and 2) to allow us to "escape the corruption *that is* in the world." These graces are necessary to lift us above the decay of human nature and unto "brotherly kindness" and "love" (v. 7). Brotherly kindness dissolves personal infighting and ungracious ignoring of one another. It allows refocusing on our real enemy—Satan. Further, to master love is to receive and release *agape* love: that Christlike, unconditional gift that is full of affection, bursting with benevolence, and that provides a love feast to all to whom we minister in the name of Jesus. This text is a promise for those yielded enough to let these gifts flow: we can actually participate in the divine nature of God, which is elevated above the corrupt, divisive spirit of the world.

(John 15:12, 13/Gen. 4:9*) D.S.

9 For he who lacks these things is
[a]shortsighted, even to blindness, and
has forgotten that he was cleansed
from his old sins.
10 Therefore, brethren, *be even more
diligent [a]to make your call and election
sure, for if you do these things you will
never stumble;
11 for so an entrance will be *supplied
to you abundantly into the everlasting
kingdom of our Lord and Savior Jesus
Christ.

Peter's Approaching Death

12 For this reason [a]I will not be negligent to remind you always of these
things, [b]though you know and are established in the present truth.
13 Yes, I think it is *right, [a]as long as

1:2 The opening phrase matches the greeting of 1 Pet. 1:2. **Knowledge** is an important term in this letter (see 1:3, 8; 2:20). The strengthened form of the Greek word (*epignosis*) indicates religious or moral insight, as used in the NT. For other uses of "knowledge" (*gnosis*), see 1:5, 6; 3:18. The frequent references may be an effort to combat a form of Gnosticism, an esoteric religious philosophy, which stressed knowledge as the way to God. Peter's message is that true knowledge is found in the God of Christ and the Scriptures.
1:3, 4 See section 3 of Truth-In-Action at the end of 2 Pet.
1:4 See section 5 of Truth-In-Action at the end of 2 Pet.
1:4 By which refers back to the "glory and virtue" of v. 3. The incarnate life of Christ has made available to believers His **exceedingly great and precious promises**. These promises surely include the Lord's Second Coming, the establishment of a new heaven and earth, and entrance into Christ's kingdom (see 1:11; 3:1–13), but would also recommend our bold acceptance "in Christ" of "all the promises of God" (2 Cor. 1:20). The purpose of the promises is that we may be sharers of a deep spiritual union with Christ, and thereby of the blessings and benefits of that relationship. The promises are also an incentive to godliness, because to share in His fullness now, as well as future glory, we must renounce **the corruption *that is* in the world**.
1:5–8 See section 2 of Truth-In-Action at the end of 2 Pet.
1:9–11 The possibility of falling into apostasy is implied here, and is amplified in 2:20–22. The believer gives evidence of his salvation by abounding in the moral graces listed in vv. 5–8 (note particularly v. 8). A person who does not grow in these virtues may lapse into **his old sins**. Peter does not suggest that salvation is by works, but exhorts believers to live in such a way that their **election** is made absolutely certain.

I am in this [1]tent, [b]to stir you up by
reminding *you,*
14 [a]knowing that shortly I *must* [1]put
off my tent, just as [b]our Lord Jesus
Christ showed me.
15 Moreover I will *be careful to ensure that you always have a reminder
of these things after my [1]decease.

The Trustworthy Prophetic Word

5 16 For we did not follow [a]cunningly
devised fables when we made known
to you the [b]power and [c]coming* of our
Lord Jesus Christ, but were [d]eye-
witnesses of His *majesty.
17 For He received from God the Father honor and glory when such a
voice came to Him from the Excellent
Glory: [a]"This is My beloved Son, in
whom I am well pleased."
18 And we heard this voice which
came from heaven when we were with
Him on [a]the holy mountain.
19 [1]And so we have the prophetic word
confirmed, which you do well to heed
as a [a]light that shines in a dark place,
[b]until [c]the day dawns and the morning
star rises in your [d]hearts;

KINGDOM DYNAMICS

1:16–19 Prophecy and the Sufficiency of God's Word, PROPHECY. When Peter encouraged believers to speak "as the oracles of God" (1 Pet. 4:11), he clearly did not mean this verbalizing of Holy Spirit-prompted words to substitute for the preaching and teaching of the Word of God. This text shows the relative importance of prophetic "words" or experiences we receive compared with the place of the Scriptures themselves. Here the apostle compares his own experience with Jesus on the Mount of Transfiguration to the abiding "prophetic word" of the Holy Scriptures (vv. 19–21). He calls the Word of the Scriptures "confirmed," and thereby makes a dramatic point for our understanding through all church history. If Peter's experience with Jesus Himself is said by Peter to be subordinate to the "more sure" Word of the Scriptures, we have both a guideline and an ultimate statement. The guideline is that no experience holds greater authority than the Word of God. This is not to discourage our experiencing the works of God's Spirit in power or blessing, but simply to remind us of the relative place of each type of "word" in our values.

There is an ultimate statement here, too. Many raise questions today as to whether we who welcome the operation of the gift of prophecy do so because of a lack of persuasion as to the "sufficiency" of God's Word. In other words, do we believe the Bible contains everything we need for salvation, for faith, and for obedient living? Of course, for the Bible believer this is never in question, for in the spirit and practical truth of Peter's words there is no comparison between the eternal Word of God and the present "words" of prophetic utterance. Prophecies are proper, biblically shown to be desirable (1 Cor. 14:1) and helpful (1 Cor. 14:3, 5). But the teaching of the Holy Scriptures are ultimate, conclusively authoritative, and "more to be desired . . . than gold"—the Eternal Word of God (Ps. 19:7–11).

(1 Cor. 14:1/Acts 21:11) J.W.H.

20 knowing this first, that [a]no *prophecy of Scripture is of any private
[1]interpretation,
21 for [a]prophecy never came by the
will of man, [b]but [1]holy men of God
spoke *as they were* moved by the Holy
Spirit.

Destructive Doctrines

2 But there were also false prophets 4
among the people, even as there
will be [a]false teachers among you, who
will secretly bring in destructive **heresies,** even denying the *Lord who
bought them, *and* bring on themselves
swift destruction.

WORD WEALTH

2:1 heresies, ***haireseis*** (*hahee*-res-is); Strong's *#139:* Compare "heresy" and

13 [b]2 Pet. 3:1 [1]Body
14 [a][2 Cor. 5:1; 2 Tim. 4:6] [b]John 13:36; 21:18, 19 [1]Die and leave this body
15 [1]Lit. *exodus, departure* *See WW at Gal. 2:10.
16 [a]1 Cor. 1:17 [b][Matt. 28:18; Eph. 1:19–22] [c][1 Pet. 5:4] [d]Matt. 17:1–5; Luke 1:2 *See WW at 1 Cor. 15:23. • See WW at Luke 9:43.
17 [a]Ps. 2:7; Is. 42:1; Matt. 17:5; Mark 9:7; Luke 1:35; 9:35
18 [a]Matt. 17:1
19 [a][John 1:4, 5, 9] [b]Prov. 4:18 [c]Rev. 2:28; 22:16 [d][2 Cor. 4:5–7] [1]Or *We also have the more sure prophetic word*
20 [a][Rom. 12:6] [1]Or *origin* *See WW at 1 Thess. 5:20.
21 [a]Jer. 23:26; [2 Tim. 3:16] [b]2 Sam. 23:2; Luke 1:70; Acts 1:16; 3:18; 1 Pet. 1:11 [1]NU *men spoke from God*

CHAPTER 2

1 [a]Matt. 24:5, 24; 1 Tim. 4:1, 2 *See WW at Jude 4.

1:16–21 See section 5 of Truth-In-Action at the end of 2 Pet.
1:16 The **power and coming** refer to the Second Advent of Christ, foreshadowed in the Transfiguration, which Peter observed (vv. 16–18).
1:19 The Transfiguration (vv. 16–18) **confirmed** the OT scriptures in general, which prophesy Christ's coming kingdom; the false teachers denied this (see 2:1; 3:1, 2). The **morning star** may allude to Num. 24:17, interpreted messianically in Judaism. When **the day dawns** (Christ's Return), the revelation of Christ in our hearts will be complete (see 1 Cor. 13:12).
1:20 This can also be translated to say that **no prophecy of Scripture is of private** *origin* (see marginal note), that is, of the prophet's own interpretation of his vision. V. 21 makes clear the reason: the prophets spoke as the Holy Spirit guided them. This answers the false teachers' interpretation, who, without the Spirit, discounted the OT prophetic word (see 2:1; 3:1–6, 16).
2:1–3 See section 4 of Truth-In-Action at the end of 2 Pet.
2:1–3 Peter warns of immoral and greedy **false teachers** who will use people as a means of reaching their own selfish goals. The NT indicates that deceptive teachers will characterize the church age and that their activities will increase "in latter times" (1 Tim. 4:1; see Matt. 24:11).

"heretical." From *haireomai,* "to choose." The word originally denoted making a choice or having an option. Progressing to having a preference because of an opinion or a sentiment, it easily slipped into a mode of disunity, choosing sides, having diversity of belief, creating dissension, and substituting self-willed opinions for submission to the truth. The dominant use in the NT is to signify sects, people professing opinions independent of the truth.

2 And many will follow their destructive ways, because of whom the way of truth will be blasphemed.
3 By covetousness they will exploit you with deceptive words; for a long time their judgment has not been idle, and their destruction [1]does not slumber.

Doom of False Teachers

4 For if God did not spare the angels who sinned, but cast *them* down to [1]hell and delivered *them* into chains of darkness, to be reserved for judgment;
5 and did not spare the ancient world, but saved Noah, *one of* eight *people,* a preacher of righteousness, bringing in the flood on the world of the ungodly;
6 and turning the cities of [a]Sodom and Gomorrah into ashes, condemned *them* to destruction, making *them* an example to those who afterward would live ungodly;
7 and [a]delivered righteous Lot, *who was* oppressed by the *filthy conduct of the wicked
8 (for that righteous man, dwelling among them, [a]tormented *his* righteous soul from day to day by seeing and hearing *their* lawless deeds)—
1 9 *then* [a]the Lord knows how to deliver the godly out of temptations and to reserve the unjust under punishment for the day of judgment,
10 and especially [a]those who walk according to the flesh in the *lust of uncleanness and despise authority. [b]*They are* presumptuous, self-willed. They are not afraid to speak evil of [1]dignitaries,
11 whereas [a]angels, who are greater in *power and might, do not bring a *reviling accusation against them before the Lord.

Depravity of False Teachers

12 But these, [a]like natural brute beasts made to be caught and destroyed, speak evil of the things they do not understand, and will utterly perish in their own corruption,
13 [a]*and* will receive the *wages of *unrighteousness, *as* those who count it pleasure [b]to [1]carouse in the daytime. [c]*They are* spots and blemishes, [2]carousing in their own deceptions while [d]they feast with you,
14 having eyes full of [1]adultery and that cannot cease from sin, enticing unstable souls. [a]*They have* a heart trained in covetous practices, *and are* accursed children.
15 They have forsaken the right way and gone astray, following the way of [a]Balaam the *son* of Beor, who loved the wages of unrighteousness;
16 but he was rebuked for his iniquity: a dumb donkey speaking with a man's voice restrained the madness of the *prophet.
17 [a]These are wells without water, [1]clouds carried by a tempest, for whom is reserved the blackness of darkness [2]forever.

Deceptions of False Teachers

18 For when they speak great swelling *words* of emptiness, they allure 4
through the lusts of the flesh, through lewdness, the ones who [1]have actually escaped from those who live in *error.

3 [1]M *will not*
4 [1]Lit. *Tartarus*
6 [a]Gen. 19:1–26; Jude 7
7 [a]Gen. 19:16, 29
*See WW at 1 Pet. 4:3.
8 [a]Ps. 119:139
9 [a]Ps.34:15–19; 1 Cor. 10:13; Rev. 3:10
10 [a]Jude 4, 7, 8 [b]Ex. 22:28; Jude 8 [1]*glorious ones,* lit. *glories*
*See WW at 2 Tim. 2:22.
11 [a]Jude 9
*See WW at Acts 4:33. • See WW at Acts 6:11.
12 [a]Jude 10
13 [a]Phil. 3:19 [b]Rom. 13:13 [c]Jude 12 [d]1 Cor. 11:20, 21 [1]*revel* [2]*reveling*
*See WW at Rev. 22:12. • See WW at John 7:18.
14 [a]Jude 11 [1]Lit. *an adulteress*
15 [a]Num. 22:5, 7; Deut. 23:4; Neh. 13:2; Jude 11; Rev. 2:14
16 *See WW at Matt. 2:5.
17 [a]Jude 12, 13 [1]NU *and mists* [2]NU omits *forever*
18 [1]NU *are barely escaping*
*See WW at Jude 11.

2:4–7 Compare note on Jude 6. The themes of sinning **angels** and the **flood** of Noah's day are also probably combined in 1 Pet. 3:19, 20. See note on 1 Pet. 3:18–20. The **judgment** in v. 4 is that of the Last Day (see 2:9; 3:7). The fact of a Last-Day setting for the warning against false teachers (see 2:1–3) is strengthened in light of Luke 17:26–29, where Noah and the flood, and the deliverance of Lot out of Sodom and Gomorrah, are models of end-time deliverance and judgment.
2:9 See section 1 of Truth-In-Action at the end of 2 Pet.
2:9 The rescues of Noah and Lot demonstrate the fact that God preserves committed believers in the midst of evil circumstances, while the destruction of evildoers demonstrates His punishment, to be pronounced in finality at **the day of judgment**.
2:10–22 Peter describes in detail the false teachers who have already infiltrated the church. The emphasis falls upon character that is sensual, arrogant, and indulgent. At this point more is said of a false life-style than of false beliefs.
2:15 The right way is contrasted with the **way of Balaam**. "The Way" was a designation for early Christianity (see Acts 9:2; 19:9, 23; 22:4; 24:14, 22). Balaam the prophet was ready to curse God's people, apparently for profit, illustrating the greed of false teachers who deceive and exploit for personal gain (see Num. 22—24; Rev. 2:14).
2:17 Wells without water are the false teachers who, instead of offering what satisfies the needs of God's people, are empty.
2:18–22 See section 4 of Truth-In-Action at the end of 2 Pet.

1 19 While they *promise them *liberty,
they themselves are slaves of [1]corrup-
tion; [a]for by whom a person is overcome, by him also he is brought into
[2]bondage.
20 For if, after they [a]have escaped the
pollutions of the world through the
knowledge of the Lord and *Savior
Jesus Christ, they are [b]again entangled
in them and overcome, the latter end
is worse for them than the beginning.
21 For [a]it would have been better for
them not to have *known the way of
righteousness, than having known *it*,
to turn from the holy commandment
delivered to them.
22 But it has happened to them according to the true proverb: [a]*"A dog re-*
turns to his own vomit," and, "a sow,
having washed, to her wallowing in the
mire."

God's Promise Is Not Slack

3 **3** Beloved, I now write to you this
second epistle (in *both of* which
[a]I stir up your **pure** *minds by way of
reminder),

WORD WEALTH

3:1 pure, *eilikrines* (eye-lik-ree-*nace*); Strong's *#1506:* Literally "tested by sunlight." The thought is that of judging something by sunlight to expose any flaws. The word described metals with alloys and liquids unadulterated with foreign substances. In the NT it is used in an ethical and moral sense, free from falsehood, pure, and without hidden motives.

2 that you may be mindful of the
words [a]which were spoken before by
the holy prophets, [b]and of the commandment of [1]us, the apostles of the
Lord and Savior,
3 knowing this first: that scoffers will
come in the last days, [a]walking according to their own lusts,
4 and saying, "Where is the promise
of His coming? For since the fathers
fell asleep, all things continue as *they*
were from the beginning of [a]cre-
ation."*
5 For this they willfully forget: that
[a]by the word of God the heavens were
of old, and the earth [b]standing out of
water and in the water,
6 [a]by which the world *that* then existed perished, being flooded with water.
7 But [a]the heavens and the earth
which are now preserved by the same
word, are reserved for [b]fire until the
day of judgment and [1]perdition of ungodly men.
8 But, beloved, do not forget this one
thing, that with the Lord one day *is* as
a thousand years, and [a]a thousand
years as one day.
9 [a]The Lord is not slack concerning
His *promise, as some count slackness,
but [b]is longsuffering toward [1]us, [c]not
willing that any should perish but
[d]that all should come to repentance.

The Day of the Lord

10 But [a]the day of the Lord will come
as a thief in the night, in which [b]the
heavens will pass away with a great
noise, and the elements will melt with
fervent heat; both the earth and the
works that are in it will be [1]burned up.
11 Therefore, since all these things will 5
be dissolved, what manner *of persons*
ought you to be [a]in holy conduct and
godliness,
12 [a]looking for and hastening the coming of the day of God, because of which
the heavens will [b]be dissolved, being
on fire, and the elements will [c]melt
with fervent heat?
13 Nevertheless we, according to His
promise, look for [a]new heavens and a

19 [a]John 8:34 [1]*depravity* [2]*slavery* *See WW at Acts 7:5. • See WW at 1 Cor. 10:29.
20 [a]Matt. 12:45 [b][Heb. 6:4–6] *See WW at John 4:42.
21 [a]Luke 12:47 *See WW at Luke 5:22.
22 [a]Prov. 26:11

CHAPTER 3

1 [a]2 Pet. 1:13 *See WW at Mark 12:30.
2 [a]2 Pet. 1:21 [b]Jude 17 [1]NU, M *the apostles of your Lord and Savior* or *your apostles of the Lord and Savior*
3 [a]2 Pet. 2:10
4 [a]Gen. 6:1–7 *See WW at Col. 1:15.
5 [a]Gen. 1:6, 9 [b]Ps. 24:2; 136:6
6 [a]Gen. 7:11, 12, 21–23
7 [a]2 Pet. 3:10, 12 [b][2 Thess. 1:8] [1]*destruction*
8 [a]Ps. 90:4
9 [a]Hab. 2:3 [b]Is. 30:18 [c]Ezek. 33:11 [d][Rom. 2:4] [1]NU *you* *See WW at Acts 13:32.
10 [a]Rev. 3:3; 16:15 [b]Ps. 102:25, 26 [1]NU *laid bare,* lit. *found*
11 [a]1 Pet. 1:15
12 [a]1 Cor. 1:7, 8 [b]Ps. 50:3 [c]Mic. 1:4
13 [a]Is. 65:17; 66:22

2:19 See section 1 of Truth-In-Action at the end of 2 Pet.
2:20, 21 The false teachers, having experienced the cleansing power of Christ, are now rejecting Him. Hence, they have returned to their former corrupt life-style and are worse off than they were before. Believers who fall into apostasy by deliberately rejecting the death and resurrection of Jesus Christ are in a more tragic position than unconverted pagans (see Heb. 6:4–6; 10:26).
3:1, 2 *See section 3 of Truth-In-Action at the end of 2 Pet.*
3:3, 4 End-time false teachers (see 2:1) ridicule the prophetic **promise** of the Lord's **coming** (see 1:19–21) in light of the apparent delay. **Fathers** refers either to the OT patriarchs or to those of first-generation Christianity.
3:8 The divine perspective on the passing of time answers the skeptics' criticism in vv. 3, 4. "Delay" of the Lord's coming is a human reaction to the divine reckoning.
3:9 A positive explanation of the temporary lack of fulfillment (vv. 3, 4) is found in the character of a merciful God. Although the wickedness of humankind calls for immediate action, God withholds His righteous wrath and delays judgment.
3:10–13 The Lord's return will be sudden and unexpected (see Matt. 24:43; Luke 12:39). Believers still look for **His promise** (v. 13), despite the scoffers (vv. 3, 4). Peter gives assurance of a new inhabitable Earth following fiery destruction of the present Earth (vv. 10, 13).
3:11–13 See section 5 of Truth-In-Action at the end of 2 Pet.
3:12 Proper Christian behavior hastens **the coming of the day of God** (see v. 11). In ways not clearly defined by the NT, the timing of the Lord's return is directly related to the condition and activity of the church (see Matt. 24:14; Acts 3:19–21).

[b]new earth in which righteousness dwells.

WORD WEALTH

3:13 promise, *epangelma* (ep-*ang*-el-mah); Strong's *#1862:* From the same root as *epangelia* (see WW at Acts 13:32). *Epangelma* signifies a promise made.

Be Steadfast

■1 14 Therefore, beloved, looking forward to these things, *be diligent [a]to be found by Him in peace, without spot and blameless;
15 and consider *that* [a]the *longsuffering of our Lord *is* salvation—as also
our beloved brother Paul, according to the wisdom given to him, has written to you,
16 as also in all his [a]epistles, speaking in them of these things, in which are some things hard to understand, which untaught and unstable *people* twist to their own destruction, as *they do* also the [b]rest of the Scriptures. ■1
17 You therefore, beloved, [a]since you know *this* beforehand, [b]beware lest you also fall from your own steadfastness, being led away with the *error of the wicked;
18 [a]but grow in the grace and knowledge of our Lord and Savior Jesus Christ. [b]To Him *be* the glory both now and forever. Amen.

13 [b]Rev. 21:1 **14** [a]1 Cor. 1:8; 15:58; [1 Thess. 3:12, 13; 5:23] *See WW at Gal. 2:10. **15** [a]Ps. 86:15; Rom. 2:4; 1 Pet. 3:20 *See WW at Heb. 6:12. **16** [a]Rom. 8:19; 1 Cor. 15:24; 1 Thess. 4:15; 2 Thess. 1:10 [b]2 Tim. 3:16 **17** [a]Mark 13:23 [b]Eph. 4:14 *See WW at Jude 11. **18** [a]Eph. 4:15 [b]Rom. 11:36; 2 Tim. 4:18; Rev. 1:6

3:14–18 See section 1 of Truth-In-Action at the end of 2 Pet.
3:16 See section 1 of Truth-In-Action at the end of 2 Pet.
3:16 The knowledge that Paul's doctrine of grace as expressed in his letters has been perverted by **untaught and unstable** persons is apparently presupposed (see Rom. 3:5–8; 6:1, 2). By the time 2 Pet. was written, Paul's letters were viewed as comparable with **the rest of the Scriptures** (meaning at least the OT), a clear evidence of an early rise of discernment in the early church on canonical and noncanonical books.

TRUTH-IN-ACTION through 2 PETER

Letting the LIFE of the Holy Spirit Bring Faith's Works Alive in You!

Truth 2 Peter Teaches	Text	**Action** 2 Peter Invites
■1 **Guidelines for Growing in Godliness** People who are controlled by the lusts of the flesh have no respect for the life-style of the godly. Such people delight in enticing others into sin. However, God knows the godly and will deliver them, as He knows the ungodly and will judge them. It is His desire that every Christian be able to appear before Him in purity.	2:9 2:19 3:14–18 3:16	**Persevere** in godliness. **Know** it is the safest place you can be. **Diligently avoid** returning to practices from which you have been delivered. **Understand** that the resulting bondage will be even greater. **Live** a blameless life. **Do not alter** your course toward Christlikeness. **Be careful** how you handle the Bible. **Recognize** that the untaught distort the truth. **Be careful** what teaching you listen to. **Measure** everything by God's Word.
■2 **Steps to Fruitfulness** Peter gives us a progressive list of Christian virtues that, when established in our lives, will cause us to be fruitful in the very knowledge of God. The life that comes from the knowledge of God can produce only good in its response to others. To fail to grow in Christ results in an inability to perceive the blessings received in initial salvation so that our identification with Jesus is forgotten or ignored.	1:5–8	**Recognize** that an effective and productive life results by sanctification (character transformation) that begins with faith and results in *love.*

Truth 2 Peter Teaches	Text	**Action** 2 Peter Invites
3 Steps to Dynamic Devotion Devotion to Jesus supplies what we need for godliness. Strong devotion results from an unyielding commitment to God's Word, which alone is the source for Christian thinking. Any other source will eventually corrupt the believer's mind.	1:3, 4 3:1, 2	**Understand** that God's power provides everything you need to live a godly life through your relationship with Jesus Christ. **Strengthen** your thinking by reading, rereading, and studying the Bible. **Understand** that wholesome thinking results from dwelling upon God's Word.
4 How to Identify the False Teacher The false teacher or false prophet is led by the flesh, seeking to obtain power or gain for himself from the ministry. Initially, his message may not be false, but his motivation in ministry is fleshly, so he appeals to the fleshly in others, offering them some carnal or soulish satisfaction. He will ultimately introduce some doctrine that is contrary to the truth. Each of us must use the Word of God to measure the words any preacher speaks, and any variation or imbalance in what is taught must be questioned. We also need to be sensitive to the prompting of the Holy Spirit in this judgment. We are to judge only the teaching. God will judge the teacher.	2:1–3 2:18–22	**Reject** any teaching that denies the lordship of Jesus. **Know** that the false teacher brings about distrust of true ministers of God. **Judge** the words of every teaching. **Let God judge** the teacher. **Beware** teaching what sounds good but means nothing. **Be established** so that you cannot be lured back into sin by false doctrine.
5 Key Lessons in Faith Logic alone cannot lead us to effective Christian living: faith is needed. The Christian life is the result of hearing God's Word, trusting it, and applying it through faithful obedience. Faith may not yield immediate dividends: its ultimate return will be realized in eternity.	1:4 1:16–21 3:11–13	**Understand** that God's promises result in our 1) sharing in God's very nature and 2) escaping moral and spiritual corruption. **Recognize** the divine origin of the Scriptures. **Understand** that any personal understanding must be scrutinized in the light of God's Word. **Understand** that the ultimate goal of the believer is not in this life. **Know** that our hope is in the new heaven and new earth. **Live** with a holy disregard for this world's values and all that controls it.

The First Epistle of JOHN

Author: The Apostle John
Date: About A.D. 90
Theme: Jesus Is the Son of God. Those Who Follow Him Must Live Righteously.
Key Words: Love, Know, Life, Light, Fellowship

Author and Recipients Although this epistle is anonymous, its style and vocabulary clearly indicate that it was written by the author of the Gospel of John. Internal evidence also points to John as the author, and ancient testimony unanimously ascribes the epistle to him.

Lack of a special dedication and salutation indicates that the letter was circular, probably sent to the churches near Ephesus, where John spent his latter years.

Date The weight of early and strong Christian tradition that John spent his latter years at Ephesus, together with the fact that the tone of the writings suggests that they are the product of a mature man who has enjoyed profound spiritual experience, points to a date near the end of the first century. In addition, the character of the heresy combated in the letter points to the same time, approximately A.D. 90.

Occasion and Purpose John states that he wrote to give assurance of eternal life to those "who believe in the name of the Son of God" (5:13). The uncertainty of his readers about their spiritual status was caused by an unsettling conflict with the teachers of a false doctrine. John refers to the teachings as deceitful (2:26; 3:7) and to the teachers as "false prophets" (4:1), liars (2:22), and antichrists (2:18, 22; 4:3). They had once been within the church, but had withdrawn (2:19) and had "gone out into the world" (4:1) to propagate their dangerous heresy.

The heresy was a forerunner of second-century Gnosticism, which taught that matter is essentially evil and spirit is essentially good. This dualistic viewpoint caused the false teachers to deny the Incarnation of Christ and, hence, the Resurrection. The true God, they taught, could never indwell a material body of flesh and blood. Therefore, the human body that Jesus supposedly possessed was not real, but merely apparent. John wrote vigorously against this error (see 2:22, 23; 4:3).

They also taught that since the evil human body was merely an envelope for the spirit within, and since nothing the body could do could affect the inner spirit, ethical distinctions ceased to be relevant. Hence, they had no sin. John answered this error with indignation (see 2:4, 6, 15–17; 3:3, 7, 9, 10; 5:18).

"Gnosticism" is a word derived from the Greek *gnosis,* meaning "knowledge." Gnostics later taught salvation by mental enlightenment, which came only to elite spiritual initiates, not to the ordinary rank and file of Christians. Hence, they substituted intellectual pursuits for faith and exalted speculation above the basic tenets of the gospel. John again reacted strenuously (see 2:20, 27), declaring that there is no private revelation reserved for a few intellectuals, and that the whole body of believers possesses the apostolic teaching.

John's purpose in writing, then, was to expose the heresy of the false teachers and to confirm the faith of the true believers.

Characteristics There are strong similarities between the Gospel of John and 1 John. The tone of the epistle is friendly and fatherly, reflecting the authority that age and apostleship bring. The style is informal and personal, revealing the apostle's intimate relationship with God and God's people.

Content First John stresses the themes of love, light, knowledge, and life in its warnings against heresy. These major elements are repeated throughout the letter, with love being the dominant note. Possessing love is clear evidence that one is a Christian, and lack of love indicates that one is in darkness (2:9–11; 3:10–23; 4:7–21).

John affirms that God is light, and fellowship with Him causes one to walk in the light in true fellowship with other believers. Fellowship with God and the brethren enables one to recognize, through the anointing of God, false doctrine and the spirit of the antichrist.

Fellowship with God necessitates walking in the light and obeying the commandments of God (1:6, 7; 2:3–5). The one "who practices righteousness is righteous, just as He is righteous" (3:7), while "whoever does not practice righteousness is not of God" (3:10). The love of the Father and the love of the world are totally incompatible (2:15–17), and no one born of God is in the habit of practicing sin (3:9; 5:18). Christ is the antithesis of sin, and He has appeared that He might take away all of our sins (3:5).

Chapter 4 continues the theme of understanding the rival spirits—the false prophets who have gone out into the world (v. 1). In order to test the spirits we must find whom they acknowledge as savior and lord. Every spirit that does not acknowledge that Jesus Christ is God in the flesh is not from God (v. 3).

The epistle ends with the testimony of Jesus the Son of God. Jesus is the One who came. The technical title of the Messiah is "He who comes" or "He who is to come" (Matt. 11:3; 1 John 5:6). John identifies Him as the One who came by water and by blood, the God who came and dwelt among us, the Word that was made flesh.

Personal Application Prominent in 1 John is the positive note of Christian certainty. Thirty-nine times the verb "know" occurs. Christian truth is beyond the realm of speculation, because it is irrevocably moored to the historical event of Jesus Christ and the apostolic witness to that event. In addition, Christians possess the anointing and witness of the Holy Spirit to assure them of the truth about God, Christ, and their own spiritual standing.

Three tests prove the genuineness of Christianity: the test of belief (4:2), the test of obedience (2:3), and the test of love (4:20). The same affirmations are stated negatively. The one who professes to be a Christian, but who cannot pass the test of belief (2:22), the test of obedience (1:6), and the test of love (4:20), is a liar. John brings all three tests together in 5:1–5, where he indicates that a profession of Christianity is false unless it is characterized by correct belief, godly obedience, and brotherly love. The same tests are valid today.

Christ Revealed John emphasizes both the deity and the humanity of Jesus, declaring that in Him God fully entered into human life. A test of Christianity is correct belief about the Incarnation (4:2, 15; 5:1).

Jesus is our Advocate with the Father (2:1). Sin is incongruous in the life of a Christian; but if he does sin, Jesus pleads his case.

Jesus is the propitiation for our sins (2:2; 4:10). See note on Romans 3:25.

Jesus is also Savior, sent by God to rescue us from sin (1:7; 3:5; 4:14). Only through Him can we have eternal life (5:11, 12).

John presents the Second Coming of Jesus as an incentive to remain firm in the faith (2:28), and he gives assurance that our complete transformation into Christ's likeness will occur at His return.

The Holy Spirit at Work John describes a threefold ministry of the Holy Spirit in this epistle. First, God's gift of the Spirit to us assures us of our relationship to Christ, both that He abides in us (3:24) and that we abide in Him (4:13). Second, the Holy Spirit testifies to the reality of the Incarnation of Christ (4:2; 5:6–8). Third, the Spirit leads true believers into a full realization of the truth concerning Jesus, that they may successfully oppose the heretics who deny that truth (2:20; 4:4).

Outline of 1 John

I. The Incarnation **1:1–10**
- A. God became flesh in human form 1:1–4
- B. God is light 1:5–10

II. The life of righteousness **2:1–29**
- A. Walking in the light 2:1–17
- B. Warning against the spirit of antichrist 2:18–29

III. The life of the children of God **3:1—4:6**
- A. Righteousness 3:1–12
- B. Love 3:13–24
- C. Belief 4:1–6

IV. The source of love **4:7–21**

V. The triumph of righteousness **5:1–5**

VI. The assurance of eternal life **5:6–12**

VII. Christian certainties **5:13–21**

What Was Heard, Seen, and Touched

THAT [a]which was from the beginning, which we have heard, which
we have [b]seen with our eyes, [c]which
we have looked upon, and [d]our hands
have handled, concerning the [e]Word
of life—
2 [a]the life [b]was manifested, and we
have seen, [c]and bear witness, and declare to you that eternal life which was
[d]with the Father and was manifested
to us—
3 that which we have seen and heard 1
we declare to you, that you also may
have *fellowship with us; and truly our
fellowship *is* [a]with the Father and with
His Son Jesus Christ.
4 And these things we write to you
[a]that [1]your joy may be full.

CHAPTER 1

1 [a][John 1:1] [b]John 1:14 [c]2 Pet. 1:16 [d]Luke 24:39 [e][John 1:1, 4, 14] **2** [a]John 1:4 [b]Rom. 16:26 [c]John 21:24 [d][John 1:1, 18; 16:28] **3** [a]1 Cor. 1:9

*See WW at Acts 2:42. **4** [a]John 15:11; 16:24 [1]NU, M *our*

1:1, 2 As the eternal Son of God, Jesus existed before His manifestation in time (see John 1:1). When He came to Earth, He assumed real manhood, a fact that was verified by those who knew Him in the flesh.
1:3, 4 See section 1 of Truth-In-Action at the end of 1 John.

Fellowship with Him and One Another

6 5 [a]This is the message which we have
heard from Him and declare to you,
that [b]God is light and in Him is no
*darkness at all.
6 [a]If we say that we have fellowship
with Him, and walk in darkness, we
lie and do not practice the truth.
7 But if we [a]walk in the light as He
is in the light, we have fellowship with
one another, and [b]the **blood** of Jesus
Christ His Son cleanses us from all
*sin.

WORD WEALTH

1:7 blood, *haima* (*hahee*-mah); Strong's *#129:* The technical word for the blood of animals and of people, but in the NT text used particularly for the atoning blood of Christ. His sacrificial blood is the agency for cleansing, forgiveness, and redemption.

8 If we say that we have no sin, we
deceive ourselves, and the *truth is not
in us.
9 If we [a]confess our sins, He is
[b]faithful and just to forgive us *our* sins
and to [c]cleanse us from all *unrighteousness.
10 If we say that we have not sinned,
we [a]make Him a liar, and His word is
not in us.

2 My little children, these things I
write to you, so that you may not
sin. And if anyone sins, [a]we have an
*Advocate with the Father, Jesus
Christ the righteous.
2 And [a]He Himself is the *propitiation for our sins, and not for ours only
but [b]also for the whole world.

5 [a]1 John 3:11 [b][1 Tim. 6:16] *See WW at John 12:46.
6 [a][1 John 2:9–11]
7 [a]Is. 2:5 [b][1 Cor. 6:11] *See WW at John 1:29.
8 *See WW at John 4:24.
9 [a]Prov. 28:13 [b][Rom. 3:24–26] [c]Ps. 51:2 *See WW at John 7:18.
10 [a]1 John 5:10

CHAPTER 2

1 [a]Heb. 7:25; 9:24 *See WW at John 15:26.
2 [a][Rom. 3:25] [b]John 1:29 *See WW at 1 John 4:10.
4 [a]Rom. 3:4
5 [a]John 14:21, 23 [b][1 John 4:12] [1]*has been completed*
6 [a]John 15:4 [b]1 Pet. 2:21
7 [a]1 John 3:11, 23; 4:21 [1]NU *Beloved* [2]NU omits *from the beginning*
8 [a]John 13:34; 15:12 [b]Rom. 13:12 [c][John 1:9; 8:12; 12:35] *See WW at Rom. 3:4. • See WW at John 12:46.
9 [a][1 Cor. 13:2]
10 [a][1 John 3:14] [b]2 Pet. 1:10 *See WW at Matt. 16:23.
11 [a][1 John 2:9; 3:15; 4:20]

The Test of Knowing Him

3 Now by this we know that we know 3
Him, if we keep His commandments.
4 He who says, "I know Him," and
does not keep His commandments, is
a [a]liar, and the truth is not in him.
5 But [a]whoever keeps His word, truly
the love of God [1]is **perfected** [b]in him.
By this we know that we are in Him.

WORD WEALTH

2:5 perfected, *teleioo* (tel-eye-*ah*-oh); Strong's *#5048:* To complete, accomplish, carry through to the end, bring to a successful conclusion, reach a goal, fulfill. In an ethical and spiritual sense, the word signifies a bringing to maturity, a perfecting.

6 [a]He who says he abides in Him
[b]ought himself also to walk just as He
walked.
7 [1]Brethren, I write no new commandment to you, but an old commandment which you have had [a]from
the beginning. The old commandment
is the word which you heard [2]from the
beginning.
8 Again, [a]a new commandment I
write to you, which thing is *true in
Him and in you, [b]because the *darkness is passing away, and [c]the true
light is already shining.
9 [a]He who says he is in the light, and 2
hates his brother, is in darkness until
now.
10 [a]He who loves his brother abides
in the light, and [b]there is no cause for
*stumbling in him.
11 But he who [a]hates his brother is in
darkness and [b]walks in *darkness, and

[b]John 12:35 *See WW at John 12:46.

1:5–10 See section 6 of Truth-In-Action at the end of 1 John.
1:5 As **light, God** reveals Himself in His perfect holiness and majesty.
1:6, 7 Our **walk in the light** is a test of **fellowship** with God, since the life of fellowship is a life that is continually cleansed from sin by **the blood of Jesus.** It also involves our relationship **with one another,** which indicates that a walk "in the light" is lived accountably before both God and man.
1:8 Anyone who walks in the light that God has revealed cannot fail to note his own sinfulness.
1:9, 10 To persevere in the false pride that denies one's sins is not only to deceive oneself (v. 8), but to accuse God of lying, since His Word declares the universality of sin. *However,* to **confess our sins** is a prerequisite to receiving the Lord's forgiveness and cleansing.
2:1, 2 Although John's purpose is to keep his readers from sinning, realistically he knows that at some time they will commit an act of sin. In His grace, God has made a twofold provision to restore sinning Christians. First, He has appointed Jesus as **an Advocate** to plead the case of sinners. He is certain to secure their pardon because He is **righteous.** Second, God has provided Jesus as **the propitiation for our sins.** See note on Rom. 3:25.
2:3–6 See section 3 of Truth-In-Action at the end of 1 John.
2:3–6 Obedience to the **commandments** of God tests one's knowledge of Him. Genuine love for God (v. 5) and a true relationship with Him (v. 6) must be evidenced by loyalty.
2:7 Another test of fellowship with God is love for the brethren, **an old commandment** that they had known since their first acquaintance with Christ.
2:8 The commandment to love is also **new** because Jesus gave it a new standard and a new motive (see John 13:34). John affirms the fact that **the true light,** which the gospel reveals, dispels **the darkness** of moral ignorance and satanic bondage.
2:9–11 See section 2 of Truth-In-Action at the end of 1 John.
2:9–11 Love is characteristic of **light,** and hate is characteristic of **darkness.** Those two are mortal enemies. Therefore, a person reveals the genuineness of his relationship with God by his relationship with others.

does not know where he is going, because the darkness has blinded his eyes.

Their Spiritual State

12 I write to you, little children,
Because [a]your sins are forgiven
you for His name's sake.
13 I write to you, fathers,
Because you have known Him
who is [a]from the beginning.
I write to you, young men,
Because you have overcome the
wicked one.
I write to you, little children,
Because you have [b]known the
Father.
14 I have written to you, fathers,
Because you have known Him
who is from the beginning.
I have written to you, young men,
Because [a]you are strong, and
the word of God abides in
you,
And you have overcome the
wicked one.

Do Not Love the World

2 15 [a]Do not love the world or the things
in the world. [b]If anyone loves the
world, the love of the Father is not in
him.
16 For all that *is* in the world—the lust
of the flesh, [a]the lust of the eyes, and
the pride of life—is not of the Father
but is of the world.
17 And [a]the world is passing away,
and the lust of it; but he who does the
will of God abides forever.

Deceptions of the Last Hour

6 18 [a]Little children, [b]it is the last hour;
and as you have heard that [c]the[1] Antichrist
is coming, [d]even now many antichrists
have come, by which we know
[e]that it is the last hour.

12 [a][1 Cor. 6:11] **13** [a]John 1:1; Rev. 22:13 [b][Rom. 8:15–17; Gal. 4:6] **14** [a]Eph. 6:10 **15** [a][Rom. 12:2]; Gal. 1:4; James 1:27 [b]Matt. 6:24; James 4:4 **16** [a][Eccl. 5:10, 11] **17** [a]1 Cor. 7:31; 1 Pet. 1:24 **18** [a]John 21:5 [b]Rom. 13:11; 1 Tim. 4:1; Heb. 1:2; 1 Pet. 4:7 [c]2 Thess. 2:3 [d]Matt. 24:5, 24; 1 John 2:22; 4:3; 2 John 7 [e]1 Tim. 4:1 [1]NU omits *the*

KINGDOM DYNAMICS

2:18 The Prophecies of Last Things, PROPHECY. Eschatology is that aspect of biblical doctrine dealing with "last things" (from Greek *eschatos,* "final"). In this text, John describes the times in which he wrote as "the last hour," evidencing that he, as vital Christians in every generation, both lived in immediate anticipation of Christ's Second Coming and saw his era as one in which the present evidence seemed to argue that his was possibly the concluding generation. This is not an unhealthy attitude: Christ Jesus desires that people expectantly anticipate His return (Matt. 25:1–13; 2 Tim. 4:8).

John not only addresses the lateness of the hour of history as he views it; he also addresses the subject of Antichrist, a commonly discussed theme when eschatology is studied. The spirit of antichrist, the Rapture of the church, the Great Tribulation, the restoration of national Israel, and the millennial reign of Christ on Earth are all among the many subjects the Bible describes as "last things." The Bible clearly says these things shall occur. However, it is not clear about the exact time; and in many cases it does not conclusively give the sequence or exact manner of the fulfillment of such events.

The *Spirit-Filled Life Bible* does not embrace any conclusive point of view concerning these popularly discussed subjects. We do affirm these things: 1) God is the Sovereign of the Universe and the God of History, which is His-Story. 2) As such, He knows the end from the beginning and at the end of history will have been verified as All-Wise and vindicated as All-Just. 3) His Son, Jesus Christ, shall come to Earth again for His church (John 14:1–3; Acts 1:11; 1 Cor. 15:50–58; 1 Thess. 4:16, 17), and shall rule on Earth (Is. 9:7; 11:6–9; Rev. 20:1–6). 4) There is a final judgment, with the reward of eternal life in heaven promised to the redeemed and the judgment of eternal loss in hell the portion of the unregenerate (Rev. 20:11–15; 21:22—22:5).

We affirm the value of the study of last

(cont. on next page)

2:12–14 John addresses different groups in the church, not according to physical age, but according to their levels of spiritual growth. His purpose is to encourage them to further progress and to warn them against the temptations that are certain to come (vv. 15–17).
2:15–17 See section 2 of Truth-In-Action at the end of 1 John.
2:15 The world does not refer to the physical creation, but to the sphere of evil operating in our world under the dominion of Satan (see 4:4; 5:19; John 12:31; 14:30; 16:11).
2:18–27 Another test of true fellowship with God is that of true belief. John distinguishes between heretics and genuine believers (vv. 18–21), describes the nature and result of the heresy (vv. 22, 23), and reminds his readers of the resources available to meet the heresy (vv. 24–27).
2:18, 19 See section 6 of Truth-In-Action at the end of 1 John.
2:18, 19 The last hour was introduced by the First Coming of Christ (see Acts 2:17; Heb. 1:1, 2; 1 Pet. 1:20). At the end of this period the one known as **the Antichrist** will come (see 2 Thess. 2:3–9), but there are already many such persons at work in the world. John identifies other **antichrists** as the heretics (deceitful, destructive, divisive "believers") who withdrew from the church (v. 19). Their withdrawal is evidence that they never really shared in the life and fellowship of the church.

(*cont. from preceding page*)
things and equally declare our conviction that differences of opinion on such matters as the Rapture, the nature of the Millennium, and so on, neither give us an advantage nor hinder us with reference to our life in Christ, as we choose to serve in His love, walk in His truth, and expect His return.

(Deut. 28:1/Rev. 4:1) J.W.H.

19 [a]They went out from us, but they
were not of us; for [b]if they had been
of us, they would have continued with
us; but *they went out* [c]that they might
be made manifest, that none of them
were of us.
20 But [a]you have an anointing [b]from
the Holy One, and [c]you[1] know all
things.
21 I have not written to you because
you do not know the truth, but because
you know it, and that no lie is of the
truth.
22 [a]Who is a liar but he who denies
that [b]Jesus is the Christ? He is antichrist who denies the Father and the
Son.
23 [a]Whoever denies the Son does not
have the [b]Father either; [c]he who acknowledges the Son has the Father
also.

Let Truth Abide in You

1 24 Therefore let that abide in you
[a]which you heard from the beginning.
If what you heard from the beginning
abides in you, [b]you also will abide in
the Son and in the Father.
25 [a]And this is the *promise that He
has *promised us—eternal life.
26 These things I have written to you
concerning those who *try to* [1]deceive
you.
27 But the [a]anointing which you have
received from Him abides in you, and
[b]you do not need that anyone teach
you; but as the same anointing
[c]teaches you concerning all things, and
is true, and is not a lie, and just as it
has taught you, you [1]will abide in Him.

The Children of God

28 And now, little children, abide in
Him, that [1]when He appears, we may
have [a]confidence and not be ashamed
before Him at His *coming.
29 [a]If you know that He is righteous, 4
you know that [b]everyone who practices righteousness is born of Him.
3 Behold [a]what manner of love the 5
Father has bestowed on us, that
[b]we should be *called children of
[1]God! Therefore the world does not
know [2]us, [c]because it did not know
Him.
2 Beloved, [a]now we are children of
God; and [b]it has not yet been revealed
what we shall be, but we know that
when He is revealed, [c]we shall be like
Him, for [d]we shall see Him as He is.
3 [a]And everyone who has this *hope
in Him purifies himself, just as He is
pure.

WORD WEALTH

3:3 pure, *hagnos* (hag-*noss*); Strong's *#53:* From the same root as *hagios,* "holy." The adjective describes a person or thing as clean, modest, pure, undefiled, morally faultless, and without blemish. Christ's ability to overcome temptation and remain pure makes Him a role model for all believers.

Sin and the Child of God

4 Whoever commits sin also commits 4
lawlessness, and [a]sin is lawlessness.
5 And you know [a]that He was manifested [b]to *take away our sins, and
[c]in Him there is no sin.

19 [a]Deut. 13:13 [b]Matt. 24:24 [c]1 Cor. 11:19
20 [a]2 Cor. 1:21 [b]Acts 3:14 [c][John 16:13] [1]NU *you all know.*
22 [a]2 John 7 [b]1 John 4:3
23 [a]John 15:23 [b]John 5:23 [c]1 John 4:15; 5:1
24 [a]2 John 5, 6 [b]John 14:23
25 [a]John 3:14–16; 6:40; 17:2, 3 *See WW at Acts 13:32. • See WW at Acts 7:5.
26 [1]*lead you astray*
27 [a][John 14:16; 16:13] [b][Jer. 31:33] [c][John 14:16] [1]NU omits *will*
28 [a]1 John 3:21; 4:17; 5:14 [1]NU *if* *See WW at 1 Cor. 15:23.
29 [a]Acts 22:14 [b]1 John 3:7, 10

CHAPTER 3

1 [a][1 John 4:10] [b][John 1:12] [c]John 15:18, 21; 16:3 [1]NU adds *And we are.* [2]M *you* *See WW at Gal. 1:6.
2 [a][Rom. 8:15, 16] [b][Rom. 8:18, 19, 23] [c]Rom. 8:29 [d][Ps. 16:11]
3 [a]1 John 4:17 *See WW at 1 Thess. 1:3.
4 [a]Rom. 4:15
5 [a]1 John 1:2; 3:8 [b]John 1:29 [c][2 Cor. 5:21] *See WW at John 16:22.

2:20, 21 In contrast to the false teachers who claimed superior knowledge, true Christians possess an understanding of spiritual realities through the illuminating ministry of the Holy Spirit.
2:22, 23 The particular error of these heretics was a denial of the Incarnation, which created a gospel of mysticism and obstructed a true understanding of the Father and personal relationship with Him (John 14:7–11).
2:24–27 Two things will protect the readers from falling victim to the seductive teachings of the heretics: 1) constantly abiding in the truth concerning Christ, which they had received from the apostles; 2) the anointing of the Holy Spirit, whose illuminating power will enable them to distinguish truth from error. To receive spiritual knowledge under the guidance of the Holy Spirit is to know truth in a way that human instruction cannot provide. The text is not an argument against the ministry of teaching (Rom. 12:7; Eph. 4:11), but an emphasis that only the Holy Spirit is able to bring revelation to the human heart (Eph. 1:17, 18).
2:24, 25 See section 1 of Truth-In-Action at the end of 1 John.
2:28, 29 Abiding in Christ is not only by faith, but by obedience.
2:29 See section 4 of Truth-In-Action at the end of 1 John.
3:1, 2 See section 5 of Truth-In-Action at the end of 1 John.
3:1 John expresses astonishment at God's love in regenerating believers, an experience **the world** cannot understand.
3:2, 3 The prospect of being transformed into the likeness of Christ motivates Christians to live righteously.
3:4–9 See section 4 of Truth-In-Action at the end of 1 John.
3:4 Sin is the spirit of rebellion against God's Law.

6 Whoever abides in Him does not
sin. Whoever sins has neither seen Him
nor *known Him.
1 7 Little children, let no one deceive
you. He who practices *righteousness
is righteous, just as He is righteous.
8 [a]He who sins is of the devil, for the
devil has sinned from the beginning.
For this purpose the Son of God was
manifested, [b]that He might destroy the
works of the devil.
9 Whoever has been [a]born of God
does not sin, for [b]His seed remains in
him; and he *cannot sin, because he
has been born of God.

The Imperative of Love

10 In this the children of God and the
children of the devil are *manifest:
Whoever does not practice righteousness is not of God, nor *is* he who
does not love his brother.
4 11 For this is the message that you
heard from the beginning, [a]that we
should love one another,
12 not as [a]Cain *who* was of the wicked
one and murdered his brother. And
why did he murder him? Because his
works were evil and his brother's righteous.
13 Do not marvel, my brethren, if
[a]the world hates you.
14 We know that we have passed from
death to life, because we love the brethren. He who does not love [1]*his* brother
abides in death.
15 [a]Whoever hates his brother is a
murderer, and you know that [b]no murderer has eternal life abiding in him.

The Outworking of Love

16 [a]By this we know love, [b]because He 4
laid down His life for us. And we also
ought to lay down *our* lives for the
brethren.
17 But [a]whoever has this world's
goods, and *sees his brother in need,
and shuts up his heart from him, how
does the love of God abide in him?
18 My little children, [a]let us not love
in word or in tongue, but in deed and
in truth.
19 And by this we [1]know [a]that we are
of the truth, and shall [2]assure* our
hearts before Him.
20 [a]For if our heart condemns us, God
is greater than our heart, and knows
all things.
21 Beloved, if our heart does not con- 5
demn us, [a]we have confidence toward
God.
22 And [a]whatever we *ask we receive
from Him, because we keep His commandments [b]and do those things that
are pleasing in His sight.
23 And this is His commandment: that
we should believe on the name of His
Son Jesus Christ [a]and love one another, as He gave [1]us commandment.

The Spirit of Truth and the Spirit of Error

24 Now [a]he who keeps His commandments [b]abides in Him, and He in him.
And [c]by this we know that He abides
in us, by the Spirit whom He has given
us.

4 Beloved, do not believe every 4
spirit, but [a]test the spirits, whether

6 *See WW at John 8:32.
7 *See WW at 2 Tim. 4:8.
8 [a]Matt. 13:38 [b]Luke 10:18
9 [a]John 1:3; 3:3 [b]1 Pet. 1:23 *See WW at Jude 24.
10 *See WW at 1 Cor. 11:19.
11 [a][John 13:34; 15:12]
12 [a]Gen. 4:4, 8
13 [a][John 15:18; 17:14]
14 [1]NU omits *his brother*
15 [a]Matt. 5:21 [b][Gal. 5:20, 21]
16 [a][John 3:16] [b]John 10:11; 15:13
17 [a]Deut. 15:7 *See WW at John 20:14.
18 [a]Ezek. 33:31
19 [a]John 18:37 [1]NU *shall know* [2]*persuade, set at rest* *See WW at 2 Thess. 3:4.
20 [a][1 Cor. 4:4, 5]
21 [a][1 John 2:28; 5:14]
22 [a]Ps. 34:15 [b]John 8:29 *See WW at Matt. 7:7.
23 [a]Matt. 22:39 [1]M omits *us*
24 [a]John 14:23 [b]John 14:21; 17:21 [c]Rom. 8:9, 14, 16

CHAPTER 4

1 [a]1 Cor. 14:29

3:6–9 John does not teach perfectionism; otherwise, he would contradict himself (see 1:8, 9). Although interpretations of this text vary, it seems John's argument is grammatically based. By using the Greek present tense he does not declare that Christians are unable to commit an occasional act of sin (see 1:8–10; 2:1), but that they are not characterized by the spirit of lawlessness (v. 4), powerlessly led into a habitual practice of sin. Sin is natural to children of the Devil, who **has sinned from the beginning,** but unnatural to children of God, who **cannot sin** without the Spirit's conviction. A constant indulgence in sin contradicts the claim to have a personal knowledge of Christ.
3:7–15 See section 1 of Truth-In-Action at the end of 1 John.
3:10–15 Love for fellow Christians is just as much a characteristic of the new nature of believers as righteous living (see John 13:35). For **hates** and **murderer,** see Matt. 5:21, 22.
3:11–15 See section 4 of Truth-In-Action at the end of 1 John.
3:16–18 See section 4 of Truth-In-Action at the end of 1 John.
3:16 The sacrifice of Christ is both the proof of His love and the standard of our own love (see Phil. 2:4–8).
3:17 Love is shown, not only in a heroic deed of self-sacrifice, but in a daily life of compassion.
3:18 See James 2:15, 16.
3:19, 20 Even when true Christians are discouraged and self-condemning, they can receive assurance that they are children of God from the objective test of God's Word.
3:21–24 See section 5 of Truth-In-Action at the end of 1 John.
3:21–23 Assurance of our standing before God gives boldness in prayer. Our prayers are not answered as a reward for obedience, but when **we keep His commandments** we give evidence that we are in harmony with God's will (see John 15:7) and thus pray accordingly.
3:24 The indwelling Holy Spirit manifests His presence outwardly in our life and conduct, giving evidence of our relationship with God.
4:1–6 See section 4 of Truth-In-Action at the end of 1 John.
4:1 Believers are not to be so gullible that they indiscriminately accept the pronouncements of all **prophets** who claim to be **of God,** that is, to speak with divine authority and under divine inspiration. A **spirit** is indeed behind every prophet, but it may be a false spirit, described as "the *spirit* of the Antichrist" (v. 3) and "the spirit of error" (v. 6), rather than "the Spirit of God" (v. 2), who is "the spirit of truth" (v. 6). Therefore, since there are many cultic and heretical

they are of God; because [b]many false
prophets have gone out into the world.
2 By this you know the Spirit of God:
[a]Every spirit that confesses that Jesus
Christ has come in the flesh is of God,
3 and every spirit that does not confess [1]that Jesus [2]Christ has come in the
flesh is not of God. And this is the *spirit*
of the Antichrist, which you have
heard was coming, and is now already
in the world.
5 4 You are of God, little children, and
have overcome them, because He who
is in you is greater than [a]he who is in
the world.
5 [a]They are of the world. Therefore
they speak *as* of the world, and [b]the
world hears them.
6 We are of God. He who knows God
hears us; he who is not of God does
not hear us. [a]By this we know the spirit
of truth and the spirit of *error.

KINGDOM DYNAMICS

4:1–6 Prophecy Not Christ-Centered Is Disqualified, PROPHECY. Since the heart of true prophecy is Christ Himself (Rev. 19:10), the word "prophecy" not only defines the Bible, but confines all prophesying that claims to be true. This text shows that John distinguished the spirit of truth and error by whether the sinless glory and saviorhood of our Lord Jesus Christ was the focus. Paul pronounced a curse upon anyone who violated this sound word of the gospel (Gal. 1:6–9). Both men were addressing the early church community and confronting the encroachment of teachers or teachings that claimed prophetic authority, but failed to present and honor Jesus Christ in a way consistent with the whole of the Scriptures.

Likewise, we should be cautious regarding groups or individuals who claim a Christian foundation: What place is Jesus Himself given? We should also reject any prophesying that preoccupies itself with mystical ideas or secondary issues. All true prophecy rests in and upon Christ, the Foundation. If that Foundation is soundly built upon, the shape of all that rises will look and sound like Jesus, God's Son.

(Rev. 19:10/Eph. 1:17–19) J.W.H.

1 [b]Matt. 24:5
2 [a][Rom. 10:8–10]; 1 Cor. 12:3; 1 John 5:1
3 [1]NU omits *that* [2]NU omits *Christ has come in the flesh*
4 [a]John 14:30; 16:11
5 [a]John 3:31 [b]John 15:19; 17:14
6 [a][1 Cor. 2:12–16] *See WW at Jude 11.
7 [a]1 John 3:10, 11, 23 [b]1 Thess. 4:9; [1 John 3:14] *See WW at Rom. 5:5.
9 [a]Rom. 5:8 [b]Is. 9:6, 7; John 3:16 *See WW at John 20:21.
10 [a]Titus 3:5 [b]1 John 2:2
11 [a]Matt. 18:33
12 [a]John 1:18; 1 Tim. 6:16; 1 John 4:20
13 [a]John 14:20

Knowing God Through Love

7 [a]Beloved, let us love one another, 1
for *love is of God; and everyone who
[b]loves is born of God and knows God.
8 He who does not love does not
know God, for God is love.
9 [a]In this the love of God was manifested toward us, that God has *sent
His only begotten [b]Son into the world,
that we might live through Him.
10 In this is love, [a]not that we loved
God, but that He loved us and sent His
Son [b]*to be* the **propitiation** for our sins.

WORD WEALTH

4:10 propitiation, *hilasmos* (hil-as-*moss*); Strong's *#2434:* Related to *hileos,* "merciful." Used in the NT only in 2:2 and 4:10, the word describes Christ, through His sacrificial death, as appeasing the wrath of God on account of sin. It also pictures His death as expiatory, providing a covering for sin. By means of the atoning death of Christ, God can be merciful to the sinner who believes in Him, and reconciliation is effected.

11 Beloved, [a]if God so loved us, we
also ought to love one another.

Seeing God Through Love

12 [a]No one has seen God at any time.
If we love one another, God abides in
us, and His love has been perfected in
us.
13 [a]By this we know that we abide in
Him, and He in us, because He has
given us of His Spirit.

teachers claiming to be spokespersons for God, we must **test the spirits** possessing them to determine their origin. Paul gives similar instructions in 1 Thess. 5:19–22.

4:2 The crux of the test is a spirit's acknowledgment or rejection of **Jesus Christ** as the incarnate Son of God. A confession of Jesus involves more than an admission of His identity (see Matt. 8:28, 29; Mark 1:24; 3:11). It is a profession of faith in Him and submission to His sovereignty. The Holy Spirit testifies to and glorifies Jesus (see John 15:26; 16:14; 1 Cor. 12:3). Therefore, a confession *proclaiming* the truth that Jesus is the incarnate Christ **is of God** testifies to both His full humanity as our Savior-Redeemer and His full deity as Lord and Sovereign King.

4:3 On the other hand, a denial of the truth concerning Jesus reveals that any claim of divine inspiration is false and that the true origin **is the *spirit* of the Antichrist.** See note on 2:18, 19.

4:4–6 That which fundamentally distinguishes the people **of the world** and the people **of God** is their respective attitudes toward Jesus Christ. By the illumination of the Holy Spirit, who **is greater** than Satan (the spirit of error), true believers may **overcome** deceiving teachers.

4:4 See section 5 of Truth-In-Action at the end of 1 John.

4:7–21 For the third time John stresses **love** as a test of the Christian life (see 2:7–11; 3:10–18). Here he traces love to its source in the nature of God as revealed at the Cross. Christians show that they are God's children by manifesting sacrificial attitudes and actions like His.

4:7–19 See section 1 of Truth-In-Action at the end of 1 John.

4:12 Although God is invisible (1 Tim. 1:17; 6:16), we manifest His nature through life-styles that reflect His love.

4:13 The **Spirit** does not indwell us because of our love; on the contrary, He enables us to love.

14 And [a]we have seen and testify that
[b]the Father has sent the Son *as* *Savior
of the world.
15 [a]Whoever confesses that Jesus is
the Son of God, God abides in him, and
he in God.
16 And we have known and believed
the love that God has for us. God is
love, and [a]he who abides in love abides
in God, and God [b]in him.

The Consummation of Love

17 Love has been *perfected among us
in this: that [a]we may have boldness in
the day of judgment; because as He is,
so are we in this world.
18 There is no **fear** in love; but *perfect
love casts out fear, because fear involves torment. But he who fears has
not been made perfect in love.

WORD WEALTH

4:18 fear, *phobos* (*fob*-oss); Strong's *#5401:* In classical Greek the word signified flight. Later it came to denote that which causes flight; hence, fear, terror, dread. In the NT *phobos* denotes both the fear of terror and the fear of reverence toward God. The English word "phobia" transliterates the Greek word.

19 [a]We love [1]Him because He first
loved us.

Obedience by Faith

20 [a]If someone says, "I love God," and
hates his brother, he is a liar; for he
who does not love his brother whom
he has seen, [1]how can he love God
[b]whom he has not seen?
21 And [a]this commandment we have
from Him: that he who loves God *must*
love his brother also.

5

Whoever believes that [a]Jesus is the 4
Christ is [b]born of God, and everyone who loves Him who begot also
loves him who is begotten of Him.
2 By this we know that we love the
children of God, when we love God and
[a]keep His commandments.
3 [a]For this is the love of God, that we
keep His commandments. And [b]His
commandments are not burdensome.
4 For [a]whatever is born of God over- 5
comes the world. And this is the victory that [b]has overcome the *world—
[1]our faith.
5 Who is he who overcomes the
world, but [a]he who believes that Jesus
is the Son of God?

The Certainty of God's Witness

6 This is He who came [a]by water and
blood—Jesus Christ; not only by water,
but by water and blood. [b]And it is the
Spirit who bears *witness, because the
Spirit is truth.
7 For there are three that bear witness [1]in heaven: the Father, [a]the Word,
and the Holy Spirit; [b]and these three
are one.
8 And there are three that bear witness on earth: [a]the Spirit, the water,
and the blood; and these three agree
as one.
9 If we receive [a]the *witness of men,
the witness of God is greater; [b]for this
is the witness of [1]God which He has
testified of His Son.
10 He who believes in the Son of God
[a]has the witness in himself; he who

14 [a]John 1:14 [b]John 3:17; 4:42 *See WW at John 4:42. **15** [a][Rom. 10:9] **16** [a][1 John 3:24] [b][John 14:23] **17** [a]1 John 2:28 *See WW at 1 John 2:5. **18** *See WW at James 3:2. **19** [a]1 John 4:10 [1]NU omits *Him* **20** [a][1 John 2:4] [b]1 John 4:12 [1]NU *he cannot* **21** [a][Matt. 5:43, 44; 22:39]

CHAPTER 5

1 [a]1 John 2:22; 4:2, 15 [b]John 1:13 **2** [a]John 15:10 **3** [a]John 14:15 [b]Matt. 11:30; 23:4 **4** [a]John 16:33 [b]1 John 2:13; 4:4 [1]M *your* *See WW at John 18:36. **5** [a]1 Cor. 15:57 **6** [a]John 1:31–34 [b][John 14:17] *See WW at Acts 26:22. **7** [a][John 1:1] [b]John 10:30 [1]NU, M omit the words from *in heaven* (v. 7) through *on earth* (v. 8). Only 4 or 5 very late mss. contain these words in Greek. **8** [a]John 15:26 **9** [a]John 5:34, 37; 8:17, 18 [b][Matt. 3:16, 17] [1]NU *God, that* *See WW at John 19:35. **10** [a][Rom. 8:16]

4:15 See vv. 1–3; 1 Cor. 12:3.
4:17–19 Possessing God's love results in fearless confidence toward God and love for the brethren. The one who knows this love has no dread of facing God at the **judgment.** Even now **in this world** we are **as He** [Christ] **is.** The comparison is that of positions, not characters. Jesus is well-pleasing to God as His Son, and we are God's children (3:1), acceptable to Him.
4:20, 21 Love for God must express itself in love for fellow believers. The "perfect love" that "casts out fear" (v. 18) sweeps away hate.
5:1–8 See section 4 of Truth-In-Action at the end of 1 John.
5:1–5 John shows how **faith, love,** and obedience are related to each other. Faith brings us into a loving relationship with God, and love for Him leads to love for other Christians and to obedience of **His commandments.** They are **not burdensome,** for the practical benefits of obedience to all God's laws are entirely contributive to human good and fulfilling to those who learn their application to life. **Our faith** brings victory over **the world,** providing a spiritual weapon by which we can combat both the temptations and the persecutions of a godless society.
5:4 See section 5 of Truth-In-Action at the end of 1 John.
5:6–13 In the previous paragraph (vv. 1, 5) John spoke of faith in the divine-human Jesus. Now he presents the basis of such belief, especially in answer to the heretics who suggested that the Spirit came upon Jesus at His baptism but left Him at His crucifixion. John insists that Christ possessed the indwelling Holy Spirit during His entire earthly life (since He was born by the power of the Spirit).
5:6 Water probably refers to the baptism of Jesus, when the Father declared His identity as the Son and anointed Him for His ministry. **Blood** refers to the Crucifixion, by which Christ completed His work. **The Spirit** testifies concerning Christ at every point of His life.
5:7, 8 The Law demanded the testimony of two or three witnesses (see Deut. 19:15; John 8:17, 18).
5:9 Behind the united testimony of the three witnesses is God Himself.
5:10 The assurance that comes to those who trust in Jesus is from the indwelling Holy Spirit (Rom. 8:16). To refuse to believe is equivalent to calling God a **liar.**

does not believe God [b]has made Him
a liar, because he has not believed the
testimony that God has given of His
Son.
11 And this is the testimony: that God
has given us eternal *life, and this life
is in His Son.
12 [a]He who has the Son has [1]life; he
who does not have the Son of God does
not have [1]life.
13 These things I have written to you
who believe in the name of the Son of
God, that you may know that you have
eternal life, [1]and that you may *con-*
tinue to believe in the name of the Son
of God.

Confidence and Compassion in Prayer

5 14 Now this is the *confidence that we
have in Him, that [a]if we ask anything
according to His will, He hears us.
15 And if we know that He hears us,
whatever we ask, we know that we
have the petitions that we have asked
of Him.

KINGDOM DYNAMICS

5:14, 15 Prayer Is Agreeing with God's Will, PRAYER. Immature faith tries to manipulate God. It looks for spiritual shortcuts and formulas guaranteed to produce an answer to any request. It regards prayer as a weapon we use to force God to make good His promises. But true prayer is not a human effort at persuading God or forcing our will on Him. True prayer is founded upon finding and coming into agreement with God's will (v. 14). We ask according to His will; then we stand in faith, confident that God hears us and that what we ask for is already ours (v. 15). Lessons: 1) To pray with authority and receive answers to your prayers, make sure you ask according to the will of God. If you do not know His will, ask Him (James 1:5). 2) Believe that God hears your petition and has already set the answer into motion. 3) Pray tenaciously and persistently until His will is accomplished. That is true prayer.

(Matt. 6:9–13/John 4:34) L.L.

10 [b]John 3:18, 33; 1 John 1:10
11 *See WW at 1 John 5:20.
12 [a][John 3:15, 36; 6:47; 17:2, 3] [1]Or *the life*
13 [1]NU omits the rest of v. 13.
14 [a][1 John 2:28; 3:21, 22] *See WW at Acts 4:31.
16 [a]Job 42:8 [b][Matt. 12:31] [c]Jer. 7:16; 14:11
17 [a]1 John 3:4 *See WW at John 7:18.
18 [a][1 Pet. 1:23]; 1 John 3:9 [b]James 1:27 [1]*guards* [2]NU *him*
19 [a]John 12:31; 17:15; Gal. 1:4
20 [a]1 John 4:2 [b]Luke 24:45 [c]John 17:3; Rev. 3:7 *See WW at Mark 12:30.

16 If anyone sees his brother sinning 4
a sin *which does* not *lead* to death, he
will ask, and [a]He will give him life for
those who commit sin not *leading* to
death. [b]There is sin *leading* to death.
[c]I do not say that he should pray about
that.
17 [a]All *unrighteousness is sin, and
there is sin not *leading* to death.

Knowing the True—Rejecting the False

18 We know that [a]whoever is born of
God does not sin; but he who has been
born of God [b]keeps[1] [2]himself, and the
wicked one does not touch him.
19 We know that we are of God, and
[a]the whole world lies *under the sway*
of the wicked one.
20 And we know that the [a]Son of God
has come and [b]has given us an *understanding, [c]that we may know Him who
is true; and we are in Him who is true,

5:11–13 John states the content of the **testimony** given by the witnesses mentioned in the previous verses. **Eternal life** signifies not only endless life, but a quality of life that comes only to those who have faith in Jesus. This life is a present possession of which we can have confident assurance.

5:14, 15 See section 5 of Truth-In-Action at the end of 1 John.

5:14, 15 Children of God may have **confidence** of free access and boldness of speech in presenting their requests to Him. There is, however, a limitation to the assurance that our prayers will be answered. The NT elsewhere bases the assurance on asking in Jesus' name (John 14:13, 14; 15:16; 16:23, 24), abiding in Christ and allowing His words to abide in us (John 15:7), having faith (Matt. 21:22; James 1:6), and being righteous in life and fervent in prayer (1 John 3:21, 22; James 5:16). Here John says that we must ask **according to His will,** which inclusively states the fundamental condition for assurance in prayer. One who abides in Christ and whose words abide in him; who prays *in the name* of Jesus, that is, in accord with His character and nature; and who is full of faith and righteousness is not inclined to pray anything contrary to His will. But more than *how* we pray, God wills and cares *that* we pray. Genuine prayer is not an attempt at precise means of getting God to meet our desires and demands; but rather, in subordinating our will to His, we open the doorway to His fullest blessings being released in our lives.

5:16, 17 See section 4 of Truth-In-Action at the end of 1 John.

5:16, 17 A specific example of prayer is intercession for a **brother sinning a sin *which does* not *lead* to death.** On the other hand, John does not encourage prayer for the restoration of those who are sinning a **sin *leading* to death.** These are the ones who, like the false teachers, have manifested the spirit of the Antichrist (2:18) in denying the Father and the Son (2:22, 23). They reveal themselves to be "children of the devil" (3:10), and they forfeit life in rejecting Christ (v. 12).

5:18 Does not sin: See note on 3:6–9, where John teaches that anyone whose life is unrepentantly characterized by sin does not belong to the family of God. The reason that a Christian does not persist unrepentantly in sin is that **he who has been born of God keeps himself,** or, as this may also be translated, "He [Jesus] who was born of God keeps him [the believer] from the relentless temptation and snare of **the wicked one.**"

5:19 John has given tests by which believers may **know** that they **are of God** as distinguished from those who belong to **the wicked one. World:** See note on 2:15. Satan exercises dominion over the world as its ruler (see John 12:31; 14:30; 16:11; 2 Cor. 4:4; Eph. 2:2; 6:12).

in His Son Jesus Christ. [d]This is the true God [e]and eternal **life.**

20 [d]Is. 9:6 [e]1 John 5:11, 12

WORD WEALTH

5:20 life, *zoe* (dzo-*ay*); Strong's *#2222:* Compare "zoology," "zoological," "Zoe." Refers to the principle of life. In the NT *zoe* denotes not only physical life, but spiritual life, which one can possess only through faith in Jesus Christ. Eternal life refers not only to duration of life, but to quality of life. It is a present life of grace and a future life of glory.

21 Little children, keep yourselves from idols. Amen. **2**

5:21 See section 2 of Truth-In-Action at the end of 1 John.
5:21 Any god, object, or pursuit other than that directed by God's revealed will and way declared in His Son (v. 20) is an idol.

TRUTH-IN-ACTION through 1 JOHN

Letting the LIFE of the Holy Spirit Bring Faith's Works Alive in You!

Truth 1 John Teaches	Text	**Action** 1 John Invites
1 Steps to Sharing the Love of God God revealed Himself to us through Jesus Christ, that we might have the light of life within by the presence of the Holy Spirit. Our mission is to let the light abide within us and shine forth to the glory of God. This produces light in the lives of others, extending the fellowship of God. Love for others is the sure sign that God lives in us and that we are in the fellowship of His love.	1:3, 4 2:24, 25 3:7–15 4:7–19	**Be full of joy. Have fellowship** with God and His people. Let God's word live in you, so that you can **live** in God. **Have eternal life!** **Understand** that righteousness manifests itself in behavior. **Understand** that righteousness manifests itself in righteous behavior. **Practice** righteousness. **Love** your brother. **Understand** that fear shows an absence of love. **Know** that Christ's presence always results in love.
2 Steps to Holiness Living in the world without partaking of the spirit of the world is the Christian's call. When the Spirit of God reveals to us the true spiritual poverty in which the world exists, it becomes easier to overcome the lures seeking to attract us back into that condition. When we understand the fullness of our inheritance in Christ, the world's offer seems poor indeed. When we truly set our affection on God, the lusts of the flesh are reduced as a problem. Unlike Lot's wife, who regretted the loss of the world, let us look ahead to the glorious hope of love, life, and light where God rules eternally.	2:9–11 2:15–17 5:21	**Recognize** that hate for others means that you are in darkness. **Do not** set your affections on, or live sacrificially on behalf of anything that 1) appeals to your fleshly appetites, 2) appeals to your covetousness or greed, or 3) fosters pride or arrogance. **Do not allow** anything to lessen even slightly your worship, service, or devotion to God.
3 A Step to Faithful Obedience Faith realizes that there is no alternative to obedience for anyone who knows Christ and has been born by His Spirit.	2:3–6	**Recognize** that only those who obey Jesus really know Him. **Understand** that obedience is the first evidence of love for God. **Know** and **believe** that only those who are learning to live like Jesus know and love Him.

Truth 1 John Teaches	Text	**Action** 1 John Invites
4 Keys to Wise Living The wise take time to discern the spirit behind any teaching or word of ministry. Unless the literal incarnation of Jesus Christ, the Virgin-born Son of God, is professed, the spirit is not from God. The outworking of faith is obedience to God's commands, and the result of obeying God is love manifested to others.	2:29	**Understand** that the best evidence for New Birth is in your conduct and behavior.
	3:4–9	**Know** that continued, willful sinning in the life contradicts a genuine conversion.
	3:11–15	**Know** that continued hatred 1) is impossible for those in Christ, and 2) will inevitably be leveled at believers by the world.
	3:16–18	**Know** that love 1) denies its own interests on behalf of others, and 2) is expressed practically.
	4:1–6	**Exercise** discernment when listening to any teaching. **Make sure** all teaching conforms to God's Word.
	5:1–8	**Understand** that one who is born again 1) loves other believers, and 2) obeys the Word of God and the Holy Spirit.
	5:16, 17	**Pray** for your brother who is in sin. **Know** that all lawlessness is sin.
5 Key Lessons in Faith Faith is based on knowledge of God's Word and His Character. The spirit of the world is in opposition to God. When we determine to stand in faith, the world loses its controlling influence over us.	3:1, 2	**Look forward** to seeing Christ at His Coming. **Know** you will **be transformed** into His likeness when He comes.
	3:21–24	**Base** your confidence on the witness of the Holy Spirit and growing obedience in your life.
	4:4	**Be assured** that victory is already ours in Christ.
	5:4	**Know** that those who are born again can never be conclusively defeated.
	5:14, 15	**Practice** the principles of faith-filled prayer. **Know** that God 1) hears all prayers that are in accord with His will, and 2) says "Yes!" to every prayer He hears.
6 Vital Keys to Dynamic Church Life Unity is a vital key to power in the local church. The Enemy seeks to destroy this unity by placing deceiving decoys within congregations to cause division and strife. When Christians refuse to accuse and reject one another, choosing instead to forgive and to love, strife is replaced by unity, and the church receives the power of the Spirit.	1:5–10	**Be open** and transparent in all you do. **Admit** your weakness to God. **Trust** Him to cleanse and forgive.
	2:18, 19	**Recognize** that the Devil brings about all separation and division in the body of Christ.

The Second Epistle of JOHN

Author: The Apostle John
Date: About A.D. 90
Theme: Warning About False Teachers
Key Words: Love, Truth

Author and Recipients Although the early testimony concerning the authorship of 2 and 3 John is not as strong as that of 1 John, they are nevertheless linked with John by the vocabulary and general subject matter. John addresses this second epistle to "the elect lady and her children," indicating that the recipient was a hospitable Christian mother whose children persevere in the faith (v. 4). John even includes greetings from her nieces and nephews (v. 13). From the designation John gives her in verse 1 (Greek *eklekte kyria*), many commentators have speculated concerning her personal name, suggesting titles such as "the elect Kyria," "the lady Electa," and "Electa Kyria." Others suggest that the designation does not denote an individual at all, but is the personification of a local church. "Her children" are the members of that church, and "the children" of her "elect sister" are the members of the local church in the place from which John is writing. A definite conclusion seems unattainable, and the question remains open.

Date The weight of evidence that John wrote all three epistles bearing his name points to about A.D. 90, shortly after 1 John was written.

Occasion and Purpose Second John is concerned with the relation of Christian truth to hospitality extended to those teachers traveling from church to church. Such hospitality was often abused. False teachers, probably from the same group that is the subject of 1 John, were confusing the fellowship of believers. John therefore gave instructions concerning which itinerant teachers to welcome and which to refuse. Genuine Christians, who could be recognized by the orthodoxy of their message (v. 10), are worthy of aid; but heretical teachers, especially those who denied the Incarnation (v. 7), are to be rejected. John also commends "the elect lady" for walking in the truth.

Content John encourages "the elect lady" to continue showing hospitality, but he also warns and guards against the abuse of Christian fellowship. Throughout the epistle he stresses truth as the basis and test of fellowship. In particular, he insists on a correct belief regarding the Incarnation of Christ, and charges that those who reject this reality have gone beyond the doctrine of Christ (v. 9). He urges readers of the letter to keep close to Christ by abiding in the truth.

Personal Application John's message is timeless in that seductive teachings continue to threaten the doctrinal stability of the church. The epistle reminds us to receive Jesus as *the* Son of God, not as *a* son of God or as *a* powerful god. John warns about those who advance beyond the doctrine of Christ, accepting new teachings and leaving apostolic doctrine behind (v. 9). To receive such people is to be identified with their evil (v. 11) and to run the risk of losing the faith (v. 8).

Christ Revealed John presents both the deity of Christ (v. 3) and His humanity (v. 7). Anyone who denies the fundamental truth concerning the divine-human Person of Christ does not have God (v. 9). John views fellowship as a distinctive feature of the Christian life, but he leaves no doubt that biblical fellowship is impossible where the apostolic doctrine of the Person and work of Christ is denied or compromised.

The Holy Spirit at Work Although the epistle does not specifically mention the Holy Spirit, His ministry is evident, particularly in bearing witness to the truth concerning the Person of Christ. The Spirit enables the true believer to discern false teachings and to "abide in the doctrine of Christ."

Outline of 2 John

Introduction	**1–3**
A. Salutation	1, 2
B. Blessing	3
I. Commendation for past loyalty	**4**
II. Exhortations	**5–11**
A. To love one another	5, 6
B. To reject error	7–11
Conclusion	**12, 13**

Greeting the Elect Lady

THE Elder,

To the [1]elect* lady and her children,
whom I love in truth, and not only I,
but also all those who have known
[a]the truth,
2 because of the truth which abides
in us and will be with us forever:

3 [a]Grace, mercy, *and* peace will be
with [1]you from God the Father and
from the Lord Jesus Christ, the Son of
the Father, in truth and love.

Walk in Christ's Commandments

■1 4 I [a]rejoiced greatly that I have found
some of your children walking in truth,
as we received commandment from the
Father.
■1 5 And now I plead with you, lady, not
as though I wrote a new commandment to you, but that which we have
had from the beginning: [a]that we love
one another.
6 [a]This is love, that we walk accord- ■1
ing to His commandments. This is the
commandment, that [b]as you have
heard from the beginning, you should
walk in it.

Beware of Antichrist Deceivers

7 For [a]many deceivers have gone out ■1
into the world [b]who do not confess
Jesus Christ *as* coming in the flesh.
[c]This is a deceiver and an antichrist.
8 [a]Look to yourselves, [b]that [1]we do
not lose those things we *worked for,
but *that* [1]we may receive a full *reward.
9 [a]Whoever* [1]transgresses and does ■1
not abide in the doctrine of Christ does
not have God. He who abides in the
doctrine of Christ has both the Father
and the Son.
10 If anyone comes to you and [a]does ■1
not bring this doctrine, do not receive
him into your house nor greet him;
11 for he who greets him shares in his
evil deeds.

1 [a]Col. 1:5 [1]*chosen* *See WW at 1 Pet. 2:9. **3** [a]1 Tim. 1:2 [1]NU, M *us* **4** [a]3 John 3, 4 **5** [a][John 13:34, 35; 15:12, 17] **6** [a]1 John 2:5; 5:3 [b]1 John 2:24 **7** [a]1 John 2:19; 4:1 [b]1 John 4:2 [c]1 John 2:22 **8** [a]Mark 13:9 [b]Gal. 3:4 [1]NU *you* *See WW at John 3:21. • See WW at Rev. 22:12. **9** [a]John 7:16; 8:31 [1]NU *goes ahead* *See WW at Acts 1:25. **10** [a]Rom. 16:17

1 The Elder: See Introduction to 3 John: Author and Recipients. **The elect lady:** See Introduction to 2 John: Author and Recipients.
2 The possession of a permanent truth is the chief reason to remain faithful and not to be led astray.
4 See section 1 of Truth-In-Action at the end of 2 John.
5 See section 1 of Truth-In-Action at the end of 2 John.
5 In one sense the command to **love** is old, because the Law of Moses demands it; in another sense it is **new,** because the example of Christ provides a new standard and a new motive. See note on 1 John 4:7–21.
6 See section 1 of Truth-In-Action at the end of 2 John.
6 Love motivates obedience.
7, 8 See section 1 of Truth-In-Action at the end of 2 John.
7 Deceivers: See Introduction to 2 John: Occasion and Purpose. **Antichrist:** See note on 1 John 2:18, 19.
9 See section 1 of Truth-In-Action at the end of 2 John.
9 The false teachers claimed superior knowledge that contradicted apostolic doctrine. In reality they had severed their relationship to God.
10 See section 1 of Truth-In-Action at the end of 2 John.
10, 11 Giving hospitality to the false teachers indicates sympathy with and support for their evil teachings. John does not forbid common courtesy, but he does prohibit action that will encourage the heretics in their work.

John's Farewell Greeting

12 [a]Having many things to write to
you, I did not wish *to do so* with paper
and ink; but I hope to come to you and
speak face to face, [b]that our joy may
be full.
13 [a]The children of your elect sister
greet you. Amen.

12 [a]3 John 13, 14 [b]John 17:13
13 [a]1 Pet. 5:13

TRUTH-IN-ACTION through 2 JOHN

Letting the LIFE of the Holy Spirit Bring Faith's Works Alive in You!

Truth 2 John Teaches	Text	**Action** 2 John Invites
1 Guidelines for Growing in Godliness Truth is to be present and active in the life of every Christian. This requires a heart that can discern error and reject it. Study of the Word, prayer, meditation, and, most importantly, the Holy Spirit are the means by which a believer receives or rejects any doctrine. Guard your heart and mind with great care.	v. 4	**Walk** in the truth of God's Word. **To know truth requires doing it.**
	v. 5	**Love;** this pleases God.
	v. 6	**Follow the commandments** of God in your behavior toward others.
	vv. 7, 8	**Receive** your full reward from God. **Confirm the confession** of anyone who is received into fellowship.
	v. 9	**Beware** of those who act presumptuously and do things God has not told them to do. **Understand** that this is as evil as doing things He has forbidden.
	v. 10	**Do not fellowship** with those who teach error. **Do not give** false teachers **access** to God's people.

The Third Epistle of JOHN

Author: The Apostle John
Date: About A.D. 90
Theme: Practicing Hospitality Toward Genuine Christian Teachers
Key Words: Love, Truth

Author and Recipients In both 2 and 3 John, the writer refers to himself as "the Elder," suggesting that he was older than the other Christians and that his personal knowledge of the faith went back much further than theirs. The strongest evidence is that all three epistles of John were written by a common author. See Introduction to 2 John: Author and Recipients.

Nothing is known about "the beloved Gaius" beyond the warm tribute John pays to him in the address of this letter. Gaius was a common name in the Roman world, and the New Testament mentions a Gaius in Corinth (Rom. 16:23; 1 Cor. 1:14), in Macedonia (Acts 19:29), and in Derbe (Acts 20:4). There is no evidence for associating the Gaius of 3 John with any of these men. Evidently he was a leader in some church of Asia.

Date John was aged both in years and experience when he wrote this letter in conjunction with 2 John near the end of his life, about A.D. 90.

Occasion and Purpose Whereas in 2 John itinerant heretics were disturbing the faith of Christians, in this epistle genuine teachers of truth are making a circuit of the churches. In the previous letter John forbade hospitality toward the false teachers; here he encourages hospitality. However, Diotrephes, a domineering person in one of the churches, opposed the authority of John. In addition, he refused hospitality to the traveling missionaries and prohibited others from entertaining them, excommunicating them when they did. John wrote to encourage Gaius in his generosity and to rebuke Diotrephes for his uncharitable conduct.

Content In fulfilling his purpose, John describes three personalities. The first is Gaius, who has demonstrated his Christian faith by his generous hospitality, even to strangers. The second is Diotrephes, whose selfish pride was disrupting the harmony of the fellowship. The third is Demetrius, whose life exemplified Christian fidelity and was worthy of imitation. These three men bear positive and negative witness to proper relationships among Christian brethren.

***Personal* Application** This letter portrays the church as a family united by bonds of love, with its members extending gracious hospitality toward one another. However, selfish ambition and factious jealousy imperil the church's fellowship, and its members must guard against such attitudes and strive to maintain a loving relationship with each other.

Christ Revealed The apostle presents Jesus as the Truth in whom we should walk. Devotion to Him motivates genuine teachers in their itinerant service (v. 7). The lives of Gaius and Demetrius exactly harmonized with the teaching of Christ, and gave strong witness to the power of His love. On the other hand, the attitude of Diotrephes shows a marked contrast to the true life in which Christ is to be first in everything.

The Holy Spirit at Work The epistle does not directly refer to the Holy Spirit, but His ministry is apparent throughout its message, particularly in enabling believers to "walk in the truth" and empowering itinerant missionaries in their ministries. The fruit of the Spirit is evident in the lives of Gaius and Demetrius.

Outline of 3 John

Salutation 1
I. Message to Gaius 2–8
A. Prayer for his health 2
B. Commendation for his adherence to the truth 3, 4
C. Commendation for his hospitality 5–8
II. Condemnation of the haughtiness of Diotrephes 9–11
III. Commendation of Demetrius 12
Conclusion 13, 14

Greeting to Gaius

THE Elder,

To the beloved Gaius, [a]whom I love in truth:

2 Beloved, I pray that you may prosper in all things and be in **health,** just as your soul prospers.

WORD WEALTH

2 health, *hugiaino* (hoog-ee-*ahee*-no); Strong's *#5198:* Compare "hygiene" and "hygienic." To be sound in body, in good health. Metaphorically, the word refers to sound doctrine (1 Tim. 1:10; 2 Tim. 4:3; Titus 2:1); sound words (1 Tim. 6:3; 2 Tim. 1:13); and soundness in the faith (Titus 1:13; 2:1).

KINGDOM DYNAMICS

2 Prosperity Is a Result, GOD'S PROSPERITY. It is clear that God wants His children to prosper. How can anyone deny that? However, prosperity should not be the end in itself. It ought to be the result of a quality of life, commitment, dedication, and action that is in line with God's Word. In this text the word "prosper" (Greek *euodoo*) literally means "to help on the road" or "succeed in reaching." It clearly implies that divine prosperity is not a momentary, passing phenomenon, but rather it is an ongoing, progressing state of success and well-being. It is intended for every area of our lives: the spiritual, the physical and emotional, and the material. However, God does not want us to unduly emphasize any one area. We must maintain a balance.

(Luke 6:38/Ps. 35:27) F.P.

3 For I [a]rejoiced greatly when brethren came and testified of the truth *that is* in you, just as you walk in the truth.
4 I have no greater [a]joy than to hear that [b]my children walk in [1]truth. 1

Gaius Commended for Generosity

5 Beloved, you do faithfully whatever you *do for the brethren [1]and for strangers, 1

1 [a]2 John 1
3 [a]2 John 4
4 [a]1 Thess. 2:19, 20; 2 John 4 [b][1 Cor. 4:15] [1]NU *the truth*
5 [1]NU *and especially for* *See WW at John 3:21.

2 See section 1 of Truth-In-Action at the end of 3 John.
2 John prays that the temporal prosperity and physical health of Gaius will be commensurate with his spiritual status, which his generosity and conduct reveal to be in a healthy and prosperous condition. Wishing the reader good **health** at the beginning of a letter was a common practice in ancient times, but John's prayer was sincere, not a matter of social convention. As such, it gives a warrant for praying for the physical, the material, and the spiritual well-being of others; and it provides a model of intercession.
4 See section 1 of Truth-In-Action at the end of 3 John.
4 As the aged apostle, John refers to his converts and other believers under his guidance as his **children.**
5–8 See section 1 of Truth-In-Action at the end of 3 John.
5 See Matt. 10:10.

6 who have borne witness of your
love before the church. *If* you send
them forward on their journey in a
manner worthy of God, you will do
well,
7 because they went forth for His
name's sake, [a]taking nothing from the
Gentiles.
8 We therefore ought to [a]receive[1]
such, that we may become fellow
workers for the truth.

Diotrephes and Demetrius

[1] 9 I wrote to the church, but Diotrephes, who loves to have the preeminence among them, does not receive
us.
10 Therefore, if I come, I will call to
mind his deeds which he does, [a]prat-
ing[1] against us with malicious words.
And not content with that, he himself
does not receive the brethren, and forbids those who wish to, putting *them*
out of the church.
11 Beloved, [a]do not imitate what is
evil, but what is good. [b]He who does
good is of God, [1]but he who does evil
has not seen [c]God.
12 Demetrius [a]has a *good* *testimony
from all, and from the truth itself. And
we also [1]bear witness, [b]and you know
that our testimony is *true.

Farewell Greeting

13 [a]I had many things to write, but I
do not wish to write to you with pen
and ink;
14 but I hope to see you *shortly, and
we shall speak face to face. Peace to
you. Our *friends greet you. Greet the
friends by name.

7 [a]1 Cor. 9:12, 15
8 [a]Matt. 10:40 [1]NU *support*
10 [a]Prov. 10:8, 10 [1]*talking nonsense*
11 [a]Ps. 34:14; 37:27 [b][1 John 2:29; 3:10] [c][1 John 3:10] [1]NU, M omit *but*
12 [a]1 Tim. 3:7 [b]John 19:35; 21:24 [1]*testify* *See WW at John 19:35. • See WW at Rom. 3:4.
13 [a]2 John 12
14 *See WW at John 6:21. • See WW at John 11:11.

6 Gaius is to treat the itinerant preachers **in a manner worthy of God.** As His messengers, they represent God, and should receive the generosity befitting their sacred calling.
7, 8 John gives three reasons for supporting the missionaries: 1) they are serving Christ; 2) to avoid all suspicion of unworthy motives in their ministry they have refused remuneration from those to whom they ministered; 3) those who support missionaries share in their work of the gospel.
9–11 See section 1 of Truth-In-Action at the end of 3 John.
9 The letter to which John refers has been lost, possibly destroyed by **Diotrephes.**
10 See Introduction to 3 John: Occasion and Purpose.
12 See Introduction to 3 John: Content.
14 **Shortly** suggests an urgency to see Gaius, perhaps to discuss the situation involving Diotrephes.

TRUTH-IN-ACTION through 3 JOHN

Letting the LIFE of the Holy Spirit Bring Faith's Works Alive in You!

Truth 3 John Teaches	Text	**Action** 3 John Invites
[1] Guidelines for Growing in Godliness The godly desire physical health, emotional stability, and prosperity to be established in the lives of others. Those who are so blessed should be eager to receive and support those ministers who are serving God.	v. 2	**Prosper** in your soul. **Understand** that health and prosperity are affected by the spirit.
	v. 4	**Be assured** that God rejoices over His children who put God's Word into practice daily.
	vv. 5–8	**Be eager and faithful** to show hospitality to those who labor in the gospel. **Recognize** that this is how God wants us to treat His servants.
	vv. 9–11	**Beware** of those who want preeminence in the church. **Reject** those who are malicious gossips. **Reprove** those who reject righteous ministry because of envy and jealousy.

The Epistle of JUDE

Author: Jude
Date: A.D. 65–80
Theme: Contending for the Faith
Key Words: Contend, the Faith, Keep

Author The author identifies himself as Jude, the "brother of James," likely the James who was the brother of our Lord and leader of the Jerusalem church (see Acts 15:13; 21:18; Gal. 1:19; 2:12). Mark 6:3 mentions Jude (Judas) as a brother of the Lord.

Date Considerations in establishing the date of this letter include whether Jude is dependent upon 2 Peter, or whether 2 Peter is dependent upon Jude, or whether both letters have drawn from a third document, which circulated as a warning against false teachers. Since most of Jude has parallels in 2 Peter (see the marginal references), some kind of interdependence is obvious. If Jude was written before 2 Peter, it may have been as early as A.D. 65. If it was written after 2 Peter, as many scholars assume, it may have been as late as A.D. 80.

Background Jude appears urgent in his purpose to warn an unknown community of Christians against false teachers. As in 2 Peter, these would-be leaders are sensual (vv. 4, 16, 18), they pervert the truth (v. 4), and they are destined for divine judgment (vv. 14, 15). They are called "dreamers" in verse 8 (perhaps given to dreams or visions), they are "clouds without water" (v. 12), and they are exposed as "not having the Spirit" in verse 19. The last reference hints that the false teachers represented themselves as those who did have the Spirit (see Matt. 7:22, 23). They may also be forerunners of Gnostic heretics in the second century who claimed spirituality.

Content The letter begins and ends with an affirmation of God's gracious action on behalf of believers, stressing divine preservation (vv. 1, 24).

However, Christians themselves are "to contend earnestly for the faith" (v. 3). *Their* responsibilities are further developed in vv. 20–23 by a series of practical exhortations. The balance of the letter exposes, especially in light of Old Testament analogies, the secret presence of false teachers within the community who seek to overthrow the faith of God's people.

Personal Application Today, perpetrators of unbiblical ethical standards, who may even claim to have the Spirit, threaten the godly commitment of Christians. However, God's power is able to keep us from falling. But *our* responsibility is to build ourselves up in the truth through praying in the Holy Spirit and to anticipate our final salvation. The Scriptures are our resource. At the same time, we are to be alert and vocal in warning those who are being swayed by false, humanistic philosophies prevalent today.

Christ Revealed The present activity of the living Christ is assumed. Jude is His servant and He preserves His own (v. 1), though false teachers deny

Him (v. 4). Believers await the future blessing of "the mercy of our Lord Jesus Christ unto eternal life" (v. 21).

The Holy Spirit at Work The Holy Spirit causes biblical teaching to come alive, so that the Christian community is built up in its "most holy faith," that is, in the apostolic teaching (see v. 20 and note on vv. 3, 4). This is accomplished through "praying in the Holy Spirit" (v. 20). Accordingly, the Spirit is important as the One through whom God preserves His own from worldly error (see vv. 1, 24). In contrast, the false teachers are devoid of the Spirit (v. 19), despite whatever claims they may make.

Outline of Jude

Greeting	**1, 2**
I. Warning against false teachers within the community	**3–19**
A. Reason for the warning	3, 4
B. Reminder of former ungodly persons	5–7
C. Character and judgment of false teachers	8–19
II. Exhortation for perseverance	**20–23**
A. Maintaining the faith	20, 21
B. Rescuing those deceived	22, 23
Doxology	**24, 25**

Greeting to the Called

JUDE, a bondservant of Jesus Christ, and [a]brother of James,

To those who are [b]called, [1]sanctified* by God the Father, and [c]preserved in Jesus Christ:

2 Mercy, [a]peace, and love be multiplied to you.

Contend for the Faith

[1] 3 Beloved, while I was very diligent to write to you [a]concerning our common salvation, I found it necessary to write to you exhorting [b]you to contend earnestly for the faith which was once for all delivered to the saints.

[1] 4 For certain men have crept in unnoticed, who long ago were marked out for this condemnation, ungodly men, who turn the grace of our God into *lewdness and deny the only **Lord** [1]God and our Lord Jesus Christ.

1 [a]Acts 1:13 [b]Rom. 1:7 [c]John 17:11,12 [1]NU *beloved* *See WW at John 10:36.
2 [a]1 Pet. 1:2; 2 Pet. 1:2
3 [a]Titus 1:4 [b]Phil. 1:27
4 [1]NU omits *God* *See WW at 1 Pet. 4:3.
5 [a]Ex. 12:51; 1 Cor. 10:5–10; Heb. 3:16
6 [1]*own*

WORD WEALTH

4 Lord, *despotes* (des-*pot*-ace); Strong's *#1203:* The origin of the English word "despot." The word signifies owner, master, one who has absolute dominion, supreme authority, and unlimited power arising from ownership. *Despotes* includes total submission on our part to God's will, not out of slavish fear or bondage, but joyfully and willingly.

Old and New Apostates

5 But I want to remind you, though you once knew this, that [a]the Lord, having saved the people out of the land of Egypt, afterward destroyed those who did not believe.

6 And the angels who did not keep their [1]proper domain, but left their own abode, He has reserved in everlasting

1 Sanctified refers to God's special action in setting apart believers for Himself. However, the proper reading here may be "beloved" (see marginal note). In either case, the divine initiative is apparent, as it is in the preceding word **called**.

3, 4 Jude apparently discontinues another letter he was writing, or is about to write, to these Christians in order to warn them of crafty false teachers who have infiltrated the church. **The faith . . . delivered to the saints** is the apostolic teaching given believers in the earliest days of the church. It is this teaching that was being perverted and for which Christians must **contend.** The corruption of "the faith" is found in self-centered and unloving behavior, immoral or sensual life-styles, and in distorted or deceitful teachings.

3 See section 1 of Truth-In-Action at the end of Jude.

4 See section 1 of Truth-In-Action at the end of Jude.

6 The angels who left their own **domain** are probably the lustful "sons of God" mentioned in Gen. 6:1–4. According to first-century Jewish teaching, especially in the apocryphal Book of 1 Enoch, angels descended and cohabited with women who lived before the Flood. Thus, the sin of these fallen angels is compared to the "sexual immorality" associated with Sodom and Gomorrah (v. 7). The early Christians knew and utilized such writings, even though they did not regard them as Holy Scripture. Although the Bible is not clear regarding precisely how these angels fell, it is clear they are now confined, awaiting the **judgment of the great day,** after Christ returns and the wicked are cast into "the everlasting fire prepared for the devil and his angels" (Matt. 25:41; see Mark 1:24). Their state exemplifies the fate of the godless.

chains under darkness for the judgment of the great day;
7 as [a]Sodom and Gomorrah, and the
cities around them in a similar manner
to these, having given themselves over
to sexual immorality and gone after
strange flesh, are set forth as an example, suffering the [1]vengeance of eternal
fire.
1 8 [a]Likewise also these dreamers defile the flesh, reject authority, and
[b]speak evil of [1]dignitaries.
9 Yet Michael the archangel, in
[1]contending with the devil, when he
disputed about the body of Moses,
dared not bring against him a reviling
accusation, but said, [a]"The Lord rebuke you!"

KINGDOM DYNAMICS

9 Archangels, ANGELS. The word "archangel" means "to be first (in political rank or power)," indicating that this is the highest rank of heavenly hosts. The only archangel specifically in the Scriptures is Michael. It is likely his shout we will hear at the Second Coming (1 Thess. 4:16). Because Gabriel is prominent in the Bible and also because his name is derived from a root word meaning "strength" or "chief" (politically), which is characteristic of archangels, some conclude that he is also an archangel. This opinion, although not supported by Scripture, was popularized by the poet John Milton.

Many scholars hold that Lucifer was an archangel before his fall (Ezek. 28). However, this is only speculation based on the position and influence he held over the angels who fell with him.

(Gen. 3:24/Is. 14:12–14) M.H.

10 [a]But these speak evil of whatever
they do not know; and whatever they

7 [a]Gen. 19:24; 2 Pet. 2:6 [1]*punishment*
8 [a]2 Pet. 2:10 [b]Ex. 22:28 [1]*glorious ones,* lit. *glories*
9 [a]Zech. 3:2 [1]*arguing*
10 [a]2 Pet. 2:12
11 [a]Gen. 4:3–8; Heb. 11:4; 1 John 3:12 [b]Num. 31:16; 2 Pet. 2:15; Rev. 2:14 [c]Num. 16:1–3, 31–35
12 [1]*stains,* or *hidden reefs* [2]NU, M *along*
13 [a]Is. 57:20 [b][Phil. 3:19] [c]2 Pet. 2:17; Jude 6
15 [a]1 Sam. 2:3 *See WW at James 5:20.

know naturally, like brute beasts, in
these things they corrupt themselves.
11 Woe to them! For they have gone
in the way [a]of Cain, [b]have run greedily
in the **error** of Balaam for profit, and
perished [c]in the rebellion of Korah.

WORD WEALTH

11 error, *plane* (*plan*-ay); Strong's *#4106:* Originally, a wandering; hence, the English word "planet." Metaphorically, the word denotes a going astray, an error. In the NT the straying is always in respect to morals and doctrine.

Apostates Depraved and Doomed

12 These are [1]spots in your love feasts,
while they feast with you without fear,
serving *only* themselves. *They are*
clouds without water, carried [2]about
by the winds; late autumn trees without fruit, twice dead, pulled up by the
roots;
13 [a]raging waves of the sea, [b]foaming
up their own shame; wandering stars
[c]for whom is reserved the blackness
of darkness forever.
14 Now Enoch, the seventh from
Adam, prophesied about these men
also, saying, "Behold, the Lord comes
with ten thousands of His saints,
15 "to execute judgment on all, to convict all who are ungodly among them
of all their ungodly deeds which they
have committed in an ungodly way,
and of all the [a]harsh things which ungodly *sinners have spoken against
Him."

Apostates Predicted

16 These are grumblers, complainers,
walking according to their own lusts;

7 Sodom and Gomorrah . . . suffering the vengeance of eternal fire is another **example** of what awaits the immoral. Their punishment is irreversible, even as was that of Sodom and Gomorrah, a paradigm of God's judgment. **The cities around them** were Admah and Zeboiim (Gen. 19:20–22; Deut. 29:23).

8–19 See section 1 of Truth-In-Action at the end of Jude.

9 Early Christian writings indicate that this account was originally in a Jewish work entitled *The Testament* (or *The Assumption*) *of Moses.* A likely explanation of the dispute **about the body of Moses** is that the Devil challenged Michael's right to bury Moses, since Moses had murdered an Egyptian (see Ex. 2:11–15). Deut. 34:5, 6 indicates that Moses' burial was divinely arranged. **The archangel** withholding **a reviling accusation** (Greek *blasphemia,* slander) even against the Devil is contrasted with the presumptuous evil speaking (Greek *blasphemeo*) of the false teachers against "dignitaries" (v. 8; see v. 10).

11 Instead of caring for his brother, **Cain** murdered him (Gen. 4:8; 1 John 3:11, 12). **Balaam** was offered money to curse Israel. After God forbade the curse, Balaam enticed Israel to sin (Num. 22—24). After leading a rebellion against Moses and Aaron, **Korah** and his followers were swallowed up by the earth (Num. 16:1–24). The judgment against false teachers is so certain that they are spoken of as having already **perished,** as did Korah.

12 Love feasts were fellowship meals of early Christians, which possibly included the Lord's Supper (see 1 Cor. 11:20–34). The false teachers are **clouds without water,** that is, promising spiritual refreshment, but not delivering.

14, 15 For **Enoch,** see Gen. 5:3–24. **The seventh from Adam** includes Adam. Jude quotes from 1 Enoch (1:9), popular in early Judaism and respected by Christians in antiquity. Enoch is not part of Holy Scriptures, but the teaching in this reference accords with biblical truth. Jude understands Enoch to prophesy the Second Coming of Christ, when the ungodly will be judged (see 2 Thess. 1:6–10). The reference to **ten thousands of His saints** is from Deut. 33:2. The saints who accompany Christ to judgment are the angels (see Matt. 16:27; 25:31).

and they [a]mouth great swelling *words,*
[b]flattering people to gain advantage.
1 17 [a]But you, beloved, remember the
words which were spoken before by
the apostles of our Lord Jesus Christ:
18 how they told you that [a]there would
be mockers in the last time who would
walk according to their own ungodly
lusts.
19 These are [1]sensual* persons, who
cause divisions, not having the Spirit.

Maintain Your Life with God

1 **20** But you, beloved, [a]building yourselves up on your most holy faith,
[b]praying in the Holy Spirit,

KINGDOM DYNAMICS

20 Benefits of Prayer in the Spirit, SPIRITUAL GIFTS. One benefit of the private, devotional practice of "tongues" is personal edification. The multiple benefits of prayer with or in the Holy Spirit may be studied, along with other aspects of His workings. See the study article on page 2018, "Holy Spirit Gifts and Power."
(Gal. 5:22, 23/1 Cor. 14:1–40) P.W.

21 keep yourselves in the love of God,
[a]looking for the mercy of our Lord
Jesus Christ unto eternal life.

16 [a]2 Pet. 2:18 [b]Prov. 28:21
17 [a]2 Pet. 3:2
18 [a]Acts 20:29; [1 Tim. 4:1]; 2 Tim. 3:1; 4:3; 2 Pet. 3:3
19 [1]*soulish* or *worldly* *See WW at James 3:15.
20 [a]Col. 2:7; 1 Thess. 5:11 [b][Rom. 8:26]
21 [a]Titus 2:13; Heb. 9:28; 2 Pet. 3:12
22 [1]NU *who are doubting* (or *making distinctions*) *See WW at Rom. 9:15. • See WW at Acts 11:12.
23 [a]Rom. 11:14 [b]Amos 4:11; Zech. 3:2; 1 Cor. 3:15 [c][Zech. 3:4, 5]; Rev. 3:4 [1]NU omits *with fear* [2]NU adds *and on some have mercy with fear* *See WW at 1 Thess. 4:17.
24 [a][Eph. 3:20] [b]Col. 1:22 [1]M *them*
25 [1]NU *the only God our*

22 And on some *have compassion,
[1]making* a distinction;
23 but [a]others save [1]with fear, [b]pull- **1**
ing* *them* out of the [2]fire, hating even
[c]the garment defiled by the flesh.

Glory to God

24 [a]Now to Him who is **able** to keep **2**
[1]you from stumbling,
And [b]to present *you* faultless
Before the presence of His glory
with exceeding joy,
25 To [1]God our *Savior,
[2]Who alone is wise,
Be *glory and majesty,
Dominion and [3]power,
Both now and forever.
Amen.

WORD WEALTH

24 able, *dunamai* (doo-nam-ahee); Strong's *#1410:* To be able, have power. The word combines power and willingness, inherent strength, and action.

[2]NU *Through Jesus Christ our Lord, Be glory* [3]NU adds *Before all time,* *See WW at John 4:42. • See WW at John 2:11. • See WW at 1 Tim. 6:16. • See WW at Mark 3:15.

17, 18 See section 1 of Truth-In-Action at the end of Jude.
20, 21 See section 1 of Truth-In-Action at the end of Jude.
20 Jude exhorts his readers to edify themselves with the apostolic teaching (see note on v. 3). A vital part of their spiritual growth is **praying in the Holy Spirit**. Such praying includes praying in one's own language as prompted by the Spirit (see Rom. 8:15), praying with "groanings which cannot be uttered" (Rom. 8:26), and praying in a tongue unknown to the one praying (see 1 Cor. 14:4, 14).
23 See section 1 of Truth-In-Action at the end of Jude.
23 The fire is perhaps the passion of lust (see v. 18), but more likely it is the fire of coming judgment (vv. 7, 15).
24, 25 See section 2 of Truth-In-Action at the end of Jude.

TRUTH-IN-ACTION through JUDE

Letting the LIFE of the Holy Spirit Bring Faith's Works Alive in You!

Truth Jude Teaches	Text	**Action** Jude Invites
1 There have always been those who attempt to divert God's people from their main purpose. Whether angels or men, God knows how to deal with the rebellious, but believers are warned not to participate with any such persons. The wicked appeals to the lusts of the eye, lusts of the flesh and to inordinate pride. They will pretend to love God, appear to do good works, but on close examination they are as fruitless as the fig tree that Jesus cursed. The wise will be able to identify those	v. 3	**Contend strongly** for biblical faith. **Accept** no form of alteration.
	v. 4	**Reject** anyone who teaches that grace is "God's permission to sin." **Understand** that such teaching is godlessness.
	vv. 8–19	**Recognize** the marks of false teachers. **Rebuke** and **reject** any teacher who . . . (1) teaches things one cannot apply. (2) practices licentious behavior. (3) speaks disrespectfully of authority.

Truth Jude Teaches	Text	**Action** Jude Invites
1 whose object is to *be* god, rather than to serve God. It will take a deeply spiritual heart to know how to reach any who are deep into evil without being contaminated—hating the sin but still loving the sinner.		(4) rejects established authority. (5) is more worried about money than the welfare of those to whom he ministers. (6) promises things he cannot and does not produce. (7) constantly changes his message; always teaches "some new thing." (8) shows no enduring fruit. (9) complains and criticizes others. (10) is motivated by personal gain. (11) is a self-promoter. (12) flatters others when it is to his advantage.
	vv. 17, 18	**Decry** and **reject** any minister who 1) follows his own desires, 2) is divisive in any way, or 3) gives no evidence of Holy Spirit life and dynamic in his life.
	vv. 20, 21	**Pray continuously** in the Spirit. **Know** that this promises a certain and holy self-edification, which is imperative if you want to build others up. **Persist** in loving attitudes and behavior through the Holy Spirit.
	v. 23	**Warn, exhort,** and **save** others from error when possible. **Do not let others fall** when it is in your power to prevent it.
2 **Key to Joyful Worship** We fully acknowledge that only by the working and grace of God is anyone able to come joyfully into His presence in blameless worship. He is the lawful Ruler of every life. Our God is King of the Universe. How blessed we are to serve Him!	vv. 24, 25	**Trust in the ability of God** to bring you blameless into His presence.

DEALING WITH "LAST THINGS"— The Rapture, Second Coming, and Millennium

Eschatology is that aspect of biblical doctrine dealing with "last things" (from Greek *eschatos*, "final"). In 1 John 2:18, John describes the times in which he wrote as "the last hour," evidencing that he lived in immediate anticipation of Christ's Second Coming, just as have Christians in every generation. He saw his era, as do many believers today, as one in which the present evidence seemed to argue that his was the concluding generation. This is not an unhealthy attitude: Christ Jesus desires that His people expectantly anticipate His return (Matt. 25:1–13; 2 Tim. 4:8).

In his first epistle, John not only writes of the lateness of the hour of history as he views it; he also addresses the subject of Antichrist, a theme commonly discussed when eschatology is studied. The spirit of antichrist, the Rapture of the church, the Great Tribulation, the restoration of national Israel, and the millennial reign of Christ on Earth are among the many subjects the Bible describes as "last things." The Bible specifically says these things shall occur. However, it is not clear about the exact time; and in many cases it does not conclusively give the sequence or precise manner of the fulfillment of such events.

The *Spirit-Filled Life® Bible* does not embrace any conclusive point of view concerning these popularly discussed subjects. Rather, it seeks to help fellow Christians clearly understand one another's viewpoints in order to assist dialogue and to dismiss bigotry. It is probably not reasonable for one Christian to be divided from another on the interpretation of things yet future, things of which neither can know the exact outcome until their actual occurrence. Both the Rapture of the church (including the Second Coming of Christ) and the Millennium (or the 1,000-year reign of Christ on Earth) are centerpieces in the prophetic future. Honesty with these two events, which are absolutely certain in the Scriptures, shows they are absolutely not precise in designating either a specific time or a conclusive method of occurrence.

The following charts are provided in a sincere effort to present each viewpoint with a simple but substantial exposure, for the sake of mutual understanding and study. Special thanks are due Robert Lightner and Marvin Rosenthal for permission to draw from the charted resources in their works. Comments enclosed in brackets, [ ], in the charts have been supplied by J.W.H.

PREMILLENNIAL PRETRIBULATIONAL VIEW

[All believers are "raptured" before the Great Tribulation. The Rapture and the Second Coming are separate events. Tribulation and Millennium are literal 7-year and 1,000-year periods.]	Rapture (1 Thess. 4:15–18)	Second Coming (2 Thess. 2:8)
	Church in heaven	
Israel and church separate programs	7-year tribulation on Earth	Earthly millennial kingdom followed by eternity (Rev. 20:1–6)

Adapted from *The Last Days Handbook*, © 1990 by Robert P. Lightner, p. 63. Published by Thomas Nelson, Inc. Used by permission.

PREMILLENNIAL POSTTRIBULATIONAL VIEW

[All believers are "raptured" at the end of the Great Tribulation. The Rapture and the Second Coming are the same event. Tribulation and Millennium are literal 7-year and 1,000-year periods.]

Rapture (1 Thess. 4:15–18) and Second Coming (2 Thess. 2:8)

Israel and church separate programs

Church in 7-year tribulation on Earth (Matt. 24:15–28)

Earthly millennial kingdom followed by eternity (Rev. 20:1–6)

Adapted from *The Last Days Handbook*, © 1990 by Robert P. Lightner, p. 65. Published by Thomas Nelson, Inc. Used by permission.

PREMILLENNIAL MIDTRIBULATIONAL VIEW

[All believers are "raptured" after 42 months (1,260 days) of the 7-year Great Tribulation. The Rapture and the Second Coming are separate events. Tribulation and Millennium are literal 7-year and 1,000-year periods.]

Rapture (1 Thess. 4:15–18)

Second Coming (2 Thess. 2:8)

Church in heaven

Israel and church separate programs

3½ years tribulation (Matt. 24:15–28)

3½ years tribulation

Earthly, millennial kingdom followed by eternity (Rev. 20:1–6)

Adapted from *The Last Days Handbook*, © 1990 by Robert P. Lightner, p. 67. Published by Thomas Nelson, Inc. Used by permission.

PREMILLENNIAL PRETRIBULATIONAL PARTIAL RAPTURE VIEW

[Only *some* believers will be "raptured" before the Great Tribulation. Those "unready" must be martyred to verify their faith. The Rapture and the Second Coming are separate events. Tribulation and Millennium are literal 7-year and 1,000-year periods.]

Partial Rapture (Matt. 25:1–13)

Second Coming

Spiritual Christians in heaven

Israel and church separate programs

7-year tribulation on Earth (Matt. 24:15–28)

Earthly kingdom followed by eternity (Rev. 20:1–6)

Adapted from *The Last Days Handbook*, © 1990 by Robert P. Lightner, p. 71. Published by Thomas Nelson, Inc. Used by permission.

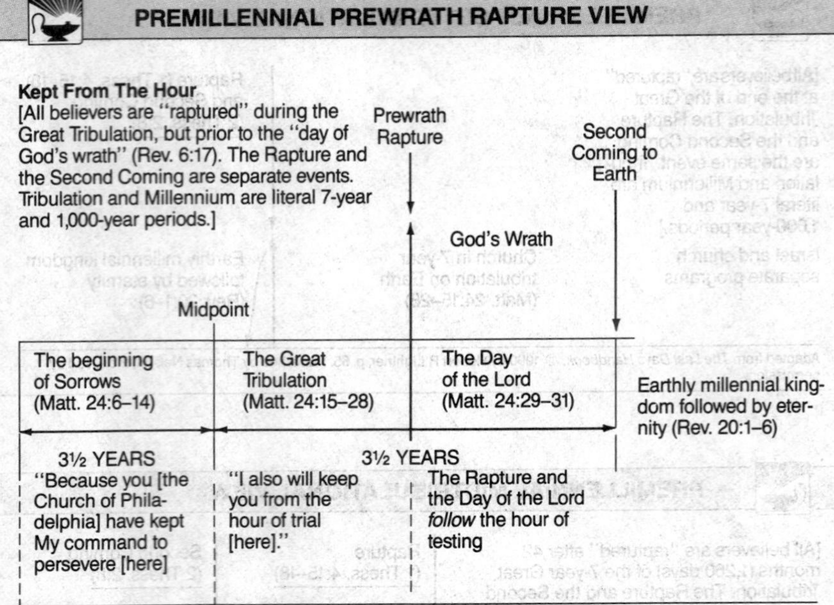
PREMILLENNIAL PREWRATH RAPTURE VIEW
Kept From The Hour
[All believers are "raptured" during the Great Tribulation, but prior to the "day of God's wrath" (Rev. 6:17). The Rapture and the Second Coming are separate events. Tribulation and Millennium are literal 7-year and 1,000-year periods.]
Prewrath Rapture
Second Coming to Earth
God's Wrath
Midpoint
The beginning of Sorrows (Matt. 24:6–14)
The Great Tribulation (Matt. 24:15–28)
The Day of the Lord (Matt. 24:29–31)
Earthly millennial kingdom followed by eternity (Rev. 20:1–6)
3½ YEARS
3½ YEARS
"Because you [the Church of Philadelphia] have kept My command to persevere [here]
"I also will keep you from the hour of trial [here]."
The Rapture and the Day of the Lord *follow* the hour of testing
Adapted from *The Prewrath Rapture of the Church*, © 1990 by Marvin J. Rosenthal, p. 241. Published by Thomas Nelson, Inc. Used by permission.

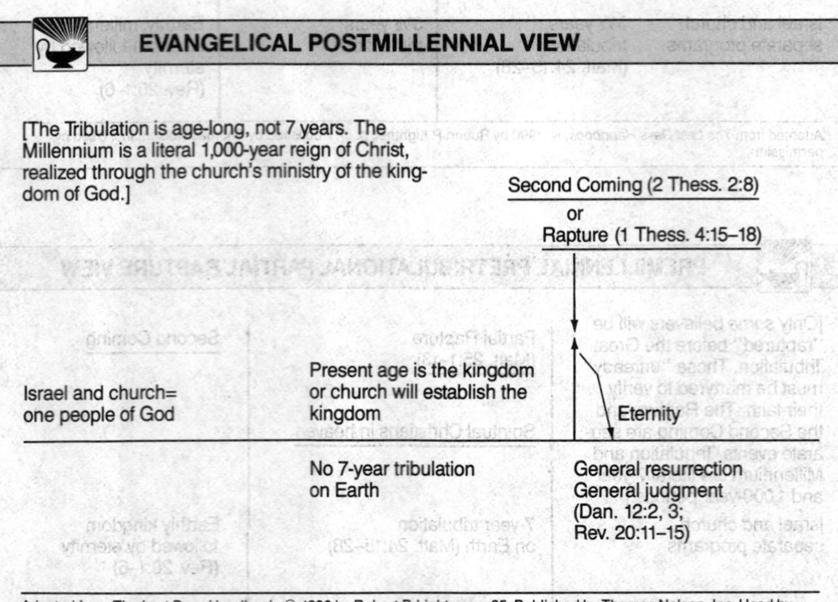
EVANGELICAL POSTMILLENNIAL VIEW
[The Tribulation is age-long, not 7 years. The Millennium is a literal 1,000-year reign of Christ, realized through the church's ministry of the kingdom of God.]
Second Coming (2 Thess. 2:8)
or
Rapture (1 Thess. 4:15–18)
Israel and church= one people of God
Present age is the kingdom or church will establish the kingdom
Eternity
No 7-year tribulation on Earth
General resurrection
General judgment
(Dan. 12:2, 3; Rev. 20:11–15)
Adapted from *The Last Days Handbook*, © 1990 by Robert P. Lightner, p. 85. Published by Thomas Nelson, Inc. Used by permission.

ST. AUGUSTINE'S AMILLENNIAL VIEW

[The Book of Revelation is symbolic of God's kingdom's triumphing through the church. The Great Tribulation and the Millennium are not 7-year and 1,000-year periods but are symbolic terms for the age-long struggle of evil against Christ's rule.]

Second Coming (2 Thess. 2:8)
or
Rapture (1 Thess. 4:15–18)

Israel and church= one people of God

Church is kingdom on Earth

Eternity

No 7-year tribulation on Earth

General resurrection
General judgment
(Dan. 12:2, 3;
Rev. 20:11–15)

Adapted from *The Last Days Handbook*, © 1990 by Robert P. Lightner, p. 78. Published by Thomas Nelson, Inc. Used by permission.

A SECOND AMILLENNIAL VIEW

[Attributed to B. B. Warfield: Same as St. Augustine's view except the kingdom of God is not seen as functioning through the church in this age.]

Kingdom promises fulfilled now in heaven

Second Coming (2 Thess. 2:8)
or
Rapture (1 Thess. 4:15–18)

Israel and church= one people of God

Church is not the kingdom on Earth

Eternity

No 7-year tribulation on Earth

General resurrection
General judgment
(Dan. 12:2, 3;
Rev. 20:11–15)

Adapted from *The Last Days Handbook*, © 1990 by Robert P. Lightner, p. 78. Published by Thomas Nelson, Inc. Used by permission.

In Studying the Book of Revelation

In determining how this wonderful book would be approached in this study Bible, the editorial team decided to take a very exciting step. We feel this will provide the reader with a most unusual and especially edifying resource in studying the Book of Revelation.

No other Bible book equals this one for variety of interpretation or the thrill of prophetic study. In order to allow virtually any believer not only to find material suited to the interpretation of their church tradition, but to afford the opportunity of comparative study with other interpretive approaches, four "helps" have been provided:

1. ***Two basic interpretive approaches are annotated throughout.*** The reader will find the **classical, historic approach** as well as the **approach of the dispensational interpreter.** At each text where the dispensational interpretation is noted for comparative study, the words ***DISPENSATIONAL INTERPRETATION*** appear, and a bracket runs the depth of the note in its margin. All other annotations are either (a) general information involving no interpretive bias, or (b) may present the interpretation of the classical, historic approach.

2. ***Two capable scholars have contributed contrasting notes.*** In the Introduction and Notes for Revelation, Dr. Earl W. Morey takes the **classical approach** to Revelation by blending the "contemporary-historical" and the "spiritual" interpretations. He affirms Revelation as a series of genuine prophetic messages that conclude with a vision of "a dynamic realized spiritual Millennium." His approach is evangelical, conservative, and consistent with the historic traditions that view the church as the body of Christ—as a people equipped with the full resources of the Holy Spirit's power to actively represent the authority of Christ the King and to extend that kingdom authority throughout the Earth, through all history.

In order to compare this classical approach with a view popular among some Christians, additional notes provide a comparative study in the **dispensational interpretation.** These have been prepared by Dr. Coleman Phillips, who also wrote the notes for the Book of Daniel.

3. ***All interpretive approaches honoring Jesus Christ and God's eternal Word are respected in this study Bible.*** Throughout church history, theories of interpretation have been numerous and widely divergent. These have been classified as the "preterist," the "continous historical," the "futurist," the "dispensational," and the "spiritual." Different views, however, often have been combined or intermingled, rendering all such classifications imprecise.

a. The "preterist," or "contemporary-historical," interpretation regards the visions of the book as referring primarily, if not exclusively, to events belonging to the closing decades of the first century, contemporary with the prophet John. The prophecy was concerned with the persecution of Christians instituted by the "beast," usually understood to be Nero or Domitian, and was continued by the Roman government, called "Babylon." Revelation was written to encourage believers with the hope that God would intervene, destroy the "beast," bring deliverance to His people, and establish His everlasting Kingdom. Some preterists advocate that Revelation is concerned solely with the destruction of Jerusalem, the temple, and the old era of apostate Judaism in A.D. 70.

b. According to the "continuous-historical" interpretation, Revelation contains visions that reveal in advance outstanding moments and events in human history from the days of Rome to the end of this present evil age. Within the book are discovered conjectured references to the various waves of barbarian invasions, the rise of Islam, the Protestant Reformation, the Counter-Reformation, the French Revolution, World War I and so on. The "beast" has been identified variously as Mohammed, the Pope, Napoleon, or some subsequent dictator. The advocates of this theory ingeniously endeavor to find in European political history the fulfillment of the various visions, considered to be in chronological order.

Even though it cannot be maintained that *specific* historical events, from the second century to the present, are prophesied *in* Revelation, nevertheless historical events and world movements do *illustrate* repeatedly the spiritual principles set forth.

c. The "futurist" interpretation sees Revelation as primarily a prophecy concerning the denouement of history as it concerns the church in the world. The seven letters are addressed to seven historical churches; and the seals represent the forces of history—however long it may last—through which God works out His redemptive and judicial purposes leading up to the end. However, beginning with chapter 8 or 16, the events described lie entirely in the future and will attend the final disposition of God's will for human history. Revelation concludes by picturing a redeemed society dwelling in a new earth that has been purged of all evil, and with God dwelling in the midst of His people, which is the goal of the long course of redemptive history. The "futurist" interpretation is premillennial, but not dispensational. It teaches that Christ will return to establish a millennial kingdom on the Earth, but this will not be a Jewish political kingdom.

d. The "dispensational" interpretation is the most recent to appear in church history. The "dispensational" scheme of redemptive history presupposes two different peoples of God throughout history—Israel and the church—and, therefore, two programs of prophecy. The seven letters to the seven churches are interpreted "prophetically" as an outline of a seven-stage church age. Revelation 4:1 is interpreted as the Rapture of the church, understood as the secret departure of all believers to heaven before "the great tribulation." The rest of the book is then seen as concerned exclusively with "the great tribulation" and the fate of Israel at the hands of the Antichrist. According to this view, Christ returns to destroy the Beast, to bind Satan, and to introduce His thousand-year reign on Earth. Dispensationalists view this Millennium as the time when the Jewish theocracy, with the temple, the sacrificial system, and the Law of Moses, is restored and the Old Testament prophecies concerning Israel's future political triumph over the Gentiles are literally—physically fulfilled.

(Interestingly, many of Pentecostal/Charistmatic tradition interpret Revelation and Daniel from this dispensational view, even though such an interpretive approach anywhere other than in prophetic scripture would dictate a denial of the present manifestation of the gifts of the Spirit.)

e. The "spiritual" or "symbolic" interpretation finds in Revelation relatively few references to *specific* events or persons of the past, present, or future, but rather the presentation of great "spiritual principles" intended to encourage and guide Christians in all geographical locations in every era of history. The successive symbolic visions set forth these principles. The living Lord Jesus Christ is victorious over the Enemy and all his allies. Those who are with Christ (the "called, chosen, and faithful," 17:14) share fully in His triumph. This reveals God as the Sovereign Ruler and Judge of the whole cosmic creation. Thus, right is ultimately vindicated in the face of wrong, justice in the face of injustice, righteousness in the face of unrighteousness. World history is moving on through tragedy and disaster to "a new heaven and a new earth."

4. ***A series of eight charts, appearing on the preceding pages, simplify comparative study and will enhance every believer's understanding.*** Finally, the reader is encouraged to note Kingdom Dynamics entries at Revelation 4:1, "Interpretive Approaches to the Book of Revelation," and 1 John 2:18, "The Prophecies of Last Things," as well as the annotation accompanying Revelation 20:1–8, which gives foundational information on different interpretive approaches to the subject of the Millennium. With these resources, it is the editors' hope that the broadening of insight will not dilute the reader's personal convictions, but will help each one understand the thinking of equally devoted Christians who view prophecy from varied perspectives.

THE REVELATION

of Jesus Christ

Writer: The Apostle John
Date: A.D. 70–95
Theme: The Lord Our God the Almighty Reigns
Key Words: Throne, Lamb, Overcomes, Seven, I Saw

Author Four times the author refers to himself as "John" (1:1, 4, 9; 22:8). He was so well known to his readers and his spiritual authority was so widely acknowledged that he did not need to establish his credentials. Early church tradition unanimously attributes this book to the apostle John.

Background and Date Evidence within Revelation indicates that it was written during a period of extreme persecution of Christians, which possibly was that begun by Nero after the great fire that nearly destroyed Rome in July of A.D. 64 and continued until his suicide in June of A.D. 68. In this view, the book thus was written before the destruction of Jerusalem in September of A.D. 70, and is an authentic prophecy concerning the continuing suffering and persecution of Christians, which would become even more intense and severe in the years ahead. On the basis of isolated statements by the early church fathers, some interpreters date the book near the end of the reign of Domitian (A.D. 81–96), after John had fled to Ephesus.

Occasion and Purpose Under the inspiration of the Spirit and the Old Testament, John had no doubt been reflecting on the horrifying events occurring both in Rome and Jerusalem when he was given "the prophecy" of what was impending—the intensification of the spiritual warfare confronting the church (1:3) perpetrated by an anti-Christian state and numerous anti-Christian religions. The purpose of this message was to provide pastoral encouragement to persecuted Christians by comforting, challenging, and proclaiming the sure and certain Christian hope, together with the assurance that in Christ they were sharing in the sovereign God's method of totally overcoming the forces of evil in all its manifestations. Revelation is also an evangelistic appeal to those who are presently living in the kingdom of darkness to enter the Kingdom of Light (22:17).

Content The central message of the Revelation is that "the Lord God Omnipotent reigns!" (19:6). This theme has been validated in history by the victory of the Lamb who is "Lord of lords and King of kings" (17:14).

Yet, those who follow the Lamb are involved in a continuing spiritual conflict, and Revelation thus provides deeper insight into the nature and tactics of the Enemy (Eph. 6:10–12). The dragon, frustrated by his defeat at the Cross and the consequent restraints placed upon his activity, and desperate to thwart the purposes of God before his inevitable doom, develops a counterfeit trinity "to make war" on the saints (12:17). The first "beast" or monster symbolizes the reality of anti-Christian government and political power (13:1–10, 13); and the second, anti-Christian religion, philosophy, and ideology (13:11–17). Together they produce the ultimately deceptive and seductive anti-Christian secular society, commerce, and culture, the harlot Babylon (chs. 17; 18), composed of those "who dwell on earth." These thus bear the "mark" of the monster, and their names are not registered in "the Lamb's Book of Life." The dragon continually delegates his restricted power and authority to the monsters and their followers in order to deceive and discourage anyone from God's creative-redemptive purpose.

NOTE: If you have not yet read the article "In Studying the Book of Revelation," which immediately precedes this introduction, it is important to your use of this resource that you do so.

Personal Application God has created the orders of community, that is, marriage and the family, economic activity, government and the state (see Rom. 13:1–7; 1 Tim. 2:1, 2). Satan, unable to create anything, tempts others to distort and misuse what God has created. Christians must discern whether a government is functioning *under* divine authority or *as* a divine authority. When the latter is the case, Christians must pray, courageously endure, and patiently accept the consequences of obeying the God whose image and seal they bear (see Mark 12:16, 17; Acts 4:19). They must do so in the confidence that after their victorious sufferings they will reign with Him.

Behind the appearances of the pomp and power of the world, there is the reality of the absolute sovereignty of the Lord God who is the Lamb, which ensures the ultimate doom of sin and evil. God is utilizing all the forces of evil, all the consequences of sin, even the suffering of His saints, to accomplish His own purposes. Believers undergoing persecution need to know that their sufferings are not meaningless, and ultimately they will be vindicated. The mainspring of Christian hope and courage is the certainty that the Enemy has been defeated and is doomed, and that followers of the Lamb are not fighting a losing cause. He has already overcome, and therefore they can and will be overcomers!

Literary Form After a preface, Revelation begins (1:4–7) and ends (22:21) as a typical New Testament letter. Although containing seven letters to the seven churches, it is clear that every member is to "hear" the message to each of the churches (2:7, 11, 17, 29; 3:6, 13, 22), as well as the message of the entire book (1:3; 22:16), in order that they might obey it (1:3; 22:9). Within this letter is "the prophecy" (1:3; 10:11; 19:10; 22:6, 7, 10, 18, 19). According to Paul, "he who prophesies speaks edification and exhortation [encouragement] and comfort to men" (1 Cor. 14:3). The prophet speaks God's Word as a call to obedience in the present and immediate future situation in the light of the ultimate future. This prophecy was not to be sealed up (22:10) because it is relevant to Christians in every generation.

Method of Communication John received these prophecies through a series of vivid visions containing symbolic images and numbers that echo those found in the prophetic books of the Old Testament. John records these visions in the chronological order in which he received them, many of them pictures of the same events from different perspectives.

He does not, however, provide a chronological order in which certain historical events are to occur. For example, Jesus is born in chapter 12, is exalted in chapter 5, and is walking in the midst of His churches in chapter 1. The beast who attacks the two witnesses in chapter 11 is not brought into existence until chapter 13. John records a series of successive visions, not a series of consecutive events.

The Revelation is a cosmic pageant—an elaborate, colorful series of tableaux, accompanied and interpreted by celestial speakers and singers. The spoken word is elevated prose, more poetic than our translations indicate. The music is similar to a cantata. Repeatedly, themes are introduced, later reintroduced, combined with other themes, and developed.

The entire message is "signified" (1:1). This is a key to the understanding of the visions, all of which contain figurative language pointing to the spiritual realities in and behind historical experience. Signs and symbols are essential because spiritual truth and unseen reality must always be communicated to human beings through their senses. Symbols point to what is ultimately indescribable. For example, the account of the demonic locusts from the abyss (9:1–12) creates a vivid, horrifying impression, even though the minute details are not intended to be interpreted.

Christ Revealed Nearly every title employed elsewhere in the New Testament to describe the divine-human nature and the redemptive work of Jesus is mentioned at least once in Revelation, which, together with numerous additional titles, provides us with our only multidimensional unveiling of the present position, continuing ministry, and ultimate victory of the exalted Christ.

Although Jesus' earthly ministry is telescoped between His Incarnation and Ascension in 12:5, Revelation asserts that the Son of God, as the Lamb, has completely finished His redemptive work (1:5, 6). By His blood sinners have been forgiven, cleansed (5:6, 9; 7:14; 12:11), liberated (1:5), and made kings and priests (1:6; 5:10). All ensuing manifestations of His applied victory are based in His finished work on the Cross; hence, Satan has been defeated (12:7–12) and bound (20:1–3). Jesus, raised from the dead, is enthroned as absolute Sovereign over all Creation (1:5; 2:27). He *is* "King of kings and Lord of lords" (17:14; 19:16), and is entitled to the same ascriptions of adoration as God the Creator (5:12–14).

The only One who is "worthy" to execute the eternal purpose of God is "the Lion of Judah," who is not a political Messiah but a sacrificed Lamb (5:5, 6). "The Lamb" is His primary title, utilized twenty-eight times in Revelation. As the One who has conquered, He has the rightful authority and the power to control all the forces of evil and their consequences for His purposes of judgment and salvation (6:1—7:17). The Lamb is on the throne (4:1—5:14; 22:3).

The Lamb, as "*One* like the Son of Man," is always in the midst of His people (1:9—3:22; 14:1), whose names are recorded in His Book of Life (3:5; 21:27). He knows them intimately, and with immeasurable holy love, He watches over, protects, disciplines, and challenges them. They share fully in His present and future victory (17:14; 19:11–16; 21:1—22:5), as well as in His present and future "marriage supper" (19:7–9; 21:2). He dwells *in* them (1:13), and they dwell *in* Him (21:22).

As *"One* like the Son of Man," He also is the Lord of the final harvest (14:14–20). He pours out His wrath in judgment upon Satan (20:10), his allies (19:20; 20:14), and the spiritually "dead" (20:12, 15)—all those who have chosen to "dwell on the earth" (3:10).

The Lamb is the God who is coming (1:7, 8; 11:17; 22:7, 20) to consummate His eternal plan, to complete the creation of the new community of His people in "a new heaven and a new earth" (21:1) and to restore the blessings of the Paradise of God (22:2–5). The Lamb is the goal of all history (22:13).

The Holy Spirit at Work The description of the Holy Spirit as "the seven Spirits of God" (1:4; 3:1; 4:5; 5:6) is distinct in the New Testament. The number seven is a symbolic, qualitative number conveying the idea of completeness and, when related to God, the idea of perfection. The Holy Spirit is thus denoted in terms of the perfection of His dynamic, manifold activity. The "seven lamps of fire" (4:5) suggest His illuminating, purifying, and energizing ministries. That the seven Spirits are before the throne (1:4; 4:5) and simultaneously are the seven eyes of the Lamb (5:6) signifies the essential triunity of God who has revealed Himself as Father, Son, and Holy Spirit. This is a mutual indwelling of the Persons without dissolving the distinctions of essential being and function.

Each of the messages to the seven churches is from the exalted Lord, yet the individual members are urged to hear "what the Spirit says" (chs. 2; 3). The Spirit only says what the Lord Jesus says.

The Spirit is thus the Spirit of prophecy. Every genuine prophecy is inspired by the Holy Spirit and bears witness to Jesus (19:10). The prophetic visions are communicated to John only when he is "in the Spirit" (1:10; 4:2; 21:10). The content of these visions is nothing less than "The Revelation of Jesus Christ" (1:1).

All genuine prophecy demands a response. "The Spirit and the bride say, 'Come!'" (22:17). Everyone either hears or refuses to hear this appeal. The Spirit is working continuously in and through the church to invite those who remain outside the City of God to enter. Only by the empowering of the Spirit is the bride enabled to witness and "patiently endure." The Spirit thus penetrates the present experience of those who hear with foretastes of the kingdom's future fulfillment.

Outline of Revelation

Prologue **1:1**

I. The letters to the seven churches **1:9—3:22**
- A. The setting: One like the Son of Man 1:9–20
- B. The letters 2:1—3:22

II. The seven seals **4:1—8:1**
- A. The setting 4:1—5:14
  - 1. The throne of God 4:1–11
  - 2. The Lamb and the scroll 5:1–14
- B. The seals 6:1—8:1
  - 1. First seal: white horse 6:1, 2
  - 2. Second seal: red horse 6:3, 4
  - 3. Third seal: black horse 6:5, 6
  - 4. Fourth seal: pale green horse 6:7, 8
  - 5. Fifth seal: souls under the altar 6:9–11
  - 6. Sixth seal: cosmic catastrophe 6:12–17
    - a. First interlude: 144,000 sealed 7:1–8
    - b. Second interlude: a great multitude 7:9–17
  - 7. Seventh seal: silence in heaven 8:1

III. The seven trumpets **8:2—11:18**
- A. The setting: the golden altar 8:2–6
- B. The trumpets 8:7—11:18
  1. First trumpet: earth 8:7
  2. Second trumpet: sea 8:8, 9
  3. Third trumpet: rivers 8:10, 11
  4. Fourth trumpet: sun 8:12
  5. Fifth trumpet: first woe—demonic locusts 8:13—9:12
  6. Sixth trumpet: second woe—cavalry 9:13–21
     - a. First interlude: the little scroll 10:1–11
     - b. Second interlude: two witnesses 11:1–14
  7. Seventh trumpet: third woe—voices in heaven 11:15–18

IV. The seven signs **11:19—15:4**
- A. The setting: the ark of the covenant 11:19
- B. The signs 12:1—15:4
  1. The woman, dragon, child, Michael 12:1–17
  2. The beast from the sea 13:1–10
  3. The beast from the earth 13:11–18
  4. The Lamb and the 144,000 14:1–5
  5. Four proclamations 14:6–13
  6. The final harvest 14:14–20
  7. The seven angels and the song of the Lamb 15:1–4

V. The seven bowls **15:5—16:21**
- A. The setting: the tent of witness 15:5—16:1
- B. Seven bowls 16:2–21
  1. First bowl: earth 16:2
  2. Second bowl: sea 16:3
  3. Third bowl: rivers 16:4–7
  4. Fourth bowl: sun 16:8, 9
  5. Fifth bowl: throne of the beast 16:10, 11
  6. Sixth bowl: Euphrates 16:12
     (Interlude: three unclean spirits) 16:13–16
  7. Seventh bowl: the cities of the nations 16:17–21

VI. The seven spectacles **17:1—20:3**
- A. The setting: a wilderness 17:1–3
- B. The spectacles 17:3—20:3
  1. A woman on a scarlet beast 17:3–5
  2. The mystery of the woman and the beast 17:6–18
  3. Seven voices: Babylon fallen 18:1—19:10
  4. King of kings and Lord of lords 19:11–16
  5. The supper of the great God 19:17, 18
  6. The war 19:19–21
  7. Satan bound 20:1–3

VII. The seven sights of the consummation **20:4—22:5**
- A. The setting 20:4–10
  1. Living and reigning with Christ 20:4–6
  2. Satan released to deceive 20:7–10
- B. The scenes 20:11—22:5
  1. The great white throne 20:11
  2. The last judgment 20:12–15
  3. The new heaven and new earth 21:1
  4. The New Jerusalem 21:2–8
  5. The bride of the Lamb 21:9–21
  6. The light of God's presence 21:22–27
  7. Paradise regained 22:1–5

Epilogue **22:6–21**
- A. Seven confirming witnesses 22:6–17
- B. Final warning and assurance 22:18–20
- C. Benediction 22:21

Introduction and Benediction

1 THE Revelation of Jesus Christ, [a]which God gave Him to show His *servants—things which must [1]shortly take place. And [b]He sent and signified *it* by His angel to His servant John,

CHAPTER 1

1 [a]John 3:32 [b]Rev. 22:6 [1]*quickly* or *swiftly* *See WW at Rev. 19:5.

KINGDOM DYNAMICS

1:1 Jesus and Angels, ANGELS. Jesus was closely associated with angels. Rev. 1:1 reveals that He commissions His angels to do His bidding. An angel was

1:1 Revelation translates the Greek word *apokalypsis,* an unveiling or disclosing of a reality that previously has not been perceived. This *apocalypse* came from God through **Jesus Christ,** whose past, present, and future position and work is the content of the revelation, communicated to **John** by an **angel** (see 22:16). The purpose of this book is **to**

used to announce Jesus' coming birth to the Virgin Mary and her fiancé, Joseph (Luke 1:26; Matt. 1:20). Angels also attended Jesus' birth and announced it to the shepherds (Luke 2:8). They protected Him from Herod's jealous wrath (Matt. 2:13, 22); and later in life, at the end of His 40-day fast, they ministered to Him and strengthened Him (Matt. 4:11).

During His agonizing struggle on the night in which He was betrayed, an angel strengthened Jesus in preparation for the Cross (Luke 22:43). These celestial creatures were present at Jesus' resurrection (Matt. 28:2) and ascension (Acts 1:10). Finally, Jesus will return "in the glory of His Father with His angels" (Matt. 16:27), and we will meet them in the air! (1 Thess. 4:16, 17).

(Ex. 3:2, 4/Rev. 12:7, 9) M.H.

2 [a]1 Cor. 1:6 [b]1 John 1:1 *See WW at John 19:35.
3 [a]Luke 11:28; Rev. 22:7 [b]James 5:8; Rev. 22:10 *See WW at 1 Thess. 5:20.
4 [a]Ex. 3:14 [b]John 1:1 [c][Is. 11:2]; Zech. 3:9; Rev. 3:1; 4:5; 5:6
5 [a]John 8:14; Prov. 14:5 [b]Is. 55:4 [c]Ps. 89:27; 1 Cor. 15:20; [Col. 1:18] [d]Rev. 17:14

2 [a]who bore witness to the word of
God, and to the *testimony of Jesus
Christ, to all things [b]that he saw.
3 [a]Blessed *is* he who reads and those **2**
who hear the words of this *prophecy,
and keep those things which are written in it; for [b]the time *is* near.

Greeting the Seven Churches

4 John, to the seven churches which
are in Asia:

Grace to you and peace from Him
[a]who is and [b]who was and who is to
come, [c]and from the seven Spirits who
are before His throne,
5 and from Jesus Christ, [a]the faithful
[b]**witness,** the [c]firstborn from the dead,
and [d]the ruler over the kings of the

show His servants, genuine believers in every age, what **must . . . take place** between the First and the Second Coming of Jesus. The events will occur **shortly** (2:5, 16; 3:11; 11:14; 22:6, 7, 12, 20), meaning they can take place at any time. The entire message is to be **signified** (revealed). This is a key to the understanding of the visions, all of which contain symbols pointing to the spiritual realities in and behind our historical experience.

1:2 John has been a true **witness,** in his life and preaching (see 1:4, 9; 21:2; 22:8), and now in this book, to what is both God's **word** to men and Jesus' **testimony** to the Father and the Truth.

1:3 See section 2 of Truth-In-Action at the end of Rev.

1:3 The first of seven *beatitudes* (see 14:13; 16:15; 19:9; 20:6; 22:7, 14) implies a reading aloud to a gathering of Christians who then are expected to obey **the words of this prophecy.** The fact that the **time** ***is*** **near** is an urgent call to obedience, not a reference to a precise historical time.

1:4 John is writing to **seven** actual **churches** in the Roman Province of **Asia,** which are representative of all local churches in every age. The blessings he pronounces have their source in the triune God. The Father is described in terms of His eternal nature (see Ex. 3:14). **The seven Spirits** picture the Holy Spirit in His manifold and perfect dynamic activity. See Introduction to Revelation: The Holy Spirit at Work.

1:5 **Jesus** is presented in terms of His redeeming sacrifice, His resurrection, and His eternal reign. Jesus as Messiah-King is a major theme in Revelation.

The Seven Churches of the Apocalypse. The churches of seven cities were recipients of an apocalyptic letter from the Lord through John. By commendation, rebuke, and warning, the people of God were exhorted to remain faithful in adversity. These churches held significant roles in the Christian experience of Asia Minor as a result of their location within a transportation network linking different parts of the region.

earth. To Him [e]who [1]loved us [f]and washed us from our sins in His own blood,
6 and has [a]made us [1]kings and priests to His God and Father, [b]to Him *be* *glory and *dominion forever and ever. Amen.

WORD WEALTH

1:5 witness, *martus* (*mar*-toos); Strong's *#3144:* Compare "martyr" and "martyrdom." One who testifies to the truth he has experienced, a witness, one who has knowledge of a fact and can give information concerning it. The word in itself does not imply death, but many of the first-century witnesses did give their lives, with the result that the word came to denote a martyr, one who witnesses for Christ by his death (Acts 22:20; Rev. 2:13; 17:6).

KINGDOM DYNAMICS

1:5, 6 Worship and Praise, WORSHIP AND THE KINGDOM. In the opening of Rev., John introduces himself as a brother and companion in the struggle we all face (v. 9). His words "in the kingdom and patience of Jesus Christ" point to the dual facts of Christ's present kingdom triumph and the ongoing presence of evil and warfare that exact the patience of the church in the kingdom advances among and through us. In prefacing the broad arenas of prophecy about to be unfolded, John addresses two very important present truths: 1) We, Christ's redeemed, are loved and are washed from our sins—a present state (v. 6). 2) We, through His glorious dominion, have been designated "kings and priests" to God—also a present calling. Thus, these dual offices give perspective on our authority and duty and how we most effectively may advance the kingdom of God.

First, we are said to be kings in the sense that under the King of kings we are the new breed—the reborn, to whom God has delegated authority to extend and administrate the powers of His rule. Of course, this involves faithful witness to the gospel in the power of the Spirit and loving service to humanity in the love of God. But it also involves confrontation with dark powers of hell, assertive prayer warfare, and an expectation of the miraculous works of God (2 Cor. 10:3–5; Eph. 6:10–20; 1 Cor. 2:4.). However, this authority is only fully accomplished in the spirit of praiseful worship, as we exercise the office of "priests." Some translations read, "a kingdom of priests," which emphasizes that the rule is only effective when the priestly mission is faithfully attended. Worship is foundational to kingdom advance. The power of the believer before God's throne, worshiping the Lamb and exalting in the Holy Spirit of praise, is mightily confounding to the Adversary. See Ex. 19:5–7 and Ps. 22:3.

(Ps. 93:2/1 Pet. 2:9) J.W.H.

7 Behold, He is coming with [a]clouds,
and every eye will see Him, even
[b]they who pierced Him. And all the
tribes of the earth will mourn because
of Him. Even so, Amen.
8 [a]"I am the Alpha and the Omega,
[1]*the* Beginning and *the* End," says the
[2]Lord, [b]"who is and who was and who
is to come, the [c]Almighty."

Vision of the Son of Man

9 I, John, [1]both your brother and
[a]companion in the tribulation and
[b]kingdom and patience of Jesus Christ,
was on the island that is called Patmos
for the word of God and for the testimony of Jesus Christ.
10 [a]I was in the Spirit on [b]the Lord's
Day, and I heard behind me [c]a loud
voice, as of a trumpet,
11 saying, [1]"I am the Alpha and the

5 [e]John 13:34 [f]Heb. 9:14 [1]NU *loves us and freed;* M *loves us and washed*
6 [a]1 Pet. 2:5, 9 [b]1 Tim. 6:16 [1]NU, M *a kingdom* *See WW at John 2:11. • See WW at 1 Tim. 6:16.
7 [a]Matt. 24:30 [b]Zech. 12:10–14; John 19:37
8 [a]Is. 41:4; Rev. 21:6; 22:13 [b]Rev. 4:8; 11:17 [c]Is. 9:6 [1]NU, M omit *the Beginning and the End* [2]NU, M *Lord God*
9 [a]Phil. 1:7 [b][Rom. 8:17; 2 Tim. 2:12] [1]NU, M omit *both*
10 [a]Acts 10:10 [b]Acts 20:7 [c]Rev. 4:1
11 [1]NU, M omit *"I am the Alpha and the Omega, the First and the Last," and,*

1:6 The sacrifice of Jesus has given to all believers the privileges that had belonged to ancient Israel (see Ex. 19:6; 29:1–9; 1 Pet. 2:9, 10). **Has made us kings and priests** is clearly a present tense reference to the believer's function *now,* in witness and in worship (see 5:10).

1:7 The Lord's return will be actual, personal, and visible (see Acts 1:9–11). **Clouds** (Dan. 7:13) symbolize God's presence, protection, and leadership. However, the emphasis here is on the Lord's coming in judgment (see Zech. 12:10; Matt. 24:30).

1:8 God seals the prophecy with the authority of His name. ***The Alpha and the Omega,*** the first and last letters of the Greek alphabet, declare that God is everything from *A* to *Z,* thus in control of all history (see Is. 44:6). As **the Almighty** One, God's power is absolute (see 4:8; 11:17; 15:3; 16:7, 14; 19:15; 21:22).

1:9 John experiences with his readers **the tribulation,** or persecution on account of their faith, with patient endurance, which is steadfast courage under unjust suffering. However, attendant to the trials involved in the Christian life is the glory of the **kingdom.** John is an exile on **Patmos,** an island 10 miles by 6 miles, located 60 miles southwest of Ephesus in the Aegean Sea. Volcanic and mostly treeless, the Romans used it as a penal colony, forcing prisoners to work in the granite quarries. John's banishment was the result of his faithful witness to the gospel.

1:10 This is the earliest reference in Christian literature to the first day of the week as **the Lord's Day.** John's experience **in the Spirit** (4:2; 17:3; 21:10) was that of a biblical prophet receiving a supernatural revelation. The **trumpet** summons and prepares John to receive a momentous message.

1:11 The seven churches were located on a major Roman postal route and are listed in the order in which a messenger would reach the towns, making a semicircular sweep from Ephesus. See note on 2:1—3:22.

Omega, the First and the Last," and,
"What you see, write in a book and
send *it* to the seven churches [2]which
are in Asia: to Ephesus, to Smyrna, to
Pergamos, to Thyatira, to Sardis, to
Philadelphia, and to Laodicea."
12 Then I turned to see the voice that
spoke with me. And having turned
[a]I saw seven golden lampstands,
13 [a]and in the midst of the seven lampstands [b]*One* like the Son of Man,
[c]clothed with a garment down to the
feet and [d]girded about the chest with
a golden band.
14 His head and [a]hair *were* white like
wool, as white as snow, and [b]His eyes
like a flame of fire;
15 [a]His feet *were* like fine brass, as if
refined in a furnace, and [b]His voice as
the sound of many waters;
16 [a]He had in His right hand seven
stars, [b]out of His mouth went a sharp
two-edged sword, [c]and His countenance *was* like the sun shining in its
strength.
17 And [a]when I saw Him, I fell at His
feet as dead. But [b]He laid His right
hand on me, saying [1]to me, "Do not
*be afraid; [c]I am the First and the Last.
18 [a]"I *am* He who lives, and was dead,
and behold, [b]I am alive forevermore.
Amen. And [c]I have the keys of [1]Hades
and of Death.
19 [1]"Write the things which you have
[a]seen, [b]and the things which are,
[c]and the things which will take place
after this.

11 [2]NU, M omit *which are in Asia*
12 [a]Ex. 25:37
13 [a]Rev. 2:1 [b]Ezek. 1:26 [c]Dan. 10:5 [d]Rev. 15:6
14 [a]Dan. 7:9 [b]Dan. 10:6
15 [a]Ezek. 1:7 [b]Ezek. 1:24; 43:2
16 [a]Rev. 1:20; 2:1; 3:1 [b]Is. 49:2 [c]Matt. 17:2
17 [a]Ezek. 1:28 [b]Dan. 8:18; 10:10, 12 [c]Is. 41:4; 44:6; 48:12 [1]NU, M omit *to me* *See WW at Matt. 10:26.
18 [a]Rom. 6:9 [b]Rev. 4:9 [c]Ps. 68:20 [1]Lit. *Unseen;* the unseen realm
19 [a]Rev. 1:9–18 [b]Rev. 2:1 [c]Rev. 4:1 [1]NU, M *Therefore, write*

1:12 The **seven golden lampstands** represent the churches (v. 20), which are lights in a dark world.
1:13–15 The clothing of the Lord symbolizes priestly royalty; the **white hair** and flaming **eyes** symbolize eternity, wisdom, and omniscience; the **fine brass** suggests immutability and omnipotence; and the **many waters** represent commanding authority.
1:16 The **seven stars** are either the pastor-messengers of the churches (1:20), or the guardian angels assigned to the churches. **In His right hand** connotes being sustained and protected. The **two-edged sword** is His Word. See 2:12, 16; 19:13, 15, 21; Heb. 4:12. The description of the Lord's **countenance** suggests indescribable glory and majesty (see Matt. 17:2).
1:17, 18 The keys of Hades and of Death: Jesus is now Lord over the realms of life and death. The power of satanic prerogatives, because of man's original rebellion, is now curbed (see Heb. 2:14, 15).
1:19 The phrase **which you have seen** refers not only to the vision of Christ John has just witnessed, but anticipates

THE SEVEN CHURCHES OF THE APOCALYPSE (1:20)

	Commendation	Criticism	Instruction	Promise
Ephesus (2:1–7)	Rejects evil, perseveres, has patience	Love for Christ no longer fervent	Do the works you did at first	The tree of life
Smyrna (2:8–11)	Gracefully bears suffering	None	Be faithful until death	The crown of life
Pergamos (2:12–17)	Keeps the faith of Christ	Tolerates immorality, idolatry, and heresies	Repent	Hidden manna and a stone with a new name
Thyatira (2:18–29)	Love, service, faith, patience is greater than at first	Tolerates cult of idolatry and immorality	Judgment coming; keep the faith	Rule over nations and receive morning star
Sardis (3:1–6)	Some have kept the faith	A dead church	Repent; strengthen what remains	Faithful honored and clothed in white
Philadelphia (3:7–13)	Perseveres in the faith	None	Keep the faith	A place in God's presence, a new name, and the New Jerusalem
Laodicea (3:14–22)	None	Indifferent	Be zealous and repent	Share Christ's throne

20 "The [1]mystery* of the seven stars
which you saw in My right hand, and
the seven golden lampstands: The
seven stars are [a]the [2]angels of the
seven churches, and [b]the seven lampstands [3]which you saw are the seven
churches.

The Loveless Church

2 "To the [1]angel of the church of
Ephesus write,
'These things says [a]He who holds
the seven stars in His right hand,
[b]who walks in the midst of the seven
golden lampstands:
2 [a]"I know your works, your labor,
your [1]patience, and that you cannot
[2]bear those who are evil. And [b]you
have tested those [c]who say they are
apostles and are not, and have found
them liars;
3 "and you have persevered and have
patience, and have labored for My
name's sake and have [a]not become
weary.
3 4 "Nevertheless I have *this* against
you, that you have *left your first love.
5 "Remember therefore from where
you have fallen; *repent and do the
first works, [a]or else I will come to you
*quickly and remove your lampstand
from its place—unless you repent.
6 "But this you have, that you hate
the deeds of the Nicolaitans, which I
also hate.
7 [a]"He who has an ear, let him hear 4
what the Spirit says to the churches.
To him who overcomes I will give
[b]to eat from [c]the tree of life, which is
in the midst of the Paradise of God." '

The Persecuted Church

8 "And to the [1]angel of the church in
Smyrna write,
'These things says [a]the First and the
Last, who was dead, and came to life:
9 "I know your works, tribulation, 4
and **poverty** (but you are [a]rich); and *I
know* the blasphemy of [b]those who say
they are Jews and are not, [c]but *are* a
[1]synagogue of Satan.

20 [a]Rev. 2:1 [b]Zech. 4:2 [1]*hidden truth* [2]Or *messengers* [3]NU, M omit *which you saw* *See WW at Mark 4:11.

CHAPTER 2

1 [a]Rev. 1:16 [b]Rev. 1:13 [1]Or *messenger*
2 [a]Ps. 1:6 [b]1 John 4:1 [c]2 Cor. 11:13 [1]*perseverance* [2]*endure*
3 [a]Gal. 6:9
4 *See WW at Mark 1:20.
5 [a]Matt. 21:41 *See WW at Matt. 3:2. • See WW at Rev. 22:20.
7 [a]Matt. 11:15 [b][Rev. 22:2, 14] [c][Gen. 2:9; 3:22]
8 [a]Rev. 1:8, 17, 18 [1]Or *messenger*
9 [a]Luke 12:21 [b]Rom. 2:17 [c]Rev. 3:9 [1]*congregation*

WORD WEALTH

2:9 poverty, ***ptocheia*** (pto-*khi*-ah); Strong's *#4432:* From a root meaning "to cower." The word indicates a state of ab-

---

visions yet to come, which will be in his past as he writes. John will therefore record both present and future events, many of which will be repeated throughout history until the climax of this age and the Age to Come (2:1—22:21).

DISPENSATIONAL INTERPRETATION makes three distinct chronological divisions in Rev. 1:19, suggesting **the things which you have seen,** refers to things past; 2) **the things which are,** to the church age (2:1—3:22); 3) **the things which will take place after this,** to matters after the church age ends (4:1—22:5).

2:1—3:22 The seven churches addressed were actual churches in the cities mentioned. They are representative of all churches of that time, as well as churches in all subsequent generations. The letters are to be interpreted historically, pastorally, and practically, with immediate application instructing the seven actual Asian churches; with ongoing application to all local churches throughout church history, giving discernment as to where they stand spiritually before the Lord; and with ongoing personal application, exhorting the individual to be an overcomer. The structure of the letters falls into a sevenfold pattern: 1) A *commission* to the messenger of the church named; 2) A *character* description of Christ; 3) A *commendation,* with the exceptions of Sardis and Laodicea; 4) A *censure,* with the exceptions of Smyrna and Philadelphia; 5) A *correction* with various imperatives; 6) A *challenge* repeated seven times. Beginning with the fourth letter, the challenge follows the covenant promise; 7) A *covenant promise,* which is a facet of Christ Himself and is a gift to every member of the body of Christ.

DISPENSATIONAL INTERPRETATION: Dispensationalists see a prophetic application in the letters, suggesting they also outline seven stages of church history, culminating with the two end-time stages seen in the churches of Philadelphia and Laodicea.

2:1–7 Ephesus: An unloving, orthodox church in the foremost city of proconsular Asia (see Acts 19; 20), and according to tradition, the residence of John before and after his imprisonment on Patmos.

2:4 See section 3 of Truth-In-Action at the end of Rev.

2:4 The spiritual vitality springing from **love** for the Lord had degenerated into orthodox routine.

2:5 I will come to you is present tense, referring not to the Second Coming, but to a spiritual coming in blessing or in judgment. **Remove your lampstand:** A congregation may continue to exist without being light in the darkness.

2:6 The name **Nicolaitans** is symbolic, meaning "Conquering the Laity." Apparently this group claimed some kind of superior status that permitted idolatry and immorality (see 2:14, 15).

2:7 See section 4 of Truth-In-Action at the end of Rev.

2:7 Overcomes is military terminology, suggesting combat against the forces of the Evil One (see Eph. 6:10-18). All believers are overcomers, but those who remain faithful in the midst of persecution and doctrinal error give proof to their faith. This is the primary emphasis in Revelation. **The tree of life** symbolizes spiritual sustenance to maintain eternal life. **Paradise** is a Persian word for garden, which was used to designate the heavenly garden of God (Luke 23:43). The symbolism suggests the perfect fellowship that God and humankind enjoyed in Eden before the Fall.

2:8–11 Smyrna was a poor, persecuted church located in a beautiful city of wealth and commercial greatness, with a large Jewish population.

2:9, 10 See section 4 of Truth-In-Action at the end of Rev.

2:9 Even though the Christians were poor, probably as a result of economic boycott, they were spiritually **rich.** Opposition from the **Jews** made life particularly difficult for Christians there. Although their official title was "Synagogue of the Lord" (see Num. 16:3), the hostile, unbelieving Jews had become **a synagogue of Satan.** The "Synagogue of the Lord" is now the church.

ject poverty, destitution, indigence. In the NT it describes the voluntary poverty that Christ experienced on our behalf (2 Cor. 8:9); the condition of saints in Macedonia (2 Cor. 8:2); and the extreme want of the church of Smyrna (Rev. 2:9).

2 10 [a]"Do not *fear any of those things
which you are about to suffer. Indeed,
the devil is about to throw *some* of you
into prison, that you may be **tested,**
and you will have tribulation ten days.
[b]Be faithful until death, and I will give
you [c]the crown of life.

WORD WEALTH

2:10 tested, *peirazo* (pie-*rad*-zoe); Strong's *#3985:* Compare "empirical" and "peirastic." To explore, test, try, assay, examine, prove, attempt, tempt. The word describes the testing of the believer's loyalty, strength, opinions, disposition, condition, faith, patience, or character. *Peirazo* determines which way one is going and what one is made of.

4 11 [a]"He who has an ear, let him hear
what the Spirit says to the churches.
He who overcomes shall not be hurt
by [b]the second death." '

The Compromising Church

12 "And to the [1]angel of the church in
Pergamos write,
'These things says [a]He who has the
sharp two-edged sword:
2 13 "I know your works, and where you
dwell, where Satan's throne *is.* And
you hold fast to My name, and did not
deny My faith even in the days in
which Antipas *was* My faithful *martyr, who was killed among you, where
Satan dwells.
14 "But I have a few things against 5
you, because you have there those who
hold the doctrine of [a]Balaam, who
taught Balak to put a *stumbling block
before the children of Israel, [b]to eat
things sacrificed to idols, [c]and to *commit sexual immorality.
15 "Thus you also have those who hold
the doctrine of the Nicolaitans, [1]which
thing I hate.
16 "Repent, or else I will come to you
*quickly and [a]will fight against them
with the sword of My mouth.
17 "He who has an ear, let him hear 4
what the Spirit says to the churches.
To him who overcomes I will give some
of the hidden [a]manna to eat. And I will
give him a white stone, and on the
stone [b]a new name written which no
one knows except him who receives
it." '

The Corrupt Church

18 "And to the [1]angel of the church in
Thyatira write,
'These things says the Son of God,
[a]who has eyes like a flame of fire, and
His feet like fine brass:
19 [a]"I know your works, love, [1]service,
faith, and your [2]patience; and *as* for
your works, the last *are* more than the
first.
20 "Nevertheless I have [1]a few things 5
against you, because you allow [2]that

10 [a]Matt. 10:22 [b]Matt. 24:13 [c]James 1:12 *See WW at Matt. 10:26.
11 [a]Rev. 13:9 [b][Rev. 20:6, 14; 21:8]
12 [a]Is. 49:2; Rev. 1:16; 2:16 [1]Or *messenger*
13 *See WW at Rev. 1:5.
14 [a]Num. 31:16 [b]Num. 25; Acts 15:29; [1 Cor. 10:20]; Rev. 2:20 [c]1 Cor. 6:13 *See WW at Matt. 16:23. • See WW at Rev. 17:2.
15 [1]NU, M *likewise.*
16 [a]Is. 11:4; 2 Thess. 2:8; Rev. 19:15 *See WW at Rev. 22:20.
17 [a]Ex. 16:33, 34; [John 6:49, 51] [b]Is. 56:5; 62:2; 65:15; Rev. 3:12
18 [a]Rev. 1:14, 15 [1]Or *messenger*
19 [a]Rev. 2:2 [1]NU, M *faith, service* [2]*perseverance*
20 [1]NU, M *against you that you tolerate* [2]M *your wife Jezebel*

2:10, 11 See section 2 of Truth-In-Action at the end of Rev.
2:10 The devil (meaning "slanderer") is behind the persecutors. **Ten days** is symbolic of a relatively short time (see Dan. 1:12). **Crown of life:** The joy of life eternal given to a victor.
2:11 See section 4 of Truth-In-Action at the end of Rev.
2:11 The second death is eternal separation from God (see 20:6, 14, 15; 21:18; Dan. 12:2; John 5:29).
2:12–17 Pergamos was a doctrinally compromising church in the oldest city of the province and the official seat of the Roman government.
2:13 See section 2 of Truth-In-Action at the end of Rev.
2:13 Satan's throne may refer to a 200-foot-high altar to Zeus or to the fact that Pergamos was the center of emperor worship. In addition, the city was the center of the worship of Aesclepius, the god of healing, whose symbol was a serpent, which to Christians symbolizes Satan. **Antipas** was evidently the first Christian in Asia to be martyred for his faith.
2:14, 15 The doctrine of Balaam and **of the Nicolaitans** were teachings that seduced the people of God into idolatry and immorality (see 2:6, 20; Num. 22—24; 25; 31:15, 16; Acts 15:28, 29; 1 Cor. 10:27–29).
2:14 See section 5 of Truth-In-Action at the end of Rev.
2:16 The Lord will purge the church with His word of judgment.
2:17 See section 4 of Truth-In-Action at the end of Rev.
2:17 Hidden manna: Jewish apocryphal mythology maintained that the pot of manna in the ark (see Ex. 16:4, 31–34) was hidden by Jeremiah, or taken by an angel to heaven, at the time of the destruction of Jerusalem in 586 B.C., where it would remain until the Messiah should come (2 Maccabees 2:4–8). Jesus is "the true bread from heaven" (7:16; see Ps. 78:24; 105:40; John 6:31–35, 48–51). Juries voted for acquittal by casting **a white stone** in an urn. Special stones were also used as tokens for various purposes, such as rewards for victors in games. **New name** refers to the imputed character of Christ (see 22:4; Is. 62:2).
2:18–29 Thyatira was a morally compromising church in a commercial city with numerous trade guilds, each with its patron deity. A city sponsoring frequent idolatrous feasts and orgies, it was famous for woolen goods and a "royal purple" dye (Acts 16:14).
2:18 The title **Son of God** expresses the relationship and fellowship, plus an equality and identity of nature between the Father and the Son.
2:20 See section 5 of Truth-In-Action at the end of Rev.
2:20, 21 Jezebel was the wife of King Ahab who promoted Canaanite religion in Israel (1 Kin. 16:29–31; 18:4, 19; 2 Kin. 9:22). Her name is used here symbolically for a false

woman [a]Jezebel, who calls herself a
prophetess, [3]to teach and seduce My
servants [b]to *commit sexual immorality and eat things sacrificed to idols.
21 "And I gave her time [a]to [1]repent of
her sexual immorality, and she did not
repent.
22 "Indeed I will cast her into a sickbed, and those who commit adultery
with her into great tribulation, unless
they repent of [1]their deeds.
23 "I will kill her children with death,
and all the churches shall know that I
am He who [a]searches[1] the minds and
hearts. And I will give to each one of
you according to your works.

WORD WEALTH

2:23 hearts, *kardia* (kar-*dee*-ah); Strong's *#2588:* From a root word meaning "to quiver" or "to palpitate" (compare "cardiac" and "pericardium"). The physical organ of the body, the center of physical life, the seat of one's personal life (both physical and spiritual), the center of one's personality, the seat of one's entire mental and moral activity, containing both rational and emotional elements. It is the seat of feelings, desires, joy, pain, and love. It is also the center for thought, understanding, and will. The human heart is the dwelling place of the Lord and the Holy Spirit. In v. 23, the omniscient Lord sees into the innermost being where all decisions concerning Him are made.

24 "Now to you I say, [1]and to the rest
in Thyatira, as many as do not have
this doctrine, who have not known the
[a]depths of Satan, as they say, [b]I
[2]will put on you no other burden.
25 "But hold fast [a]what you have till I
come.
26 "And he who overcomes, and keeps
[a]My works until the end, [b]to him I will
give power over the nations—

20 [a]1 Kin. 16:31; 21:25 [b]Ex. 34:15 [3]NU, M *and teaches and seduces* *See WW at Rev. 17:2.
21 [a]Rev. 9:20; 16:9, 11 [1]NU, M *repent, and she does not want to repent of her sexual immorality.*
22 [1]NU, M *her*
23 [a]Jer. 11:20; 17:10 [1]*examines*
24 [a]2 Tim. 3:1–9 [b]Acts 15:28 [1]NU, M omit *and* [2]NU, M omit *will*
25 [a]Rev. 3:11
26 [a][John 6:29] [b][Matt. 19:28]
27 [a]Ps. 2:8, 9 *See WW at Rom. 16:28.
28 [a]2 Pet. 1:19

CHAPTER 3

1 [a]Rev. 1:4, 16 [1]Or *messenger*
2 [1]NU, M *My God*
3 [a]1 Tim. 6:20 [b]Rev. 3:19 [c]Matt. 24:42, 43 [d][Rev. 16:15]
4 [a]Acts 1:15 [b][Jude 23] [c]Rev. 4:4; 6:11 [1]NU, M *Nevertheless you* [2]NU, M omit *even*
5 [a][Rev. 19:8] [b]Ex. 32:32 [c]Phil. 4:3 [d]Luke 12:8 *See WW at Col. 2:14.
6 [a]Rev. 2:7
7 [1]Or *messenger*

27 *'He[a] shall rule them with a rod of*
iron;
*They shall be *dashed to pieces*
like the potter's vessels'—
as I also have received from My Father;
28 "and I will give him [a]the morning
star.
29 "He who has an ear, let him hear 4
what the Spirit says to the churches." '

The Dead Church

3 "And to the [1]angel of the church 6
in Sardis write,
'These things says He who [a]has the
seven Spirits of God and the seven
stars: "I know your works, that you
have a name that you are alive, but you
are dead.
2 "Be watchful, and strengthen the
things which remain, that are ready to
die, for I have not found your works
perfect before [1]God.
3 [a]"Remember therefore how you
have received and heard; hold fast and
[b]repent. [c]Therefore if you will not
watch, I will come upon you [d]as a thief,
and you will not know what hour I will
come upon you.
4 [1]"You have [a]a few names [2]even in
Sardis who have not [b]defiled their garments; and they shall walk with Me
[c]in white, for they are worthy.
5 "He who overcomes [a]shall be
clothed in white garments, and I will
not [b]blot* out his name from the
[c]Book of Life; but [d]I will confess his
name before My Father and before His
angels.
6 [a]"He who has an ear, let him hear 4
what the Spirit says to the churches." '

The Faithful Church

7 "And to the [1]angel of the church in
Philadelphia write,

prophetess who led people into literal and spiritual fornication.
2:22–24 Sickbed: Punishment for sin *may* be experienced in the physical body, even resulting in premature death. **Her children** are her followers. **The depths of Satan** is a biting sarcastic castigation of this heretical teaching (Rom. 6:1–23).
2:26, 27 The overcomer will share in Christ's triumph over all evil and evildoers, and in His messianic rule (see Ps. 2:8, 9), which was inaugurated at His First Coming (see 1:6).
2:28 The morning star: Jesus Himself, heralding the dawn of a new day, is our ultimate reward (22:16; 2 Pet. 1:19).
2:29 See section 4 of Truth-In-Action at the end of Rev.
3:1–6 Sardis was a dead church in the ancient capital of the kingdom of Lydia, and of King Croesus (560–546 B.C.) who issued the first gold coins; here it represents a decadent city of luxury, apathy, and licentious religiosity.
3:1–5 See section 6 of Truth-In-Action at the end of Rev.
3:3 I will come . . . as a thief refers to an unexpected historical judgment, not the Second Coming (see note on 2:5).
3:4 The only commendation of this church is recognition of the **few** who are faithful.
3:5 White garments are the robes of the righteousness of Jesus Christ, and thus of victorious joy. **I will not blot out his name** assures the certainty of the Lord's promise. **Book of Life** is God's eternal record of the redeemed (see 13:8; 17:8; 20:12, 15; Ex. 32:32; Ps. 69:28; Dan. 12:1; Mal. 3:16; Luke 10:20; Phil. 4:3).
3:6 See section 4 of Truth-In-Action at the end of Rev.
3:7–13 Philadelphia was a faithful church in a small town that was established to be a center for Greek culture. The town was renowned for its surrounding vineyards but subject to frequent earthquakes.

'These things says [a]He who is holy,
[b]He who is true, [c]"*He who has the*
key of David, [d]*He who opens and no*
one shuts, and [e]*shuts and no one*
opens":
8 [a]"I know your works. See, I have
set before you [b]an open door, [1]and no
one can shut it; for you have a little
strength, have kept My word, and have
not denied My name.
9 "Indeed I will make [a]*those* of the
synagogue of Satan, who say they are
Jews and are not, but lie—indeed
[b]I will make them come and *worship
before your feet, and to know that I
have loved you.
10 "Because you have kept [1]My command to persevere, [a]I also will keep
you from the hour of trial which shall
come upon [b]the whole world, to *test
those who dwell [c]on the earth.
11 [1]"Behold, [a]I am coming *quickly!
[b]Hold fast what you have, that no one
may take [c]your crown.
12 "He who overcomes, I will make
him [a]a pillar in the temple of My God,
and he shall [b]go out no more. [c]I will
write on him the name of My God and
the name of the city of My God, the
[d]New Jerusalem, which [e]comes down
out of *heaven from My God. [f]*And I*
will write on him My new name.
4 13 [a]"He who has an ear, let him hear
what the Spirit says to the churches."'

7 [a]Acts 3:14 [b]1 John 5:20 [c]Is. 9:7; 22:22 [d][Matt. 16:19] [e]Job 12:14
8 [a]Rev. 3:1 [b]1 Cor. 16:9 [1]NU, M *which no one can shut*
9 [a]Rev. 2:9 [b]Is. 45:14; 49:23; 60:14 *See WW at Rev. 4:10.
10 [a]2 Pet. 2:9 [b]Luke 2:1 [c]Is. 24:17 [1]Lit. *the word of My patience* *See WW at Rev. 2:10.
11 [a]Phil. 4:5 [b]Rev. 2:25 [c][Rev. 2:10] [1]NU, M omit *Behold* *See WW at Rev. 22:20.
12 [a]1 Kin. 7:21 [b]Ps. 23:6 [c][Rev. 14:1; 22:4] [d][Heb. 12:22] [e]Rev. 21:2 [f][Rev. 2:17; 22:4] *See WW at Rev. 21:1.
13 [a]Rev. 2:7
14 [a]2 Cor. 1:20 [b]Rev. 1:5; 3:7; 19:11 [c][Col. 1:15] [1]Or *messenger*

The Lukewarm Church

14 "And to the [1]angel of the church
[2]of the Laodiceans write,
[a]'These things says the Amen,
[b]the Faithful and True Witness, [c]the
Beginning of the *creation of God:
15 [a]"I know your works, that you are 3
neither cold nor hot. I could wish you
were cold or hot.
16 "So then, because you are lukewarm, and neither [1]cold nor hot, I will
vomit you out of My mouth.
17 "Because you say, [a]'I am rich, have 1
become wealthy, and have need of
nothing'—and do not know that you
are wretched, miserable, poor, blind,
and naked—
18 "I counsel you [a]to buy from Me gold 1
refined in the fire, that you may be
rich; and [b]white garments, that you
may be clothed, *that* the shame of your
nakedness may not be revealed; and
anoint your eyes with eye salve, that
you may see.
19 [a]"As many as I *love, I rebuke and 3
[b]chasten.[1] Therefore be [2]zealous* and
repent.
20 "Behold, [a]I stand at the door and

[2]NU, M *in Laodicea* *See WW at Col. 1:15. **15** [a]Rev. 3:1 **16** [1]NU, M *hot nor cold* **17** [a]Hos. 12:8 **18** [a]Is. 55:1 [b]2 Cor. 5:3 **19** [a]Job 5:17 [b]Heb. 12:6 [1]*discipline* [2]*eager* *See WW at John 21:15. • See WW at 1 Cor. 14:1. **20** [a]Song 5:2

3:7 The key of David symbolizes authority (see 5:5; 22:16; Is. 22:22).
3:8 An open door: Either of service and evangelistic opportunity (1 Cor. 16:9; 2 Cor. 2:12) or of entrance into the consummated kingdom.
3:9 See note on 2:9.
3:10 I will keep you is the Lord's assurance that according to John 17:6, 11, 12, 15, He is able to preserve His people **from the hour of trial,** the climactic trial, which has been and will continue to be anticipated through many historical manifestations (including such times as Jesus prophesied in Matt. 24:21, 22). **Those who dwell on the earth** describes humankind in opposition to God (6:10; 8:13; 11:10; 13:3, 8, 12, 14; l4:3, 6; 17:2, 8).

DISPENSATIONAL INTERPRETATION: The church will be raptured before the Great Tribulation period (see note on 1 Thess. 4:17). Christians do suffer and will continue to suffer persecution and tribulation in general, but God's **I also will keep you from** [Greek "out of"] **the hour of trial** is a clear, literal promise to believers for deliverance from the coming Great Tribulation (6:1—19:10). It does not indicate a preservation *in,* but a complete exemption *from,* the Earth's final distresses.

3:11 I am coming quickly is a warning to the oppressors, and an encouragement to the oppressed (see note on 1:1).
3:12 A city often honored a notable citizen by erecting **a pillar** in a temple with his name inscribed on it. Thus, the Lord will honor His faithful permanently (**go out no more**) by inscribing on them **the name of My God,** of **the New Jerusalem,** and of Christ, indicating identification with and possession by God, a spiritual citizenship, and a reflection of the character of Christ. See note on 2:17.
3:13 See section 4 of Truth-In-Action at the end of Rev.
3:14–22 Laodicea was an arrogant, self-sufficient church in an affluent city.
3:14 The Amen is the God of Truth (see 1:6; Is. 65:16) and the Guarantor of all God's promises (see 2 Cor. 1:20). **The Beginning of the creation of God** refers to the source and cause of creation (see John 1:3; Col. 1:15–18; Heb. 1:2).
3:15, 16 Neither cold nor hot: Cold springs are refreshing; hot mineral springs are medicinal; **lukewarm** is nauseating.
3:15 See section 3 of Truth-In-Action at the end of Rev.
3:17, 18 Gold . . . white garments . . . eye salve: Laodicea was noted for being a banking center, for the production of a glossy black wool used in clothing and carpets, and for producing a salve for the curing of eye disorders. The church desperately needed the grace that regenerates, the garments of Christ's righteousness, and Spirit-illumined eyes of the heart.
3:17 See section 1 of Truth-In-Action at the end of Rev.
3:18 See section 1 of Truth-In-Action at the end of Rev.
3:19 See section 3 of Truth-In-Action at the end of Rev.
3:20 Behold, I stand at the door and knock is addressed to a complacent church. Individuals may still open the door and enjoy intimate fellowship with the Lord. That He *waits* for the door to be opened shows the paradox of grace and personal responsibility.

DISPENSATIONAL INTERPRETATION sees the church in Philadelphia and the church of the Laodiceans (vv. 7–22) as representing the church during the period just prior to the Rapture, Philadelphia as picturing the end-time church characterized by revival, and Laodicea as the apostate "church" just prior to the Rapture.

knock. [b]If anyone hears My voice and
opens the door, [c]I will come in to him
and dine with him, and he with Me.
21 "To him who overcomes [a]I will
grant to sit with Me on My throne, as
I also overcame and sat down with My
Father on His throne.
 22 [a]"He who has an ear, let him
hear what the Spirit says to the
churches." ' "

20 [b]Luke 12:36, 37; John 10:3 [c][John 14:23]
21 [a]Matt. 19:28; 2 Tim. 2:12; [Rev. 2:26; 20:4]
22 [a]Rev. 2:7

The Throne Room of Heaven

CHAPTER 4

4 After these things I looked, and behold, a door *standing* [a]open in heaven. And the first voice which I heard *was* like a [b]trumpet speaking with me, saying, "Come up here, and I will show you things which must take place after this."

1 [a]Ezek. 1:1; Rev. 19:11 [b]Rev. 1:10

KINGDOM DYNAMICS

4:1 Interpretive Approaches to the Book of Revelation, PROPHECY. Many devoted Christians are surprised to discover that other equally dedicated believers view the prophecies of the Book of Revelation differently from them. The book tolerates a wide spectrum of approaches, but the common denominator of all is the ultimate triumph of Jesus Christ, who culminates history with His final coming and reigns with and through His church forever.

The most popularized and widely discussed approach is called the Dispensationalist interpretation. This proposes that the Rapture of the church is referred to in v. 1, at which time the redeemed in Christ are translated into heaven at His coming "in the air" (1 Thess. 4:17). Rev. 6—18 are perceived as the Great Tribulation (Matt. 24:21) or the wrath of God (1 Thess. 5:9) from which believers are kept (Rev. 3:10). This approach sees national Israel as God's people on Earth at this time (the church having been raptured), restored to Jerusalem, protected by divine seal (7:1–8), worshiping in a rebuilt temple (11:1–3), and suffering at the hand of the Antichrist.

Not as widely published but at least equally widely believed is the Moderate Futurist view. This proposes the Book of Revelation as summarizing the conclusion of the church's agelong procession through tribulation and triumph, warfare, and victory, and consummating in the climactic return of Jesus Christ for His church. The tribulation is generally viewed as agelong, but increasing in intensity, so that the church is understood as present through much of Earth's turmoil until just prior to the outpouring of the "bowls full of the wrath of God" (15:7). This occurs during ch. 16 and culminates in the collapse of the present world order (chs. 17; 18).

Among other views are these: 1) The Historic position sees Rev. as a symbolic prophecy of the whole of church history, with the events of the book a picture of the events and movements that have shaped the conflict and progress of the Christian church. 2) The Preterist views Rev. as a message of hope and comfort to first-century believers only, offering them an expectation of their deliverance from Roman persecution and oppression. 3) The Idealist formulates no particular historical focus or effort at interpreting specifics of the book, rather seeing it as a broad, poetic portrayal of the conflict between the kingdom of God and the powers of Satan.

(1 John 2:18/Obad. 15) J.W.H.

2 Immediately [a]I was in the Spirit;
and behold, [b]a throne set in heaven,
and *One* sat on the throne.
3 [1]And He who sat there was [a]like a
jasper and a sardius stone in appearance; [b]and *there was* a rainbow
around the throne, in appearance like
an emerald.

2 [a]Rev. 1:10 [b]1 Kin. 22:19; Is. 6:1; Ezek. 1:26; Dan. 7:9; Rev. 3:21; 4:9
3 [a]Matt. 5:8; Rev. 21:11 [b]Gen. 9:13–17; Ezek. 1:28; Rev. 10:1 [1]M omits *And He who sat there was,* making the following a description of the throne.

3:22 See section 4 of Truth-In-Action at the end of Rev.

4:1—5:14 The visions recorded in these chapters prepare for the opening of the seven seals by declaring the power of God as Creator and the love of God as Redeemer.

4:1 A door *standing* open in heaven is the door of prophetic revelation. **The first voice** was that of the Lord Jesus Christ (1:10). The Lord summoned John to **come** in order that he might receive a heavenly perspective of **things which must take place** on Earth. John did not record the events in chronological order.

The recurrences of the **after these things** (for example, v. 1; 7:1, 9) and such phrases as "and I saw . . ." (10:1), "*Then I was . . .* " (11:1), and "Now a great sign . . ." (12:1) refer only to the sequence of John's receiving them. This is the same as is commonly found among all biblical prophets, who report when they saw a vision (for example, Is. 6:1; Jer. 25:1; Ezek. 20:1). The order in their reporting the prophetic vision is not necessarily intended to suggest a sequential order with the occurrences of fulfillment.

DISPENSATIONAL INTERPRETATION: This chapter division is critical for interpreting the remainder of Rev. See note on 1:19. John's hearing **a trumpet** and being asked to **come up** to the throne are seen as symbolic of the "catching away" (Rapture) of the church prior to the Great Tribulation. (See note on 3:10, "Dispensational Interpretation." This interpretation views the church's departure to heaven at this point [4:1] as the reason that the word "church" does not appear again until 22:16. Alternate views of the timing of the Rapture are noted at 6:17 and 19:14.)

4:2 I was in the Spirit denotes a state of heightened spiritual sensitivity (1:10). The ***One*** who **sat on the throne** is identified in v. 8 as God, who is described not in form, but in terms of brilliance and glory (see Ezek. 1:16–28).

4:3 Jasper is probably a diamond (see 21:11), suggesting purity or holiness. **Sardius** is carnelian, deep red, picturing God's avenging wrath. **Emerald** is green, the dominant color in a **rainbow,** symbolizing mercy (Gen. 9:12–15).

4 [a]Around the throne *were* twenty-
four thrones, and on the thrones I saw
twenty-four elders sitting, [b]clothed in
white [1]robes; and they had crowns of
gold on their heads.
5 And from the throne proceeded
[a]lightnings, [1]thunderings, and voices.
[b]Seven lamps of fire *were* burning before the throne, which are [c]the[2] seven
Spirits of God.
6 Before the throne *there* [1]*was* [a]a
sea of glass, like crystal. [b]And in
the midst of the throne, and around the
throne, *were* four living creatures full
of eyes in front and in back.
7 [a]The first living creature *was* like
a lion, the second living creature like
a calf, the third living creature had a
face like a man, and the fourth living
creature *was* like a flying eagle.
8 *The* four living creatures, each having [a]six wings, were full of eyes around
and within. And they do not rest day
or night, saying:

[b]"Holy,[1] holy, holy,
[c]Lord God Almighty,
[d]Who was and is and is to come!"

9 Whenever the living creatures give
glory and honor and thanks to Him
who sits on the throne, [a]who lives forever and ever,
10 [a]the twenty-four elders fall down
before Him who sits on the throne and
worship Him who lives forever and
ever, and cast their crowns before the
throne, saying:

11 "You[a] are worthy, [1]O Lord,
To receive glory and honor and
power;
[b]For You created all things,
And by [c]Your will they [2]exist and
were created."

4 [a]Rev. 11:16 [b]Rev. 3:4, 5 [1]NU, M *robes, with crowns*
5 [a]Rev. 8:5; 11:19; 16:18 [b]Ex. 37:23 [c][Rev. 1:4] [1]NU, M *voices, and thunderings.* [2]M omits *the*
6 [a]Rev. 15:2 [b]Ezek. 1:5 [1]NU, M add *something like*
7 [a]Ezek. 1:10; 10:14
8 [a]Is. 6:2 [b]Is. 6:3 [c]Rev. 1:8 [d]Rev. 1:4 [1]M has *holy* nine times.
9 [a]Rev. 1:18
10 [a]Rev. 5:8, 14; 7:11; 11:16; 19:4
11 [a]Rev. 1:6; 5:12 [b]Gen. 1:1 [c]Col. 1:16 [1]NU, M *our Lord and God* [2]NU, M *existed*

CHAPTER 5

1 [a]Ezek. 2:9, 10 [b]Is. 29:11
2 [a]Rev. 4:11; 5:9
3 *See WW at Jude 24.
4 [1]NU, M omit *and read* *See WW at Mark 13:14.
5 [a]Gen. 49:9 [b]Heb. 7:14 [c]Is. 11:1, 10 [d]Rev. 3:21 [e]Rev. 6:1 [1]NU, M omit *to loose*
6 [1]NU, M *I saw in the midst . . . a Lamb standing*

WORD WEALTH

4:10 worship, *proskuneo* (pros-koo-*neh*-oh); Strong's *#4352:* From *pros,* "toward," and *kuneo,* "to kiss." To prostrate oneself, bow down, do obeisance, show reverence, do homage, worship, adore. In the NT the word especially denotes homage rendered to God and the ascended Christ. All believers have a one-dimensional worship, to the only Lord and Savior. We do not worship angels, saints, shrines, relics, or religious personages.

The Lamb Takes the Scroll

5 And I saw in the right *hand* of Him
who sat on the throne [a]a scroll
written inside and on the back, [b]sealed
with seven seals.
2 Then I saw a strong angel proclaiming with a loud voice, [a]"Who is
worthy to open the scroll and to loose
its seals?"
3 And no one in heaven or on the
earth or under the earth *was able to
open the scroll, or to look at it.
4 So I wept much, because no one
was found worthy to open [1]and *read
the scroll, or to look at it.
5 But one of the elders said to me,
"Do not weep. Behold, [a]the Lion of the
tribe of [b]Judah, [c]the Root of David, has
[d]prevailed to open the scroll [e]and
[1]to loose its seven seals."
6 And I looked, [1]and behold, in the
midst of the throne and of the four living creatures, and in the midst of the

4:4 Twenty-four elders are the celestial representatives of all the redeemed, glorified and enthroned, who worship continuously. **White robes** symbolize purity. The **crowns** suggest victory and joy, not political authority.
4:5 Lightnings and **thunderings** describe the awesome and wondrous power of God. **Seven lamps of fire** represent **the seven Spirits of God,** the Holy Spirit. See note on 1:4.
4:6 Sea of glass, like crystal denotes the unapproachableness and majesty of God (see Ex. 24:10; Ezek. 1:26). **Four living creatures** are cherubim, the highest ranking celestial beings; they represent all the vital forces of creation whose primary function is worship. **Full of eyes** symbolizes unceasing watchfulness.
4:7 The four symbols suggest majestic courage, strength, intelligence, and speed in the service of the Creator. There is no biblical basis for the tradition attributing these symbols to the four Gospels.
4:8 The holiness, omnipotence, and eternity of God are praised in this first of 20 chorales, which interpret the meaning of many of the visions throughout Revelation.
4:9–11 The twenty-four elders reverentially acknowledge the One from whom all blessings flow, and join in an antiphonal praise to God as Creator. See note on v. 4.

DISPENSATIONAL INTERPRETATION sees in vv. 4–11 evidence of the church's exemption from the Great Tribulation in that these **elders,** who are seen as representative of the faithful overcomers of the church, are already glorified, enthroned, and crowned (see 3:10; John 5:24; 1 Thess. 1:1–10; 5:1–11).

5:1 The right *hand* is the symbol of power and authority. The **scroll** is the redemptive plan of God, foreshadowed in the OT, inaugurated in Jesus Christ and now revealed in its victorious consummation (see Ezek. 2:9, 10; Heb. 2:5–10). **Written inside and on the back** and **sealed with seven seals** indicates that nothing can be added to God's Last Will and Testament.
5:2–4 No creature, celestial or earthly, **is worthy** to reveal or execute God's plan for "the fullness of the times" (Eph. 1:9, 10).
5:5 The Lion: Christ is the greatest member **of the tribe of Judah** (see Gen. 49:9, 10). **The Root of David:** Messianic prophecy spoke of an ideal king of David's line who would combine power and goodness (see Is. 11:1, 10; Jer. 23:5; Zech. 3:8).
5:6 Instead of a Lion, the emblem of strength, John saw **a Lamb,** the symbol of meekness and of sacrificial offering.

elders, stood [a]a *Lamb as though it had
been slain, having seven horns and
[b]seven eyes, which are [c]the seven
Spirits of God sent out into all the
earth.
7 Then He came and took the scroll
out of the right hand [a]of Him who sat
on the throne.

Worthy Is the Lamb

8 Now when He had taken the scroll,
[a]the four living creatures and the
twenty-four elders fell down before the
Lamb, each having a harp, and golden
bowls full of incense, which are the
[b]prayers of the saints.
9 And [a]they sang a new song, saying:

[b]"You are worthy to take the scroll,
And to open its seals;
For You were slain,
And [c]have redeemed us to God
[d]by Your blood
Out of every tribe and tongue and
people and nation,
10 And have made [1]us [a]kings[2] and
[b]priests to our God;
And [3]we shall reign on the earth."

KINGDOM DYNAMICS

5:8–10 Destined for Victory, WORLD EVANGELISM. The Book of Revelation prophetically describes the depth of penetration the gospel will have on the nations. 1) In vv. 8–10 John's vision assures people out of every tribe, tongue, people and nation will be redeemed by the blood of Christ; and 2) that they will learn their role of intercession and authority as believers as they function as kings and priests, reigning "in Christ" while on Earth, in His kingdom authority (vv. 8, 10). Further, Rev. unveils the fact that the spiritual war will continue until "the kingdoms of this world have become *the kingdoms* of our Lord and of His Christ, and He shall reign forever and ever" (11:15). The messenger (the evangel) is to go to all who dwell on Earth—to every nation, tribe, tongue, and people (14:6, 7). Rev. 7:9–12 forecasts the ultimate consummation of the Great Commission at work as a countless number from every people gather at God's eternal throne. Let this profound prophetic vision motivate us as we embrace Jesus. We are destined for triumph!

(Gal. 6:7, 8/Ps. 2:8*) G.C.

6 [a]Is. 53:7; [John 1:29; 1 Pet. 1:19] [b]Zech. 3:9; 4:10 [c]Rev. 1:4; 3:1; 4:5 *See WW at Rev. 6:1.
7 [a]Rev. 4:2
8 [a]Rev. 4:8–10; 19:4 [b]Ps. 141:2; Rev. 8:3
9 [a]Rev. 14:3 [b]Rev. 4:11 [c]John 1:29 [d][Heb. 9:12; 1 Pet. 1:18, 19]
10 [a]Ex. 19:6 [b]Is. 61:6 [1]NU, M *them* [2]NU *a kingdom* [3]NU, M *they*
12 *See WW at Acts 6:10.
13 [a]Phil. 2:10; Rev. 5:3 [b]1 Chr. 29:11; Rom. 9:5; 1 Tim. 6:16; 1 Pet. 4:11 [c]Rev. 4:2, 3; 6:16; 20:11 [1]M adds *Amen* *See WW at 1 Tim. 6:16.

11 Then I looked, and I heard the voice
of many angels around the throne, the
living creatures, and the elders; and
the number of them was ten thousand
times ten thousand, and thousands of
thousands,
12 saying with a loud voice:

"Worthy is the Lamb who was
slain
To receive power and riches and
*wisdom,
And strength and honor and glory
and blessing!"

13 And [a]every **creature** which is in
heaven and on the earth and under the
earth and such as are in the sea, and
all that are in them, I heard saying:

[b]"Blessing and honor and glory and
*power
Be to Him [c]who sits on the throne,
And to the Lamb, forever and
[1]ever!"

WORD WEALTH

5:13 creature, *ktisma* (*ktis*-mah); Strong's *#2938:* The created thing, formation, product, the thing founded. In nonbiblical Greek it described founding a town, building it, and then colonizing it. The word comes from *ktizo,* "to build." *Ktisma* denotes the component parts of creation. The Creator called every one of them into existence. In v. 13, heaven as well as Earth's creatures exist only to glorify God and the Lamb of God.

The fact that the Lamb was **slain,** but is living, shows that He has overcome. God's purpose, concealed for ages, can now be revealed and accomplished (see Is. 53; John 1:29, 36). **Seven horns** denote complete and perfect power. **Seven eyes** represent complete and perfect knowledge and insight. **Seven Spirits:** See Introduction to Revelation: The Holy Spirit at Work.

5:7 *This picture is the fulfillment of Dan.* 7:9–14. Compare the description of "the Ancient of Days" in Dan. with the "*One* like the Son of Man" in Rev. 1:13–16.

5:8 Incense represents (Ps. 141:2) and purifies **the prayers of the saints,** redeemed sinners, which are presented by **the twenty-four elders.**

5:9 They sang a new song (Ps. 33:3; 40:3; 96:1; 98:1; 144:9; 149:1; Is. 42:1–13) in response to God's new redemptive act in history: God in Christ has inaugurated the church age (14:1–5). The same ascription of praise is accorded to the Lamb as to the Creator (4:11).

5:10 As a royal priesthood the saints **reign** *now* with Christ **on the earth** by their worship, their prayers, and their witness in word and deed. This sense of praise is in progress *now* and throughout redemptive history (see 1:6).

5:13, 14 Every created being joins the cosmic chorus, and ascribes to **the Lamb** every attribute of God. All history is moving toward the predestined goal of the eventual and ultimate universal recognition of the lordship of Jesus Christ (see Phil. 2:10, 11). **Amen:** "Yes, it is true!"

14 Then the four living creatures said,
"Amen!" And the [1]twenty-four elders
fell down and *worshiped [2]Him who
lives forever and ever.

First Seal: The Conqueror

6 Now [a]I saw when the **Lamb** opened
one of the [1]seals; and I heard
[b]one of the four living creatures saying
with a voice like thunder, "Come and
see."

WORD WEALTH

6:1 Lamb, *arnion* (ar-*nee*-on); Strong's *#721:* Originally, a little lamb, but the diminutive force is largely missing in the NT. In John 21:15, *arnion* is used of young believers, while 29 times in Rev. it is the title of the exalted Christ. *Arnion* is in direct contrast to the beast. The beast is savage, cruel, hostile, and destructive. By contradistinction our Lord as a lamb is gentle, compassionate, loving, and kind, innocently suffering and dying to atone for our sins. In Rev., lion and lamb combine the two elements of majesty and meekness.

2 And I looked, and behold, [a]a white
horse. [b]He who sat on it had a bow;
[c]and a crown was given to him, and
he went out [d]conquering and to conquer.

Second Seal: Conflict on Earth

3 When He opened the second seal,
[a]I heard the second living creature saying, "Come [1]and see."

14 [1]NU, M omit *twenty-four* [2]NU, M omit *Him who lives forever and ever*
*See WW at Rev. 4:10.

CHAPTER 6

1 [a]Is. 53:7; [John 1:29; Rev. 5:5–7, 12; 13:8] [b]Rev. 4:7 [1]NU, M *seven seals*
2 [a]Zech. 1:8; 6:3 [b]Ps. 45:4, 5, LXX [c]Zech. 6:11; Rev. 9:7; 14:14; 19:12 [d]Matt. 24:5; Rev. 3:21
3 [a]Rev. 4:7 [1]NU, M omit *and see*
4 [a]Zech. 1:8; 6:2 [b]Matt. 24:6, 7
5 [a]Rev. 4:7 [b]Zech. 6:2, 6 [c]Matt. 24:7 [1]*balances*
6 [a]Rev. 7:3; 9:4 [1]Gr. *choinix,* about 1 quart [2]About 1 day's wage for a worker
*See WW at Acts 25:10.
7 [a]Rev. 4:7
8 [a]Zech. 6:3 [b]Jer. 14:12; 15:2; 24:10; 29:17; Ezek. 5:12, 17; 14:21; 29:5; Matt. 24:9 [c]Lev. 26:22 [1]*authority*
9 [a]Rev. 8:3 [b][Rev. 20:4] [c]Rev. 1:2, 9

4 [a]Another horse, fiery red, went out.
And it was granted to the one who sat
on it to [b]take peace from the earth, and
that *people* should kill one another;
and there was given to him a great
sword.

Third Seal: Scarcity on Earth

5 When He opened the third seal,
[a]I heard the third living creature say,
"Come and see." So I looked, and behold, [b]a black horse, and he who sat
on it had a pair of [c]scales[1] in his hand.
6 And I heard a voice in the midst of
the four living creatures saying, "A
[1]quart of wheat for a [2]denarius, and
three quarts of barley for a denarius;
and [a]do not *harm the oil and the
wine."

Fourth Seal: Widespread Death on Earth

7 When He opened the fourth seal,
[a]I heard the voice of the fourth living
creature saying, "Come and see."
8 [a]So I looked, and behold, a pale
horse. And the name of him who sat
on it was Death, and Hades followed
with him. And [1]power was given to
them over a fourth of the earth,
[b]to kill with sword, with hunger, with
death, [c]and by the beasts of the earth.

Fifth Seal: The Cry of the Martyrs

9 When He opened the fifth seal, I
saw under [a]the altar [b]the souls of those
who had been slain [c]for the word of

6:1—8:1 The seals: The scroll cannot be unrolled until all seven seals are broken. Zechariah's visions of the four horsemen who patrol the Earth (see Zech. 1:8–10; 6:1–7) may have been creatively utilized here. An alternate Greek textual reading, **Come!,** which is a command addressed to each of the horsemen, is preferred by many to the **come and see** addressed here to John. The One on the throne is in complete control of the tragic consequences of sin in history and uses them to accomplish His purposes (Ezek. 14:21).

6:1, 2 Many see the rider on the **white horse** as the symbol of international power politics in the form of military conquest. Some others see the white horse rider as Christ continuing to move in triumph through His church during the throes of the following events, **conquering** through tribulation **and to conquer** ultimately over all (19:11—see 19:1–16).

DISPENSATIONAL INTERPRETATION: Dispensationalists view v. 1 as the beginning of the Great Tribulation, and the white horse rider (v. 2) as a counterfeit christ riding to win the world's adulation and submission (see Dan. 7:7).

6:3, 4 The rider on the **horse, fiery red,** is the symbol of civil war and strife.

6:5, 6 The rider on the **black horse** is the symbol of economic disruption. The problem is not famine, but inflation and scarcity. A **denarius** was the daily wage for a laborer, which ordinarily would buy eight times the amount of **wheat** and **barley** as under these conditions. **The oil and the wine,** symbolic of luxuries, likely means the famine is viewed as limited. It does not depict worldwide, rampant starvation.

6:7, 8 Pale, a yellowish-green color, represents disease and death. **Hades:** The grave. **Over a fourth:** The devastation is limited in scope.

6:9–11 Under the altar: In ancient sacrifices, the blood, which symbolized life, was poured out at the base of the altar. John saw **the souls of** all the Christian martyrs up until the time of the writing of Rev., and by implication, until the Second Coming of Christ. They were praying for the vindication of God's justice, not for vengeance. **Those who dwell on the earth:** See note on 3:10. **White robe** represents purity and victory. **Rest a little while longer:** God patiently delays the Final Judgment to give evildoers the opportunity to repent, even though His saints continue to suffer. God is concerned for justice, but even more for mercy.

The five seals refer to military conflict and conquest, civil war, economic disruption, pestilence, murder, accidents, and persecutions (see Luke 21:9).

DISPENSATIONAL INTERPRETATION: The martyred **souls** (vv. 9–11) represent some of the Great Tribulation

God and for [d]the *testimony which they held.

10 And they cried with a loud voice, saying, [a]"How long, O *Lord, [b]holy and true, [c]until You judge and avenge our blood on those who dwell on the earth?"

11 Then a [a]white robe was given to each of them; and it was said to them [b]that they should *rest a little while longer, until both *the number of* their fellow servants and their brethren, who would be killed as they *were*, was completed.

Sixth Seal: Cosmic Disturbances

12 I looked when He opened the sixth seal, [a]and [1]behold, there was a great earthquake; and [b]the sun became black as sackcloth of hair, and the [2]moon became like blood.

13 [a]And the stars of heaven fell to the earth, as a fig tree drops its late figs when it is shaken by a mighty wind.

14 [a]Then the sky [1]receded as a scroll when it is rolled up, and [b]every mountain and island was moved out of its place.

15 And the [a]kings of the earth, the great men, [1]the rich men, the commanders, the mighty men, every slave and every **free** man, [b]hid themselves in the caves and in the rocks of the mountains,

9 [d]2 Tim. 1:8 *See WW at John 19:35.
10 [a]Zech. 1:12 [b]Rev. 3:7 [c]Rev. 11:18 *See WW at Jude 4.
11 [a]Rev. 3:4, 5; 7:9 [b]Heb. 11:40 *See WW at Rev. 14:13.
12 [a]Matt. 24:7 [b]Joel 2:10, 31; 3:15 [1]NU, M omit *behold* [2]NU, M *whole moon*
13 [a]Rev. 8:10; 9:1
14 [a]Is. 34:4 [b]Rev. 16:20 [1]Or *split apart*
15 [a]Ps. 2:2–4 [b]Is. 2:10, 19, 21; 24:21 [1]NU, M *the commanders, the rich men,*
16 [a]Luke 23:29, 30 [b]Rev. 20:11
17 [a]Zeph. 1:14

CHAPTER 7

1 [a]Dan. 7:2 [b]Rev. 7:3; 8:7; 9:4 *See WW at Matt. 4:11.
3 [a]Rev. 6:6 [b]Rev. 22:4
4 [a]Rev. 9:16 [b]Rev. 14:1, 3

WORD WEALTH

6:15 free, *eleutheros* (el-yoo-ther-oss); Strong's *#1658:* Freeborn, exempt from legal obligation, unconstrained. It is the opposite of enslaved. The word is derived from the verb *eleuthomai,* "to come, go," thus describing the freedom to go where one chooses.

16 [a]and said to the mountains and rocks, "Fall on us and hide us from the face of Him who [b]sits on the throne and from the wrath of the Lamb!

17 "For the great day of His wrath has come, [a]and who is able to stand?"

The Sealed of Israel

7 After these things I saw four *angels standing at the four corners of the earth, [a]holding the four winds of the earth, [b]that the wind should not blow on the earth, on the sea, or on any tree.

2 Then I saw another angel ascending from the east, having the seal of the living God. And he cried with a loud voice to the four angels to whom it was granted to harm the earth and the sea,

3 saying, [a]"Do not harm the earth, the sea, or the trees till we have sealed the servants of our God [b]on their foreheads."

4 [a]And I heard the number of those who were sealed. [b]One hundred *and*

saints. It seems obvious that all who receive Jesus Christ during this time are martyred, except the remnant of Israel who are sealed for protection. See notes on 7:4–8 and 7:9–17, "Dispensational Interpretation."

6:12–17 The sixth seal describes a cosmic catastrophe inconceivable to the human mind; it is not to be interpreted literally. Seven structures of creation and seven classes of men are affected (see Heb. 12:27; Luke 23:27–30; Is. 2:2, 17; Hos. 10:8). This appears to be the final Day of the Lord, **the great day of His wrath.** See note on Obad. 15. But it has its precursors in social upheavals and the rise and fall of empires and civilizations throughout history. **Fall . . . hide us:** The unsaved do not repent, but "pray" to "nature" for deliverance. The question **who is able to stand?** is answered in the two interlude visions.

6:17 The great day of His wrath: The "prewrath Rapture" view sees the promise of 1 Thess. 4:17 and Rev. 4:10 being fulfilled just prior to this event. The church is "kept out of" this hour of consummate judgment upon the Earth, but is present during the earlier segments of the Great Tribulation (6:1–12) in accordance with Jesus' words in Matt. 24:29–31.

7:1–8 *The first interlude pictures the sealing of the redeemed in order that they may survive the terrors associated with the day of wrath.*

7:1 The four winds of the earth are evil forces of devastation controlled by **four angels.**

7:2, 3 The east symbolizes the source of blessing. **The seal** is the invisible sign of God's protection, not from tribulation and death, but from God's wrath. See Ezek. 9:4–6; Eph. 1:13. Those sealed by the Holy Spirit are God's possession, in dramatic contrast to those who bear "the mark of the beast" (see note on 13:6, 17).

7:4–17 In the first interlude (vv. 4–8), **one hundred and forty-four thousand** symbolizes completeness. A thousand was the basic military division in the camp of Israel (Num. 31:4, 5), the result of 10x10x10, a perfect cube symbolizing completeness, multiplied by 144, or 12x12, symbolizing the faithful remnant of the Old plus the New Israel (that is, the church—including believing Jews and Gentiles). This results in the complete spiritual Israel (see note on Gal. 6:16)—the entire church militant upon the Earth (14:1–5).

The second interlude (vv. 9–17) pictures the blessed state of the redeemed in heaven. This is the church triumphant, the innumerable cloud of witnesses constantly surrounding the church militant (Heb. 12:1).

DISPENSATIONAL INTERPRETATION: According to this viewpoint, the sealing of the 144,000 (vv. 4–8) is that of a literal band of Jews, alive at that time and the godly remnant of national Israel on Earth during the Great Tribulation. That they are physical Jews (as opposed to "spiritual") is noted by the fact a detailed listing of the 12 tribes is given (vv. 5–8). The Scriptures teach that the Lord will sovereignly deal with national Israel before the kingdom is consummated (see Zech. 12:10–13; Rom. 11:26–32). Without this seal, all who witness to the true God during the Great Tribulation will be martyred, except the 144,000 "sealed" Jewish remnant.

forty-four thousand [c]of all the tribes of the children of Israel *were* sealed:

5 of the tribe of Judah
twelve thousand *were* sealed;
of the tribe of Reuben
twelve thousand *were* [1]sealed;
of the tribe of Gad
twelve thousand *were* sealed;
6 of the tribe of Asher
twelve thousand *were* sealed;
of the tribe of Naphtali
twelve thousand *were* sealed;
of the tribe of Manasseh
twelve thousand *were* sealed;
7 of the tribe of Simeon
twelve thousand *were* sealed;
of the tribe of Levi
twelve thousand *were* sealed;
of the tribe of Issachar
twelve thousand *were* sealed;
8 of the tribe of Zebulun
twelve thousand *were* sealed;
of the tribe of Joseph
twelve thousand *were* sealed;
of the tribe of Benjamin
twelve thousand *were* sealed.

A Multitude from the Great Tribulation

9 After these things I looked, and behold, [a]a great multitude which no one could number, [b]of all nations, tribes, peoples, and tongues, standing before the throne and before the Lamb, [c]clothed with white robes, with palm branches in their hands,
10 and crying out with a loud voice, saying, [a]"Salvation *belongs* to our God [b]who sits on the throne, and to the Lamb!"
11 [a]All the angels stood around the throne and the elders and the four living creatures, and fell on their faces before the throne and [b]worshiped God,
12 [a]saying:

"Amen! Blessing and glory and wisdom,
Thanksgiving and honor and power and might,
Be to our God forever and ever. Amen."

13 Then one of the elders answered, saying to me, "Who are these arrayed in [a]white robes, and where did they come from?"
14 And I said to him, [1]"Sir, you know." So he said to me, [a]"These are the ones who come out of the great *tribulation, and [b]washed their robes and made them white in the blood of the *Lamb.
15 "Therefore they are before the throne of God, and serve Him day and night in His temple. And He who sits on the throne will [a]dwell among them.
16 [a]"They shall neither hunger anymore nor thirst anymore; [b]the sun shall not strike them, nor any heat;
17 "for the Lamb who is in the midst of the throne [a]will shepherd them and lead them to [1]living fountains of waters. [b]And God will *wipe away every tear from their eyes."

Seventh Seal: Prelude to the Seven Trumpets

8 When[a] He opened the seventh seal, there was silence in heaven for about half an hour.
2 [a]And I saw the seven angels who stand before God, [b]and to them were given seven trumpets.
3 Then another angel, having a golden censer, came and stood at the

4 [c]Gen. 49:1–27
5 [1]NU, M omit *sealed* in vv. 5b–8b.
9 [a]Is. 60:1–5; Rom. 11:25 [b]Rev. 5:9 [c]Rev. 3:5, 18; 4:4; 6:11
10 [a]Ps. 3:8; Is. 43:11; Jer. 3:23; Hos. 13:4; Rev. 19:1 [b]Rev. 5:13
11 [a]Rev. 4:6 [b]Rev. 4:11; 5:9, 12, 14; 11:16
12 [a]Rev. 5:13, 14
13 [a]Rev. 7:9
14 [a]Rev. 6:9 [b]Is. 1:18; Zech. 3:3–5; [Heb. 9:14] [1]NU, M *My lord* *See WW at John 16:33. • See WW at Rev. 6:1.
15 [a]Is. 4:5, 6; Rev. 21:3
16 [a]Ps. 121:5; Is. 49:10 [b]Ps. 121:6; Rev. 21:4
17 [a]Ps. 23:1; Matt. 2:6; [John 10:11, 14] [b]Is. 25:8; Matt. 5:4; Rev. 21:4 [1]NU, M *fountains of the waters of life* *See WW at Col. 2:14.

CHAPTER 8

1 [a]Rev. 6:1
2 [a][Matt. 18:10]; Luke 1:19 [b]2 Chr. 29:25–28

7:9 A great multitude is all the redeemed out of all people groups throughout all of history. **White robes** and **palm branches** symbolize righteousness and victory.
7:11, 12 A sevenfold ascription of adoration.
7:14 The ones who come out of: Literally, "ones coming out," a present participle, expressing a continuous and repeated action, not a once-for-all action. This is not a postconsummation picture. Therefore, tribulation is to some degree taking place throughout the entire church age (see 1:9; 2:9, 22; Matt. 13:21; John 16:33; Acts 14:22; Rom. 8:35, 36; 12:12. The **great tribulation** describes the acceleration and intensification of troublesome times as this Age comes to an end, climaxing with the Rapture and Second Coming. **Made them white** represents the imputed righteousness of Christ.
7:15 Dwell: Literally "spread His tabernacle over them."
7:17 The Lamb is the **shepherd:** See Ps. 23:2; Is. 25:8; Ezek. 34:23.
8:1 All **heaven** waits in awestruck anticipation for the fulfillment of God's purpose. **About half an hour** signifies a brief, limited period.
DISPENSATIONAL INTERPRETATION: **The seventh seal** (v. 1) comprises the seven trumpet judgments (8:7—9:21; 11:15–19).
8:2—11:18 The **seven trumpets** announce severe judgment in response to the prayers of the saints. It was a common belief in intertestamental Judaism that **seven angels** "presented the prayers of the saints" (see Tobit 12:15). **Trumpets** are a warning signal and summons to repentance (see Ex. 19:16, 19). The plagues released by the blowing of the **trumpets** are reminiscent of the plagues of Egypt (see Ex. 7:17–21; 9:23–25; 10:21–23). The first four affect the natural world, and the last three affect the unredeemed. These calamities are symbolic, not literal; they are repetitive throughout history rather than consecutive; again, they will intensify as this Age closes. See note on 7:14.
8:3 The golden altar was the altar of incense (see 6:9; Ps. 141:2; Luke 1:8–10). **The prayers of all the saints** avail to bring upon the Earth God's judgments, which summon

altar. He was given much incense, that
he should offer *it* with [a]the prayers of
all the saints upon [b]the golden altar
which was before the throne.
4 And [a]the smoke of the incense, with
the prayers of the saints, ascended before God from the angel's hand.
5 Then the angel took the censer,
filled it with fire from the altar, and
threw *it* to the earth. And [a]there were
noises, thunderings, [b]lightnings, [c]and
an earthquake.
6 So the seven angels who had the
seven trumpets *prepared themselves
to sound.

First Trumpet: Vegetation Struck

7 The first angel sounded: [a]And hail
and fire followed, mingled with blood,
and they were thrown [b]to the [1]earth.
And a third [c]of the trees were burned
up, and all green grass was burned
up.

Second Trumpet: The Seas Struck

8 Then the second angel sounded:
[a]And *something* like a great mountain
burning with fire was thrown into the
sea, [b]and a third of the sea [c]became
blood.
9 [a]And a third of the living *creatures
in the sea died, and a third of the ships
were destroyed.

Third Trumpet: The Waters Struck

10 Then the third angel sounded:
[a]And a great star fell from heaven,
burning like a torch, [b]and it fell on a
third of the rivers and on the springs
of water.
11 [a]The name of the star is Wormwood. [b]A third of the waters became
wormwood, and many men died from
the water, because it was made bitter.

Fourth Trumpet: The Heavens Struck

12 [a]Then the fourth angel sounded:
And a third of the sun was struck, a
third of the moon, and a third of the
stars, so that a third of them were darkened. A third of the day [1]did not shine,
and likewise the night.
13 And I looked, [a]and I heard an
[1]angel flying through the midst of
heaven, saying with a loud voice,
[b]"Woe, woe, woe to the inhabitants of
the earth, because of the remaining
blasts of the trumpet of the three angels who are about to sound!"

Fifth Trumpet: The Locusts from the Bottomless Pit

9 Then the fifth angel sounded:
[a]And I saw a star fallen from
heaven to the earth. To him was given
the key to [b]the [1]bottomless pit.
2 And he opened the bottomless pit,
and smoke arose out of the pit like the
smoke of a great furnace. So the
[a]sun and the air were darkened because of the smoke of the pit.
3 Then out of the smoke locusts came
upon the earth. And to them was given
power, [a]as the scorpions of the earth
have power.
4 They were commanded [a]not to
*harm [b]the grass of the earth, or any
green thing, or any tree, but only those
men who do not have [c]the seal of God
on their foreheads.
5 And [1]they were not given *authority*
to kill them, [a]but to torment them *for*
five months. Their torment *was* like the
torment of a scorpion when it strikes
a man.
6 In those days [a]men will seek death
and will not find it; they will desire to
die, and death will flee from them.
7 [a]The shape of the locusts was like
horses prepared for battle. [b]On their

3 [a]Rev. 5:8 [b]Ex. 30:1
4 [a]Ps. 141:2
5 [a]Rev. 11:19; 16:18 [b]Rev. 4:5 [c]2 Sam. 22:8
6 *See WW at Rev. 21:2.
7 [a]Ezek. 38:22 [b]Rev. 16:2 [c]Rev. 9:4, 15–18 [1]NU, M add *and a third of the earth was burned up*
8 [a]Jer. 51:25 [b]Ex. 7:17 [c]Ezek. 14:19
9 [a]Rev. 16:3 *See WW at Rev. 5:13.
10 [a]Is. 14:12 [b]Rev. 14:7; 16:4
11 [a]Ruth 1:20 [b]Ex. 15:23
12 [a]Is. 13:10 [1]*had no light*
13 [a]Rev. 14:6; 19:17 [b]Rev. 9:12; 11:14; 12:12 [1]NU, M *eagle*

CHAPTER 9

1 [a]Rev. 8:10 [b]Luke 8:31 [1]Lit. *shaft of the abyss*
2 [a]Joel 2:2, 10
3 [a]Judg. 7:12
4 [a]Rev. 6:6 [b]Rev. 8:7 [c]Rev. 7:2, 3 *See WW at Acts 25:10.
5 [a][Rev. 9:10; 11:7] [1]The locusts
6 [a]Jer. 8:3
7 [a]Joel 2:4 [b]Nah. 3:17

the rebellious to repentance and partially vindicate God's justice.

8:7 A third, a significant minority of **the earth** and its vegetation, man's environment, is devastated.

8:8, 9 A great mountain burning with fire suggests a volcano whose ashes pollute **the sea.**

8:10, 11 The fresh waters are polluted. **Wormwood:** A bitter herb, sometimes poisonous, symbolizes the tragic results of sin (see Jer. 9:15; 23:15).

8:12 These symbolic cosmic convulsions are partial *disruptions, not to be compared with the Final Coming of* Jesus.

8:13 An angel: The preferred marginal reading of "eagle" refers to a "vulture," a bird of prey.

9:1 A star fallen from heaven refers to an unidentified demonic being, possibly Satan himself, a fallen angel (see 9:11; 12:7–12; Is. 14:12–14; Ezek. 28:11–17). **The bottomless pit,** literally "the shaft of the abyss," is the reservoir of evil (see 9:11; 11:7; 17:8; 20:1–3).

9:2 Smoke is a symbol of deception.

9:3 Locusts symbolize demonic beings (see Ex. 10:12–15; Joel 1:1—2:11). **As the scorpions** is a simile indicating excruciating pain (Luke 10:19).

9:4 Demons cannot harm those who are sealed by God (Eph. 1:13).

DISPENSATIONAL INTERPRETATION: All people except the 144,000 Jewish remnant are exposed to these judgments. See note on 7:4–17, "Dispensational Interpretation."

9:5, 6 Five months represent a limited period of time, corresponding to the life cycle of a locust. **Torment:** The purpose is not to destroy, but to lead to repentance.

9:7–10 Locusts actually resemble little horses. The vivid symbolic description is intended to terrify.

heads were crowns of something like
gold, [c]and their faces *were* like the
faces of men.
8 They had hair like women's hair,
and [a]their teeth were like lions' *teeth.*
9 And they had breastplates like
breastplates of iron, and the sound of
their wings *was* [a]like the sound of
chariots with many horses running
into battle.
10 They had tails like scorpions, and
there were stings in their tails. Their
power *was* to hurt men five months.
11 And they had as king over them
[a]the angel of the bottomless pit, whose
name in Hebrew *is* [1]Abaddon, but in
Greek he has the name [2]Apollyon.
12 [a]One woe is past. Behold, still two
more woes are coming after these
things.

Sixth Trumpet: The Angels from the Euphrates

13 Then the sixth angel sounded: And
I heard a voice from the four horns of
the [a]golden altar which is before God,
14 saying to the sixth angel who had
the trumpet, "Release the four angels
who are bound [a]at the great river Euphrates."
15 So the four angels, who had been
prepared for the hour and day and
month and year, were released to kill
a [a]third of mankind.
16 Now [a]the number of the army
[b]of the horsemen *was* two hundred
million; [c]I heard the number of them.
17 And thus I saw the horses in the vision: those who sat on them had
breastplates of fiery red, hyacinth blue,
and sulfur yellow; [a]and the heads of
the horses *were* like the heads of lions;
and out of their mouths came fire,
smoke, and brimstone.
18 By these three *plagues* a third of
mankind was killed—by the fire and
the smoke and the brimstone which
came out of their mouths.
19 For [1]their power is in their mouth
and in their tails; [a]for their tails *are*
like serpents, having heads; and with
them they do harm.
20 But the rest of mankind, who were
not killed by these plagues, [a]did not
repent of the works of their hands, that
they should not worship [b]demons,
[c]and idols of gold, silver, brass, stone,
and wood, which can neither see nor
hear nor walk.
21 And they did not repent of their
murders [a]or their [1]**sorceries** or their
sexual immorality or their thefts.

7 [c]Dan. 7:8
8 [a]Joel 1:6
9 [a]Jer. 47:3; Joel 2:5–7
11 [a]Eph. 2:2 [1]Lit. *Destruction* [2]Lit. *Destroyer*
12 [a]Rev. 8:13; 11:14
13 [a]Rev. 8:3
14 [a]Gen. 15:18; Deut. 1:7; Josh. 1:4; Rev. 16:12
15 [a]Rev. 8:7–9; 9:18
16 [a]Ps. 68:17; Dan. 7:10 [b]Ezek. 38:4 [c]Rev. 7:4
17 [a]1 Chr. 12:8; Is. 5:28, 29
19 [a]Is. 9:15 [1]NU, M *the power of the horses*
20 [a]Deut. 31:29 [b]Lev. 17:7; Deut. 32:17; Ps. 106:37; 1 Cor. 10:20 [c]Ps. 115:4–7; 135:15–17; Dan. 5:23
21 [a]Rev. 21:8; 22:15 [1]NU, M *drugs*

CHAPTER 10

1 [a]Ezek. 1:26–28; Rev. 4:3 [b]Matt. 17:2; Rev. 1:16 [c]Rev. 1:15
2 [a]Ps. 95:5; Matt. 28:18
3 [a]Ps. 29:3–9; Rev. 4:5; 8:5
4 [a]Dan. 8:26; 12:4, 9; Rev. 22:10 [1]NU, M *sounded,* [2]NU, M omit *to me*

WORD WEALTH

9:21 sorceries, *pharmakeia* (far-mak-*eye*-ah); Strong's *#5331:* Compare "pharmacy" and "pharmacist." Generally described the use of medicine, drugs, or spells. Later the word was used of poisoning, and then of sorcery, accompanied by drugs, incantations, charms, and magic.

The Mighty Angel with the Little Book

10 I saw still another mighty angel
coming down from heaven,
clothed with a cloud. [a]And a rainbow
was on [b]his head, his face *was* like
the sun, and [c]his feet like pillars of
fire.
2 He had a little book open in his
hand. [a]And he set his right foot on the
sea and *his* left *foot* on the land,
3 and cried with a loud voice, as *when*
a lion roars. When he cried out,
[a]seven thunders uttered their voices.
4 Now when the seven thunders
[1]uttered their voices, I was about to
write; but I heard a voice from heaven
saying [2]to me, [a]"Seal up the things
which the seven thunders uttered, and
do not write them."

9:11, 12 These are not physical locusts (see Prov. 30:27), but demonic forces under the direction of **the angel** (see note on v. 1) named **Abaddon,** "Destruction" (see Job 26:6) or **Apollyon,** "Destroyer" (see 1 Cor. 10:10).
9:13 A voice comes in response to the prayers of the saints (see 6:10; 8:2–6).
9:14, 15 Release: God controls the time and the extent of the plague. **Euphrates:** Traditionally, the eastern boundary of the people of God, and also of the Roman Empire, the Euphrates is a symbolic restraint upon the forces of evil. **Angels . . . were released,** resulting in universal spiritual warfare.
9:16–19 I heard the number: John is unable to count the **two hundred million** of this demonic cavalry. Again, the description is intended to terrify.
DISPENSATIONAL INTERPRETATION: Literal armies from the East move toward national Israel in preparation for the Battle of Armageddon. See note on 16:12–16, "Dispensational Interpretation."
9:20, 21 The purpose of **these plagues** is to lead people to repentance. The unfortunate effect is the hardening of hearts (see Ex. 8:15–19).
10:1–11 Between the sounding of the sixth and the seventh trumpet a dramatic interlude reveals the mission of the church while the warning trumpets are being sounded.
10:1, 2 The **mighty angel,** similar in appearance to the "*One* like the Son of Man" (1:13–16), is obviously His special envoy. His stance indicates that he has a message for the whole world.
10:3 Seven thunders: The voice of the Lord (see John 12:27–31; Ps. 29).
10:4 The whole counsel of God has not been revealed (see Deut. 29:29; 1 Cor. 13:8–12).

5 The angel whom I saw standing on
the sea and on the land [a]raised* up his
[1]hand to heaven
6 and swore by Him who lives forever
and ever, [a]who created heaven and the
things that are in it, the earth and the
things that are in it, and the sea and
the things that are in it, [b]that there
should be delay no longer,
7 but [a]in the days of the sounding of
the seventh angel, when he is about to
sound, the mystery of God would be
finished, as He declared to His servants
the prophets.

John Eats the Little Book

8 Then the voice which I heard from
heaven spoke to me again and said,
"Go, take the little book which is open
in the hand of the angel who stands
on the sea and on the earth."
9 So I went to the angel and said to
him, "Give me the little book." And he
said to me, [a]"Take and eat it; and it
will make your stomach bitter, but it
will be as sweet as honey in your
mouth."
10 Then I took the little book out of
the angel's hand and ate it, [a]and it was
as sweet as honey in my mouth. But
when I had eaten it, [b]my stomach became bitter.
11 And [1]he said to me, "You must
prophesy again about many peoples,
nations, tongues, and kings."

The Two Witnesses

11 Then I was given [a]a reed like a
measuring rod. [1]And the angel
stood, saying, [b]"Rise and measure the
temple of God, the altar, and those who
worship there.
2 "But leave out [a]the court which is
outside the temple, and do not measure
it, [b]for it has been given to the Gentiles.
And they will [c]tread the holy city
underfoot *for* [d]forty-two months.
3 "And I will give *power* to my two
[a]witnesses, [b]and they will prophesy
[c]one thousand two hundred and sixty
days, clothed in sackcloth."
4 These are the [a]two olive trees and
the two lampstands standing before
the [1]God of the earth.
5 And if anyone wants to harm them,
[a]fire proceeds from their mouth and

5 [a]Dan. 12:7 [1]NU, M *right hand* *See WW at John 16:22.
6 [a]Rev. 4:11 [b]Rev. 16:17
7 [a]Rev. 11:15
9 [a]Jer. 15:16
10 [a]Ezek. 3:3 [b]Ezek. 2:10
11 [1]NU, M *they*

CHAPTER 11

1 [a]Ezek. 40:3—42:20 [b]Num. 23:18 [1]NU, M omit *And the angel stood*
2 [a]Ezek. 40:17, 20 [b]Ps. 79:1 [c]Dan. 8:10 [d]Rev. 12:6; 13:5
3 [a]Rev. 20:4 [b]Rev. 19:10 [c]Rev. 12:6
4 [a]Zech. 4:2, 3, 11, 14 [1]NU, M *Lord*
5 [a]2 Kin. 1:10–12

10:5–7 There is much that God does want us to know (see Deut. 29:29). **Raised up his hand** represents a solemn oath. **Delay no longer** refers to the fulfillment of God's purpose. **Mystery of God:** See 11:15–18; Rom. 16:25, 26; Eph. 1:9, 10; 3:1–11.

DISPENSATIONAL INTERPRETATION: **The mystery of God would be finished:** V. 7 correlates with Dan. 9:24, the finishing of God's final purpose concerning national Israel and the city of Jerusalem. Even though national Israel is promised deliverance, she must first experience suffering and judgment (see Jer. 15:10; 20:14–18). See also the note on Dan. 9:24, 26.

10:8 The little book is not the scroll which only the Lamb could unseal (see 5:1–14), since it is **open** (see v. 2). "The little book" is the gospel that John and the two witnesses are to proclaim (10:11; 11:3, 6, 7). It is possible, but improbable, that the reference is to chs. 12—22.

10:9–11 Eat: The message must saturate the personality of the proclaimer. **Bitter . . . sweet:** The message brings God's grace, love, and mercy; but when rejected it brings inevitable judgment (see Jer. 15:16; Ezek. 2:8; 3:1–3).

11:1–14 A second interlude presents another perspective on the witnessing church, especially amid tribulation and persecution.

11:1, 2 The **measuring rod** symbolizes either preservation or destruction (see Zech. 2:1—5:11; Ezek. 40:3—42:20); the context indicates preservation. **The temple of God** refers to the people of God, the body of Christ (see 1 Cor. 3:16; 2 Cor. 6:16; Eph. 2:19–22), not Herod's temple in Jerusalem, destroyed in A.D. 70, nor one purported to be rebuilt in the future. **The altar** is the altar of incense, symbolizing the prayers of the saints (see 5:8). **Those who worship there** are all the preserved saints. **The court . . .** of **the Gentiles** is not to be measured for protection. **Forty-two months,** or three and one-half years, suggests a limited time rather than literal time (see v. 3; 12:14). The horrible tribulation suffered by the Jews under Antiochus Epiphanes, which lasted from 168 to 165 B.C. (Dan. 7:25; 8:9–26; 9:24–27; 11:1–45; 12:7–12), became the symbol for all subsequent persecution of the faithful.

DISPENSATIONAL INTERPRETATION: Vv. 1, 2 depict Jewish **temple** worship restored in the first three and one-half years of the Great Tribulation, also known as Daniel's Seventieth Week. See note on Dan. 9:24–27. This is followed by "the abomination of desolation," a time when the Beast will demand that temple sacrifices cease, and his image be placed in the temple to be worshiped. See note on Dan. 9:26, 27. **They will tread . . . forty-two months:** This began about 605 B.C. with Judah's captivity under Nebuchadnezzar and will likely not end until the Second Coming (see 19:20, 21; Dan. 2:34, 35). Some interpreters, however, believe this was completed in 1967, when Israel captured Old Jerusalem in the Six Day War (see Luke 21:24).

Forty-two months as a time frame shows perfect harmony between Dan. and Rev. Daniel speaks of "70 weeks of years" (9:24–27), revealing that all prophetic history for this age will culminate in a final seventieth week of years. During this final seven-year period, every prophecy concerning national Israel and Jerusalem would be fulfilled literally. However, he spoke about this final week of years as being divided into two distinct three and one-half-year periods (Dan. 9:27), the last half being the Great Tribulation. This is the significance of Revelation's 42 months (11:2), 1,260 days (11:3; 12:6), and "time and times and half a time" (12:14). See note on Dan. 9:24, 26.

11:3–6 The **two witnesses,** identified as **the two olive trees** and **the two lampstands** are symbols of the witnessing church militant (see Zech. 4:1–4, 6, 10, 14), proclaiming the gospel accompanied by signs and wonders. They are purposely not identified as individuals, although they are reminiscent of Zerubbabel and Joshua (see Zech. 3:1—4:14), as well as Elijah (see 1 Kin. 17:1; 2 Kin. 1:10) and Moses (see Ex. 7—12). **Sackcloth:** Like the trumpet warnings, God's Word is a call to repentance (see Jer. 5:14).

devours their enemies. [b]And if anyone
wants to harm them, he must be killed
in this manner.
6 These [a]have power to shut heaven,
so that no rain falls in the days of their
prophecy; and they have power over
waters to turn them to blood, and to
strike the earth with all plagues, as often as they desire.

The Witnesses Killed

7 When they [a]finish their testimony,
[b]the beast that ascends [c]out of the
bottomless pit [d]will make war against
them, overcome them, and kill them.
8 And their dead bodies *will lie* in the
street of [a]the great city which **spiritually** is called Sodom and Egypt,
[b]where also [1]our Lord was crucified.

WORD WEALTH

11:8 spiritually, *pneumatikos* (pnyoo-mat-ik-*oce*); Strong's *#4153:* Compare "pneumonia," "pneumatic," "pneumatology." An adverb denoting a symbolical or spiritual sense. In 1 Cor. 2:14, the word is used to describe why natural reasoning cannot comprehend things of the spirit. They are discerned *pneumatikos,* with the aid of the Holy Spirit. Here Jerusalem is called "Sodom" for its gross spiritual perversity and "Egypt" for opposing God's plans and purposes.

9 [a]Then *those* from the peoples,
tribes, tongues, and nations [1]will see
their dead bodies three-and-a-half
days, [b]and not allow their dead bodies
to be put into graves.
10 [a]And those who dwell on the earth
will rejoice over them, make merry,
[b]and send gifts to one another, [c]be-
cause these two prophets tormented
those who dwell on the earth.

The Witnesses Resurrected

11 [a]Now after the three-and-a-half
days [b]the breath of life from God entered them, and they stood on their
feet, and great fear fell on those who
*saw them.
12 And [1]they heard a loud voice from
heaven saying to them, "Come up
here." [a]And they ascended to heaven
[b]in a cloud, [c]and their enemies saw
them.
13 In the same hour [a]there was a great
earthquake, [b]and a tenth of the city
fell. In the earthquake seven thousand
people were killed, and the rest were
afraid [c]and gave glory to the God of
heaven.
14 [a]The second woe is past. Behold,
the third woe is coming *quickly.

Seventh Trumpet: The Kingdom Proclaimed

15 Then [a]the seventh angel sounded:
[b]And there were loud voices in heaven,
saying, [c]"The [1]kingdoms of this *world
have become *the kingdoms* of our Lord

5 [b]Num. 16:29
6 [a]1 Kin. 17:1
7 [a]Luke 13:32 [b]Rev. 13:1, 11; 17:8 [c]Rev. 9:1, 2 [d]Dan. 7:21
8 [a]Rev. 14:8 [b]Heb. 13:12 [1]NU, M *their*
9 [a]Rev. 17:15 [b]Ps. 79:2, 3 [1]NU, M *see . . . and will not allow*
10 [a]Rev. 12:12 [b]Esth. 9:19, 22 [c]Rev. 16:10
11 [a]Rev. 11:9 [b]Ezek. 37:5, 9, 10 *See WW at John 20:14.
12 [a]Is. 14:13 [b]Acts 1:9 [c]2 Kin. 2:11, 12 [1]M *I*
13 [a]Rev. 6:12; 8:5; 11:19; 16:18 [b]Rev. 16:19 [c]Rev. 14:7; 16:9; 19:7
14 [a]Rev. 8:13; 9:12 *See WW at Rev. 22:20.
15 [a]Rev. 8:2; 10:7 [b]Is. 27:13 [c]Rev. 12:10 [1]NU, M *kingdom . . . has become the kingdom* *See WW at John 18:36.

11:7 The beast from the **bottomless pit** is pictured as actually functioning before the description of his origin, which is additional evidence that the visions are not in chronological order (see 13:1–10; 17:6–18). **Make war** is an appropriate description of the persecution of the church militant, not of just two individual prophets.
11:8 Their dead bodies: Literally "their corpse," in the singular, not plural, symbolizes the body of Christ that now appears to have been overcome (v. 7). **The great city** is not literally the physical city of Jerusalem, but **spiritually** the world in rebellion against God. **Sodom** symbolizes immorality, and **Egypt** symbolizes the political oppression of the people of God in this world where **our Lord was crucified.**
11:9, 10 Their dead bodies is literally "their corpse," singular again. **Three-and-a-half days** describes a very brief time, in contrast to the period of persecution (see 20:7–10). The second occurrence of **their dead bodies** is plural, indicating the individual members of the body of Christ. The final indignity was to leave them unburied. **Those who dwell on the earth:** See note on 3:10.
11:11, 12 Come up here: The witnessing church, symbolized by the two witnesses, is resurrected. In historical times and places the witnessing church has appeared to be destroyed, only to be resuscitated and revived by God (see Ezek. 37:1–14). With reference to the final resurrection of the church, this event is proleptic and not sequential (see 1 Thess. 4:13–17).
11:13 God's judgment falls on the world because of the persecution of His people (18:1—19:10). **Seven thousand** is a symbolic, not a literal, number, representing that which is complete but limited. **The rest** still have an opportunity to repent, but apparently they do not. They respond with fear and give **glory** to God only because of the tremendous manifestations of His power.
11:14 The third woe is only for "those who destroy the earth" (v. 18).

DISPENSATIONAL INTERPRETATION: Dispensationalists view vv. 3–14 as follows: **My two witnesses** are believed to be either Moses and Enoch or Moses and Elijah. Enoch and Elijah escaped physical death by translation; Moses was sovereignly taken from the grave and glorified (see Gen. 5:24; 2 Kin. 2:11; Matt. 17:3; Jude 9). There are some dispensational authors who feel this view is not consistent with the context because the two witnesses are killed and then resurrected. They feel this is unlikely with respect to the glorified men.

Whether or not they are literally Moses and Enoch or Moses and Elijah, these two men will certainly manifest power equal to these OT prophets. This is confirmed in the various symbolisms: **fire proceeds from their mouth,** they **shut heaven, so that no rain falls, they turn** [waters] **to blood,** and they work many other signs and miracles. **The beast** (who is the leader of a coalition, which will be termed "The United States of Europe") finally kills them, but not until **they finish their testimony** (v. 7).
11:15–18 The seventh trumpet presents the consummation of God's reign (10:6, 7).

and of His Christ, [d]and He shall reign
forever and ever!"
16 And [a]the twenty-four elders who
sat before God on their thrones fell on
their faces and [b]worshiped God,
17 saying:

"We *give You thanks, O Lord God
Almighty,
The One [a]who is and who was
[1]and who is to come,
Because You have taken Your
great power [b]and reigned.
18 The nations were [a]angry,* and
Your [1]wrath has come,
And the time of the [b]dead, that
they should be judged,
And that You should *reward
Your servants the prophets and
the saints,
And those who fear Your name,
small and great,
And should destroy those who
destroy the earth."

19 Then [a]the temple of God was
opened in heaven, and the ark of
[1]His covenant was seen in His temple.
And [b]there were lightnings, noises,
thunderings, an earthquake, [c]and
great hail.

15 [d]Ex. 15:18
16 [a]Rev. 4:4
[b]Rev. 4:11; 5:9, 12, 14; 7:11
17 [a]Rev. 16:5
[b]Rev. 19:6 [1]NU, M omit *and who is to come*
*See WW at John 6:11.
18 [a]Ps. 2:1
[b]Dan. 7:10
[1]*anger*
*See WW at Rev. 12:17. • See WW at Rev. 22:12.
19 [a]Rev. 4:1; 15:5, 8 [b]Rev. 8:5
[c]Rev. 16:21 [1]M *the covenant of the Lord*

CHAPTER 12

1 *See WW at Rev. 16:14. • See WW at Rev. 21:1.
2 [a]Is. 26:17; 66:6–9
3 [a]Rev. 13:1; 17:3, 7, 9
4 [a]Rev. 9:10, 19
[b]Rev. 8:7, 12
[c]Dan. 8:10
[d]Rev. 12:2
[e]Matt. 2:16
5 [a]Ps. 2:9 [b]Acts 1:9–11

The Woman, the Child, and the Dragon

12 Now a great *sign appeared in
*heaven: a woman clothed with
the sun, with the moon under her feet,
and on her head a garland of twelve
stars.
2 Then being with child, she cried out
[a]in labor and in pain to give birth.
3 And another sign appeared in
heaven: behold, [a]a great, fiery red
dragon having seven heads and ten
horns, and seven diadems on his
heads.
4 [a]His tail drew a third [b]of the stars
of heaven [c]and threw them to the
earth. And the dragon stood [d]before
the woman who was ready to give
birth, [e]to devour her Child as soon as
it was born.
5 She bore a male Child [a]who was to
rule all nations with a rod of iron. And
her Child was [b]caught* up to God and
His throne.
6 Then [a]the woman fled into the wilderness, where she has a place *prepared by God, that they should feed
her there [b]one thousand two hundred
and sixty days.

*See WW at 1 Thess. 4:17. 6 [a]Rev. 12:4, 14 [b]Rev. 11:3; 13:5 *See WW at Rev. 21:2.

DISPENSATIONAL INTERPRETATION: In spite of the fact that much heavy judgment and suffering must come, vv. 15–19 anticipate the glory of the coming reign of **Christ** on Earth.

11:15 The kingdoms: Literally "kingdom," in the singular, represents all "who dwell on the earth." See note on 3:10.

11:19 John reminds his readers that they are continuously in the presence of the throne, in **the temple of God . . . in heaven.** The throne is **the ark of His covenant,** specifically the Mercy Seat (see Ex. 25:8, 9, 10–22; Heb. 9:23–26), a reminder of God's faithfulness in remembering His people.

12:1–17 In this series of visions, specific events are pictured symbolically. We are thus enabled to see the spiritual reality and meaning of events in our historical experience, such as the birth of the Messiah, together with Satan's continuous attempts to destroy Him before He completed His redemptive work, and His exaltation, followed by the resultant persecution of His church. Knowing that they share in His victory will enable His people to endure patiently any future afflictions.

12:1–4 A great sign points to a genuine reality. The **woman** symbolizes God's people, the faithful remnant of Old-Covenant Israel (see Gen. 37:9; Is. 7:14; 26:17, 18; 49:1–13; 66:7, 8), through whom the Messiah came forth (12:4, 5).

The **red dragon** of v. 3 is identified in v. 9 as the Devil (see Is. 27:1). **Seven heads** represent complete authority, intelligence, and cleverness, but not wisdom (see Prov. 1:7). ***Ten*** *represents earthly completeness, which is therefore* limited. **Horns** are a symbol of physical or political strength. **Seven diadems** represent political authority.

A third of the stars of heaven (v. 4) is a symbolic representation of angelic beings (see 2 Pet. 2:4; Jude 6; Ezek. 28:1–19). From the beginning (see Gen. 3:15), the obsession of **the dragon** has been to thwart the purpose of God being worked out through **the woman,** the messianic community, and through the Messiah, **her Child.**

DISPENSATIONAL INTERPRETATION: **A woman** is national Israel. The **twelve stars** symbolize the 12 tribes. She is pictured as a married woman **in labor,** about to **give birth** to a faithful Jewish remnant. **In pain** indicates the remnant's agony throughout Jewish history.

The **red dragon** is Satan. **Seven diadems** identify him with the last of the Gentile rulers who will be represented by the Beast (see 13:1–10; Dan. 7:8). Some scholars feel that **a third of the stars of heaven** is symbolic of the angels who cast their lot with Satan in his rebellion against God. They are the "principalities and powers" against whom all believers "wrestle" (see Eph. 6:12).

12:5 The **Child** was sent **to rule,** literally, "to shepherd," **with a rod of iron,** a symbol of firmness, but not tyranny (see Ps. 2:7–9; Dan. 7:13, 14; Acts 1:9). The total revelational event of Jesus Christ is here telescoped between His birth and His enthronement.

DISPENSATIONAL INTERPRETATION: From the Jewish remnant (v. 2), Christ the **male Child** is born **to rule all nations.** The remnant will be intimately identified with the throne of Christ in the millennial kingdom.

12:6 The woman no longer represents the messianic community that brought forth the Messiah, but is now the church that the Messiah brought forth. The reason for the flight is given in v. 13. **A place prepared by God** is where He protects and lovingly provides for His people. **One thousand two hundred and sixty days** is the consistent symbol for affliction and persecution of the witnessing church. See notes on 11:3; 12:14.

DISPENSATIONAL INTERPRETATION: National Israel is evidently to be providentially protected during the Great Tribulation by some type of flight. **The wilderness** here could be Petra in Edom (see Dan. 11:41; Matt. 24:16).

Satan Thrown Out of Heaven

7 And war broke out in heaven:
[a]Michael and his angels fought [b]with
the dragon; and the dragon and his angels fought,

KINGDOM DYNAMICS

12:7–11 Angelic Activity in Spiritual Warfare, FAITH'S WARFARE. The casting down of Satan results from a great battle between the hosts of heaven and the hordes of hell. In this battle, heaven's warriors force Satan and his demons forever from the heavenly realm. But we must note that victory is not achieved solely by the angels, but also by believers' use of spiritual weapons. The angels fight, but God's saints provide the "firepower." This is clearly shown by v. 11, "They overcame him by the blood of the Lamb and by the word of their testimony." The angels did not overcome the Accuser alone; the saints were in partnership through prayer-warfare; the angels were God's means for administering the victory, which prayer enforced.

Notice the mention of Michael, the archangel (v. 7, one of four places where he is mentioned in Scripture). In each mention, spiritual warfare is clearly implied. This is true in Dan. 10 where Michael's involvement in battle to victory is the direct result of Daniel's fasting and prayer (see Dan. 10:1–4, 12, 13).

(Ezra 8:21–23/Mark 11:20–24) D.E.

KINGDOM DYNAMICS

12:7, 9 Fallen Angels, ANGELS. The Scriptures reveal both good angels and evil angels. The evil entities are those angels who rebelled with Lucifer and were cast out of heaven with him. Their minds and understanding have been covered with the horrible darkness of deception—the same tactic Satan still uses to lead his victims astray. They were created in God's original order to do His will, as those angels who continue in obedience to His throne. But these "did not keep their proper domain" (Jude 6) and are now agents of the Adversary, bound under his dark dominion and serving Satan's rebellious enterprises.

(Rev. 1:1/Heb. 1:14) M.H.

7 [a]Dan. 10:13, 21; 12:1; Jude 9 [b]Rev. 20:2

8 [1]*were not strong enough* [2]M *him*

9 [a]Luke 10:18; John 12:31 [b]Gen. 3:1, 4; 2 Cor. 11:3; Rev. 12:15; 20:2 [c]Rev. 20:3 [d]Rev. 9:1

10 [a]Rev. 11:15 [b]Job 1:9, 11; 2:5; Zech. 3:1

11 [a]Rom. 16:20 [b]Luke 14:26; [Rev. 2:10] *See WW at Rev. 6:1.

8 but they [1]did not prevail, nor was
a place found for [2]them in heaven any
longer.
9 So [a]the great dragon was cast out,
[b]that serpent of old, called the Devil
and Satan, [c]who deceives the whole
world; [d]he was cast to the earth, and
his angels were cast out with him.
10 Then I heard a loud voice saying
in heaven, [a]"Now salvation, and
strength, and the kingdom of our God,
and the power of His Christ have come,
for the accuser of our brethren, [b]who
accused them before our God day and
night, has been cast down.
11 "And [a]they overcame him by the 7
blood of the *Lamb and by the word
of their testimony, [b]and they did not
love their lives to the death.

KINGDOM DYNAMICS

12:10, 11 NT: Agelong Warfare, PROPHECY AND THE KINGDOM. John's prophecy in ch. 12 conveys the same essential message as Dan. 7, the primary difference being that John writes after Christ's first coming, victorious death, resurrection, and ascension (v. 5). Vv. 1–17 relate: 1) the ongoing warfare on Earth (v. 9); 2) the overcoming ability of the redeemed because "the kingdom" has come (v. 10); 3) the two-edged truth that their victories often cost martyrdom (v. 11); and 4) the basis of their triumph: the Cross ("the blood of the Lamb") and the authority of God's Word ("the word of their testimony"—v. 12). Various interpretive systems see this at different times within redemptive history. The mixture of pre-, a-, and postmillennial viewpoints has often fragmented the church, rather than providing a common base of wisdom for each group to receive while embracing one another as, presently, we all face a common Adversary (v. 9). Seeing that no complete interpretive scheme will be verified until after Christ comes, our wisdom is to embrace the Cross as our salvation and our source of overcoming victory. Then we can enter the conflict in confidence, knowing we shall triumph even though circumstances temporarily

(*cont. on next page*)

12:7–12 The same spiritual conflict, contemporaneous with vv. 1–6, is now described in the heavenly realm. **Michael,** in the tradition of Judaism, is one of seven archangels and the guardian champion of Israel (see Dan. 10:13, 21; 12:1; Jude 9). **The dragon and his angels** were defeated by the total event of Jesus Christ (see Matt. 12:28; 28:18; Luke 10:17–19; John 12:31, 32; Col. 2:15).

DISPENSATIONAL INTERPRETATION: **Michael** has a unique place in the destiny of national Israel (see Dan. 12:1). Here, Michael is involved in the expulsion of Satan from **heaven . . . to the earth** in the middle of the Great Tribulation (see Dan. 10:10–14).

12:10 Now refers to the First Advent (v. 5). This is His kingdom "not of this world"; it must *not* be understood in terms of an earthly political kingdom. **The accuser:** See notes on Job 1:6—2:7 and 1:6.

12:11 See section 7 of Truth-In-Action at the end of Rev.

12:11 They overcame him by appropriating the victory of the finished work of Christ, by the public confession of their faith and patient endurance (see note on 1:9), even in the face of martyrdom (see 13:10). The church's constant posture under the authority of the Cross's victory **by the blood of the Lamb** and steadfastness to the promise and authority of God's Word—**the word of their testimony**—is the key to their overcoming.

(*cont. from preceding page*)
set us back. In the time of conflict, it will make no difference who was "right," but only that we were on the Messiah's side in this agelong spiritual struggle.

The text provides two indisputable facts: 1) the kingdom of God has already established triumph over the Serpent (vv. 9, 10); 2) still, those engaged in conflict in the name of the Lamb sometimes are vanquished to death (v. 11). Breadth and balance is given to our perspective. The presence of the kingdom at this time calls each believer to responsible spiritual warfare and anticipated victories. Yet, at the same time, the presence of evil struggles for survival; though "cast down," the Serpent writhes viciously. Thus our temporal situation is often a fierce and sometimes painful struggle, seeming to issue in an indeterminate standoff before our Enemy. But he only has "a short time," until finally the kingdom to come (v. 10) shall become the kingdom accomplished (Rev. 19—22). Let us do battle in faith and with faithfulness and, looking to that day of His ultimate kingdom, know the Holy Spirit is preparing us for kingdom victories today. See Dan. 7:21, 22. (Dan. 7:21, 22/Gen. 1:1) J.W.H.

 **KINGDOM DYNAMICS**

12:11 Declaring the Ultimate Victory in Christ, FAITH'S CONFESSION. There is no greater biblical declaration of faith's confession. Those facing the cataclysmic travail of the last days endure it with a constant statement of the overcoming power of the blood of the Lamb and of the word of their transforming faith in Christ. Some of those declaring Christ's ultimate victory with their own lips (6:9; 11:7) face the fury of Satan's most vicious and personal attacks against them. Yet, their faith is unwavering, the result of an abiding relationship with Jesus Christ. This is the heart of faith's confession, based in God's Word and the blood of the Lamb, whose victory has provided the eternal conquest of Satan.

With Christ's victory over Satan, we see these who have maintained their confession of faith and thereby share in His victory. With their sins blotted out and their declaration of Jesus' redemptive work in their lives, they silence the attempts of the prince of darkness to intimidate God's children. His accusing voice of condemnation and guilt is swallowed up in the triumph of Calvary. Declare your abiding faith in the accomplished work of the Cross, and constantly participate in Jesus' ultimate victory, overcoming Satan by the power of the Cross and the steadfastness of your confession of faith in Christ's triumph.
(Heb. 11:13–16/Gen. 17:5*) R.H.

 **KINGDOM DYNAMICS**

12:11 The Weapon of the Blood, THE BLOOD. This passage portrays Satan as cast down to the Earth, confronting and accusing the citizens of the kingdom of God. The primary weapon of the people of God against Satan is the blood of the Lamb. The blood of Christ, the Lamb, causes the people of God to prevail because it answers all of the Enemy's accusations. Satan controls and defeats humankind through guilt and accusations. He is a "blackmailer." However, the saints know that the blood has satisfied all of the charges against them, joined them to God, and provided them with every necessary provision to defeat Satan. The blood has established an unassailable bond with a sovereign God that prevents Satan from separating the embattled Christian from God's eternal and complete resources. God has declared us righteous and victorious through the blood of Christ.
(Rom. 5:9/1 Cor. 10:16) C.S.

12 "Therefore [a]rejoice, O heavens, and
you who dwell in them! [b]Woe to the
inhabitants of the earth and the sea!
For the devil has come down to you,
having great *wrath, [c]because he
knows that he has a short time."

The Woman Persecuted

13 Now when the dragon saw that he
had been cast to the earth, he persecuted [a]the woman who gave birth to
the male *Child.*

12 [a]Ps. 96:11; Is. 44:23; Rev. 18:20 [b]Rev. 8:13 [c]Rev. 10:6 *See WW at Luke 4:28.
13 [a]Rev. 12:5

12:12 The defeat of the Devil causes rejoicing among God's people, but **woe** among people of the world. Note the intensification of evil workings of hell as the Age progresses and the Adversary knows he has a short time.
12:13–17 The dragon (v. 13), because he has already been defeated (Col. 2:14, 15), is relentless in retaliative efforts, *struggling to retain claim* on the planet he has lost. Thus, he **persecuted the woman,** the witnessing church (vv. 4–6; John 15:18–21). **Two wings of a great eagle** (v. 14): The prototype was God's protecting and nourishing His people in their deliverance from bondage in Egypt (see Ex. 19:4). In vv. 15, 16 **the serpent** utilizes all resources to destroy **the woman.** The **flood** symbolizes the peoples of the world (see 17:15; Is. 17:12). **The earth:** God's creation is one of His resources to preserve His people (see Ex. 15:12). Frustrated in his failure to destroy both the Messiah and His community, **the dragon** makes **war with** individual members of the witnessing church (v. 17).
DISPENSATIONAL INTERPRETATION: According to this view of vv. 13–17, when **the dragon** is cast forth upon the Earth, he immediately begins to persecute Israel; however, as previously noted, Israel is given divine deliverance in **her place,** prepared for protection. When he realizes he cannot touch national Israel, he pursues **the rest of her offspring** who are openly and actively ministering as witnesses of Jesus Christ (see 7:3–8; Matt. 24:15–20).

14 [a]But the woman was given two
wings of a great eagle, [b]that she might
fly [c]into the wilderness to her place,
where she is nourished [d]for a *time and
times and half a time, from the presence of the serpent.
15 So the serpent [a]spewed water out
of his mouth like a flood after the
woman, that he might cause her to be
carried away by the flood.
16 But the earth helped the woman,
and the earth opened its mouth
and swallowed up the flood which
the dragon had spewed out of his
mouth.
17 And the dragon was **enraged** with
the woman, and he went to make war
with the rest of her offspring, who keep
the commandments of God and have
the testimony of Jesus [1]Christ.

WORD WEALTH

12:17 enraged, *orgizo* (or-*gid*-zoe); Strong's *#3710:* Compare "orgy" and "orgiastic." To provoke to anger. In the NT the verb is always in the passive, "to be provoked to anger." The word describes a passion that is furious and raging with a desire for revenge. It is so intense a passion that it will terminate by attempting to kill. Christians are to avoid that kind of intense wrath (Matt. 5:22; Eph. 4:26).

The Beast from the Sea

13 Then [1]I stood on the sand of the
sea. And I saw [a]a beast rising
up out of the sea, [b]having [2]seven heads
and ten horns, and on his horns ten
crowns, and on his heads a [c]blasphe-
mous name.
2 Now the beast which I saw was like
a leopard, his feet were like *the feet
of* a bear, and his mouth like the mouth
of a lion. The [a]dragon gave him his
power, his throne, and great authority.
3 And *I saw* one of his heads [a]as if it
had been mortally wounded, and his
deadly wound was *healed. And
[b]all the world marveled and followed
the beast.
4 So they worshiped the dragon who
gave authority to the beast; and they
worshiped the beast, saying, [a]"Who *is*
like the beast? Who is able to make
war with him?"
5 And he was given [a]a mouth speaking great things and blasphemies, and
he was given authority to [1]continue for
[b]forty-two months.
6 Then he opened his mouth in blasphemy against God, to blaspheme His
name, [a]His tabernacle, and those who
dwell in heaven.
7 It was granted to him [a]to make war
with the saints and to overcome them.
And [b]authority was given him over
every [1]tribe, tongue, and nation.
8 All who dwell on the earth will worship him, [a]whose names have not been
written in the Book of Life of the
*Lamb slain [b]from the foundation of
the world.
9 [a]If anyone has an ear, let him hear.
10 [a]He who leads into captivity shall 2
go into captivity; [b]he who kills with the
sword must be killed with the sword.
[c]Here is the [1]patience and the faith of
the saints.

The Beast from the Earth

11 Then I saw another beast [a]coming
up out of the earth, and he had two

14 [a]Ex. 19:4; Deut. 32:11; Is. 40:31 [b]Rev. 12:6 [c]Rev. 17:3 [d]Dan. 7:25; 12:7 *See WW at Col. 4:5. **15** [a]Is. 59:19 **17** [1]NU, M omit *Christ*

CHAPTER 13

1 [a]Dan. 7:2, 7 [b]Rev. 12:3 [c]Dan. 7:8; 11:36; Rev. 17:3 [1]NU *he* [2]NU, M *ten horns and seven heads* **2** [a]Rev. 12:3, 9; 13:4, 12 **3** [a]Rev. 13:12, 14 [b]Rev. 17:8 *See WW at Matt. 12:22. **4** [a]Ex. 15:11; Is. 46:5; Rev. 18:18 **5** [a]Dan. 7:8, 11, 20, 25; 11:36; 2 Thess. 2:3 [b]Rev. 11:2 [1]M *make war* **6** [a][John 1:14; Col. 2:9] **7** [a]Dan. 7:21; Rev. 11:7 [b]Rev. 11:18 [1]NU, M add *and people* **8** [a]Ex. 32:32; [Rev. 20:12–15] [b]Matt. 25:34; Rev. 17:8 *See WW at Rev. 6:1. **9** [a]Rev. 2:7 **10** [a]Is. 33:1; Jer. 15:2; 43:11 [b]Gen. 9:6; Matt. 26:52; Rev. 11:18 [c]Heb. 6:12; Rev. 14:12 [1]*perseverance* **11** [a]Rev. 11:7

13:1 I stood: The preferred reading (see marginal note) is "he stood" (that is, the dragon). **A beast rising up out of the sea** is a mirror-image of the dragon, called forth from the peoples of the world (17:15) as an ally in his war against the saints (v. 7). The **crowns** are on the **ten horns** (political power), not on the **seven heads** (the source of authority), which is the dragon who delegates his authority to the monster (vv. 4, 7). **The beast** represents an incarnation of politico-social evil (see Introduction to Revelation: Content).
13:2 This monster is a composite of Daniel's pictures of past political powers (see Dan. 7:2–7).
13:3, 4 One of his heads . . . wounded is a parody of the Lamb. The symbol represents either empires or individual emperors (17:10; see Introduction to Revelation: Content). The spiritual principle is the same with either interpretation.
13:5 He was given . . . blasphemies by the dragon. **He was given authority** by God (v. 7), over those "who dwell on the earth" (vv. 7, 8; see note on 3:10). **Forty-two months:** See note on 11:2.
13:6–8 Blasphemy is irreverent speech that calls what is human "divine," what is evil "good," and what is good "evil." **His name** is the character of God revealed in the Person of the Lord Jesus Christ. **And** may also be translated "even" or "that is." **His tabernacle, those who dwell in heaven,** are God's people, the church. They are not those who **dwell on the earth** (v. 8; see note on 3:10).
13:7 See note on 11:7.
13:8 The Book of Life is God's register of the redeemed. See note on 3:5. **From the foundation of the world** refers to before the Creation (1 Pet. 1:20).
13:9, 10 The Lord's words of judgment upon Judah (see Jer. 15:2, 3) become words of counsel and encouragement. The persecuted are to maintain a patient trust in God to work out His purposes, and are not to adopt the methods of the Beast and the dragon.
13:10 See section 2 of Truth-In-Action at the end of Rev.
13:11–18 Another beast, identified as the False Prophet (16:13; 19:20; 20:10), is **like a lamb,** a symbol of the priesthood of the imperial cult, enforcing the worship of Caesar, performing **great signs** (v. 13), such as demonic magic and ventriloquism, which deceive **those who dwell on the earth** (see Deut. 13:1–5; Matt. 24:24; 2 Thess. 2:9). **Out of the earth** (v. 11): The imperial cult first arose in provincial Asia. The **mark** (v. 16) is a counterfeit of "the

horns like a lamb and spoke like a
dragon.
12 And he exercises all the authority
of the first beast in his presence, and
causes the earth and those who dwell
in it to worship the first beast, [a]whose
deadly wound was healed.
13 [a]He performs great signs, [b]so that
he even makes fire come down from
heaven on the earth in the sight of
men.
14 [a]And he deceives [1]those who dwell
on the earth [b]by those signs which he
was granted to do in the sight of the
beast, telling those who dwell on the
earth to make an image to the beast
who was wounded by the sword
[c]and lived.
15 He was granted *power* to give
breath to the image of the beast, that
the image of the beast should both
speak [a]and cause as many as would
not worship the image of the beast to
be killed.
1 16 He causes all, both small and great,
rich and poor, *free and slave, [a]to receive a mark on their right hand or on
their foreheads,
17 and that no one may buy or sell except one who has [1]the mark or [a]the
name of the beast, [b]or the number of
his name.
18 [a]Here is wisdom. Let him who has
[b]understanding calculate [c]the number
of the beast, [d]for it is the number of a
man: His number *is* 666.

12 [a]Rev. 13:3, 4
13 [a]Matt. 24:24 [b]1 Kin. 18:38
14 [a]Rev. 12:9 [b]2 Thess. 2:9 [c]2 Kin. 20:7 [1]M *my own people*
15 [a]Rev. 16:2
16 [a]Rev. 7:3; 14:9; 20:4 *See WW at Rev. 6:15.
17 [a]Rev. 14:9–11 [b]Rev. 15:2 [1]NU, M *the mark, the name*
18 [a]Rev. 17:9 [b][1 Cor. 2:14] [c]Rev. 15:2 [d]Rev. 21:17

KINGDOM DYNAMICS

13:18 12. What Is the Mark of the Beast?, SPIRITUAL ANSWERS. For the answer to this and other questions about God and the power life in His kingdom, see the study article "Spiritual Answers to Hard Questions," which begins on page 1996. P.R.

The Lamb and the 144,000

14 Then I looked, and behold,
[1]a [a]Lamb* standing on Mount
Zion, and with Him [b]one hundred *and*
forty-four thousand, [2]having His Father's name [c]written on their foreheads.
2 And I heard a voice from heaven,
[a]like the voice of many waters, and like
the voice of loud thunder. And I heard
the sound of [b]harpists playing their
harps.

CHAPTER 14

1 [a]Rev. 5:6 [b]Rev. 7:4; 14:3 [c]Rev. 7:3; 22:4 [1]NU, M *the* [2]NU, M add *His name and* *See WW at Rev. 6:1.
2 [a]Rev. 1:15; 19:6 [b]Rev. 5:8

seal of the living God" (7:2–4), validating a citizen's loyalty to the emperor.

DISPENSATIONAL INTERPRETATION: In vv. 1–18 dispensationalists see the emergence of the **beast** and his false prophet. This phase of world history will be characterized by the following conditions: 1) A world ruler is empowered by Satan (vv. 2, 4); 2) he and Satan share the worship and adulation of most of the world (vv. 4, 8, 12, 15); 3) the ruler emerges as the ultimate military power (v. 4); 4) his power and authority extend throughout the Earth (v. 7); 5) he harasses and persecutes all those whose faith is in Jesus Christ (vv. 6, 7).

The **beast** (v. 1) is the Antichrist. He is the last great ruler of the Gentile world powers. **Rising up out of the sea** (v. 1) is symbolic of his arising out of chaotic political events (see Is. 7:20). He is in complete rebellion against the true God and certainly parallels the satanic ruler of Dan. 7. **His deadly wound** (v. 3), said to be **healed,** most likely refers to the resurrection of an imperial form of government thought extinct. Because of the intensity of the antichrist spirit of the Beast himself, coupled with the system he represents, it seems highly unlikely, however, that he represents any form of Christianity. In every dimension, he is antichrist (see 2 Thess. 2:3–12; 1 John 2:22; 4:3).

Another beast . . . out of the earth (v. 11) is the False Prophet. He serves as the Antichrist's mouthpiece. He poses as a true prophet, but directs people **to worship the first beast** (vv. 12–14). It is interesting that the most significant sign of the Antichrist is attributed to the False Prophet, *namely, the physical sealing with* **the mark . . . of the beast, his number . . . 666** (v. 18).

13:16 See section 1 of Truth-In-Action at the end of Rev.

13:18 Since neither the Hebrew nor Greek language possessed a separate numerical system, the letters of their alphabets carried numerical value. Hence, the symbolic **number of the beast** is the sum of the numerical values of the separate letters of his name. The monster may be the last of many pseudo-messiahs (see Matt. 24:24; Mark 13:22) to arise in history who manifest the spirit of antichrist. See 1 John 2:18, 19, 22; 4:3; 2 John 7.

The dragon has developed a counterfeit trinity in his spiritual warfare against the church (see Introduction to Revelation: Content). Opposed to this is the reality of the true Trinity-Unity: God the Father who sends His Son, the Lamb, who pours out His Holy Spirit and seals His saints, represented by the woman and her offspring, who dwell in heaven and whose names are written in the Lamb's Book of Life. The spiritual warfare and the tribulation will continue until the Second Coming of Christ.

14:1–5 The vision of persecution abruptly changes to a vision of the church in glory.

DISPENSATIONAL INTERPRETATION: Insights into the culmination of the Great Tribulation (vv. 1–20).

14:1 The **one hundred *and* forty-four thousand** symbolize all faithful saints (see note on 7:4–8). **Mount Zion** is a spiritual reality (see Heb. 12:22–24) expressing the communion of the saints, not a geographical location. The **Father's name** is a deliberate contrast with "the name of the beast" (13:16, 17).

DISPENSATIONAL INTERPRETATION: The 144,000 represent the Jewish remnant sealed and consequently spared from the Great Tribulation. They are closely identified with **the Lamb** (Jesus Christ) and **Mount Zion,** typical of the seat of kingdom power in Jerusalem. They are the same as those referred to in 7:1–8.

14:2–5 The **new song** is a song of redemption, which only the **redeemed** can understand. They are spiritual **virgins** who have remained true to the Lord, not having prostituted themselves through idolatry. **They are without fault,** unblemished because they are in Christ and are thus an acceptable sacrifice.

3 They sang as it were a new song
before the throne, before the four living creatures, and the elders; and no
one could learn that song [a]except the
hundred *and* forty-four thousand who
were redeemed from the earth.
5 4 These are the ones who were not
defiled with women, [a]for they are virgins. These are the ones [b]who follow
the Lamb wherever He goes. These
[c]were [1]redeemed from *among* men,
[d]*being* firstfruits to God and to the
Lamb.
5 And [a]in their mouth was found no
[1]deceit, for [b]they are without fault
[2]before the throne of God.

The Proclamations of Three Angels

6 Then I saw another angel [a]flying in
the midst of heaven, [b]having the **everlasting** *gospel to preach to those who
dwell on the earth—[c]to every nation,
tribe, tongue, and people—

WORD WEALTH

14:6 everlasting, *aionios* (ahee-oh-nee-oss); Strong's *#166:* Compare "eon." Perpetual, unchanging, of unlimited duration, eternal, agelong, unending. The word may denote that which is without either beginning or end (Rom. 16:26; Heb. 9:14); without beginning (Rom. 16:25; 2 Tim. 1:9); without end (Luke 16:9; 2 Cor. 5:1; Rev. 14:6).

7 saying with a loud voice, [a]"Fear
God and give glory to Him, for the hour
of His *judgment has come; [b]and *worship Him who made heaven and earth,
the sea and springs of water."
8 And another angel followed, say-
ing, [a]"Babylon[1] is fallen, is fallen, that
great city, because [b]she has made all
nations drink of the wine of the *wrath
of her fornication."
9 Then a third angel followed them,
saying with a loud voice, [a]"If anyone
worships the beast and his image, and
receives *his* [b]mark on his forehead or
on his hand,
10 "he himself [a]shall also drink of the
wine of the wrath of God, which is
[b]poured out full strength into [c]the cup
of His indignation. [d]He shall be tormented with [e]fire and brimstone in the
presence of the holy angels and in the
presence of the Lamb.
11 "And [a]the smoke of their torment
ascends forever and ever; and they
have no rest day or night, who worship
the beast and his image, and whoever
receives the mark of his name."
12 [a]Here is the [1]patience of the saints; 2
[b]here[2] *are* those who keep the commandments of God and the faith of
Jesus.
13 Then I heard a voice from heaven
saying [1]to me, "Write: [a]'Blessed* *are*
the dead [b]who die in the Lord from
now on.'" "Yes," says the Spirit,
[c]"that they may **rest** from their labors,
and their works follow [d]them."

WORD WEALTH

14:13 rest, *anapauo* (an-ap-ow-oh); Strong's *#373:* From *ana,* "up," and *pauo,* "to make to cease." The word describes a cessation from toil, a refreshment, an intermission.

Reaping the Earth's Harvest

14 Then I looked, and behold, a white
cloud, and on the cloud sat *One* like
the Son of Man, having on His head a

3 [a]Rev. 5:9
4 [a][2 Cor. 11:2] [b]Rev. 3:4; 7:17 [c]Rev. 5:9 [d]James 1:18 [1]M adds *by Jesus*
5 [a]Ps. 32:2 [b]Eph. 5:27 [1]NU, M *falsehood* [2]NU, M omit the rest of v. 5.
6 [a]Rev. 8:13 [b]Eph. 3:9 [c]Rev. 13:7 *See WW at Mark 1:1.
7 [a]Rev. 11:18 [b]Neh. 9:6 *See WW at Matt. 5:22. • See WW at Rev. 4:10.
8 [a]Is. 21:9 [b]Jer. 51:7 [1]NU *Babylon the great is fallen, is fallen, which has made;* M *Babylon the great is fallen. She has made* *See WW at Luke 4:28.
9 [a]Rev. 13:14, 15; 14:11 [b]Rev. 13:16
10 [a]Ps. 75:8 [b]Rev. 18:6 [c]Rev. 16:19 [d]Rev. 20:10 [e]2 Thess. 1:7
11 [a]Is. 34:8–10
12 [a]Rev. 13:10 [b]Rev. 12:17 [1]*steadfastness, perseverance* [2]NU, M omit *here are those*
13 [a]Eccl. 4:1, 2 [b]1 Cor. 15:18 [c]Heb. 4:9, 10 [d][1 Cor. 3:11–15; 15:58] [1]NU, M omit *to me* *See WW at Matt. 5:3.

14:4, 5 See section 5 of Truth-In-Action at the end of Rev.
14:6, 7 The gospel is **everlasting,** in contrast to the provisional Old Covenant, and is intended to be heard universally. It is good news to those who respond to it but judgment to those who refuse it.
14:8 In the OT, **Babylon** was a center of idolatry, the occult, and immorality. See note on 18:1—19:10. In the NT, it is sometimes a cryptic name for Rome (see 18:9, 10; 1 Pet. 5:13). From the perspective of the eternal God, **that great city,** the world in every generation, has already been judged and is **fallen** (see Is. 13; 21:9; Jer. 51). **The wine of the wrath of her fornication:** Idolatry, worshiping the monster, inevitably results in the drinking of the cup of God's wrath in judgment (see Ps. 75:8; Jer. 25:15, 16; 51:7).
DISPENSATIONAL INTERPRETATION: In this view of vv. 6–8, although **Babylon** is a symbol of the satanic world system, it is possible such a system could be centered in a literal city. Historically, there has been speculation that geographical Babylon may be restored in modern-day Iraq. Whether symbolic or literal, Babylon will have great religious and political significance in the last days (see chs. 17; 18; Is. 13).
14:9–11 Tormented with fire: There can be no compromise in the spiritual conflict (see 19:20; 20:10; Matt. 18:8, 9; Mark 9:43–48).
14:12 See section 2 of Truth-In-Action at the end of Rev.
14:12 Here: The fact of judgment (vv. 9–11) shows the need for **patience** in faith and obedience. See note on 1:9.
14:13 The **voice from heaven** is perhaps that of the Lamb proclaiming the second of the seven beatitudes. **From now on** is from the moment of the Lamb's finished work and victory (see 5:6–14; 12:5, 11). **The Spirit** may be the voice, or this may be an antiphonal response by the Holy Spirit. **Rest** represents a dramatic contrast to v. 11.
DISPENSATIONAL INTERPRETATION: In vv. 9–13 **a third angel** announces the full fury of **the wrath of God** on all those who worship **the beast.** The believing Jewish martyrs will suffer physical death, but those who worship the Antichrist will experience eternal punishment (see 20:10–15).
14:14–20 John views a picture of the Final Judgment, first of believers (see 1 Thess. 4:15–17; John 5:28, 29), followed immediately by that of unbelievers (see Joel 3:13).

golden crown, and in His hand a sharp
sickle.
15 And another angel [a]came out of the
temple, crying with a loud voice to Him
who sat on the cloud, [b]"Thrust in Your
sickle and reap, for the time has come
[1]for You to reap, for the harvest
[c]of the earth is ripe."
16 So He who sat on the cloud thrust
in His sickle on the earth, and the earth
was reaped.

Reaping the Grapes of Wrath

17 Then another angel came out of the
temple which is in heaven, he also having a sharp sickle.
18 And another angel came out from
the altar, [a]who had power over fire,
and he cried with a loud cry to him
who had the sharp sickle, saying,
[b]"Thrust in your sharp sickle and
gather the clusters of the vine of the
earth, for her grapes are fully ripe."
19 So the angel thrust his sickle into
the earth and gathered the vine of the
earth, and threw *it* into [a]the great
winepress of the wrath of God.
20 And [a]the winepress was trampled
[b]outside the city, and blood came out
of the winepress, [c]up to the horses' bri-
dles, for one thousand six hundred
[1]furlongs.

Prelude to the Bowl Judgments

15 Then [a]I saw another *sign in
heaven, great and marvelous:
[b]seven angels having the seven last
plagues, [c]for in them the wrath of God
is complete.
2 And I saw *something* like [a]a sea of
glass [b]mingled with fire, and those
who have the victory over the beast,
[c]over his image and [1]over his mark *and*

15 [a]Rev. 16:17 [b]Joel 3:13 [c]Jer. 51:33 [1]NU, M omit *for You*
18 [a]Rev. 16:8 [b]Joel 3:13
19 [a]Rev. 19:15
20 [a]Is. 63:3 [b]Heb. 13:12 [c]Is. 34:3 [1]Lit. *stadia*, about 184 miles in all

CHAPTER 15

1 [a]Rev. 12:1, 3 [b]Rev. 21:9 [c]Rev. 14:10 *See WW at Rev. 16:14.
2 [a]Rev. 4:6 [b][Matt. 3:11] [c]Rev. 13:14, 15 [d]Rev. 13:17 [e]Rev. 5:8 [1]NU, M omit *over his mark*
3 [a]Ex. 15:1–21 [b]Rev. 15:3 [c]Deut. 32:3, 4 [d]Ps. 145:17 [1]NU, M *nations* *See WW at Rev. 6:1.
4 [a]Ex. 15:14 [b]Lev. 11:44 [c]Is. 66:23
5 [a]Num. 1:50 [1]NU, M omit *behold* [2]*sanctuary*, the inner shrine
6 [a]Ex. 28:6 [1]*sanctuary*, the inner shrine *See WW at Matt. 5:8.
7 [a]Rev. 4:6 [b]1 Thess. 1:9
8 [a]Ex. 19:18; 40:34

over the [d]number of his name, standing on the sea of glass, [e]having harps
of God.
3 They sing [a]the song of Moses, the
servant of God, and the song of the
[b]Lamb,* saying:

[c]"Great and marvelous *are* Your
works,
Lord God Almighty!
[d]Just and true *are* Your ways,
O King of the [1]saints!
4 [a]Who shall not fear You, O Lord,
and glorify Your name?
For *You* alone *are* [b]holy.
For [c]all nations shall come and
worship before You,
For Your judgments have been
manifested."

5 After these things I looked, and
[1]behold, [a]the [2]temple of the tabernacle
of the **testimony** in heaven was
opened.

> **WORD WEALTH**
>
> **15:5 testimony,** *marturion* (mar-*too*-ree-on); Strong's *#3142:* Compare "martyr" and "martyrology." Proof, evidence, witness, proclamation of personal experience. The tabernacle, which evidences God's presence, is a testimony to the covenant between Him and His people.

6 And out of the [1]temple came the
seven angels having the seven plagues,
[a]clothed in *pure bright linen, and having their chests girded with golden
bands.
7 [a]Then one of the four living creatures gave to the seven angels seven
golden bowls full of the wrath of God
[b]who lives forever and ever.
8 [a]The temple was filled with smoke

DISPENSATIONAL INTERPRETATION: The scope of the coming judgments and preview of Armageddon are revealed. This passage depicts a time of separation of the wicked from the righteous, and the focus will be God's final dealing with Earth-dwellers (see Matt. 25:31–46).

14:15, 16 Another angel delivered the command of the Judgment from **the temple,** possibly because Jesus specifically disclaimed any knowledge of the time of this event (see Matt. 24:36; Mark 13:32).

14:18 Another angel came in answer to the cries of those under **the altar.** See note on 6:10.

14:20 Outside the city suggests retribution for those who *compelled Jesus to suffer "outside the gate"* (see Heb. 13:12, 13). The number associated with the amount of **blood** should be regarded as qualitative, not quantitative, heightening the utter gruesomeness of the scene (see Is. 63:2–6).

15:1–4 Preparation is made for the consummation of the Judgment with the introduction of **seven angels** who will empty the seven bowls (16:1–21). While the seals and the trumpets picture partial judgments, the seven bowls picture judgments that are about to be consummated, and thus are the last.

15:2 Like indicates a simile. **A sea of glass mingled with fire** is suggestive of the deliverance of Israel at the Red Sea, with its waters reddened by the pillar of fire. The emphasis is on the safety of the redeemed.

15:3, 4 Moses sang a **song** of redemption following the crossing of the Red Sea (see Ex. 15:1–18), which is now **the song of the Lamb,** a celebration of God's judgment, power, and sovereignty.

15:5—16:1 The tabernacle of the testimony is, literally, "the tent of witness," the exact word describing the ancient tabernacle in the Greek text of Ex. 40:34, 35. From this heavenly counterpart of the earthly tabernacle, **the seven angels** come forth to execute judgment.

15:6, 7 The angels are dressed as priests.

15:8 Smoke: See Is. 6:1–4. **Glory:** See Ex. 40:34, 35; 1 Kin. 8:10, 11. **No one was able to enter:** The mercy seat

[b]from the glory of God and from His
power, and no one was able to enter
the temple till the seven plagues of the
seven angels were completed.

16 Then I heard a loud voice from
the temple saying [a]to the seven
angels, "Go and pour out the [1]bowls
[b]of the wrath of God on the earth."

First Bowl: Loathsome Sores

2 So the first went and poured out his
bowl [a]upon the earth, and a [1]foul and
[b]loathsome sore came upon the men
[c]who had the mark of the beast and
those [d]who worshiped his image.

Second Bowl: The Sea Turns to Blood

3 Then the second angel poured out
his bowl [a]on the sea, and [b]it became
blood as of a dead *man;* [c]and every living creature in the sea died.

Third Bowl: The Waters Turn to Blood

4 Then the third angel poured out his
bowl [a]on the rivers and springs of water, [b]and they became blood.
5 And I heard the angel of the waters
saying:

[a]"You are righteous, [1]O Lord,
The One [b]who is and who
[2]was and who is to be,
Because You have judged these
things.
6 For [a]they have shed the blood
[b]of saints and prophets,
[c]And You have given them blood
to drink.
[1]For it is their just due."

7 And I heard [1]another from the altar
saying, "Even so, [a]Lord God Almighty,
[b]true and righteous *are* Your judgments."

Fourth Bowl: Men Are Scorched

8 Then the fourth angel poured out
his bowl [a]on the sun, [b]and power was
given to him to scorch men with fire.
9 And men were scorched with great
heat, and they [a]blasphemed the name
of God who has power over these
plagues; [b]and they did not repent
[c]and give Him glory.

Fifth Bowl: Darkness and Pain

10 Then the fifth angel poured out his
bowl [a]on the throne of the beast,
[b]and his kingdom became full of darkness; [c]and they gnawed their tongues
because of the pain.
11 They blasphemed the God of
heaven because of their pains and their
sores, and did not repent of their deeds.

Sixth Bowl: Euphrates Dried Up

12 Then the sixth angel poured out his
bowl [a]on the great river Euphrates,
[b]and its water was dried up, [c]so that
the way of the kings from the east
might be prepared.
13 And I saw three unclean [a]spirits
like frogs *coming* out of the mouth of
[b]the dragon, out of the mouth of the
beast, and out of the mouth of [c]the
false prophet.
14 For they are spirits of demons,
[a]performing **signs,** *which* go out to the
kings [1]of the earth and of [b]the whole
world, to gather them to [c]the battle of
that great day of God Almighty.

8 [b]2 Thess. 1:9

CHAPTER 16

1 [a]Rev. 15:1 [b]Rev. 14:10 [1]NU, M *seven bowls*
2 [a]Rev. 8:7 [b]Ex. 9:9–11 [c]Rev. 13:15–17; 14:9 [d]Rev. 13:14 [1]*severe and malignant,* lit. *bad and evil*
3 [a]Rev. 8:8; 11:6 [b]Ex. 7:17–21 [c]Rev. 8:9
4 [a]Rev. 8:10 [b]Ex. 7:17–20
5 [a]Rev. 15:3, 4 [b]Rev. 1:4, 8 [1]NU, M omit *O Lord* [2]NU, M *was, the Holy One*
6 [a]Matt. 23:34 [b]Rev. 11:18 [c]Is. 49:26 [1]NU, M omit *For*
7 [a]Rev. 15:3 [b]Rev. 13:10; 19:2 [1]NU, M omit *another from*
8 [a]Rev. 8:12 [b]Rev. 9:17, 18
9 [a]Rev. 16:11 [b]Dan. 5:22 [c]Rev. 11:13
10 [a]Rev. 13:2 [b]Rev. 8:12; 9:2 [c]Rev. 11:10
12 [a]Rev. 9:14 [b]Jer. 50:38 [c]Is. 41:2, 25; 46:11
13 [a]1 John 4:1 [b]Rev. 12:3, 9 [c]Rev. 13:11, 14; 19:20; 20:10
14 [a]2 Thess. 2:9 [b]Luke 2:1 [c]Rev. 17:14; 19:19; 20:8 [1]NU, M omit *of the earth and*

is now inaccessible. No further petitions or intercessions will be heard until the Final Judgment is completed.

16:1 God Himself commands the Final Judgment.

16:2–21 While the seven bowls have certain similarities to the seven trumpets, there are pronounced differences. The plagues introduced by the trumpets were partial and constituted a call to repentance. The bowls are the execution of total judgment when there is no more hope of repentance. The first four bowls affect the environment; the last three, the realm of the monster. The brief, rapid descriptions suggest simultaneous, rather than successive, actions. The descriptive details are not to be understood physically, but as terrifying calamities.

16:2 The first judgment is similar to the sixth Egyptian plague (see Ex. 9:9–11).

16:3 This plague is similar to the first one in Egypt (see Ex. 7:17–21).

16:4 Unlike the Egyptian plague, which affected only the waters of Egypt, every source of Earth's fresh water is now affected, indicating complete judgment.

16:6 God's judgment is retributive justice, of equal weight with the crime.

16:7 The voice of the martyrs (see 6:9, 10; 8:3) affirms the right of God to vindicate them.

16:8, 9 No matter how intense the suffering, the people, having lost the capacity, **did not repent.** Like Pharaoh their hearts are stubbornly defiant.

16:10, 11 **The throne of the beast** for John and his readers was the capital of the empire, Rome (see 2:13; 13:2).

16:12–14 The **Euphrates,** the last barrier to total destruction, is removed (9:14–21), clearing the way for invasion **from the east.** The Parthians from beyond the Euphrates symbolize all future military invasions that would destroy the empire. **Frogs** symbolize the demonic work of this unholy, counterfeit trinity. **The false prophet:** See 13:11–18; 19:20; 20:10. Although totally unaware of it, they are being used by God to accomplish His purpose, **to gather them to the battle** (see 19:19–21; 20:7–10). **That great day** is when the total redemptive purpose of God will be consummated in both salvation and judgment.

WORD WEALTH

16:14 signs, *semeion* (say-*mi*-on); Strong's *#4592:* Compare "semiology," "semiotic," "semaphore." A sign, mark, token. The word is used to distinguish between persons or objects (Matt. 26:48; Luke 2:12); to denote a warning or admonition (Matt. 12:39; 16:4); as an omen portending future events (Mark 13:4; Luke 21:7); to describe miracles and wonders, whether indicating divine authority (Matt. 12:38, 39; Mark 8:11, 12) or ascribed to false teachers and demons (Matt. 24:24; Rev. 16:14).

15 [a]"Behold, I am coming as a thief.
Blessed *is* he who watches, and keeps
his garments, [b]lest he walk naked and
they see his shame."
16 [a]And they gathered them together
to the place called in Hebrew,
[1]Armageddon.

Seventh Bowl: The Earth Utterly Shaken

17 Then the seventh angel poured out
his bowl into the air, and a loud voice
came out of the temple of heaven, from
the throne, saying, [a]"It is done!"
18 And [a]there were noises and thunderings and lightnings; [b]and there was
a great earthquake, such a mighty and
great earthquake [c]as had not occurred
since men were on the earth.
19 Now [a]the great city was divided
into three parts, and the cities of the
nations fell. And [b]great Babylon
[c]was remembered before God, [d]to give
her the cup of the wine of the fierceness of His wrath.

15 [a]Matt. 24:43; Luke 12:39; Rev. 3:3, 11 [b]2 Cor. 5:3
16 [a]Rev. 19:19 [1]Lit. *Mount Megiddo;* M *Megiddo*
17 [a]Rev. 10:6; 21:6
18 [a]Rev. 4:5 [b]Rev. 11:13 [c]Dan. 12:1; Matt. 24:21
19 [a]Rev. 14:8 [b]Rev. 17:5, 18 [c]Rev. 14:8; 18:5 [d]Is. 51:17; Rev. 14:10
20 [a]Rev. 6:14; 20:11

CHAPTER 17

1 [a]Rev. 1:1; 21:9 [b]Rev. 16:19 [c]Is. 1:21; Jer. 2:20; Nah. 3:4; Rev. 17:5, 15; 19:2 [d]Jer. 51:13; Rev. 17:15 [1]NU, M omit *to me* *See WW at Rev. 20:4.
2 [a]Rev. 2:22; 18:3, 9 [b]Jer. 51:7; Rev. 14:8
3 [a]Rev. 12:6, 14; 21:10 [b]Rev. 12:3 [c]Rev. 13:1

20 Then [a]every island fled away, and
the mountains were not found.
21 And great hail from heaven fell
upon men, *each hailstone* about the
weight of a talent. Men blasphemed
God because of the plague of the hail,
since that plague was exceedingly
great.

The Scarlet Woman and the Scarlet Beast

17 Then [a]one of the seven angels
who had the seven bowls came
and talked with me, saying [1]to me,
"Come, [b]I will show you the *judgment
of [c]the great harlot [d]who sits on many
waters,
2 [a]"with whom the kings of the earth
committed fornication, and [b]the inhabitants of the earth were made drunk
with the wine of her fornication."

WORD WEALTH

17:2 committed fornication, *porneuo* (porn-yoo-oh); Strong's *#4203:* Compare "pornographic" and "pornography." To engage in illicit sexual intercourse, be unfaithful, play the harlot, prostitute oneself. The word is used literally (Mark 10:19; 1 Cor. 6:18; 10:8; Rev. 2:14, 20) and metaphorically to describe spiritual fornication, that is, idolatry (Rev. 17:2; 18:3, 9).

3 So he carried me away in the Spirit
[a]into the wilderness. And I saw a
woman sitting [b]on a scarlet beast
which was full of [c]names of blasphemy, having seven heads and ten
horns.

16:15 The Day of the Lord will come unexpectedly and demands watchfulness on the part of the followers of Christ. It will be an indescribable blessing to those who are spiritually prepared. See note on Matt. 24:42; 1 Thess. 4:18—5:2.

16:16 They are the demonic frogs. **Armageddon,** or "Harmageddon," may refer to the Mount of Megiddo, at the upper entrance to the Plain of Esdraelon, Israel's chief battlefield in ancient time (see Judg. 5:19; 2 Kin. 9:27; 23:29; Zech. 12:11). The thought is not necessarily a literal military conflict, but, in any case, is a spiritually decisive conflict involving the final overthrow of the enemy by the power of almighty God.

DISPENSATIONAL INTERPRETATION: Vv. 12–16 present a parenthetical view of the final end-times world war, known as "the Battle of Armageddon." Demonic spirits, under the control of Satan, Antichrist, and the False Prophet, work deceptive miracles and manipulate the rulers of the world, causing them to gather in a great show of military strength against national Israel. See note on 19:17–21, "Dispensational Interpretation." Armageddon is located in the northern part of the plains of Jezreel.

16:17–21 Into the air: The Judgment is universal. **It is done:** The Judgment is complete. **The great city,** called **Babylon,** was initially Rome, the empire and its capital, symbolizing the judgment of God in the rise and fall of nations and empires throughout history, as well as at the end. People who have hardened their hearts choose to curse God rather than to repent.

17:1 The judgment is detailed, close-up pictures of the events of 16:17–21. **The great harlot** is Babylon (see 7:5; 18:2), symbolic of the ancient city of Rome, a type of every idolatrous system opposed to Christ. The **many waters** are the people groups over whom the harlot reigns (v. 15). See note on 18:1—19:10.

17:3 John is taken **into the wilderness** in order that he may view the scene from a proper perspective, as well as for protection. The **woman** is the harlot, identified in v. 18 as the ancient city of Rome. The **scarlet beast** is the beast that rose out of the sea (13:1). Its **heads** and **horns** symbolize the power of the empire which supports the harlot. **Sitting on:** Anti-Christian civilization is undergirded by anti-Christian political power (13:1–10). **Names of blasphemy:** Divine titles appropriated by an emperor or a state civil religion.

4 The woman [a]was arrayed in purple
and scarlet, [b]and adorned with gold
and precious stones and pearls, [c]hav-
ing in her hand a golden cup [d]full of
abominations and the filthiness of
[1]her fornication.
5 And on her forehead a name *was*
written:

[a]MYSTERY,
BABYLON THE GREAT,
THE MOTHER OF HARLOTS
AND OF THE
ABOMINATIONS OF THE
EARTH.

6 I saw [a]the woman, drunk [b]with the
blood of the saints and with the blood
of [c]the martyrs of Jesus. And when I
saw her, I marveled with great
amazement.

The Meaning of the Woman and the Beast

7 But the angel said to me, "Why did
you marvel? I will tell you the [1]mystery
of the woman and of the beast that carries her, which has the seven heads
and the ten horns.
8 "The beast that you saw was, and
is not, and [a]will ascend out of the
bottomless pit and [b]go to [1]perdition.
And those who [c]dwell on the earth
[d]will marvel, [e]whose names are not
written in the Book of Life from the
foundation of the world, when they see
the beast that was, and is not, and
[2]yet is.
9 [a]"Here *is* the mind which has wisdom: [b]The seven heads are seven
mountains on which the woman sits.

4 [a]Rev. 18:12, 16 [b]Dan. 11:38 [c]Jer. 51:7 [d]Rev. 14:8 [1]M *the fornication of the earth*
5 [a]2 Thess. 2:7
6 [a]Rev. 18:24 [b]Rev. 13:15 [c]Rev. 6:9, 10
7 [1]*hidden truth*
8 [a]Rev. 11:7 [b]Rev. 13:10; 17:11 [c]Rev. 3:10 [d]Rev. 13:3 [e]Rev. 13:8 [1]*destruction* [2]NU, M *shall be present*
9 [a]Rev. 13:18 [b]Rev. 13:1
10 [a]Rev. 13:5
11 [a]Rev. 13:3, 12, 14; 17:8 [1]*destruction*
12 [a]Dan. 7:20
14 [a]Rev. 16:14; 19:19 [b]Rev. 19:20 [c]1 Tim. 6:15 [d]Jer. 50:44 *See WW at Rev. 6:1. • See WW at 1 Pet. 2:9.
15 [a]Is. 8:7 [b]Rev. 13:7
16 [a]Jer. 50:41 [b]Rev. 18:17, 19 [c]Ezek. 16:37, 39 [d]Rev. 18:8 [1]NU, M *saw, and the beast*
17 [a]2 Thess. 2:11 [b]Rev. 10:7 *See WW at Rev. 2:23.
18 [a]Rev. 11:8; 16:19 [b]Rev. 12:4

CHAPTER 18

1 [a]Rev. 17:1, 7 [b]Ezek. 43:2

10 "There are also seven kings. Five
have fallen, one is, *and* the other has
not yet come. And when he comes, he
must [a]continue a short time.
11 "The [a]beast that was, and is not, is
himself also the eighth, and is of the
seven, and is going to [1]perdition.
12 [a]"The ten horns which you saw are
ten kings who have received no kingdom as yet, but they receive authority
for one hour as kings with the beast.
13 "These are of one mind, and they
will give their power and authority to
the beast.
14 [a]"These will make war with the
*Lamb, and the Lamb will [b]overcome
them, [c]for He is Lord of lords and King
of kings; [d]and those *who are* with Him
are called, *chosen, and faithful."
15 Then he said to me, [a]"The waters
which you saw, where the harlot sits,
[b]are peoples, multitudes, nations, and
tongues.
16 "And the ten horns which you
[1]saw on the beast, [a]these will hate the
harlot, make her [b]desolate [c]and naked,
eat her flesh and [d]burn her with fire.
17 [a]"For God has put it into their
*hearts to fulfill His purpose, to be of
one mind, and to give their kingdom
to the beast, [b]until the words of God
are fulfilled.
18 "And the woman whom you saw
[a]is that great city [b]which reigns over
the kings of the earth."

The Fall of Babylon the Great

18 After[a] these things I saw another angel coming down from
heaven, having great authority, [b]and

17:4 The gaudy adornment of the woman suggests her wealth and earthly glory. **Abominations** are idol worship and its defilements.
17:5 Roman prostitutes were required to wear a label with their names on their foreheads. **BABYLON:** See note on 18:1—19:10. To the early Christians, Rome was Babylon (see v. 9; 1 Pet. 5:13), **THE MOTHER** of idolatry and all its evils.

DISPENSATIONAL INTERPRETATION: **BABYLON THE GREAT, THE MOTHER OF HARLOTS,** has used all peoples of the Earth for her own selfish interests. In vv. 1–6 she represents the ultimate religious and moral prostitute, which merges with and manipulates governmental power whenever it is to her advantage. She therefore symbolizes and heads up the religious apostasy of the last days.

17:9 The city of Rome sits on seven hills.

DISPENSATIONAL INTERPRETATION: The **seven mountains** have caused some to identify **the woman** with Rome and its papacy.

17:10 Seven kings represent the complete number of Roman emperors, however many there might be, and by implication the complete number of political powers that persecute God's people throughout history.
17:12, 13 Ten horns: Some see the governors of the chief provinces of the Roman Empire, who **for one hour** (A.D. June 68 to A.D. December 69), were involved in the bloody civil strife that nearly destroyed Rome as an illustration of the spiritual principle that anti-Christian political and military power inevitably destroy the economy and the nation or civilization that they undergird, thus inducing their own retribution and fulfilling the purposes of God (vv. 16, 17).
17:14 This verse summarizes the message of the Revelation.

DISPENSATIONAL INTERPRETATION: In vv. 7–18 **the woman** is destroyed by the very **beast** (forces of Antichrist) upon whom she rode into influence and power. All of this will be performed by God's providence to fulfill His word.

18:1—19:10 Seven voices describe the fall of **Babylon** as an accomplished fact, some in thanksgiving and others in dismay. Babylon in the NT is a symbol of sinful humanity and its capacity for self-delusion, ambition, sinful pride, and demonized depravity. It thus represents world culture in rebellion against God. Babylon stands in contrast to the church as a society that persecutes God's people and thus inevitably will be destroyed.

DISPENSATIONAL INTERPRETATION: **Babylon** in 18:1–24 represents the satanic world system in all of its industrial, economic, and godless commercialism in contrast to what

the earth was illuminated with his glory.
2 And he cried [1]mightily with a loud
voice, saying, [a]"Babylon the great is
fallen, is fallen, and [b]has become a
dwelling place of demons, a prison for
every foul spirit, and [c]a cage for every
unclean and hated bird!
3 "For all the nations [a]have drunk of
the wine of the wrath of her fornication, the kings of the earth have *committed fornication with her, [b]and the
merchants of the earth have become
rich through the [1]abundance of her
luxury."
4 And I heard another voice from
heaven saying, [a]"Come out of her, my
people, lest you share in her sins, and
lest you receive of her plagues.
5 [a]"For her sins [1]have reached to
heaven, and [b]God has remembered her
iniquities.
6 [a]"Render to her just as she rendered [1]to you, and repay her double
according to her works; [b]in the cup
which she has mixed, [c]mix double for
her.
7 [a]"In the measure that she glorified
herself and lived [1]luxuriously, in the
same measure give her torment and
sorrow; for she says in her heart, 'I sit
as [b]queen, and am no widow, and will
not see sorrow.'
8 "Therefore her plagues will come
[a]in one day—death and mourning and
famine. And [b]she will be utterly
burned with fire, [c]for strong *is* the Lord
God who [1]judges her.

The World Mourns Babylon's Fall

9 [a]"The kings of the earth *who committed fornication and lived luxuriously with her [b]will weep and lament
for her, [c]when they see the smoke of
her burning,
10 "standing at a distance for fear of
her torment, saying, [a]'Alas, alas, that
great city Babylon, that mighty city!
[b]For in one hour your judgment has
come.'
11 "And [a]the merchants of the earth
will weep and **mourn** over her, for no
one buys their merchandise anymore:

WORD WEALTH

18:11 mourn, *pentheo* (pen-*theh*-oh); *Strong's #3996:* Compare "nepenthe," a drug that removes grief. To grieve, lament, mourn. In vv. 11, 15, and 19, *pentheo* is used of merchants who mourn the destruction of Babylon. The ungodly will experience great sorrow at the overthrow of the world system.

12 [a]"merchandise of gold and silver,
precious stones and pearls, fine linen
and purple, silk and scarlet, every kind
of citron wood, every kind of object of
ivory, every kind of object of most precious wood, bronze, iron, and marble;
13 "and cinnamon and incense, fragrant oil and frankincense, wine and
oil, fine flour and wheat, cattle and
sheep, horses and chariots, and bodies
and [a]souls of men.
14 "The fruit that your soul longed for
has gone from you, and all the things
which are rich and splendid have
[1]gone from you, and you shall find
them no more at all.
15 "The merchants of these things,
who became rich by her, will stand at
a distance for fear of her torment,
weeping and *wailing,
16 "and saying, 'Alas, alas, [a]that great
city [b]that was clothed in fine linen, purple, and scarlet, and adorned with gold
and precious stones and pearls!
17 [a]'For in one hour such great riches
[1]came to nothing.' [b]Every shipmaster,
all who travel by ship, sailors, and as
many as *trade on the sea, stood at a
distance
18 [a]"and cried out when they saw the
smoke of her burning, saying, [b]'What
is like this great city?'
19 [a]"They threw dust on their heads
and cried out, weeping and *wailing,
and saying, 'Alas, alas, that great city,
in which all who had ships on the sea
became rich by her wealth! [b]For in one
hour she [1]is made desolate.'
20 [a]"Rejoice over her, O heaven, and
you [1]holy apostles and prophets, for
[b]God has avenged you on her!"

Finality of Babylon's Fall

21 Then a mighty angel took up a stone
like a great millstone and threw *it* into
the sea, saying, [a]"Thus with violence
the great city Babylon shall be thrown
down, and [b]shall not be found anymore.
22 [a]"The sound of harpists, musicians,
flutists, and trumpeters shall not be

---

2 [a]Is. 13:19; 21:9 [b]Is. 13:21; 34:11, 13–15 [c]Is. 14:23 [1]NU, M omit *mightily*
3 [a]Rev. 14:8 [b]Is. 47:15 [1]Lit. *strengths* *See WW at Rev. 17:2.
4 [a]Is. 48:20
5 [a]Gen. 18:20 [b]Rev. 16:19 [1]NU, M *have been heaped up*
6 [a]Ps. 137:8 [b]Rev. 14:10 [c]Rev. 16:19 [1]NU, M omit *to you*
7 [a]Ezek. 28:2–8 [b]Is. 47:7, 8 [1]*sensually*
8 [a]Rev. 18:10 [b]Rev. 17:16 [c]Jer. 50:34 [1]NU, M *has judged*
9 [a]Ezek. 26:16; 27:35 [b]Jer. 50:46 [c]Rev. 19:3 *See WW at Rev. 17:2.
10 [a]Is. 21:9 [b]Rev. 18:17, 19
11 [a]Ezek. 27:27–34
12 [a]Rev. 17:4
13 [a]Ezek. 27:13
14 [1]NU, M *been lost to you*
15 *See WW at Rev. 18:11.
16 [a]Rev. 17:18 [b]Rev. 17:4
17 [a]Rev. 18:10 [b]Is. 23:14 [1]*have been laid waste* *See WW at John 3:21.
18 [a]Ezek. 27:30 [b]Rev. 13:4
19 [a]Josh. 7:6 [b]Rev. 18:8 [1]*have been laid waste* *See WW at Rev. 18:11.
20 [a]Jer. 51:48 [b]Luke 11:49 [1]NU, M *saints and apostles*
21 [a]Jer. 51:63, 64 [b]Rev. 12:8; 16:20
22 [a]Jer. 7:34; 16:9; 25:10

---

last-days apostate, religious forces she symbolizes in ch. 17. See note on 17:1–6, "Dispensational Interpretation."
18:9, 10 The voices of **the kings** who are allied with Rome lament the fall of the **mighty city.**
18:11–20 The voices of **the merchants** selfishly lament the loss of their commerce and markets.
18:21 Great millstone is prophetic symbolic action indicating total destruction (see Jer. 51:63, 64; Luke 17:2).

heard in you anymore. No craftsman
of any craft shall be found in you anymore, and the sound of a millstone
shall not be heard in you anymore.
23 [a]"The light of a lamp shall not shine
in you anymore, [b]and the voice of
bridegroom and bride shall not be
heard in you anymore. For [c]your merchants were the great men of the earth,
[d]for by your *sorcery all the nations
were deceived.
24 "And [a]in her was found the blood
of prophets and saints, and of all who
[b]were slain on the earth."

Heaven Exults over Babylon

19 After these things [a]I [1]heard a
loud voice of a great multitude
in heaven, saying, "Alleluia!
[b]Salvation and glory and honor and
*power *belong* to [2]the Lord our God!
2 "For [a]true and righteous *are* His
judgments, because He has judged the
great harlot who corrupted the earth
with her fornication; and He [b]has
avenged on her the blood of His servants *shed* by her."
3 Again they said, "Alleluia! [a]Her
smoke rises up forever and ever!"
4 And [a]the twenty-four elders and the
four living creatures fell down and
worshiped God who sat on the throne,
saying, [b]"Amen! Alleluia!"
5 Then a voice came from the throne,
saying, [a]"Praise our God, all you His
servants and those who fear Him,
[b]both[1] small and great!"

WORD WEALTH

19:5 servants, *doulos* (*doo*-loss); Strong's *#1401:* From *deo,* "to bind." The word denotes one in bondage to or subject to another, and is usually translated "slave" or "servant." Often the service involved is voluntary, in which a person willingly offers obedience, devotion, and loyalty to another, subordinating his will to him. The word is used of natural conditions (Matt. 8:9; 18:23), and metaphorically to describe servants of Christ (Rom. 1:1; 1 Cor. 7:22), of God (Acts 16:17; Titus 1:1), of sin (John 8:34; Rom. 6:17, 20), of corruption (2 Pet. 2:19), and of evil (Matt. 18:32; 24:48).

23 [a]Jer. 25:10 [b]Jer. 7:34; 16:9 [c]Is. 23:8; Rev. 6:15; 18:3 [d]2 Kin. 9:22 *See WW at Rev. 9:21. **24** [a]Rev. 16:6; 17:6 [b]Jer. 51:49

CHAPTER 19

1 [a]Jer. 51:48; Rev. 11:15; 19:6 [b]Rev. 4:11 [1]NU, M add *something like* [2]NU, M omit *the Lord* *See WW at Acts 4:33. **2** [a]Rev. 15:3; 16:7 [b]Deut. 32:43; 2 Kin. 9:7; Luke 18:7, 8; Rev. 6:10 **3** [a]Is. 34:10; Rev. 14:11 **4** [a]Rev. 4:4, 6, 10 [b]1 Chr. 16:36 **5** [a]Ps. 134:1 [b]Rev. 11:18 [1]NU, M omit *both*

6 [a]Ezek. 1:24; Rev. 1:15; 14:2 [b]Rev. 11:15 [1]NU, M *our* **7** [a][Matt. 22:2; 25:10]; Luke 12:36; John 3:29; [2 Cor. 11:2]; Eph. 5:23, 32; Rev. 19:9 *See WW at Rev. 6:1. **8** [a]Ps. 45:13; Ezek. 16:10 [b]Ps. 132:9 **9** [a]Matt. 22:2; Luke 14:15 [b]Rev. 22:6 **10** [a]Rev. 22:8 [b]Acts 10:26; Rev. 22:9 [c][Heb. 1:14] [d]1 John 5:10 [e]Luke 24:27; John 5:39 *See WW at John 19:35.

6 [a]And I heard, as it were, the voice
of a great multitude, as the sound of
many waters and as the sound of
mighty thunderings, saying, "Alleluia!
For [b]the[1] Lord God Omnipotent reigns!
7 "Let us be glad and rejoice and give
Him glory, for [a]the marriage of the
*Lamb has come, and His wife has
made herself ready."
8 And [a]to her it was granted to be arrayed in fine linen, clean and bright,
[b]for the fine linen is the righteous acts
of the saints.
9 Then he said to me, "Write:
[a]'Blessed *are* those who are called to
the marriage supper of the Lamb!'"
And he said to me, [b]"These are the true
sayings of God."

KINGDOM DYNAMICS

19:7–9 Restoration of Intimacy with God, RESTORATION. This text promises restored intimacy with God as His purpose develops in His people. The entire concept of "The Holy Spirit and Restoration" is developed in the study article, which begins on page 2012.

(Is. 4:2, 3/Joel 2:28, 29) J.R.

10 And [a]I fell at his feet to worship
him. But he said to me, [b]"See *that you*
do not *do that!* I am your [c]fellow servant, and of your brethren [d]who have
the testimony of Jesus. Worship God!
For the [e]testimony* of Jesus is the
spirit of prophecy."

KINGDOM DYNAMICS

19:10 The Holy Scriptures and the Spirit of Prophecy, PROPHECY. The entire

(*cont. on next page*)

19:1–6 The **voice of a great multitude** exults over the triumph of righteousness and truth. The word **Alleluia** ("praise the Lord") occurs only in this passage in the NT.

19:6–10 The voice of a great multitude announces **the marriage supper of the Lamb.** Again, this is not sequential; the consummation of the kingdom, already proleptically announced in 11:15, is once again so announced.

19:7 In the OT (see Is. 54:1–6; Hos. 2:19; 11:8, 9), Israel is called God's **wife,** but in the NT (Eph. 5:23–32), this metaphor is transferred to the church.

19:8 Granted . . . fine linen: By God's grace. **The righteous acts:** The good works that are the fruit of being justified by faith in Jesus Christ.

19:9 Marriage supper of the Lamb is the fellowship of eternal blessedness, foreshadowed by the Lord's Supper, rather than a literal meal.

19:10 John's temptation to worship the angel, repeated for emphasis (22:8, 9), warns that idolatry may arise within the church when the messenger, or even the message, is idolized. The essence of every genuine **prophecy** is its **testimony of Jesus,** the witness borne to Him.

***DISPENSATIONAL INTERPRETATION:* The marriage supper of the Lamb** (vv. 7–10), an actual meal in heaven, is the final manifestation of the marriage of Christ and **His wife.** This culminates their initial relationship, likened to an engagement, which was a legal arrangement in Jewish culture. This follows the coming of Christ as Bridegroom in the Rapture of the church before the Great Tribulation and precedes His return seven years later to establish His millennial kingdom.

(*cont. from preceding page*)
Bible is a product of the Holy Spirit, who is not only "the Spirit of truth" (John 16:13), but "the spirit of prophecy" (Rev. 19:10). The verb "to prophesy" (derived from Greek preposition *pro* and verb *phemi*) means "to speak forth before." The preposition "before" in this use may mean 1) "in advance" and/or 2) "in front of." Thus, "to prophesy" is a proper term to describe the proclamation of God's Word as it forecasts events. It may also describe the declaration of God's Word forthrightly, boldly, or confrontingly before a group or individual—telling forth God's truth and will. So, in both respects, the Bible is prophetic: a Book that reveals God's will through His Word and His works, as well as a Book that reveals God's plans and predictions.

This text defines the witness or testimony of Jesus Himself as being synonymous with, or at the heart of, the spirit of prophecy. These words not only define Scripture; they also confine all utterances that claim to be true prophecy: Jesus Christ will be at the center of it all, as He is in the whole Bible. 1) The OT exists to reveal Christ (Luke 24:27; John 5:39; 1 Pet. 1:10–12); and 2) the NT is inspired by the Holy Spirit for the same purpose (John 14:26; 16:13–15).

(*/1 John 4:1–6) J.W.H.

Christ on a White Horse

11 [a]Now I saw heaven opened, and behold, [b]a white horse. And He who sat
on him *was* called [c]Faithful and True,
and [d]in righteousness He judges and
makes war.
12 [a]His eyes *were* like a flame of fire,
and on His head *were* many crowns.
[b]He [1]had a name written that no one
knew except Himself.
13 [a]He *was* clothed with a robe dipped
in blood, and His name is called
[b]The Word of God.
14 [a]And the armies in heaven, [b]clothed
in [1]fine linen, white and clean, *followed Him on white horses.
15 Now [a]out of His mouth goes a
[1]sharp sword, that with it He should
strike the nations. And [b]He Himself
will rule them with a rod of iron.
[c]He Himself treads the winepress of
the fierceness and *wrath of Almighty
God.
16 And [a]He has on *His* robe and on
His thigh a name written:

[b]KING OF KINGS
AND LORD OF LORDS.

The Beast and His Armies Defeated

17 Then I saw an angel standing in the
sun; and he cried with a loud voice,
saying to all the birds that fly in the
midst of heaven, [a]"Come and gather
together for the [1]supper of the great
God,
18 [a]"that you may eat the flesh of

11 [a]Rev. 15:5 [b]Ps. 45:3, 4; Rev. 6:2; 19:19, 21 [c]Rev. 3:7, 14 [d]Ps. 96:13; Is. 11:4
12 [a]Dan. 10:6; Rev. 1:14 [b]Rev. 2:17; 19:16 [1]M adds *names written, and*
13 [a]Is. 63:2, 3 [b][John 1:1, 14]
14 [a]Rev. 14:20 [b]Matt. 28:3 [1]NU, M *pure white linen* *See WW at John 13:36.
15 [a]Is. 11:4; 2 Thess. 2:8; Rev. 1:16 [b]Ps. 2:8, 9 [c]Is. 63:3–6; Rev. 14:20 [1]M *sharp two-edged* *See WW at Luke 4:28.
16 [a]Rev. 2:17; 19:12 [b]Dan. 2:47
17 [a]1 Sam. 17:44; Jer. 12:9; Ezek. 39:17 [1]NU, M *great supper of God*
18 [a]Ezek. 39:18–20

19:11 The **white horse** symbolizes victory. **Faithful and True** describes Jesus, whose final victory in the **war** to come serves only to make clear to those "who dwell on the earth" what has been seen by the eyes of faith in His Cross and Resurrection. His standards and methods are qualitatively different from those of the dragon and his allies. He judges in the law court, not on the battlefield (see Is. 11:1–5). He conducts a spiritual warfare, not a military one.
19:12 His eyes: See note on 1:14. **Many crowns** represent unlimited diadems of sovereign authority (11:15), far surpassing the limited number usurped by the dragon (12:3) and the Beast (13:1). **Name written:** See note on v. 16. **No one knew:** The fullness of the Person of Jesus is beyond human comprehension (see 2:17; 3:12, 13).
19:13 Christ's **robe** is **dipped in** His atoning **blood,** not that of His enemies, since the battle has not yet taken place. **The Word of God:** Jesus reveals the character and purpose of God (see John 1:1, 14, 18; 10:30; 14:9; 1 John 1:1).
19:14 The **armies in heaven** are glorified saints described in similar terms of purity in v. 8. This is best seen as the time of the Rapture, as the church triumphant rises to meet Christ and the other returning saints (who have died) in the air at His return. See notes on v. 11 and 1 Thess. 4:17. *The raptured saints shall then immediately return to Earth* with Christ and the others. (For an alternate view on the time of the Rapture, see note on 4:1, "Dispensational Interpretation.")
19:15 The **sword** coming **out of His mouth** is the Word of God (see Heb. 4:12). **Rod of iron:** See note on 12:5. **Treads the winepress:** See 14:19, 20.
19:16 This awesome title (see 17:14; Deut. 10:17), earned by Christ's completed work and victory on the Cross (Phil. 2:5–11), is the basis for His consummating the victory over the dragon and his allies.

DISPENSATIONAL INTERPRETATION: In vv. 11–16 Christ leaves heaven with His saints and angels prior to His destruction of the Beast's forces. He fights for Israel to consummate the Battle of Armageddon. See Dan. 2:34, 35; Joel 3:9–16; Zech. 12:1–9; 14:1–4; Matt. 24:27–30.

Christ's return to Earth (v. 11) is seen as literal and premillennial (see note on 20:1–8). It is apocalyptic, necessary to inaugurate the next phase of His reign. Although the symbolic nature of the Bible's prophetic language makes it difficult to determine exactly what will be transpiring on Earth, it is clear Antichrist will be ruling with destruction, and Christ's return will destroy him. See note on vv. 19–21.
19:17–21 The victory is announced before the battle is fought (vv. 17, 18). **Birds** of prey are invited to a grisly feast, a solemn contrast to the marriage supper of the Lamb (see Ezek. 39:17–20).

The brief account of the final battle in vv. 19–21 is almost anticlimatic. **The beast** (see 13:1–10) and **the false prophet** (see 13:11–17) are seized and **cast alive into the lake of fire** (see 20:14; Dan. 7:11). Their allies are slain by the Word of the Lord, which has power to overcome all evil. The principle taught here applies in all generations. Any system which sets itself in opposition to Christ is doomed to defeat.

DISPENSATIONAL INTERPRETATION: The Battle of Armageddon: See note on 16:12–16, "Dispensational

kings, the flesh of captains, the flesh
of mighty men, the flesh of horses and
of those who sit on them, and the flesh
of all *people*, [1]free* and slave, both
small and great."
19 [a]And I saw the beast, the kings of
the earth, and their armies, gathered
together to make war against Him who
sat on the horse and against His army.
20 [a]Then the beast was captured, and
with him the false prophet who worked
signs in his presence, by which he deceived those who received the mark of
the beast and [b]those who worshiped
his image. [c]These two were cast alive
into the lake of fire [d]burning with
brimstone.
21 And the rest [a]were killed with the
sword which proceeded from the
mouth of Him who sat on the horse.
[b]And all the birds [c]were *filled with
their flesh.

Satan Bound 1000 Years

20 Then I saw an angel coming
down from heaven, [a]having the
key to the bottomless pit and a great
chain in his hand.
2 He laid hold of [a]the dragon, that
serpent of old, who is *the* Devil and
Satan, and bound him for a thousand
years;
3 and he cast him into the bottomless
pit, and shut him up, and [a]set a seal
on him, [b]so that he should deceive the
nations no more till the thousand years
were finished. But after these things he
must be released for a little while.

KINGDOM DYNAMICS

20:2, 3 13. What Is the Millennium?, SPIRITUAL ANSWERS. For the answer to this and other probing questions about God and the power life in His kingdom, see the study article "Spiritual Answers to Hard Questions," which begins on page 1996. P.R.

The Saints Reign with Christ 1000 Years

4 And I saw [a]thrones, and they sat
on them, and [b]**judgment** was committed to them. Then *I saw* [c]the souls of
those who had been beheaded for their
witness to Jesus and for the word of
God, [d]who had not worshiped the
beast [e]or his image, and had not received *his* mark on their foreheads or
on their hands. And they [f]lived and
[g]reigned with Christ for [1]a thousand
years.

WORD WEALTH

20:4 judgment, *krima* (*kree*-mah); Strong's *#2917:* Compare "crime" and *(cont. on next page)*

18 [1]NU, M *both free* *See WW at Rev. 6:15. **19** [a]Rev. 16:13–16 **20** [a]Rev. 16:13 [b]Rev. 13:8, 12, 13 [c]Is. 30:33; Dan. 7:11 [d]Rev. 14:10 **21** [a]Rev. 19:15 [b]Rev. 19:17, 18 [c]Rev. 17:16 *See WW at Matt. 15:33.

CHAPTER 20

1 [a]Rev. 1:18; 9:1 **2** [a]Is. 24:22; 2 Pet. 2:4; Jude 6 **3** [a]Dan. 6:17; Matt. 27:66 [b]Rev. 12:9; 20:8, 10

4 [a]Dan. 7:9; Matt. 19:28; Luke 22:30 [b]Dan. 7:22; [1 Cor. 6:2, 3] [c]Rev. 6:9 [d]Rev. 13:12 [e]Rev. 13:15 [f]John 14:19 [g]Rom. 8:17; 2 Tim. 2:12 [1]M *the*

Interpretation." West of Jordan, in the plain of Jezreel called Megiddo, the military forces of the Beast and False Prophet will be totally destroyed by the return of Christ. Anti-Semitism will reach a level not previously seen in history. **The kings of the earth** will gather against national Israel in great numbers. Only Christ's return to Earth destroys them (see Zech. 12:1–9; 14:1–4).

The beast (vv. 19, 20), a man, not a computer or government system, is the same power as "another horn, a little one" of Dan. 7:8, the "desolator" of Dan. 9:27, the "abomination of desolation" of Matt. 24:15, and "the lawless one" of 2 Thess. 2:8. Though destroyed, he is not annihilated.

20:1–8 EDITORIAL NOTE: There are basically two broad positions regarding the reign of Christ during this 1,000-year period, or Millennium. The *premillennial view* holds that after the victory of ch. 19, Christ will set up an earthly kingdom and will reign with the resurrected saints in peace and righteousness for 1,000 years, which may be a literal period or may be symbolic of an undetermined period. At the end of this period Satan will lead a final rebellion which will fail, and the world to come begins.

The *realized millennial view* (also called amillennial or present millennial) holds that the 1,000 years symbolize the period between the two advents of Christ, either as fully or progressively being realized. In this view, the millennial kingdom is a spiritual, not a political, reign of saints, being realized with Christ now, whether the believer is in heaven or on Earth.

The charts beginning on page 1948 elaborate and define distinctives to these views and detailed differences of position even within those two schools of thought.

20:1–3 The Devil, who empowered the Beast and the False Prophet, shares their doom. In the first stage of his judgment, he is **bound for a thousand years** in **the bottomless pit.** Whatever one's interpretation of the Millennium, the central truth of the defeat of Satan in stages remains the same. The purpose of the binding of the Devil is **that he should deceive the nations no more.** From the time of Jesus' First Advent and the outpouring of the Holy Spirit, it has no longer been possible for Satan to keep the peoples of the world in darkness without contest (Luke 2:29–32), as disciples proclaim the gospel to "all nations" (see Matt. 28:18–20).

***DISPENSATIONAL INTERPRETATION:* An angel coming down from heaven . . . laid hold of the dragon** signifies that Satan is uniquely at work on Earth after the events of 12:9. He is **bound** for the length of the Millennium in order that Christ might establish divine authority.

20:4–6 The plural **thrones** is used only four times in Rev. (see 4:4; 11:16), and those seated on them are always the twenty-four elders. **Judgment was committed to them** as representatives of the church in heaven and on Earth (see Dan. 7:9, 22, 27; Matt. 19:28; Luke 22:30; Heb. 12:1, 2). **Souls:** The vision is of a time before the final Resurrection (1 Cor. 15:42–58). **Beheaded** is symbolic of all martyrs.

***DISPENSATIONAL INTERPRETATION:* The first resurrection** includes the resurrection of 1) Jesus Christ, 2) many dead saints of OT times (Matt. 27:52, 53), 3) the dead saints of the church, 4) the rapture of the living saints (1 Thess. 4:16, 17), and 5) those who are martyred for their testimony during the Great Tribulation.

(*cont. from preceding page*)
"criminal." A legal term describing the judicial process of deciding guilt or innocence. The word is used chiefly for the verdict itself, reached after an investigation. The Lord forbids faultfinding decisions in Matt. 7:2, while in 1 Cor. 6:7, Paul discourages lawsuits against fellow Christians. *Krima* is used frequently of the judgment of God against wrongdoing.

5 But the rest of the dead did not live
again until the thousand years were
finished. This *is* the first *resurrection.
6 Blessed and holy *is* he who has part
in the first resurrection. Over such
[a]the second death has no power, but
they shall be [b]priests of God and of
Christ, [c]and shall reign with Him a
thousand years.

Satanic Rebellion Crushed

7 Now when the thousand years have
expired, Satan will be released from
his prison
8 and will go out [a]to deceive the nations which are in the four corners of
the earth, [b]Gog and Magog, [c]to gather
them together to battle, whose number
is as the sand of the sea.
9 [a]They went up on the breadth of the
earth and surrounded the camp of the
saints and the beloved city. And fire
came down from God out of heaven
and devoured them.
10 The devil, who deceived them, was
cast into the lake of fire and brimstone
[a]where[1] the beast and the false prophet
are. And they [b]will be tormented day
and night forever and ever.

The Great White Throne Judgment

11 Then I saw a great white throne and
Him who sat on it, from whose face
[a]the earth and the heaven fled away.
[b]And there was found no place for
them.
12 And I saw the dead, [a]small and
great, standing before [1]God, [b]and
books were opened. And another
[c]book was opened, which is *the Book*
of Life. And the dead were judged
[d]according to their works, by the
things which were written in the
books.
13 The sea gave up the dead who were
in it, [a]and Death and Hades delivered
up the dead who were in them. [b]And
they were judged, each one according
to his works.
14 Then [a]Death and Hades were cast
into the lake of fire. [b]This is the second
[1]death.
15 And anyone not found written in
the Book of Life [a]was cast into the lake
of fire.

All Things Made New

21 Now [a]I saw a *new **heaven** and
a new earth, [b]for the first
heaven and the first earth had passed
away. Also there was no more sea.

WORD WEALTH

21:1 heaven, *ouranos* (oo-ran-*oss*); Strong's #3772: Compare "uranography" and "Uranus." A word, often used in the plural, to denote the sky and the regions above the Earth (Heb. 1:10; 2 Pet. 3:5, 10) and the abode of God (Matt. 5:34; Rom. 1:18), Christ (Luke 24:51; Acts 3:21), angels (Matt. 24:36; Mark 12:25), and resurrected saints (2 Cor. 5:1). By metonymy the word refers to God (Matt. 21:25; Luke 15:18) and to the inhabitants of heaven (Rev. 18:20).

2 Then I, [1]John, saw [a]the holy city,
New Jerusalem, coming down out of

---

5 *See WW at Acts 23:6.
6 [a][Rev. 2:11; 20:14] [b]Is. 61:6; 1 Pet. 2:9; Rev. 1:6 [c]Rev. 20:4
8 [a]Rev. 12:9; 20:3, 10 [b]Ezek. 38:2; 39:1, 6 [c]Rev. 16:14
9 [a]Is. 8:8; Ezek. 38:9, 16
10 [a]Rev. 19:20; 20:14, 15 [b]Rev. 14:10 [1]NU, M *where also*
11 [a]2 Pet. 3:7; Rev. 21:1 [b]Dan. 2:35; Rev. 12:8
12 [a]Rev. 19:5 [b]Dan. 7:10 [c]Ps. 69:28; Dan. 12:1; Phil. 4:3; Rev. 3:5 [d]Jer. 17:10; Matt. 16:27; Rom. 2:6; Rev. 2:23; 20:12 [1]NU, M *the throne*
13 [a]1 Cor. 15:26; Rev. 1:18; 6:8; 21:4 [b]Matt. 16:27; Rev. 2:23; 20:12
14 [a]1 Cor. 15:26; Rev. 1:18; 6:8; 21:4 [b]Rev. 21:8 [1]NU, M *death, the lake of fire.*
15 [a]Rev. 19:20

CHAPTER 21

1 [a]Is. 65:17; 66:22; [2 Pet. 3:13] [b][2 Pet. 3:10]; Rev. 20:11 *See WW at 2 Cor. 5:17.
2 [a]Is. 52:1; [Gal. 4:26]; Heb. 11:10 [1]NU, M omit *John*

20:7–10 Satan's desire is to hasten the day of the **battle** (v. 8) in order to frustrate God's purpose by limiting the scope of His salvation (2 Pet. 3:8–10), but he is bound until God sovereignly determines to release him. He then will make one last effort to destroy Christ and His people. **Four corners** connotes worldwide. In Ezek. 38 and 39 **Gog** is the prince of the land of **Magog.** They represent rulers and their peoples who ally with Satan in rebellion against God. **The camp of the saints** is **the beloved city,** or the "New Jerusalem" (21:2), the residence of the saints. There is no military battle. This is spiritual warfare, and the enemy cannot withstand the overwhelming power of God.

DISPENSATIONAL INTERPRETATION: At the end of the 1,000 years, **Satan will be released** in the Earth again **to deceive.** It appears that many who submitted to Christ's rule during the Millennium did so without inner commitment to His lordship. The final deception of Satan separates these from those who have sincerely submitted. This is the last insurrection that the Lord will tolerate. Satan will next be **cast into the lake of fire** and **tormented . . . forever.**

20:11–15 History has ended, and only Final Judgment is left to complete the drama of redemption. The Final Judgment is concerned with the spiritually **dead,** not the saints. ***The Book* of Life was opened** to reveal that the names of the **dead** do not appear in it. "The last enemy" to be destroyed is **Death and Hades,** the temporary abode of the dead until the Final Judgment. They are ultimately as powerless as the other forces of evil.

DISPENSATIONAL INTERPRETATION: This judgment (vv. 11–15) closes the millennial period and opens the Age to Come. It is the greatest of all judgments because it encompasses all the wicked from the beginning of man's history. Jesus Christ is the One sitting on the **great white throne,** fulfilling John 5:22. Those who are judged are lost because they refused God's salvation in Christ by grace through faith. Their doom is **the second death.**

21:2 The holy city is the **bride** of Christ, the church (see vv. 9, 10), as well as the abode of the saints.

heaven from God, **prepared** [b]as a bride
*adorned for her husband.

WORD WEALTH

21:2 prepared, *hetoimazo* (het-oy-*mad*-zoe); Strong's *#2090:* To make ready, prepare, make arrangements. In addition to its normal use describing preparation for coming events, the word is used of preparation for the Messiah (Matt. 3:3; Mark 1:3; Luke 1:76), of blessings that God has ordained (Matt. 20:23; 25:34), and of judgment (Matt. 25:41).

3 And I heard a loud voice from
heaven saying, "Behold, [a]the tabernacle of God *is* with men, and He will
dwell with them, and they shall be His
people. God Himself will be with them
and be their God.
4 [a]"And God will *wipe away every
tear from their eyes; [b]there shall be no
more death, [c]nor sorrow, nor crying.
There shall be no more pain, for the
former things have passed away."
5 Then [a]He who sat on the throne
said, [b]"Behold, I make all things new."
And He said [1]to me, "Write, for
[c]these words are true and faithful."
6 And He said to me, [a]"It[1] is done!
[b]I am the Alpha and the Omega, the
Beginning and the End. [c]I will give of
the fountain of the water of life freely
to him who thirsts.
7 "He who overcomes [1]shall inherit
all things, and [a]I will be his God and
he shall be My son.
8 [a]"But the cowardly, [1]unbelieving,
abominable, murderers, sexually immoral, sorcerers, idolaters, and all liars
shall have their part in [b]the lake which
burns with fire and brimstone, which
is the second death."

The New Jerusalem

9 Then one of [a]the seven angels who
had the seven bowls filled with the
seven last plagues came [1]to me and
talked with me, saying, "Come, I will
show you [b]the [2]bride, the Lamb's
wife."
10 And he carried me away [a]in the
Spirit to a great and high mountain,
and showed me [b]the [1]great city, the
[2]holy Jerusalem, descending out of
heaven from God,
11 [a]having the glory of God. Her light
was like a most precious stone, like a
jasper stone, clear as crystal.
12 Also she had a great and high wall
with [a]twelve gates, and twelve angels
at the gates, and names written on
them, which are *the names* of the
twelve tribes of the children of Israel:
13 [a]three gates on the east, three gates
on the north, three gates on the south,
and three gates on the west.
14 Now the wall of the city had twelve
foundations, and [a]on them were the
[1]names of the twelve *apostles of the
Lamb.
15 And he who talked with me [a]had a
gold reed to measure the city, its gates,
and its wall.
16 The city is laid out as a square; its
length is as great as its breadth. And
he measured the city with the reed:
twelve thousand [1]furlongs. Its length,
breadth, and height are equal.
17 Then he measured its wall: one hundred *and* forty-four cubits, *according*
to the measure of a man, that is, of an
angel.
18 The construction of its wall was *of*
jasper; and the city *was* pure gold, like
clear glass.
19 [a]The foundations of the wall of the
city *were* *adorned with all kinds of
precious stones: the first foundation
was jasper, the second sapphire, the
third chalcedony, the fourth emerald,
20 the fifth sardonyx, the sixth sardius,
the seventh chrysolite, the eighth
beryl, the ninth topaz, the tenth chrys-
oprase, the eleventh jacinth, and the
twelfth amethyst.
21 The twelve gates *were* twelve
[a]pearls: each individual gate was of

2 [b]2 Cor. 11:2 *See WW at Matt. 25:7.
3 [a]Lev. 26:11
4 [a]Is. 25:8 [b]1 Cor. 15:26 [c]Is. 35:10; 51:11; 65:19 *See WW at Col. 2:14.
5 [a]Rev. 4:2, 9; 20:11 [b]Is. 43:19 [c]Rev. 19:9; 22:6 [1]NU, M omit *to me*
6 [a]Rev. 10:6; 16:17 [b]Rev. 1:8; 22:13 [c]John 4:10 [1]M omits *It is done*
7 [a]Zech. 8:8 [1]M *I shall give him these things*
8 [a]1 Cor. 6:9 [b]Rev. 20:14 [1]M adds *and sinners,*
9 [a]Rev. 15:1 [b]Rev. 19:7; 21:2 [1]NU, M omit *to me* [2]M *woman, the Lamb's bride*
10 [a]Rev. 1:10 [b]Ezek. 48 [1]NU, M omit *great* [2]NU, M *holy city, Jerusalem*
11 [a]Rev. 15:8; 21:23; 22:5
12 [a]Ezek. 48:31–34
13 [a]Ezek. 48:31–34
14 [a]Eph. 2:20 [1]NU, M *twelve names* *See WW at 1 Cor. 12:28.
15 [a]Ezek. 40:3
16 [1]Lit. *stadia,* about 1,380 miles in all
19 [a]Is. 54:11 *See WW at Matt. 25:7.
21 [a]Matt. 13:45, 46

21:3, 4 The tabernacle and the accompanying description of the bliss of the saints indicate the unbroken fellowship between God and His people. Because of His presence there is no more sorrow. See note on Ezek. 40:1—48:35.
21:5, 6 God proclaims the completion of the **new** as well as the destruction of the old (16:17).
21:8 Cowardly: Courage and patient endurance are indispensable in the conflict between the Lamb and the dragon. **Unbelieving** is the opposite of faithfulness. **Abominable** means polluted by the Earth's abominations (17:5). **Sorcerers:** The literal Greek refers to those dealing in drugs. **Liars** are those who deviate from the truth and join the deceivers.
21:10 High mountain does not refer to perspective, but to the actual site of **the holy Jerusalem** (see Ps. 48:1, 2; Is. 2:2; Ezek. 40:2; 48:12–16; Mic. 4:1; Zech. 8:22; 14:16).
21:11–14 Jasper: See note on 4:3. The **twelve gates** are open in all directions to all peoples (vv. 24, 25). **The twelve tribes** (see 7:1–8) plus **the twelve apostles** are the combined people of God, incorporating the Old and New, built on **twelve foundations,** the testimony of the eyewitnesses to the revelation of God (see Eph. 2:20).
21:15–17 The city is a perfect cube, a symbol of perfection, as was the Most Holy Place (see 1 Kin. 6:20). The dimensions of 12 and 1,000 indicate that there will be perfect room for all the redeemed.
21:18–21 The precious materials used in the construction of **the city** magnify its beauty and glory.

one pearl. [b]And the street of the city
was pure gold, like transparent glass.

The Glory of the New Jerusalem

22 [a]But I saw no temple in it, for the
Lord God Almighty and the Lamb are
its temple.
23 [a]The city had no need of the sun
or of the moon to shine [1]in it, for the
[2]glory of God illuminated it. The Lamb
is its light.
24 [a]And the nations [1]of those who are
saved shall walk in its light, and the
kings of the earth bring their glory and
honor [2]into it.
25 [a]Its gates shall not be shut at all by
day [b](there shall be no night there).
26 [a]And they shall bring the glory and
the honor of the nations into [1]it.
27 But [a]there shall by no means enter
it anything [1]that defiles, or causes an
abomination or a lie, but only those
who are written in the Lamb's [b]Book
of Life.

The River of Life

22 And he showed me [a]a [1]pure*
river of water of life, clear as
crystal, proceeding from the throne of
God and of the *Lamb.
2 [a]In the middle of its street, and on
either side of the river, *was* [b]the tree
of life, which bore twelve fruits, each
tree *yielding its fruit every month.
The leaves of the tree *were* [c]for the
healing of the nations.
3 And [a]there shall be no more curse,
[b]but the throne of God and of the Lamb
shall be in it, and His [c]servants shall
serve Him.
4 [a]They shall see His face, and
[b]His name *shall be* on their foreheads.
5 [a]There shall be no night there: They
need no lamp nor [b]light of the sun, for
[c]the Lord God gives them light.
[d]And they shall reign forever and ever.

The Time Is Near

6 Then he said to me, [a]"These words
are faithful and true." And the Lord
God of the [1]holy prophets [b]sent His angel to show His servants the things
which must [c]shortly take place.
7 [a]"Behold, I am coming *quickly!
[b]Blessed* *is* he who keeps the words
of the prophecy of this book."
8 Now I, John, [1]saw and heard these
things. And when I heard and saw,
[a]I fell down to worship before the feet
of the angel who showed me these
things.
9 Then he said to me, [a]"See *that you*
do not *do that*. [1]For I am your fellow
servant, and of your brethren the
prophets, and of those who keep the
words of this book. *Worship God."
10 [a]And he said to me, "Do not seal
the words of the prophecy of this book,
[b]for the time is at hand.
11 "He who is unjust, let him be unjust
still; he who is filthy, let him be filthy
still; he who is righteous, let him
[1]be righteous still; he who is *holy, let
him be holy still."

Jesus Testifies to the Churches

12 "And behold, I am coming quickly,
and [a]My **reward** *is* with Me, [b]to give
to every one according to his work.

21 [b]Rev. 22:2
22 [a]John 4:21, 23
23 [a]Is. 24:23; 60:19, 20 [1]NU, M omit *in it* [2]M *very glory*
24 [a]Is. 60:3, 5; 66:12 [1]NU, M omit *of those who are saved* [2]M *of the nations to Him*
25 [a]Is. 60:11 [b]Is. 60:20
26 [a]Rev. 21:24 [1]M adds *that they may enter in.*
27 [a]Joel 3:17 [b]Phil. 4:3 [1]NU, M *profane, nor one who causes*

CHAPTER 22

1 [a]Ezek. 47:1 [1]NU, M omit *pure* *See WW at Matt. 5:8. • See WW at Rev. 6:1.
2 [a]Ezek. 47:12 [b]Gen. 2:9 [c]Rev. 21:24 *See WW at Matt. 22:21.
3 [a]Zech. 14:11 [b]Ezek. 48:35 [c]Rev. 7:15
4 [a][Matt. 5:8] [b]Rev. 14:1
5 [a]Rev. 21:23 [b]Rev. 7:15 [c]Ps. 36:9 [d]Dan. 7:18, 27
6 [a]Rev. 19:9 [b]Rev. 1:1 [c]Heb. 10:37 [1]NU, M *spirits of the prophets*
7 [a][Rev. 3:11] [b]Rev. 1:3 *See WW at Rev. 22:20. • See WW at Matt. 5:3.
8 [a]Rev. 19:10 [1]NU, M *am the one who heard and saw*
9 [a]Rev. 19:10 [1]NU, M omit *For* *See WW at Rev. 4:10.
10 [a]Dan. 8:26 [b]Rev. 1:3
11 [1]NU, M *do right* *See WW at John 10:36.
12 [a]Is. 40:10; 62:11 [b]Rev. 20:12

21:22, 23 Neither **temple** nor created light is needed, because of the presence of **God** and **the Lamb.**
21:24–26 The city is perfect it its universality and in its holiness.
22:1 The **river** symbolizes the blessings of God (see Gen. 2:9–14; Ps. 46:4; Ezek. 47:1–12).
22:2 The **tree of life** suggests abundant life. Everything necessary to sustain life, including perpetual health, is provided (see 2:7; Gen. 2:9; 3:22; Ezek. 47:12).
22:3 God's **curse** (see Gen. 3:17) is removed forever (see Ezek. 36:33–36; Zech. 14:11). There will be perfect divine government, and the saints will delight to **serve** God.
22:4 See His face: The redeemed enjoy perfect fellowship with God and the Lamb. **On their foreheads:** See note on 3:12.
22:6–20 There are seven confirming witnesses testifying to the authenticity of the message.
22:6 The first witness is that of God through **His angel. These words** refer to the content of Rev. **The holy prophets** is literally, "the spirits of the prophets," their natural faculties under supernatural inspiration. **Which must shortly take place** refers to the spiritual conflict (see 17:14).
22:7 A parenthetical response by Jesus. **Coming quickly** means inevitably, according to God's time, not man's. See note on 1:1.
22:8, 9 The second witness is John's personal deposition (see 19:10).
22:10, 11 The third witness is the witness of the angel (see Heb. 1:14). **Do not seal:** The visions are not to be kept secret for a later generation, but are relevant to all Christians until the consummation of the kingdom. The deliberate choice that one makes fixes one's unalterable fate. Character produces its inevitable fruit.
22:12–16 The fourth witness is the Lord Jesus. **Quickly:** However long the era of the Spirit continues, the next act in God's universal drama is the consummation of the ages. **The Alpha and the Omega:** Jesus applies God's title to Himself. See note on 1:8. All who have obeyed the Lord **may enter . . . the city,** but all others are excluded (v. 15). **The Root and the Offspring:** Jesus is not only the promised

WORD WEALTH

22:12 reward, *misthos* (mis-*thoss*); Strong's *#3408:* Pay, wages, salary, recompense for service. The word especially describes divine rewards given to believers for the moral quality of their actions. The reward can be one and the same in all cases, but its value to the individual worker will vary according to the work he has done.

13 [a]"I am the Alpha and the Omega,
the [1]Beginning and *the* End, the First
and the Last."
14 [a]Blessed *are* those who [1]do His
commandments, that they may have
the right [b]to the tree of life, [c]and may
enter through the gates into the city.
15 [1]But [a]outside *are* [b]dogs and sorcerers and sexually immoral and murderers and idolaters, and whoever
*loves and practices a lie.
16 [a]"I, Jesus, have sent My angel to
testify to you these things in the
churches. [b]I am the Root and the Offspring of David, [c]the Bright and Morning Star."
17 And the Spirit and [a]the bride say,
"Come!" And let him who hears say,
"Come!" [b]And let him who thirsts
come. Whoever desires, let him take
the water of life freely.

A Warning

18 [1]For I testify to everyone who hears
the words of the prophecy of this book:
[a]If anyone adds to these things,
[2]God will add to him the plagues that
are written in this book;
19 and if anyone takes away from the
*words of the book of this *prophecy,
[a]God[1] shall take away his part from
the [2]Book of Life, from the holy city,
and *from* the things which are written
in this book.

I Am Coming Quickly

20 He who testifies to these things
says, "Surely I am coming **quickly.**"
Amen. Even so, come, Lord Jesus!
21 The grace of our Lord Jesus Christ
be [1]with you all. Amen.

13 [a]Is. 41:4 [1]NU, M *First and the Last, the Beginning and the End.*
14 [a]Dan. 12:12; [1 John 3:24] [b][Prov. 11:30]; Rev. 2:7 [c]Rev. 21:27 [1]NU *wash their robes,*
15 [a]Matt. 8:12; 1 Cor. 6:9; Gal. 5:19; Col. 3:6; Rev. 21:8 [b]Deut. 23:18; Matt. 7:6; Phil. 3:2 [1]NU, M omit *But* *See WW at John 21:15.
16 [a]Rev. 1:1 [b]2 Sam. 7:12; Is. 9:7; Jer. 23:5; Rev. 5:5 [c]Num. 24:17; Luke 1:78; 2 Pet. 1:19
17 [a][Rev. 21:2, 9] [b]Is. 55:1; Rev. 21:6
18 [a]Deut. 4:2; 12:32; Prov. 30:6 [1]NU, M omit *For* [2]M *may God add*
19 [a]Ex. 32:33 [1]M *may God take away* [2]NU, M *tree of life* *See WW at Acts 19:20. • See WW at 1 Thess. 5:20.
21 [1]NU *with all;* M *with all the saints*

WORD WEALTH

22:20 quickly, *tachu* (takh-*oo*); Strong's *#5035:* Compare "tachometer." Immediately, speedily, shortly, hastily. The word is especially used in the Book of Revelation in relation to the imminent return of Christ.

KINGDOM DYNAMICS

22:20 "Surely I Am Coming Quickly," MESSIAH'S COMING. Among the very last words of the Bible is this promise from the Lord Jesus, "Surely I am coming quickly." This blessed hope, which was declared by angels and spoken of by the apostles, is tenderly reiterated by the Lord at the very end of His Word. It is as if He wished to say, "There is much in My Word that you need attend to, but do not let this hope be overshadowed: I am coming back soon." Together with John, let us say, "Even so, come, Lord Jesus!"

(Matt. 25:13/Gen. 3:15*) J.H.

King of the lineage of David, whose kingdom would be established forever (see 2 Sam. 7:13, 14), but the Creator of David (see Ps. 110:1; Is. 11:1, 10). **The Bright and Morning Star** connotes the dawn of the new, eternal Day (see 2:28; Num. 24:17).

22:17 The fifth, sixth, and seventh witnesses are **the Spirit, the bride,** and **him who hears.** The climactic focus of the Revelation is an evangelistic appeal, **Come,** addressed to those who still remain outside (22:15). The Spirit without the bride does not issue the invitation. The bride without the Spirit cannot.

22:18, 19 This solemn warning is directed against any perversion in interpretation of **the prophecy of this book,** made by those who read into Rev. what the Holy Spirit never intended to teach.

22:20 Jesus again gives assurance of His return, to which John adds his affirming word (see 1 Cor. 16:22).

TRUTH-IN-ACTION through REVELATION

Letting the LIFE of the Holy Spirit Bring Faith's Works Alive in You!

Truth Revelation Teaches	Text	**Action** Revelation Invites
1 Steps to Holiness Jesus calls His people to be fully separated from the world's value system and to be totally committed to Him. They are to find the spiritual power source in their lives in Christ, not in occult practices. The believer is to gauge success by the measuring rod of God, rather than by the world's social and financial standard. When the Christian understands God's view from the eternal, the present comes into correct perspective.	3:17 3:18 13:16	**Do not value** worldly success. **Do not trust** worldly wealth. **Repent** wherever you have done these things. **Recognize** that worldly assets have no spiritual or heavenly value! **Return** to a spiritual value system wherever you have departed. **Do not adopt** the world's way of thinking or its standards of behavior.
2 Key Lessons in Faith Faith is established in the knowledge of God, trusting Him for understanding and wisdom in the face of persecution. Faith's commitment to overcome, based on the shed blood of Jesus, does not fear even death.	1:3 2:10, 11 2:13 13:10; 14:12	**Trust God for understanding** when you read Rev. **Be faithful to Jesus** when confronted with persecution and death. **Never renounce** faith in Jesus. **Understand** that the Lord calls His people to faithfulness and patient endurance. **Never give up!**
3 Steps to Dynamic Devotion Jesus requires absolute devotion and rejects lackadaisical, half-hearted followers. Zeal for the Lord is not optional for His disciples. Devotion willingly submits to Jesus' discipline because it recognizes His love in it.	2:4 3:15 3:19	**Give** your love for Jesus first place in your life. **Commit** yourself both emotionally and intellectually to Christ. **Avoid** lukewarmness; **stir up** your zeal for the Lord. **Repent quickly** whenever the Spirit convicts you of sin.
4 Keys to Wise Living The wise believer takes the time to listen with his spiritual hearing to what the Spirit is saying to the church. This is as needed today as it was in the first century. One who hears and follows the voice of the Holy Spirit does not need to fear the deception that leads to apostasy. Rather, he will walk where Jesus requires and will grow in the things of the Spirit of God, which produce healthy, vibrant, Spirit-filled churches capable of preaching Jesus to all the world.	2:7, 11, 17, 29; 3:6, 13, 22 2:9, 10	**Develop** your spiritual ear. **Listen** to what the Spirit is saying to the church. When forced to choose, **obey** God, not man! **Understand** that one may be rich in the Spirit but poor in the world's eyes. **Be faithful** and **receive** the crown of life.
5 Keys to Moral Purity The church is pictured as the bride of Christ; thus sexual impurity and apostasy are linked. Christians are required to be faithful to Christ, being sexually pure, worshiping no carnal idol.	2:14, 20 14:4, 5	**Reject** any teaching or practice that allows sexual immorality among God's people. **Maintain** sexual purity. **Practice** absolute obedience to Jesus. **Live** a blameless life.

Truth Revelation Teaches	Text	**Action** Revelation Invites
6 Steps in Developing Humility The believer is constantly to strengthen the things of God that have become established in his life. Being ready to repent for any failure, to make right any sin, will cause the believer to refine his walk in the Spirit. Outward works do not always indicate a right condition of heart, but a right condition of heart produces good works.	3:1–5	**Do not be** lulled to sleep because of a good reputation. **Keep on pressing** into Jesus. **Make sure** you practice the teachings you have received. **Obey** God's word to you.
7 Guidelines to Gaining Victory Spiritual victory is something we enter into. Jesus Christ has already won the victory through His death, burial, and resurrection.	12:11	**Conduct spiritual warfare** on the basis of Jesus' shed blood and through the declaration that He died for your sins and rose again for your justification. **Love** Jesus more than life itself.

Spiritual Answers to Hard Questions

Answering Essential Questions About God and the Power Life in His Kingdom

by Pat Robertson

These thirty-eight crucial and interesting questions have been selected because of the frequency of their occurrence and the teaching value the answers provide. They are distilled from *Answers to 200 of Life's Most Probing Questions,* copyright © 1984 by Pat Robertson (published by Thomas Nelson and used by permission).

Questions on God's Nature and Our Salvation

1. *What is God like?* (Acts 17:23)

Theologians have tried to describe God in many ways. He is the substance of all human virtues. He is all-wise and all-knowing. He can do anything and everything we cannot do, and He is everything good that we would like to be. So we say that He is *omnipotent* (all-powerful) or *omniscient* (all-knowing) or *omnipresent* (present everywhere).

On the other hand, we can describe God by contrasting Him with our human limitations. For example, we are mortal, but God is immortal. We are fallible, but God is infallible.

God is a Spirit: eternal and ever-living. He has no beginning or end. He is a Person who is totally self-aware—"I am"; totally moral—"I ought"; and totally self-assertive—"I will." He is the essence of love, and He is loving. He is also a righteous judge—totally fair and just.

God is the Father of all creation, the Creator of all. He is all-powerful and sustains the universe. He exists outside the universe (theologians call this *transcendence*), yet He is present throughout the universe (theologians say He is *immanent*) and is its ruler. He exists in nature, but He is not nature, nor is He bound by the laws of nature as the pantheists assert. He is the source of all life and everything that is.

The best description of God is the name that He gave for Himself to the early Israelites, *Yahweh. Yahweh* is usually translated "Jehovah" or "LORD." Scholars believe that this is the *hiphil* tense of the Hebrew verb "to be" and literally means "He who causes (everything else) to be."

2. *What does the Bible say about the Trinity?* (2 Cor. 13:14)

The Trinity is one of the great theological mysteries. There are some who think that because we believe in monotheism, one God, we cannot accept the concept of the Trinity. Yet the Bible teaches that the Godhead consists of three divine Persons—Father, Son, and Holy Spirit—each fully God, each showing fully the divine nature (Luke 3:21, 22).

The Father is the fountainhead of the Trinity, the Creator, the first cause. He is the primary thought, the concept of all that has been and will be created. Jesus said, "My Father has been working until now, and I have been working" (John 5:17).

The Son is the "Logos" or expression of God—the "only begotten" of the Father—and He Himself is God. Further, as God incarnate, He reveals the Father to us (John 14:9). The Son of God is both the agent of creation and mankind's only Redeemer.

The Holy Spirit, the third Person of the Trinity, proceeds from the Father and is worshiped and glorified together with the Father and the Son. He inspired the *Scriptures*, empowers God's people, and convicts the world "of sin, and of righteousness, and of judgment" (John 16:8).

All three Persons of the Godhead are eternal. The Father exists and has existed forever. With Him always existed His expression, the Son. Always the Father loved the Son, and the Son loved and served the Father. From that relationship of love exists the

Spirit of God, who is eternal and has existed forever. The Father did not exist first, then later the Son, and still later the Spirit. They all three have existed from before there was anything that could begin—three distinct Persons all functioning as One. Upon the occasion of Jesus' baptism, all three Persons in the Trinity were present and active. The Father spoke from heaven, the Son was fulfilling all righteousness, and the Spirit descended upon the Son like a dove (Matt. 3:16, 17).

The existence of the Trinity is a mystery that one day we will understand clearly. For now, we know that the Bible teaches it and Jesus revealed it, and the Christian church from the beginning has confessed and safeguarded this precious truth (1 Cor. 12:4–6; 2 Cor. 13:14; Eph. 4:4–6; 2 Thess. 2:13, 14).

3. *What do I have to do to be saved?* (John 3:3)

To be saved you must turn away from sin, believe in the death and resurrection of Jesus, and receive Him as Lord and Savior of your life.

Here is the step-by-step process. First, you must consider your life and then turn away from everything in it that is contrary to what God wants. This turning away from selfishness and toward God is called *repentance* (Matt. 3:7–10; Acts 3:19).

Second, you must acknowledge that Jesus Christ died on the Cross to forgive you of sin. You take Him as your Savior to cleanse you from sin—as the substitute who paid the price due for your sin (Rom. 5:9, 10; Titus 2:14).

Third, you must ask Him to be Lord of your life, acknowledging openly and verbally that Jesus is not only your Savior but your Lord (1 John 2:23).

The Bible says that as many as received Him were given the power to become the sons of God (John 1:12). So when you open your heart and receive Him, He comes into your heart—your inner person—through His Holy Spirit, and begins to live His life in you. From that point it is your privilege and call to confess what God has done (Rom. 10:9).

4. *If I sin, will I lose my salvation?* (Heb. 6:4–6)

An act of sin does not cost you your salvation. There are people who teach that if you sin once after you have accepted Jesus, you must be saved again. But this is not what the Bible teaches.

Can you conceive of somebody adopting a child and then throwing it out on the street because it falls while learning to walk? When we are saved, we are adopted into the family of God. We must, out of love on one hand and godly fear on the other, seek to live a life that is pleasing to Him. But the idea that one act of sin would cause someone to be thrown out of God's family is not in the Bible (1 John 1:7, 9). However, acts of sin or rebellion will take away the joy of your salvation. When David sinned he had no joy, because he had rebelled against God (Ps. 51:12). He said, "Do not take Your Holy Spirit from me" (Ps. 51:11). Even though he had committed adultery and had been responsible for an innocent man's death, by this clear statement we are shown that he still had the Holy Spirit. Though punishment came due to his sin, nevertheless, God forgave and loved him because David was repentant before the Lord.

If one continues in a course of known sin, assurance of one's salvation may be lost, but that is not the same as an actual loss of one's salvation. When the Scripture says, "Whoever is born of God does not sin" (1 John 5:18), the sense of the Greek is not that a Christian never commits an act of sin, but that he does not continue in a course of sin, refusing to confess and repent of his sins. A person born of the Spirit of God will be drawn back to repentance every time he sins.

Beyond that, we do read in Hebrews 10:29 that if somebody actually says the blood of Jesus Christ is a common (unholy) thing and renounces the salvation he has received, then that person may have lost it all. But the same book says, "But, beloved, we are confident of better things concerning you" (Heb. 6:9). It is very hard to believe that someone who has been born again would turn that far away from God.

But one might ask, if we are new creatures in Christ, why do we even still have the capacity to sin? The answer is that perfection for the Christian awaits us in heaven (1 Cor. 15:54). Now, we are united with Jesus at salvation, but we are being progressively transformed into His image (2 Cor. 3:18). We are being changed throughout our lives, but there is no final moment, short of death, when the believer becomes sinlessly perfect (1 John 1:8).

Questions on Spirit-Filled Living

5. *How do I receive the baptism in the Holy Spirit?* (Acts 2:38, 39)

You need to do a number of things in order to receive this blessing. First, you need to be born again. The person who is going to be filled with the Spirit must have the indwelling Spirit and must belong to Jesus (Rom. 8:9).

The second thing you have to do is ask. The Bible says, if we ask for the Holy Spirit, that prayer will be answered (Luke 11:8).

The third thing you have to do is surrender. The apostle Paul made this need clear in the Book of Romans when he said, "Present your bodies a living sacrifice" (Rom. 12:1).

Fourth, you must be willing to obey the Spirit. God does not give this power to someone and then say, "You can take the part you like and leave the part you do not like." If you want to be immersed in the Holy Spirit, you need to be prepared to obey the Spirit (Acts 5:32).

Fifth, you need to believe. The apostle Paul said, "Did you receive the Spirit by the works of the law, or by the hearing of faith?" (Gal. 3:2). The answer, obviously, is *faith.* You have to believe that if you ask, you will receive.

Finally, you have to exercise what God has given you. Having asked, having received, having been willing to obey, and having believed, you need to respond in a biblical fashion.

The Bible says those baptized with the Holy Spirit on the Day of Pentecost "began to speak with other tongues, as the Spirit gave them utterance" (Acts 2:4). This means they spoke the words that the Spirit gave them. The Holy Spirit gave the words, but the apostles and disciples voluntarily responded. There was action based on faith, not merely passive acceptance of the blessing. That is the way it is with God. God is offering the baptism in the Holy Spirit to people who need only to reach out and take it and then enjoy the blessing.

6. *Can I live a holy life?* (Matt. 5:8)

If it were not possible to live a holy life, God would not have commanded it. He said, "You shall be holy, for I the LORD your God *am* holy" (Lev. 19:2). To be holy means to be separated to God. God's nature itself defines holiness. Being set apart to God makes us holy.

We are *not* made holy by doing good things. We *are* made holy by faith in Christ, just as we are saved by faith. Little by little, as we grow and live with the Lord, we will become more like Him (2 Cor. 3:18).

As we look to the Lord Jesus, think about Jesus, study about Jesus, pray to Jesus, and seek to follow His example, we become like Him. We begin to think like Him and act like Him. We become like Him because we are set apart to Him. This is true holiness.

If you are a Christian, ten years from now your life should be considerably different from what it is now. Your motives and desires, as you draw closer to Him, should be continuously more holy.

Jesus said, "Blessed are the pure in heart, for they shall see God" (Matt. 5:8). We can achieve a degree of purity in this life. It comes from God, as we grow closer to Him and are more like Him. Although perfection is not totally attainable in this life, it is something we should constantly strive toward and aim for, for Christian maturity and holy living constitute being a responsible son or daughter of God. Holiness is also practical. Mature holiness is seen in people who have stopped being concerned about their own needs and pursuits and have entered into the global vision of their Father so that they may transform a hurting world. Holiness begets the maturity in which we go out as Christ's agents in order to accomplish the aims of the Lord's Prayer (Matt. 6:10).

7. *How can I know God's will?* (Rom. 12:2)

The best way to know God's will is to be familiar with the Bible. That is because virtually everything you need to know concerning the will of God is in the Bible. If you get to know God's Word and understand it clearly, you can know the will of God (Ps. 119:6, 7, 9, 105).

Another way you can know the will of God is through prayer, when you commune with God and learn what pleases Him. The Bible says, "Let the peace of God rule in your hearts" (Col. 3:15). This means that the peace of God is like a regulator, so that when you violate the will of God, His peace leaves you and you have inner turmoil, immediately discovering you are going against God's will. Knowing God's Word and knowing the peace that comes about through a continuous relationship with Him are the best ways of knowing God's will (John 15:4).

It is also true, however, that God will show us His will through a number of other means. He will show us His will through godly counselors (Prov. 19:20; 20:18; 24:6). We can also discern God's will in part through circumstances; through the inner voice of the Spirit of God speaking to us; or through visions or dreams (Is. 1:1; Acts 2:17). He can reveal His will to us in many ways.

The key is to be sure that we are submitted to Him and are willing to do whatever He shows us. If we purpose to do His will, we will know His leading.

Finally, for people who seemingly are unable to discern God's positive directions, I recommend "negative" guidance. Say, "Father, I want Your will above all else. Please do not let me miss Your plan and purpose for my life." Such surrender has the guarantee of His guidance (Prov. 3:5, 6).

8. *How do I pray for a miracle?* (Matt. 17:20)

When we are faced with a great need, either for ourselves or for others, we should begin by humbly seeking to know God's will in the matter: "Father, what do You want to do in this situation?" Jesus said, "My Father has been working until now, and I have been working" (John 5:17). He listened to the voice of the Father, and He watched Him. Be careful not to start or end a prayer by saying blindly, "If it be Your will." Rather, you should seek to *know* God's will in the situation and then base your prayer upon it. Praying for a miracle is welcoming a gift of the Holy Spirit to manifest. When His will is to work one, He will witness that to your heart. Then you can ask Him to perform the miracle that you know He wants to bring about.

It is often important to exercise a key to the miraculous—the spoken word. God has given us authority over disease, demons, sickness, storms, and finances (Matt. 10:1; Luke 10:19). Often, we may keep asking God to act, when, in fact, He calls us to employ His authority by our action with divinely empowered speech. Then we may declare that authority in Jesus' name: we may command needed funds to come to us, command a storm to be stilled, command a demon to come out, command any affliction to leave, command a sickness to depart.

Jesus said, "Whoever says to this mountain, 'Be removed and be cast into the sea,' and does not doubt in his heart, but believes that those things he says will be done, he will have whatever he says" (Mark 11:23). Believe in your heart that it has already happened! With the anointing of faith that God gives you, speak it forth. But remember, miracles come by faith in God's present power, not by a ritual or formula of human works or willpower.

9. *What is the unpardonable sin?* (Matt. 12:31)

The concept of an unpardonable sin has been a source of difficulty for many because it seems to go against the Bible's teachings about grace. We understand that God's grace forgives every sin, but our Lord mentioned one sin that cannot be forgiven.

The religious leaders had come out to hear Him, but they opposed virtually everything He said. As He was casting out demons, they accused Him of doing this by satanic means (Matt. 12:24).

Those people were so blind spiritually that they were attributing the work of the Holy Spirit to Satan. Furthermore, they were rejecting the Holy Spirit's work in their own lives. In essence, the Holy Spirit was saying of Jesus, "This is the Son of God. This is God," and they were saying, "He is not God! He is Satan's agent." It was then Jesus said, "Every sin and blasphemy will be forgiven men, but the blasphemy *against* the Spirit will not be forgiven" (Matt. 12:31).

Obviously, the unpardonable sin is not merely saying an unkind thing about the Holy Spirit. The religious leaders involved had turned totally against the revelation of God. They were so far into their own wickedness that they rejected not only Jesus Christ, but also the Holy Spirit. They were saying that good was evil and evil was good. They called the Spirit of God, Satan!

Once they had rejected Jesus, the one source of forgiveness, there was now no forgiveness. A person who turns away from Jesus Christ can receive no forgiveness, and that is what these had done.

If you want to obey God but are concerned that you may have committed the unpardonable sin, you have not committed it. If anyone today has committed this sin, it would be one who is hard-hearted, who has turned against Jesus, reviled Him, and become so depraved that he would claim that God's Spirit is Satan.

Questions on the End Times

10. *When is Jesus Christ coming again?* (Matt. 24:42)

Nobody can say with any degree of certainty when Jesus is coming again, because He said clearly that even the angels in heaven do not know that day (Mark 13:32). No man knows that day, and the Son of God, when He was on the Earth, did not know either. This knowledge, the Lord Jesus said, was strictly reserved for the Father.

We can see certain signs, or clues, that His coming is approaching (Matt. 24:3; Luke 21:7). Jesus said there would be wars and rumors of wars, revolutions, widespread famine, disease, and earthquakes in many different places (Matt. 24:6, 7; Luke 21:10, 11). There would be an increase of lawlessness and anarchy, and finally an appearance of the Antichrist (2 Thess. 2:3, 4). Along with the "man of sin" will come what is called an apostasy, or a falling away. Many of the believing people will grow cold in their faith (Matt. 24:12). There will be persecution of Christians and a time of general trouble. All these things are already happening with increasing frequency.

Another event most believe had to happen before Jesus could return was the reestablishment of the state of Israel. The original Israel disappeared from the globe centuries ago, but in 1948 the new state of Israel was established. The regathering of Jews to Israel is a clear sign, in both the Old and New Testaments, that our age is just about over (Luke 21:24). On June 6, 1967, the Jews, for the first time since Jerusalem was captured by Nebuchadnezzar in 586 B.C. took over control of the entire city of Jerusalem, thus *signaling the* approaching end of Gentile world power.

Jesus said, however, that the one major thing that would herald His coming would be the proclamation of the gospel (Matt. 24:14).

These are signs of the times. We are always to be ready for our Lord's return, but nobody knows the day and hour when that will be.

11. *Who is the Antichrist?* (2 Thess. 2:2, 3)

In the Book of Revelation we are told that a world dictator will arise who will be endued with the power of Satan himself and will claim for himself the prerogatives of God (Rev. 13:1–18; 2 Thess. 2:4). Assisting him will be a False Prophet who will do signs in this dictator's name (Rev. 13:13–15; 19:20).

We do know that the Book of Revelation was written during a time when Christians were being persecuted in the Roman Empire. We also know that the Roman emperors liked to think of themselves as gods, making statues of themselves and requiring worship of themselves. I believe those earlier dictators were representations of the final world dictator. There is always the possibility that the Antichrist is already in the world. This man will appear as a great leader, speaking great words of wisdom, and will draw all of the non-Christian people to worship him. To them he will be the sum of wisdom, with the answers to all their problems (Rev. 13:18).

For an antichrist figure to come into the modern world, there must be a breakdown of the world system as we know it now. There would have to be breakdowns in currency, in law and order, and in the power structures of national states.

A financial panic could help pave the way for him. So could a nuclear war. Such disasters could leave people crying out for a man of peace, who will be Satan's counterfeit to Jesus Christ. This man will seem to be like Jesus, until such time as he is ready to show his true self. Then he will be incredibly cruel (Dan. 7; 8). The Antichrist will be the most hideous example of dictatorial power that the world has ever known.

Remember that the antichrist spirit is in anybody who tries to draw people away from Jesus, saying, "Worship me." The antichrist spirit is often present now in the worship and veneration we give to governments, dictators, military leaders, and various other human figures. Systems being taught in our schools, media, and intellectual circles are often much like that which will ultimately lead people to the Antichrist, because he will be the consummate figure of humanism.

12. *What is the mark of the Beast?* (Rev. 13:18)

In the Book of Revelation there is reference to the number of the Antichrist, which is 666 (Rev. 13:18). *Six* in biblical numerology is the number of man—just short of perfection, whereas *seven* is the number of perfection. So 666 may refer to the quintessential humanist. Revelation tells us that the number 666, or the mark of the Antichrist, is going to be stamped upon the hand and the forehead of every person in the world during the reign of the Antichrist.

The forehead represents our wills, our volition, while the hand represents our activities. Somehow the Antichrist will get his imprint on people everywhere, causing them, through their wills and their actions, to serve him. It is not farfetched to think that the Antichrist could impose population control by some global means (Rev. 13:16, 17).

The Bible warns us that if we have the mark of the Beast, we will then share the terrible fate of the Beast (Rev. 14:11). No one should fear "accidentally" taking the mark of the Beast. To do so involves "worshiping" the Beast (Rev. 13:15), and the decision will be clear enough that it will be a life-and-death matter. However, we should still be sensitive today, for if we regard the forehead as the center of the will and the hand as being symbolic of what we do, it seems that the mark is more than some technological device. What we are really talking about here is who gets our allegiance. In a real respect the spirit of antichrist is active already (1 John 2:18). Will we give the spirit of the world our minds and our work? If our allegiance is to God, we will not serve the Antichrist, and we will not take his mark upon us.

13. *What is the Millennium?* (Rev. 20:2, 3)

A millennium is one thousand years. The biblical Millennium will be a period of peace, love, and brotherhood when all nature lives in the harmony that was intended in the Garden of Eden. The Book of Isaiah (11:6–9) speaks of a time when the wild animals will live at peace with domestic animals, when the serpents will no longer bite. A little child will be able to play by a cobra's den or lead wild beasts around and not be harmed. Military schools will close, and implements of war will no longer be manufactured. The money and resources that now go into warfare will then be devoted to peaceful pursuits. When this day comes, every person will have his own plot of ground, his own home. All will live in harmony with their neighbors. No one will be afraid that someone will try to steal his belongings. There will be universal peace, for the knowledge of the Lord will cover the Earth as the waters cover the sea.

I believe the Millennium is a transition period, when Jesus Christ comes back to Earth to show mankind what it would have been like if sin had never entered the world. It will be a time when Jesus Christ will reign as king, and the kingdom of God will be established on Earth. There will be a one-world government under the leadership of Jesus with nation-states subject to Him. The Bible says representatives of the nations of the Earth will come to Jerusalem each year (Is. 2:2–4; Zech. 14:16).

14. *Will I have my family in heaven?* (Eph. 6:1)

There is no reason to suppose that there could not be families in heaven. However, all Christians are part of God's family now, and the bonds that draw human families together probably will not be necessary in heaven. There, we will all be part of one enormous family, and we will all feel a deep love for everyone else. There will not be the idea that "I am here with my wife and the two of us are separate from everyone else." We will all be one in Christ (Eph. 3:14, 15).

Though we will probably have families in heaven, note two things: First, your husband or wife or child or parent will be in heaven with you—if you are a Christian—only if they have been born again by the Spirit of God (John 3:3, 5). Your closeness to God will not save the members of your family. They must have their own personal relationships with Jesus Christ (Acts 16:31). Second, Jesus said there will no longer be human procreation in heaven, and the necessity of mating and child nurture will cease (Mark 12:25).

15. *What is hell like?* (Luke 16:23)

There are two descriptions of hell in the Bible. One is of a burning fire. Jesus often used the word *Gehenna* to describe hell. Gehenna was the refuse dump outside Jerusalem that was always on fire. Jesus said hell was a place of worms, maggots, fire, and trouble. From that we get the image of a lake of fire and the concept of perpetual burning. The evil ones there are full of remorse and torment (Mark 9:43–48).

Jesus also said that hell would be "outer darkness…weeping and gnashing of teeth" (Matt. 8:12). Here the image is one of terrible loneliness: separation from God and man. Those who are consigned to hell will be put out into the inky blackness of eternity, with nobody to turn to or talk to—constantly alone. They will suffer the remorse of knowing they had the opportunity to come into heaven with God but turned it down.

The Bible speaks of a lake of fire reserved for the Devil and his angels (Matt. 25:41). Human beings were never intended to go into hell. But the ones who choose to reject God will one day follow Satan right into this eternal torment.

There will be no exit from hell, no way out, no second chance. That is why it is so important in this life to receive the pardon that God extends to all men through the Cross of Jesus Christ (Rev. 20:11–15).

Questions on Morality and Ethics

16. *What does the Bible say about homosexuality?* (Rom. 1:27)

The Bible says that it is an abomination for a man to lie with a man as with a woman, or a woman to lie with a woman as with a man (Lev. 18:22; 20:13). The Bible says that because of certain abominations such as homosexuality, a land will vomit out its inhabitants (Lev. 18:25). The apostle Paul called it "shameful," the result of being given up by God to "vile passions" (Rom. 1:24–27).

In the Old Testament, those who practiced these things were removed from the congregation of Israel by execution. We are told in the New Testament that those who practice homosexuality will not enter the kingdom of God (1 Cor. 6:9, 10). The apostle Paul shows homosexuality as a final order of rebellion against God. When people exchange the truth of God for a lie, and begin to worship the creature instead of the Creator, they are given up to evil. When values are turned upside down and moral anarchy appears, men burn with lust for other men and women burn for women, and they will receive in their own bodies the punishment for their actions (Rom. 1:22–27). From a biblical standpoint, the rise of homosexuality is a sign that a society is in the last stages of decay.

17. *Is abortion wrong?* (Ps. 139:13)

Abortion is definitely wrong. It is the taking of a human life, for the Bible shows that life begins at conception. God fashions us while we are in our mother's womb (Ps. 139:13). The prophet Jeremiah and the apostle Paul were called by God before they were born (Jer. 1:5; Gal. 1:15). John the Baptist leaped in his mother's womb when the voice of Mary, the mother of the Lord, was heard (Luke 1:44). Obviously children in the womb have spiritual identity.

From the moment of conception there is a progression of development that continues through adulthood. God condemned the Israelites who were offering their children as sacrifices to the heathen god Molech. Such children were burned up in the fires of sacrifice (Lev. 20:2), offered to a god of sensuality and convenience. The same is occurring today, and by acting in this way we are saying that human beings are not worth anything. This is a terrible blot on our society.

The Bible is not more specific on the matter of abortion because such a practice would have been unthinkable to the people of God. For instance, when Israel was in Egypt, a cruel Pharaoh forced the Israelites to kill their newborn babies. In the Bible this was looked upon as the height of cruel oppression (Ex. 1:15–22). The idea of killing their own children would have been anathema to the Hebrews. All through the Old Testament, women yearned for children. Children were considered a gift from God. Women prayed not to be barren. How could a righteous woman turn against her own children to destroy them? Abortion is not only unthinkable, it is also the height of pagan barbarity.

18. *What is the difference between adultery and fornication?* (Matt. 5:27)

Sexual intercourse between a married person and someone who is not his or her mate is adultery.

The Ten Commandments contain the prohibition against adultery: "You shall not commit adultery" (Ex. 20:14). The reason is simple: marriage is the foundation of society, and with it comes the responsibility of child-rearing. Casual sex outside marriage not only imperils marriage but also destroys the paternal or maternal feeling for the children of the marriage, and blurs the lines of family relationships.

Fornication is sex between two unmarried people. The apostle Paul said this is a sin against the body. He commands Christians to flee fornication as a sin against self and God, for the believer's body is the temple of the Holy Spirit (1 Cor. 6:18, 19). Paul says that if a believer takes his body and joins it to a harlot (or someone who is immoral), he is joining Jesus Christ to that person (1 Cor. 6:15, 16).

It is very important to understand that neither fornicators nor adulterers will enter the kingdom of heaven (1 Cor. 6:9, 10). In today's world, the term *fornication* is rarely used and immorality between unmarried people is commonly accepted as a life-style. But immorality, however commonplace, is a sin that will keep millions of people out of heaven, unless they repent.

19. *Should a Christian be involved in police or military service?* (Rom. 13:3, 4)

There are some who do not believe that Christians can be soldiers or policemen, but the apostle Paul shows that such "rulers," if they serve good and do justly, are

"God's ministers" (Rom. 13:2–7) because they restrain evil. The police, as God's ministers, provide an essential service to society. As long as there are sinful people, we will need policemen. As long as men and women will not submit voluntarily to the righteous commands of God, force will be necessary to keep them from murdering, raping, kidnapping, stealing—from victimizing innocent people. Thus, it is proper if a Christian is involved in police work or in military service. There must be law and order, for no one is safe when there is anarchy.

There are those who, because of sincere religious beliefs, feel that they could never kill another human being, even in war. Society must accommodate the views of such people, but the Bible does not mandate that a Christian be a conscientious objector.

20. *When should a Christian disobey the civil government?* (Rom. 13:7; Acts 5:27–29)

When a civil government refuses people the liberty to worship and obey God freely, it has lost its mandate of authority from God. Then the Christian should feel justified in disobeying.

Thomas Jefferson believed that when a government began to be tyrannical, it was the right and even the *duty* of the citizens to rebel against that government. The Christian, however, is called to bear with his government wherever possible. Jesus did not call for revolution against Rome, even though it was an oppressive conqueror of Israel. On the other hand, the apostles refused to obey an order not to preach and teach in Jesus' name (Acts 5:27–29). Whenever the civil government forbids the practice of things that God has commanded us to do, or tells us to do things He has commanded us not to do, then we are on solid ground in disobeying the government. Blind obedience to government is never right. However difficult or costly it may be, we all must reserve the right to say no to things that we consider oppressive or immoral.

21. *Do people have to be poor in order to be holy?* (Luke 18:22)

It has been taught for many years that holiness and poverty go hand in hand. The apostle Paul said, "I know how to be abased, and I know how to abound." Then he added, "I can do all things through Christ who strengthens me" (Phil. 4:12, 13).

You can be just as holy when you are financially comfortable as you can be when you are poor. Perhaps it is easier to cry out to God for help when you are in need. But if Christians sanctify God in their hearts ahead of material concern, they should be able to live above their circumstances whether that involves prosperity or poverty.

Poverty is a curse, not a blessing. It is certainly not equated with righteousness. It comes sometimes because of the horrors of war, sometimes because of unjust or unwise government, sometimes because of oppression by the greedy and the ruthless, sometimes because of disobedience to God's commandments, and sometimes because of lack of knowledge of God's principles of blessing. Sometimes temporary poverty follows a satanic attack or a serious and unexplainable calamity. Whatever its cause, poverty is not equated with holiness.

Some voluntarily take a vow of poverty so that they can give themselves totally to God. In that situation, poverty becomes a blessing for those people, because they have given up material riches for God. However, simply being poor is not a sign of holiness. Of course, neither is being wealthy. Godly people are those who are content wherever God has placed them and who are serving Him to the best of their abilities, irrespective of material circumstances (1 Tim. 6:6, 17–19).

22. *How do I forgive my enemies?* (Matt. 5:43, 44)

The *first* step in forgiveness is to recognize your resentment against an enemy. You must understand who the enemy is and what he has done to hurt you. Then you must consciously say, "I forgive that person for the following wrongs against me." Then repent of your feelings against your enemy and ask God to forgive you, as Jesus said (Luke 11:4).

After that, begin to pray actively for your enemy's good. Jesus told us to pray for our enemies and that doing this will help to fill us with love for them (Matt. 5:43–48). When you pray for your enemies, asking God to meet their needs and manifest Himself to them, you are overcoming evil with good. Instead of fighting negative thoughts in your mind, you are filling your mind with positive thoughts of God's love for that person. You are now on the side of your enemy; you have a spiritual stake in his well-being. If God answers your prayer, which you want Him to do, the person prayed for will be blessed, and you will learn about redemption—the ultimate form of forgiveness (Matt. 18:21–35). So if you ask God to bless someone who has wronged you, the result may well be a repentant sinner and a new brother or sister in the Lord!

23. *How can I quit drinking or depending on drugs?* (Rom. 13:13, 14)

In both of these instances a person has to make up his mind to quit. I do not believe in gradually tapering off of cigarettes, narcotics, or alcohol. You need to make a total break. That means you should get rid of anything you have that might tempt you (Rom. 13:13, 14).

In my case, when I found Jesus, I poured some expensive liquor down the drain, to the consternation of my wife, who had not yet made the same commitment. That was a definite break for me. From that moment on, I was not going to drink anymore. I believe this is the case with any habit a person regards as sinful. He or she must say, "That's it. That's the last one. No more." And from that moment on, ask God to help you.

You must confess that you have been doing something you consider wrong, and that you have been defiling the temple of God (1 Cor. 6:19, 20). You must tell God that you want and need His forgiveness and deliverance. You must renounce your habit and cast the spirit of alcohol, the spirit of narcotics, or the spirit of nicotine from your body. Command it to leave you and resolve that, with God's help, you will never again smoke another cigarette, another joint of marijuana, or whatever it may be that you are giving up.

After that, do not consort with those who helped to get you into trouble or who would soon have you back where you used to be. It may be hard to do that, but it is necessary. Instead, you should try to find some others, preferably Christians, who have given up the same habit themselves, to support you during the first days of quitting.

It takes about thirty days to establish a new habit. It will take about the same length of time for your body to clean out the poisons and the chemical dependency. Keep full of the Holy Spirit. Replace what has controlled you with a new dimension of the Holy Spirit's fullness (Eph. 5:18).

24. *Is there anything wrong with gambling?* (Luke 4:12)

In the Bible, the sacred lot was cast as a means of determining the mind of God (Lev. 16:7–10; Jon. 1:7; Acts 1:24–26). In ancient Israel it was assumed that God was in control of the dice and that He would speak to His people this way. Although there is no such thing as luck and God is in control of everything, when somebody takes money that belongs to God (because everything we have belongs to God) and bets it on the turn of a roulette wheel, or a turn of a card, he is asking for trouble. He is saying by his actions, "God, I am risking Your money and my faith on the hope that You'll 'make it happen!' " When you act like that, you are putting the Lord to the test. You are tempting God, and that is a sin (Deut. 6:16; Luke 4:10–12).

Gambling can destroy a person, becoming an obsession and a compulsion just like alcoholism. The habitual gambler ruins his family and his life, and some have stolen to get money for gambling. It can become a disease that has destroyed literally tens of thousands of people.

The pervasiveness of gambling in our society teaches people that fame, success, and fortune are available without work or struggle. The virtues of industry, thrift, careful investment, and patience are all undermined by this vice. In their place come human greed, lust, avarice, sloth, and a live-for-the-moment mentality. How tragic to see legislatures link their budgetary futures to legalized gambling and lotteries that will undermine the very virtues their citizens need for true long-range growth and prosperity!

Questions on the Demonic

25. *What is a demon?* (Mark 5:2–5)

A demon is a fallen angel. When Satan, who was the very highest angel, rebelled against God, he took a large number of the angels with him in rebellion (Is. 14:12–15; Rev. 12:3, 4). When their rebellion failed, they were cast out of heaven. Those angels are now demons. As angels can ascend the heights of spirituality, demons reach the depths of hatred, bitterness, and perversion. Demons torment people, possess them, and lead them from God and His truth (Mark 5:2–5; Acts 13:6–12).

Although lust, homosexuality, drunkenness, gluttony, and witchcraft are expressions of sinful flesh, these are among practices that can also be expressions of demonic activity in the lives of people. Grossly perverted sexual practices, such as sadomasochism and pedophilia, have demonic roots. In a similar manner, schizophrenia can be a mental disease, but it can also be caused by demon possession.

Just as the angels have archangels and higher powers, the demons have what are called "principalities and powers." It is possible that various demon princes are in charge of specific cities or regions in the world.

There is conflict in the invisible world between God's loyal messengers and the demonic hosts. Somehow in God's wonderful order, He uses the prayers of His people to restrain demonic activity and to direct the action of angelic powers to control demons (see Dan. 10).

26. *What power do Christians have over demons?* (Matt. 10:8)

The Bible says, "He who is in you is greater than he who is in the world" (1 John 4:4). The Christian believer, by having the Holy Spirit within him, has power over all demons. When Jesus Christ sent His apostles out on their mission, He said He was giving them authority *(exousia)* over all the power *(dunamis)* of the enemy (Luke 10:19). Jesus' authority is greater than satanic power. When the disciples said, "Lord, even the demons are subject to us in Your name," Jesus replied, "Do not rejoice in this, that the spirits are subject to you, but rather rejoice because your names are written in heaven" (Luke 10:17, 20). The Christian believer has unlimited authority over demons in the name of Jesus, but that authority is nothing compared to the glory and authority we will know in heaven.

27. *What is exorcism?* (Acts 19:13)

Exorcism is commanding, in the name of Jesus, a demon to come out of an individual, a house, or wherever the demon happens to be. Exorcism is accomplished by the spoken word, in the name of Jesus, through the power of the Holy Spirit, and it is done simply and quickly (Acts 16:16–18).

The person who is doing the exorcism should be filled with God's Spirit. He should not have any unsurrendered sin in his life, because the demon will take advantage of any weakness (Acts 19:13–16). So, this person should be pure of ulterior motives, sexual impurities, greed, and anything that would leave him open to some charge by the Devil, who is the accuser of the brethren.

Another word of caution: People should not go out looking for demons or make up demons where they do not exist. A believer should be prepared to confront demons when the need arises, but he or she should not seek this kind of encounter.

28. *What about mind control and mind-science beliefs?* (Col. 2:8)

Such cults focus on the "universal consciousness" concept that human beings: 1) are part of a vast, timeless consciousness; 2) are ultimately divine; 3) will live forever in various forms (reincarnation, and so on); 4) can communicate with the dead or other spirits; and 5) can receive power through psychic or even bodily exercises to transcend nature, understand mysteries, and affect their own destinies or the lives of those around them.

These groups, in the name of "research and enlightenment," "psychic research," "transcendental meditation," "yoga," and so on, are actually not in touch with some great "God consciousness" or psychic power, but with Satan and demons.

The Greek word *psuche* is translated "soul," from which we derive the word *psychic*. Most mind-science groups deal with psychic, or soulish, phenomena. First Corinthians 2:14 says the *psuchikos* or "soulish" person ("the natural man") will not receive the things of the Spirit of God, for they are foolishness to him. Mind control and New Age movement teachings all appeal to the soulish man, because they do not require repentance and being born again (John 3:3, 5). A concept prevalent in these groups is that if a person gains sufficient knowledge, he can dominate or control events because he is *part* of god or *is* god.

We must remember that the soulish realm is the realm of demons. Demons can and often do enter into this psychic area. The people who are in touch with the dead or "the other world" are not tapping into some universal consciousness. They are in touch with demons. Demons lurk behind many of the oriental religions, as well as behind the mind control teachings.

Questions on the Laws of the Kingdom of God

29. *What is the kingdom of God?* (Luke 17:21)

A kingdom is a place where a king rules. The kingdom of God is wherever God reigns over the lives of His subjects. The kingdom of God is not visible because God is not visible. It is a spiritual kingdom, not a visible one. Jesus Christ said, "The kingdom of God is within you" (Luke 17:21).

Jesus gave us, in the Lord's Prayer, a petition to God: "Your kingdom come. Your will be done on earth as *it is* in heaven" (Matt. 6:10). This prayer shows the priority Jesus gave to the kingdom of God. Can we not say that the kingdom of God will come on Earth when the will of God is as respected here as it is in heaven, when the visible world totally reflects the invisible world? I think we can. In the kingdom of God, everything is subject to God's power, instantly, with no question. In the visible world, there is resistance to God's will.

The kingdom of God is eternal. At the present time, it is an invisible kingdom here in our midst. Wherever there are those who honor Jesus Christ, the King, and wherever the Spirit of the King is, there is the kingdom of God. (See also Kingdom Dynamics: The Kingdom of God, beginning at Genesis 1:1.)

30. *What is the greatest virtue in the kingdom?* (Matt. 18:1–4)

If pride is the greatest sin—and it is—then humility must be the greatest virtue. It is humility that allows me to acknowledge that God has a claim on my life, that I am a fallible, mortal creature, and that God is the Master of the universe. It is humility that says, "I am a sinner, and I need to be saved." Humility is the beginning of wisdom (Prov. 22:4). The truths of the kingdom are only perceived by those who are humble. No one who is proud will ever gain anything from God, because "God resists the proud, but gives grace to the humble" (James 4:6). Those who are humble receive the grace of God and are given the secrets of the kingdom, because they come as beggars. Jesus Christ said, "Blessed *are* the poor in spirit, for theirs is the kingdom of heaven" (Matt. 5:3).

31. *What is the greatest sin in the kingdom?* (Matt. 23:2–12)

The greatest sin is pride—for a number of reasons (Ps. 59:12; Prov. 8:13; 16:18; 29:23). First, pride was the fundamental sin of Satan when he first sinned. Pride says, "I can do it better than God," and Satan thought he could do a better job of running the universe than God could (Is. 14:12–14; Ezek. 28:12–19)! Second, pride inevitably leads to the sin of rebellion. By proudly carrying on our plan for our lives and those around us, we necessarily come into conflict with God's plan. That is why the Bible says, "God resists the proud, but gives grace to the humble" (James 4:6).

There is no way of being neutral in the kingdom. One is either for Jesus or against Him. The proud are automatically against Him, because their life is not yielded to Him and to what He wants to accomplish.

Finally, pride leads to a sense of self-sufficiency, making us unwilling to learn or receive from God or man. Jesus said to be converted and become as little children (Matt. 18:3, 4). Children are trusting and they are teachable. They always want to learn from the Father.

But once a person becomes proud he supposes self-sufficiency and cannot learn, while the good things of the kingdom of God are given to those who ask. If you do not ask, you do not receive.

God's name reveals this truth. He is "I AM" (Ex. 3:14). I am what? The answer—I am the supply of your need. I am healing, wisdom, sanctification, provision, victory, and salvation. His great power extends to His people like a blank check. We are to fill in the blank according to our need. It is only when you realize that you are needy that you can truly experience God. If we feel that we have no needs, if we are totally self-sufficient, then we have closed God out of our lives. That is why pride cuts off all of the blessings of the kingdom. By pride we sin against God and against ourselves.

32. *What kingdom law underlies all personal and corporate development?* (Matt. 25:14–30)

This is called the "law of use." Jesus told about a rich man who was going away on a trip and distributed different resources to each of his servants (Matt. 25:14–30). Then he said, "Do business with these until I come back." Two servants invested what they were given, but the third did not. When the master came back, he asked for an accounting. The first two were praised and rewarded for their diligence, but when Jesus told this story, the ending seemed unfair. He took away from the man who did not invest and gave his talent to the most fruitful investor, firmly announcing this law of the kingdom: "To everyone who has, more will be given . . . but from him who does not have, even what he has will be taken away" (Matt. 25:29). In other words, if you use what is given to you, you will gain more. If you fail to use what is given to you, you will lose even what you think you have. Whether in physical, intellectual, financial, or relational dealings, whatever is given you, however small it is, use it. Use it diligently and use it on an ever-increasing scale. Set goals to increase whatever you do. This is the secret of the kingdom, which guarantees success to any Christian who applies it.

33. *What kingdom law is at the heart of all relationships?* (Matt. 7:12)

Jesus Christ gave a law that is so profound that it should be adopted by every society. It is the law of reciprocity. I use the term "law" because it is a universal principle: "Whatever you want men to do to you, do also to them" (Matt. 7:12). How profound an effect this "golden rule" would have if applied at every level in our world!

You would not want a neighbor to steal your tools, so do not take his. You would not like to be struck by a reckless driver, so do not drive recklessly. You would want a helping hand in time of need, so help others in need. In industry, we would not want the person upstream from us polluting the river, so we should not do it to the person downstream from us. We would not want to breathe chemically polluted air, so we should not pollute someone else's air. In the workplace, we would not want to be oppressed, so we should not oppress our employees. If applied, this kingdom law would remove the need for armies, jails, and prisons; problems would be relieved, the burden of government reduced and the productive energies of all the people released. "Do unto others as you would have them do unto you," if put into practice, would revolutionize our society. This is the kingdom foundation for all social relationships.

34. *What kingdom law is necessary for the laws of reciprocity and use to work?* (Matt. 7:7, 8)

Jesus taught the law of constant prayer (to God) and steadfast persistence (in human endeavor): He said, "Ask, and keep on asking; seek and keep on seeking; and knock and keep on knocking" (Matt. 7:7, 8, paraphrased). The Greek present tense emphasizes continuous action: Jesus was not saying knock once and stop, but keep on knocking until the door is opened. God, in His wonderful wisdom, has built the world in such a fashion that only those who are diligent and who persevere win the highest prizes. The person who is determined to achieve his God-given goal, despite all obstacles, will wind up a winner. Those who are fainthearted and faltering, whose minds are not made up about something, will always lose.

God makes us reach high for the better things. Only a few will strive hard enough to win them. Those who keep going in spite of problems, pain, and difficulty will eventually overcome them.

It is necessary to keep at something long enough to let the laws of use and reciprocity work for you. The apostle Paul proudly declared, "I have fought the good fight, I have finished the race, I have kept the faith" (2 Tim. 4:7). He wrote to the Galatians, "Let us not grow weary while doing good, for in due season we shall reap if we do not lose heart" (Gal. 6:9). In whatever task God places you, do not quit, but stay the course.

35. *What law guarantees the possibility of accomplishing impossible things?* (Mark 11:22, 23)

The law of miracles guarantees the performance of impossible things. Miracles take place in Jesus' name, with power flowing from the invisible world where God is, through the spirit of man, where the center of our being is, through the mind of man, where doubts can arise, and out into the world around us through thoughts and the spoken word (see Question #8 for steps to take).

But a condition must be noted. Do not doubt in your heart (Mark 11:22–24). Those who are double-minded will not receive anything (James 1:6–8). Further, Jesus goes on to say, "Whenever you stand praying, and you have anything against anyone, forgive him, that your Father in heaven may also forgive you" (Mark 11:25). The great hindrance to miracles is a lack of forgiveness. Whether or not the attitude is justified by the circumstances, there must be freedom from bitterness and resentment or there will be no mountain-moving miracles. There can be no resentment, no bitterness, no jealousy, no envy—none of these things. To see miracles, there must be forgiveness and love.

36. *How is it possible that a kingdom can be destroyed?* (Luke 11:17, 18)

Jesus said, "Every kingdom divided against itself is brought to desolation, and a house *divided* against a house falls" (Luke 11:17, 18).

This is a universal truth. The best of all plans can be destroyed if we lack unity. When there is division, plans *cannot* succeed. This the reason Satan does everything he can to cause division among Christians. Because we are so divided, suspicious, and focused on each other's weak points, we are breaking the most important key for corporate success: unity.

Jesus said that the world would know that God had sent Him if His disciples were one (John 17:20–23). Unity is "exhibit A" to the world, showing the supernatural origins of the Christian church. "How these Christians love one another!" was the amazed observation of the people of the Roman Empire. With unity, the church can win the world. Without unity, the church is powerless. Even evil men can find success through unity. God looked down on the tower of Babel and said, "Indeed the people *are* one and they all have one language . . . now nothing that they propose to do will be withheld from them" (Gen. 11:6). This is God's own appraisal of mankind in unity. Unity brings incredible strength! Nothing is impossible for people working in unity.

In Old Testament times, when God desired to destroy the enemies of Israel, He sent division among them and caused them to fight themselves. Israel often did not have to go into battle to fight because the enemy destroyed itself. Any time an organization begins to fight itself, it will go down. Unless it moves in unity, there is absolutely nothing it can do—for good or evil. Think what God's people working in unity under His blessing can accomplish according to the laws of His kingdom!

37. *How does one become great in the kingdom of God?* (Luke 22:25–27)

The Lord Jesus chose men—ordinary fallible human beings—to be His disciples. Like people everywhere, they wrestled with pride and ambition (Matt. 20:20–23). Realizing their striving, Jesus set a little child down in their midst, saying that in the kingdom, the great are like children—humble, trusting, and teachable (Matt. 18:4). Later, when their concern for status surfaced again, He elaborated this law, saying that the greatest is the servant of all (Luke 22:25–27). This standard works today! The great in our society are people who serve the sick, the needy, and the wounded. These are great because they have given themselves to serve others. Jesus Christ leads the list. He is the greatest of all because He gave Himself for the sins of the world (Phil. 2:1–11).

There is a very practical outworking of the law of greatness in the everyday world. Those who do serve the most people may often become the most famous and prosperous. But this was not their motive; rather, recognition seems to be the inevitable fruit of self-giving, childlike service to mankind.

38. *What sin particularly blocks the flow of kingdom power?* (Matt. 18:21–35)

Lack of forgiveness blocks access to the kingdom and to its marvelous power. (See also Matt. 6:5–15; Mark 11:22–26.)

The first person you probably have not forgiven is yourself. More people lack forgiveness toward themselves than toward anybody else. They are unwilling to forgive themselves and to recognize that God says, "As far as the east is from the west, *so* far has He removed our transgressions from us" (Ps. 103:12). If you are a believer, He has already cleansed your conscience from dead works so that you might serve the living God (Heb. 9:14). God cleanses us for service in order not to leave us with the guilt of past sin. That should be dead, buried, and forgotten.

"If our heart does not condemn us," the Bible says, "we have confidence toward God" (1 John 3:21). Obviously, we cannot have continuing sin in our lives and expect forgiveness. We have to be free from ongoing conscious sin and rebellion against God. But if we are walking in the light, and walking in forgiveness, then the blood of Jesus Christ is continuously cleansing us from all sin (1 John 1:7).

The second person we have to "forgive," if we have bitterness, is God Himself. There are people who blame God because a child died, because a husband ran away, because they have been sick, because they have not had enough money. Consciously or unconsciously they think all of these things are God's fault. There is deep-seated resentment; yet you cannot be resentful toward God and experience kingdom power flowing in your life: you have to rid yourself of any bitterness toward God. That may take some soul-searching. You must ask yourself, "Am I blaming God for my situation?"

The third person you may have to forgive is a member of your family. You have to get rid of resentment, especially toward those closest to you. The husbands, the wives, the children, and the parents—all must be forgiven when slights and resentments have built up in family situations. Many people say, "Well, I didn't think that counted. I thought that was just a family matter." All lack of forgiveness has to be eliminated, especially toward every family member.

Finally, there has to be forgiveness for anybody else who has ever done anything against you. It may be that your resentment is justified. The person may have done a very evil, terrible thing to you. You may have every legal and intellectual right to hold a grudge and to hate that person. But if you want to see kingdom life and power flow in your life, it is absolutely imperative that you forgive.

Forgive them to the point where you actually feel yourself cleansed of resentment and bitterness and are actually praying for them. If you do not, the lack of forgiveness will make it impossible for God's power to be released to and in you. The miracle life depends 100 percent on your relationship to God the Father. That relationship is built strictly on the strength of His forgiveness of your sin.

Forgiveness is the key. Other sins can be present, and if your heart condemns you for something else, then of course you do not have confidence before God. But it is lack of forgiveness that most often comes between people and God.

The Holy Spirit and Restoration

by James Robison

New Testament Prophecy of Restoration (Acts 3:19–21)

Restoration in every dimension of human experience is at the heart of the Christian gospel. It is woven through all the Scriptures and must be at the forefront of our ministry of the truth.

Acts 3:19–21 makes the most pointed reference to restoration in the New Testament. Peter urges a return to God for cleansing from sins. He adds that this returning would pave the way for a period of refreshing renewal that would result from the presence of the Lord with His people. It would also prepare for the return of Christ, whom, Peter said, "heaven must receive [or retain] until the times of restoration of all things, which God has spoken by the mouth of all His holy prophets since the world began" (Acts 3:21).

Many feel it is now, in these last days, that "all things" prophesied will be fulfilled and restoration completed. The ultimate restoration is the return of the church, the bride of Christ, to the majesty and glory God intended for her. To accomplish this restoration, God has begun to release His power and purity without measure through the church. The sifting has begun in order that the unshakable kingdom may be revealed (Heb. 12:27, 28).

The Biblical Definition of Restoration (Job 42:10–12)

According to the dictionary, "to restore" means to "bring back to a former or original condition." When something is restored in the Scriptures, however, it is always increased, multiplied or improved so that its latter state is significantly better than its original state (see Joel 2:21–26).

For example, under the Law of Moses, if someone stole an ox or a sheep, it was not sufficient for him simply to restore the animal he had taken. He had to pay back five oxen or four sheep (Ex. 22:1). When God restored Job after the terrible trials he endured, He gave him twice what he had lost and blessed him more in his latter days than in the beginning (Job 42:10–12). Jesus told His disciples that anyone who gave up anything to follow Him would have it restored a hundredfold (Mark 10:29, 30).

God multiplies when He restores. And so, in His restoration work today, God is not simply restoring the church to the glory it displayed in New Testament times. He is seeking to restore it to a state more powerful, majestic, and glorious than anything the world has yet seen!

Restoration "In the Beginning" (Gen. 1—3)

The beginning of the Bible's restoration theme is found at the beginning of all things—in the Book of Genesis. God created man in His own image—male and female. Man enjoyed the image of God, the intimacy of God, and unbroken fellowship with God.

However, man chose to eat of the tree of the knowledge of good and evil. In so doing, he decided to take his life into his own hands. Instead of living from the wisdom, righteousness, and resources of God, he would live from his own limited resources—working things out for himself.

With that tragic decision, man lost his God-image (that is, godliness), as well as his intimacy and his fellowship with the Lord, His Creator. But God's restoration work began immediately. As the now self-conscious man tried the work of his own hands to make coverings for his nakedness, God provided clothing made from an animal skin. This clearly revealed God's plan of redemption and restoration for fallen man. That first sacrifice, providing clothing, pointed toward the ultimate sacrificial Lamb of God—Jesus Himself.

Man's Plunge into Degradation (Gen. 4—12)

After being dismissed from the Garden and barred from the Tree of Life that stood in its midst, Adam begot children that were in his own image of self-centered disobedience, rather than in the image of God. From that point man fell deeper and deeper into depravity, until the Lord deemed it necessary to destroy the race and start over with a single family, that of Noah.

The covenant of the rainbow (Gen. 9:13) was one of the most important of many signs God gave during this period of time—a sign by which He indicated His intent to restore what had been lost through Adam and Eve. It is a timeless reminder of God's plan to bring man beyond judgment into His purpose.

With the call of Abram (Gen. 12), that purpose began to unfold as God's program for man's restoration became expressed through a specific individual. The "great nation" He promised to bring forth through Abram began with Israel, but was destined to become the church, the household of God. Although there are many prophecies concerning Israel, we can rest assured that for their fulfillment God had the church at heart from the beginning. The church is no more an afterthought than was God's promise of His Messiah—Jesus Christ.

Restoration Foreshadowed (Joseph: Gen. 37—46)

The outline of God's restoration work stands out vividly in the life of Joseph. Joseph was *forsaken, falsely accused,* and *forgotten.* But finally he was *favored* by God and restored to the rule God had ordained for him.

1. *Forsaken.* When Joseph revealed to his brothers that God had called him to rule over them, they reacted with vicious envy, selling him into slavery in Egypt.
2. *Falsely Accused.* God prospered Joseph—even in slavery, so that his master put him in charge of his estate. But then his master's wife falsely accused Joseph of assaulting her, and he was thrown into prison.
3. *Forgotten.* While in prison, Joseph interpreted the dreams of Pharaoh's butler and baker. The butler was elated at hearing he would be set free, and Joseph asked him to speak a good word for him to Pharaoh. But, once out of prison and doing well, the butler forgot Joseph.
4. *Favored.* God did not forget, however. Two years later Pharaoh had a dream. The butler remembered Joseph and told Pharaoh about him. Joseph interpreted the dream, warning Pharaoh of seven years of famine. Grateful for the warning, Pharaoh put Joseph in control of all the wealth of Egypt. Not only was Joseph restored by this act, but, when the drought struck, he was in a position to save his people.

Man's Futile Efforts at Self-Restoration (Jer. 8—10; Lam. 2)

God promised to send a prophet like Moses to the Israelites to assure their ultimate deliverance. This was necessary because they had refused to hear God for themselves, insisting that He speak directly only to Moses (Deut. 18:15, 16). Their fear of listening to Him put them under the letter of the law, where human effort labored to gain and keep divine acceptance. But God, knowing the limits of the law, instituted the Mosaic system of animal sacrifices to atone for their sins. He also placed the law as a schoolteacher to point to the ultimate deliverance through the shed blood of Jesus, the ultimate sacrifice (Heb. 10:10).

The failure of their efforts is presented most graphically in Jeremiah 8—10 and Lamentations 2, in the destruction of Jerusalem and the scattering of the people. These chapters paint a grim picture of human stubbornness, and the rebellion, immorality, idolatry, and general corruption afflicting the entire nation of Israel. They had forced God to such extremes of discipline that He had become like an enemy to them (Lam. 2:5).

Jeremiah 9:3 summarizes their plight, which resembles that of many in today's church: "And they do not know Me." Despite their most determined self-effort, they still did not have a personal relationship with God.

The Corruption of Leadership (Ezek. 34:1–10)

Having chosen to hear men rather than God, the people soon were hearing lies (Jer. 9:3). Ezekiel 34:1–10 exposes the wickedness and depravity into which the leaders had sunk. They used their offices and ministries only for what they could get for themselves, not to serve the people. They did not feed the flock, but rather they fed themselves. In His fury, God set Himself against these evil shepherds, vowing to take the sheep from them and put an end to this ruthless exploitation.

The shepherd analogy is retained in the restoration promise with which God follows these censuring statements. "For thus says the Lord GOD: 'Indeed I Myself will search for My sheep and seek them out. As a shepherd seeks out his flock . . . so will I seek out My sheep' " (vv. 11, 12). God, then and now, wants His people to be directly related to Him, hearing Him, responding to Him, and living from His abundant life. He has never wavered from His commitment to restore the intimate love relationship that was lost in Eden.

The Futility of Religious Ritual (Amos 5:21–23)

Because man consistently has thought to earn God's acceptance by his own performance, men came to think even of their spiritual relationship with God only in terms of externals. They thought that just by observing certain rules and regulations, performing certain rituals, and speaking certain words, they could stay in favor with God.

The Lord set them straight concerning this misconception in the words of the prophets. He let them know that He despised their ritualistic worship and empty sacrifices (Amos 5:21, 22), mock solemnity (Is. 58:4, 5), and lip-service devotion (Jer. 7:4). He had become sick of their singing, in which they only mouthed deceptive words that meant nothing to them (Amos 5:23). He vowed to turn their singing into wailing and cause their songs to become songs of lamentation and mourning (Jer. 7:34).

The Shaking of the Works of Men's Hands (Heb. 12:26, 27)

Everything Israel and Judah built up in generations of self-effort was an abomination to God, and He systematically gave over for destruction all they had accomplished by "the works of their own hands" (Jer. 1:16; 32:29–36).

The message of their misconception speaks to us today, and the apostle Paul summarizes the shaking God is determined to perform (Heb. 12:26, 27). Everything built by the hand of man, in the energy and wisdom of the flesh, He has vowed to shake down. Only the things that cannot be shaken—the things built in His eternal power and wisdom—will remain.

The great shaking Paul prophesied has begun and is continuing in the church today. For the same evils that plagued Israel—seeking to please God by external performance, lapsing into idolatry and moral decay, corruption in leadership, and worshiping the works of men's hands—are too present even in the church. Their removal is an essential part of the restoration process.

The Place of Repentance in Restoration (Is. 58:1–14)

After pronouncing fierce judgment and chastisement on the people because of their apostasy, God presents wonderful promises of restoration. He says He will bring forth their righteousness as the noonday, and they will become like a watered garden. He will take away their iniquity, heal their apostasy, and love them freely (see Is. 58; Jer. 31—33; Hos. 14).

Between His voice of judgment and His promise of restoration, however, God's prophets consistently impose one vital exhortation: Repent! In Isaiah 58 it is indicated: "If you turn from your ritual fasts and submit to the true fast." It is contained in the voice of grieving Ephraim in Jeremiah 31:19: "I turned back, I repented." And in Hosea 14:1, it is couched in the pleading words, "Return, O Israel."

"Repent" did not mean to return to more dedicated efforts to please God by keeping the law or performing better works. The plea has always been simply to *turn to God Himself*—to allow Him to cleanse and restore.

Restoration of the Tabernacle of David (Acts 15:16–18)

In Acts 15:1–29 a question was raised as to whether Gentiles could be accepted as Christians without submitting to the Law of Moses. Peter responded by noting that neither the Jews nor their fathers had been able to bear the burden of the Law; therefore, it made no sense to burden the Gentiles with it. "We believe that through the grace of the Lord Jesus Christ we shall be saved in the same manner as they [the Gentiles]" (v. 11). James confirmed Peter's statement by quoting a passage from Amos, in which God promises to "rebuild the tabernacle of David . . . so that the rest of mankind may seek the LORD" (Acts 15:16, 17).

Many other Scriptures refer to the tabernacle of David, though not always by that name. The name often used is "Zion," Jerusalem's mount where the tabernacle stood and where God dwelt among His people.

Joel 2 begins with the thrilling cry, "Blow the trumpet in Zion, and sound an alarm in My holy mountain!" Hebrews 12:22 says: "But you have come to Mount Zion." Both refer to the tabernacle of David. An understanding of the concept of God's restoration of this tabernacle is essential, for it affords a clear, biblical view of what God is doing in the church today.

The Tabernacle of David: Origin and Description

The tabernacle of David was established shortly after David succeeded Saul as king. The ark of the covenant, which represented the presence and power of God, had been captured by the Philistines. After a series of plagues, the Philistines returned it to Kirjath Jearim, where it remained at the house of Abinadab (1 Sam. 4:1—7:1). David coveted God's manifest presence with him and the people of Israel, so he sought to return the ark to Jerusalem and place it in a tent on Mount Zion (2 Sam. 6; 1 Chr. 13—16).

Prior to its capture, the ark had been housed in the tabernacle of Moses—resting in the inner chamber called the Most Holy Place. No one but the high priest was allowed to enter into the presence of the ark, and he only once a year to sprinkle the blood of a sacrificed animal on the mercy seat that covered the ark (Heb. 9:1–7). The people could approach only to the outer court of the tabernacle to present their sacrifices and worship God.

The tabernacle of David marked a revolutionary departure from this system of separating God from the people. Without violating the spirit of the Law of Moses, David cultivated a spirit of intimacy again between the people and the Lord.

The Significance of the Restoration of the Tabernacle of David

The great significance of the tabernacle of David lay in the fact that the ark, the very presence of God, was back in the midst of the people in Jerusalem. The people were taught by David to worship God with praise, thanksgiving, and rejoicing. Some sixteen ministries were ordained to be performed twenty-four hours a day, seven days a week. None of these ministries were related to guilt or condemnation; all reflected recognition of the mercy and lovingkindness of God and His unconditional acceptance of all who approached Him in faith.

Restoration of the tabernacle of David today means doing away with legalism, judgmentalism, and condemnation, and turning to the hurting people of the church and the world with the open and accepting arms of a loving God (Heb. 10:1–25). The Lord is inviting all to turn to Him, to let Him wipe their sins away, and to receive the refreshing that comes from being in the very presence of the Lord (Acts 3:19).

Restoration of the God-Image (Is. 4:2, 3)

Just as the tabernacle of David represents restoration of the fellowship with God that was lost in Eden, so the analogy of the Branch symbolizes restoration of the God-image—godliness and the family tie with God. Isaiah 4:2, 3 speaks of a "righteous Branch of David" that will spring forth. That Branch is Christ, the Head of the true church, consisting of those who have received salvation and the new birth by grace through faith. Jesus identified Himself as the Vine and His disciples as the branches and He said they would bring forth much fruit if they would abide in Him (John 15:5).

Numerous other Scriptures denote that, in Christ Jesus, God restores His people to the Father-child relationship that was broken by Adam's disobedience. All who believe in Him are brought back into the household of God (Eph. 2:19) and are destined to be conformed to His image (Rom. 8:29).

Restoration of Intimacy with God (Rev. 19:7–9)

The Lord illustrates the restoration of His intimacy with His people through the analogy of the Bride and Bridegroom. The passage in Revelation 19:7–9 depicts the wedding feast of the Lamb, Jesus, when He claims His bride, the church, after she has made herself ready for Him. In his letter to the Ephesians, Paul explains how the bride will prepare herself: by submitting to God and allowing herself to be cleansed by the washing of His Word, so that she may be presented to the Bridegroom without spot, wrinkle, or blemish (Eph. 5:25–27).

When the bride is prepared and Jesus returns for her, the intimacy broken in the Garden will be completely restored, and man will again become one with Christ and with God, as Jesus prayed in John 17. But, as in the first "marriage," the bride must be bone of His bones and flesh of His flesh—that is, she must be like Him. He will not return for a defiled, defeated bride. In these days of restoration, God is preparing the bride with beauty and power and dressing her in His glory.

The Holy Spirit: The Agent of Restoration (Joel 2:28, 29)

God's work of restoration is a work of the Holy Spirit in and through the lives of those who have believed in Jesus and have been born from above (John 3:3). The prophet Joel foretold a day when God would pour out His Spirit "on all flesh" (Joel 2:28, 29). Thus, His power would be shared with all His people and not limited to one chosen individual. This explains why Christ told His disciples it was to their advantage for Him to leave them and go to the Father (John 16:7), because then the Spirit could be sent to indwell each of them, to fill them and to enable the supernatural works of God to be done through them.

Titus 3:5, 6 reveals that even salvation—the regeneration of the dead spirit of man and the cleansing that makes the new man acceptable to God—is the work of the Holy Spirit.

Finally, in Acts 1:8, Jesus tells the disciples to do nothing until the Holy Spirit has come. Then, He promises, they will be empowered to witness of Him and their witness will spread the Good News throughout the world.

What Restoration Means to the Individual (John 10:10)

Perhaps the best way to summarize all that restoration means to the individual believer would be to use the simple word God used in both the Old Testament and the New Testament: *life.* In Deuteronomy 30:20, Moses said of the Lord, "He *is* your life." In Colossians 3:4, Paul speaks of "Christ *who is* our life." And Jesus said, "I have come that they may have life, and that they may have *it* more abundantly" (John 10:10). But no words exceed the splendor or completeness of David's when he said of the Lord, "He restores my soul" (Ps. 23:3).

Restoration, to the individual, means the replacing of spiritual death with spiritual life. Ezekiel 36:25–28 graphically describes just such a transplant. But not only do we receive a new type and quality of life, but we must also grow in it. In many verses we see that process of growth as a work of the Holy Spirit (John 16:23; 17:22; Rom. 8:13; Phil. 1:6; 2:13; Col. 1:27). By His Holy Spirit, God continues and perfects the work He began in us at salvation.

What Restoration Means to the Church (John 13:34, 35)

To the church as a whole, restoration means more than becoming a reproduction of the New Testament church. It means becoming all God originally intended the church to be. Remember, restoration means the establishment of something more and better than the original.

First, restoration means that the church will display the kind of love Jesus demonstrated during His ministry on Earth. By this love, He said, all men would know His disciples (John 13:34, 35). Restoration also means the release of God's power without measure through the church. That release will come through His people as the gifts of the Spirit operate without restraint or restriction under the direction of the Holy Spirit—and in the holy spirit of God's love.

Through the full operation of the gifts and ministries that God appoints, and operating in the love essential to His own nature, the church will reach a level of maturity and unity that can be measured only in terms of "the stature of the fullness of Christ" (Eph. 4:13). As the church becomes a spiritual house (Eph. 2:20) inhabited by a holy priesthood, offering up spiritual sacrifices acceptable to God through Jesus Christ (1 Pet. 2:5), all men will be drawn to Him; the world will at last see the glory of God through this restored church.

Holy Spirit Gifts and Power

by Paul Walker

Without a doubt, the Pentecostal revival of the early 1900s and the Charismatic renewal, which had its beginning in the late 1950s, together constitute one of the most innovative and impactive spiritual renovations in history. But when we investigate this phenomenon we must ask: 1) Why has this happened? 2) What is this doing? and 3) How can spiritual integrity be maintained?

Why Has This Happened?

The first reason has been an evident need for renewal of mission and purpose throughout the church and among its individual members.

Second, in view of this need for renewal, there has been a definite movement on the part of sincere believers to recover the dynamic power of the Holy Spirit, which transformed and empowered the early Christians. Emerging from this movement has been an inbreaking of the Holy Spirit, accompanied by speaking in tongues, among believers in every major denomination, demonstrating that the baptism in the Holy Spirit is not a denomination or a movement but an experience that brings enduement of spiritual power for intensified service.

Third, this inbreaking of the Holy Spirit has linked both the mainline Protestant and the traditional Pentecostal movement to the worship practices of the first century through what has appropriately been referred to as the Charismatic movement (derived from *charismata,* the Greek word used, for example, in 1 Cor. 12:4, 30 for the gifts of the Holy Spirit).

What Is This Doing?

Renewal then raises the question, What really happens when the gifts go to church? In attempting to answer, attention must be given to the scriptural foundation, the traditional context, and the contemporary witness.

The Scripture Is Being Fulfilled

First, the Bible unequivocally declares, "Be filled with the Spirit" (Eph. 5:18). An analysis of the Greek verb translated "be filled" shows that it is in the present tense, indicating that this blessing is one that we may experience and enjoy now. The fact that the verb is a command (imperative mood) does not leave the responsive disciple an option in the matter. However, since the verb is in the passive voice, it is clear that being filled with the Spirit is not something the Christian achieves through his own efforts, but is something that is done for him and to which he submits. Hence, the Scriptures depict a theocentric view of the Holy Spirit's filling, in which the Higher reaches down to gather up the lower into ultimate communion. Clarity on this point dismisses the criticism or misunderstanding of some who seem to see this experience as something merely conjured up by human suggestion, proposition, or excitement.

The Person of the Holy Spirit Is at Work

Second, the Bible reveals that the Person of the Holy Spirit has been the primary agent in all of the ministry of the Word throughout the centuries. The Scripture states clearly that the triune Godhead operates coequally, coeternally, coexistently, as one unit. But it also has been suggested, and with validity, that we might view this unity of activity with an eye toward the special function of each member of the Trinity: the executive is the Father, the architect is the Son, and the contractor is the Holy Spirit.

Thus, the Scriptures show the Holy Spirit uniquely and distinctly at work in these roles: ***1) He is the Author of the Old Testament*** (2 Sam. 23:2; Is. 59:21; Jer. 1:9; 2 Tim. 3:15–17; 2 Pet. 1:21) ***and the New Testament*** (John 14:25, 26; 1 Cor. 2:13; 1 Thess. 4:15; Rev. 1:10, 11; 2:7). ***2) He is the Old Testament Anointer.*** The Scriptures name no less than sixteen Old Testament leaders in Israel who received this anointing: Joseph

(Gen. 41:38); Moses (Num. 11:17); Joshua (Num. 27:18); Othniel (Judg. 3:10); Gideon (Judg. 6:34); Jephthah (Judg. 11:29); Samson (Judg. 14:6, 19; 15:14, 15); Saul (1 Sam. 10:10; 11:6); David (1 Sam. 16:13); Elijah (1 Kin. 8:12, 2 Kin. 2:16); Elisha (2 Kin. 2:15); Azariah (2 Chr. 15:1); Zechariah (2 Chr. 24:20); Ezekiel (Ezek. 2:2); Daniel (Dan. 4:9; 5:11; 6:3); Micah (Mic. 3:8).

Thus, the Holy Spirit, as contractor, anointed the Old Testament prophets Isaiah and Joel to write—to prophesy of the day when He would be outpoured and when His gifts would be exercised in the church, throughout the whole church age (Joel 2:28–32; Acts 2:17–21). In Isaiah 28:11, 12, God used Isaiah to tell Judah that He would teach them in a manner they did not like and that He would give them knowledge through the language of foreigners as a sign of their unbelief. Centuries later the apostle Paul expands the intent of this passage, referring it to the gift of speaking in tongues in the church as a manifestation or sign to unbelievers (1 Cor. 14:21, 22). This sign could be in languages either known or unknown to human beings (compare 1 Cor. 14 with Acts 2:1–11; 10:45, 46).

In all these respects, we see the Holy Spirit as one who operates in the church as a definite personality—a Person given as a gift to the church to assure that the continued ministry of the resurrected Christ is expressed and verified. The Holy Spirit, then, has all the characteristics of a person:

1. He possesses the attributes of mind (Rom. 8:27), will (1 Cor. 12:11), and feeling (Eph. 4:30).

2. He engages in such activities as revealing (2 Pet. 1:21), teaching (John 14:26), witnessing (Heb. 10:15), interceding (Rom. 8:26), speaking (Rev. 2:7), commanding (Acts 16:6, 7), and testifying (John 15:26).

3. He has a relationship with human persons: He can be grieved (Eph. 4:30), lied to (Acts 5:3), and blasphemed (Matt. 12:31, 32).

4. The Holy Spirit possesses the divine attributes of the Godhead: He is eternal (Heb. 9:14), omnipresent (Ps. 139:7–10), omnipotent (Luke 1:35), and omniscient (1 Cor. 2:10, 11).

5. He is referred to by such names as the Spirit of God, the Spirit of Christ, the Comforter, the Holy Spirit, the Holy Spirit of promise, the Spirit of truth, the Spirit of grace, the Spirit of life, the Spirit of adoption, and the Spirit of holiness.

6. He is illustrated with such symbols as fire (Acts 2:1, 2), wind (Acts 2:1, 2), water (John 7:37–39), a seal (Eph. 1:13), oil (Acts 10:38), and a dove (John 1:32).

All this unfolds something of the vast realm or sphere of the operation of the Holy Spirit in the Old and New Testament and in the contemporary church.

Accounts in Acts Are Being Rediscovered and Applied

Third, the Book of Acts provides five accounts of people receiving the fullness or infilling or baptism in the Holy Spirit (Acts 2:4; 8:14–25; 9:17–20; 10:44–48; 19:1–7). In these accounts five factors are manifest: 1) There was an overwhelming inbreaking of God's presence experienced by all who were present. 2) There was an evident transformation in the lives and witness of the disciples who were filled. 3) That which was experienced became the impetus for the growth of the church, as "daily in the temple, and in every house, they did not cease teaching and preaching Jesus as the Christ" (Acts 5:42). 4) The immediate evidence in three of the five accounts was glossolalia: For they heard them speak with tongues and magnify God" (Acts 10:46). [*Glossolalia* is a coined term derived from the Greek *glossa* ("tongue") and *laleo* ("to speak").] 5) The ultimate purpose of this experience was empowered witnessing (Acts 1:8) and a deeper dimension of Christian commitment for the achievement of happiness (Eph. 5:19), gratitude (Eph. 5:20), humility (Eph. 5:21), and fruitfulness (Gal. 5:22, 23).

Together, the above facts demonstrate what the present Pentecostal/Charismatic renewal is experiencing through the Holy Spirit at work in the church. The problem is that too frequently the elements of this renewal are misunderstood or misapplied for lack of a biblical understanding of "tongues" and the function of the gifts of the

Spirit. Although there are varying theological and ethical viewpoints among some in the Neo-Pentecostal/Charismatic movement, a common bond of unity in the Spirit-filled renewal is the practice of "speaking with tongues" in prayer and worship, together with an acceptance and welcoming of the operation of the Holy Spirit's gifts in their midst. Thus, to fully understand this phenomenon, it is necessary to see the Pentecostal/Charismatic view as they have learned to implement the Book of Acts' manifestations of the Holy Spirit's power-workings, applying the controls taught in 1 Corinthians 12—14.

How Can Spiritual Integrity Be Maintained?

Establishing Our Perspective

First, the Pentecostal or Charismatic sees the baptism or infilling of the Holy Spirit as an experience subsequent to Christian conversion: one that comes about through a process of yielding the complete person into the guidance and indwelling of the Holy Spirit. We agree that the Holy Spirit is operative in *every* believer and in the varied ministries of the church. Still every believer must answer the question of Acts 19:2, "Have you received the Holy Spirit since you believed?"

Two expressions should be qualified here:

1. It should be understood that by "baptism in the Holy Spirit" the traditional Pentecostal/Charismatic does not refer to that baptism *of* the Holy Spirit accomplished at conversion, whereby the believer is placed *into* the body of Christ by faith in His redeeming work on the Cross (1 Cor. 12:13). Thus, no biblically oriented Charismatic ever views a non-Charismatic as "less saved" or less spiritual than himself. The baptism in or with the Holy Spirit (John 1:33; Acts 1:5) was and is directed by the Lord Jesus to be "received" (John 20:22; Acts 1:8) as a "gift" given following His ascension (John 7:39; Acts 2:38, 39). However, should any prefer to dismiss this terminology, we contend that to experience the Holy Spirit's fullness in the spirit of unity is more important than to separate company or diminish our passion for His fullness over differences in theological wording or practice.

2. By "a process of yielding the complete person" the Pentecostal/Charismatic does not mean either (a) a passivity of mind or (b) a self-hypnotic or trancelike state. Rather, this terminology refers to an assertive prayerful, heartfelt quest for God. The *mind* is active, worshiping Jesus Christ, the Baptizer with the Holy Spirit (John 1:33). The *emotions* are warmed, as the love of God is poured forth into our hearts (Rom. 5:5). One's *physical* being participates, as worship is spoken and expressed, with upraised voice in prayer (Acts 4:24) or upraised hands of adoration (Ps. 63:1–5).

The Twofold Function of the Gift of Tongues

In regard to those who have "received," the Bible describes two basic functions of "tongues": it is for personal edification and for public exhortation.

In the experience of the baptism in or infilling of the Holy Spirit, "tongues" functions as a sign of the Holy Spirit's presence. Jesus prophesied it as a sign (Mark 16:17), Paul referred to it as a sign (1 Cor. 14:22), and Peter noted its uniformity as a sign-gift in confirming the validity of the Gentiles' experience in the Holy Spirit. (Compare Acts 10:44–46 with 11:16, 17 and 15:7–9). Thus, speaking with tongues is a properly expected sign, affirming the Holy Spirit's abiding presence and assuring the believer of an invigorated living witness. It is not viewed as a *qualification for* fullness of the Holy Spirit, but as one *indication of* that fullness.

Tongues for Personal Edification

First, "speaking in tongues" is a private affair for self-edification (1 Cor. 14:2–4). Thus, glossolalia is practiced devotionally by the believer in his most intimate and intercessory moments of communication with God as he is moved upon by the Holy Spirit. This "devotional" application may also be practiced by corporate agreement, in group gatherings where no unbelievers or uninformed people are present (1 Cor. 14:23). In line with this understanding, the following reasons are propounded for speaking with tongues:

1. Speaking with tongues as the Holy Spirit gives utterance is the unique spiritual gift identified with the church of Jesus Christ. All other gifts, miracles, and spiritual manifestations were in evidence during Old Testament times, before the Day of Pentecost. This new phenomenon came into evidence and became uniquely identified with the church and was ordained by God for the church (1 Cor. 12:28; 14:21).

2. Speaking with tongues is a specific fulfillment of prophecies by Isaiah and Jesus. Compare Isaiah 28:11 with 1 Corinthians 14:21, and Mark 16:17 with Acts 2:4; 10:46; 19:6; and 1 Corinthians 14:5, 14–18, 39.

3. Speaking with tongues is a proof of the resurrection and glorification of Jesus Christ (John 16:7; Acts 2:26).

4. Speaking with tongues is an evidence of the baptism in or infilling of the Holy Spirit (Acts 2:4; 10:45, 46; 19:6).

5. Speaking with tongues is a spiritual gift for self-edification (1 Cor. 14:4; Jude 20).

6. Speaking with tongues is a spiritual gift for spiritual edification of the church when accompanied by interpretation (1 Cor. 14:5).

7. Speaking with tongues is a spiritual gift for communication with God in private worship (1 Cor. 14:15).

8. Speaking with tongues is a means by which the Holy Spirit intercedes through us in prayer (Rom. 8:26; 1 Cor. 14:14; Eph. 6:18).

9. Speaking with tongues is a spiritual means for rejoicing (1 Cor. 14:15; Eph. 5:18, 19).

10. Paul's application of Isaiah's prophecy seems to indicate that speaking with tongues is also intended as a means of "rest" or "refreshing" (Is. 28:12; 1 Cor. 14:21).

11. Tongues follow as one confirmation of the Word of God when it is preached (Mark 16:17, 20; 1 Cor. 14:22).

Tongues for Public Exhortation

Turning to the second function of "tongues"—public exhortation—1 Corinthians 14 bases the gifts of the Spirit on the one sure foundation of love (1 Cor. 14:1). Public "tongues" also calls for integrity in practice as the key for the preservation of order in our fellowship and the worship services. Conceding that there have been those who have abused the gift as an occasion for fleshly pride, we must recognize that it can be a vital and valuable part of worship when placed in its proper setting for the edification of the body (1 Cor. 14:12, 13).

However, the sincere Spirit-filled believer will not be preoccupied with this gift alone, for he sees it as only one of many gifts given for the "wholeness" of the church; therefore, he does not worship or meet with others just to speak in tongues for the mere sake of the practice itself. Such motivation would be immature, vain, and idolatrous. Rather, sincere believers gather to worship God and to be thoroughly equipped for every good work through the teaching of His Word (2 Tim. 3:16, 17). Consequently, the scripturally sensitive believer recognizes the following New Testament direction regarding spiritual gifts:

1. Speaking in "tongues" only edifies public worship when it is interpreted; thus, the worshiper is to pray for the interpretation and if it is withheld, he keeps silent, unless someone who functions in the gift of interpretation is known to be present (1 Cor. 14:5, 28).

2. The Spirit works only to edify; thus, whenever He is truly present all things are in order and devoid of embarrassment or uneasiness (1 Cor. 14:26, 40).

3. The "spirits of the prophets are subject to the prophets" (1 Cor. 14:32). That is, each truly Spirit-filled person *can* exercise self-control; thus, confusion can and should be avoided so that decency with unity may prevail (1 Cor. 14:40).

4. The basis of all gifts is love. *Love,* not the experience of a gift, is the qualifying factor for those who would exercise spiritual gifts. Thus, in the administration of spiritual authority in the local congregation, the Word demands that we "judge" (1 Cor. 14:29) to confirm that those who exercise gifts actually do "pursue love, and desire spiritual *gifts*" (1 Cor. 13:1–13; 14:1).

5. The Author and Dispenser of the gifts is the Holy Spirit, who divides them as He wills; thus, no gift becomes the exclusive possession of any believer for his personal edification and pride. Rather, the gifts are placed in the church to be exercised by the body for the mutual edification of the believers (1 Cor. 12:1–11) and as a means for expanded ministry.

6. The exercise of tongues is to be limited to sequences of two or three at the most (1 Cor. 14:27). While many hold this to be a rigid number, others understand it to be a guideline to keep the worship service in balance. In actuality, the Holy Spirit rarely moves beyond these limitations; however, on occasions, for special reasons to meet special needs, there may be more than one sequence of two or three appropriately spaced apart in a given service. The overarching guideline is, "Let all things be done decently and in order" (1 Cor. 14:40).

The Contemporary Witness

Moving beyond one's fullness in the Holy Spirit, it is important to understand the impact of the Spirit's full operation of gifts in and through the life and witness of the church.

The Spirit-filled experience is more than just "speaking in tongues." In reality it is coming into the fullness of the gifts and fruit of the Spirit as outlined in the New Testament (1 Cor. 12:7-11; Gal. 5:22, 23). It also encompasses the broader scope of exercising God's gifts of spiritual enablement described in Romans 12:3–8 and Ephesians 4:7–12.

The Greek word *charisma* (singular) or *charismata* (plural) is used to designate spiritual gifts, and in the most technical sense mean "gifts of holy grace." In Ephesians 4:11–13 the words *dorea* and *doma* are also used to designate "gifts," referring to these gifts as "enablers" or "equippers" for personal service in the kingdom of God. Also, the word *pneumatika* employed in 1 Corinthians 12:1 is used to describe the gifts as "things belonging to the Spirit." The point is that each of these words gives a contemporary meaning to the supernatural work of the Spirit in our lives as He prepares us for kingdom service and growth in grace. For this to happen we are called upon to "earnestly desire the best gifts" (1 Cor. 12:31). Thus removing the cloak of passivity and ardently seeking to understand the operation of and appropriate response to *all* spiritual gifts is biblically proper.

In speaking of the gifts, however, exclusivism is never implied. The gifts are placed in the church as resources to be utilized at the point of need for ministry in the body. This means that not every believer will have the same gifts as every other believer. Rather, the Holy Spirit is the Author and Dispenser of the gifts to bring about integrity in worship and kingdom expression.

The Gifts of the Godhead

For many, clarification of the distinct role each member of the Godhead plays in giving gifts to mankind is helpful. Foundationally, of course, our existence—human life—is given by the Father (Gen. 2:7; Heb. 12:9), who also gave His only begotten Son as the Redeemer for mankind (John 3:16). Redemptively, Jesus is the giver of eternal life (John 5:38–40; 10:27, 28): He gave His life and shed His blood to gain that privilege *(John 10:17, 18;* Eph. 5:25–27). Further, the Father and Son have jointly sent the Holy Spirit (Acts 2:17, 33) to advance the work of redemption through the church's ministry of worship, growth, and evangelism.

In sequence, then, we find Romans 12:3–8 describing gifts given by God as Father. They seem to characterize basic "motivations," that is, inherent tendencies that characterize each different person by reason of the Creator's unique workmanship in their initial gifting. While only seven categories are listed, observation indicates that few people are fully described by only one. More commonly a mix is found, with different traits of each gift present to some degree, while usually one will be the dominant trait of that person. It would be a mistake to suppose that an individual's learning to respond to the Creator's gifting of them in one or more of these categories fulfills the Bible's call to "earnestly desire the best gifts" (1 Cor. 12:31). These gifts of our place in God's created order are foundational.

Second, in 1 Corinthians 12:7–11, the nine gifts of the Holy Spirit are listed. Their purpose is specific—to "profit" the body of the church. ("Profit," Greek *sumphero,* means "to bring together, to benefit, to be advantageous," which is experienced as the body is strengthened in its life together and expanded through its ministry of evangelism.) These nine gifts are specifically available to *every* believer as the Holy Spirit distributes them (1 Cor. 12:11). They are not to be merely acknowledged in a passive way, but rather are to be actively welcomed and expected (1 Cor. 13:1; 14:1).

Third, the gifts which the Son of God has given are pivotal in assuring that the first two categories of gifts are applied in the body of the church. Ephesians 4:7–16 not only indicates the "office gifts" Christ has placed in the church along with their purpose. The ministry of these leaders is to "equip" the body by assisting each person: 1) to perceive the *place* the Creator has made him to fill, by His creative workmanship in him, and the possibilities that salvation now opens to his realization of what he was made to be; and 2) to receive the *power* of the Holy Spirit, and begin to respond to His gifts, which are given to expand each believer's capabilities *beyond* the created order and toward the redemptive dimension of ministry, for edifying the church and evangelizing the world.

In this light, we examine these clearly designated categories of giftings: the Father's (Rom. 12:6–8), the Son's (Eph. 4:11) and the Holy Spirit's (1 Cor. 12:8–10). While the study expands beyond those listings and beyond the above outlined structure of the gifts of the Godhead, this general outline will help in two ways. First, it assists us by noting the distinct interest and work of each member of the Trinity in providing for our unique purpose and fulfillment. Second, it prevents us from confusing our foundational motivation in life and service for God with our purposeful quest for and openness to His Holy Spirit's full resources and power for service and ministry.

Romans 12:3–8: Gifts of the Father (Basic Life Purpose and Motivation)

1. PROPHECY
   a. To speak with forthrightness and insight, especially when enabled by the Spirit of God (Joel 2:28).
   b. To demonstrate moral boldness and uncompromising commitment to worthy values.
   c. To influence others in one's arena of influence with a positive spirit of social or spiritual righteousness.
   NOTE: Because all three categories of gifts—the Father's, the Holy Spirit's, involve some expression of "prophecy," it is helpful to differentiate. In this category (Rom. 12) the focus is *general,* characterized by that level of the prophetic gift which would belong to *every* believer—"all flesh." The Holy Spirit's "gift of prophecy" (1 Cor. 12) refers to supernatural prompting, so much so that tongues with interpretation is equated with its operation (1 Cor. 14:5). The office-gift of the prophet, which Christ gives to His church through individual ministries, is yet another expression of prophecy: those holding this office must meet *both* the Old Testament requirements of a prophet's accuracy in his message, and the New Testament standards of life and character required of spiritual leadership.
2. MINISTRY
   a. To minister and render loving, general service to meet the needs of others.
   b. Illustrated in the work and office of the deacon (Matt. 20:26).

3. TEACHING
   a. The supernatural ability to explain and apply the truths received from God for the church.
   b. Presupposes study and the Spirit's illumination providing the ability to make divine truth clear to the people of God.
   c. Considered distinct from the work of the prophet who speaks as the direct mouthpiece of God.
4. EXHORTATION
   a. Literally means to call aside for the purpose of making an appeal.
   b. In a broader sense it means to entreat, comfort, or instruct (Acts 4:36; Heb. 10:25).
5. GIVING
   a. The essential meaning is to give out of a spirit of generosity.
   b. In a more technical sense it refers to those with resources aiding those without such resources (2 Cor. 8:2; 9:11–13).
   c. This gift is to be exercised without outward show or pride and with liberality. (2 Cor. 1:12; 8:2; 9:11, 13)
6. LEADERSHIP
   a. Refers to the one "standing in front."
   b. Involves the exercise of the Holy Spirit in modeling, superintending, and developing the body of Christ.
   c. Leadership is to be exercised with diligence.
7. MERCY
   a. To feel sympathy with the misery of another.
   b. To relate to others in empathy, respect, and honesty.
   c. To be effective, this gift is to be exercised with kindness and cheerfulness—not as a matter of duty.

1 Corinthians 12:8–10, 28: Gifts of the Holy Spirit

1. WORD OF WISDOM
   a. Supernatural perspective to ascertain the divine means for accomplishing God's will in given situations.
   b. Divinely given power to appropriate spiritual intuition in problem solving.
   c. Sense of divine direction.
   d. Being led by the Holy Spirit to act appropriately in a given set of circumstances.
   e. Knowledge rightly applied: wisdom works interactively with knowledge and discernment.
2. WORD OF KNOWLEDGE
   a. Supernatural revelation of the divine will and plan.
   b. Supernatural insight or understanding of circumstances or a body of facts by revelation: that is, without assistance of any human resource but solely by divine aid.
   c. Implies a deeper and more advanced understanding of the communicated acts of God.
   d. Involves moral wisdom for right living and relationships.
   e. Requires objective understanding concerning divine things in human duties.
   f. May also refer to knowledge of God or of the things that belong to God, as related in the gospel.
3. FAITH
   a. Supernatural ability to believe God without doubt.
   b. Supernatural ability to combat unbelief.
   c. Supernatural ability to meet adverse circumstances with trust in God's messages and words.
   d. Inner conviction impelled by an urgent and higher calling.
4. GIFTS OF HEALINGS
   a. Refers to supernatural healing without human aid.

b. May include divinely assisted application of human instrumentation and medical means of treatment.
c. Does not discount the use of God's creative gifts.

5. WORKING OF MIRACLES
a. Supernatural power to intervene and counteract earthly and evil forces.
b. Literally means a display of power giving the ability to go beyond the natural.
c. Operates closely with the gifts of faith and healings to bring authority over sin, Satan, sickness and the binding forces of this age.

6. PROPHECY
a. Divinely inspired and anointed utterance.
b. Supernatural proclamation in a known language.
c. Manifestation of the Spirit of God—not of intellect (1 Cor. 12:7).
d. May be possessed and operated by all who have the infilling of the Holy Spirit (1 Cor. 14:31).
e. Intellect, faith, and will are operative in this gift, but its exercise is not intellectually based. It is calling forth words from the Spirit of God.

7. DISCERNING OF SPIRITS
a. Supernatural power to detect the realm of the spirits and their activities.
b. Implies the power of spiritual insight—supernatural revelation of plans and purposes of the Enemy and his forces.

8. DIFFERENT KINDS OF TONGUES
a. Supernatural utterance in languages not known to the speaker: these languages may be existent in the world, revived from some past culture, or "unknown" in the sense that they are a means of communication inspired by the Holy Spirit (Is. 28:11; Mark 16:17; Acts 2:4; 10:44–48; 19:1–7; 1 Cor. 12:10, 28–31; 13:1–3; 14:2, 4–22, 26–32).
b. Serve as an evidence and sign of the indwelling and working of the Holy Spirit.

9. INTERPRETATION OF TONGUES
a. Supernatural power to reveal the meaning of tongues.
b. Functions not as an operation of the mind of man but as the mind of the Spirit.
c. Does not serve as a translation (interpreter never understands the tongue he is interpreting), but rather is a declaration of meaning.
d. Is exercised as a miraculous and supernatural phenomenon as are the gift of speaking in tongues and the gift of prophecy.

Ephesians 4:11 (Also 1 Cor. 12:28): Gifts of the Son (To Facilitate and Equip the Body of the Church)

1. APOSTLES
a. In apostolic days referred to a select group chosen to carry out directly the ministry of Christ; included the assigned task given to a few to complete the sacred canon of the Holy Scriptures.
b. Implies the exercise of a distinct representative role of broader leadership given by Christ.
c. Functions as a messenger or spokesman of God.
d. In contemporary times refers to those who have the spirit of apostleship in remarkably extending the work of the church, opening fields to the gospel, and overseeing larger sections of the body of Jesus Christ.

2. PROPHET
a. A spiritually mature spokesman/proclaimer with a special, divinely focused message to the church or the world.
b. A person uniquely gifted at times with insight into future events.

3. EVANGELIST
a. Refers primarily to a special gift of preaching or witnessing in a way that brings unbelievers into the experience of salvation.

b. Functionally, the gift of evangelist operates for the establishment of new works, while pastors and teachers follow up to organize and sustain.
c. Essentially, the gift of evangelist operates to establish converts and to gather them spiritually and literally into the body of Christ.

4. PASTOR/TEACHER
a. The word "pastor" comes from a root meaning "to protect," from which we get the word "shepherd."
b. Implies the function of a shepherd/leader to nurture, teach, and care for the spiritual needs of the body.

5. MISSIONARY (some see "apostle" or "evangelist" in this light)
a. Implies the unfolding of a plan for making the gospel known to all the world (Rom. 1:16).
b. Illustrates an attitude of humility necessary for receiving a call to remote areas and unknown situations (Is. 6:1–13).
c. Connotes an inner compulsion to lead the whole world to an understanding of Jesus Christ (2 Cor. 5:14–20).

Special Graces

1. HOSPITALITY
a. Literally means to love, to do, or to do with pleasure.
b. Illustrates Peter's notion of one of the two categories of gifts: 1) teaching, 2) practical service (1 Pet. 4:10, 11).
c. Was utilized in caring for believers and workers who visited to worship, work, and become involved in the body of Christ.
d. Illustrated in the teaching of Jesus concerning judgment (Matt. 25:35, 40).

2. CELIBACY (Matt. 19:10; 1 Cor. 7:7–9, 27; 1 Tim. 4:3; Rev. 14:4).
a. The Bible considers marriage to be honorable, ordained of God, and a need for every person.
b. Implies a special gift of celibacy, which frees the individual from the duties, pressures, and preoccupations of family life, allowing undivided attention to the Lord's work.

3. MARTYRDOM (1 Pet. 4:12, 13)
a. Illustrated in the spirit of Stephen (Acts 7:59, 60).
b. Fulfilled in the attitude of Paul (2 Tim. 4:6–8).

Concordance

The Concordance includes proper names and significant topics, defined by phrases and scripture references. Occasionally, a keyword applies to more than one Bible person, place, or topic. This is the case with "Abijah," for whom the Concordance lists four different persons by that name. The second, third, and following occurrences are distinguished by the dash ("———").

AARON
Ancestry and family of, Ex 6:16–20, 23
Helper and prophet to Moses, Ex 4:13–31; 7:1, 2
Appears before Pharaoh, Ex 5:1–4
Performs miracles, Ex 7:9, 10, 19, 20
Supports Moses' hands, Ex 17:10–12
Ascends Mt. Sinai; sees God's glory, Ex 19:24; 24:1, 9, 10
Judges Israel in Moses' absence, Ex 24:14
Chosen by God as priest, Ex 28:1
Consecrated, Ex 29; Lev 8
Duties prescribed, Ex 30:7–10
Tolerates Israel's idolatry, Ex 32
Priestly ministry begins, Lev 9
Sons offer profane fire; Aaron's humble response, Lev 10
Conspires against Moses, Num 12:1–16
Rebelled against by Korah, Num 16
Intercedes to stop plague, Num 16:45–48
Rod buds to confirm his authority, Num 17:1–10
With Moses, fails at Meribah, Num 20:1–13
Dies; son succeeds him as priest, Num 20:23–29
His priesthood compared:
with Melchizedek's, Heb 7:11–19
with Christ's, Heb 9:6–15, 23–28

ABADDON
Angel of the bottomless pit, Rev 9:11

ABBA
And He said, "*A* ... Mark 14:36
by whom we cry out, "*A* ... Rom 8:15
crying out, "*A* ... Gal 4:6

ABED-NEGO
Name given to Azariah, a Hebrew captive, Dan 1:7
Appointed by Nebuchadnezzar, Dan 2:49
Refuses to serve idols; cast into furnace but delivered, Dan 3:12–30

ABEL
Adam's second son, Gen 4:2
His offering accepted, Gen 4:4
Murdered by Cain, Gen 4:8
His sacrifice offered by faith, Heb 11:4

ABHOR
My soul shall not *a* ... Lev 26:11
Therefore I *a* myself ... Job 42:6
nations will *a* him ... Prov 24:24
a the pride of Jacob ... Amos 6:8
A what is evil ... Rom 12:9

ABHORRED
a His own inheritance ... Ps 106:40
he who is *a* by the ... Prov 22:14
and their soul also *a* ... Zech 11:8

ABIATHAR
A priest who escapes Saul at Nob, 1 Sam 22:20–23
Becomes high priest under David, 1 Sam 23:6, 9–12
Remains faithful to David, 2 Sam 15:24–29
Informs David about Ahithophel, 2 Sam 15:34–36
Supports Adonijah's usurpation, 1 Kin 1:7, 9, 25
Deposed by Solomon, 1 Kin 2:26, 27, 35

ABIDE
nor *a* in its paths ... Job 24:13
LORD, who may *a* ... Ps 15:1
He shall *a* before God ... Ps 61:7
the Most High shall *a* ... Ps 91:1
"If you *a* in My word ... John 8:31
And a slave does not *a* ... John 8:35
Helper, that He may *a* ... John 14:16
A in Me and I in you ... John 15:4
If you *a* in Me ... John 15:7
a in My love ... John 15:9
And now *a* faith ... 1 Cor 13:13
does the love of God *a* ... 1 John 3:17
by this we know that we *a* ... 1 John 4:13

ABIDES
even He who *a* from of old ... Ps 55:19
He who *a* in Me ... John 15:5
lives and *a* forever ... 1 Pet 1:23
will of God *a* forever ... 1 John 2:17

ABIDING
not have His word *a* ... John 5:38
has eternal life *a* ... 1 John 3:15

ABIGAIL
Wise wife of foolish Nabal, 1 Sam 25:3
Appeases David and becomes his wife, 1 Sam 25:14–42
Mother of Chileab, 2 Sam 3:3

ABIHU
Second son of Aaron, Ex 6:23
Offers profane fire and dies, Lev 10:1–7

ABIJAH
Samuel's second son; follows corrupt ways, 1 Sam 8:2, 3
——— Descendant of Aaron; head of an office of priests, 1 Chr 24:3, 10
Zechariah belongs to division of, Luke 1:5
——— Son of Jeroboam I, 1 Kin 14:1–18
——— Another name for King Abijam, 2 Chr 11:20

ABIJAM (or Abijah)
King of Judah, 1 Kin 14:31
Follows the sins of his father, 1 Kin 15:1–7
Defeats Jeroboam and takes cities, 2 Chr 13:13–20

ABILITY
who had *a* to serve ... Dan 1:4
according to his own *a* ... Matt 25:15
and beyond their *a* ... 2 Cor 8:3
a which God supplies ... 1 Pet 4:11

ABIMELECH
King of Gerar; takes Sarah in ignorance, Gen 20:1–18
Makes treaty with Abraham, Gen 21:22–34
——— A second king of Gerar; sends Isaac away, Gen 26:1–16
Makes treaty with Isaac, Gen 26:17–33
——— Gideon's son by a concubine, Judg 8:31
Conspires to become king, Judg 9

ABINADAB
A man of Kirjath Jearim in whose house the ark was kept, 1 Sam 7:1, 2
——— The second of Jesse's eight sons, 1 Sam 16:8
Serves in Saul's army, 1 Sam 17:13
——— A son of Saul slain at Mt. Gilboa, 1 Sam 31:1–8
Bones of, buried by men of Jabesh, 1 Chr 10:1–12

ABIRAM
Reubenite who conspired against Moses, Num 16:1–50

ABISHAG
A Shunammite employed as David's nurse, 1 Kin 1:1–4, 15
Witnessed David's choice of Solomon as successor, 1 Kin 1:15–31
Adonijah slain for desiring to marry her, 1 Kin 2:13–25

ABISHAI
David's nephew; joins Joab in blood revenge against Abner, 2 Sam 2:18–24
Loyal to David during Absalom's and Sheba's rebellion, 2 Sam 16:9–12; 20:1–6, 10
Rebuked by David, 2 Sam 16:9–12; 19:21–23
His exploits, 2 Sam 21:16, 17; 23:18; 1 Chr 18:12, 13

ABLE
you are *a* to number ... Gen 15:5
shall give as he is *a* ... Deut 16:17
For who is *a* to judge ... 1 Kin 3:9
"The LORD is *a* ... 2 Chr 25:9
Who then is *a* to stand ... Job 41:10
God whom we serve is *a* ... Dan 3:17
God is *a* to raise up ... Matt 3:9
believe that I am *a* ... Matt 9:28
fear Him who is *a* ... Matt 10:28
Are you *a* to drink the ... Matt 20:22
beyond what you are *a* ... 1 Cor 10:13
And God is *a* to make ... 2 Cor 9:8
may be *a* to comprehend ... Eph 3:18
persuaded that He is *a* ... 2 Tim 1:12
learning and never *a* ... 2 Tim 3:7
being tempted, He is *a* ... Heb 2:18
that God was *a* to ... Heb 11:19
to Him who is *a* ... Jude 24
has come, and who is *a* ... Rev 6:17

ABNER
Saul's cousin; commander of his army, 1 Sam 14:50, 51
Rebuked by David, 1 Sam 26:5, 14–16
Supports Ishbosheth; defeated by David's men; kills Asahel, 2 Sam 2:8–32
Makes covenant with David, 2 Sam 3:6–21
Killed by Joab; mourned by David, 2 Sam 3:22–39

ABOLISHED
your works may be *a* ... Ezek 6:6
having *a* in His flesh ... Eph 2:15
Christ, who has *a* ... 2 Tim 1:10

ABOMINABLE
not make yourselves *a* ... Lev 11:43
They have done *a* ... Ps 14:1
your grave like an *a* ... Is 14:19
Oh, do not do this *a* ... Jer 44:4

they deny Him, being *a* ....Titus 1:16
and *a* idolatries ....1 Pet 4:3
unbelieving, *a* ....Rev 21:8

ABOMINATION

every shepherd is an *a* ....Gen 46:34
If we sacrifice the *a* ....Ex 8:26
You have made me an *a* ....Ps 88:8
yes, seven are an *a* ....Prov 6:16
wickedness is an *a* ....Prov 8:7
Dishonest scales are an *a* ....Prov 11:1
the scoffer is an *a* ....Prov 24:9
prayer is an *a* ....Prov 28:9
An unjust man is an *a* ....Prov 29:27
incense is an *a* ....Is 1:13
and place there the *a* ....Dan 11:31
the *a* of desolation ....Dan 12:11
the '*a* of desolation,' ....Matt 24:15
among men is an *a* ....Luke 16:15

ABOMINATIONS

to follow the *a* ....Deut 18:9
delights in their *a* ....Is 66:3
will put away your *a* ....Jer 4:1
your harlotry, your *a* ....Jer 13:27
will see greater *a* ....Ezek 8:6
a which they commit ....Ezek 8:17
you, throw away the *a* ....Ezek 20:7
show her all her *a* ....Ezek 22:2
a golden cup full of *a* ....Rev 17:4
of the *a* of the earth ....Rev 17:5

ABOUND

lawlessness will *a* ....Matt 24:12
the offense might *a* ....Rom 5:20
sin that grace may *a* ....Rom 6:1
thanksgiving to *a* ....2 Cor 4:15
to make all grace *a* ....2 Cor 9:8
and I know how to *a* ....Phil 4:12
that you should *a* ....1 Thess 4:1
things are yours and *a* ....2 Pet 1:8

ABOUNDED

But where sin *a* ....Rom 5:20

ABOUNDING

and *a* in mercy ....Ps 103:8
immovable, always *a* ....1 Cor 15:58

ABOVE

that is in heaven *a* ....Ex 20:4
"He sent from *a* ....2 Sam 22:17
A it stood seraphim ....Is 6:2
nor a servant *a* his master .....Matt 10:24
He who comes from *a* ....John 3:31
I am from *a* ....John 8:23
been given you from *a* ....John 19:11
who is *a* all ....Eph 4:6
the name which is *a* ....Phil 2:9
things which are *a* ....Col 3:1
perfect gift is from *a* ....James 1:17

ABRAHAM

Ancestry and family, Gen 11:26–31
Receives God's call; enters Canaan, Gen 12:1–6
Promised Canaan by God; pitched tent near Bethel, Gen 12:7, 8
Deceives Egyptians concerning Sarai, Gen 12:11–20
Separates from Lot; inherits Canaan, Gen 13
Rescues Lot from captivity, Gen 14:11–16
Gives a tithe to Melchizedek; refuses spoil, Gen 14:18–24
Covenant renewed; promised a son, Gen 15
Takes Hagar as concubine; Ishmael born, Gen 16
Name changed from Abram; circumcision commanded, Gen 17
Entertains Lord and angels, Gen 18:1–15
Intercedes for Sodom, Gen 18:16–33
Deceives Abimelech concerning Sarah, Gen 20
Birth of Isaac, Gen 21:1–7
Sends Hagar and Ishmael away, Gen 21:9–14
Offers Isaac in obedience to God, Gen 22:1–19
Finds wife for Isaac, Gen 24
Marries Keturah; fathers other children; dies, Gen 25:1–10
Friend of God, 2 Chr 20:7
Justified by faith, Rom 4:1–12
Father of true believers, Rom 4:11–25
In the line of faith, Heb 11:8–10
Eternal home of, in heaven, Luke 16:19–25

ABRAM

See ABRAHAM

ABSALOM

Son of David, 2 Sam 3:3
Kills Amnon for raping Tamar; flees from David, 2 Sam 13:20–39
Returns through Joab's intrigue; reconciled to David, 2 Sam 14
Attempts to usurp throne, 2 Sam 15:1—18:8
Caught and killed by Joab, 2 Sam 18:9–18
Mourned by David, 2 Sam 18:19—19:8

ABSTAIN

we write to them to *a* ....Acts 15:20
A from every form ....1 Thess 5:22
and commanding to *a* ....1 Tim 4:3
a from fleshly lusts ....1 Pet 2:11

ABUNDANCE

is the sound of *a* ....1 Kin 18:41
workmen with you in *a* ....1 Chr 22:15
and *a* of peace ....Ps 72:7
eyes bulge with *a* ....Ps 73:7
nor he who loves *a* ....Eccl 5:10
delight itself in *a* ....Is 55:2
For out of the *a* ....Matt 12:34
put in out of their *a* ....Mark 12:44
not consist in the *a* ....Luke 12:15
of affliction the *a* ....2 Cor 8:2
above measure by the *a* ....2 Cor 12:7
rich through the *a* ....Rev 18:3

ABUNDANT

Longsuffering and *a* ....Ps 86:15
slow to anger and *a* ....Jon 4:2
in labors more *a* ....2 Cor 11:23
Lord was exceedingly *a* ....1 Tim 1:14
a mercy has begotten ....1 Pet 1:3

ABUNDANTLY

a satisfied with the ....Ps 36:8
may have it more *a* ....John 10:10
to do exceedingly *a* ....Eph 3:20
to show more *a* to the ....Heb 6:17

ACACIA GROVE

Spies sent from, Josh 2:1
Israel's last camp before crossing the Jordan, Josh 3:1

ACCEPT

For I will *a* him ....Job 42:8
a your burnt sacrifice ....Ps 20:3
offering, I will not *a* ....Jer 14:12
Should I *a* this from ....Mal 1:13

ACCEPTABLE

sought to find *a* ....Eccl 12:10
a time I have heard ....Is 49:8
proclaim the *a* year ....Is 61:2
proclaim the *a* year ....Luke 4:19
is that good and *a* ....Rom 12:2
finding out what is *a* ....Eph 5:10
For this is good and *a* ....1 Tim 2:3
spiritual sacrifices *a* ....1 Pet 2:5

ACCEPTED

Behold, now is the *a* ....2 Cor 6:2
by which He made us *a* ....Eph 1:6

ACCESS

we have *a* by faith ....Rom 5:2
we have boldness and *a* ....Eph 3:12

ACCOMPLISHED

today the LORD has *a* ....1 Sam 11:13
A desire *a* is sweet to ....Prov 13:19
must still be *a* ....Luke 22:37
all things were now *a* ....John 19:28

ACCORD

and Israel with one *a* ....Josh 9:2
serve Him with one *a* ....Zeph 3:9
continued with one *a* ....Acts 1:14
daily with one *a* ....Acts 2:46
what *a* has Christ with ....2 Cor 6:15
love, being of one *a* ....Phil 2:2

ACCOUNT

they will give *a* ....Matt 12:36
The former *a* I made ....Acts 1:1
each of us shall give *a* ....Rom 14:12
put that on my *a* ....Philem 18
those who must give *a* ....Heb 13:17

ACCOUNTED

and He *a* it to him ....Gen 15:6
And that was *a* to him ....Ps 106:31
his faith is *a* ....Rom 4:5
a as sheep for the ....Rom 8:36
and it was *a* to him ....Gal 3:6
and it was *a* to him ....James 2:23

ACCURSED

he who is hanged is *a* ....Deut 21:23
regarding the *a* things ....Josh 7:1
years old shall be *a* ....Is 65:20
not know the law is *a* ....John 7:49
that I myself were *a* ....Rom 9:3
calls Jesus *a*, and no one ....1 Cor 12:3
let him be *a* ....Gal 1:8

ACCUSATION

they wrote an *a* against ....Ezra 4:6
over His head the *a* ....Matt 27:37
they might find an *a* ....Luke 6:7
Do not receive an *a* ....1 Tim 5:19
not bring a reviling *a* ....2 Pet 2:11

ACCUSE

anyone or *a* falsely ....Luke 3:14
they began to *a* Him ....Luke 23:2
think that I shall *a* ....John 5:45

ACCUSED

forward and *a* the Jews ....Dan 3:8
while He was being *a* ....Matt 27:12

ACCUSER

a of our brethren ....Rev 12:10

ACHAIA

Visited by Paul, Acts 18:1, 12
Apollos preaches in, Acts 18:24–28
Gospel proclaimed throughout, 1 Thess 1:7, 8

ACHAN (or Achar)

Sin of, caused Israel's defeat, Josh 7:1–15
Stoned to death, Josh 7:16–25
Sin of, recalled, Josh 22:20
Also called Achar, 1 Chr 2:7

ACHISH

A king of Gath, 1 Sam 21:10–15
David seeks refuge with, 1 Sam 27:1–12
Forced by Philistine lords to expel David, 1 Sam 29:1–11
Receives Shimei's servants, 1 Kin 2:39, 40

ACHOR, VALLEY OF

Site of Achan's stoning, Josh 7:24–26

On Judah's boundary, Josh 15:7
Promises concerning, Is 65:10

ACHSAH
A daughter of Caleb, 1 Chr 2:49
Given to Othniel, Josh 15:16–19
Given springs of water, Judg 1:12–15

ACKNOWLEDGE
did he *a* his brothers .... Deut 33:9
a my transgressions .... Ps 51:3
in all your ways *a* .... Prov 3:6
and Israel does not *a* .... Is 63:16
a your iniquity .... Jer 3:13
let him *a* that the things ...... 1 Cor 14:37

ACKNOWLEDGED
of Israel, and God *a* them .... Ex 2:25
a my sin to You .... Ps 32:5

ACQUAINTED
and are *a* with all my ways .... Ps 139:3
a Man of sorrows and *a* .... Is 53:3

ACT
seen every great *a* .... Deut 11:7
is time for You to *a* .... Ps 119:126
His *a*, His unusual *a* .... Is 28:21
in the very *a* .... John 8:4

ACTIONS
by Him *a* are weighed .... 1 Sam 2:3

ACTS
LORD, the righteous *a* .... Judg 5:11
His *a* to the children .... Ps 103:7
declare Your mighty *a* .... Ps 145:4
of Your awesome *a* .... Ps 145:6

ADAM
Creation of, Gen 1:26, 27; 2:7
Given dominion over the earth, Gen 1:28–30
Given a wife, Gen 2:18–25
Temptation, fall, and exile from Eden, Gen 3
Children of, Gen 4:1, 2; 5:3, 4
Transgression results in sin and death, Rom 5:12–14
—— Last or second Adam, an appellation of Christ, Rom 5:14, 15; 1 Cor 15:20–24, 45–48

ADD
You shall not *a* .... Deut 4:2
Do not *a* to His words .... Prov 30:6

ADDED
things shall be *a* .... Matt 6:33
And the Lord *a* to the .... Acts 2:47
many people were *a* .... Acts 11:24
It was *a* because of .... Gal 3:19

ADMONISH
also to *a* one another .... Rom 15:14
a him as a brother .... 2 Thess 3:15

ADMONISHED
further, my son, be *a* .... Eccl 12:12
Angel of the LORD *a* .... Zech 3:6

ADMONISHING
a one another in .... Col 3:16

ADMONITION
were written for our *a* .... 1 Cor 10:11
in the training and *a* .... Eph 6:4

ADONIJAH
David's fourth son, 2 Sam 3:2, 4
Attempts to usurp throne, 1 Kin 1:5–53
Desires Abishag as wife, 1 Kin 2:13–18
Executed by Solomon, 1 Kin 2:19–25

ADONI-ZEDEK
An Amorite king of Jerusalem, Josh 10:1–5
Defeated and slain by Joshua, Josh 10:6–27

ADONIRAM (or Adoram)
Official under David, Solomon, and Rehoboam, 2 Sam 20:24; 1 Kin 5:14; 12:18
Stoned by angry Israelites, 1 Kin 12:18
Called Hadoram, 2 Chr 10:18

ADOPTION
the Spirit of *a* .... Rom 8:15
waiting for the *a* .... Rom 8:23
to whom pertain the *a* .... Rom 9:4
we might receive the *a* .... Gal 4:5
a as sons by Jesus .... Eph 1:5

ADORN
a the monuments .... Matt 23:29
also, that the women *a* .... 1 Tim 2:9

ADORNED
By His Spirit He *a* .... Job 26:13
You shall again be *a* .... Jer 31:4
temple, how it was *a* .... Luke 21:5
also *a* themselves .... 1 Pet 3:5
prepared as a bride *a* .... Rev 21:2

ADULTERER
the *a* and the adulteress .... Lev 20:10
The eye of the *a* .... Job 24:15

ADULTERERS
the land is full of *a* .... Jer 23:10
nor idolaters, nor *a* .... 1 Cor 6:9
a God will judge .... Heb 13:4
A and adulteresses .... James 4:4

ADULTERIES
I have seen your *a* .... Jer 13:27
her sight, and her *a* .... Hos 2:2
evil thoughts, *a* .... Mark 7:21

ADULTEROUS
evil and *a* generation .... Matt 12:39

ADULTERY
You shall not commit *a* .... Ex 20:14
Whoever commits *a* .... Prov 6:32
Israel had committed *a* .... Jer 3:8
already committed *a* .... Matt 5:28
is divorced commits *a* .... Matt 5:32
another commits *a* .... Mark 10:11
a woman caught in *a* .... John 8:3
those who commit *a* .... Rev 2:22

ADVANTAGE
a will it be to You .... Job 35:3
man has no *a* over .... Eccl 3:19
a that I go away .... John 16:7
What *a* then has the .... Rom 3:1
Satan should take *a* .... 2 Cor 2:11
no one should take *a* .... 1 Thess 4:6
people to gain *a* .... Jude 16

ADVERSARIES
The *a* of the LORD .... 1 Sam 2:10
rid Myself of My *a* .... Is 1:24
a will not be able .... Luke 21:15
and there are many *a* .... 1 Cor 16:9
terrified by your *a* .... Phil 1:28
will devour the *a* .... Heb 10:27

ADVERSARY
in the way as an *a* .... Num 22:22
battle he become our *a* .... 1 Sam 29:4
how long will the *a* .... Ps 74:10
a has spread his hand .... Lam 1:10
Agree with your *a* .... Matt 5:25
justice for me from my *a* .... Luke 18:3
opportunity to the *a* .... 1 Tim 5:14
your *a* the devil walks .... 1 Pet 5:8

ADVERSITIES
you from all your *a* .... 1 Sam 10:19
known my soul in *a* .... Ps 31:7

ADVERSITY
them with every *a* .... 2 Chr 15:6
I shall never be in *a* .... Ps 10:6
from the days of *a* .... Ps 94:13
brother is born for *a* .... Prov 17:17
faint in the day of *a* .... Prov 24:10
the day of *a* consider .... Eccl 7:14
you the bread of *a* .... Is 30:20

ADVICE
And blessed is your *a* .... 1 Sam 25:33
in this I give my *a* .... 2 Cor 8:10

ADVOCATE
we have an *A* with the .... 1 John 2:1

AFAR
and worship from *a* .... Ex 24:1
sons shall come from *a* .... Is 60:4
and not a God *a* .... Jer 23:23
and saw Abraham *a* .... Luke 16:23
to all who are *a* .... Acts 2:39
to you who were *a* .... Eph 2:17
but having seen them *a* .... Heb 11:13

AFFAIRS
he will guide his *a* .... Ps 112:5
I may hear of your *a* .... Phil 1:27
himself with the *a* .... 2 Tim 2:4

AFFECTION
to his wife the *a* .... 1 Cor 7:3
for you all with the *a* .... Phil 1:8
if any *a* and mercy .... Phil 2:1

AFFECTIONATE
Be kindly *a* to one .... Rom 12:10

AFFLICT
a them with their .... Ex 1:11
oath to *a* her soul .... Num 30:13
may be bound to *a* you .... Judg 16:6
a the descendants .... 1 Kin 11:39
will hear, and *a* them .... Ps 55:19
a Your heritage .... Ps 94:5
a man to *a* his soul .... Is 58:5
to destroy, and to *a* .... Jer 31:28
For He does not *a* .... Lam 3:33
deal with all who *a* .... Zeph 3:19

AFFLICTED
"Why have You *a* .... Num 11:11
and the Almighty has *a* .... Ruth 1:21
To him who is *a* .... Job 6:14
hears the cry of the *a* .... Job 34:28
You *a* the peoples .... Ps 44:2
Before I was *a* .... Ps 119:67
I am *a* very much .... Ps 119:107
Many a time they have *a* .... Ps 129:1
the cause of the *a* .... Ps 140:12
days of the *a* are evil .... Prov 15:15
Smitten by God, and *a* .... Is 53:4
oppressed and He was *a* .... Is 53:7
"O you *a* one .... Is 54:11
Why have we *a* our .... Is 58:3
and satisfy the *a* .... Is 58:10
her virgins are *a* .... Lam 1:4
she has relieved the *a* .... 1 Tim 5:10
being destitute, *a* .... Heb 11:37

AFFLICTION
in the land of my *a* .... Gen 41:52
the bread of *a* .... Deut 16:3
indeed look on the *a* .... 1 Sam 1:11
LORD saw that the *a* .... 2 Kin 14:26
a take hold of me .... Job 30:16
days of *a* confront me .... Job 30:27
held in the cords of *a* .... Job 36:8
of death, bound in *a* .... Ps 107:10
is my comfort in my *a* .... Ps 119:50
and it is an evil *a* .... Eccl 6:2
a He was afflicted .... Is 63:9
refuge in the day of *a* .... Jer 16:19
"O LORD, behold my *a* .... Lam 1:9
not grieved for the *a* .... Amos 6:6
For our light *a* .... 2 Cor 4:17

supposing to add *a* ....Phil 1:16
the word in much *a* ....1 Thess 1:6

AFRAID
garden, and I was *a* ....Gen 3:10
saying, "Do not be *a* ....Gen 15:1
his face, for he was *a* ....Ex 3:6
none will make you *a* ....Lev 26:6
of whom you are *a* ....Deut 7:19
I will not be *a* ....Ps 3:6
ungodliness made me *a* ....Ps 18:4
Do not be *a* when one ....Ps 49:16
Whenever I am *a* ....Ps 56:3
farthest parts are *a* ....Ps 65:8
nor be *a* of their threats ....Is 8:12
no one will make them *a* ....Is 17:2
that you should be *a* ....Is 51:12
dream which made me *a* ....Dan 4:5
do not be *a* ....Matt 14:27
if you do evil, be *a* ....Rom 13:4
do good and are not *a* ....1 Pet 3:6

AFTERWARD
A he will let you go ....Ex 11:1
a we will speak ....Job 18:2
a receive me to glory ....Ps 73:24
you shall follow Me *a* ....John 13:36
the firstfruits, *a* ....1 Cor 15:23

AGAG
A king of Amalek in Balaam's prophecy, Num 24:7
——— Amalekite king spared by Saul, but slain by Samuel, 1 Sam 15:8, 9, 20–24, 32, 33

AGAIN
day He will rise *a* ....Matt 20:19
'You must be born *a* ....John 3:7
to renew them *a* ....Heb 6:6
having been born *a* ....1 Pet 1:23

AGAINST
his hand shall be *a* ....Gen 16:12
I will set My face *a* ....Lev 20:3
come to 'set a man *a* ....Matt 10:35
or house divided *a* ....Matt 12:25
not with Me is *a* Me ....Matt 12:30
blasphemy *a* the Spirit ....Matt 12:31
For nation will rise *a* ....Matt 24:7
out, as *a* a robber ....Matt 26:55
I have sinned *a* ....Luke 15:18
lifted up his heel *a* ....John 13:18
LORD and *a* His Christ ....Acts 4:26
to kick *a* the goads ....Acts 9:5
all men everywhere *a* ....Acts 21:28
let us not fight *a* ....Acts 23:9
a the promises of God ....Gal 3:21
we do not wrestle *a* ....Eph 6:12
I have a few things *a* ....Rev 2:20

AGE
well advanced in *a* ....Gen 18:11
Israel were dim with *a* ....Gen 48:10
the flower of their *a* ....1 Sam 2:33
the grave at a full *a* ....Job 5:26
a is as nothing ....Ps 39:5
and in the *a* to come ....Mark 10:30
"The sons of this *a* ....Luke 20:34
He is of *a* ....John 9:21
who are of full *a* ....Heb 5:14
the powers of the *a* ....Heb 6:5

AGES
ordained before the *a* ....1 Cor 2:7
in other *a* was not ....Eph 3:5
at the end of the *a* ....Heb 9:26

AGONY
And being in *a* ....Luke 22:44

AGREE
A with your adversary ....Matt 5:25
that if two of you *a* ....Matt 18:19
testimonies did not *a* ....Mark 14:56
and these three *a* ....1 John 5:8

AGREED
unless they are *a* ....Amos 3:3
they were glad, and *a* ....Luke 22:5

AHAB
A wicked king of Israel, 1 Kin 16:29
Marries Jezebel; promotes Baal worship, 1 Kin 16:31–33; 18:17–46
Denounced by Elijah, 1 Kin 17:1
Wars against Ben-Hadad, 1 Kin 20:1–43
Covets Naboth's vineyard, 1 Kin 21:1–16
Death predicted; repentance delays judgment, 1 Kin 21:17–29
Goes to war in spite of Micaiah's warning; killed in battle, 1 Kin. 22:1–37
Prophecy concerning, fulfilled, 1 Kin 22:38
——— Lying prophet, Jer 29:21–23

AHASUERUS
The father of Darius the Mede, Dan 9:1
——— Persian king, probably Xerxes I, 486–465 B.C., Ezra 4:6; Esth 1:1
Makes Esther queen, Esth 2:16, 17
Orders Jews annihilated, by Haman's advice, Esth 3:8–15
Reverses decree at Esther's request, Esth 7; 8
Exalts Mordecai, Esth 10:1–3

AHAZ
King of Judah; pursues idolatry; submits to Assyrian rule; desecrates the temple, 2 Kin 16
Defeated by Syria and Israel, 2 Chr 28:5–15
Comforted by Isaiah; refuses to ask a sign, Is 7:1–17

AHAZIAH
King of Israel; son of Ahab and Jezebel; worships Baal, 1 Kin 22:51–53
Falls through lattice; calls on Baal-Zebub; dies according to Elijah's word, 2 Kin 1:2–18
——— King of Judah; Ahab's son-in-law; reigns wickedly, 2 Kin 8:25–29; 2 Chr 22:1–6
Killed by Jehu, 2 Kin 9:27–29; 2 Chr 22:7–9

AHIJAH
A prophet of Shiloh who foretells division of Solomon's kingdom, 1 Kin 11:29–39
Foretells elimination of Jeroboam's line, 1 Kin 14:1–18
A writer of prophecy, 2 Chr 9:29

AHIKAM
Sent in Josiah's mission to Huldah, 2 Kin 22:12–14
Protects Jeremiah, Jer 26:24
The father of Gedaliah, governor under Nebuchadnezzar, 2 Kin 25:22; Jer 39:14

AHIMAAZ
A son of Zadok the high priest, 1 Chr 6:8, 9
Warns David of Absalom's plans, 2 Sam 15:27, 36
First to tell David of Absalom's defeat, 2 Sam 18:19–30

AHIMELECH
High priest in Saul's reign; helps David, 1 Sam 21:1–9
Betrayed and killed by Doeg; son Abiathar escapes, 1 Sam 22:9–20
David writes concerning, Ps 52:title

AHINOAM
Wife of David, 1 Sam 25:43; 27:3; 30:5, 18
Mother of Amnon, 2 Sam 3:2

AHITHOPHEL
David's counselor, 2 Sam 15:12
Joins Absalom's insurrection; counsels him, 2 Sam 15:31; 16:20–23
His counsel rejected; commits suicide, 2 Sam 17:1–23

AI
Israel defeated at, Josh 7:2–5
Israel destroys completely, Josh 8:1–28

AIJALON
Amorites not driven from, Judg 1:35
Miracle there, Josh 10:12, 13
City of refuge, 1 Chr 6:66–69
Fortified by Rehoboam, 2 Chr 11:5, 10
Captured by Philistines, 2 Chr 28:18

AIR
the birds of the *a* ....Gen 1:26
of the *a* have nests ....Luke 9:58
as one who beats the *a* ....1 Cor 9:26
be speaking into the *a* ....1 Cor 14:9
of the power of the *a* ....Eph 2:2
meet the Lord in the *a* ....1 Thess 4:17
his bowl into the *a* ....Rev 16:17

AKEL DAMA
Field called "Field of Blood," Acts 1:19

ALARM
to sound the *a* against ....2 Chr 13:12
A day of trumpet and *a* ....Zeph 1:16

ALEXANDER
A member of the high-priestly family, Acts 4:6
——— A Jew in Ephesus, Acts 19:33, 34
——— An apostate condemned by Paul, 1 Tim 1:19, 20

ALEXANDRIA
Men of, persecute Stephen, Acts 6:9
Paul sails in ship of, Acts 27:6

ALIEN
because you were an *a* ....Deut 23:7
I am an *a* in their ....Job 19:15
who turn away an *a* ....Mal 3:5

ALIENATED
a herself from them ....Ezek 23:17
darkened, being *a* ....Eph 4:18
you, who once were *a* ....Col 1:21

ALIENS
For we are *a* and ....1 Chr 29:15
For I have loved *a* ....Jer 2:25
A have devoured his ....Hos 7:9
without Christ, being *a* ....Eph 2:12
the armies of the *a* ....Heb 11:34

ALIVE
in the ark remained *a* ....Gen 7:23
with them went down *a* ....Num 16:33
LORD your God are *a* ....Deut 4:4
I kill and I make *a* ....Deut 32:39
Let them go down *a* ....Ps 55:15
he preserves himself *a* ....Ezek 18:27
heard that He was *a* ....Mark 16:11
son was dead and is *a* ....Luke 15:24
presented Himself *a* ....Acts 1:3
dead indeed to sin, but *a* ....Rom 6:11
I was *a* once without ....Rom 7:9
all shall be made *a* ....1 Cor 15:22
trespasses, made us *a* ....Eph 2:5
flesh, He has made *a* ....Col 2:13
that we who are *a* ....1 Thess 4:15
the flesh but made *a* ....1 Pet 3:18
and behold, I am *a* ....Rev 1:18
a name that you are *a* ....Rev 3:1
These two were cast *a* ....Rev 19:20

ALLELUIA
Again they said, "*A* ....Rev 19:3

ALLOW
a Your Holy One . . . . .Ps 16:10
a My faithfulness . . . . .Ps 89:33
nor do you *a* those . . . . .Matt 23:13
a Your Holy One . . . . .Acts 2:27
who will not *a* . . . . .1 Cor 10:13

ALMOND
a blossoms on one . . . . .Ex 25:33
a tree blossoms . . . . .Eccl 12:5

ALMOST
for me, my feet had *a* . . . . .Ps 73:2
a persuade me to . . . . .Acts 26:28
a all things are . . . . .Heb 9:22

ALMS
But rather give *a* . . . . .Luke 11:41
you have and give *a* . . . . .Luke 12:33
I came to bring *a* . . . . .Acts 24:17

ALOES
with myrrh and *a* . . . . .Ps 45:8
my bed with myrrh, *a* . . . . .Prov 7:17
mixture of myrrh and *a* . . . . . . .John 19:39

ALPHA
I am the *A* and the . . . . .Rev 1:8
I am the *A* and the . . . . .Rev 22:13

ALTAR
Then Noah built an *a* . . . . .Gen 8:20
An *a* of earth you . . . . .Ex 20:24
a shall be kept . . . . .Lev 6:9
it to you upon the *a* . . . . .Lev 17:11
offering for the *a* . . . . .Num 7:84
called the *a* Witness . . . . .Josh 22:34
and tear down the *a* . . . . .Judg 6:25
"Go up, erect an *a* . . . . .2 Sam 24:18
cried out against the *a* . . . . .1 Kin 13:2
I will go to the *a* . . . . .Ps 43:4
there will be an *a* . . . . .Is 19:19
Lord has spurned His *a* . . . . .Lam 2:7
you cover the *a* . . . . .Mal 2:13
your gift to the *a* . . . . .Matt 5:23
swears by the *a* . . . . .Matt 23:18
I even found an *a* . . . . .Acts 17:23
the offerings of the *a* . . . . .1 Cor 9:13
partakers of the *a* . . . . .1 Cor 10:18
We have an *a* from . . . . .Heb 13:10
Isaac his son on the *a* . . . . .James 2:21
and stood at the *a* . . . . .Rev 8:3

ALTARS
a Hezekiah has taken . . . . .2 Kin 18:22
Even Your *a*, O LORD . . . . .Ps 84:3
on the horns of your *a* . . . . .Jer 17:1
a shall be broken . . . . .Ezek 6:4
has made many *a* . . . . .Hos 8:11
a shall be heaps . . . . .Hos 12:11
destruction on the *a* . . . . .Amos 3:14
and torn down Your *a* . . . . .Rom 11:3

ALWAYS
delight, rejoicing *a* . . . . .Prov 8:30
the poor with you *a* . . . . .Matt 26:11
Me you do not have *a* . . . . .Matt 26:11
lo, I am with you *a* . . . . .Matt 28:20
'Son, you are *a* . . . . .Luke 15:31
men *a* ought to pray . . . . .Luke 18:1
immovable, *a* abounding . . . . . .1 Cor 15:58
Rejoice in the Lord *a* . . . . .Phil 4:4
thus we shall *a* . . . . .1 Thess 4:17
a be ready to give a . . . . .1 Pet 3:15

AM
to Moses, "I *A* WHO I *A* . . . . .Ex 3:14
First and I *a* the Last . . . . .Is 44:6
in My name, I *a* there . . . . .Matt 18:20
I *a* the bread of life . . . . .John 6:35
I *a* the light of the . . . . .John 8:12
I *a* from above . . . . .John 8:23
Abraham was, I *A* . . . . .John 8:58
I *a* the door . . . . .John 10:9
I *a* the good shepherd . . . . John 10:11
I *a* the resurrection . . . . .John 11:25
to him, "I *a* the way . . . . .John 14:6
of God I *a* what I *a* . . . . .1 Cor 15:10

AMALEK
Grandson of Esau, Gen 36:11, 12
A chief of Edom, Gen 36:16
First among nations, Num 24:20

AMALEKITES
Destruction predicted, Ex 17:14; Deut 25:17–19
Defeated by Israel, Ex 17:8–13; Judg 7:12–25; 1 Sam 14:47, 48; 27:8, 9; 1 Chr 4:42, 43
Overcome Israel, Num 14:39–45; Judg 3:13

AMASA
Commands Absalom's rebels, 2 Sam 17:25
Made David's commander, 2 Sam 19:13
Treacherously killed by Joab, 2 Sam 20:9–12
Death avenged, 1 Kin 2:28–34

AMAZIAH
King of Judah; kills his father's assassinators, 2 Kin 14:1–6; 2 Chr 25:1–4
Hires troops from Israel; is rebuked by a man of God; sends troops home, 2 Chr 25:5–10
Defeats Edomites; worships their gods, 2 Chr 25:11–16
Wars with Israel, 2 Kin 14:8–14; 2 Chr 25:17–24
Killed by conspirators, 2 Chr 25:25–28

AMBASSADOR
but a faithful *a* . . . . .Prov 13:17
for which I am an *a* . . . . .Eph 6:20

AMBASSADORS
which sends *a* by sea . . . . .Is 18:2
cry outside, the *a* . . . . .Is 33:7
we are *a* for Christ . . . . .2 Cor 5:20

AMBITION
Christ from selfish *a* . . . . .Phil 1:16
through selfish *a* . . . . .Phil 2:3

AMEN
uninformed say "*A* . . . . .1 Cor 14:16
are Yes, and in Him *A* . . . . .2 Cor 1:20
creatures said, "*A* . . . . .Rev 5:14

AMEND
A your ways and your . . . . Jer 7:3
from his evil way, *a* . . . . .Jer 35:15

AMMON
A nation fathered by Lot, Gen 19:36, 38

AMMONITES
Excluded from assembly for hostility to Israel, Deut 23:3–6
Propose cruel treaty; conquered by Saul, 1 Sam 11:1–3, 11
Abuse David's ambassadors; conquered by his army, 2 Sam 10:1–14
Harass postexilic Jews, Neh 4:3, 7, 8
Defeated by Israel and Judah, Judg 11:4–33; 2 Chr 20:1–25; 27:5, 6
Prophecies concerning, Ps 83:1–18; Jer 25:9–21; Ezek 25:1–7; Amos 1:13–15; Zeph 2:9–11

AMNON
A son of David, 2 Sam 3:2
Rapes his half sister, 2 Sam 13:1–18
Killed by Absalom, 2 Sam 13:19–29

AMON
King of Judah, 2 Kin 21:18, 19
Follows evil, 2 Chr 33:22, 23
Killed by conspiracy, 2 Kin 21:23, 24
——— A governor of Samaria, 1 Kin 22:10, 26

AMORITES
Defeated by Joshua, Josh 10:1–43
Not driven out of Canaan, Judg 1:34–36
Put to forced labor under Solomon, 1 Kin 9:20, 21

AMOS
A prophet of Israel, Amos 1:1
Pronounces judgment against nations, Amos 1:1–3, 15
Denounces Israel's sins, Amos 4:1—7:9
Condemns Amaziah, the priest of Bethel, Amos 7:10–17
Predicts Israel's downfall, Amos 9:1–10
Foretells great blessings, Amos 9:11–15

AMRAM
Son of Kohath, Num 3:17–19
The father of Aaron, Moses and Miriam, Ex 6:18–20; 1 Chr 6:3

ANAKIM
A race of giants; very strong, Num 13:28–33; Deut 2:10, 11, 21
Defeated
by Joshua, Josh 10:36–39; 11:21
by Caleb, Josh 14:6–15

ANANIAS
Disciple at Jerusalem; slain for lying to God, Acts 5:1–11
——— A Christian disciple at Damascus, Acts 9:10–19; 22:12–16
——— A Jewish high priest, Acts 23:1–5

ANATHOTH
A Levitical city in Benjamin, Josh 21:18
Jeremiah's birthplace; he buys property there, Jer 1:1; 32:6–15
To be invaded by Assyria, Is 10:30

ANCHOR
hope we have as an *a* . . . . .Heb 6:19

ANCIENT
Do not remove the *a* . . . . .Prov 23:10
a times that I . . . . .Is 37:26
until the *A* of Days . . . . .Dan 7:22

ANDREW
A disciple of John the Baptist, then of Christ, Matt 4:18, 19; John 1:40–42
Enrolled among the Twelve, Matt 10:2
Mentioned, Mark 13:3, 4; John 6:8, 9; 12:20–22; Acts 1:13

ANGEL
Now the *A* of the LORD . . . . .Gen 16:7
A who has redeemed me . . . . . . .Gen 48:16
"Behold, I send an *A* . . . . .Ex 23:20
the donkey saw the *A* . . . . .Num 22:23
For I have seen the *A* . . . . Judg 6:22
Manoah said to the *A* . . . . Judg 13:17
in my sight as an *a* . . . . .1 Sam 29:9
a who was destroying . . . . .2 Sam 24:16
night that the *a* . . . . .2 Kin 19:35
the *A* of His Presence . . . . .Is 63:9
struggled with the *A* . . . . .Hos 12:4
standing before the *A* . . . . .Zech 3:3
like God, like the *A* . . . . .Zech 12:8
things, behold, an *a* . . . . .Matt 1:20
for an *a* of the Lord . . . . .Matt 28:2
Then an *a* of the Lord . . . . .Luke 1:11
And behold, an *a* . . . . .Luke 2:9
a appeared to Him from . . . . . . .Luke 22:43
For an *a* went down at . . . . John 5:4
a has spoken to Him . . . . John 12:29
But at night an *a* . . . . .Acts 5:19
A who appeared to him . . . . .Acts 7:35
Then immediately an *a* . . . . .Acts 12:23
and no *a* or spirit . . . . .Acts 23:8

a has spoken to him ... Acts 23:9
by me this night an *a* ... Acts 27:23
himself into an *a* ... 2 Cor 11:14
even if we, or an *a* ... Gal 1:8
Then I saw a strong *a* ... Rev 5:2
over them the *a* ... Rev 9:11
Then I saw an *a* ... Rev 19:17
Jesus, have sent My *a* ... Rev 22:16

ANGELS

If He charges His *a* ... Job 4:18
lower than the *a* ... Ps 8:5
He shall give His *a* ... Ps 91:11
Praise Him, all His *a* ... Ps 148:2
He shall give His *a* ... Matt 4:6
a will come forth ... Matt 13:49
a always see the face ... Matt 18:10
but are like *a* ... Matt 22:30
not even the *a* ... Matt 24:36
and all the holy *a* ... Matt 25:31
twelve legions of *a* ... Matt 26:53
the presence of the *a* ... Luke 15:10
was carried by the *a* ... Luke 16:22
are equal to the *a* ... Luke 20:36
And she saw two *a* ... John 20:12
that we shall judge *a* ... 1 Cor 6:3
head, because of the *a* ... 1 Cor 11:10
and worship of *a* ... Col 2:18
with His mighty *a* ... 2 Thess 1:7
the Spirit, seen by *a* ... 1 Tim 3:16
much better than the *a* ... Heb 1:4
does not give aid to *a* ... Heb 2:16
company of *a* ... Heb 12:22
entertained *a* ... Heb 13:2
things which *a* desire ... 1 Pet 1:12
did not spare the *a* ... 2 Pet 2:4
a who did not keep ... Jude 6
Michael and his *a* ... Rev 12:7

ANGER

Cursed be their *a* ... Gen 49:7
sun, that the fierce *a* ... Num 25:4
fierceness of His *a* ... Deut 13:17
of this great *a* ... Deut 29:24
So the *a* of the LORD ... Judg 10:7
to provoke Me to *a* ... 1 Kin 16:2
For His *a* is but for a ... Ps 30:5
let Your wrathful *a* ... Ps 69:24
a time He turned His *a* ... Ps 78:38
made a path for His *a* ... Ps 78:50
You prolong Your *a* ... Ps 85:5
the power of Your *a* ... Ps 90:11
gracious, slow to *a* ... Ps 103:8
Nor will He keep His *a* ... Ps 103:9
harsh word stirs up *a* ... Prov 15:1
a sins against his own ... Prov 20:2
a rests in the bosom ... Eccl 7:9
a the Holy One of ... Is 1:4
a is not turned away ... Is 5:25
a is turned away ... Is 12:1
'I will not cause My *a* ... Jer 3:12
For great is the *a* ... Jer 36:7
and I will send My *a* ... Ezek 7:3
does not retain His *a* ... Mic 7:18
fierceness of His *a* ... Nah 1:6
a is kindled against ... Zech 10:3
around at them with *a* ... Mark 3:5
bitterness, wrath, *a* ... Eph 4:31

ANGRY

Cain, "Why are you a ... Gen 4:6
"Let not the Lord be *a* ... Gen 18:30
the Son, lest He be *a* ... Ps 2:12
judge, and God is *a* ... Ps 7:11
When once You are *a* ... Ps 76:7
Will you be *a* forever ... Ps 79:5
friendship with an *a* ... Prov 22:24
backbiting tongue an *a* ... Prov 25:23
a man stirs up strife ... Prov 29:22
in your spirit to be *a* ... Eccl 7:9
I was *a* with My people ... Is 47:6
nor will I always be *a* ... Is 57:16
covetousness I was *a* ... Is 57:17
right for you to be *a* ... Jon 4:4
LORD has been very *a* ... Zech 1:2
I am exceedingly *a* ... Zech 1:15
you that whoever is *a* ... Matt 5:22
"Be *a*, and do not sin" ... Eph 4:26
Therefore I was *a* ... Heb 3:10
with whom was He *a* ... Heb 3:17
The nations were *a* ... Rev 11:18

ANGUISH

a has come upon me ... 2 Sam 1:9
a make him afraid ... Job 15:24
I will be in *a* over my ... Ps 38:18
trouble and *a* have overtaken ... Ps 119:143
longer remembers the *a* ... John 16:21
tribulation and *a* ... Rom 2:9
much affliction and *a* ... 2 Cor 2:4

ANIMAL

of every clean *a* ... Gen 7:2
Whoever kills an *a* ... Lev 24:18
the life of his *a* ... Prov 12:10
set him on his own *a* ... Luke 10:34

ANIMALS

of *a* after their kind ... Gen 6:20
sacrifices of fat *a* ... Ps 66:15
of four-footed *a* ... Acts 10:12
and four-footed *a* ... Rom 1:23

ANNA

Aged prophetess, Luke 2:36–38

ANNAS

A Jewish high priest, Luke 3:2
Christ appeared before, John 18:12–24
Peter and John appeared before, Acts 4:6

ANOINT

You shall *a* them ... Ex 28:41
but you shall not *a* ... Deut 28:40
you shall *a* for Me the ... 1 Sam 16:3
a yourself with oil ... 2 Sam 14:2
a my head with oil ... Ps 23:5
Arise, you princes, *a* ... Is 21:5
a the Most Holy ... Dan 9:24
when you fast, *a* ... Matt 6:17
a My body for burial ... Mark 14:8
they might come and *a* ... Mark 16:1
a your eyes with eye ... Rev 3:18

ANOINTED

the priest, who is *a* ... Lev 16:32
"Surely the LORD's *a* ... 1 Sam 16:6
destroy the LORD's *a* ... 2 Sam 1:14
he cursed the LORD's *a* ... 2 Sam 19:21
shows mercy to His *a* ... 2 Sam 22:51
"Do not touch My *a* ... 1 Chr 16:22
the LORD saves His *a* ... Ps 20:6
because the LORD has *a* ... Is 61:1
"These are the two *a* ... Zech 4:14
Because He has *a* ... Luke 4:18
but this woman has *a* ... Luke 7:46
a the eyes of the ... John 9:6
It was that Mary who *a* ... John 11:2
Jesus, whom You *a* ... Acts 4:27
and has *a* us is God ... 2 Cor 1:21

ANOINTING

also made the holy *a* ... Ex 37:29
pray over him, *a* him ... James 5:14
But you have an *a* ... 1 John 2:20
but as the same *a* ... 1 John 2:27

ANOTHER

that you love one *a* ... John 13:34
and He will give you *a* ... John 14:16
'Let *a* take his ... Acts 1:20

ANSWER

will give Pharaoh an *a* ... Gen 41:16
a I should take back ... 2 Sam 24:13
Him, he could not *a* ... Job 9:3
Call, and I will *a* ... Job 13:22
how shall I *a* Him ... Job 31:14
and you shall *a* ... Job 40:7
the day that I call, *a* ... Ps 102:2
In Your faithfulness *a* ... Ps 143:1
a turns away wrath ... Prov 15:1
A man has joy by the *a* ... Prov 15:23
He who gives a right *a* ... Prov 24:26
a a fool according ... Prov 26:4
was there none to *a* ... Is 50:2
for there is no *a* ... Mic 3:7
or what you should *a* ... Luke 12:11
you may have an *a* ... 2 Cor 5:12
ought to *a* each one ... Col 4:6

ANT

Go to the *a* ... Prov 6:6

ANTICHRIST

heard that the *A* ... 1 John 2:18
a who denies the ... 1 John 2:22
is the spirit of the *A* ... 1 John 4:3
is a deceiver and an *a* ... 2 John 7

ANTIOCH

——— In Syria:
First Gentile church established, Acts 11:19–21
Disciples first called "Christians" in, Acts 11:26
Church commissions Paul, Acts 13:1–4; 15:35–41
Church troubled by Judaizers, Acts 15:1–4; Gal 2:11–21
——— In Pisidia:
Paul visits; Jews reject the gospel, Acts 13:14, 42–51

ANXIETIES

the multitude of my *a* ... Ps 94:19
Try me, and know my *a* ... Ps 139:23

ANXIETY

A in the heart of man ... Prov 12:25
eat their bread with *a* ... Ezek 12:19

ANXIOUS

drink, nor have an *a* ... Luke 12:29
Be *a* for nothing ... Phil 4:6

APART

that you shall set *a* ... Ex 13:12
she shall be set *a* ... Lev 15:19
the LORD has set *a* ... Ps 4:3
justified by faith *a* ... Rom 3:28

APHEK

A town in the Plain of Sharon, Josh 12:18
Site of Philistine camp, 1 Sam 4:1; 29:1
——— A city in Jezreel, 1 Kin 20:26–30
Syria's defeat prophesied here, 2 Kin 13:14–19

APOLLOS

An Alexandrian Jew; instructed by Aquila and Priscilla and sent to Achaia, Acts 18:24–28
Referred to as having ministered in Corinth, 1 Cor 1:12; 3:4, 22; 4:6; 16:12

APOLLYON

Angel of the bottomless pit, Rev 9:11

APOSTLE

called to be an *a* ... Rom 1:1
inasmuch as I am an *a* ... Rom 11:13
Am I not an *a* ... 1 Cor 9:1
the signs of an *a* were ... 2 Cor 12:12
a preacher and an *a* ... 1 Tim 2:7
consider the *A* ... Heb 3:1

APOSTLES

of the twelve *a* ... Matt 10:2

whom He also named *a* ....Luke 6:13
displayed us, the *a* ....1 Cor 4:9
am the least of the *a* ....1 Cor 15:9
to the most eminent *a* ....2 Cor 11:5
themselves into *a* ....2 Cor 11:13
none of the other *a* ....Gal 1:19
gave some to be *a* ....Eph 4:11
who say they are *a* ....Rev 2:2
heaven, and you holy *a* ....Rev 18:20

APOSTLESHIP

in this ministry and *a* ....Acts 1:25
received grace and *a* ....Rom 1:5
are the seal of my *a* ....1 Cor 9:2
in Peter for the *a* ....Gal 2:8

APPAREL

is glorious in His *a* ....Is 63:1
clothed with foreign *a* ....Zeph 1:8
by them in white *a* ....Acts 1:10
themselves in modest *a* ....1 Tim 2:9
gold rings, in fine *a* ....James 2:2
or putting on fine *a* ....1 Pet 3:3

APPEAR

and let the dry land *a* ....Gen 1:9
all your males shall *a* ....Ex 23:17
all Israel comes to *a* ....Deut 31:11
shall I come and *a* ....Ps 42:2
Let Your work *a* ....Ps 90:16
He shall *a* in His ....Ps 102:16
doings your sins *a* ....Ezek 21:24
faces that they may *a* ....Matt 6:16
also outwardly *a* ....Matt 23:28
kingdom of God would *a* .....Luke 19:11
For we must all *a* ....2 Cor 5:10
for Him He will *a* ....Heb 9:28
and the sinner *a* ....1 Pet 4:18

APPEARANCE

Do not look at his *a* ....1 Sam 16:7
a is blacker than soot ....Lam 4:8
As He prayed, the *a* ....Luke 9:29
judge according to *a* ....John 7:24
those who boast in *a* ....2 Cor 5:12
to the outward *a* ....2 Cor 10:7
found in *a* as a man ....Phil 2:8
indeed have an *a* ....Col 2:23

APPEARED

an angel of the Lord *a* ....Luke 1:11
who *a* in glory and ....Luke 9:31
brings salvation has *a* ....Titus 2:11
of the ages, He has *a* ....Heb 9:26

APPEARING

Lord Jesus Christ's *a* ....1 Tim 6:14
been revealed by the *a* ....2 Tim 1:10
and the dead at His *a* ....2 Tim 4:1
who have loved His *a* ....2 Tim 4:8
hope and glorious *a* ....Titus 2:13

APPEARS

can stand when He *a* ....Mal 3:2
who is our life *a* ....Col 3:4
the Chief Shepherd *a* ....1 Pet 5:4
in Him, that when He *a* ....1 John 2:28

APPLE

He kept him as the *a* ....Deut 32:10
And my law as the *a* ....Prov 7:2
Like an *a* tree among ....Song 2:3
touches the *a* of His eye ....Zech 2:8

APPLES

fitly spoken is like *a* ....Prov 25:11
refresh me with *a* ....Song 2:5

APPOINT

I will even *a* terror ....Lev 26:16
a each of them to his ....Num 4:19
a me ruler over the ....2 Sam 6:21
a salvation for walls ....Is 26:1
For God did not *a* ....1 Thess 5:9
a elders in every city ....Titus 1:5

APPOINTED

You have *a* his limits ....Job 14:5
To release those *a* ....Ps 102:20
And as it is *a* for men ....Heb 9:27

APPROACH

a anyone who is near ....Lev 18:6
And cause to *a* You ....Ps 65:4
year, make those who *a* ....Heb 10:1

APPROACHING

take delight in *a* God ....Is 58:2
as you see the Day *a* ....Heb 10:25

APPROVE

their posterity who *a* ....Ps 49:13
do the same but also *a* ....Rom 1:32
a the things that ....Rom 2:18
a the things that are ....Phil 1:10

APPROVED

to God and *a* by men ....Rom 14:18
to present yourself *a* ....2 Tim 2:15
when he has been *a* ....James 1:12

AQUILA

Paul's host in Corinth, Acts 18:2, 3
Travels to Syria and Ephesus with Paul, Acts 18:18, 19
Instructs Apollos, Acts 18:24–26
Esteemed by Paul, Rom 16:3, 4

AR

A chief Moabite city, Num 21:15
On Israel's route, Deut 2:18
Destroyed by Sihon, Num 21:28
Destroyed by God, Is 15:1

ARABIA

Pays tribute to Solomon, 1 Kin 10:14, 15
Plunders Jerusalem, 2 Chr 21:16, 17
Defeated by Uzziah, 2 Chr 26:1, 7
Denounced by prophets, Is 21:13–17

ARARAT

Site of ark's landing, Gen 8:4
Assassins flee to, 2 Kin 19:37; Is 37:38

ARAUNAH (or Ornan)

A Jebusite, 2 Sam 24:15–25
His threshing floor bought by David, 2 Sam 24:18–25
becomes site of temple, 2 Chr 3:1
Also called Ornan, 1 Chr 21:18–28

ARCHANGEL

with the voice of an *a* ....1 Thess 4:16
Yet Michael the *a* ....Jude 9

ARCHELAUS

Son of Herod the Great, Matt 2:22

AREOPAGUS

Paul preaches at, Acts 17:18–34

ARGUMENTS

fill my mouth with *a* ....Job 23:4
casting down *a* and ....2 Cor 10:5

ARISE

needy, now I will *a* ....Ps 12:5
A for our help ....Ps 44:26
Let God *a* ....Ps 68:1
A, shine; for your light ....Is 60:1
But the LORD will *a* ....Is 60:2
Righteousness shall *a* ....Mal 4:2
I will *a* and go to ....Luke 15:18
you who sleep, *a* ....Eph 5:14

ARISTARCHUS

A Macedonian Christian, Acts 19:29
Accompanies Paul, Acts 20:1, 4
Imprisoned with Paul, Col 4:10

ARK

Make yourself an *a* ....Gen 6:14
she took an *a* of bulrushes ....Ex 2:3
Bezalel made the *a* ....Ex 37:1
seat which is on the *a* ....Lev 16:2
Let us bring the *a* ....1 Sam 4:3
golden censer and the *a* ....Heb 9:4
of Noah, while the *a* ....1 Pet 3:20
in heaven, and the *a* ....Rev 11:19

ARM

with an outstretched *a* ....Ex 6:6
"Has the LORD's *a* ....Num 11:23
With him is an *a* ....2 Chr 32:8
a that has no strength ....Job 26:2
Have you an *a* like God ....Job 40:9
Break the *a* of the ....Ps 10:15
You have a mighty *a* ....Ps 89:13
a have gained Him the ....Ps 98:1
a shall rule for Him ....Is 40:10
therefore His own *a* ....Is 59:16
strength with His *a* ....Luke 1:51
with an uplifted *a* ....Acts 13:17
a yourselves also with ....1 Pet 4:1

ARMAGEDDON

See MEGIDDO
Possible site of final battle, Rev 16:16

ARMED

You have *a* me with ....2 Sam 22:40
a strong man, fully *a* ....Luke 11:21

ARMIES

make captains of the *a* ....Deut 20:9
"I defy the *a* ....1 Sam 17:10
any number to His *a* ....Job 25:3
not go out with our *a* ....Ps 60:10
And he sent out his *a* ....Matt 22:7
surrounded by *a* ....Luke 21:20
And the *a* in heaven ....Rev 19:14
the earth, and their *a* ....Rev 19:19

ARMOR

but he put his *a* ....1 Sam 17:54
spears, put on the *a* ....Jer 46:4
let us put on the *a* ....Rom 13:12
Put on the whole *a* ....Eph 6:11

ARMS

are the everlasting *a* ....Deut 33:27
into the clash of *a* ....Job 39:21
It is God who *a* ....Ps 18:32
My *a* will judge the ....Is 51:5
wounds between your *a* ....Zech 13:6
took them up in His *a* ....Mark 10:16
took Him up in his *a* ....Luke 2:28

ARMY

the multitude of an *a* ....Ps 33:16
an exceedingly great *a* ....Ezek 37:10
the number of the *a* ....Rev 9:16

ARNON

Boundary between Moab and Ammon, Num 21:13, 26
Border of Reuben, Deut 3:12, 16
Ammonites reminded of, Judg 11:18–26

AROMA

smelled a soothing *a* ....Gen 8:21
To the one we are the *a* ....2 Cor 2:16
for a sweet-smelling *a* ....Eph 5:2
a sweet-smelling *a* ....Phil 4:18

AROUSED

the LORD was greatly *a* ....Num 11:10
his wrath was *a* ....Job 32:2
Then Joseph, being *a* ....Matt 1:24

ARPHAXAD

A son of Shem, Gen 10:22, 24
Born two years after the flood, Gen 11:10–13
An ancestor of Christ, Luke 3:36

ARRAYED

his glory was not *a* ....Matt 6:29

"Who are these *a* .... Rev 7:13
The woman was *a* .... Rev 17:4

ARROW

deliverance and the *a* .... 2 Kin 13:17
a cannot make him flee .... Job 41:28
make ready their *a* .... Ps 11:2
a that flies by day .... Ps 91:5
a sword, and a sharp *a* .... Prov 25:18
Their tongue is an *a* .... Jer 9:8
as a target for the *a* .... Lam 3:12

ARROWS

He sent out *a* and .... 2 Sam 22:15
a pierce me deeply .... Ps 38:2
There He broke the *a* .... Ps 76:3
Like *a* in the hand of .... Ps 127:4
He has caused the *a* .... Lam 3:13
were sworn over Your *a* .... Hab 3:9

ARTAXERXES

Artaxerxes I, king of Persia (465–425 B.C.), authorizes Ezra's mission to Jerusalem, Ezra 7:1–28
Temporarily halts rebuilding program at Jerusalem, Ezra 4:7–23
Authorizes Nehemiah's mission, Neh 2:1–10
Permits Nehemiah to return, Neh 13:6

ARTEMIS

Worship of, at Ephesus, creates uproar, Acts 19:23–41

ASA

Third king of Judah; restores true worship, 1 Kin 15:8–15; 2 Chr 14; 15
Hires Ben-Hadad against Baasha; rebuked by a prophet, 1 Kin 15:16–22; 2 Chr 16:1–10
Diseased, seeks physicians rather than the Lord, 2 Chr 16:12
Death and burial, 2 Chr 16:13, 14

ASAHEL

David's nephew; captain in his army; noted for valor, 2 Sam 2:18; 23:24; 1 Chr 2:16; 27:7
Killed by Abner, 2 Sam 2:19–23
Avenged by Joab, 2 Sam 3:27, 30

ASAPH

A Levite choir leader under David and Solomon, 1 Chr 15:16–19; 16:1–7; 2 Chr 5:6, 12
Twelve Psalms assigned to, 2 Chr 29:30; Ps 50; 73—83

ASCEND

Who may *a* into the .... Ps 24:3
If I *a* into heaven .... Ps 139:8
'I will *a* into heaven .... Is 14:13
a as high as the eagle .... Obad 4
see the Son of Man *a* .... John 6:62

ASCENDED

You have *a* on high .... Ps 68:18
Who has *a* into heaven .... Prov 30:4
No one has *a* .... John 3:13
"When He *a* on high .... Eph 4:8
also the One who *a* .... Eph 4:10
And they *a* to heaven .... Rev 11:12

ASCENDING

angels of God were *a* .... Gen 28:12
the angels of God *a* .... John 1:51

ASCRIBE

a greatness to our God .... Deut 32:3
a righteousness .... Job 36:3
A strength to God .... Ps 68:34

ASENATH

Daughter of Poti-Pherah and wife of Joseph, Gen 41:45
Mother of Manasseh and Ephraim, Gen 41:50–52; 46:20

ASHAMED

I am too *a* and .... Ezra 9:6
all my enemies be *a* .... Ps 6:10
Let me not be *a* .... Ps 25:2
who waits on You be *a* .... Ps 25:3
The wise men are *a* .... Jer 8:9
forsake You shall be *a* .... Jer 17:13
And Israel shall be *a* .... Hos 10:6
For whoever is *a* .... Mark 8:38
am not *a* of the gospel .... Rom 1:16
nothing I shall be *a* .... Phil 1:20
Therefore God is not *a* .... Heb 11:16
in Christ may be *a* .... 1 Pet 3:16
let him not be *a* .... 1 Pet 4:16
and not be *a* before .... 1 John 2:28

ASHDOD

One of five Philistine cities, Josh 13:3
Seat of Dagon worship, 1 Sam 5:1–8
Opposes Nehemiah, Neh 4:7
Women of, marry Jews, Neh 13:23, 24
Called Azotus, Acts 8:40

ASHER

Jacob's second son by Zilpah, Gen 30:12, 13
Goes to Egypt with Jacob, Gen 46:8, 17
Blessed by Jacob, Gen 49:20
——— Tribe of:
Census of, Num 1:41; 26:47
Slow to fight against Canaanites, Judg 1:31, 32; 5:17
Among Gideon's army, Judg 6:35; 7:23
A godly remnant among, 2 Chr 30:11

ASHERAH

The female counterpart of Baal, Judg 3:7; 1 Kin 18:19
Image of, erected by Manasseh in the temple, 2 Kin 21:7
Vessels of, destroyed by Josiah, 2 Kin 23:4
——— Translated "wooden images," idols used in the worship of Asherah, Ex 34:13; Deut 12:3; 16:21; 1 Kin 16:32, 33; 2 Kin 23:6, 7

ASHES

are proverbs of *a* .... Job 13:12
become like dust and *a* .... Job 30:19
For I have eaten *a* .... Ps 102:9
He feeds on *a* .... Is 44:20
sackcloth and sat in *a* .... Jon 3:6
in sackcloth and *a* .... Luke 10:13
and the *a* of a heifer .... Heb 9:13

ASHKELON

One of five Philistine cities, Josh 13:3; Jer 47:5, 7
Captured by Judah, Judg 1:18
Men of, killed by Samson, Judg 14:19, 20
Repossessed by Philistines, 1 Sam 6:17; 2 Sam 1:20
Doom of, pronounced by the prophets, Jer 47:5, 7; Amos 1:8; Zeph 2:4, 7; Zech 9:5

ASHTAROTH

A city in Bashan; residence of King Og, Deut 1:4; Josh 12:4
Captured by Israel, Josh 9:10
——— A general designation of the Canaanite female deities, 1 Sam 7:3, 4; 31:10

ASHTORETH

A mother-goddess worshiped by the Philistines, 1 Sam 31:10
Israel ensnared by, Judg 2:13; 10:6
Worshiped by Solomon, 1 Kin 11:5, 33
Destroyed by Josiah, 2 Kin 23:13

ASIA

Paul forbidden to preach in, Acts 16:6
Paul's later ministry in, Acts 19:1–26
Seven churches of, Rev 1:4, 11

ASK

"Why is it that you *a* .... Gen 32:29
when your children *a* .... Josh 4:6
"*A* a sign for yourself .... Is 7:11
They shall *a* the way .... Jer 50:5
the young children *a* .... Lam 4:4
A the LORD for rain in .... Zech 10:1
whatever things you *a* .... Matt 21:22
a, and it will be .... Luke 11:9
that whatever You *a* .... John 11:22
a anything in My .... John 14:14
in that day you will *a* .... John 16:23
something, let them *a* .... 1 Cor 14:35
above all that we *a* .... Eph 3:20
wisdom, let him *a* .... James 1:5
But let him *a* in faith .... James 1:6
because you do not *a* .... James 4:2
hears us, whatever we *a* .... 1 John 5:15

ASKS

For everyone who *a* .... Matt 7:8
if his son *a* for bread .... Matt 7:9
Or if he *a* for a fish .... Luke 11:11

ASLEEP

down, and was fast *a* .... Jon 1:5
But He was *a* .... Matt 8:24
but some have fallen *a* .... 1 Cor 15:6
those who are *a* .... 1 Thess 4:15
the fathers fell *a* .... 2 Pet 3:4

ASSEMBLED

of the God of Israel *a* .... Ezra 9:4
behold, the kings *a* .... Ps 48:4

ASSEMBLING

not forsaking the *a* .... Heb 10:25

ASSEMBLY

to kill this whole *a* .... Ex 16:3
It is a sacred *a* .... Lev 23:36
a I will praise You .... Ps 22:22
I have hated the *a* .... Ps 26:5
also in the *a* of the .... Ps 89:5
to be feared in the *a* .... Ps 89:7
will rest in the *a* of the .... Prov 21:16
fast, call a sacred *a* .... Joel 1:14
people, sanctify the *a* .... Joel 2:16
a I will sing praise .... Heb 2:12
to the general *a* .... Heb 12:23
come into your *a* .... James 2:2

ASSHUR

One of the sons of Shem; progenitor of the Assyrians, Gen 10:22; 1 Chr 1:17
——— The chief god of the Assyrians; seen in names like Ashurbanipal (Osnapper), Ezra 4:10
——— A city in Assyria or the nation of Assyria, Num 24:22, 24

ASSURANCE

night, and have no *a* .... Deut 28:66
riches of the full *a* .... Col 2:2
Spirit and in much *a* .... 1 Thess 1:5
to the full *a* of hope .... Heb 6:11
a true heart in full *a* .... Heb 10:22

ASSYRIA (or Asshur)

Founded by Nimrod, Gen 10:8–12; Mic 5:6
Agent of God's purposes, Is 7:17–20; 10:5, 6
Attacks and finally conquers Israel, 2 Kin 15:19, 20, 29; 17:3–41
Invades and threatens Judah, 2 Kin 18:13–37
Hezekiah prays for help against; army miraculously slain, 2 Kin 19:1–35
Prophecies concerning, Num 24:22–24; Is 10:12–19; 14:24, 25; 19:23–25; Hos 10:6; 11:5; Nah 3:1–19

ASTONISHED
Just as many were *a* ....Is 52:14
that the people were *a* ....Matt 7:28
who heard Him were *a* ....Luke 2:47

ASTONISHMENT
you shall become an *a* ....Deut 28:37
a has taken hold ....Jer 8:21

ASTRAY
is a people who go *a* ....Ps 95:10
a fool, shall not go *a* ....Is 35:8
Their lies lead them *a* ....Amos 2:4
and one of them goes *a* ....Matt 18:12
'They always go *a* ....Heb 3:10
like sheep going *a* ....1 Pet 2:25

ATHALIAH
Daughter of Ahab and Jezebel, 2 Kin 8:18, 26; 2 Chr 22:2, 3
Kills royal children; usurps throne, 2 Kin 11:1–3; 2 Chr 22:10, 11
Killed in priestly uprising, 2 Kin 11:4–16; 2 Chr 23:1–21

ATHENS
Paul preaches in, Acts 17:15–34
Paul resides in, 1 Thess 3:1

ATONEMENT
a year he shall make *a* ....Ex 30:10
priest shall make *a* ....Lev 16:30
the blood that makes *a* ....Lev 17:11
for it is the Day of *A* ....Lev 23:28
what shall I make *a* ....2 Sam 21:3
offerings to make *a* ....Neh 10:33
a is provided for ....Prov 16:6
there will be no *a* ....Is 22:14
I provide you an *a* ....Ezek 16:63

ATTAIN
It is high, I cannot *a* ....Ps 139:6
understanding will *a* ....Prov 1:5
How long until they *a* ....Hos 8:5
worthy to *a* that age ....Luke 20:35
by any means, I may *a* ....Phil 3:11

ATTEND
just cause, O LORD, *a* ....Ps 17:1
And *a* to the voice of ....Ps 86:6
behold, I will *a* ....Jer 23:2

ATTENTION
My son, give *a* to my ....Prov 4:20
Till I come, give *a* ....1 Tim 4:13
and you pay *a* to the ....James 2:3

ATTENTIVE
Let Your ears be *a* ....Ps 130:2
the people were very *a* ....Luke 19:48

AUTHOR
For God is not the *a* ....1 Cor 14:33
He became the *a* ....Heb 5:9
unto Jesus, the *a* ....Heb 12:2

AUTHORITIES
a that exist are ....Rom 13:1
of God, angels and *a* ....1 Pet 3:22

AUTHORITY
Jew, wrote with full *a* ....Esth 9:29
the righteous are in *a* ....Prov 29:2
them as one having *a* ....Matt 7:29
who are great exercise *a* ......Matt 20:25
"All *a* has been given ....Matt 28:18
a I will give You ....Luke 4:6
and has given Him *a* ....John 5:27
You have given Him *a* ....John 17:2
has put in His own *a* ....Acts 1:7
For there is no *a* ....Rom 13:1
to have a symbol of *a* ....1 Cor 11:10
and all who are in *a* ....1 Tim 2:2
and rebuke with all *a* ....Titus 2:15
defile the flesh, reject *a* ....Jude 8

AVAILS
nor uncircumcision *a* ....Gal 5:6
of a righteous man *a* ....James 5:16

AVEN
The city of On in Egypt near Cairo; known as Heliopolis, Gen 41:45; Ezek 30:17
——— A name contemptuously applied to Bethel, Hos 10:5, 8
——— Valley in Syria, Amos 1:5

AVENGE
for He will *a* the ....Deut 32:43
you that He will *a* ....Luke 18:8
Beloved, do not *a* ....Rom 12:19
a our blood on those ....Rev 6:10

AVENGER
The *a* of blood ....Num 35:19
the enemy and the *a* ....Ps 8:2
God's minister, an *a* ....Rom 13:4
the Lord is the *a* ....1 Thess 4:6

AVENGES
It is God who *a* ....2 Sam 22:48
When He *a* blood ....Ps 9:12

AWAKE
be satisfied when I *a* ....Ps 17:15
I lie *a* ....Ps 102:7
A, lute and harp ....Ps 108:2
My eyes are *a* through ....Ps 119:148
A, O north wind ....Song 4:16
but my heart is *a* ....Song 5:2
of the earth shall *a* ....Dan 12:2
it is high time to *a* ....Rom 13:11
A to righteousness ....1 Cor 15:34
"*A*, you who sleep ....Eph 5:14

AWAY
the wind drives *a* ....Ps 1:4
Do not cast me *a* ....Ps 51:11
A time to cast *a* ....Eccl 3:5
fair one, and come *a* ....Song 2:10
and the shadows flee *a* ....Song 2:17
minded to put her *a* ....Matt 1:19
and earth will pass *a* ....Matt 24:35
and steal Him *a* ....Matt 27:64
the rich He has sent *a* ....Luke 1:53
of God who takes *a* ....John 1:29
"I am going *a* ....John 8:21
they cried out, "*A* ....John 19:15
"They have taken *a* ....John 20:2
crying out, "*A* ....Acts 21:36
the veil is taken *a* ....2 Cor 3:14
Barnabas was carried *a* ....Gal 2:13
unless the falling *a* ....2 Thess 2:3
in Asia have turned *a* ....2 Tim 1:15
heard, lest we drift *a* ....Heb 2:1
if they fall *a* ....Heb 6:6
which can never take *a* ....Heb 10:11
that does not fade *a* ....1 Pet 5:4
the world is passing *a* ....1 John 2:17
and the heaven fled *a* ....Rev 20:11
if anyone takes *a* ....Rev 22:19
God shall take *a* ....Rev 22:19

AWE
the world stand in *a* ....Ps 33:8
my heart stands in *a* ....Ps 119:161

AWESOME
a is this place ....Gen 28:17
a thing that I will do ....Ex 34:10
God, the great and *a* ....Deut 7:21
God, mighty and *a* ....Deut 10:17
Angel of God, very *a* ....Judg 13:6
a deeds for Your land ....2 Sam 7:23
heaven, O great and *a* ....Neh 1:5
hand shall teach You *a* ....Ps 45:4
By *a* deeds in ....Ps 65:5
a are Your works ....Ps 66:3
He is *a* in His doing ....Ps 66:5
O God, You are more *a* ....Ps 68:35
He is *a* to the kings ....Ps 76:12
Your great and *a* name ....Ps 99:3
of the might of Your *a* ....Ps 145:6
When You did *a* things ....Is 64:3
with me as a mighty, *a* ....Jer 20:11
her collapse was *a* ....Lam 1:9
"O Lord, great and *a* ....Dan 9:4

AX
a stroke with the *a* ....Deut 19:5
Abimelech took an *a* ....Judg 9:48
a tree, the iron *a* ....2 Kin 6:5
If the *a* is dull ....Eccl 10:10
a boast itself against ....Is 10:15
And even now the *a* ....Matt 3:10

AZARIAH
A prophet who encourages King Asa, 2 Chr 15:1–8
——— Son of King Jehoshaphat, 2 Chr 21:2
——— King of Judah, 2 Kin 15:1
——— A high priest who rebukes King Uzziah, 2 Chr 26:16–20
——— Chief priest in the time of Hezekiah, 2 Chr 31:9, 10
——— The Hebrew name of Abed-Nego, Dan 1:7

AZEKAH
Camp of Goliath, 1 Sam 17:1, 4, 17
Besieged by Nebuchadnezzar, Jer 34:7

AZMAVETH
A village near Jerusalem, Neh 12:29
Also called Beth Azmaveth, Neh 7:28

BAAL (or Baals)
Deities of Canaanite polytheism, Judg 10:10–14
The male god of the Phoenicians and Canaanites; the counterpart of the female Ashtaroth, 2 Kin 23:5
Nature of the worship of, 1 Kin 18:26, 28; 19:18; Ps 106:28; Jer 7:9; 19:5; Hos 9:10; 13:1, 2
Worshiped by Israelites, Num 25:1–5; Judg 2:11–14; 3:7; 6:28–32; 1 Kin 16:31, 32; 2 Kin 21:3; Jer 11:13; Hos 2:8
Ahaz makes images to, 2 Chr 28:1–4
Overthrown by Elijah, 1 Kin 18:17–40 by Josiah, 2 Kin 23:4, 5
Denounced by prophets, Jer 19:4–6; Ezek 16:1, 2, 20, 21
Historic retrospect, Rom 11:4

BAAL PEOR (or Baal of Peor)
A Moabite god; worshiped by Israelites, Num 25:1–9

BAAL PERAZIM
Site of David's victory over the Philistines, 2 Sam 5:18–20
Same as Perazim, Is 28:21

BAAL-ZEBUB
A Philistine god at Ekron, 2 Kin 1:2
Ahaziah inquires of, 2 Kin 1:2, 6, 16
Also called Beelzebub, Matt 10:25; 12:24

BAALS
Deities of Canaanite polytheism, Judg 10:10–14
Ensnare Israelites, Judg 2:11–14; 3:7
Ahaz makes images to, 2 Chr 28:1–4

BAANAH
A murderer of Ishbosheth, 2 Sam 4:1–12

BAASHA
Usurps throne of Israel; his evil reign; wars with Judah, 1 Kin 15:16—16:7

BABE
the *b* leaped in my ....Luke 1:44

You will find a *B* .... Luke 2:12
for he is a *b* .... Heb 5:13

BABEL, TOWER OF
A huge brick structure intended to magnify man and preserve the unity of the race, Gen 11:1–4
Objectives of, thwarted by God, Gen 11:5–9

BABES
Out of the mouth of *b* .... Ps 8:2
b shall rule over them .... Is 3:4
revealed them to *b* .... Matt 11:25
'Out of the mouth of *b* .... Matt 21:16
a teacher of *b* .... Rom 2:20
as to carnal, as to *b* .... 1 Cor 3:1
as newborn *b* .... 1 Pet 2:2

BABYLON
Built by Nimrod; Tower of Babel, Gen 10:8–10; 11:1–9
Descriptions of, Is 13:19; 14:4; Jer 51:44; Dan 4:30
Jews carried captive to, 2 Kin 25:1–21; 2 Chr 36:5–21
Inhabitants of, described, Is 47:1, 9–13; Jer 50:35–38; Dan 5:1–3
Prophecies concerning, Is 13:1–22; Jer 21:1–7; 25:9–12; 27:5–8; 29:10; Jer 50:1–46; Dan 2:31–38; 7:2–4
The prophetic city, Rev 14:8; 16:19; 17:1—18:24

BACK
Jordan turned *b* .... Ps 114:3
but a rod is for the *b* .... Prov 10:13
for the fool's *b* .... Prov 26:3
I gave My *b* to those .... Is 50:6
cast Me behind your *b* .... Ezek 23:35
found Him, bring *b* word .... Matt 2:8
plow, and looking *b* .... Luke 9:62
they drew *b* and fell .... John 18:6
I am sending him *b* .... Philem 12
of those who draw *b* .... Heb 10:39
someone turns him *b* .... James 5:19
inside and on the *b* .... Rev 5:1

BACKBITERS
b, haters of God .... Rom 1:30

BACKBITING
b tongue an angry .... Prov 25:23

BACKSLIDER
The *b* in heart will be .... Prov 14:14

BACKSLIDINGS
b will rebuke you .... Jer 2:19
And I will heal your *b* .... Jer 3:22
b have increased .... Jer 5:6
for our *b* are many .... Jer 14:7

BACKWARD
fell off the seat *b* .... 1 Sam 4:18
shadow ten degrees *b* .... 2 Kin 20:11

BAD
speak to you either *b* .... Gen 24:50
good for *b* or *b* for good .... Lev 27:10
b tree bears *b* fruit .... Matt 7:17

BAG
is sealed up in a *b* .... Job 14:17
wages to put into a *b* .... Hag 1:6
nor *b* for your .... Matt 10:10

BALAAM
Sent by Balak to curse Israel, Num 22:5–7; Josh 24:9
Hindered by talking donkey, Num 22:22–35; 2 Pet 2:16
Curse becomes a blessing, Deut 23:4, 5; Josh 24:10
Prophecies of, Num 23:7–10, 18–24; 24:3–9, 15–24
NT references to, 2 Pet 2:15, 16; Jude 11; Rev 2:14

BALAK
A Moabite king, Num 22:4
Hires Balaam to curse Israel, Num 22—24

BALANCE
b is an abomination .... Prov 11:1
small dust on the *b* .... Is 40:15

BALANCES
falsifying the *b* .... Amos 8:5

BALD
shall not make any *b* .... Lev 21:5
every head shall be *b* .... Jer 48:37
completely *b* because .... Ezek 27:31

BALDHEAD
Go up, you *b* .... 2 Kin 2:23

BALM
a little *b* and a .... Gen 43:11
no *b* in Gilead .... Jer 8:22

BAND
A *b* of robbers takes .... Hos 7:1
with a golden *b* .... Rev 1:13

BANDAGED
him, and *b* his wounds .... Luke 10:34

BANKERS
my money with the *b* .... Matt 25:27

BANNERS
we will set up our *b* .... Ps 20:5
They set up their *b* .... Ps 74:4
as an army with *b* .... Song 6:4

BANQUET
b that I have prepared .... Esth 5:4
companions make a *b* .... Job 41:6
lords, came to the *b* .... Dan 5:10

BANQUETING
He brought me to the *b* .... Song 2:4

BANQUETS
b shall be removed .... Amos 6:7

BAPTISM
coming to his *b* .... Matt 3:7
b that I am baptized .... Matt 20:22
The *b* of John .... Matt 21:25
But I have a *b* .... Luke 12:50
said, "Into John's *b* .... Acts 19:3
with Him through *b* .... Rom 6:4
Lord, one faith, one *b* .... Eph 4:5
buried with Him in *b* .... Col 2:12
now saves us—*b* .... 1 Pet 3:21

BAPTISMS
of the doctrine of *b* .... Heb 6:2

BAPTIZE
I indeed *b* you with .... Matt 3:11
"Why then do you *b* .... John 1:25
Himself did not *b* .... John 4:2
did not send me to *b* .... 1 Cor 1:17

BAPTIZED
"I need to be *b* .... Matt 3:14
b will be saved .... Mark 16:16
b more disciples .... John 4:1
every one of you be *b* .... Acts 2:38
all his family were *b* .... Acts 16:33
believed and were *b* .... Acts 18:8
Arise and be *b* .... Acts 22:16
were *b* into Christ .... Rom 6:3
I thank God that I *b* .... 1 Cor 1:14
b the household .... 1 Cor 1:16
all were *b* into Moses .... 1 Cor 10:2
Spirit we were all *b* .... 1 Cor 12:13
who are *b* for the dead .... 1 Cor 15:29
as many of you as were *b* .... Gal 3:27

BAPTIZING
b them in the name of .... Matt 28:19
therefore I came *b* .... John 1:31

BAR-JESUS (or Elymas)
A Jewish false prophet, Acts 13:6–12

BAR-JONAH
Surname of Simon (Peter), Matt 16:17

BARABBAS
A murderer released in place of Jesus, Matt 27:16–26; Acts 3:14, 15

BARAK
Defeats Jabin, Judg 4:1–24
A man of faith, Heb 11:32

BARBARIAN
nor uncircumcised, *b* .... Col 3:11

BARE
make yourselves *b* .... Is 32:11
The LORD has made *b* .... Is 52:10

BARLEY
a land of wheat and *b* .... Deut 8:8
loaf of *b* bread tumbled .... Judg 7:13
beginning of *b* harvest .... Ruth 1:22
who has five *b* loaves .... John 6:9
and three quarts of *b* .... Rev 6:6

BARN
seed still in the *b* .... Hag 2:19
the wheat into my *b* .... Matt 13:30
storehouse nor *b* .... Luke 12:24

BARNABAS
A disciple from Cyprus; gives property, Acts 4:36, 37
Supports Paul, Acts 9:27
Ministers in Antioch, Acts 11:22–30
Travels with Paul, Acts 12:25; 13—15
Breaks with Paul over John Mark, Acts 15:36–39

BARNS
b will be filled .... Prov 3:10
b are broken down .... Joel 1:17
reap nor gather into *b* .... Matt 6:26
I will pull down my *b* .... Luke 12:18

BARREN
But Sarai was *b* .... Gen 11:30
b has borne seven .... 1 Sam 2:5
He grants the *b* .... Ps 113:9
"Sing, O *b* .... Is 54:1
'Blessed are the *b* .... Luke 23:29
"Rejoice, O *b* .... Gal 4:27
you will be neither *b* .... 2 Pet 1:8

BARSABAS
Nominated to replace Judas, Acts 1:23
Sent to Antioch, Acts 15:22

BARTHOLOMEW
Called Nathanael, John 1:45, 46
One of the twelve apostles, Matt 10:3; Acts 1:13

BARTIMAEUS
Blind beggar healed by Jesus, Mark 10:46–52

BARUCH
Son of Neriah, Jer 32:12, 13
Jeremiah's faithful friend and scribe, Jer 36:4–32

BARZILLAI
Supplies David with food, 2 Sam 17:27–29
Age restrains him from following David, 2 Sam 19:31–39

BASHAN
Conquered by Israel, Num 21:33–35
Assigned to Manasseh, Deut 3:13
Conquered by Hazael, king of Syria, 2 Kin 10:32, 33

BEHOLDING
with unveiled face, *b* ....2 Cor 3:18

BEING
man became a living *b* ....Gen 2:7
God while I have my *b* ....Ps 104:33
move and have our *b* ....Acts 17:28
who, *b* in the form of ....Phil 2:6

BEL
Patron god of Babylon, Is 46:1; Jer 50:2; 51:44

BELIEF
by the Spirit and *b* ....2 Thess 2:13

BELIEVE
B in the LORD your God ....2 Chr 20:20
tears, "Lord, I *b* ....Mark 9:24
b that you receive ....Mark 11:24
because they did not *b* ....Mark 16:14
have no root, who *b* ....Luke 8:13
and slow of heart to *b* ....Luke 24:25
to those who *b* ....John 1:12
how will you *b* ....John 3:12
sent, Him you do not *b* ....John 5:38
we may see it and *b* ....John 6:30
to him, "Do you *b* ....John 9:35
this, that they may *b* ....John 11:42
you *b* in God ....John 14:1
written that you may *b* ....John 20:31
King Agrippa, do you *b* ....Acts 26:27
the Lord Jesus and *b* ....Rom 10:9
And how shall they *b* ....Rom 10:14
a wife who does not *b* ....1 Cor 7:12
I spoke," we also *b* ....2 Cor 4:13
given to those who *b* ....Gal 3:22
Christ, not only to *b* ....Phil 1:29
comes to God must *b* ....Heb 11:6
b that there is one ....James 2:19
Even the demons *b* ....James 2:19
Beloved, do not *b* ....1 John 4:1

BELIEVED
And he *b* in the LORD ....Gen 15:6
b that I would see the ....Ps 27:13
Who has *b* our report ....Is 53:1
of that city *b* in Him ....John 4:39
seen Me, you have *b* ....John 20:29
who heard the word *b* ....Acts 4:4
of those who *b* were of ....Acts 4:32
Holy Spirit when you *b* ....Acts 19:2
"Abraham *b* God ....Rom 4:3
I know whom I have *b* ....2 Tim 1:12

BELIEVERS
be an example to the *b* ....1 Tim 4:12
are benefited are *b* ....1 Tim 6:2

BELIEVES
The simple *b* every ....Prov 14:15
He who *b* and is ....Mark 16:16
that whoever *b* in Him ....John 3:16
He who *b* in the Son ....John 3:36
with the heart one *b* ....Rom 10:10
b all things ....1 Cor 13:7

BELIEVING
you ask in prayer, *b* ....Matt 21:22
blessed with *b* Abraham ....Gal 3:9

BELLY
On your *b* you shall go ....Gen 3:14
And Jonah was in the *b* ....Jon 1:17
three nights in the *b* ....Matt 12:40
whose god is their *b* ....Phil 3:19

BELONG
To the Lord our God *b* ....Dan 9:9
My name, because you *b* ....Mark 9:41

BELOVED
"The *b* of the Lord ....Deut 33:12
so He gives His *b* ....Ps 127:2
of myrrh is my *b* ....Song 1:13
My *b* is mine ....Song 2:16
b more than another ....Song 5:9
Where has your *b* ....Song 6:1
leaning upon her *b* ....Song 8:5
a song of my *B* ....Is 5:1
for you are greatly *b* ....Dan 9:23
"This is My *b* ....Matt 3:17
election they are *b* ....Rom 11:28
us accepted in the *B* ....Eph 1:6
Luke the *b* physician ....Col 4:14
than a slave as a *b* ....Philem 16
"This is My *b* ....2 Pet 1:17
our *b* brother Paul ....2 Pet 3:15
the saints and the *b* ....Rev 20:9

BELSHAZZAR
King of Babylon; Daniel interprets his dream, Dan 5

BELT
with a leather *b* ....Matt 3:4
us, he took Paul's *b* ....Acts 21:11

BELTESHAZZAR
Daniel's Babylonian name, Dan 1:7

BEMOAN
Or who will *b* you ....Jer 15:5
for the dead, nor *b* ....Jer 22:10

BEN-AMMI
Son of Lot; father of the Ammonites, Gen 19:38

BEN-HADAD
Ben-Hadad I, king of Damascus; hired by Asa, king of Judah, to attack Baasha, king of Israel, 1 Kin 15:18–21
——— Ben-Hadad II, king of Damascus; makes war on Ahab, king of Israel, 1 Kin 20
Falls in siege against Samaria, 2 Kin 6:24–33; 7:6–20
Killed by Hazael, 2 Kin 8:7–15
——— Ben-Hadad III, king of Damascus; loses all Israelite conquests made by Hazael, his father, 2 Kin 13:3–25

BENAIAH
The son of Jehoiada; a mighty man, 2 Sam 23:20–23
Faithful to David, 2 Sam 15:18; 20:23
Escorts Solomon to the throne, 1 Kin 1:38–40
Executes Adonijah, Joab and Shimei, 1 Kin 2:25, 29–34, 46
——— A Pirathonite; another of David's mighty men, 2 Sam 23:30
Divisional commander, 1 Chr 27:14

BENEATH
and on the earth *b* ....Deut 4:39
"You are from *b* ....John 8:23

BENEFIT
That I may see the *b* ....Ps 106:5
people who could not *b* ....Is 30:5
might have a second *b* ....2 Cor 1:15

BENJAMIN
Jacob's youngest son, Gen 35:16–20
Taken to Egypt against Jacob's wishes, Gen 42—45
Jacob's prophecy concerning, Gen 49:27
——— Tribe of:
Families of, Num 26:38–41
Territory allotted to, Josh 18:11–28
Attacked by remaining tribes for condoning sin of Gibeah, Judg 20:12–48
Wives provided for remnant of, Judg 21:1–23
Tribe of Saul, 1 Sam 9:1, 2
of Paul, Phil 3:5

BEREA
A city of Macedonia; visited by Paul, Acts 17:10–15

BEREAVE
I will *b* them of ....Jer 15:7
no more shall you *b* ....Ezek 36:12
children, yet I will *b* ....Hos 9:12

BERNICE
Sister of Herod Agrippa II, Acts 25:13, 23
Hears Paul's defense, Acts 26:1–30

BERODACH-BALADAN
See MERODACH-BALADAN
A king of Babylon, 2 Kin 20:12–19

BESEECH
Return, we *b* You ....Ps 80:14
b you therefore ....Rom 12:1
of the LORD, *b* you to ....Eph 4:1

BESIDE
He leads me *b* the ....Ps 23:2
"Paul, you are *b* ....Acts 26:24
For if we are *b* ....2 Cor 5:13

BEST
with the *b* ointments ....Amos 6:6
'Bring out the *b* ....Luke 15:22
earnestly desire the *b* ....1 Cor 12:31

BETH HORON
Twin towns of Ephraim, Josh 16:3, 5
Fortified by Solomon, 2 Chr 8:3–5
Prominent in battles, Josh 10:10–14; 1 Sam 13:18

BETH PEOR
Town near Pisgah, Deut 3:29
Moses buried near, Deut 34:6
Assigned to Reubenites, Josh 13:15, 20

BETH SHAN (or Beth Shean)
A town in Issachar, Josh 17:11–16
Saul's corpse hung up at, 1 Sam 31:10–13; 2 Sam 21:12–14

BETH SHEMESH
Ark brought to, 1 Sam 6:12–19
Joash defeats Amaziah at, 2 Kin 14:11
Taken by Philistines, 2 Chr 28:18

BETHABARA
A place beyond the Jordan where John baptized, John 1:28

BETHANY
A town on the Mt. of Olives, Luke 19:29
Home of Lazarus, John 11:1
Home of Simon, the leper, Matt 26:6
Jesus visits there, Mark 11:1, 11, 12
Scene of the Ascension, Luke 24:50, 51

BETHEL
Abram settles near, Gen 12:7, 8
Site of Abram's altar, Gen 13:3, 4
Site of Jacob's vision of the ladder, Gen 28:10–19
Jacob returns to, Gen 35:1–15
Samuel judges there, 1 Sam 7:15, 16
Site of worship and sacrifice, 1 Sam 10:3
Center of idolatry, 1 Kin 12:28–33
Josiah destroys altars of, 2 Kin 23:4, 15–20
Denounced by prophets, 1 Kin 13:1–10; Amos 7:10–13; Jer 48:13; Hos 10:15

BETHESDA
Jerusalem pool, John 5:2–4

BETHLEHEM
Originally called Ephrath, Gen 35:16
Rachel buried there, Gen 35:19
Home of Naomi and Boaz, Ruth 1:1, 19; 4:9–11
Home of David, 1 Sam 16:1–18
Predicted place of Messiah's birth, Mic 5:2

B those who persecute . . . . .Rom 12:14
Being reviled, we *b* . . . . .1 Cor 4:12
With it we *b* our God . . . . James 3:9

BLESSED

And God *b* them . . . . .Gen 1:22
the earth shall be *b* . . . . .Gen 12:3
b be those who . . . . .Gen 27:29
indeed he shall be *b* . . . . .Gen 27:33
B is he who . . . . .Num 24:9
B shall be the . . . . .Deut 28:4
You have *b* the work of . . . . .Job 1:10
B is the man who walks . . . . .Ps 1:1
B is the man to whom . . . . .Ps 32:2
B is the nation whose . . . . .Ps 33:12
B is he who considers . . . . .Ps 41:1
B are those who keep . . . . .Ps 106:3
B is he who comes . . . . .Ps 118:26
b who fears the LORD . . . . .Ps 128:4
rise up and call her *b* . . . . .Prov 31:28
will call you *b* . . . . .Mal 3:12
B are the poor in . . . . .Matt 5:3
B are those who mourn . . . . .Matt 5:4
B are the meek . . . . .Matt 5:5
B are those who hunger . . . . .Matt 5:6
B are the merciful . . . . .Matt 5:7
B are the pure in . . . . .Matt 5:8
B are the peacemakers . . . . .Matt 5:9
B are those who are . . . . .Matt 5:10
B are you when they . . . . .Matt 5:11
b is he who is . . . . .Matt 11:6
b are your eyes . . . . .Matt 13:16
B is He who comes . . . . .Matt 21:9
hand, 'Come, you *b* . . . . .Matt 25:34
Jesus took bread, *b* . . . . .Matt 26:26
b are you among women . . . . . . .Luke 1:28
know these things, *b* . . . . John 13:17
B are those who have . . . . .John 20:29
'It is more *b* to give . . . . .Acts 20:35
the Creator, who is *b* . . . . .Rom 1:25
all, the eternally *b* . . . . .Rom 9:5
B be the God and . . . . .Eph 1:3
b God which was . . . . .1 Tim 1:11
the lesser is *b* . . . . .Heb 7:7
this one will be *b* . . . . James 1:25
B is he who reads . . . . .Rev 1:3
'*B* are the dead who . . . . .Rev 14:13
B is he who watches . . . . .Rev 16:15
B are those who are . . . . .Rev 19:9
B and holy is he who . . . . .Rev 20:6
B is he who keeps the . . . . .Rev 22:7
B are those who do His . . . . .Rev 22:14

BLESSING

and you shall be a *b* . . . . .Gen 12:2
I will command My *b* . . . . .Lev 25:21
before you today a *b* . . . . .Deut 11:26
The *b* of a perishing . . . . .Job 29:13
Your *b* is upon Your . . . . .Ps 3:8
The *b* of the LORD . . . . .Prov 10:22
shall be showers of *b* . . . . .Ezek 34:26
relent, and leave a *b* . . . . .Joel 2:14
and you shall be a *b* . . . . .Zech 8:13
the fullness of the *b* . . . . .Rom 15:29
b which we bless . . . . .1 Cor 10:16
that the *b* of Abraham . . . . .Gal 3:14
with every spiritual *b* . . . . .Eph 1:3
cultivated, receives *b* . . . . .Heb 6:7
to inherit the *b* . . . . .Heb 12:17
honor and glory and *b* . . . . .Rev 5:12

BLESSINGS

of the law, the *b* . . . . .Josh 8:34
B are on the head of . . . . .Prov 10:6

BLIGHT

"I blasted you with *b* . . . . .Amos 4:9
I struck you with *b* . . . . .Hag 2:17

BLIND

I was eyes to the *b* . . . . .Job 29:15
B yourselves and be . . . . .Is 29:9
To open *b* eyes . . . . .Is 42:7
I will bring the *b* . . . . .Is 42:16
b people who have eyes . . . . .Is 43:8
His watchmen are *b* . . . . .Is 56:10
They wandered *b* . . . . .Lam 4:14
when you offer the *b* . . . . .Mal 1:8
The *b* see . . . . .Matt 11:5
b leads the *b* . . . . .Matt 15:14
of sight to the *b* . . . . .Luke 4:18
to Him, "Are we *b* . . . . .John 9:40
miserable, poor, *b* . . . . .Rev 3:17

BLINDED

b their eyes and . . . . .John 12:40
and the rest were *b* . . . . .Rom 11:7
of this age has *b* . . . . .2 Cor 4:4
the darkness has *b* . . . . .1 John 2:11

BLOOD

of your brother's *b* . . . . .Gen 4:10
b shall be shed . . . . .Gen 9:6
you are a husband of *b* . . . . .Ex 4:25
b that makes atonement . . . . .Lev 17:11
b sustains its life . . . . .Lev 17:14
do not cover my *b* . . . . .Job 16:18
is there in my *b* . . . . .Ps 30:9
And condemn innocent *b* . . . . .Ps 94:21
hands are full of *b* . . . . .Is 1:15
also disclose her *b* . . . . .Is 26:21
And the moon into *b* . . . . Joel 2:31
For this is My *b* . . . . .Matt 26:28
called the Field of *B* . . . . .Matt 27:8
"His *b* be on us and . . . . .Matt 27:25
new covenant in My *b* . . . . .Luke 22:20
were born, not of *b* . . . . John 1:13
b has eternal life . . . . John 6:54
b every nation of men . . . . .Acts 17:26
with His own *b* . . . . .Acts 20:28
propitiation by His *b* . . . . .Rom 3:25
justified by His *b* . . . . .Rom 5:9
through His *b* . . . . .Eph 1:7
brought near by the *b* . . . . .Eph 2:13
against flesh and *b* . . . . .Eph 6:12
peace through the *b* . . . . .Col 1:20
"This is the *b* . . . . .Heb 9:20
are purified with *b* . . . . .Heb 9:22
of *b* there is no . . . . .Heb 9:22
the Holiest by the *b* . . . . .Heb 10:19
sprinkling of the *b* . . . . .1 Pet 1:2
with the precious *b* . . . . .1 Pet 1:19
b of Jesus Christ His . . . . .1 John 1:7
our sins in His own *b* . . . . .Rev 1:5
us to God by Your *b* . . . . .Rev 5:9
them white in the *b* . . . . .Rev 7:14
overcame him by the *b* . . . . .Rev 12:11
a robe dipped in *b* . . . . .Rev 19:13

BLOODSHED

me from the guilt of *b* . . . . .Ps 51:14
the land is full of *b* . . . . .Ezek 9:9
build up Zion with *b* . . . . .Mic 3:10

BLOODTHIRSTY

The LORD abhors the *b* . . . . .Ps 5:6
B and deceitful men . . . . .Ps 55:23

BLOSSOM

Israel shall *b* and bud . . . . .Is 27:6
and *b* as the rose . . . . .Is 35:1
the fig tree may not *b* . . . . .Hab 3:17

BLOT

say that He would *b* . . . . .2 Kin 14:27
from my sins, and *b* . . . . .Ps 51:9
and I will not *b* . . . . .Rev 3:5

BLOTTED

Let them be *b* out of . . . . .Ps 69:28
I have *b* out . . . . .Is 44:22
your sins may be *b* . . . . .Acts 3:19

BLOW

an east wind to *b* . . . . .Ps 78:26
B upon my garden . . . . .Song 4:16
with a very severe *b* . . . . .Jer 14:17

BLOWS

B that hurt cleanse . . . . .Prov 20:30
breath of the LORD *b* . . . . .Is 40:7
The wind *b* where it . . . . John 3:8

BOANERGES

Surname of James and John, Mark 3:17

BOAST

puts on his armor *b* . . . . .1 Kin 20:11
soul shall make its *b* . . . . .Ps 34:2
God we *b* all day long . . . . .Ps 44:8
and make your *b* . . . . .Rom 2:17
that we are your *b* . . . . .2 Cor 1:14
you, and not to *b* . . . . .2 Cor 10:16
that I also may *b* . . . . .2 Cor 11:16
lest anyone should *b* . . . . .Eph 2:9
your hearts, do not *b* . . . . James 3:14

BOASTERS

God, violent, proud, *b* . . . . .Rom 1:30
lovers of money, *b* . . . . .2 Tim 3:2

BOASTFUL

b shall not stand . . . . .Ps 5:5
I was envious of the *b* . . . . .Ps 73:3

BOASTING

Where is *b* then . . . . .Rom 3:27
should make my *b* . . . . .1 Cor 9:15
you, great is my *b* . . . . .2 Cor 7:4
All such *b* is evil . . . . James 4:16

BOAZ

A wealthy Bethlehemite, Ruth 2:1, 4–18
Husband of Ruth, Ruth 4:10–13
Ancestor of Christ, Matt 1:5
——— Pillar of the temple, 1 Kin 7:21

BODIES

valley of the dead *b* . . . . .Jer 31:40
b a living sacrifice . . . . .Rom 12:1
not know that your *b* . . . . .1 Cor 6:15
also celestial *b* . . . . .1 Cor 15:40
wives as their own *b* . . . . .Eph 5:28
and chariots, and *b* . . . . .Rev 18:13

BODILY

b form like a dove . . . . .Luke 3:22
b presence is weak . . . . .2 Cor 10:10
of the Godhead *b* . . . . .Col 2:9
b exercise . . . . .1 Tim 4:8

BODY

b clings to the ground . . . . .Ps 44:25
b is carved ivory . . . . .Song 5:14
b was wet with the dew . . . . .Dan 4:33
of the *b* is the eye . . . . .Matt 6:22
those who kill the *b* . . . . .Matt 10:28
this is My *b* . . . . .Matt 26:26
and asked for the *b* . . . . .Matt 27:58
around his naked *b* . . . . .Mark 14:51
of the temple of His *b* . . . . .John 2:21
deliver me from this *b* . . . . .Rom 7:24
redemption of our *b* . . . . .Rom 8:23
members in one *b* . . . . .Rom 12:4
and the Lord for the *b* . . . . .1 Cor 6:13
against his own *b* . . . . .1 Cor 6:18
not know that your *b* . . . . .1 Cor 6:19
glorify God in your *b* . . . . .1 Cor 6:20
But I discipline my *b* . . . . .1 Cor 9:27
one bread and one *b* . . . . .1 Cor 10:17
b which is broken . . . . .1 Cor 11:24
be guilty of the *b* . . . . .1 Cor 11:27
For as the *b* is one . . . . .1 Cor 12:12
baptized into one *b* . . . . .1 Cor 12:13
b is not one member . . . . .1 Cor 12:14
are the *b* of Christ . . . . .1 Cor 12:27
though I give my *b* . . . . .1 Cor 13:3

It is sown a natural *b* ....1 Cor 15:44
both to God in one *b* ....Eph 2:16
be magnified in my *b* ....Phil 1:20
in the *b* of His flesh ....Col 1:22
by putting off the *b* ....Col 2:11
and neglect of the *b* ....Col 2:23
were called in one *b* ....Col 3:15
b You have prepared ....Heb 10:5
the offering of the *b* ....Heb 10:10
For as the *b* without ....James 2:26
our sins in His own *b* ....1 Pet 2:24

BOLD
the righteous are *b* ....Prov 28:1
whatever anyone is *b* ....2 Cor 11:21
are much more *b* ....Phil 1:14

BOLDLY
I may open my mouth *b* ....Eph 6:19
therefore come *b* ....Heb 4:16
So we may *b* say ....Heb 13:6

BOLDNESS
Great is my *b* of ....2 Cor 7:4
in whom we have *b* ....Eph 3:12
but with all *b* ....Phil 1:20
standing and great *b* ....1 Tim 3:13
brethren, having *b* ....Heb 10:19
that we may have *b* ....1 John 4:17

BOND
bring you into the *b* ....Ezek 20:37
of the Spirit in the *b* ....Eph 4:3
love, which is the *b* ....Col 3:14

BONDAGE
because of the *b* ....Ex 2:23
out of the house of *b* ....Ex 13:14
the spirit of *b* ....Rom 8:15
might bring us into *b* ....Gal 2:4
which gives birth to *b* ....Gal 4:24
again with a yoke of *b* ....Gal 5:1
lifetime subject to *b* ....Heb 2:15
he is brought into *b* ....2 Pet 2:19

BONDSERVANTS
B, be obedient to ....Eph 6:5
Masters, give your *b* ....Col 4:1
for vice, but as *b* ....1 Pet 2:16

BONDWOMAN
"Cast out this *b* ....Gen 21:10
the one by a *b* ....Gal 4:22

BONE
"This is now *b* ....Gen 2:23
b clings to my skin ....Job 19:20
bonds came together, *b* ....Ezek 37:7

BONES
shall carry up my *b* ....Gen 50:25
which made all my *b* ....Job 4:14
His *b* are like beams ....Job 40:18
I can count all My *b* ....Ps 22:17
and my *b* waste away ....Ps 31:10
I kept silent, my *b* ....Ps 32:3
the wind, or how the *b* ....Eccl 11:5
say to them, 'O dry *b* ....Ezek 37:4
b are the whole house ....Ezek 37:11
of dead men's *b* ....Matt 23:27
b shall be broken ....John 19:36
concerning his *b* ....Heb 11:22

BOOK
you will find in the *b* ....Ezra 4:15
distinctly from the *b* ....Neh 8:8
were inscribed in a *b* ....Job 19:23
"Search from the *b* ....Is 34:16
'Write in a *b* for ....Jer 30:2
found written in the *b* ....Dan 12:1
so a *b* of remembrance ....Mal 3:16
are written in the *b* ....Gal 3:10
sprinkled both the *b* ....Heb 9:19
in the Lamb's *B* ....Rev 21:27
the prophecy of this *b* ....Rev 22:18
the words of the *b* ....Rev 22:19

BOOKS
b there is no end ....Eccl 12:12
not contain the *b* ....John 21:25
magic brought their *b* ....Acts 19:19
God, and *b* were opened ....Rev 20:12

BORDERS
and enlarge your *b* ....Ex 34:24
makes peace in your *b* ....Ps 147:14
and enlarge the *b* ....Matt 23:5

BORE
conceived and *b* Cain ....Gen 4:1
And to Sarah who *b* ....Is 51:2
b the sin of many ....Is 53:12
and He *b* them and ....Is 63:9
b our sicknesses ....Matt 8:17
who Himself *b* our sins ....1 Pet 2:24
b a male Child who was ....Rev 12:5

BORN
"Every son who is *b* ....Ex 1:22
yet man is *b* to ....Job 5:7
"Man who is *b* ....Job 14:1
'This one was *b* ....Ps 87:4
A time to be *b* ....Eccl 3:2
unto us a Child is *b* ....Is 9:6
Or shall a nation be *b* ....Is 66:8
b Jesus who is called ....Matt 1:16
For there is *b* ....Luke 2:11
unless one is *b* again ....John 3:3
That which is *b* ....John 3:6
For this cause I was *b* ....John 18:37
me also, as by one *b* ....1 Cor 15:8
of the bondwoman was *b* ....Gal 4:23
having been *b* again ....1 Pet 1:23
who loves is *b* of God ....1 John 4:7
is the Christ is *b* ....1 John 5:1
know that whoever is *b* ....1 John 5:18

BORROWER
b is servant to the ....Prov 22:7
lender, so with the *b* ....Is 24:2

BOSOM
man take fire to his *b* ....Prov 6:27
consolation of her *b* ....Is 66:11
angels to Abraham's *b* ....Luke 16:22
Son, who is in the *b* ....John 1:18
leaning on Jesus' *b* ....John 13:23

BOTTOMLESS
given the key to the *b* ....Rev 9:1
ascend out of the *b* ....Rev 17:8
the key to the *b* ....Rev 20:1

BOUGHS
cedars with its *b* ....Ps 80:10
She sent out her *b* ....Ps 80:11

BOUGHT
the hand of him who *b* ....Lev 25:28
not your Father, who *b* ....Deut 32:6
b the threshing floor ....2 Sam 24:24
b the field from ....Jer 32:9
all that he had and *b* ....Matt 13:46
For you were *b* at a ....1 Cor 6:20
denying the Lord who *b* ....2 Pet 2:1

BOUND
of the wicked have *b* ....Ps 119:61
b the waters in a ....Prov 30:4
not been closed or *b* ....Is 1:6
on earth will be *b* ....Matt 16:19
b hand and foot with ....John 11:44
And see, now I go *b* ....Acts 20:22
of Israel I am *b* ....Acts 28:20
who has a husband is *b* ....Rom 7:2
Are you *b* to a wife ....1 Cor 7:27
Devil and Satan, and *b* ....Rev 20:2

BOUNTIFUL
the miser said to be *b* ....Is 32:5
you into a *b* country ....Jer 2:7

BOUNTIFULLY
Because He has dealt *b* ....Ps 13:6
and he who sows *b* ....2 Cor 9:6

BOW
b remained in strength ....Gen 49:24
You shall not *b* ....Ex 23:24
to serve them and *b* ....Judg 2:19
b is renewed in my ....Job 29:20
will not trust in my *b* ....Ps 44:6
He breaks the *b* ....Ps 46:9
like a deceitful *b* ....Ps 78:57
let us worship and *b* ....Ps 95:6
B down Your heavens ....Ps 144:5
not save them by *b* ....Hos 1:7
who sat on it had a *b* ....Rev 6:2

BOWED
stood all around and *b* ....Gen 37:7
b the heavens also ....2 Sam 22:10
whose knees have not *b* ....1 Kin 19:18
They have *b* down and ....Ps 20:8
And they *b* the knee ....Matt 27:29
men who have not *b* ....Rom 11:4

BOWL
his hand in the *b* ....Prov 19:24
or the golden *b* ....Eccl 12:6
and poured out his *b* ....Rev 16:2

BOWLS
who drink wine from *b* ....Amos 6:6
a harp, and golden *b* ....Rev 5:8
Go and pour out the *b* ....Rev 16:1
who had the seven *b* ....Rev 21:9

BOZRAH
City of Edom, Gen 36:33
Destruction of, foretold, Amos 1:12
Figurative of Messiah's victory, Is 63:1

BRANCH
blossoms on one *b* ....Ex 25:33
b will not be green ....Job 15:32
from Israel, palm *b* ....Is 9:14
B shall grow out of ....Is 11:1
raise to David a *B* ....Jer 23:5
grow up to David a *B* ....Jer 33:15
forth My Servant the *B* ....Zech 3:8
whose name is the *B* ....Zech 6:12
b has already become ....Matt 24:32
b that bears fruit He ....John 15:2
b cannot bear fruit ....John 15:4
he is cast out as a *b* ....John 15:6

BRANCHES
in the sun, and his *b* ....Job 8:16
and bring forth *b* ....Job 14:9
and cut down the *b* ....Is 18:5
and its *b* are broken ....Jer 11:16
His *b* shall spread ....Hos 14:6
vine, you are the *b* ....John 15:5
b were broken off ....Rom 11:17

BRASS
become sounding *b* ....1 Cor 13:1
feet were like fine *b* ....Rev 1:15

BRAVE
in the faith, be *b* ....1 Cor 16:13

BREAD
face you shall eat *b* ....Gen 3:19
of Salem brought out *b* ....Gen 14:18
"Behold, I will rain *b* ....Ex 16:4
shall eat unleavened *b* ....Ex 23:15
not live by *b* alone ....Deut 8:3
lives, I do not have *b* ....1 Kin 17:12
new wine, a land of *b* ....2 Kin 18:32
that his life abhors *b* ....Job 33:20
people as they eat *b* ....Ps 14:4

Can He give *b* also . . . . . Ps 78:20
up late, to eat the *b* . . . . . Ps 127:2
her poor with *b* . . . . . Ps 132:15
For they eat the *b* . . . . . Prov 4:17
b eaten in secret is . . . . . Prov 9:17
B gained by deceit is . . . . . Prov 20:17
Go, eat your *b* with . . . . . Eccl 9:7
Cast your *b* upon the . . . . . Eccl 11:1
b will be given him . . . . . Is 33:16
for what is not *b* . . . . . Is 55:2
to share your *b* . . . . . Is 58:7
We get our *b* at the . . . . . Lam 5:9
who give me my *b* . . . . . Hos 2:5
For their *b* shall be . . . . . Hos 9:4
And lack of *b* in all . . . . . Amos 4:6
these stones become *b* . . . . . Matt 4:3
not live by *b* alone . . . . . Matt 4:4
this day our daily *b* . . . . . Matt 6:11
eating, Jesus took *b* . . . . . Matt 26:26
no bag, no *b* . . . . . Mark 6:8
is he who shall eat *b* . . . . . Luke 14:15
gives you the true *b* . . . . . John 6:32
I am the *b* of life . . . . . John 6:48
having dipped the *b* . . . . . John 13:26
b which we break . . . . . 1 Cor 10:16
He was betrayed took *b* . . . . . 1 Cor 11:23
as you eat this *b* . . . . . 1 Cor 11:26
did we eat anyone's *b* . . . . . 2 Thess 3:8
and eat their own *b* . . . . . 2 Thess 3:12

BREAK

b their bones and . . . . . Num 24:6
torment my soul, and *b* . . . . . Job 19:2
They *b* up my path . . . . . Job 30:13
B their teeth in their . . . . . Ps 58:6
And now they *b* down . . . . . Ps 74:6
b My statutes and do . . . . . Ps 89:31
covenant I will not *b* . . . . . Ps 89:34
Remember, do not *b* . . . . . Jer 14:21
together to *b* bread . . . . . Acts 20:7

BREAKING

in the *b* of bread . . . . . Acts 2:42
b bread from house to . . . . . Acts 2:46
weeping and *b* my heart . . . . . Acts 21:13
dishonor God through *b* . . . . . Rom 2:23

BREAKS

He *b* in pieces mighty . . . . . Job 34:24
My soul *b* with longing . . . . . Ps 119:20
Until the day *b* . . . . . Song 2:17
Whoever therefore *b* . . . . . Matt 5:19

BREAST

back on Jesus' *b* . . . . . John 13:25

BREASTPLATE

a *b*, an ephod . . . . . Ex 28:4
righteousness as a *b* . . . . . Is 59:17
having put on the *b* . . . . . Eph 6:14

BREASTS

blessings of the *b* . . . . . Gen 49:25
on My mother's *b* . . . . . Ps 22:9
doe, let her *b* satisfy . . . . . Prov 5:19
Your two *b* are like . . . . . Song 4:5
b which nursed You . . . . . Luke 11:27
done, beat their *b* . . . . . Luke 23:48

BREATH

nostrils the *b* of life . . . . . Gen 2:7
at the blast of the *b* . . . . . 2 Sam 22:16
that there was no *b* . . . . . 1 Kin 17:17
perish, and by the *b* . . . . . Job 4:9
as long as my *b* . . . . . Job 27:3
has made me, and the *b* . . . . . Job 33:4
You take away their *b* . . . . . Ps 104:29
Man is like a *b* . . . . . Ps 144:4
everything that has *b* . . . . . Ps 150:6
they all have one *b* . . . . . Eccl 3:19
from it, who gives *b* . . . . . Is 42:5
"Surely I will cause *b* . . . . . Ezek 37:5
God who holds your *b* . . . . . Dan 5:23
gives to all life, *b* . . . . . Acts 17:25
consume with the *b* . . . . . 2 Thess 2:8
power to give *b* . . . . . Rev 13:15

BREATHE

me, and such as *b* . . . . . Ps 27:12
winds, O breath, and *b* . . . . . Ezek 37:9

BREATHES

indeed he *b* his last . . . . . Job 14:10

BRETHREN

presence of all his *b* . . . . . Gen 16:12
be lifted above his *b* . . . . . Deut 17:20
and you are all *b* . . . . . Matt 23:8
least of these My *b* . . . . . Matt 25:40
Go and tell My *b* . . . . . Matt 28:10
firstborn among many *b* . . . . . Rom 8:29
to judge between his *b* . . . . . 1 Cor 6:5
thus sin against the *b* . . . . . 1 Cor 8:12
over five hundred *b* . . . . . 1 Cor 15:6
perils among false *b* . . . . . 2 Cor 11:26
b secretly brought . . . . . Gal 2:4
to be made like His *b* . . . . . Heb 2:17
sincere love of the *b* . . . . . 1 Pet 1:22
because we love the *b* . . . . . 1 John 3:14
our lives for the *b* . . . . . 1 John 3:16
does not receive the *b* . . . . . 3 John 10
of your *b* the prophets . . . . . Rev 22:9

BRIBE

you shall take no *b* . . . . . Ex 23:8
b blinds the eyes . . . . . Deut 16:19
b debases the heart . . . . . Eccl 7:7

BRIBES

hand is full of *b* . . . . . Ps 26:10
but he who hates *b* . . . . . Prov 15:27
but he who receives *b* . . . . . Prov 29:4
everyone loves *b* . . . . . Is 1:23
the just and taking *b* . . . . . Amos 5:12

BRICK

people straw to make *b* . . . . . Ex 5:7
incense on altars of *b* . . . . . Is 65:3
Make strong the *b* . . . . . Nah 3:14

BRICKS

"Come, let us make *b* . . . . . Gen 11:3
b which they made . . . . . Ex 5:8
deliver the quota of *b* . . . . . Ex 5:18
b have fallen down . . . . . Is 9:10

BRIDE

them on you as a *b* . . . . . Is 49:18
He who has the *b* . . . . . John 3:29
I will show you the *b* . . . . . Rev 21:9
the Spirit and the *b* . . . . . Rev 22:17

BRIDEGROOM

righteousness, as a *b* . . . . . Is 61:10
and as the *b* rejoices . . . . . Is 62:5
mourn as long as the *b* . . . . . Matt 9:15
b will be taken away . . . . . Matt 9:15
went out to meet the *b* . . . . . Matt 25:1
b fast while the . . . . . Mark 2:19
the friend of the *b* . . . . . John 3:29

BRIDLE

with bit and *b* . . . . . Ps 32:9
b the whole body . . . . . James 3:2

BRIER

b shall come up the . . . . . Is 55:13
longer be a pricking *b* . . . . . Ezek 28:24
of them is like a *b* . . . . . Mic 7:4

BRIERS

there shall come up *b* . . . . . Is 5:6
their words, though *b* . . . . . Ezek 2:6

BRIGHTER

Her Nazirites were *b* . . . . . Lam 4:7
a light from heaven, *b* . . . . . Acts 26:13

BRIGHTNESS

From the *b* before Him . . . . . 2 Sam 22:13
and kings to the *b* . . . . . Is 60:3
goes forth as *b* . . . . . Is 62:1
very dark, with no *b* . . . . . Amos 5:20
who being the *b* . . . . . Heb 1:3

BRIMSTONE

Then the LORD rained *b* . . . . . Gen 19:24
b is scattered on his . . . . . Job 18:15
fire, smoke, and *b* . . . . . Rev 9:17
the lake of fire and *b* . . . . . Rev 20:10

BRING

LORD your God will *b* . . . . . Deut 30:3
b back his soul . . . . . Job 33:30
for they *b* down . . . . . Ps 55:3
Lord said, "I will *b* . . . . . Ps 68:22
B forth your . . . . . Is 41:21
b forth justice . . . . . Is 42:3
b My righteousness . . . . . Is 46:13
Though they *b* up their . . . . . Hos 9:12
And she will *b* . . . . . Matt 1:21
b no fruit to maturity . . . . . Luke 8:14
b this Man's blood . . . . . Acts 5:28
Who shall *b* a charge . . . . . Rom 8:33
b Christ down from . . . . . Rom 10:6
b Christ up from the . . . . . Rom 10:7
even so God will *b* . . . . . 1 Thess 4:14

BROAD

set me in a *b* place . . . . . Ps 118:5
b is the way that . . . . . Matt 7:13
their phylacteries *b* . . . . . Matt 23:5

BROKE

b them at the foot of . . . . . Ex 32:19
b open the fountain . . . . . Ps 74:15
covenant which they *b* . . . . . Jer 31:32
He blessed and *b* . . . . . Matt 14:19
b the flask and poured . . . . . Mark 14:3
b the legs of the . . . . . John 19:32

BROKEN

he has *b* My covenant . . . . . Gen 17:14
I am like a *b* vessel . . . . . Ps 31:12
their bows shall be *b* . . . . . Ps 37:15
He has *b* his covenant . . . . . Ps 55:20
heart the spirit is *b* . . . . . Prov 15:13
b spirit dries the . . . . . Prov 17:22
but who can bear a *b* . . . . . Prov 18:14
in the staff of this *b* . . . . . Is 36:6
heart within me is *b* . . . . . Jer 23:9
is oppressed and *b* . . . . . Hos 5:11
this stone will be *b* . . . . . Matt 21:44
Scripture cannot be *b* . . . . . John 10:35
is My body which is *b* . . . . . 1 Cor 11:24

BROKENHEARTED

He heals the *b* and . . . . . Ps 147:3

BRONZE

So Moses made a *b* . . . . . Num 21:9
your head shall be *b* . . . . . Deut 28:23
b serpent that Moses . . . . . 2 Kin 18:4
Or is my flesh *b* . . . . . Job 6:12
b as rotten wood . . . . . Job 41:27
broken the gates of *b* . . . . . Ps 107:16
b I will bring . . . . . Is 60:17
b walls against the . . . . . Jer 1:18
people a fortified *b* . . . . . Jer 15:20
a third kingdom of *b* . . . . . Dan 2:39
make your hooves *b* . . . . . Mic 4:13
were mountains of *b* . . . . . Zech 6:1

BROOD

The *b* of evildoers . . . . . Is 14:20
B of vipers . . . . . Matt 12:34
hen gathers her *b* . . . . . Luke 13:34

BROOK

stones from the *b* . . . . . 1 Sam 17:40
shall drink of the *b* . . . . . Ps 110:7
disciples over the *B* . . . . . John 18:1

BROOKS
good land, a land of *b* ... Deut 8:7
b that pass away ... Job 6:15
for the water *b* ... Ps 42:1

BROTHER
"Where is Abel your *b* ... Gen 4:9
he were my friend or *b* ... Ps 35:14
speak against your *b* ... Ps 50:20
and a *b* is born for ... Prov 17:17
b offended is harder ... Prov 18:19
has neither son nor *b* ... Eccl 4:8
and do not trust any *b* ... Jer 9:4
he pursued his *b* ... Amos 1:11
Was not Esau Jacob's *b* ... Mal 1:2
b will deliver up ... Matt 10:21
how often shall my *b* ... Matt 18:21
"Teacher, tell my *b* ... Luke 12:13
b will rise again ... John 11:23
do you judge your *b* ... Rom 14:10
b goes to law against ... 1 Cor 6:6
shall the weak *b* ... 1 Cor 8:11
slave—a beloved *b* ... Philem 16
He who loves his *b* ... 1 John 2:10
and murdered his *b* ... 1 John 3:12
Whoever hates his *b* ... 1 John 3:15
b sinning a sin which ... 1 John 5:16
I, John, both your *b* ... Rev 1:9

BROTHERHOOD
the covenant of *b* ... Amos 1:9
I might break the *b* ... Zech 11:14
Love the *b* ... 1 Pet 2:17
experienced by your *b* ... 1 Pet 5:9

BROTHERLY
to one another with *b* ... Rom 12:10
b love continue ... Heb 13:1

BROTHER'S
Am I my *b* keeper ... Gen 4:9
at the speck in your *b* ... Matt 7:3

BROTHERS
My *b* have dealt ... Job 6:15
a stranger to my *b* ... Ps 69:8
is My mother, or My *b* ... Mark 3:33
b are these who hear ... Luke 8:21
b did not believe ... John 7:5
love as *b* ... 1 Pet 3:8

BROUGHT
He *b* out His people ... Ps 105:48
The king has *b* me into ... Song 1:4
to heaven, will be *b* ... Luke 10:15

BRUISE
He shall *b* your head ... Gen 3:15
LORD binds up the *b* ... Is 30:26
the LORD to *b* Him ... Is 53:10

BRUISED
b reed He will not ... Is 42:3
He was *b* for our ... Is 53:5
b reed He will not ... Matt 12:20

BUILD
b ourselves a city ... Gen 11:4
"Would you *b* a house ... 2 Sam 7:5
b a temple for the name ... 1 Kin 8:17
that the LORD will *b* ... 1 Chr 17:10
Solomon who shall *b* ... 1 Chr 28:6
able to *b* Him a temple ... 2 Chr 2:6
labor in vain who *b* ... Ps 127:1
down, and a time to *b* ... Eccl 3:3
house that you will *b* ... Is 66:1
I will *b* them and not ... Jer 24:6
Who *b* up Zion with ... Mic 3:10
b the desolate ... Mal 1:4
'This man began to *b* ... Luke 14:30
What house will you *b* ... Acts 7:49
b you up and give you ... Acts 20:32
named, lest I should *b* ... Rom 15:20
For if I *b* again ... Gal 2:18

BUILDER
me, as a wise master *b* ... 1 Cor 3:10
foundations, whose *b* ... Heb 11:10

BUILDING
field, you are God's *b* ... 1 Cor 3:9
destroyed, we have a *b* ... 2 Cor 5:1
in whom the whole *b* ... Eph 2:21
But you, beloved, *b* ... Jude 20

BUILDS
The LORD *b* up ... Ps 147:2
The wise woman *b* ... Prov 14:1
one take heed how he *b* ... 1 Cor 3:10

BUILT
Wisdom has *b* her house ... Prov 9:1
my works great, I *b* ... Eccl 2:4
Babylon, that I have *b* ... Dan 4:30
to a wise man who *b* ... Matt 7:24
a foolish man who *b* ... Matt 7:26
work which he has *b* ... 1 Cor 3:14
having been *b* on the ... Eph 2:20
rooted and *b* up in Him ... Col 2:7
For every house is *b* ... Heb 3:4
stones, are being *b* ... 1 Pet 2:5

BULLS
in the blood of *b* ... Is 1:11
For if the blood of *b* ... Heb 9:13

BULWARKS
Mark well her *b* ... Ps 48:13
for walls and *b* ... Is 26:1

BURDEN
You have laid the *b* ... Num 11:11
one knows his own *b* ... 2 Chr 6:29
so that I am a *b* ... Job 7:20
Cast your *b* on the ... Ps 55:22
the grasshopper is a *b* ... Eccl 12:5
in that day that his *b* ... Is 10:27
its reproach is a *b* ... Zeph 3:18
easy and My *b* is light ... Matt 11:30
as it may, I did not *b* ... 2 Cor 12:16
we might not be a *b* ... 1 Thess 2:9
on you no other *b* ... Rev 2:24

BURDENS
and looked at their *b* ... Ex 2:11
For they bind heavy *b* ... Matt 23:4
Bear one another's *b* ... Gal 6:2

BURDENSOME
b task God has given ... Eccl 1:13
his life will be *b* ... Is 15:4
I myself was not *b* ... 2 Cor 12:13
commandments are not *b* ... 1 John 5:3

BURIAL
indeed he has no *b* ... Eccl 6:3
she did it for My *b* ... Matt 26:12
for the day of My *b* ... John 12:7
Stephen to his *b* ... Acts 8:2

BURIED
and there will I be *b* ... Ruth 1:17
I saw the wicked *b* ... Eccl 8:10
away the body and *b* ... Matt 14:12
also died and was *b* ... Luke 16:22
Therefore we were *b* ... Rom 6:4
and that He was *b* ... 1 Cor 15:4
b with Him in baptism ... Col 2:12

BURN
the bush does not *b* ... Ex 3:3
that My wrath may *b* ... Ex 32:10
b their chariots ... Josh 11:6
both will *b* together ... Is 1:31
"Did not our heart *b* ... Luke 24:32
eat her flesh and *b* ... Rev 17:16

BURNED
If anyone's work is *b* ... 1 Cor 3:15
my body to be *b* ... 1 Cor 13:3
whose end is to be *b* ... Heb 6:8
be touched and that *b* ... Heb 12:18
are *b* outside the camp ... Heb 13:11
in it will be *b* ... 2 Pet 3:10
all green grass was *b* ... Rev 8:7

BURNING
b torch that passed ... Gen 15:17
with severe *b* fever ... Deut 28:22
on his lips like a *b* ... Prov 16:27
b fire shut up in my ... Jer 20:9
b jealousy against the ... Ezek 36:5
plucked from the *b* ... Amos 4:11
a great mountain *b* ... Rev 8:8
fell from heaven, *b* ... Rev 8:10

BURNT
lamb for a *b* offering ... Gen 22:7
delight in *b* offering ... Ps 51:16
b offerings are not ... Jer 6:20
Though you offer Me *b* ... Amos 5:22

BURST
it is ready to *b* ... Job 32:19
with doors, when it *b* ... Job 38:8
the new wine will *b* ... Luke 5:37
falling headlong, he *b* ... Acts 1:18

BURY
b your dead in the ... Gen 23:6
was no one to *b* them ... Ps 79:3
go and *b* my father ... Matt 8:21
and let the dead *b* ... Matt 8:22

BUSH
from the midst of a *b* ... Ex 3:2
Him who dwelt in the *b* ... Deut 33:16
to him in the *b* ... Acts 7:35

BUSINESS
in ships, who do *b* ... Ps 107:23
farm, another to his *b* ... Matt 22:5
about My Father's *b* ... Luke 2:49

BUSYBODIES
at all, but are *b* ... 2 Thess 3:11
but also gossips and *b* ... 1 Tim 5:13

BUTTER
So he took *b* and milk ... Gen 18:8
were smoother than *b* ... Ps 55:21
of milk produces *b* ... Prov 30:33

BUY
in Egypt to *b* grain ... Gen 41:57
B the truth ... Prov 23:23
Yes, come, *b* wine and ... Is 55:1
that we may *b* the poor ... Amos 8:6
b food for all these ... Luke 9:18
"*B* those things we ... John 13:29
rejoice, those who *b* ... 1 Cor 7:30
spend a year there, *b* ... James 4:13
I counsel you to *b* ... Rev 3:18
and that no one may *b* ... Rev 13:17

BUYER
nothing," cries the *b* ... Prov 20:14
as with the *b* ... Is 24:2
'Let not the *b* ... Ezek 7:12

BUYS
a field and *b* it ... Prov 31:16
has and *b* that field ... Matt 13:44
b their merchandise ... Rev 18:11

BYWORD
But He has made me a *b* ... Job 17:6
You made us a *b* ... Ps 44:14

CAESAR
——— Augustus Caesar (31 B.C.–A.D. 14):
Decree of brings Joseph and Mary to Bethlehem, Luke 2:1
——— Tiberius Caesar (A.D. 14–37):
Christ's ministry dated by, Luke 3:1–23

Tribute paid to, Matt 22:17–21
Jews side with, John 19:12
——— Claudius Caesar (A.D. 41–54):
Famine in time of, Acts 11:28
Banished Jews from Rome, Acts 18:2
——— Nero Caesar (A.D. 54–68):
Paul appealed to, Acts 25:8–12
Christian converts in household of, Phil 4:22
Paul tried before, 2 Tim 4:16–18
Called Augustus, Acts 25:21

CAESAREA

Roman capital of Palestine, Acts 12:19; 23:33
Paul escorted to, Acts 23:23–33
Paul imprisoned at; appeals to Caesar, Acts 25:4, 8–13
Peter preaches at, Acts 10:34–43
Paul preaches at, Acts 9:26–30; 18:22; 21:8

CAESAREA PHILIPPI

A city in northern Palestine; scene of Peter's great confession, Matt 16:13–20
Probable site of the Transfiguration, Matt 17:1–3

CAGE

c is full of birds .... Jer 5:27
foul spirit, and a *c* .... Rev 18:2

CAIAPHAS

Son-in-law of Annas; high priest, John 18:13
Makes prophecy, John 11:49–52
Jesus appears before, John 18:23, 24
Apostles appear before, Acts 4:1–22

CAIN

Adam's first son, Gen 4:1
His offering rejected, Gen 4:2–7; Heb 11:4
Murders Abel; is exiled; settles in Nod, Gen 4:8–17
A type of evil, Jude 11

CAKES

Sustain me with *c* .... Song 2:5
and love the raisin *c* .... Hos 3:1

CALAMITIES

refuge, until these *c* .... Ps 57:1

CALAMITY

for the day of their *c* .... Deut 32:35
will laugh at your *c* .... Prov 1:26
c shall come suddenly .... Prov 6:15
If there is *c* in a .... Amos 3:6

CALEB

Sent as spy; gives good report; rewarded, Num 13:2, 6, 27, 30; 14:5–9, 24–38
Inherits Hebron, Josh 14:6–15
Conquers his territory with Othniel's help, Josh 15:13–19

CALF

and made a molded *c* .... Ex 32:4
They made a *c* in Horeb .... Ps 106:19
is, than a fatted *c* .... Prov 15:17
like a stubborn *c* .... Hos 4:16
Your *c* is rejected .... Hos 8:5
And bring the fatted *c* .... Luke 15:23
creature like a *c* .... Rev 4:7

CALL

I will *c* to the LORD .... 1 Sam 12:17
c their lands after .... Ps 49:11
To you, O men, I *c* .... Prov 8:4
c upon Him while He .... Is 55:6
'*C* to Me .... Jer 33:3
Arise, *c* on your God .... Jon 1:6
They will *c* on My name .... Zech 13:9
c His name JESUS .... Matt 1:21
c the righteous .... Matt 9:13
Lord our God will *c* .... Acts 2:39
c them My people .... Rom 9:25
then shall they *c* .... Rom 10:14
For God did not *c* .... 1 Thess 4:7
c and election sure .... 2 Pet 1:10

CALLED

c the light Day .... Gen 1:5
c his wife's name Eve .... Gen 3:20
"I, the LORD, have *c* .... Is 42:6
I have *c* you by your .... Is 43:1
The LORD has *c* Me from .... Is 49:1
and out of Egypt I *c* .... Hos 11:1
"Out of Egypt I *c* .... Matt 2:15
a city *c* Nazareth .... Matt 2:23
For many are *c* .... Matt 20:16
to those who are the *c* .... Rom 8:28
these He also *c* .... Rom 8:30
But God has *c* us to .... 1 Cor 7:15
praises of Him who *c* .... 1 Pet 2:9
knowledge of Him who *c* .... 2 Pet 1:3
c children of God .... 1 John 3:1

CALLING

the gifts and the *c* .... Rom 11:29
For you see your *c* .... 1 Cor 1:26
remain in the same *c* .... 1 Cor 7:20
to walk worthy of the *c* .... Eph 4:1
in one hope of your *c* .... Eph 4:4
us with a holy *c* .... 2 Tim 1:9
of the heavenly *c* .... Heb 3:1

CALLS

c them all by name .... Ps 147:4
there is no one who *c* .... Is 64:7
David himself *c* .... Mark 12:37
c his own sheep .... John 10:3
For "whoever *c* .... Rom 10:13

CALM

the sea will become *c* .... Jon 1:12
there was a great *c* .... Matt 8:26

CALVARY

Christ crucified there, Luke 23:33
Same as "Golgotha" in Hebrew, John 19:17

CALVES

made two *c* of gold .... 1 Kin 12:28
their cow *c* without .... Job 21:10
like stall-fed *c* .... Mal 4:2
blood of goats and *c* .... Heb 9:12
he took the blood of *c* .... Heb 9:19

CAMEL

it is easier for a *c* .... Matt 19:24
and swallow a *c* .... Matt 23:24

CAMP

"This is God's *c* .... Gen 32:2
who went before the *c* .... Ex 14:19
to Him, outside the *c* .... Heb 13:13

CANA

A village of upper Galilee; home of Nathanael, John 21:2
Site of Christ's first miracle, John 2:1–11
Healing at, John 4:46–54

CANAAN

A son of Ham, Gen 10:6
Cursed by Noah, Gen 9:20–25
——— Promised Land, Gen 12:5
Boundaries of, Gen 10:19
God's promises concerning, given to Abraham, Gen 12:1–3
to Isaac, Gen 26:2, 3
to Jacob, Gen 28:10–13
to Israel, Ex 3:8
Conquest of, announced, Gen 15:7–21
preceded by spying expedition, Num 13:1–33
delayed by unbelief, Num 14:1–35
accomplished by the Lord, Josh 23:1–16
achieved only in part, Judg 1:21, 27–36

CANAANITES

Israelites commanded to:
drive them out; not serve their gods, Ex 23:23–33
shun their abominations, Lev 18:24–30
not make covenants or intermarry with them, Deut 7:1–3

CAPERNAUM

Simon Peter's home, Mark 1:21, 29
Christ performs healings there, Matt 8:5–17; 9:1–8; Mark 1:21–28; John 4:46–54
preaches there, Mark 9:33–50; John 6:24–71
uses as headquarters, Matt 4:13–17
pronounces judgment upon, Matt 11:23, 24

CAPPADOCIA

Jews from, at Pentecost, Acts 2:1, 9
Christians of, addressed by Peter, 1 Pet 1:1

CAPTAIN

which, having no *c* .... Prov 6:7

CAPTIVE

have led captivity *c* .... Ps 68:18
of your neck, O *c* .... Is 52:2
they shall now go *c* .... Amos 6:7
and be led away *c* .... Luke 21:24
He led captivity *c* .... Eph 4:8

CAPTIVES

will bring back the *c* .... Amos 9:14
and return their *c* .... Zeph 2:7
make *c* of gullible women .... 2 Tim 3:6

CAPTIVITY

bring you back from *c* .... Deut 30:3
high, You have led *c* .... Ps 68:18
Judah has gone into *c* .... Lam 1:3
from David until the *c* .... Matt 1:17
and bringing me into *c* .... Rom 7:23
every thought into *c* .... 2 Cor 10:5
on high, He led *c* .... Eph 4:8
shall go into *c* .... Rev 13:10

CARCASS

honey were in the *c* .... Judg 14:8
For wherever the *c* .... Matt 24:28

CARE

"Lord, do You not *c* .... Luke 10:40
you to be without *c* .... 1 Cor 7:32
who will sincerely *c* .... Phil 2:20
how will he take *c* .... 1 Tim 3:5
casting all your *c* .... 1 Pet 5:7

CARED

he said, not that he *c* .... John 12:6

CAREFULLY

c keep all these .... Deut 11:22
I shall walk *c* all my .... Is 38:15

CARELESS

but he who is *c* .... Prov 19:16

CARES

no one *c* for my soul .... Ps 142:4
and are choked with *c* .... Luke 8:14
He who is unmarried *c* .... 1 Cor 7:32
for He *c* for you .... 1 Pet 5:7

CARMEL

City of Judah, Josh 15:55
Site of Saul's victory, 1 Sam 15:12
——— A mountain of Palestine, Josh 19:26
Scene of Elijah's triumph, 1 Kin 18:19–45
Elisha visits, 2 Kin 2:25

CARNAL

spiritual, but I am *c* .... Rom 7:14
c mind is enmity .... Rom 8:7
for you are still *c* .... 1 Cor 3:3
our warfare are not *c* .... 2 Cor 10:4

How could one *c* ....Deut 32:30
angel of the LORD *c* ....Ps 35:5

CHASTE
may present you as a *c* ....2 Cor 11:2
to be discreet, *c* ....Titus 2:5
c conduct accompanied ....1 Pet 3:2

CHASTEN
C your son while there ....Prov 19:18
is My desire, I will *c* ....Hos 10:10
a father does not *c* ....Heb 12:7
I love, I rebuke and *c* ....Rev 3:19

CHASTENED
c my soul with fasting ....Ps 69:10
c every morning ....Ps 73:14
The LORD has *c* me ....Ps 118:18
In vain I have *c* ....Jer 2:30
c us as seemed best ....Heb 12:10

CHASTENING
have not seen the *c* ....Deut 11:2
do not despise the *c* ....Job 5:17
'I have borne *c* ....Job 34:31
a prayer when Your *c* ....Is 26:16
if you are without *c* ....Heb 12:8
Now no *c* seems to be ....Heb 12:11

CHASTENS
the LORD loves He *c* ....Heb 12:6

CHASTISE
and I, even I, will *c* ....Lev 26:28
c them according ....Hos 7:12
I will therefore *c* ....Luke 23:22

CHASTISEMENT
the *c* for our peace ....Is 53:5

CHEAT
'You shall not *c* ....Lev 19:13
Beware lest anyone *c* ....Col 2:8

CHEATED
let yourselves be *c* ....1 Cor 6:7
we have *c* no one ....2 Cor 7:2

CHEBAR
River in Babylonia, Ezek 1:3
Site of Ezekiel's visions, Ezek 10:15, 20

CHEDORLAOMER
A king of Elam; invaded Canaan, Gen 14:1–16

CHEEK
Let him give his *c* ....Lam 3:30
with a rod on the *c* ....Mic 5:1
on your right *c* ....Matt 5:39

CHEEKBONE
my enemies on the *c* ....Ps 3:7

CHEEKS
c are lovely with ....Song 1:10
His *c* are like a bed ....Song 5:13
struck Me, and My *c* ....Is 50:6

CHEER
and let your heart *c* ....Eccl 11:9
"Son, be of good *c* ....Matt 9:2

CHEERFUL
for God loves a *c* ....2 Cor 9:7
Is anyone *c* ....James 5:13

CHEERFULNESS
shows mercy, with *c* ....Rom 12:8

CHEMOSH
The god of the Moabites, Num 21:29
Children sacrificed to, 2 Kin 3:26, 27
Solomon builds altars to, 1 Kin 11:7
Josiah destroys altars of, 2 Kin 23:13

CHERISHES
but nourishes and *c* ....Eph 5:29
as a nursing mother *c* ....1 Thess 2:7

CHERUB
He rode upon a *c* ....2 Sam 22:11

CHERUBIM
and He placed *c* ....Gen 3:24
dwell between the *c* ....Ps 80:1
fire from among the *c* ....Ezek 10:2
above it were the *c* ....Heb 9:5

CHIEF
is white and ruddy, *c* ....Song 5:10
of whom I am *c* ....1 Tim 1:15
Zion a *c* cornerstone ....1 Pet 2:6
has become the *c* ....1 Pet 2:7
C Shepherd appears ....1 Pet 5:4

CHILD
Like a weaned *c* ....Ps 131:2
c is known by his ....Prov 20:11
Train up a *c* in the ....Prov 22:6
For unto us a *C* ....Is 9:6
c shall lead them ....Is 11:6
When Israel was a *c* ....Hos 11:1
virgin shall be with *c* ....Matt 1:23
He took a little *c* ....Mark 9:36
of God as a little *c* ....Mark 10:15
kind of *c* will this be ....Luke 1:66
So the *c* grew and ....Luke 1:80
When I was a *c* ....1 Cor 13:11
She bore a male *C* ....Rev 12:5

CHILDBEARING
she will be saved in *c* ....1 Tim 2:15

CHILDBIRTH
pain as a woman in *c* ....Is 13:8

CHILDHOOD
from your flesh, for *c* ....Eccl 11:10
And he said, "From *c* ....Mark 9:21
c you have known ....2 Tim 3:15

CHILDLESS
give me, seeing I go *c* ....Gen 15:2
this man down as *c* ....Jer 22:30

CHILDREN
she bore Jacob no *c* ....Gen 30:1
and all of you are *c* ....Ps 82:6
c are a heritage ....Ps 127:3
He has blessed your *c* ....Ps 147:13
let the *c* of Zion be ....Ps 149:2
c are blessed after ....Prov 20:7
c rise up and call her ....Prov 31:28
c are their oppressors ....Is 3:12
c whom the LORD has ....Is 8:18
be the peace of your *c* ....Is 54:13
they are My people, *c* ....Is 63:8
the hearts of the *c* ....Mal 4:6
c will rise up against ....Matt 10:21
and become as little *c* ....Matt 18:3
c were brought to Him ....Matt 19:13
"Let the little *c* ....Matt 19:14
the right to become *c* ....John 1:12
you were Abraham's *c* ....John 8:39
spirit that we are *c* ....Rom 8:16
but as my beloved *c* ....1 Cor 4:14
Brethren, do not be *c* ....1 Cor 14:20
c ought not to lay up ....2 Cor 12:14
and were by nature *c* ....Eph 2:3
should no longer be *c* ....Eph 4:14
Walk as *c* of light ....Eph 5:8
and harmless, *c* ....Phil 2:15
now we are *c* of God ....1 John 3:2
that we love the *c* ....1 John 5:2
to hear that my *c* ....3 John 4

CHILION
Elimelech's son, Ruth 1:2
Orpah's deceased husband, Ruth 1:4, 5
Boaz redeems his estate, Ruth 4:9

CHINNERETH (or Chinneroth)
Fortified city in Naphtali, Deut 3:17
A region bordering the Sea of Galilee, 1 Kin 15:20
Same as the plain of Gennesaret, Matt 14:34
——— The OT name for the Sea of Galilee, Num 34:11
Also called Lake of Gennesaret, Luke 5:1

CHOOSE
therefore *c* life ....Deut 30:19
c none of his ways ....Prov 3:31
evil and *c* the good ....Is 7:15
will still *c* Israel ....Is 14:1
will again *c* Jerusalem ....Zech 1:17
You did not *c* ....John 15:16
yet what I shall *c* ....Phil 1:22

CHOSEN
of Jacob, His *c* ....1 Chr 16:13
people He has *c* ....Ps 33:12
a covenant with My *c* ....Ps 89:3
c the way of truth ....Ps 119:30
servant whom I have *c* ....Is 43:10
c that good part ....Luke 10:42
I know whom I have *c* ....John 13:18
c you that you should ....Acts 22:14
c the foolish things ....1 Cor 1:27
Has God not *c* the poor ....James 2:5
But you are a *c* ....1 Pet 2:9

CHRIST
genealogy of Jesus *C* ....Matt 1:1
Jesus who is called *C* ....Matt 1:16
"You are the *C* ....Matt 16:16
if You are the *C* ....Matt 26:63
a Savior, who is *C* ....Luke 2:11
that He Himself is *C* ....Luke 23:2
the law that the *C* ....John 12:34
he preached the *C* ....Acts 9:20
have the Spirit of *C* ....Rom 8:9
It is *C* who died ....Rom 8:34
C did not please ....Rom 15:3
Is *C* divided ....1 Cor 1:13
Him you are in *C* Jesus ....1 Cor 1:30
to be justified by *C* ....Gal 2:17
been crucified with *C* ....Gal 2:20
but *C* lives in me ....Gal 2:20
your Seed," who is *C* ....Gal 3:16
before by God in *C* ....Gal 3:17
C may dwell in your ....Eph 3:17
C will give you ....Eph 5:14
C is head of the ....Eph 5:23
to me, to live is *C* ....Phil 1:21
confess that Jesus *C* ....Phil 2:11
C who strengthens ....Phil 4:13
which is *C* in you ....Col 1:27
C who is our ....Col 3:4
C is all and in all ....Col 3:11
and men, the Man *C* ....1 Tim 2:5
Jesus *C* is the same ....Heb 13:8
C His Son cleanses us ....1 John 1:7
that Jesus is the *C* ....1 John 5:1
of His *C* have come ....Rev 12:10
and reigned with *C* ....Rev 20:4

CHRISTIAN
me to become a *C* ....Acts 26:28
anyone suffers as a *C* ....1 Pet 4:16

CHRISTIANS
were first called *C* ....Acts 11:26

CHRISTS
For false *c* and ....Matt 24:24

CHURCH
rock I will build My *c* ....Matt 16:18
them, tell it to the *c* ....Matt 18:17
c daily those who were ....Acts 2:47
elders in every *c* ....Acts 14:23
do you despise the *c* ....1 Cor 11:22
be made known by the *c* ....Eph 3:10

also loved the *c* ....Eph 5:25
Himself a glorious *c* ....Eph 5:27
as the Lord does the *c* ....Eph 5:29
body, which is the *c* ....Col 1:24
and do not let the *c* ....1 Tim 5:16
general assembly and *c* ....Heb 12:23
To the angel of the *c* ....Rev 2:1

CHURCHES

strengthening the *c* ....Acts 15:41
The *c* of Christ greet ....Rom 16:16
imitators of the *c* ....1 Thess 2:14
John, to the seven *c* ....Rev 1:4
angels of the seven *c* ....Rev 1:20
these things in the *c* ....Rev 22:16

CILICIA

Paul's homeland, Acts 21:39
Students from, argued with Stephen, Acts 6:9
Paul labors in, Gal 1:21

CIRCLE

He walks above the *c* ....Job 22:14
when He drew a *c* ....Prov 8:27
who sits above the *c* ....Is 40:22

CIRCUIT

of heaven, and its *c* ....Ps 19:6
comes again on its *c* ....Eccl 1:6

CIRCUMCISE

c the foreskin of your ....Deut 10:16
LORD your God will *c* ....Deut 30:6
C yourselves to the ....Jer 4:4
is necessary to *c* them ....Acts 15:5

CIRCUMCISED

among you shall be *c* ....Gen 17:10
who will justify the *c* ....Rom 3:30
While he was *c* ....Rom 4:10
the gospel for the *c* ....Gal 2:7
if you become *c* ....Gal 5:2
c the eighth day ....Phil 3:5
In Him you were also *c* ....Col 2:11

CIRCUMCISION

him the covenant of *c* ....Acts 7:8
c that which is outward ....Rom 2:28
c is that of the heart ....Rom 2:29
a servant to the *c* ....Rom 15:8
C is nothing and ....1 Cor 7:19
Christ Jesus neither *c* ....Gal 5:6
For we are the *c* ....Phil 3:3
circumcised with the *c* ....Col 2:11
those of the *c* ....Titus 1:10

CIRCUMSPECTLY

then that you walk *c* ....Eph 5:15

CISTERN

waters of his own *c* ....2 Kin 18:31
from your own *c* ....Prov 5:15

CITIES

He overthrew those *c* ....Gen 19:25
repair the ruined *c* ....Is 61:4
c are a wilderness ....Is 64:10
c will be laid waste ....Jer 4:7
three parts, and the *c* ....Rev 16:19

CITIZEN

But I was born a *c* ....Acts 22:28

CITIZENS

But his *c* hated him ....Luke 19:14
but fellow *c* with the ....Eph 2:19

CITIZENSHIP

sum I obtained this *c* ....Acts 22:28
For our *c* is in heaven ....Phil 3:20

CITY

And he built a *c* ....Gen 4:17
shall make glad the *c* ....Ps 46:4
c shall flourish ....Ps 72:16
They found no *c* ....Ps 107:4
c that is compact ....Ps 122:3
the LORD guards the *c* ....Ps 127:1
at the entry of the *c* ....Prov 8:3
c has become a harlot ....Is 1:21
upon Zion, the *c* ....Is 33:20
after the holy *c* ....Is 48:2
How lonely sits the *c* ....Lam 1:1
Nineveh, that great *c* ....Jon 4:11
c that dwelt securely ....Zeph 2:15
to the oppressing *c* ....Zeph 3:1
c called Nazareth ....Matt 2:23
c that is set on a ....Matt 5:14
He has prepared a *c* ....Heb 11:16
Zion and to the *c* ....Heb 12:22
have no continuing *c* ....Heb 13:14
will tread the holy *c* ....Rev 11:2
fallen, that great *c* ....Rev 14:8
and the beloved *c* ....Rev 20:9
John, saw the holy *c* ....Rev 21:2
c was pure gold ....Rev 21:18
c had no need of the ....Rev 21:23
the gates into the *c* ....Rev 22:14

CLAP

c their hands at him ....Job 27:23
Oh, *c* your hands ....Ps 47:1
let the rivers *c* ....Ps 98:8
of the field shall *c* ....Is 55:12

CLAUDIUS LYSIAS

Roman commander who protected Paul, Acts 24:22–24, 26

CLAY

dwell in houses of *c* ....Job 4:19
have made me like *c* ....Job 10:9
are defenses of *c* ....Job 13:12
been formed out of *c* ....Job 33:6
takes on form like *c* ....Job 38:14
pit, out of the miry *c* ....Ps 40:2
be esteemed as the *c* ....Is 29:16
Shall the *c* say to him ....Is 45:9
We are the *c* ....Is 64:8
"Look, as the *c* ....Jer 18:6
iron and partly of *c* ....Dan 2:33
blind man with the *c* ....John 9:6
have power over the *c* ....Rom 9:21

CLEAN

seven each of every *c* ....Gen 7:2
between unclean and *c* ....Lev 10:10
wash in them and be *c* ....2 Kin 5:12
Who can bring a *c* ....Job 14:4
He who has *c* hands and ....Ps 24:4
make yourselves *c* ....Is 1:16
Then I will sprinkle *c* ....Ezek 36:25
c out His threshing ....Matt 3:12
You can make me *c* ....Matt 8:2
all things are *c* ....Luke 11:41
but is completely *c* ....John 13:10
"You are not all *c* ....John 13:11
You are already *c* ....John 15:3
in fine linen, *c* ....Rev 19:8

CLEANSE

You shall *c* the altar ....Ex 29:36
C me from secret ....Ps 19:12
and *c* me from my sin ....Ps 51:2
How can a young man *c* ....Ps 119:9
I will *c* you from all ....Ezek 36:25
c the lepers, raise ....Matt 10:8
might sanctify and *c* ....Eph 5:26
c your conscience ....Heb 9:14
C your hands ....James 4:8
us our sins and to *c* ....1 John 1:9

CLEANSED

Surely I have *c* ....Ps 73:13
and you were not *c* ....Ezek 24:13
the lepers are *c* ....Matt 11:5
"Were there not ten *c* ....Luke 17:17

CLEANSES

Therefore if anyone *c* ....2 Tim 2:21
Jesus Christ His Son *c* ....1 John 1:7

CLEAR

c shining after rain ....2 Sam 23:4
fair as the moon, *c* ....Song 6:10
yourselves to be *c* ....2 Cor 7:11
like a jasper stone, *c* ....Rev 21:11
of life, *c* as crystal ....Rev 22:1

CLEFTS

to go into the *c* ....Is 2:21
valleys and in the *c* ....Is 7:19
you who dwell in the *c* ....Jer 49:16

CLIMB

go into thickets and *c* ....Jer 4:29
mighty men, they *c* ....Joel 2:7
though they *c* up to ....Amos 9:2

CLING

and that you may *c* ....Deut 30:20
to her, "Do not *c* ....John 20:17
C to what is good ....Rom 12:9

CLINGS

and My tongue *c* ....Ps 22:15
My soul *c* to the dust ....Ps 119:25

CLOAK

c You will change them ....Ps 102:26
let him have your *c* ....Matt 5:40
c You will fold them ....Heb 1:12
using liberty as a *c* ....1 Pet 2:16

CLOTH

a piece of unshrunk *c* ....Matt 9:16
in a clean linen *c* ....Matt 27:59

CLOTHE

c them with tunics ....Ex 40:14
c me with skin and ....Job 10:11
c her priests with ....Ps 132:16
His enemies I will *c* ....Ps 132:18
Though you *c* yourself ....Jer 4:30
He not much more *c* ....Matt 6:30

CLOTHED

of skin, and *c* them ....Gen 3:21
Have you *c* his neck ....Job 39:19
off my sackcloth and *c* ....Ps 30:11
The pastures are *c* ....Ps 65:13
the LORD is *c* ....Ps 93:1
You are *c* with honor ....Ps 104:1
c himself with cursing ....Ps 109:18
Let Your priests be *c* ....Ps 132:9
all her household is *c* ....Prov 31:21
c you with fine linen ....Ezek 16:10
A man *c* in soft ....Matt 11:8
I was naked and you *c* ....Matt 25:36
legion, sitting and *c* ....Mark 5:15
And they *c* Him with ....Mark 15:17
rich man who was *c* ....Luke 16:19
desiring to be *c* ....2 Cor 5:2
that you may be *c* ....Rev 3:18
a woman *c* with the sun ....Rev 12:1
He was *c* with a robe ....Rev 19:13

CLOTHES

c will abhor me ....Job 9:31
c became shining ....Mark 9:3
many spread their *c* ....Luke 19:36
laid down their *c* ....Acts 7:58
and tore off their *c* ....Acts 22:23
a poor man in filthy *c* ....James 2:2

CLOTHING

c they cast lots ....Ps 22:18
c is woven with gold ....Ps 45:13
will provide your *c* ....Prov 27:26
and honor are her *c* ....Prov 31:25
of vengeance for *c* ....Is 59:17
the body more than *c* ....Matt 6:25
do you worry about *c* ....Matt 6:28

But Jesus did not *c* .... John 2:24
c sexual immorality .... 1 Cor 10:8
c these to faithful .... 2 Tim 2:2
c their souls to Him .... 1 Pet 4:19
c sin not leading .... 1 John 5:16

COMMITS
to you, whoever *c* .... John 8:34
sin also *c* lawlessness .... 1 John 3:4

COMMITTED
For My people have *c* .... Jer 2:13
c things deserving .... Luke 12:48
For God has *c* them all .... Rom 11:32
Guard what was *c* .... 1 Tim 6:20
"Who *c* no sin .... 1 Pet 2:22
c Himself to Him who .... 1 Pet 2:23

COMMON
of the *c* people sins .... Lev 4:27
poor have this in *c* .... Prov 22:2
c people heard Him .... Mark 12:37
had all things in *c* .... Acts 2:44
never eaten anything *c* .... Acts 10:14
not call any man *c* .... Acts 10:28
a true son in our *c* .... Titus 1:4
concerning our *c* .... Jude 3

COMMUNION
bless, is it not the *c* .... 1 Cor 10:16
c has light with .... 2 Cor 6:14
c of the Holy Spirit .... 2 Cor 13:14

COMPANION
a man my equal, My *c* .... Ps 55:13
I am a *c* of all who .... Ps 119:63
the Man who is My *C* .... Zech 13:7
urge you also, true *c* .... Phil 4:3
your brother and *c* .... Rev 1:9

COMPANIONS
are rebellious, and *c* .... Is 1:23
and calling to their *c* .... Matt 11:16
more than Your *c* .... Heb 1:9
while you became *c* .... Heb 10:33

COMPANY
great was the *c* .... Ps 68:11
epistle not to keep *c* .... 1 Cor 5:9
c corrupts good habits .... 1 Cor 15:33
and do not keep *c* .... 2 Thess 3:14
to an innumerable *c* .... Heb 12:22

COMPARE
may desire cannot *c* .... Prov 3:15
c ourselves with those .... 2 Cor 10:12

COMPARED
the heavens can be *c* .... Ps 89:6
may desire cannot be *c* .... Prov 8:11
are not worthy to be *c* .... Rom 8:18

COMPASSION
show you mercy, have *c* .... Deut 13:17
His people and have *c* .... Deut 32:36
He, being full of *c* .... Ps 78:38
are a God full of *c* .... Ps 86:15
will return and have *c* .... Jer 12:15
yet He will show *c* .... Lam 3:32
c everyone to his .... Zech 7:9
He was moved with *c* .... Matt 9:36
also have had *c* .... Matt 18:33
"I have *c* on the .... Mark 8:2
whomever I will have *c* .... Rom 9:15
He can have *c* on those .... Heb 5:2
of one mind, having *c* .... 1 Pet 3:8
And on some have *c* .... Jude 22

COMPASSIONATE
c women have cooked .... Lam 4:10
the Lord is very *c* .... James 5:11

COMPASSIONS
because His *c* fail not .... Lam 3:22

C[illegible]
c t[illegible] .... Luke 14:23

COMP[illegible]
Macedo[illegible] .... Acts 18:5

COMPELS
the spirit with[illegible] .... Job 32:18
And whoever *c* .... Matt 5:41
the love of Christ *c* .... 2 Cor 5:14

COMPLACENCY
slay them, and the *c* .... Prov 1:32
who are settled in *c* .... [illegible]ph 1:12

COMPLAIN
should a living man *c* .... [illegible]:39

COMPLAINED
and you *c* in your .... Deut 1[illegible]
but *c* in their tents .... Ps 106:25
some of them also *c* .... 1 Cor 10:10

COMPLAINERS
These are grumblers, *c* .... Jude 16

COMPLAINING
all things without *c* .... Phil 2:14

COMPLAINT
"Even today my *c* .... Job 23:2
I pour out my *c* .... Ps 142:2
for the LORD has a *c* .... Mic 6:2
if anyone has a *c* .... Col 3:13

COMPLAINTS
Who has *c* .... Prov 23:29
laid many serious *c* .... Acts 25:7

COMPLETE
that you may be made *c* .... 2 Cor 13:9
work in you will *c* .... Phil 1:6
and you are *c* in Him .... Col 2:10
of God may be *c* .... 2 Tim 3:17
make you *c* in every .... Heb 13:21
the wrath of God is *c* .... Rev 15:1

COMPLETELY
I made a man *c* well .... John 7:23
Himself sanctify you *c* .... 1 Thess 5:23

COMPREHEND
which we cannot *c* .... Job 37:5
c my path and my lying .... Ps 139:3
the darkness did not *c* .... John 1:5
may be able to *c* .... Eph 3:18

CONCEAL
Almighty I will not *c* .... Job 27:11
c pride from man .... Job 33:17
of God to *c* a matter .... Prov 25:2

CONCEALED
c Your lovingkindness .... Ps 40:10
than love carefully *c* .... Prov 27:5

CONCEIT
selfish ambition or *c* .... Phil 2:3

CONCEITED
Let us not become *c* .... Gal 5:26

CONCEIVE
the virgin shall *c* .... Is 7:14
And behold, you will *c* .... Luke 1:31

CONCEIVED
in sin my mother *c* .... Ps 51:5
when desire has *c* .... James 1:15

CONCERN
Neither do I *c* myself .... Ps 131:1
the things which *c* .... Acts 28:31
my deep *c* for all the .... 2 Cor 11:28

CONCLUSION
Let us hear the *c* .... Eccl 12:13

CONDEMN
say to God, 'Do not *c* .... Job 10:2
world to *c* the world .... John 3:17
her, "Neither do I *c* .... John 8:11
judge another you *c* .... Rom 2:1
our heart does not *c* .... 1 John 3:21

CONDEMNATION
will receive greater *c* .... Matt 23:14
can you escape the *c* .... Matt 23:33
subject to eternal *c* .... Mark 3:29
And this is the *c* .... John 3:19
the resurrection of *c* .... John 5:29
Their *c* is just .... Rom 3:8
therefore now no *c* .... Rom 8:1
of *c* had glory .... 2 Cor 3:9
having *c* because they .... 1 Tim 5:12
marked out for this *c* .... Jude 4

CONDEMNED
words you will be *c* .... Matt 12:37
does not believe is *c* .... John 3:18
sin in the flesh .... Rom 8:3

CONDEMNS
Who is he who *c* .... Rom 8:34
For if our heart *c* .... 1 John 3:20

CONDUCT
c yourselves like men .... 1 Sam 4:9
who are of upright *c* .... Ps 37:14
c yourself in the [illegible] .... 1 Tim 3:15
c that his works are .... James 3:13
to each one's work *c* .... 1 Pet 1:17
from your aimless *c* .... 1 Pet 1:18
may be won by the *c* .... 1 Pet 3:1

CONFESS
c my transgressions .... Ps 32:5
that if you *c* with .... Rom 10:9
every tongue shall *c* .... Rom 14:11
C your trespasses .... James 5:16
If we *c* our sins .... 1 John 1:9
but I will *c* his name .... Rev 3:5

CONFESSED
c that He was Christ .... John 9:22
c the good confession .... 1 Tim 6:12

CONFESSES
prosper, but whoever *c* .... Prov 28:13
c that Jesus is the .... 1 John 4:15

CONFESSION
of Israel, and make *c* .... Josh 7:19
with the mouth *c* .... Rom 10:10
confessed the good *c* .... 1 Tim 6:12
witnessed the good *c* .... 1 Tim 6:13
High Priest of our *c* .... Heb 3:1
let us hold fast our *c* .... Heb 4:14

CONFIDENCE
You who are the *c* .... Ps 65:5
the LORD than to put *c* .... Ps 118:8
c shall be your .... Is 30:15
Jesus, and have no *c* .... Phil 3:3
if we hold fast the *c* .... Heb 3:6
appears, we may have *c* .... 1 John 2:28

CONFINED
saying, "I am *c* .... Jer 36:5
the Scripture has *c* .... Gal 3:22

CONFIRM
c the promises .... Rom 15:8
who will also *c* .... 1 Cor 1:8

CONFIRMED
covenant that was *c* .... Gal 3:17
by the Lord, and was *c* .... Heb 2:3
c it by an oath .... Heb 6:17
prophetic word *c* .... 2 Pet 1:19

CONFIRMING
c the word through the .... Mark 16:20

CONFLICT
having the same *c* .... Phil 1:30
to know what a great *c* .... Col 2:1

CONFLICTS
Outside were *c* ....2 Cor 7:5

CONFORMED
predestined to be *c* ....Rom 8:29
And do not be *c* ....Rom 12:2
sufferings, being *c* ....Phil 3:10
body that it may be *c* ....Phil 3:21

CONFUSE
c their language ....Gen 11:7

CONFUSED
there the LORD *c* ....Gen 11:9
the assembly was *c* ....Acts 19:32

CONFUSION
c who plot my hurt ....Ps 35:4
us drink the wine of *c* ....Ps 60:3

CONGREGATION
Nor sinners in the *c* ....Ps 1:5
the *c* of the wicked ....Ps 22:16
God stands in the *c* ....Ps 82:1

CONIAH
King of Judah, Jer 22:24, 28
Same as Jehoiachin, 2 Kin 24:8

CONQUER
conquering and to *c* ....Rev 6:2

CONQUERORS
we are more than *c* ....Rom 8:37

CONSCIENCE
convicted by their *c* ....John 8:9
strive to have a *c* ....Acts 24:16
I am not lying, my *c* ....Rom 9:1
wrath but also for *c* ....Rom 13:5
no questions for *c* ....1 Cor 10:25
faith with a pure *c* ....1 Tim 3:9
having their own *c* ....1 Tim 4:2
to God, cleanse your *c* ....Heb 9:14
from an evil *c* and our ....Heb 10:22
having a good *c* ....1 Pet 3:16

CONSECRATE
"*C* to Me all the ....Ex 13:2
c himself this day ....1 Chr 29:5
the trumpet in Zion, *c* ....Joel 2:15
c their gain to the ....Mic 4:13

CONSECRATED
c this house which you ....1 Kin 9:3

CONSENT
entice you, do not *c* ....Prov 1:10
and does not *c* to ....1 Tim 6:3

CONSENTED
you saw a thief, you *c* ....Ps 50:18
He had not *c* to their ....Luke 23:51

CONSENTING
Now Saul was *c* to his ....Acts 8:1

CONSIDER
When I *c* Your heavens ....Ps 8:3
c her palaces ....Ps 48:13
c carefully what is ....Prov 23:1
C the work of God ....Eccl 7:13
My people do not *c* ....Is 1:3
c the operation ....Is 5:12
your God will *c* ....Jon 1:6
"*C* your ways ....Hag 1:5
C the lilies of the ....Matt 6:28
C the ravens ....Luke 12:24
Let a man so *c* us ....1 Cor 4:1
c how great this man ....Heb 7:4
c one another in order ....Heb 10:24
c Him who endured ....Heb 12:3

CONSIST
in Him all things *c* ....Col 1:17

CONSOLATION
waiting for the *C* ....Luke 2:25
have received your *c* ....Luke 6:24
24 .2 Cor 1:5
....Phil 2:1
abound in us, so ou .2 Thess 2:16
if there is any *c* ....Heb 6:18
given us everlas
we might have

CONSOLAT
..........Job 15:11
Are the *c* o

CONSO
rn ....Is 61:3
c those

CONS
.....................Acts 12:5
c pr

ME

CO idst, lest I *c* ....Ex 33:3
great fire will *c* ....Deut 5:25
them in wrath ....Ps 59:13
whom the Lord will *c* ....2 Thess 2:8

CONSUMED
but the bu... was not *c* ....Ex 3:2
c the ...urnt ....1 Kin 18:38
...or we have been *c* ....Ps 90:7
mercies we are not *c* ....Lam 3:22
beware lest you be *c* ....Gal 5:15

CONSUMING
the LORD was like a *c* ....Ex 24:17
before you as a *c* ....Deut 9:3
our God is a *c* fire ....Heb 12:29

CONTAIN
of heavens cannot *c* ....2 Chr 2:6
c the books that ....John 21:25

CONTEMPT
He pours *c* on princes ....Job 12:21
wicked comes, *c* comes ....Prov 18:3
and everlasting *c* ....Dan 12:2
and be treated with *c* ....Mark 9:12

CONTEMPTIBLE
of the LORD is *c* ....Mal 1:7
also have made you *c* ....Mal 2:9
and his speech *c* ....2 Cor 10:10

CONTEND
show me why You *c* ....Job 10:2
Will you *c* for God ....Job 13:8
let us *c* together ....Is 43:26
for I will *c* with him ....Is 49:25
then how can you *c* ....Jer 12:5
c earnestly for the ....Jude 3

CONTENT
state I am, to be *c* ....Phil 4:11
these we shall be *c* ....1 Tim 6:8
covetousness; be *c* ....Heb 13:5

CONTENTION
lips enter into *c* ....Prov 18:6
and *c* will leave ....Prov 22:10
strife and a man of *c* ....Jer 15:10

CONTENTIONS
Casting lots causes *c* ....Prov 18:18
sorcery, hatred, *c* ....Gal 5:20
genealogies, *c* ....Titus 3:9

CONTENTIOUS
than with a *c* and ....Prov 21:19
shared with a *c* woman ....Prov 25:24
anyone seems to be *c* ....1 Cor 11:16

CONTENTMENT
c is great gain ....1 Tim 6:6

CONTINUAL
a merry heart has a *c* ....Prov 15:15
in wrath with a *c* ....Is 14:6
c coming she weary me ....Luke 18:5
c grief in my heart ....Rom 9:2

CONTINUALLY
heart was only evil *c* ....Gen 6:5
His praise shall *c* ....Ps 34:1
and Your truth *c* ....Ps 40:11
of God endures *c* ....Ps 52:1
I keep Your law *c* ....Ps 119:44
Before Me *c* are grief ....Jer 6:7
and wait on your God *c* ....Hos 12:6
will give ourselves *c* ....Acts 6:4
remains a priest *c* ....Heb 7:3
c offer the sacrifice ....Heb 13:15

CONTINUE
tells lies shall not *c* ....Ps 101:7
persuaded them to *c* ....Acts 13:43
Shall we *c* in sin that ....Rom 6:1
who does not *c* in all ....Gal 3:10
C earnestly in prayer ....Col 4:2
because they did not *c* ....Heb 8:9
Let brotherly love *c* ....Heb 13:1
asleep, all things *c* ....2 Pet 3:4

CONTINUED
c steadfastly in the ....Acts 2:42
us, they would have *c* ....1 John 2:19

CONTINUES
But He, because He *c* ....Heb 7:24
law of liberty and *c* ....James 1:25

CONTRADICTIONS
idle babblings and *c* ....1 Tim 6:20

CONTRARY
to worship God *c* ....Acts 18:13
and these are *c* ....Gal 5:17
please God and are *c* ....1 Thess 2:15
other thing that is *c* ....1 Tim 1:10

CONTRIBUTION
to make a certain *c* ....Rom 15:26

CONTRITE
saves such as have a *c* ....Ps 34:18
a broken and a *c* ....Ps 51:17
with him who has a *c* ....Is 57:15
poor and of a *c* spirit ....Is 66:2

CONTROVERSY
another, matters of *c* ....Deut 17:8
For the LORD has a *c* ....Jer 25:31
c great is ....1 Tim 3:16

CONVERSION
describing the *c* ....Acts 15:3

CONVERTED
unless you are *c* ....Matt 18:3

CONVICT
He has come, He will *c* ....John 16:8
c those who ....Titus 1:9
c all who are ungodly ....Jude 15

CONVICTS
Which of you *c* ....John 8:46

COOKED
c their own children ....Lam 4:10

COOL
in the garden in the *c* ....Gen 3:8
and *c* my tongue ....Luke 16:24

COPIES
necessary that the *c* ....Heb 9:23
hands, which are *c* ....Heb 9:24

COPPER
hills you can dig *c* ....Deut 8:9
of cups, pitchers, *c* ....Mark 7:4
sold for two *c* coins ....Luke 12:6

COPPERSMITH
c did me much harm ....2 Tim 4:14

CORD
this line of scarlet *c* ....Josh 2:18
And a threefold *c* ....Eccl 4:12
before the silver *c* ....Eccl 12:6

CORDS
in pieces the *c* ....Ps 129:4
he is caught in the *c* ....Prov 5:22
draw iniquity with *c* ....Is 5:18

them with gentle *c* ....Hos 11:4
had made a whip of *c* ....John 2:15

CORINTH
Paul labors at, Acts 18:1–18
Site of church, 1 Cor 1:2
Visited by Apollos, Acts 19:1

CORNELIUS
A religious Gentile, Acts 10:1–48

CORNER
was not done in a *c* ....Acts 26:26

CORNERSTONE
Or who laid its *c* ....Job 38:6
has become the chief *c* ....Ps 118:22
stone, a precious *c* ....Is 28:16
become the chief *c* ....Matt 21:42
in Zion a chief *c* ....1 Pet 2:6

CORPSE
c was thrown on the ....1 Kin 13:24
c trodden underfoot ....Is 14:19

CORRECT
with rebukes You *c* ....Ps 39:11
C your son ....Prov 29:17
But I will *c* you in ....Jer 30:11

CORRECTED
human fathers who *c* ....Heb 12:9

CORRECTION
nor detest His *c* ....Prov 3:11
but he who refuses *c* ....Prov 10:17
but he who hates *c* ....Prov 12:1
c will drive it ....Prov 22:15
Do not withhold *c* ....Prov 23:13
they received no *c* ....Jer 2:30
for reproof, for *c* ....2 Tim 3:16

CORRECTS
is the man whom God *c* ....Job 5:17
the LORD LOVES HE *c* ....Prov 3:12

CORRUPT
have together become *c* ....Ps 14:3
have together become *c* ....Ps 53:3
old man which grows *c* ....Eph 4:22
men of *c* minds ....2 Tim 3:8
in these things they *c* ....Jude 10

CORRUPTED
for all flesh had *c* ....Gen 6:12
we have *c* no one ....2 Cor 7:2
so your minds may be *c* ....2 Cor 11:3
Your riches are *c* ....James 5:2
the great harlot who *c* ....Rev 19:2

CORRUPTIBLE
For this *c* must put on ....1 Cor 15:53
redeemed with *c* things ....1 Pet 1:18

CORRUPTION
Your Holy One to see *c* ....Ps 16:10
God raised up saw no *c* ....Acts 13:37
from the bondage of *c* ....Rom 8:21
The body is sown in *c* ....1 Cor 15:42
c inherit incorruption ....1 Cor 15:50
of the flesh reap *c* ....Gal 6:8
having escaped the *c* ....2 Pet 1:4
perish in their own *c* ....2 Pet 2:12

COST
and count the *c* ....Luke 14:28

COULD
has done what she *c* ....Mark 14:8
c remove mountains ....1 Cor 13:2
which no one *c* number ....Rev 7:9

COUNCILS
deliver you up to *c* ....Mark 13:9

COUNSEL
and strength, He has *c* ....Job 12:13
the *c* of the wicked is ....Job 21:16
when the friendly *c* ....Job 29:4
is this who darkens *c* ....Job 38:2
who walks not in the *c* ....Ps 1:1
We took sweet *c* ....Ps 55:14
guide me with Your *c* ....Ps 73:24
you disdained all my *c* ....Prov 1:25
have none of my *c* ....Prov 1:30
Where there is no *c* ....Prov 11:14
C in the heart of man ....Prov 20:5
by wise *c* wage war ....Prov 20:18
whom did He take *c* ....Is 40:14
You are great in *c* ....Jer 32:19
according to the *c* ....Eph 1:11
immutability of His *c* ....Heb 6:17
I *c* you to buy from ....Rev 3:18

COUNSELOR
be called Wonderful, *C* ....Is 9:6
but there was no *c* ....Is 41:28
Has your *c* perished ....Mic 4:9
who has become His *c* ....Rom 11:34

COUNSELORS
c there is safety ....Prov 11:14

COUNT
c the people of Israel ....2 Sam 24:4
c my life dear to ....Acts 20:24
c me as a partner ....Philem 17
His promise, as some *c* ....2 Pet 3:9

COUNTED
Even a fool is *c* ....Prov 17:28
c as the small dust ....Is 40:15
the wages are not *c* ....Rom 4:4
He *c* me faithful ....1 Tim 1:12
who rule well be *c* ....1 Tim 5:17

COUNTENANCE
The LORD lift up His *c* ....Num 6:26
c they did not cast ....Job 29:24
up the light of Your *c* ....Ps 4:6
His *c* is like Lebanon ....Song 5:15
with a sad *c* ....Matt 6:16
His *c* was like ....Matt 28:3
of the glory of his *c* ....2 Cor 3:7
sword, and His *c* ....Rev 1:16

COUNTRY
"Get out of your *c* ....Gen 12:1
good news from a far *c* ....Prov 25:25
and went into a far *c* ....Matt 21:33
as in a foreign *c* ....Heb 11:9
that is, a heavenly *c* ....Heb 11:16

COURAGE
strong and of good *c* ....Deut 31:6
thanked God and took *c* ....Acts 28:15

COURT
appoint my day in *c* ....Job 9:19
by you or by a human *c* ....1 Cor 4:3
They zealously *c* ....Gal 4:17

COURTEOUS
be tenderhearted, be *c* ....1 Pet 3:8

COURTS
he may dwell in Your *c* ....Ps 65:4
even faints for the *c* ....Ps 84:2
flourish in the *c* ....Ps 92:13
and into His *c* ....Ps 100:4
drink it in My holy *c* ....Is 62:9

COVENANT
I will establish My *c* ....Gen 6:18
the LORD made a *c* ....Gen 15:18
for Me, behold, My *c* ....Gen 17:4
as a perpetual *c* ....Ex 31:16
it is a *c* of salt ....Num 18:19
Remember His *c* forever ......1 Chr 16:15
"I have made a *c* ....Job 31:1
will show them His *c* ....Ps 25:14
c shall stand firm ....Ps 89:28
sons will keep My *c* ....Ps 132:12
and give You as a *C* ....Is 42:6
the words of this *c* ....Jer 11:2
I will make a new *c* ....Jer 31:31
'I made a *c* with your ....Jer 34:13
I might break the *c* ....Zech 11:10
the Messenger of the *c* ....Mal 3:1
cup is the new *c* ....Luke 22:20
c that was confirmed ....Gal 3:17
Mediator of a better *c* ....Heb 8:6
c had been faultless ....Heb 8:7
He says, "A new *c* ....Heb 8:13
Mediator of the new *c* ....Heb 12:24
of the everlasting *c* ....Heb 13:20

COVENANTS
the glory, the *c* ....Rom 9:4
these are the two *c* ....Gal 4:24

COVER
the rock, and will *c* ....Ex 33:22
He shall *c* you with ....Ps 91:4
c Yourself with light ....Ps 104:2
LORD as the waters *c* ....Is 11:9
and will no more *c* ....Is 26:21
from the wind and a *c* ....Is 32:2
not to *c* his head ....1 Cor 11:7
c a multitude of sins ....James 5:20

COVERED
The depths have *c* ....Ex 15:5
c my transgressions as ....Job 31:33
Whose sin is *c* ....Ps 32:1
the wings of a dove *c* ....Ps 68:13
c all their sin ....Ps 85:2
You *c* me in my ....Ps 139:13
with two he *c* his face ....Is 6:2
of Jacob will be *c* ....Is 27:9
You have *c* Yourself ....Lam 3:44
For there is nothing *c* ....Matt 10:26

COVERING
spread a cloud for a *c* ....Ps 105:39
make sackcloth their *c* ....Is 50:3
given to her for a *c* ....1 Cor 11:15

COVERINGS
and made themselves *c* ....Gen 3:7

COVET
"You shall not *c* ....Ex 20:17
c fields and take them ....Mic 2:2
You murder and *c* ....James 4:2

COVETED
c no one's silver ....Acts 20:33

COVETOUS
nor thieves, nor *c* ....1 Cor 6:10
trained in *c* practices ....2 Pet 2:14

COVETOUSNESS
but he who hates *c* ....Prov 28:16
for nothing but your *c* ....Jer 22:17
heed and beware of *c* ....Luke 12:15
would not have known *c* ....Rom 7:7
all uncleanness or *c* ....Eph 5:3
conduct be without *c* ....Heb 13:5

COWARDLY
the *c*, unbelieving ....Rev 21:8

CRAFTINESS
wise in their own *c* ....Job 5:13
not walking in *c* ....2 Cor 4:2
deceived Eve by his *c* ....2 Cor 11:3
in the cunning *c* ....Eph 4:14

CRAFTSMAN
instructor of every *c* ....Gen 4:22
c encouraged the ....Is 41:7
c stretches out his ....Is 44:13

CRAFTY
Jonadab was a very *c* ....2 Sam 13:3
the devices of the *c* ....Job 5:12
They have taken *c* ....Ps 83:3

of a harlot, and a *c* ....Prov 7:10
Nevertheless, being *c* ....2 Cor 12:16

CREAM
she brought out *c* ....Judg 5:25
were bathed with *c* ....Job 29:6

CREATE
peace and *c* calamity ....Is 45:7
For behold, I *c* ....Is 65:17

CREATED
So God *c* man in His ....Gen 1:27
Spirit, they are *c* ....Ps 104:30
and they were *c* ....Ps 148:5
and see who has *c* ....Is 40:26
of Israel has *c* ....Is 41:20
For the LORD has *c* ....Jer 31:22
Has not one God *c* ....Mal 2:10
Nor was man *c* for the ....1 Cor 11:9
c in Christ Jesus ....Eph 2:10
hidden in God who *c* ....Eph 3:9
new man which was *c* ....Eph 4:24
Him all things were *c* ....Col 1:16
from foods which God *c* ....1 Tim 4:3
for You *c* all things ....Rev 4:11

CREATION
c which God ....Mark 13:19
c was subjected ....Rom 8:20
know that the whole *c* ....Rom 8:22
Christ, he is a new *c* ....2 Cor 5:17
anything, but a new *c* ....Gal 6:15
firstborn over all *c* ....Col 1:15

CREATOR
Remember now your *C* ....Eccl 12:1
God, the LORD, the *C* ....Is 40:28
rather than the *C* ....Rom 1:25
to a faithful *C* ....1 Pet 4:19

CREATURE
the gospel to every *c* ....Mark 16:15
For every *c* of God is ....1 Tim 4:4
And there is no *c* ....Heb 4:13
And every *c* which is ....Rev 5:13
and every living *c* ....Rev 16:3

CREATURES
created great sea *c* ....Gen 1:21
firstfruits of His *c* ....James 1:18
were four living *c* ....Rev 4:6

CREDIT
who love you, what *c* ....Luke 6:32
For what *c* is it if ....1 Pet 2:20

CREDITOR
Every *c* who has lent ....Deut 15:2
c is coming to take my ....2 Kin 4:1
c seize all that he ....Ps 109:11
There was a certain *c* ....Luke 7:41

CREEP
of the forest *c* ....Ps 104:20
sort are those who *c* ....2 Tim 3:6

CREEPING
c thing and beast of ....Gen 1:24
every sort of *c* thing ....Ezek 8:10

CRETE
Paul visits, Acts 27:7–21
Titus dispatched to, Titus 1:5
Inhabitants of, evil and lazy, Titus 1:12

CRIED
the poor who *c* out ....Job 29:12
They *c* to You ....Ps 22:5
of the depths I have *c* ....Ps 130:1

CRIES
your brother's blood *c* ....Gen 4:10
with vehement *c* ....Heb 5:7

CRIMES
land is filled with *c* ....Ezek 7:23

CRIMINALS
also two others, *c* ....Luke 23:32

CRISPUS
Chief ruler of synagogue of Corinth, Acts 18:8
Baptized by Paul, 1 Cor 1:14

CROOKED
turn aside to their *c* ....Ps 125:5
whose ways are *c* ....Prov 2:15
c places shall be made ....Is 40:4
c places straight ....Is 45:2
c places shall be made ....Luke 3:5
in the midst of a *c* ....Phil 2:15

CROSS
does not take his *c* ....Matt 10:38
to bear His *c* ....Matt 27:32
down from the *c* ....Matt 27:40
lest the *c* of Christ ....1 Cor 1:17
persecution for the *c* ....Gal 6:12
boast except in the *c* ....Gal 6:14
one body through the *c* ....Eph 2:16
the enemies of the *c* ....Phil 3:18
Him endured the *c* ....Heb 12:2

CROWN
You set a *c* of pure ....Ps 21:3
c the year with Your ....Ps 65:11
have profaned his *c* ....Ps 89:39
upon Himself His *c* ....Ps 132:18
The *c* of the wise is ....Prov 14:24
head is a *c* of glory ....Prov 16:31
Woe to the *c* of pride ....Is 28:1
hosts will be for a *c* ....Is 28:5
c has fallen from our ....Lam 5:16
they had twisted a *c* ....Matt 27:29
obtain a perishable *c* ....1 Cor 9:25
brethren, my joy and *c* ....Phil 4:1
laid up for me the *c* ....2 Tim 4:8
he will receive the *c* ....James 1:12
no one may take your *c* ....Rev 3:11
on His head a golden *c* ....Rev 14:14

CROWNED
angels, and You have *c* ....Ps 8:5
but the prudent are *c* ....Prov 14:18
athletics, he is not *c* ....2 Tim 2:5
You have *c* him with glory ....Heb 2:7

CROWNS
and they had *c* of gold ....Rev 4:4
on his horns ten *c* ....Rev 13:1
His head were many *c* ....Rev 19:12

CRUCIFIED
"Let Him be *c* ....Matt 27:22
Calvary, there they *c* ....Luke 23:33
lawless hands, have *c* ....Acts 2:23
that our old man was *c* ....Rom 6:6
Was Paul *c* for you ....1 Cor 1:13
Jesus Christ and Him *c* ....1 Cor 2:2
they would not have *c* ....1 Cor 2:8
though He was *c* ....2 Cor 13:4
I have been *c* ....Gal 2:20

CRUCIFY
out again, "*C* Him ....Mark 15:13
I have power to *c* You ....John 19:10
since they *c* again ....Heb 6:6

CRUEL
wrath, for it is *c* ....Gen 49:7
spirit and *c* bondage ....Ex 6:9
hate me with *c* hatred ....Ps 25:19
of the wicked are *c* ....Prov 12:10

CRUELTY
of *c* are in their ....Gen 49:5
the haunts of *c* ....Ps 74:20
c you have ruled ....Ezek 34:4

CRY
and their *c* came up to ....Ex 2:23
of oppressions they *c* ....Job 35:9
heart and my flesh *c* ....Ps 84:2
I *c* out with my whole ....Ps 119:145
Does not wisdom *c* ....Prov 8:1
"What shall I *c* ....Is 40:6
nor lift up a *c* ....Jer 7:16
c mightily to God ....Jon 3:8
at midnight a *c* ....Matt 25:6
His own elect who *c* ....Luke 18:7

CRYING
"The voice of one *c* ....Matt 3:3
nor sorrow, nor *c* ....Rev 21:4

CRYSTAL
nor *c* can equal it ....Job 28:17
your gates of *c* ....Is 54:12
of an awesome *c* ....Ezek 1:22
a sea of glass, like *c* ....Rev 4:6

CUBIT
shall finish it to a *c* ....Gen 6:16
can add one *c* ....Matt 6:27

CUCUMBERS
in Egypt, the *c* ....Num 11:5
a hut in a garden of *c* ....Is 1:8

CUNNING
the serpent was more *c* ....Gen 3:1
c comes quickly ....Job 5:13
c craftiness of deceitful ....Eph 4:14

CUP
My *c* runs over ....Ps 23:5
waters of a full *c* are ....Ps 73:10
the LORD there is a *c* ....Ps 75:8
I will take up the *c* ....Ps 116:13
the dregs of the *c* ....Is 51:17
men give them the *c* ....Jer 16:7
"Take this wine *c* ....Jer 25:15
The *c* of the LORD's ....Hab 2:16
make Jerusalem a *c* ....Zech 12:2
little ones only a *c* ....Matt 10:42
Then He took the *c* ....Matt 26:27
possible, let this *c* ....Matt 26:39
c is the new covenant ....Luke 22:20
cannot drink the *c* ....1 Cor 10:21
c is the new ....1 Cor 11:25
to give her the *c* ....Rev 16:19

CURE
but they could not *c* ....Matt 17:16
and to *c* diseases ....Luke 9:1

CURSE
c the ground for man's ....Gen 8:21
c a ruler of your ....Ex 22:28
You shall not *c* ....Lev 19:14
c this people for me ....Num 22:6
Balaam, "Neither *c* ....Num 23:25
your God turned the *c* ....Deut 23:5
said to him, '*C* David ....2 Sam 16:10
C God and die ....Job 2:9
mouth, but they *c* ....Ps 62:4
The *c* of the LORD is ....Prov 3:33
Do not *c* the king ....Eccl 10:20
do not *c* the rich ....Eccl 10:20
"I will send a *c* ....Mal 2:2
are cursed with a *c* ....Mal 3:9
law are under the *c* ....Gal 3:10

CURSED
c more than all cattle ....Gen 3:14
C is the man who ....Jer 17:5
c is he who keeps ....Jer 48:10
'Depart from Me, you *c* ....Matt 25:41
and near to being *c* ....Heb 6:8

CURSES
I will curse him who *c* ....Gen 12:3
'For everyone who *c* ....Lev 20:9
c his father or his ....Prov 20:20

CURSINGS
by the sword for the *c* . . . . Hos 7:16

CURTAIN
of each *c* shall be . . . . Ex 26:2
the heavens like a *c* . . . . Ps 104:2

CUSH
Ham's oldest son, 1 Chr 1:8–10
——— Another name for Ethiopia, Is 18:1

CUSHAN-RISHATHAIM
Mesopotamian king; oppresses Israel, Judg 3:8
Othniel delivers Israel from, Judg 3:9, 10

CUSTOM
to me, as Your *c* . . . . Ps 119:132
according to the *c* . . . . Acts 15:1
we have no such *c* . . . . 1 Cor 11:16

CUT
confidence shall be *c* . . . . Job 8:14
evildoers shall be *c* . . . . Ps 37:9
the wicked will be *c* . . . . Prov 2:22
causes you to sin, *c* . . . . Matt 5:30
and will *c* him in . . . . Matt 24:51
him whose ear Peter *c* . . . . John 18:26
He had his hair *c* . . . . Acts 18:18

CYMBAL
or a clanging *c* . . . . 1 Cor 13:1

CYPRUS
Mentioned in prophecies, Num 24:24; Is 23:1–12; Jer 2:10
Christians preach to Jews of, Acts 11:19, 20
Paul and Barnabas visit, Acts 13:4–13; 15:39

CYRENE
A Greek colonial city in North Africa; home of Simon the cross-bearer, Matt 27:32
Synagogue of, Acts 6:9
Christians from, become missionaries, Acts 11:20

CYRUS
King of Persia, referred to as God's anointed, Is 44:28—45:1

DAGON
The national god of the Philistines, Judg 16:23
Falls before ark, 1 Sam 5:1–5

DAILY
much as they gather *d* . . . . Ex 16:5
d He shall be . . . . Ps 72:15
to me, watching *d* . . . . Prov 8:34
Yet they seek Me *d* . . . . Is 58:2
Give us this day our *d* . . . . Matt 6:11
I sat *d* with you . . . . Matt 26:55
take up his cross *d* . . . . Luke 9:23
the Scriptures *d* . . . . Acts 17:11
our Lord, I die *d* . . . . 1 Cor 15:31
stands ministering *d* . . . . Heb 10:11

DALMATIA
A region east of the Adriatic Sea; Titus departs for, 2 Tim 4:10

DAMASCUS
Capital of Syria; captured by David; ruled by enemy kings, 2 Sam 8:5, 6; 1 Kin 11:23, 24; 15:18
Elisha's prophecy in, 2 Kin 8:7–15
Taken by Assyrians, 2 Kin 16:9
Prophecy concerning, Is 8:3, 4
Paul converted on road to; first preaches there, Acts 9:1–22
escapes from, 2 Cor 11:32, 33
revisits, Gal 1:17

DAN
Jacob's son by Bilhah, Gen 30:5, 6
Prophecy concerning, Gen 49:16, 17
——— Tribe of:
Numbered, Num 1:38, 39
Blessed, Deut 33:22
Receive their inheritance, Josh 19:40–47
Fall into idolatry, Judg 18:1–31
——— Town, northern boundary of Israel, Judg 20:1
Called Leshem; captured by Danites, Josh 19:47
Center of idolatry, 1 Kin 12:28–30
Destroyed by Ben-Hadad, 1 Kin 15:20

DANCE
and their children *d* . . . . Job 21:11
His name with the *d* . . . . Ps 149:3
mourn, and a time to *d* . . . . Eccl 3:4
d has turned into . . . . Lam 5:15
and you did not *d* . . . . Matt 11:17

DANCED
Then David *d* before . . . . 2 Sam 6:14
daughter of Herodias *d* . . . . Matt 14:6

DANCING
saw the calf and the *d* . . . . Ex 32:19
me my mourning into *d* . . . . Ps 30:11
he heard music and *d* . . . . Luke 15:25

DANIEL
Taken to Babylon; refuses Nebuchadnezzar's foods, Dan 1
Interprets dreams; honored by king, Dan 2
Interprets handwriting on wall; honored by Belshazzar, Dan 5:10–29
Appointed to high office; conspired against and thrown to lions, Dan 6:1–23
Visions of four beasts, ram and goat, Dan 7; 8
Intercedes for Israel, Dan 9:1–19
Further visions, Dan 9:20—12:13

DARIUS
Darius the Mede, son of Ahasuerus; made king of the Chaldeans, Dan 9:1
Succeeds Belshazzar, Dan 5:30, 31
Co-ruler with Cyrus, Dan 6:28
——— Darius Hystaspis (522–486 B.C.), king of all Persia; temple work dated by his reign, Ezra 4:5, 24
Confirms Cyrus's royal edict, Ezra 6:1–14
——— Darius the Persian (423–404 B.C.); priestly records kept during his reign, Neh 12:22

DARK
dwell in the *d* cloud . . . . 1 Kin 8:12
I am *d* . . . . Song 1:5
d place of the earth . . . . Is 45:19
d places like the dead . . . . Lam 3:6
and makes the day *d* . . . . Amos 5:8
and the day shall be *d* . . . . Mic 3:6
I tell you in the *d* . . . . Matt 10:27
while it was still *d* . . . . John 20:1
shines in a *d* place . . . . 2 Pet 1:19

DARKENED
so that the land was *d* . . . . Ex 10:15
Let their eyes be *d* . . . . Ps 69:23
their understanding *d* . . . . Eph 4:18

DARKNESS
d He called Night . . . . Gen 1:5
shall enlighten my *d* . . . . 2 Sam 22:29
through the deep *d* . . . . Job 22:13
Those who sat in *d* . . . . Ps 107:10
d shall not hide . . . . Ps 139:12
d have seen a . . . . Is 9:2
I will make *d* light . . . . Is 42:16
and deep *d* the people . . . . Is 60:2
Israel, or a land of *d* . . . . Jer 2:31
body will be full of *d* . . . . Matt 6:23
cast out into outer *d* . . . . Matt 8:12
and the power of *d* . . . . Luke 22:53
d rather than light . . . . John 3:19
d does not know . . . . John 12:35
For you were once *d* . . . . Eph 5:8
the rulers of the *d* . . . . Eph 6:12
us from the power of *d* . . . . Col 1:13
of the night nor of *d* . . . . 1 Thess 5:5
and to blackness and *d* . . . . Heb 12:18
called you out of *d* . . . . 1 Pet 2:9
d is reserved . . . . 2 Pet 2:17
and in Him is no *d* . . . . 1 John 1:5
Him, and walk in *d* . . . . 1 John 1:6
d is passing away . . . . 1 John 2:8
blackness of *d* forever . . . . Jude 13

DATHAN
Joins Korah's rebellion, Num 16:1–35
Swallowed up by the earth, Ps 106:17

DAUGHTER
had neither son nor *d* . . . . Judg 11:34
"Rejoice greatly, O *d* . . . . Zech 9:9
"Fear not, *d* of Zion . . . . John 12:15
the son of Pharaoh's *d* . . . . Heb 11:24

DAUGHTERS
he had sons and *d* . . . . Gen 5:4
of God saw the *d* . . . . Gen 6:2
a bird, and all the *d* . . . . Eccl 12:4
d shall prophesy . . . . Acts 2:17
man had four virgin *d* . . . . Acts 21:9
shall be My sons and *d* . . . . 2 Cor 6:18

DAVID
Anointed by Samuel, 1 Sam 16:1–13
Becomes royal harpist, 1 Sam 16:14–23
Defeats Goliath, 1 Sam 17
Makes covenant with Jonathan, 1 Sam 18:1–4
Honored by Saul; loved by the people; Saul becomes jealous, 1 Sam 18:5–16
Wins Michal as wife, 1 Sam 18:17–30
Flees from Saul, 1 Sam 19; 20; 21:10—22:5; 23:14–29
Eats the holy bread, 1 Sam 21:1–6; Matt 12:3, 4
Saves Keilah from Philistines, 1 Sam 23:1–13
Twice spares Saul's life, 1 Sam 24:1–22; 26:1–25
Anger at Nabal appeased by Abigail; marries her, 1 Sam 25:2–42
Allies with the Philistines, 1 Sam 27:1—28:2
Rejected by them, 1 Sam 29
Avenges destruction of Ziklag, 1 Sam 30
Mourns death of Saul and Jonathan, 2 Sam 1
Anointed king of Judah, 2 Sam 2:1–7
War with Saul's house; Abner defects to David, 2 Sam 3:1, 6–21
Mourns Abner's death, 2 Sam 3:28–39
Punishes Ishbosheth's murderers, 2 Sam 4
Anointed king of all Israel, 2 Sam 5:1–5
Conquers Jerusalem; makes it his capital, 2 Sam 5:6–16
Defeats Philistines, 2 Sam 5:17–25
Brings ark to Jerusalem, 2 Sam 6
Receives eternal covenant, 2 Sam 7
Further conquests, 2 Sam 8; 10
Shows mercy to Mephibosheth, 2 Sam 9
Commits adultery and murder, 2 Sam 11
Rebuked by Nathan; repents, 2 Sam 12:1–23; Ps 32; 51
Absalom's rebellion, 2 Sam 15—18
Mourns Absalom's death, 2 Sam 18:33—19:8
Shows himself merciful, 2 Sam 19:18–39
Sheba's rebellion, 2 Sam 19:40—20:22

Avenges the Gibeonites, 2 Sam 21:1–14
Song of deliverance, 2 Sam 22
Sins by numbering the people, 2 Sam 24:1–17
Buys threshing floor to build altar, 2 Sam 24:18–25
Secures Solomon's succession, 1 Kin 1:5–53
Instructions to Solomon, 1 Kin 2:1–11
Last words, 2 Sam 23:1–7
Inspired by Spirit, Matt 22:43
As prophet, Acts 2:29–34
Faith of, Heb 11:32–34

DAY

God called the light *D* .... Gen 1:5
and *d* and night .... Gen 8:22
shall observe this *d* .... Ex 12:17
Remember the Sabbath *d* .... Ex 20:8
and cursed the *d* .... Job 3:1
d utters speech .... Ps 19:2
For a *d* in Your courts .... Ps 84:10
d the LORD has .... Ps 118:24
not strike you by *d* .... Ps 121:6
night shines as the *d* .... Ps 139:12
do not know what a *d* .... Prov 27:1
For the *d* of the LORD .... Joel 2:11
who put far off the *d* .... Amos 6:3
for the *d* of the LORD .... Zeph 1:7
who has despised the *d* .... Zech 4:10
who can endure the *d* .... Mal 3:2
d our daily bread .... Matt 6:11
and Gomorrah in the *d* .... Matt 10:15
sent Me while it is *d* .... John 9:4
great and awesome *d* .... Acts 2:20
person esteems one *d* .... Rom 14:5
D will declare it .... 1 Cor 3:13
again the third *d* .... 1 Cor 15:4
perfectly that the *d* .... 1 Thess 5:2
and sons of the *d* .... 1 Thess 5:5
with the Lord one *d* .... 2 Pet 3:8

DAYS

d are swifter than a .... Job 7:6
Let me alone, for my *d* .... Job 7:16
of woman is of few *d* .... Job 14:1
blessed the latter *d* .... Job 42:12
The *d* of our lives are .... Ps 90:10
for length of *d* .... Prov 3:2
"Why were the former *d* .... Eccl 7:10
Before the difficult *d* .... Eccl 12:1
and tested them ten *d* .... Dan 1:14
had shortened those *d* .... Mark 13:20
raise it up in three *d* .... John 2:20
You observe *d* and .... Gal 4:10
life and see good *d* .... 1 Pet 3:10

DEACONS

with the bishops and *d* .... Phil 1:1
d must be reverent .... 1 Tim 3:8
d be the husbands .... 1 Tim 3:12

DEAD

"We shall all be *d* .... Ex 12:33
he stood between the *d* .... Num 16:48
work wonders for the *d* .... Ps 88:10
who have long been *d* .... Ps 143:3
But the *d* know nothing .... Eccl 9:5
shall cast out the *d* .... Is 26:19
d bury their own *d* .... Matt 8:22
d are raised up and .... Matt 11:5
not the God of the *d* .... Matt 22:32
for this my son was *d* .... Luke 15:24
d will hear the voice .... John 5:25
was raised from the *d* .... Rom 6:4
yourselves to be *d* .... Rom 6:11
from the law sin was *d* .... Rom 7:8
be Lord of both the *d* .... Rom 14:9
resurrection of the *d* .... 1 Cor 15:12
baptized for the *d* .... 1 Cor 15:29
made alive, who were *d* .... Eph 2:1
And the *d* in Christ .... 1 Thess 4:16
d while she lives .... 1 Tim 5:6
without works is *d* .... James 2:26
d did not live again .... Rev 20:5
And the *d* were judged .... Rev 20:12

DEAD SEA

Called the:
Salt Sea, Gen 14:3
Sea of the Arabah, Deut 3:17

DEADLY

they drink anything *d* .... Mark 16:18
evil, full of *d* poison .... James 3:8
d wound was healed .... Rev 13:3

DEADNESS

the *d* of Sarah's womb .... Rom 4:19

DEAF

makes the mute, the *d* .... Ex 4:11
d shall hear the words .... Is 29:18
d shall be unstopped .... Is 35:5
d as My messenger .... Is 42:19
d who have ears .... Is 43:8
their ears shall be *d* .... Mic 7:16
are cleansed and the *d* .... Matt 11:5

DEATH

Let me die the *d* .... Num 23:10
d parts you and me .... Ruth 1:17
and the shadow of *d* .... Job 10:21
You will bring me to *d* .... Job 30:23
For in *d* there is no .... Ps 6:5
I sleep the sleep of *d* .... Ps 13:3
of the shadow of *d* .... Ps 23:4
my soul from *d* .... Ps 56:13
can live and not see *d* .... Ps 89:48
house leads down to *d* .... Prov 2:18
who hate me love *d* .... Prov 8:36
D and life are in the .... Prov 18:21
swallow up *d* forever .... Is 25:8
no pleasure in the *d* .... Ezek 18:32
redeem them from *d* .... Hos 13:14
turns the shadow of *d* .... Amos 5:8
who shall not taste *d* .... Matt 16:28
but has passed from *d* .... John 5:24
he shall never see *d* .... John 8:51
Nevertheless *d* reigned .... Rom 5:14
as sin reigned in *d* .... Rom 5:21
D no longer has .... Rom 6:9
the wages of sin is *d* .... Rom 6:23
to bear fruit to *d* .... Rom 7:5
proclaim the Lord's *d* .... 1 Cor 11:26
since by man came *d* .... 1 Cor 15:21
D is swallowed up in .... 1 Cor 15:54
The sting of *d* is sin .... 1 Cor 15:56
we are the aroma of *d* .... 2 Cor 2:16
d is working in us .... 2 Cor 4:12
the world produces *d* .... 2 Cor 7:10
to the point of *d* .... Phil 2:8
d crowned with glory .... Heb 2:9
who had the power of *d* .... Heb 2:14
that he did not see *d* .... Heb 11:5
brings forth *d* .... James 1:15
to God, being put to *d* .... 1 Pet 3:18
is sin leading to *d* .... 1 John 5:16
Be faithful until *d* .... Rev 2:10
Over such the second *d* .... Rev 20:6
shall be no more *d* .... Rev 21:4
which is the second *d* .... Rev 21:8

DEBIR

City of Judah; captured by Joshua, Josh 10:38, 39
Recaptured by Othniel; formerly called Kirjath Sepher, Josh 15:15–17; Judg 1:11–13

DEBORAH

A prophetess and judge, Judg 4:4–14
Composed song of triumph, Judg 5:1–31

DEBTOR

I am a *d* both to .... Rom 1:14
that he is a *d* to keep .... Gal 5:3

DEBTORS

as we forgive our *d* .... Matt 6:12
of his master's *d* .... Luke 16:5
brethren, we are *d* .... Rom 8:12
and they are their *d* .... Rom 15:27

DECEIT

spirit there is no *d* .... Ps 32:2
from speaking *d* .... Ps 34:13
d shall not dwell .... Ps 101:7
D is in the heart of .... Prov 12:20
Nor was any *d* in His .... Is 53:9
They hold fast to *d* .... Jer 8:5
in whom is no *d* .... John 1:47
"O full of all *d* .... Acts 13:10
philosophy and empty *d* .... Col 2:8
no sin, nor was *d* .... 1 Pet 2:22
mouth was found no *d* .... Rev 14:5

DECEITFUL

deliver me from the *d* .... Ps 43:1
d men shall not .... Ps 55:23
of the wicked are *d* .... Prov 12:5
of an enemy are *d* .... Prov 27:6
"The heart is *d* .... Jer 17:9
are false apostles, *d* .... 2 Cor 11:13

DECEITFULLY

an idol, nor sworn *d* .... Ps 24:4
the word of God *d* .... 2 Cor 4:2

DECEITFULNESS

this world and the *d* .... Matt 13:22
hardened through the *d* .... Heb 3:13

DECEIVE

'Do not *d* yourselves .... Jer 37:9
rise up and *d* many .... Matt 24:11
wonders to *d* .... Matt 24:24
Let no one *d* himself .... 1 Cor 3:18
Let no one *d* you with .... Eph 5:6
we have no sin, we *d* .... 1 John 1:8

DECEIVED

"The serpent *d* .... Gen 3:13
d heart has turned him .... Is 44:20
by the commandment, *d* .... Rom 7:11
as the serpent *d* .... 2 Cor 11:3
but the woman being *d* .... 1 Tim 2:14
deceiving and being *d* .... 2 Tim 3:13

DECEIVER

"But cursed be the *d* .... Mal 1:14
how that *d* said .... Matt 27:63
This is a *d* and an .... 2 John 7

DECENTLY

all things be done *d* .... 1 Cor 14:40

DECISION

but its every *d* .... Prov 16:33
in the valley of *d* .... Joel 3:14

DECLARE

The heavens *d* the .... Ps 19:1
d Your name to My .... Ps 22:22
d what He had done .... Ps 66:16
d that the LORD is .... Ps 92:15
d His generation .... Is 53:8
"I will *d* Your name .... Heb 2:12
seen and heard we *d* .... 1 John 1:3

DECLARED

the Father, He has *d* .... John 1:18
and *d* to be the Son of .... Rom 1:4

DECREE

"I will declare the *d* .... Ps 2:7
d which shall not pass .... Ps 148:6
in those days that a *d* .... Luke 2:1

DEDICATED

house and has not *d* .... Deut 20:5

every *d* thing in ....Ezek 44:29
first covenant was *d* ....Heb 9:18

DEDICATION
sacrifices at the *d* ....Ezra 6:17
it was the Feast of *D* ....John 10:22

DEED
d has been done ....Judg 19:30
you do a charitable *d* ....Matt 6:2
you do in word or *d* ....Col 3:17

DEEDS
Declare His *d* among ....Ps 9:11
vengeance on their *d* ....Ps 99:8
harlot by their own *d* ....Ps 106:39
declare His *d* among ....Is 12:4
they surpass the *d* ....Jer 5:28
because their *d* ....John 3:19
You do the *d* ....John 8:41
one according to his *d* ....Rom 2:6
you put to death the *d* ....Rom 8:13
shares in his evil *d* ....2 John 11

DEEP
LORD God caused a *d* ....Gen 2:21
He lays up the *d* ....Ps 33:7
D calls unto *d* ....Ps 42:7
In His hand are the *d* ....Ps 95:4
His wonders in the *d* ....Ps 107:24
put out in *d* darkness ....Prov 20:20
led them through the *d* ....Is 63:13
d closed around me ....Jon 2:5
d uttered its voice ....Hab 3:10
"Launch out into the *d* ....Luke 5:4
I have been in the *d* ....2 Cor 11:25

DEER
"Naphtali is a *d* ....Gen 49:21
As the *d* pants for the ....Ps 42:1
shall leap like a *d* ....Is 35:6

DEFEND
'For I will *d* this ....2 Kin 19:34
d my own ways before ....Job 13:15
D the poor and ....Ps 82:3
d the fatherless ....Is 1:17
of hosts *d* Jerusalem ....Is 31:5

DEFENDER
a *d* of widows ....Ps 68:5

DEFENSE
For wisdom is a *d* ....Eccl 7:12
d will be the ....Is 33:16
am appointed for the *d* ....Phil 1:17
d no one stood with me ....2 Tim 4:16
be ready to give a *d* ....1 Pet 3:15

DEFILE
the heart, and they *d* ....Matt 15:18
also these dreamers *d* ....Jude 8

DEFILED
d the dwelling place ....Ps 74:7
For your hands are *d* ....Is 59:3
lest they should be *d* ....John 18:28
to those who are *d* ....Titus 1:15
and conscience are *d* ....Titus 1:15
even the garment *d* ....Jude 23

DEFILES
mouth, this *d* a man ....Matt 15:11
d the temple of God ....1 Cor 3:17
it anything that *d* ....Rev 21:27

DEFRAUD
d his brother in this ....1 Thess 4:6

DEGENERATE
before Me into the *d* ....Jer 2:21
d is your heart ....Ezek 16:30

DEGREES
go forward ten *d* ....2 Kin 20:9

DELICACIES
let me eat of their *d* ....Ps 141:4

Do not desire his *d* ....Prov 23:3
of the king's *d* ....Dan 1:5

DELICATE
be called tender and *d* ....Is 47:1
a lovely and *d* woman ....Jer 6:2

DELIGHT
the LORD as great *d* ....1 Sam 15:22
And his heart took *d* ....2 Chr 17:6
Will he *d* himself in ....Job 27:10
But his *d* is in the ....Ps 1:2
D yourself also in the ....Ps 37:4
I *d* to do Your will ....Ps 40:8
Your law had been my *d* ....Ps 119:92
d ourselves with love ....Prov 7:18
And I was daily His *d* ....Prov 8:30
truthfully are His *d* ....Prov 12:22
And let your soul *d* ....Is 55:2
call the Sabbath a *d* ....Is 58:13
For I *d* in the law of ....Rom 7:22

DELIGHTS
O love, with your *d* ....Song 7:6
For the LORD *d* in you ....Is 62:4
forever, because He *d* ....Mic 7:18

DELILAH
Deceives Samson, Judg 16:4–22

DELIVER
d them out of the hand ....Ex 3:8
He shall *d* you in six ....Job 5:19
is no one who can *d* ....Job 10:7
'*D* him from going down ....Job 33:24
Let Him *d* Him ....Ps 22:8
d their soul from ....Ps 33:19
I will *d* him and honor ....Ps 91:15
d you from the immoral ....Prov 2:16
wickedness will not *d* ....Eccl 8:8
have I no power to *d* ....Is 50:2
we serve is able to *d* ....Dan 3:17
into temptation, but *d* ....Matt 6:13
let Him *d* Him now if ....Matt 27:43
d such a one to Satan ....1 Cor 5:5
And the Lord will *d* ....2 Tim 4:18
d the godly out of ....2 Pet 2:9

DELIVERANCE
d He gives to His king ....Ps 18:50
but *d* is of the LORD ....Prov 21:31
not accepting *d* ....Heb 11:35

DELIVERED
d the poor who cried ....Job 29:12
for You have *d* my soul ....Ps 56:13
For He has *d* the life ....Jer 20:13
All things have been *d* ....Matt 11:27
who was *d* up because ....Rom 4:25
But now we have been *d* ....Rom 7:6
who *d* us from so great ....2 Cor 1:10
was once for all *d* ....Jude 3

DELIVERER
the LORD raised up a *d* ....Judg 3:9
LORD gave Israel a *d* ....2 Kin 13:5
D will come out of ....Rom 11:26

DELIVERS
d the kingdom to God ....1 Cor 15:24
even Jesus who *d* ....1 Thess 1:10

DEMAS
Follows Paul, Col 4:14
Forsakes Paul, 2 Tim 4:10

DEMETRIUS
A silversmith at Ephesus, Acts 19:24–31
—— A good Christian, 3 John 12

DEMON
Jesus rebuked the *d* ....Matt 17:18
you say, 'He has a *d* ....Luke 7:33
and have a *d* ....John 8:48

DEMONS
They sacrificed to *d* ....Deut 32:17
their daughters to *d* ....Ps 106:37
authority over all *d* ....Luke 9:1
the *d* are subject ....Luke 10:17
Lord and the cup of *d* ....1 Cor 10:21
Even the *d* believe ....James 2:19
a dwelling place of *d* ....Rev 18:2

DEMONSTRATE
faith, to *d* His ....Rom 3:25

DEMONSTRATES
d His own love toward ....Rom 5:8

DEN
in the viper's *d* ....Is 11:8
by My name, become a *d* ....Jer 7:11
cast him into the *d* ....Dan 6:16
it a '*d* of thieves ....Matt 21:13

DENARIUS
the laborers for a *d* ....Matt 20:2
they brought Him a *d* ....Matt 22:19
quart of wheat for a *d* ....Rev 6:6

DENIED
before men will be *d* ....Luke 12:9
Peter then *d* again ....John 18:27
d the Holy One and the ....Acts 3:14
things cannot be *d* ....Acts 19:36
household, he has *d* ....1 Tim 5:8
word, and have not *d* ....Rev 3:8

DENIES
But whoever *d* ....Matt 10:33
d that Jesus is the ....1 John 2:22

DENS
lie down in their *d* ....Ps 104:22
and mountains, in *d* ....Heb 11:38

DENY
lest I be full and *d* ....Prov 30:9
let him *d* himself ....Matt 16:24
He cannot *d* Himself ....2 Tim 2:13
in works they *d* ....Titus 1:16
d the only Lord ....Jude 4
d My faith even ....Rev 2:13

DENYING
but *d* its power ....2 Tim 3:5
d ungodliness and ....Titus 2:12
d the Lord who bought ....2 Pet 2:1

DEPART
scepter shall not *d* ....Gen 49:10
they say to God, '*D* ....Job 21:14
D from evil ....Ps 34:14
fear the LORD and *d* ....Prov 3:7
the mountains, shall *d* ....Is 54:10
on the left hand, '*D* ....Matt 25:41
will *d* from the faith ....1 Tim 4:1

DEPARTURE
d savage wolves will ....Acts 20:29
and the time of my *d* ....2 Tim 4:6

DEPRESSION
of man causes *d* ....Prov 12:25

DEPRIVE
d myself of good ....Eccl 4:8
d one another except ....1 Cor 7:5

DEPTH
because they had no *d* ....Matt 13:5
nor height nor *d* ....Rom 8:39
Oh, the *d* of the ....Rom 11:33
width and length and *d* ....Eph 3:18

DEPTHS
d have covered them ....Ex 15:5
The *d* also trembled ....Ps 77:16
my soul from the *d* ....Ps 86:13
led them through the *d* ....Ps 106:9
go down again to the *d* ....Ps 107:26

d I was brought forth .... Prov 8:24
our sins into the *d* .... Mic 7:19
have not known the *d* .... Rev 2:24

DERBE
Paul visits, Acts 14:6, 20
Paul meets Timothy at, Acts 16:1

DERISION
shall hold them in *d* .... Ps 2:4
I am in *d* daily .... Jer 20:7

DESCEND
His glory shall not *d* .... Ps 49:17
d now from the cross .... Mark 15:32
Lord Himself will *d* .... 1 Thess 4:16
This wisdom does not *d* .... James 3:15

DESCENDANTS
All you *d* of Jacob .... Ps 22:23
d shall inherit the .... Ps 25:13
In the LORD all the *d* .... Is 45:25
"We are Abraham's *d* .... John 8:33

DESCENDED
because the LORD *d* .... Ex 19:18
that He also first *d* .... Eph 4:9
He who *d* is also the .... Eph 4:10

DESCENDING
were ascending and *d* .... Gen 28:12
"I saw the Spirit *d* .... John 1:32
God ascending and *d* .... John 1:51
the holy Jerusalem, *d* .... Rev 21:10

DESERT
d shall rejoice .... Is 35:1
and rivers in the *d* .... Is 43:19
'Look, He is in the *d* .... Matt 24:26

DESERTED
d place by Himself .... Matt 14:13

DESERTS
led them through the *d* .... Is 48:21
They wandered in *d* .... Heb 11:38

DESERVE
to them what they *d* .... Ps 28:4
d I will judge them .... Ezek 7:27

DESIGN
with an artistic *d* .... Ex 26:31
may keep its whole *d* .... Ezek 43:11

DESIRABLE
the eyes, and a tree *d* .... Gen 3:6
d that we should leave .... Acts 6:2

DESIRE
d shall be for your .... Gen 3:16
for we do not *d* .... Job 21:14
him his heart's *d* .... Ps 21:2
Behold, You *d* truth in .... Ps 51:6
upon earth that I *d* .... Ps 73:25
the *d* of the wicked .... Ps 112:10
and satisfy the *d* .... Ps 145:16
The *d* of the lazy .... Prov 21:25
a burden, and *d* fails .... Eccl 12:5
the *d* of our soul is .... Is 26:8
d I have desired .... Luke 22:15
"Father, I *d* that .... John 17:24
all manner of evil *d* .... Rom 7:8
Brethren, my heart's *d* .... Rom 10:1
d the best gifts .... 1 Cor 12:31
d spiritual gifts .... 1 Cor 14:1
the two, having a *d* .... Phil 1:23
passion, evil *d* .... Col 3:5
d has conceived .... James 1:15

DESIRED
d are they than gold .... Ps 19:10
One thing I have *d* .... Ps 27:4
guides them to their *d* .... Ps 107:30
What is *d* in a man is .... Prov 19:22
Whatever my eyes *d* .... Eccl 2:10
desire I have *d* .... Luke 22:15

DESIRES
Who is the man who *d* .... Ps 34:12
shall give you the *d* .... Ps 37:4
the devil, and the *d* .... John 8:44
fulfilling the *d* .... Eph 2:3
not come from your *d* .... James 4:1

DESOLATE
on me, for I am *d* .... Ps 25:16
the wilderness in a *d* .... Ps 107:4
my children and am *d* .... Is 49:21
any more be termed *D* .... Is 62:4
to make your land *d* .... Jer 4:7
house is left to you *d* .... Matt 23:38
one hour she is made *d* .... Rev 18:19

DESOLATION
the 'abomination of *d* .... Matt 24:15
then know that its *d* .... Luke 21:20

DESPAIRED
turned my heart and *d* .... Eccl 2:20
strength, so that we *d* .... 2 Cor 1:8

DESPISE
if you *d* My statutes .... Lev 26:15
d Me shall be lightly .... 1 Sam 2:30
d your mother when she .... Prov 23:22
d your feast days .... Amos 5:21
to you priests who *d* .... Mal 1:6
one and *d* the other .... Matt 6:24
d the riches of His .... Rom 2:4
d the church of God .... 1 Cor 11:22
and *d* authority .... 2 Pet 2:10

DESPISED
poor man's wisdom is *d* .... Eccl 9:16
d the word of the Holy .... Is 5:24
He is *d* and rejected .... Is 53:3
the things which are *d* .... 1 Cor 1:28

DESPISES
wisdom *d* his neighbor .... Prov 11:12
d the word will be .... Prov 13:13
d his neighbor sins .... Prov 14:21
but a foolish man *d* .... Prov 15:20
d the scepter of My .... Ezek 21:10

DESPISING
the cross, *d* the shame .... Heb 12:2

DESTITUTE
the prayer of the *d* .... Ps 102:17
of corrupt minds and *d* .... 1 Tim 6:5
sister is naked and *d* .... James 2:15

DESTROY
d the righteous .... Gen 18:23
d all the wicked .... Ps 101:8
of the LORD I will *d* .... Ps 118:10
the wicked He will *d* .... Ps 145:20
Why should you *d* .... Eccl 7:16
shall not hurt nor *d* .... Is 11:9
have mercy, but will *d* .... Jer 13:14
d them with double .... Jer 17:18
I did not come to *d* .... Matt 5:17
Him who is able to *d* .... Matt 10:28
Barabbas and *d* Jesus .... Matt 27:20
d this temple .... Mark 14:58
to save life or to *d* .... Luke 6:9
d men's lives but to .... Luke 9:56
d the work of God for .... Rom 14:20
d the wisdom of the .... 1 Cor 1:19
foods, but God will *d* .... 1 Cor 6:13
able to save and to *d* .... James 4:12

DESTROYED
d all living things .... Gen 7:23
d those who hated me .... 2 Sam 22:41
My people are *d* .... Hos 4:6
"O Israel, you are *d* .... Hos 13:9
house, this tent, is *d* .... 2 Cor 5:1

DESTROYER
the paths of the *d* .... Ps 17:4
him who is a great *d* .... Prov 18:9
destroyed by the *d* .... 1 Cor 10:10

DESTRUCTION
not be afraid of *d* .... Job 5:21
D has no covering .... Job 26:6
d come upon him .... Ps 35:8
cast them down to *d* .... Ps 73:18
You turn man to *d* .... Ps 90:3
d that lays waste .... Ps 91:6
your life from *d* .... Ps 103:4
d will come to the .... Prov 10:29
Pride goes before *d* .... Prov 16:18
d the heart of a man .... Prov 18:12
called the City of *D* .... Is 19:18
neither wasting nor *d* .... Is 60:18
heifer, but *d* comes .... Jer 46:20
wrath prepared for *d* .... Rom 9:22
one to Satan for the *d* .... 1 Cor 5:5
whose end is *d* .... Phil 3:19
then sudden *d* .... 1 Thess 5:3
with everlasting *d* .... 2 Thess 1:9
which drown men in *d* .... 1 Tim 6:9
twist to their own *d* .... 2 Pet 3:16

DETERMINED
Since his days are *d* .... Job 14:5
of hosts will make a *d* .... Is 10:23
"Seventy weeks are *d* .... Dan 9:24
d their preappointed .... Acts 17:26
For I *d* not to know .... 1 Cor 2:2

DEVIL
to be tempted by the *d* .... Matt 4:1
prepared for the *d* .... Matt 25:41
forty days by the *d* .... Luke 4:2
then the *d* comes and .... Luke 8:12
and one of you is a *d* .... John 6:70
of your father the *d* .... John 8:44
d having already put .... John 13:2
give place to the *d* .... Eph 4:27
the wiles of the *d* .... Eph 6:11
the snare of the *d* .... 2 Tim 2:26
Resist the *d* and he .... James 4:7
the works of the *d* .... 1 John 3:8
contending with the *d* .... Jude 9
Indeed, the *d* is about .... Rev 2:10

DEVISE
Do not *d* evil against .... Prov 3:29
Woe to those who *d* .... Mic 2:1

DEVISES
d wickedness on his .... Ps 36:4
he *d* evil continually .... Prov 6:14
d wicked plans to .... Is 32:7
But a generous man *d* .... Is 32:8

DEVOTED
d offering is most .... Lev 27:28
"Every *d* thing in .... Num 18:14
Your servant, who is *d* .... Ps 119:38

DEVOUR
A fire shall *d* before .... Ps 50:3
For you *d* widows' .... Matt 23:14
bite and *d* one another .... Gal 5:15
seeking whom he may *d* .... 1 Pet 5:8
d her Child as .... Rev 12:4

DEVOURED
Some wild beast has *d* .... Gen 37:20
rebel, you shall be *d* .... Is 1:20
the curse has *d* .... Is 24:6
Your sword has *d* .... Jer 2:30
For shame has *d* .... Jer 3:24
have *d* their judges .... Hos 7:7
trees, the locust *d* .... Amos 4:9
birds came and *d* them .... Matt 13:4
of heaven and *d* them .... Rev 20:9

DEVOURING
You love all *d* words .... Ps 52:4
the flame of *d* fire .... Is 29:6

DISSOLVED
of heaven shall be *d* . . . . . Is 34:4
the heavens will be *d* . . . . . 2 Pet 3:12

DISTINCTION
and made no *d* . . . . . Acts 15:9
For there is no *d* . . . . . Rom 10:12
compassion, making a *d* . . . . . Jude 22

DISTRESS
me in the day of my *d* . . . . . Gen 35:3
When you are in *d* . . . . . Deut 4:30
my life from every *d* . . . . . 1 Kin 1:29
you out of dire *d* . . . . . Job 36:16
keep you from *d* . . . . . Job 36:19
d them in His deep . . . . . Ps 2:5
on the LORD in *d* . . . . . Ps 118:5
a whirlwind, when *d* . . . . . Prov 1:27
and on the earth *d* . . . . . Luke 21:25
tribulation, or *d* . . . . . Rom 8:35
of the present *d* . . . . . 1 Cor 7:26

DISTRESSED
heart within me is *d* . . . . . Ps 143:4
troubled and deeply *d* . . . . . Mark 14:33

DISTRESSES
bring me out of my *d* . . . . . Ps 25:17

DISTRIBUTE
that you have and *d* . . . . . Luke 18:22

DISTRIBUTED
and they *d* to each as . . . . . Acts 4:35
But as God has *d* . . . . . 1 Cor 7:17

DISTRIBUTING
d to the needs of the . . . . . Rom 12:13

DIVERSITIES
There are *d* . . . . . 1 Cor 12:4

DIVIDE
D the living child . . . . . 1 Kin 3:25
d their tongues . . . . . Ps 55:9
d the spoil with the . . . . . Prov 16:19
d the inheritance . . . . . Luke 12:13
"Take this and *d* . . . . . Luke 22:17

DIVIDED
and the waters were *d* . . . . . Ex 14:21
death they were not *d* . . . . . 2 Sam 1:23
And You *d* the sea . . . . . Neh 9:11
"Who has *d* a channel . . . . . Job 38:25
shall they ever be *d* . . . . . Ezek 37:22
kingdom has been *d* . . . . . Dan 5:28
your land shall be *d* . . . . . Amos 7:17
"Every kingdom *d* . . . . . Matt 12:25
and a house *d* against . . . . . Luke 11:17
in one house will be *d* . . . . . Luke 12:52
So he *d* to them his . . . . . Luke 15:12
appeared to them *d* . . . . . Acts 2:3
d them among all . . . . . Acts 2:45
Is Christ *d* . . . . . 1 Cor 1:13
the great city was *d* . . . . . Rev 16:19

DIVIDING
rightly *d* the word of . . . . . 2 Tim 2:15

DIVINATION
shall you practice *d* . . . . . Lev 19:26
D is on . . . . . Prov 16:10
darkness without *d* . . . . . Mic 3:6
a spirit of *d* met us . . . . . Acts 16:16

DIVINE
futility and who *d* . . . . . Ezek 13:9
and her prophets *d* . . . . . Mic 3:11
d service and the . . . . . Heb 9:1
d power has given . . . . . 2 Pet 1:3

DIVINERS
your prophets, your *d* . . . . . Jer 27:9

DIVISION
So there was a *d* . . . . . John 7:43
piercing even to the *d* . . . . . Heb 4:12

DIVISIONS
note those who cause *d* . . . . . Rom 16:17
and that there be no *d* . . . . . 1 Cor 1:10
envy, strife, and *d* . . . . . 1 Cor 3:3
hear that there are *d* . . . . . 1 Cor 11:18
persons, who cause *d* . . . . . Jude 19

DIVISIVE
Reject a *d* man after . . . . . Titus 3:10

DIVORCE
her a certificate of *d* . . . . . Deut 24:1
of your mother's *d* . . . . . Is 50:1
a certificate of *d* . . . . . Mark 10:4

DO
set in them to *d* evil . . . . . Eccl 8:11
I will also *d* it . . . . . Is 46:11
men to *d* to you, *d* . . . . . Matt 7:12
d this and you will . . . . . Luke 10:28
He sees the Father *d* . . . . . John 5:19
without Me you can *d* . . . . . John 15:5
"Sirs, what must I *d* . . . . . Acts 16:30
d evil that good may . . . . . Rom 3:8
For what I will to *d* . . . . . Rom 7:15
good that I will to *d* . . . . . Rom 7:19
or whatever you *d*, *d* . . . . . 1 Cor 10:31
d all things through . . . . . Phil 4:13
d in word or deed, *d* . . . . . Col 3:17
d good and to share . . . . . Heb 13:16
and *d* this or that . . . . . James 4:15

DOCTRINE
said, 'My *d* is pure . . . . . Job 11:4
for I give you good *d* . . . . . Prov 4:2
idol is a worthless *d* . . . . . Jer 10:8
of bread, but of the *d* . . . . . Matt 16:12
What new *d* is this . . . . . Mark 1:27
"My *d* is not Mine . . . . . John 7:16
Jerusalem with your *d* . . . . . Acts 5:28
heart that form of *d* . . . . . Rom 6:17
with every wind of *d* . . . . . Eph 4:14
is contrary to sound *d* . . . . . 1 Tim 1:10
followed my *d* . . . . . 2 Tim 3:10
is profitable for *d* . . . . . 2 Tim 3:16
not endure sound *d* . . . . . 2 Tim 4:3
in *d* showing . . . . . Titus 2:7
they may adorn the *d* . . . . . Titus 2:10
not abide in the *d* . . . . . 2 John 9

DOCTRINES
the commandments and *d* . . . . . Col 2:22
spirits and *d* of . . . . . 1 Tim 4:1
various and strange *d* . . . . . Heb 13:9

DOEG
An Edomite; chief of Saul's herdsmen, 1 Sam 21:7
Betrays David, 1 Sam 22:9, 10
Kills 85 priests, 1 Sam 22:18, 19

DOERS
of God, but the *d* . . . . . Rom 2:13
But be *d* of the word . . . . . James 1:22

DOG
to David, "Am I a *d* . . . . . 1 Sam 17:43
they growl like a *d* . . . . . Ps 59:6
d returns to his own . . . . . Prov 26:11
d is better than a . . . . . Eccl 9:4
d returns to his own . . . . . 2 Pet 2:22

DOGS
Yes, they are greedy *d* . . . . . Is 56:11
what is holy to the *d* . . . . . Matt 7:6
d eat the crumbs which . . . . . Matt 15:27
Moreover the *d* came . . . . . Luke 16:21
But outside are *d* . . . . . Rev 22:15

DOMINION
let them have *d* . . . . . Gen 1:26
"*D* and fear belong . . . . . Job 25:2
made him to have *d* . . . . . Ps 8:6
let them not have *d* . . . . . Ps 19:13
besides You have had *d* . . . . . Is 26:13
d is an everlasting . . . . . Dan 4:34
sin shall not have *d* . . . . . Rom 6:14
Not that we have *d* . . . . . 2 Cor 1:24
glory and majesty, *d* . . . . . Jude 25

DONKEY
d saw the Angel . . . . . Num 22:23
Does the wild *d* . . . . . Job 6:5
d its master's crib . . . . . Is 1:3
and riding on a *d* . . . . . Zech 9:9
colt, the foal of a *d* . . . . . Matt 21:5
He had found a young *d* . . . . . John 12:14
d speaking with a . . . . . 2 Pet 2:16

DONKEYS
d quench their thirst . . . . . Ps 104:11
a chariot of *d* . . . . . Is 21:7
And the wild *d* stood . . . . . Jer 14:6

DOOR
sin lies at the *d* . . . . . Gen 4:7
keep watch over the *d* . . . . . Ps 141:3
d turns on its hinges . . . . . Prov 26:14
stone against the *d* . . . . . Matt 27:60
to you, I am the *d* . . . . . John 10:7
and effective *d* . . . . . 1 Cor 16:9
d was opened to me by . . . . . 2 Cor 2:12
would open to us a *d* . . . . . Col 4:3
is standing at the *d* . . . . . James 5:9
before you an open *d* . . . . . Rev 3:8
I stand at the *d* . . . . . Rev 3:20
and behold, a *d* . . . . . Rev 4:1

DOORKEEPER
I would rather be a *d* . . . . . Ps 84:10
To him the *d* . . . . . John 10:3

DOORPOSTS
write them on the *d* . . . . . Deut 6:9
"Strike the *d* . . . . . Amos 9:1

DOORS
up, you everlasting *d* . . . . . Ps 24:7
the entrance of the *d* . . . . . Prov 8:3
when the *d* are shut in . . . . . Eccl 12:4
who would shut the *d* . . . . . Mal 1:10

DORCAS
Disciple at Joppa, also called Tabitha; raised to life, Acts 9:36–42

DOUBLE
from the LORD's hand *d* . . . . . Is 40:2
first I will repay *d* . . . . . Jer 16:18
worthy of *d* honor . . . . . 1 Tim 5:17
and repay her *d* . . . . . Rev 18:6

DOUBLE-MINDED
I hate the *d* . . . . . Ps 119:113
he is a *d* man . . . . . James 1:8
your hearts, you *d* . . . . . James 4:8

DOUBT
life shall hang in *d* . . . . . Deut 28:66
faith, why did you *d* . . . . . Matt 14:31

DOUBTING
without wrath and *d* . . . . . 1 Tim 2:8
in faith, with no *d* . . . . . James 1:6

DOUBTS
And why do *d* arise in . . . . . Luke 24:38
for I have *d* about you . . . . . Gal 4:20
doubting, for he who *d* . . . . . James 1:6

DOVE
d found no resting . . . . . Gen 8:9
I had wings like a *d* . . . . . Ps 55:6
I mourned like a *d* . . . . . Is 38:14
also is like a silly *d* . . . . . Hos 7:11
descending like a *d* . . . . . Matt 3:16

DOVES
and moan sadly like *d* . . . . . Is 59:11
and harmless as *d* . . . . . Matt 10:16
of those who sold *d* . . . . . Matt 21:12

DRAGNET
gather them in their *d* .....Hab 1:15
d that was cast .....Matt 13:47

DRAGON
a great, fiery red *d* .....Rev 12:3
fought with the *d* .....Rev 12:7
they worshiped the *d* .....Rev 13:4
He laid hold of the *d* .....Rev 20:2

DRANK
them, and they all *d* .....Mark 14:23
d the same spiritual .....1 Cor 10:4

DRAW
d honey from the rock .....Deut 32:13
me to *d* near to God .....Ps 73:28
and the years *d* .....Eccl 12:1
D me away .....Song 1:4
Woe to those who *d* .....Is 5:18
with joy you will *d* .....Is 12:3
"*D* some out now .....John 2:8
You have nothing to *d* .....John 4:11
will *d* all peoples .....John 12:32
let us *d* near with a .....Heb 10:22
D near to God and He .....James 4:8

DRAWN
The wicked have *d* .....Ps 37:14
tempted when he is *d* .....James 1:14

DRAWS
and my life *d* near to .....Ps 88:3
your redemption *d* .....Luke 21:28

DREAD
fear of you and the *d* .....Gen 9:2
begin to put the *d* .....Deut 2:25

DREADFUL
of the great and *d* .....Mal 4:5

DREAM
Now Joseph had a *d* .....Gen 37:5
I speak to him in a *d* .....Num 12:6
will fly away like a *d* .....Job 20:8
As a *d* when one awakes .....Ps 73:20
like those who *d* .....Ps 126:1
For a *d* comes through .....Eccl 5:3
her, shall be as a *d* .....Is 29:7
prophet who has a *d* .....Jer 23:28
do not let the *d* .....Dan 4:19
your old men shall *d* .....Joel 2:28
to Joseph in a *d* .....Matt 2:13
things today in a *d* .....Matt 27:19
your old men shall *d* .....Acts 2:17

DREAMS
in the multitude of *d* .....Eccl 5:7
when a hungry man *d* .....Is 29:8
Nebuchadnezzar had *d* .....Dan 2:1

DREGS
d shall all the wicked .....Ps 75:8
has settled on his *d* .....Jer 48:11

DRIED
My strength is *d* .....Ps 22:15
of her blood was *d* .....Mark 5:29
saw the fig tree *d* .....Mark 11:20
and its water was *d* .....Rev 16:12

DRINK
"What shall we *d* .....Ex 15:24
"Do not *d* wine or .....Lev 10:9
and let him *d* of the .....Job 21:20
gave me vinegar to *d* .....Ps 69:21
D water from your own .....Prov 5:15
mocker, strong *d* .....Prov 20:1
lest they *d* and forget .....Prov 31:5
Give strong *d* to him .....Prov 31:6
Let him *d* and forget .....Prov 31:7
d your wine with a .....Eccl 9:7
follow intoxicating *d* .....Is 5:11
mixing intoxicating *d* .....Is 5:22
d the milk of the .....Is 60:16
My servants shall *d* .....Is 65:13
bosom, that you may *d* .....Is 66:11
d water by measure .....Ezek 4:11
"Bring wine, let us *d* .....Amos 4:1
to you of wine and *d* .....Mic 2:11
and you gave Me no *d* .....Matt 25:42
that day when I *d* .....Matt 26:29
mingled with gall to *d* .....Matt 27:34
with myrrh to *d* .....Mark 15:23
to her, "Give Me a *d* .....John 4:7
him come to Me and *d* .....John 7:37
d wine nor do anything .....Rom 14:21
do, as often as you *d* .....1 Cor 11:25
all been made to *d* .....1 Cor 12:13
No longer *d* only water .....1 Tim 5:23
has made all nations *d* .....Rev 14:8

DRINKS
to her, "Whoever *d* .....John 4:13
d My blood has .....John 6:54
For he who eats and *d* .....1 Cor 11:29
For the earth which *d* .....Heb 6:7

DRIPPING
wife are a continual *d* .....Prov 19:13
His lips are lilies, *d* .....Song 5:13

DRIVE
of the wicked *d* .....Ps 36:11
They shall *d* you from .....Dan 4:25
temple and began to *d* .....Mark 11:15

DRIVEN
They were *d* out from .....Job 30:5
Let them be *d* backward .....Ps 40:14
sail and so were *d* .....Acts 27:17
a wave of the sea *d* .....James 1:6

DROP
They *d* on the pastures .....Ps 65:12
the nations are as a *d* .....Is 40:15

DROSS
of the earth like *d* .....Ps 119:119
Take away the *d* .....Prov 25:4
purge away your *d* .....Is 1:25
of Israel has become *d* .....Ezek 22:18

DROUGHT
through a land of *d* .....Jer 2:6
in the year of *d* .....Jer 17:8
For I called for a *d* .....Hag 1:11

DROVE
So He *d* out the man .....Gen 3:24
temple of God and *d* .....Matt 21:12
a whip of cords, He *d* .....John 2:15

DROWN
nor can the floods *d* .....Song 8:7
harmful lusts which *d* .....1 Tim 6:9

DRUNK
of the wine and was *d* .....Gen 9:21
d my wine with my milk .....Song 5:1
you afflicted, and *d* .....Is 51:21
My anger, made them *d* .....Is 63:6
be satiated and made *d* .....Jer 46:10
the guests have well *d* .....John 2:10
For these are not *d* .....Acts 2:15
and another is *d* .....1 Cor 11:21
And do not be *d* .....Eph 5:18
and those who get *d* .....1 Thess 5:7
the earth were made *d* .....Rev 17:2
I saw the woman, *d* .....Rev 17:6

DRUNKARD
d could be included .....Deut 29:19
d is a proverb in the .....Prov 26:9
to and fro like a *d* .....Is 24:20
or a reviler, or a *d* .....1 Cor 5:11

DRUNKEN
I am like a *d* man .....Jer 23:9

DRUNKENNESS
will be filled with *d* .....Ezek 23:33
Jerusalem a cup of *d* .....Zech 12:2
with carousing, *d* .....Luke 21:34
not in revelry and *d* .....Rom 13:13
envy, murders, *d* .....Gal 5:21
lusts, *d* .....1 Pet 4:3

DRY
place, and let the *d* .....Gen 1:9
made the sea into *d* .....Ex 14:21
It was *d* on the fleece .....Judg 6:40
I will *d* up her sea .....Jer 51:36
d tree flourish .....Ezek 17:24
will make the rivers *d* .....Ezek 30:12
will be done in the *d* .....Luke 23:31

DUE
because it is your *d* .....Lev 10:13
their food in *d* season .....Ps 104:27
pay all that was *d* .....Matt 18:34
d time Christ died .....Rom 5:6
to whom taxes are *d* .....Rom 13:7
d season we shall .....Gal 6:9
exalt you in *d* time .....1 Pet 5:6

DULL
heart of this people *d* .....Is 6:10
people have grown *d* .....Matt 13:15
you have become *d* .....Heb 5:11

DUMB
the tongue of the *d* .....Is 35:6
"Deaf and *d* spirit .....Mark 9:25

DUNGHILL
the land nor for the *d* .....Luke 14:35

DUST
formed man of the *d* .....Gen 2:7
d you shall return .....Gen 3:19
descendants as the *d* .....Gen 13:16
now, I who am but *d* .....Gen 18:27
"Who can count the *d* .....Num 23:10
lay your gold in the *d* .....Job 22:24
and repent in *d* .....Job 42:6
Will the *d* praise You .....Ps 30:9
like the whirling *d* .....Ps 83:13
show favor to her *d* .....Ps 102:14
that we are *d* .....Ps 103:14
or the primal *d* .....Prov 8:26
all are from the *d* .....Eccl 3:20
counted as the small *d* .....Is 40:15
They shall lick the *d* .....Mic 7:17
city, shake off the *d* .....Matt 10:14
image of the man of *d* .....1 Cor 15:49

DWELL
O LORD, make me *d* .....Ps 4:8
Who may *d* in Your holy .....Ps 15:1
He himself shall *d* .....Ps 25:13
d in the land .....Ps 37:3
the LORD God might *d* .....Ps 68:18
of my God than *d* .....Ps 84:10
Him, that glory may *d* .....Ps 85:9
Woe is me, that I *d* .....Ps 120:5
he will *d* on high .....Is 33:16
into Egypt to *d* there .....Is 52:4
"I *d* in the high and .....Is 57:15
"They shall no longer *d* .....Lam 4:15
they enter and *d* there .....Matt 12:45
of Judea and all who *d* .....Acts 2:14
"I will *d* in them .....2 Cor 6:16
that Christ may *d* .....Eph 3:17
the fullness should *d* .....Col 1:19
the word of Christ *d* .....Col 3:16
men, and He will *d* .....Rev 21:3

DWELLING
A people *d* alone .....Num 23:9
is the way to the *d* .....Job 38:19
built together for a *d* .....Eph 2:22
a foreign country, *d* .....Heb 11:9

DWELLS
He who *d* in the secret . . . . Ps 91:1
but the Father who *d* . . . . John 14:10
do it, but sin that *d* . . . . Rom 7:17
the Spirit of God *d* . . . . Rom 8:9
from the dead *d* . . . . Rom 8:11
the Spirit of God *d* . . . . 1 Cor 3:16
d all the fullness . . . . Col 2:9
which righteousness *d* . . . . 2 Pet 3:13
you, where Satan *d* . . . . Rev 2:13

DWELT
Egypt, and Jacob *d* . . . . Ps 105:23
became flesh and *d* . . . . John 1:14
By faith he *d* in the . . . . Heb 11:9

DYING
I do not object to *d* . . . . Acts 25:11
in the body the *d* . . . . 2 Cor 4:10
Jacob, when he was *d* . . . . Heb 11:21

EAGLE
As an *e* stirs up its . . . . Deut 32:11
e swooping on its prey . . . . Job 9:26
fly away like an *e* . . . . Prov 23:5
The way of an *e* . . . . Prov 30:19
nest as high as the *e* . . . . Jer 49:16
had the face of an *e* . . . . Ezek 1:10
like a flying *e* . . . . Rev 4:7
two wings of a great *e* . . . . Rev 12:14

EAGLES
up with wings like *e* . . . . Is 40:31
are swifter than *e* . . . . Jer 4:13
e will be gathered . . . . Matt 24:28

EAGLES'
how I bore you on *e* . . . . Ex 19:4

EAR
shall pierce his *e* . . . . Ex 21:6
Does not the *e* test . . . . Job 12:11
Bow down Your *e* . . . . Ps 31:2
And the *e* of the wise . . . . Prov 18:15
He awakens My *e* . . . . Is 50:4
e is uncircumcised . . . . Jer 6:10
what you hear in the *e* . . . . Matt 10:27
cut off his right *e* . . . . John 18:10
not seen, nor *e* heard . . . . 1 Cor 2:9
if the *e* should say . . . . 1 Cor 12:16
He who has an *e* . . . . Rev 2:7

EARNEST
must give the more *e* . . . . Heb 2:1

EARNESTLY
if you *e* obey My . . . . Deut 11:13
He prayed more *e* . . . . Luke 22:44
in this we groan, *e* . . . . 2 Cor 5:2
e that it would not . . . . James 5:17
you to contend *e* . . . . Jude 3

EARS
both his *e* will tingle . . . . 2 Kin 21:12
Whoever shuts his *e* . . . . Prov 21:13
And hear with their *e* . . . . Is 6:10
He who has *e* . . . . Matt 11:15
e are hard of hearing . . . . Matt 13:15
they have itching *e* . . . . 2 Tim 4:3
e are open to their . . . . 1 Pet 3:12

EARTH
e which is under you . . . . Deut 28:23
e are the LORD's . . . . 1 Sam 2:8
coming to judge the *e* . . . . 1 Chr 16:33
service for man on *e* . . . . Job 7:1
He hangs the *e* on . . . . Job 26:7
foundations of the *e* . . . . Job 38:4
e is the LORD's . . . . Ps 24:1
the shields of the *e* . . . . Ps 47:9
You visit the *e* . . . . Ps 65:9
You had formed the *e* . . . . Ps 90:2
let the *e* be moved . . . . Ps 99:1
glory is above the *e* . . . . Ps 148:13
wisdom founded the *e* . . . . Prov 3:19
there was ever an *e* . . . . Prov 8:23
For three things the *e* . . . . Prov 30:21
e abides forever . . . . Eccl 1:4
for the meek of the *e* . . . . Is 11:4
e is My footstool . . . . Is 66:1
and the *e* shone with . . . . Ezek 43:2
I will darken the *e* . . . . Amos 8:9
e will be filled . . . . Hab 2:14
shall inherit the *e* . . . . Matt 5:5
heaven and *e* pass away . . . . Matt 5:18
e as it is in heaven . . . . Matt 6:10
treasures on *e* . . . . Matt 6:19
then shook the *e* . . . . Heb 12:26
"Do not harm the *e* . . . . Rev 7:3
from whose face the *e* . . . . Rev 20:11
new heaven and a new *e* . . . . Rev 21:1

EARTHLY
If I have told you *e* . . . . John 3:12
that if our *e* house . . . . 2 Cor 5:1
their mind on *e* things . . . . Phil 3:19
from above, but is *e* . . . . James 3:15

EARTHQUAKE
after the wind an *e* . . . . 1 Kin 19:11
as you fled from the *e* . . . . Zech 14:5
there was a great *e* . . . . Matt 28:2
there was a great *e* . . . . Rev 6:12

EASE
I was at *e* . . . . Job 16:12
you women who are at *e* . . . . Is 32:9
to you who are at *e* . . . . Amos 6:1
take your *e* . . . . Luke 12:19

EASIER
Which is *e*, to say . . . . Mark 2:9
It is *e* for a camel . . . . Mark 10:25

EAST
goes toward the *e* . . . . Gen 2:14
the LORD brought an *e* . . . . Ex 10:13
e wind scattered . . . . Job 38:24
As far as the *e* . . . . Ps 103:12
descendants from the *e* . . . . Is 43:5
wise men from the *E* . . . . Matt 2:1
many will come from *e* . . . . Matt 8:11
will come from the *e* . . . . Luke 13:29
e might be prepared . . . . Rev 16:12

EAT
you may freely *e* . . . . Gen 2:16
'You shall not *e* . . . . Gen 3:17
my people as they *e* . . . . Ps 53:4
good to *e* much honey . . . . Prov 25:27
e this scroll . . . . Ezek 3:1
on your couches, *e* . . . . Amos 6:4
e the flesh of My . . . . Mic 3:3
life, what you will *e* . . . . Matt 6:25
You to *e* the Passover . . . . Matt 26:17
give us His flesh to *e* . . . . John 6:52
one believes he may *e* . . . . Rom 14:2
e meat nor drink wine . . . . Rom 14:21
I will never again *e* . . . . 1 Cor 8:13
neither shall he *e* . . . . 2 Thess 3:10
e your flesh like fire . . . . James 5:3

EATEN
Have you *e* from the . . . . Gen 3:11
e my honeycomb with my . . . . Song 5:1
e the fruit of lies . . . . Hos 10:13
And he was *e* by worms . . . . Acts 12:23

EATS
The righteous *e* . . . . Prov 13:25
receives sinners and *e* . . . . Luke 15:2
Whoever *e* My flesh . . . . John 6:54
e this bread will live . . . . John 6:58
e despise him who does . . . . Rom 14:3
He who *e*, *e* to the . . . . Rom 14:6
an unworthy manner *e* . . . . 1 Cor 11:29

EBAL
Mountain in Samaria, Deut 27:12, 13
Stones of the law erected upon, Deut 27:1–8; Josh 8:30–35

EBED-MELECH
Ethiopian eunuch; rescues Jeremiah, Jer 38:7–13
Promised divine protection, Jer 39:15–18

EBENEZER
Site of Israel's defeat, 1 Sam 4:1–10
Ark transferred from, 1 Sam 5:1
Site of memorial stone, 1 Sam 7:10, 12

EBER
Great-grandson of Shem, Gen 10:21–24; 1 Chr 1:25
Progenitor of the:
Hebrews, Gen 11:16–26
Arabians and Arameans, Gen 10:25–30
Ancestor of Christ, Luke 3:35

EDEN
First home of mankind, Gen 2:8–15
Zion becomes like, Is 51:3
Called the "garden of God," Ezek 28:13

EDIFICATION
his good, leading to *e* . . . . Rom 15:2
prophesies speaks *e* . . . . 1 Cor 14:3
things be done for *e* . . . . 1 Cor 14:26
the Lord gave us for *e* . . . . 2 Cor 10:8
has given me for *e* . . . . 2 Cor 13:10
rather than godly *e* . . . . 1 Tim 1:4

EDIFIES
puffs up, but love *e* . . . . 1 Cor 8:1
he who prophesies *e* . . . . 1 Cor 14:4

EDIFY
but not all things *e* . . . . 1 Cor 10:23
and *e* one another . . . . 1 Thess 5:11

EDIFYING
of the body for the *e* . . . . Eph 4:16

EDOM
Name given to Esau, Gen 25:30
——— Land of Esau; called Seir, Gen 32:3
Called Edom and Idumea, Mark 3:8
People of, cursed, Is 34:5, 6

EDOMITES
Descendants of Esau, Gen 36:9
Refuse passage to Israel, Num 20:18–20
Hostile to Israel, Gen 27:40; 1 Sam 14:47; 2 Chr 20:10; Ps 137:7
Prophecies concerning, Gen 27:37; Is 34:5–17; Ezek 25:12–14; 35:5–7; Amos 9:11, 12

EFFECTIVELY
for He who worked *e* . . . . Gal 2:8
e works in you who . . . . 1 Thess 2:13

EGYPT
Abram visits, Gen 12:10
Joseph sold into, Gen 37:28, 36
Joseph becomes leader in, Gen 39:1–4
Hebrews move to, Gen 46:5–7
Hebrews persecuted in, Ex 1:15–22
Plagues on, Ex 7—11
Israel leaves, Ex 12:31–33
Army of, perishes, Ex 14:26–28
Prophecies concerning, Gen 15:13; Is 19:18–25; Ezek 29:14, 15; 30:24, 25; Matt 2:15

EHUD
Son of Gera, Judg 3:15
Slays Eglon, Judg 3:16–26

EKRON
Philistine city, Josh 13:3
Captured by Judah, Judg 1:18
Assigned to Dan, Josh 19:40, 43

Ark sent to, 1 Sam 5:10
Denounced by the prophets, Jer 25:9, 20

ELAH
King of Israel, 1 Kin 16:6, 8–10

ELAMITES
Descendants of Shem, Gen 10:22
Destruction of, Jer 49:34–39
In Persian Empire, Ezra 4:9
Jews from, at Pentecost, Acts 2:9

ELATH
Seaport on Red Sea, 1 Kin 9:26
Built by Azariah, 2 Kin 14:21, 22
Captured by Syrians, 2 Kin 16:6
Same as Ezion Geber, 2 Chr 8:17

EL BETHEL
Site of Jacob's altar, Gen 35:6, 7

ELDER
The *e* and honorable . . . . .Is 9:15
against an *e* except . . . . .1 Tim 5:19
I who am a fellow *e* . . . . .1 Pet 5:1

ELDERS
and seventy of the *e* . . . . .Ex 24:1
And teach his *e* . . . . .Ps 105:22
and counsel from the *e* . . . . .Ezek 7:26
the tradition of the *e* . . . . .Matt 15:2
be rejected by the *e* . . . . .Luke 9:22
they had appointed *e* . . . . .Acts 14:23
and called for the *e* . . . . .Acts 20:17
e who rule well be . . . . .1 Tim 5:17
lacking, and appoint *e* . . . . .Titus 1:5
e obtained a good . . . . .Heb 11:2
Let him call for the *e* . . . . .James 5:14
e who are among you I . . . . .1 Pet 5:1
I saw twenty-four *e* . . . . .Rev 4:4

ELEAZAR
Son of Aaron; succeeds him as high priest, Ex 6:23, 25; 28:1; Lev 10:6, 7; Num 3:32; 20:25–28; Josh 14:1; 24:33

ELECT
whom I uphold, My *E* . . . . .Is 42:1
and Israel My *e* . . . . .Is 45:4
e shall long enjoy the . . . . .Is 65:22
gather together His *e* . . . . .Matt 24:31
e have obtained it . . . . .Rom 11:7
e according to the . . . . .1 Pet 1:2
a chief cornerstone, *e* . . . . .1 Pet 2:6
e sister greet you . . . . .2 John 13

ELECTION
e they are beloved . . . . .Rom 11:28
call and *e* sure . . . . .2 Pet 1:10

ELEMENTS
weak and beggarly *e* . . . . .Gal 4:9
e will melt with . . . . .2 Pet 3:10

ELEVEN
and his *e* sons . . . . .Gen 32:22
e disciples went away . . . . .Matt 28:16
numbered with the *e* . . . . .Acts 1:26

ELI
Officiates in Shiloh, 1 Sam 1:3
Blesses Hannah, 1 Sam 1:12–19
Becomes Samuel's guardian, 1 Sam 1:20–28
Samuel ministers before, 1 Sam 2:11
Sons of, 1 Sam 2:12–17
Rebukes sons, 1 Sam 2:22–25
Rebuked by a man of God, 1 Sam 2:27–36
Instructs Samuel, 1 Sam 3:1–18
Death of, 1 Sam 4:15–18

ELIAB
Brother of David, 1 Sam 16:5–13
Fights in Saul's army, 1 Sam 17:13
Discounts David's worth, 1 Sam 17:28, 29

ELIAKIM
Son of Hilkiah, 2 Kin 18:18
Confers with Rabshakeh, Is 36:4, 11–22
Sent to Isaiah, Is 37:2–5
Becomes type of the Messiah, Is 22:20–25
—— Son of King Josiah, 2 Kin 23:34
Name changed to Jehoiakim, 2 Chr 36:4

ELIASHIB
High priest, Neh 12:10
Rebuilds Sheep Gate, Neh 3:1, 20, 21
Allies with foreigners, Neh 13:4, 5, 28

ELIHU
David's brother, 1 Chr 27:18
Called Eliab, 1 Sam 16:6
—— One who reproved Job and his friends, Job 32:2, 4–6

ELIJAH
Denounces Ahab; goes into hiding; fed by ravens, 1 Kin 17:1–7
Dwells with widow; performs miracles for her, 1 Kin 17:8–24
Sends message to Ahab; overthrows prophets of Baal, 1 Kin 18:1–40
Brings rain, 1 Kin 18:41–45
Flees from Jezebel; fed by angels, 1 Kin 19:1–8
Receives revelation from God, 1 Kin 19:9–18
Condemns Ahab, 1 Kin 21:15–29
Condemns Ahaziah; fire consumes troops sent against him, 2 Kin 1:1–16
Taken up to heaven, 2 Kin 2:1–15
Appears with Christ in Transfiguration, Matt 17:1–4
Type of John the Baptist, Mal 4:5, 6; Luke 1:17

ELIMELECH
Naomi's husband, Ruth 1:1–3; 2:1, 3; 4:3–9

ELIPHAZ
One of Job's friends, Job 2:11
Rebukes Job, Job 4:1, 5
Is forgiven, Job 42:7–9

ELISHA
Chosen as Elijah's successor; follows him, 1 Kin 19:16–21
Witnesses Elijah's translation; receives his spirit and mantle, 2 Kin 2:1–18
Performs miracles, 2 Kin 2:19–25; 4:1—6:23
Prophesies victory over Moab; fulfilled, 2 Kin 3:11–27
Prophesies end of siege; fulfilled, 2 Kin 7
Prophesies death of Ben-Hadad, 2 Kin 8:7–15
Sends servant to anoint Jehu, 2 Kin 9:1–3
Last words and death; miracle performed by his bones, 2 Kin 13:14–21

ELIZABETH
Barren wife of Zacharias, Luke 1:5–7
Conceives a son, Luke 1:13, 24, 25
Salutation to Mary, Luke 1:36–45
Mother of John the Baptist, Luke 1:57–60

ELKANAH
Father of Samuel, 1 Sam 1:1–23
—— Son of Korah, Ex 6:24
Escapes judgment, Num 26:11

ELNATHAN
Father of Nehushta, 2 Kin 24:8
Goes to Egypt, Jer 26:22
Entreats with king, Jer 36:25

ELOQUENT
"O my Lord, I am not *e* . . . . .Ex 4:10
an *e* man and mighty . . . . .Acts 18:24

ELYMAS
Arabic name of Bar-Jesus, a false prophet, Acts 13:6–12

EMMAUS
Town near Jerusalem, Luke 24:13–18

EMPTY
appear before Me *e* . . . . .Ex 23:15
e things which . . . . .1 Sam 12:21
not listen to *e* talk . . . . .Job 35:13
LORD makes the earth *e* . . . . .Is 24:1
comes, he finds it *e* . . . . .Matt 12:44
He has sent away *e* . . . . .Luke 1:53
you with *e* words . . . . .Eph 5:6

EN GEDI
Occupied by the Amorites, Gen 14:7
Assigned to Judah, Josh 15:62, 63
David's hiding place, 1 Sam 23:29
Noted for vineyards, Song 1:14

EN HAKKORE
Miraculous spring, Judg 15:14–19

EN ROGEL
Fountain outside Jerusalem, 2 Sam 17:17
Seat of Adonijah's plot, 1 Kin 1:5–9

ENCOURAGED
is, that I may be *e* . . . . .Rom 1:12
and all may be *e* . . . . .1 Cor 14:31
their hearts may be *e* . . . . .Col 2:2

END
yet your latter *e* . . . . .Job 8:7
make me to know my *e* . . . . .Ps 39:4
shall keep it to the *e* . . . . .Ps 119:33
e is the way of death . . . . .Prov 14:12
There was no *e* of all . . . . .Eccl 4:16
Declaring the *e* . . . . .Is 46:10
Our *e* was near . . . . .Lam 4:18
whose iniquity shall *e* . . . . .Ezek 21:25
what shall be the *e* . . . . .Dan 12:8
e has come upon my . . . . .Amos 8:2
the harvest is the *e* . . . . .Matt 13:39
to pass, but the *e* . . . . .Matt 24:6
always, even to the *e* . . . . .Matt 28:20
He loved them to the *e* . . . . .John 13:1
For Christ is the *e* . . . . .Rom 10:4
the hope firm to the *e* . . . . .Heb 3:6
but now, once at the *e* . . . . .Heb 9:26
of Job and seen the *e* . . . . .James 5:11
But the *e* of all . . . . .1 Pet 4:7
what will be the *e* . . . . .1 Pet 4:17
the latter *e* is worse . . . . .2 Pet 2:20
My works until the *e* . . . . .Rev 2:26
Beginning and the *E* . . . . .Rev 22:13

ENDEAVORING
e to keep the unity . . . . .Eph 4:3

ENDLESS
and *e* genealogies . . . . .1 Tim 1:4
to the power of an *e* . . . . .Heb 7:16

ENDS
All the *e* of the world . . . . .Ps 22:27
established all the *e* . . . . .Prov 30:4
she came from the *e* . . . . .Matt 12:42
to the *e* of the . . . . .Acts 13:47
their words to the *e* . . . . .Rom 10:18

ENDURANCE
For you have need of *e* . . . . .Heb 10:36
e the race that . . . . .Heb 12:1

ENDURE
But the LORD shall *e* . . . . .Ps 9:7
as the sun and moon *e* . . . . .Ps 72:5
His name shall *e* . . . . .Ps 72:17
nor does a crown *e* . . . . .Prov 27:24
Can your heart *e* . . . . .Ezek 22:14
persecuted, we *e* . . . . .1 Cor 4:12
Therefore I *e* all . . . . .2 Tim 2:10
them blessed who *e* . . . . .James 5:11

ENDURED
what persecutions I *e* . . . . .2 Tim 3:11

suffer trouble as an *e* ... 2 Tim 2:9
a thief, an *e* ... 1 Pet 4:15

EVILDOERS
e shall be cut off ... Ps 37:9
Depart from me, you *e* ... Ps 119:115
iniquity, a brood of *e* ... Is 1:4
e shall never be ... Is 14:20
against you as *e* ... 1 Pet 2:12

EVILS
e have surrounded me ... Ps 40:12
have committed two *e* ... Jer 2:13

EXALT
God, and I will *e* ... Ex 15:2
e the horn of His ... 1 Sam 2:10
e His name together ... Ps 34:3
E the LORD our God ... Ps 99:5
are my God, I will *e* ... Ps 118:28
if I do not *e* ... Ps 137:6
into heaven, I will *e* ... Is 14:13
E the humble ... Ezek 21:26
and he shall *e* himself ... Dan 8:25

EXALTATION
e comes neither from ... Ps 75:6
who rejoice in My *e* ... Is 13:3
brother glory in his *e* ... James 1:9

EXALTED
Let God be *e* ... 2 Sam 22:47
built You an *e* ... 2 Chr 6:2
name, which is *e* ... Neh 9:5
when vileness is *e* ... Ps 12:8
I will be *e* among the ... Ps 46:10
righteous shall be *e* ... Ps 75:10
favor our horn is *e* ... Ps 89:17
You are *e* far above ... Ps 97:9
His name alone is *e* ... Ps 148:13
upright the city is *e* ... Prov 11:11
LORD alone shall be *e* ... Is 2:11
valley shall be *e* ... Is 40:4
Him God has *e* ... Acts 5:31
And lest I should be *e* ... 2 Cor 12:7
also has highly *e* ... Phil 2:9

EXALTS
Righteousness *e* ... Prov 14:34
high thing that *e* ... 2 Cor 10:5
e himself above all ... 2 Thess 2:4

EXAMINE
E me, O LORD ... Ps 26:2
But let a man *e* ... 1 Cor 11:28
But let each one *e* ... Gal 6:4

EXAMPLE
to make her a public *e* ... Matt 1:19
I have given you an *e* ... John 13:15
in following my *e* ... Phil 3:17
to make ourselves an *e* ... 2 Thess 3:9
youth, but be an *e* ... 1 Tim 4:12
us, leaving us an *e* ... 1 Pet 2:21
making them an *e* ... 2 Pet 2:6
are set forth as an *e* ... Jude 7

EXAMPLES
happened to them as *e* ... 1 Cor 10:11
so that you became *e* ... 1 Thess 1:7
to you, but being *e* ... 1 Pet 5:3

EXCEEDING
He might show the *e* ... Eph 2:7

EXCEEDINGLY
for the LORD must be *e* ... 1 Chr 22:5
You have made him *e* ... Ps 21:6
is far off and *e* deep ... Eccl 7:24
e high mountain ... Matt 4:8
Rejoice and be *e* ... Matt 5:12

EXCEL
you His angels, who *e* ... Ps 103:20
but you *e* them all ... Prov 31:29
that you seek to *e* ... 1 Cor 14:12

EXCELLENCE
e You have overthrown ... Ex 15:7
did not come with *e* ... 1 Cor 2:1

EXCELLENT
He is *e* in power ... Job 37:23
It shall be as *e* ... Ps 141:5
will speak of *e* things ... Prov 8:6
like Lebanon, *e* ... Song 5:15
for He has done *e* ... Is 12:5
in counsel and *e* ... Is 28:29
Inasmuch as an *e* ... Dan 5:12
the things that are *e* ... Rom 2:18
the things that are *e* ... Phil 1:10
e sacrifice than Cain ... Heb 11:4
came to Him from the *E* ... 2 Pet 1:17

EXCELS
Do you see a man who *e* ... Prov 22:29
I saw that wisdom *e* ... Eccl 2:13
of the glory that *e* ... 2 Cor 3:10

EXCHANGE
man give in *e* for his soul ... Matt 16:26

EXCHANGED
Nor can it be *e* ... Job 28:17
e the truth of God for ... Rom 1:25
For even their women *e* ... Rom 1:26

EXCUSE
God be angry at your *e* ... Eccl 5:6
but now they have no *e* ... John 15:22
they are without *e* ... Rom 1:20
do you think that we *e* ... 2 Cor 12:19

EXCUSES
began to make *e* ... Luke 14:18

EXECUTE
e vengeance on the ... Ps 149:7
if you thoroughly *e* ... Jer 7:5
e the fierceness ... Hos 11:9
e judgment also ... John 5:27
e wrath on him who ... Rom 13:4

EXECUTES
by the judgment He *e* ... Ps 9:16
e righteousness ... Ps 103:6
e justice for the ... Ps 146:7
e justice for me ... Mic 7:9

EXERCISE
those who are great *e* ... Matt 20:25
e yourself toward ... 1 Tim 4:7
e profits a little ... 1 Tim 4:8

EXHORT
we command and *e* ... 2 Thess 3:12
e him as a father ... 1 Tim 5:1
and *e* these things ... 1 Tim 6:2
doctrine, both to *e* ... Titus 1:9
Speak these things, *e* ... Titus 2:15
e one another ... Heb 3:13

EXHORTATION
you have any word of *e* ... Acts 13:15
he who exhorts, in *e* ... Rom 12:8
to reading, to *e* ... 1 Tim 4:13
with the word of *e* ... Heb 13:22

EXHORTED
For I earnestly *e* ... Jer 11:7
e and strengthened ... Acts 15:32
as you know how we *e* ... 1 Thess 2:11

EXILE
and also an *e* from ... 2 Sam 15:19
The captive *e* hastens ... Is 51:14

EXIST
things which do not *e* ... Rom 4:17
by Your will they *e* ... Rev 4:11

EXPECT
an hour you do not *e* ... Luke 12:40

EXPECTATION
The *e* of the poor ... Ps 9:18
God alone, for my *e* ... Ps 62:5
the people were in *e* ... Luke 3:15
a certain fearful *e* ... Heb 10:27

EXPERT
and the *e* enchanter ... Is 3:3
those of an *e* warrior ... Jer 50:9
because you are *e* ... Acts 26:3

EXPLAIN
was no one who could *e* ... Gen 41:24
days they could not *e* ... Judg 14:14
"*E* this parable to us ... Matt 15:15
to say, and hard to *e* ... Heb 5:11

EXPLOIT
e all your ... Is 58:3
against those who *e* ... Mal 3:5
they will *e* you with ... 2 Pet 2:3

EXPOSED
his deeds should be *e* ... John 3:20
all things that are *e* ... Eph 5:13

EXPOUNDED
He *e* to them in all ... Luke 24:27

EXPRESS
man cannot *e* it ... Eccl 1:8
of His glory and the *e* ... Heb 1:3

EXPRESSLY
of the LORD came *e* ... Ezek 1:3
Now the Spirit *e* ... 1 Tim 4:1

EXTEND
none to *e* mercy to him ... Ps 109:12
"Behold, I will *e* ... Is 66:12
did not *e* to you ... 2 Cor 10:14

EXTINGUISHED
broken, my days are *e* ... Job 17:1
They are *e* ... Is 43:17

EXTOL
I will *e* You ... Ps 30:1
e Him who rides ... Ps 68:4

EXTORTION
e gathers it for him ... Prov 28:8
your neighbors by *e* ... Ezek 22:12
they are full of *e* ... Matt 23:25

EXTORTIONERS
e will inherit ... 1 Cor 6:10

EYE
e for *e* ... Ex 21:24
the ear, but now my *e* ... Job 42:5
guide you with My *e* ... Ps 32:8
Behold, the *e* of the ... Ps 33:18
He who formed the *e* ... Ps 94:9
and the seeing *e* ... Prov 20:12
who has a generous *e* ... Prov 22:9
A man with an evil *e* ... Prov 28:22
e that mocks his ... Prov 30:17
e is not satisfied ... Eccl 1:8
labors, nor is his *e* ... Eccl 4:8
for they shall see *e* ... Is 52:8
e seen any God besides ... Is 64:4
the apple of His *e* ... Zech 2:8
if your right *e* ... Matt 5:29
it was said, 'An *e* ... Matt 5:38
plank in your own *e* ... Matt 7:3
e causes you to sin ... Matt 18:9
Or is your *e* evil ... Matt 20:15
e causes you to sin ... Mark 9:47
the *e* of a needle ... Luke 18:25
"Because I am not an *e* ... 1 Cor 12:16
whole body were an *e* ... 1 Cor 12:17
the twinkling of an *e* ... 1 Cor 15:52

every *e* will see Him ....Rev 1:7
your eyes with *e* salve ....Rev 3:18

EYELIDS
His eyes behold, His *e* ....Ps 11:4
e look right before ....Prov 4:25

EYES
e will be opened ....Gen 3:5
and you can be our *e* ....Num 10:31
she put paint on her *e* ....2 Kin 9:30
For the *e* of the ....2 Chr 16:9
Do You have *e* of flesh ....Job 10:4
And my *e* shall behold ....Job 19:27
I was *e* to the blind ....Job 29:15
e observe from afar ....Job 39:29
e are secretly fixed ....Ps 10:8
e are ever toward the ....Ps 25:15
The *e* of the LORD are ....Ps 34:15
e fail while I wait ....Ps 69:3
e shall you look ....Ps 91:8
I will lift up my *e* ....Ps 121:1
not give sleep to my *e* ....Ps 132:4
e saw my substance ....Ps 139:16
e look straight ahead ....Prov 4:25
but the *e* of a fool ....Prov 17:24
Will you set your *e* ....Prov 23:5
Who has redness of *e* ....Prov 23:29
be wise in his own *e* ....Prov 26:5
so the *e* of man are ....Prov 27:20
The wise man's *e* ....Eccl 2:14
e than the wandering ....Eccl 6:9
You have dove's *e* ....Song 1:15
e have seen the King ....Is 6:5
of the book, and the *e* ....Is 29:18
e fail from looking ....Is 38:14
O LORD, are not Your *e* ....Jer 5:3
Who have *e* and see ....Jer 5:21
e will weep bitterly ....Jer 13:17
For I will set My *e* ....Jer 24:6
rims were full of *e* ....Ezek 1:18
full of *e* all around ....Ezek 10:12
that horn which had *e* ....Dan 7:20
horn between his *e* ....Dan 8:5
You are of purer *e* ....Hab 1:13
But blessed are your *e* ....Matt 13:16
"He put clay on my *e* ....John 9:15
e they have closed ....Acts 28:27
e that they should not ....Rom 11:8
plucked out your own *e* ....Gal 4:15
have seen with our *e* ....1 John 1:1
the lust of the *e* ....1 John 2:16
as snow, and His *e* ....Rev 1:14
and anoint your *e* ....Rev 3:18
creatures full of *e* ....Rev 4:6
horns and seven *e* ....Rev 5:6
tear from their *e* ....Rev 21:4

EYESERVICE
not with *e* ....Eph 6:6
the flesh, not with *e* ....Col 3:22

EYEWITNESSES
the beginning were *e* ....Luke 1:2
e of His majesty ....2 Pet 1:16

EZEKIEL
Sent to rebellious Israel, Ezek 2; 3
Prophesies by symbolic action:
siege of Jerusalem, Ezek 4
destruction of Jerusalem, Ezek 5
captivity of Judah, Ezek 12:1–20
destruction of the temple, Ezek 24:15–27
Visions of:
God's glory, Ezek 1:4–28
abominations, Ezek 8:5–18
valley of dry bones, Ezek 37:1–14
messianic times, Ezek 40—48
river of life, Ezek 47:1–5
Parables, allegories, dirges of, Ezek 15; 16; 17; 19; 23; 24

EZION GEBER
See ELATH
Town on the Red Sea, 1 Kin 9:26
Israelite encampment, Num 33:35
Seaport of Israel's navy, 1 Kin 22:48

EZRA
Scribe, priest and reformer of postexilic times; commissioned by Artaxerxes, Ezra 7
Returns with exiles to Jerusalem, Ezra 8
Institutes reforms, Ezra 9
Reads the Law, Neh 8
Assists in dedication of wall, Neh 12:27–43

FABLES
nor give heed to *f* ....1 Tim 1:4
be turned aside to *f* ....2 Tim 4:4
cunningly devised *f* ....2 Pet 1:16

FACE
"For I have seen God *f* ....Gen 32:30
f shone while he ....Ex 34:29
he put a veil on his *f* ....Ex 34:33
the LORD make His *f* ....Num 6:25
Then he turned his *f* ....2 Kin 20:2
curse You to Your *f* ....Job 1:11
me, I will see Your *f* ....Ps 17:15
Why do You hide Your *f* ....Ps 44:24
and cause His *f* ....Ps 67:1
of his *f* is changed ....Eccl 8:1
sins have hidden His *f* ....Is 59:2
I have made your *f* ....Ezek 3:8
but to us shame of *f* ....Dan 9:7
before Your *f* who ....Matt 11:10
f shone like the sun ....Matt 17:2
always before my *f* ....Acts 2:25
dimly, but then *f* ....1 Cor 13:12
look steadily at the *f* ....2 Cor 3:7
with unveiled *f* ....2 Cor 3:18
withstood him to his *f* ....Gal 2:11
his natural *f* in a ....James 1:23
but the *f* of the LORD ....1 Pet 3:12
They shall see His *f* ....Rev 22:4

FACES
f were not ashamed ....Ps 34:5
hid, as it were, our *f* ....Is 53:3
be afraid of their *f* ....Jer 1:8
and all *f* turned pale ....Jer 30:6
they disfigure their *f* ....Matt 6:16

FADE
we all *f* as a leaf ....Is 64:6
and the leaf shall *f* ....Jer 8:13
rich man also will *f* ....James 1:11
and that does not *f* ....1 Pet 1:4

FADES
withers, the flower *f* ....Is 40:7

FAIL
eyes shall look and *f* ....Deut 28:32
flesh and my heart *f* ....Ps 73:26
of the thirsty to *f* ....Is 32:6
their tongues *f* ....Is 41:17
whose waters do not *f* ....Is 58:11
have caused wine to *f* ....Jer 48:33
of the olive may *f* ....Hab 3:17
nor shall the vine *f* ....Mal 3:11
that when you *f* ....Luke 16:9
tittle of the law to *f* ....Luke 16:17
faith should not *f* ....Luke 22:32
they will *f* ....1 Cor 13:8
Your years will not *f* ....Heb 1:12
For the time would *f* ....Heb 11:32

FAILED
Not a word *f* of any ....Josh 21:45
My relatives have *f* ....Job 19:14
refuge has *f* me ....Ps 142:4

FAILS
my strength *f* because ....Ps 31:10
my spirit *f* ....Ps 143:7
and every vision *f* ....Ezek 12:22
Love never *f* ....1 Cor 13:8

FAINT
the youths shall *f* ....Is 40:30
shall walk and not *f* ....Is 40:31
my heart is *f* in me ....Jer 8:18
and the infants *f* ....Lam 2:11

FAINTED
thirsty, their soul *f* ....Ps 107:5

FAINTS
longs, yes, even *f* ....Ps 84:2
My soul *f* for Your ....Ps 119:81
And the whole heart *f* ....Is 1:5
the earth, neither *f* ....Is 40:28

FAIR
Behold, you are *f* ....Song 1:15
of the Lord is not *f* ....Ezek 18:25
to a place called *F* ....Acts 27:8
what is just and *f* ....Col 4:1

FAIREST
another beloved, O *f* ....Song 5:9
your beloved gone, O *f* ....Song 6:1

FAITH
in whom is no *f* ....Deut 32:20
shall live by his *f* ....Hab 2:4
you, O you of little *f* ....Matt 6:30
not found such great *f* ....Matt 8:10
f as a mustard seed ....Matt 17:20
that you have no *f* ....Mark 4:40
to them, "Have *f* ....Mark 11:22
"Increase our *f* ....Luke 17:5
will He really find *f* ....Luke 18:8
a man full of *f* ....Acts 6:5
are sanctified by *f* ....Acts 26:18
for obedience to the *f* ....Rom 1:5
God is revealed from *f* ....Rom 1:17
God, through *f* ....Rom 3:22
f apart from the deeds ....Rom 3:28
his *f* is accounted for ....Rom 4:5
f is made void and the ....Rom 4:14
those who are of the *f* ....Rom 4:16
f which we preach ....Rom 10:8
f comes by hearing ....Rom 10:17
and you stand by *f* ....Rom 11:20
in proportion to our *f* ....Rom 12:6
Do you have *f* ....Rom 14:22
he does not eat from *f* ....Rom 14:23
though I have all *f* ....1 Cor 13:2
And now abide *f* ....1 Cor 13:13
For we walk by *f* ....2 Cor 5:7
the flesh I live by *f* ....Gal 2:20
or by the hearing of *f* ....Gal 3:2
f are sons of Abraham ....Gal 3:7
the law is not of *f* ....Gal 3:12
But after *f* has come ....Gal 3:25
f working through love ....Gal 5:6
of the household of *f* ....Gal 6:10
been saved through *f* ....Eph 2:8
one Lord, one *f* ....Eph 4:5
to the unity of the *f* ....Eph 4:13
taking the shield of *f* ....Eph 6:16
your work of *f* ....1 Thess 1:3
for not all have *f* ....2 Thess 3:2
having *f* and a good ....1 Tim 1:19
the mystery of the *f* ....1 Tim 3:9
he has denied the *f* ....1 Tim 5:8
I have kept the *f* ....2 Tim 4:7
in our common *f* ....Titus 1:4
not being mixed with *f* ....Heb 4:2
f is the substance ....Heb 11:1
without *f* it is ....Heb 11:6
someone says he has *f* ....James 2:14

Show me your *f* . . . James 2:18
and not by *f* only . . . James 2:24
f will save the sick . . . James 5:15
add to your *f* virtue . . . 2 Pet 1:5
on your most holy *f* . . . Jude 20
the patience and the *f* . . . Rev 13:10
of God and the *f* . . . Rev 14:12

FAITHFUL

God, He is God, the *f* . . . Deut 7:9
f disappear from among . . . Ps 12:1
LORD preserves the *f* . . . Ps 31:23
whose spirit was not *f* . . . Ps 78:8
eyes shall be on the *f* . . . Ps 101:6
f spirit conceals a . . . Prov 11:13
But who can find a *f* . . . Prov 20:6
f witness between us . . . Jer 42:5
the Holy One who is *f* . . . Hos 11:12
"Who then is a *f* . . . Matt 24:45
good and *f* servant . . . Matt 25:23
He who is *f* in what . . . Luke 16:10
if you have not been *f* . . . Luke 16:12
have judged me to be *f* . . . Acts 16:15
God is *f* . . . 1 Cor 1:9
is my beloved and *f* . . . 1 Cor 4:17
But as God is *f* . . . 2 Cor 1:18
f brethren in Christ . . . Col 1:2
He who calls you is *f* . . . 1 Thess 5:24
This is a *f* saying and . . . 1 Tim 1:15
f High Priest in . . . Heb 2:17
as Moses also was *f* . . . Heb 3:2
He who promised is *f* . . . Heb 10:23
He is *f* and just to . . . 1 John 1:9
Be *f* until death . . . Rev 2:10
words are true and *f* . . . Rev 21:5

FAITHFULNESS

I have declared Your *f* . . . Ps 40:10
f You shall establish . . . Ps 89:2
Your *f* also surrounds . . . Ps 89:8
and Your *f* every night . . . Ps 92:2
f endures to all . . . Ps 119:90
In Your *f* answer me . . . Ps 143:1
counsels of old are *f* . . . Is 25:1
great is Your *f* . . . Lam 3:23
unbelief make the *f* . . . Rom 3:3

FAITHLESS

"O *f* generation . . . Mark 9:19
If we are *f* . . . 2 Tim 2:13

FALL

a deep sleep to *f* . . . Gen 2:21
but do not let me *f* . . . 2 Sam 24:14
Let them *f* by their . . . Ps 5:10
For I am ready to *f* . . . Ps 38:17
Yes, all kings shall *f* . . . Ps 72:11
righteous man may *f* . . . Prov 24:16
but the wicked shall *f* . . . Prov 24:16
digs a pit will *f* . . . Prov 26:27
all their host shall *f* . . . Is 34:4
men shall utterly *f* . . . Is 40:30
of music, you shall *f* . . . Dan 3:5
And great was its *f* . . . Matt 7:27
the blind, both will *f* . . . Matt 15:14
the stars will *f* . . . Matt 24:29
"I saw Satan *f* . . . Luke 10:18
that they should *f* . . . Rom 11:11
take heed lest he *f* . . . 1 Cor 10:12
with pride he *f* . . . 1 Tim 3:6
if they *f* away . . . Heb 6:6
lest anyone *f* short of . . . Heb 12:15
it all joy when you *f* . . . James 1:2
and rocks, "*F* on us . . . Rev 6:16

FALLEN

"Babylon is *f* . . . Is 21:9
you have *f* from grace . . . Gal 5:4
And I saw a star *f* . . . Rev 9:1
"Babylon is *f* . . . Rev 14:8

FALLING

great drops of blood *f* . . . Luke 22:44
f away comes first . . . 2 Thess 2:3

FALLS

who is alone when he *f* . . . Eccl 4:10
And whoever *f* . . . Matt 21:44
master he stands or *f* . . . Rom 14:4
its flower *f* . . . James 1:11
so that no rain *f* . . . Rev 11:6

FALSE

"You shall not bear *f* . . . Ex 20:16
I hate every *f* way . . . Ps 119:104
gives heed to *f* lips . . . Prov 17:4
f witness shall perish . . . Prov 21:28
and do not love a *f* . . . Zech 8:17
"Beware of *f* prophets . . . Matt 7:15
f christs and *f* . . . Matt 24:24
and we are found *f* . . . 1 Cor 15:15
among *f* brethren . . . 2 Cor 11:26
of *f* brethren . . . Gal 2:4
f prophets have gone . . . 1 John 4:1
mouth of the *f* prophet . . . Rev 16:13

FALSEHOOD

those who speak *f* . . . Ps 5:6
and brings forth *f* . . . Ps 7:14
For their deceit is *f* . . . Ps 119:118
remove *f* and lies far . . . Prov 30:8
under *f* we have hidden . . . Is 28:15
offspring of *f* . . . Is 57:4

FALSELY

it, and swears *f* . . . Lev 6:3
nor have we dealt *f* . . . Ps 44:17
surely they swear *f* . . . Jer 5:2
words, swearing *f* . . . Hos 10:4
of evil against you *f* . . . Matt 5:11
f called knowledge . . . 1 Tim 6:20

FAME

Sheba heard of the *f* . . . 1 Kin 10:1
Your *f* went out . . . Ezek 16:14
them for praise and *f* . . . Zeph 3:19
Then His *f* went . . . Matt 4:24

FAMILIES

in you all the *f* . . . Gen 12:3
and makes their *f* . . . Ps 107:41
the God of all the *f* . . . Jer 31:1
f which the LORD has . . . Jer 33:24
in your seed all the *f* . . . Acts 3:25

FAMILY

shall mourn, every *f* . . . Zech 12:12
f were baptized . . . Acts 16:33
from whom the whole *f* . . . Eph 3:15

FAMINE

Now there was a *f* . . . Gen 12:10
keep them alive in *f* . . . Ps 33:19
He called for a *f* . . . Ps 105:16
send the sword, the *f* . . . Jer 24:10
of the fever of *f* . . . Lam 5:10
I will increase the *f* . . . Ezek 5:16
there arose a severe *f* . . . Luke 15:14

FAN

not to *f* or to cleanse . . . Jer 4:11
His winnowing *f* . . . Matt 3:12

FAR

removed my brothers *f* . . . Job 19:13
Your judgments are *f* . . . Ps 10:5
Be not *f* from Me . . . Ps 22:11
those who are *f* . . . Ps 73:27
The LORD is *f* from the . . . Prov 15:29
but it was *f* from me . . . Eccl 7:23
removed their hearts *f* . . . Is 29:13
Those near and those *f* . . . Ezek 22:5
their heart is *f* from . . . Matt 15:8
going to a *f* country . . . Mark 13:34
though He is not *f* . . . Acts 17:27
you who once were *f* . . . Eph 2:13

FARMER

The hard-working *f* . . . 2 Tim 2:6
See how the *f* waits . . . James 5:7

FAST

f as you do this day . . . Is 58:4
f that I have chosen . . . Is 58:5
"Moreover, when you *f* . . . Matt 6:16
disciples do not *f* . . . Matt 9:14
I *f* twice a week . . . Luke 18:12

FASTED

'Why have we *f* . . . Is 58:3
'When you *f* and . . . Zech 7:5
And when He had *f* . . . Matt 4:2

FASTENED

were its foundations *f* . . . Job 38:6
'the peg that is *f* . . . Is 22:25

FASTING

humbled myself with *f* . . . Ps 35:13
are weak through *f* . . . Ps 109:24
house on the day of *f* . . . Jer 36:6
except by prayer and *f* . . . Matt 17:21
give yourselves to *f* . . . 1 Cor 7:5

FASTINGS

in sleeplessness, in *f* . . . 2 Cor 6:5

FAT

and you will eat the *f* . . . Gen 45:18
f is the LORD's . . . Lev 3:16
Now Eglon was a very *f* . . . Judg 3:17
have closed up their *f* . . . Ps 17:10

FATHER

man shall leave his *f* . . . Gen 2:24
and you shall be a *f* . . . Gen 17:4
'You are my *f* . . . Job 17:14
I was a *f* to the poor . . . Job 29:16
A *f* of the fatherless . . . Ps 68:5
f pities his children . . . Ps 103:13
the instruction of a *f* . . . Prov 4:1
God, Everlasting *F* . . . Is 9:6
You, O LORD, are our *F* . . . Is 63:16
time cry to Me, My *F* . . . Jer 3:4
for I am a *F* to Israel . . . Jer 31:9
"A son honors his *f* . . . Mal 1:6
Have we not all one *F* . . . Mal 2:10
Our *F* in heaven . . . Matt 6:9
He who loves *f* . . . Matt 10:37
does anyone know the *F* . . . Matt 11:27
'He who curses *f* . . . Matt 15:4
for One is your *F* . . . Matt 23:9
F will be divided . . . Luke 12:53
F loves the Son . . . John 3:35
F has been working . . . John 5:17
F raises the dead . . . John 5:21
F judges no one . . . John 5:22
He has seen the *F* . . . John 6:46
F who sent Me bears . . . John 8:18
we have one *F* . . . John 8:41
of your *f* the devil . . . John 8:44
I and My *F* are one . . . John 10:30
and believe that the *F* . . . John 10:38
'I am going to the *F* . . . John 14:28
F is the vinedresser . . . John 15:1
came forth from the *F* . . . John 16:28
that he might be the *f* . . . Rom 4:11
"I have made you a *f* . . . Rom 4:17
"I will be a *F* . . . 2 Cor 6:18
one God and *F* of all . . . Eph 4:6
but exhort him as a *f* . . . 1 Tim 5:1
"I will be to Him a *F* . . . Heb 1:5
without *f*, without mother . . . Heb 7:3
comes down from the *F* . . . James 1:17
if you call on the *F* . . . 1 Pet 1:17
and testify that the *F* . . . 1 John 4:14

FATHER'S
you in My *F* kingdom . . . Matt 26:29
I must be about My *F* . . . Luke 2:49
F house are many . . . John 14:2
that a man has his *f* . . . 1 Cor 5:1

FATHERLESS
my hand against the *f* . . . Job 31:21
the helper of the *f* . . . Ps 10:14
to do justice to the *f* . . . Ps 10:18
He relieves the *f* . . . Ps 146:9
the fields of the *f* . . . Prov 23:10
do not defend the *f* . . . Is 1:23
they may rob the *f* . . . Is 10:2
You the *f* finds mercy . . . Hos 14:3

FATHERS
the LORD God of our *f* . . . Ezra 7:27
f trusted in You . . . Ps 22:4
our ears, O God, our *f* . . . Ps 44:1
have sinned with our *f* . . . Ps 106:6
f ate the manna . . . John 6:31
of whom are the *f* . . . Rom 9:5
you do not have many *f* . . . 1 Cor 4:15
unaware that all our *f* . . . 1 Cor 10:1

FATNESS
as with marrow and *f* . . . Ps 63:5
of the root and *f* . . . Rom 11:17

FATTED
f cattle are . . . Matt 22:4
has killed the *f* . . . Luke 15:27

FAULT
find no charge or *f* . . . Dan 6:4
I have found no *f* . . . Luke 23:14
does He still find *f* . . . Rom 9:19
of God without *f* . . . Phil 2:15
for they are without *f* . . . Rev 14:5

FAULTLESS
covenant had been *f* . . . Heb 8:7
to present you *f* . . . Jude 24

FAULTS
"I remember my *f* . . . Gen 41:9
me from secret *f* . . . Ps 19:12
are beaten for your *f* . . . 1 Pet 2:20

FAVOR
granted me life and *f* . . . Job 10:12
f You will . . . Ps 5:12
His *f* is for life . . . Ps 30:5
A good man obtains *f* . . . Prov 12:2
but his *f* is like dew . . . Prov 19:12
and seek the LORD's *f* . . . Jer 26:19
and stature, and in *f* . . . Luke 2:52
God and having *f* . . . Acts 2:47
to do the Jews a *f* . . . Acts 24:27

FAVORABLE
And will He be *f* . . . Ps 77:7
LORD, You have been *f* . . . Ps 85:1

FAVORED
because You *f* them . . . Ps 44:3
"Rejoice, highly *f* . . . Luke 1:28

FAVORITISM
do not show personal *f* . . . Luke 20:21
God shows personal *f* . . . Gal 2:6

FEAR
this and live, for I *f* God . . . Gen 42:18
f the people of the . . . Num 14:9
to put the dread and *f* . . . Deut 2:25
f Me all the days . . . Deut 4:10
f the LORD your God . . . Deut 6:2
book, that you may *f* . . . Deut 28:58
said, "Does Job *f* . . . Job 1:9
Yes, you cast off *f* . . . Job 15:4
Surely no *f* of me will . . . Job 33:7
He mocks at *f* . . . Job 39:22
they are in great *f* . . . Ps 14:5
The *f* of the LORD is . . . Ps 19:9
of death, I will *f* . . . Ps 23:4
whom shall I *f* . . . Ps 27:1
Let all the earth *f* . . . Ps 33:8
Oh, *f* the LORD . . . Ps 34:9
there is no *f* of God . . . Ps 36:1
they are in great *f* . . . Ps 53:5
hear, all you who *f* . . . Ps 66:16
f You as long as the . . . Ps 72:5
heart to *f* Your name . . . Ps 86:11
The *f* of the LORD is . . . Ps 111:10
f You will be glad . . . Ps 119:74
f the LORD and depart . . . Prov 3:7
The *f* of man brings a . . . Prov 29:25
it, that men should *f* . . . Eccl 3:14
F God and keep His . . . Eccl 12:13
let Him be your *f* . . . Is 8:13
"Be strong, do not *f* . . . Is 35:4
Do you not *f* Me . . . Jer 5:22
who would not *f* . . . Jer 10:7
but I will put My *f* . . . Jer 32:40
who *f* My name the Sun . . . Mal 4:2
f Him who is able . . . Matt 10:28
"Do not *f* . . . Luke 12:32
a judge who did not *f* . . . Luke 18:2
"Do you not even *f* . . . Luke 23:40
And walking in the *f* . . . Acts 9:31
the rest also may *f* . . . 1 Tim 5:20
given us a spirit of *f* . . . 2 Tim 1:7
those who through *f* . . . Heb 2:15
His rest, let us *f* . . . Heb 4:1
because of His godly *f* . . . Heb 5:7
F God . . . 1 Pet 2:17
love casts out *f* . . . 1 John 4:18
Do not *f* any of . . . Rev 2:10

FEARED
But the midwives *f* . . . Ex 1:17
He is also to be *f* . . . 1 Chr 16:25
f God more than . . . Neh 7:2
Yourself, are to be *f* . . . Ps 76:7
Then those who *f* . . . Mal 3:16

FEARFUL
f in praises, doing . . . Ex 15:11
them, "Why are you *f* . . . Matt 8:26
It is a *f* thing to . . . Heb 10:31

FEARFULLY
f and wonderfully made . . . Ps 139:14

FEARFULNESS
F and trembling have . . . Ps 55:5
f has seized the . . . Is 33:14

FEARING
is devoted to *f* You . . . Ps 119:38
sincerity of heart, *f* . . . Col 3:22
forsook Egypt, not *f* . . . Heb 11:27

FEARS
upright man, one who *f* . . . Job 1:8
Who is the man that *f* . . . Ps 25:12
me from all my *f* . . . Ps 34:4
an oath as he who *f* . . . Eccl 9:2
every nation whoever *f* . . . Acts 10:35
f has not been made . . . 1 John 4:18

FEAST
Then he made them a *f* . . . Gen 19:3
and you shall keep a *f* . . . Num 29:12
f is made for laughter . . . Eccl 10:19
f day the terrors that . . . Lam 2:22
hate, I despise your *f* . . . Amos 5:21
every year at the *F* . . . Luke 2:41
when you give a *f* . . . Luke 14:13
Now the Passover, a *f* . . . John 6:4
great day of the *f* . . . John 7:37
let us keep the *f* . . . 1 Cor 5:8

FEASTING
go to the house of *f* . . . Eccl 7:2

FEASTS
I will turn your *f* . . . Amos 8:10
the best places at *f* . . . Luke 20:46
spots in your love *f* . . . Jude 12

FED
f me all my life long . . . Gen 48:15
and *f* you with manna . . . Deut 8:3
but the shepherds *f* . . . Ezek 34:8
f you with milk and . . . 1 Cor 3:2

FEEBLE
strengthened the *f* . . . Job 4:4
And there was none *f* . . . Ps 105:37
And my flesh is *f* . . . Ps 109:24
Every hand will be *f* . . . Ezek 7:17
hang down, and the *f* . . . Heb 12:12

FEED
ravens to *f* you there . . . 1 Kin 17:4
death shall *f* on them . . . Ps 49:14
of the righteous *f* . . . Prov 10:21
and *f* your flocks . . . Is 61:5
to him, "*F* My lambs . . . John 21:15
to him, "*F* My sheep . . . John 21:17
your enemy hungers, *f* . . . Rom 12:20
my goods to *f* the poor . . . 1 Cor 13:3

FEEDS
"Ephraim *f* on the wind . . . Hos 12:1
your heavenly Father *f* . . . Matt 6:26

FEET
So she lay at his *f* . . . Ruth 3:14
so my *f* did not slip . . . 2 Sam 22:37
f they hang far . . . Job 28:4
I was *f* to the lame . . . Job 29:15
all things under his *f* . . . Ps 8:6
He makes my *f* like the . . . Ps 18:33
You have set my *f* . . . Ps 31:8
does not allow our *f* . . . Ps 66:9
f had almost stumbled . . . Ps 73:2
f have been standing . . . Ps 122:2
For their *f* run to . . . Prov 1:16
Her *f* go down to death . . . Prov 5:5
sandals off your *f* . . . Is 20:2
called him to His *f* . . . Is 41:2
up the dust of your *f* . . . Is 49:23
mountains are the *f* . . . Is 52:7
place of My *f* glorious . . . Is 60:13
are the dust of His *f* . . . Nah 1:3
in that day His *f* . . . Zech 14:4
two hands or two *f* . . . Matt 18:8
began to wash His *f* . . . Luke 7:38
also sat at Jesus' *f* . . . Luke 10:39
wash the disciples' *f* . . . John 13:5
at the apostles' *f* . . . Acts 4:35
f are swift to shed . . . Rom 3:15
beautiful are the *f* . . . Rom 10:15
all things under His *f* . . . 1 Cor 15:27
and having shod your *f* . . . Eph 6:15
fell at His *f* as dead . . . Rev 1:17
And I fell at his *f* . . . Rev 19:10

FELIX
Governor of Judea; letter addressed to, Acts 23:24–30
Paul's defense before, Acts 24:1–27

FELLOW
f servants who owed . . . Matt 18:28
begins to beat his *f* . . . Matt 24:49
f worker concerning . . . 2 Cor 8:23
f citizens with the . . . Eph 2:19
Gentiles should be *f* . . . Eph 3:6
rest of my *f* workers . . . Phil 4:3
These are my only *f* . . . Col 4:11
that we may become *f* . . . 3 John 8
I am your *f* servant . . . Rev 19:10

FELLOWSHIP
doctrine and *f* . . . Acts 2:42
were called into the *f* . . . 1 Cor 1:9
not want you to have *f* . . . 1 Cor 10:20
f has righteousness . . . 2 Cor 6:14

the right hand of *f* ..... Gal 2:9
And have no *f* with the ..... Eph 5:11
for your *f* in the ..... Phil 1:5
of love, if any *f* ..... Phil 2:1
and the *f* of His ..... Phil 3:10
also may have *f* ..... 1 John 1:3
we say that we have *f* ..... 1 John 1:6
the light, we have *f* ..... 1 John 1:7

FERVENT
and being *f* in spirit ..... Acts 18:25
f prayer of a ..... James 5:16
all things have *f* ..... 1 Pet 4:8
will melt with *f* ..... 2 Pet 3:10

FERVENTLY
you, always laboring *f* ..... Col 4:12
love one another *f* ..... 1 Pet 1:22

FESTUS
Governor of Judea, Acts 24:27
Paul's defense made to, Acts 25:1–22

FEVER
f which shall ..... Lev 26:16
my bones burn with *f* ..... Job 30:30
and rebuked the *f* ..... Luke 4:39

FEW
f and evil have been ..... Gen 47:9
f days and full of ..... Job 14:1
Let his days be *f* ..... Ps 109:8
let your words be *f* ..... Eccl 5:2
and there are *f* ..... Matt 7:14
but the laborers are *f* ..... Matt 9:37
called, but *f* chosen ..... Matt 20:16
"Lord, are there *f* ..... Luke 13:23
prepared, in which a *f* ..... 1 Pet 3:20
I have a *f* things ..... Rev 2:20

FIDELITY
but showing all good *f* ..... Titus 2:10

FIELD
Let the *f* be joyful ..... Ps 96:12
to house; they add *f* ..... Is 5:8
becomes a fruitful *f* ..... Is 32:15
The *f* is the world ..... Matt 13:38
and buys that *f* ..... Matt 13:44
f has been called the ..... Matt 27:8
you are God's *f* ..... 1 Cor 3:9

FIELD OF BLOOD
A field bought as a cemetery for Judas's burial, Matt 27:1–10
Predicted in the OT, Zech 11:12, 13

FIELDS
f yield no food ..... Hab 3:17
living out in the *f* ..... Luke 2:8
eyes and look at the *f* ..... John 4:35

FIERCENESS
f has deceived you ..... Jer 49:16
the winepress of the *f* ..... Rev 19:15

FIERY
the LORD sent *f* serpents ..... Num 21:6
right hand came a *f* ..... Deut 33:2
shall make them as a *f* ..... Ps 21:9
offspring will be a *f* ..... Is 14:29
burning *f* furnace ..... Dan 3:6
concerning the *f* ..... 1 Pet 4:12
f red dragon having ..... Rev 12:3

FIG
f leaves together ..... Gen 3:7
his vine and his *f* ..... 1 Kin 4:25
fruit falling from a *f* ..... Is 34:4
f tree may not blossom ..... Hab 3:17
fruit on this *f* ..... Luke 13:7
"Look at the *f* ..... Luke 21:29
'I saw you under the *f* ..... John 1:50
Can a *f* tree ..... James 3:12
f tree drops its late ..... Rev 6:13

FIGHT
The LORD will *f* ..... Ex 14:14
you go with me to *f* ..... 1 Kin 22:4
Our God will *f* for us ..... Neh 4:20
My servants would *f* ..... John 18:36
to him, let us not *f* ..... Acts 23:9
F the good *f* ..... 1 Tim 6:12
have fought the good *f* ..... 2 Tim 4:7
You *f* and war ..... James 4:2

FIGHTS
your God is He who *f* ..... Josh 23:10
because my lord *f* ..... 1 Sam 25:28
f come from among ..... James 4:1

FIGS
puts forth her green *f* ..... Song 2:13
f set before the ..... Jer 24:1
from thornbushes or *f* ..... Matt 7:16
men do not gather *f* ..... Luke 6:44
or a grapevine bear *f* ..... James 3:12

FILL
f the earth and subdue ..... Gen 1:28
wealth, that I may *f* ..... Prov 8:21
"Do I not *f* heaven ..... Jer 23:24
f this temple with ..... Hag 2:7
"*F* the waterpots ..... John 2:7
that He might *f* ..... Eph 4:10
so as always to *f* ..... 1 Thess 2:16

FILLED
the whole earth be *f* ..... Ps 72:19
Then our mouth was *f* ..... Ps 126:2
for they shall be *f* ..... Matt 5:6
"Let the children be *f* ..... Mark 7:27
he would gladly have *f* ..... Luke 15:16
being *f* with all ..... Rom 1:29
full of goodness, *f* ..... Rom 15:14
that you may be *f* ..... Eph 3:19
but be *f* with the ..... Eph 5:18
being *f* with the ..... Phil 1:11
peace, be warmed and *f* ..... James 2:16

FILTH
has washed away the *f* ..... Is 4:4
been made as the *f* ..... 1 Cor 4:13
the removal of the *f* ..... 1 Pet 3:21

FILTHINESS
from all your *f* ..... Ezek 36:25
ourselves from all *f* ..... 2 Cor 7:1
lay aside all *f* ..... James 1:21
abominations and the *f* ..... Rev 17:4

FILTHY
is abominable and *f* ..... Job 15:16
with *f* garments ..... Zech 3:3
malice, blasphemy, *f* ..... Col 3:8
poor man in *f* clothes ..... James 2:2
oppressed by the *f* ..... 2 Pet 2:7
let him be *f* ..... Rev 22:11

FIND
sure your sin will *f* ..... Num 32:23
Almighty, we cannot *f* ..... Job 37:23
life to those who *f* ..... Prov 4:22
that no one can *f* ..... Eccl 3:11
waters, for you will *f* ..... Eccl 11:1
seek, and you will *f* ..... Matt 7:7
for My sake will *f* ..... Matt 10:39
when he comes, will *f* ..... Matt 24:46
f a Babe wrapped ..... Luke 2:12
f no fault in this Man ..... Luke 23:4
I *f* then a law ..... Rom 7:21
f grace to help in ..... Heb 4:16

FINDING
great things past *f* ..... Job 9:10
and *f* none ..... Luke 11:24
and His ways past *f* ..... Rom 11:33

FINDS
f me *f* life ..... Prov 8:35
f a wife *f* a good ..... Prov 18:22
Whatever your hand *f* ..... Eccl 9:10
and he who seeks *f* ..... Matt 7:8
f his life will lose ..... Matt 10:39
and he who seeks *f* ..... Luke 11:10

FINE
Then I beat them as *f* ..... 2 Sam 22:43
gold, yea, than much *f* ..... Ps 19:10
f gold is a wise ..... Prov 25:12
set on bases of *f* gold ..... Song 5:15
more rare than *f* ..... Is 13:12
and for *f* clothing ..... Is 23:18
how changed the *f* ..... Lam 4:1
rings, in *f* apparel ..... James 2:2
for the *f* linen is the ..... Rev 19:8

FINGER
written with the *f* ..... Ex 31:18
f shall be thicker ..... 1 Kin 12:10
the pointing of the *f* ..... Is 58:9
dip the tip of his *f* ..... Luke 16:24
the ground with His *f* ..... John 8:6
"Reach your *f* ..... John 20:27

FINGERS
the work of Your *f* ..... Ps 8:3
he points with his *f* ..... Prov 6:13
that which their own *f* ..... Is 2:8
with one of their *f* ..... Matt 23:4

FINISH
city, to *f* the ..... Dan 9:24
he has enough to *f* ..... Luke 14:28
has given Me to *f* ..... John 5:36
so that I may *f* ..... Acts 20:24

FINISHED
f the work which You ..... John 17:4
He said, "It is *f* ..... John 19:30
I have *f* the race ..... 2 Tim 4:7
thousand years were *f* ..... Rev 20:3

FIRE
rained brimstone and *f* ..... Gen 19:24
to him in a flame of *f* ..... Ex 3:2
by day, and *f* was over ..... Ex 40:38
God, who answers by *f* ..... 1 Kin 18:24
LORD was not in the *f* ..... 1 Kin 19:12
I was musing, the *f* ..... Ps 39:3
we went through *f* ..... Ps 66:12
they have set *f* ..... Ps 74:7
f goes before Him ..... Ps 97:3
f and hail ..... Ps 148:8
burns as the *f* ..... Is 9:18
says the LORD, whose *f* ..... Is 31:9
you walk through the *f* ..... Is 43:2
f that burns all the ..... Is 65:5
on whose bodies the *f* ..... Dan 3:27
He break out like *f* ..... Amos 5:6
for conflict by *f* ..... Amos 7:4
like a refiner's *f* ..... Mal 3:2
the Holy Spirit and *f* ..... Matt 3:11
f is not quenched ..... Mark 9:44
"I came to send *f* ..... Luke 12:49
tongues, as of *f* ..... Acts 2:3
f taking vengeance ..... 2 Thess 1:8
and that burned with *f* ..... Heb 12:18
And the tongue is a *f* ..... James 3:6
vengeance of eternal *f* ..... Jude 7
f came down from God ..... Rev 20:9
into the lake of *f* ..... Rev 20:14

FIREBRANDS
a madman who throws *f* ..... Prov 26:18
two stubs of smoking *f* ..... Is 7:4

FIRM
their strength is *f* ..... Ps 73:4
f the feeble knees ..... Is 35:3
of the hope *f* to the ..... Heb 3:6

FIRMAMENT
Thus God made the *f* ..... Gen 1:7

f shows His handiwork ....Ps 19:1
in His mighty *f* ....Ps 150:1
brightness of the *f* ....Dan 12:3

FIRST
The *f* one to plead his ....Prov 18:17
f father sinned ....Is 43:27
desires to be *f* ....Matt 20:27
f shall be slave ....Mark 10:44
And the gospel must *f* ....Mark 13:10
evil, of the Jew *f* ....Rom 2:9
"Or who has *f* ....Rom 11:35
f man Adam became a ....1 Cor 15:45
f a willing mind ....2 Cor 8:12
that we who *f* trusted ....Eph 1:12
For Adam was formed *f* ....1 Tim 2:13
f covenant had been ....Heb 8:7
love Him because He *f* ....1 John 4:19
I am the *F* and the ....Rev 1:17
you have left your *f* ....Rev 2:4
is the *f* resurrection ....Rev 20:5

FIRSTBORN
LORD struck all the *f* ....Ex 12:29
I will make him My *f* ....Ps 89:27
Shall I give my *f* ....Mic 6:7
brought forth her *f* ....Matt 1:25
that He might be the *f* ....Rom 8:29
invisible God, the *f* ....Col 1:15
the beginning, the *f* ....Col 1:18
witness, the *f* from ....Rev 1:5

FIRSTFRUIT
For if the *f* is holy ....Rom 11:16

FIRSTFRUITS
and with the *f* ....Prov 3:9
also who have the *f* ....Rom 8:23
and has become the *f* ....1 Cor 15:20
Christ the *f* ....1 Cor 15:23
might be a kind of *f* ....James 1:18
among men, being *f* ....Rev 14:4

FISH
f taken in a cruel net ....Eccl 9:12
had prepared a great *f* ....Jon 1:17
do You make men like *f* ....Hab 1:14
Or if he asks for a *f* ....Matt 7:10
belly of the great *f* ....Matt 12:40
five loaves and two *f* ....Matt 14:17
and likewise the *f* ....John 21:13

FISHERMEN
The *f* also will mourn ....Is 19:8
I will send for many *f* ....Jer 16:16

FISHERS
and I will make you *f* ....Matt 4:19

FIT
and looking back, is *f* ....Luke 9:62

FITTING
Is it *f* to say to a ....Job 34:18
Luxury is not *f* ....Prov 19:10
so honor is not *f* ....Prov 26:1
things which are not *f* ....Rom 1:28
a High Priest was *f* ....Heb 7:26

FIVE
f smooth stones ....1 Sam 17:40
about *f* thousand men ....Matt 14:21
and *f* were foolish ....Matt 25:2

FIXED
f My limit for it ....Job 38:10
is a great gulf *f* ....Luke 16:26

FLAME
appeared to him in a *f* ....Ex 3:2
f will dry out his ....Job 15:30
f consumes the chaff ....Is 5:24
and tempest and the *f* ....Is 29:6
nor shall the *f* ....Is 43:2
behind them a *f* ....Joel 2:3
am tormented in this *f* ....Luke 16:24
and His ministers a *f* ....Heb 1:7
and His eyes like a *f* ....Rev 1:14

FLAMES
the LORD divides the *f* ....Ps 29:7

FLAMING
f sword which turned ....Gen 3:24
f fire in their land ....Ps 105:32
in *f* fire taking ....2 Thess 1:8

FLATTER
I do not know how to *f* ....Job 32:22
They *f* with their ....Ps 5:9

FLATTERING
f mouth works ruin ....Prov 26:28
f speech deceive ....Rom 16:18
any time did we use *f* ....1 Thess 2:5
swelling words, *f* ....Jude 16

FLATTERS
with one who *f* with ....Prov 20:19
f his neighbor spreads ....Prov 29:5

FLAVOR
the salt loses its *f* ....Matt 5:13

FLAX
f He will not quench ....Is 42:3
f He will not quench ....Matt 12:20

FLED
The sea saw it and *f* ....Ps 114:3
who have *f* for refuge ....Heb 6:18

FLEE
f away secretly ....Gen 31:27
those who hate You *f* ....Num 10:35
such a man as I *f* ....Neh 6:11
who see me outside *f* ....Ps 31:11
Or where can I *f* ....Ps 139:7
And the shadows *f* ....Song 2:17
who are in Judea *f* ....Matt 24:16
F sexual immorality ....1 Cor 6:18
f these things and ....1 Tim 6:11
devil and he will *f* ....James 4:7

FLESH
bone of my bones and *f* ....Gen 2:23
shall become one *f* ....Gen 2:24
f had corrupted their ....Gen 6:12
f I shall see God ....Job 19:26
My *f* also will rest in ....Ps 16:9
that they were but *f* ....Ps 78:39
my heart and my *f* ....Ps 84:2
f shall bless His holy ....Ps 145:21
is wearisome to the *f* ....Eccl 12:12
And all *f* shall see it ....Is 40:5
"All *f* is grass ....Is 40:6
out My Spirit on all *f* ....Joel 2:28
Simon Bar-Jonah, for *f* ....Matt 16:17
two shall become one *f* ....Matt 19:5
were shortened, no *f* ....Matt 24:22
shall become one *f* ....Mark 10:8
f shall see the ....Luke 3:6
And the Word became *f* ....John 1:14
I shall give is My *f* ....John 6:51
unless you eat the *f* ....John 6:53
f profits nothing ....John 6:63
according to the *f* ....John 8:15
when we were in the *f* ....Rom 7:5
of God, but with the *f* ....Rom 7:25
on the things of the *f* ....Rom 8:5
you are not in the *f* ....Rom 8:9
to the *f* you will die ....Rom 8:13
f should glory in His ....1 Cor 1:29
"shall become one *f* ....1 Cor 6:16
there is one kind of *f* ....1 Cor 15:39
For the *f* lusts ....Gal 5:17
have crucified the *f* ....Gal 5:24
good showing in the *f* ....Gal 6:12
may boast in your *f* ....Gal 6:13
f has ceased from sin ....1 Pet 4:1
of his time in the *f* ....1 Pet 4:2
the lust of the *f* ....1 John 2:16
has come in the *f* ....1 John 4:2
dreamers defile the *f* ....Jude 8

FLESHLY
f wisdom but by the ....2 Cor 1:12
law of a *f* commandment ....Heb 7:16
f lusts which ....1 Pet 2:11

FLIES
will send swarms of *f* ....Ex 8:21
He sent swarms of *f* ....Ps 78:45
Dead *f* putrefy the ....Eccl 10:1

FLIGHT
f shall perish from ....Amos 2:14
And pray that your *f* ....Matt 24:20

FLINT
will seem like *f* ....Is 5:28
set My face like a *f* ....Is 50:7

FLOCK
Your people like a *f* ....Ps 77:20
wilderness like a *f* ....Ps 78:52
lead Joseph like a *f* ....Ps 80:1
the footsteps of the *f* ....Song 1:8
He will feed His *f* ....Is 40:11
you do not feed the *f* ....Ezek 34:3
are My *f*, the *f* ....Ezek 34:31
though the *f* be cut ....Hab 3:17
my God, "Feed the *f* ....Zech 11:4
sheep of the *f* ....Matt 26:31
"Do not fear, little *f* ....Luke 12:32
there will be one *f* ....John 10:16
of the milk of the *f* ....1 Cor 9:7
Shepherd the *f* of God ....1 Pet 5:2
examples to the *f* ....1 Pet 5:3

FLOOD
the waters of the *f* ....Gen 7:10
sat enthroned at the *F* ....Ps 29:10
them away like a *f* ....Ps 90:5
will you do in the *f* ....Jer 12:5
the days before the *f* ....Matt 24:38
bringing in the *f* ....2 Pet 2:5
of his mouth like a *f* ....Rev 12:15

FLOODS
me, and the *f* of ....Ps 18:4
f on the dry ground ....Is 44:3
rain descended, the *f* ....Matt 7:25

FLOURISH
the righteous shall *f* ....Ps 72:7

FLOURISHED
your care for me has *f* ....Phil 4:10

FLOURISHES
In the morning it *f* ....Ps 90:6

FLOW
f away as waters which ....Ps 58:7
and the waters *f* ....Ps 147:18
that its spices may *f* ....Song 4:16
all nations shall *f* ....Is 2:2
of his heart will *f* ....John 7:38

FLOWER
comes forth like a *f* ....Job 14:2
as a *f* of the field ....Ps 103:15
beauty is a fading *f* ....Is 28:4
is like the *f* of the ....Is 40:6
grass withers, the *f* ....Is 40:7
if she is past the *f* ....1 Cor 7:36
of man as the *f* ....1 Pet 1:24

FLOWERS
f appear on the earth ....Song 2:12

FLOWING
'a land *f* with milk ....Deut 6:3
of wisdom is a *f* ....Prov 18:4
the Gentiles like a *f* ....Is 66:12

to repay, he freely *f* . . . . Luke 7:42
God in Christ *f* . . . . Eph 4:32
even as Christ *f* . . . . Col 3:13

FORGET
"For God has made me *f* . . . . Gen 41:51
yourselves, lest you *f* . . . . Deut 4:23
f the covenant of your . . . . Deut 4:31
f the LORD who brought . . . . Deut 6:12
the paths of all who *f* . . . . Job 8:13
all the nations that *f* . . . . Ps 9:17
this, you who *f* . . . . Ps 50:22
f the works of God . . . . Ps 78:7
I will not *f* Your word . . . . Ps 119:16
If I *f* you . . . . Ps 137:5
My son, do not *f* . . . . Prov 3:1
f her nursing child . . . . Is 49:15
f the LORD your Maker . . . . Is 51:13
f her ornaments . . . . Jer 2:32
f your work and labor . . . . Heb 6:10

FORGETS
f the covenant of her . . . . Prov 2:17
and immediately *f* . . . . James 1:24

FORGETTING
f those things which . . . . Phil 3:13

FORGIVE
dwelling place, and *f* . . . . 1 Kin 8:39
f their sin and heal . . . . 2 Chr 7:14
good, and ready to *f* . . . . Ps 86:5
And *f* us our debts . . . . Matt 6:12
Father will also *f* . . . . Matt 6:14
f men their trespasses . . . . Matt 6:15
his heart, does not *f* . . . . Matt 18:35
Who can *f* sins but God . . . . Mark 2:7
f the sins of any . . . . John 20:23
you ought rather to *f* . . . . 2 Cor 2:7
anything, I also *f* . . . . 2 Cor 2:10
F me this wrong . . . . 2 Cor 12:13
f us our sins and to . . . . 1 John 1:9

FORGIVEN
transgression is *f* . . . . Ps 32:1
sins be *f* them . . . . Mark 4:12
to whom little is *f* . . . . Luke 7:47
indeed I have *f* . . . . 2 Cor 2:10
f you all trespasses . . . . Col 2:13
sins, he will be *f* . . . . James 5:15
your sins are *f* . . . . 1 John 2:12

FORGIVENESS
But there is *f* with . . . . Ps 130:4
God belong mercy and *f* . . . . Dan 9:9
preached to you the *f* . . . . Acts 13:38
they may receive *f* . . . . Acts 26:18
His blood, the *f* . . . . Eph 1:7

FORGIVES
f all your iniquities . . . . Ps 103:3
"Who is this who even *f* . . . . Luke 7:49

FORGIVING
tenderhearted, *f* . . . . Eph 4:32
and *f* one another . . . . Col 3:13

FORGOT
remember Joseph, but *f* . . . . Gen 40:23
f the LORD their God . . . . Judg 3:7
f His works and His . . . . Ps 78:11
They soon *f* His works . . . . Ps 106:13

FORGOTTEN
f the God who fathered . . . . Deut 32:18
"Why have You *f* . . . . Ps 42:9
If we had *f* the name . . . . Ps 44:20
memory of them is *f* . . . . Eccl 9:5
you will not be *f* . . . . Is 44:21
And my Lord has *f* . . . . Is 49:14
I have *f* prosperity . . . . Lam 3:17
not one of them is *f* . . . . Luke 12:6
f the exhortation . . . . Heb 12:5
f that he was cleansed . . . . 2 Pet 1:9

FORM
earth was without *f* . . . . Gen 1:2
Who would *f* a god or . . . . Is 44:10
f the light and create . . . . Is 45:7
descended in bodily *f* . . . . Luke 3:22
time, nor seen His *f* . . . . John 5:37
For the *f* of this . . . . 1 Cor 7:31
who, being in the *f* . . . . Phil 2:6
Abstain from every *f* . . . . 1 Thess 5:22
having a *f* of . . . . 2 Tim 3:5

FORMED
And the LORD God *f* . . . . Gen 2:7
And His hands *f* . . . . Ps 95:5
f my inward parts . . . . Ps 139:13
f everything gives the . . . . Prov 26:10
say of him who *f* . . . . Is 29:16
Me there was no God *f* . . . . Is 43:10
This people I have *f* . . . . Is 43:21
"Before I *f* you in . . . . Jer 1:5
Will the thing *f* . . . . Rom 9:20
say to him who *f* . . . . Rom 9:20
until Christ is *f* . . . . Gal 4:19
For Adam was *f* first . . . . 1 Tim 2:13

FORMER
f lovingkindness . . . . Ps 89:49
f days better than . . . . Eccl 7:10
f rain to the earth . . . . Hos 6:3
f prophets preached . . . . Zech 1:4
f conduct in Judaism . . . . Gal 1:13
your *f* conduct . . . . Eph 4:22
f things have passed . . . . Rev 21:4

FORNICATION
"We were not born of *f* . . . . John 8:41
of the wrath of her *f* . . . . Rev 14:8

FORNICATOR
you know, that no *f* . . . . Eph 5:5
lest there be any *f* . . . . Heb 12:16

FORNICATORS
but *f* and adulterers . . . . Heb 13:4

FORSAKE
but if you *f* Him . . . . 2 Chr 15:2
"If his sons *f* . . . . Ps 89:30
f His inheritance . . . . Ps 94:14
But I did not *f* . . . . Ps 119:87
father, and do not *f* . . . . Prov 1:8
worthless idols *f* . . . . Jon 2:8
of you does not *f* . . . . Luke 14:33
never leave you nor *f* . . . . Heb 13:5

FORSAKEN
My God, why have You *f* . . . . Ps 22:1
seen the righteous *f* . . . . Ps 37:25
you dread will be *f* . . . . Is 7:16
cities will be as a *f* . . . . Is 17:9
a mere moment I have *f* . . . . Is 54:7
no longer be termed *F* . . . . Is 62:4
they have *f* Me . . . . Jer 2:13
My God, why have You *f* . . . . Matt 27:46
persecuted, but not *f* . . . . 2 Cor 4:9
for Demas has *f* . . . . 2 Tim 4:10
f the right way . . . . 2 Pet 2:15

FORSAKING
f the assembling . . . . Heb 10:25

FORSOOK
f God who made him . . . . Deut 32:15
all the disciples *f* . . . . Matt 26:56
with me, but all *f* . . . . 2 Tim 4:16
By faith he *f* Egypt . . . . Heb 11:27

FORTRESS
LORD is my rock, my *f* . . . . 2 Sam 22:2
my rock of refuge, a *f* . . . . Ps 31:2

FOUL
My wounds are *f* . . . . Ps 38:5
f weather today . . . . Matt 16:3
a prison for every *f* . . . . Rev 18:2

FOUND
f a helper comparable . . . . Gen 2:20
where can wisdom be *f* . . . . Job 28:12
when You may be *f* . . . . Ps 32:6
f My servant David . . . . Ps 89:20
a thousand I have *f* . . . . Eccl 7:28
this only I have *f* . . . . Eccl 7:29
f the one I love . . . . Song 3:4
LORD while He may be *f* . . . . Is 55:6
your fruit is *f* . . . . Hos 14:8
fruit on it and *f* none . . . . Luke 13:6
he was lost and is *f* . . . . Luke 15:24
f the Messiah" (which . . . . John 1:41
I *f* to bring death . . . . Rom 7:10
and be *f* in Him . . . . Phil 3:9
be diligent to be *f* . . . . 2 Pet 3:14

FOUNDATION
he shall lay its *f* . . . . Josh 6:26
His *f* is in the holy . . . . Ps 87:1
and justice are the *f* . . . . Ps 89:14
Of old You laid the *f* . . . . Ps 102:25
has an everlasting *f* . . . . Prov 10:25
deep and laid the *f* . . . . Luke 6:48
the earth without a *f* . . . . Luke 6:49
loved Me before the *f* . . . . John 17:24
I have laid the *f* . . . . 1 Cor 3:10
f can anyone lay than . . . . 1 Cor 3:11
us in Him before the *f* . . . . Eph 1:4
the solid *f* of God . . . . 2 Tim 2:19
not laying again the *f* . . . . Heb 6:1
Lamb slain from the *f* . . . . Rev 13:8
the first *f* was jasper . . . . Rev 21:19

FOUNDATIONS
when I laid the *f* . . . . Job 38:4
f are destroyed . . . . Ps 11:3
You who laid the *f* . . . . Ps 104:5
shall raise up the *f* . . . . Is 58:12
The *f* of the wall . . . . Rev 21:19

FOUNDED
For He has *f* it upon . . . . Ps 24:2
shake it, for it was *f* . . . . Luke 6:48

FOUNTAIN
will become in him a *f* . . . . John 4:14

FOUNTAINS
on that day all the *f* . . . . Gen 7:11
f be dispersed abroad . . . . Prov 5:16
when there were no *f* . . . . Prov 8:24
lead them to living *f* . . . . Rev 7:17

FOX
build, if even a *f* . . . . Neh 4:3
"Go, tell that *f* . . . . Luke 13:32

FOXES
caught three hundred *f* . . . . Judg 15:4
f that spoil the vines . . . . Song 2:15
F have holes and birds . . . . Luke 9:58

FRAGMENTS
f that remained . . . . Matt 14:20
of the leftover *f* . . . . Luke 9:17
baskets with the *f* . . . . John 6:13

FRAGRANCE
garments is like the *f* . . . . Song 4:11
was filled with the *f* . . . . John 12:3
we are to God the *f* . . . . 2 Cor 2:15

FRAME
For He knows our *f* . . . . Ps 103:14
f was not hidden . . . . Ps 139:15

FREE
and the servant is *f* . . . . Job 3:19
let the oppressed go *f* . . . . Is 58:6
'You will be made *f* . . . . John 8:33
if the Son makes you *f* . . . . John 8:36
And having been set *f* . . . . Rom 6:18
now having been set *f* . . . . Rom 6:22
Jesus has made me *f* . . . . Rom 8:2

Am I not *f* ....1 Cor 9:1
is neither slave nor *f* ....Gal 3:28
Jerusalem above is *f* ....Gal 4:26
Christ has made us *f* ....Gal 5:1
he is a slave or *f* ....Eph 6:8
poor, *f* and slave ....Rev 13:16

FREELY
the garden you may *f* ....Gen 2:16
I will love them *f* ....Hos 14:4
F you have received ....Matt 10:8
f give us all ....Rom 8:32
that have been *f* ....1 Cor 2:12
the water of life *f* ....Rev 22:17

FRESH
My glory is *f* within ....Job 29:20
They shall be *f* ....Ps 92:14
both salt water and *f* ....James 3:12

FRIEND
a man speaks to his *f* ....Ex 33:11
of Abraham Your *f* ....2 Chr 20:7
though he were my *f* ....Ps 35:14
f You have put ....Ps 88:18
f loves at all times ....Prov 17:17
f who sticks closer ....Prov 18:24
not forsake your own *f* ....Prov 27:10
a *f* of tax collectors ....Matt 11:19
of you shall have a *f* ....Luke 11:5
f Lazarus sleeps ....John 11:11
you are not Caesar's *f* ....John 19:12
Philemon our beloved *f* ....Philem 1
he was called the *f* ....James 2:23
wants to be a *f* ....James 4:4

FRIENDS
and hate your *f* ....2 Sam 19:6
My *f* scorn me ....Job 16:20
f have forgotten me ....Job 19:14
the rich has many *f* ....Prov 14:20
one's life for his *f* ....John 15:13
You are My *f* ....John 15:14
I have called you *f* ....John 15:15
to forbid any of his *f* ....Acts 24:23

FROGS
your territory with *f* ....Ex 8:2
f coming out of the ....Rev 16:13

FRONTLETS
on your hand and as *f* ....Ex 13:16
and they shall be as *f* ....Deut 6:8

FRUIT
and showed them the *f* ....Num 13:26
Blessed shall be the *f* ....Deut 28:4
brings forth its *f* ....Ps 1:3
f is better than gold ....Prov 8:19
The *f* of the righteous ....Prov 11:30
with good by the *f* ....Prov 12:14
f was sweet to my ....Song 2:3
they shall eat the *f* ....Is 3:10
like the first *f* ....Is 28:4
"I create the *f* ....Is 57:19
f is found in Me ....Hos 14:8
does not bear good *f* ....Matt 3:10
good tree bears good *f* ....Matt 7:17
not drink of this *f* ....Matt 26:29
and blessed is the *f* ....Luke 1:42
life, and bring no *f* ....Luke 8:14
and he came seeking *f* ....Luke 13:6
And if it bears *f* ....Luke 13:9
branch that bears *f* ....John 15:2
that you bear much *f* ....John 15:8
should go and bear *f* ....John 15:16
f did you have then in ....Rom 6:21
God, you have your *f* ....Rom 6:22
that we should bear *f* ....Rom 7:4
But the *f* of the ....Gal 5:22
but I seek the *f* ....Phil 4:17
yields the peaceable *f* ....Heb 12:11
Now the *f* of ....James 3:18
autumn trees without *f* ....Jude 12
tree yielding its *f* ....Rev 22:2

FRUITFUL
them, saying, "Be *f* ....Gen 1:22
a *f* bough, a *f* ....Gen 49:22
wife shall be like a *f* ....Ps 128:3
heaven and *f* seasons ....Acts 14:17
pleasing Him, being *f* ....Col 1:10

FRUITS
Therefore bear *f* ....Matt 3:8
know them by their *f* ....Matt 7:16
and increase the *f* ....2 Cor 9:10
of mercy and good *f* ....James 3:17
which bore twelve *f* ....Rev 22:2

FUEL
people shall be as *f* ....Is 9:19
into the fire for *f* ....Ezek 15:4

FULFILL
the LORD, to *f* his vow ....Lev 22:21
And you shall *f* ....1 Kin 5:9
f all your petitions ....Ps 20:5
f the desire of those ....Ps 145:19
for us to *f* all ....Matt 3:15
f the law of Christ ....Gal 6:2
f my joy by being ....Phil 2:2
and *f* all the good ....2 Thess 1:11
If you really *f* ....James 2:8

FULFILLED
the law till all is *f* ....Matt 5:18
of the Gentiles are *f* ....Luke 21:24
all things must be *f* ....Luke 24:44
of the law might be *f* ....Rom 8:4
loves another has *f* ....Rom 13:8
For all the law is *f* ....Gal 5:14

FULFILLMENT
for there will be a *f* ....Luke 1:45
love is the *f* of the ....Rom 13:10

FULL
I went out *f* ....Ruth 1:21
For I am *f* of words ....Job 32:18
of the LORD is *f* ....Ps 29:4
who has his quiver *f* ....Ps 127:5
Lest I be *f* and deny ....Prov 30:9
yet the sea is not *f* ....Eccl 1:7
the whole earth is *f* ....Is 6:3
and it was *f* of bones ....Ezek 37:1
But truly I am *f* ....Mic 3:8
whole body will be *f* ....Matt 6:22
of the Father, *f* ....John 1:14
your joy may be *f* ....John 15:11
chose Stephen, a man *f* ....Acts 6:5
You are already *f* ....1 Cor 4:8
learned both to be *f* ....Phil 4:12
I am *f*, having received ....Phil 4:18

FULL-GROWN
and sin, when it is *f* ....James 1:15

FULLNESS
satisfied with the *f* ....Ps 36:8
f we have all received ....John 1:16
to Israel until the *f* ....Rom 11:25
But when the *f* of the ....Gal 4:4
dispensation of the *f* ....Eph 1:10
filled with all the *f* ....Eph 3:19
Him dwells all the *f* ....Col 2:9

FURIOUS
You have been *f* ....Ps 89:38
f man do not go ....Prov 22:24
fury and in *f* rebukes ....Ezek 5:15
LORD avenges and is *f* ....Nah 1:2
this, they were *f* ....Acts 5:33

FURNACE
you out of the iron *f* ....Deut 4:20
tested you in the *f* ....Is 48:10
of a burning fiery *f* ....Dan 3:6
cast them into the *f* ....Matt 13:42
the smoke of a great *f* ....Rev 9:2

FURNISHED
also *f* her table ....Prov 9:2
a large upper room, *f* ....Mark 14:15

FURY
F is not in Me ....Is 27:4
they are full of the *f* ....Is 51:20
f to His adversaries ....Is 59:18
and My own *f* ....Is 63:5
even in anger and *f* ....Jer 21:5
and I will cause My *f* ....Ezek 5:13
Thus will I spend My *f* ....Ezek 6:12
in anger and *f* on the ....Mic 5:15

FUTILE
For it is not a *f* ....Deut 32:47
of the peoples are *f* ....Jer 10:3
wise, that they are *f* ....1 Cor 3:20
risen, your faith is *f* ....1 Cor 15:17

FUTILITY
allotted months of *f* ....Job 7:3
f have You created all ....Ps 89:47
was subjected to *f* ....Rom 8:20

FUTURE
for the *f* of that man ....Ps 37:37
the *f* of the wicked ....Ps 37:38
to give you a *f* ....Jer 29:11

GAAL
Son of Ebed; vilifies Abimelech, Judg 9:26–41

GAASH
Hill of Ephraim, Judg 2:9
Joshua buried near, Josh 24:30

GABBATHA
Place of Pilate's court, John 19:13

GABRIEL
Messenger archangel; interprets Daniel's vision, Dan 8:16–27
Reveals the prophecy of 70 weeks, Dan 9:21–27
Announces John's birth, Luke 1:11–22
Announces Christ's birth, Luke 1:26–38
Stands in God's presence, Luke 1:19

GAD
Son of Jacob by Zilpah, Gen 30:10, 11
Blessed by Jacob, Gen 49:19
——— Tribe of:
Census of, Num 1:24, 25
Territory of, Num 32:20–36
Captivity of, 1 Chr 5:26
Later references to, Rev 7:5
——— Prophet in David's reign, 1 Sam 22:5
Message of, to David, 2 Sam 24:10–16

GADARENES (or Gergesenes)
People east of the Sea of Galilee, Mark 5:1
Healing of demon-possessed in territory of, Matt 8:28–34

GAIN
g than fine gold ....Prov 3:14
will have no lack of *g* ....Prov 31:11
a time to *g* ....Eccl 3:6
to get dishonest *g* ....Ezek 22:27
him who covets evil *g* ....Hab 2:9
and to die is *g* ....Phil 1:21
rubbish, that I may *g* ....Phil 3:8
is a means of *g* ....1 Tim 6:5
contentment is great *g* ....1 Tim 6:6
for dishonest *g* ....1 Pet 5:2

GAINS
g the whole world ....Matt 16:26

GAIUS
Companion of Paul, Acts 19:29
——— Convert at Derbe, Acts 20:4
——— Paul's host at Corinth, Rom 16:23; 1 Cor 1:14

GALATIA
Paul visits, Acts 16:6; 18:23
Paul writes to Christians in, Gal 1:1
Peter writes to Christians in, 1 Pet 1:1

GALILEANS
Speech of, Mark 14:70
Faith of, John 4:45
Pilate's cruelty toward, Luke 13:1, 2

GALILEE
Prophecies concerning, Deut 33:18–23; Is 9:1, 2
Dialect of, distinctive, Matt 26:73
Herod's jurisdiction over, Luke 3:1
Christ's contacts with, Matt 2:22; 4:12–25; 26:32; 27:55; John 4:1, 3

GALILEE, SEA OF
Scene of many events in Christ's life, Mark 7:31
Called Chinnereth, Num 34:11
Later called Gennesaret, Luke 5:1

GALL
They also gave me *g* . . . . Ps 69:21
the wormwood and the *g* . . . . Lam 3:19
turned justice into *g* . . . . Amos 6:12
wine mingled with *g* . . . . Matt 27:34

GALLIO
Roman proconsul of Achaia, dismisses charges against Paul, Acts 18:12–17

GAMALIEL
Famous Jewish teacher, Acts 22:3
Respected by people, Acts 5:34–39

GARDEN
LORD God planted a *g* . . . . Gen 2:8
g enclosed is my . . . . Song 4:12
like a watered *g* . . . . Is 58:11
Eden, the *g* of God . . . . Ezek 28:13
raise up for them a *g* . . . . Ezek 34:29
where there was a *g* . . . . John 18:1
in the *g* a new tomb . . . . John 19:41

GARMENT
beautiful Babylonian *g* . . . . Josh 7:21
g that is moth-eaten . . . . Job 13:28
made sackcloth my *g* . . . . Ps 69:11
with light as with a *g* . . . . Ps 104:2
one who takes away a *g* . . . . Prov 25:20
the hem of His *g* . . . . Matt 9:20
have on a wedding *g* . . . . Matt 22:11
cloth on an old *g* . . . . Mark 2:21
all grow old like a *g* . . . . Heb 1:11
hating even the *g* . . . . Jude 23

GARMENTS
g did not wear out on . . . . Deut 8:4
Why are your *g* hot . . . . Job 37:17
They divide My *g* . . . . Ps 22:18
g always be white . . . . Eccl 9:8
g rolled in blood . . . . Is 9:5
from Edom, with dyed *g* . . . . Is 63:1
Take away the filthy *g* . . . . Zech 3:4
man clothed in soft *g* . . . . Matt 11:8
spread their *g* on the . . . . Matt 21:8
and divided His *g* . . . . Matt 27:35
by them in shining *g* . . . . Luke 24:4
g are moth-eaten . . . . James 5:2
be clothed in white *g* . . . . Rev 3:5

GARRISON
gathered the whole *g* . . . . Matt 27:27
Damascenes with a *g* . . . . 2 Cor 11:32

GATE
This is the *g* of the . . . . Ps 118:20
by the narrow *g* . . . . Matt 7:13
by the Sheep *G* a pool . . . . John 5:2
laid daily at the *g* . . . . Acts 3:2
suffered outside the *g* . . . . Heb 13:12
each individual *g* . . . . Rev 21:21

GATES
possess the *g* of those . . . . Gen 24:60
g are burned with fire . . . . Neh 1:3
they go down to the *g* . . . . Job 17:16
up your heads, O you *g* . . . . Ps 24:7
The LORD loves the *g* . . . . Ps 87:2
Open to me the *g* . . . . Ps 118:19
is known in the *g* . . . . Prov 31:23
go through the *g* . . . . Is 62:10
and the *g* of Hades . . . . Matt 16:18
wall with twelve *g* . . . . Rev 21:12
g were twelve pearls . . . . Rev 21:21
g shall not be shut . . . . Rev 21:25

GATH
Philistine city, 1 Sam 6:17
Ark carried to, 1 Sam 5:8
David takes refuge in, 1 Sam 21:10–15
David's second flight to, 1 Sam 27:3–12
Captured by David, 1 Chr 18:1
Destruction of, prophetic, Amos 6:1–3
Name becomes proverbial, Mic 1:10

GATHER
g my soul with sinners . . . . Ps 26:9
G My saints . . . . Ps 50:5
and a time to *g* stones . . . . Eccl 3:5
g the lambs with His . . . . Is 40:11
g His wheat into the . . . . Matt 3:12
sow nor reap nor *g* . . . . Matt 6:26
Do men *g* grapes from . . . . Matt 7:16
g where I have not . . . . Matt 25:26
g together His . . . . Mark 13:27

GATHERED
g little had no lack . . . . Ex 16:18
And *g* out of the lands . . . . Ps 107:3
g some of every kind . . . . Matt 13:47
the nations will be *g* . . . . Matt 25:32

GATHERING
g together of the . . . . Gen 1:10
g together to Him . . . . 2 Thess 2:1

GATHERS
g the waters of the . . . . Ps 33:7
His heart *g* iniquity . . . . Ps 41:6
g her food in the . . . . Prov 6:8
The Lord GOD, who *g* . . . . Is 56:8
together, as a hen *g* . . . . Matt 23:37

GAVE
to be with me, she *g* . . . . Gen 3:12
g You this authority . . . . Matt 21:23
that He *g* His only . . . . John 3:16
Those whom You *g* . . . . John 17:12
but God *g* the increase . . . . 1 Cor 3:6
g Himself for our sins . . . . Gal 1:4
g Himself for me . . . . Gal 2:20
g Himself for it . . . . Eph 5:25
The sea *g* up the dead . . . . Rev 20:13

GAZA
Philistine city, Josh 13:3
Samson removes the gates of, Judg 16:1–3
Samson taken there as prisoner; his revenge, Judg 16:21–31
Sin of, condemned, Amos 1:6, 7
Philip journeys to, Acts 8:26

GAZED
g into heaven and saw . . . . Acts 7:55

GAZING
why do you stand *g* . . . . Acts 1:11

GEDALIAH
Made governor of Judah, 2 Kin 25:22–26
Befriends Jeremiah, Jer 40:5, 6
Murdered by Ishmael, Jer 41:2, 18

GEHAZI
Elisha's servant; seeks reward from Naaman, 2 Kin 5:20–24
Afflicted with leprosy, 2 Kin 5:25–27
Relates Elisha's deeds to Jehoram, 2 Kin 8:4–6

GENEALOGIES
fables and endless *g* . . . . 1 Tim 1:4

GENEALOGY
The book of the *g* . . . . Matt 1:1
mother, without *g* . . . . Heb 7:3

GENERATION
perverse and crooked *g* . . . . Deut 32:5
The *g* of the upright . . . . Ps 112:2
g shall praise Your . . . . Ps 145:4
g that curses its . . . . Prov 30:11
g that is pure in its . . . . Prov 30:12
One *g* passes away . . . . Eccl 1:4
g it shall lie . . . . Is 34:10
who will declare His *g* . . . . Is 53:8
and adulterous *g* . . . . Matt 12:39
this *g* will by no . . . . Matt 24:34
from this perverse *g* . . . . Acts 2:40
But you are a chosen *g* . . . . 1 Pet 2:9

GENERATIONS
be remembered in all *g* . . . . Ps 45:17
Your praise to all *g* . . . . Ps 79:13
for a thousand *g* . . . . Ps 105:8
g will call me blessed . . . . Luke 1:48

GENEROUS
g soul will be made . . . . Prov 11:25
g eye will be blessed . . . . Prov 22:9
no longer be called *g* . . . . Is 32:5
g man devises *g* . . . . Is 32:8

GENTILES
G were separated . . . . Gen 10:5
as a light to the *G* . . . . Is 42:6
G shall come to your . . . . Is 60:3
the riches of the *G* . . . . Is 61:6
all these things the *G* . . . . Matt 6:32
into the way of the *G* . . . . Matt 10:5
revelation to the *G* . . . . Luke 2:32
G are fulfilled . . . . Luke 21:24
bear My name before *G* . . . . Acts 9:15
poured out on the *G* . . . . Acts 10:45
a light to the *G* . . . . Acts 13:47
blasphemed among the *G* . . . . Rom 2:24
also the God of the *G* . . . . Rom 3:29
even named among the *G* . . . . 1 Cor 5:1
mystery among the *G* . . . . Col 1:27
a teacher of the *G* . . . . 1 Tim 2:7
nothing from the *G* . . . . 3 John 7

GENTLE
g tongue breaks a bone . . . . Prov 25:15
from Me, for I am *g* . . . . Matt 11:29
But we were *g* among . . . . 1 Thess 2:7
to be peaceable, *g* . . . . Titus 3:2
only to the good and *g* . . . . 1 Pet 2:18
ornament of a *g* . . . . 1 Pet 3:4

GENTLENESS
g has made me great . . . . Ps 18:35
love and a spirit of *g* . . . . 1 Cor 4:21
g, self-control . . . . Gal 5:23
all lowliness and *g* . . . . Eph 4:2
Let your *g* be known to . . . . Phil 4:5
love, patience, *g* . . . . 1 Tim 6:11

GERAR
Town of Philistia, Gen 10:19
Visited by Abraham, Gen 20:1–18
Visited by Isaac, Gen 26:1–17
Abimelech, king of, Gen 26:1, 26

GERSHOM (or Gershon)
Son of Moses, Ex 2:21, 22
Circumcised, Ex 4:25
Founder of Levite family, 1 Chr 23:14–16

GESHUR
Inhabitants of, not expelled by Israel, Josh 13:13
Talmai, king of, grandfather of Absalom, 2 Sam 3:3
Absalom flees to, 2 Sam 13:37, 38

GETHSEMANE
Garden near Jerusalem, Matt 26:30, 36
Often visited by Christ, Luke 22:39
Scene of Christ's agony and betrayal, Matt 26:36–56; John 18:1–12

GEZER
Canaanite city, Josh 10:33
Inhabitants not expelled, Josh 16:10
Given as dowry of Pharaoh's daughter, 1 Kin 9:15–17

GIBEAH
Town of Benjamin; known for wickedness, Judg 19:12–30
Destruction of, Judg 20:1–48
Saul's birthplace, 1 Sam 10:26
Saul's political capital, 1 Sam 15:34
Wickedness of, long remembered, Hos 9:9

GIBEON
Sun stands still at, Josh 10:12
Location of tabernacle, 1 Chr 16:39
Joab struck Amasa at, 2 Sam 20:8–10
Joab killed at, 1 Kin 2:28–34
Site of Solomon's sacrifice and dream, 1 Kin 3:5–15

GIBEONITES
Trick Joshua into making treaty; subjected to forced labor, Josh 9:3–27
Rescued by Joshua, Josh 10
Massacred by Saul; avenged by David, 2 Sam 21:1–9

GIDEON
Called by an angel, Judg 6:11–24
Destroys Baal's altar, Judg 6:25–32
Fleece confirms call from God, Judg 6:36–40
Miraculous victory over the Midianites, Judg 7
Takes revenge on Succoth and Penuel, Judg 8:4–21
Refuses kingship; makes an ephod, Judg 8:22–28
Fathers seventy-one sons; dies, Judg 8:29–35

GIFT
g makes room for him . . . . Prov 18:16
A *g* in secret pacifies . . . . Prov 21:14
it is the *g* of God . . . . Eccl 3:13
is Corban"—'(that is, a *g* . . . . Mark 7:11
"If you knew the *g* . . . . John 4:10
But the free *g* is not . . . . Rom 5:15
but the *g* of God is . . . . Rom 6:23
each one has his own *g* . . . . 1 Cor 7:7
though I have the *g* . . . . 1 Cor 13:2
it is the *g* of God . . . . Eph 2:8
Not that I seek the *g* . . . . Phil 4:17
Do not neglect the *g* . . . . 1 Tim 4:14
you to stir up the *g* . . . . 2 Tim 1:6
tasted the heavenly *g* . . . . Heb 6:4
Every good *g* and every . . . . James 1:17
one has received a *g* . . . . 1 Pet 4:10

GIFTS
g you shall offer . . . . Num 18:29
You have received *g* . . . . Ps 68:18
and Seba will offer *g* . . . . Ps 72:10
though you give many *g* . . . . Prov 6:35
to one who gives *g* . . . . Prov 19:6
how to give good *g* . . . . Matt 7:11
rich putting their *g* . . . . Luke 21:1
g differing . . . . Rom 12:6
are diversities of *g* . . . . 1 Cor 12:4
and desire spiritual *g* . . . . 1 Cor 14:1
captive, and gave *g* . . . . Eph 4:8

GIHON
River of Eden, Gen 2:13
——— Spring outside Jerusalem, 1 Kin 1:33–45
Source of water supply, 2 Chr 32:30

GILBOA
Range of limestone hills in Issachar, 1 Sam 28:4
Scene of Saul's death, 1 Sam 31:1–9
Under David's curse, 2 Sam 1:17, 21

GILEAD
Plain east of the Jordan; taken from the Amorites and assigned to Gad, Reuben, and Manasseh, Num 21:21–35; 32:33–40; Deut 3:12, 13; Josh 13:24–28
Ishbosheth rules over, 2 Sam 2:8, 9
David takes refuge in, 2 Sam 17:21–26
Conquered by Hazael, 2 Kin 10:32, 33
Balm of, figurative of national healing, Jer 8:22

GILGAL
Site of memorial stones, circumcision, first Passover in the Promised Land, Josh 4:19—5:12
Site of Gibeonite covenant, Josh 9:3–15
One location on Samuel's circuit, 1 Sam 7:15, 16
Saul made king and later rejected, 1 Sam 11:15; 13:4–15
Denounced for idolatry, Hos 9:15

GIRD
G Your sword upon Your . . . . Ps 45:3
of wrath You shall *g* . . . . Ps 76:10
I will *g* you . . . . Is 45:5
and another will *g* . . . . John 21:18
Therefore *g* up the . . . . 1 Pet 1:13

GIRDED
a towel and *g* Himself . . . . John 13:4
down to the feet and *g* . . . . Rev 1:13

GIRGASHITES
Descendants of Canaan, Gen 10:15, 16
Land of, given to Abraham's descendants, Gen 15:18, 21
Delivered to Israel, Josh 24:11

GITTITES
600 follow David, 2 Sam 15:18–23

GIVE
g thanks to the LORD . . . . 1 Chr 16:8
g me wisdom and . . . . 2 Chr 1:10
G ear to my prayer . . . . Ps 17:1
G to them according . . . . Ps 28:4
g you the desires . . . . Ps 37:4
Yes, the LORD will *g* . . . . Ps 85:12
G me understanding . . . . Ps 119:34
g me your heart . . . . Prov 23:26
You will *g* truth to . . . . Mic 7:20
G to him who asks . . . . Matt 5:42
G us this day our . . . . Matt 6:11
what you have and *g* . . . . Matt 19:21
authority I will *g* . . . . Luke 4:6
g them eternal life . . . . John 10:28
A new commandment I *g* . . . . . . John 13:34
but what I do have I *g* . . . . Acts 3:6
g us all things . . . . Rom 8:32
G no offense . . . . 1 Cor 10:32
So let each one *g* . . . . 2 Cor 9:7
g him who has need . . . . Eph 4:28
g thanks to God always . . . . 2 Thess 2:13
g yourself entirely . . . . 1 Tim 4:15
good works, ready to *g* . . . . 1 Tim 6:18

GIVEN
to him more will be *g* . . . . Matt 13:12
has, more will be *g* . . . . Matt 25:29
to whom much is *g* . . . . Luke 12:48
g Me I should lose . . . . John 6:39
Spirit was not yet *g* . . . . John 7:39
have been freely *g* . . . . 1 Cor 2:12
not *g* to wine . . . . 1 Tim 3:3

GIVES
He who *g* to the poor . . . . Prov 28:27
For God *g* wisdom and . . . . Eccl 2:26
g life to the world . . . . John 6:33
All that the Father *g* . . . . John 6:37
The good shepherd *g* . . . . John 10:11
not as the world *g* . . . . John 14:27
g us richly all things . . . . 1 Tim 6:17
who *g* to all liberally . . . . James 1:5
But He *g* more grace . . . . James 4:6
g grace to the humble . . . . James 4:6

GLAD
I will be *g* and . . . . Ps 9:2
my heart is *g* . . . . Ps 16:9
Be *g* in the LORD and . . . . Ps 32:11
streams shall make *g* . . . . Ps 46:4
And wine that makes *g* . . . . Ps 104:15
I was *g* when they said . . . . Ps 122:1
make merry and be *g* . . . . Luke 15:32
he saw it and was *g* . . . . John 8:56

GLADNESS
in the day of your *g* . . . . Num 10:10
day of feasting and *g* . . . . Esth 9:17
You have put *g* in my . . . . Ps 4:7
me hear joy and *g* . . . . Ps 51:8
Serve the LORD with *g* . . . . Ps 100:2
shall obtain joy and *g* . . . . Is 35:10
over you with *g* . . . . Zeph 3:17
receive it with *g* . . . . Mark 4:16

GLORIFIED
the people I must be *g* . . . . Lev 10:3
and they *g* the God of . . . . Matt 15:31
Jesus was not yet *g* . . . . John 7:39
when Jesus was *g* . . . . John 12:16
By this My Father is *g* . . . . John 15:8
I have *g* You on the . . . . John 17:4
g His Servant Jesus . . . . Acts 3:13
these He also *g* . . . . Rom 8:30
things God may be *g* . . . . 1 Pet 4:11

GLORIFY
My altar, and I will *g* . . . . Is 60:7
g your Father in . . . . Matt 5:16
Father, *g* Your name . . . . John 12:28
He will *g* Me . . . . John 16:14
And now, O Father, *g* . . . . John 17:5
what death he would *g* . . . . John 21:19
God, they did not *g* . . . . Rom 1:21
therefore *g* God in . . . . 1 Cor 6:20
also Christ did not *g* . . . . Heb 5:5
ashamed, but let him *g* . . . . 1 Pet 4:16

GLORIOUS
daughter is all *g* . . . . Ps 45:13
And blessed be His *g* . . . . Ps 72:19
G things are spoken . . . . Ps 87:3
is honorable and *g* . . . . Ps 111:3
g splendor of Your . . . . Ps 145:5
habitation, holy and *g* . . . . Is 63:15
it to Himself a *g* . . . . Eph 5:27
be conformed to His *g* . . . . Phil 3:21
g appearing of our . . . . Titus 2:13

GLORY
"Please, show me Your *g* . . . . Ex 33:18
g has departed from . . . . 1 Sam 4:21
G in His holy name . . . . 1 Chr 16:10

a shield for me, my *g* ....Ps 3:3
who have set Your *g* ....Ps 8:1
Who is this King of *g* ....Ps 24:8
the place where Your *g* ....Ps 26:8
Your power and Your *g* ....Ps 63:2
shall speak of the *g* ....Ps 145:11
wise shall inherit *g* ....Prov 3:35
The *g* of young men is ....Prov 20:29
It is the *g* of God to ....Prov 25:2
"*G* to the righteous ....Is 24:16
g I will not give ....Is 42:8
g will be seen upon ....Is 60:2
then be likened in *g* ....Ezek 31:18
I will change their *g* ....Hos 4:7
and I will be the *g* ....Zech 2:5
He shall bear the *g* ....Zech 6:13
that they may have *g* ....Matt 6:2
the power and the *g* ....Matt 6:13
g was not arrayed ....Matt 6:29
Man will come in the *g* ....Matt 16:27
with power and great *g* ....Matt 24:30
"*G* to God in the ....Luke 2:14
and we beheld His *g* ....John 1:14
and manifested His *g* ....John 2:11
I do not seek My own *g* ....John 8:50
"Give God the *g* ....John 9:24
g which I had with You ....John 17:5
g which You gave Me I ....John 17:22
he did not give *g* ....Acts 12:23
doing good seek for *g* ....Rom 2:7
fall short of the *g* ....Rom 3:23
in faith, giving *g* ....Rom 4:20
the adoption, the *g* ....Rom 9:4
the riches of His *g* ....Rom 9:23
God, alone wise, be *g* ....Rom 16:27
who glories, let him *g* ....1 Cor 1:31
but woman is the *g* ....1 Cor 11:7
of the *g* that excels ....2 Cor 3:10
of the gospel of the *g* ....2 Cor 4:4
eternal weight of *g* ....2 Cor 4:17
who glories, let him *g* ....2 Cor 10:17
to His riches in *g* ....Phil 4:19
appear with Him in *g* ....Col 3:4
For you are our *g* ....1 Thess 2:20
many sons to *g* ....Heb 2:10
grass, and all the *g* ....1 Pet 1:24
to whom belong the *g* ....1 Pet 4:11
for the Spirit of *g* ....1 Pet 4:14
the presence of His *g* ....Jude 24
O Lord, to receive *g* ....Rev 4:11
g of God illuminated ....Rev 21:23

GO

He said, "Let Me *g* ....Gen 32:26
'Let My people *g* ....Ex 5:1
Presence does not *g* ....Ex 33:15
for wherever you *g* ....Ruth 1:16
"Look, I *g* forward ....Job 23:8
For I used to *g* ....Ps 42:4
g astray as soon as ....Ps 58:3
I will *g* in the ....Ps 71:16
Those who *g* down to ....Ps 107:23
Where can I *g* from ....Ps 139:7
G to the ant ....Prov 6:6
All *g* to one place ....Eccl 3:20
of mourning than to *g* ....Eccl 7:2
of Zion shall *g* ....Is 2:3
You wherever You *g* ....Matt 8:19
do not *g* out ....Matt 24:26
He said to them, "*G* ....Mark 16:15
And I say to one, '*G* ....Luke 7:8
also want to *g* away ....John 6:67
to whom shall we *g* ....John 6:68
g you cannot come ....John 8:21
I *g* to prepare a place ....John 14:2
will do, because I *g* ....John 14:12
seek Me, let these *g* ....John 18:8
and he shall *g* out no more ......Rev 3:12

GOAL

I press toward the *g* ....Phil 3:14

GOATS

drink the blood of *g* ....Ps 50:13
his sheep from the *g* ....Matt 25:32
with the blood of *g* ....Heb 9:12
g could take away ....Heb 10:4

GOD

G created the heavens ....Gen 1:1
Abram of *G* Most High ....Gen 14:19
and I will be their *G* ....Gen 17:8
of the Mighty *G* ....Gen 49:24
the *G* of Abraham ....Ex 3:6
He is my *G* ....Ex 15:2
Stand before *G* for the ....Ex 18:19
"I am the LORD your *G* ....Ex 20:2
"This is your *g* ....Ex 32:4
G is not a man ....Num 23:19
G is a consuming fire ....Deut 4:24
great and awesome *G* ....Deut 7:21
my people, and your *G* ....Ruth 1:16
know that there is a *G* ....1 Sam 17:46
a rock, except our *G* ....2 Sam 22:32
If the LORD is *G* ....1 Kin 18:21
G is greater than all ....2 Chr 2:5
G is greater than ....Job 33:12
"Behold, *G* is mighty ....Job 36:5
"Behold, *G* is great ....Job 36:26
You have been My *G* ....Ps 22:10
"Where is your *G* ....Ps 42:3
G is our refuge ....Ps 46:1
G is in the midst of ....Ps 46:5
G is the King of all ....Ps 47:7
The Mighty One, *G* ....Ps 50:1
I am *G* ....Ps 50:7
me a clean heart, O *G* ....Ps 51:10
Our *G* is the *G* ....Ps 68:20
Who is so great a *G* ....Ps 77:13
Restore us, O *G* ....Ps 80:7
You alone are *G* ....Ps 86:10
Exalt the LORD our *G* ....Ps 99:9
Yes, our *G* is merciful ....Ps 116:5
give thanks to the *G* ....Ps 136:26
For *G* is in heaven ....Eccl 5:2
Counselor, Mighty *G* ....Is 9:6
G is my salvation ....Is 12:2
Behold, this is our *G* ....Is 25:9
"Behold your *G* ....Is 40:9
Is there a *G* besides ....Is 44:8
to Zion, "Your *G* ....Is 52:7
stricken, smitten by *G* ....Is 53:4
and I will be their *G* ....Jer 31:33
and I saw visions of *G* ....Ezek 1:1
Who is a *G* like You ....Mic 7:18
"*G* with us ....Matt 1:23
in *G* my Savior ....Luke 1:47
the Word was with *G* ....John 1:1
enter the kingdom of *G* ....John 3:5
For *G* so loved the ....John 3:16
has certified that *G* ....John 3:33
G is Spirit ....John 4:24
"My Lord and my *G* ....John 20:28
Christ is the Son of *G* ....Acts 8:37
To the Unknown *G* ....Acts 17:23
Indeed, let *G* be true ....Rom 3:4
If *G* is for us ....Rom 8:31
G is faithful ....1 Cor 1:9
us there is one *G* ....1 Cor 8:6
G shall supply all ....Phil 4:19
and I will be their *G* ....Heb 8:10
G is a consuming fire ....Heb 12:29
G is greater than our ....1 John 3:20
for *G* is love ....1 John 4:8
No one has seen *G* ....1 John 4:12
in the temple of My *G* ....Rev 3:12
gave glory to the *G* ....Rev 11:13
G Himself will be ....Rev 21:3
and I will be his *G* ....Rev 21:7

GODDESS

after Ashtoreth the *g* ....1 Kin 11:5
of the great *g* Diana ....Acts 19:35

GODHEAD

eternal power and *G* ....Rom 1:20
the fullness of the *G* ....Col 2:9

GODLINESS

is the mystery of *g* ....1 Tim 3:16
g is profitable ....1 Tim 4:8
Now *g* with contentment ....1 Tim 6:6
having a form of *g* ....2 Tim 3:5
pertain to life and *g* ....2 Pet 1:3
to perseverance *g* ....2 Pet 1:6

GODLY

Himself him who is *g* ....Ps 4:3
everyone who is *g* ....Ps 32:6
who desire to live *g* ....2 Tim 3:12
righteously, and *g* ....Titus 2:12
reverence and *g* fear ....Heb 12:28
to deliver the *g* ....2 Pet 2:9

GODS

your God is God of *g* ....Deut 10:17
the household *g* ....2 Kin 23:24
He judges among the *g* ....Ps 82:1
I said, "You are *g* ....Ps 82:6
yourselves with *g* ....Is 57:5
If He called them *g* ....John 10:35
g have come down to ....Acts 14:11

GOG

Prince of Rosh, Meshech, and Tubal, Ezek 38:2, 3
——— Leader of the final battle, Rev 20:8–15

GOLD

And the *g* of that land ....Gen 2:12
a mercy seat of pure *g* ....Ex 25:17
multiply silver and *g* ....Deut 17:17
"If I have made *g* ....Job 31:24
yea, than much fine *g* ....Ps 19:10
is like apples of *g* ....Prov 25:11
is Mine, and the *g* ....Hag 2:8
g I do not have ....Acts 3:6
with braided hair or *g* ....1 Tim 2:9
a man with *g* rings ....James 2:2
Your *g* and silver are ....James 5:3
more precious than *g* ....1 Pet 1:7
like silver or *g* ....1 Pet 1:18
of the city was pure *g* ....Rev 21:21

GOLGOTHA

Where Jesus died, Matt 27:33–35

GOLIATH

Giant of Gath, 1 Sam 17:4
Killed by David, 1 Sam 17:50
——— Brother of above; killed by Elhanan, 2 Sam 21:19

GOMER

Son of Japheth, Gen 10:2, 3; 1 Chr 1:5, 6
Northern nation, Ezek 38:6
——— Wife of Hosea, Hos 1:2, 3

GOMORRAH

With Sodom, defeated by Chedorlaomer; Lot captured, Gen 14:8–12
Destroyed by God, Gen 19:23–29
Later references to, Is 1:10; Amos 4:11; Matt 10:15

GOOD

God saw that it was *g* ....Gen 1:10
but God meant it for *g* ....Gen 50:20
LORD has promised *g* ....Num 10:29
you have spoken is *g* ....2 Kin 20:19
seeking the *g* of his ....Esth 10:3
indeed accept *g* ....Job 2:10
"Who will show us any *g* ....Ps 4:6

is none who does *g* ... Ps 14:1
G and upright is the ... Ps 25:8
that he may see *g* ... Ps 34:12
Truly God is *g* to ... Ps 73:1
g man deals graciously ... Ps 112:5
Your Spirit is *g* ... Ps 143:10
g man obtains favor ... Prov 12:2
g word makes it glad ... Prov 12:25
on the evil and the *g* ... Prov 15:3
A merry heart does *g* ... Prov 17:22
who knows what is *g* ... Eccl 6:12
learn to do *g* ... Is 1:17
Zion, you who bring *g* ... Is 40:9
tidings of *g* things ... Is 52:7
talked to me, with *g* ... Zech 1:13
they may see your *g* ... Matt 5:16
said, "Be of *g* cheer ... Matt 9:22
A *g* man out of the ... Matt 12:35
"*G* Teacher, what *g* ... Matt 19:16
No one is *g* but One ... Matt 19:17
For she has done a *g* ... Matt 26:10
behold, I bring you *g* ... Luke 2:10
love your enemies, do *g* ... Luke 6:35
"Can anything *g* ... John 1:46
Some said, "He is *g* ... John 7:12
g works I have shown ... John 10:32
who went about doing *g* ... Acts 10:38
For he was a *g* man ... Acts 11:24
in that He did *g* ... Acts 14:17
g man someone would ... Rom 5:7
in my flesh) nothing *g* ... Rom 7:18
overcome evil with *g* ... Rom 12:21
Jesus for *g* works ... Eph 2:10
fruitful in every *g* ... Col 1:10
know that the law is *g* ... 1 Tim 1:8
For this is *g* and ... 1 Tim 2:3
bishop, he desires a *g* ... 1 Tim 3:1
for this is *g* and ... 1 Tim 5:4
be rich in *g* works ... 1 Tim 6:18
prepared for every *g* ... 2 Tim 2:21
and have tasted the *g* ... Heb 6:5
Every *g* gift and every ... James 1:17
g works which they ... 1 Pet 2:12
to suffer for doing *g* ... 1 Pet 3:17

GOODNESS

"I will make all My *g* ... Ex 33:19
and abounding in *g* ... Ex 34:6
"You are my Lord, my *g* ... Ps 16:2
Surely *g* and mercy ... Ps 23:6
that I would see the *g* ... Ps 27:13
how great is Your *g* ... Ps 31:19
The *g* of God endures ... Ps 52:1
how great is its *g* ... Zech 9:17
the riches of His *g* ... Rom 2:4
consider the *g* and ... Rom 11:22
kindness, *g* ... Gal 5:22

GOODS

When *g* increase ... Eccl 5:11
and plunder his *g* ... Matt 12:29
ruler over all his *g* ... Matt 24:47
"Soul, you have many *g* ... Luke 12:19
man was wasting his *g* ... Luke 16:1
I give half of my *g* ... Luke 19:8
has this world's *g* ... 1 John 3:17

GOSHEN

District of Egypt where Israel lived; the best of the land, Gen 45:10; 46:28, 29; 47:1–11

GOSPEL

The beginning of the *g* ... Mark 1:1
and believe in the *g* ... Mark 1:15
g must first be ... Mark 13:10
to testify to the *g* ... Acts 20:24
separated to the *g* ... Rom 1:1
not ashamed of the *g* ... Rom 1:16
should live from the *g* ... 1 Cor 9:14
if our *g* is veiled ... 2 Cor 4:3
to a different *g* ... Gal 1:6
of truth, the *g* ... Eph 1:13
the mystery of the *g* ... Eph 6:19
g which you heard ... Col 1:23
the everlasting *g* ... Rev 14:6

GOVERNMENT

and the *g* will be upon ... Is 9:6

GRACE

But Noah found *g* ... Gen 6:8
G is poured upon Your ... Ps 45:2
The LORD will give *g* ... Ps 84:11
the Spirit of *g* ... Zech 12:10
and the *g* of God was ... Luke 2:40
g and truth came ... John 1:17
And great *g* was upon ... Acts 4:33
G to you and peace ... Rom 1:7
receive abundance of *g* ... Rom 5:17
g is no longer *g* ... Rom 11:6
The *g* of our Lord ... Rom 16:20
For you know the *g* ... 2 Cor 8:9
g is sufficient ... 2 Cor 12:9
The *g* of the Lord ... 2 Cor 13:14
you have fallen from *g* ... Gal 5:4
to the riches of His *g* ... Eph 1:7
g you have been ... Eph 2:8
dispensation of the *g* ... Eph 3:2
g was given according ... Eph 4:7
G be with all those ... Eph 6:24
shaken, let us have *g* ... Heb 12:28
But He gives more *g* ... James 4:6
this is the true *g* ... 1 Pet 5:12
but grow in the *g* ... 2 Pet 3:18

GRACIOUS

he said, "God be *g* ... Gen 43:29
I will be *g* to whom I ... Ex 33:19
then He is *g* to him ... Job 33:24
wise man's mouth are *g* ... Eccl 10:12
of hosts will be *g* ... Amos 5:15
know that You are a *g* ... Jon 4:2
that He may be *g* ... Mal 1:9
at the *g* words which ... Luke 4:22
that the Lord is *g* ... 1 Pet 2:3

GRAIN

Israel went to buy *g* ... Gen 42:5
it treads out the *g* ... Deut 25:4
You provide their *g* ... Ps 65:9
be an abundance of *g* ... Ps 72:16
him who withholds *g* ... Prov 11:26
be revived like *g* ... Hos 14:7
G shall make the young ... Zech 9:17
to pluck heads of *g* ... Matt 12:1
unless a *g* of wheat ... John 12:24
it treads out the *g* ... 1 Cor 9:9

GRANT

and *g* us Your ... Ps 85:7
G that these two ... Matt 20:21
who overcomes I will *g* ... Rev 3:21

GRAPES

in the blood of *g* ... Gen 49:11
their *g* are *g* of gall ... Deut 32:32
g give a good smell ... Song 2:13
vines have tender *g* ... Song 2:15
brought forth wild *g* ... Is 5:2
Yet gleaning *g* will be ... Is 17:6
"No *g* shall be ... Jer 8:13
have eaten sour *g* ... Ezek 18:2
Do men gather *g* ... Matt 7:16
g are fully ripe ... Rev 14:18

GRASS

they were as the *g* ... 2 Kin 19:26
offspring like the *g* ... Job 5:25
g which grows up ... Ps 90:5
his days are like *g* ... Ps 103:15
The *g* withers ... Is 40:7
so clothes the *g* ... Matt 6:30
to sit down on the *g* ... Matt 14:19
"All flesh is as *g* ... 1 Pet 1:24

GRASSHOPPERS

inhabitants are like *g* ... Is 40:22
generals like great *g* ... Nah 3:17

GRAVE

g does not come ... Job 7:9
for the *g* as my house ... Job 17:13
my soul up from the *g* ... Ps 30:3
the power of the *g* ... Ps 49:15
or wisdom in the *g* ... Eccl 9:10
And they made His *g* ... Is 53:9
the power of the *g* ... Hos 13:14

GRAVES

there were no *g* ... Ex 14:11
and the *g* were opened ... Matt 27:52
g which are not ... Luke 11:44
g will hear His voice ... John 5:28

GRAY

would bring down my *g* ... Gen 42:38
the man of *g* hairs ... Deut 32:25
of old men is their *g* ... Prov 20:29

GREAT

and make your name *g* ... Gen 12:2
He has done us this *g* ... 1 Sam 6:9
For the LORD is *g* ... 1 Chr 16:25
I build will be *g* ... 2 Chr 2:5
"The work is *g* ... Neh 4:19
Who does *g* things ... Job 5:9
G men are not always ... Job 32:9
in the *g* assembly ... Ps 22:25
g are Your works ... Ps 92:5
my God, You are very *g* ... Ps 104:1
"The LORD has done *g* ... Ps 126:2
g is the sum of them ... Ps 139:17
in the place of the *g* ... Prov 25:6
g is the Holy One ... Is 12:6
And do you seek *g* ... Jer 45:5
g is Your faithfulness ... Lam 3:23
The *g* day of the LORD ... Zeph 1:14
he shall be called *g* ... Matt 5:19
one pearl of *g* price ... Matt 13:46
desires to become *g* ... Matt 20:26
g drops of blood ... Luke 22:44
that he was someone *g* ... Acts 8:9
"*G* is Diana of the ... Acts 19:28
that I have *g* sorrow ... Rom 9:2
without controversy *g* ... 1 Tim 3:16
with contentment is *g* ... 1 Tim 6:6
But in a *g* house ... 2 Tim 2:20
appearing of our *g* ... Titus 2:13
See how *g* a forest ... James 3:5
g men, the rich men ... Rev 6:15
Babylon the *G* ... Rev 17:5
Then I saw a *g* white ... Rev 20:11
the dead, small and *g* ... Rev 20:12

GREATER

the throne will I be *g* ... Gen 41:40
g than all the gods ... Ex 18:11
whose appearance was *g* ... Dan 7:20
kingdom of heaven is *g* ... Matt 11:11
place there is One *g* ... Matt 12:6
g than Jonah is here ... Matt 12:41
g than Solomon is here ... Matt 12:42
g things than these ... John 1:50
g than our father ... John 4:12
a servant is not *g* ... John 13:16
g than he who sent him ... John 13:16
G love has no one ... John 15:13
'A servant is not *g* ... John 15:20
parts have *g* modesty ... 1 Cor 12:23
he who prophesies is *g* ... 1 Cor 14:5
swear by no one *g* ... Heb 6:13
condemns us, God is *g* ... 1 John 3:20
witness of God is *g* ... 1 John 5:9

GREATEST
little child is the *g* ....Matt 18:4
be considered the *g* ....Luke 22:24
but the *g* of these is ....1 Cor 13:13

GREATNESS
And in the *g* of Your ....Ex 15:7
According to the *g* ....Ps 79:11
g is unsearchable ....Ps 145:3
I will declare Your *g* ....Ps 145:6
I have attained *g* ....Eccl 1:16
traveling in the *g* ....Is 63:1
is the exceeding *g* ....Eph 1:19

GREECE
Paul preaches in, Acts 17:16–31
Daniel's vision of, Dan 8:21

GREED
part is full of *g* ....Luke 11:39

GREEDINESS
all uncleanness with *g* ....Eph 4:19
the faith in their *g* ....1 Tim 6:10

GREEDY
of everyone who is *g* ....Prov 1:19
not violent, not *g* ....1 Tim 3:3
not violent, not *g* ....Titus 1:7

GREEK
written in Hebrew, *G* ....John 19:20
and also for the *G* ....Rom 1:16
with me, being a *G* ....Gal 2:3
is neither Jew nor *G* ....Gal 3:28

GREEKS
Natives of Greece, Joel 3:6; Acts 16:1
Spiritual state of, Rom 10:12
Some believe, Acts 14:1

GREET
g your brethren only ....Matt 5:47
G one another with a ....1 Cor 16:20
into your house nor *g* ....2 John 10
G the friends by name ....3 John 14

GREW
And the Child *g* ....Luke 2:40
But the word of God *g* ....Acts 12:24
the word of the Lord *g* ....Acts 19:20

GRIEF
burden and his own *g* ....2 Chr 6:29
g were fully weighed ....Job 6:2
Though I speak, my *g* ....Job 16:6
observe trouble and *g* ....Ps 10:14
of mirth may be *g* ....Prov 14:13
much wisdom is much *g* ....Eccl 1:18
and acquainted with *g* ....Is 53:3
joy and not with *g* ....Heb 13:17

GRIEVE
g the children of men ....Lam 3:33
g the Holy Spirit ....Eph 4:30

GRIEVED
earth, and He was *g* ....Gen 6:6
Has not my soul *g* ....Job 30:25
forty years I was *g* ....Ps 95:10
a woman forsaken and *g* ....Is 54:6
g His Holy Spirit ....Is 63:10
with anger, being *g* ....Mark 3:5
Peter was *g* because ....John 21:17

GRINDING
the sound of *g* is low ....Eccl 12:4
g the faces of the ....Is 3:15
Two women will be *g* ....Matt 24:41

GROAN
The dying *g* in the ....Job 24:12
even we ourselves *g* ....Rom 8:23
who are in this tent *g* ....2 Cor 5:4

GROANING
So God heard their *g* ....Ex 2:24
I am weary with my *g* ....Ps 6:6
Then Jesus, again *g* ....John 11:38

GROANINGS
g which cannot ....Rom 8:26

GROPE
And you shall *g* ....Deut 28:29
They *g* in the dark ....Job 12:25
We *g* for the wall like ....Is 59:10
hope that they might *g* ....Acts 17:27

GROUND
"Cursed is the *g* ....Gen 3:17
you stand is holy *g* ....Ex 3:5
up your fallow *g* ....Jer 4:3
give its fruit, the *g* ....Zech 8:12
others fell on good *g* ....Matt 13:8
bought a piece of *g* ....Luke 14:18
God, the pillar and *g* ....1 Tim 3:15

GROUNDED
being rooted and *g* ....Eph 3:17

GROW
they will all *g* ....Ps 102:26
the horn of David *g* ....Ps 132:17
the earth will *g* ....Is 51:6
you shall go out and *g* ....Mal 4:2
truth in love, may *g* ....Eph 4:15
and they will all *g* ....Heb 1:11
but *g* in the grace and ....2 Pet 3:18

GUARANTEE
in our hearts as a *g* ....2 Cor 1:22
us the Spirit as a *g* ....2 Cor 5:5
who is the *g* of our ....Eph 1:14

GUARD
g the way to the tree ....Gen 3:24
will be your rear *g* ....Is 52:12
g the doors of your ....Mic 7:5
we were kept under *g* ....Gal 3:23
G what was committed ....1 Tim 6:20

GUARDS
Unless the LORD *g* ....Ps 127:1
And the *g* shook for ....Matt 28:4

GUIDANCE
and excellent in *g* ....Is 28:29

GUIDE
He will be our *g* ....Ps 48:14
Father, You are the *g* ....Jer 3:4
g our feet into the ....Luke 1:79
has come, He will *g* ....John 16:13
Judas, who became a *g* ....Acts 1:16
you yourself are a *g* ....Rom 2:19

GUIDES
to you, blind *g* ....Matt 23:16
unless someone *g* ....Acts 8:31

GUILT
they accept their *g* ....Lev 26:41
g has grown up to the ....Ezra 9:6
of your fathers' *g* ....Matt 23:32

GUILTLESS
g who takes His name ....Ex 20:7
have condemned the *g* ....Matt 12:7

GUILTY
"We are truly *g* ....Gen 42:21
we have been very *g* ....Ezra 9:7
the world may become *g* ....Rom 3:19
in one point, he is *g* ....James 2:10

GULF
you there is a great *g* ....Luke 16:26

HABAKKUK
Prophet in Judah just prior to Babylonian invasion, Hab 1:1
Prayer of, in praise of God, Hab 3:1–19

HABITATION
to Your holy *h* ....Ex 15:13
your rightful *h* ....Job 8:6
Is God in His holy *h* ....Ps 68:5
their *h* be desolate ....Ps 69:25
the Most High, your *h* ....Ps 91:9
go to a city for *h* ....Ps 107:7
establish a city for *h* ....Ps 107:36
but He blesses the *h* ....Prov 3:33
in a peaceful *h* ....Is 32:18
Jerusalem, a quiet *h* ....Is 33:20
from His holy *h* ....Zech 2:13
'Let his *h* be ....Acts 1:20
be clothed with our *h* ....2 Cor 5:2

HADASSAH
Esther's Jewish name, Esth 2:7

HADES
be brought down to *H* ....Matt 11:23
H shall not ....Matt 16:18
being in torments in *H* ....Luke 16:23
not leave my soul in *H* ....Acts 2:27
I have the keys of *H* ....Rev 1:18
H were cast into the ....Rev 20:14

HAGAR
Sarah's servant; bears Ishmael to Abraham, Gen 16
Abraham sends her away; God comforts her, Gen 21:9–21
Paul explains symbolic meaning of, Gal 4:22–31

HAGGAI
Postexilic prophet; contemporary of Zechariah, Ezra 5:1, 2; 6:14; Hag 1:1

HAGGITH
One of David's wives, 2 Sam 3:4
Mother of Adonijah, 1 Kin 1:5

HAIL
cause very heavy *h* ....Ex 9:18
seen the treasury of *h* ....Job 38:22
He casts out His *h* ....Ps 147:17
h will sweep away the ....Is 28:17
of the plague of the *h* ....Rev 16:21

HAIR
bring down my gray *h* ....Gen 42:38
the *h* on my body stood ....Job 4:15
Your *h* is like a flock ....Song 4:1
you cannot make one *h* ....Matt 5:36
But not a *h* of your ....Luke 21:18
if a woman has long *h* ....1 Cor 11:15
not with braided *h* ....1 Tim 2:9
h like women's *h* ....Rev 9:8

HAIRS
are more than the *h* ....Ps 40:12
h I will carry you ....Is 46:4
yes, gray *h* are here ....Hos 7:9
But the very *h* ....Matt 10:30

HAIRY
h garment all over ....Gen 25:25
him, "A *h* man ....2 Kin 1:8

HAKKOZ
Descendant of Aaron, 1 Chr 24:1, 10
Called Koz, Ezra 2:61, 62
Descendants of, kept from priesthood, Neh 7:63, 64

HALLOW
hosts, Him you shall *h* ....Is 8:13
h the Holy One of ....Is 29:23
h the Sabbath day ....Jer 17:24

HALLOWED
the Sabbath day and *h* ....Ex 20:11
but I will be *h* ....Lev 22:32
who is holy shall be *h* ....Is 5:16
heaven, *h* be Your name ....Matt 6:9

HAM
Noah's youngest son, Gen 5:32
Enters ark, Gen 7:7
His immoral behavior merits Noah's curse, Gen 9:22–25
Father of descendants of repopulated earth, Gen 10:6–20

HAMAN
Plots to destroy Jews, Esth 3:3–15
Invited to Esther's banquet, Esth 5:1–14
Forced to honor Mordecai, Esth 6:5–14
Hanged on his own gallows, Esth 7:1–10

HAMATH
Israel's northern boundary, Num 34:8; 1 Kin 8:65; Ezek 47:16–20
Conquered, 2 Kin 18:34; Jer 49:23
Israelites exiled there, Is 11:11

HAMMER
h that breaks the rock . . . . Jer 23:29
How the *h* of the whole . . . . Jer 50:23

HAMOR
Sells land to Jacob, Gen 33:18–20; Acts 7:16
Killed by Jacob's sons, Gen 34:1–31

HANANI
Father of Jehu the prophet, 1 Kin 16:1, 7
Rebukes Asa; confined to prison, 2 Chr 16:7–10
——— Nehemiah's brother; brings news concerning the Jews, Neh 1:2
Becomes a governor of Jerusalem, Neh 7:2

HANANIAH
False prophet who contradicts Jeremiah, Jer 28:1–17
——— Hebrew name of Shadrach, Dan 1:6, 7, 11

HAND
h shall be against . . . . Gen 16:12
tooth for tooth, *h* . . . . Ex 21:24
the *h* of God was . . . . 1 Sam 5:11
and strengthened his *h* . . . . 1 Sam 23:16
Uzzah put out his *h* . . . . 2 Sam 6:6
let us fall into the *h* . . . . 2 Sam 24:14
Then, by the good *h* . . . . Ezra 8:18
He would loose His *h* . . . . Job 6:9
he stretches out his *h* . . . . Job 15:25
that your own right *h* . . . . Job 40:14
h has held me up . . . . Ps 18:35
My times are in Your *h* . . . . Ps 31:15
and night Your *h* . . . . Ps 32:4
Your right *h* is full . . . . Ps 48:10
Let Your *h* be upon the . . . . Ps 80:17
h shall be established . . . . Ps 89:21
"Sit at My right *h* . . . . Ps 110:1
days is in her right *h* . . . . Prov 3:16
heart is in the *h* . . . . Prov 21:1
Whatever your *h* . . . . Eccl 9:10
is at his right *h* . . . . Eccl 10:2
do not withhold your *h* . . . . Eccl 11:6
His left *h* is under my . . . . Song 8:3
My *h* has laid the . . . . Is 48:13
Behold, the LORD's *h* . . . . Is 59:1
are the work of Your *h* . . . . Is 64:8
Am I a God near at *h* . . . . Jer 23:23
of heaven is at *h* . . . . Matt 3:2
if your right *h* . . . . Matt 5:30
do not let your left *h* . . . . Matt 6:3
h causes you to sin . . . . Mark 9:43
sitting at the right *h* . . . . Mark 14:62
delivered from the *h* . . . . Luke 1:74
at the right *h* of God . . . . Acts 7:55
is even at the right *h* . . . . Rom 8:34
with my own *h* . . . . 1 Cor 16:21
to you with my own *h* . . . . Gal 6:11
The Lord is at *h* . . . . Phil 4:5
"Sit at My right *h* . . . . Heb 1:13
down at the right *h* . . . . Heb 10:12
stars in His right *h* . . . . Rev 2:1

HANDS
the *h* are the *h* . . . . Gen 27:22
here we are, in your *h* . . . . Josh 9:25
took his life in his *h* . . . . 1 Sam 19:5
put my life in my *h* . . . . 1 Sam 28:21
but His *h* make whole . . . . Job 5:18
and cleanse my *h* . . . . Job 9:30
h have made me and . . . . Job 10:8
They pierced My *h* . . . . Ps 22:16
h formed the dry land . . . . Ps 95:5
stretches out her *h* . . . . Prov 31:19
say, 'He has no *h* . . . . Is 45:9
than having two *h* . . . . Matt 18:8
Behold My *h* and My . . . . Luke 24:39
only, but also my *h* . . . . John 13:9
h the print of the . . . . John 20:25
know that these *h* . . . . Acts 20:34
his *h* what is good . . . . Eph 4:28
lifting up holy *h* . . . . 1 Tim 2:8
the laying on of the *h* . . . . 1 Tim 4:14
to fall into the *h* . . . . Heb 10:31

HANDWRITING
having wiped out the *h* . . . . Col 2:14

HANGED
for he who is *h* . . . . Deut 21:23
went and *h* himself . . . . Matt 27:5

HANGS
h the earth on nothing . . . . Job 26:7
is everyone who *h* . . . . Gal 3:13

HANNAH
Barren wife of Elkanah; prays for a son, 1 Sam 1:1–18
Bears Samuel and dedicates him to the Lord, 1 Sam 1:19–28
Magnifies God, 1 Sam 2:1–10

HANUN
King of Ammon; disgraces David's ambassadors and is defeated by him, 2 Sam 10:1–14

HAPPY
H is the man who has . . . . Ps 127:5
H are the people who . . . . Ps 144:15
H is the man who finds . . . . Prov 3:13
mercy on the poor, *h* . . . . Prov 14:21
trusts in the LORD, *h* . . . . Prov 16:20
h is he who keeps . . . . Prov 29:18
H is he who does not . . . . Rom 14:22

HARAN
Abraham's younger brother, Gen 11:26–31
City of Mesopotamia, Gen 11:31
Abraham leaves, Gen 12:4, 5
Jacob dwells at, Gen 29:4–35

HARASS
and Judah shall not *h* . . . . Is 11:13
h some from the church . . . . Acts 12:1

HARD
Is anything too *h* . . . . Gen 18:14
His heart is as *h* . . . . Job 41:24
shown Your people *h* . . . . Ps 60:3
I knew you to be a *h* . . . . Matt 25:24
"This is a *h* saying . . . . John 6:60
are some things *h* . . . . 2 Pet 3:16

HARDEN
But I will *h* his heart . . . . Ex 4:21
Do not *h* your hearts . . . . Ps 95:8
h your hearts as . . . . Heb 3:8

HARDENED
But Pharaoh *h* his . . . . Ex 8:32
Who has *h* himself . . . . Job 9:4
their heart was *h* . . . . Mark 6:52
eyes and *h* their hearts . . . . John 12:40
lest any of you be *h* . . . . Heb 3:13

HARDENS
A wicked man *h* his . . . . Prov 21:29
h his heart will fall . . . . Prov 28:14
whom He wills He *h* . . . . Rom 9:18

HARDSHIP
h that has befallen us . . . . Num 20:14
h as a good soldier . . . . 2 Tim 2:3

HARLOT
of a *h* named Rahab . . . . Josh 2:1
h is a deep pit . . . . Prov 23:27
h is one body with . . . . 1 Cor 6:16
h Rahab did not perish . . . . Heb 11:31
of the great *h* who . . . . Rev 17:1

HARLOTRIES
the land with your *h* . . . . Jer 3:2
Let her put away her *h* . . . . Hos 2:2

HARLOTRY
through her casual *h* . . . . Jer 3:9
the lewdness of your *h* . . . . Jer 13:27
let them put their *h* . . . . Ezek 43:9
are the children of *h* . . . . Hos 2:4
Ephraim, you commit *h* . . . . Hos 5:3
for the spirit of *h* . . . . Hos 5:4

HARLOTS
his blood while the *h* . . . . 1 Kin 22:38
h enter the . . . . Matt 21:31
Great, The Mother of *H* . . . . Rev 17:5

HARM
do My prophets no *h* . . . . 1 Chr 16:22
and I will not *h* . . . . Jer 25:6
and do not *h* the oil . . . . Rev 6:6

HARMLESS
become blameless and *h* . . . . Phil 2:15
for us, who is holy, *h* . . . . Heb 7:26

HARMONIOUS
the harp, with *h* sound . . . . Ps 92:3

HARP
those who play the *h* . . . . Gen 4:21
with the lute and *h* . . . . Ps 150:3
Lamb, each having a *h* . . . . Rev 5:8

HARPS
We hung our *h* upon the . . . . Ps 137:2
playing their *h* . . . . Rev 14:2

HARSH
"Your words have been *h* . . . . Mal 3:13
but also to the *h* . . . . 1 Pet 2:18

HARVEST
seedtime and *h* . . . . Gen 8:22
to the joy of *h* . . . . Is 9:3
shall eat up your *h* . . . . Jer 5:17
"The *h* is past . . . . Jer 8:20
of her *h* will come . . . . Jer 51:33
h truly is plentiful . . . . Matt 9:37
pray the Lord of the *h* . . . . Matt 9:38
sickle, because the *h* . . . . Mark 4:29
already white for *h* . . . . John 4:35
the *h* of the earth is . . . . Rev 14:15

HASTE
you shall eat it in *h* . . . . Ex 12:11
For I said in my *h* . . . . Ps 31:22
And they came with *h* . . . . Luke 2:16
"Zacchaeus, make *h* . . . . Luke 19:5

HASTEN
be multiplied who *h* . . . . Ps 16:4
Do not *h* in your . . . . Eccl 7:9
I, the LORD, will *h* . . . . Is 60:22

HASTENS
and he sins who *h* . . . . Prov 19:2
with an evil eye *h* . . . . Prov 28:22
is near and *h* quickly . . . . Zeph 1:14

HASTILY
utter anything *h* . . . . .Eccl 5:2
lay hands on anyone *h* . . . . .1 Tim 5:22

HATE
'You shall not *h* . . . . .Lev 19:17
h all workers of . . . . .Ps 5:5
h the righteous shall . . . . .Ps 34:21
love the LORD, *h* evil . . . . .Ps 97:10
h every false way . . . . .Ps 119:104
h the double-minded . . . . .Ps 119:113
I *h* and abhor lying . . . . .Ps 119:163
love, and a time to *h* . . . . .Eccl 3:8
h robbery for burnt . . . . .Is 61:8
You who *h* good and . . . . .Mic 3:2
either he will *h* . . . . .Matt 6:24

HATED
Therefore I *h* life . . . . .Eccl 2:17
h all my labor in . . . . .Eccl 2:18
but Esau I have *h* . . . . .Mal 1:3
And you will be *h* . . . . .Matt 10:22
have seen and also *h* . . . . .John 15:24
but Esau I have *h* . . . . .Rom 9:13
For no one ever *h* . . . . .Eph 5:29
and *h* lawlessness . . . . .Heb 1:9

HATEFUL
h woman when she is . . . . .Prov 30:23
in malice and envy, *h* . . . . .Titus 3:3

HATERS
The *h* of the LORD . . . . .Ps 81:15
backbiters, *h* of God . . . . .Rom 1:30

HATES
six things the LORD *h* . . . . .Prov 6:16
lose it, and he who *h* . . . . .John 12:25
"If the world *h* . . . . .John 15:18
h his brother is . . . . .1 John 2:11

HAUGHTY
Your eyes are on the *h* . . . . . . .2 Sam 22:28
bring down *h* looks . . . . .Ps 18:27
my heart is not *h* . . . . .Ps 131:1
h spirit before a fall . . . . .Prov 16:18
A proud and *h* man . . . . .Prov 21:24
Do not be *h* . . . . .Rom 11:20
age not to be *h* . . . . .1 Tim 6:17

HAZAEL
Anointed king of Syria by Elijah, 1 Kin 19:15–17
Elisha predicts his taking the throne, 2 Kin 8:7–15
Oppresses Israel, 2 Kin 8:28, 29; 10:32, 33; 12:17, 18; 13:3–7, 22

HAZOR
Royal Canaanite city destroyed by Joshua, Josh 11:1–13
Rebuilt and assigned to Naphtali, Josh 19:32, 36
Army of, defeated by Deborah and Barak, Judg 4:1–24

HEAD
He shall bruise your *h* . . . . .Gen 3:15
my skin, and laid my *h* . . . . .Job 16:15
return upon his own *h* . . . . .Ps 7:16
h is covered with dew . . . . .Song 5:2
The whole *h* is sick . . . . .Is 1:5
it to bow down his *h* . . . . .Is 58:5
could lift up his *h* . . . . .Zech 1:21
you swear by your *h* . . . . .Matt 5:36
having his *h* covered . . . . .1 Cor 11:4
and gave Him to be *h* . . . . .Eph 1:22
For the husband is *h* . . . . .Eph 5:23
His *h* and his hair . . . . .Rev 1:14

HEADS
men to ride over our *h* . . . . .Ps 66:12
Him, wagging their *h* . . . . .Matt 27:39
dragon having seven *h* . . . . .Rev 12:3

HEAL
I wound and I *h* . . . . .Deut 32:39
O LORD, *h* me . . . . .Ps 6:2
sent Me to *h* the . . . . .Is 61:1
h your backslidings . . . . .Jer 3:22
who can *h* you . . . . .Lam 2:13
torn, but He will *h* . . . . .Hos 6:1
H the sick . . . . .Matt 10:8
so that I should *h* . . . . .Matt 13:15
sent Me to *h* the . . . . .Luke 4:18
Physician, *h* yourself . . . . .Luke 4:23

HEALED
His word and *h* them . . . . .Ps 107:20
And return and be *h* . . . . .Is 6:10
His stripes we are *h* . . . . .Is 53:5
h the hurt of My . . . . .Jer 6:14
When I would have *h* . . . . .Hos 7:1
and He *h* them . . . . .Matt 4:24
he had faith to be *h* . . . . .Acts 14:9
that you may be *h* . . . . .James 5:16
his deadly wound was *h* . . . . .Rev 13:3

HEALING
h shall spring forth . . . . .Is 58:8
so that there is no *h* . . . . .Jer 14:19
Your injury has no *h* . . . . .Nah 3:19
shall arise with *h* . . . . .Mal 4:2
and *h* all kinds of . . . . .Matt 4:23
tree were for the *h* . . . . .Rev 22:2

HEALINGS
to another gifts of *h* . . . . .1 Cor 12:9
Do all have gifts of *h* . . . . .1 Cor 12:30

HEALS
h all your diseases . . . . .Ps 103:3
h the stroke of their . . . . .Is 30:26
Jesus the Christ *h* . . . . .Acts 9:34

HEALTH
to the soul and *h* . . . . .Prov 16:24
and for a time of *h* . . . . .Jer 8:15
no recovery for the *h* . . . . .Jer 8:22
all things and be in *h* . . . . .3 John 2

HEAR
"*H*, O Israel . . . . .Deut 6:4
Him you shall *h* . . . . .Deut 18:15
H me when I call . . . . .Ps 4:1
O You who *h* prayer . . . . .Ps 65:2
h what God the LORD . . . . .Ps 85:8
ear, shall He not *h* . . . . .Ps 94:9
h the words of the . . . . .Prov 22:17
h rather than to give . . . . .Eccl 5:1
H, O heavens . . . . .Is 1:2
H, you who are afar . . . . .Is 33:13
Let the earth *h* . . . . .Is 34:1
I spoke, you did not *h* . . . . .Is 65:12
'Hearing you will *h* . . . . .Matt 13:14
if he will not *h* . . . . .Matt 18:16
"Take heed what you *h* . . . . .Mark 4:24
ears, do you not *h* . . . . .Mark 8:18
h the sound of it . . . . .John 3:8
that God does not *h* . . . . .John 9:31
And how shall they *h* . . . . .Rom 10:14
man be swift to *h* . . . . .James 1:19
h what the Spirit says . . . . .Rev 2:7

HEARD
h the sound of the . . . . .Gen 3:8
h their cry because of . . . . .Ex 3:7
you only *h* a voice . . . . .Deut 4:12
certainly God has *h* . . . . .Ps 66:19
quietly, should be *h* . . . . .Eccl 9:17
Have you not *h* . . . . .Is 40:21
world men have not *h* . . . . .Is 64:4
Who has *h* such a thing . . . . .Is 66:8
h Ephraim bemoaning . . . . .Jer 31:18
that they will be *h* . . . . .Matt 6:7
h the word believed . . . . .Acts 4:4
I say, have they not *h* . . . . .Rom 10:18
not seen, nor ear *h* . . . . .1 Cor 2:9
h inexpressible . . . . .2 Cor 12:4
things that you have *h* . . . . .2 Tim 2:2
the things we have *h* . . . . .Heb 2:1
the word which they *h* . . . . .Heb 4:2
from death, and was *h* . . . . .Heb 5:7
which we have *h* . . . . .1 John 1:1
Lord's Day, and I *h* . . . . .Rev 1:10

HEARER
if anyone is a *h* . . . . .James 1:23
is not a forgetful *h* . . . . .James 1:25

HEARERS
for not the *h* of the . . . . .Rom 2:13
impart grace to the *h* . . . . .Eph 4:29
of the word, and not *h* . . . . .James 1:22

HEARING
and read in the *h* . . . . .Ex 24:7
Book of Moses in the *h* . . . . .Neh 13:1
Do not speak in the *h* . . . . .Prov 23:9
'Keep on *h* . . . . .Is 6:9
h they do not . . . . .Matt 13:13
h they may hear . . . . .Mark 4:12
If the whole were *h* . . . . .1 Cor 12:17
or by the *h* of faith . . . . .Gal 3:2
have become dull of *h* . . . . .Heb 5:11

HEARS
for Your servant *h* . . . . .1 Sam 3:9
out, and the LORD *h* . . . . .Ps 34:17
He who *h* you *h* Me . . . . .Luke 10:16
of God *h* God's words . . . . .John 8:47
And if anyone *h* . . . . .John 12:47
who is of the truth *h* . . . . .John 18:37
He who knows God *h* . . . . .1 John 4:6
And let him who *h* . . . . .Rev 22:17

HEART
h was only evil . . . . .Gen 6:5
for you know the *h* . . . . .Ex 23:9
great searchings of *h* . . . . .Judg 5:16
h rejoices in the LORD . . . . .1 Sam 2:1
God gave him another *h* . . . . . . .1 Sam 10:9
LORD looks at the *h* . . . . .1 Sam 16:7
his wives turned his *h* . . . . .1 Kin 11:4
He pierces my *h* . . . . .Job 16:13
How my *h* yearns within . . . . .Job 19:27
For God made my *h* . . . . .Job 23:16
My *h* is in turmoil and . . . . .Job 30:27
My *h* also instructs me . . . . .Ps 16:7
your *h* live forever . . . . .Ps 22:26
h is overflowing . . . . .Ps 45:1
My *h* is steadfast . . . . .Ps 57:7
Thus my *h* was grieved . . . . .Ps 73:21
my *h* and my flesh cry . . . . .Ps 84:2
h shall depart from me . . . . .Ps 101:4
look and a proud *h* . . . . .Ps 101:5
with my whole *h* . . . . .Ps 111:1
h is not haughty . . . . .Ps 131:1
h makes a cheerful . . . . .Prov 15:13
The king's *h* is in the . . . . .Prov 21:1
as he thinks in his *h* . . . . .Prov 23:7
with a wicked *h* . . . . .Prov 26:23
h reveals the man . . . . .Prov 27:19
trusts in his own *h* . . . . .Prov 28:26
The *h* of the wise is . . . . .Eccl 7:4
and a wise man's *h* . . . . .Eccl 8:5
h yearned for him . . . . .Song 5:4
and the whole *h* . . . . .Is 1:5
h shall resound . . . . .Is 16:11
the yearning of Your *h* . . . . .Is 63:15
the mind and the *h* . . . . .Jer 11:20
h is deceitful above . . . . .Jer 17:9
I will give them a *h* . . . . .Jer 24:7
therefore My *h* yearns . . . . .Jer 31:20
and take the stony *h* . . . . .Ezek 11:19
get yourselves a new *h* . . . . .Ezek 18:31
uncircumcised in *h* . . . . .Ezek 44:7
are the pure in *h* . . . . .Matt 5:8

is, there your *h* . . . . .Matt 6:21
of the *h* proceed evil . . . . .Matt 15:19
h will flow rivers . . . . John 7:38
"Let not your *h* . . . . John 14:1
believed were of one *h* . . . . .Acts 4:32
Satan filled your *h* . . . . .Acts 5:3
h is not right in the . . . . .Acts 8:21
h that God has raised . . . . .Rom 10:9
in sincerity of *h* . . . . .Eph 6:5
refresh my *h* in the . . . . .Philem 20
and shuts up his *h* . . . . .1 John 3:17
if our *h* condemns us . . . . .1 John 3:20

HEARTILY

you do, do it *h* . . . . .Col 3:23

HEARTS

God tests the *h* . . . . .Ps 7:9
who seek God, your *h* . . . . .Ps 69:32
let the *h* of those . . . . .Ps 105:3
And he will turn the *h* . . . . .Mal 4:6
h failing them from . . . . .Luke 21:26
purifying their *h* . . . . .Acts 15:9
will guard your *h* . . . . .Phil 4:7
of God rule in your *h* . . . . .Col 3:15

HEATHEN

repetitions as the *h* . . . . .Matt 6:7
him be to you like a *h* . . . . .Matt 18:17

HEAVEN

called the firmament *H* . . . . .Gen 1:8
precious things of *h* . . . . .Deut 33:13
LORD looks down from *h* . . . . .Ps 14:2
word is settled in *h* . . . . .Ps 119:89
For God is in *h* . . . . .Eccl 5:2
"*H* is My throne . . . . .Is 66:1
"If *h* above can be . . . . .Jer 31:37
and the birds of the *h* . . . . .Dan 2:38
come to know that *H* . . . . .Dan 4:26
for the kingdom of *h* . . . . .Matt 3:2
your Father in *h* . . . . .Matt 5:16
on earth as it is in *h* . . . . .Matt 6:10
H and earth will . . . . .Matt 24:35
from Him a sign from *h* . . . . .Mark 8:11
have sinned against *h* . . . . .Luke 15:18
you shall see *h* . . . . John 1:51
one has ascended to *h* . . . . John 3:13
the true bread from *h* . . . . John 6:32
a voice came from *h* . . . . John 12:28
sheet, let down from *h* . . . . .Acts 11:5
the whole family in *h* . . . . .Eph 3:15
laid up for you in *h* . . . . .Col 1:5
and the *h* gave rain . . . . James 5:18
there was silence in *h* . . . . .Rev 8:1
sign appeared in *h* . . . . .Rev 12:1
Now I saw a new *h* . . . . .Rev 21:1

HEAVENLY

your *h* Father will . . . . .Matt 6:14
h host praising God . . . . .Luke 2:13
if I tell you *h* things . . . . John 3:12
are those who are *h* . . . . .1 Cor 15:48
blessing in the *h* . . . . .Eph 1:3
and have tasted the *h* . . . . .Heb 6:4
h things themselves . . . . .Heb 9:23
a better, that is, a *h* . . . . .Heb 11:16
the living God, the *h* . . . . .Heb 12:22

HEAVENS

I will make your *h* . . . . .Lev 26:19
and the highest *h* . . . . .Deut 10:14
h cannot contain . . . . .1 Kin 8:27
the LORD made the *h* . . . . .1 Chr 16:26
Till the *h* are no more . . . . Job 14:12
in the *h* shall laugh . . . . .Ps 2:4
h declare the glory . . . . .Ps 19:1
Let the *h* declare His . . . . .Ps 50:6
h can be compared . . . . .Ps 89:6
The *h* are Yours . . . . .Ps 89:11
For as the *h* are high . . . . .Ps 103:11
When He prepared the *h* . . . . . . .Prov 8:27

h are higher than the . . . . .Is 55:9
behold, I create new *h* . . . . .Is 65:17
and behold, the *h* . . . . .Matt 3:16
h will be shaken . . . . .Matt 24:29
h are the work of Your . . . . .Heb 1:10
h will pass away . . . . .2 Pet 3:10

HEBREW

Term applied to:
Abram, Gen 14:13
Israelites, 1 Sam 4:6, 9
Jews, Acts 6:1
Paul, Phil 3:5

HEBRON

Abram, Isaac, and Jacob dwell there, Gen 13:18; 23:2–20; 35:27
Visited by spies, Num 13:21, 22
Defeated by Joshua, Josh 10:1–37
Caleb's inheritance, Josh 14:12–15
David's original capital; sons born there, 2 Sam 2:1–3, 11; 3:2–5
Site of Absalom's rebellion, 2 Sam 15:7–10

HEDGE

behold, I will *h* . . . . .Hos 2:6
sharper than a thorn *h* . . . . .Mic 7:4
a vineyard and set a *h* . . . . .Mark 12:1

HEDGED

and whom God has *h* . . . . Job 3:23
You have *h* me behind . . . . .Ps 139:5
He has *h* me in so that . . . . .Lam 3:7

HEED

By taking *h* according . . . . .Ps 119:9
if you *h* Me .Jer 17:24
and let us not give *h* . . . . .Jer 18:18
nor give *h* to fables . . . . .1 Tim 1:4
the more earnest *h* . . . . .Heb 2:1

HEEL

you shall bruise His *h* . . . . .Gen 3:15
took hold of Esau's *h* . . . . .Gen 25:26
has lifted up his *h* . . . . .Ps 41:9
Me has lifted up his *h* . . . . John 13:18

HEIGHT

"Is not God in the *h* . . . . Job 22:12
looked down from the *h* . . . . .Ps 102:19
nor *h* nor depth . . . . .Rom 8:39
length and depth and *h* . . . . .Eph 3:18

HEIR

Has he no *h* . . . . .Jer 49:1
Now I say that the *h* . . . . .Gal 4:1
if a son, then an *h* . . . . .Gal 4:7
He has appointed *h* . . . . .Heb 1:2
the world and became *h* . . . . .Heb 11:7

HEIRS

if children, then *h* . . . . .Rom 8:17
of God and joint *h* . . . . .Rom 8:17
should be fellow *h* . . . . .Eph 3:6
be rich in faith and *h* . . . . James 2:5
vessel, and as being *h* . . . . .1 Pet 3:7

HELL

shall be turned into *h* . . . . .Ps 9:17
go down alive into *h* . . . . .Ps 55:15
house is the way to *h* . . . . .Prov 7:27
his soul from *h* . . . . .Prov 23:14
H and Destruction are . . . . .Prov 27:20
"*H* from beneath is . . . . .Is 14:9
be in danger of *h* fire . . . . .Matt 5:22
to be cast into *h* . . . . .Matt 18:9
the condemnation of *h* . . . . .Matt 23:33
power to cast into *h* . . . . .Luke 12:5
it is set on fire by *h* . . . . James 3:6

HELLENISTS

Greek-speaking Jews, Acts 6:1
Hostile to Paul, Acts 9:29
Gospel preached to, Acts 11:20

HELMET

a breastplate, and a *h* . . . . .Is 59:17
And take the *h* of . . . . .Eph 6:17
and love, and as a *h* . . . . .1 Thess 5:8

HELP

the shield of your *h* . . . . .Deut 33:29
Is my *h* not within me . . . . Job 6:13
"There is no *h* . . . . .Ps 3:2
May He send you *h* . . . . .Ps 20:2
He is our *h* and our . . . . .Ps 33:20
yet praise Him, the *h* . . . . .Ps 42:11
A very present *h* . . . . .Ps 46:1
Give us *h* from trouble . . . . .Ps 60:11
God, make haste to *h* . . . . .Ps 71:12
"I have given *h* . . . . .Ps 89:19
the LORD had been my *h* . . . . .Ps 94:17
there was none to *h* . . . . .Ps 107:12
He is their *h* and . . . . .Ps 115:9
Our *h* is in the name . . . . .Ps 124:8
let no one *h* him . . . . .Prov 28:17
h my unbelief . . . . .Mark 9:24
tell her to *h* me . . . . .Luke 10:40
and find grace to *h* . . . . .Heb 4:16

HELPED

far the LORD has *h* . . . . .1 Sam 7:12
fall, but the LORD *h* . . . . .Ps 118:13
of salvation I have *h* . . . . .Is 49:8
h His servant Israel . . . . .Luke 1:54

HELPER

I will make him a *h* . . . . .Gen 2:18
Behold, God is my *h* . . . . .Ps 54:4
give you another *H* . . . . John 14:16
"But when the *H* . . . . John 15:26
she has been a *h* . . . . .Rom 16:2
"The LORD is my *h* . . . . .Heb 13:6

HELPS

the Spirit also *h* . . . . .Rom 8:26
gifts of healings, *h* . . . . .1 Cor 12:28

HEM

and touched the *h* . . . . .Matt 9:20
might only touch the *h* . . . . .Matt 14:36

HEMAN

Composer of a Psalm, Ps 88:title

HERESIES

dissensions, *h* . . . . .Gal 5:20
in destructive *h* . . . . .2 Pet 2:1

HERITAGE

give it to you as a *h* . . . . .Ex 6:8
have given me the *h* . . . . .Ps 61:5
for that is his *h* . . . . .Eccl 3:22
for it is his *h* . . . . .Eccl 5:18
This is the *h* of the . . . . .Is 54:17
of My people, My *h* . . . . Joel 3:2
The flock of Your *h* . . . . .Mic 7:14

HERMES

Paul acclaimed as, Acts 14:12

HERMON

Highest mountain (9,166 ft.) in Syria; also called Sirion, Shenir, Deut 3:8, 9

HEROD

——— Herod the Great, procurator of Judea (37–4 B.C.), Luke 1:5
Inquires about Jesus' birth, Matt 2:3–8
Slays infants of Bethlehem, Matt 2:12–18
——— Herod Antipas, the tetrarch, ruler of Galilee and Perea (4 B.C.–A.D. 39), Luke 3:1
Imprisons John the Baptist, Luke 3:18–21
Has John the Baptist beheaded, Matt 14:1–12
Disturbed about Jesus, Luke 9:7–9
Jesus sent to him, Luke 23:7–11
——— Herod Agrippa I (A.D. 37–44), Acts 12:1, 19

Kills James, Acts 12:1, 2
Imprisons Peter, Acts 12:3–11, 19
Slain by an angel, Acts 12:20–23
——— Herod Agrippa II (A.D. 53–70); called Agrippa and King Agrippa, Acts 25:22–24, 26
Festus tells him about Paul, Acts 25:13–27
Paul makes a defense before, Acts 26:1–32

HERODIANS
Join Pharisees against Jesus, Mark 3:6
Seek to trap Jesus, Matt 22:15–22
Jesus warns against, Mark 8:15

HERODIAS
Granddaughter of Herod the Great; plots John's death, Matt 14:3–12
Married her uncle, Mark 6:17, 18

HESHBON
Ancient Moabite city; taken by Moses, Num 21:23–34
Assigned to Reubenites, Num 32:1–37
Prophecies concerning, Is 15:1–4; 16:8–14; Jer 48:2, 34, 35

HETH
Son of Canaan, Gen 10:15
Abraham buys field from sons of, Gen 23:3–20
Esau marries daughters of, Gen 27:46

HEZEKIAH
Righteous king of Judah; reforms temple and worship, 2 Chr 29—31
Wars with Assyria; prayer for deliverance is answered, 2 Kin 18:7—19:37
His sickness and recovery; thanksgiving, 2 Kin 20:1–11; Is 38:9–22
Boasts to Babylonian ambassadors, 2 Kin 20:12–19
Death, 2 Kin 20:20, 21

HIDDEKEL
Hebrew name of the river Tigris, Gen 2:14; Dan 10:4

HIDDEN
and the LORD has *h* ... 2 Kin 4:27
It is *h* from the eyes ... Job 28:21
h Your righteousness ... Ps 40:10
and my sins are not *h* ... Ps 69:5
Your word I have *h* ... Ps 119:11
h riches of secret ... Is 45:3
there His power was *h* ... Hab 3:4
h that will not ... Matt 10:26
the *h* wisdom which God ... 1 Cor 2:7
bring to light the *h* ... 1 Cor 4:5
have renounced the *h* ... 2 Cor 4:2
rather let it be the *h* ... 1 Pet 3:4
give some of the *h* ... Rev 2:17

HIDE
H me under the shadow ... Ps 17:8
You shall *h* them in ... Ps 31:20
O God, and do not *h* ... Ps 55:1
You *h* Your face ... Ps 104:29
darkness shall not *h* ... Ps 139:12
You are God, who *h* ... Is 45:15
h yourself from your ... Is 58:7
"Fall on us and *h* ... Rev 6:16

HIDING
You are my *h* place ... Ps 32:7
A man will be as a *h* ... Is 32:2

HIEL
Native of Bethel; rebuilds Jericho, 1 Kin 16:34
Fulfills Joshua's curse, Josh 6:26

HIGH
priest of God Most *H* ... Gen 14:18
For the LORD Most *H* ... Ps 47:2
h is Your right ... Ps 89:13
are on *h* forevermore ... Ps 92:8
the LORD is on *h* ... Ps 138:6
"I dwell in the *h* ... Is 57:15
know that the Most *H* ... Dan 4:17
whose habitation is *h* ... Obad 3
up on a *h* mountain by ... Matt 17:1
your mind on *h* things ... Rom 12:16
h thing that exalts ... 2 Cor 10:5
and faithful *H* Priest ... Heb 2:17

HIGHER
They are *h* than heaven ... Job 11:8
you, 'Friend, go up *h* ... Luke 14:10
h than the heavens ... Heb 7:26

HIGHWAY
of the upright is a *h* ... Prov 15:19
in the desert a *h* ... Is 40:3
up, build up the *h* ... Is 62:10

HIGHWAYS
h shall be elevated ... Is 49:11
go into the *h* ... Matt 22:9

HILKIAH
Shallum's son, 1 Chr 6:13
High priest in Josiah's reign, 2 Chr 34:9–22
Oversees temple work, 2 Kin 22:4–7
Finds the Book of the Law, 2 Kin 22:8–14
Aids in reformation, 2 Kin 23:4

HILL
My King on My holy *h* ... Ps 2:6
h cannot be hidden ... Matt 5:14
and *h* brought low ... Luke 3:5
to the brow of the *h* ... Luke 4:29

HILLS
of the everlasting *h* ... Gen 49:26
possess is a land of *h* ... Deut 11:11
of the *h* are His also ... Ps 95:4
up my eyes to the *h* ... Ps 121:1
settled, before the *h* ... Prov 8:25

HINDERED
come to you (but was *h* ... Rom 1:13
Who *h* you from obeying ... Gal 5:7
prayers may not be *h* ... 1 Pet 3:7

HINNOM, VALLEY OF THE SON OF
See TOPHET
Place near Jerusalem used for human sacrifice, 2 Kin 23:10; 2 Chr 28:3; Jer 7:31, 32; 19:1–15

HIRAM
King of Tyre; provided for David's palace and Solomon's temple, 2 Sam 5:11; 1 Kin 5:1–12; 9:10–14, 26–28; 10:11; 1 Chr 14:1

HIRE
h laborers for his ... Matt 20:1

HIRED
h man who eagerly ... Job 7:2
h servants have bread ... Luke 15:17

HITTITES
One of seven Canaanite nations, Deut 7:1
Israelites intermarry with, Judg 3:5, 6; 1 Kin 11:1; Ezra 9:1, 2

HIVITES
One of seven Canaanite nations, Deut 7:1
Esau intermarries with, Gen 36:2
Gibeonites belong to, Josh 9:3, 7

HOLD
h my eyelids open ... Ps 77:4
right hand shall *h* ... Ps 139:10
LORD your God, will *h* ... Is 41:13
I cannot *h* my peace ... Jer 4:19
h fast that word ... 1 Cor 15:2
h fast our confession ... Heb 4:14
h fast and repent ... Rev 3:3

HOLES
"Foxes have *h* ... Matt 8:20

HOLIEST
the way into the *H* ... Heb 9:8
to enter the *H* by the ... Heb 10:19

HOLINESS
You, glorious in *h* ... Ex 15:11
has spoken in His *h* ... Ps 60:6
I have sworn by My *h* ... Ps 89:35
h adorns Your house ... Ps 93:5
the Highway of *H* ... Is 35:8
to the Spirit of *h* ... Rom 1:4
spirit, perfecting *h* ... 2 Cor 7:1
uncleanness, but in *h* ... 1 Thess 4:7
be partakers of His *h* ... Heb 12:10

HOLY
where you stand is *h* ... Ex 3:5
priests and a *h* nation ... Ex 19:6
day, to keep it *h* ... Ex 20:8
distinguish between *h* ... Lev 10:10
the LORD your God am *h* ... Lev 19:2
"No one is *h* ... 1 Sam 2:2
h seed is mixed ... Ezra 9:2
h ones will you turn ... Job 5:1
God sits on His *h* ... Ps 47:8
God, in His *h* mountain ... Ps 48:1
my life, for I am *h* ... Ps 86:2
"*H*, *h*, *h* is the LORD ... Is 6:3
child of the *H* Spirit ... Matt 1:18
baptize you with the *H* ... Mark 1:8
who speak, but the *H* ... Mark 13:11
H Spirit will come ... Luke 1:35
H Spirit descended ... Luke 3:22
Father give the *H* ... Luke 11:13
H Spirit will teach ... Luke 12:12
H Spirit was not ... John 7:39
H Spirit has come ... Acts 1:8
all filled with the *H* ... Acts 2:4
apostles' hands the *H* ... Acts 8:18
to speak, the *H* Spirit ... Acts 11:15
good to the *H* Spirit ... Acts 15:28
receive the *H* Spirit ... Acts 19:2
if the firstfruit is *h* ... Rom 11:16
peace and joy in the *H* ... Rom 14:17
one another with a *h* ... Rom 16:16
H Spirit teaches ... 1 Cor 2:13
that we should be *h* ... Eph 1:4
were sealed with the *H* ... Eph 1:13
partakers of the *H* ... Heb 6:4
has not entered the *h* ... Heb 9:24
H Spirit sent from ... 1 Pet 1:12
He who called you is *h* ... 1 Pet 1:15
it is written, "Be *h* ... 1 Pet 1:16
moved by the *H* Spirit ... 2 Pet 1:21
anointing from the *H* ... 1 John 2:20
says He who is *h* ... Rev 3:7
For You alone are *h* ... Rev 15:4
is *h*, let him be *h* ... Rev 22:11

HOME
LORD has brought me *h* ... Ruth 1:21
sparrow has found a *h* ... Ps 84:3
the stork has her *h* ... Ps 104:17
to his eternal *h* ... Eccl 12:5
said to him, "Go *h* ... Mark 5:19
into an everlasting *h* ... Luke 16:9
to him and make Our *h* ... John 14:23
took her to his own *h* ... John 19:27
let him eat at *h* ... 1 Cor 11:34
own husbands at *h* ... 1 Cor 14:35
that while we are at *h* ... 2 Cor 5:6
to show piety at *h* ... 1 Tim 5:4

HOMEMAKERS
be discreet, chaste, *h* ... Titus 2:5

HONEY
"What is sweeter than *h* ... Judg 14:18
and with *h* from the ... Ps 81:16

My son, eat *h* because ... Prov 24:13
not good to eat much *h* ... Prov 25:27
h and milk are under ... Song 4:11
was locusts and wild *h* ... Matt 3:4

HONEYCOMB
than honey and the *h* ... Ps 19:10
words are like a *h* ... Prov 16:24
fish and some *h* ... Luke 24:42

HONOR
H your father and your ... Ex 20:12
both riches and *h* ... 1 Kin 3:13
the king delights to *h* ... Esth 6:6
earth, and lay my *h* ... Ps 7:5
A man who is in *h* ... Ps 49:20
Sing out the *h* of His ... Ps 66:2
will deliver him and *h* ... Ps 91:15
H and majesty are ... Ps 96:6
h have all His saints ... Ps 149:9
H the LORD with your ... Prov 3:9
before *h* is humility ... Prov 15:33
h is not fitting ... Prov 26:1
spirit will retain *h* ... Prov 29:23
Father, where is My *h* ... Mal 1:6
is not without *h* ... Matt 13:57
'*H* your father and your ... Matt 15:4
h the Son just as they ... John 5:23
"I do not receive *h* ... John 5:41
but I *h* My Father ... John 8:49
"If I *h* Myself ... John 8:54
him My Father will *h* ... John 12:26
make one vessel for *h* ... Rom 9:21
to whom fear, *h* ... Rom 13:7
we bestow greater *h* ... 1 Cor 12:23
sanctification and *h* ... 1 Thess 4:4
alone is wise, be *h* ... 1 Tim 1:17
worthy of double *h* ... 1 Tim 5:17
and clay, some for *h* ... 2 Tim 2:20
no man takes this *h* ... Heb 5:4
H the king ... 1 Pet 2:17
from God the Father *h* ... 2 Pet 1:17
give glory and *h* ... Rev 4:9

HONORABLE
of God, and he is an *h* ... 1 Sam 9:6
His work is *h* and ... Ps 111:3
It is *h* for a man to ... Prov 20:3
traders are the *h* ... Is 23:8
holy day of the LORD *h* ... Is 58:13
providing *h* things ... 2 Cor 8:21
Marriage is *h* among ... Heb 13:4
having your conduct *h* ... 1 Pet 2:12

HONORS
h those who fear the ... Ps 15:4
'This people *h* Me ... Mark 7:6
It is My Father who *h* ... John 8:54

HOPE
I should say I have *h* ... Ruth 1:12
are spent without *h* ... Job 7:6
so You destroy the *h* ... Job 14:19
where then is my *h* ... Job 17:15
h He has uprooted ... Job 19:10
also will rest in *h* ... Ps 16:9
heart, all you who *h* ... Ps 31:24
My *h* is in You ... Ps 39:7
For You are my *h* ... Ps 71:5
I *h* in Your word ... Ps 119:147
O Israel, *h* in the ... Ps 130:7
h will not be cut ... Prov 23:18
There is more *h* ... Prov 26:12
the living there is *h* ... Eccl 9:4
O the *H* of Israel ... Jer 14:8
good that one should *h* ... Lam 3:26
Achor as a door of *h* ... Hos 2:15
you prisoners of *h* ... Zech 9:12
I have *h* in God ... Acts 24:15
to *h*, in *h* believed ... Rom 4:18
and rejoice in *h* ... Rom 5:2
h does not disappoint ... Rom 5:5
were saved in this *h* ... Rom 8:24
h that is seen is ... Rom 8:24
But if we *h* for what ... Rom 8:25
And now abide faith, *h* ... 1 Cor 13:13
life only we have *h* ... 1 Cor 15:19
may know what is the *h* ... Eph 1:18
were called in one *h* ... Eph 4:4
h which is laid ... Col 1:5
Christ in you, the *h* ... Col 1:27
For what is our *h* ... 1 Thess 2:19
others who have no *h* ... 1 Thess 4:13
and as a helmet the *h* ... 1 Thess 5:8
Jesus Christ, our *h* ... 1 Tim 1:1
in *h* of eternal life ... Titus 1:2
for the blessed *h* ... Titus 2:13
to lay hold of the *h* ... Heb 6:18
of a better *h* ... Heb 7:19
us again to a living *h* ... 1 Pet 1:3
you a reason for the *h* ... 1 Pet 3:15
who has this *h* in Him ... 1 John 3:3

HOPHNI
Wicked son of Eli, 1 Sam 1:3; 2:12–17, 22–25
Prophecy against, 1 Sam 2:27–36; 3:11–14
Carries ark into battle; killed, 1 Sam 4:1–11

HOR
Mountain of Edom; scene of Aaron's death, Num 20:22–29; 33:37–39

HOREB
See SINAI
God appears to Moses at, Ex 3:1–22
Water flows from, Ex 17:6
Elijah lodged here 40 days, 1 Kin 19:8, 9

HORITES
Inhabitants of Mt. Seir, Gen 36:20
Defeated by Chedorlaomer, Gen 14:5, 6
Driven out by Esau's descendants, Gen 36:20–29; Deut 2:12, 22

HORN
my shield and the *h* ... Ps 18:2
h will be exalted ... Ps 112:9
goat had a notable *h* ... Dan 8:5
and has raised up a *h* ... Luke 1:69

HORRIBLE
h thing has been ... Jer 5:30
I have seen a *h* ... Hos 6:10

HORROR
and behold, *h* and ... Gen 15:12
sorrow, the cup of *h* ... Ezek 23:33
you will become a *h* ... Ezek 27:36

HORSE
The *h* and its rider He ... Ex 15:1
Have you given the *h* ... Job 39:19
h is a vain hope ... Ps 33:17
the strength of the *h* ... Ps 147:10
h is prepared for the ... Prov 21:31
and behold, a white *h* ... Rev 6:2
and behold, a black *h* ... Rev 6:5
and behold, a pale *h* ... Rev 6:8
and behold, a white *h* ... Rev 19:11

HORSES
seen servants on *h* ... Eccl 10:7
h are swifter than ... Jer 4:13
Do *h* run on rocks ... Amos 6:12
we put bits in *h* ... James 3:3

HOSANNA
H in the highest ... Matt 21:9

HOSEA
Son of Beeri, prophet of the northern kingdom, Hos 1:1

HOSHEA
Original name of Joshua, the son of Nun, Deut 32:44; Num 13:8, 16
—— Israel's last king; usurps throne, 2 Kin 15:30
Reigns wickedly; Israel taken to Assyria during reign, 2 Kin 17:1–23

HOSPITABLE
of good behavior, *h* ... 1 Tim 3:2
Be *h* to one another ... 1 Pet 4:9

HOST
who brings out their *h* ... Is 40:26
of the heavenly *h* ... Luke 2:13

HOSTS
name of the LORD of *h* ... 1 Sam 17:45
As the LORD of *h* lives ... 1 Kin 18:15
The LORD of *h* is with ... Ps 46:7
LORD, all you His *h* ... Ps 103:21
praise Him, all His *h* ... Ps 148:2
word of the LORD of *h* ... Is 39:5
LORD of *h* is His name ... Is 47:4
against spiritual *h* ... Eph 6:12

HOT
of the LORD was *h* ... Judg 2:14
My heart was *h* within ... Ps 39:3
are neither cold nor *h* ... Rev 3:15

HOUR
h what you should ... Matt 10:19
day and *h* no one knows ... Matt 24:36
Man is coming at an *h* ... Matt 24:44
Behold, the *h* is at ... Matt 26:45
But this is your *h* ... Luke 22:53
h has not yet come ... John 2:4
But the *h* is coming ... John 4:23
h has come that the ... John 12:23
save Me from this *h* ... John 12:27
"Father, the *h* ... John 17:1
will not know what *h* ... Rev 3:3
keep you from the *h* ... Rev 3:10

HOUSE
from your father's *h* ... Gen 12:1
But as for me and my *h* ... Josh 24:15
h appointed for all ... Job 30:23
with them to the *h* ... Ps 42:4
the goodness of Your *h* ... Ps 65:4
For her *h* leads down ... Prov 2:18
Through wisdom a *h* ... Prov 24:3
better to go to the *h* ... Eccl 7:2
of the *h* tremble ... Eccl 12:3
to the *h* of the God of ... Is 2:3
to those who join *h* ... Is 5:8
h was filled with ... Is 6:4
'Set your *h* in order ... Is 38:1
h shall be called a ... Is 56:7
and beat on that *h* ... Matt 7:25
h divided against ... Matt 12:25
h shall be called a ... Matt 21:13
h may be filled ... Luke 14:23
make My Father's *h* ... John 2:16
h are many mansions ... John 14:2
publicly and from *h* ... Acts 20:20
in his own rented *h* ... Acts 28:30
who rules his own *h* ... 1 Tim 3:4
the church in your *h* ... Philem 2
For every *h* is built ... Heb 3:4
His own *h*, whose *h* ... Heb 3:6
him into your *h* ... 2 John 1:10

HOUSEHOLD
over the ways of her *h* ... Prov 31:27
If the *h* is worthy ... Matt 10:13
be those of his own *h* ... Matt 10:36
h were baptized ... Acts 16:15
saved, you and your *h* ... Acts 16:31
also baptized the *h* ... 1 Cor 1:16
those who are of the *h* ... Gal 6:10
who are of Caesar's *h* ... Phil 4:22

HOUSES
h are safe from fear ... Job 21:9

IMAGE
Us make man in Our *i* .... Gen 1:26
yourselves a carved *i* .... Deut 4:16
shall despise their *i* .... Ps 73:20
the king made an *i* .... Dan 3:1
to them, "Whose *i* .... Matt 22:20
since he is the *i* .... 1 Cor 11:7
He is the *i* of the .... Col 1:15
and not the very *i* .... Heb 10:1
the beast and his *i* .... Rev 14:9
who worshiped his *i* .... Rev 19:20

IMITATE
I urge you, *i* me .... 1 Cor 4:16
as I also *i* Christ .... 1 Cor 11:1
i those who through .... Heb 6:12

IMMANUEL
shall call His name *I* .... Is 7:14
shall call His name *I* .... Matt 1:23

IMMEDIATELY
i the Spirit .... Mark 1:12
hear, Satan comes *i* .... Mark 4:15
i forgets what .... James 1:24
I I was in the Spirit .... Rev 4:2

IMMORAL
i woman is a deep pit .... Prov 22:14
murderers, sexually *i* .... Rev 21:8

IMMORALITY
except sexual *i* .... Matt 5:32
i as is not even named .... 1 Cor 5:1
abstain from sexual *i* .... 1 Thess 4:3

IMMORTAL
to the King eternal, *i* .... 1 Tim 1:17

IMMORTALITY
glory, honor, and *i* .... Rom 2:7
mortal must put on *i* .... 1 Cor 15:53
who alone has *i* .... 1 Tim 6:16
and brought life and *i* .... 2 Tim 1:10

IMMOVABLE
be steadfast, *i* .... 1 Cor 15:58

IMPART
see you, that I may *i* .... Rom 1:11
that it may *i* grace .... Eph 4:29

IMPOSSIBLE
and nothing will be *i* .... Matt 17:20
"With men this is *i* .... Matt 19:26
God nothing will be *i* .... Luke 1:37
without faith it is *i* .... Heb 11:6

IMPOSTORS
i will grow worse .... 2 Tim 3:13

IMPRISONMENT
and of chains and *i* .... Heb 11:36

IMPRISONMENTS
in stripes, in *i* .... 2 Cor 6:5

IMPURITY
a woman during her *i* .... Ezek 18:6

IMPUTE
"Do not let my lord *i* .... 2 Sam 19:19
the LORD does not *i* .... Ps 32:2
the LORD shall not *i* .... Rom 4:8

IMPUTED
bloodshed shall be *i* .... Lev 17:4
might be *i* to them .... Rom 4:11
alone that it was *i* .... Rom 4:23
but sin is not *i* .... Rom 5:13

INCENSE
golden bowls full of *i* .... Rev 5:8

INCLINE
i your heart to the .... Josh 24:23
i my heart to any evil .... Ps 141:4

INCORRUPTIBLE
the glory of the *i* .... Rom 1:23
dead will be raised *i* .... 1 Cor 15:52
to an inheritance *i* .... 1 Pet 1:4
corruptible seed but *i* .... 1 Pet 1:23

INCORRUPTION
it is raised in *i* .... 1 Cor 15:42
corruption inherit *i* .... 1 Cor 15:50
must put on *i* .... 1 Cor 15:53

INCREASE
if riches *i* .... Ps 62:10
the LORD give you *i* .... Ps 115:14
hear and *i* learning .... Prov 1:5
When goods *i* .... Eccl 5:11
Of the *i* of His .... Is 9:7
and knowledge shall *i* .... Dan 12:4
Lord, "*I* our faith .... Luke 17:5
He must *i* .... John 3:30
but God gave the *i* .... 1 Cor 3:6
grows with the *i* .... Col 2:19
for they will *i* .... 2 Tim 2:16

INCREASED
The waters *i* and .... Gen 7:17
i your mercy which you .... Gen 19:19
nation and *i* its joy .... Is 9:3
And Jesus *i* in wisdom .... Luke 2:52

INCREASES
i knowledge *i* .... Eccl 1:18
who have no might He *i* .... Is 40:29

INCURABLE
My wound is *i* .... Job 34:6
'Your affliction is *i* .... Jer 30:12
Your sorrow is *i* .... Jer 30:15

INDEED
i it was very .... Gen 1:31
"But will God *i* .... 1 Kin 8:27
"Behold, an Israelite *i* .... John 1:47

INDIA
Eastern limit of Persian Empire, Esth 1:1

INDICATING
the Holy Spirit *i* .... Heb 9:8
who was in them was *i* .... 1 Pet 1:11

INDIGNANT
saw it, they were *i* .... Matt 26:8

INDIGNATION
of His anger, wrath, *i* .... Ps 78:49
I has taken hold .... Ps 119:53
in whose hand is My *i* .... Is 10:5
For the *i* of the LORD .... Is 34:2
have filled me with *i* .... Jer 15:17
can stand before His *i* .... Nah 1:6
i which will devour .... Heb 10:27
into the cup of His *i* .... Rev 14:10

INDUCED
O LORD, You *i* me .... Jer 20:7
if the prophet is *i* .... Ezek 14:9
I the LORD have *i* .... Ezek 14:9

INEXCUSABLE
Therefore you are *i* .... Rom 2:1

INEXPRESSIBLE
Paradise and heard *i* .... 2 Cor 12:4
you rejoice with joy *i* .... 1 Pet 1:8

INFALLIBLE
suffering by many *i* .... Acts 1:3

INFANTS
i who never saw .... Job 3:16
they also brought *i* .... Luke 18:15

INFERIOR
another kingdom *i* .... Dan 2:39
that I am not at all *i* .... 2 Cor 11:5

INFIRMITIES
"He Himself took our *i* .... Matt 8:17
boast, except in my *i* .... 2 Cor 12:5
and your frequent *i* .... 1 Tim 5:23

INHABIT
the wicked will not *i* .... Prov 10:30
cities and *i* them .... Amos 9:14

INHABITANT
Cry out and shout, O *i* .... Is 12:6
And the *i* will not say .... Is 33:24

INHABITANTS
He looks on all the *i* .... Ps 33:14
give ear, all *i* .... Ps 49:1
Let the *i* of Sela sing .... Is 42:11
Woe to the *i* of the .... Rev 12:12

INHABITED
rejoicing in His *i* .... Prov 8:31
'You shall be *i* .... Is 44:26
who formed it to be *i* .... Is 45:18

INHERIT
i the iniquities .... Job 13:26
descendants shall *i* .... Ps 25:13
The righteous shall *i* .... Ps 37:29
The wise shall *i* .... Prov 3:35
love me to *i* wealth .... Prov 8:21
The simple *i* folly .... Prov 14:18
the blameless will *i* .... Prov 28:10
i the kingdom prepared .... Matt 25:34
I do that I may *i* .... Mark 10:17
unrighteous will not *i* .... 1 Cor 6:9
you may *i* a blessing .... 1 Pet 3:9
who overcomes shall *i* .... Rev 21:7

INHERITANCE
"You shall have no *i* .... Num 18:20
is the place of His *i* .... Deut 32:9
the portion of my *i* .... Ps 16:5
yes, I have a good *i* .... Ps 16:6
i shall be forever .... Ps 37:18
He will choose our *i* .... Ps 47:4
You confirmed Your *i* .... Ps 68:9
the tribe of Your *i* .... Ps 74:2
i gained hastily .... Prov 20:21
right of *i* is yours .... Jer 32:8
i has been turned .... Lam 5:2
will arise to your *i* .... Dan 12:13
And God gave him no *i* .... Acts 7:5
and give you an *i* .... Acts 20:32
For if the *i* is of the .... Gal 3:18
we have obtained an *i* .... Eph 1:11
be partakers of the *i* .... Col 1:12
receive as an *i* .... Heb 11:8
i incorruptible .... 1 Pet 1:4

INIQUITIES
How many are my *i* .... Job 13:23
i have overtaken me .... Ps 40:12
I prevail against me .... Ps 65:3
forgives all your *i* .... Ps 103:3
LORD, should mark *i* .... Ps 130:3
was bruised for our *i* .... Is 53:5
He shall bear their *i* .... Is 53:11
i have separated you .... Is 59:2

INIQUITY
God, visiting the *i* of the .... Ex 20:5
He has not observed *i* .... Num 23:21
wicked brings forth *i* .... Ps 7:14
O LORD, pardon my *i* .... Ps 25:11
i I have not hidden .... Ps 32:5
was brought forth in *i* .... Ps 51:5
If I regard *i* in my .... Ps 66:18
Add *i* to their .... Ps 69:27
workers of *i* flourish .... Ps 92:7
i boast in themselves .... Ps 94:4
Shall the throne of *i* .... Ps 94:20
i have dominion .... Ps 119:133
i will reap sorrow .... Prov 22:8
a people laden with *i* .... Is 1:4
i is taken away .... Is 6:7
has laid on Him the *i* .... Is 53:6
will remember their *i* .... Hos 9:9

to those who devise *i* .... Mic 2:1
like You, pardoning *i* .... Mic 7:18
all you workers of *i* .... Luke 13:27
a fire, a world of *i* .... James 3:6

INJUSTICE
of truth and without *i* .... Deut 32:4
i shuts her mouth .... Job 5:16
i have your fathers .... Jer 2:5

INN
room for them in the *i* .... Luke 2:7
brought him to an *i* .... Luke 10:34

INNOCENCE
of my heart and *i* .... Gen 20:5
washed my hands in *i* .... Ps 73:13

INNOCENT
do not kill the *i* .... Ex 23:7
a bribe to slay an *i* .... Deut 27:25
i will divide the .... Job 27:17
a bribe against the *i* .... Ps 15:5
because I was found *i* .... Dan 6:22
saying, "I am *i* .... Matt 27:24
this day that I am *i* .... Acts 20:26

INNUMERABLE
i as the sand which is .... Heb 11:12
i company of angels .... Heb 12:22

INQUIRED
children of Israel *i* .... Judg 20:27
Therefore David *i* .... 1 Sam 23:2
the LORD, nor *i* of Him .... Zeph 1:6
the prophets have *i* .... 1 Pet 1:10

INSANE
images, and they are *i* .... Jer 50:38
the spiritual man is *i* .... Hos 9:7

INSCRIBED
Oh, that they were *i* .... Job 19:23
See, I have *i* you on .... Is 49:16

INSPIRATION
is given by *i* of God .... 2 Tim 3:16

INSTRUCT
good Spirit to *i* them .... Neh 9:20
I will *i* you and teach .... Ps 32:8
the LORD that he may *i* .... 1 Cor 2:16

INSTRUCTED
Surely you have *i* .... Job 4:3
counsel, and who *i* .... Is 40:14
This man had been *i* .... Acts 18:25
are excellent, being *i* .... Rom 2:18
Moses was divinely *i* .... Heb 8:5

INSTRUCTION
seeing you hate *i* .... Ps 50:17
despise wisdom and *i* .... Prov 1:7
Take firm hold of *i* .... Prov 4:13
Hear *i* and be wise .... Prov 8:33
Give *i* to a wise man .... Prov 9:9
i loves knowledge .... Prov 12:1
Cease listening to *i* .... Prov 19:27
Apply your heart to *i* .... Prov 23:12
for correction, for *i* .... 2 Tim 3:16

INSTRUMENT
to Him with an *i* .... Ps 33:2
on an *i* of ten strings .... Ps 92:3

INSTRUMENTS
i of cruelty are in .... Gen 49:5
with stringed *i* .... Ps 150:4
i of unrighteousness .... Rom 6:13
i of righteousness .... Rom 6:13

INSUBORDINATE
for the lawless and *i* .... 1 Tim 1:9
For there are many *i* .... Titus 1:10

INSUBORDINATION
of dissipation or *i* .... Titus 1:6

INSULTED
will be mocked and *i* .... Luke 18:32
i the Spirit of grace .... Heb 10:29

INSULTS
nor be afraid of their *i* .... Is 51:7

INTEGRITY
In the *i* of my heart .... Gen 20:5
he holds fast to his *i* .... Job 2:3
that God may know my *i* .... Job 31:6
I have walked in my *i* .... Ps 26:1
You uphold me in my *i* .... Ps 41:12
The *i* of the upright .... Prov 11:3
in doctrine showing *i* .... Titus 2:7

INTERCEDE
the LORD, who will *i* .... 1 Sam 2:25

INTERCESSION
of many, and made *i* .... Is 53:12
Spirit Himself makes *i* .... Rom 8:26
always lives to make *i* .... Heb 7:25

INTERCESSOR
that there was no *i* .... Is 59:16

INTEREST
shall not charge him *i* .... Ex 22:25
men lent to me for *i* .... Jer 15:10
collected it with *i* .... Luke 19:23

INTERPRET
Do all *i* .... 1 Cor 12:30
pray that he may *i* .... 1 Cor 14:13
in turn, and let one *i* .... 1 Cor 14:27

INTERPRETATION
"This is the *i* .... Gen 40:12
to another the *i* .... 1 Cor 12:10
a revelation, has an *i* .... 1 Cor 14:26
of any private *i* .... 2 Pet 1:20

INTERPRETATIONS
Do not *i* belong to God .... Gen 40:8
that you can give *i* .... Dan 5:16

INTRIGUE
seize the kingdom by *i* .... Dan 11:21
join with them by *i* .... Dan 11:34

INVISIBLE
of the world His *i* .... Rom 1:20
is the image of the *i* .... Col 1:15
eternal, immortal, *i* .... 1 Tim 1:17
as seeing Him who is *i* .... Heb 11:27

INWARD
i part is destruction .... Ps 5:9
Both the *i* thought .... Ps 64:6
You have formed my *i* .... Ps 139:13
God according to the *i* .... Rom 7:22
i man is being renewed .... 2 Cor 4:16

INWARDLY
i they are .... Matt 7:15
is a Jew who is one *i* .... Rom 2:29

IRON
He regards *i* as straw .... Job 41:27
i sharpens *i* .... Prov 27:17
and your neck was an *i* .... Is 48:4
its feet partly of *i* .... Dan 2:33

ISAAC
Promised heir of the covenant, Gen 17:16–21
Born and circumcised, Gen 21:1–7
Offered up as a sacrifice, Gen 22:1–19
Marries Rebekah, Gen 24:62–67
Prays for children; prefers Esau, Gen 25:21–28
Dealings with Abimelech, king of Gerar, Gen 26:1–31
Mistakenly blesses Jacob, Gen 27:1—28:5
Dies in his old age, Gen 35:28, 29
NT references to, Luke 3:34; Gal 4:21–31; Heb 11:9, 20

ISAIAH
Prophet during reigns of Uzziah, Jotham, Ahaz and Hezekiah, Is 1:1
Responds to prophetic call, Is 6:1–13
Prophesies to Hezekiah, 2 Kin 19; 20
Writes Uzziah's biography, 2 Chr 26:22
Writes Hezekiah's biography, 2 Chr 32:32
Quoted in NT, Matt 1:22, 23; 3:3; 8:17; 12:17–21; Luke 4:17–19; Acts 13:34; Rom 9:27, 29; 10:16, 20, 21; 11:26, 27; 15:12; 1 Pet 2:22

ISCARIOT, JUDAS
Listed among the Twelve, Mark 3:14, 19; Luke 6:16
Criticizes Mary, John 12:3–6
Identified as betrayer, John 13:21–30
Takes money to betray Christ, Matt 26:14–16
Betrays Christ with a kiss, Mark 14:43–45
Repents and commits suicide, Matt 27:3–10
His place filled, Acts 1:15–26

ISHBOSHETH
One of Saul's sons; made king, 2 Sam 2:8–10
Offends Abner, 2 Sam 3:7–11
Slain; his assassins executed, 2 Sam 4:1–12

ISHMAEL
Abram's son by Hagar, Gen 16:3, 4, 11–16
Circumcised, Gen 17:25
Scoffs at Isaac's feast; exiled with his mother, Gen 21:8–21
His sons; his death, Gen 25:12–18
——— Son of Nethaniah; kills Gedaliah, 2 Kin 25:22–26

ISHMAELITES
Settle at Havilah, Gen 25:17, 18
Joseph sold to, Gen 37:25–28
Sell Joseph to Potiphar, Gen 39:1

ISRAEL
Used to refer to:
- Jacob, Gen 32:28
- descendants of Jacob, Gen 49:16, 28
- ten northern tribes (in contrast to Judah), 1 Sam 11:8
- restored nation after exile, Ezra 9:1
- true church, Gal 6:16

ISRAEL
be called Jacob, but *I* .... Gen 32:28
"Hear, O *I* .... Deut 6:4
shepherd My people *I* .... 2 Sam 7:7
Truly God is good to *I* .... Ps 73:1
helped His servant *I* .... Luke 1:54
For they are not all *I* .... Rom 9:6
and upon the *I* of God .... Gal 6:16

ISRAELITES
Afflicted in Egypt, Ex 1:12–22
Escape from Egypt, Ex 12:29–42, 50; 13:17–22
Receive law at Sinai, Ex 19
Idolatry and rebellion of, Ex 32; Num 13; 14
Wander in the wilderness, Num 14:26–39
Cross Jordan; conquer Canaan, Josh 4; 12
Ruled by judges, Judg 2
Saul chosen as king, 1 Sam 10
Kingdom divided, 1 Kin 12
Northern kingdom carried captive, 2 Kin 17
Southern kingdom carried captive, 2 Kin 24
70 years in exile, 2 Chr 36:20, 21
Return after exile, Ezra 1:1–5
Nation rejects Christ, Matt 27:20–27
Nation destroyed, Luke 21:20–24

ISSACHAR
Jacob's fifth son, Gen 30:17, 18
——— Tribe of:
Genealogy of, 1 Chr 7:1–5
Prophecy concerning, Gen 49:14, 15
Census at Sinai, Num 1:28, 29
Inheritance of, Josh 19:17–23

ITALY
Jews expelled from, Acts 18:2
Paul sails for, Acts 27:1, 6
Christians in, Acts 28:14

ITHAMAR
Youngest son of Aaron, Ex 6:23
Consecrated as priest, Ex 28:1
Duty entrusted to, Ex 38:21
Jurisdiction over Gershonites and Merarites, Num 4:21–33

JABBOK
River entering the Jordan about 20 miles north of the Dead Sea, Num 21:24
Scene of Jacob's conflict, Gen 32:22–32
Boundary marker, Deut 3:16

JABESH GILEAD
Consigned to destruction, Judg 21:8–15
Saul defeats the Ammonites at, 1 Sam 11:1–11
Citizens of, rescue Saul's body, 1 Sam 31:11–13
David thanks citizens of, 2 Sam 2:4–7

JABIN
Canaanite king of Hazor; leads confederacy against Joshua, Josh 11:1–14
——— Another king of Hazor; oppresses Israelites, Judg 4:2
Defeated by Deborah and Barak, Judg 4:3–24
Immortalized in poetry, Judg 5:1–31

JACOB
Son of Isaac and Rebekah; Rebekah's favorite, Gen 25:21–28
Obtains birthright, Gen 25:29–34
Obtains blessing meant for Esau; flees, Gen 27:1—28:5
Sees vision of ladder, Gen 28:10–22
Serves Laban for Rachel and Leah, Gen 29:1–30
Fathers children, Gen 29:31—30:24
Flees from, makes covenant with Laban, Gen 30:25—31:55
Makes peace with Esau, Gen 32:1–21; 33:1–17
Wrestles with God, Gen 32:22–32
Returns to Bethel; renamed Israel, Gen 35:1–15
Shows preference for Joseph, Gen 37:3
Mourns Joseph's disappearance, Gen 37:32–35
Sends sons to Egypt for food, Gen 42:1–5
Reluctantly allows Benjamin to go, Gen 43:1–15
Moves his household to Egypt, Gen 45:25—47:12
Blesses his sons and grandsons; dies, Gen 48; 49
Buried in Canaan, Gen 50:1–14

JACOB'S WELL
Christ teaches a Samaritan woman at, John 4:5–26

JAEL
Wife of Heber the Kenite; kills Sisera, Judg 4:17–22
Praised by Deborah, Judg 5:24–27

JAIR
Manassite warrior; conquers towns in Gilead, Num 32:41; Deut 3:14
——— Eighth judge of Israel, Judg 10:3–5

JAIRUS
Ruler of the synagogue; Jesus raises his daughter, Mark 5:22–24, 35–43

JAMES
Son of Zebedee, called as disciple, Matt 4:21, 22; Luke 5:10, 11
One of the Twelve, Matt 10:2; Mark 3:17
Zealous for the Lord, Luke 9:52–54
Ambitious for honor, Mark 10:35–45
Witnesses Transfiguration, Matt 17:1–9
Martyred by Herod Agrippa, Acts 12:2
——— Son of Alphaeus; one of the Twelve, Matt 10:3, 4
Called "the Less," Mark 15:40
——— Jesus' half brother, Matt 13:55, 56; Gal 1:19
Becomes leader of Jerusalem Council and Jerusalem church, Acts 15:13–22; Gal 2:9
Author of an epistle, James 1:1

JANNES AND JAMBRES
Two Egyptian magicians; oppose Moses, Ex 7:11–22; 2 Tim 3:8

JAPHETH
One of Noah's three sons, Gen 5:32
Receives blessing, Gen 9:20–27
His descendants occupy Asia Minor and Europe, Gen 10:2–5

JARED
Father of Enoch, Gen 5:15–20
Ancestor of Noah, 1 Chr 1:2
Ancestor of Christ, Luke 3:37

JASHER
Book of, quoted, Josh 10:13

JASON
Welcomes Paul at Thessalonica, Acts 17:5–9
Described as Paul's kinsman, Rom 16:21

JAVAN
Son of Japheth, Gen 10:2, 4
Descendants of, to receive good news, Is 66:19, 20

JEALOUS
your God, am a *j* God . . . . .Ex 20:5
LORD, whose name is *J* . . . . .Ex 34:14
a consuming fire, a *j* . . . . .Deut 4:24
For I am *j* for you . . . . .2 Cor 11:2

JEALOUSY
They provoked Him to *j* . . . . . . .Deut 32:16
Will Your *j* burn like . . . . .Ps 79:5
j is a husband's . . . . .Prov 6:34
as strong as death, *j* . . . . .Song 8:6
will provoke you to *j* . . . . .Rom 10:19
for you with godly *j* . . . . .2 Cor 11:2

JEBUS
Canaanite name of Jerusalem before captured by David, 1 Chr 11:4–8

JEBUSITES
Descendants of Canaan, Gen 15:18–21; Num 13:29
Defeated by Joshua, Josh 11:1–12
Not driven from Jerusalem; later conquered by David, Judg 1:21; 2 Sam 5:6–8
Put to forced labor under Solomon, 1 Kin 9:20, 21

JECONIAH
See JEHOIACHIN
Variant form of Jehoiachin, 1 Chr 3:16, 17
Abbreviated to Coniah, Jer 22:24, 28

JEDIDIAH
Name given to Solomon by Nathan, 2 Sam 12:24, 25

JEDUTHUN
Levite musician appointed by David, 1 Chr 16:41, 42
Heads a family of musicians, 2 Chr 5:12
Name appears in Psalm titles, Ps 39; 62; 77

JEGAR SAHADUTHA
Name given by Laban to memorial stones, Gen 31:46, 47

JEHOAHAZ
Son and successor of Jehu, king of Israel, 2 Kin 10:35
Seeks the Lord in defeat, 2 Kin 13:2–9
——— Son and successor of Josiah, king of Judah, 2 Kin 23:30–34
Called Shallum, 1 Chr 3:15
——— Another form of Ahaziah, youngest son of King Joram, 2 Chr 21:17

JEHOASH
See JOASH

JEHOIACHIN
Son of Jehoiakim; next to the last king of Judah, 2 Kin 24:8
Deported to Babylon, 2 Kin 24:8–16
Liberated by Evil-Merodach, Jer 52:31–34

JEHOIADA
High priest during reign of Joash, 2 Kin 11:4—12:16
Instructs Joash, 2 Kin 12:2

JEHOIAKIM
Wicked king of Judah; son of Josiah; serves Pharaoh and Nebuchadnezzar, 2 Kin 23:34—24:7
Taken captive to Babylon, 2 Chr 36:6–8
Kills prophet Urijah, Jer 26:20–23
Destroys Jeremiah's scroll; cursed by God, Jer 36

JEHORAM (or Joram)
Wicked king of Judah; son of Jehoshaphat, 2 Kin 8:16–24
Marries Athaliah, 2 Kin 8:18, 19
Kills his brothers, 2 Chr 21:2, 4
Elijah prophesies against him; prophecy fulfilled, 2 Chr 21:12–20
——— Wicked king of Israel; son of Ahab, 2 Kin 3:1–3
Counseled by Elisha, 2 Kin 3; 5:8; 6:8–12
Wounded in battle, 2 Kin 8:28, 29
Killed by Jehu, 2 Kin 9:14–26

JEHOSHAPHAT
Righteous king of Judah; son of Asa, 1 Kin 22:41–50
Goes to war with Ahab against Syria, 1 Kin 22:1–36
Institutes reforms; sends out teachers of the Law, 2 Chr 17:6–9; 19
His enemies defeated through his faith, 2 Chr 20:1–30

JEHOZABAD
Son of a Moabitess; assassinates Joash, 2 Kin 12:20, 21
Put to death, 2 Chr 25:3

JEHU
Prophet; denounces Baasha, 1 Kin 16:1–7
Rebukes Jehoshaphat, 2 Chr 19:2, 3
——— Commander under Ahab; anointed king, 1 Kin 19:16; 2 Kin 9:1–13
Destroys the house of Ahab, 2 Kin 9:14—10:30
Turns away from the Lord; dies, 2 Kin 10:31–36

JEHUDI
Reads Jeremiah's scroll, Jer 36:14, 21, 23

JEPHTHAH
Gilead's son by a harlot, Judg 11:1
Driven out, then brought back to command army against Ammonites, Judg 11:2–28
Sacrifices his daughter to fulfill a vow, Judg 11:29–40
Chastises Ephraim, Judg 12:1–7

JEREMIAH
Prophet under Josiah, Jehoiakim, and Zedekiah, Jer 1:1–3
Called by God, Jer 1:4–9
Forbidden to marry, Jer 16:2
Imprisoned by Pashhur, Jer 20:1–6
Prophecy written, destroyed, rewritten, Jer 36
Accused of defection and imprisoned; released by Zedekiah, Jer 37
Cast into dungeon; rescued; prophesies to Zedekiah, Jer 38
Set free by Nebuchadnezzar, Jer 39:11—40:6
Forcibly taken to Egypt, Jer 43:5–7

JERICHO
City near the Jordan, Num 22:1
Called the city of palm trees, Deut 34:3; 2 Chr 28:15
Miraculously defeated by Joshua, Josh 6
Rebuilt by Hiel, 1 Kin 16:34
Visited by Jesus, Matt 20:29–34; Luke 19:1–10

JEROBOAM
Son of Nebat; receives prophecy that he will be king, 1 Kin 11:26–40
Made king; leads revolt against Rehoboam, 1 Kin 12:1–24
Sets up idols, 1 Kin 12:25–33
Rebuked by a man of God, 1 Kin 13:1–10
Judgment on house of, 1 Kin 13:33—14:20
——— Wicked king of Israel; son of Joash; successful in war, 2 Kin 14:23–29
Prophecy concerning, by Amos, Amos 7:7–13

JERUBBAAL
Name given to Gideon for destroying Baal's altar, Judg 6:32

JERUSALEM
Originally called Salem, Gen 14:18
Jebusite city, Josh 15:8; Judg 1:8, 21
King of, defeated by Joshua, Josh 10:5–23
Conquered by David; made capital, 2 Sam 5:6–9
Ark brought to, 2 Sam 6:12–17; 1 Kin 8:1–13
Saved from plague, 2 Sam 24:16
Temple built and dedicated here, 1 Kin 6; 8:14–66
Suffers in war, 1 Kin 14:25–27; 2 Kin 14:13, 14; Is 7:1
Miraculously saved, 2 Kin 19:31–36
Captured by Babylon, 2 Kin 24:10—25:21; Jer 39:1–8
Exiles return and rebuild temple, Ezra 1:1–4; 2:1
Walls of, dedicated, Neh 12:27–47
Christ enters as king, Matt 21:4–11
Christ laments for, Matt 23:37; Luke 19:41–44
Church born in, Acts 2
Christians of, persecuted, Acts 4

JESHIMON
Wilderness west of the Dead Sea, 1 Sam 23:19, 24

JESHUA (or Joshua)
Postexilic high priest; returns with Zerubbabel, Ezra 2:2
Aids in rebuilding temple, Ezra 3:2–8
Also called Joshua; seen in vision, Zech 3:1–10

JESHURUN
Poetic name of endearment for Israel, Deut 32:15

JESSE
Grandson of Ruth and Boaz, Ruth 4:17–22
Father of David, 1 Sam 16:1–13
Mentioned in prophecy, Is 11:1, 10

JESUS
J Christ was as .... Matt 1:18
shall call His name *J* .... Matt 1:21
J was led up by the .... Matt 4:1
These twelve *J* sent .... Matt 10:5
and laid hands on *J* .... Matt 26:50
Barabbas and destroy *J* .... Matt 27:20
we to do with You, *J* .... Mark 1:24
J withdrew with His .... Mark 3:7
J went into Jerusalem .... Mark 11:11
as they were eating, *J* .... Mark 14:22
and he delivered *J* .... Mark 15:15
J rebuked the .... Luke 9:42
truth came through *J* .... John 1:17
J lifted up His eyes .... John 6:5
J wept .... John 11:35
J was crucified .... John 19:20
This *J* God has raised .... Acts 2:32
of Your holy Servant *J* .... Acts 4:30
believed on the Lord *J* .... Acts 11:17
baptized into Christ *J* .... Rom 6:3
your mouth the Lord *J* .... Rom 10:9
among you except *J* .... 1 Cor 2:2
the day of the Lord *J* .... 1 Cor 5:5
perfect in Christ *J* .... Col 1:28
J who is called .... Col 4:11
exhort in the Lord *J* .... 1 Thess 4:1
But we see *J* .... Heb 2:9
looking unto *J* .... Heb 12:2
J Christ the righteous .... 1 John 2:1
Revelation of *J* Christ .... Rev 1:1
so, come, Lord *J* .... Rev 22:20

JETHRO
Priest of Midian; becomes Moses' father-in-law, Ex 2:16–22
Blesses Moses' departure, Ex 4:18
Visits and counsels Moses, Ex 18
Also called Reuel, Num 10:29

JEWELS
your thighs are like *j* .... Songs 7:1
that I make them My *j* .... Mal 3:17

JEWS
Jesus born King of the, Matt 2:2
Salvation comes through the, John 4:22; Acts 11:19; Rom 1:16; 2:9, 10
Reject Christ, Matt 27:21–25
Reject the gospel, Acts 13:42–46

JEZEBEL
Ahab's idolatrous wife, 1 Kin 16:31
Her abominable acts, 1 Kin 18:4, 13; 19:1, 2; 21:1–16
Death prophesied; prophecy fulfilled, 1 Kin 21:23; 2 Kin 9:7, 30–37
——— Type of paganism in the church, Rev 2:20

JEZREEL
Ahab's capital, 1 Kin 18:45; 21:1
Ahab's family destroyed at, 1 Kin 21:23; 2 Kin 9:30–37; 10:1–11

JOAB
David's nephew; commands his army, 2 Sam 2:10–32; 8:16; 10:1–14; 11:1, 14–25; 20:1–23
Kills Abner, 2 Sam 3:26, 27
Intercedes for Absalom, 2 Sam 14:1–33
Remains loyal to David; kills Absalom, 2 Sam 18:1–5, 9–17
Demoted; kills Amasa, 2 Sam 19:13; 20:8–10
Opposes census, 2 Sam 24:1–9; 1 Chr 21:1–6
Supports Adonijah, 1 Kin 1:7
Solomon orders his death in obedience to David's command, 1 Kin 2:1–6, 28–34

JOANNA
Wife of Chuza, Herod's steward, Luke 8:1–3
With others, heralds Christ's resurrection, Luke 23:55, 56

JOASH (or Jehoash)
Son of Ahaziah; saved from Athaliah's massacre and crowned by Jehoiada, 2 Kin 11:1–12
Repairs the temple, 2 Kin 12:1–16
Turns away from the Lord and is killed, 2 Chr 24:17–25
——— Wicked king of Israel; son of Jehoahaz, 2 Kin 13:10–25
Defeats Amaziah in battle, 2 Kin 14:8–15; 2 Chr 25:17–24

JOB
Model of righteousness, Job 1:1–5
His faith tested, Job 1:6—2:10
Debates with his three friends; complains to God, Job 3—33
Elihu intervenes, Job 34—37
God's answer, Job 38—41
Humbles himself and repents, Job 42:1–6
Restored to prosperity, Job 42:10–17

JOCHEBED
Daughter of Levi; mother of Miriam, Aaron, and Moses, Ex 6:20

JOEL
Preexilic prophet, Joel 1:1
Quoted in NT, Acts 2:16

JOHANAN
Military leader of Judah; warns Gedaliah of Ishmael's plot, Jer 40:13–16
Avenges Gedaliah; takes the people to Egypt, Jer 41:11–18

JOHN
The apostle, son of Zebedee; called as disciple, Matt 4:21, 22; Luke 5:1–11
Chosen as one of the Twelve, Matt 10:2
Especially close to Christ, Matt 17:1–9; Mark 13:3; John 13:23–25; 19:26, 27; 20:2–8; 21:7, 20
Ambitious and overzealous, Mark 10:35–41; Luke 9:54–56
Sent to prepare the Passover, Luke 22:8–13
With Peter, heals a man and is arrested, Acts 3:1—4:22
Goes on missionary trip with Peter, Acts 8:14–25
Exiled on Patmos, Rev 1:9
Author of Gospel, three epistles, and the Revelation, John 21:23–25; 1 John; 2 John; 3 John; Rev 1:1
——— The Baptist; OT prophecy concerning, Is 40:3–5; Mal 4:5
His birth announced and accomplished, Luke 1:11–20, 57–80
Preaches repentance, Luke 3:1–20
Bears witness to Christ, John 1:19–36; 3:25–36
Baptizes Jesus, Matt 3:13–17

Jesus speaks about, Matt 11:7–19
Identified with Elijah, Matt 11:13, 14
Herod imprisons and kills, Matt 14:3–12
——— Surnamed Mark: *see* MARK

JOINED

and mother and be *j* .... Gen 2:24
for him who is *j* .... Eccl 9:4
"Ephraim is *j* .... Hos 4:17
what God has *j* .... Matt 19:6
you be perfectly *j* .... 1 Cor 1:10
But he who is *j* .... 1 Cor 6:17
the whole body, *j* .... Eph 4:16

JOINT

j as He wrestled .... Gen 32:25
My bones are out of *j* .... Ps 22:14
j heirs with Christ .... Rom 8:17
by what every *j* .... Eph 4:16

JONADAB (or Jehonadab)

David's nephew; encourages Amnon in sin, 2 Sam 13:3–5, 32–36
——— Son of Rechab; father of the Rechabites, Jer 35:5–19
Helps Jehu overthrow Baal, 2 Kin 10:15–28

JONAH

Prophet sent to Nineveh; rebels and is punished, Jon 1
Repents and is saved, Jon 2
Preaches in Nineveh, Jon 3
Becomes angry at God's mercy, Jon 4
Type of Christ's resurrection, Matt 12:39, 40

JONATHAN

King Saul's eldest son; his exploits in battle, 1 Sam 13:2, 3; 14:1–14, 49
Saved from his father's wrath, 1 Sam 14:24–45
Makes covenant with David; protects him from Saul, 1 Sam 18:1–4; 19:1–7; 20:1–42; 23:15–18
Killed by Philistines, 1 Sam 31:2, 8
Mourned by David; his son provided for, 2 Sam 1:17–27; 9:1–8
——— Son of high priest Abiathar; faithful to David, 2 Sam 15:26–36; 17:15–22
Informs Adonijah of Solomon's coronation, 1 Kin 1:41–49

JOPPA

Scene of Peter's vision, Acts 10:5–23, 32

JORDAN RIVER

Lot dwells near, Gen 13:8–13
Canaan's eastern boundary, Num 34:12
Moses forbidden to cross, Deut 3:27
Miraculous dividing of, for Israel, Josh 3:1–17
by Elijah, 2 Kin 2:5–8
by Elisha, 2 Kin 2:13,14
Naaman healed in, 2 Kin 5:10–14
John baptizes in, Matt 3:6, 13–17

JOSEPH

Son of Jacob by Rachel, Gen 30:22–24
Loved by Jacob; hated by his brothers, Gen 37:3–11
Sold into slavery, Gen 37:12–36
Unjustly imprisoned in Egypt, Gen 39:1–23
Interprets dreams in prison, Gen 40:1–23
Wins Pharaoh's favor, Gen 41:1–44
Prepares Egypt for famine, Gen 41:45–57
Sells grain to his brothers, Gen 42—44
Reveals identity and reconciles with brothers; sends for Jacob, Gen 45:1–28
Settles family in Egypt, Gen 47:1–12
His sons blessed by Jacob, Gen 48:1–22
Blessed by Jacob, Gen 49:22–26
Buries his father; reassures his brothers, Gen 50:1–21
His death, Gen 50:22–26
——— Husband of Mary, Jesus' mother, Matt 1:16
Visited by angel, Matt 1:19–25
Takes Mary to Bethlehem, Luke 2:3–7
Protects Jesus from Herod, Matt 2:13–23
Jesus subject to, Luke 2:51
——— Secret disciple from Arimathea; donates tomb and assists in Christ's burial, Mark 15:42–46; Luke 23:50–53; John 19:38–42

JOSES

One of Jesus' half brothers, Matt 13:55
——— The name of Barnabas, Acts 4:36

JOSHUA

See JESHUA
——— Leader of Israel succeeding Moses, Num 27:18–23
Leads battle against Amalek, Ex 17:8–16
Sent as spy into Canaan; reports favorably, Num 13:16–25; 14:6–9
Assumes command, Josh 1:1–18
Sends spies to Jericho, Josh 2:1
Leads Israel across Jordan, Josh 3:1–17
Sets up commemorative stones, Josh 4:1–24
Circumcises the people, Josh 5:2–9
Conquers Jericho, Josh 5:13—6:27
Punishes Achan, Josh 7:10–26
Conquers Canaan, Josh 8—12
Divides the land, Josh 13—19
Addresses rulers, Josh 23:1–16
Addresses the people, Josh 24:1–28
His death, Josh 24:29, 30

JOSIAH

Righteous king of Judah; son of Amon, 2 Kin 22:1, 2
Repairs the temple, 2 Kin 22:3–9
Hears the Law; spared for his humility, 2 Kin 22:10–20
Institutes reforms, 2 Kin 23:1–25
Killed in battle, 2 Chr 35:20–25

JOTHAM

Gideon's youngest son; escapes Abimelech's massacre, Judg 9:5
Utters prophetic parable, Judg 9:7–21
——— Righteous king of Judah; son of Azariah, 2 Kin 15:32–38; 2 Chr 27:1–9

JOURNEY

us go three days' *j* .... Ex 3:18
busy, or he is on a *j* .... 1 Kin 18:27
Nevertheless I must *j* .... Luke 13:33
wearied from His *j* .... John 4:6

JOY

LORD your God with *j* .... Deut 28:47
heart to sing for *j* .... Job 29:13
is fullness of *j* .... Ps 16:11
j comes in the morning .... Ps 30:5
To God my exceeding *j* .... Ps 43:4
You according to the *j* .... Is 9:3
j you will draw .... Is 12:3
ashes, the oil of *j* .... Is 61:3
j shall be theirs .... Is 61:7
shall sing for *j* .... Is 65:14
word was to me the *j* .... Jer 15:16
receives it with *j* .... Matt 13:20
Enter into the *j* .... Matt 25:21
in my womb for *j* .... Luke 1:44
there will be more *j* .... Luke 15:7
did not believe for *j* .... Luke 24:41
My *j* may remain in .... John 15:11
they may have My *j* .... John 17:13
fill you with all *j* .... Rom 15:13
that my *j* is the *j* .... 2 Cor 2:3
the Spirit is love, *j* .... Gal 5:22
brethren, my *j* and .... Phil 4:1
longsuffering with *j* .... Col 1:11
are our glory and *j* .... 1 Thess 2:20
j that was set before .... Heb 12:2
count it all *j* .... James 1:2
j inexpressible .... 1 Pet 1:8
with exceeding *j* .... 1 Pet 4:13
I have no greater *j* .... 3 John 4

JOYFUL

And my soul shall be *j* .... Ps 35:9
Make a *j* shout to the .... Ps 100:1
of prosperity be *j* .... Eccl 7:14
and make them *j* .... Is 56:7
I am exceedingly *j* .... 2 Cor 7:4

JOZACHAR

Assassin of Joash, 2 Kin 12:19–21
Called Zabad, 2 Chr 24:26

JUBAL

Son of Lamech, Gen 4:21

JUDAH

Son of Jacob and Leah, Gen 29:30–35
Intercedes for Joseph, Gen 37:26, 27
Fails in duty to Tamar, Gen 38:1–30
Offers himself as Benjamin's ransom, Gen 44:18–34
Jacob bestows birthright on, Gen 49:3–10
Ancestor of Christ, Matt 1:3, 16
——— Tribe of:
Prophecy concerning, Gen 49:8–12
Numbered at Sinai, Num 1:26, 27
Territory assigned to, Josh 15:1–63
Leads in conquest of Canaan, Judg 1:1–19
Makes David king, 2 Sam 2:1–11
Loyal to David and his house, 2 Sam 20:1, 2; 1 Kin 12:20
Becomes leader of southern kingdom, 1 Kin 14:21, 22
Taken to Babylon, 2 Kin 24:1–16
Returns after exile, 2 Chr 36:20–23

JUDAS

Judas Lebbaeus, surnamed Thaddaeus, Matt 10:3
One of Christ's apostles, Luke 6:13, 16
Offers a question, John 14:22
——— Judas Barsabas, a chief deputy, Acts 15:22–32
——— Betrayer of Christ: *see* ISCARIOT

JUDE (or Judas)

Half brother of Christ, Matt 13:55
Does not believe in Christ, John 7:5
Becomes Christ's disciple, Acts 1:14
Writes an epistle, Jude 1

JUDEA

Christ born in, Matt 2:1, 5, 6
Hostile toward Christ, John 7:1
Gospel preached in, Acts 8:1, 4
Churches established in, Acts 9:31

JUDGE

The LORD *j* between .... Gen 16:5
For the LORD will *j* .... Deut 32:36
coming to *j* the earth .... 1 Chr 16:33
Rise up, O *J* of the .... Ps 94:2
sword the LORD will *j* .... Is 66:16
deliver you to the *j* .... Matt 5:25
"*J* not, that you be not .... Matt 7:1
"Man, who made Me a *j* .... Luke 12:14
j who did not fear God .... Luke 18:2
As I hear, I *j* .... John 5:30
Do not *j* according .... John 7:24
I *j* no one .... John 8:15
j the world but to .... John 12:47
this, O man, you who *j* .... Rom 2:3
then how will God *j* .... Rom 3:6
Therefore let us not *j* .... Rom 14:13
Christ, who will *j* .... 2 Tim 4:1
Lord, the righteous *J* .... 2 Tim 4:8
heaven, to God the *J* .... Heb 12:23

But if you *j* the law ....James 4:11
are you to *j* another ....James 4:12

JUDGES

j who delivered ....Judg 2:16
in the days when the *j* ....Ruth 1:1
Surely He is God who *j* ....Ps 58:11
He *j* among the gods ....Ps 82:1
He makes the *j* of the ....Is 40:23
j are evening wolves ....Zeph 3:3
For the Father *j* ....John 5:22
he who is spiritual *j* ....1 Cor 2:15
j me is the Lord ....1 Cor 4:4
Him who *j* righteously ....1 Pet 2:23

JUDGMENT

show partiality in *j* ....Deut 1:17
Teach me good *j* ....Ps 119:66
him in right *j* ....Is 28:26
from prison and from *j* ....Is 53:8
I will also speak *j* ....Jer 4:12
j was made in favor of ....Dan 7:22
be in danger of the *j* ....Matt 5:21
will rise up in the *j* ....Matt 12:42
shall not come into *j* ....John 5:24
and My *j* is righteous ....John 5:30
if I do judge, My *j* ....John 8:16
Now is the *j* ....John 12:31
the righteous *j* ....Rom 1:32
j which came from one ....Rom 5:16
all stand before the *j* ....Rom 14:10
eats and drinks *j* ....1 Cor 11:29
appear before the *j* ....2 Cor 5:10
after this the *j* ....Heb 9:27
For *j* is without mercy ....James 2:13
receive a stricter *j* ....James 3:1
time has come for *j* ....1 Pet 4:17
a long time their *j* ....2 Pet 2:3
darkness for the *j* ....Jude 6

JUDGMENTS

The *j* of the LORD are ....Ps 19:9
j are a great deep ....Ps 36:6
I dread, for Your *j* ....Ps 119:39
unsearchable are His *j* ....Rom 11:33
righteous are His *j* ....Rev 19:2

JULIUS

Roman centurion assigned to guard Paul, Acts 27:1–44

JUST

Noah was a *j* man ....Gen 6:9
Hear a *j* cause ....Ps 17:1
It is a joy for the *j* ....Prov 21:15
j man who perishes ....Eccl 7:15
For there is not a *j* ....Eccl 7:20
j is uprightness ....Is 26:7
the blood of the *j* ....Lam 4:13
j shall live by his ....Hab 2:4
He is *j* and having ....Zech 9:9
her husband, being a *j* ....Matt 1:19
resurrection of the *j* ....Luke 14:14
j persons who need no ....Luke 15:7
the Holy One and the *J* ....Acts 3:14
dead, both of the *j* ....Acts 24:15
j shall live by faith ....Rom 1:17
that He might be *j* ....Rom 3:26
whatever things are *j* ....Phil 4:8
j men made perfect ....Heb 12:23
have murdered the *j* ....James 5:6
He is faithful and *j* ....1 John 1:9
J and true are Your ....Rev 15:3

JUSTICE

for all His ways are *j* ....Deut 32:4
the Almighty pervert *j* ....Job 8:3
j as the noonday ....Ps 37:6
and Your poor with *j* ....Ps 72:2
He will bring *j* ....Ps 72:4
Do *j* to the afflicted ....Ps 82:3
and *j* are the ....Ps 89:14
revenues without *j* ....Prov 16:8
do not understand *j* ....Prov 28:5
j the measuring line ....Is 28:17
the LORD is a God of *j* ....Is 30:18
He will bring forth *j* ....Is 42:1
No one calls for *j* ....Is 59:4
J is turned back ....Is 59:14
I, the LORD, love *j* ....Is 61:8
you, O home of *j* ....Jer 31:23
plundering, execute *j* ....Ezek 45:9
truth, and His ways *j* ....Dan 4:37
observe mercy and *j* ....Hos 12:6
'Execute true *j* ....Zech 7:9
"Where is the God of *j* ....Mal 2:17
And He will declare *j* ....Matt 12:18
His humiliation His *j* ....Acts 8:33

JUSTIFICATION

because of our *j* ....Rom 4:25
offenses resulted in *j* ....Rom 5:16
men, resulting in *j* ....Rom 5:18

JUSTIFIED

Me that you may be *j* ....Job 40:8
of Israel shall be *j* ....Is 45:25
words you will be *j* ....Matt 12:37
But wisdom is *j* ....Luke 7:35
j rather than the ....Luke 18:14
who believes is *j* ....Acts 13:39
"That You may be *j* ....Rom 3:4
law no flesh will be *j* ....Rom 3:20
j freely by His grace ....Rom 3:24
having been *j* by ....Rom 5:1
these He also *j* ....Rom 8:30
but you were *j* ....1 Cor 6:11
that we might be *j* ....Gal 2:16
no flesh shall be *j* ....Gal 2:16
who attempt to be *j* ....Gal 5:4
j in the Spirit ....1 Tim 3:16
then that a man is *j* ....James 2:24
the harlot also *j* ....James 2:25

JUSTIFY

j the wicked for a ....Is 5:23
wanting to *j* himself ....Luke 10:29
"You are those who *j* ....Luke 16:15
is one God who will *j* ....Rom 3:30
that God would *j* ....Gal 3:8

JUSTLY

of you but to do *j* ....Mic 6:8
And we indeed *j* ....Luke 23:41
how devoutly and *j* ....1 Thess 2:10

JUSTUS

Surname of Joseph, a disciple, Acts 1:23
——— Man of Corinth; befriends Paul, Acts 18:7

KADESH

Spies sent from, Num 13:3, 26
Moses strikes rock at, Num 20:1–13
Boundary in the new Israel, Ezek 47:19

KADESH BARNEA

Boundary of Promised Land, Num 34:1–4
Limit of Joshua's military campaign, Josh 10:41

KEEP

k you wherever you ....Gen 28:15
day, to *k* it holy ....Ex 20:8
and *k* My judgments ....Lev 25:18
k all My commandments ....1 Kin 6:12
and that You would *k* ....1 Chr 4:10
Even he who cannot *k* ....Ps 22:29
K my soul ....Ps 25:20
do not *k* silence ....Ps 35:22
k Your righteous ....Ps 119:106
k them in the midst of ....Prov 4:21
K your heart with all ....Prov 4:23
a time to *k* silence ....Eccl 3:7
Let all the earth *k* ....Hab 2:20
k the commandments ....Matt 19:17
If you love Me, *k* ....John 14:15
k through Your name ....John 17:11
orderly and *k* the law ....Acts 21:24
Let your women *k* ....1 Cor 14:34
k the unity of the ....Eph 4:3
k yourself pure ....1 Tim 5:22
k His commandments ....1 John 2:3
k yourselves in the ....Jude 21
k you from stumbling ....Jude 24
k those things ....Rev 1:3

KEEPER

Am I my brother's *k* ....Gen 4:9
The LORD is your *k* ....Ps 121:5

KEEPS

the faithful God who *k* ....Deut 7:9
k truth forever ....Ps 146:6
k his way preserves ....Prov 16:17
k the commandment ....Prov 19:16
Whoever *k* the law is a ....Prov 28:7
none of you *k* the law ....John 7:19
born of God *k* himself ....1 John 5:18
and *k* his garments ....Rev 16:15

KEILAH

Town of Judah; rescued from Philistines by David, 1 Sam 23:1–5
Prepares to betray David; he escapes, 1 Sam 23:6–13

KENITES

Canaanite tribe whose land is promised to Abraham's seed, Gen 15:19
Subjects of Balaam's prophecy, Num 24:20–22
Settle with Judahites, Judg 1:16
Spared by Saul in war with Amalekites, 1 Sam 15:6

KEPT

For I have *k* the ways ....2 Sam 22:22
vineyard I have not *k* ....Song 1:6
these things I have *k* ....Matt 19:20
all these things I have *k* ....Mark 10:20
k all these things ....Luke 2:19
love, just as I have *k* ....John 15:10
k back part of the ....Acts 5:2
I have *k* the faith ....2 Tim 4:7
who are *k* by the power ....1 Pet 1:5
which now exist are *k* ....2 Pet 3:7

KETURAH

Abraham's second wife, Gen 25:1
Sons of:
Listed, Gen 25:1, 2
Given gifts and sent away, Gen 25:6

KEY

The *k* of the house of ....Is 22:22
have taken away the *k* ....Luke 11:52
"He who has the *k* ....Rev 3:7
heaven, having the *k* ....Rev 20:1

KEYS

I will give you the *k* ....Matt 16:19
And I have the *k* ....Rev 1:18

KIBROTH HATTAAVAH

Burial site of Israelites slain by God, Num 11:33–35

KIDRON

Valley near Jerusalem; crossed by David and Christ, 2 Sam 15:23; John 18:1
Idols dumped there, 2 Chr 29:16

KILL

who finds me will *k* ....Gen 4:14
k the Passover ....Ex 12:21
I *k* and I make alive ....Deut 32:39
"Am I God, to *k* ....2 Kin 5:7
a time to *k* ....Eccl 3:3

k rather than ... Prov 8:10
Wise people store up *k* ... Prov 10:14
k is easy to him who ... Prov 14:6
k spares his words ... Prov 17:27
a soul to be without *k* ... Prov 19:2
and he who increases *k* ... Eccl 1:18
k is that wisdom ... Eccl 7:12
no work or device or *k* ... Eccl 9:10
Whom will he teach *k* ... Is 28:9
k shall increase ... Dan 12:4
you have rejected *k* ... Hos 4:6
having more accurate *k* ... Acts 24:22
having the form of *k* ... Rom 2:20
by the law is the *k* of sin ... Rom 3:20
K puffs up ... 1 Cor 8:1
whether there is *k* ... 1 Cor 13:8
Christ which passes *k* ... Eph 3:19
is falsely called *k* ... 1 Tim 6:20
in the grace and *k* ... 2 Pet 3:18

KNOWN
In Judah God is *k* ... Ps 76:1
my mouth will I make *k* ... Ps 89:1
If you had *k* Me ... John 8:19
My sheep, and am *k* ... John 10:14
The world has not *k* ... John 17:25
peace they have not *k* ... Rom 3:17
I would not have *k* ... Rom 7:7
"For who has *k* ... Rom 11:34
after you have *k* ... Gal 4:9
requests be made *k* ... Phil 4:6
k the Holy Scriptures ... 2 Tim 3:15

KNOWS
For God *k* that in ... Gen 3:5
k the secrets of the ... Ps 44:21
he understands and *k* ... Jer 9:24
k what is in the ... Dan 2:22
k those who trust ... Nah 1:7
k the things you have ... Matt 6:8
and hour no one *k* ... Matt 24:36
k who the Son is ... Luke 10:22
but God *k* your hearts ... Luke 16:15
searches the hearts *k* ... Rom 8:27
k the things of God ... 1 Cor 2:11
k those who are His ... 2 Tim 2:19
to him who *k* to do ... James 4:17
and *k* all things ... 1 John 3:20
written which no one *k* ... Rev 2:17

KOHATH
Second son of Levi, Gen 46:8, 11
Brother of Jochebed, mother of Aaron and Moses, Ex 6:16–20

KOHATHITES
Numbered, Num 3:27, 28
Duties assigned to, Num 4:15–20
Leaders of temple music, 1 Chr 6:31–38; 2 Chr 20:19

KORAH
Leads rebellion against Moses and Aaron; supernaturally destroyed, Num 16:1–35
Sons of, not destroyed, Num 26:9–11

LABAN
Son of Bethuel; brother of Rebekah; father of Leah and Rachel, Gen 24:15, 24, 29; 29:16
Agrees to Rebekah's marriage to Isaac, Gen 24:50, 51
Entertains Jacob, Gen 29:1–14
Substitutes Leah for Rachel, Gen 29:15–30
Agrees to division of cattle; grows resentful of Jacob, Gen 30:25—31:2
Pursues Jacob and makes covenant with him, Gen 31:21–55

LABOR
Six days you shall *l* ... Ex 20:9
why then do I *l* ... Job 9:29
their boast is only *l* ... Ps 90:10
The *l* of the righteous ... Prov 10:16
l will increase ... Prov 13:11
l there is profit ... Prov 14:23
things are full of *l* ... Eccl 1:8
has man for all his *l* ... Eccl 2:22
He shall see the *l* ... Is 53:11
"Before she was in *l* ... Is 66:7
from the womb to see *l* ... Jer 20:18
to Me, all you who *l* ... Matt 11:28
Do not *l* for the ... John 6:27
knowing that your *l* ... 1 Cor 15:58
but rather let him *l* ... Eph 4:28
mean fruit from my *l* ... Phil 1:22
your work of faith, *l* ... 1 Thess 1:3
forget your work and *l* ... Heb 6:10
your works, your *l* ... Rev 2:2

LABORERS
but the *l* are few ... Matt 9:37

LABORS
The person who *l* ... Prov 16:26
is no end to all his *l* ... Eccl 4:8
entered into their *l* ... John 4:38
creation groans and *l* ... Rom 8:22
l more abundant ... 2 Cor 11:23
may rest from their *l* ... Rev 14:13

LACHISH
Defeated by Joshua, Josh 10:3–33
Taken by Sennacherib, 2 Kin 18:13–17; Is 36:1, 2; 37:8

LACK
anyone perish for *l* ... Job 31:19
the LORD shall not *l* ... Ps 34:10
to the poor will not *l* ... Prov 28:27
What do I still *l* ... Matt 19:20
"One thing you *l* ... Mark 10:21

LADEN
nation, a people *l* ... Is 1:4
and are heavy *l* ... Matt 11:28

LADIES
wisest *l* answered her ... Judg 5:29
very day the noble *l* ... Esth 1:18

LADY
'I shall be a *l* ... Is 47:7
To the elect *l* ... 2 John 1

LAHAI ROI
Name of a well, Gen 16:7, 14
Same as Beer Lahai Roi, Gen 24:62

LAID
But man dies and is *l* ... Job 14:10
the place where they *l* ... Mark 16:6
"Where have you *l* ... John 11:34

LAISH
Called Leshem, Josh 19:47; Judg 18:29
Taken by Danites, Judg 18:7, 14, 27

LAMB
but where is the *l* ... Gen 22:7
took the poor man's *l* ... 2 Sam 12:4
shall dwell with the *l* ... Is 11:6
He was led as a *l* ... Is 53:7
l shall feed together ... Is 65:25
The *L* of God who takes ... John 1:29
of Christ, as of a *l* ... 1 Pet 1:19
the elders, stood a *L* ... Rev 5:6
"Worthy is the *L* ... Rev 5:12
by the blood of the *L* ... Rev 12:11
Book of Life of the *L* ... Rev 13:8
supper of the *L* ... Rev 19:9

LAME
l take the prey ... Is 33:23
l shall leap like a ... Is 35:6
when you offer the *l* ... Mal 1:8
blind see and the *l* ... Matt 11:5
And a certain man *l* ... Acts 3:2
so that what is *l* ... Heb 12:13

LAMECH
Son of Methushael, of Cain's race, Gen 4:17, 18
——— Son of Methuselah; father of Noah, Gen 5:25–31

LAMENTATION
was heard in Ramah, *l* ... Jer 31:15
was heard in Ramah, *l* ... Matt 2:18
and made great *l* ... Acts 8:2

LAMP
For You are my *l* ... 2 Sam 22:29
"How often is the *l* ... Job 21:17
You will light my *l* ... Ps 18:28
Your word is a *l* ... Ps 119:105
the *l* of the wicked ... Prov 13:9
his *l* will be put out ... Prov 20:20
Nor do they light a *l* ... Matt 5:15
"The *l* of the body ... Matt 6:22
when he has lit a *l* ... Luke 8:16
l gives you light ... Luke 11:36
does not light a *l* ... Luke 15:8
burning and shining *l* ... John 5:35
l shall not shine ... Rev 18:23
They need no *l* nor ... Rev 22:5

LAMPS
he made its seven *l* ... Ex 37:23
Jerusalem with *l* ... Zeph 1:12
and trimmed their *l* ... Matt 25:7
Seven *l* of fire ... Rev 4:5

LAMPSTAND
branches of the *l* ... Ex 25:32
and there is a *l* ... Zech 4:2
a basket, but on a *l* ... Matt 5:15
in which was the *l* ... Heb 9:2
and remove your *l* ... Rev 2:5

LAND
l that I will show you ... Gen 12:1
l flowing with milk ... Ex 3:8
l which I am giving ... Josh 1:2
is heard in our *l* ... Song 2:12
they will see the *l* ... Is 33:17
Bethlehem, in the *l* ... Matt 2:6

LANDMARK
your neighbor's *l* ... Deut 19:14
remove the ancient *l* ... Prov 22:28
those who remove a *l* ... Hos 5:10

LANGUAGE
whole earth had one *l* ... Gen 11:1
is no speech nor *l* ... Ps 19:3
a people of strange *l* ... Ps 114:1
the peoples a pure *l* ... Zeph 3:9
speak in his own *l* ... Acts 2:6
blasphemy, filthy *l* ... Col 3:8

LAODICEA
Paul's concern for, Col 2:1; 4:12–16
Letter to church of, Rev 3:14–22

LAST
He shall stand at *l* ... Job 19:25
First and I am the *L* ... Is 44:6
l man the same as ... Matt 20:14
l will be first ... Matt 20:16
children, it is the *l* ... 1 John 2:18
the First and the *L* ... Rev 1:11

LAUGH
Why did Sarah *l* ... Gen 18:13
"God has made me *l* ... Gen 21:6
You, O LORD, shall *l* ... Ps 59:8
Woe to you who *l* ... Luke 6:25

LAUGHS
he *l* at the threat of ... Job 41:29
The Lord *l* at him ... Ps 37:13

LAUGHTER
was filled with *l* . . . . Ps 126:2
your *l* be turned to . . . . James 4:9

LAW
stones a copy of the *l* . . . . Josh 8:32
When He made a *l* . . . . Job 28:26
The *l* of the LORD is . . . . Ps 19:7
The *l* of his God is in . . . . Ps 37:31
I delight in Your *l* . . . . Ps 119:70
The *l* of Your mouth is . . . . Ps 119:72
l is my delight . . . . Ps 119:77
Oh, how I love Your *l* . . . . Ps 119:97
And Your *l* is truth . . . . Ps 119:142
and the *l* a light . . . . Prov 6:23
shall go forth the *l* . . . . Is 2:3
l will proceed from Me . . . . Is 51:4
in whose heart is My *l* . . . . Is 51:7
the *L* is no more . . . . Lam 2:9
The *l* of truth was in . . . . Mal 2:6
to destroy the *L* . . . . Matt 5:17
for this is the *L* . . . . Matt 7:12
hang all the *L* and the . . . . Matt 22:40
"The *l* and the . . . . Luke 16:16
l was given through . . . . John 1:17
"Does our *l* judge a . . . . John 7:51
l is the knowledge . . . . Rom 3:20
because the *l* brings . . . . Rom 4:15
when there is no *l* . . . . Rom 5:13
you are not under *l* . . . . Rom 6:14
Is the *l* sin . . . . Rom 7:7
For we know that the *l* . . . . Rom 7:14
warring against the *l* . . . . Rom 7:23
For what the *l* could . . . . Rom 8:3
who are without *l* . . . . 1 Cor 9:21
l that I might live . . . . Gal 2:19
under guard by the *l* . . . . Gal 3:23
born under the *l* . . . . Gal 4:4
l is fulfilled in one . . . . Gal 5:14
l is not made for a . . . . 1 Tim 1:9
into the perfect *l* . . . . James 1:25
fulfill the royal *l* . . . . James 2:8

LAWFUL
doing what is not *l* . . . . Matt 12:2
Is it *l* to pay taxes . . . . Matt 22:17
All things are *l* . . . . 1 Cor 6:12

LAWGIVER
Judah is My *l* . . . . Ps 60:7
the LORD is our *L* . . . . Is 33:22
There is one *L* . . . . James 4:12

LAWLESS
l one will be revealed . . . . 2 Thess 2:8
and hearing their *l* . . . . 2 Pet 2:8

LAWLESSNESS
Me, you who practice *l* . . . . Matt 7:23
l is already at work . . . . 2 Thess 2:7
and hated *l* . . . . Heb 1:9
and sin is *l* . . . . 1 John 3:4

LAWYERS
l rejected the will of . . . . Luke 7:30
Woe to you also, *l* . . . . Luke 11:46

LAY
nowhere to *l* His head . . . . Matt 8:20
l hands may receive . . . . Acts 8:19
Do not *l* hands on . . . . 1 Tim 5:22
l aside all . . . . James 1:21

LAZARUS
Beggar described in a parable, Luke 16:20–25
——— Brother of Mary and Martha; raised from the dead, John 11:1–44
Attends a supper, John 12:1, 2
Jews seek to kill, John 12:9–11

LAZINESS
L casts one into a . . . . Prov 19:15
l the building decays . . . . Eccl 10:18

LAZY
l man will be put to . . . . Prov 12:24
l man does not roast . . . . Prov 12:27
soul of a *l* man desires . . . . Prov 13:4
l man buries his hand . . . . Prov 19:24
by the field of the *l* . . . . Prov 24:30
l man is wiser in his . . . . Prov 26:16
wicked and *l* servant . . . . Matt 25:26
liars, evil beasts, *l* . . . . Titus 1:12

LEAD
they sank like *l* . . . . Ex 15:10
L me in Your truth and . . . . Ps 25:5
L me and guide me . . . . Ps 31:3
Your hand shall *l* . . . . Ps 139:10
And do not *l* us into . . . . Matt 6:13
"Can the blind *l* . . . . Luke 6:39

LEADS
He *l* me beside the . . . . Ps 23:2
He *l* me in the paths . . . . Ps 23:3
And if the blind *l* . . . . Matt 15:14
by name and *l* them out . . . . John 10:3
the goodness of God *l* . . . . Rom 2:4

LEAF
plucked olive *l* . . . . Gen 8:11
Will You frighten a *l* . . . . Job 13:25
l will be green . . . . Jer 17:8

LEAH
Laban's eldest daughter; given to Jacob deceitfully, Gen 29:16–27
Unloved by Jacob, but bears children, Gen 29:30–35; 30:16–21

LEAN
all your heart, and *l* . . . . Prov 3:5
Yet they *l* on the LORD . . . . Mic 3:11

LEANNESS
request, but sent *l* . . . . Ps 106:15
of hosts, will send *l* . . . . Is 10:16

LEAP
by my God I can *l* . . . . Ps 18:29
Then the lame shall *l* . . . . Is 35:6

LEARN
it, may hear and *l* . . . . Deut 31:13
l Your statutes . . . . Ps 119:71
lest you *l* his ways . . . . Prov 22:25
l to do good . . . . Is 1:17
neither shall they *l* . . . . Is 2:4
My yoke upon you and *l* . . . . Matt 11:29
Let a woman *l* in . . . . 1 Tim 2:11
let our people also *l* . . . . Titus 3:14

LEARNED
Me the tongue of the *l* . . . . Is 50:4
who has heard and *l* . . . . John 6:45
have not so *l* Christ . . . . Eph 4:20
in all things I have *l* . . . . Phil 4:12
l obedience by the . . . . Heb 5:8

LEARNING
hear and increase *l* . . . . Prov 1:5
l is driving you mad . . . . Acts 26:24
were written for our *l* . . . . Rom 15:4

LEAST
Judah, are not the *l* . . . . Matt 2:6
so, shall be called *l* . . . . Matt 5:19
For I am the *l* of the . . . . 1 Cor 15:9

LEAVE
a man shall *l* his . . . . Gen 2:24
He will not *l* you nor . . . . Deut 31:6
For You will not *l* . . . . Ps 16:10
do not *l* me nor . . . . Ps 27:9
"I will never *l* . . . . Heb 13:5

LEAVEN
day you shall remove *l* . . . . Ex 12:15
of heaven is like *l* . . . . Matt 13:33
and beware of the *l* . . . . Matt 16:6
know that a little *l* . . . . 1 Cor 5:6
l leavens the whole . . . . Gal 5:9

LEAVES
and they sewed fig *l* . . . . Gen 3:7
nothing on it but *l* . . . . Matt 21:19
l the sheep and flees . . . . John 10:12
The *l* of the tree . . . . Rev 22:2

LEBANON
Part of Israel's inheritance, Josh 13:5–7
Not completely conquered, Judg 3:1–3
Source of materials for temple, 1 Kin 5:2–18; Ezra 3:7
Mentioned in prophecy, Is 10:34; 29:17; 35:2; Ezek 17:3; Hos 14:5–7

LEBBAEUS
See JUDAS
Surname of Judas (Jude), Matt 10:3

LED
l the people around by . . . . Ex 13:18
so the LORD alone *l* . . . . Deut 32:12
l them forth by the . . . . Ps 107:7
l them by the right . . . . Is 63:12
For as many as are *l* . . . . Rom 8:14
l captivity captive . . . . Eph 4:8
l away by various . . . . 2 Tim 3:6

LEFT
l hand know what your . . . . Matt 6:3
"See, we have *l* . . . . Matt 19:27
And everyone who has *l* . . . . Matt 19:29

LEMUEL
King taught by his mother, Prov 31:1–31

LEND
"If you *l* money to . . . . Ex 22:25
l him sufficient . . . . Deut 15:8
And if you *l* . . . . Luke 6:34
l me three loaves . . . . Luke 11:5

LENDER
is servant to the *l* . . . . Prov 22:7
as with the *l* . . . . Is 24:2

LENDS
ever merciful, and *l* . . . . Ps 37:26
deals graciously and *l* . . . . Ps 112:5
has pity on the poor *l* . . . . Prov 19:17

LENGTH
The *l* of the ark shall . . . . Gen 6:15
is your life and the *l* . . . . Deut 30:20
L of days is in her . . . . Prov 3:16
l is as great as its . . . . Rev 21:16

LEOPARD
the *l* shall lie down . . . . Is 11:6
or the *l* its spots . . . . Jer 13:23

LEPERS
And when these *l* . . . . 2 Kin 7:8
And many *l* were in . . . . Luke 4:27

LETTER
the oldness of the *l* . . . . Rom 7:6
for the *l* kills . . . . 2 Cor 3:6
you sorry with my *l* . . . . 2 Cor 7:8
or by word or by *l* . . . . 2 Thess 2:2

LETTERS
does this Man know *l* . . . . John 7:15
or *l* of commendation . . . . 2 Cor 3:1
"For his *l*," they say . . . . 2 Cor 10:10
with what large *l* . . . . Gal 6:11

LEVI
Third son of Jacob and Leah, Gen 29:34
Avenges rape of Dinah, Gen 34:25–31
Jacob's prophecy concerning, Gen 49:5–7
Ancestor of Moses and Aaron, Ex 6:16–27

LEVIATHAN
"Can you draw out *L* . . . . Job 41:1
L which You have made . . . . Ps 104:26

LEVITE
"Is not Aaron the *L* .Ex 4:14
Likewise a *L* .Luke 10:32
a *L* of the country of .Acts 4:36

LEVITES
Rewarded for dedication, Ex 32:26–29
Appointed over tabernacle, Num 1:47–54
Substituted for Israel's firstborn, Num 3:12–45
Consecrated to the Lord's service, Num 8:5–26
Cities assigned to, Num 35:2–8; Josh 14:3, 4; 1 Chr 6:54–81
Organized for temple service, 1 Chr 9:14–34; 23:1—26:28

LEWDNESS
wickedness, deceit, *l* .Mark 7:22
drunkenness, not in *l* .Rom 13:13
themselves over to *l* .Eph 4:19
when we walked in *l* .1 Pet 4:3

LIAR
for he is a *l* and the .John 8:44
but every man a *l* .Rom 3:4
we make Him a *l* .1 John 1:10
Who is a *l* but he who .1 John 2:22
his brother, he is a *l* .1 John 4:20
God has made Him a *l* .1 John 5:10

LIARS
"All men are *l* .Ps 116:11
Cretans are always *l* .Titus 1:12
and have found them *l* .Rev 2:2
l shall have their .Rev 21:8

LIBERALITY
he who gives, with *l* .Rom 12:8
the riches of their *l* .2 Cor 8:2

LIBERALLY
who gives to all *l* .James 1:5

LIBERTY
year, and proclaim *l* .Lev 25:10
And I will walk at *l* .Ps 119:45
to proclaim *l* to the .Is 61:1
to proclaim *l* to the .Luke 4:18
into the glorious *l* .Rom 8:21
For why is my *l* .1 Cor 10:29
Lord is, there is *l* .2 Cor 3:17
therefore in the *l* .Gal 5:1
l as an opportunity .Gal 5:13
the perfect law of *l* .James 1:25
yet not using *l* .1 Pet 2:16

LIBNAH
Canaanite city, captured by Joshua, Josh 10:29, 30
Given to Aaron's descendants, Josh 21:13

LIBYA
Mentioned in prophecy, Ezek 30:5; Dan 11:43
Jews from, present at Pentecost, Acts 2:1–10

LIE
man, that He should *l* .Num 23:19
For now I will *l* .Job 7:21
I will not *l* to David .Ps 89:35
Do not *l* to one .Col 3:9
God, who cannot *l* .Titus 1:2
do not boast and *l* .James 3:14
know it, and that no *l* .1 John 2:21
an abomination or a *l* .Rev 21:27

LIED
They have *l* about the .Jer 5:12
You have not *l* to men .Acts 5:4

LIES
sin *l* at the door .Gen 4:7
and he who speaks *l* .Prov 19:5
speaking *l* in .1 Tim 4:2
and the whole world *l* .1 John 5:19

LIFE
the breath of *l* .Gen 2:7
l was also in the .Gen 2:9
then you shall give *l* .Ex 21:23
For the *l* of the .Lev 17:11
before you today *l* .Deut 30:15
You have granted me *l* .Job 10:12
in whose hand is the *l* .Job 12:10
God takes away his *l* .Job 27:8
with the light of *l* .Job 33:30
He will redeem their *l* .Ps 72:14
word has given me *l* .Ps 119:50
regain the paths of *l* .Prov 2:19
She is a tree of *l* .Prov 3:18
so they will be *l* .Prov 3:22
finds me finds *l* .Prov 8:35
l winds upward for the .Prov 15:24
thief hates his own *l* .Prov 29:24
is that wisdom gives *l* .Eccl 7:12
I have cut off my *l* .Is 38:12
you the way of *l* .Jer 21:8
l shall be as a prize .Jer 39:18
not worry about your *l* .Matt 6:25
l does not consist .Luke 12:15
L is more than .Luke 12:23
l was the light .John 1:4
so the Son gives *l* .John 5:21
as the Father has *l* .John 5:26
spirit, and they are *l* .John 6:63
have the light of *l* .John 8:12
and I lay down My *l* .John 10:15
resurrection and the *l* .John 11:25
you lay down your *l* .John 13:38
God, who gives *l* .Rom 4:17
that pertain to this *l* .1 Cor 6:3
Lord Jesus, that the *l* .2 Cor 4:10
l which I now live .Gal 2:20
l is hidden with .Col 3:3
of God who gives *l* .1 Tim 6:13
For what is your *l* .James 4:14
that pertain to *l* .2 Pet 1:3
l was manifested .1 John 1:2
and the pride of *l* .1 John 2:16
has given us eternal *l* .1 John 5:11
who has the Son has *l* .1 John 5:12
the Lamb's Book of *L* .Rev 21:27
right to the tree of *l* .Rev 22:14
the water of *l* freely .Rev 22:17
from the Book of *L* .Rev 22:19

LIFT
I will *l* up my hands .Ps 63:4
I will *l* up my eyes to .Ps 121:1
l up your voice like a .Is 58:1
l our hearts and hands .Lam 3:41
Lord, and He will *l* .James 4:10

LIFTED
O LORD, for You have *l* .Ps 30:1
your heart is *l* .Ezek 28:2
in Hades, he *l* up his .Luke 16:23
the Son of Man be *l* .John 3:14
And I, if I am *l* .John 12:32
of Man must be *l* .John 12:34

LIGHT
"Let there be *l* .Gen 1:3
"The *l* of the wicked .Job 18:5
l will shine on your .Job 22:28
the wicked their *l* .Job 38:15
to the dwelling of *l* .Job 38:19
LORD, lift up the *l* .Ps 4:6
The LORD is my *l* .Ps 27:1
Oh, send out Your *l* .Ps 43:3
L is sown for the .Ps 97:11
and He has given us *l* .Ps 118:27
and a *l* to my path .Ps 119:105
The *l* of the righteous .Prov 13:9
The *l* of the eyes .Prov 15:30
The LORD gives *l* .Prov 29:13
Truly the *l* is sweet .Eccl 11:7
let us walk in the *l* .Is 2:5
l is darkened by the .Is 5:30
because there is no *l* .Is 8:20
moon will be as the *l* .Is 30:26
l shall break forth .Is 58:8
for your *l* has come .Is 60:1
be your everlasting *l* .Is 60:20
gives the sun for a *l* .Jer 31:35
l that goes .Hos 6:5
"You are the *l* .Matt 5:14
Let your *l* so shine .Matt 5:16
body will be full of *l* .Matt 6:22
than the sons of *l* .Luke 16:8
and the life was the *l* .John 1:4
That was the true *L* .John 1:9
darkness rather than *l* .John 3:19
evil hates the *l* .John 3:20
truth comes to the *l* .John 3:21
saying, "I am the *l* .John 8:12
believe in the *l* .John 12:36
I have come as a *l* .John 12:46
l the hidden .1 Cor 4:5
God who commanded *l* .2 Cor 4:6
Walk as children of *l* .Eph 5:8
You are all sons of *l* .1 Thess 5:5
and immortality to *l* .2 Tim 1:10
into His marvelous *l* .1 Pet 2:9
do well to heed as a *l* .2 Pet 1:19
to you, that God is *l* .1 John 1:5
l as He is in the .1 John 1:7
says he is in the *l* .1 John 2:9
The Lamb is its *l* .Rev 21:23
Lord God gives them *l* .Rev 22:5

LIGHTNING
For as the *l* .Matt 24:27
countenance was like *l* .Matt 28:3
saw Satan fall like *l* .Luke 10:18

LIGHTNINGS
were thunderings and *l* .Ex 19:16
the *l* lit up the world .Ps 77:18
l light the world .Ps 97:4
the throne proceeded *l* .Rev 4:5

LIGHTS
"Let there be *l* .Gen 1:14
Him who made great *l* .Ps 136:7
whom you shine as *l* .Phil 2:15
from the Father of *l* .James 1:17

LIKE-MINDED
grant you to be *l* .Rom 15:5
For I have no one *l* .Phil 2:20

LIKENESS
according to Our *l* .Gen 1:26
carved image—any *l* .Ex 20:4
when I awake in Your *l* .Ps 17:15
His own Son in the *l* .Rom 8:3
and coming in the *l* .Phil 2:7

LILY
the *l* of the valleys .Song 2:1
Like a *l* among thorns .Song 2:2
shall grow like the *l* .Hos 14:5

LINE
l has gone out through .Ps 19:4
upon precept, *l* upon *l* .Is 28:10
I am setting a plumb *l* .Amos 7:8

LINEAGE
was of the house and *l* .Luke 2:4

LINEN
her clothing is fine *l* .Prov 31:22
wrapped Him in the *l* .Mark 15:46
l is the righteous .Rev 19:8

LION
he lies down as a *l* . . . . .Gen 49:9
like a fierce *l* . . . . .Job 10:16
l shall eat straw . . . . .Is 11:7
For I will be like a *l* . . . . .Hos 5:14

LIONS
My soul is among *l* . . . . .Ps 57:4
the mouths of *l* . . . . .Heb 11:33

LIPS
of uncircumcised *l* . . . . .Ex 6:12
off all flattering *l* . . . . .Ps 12:3
Let the lying *l* . . . . .Ps 31:18
The *l* of the righteous . . . . .Prov 10:21
but the *l* of knowledge . . . . .Prov 20:15
am a man of unclean *l* . . . . .Is 6:5
asps is under their *l* . . . . .Rom 3:13
other *l* I will speak . . . . .1 Cor 14:21
from evil, and his *l* . . . . .1 Pet 3:10

LISTEN
L carefully to Me . . . . .Is 55:2
O Lord, *l* and act . . . . .Dan 9:19
you are not able to *l* . . . . .John 8:43
Why do you *l* to Him . . . . .John 10:20
you who fear God, *l* . . . . .Acts 13:16

LITTLE
l foxes that spoil the . . . . .Song 2:15
We have a *l* sister . . . . .Song 8:8
upon line, here a *l* . . . . .Is 28:10
though you are *l* . . . . .Mic 5:2
indeed it came to *l* . . . . .Hag 1:9
for I was a *l* angry . . . . .Zech 1:15
l ones only a cup . . . . .Matt 10:42
"O you of *l* faith . . . . .Matt 14:31
Whoever receives one *l* . . . . .Matt 18:5
to whom *l* is forgiven . . . . .Luke 7:47
faithful in a very *l* . . . . .Luke 19:17
exercise profits a *l* . . . . .1 Tim 4:8

LIVE
eat, and *l* forever . . . . .Gen 3:22
a man does, he shall *l* . . . . .Lev 18:5
I would not *l* forever . . . . .Job 7:16
L joyfully with the . . . . .Eccl 9:9
by these things men *l* . . . . .Is 38:16
sin, he shall surely *l* . . . . .Ezek 3:21
"Seek Me and *l* . . . . .Amos 5:4
but the just shall *l* . . . . .Hab 2:4
l by bread alone . . . . .Matt 4:4
who feeds on Me will *l* . . . . .John 6:57
for in Him we *l* . . . . .Acts 17:28
l peaceably with all . . . . .Rom 12:18
the life which I now *l* . . . . .Gal 2:20
If we *l* in the Spirit . . . . .Gal 5:25
to me, to *l* is Christ . . . . .Phil 1:21
l godly in Christ . . . . .2 Tim 3:12
to *l* honorably . . . . .Heb 13:18
l according to God in . . . . .1 Pet 4:6

LIVES
but man *l* by every . . . . .Deut 8:3
have risked their *l* . . . . .Acts 15:26
He *l* to God . . . . .Rom 6:10
For none of us *l* . . . . .Rom 14:7
but Christ *l* in me . . . . .Gal 2:20
to lay down our *l* . . . . .1 John 3:16
I am He who *l* . . . . .Rev 1:18

LIVING
and man became a *l* . . . . .Gen 2:7
in the light of the *l* . . . . .Ps 56:13
l will take it to . . . . .Eccl 7:2
l know that they will . . . . .Eccl 9:5
Why should a *l* man . . . . .Lam 3:39
the dead, but of the *l* . . . . .Matt 22:32
Why do you seek the *l* . . . . .Luke 24:5
to be Judge of the *l* . . . . .Acts 10:42
who will judge the *l* . . . . .2 Tim 4:1
the word of God is *l* . . . . .Heb 4:12
ready to judge the *l* . . . . .1 Pet 4:5
l creature was like a . . . . .Rev 4:7

LO-AMMI
Symbolic name of Hosea's son, Hos 1:8, 9

LO-RUHAMAH
Symbolic name of Hosea's daughter, Hos 1:6

LOATHE
I *l* my life . . . . .Job 7:16
l themselves for the . . . . .Ezek 6:9

LOATHSOME
but a wicked man is *l* . . . . .Prov 13:5

LOAVES
have here only five *l* . . . . .Matt 14:17
He took the seven *l* . . . . .Matt 15:36
lend me three *l* . . . . .Luke 11:5
you ate of the *l* . . . . .John 6:26

LOCUST
What the chewing *l* . . . . .Joel 1:4
left, the swarming *l* . . . . .Joel 1:4

LOCUSTS
as numerous as *l* . . . . .Judg 7:12
He spoke, and *l* came . . . . .Ps 105:34
the *l* have no king . . . . .Prov 30:27
and his food was *l* . . . . .Matt 3:4
waist, and he ate *l* . . . . .Mark 1:6
out of the smoke *l* . . . . .Rev 9:3

LOFTY
haughty, nor my eyes *l* . . . . .Ps 131:1
Wisdom is too *l* . . . . .Prov 24:7
l are their eyes . . . . .Prov 30:13
and *L* One who . . . . .Is 57:15

LONG
your days may be *l* . . . . .Deut 5:16
who *l* for death . . . . .Job 3:21
me the thing that I *l* . . . . .Job 6:8
I *l* for Your salvation . . . . .Ps 119:174
go around in *l* robes . . . . .Mark 12:38
how greatly I *l* . . . . .Phil 1:8

LONGSUFFERING
and gracious, *l* . . . . .Ps 86:15
is love, joy, peace, *l* . . . . .Gal 5:22
and gentleness, with *l* . . . . .Eph 4:2
for all patience and *l* . . . . .Col 1:11
might show all *l* . . . . .1 Tim 1:16
when once the Divine *l* . . . . .1 Pet 3:20
and consider that the *l* . . . . .2 Pet 3:15

LOOK
Do not *l* behind you . . . . .Gen 19:17
who has a haughty *l* . . . . .Ps 101:5
A proud *l* .Prov 6:17
that day a man will *l* . . . . .Is 17:7
L upon Zion . . . . .Is 33:20
"*L* to Me . . . . .Is 45:22
we *l* for light . . . . .Is 59:9
we *l* for justice . . . . .Is 59:11
l on Me whom they . . . . .Zech 12:10
say to you, '*L* here . . . . .Luke 17:23
of Israel could not *l* . . . . .2 Cor 3:7
while we do not *l* . . . . .2 Cor 4:18
Let each of you *l* . . . . .Phil 2:4
L to yourselves . . . . .2 John 8

LOOKED
But when I *l* for good . . . . .Job 30:26
They *l* to Him and were . . . . .Ps 34:5
For He *l* down from the . . . . .Ps 102:19
He *l* for justice . . . . .Is 5:7
"We *l* for peace . . . . .Jer 8:15
"You *l* for much . . . . .Hag 1:9
the Lord turned and *l* . . . . .Luke 22:61
for he *l* to the reward . . . . .Heb 11:26

LOOKING
the plow, and *l* back . . . . .Luke 9:62
l for the blessed hope . . . . .Titus 2:13
l unto Jesus . . . . .Heb 12:2
l carefully lest . . . . .Heb 12:15
l for the mercy of . . . . .Jude 21

LOOKS
Absalom for his good *l* . . . . .2 Sam 14:25
Then he *l* at men and . . . . .Job 33:27
God *l* down from heaven . . . . .Ps 53:2
The lofty *l* of man . . . . .Is 2:11
to you that whoever *l* . . . . .Matt 5:28

LOOSE
l the armor of kings . . . . .Is 45:1
and whatever you *l* . . . . .Matt 16:19
said to them, "*L* him . . . . .John 11:44

LOOSED
You have *l* my bonds . . . . .Ps 116:16
the silver cord is *l* . . . . .Eccl 12:6

LORD
L is my strength . . . . .Ex 15:2
L is a man of war . . . . .Ex 15:3
L our God, the *L* . . . . .Deut 6:4
sacrifice to the *L* your God . . . . . . .Deut 17:1
may know that the *L* . . . . .1 Kin 8:60
If the *L* is God . . . . .1 Kin 18:21
You alone are the *L* . . . . .Neh 9:6
The *L* of hosts . . . . .Ps 24:10
belongs to the *L* . . . . .Ps 89:18
let us sing to the *L* . . . . .Ps 95:1
L is the great God . . . . .Ps 95:3
Gracious is the *L* . . . . .Ps 116:5
L surrounds His people . . . . .Ps 125:2
The *L* is righteous . . . . .Ps 129:4
L is near to all who . . . . .Ps 145:18
L is a God of justice . . . . .Is 30:18
L Our Righteousness . . . . .Jer 23:6
L has done marvelous . . . . .Joel 2:21
L God is my strength . . . . .Hab 3:19
"The *L* is one . . . . .Zech 14:9
shall not tempt the *L* . . . . .Matt 4:7
shall worship the *L* . . . . .Matt 4:10
Son of Man is also *L* . . . . .Mark 2:28
who is Christ the *L* . . . . .Luke 2:11
why do you call Me '*L* . . . . .Luke 6:46
L is risen indeed . . . . .Luke 24:34
call Me Teacher and *L* . . . . .John 13:13
He is *L* of all . . . . .Acts 10:36
'Who are You, *L* . . . . .Acts 26:15
with your mouth the *L* . . . . .Rom 10:9
Greek, for the same *L* . . . . .Rom 10:12
say that Jesus is *L* . . . . .1 Cor 12:3
second Man is the *L* . . . . .1 Cor 15:47
the Spirit of the *L* . . . . .2 Cor 3:17
that Jesus Christ is *L* . . . . .Phil 2:11
and deny the only *L* . . . . .Jude 4
L God Omnipotent . . . . .Rev 19:6

LORDS
many gods and many *l* . . . . .1 Cor 8:5
nor as being *l* over . . . . .1 Pet 5:3
for He is Lord of *l* . . . . .Rev 17:14

LOSE
gain, and a time to *l* . . . . .Eccl 3:6
save his life will *l* . . . . .Matt 16:25
reap if we do not *l* . . . . .Gal 6:9
that we do not *l* . . . . .2 John 8

LOSES
but if the salt *l* . . . . .Matt 5:13
and *l* his own soul . . . . .Matt 16:26
if she *l* one coin . . . . .Luke 15:8
l his life will . . . . .Luke 17:33

LOSS
he will suffer *l* . . . . .1 Cor 3:15
count all things *l* . . . . .Phil 3:8

LOST
are dry, our hope is *l* . . . . .Ezek 37:11
save that which was *l* . . . . .Matt 18:11

the one which is *l* .... Luke 15:4
my sheep which was *l* .... Luke 15:6
the piece which I *l* .... Luke 15:9
and none of them is *l* .... John 17:12
You gave Me I have *l* .... John 18:9

LOT

Abram's nephew; accompanies him, Gen 11:27—12:5; 13:1
Separates from Abram, Gen 13:5–12
Rescued by Abram, Gen 14:12–16
Saved from Sodom for his hospitality, Gen 19:1–29
Tricked into committing incest, Gen 19:30–38

LOT

shall be divided by *l* .... Num 26:55
You maintain my *l* .... Ps 16:5
cast in your *l* among .... Prov 1:14
l is cast into the lap .... Prov 16:33

LOT'S WIFE

Disobedient, becomes pillar of salt, Gen 19:26
Event to be remembered, Luke 17:32

LOTS

l causes contentions .... Prov 18:18
garments, casting *l* .... Mark 15:24
And they cast their *l* .... Acts 1:26

LOUD

I cried out with a *l* .... Gen 39:14
Him with *l* cymbals .... Ps 150:5
cried out with a *l* .... Matt 27:46
I heard behind me a *l* .... Rev 1:10

LOVE

l your neighbor as .... Lev 19:18
l the LORD your God .... Deut 6:5
your *l* to me was .... 2 Sam 1:26
How long will you *l* .... Ps 4:2
Oh, *l* the LORD .... Ps 31:23
l righteousness .... Ps 45:7
he has set his *l* .... Ps 91:14
Oh, how I *l* Your law .... Ps 119:97
peace have those who *l* .... Ps 119:165
preserves all who *l* .... Ps 145:20
us take our fill of *l* .... Prov 7:18
l covers all sins .... Prov 10:12
a time to *l* .... Eccl 3:8
People know neither *l* .... Eccl 9:1
l is better than wine .... Song 1:2
banner over me was *l* .... Song 2:4
stir up nor awaken *l* .... Song 3:5
I will give you my *l* .... Song 7:12
l is as strong as .... Song 8:6
waters cannot quench *l* .... Song 8:7
time was the time of *l* .... Ezek 16:8
backsliding, I will *l* .... Hos 14:4
do justly, to *l* mercy .... Mic 6:8
to you, *l* your enemies .... Matt 5:44
l those who *l* you .... Matt 5:46
which of them will *l* .... Luke 7:42
you do not have the *l* .... John 5:42
if you have *l* for one .... John 13:35
"If you *l* Me .... John 14:15
and My Father will *l* .... John 14:23
l one another as I .... John 15:12
l has no one than this .... John 15:13
l Me more than these .... John 21:15
of Jonah, do you *l* .... John 21:16
You know that I *l* .... John 21:16
because the *l* of God .... Rom 5:5
Let *l* be without .... Rom 12:9
to *l* one another .... Rom 13:8
L does no harm to a .... Rom 13:10
up, but *l* edifies .... 1 Cor 8:1
L suffers long and is .... 1 Cor 13:4
l does not envy .... 1 Cor 13:4
l does not parade .... 1 Cor 13:4
L never fails .... 1 Cor 13:8
greatest of these is *l* .... 1 Cor 13:13
For the *l* of Christ .... 2 Cor 5:14
and the God of *l* .... 2 Cor 13:11
of the Spirit is *l* .... Gal 5:22
Husbands, *l* your wives .... Eph 5:25
of the Son of His *l* .... Col 1:13
l your wives and do .... Col 3:19
the commandment is *l* .... 1 Tim 1:5
continue in faith, *l* .... 1 Tim 2:15
word, in conduct, in *l* .... 1 Tim 4:12
For the *l* of money is .... 1 Tim 6:10
l their husbands .... Titus 2:4
Let brotherly *l* .... Heb 13:1
having not seen you *l* .... 1 Pet 1:8
L the brotherhood .... 1 Pet 2:17
for "*l* will cover a .... 1 Pet 4:8
with a kiss of *l* .... 1 Pet 5:14
brotherly kindness *l* .... 2 Pet 1:7
loves the world, the *l* .... 1 John 2:15
we *l* the brethren .... 1 John 3:14
By this we know *l* .... 1 John 3:16
him, how does the *l* .... 1 John 3:17
Beloved, let us *l* .... 1 John 4:7
know God, for God is *l* .... 1 John 4:8
In this is *l* .... 1 John 4:10
If we *l* one another .... 1 John 4:12
L has been perfected .... 1 John 4:17
There is no fear in *l* .... 1 John 4:18
l Him because He first .... 1 John 4:19
who loves God must *l* .... 1 John 4:21
For this is the *l* .... 1 John 5:3
have left your first *l* .... Rev 2:4
and they did not *l* .... Rev 12:11

LOVED

Because the LORD has *l* .... 1 Kin 10:9
L one and friend You .... Ps 88:18
"I have *l* you .... Mal 1:2
Yet Jacob I have *l* .... Mal 1:2
forgiven, for she *l* .... Luke 7:47
so *l* the world that .... John 3:16
"See how He *l* .... John 11:36
whom Jesus *l* .... John 13:23
"As the Father *l* .... John 15:9
l them as You have .... John 17:23
"Jacob I have *l* .... Rom 9:13
the Son of God, who *l* .... Gal 2:20
l the church and gave .... Eph 5:25
l righteousness .... Heb 1:9
God, but that He *l* .... 1 John 4:10
Beloved, if God so *l* .... 1 John 4:11
To Him who *l* us and .... Rev 1:5

LOVELY

l is Your tabernacle .... Ps 84:1
l woman who lacks .... Prov 11:22
he is altogether *l* .... Song 5:16
whatever things are *l* .... Phil 4:8

LOVES

l righteousness .... Ps 33:5
life, and *l* many days .... Ps 34:12
A friend *l* at all .... Prov 17:17
He who *l* father or .... Matt 10:37
l his life will lose .... John 12:25
l Me will be loved .... John 14:21
l a cheerful giver .... 2 Cor 9:7
who *l* his wife *l* .... Eph 5:28
If anyone *l* the world .... 1 John 2:15
l God must love his .... 1 John 4:21
l him who is .... 1 John 5:1

LOVINGKINDNESS

not concealed Your *l* .... Ps 40:10
l is better than life .... Ps 63:3
to declare Your *l* .... Ps 92:2
l I have drawn .... Jer 31:3

LOW

He brings *l* and lifts .... 1 Sam 2:7
both *l* and high .... Ps 49:2
it *l*, He lays it *l* .... Is 26:5
and hill brought *l* .... Luke 3:5

LOWER

made him a little *l* .... Ps 8:5
shall go into the *l* .... Ps 63:9
made him a little *l* .... Heb 2:7

LOWLINESS

with all *l* and .... Eph 4:2
or conceit, but in *l* .... Phil 2:3

LOWLY

yet He regards the *l* .... Ps 138:6
for I am gentle and *l* .... Matt 11:29
He has regarded the *l* .... Luke 1:48
and exalted the *l* .... Luke 1:52
in presence am *l* .... 2 Cor 10:1
l body that it may be .... Phil 3:21
l brother glory .... James 1:9

LOYAL

or else he will be *l* .... Matt 6:24

LUCIFER

Name applied to Satan, Is 14:12

LUKE

"The beloved physician," Col 4:14
Paul's last companion, 2 Tim 4:11

LUKEWARM

because you are *l* .... Rev 3:16

LUMP

from the same *l* .... Rom 9:21
you may be a new *l* .... 1 Cor 5:7

LUST

Do not *l* after her .... Prov 6:25
caught by their *l* .... Prov 11:6
looks at a woman to *l* .... Matt 5:28
not fulfill the *l* .... Gal 5:16
not in passion of *l* .... 1 Thess 4:5
You *l* and do not have .... James 4:2
the *l* of the flesh .... 1 John 2:16

LUSTS

to fulfill its *l* .... Rom 13:14
l which drown men .... 1 Tim 6:9
also youthful *l* .... 2 Tim 2:22
and worldly *l* .... Titus 2:12
to the former *l* .... 1 Pet 1:14
abstain from fleshly *l* .... 1 Pet 2:11
to their own ungodly *l* .... Jude 18

LUTE

Awake, *l* and harp .... Ps 57:8
l I will praise You .... Ps 71:22
harp with the *l* .... Ps 81:2
ten strings, on the *l* .... Ps 92:3
Awake, *l* and harp .... Ps 108:2
Praise Him with the *l* .... Ps 150:3

LUXURY

L is not fitting .... Prov 19:10
l are in kings' courts .... Luke 7:25
in pleasure and *l* .... James 5:5
the abundance of her *l* .... Rev 18:3

LYDDA

Aeneas healed at, Acts 9:32–35

LYDIA

Woman of Thyatira; Paul's first European convert, Acts 16:14, 15, 40
—— District of Asia Minor containing Ephesus, Smyrna, Thyatira, and Sardis, Rev 1:11

LYING

I hate and abhor *l* .... Ps 119:163
righteous man hates *l* .... Prov 13:5
not trust in these *l* .... Jer 7:4
in swaddling cloths, *l* .... Luke 2:12
saw the linen cloths *l* .... John 20:5

putting away *l* .... Eph 4:25
signs, and *l* wonders .... 2 Thess 2:9

LYSTRA

Paul visits; is worshiped by people of and stoned by Jews, Acts 14:6–20
Home of Timothy, Acts 16:1, 2

MAACAH (or Maachah)

Small Syrian kingdom near Mt. Hermon, Deut 3:14
Not possessed by Israel, Josh 13:13
——— David's wife; mother of Absalom, 2 Sam 3:3
——— Wife of Rehoboam; mother of King Abijah, 2 Chr 11:18–21
Makes idol; is deposed as queen mother, 1 Kin 15:13

MACEDONIA

Paul preaches in, Acts 16:9—17:14
Paul's troubles in, 2 Cor 7:5
Churches of, generous, Rom 15:26; 2 Cor 8:1–5

MACHIR

Manasseh's only son, Gen 50:23
Founder of the family of Machirites, Num 26:29
Conqueror of Gilead, Num 32:39, 40

MACHPELAH

Field containing a cave; bought by Abraham, Gen 23:9–18
Sarah and Abraham buried here, Gen 23:19; 25:9, 10
Isaac, Rebekah, Leah, and Jacob buried here, Gen 49:29–31

MADE

m the stars also .... Gen 1:16
wife the LORD God *m* .... Gen 3:21
hear long ago how I *m* .... Is 37:26
things My hand has *m* .... Is 66:2
All things were *m* .... John 1:3

MADNESS

before them, *m* .... 1 Sam 21:13
wisdom and to know *m* .... Eccl 1:17
m is in their hearts .... Eccl 9:3

MAGIC

women who sew *m* .... Ezek 13:18
m brought their books .... Acts 19:19

MAGNIFICENCE

m I cannot endure .... Job 31:23

MAGNIFIED

So let Your name be *m* .... 2 Sam 7:26
"Let the LORD be *m* .... Ps 35:27
for You have *m* Your .... Ps 138:2
the Lord Jesus was *m* .... Acts 19:17
also Christ will be *m* .... Phil 1:20

MAGNIFIES

"My soul *m* the Lord .... Luke 1:46

MAGNIFY

m the LORD with me .... Ps 34:3
m himself above every .... Dan 11:36

MAGOG

People among Japheth's descendants, Gen 10:2
Associated with Gog, Ezek 38:2
Representatives of final enemies, Rev 20:8

MAHANAIM

Name given by Jacob to a sacred site, Gen 32:2
Becomes Ishbosheth's capital, 2 Sam 2:8–29
David flees to, during Absalom's rebellion, 2 Sam 17:24, 27

MAHER-SHALAL-HASH-BAZ

Symbolic name of Isaiah's second son; prophetic of the fall of Damascus and Samaria, Is 8:1–4

MAHLON

Husband of Ruth; without child, Ruth 1:2–5

MAIDENS

Both young men and *m* .... Ps 148:12
She has sent out her *m* .... Prov 9:3

MAIDSERVANT

"I am Ruth, your *m* .... Ruth 3:9
save the son of Your *m* .... Ps 86:16
"Behold the *m* .... Luke 1:38
lowly state of His *m* .... Luke 1:48

MAIDSERVANTS

m shall lead her as .... Nah 2:7
m I will pour out My .... Acts 2:18

MAIMED

to enter into life *m* .... Mark 9:43
the poor and the *m* .... Luke 14:21

MAJESTY

with God is awesome *m* .... Job 37:22
splendor of Your *m* .... Ps 145:5
right hand of the *M* .... Heb 1:3
eyewitnesses of His *m* .... 2 Pet 1:16
wise, be glory and *m* .... Jude 25

MAKE

"Let Us *m* man in Our .... Gen 1:26
let us *m* a name for .... Gen 11:4
m you a great nation .... Gen 12:2
"You shall not *m* .... Ex 20:4
m Our home with him .... John 14:23

MAKER

where is God my *M* .... Job 35:10
man will look to his *M* .... Is 17:7
who strives with his *M* .... Is 45:9
M is your husband .... Is 54:5
has forgotten his *M* .... Hos 8:14
builder and *m* is God .... Heb 11:10

MALACHI

Prophet and writer, Mal 1:1

MALCHISHUA

Son of King Saul, 1 Sam 14:49
Killed at Gilboa, 1 Sam 31:2

MALCHUS

Servant of the high priest, John 18:10

MALICE

in *m* be babes .... 1 Cor 14:20
pleasures, living in *m* .... Titus 3:3
laying aside all *m* .... 1 Pet 2:1

MALTA

Paul's shipwreck, Acts 28:1–8

MAMRE

Town or district near Hebron, Gen 23:19
Abram dwells by the oaks of, Gen 13:18

MAN

"Let Us make *m* .... Gen 1:26
"You are the *m* .... 2 Sam 12:7
"What is *m* .... Job 7:17
For an empty-headed *m* .... Job 11:12
"Are you the first *m* .... Job 15:7
m that You are mindful .... Ps 8:4
What can *m* do to me .... Ps 118:6
coming of the Son of *M* .... Matt 24:27
"Behold the *M* .... John 19:5
m is not from woman .... 1 Cor 11:8
since by *m* came death .... 1 Cor 15:21
though our outward *m* .... 2 Cor 4:16
in Himself one new *m* .... Eph 2:15
that the *m* of God may .... 2 Tim 3:17
is the number of a *m* .... Rev 13:18

MANASSEH

Joseph's firstborn son, Gen 41:50, 51
Adopted by Jacob, Gen 48:5, 6
Loses his birthright to Ephraim, Gen 48:13–20
——— Tribe of:
Numbered, Num 1:34, 35
Half-tribe of, settle east of Jordan, Num 32:33–42; Deut 3:12–15
Help Joshua against Canaanites, Josh 1:12–18
Land assigned to western half-tribe, Josh 17:1–13
Eastern half-tribe builds altar, Josh 22:9–34
Some of, help David, 1 Chr 12:19–31
——— Wicked king of Judah; son of Hezekiah, 2 Kin 21:1–18; 2 Chr 33:1–9
Captured and taken to Babylon; repents and is restored, 2 Chr 33:10–13
Removes idols and altars, 2 Chr 33:14–20

MANGER

Will he bed by your *m* .... Job 39:9
and laid Him in a *m* .... Luke 2:7
the Babe lying in a *m* .... Luke 2:16

MANIFEST

m Myself to him .... John 14:21
is it that You will *m* .... John 14:22

MANIFESTATION

But the *m* of the .... 1 Cor 12:7
deceitfully, but by *m* .... 2 Cor 4:2

MANIFESTED

"I have *m* Your name .... John 17:6
God was *m* in the flesh .... 1 Tim 3:16
the life was *m* .... 1 John 1:2
the love of God was *m* .... 1 John 4:9

MANIFOLD

m are Your works .... Ps 104:24
the *m* wisdom of God .... Eph 3:10
good stewards of the *m* .... 1 Pet 4:10

MANNA

of Israel ate *m* .... Ex 16:35
had rained down *m* .... Ps 78:24
Our fathers ate the *m* .... John 6:31
of the hidden *m* .... Rev 2:17

MANNER

Is this the *m* of man .... 2 Sam 7:19
in an unworthy *m* .... 1 Cor 11:27
sorrowed in a godly *m* .... 2 Cor 7:11
as is the *m* of some .... Heb 10:25
what *m* of persons .... 2 Pet 3:11
Behold what *m* of love .... 1 John 3:1
m worthy of God .... 3 John 6

MANOAH

Danite; father of Samson, Judg 13:1–25

MANSIONS

house are many *m* .... John 14:2

MANTLE

Then he took the *m* .... 2 Kin 2:14

MARA

Name chosen by Naomi, Ruth 1:20

MARAH

First Israelite camp after passing through the Red Sea, Num 33:8, 9

MARK (John)

Son of Mary of Jerusalem; travels with Barnabas and Saul, Acts 12:12, 25
Leaves Paul at Perga, Acts 13:13
Barnabas and Paul separate because of him, Acts 15:37–40
Later approved by Paul, Col 4:10; 2 Tim 4:11
Companion of Peter, 1 Pet 5:13
Author of the second Gospel, Mark 1:1

MARK
And the LORD set a *m* .... Gen 4:15
M the blameless man .... Ps 37:37
slave, to receive a *m* .... Rev 13:16
whoever receives the *m* .... Rev 14:11

MARRED
so His visage was *m* .... Is 52:14
he made of clay was *m* .... Jer 18:4

MARRIAGE
nor are given in *m* .... Matt 22:30
her in *m* does well .... 1 Cor 7:38
M is honorable among .... Heb 13:4
the *m* of the Lamb has .... Rev 19:7

MARRIED
"for I am *m* to you .... Jer 3:14
But he who is *m* .... 1 Cor 7:33
But she who is *m* .... 1 Cor 7:34

MARROW
and of joints and *m* .... Heb 4:12

MARRY
it is better not to *m* .... Matt 19:10
they neither *m* nor are .... Matt 22:30
let them *m* .... 1 Cor 7:9
forbidding to *m* .... 1 Tim 4:3
the younger widows *m* .... 1 Tim 5:14

MARRYING
and drinking, *m* .... Matt 24:38

MARTHA
Sister of Mary and Lazarus; loved by Jesus, John 11:1–5
Affirms her faith, John 11:19–28
Offers hospitality to Jesus, Luke 10:38; John 12:1, 2
Gently rebuked by Christ, Luke 10:39–42

MARTYR
m Stephen was shed .... Acts 22:20
was My faithful *m* .... Rev 2:13

MARTYRS
the blood of the *m* .... Rev 17:6

MARVEL
Do not *m* at this .... John 5:28

MARVELED
Jesus heard it, He *m* .... Matt 8:10
And the multitudes *m* .... Matt 9:33
so that Pilate *m* .... Mark 15:5
And all the world *m* .... Rev 13:3
when I saw her, I *m* .... Rev 17:6

MARVELOUS
m things He did .... Ps 78:12
It is *m* in our eyes .... Ps 118:23
M are Your works .... Ps 139:14
of darkness into His *m* .... 1 Pet 2:9

MARY
Mother of Christ, Matt 1:16
Visited by angel, Luke 1:26–38
Visits Elizabeth and offers praise, Luke 1:39–56
Gives birth to Jesus, Luke 2:6–20
Flees to Egypt, Matt 2:13–18
Visits Jerusalem with Jesus, Luke 2:41–52
Entrusted to John's care, John 19:25–27
——— Mother of James and Joses; present at crucifixion and burial, Matt 27:55–61
Sees the risen Lord; informs disciples, Matt 28:1–10
——— Magdalene; delivered from seven demons; supports Christ's ministry, Luke 8:2, 3
Present at crucifixion and burial, Matt 27:55–61
First to see the risen Lord, Mark 16:1–10; John 20:1–18
——— Sister of Martha and Lazarus; loved by Jesus, John 11:1–5
Grieves for Lazarus, John 11:19, 20, 28–33
Anoints Jesus, Matt 26:6–13; John 12:1–8
Commended by Jesus, Luke 10:38–42
——— Mark's mother, Acts 12:12–17

MASSAH AND MERIBAH
First, at Rephidim, Israel just out of Egypt, Ex 17:1–7
Second, at Kadesh Barnea, 40 years later, Num 20:1–13

MASTER
of Abraham his *m* .... Gen 24:9
a servant like his *m* .... Matt 10:25
greater than his *m* .... John 15:20
m builder I have laid .... 1 Cor 3:10
and useful for the *M* .... 2 Tim 2:21

MASTERS
m besides You have .... Is 26:13
can serve two *m* .... Luke 16:13
M, give your bondservants .... Col 4:1
who have believing *m* .... 1 Tim 6:2

MATTANIAH
King Zedekiah's original name, 2 Kin 24:17

MATTER
m is found in me .... Job 19:28
He who answers a *m* .... Prov 18:13

MATTERS
the weightier *m* .... Matt 23:23
judge the smallest *m* .... 1 Cor 6:2

MATTHEW
Becomes Christ's follower, Matt 9:9
Chosen as one of the Twelve, Matt 10:2, 3
Called Levi, the son of Alphaeus, Mark 2:14
Author of the first Gospel, Matt (title)

MATTHIAS
Chosen by lot to replace Judas, Acts 1:15–26

MATURE
among those who are *m* .... 1 Cor 2:6
understanding be *m* .... 1 Cor 14:20
us, as many as are *m* .... Phil 3:15

MEASURE
a perfect and just *m* .... Deut 25:15
apportion the waters by *m* .... Job 28:25
and the short *m* .... Mic 6:10
give the Spirit by *m* .... John 3:34
to each one a *m* .... Rom 12:3
m the temple of God .... Rev 11:1

MEASURED
m the waters in the .... Is 40:12
you use, it will be *m* .... Matt 7:2
Then he *m* its wall .... Rev 21:17

MEASURES
your house differing *m* .... Deut 25:14
weights and diverse *m* .... Prov 20:10

MEASURING
the man's hand was a *m* .... Ezek 40:5
behold, a man with a *m* .... Zech 2:1
m themselves by .... 2 Cor 10:12
given a reed like a *m* .... Rev 11:1

MEAT
Can He provide *m* .... Ps 78:20
He also rained *m* .... Ps 78:27
good neither to eat *m* .... Rom 14:21
will never again eat *m* .... 1 Cor 8:13
is sold in the *m* .... 1 Cor 10:25

MEDDLE
why should you *m* .... 2 Kin 14:10

MEDES, MEDIA
Part of Medo-Persian Empire, Esth 1:19
Israel deported to, 2 Kin 17:6
Babylon falls to, Dan 5:30, 31
Daniel rises high in kingdom of, Dan 6:1–28
Cyrus, king of, allows Jews to return, 2 Chr 36:22, 23
Agents in Babylon's fall, Is 13:17–19

MEDIATOR
Nor is there any *m* .... Job 9:33
by the hand of a *m* .... Gal 3:19
is one God and one *M* .... 1 Tim 2:5
as He is also *M* .... Heb 8:6
to Jesus the *M* of the .... Heb 12:24

MEDICINE
does good, like *m* .... Prov 17:22

MEDITATE
Isaac went out to *m* .... Gen 24:63
but you shall *m* .... Josh 1:8
M within your heart on .... Ps 4:4
I *m* within my heart .... Ps 77:6
I will *m* on Your .... Ps 119:15
Your heart will *m* .... Is 33:18
m beforehand on what .... Luke 21:14
m on these things .... Phil 4:8

MEDITATES
in His law he *m* .... Ps 1:2

MEDITATION
of my mouth and the *m* .... Ps 19:14
m be sweet to Him .... Ps 104:34
It is my *m* all the day .... Ps 119:97

MEDITERRANEAN SEA
Described as:
Sea, Gen 49:13
Great Sea, Josh 1:4; 9:1
Sea of the Philistines, Ex 23:31
Western Sea, Deut 11:24; Joel 2:20; Zech 14:8

MEDIUM
a woman who is a *m* .... Lev 20:27
a woman who is a *m* .... 1 Sam 28:7

MEDIUMS
"Seek those who are *m* .... Is 8:19

MEEK
with equity for the *m* .... Is 11:4
Blessed are the *m* .... Matt 5:5

MEEKNESS
with you by the *m* .... 2 Cor 10:1
are done in the *m* .... James 3:13

MEET
For You *m* him with the .... Ps 21:3
prepare to *m* your God .... Amos 4:12
go out to *m* him .... Matt 25:6
m the Lord in the air .... 1 Thess 4:17

MEETING
In the tabernacle of *m* .... Ex 27:21
burned up all the *m* .... Ps 74:8

MEGIDDO
City of Canaan; scene of battles, Judg 5:19–21; 2 Kin 23:29, 30
Fortified by Solomon, 1 Kin 9:15
Possible site of Armageddon, Rev 16:16

MELCHIZEDEK
Priest and king of Salem, Gen 14:18–20
Type of Christ's eternal priesthood, Heb 7:1–22

MELODY
make sweet *m* .... Is 23:16
singing and making *m* .... Eph 5:19

MELT
You make his beauty *m* .... Ps 39:11
man's heart will *m* .... Is 13:7
the elements will *m* .... 2 Pet 3:10

MEMBER
body is not one *m* . . . . .1 Cor 12:14
tongue is a little *m* . . . . James 3:5

MEMBERS
you that one of your *m* . . . . Matt 5:29
do not present your *m* . . . . .Rom 6:13
that your bodies are *m* . . . . .1 Cor 6:15
neighbor, for we are *m* . . . . .Eph 4:25

MEMORIAL
and this is My *m* . . . . .Ex 3:15
also be told as a *m* . . . . Matt 26:13
be told of as a *m* . . . . .Mark 14:9

MEMORY
The *m* of him perishes . . . . Job 18:17
He may cut off the *m* . . . . .Ps 109:15
The *m* of the righteous . . . . .Prov 10:7

MEMPHIS (or Noph)
Ancient capital of Egypt, Hos 9:6
Prophesied against by Isaiah, Is 19:13
Jews flee to, Jer 44:1
Denounced by the prophets, Jer 46:19

MEN
m began to call on the . . . . .Gen 4:26
saw the daughters of *m* . . . . .Gen 6:2
you shall die like *m* . . . . .Ps 82:7
the Egyptians are *m* . . . . .Is 31:3
make you fishers of *m* . . . . .Matt 4:19
goodwill toward *m* . . . . .Luke 2:14
from heaven or from *m* . . . . Luke 20:4
Likewise also the *m* . . . . .Rom 1:27
let no one boast in *m* . . . . .1 Cor 3:21
the Lord, and not to *m* . . . . .Eph 6:7
between God and *m* . . . . .1 Tim 2:5

MENAHEM
Cruel king of Israel, 2 Kin 15:14–18

MENSERVANTS
And also on My *m* . . . . .Joel 2:29
And on My *m* and on My . . . . . . Acts 2:18

MENTION
I will make *m* of Your . . . . .Ps 71:16
by You only we make *m* . . . . .Is 26:13
You who make *m* of the . . . . .Is 62:6
he was dying, made *m* . . . . Heb 11:22

MEPHIBOSHETH
Son of King Saul, 2 Sam 21:8
—— Grandson of King Saul; crippled son of Jonathan, 2 Sam 4:4–6
Sought out and honored by David, 2 Sam 9:1–13
Accused by Ziba, 2 Sam 16:1–4
Later explains himself to David, 2 Sam 19:24–30
Spared by David, 2 Sam 21:7

MERAB
King Saul's eldest daughter, 1 Sam 14:49
Saul promises her to David, but gives her to Adriel, 1 Sam 18:17–19

MERARI
Third son of Levi, Gen 46:11
—— Descendants of, called Merarites:
Duties in the tabernacle, Num 3:35–37
Cities assigned to, Josh 21:7, 34–40
Duties in the temple, 1 Chr 26:10–19
Assist Ezra after exile, Ezra 8:18, 19

MERCHANDISE
perceives that her *m* . . . . .Prov 31:18
house a house of *m* . . . . John 2:16

MERCHANTS
set it in a city of *m* . . . . .Ezek 17:4
have multiplied your *m* . . . . .Nah 3:16
m were the great men . . . . Rev 18:23

MERCIES
for His *m* are great . . . . 2 Sam 24:14
and His tender *m* . . . . .Ps 145:9
give you the sure *m* . . . . .Acts 13:34
the Father of *m* . . . . .2 Cor 1:3

MERCIFUL
LORD, the LORD God, *m* . . . . .Ex 34:6
He is ever *m* .Ps 37:26
God be *m* to us and . . . . .Ps 67:1
Blessed are the *m* . . . . Matt 5:7
saying, 'God be *m* . . . . .Luke 18:13
For I will be *m* . . . . .Heb 8:12
compassionate and *m* . . . . James 5:11

MERCY
but showing *m* to . . . . .Ex 20:6
and abundant in *m* . . . . Num 14:18
m endures forever . . . . 1 Chr 16:34
to Your *m* remember me . . . . .Ps 25:7
I trust in the *m* .Ps 52:8
shall send forth His *m* . . . . .Ps 57:3
You, O Lord, belongs *m* . . . . Ps 62:12
m ceased forever . . . . .Ps 77:8
M and truth have met . . . . .Ps 85:10
M shall be built . . . . .Ps 89:2
m and truth go before . . . . Ps 89:14
m is everlasting . . . . .Ps 100:5
I will sing of *m* . . . . Ps 101:1
For Your *m* is great . . . . .Ps 108:4
is full of Your *m* . . . . Ps 119:64
the LORD there is *m* . . . . Ps 130:7
Let not *m* and truth . . . . .Prov 3:3
who honors Him has *m* . . . . .Prov 14:31
cruel and have no *m* . . . . Jer 6:23
Lord our God belong *m* . . . . .Dan 9:9
For I desire *m* and not . . . . Hos 6:6
do justly, to love *m* . . . . Mic 6:8
'I desire *m* and not . . . . Matt 9:13
And His *m* is on those . . . . Luke 1:50
"I will have *m* . . . . .Rom 9:15
of God who shows *m* . . . . .Rom 9:16
that He might have *m* . . . . .Rom 11:32
m has made trustworthy . . . . 1 Cor 7:25
as we have received *m* . . . . 2 Cor 4:1
God, who is rich in *m* . . . . .Eph 2:4
but I obtained *m* . . . . .1 Tim 1:13
that he may find *m* . . . . .2 Tim 1:18
to His *m* He saved us . . . . Titus 3:5
that we may obtain *m* . . . . .Heb 4:16
judgment is without *m* . . . . James 2:13
God, looking for the *m* . . . . Jude 21

MERIB-BAAL
Another name for Mephibosheth, 1 Chr 8:34

MERODACH
Supreme deity of the Babylonians, Jer 50:2
Otherwise called Bel, Is 46:1

MERODACH-BALADAN
Sends ambassadors to Hezekiah, Is 39:1–8
Also called Berodach-Baladan, 2 Kin 20:12

MERRY
m heart makes a . . . . Prov 15:13
eat, drink, and be *m* . . . . Eccl 8:15
we should make *m* . . . . .Luke 15:32

MESHACH
Name given to Mishael, Dan 1:7
Advanced to high position, Dan 2:49
Remains faithful in testing, Dan 3:13–30

MESHECH
Son of Japheth, Gen 10:2
His descendants, mentioned in prophecy, Ezek 27:13; 32:26; 38:2, 3

MESOPOTAMIA
Home of Abraham's relatives, Gen 24:4, 10, 15
Called Padan Aram and Syria, Gen 25:20; 31:20, 24
Israel enslaved to, Judg 3:8–10
Jews from, present at Pentecost, Acts 2:9

MESSAGE
I have heard a *m* . . . . .Jer 49:14
For the *m* of the cross . . . . 1 Cor 1:18

MESSENGER
is a faithful *m* . . . . .Prov 25:13
"Behold, I send My *m* . . . . .Mal 3:1
'Behold, I send My *m* . . . . .Matt 11:10

MESSIAH
until *M* the Prince . . . . .Dan 9:25
"We have found the *M* . . . . John 1:41

METHUSELAH
Oldest man on record, Gen 5:27

MICAH
Prophet, contemporary of Isaiah, Is 1:1; Mic 1:1

MICAIAH (or Michaiah)
Prophet who predicts Ahab's death, 1 Kin 22:8–28
—— Contemporary of Jeremiah, Jer 36:11–13

MICHAEL
Chief prince, Dan 10:13, 21
Disputes with Satan, Jude 9
Fights the dragon, Rev 12:7–9

MICHAL
Daughter of King Saul, 1 Sam 14:49
Loves and marries David, 1 Sam 18:20–28
Saves David from Saul, 1 Sam 19:9–17
Given to Palti, 1 Sam 25:44
David demands her from Abner, 2 Sam 3:13–16
Ridicules David; becomes barren, 2 Sam 6:16–23

MICHMASH
Site of battle with Philistines, 1 Sam 13:5, 11, 16, 23
Scene of Jonathan's victory, 1 Sam 14:1–16

MIDIAN
Son of Abraham by Keturah, Gen 25:1–4
—— Region in the Arabian desert occupied by the Midianites, Gen 25:6; Ex 2:15

MIDIANITES
Descendants of Abraham by Keturah, Gen 25:1, 2
Moses flees to, Ex 2:15
Join Moab in cursing Israel, Num 22:4–7
Intermarriage with incurs God's wrath, Num 25:1–18
Defeated by Israel, Num 31:1–10
Oppress Israel; defeated by Gideon, Judg 6; 7

MIDST
God is in the *m* . . . . .Ps 46:5
that I am in the *m* . . . . .Joel 2:27
I am there in the *m* . . . . .Matt 18:20

MIGHT
'My power and the *m* . . . . Deut 8:17
shall speak of the *m* . . . . .Ps 145:6
the greatness of His *m* . . . . Is 40:26
man glory in his *m* . . . . Jer 9:23
their *m* has failed . . . . .Jer 51:30
'Not by *m* nor by . . . . .Zech 4:6
in the power of His *m* . . . . .Eph 6:10
greater in power and *m* . . . . .2 Pet 2:11
honor and power and *m* . . . . .Rev 7:12

MIGHTY
He was a *m* hunter . . . . Gen 10:9
for they are too *m* . . . . Num 22:6
How the *m* have fallen . . . . 2 Sam 1:19
is wise in heart and *m* . . . . Job 9:4

The LORD *m* in battle . . . . .Ps 24:8
their Redeemer is *m* . . . . .Prov 23:11
Woe to men *m* at . . . . .Is 5:22
great in counsel and *m* . . . . Jer 32:19
m men are made red . . . . .Nah 2:3
m has done great . . . . .Luke 1:49
He has put down the *m* . . . . .Luke 1:52
the flesh, not many *m* . . . . .1 Cor 1:26
the working of His *m* . . . . .Eph 1:19
from heaven with His *m* . . . . . .2 Thess 1:7

MILCOM

Solomon went after, 1 Kin 11:5
Altar destroyed by Josiah, 2 Kin 23:12, 13

MILETUS

Paul meets Ephesian elders here, Acts 20:15–38
Paul leaves Trophimus here, 2 Tim 4:20

MILK

for water, she gave *m* . . . . Judg 5:25
honey and *m* are under . . . . .Song 4:11
come, buy wine and *m* . . . . .Is 55:1
and whiter than *m* . . . . .Lam 4:7
shall flow with *m* . . . . Joel 3:18
have come to need *m* . . . . .Heb 5:12
m is unskilled in the . . . . .Heb 5:13
desire the pure *m* . . . . .1 Pet 2:2

MILLO

Fort at Jerusalem, 2 Sam 5:9
Prepared by Solomon, 1 Kin 9:15
Strengthened by Hezekiah, 2 Chr 32:5
Scene of Joash's death, 2 Kin 12:20, 21

MILLSTONE

m were hung around his . . . . . . .Matt 18:6
a stone like a great *m* . . . . .Rev 18:21

MIND

put wisdom in the *m* . . . . Job 38:36
perfect peace, whose *m* . . . . .Is 26:3
nor have an anxious *m* . . . . .Luke 12:29
m I myself serve the . . . . .Rom 7:25
who has known the *m* . . . . .Rom 11:34
Be of the same *m* . . . . .Rom 12:16
convinced in his own *m* . . . . .Rom 14:5
"who has known the *m* . . . . .1 Cor 2:16
you are out of your *m* . . . . .1 Cor 14:23
Let this *m* be in you . . . . .Phil 2:5
to *m* your own . . . . .1 Thess 4:11
love and of a sound *m* . . . . .2 Tim 1:7

MINDFUL

is man that You are *m* . . . . .Ps 8:4
The LORD has been *m* . . . . .Ps 115:12
for you are not *m* . . . . .Matt 16:23
is man that You are *m* . . . . .Heb 2:6

MINDS

people change their *m* . . . . .Ex 13:17
put My law in their *m* . . . . .Jer 31:33
I stir up your pure *m* . . . . .2 Pet 3:1
He who searches the *m* . . . . .Rev 2:23

MINISTER

to make you a *m* . . . . .Acts 26:16
for he is God's *m* . . . . .Rom 13:4
you will be a good *m* . . . . .1 Tim 4:6
a *M* of the sanctuary . . . . .Heb 8:2

MINISTERED

But the child *m* . . . . .1 Sam 2:11
a thousand thousands *m* . . . . .Dan 7:10
As they *m* to the Lord . . . . .Acts 13:2

MINISTERS

angels spirits, His *m* . . . . .Ps 104:4
for they are God's *m* . . . . .Rom 13:6
commend ourselves as *m* . . . . . . .2 Cor 6:4
Are they *m* of Christ . . . . .2 Cor 11:23
If anyone *m* . . . . .1 Pet 4:11

MINISTRIES

are differences of *m* . . . . .1 Cor 12:5

MINISTRY

I magnify my *m* . . . . .Rom 11:13
But if the *m* of death . . . . .2 Cor 3:7
since we have this *m* . . . . .2 Cor 4:1
and has given us the *m* . . . . .2 Cor 5:18
for the work of *m* . . . . .Eph 4:12
m which you have . . . . .Col 4:17
fulfill your *m* . . . . .2 Tim 4:5
a more excellent *m* . . . . .Heb 8:6

MINT

For you pay tithe of *m* . . . . .Matt 23:23

MIRACLE

saying, 'Show a *m* . . . . .Ex 7:9
no one who works a *m* . . . . .Mark 9:39
that a notable *m* . . . . .Acts 4:16

MIRACLES

God worked unusual *m* . . . . .Acts 19:11
the working of *m* . . . . .1 Cor 12:10
Are all workers of *m* . . . . .1 Cor 12:29
with various *m* . . . . .Heb 2:4

MIRIAM

Sister of Aaron and Moses, Num 26:59
Chosen by God; called a prophetess, Ex 15:20
Punished for rebellion, Num 12:1–16
Buried at Kadesh, Num 20:1

MIRTH

I will test you with *m* . . . . .Eccl 2:1
is in the house of *m* . . . . .Eccl 7:4
joy is darkened, the *m* . . . . .Is 24:11

MITES

widow putting in two *m* . . . . .Luke 21:2

MIZPAH

Site of covenant between Jacob and Laban, Gen 31:44–53
—— Town of Benjamin; outraged Israelites gather here, Josh 18:21, 26; Judg 20:1, 3
Samuel gathers Israel, 1 Sam 7:5–16; 10:17–25
Residence of Gedaliah, 2 Kin 25:23, 25

MOAB

Son of Lot, Gen 19:33–37
—— Country of the Moabites, Deut 1:5

MOABITES

Descendants of Lot, Gen 19:36, 37
Join Midian in cursing Israel, Num 22:4
Excluded from Israel, Deut 23:3–6
Kindred of Ruth, Ruth 1:4
Subdued by Israel, 1 Sam 14:47; 2 Sam 8:2; 2 Kin 3:4–27
Women of, lead Solomon astray, 1 Kin 11:1–8
Prophecies concerning, Is 11:14; 15:1–9; Jer 48:1–47; Amos 2:1–3

MOCK

I will *m* when your . . . . .Prov 1:26
Fools *m* at sin . . . . .Prov 14:9
to the Gentiles to *m* . . . . .Matt 20:19

MOCKED

at noon, that Elijah *m* . . . . .1 Kin 18:27
"I am one *m* by his . . . . .Job 12:4
knee before Him and *m* . . . . .Matt 27:29
deceived, God is not *m* . . . . .Gal 6:7

MOCKER

Wine is a *m* . . . . .Prov 20:1

MOCKERS

that there would be *m* . . . . .Jude 18

MOCKINGS

others had trial of *m* . . . . .Heb 11:36

MOCKS

He who *m* the poor . . . . .Prov 17:5

MOLECH

God of the Ammonites; worshiped by Solomon, 1 Kin 11:7
Human sacrifice made to, Lev 18:21; 2 Kin 23:10

MOMENT

consume them in a *m* . . . . .Num 16:21
In a *m* they die . . . . .Job 34:20
face from you for a *m* . . . . .Is 54:8
in a *m*, in the . . . . .1 Cor 15:52
which is but for a *m* . . . . .2 Cor 4:17

MONEY

does not put out his *m* . . . . .Ps 15:5
m answers every . . . . .Eccl 10:19
be redeemed without *m* . . . . .Is 52:3
and you who have no *m* . . . . .Is 55:1
of the *m* changers . . . . .Matt 21:12
and hid his lord's *m* . . . . .Matt 25:18
promised to give him *m* . . . . .Mark 14:11
Carry neither *m* . . . . .Luke 10:4
I sent you without *m* . . . . .Luke 22:35
the *m* changers doing . . . . .John 2:14
be purchased with *m* . . . . .Acts 8:20
not greedy for *m* . . . . .1 Tim 3:3
m is a root of all . . . . .1 Tim 6:10
not greedy for *m* . . . . .Titus 1:7

MONSTER

me up like a *m* . . . . .Jer 51:34
of Egypt, O great *m* . . . . .Ezek 29:3

MOON

until the *m* is no more . . . . .Ps 72:7
morning, fair as the *m* . . . . .Song 6:10
sun and *m* grow dark . . . . .Joel 2:10
m will not give its . . . . .Mark 13:24

MORDECAI

Esther's guardian; advises her, Esth 2:5–20
Reveals plot to kill the king, Esth 2:21–23
Refuses homage to Haman, Esth 3:1–6
Honored by the king, Esth 6:1–12
Exalted highly, Esth 8:15; 9:4
Institutes feast of Purim, Esth 9:20–31

MORIAH

God commands Abraham to sacrifice Isaac here, Gen 22:1–13
Site of Solomon's temple, 2 Chr 3:1

MORNING

the eyelids of the *m* . . . . .Job 41:18
Evening and *m* and at . . . . .Ps 55:17
the wings of the *m* . . . . .Ps 139:9
looks forth as the *m* . . . . .Song 6:10
Lucifer, son of the *m* . . . . .Is 14:12
established as the *m* . . . . .Hos 6:3
very early in the *m* . . . . .Luke 24:1
the Bright and *M* Star . . . . .Rev 22:16

MORSEL

or eaten my *m* by . . . . .Job 31:17
Better is a dry *m* . . . . .Prov 17:1
Esau, who for one *m* . . . . .Heb 12:16

MORTAL

sin reign in your *m* . . . . .Rom 6:12
and this *m* must put . . . . .1 Cor 15:53

MORTALITY

m may be swallowed . . . . .2 Cor 5:4

MOSES

Born; hidden by mother; adopted by Pharaoh's daughter, Ex 2:1–10
Kills Egyptian and flees to Midian, Ex 2:11–22
Receives call from God, Ex 3:1—4:17
Returns to Israelites in Egypt, Ex 4:18–31
Wins Israel's deliverance with plagues, Ex 5:1—6:13; 6:28—11:10; 12:29–42
Leads Israel out of Egypt and through the Red Sea, Ex 13:17—14:31

His song of praise, Ex 15:1–18
Provides miraculously for the people, Ex 15:22—17:7
Appoints judges, Ex 18
Receives the law on Mount Sinai, Ex 19—23
Receives instructions for tabernacle, Ex 25—31
Intercedes for Israel's sin, Ex 32
Recommissioned and encouraged, Ex 33; 34
Further instructions and building of the tabernacle, Ex 35—40
Consecrates Aaron, Lev 8:1–36
Takes census, Num 1:1–54
Resumes journey to Canaan, Num 10:11–36
Complains; 70 elders appointed, Num 11:1–35
Intercedes for people when they refuse to enter Canaan, Num 14:11–25
Puts down Korah's rebellion, Num 16
Sins in anger, Num 20:1–13
Makes bronze serpent, Num 21:4–9
Travels toward Canaan, Num 21:10–20
Takes second census, Num 26
Commissions Joshua as his successor, Num 27:12–23
Receives further laws, Num 28—30
Commands conquest of Midian, Num 31
Final instructions, Num 32—36
Forbidden to enter Promised Land, Deut 3:23–28
Gives farewell messages, Deut 32; 33
Sees Promised Land; dies, Deut 34:1–7
Is mourned and extolled, Deut 34:8–12
Appears with Christ at Transfiguration, Matt 17:1–3

MOTH
m will eat them . . . . Is 50:9
where *m* and rust . . . . Matt 6:19

MOTHER
because she was the *m* . . . . Gen 3:20
like a joyful *m* . . . . Ps 113:9
the only one of her *m* . . . . Song 6:9
m might have been my . . . . Jer 20:17
leave his father and *m* . . . . Matt 19:5
"Behold your *m* . . . . John 19:27
free, which is the *m* . . . . Gal 4:26
The *M* of Harlots . . . . Rev 17:5

MOUNT
come up to *M* Sinai . . . . Ex 19:23
you like *M* Carmel . . . . Song 7:5
they shall *m* up with . . . . Is 40:31
for this Hagar is *M* . . . . Gal 4:25

MOUNT CARMEL
Prophets gather at, 1 Kin 18:19, 20
Elisha journeys to, 2 Kin 2:25
Shunammite woman comes to Elisha at, 2 Kin 4:25

MOUNT EBAL
Cursed by God, Deut 11:29
Joshua builds an altar on, Josh 8:30

MOUNT GERIZIM
Mount of blessing, Deut 11:29; 27:12
Jotham speaks to people of Shechem here, Judg 9:7
Samaritans' sacred mountain, John 4:20, 21

MOUNT GILBOA
Men of Israel slain at, 1 Sam 31:1
Saul and his sons slain at, 1 Sam 31:8

MOUNT GILEAD
Gideon divides the people for battle at, Judg 7:3

MOUNT HOR
Lord speaks to Moses and Aaron on, Num 20:23
Aaron dies on, Num 20:25–28

MOUNT HOREB
Sons of Israel stripped of ornaments at, Ex 33:6
The same as Sinai, Ex 3:1

MOUNT OF OLIVES
See OLIVES, MOUNT OF

MOUNT SINAI
Lord descends upon, in fire, Ex 19:18
Lord calls Moses to the top of, Ex 19:20
The glory of the Lord rests on, for six days, Ex 24:16

MOUNT TABOR
Deborah sends Barak there to defeat Canaanites, Judg 4:6–14

MOUNT ZION
Survivors shall go out from, 2 Kin 19:31

MOUNTAIN
to Horeb, the *m* . . . . Ex 3:1
"But as a *m* falls . . . . Job 14:18
You have made my *m* . . . . Ps 30:7
of many peaks is the *m* . . . . Ps 68:15
let us go up to the *m* . . . . Is 2:3
image became a great *m* . . . . Dan 2:35
Who are you, O great *m* . . . . Zech 4:7
you will say to this *m* . . . . Matt 17:20
with Him on the holy *m* . . . . 2 Pet 1:18

MOUNTAINS
He removes the *m* . . . . Job 9:5
Surely the *m* yield . . . . Job 40:20
m will bring peace . . . . Ps 72:3
excellent than the *m* . . . . Ps 76:4
m were brought forth . . . . Ps 90:2
m melt like wax at the . . . . Ps 97:5
m skipped like rams . . . . Ps 114:4
m surround Jerusalem . . . . Ps 125:2
m shall depart and the . . . . Is 54:10
in Judea flee to the *m* . . . . Matt 24:16
that I could remove *m* . . . . 1 Cor 13:2
m were not found . . . . Rev 16:20

MOURN
and you *m* at last . . . . Prov 5:11
a time to *m* . . . . Eccl 3:4
are those who *m* . . . . Matt 5:4
Lament and *m* and weep . . . . James 4:9
of the earth will *m* . . . . Rev 1:7

MOURNING
This is a deep *m* . . . . Gen 50:11
m all the day long . . . . Ps 38:6
m shall be ended . . . . Is 60:20
men break bread in *m* . . . . Jer 16:7
I will turn their *m* . . . . Jer 31:13
shall be a great *m* . . . . Zech 12:11
be turned to *m* and . . . . James 4:9

MOURNS
heavily, as one who *m* . . . . Ps 35:14
The earth *m* and fades . . . . Is 24:4
for Him as one *m* . . . . Zech 12:10

MOUTH
"Who has made man's *m* . . . . Ex 4:11
Out of the *m* of babes . . . . Ps 8:2
The *m* of the righteous . . . . Ps 37:30
m shall speak wisdom . . . . Ps 49:3
iniquity stops its *m* . . . . Ps 107:42
knowledge, but the *m* . . . . Prov 10:14
m preserves his life . . . . Prov 13:3
The *m* of an immoral . . . . Prov 22:14
and a flattering *m* . . . . Prov 26:28
m speaking pompous . . . . Dan 7:8
the doors of your *m* . . . . Mic 7:5
m defiles a man . . . . Matt 15:11
m I will judge you . . . . Luke 19:22
I will give you a *m* . . . . Luke 21:15
m confession is made . . . . Rom 10:10
m great swelling words . . . . Jude 16
vomit you out of My *m* . . . . Rev 3:16

MOVE
and the earth will *m* . . . . Is 13:13
the mountain shall *m* . . . . Zech 14:4
in Him we live and *m* . . . . Acts 17:28

MOVED
shall never be *m* . . . . Ps 15:5
she shall not be *m* . . . . Ps 46:5
spoke as they were *m* . . . . 2 Pet 1:21

MUCH
m study is . . . . Eccl 12:12
m better than wine is . . . . Song 4:10
to whom *m* is given . . . . Luke 12:48
M more then . . . . Rom 5:9

MULTIPLIED
sorrows shall be *m* . . . . Ps 16:4
of the disciples *m* . . . . Acts 6:7
word of God grew and *m* . . . . Acts 12:24

MULTIPLY
"Be fruitful and *m* . . . . Gen 1:22
m your descendants . . . . Gen 16:10
m my days as the . . . . Job 29:18
m the descendants . . . . Jer 33:22

MULTITUDE
stars of heaven in *m* . . . . Deut 1:10
Your house in the *m* . . . . Ps 5:7
m that kept a pilgrim . . . . Ps 42:4
In the *m* of words sin . . . . Prov 10:19
In a *m* of people is a . . . . Prov 14:28
compassion on the *m* . . . . Matt 15:32
with the angel a *m* . . . . Luke 2:13
"love will cover a *m* . . . . 1 Pet 4:8
and behold, a great *m* . . . . Rev 7:9

MURDER
"You shall not *m* . . . . Ex 20:13
'You shall not *m* . . . . Matt 5:21
threats and *m* against . . . . Acts 9:1
You *m* and covet and . . . . James 4:2

MURDERED
sons of those who *m* . . . . Matt 23:31
Jesus whom you *m* . . . . Acts 5:30
one and *m* his brother . . . . 1 John 3:12

MURDERER
He was a *m* from the . . . . John 8:44
and asked for a *m* . . . . Acts 3:14
of you suffer as a *m* . . . . 1 Pet 4:15
his brother is a *m* . . . . 1 John 3:15

MURDERERS
in it, but now *m* . . . . Is 1:21
and profane, for *m* . . . . 1 Tim 1:9
abominable, *m* . . . . Rev 21:8

MURDERS
evil thoughts, *m* . . . . Matt 15:19
envy, *m*, drunkenness . . . . Gal 5:21

MUSIC
So David played *m* . . . . 1 Sam 18:10
m are brought low . . . . Eccl 12:4
the house, he heard *m* . . . . Luke 15:25

MUTE
Or who makes the *m* . . . . Ex 4:11
m who does not open . . . . Ps 38:13
I was *m* with silence . . . . Ps 39:2
I was *m* . . . . Ps 39:9

MUZZLE
"You shall not *m* . . . . Deut 25:4
"You shall not *m* . . . . 1 Tim 5:18

MYSTERIES
to you to know the *m* . . . . Matt 13:11

and understand all *m* .... 1 Cor 13:2
the spirit he speaks *m* .... 1 Cor 14:2

MYSTERY

given to know the *m* .... Mark 4:11
wisdom of God in a *m* .... 1 Cor 2:7
Behold, I tell you a *m* .... 1 Cor 15:51
made known to us the *m* .... Eph 1:9
This is a great *m* .... Eph 5:32
m which has been .... Col 1:26
the *m* of godliness .... 1 Tim 3:16

NAAMAN

Captain in the Syrian army, 2 Kin 5:1–11
Healed of his leprosy, 2 Kin 5:14–17
Referred to by Christ, Luke 4:27

NABAL

Refuses David's request, 1 Sam 25:2–12
Escapes David's wrath but dies of a stroke, 1 Sam 25:13–39

NABOTH

Murdered for his vineyard by King Ahab, 1 Kin 21:1–16
His murder avenged, 1 Kin 21:17–25

NADAB

Eldest of Aaron's four sons, Ex 6:23
Takes part in affirming covenant, Ex 24:1, 9–12
Becomes priest, Ex 28:1
Consumed by fire, Lev 10:1–7
——— King of Israel, 1 Kin 14:20
Killed by Baasha, 1 Kin 15:25–31

NAHASH

King of Ammon; makes impossible demands, 1 Sam 11:1–15

NAHOR

Grandfather of Abraham, Gen 11:24–26
——— Son of Terah, brother of Abraham, Gen 11:17

NAHUM

Inspired prophet to Judah concerning Nineveh, Nah 1:1

NAIN

Village south of Nazareth; Jesus raises widow's son here, Luke 7:11–17

NAIOTH

Prophets' school in Ramah, 1 Sam 19:18, 19, 22, 23

NAKED

And they were both *n* .... Gen 2:25
knew that they were *n* .... Gen 3:7
"*N* I came from my .... Job 1:21
Isaiah has walked *n* .... Is 20:3
I was *n* and you .... Matt 25:36
and fled from them *n* .... Mark 14:52
shall not be found *n* .... 2 Cor 5:3
but all things are *n* .... Heb 4:13
brother or sister is *n* .... James 2:15
poor, blind, and *n* .... Rev 3:17

NAKEDNESS

of Canaan, saw the *n* .... Gen 9:22
or famine, or *n* .... Rom 8:35
often, in cold and *n* .... 2 Cor 11:27
n may not be revealed .... Rev 3:18

NAME

Abram called on the *n* .... Gen 13:4
Israel shall be your *n* .... Gen 35:10
This is My *n* forever .... Ex 3:15
shall not take the *n* .... Ex 20:7
are called by the *n* .... Deut 28:10
glorious and awesome *n* .... Deut 28:58
by My *n* will humble .... 2 Chr 7:14
and he has no *n* .... Job 18:17
excellent is Your *n* .... Ps 8:1
n will put their trust .... Ps 9:10
be His glorious *n* .... Ps 72:19
n is great in Israel .... Ps 76:1
do not call on Your *n* .... Ps 79:6
to Your *n* give glory .... Ps 115:1
above all Your *n* .... Ps 138:2
He calls them all by *n* .... Ps 147:4
The *n* of the LORD is a .... Prov 18:10
A good *n* is to be .... Prov 22:1
what is His Son's *n* .... Prov 30:4
make mention of Your *n* .... Is 26:13
the LORD, that is My *n* .... Is 42:8
be to the LORD for a *n* .... Is 55:13
be called by a new *n* .... Is 62:2
Everlasting is Your *n* .... Is 63:16
who calls on Your *n* .... Is 64:7
it shall be to Me a *n* .... Jer 33:9
and made Yourself a *n* .... Dan 9:15
we will walk in the *n* .... Mic 4:5
They will call on My *n* .... Zech 13:9
n shall be great .... Mal 1:11
to you who fear My *n* .... Mal 4:2
you shall call His *n* .... Matt 1:21
hallowed be Your *n* .... Matt 6:9
prophesied in Your *n* .... Matt 7:22
righteous man in the *n* .... Matt 10:41
n Gentiles will trust .... Matt 12:21
together in My *n* .... Matt 18:20
will come in My *n* .... Matt 24:5
"My *n* is Legion .... Mark 5:9
The virgin's *n* was .... Luke 1:27
"His *n* is John .... Luke 1:63
and cast out your *n* .... Luke 6:22
who believe in His *n* .... John 1:12
comes in his own *n* .... John 5:43
his own sheep by *n* .... John 10:3
through faith in His *n* .... Acts 3:16
there is no other *n* .... Acts 4:12
suffer shame for His *n* .... Acts 5:41
which is above every *n* .... Phil 2:9
deed, do all in the *n* .... Col 3:17
a more excellent *n* .... Heb 1:4
blaspheme that noble *n* .... James 2:7
reproached for the *n* .... 1 Pet 4:14
you hold fast to My *n* .... Rev 2:13
n that you are alive .... Rev 3:1
having His Father's *n* .... Rev 14:1
and glorify Your *n* .... Rev 15:4
n written that no one .... Rev 19:12

NAMED

let my name be *n* .... Gen 48:16
I have *n* you .... Is 45:4

NAOMI

Widow of Elimelech, Ruth 1:1–3
Returns to Bethlehem with Ruth, Ruth 1:14–19
Arranges Ruth's marriage to Boaz, Ruth 3; 4

NAPHTALI

Son of Jacob by Bilhah, Gen 30:1–8
Receives Jacob's blessing, Gen 49:21, 28
——— Tribe of:
Numbered, Num 1:42, 43
Territory assigned to, Josh 19:32–39
Joins Gideon's army, Judg 7:23
Attacked by Ben-Hadad and Tiglath-Pileser, 1 Kin 15:20; 2 Kin 15:29
Prophecy of great light in; fulfilled in Christ's ministry, Is 9:1–7; Matt 4:12–16

NARROW

"Enter by the *n* gate .... Matt 7:13
n is the gate and .... Matt 7:14

NATHAN

Son of David, 2 Sam 5:14
Mary's lineage traced through, Zech 12:12
——— Prophet under David and Solomon, 1 Chr 29:29
Reveals God's plan to David, 2 Sam 7:2–29
Rebukes David's sin, 2 Sam 12:1–15
Reveals Adonijah's plot, 1 Kin 1:10–46

NATHANAEL

One of Christ's disciples, John 1:45–51

NATION

make you a great *n* .... Gen 12:2
You slay a righteous *n* .... Gen 20:4
priests and a holy *n* .... Ex 19:6
dealt thus with any *n* .... Ps 147:20
exalts a *n* .... Prov 14:34
lift up sword against *n* .... Is 2:4
that the righteous *n* .... Is 26:2
a small one a strong *n* .... Is 60:22
n that was not called .... Is 65:1
n changed its gods .... Jer 2:11
I will make them one *n* .... Ezek 37:22
since there was a *n* .... Dan 12:1
n will rise against .... Matt 24:7
for he loves our *n* .... Luke 7:5
those who are not a *n* .... Rom 10:19
tribe, tongue, and *n* .... Rev 13:7

NATIONS

itself among the *n* .... Num 23:9
Why do the *n* rage .... Ps 2:1
I will give You the *n* .... Ps 2:8
n shall serve Him .... Ps 72:11
n shall call Him .... Ps 72:17
n shall fear the name .... Ps 102:15
is high above all *n* .... Ps 113:4
All *n* before Him are .... Is 40:17
n who do not know .... Is 55:5
the wise men of the *n* .... Jer 10:7
n shall be joined .... Zech 2:11
disciples of all the *n* .... Matt 28:19
who was to rule all *n* .... Rev 12:5
the healing of the *n* .... Rev 22:2

NATURAL

women exchanged the *n* .... Rom 1:26
the men, leaving the *n* .... Rom 1:27
did not spare the *n* .... Rom 11:21
n man does not receive .... 1 Cor 2:14
It is sown a *n* body .... 1 Cor 15:44
not first, but the *n* .... 1 Cor 15:46

NATURE

for what is against *n* .... Rom 1:26
n itself teach you .... 1 Cor 11:14
We who are Jews by *n* .... Gal 2:15
by *n* children of wrath .... Eph 2:3
of the divine *n* .... 2 Pet 1:4

NAZARENE

Jesus to be called, Matt 2:23
Descriptive of Jesus' followers, Acts 24:5

NAZARETH

Town in Galilee; considered obscure, John 1:46
City of Jesus' parents, Matt 2:23
Early home of Jesus, Luke 2:39–51
Jesus rejected by, Luke 4:16–30

NEAR

that has God so *n* to it .... Deut 4:7
But the word is very *n* .... Deut 30:14
The LORD is *n* to all .... Ps 145:18
upon Him while He is *n* .... Is 55:6
know that it is *n* .... Matt 24:33
kingdom of God is *n* .... Luke 21:31
"The word is *n* .... Rom 10:8
to those who were *n* .... Eph 2:17
for the time is *n* .... Rev 1:3

NEBO

Babylonian god, Is 46:1
——— Summit of Pisgah; Moses dies here, Deut 32:49; 34:1, 5

NEBUCHADNEZZAR
Monarch of the Neo-Babylonian Empire (605–562 B.C.); carries Jews captive to Babylon, Dan 1:1–3
Crushes Jehoiachin's revolt, 2 Kin 24:10–17
Destroys Jerusalem; captures Zedekiah, Jer 39:5–8
Prophecies concerning, Is 14:4–27; Jer 21:7–10; 25:8, 9; 27:4–11; 32:28–36; 43:10–13; Ezek 26:7–12

NEBUZARADAN
Nebuchadnezzar's captain at siege of Jerusalem, 2 Kin 25:8–20
Protects Jeremiah, Jer 39:11–14

NECESSARY
mouth more than my *n* . . . . Job 23:12
and thus it was *n* . . . . Luke 24:46
burden than these *n* . . . . Acts 15:28
I found it *n* to write . . . . Jude 3

NECESSITIES
have provided for my *n* . . . . Acts 20:34
and again for my *n* . . . . Phil 4:16

NECESSITY
n is laid upon me . . . . 1 Cor 9:16
not grudgingly or of *n* . . . . 2 Cor 9:7

NECK
smooth part of his *n* . . . . Gen 27:16
and grace to your *n* . . . . Prov 3:22
n was an iron sinew . . . . Is 48:4
were hung around his *n* . . . . Matt 18:6
ran and fell on his *n* . . . . Luke 15:20

NECKS
stiffened their *n* . . . . Neh 9:29
with outstretched *n* . . . . Is 3:16
who risked their own *n* . . . . Rom 16:4

NEED
in nakedness, and in *n* . . . . Deut 28:48
a prowler, and your *n* . . . . Prov 24:34
the things you have *n* . . . . Matt 6:8
'The Lord has *n* . . . . Matt 21:3
each as anyone had *n* . . . . Acts 4:35
hand, "I have no *n* . . . . 1 Cor 12:21
who ministered to my *n* . . . . Phil 2:25
supply all your *n* . . . . Phil 4:19
to help in time of *n* . . . . Heb 4:16
sees his brother in *n* . . . . 1 John 3:17
The city had no *n* . . . . Rev 21:23

NEEDY
your poor and your *n* . . . . Deut 15:11
They push the *n* . . . . Job 24:4
n shall not always be . . . . Ps 9:18
He will deliver the *n* . . . . Ps 72:12
and lifts the *n* . . . . Ps 113:7
to rob the *n* of . . . . Is 10:2
n will lie down in . . . . Is 14:30
a strength to the *n* . . . . Is 25:4

NEGLECT
n the gift that is . . . . 1 Tim 4:14
if we *n* so great a . . . . Heb 2:3

NEGLECTED
n the weightier . . . . Matt 23:23
their widows were *n* . . . . Acts 6:1

NEHEMIAH
Jewish cupbearer to King Artaxerxes; prays for restoration of Jerusalem, Neh 1:4–11
King commissions him to rebuild walls, Neh 2:1–8
Overcomes opposition and accomplishes rebuilding, Neh 4—6
Appointed governor, Neh 5:14
Participates with Ezra in restored worship, Neh 8—10
Registers the people and the priests and Levites, Neh 11:1—12:26
Dedicates the wall, Neh 12:27–43
Returns to Jerusalem after absence and institutes reforms, Neh 13:4–31

NEIGHBOR
you shall love your *n* . . . . Lev 19:18
for better is a *n* . . . . Prov 27:10
every man teach his *n* . . . . Jer 31:34
gives drink to his *n* . . . . Hab 2:15
'You shall love your *n* . . . . Matt 5:43
"And who is my *n* . . . . Luke 10:29
"You shall love your *n* . . . . Rom 13:9

NEST
and make its *n* . . . . Job 39:27
n is a man who wanders . . . . Prov 27:8
though you set your *n* . . . . Obad 4
that he may set his *n* . . . . Hab 2:9

NET
me with His *n* . . . . Job 19:6
have hidden their *n* . . . . Ps 35:7
They have prepared a *n* . . . . Ps 57:6
an antelope in a *n* . . . . Is 51:20
catch in their *n* . . . . Hab 1:15
I will let down the *n* . . . . Luke 5:5
to them, "Cast the *n* . . . . John 21:6

NETHINIM
Servants of the Levites, Ezra 8:20
Possible origins of:
Gibeonites, Josh 9:23–27
Solomon's forced laborers, 1 Kin 9:20, 21
Mentioned, 1 Chr 9:2; Ezra 2:43–54; 7:24; 8:17; Neh 3:31; 7:46–60, 73; 10:28, 29; 11:21

NEVER
in Me shall *n* thirst . . . . John 6:35
in Me shall *n* die . . . . John 11:26
Love *n* fails . . . . 1 Cor 13:8
n take away sins . . . . Heb 10:11
"I will *n* leave you . . . . Heb 13:5
prophecy *n* came by . . . . 2 Pet 1:21

NEW
Now there arose a *n* . . . . Ex 1:8
the LORD creates a *n* . . . . Num 16:30
They chose *n* gods . . . . Judg 5:8
and there is nothing *n* . . . . Eccl 1:9
Behold, I will do a *n* . . . . Is 43:19
For behold, I create *n* . . . . Is 65:17
when I will make a *n* . . . . Jer 31:31
n every morning . . . . Lam 3:23
wine into *n* wineskins . . . . Matt 9:17
of the *n* covenant . . . . Matt 26:28
n commandment I give . . . . John 13:34
tell or to hear some *n* . . . . Acts 17:21
he is a *n* creation . . . . 2 Cor 5:17
n man who is renewed . . . . Col 3:10
when I will make a *n* . . . . Heb 8:8
n heavens and a *n* . . . . 2 Pet 3:13
n name written which . . . . Rev 2:17
And they sang a *n* . . . . Rev 5:9
And I saw a *n* heaven . . . . Rev 21:1
I make all things *n* . . . . Rev 21:5

NEWNESS
also should walk in *n* . . . . Rom 6:4
should serve in the *n* . . . . Rom 7:6

NEWS
heard this bad *n* . . . . Ex 33:4
soul, so is good *n* . . . . Prov 25:25
him who brings good *n* . . . . Is 52:7

NICANOR
One of the first seven deacons, Acts 6:1–5

NICODEMUS
Pharisee; converses with Jesus, John 3:1–12
Protests unfairness of Christ's trial, John 7:50–52
Brings gifts to anoint Christ's body, John 19:39, 40

NICOLAITANS
Group teaching moral laxity, Rev 2:6–15

NICOLAS
One of the first seven deacons, Acts 6:5

NIGHT
darkness He called *N* . . . . Gen 1:5
It is a *n* of solemn . . . . Ex 12:42
pillar of fire by *n* . . . . Ex 13:22
and the *n* be ended . . . . Job 7:4
gives songs in the *n* . . . . Job 35:10
n reveals knowledge . . . . Ps 19:2
awake through the *n* . . . . Ps 119:148
and stars to rule by *n* . . . . Ps 136:9
desired You in the *n* . . . . Is 26:9
and perished in a *n* . . . . Jon 4:10
and continued all *n* . . . . Luke 6:12
man came to Jesus by *n* . . . . John 3:2
n is coming when no . . . . John 9:4
came to Jesus by *n* . . . . John 19:39
The *n* is far spent . . . . Rom 13:12
as a thief in the *n* . . . . 1 Thess 5:2
We are not of the *n* . . . . 1 Thess 5:5
there shall be no *n* . . . . Rev 21:25
there shall be no *n* . . . . Rev 22:5

NILE
Hebrew children drowned in, Ex 1:22
Moses hidden in, Ex 2:3–10
Water of, turned to blood, Ex 7:14–21
Mentioned in prophecies, Is 19:5–8; 23:3; 27:12; Jer 46:7–9; Amos 9:5

NIMROD
Ham's grandson, Gen 10:6–12

NINETY-NINE
he not leave the *n* . . . . Matt 18:12
n just persons . . . . Luke 15:7

NINEVEH
Capital of Assyria, 2 Kin 19:36
Jonah preaches to; people repent, Jon 3:1–10; Matt 12:41
Prophecy against, Nah 2:13—3:19; Zeph 2:13–15

NOAH
Son of Lamech, Gen 5:28–32
Finds favor with God; commissioned to build the ark, Gen 6:8–22
Fills ark and survives flood, Gen 7
Leaves ark; builds altar; receives God's promise, Gen 8
God's covenant with, Gen 9:1–17
Blesses and curses his sons; dies, Gen 9:18–29

NO AMON (or Thebes)
Nineveh compared to, Nah 3:8

NOB
City of priests; David flees to, 1 Sam 21:1–9
Priests of, killed by Saul, 1 Sam 22:9–23

NOBLE
whatever things are *n* . . . . Phil 4:8
not blaspheme that *n* . . . . James 2:7

NOD
Place (east of Eden) of Cain's exile, Gen 4:16, 17

NOISE
The *n* of a multitude . . . . Is 13:4
people who make a *n* . . . . Is 17:12
of Egypt, is but a *n* . . . . Jer 46:17
They have made a *n* . . . . Lam 2:7
away with a great *n* . . . . 2 Pet 3:10

NOSTRILS
n the breath of life .... Gen 2:7
breath of God in my *n* .... Job 27:3
breath is in his *n* .... Is 2:22

NOTHING
For now you are *n* .... Job 6:21
rich, yet has *n* .... Prov 13:7
"It is good for *n* .... Prov 20:14
before Him are as *n* .... Is 40:17
their works are *n* .... Is 41:29
I can of Myself do *n* .... John 5:30
Me you can do *n* .... John 15:5
men, it will come to *n* .... Acts 5:38
bring to *n* the things .... 1 Cor 1:28
For I know of *n* against .... 1 Cor 4:4
have not love, I am *n* .... 1 Cor 13:2
love, it profits me *n* .... 1 Cor 13:3
Be anxious for *n* .... Phil 4:6
For we brought *n* .... 1 Tim 6:7
complete, lacking *n* .... James 1:4
name's sake, taking *n* .... 3 John 7

NOURISHED
"I have *n* and .... Is 1:2
n and knit together .... Col 2:19
n in the words of .... 1 Tim 4:6

NOURISHES
n and cherishes it .... Eph 5:29

NUMBER
if a man could *n* .... Gen 13:16
that I may know the *n* .... 2 Sam 24:2
things without *n* .... Job 5:9
For now You *n* my steps .... Job 14:16
n the clouds by wisdom .... Job 38:37
teach us to *n* our days .... Ps 90:12
He counts the *n* .... Ps 147:4
which no one could *n* .... Rev 7:9
His *n* is 666 .... Rev 13:18

NUMBERED
are more than can be *n* .... Ps 40:5
God has *n* your kingdom .... Dan 5:26
'And He was *n* with .... Luke 22:37

OATH
people feared the *o* .... 1 Sam 14:26
for the sake of your *o* .... Eccl 8:2
I may establish the *o* .... Jer 11:5
And you shall be an *o* .... Jer 42:18
he denied with an *o* .... Matt 26:72
o which He swore .... Luke 1:73
themselves under an *o* .... Acts 23:12

OATHS
shall perform your *o* .... Matt 5:33
because of the *o* .... Matt 14:9

OBADIAH
King Ahab's steward, 1 Kin 18:3–16
—— Prophet of Judah, Obad 1

OBED
Son of Boaz and Ruth, Ruth 4:17–22

OBED-EDOM
Philistine from Gath; ark of the Lord left in his house, 2 Sam 6:10–12; 1 Chr 13:13, 14

OBEDIENCE
and apostleship for *o* .... Rom 1:5
o many will be made .... Rom 5:19
captivity to the *o* .... 2 Cor 10:5
confidence in your *o* .... Philem 21
yet He learned *o* .... Heb 5:8
for *o* and sprinkling .... 1 Pet 1:2

OBEDIENT
you are willing and *o* .... Is 1:19
of the priests were *o* .... Acts 6:7
make the Gentiles *o* .... Rom 15:18
bondservants, be *o* to .... Eph 6:5
Himself and became *o* .... Phil 2:8
homemakers, good, *o* .... Titus 2:5
as *o* children .... 1 Pet 1:14

OBEY
LORD, that I should *o* .... Ex 5:2
God and *o* His voice .... Deut 4:30
o the commandments .... Deut 11:27
His voice we will *o* .... Josh 24:24
o is better than .... 1 Sam 15:22
they hear of me they *o* .... Ps 18:44
if you diligently *o* .... Zech 6:15
o God rather than men .... Acts 5:29
and do not *o* the truth .... Rom 2:8
yourselves slaves to *o* .... Rom 6:16
o your parents in all .... Col 3:20
Bondservants, *o* in all .... Col 3:22
on those who do not *o* .... 2 Thess 1:8
O those who rule .... Heb 13:17
if some do not *o* .... 1 Pet 3:1

OBEYED
of sin, yet you *o* .... Rom 6:17
they have not all *o* .... Rom 10:16
By faith Abraham *o* .... Heb 11:8
as Sarah *o* Abraham .... 1 Pet 3:6

OBSERVE
man, and *o* the upright .... Ps 37:37
and let your eyes *o* .... Prov 23:26
o mercy and justice .... Hos 12:6
teaching them to *o* all .... Matt 28:20
o days and months and .... Gal 4:10
o your chaste conduct .... 1 Pet 3:2

OBSERVES
o the wind will not .... Eccl 11:4
He who *o* the day .... Rom 14:6

OBSTINATE
and made his heart *o* .... Deut 2:30
I knew that you were *o* .... Is 48:4

OBTAIN
They shall *o* joy and .... Is 35:10
they also may *o* mercy .... Rom 11:31
o salvation through .... 1 Thess 5:9
and covet and cannot *o* .... James 4:2

OBTAINED
o a part in this .... Acts 1:17
yet have now *o* mercy .... Rom 11:30
endured, he *o* the .... Heb 6:15
To those who have *o* .... 2 Pet 1:1

OBTAINS
o favor from the LORD .... Prov 8:35

ODED
Prophet of Samaria, 2 Chr 28:9–15

OFFEND
I will *o* no more .... Job 34:31
that devour him will *o* .... Jer 2:3
lest we *o* them .... Matt 17:27
than that he should *o* .... Luke 17:2
them, "Does this *o* .... John 6:61

OFFENDED
So they were *o* at Him .... Matt 13:57
stumbles or is *o* .... Rom 14:21

OFFENDER
who make a man an *o* .... Is 29:21
For if I am an *o* .... Acts 25:11

OFFENSE
and a rock of *o* .... Is 8:14
You are an *o* to Me .... Matt 16:23
by the one man's *o* .... Rom 5:17
Give no *o* .... 1 Cor 10:32
the *o* of the cross .... Gal 5:11
sincere and without *o* .... Phil 1:10
and a rock of *o* .... 1 Pet 2:8

OFFENSES
For *o* must come .... Matt 18:7
impossible that no *o* .... Luke 17:1
up because of our *o* .... Rom 4:25

OFFER
o the blind as a .... Mal 1:8
come and *o* your gift .... Matt 5:24
let us continually *o* .... Heb 13:15

OFFERED
to eat those things *o* .... 1 Cor 8:10
the eternal Spirit *o* .... Heb 9:14
so Christ was *o* .... Heb 9:28
o one sacrifice .... Heb 10:12
By faith Abel *o* .... Heb 11:4

OFFERING
you shall bring your *o* .... Lev 1:2
o You did not require .... Ps 40:6
You make His soul an *o* .... Is 53:10
to the LORD an *o* .... Mal 3:3
Himself for us, an *o* .... Eph 5:2
out as a drink *o* .... Phil 2:17
o You did not .... Heb 10:5
o He has perfected .... Heb 10:14
is no longer an *o* .... Heb 10:18

OFFERINGS
and offered burnt *o* .... Gen 8:20
He remember all your *o* .... Ps 20:3
In burnt *o* and .... Heb 10:6

OFFICE
let another take his *o* .... Ps 109:8
sitting at the tax *o* .... Matt 9:9

OFFSCOURING
You have made us an *o* .... Lam 3:45
the *o* of all things .... 1 Cor 4:13

OFFSPRING
My blessing on your *o* .... Is 44:3
He seeks godly *o* .... Mal 2:15
wife and raise up *o* .... Matt 22:24
For we are also His *o* .... Acts 17:28
am the Root and the *O* .... Rev 22:16

OFTEN
o I wanted to gather .... Luke 13:34
as *o* as you eat this .... 1 Cor 11:26
in sleeplessness *o* .... 2 Cor 11:27
should offer Himself *o* .... Heb 9:25

OG
Amorite king of Bashan, Deut 3:1–13
Defeated and killed by Israel, Num 21:32–35

OHOLAH
Symbolic name of Samaria, Ezek 23:4, 5, 36

OIL
for the anointing *o* .... Ex 25:6
I cease giving my *o* .... Judg 9:9
a bin, and a little *o* .... 1 Kin 17:12
poured out rivers of *o* .... Job 29:6
anointed with fresh *o* .... Ps 92:10
the heart of man, *o* .... Ps 104:15
like the precious *o* .... Ps 133:2
be as excellent *o* .... Ps 141:5
thousand rivers of *o* .... Mic 6:7
very costly fragrant *o* .... Matt 26:7
o might have been sold .... Matt 26:9
anointing him with *o* .... James 5:14
and do not harm the *o* .... Rev 6:6

OINTMENT
O and perfume delight .... Prov 27:9
your name is *o* .... Song 1:3

OLD
young, and now am *o* .... Ps 37:25
all manner, new and *o* .... Song 7:13
was said to those of *o* .... Matt 5:21
yet fifty years *o* .... John 8:57

but when you are *o* .... John 21:18
Your *o* men shall dream .... Acts 2:17
o man was crucified .... Rom 6:6
of the *O* Testament .... 2 Cor 3:14
o things have passed .... 2 Cor 5:17
have put off the *o* man .... Col 3:9
obsolete and growing *o* .... Heb 8:13
that serpent of *o* .... Rev 20:2

OLDER
o shall serve the .... Gen 25:23
o than your father .... Job 15:10
"Now his *o* son was .... Luke 15:25
not rebuke an *o* man .... 1 Tim 5:1
o women as mothers .... 1 Tim 5:2

OLIVE
a freshly plucked *o* .... Gen 8:11
I am like a green *o* .... Ps 52:8
of the *o* may fail .... Hab 3:17
o tree which is wild .... Rom 11:24

OLIVES, MOUNT OF
David flees to, 2 Sam 15:30
Prophecy concerning, Zech 14:4
Christ's triumphal entry from, Matt 21:1
Prophetic discourse delivered from, Matt 24:3
Christ's ascension from, Acts 1:9–12

OMNIPOTENT
For the Lord God *O* .... Rev 19:6

OMRI
Made king of Israel by army, 1 Kin 16:16, 21, 22
Builds Samaria; reigns wickedly, 1 Kin 16:23–27

ON
City of Lower Egypt; center of sun worship, Gen 41:45, 50
Called Beth Shemesh, Jer 43:13

ONAN
Second son of Judah; slain for failure to give his brother an heir, Gen 38:8–10

ONCE
died, He died to sin *o* .... Rom 6:10
for men to die *o* .... Heb 9:27
also suffered *o* .... 1 Pet 3:18

ONE
God may speak in *o* way .... Job 33:14
Two are better than *o* .... Eccl 4:9
you will be gathered *o* .... Is 27:12
"*O* thing you lack .... Mark 10:21
o thing is needed .... Luke 10:42
I and My Father are *o* .... John 10:30
Me, that they may be *o* .... John 17:11
o accord in the temple .... Acts 2:46
for you are all *o* .... Gal 3:28
to create in Himself *o* .... Eph 2:15
o body and *o* Spirit .... Eph 4:4
o hope of your calling .... Eph 4:4
o Lord, *o* faith, *o* .... Eph 4:5
o God and Father of .... Eph 4:6
For there is *o* God and .... 1 Tim 2:5
o Mediator between God .... 1 Tim 2:5
the husband of *o* wife .... 1 Tim 3:2
a thousand years as *o* .... 2 Pet 3:8
and these three are *o* .... 1 John 5:7

ONESIMUS
Slave of Philemon converted by Paul in Rome, Philem 10–17
With Tychicus, carries Paul's letters to Colosse and to Philemon, Col 4:7–9

ONESIPHORUS
Ephesian Christian commended for his service, 2 Tim 1:16–18

OPEN
o His lips against you .... Job 11:5
You *o* Your hand .... Ps 104:28
O your mouth for the .... Prov 31:8
and no one shall *o* .... Is 22:22
a lamb in *o* country .... Hos 4:16
Can a demon *o* the eyes ...... John 10:21
our heart is wide *o* .... 2 Cor 6:11
things are naked and *o* .... Heb 4:13
o the scroll and to .... Rev 5:2

OPENED
o not His mouth .... Is 53:7
Then their eyes were *o* .... Luke 24:31
o the Scriptures .... Luke 24:32
o their understanding .... Luke 24:45
effective door has *o* .... 1 Cor 16:9
when the Lamb *o* .... Rev 6:1
Now I saw heaven *o* .... Rev 19:11

OPENS
o the ears of men .... Job 33:16
The LORD *o* the eyes of .... Ps 146:8
him the doorkeeper *o* .... John 10:3
and shuts and no one *o* .... Rev 3:7

OPHIR
Famous for gold, 1 Chr 29:4

OPHRAH
Town in Manasseh; home of Gideon, Judg 6:11, 15
Site of Gideon's burial, Judg 8:32

OPINION
dared not declare my *o* .... Job 32:6
be wise in your own *o* .... Rom 11:25

OPPORTUNITY
But sin, taking *o* .... Rom 7:8
as we have *o* .... Gal 6:10
but you lacked *o* .... Phil 4:10
they would have had *o* .... Heb 11:15

OPPRESS
you shall not *o* .... Lev 25:17
You that You should *o* .... Job 10:3
He does not *o* .... Job 37:23
he loves to *o* .... Hos 12:7
o the widow or the .... Zech 7:10
Do not the rich *o* .... James 2:6

OPPRESSED
Whom have I *o* .... 1 Sam 12:3
For he has *o* and .... Job 20:19
fatherless and the *o* .... Ps 10:18
for all who are *o* .... Ps 103:6
The tears of the *o* .... Eccl 4:1
He was *o* and He was .... Is 53:7
her midst, and the *o* .... Amos 3:9
healing all who were *o* .... Acts 10:38
Lot, who was *o* by .... 2 Pet 2:7

OPPRESSES
o the poor reproaches .... Prov 14:31
o the poor to increase .... Prov 22:16
A poor man who *o* .... Prov 28:3

OPPRESSION
have surely seen the *o* .... Ex 3:7
"For the *o* of the .... Ps 12:5
Do not trust in *o* .... Ps 62:10
their life from *o* .... Ps 72:14
brought low through *o* .... Ps 107:39
Redeem me from the *o* .... Ps 119:134
considered all the *o* .... Eccl 4:1
o destroys a wise .... Eccl 7:7
justice, but behold, *o* .... Is 5:7
surely seen the *o* .... Acts 7:34

OPPRESSOR
the voice of the *o* .... Job 3:18
Do not envy the *o* .... Prov 3:31
is a great *o* .... Prov 28:16
of the fury of the *o* .... Is 51:13
No more shall an *o* .... Zech 9:8

ORACLES
received the living *o* .... Acts 7:38
were committed the *o* .... Rom 3:2
principles of the *o* .... Heb 5:12
let him speak as the *o* .... 1 Pet 4:11

ORDAINED
infants You have *o* .... Ps 8:2
o you a prophet .... Jer 1:5
the Man whom He has *o* ...... Acts 17:31

ORDER
'Set your house in *o* .... 2 Kin 20:1
set your words in *o* .... Job 33:5
you, and set them in *o* .... Ps 50:21
swept, and put in *o* .... Matt 12:44
done decently and in *o* .... 1 Cor 14:40
each one in his own *o* .... 1 Cor 15:23
to see your good *o* .... Col 2:5
according to the *o* .... Heb 5:6

ORDINANCE
resists the *o* of God .... Rom 13:2
yourselves to every *o* .... 1 Pet 2:13

ORDINANCES
Do you know the *o* .... Job 38:33
"If those *o* depart .... Jer 31:36
not appointed the *o* .... Jer 33:25
gone away from My *o* .... Mal 3:7
and fleshly *o* imposed .... Heb 9:10

ORION
Brilliant constellation, Job 9:9

ORNAMENT
will be a graceful *o* .... Prov 1:9
of gold and an *o* .... Prov 25:12
with them all as an *o* .... Is 49:18

ORPAH
Ruth's sister-in-law, Ruth 1:4, 14

ORPHANS
We have become *o* .... Lam 5:3
I will not leave you *o* .... John 14:18
to visit *o* and widows .... James 1:27

OSNAPPER
Called "the great and noble," Ezra 4:10

OSTRICHES
o will dwell there .... Is 13:21
is cruel, like *o* .... Lam 4:3
a mourning like the *o* .... Mic 1:8

OTHNIEL
Son of Kenaz, Caleb's youngest brother, Judg 1:13
Captures Kirjath Sepher; receives Caleb's daughter as wife, Josh 15:15–17
First judge of Israel, Judg 3:9–11

OUGHT
what Israel *o* to do .... 1 Chr 12:32
These you *o* to have .... Matt 23:23
pray for as we *o* .... Rom 8:26
how you *o* to conduct .... 1 Tim 3:15
which they *o* not .... 1 Tim 5:13
persons *o* you to be .... 2 Pet 3:11

OUTCAST
they called you an *o* .... Jer 30:17

OUTCASTS
gathers together the *o* .... Ps 147:2
will assemble the *o* .... Is 11:12
hide the *o* .... Is 16:3
Let My *o* dwell with .... Is 16:4

OUTCRY
that there be no *o* .... Ps 144:14

OUTSIDE
and dish, that the *o* .... Matt 23:26
Pharisees make the *o* .... Luke 11:39
toward those who are *o* .... Col 4:5

to Him, *o* the camp .... Heb 13:13
But *o* are dogs and .... Rev 22:15

OUTSTRETCHED
and with an *o* arm .... Deut 26:8
against you with an *o* .... Jer 21:5

OUTWARD
at the *o* appearance .... 1 Sam 16:7
adornment be merely *o* .... 1 Pet 3:3

OUTWARDLY
appear beautiful *o* .... Matt 23:27
not a Jew who is one *o* .... Rom 2:28

OVEN
make them as a fiery *o* .... Ps 21:9
burning like an *o* .... Mal 4:1
is thrown into the *o* .... Matt 6:30

OVERCAME
My throne, as I also *o* .... Rev 3:21
And they *o* him by .... Rev 12:11

OVERCOME
good cheer, I have *o* .... John 16:33
o evil with good .... Rom 12:21
because you have *o* .... 1 John 2:13
and the Lamb will *o* .... Rev 17:14

OVERCOMES
of God *o* the world .... 1 John 5:4
o I will give to eat .... Rev 2:7
o shall not be hurt .... Rev 2:11
o shall inherit all .... Rev 21:7

OVERFLOWING
My heart is *o* with a .... Ps 45:1

OVERSEER
Then he made him *o* .... Gen 39:4
having no captain, *o* .... Prov 6:7
to the Shepherd and *O* .... 1 Pet 2:25

OVERSEERS
Spirit has made you *o* .... Acts 20:28
you, serving as *o* .... 1 Pet 5:2

OVERTAKE
does righteousness *o* .... Is 59:9
you feared shall *o* .... Jer 42:16
and *o* this chariot .... Acts 8:29
that this Day should *o* .... 1 Thess 5:4

OVERTAKEN
No temptation has *o* .... 1 Cor 10:13
if a man is *o* in any .... Gal 6:1

OVERTHREW
So He *o* those cities .... Gen 19:25
will be as when God *o* .... Is 13:19
As God *o* Sodom and .... Jer 50:40
"I *o* some of you .... Amos 4:11

OVERTHROW
you shall utterly *o* .... Ex 23:24
o the righteous in .... Prov 18:5
o the throne of .... Hag 2:22
o the faith of some .... 2 Tim 2:18

OVERTHROWN
Their judges are *o* .... Ps 141:6
of Sodom, which was *o* .... Lam 4:6
I will make it *o* .... Ezek 21:27
and Nineveh shall be *o* .... Jon 3:4

OVERTHROWS
and *o* the mighty .... Job 12:19
o them in the night .... Job 34:25
o the words of the .... Prov 22:12

OVERTURNED
my heart is *o* within .... Lam 1:20
o the tables of the .... Matt 21:12
money and *o* the tables .... John 2:15

OVERWHELM
o the fatherless .... Job 6:27
sends them out, they *o* .... Job 12:15

OVERWHELMED
when my heart is *o* .... Ps 61:2
and my spirit was *o* .... Ps 77:3
o their enemies .... Ps 78:53
waters would have *o* .... Ps 124:4
my spirit is *o* within .... Ps 143:4

OWE
'How much do you *o* .... Luke 16:5
O no one anything .... Rom 13:8
o me even your own .... Philem 19

OWED
o him ten thousand .... Matt 18:24
fellow servants who *o* .... Matt 18:28
o five hundred denarii .... Luke 7:41

OWN
He came to His *o* .... John 1:11
having loved His *o* .... John 13:1
world would love its *o* .... John 15:19
and you are not your *o* .... 1 Cor 6:19
But each one has his *o* .... 1 Cor 7:7
For all seek their *o* .... Phil 2:21
from our sins in His *o* .... Rev 1:5

OX
shall not muzzle an *o* .... Deut 25:4
"Will the wild *o* .... Job 39:9
you bind the wild *o* .... Job 39:10
like a young wild *o* .... Ps 29:6
exalted like a wild *o* .... Ps 92:10
o knows its owner .... Is 1:3
had the face of an *o* .... Ezek 1:10
Sabbath loose his *o* .... Luke 13:15
shall not muzzle an *o* .... 1 Cor 9:9

PACIFIES
A gift in secret *p* .... Prov 21:14
for conciliation *p* .... Eccl 10:4

PADAN ARAM
Same as Mesopotamia, Gen 24:10; *see* MESOPOTAMIA
Home of Isaac's wife, Gen 25:20
Jacob flees to, Gen 28:2–7
Jacob returns from, Gen 31:17, 18
People of, called Syrians, Gen 31:24
Language of, called Aramaic, 2 Kin 18:26

PAIN
p you shall bring .... Gen 3:16
p as a woman in .... Is 13:8
are filled with *p* .... Is 21:3
before her *p* came .... Is 66:7
Why is my *p* perpetual .... Jer 15:18
shall be no more *p* .... Rev 21:4

PAINED
My heart is severely *p* .... Ps 55:4
I am *p* in my very .... Jer 4:19

PAINFUL
this, it was too *p* .... Ps 73:16
for the present, but *p* .... Heb 12:11

PAINS
The *p* of death .... Ps 116:3
having loosed the *p* .... Acts 2:24
upon them, as labor *p* .... 1 Thess 5:3

PAINT
and she put *p* on her .... 2 Kin 9:30
your eyes with *p* .... Jer 4:30

PALACE
enter the King's *p* .... Ps 45:15
a *p* of foreigners .... Is 25:2
guards his own *p* .... Luke 11:21
evident to the whole *p* .... Phil 1:13

PALACES
out of the ivory *p* .... Ps 45:8
God is in her *p* .... Ps 48:3
has entered our *p* .... Jer 9:21

PALE
his face now grow *p* .... Is 29:22
and all faces turned *p* .... Jer 30:6
behold, a *p* horse .... Rev 6:8

PALM
of water and seventy *p* .... Ex 15:27
p trees and went out .... John 12:13
p branches in their .... Rev 7:9

PALMS
struck Him with the *p* .... Matt 26:67

PALTI (or Paltiel)
Man to whom Saul gives Michal, David's wife, in marriage, 1 Sam 25:44; 2 Sam 3:15

PAMPHYLIA
People from, at Pentecost, Acts 2:10
Paul visits; John Mark returns home from, Acts 13:13; 15:38
Paul preaches in cities of, Acts 14:24, 25

PANGS
The *p* of death .... Ps 18:4
P and sorrows will .... Is 13:8
labors with birth *p* .... Rom 8:22

PANT
They *p* after the dust .... Amos 2:7

PANTS
As the deer *p* for the .... Ps 42:1

PAPHOS
Paul blinds Elymas at, Acts 13:6–13

PARABLE
open my mouth in a *p* .... Ps 78:2
p He did not speak .... Matt 13:34
do You speak this *p* .... Luke 12:41

PARABLES
'Does he not speak *p* .... Ezek 20:49
understand all the *p* .... Mark 4:13
rest it is given in *p* .... Luke 8:10

PARADISE
will be with Me in *P* .... Luke 23:43
was caught up into *P* .... 2 Cor 12:4
in the midst of the *P* .... Rev 2:7

PARAN
Residence of exiled Ishmael, Gen 21:21
Israelites camp in, Num 10:12
Headquarters of spies, Num 13:3, 26
Site of David's refuge, 1 Sam 25:1

PARCHMENTS
especially the *p* .... 2 Tim 4:13

PARDON
p your transgressions .... Ex 23:21
O LORD, *p* my iniquity .... Ps 25:11
He will abundantly *p* .... Is 55:7
p all their iniquities .... Jer 33:8

PARDONING
is a God like You, *p* .... Mic 7:18

PARENTS
will rise up against *p* .... Matt 10:21
has left house or *p* .... Luke 18:29
disobedient to *p* .... Rom 1:30
to lay up for the *p* .... 2 Cor 12:14

PARMENAS
One of the first seven deacons, Acts 6:5

PART
You have no *p* in the .... Josh 22:25
has chosen that good *p* .... Luke 10:42
you, you have no *p* .... John 13:8
For we know in *p* .... 1 Cor 13:9
p has a believer .... 2 Cor 6:15
shall take away his *p* .... Rev 22:19

PARTAKE
for we all *p* of that .... 1 Cor 10:17
you cannot *p* of the .... 1 Cor 10:21

PARTAKER
and have been a *p* ... Ps 50:18
in hope should be *p* ... 1 Cor 9:10
Christ, and also a *p* ... 1 Pet 5:1

PARTAKERS
Gentiles have been *p* ... Rom 15:27
of the sacrifices *p* ... 1 Cor 10:18
know that as you are *p* ... 2 Cor 1:7
gospel, you all are *p* ... Phil 1:7
qualified us to be *p* ... Col 1:12
For we have become *p* ... Heb 3:14

PARTED
them, that He was *p* ... Luke 24:51
so sharp that they *p* ... Acts 15:39

PARTIALITY
You shall not show *p* ... Deut 1:17
unjustly, and show *p* ... Ps 82:2
is not good to show *p* ... Prov 18:5
but have shown *p* ... Mal 2:9
that God shows no *p* ... Acts 10:34
For there is no *p* ... Rom 2:11
doing nothing with *p* ... 1 Tim 5:21
but if you show *p* ... James 2:9
good fruits, without *p* ... James 3:17

PARTITION
the Testimony, and *p* ... Ex 40:3

PARTNER
Whoever is a *p* with a ... Prov 29:24
you count me as a *p* ... Philem 17

PARTS
anything but death *p* ... Ruth 1:17
in the inward *p* ... Ps 51:6
Shout, you lower *p* ... Is 44:23
but our presentable *p* ... 1 Cor 12:24
into the lower *p* ... Eph 4:9

PASHHUR
Official opposing Jeremiah, Jer 21:1; 38:1–13
——— Priest who puts Jeremiah in jail, Jer 20:1–6

PASS
I will *p* over you ... Ex 12:13
of the sea that *p* ... Ps 8:8
When you *p* through the ... Is 43:2
"I will make you *p* ... Ezek 20:37
I will not *p* by them ... Amos 7:8
and earth will *p* ... Matt 24:35

PASSED
And behold, the LORD *p* ... 1 Kin 19:11
forbearance God had *p* ... Rom 3:25
High Priest who has *p* ... Heb 4:14
know that we have *p* ... 1 John 3:14

PASSES
For the wind *p* over it ... Ps 103:16
of Christ which *p* ... Eph 3:19

PASSION
than to burn with *p* ... 1 Cor 7:9
uncleanness, *p*, evil ... Col 3:5

PASSIONS
gave them up to vile *p* ... Rom 1:26

PASSOVER
It is the LORD'S *P* ... Ex 12:11
of King Josiah this *P* ... 2 Kin 23:23
I will keep the *P* ... Matt 26:18
indeed Christ, our *P* ... 1 Cor 5:7
By faith he kept the *P* ... Heb 11:28

PAST
My days are *p* ... Job 17:11
lo, the winter is *p* ... Song 2:11
and His ways *p* finding ... Rom 11:33
ways spoke in time *p* ... Heb 1:1
p lifetime in doing ... 1 Pet 4:3

PASTORS
and some *p* and ... Eph 4:11

PASTURE
the sheep of Your *p* ... Ps 74:1
the people of His *p* ... Ps 95:7
feed them in good *p* ... Ezek 34:14
in and out and find *p* ... John 10:9

PASTURES
to lie down in green *p* ... Ps 23:2

PATH
p no bird knows ... Job 28:7
You will show me the *p* ... Ps 16:11
lead me in a smooth *p* ... Ps 27:11
But the *p* of the just ... Prov 4:18
way in the sea and a *p* ... Is 43:16

PATHROS
Described as a lowly kingdom, Ezek 29:14–16
Refuge for dispersed Jews, Jer 44:1–15
Jews to be regathered from, Is 11:11

PATHS
He leads me in the *p* ... Ps 23:3
Teach me Your *p* ... Ps 25:4
and all her *p* are ... Prov 3:17
p they have not ... Is 42:16
themselves crooked *p* ... Is 59:8
Make His *p* straight ... Matt 3:3
and make straight *p* ... Heb 12:13

PATIENCE
'Master, have *p* ... Matt 18:26
and bear fruit with *p* ... Luke 8:15
Now may the God of *p* ... Rom 15:5
labor of love, and *p* ... 1 Thess 1:3
faith, love, *p* ... 1 Tim 6:11
your faith produces *p* ... James 1:3
p have its perfect ... James 1:4
in the kingdom and *p* ... Rev 1:9
Here is the *p* and the ... Rev 13:10

PATIENT
rejoicing in hope, *p* ... Rom 12:12
uphold the weak, be *p* ... 1 Thess 5:14

PATIENTLY
the LORD, and wait *p* ... Ps 37:7
if you take it *p* ... 1 Pet 2:20

PATMOS
John, banished here, receives the Revelation, Rev 1:9

PATRIARCHS
begot the twelve *p* ... Acts 7:8

PATTERN
p which you were ... Ex 26:30
as you have us for a *p* ... Phil 3:17
Hold fast the *p* ... 2 Tim 1:13
p shown you on the ... Heb 8:5

PAUL
Roman citizen from Tarsus; studied under Gamaliel, Acts 22:3, 25–28
Originally called Saul; persecutes the church, Acts 7:58; 8:1, 3; 9:1, 2
Converted on road to Damascus, Acts 9:3–19
Preaches in Damascus; escapes to Jerusalem and then to Tarsus, Acts 9:20–30
Ministers in Antioch; sent to Jerusalem, Acts 11:25–30
First missionary journey, Acts 13; 14
Speaks for Gentiles at Jerusalem Council, Acts 15:1–5, 12
Second missionary journey, Acts 15:36—18:22
Third missionary journey, Acts 18:23—21:14
Arrested in Jerusalem; defense before Roman authorities, Acts 21:15—26:32
Sent to Rome, Acts 27:1—28:31
His epistles, Rom; 1 and 2 Cor; Gal; Eph; Phil; Col; 1 and 2 Thess; 1 and 2 Tim; Titus; Philem

PAULUS, SERGIUS
Roman proconsul of Cyprus, Acts 13:4, 7

PAVILION
shall hide me in His *p* ... Ps 27:5
them secretly in a *p* ... Ps 31:20

PAY
with which to *p* ... Prov 22:27
priests teach for *p* ... Mic 3:11
with me, and I will *p* ... Matt 18:26
p taxes to Caesar ... Matt 22:17
For you *p* tithe of ... Matt 23:23

PEACE
"These men are at *p* ... Gen 34:21
I will give *p* in the ... Lev 26:6
you, and give you *p* ... Num 6:26
'Make *p* with me by a ... 2 Kin 18:31
field shall be at *p* ... Job 5:23
both lie down in *p* ... Ps 4:8
seek *p* and pursue it ... Ps 34:14
for He will speak *p* ... Ps 85:8
p have those who ... Ps 119:165
I am for *p* ... Ps 120:7
for the *p* of Jerusalem ... Ps 122:6
P be within your walls ... Ps 122:7
P be upon Israel ... Ps 125:5
war, and a time of *p* ... Eccl 3:8
Father, Prince of *P* ... Is 9:6
keep him in perfect *p* ... Is 26:3
p they have not ... Is 59:8
slightly, saying, '*P* ... Jer 6:14
"We looked for *p* ... Jer 8:15
give you assured *p* ... Jer 14:13
they will seek *p* ... Ezek 7:25
P be multiplied ... Dan 4:1
this One shall be *p* ... Mic 5:5
place I will give *p* ... Hag 2:9
is worthy, let your *p* ... Matt 10:13
that I came to bring *p* ... Matt 10:34
and on earth *p* ... Luke 2:14
if a son of *p* is there ... Luke 10:6
that make for your *p* ... Luke 19:42
I leave with you, My *p* ... John 14:27
in Me you may have *p* ... John 16:33
Grace to you and *p* ... Rom 1:7
by faith, we have *p* ... Rom 5:1
God has called us to *p* ... 1 Cor 7:15
p will be with you ... 2 Cor 13:11
Spirit is love, joy, *p* ... Gal 5:22
He Himself is our *p* ... Eph 2:14
and the *p* of God ... Phil 4:7
heaven, having made *p* ... Col 1:20
And let the *p* of God ... Col 3:15
Be at *p* among ... 1 Thess 5:13
faith, love, *p* ... 2 Tim 2:22
meaning "king of *p*," ... Heb 7:2
is sown in *p* by those ... James 3:18
p be multiplied ... 2 Pet 1:2

PEACEABLE
and *p* life in all ... 1 Tim 2:2
is first pure, then *p* ... James 3:17

PEACEABLY
on you, live *p* ... Rom 12:18

PEACEMAKERS
Blessed are the *p* ... Matt 5:9

PEARL
had found one *p* ... Matt 13:46
gate was of one *p* ... Rev 21:21

PEARLS
nor cast your *p* ... Matt 7:6

hair or gold or *p* . . . 1 Tim 2:9
gates were twelve *p* . . . Rev 21:21

PEG
wife, took a tent *p* . . . Judg 4:21
will fasten him as a *p* . . . Is 22:23

PEKAH
Son of Remaliah; usurps Israel's throne, 2 Kin 15:25–28
Forms alliance with Rezin of Syria against Ahaz, Is 7:1–9
Alliance defeated; captives returned, 2 Kin 16:5–9
Territory of, overrun by Tiglath-Pileser, 2 Kin 15:29
Assassinated by Hoshea, 2 Kin 15:30

PEKAHIAH
Son of Menahem; king of Israel, 2 Kin 15:22–26
Assassinated by Pekah, 2 Kin 15:23–25

PEN
My tongue is the *p* . . . Ps 45:1
on it with a man's *p* . . . Is 8:1
to write to you with *p* . . . 3 John 13

PENTECOST
P had fully come . . . Acts 2:1

PENUEL
Place east of Jordan; site of Jacob's wrestling with angel, Gen 32:24–31
Inhabitants of, slain by Gideon, Judg 8:8, 9, 17

PEOPLE
will take you as My *p* . . . Ex 6:7
Who is like you, a *p* . . . Deut 33:29
p shall be my *p* . . . Ruth 1:16
p who know the joyful . . . Ps 89:15
We are His *p* and the . . . Ps 100:3
Happy are the *p* . . . Ps 144:15
"Blessed is Egypt My *p* . . . Is 19:25
this is a rebellious *p* . . . Is 30:9
p who provoke Me . . . Is 65:3
and they shall be My *p* . . . Jer 24:7
for you are not My *p* . . . Hos 1:9
like *p*, like priest . . . Hos 4:9
to make ready a *p* . . . Luke 1:17
take out of them a *p* . . . Acts 15:14
who were not My *p* . . . Rom 9:25
and they shall be My *p* . . . 2 Cor 6:16
His own special *p* . . . Titus 2:14
LORD will judge His *p* . . . Heb 10:30
but are now the *p* . . . 1 Pet 2:10
tribe and tongue and *p* . . . Rev 5:9
they shall be His *p* . . . Rev 21:3

PEOR
Mountain of Moab opposite Jericho, Num 23:28
Israel's camp seen from, Num 24:2
——— Moabite god called Baal of Peor, Num 25:3, 5, 18
Israelites punished for worship of, Num 31:16

PERCEIVE
given you a heart to *p* . . . Deut 29:4
but I cannot *p* . . . Job 23:8
seeing, but do not *p* . . . Is 6:9
may see and not *p* . . . Mark 4:12

PERDITION
except the son of *p* . . . John 17:12
to them a proof of *p* . . . Phil 1:28
revealed, the son of *p* . . . 2 Thess 2:3
who draw back to *p* . . . Heb 10:39
day of judgment and *p* . . . 2 Pet 3:7

PEREZ
One of Judah's twin sons by Tamar, Gen 38:24–30

PERFECT
Noah was a just man, *p* . . . Gen 6:9
one who is *p* in . . . Job 36:4
for God, His way is *p* . . . Ps 18:30
You were *p* in your . . . Ezek 28:15
Father in heaven is *p* . . . Matt 5:48
"If you want to be *p* . . . Matt 19:21
they may be made *p* . . . John 17:23
and *p* will of God . . . Rom 12:2
when that which is *p* . . . 1 Cor 13:10
present every man *p* . . . Col 1:28
the law made nothing *p* . . . Heb 7:19
of just men made *p* . . . Heb 12:23
good gift and every *p* . . . James 1:17
in word, he is a *p* . . . James 3:2
p love casts out fear . . . 1 John 4:18

PERFECTED
third day I shall be *p* . . . Luke 13:32
or am already *p* . . . Phil 3:12
the Son who has been *p* . . . Heb 7:28
the love of God is *p* . . . 1 John 2:5

PERFECTION
the *p* of beauty . . . Ps 50:2
consummation of all *p* . . . Ps 119:96
let us go on to *p* . . . Heb 6:1

PERGA
Visited by Paul, Acts 13:13, 14; 14:25

PERGAMOS
Site of one of the seven churches, Rev 1:11
Special message to, Rev 2:12–17

PERILOUS
from the *p* pestilence . . . Ps 91:3
in the last days *p* . . . 2 Tim 3:1

PERILS
journeys often, in *p* . . . 2 Cor 11:26

PERISH
"Surely we die, we *p* . . . Num 17:12
All flesh would *p* . . . Job 34:15
they *p* at the rebuke . . . Ps 80:16
very day his plans *p* . . . Ps 146:4
so that we may not *p* . . . Jon 1:6
little ones should *p* . . . Matt 18:14
will all likewise *p* . . . Luke 13:3
in Him should not *p* . . . John 3:16
they shall never *p* . . . John 10:28
concern things which *p* . . . Col 2:22
among those who *p* . . . 2 Thess 2:10
that any should *p* . . . 2 Pet 3:9

PERISHED
p being innocent . . . Job 4:7
Truth has *p* and has . . . Jer 7:28
The faithful man has *p* . . . Mic 7:2

PERISHING
We are *p* . . . Matt 8:25
to those who are *p* . . . 2 Cor 4:3

PERIZZITES
One of seven Canaanite nations, Deut 7:1
Possessed Palestine in Abraham's time, Gen 13:7
Jacob's fear of, Gen 34:30
Many of, slain by Judah, Judg 1:4, 5

PERMIT
the Spirit did not *p* . . . Acts 16:7
I do not *p* a woman . . . 1 Tim 2:12

PERMITS
you, if the Lord *p* . . . 1 Cor 16:7
we will do if God *p* . . . Heb 6:3

PERPETUATED
Your name shall be *p* . . . Nah 1:14

PERPLEXED
at one another, *p* . . . John 13:22
we are *p* . . . 2 Cor 4:8

PERSECUTE
p me as God does . . . Job 19:22
p me wrongfully . . . Ps 119:86
when they revile and *p* . . . Matt 5:11
Bless those who *p* . . . Rom 12:14

PERSECUTED
p the poor and needy . . . Ps 109:16
p the prophets who . . . Matt 5:12
If they *p* Me . . . John 15:20
p the church of God . . . 1 Cor 15:9
p, but not forsaken . . . 2 Cor 4:9
p us now preaches the . . . Gal 1:23

PERSECUTION
p arises because of . . . Matt 13:21
At that time a great *p* . . . Acts 8:1
do I still suffer *p* . . . Gal 5:11

PERSECUTOR
a blasphemer, a *p* . . . 1 Tim 1:13

PERSEVERANCE
tribulation produces *p* . . . Rom 5:3
to this end will all *p* . . . Eph 6:18
longsuffering, love, *p* . . . 2 Tim 3:10
to self-control *p* . . . 2 Pet 1:6

PERSEVERE
kept My command to *p* . . . Rev 3:10

PERSON
In whose eyes a vile *p* . . . Ps 15:4
p will suffer hunger . . . Prov 19:15
do not regard the *p* . . . Matt 22:16
express image of His *p* . . . Heb 1:3
let it be the hidden *p* . . . 1 Pet 3:4

PERSUADE
"You almost *p* me . . . Acts 26:28
the Lord, we *p* men . . . 2 Cor 5:11
For do I now *p* men . . . Gal 1:10

PERSUADED
a ruler is *p* . . . Prov 25:15
neither will they be *p* . . . Luke 16:31
p that He is able . . . 2 Tim 1:12

PERSUASIVE
p words of human . . . 1 Cor 2:4
you with *p* words . . . Col 2:4

PERTAINING
Priest in things *p* . . . Heb 2:17
for men in things *p* . . . Heb 5:1

PERVERSE
your way is *p* . . . Num 22:32
for the *p* person is an . . . Prov 3:32
p lips far from you . . . Prov 4:24
p heart will be . . . Prov 12:8
p man sows strife . . . Prov 16:28
but he who is *p* . . . Prov 28:18
from this *p* generation . . . Acts 2:40

PERVERT
You shall not *p* . . . Deut 16:19
and *p* all equity . . . Mic 3:9
p the gospel of Christ . . . Gal 1:7

PERVERTING
We found this fellow *p* . . . Luke 23:2
will you not cease *p* . . . Acts 13:10

PERVERTS
p the words of the . . . Ex 23:8
p his ways will become . . . Prov 10:9

PESTILENCE
from the perilous *p* . . . Ps 91:3
p that walks in . . . Ps 91:6
Before Him went *p* . . . Hab 3:5

PESTILENCES
will be famines, *p* . . . Matt 24:7

PETER
Fisherman; called to discipleship, Matt 4:18–20; John 1:40–42

Called as apostle, Matt 10:2–4
Walks on water, Matt 14:28–33
Confesses Christ's deity, Matt 16:13–19
Rebuked by Christ, Matt 16:21–23
Witnesses Transfiguration, Matt 17:1–8; 2 Pet 1:16–18
Denies Christ three times, Matt 26:69–75
Commissioned to feed Christ's sheep, John 21:15–17
Leads disciples, Acts 1:15–26
Preaches at Pentecost, Acts 2:1–41
Performs miracles, Acts 3:1–11; 5:14–16; 9:32–43
Called to minister to Gentiles, Acts 10
Defends his visit to Gentiles, Acts 11:1–18
Imprisoned and delivered, Acts 12:3–19
Speaks at Jerusalem Council, Acts 15:7–14
Writes epistles, 1 Pet 1:1; 2 Pet 1:1

PETITION
of Israel grant your *p* ....1 Sam 1:17

PETITIONS
fulfill all your *p* ....Ps 20:5
p that we have asked ....1 John 5:15

PHARAOH
Kings of Egypt, contemporaries of:
Abraham, Gen 12:15–20
Joseph, Gen 40; 41
Moses in youth, Ex 1:8–11
the Exodus, Ex 5—14
Solomon, 1 Kin 3:1; 11:17–20
Other Pharaohs, 1 Kin 14:25, 26; 2 Kin 17:4; 18:21; 19:9; 23:29; Jer 44:30

PHARISEE
to pray, one a *P* ....Luke 18:10
and brethren, I am a *P* ....Acts 23:6

PHILADELPHIA
City of Lydia in Asia Minor; church established here, Rev 1:11

PHILEMON
Christian at Colosse to whom Paul writes, Philem 1
Paul appeals to him to receive Onesimus, Philem 9–21

PHILIP
Son of Herod the Great, Matt 14:3
——— One of the twelve apostles, Matt 10:3
Brings Nathanael to Christ, John 1:43–48
Tested by Christ, John 6:5–7
Introduces Greeks to Christ, John 12:20–22
Gently rebuked by Christ, John 14:8–12
——— One of the first seven deacons, Acts 6:5
Called an evangelist, Acts 21:8
Preaches in Samaria, Acts 8:5–13
Leads the Ethiopian eunuch to Christ, Acts 8:26–40

PHILIPPI
City of Macedonia (named after Philip of Macedon); visited by Paul, Acts 16:12; 20:6
Paul writes letter to church of, Phil 1:1

PHILISTIA
The land of the Philistines, Gen 21:32, 34; Josh 13:2; Ps 60:8

PHILISTINES
Not attacked by Joshua, Josh 13:1–3
Left to test Israel, Judg 3:1–4
God delivers Israel to, as punishment, Judg 10:6, 7
Israel delivered from, by Samson, Judg 13—16
Capture, then return the ark of the Lord, 1 Sam 4—6
Wars and dealings with Saul and David, 1 Sam 13:15—14:23; 17:1–52; 18:25–27; 21:10–15; 27:1—28:6; 29:1–11; 31:1–13; 2 Sam 5:17–25
Originally on the island of Caphtor, Jer 47:4
Prophecies concerning, Is 9:11, 12; Jer 25:15–20; 47:1–7; Ezek 25:15–17; Zeph 2:4–6

PHINEHAS
Aaron's grandson; executes God's judgment, Num 25:1–18; Ps 106:30, 31
Settles dispute over memorial altar, Josh 22:11–32
——— Younger son of Eli; abuses his office, 1 Sam 1:3; 2:12–17, 22–36
Killed by Philistines, 1 Sam 4:11, 17

PHOENICIA
Mediterranean coastal region including the cities of Ptolemais, Tyre, Zarephath and Sidon; evangelized by early Christians, Acts 11:19
Jesus preaches here, Matt 15:21

PHRYGIA
Jews from, at Pentecost, Acts 2:1, 10
Visited twice by Paul, Acts 16:6

PHYLACTERIES
They make their *p* ....Matt 23:5

PHYSICIAN
Gilead, is there no *p* ....Jer 8:22
have no need of a *p* ....Matt 9:12
Luke the beloved *p* ....Col 4:14

PHYSICIANS
are all worthless *p* .... Job 13:4
her livelihood on *p* ....Luke 8:43

PI HAHIROTH
Israel camps there before crossing the Red Sea, Ex 14:2, 9; Num 33:7, 8

PIECES
for my wages thirty *p* ....Zech 11:12
they took the thirty *p* ....Matt 27:9
shall be dashed to *p* ....Rev 2:17

PIERCE
and his master shall *p* ....Ex 21:6
a sword will *p* ....Luke 2:35

PIERCED
p My hands and My feet ....Ps 22:16
on Me whom they have *p* ......Zech 12:10
of the soldiers *p* ....John 19:34
p themselves through ....1 Tim 6:10
and they also who *p* ....Rev 1:7

PIERCING
p even to the division ....Heb 4:12

PIETY
first learn to show *p* ....1 Tim 5:4

PILATE, PONTIUS
Governor of Judea (A.D. 26–36), Luke 3:1
Questions Jesus and delivers Him to Jews, Matt 27:2, 11–26; John 18:28—19:16

PILGRIMAGE
heart is set on *p* ....Ps 84:5
In the house of my *p* ....Ps 119:54

PILGRIMS
we are aliens and *p* ....1 Chr 29:15
were strangers and *p* ....Heb 11:13

PILLAR
and she became a *p* ....Gen 19:26
and by night in a *p* ....Ex 13:21
the living God, the *p* ....1 Tim 3:15

PILLARS
break their sacred *p* ....Ex 34:13
I set up its *p* firmly ....Ps 75:3
out her seven *p* ....Prov 9:1
blood and fire and *p* ....Joel 2:30
and his feet like *p* ....Rev 10:1

PINNACLE
set Him on the *p* ....Luke 4:9

PISGAH
Balaam offers sacrifice upon, Num 23:14
Moses views Promised Land from, Deut 3:27
Site of Moses' death, Deut 34:1–7

PISHON
One of Eden's four rivers, Gen 2:10, 11

PISIDIA
Twice visited by Paul, Acts 13:13, 14; 14:24

PITHOM
Egyptian city built by Hebrew slaves, Ex 1:11

PIT
cast him into some *p* ....Gen 37:20
soul draws near the *P* ....Job 33:22
who go down to the *p* ....Ps 28:1
woman is a deep *p* ....Prov 22:14
a harlot is a deep *p* ....Prov 23:27
fall into his own *p* ....Prov 28:10
my life in the *p* ....Lam 3:53
who descend into the *P* ....Ezek 31:16
up my life from the *p* ....Jon 2:6
from the waterless *p* ....Zech 9:11
if it falls into a *p* ....Matt 12:11
into the bottomless *p* ....Rev 20:3

PITCHERS
hand, with empty *p* ....Judg 7:16
the washing of cups, *p* ....Mark 7:4

PITY
eye shall have no *p* ....Deut 7:16
"Have *p* on me ....Job 19:21
for someone to take *p* ....Ps 69:20
He who has *p* on the ....Prov 19:17
p He redeemed them ....Is 63:9
land, and *p* His people ....Joel 2:18
And should I not *p* ....Jon 4:11
just as I had *p* ....Matt 18:33

PLACE
p know him anymore ....Job 7:10
All go to one *p* ....Eccl 3:20
return again to My *p* ....Hos 5:15
Come, see the *p* ....Matt 28:6
My word has no *p* ....John 8:37
I go to prepare a *p* ....John 14:2
might go to his own *p* ....Acts 1:25

PLACES
set them in slippery *p* ....Ps 73:18
dark *p* of the earth ....Ps 74:20
and the rough *p* ....Is 40:4
They love the best *p* ....Matt 23:6
in the heavenly *p* ....Eph 1:3

PLAGUE
bring yet one more *p* ....Ex 11:1
p come near your ....Ps 91:10
and the *p* was stopped ....Ps 106:30

PLAGUES
I will send all My *p* ....Ex 9:14
I will be your *p* ....Hos 13:14
p that are written ....Rev 22:18

PLAINLY
the Christ, tell us *p* ....John 10:24
now You are speaking *p* ....John 16:29
such things declare *p* ....Heb 11:14

PLAN
p evil things in their ....Ps 140:2
Let none of you *p* ....Zech 7:10

PLANK
First remove the *p* ....Matt 7:5

PLANS
He makes the *p* of the ....Ps 33:10
in that very day his *p* ....Ps 146:4
that devises wicked *p* ....Prov 6:18
A man's heart *p* ....Prov 16:9
P are established ....Prov 20:18

PLANT
A time to *p* ....Eccl 3:2
Him as a tender *p* ....Is 53:2
they shall *p* vineyards ....Is 65:21
p of an alien vine ....Jer 2:21
p which My heavenly ....Matt 15:13

PLANTED
shall be like a tree *p* ....Ps 1:3
Your right hand has *p* ....Ps 80:15
shall they be *p* ....Is 40:24
by the roots and be *p* ....Luke 17:6
I *p*, Apollos watered ....1 Cor 3:6

PLANTS
our sons may be as *p* ....Ps 144:12
down its choice *p* ....Is 16:8
neither he who *p* ....1 Cor 3:7

PLAY
and rose up to *p* ....Ex 32:6
p skillfully with a ....Ps 33:3
nursing child shall *p* ....Is 11:8
and rose up to *p* ....1 Cor 10:7

PLEAD
the one who would *p* ....Judg 6:31
Oh, that one might *p* ....Job 16:21
p my cause against an ....Ps 43:1
p with your friend ....Prov 6:3
Behold, I will *p* ....Jer 2:35
p His case with all...............Jer 25:31

PLEADED
Then Moses *p* with the ....Ex 32:11
this thing I *p* with ....2 Cor 12:8

PLEASANT
food, that it was *p* ....Gen 3:6
they despised the *p* ....Ps 106:24
how good and how *p* ....Ps 133:1
and knowledge is *p* ....Prov 2:10
P words are like a ....Prov 16:24
p places of the ....Jer 23:10
Is he a *p* child ....Jer 31:20
I ate no *p* food ....Dan 10:3

PLEASE
When a man's ways *p* ....Prov 16:7
do those things that *p* ....John 8:29
in the flesh cannot *p* ....Rom 8:8
p his neighbor for his ....Rom 15:2
how he may *p* the Lord ....1 Cor 7:32
Or do I seek to *p* men ....Gal 1:10
is impossible to *p* Him ....Heb 11:6

PLEASED
Then You shall be *p* ....Ps 51:19
The LORD is well *p* ....Is 42:21
Would he be *p* with you ....Mal 1:8
in whom I am well *p* ....Matt 3:17
God was not well *p* ....1 Cor 10:5
testimony, that he *p* ....Heb 11:5
in whom I am well *p* ....2 Pet 1:17

PLEASES
He does whatever He *p* ....Ps 115:3
Whatever the LORD *p* ....Ps 135:6

PLEASING
sacrifice, well *p* ....Phil 4:18
for this is well *p* ....Col 3:20
in you what is well *p* ....Heb 13:21

PLEASURE
not a God who takes *p* ....Ps 5:4
Do good in Your good *p* ....Ps 51:18
Your servants take *p* ....Ps 102:14
p will be a poor man ....Prov 21:17
for He has no *p* ....Eccl 5:4
shall perform all My *p* ....Is 44:28
your fast you find *p* ....Is 58:3
nor finding your own *p* ....Is 58:13
Do I have any *p* ....Ezek 18:23
I have no *p* in you ....Mal 1:10
your Father's good *p* ....Luke 12:32
to the good *p* of His ....Eph 1:5
fulfill all the good *p* ....2 Thess 1:11
p is dead while ....1 Tim 5:6
for sin You had no *p* ....Heb 10:6
back, My soul has no *p* ....Heb 10:38
p that war in your ....James 4:1
on the earth in *p* ....James 5:5

PLEASURES
Your right hand are *p* ....Ps 16:11
cares, riches, and *p* ....Luke 8:14
to enjoy the passing *p* ....Heb 11:25

PLEIADES
Part of God's creation, Job 9:9; Amos 5:8

PLENTIFUL
You, O God, sent a *p* ....Ps 68:9
The harvest truly is *p* ....Matt 9:37

PLENTIFULLY
rich man yielded *p* ....Luke 12:16

PLENTY
p which were in the ....Gen 41:53
LORD will grant you *p* ....Deut 28:11
his land will have *p* ....Prov 28:19

PLOT
and the people *p* ....Ps 2:1
p became known to Saul ....Acts 9:24

PLOTTED
and *p* to take Jesus by ....Matt 26:4
chief priests *p* ....John 12:10

PLOW
lazy man will not *p* ....Prov 20:4
Does one *p* there with ....Amos 6:12
put his hand to the *p*..........Luke 9:62
he who plows should *p* ....1 Cor 9:10

PLOWED
"Zion shall be *p* ....Jer 26:18
You have *p* wickedness ....Hos 10:13
of you Zion shall be *p* ....Mic 3:12

PLUCK
grain, you may *p* ....Deut 23:25
who pass by the way *p* ....Ps 80:12
obey, I will utterly *p* ....Jer 12:17
p the heads of grain ....Mark 2:23

PLUCKED
p the victim from his ....Job 29:17
cheeks to those who *p* ....Is 50:6
And His disciples *p* ....Luke 6:1
you would have *p* ....Gal 4:15

PLUMB
a *p* line, with a *p* ....Amos 7:7
rejoice to see the *p* ....Zech 4:10

PLUNDER
p the Egyptians ....Ex 3:22
who pass by the way *p* ....Ps 89:41
The *p* of the poor is ....Is 3:14
p you shall become ....Jer 30:16
house and *p* his goods ....Matt 12:29

PLUNDERED
stouthearted were *p* ....Ps 76:5
a people robbed and *p* ....Is 42:22
"And when you are *p* ....Jer 4:30
Because you have *p* ....Hab 2:8

PLUNDERING
me because of the *p* ....Is 22:4
accepted the *p* of your ....Heb 10:34

POISON
the *p* of asps is under ....Ps 140:3
"The *p* of asps is ....Rom 3:13
evil, full of deadly *p* ....James 3:8

POISONED
p by bitterness ....Acts 8:23
p their minds against ....Acts 14:2

POMP
multitude and their *p* ....Is 5:14
p is brought down to ....Is 14:11
had come with great *p* ....Acts 25:23

POMPOUS
and a mouth speaking *p* ....Dan 7:8

PONDER
P the path of your ....Prov 4:26

PONDERED
p them in her heart...........Luke 2:19

PONDERS
p all his paths ....Prov 5:21

PONTUS
Jews from, at Pentecost, Acts 2:5, 9
Home of Aquila, Acts 18:2
Christians of, addressed by Peter, 1 Pet 1:1

POOL
the wilderness a *p* ....Is 41:18
by the Sheep Gate a *p* ....John 5:2

POOLS
also covers it with *p* ....Ps 84:6
a wilderness into *p* ....Ps 107:35
your eyes like the *p* ....Song 7:4

POOR
p shall not give less ....Ex 30:15
be partial to the *p* ....Lev 19:15
p will never cease ....Deut 15:11
So the *p* have hope ....Job 5:16
and forsaken the *p* ....Job 20:19
I delivered the *p* ....Job 29:12
soul grieved for the *p* ....Job 30:25
p shall eat and be ....Ps 22:26
p man cried out ....Ps 34:6
But I am *p* and needy ....Ps 40:17
goodness for the *p* ....Ps 68:10
Let the *p* and needy ....Ps 74:21
yet He sets the *p* ....Ps 107:41
He raises the *p* ....Ps 113:7
a slack hand becomes *p* ....Prov 10:4
p man is hated even ....Prov 14:20
has mercy on the *p* ....Prov 14:21
who oppresses the *p* ....Prov 14:31
p reproaches his Maker ....Prov 17:5
p man is better than a ....Prov 19:22
p have this in common ....Prov 22:2
Do not rob the *p* ....Prov 22:22
p man who oppresses ....Prov 28:3
remembered that same *p* ....Eccl 9:15
for silver, and the *p* ....Amos 2:6
the alien or the *p* ....Zech 7:10
in particular the *p* ....Zech 11:7
"Blessed are the *p* ....Matt 5:3
p have the gospel ....Matt 11:5
For you have the *p* ....Matt 26:11
your sakes He became *p* ....2 Cor 8:9
should remember the *p* ....Gal 2:10
God not chosen the *p* ....James 2:5
have dishonored the *p* ....James 2:6
wretched, miserable, *p* ....Rev 3:17

PORCIUS FESTUS
Paul stands trial before, Acts 25:1–22

PORTION
For the LORD's *p* ....Deut 32:9
This is the *p* from God ....Job 20:29
O LORD, You are the *p* ....Ps 16:5
heart and my *p* forever ....Ps 73:26

You are my *p* . . . . .Ps 119:57
I will divide Him a *p* . . . . .Is 53:12
rejoice in their *p* . . . . .Is 61:7
The *P* of Jacob is not . . . . Jer 10:16
they have trodden My *p* . . . . Jer 12:10
"The LORD is my *p* . . . . .Lam 3:24
and appoint him his *p* . . . . .Matt 24:51
to give them their *p* . . . . .Luke 12:42
give me the *p* . . . . .Luke 15:12

POSSESS
descendants shall *p* . . . . .Gen 22:17
p the land which . . . . Josh 1:11
By your patience *p* . . . . .Luke 21:19
p his own vessel . . . . .1 Thess 4:4

POSSESSED
much land yet to be *p* . . . . Josh 13:1
"The LORD *p* me at . . . . .Prov 8:22
of the things he *p* . . . . .Acts 4:32

POSSESSING
and yet *p* all things . . . . .2 Cor 6:10

POSSESSION
as an everlasting *p* . . . . .Gen 17:8
the rest of their *p* . . . . .Ps 17:14
they did not gain *p* . . . . .Ps 44:3
of the purchased *p* . . . . .Eph 1:14
and an enduring *p* . . . . .Heb 10:34

POSSESSIONS
is full of Your *p* . . . . .Ps 104:24
kinds of precious *p* . . . . .Prov 1:13
Yes, I had greater *p* . . . . .Eccl 2:7
for he had great *p* . . . . .Mark 10:22
and there wasted his *p* . . . . . . .Luke 15:13
and sold their *p* . . . . .Acts 2:45

POSSIBLE
God all things are *p* . . . . .Matt 19:26
p that the blood . . . . .Heb 10:4

POSTERITY
to preserve a *p* . . . . .Gen 45:7
p shall serve Him . . . . .Ps 22:30
p who approve their . . . . .Ps 49:13

POT
to Aaron, "Take a *p* . . . . .Ex 16:33
from a boiling *p* . . . . .Job 41:20
The refining *p* is for . . . . .Prov 17:3
p that had the manna . . . . .Heb 9:4

POTENTATE
the blessed and only *P* . . . . .1 Tim 6:15

POTI-PHERAH
Egyptian priest of On (Heliopolis), Gen 41:45–50
Father of Asenath, Joseph's wife, Gen 46:20

POTIPHAR
High Egyptian officer, Gen 39:1
Puts Joseph in jail, Gen 39:20

POTS
when we sat by the *p* . . . . .Ex 16:3
also took away the *p* . . . . .Jer 52:18
are regarded as clay *p* . . . . .Lam 4:2

POTSHERD
for himself a *p* . . . . .Job 2:8
is dried up like a *p* . . . . .Ps 22:15
Let the *p* strive with . . . . .Is 45:9

POTTER'S FIELD
Judas's money used for purchase of, Matt 27:7, 8

POUR
p out your heart . . . . .Ps 62:8
P out Your wrath . . . . .Ps 79:6
p My Spirit on your . . . . .Is 44:3
and let the skies *p* . . . . .Is 45:8
P out Your fury . . . . Jer 10:25
that I will *p* out My . . . . Joel 2:28
"And I will *p* . . . . .Zech 12:10
angels, "Go and *p* . . . . .Rev 16:1

POURED
And now my soul is *p* . . . . Job 30:16
I am *p* out like water . . . . .Ps 22:14
grace is *p* upon Your . . . . .Ps 45:2
name is ointment *p* . . . . .Song 1:3
visited You, they *p* . . . . .Is 26:16
strong, because He *p* . . . . .Is 53:12
and My fury will be *p* . . . . .Jer 7:20
His fury is *p* out like . . . . .Nah 1:6
broke the flask and *p* . . . . .Mark 14:3
of God has been *p* . . . . .Rom 5:5
if I am being *p* . . . . .Phil 2:17
I am already being *p* . . . . .2 Tim 4:6
whom He *p* out on us . . . . .Titus 3:6

POVERTY
of the poor is their *p* . . . . .Prov 10:15
but it leads to *p* . . . . .Prov 11:24
P and shame will come . . . . .Prov 13:18
leads only to *p* . . . . .Prov 14:23
lest you come to *p* . . . . .Prov 20:13
give me neither *p* . . . . .Prov 30:8
p put in all the . . . . .Luke 21:4
and their deep *p* . . . . .2 Cor 8:2
p might become rich . . . . .2 Cor 8:9
tribulation, and *p* . . . . .Rev 2:9

POWER
that I may show My *p* . . . . .Ex 9:16
become glorious in *p* . . . . .Ex 15:6
for God has *p* to help . . . . .2 Chr 25:8
him who is without *p* . . . . Job 26:2
p who can understand . . . . Job 26:14
p belongs to God . . . . .Ps 62:11
p Your enemies shall . . . . .Ps 66:3
gives strength and *p* . . . . .Ps 68:35
a king is, there is *p* . . . . .Eccl 8:4
No one has *p* over the . . . . .Eccl 8:8
the strength of His *p* . . . . .Is 40:26
truly I am full of *p* . . . . .Mic 3:8
anger and great in *p* . . . . .Nah 1:3
'Not by might nor by *p* . . . . .Zech 4:6
the kingdom and the *p* . . . . .Matt 6:13
the Son of Man has *p* . . . . .Matt 9:6
who had given such *p* . . . . .Matt 9:8
Scriptures nor the *p* . . . . .Matt 22:29
And the *p* of the Lord . . . . .Luke 5:17
p went out from Him . . . . .Luke 6:19
you are endued with *p* . . . . .Luke 24:49
I have *p* to lay it . . . . John 10:18
not know that I have *p* . . . . John 19:10
"You could have no *p* . . . . John 19:11
you shall receive *p* . . . . .Acts 1:8
as though by our own *p* . . . . .Acts 3:12
man is the great *p* . . . . .Acts 8:10
"Give me this *p* . . . . .Acts 8:19
for it is the *p* . . . . .Rom 1:16
even His eternal *p* . . . . .Rom 1:20
saved it is the *p* . . . . .1 Cor 1:18
Greeks, Christ the *p* . . . . .1 Cor 1:24
be brought under the *p* . . . . .1 Cor 6:12
that the *p* of Christ . . . . .2 Cor 12:9
greatness of His *p* . . . . .Eph 1:19
working of His *p* . . . . .Eph 3:7
the Lord and in the *p* . . . . .Eph 6:10
to His glorious *p* . . . . .Col 1:11
the glory of His *p* . . . . .2 Thess 1:9
of fear, but of *p* . . . . .2 Tim 1:7
by the word of His *p* . . . . .Heb 1:3
p of death, that . . . . .Heb 2:14
but according to the *p* . . . . .Heb 7:16
as His divine *p* . . . . .2 Pet 1:3
dominion and *p* . . . . .Jude 25
to him I will give *p* . . . . .Rev 2:26
glory and honor and *p* . . . . .Rev 4:11
honor and glory and *p* . . . . .Rev 5:13

POWERFUL
of the LORD is *p* . . . . .Ps 29:4
of God is living and *p* . . . . .Heb 4:12

POWERS
principalities and *p* . . . . .Col 2:15
word of God and the *p* . . . . .Heb 6:5

PRAETORIUM
Pilate's, in Jerusalem, Mark 15:16; John 18:28; Matt 27:27
——— Herod's palace at Caesarea, Acts 23:35

PRAISE
your brothers shall *p* . . . . .Gen 49:8
He is your *p* . . . . .Deut 10:21
I will sing *p* to the . . . . .Judg 5:3
p shall be of You in . . . . .Ps 22:25
For *p* from the upright . . . . .Ps 33:1
p shall continually be . . . . .Ps 34:1
the people shall *p* . . . . .Ps 45:17
Whoever offers *p* . . . . .Ps 50:23
P is awaiting You . . . . .Ps 65:1
make His *p* glorious . . . . .Ps 66:2
let all the peoples *p* . . . . .Ps 67:3
Let heaven and earth *p* . . . . .Ps 69:34
p shall be continually . . . . .Ps 71:6
And the heavens will *p* . . . . .Ps 89:5
silent, O God of my *p* . . . . .Ps 109:1
Seven times a day I *p* . . . . .Ps 119:164
All Your works shall *p* . . . . .Ps 145:10
shall speak the *p* . . . . .Ps 145:21
P the LORD . . . . .Ps 148:1
that has breath *p* . . . . .Ps 150:6
Let another man *p* . . . . .Prov 27:2
let her own works *p* . . . . .Prov 31:31
And your gates *P* . . . . .Is 60:18
He makes Jerusalem a *p* . . . . .Is 62:7
For You are my *p* . . . . .Jer 17:14
Me a name of joy, a *p* . . . . .Jer 33:9
give you fame and *p* . . . . .Zeph 3:20
You have perfected *p* . . . . .Matt 21:16
of men more than the *p* . . . . .John 12:43
p is not from men but . . . . .Rom 2:29
Then each one's *p* . . . . .1 Cor 4:5
the brother whose *p* . . . . .2 Cor 8:18
should be to the *p* . . . . .Eph 1:12
to the glory and *p* . . . . .Phil 1:11
I will sing *p* to You . . . . .Heb 2:12
the sacrifice of *p* . . . . .Heb 13:15
and for the *p* of those . . . . .1 Pet 2:14
saying, "*P* our God . . . . .Rev 19:5

PRAISED
who is worthy to be *p* . . . . .2 Sam 22:4
daily He shall be *p* . . . . .Ps 72:15
LORD's name is to be *p* . . . . .Ps 113:3
and greatly to be *p* . . . . .Ps 145:3
where our fathers *p* . . . . .Is 64:11
the Most High and *p* . . . . .Dan 4:34

PRAISES
enthroned in the *p* . . . . .Ps 22:3
it is good to sing *p* . . . . .Ps 147:1
and he *p* her . . . . .Prov 31:28
shall proclaim the *p* . . . . .Is 60:6
you may proclaim the *p* . . . . .1 Pet 2:9

PRAISEWORTHY
if there is anything *p* . . . . .Phil 4:8

PRAISING
they will still be *p* . . . . .Ps 84:4
of the heavenly host *p* . . . . .Luke 2:13
in the temple *p* . . . . .Luke 24:53

PRAY
LORD in ceasing to *p* . . . . .1 Sam 12:23
at noon I will *p* . . . . .Ps 55:17
who hate you, and *p* . . . . .Matt 5:44
"And when you *p* . . . . .Matt 6:5
But you, when you *p* . . . . .Matt 6:6

- manner, therefore, *p* . . . Matt 6:9
- Watch and *p* . . . Matt 26:41
- to the mountain to *p* . . . Mark 6:46
- "Lord, teach us to *p* . . . Luke 11:1
- men always ought to *p* . . . Luke 18:1
- And I will *p* . . . John 14:16
- I do not *p* for the . . . John 17:9
- "I do not *p* for . . . John 17:20
- know what we should *p* . . . Rom 8:26
- I will *p* with the . . . 1 Cor 14:15
- *p* without ceasing . . . 1 Thess 5:17
- Brethren, *p* for us . . . 1 Thess 5:25
- therefore that the men *p* . . . 1 Tim 2:8
- Let him *p* . . . James 5:13
- to one another, and *p* . . . James 5:16
- say that he should *p* . . . 1 John 5:16
- *p* that you may prosper . . . 3 John 2

PRAYED

- Pharisee stood and *p* . . . Luke 18:11
- *p* more earnestly . . . Luke 22:44
- *p* earnestly that it . . . James 5:17

PRAYER

- in heaven their *p* . . . 1 Kin 8:45
- *p* made in this place . . . 2 Chr 7:15
- fear, and restrain *p* . . . Job 15:4
- And my *p* is pure . . . Job 16:17
- *p* would return to my . . . Ps 35:13
- A *p* to the God of my . . . Ps 42:8
- *P* also will be made . . . Ps 72:15
- Let my *p* come before . . . Ps 88:2
- He shall regard the *p* . . . Ps 102:17
- but I give myself to *p* . . . Ps 109:4
- to the LORD, but the *p* . . . Prov 15:8
- not go out except by *p* . . . Matt 17:21
- all night in *p* to God . . . Luke 6:12
- continually to *p* . . . Acts 6:4
- where *p* was . . . Acts 16:13
- steadfastly in *p* . . . Rom 12:12
- to fasting and *p* . . . 1 Cor 7:5
- always with all *p* . . . Eph 6:18
- but in everything by *p* . . . Phil 4:6
- the word of God and *p* . . . 1 Tim 4:5
- And the *p* of faith . . . James 5:15

PRAYERS

- though you make many *p* . . . Is 1:15
- pretense make long *p* . . . Matt 23:14
- fervently for you in *p* . . . Col 4:12
- that supplications, *p* . . . 1 Tim 2:1
- *p* may not be hindered . . . 1 Pet 3:7
- are open to their *p* . . . 1 Pet 3:12
- and watchful in your *p* . . . 1 Pet 4:7
- which are the *p* . . . Rev 5:8

PREACH

- that great city, and *p* . . . Jon 3:2
- time Jesus began to *p* . . . Matt 4:17
- you hear in the ear, *p* . . . Matt 10:27
- *P* the gospel to the . . . Luke 4:18
- *p* the kingdom of God . . . Luke 9:60
- And how shall they *p* . . . Rom 10:15
- *p* Christ crucified . . . 1 Cor 1:23
- is me if I do not *p* . . . 1 Cor 9:16
- I or they, so we *p* . . . 1 Cor 15:11
- For we do not *p* . . . 2 Cor 4:5
- *p* Christ even from . . . Phil 1:15
- *P* the word . . . 2 Tim 4:2

PREACHED

- *p* that people . . . Mark 6:12
- out and *p* everywhere . . . Mark 16:20
- of sins should be *p* . . . Luke 24:47
- *p* Christ to them . . . Acts 8:5
- through this Man is *p* . . . Acts 13:38
- lest, when I have *p* . . . 1 Cor 9:27
- whom we have not *p* . . . 2 Cor 11:4
- than what we have *p* . . . Gal 1:8
- in truth, Christ is *p* . . . Phil 1:18
- the gospel was *p* . . . Heb 4:2
- also He went and *p* . . . 1 Pet 3:19

PREACHER

- The words of the *P* . . . Eccl 1:1
- they hear without a *p* . . . Rom 10:14
- I was appointed a *p* . . . 1 Tim 2:7
- of eight people, a *p* . . . 2 Pet 2:5

PREACHES

- the Jesus whom Paul *p* . . . Acts 19:13
- *p* another Jesus whom . . . 2 Cor 11:4
- *p* any other gospel . . . Gal 1:9
- *p* the faith which he . . . Gal 1:23

PREACHING

- *p* Jesus as the . . . Acts 5:42
- to my gospel and the *p* . . . Rom 16:25
- not risen, then our *p* . . . 1 Cor 15:14

PRECEPT

- *p* must be upon *p* . . . Is 28:10

PRECEPTS

- and commanded them *p* . . . Neh 9:14
- all His *p* are sure . . . Ps 111:7
- us to keep Your *p* . . . Ps 119:4
- how I love Your *p* . . . Ps 119:159
- and kept all his *p* . . . Jer 35:18

PRECIOUS

- because my life was *p* . . . 1 Sam 26:21
- *P* in the sight of the . . . Ps 116:15
- How *p* also are Your . . . Ps 139:17
- She is more *p* than . . . Prov 3:15
- Since you were *p* . . . Is 43:4
- *p* things shall not . . . Is 44:9
- if you take out the *p* . . . Jer 15:19
- The *p* sons of Zion . . . Lam 4:2
- farmer waits for the *p* . . . James 5:7
- more *p* than gold . . . 1 Pet 1:7
- who believe, He is *p* . . . 1 Pet 2:7
- *p* in the sight of . . . 1 Pet 3:4

PREDESTINED

- He foreknew, He also *p* . . . Rom 8:29
- having *p* us to . . . Eph 1:5
- inheritance, being *p* . . . Eph 1:11

PREEMINENCE

- He may have the *p* . . . Col 1:18
- loves to have the *p* . . . 3 John 9

PREPARATION

- Now it was the *P* . . . John 19:14
- your feet with the *p* . . . Eph 6:15

PREPARE

- *p* your hearts for the . . . 1 Sam 7:3
- *p* a table before me in . . . Ps 23:5
- *p* mercy and truth . . . Ps 61:7
- *P* the way of the LORD . . . Is 40:3
- *P* the way for the . . . Is 62:10
- *P* the way of the LORD . . . Mark 1:3
- will, and did not *p* . . . Luke 12:47
- *p* a place for you . . . John 14:2

PREPARED

- place which I have *p* . . . Ex 23:20
- You *p* room for it . . . Ps 80:9
- When He *p* the heavens . . . Prov 8:27
- for the LORD has *p* . . . Zeph 1:7
- for whom it is *p* . . . Matt 20:23
- which You have *p* . . . Luke 2:31
- mercy, which He had *p* . . . Rom 9:23
- things which God has *p* . . . 1 Cor 2:9
- Now He who has *p* . . . 2 Cor 5:5
- *p* beforehand that we . . . Eph 2:10
- God, for He has *p* . . . Heb 11:16

PRESENCE

- themselves from the *p* . . . Gen 3:8
- went out from the *p* . . . Gen 4:16
- we die in your *p* . . . Gen 47:15
- *P* will go with you . . . Ex 33:14
- and honor the *p* . . . Lev 19:32
- afraid in any man's *p* . . . Deut 1:17
- am terrified at His *p* . . . Job 23:15
- *p* is fullness of joy . . . Ps 16:11
- shall dwell in Your *p* . . . Ps 140:13
- not tremble at My *p* . . . Jer 5:22
- shall shake at My *p* . . . Ezek 38:20
- Be silent in the *p* . . . Zeph 1:7
- and drank in Your *p* . . . Luke 13:26
- full of joy in Your *p* . . . Acts 2:28
- but his bodily *p* . . . 2 Cor 10:10
- obeyed, not as in my *p* . . . Phil 2:12

PRESENT

- we are all *p* before . . . Acts 10:33
- evil is *p* with me . . . Rom 7:21
- *p* your bodies a living . . . Rom 12:1
- or death, or things *p* . . . 1 Cor 3:22
- absent in body but *p* . . . 1 Cor 5:3
- not only when I am *p* . . . Gal 4:18
- that He might *p* . . . Eph 5:27
- to *p* yourself . . . 2 Tim 2:15
- *p* you faultless . . . Jude 24

PRESENTED

- treasures, they *p* . . . Matt 2:11
- For just as you *p* . . . Rom 6:19

PRESERVE

- before you to *p* life . . . Gen 45:5
- You shall *p* me from . . . Ps 32:7
- O LORD, You *p* man and . . . Ps 36:6
- He shall *p* your soul . . . Ps 121:7
- The LORD shall *p* . . . Ps 121:8
- children, I will *p* . . . Jer 49:11
- pardon those whom I *p* . . . Jer 50:20
- loses his life will *p* . . . Luke 17:33
- every evil work and *p* . . . 2 Tim 4:18

PRESERVED

- and my life is *p* . . . Gen 32:30
- soul, and body be *p* . . . 1 Thess 5:23

PRESERVES

- For the LORD *p* the . . . Ps 31:23
- *p* the souls of His . . . Ps 97:10
- The LORD *p* the simple . . . Ps 116:6
- who guards his mouth *p* . . . Prov 13:3
- he who keeps his way *p* . . . Prov 16:17

PRESS

- I *p* toward the goal . . . Phil 3:14

PRESSED

- *p* her virgin bosom . . . Ezek 23:8
- We are hard *p* on every . . . 2 Cor 4:8
- For I am hard *p* . . . Phil 1:23

PRETENSE

- whole heart, but in *p* . . . Jer 3:10
- *p* make long prayers . . . Matt 23:14

PREVAIL

- no man shall *p* . . . 1 Sam 2:9
- our tongue we will *p* . . . Ps 12:4
- but they shall not *p* . . . Jer 1:19
- of Hades shall not *p* . . . Matt 16:18

PREVAILED

- hand, that Israel *p* . . . Ex 17:11
- with the Angel and *p* . . . Hos 12:4
- grew mightily and *p* . . . Acts 19:20

PREY

- the mountains of *p* . . . Ps 76:4
- has not given us as *p* . . . Ps 124:6
- Shall the *p* be taken . . . Is 49:24
- evil makes himself a *p* . . . Is 59:15
- shall no longer be a *p* . . . Ezek 34:22
- when he has no *p* . . . Amos 3:4

PRICE

- be weighed for its *p* . . . Job 28:15
- a fool the purchase *p* . . . Prov 17:16
- one pearl of great *p* . . . Matt 13:46
- back part of the *p* . . . Acts 5:3
- you were bought at a *p* . . . 1 Cor 6:20

PUNISHED
You our God have *p* ...Ezra 9:13
because He has not *p* ...Job 35:15
p them often in every ...Acts 26:11
These shall be *p* ...2 Thess 1:9

PUNISHMENT
p is greater than I ...Gen 4:13
you do in the day of *p* ...Is 10:3
p they shall be cast ...Jer 8:12
p they shall perish ...Jer 10:15
a man for the *p* ...Lam 3:39
The *p* of the iniquity ...Lam 4:6
days of *p* have come ...Hos 9:7
not turn away its *p* ...Amos 1:3
into everlasting *p* ...Matt 25:46
p which was inflicted ...2 Cor 2:6
Of how much worse *p* ...Heb 10:29
sent by him for the *p* ...1 Pet 2:14
the unjust under *p* ...2 Pet 2:9

PURCHASED
of God could be *p* ...Acts 8:20
of the *p* possession ...Eph 1:14

PURE
a mercy seat of *p* gold ...Ex 25:17
Can a man be more *p* ...Job 4:17
if you were *p* and ...Job 8:6
'My doctrine is *p* ...Job 11:4
that he could be *p* ...Job 15:14
the heavens are not *p* ...Job 15:15
the stars are not *p* ...Job 25:5
of the LORD are *p* ...Ps 12:6
will show Yourself *p* ...Ps 18:26
To such as are *p* ...Ps 73:1
of the *p* are pleasant ...Prov 15:26
ways of a man are *p* ...Prov 16:2
my heart clean, I am *p* ...Prov 20:9
but as for the *p* ...Prov 21:8
a generation that is *p* ...Prov 30:12
Shall I count *p* ...Mic 6:11
things indeed are *p* ...Rom 14:20
whatever things are *p* ...Phil 4:8
keep yourself *p* ...1 Tim 5:22
p all things are *p* ...Titus 1:15
above is first *p* ...James 3:17
babes, desire the *p* ...1 Pet 2:2
just as He is *p* ...1 John 3:3

PURGE
P me with hyssop ...Ps 51:7
p them as gold and ...Mal 3:3

PURGED
away, and your sin *p* ...Is 6:7
He had by Himself *p* ...Heb 1:3

PURIFICATION
for the water of *p* ...Num 19:9
with the water of *p* ...Num 31:23

PURIFIED
earth, *p* seven times ...Ps 12:6
all things are *p* ...Heb 9:22
Since you have *p* ...1 Pet 1:22

PURIFIES
hope in Him *p* himself ...1 John 3:3

PURIFY
p the sons of Levi ...Mal 3:3
and *p* your hearts ...James 4:8

PURIFYING
thus *p* all foods ...Mark 7:19
p their hearts by ...Acts 15:9
sanctifies for the *p* ...Heb 9:13

PURIM
called these days *P* ...Esth 9:26

PURITY
be delivered by the *p* ...Job 22:30
He who loves *p* of ...Prov 22:11
by *p*, by knowledge ...2 Cor 6:6
spirit, in faith, in *p* ...1 Tim 4:12

PURPLE
who was clothed in *p* ...Luke 16:19
they put on Him a *p* ...John 19:2
She was a seller of *p* ...Acts 16:14

PURPOSE
and fulfill all your *p* ...Ps 20:4
A time for every *p* ...Eccl 3:1
p that is purposed ...Is 14:26
But for this *p* I came ...John 12:27
by the determined *p* ...Acts 2:23
them all that with *p* ...Acts 11:23
to the eternal *p* ...Eph 3:11
Now the *p* of the ...1 Tim 1:5
to fulfill His *p* ...Rev 17:17

PURPOSED
For the LORD had *p* ...2 Sam 17:14
LORD of hosts has *p* ...Is 23:9
But Daniel *p* in his ...Dan 1:8
pleasure which He *p* ...Eph 1:9

PURSUE
And will You *p* dry ...Job 13:25
p my honor as the wind ...Job 30:15
The sword shall *p* ...Jer 48:2
but their hearts *p* ...Ezek 33:31
Let us know, let us *p* ...Hos 6:3
p righteousness ...Rom 9:30
P love, and desire ...1 Cor 14:1
p righteousness ...1 Tim 6:11
him seek peace and *p* ...1 Pet 3:11

PURSUES
Evil *p* sinners ...Prov 13:21
flee when no one *p* ...Prov 28:1

PUT
Also He has *p* eternity ...Eccl 3:11
pride He is able to *p* down ...Dan 4:37
what you will *p* on ...Matt 6:25
p my hand into His ...John 20:25
But *p* on the Lord ...Rom 13:14

QUAIL
and it brought *q* ...Num 11:31
and He brought *q* ...Ps 105:40

QUAKED
the whole mountain *q* ...Ex 19:18
and the earth *q* ...Matt 27:51

QUAKES
The earth *q* before ...Joel 2:10

QUALIFIED
the Father who has *q* ...Col 1:12

QUARREL
see how he seeks a *q* ...2 Kin 5:7
any fool can start a *q* ...Prov 20:3
He will not *q* nor cry ...Matt 12:19
of the Lord must not *q* ...2 Tim 2:24

QUARRELSOME
but gentle, not *q* ...1 Tim 3:3

QUEEN
Q Vashti also made a ...Esth 1:9
stands the *q* in gold ...Ps 45:9
burn incense to the *q* ...Jer 44:17
The *q* of the South ...Matt 12:42
under Candace the *q* ...Acts 8:27
heart, 'I sit as *q* ...Rev 18:7

QUEENS
There are sixty *q* ...Song 6:8
q your nursing mothers ...Is 49:23

QUENCH
Many waters cannot *q* ...Song 8:7
so that no one can *q* ...Jer 4:4
flax He will not *q* ...Matt 12:20
q all the fiery ...Eph 6:16
Do not *q* the Spirit ...1 Thess 5:19

QUENCHED
LORD, the fire was *q* ...Num 11:2
they were *q* like a ...Ps 118:12
their fire is not *q* ...Is 66:24
that shall never be *q* ...Mark 9:43
and the fire is not *q* ...Mark 9:44
q the violence of fire ...Heb 11:34

QUESTIONS
test him with hard *q* ...1 Kin 10:1
and asking them *q* ...Luke 2:46
market, asking no *q* ...1 Cor 10:25

QUICK-TEMPERED
q man acts foolishly ...Prov 14:17
not self-willed, not *q* ...Titus 1:7

QUICKLY
have turned aside *q* ...Ex 32:8
with your adversary *q* ...Matt 5:25
"What you do, do *q* ...John 13:27
Behold, I am coming *q* ...Rev 3:11
"Surely I am coming *q* ...Rev 22:20

QUIET
lain still and been *q* ...Job 3:13
'Take heed, and be *q* ...Is 7:4
earth is at rest and *q* ...Is 14:7
gladness, He will *q* ...Zeph 3:17
warned him to be *q* ...Mark 10:48
aspire to lead a *q* ...1 Thess 4:11
we may lead a *q* and ...1 Tim 2:2
a gentle and *q* spirit ...1 Pet 3:4

QUIETED
calmed and *q* my soul ...Ps 131:2
the city clerk had *q* ...Acts 19:35

QUIETNESS
will give peace and *q* ...1 Chr 22:9
When He gives *q* ...Job 34:29
a handful with *q* ...Eccl 4:6
in *q* and confidence ...Is 30:15
of righteousness, *q* ...Is 32:17
that they work in *q* ...2 Thess 3:12

QUIETS
q the earth by the ...Job 37:17

QUIVER
q rattles against him ...Job 39:23
the man who has his *q* ...Ps 127:5
q He has hidden Me ...Is 49:2
Their *q* is like an ...Jer 5:16

RAAMSES
Treasure city built by Hebrew slaves, Ex 1:11

RABBAH
Capital of Ammon, Amos 1:14
Besieged by Joab; defeated and enslaved by David, 2 Sam 12:26–31
Destruction of, foretold, Jer 49:2, 3

RABBI
be called by men, '*R* ...Matt 23:7
do not be called '*R* ...Matt 23:8

RABBONI
Mary addresses Christ as, John 20:16

RABSARIS
Title applied to:
Assyrian officials sent by Sennacherib, 2 Kin 18:17
Babylonian prince, Jer 39:3, 13

RABSHAKEH
Sent by king of Assyria to threaten Hezekiah, 2 Kin 18:17–37; Is 36:2–22
The Lord sends rumor to take him away, 2 Kin 19:6–8; Is 37:6–8

RACA
to his brother, '*R* .... Matt 5:22

RACE
man to run its *r* .... Ps 19:5
r is not to the swift .... Eccl 9:11
who run in a *r* all run .... 1 Cor 9:24
I have finished the *r* .... 2 Tim 4:7
with endurance the *r* .... Heb 12:1

RACHEL
Laban's younger daughter; Jacob's favorite wife, Gen 29:28–30
Supports her husband's position, Gen 31:14–16
Mother of Joseph and Benjamin, Gen 30:22–25
Prophecy concerning; quoted, Jer 31:15; Matt 2:18

RAGE
Disperse the *r* of your .... Job 40:11
Why do the nations *r* .... Ps 2:1
'Why did the nations *r* .... Acts 4:25

RAHAB
Prostitute in Jericho; helps Joshua's spies, Josh 2:1–21
Spared in battle, Josh 6:17–25
Mentioned in the NT, Matt 1:5; Heb 11:31; James 2:25
——— Used figuratively of Egypt, Ps 87:4

RAIN
had not caused it to *r* .... Gen 2:5
And the *r* was on the .... Gen 7:12
He gives *r* on the .... Job 5:10
to the gentle *r* .... Job 37:6
sent a plentiful *r* .... Ps 68:9
clouds, who prepares *r* .... Ps 147:8
snow in summer and *r* .... Prov 26:1
r which leaves no food .... Prov 28:3
not return after the *r* .... Eccl 12:2
the *r* is over and gone .... Song 2:11
our God, who gives *r* .... Jer 5:24
I will *r* down on him .... Ezek 38:22
given you the former *r* .... Joel 2:23
there will be no *r* .... Zech 14:17
the good, and sends *r* .... Matt 5:45
and the *r* descended .... Matt 7:25
He did good, gave us *r* .... Acts 14:17
r that often comes .... Heb 6:7
that it would not *r* .... James 5:17
and the heaven gave *r* .... James 5:18

RAINBOW
I set My *r* in the .... Gen 9:13
and there was a *r* .... Rev 4:3

RAINED
had *r* down manna on .... Ps 78:24
r fire and brimstone .... Luke 17:29

RAISE
third day He will *r* .... Hos 6:2
that God is able to *r* .... Matt 3:9
in three days I will *r* .... John 2:19
and I will *r* him up at .... John 6:40
Lord and will also *r* .... 1 Cor 6:14
and the Lord will *r* .... James 5:15

RAISED
this purpose I have *r* .... Ex 9:16
be killed, and be *r* .... Matt 16:21
whom God *r* up .... Acts 2:24
just as Christ was *r* .... Rom 6:4
Spirit of Him who *r* .... Rom 8:11
And God both *r* up the .... 1 Cor 6:14
"How are the dead *r* .... 1 Cor 15:35
and the dead will be *r* .... 1 Cor 15:52
and *r* us up together .... Eph 2:6
then you were *r* .... Col 3:1

RAISES
r the poor out of the .... Ps 113:7
r those who are bowed .... Ps 146:8
For as the Father *r* .... John 5:21
but in God who *r* .... 2 Cor 1:9

RAM
r which had two horns .... Dan 8:3

RAMAH
Fortress built, 1 Kin 15:17–22
Samuel's headquarters, 1 Sam 7:15, 17
David flees to, 1 Sam 19:18–23

RAMOTH GILEAD
City of refuge east of Jordan, Deut 4:43; Josh 20:8; 1 Chr 6:80
Site of Ahab's fatal conflict with Syrians, 1 Kin 22:1–39

RAMS
the sweet aroma of *r* .... Ps 66:15
r of Nebaioth shall .... Is 60:7

RANSOM
r would not help you .... Job 36:18
nor give to God a *r* .... Ps 49:7
The *r* of a man's life .... Prov 13:8
"I will *r* them from .... Hos 13:14
to give His life a *r* .... Mark 10:45
who gave Himself a *r* .... 1 Tim 2:6

RANSOMED
and the *r* of the LORD .... Is 35:10
redeemed Jacob, and *r* .... Jer 31:11

RARE
of the LORD was *r* .... 1 Sam 3:1
make a mortal more *r* .... Is 13:12

RASH
Do not be *r* with your .... Eccl 5:2

RASHLY
so that he spoke *r* .... Ps 106:33
and do nothing *r* .... Acts 19:36

RAVEN
food for the *r* .... Job 38:41
and black as a *r* .... Song 5:11

RAVENS
and to the young *r* .... Ps 147:9
Consider the *r* .... Luke 12:24

RAVISHED
You have *r* my heart .... Song 4:9
r the women in Zion .... Lam 5:11

REACHED
earth, and its top *r* .... Gen 28:12
For her sins have *r* .... Rev 18:5

REACHING
r forward to those .... Phil 3:13

READ
"Have you never *r* .... Matt 21:42
day, and stood up to *r* .... Luke 4:16
hearts, known and *r* .... 2 Cor 3:2
when Moses is *r* .... 2 Cor 3:15
when this epistle is *r* .... Col 4:16

READINESS
the word with all *r* .... Acts 17:11
that as there was a *r* .... 2 Cor 8:11

READING
r the prophet Isaiah .... Acts 8:30
give attention to *r* .... 1 Tim 4:13

READS
that he may run who *r* .... Hab 2:2
Blessed is he who *r* .... Rev 1:3

READY
"The LORD was *r* .... Is 38:20
and those who were *r* .... Matt 25:10
"Lord, I am *r* .... Luke 22:33
and being *r* to punish .... 2 Cor 10:6
Be *r* in season and out .... 2 Tim 4:2
and always be *r* .... 1 Pet 3:15

REAP
in tears shall *r* .... Ps 126:5
r the whirlwind .... Hos 8:7
they neither sow nor *r* .... Matt 6:26
you knew that I *r* .... Matt 25:26
that he will also *r* .... Gal 6:7
due season we shall *r* .... Gal 6:9

REAPED
wheat but *r* thorns .... Jer 12:13
you have *r* iniquity .... Hos 10:13

REAPER
r does not fill his .... Ps 129:7

REAPERS
I will say to the *r* .... Matt 13:30
r are the angels .... Matt 13:39

REAPING
r what I did not .... Luke 19:22

REAPS
One sows and another *r* .... John 4:37

REASON
out wisdom and the *r* .... Eccl 7:25
Come now, and let us *r* .... Is 1:18
faith, why do you *r* .... Matt 16:8
words of truth and *r* .... Acts 26:25
who asks you a *r* .... 1 Pet 3:15

REASONED
for three Sabbaths *r* .... Acts 17:2
r about righteousness .... Acts 24:25

REBEKAH
Great-niece of Abraham, Gen 22:20–23
Becomes Isaac's wife, Gen 24:15–67
Mother of Esau and Jacob, Gen 25:21–28
Encourages Jacob to deceive Isaac, then to flee, Gen 27:1–29, 42–46

REBEL
Only do not *r* .... Num 14:9
Will you *r* against the .... Neh 2:19
There are those who *r* .... Job 24:13
and they did not *r* .... Ps 105:28
if you refuse and *r* .... Is 1:20

REBELLION
r is as the sin .... 1 Sam 15:23
For he adds *r* to his .... Job 34:37
evil man seeks only *r* .... Prov 17:11
you have taught *r* .... Jer 28:16
hearts as in the *r* .... Heb 3:8
and perished in the *r* .... Jude 11

REBELLIOUS
r exalt themselves .... Ps 66:7
but the *r* dwell in a .... Ps 68:6
day long to a *r* people .... Is 65:2
a defiant and *r* heart .... Jer 5:23
their princes are *r* .... Hos 9:15

REBUILD
God, to *r* its ruins .... Ezra 9:9
tombs, that I may *r* .... Neh 2:5
r it as in the days of .... Amos 9:11

REBUKE
He will surely *r* .... Job 13:10
astonished at His *r* .... Job 26:11
they perish at the *r* .... Ps 80:16
At Your *r* they fled .... Ps 104:7
And let him *r* me .... Ps 141:5
Turn at my *r* .... Prov 1:23
r a wise man .... Prov 9:8
R is more effective .... Prov 17:10
r is better than love .... Prov 27:5
better to hear the *r* .... Eccl 7:5
r the oppressor .... Is 1:17
sake I have suffered *r* .... Jer 15:15

r strong nations . . . . Mic 4:3
sins against you, *r* . . . . Luke 17:3
r Your disciples . . . . Luke 19:39
Do not *r* an older man . . . . 1 Tim 5:1
who are sinning *r* . . . . 1 Tim 5:20
r them sharply . . . . Titus 1:13
"The Lord *r* you . . . . Jude 9
As many as I love, I *r* . . . . Rev 3:19

REBUKED
r the winds and the . . . . Matt 8:26
r their unbelief . . . . Mark 16:14
when you are *r* by Him . . . . Heb 12:5
but he was *r* for his . . . . 2 Pet 2:16

REBUKES
with *r* You correct . . . . Ps 39:11
r a wicked man . . . . Prov 9:7
ear that hears the *r* . . . . Prov 15:31
r a man will find more . . . . Prov 28:23

RECEIVE
He shall *r* blessing . . . . Ps 24:5
r us graciously . . . . Hos 14:2
you are willing to *r* . . . . Matt 11:14
believing, you will *r* . . . . Matt 21:22
and His own did not *r* . . . . John 1:11
"I do not *r* honor . . . . John 5:41
will come again and *r* . . . . John 14:3
the world cannot *r* . . . . John 14:17
Ask, and you will *r* . . . . John 16:24
"*R* the Holy Spirit . . . . John 20:22
"Lord Jesus, *r* . . . . Acts 7:59
r the Holy Spirit . . . . Acts 19:2
R one who is weak . . . . Rom 14:1
that each one may *r* . . . . 2 Cor 5:10
r the grace of God in . . . . 2 Cor 6:1
r the Spirit by the . . . . Gal 3:2
R him therefore in the . . . . Phil 2:29
suppose that he will *r* . . . . James 1:7
whatever we ask we *r* . . . . 1 John 3:22

RECEIVED
r your consolation . . . . Luke 6:24
in your lifetime you *r* . . . . Luke 16:25
But as many as *r* . . . . John 1:12
for God has *r* him . . . . Rom 14:3
For I *r* from the Lord . . . . 1 Cor 11:23
have *r* Christ Jesus . . . . Col 2:6
r up in glory . . . . 1 Tim 3:16
For He *r* from God the . . . . 2 Pet 1:17

RECEIVES
r correction is prudent . . . . Prov 15:5
r you *r* Me . . . . Matt 10:40
r one little child . . . . Matt 18:5
and whoever *r* Me . . . . Mark 9:37

RECHAB
Assassin of Ishbosheth, 2 Sam 4:2, 6
——— Father of Jehonadab, founder of the Rechabites, 2 Kin 10:15–23
Related to the Kenites, 1 Chr 2:55

RECHABITES
Kenite clan fathered by Rechab, committed to nomadic life, Jer 35:1–19

RECOMPENSE
He will accept no *r* . . . . Prov 6:35
not say, "I will *r* . . . . Prov 20:22
days of *r* have come . . . . Hos 9:7

RECOMPENSED
of my hands He has *r* . . . . 2 Sam 22:21
the LORD has *r* me . . . . 2 Sam 22:25

RECONCILE
and that He might *r* . . . . Eph 2:16
r all things to . . . . Col 1:20

RECONCILED
First be *r* to your . . . . Matt 5:24
were enemies we were *r* . . . . Rom 5:10
Christ's behalf, be *r* . . . . 2 Cor 5:20

RECONCILIATION
now received the *r* . . . . Rom 5:11
to us the word of *r* . . . . 2 Cor 5:19

RECONCILING
cast away is the *r* . . . . Rom 11:15
God was in Christ *r* . . . . 2 Cor 5:19

RED
the first came out *r* . . . . Gen 25:25
though they are *r* . . . . Is 1:18
Why is Your apparel *r* . . . . Is 63:2
for the sky is *r* . . . . Matt 16:2

RED SEA
Divided for Israelites, Ex 14:15–31
Boundary of Promised Land, Ex 23:31

REDEEM
man you shall surely *r* . . . . Num 18:15
in our power to *r* them . . . . Neh 5:5
In famine He shall *r* . . . . Job 5:20
R me from the hand of . . . . Job 6:23
can by any means *r* . . . . Ps 49:7
But God will *r* my soul . . . . Ps 49:15
r their life from . . . . Ps 72:14
And He shall *r* Israel . . . . Ps 130:8
all that it cannot *r* . . . . Is 50:2
I will *r* them from . . . . Hos 13:14
was going to *r* Israel . . . . Luke 24:21
r those who were . . . . Gal 4:5
us, that He might *r* . . . . Titus 2:14

REDEEMED
people whom You have *r* . . . . Ex 15:13
r them from the hand . . . . Ps 106:10
Let the *r* of the LORD . . . . Ps 107:2
r shall walk there . . . . Is 35:9
sea a road for the *r* . . . . Is 51:10
and you shall be *r* . . . . Is 52:3
and *r* His people . . . . Luke 1:68
Christ has *r* us from . . . . Gal 3:13
that you were not *r* . . . . 1 Pet 1:18
were slain, and have *r* . . . . Rev 5:9
These were *r* from . . . . Rev 14:4

REDEEMER
For I know that my *R* . . . . Job 19:25
Most High God their *R* . . . . Ps 78:35
for their *R* is mighty . . . . Prov 23:11
the LORD and your *R* . . . . Is 41:14
R will come to Zion . . . . Is 59:20
our *R* from Everlasting . . . . Is 63:16
Their *R* is strong . . . . Jer 50:34

REDEEMING
r the time . . . . Eph 5:16

REDEMPTION
For the *r* of their . . . . Ps 49:8
with Him is abundant *r* . . . . Ps 130:7
r is yours to buy it . . . . Jer 32:7
those who looked for *r* . . . . Luke 2:38
your *r* draws near . . . . Luke 21:28
grace through the *r* . . . . Rom 3:24
the adoption, the *r* . . . . Rom 8:23
sanctification and *r* . . . . 1 Cor 1:30
In Him we have *r* . . . . Eph 1:7
for the day of *r* . . . . Eph 4:30
obtained eternal *r* . . . . Heb 9:12

REED
r He will not break . . . . Is 42:3
r shaken by the wind . . . . Matt 11:7
on the head with a *r* . . . . Mark 15:19

REEDS
r flourish without . . . . Job 8:11
the beasts of the *r* . . . . Ps 68:30

REFINED
where gold is *r* . . . . Job 28:1
us as silver is *r* . . . . Ps 66:10

REFINER
He will sit as a *r* . . . . Mal 3:3

REFRAIN
R from meddling with . . . . 2 Chr 35:21
who have no right to *r* . . . . 1 Cor 9:6
good days, let him *r* . . . . 1 Pet 3:10

REFRESH
bread, that you may *r* . . . . Gen 18:5
r my heart in the Lord . . . . Philem 20

REFRESHED
of God, and may be *r* . . . . Rom 15:32
r my spirit and yours . . . . 1 Cor 16:18
his spirit has been *r* . . . . 2 Cor 7:13
for he often *r* . . . . 2 Tim 1:16

REFUGE
six cities of *r* . . . . Num 35:6
eternal God is your *r* . . . . Deut 33:27
you have come for *r* . . . . Ruth 2:12
but the LORD is his *r* . . . . Ps 14:6
God is our *r* and . . . . Ps 46:1
wings I will make my *r* . . . . Ps 57:1
God is a *r* for us . . . . Ps 62:8
You are my strong *r* . . . . Ps 71:7
who have fled for *r* . . . . Heb 6:18

REFUSE
r the evil and choose . . . . Is 7:15
through deceit they *r* . . . . Jer 9:6
hear or whether they *r* . . . . Ezek 2:5
See that you do not *r* . . . . Heb 12:25

REFUSES
My soul *r* to touch . . . . Job 6:7
And if he *r* to hear . . . . Matt 18:17

REGARD
r the rich more than . . . . Job 34:19
r iniquity in my heart . . . . Ps 66:18
r the prayer of the . . . . Ps 102:17
did not fear God nor *r* . . . . Luke 18:2

REGARDED
my hand and no one *r* . . . . Prov 1:24
r the lowly state . . . . Luke 1:48

REGARDS
r a rebuke will be . . . . Prov 13:18
He no longer *r* them . . . . Lam 4:16

REGENERATION
to you, that in the *r* . . . . Matt 19:28
the washing of *r* . . . . Titus 3:5

REGISTERED
So all went to be *r* . . . . Luke 2:3
firstborn who are *r* . . . . Heb 12:23

REHOBOAM
Son and successor of Solomon; refuses reform, 1 Kin 11:43—12:15
Ten tribes revolt against, 1 Kin 12:16–24
Reigns over Judah 17 years, 1 Kin 14:21–31; 2 Chr 11:5–23
Apostasizes, then repents, 2 Chr 12:1–16

REHOBOTH
Name of a well dug by Isaac, Gen 26:22

REIGN
but a king shall *r* . . . . 1 Sam 12:12
hypocrite should not *r* . . . . Job 34:30
so the LORD will *r* . . . . Mic 4:7
And He will *r* . . . . Luke 1:33
not have this man to *r* . . . . Luke 19:14
righteousness will *r* . . . . Rom 5:17
so grace might *r* . . . . Rom 5:21
do not let sin *r* . . . . Rom 6:12
For He must *r* till He . . . . 1 Cor 15:25
and we shall *r* on the . . . . Rev 5:10
of Christ, and shall *r* . . . . Rev 20:6

REIGNED
so that as sin *r* . . . . Rom 5:21
You have *r* as kings . . . . 1 Cor 4:8
And they lived and *r* . . . . Rev 20:4

REIGNS
God *r* over the nations ....Ps 47:8
The LORD *r* ....Ps 93:1
to Zion, "Your God *r* ....Is 52:7
Lord God Omnipotent *r* ....Rev 19:6

REJECT
will these people *r* ....Num 14:11
r all those who stray ....Ps 119:118
"All too well you *r* ....Mark 7:9
R a divisive man ....Titus 3:10

REJECTED
r has become the chief ....Ps 118:22
He is despised and *r* ....Is 53:3
Israel has *r* the ....Hos 8:3
r has become the chief ....Matt 21:42
many things and be *r* ....Luke 17:25
This Moses whom they *r* ....Acts 7:35
to a living stone, *r* ....1 Pet 2:4
r has become the chief ....1 Pet 2:7

REJECTION
you shall know My *r* ....Num 14:34

REJECTS
he who *r* Me *r* ....Luke 10:16
r this does not reject ....1 Thess 4:8

REJOICE
so the LORD will *r* ....Deut 28:63
let the field *r* ....1 Chr 16:32
and let Your saints *r* ....2 Chr 6:41
r who put their trust ....Ps 5:11
people, let Jacob *r* ....Ps 14:7
R in the LORD ....Ps 33:1
mutual confusion who *r* ....Ps 35:26
The righteous shall *r* ....Ps 58:10
of Your wings I will *r* ....Ps 63:7
But the king shall *r* ....Ps 63:11
Let them *r* before God ....Ps 68:3
In Your name they *r* ....Ps 89:16
Let the heavens *r* ....Ps 96:11
Let the earth *r* ....Ps 97:1
righteous see it and *r* ....Ps 107:42
we will *r* and be glad ....Ps 118:24
who *r* in doing evil ....Prov 2:14
be blessed, and *r* ....Prov 5:18
she shall *r* in time to ....Prov 31:25
R, O young man ....Eccl 11:9
We will be glad and *r* ....Song 1:4
among men shall *r* ....Is 29:19
I will greatly *r* ....Is 61:10
My servants shall *r* ....Is 65:13
your heart shall *r* ....Is 66:14
Yes, I will *r* ....Jer 32:41
Do not *r* over me ....Mic 7:8
He will *r* over you ....Zeph 3:17
do not *r* in this ....Luke 10:20
loved Me, you would *r* ....John 14:28
but the world will *r* ....John 16:20
and your heart will *r* ....John 16:22
R with those who ....Rom 12:15
and in this I *r* ....Phil 1:18
faith, I am glad and *r* ....Phil 2:17
R in the Lord always ....Phil 4:4
R always ....1 Thess 5:16
yet believing, you *r* ....1 Pet 1:8

REJOICED
for good as He *r* ....Deut 30:9
for my heart *r* ....Eccl 2:10
and my spirit has *r* ....Luke 1:47
In that hour Jesus *r* ....Luke 10:21
Your father Abraham *r* ....John 8:56
But I *r* in the Lord ....Phil 4:10

REJOICES
glad, and my glory *r* ....Ps 16:9
but *r* in the truth ....1 Cor 13:6

REJOICING
His works with *r* ....Ps 107:22
The voice of *r* and ....Ps 118:15
for they are the *r* ....Ps 119:111
come again with *r* ....Ps 126:6
r in His inhabited ....Prov 8:31
he went on his way *r* ....Acts 8:39
yet always *r* ....2 Cor 6:10
or joy, or crown of *r* ....1 Thess 2:19
confidence and the *r* ....Heb 3:6

RELEASE
do you want me to *r* ....Matt 27:17
and power to *r* You ....John 19:10
"*R* the four angels ....Rev 9:14

RELENT
sworn and will not *r* ....Ps 110:4
and will not *r* ....Jer 4:28
then the LORD will *r* ....Jer 26:13
if He will turn and *r* ....Joel 2:14
sworn and will not *r* ....Heb 7:21

RELENTED
So the LORD *r* from the ....Ex 32:14
the LORD looked and *r* ....1 Chr 21:15
and God *r* from the ....Jon 3:10

RELIEF
saw that there was *r* ....Ex 8:15
that I may find *r* ....Job 32:20

RELIEVE
of my lips would *r* ....Job 16:5
r those who are really ....1 Tim 5:16

RELIGION
about their own *r* ....Acts 25:19
in self-imposed *r* ....Col 2:23
heart, this one's *r* ....James 1:26
and undefiled *r* ....James 1:27

RELIGIOUS
things you are very *r* ....Acts 17:22
you thinks he is *r* ....James 1:26

RELY
name of the LORD and *r* ....Is 50:10
You *r* on your sword ....Ezek 33:26

REMAIN
shall let none of it *r* ....Ex 12:10
r angry forever ....Jer 3:5
and this city shall *r* ....Jer 17:25
that if ten men *r* ....Amos 6:9
you, that My joy may *r* ....John 15:11
your fruit should *r* ....John 15:16
"If I will that he *r* ....John 21:22
the greater part *r* ....1 Cor 15:6
Nevertheless to *r* ....Phil 1:24
we who are alive and *r* ....1 Thess 4:15
the things which *r* ....Rev 3:2

REMAINDER
with the *r* of wrath ....Ps 76:10
I am deprived of the *r* ....Is 38:10

REMAINED
Also my wisdom *r* ....Eccl 2:9
And Mary *r* with her ....Luke 1:56
like a dove, and He *r* ....John 1:32

REMAINS
"While the earth *r* ....Gen 8:22
Therefore your sin *r* ....John 9:41
There *r* therefore a ....Heb 4:9
sin, for His seed *r* ....1 John 3:9

REMEMBER
But *r* me when it is ....Gen 40:14
R the Sabbath day ....Ex 20:8
r that you were a ....Deut 15:15
R His marvelous works ....1 Chr 16:12
but we will *r* the name ....Ps 20:7
r the sins of my youth ....Ps 25:7
r Your name in the ....Ps 119:55
R now your Creator ....Eccl 12:1
r your love more than ....Song 1:4
r the former things ....Is 43:18
"I *r* you, the kindness ....Jer 2:2
and their sin I will *r* ....Jer 31:34
r the covenant of ....Amos 1:9
in wrath *r* mercy ....Hab 3:2
and to *r* His holy ....Luke 1:72
R Lot's wife ....Luke 17:32
r the words of the ....Acts 20:35
R my chains ....Col 4:18
R that Jesus Christ ....2 Tim 2:8
R those who rule ....Heb 13:7

REMEMBERED
Then God *r* Noah ....Gen 8:1
r His covenant with ....Ex 2:24
I *r* God ....Ps 77:3
r His covenant forever ....Ps 105:8
r Your judgments ....Ps 119:52
Who *r* us in our lowly ....Ps 136:23
yea, we wept when we *r* ....Ps 137:1
r that same poor man ....Eccl 9:15
r the days of old ....Is 63:11
And Peter *r* the word ....Matt 26:75
r the word of the Lord ....Acts 11:16

REMEMBRANCE
in death there is no *r* ....Ps 6:5
I call to *r* my song ....Ps 77:6
There is no *r* of ....Eccl 1:11
Put Me in *r* ....Is 43:26
do this in *r* of Me ....Luke 22:19
do this in *r* of Me ....1 Cor 11:24

REMIND
r you always of these ....2 Pet 1:12
But I want to *r* you ....Jude 5

REMINDER
there is a *r* of sins ....Heb 10:3
you always have a *r* ....2 Pet 1:15
pure minds by way of *r* ....2 Pet 3:1

REMISSION
repentance for the *r* ....Mark 1:4
Jesus Christ for the *r* ....Acts 2:38
where there is *r* ....Heb 10:18

REMNANT
to us a very small *r* ....Is 1:9
The *r* will return ....Is 10:21
be well with your *r* ....Jer 15:11
I will gather the *r* ....Jer 23:3
and all the *r* of Judah ....Jer 44:28
Yet I will leave a *r* ....Ezek 6:8
r whom the LORD calls ....Joel 2:32
I will not treat the *r* ....Zech 8:11
time there is a *r* ....Rom 11:5

REMOVE
R Your plague from me ....Ps 39:10
R Your gaze from me ....Ps 39:13
r your foot from evil ....Prov 4:27
r falsehood and lies ....Prov 30:8
Therefore *r* sorrow ....Eccl 11:10
r this cup from Me ....Luke 22:42
r your lampstand ....Rev 2:5

REMOVED
Though the earth be *r* ....Ps 46:2
r our transgressions ....Ps 103:12
will never be *r* ....Prov 10:30
and the hills be *r* ....Is 54:10
this mountain, 'Be *r* ....Matt 21:21

REND
So *r* your heart ....Joel 2:13

RENDER
What shall I *r* to the ....Ps 116:12
who will *r* to him the ....Matt 21:41
"*R* therefore to Caesar ....Matt 22:21

RENEW
r a steadfast ....Ps 51:10

r the face of the ... Ps 104:30
on the LORD shall *r* ... Is 40:31

RENEWED
that your youth is *r* ... Ps 103:5
inward man is being *r* ... 2 Cor 4:16
and be *r* in the spirit ... Eph 4:23
the new man who is *r* ... Col 3:10

RENEWING
transformed by the *r* ... Rom 12:2
of regeneration and *r* ... Titus 3:5

RENOUNCE
Why do the wicked *r* ... Ps 10:13

RENOUNCED
r the covenant of Your ... Ps 89:39
r the hidden things ... 2 Cor 4:2

RENOUNCES
greedy and *r* the LORD ... Ps 10:3

RENOWN
were of old, men of *r* ... Gen 6:4

REPAID
done, so God has *r* ... Judg 1:7
And he has *r* me evil ... 1 Sam 25:21
good shall be *r* ... Prov 13:21
Shall evil be *r* ... Jer 18:20

REPAIR
r the house of your ... 2 Chr 24:5
r the ruined cities ... Is 61:4

REPAY
He will *r* him to his ... Deut 7:10
silence, but will *r* ... Is 65:6
He will surely *r* ... Jer 51:56
again, I will *r* ... Luke 10:35
because they cannot *r* ... Luke 14:14
R no one evil for evil ... Rom 12:17
is Mine, I will *r* ... Rom 12:19
r their parents ... 1 Tim 5:4
I will *r* ... Philem 19

REPAYS
and who *r* him for what ... Job 21:31
r the proud person ... Ps 31:23
shall he be who *r* ... Ps 137:8
the LORD, who fully *r* ... Is 66:6

REPENT
I abhor myself, and *r* ... Job 42:6
"*R*, for the kingdom ... Matt 3:2
you *r* you will all ... Luke 13:3
said to them, "*R* ... Acts 2:38
men everywhere to *r* ... Acts 17:30
be zealous and *r* ... Rev 3:19

REPENTANCE
you with water unto *r* ... Matt 3:11
a baptism of *r* for the ... Mark 1:4
persons who need no *r* ... Luke 15:7
sorrow produces *r* ... 2 Cor 7:10
will grant them *r* ... 2 Tim 2:25
renew them again to *r* ... Heb 6:6
found no place for *r* ... Heb 12:17
all should come to *r* ... 2 Pet 3:9

REPENTED
No man *r* of his ... Jer 8:6
after my turning, I *r* ... Jer 31:19
it, because they *r* ... Matt 12:41

REPHAIM
Valley near Jerusalem, 2 Sam 23:13, 14
Scene of Philistine defeats, 2 Sam 5:18–22

REPHIDIM
Israelite camp, Num 33:12–15
Moses strikes rock at, Ex 17:1–7
Amalek defeated at, Ex 17:8–16

REPORT
circulate a false *r* ... Ex 23:1
For it is not a good *r* ... 1 Sam 2:24
r makes the bones ... Prov 15:30
Who has believed our *r* ... Is 53:1
who has believed our *r* ... Rom 10:16
things are of good *r* ... Phil 4:8

REPROACH
r me as long as I live ... Job 27:6
does he take up a *r* ... Ps 15:3
You make us a *r* ... Ps 44:13
sake I have borne *r* ... Ps 69:7
R has broken my heart ... Ps 69:20
nation, but sin is a *r* ... Prov 14:34
with dishonor comes *r* ... Prov 18:3
do not fear the *r* ... Is 51:7
not remember the *r* ... Is 54:4
bring an everlasting *r* ... Jer 23:40
because I bore the *r* ... Jer 31:19
you shall bear the *r* ... Mic 6:16
these things You *r* ... Luke 11:45
lest he fall into *r* ... 1 Tim 3:7
esteeming the *r* ... Heb 11:26
and without *r* ... James 1:5

REPROACHES
is not an enemy who *r* ... Ps 55:12
oppresses the poor *r* ... Prov 14:31
curse, and Israel to *r* ... Is 43:28
in infirmities, in *r* ... 2 Cor 12:10

REPROOF
for doctrine, for *r* ... 2 Tim 3:16

REPROOFS
R of instruction are ... Prov 6:23

REPUTATION
seven men of good *r* ... Acts 6:3
to those who were of *r* ... Gal 2:2
made Himself of no *r* ... Phil 2:7

REQUEST
not withheld the *r* ... Ps 21:2
He gave them their *r* ... Ps 106:15
the Lord God to make *r* ... Dan 9:3
For Jews *r* a sign ... 1 Cor 1:22
of mine making *r* ... Phil 1:4

REQUESTS
r be made known ... Phil 4:6

REQUIRE
the LORD your God *r* ... Deut 10:12
a foreigner you may *r* ... Deut 15:3
"You will not *r* ... Ps 10:13
offering You did not *r* ... Ps 40:6
what does the LORD *r* ... Mic 6:8

REQUIRED
of the world may be *r* ... Luke 11:50
your soul will be *r* ... Luke 12:20
him much will be *r* ... Luke 12:48
Moreover it is *r* ... 1 Cor 4:2

REQUIREMENTS
keeps the righteous *r* ... Rom 2:26
r that was against us ... Col 2:14

RESCUE
R me from their ... Ps 35:17
and no one shall *r* ... Hos 5:14

RESERVED
which I have *r* for the ... Job 38:23
"I have *r* for Myself ... Rom 11:4
r in heaven for you ... 1 Pet 1:4
of darkness, to be *r* ... 2 Pet 2:4
habitation, He has *r* ... Jude 6

RESIST
r an evil person ... Matt 5:39
r the Holy Spirit ... Acts 7:51
R the devil and he ... James 4:7

RESISTED
For who has *r* His will ... Rom 9:19
Jannes and Jambres *r* ... 2 Tim 3:8
for he has greatly *r* ... 2 Tim 4:15
You have not yet *r* ... Heb 12:4

RESISTS
"God *r* the proud ... James 4:6
for "God *r* the proud ... 1 Pet 5:5

RESPECT
Have *r* to the covenant ... Ps 74:20
his eyes will have *r* ... Is 17:7
saying, 'They will *r* ... Matt 21:37
of the law held in *r* ... Acts 5:34
and we paid them *r* ... Heb 12:9

RESPECTED
And the LORD *r* Abel ... Gen 4:4
little folly to one *r* ... Eccl 10:1

REST
is the Sabbath of *r* ... Ex 31:15
you shall find no *r* ... Deut 28:65
to build a house of *r* ... 1 Chr 28:2
I would have been at *r* ... Job 3:13
the weary are at *r* ... Job 3:17
R in the LORD ... Ps 37:7
fly away and be at *r* ... Ps 55:6
of the LORD shall *r* ... Is 11:2
whole earth is at *r* ... Is 14:7
"This is the *r* ... Is 28:12
sake I will not *r* ... Is 62:1
is the place of My *r* ... Is 66:1
then you will find *r* ... Jer 6:16
and I will give you *r* ... Matt 11:28
and you will find *r* ... Matt 11:29
shall not enter My *r* ... Heb 3:11
remains therefore a *r* ... Heb 4:9
to enter that *r* ... Heb 4:11
And they do not *r* ... Rev 4:8
that they should *r* ... Rev 6:11
"that they may *r* ... Rev 14:13
But the *r* of the dead ... Rev 20:5

RESTED
He had done, and He *r* ... Gen 2:2
glory of the LORD *r* ... Ex 24:16
when the Spirit *r* ... Num 11:25
"And God *r* on the ... Heb 4:4

RESTING
do not plunder his *r* ... Prov 24:15
r place shall be ... Is 11:10
all the earth is *r* ... Zech 1:11
still sleeping and *r* ... Matt 26:45

RESTLESS
I am *r* in my complaint ... Ps 55:2

RESTORATION
until the times of *r* ... Acts 3:21

RESTORE
R to me the joy ... Ps 51:12
I still must *r* ... Ps 69:4
r your judges as ... Is 1:26
r them to this place ... Jer 27:22
For I will *r* health to ... Jer 30:17
"So I will *r* to you ... Joel 2:25
declare that I will *r* ... Zech 9:12
and will *r* all things ... Matt 17:11
I *r* fourfold ... Luke 19:8
You at this time *r* ... Acts 1:6
who are spiritual *r* ... Gal 6:1

RESTORER
may he be to you a *r* ... Ruth 4:15

RESTORES
with joy, for He *r* ... Job 33:26
He *r* my soul ... Ps 23:3

RESTRAIN
now *r* Your hand ... 2 Sam 24:16
Therefore I will not *r* ... Job 7:11
Will You *r* Yourself ... Is 64:12
no one can *r* His hand ... Dan 4:35

He swallows down *r* ... Job 20:15
he heaps up *r* ... Ps 39:6
the abundance of his *r* ... Ps 52:7
if *r* increase ... Ps 62:10
r will be in his house ... Ps 112:3
in her left hand *r* ... Prov 3:16
R and honor are ... Prov 8:18
R do not profit ... Prov 11:4
in his *r* will fall ... Prov 11:28
yet has great *r* ... Prov 13:7
of the wise is their *r* ... Prov 14:24
and *r* are an ... Prov 19:14
of the LORD are *r* ... Prov 22:4
r are not forever ... Prov 27:24
r kept for their owner ... Eccl 5:13
darkness and hidden *r* ... Is 45:3
you shall eat the *r* ... Is 61:6
so is he who gets *r* ... Jer 17:11
have increased your *r* ... Ezek 28:5
for those who have *r* ... Mark 10:23
do you despise the *r* ... Rom 2:4
might make known the *r* ... Rom 9:23
what are the *r* ... Eph 1:18
show the exceeding *r* ... Eph 2:7
the unsearchable *r* ... Eph 3:8
trust in uncertain *r* ... 1 Tim 6:17
r than the treasures ... Heb 11:26
r are corrupted ... James 5:2
to receive power and *r* ... Rev 5:12

RICHLY
Christ dwell in you *r* ... Col 3:16
God, who gives us *r* ... 1 Tim 6:17

RIDE
wind and cause me to *r* ... Job 30:22
in Your majesty *r* ... Ps 45:4
have caused men to *r* ... Ps 66:12

RIDER
r He has thrown ... Ex 15:1
the horse and its *r* ... Job 39:18

RIDICULE
those who see Me *r* Me ... Ps 22:7
Whom do you *r* ... Is 57:4

RIDICULED
they *r* Him ... Matt 9:24

RIGHT
you shall do what is *r* ... Deut 6:18
the *r* of the firstborn ... Deut 21:17
did what was *r* in his ... Judg 21:25
"Is your heart *r* ... 2 Kin 10:15
them forth by the *r* ... Ps 107:7
Lord, "Sit at My *r* ... Ps 110:1
is a way which seems *r* ... Prov 14:12
way of a man is *r* ... Prov 21:2
things that are *r* ... Is 45:19
until He comes whose *r* ... Ezek 21:27
of the LORD are *r* ... Hos 14:9
do not know to do *r* ... Amos 3:10
and whatever is *r* ... Matt 20:4
clothed and in his *r* ... Mark 5:15
not judge what is *r* ... Luke 12:57
to them He gave the *r* ... John 1:12
your heart is not *r* ... Acts 8:21
Do we have no *r* ... 1 Cor 9:4
seven stars in His *r* ... Rev 2:1

RIGHTEOUS
also destroy the *r* ... Gen 18:23
and they justify the *r* ... Deut 25:1
"You are more *r* ... 1 Sam 24:17
that he could be *r* ... Job 15:14
r will hold to his way ... Job 17:9
"The *r* see it and ... Job 22:19
knows the way of the *r* ... Ps 1:6
LORD, will bless the *r* ... Ps 5:12
r God tests the hearts ... Ps 7:9
what can the *r* ... Ps 11:3
The *r* cry out ... Ps 34:17
the LORD upholds the *r* ... Ps 37:17
r shows mercy and ... Ps 37:21
I have not seen the *r* ... Ps 37:25
the *r* will be in ... Ps 112:6
The LORD is *r* in all ... Ps 145:17
the LORD loves the *r* ... Ps 146:8
will not allow the *r* ... Prov 10:3
r is a well of life ... Prov 10:11
The labor of the *r* ... Prov 10:16
r will be gladness ... Prov 10:28
r is delivered from ... Prov 11:8
r will be delivered ... Prov 11:21
r will flourish ... Prov 11:28
r will be recompensed ... Prov 11:31
r man regards the life ... Prov 12:10
r should choose his ... Prov 12:26
r there is much ... Prov 15:6
the prayer of the *r* ... Prov 15:29
the *r* run to it and ... Prov 18:10
r are bold as a lion ... Prov 28:1
When the *r* are in ... Prov 29:2
r considers the cause ... Prov 29:7
Do not be overly *r* ... Eccl 7:16
event happens to the *r* ... Eccl 9:2
r that it shall be ... Is 3:10
the gates, that the *r* ... Is 26:2
with My *r* right hand ... Is 41:10
By His knowledge My *r* ... Is 53:11
The *r* perishes ... Is 57:1
people shall all be *r* ... Is 60:21
R are You ... Jer 12:1
your sins by being *r* ... Dan 4:27
they sell the *r* ... Amos 2:6
not come to call the *r* ... Matt 9:13
r men desired to see ... Matt 13:17
r will shine forth as ... Matt 13:43
And they were both *r* ... Luke 1:6
that they were *r* ... Luke 18:9
"Certainly this was a *r* ... Luke 23:47
"There is none *r* ... Rom 3:10
r man will one die ... Rom 5:7
witness that he was *r* ... Heb 11:4
Jesus Christ the *r* ... 1 John 2:1
just as He is *r* ... 1 John 3:7
r are Your ... Rev 16:7
fine linen is the *r* ... Rev 19:8

RIGHTEOUSLY
judge the people *r* ... Ps 67:4
He who walks *r* and ... Is 33:15
should live soberly, *r* ... Titus 2:12
to Him who judges *r* ... 1 Pet 2:23

RIGHTEOUSNESS
it to him for *r* ... Gen 15:6
My *r* I hold fast ... Job 27:6
I put on *r* ... Job 29:14
I will ascribe *r* ... Job 36:3
I call, O God of my *r* ... Ps 4:1
righteous, He loves *r* ... Ps 11:7
from the LORD, and *r* ... Ps 24:5
shall speak of Your *r* ... Ps 35:28
the good news of *r* ... Ps 40:9
You love *r* and hate ... Ps 45:7
heavens declare His *r* ... Ps 50:6
sing aloud of Your *r* ... Ps 51:14
r and peace have ... Ps 85:10
R will go before Him ... Ps 85:13
r they are exalted ... Ps 89:16
will return to *r* ... Ps 94:15
r and justice are the ... Ps 97:2
and he who does *r* ... Ps 106:3
r endures forever ... Ps 111:3
r is an everlasting ... Ps 119:142
r delivers from death ... Prov 10:2
The *r* of the blameless ... Prov 11:5
The *r* of the upright ... Prov 11:6
r leads to life ... Prov 11:19
the way of *r* is life ... Prov 12:28
R guards him whose way ... Prov 13:6
R exalts a nation ... Prov 14:34
found in the way of *r* ... Prov 16:31
He who follows *r* ... Prov 21:21
r lodged in it ... Is 1:21
r He shall judge ... Is 11:4
R shall be the belt ... Is 11:5
he will not learn *r* ... Is 26:10
and *r* the plummet ... Is 28:17
r will be peace ... Is 32:17
in the LORD I have *r* ... Is 45:24
who are far from *r* ... Is 46:12
r will be forever ... Is 51:8
I will declare your *r* ... Is 57:12
and His own *r* ... Is 59:16
r as a breastplate ... Is 59:17
be called trees of *r* ... Is 61:3
r goes forth as ... Is 62:1
The LORD Our *R* ... Jer 23:6
to David a Branch of *r* ... Jer 33:15
has revealed our *r* ... Jer 51:10
The *r* of the righteous ... Ezek 18:20
O Lord, *r* belongs ... Dan 9:7
in everlasting *r* ... Dan 9:24
who turn many to *r* ... Dan 12:3
for yourselves *r* ... Hos 10:12
to fulfill all *r* ... Matt 3:15
exceeds the *r* of the ... Matt 5:20
to you in the way of *r* ... Matt 21:32
in holiness and *r* ... Luke 1:75
For in it the *r* ... Rom 1:17
even the *r* of God ... Rom 3:22
a seal of the *r* ... Rom 4:11
accounted to him for *r* ... Rom 4:22
r will reign in life ... Rom 5:17
might reign through *r* ... Rom 5:21
is life because of *r* ... Rom 8:10
who did not pursue *r* ... Rom 9:30
pursuing the law of *r* ... Rom 9:31
ignorant of God's *r* ... Rom 10:3
we might become the *r* ... 2 Cor 5:21
r comes through the ... Gal 2:21
the breastplate of *r* ... Eph 6:14
not having my own *r* ... Phil 3:9
things and pursue *r* ... 1 Tim 6:11
r which we have ... Titus 3:5
r which is according ... Heb 11:7
does not produce the *r* ... James 1:20
should suffer for *r* ... 1 Pet 3:14
a preacher of *r* ... 2 Pet 2:5
a new earth in which *r* ... 2 Pet 3:13
who practices *r* ... 1 John 2:29
He who practices *r* ... 1 John 3:7
does not practice *r* ... 1 John 3:10

RIGHTLY
wise uses knowledge *r* ... Prov 15:2
R do they love you ... Song 1:4
"You have answered *r* ... Luke 10:28
r dividing the word ... 2 Tim 2:15

RISE
is vain for you to *r* ... Ps 127:2
"Now I will *r* ... Is 33:10
for He makes His sun *r* ... Matt 5:45
of Nineveh will *r* ... Matt 12:41
third day He will *r* ... Matt 20:19
false prophets will *r* ... Matt 24:24
persuaded though one *r* ... Luke 16:31
third day He will *r* ... Luke 18:33
had to suffer and *r* ... Acts 17:3
be the first to *r* ... Acts 26:23
fact the dead do not *r* ... 1 Cor 15:15
in Christ will *r* ... 1 Thess 4:16

RISEN
of the LORD is *r* ... Is 60:1
women there has not *r* ... Matt 11:11
disciples that He is *r* ... Matt 28:7

"The Lord is *r* .... Luke 24:34
furthermore is also *r* .... Rom 8:34
then Christ is not *r* .... 1 Cor 15:13
if Christ is not *r* .... 1 Cor 15:17
But now Christ is *r* .... 1 Cor 15:20

RISING
may know from the *r* .... Is 45:6
questioning what the *r* .... Mark 9:10
for the fall and *r* .... Luke 2:34

RIVER
Indeed the *r* may rage .... Job 40:23
them drink from the *r* .... Ps 36:8
r whose streams shall .... Ps 46:4
the *r* of God is full .... Ps 65:9
went through the *r* .... Ps 66:6
peace to her like a *r* .... Is 66:12
in the Jordan *R* .... Mark 1:5
he showed me a pure *r* .... Rev 22:1

RIVERS
He turns *r* into a .... Ps 107:33
R of water run down .... Ps 119:136
By the *r* of Babylon .... Ps 137:1
All the *r* run into the .... Eccl 1:7
us a place of broad *r* .... Is 33:21
the wilderness and *r* .... Is 43:19
the sea, I make the *r* .... Is 50:2
his heart will flow *r* .... John 7:38

RIZPAH
Saul's concubine taken by Abner, 2 Sam 3:6–8
Sons of, killed, 2 Sam 21:8, 9
Grief-stricken, cares for corpses, 2 Sam 21:10–14

ROAD
I will even make a *r* .... Is 43:19
depths of the sea a *r* .... Is 51:10
seen the Lord on the *r* .... Acts 9:27

ROAR
Let the sea *r* .... 1 Chr 16:32
though its waters *r* .... Ps 46:3
The young lions *r* .... Ps 104:21
'The LORD will *r* .... Jer 25:30
He will *r* like a lion .... Hos 11:10
The LORD also will *r* .... Joel 3:16
Will a lion *r* in the .... Amos 3:4

ROARING
wrath is like the *r* .... Prov 19:12
Like a *r* lion and a .... Prov 28:15
and the waves *r* .... Luke 21:25
walks about like a *r* .... 1 Pet 5:8

ROARS
their voice *r* like the .... Jer 6:23
"The LORD *r* from .... Amos 1:2
as when a lion *r* .... Rev 10:3

ROB
r the poor because he .... Prov 22:22
r the needy of justice .... Is 10:2
"Will a man *r* God .... Mal 3:8
do you *r* temples .... Rom 2:22

ROBBED
r their treasuries .... Is 10:13
But this is a people *r* .... Is 42:22
Yet you have *r* Me .... Mal 3:8
r other churches .... 2 Cor 11:8

ROBBER
a son who is a *r* .... Ezek 18:10
is a thief and a *r* .... John 10:1
Barabbas was a *r* .... John 18:40

ROBBERS
and Israel to the *r* .... Is 42:24
also crucified two *r* .... Mark 15:27
Me are thieves and *r* .... John 10:8
here who are neither *r* .... Acts 19:37
waters, in perils of *r* .... 2 Cor 11:26

ROBBERY
nor vainly hope in *r* .... Ps 62:10
I hate *r* for burnt .... Is 61:8
did not consider it *r* .... Phil 2:6

ROBE
justice was like a *r* .... Job 29:14
instead of a rich *r* .... Is 3:24
covered me with the *r* .... Is 61:10
'Bring out the best *r* .... Luke 15:22
on Him a purple *r* .... John 19:2
Then a white *r* was .... Rev 6:11

ROBES
to the King in *r* .... Ps 45:14
have stained all My *r* .... Is 63:3
clothe you with rich *r* .... Zech 3:4
go around in long *r* .... Luke 20:46
clothed with white *r* .... Rev 7:9

ROCK
you shall strike the *r* .... Ex 17:6
and struck the *r* .... Num 20:11
R who begot you .... Deut 32:18
For their *r* is not .... Deut 32:31
nor is there any *r* .... 1 Sam 2:2
"The LORD is my *r* .... 2 Sam 22:2
And who is a *r* .... 2 Sam 22:32
Blessed be my *R* .... 2 Sam 22:47
away, and as a *r* .... Job 14:18
set me high upon a *r* .... Ps 27:5
For You are my *r* .... Ps 31:3
r that is higher than .... Ps 61:2
and my God the *r* .... Ps 94:22
who turned the *r* .... Ps 114:8
been mindful of the *R* .... Is 17:10
shadow of a great *r* .... Is 32:2
his house on the *r* .... Matt 7:24
r I will build My .... Matt 16:18
Some fell on *r* .... Luke 8:6
stumbling stone and *r* .... Rom 9:33
R that followed them .... 1 Cor 10:4

ROCKS
and the *r* were split .... Matt 27:51
to the mountains and *r* .... Rev 6:16

ROD
And Moses took the *r* .... Ex 4:20
chasten him with the *r* .... 2 Sam 7:14
Your *r* and Your staff .... Ps 23:4
The *r* and rebuke give .... Prov 29:15
shall come forth a *R* .... Is 11:1
you pass under the *r* .... Ezek 20:37
I come to you with a *r* .... 1 Cor 4:21
rule them with a *r* .... Rev 2:27

ROLLED
the heavens shall be *r* .... Is 34:4
the stone had been *r* .... Mark 16:4

ROME
Jews expelled from, Acts 18:2
Paul:
- Writes to Christians of, Rom 1:7
- Desires to go to, Acts 19:21
- Comes to, Acts 28:14
- Imprisoned in, Acts 28:16

ROOM
You prepared *r* for it .... Ps 80:9
until no more *r* .... Zech 10:10
you a large upper *r* .... Mark 14:15
no *r* for them in the .... Luke 2:7
still there is *r* .... Luke 14:22
into the upper *r* .... Acts 1:13

ROOMS
make *r* in the ark .... Gen 6:14
He is in the inner *r* .... Matt 24:26

ROOSTER
him, "Before the *r* .... Matt 26:75

ROOT
r bearing bitterness .... Deut 29:18
the foolish taking *r* .... Job 5:3
r may grow old in the .... Job 14:8
day there shall be a *R* .... Is 11:10
shall again take *r* .... Is 37:31
because they had no *r* .... Matt 13:6
and if the *r* is holy .... Rom 11:16
of money is a *r* .... 1 Tim 6:10
lest any *r* of .... Heb 12:15
I am the *R* and the .... Rev 22:16

ROOTED
that you, being *r* .... Eph 3:17
r and built up in Him .... Col 2:7

ROOTS
because its *r* reached .... Ezek 31:7
and lengthen his *r* .... Hos 14:5
dried up from the *r* .... Mark 11:20
pulled up by the *r* .... Jude 12

ROSE
I am the *r* of Sharon .... Song 2:1
and blossom as the *r* .... Is 35:1
end Christ died and *r* .... Rom 14:9
buried, and that He *r* .... 1 Cor 15:4
that Jesus died and *r* .... 1 Thess 4:14

RUBIES
of wisdom is above *r* .... Job 28:18
more precious than *r* .... Prov 3:15
is better than *r* .... Prov 8:11
worth is far above *r* .... Prov 31:10
your pinnacles of *r* .... Is 54:12
ruddy in body than *r* .... Lam 4:7

RUDDY
Now he was *r* .... 1 Sam 16:12
beloved is white and *r* .... Song 5:10

RUIN
r those two can bring .... Prov 24:22
have made a city a *r* .... Is 25:2
will not be your *r* .... Ezek 18:30
And the *r* of that .... Luke 6:49
to no profit, to the *r* .... 2 Tim 2:14

RUINED
shall be utterly *r* .... Is 60:12
the mighty trees are *r* .... Zech 11:2
wineskins will be *r* .... Luke 5:37

RULE
and he shall *r* .... Gen 3:16
r the raging of the .... Ps 89:9
A wise servant will *r* .... Prov 17:2
Yet he will *r* over all .... Eccl 2:19
puts an end to all *r* .... 1 Cor 15:24
us walk by the same *r* .... Phil 3:16
let the peace of God *r* .... Col 3:15
Let the elders who *r* .... 1 Tim 5:17
Remember those who *r* .... Heb 13:7

RULER
the sheep, to be *r* .... 2 Sam 7:8
down to eat with a *r* .... Prov 23:1
bear is a wicked *r* .... Prov 28:15
r pays attention .... Prov 29:12
to Me the One to be *r* .... Mic 5:2
by Beelzebub, the *r* .... Matt 12:24
I will make you *r* .... Matt 25:21
the *r* of this world .... John 12:31
because the *r* of this .... John 16:11
'Who made you a *r* .... Acts 7:27
speak evil of a *r* .... Acts 23:5

RULERS
and the *r* take counsel .... Ps 2:2
r decree justice .... Prov 8:15
"You know that the *r* .... Matt 20:25
Have any of the *r* .... John 7:48
r are not a .... Rom 13:3
which none of the *r* .... 1 Cor 2:8

powers, against the *r* … Eph 6:12
to be subject to *r* … Titus 3:1

RULES
'He who *r* over men … 2 Sam 23:3
them know that God *r* … Ps 59:13
He *r* by His power … Ps 66:7
r his spirit than he … Prov 16:32
that the Most High *r* … Dan 4:17
that the Most High *r* … Dan 4:32
r his own house well … 1 Tim 3:4
according to the *r* … 2 Tim 2:5

RUMOR
r will be upon *r* … Ezek 7:26

RUMORS
hear of wars and *r* … Matt 24:6
you hear of wars and *r* … Mark 13:7

RUN
I will *r* the course of … Ps 119:32
r and not be weary … Is 40:31
many shall *r* to and … Dan 12:4
Therefore I *r* thus … 1 Cor 9:26
I might *r*, or had *r* … Gal 2:2
that I have not *r* … Phil 2:16
us, and let us *r* … Heb 12:1
that you do not *r* … 1 Pet 4:4

RUNNER
are swifter than a *r* … Job 9:25
r will run to meet … Jer 51:31

RUTH
Moabitess, Ruth 1:4
Follows Naomi, Ruth 1:6–18
Marries Boaz, Ruth 4:9–13
Ancestress of Christ, Ruth 4:13, 21, 22

SABAOTH
S had left us a … Rom 9:29
ears of the Lord of *S* … James 5:4

SABBATH
'Tomorrow is a *S* … Ex 16:23
"Remember the *S* … Ex 20:8
S was made for man … Mark 2:27
is also Lord of the *S* … Mark 2:28
not only broke the *S* … John 5:18

SABBATHS
S you shall keep … Ex 31:13
The New Moons, the *S* … Is 1:13
also gave them My *S* … Ezek 20:12

SACKCLOTH
You have put off my *s* … Ps 30:11
and remove the *s* … Is 20:2

SACRED
iniquity and the *s* … Is 1:13

SACRIFICE
do you kick at My *s* … 1 Sam 2:29
S and offering You did … Ps 40:6
offer to You the *s* … Ps 116:17
to the LORD than *s* … Prov 21:3
For the LORD has a *s* … Is 34:6
who will bring the *s* … Jer 33:11
of My offerings they *s* … Hos 8:13
But I will *s* to You … Jon 2:9
LORD has prepared a *s* … Zeph 1:7
offer the blind as a *s* … Mal 1:8
desire mercy and not *s* … Matt 9:13
s will be seasoned … Mark 9:49
an offering and a *s* … Eph 5:2
aroma, an acceptable *s* … Phil 4:18
put away sin by the *s* … Heb 9:26
He had offered one *s* … Heb 10:12
no longer remains a *s* … Heb 10:26
God a more excellent *s* … Heb 11:4
offer the *s* of praise … Heb 13:15

SACRIFICED
s their sons and their … Ps 106:37
to eat things *s* … Rev 2:14

SACRIFICES
The *s* of God are a … Ps 51:17
multitude of your *s* … Is 1:11
Bring no more futile *s* … Is 1:13
he who *s* a lamb … Is 66:3
acceptable, nor your *s* … Jer 6:20
by him the daily *s* … Dan 8:11
burnt offerings and *s* … Mark 12:33
priests, to offer up *s* … Heb 7:27
s God is well pleased … Heb 13:16
offer up spiritual *s* … 1 Pet 2:5

SAD
"Why is your face *s* … Neh 2:2
s countenance the … Eccl 7:3
whom I have not made *s* … Ezek 13:22
as you walk and are *s* … Luke 24:17

SADDUCEES
Rejected by John, Matt 3:7
Test Jesus, Matt 16:1–12
Silenced by Jesus, Matt 22:23–34
Disturbed by teaching of resurrection, Acts 4:1, 2
Oppose apostles, Acts 5:17–40

SAFE
and I shall be *s* … Ps 119:117
in the LORD shall be *s* … Prov 29:25
he has received him *s* … Luke 15:27

SAFELY
And He led them on *s* … Ps 78:53
make them lie down *s* … Hos 2:18

SAFETY
sons are far from *s* … Job 5:4
take your rest in *s* … Job 11:18
will set him in the *s* … Ps 12:5
say, "Peace and *s* … 1 Thess 5:3

SAINTS
ten thousands of *s* … Deut 33:2
the feet of His *s* … 1 Sam 2:9
puts no trust in His *s* … Job 15:15
s who are on the earth … Ps 16:3
does not forsake His *s* … Ps 37:28
"Gather My *s* … Ps 50:5
the souls of His *s* … Ps 97:10
is the death of His *s* … Ps 116:15
the way of His *s* … Prov 2:8
war against the *s* … Dan 7:21
shall persecute the *s* … Dan 7:25
Jesus, called to be *s* … 1 Cor 1:2
the least of all the *s* … Eph 3:8
Christ with all His *s* … 1 Thess 3:13
be glorified in His *s* … 2 Thess 1:10
all delivered to the *s* … Jude 3
ways, O King of the *s* … Rev 15:3
shed the blood of *s* … Rev 16:6
the camp of the *s* … Rev 20:9

SALEM
Jerusalem's original name, Gen 14:18
Used poetically, Ps 76:2

SALOME
One of the ministering women, Mark 15:40, 41
Visits empty tomb, Mark 16:1
——— Herodias' daughter (not named in the Bible), Matt 14:6–11

SALT
shall season with *s* … Lev 2:13
"You are the *s* … Matt 5:13
s loses its flavor … Mark 9:50

SALT SEA
OT name for the Dead Sea, Gen 14:3; Num 34:3, 12

SALVATION
still, and see the *s* … Ex 14:13
For this is all my *s* … 2 Sam 23:5
the good news of His *s* … 1 Chr 16:23
S belongs to the LORD … Ps 3:8
is my light and my *s* … Ps 27:1
on earth, Your *s* … Ps 67:2
God is the God of *s* … Ps 68:20
and Your *s* all the day … Ps 71:15
Surely His *s* is near … Ps 85:9
and He has become my *s* … Ps 118:14
S is far from the … Ps 119:155
God will appoint *s* … Is 26:1
with an everlasting *s* … Is 45:17
for My *s* is about to … Is 56:1
call your walls *S* … Is 60:18
s as a lamp that burns … Is 62:1
LORD our God is the *s* … Jer 3:23
joy in the God of my *s* … Hab 3:18
is just and having *s* … Zech 9:9
raised up a horn of *s* … Luke 1:69
eyes have seen Your *s* … Luke 2:30
to him, "Today *s* … Luke 19:9
what we worship, for *s* … John 4:22
Nor is there *s* … Acts 4:12
you should be for *s* … Acts 13:47
the power of God to *s* … Rom 1:16
s is nearer than … Rom 13:11
now is the day of *s* … 2 Cor 6:2
work out your own *s* … Phil 2:12
wrath, but to obtain *s* … 1 Thess 5:9
chose you for *s* … 2 Thess 2:13
also may obtain the *s* … 2 Tim 2:10
of God that brings *s* … Titus 2:11
neglect so great a *s* … Heb 2:3
s the prophets have … 1 Pet 1:10

SAMARIA
Capital of Israel, 1 Kin 16:24–29
Besieged by Ben-Hadad, 1 Kin 20:1–21
Besieged again; miraculously delivered, 2 Kin 6:24—7:20
Inhabitants deported by Assyria; repopulated with foreigners, 2 Kin 17:5, 6, 24–41
——— District of Palestine in Christ's time, Luke 17:11–19
Disciples forbidden to preach in, Matt 10:5
Gospel preached there after the Ascension, Acts 1:8; 9:31; 15:3

SAMARITAN
But a certain *S* … Luke 10:33
a drink from me, a *S* … John 4:9

SAMARITANS
People of mixed heredity, 2 Kin 17:24–41
Christ preaches to, John 4:5–42
Story of "the good Samaritan," Luke 10:30–37
Converts among, Acts 8:5–25

SAMSON
Birth predicted and accomplished, Judg 13:2–25
Marries Philistine; avenges betrayal, Judg 14
Defeats Philistines singlehandedly, Judg 15
Betrayed by Delilah; loses strength, Judg 16:4–22
Destroys many in his death, Judg 16:23–31

SAMUEL
Born in answer to prayer; dedicated to God, 1 Sam 1:1–28
Receives revelation; recognized as prophet, 1 Sam 3:1–21
Judges Israel, 1 Sam 7:15–17
Warns Israel against a king, 1 Sam 8:10–18
Anoints Saul, 1 Sam 9:15—10:1

- Rebukes Saul, 1 Sam 15:10–35
- Anoints David, 1 Sam 16:1–13
- Death of, 1 Sam 25:1

SANBALLAT
- Influential Samaritan; attempts to thwart Nehemiah's plans, Neh 2:10; 4:7, 8; 6:1–14

SANCTIFICATION
- righteousness and *s* .... 1 Cor 1:30
- will of God, your *s* .... 1 Thess 4:3
- salvation through *s* .... 2 Thess 2:13

SANCTIFIED
- I have commanded My *s* .... Is 13:3
- you were born I *s* .... Jer 1:5
- Him whom the Father *s* .... John 10:36
- they also may be *s* .... John 17:19
- might be acceptable, *s* .... Rom 15:16
- to those who are *s* .... 1 Cor 1:2
- washed, but you were *s* .... 1 Cor 6:11
- husband is *s* by the .... 1 Cor 7:14
- for it is *s* by the .... 1 Tim 4:5
- those who are being *s* .... Heb 2:11
- will we have been *s* .... Heb 10:10
- who are called, *s* .... Jude 1

SANCTIFIES
- or the temple that *s* .... Matt 23:17
- For both He who *s* .... Heb 2:11

SANCTIFY
- would send and *s* them .... Job 1:5
- *s* My great name .... Ezek 36:23
- that I, the LORD, *s* .... Ezek 37:28
- Myself and *s* Myself .... Ezek 38:23
- *S* them by Your .... John 17:17
- for their sakes I *s* .... John 17:19
- that He might *s* .... Eph 5:26

SANCTUARY
- let them make Me a *s* .... Ex 25:8
- I went into the *s* .... Ps 73:17
- set fire to Your *s* .... Ps 74:7
- O God, is in the *s* .... Ps 77:13
- He will be as a *s* .... Is 8:14
- He has abandoned His *s* .... Lam 2:7
- I shall be a little *s* .... Ezek 11:16
- to shine on Your *s* .... Dan 9:17
- and the earthly *s* .... Heb 9:1

SAND
- descendants as the *s* .... Gen 32:12
- be heavier than the *s* .... Job 6:3
- in number than the *s* .... Ps 139:18
- O Israel, be as the *s* .... Is 10:22
- innumerable as the *s* .... Heb 11:12

SAPPHIRA
- Wife of Ananias; struck dead for lying, Acts 5:1–11

SARAH (or Sarai)
- Barren wife of Abram, Gen 11:29–31
- Represented as Abram's sister, Gen 12:10–20
- Gives Abram her maid, Gen 16:1–3
- Receives promise of a son, Gen 17:15–21
- Gives birth to Isaac, Gen 21:1–8

SARDIS
- Site of one of the seven churches, Rev 1:11

SAT
- of Babylon, there we *s* .... Ps 137:1
- I *s* down in his shade .... Song 2:3
- *s* alone because of .... Jer 15:17
- into heaven, and *s* .... Mark 16:19
- And He who *s* there was .... Rev 4:3

SATAN
- *S* stood up against .... 1 Chr 21:1
- before the LORD, and *S* .... Job 1:6
- And the LORD said to *S* .... Zech 3:2
- "Away with you, *S* .... Matt 4:10
- "Get behind Me, *S* .... Matt 16:23
- "How can *S* cast out .... Mark 3:23
- to them, "I saw *S* .... Luke 10:18
- *S* has asked for you .... Luke 22:31
- *S* filled your heart .... Acts 5:3
- such a one to *S* .... 1 Cor 5:5
- For *S* himself .... 2 Cor 11:14
- to the working of *S* .... 2 Thess 2:9
- are a synagogue of *S* .... Rev 2:9
- you, where *S* dwells .... Rev 2:13
- known the depths of *S* .... Rev 2:24
- called the Devil and *S* .... Rev 12:9
- years have expired, *S* .... Rev 20:7

SATISFIED
- I shall be *s* when I .... Ps 17:15
- his land will be *s* .... Prov 12:11
- a good man will be *s* .... Prov 14:14
- *s* soul loathes the .... Prov 27:7
- that are never *s* .... Prov 30:15
- silver will not be *s* .... Eccl 5:10
- left hand and not be *s* .... Is 9:20
- of His soul, and be *s* .... Is 53:11
- My people shall be *s* .... Jer 31:14
- still were not *s* .... Ezek 16:28
- but they were not *s* .... Amos 4:8
- and cannot be *s* .... Hab 2:5

SATISFIES
- *s* your mouth with good .... Ps 103:5
- *s* the longing soul .... Ps 107:9

SATISFY
- *s* us early with Your .... Ps 90:14
- long life I will *s* .... Ps 91:16
- *s* her poor with bread .... Ps 132:15
- for what does not *s* .... Is 55:2

SAUL
- Becomes first king of Israel, 1 Sam 9—11
- Sacrifices unlawfully, 1 Sam 13:1–14
- Wars with Philistines, 1 Sam 13:15—14:52
- Disregards the Lord's command; rejected by God, 1 Sam 15
- Suffers from distressing spirits, 1 Sam 16:14–23
- Becomes jealous of David; attempts to kill him, 1 Sam 18:5—19:22
- Pursues David; twice spared by him, 1 Sam 22—24; 26
- Consults medium, 1 Sam 28:7–25
- Defeated, commits suicide; buried, 1 Sam 31
- —— of Tarsus, apostle to the Gentiles: *see* PAUL

SAVE
- the LORD does not *s* .... 1 Sam 17:47
- there was none to *s* .... 2 Sam 22:42
- *s* the humble person .... Job 22:29
- Oh, *s* me for Your .... Ps 6:4
- *S* Your people .... Ps 28:9
- send from heaven and *s* .... Ps 57:3
- *s* the children of the .... Ps 72:4
- *s* the souls of the .... Ps 72:13
- LORD, AND HE WILL *S* .... Prov 20:22
- He will come and *s* .... Is 35:4
- LORD was ready to *s* .... Is 38:20
- *s* your children .... Is 49:25
- that it cannot *s* .... Is 59:1
- mighty to *s* .... Is 63:1
- one who cannot *s* .... Jer 14:9
- *s* you and deliver you .... Jer 15:20
- *s* me, and I shall be .... Jer 17:14
- O LORD, *s* Your people .... Jer 31:7
- other, That he may *s* .... Hos 13:10
- Assyria shall not *s* .... Hos 14:3
- the Mighty One, will *s* .... Zeph 3:17
- JESUS, for He will *s* .... Matt 1:21
- *s* his life will .... Matt 16:25
- *s* that which was .... Matt 18:11
- *s* life or to kill .... Mark 3:4
- let Him *s* Himself if .... Luke 23:35
- You are the Christ, *s* .... Luke 23:39
- 'Father, *s* Me from .... John 12:27
- but to *s* the world .... John 12:47
- and *s* some of them .... Rom 11:14
- the world to *s* sinners .... 1 Tim 1:15
- doing this you will *s* .... 1 Tim 4:16
- able to *s* your souls .... James 1:21
- Can faith *s* him .... James 2:14

SAVED
- like you, a people *s* .... Deut 33:29
- But You have *s* us from .... Ps 44:7
- and we are not *s* .... Jer 8:20
- "Who then can be *s* .... Matt 19:25
- "He *s* others .... Matt 27:42
- That we should be *s* .... Luke 1:71
- "Your faith has *s* .... Luke 7:50
- through Him might be *s* .... John 3:17
- them, saying, "Be *s* .... Acts 2:40
- what must I do to be *s* .... Acts 16:30
- For we were *s* in this .... Rom 8:24
- is that they may be *s* .... Rom 10:1
- all Israel will be *s* .... Rom 11:26
- his spirit may be *s* .... 1 Cor 5:5
- which also you are *s* .... 1 Cor 15:2
- those who are being *s* .... 2 Cor 2:15
- grace you have been *s* .... Eph 2:8
- all men to be *s* .... 1 Tim 2:4
- she will be *s* in .... 1 Tim 2:15
- to His mercy He *s* .... Titus 3:5
- eight souls, were *s* .... 1 Pet 3:20
- of those who are *s* .... Rev 21:24

SAVES
- *s* the needy from the .... Job 5:15
- *s* such as have a .... Ps 34:18
- antitype which now *s* .... 1 Pet 3:21

SAVIOR
- forgot God their *S* .... Ps 106:21
- He will send them a *S* .... Is 19:20
- of Israel, your *S* .... Is 43:3
- Me, a just God and a *S* .... Is 45:21
- I, the LORD, am your *S* .... Is 60:16
- So He became their *S* .... Is 63:8
- for there is no *s* .... Hos 13:4
- rejoiced in God my *S* .... Luke 1:47
- the city of David a *S* .... Luke 2:11
- the Christ, the *S* .... John 4:42
- to be Prince and *S* .... Acts 5:31
- up for Israel a *S* .... Acts 13:23
- and He is the *S* .... Eph 5:23
- of God our *S* and the .... 1 Tim 1:1
- God, who is the *S* .... 1 Tim 4:10
- of our *S* Jesus Christ .... 2 Tim 1:10
- God and *S* Jesus Christ .... Titus 2:13

SAWN
- stoned, they were *s* .... Heb 11:37

SAY
- But I *s* to you that .... Matt 5:22
- "But who do you *s* .... Matt 16:15
- *s* that we have no sin .... 1 John 1:8

SAYING
- disclose my dark *s* .... Ps 49:4
- cannot accept this *s* .... Matt 19:11
- "This is a hard *s* .... John 6:60
- This is a faithful *s* .... 1 Tim 1:15

SAYINGS
- I will utter dark *s* .... Ps 78:2
- whoever hears these *s* .... Matt 7:24

SCALES
- You shall have honest *s* .... Lev 19:36
- be weighed on honest *s* .... Job 31:6
- deceitful *s* are in his .... Hos 12:7
- on it had a pair of *s* .... Rev 6:5

You said, "*S* My face ....Ps 27:8
early will I *s* You ....Ps 63:1
s me diligently will ....Prov 8:17
s one's own glory ....Prov 25:27
s justice, rebuke ....Is 1:17
Should they *s* the dead ....Is 8:19
the Gentiles shall *s* ....Is 11:10
Jacob, '*S* Me in vain ....Is 45:19
S the LORD while He ....Is 55:6
Yet they *s* Me daily ....Is 58:2
s great things for ....Jer 45:5
s what was lost ....Ezek 34:16
"*S* Me and live ....Amos 5:4
and people should *s* ....Mal 2:7
things the Gentiles *s* ....Matt 6:32
s, and you will find ....Matt 7:7
of Man has come to *s* ....Luke 19:10
because I do not *s* ....John 5:30
You will *s* Me and ....John 7:34
in doing good *s* ....Rom 2:7
Because they did not *s* ....Rom 9:32
Let no one *s* his own ....1 Cor 10:24
for I do not *s* yours ....2 Cor 12:14
For all *s* their own ....Phil 2:21
s those things which ....Col 3:1
s the one to come ....Heb 13:14

SEEKING
run to and fro, *s* ....Amos 8:12
and he came *s* fruit ....Luke 13:6
for the Father is *s* ....John 4:23
like a roaring lion, *s* ....1 Pet 5:8

SEEKS
no one *s* her ....Jer 30:17
receives, and he who *s* ....Matt 7:8
There is none who *s* ....Rom 3:11

SEEMS
There is a way which *s* ....Prov 14:12
have, even what he *s* ....Luke 8:18
If anyone among you *s* ....1 Cor 3:18

SEEN
s God face to face ....Gen 32:30
All this I have *s* ....Eccl 8:9
s the one I love ....Song 3:3
Who has *s* such things ....Is 66:8
s strange things today ....Luke 5:26
No one has *s* God at ....John 1:18
time, nor *s* His form ....John 5:37
I speak what I have *s* ....John 8:38
s Me has *s* the ....John 14:9
things which we have *s* ....Acts 4:20
s Jesus Christ our ....1 Cor 9:1
things which are not *s* ....2 Cor 4:18
whom no man has *s* ....1 Tim 6:16
heard, which we have *s* ....1 John 1:1

SEES
here seen Him who *s* ....Gen 16:13
s all the sons of men ....Ps 33:13
s his brother in need ....1 John 3:17
s his brother sinning ....1 John 5:16

SEIR
Home of Esau, Gen 32:3
Horites of, dispossessed by Esau's descendants, Deut 2:12
Desolation of, Ezek 35:15

SELF-CONTROL
about righteousness, *s* ....Acts 24:25
they cannot exercise *s* ....1 Cor 7:9
gentleness, *s* ....Gal 5:23
slanderers, without *s* ....2 Tim 3:3
to knowledge *s* ....2 Pet 1:6

SELL
said, "*S* me your ....Gen 25:31
S Your people for ....Ps 44:12
s the righteous ....Amos 2:6
s whatever you have ....Mark 10:21
no sword, let him *s* ....Luke 22:36
no one may buy or *s* ....Rev 13:17

SEND
He shall *s* from heaven ....Ps 57:3
"Whom shall I *s* ....Is 6:8
s them a Savior ....Is 19:20
"Behold, I *s* you out ....Matt 10:16
The Son of Man will *s* ....Matt 13:41
s Lazarus that he ....Luke 16:24
whom the Father will *s* ....John 14:26
has sent Me, I also *s* ....John 20:21

SENNACHERIB
Assyrian king (705–681 B.C.); son and successor of Sargon II, 2 Kin 18:13
Death of, by assassination, 2 Kin 19:36, 37

SENSES
of use have their *s* ....Heb 5:14

SENSUAL
but is earthly, *s* ....James 3:15
These are *s* persons ....Jude 19

SENT
and His Spirit have *s* ....Is 48:16
s these prophets ....Jer 23:21
As the Father has *s* ....John 20:21
unless they are *s* ....Rom 10:15
s His Son to be the ....1 John 4:10

SEPARATE
he shall *s* himself ....Num 6:3
s yourselves from the ....Ezra 10:11
let not man *s* ....Matt 19:6
Who shall *s* us from ....Rom 8:35
harmless, undefiled, *s* ....Heb 7:26

SEPARATED
but the poor is *s* ....Prov 19:4
"The LORD has utterly *s* ....Is 56:3
to be an apostle, *s* ....Rom 1:1
it pleased God, who *s* ....Gal 1:15

SEPARATES
who repeats a matter *s* ....Prov 17:9

SEPARATION
the middle wall of *s* ....Eph 2:14

SERAPHIM
Above it stood *s* ....Is 6:2

SERGIUS PAULUS
Roman proconsul of Cyprus, converted by Paul, Acts 13:7–12

SERPENT
s was more cunning ....Gen 3:1
"The *s* deceived me ....Gen 3:13
"Make a fiery *s* ....Num 21:8
like the poison of a *s* ....Ps 58:4
s you shall trample ....Ps 91:13
their tongues like a *s* ....Ps 140:3
air, the way of a *s* ....Prov 30:19
s may bite when it is ....Eccl 10:11
be a fiery flying *s* ....Is 14:29
and wounded the *s* ....Is 51:9
will he give him a *s* ....Matt 7:10
Moses lifted up the *s* ....John 3:14
was cast out, that *s* ....Rev 12:9

SERPENTS
is the poison of *s* ....Deut 32:33
be wise as *s* ....Matt 10:16
to trample on *s* ....Luke 10:19

SERVANT
a *s* of servants he ....Gen 9:25
s who earnestly ....Job 7:2
and the fool will be *s* ....Prov 11:29
s will rule over a son ....Prov 17:2
A *s* will not be ....Prov 29:19
Who is blind but My *s* ....Is 42:19
"Is Israel a *s* ....Jer 2:14
and a *s* his master ....Mal 1:6
you, let him be your *s* ....Matt 20:26
good and faithful *s* ....Matt 25:21
'You wicked and lazy *s* ....Matt 25:26
the unprofitable *s* ....Matt 25:30
that *s* who knew his ....Luke 12:47
s does not know what ....John 15:15
against Your holy *S* ....Acts 4:27

SERVANTS
puts no trust in His *s* ....Job 4:18
for all your *s* ....Ps 119:91
on the ground like *s* ....Eccl 10:7
shall call you the *s* ....Is 61:6
S rule over us ....Lam 5:8
are unprofitable *s* ....Luke 17:10
longer do I call you *s* ....John 15:15
so consider us, as *s* ....1 Cor 4:1

SERVE
LORD your God and *s* ....Deut 6:13
land, so you shall *s* aliens ....Jer 5:19
s Him with one accord ....Zeph 3:9
You cannot *s* God and ....Matt 6:24
to be served, but to *s* ....Matt 20:28
the mind I myself *s* ....Rom 7:25
but through love *s* ....Gal 5:13
s the LORD Christ ....Col 3:24
s the living God ....Heb 9:14
s Him day and night in ....Rev 7:15

SERVICE
do you mean by this *s* ....Ex 12:26
that he offers God *s* ....John 16:2
is your reasonable *s* ....Rom 12:1
with goodwill doing *s* ....Eph 6:7
your works, love, *s* ....Rev 2:19

SERVING
years I have been *s* ....Luke 15:29
s the Lord with all ....Acts 20:19
fervent in spirit, *s* ....Rom 12:11
you, *s* as overseers ....1 Pet 5:2

SET
"See, I have *s* ....Deut 30:15
s the LORD always ....Ps 16:8
I will *s* him on high ....Ps 91:14
s aside the grace ....Gal 2:21

SETH
Third son of Adam, Gen 4:25
In Christ's ancestry, Luke 3:38

SETTLED
and my speech *s* ....Job 29:22
O LORD, Your word is *s* ....Ps 119:89
the mountains were *s* ....Prov 8:25
s accounts with them ....Matt 25:19

SEVEN
S times a day I praise ....Ps 119:164
s other spirits more ....Luke 11:26
s times in a day ....Luke 17:4
out from among you *s* ....Acts 6:3
s churches which are ....Rev 1:4

SEVENTY
S weeks are ....Dan 9:24
up to *s* times seven ....Matt 18:22
Then the *s* returned ....Luke 10:17

SEVERE
My wound is *s* ....Jer 10:19
not to be too *s* ....2 Cor 2:5

SHADE
I sat down in his *s* ....Song 2:3
be a tabernacle for *s* ....Is 4:6
may nest under its *s* ....Mark 4:32

SHADOW
May darkness and the *s* ....Job 3:5
He flees like a *s* ....Job 14:2
hide me under the *s* ....Ps 17:8
walks about like a *s* ....Ps 39:6
like a passing *s* ....Ps 144:4

he passes like a *s* ... Eccl 6:12
and to trust in the *s* ... Is 30:2
In the *s* of His hand ... Is 49:2
which are a *s* of ... Col 2:17
the law, having a *s* ... Heb 10:1
is no variation or *s* ... James 1:17

SHADOWS
my members are like *s* ... Job 17:7
and the *s* flee away ... Song 2:17

SHADRACH
Hananiah's Babylonian name, Dan 1:3, 7
Cast into the fiery furnace, Dan 3:1–28

SHAKE
Who is he who will *s* ... Job 17:3
s the earth ... Is 2:19
S yourself from the ... Is 52:2
s their heads at the ... Lam 2:15
and the knees *s* ... Nah 2:10
hiss and *s* his fist ... Zeph 2:15
I will *s* all nations ... Hag 2:7
s not only the earth ... Heb 12:26

SHAKEN
he will never be *s* ... Ps 112:6
together was *s* ... Acts 4:31
not to be soon *s* ... 2 Thess 2:2

SHAKES
s the earth out of its ... Job 9:6
s the Wilderness ... Ps 29:8

SHALLUM
King of Israel, 2 Kin 15:10–15

SHALMANESER
Assyrian king, 2 Kin 17:3

SHAME
you turn my glory to *s* ... Ps 4:2
let them be put to *s* ... Ps 83:17
s who serve carved ... Ps 97:7
hate Zion be put to *s* ... Ps 129:5
s shall be the ... Prov 3:35
is a son who causes *s* ... Prov 10:5
hide My face from *s* ... Is 50:6
S has covered our ... Jer 51:51
their glory into *s* ... Hos 4:7
never be put to *s* ... Joel 2:26
the unjust knows no *s* ... Zeph 3:5
worthy to suffer *s* ... Acts 5:41
will not be put to *s* ... Rom 9:33
to put to *s* the wise ... 1 Cor 1:27
I say this to your *s* ... 1 Cor 6:5
glory is in their *s* ... Phil 3:19
put Him to an open *s* ... Heb 6:6

SHAMEFUL
committing what is *s* ... Rom 1:27
for it is *s* for women ... 1 Cor 14:35
For it is *s* even to ... Eph 5:12

SHAMGAR
Judge of Israel; strikes down 600 Philistines, Judg 3:31

SHAMMAH
Son of Jesse, 1 Sam 16:9
Called Shimea, 1 Chr 2:13
——— One of David's mighty men, 2 Sam 23:11
Also called Shammoth the Harorite, 1 Chr 11:27

SHAPHAN
Scribe under Josiah, 2 Kin 22:3–14

SHARE
a stranger does not *s* ... Prov 14:10
s your bread with the ... Is 58:7
is taught the word *s* ... Gal 6:6
to give, willing to *s* ... 1 Tim 6:18
to do good and to *s* ... Heb 13:16

SHARON
Coastal plain between Joppa and Mt. Carmel, 1 Chr 27:29
Famed for roses, Song 2:1
Inhabitants of, turn to the Lord, Acts 9:35

SHARP
S as a two-edged sword ... Prov 5:4

SHARPEN
s their tongue like a ... Ps 64:3
and one does not *s* ... Eccl 10:10

SHATTERED
at ease, but He has *s* ... Job 16:12

SHEALTIEL
Son of King Jeconiah and father of Zerubbabel, 1 Chr 3:17

SHEAR-JASHUB
Symbolic name given to Isaiah's son, Is 7:3

SHEATH
'Return it to its *s* ... Ezek 21:30
your sword into the *s* ... John 18:11

SHEAVES
bringing his *s* ... Ps 126:6
nor he who binds *s* ... Ps 129:7
gather them like *s* ... Mic 4:12

SHEBA
Land of, occupied by Sabeans, famous traders, Job 1:15; Ps 72:10
Queen of, visits Solomon; marvels at his wisdom, 1 Kin 10:1–13
Mentioned by Christ, Matt 12:42

SHEBAH
Name given to a well and town (Beersheba), Gen 26:31–33

SHEBNA
Treasurer under Hezekiah, Is 22:15
Demoted to position of scribe, 2 Kin 19:2
Man of pride and luxury, replaced by Eliakim, Is 22:19–21

SHECHEM
Son of Hamor; rapes Dinah, Jacob's daughter, Gen 34:1–31
——— Ancient city of Ephraim, Gen 33:18
Joshua's farewell address delivered at, Josh 24:1–25
Supports Abimelech; destroyed, Judg 9
Rebuilt by Jeroboam I, 1 Kin 12:25

SHED
which is *s* for many ... Matt 26:28

SHEDDING
blood, and without *s* ... Heb 9:22

SHEEP
astray like a lost *s* ... Ps 119:176
slaughter, and as a *s* ... Is 53:7
Pull them out like *s* ... Jer 12:3
have been lost *s* ... Jer 50:6
will search for My *s* ... Ezek 34:11
shall judge between *s* ... Ezek 34:17
s will be scattered ... Zech 13:7
rather to the lost *s* ... Matt 10:6
I send you out as *s* ... Matt 10:16
And He will set the *s* ... Matt 25:33
having a hundred *s* ... Luke 15:4
and he calls his own *s* ... John 10:3
and I know My *s* ... John 10:14
s I have which are not ... John 10:16
"He was led as a *s* ... Acts 8:32
like *s* going astray ... 1 Pet 2:25

SHEEPFOLDS
lie down among the *s* ... Ps 68:13

SHELTER
I will trust in the *s* ... Ps 61:4
in You I take *s* ... Ps 143:9
the LORD will be a *s* ... Joel 3:16

SHELTERS
s him all the day long ... Deut 33:12
be pastures, with *s* ... Zeph 2:6

SHEM
Oldest son of Noah, Gen 5:32
Escapes the flood, Gen 7:13
Receives a blessing, Gen 9:23, 26
Ancestor of Semitic people, Gen 10:22–32

SHEMAIAH
Prophet of Judah, 1 Kin 12:22–24
Explains Shishak's invasion as divine punishment, 2 Chr 12:5–8
Records Rehoboam's reign, 2 Chr 12:15

SHEMER
Sells Omri the hill on which Samaria is built, 1 Kin 16:23, 24

SHEOL
down to the gates of *S* ... Job 17:16
not leave my soul in *S* ... Ps 16:10
S laid hold of me ... Ps 116:3
S cannot thank ... Is 38:18
the belly of *S* I cried ... Jon 2:2

SHEPHERD
s is an abomination ... Gen 46:34
s My people Israel ... 2 Sam 5:2
The LORD is my *s* ... Ps 23:1
s Jacob His people ... Ps 78:71
His flock like a *s* ... Is 40:11
of Cyrus, 'He is My *s* ... Is 44:28
s who follows You ... Jer 17:16
because there was no *s* ... Ezek 34:5
I will establish one *s* ... Ezek 34:23
"As a *s* takes from ... Amos 3:12
to the worthless *s* ... Zech 11:17
'I will strike the *S* ... Matt 26:31
"I am the good *s* ... John 10:11
s the church of God ... Acts 20:28
the dead, that great *S* ... Heb 13:20
S the flock of God ... 1 Pet 5:2
when the Chief *S* ... 1 Pet 5:4
of the throne will *s* ... Rev 7:17

SHEPHERDS
your sons shall be *s* ... Num 14:33
And they are *s* who ... Is 56:11
And I will give you *s* ... Jer 3:15
s who destroy and ... Jer 23:1
s who feed My people ... Jer 23:2
s have led them astray ... Jer 50:6
s fed themselves ... Ezek 34:8
in the same country *s* ... Luke 2:8

SHESHACH
Symbolic of Babylon, Jer 25:26

SHESHBAZZAR
Prince of Judah, Ezra 1:8, 11

SHIELD
I am your *s* ... Gen 15:1
He is a *s* to all who ... 2 Sam 22:31
my *s* and the horn of ... Ps 18:2
God is a sun and *s* ... Ps 84:11
truth shall be your *s* ... Ps 91:4
all, taking the *s* ... Eph 6:16

SHIHOR
Name given to the Nile, Is 23:3
Israel's southwestern border, Josh 13:3

SHILOH
Center of worship, Judg 18:31
Headquarters for division of Promised Land, Josh 18:1, 10
Benjamites seize women of, Judg 21:19–23
Ark of the covenant taken from, 1 Sam 4:3–11

Punishment given to, Jer 7:12–15
——— Messianic title, Gen 49:10

SHIMEI
Benjamite; insults David, 2 Sam 16:5–13
Pardoned, but confined, 2 Sam 19:16–23
Breaks agreement; executed by Solomon, 1 Kin 2:39–46

SHIMSHAI
Scribe opposing the Jews, Ezra 4:8–24

SHINAR
Tower built at, Gen 11:2–9

SHINE
LORD make His face *s* .... Num 6:25
cause His face to *s* .... Ps 67:1
the cherubim, *s* .... Ps 80:1
Make Your face *s* .... Ps 119:135
who are wise shall *s* .... Dan 12:3
the righteous will *s* .... Matt 13:43
among whom you *s* .... Phil 2:15

SHINING
the earth, by clear *s* .... 2 Sam 23:4
His clothes became *s* .... Mark 9:3
light is already *s* .... 1 John 2:8
was like the sun *s* .... Rev 1:16

SHIPHRAH
Hebrew midwife, Ex 1:15

SHIPS
pass by like swift *s* .... Job 9:26
down to the sea in *s* .... Ps 107:23
like the merchant *s* .... Prov 31:14
Look also at *s* .... James 3:4

SHIPWRECK
faith have suffered *s* .... 1 Tim 1:19

SHOOT
they *s* out the lip .... Ps 22:7
But God shall *s* .... Ps 64:7

SHORT
have sinned and fall *s* .... Rom 3:23
the work and cut it *s* .... Rom 9:28

SHORTENED
his youth You have *s* .... Ps 89:45
the wicked will be *s* .... Prov 10:27
those days were *s* .... Matt 24:22

SHOUT
s joyfully to the Rock .... Ps 95:1
S joyfully to the LORD .... Ps 98:4
Make a joyful *s* .... Ps 100:1
from heaven with a *s* .... 1 Thess 4:16

SHOW
a land that I will *s* .... Gen 12:1
S me Your ways .... Ps 25:4
s yourselves men .... Is 46:8
s Him greater works .... John 5:20
s us the Father .... John 14:8

SHOWBREAD
you shall set the *s* .... Ex 25:30
s which had been taken .... 1 Sam 21:6
s which was not lawful .... Matt 12:4

SHOWERS
make it soft with *s* .... Ps 65:10
s have been withheld .... Jer 3:3
can the heavens give *s* .... Jer 14:22
from the LORD, like *s* .... Mic 5:7

SHRINES
who made silver *s* .... Acts 19:24

SHULAMITE
Beloved of the bridegroom king, Song 6:13

SHUNAMMITE
Abishag, David's nurse, 1 Kin 1:3, 15
——— Woman who cared for Elisha, 2 Kin 4:8–12

SHUSHAN
Residence of Persian monarchs, Esth 1:2

SHUT
"Or who *s* in the sea .... Job 38:8
Has He in anger *s* .... Ps 77:9
For you *s* up the .... Matt 23:13

SHUTS
s his ears to the cry .... Prov 21:13
s his eyes from seeing .... Is 33:15
brother in need, and *s* .... 1 John 3:17
who opens and no one *s* .... Rev 3:7

SICK
have made him *s* .... Hos 7:5
I was *s* and you .... Matt 25:36
he whom You love is *s* .... John 11:3
many are weak and *s* .... 1 Cor 11:30
have left in Miletus *s* .... 2 Tim 4:20
faith will save the *s* .... James 5:15

SICKLE
Put in the *s* .... Joel 3:13
"Thrust in Your *s* .... Rev 14:15

SICKNESS
will sustain him in *s* .... Prov 18:14
"This *s* is not unto .... John 11:4

SIDE
The LORD is on my *s* .... Ps 118:6
the net on the right *s* .... John 21:6

SIDON
Canaanite city; inhabitants not expelled, Judg 1:31
Hostile relations with Israel, Judg 10:12; Is 23:12; Joel 3:4–6
Jesus preaches to, Matt 15:21; Luke 6:17

SIFT
s the nations with the .... Is 30:28
s the house of Israel .... Amos 9:9
for you, that he may *s* .... Luke 22:31

SIGH
our years like a *s* .... Ps 90:9
the merry-hearted *s* .... Is 24:7
of the men who *s* .... Ezek 9:4

SIGHING
For my *s* comes before .... Job 3:24
s is not hidden .... Ps 38:9

SIGHT
and see this great *s* .... Ex 3:3
seemed good in Your *s* .... Matt 11:26
by faith, not by *s* .... 2 Cor 5:7

SIGN
Show me a *s* for good .... Ps 86:17
will give you a *s* .... Is 7:14
for an everlasting *s* .... Is 55:13
we want to see a *s* .... Matt 12:38
seeks after a *s* .... Matt 12:39
And what will be the *s* .... Matt 24:3
s which will be spoken .... Luke 2:34
again is the second *s* .... John 4:54
For Jews request a *s* .... 1 Cor 1:22
Now a great *s* appeared .... Rev 12:1

SIGNS
and let them be for *s* .... Gen 1:14
you not know their *s* .... Job 21:29
They performed His *s* .... Ps 105:27
We are for *s* and .... Is 8:18
How great are His *s* .... Dan 4:3
cannot discern the *s* .... Matt 16:3
the accompanying *s* .... Mark 16:20
s Jesus did in Cana of .... John 2:11
no one can do these *s* .... John 3:2
you people see *s* .... John 4:48
because you saw the *s* .... John 6:26
is a sinner do such *s* .... John 9:16
this Man works many *s* .... John 11:47
Jesus did many other *s* .... John 20:30
demons, performing *s* .... Rev 16:14

SIHON
Amorite king; defeated by Israel, Num 21:21–32
Territory of, assigned to Reuben and Gad, Num 32:1–38

SILAS (or Silvanus)
Leader in Jerusalem church; sent to Antioch, Acts 15:22–35
Travels with Paul, Acts 15:40, 41
Jailed and released, Acts 16:25–40
Mentioned in epistles, 2 Cor 1:19; 1 Thess 1:1; 2 Thess 1:1; 1 Pet 5:12

SILENCE
that You may *s* .... Ps 8:2
I was mute with *s* .... Ps 39:2
soon have settled in *s* .... Ps 94:17
"Sit in *s* .... Is 47:5
seal, there was *s* .... Rev 8:1

SILENT
the wicked shall be *s* .... 1 Sam 2:9
season, and am not *s* .... Ps 22:2
Do not be *s* to me .... Ps 28:1
Let them be *s* in the .... Ps 31:17
Be *s* in the presence .... Zeph 1:7
Let your women keep *s* .... 1 Cor 14:34

SILOAM
Tower of, falls and kills 18 people, Luke 13:4
Blind man washes in pool of, John 9:1–11

SILVER
and your precious *s* .... Job 22:25
Though he heaps up *s* .... Job 27:16
s tried in a furnace .... Ps 12:6
have refined us as *s* .... Ps 66:10
than the profits of *s* .... Prov 3:14
chosen rather than *s* .... Prov 16:16
refining pot is for *s* .... Prov 17:3
He who loves *s* will .... Eccl 5:10
s has become dross .... Is 1:22
call them rejected *s* .... Jer 6:30
may buy the poor for *s* .... Amos 8:6
him thirty pieces of *s* .... Matt 26:15

SIMEON
Son of Jacob by Leah, Gen 29:32, 33
Avenged his sister's dishonor, Gen 34:25–31
Held hostage by Joseph, Gen 42:18–20, 24
Rebuked by Jacob, Gen 49:5–7
——— Tribe of:
Numbered, Num 1:23; 26:12–14
Receive inheritance, Josh 19:1–9
Fight Canaanites with Judah, Judg 1:1–3, 17–20
——— Just man; blesses infant Jesus, Luke 2:25–35

SIMON
Simon Peter: *see* PETER
——— One of the Twelve; called "the Cananite," Matt 10:4
——— One of Jesus' half brothers, Matt 13:55
——— Pharisee, Luke 7:36–40
——— Man of Cyrene, Matt 27:32
——— Sorcerer, Acts 8:9–24
——— Tanner in Joppa, Acts 9:43

SIMPLE
making wise the *s* .... Ps 19:7
LORD preserves the *s* .... Ps 116:6
understanding to the *s* .... Ps 119:130
s believes every word .... Prov 14:15
the hearts of the *s* .... Rom 16:18

SIMPLICITY
ones, will you love *s* .... Prov 1:22

in the world in *s* .... 2 Cor 1:12
corrupted from the *s* .... 2 Cor 11:3

SIN

committed a great *s* .... Ex 32:20
he died in his own *s* .... Num 27:3
and be sure your *s* .... Num 32:23
to death for his own *s* .... Deut 24:16
all this Job did not *s* .... Job 2:10
and search out my *s* .... Job 10:6
Be angry, and do not *s* .... Ps 4:4
my ways, lest I *s* .... Ps 39:1
s is always before me .... Ps 51:3
in *s* my mother .... Ps 51:5
s is a reproach .... Prov 14:34
good and does not *s* .... Eccl 7:20
soul an offering for *s* .... Is 53:10
And He bore the *s* .... Is 53:12
s I will remember no .... Jer 31:34
They eat up the *s* .... Hos 4:8
Now they *s* more and .... Hos 13:2
who believe in Me to *s* .... Matt 18:6
who takes away the *s* .... John 1:29
S no more .... John 5:14
"He who is without *s* .... John 8:7
convict the world of *s* .... John 16:8
they are all under *s* .... Rom 3:9
s entered the world .... Rom 5:12
s is not imputed .... Rom 5:13
s that grace may .... Rom 6:1
died to *s* once for all .... Rom 6:10
s shall not have .... Rom 6:14
Shall we *s* because we .... Rom 6:15
s that dwells in me .... Rom 7:17
Him who knew no *s* .... 2 Cor 5:21
man of *s* is revealed .... 2 Thess 2:3
we are, yet without *s* .... Heb 4:15
appeared to put away *s* .... Heb 9:26
s willfully after we .... Heb 10:26
it gives birth to *s* .... James 1:15
do it, to him it is *s* .... James 4:17
"Who committed no *s* .... 1 Pet 2:22
say that we have no *s* .... 1 John 1:8
that you may not *s* .... 1 John 2:1
s is lawlessness .... 1 John 3:4
in Him there is no *s* .... 1 John 3:5
and he cannot *s* .... 1 John 3:9
for those who commit *s* .... 1 John 5:16
unrighteousness is *s* .... 1 John 5:17

SINAI

Mountain (same as Horeb) where the law was given, Ex 19:1–25
Used allegorically by Paul, Gal 4:24, 25

SINCERE

Holy Spirit, by *s* love .... 2 Cor 6:6
and from *s* faith .... 1 Tim 1:5
s love of the brethren .... 1 Pet 1:22

SINCERITY

LORD, serve Him in *s* .... Josh 24:14
unleavened bread of *s* .... 1 Cor 5:8
simplicity and godly *s* .... 2 Cor 1:12
men-pleasers, but in *s* .... Col 3:22

SINFUL

Alas, *s* nation .... Is 1:4
and *s* generation .... Mark 8:38
from me, for I am a *s* .... Luke 5:8
the hands of *s* men .... Luke 24:7
become exceedingly *s* .... Rom 7:13
likeness of *s* flesh .... Rom 8:3

SING

"*S* to the LORD .... Ex 15:21
the widow's heart to *s* .... Job 29:13
S out the honor .... Ps 66:2
I will *s* of mercy and .... Ps 101:1
"*S* us one of the songs .... Ps 137:3
My servants shall *s* .... Is 65:14
I will *s* with the .... 1 Cor 14:15
assembly I will *s* .... Heb 2:12
Let him *s* psalms .... James 5:13

SINGERS

The *s* went before .... Ps 68:25
male and female *s* .... Eccl 2:8

SINGING

His presence with *s* .... Ps 100:2
and our tongue with *s* .... Ps 126:2
the time of *s* has come .... Song 2:12
break forth into *s* .... Is 14:7
even with joy and *s* .... Is 35:2
come to Zion with *s* .... Is 35:10
and spiritual songs, *s* .... Eph 5:19

SINK

I *s* in deep mire .... Ps 69:2
to *s* he cried out .... Matt 14:30

SINNED

You only, have I *s* .... Ps 51:4
Jerusalem has *s* .... Lam 1:8
Our fathers *s* and are .... Lam 5:7
"Father, I have *s* .... Luke 15:18
"Rabbi, who *s* .... John 9:2
For as many as have *s* .... Rom 2:12
for all have *s* and .... Rom 3:23
marries, she has not *s* .... 1 Cor 7:28
say that we have not *s* .... 1 John 1:10
for the devil has *s* .... 1 John 3:8

SINNER

s He gives the work .... Eccl 2:26
s does evil a hundred .... Eccl 8:12
s destroys much good .... Eccl 9:18
the city who was a *s* .... Luke 7:37
s who repents than .... Luke 15:7
can a man who is a *s* .... John 9:16
the ungodly and the *s* .... 1 Pet 4:18

SINNERS

in the path of *s* .... Ps 1:1
therefore He teaches *s* .... Ps 25:8
soul with *s* .... Ps 26:9
s be consumed from the .... Ps 104:35
son, if *s* entice you .... Prov 1:10
The *s* in Zion are .... Is 33:14
the righteous, but *s* .... Matt 9:13
tax collectors and *s* .... Matt 11:19
s love those who love .... Luke 6:32
Galileans were worse *s* .... Luke 13:2
God does not hear *s* .... John 9:31
while we were still *s* .... Rom 5:8
many were made *s* .... Rom 5:19
the ungodly and for *s* .... 1 Tim 1:9
the world to save *s* .... 1 Tim 1:15
separate from *s* .... Heb 7:26
such hostility from *s* .... Heb 12:3
things which ungodly *s* .... Jude 15

SINS

my iniquities and *s* .... Job 13:23
from presumptuous *s* .... Ps 19:13
You, our secret *s* .... Ps 90:8
but he who *s* against .... Prov 8:36
s have hidden His face .... Is 59:2
the soul who *s* shall .... Ezek 18:4
to make an end of *s* .... Dan 9:24
if your brother *s* .... Matt 18:15
I take away their *s* .... Rom 11:27
s according to the .... 1 Cor 15:3
are still in your *s* .... 1 Cor 15:17
the forgiveness of *s* .... Eph 1:7
s are clearly evident .... 1 Tim 5:24
once to bear the *s* .... Heb 9:28
If we confess our *s* .... 1 John 1:9
propitiation for our *s* .... 1 John 2:2
s are forgiven you .... 1 John 2:12
Whoever *s* has neither .... 1 John 3:6
you share in her *s* .... Rev 18:4

SION

See ZION
Name given to all or part of Mt. Hermon, Deut 4:48

SISERA

Canaanite commander of Jabin's army; slain by Jael, Judg 4:2–22

SISTER

are my mother and my *s* .... Job 17:14
We have a little *s* .... Song 8:8
is My brother and *s* .... Matt 12:50
to you Phoebe our *s* .... Rom 16:1
s is not under bondage .... 1 Cor 7:15

SIT

Those who *s* in the .... Ps 69:12
"Come down and *s* .... Is 47:1
"Why do we *s* still .... Jer 8:14
but to *s* on My right .... Matt 20:23
and the Pharisees *s* .... Matt 23:2
"*S* at My right hand .... Heb 1:13
say to him, "You *s* .... James 2:3
I will grant to *s* .... Rev 3:21
heart, 'I *s* as queen .... Rev 18:7

SITS

God *s* on His holy .... Ps 47:8
It is He who *s* above .... Is 40:22
so that he *s* as God .... 2 Thess 2:4
where the harlot *s* .... Rev 17:15

SITTING

You know my *s* down and .... Ps 139:2
see the Son of Man *s* .... Mark 14:62
where Christ is, *s* .... Col 3:1

SKILL

hand forget its *s* .... Ps 137:5
nor favor to men of *s* .... Eccl 9:11
them knowledge and *s* .... Dan 1:17
forth to give you *s* .... Dan 9:22

SKIN

God made tunics of *s* .... Gen 3:21
LORD and said, "*S* .... Job 2:4
have escaped by the *s* .... Job 19:20
Ethiopian change his *s* .... Jer 13:23
s is hot as an oven .... Lam 5:10

SKULL

to say, Place of a *S* .... Matt 27:33

SLACK

He will not be *s* .... Deut 7:10
s hand becomes poor .... Prov 10:4
The Lord is not *s* .... 2 Pet 3:9

SLAIN

s his thousands .... 1 Sam 18:7
beauty of Israel is *s* .... 2 Sam 1:19
the dead, like the *s* .... Ps 88:5
and all who were *s* .... Prov 7:26
I shall be *s* in the .... Prov 22:13
s men are not *s* .... Is 22:2
no more cover her *s* .... Is 26:21
and the *s* of the LORD .... Is 66:16
and night for the *s* .... Jer 9:1
Those *s* by the sword .... Lam 4:9
the prophets, I have *s* .... Hos 6:5
is the Lamb who was *s* .... Rev 5:12

SLANDER

s your own mother's .... Ps 50:20
and whoever spreads *s* .... Prov 10:18

SLANDERERS

be reverent, not *s* .... 1 Tim 3:11
unforgiving, *s* .... 2 Tim 3:3
in behavior, not *s* .... Titus 2:3

SLAUGHTER

as sheep for the *s* .... Ps 44:22
led as a lamb to the *s* .... Is 53:7
but the Valley of *S* .... Jer 7:32

heaven, O Lucifer, *s* . . . . . Is 14:12
fourth is like the *S* . . . . . Dan 3:25
He is an unwise *s* . . . . . Hos 13:13
prophet, nor was I a *s* . . . . . Amos 7:14
s honors his father . . . . . Mal 1:6
will bring forth a *S* . . . . . Matt 1:21
"This is My beloved *S* . . . . . Matt 3:17
Jesus, You *S* of God . . . . . Matt 8:29
not the carpenter's *s* . . . . . Matt 13:55
You are the *S* of God . . . . . Matt 14:33
are the Christ, the *S* . . . . . Matt 16:16
of all he sent his *s* . . . . . Matt 21:37
Whose *S* is He . . . . . Matt 22:42
'Lord,' how is He his *S* . . . . . Matt 22:45
as much a *s* of hell . . . . . Matt 23:15
of the *S* of Man . . . . . Matt 24:37
'I am the *S* of God . . . . . Matt 27:43
"Truly this was the *S* . . . . . Matt 27:54
of Jesus Christ, the *S* . . . . . Mark 1:1
called the *S* of the . . . . . Luke 1:32
out, the only *s* . . . . . Luke 7:12
And if a *s* of peace . . . . . Luke 10:6
to be called your *s* . . . . . Luke 15:19
because he also is a *s* . . . . . Luke 19:9
The only begotten *S* . . . . . John 1:18
that this is the *S* . . . . . John 1:34
of the only begotten *S* . . . . . John 3:18
S can do nothing . . . . . John 5:19
s abides forever . . . . . John 8:35
you believe in the *S* . . . . . John 9:35
I said, 'I am the *S* . . . . . John 10:36
"Woman, behold your *s* . . . . . John 19:26
Jesus Christ is the *S* . . . . . Acts 8:37
declared to be the *S* . . . . . Rom 1:4
in the gospel of His *S* . . . . . Rom 1:9
by sending His own *S* . . . . . Rom 8:3
not spare His own *S* . . . . . Rom 8:32
S Himself will also be . . . . . 1 Cor 15:28
live by faith in the *S* . . . . . Gal 2:20
God sent forth His *S* . . . . . Gal 4:4
longer a slave but a *s* . . . . . Gal 4:7
the knowledge of the *S* . . . . . Eph 4:13
you for my *s* Onesimus . . . . . Philem 10
"You are My *S* . . . . . Heb 1:5
but Christ as a *S* over His . . . . . Heb 3:6
though He was a *S* . . . . . Heb 5:8
but made like the *S* . . . . . Heb 7:3
to be called the *s* . . . . . Heb 11:24
"This is My beloved *S* . . . . . 2 Pet 1:17
Whoever denies the *S* . . . . . 1 John 2:23
God has given of His *S* . . . . . 1 John 5:10
One like the *S* of Man . . . . . Rev 1:13

SONG

is my strength and *s* . . . . . Ex 15:2
Sing to Him a new *s* . . . . . Ps 33:3
He has put a new *s* . . . . . Ps 40:3
in the night His *s* . . . . . Ps 42:8
me, and I am the *s* . . . . . Ps 69:12
asked of us a *s* . . . . . Ps 137:3
I will sing a new *s* . . . . . Ps 144:9
to my Well-beloved a *s* . . . . . Is 5:1
their taunting *s* . . . . . Lam 3:14
I am their taunting *s* . . . . . Lam 3:63
as a very lovely *s* . . . . . Ezek 33:32
They sang a new *s* . . . . . Rev 5:9
And they sing the *s* . . . . . Rev 15:3

SONGS

my Maker, who gives *s* . . . . . Job 35:10
surround me with *s* . . . . . Ps 32:7
have been my *s* in the . . . . . Ps 119:54
Sing us one of the *s* . . . . . Ps 137:3
is one who sings *s* . . . . . Prov 25:20
and spiritual *s* . . . . . Eph 5:19

SONS

s come to honor . . . . . Job 14:21
shall be Your *s* . . . . . Ps 45:16
my beloved among the *s* . . . . . Song 2:3
s shall come from afar . . . . . Is 60:4
"Has Israel no *s* . . . . . Jer 49:1
The precious *s* of Zion . . . . . Lam 4:2
'You are the *s* . . . . . Hos 1:10
He will purify the *s* . . . . . Mal 3:3
to him, "Then the *s* . . . . . Matt 17:26
and you will be *s* . . . . . Luke 6:35
that you may become *s* . . . . . John 12:36
You are *s* of the . . . . . Acts 3:25
of God, these are *s* . . . . . Rom 8:14
who are of faith are *s* . . . . . Gal 3:7
the adoption as *s* . . . . . Gal 4:5
because you are *s* . . . . . Gal 4:6
You are all *s* of light . . . . . 1 Thess 5:5
in bringing many *s* . . . . . Heb 2:10
speaks to you as to *s* . . . . . Heb 12:5
illegitimate and not *s* . . . . . Heb 12:8

SOON

for it is *s* cut off . . . . . Ps 90:10
s forgot His works . . . . . Ps 106:13

SORCERER

omens, or a *s* . . . . . Deut 18:10
But Elymas the *s* . . . . . Acts 13:8

SORCERERS

soothsayers, or your *s* . . . . . Jer 27:9
outside are dogs and *s* . . . . . Rev 22:15

SORCERESS

shall not permit a *s* . . . . . Ex 22:18

SORCERY

For there is no *s* . . . . . Num 23:23
idolatry, *s* . . . . . Gal 5:20

SORES

and putrefying *s* . . . . . Is 1:6
Lazarus, full of *s* . . . . . Luke 16:20

SORROW

multiply your *s* . . . . . Gen 3:16
s dances before him . . . . . Job 41:22
in my soul, having *s* . . . . . Ps 13:2
s is continually . . . . . Ps 38:17
I found trouble and *s* . . . . . Ps 116:3
And He adds no *s* . . . . . Prov 10:22
the heart may *s* . . . . . Prov 14:13
S is better than . . . . . Eccl 7:3
Therefore remove *s* . . . . . Eccl 11:10
and desperate *s* . . . . . Is 17:11
you shall cry for *s* . . . . . Is 65:14
to see labor and *s* . . . . . Jer 20:18
Your *s* is incurable . . . . . Jer 30:15
added grief to my *s* . . . . . Jer 45:3
gather those who *s* . . . . . Zeph 3:18
them sleeping from *s* . . . . . Luke 22:45
s has filled your . . . . . John 16:6
s will be turned . . . . . John 16:20
that I have great *s* . . . . . Rom 9:2
s produces repentance . . . . . 2 Cor 7:10
lest I should have *s* . . . . . Phil 2:27
s as others who have . . . . . 1 Thess 4:13
no more death, nor *s* . . . . . Rev 21:4

SORROWFUL

am a woman of *s* spirit . . . . . 1 Sam 1:15
But I am poor and *s* . . . . . Ps 69:29
For all his days are *s* . . . . . Eccl 2:23
replenished every *s* . . . . . Jer 31:25
were exceedingly *s* . . . . . Matt 17:23
saying, he went away *s* . . . . . Matt 19:22
soul is exceedingly *s* . . . . . Matt 26:38
and went away *s* . . . . . Mark 10:22
and you will be *s* . . . . . John 16:20
if I make you *s* . . . . . 2 Cor 2:2
and I may be less *s* . . . . . Phil 2:28

SORROWS

the *s* of Sheol . . . . . 2 Sam 22:6
s God distributes . . . . . Job 21:17
s shall be multiplied . . . . . Ps 16:4
by men, a Man of *s* . . . . . Is 53:3
are the beginning of *s* . . . . . Matt 24:8
through with many *s* . . . . . 1 Tim 6:10

SORRY

s that He had made man . . . . . Gen 6:6
who will be *s* for you . . . . . Is 51:19
And the king was *s* . . . . . Matt 14:9
For you were made *s* . . . . . 2 Cor 7:9

SOSTHENES

Ruler of the synagogue at Corinth, Acts 18:17

——— Paul's Christian brother, 1 Cor 1:1

SOUGHT

I *s* the LORD . . . . . Ps 34:4
whole heart I have *s* . . . . . Ps 119:10
s the one I love . . . . . Song 3:1
shall be called *S* Out . . . . . Is 62:12
So I *s* for a man . . . . . Ezek 22:30
s what was lost . . . . . Ezek 34:4
s favor from Him . . . . . Hos 12:4
LORD, and have not *s* . . . . . Zeph 1:6
s it diligently . . . . . Heb 12:17

SOUL

s enter their council . . . . . Gen 49:6
with all your *s* . . . . . Deut 6:5
was knit to the *s* . . . . . 1 Sam 18:1
your heart and your *s* . . . . . 1 Chr 22:19
"My *s* loathes my life . . . . . Job 10:1
as you do, if your *s* . . . . . Job 16:4
s draws near the Pit . . . . . Job 33:22
will not leave my *s* . . . . . Ps 16:10
converting the *s* . . . . . Ps 19:7
He restores my *s* . . . . . Ps 23:3
s shall make its boast . . . . . Ps 34:2
s shall be joyful . . . . . Ps 35:9
you cast down, O my *s* . . . . . Ps 42:5
s silently waits . . . . . Ps 62:1
He has done for my *s* . . . . . Ps 66:16
Let my *s* live . . . . . Ps 119:175
s knows very well . . . . . Ps 139:14
No one cares for my *s* . . . . . Ps 142:4
so destroys his own *s* . . . . . Prov 6:32
me wrongs his own *s* . . . . . Prov 8:36
it is not good for a *s* . . . . . Prov 19:2
A satisfied *s* loathes . . . . . Prov 27:7
When You make His *s* . . . . . Is 53:10
s delight itself . . . . . Is 55:2
and your *s* shall live . . . . . Is 55:3
you have heard, O my *s* . . . . . Jer 4:19
the *s* of the father as . . . . . Ezek 18:4
the proud, his *s* . . . . . Hab 2:4
able to destroy both *s* . . . . . Matt 10:28
and loses his own *s* . . . . . Matt 16:26
with all your *s* . . . . . Matt 22:37
Now My *s* is troubled . . . . . John 12:27
of one heart and one *s* . . . . . Acts 4:32
your whole spirit, *s* . . . . . 1 Thess 5:23
to the saving of the *s* . . . . . Heb 10:39
his way will save a *s* . . . . . James 5:20
his righteous *s* . . . . . 2 Pet 2:8
health, just as your *s* . . . . . 3 John 2

SOULS

and will save the *s* . . . . . Ps 72:13
and he who wins *s* . . . . . Prov 11:30
s shall be like a . . . . . Jer 31:12
who made our very *s* . . . . . Jer 38:16
unsettling your *s* . . . . . Acts 15:24
is able to save your *s* . . . . . James 1:21

SOUND

s heart is life . . . . . Prov 14:30
one rises up at the *s* . . . . . Eccl 12:4
voice was like the *s* . . . . . Ezek 43:2
s an alarm in My holy . . . . . Joel 2:1
do not *s* a trumpet . . . . . Matt 6:2
s words which you . . . . . 2 Tim 1:13
that they may be *s* . . . . . Titus 1:13

SOUNDNESS
There is no *s* in my ....Ps 38:3
him this perfect *s* ....Acts 3:16

SOW
s trouble reap ....Job 4:8
then let me *s* ....Job 31:8
s fields and plant ....Ps 107:37
Those who *s* in tears ....Ps 126:5
the wind will not *s* ....Eccl 11:4
Blessed are you who *s* ....Is 32:20
ground, and do not *s* ....Jer 4:3
"They *s* the wind ....Hos 8:7
S for yourselves ....Hos 10:12
s is not made alive ....1 Cor 15:36

SOWER
may give seed to the *s* ....Is 55:10
"Behold, a *s* went ....Matt 13:3

SOWN
shall they be *s* ....Is 40:24
a land not *s* ....Jer 2:2
"You have *s* much ....Hag 1:6
s spiritual things ....1 Cor 9:11
It is *s* in weakness ....1 Cor 15:43
of righteousness is *s* ....James 3:18

SOWS
s righteousness will ....Prov 11:18
s the good seed is the ....Matt 13:37
'One *s* and another ....John 4:37
s sparingly will ....2 Cor 9:6
for whatever a man *s* ....Gal 6:7

SPARE
The LORD would not *s* ....Deut 29:20
hand, but *s* his life ....Job 2:6
S the poor and needy ....Ps 72:13
I will not pity nor *s* ....Jer 13:14
say, "*S* Your people ....Joel 2:17
s them as a man spares ....Mal 3:17
He who did not *s* ....Rom 8:32
s the natural branches ....Rom 11:21
branches, He may not *s* ....Rom 11:21
flesh, but I would *s* ....1 Cor 7:28
if God did not *s* ....2 Pet 2:4

SPARES
s his rod hates his ....Prov 13:24

SPARKLES
it is red, when it *s* ....Prov 23:31

SPARROW
s has found a home ....Ps 84:3
awake, and am like a *s* ....Ps 102:7

SPARROWS
more value than many *s* ....Matt 10:31

SPAT
Then they *s* on Him ....Matt 27:30
in his ears, and He *s* ....Mark 7:33

SPEAK
only the word that I *s* ....Num 22:35
s just once more ....Judg 6:39
s good words to them ....1 Kin 12:7
oh, that God would *s* ....Job 11:5
Will you *s* wickedly ....Job 13:7
For God may *s* in one ....Job 33:14
Will he *s* softly to ....Job 41:3
Do not *s* in the ....Prov 23:9
and a time to *s* ....Eccl 3:7
If they do not *s* ....Is 8:20
tongue He will *s* ....Is 28:11
s anymore in His name ....Jer 20:9
at the end it will *s* ....Hab 2:3
s each man the truth ....Zech 8:16
or what you should *s* ....Matt 10:19
it is not you who *s* ....Matt 10:20
to you when all men *s* ....Luke 6:26
s what We know and ....John 3:11
s what I have seen ....John 8:38
He hears He will *s* ....John 16:13
Spirit and began to *s* ....Acts 2:4
Do all *s* with tongues ....1 Cor 12:30
I would rather *s* ....1 Cor 14:19
So *s* and so do as ....James 2:12

SPEAKING
s your own words ....Is 58:13
while they are still *s* ....Is 65:24
a proof of Christ *s* ....2 Cor 13:3
envy, and all evil *s* ....1 Pet 2:1

SPEAKS
to face, as a man *s* ....Ex 33:11
this day that God *s* ....Deut 5:24
day that I am He who *s* ....Is 52:6
He whom God has sent *s* ....John 3:34
When he *s* a lie ....John 8:44
he being dead still *s* ....Heb 11:4
of sprinkling that *s* ....Heb 12:24

SPEAR
lay hold on bow and *s* ....Jer 6:23
His side with a *s* ....John 19:34

SPEARS
whose teeth are *s* ....Ps 57:4
and their *s* into ....Is 2:4
pruning hooks into *s* ....Joel 3:10

SPECK
do you look at the *s* ....Matt 7:3

SPECTACLE
and make you a *s* ....Nah 3:6
we have been made a *s* ....1 Cor 4:9
He made a public *s* ....Col 2:15
you were made a *s* ....Heb 10:33

SPEECH
one language and one *s* ....Gen 11:1
drop as the rain, my *s* ....Deut 32:2
s settled on them as ....Job 29:22
There is no *s* nor ....Ps 19:3
s is not becoming ....Prov 17:7
your *s* shall be low ....Is 29:4
a people of obscure *s* ....Is 33:19
not understand My *s* ....John 8:43
s deceive the hearts ....Rom 16:18
and his *s* contemptible ....2 Cor 10:10
I am untrained in *s* ....2 Cor 11:6
s always be with grace ....Col 4:6

SPEECHLESS
your mouth for the *s* ....Prov 31:8
And he was *s* ....Matt 22:12

SPEED
they shall come with *s* ....Is 5:26

SPEEDILY
judgment be executed *s* ....Ezra 7:26
to me, deliver me *s* ....Ps 31:2
I call, answer me *s* ....Ps 102:2

SPEND
Why do you *s* money for ....Is 55:2
whatever more you *s* ....Luke 10:35
I will very gladly *s* ....2 Cor 12:15
amiss, that you may *s* ....James 4:3

SPENT
strength shall be *s* ....Lev 26:20
For my life is *s* ....Ps 31:10
in vain, I have *s* ....Is 49:4
"But when he had *s* ....Luke 15:14

SPEW
nor hot, I will *s* ....Rev 3:16

SPIES
to them, "You are *s* ....Gen 42:9
men who had been *s* ....Josh 6:23
s who pretended ....Luke 20:20

SPIRIT
And the *S* of God was ....Gen 1:2
S shall not strive ....Gen 6:3
in whom is the *S* ....Gen 41:38
and everyone whose *s* ....Ex 35:21
S that is upon you ....Num 11:17
And the *S* rested upon ....Num 11:26
LORD would put His *S* ....Num 11:29
he has a different *s* ....Num 14:24
in whom is the *S* ....Num 27:18
portion of your *s* ....2 Kin 2:9
there was no more *s* ....2 Chr 9:4
s came forward and ....2 Chr 18:20
also gave Your good *S* ....Neh 9:20
against them by Your *S* ....Neh 9:30
Then a *s* passed before ....Job 4:15
And whose *s* came from ....Job 26:4
The *S* of God has made ....Job 33:4
hand I commit my *s* ....Ps 31:5
s was not faithful ....Ps 78:8
You send forth Your *S* ....Ps 104:30
Your *S* is good ....Ps 143:10
The *s* of a man is the ....Prov 20:27
Who knows the *s* ....Eccl 3:21
s will return to God ....Eccl 12:7
night, yes, by my *s* ....Is 26:9
out on you the *s* ....Is 29:10
are flesh, and not *s* ....Is 31:3
S has gathered them ....Is 34:16
is the life of my *s* ....Is 38:16
I have put My *S* ....Is 42:1
and His *S* have sent Me ....Is 48:16
s would fail before Me ....Is 57:16
"The *S* of the Lord ....Is 61:1
S entered me when He ....Ezek 2:2
the *S* lifted me up ....Ezek 3:12
who follow their own *s* ....Ezek 13:3
new heart and a new *s* ....Ezek 18:31
be feeble, every *s* ....Ezek 21:7
I will put My *S* ....Ezek 36:27
in him is the *S* ....Dan 4:8
as an excellent *s* ....Dan 5:12
walk in a false *s* ....Mic 2:11
and forms the *s* ....Zech 12:1
and He saw the *S* ....Matt 3:16
I will put My *S* ....Matt 12:18
S descending upon Him ....Mark 1:10
Immediately the *S* ....Mark 1:12
s indeed is willing ....Mark 14:38
go before Him in the *s* ....Luke 1:17
in the power of the *S* ....Luke 4:14
manner of *s* you are of ....Luke 9:55
hands I commit My *s* ....Luke 23:46
they had seen a *s* ....Luke 24:37
s does not have flesh ....Luke 24:39
God is *S* ....John 4:24
I speak to you are *s* ....John 6:63
He was troubled in *s* ....John 13:21
the *S* of truth ....John 14:17
when He, the *S* ....John 16:13
but if a *s* or an angel ....Acts 23:9
whom I serve with my *s* ....Rom 1:9
according to the *S* ....Rom 8:5
the flesh but in the *S* ....Rom 8:9
does not have the *S* ....Rom 8:9
s that we are children ....Rom 8:16
what the mind of the *S* ....Rom 8:27
to us through His *S* ....1 Cor 2:10
also have the *S* ....1 Cor 7:40
gifts, but the same *S* ....1 Cor 12:4
in a tongue, my *s* ....1 Cor 14:14
but the *S* gives life ....2 Cor 3:6
Now the Lord is the *S* ....2 Cor 3:17
we have the same *s* ....2 Cor 4:13
Having begun in the *S* ....Gal 3:3
has sent forth the *S* ....Gal 4:6
he who sows to the *S* ....Gal 6:8
with the Holy *S* ....Eph 1:13
may give to you the *s* ....Eph 1:17
the unity of the *S* ....Eph 4:3

is one body and one *S* . . . Eph 4:4
stand fast in one *s* . . . Phil 1:27
yet I am with you in *s* . . . Col 2:5
and may your whole *s* . . . 1 Thess 5:23
S expressly says that . . . 1 Tim 4:1
division of soul and *s* . . . Heb 4:12
through the eternal *S* . . . Heb 9:14
S who dwells in us . . . James 4:5
made alive by the *S* . . . 1 Pet 3:18
S whom He has given . . . 1 John 3:24
do not believe every *s* . . . 1 John 4:1
By this you know the *S* . . . 1 John 4:2
By this we know the *s* . . . 1 John 4:6
has given us of His *S* . . . 1 John 4:13
S who bears witness . . . 1 John 5:6
not having the *S* . . . Jude 19
I was in the *S* on the . . . Rev 1:10
him hear what the *S* . . . Rev 2:7
And the *S* and the . . . Rev 22:17

SPIRITS
God, the God of the *s* . . . Num 16:22
who makes His angels *s* . . . Ps 104:4
the LORD weighs the *s* . . . Prov 16:2
power over unclean *s* . . . Matt 10:1
heed to deceiving *s* . . . 1 Tim 4:1
not all ministering *s* . . . Heb 1:14
to the Father of *s* . . . Heb 12:9
and preached to the *s* . . . 1 Pet 3:19
spirit, but test the *s* . . . 1 John 4:1

SPIRITUAL
s judges all things . . . 1 Cor 2:15
s people but as to . . . 1 Cor 3:1
to be a prophet or *s* . . . 1 Cor 14:37
However, the *s* is not . . . 1 Cor 15:46
s restore such a one . . . Gal 6:1

SPIRITUALLY
s minded is life . . . Rom 8:6
because they are *s* . . . 1 Cor 2:14

SPITEFULLY
for those who *s* . . . Matt 5:44

SPLENDOR
on the glorious *s* . . . Ps 145:5
of Zion all her *s* . . . Lam 1:6

SPOIL
hate us have taken *s* . . . Ps 44:10
when they divide the *s* . . . Is 9:3
He shall divide the *s* . . . Is 53:12
Take *s* of silver . . . Nah 2:9
s will be divided . . . Zech 14:1

SPOKE
s they did not hear . . . Is 66:4
who feared the LORD *s* . . . Mal 3:16
"No man ever *s* . . . John 7:46
We know that God *s* . . . John 9:29
I was a child, I *s* . . . 1 Cor 13:11
in various ways *s* . . . Heb 1:1
s as they were moved . . . 2 Pet 1:21

SPOKEN
'just as you have *s* . . . Num 14:28
God has *s* once . . . Ps 62:11
I have not *s* in secret . . . Is 45:19
'What have we *s* . . . Mal 3:13
why am I evil *s* . . . 1 Cor 10:30

SPONGE
them ran and took a *s* . . . Matt 27:48

SPOT
and there is no *s* . . . Song 4:7
church, not having *s* . . . Eph 5:27
commandment without *s* . . . 1 Tim 6:14
Himself without *s* . . . Heb 9:14

SPREAD
fell on my knees and *s* . . . Ezra 9:5
they have *s* a net by . . . Ps 140:5
Then He *s* it before me . . . Ezek 2:10
Then the word of God *s* . . . Acts 6:7
the Lord was being *s* . . . Acts 13:49
their message will *s* . . . 2 Tim 2:17

SPREADS
He alone *s* out the . . . Job 9:8
s them out like a tent . . . Is 40:22
Zion *s* out her hands . . . Lam 1:17

SPRING
Truth shall *s* out of . . . Ps 85:11
is like a murky *s* . . . Prov 25:26
sister, my spouse, a *s* . . . Song 4:12
s forth I tell you . . . Is 42:9
of Israel to *s* forth . . . Ezek 29:21
s shall become dry . . . Hos 13:15
s send forth fresh . . . James 3:11

SPRINGING
a fountain of water *s* . . . John 4:14
of bitterness *s* . . . Heb 12:15

SPRINGS
"Have you entered the *s* . . . Job 38:16
He sends the *s* into . . . Ps 104:10
and the thirsty land *s* . . . Is 35:7
and the dry land *s* . . . Is 41:18

SPRINKLED
s dust on his head . . . Job 2:12
and hyssop, and *s* . . . Heb 9:19
having our hearts *s* . . . Heb 10:22

SPROUT
down, that it will *s* . . . Job 14:7
and the seed should *s* . . . Mark 4:27

STAFF
this Jordan with my *s* . . . Gen 32:10
your feet, and your *s* . . . Ex 12:11
Your rod and Your *s* . . . Ps 23:4
LORD has broken the *s* . . . Is 14:5
'How the strong *s* . . . Jer 48:17
they have been a *s* . . . Ezek 29:6
on the top of his *s* . . . Heb 11:21

STAGGER
and He makes them *s* . . . Job 12:25
they will drink and *s* . . . Jer 25:16

STAGGERS
as a drunken man *s* . . . Is 19:14

STAMMERERS
s will be ready . . . Is 32:4

STAMMERING
For with *s* lips and . . . Is 28:11
s tongue that you . . . Is 33:19

STAND
one shall be able to *s* . . . Deut 7:24
"Who is able to *s* . . . 1 Sam 6:20
but it does not *s* . . . Job 8:15
lives, and He shall *s* . . . Job 19:25
ungodly shall not *s* . . . Ps 1:5
Why do You *s* afar off . . . Ps 10:1
Or who may *s* in His . . . Ps 24:3
Who will *s* up for me . . . Ps 94:16
and let an accuser *s* . . . Ps 109:6
he will not *s* before . . . Prov 22:29
Do not take your *s* . . . Eccl 8:3
"It shall not *s* . . . Is 7:7
"*S* in the ways and . . . Jer 6:16
not lack a man to *s* . . . Jer 35:19
whose words will *s* . . . Jer 44:28
and it shall *s* . . . Dan 2:44
but she shall not *s* . . . Dan 11:17
Who can *s* before His . . . Nah 1:6
And who can *s* when He . . . Mal 3:2
that kingdom cannot *s* . . . Mark 3:24
he will be made to *s* . . . Rom 14:4
Watch, *s* fast in the . . . 1 Cor 16:13
for by faith you *s* . . . 2 Cor 1:24
having done all, to *s* . . . Eph 6:13
S therefore . . . Eph 6:14
s fast in the Lord . . . Phil 4:1
now we live, if you *s* . . . 1 Thess 3:8
of God in which you *s* . . . 1 Pet 5:12
Behold, I *s* at the . . . Rev 3:20

STANDARD
LORD will lift up a *s* . . . Is 59:19
Set up the *s* toward . . . Jer 4:6

STANDING
the LORD, and Satan *s* . . . Zech 3:1
they love to pray *s* . . . Matt 6:5
and the Son of Man *s* . . . Acts 7:56
Then I saw an angel *s* . . . Rev 19:17

STANDS
The LORD *s* up to plead . . . Is 3:13
him who thinks he *s* . . . 1 Cor 10:12

STAR
S shall come out of . . . Num 24:17
For we have seen His *s* . . . Matt 2:2
for one *s* differs from . . . 1 Cor 15:41
give him the morning *s* . . . Rev 2:28
And a great *s* fell . . . Rev 8:10
Bright and Morning *S* . . . Rev 22:16

STARS
He made the *s* also . . . Gen 1:16
s are not pure in His . . . Job 25:5
when the morning *s* . . . Job 38:7
the moon and the *s* . . . Ps 8:3
praise Him, all you *s* . . . Ps 148:3
born as many as the *s* . . . Heb 11:12
wandering *s* for whom . . . Jude 13
a garland of twelve *s* . . . Rev 12:1

STATE
man at his best *s* . . . Ps 39:5
us in our lowly *s* . . . Ps 136:23
and the last *s* of that . . . Matt 12:45
learned in whatever *s* . . . Phil 4:11

STATURE
add one cubit to his *s* . . . Matt 6:27
in wisdom and *s* . . . Luke 2:52
the measure of the *s* . . . Eph 4:13

STATUTE
shall be a perpetual *s* . . . Lev 3:17

STATUTES
the *s* of the LORD are . . . Ps 19:8
Teach me Your *s* . . . Ps 119:12
s have been my songs . . . Ps 119:54
not walked in My *s* . . . Ezek 5:6

STAY
her feet would not *s* . . . Prov 7:11
S here and watch with . . . Matt 26:38
for today I must *s* . . . Luke 19:5
the time of your *s* . . . 1 Pet 1:17

STEADFAST
yes, you could be *s* . . . Job 11:15
O God, my heart is *s* . . . Ps 57:7
their heart was not *s* . . . Ps 78:37
his heart is *s* . . . Ps 112:7
God, and *s* forever . . . Dan 6:26
brethren, be *s* . . . 1 Cor 15:58
faith, grounded and *s* . . . Col 1:23
angels proved *s* . . . Heb 2:2
of our confidence *s* . . . Heb 3:14
soul, both sure and *s* . . . Heb 6:19
Resist him, *s* in the . . . 1 Pet 5:9

STEADFASTLY
s set His face to go . . . Luke 9:51
And they continued *s* . . . Acts 2:42
continuing *s* in . . . Rom 12:12

STEADFASTNESS
good order and the *s* . . . Col 2:5
from your own *s* . . . 2 Pet 3:17

STEAL
"You shall not *s* . . . Ex 20:15

STREETS
- the corners of the *s* ... Matt 6:5
- You taught in our *s* ... Luke 13:26
- out quickly into the *s* ... Luke 14:21

STRENGTH
- for by *s* of hand the ... Ex 13:3
- just as my *s* was then ... Josh 14:11
- my soul, march on in *s* ... Judg 5:21
- a man is, so is his *s* ... Judg 8:21
- *s* no man shall ... 1 Sam 2:9
- the God of my *s* ... 2 Sam 22:3
- have armed me with *s* ... 2 Sam 22:40
- the LORD glory and *s* ... 1 Chr 16:28
- Is my *s* the *s* ... Job 6:12
- Him are wisdom and *s* ... Job 12:13
- him because his *s* ... Job 39:11
- You have ordained *s* ... Ps 8:2
- love You, O LORD, my *s* ... Ps 18:1
- The LORD is the *s* ... Ps 27:1
- The LORD is their *s* ... Ps 28:8
- The LORD will give *s* ... Ps 29:11
- delivered by great *s* ... Ps 33:16
- He is their *s* in the ... Ps 37:39
- are the God of my *s* ... Ps 43:2
- is our refuge and *s* ... Ps 46:1
- is He who gives *s* ... Ps 68:35
- I will go in the *s* ... Ps 71:16
- but God is the *s* ... Ps 73:26
- They go from *s* to ... Ps 84:7
- the glory of their *s* ... Ps 89:17
- *s* and beauty are in ... Ps 96:6
- made me bold with *s* ... Ps 138:3
- of the LORD is *s* ... Prov 10:29
- knowledge increases *s* ... Prov 24:5
- *S* and honor are her ... Prov 31:25
- is better than *s* ... Eccl 9:16
- for *s* and not for ... Eccl 10:17
- For You have been a *s* ... Is 25:4
- him take hold of My *s* ... Is 27:5
- of His might and the *s* ... Is 40:26
- might He increases *s* ... Is 40:29
- works it with the *s* ... Is 44:12
- righteousness and *s* ... Is 45:24
- Put on your *s* ... Is 52:1
- O LORD, my *s* and my ... Jer 16:19
- I will destroy the *s* ... Hag 2:22
- He has shown *s* with ... Luke 1:51
- were still without *s* ... Rom 5:6
- *s* is made perfect ... 2 Cor 12:9
- you have a little *s* ... Rev 3:8

STRENGTHEN
- and He shall *s* ... Ps 27:14
- *S* the weak hands ... Is 35:3
- "So I will *s* them in ... Zech 10:12
- *s* your brethren ... Luke 22:32
- *s* the hands ... Heb 12:12
- *s* the things ... Rev 3:2

STRENGTHENED
- weak you have not *s* ... Ezek 34:4
- unbelief, but was *s* ... Rom 4:20
- of His glory, to be *s* ... Eph 3:16
- stood with me and *s* ... 2 Tim 4:17

STRENGTHENS
- *s* the wise more than ... Eccl 7:19
- through Christ who *s* ... Phil 4:13

STRETCH
- will quickly *s* out her ... Ps 68:31
- said to the man, "*S* ... Matt 12:13
- are old, you will *s* ... John 21:18

STRETCHED
- I have *s* out my hands ... Ps 88:9
- His wisdom, and has *s* ... Jer 10:12
- "All day long I have *s* ... Rom 10:21

STRETCHES
- For he *s* out his hand ... Job 15:25

STRICKEN
- My heart is *s* and ... Ps 102:4
- yet we esteemed Him *s* ... Is 53:4
- of My people He was *s* ... Is 53:8
- You have *s* them ... Jer 5:3
- He has *s*, but He will ... Hos 6:1

STRIFE
- let there be no *s* ... Gen 13:8
- You have made us a *s* ... Ps 80:6
- at the waters of *s* ... Ps 106:32
- Hatred stirs up *s* ... Prov 10:12
- comes nothing but *s* ... Prov 13:10
- man stirs up *s* ... Prov 15:18
- transgression loves *s* ... Prov 17:19
- borne me, a man of *s* ... Jer 15:10
- and lust, not in *s* ... Rom 13:13
- even from envy and *s* ... Phil 1:15
- which come envy, *s* ... 1 Tim 6:4

STRIKE
- said, "*S* this people ... 2 Kin 6:18
- The sun shall not *s* ... Ps 121:6
- Let the righteous *s* ... Ps 141:5
- *S* a scoffer ... Prov 19:25
- *s* your hands ... Ezek 21:14
- *s* the waves of the sea ... Zech 10:11
- "*S* the Shepherd ... Zech 13:7
- *s* the earth with a ... Mal 4:6
- 'I will *s* the Shepherd ... Matt 26:31
- if well, why do you *s* ... John 18:23
- the sun shall not *s* ... Rev 7:16
- *s* the earth with all ... Rev 11:6

STRINGED
- of your *s* instruments ... Is 14:11
- of your *s* instruments ... Amos 5:23

STRIP
- *S* yourselves ... Is 32:11
- *s* her naked and expose ... Hos 2:3

STRIPES
- their iniquity with *s* ... Ps 89:32
- *s* we are healed ... Is 53:5
- be beaten with many *s* ... Luke 12:47
- I received forty *s* ... 2 Cor 11:24
- *s* you were healed ... 1 Pet 2:24

STRIVE
- "My Spirit shall not *s* ... Gen 6:3
- He will not always *s* ... Ps 103:9
- Do not *s* with a man ... Prov 3:30
- Let the potsherd *s* ... Is 45:9
- "*S* to enter through ... Luke 13:24
- the Lord not to *s* ... 2 Tim 2:14

STRONG
- Be *s* and conduct ... 1 Sam 4:9
- indeed He is *s* ... Job 9:19
- The LORD *s* and mighty ... Ps 24:8
- bring me to the *s* ... Ps 60:9
- *s* is Your hand ... Ps 89:13
- A wise man is *s* ... Prov 24:5
- *s* shall be as tinder ... Is 1:31
- "We have a *s* city ... Is 26:1
- the weak say, 'I am *s* ... Joel 3:10
- When a *s* man ... Luke 11:21
- We then who are *s* ... Rom 15:1
- I am weak, then I am *s* ... 2 Cor 12:10
- are weak and you are *s* ... 2 Cor 13:9
- my brethren, be *s* ... Eph 6:10
- weakness were made *s* ... Heb 11:34
- *s* is the Lord God ... Rev 18:8

STRONGHOLD
- of my salvation, my *s* ... Ps 18:2
- down the trusted *s* ... Prov 21:22

STRUCK
- *s* the rock twice ... Num 20:11
- the hand of God has *s* ... Job 19:21
- *s* all my enemies ... Ps 3:7
- Behold, He *s* the rock ... Ps 78:20
- I was angry and *s* ... Is 57:17
- in My wrath I *s* ... Is 60:10
- *s* the head from the ... Hab 3:13
- I *s* you with blight ... Hag 2:17
- took the reed and *s* ... Matt 27:30
- Him, they *s* Him on the ... Luke 22:64

STUBBLE
- shall bring forth *s* ... Is 33:11
- his sword, as driven *s* ... Is 41:2
- they shall be as *s* ... Is 47:14
- *s* that passes ... Jer 13:24
- do wickedly will be *s* ... Mal 4:1

STUBBORN
- If a man has a *s* ... Deut 21:18
- and *s* children ... Ezek 2:4

STUMBLE
- causes them to *s* ... Ps 119:165
- to make my steps *s* ... Ps 140:4
- your foot will not *s* ... Prov 3:23
- know what makes them *s* ... Prov 4:19
- one will be weary or *s* ... Is 5:27
- among them shall *s* ... Is 8:15
- we *s* at noonday as at ... Is 59:10
- that they might not *s* ... Is 63:13
- before your feet *s* ... Jer 13:16
- they will *s* and fall ... Jer 46:6
- have caused many to *s* ... Mal 2:8
- you will be made to *s* ... Matt 26:31
- if all are made to *s* ... Matt 26:33
- immediately they *s* ... Mark 4:17
- who believe in Me to *s* ... Mark 9:42
- the day, he does not *s* ... John 11:9
- Who is made to *s* ... 2 Cor 11:29
- whole law, and yet *s* ... James 2:10
- For we all *s* in many ... James 3:2

STUMBLED
- and those who *s* ... 1 Sam 2:4
- God, for you have *s* ... Hos 14:1
- *s* that they should ... Rom 11:11

STUMBLING
- the deaf, nor put a *s* ... Lev 19:14
- but a stone of *s* ... Is 8:14
- Behold, I will lay *s* ... Jer 6:21
- watched for my *s* ... Jer 20:10
- it became their *s* ... Ezek 7:19
- stumbled at that *s* ... Rom 9:32
- I lay in Zion a *s* ... Rom 9:33
- this, not to put a *s* ... Rom 14:13
- to the Jews a *s* ... 1 Cor 1:23
- of yours become a *s* ... 1 Cor 8:9
- and "A stone of *s* ... 1 Pet 2:8
- is no cause for *s* ... 1 John 2:10
- to keep you from *s* ... Jude 24

STUPID
- and regarded as *s* ... Job 18:3
- who hates correction is *s* ... Prov 12:1
- Surely I am more *s* ... Prov 30:2

SUBDUE
- *s* the peoples under us ... Ps 47:3
- shall *s* three kings ... Dan 7:24
- *s* our iniquities ... Mic 7:19
- *s* all things to ... Phil 3:21

SUBJECT
- for it is not *s* ... Rom 8:7
- Let every soul be *s* ... Rom 13:1
- all things are made *s* ... 1 Cor 15:28
- Himself will also be *s* ... 1 Cor 15:28
- Remind them to be *s* ... Titus 3:1
- all their lifetime *s* ... Heb 2:15
- having been made *s* ... 1 Pet 3:22

SUBJECTION
- put all things in *s* ... Heb 2:8
- more readily be in *s* ... Heb 12:9

And I will send a *s* .... Jer 9:16
will die by the *s* .... Ezek 7:15
'A *s*, a *s* is sharpened .... Ezek 21:9
'A *s*, a *s* is drawn .... Ezek 21:28
Bow and *s* of battle I .... Hos 2:18
"Awake, O *s* .... Zech 13:7
to bring peace but a *s* .... Matt 10:34
for all who take the *s* .... Matt 26:52
s will pierce through .... Luke 2:35
he does not bear the *s* .... Rom 13:4
the *s* of the Spirit .... Eph 6:17
than any two-edged *s* .... Heb 4:12
a sharp two-edged *s* .... Rev 1:16
mouth goes a sharp *s* .... Rev 19:15

SWORDS
yet they were drawn *s* .... Ps 55:21
shall beat their *s* .... Is 2:4
look, here are two *s* .... Luke 22:38

SWORE
So I *s* in My wrath .... Ps 95:11
So I *s* in My wrath .... Heb 3:11
and *s* by Him who lives .... Rev 10:6

SWORN
"By Myself I have *s* .... Gen 22:16
The LORD has *s* in .... Ps 132:11
I have *s* by Myself .... Is 45:23
"The LORD has *s* .... Heb 7:21

SYMBOLIC
which things are *s* .... Gal 4:24
It was *s* for the .... Heb 9:9

SYMPATHIZE
Priest who cannot *s* .... Heb 4:15

SYMPATHY
My *s* is stirred .... Hos 11:8

SYNAGOGUE
He went into the *s* .... Luke 4:16
but are a *s* of Satan .... Rev 2:9

SYRIANS
Abraham's kindred, Gen 22:20–23; 25:20
Hostile to Israel, 2 Sam 8:11–13; 10:6–19; 1 Kin 20:1–34; 22:1–38; 2 Kin 6:8—7:7
Defeated by Assyria, 2 Kin 16:9
Destruction of, foretold, Is 17:1–3
Gospel preached to, Acts 15:23, 41

SYRO-PHOENICIAN
Daughter of, freed of demon, Mark 7:25–31

TABERAH
Israelite camp; fire destroys many there, Num 11:1–3

TABERNACLE
you shall make the *t* .... Ex 26:1
t He shall hide me .... Ps 27:5
I will abide in Your *t* .... Ps 61:4
In Salem also is His *t* .... Ps 76.2
How lovely is Your *t* .... Ps 84:1
quiet home, a *t* .... Is 33:20
You also took up the *t* .... Acts 7:43
and will rebuild the *t* .... Acts 15:16
and more perfect *t* .... Heb 9:11
Behold, the *t* .... Rev 21:3

TABERNACLES
us make here three *t* .... Matt 17:4
Feast of *T* was at hand .... John 7:2

TABITHA
See DORCAS

TABLE
shall also make a *t* .... Ex 25:23
prepare a *t* before me .... Ps 23:5
t become a snare .... Ps 69:22
dogs under the *t* .... Mark 7:28
t become a snare .... Rom 11:9
of the Lord's *t* .... 1 Cor 10:21

TABLES
t are full of vomit .... Is 28:8
and overturned the *t* .... Matt 21:12
of God and serve *t* .... Acts 6:2

TABLET
write them on the *t* .... Prov 3:3
is engraved on the *t* .... Jer 17:1

TABOR
Scene of rally against Sisera, Judg 4:6, 12, 14

TAHPANHES (or Tehaphnehes)
City of Egypt; refuge of fleeing Jews, Jer 2:16; 44:1; Ezek 30:18

TAIL
the head and not the *t* .... Deut 28:13
t drew a third of the .... Rev 12:4

TAKE
T your sandal off your .... Josh 5:15
t Your Holy Spirit .... Ps 51:11
t not the word of .... Ps 119:43
in You I *t* shelter .... Ps 143:9
t words with you .... Hos 14:2
T My yoke upon .... Matt 11:29
T what is yours and .... Matt 20:14
and *t* up his cross .... Mark 8:34
T this cup away .... Mark 14:36
My life that I may *t* .... John 10:17
I urge you to *t* heart .... Acts 27:22

TAKEN
you are *t* by the words .... Prov 6:2
He was *t* from prison .... Is 53:8
one will be *t* and the .... Matt 24:40
what he has will be *t* .... Mark 4:25
He was *t* up .... Acts 1:9
until He is *t* out of .... 2 Thess 2:7
By faith Enoch was *t* away ...... Heb 11:5

TALEBEARER
not go about as a *t* .... Lev 19:16
t reveals secrets .... Prov 11:13

TALENT
went and hid your *t* .... Matt 25:25

TALK
shall *t* of them when .... Deut 6:7
t be vindicated .... Job 11:2
with unprofitable *t* .... Job 15:3
My tongue also shall *t* .... Ps 71:24
entangle Him in His *t* .... Matt 22:15
I will no longer *t* .... John 14:30
turned aside to idle *t* .... 1 Tim 1:6

TAMAR
Wife of Er and mother of Perez and Zerah, Gen 38:6–30
—— Absalom's sister, 2 Sam 13:1–32

TAMBOURINE
They sing to the *t* .... Job 21:12
The mirth of the *t* .... Is 24:8

TARES
the *t* also appeared .... Matt 13:26

TARGET
You set me as Your *t* .... Job 7:20
and set me up as a *t* .... Lam 3:12

TARRY
who turns aside to *t* .... Jer 14:8
come and will not *t* .... Heb 10:37

TARSHISH
City at a great distance from Palestine, Jon 1:3
Ships of, noted in commerce, Ps 48:7

TARSUS
Paul's birthplace, Acts 21:39
Saul sent to, Acts 9:30
Visited by Barnabas, Acts 11:25

TARTAN
Sent to fight against Jerusalem, 2 Kin 18:17

TASTE
and its *t* was like the .... Num 11:8
Oh, *t* and see that the .... Ps 34:8
are Your words to my *t* .... Ps 119:103
was sweet to my *t* .... Song 2:3
Do not touch, do not *t* .... Col 2:21
might *t* death for .... Heb 2:9

TASTED
But when He had *t* .... Matt 27:34
t the heavenly gift .... Heb 6:4
t the good word .... Heb 6:5
t that the Lord is .... 1 Pet 2:3

TATTENAI
Persian governor opposing the Jews, Ezra 5:3, 6

TAUGHT
O God, You have *t* .... Ps 71:17
as His counselor has *t* .... Is 40:13
presence, and You *t* .... Luke 13:26
they shall all be *t* .... John 6:45
but as My Father *t* .... John 8:28
from man, nor was I *t* .... Gal 1:12

TAX
t collectors do the .... Matt 5:46
received the temple *t* .... Matt 17:24
I say to you that *t* .... Matt 21:31
Show Me the *t* .... Matt 22:19

TAXES
take customs or *t* .... Matt 17:25
Is it lawful to pay *t* .... Matt 22:17
forbidding to pay *t* .... Luke 23:2
t to whom *t* .... Rom 13:7

TEACH
t them diligently .... Deut 6:7
t Jacob Your judgments .... Deut 33:10
t you the good and the .... 1 Sam 12:23
"Can anyone *t* .... Job 21:22
"I will *t* you about .... Job 27:11
t me what I do not see .... Job 34:32
t me Your paths .... Ps 25:4
T me Your way .... Ps 27:11
t you the fear of the .... Ps 34:11
t You awesome things .... Ps 45:4
t transgressors Your .... Ps 51:13
So *t* us to number our .... Ps 90:12
He will *t* us His ways .... Is 2:3
"Whom will he *t* .... Is 28:9
a bribe, her priests *t* .... Mic 3:11
t the way of God in .... Matt 22:16
in My name, He will *t* .... John 14:26
even nature itself *t* .... 1 Cor 11:14
permit a woman to *t* .... 1 Tim 2:12
things command and *t* .... 1 Tim 4:11
T and exhort these .... 1 Tim 6:2
t you again the first .... Heb 5:12

TEACHER
for One is your *T* .... Matt 23:8
asked Him, "Good *T* .... Mark 10:17
know that You are a *t* .... John 3:2
You call Me *T* .... John 13:13
named Gamaliel, a *t* .... Acts 5:34
a *t* of babes, having .... Rom 2:20
a *t* of the Gentiles in .... 1 Tim 2:7

TEACHERS
than all my *t* .... Ps 119:99
t will not be moved .... Is 30:20
prophets, third *t* .... 1 Cor 12:28
and some pastors and *t* .... Eph 4:11
desiring to be *t* .... 1 Tim 1:7
time you ought to be *t* .... Heb 5:12
of you become *t* .... James 3:1
there will be false *t* .... 2 Pet 2:1

TEACHES
therefore He *t* sinners . . . . .Ps 25:8
the Holy Spirit *t* . . . . .1 Cor 2:13
If anyone *t* otherwise . . . . .1 Tim 6:3
the same anointing *t* . . . . .1 John 2:27

TEACHING
t them to observe all . . . . .Matt 28:20
they did not cease *t* . . . . .Acts 5:42
he who teaches, in *t* . . . . .Rom 12:7
t every man in all . . . . .Col 1:28
t things which they . . . . .Titus 1:11
t us that . . . . .Titus 2:12

TEAR
t yourself in anger . . . . .Job 18:4
lest they *t* me like a . . . . .Ps 7:2
I, even I, will *t* . . . . .Hos 5:14
feet, and turn and *t* . . . . .Matt 7:6
will wipe away every *t* . . . . .Rev 21:4

TEARS
I have seen your *t* . . . . .2 Kin 20:5
my couch with my *t* . . . . .Ps 6:6
t have been my food . . . . .Ps 42:3
with the bread of *t* . . . . .Ps 80:5
drench you with my *t* . . . . .Is 16:9
GOD will wipe away *t* . . . . .Is 25:8
eyes may run with *t* . . . . Jer 9:18
My eyes fail with *t* . . . . .Lam 2:11
His feet with her *t* . . . . .Luke 7:38
night and day with *t* . . . . .Acts 20:31
mindful of your *t* . . . . .2 Tim 1:4
vehement cries and *t* . . . . .Heb 5:7
it diligently with *t* . . . . .Heb 12:17

TEETH
t whiter than milk . . . . .Gen 49:12
by the skin of my *t* . . . . .Job 19:20
You have broken the *t* . . . . .Ps 3:7
As vinegar to the *t* . . . . .Prov 10:26
you cleanness of *t* . . . . .Amos 4:6

TEKOA
Home of a wise woman, 2 Sam 14:2, 4, 9
Home of Amos, Amos 1:1

TELL
that you may *t* it to . . . . .Ps 48:13
the message that I *t* . . . . .Jon 3:2
Who can *t* if God . . . . .Jon 3:9
t him his fault . . . . .Matt 18:15
whatever they *t* . . . . .Matt 23:3
He comes, He will *t* . . . . .John 4:25

TEMAN
Tribe in northeast Edom, Gen 36:34
Judgment pronounced against, Amos 1:12
God appears from, Hab 3:3

TEMPERATE
for the prize is *t* in all . . . . .1 Cor 9:25
husband of one wife, *t* . . . . .1 Tim 3:2

TEMPEST
the windy storm and *t* . . . . .Ps 55:8
one, tossed with *t* . . . . .Is 54:11
And suddenly a great *t* . . . . .Matt 8:24

TEMPLE
So Solomon built the *t* . . . . .1 Kin 6:14
LORD is in His holy *t* . . . . .Ps 11:4
to inquire in His *t* . . . . .Ps 27:4
suddenly come to His *t* . . . . .Mal 3:1
One greater than the *t* . . . . .Matt 12:6
murdered between the *t* . . . . . . .Matt 23:35
found Him in the *t* . . . . .Luke 2:46
"Destroy this *t* . . . . .John 2:19
was speaking of the *t* . . . . .John 2:21
one accord in the *t* . . . . .Acts 2:46
that you are the *t* . . . . .1 Cor 3:16
your body is the *t* . . . . .1 Cor 6:19
grows into a holy *t* . . . . .Eph 2:21
sits as God in the *t* . . . . .2 Thess 2:4
Then the *t* of God was . . . . .Rev 11:19
But I saw no *t* in it . . . . .Rev 21:22
and the Lamb are its *t* . . . . .Rev 21:22

TEMPLES
t made with hands . . . . .Acts 7:48

TEMPORARY
which are seen are *t* . . . . .2 Cor 4:18

TEMPT
Why do you *t* the LORD . . . . .Ex 17:2
they even *t* God . . . . .Mal 3:15
t the LORD your God . . . . .Matt 4:7
that Satan does not *t* . . . . .1 Cor 7:5
nor let us *t* Christ . . . . .1 Cor 10:9
nor does He Himself *t* . . . . .James 1:13

TEMPTATION
do not lead us into *t* . . . . .Matt 6:13
lest you enter into *t* . . . . .Matt 26:41
in time of *t* fall away . . . . .Luke 8:13
t has overtaken you . . . . .1 Cor 10:13
to be rich fall into *t* . . . . .1 Tim 6:9
the man who endures *t* . . . . .James 1:12

TEMPTED
forty days, *t* by Satan . . . . .Mark 1:13
not allow you to be *t* . . . . .1 Cor 10:13
lest you also be *t* . . . . .Gal 6:1
has suffered, being *t* . . . . .Heb 2:18
in all points *t* . . . . .Heb 4:15
But each one is *t* . . . . .James 1:14

TEMPTER
Now when the *t* came . . . . .Matt 4:3

TENDER
your heart was *t* . . . . .2 Kin 22:19
t shoots will not . . . . .Job 14:7
no more be called *t* . . . . .Is 47:1
through the *t* mercy of . . . . .Luke 1:78
put on *t* mercies . . . . .Col 3:12

TENDERHEARTED
to one another, *t* . . . . .Eph 4:32
love as brothers, be *t* . . . . .1 Pet 3:8

TENT
shall know that your *t* . . . . .Job 5:24
like a shepherd's *t* . . . . .Is 38:12
the place of your *t* . . . . .Is 54:2
My *t* is plundered . . . . .Jer 10:20
earthly house, this *t* . . . . .2 Cor 5:1
long as I am in this *t* . . . . .2 Pet 1:13
I must put off my *t* . . . . .2 Pet 1:14

TENTMAKERS
occupation they were *t* . . . . .Acts 18:3

TENTS
those who dwell in *t* . . . . .Gen 4:20
"How lovely are your *t* . . . . .Num 24:5
The *t* of robbers . . . . .Job 12:6
than dwell in the *t* . . . . .Ps 84:10
I dwell among the *t* . . . . .Ps 120:5
LORD will save the *t* . . . . .Zech 12:7

TERAH
Father of Abram, Gen 11:26
Idolater, Josh 24:2
Dies in Haran, Gen 11:25–32

TERRESTRIAL
bodies and *t* bodies . . . . .1 Cor 15:40

TERRIBLE
t wilderness .Deut 1:19
haughtiness of the *t* . . . . .Is 13:11
is great and very *t* . . . . .Joel 2:11

TERRIFIED
to you, 'Do not be *t* . . . . .Deut 1:29
But they were *t* . . . . .Luke 24:37
and not in any way *t* . . . . .Phil 1:28

TERRIFIES
and the Almighty *t* . . . . .Job 23:16

TERRIFY
me with dreams and *t* . . . . .Job 7:14
not let dread of Him *t* . . . . .Job 9:34
are coming to *t* them . . . . .Zech 1:21

TERROR
there shall be *t* . . . . .Deut 32:25
are nothing, you see *t* . . . . .Job 6:21
from God is a *t* . . . . .Job 31:23
not be afraid of the *t* . . . . .Ps 91:5
I will make you a *t* . . . . .Jer 20:4
but a great *t* fell . . . . .Dan 10:7

TERRORS
the *t* of God are . . . . .Job 6:4
T frighten him on . . . . .Job 18:11
before the king of *t* . . . . .Job 18:14
T overtake him like a . . . . .Job 27:20
consumed with *t* . . . . .Ps 73:19

TERTULLUS
Orator who accuses Paul, Acts 24:1–8

TEST
God has come to *t* you . . . . .Ex 20:20
t him with hard . . . . .1 Kin 10:1
behold, His eyelids *t* . . . . .Ps 11:4
t them as gold is . . . . .Zech 13:9
said, "Why do you *t* . . . . .Matt 22:18
t the Spirit of the . . . . .Acts 5:9
why do you *t* God by . . . . .Acts 15:10
and the fire will *t* . . . . .1 Cor 3:13
T yourselves . . . . .2 Cor 13:5
T all things . . . . .1 Thess 5:21
but *t* the spirits . . . . .1 John 4:1

TESTAMENT
where there is a *t* . . . . .Heb 9:16
For a *t* is in force . . . . .Heb 9:17

TESTED
that God *t* Abraham . . . . .Gen 22:1
You have *t* my heart . . . . .Ps 17:3
And they *t* God in . . . . .Ps 78:18
t you at the waters of . . . . .Ps 81:7
When your fathers *t* . . . . .Ps 95:9
t them ten days . . . . .Dan 1:14
also first be *t* . . . . .1 Tim 3:10
Where your fathers *t* . . . . .Heb 3:9
though it is *t* by fire . . . . .1 Pet 1:7
t those who say they . . . . .Rev 2:2

TESTIFIED
Yet the LORD *t* against . . . . .2 Kin 17:13
he who has seen has *t* . . . . .John 19:35
for as you have *t* . . . . .Acts 23:11
t beforehand the . . . . .1 Pet 1:11
of God which He has *t* . . . . .1 John 5:9

TESTIFIES
and heard, that He *t* . . . . .John 3:32
that the Holy Spirit *t* . . . . .Acts 20:23

TESTIFY
yes, your own lips *t* . . . . .Job 15:6
You, and our sins *t* . . . . .Is 59:12
T against Me . . . . .Mic 6:3
t what We have . . . . .John 3:11
these are they which *t* . . . . .John 5:39
t that the Father . . . . .1 John 4:14
sent My angel to *t* . . . . .Rev 22:16

TESTIFYING
was righteous, God *t* . . . . .Heb 11:4
t that this is .1 Pet 5:12

TESTIMONIES
those who keep His *t* . . . . .Ps 119:2
for I have kept Your *t* . . . . .Ps 119:22
t are my meditation . . . . .Ps 119:99
I love Your *t* . . . . .Ps 119:119
t are wonderful . . . . .Ps 119:129

TESTIMONY
two tablets of the *T* . . . . .Ex 31:18

For He established a *t* . . . . .Ps 78:5
that I may keep the *t* . . . . .Ps 119:88
Bind up the *t* . . . . .Is 8:16
under your feet as a *t* . . . . .Mark 6:11
Now this is the *t* . . . . John 1:19
no one receives His *t* . . . . John 3:32
who has received His *t* . . . . John 3:33
in your law that the *t* . . . . John 8:17
and we know that his *t* . . . . .John 21:24
declaring to you the *t* . . . . .1 Cor 2:1
obtained a good *t* . . . . .Heb 11:2
he had this *t* . . . . .Heb 11:5
not believed the *t* . . . . .1 John 5:10
And this is the *t* . . . . .1 John 5:11
For the *t* of Jesus is . . . . .Rev 19:10

TESTING
came to Him, *t* Him . . . . .Matt 19:3
knowing that the *t* . . . . James 1:3

TESTS
the righteous God *t* . . . . .Ps 7:9
gold, but the LORD *t* . . . . .Prov 17:3
men, but God who *t* . . . . .1 Thess 2:4

THADDAEUS
One of the Twelve, Mark 3:18

THANK
"I *t* You and praise . . . . .Dan 2:23
"I *t* You, Father . . . . .Matt 11:25
t that servant because . . . . .Luke 17:9
t You that I am not . . . . .Luke 18:11
First, I *t* my God . . . . .Rom 1:8
t Christ Jesus our . . . . .1 Tim 1:12

THANKFUL
Be *t* to Him .Ps 100:4
Him as God, nor were *t* . . . . .Rom 1:21

THANKFULNESS
Felix, with all *t* . . . . .Acts 24:3

THANKS
the cup, and gave *t* . . . . .Matt 26:27
t He distributed them . . . . John 6:11
for he gives God *t* . . . . .Rom 14:6
T be to God for His . . . . .2 Cor 9:15
giving *t* always for . . . . Eph 5:20
t can we render . . . . .1 Thess 3:9

THANKSGIVING
with the voice of *t* . . . . .Ps 26:7
Offer to God *t* . . . . .Ps 50:14
His presence with *t* . . . . .Ps 95:2
into His gates with *t* . . . . .Ps 100:4
the sacrifices of *t* . . . . .Ps 107:22
supplication, with *t* . . . . .Phil 4:6
vigilant in it with *t* . . . . .Col 4:2
to be received with *t* . . . . .1 Tim 4:3

THEOPHILUS
Luke addresses his writings to, Luke 1:3; Acts 1:1

THESSALONICA
Paul preaches in, Acts 17:1–13
Paul writes letters to churches of, 1 Thess 1:1

THIEF
When you saw a *t* . . . . .Ps 50:18
do not despise a *t* . . . . .Prov 6:30
t hates his own life . . . . .Prov 29:24
t is ashamed when he . . . . Jer 2:26
the windows like a *t* . . . . Joel 2:9
t shall be expelled . . . . .Zech 5:3
known what hour the *t* . . . . .Matt 24:43
t approaches nor moth . . . . .Luke 12:33
way, the same is a *t* . . . . John 10:1
because he was a *t* . . . . John 12:6
Lord will come as a *t* . . . . .2 Pet 3:10
upon you as a *t* . . . . .Rev 3:3

THIEVES
And companions of *t* . . . . .Is 1:23
destroy and where *t* . . . . .Matt 6:19
before Me and *t* . . . . .John 10:8

THIGH
them hip and *t* with a . . . . Judg 15:8
good piece, the *t* . . . . .Ezek 24:4

THINGS
in heaven give good *t* . . . . .Matt 7:11
evil, speak good *t* . . . . .Matt 12:34
kept all these *t* . . . . .Luke 2:51
Lazarus evil *t* . . . . .Luke 16:25
the Scriptures the *t* . . . . .Luke 24:27
share in all good *t* . . . . .Gal 6:6

THINK
nor does his heart *t* . . . . .Is 10:7
t that they will be . . . . .Matt 6:7
t you have eternal . . . . John 5:39
not to *t* of himself . . . . .Rom 12:3
of ourselves to *t* . . . . .2 Cor 3:5
all that we ask or *t* . . . . Eph 3:20

THINKS
yet the LORD *t* upon me . . . . .Ps 40:17
for as he *t* in his . . . . .Prov 23:7
t that he knows . . . . .1 Cor 8:2
t he stands take heed . . . . .1 Cor 10:12
For if anyone *t* . . . . .Gal 6:3
t he is religious . . . . .James 1:26

THIRST
tongues fail for *t* . . . . .Is 41:17
those who hunger and *t* . . . . .Matt 5:6
in Me shall never *t* . . . . John 6:35
said, "I *t*!" . . . . John 19:28
we both hunger and *t* . . . . .1 Cor 4:11
anymore nor *t* anymore . . . . .Rev 7:16

THIRSTS
My soul *t* for God . . . . .Ps 42:2
saying, "If anyone *t* . . . . .John 7:37
if he *t* . . . . .Rom 12:20
freely to him who *t* . . . . .Rev 21:6
And let him who *t* . . . . .Rev 22:17

THIRSTY
and if he is *t* . . . . .Prov 25:21
as when a *t* man dreams . . . . .Is 29:8
the drink of the *t* . . . . .Is 32:6
t land springs of . . . . .Is 35:7
on him who is *t* . . . . .Is 44:3
but you shall be *t* . . . . .Is 65:13
I was *t* and you gave . . . . .Matt 25:35
we see You hungry or *t* . . . . .Matt 25:44

THISTLES
t grow instead of . . . . .Job 31:40
or figs from *t* . . . . .Matt 7:16

THOMAS
Apostle of Christ, Matt 10:3
Ready to die with Christ, John 11:16
Doubts Christ's resurrection, John 20:24–29

THORN
t that goes into the . . . . .Prov 26:9
t shall come up the . . . . .Is 55:13
a *t* in the flesh was . . . . .2 Cor 12:7

THORNS
Both *t* and thistles it . . . . .Gen 3:18
T and snares are . . . . .Prov 22:5
all overgrown with *t* . . . . .Prov 24:31
the crackling of *t* . . . . .Eccl 7:6
Like a lily among *t* . . . . .Song 2:2
and do not sow among *t* . . . . Jer 4:3
wheat but reaped *t* . . . . Jer 12:13
And some fell among *t* . . . . .Matt 13:7
wearing the crown of *t* . . . . John 19:5

THOUGHT
t is that their houses . . . . .Ps 49:11
You *t* that I was . . . . .Ps 50:21
Both the inward *t* . . . . .Ps 64:6
I *t* about my ways . . . . .Ps 119:59
You understand my *t* . . . . .Ps 139:2
"Surely, as I have *t* . . . . .Is 14:24
to man what his *t* . . . . .Amos 4:13
perceiving the *t* . . . . .Luke 9:47
And he *t* within . . . . .Luke 12:17
I *t* as a child . . . . .1 Cor 13:11

THOUGHTS
the intent of the *t* . . . . .1 Chr 28:9
is in none of his *t* . . . . .Ps 10:4
t toward us . . . . .Ps 40:5
t are very deep . . . . .Ps 92:5
The LORD knows the *t* . . . . .Ps 94:11
t will be established . . . . .Prov 16:3
unrighteous man his *t* . . . . .Is 55:7
For My *t* are not your . . . . .Is 55:8
long shall your evil *t* . . . . Jer 4:14
they do not know the *t* . . . . .Mic 4:12
Jesus, knowing their *t* . . . . .Matt 9:4
heart proceed evil *t* . . . . .Matt 15:19
futile in their *t* . . . . .Rom 1:21
The LORD knows the *t* . . . . .1 Cor 3:20

THREATS
Lord, look on their *t* . . . . .Acts 4:29
still breathing *t* . . . . .Acts 9:1

THREE
you will deny Me *t* . . . . .Matt 26:34
hope, love, these *t* . . . . .1 Cor 13:13
and these *t* are one . . . . .1 John 5:7

THRESH
he does not *t* it . . . . .Is 28:28
t the mountains . . . . .Is 41:15
it is time to *t* her . . . . Jer 51:33
"Arise and *t* . . . . .Mic 4:13

THRESHING
t shall last till the . . . . .Lev 26:5
like the dust at *t* . . . . .2 Kin 13:7
Oh, my *t* and the grain . . . . .Is 21:10

THROAT
t is an open tomb . . . . .Ps 5:9
put a knife to your *t* . . . . .Prov 23:2
unshod, and your *t* . . . . Jer 2:25
t is an open tomb . . . . .Rom 3:13

THRONE
LORD sitting on His *t* . . . . .1 Kin 22:19
He has prepared His *t* . . . . .Ps 9:7
temple, the LORD's *t* . . . . .Ps 11:4
Your *t*, O God, is . . . . .Ps 45:6
has established His *t* . . . . .Ps 103:19
he upholds his *t* . . . . .Prov 20:28
Lord sitting on a *t* . . . . .Is 6:1
"Heaven is My *t* . . . . .Is 66:1
shall be called The *T* . . . . Jer 3:17
do not disgrace the *t* . . . . Jer 14:21
A glorious high *t* . . . . Jer 17:12
t was a fiery flame . . . . .Dan 7:9
sit and rule on His *t* . . . . .Zech 6:13
for it is God's *t* . . . . .Matt 5:34
will give Him the *t* . . . . .Luke 1:32
"Your *t*, O God, is . . . . .Heb 1:8
come boldly to the *t* . . . . .Heb 4:16
where Satan's *t* . . . . .Rev 2:13
My Father on His *t* . . . . .Rev 3:21
I saw a great white *t* . . . . .Rev 20:11

THRONES
t are set there . . . . .Ps 122:5
also sit on twelve *t* . . . . .Matt 19:28
mighty from their *t* . . . . .Luke 1:52
invisible, whether *t* . . . . .Col 1:16
t I saw twenty-four . . . . .Rev 4:4

THRONG
house of God in the *t* . . . . .Ps 55:14

THROW
of your land and *t* . . . . .Mic 5:11

t Yourself down ....Matt 4:6
children's bread and *t* ....Matt 15:26

THROWN
their slain shall be *t* ....Is 34:3
neck, and he were *t* ....Mark 9:42

THUNDER
But the *t* of His power ....Job 26:14
The voice of Your *t* ....Ps 77:18
the secret place of *t* ....Ps 81:7
t they hastened away ....Ps 104:7
that is, "Sons of *T*" ....Mark 3:17
the voice of loud *t* ....Rev 14:2

THUNDERED
"The LORD *t* from ....2 Sam 22:14
The LORD *t* ....Ps 18:13

THUNDERINGS
people witnessed the *t* ....Ex 20:18
the sound of mighty *t* ....Rev 19:6

THUNDERS
t marvelously with His ....Job 37:5
The God of glory *t* ....Ps 29:3

THYATIRA
Residence of Lydia, Acts 16:14
Site of one of the seven churches, Rev 2:18–24

TIBERIAS
Sea of Galilee called, John 6:1, 23

TIDINGS
be afraid of evil *t* ....Ps 112:7
I bring you good *t* ....Luke 2:10
who bring glad *t* ....Rom 10:15

TIGLATH-PILESER
Powerful Assyrian king who invades Samaria, 2 Kin 15:29

TILL
no man to *t* the ground ....Gen 2:5

TILLER
but Cain was a *t* ....Gen 4:2

TILLS
t his land will be ....Prov 12:11
t his land will have ....Prov 28:19

TIME
pray to You in a *t* ....Ps 32:6
ashamed in the evil *t* ....Ps 37:19
how short my *t* is ....Ps 89:47
A *t* to be born ....Eccl 3:2
but *t* and chance ....Eccl 9:11
your *t* was the *t* ....Ezek 16:8
you did not know the *t* ....Luke 19:44
t has not yet come ....John 7:6
I have a convenient *t* ....Acts 24:25
for the *t* is near ....Rev 1:3

TIMES
understanding of the *t* ....1 Chr 12:32
t are not hidden ....Job 24:1
t are in Your hand ....Ps 31:15
the signs of the *t* ....Matt 16:3
Gentiles until the *t* ....Luke 21:24
not for you to know *t* ....Acts 1:7
their preappointed *t* ....Acts 17:26
last days perilous *t* ....2 Tim 3:1
God, who at various *t* ....Heb 1:1

TIMON
One of the first seven deacons, Acts 6:1–5

TIMOTHY
Paul's companion, Acts 16:1–3; 18:5; 20:4, 5; 2 Cor 1:19; Phil 1:1; 2 Tim 4:9, 21
Ministers independently, Acts 17:14, 15; 19:22; 1 Cor 4:17; Phil 2:19, 23; 1 Thess 3:1–6; 1 Tim 1:1–3; 4:14

TIRZAH
Seat of Jeroboam's rule, 1 Kin 14:17
Capital of Israel until Omri's reign, 1 Kin 16:6–23

TITHE
And he gave him a *t* ....Gen 14:20
LORD, a tenth of the *t* ....Num 18:26
"You shall truly *t* ....Deut 14:22
shall bring out the *t* ....Deut 14:28
laying aside all the *t* ....Deut 26:12
in abundantly the *t* ....2 Chr 31:5
Judah brought the *t* ....Neh 13:12
For you pay *t* of mint ....Matt 23:23

TITHES
to redeem any of his *t* ....Lev 27:31
t which you receive ....Num 18:28
and to bring the *t* ....Neh 10:37
firstfruits, and the *t* ....Neh 12:44
the articles, the *t* ....Neh 13:5
Bring all the *t* ....Mal 3:10
I give *t* of all that I ....Luke 18:12
to receive *t* from the ....Heb 7:5
mortal men receive *t* ....Heb 7:8
Levi, who receives *t* ....Heb 7:9

TITTLE
away, one jot or one *t* ....Matt 5:18

TITUS
Ministers in Crete, Titus 1:4, 5
Paul's representative in Corinth, 2 Cor 7:6, 7, 13, 14; 8:6–23

TOBIAH
Ammonite servant; ridicules the Jews, Neh 2:10

TODAY
t I have begotten You ....Ps 2:7
of the field, which *t* ....Matt 6:30
the grass, which *t* ....Luke 12:28
t you will be with Me ....Luke 23:43
t I have begotten You ....Heb 1:5
"*T*, if you will hear ....Heb 3:7
the same yesterday, *t* ....Heb 13:8

TOIL
t you shall eat of ....Gen 3:17
they neither *t* nor ....Matt 6:28
our labor and *t* ....1 Thess 2:9

TOILED
"Master, we have *t* ....Luke 5:5

TOLD
Behold, I have *t* ....Matt 28:7
things which were *t* ....Luke 2:18
t me all things that I ....John 4:29
t you the truth which ....John 8:40
so, I would have *t* ....John 14:2
"And now I have *t* ....John 14:29

TOMB
throat is an open *t* ....Ps 5:9
in the garden a new *t* ....John 19:41
throat is an open *t* ....Rom 3:13

TOMBS
like whitewashed *t* ....Matt 23:27
you build the *t* ....Matt 23:29
For you build the *t* ....Luke 11:47

TOMORROW
drink, for *t* we die ....Is 22:13
t will be as today ....Is 56:12
t is thrown into the ....Matt 6:30
do not worry about *t* ....Matt 6:34
drink, for *t* we die ....1 Cor 15:32
what will happen *t* ....James 4:14

TONGUE
the scourge of the *t* ....Job 5:21
hides it under his *t* ....Job 20:12
Keep your *t* from evil ....Ps 34:13
t shall speak of Your ....Ps 35:28
lest I sin with my *t* ....Ps 39:1
to you, you false *t* ....Ps 120:3
laughter, and our *t* ....Ps 126:2
remember you, let my *t* ....Ps 137:6
is not a word on my *t* ....Ps 139:4
but the perverse *t* ....Prov 10:31
forever, but a lying *t* ....Prov 12:19
A wholesome *t* is a ....Prov 15:4
t keeps his soul ....Prov 21:23
t breaks a bone ....Prov 25:15
t shall take an oath ....Is 45:23
GOD has given Me the *t* ....Is 50:4
t should confess that ....Phil 2:11
does not bridle his *t* ....James 1:26
t is a little member ....James 3:5
And the *t* is a fire ....James 3:6
no man can tame the *t* ....James 3:8
love in word or in *t* ....1 John 3:18
every nation, tribe, *t* ....Rev 14:6

TONGUES
From the strife of *t* ....Ps 31:20
speak with new *t* ....Mark 16:17
to them divided *t*, as of fire ....Acts 2:3
and they spoke with *t* ....Acts 19:6
I speak with the *t* ....1 Cor 13:1
Therefore *t* are for a ....1 Cor 14:22

TOOTH
eye for eye, *t* ....Ex 21:24
is like a bad *t* ....Prov 25:19
eye for an eye and a *t* ....Matt 5:38

TOPHET
See HINNOM, VALLEY OF THE SON OF
T was established ....Is 30:33
the high places of *T* ....Jer 7:31
make this city like *T* ....Jer 19:12
like the place of *T* ....Jer 19:13

TORCH
and like a fiery *t* ....Zech 12:6

TORCHES
When he had set the *t* ....Judg 15:5
his eyes like *t* ....Dan 10:6
come with flaming *t* ....Nah 2:3

TORMENT
"How long will you *t* ....Job 19:2
shall lie down in *t* ....Is 50:11
You come here to *t* ....Matt 8:29
to this place of *t* ....Luke 16:28
fear involves *t* ....1 John 4:18
t ascends forever ....Rev 14:11

TORMENTED
for I am *t* in this ....Luke 16:24
And they will be *t* ....Rev 20:10

TORMENTS
And being in *t* ....Luke 16:23

TORN
aside my ways and *t* ....Lam 3:11
for He has *t* ....Hos 6:1
of the temple was *t* ....Matt 27:51

TOSSED
t with tempest ....Is 54:11
t to and fro and ....Eph 4:14

TOUCH
seven no evil shall *t* ....Job 5:19
t no unclean thing ....Is 52:11
"If only I may *t* ....Matt 9:21
that they might only *t* ....Matt 14:36
a man not to *t* a woman ....1 Cor 7:1
wicked one does not *t* ....1 John 5:18

TOUCHED
whose hearts God had *t* ......1 Sam 10:26
t my mouth with it ....Is 6:7
hand and *t* my mouth ....Jer 1:9
mountain that may be *t* ....Heb 12:18

TOUCHES
- He *t* the hills ... Ps 104:32
- *t* you *t* the ... Zech 2:8

TOWER
- *t* whose top is in the ... Gen 11:4
- for me, a strong *t* ... Ps 61:3
- my fortress, my high *t* ... Ps 144:2
- like an ivory *t* ... Song 7:4
- a watchman in the *t* ... Is 21:5
- in it and built a *t* ... Matt 21:33

TRADITION
- transgress the *t* ... Matt 15:2
- of no effect by your *t* ... Matt 15:6
- according to the *t* ... Col 2:8
- *t* which he received ... 2 Thess 3:6
- conduct received by *t* ... 1 Pet 1:18

TRADITIONS
- zealous for the *t* ... Gal 1:14
- *t* which you were ... 2 Thess 2:15

TRAIN
- *T* up a child in the ... Prov 22:6
- *t* of His robe filled ... Is 6:1

TRAINED
- who is perfectly *t* ... Luke 6:40
- those who have been *t* ... Heb 12:11

TRAINING
- bring them up in the *t* ... Eph 6:4

TRAITOR
- also became a *t* ... Luke 6:16

TRAITORS
- *t*, headstrong ... 2 Tim 3:4

TRAMPLE
- Your name we will *t* ... Ps 44:5
- serpent you shall *t* ... Ps 91:13
- hand, to *t* My courts ... Is 1:12
- You shall *t* the wicked ... Mal 4:3
- swine, lest they *t* ... Matt 7:6
- you the authority to *t* ... Lk 10:19

TRAMPLED
- *t* them in My fury ... Is 63:3
- now she will be *t* ... Mic 7:10
- *t* the nations in anger ... Hab 3:12
- Jerusalem will be *t* ... Luke 21:24
- *t* the Son of God ... Heb 10:29
- the winepress was *t* ... Rev 14:20

TRANCE
- he fell into a *t* ... Acts 10:10
- *t* I saw a vision ... Acts 11:5

TRANSFIGURED
- and was *t* before them ... Matt 17:2

TRANSFORMED
- this world, but be *t* ... Rom 12:2
- the Lord, are being *t* ... 2 Cor 3:18

TRANSGRESS
- *t* the command of the ... Num 14:41
- the LORD's people *t* ... 1 Sam 2:24
- my mouth shall not *t* ... Ps 17:3
- his mouth must not *t* ... Prov 16:10
- of bread a man will *t* ... Prov 28:21
- do Your disciples *t* ... Matt 15:2

TRANSGRESSED
- *t* My covenant ... Josh 7:11
- your mediators have *t* ... Is 43:27
- the rulers also *t* ... Jer 2:8
- their fathers have *t* ... Ezek 2:3
- Yes, all Israel has *t* ... Dan 9:11
- *t* your commandment ... Luke 15:29

TRANSGRESSES
- "Indeed, because he *t* ... Hab 2:5
- Whoever *t* and does not ... 2 John 9

TRANSGRESSION
- iniquity and *t* and sin ... Ex 34:7
- Make me know my *t* ... Job 13:23
- *t* is sealed up in a ... Job 14:17
- be innocent of great *t* ... Ps 19:13
- because of their *t* ... Ps 107:17
- He who covers a *t* ... Prov 17:9
- He who loves *t* loves ... Prov 17:19
- tell My people their *t* ... Is 58:1
- at Gilgal multiply *t* ... Amos 4:4
- my firstborn for my *t* ... Mic 6:7
- and passing over the *t* ... Mic 7:18
- no law there is no *t* ... Rom 4:15
- deceived, fell into *t* ... 1 Tim 2:14
- steadfast, and every *t* ... Heb 2:2

TRANSGRESSIONS
- if I have covered my *t* ... Job 31:33
- "I will confess my *t* ... Ps 32:5
- me from all my *t* ... Ps 39:8
- mercies, blot out my *t* ... Ps 51:1
- For I acknowledge my *t* ... Ps 51:3
- has He removed our *t* ... Ps 103:12
- who blots out your *t* ... Is 43:25
- was wounded for our *t* ... Is 53:5
- for the *t* of My people ... Is 53:8
- from you all the *t* ... Ezek 18:31
- was added because of *t* ... Gal 3:19
- redemption of the *t* ... Heb 9:15

TRANSGRESSOR
- and were called a *t* ... Is 48:8
- I make myself a *t* ... Gal 2:18

TRANSGRESSORS
- Then I will teach *t* ... Ps 51:13
- to any wicked *t* ... Ps 59:5
- numbered with the *t* ... Is 53:12
- numbered with the *t* ... Mark 15:28

TRAP
- of Israel, as a *t* ... Is 8:14
- where there is no *t* ... Amos 3:5

TRAPS
- they have set *t* ... Ps 140:5
- for me, and from the *t* ... Ps 141:9

TREACHEROUS
- the *t* dealer deals ... Is 21:2
- an assembly of *t* men ... Jer 9:2
- are insolent, *t* ... Zeph 3:4

TREACHEROUSLY
- and you who deal *t* ... Is 33:1
- happy who deal so *t* ... Jer 12:1
- even they have dealt *t* ... Jer 12:6
- They have dealt *t* ... Hos 5:7
- Why do we deal *t* ... Mal 2:10
- that you do not deal *t* ... Mal 2:16
- This man dealt *t* ... Acts 7:19

TREAD
- *t* down the wicked in ... Job 40:12
- it is He who shall *t* ... Ps 60:12
- You shall *t* upon the ... Ps 91:13
- shout, as those who *t* ... Jer 25:30
- will come down and *t* ... Mic 1:3
- And they will *t* ... Rev 11:2

TREADS
- like one who *t* in the ... Is 63:2
- *t* the high places ... Amos 4:13
- an ox while it *t* ... 1 Tim 5:18
- *t* the winepress ... Rev 19:15

TREASURE
- to you His good *t* ... Deut 28:12
- one who finds great *t* ... Ps 119:162
- for His special *t* ... Ps 135:4
- there is much *t* ... Prov 15:6
- There is desirable *t* ... Prov 21:20
- of the LORD is His *t* ... Is 33:6
- For where your *t* ... Matt 6:21
- *t* brings forth evil ... Matt 12:35
- *t* things new and old ... Matt 13:52
- and you will have *t* ... Matt 19:21
- So is he who lays up *t* ... Luke 12:21
- But we have this *t* ... 2 Cor 4:7
- You have heaped up *t* ... James 5:3

TREASURES
- sealed up among My *t* ... Deut 32:34
- it more than hidden *t* ... Job 3:21
- her as for hidden *t* ... Prov 2:4
- *t* of wickedness profit ... Prov 10:2
- Getting *t* by a lying ... Prov 21:6
- is no end to their *t* ... Is 2:7
- I will give you the *t* ... Is 45:3
- Are there yet the *t* ... Mic 6:10
- for yourselves *t* ... Matt 6:19
- are hidden all the *t* ... Col 2:3
- riches than the *t* ... Heb 11:26

TREATY
- Now Solomon made a *t* ... 1 Kin 3:1

TREE
- but of the *t* ... Gen 2:17
- you eaten from the *t* ... Gen 3:11
- there is hope for a *t* ... Job 14:7
- *t* planted by the ... Ps 1:3
- like a native green *t* ... Ps 37:35
- *t* falls to the south ... Eccl 11:3
- Like an apple *t* ... Song 2:3
- for as the days of a *t* ... Is 65:22
- *t* planted by the ... Jer 17:8
- *t* bears good fruit ... Matt 7:17
- His own body on the *t* ... 1 Pet 2:24
- give to eat from the *t* ... Rev 2:7
- the river, was the *t* ... Rev 22:2

TREES
- *t* once went forth ... Judg 9:8
- Also he spoke of *t* ... 1 Kin 4:33
- Then all the *t* of the ... Ps 96:12
- The *t* of the LORD are ... Ps 104:16
- all kinds of fruit *t* ... Eccl 2:5
- they may be called *t* ... Is 61:3
- and on beast, on the *t* ... Jer 7:20
- so that all the *t* ... Ezek 31:9
- "I see men like *t* ... Mark 8:24
- late autumn *t* without ... Jude 12
- the sea, or the *t* ... Rev 7:3

TREMBLE
- *T* before Him ... 1 Chr 16:30
- have made the earth *t* ... Ps 60:2
- let the peoples *t* ... Ps 99:1
- who made the earth *t* ... Is 14:16
- That the nations may *t* ... Is 64:2
- 'Will you not *t* ... Jer 5:22
- wrath the earth will *t* ... Jer 10:10
- they shall fear and *t* ... Jer 33:9
- my kingdom men must *t* ... Dan 6:26

TREMBLED
- of Edom, the earth *t* ... Judg 5:4
- for his heart *t* ... 1 Sam 4:13
- Then everyone who *t* ... Ezra 9:4
- the earth shook and *t* ... Ps 18:7
- and indeed they *t* ... Jer 4:24

TREMBLING
- it was a very great *t* ... 1 Sam 14:15
- your water with *t* ... Ezek 12:18
- in fear, and in much *t* ... 1 Cor 2:3
- *t* you received ... 2 Cor 7:15
- flesh, with fear and *t* ... Eph 6:5
- with fear and *t* ... Phil 2:12

TRESPASSES
- still goes on in his *t* ... Ps 68:21
- forgive men their *t* ... Matt 6:14
- not imputing their *t* ... 2 Cor 5:19
- who were dead in *t* ... Eph 2:1
- forgiven you all *t* ... Col 2:13

TRIAL
- as in the day of *t* ... Ps 95:8

in the day of *t* .....Heb 3:8
concerning the fiery *t* .....1 Pet 4:12
t which shall come .....Rev 3:10

TRIBE

of old, the *t* of Your .....Ps 74:2
belongs to another *t* .....Heb 7:13
the Lion of the *t* .....Rev 5:5
blood out of every *t* .....Rev 5:9

TRIBES

where the *t* go up .....Ps 122:4
to raise up the *t* .....Is 49:6
promise our twelve *t* .....Acts 26:7
t which are scattered .....James 1:1

TRIBULATION

there will be great *t* .....Matt 24:21
world you will have *t* .....John 16:33
in hope, patient in *t* .....Rom 12:12
joyful in all our *t* .....2 Cor 7:4
that we would suffer *t* .....1 Thess 3:4
t those who .....2 Thess 1:6
and you will have *t* .....Rev 2:10
with her into great *t* .....Rev 2:22
out of the great *t* .....Rev 7:14

TRIBULATIONS

t enter the kingdom .....Acts 14:22
but we also glory in *t* .....Rom 5:3
not lose heart at my *t* .....Eph 3:13
t that you endure .....2 Thess 1:4

TRIED

You have *t* me and have .....Ps 17:3
a *t* stone, a precious .....Is 28:16

TRIMMED

and *t* their lamps .....Matt 25:7

TRIUMPH

Let not my enemies *t* .....Ps 25:2
I will *t* in the works .....Ps 92:4
always leads us in *t* .....2 Cor 2:14

TRIUMPHED

the LORD, for He has *t* .....Ex 15:1

TROAS

Paul receives vision at, Acts 16:8–11

TROUBLE

that they were in *t* .....Ex 5:19
no rest, for *t* comes .....Job 3:26
few days and full of *t* .....Job 14:1
for the time of *t* .....Job 38:23
have increased who *t* .....Ps 3:1
under his tongue is *t* .....Ps 10:7
from Me, for *t* is near .....Ps 22:11
t He shall hide me .....Ps 27:5
O LORD, for I am in *t* .....Ps 31:9
not in *t* as other men .....Ps 73:5
will be with him in *t* .....Ps 91:15
walk in the midst of *t* .....Ps 138:7
is delivered from *t* .....Prov 11:8
of the wicked is *t* .....Prov 15:6
t they have .....Is 26:16
also in the time of *t* .....Is 33:2
and there was *t* .....Jer 8:15
Savior in time of *t* .....Jer 14:8
such will have *t* .....1 Cor 7:28
there are some who *t* .....Gal 1:7

TROUBLED

Your face, and I was *t* .....Ps 30:7
Your face, they are *t* .....Ps 104:29
wicked are like the *t* .....Is 57:20
You are worried and *t* .....Luke 10:41
to give you who are *t* .....2 Thess 1:7
shaken in mind or *t* .....2 Thess 2:2

TROUBLES

"What *t* the people .....1 Sam 11:5
deliver you in six *t* .....Job 5:19
The *t* of my heart have .....Ps 25:17
out of all their *t* .....Ps 25:22
my soul is full of *t* .....Ps 88:3
because the former *t* .....Is 65:16
will be famines and *t* .....Mark 13:8
him out of all his *t* .....Acts 7:10

TROUBLING

spirit from God is *t* .....1 Sam 16:15
wicked cease from *t* .....Job 3:17

TRUE

and Your words are *t* .....2 Sam 7:28
But the LORD is the *t* .....Jer 10:10
"Let the LORD be a *t* .....Jer 42:5
we know that You are *t* .....Matt 22:16
He who sent Me is *t* .....John 7:28
about this Man were *t* .....John 10:41
Indeed, let God be *t* .....Rom 3:4
whatever things are *t* .....Phil 4:8
may know Him who is *t* .....1 John 5:20
is holy, He who is *t* .....Rev 3:7
"These are the *t* .....Rev 19:9
for these words are *t* .....Rev 21:5

TRUMPET

Blow the *t* at the time .....Ps 81:3
"Blow the *t* in the .....Jer 4:5
deed, do not sound a *t* .....Matt 6:2
t makes an uncertain .....1 Cor 14:8
For the *t* will sound .....1 Cor 15:52
loud voice, as of a *t* .....Rev 1:10

TRUST

t is a spider's web .....Job 8:14
If God puts no *t* .....Job 15:15
T in the LORD .....Ps 37:3
You are my *t* from my .....Ps 71:5
T in the LORD with all .....Prov 3:5
my salvation, I will *t* .....Is 12:2
Let him *t* in the name .....Is 50:10
Do not *t* in these .....Jer 7:4
Do not *t* in a friend .....Mic 7:5
those who *t* in riches .....Mark 10:24
committed to your *t* .....1 Tim 6:20

TRUSTED

"He *t* in the LORD .....Ps 22:8
He *t* in God .....Matt 27:43
that we who first *t* .....Eph 1:12
the holy women who *t* .....1 Pet 3:5

TRUSTS

But he who *t* in the .....Ps 32:10
He who *t* in his own .....Prov 28:26

TRUTH

led me in the way of *t* .....Gen 24:48
justice, a God of *t* .....Deut 32:4
and speaks the *t* .....Ps 15:2
t continually preserve .....Ps 40:11
Behold, You desire *t* .....Ps 51:6
T shall spring out of .....Ps 85:11
t shall be your shield .....Ps 91:4
t utterly out of my .....Ps 119:43
and Your law is *t* .....Ps 119:142
of Your word is *t* .....Ps 119:160
t is fallen in the .....Is 59:14
not valiant for the *t* .....Jer 9:3
"There is no *t* .....Hos 4:1
called the City of *T* .....Zech 8:3
speak each man the *t* .....Zech 8:16
t was in his mouth .....Mal 2:6
you shall know the *t* .....John 8:32
"I am the way, the *t* .....John 14:6
He, the Spirit of *t* .....John 16:13
to Him, "What is *t* .....John 18:38
speak the words of *t* .....Acts 26:25
who suppress the *t* .....Rom 1:18
of sincerity and *t* .....1 Cor 5:8
but, speaking the *t* .....Eph 4:15
your waist with *t* .....Eph 6:14
in the word of the *t* .....Col 1:5
the love of the *t* .....2 Thess 2:10
I am speaking the *t* .....1 Tim 2:7
they may know the *t* .....2 Tim 2:25
the knowledge of the *t* .....2 Tim 3:7
in the present *t* .....2 Pet 1:12
way of *t* will be .....2 Pet 2:2
that we are of the *t* .....1 John 3:19
the Spirit is *t* .....1 John 5:6
t that is in you .....3 John 3

TRY

t my mind and my heart .....Ps 26:2
refine them and *t* them .....Jer 9:7
t Me now in this .....Mal 3:10
which is to *t* you .....1 Pet 4:12

TUBAL

Son of Japheth, Gen 10:2
—— Tribe associated with Javan and Meshech, Is 66:19
In Gog's army, Ezek 38:2, 3
Punishment of, Ezek 32:26, 27

TUBAL-CAIN

Son of Lamech, Gen 4:19–22

TUMULT

their waves, and the *t* .....Ps 65:7
Your enemies make a *t* .....Ps 83:2

TUNIC

Also he made him a *t* .....Gen 37:3
and take away your *t* .....Matt 5:40

TUNICS

the LORD God made *t* .....Gen 3:21
not to put on two *t* .....Mark 6:9
weeping, showing the *t* .....Acts 9:39

TURBAN

like a robe and a *t* .....Job 29:14
"Remove the *t* .....Ezek 21:26

TURN

you shall not *t* .....Deut 17:11
Then we will not *t* .....Ps 80:18
but let them not *t* .....Ps 85:8
yet I do not *t* .....Ps 119:51
T at my rebuke .....Prov 1:23
not let your heart *t* .....Prov 7:25
'*T* now everyone from .....Jer 35:15
"Repent, *t* away from .....Ezek 14:6
yes, let every one *t* .....Jon 3:8
"*T* now from your evil .....Zech 1:4
on your right cheek, *t* .....Matt 5:39
t the hearts of the .....Luke 1:17
you that you should *t* .....Acts 14:15
t them from darkness .....Acts 26:18
Let him *t* away from .....1 Pet 3:11

TURNED

kept His way and not *t* .....Job 23:11
The wicked shall be *t* .....Ps 9:17
let them be *t* back and .....Ps 70:2
t my feet to Your .....Ps 119:59
of Israel, they have *t* .....Is 1:4
number believed and *t* .....Acts 11:21
and how you *t* to God .....1 Thess 1:9

TURNING

marvel that you are *t* .....Gal 1:6
or shadow of *t* .....James 1:17

TURNS

of the wicked He *t* .....Ps 146:9
A soft answer *t* .....Prov 15:1
but no one *t* back .....Nah 2:8
that he who *t* .....James 5:20

TURTLEDOVE

the life of Your *t* .....Ps 74:19
t is heard in our land .....Song 2:12

TUTOR

the law was our *t* .....Gal 3:24
no longer under a *t* .....Gal 3:25

TWIST
All day they *t* my ....Ps 56:5
unstable people *t* to ....2 Pet 3:16

TWO
the ark to Noah, *t* ....Gen 7:15
t young pigeons ....Lev 12:8
T are better than one ....Eccl 4:9
t he covered his ....Is 6:2
t shall become one ....Matt 19:5
t young pigeons.................Luke 2:24
new man from the *t* ....Eph 2:15

TYCHICUS
Paul's companion, Acts 20:1, 4
Paul's messenger, Eph 6:21, 22; Col 4:7–9; 2 Tim 4:12

UNBELIEF
because of their *u* ....Matt 13:58
help my *u* ....Mark 9:24
and He rebuked their *u* ....Mark 16:14
did it ignorantly in *u* ....1 Tim 1:13
you an evil heart of *u* ....Heb 3:12
enter in because of *u* ....Heb 3:19

UNBELIEVERS
who believe but to *u* ....1 Cor 14:22
are uninformed or *u* ....1 Cor 14:23
yoked together with *u* ....2 Cor 6:14

UNBELIEVING
Do not be *u* ....John 20:27
u Jews stirred up the ....Acts 14:2
For the *u* husband is ....1 Cor 7:14
u nothing is pure ....Titus 1:15
But the cowardly, *u* ....Rev 21:8

UNCIRCUMCISED
You stiff-necked and *u* ....Acts 7:51
not the physically *u* ....Rom 2:27
by faith and the *u* ....Rom 3:30
u had been committed ....Gal 2:7

UNCLEAN
of animals that are *u* ....Gen 7:2
who touches any *u* ....Lev 7:21
I am a man of *u* lips ....Is 6:5
u shall no longer come ....Is 52:1
He commands even the *u* ......Mark 1:27
He rebuked the *u* ....Mark 9:25
any man common or *u* ....Acts 10:28
there is nothing *u* ....Rom 14:14
Do not touch what is *u* ....2 Cor 6:17
that no fornicator, *u* ....Eph 5:5

UNCLEANNESS
men's bones and all *u* ....Matt 23:27
members as slaves of *u* ....Rom 6:19
did not call us to *u* ....1 Thess 4:7
flesh in the lust of *u* ....2 Pet 2:10

UNDEFILED
Blessed are the *u* ....Ps 119:1
all, and the bed *u* ....Heb 13:4
incorruptible and *u* ....1 Pet 1:4

UNDERSTAND
u one another's speech ....Gen 11:7
if there are any who *u* ....Ps 14:2
in Egypt did not *u* ....Ps 106:7
is to *u* his way ....Prov 14:8
Evil men do not *u* ....Prov 28:5
hearing, but do not *u* ....Is 6:9
and quick to *u* ....Dan 1:4
set your heart to *u* ....Dan 10:12
u shall instruct many ....Dan 11:33
of the wicked shall *u* ....Dan 12:10
people who do not *u* ....Hos 4:14
Let him *u* these things ....Hos 14:9
Why do you not *u* ....John 8:43
u what you are reading ....Acts 8:30
lest they should *u* ....Acts 28:27
u all mysteries ....1 Cor 13:2
some things hard to *u* ....2 Pet 3:16

UNDERSTANDING
asked for yourself *u* ....1 Kin 3:11
He has counsel and *u* ....Job 12:13
is the place of *u* ....Job 28:12
depart from evil is *u* ....Job 28:28
Almighty gives him *u* ....Job 32:8
not endow her with *u* ....Job 39:17
my heart shall give *u* ....Ps 49:3
Give me *u* ....Ps 119:34
Your precepts I get *u* ....Ps 119:104
His *u* is infinite ....Ps 147:5
apply your heart to *u* ....Prov 2:2
lean not on your own *u* ....Prov 3:5
u He established ....Prov 3:19
and go in the way of *u* ....Prov 9:6
of the Holy One is *u* ....Prov 9:10
a man of *u* has wisdom ....Prov 10:23
U is a wellspring ....Prov 16:22
u will find good ....Prov 19:8
and instruction and *u* ....Prov 23:23
but the poor who has *u* ....Prov 28:11
Spirit of wisdom and *u* ....Is 11:2
His *u* is unsearchable ....Is 40:28
the heaven by His *u* ....Jer 51:15
also still without *u* ....Matt 15:16
And He opened their *u* ....Luke 24:45
also pray with the *u* ....1 Cor 14:15
five words with my *u* ....1 Cor 14:19
and spiritual *u* ....Col 1:9
the Lord give you *u* ....2 Tim 2:7
Who is wise and *u* ....James 3:13
and has given us an *u* ....1 John 5:20

UNDERSTANDS
all plain to him who *u* ....Prov 8:9
is easy to him who *u* ....Prov 14:6
there is none who *u* ....Rom 3:11

UNDERSTOOD
Then I *u* their end ....Ps 73:17
My heart has *u* great ....Eccl 1:16
Have you not *u* from ....Is 40:21
u all these things ....Matt 13:51
clearly seen, being *u* ....Rom 1:20

UNDONE
"Woe is me, for I am *u* ....Is 6:5
leaving the others *u* ....Matt 23:23

UNFAITHFUL
u will be uprooted ....Prov 2:22
way of the *u* is hard ....Prov 13:15

UNFORGIVING
unloving, *u* ....Rom 1:31

UNFORMED
substance, being yet *u* ....Ps 139:16

UNFRUITFUL
and it becomes *u* ....Mark 4:19
that they may not be *u* ....Titus 3:14

UNGODLINESS
u made me afraid ....Ps 18:4
heaven against all *u* ....Rom 1:18
He will turn away *u* ....Rom 11:26

UNGODLY
delivered me to the *u* ....Job 16:11
u shall not stand ....Ps 1:5
of the *u* shall perish ....Ps 1:6
my cause against an *u* ....Ps 43:1
u man digs up evil ....Prov 16:27
who justifies the *u* ....Rom 4:5
Christ died for the *u* ....Rom 5:6
and perdition of *u* men ....2 Pet 3:7
convict all who are *u* ....Jude 15

UNHOLY
the holy and *u* ....Ezek 22:26
for sinners, for the *u* ....1 Tim 1:9

UNINTENTIONALLY
kills his neighbor *u* ....Deut 4:42

UNITE
U my heart to fear ....Ps 86:11

UNITY
to dwell together in *u* ....Ps 133:1
to keep the *u* of the ....Eph 4:3
we all come to the *u* ....Eph 4:13

UNJUST
hope of the *u* perishes ....Prov 11:7
u knows no shame ....Zeph 3:5
commended the *u* ....Luke 16:8
extortioners, *u* ....Luke 18:11
of the just and the *u* ....Acts 24:15
u who inflicts wrath ....Rom 3:5
For God is not *u* ....Heb 6:10
the just for the *u* ....1 Pet 3:18
let him be *u* still ....Rev 22:11

UNJUSTLY
long will you judge *u* ....Ps 82:2
he will deal *u* ....Is 26:10

UNKNOWN
not stand before *u* ....Prov 22:29
To The *U* God ....Acts 17:23
And I was *u* by face to ....Gal 1:22

UNLEAVENED
the Feast of *U* Bread ....Ex 12:17
the Feast of *U* Bread ....Mark 14:1
since you truly are *u* ....1 Cor 5:7

UNLOVING
untrustworthy, *u* ....Rom 1:31

UNMERCIFUL
unforgiving, *u* ....Rom 1:31

UNPREPARED
with me and find you *u* ....2 Cor 9:4

UNPROFITABLE
And cast the *u* ....Matt 25:30
'We are *u* servants ....Luke 17:10
have together become *u* ....Rom 3:12
who once was *u* to you ....Philem 11
for that would be *u* ....Heb 13:17

UNPUNISHED
wicked will not go *u* ....Prov 11:21
be rich will not go *u* ....Prov 28:20

UNQUENCHABLE
up the chaff with *u* ....Matt 3:12
He will burn with *u* ....Luke 3:17

UNRIGHTEOUS
u man his thoughts ....Is 55:7
been faithful in the *u* ....Luke 16:11
u will not inherit the ....1 Cor 6:9

UNRIGHTEOUSNESS
and there is no *u* ....Ps 92:15
builds his house by *u* ....Jer 22:13
Him is true, and no *u* ....John 7:18
all ungodliness and *u* ....Rom 1:18
the truth, but obey *u* ....Rom 2:8
Is there *u* with God ....Rom 9:14
cleanse us from all *u* ....1 John 1:9
All *u* is sin ....1 John 5:17

UNRULY
those who are *u* ....1 Thess 5:14
It is an *u* evil ....James 3:8

UNSEARCHABLE
heart of kings is *u* ....Prov 25:3
u are His judgments ....Rom 11:33

UNSPOTTED
to keep oneself *u* ....James 1:27

UNSTABLE
U as water ....Gen 49:4

VINE
to the choice *v* ....Gen 49:11
their *v* is of the *v* ....Deut 32:32
You have brought a *v* ....Ps 80:8
planted you a noble *v* ....Jer 2:21
grapes shall be on the *v* ....Jer 8:13
Israel empties his *v* ....Hos 10:1
shall sit under his *v* ....Mic 4:4
of this fruit of the *v* ....Matt 26:29
"I am the true *v* ....John 15:1

VINEDRESSER
and My Father is the *v* ....John 15:1

VINEGAR
As *v* to the teeth and ....Prov 10:26
weather, and like *v* ....Prov 25:20

VINES
foxes that spoil the *v* ....Song 2:15
nor fruit be on the *v* ....Hab 3:17

VINEYARD
v which Your right ....Ps 80:15
laborers for his *v* ....Matt 20:1
Who plants a *v* and ....1 Cor 9:7

VIOLENCE
was filled with *v* ....Gen 6:11
You save me from *v* ....2 Sam 22:3
the one who loves *v* ....Ps 11:5
such as breathe out *v* ....Ps 27:12
from oppression and *v* ....Ps 72:14
v covers the ....Prov 10:6
He had done no *v* ....Is 53:9
and *v* in the land ....Jer 51:46
cause the seat of *v* ....Amos 6:3
way and from the *v* ....Jon 3:8
rich men are full of *v* ....Mic 6:12
For plundering and *v* ....Hab 1:3
one's garment with *v* ....Mal 2:16
of heaven suffers *v* ....Matt 11:12

VIOLENT
me from the *v* man ....Ps 18:48
let evil hunt the *v* ....Ps 140:11
violence, and the *v* ....Matt 11:12
haters of God, *v* ....Rom 1:30
given to wine, not *v* ....1 Tim 3:3

VIPER
and stings like a *v* ....Prov 23:32
will come forth a *v* ....Is 14:29
which is crushed a *v* ....Is 59:5

VIPERS
to them, "Brood of *v* ....Matt 3:7

VIRGIN
v shall conceive ....Is 7:14
O you oppressed *v* ....Is 23:12
v daughter of my ....Jer 14:17
The *v* of Israel has ....Amos 5:2
"Behold, the *v* shall ....Matt 1:23
between a wife and a *v* ....1 Cor 7:34
you as a chaste *v* ....2 Cor 11:2

VIRGINS
v who took their lamps ....Matt 25:1
women, for they are *v* ....Rev 14:4

VIRTUE
if there is any *v* ....Phil 4:8
us by glory and *v* ....2 Pet 1:3
to your faith *v* ....2 Pet 1:5

VISAGE
v was marred more than ....Is 52:14

VISIBLE
that are on earth, *v* ....Col 1:16
of things which are *v* ....Heb 11:3

VISION
chased away like a *v* ....Job 20:8
Then You spoke in a *v* ....Ps 89:19
the Valley of *V* ....Is 22:1
a dream of a night *v* ....Is 29:7
her prophets find no *v* ....Lam 2:9
have night without *v* ....Mic 3:6
they had also seen a *v* ....Luke 24:23
in a trance I saw a *v* ....Acts 11:5
v appeared to Paul in ....Acts 16:9
to the heavenly *v* ....Acts 26:19

VISIONS
thoughts from the *v* ....Job 4:13
young men shall see *v* ....Joel 2:28
I will come to *v* ....2 Cor 12:1

VISIT
but God will surely *v* ....Gen 50:24
in the day when I *v* ....Ex 32:34
v the earth and water ....Ps 65:9
Oh, *v* me with Your ....Ps 106:4
v orphans and widows ....James 1:27

VISITATION
the time of your *v* ....Luke 19:44
God in the day of *v* ....1 Pet 2:12

VISITED
he will not be *v* ....Prov 19:23
Israel, for He has *v* ....Luke 1:68
how God at the first *v* ....Acts 15:14

VOICE
"I heard Your *v* ....Gen 3:10
v is Jacob's *v* ....Gen 27:22
I should obey His *v* ....Ex 5:2
fire a still small *v* ....1 Kin 19:12
and my flute to the *v* ....Job 30:31
you thunder with a *v* ....Job 40:9
He uttered His *v* ....Ps 46:6
He sends out His *v* ....Ps 68:33
have lifted up their *v* ....Ps 93:3
if you will hear His *v* ....Ps 95:7
word, heeding the *v* ....Ps 103:20
for your *v* is sweet ....Song 2:14
The *v* of one crying in ....Is 40:3
the *v* of weeping shall ....Is 65:19
A *v* from the temple ....Is 66:6
v was heard in Ramah ....Jer 31:15
who has a pleasant *v* ....Ezek 33:32
v was heard in Ramah ....Matt 2:18
"The *v* of one crying ....Matt 3:3
And suddenly a *v* ....Matt 3:17
will anyone hear His *v* ....Matt 12:19
and suddenly a *v* ....Matt 17:5
for they know his *v* ....John 10:4
v did not come because ......John 12:30
the truth hears My *v* ....John 18:37
the *v* of an archangel ....1 Thess 4:16
whose *v* then shook the ....Heb 12:26
glory when such a *v* ....2 Pet 1:17
If anyone hears My *v* ....Rev 3:20

VOICES
shall lift up their *v* ....Is 52:8
And there were loud *v* ....Rev 11:15

VOID
they are a nation *v* ....Deut 32:28
the LORD had made a *v* ....Judg 21:15
regarded Your law as *v* ....Ps 119:126
Do we then make *v* ....Rom 3:31
heirs, faith is made *v* ....Rom 4:14
make my boasting *v* ....1 Cor 9:15

VOLUME
in the *v* of the book ....Heb 10:7

VOMIT
lest the land *v* ....Lev 18:28
man staggers in his *v* ....Is 19:14
returns to his own *v* ....2 Pet 2:22

VOW
Then Jacob made a *v* ....Gen 28:20
And Jephthah made a *v* ....Judg 11:30
he carried out his *v* ....Judg 11:39
v shall be performed ....Ps 65:1
When you make a *v* ....Eccl 5:4
not to *v* than to *v* ....Eccl 5:5
for he had taken a *v* ....Acts 18:18
men who have taken a *v* ....Acts 21:23

VOWS
you will pay your *v* ....Job 22:27
I will pay My *v* ....Ps 22:25
V made to You are ....Ps 56:12
Make *v* to the LORD ....Ps 76:11
today I have paid my *v* ....Prov 7:14
to reconsider his *v* ....Prov 20:25
And what, son of my *v* ....Prov 31:2
to the LORD and took *v* ....Jon 1:16

WAGE
those who exploit *w* ....Mal 3:5
w the good warfare ....1 Tim 1:18

WAGES
I will give you your *w* ....Ex 2:9
the *w* of the wicked ....Prov 10:16
w will be troubled ....Is 19:10
and he who earns *w* ....Hag 1:6
to you, give me my *w* ....Zech 11:12
and give them their *w* ....Matt 20:8
be content with your *w* ....Luke 3:14
is worthy of his *w* ....Luke 10:7
him who works, the *w* ....Rom 4:4
For the *w* of sin is ....Rom 6:23
is worthy of his *w* ....1 Tim 5:18
Indeed the *w* of the ....James 5:4

WAIL
My heart shall *w* ....Jer 48:36
"Son of man, *w* ....Ezek 32:18

WAILING
w is heard from Zion ....Jer 9:19
of heart and bitter *w* ....Ezek 27:31
There will be *w* ....Matt 13:42

WAIT
hard service I will *w* ....Job 14:14
If I *w* for the grave ....Job 17:13
W on the LORD ....Ps 27:14
w patiently for Him ....Ps 37:7
my eyes fail while I *w* ....Ps 69:3
These all *w* for You ....Ps 104:27
And I will *w* on the ....Is 8:17
the LORD will *w* ....Is 30:18
those who *w* on the ....Is 40:31
not be ashamed who *w* ....Is 49:23
w quietly for the ....Lam 3:26
I will *w* for the God ....Mic 7:7
be like men who *w* ....Luke 12:36
see, we eagerly *w* ....Rom 8:25
w for one another ....1 Cor 11:33
the Spirit eagerly *w* ....Gal 5:5
we also eagerly *w* ....Phil 3:20
and to *w* for His Son ....1 Thess 1:10
To those who eagerly *w* ....Heb 9:28

WAITED
and when I *w* for light ....Job 30:26
w patiently for the ....Ps 40:1
we have *w* for Him ....Is 25:9
And the people *w* ....Luke 1:21
day you have *w* and ....Acts 27:33
Divine longsuffering *w* ....1 Pet 3:20

WAITING
w at the posts of my ....Prov 8:34
w for the Consolation ....Luke 2:25
who himself was also *w* ....Luke 23:51
ourselves, eagerly *w* ....Rom 8:23
from that time *w* ....Heb 10:13

WAITS
of the adulterer *w* ....Job 24:15
my soul silently *w* ....Ps 62:1
My soul *w* for the Lord ....Ps 130:6

for the one who *w* ... Is 64:4
the creation eagerly *w* ... Rom 8:19

WALK
w before Me and be ... Gen 17:1
in which they must *w* ... Ex 18:20
You shall *w* in all ... Deut 5:33
Yea, though I *w* ... Ps 23:4
W about Zion ... Ps 48:12
that Israel would *w* ... Ps 81:13
I will *w* within my ... Ps 101:2
I will *w* before the ... Ps 116:9
Though I *w* in the ... Ps 138:7
W prudently when you ... Eccl 5:1
w in the ways of your ... Eccl 11:9
come and let us *w* ... Is 2:5
"This is the way, *w* ... Is 30:21
be weary, they shall *w* ... Is 40:31
w in the light of your ... Is 50:11
people, who *w* in a way ... Is 65:2
commit adultery and *w* ... Jer 23:14
the righteous *w* ... Hos 14:9
w humbly with your God ... Mic 6:8
take up your bed and *w* ... John 5:8
W while you have the ... John 12:35
so we also should *w* ... Rom 6:4
Let us *w* properly ... Rom 13:13
For we *w* by faith ... 2 Cor 5:7
W in the Spirit ... Gal 5:16
that we should *w* ... Eph 2:10
And *w* in love ... Eph 5:2
W as children of light ... Eph 5:8
attained, let us *w* ... Phil 3:16
note those who so *w* ... Phil 3:17
that you may *w* worthy ... Col 1:10
Jesus the Lord, so *w* ... Col 2:6
us how you ought to *w* ... 1 Thess 4:1
w just as He ... 1 John 2:6
and they shall *w* ... Rev 3:4

WALKED
Enoch *w* with God ... Gen 5:22
by His light I *w* ... Job 29:3
The people who *w* ... Is 9:2
He *w* with Me in peace ... Mal 2:6
Jesus no longer *w* ... John 11:54
w according to the ... 2 Cor 10:2
in which you once *w* ... Eph 2:2
to walk just as He *w* ... 1 John 2:6

WALKING
of the LORD God *w* ... Gen 3:8
see four men loose, *w* ... Dan 3:25
before God, *w* in all ... Luke 1:6
they saw Jesus *w* ... John 6:19
And *w* in the fear of ... Acts 9:31
you are no longer *w* ... Rom 14:15
not *w* in craftiness ... 2 Cor 4:2
of your children *w* ... 2 John 4

WALKS
the LORD your God *w* ... Deut 23:14
is the man who *w* ... Ps 1:1
He who *w* uprightly ... Ps 15:2
He who *w* with ... Prov 10:9
He who *w* with wise men ... Prov 13:20
w blamelessly will be ... Prov 28:18
w wisely will be ... Prov 28:26
Whoever *w* the road ... Is 35:8
Who *w* in darkness and ... Is 50:10
it is not in man who *w* ... Jer 10:23
do good to him who *w* ... Mic 2:7
If anyone *w* in the day ... John 11:9
he who *w* in darkness ... John 12:35
adversary the devil *w* ... 1 Pet 5:8
is in darkness and *w* ... 1 John 2:11

WALL
then the *w* of the city ... Josh 6:5
his face toward the *w* ... 2 Kin 20:2
like a leaning *w* ... Ps 62:3
and like a high *w* ... Prov 18:11
If she is a *w* ... Song 8:9
We grope for the *w* ... Is 59:10
you, you whitewashed *w* ... Acts 23:3
a window in the *w* ... 2 Cor 11:33
down the middle *w* ... Eph 2:14
Now the *w* of the city ... Rev 21:14

WALLS
broken down, without *w* ... Prov 25:28
salvation for *w* ... Is 26:1
you shall call your *w* ... Is 60:18
By faith the *w* of ... Heb 11:30

WANDER
and makes them *w* ... Job 12:24
ones cry to God, and *w* ... Job 38:41
Indeed, I would *w* ... Ps 55:7
Oh, let me not *w* ... Ps 119:10
they have loved to *w* ... Jer 14:10

WANDERED
w blind in the streets ... Lam 4:14
My sheep *w* through ... Ezek 34:6
They *w* in deserts and ... Heb 11:38

WANDERS
He *w* about for bread ... Job 15:23
Like a bird that *w* ... Prov 27:8
if anyone among you *w* ... James 5:19

WANT
I shall not *w* ... Ps 23:1
he began to be in *w* ... Luke 15:14

WANTING
balances, and found *w* ... Dan 5:27

WANTON
necks and *w* eyes ... Is 3:16
have begun to grow *w* ... 1 Tim 5:11

WAR
"There is a noise of *w* ... Ex 32:17
the LORD for the *w* ... Num 32:20
my hands to make *w* ... 2 Sam 22:35
day of battle and *w* ... Job 38:23
w may rise against ... Ps 27:3
speak, they are for *w* ... Ps 120:7
by wise counsel wage *w* ... Prov 20:18
will wage your own *w* ... Prov 24:6
shall they learn *w* ... Is 2:4
from the distress of *w* ... Is 21:15
we shall see no *w* ... Jer 42:14
same horn was making *w* ... Dan 7:21
men returned from *w* ... Mic 2:8
king, going to make *w* ... Luke 14:31
Who ever goes to *w* ... 1 Cor 9:7
for pleasure that *w* ... James 4:1
You fight and *w* ... James 4:2
fleshly lusts which *w* ... 1 Pet 2:11
w broke out in heaven ... Rev 12:7
He judges and makes *w* ... Rev 19:11

WARFARE
to her, that her *w* ... Is 40:2
w are not carnal ... 2 Cor 10:4
may wage the good *w* ... 1 Tim 1:18
w entangles ... 2 Tim 2:4

WARM
they will keep *w* ... Eccl 4:11
but no one is *w* ... Hag 1:6

WARMED
w himself at the fire ... Mark 14:54
Depart in peace, be *w* ... James 2:16

WARMS
w them in the dust ... Job 39:14
He even *w* himself and ... Is 44:16

WARN
w the wicked from his ... Ezek 3:18
w everyone night ... Acts 20:31
beloved children I *w* ... 1 Cor 4:14
w those who are ... 1 Thess 5:14

WARNED
"The man solemnly *w* ... Gen 43:3
them Your servant is *w* ... Ps 19:11
Then, being divinely *w* ... Matt 2:12
Who *w* you to flee ... Matt 3:7
Noah, being divinely *w* ... Heb 11:7

WARNING
w every man and ... Col 1:28

WARRING
w against the law of ... Rom 7:23

WARRIOR
He runs at me like a *w* ... Job 16:14

WARS
He makes *w* cease to ... Ps 46:9
And you will hear of *w* ... Matt 24:6
Where do *w* and fights ... James 4:1

WASH
w myself with snow ... Job 9:30
I will *w* my hands in ... Ps 26:6
W me thoroughly ... Ps 51:2
he shall *w* his feet in ... Ps 58:10
"*W* yourselves ... Is 1:16
O Jerusalem, *w* your ... Jer 4:14
head and *w* your face ... Matt 6:17
For they do not *w* ... Matt 15:2
not eat unless they *w* ... Mark 7:3
w His feet with her ... Luke 7:38
said to him, "Go, *w* ... John 9:7
w the disciples' ... John 13:5
"You shall never *w* ... John 13:8
w one another's ... John 13:14
w away your sins ... Acts 22:16

WASHED
and *w* my hands in ... Ps 73:13
When the Lord has *w* ... Is 4:4
cut, nor were you *w* ... Ezek 16:4
w his hands before the ... Matt 27:24
My feet, but she has *w* ... Luke 7:44
So when He had *w* ... John 13:12
w their stripes ... Acts 16:33
But you were *w* ... 1 Cor 6:11
if she has *w* the ... 1 Tim 5:10
Him who loved us and *w* ... Rev 1:5
w their robes and made ... Rev 7:14

WASHING
cleanse her with the *w* ... Eph 5:26
us, through the *w* ... Titus 3:5

WASTE
who are left shall *w* ... Lev 26:39
the cities are laid *w* ... Is 6:11
empty and makes it *w* ... Is 24:1
w the mountains ... Is 42:15
"Why this *w* ... Matt 26:8

WASTED
The field is *w* ... Joel 1:10
this fragrant oil *w* ... Mark 14:4
w his possessions ... Luke 15:13

WASTING
w and destruction are ... Is 59:7
that this man was *w* ... Luke 16:1

WATCH
of them we set a *w* ... Neh 4:9
my steps, but do not *w* ... Job 14:16
is past, and like a *w* ... Ps 90:4
keep *w* over the door ... Ps 141:3
and all who *w* for ... Is 29:20
W the road ... Nah 2:1
W therefore, for you ... Matt 24:42
"What! Could you not *w* ... Matt 26:40
W and pray, lest you ... Matt 26:41
W, stand fast in the ... 1 Cor 16:13
submissive, for they *w* ... Heb 13:17

WATCHED
in the days when God *w* .... Job 29:2
come, he would have *w* .... Matt 24:43

WATCHES
w the righteous .... Ps 37:32
She *w* over the ways of .... Prov 31:27
Blessed is he who *w* .... Rev 16:15

WATCHFUL
But you be *w* in all .... 2 Tim 4:5
be serious and *w* .... 1 Pet 4:7

WATCHING
who listens to me, *w* .... Prov 8:34
the flock, who were *w* .... Zech 11:11
he comes, will find *w* .... Luke 12:37

WATCHMAN
guards the city, the *w* .... Ps 127:1
W, what of the night .... Is 21:11
I have made you a *w* .... Ezek 3:17
the day of your *w* .... Mic 7:4

WATCHMEN
w who go about the .... Song 3:3
w shall lift up their .... Is 52:8
His *w* are blind .... Is 56:10
I have set *w* on your .... Is 62:6
Also, I set *w* over you .... Jer 6:17
strong, set up the *w* .... Jer 51:12

WATER
Eden to *w* the garden .... Gen 2:10
Unstable as *w* .... Gen 49:4
your bread and your *w* .... Ex 23:25
of affliction and *w* .... 1 Kin 22:27
w disappears from the .... Job 14:11
w wears away stones .... Job 14:19
drinks iniquity like *w* .... Job 15:16
not given the weary *w* .... Job 22:7
He binds up the *w* .... Job 26:8
I am poured out like *w* .... Ps 22:14
where there is no *w* .... Ps 63:1
they have shed like *w* .... Ps 79:3
Drink *w* from your own .... Prov 5:15
"Stolen *w* is sweet .... Prov 9:17
the whole supply of *w* .... Is 3:1
and needy seek *w* .... Is 41:17
For I will pour *w* .... Is 44:3
silence and given us *w* .... Jer 8:14
eye overflows with *w* .... Lam 1:16
will be as weak as *w* .... Ezek 7:17
w the land with the .... Ezek 32:6
you gave Me no *w* .... Luke 7:44
there was much *w* .... John 3:23
given you living *w* .... John 4:10
rivers of living *w* .... John 7:38
blood and *w* came out .... John 19:34
"Can anyone forbid *w* .... Acts 10:47
with the washing of *w* .... Eph 5:26
can yield both salt *w* .... James 3:12
were saved through *w* .... 1 Pet 3:20
is He who came by *w* .... 1 John 5:6
the Spirit, the *w* .... 1 John 5:8
are clouds without *w* .... Jude 12
let him take the *w* .... Rev 22:17

WATERED
w the whole face .... Gen 2:6
that it was well *w* .... Gen 13:10
I planted, Apollos *w* .... 1 Cor 3:6

WATERS
and struck the *w* .... Ex 7:20
If He withholds the *w* .... Job 12:15
me beside the still *w* .... Ps 23:2
though its *w* roar and .... Ps 46:3
w have come up to my .... Ps 69:1
then the *w* would have .... Ps 124:4
rich, and he who *w* .... Prov 11:25
Who has bound the *w* .... Prov 30:4
your bread upon the *w* .... Eccl 11:1
a well of living *w* .... Song 4:15
w cannot quench love .... Song 8:7
of the LORD as the *w* .... Is 11:9
w will fail from the .... Is 19:5
because I give *w* .... Is 43:20
have sworn that the *w* .... Is 54:9
thirsts, come to the *w* .... Is 55:1
fountain of living *w* .... Jer 2:13
w flowed over my head .... Lam 3:54
the sound of many *w* .... Ezek 43:2
w surrounded me .... Jon 2:5
shall be that living *w* .... Zech 14:8
often, in perils of *w* .... 2 Cor 11:26
living fountains of *w* .... Rev 7:17
w became wormwood .... Rev 8:11

WAVER
He did not *w* at the .... Rom 4:20

WAVERING
of our hope without *w* .... Heb 10:23

WAVES
and here your proud *w* .... Job 38:11
all Your *w* and billows .... Ps 42:7
the noise of their *w* .... Ps 65:7
the multitude of its *w* .... Jer 51:42
was covered with the *w* .... Matt 8:24
sea, tossed by the *w* .... Matt 14:24
raging *w* of the sea .... Jude 13

WAX
My heart is like *w* .... Ps 22:14
w melts before the .... Ps 68:2
mountains melt like *w* .... Ps 97:5

WAY
and show them the *w* .... Ex 18:20
day I am going the *w* .... Josh 23:14
and the right *w* .... 1 Sam 12:23
As for God, His *w* .... 2 Sam 22:31
to a man whose *w* .... Job 3:23
But He knows the *w* .... Job 23:10
"Where is the *w* .... Job 38:19
the LORD knows the *w* .... Ps 1:6
you perish in the *w* .... Ps 2:12
Teach me Your *w* .... Ps 27:11
This is the *w* of those .... Ps 49:13
w may be known on .... Ps 67:2
Your *w* was in the sea .... Ps 77:19
where there is no *w* .... Ps 107:40
I have chosen the *w* .... Ps 119:30
I hate every false *w* .... Ps 119:104
in the *w* everlasting .... Ps 139:24
and preserves the *w* .... Prov 2:8
The *w* of the wicked is .... Prov 4:19
instruction are the *w* .... Prov 6:23
w that seems right .... Prov 14:12
not know what is the *w* .... Eccl 11:5
of terrors in the *w* .... Eccl 12:5
The *w* of the just is .... Is 26:7
"This is the *w* .... Is 30:21
LORD, who makes a *w* .... Is 43:16
wicked forsake his *w* .... Is 55:7
O LORD, I know the *w* .... Jer 10:23
one heart and one *w* .... Jer 32:39
Israel, is it not My *w* .... Ezek 18:25
w which is not fair .... Ezek 33:17
and pervert the *w* .... Amos 2:7
the LORD has His *w* .... Nah 1:3
he will prepare the *w* .... Mal 3:1
and broad is the *w* .... Matt 7:13
and difficult is the *w* .... Matt 7:14
will prepare Your *w* .... Matt 11:10
and teach the *w* .... Matt 22:16
and the *w* you know .... John 14:4
to him, "I am the *w* .... John 14:6
proclaim to us the *w* .... Acts 16:17
explained to him the *w* .... Acts 18:26
you a more excellent *w* .... 1 Cor 12:31
w which He consecrated .... Heb 10:20
forsaken the right *w* .... 2 Pet 2:15
to have known the *w* .... 2 Pet 2:21
have gone in the *w* .... Jude 11

WAYS
for all His *w* are .... Deut 32:4
they do not know its *w* .... Job 24:13
is the first of the *w* .... Job 40:19
Show me Your *w* .... Ps 25:4
transgressors Your *w* .... Ps 51:13
would walk in My *w* .... Ps 81:13
w were directed .... Ps 119:5
I thought about my *w* .... Ps 119:59
righteous in all His *w* .... Ps 145:17
For the *w* of man are .... Prov 5:21
w please the LORD .... Prov 16:7
He will teach us His *w* .... Is 2:3
nor are your *w* .... Is 55:8
"Stand in the *w* .... Jer 6:16
"Amend your *w* .... Jer 7:3
and examine our *w* .... Lam 3:40
and owns all your *w* .... Dan 5:23
w are everlasting .... Hab 3:6
misery are in their *w* .... Rom 3:16
judgments and His *w* .... Rom 11:33
unstable in all his *w* .... James 1:8
their destructive *w* .... 2 Pet 2:2
and true are Your *w* .... Rev 15:3

WEAK
then I shall become *w* .... Judg 16:7
And I am *w* today .... 2 Sam 3:39
me, O LORD, for I am *w* .... Ps 6:2
gives power to the *w* .... Is 40:29
knee will be as *w* .... Ezek 7:17
let the *w* say .... Joel 3:10
not your hands be *w* .... Zeph 3:16
but the flesh is *w* .... Matt 26:41
And not being *w* .... Rom 4:19
Receive one who is *w* .... Rom 14:1
God has chosen the *w* .... 1 Cor 1:27
We are *w*, but you are .... 1 Cor 4:10
to the *w* I became as *w* .... 1 Cor 9:22
this reason many are *w* .... 1 Cor 11:30
For when I am *w* .... 2 Cor 12:10

WEAKENED
w my strength in the .... Ps 102:23
the ground, you who *w* .... Is 14:12

WEAKER
house of Saul grew *w* .... 2 Sam 3:1
the wife, as to the *w* .... 1 Pet 3:7

WEAKNESS
than men, and the *w* .... 1 Cor 1:25
I was with you in *w* .... 1 Cor 2:3
It is sown in *w* .... 1 Cor 15:43
is also subject to *w* .... Heb 5:2
w were made strong .... Heb 11:34

WEAKNESSES
also helps in our *w* .... Rom 8:26
sympathize with our *w* .... Heb 4:15

WEALTH
have gained me this *w* .... Deut 8:17
a man of great *w* .... Ruth 2:
not asked riches or *w* .... 2 Chr 1:11
who trust in their *w* .... Ps 49:6
w is his strong city .... Prov 10:15
W gained by dishonesty .... Prov 13:11
W makes many friends .... Prov 19:4
may bring to you the *w* .... Is 60:11

WEALTHY
w nation that dwells .... Jer 49:31
rich, have become *w* .... Rev 3:17

WEANED
w child shall put his .... Is 11:8
Those just *w* from milk .... Is 28:9

WEAPON
w formed against you ... Is 54:17
with a deadly *w* ... Ezek 9:1

WEAPONS
is better than *w* ... Eccl 9:18
the LORD and His *w* ... Is 13:5
For the *w* of our ... 2 Cor 10:4

WEAR
but the just will *w* ... Job 27:17
'What shall we *w* ... Matt 6:31

WEARIED
you have *w* Me with ... Is 43:24
You are *w* in the ... Is 57:10
and they have *w* ... Jer 12:5
You have *w* the LORD ... Mal 2:17
therefore, being *w* ... John 4:6

WEARINESS
say, 'Oh, what a *w* ... Mal 1:13
in *w* and toil ... 2 Cor 11:27

WEARY
to Isaac, "I am *w* ... Gen 27:46
lest he become *w* ... Prov 25:17
As cold water to a *w* ... Prov 25:25
No one will be *w* ... Is 5:27
you may cause the *w* ... Is 28:12
shall run and not be *w* ... Is 40:31
to him who is *w* ... Is 50:4
I am *w* of holding it ... Jer 6:11
w themselves to commit ... Jer 9:5
I was *w* of holding it ... Jer 20:9
continual coming she *w* ... Luke 18:5
And let us not grow *w* ... Gal 6:9
do not grow *w* in ... 2 Thess 3:13
lest you become *w* ... Heb 12:3

WEATHER
a garment in cold *w* ... Prov 25:20
'It will be fair *w* ... Matt 16:2

WEDDING
were invited to the *w* ... Matt 22:3
Come to the *w* ... Matt 22:4
find, invite to the *w* ... Matt 22:9
in with him to the *w* ... Matt 25:10
day there was a *w* ... John 2:1

WEEK
with many for one *w* ... Dan 9:27
the first day of the *w* ... Matt 28:1
the first day of the *w* ... Acts 20:7
the first day of the *w* ... 1 Cor 16:2

WEEKS
w are determined ... Dan 9:24
w Messiah shall be cut ... Dan 9:26

WEEP
"Hannah, why do you *w* ... 1 Sam 1:8
a time to *w* ... Eccl 3:4
you shall *w* no more ... Is 30:19
it, my soul will *w* ... Jer 13:17
W not for the dead ... Jer 22:10
to the LORD, *w* between ... Joel 2:17
this commotion and *w* ... Mark 5:39
Blessed are you who *w* ... Luke 6:21
to her, "Do not *w* ... Luke 7:13
and you did not *w* ... Luke 7:32
of Jerusalem, do not *w* ... Luke 23:28
to the tomb to *w* there ... John 11:31
w with those who *w* ... Rom 12:15
those who *w* as though ... 1 Cor 7:30

WEEPING
of Israel, who were *w* ... Num 25:6
w as they went up ... 2 Sam 15:30
the noise of the *w* ... Ezra 3:13
face is flushed from *w* ... Job 16:16
the voice of my *w* ... Ps 6:8
my drink with *w* ... Ps 102:9
of hosts called for *w* ... Is 22:12
w shall no longer ... Is 65:19
They shall come with *w* ... Jer 31:9
w they shall come ... Jer 50:4
were sitting there *w* ... Ezek 8:14
with fasting, with *w* ... Joel 2:12
with tears, with *w* ... Mal 2:13
There will be *w* ... Matt 8:12
outside by the tomb *w* ... John 20:11
"Woman, why are you *w* ... John 20:13
"What do you mean by *w* ... Acts 21:13

WEIGH
You *w* out the violence ... Ps 58:2
O Most Upright, You *w* ... Is 26:7

WEIGHED
nor can silver be *w* ... Job 28:15
W the mountains ... Is 40:12
You have been *w* ... Dan 5:27
lest your hearts be *w* ... Luke 21:34

WEIGHS
eyes, but the LORD *w* ... Prov 16:2
Where is he who *w* ... Is 33:18

WEIGHT
a perfect and just *w* ... Deut 25:15
a just *w* is His delight ... Prov 11:1
and eternal *w* of glory ... 2 Cor 4:17
us lay aside every *w* ... Heb 12:1

WELL
If you do *w* ... Gen 4:7
that it may go *w* ... Deut 4:40
you when you do *w* ... Ps 49:18
daughters have done *w* ... Prov 31:29
know that it will be *w* ... Eccl 8:12
wheel broken at the *w* ... Eccl 12:6
that it shall be *w* ... Is 3:10
"Those who are *w* ... Matt 9:12
said to him, '*W* done ... Matt 25:21
faith has made you *w* ... Mark 5:34
Now Jacob's *w* was ... John 4:6
the elders who rule *w* ... 1 Tim 5:17

WELL-BEING
them, and their *w* ... Ps 69:22
each one the other's *w* ... 1 Cor 10:24

WELLS
draw water from the *w* ... Is 12:3
These are *w* without ... 2 Pet 2:17

WEPT
and the man of God *w* ... 2 Kin 8:11
for the people *w* ... Ezra 10:1
that I sat down and *w* ... Neh 1:4
Have I not *w* for him ... Job 30:25
down, yea, we *w* ... Ps 137:1
out and *w* bitterly ... Matt 26:75
He saw the city and *w* ... Luke 19:41
Jesus *w* ... John 11:35
So I *w* much ... Rev 5:4

WHEAT
with the finest of *w* ... Ps 81:16
we may trade *w* ... Amos 8:5
even sell the bad *w* ... Amos 8:6
but gather the *w* ... Matt 13:30
w falls into the ... John 12:24
perhaps *w* or some ... 1 Cor 15:37
oil, fine flour and *w* ... Rev 18:13

WHEEL
brings the threshing *w* ... Prov 20:26
the fountain, or the *w* ... Eccl 12:6
in the middle of a *w* ... Ezek 1:16

WHEELS
off their chariot *w* ... Ex 14:25
the rumbling of his *w* ... Jer 47:3
appearance of the *w* ... Ezek 1:16
noise of rattling *w* ... Nah 3:2

WHIP
A *w* for the horse ... Prov 26:3
The noise of a *w* ... Nah 3:2

WHIRLWIND
Elijah went up by a *w* ... 2 Kin 2:11
Job out of the *w* ... Job 38:1
them away as with a *w* ... Ps 58:9
w will take them away ... Is 40:24
w shall scatter them ... Is 41:16
w shall be raised ... Jer 25:32
has His way in the *w* ... Nah 1:3

WHISPER
my ear received a *w* ... Job 4:12
and wizards, who *w* ... Is 8:19

WHISPERER
w separates the best ... Prov 16:28

WHISPERERS
they are *w* ... Rom 1:29

WHISPERINGS
backbitings, *w* ... 2 Cor 12:20

WHITE
My beloved is *w* ... Song 5:10
and make them *w* ... Dan 11:35
be purified, made *w* ... Dan 12:10
for they are already *w* ... John 4:35
walk with Me in *w* ... Rev 3:4
clothed in *w* garments ... Rev 3:5
behold, a *w* horse ... Rev 6:2
and made them *w* ... Rev 7:14
Then I saw a great *w* ... Rev 20:11

WHOLESOME
w tongue is a tree ... Prov 15:4
not consent to *w* words ... 1 Tim 6:3

WHOLLY
w followed the LORD ... Deut 1:36
I will not leave you *w* ... Jer 46:28

WICKED
w shall be silent ... 1 Sam 2:9
Should you help the *w* ... 2 Chr 19:2
Why do the *w* live and ... Job 21:7
w are reserved for the ... Job 21:30
to nobles, 'You are *w* ... Job 34:18
with the *w* every day ... Ps 7:11
w is snared in the ... Ps 9:16
w shall be turned ... Ps 9:17
do the *w* renounce God ... Ps 10:13
w bend their bow ... Ps 11:2
w He will rain coals ... Ps 11:6
Evil shall slay the *w* ... Ps 34:21
w shall be no more ... Ps 37:10
The *w* watches the ... Ps 37:32
how long will the *w* ... Ps 94:3
and the *w* be no more ... Ps 104:35
is far from the *w* ... Ps 119:155
if there is any *w* ... Ps 139:24
w will be cut off from ... Prov 2:22
w will fall by his own ... Prov 11:5
LORD is far from the *w* ... Prov 15:29
w flee when no one ... Prov 28:1
Do not be overly *w* ... Eccl 7:17
not be well with the *w* ... Eccl 8:13
w forsake his way ... Is 55:7
But the *w* are like the ... Is 57:20
and desperately *w* ... Jer 17:9
w shall do wickedly ... Dan 12:10
at all acquit the *w* ... Nah 1:3
w one does not touch ... 1 John 5:18
the sway of the *w* ... 1 John 5:19

WICKEDLY
Will you speak *w* ... Job 13:7
God will never do *w* ... Job 34:12
Those who do *w* ... Dan 11:32
yes, all who do *w* ... Mal 4:1

WICKEDNESS
LORD saw that the *w* ... Gen 6:5
can I do this great *w* ... Gen 39:9
'*W* proceeds from the ... 1 Sam 24:13
w oppress them ... 2 Sam 7:10
Is not your *w* great ... Job 22:5
Oh, let the *w* of the ... Ps 7:9
alive into hell, for *w* ... Ps 55:15
in the tents of *w* ... Ps 84:10
I will not know *w* ... Ps 101:4
eat the bread of *w* ... Prov 4:17
w is an abomination ... Prov 8:7
w will not deliver ... Eccl 8:8
w burns as the ... Is 9:18
have trusted in your *w* ... Is 47:10
w will correct you ... Jer 2:19
wells up with her *w* ... Jer 6:7
man repented of his *w* ... Jer 8:6
not turn from his *w* ... Ezek 3:19
You have plowed *w* ... Hos 10:13
and cannot look on *w* ... Hab 1:13
for those who do *w* ... Mal 3:15
is full of greed and *w* ... Luke 11:39
sexual immorality, *w* ... Rom 1:29
spiritual hosts of *w* ... Eph 6:12
and overflow of *w* ... James 1:21

WIDE
shall open your hand *w* ... Deut 15:8
opened their mouth *w* ... Job 29:23
w his lips shall have ... Prov 13:3
will build myself a *w* ... Jer 22:14
w is the gate and ... Matt 7:13
to you, our heart is *w* ... 2 Cor 6:11

WIDOW
does no good for the *w* ... Job 24:21
They slay the *w* ... Ps 94:6
and his wife a *w* ... Ps 109:9
the fatherless and *w* ... Ps 146:9
plead for the *w* ... Is 1:17
How like a *w* is she ... Lam 1:1
Then one poor *w* ... Mark 12:42
w has children or ... 1 Tim 5:4
Do not let a *w* under ... 1 Tim 5:9

WIDOWS
a defender of *w* ... Ps 68:5
and let your *w* trust ... Jer 49:11
w were neglected ... Acts 6:1
that the younger *w* ... 1 Tim 5:14
to visit orphans and *w* ... James 1:27

WIFE
and be joined to his *w* ... Gen 2:24
an excellent *w* is the ... Prov 12:4
w finds a good thing ... Prov 18:22
but a prudent *w* ... Prov 19:14
w whom you love all ... Eccl 9:9
like a youthful *w* ... Is 54:6
"Go, take yourself a *w* ... Hos 1:2
for a *w* he tended sheep ... Hos 12:12
with the *w* of his ... Mal 2:15
"Whoever divorces his *w* ... Mark 10:11
'I have married a *w* ... Luke 14:20
Remember Lot's *w* ... Luke 17:32
all seven had her as *w* ... Luke 20:33
so love his own *w* ... Eph 5:33
the husband of one *w* ... Titus 1:6
giving honor to the *w* ... 1 Pet 3:7
bride, the Lamb's *w* ... Rev 21:9

WILD
locusts and *w* honey ... Matt 3:4
olive tree which is *w* ... Rom 11:24

WILDERNESS
wasteland, a howling *w* ... Deut 32:10
w yields food for them ... Job 24:5
coming out of the *w* ... Song 3:6
made the world as a *w* ... Is 14:17
I will make the *w* ... Is 41:18
Let the *w* and its ... Is 42:11
Have I been a *w* ... Jer 2:31
of one crying in the *w* ... Matt 3:3
the serpent in the *w* ... John 3:14
congregation in the *w* ... Acts 7:38

WILES
to stand against the *w* ... Eph 6:11

WILL
w be done on earth as ... Matt 6:10
but he who does the *w* ... Matt 7:21
of the two did the *w* ... Matt 21:31
nevertheless not My *w* ... Luke 22:42
flesh, nor of the *w* ... John 1:13
I do not seek My own *w* ... John 5:30
not to do My own *w* ... John 6:38
This is the *w* ... John 6:39
wills to do His *w* ... John 7:17
w is present with me ... Rom 7:18
and perfect *w* of God ... Rom 12:2
works in you both to *w* ... Phil 2:13
the knowledge of His *w* ... Col 1:9
according to His own *w* ... Heb 2:4
come to do Your *w* ... Heb 10:9
good work to do His *w* ... Heb 13:21
but he who does the *w* ... 1 John 2:17

WILLFULLY
For if we sin *w* ... Heb 10:26
For this they *w* ... 2 Pet 3:5

WILLING
is of a *w* heart ... Ex 35:5
If you are *w* and ... Is 1:19
him, saying, "I am *w* ... Matt 8:3
The spirit indeed is *w* ... Matt 26:41
The spirit indeed is *w* ... Mark 14:38
if there is first a *w* ... 2 Cor 8:12
w that any should ... 2 Pet 3:9

WILLINGLY
to futility, not *w* ... Rom 8:20
For if I do this *w* ... 1 Cor 9:17
by compulsion but *w* ... 1 Pet 5:2

WILLS
to whom the Son *w* ... Matt 11:27
it is not of him who *w* ... Rom 9:16
say, "If the Lord *w* ... James 4:15

WIN
w one proselyte ... Matt 23:15
to all, that I might *w* ... 1 Cor 9:19

WIND
LORD was not in the *w* ... 1 Kin 19:11
w carries him away ... Job 27:21
the chaff which the *w* ... Ps 1:4
He causes His *w* ... Ps 147:18
will inherit the *w* ... Prov 11:29
He who observes the *w* ... Eccl 11:4
is the way of the *w* ... Eccl 11:5
Awake, O north *w* ... Song 4:16
the prophets become *w* ... Jer 5:13
He brings the *w* ... Jer 51:16
Ephraim feeds on the *w* ... Hos 12:1
and creates the *w* ... Amos 4:13
A reed shaken by the *w* ... Matt 11:7
And the *w* ceased and ... Mark 4:39
and rebuked the *w* ... Luke 8:24
The *w* blows where ... John 3:8
of a rushing mighty *w* ... Acts 2:2
about with every *w* ... Eph 4:14

WINDOWS
looking through the *w* ... Song 2:9
has come through our *w* ... Jer 9:21
upper room, with his *w* ... Dan 6:10
not open for you the *w* ... Mal 3:10

WINDS
from the four *w* ... Ezek 37:9
be, that even the *w* ... Matt 8:27
holding the four *w* ... Rev 7:1

WINE
Noah awoke from his *w* ... Gen 9:24
w that makes glad ... Ps 104:15
W is a mocker ... Prov 20:1
Do not look on the *w* ... Prov 23:31
love is better than *w* ... Song 1:2
w inflames them ... Is 5:11
Yes, come, buy *w* ... Is 55:1
they gave Him sour *w* ... Matt 27:34
when they ran out of *w* ... John 2:3
do not be drunk with *w* ... Eph 5:18
but use a little *w* ... 1 Tim 5:23
not given to much *w* ... Titus 2:3
her the cup of the *w* ... Rev 16:19

WINEBIBBERS
Do not mix with *w* ... Prov 23:20

WINEPRESS
"I have trodden the *w* ... Is 63:3
for the *w* is full ... Joel 3:13
into the great *w* ... Rev 14:19
Himself treads the *w* ... Rev 19:15

WINESKIN
I have become like a *w* ... Ps 119:83

WINESKINS
new wine into old *w* ... Matt 9:17

WING
One *w* of the cherub ... 1 Kin 6:24
so I spread My *w* ... Ezek 16:8

WINGS
w you have come ... Ruth 2:12
He flew upon the *w* ... Ps 18:10
the shadow of Your *w* ... Ps 36:7
If I take the *w* ... Ps 139:9
each one had six *w* ... Is 6:2
with healing in His *w* ... Mal 4:2
woman was given two *w* ... Rev 12:14

WINS
w souls is wise ... Prov 11:30

WINTER
have made summer and *w* ... Ps 74:17
For lo, the *w* is past ... Song 2:11
w it shall occur ... Zech 14:8
flight may not be in *w* ... Matt 24:20

WIPE
the Lord GOD will *w* ... Is 25:8
w them with the towel ... John 13:5
w away every tear ... Rev 21:4

WISDOM
for this is your *w* ... Deut 4:6
w will die with you ... Job 12:2
will make me to know *w* ... Ps 51:6
is the man who finds *w* ... Prov 3:13
Get *w*! Get understanding! ... Prov 4:5
W is the principal ... Prov 4:7
is the beginning of *w* ... Prov 9:10
to get *w* than gold ... Prov 16:16
w loves his own soul ... Prov 19:8
W is too lofty for a ... Prov 24:7
w is much grief ... Eccl 1:18
W is better than ... Eccl 9:16
w is justified by her ... Matt 11:19
Jesus increased in *w* ... Luke 2:52
riches both of the *w* ... Rom 11:33
the gospel, not with *w* ... 1 Cor 1:17
Greeks seek after *w* ... 1 Cor 1:22
For the *w* of this world ... 1 Cor 3:19
not with fleshly *w* ... 2 Cor 1:12
now the manifold *w* ... Eph 3:10
all the treasures of *w* ... Col 2:3
Walk in *w* toward those ... Col 4:5
If any of you lacks *w* ... James 1:5

with which I was *w* . . . . Zech 13:6
to the beast who was *w* . . . . Rev 13:14

WOUNDS
and binds up their *w* . . . . Ps 147:3
Faithful are the *w* . . . . Prov 27:6
and bandaged his *w* . . . . Luke 10:34

WRATH
w has gone out from . . . . Num 16:46
provoked the LORD to *w* . . . . Deut 9:22
Had I not feared the *w* . . . . Deut 32:27
w kills a foolish . . . . Job 5:2
speak to them in His *w* . . . . Ps 2:5
living and burning *w* . . . . Ps 58:9
Surely the *w* of man . . . . Ps 76:10
Your fierce *w* has gone . . . . Ps 88:16
Will Your *w* burn like . . . . Ps 89:46
w we are terrified . . . . Ps 90:7
So I swore in My *w* . . . . Ps 95:11
in the day of His *w* . . . . Ps 110:5
death is the king's *w* . . . . Prov 16:14
The king's *w* is like . . . . Prov 19:12
of great *w* will suffer . . . . Prov 19:19
w is heavier than . . . . Prov 27:3
W is cruel and anger a . . . . Prov 27:4
w I will give him . . . . Is 10:6
With a little *w* . . . . Is 54:8
in My *w* I struck you . . . . Is 60:10
I will pour out my *w* . . . . Hos 5:10
w remember mercy . . . . Hab 3:2
you to flee from the *w* . . . . Matt 3:7
see life, but the *w* . . . . John 3:36
For the *w* of God is . . . . Rom 1:18
up for yourself *w* . . . . Rom 2:5
the law brings about *w* . . . . Rom 4:15
wanting to show His *w* . . . . Rom 9:22
rather give place to *w* . . . . Rom 12:19
not only because of *w* . . . . Rom 13:5
outbursts of *w* . . . . 2 Cor 12:20
nature children of *w* . . . . Eph 2:3
sun go down on your *w* . . . . Eph 4:26
Let all bitterness, *w* . . . . Eph 4:31
delivers us from the *w* . . . . 1 Thess 1:10
w has come upon them . . . . . . 1 Thess 2:16
holy hands, without *w* . . . . 1 Tim 2:8
So I swore in My *w* . . . . Heb 3:11
not fearing the *w* . . . . Heb 11:27
for the *w* of man does . . . . James 1:20
throne and from the *w* . . . . Rev 6:16
to you, having great *w* . . . . Rev 12:12
of the wine of the *w* . . . . Rev 14:8
winepress of the *w* . . . . Rev 14:19
for in them the *w* . . . . Rev 15:1
fierceness of His *w* . . . . Rev 16:19

WRATHFUL
w man stirs up strife . . . . Prov 15:18

WRESTLE
For we do not *w* . . . . Eph 6:12

RETCHED
w man that I am . . . . Rom 7:24
know that you are *w* . . . . Rev 3:17

RINGING
w the nose produces . . . . Prov 30:33

RINKLE
not having spot or *w* . . . . Eph 5:27

RITE
"*W* these words . . . . Ex 34:27
w bitter things . . . . Job 13:26
w them on the tablet . . . . Prov 7:3
W this man down as . . . . Jer 22:30
w them on their hearts . . . . Heb 8:10
their minds I will *w* . . . . Heb 10:16
I had many things to *w* . . . . 3 John 13

RITTEN
tablets of stone, *w* . . . . Ex 31:18
Have I not *w* to you . . . . Prov 22:20

your names are *w* . . . . Luke 10:20
"What I have *w* . . . . John 19:22
ministered by us, *w* . . . . 2 Cor 3:3
the stone a new name *w* . . . . Rev 2:17
the plagues that are *w* . . . . Rev 22:18

WRONG
sinned, we have done *w* . . . . 2 Chr 6:37
I cry out concerning *w* . . . . Job 19:7
not charge them with *w* . . . . Job 24:12
no one to do them *w* . . . . Ps 105:14
Do no *w* and do no . . . . Jer 22:3
I am doing you no *w* . . . . Matt 20:13
Man has done nothing *w* . . . . . . Luke 23:41
Jews I have done no *w* . . . . Acts 25:10
Forgive me this *w* . . . . 2 Cor 12:13
But he who does *w* . . . . Col 3:25

WRONGED
then that God has *w* . . . . Job 19:6
We have *w* no one . . . . 2 Cor 7:2

WROTE
of the hand that *w* . . . . Dan 5:5
stooped down and *w* . . . . John 8:6

WROUGHT
And skillfully *w* . . . . Ps 139:15

YEAR
first month of the *y* . . . . Ex 12:2
In the *Y* of Jubilee . . . . Lev 27:24
the acceptable *y* . . . . Is 61:2
be his until the *y* . . . . Ezek 46:17
to Jerusalem every *y* . . . . Luke 2:41
went alone once a *y* . . . . Heb 9:7
of sins every *y* . . . . Heb 10:3

YEARS
Are Your *y* like the . . . . Job 10:5
y should teach . . . . Job 32:7
I will remember the *y* . . . . Ps 77:10
For a thousand *y* . . . . Ps 90:4
lives are seventy *y* . . . . Ps 90:10
y will have no end . . . . Ps 102:27
when He was twelve *y* . . . . Luke 2:42
are not yet fifty *y* . . . . John 8:57
y will not fail . . . . Heb 1:12
with Him a thousand *y* . . . . Rev 20:6

YES
let your '*Y*' be '*Y*,' . . . . Matt 5:37
No, but in Him was *Y* . . . . 2 Cor 1:19

YOKE
you shall break his *y* . . . . Gen 27:40
and He will put a *y* . . . . Deut 28:48
Your father made our *y* . . . . 1 Kin 12:4
You have broken the *y* . . . . Is 9:4
Take My *y* upon you . . . . Matt 11:29

YOKED
Do not be unequally *y* . . . . 2 Cor 6:14

YOUNG
His flesh shall be *y* . . . . Job 33:25
I have been *y* . . . . Ps 37:25
she may lay her *y* . . . . Ps 84:3
y ones shall lie . . . . Is 11:7
dream dreams, your *y* . . . . Joel 2:28
y man followed Him . . . . Mark 14:51
I write to you, *y* . . . . 1 John 2:13

YOUNGER
they mock at me, men *y* . . . . Job 30:1
y son gathered all . . . . Luke 15:13
let him be as the *y* . . . . Luke 22:26
y women as sisters . . . . 1 Tim 5:2
Likewise you *y* people . . . . 1 Pet 5:5

YOURS
all that I have are *y* . . . . 1 Kin 20:4
the battle is not *y* . . . . 2 Chr 20:15
I am *Y*, save me . . . . Ps 119:94
Y is the kingdom . . . . Matt 6:13

Take what is *y* . . . . Matt 20:14
y is the kingdom . . . . Luke 6:20
And all Mine are *Y* . . . . John 17:10
For all things are *y* . . . . 1 Cor 3:21
for I do not seek *y* . . . . 2 Cor 12:14

YOUTH
for he was only a *y* . . . . 1 Sam 17:42
the LORD from my *y* . . . . 1 Kin 18:12
the sins of my *y* . . . . Ps 25:7
the companion of her *y* . . . . Prov 2:17
in the days of your *y* . . . . Eccl 11:9
the shame of your *y* . . . . Is 54:4
speak, for I am a *y* . . . . Jer 1:6
I have kept from my *y* . . . . Matt 19:20
no one despise your *y* . . . . 1 Tim 4:12

YOUTHFUL
Flee also *y* lusts . . . . 2 Tim 2:22

ZACCHAEUS
Wealthy tax collector converted to Christ, Luke 19:1–10

ZACHARIAS
Father of John the Baptist, Luke 1:5–17

ZADOK
Co-priest with Abiathar; remains loyal to David, 2 Sam 15:24–29; 20:25
Rebuked by David, 2 Sam 19:11, 12
Does not follow Adonijah; anoints Solomon, 1 Kin 1:8–45
Takes Abiathar's place, 1 Kin 2:35

ZAREPHATH
Town of Sidon where Elijah revives widow's son, 1 Kin 17:8–24; Luke 4:26

ZEAL
The *z* of the LORD of . . . . 2 Kin 19:31
z has consumed me . . . . Ps 119:139
He shall stir up His *z* . . . . Is 42:13
have spoken it in My *z* . . . . Ezek 5:13
for Zion with great *z* . . . . Zech 8:2
"*Z* for Your house has . . . . John 2:17
that they have a *z* . . . . Rom 10:2
z has stirred up the . . . . 2 Cor 9:2

ZEALOUS
"I have been very *z* . . . . 1 Kin 19:10
'I am *z* for Zion with . . . . Zech 8:2
since you are *z* . . . . 1 Cor 14:12
But it is good to be *z* . . . . Gal 4:18
z for good works . . . . Titus 2:14

ZEBAH
King of Midian killed by Gideon, Judg 8:4–28

ZEBEDEE
Galilean fisherman; father of James and John, Matt 4:21, 22

ZEBULUN
Sixth son of Jacob and Leah, Gen 30:19, 20
Prophecy concerning, Gen 49:13
—— Tribe of:
Numbered, Num 1:30, 31; 26:27
Territory assigned to, Josh 19:10–16
Joins Gideon in battle, Judg 6:34, 35
Some respond to Hezekiah's reforms, 2 Chr 30:10–18
Christ visits territory of, Matt 4:13–16

ZECHARIAH
King of Israel; last ruler of Jehu's dynasty, 2 Kin 15:8–12
—— Postexilic prophet and priest, Ezra 5:1; Zech 1:1, 7

ZEDEKIAH
Last king of Judah; uncle and successor of Jehoiachin; reigns wickedly, 2 Kin 24:17–19; 2 Chr 36:10

Rebels against Nebuchadnezzar, 2 Chr 36:11–13
Denounced by Jeremiah, Jer 34:1–22
Consults Jeremiah, Jer 37; 38
Captured and taken to Babylon, 2 Kin 25:1–7; Jer 39:1–7

ZELOPHEHAD
Manassite whose five daughters secure female rights, Num 27:1–7

ZEPHANIAH
Author of Zephaniah, Zeph 1:1
——— Priest and friend of Jeremiah during Zedekiah's reign, Jer 21:1

ZERUBBABEL
Descendant of David, 1 Chr 3:1–19
Leader of Jewish exiles, Neh 7:6, 7; Hag 2:21–23
Rebuilds the temple, Ezra 3:1–10; Zech 4:1–14

ZIBA
Saul's servant, 2 Sam 9:9
Befriends David, 2 Sam 16:1–4
Accused of deception by Mephibosheth, 2 Sam 19:17–30

ZIKLAG
City on the border of Judah, Josh 15:1, 31
Held by David, 1 Sam 27:6
Overthrown by Amalekites, 1 Sam 30:1–31

ZILPAH
Leah's maid, Gen 29:24
Mother of Gad and Asher, Gen 30:9–13

ZIMRI
Simeonite prince slain by Phinehas, Num 25:6–14
——— King of Israel for seven days, 1 Kin 16:8–20

ZIN
Wilderness through which the Israelites passed, Num 20:1
Border between Judah and Edom, Josh 15:1–3

ZION
Literally, an area in Jerusalem; called the City of David, 2 Sam 5:6–9; 2 Chr 5:2
Used figuratively of God's kingdom, Ps 125:1; Heb 12:22; Rev 14:1

ZIPPORAH
Daughter of Jethro; wife of Moses, Ex 18:1, 2

ZOAR
Ancient city of Canaan originally named Bela, Gen 14:2, 8
Spared destruction at Lot's request, Gen 19:20–23

ZOPHAR
Naamathite; friend of Job, Job 2:11